2024

Harris
North Carolina
Manufacturers Directory

Published May 2024 next update May 2025

WARNING: Purchasers and users of this directory may not use this directory to compile mailing lists, other marketing aids and other types of data, which are sold or otherwise provided to third parties. Such use is wrongful, illegal and a violation of the federal copyright laws.

CAUTION: Because of the many thousands of establishment listings contained in this directory and the possibilities of both human and mechanical error in processing this information, Mergent Inc. cannot assume liability for the correctness of the listings or information on which they are based. Hence, no information contained in this work should be relied upon in any instance where there is a possibility of any loss or damage as a consequence of any error or omission in this volume.

Publisher
Mergent Inc.
444 Madison Ave
New York, NY 10022

©Mergent Inc All Rights Reserved
2024 Mergent Business Press
ISSN 1080-2614
ISBN 979-8-89251-107-0

TABLE OF CONTENTS

Summary of Contents & Explanatory Notes 4
User's Guide to Listings 6

Geographic Section
County/City Cross-Reference Index 9
Firms Listed by Location City 13

Standard Industrial Classification (SIC) Section
SIC Alphabetical Index 693
SIC Numerical Index 697
Firms Listed by SIC 703

Alphabetic Section
Firms Listed by Firm Name 947

Product Section
Industrial Product Index 1221
Firms Listed by Product Category 1235

SUMMARY OF CONTENTS

Number of Companies 17,156
Number of Decision Makers 21,316
Minimum Number of Employees 4

EXPLANATORY NOTES

How to Cross-Reference in This Directory

Sequential Entry Numbers. Each establishment in the Geographic Section is numbered sequentially (G-0000). The number assigned to each establishment is referred to as its "entry number." To make cross-referencing easier, each listing in the Geographic, SIC, Alphabetic and Product Sections includes the establishment's entry number. To facilitate locating an entry in the Geographic Section, the entry numbers for the first listing on the left page and the last listing on the right page are printed at the top of the page next to the city name.

Source Suggestions Welcome

Although all known sources were used to compile this directory, it is possible that companies were inadvertently omitted. Your assistance in calling attention to such omissions would be greatly appreciated. A special form on the facing page will help you in the reporting process.

Analysis

Every effort has been made to contact all firms to verify their information. The one exception to this rule is the annual sales figure, which is considered by many companies to be confidential information. Therefore, estimated sales have been calculated by multiplying the nationwide average sales per employee for the firm's major SIC/NAICS code by the firm's number of employees. Nationwide averages for sales per employee by SIC/NAICS codes are provided by the U.S. Department of Commerce and are updated annually. All sales—sales (est)—have been estimated by this method. The exceptions are parent companies (PA), division headquarters (DH) and headquarter locations (HQ) which may include an actual corporate sales figure—sales (corporate-wide) if available.

Types of Companies

Descriptive and statistical data are included for companies in the entire state. These comprise manufacturers, machine shops, fabricators, assemblers and printers. Also identified are corporate offices in the state.

Employment Data

This directory contains companies with 4 or more employees. The employment figure shown in the Geographic Section includes male and female employees and embraces all levels of the company: administrative, clerical, sales and maintenance. This figure is for the facility listed and does not include other plants or offices. It should be recognized that these figures represent an approximate year-round average. These employment figures are broken into codes A through G and used in the Product and SIC Sections to further help you in qualifying a company. Be sure to check the footnotes on the bottom of pages for the code breakdowns.

Standard Industrial Classification (SIC)

The Standard Industrial Classification (SIC) system used in this directory was developed by the federal government for use in classifying establishments by the type of activity they are engaged in. The SIC classifications used in this directory are from the 1987 edition published by the U.S. Government's Office of Management and Budget. The SIC system separates all activities into broad industrial divisions (e.g., manufacturing, mining, retail trade). It further subdivides each division. The range of manufacturing industry classes extends from two-digit codes (major industry group) to four-digit codes (product).

For example:

Industry Breakdown	Code	Industry, Product, etc.
*Major industry group	20	Food and kindred products
Industry group	203	Canned and frozen foods
*Industry	2033	Fruits and vegetables, etc.

*Classifications used in this directory

Only two-digit and four-digit codes are used in this directory.

Arrangement

1. The **Geographic Section** contains complete in-depth corporate data. This section is sorted by cities listed in alphabetical order and companies listed alphabetically within each city. A County/City Index for referencing cities within counties precedes this section.

> IMPORTANT NOTICE: It is a violation of both federal and state law to transmit an unsolicited advertisement to a facsimile machine. Any user of this product that violates such laws may be subject to civil and criminal penalties, which may exceed $500 for each transmission of an unsolicited facsimile. Mergent Inc. provides fax numbers for lawful purposes only and expressly forbids the use of these numbers in any unlawful manner.

2. The **Standard Industrial Classification (SIC) Section** lists companies under approximately 500 four-digit SIC codes. An alphabetical and a numerical index precedes this section. A company can be listed under several codes. The codes are in numerical order with companies listed alphabetically under each code.

3. The **Alphabetic Section** lists all companies with their full physical or mailing addresses and telephone number.

4. The **Product Section** lists companies under unique Harris categories. An index preceding this section lists all product categories in alphabetical order. Companies can be listed under several categories.

USER'S GUIDE TO LISTINGS

GEOGRAPHIC SECTION

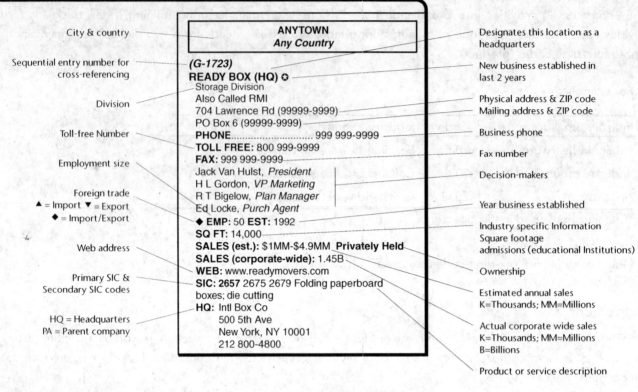

ANYTOWN
Any Country

(G-1723)
READY BOX (HQ) ✪
Storage Division
Also Called RMI
704 Lawrence Rd (99999-9999)
PO Box 6 (99999-9999)
PHONE............................999 999-9999
TOLL FREE: 800 999-9999
FAX: 999 999-9999
Jack Van Hulst, *President*
H L Gordon, *VP Marketing*
R T Bigelow, *Plan Manager*
Ed Locke, *Purch Agent*
◆ **EMP:** 50 **EST:** 1992
SQ FT: 14,000
SALES (est.): $1MM-$4.9MM **Privately Held**
SALES (corporate-wide): 1.45B
WEB: www.readymovers.com
SIC: 2657 2675 2679 Folding paperboard boxes; die cutting
HQ: Intl Box Co
500 5th Ave
New York, NY 10001
212 800-4800

City & country
Sequential entry number for cross-referencing
Division
Toll-free Number
Employment size
Foreign trade
▲ = Import ▼ = Export
◆ = Import/Export
Web address
Primary SIC & Secondary SIC codes
HQ = Headquarters
PA = Parent company

Designates this location as a headquarters
New business established in last 2 years
Physical address & ZIP code
Mailing address & ZIP code
Business phone
Fax number
Decision-makers
Year business established
Industry specific Information
Square footage
admissions (educational Institutions)
Ownership
Estimated annual sales
K=Thousands; MM=Millions
Actual corporate wide sales
K=Thousands; MM=Millions
B=Billions
Product or service description

SIC SECTION

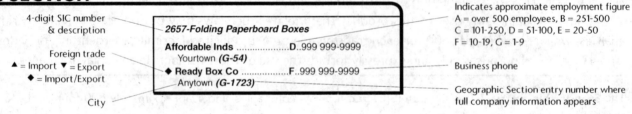

2657-Folding Paperboard Boxes

Affordable Inds ....**D**..999 999-9999
Yourtown ***(G-54)***
◆ **Ready Box Co** ....**F**..999 999-9999
Anytown ***(G-1723)***

4-digit SIC number & description
Foreign trade
▲ = Import ▼ = Export
◆ = Import/Export
City

Indicates approximate employment figure
A = over 500 employees, B = 251-500
C = 101-250, D = 51-100, E = 20-50
F = 10-19, G = 1-9
Business phone
Geographic Section entry number where full company information appears

ALPHABETIC SECTION

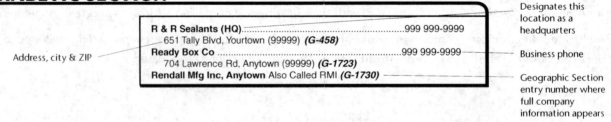

R & R Sealants (HQ)...999 999-9999
651 Tally Blvd, Yourtown (99999) ***(G-458)***
Ready Box Co 999 999-9999
704 Lawrence Rd, Anytown (99999) ***(G-1723)***
Rendall Mfg Inc, Anytown Also Called RMI ***(G-1730)***

Address, city & ZIP

Designates this location as a headquarters
Business phone
Geographic Section entry number where full company information appears

PRODUCT SECTION

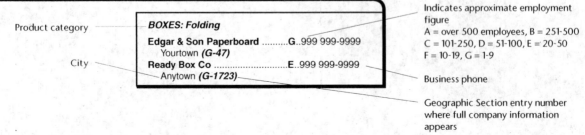

BOXES: Folding

Edgar & Son Paperboard ....**G**..999 999-9999
Yourtown ***(G-47)***
Ready Box Co ....**E**..999 999-9999
Anytown ***(G-1723)***

Product category
City

Indicates approximate employment figure
A = over 500 employees, B = 251-500
C = 101-250, D = 51-100, E = 20-50
F = 10-19, G = 1-9
Business phone
Geographic Section entry number where full company information appears

GEOGRAPHIC SECTION

Companies sorted by city in alphabetical order
In-depth company data listed

STANDARD INDUSTRIAL CLASSIFICATIONS

Alphabetical index of classification descriptions
Numerical index of classification descriptions
Companies sorted by SIC product groupings

ALPHABETIC SECTION

Company listings in alphabetical order

PRODUCT INDEX

Product categories listed in alphabetical order

PRODUCT SECTION

Companies sorted by product and manufacturing service classifications

COUNTY/CITY CROSS-REFERENCE INDEX

Alamance
- Alamance .... (G-68)
- Altamahaw .... (G-122)
- Burlington .... (G-1360)
- Elon .... (G-5656)
- Elon College .... (G-5664)
- Graham .... (G-6677)
- Haw River .... (G-7749)
- Mebane .... (G-10396)
- Saxapahaw .... (G-14217)
- Snow Camp .... (G-14495)
- Swepsonville .... (G-15050)

Alexander
- Hiddenite .... (G-8213)
- Stony Point .... (G-14971)
- Taylorsville .... (G-15126)

Alleghany
- Ennice .... (G-5685)
- Glade Valley .... (G-6573)
- Laurel Springs .... (G-9466)
- Sparta .... (G-14587)

Anson
- Ansonville .... (G-152)
- Lilesville .... (G-9835)
- Mc Farlan .... (G-10381)
- Morven .... (G-11471)
- Peachland .... (G-12173)
- Polkton .... (G-12382)
- Wadesboro .... (G-15500)

Ashe
- Creston .... (G-4623)
- Crumpler .... (G-4628)
- Fleetwood .... (G-5974)
- Jefferson .... (G-9087)
- Lansing .... (G-9454)
- Todd .... (G-15323)
- Warrensville .... (G-15653)
- West Jefferson .... (G-15936)

Avery
- Banner Elk .... (G-892)
- Beech Mountain .... (G-972)
- Newland .... (G-11881)

Beaufort
- Aurora .... (G-831)
- Bath .... (G-914)
- Chocowinity .... (G-3894)
- Pantego .... (G-12162)
- Pinetown .... (G-12243)
- Washington .... (G-15678)

Bertie
- Aulander .... (G-830)
- Colerain .... (G-4139)
- Lewiston Woodville ... (G-9662)
- Merry Hill .... (G-10440)
- Roxobel .... (G-13829)
- Windsor .... (G-16564)

Bladen
- Bladenboro .... (G-1143)
- Clarkton .... (G-3948)
- Dublin .... (G-4837)
- Elizabethtown .... (G-5583)
- Kelly .... (G-9137)
- Tar Heel .... (G-15089)
- White Oak .... (G-15958)

Brunswick
- Ash .... (G-395)
- Belville .... (G-1023)
- Bolivia .... (G-1162)
- Calabash .... (G-1552)
- Leland .... (G-9523)
- Navassa .... (G-11757)
- Oak Island .... (G-12048)
- Ocean Isle Beach .... (G-12086)
- Shallotte .... (G-14270)
- Southport .... (G-14563)
- Sunset Beach .... (G-14999)
- Supply .... (G-15005)
- Winnabow .... (G-16580)

Buncombe
- Alexander .... (G-117)
- Arden .... (G-306)
- Asheville .... (G-512)
- Barnardsville .... (G-906)
- Biltmore Lake .... (G-1100)
- Black Mountain .... (G-1118)
- Candler .... (G-1566)
- Enka .... (G-5683)
- Fairview .... (G-5706)
- Leicester .... (G-9506)
- Swannanoa .... (G-15017)
- Weaverville .... (G-15836)

Burke
- Connelly Springs ...... (G-4397)
- Drexel .... (G-4836)
- Hildebran .... (G-8619)
- Icard .... (G-8916)
- Morganton .... (G-11196)
- Rutherford College .. (G-13858)
- Valdese .... (G-15442)

Cabarrus
- Concord .... (G-4184)
- Harrisburg .... (G-7699)
- Kannapolis .... (G-9110)
- Midland .... (G-10456)
- Mount Pleasant .... (G-11672)

Caldwell
- Granite Falls .... (G-6720)
- Hudson .... (G-8759)
- Lenoir .... (G-9566)

Camden
- Camden .... (G-1555)
- Shiloh .... (G-14391)
- South Mills .... (G-14524)

Carteret
- Atlantic .... (G-827)
- Atlantic Beach .... (G-828)
- Beaufort .... (G-943)
- Davis .... (G-4707)
- Emerald Isle .... (G-5669)
- Gloucester .... (G-6574)
- Marshallberg .... (G-10209)
- Morehead City .... (G-11148)
- Newport .... (G-11896)
- Smyrna .... (G-14490)
- Stella .... (G-14938)

Caswell
- Blanch .... (G-1151)
- Leasburg .... (G-9505)
- Milton .... (G-10515)
- Pelham .... (G-12177)
- Prospect Hill .... (G-12407)
- Yanceyville .... (G-17065)

Catawba
- Catawba .... (G-1963)
- Claremont .... (G-3899)
- Conover .... (G-4412)
- Hickory .... (G-7926)
- Maiden .... (G-10099)
- Newton .... (G-11911)
- Sherrills Ford .... (G-14383)
- Terrell .... (G-15179)

Chatham
- Bear Creek .... (G-936)
- Bennett .... (G-1027)
- Goldston .... (G-6672)
- Moncure .... (G-10611)
- Pittsboro .... (G-12331)
- Siler City .... (G-14394)

Cherokee
- Andrews .... (G-123)
- Marble .... (G-10133)
- Murphy .... (G-11704)
- Topton .... (G-15325)

Chowan
- Edenton .... (G-5504)
- Tyner .... (G-15433)

Clay
- Brasstown .... (G-1266)
- Hayesville .... (G-7759)

Cleveland
- Boiling Springs .... (G-1158)
- Casar .... (G-1933)
- Fallston .... (G-5728)
- Grover .... (G-7605)
- Kings Mountain .... (G-9288)
- Lattimore .... (G-9457)
- Lawndale .... (G-9500)
- Mooresboro .... (G-10838)
- Shelby .... (G-14281)

Columbus
- Bolton .... (G-1167)
- Chadbourn .... (G-1974)
- Clarendon .... (G-3946)
- Delco .... (G-4718)
- Evergreen .... (G-5696)
- Fair Bluff .... (G-5699)
- Lake Waccamaw ...... (G-9448)
- Nakina .... (G-11731)
- Riegelwood .... (G-13557)
- Tabor City .... (G-15077)
- Whiteville .... (G-15959)

Craven
- Bridgeton .... (G-1294)
- Cherry Point .... (G-3857)
- Cove City .... (G-4597)
- Dover .... (G-4834)
- Ernul .... (G-5686)
- Havelock .... (G-7738)
- New Bern .... (G-11765)
- Trent Woods .... (G-15328)
- Vanceboro .... (G-15474)

Cumberland
- Eastover .... (G-5481)
- Falcon .... (G-5727)
- Fayetteville .... (G-5744)
- Fort Bragg .... (G-6089)
- Hope Mills .... (G-8730)
- Linden .... (G-9938)
- Spring Lake .... (G-14624)
- Stedman .... (G-14933)

Currituck
- Aydlett .... (G-861)
- Currituck .... (G-4632)
- Grandy .... (G-6718)
- Harbinger .... (G-7683)
- Jarvisburg .... (G-9083)
- Knotts Island .... (G-9435)
- Moyock .... (G-11691)
- Point Harbor .... (G-12380)
- Powells Point .... (G-12396)

Dare
- Avon .... (G-843)
- Frisco .... (G-6176)
- Hatteras .... (G-7737)
- Kill Devil Hills .... (G-9254)
- Kitty Hawk .... (G-9399)
- Manns Harbor .... (G-10122)
- Manteo .... (G-10126)
- Nags Head .... (G-11719)
- Rodanthe .... (G-13756)
- Southern Shores ..... (G-14561)
- Wanchese .... (G-15641)

Davidson
- Denton .... (G-4725)
- Lexington .... (G-9676)
- Linwood .... (G-9943)
- Southmont .... (G-14562)
- Thomasville .... (G-15181)
- Welcome .... (G-15871)

Davie
- Advance .... (G-37)
- Mocksville .... (G-10550)

Duplin
- Albertson .... (G-114)
- Beulaville .... (G-1091)
- Chinquapin .... (G-3891)
- Faison .... (G-5721)
- Kenansville .... (G-9140)
- Magnolia .... (G-10098)
- Rose Hill .... (G-13773)
- Teachey .... (G-15177)
- Wallace .... (G-15618)
- Warsaw .... (G-15664)

Durham
- Bahama .... (G-863)
- Durham .... (G-4892)
- Research Triangle Pa (G-13548)
- Rougemont .... (G-13787)
- Rtp .... (G-13830)

Edgecombe
- Battleboro .... (G-918)
- Macclesfield .... (G-10064)
- Pinetops .... (G-12239)
- Princeville .... (G-12406)
- Rocky Mount .... (G-13663)
- Tarboro .... (G-15093)

Forsyth
- Belews Creek .... (G-973)
- Clemmons .... (G-4023)
- Kernersville .... (G-9158)
- Lewisville .... (G-9664)
- Pfafftown .... (G-12187)
- Rural Hall .... (G-13832)
- Tobaccoville .... (G-15316)
- Walkertown .... (G-15613)
- Winston Salem .... (G-16584)

Franklin
- Bunn .... (G-1327)
- Franklinton .... (G-6151)
- Louisburg .... (G-9978)
- Youngsville .... (G-17066)

Gaston
- Alexis .... (G-121)
- Belmont .... (G-974)
- Bessemer City .... (G-1048)
- Cherryville .... (G-3861)
- Cramerton .... (G-4600)
- Dallas .... (G-4634)
- Gastonia .... (G-6333)
- Lowell .... (G-10007)
- Mc Adenville .... (G-10377)
- Mount Holly .... (G-11617)
- Stanley .... (G-14683)

Gates
- Gates .... (G-6545)
- Gatesville .... (G-6546)
- Hobbsville .... (G-8674)
- Sunbury .... (G-14995)

Graham
- Robbinsville .... (G-13604)

Granville
- Bullock .... (G-1326)
- Butner .... (G-1540)
- Creedmoor .... (G-4601)
- Oxford .... (G-12119)
- Stem .... (G-14939)

COUNTY/CITY CROSS-REFERENCE

Greene
- Hookerton .... (G-8728)
- Snow Hill .... (G-14498)
- Walstonburg .... (G-15637)

Guilford
- Archdale .... (G-265)
- Browns Summit .... (G-1298)
- Climax .... (G-4086)
- Colfax .... (G-4141)
- Gibsonville .... (G-6556)
- Greensboro .... (G-6766)
- High Point .... (G-8228)
- Jamestown .... (G-9048)
- Julian .... (G-9104)
- Mc Leansville .... (G-10383)
- Oak Ridge .... (G-12057)
- Pleasant Garden .... (G-12356)
- Stokesdale .... (G-14940)
- Summerfield .... (G-14974)
- Whitsett .... (G-15982)

Halifax
- Enfield .... (G-5673)
- Halifax .... (G-7610)
- Hollister .... (G-8677)
- Littleton .... (G-9949)
- Roanoke Rapids .... (G-13564)
- Scotland Neck .... (G-14218)
- Weldon .... (G-15879)

Harnett
- Angier .... (G-130)
- Bunnlevel .... (G-1329)
- Cameron .... (G-1560)
- Coats .... (G-4129)
- Dunn .... (G-4846)
- Erwin .... (G-5687)
- Lillington .... (G-9842)

Haywood
- Canton .... (G-1599)
- Clyde .... (G-4120)
- Maggie Valley .... (G-10093)
- Waynesville .... (G-15791)

Henderson
- Dana .... (G-4662)
- East Flat Rock .... (G-5472)
- Etowah .... (G-5691)
- Flat Rock .... (G-5959)
- Fletcher .... (G-5978)
- Hendersonville .... (G-7817)
- Horse Shoe .... (G-8739)
- Mills River .... (G-10497)
- Mountain Home .... (G-11689)
- Zirconia .... (G-17150)

Hertford
- Ahoskie .... (G-54)
- Cofield .... (G-4135)
- Como .... (G-4183)
- Harrellsville .... (G-7698)
- Murfreesboro .... (G-11698)
- Winton .... (G-17020)

Hoke
- Raeford .... (G-12414)

Hyde
- Ocracoke .... (G-12096)
- Swanquarter .... (G-15039)

Iredell
- Harmony .... (G-7685)
- Mooresville .... (G-10844)
- Olin .... (G-12107)
- Statesville .... (G-14732)
- Troutman .... (G-15363)
- Union Grove .... (G-15435)

Jackson
- Cashiers .... (G-1935)
- Cullowhee .... (G-4631)
- Dillsboro .... (G-4817)
- Sylva .... (G-15051)
- Whittier .... (G-16007)

Johnston
- Benson .... (G-1029)
- Clayton .... (G-3949)
- Four Oaks .... (G-6099)
- Kenly .... (G-9146)
- Pine Level .... (G-12207)
- Princeton .... (G-12399)
- Selma .... (G-14250)
- Smithfield .... (G-14447)

Jones
- Maysville .... (G-10369)
- Pollocksville .... (G-12391)
- Trenton .... (G-15332)

Lee
- Broadway .... (G-1296)
- Sanford .... (G-14080)

Lenoir
- Deep Run .... (G-4715)
- Kinston .... (G-9339)
- La Grange .... (G-9438)
- Pink Hill .... (G-12314)

Lincoln
- Crouse .... (G-4627)
- Denver .... (G-4757)
- Iron Station .... (G-8973)
- Lincolnton .... (G-9863)
- Vale .... (G-15462)

Macon
- Franklin .... (G-6114)
- Highlands .... (G-8611)
- Otto .... (G-12118)

Madison
- Hot Springs .... (G-8744)
- Mars Hill .... (G-10191)
- Marshall .... (G-10199)

Martin
- Everetts .... (G-5695)
- Hamilton .... (G-7613)
- Jamesville .... (G-9077)
- Robersonville .... (G-13614)
- Williamston .... (G-16056)

Mcdowell
- Little Switzerland .... (G-9948)
- Marion .... (G-10137)
- Nebo .... (G-11759)
- Old Fort .... (G-12098)

Mecklenburg
- Charlotte .... (G-2106)
- Cornelius .... (G-4519)
- Davidson .... (G-4664)
- Huntersville .... (G-8784)
- Matthews .... (G-10230)
- Mint Hill .... (G-10520)
- Paw Creek .... (G-12172)
- Pineville .... (G-12252)

Mitchell
- Bakersville .... (G-880)
- Spruce Pine .... (G-14629)

Montgomery
- Biscoe .... (G-1103)
- Candor .... (G-1593)
- Ether .... (G-5690)
- Mount Gilead .... (G-11599)
- Star .... (G-14714)
- Troy .... (G-15400)

Moore
- Aberdeen .... (G-1)
- Carthage .... (G-1659)
- Eagle Springs .... (G-5461)
- Jackson Springs .... (G-8983)
- Pinebluff .... (G-12213)
- Pinehurst .... (G-12217)
- Robbins .... (G-13596)
- Southern Pines .... (G-14526)
- Vass .... (G-15490)
- West End .... (G-15927)
- Whispering Pines .... (G-15953)

Nash
- Bailey .... (G-868)
- Castalia .... (G-1939)
- Middlesex .... (G-10444)
- Nashville .... (G-11733)
- Rocky Mount .... (G-13678)
- Sharpsburg .... (G-14280)
- Spring Hope .... (G-14612)
- Whitakers .... (G-15956)

New Hanover
- Carolina Beach .... (G-1631)
- Castle Hayne .... (G-1941)
- Kure Beach .... (G-9436)
- Wilmington .... (G-16086)
- Wrightsville Beach .... (G-17025)

Northampton
- Conway .... (G-4516)
- Garysburg .... (G-6329)
- Gaston .... (G-6330)
- Jackson .... (G-8982)
- Margarettsville .... (G-10136)
- Pendleton .... (G-12185)
- Pleasant Hill .... (G-12364)
- Potecasi .... (G-12395)
- Seaboard .... (G-14226)
- Severn .... (G-14268)
- Woodland .... (G-17022)

Onslow
- Cape Carteret .... (G-1630)
- Holly Ridge .... (G-8678)
- Hubert .... (G-8747)
- Jacksonville .... (G-8984)
- Richlands .... (G-13555)
- Sneads Ferry .... (G-14491)
- Surf City .... (G-15015)
- Swansboro .... (G-15041)

Orange
- Carrboro .... (G-1644)
- Cedar Grove .... (G-1970)
- Chapel Hill .... (G-1978)
- Efland .... (G-5524)
- Hillsborough .... (G-8630)

Pamlico
- Arapahoe .... (G-262)
- Bayboro .... (G-935)
- Grantsboro .... (G-6763)
- Lowland .... (G-10014)
- Merritt .... (G-10439)
- Oriental .... (G-12109)
- Vandemere .... (G-15489)

Pasquotank
- Elizabeth City .... (G-5529)

Pender
- Atkinson .... (G-826)
- Burgaw .... (G-1332)
- Hampstead .... (G-7635)
- Maple Hill .... (G-10131)
- Rocky Point .... (G-13743)
- Watha .... (G-15742)
- Willard .... (G-16054)

Perquimans
- Belvidere .... (G-1021)
- Hertford .... (G-7916)

Person
- Hurdle Mills .... (G-8909)
- Roxboro .... (G-13792)
- Semora .... (G-14264)
- Timberlake .... (G-15313)

Pitt
- Ayden .... (G-847)
- Bethel .... (G-1089)
- Farmville .... (G-5731)
- Fountain .... (G-6092)
- Greenville .... (G-7477)
- Grifton .... (G-7599)
- Grimesland .... (G-7604)
- Simpson .... (G-14437)
- Winterville .... (G-16993)

Polk
- Columbus .... (G-4172)
- Lynn .... (G-10063)
- Mill Spring .... (G-10483)
- Saluda .... (G-14070)
- Tryon .... (G-15421)

Randolph
- Asheboro .... (G-397)
- Cedar Falls .... (G-1969)
- Franklinville .... (G-6167)
- Liberty .... (G-9804)
- Ramseur .... (G-13439)
- Randleman .... (G-13452)
- Seagrove .... (G-14231)
- Sophia .... (G-14513)
- Staley .... (G-14663)
- Trinity .... (G-15338)

Richmond
- Cordova .... (G-4517)
- Ellerbe .... (G-5641)
- Hamlet .... (G-7615)
- Hoffman .... (G-8676)
- Marston .... (G-10229)
- Rockingham .... (G-13617)

Robeson
- Fairmont .... (G-5700)
- Lumber Bridge .... (G-10020)
- Lumberton .... (G-10023)
- Maxton .... (G-10353)
- Orrum .... (G-12115)
- Parkton .... (G-12171)
- Pembroke .... (G-12180)
- Red Springs .... (G-13495)
- Rowland .... (G-13789)
- Saint Pauls .... (G-13904)

Rockingham
- Eden .... (G-5484)
- Madison .... (G-10069)
- Mayodan .... (G-10363)
- Reidsville .... (G-13504)
- Stoneville .... (G-14953)

Rowan
- China Grove .... (G-3880)
- Cleveland .... (G-4067)
- Faith .... (G-5726)
- Gold Hill .... (G-6580)
- Granite Quarry .... (G-6760)
- Landis .... (G-9450)
- Mount Ulla .... (G-11681)
- Rockwell .... (G-13647)
- Salisbury .... (G-13911)
- Spencer .... (G-14601)
- Woodleaf .... (G-17023)

Rutherford
- Bostic .... (G-1259)
- Chimney Rock .... (G-3879)
- Cliffside .... (G-4084)
- Ellenboro .... (G-5634)
- Forest City .... (G-6056)
- Lake Lure .... (G-9447)
- Rutherfordton .... (G-13860)
- Spindale .... (G-14603)
- Union Mills .... (G-15439)

Sampson
- Autryville .... (G-840)
- Clinton .... (G-4088)
- Garland .... (G-6241)
- Godwin .... (G-6575)
- Harrells .... (G-7691)
- Ivanhoe .... (G-8979)
- Newton Grove .... (G-11987)
- Roseboro .... (G-13782)

Scotland
- Gibson .... (G-6555)
- Laurel Hill .... (G-9459)
- Laurinburg .... (G-9469)
- Wagram .... (G-15521)

Stanly
- Albemarle .... (G-70)
- Badin .... (G-862)
- Locust .... (G-9955)

COUNTY/CITY CROSS-REFERENCE

New London .... (G-11866)
Norwood .... (G-12036)
Oakboro .... (G-12068)
Richfield .... (G-13552)
Stanfield .... (G-14673)

Stokes
Danbury .... (G-4663)
Germanton .... (G-6550)
King .... (G-9264)
Lawsonville .... (G-9503)
Pine Hall .... (G-12206)
Pinnacle .... (G-12319)
Sandy Ridge .... (G-14076)
Walnut Cove .... (G-15630)

Surry
Ararat .... (G-263)
Dobson .... (G-4818)
Elkin .... (G-5608)
Lowgap .... (G-10013)
Mount Airy .... (G-11472)
Pilot Mountain .... (G-12196)
State Road .... (G-14726)
Westfield .... (G-15950)

Swain
Bryson City .... (G-1319)
Cherokee .... (G-3853)

Transylvania
Balsam Grove .... (G-891)
Brevard .... (G-1269)
Penrose .... (G-12186)
Pisgah Forest .... (G-12323)
Rosman .... (G-13786)
Sapphire .... (G-14213)

Tyrrell
Columbia .... (G-4165)

Union
Indian Trail .... (G-8917)
Marshville .... (G-10210)
Matthews .... (G-10300)
Mineral Springs .... (G-10517)
Monroe .... (G-10631)
Stallings .... (G-14671)
Waxhaw .... (G-15743)
Wingate .... (G-16574)

Vance
Henderson .... (G-7774)
Kittrell .... (G-9394)

Manson .... (G-10124)
Middleburg .... (G-10443)

Wake
Apex .... (G-156)
Cary .... (G-1669)
Fuquay Varina .... (G-6177)
Garner .... (G-6248)
Holly Springs .... (G-8686)
Knightdale .... (G-9409)
Morrisville .... (G-11271)
New Hill .... (G-11860)
Raleigh .... (G-12446)
Rolesville .... (G-13757)
Wake Forest .... (G-15525)
Wendell .... (G-15891)
Willow Spring .... (G-16075)
Zebulon .... (G-17117)

Warren
Macon .... (G-10068)
Norlina .... (G-11995)
Warrenton .... (G-15654)

Washington
Creswell .... (G-4626)

Plymouth .... (G-12365)
Roper .... (G-13770)

Watauga
Blowing Rock .... (G-1154)
Boone .... (G-1172)
Deep Gap .... (G-4708)
Vilas .... (G-15495)
Zionville .... (G-17148)

Wayne
Dudley .... (G-4840)
Fremont .... (G-6172)
Goldsboro .... (G-6587)
Mount Olive .... (G-11653)
Pikeville .... (G-12191)
Seven Springs .... (G-14266)
Sjafb .... (G-14446)

Wilkes
Boomer .... (G-1169)
Ferguson .... (G-5956)
Hays .... (G-7773)
Mc Grady .... (G-10382)
Millers Creek .... (G-10492)
Moravian Falls .... (G-11141)

North Wilkesboro .... (G-11996)
Purlear .... (G-12410)
Roaring River .... (G-13592)
Ronda .... (G-13763)
Thurmond .... (G-15310)
Traphill .... (G-15327)
Wilkesboro .... (G-16011)

Wilson
Elm City .... (G-5646)
Lucama .... (G-10016)
Saratoga .... (G-14216)
Sims .... (G-14439)
Stantonsburg .... (G-14711)
Wilson .... (G-16461)

Yadkin
Boonville .... (G-1252)
East Bend .... (G-5464)
Hamptonville .... (G-7665)
Jonesville .... (G-9094)
Yadkinville .... (G-17029)

Yancey
Burnsville .... (G-1521)
Micaville .... (G-10442)

GEOGRAPHIC SECTION

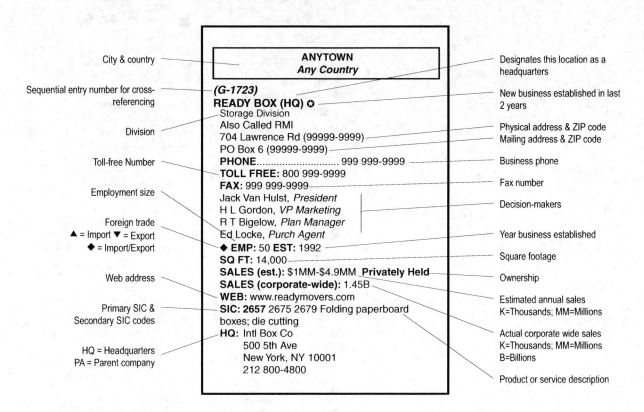

See footnotes for symbols and codes identification.
- This section is in alphabetical order by city.
- Companies are sorted alphabetically under their respective cities.
- To locate cities within a county refer to the County/City Cross Reference Index.

IMPORTANT NOTICE: It is a violation of both federal and state law to transmit an unsolicited advertisement to a facsimile machine. Any user of this product that violates such laws may be subject to civil and criminal penalties which may exceed $500 for each transmission of an unsolicited facsimile. Harris InfoSource provides fax numbers for lawful purposes only and expressly forbids the use of these numbers in any unlawful manner.

Aberdeen
Moore County

(G-1)
ABERDEEN COCA-COLA BTLG CO INC
203 W South St (28315-2709)
P.O. Box 518 (28315-0518)
PHONE..................910 944-2305
Gary Alan Moon, *Pr*
Doris B Moon, *VP*
EMP: 24 **EST:** 1913
SQ FT: 4,800
SALES (est): 1.96MM **Privately Held**
Web: www.aberdeencocacola.com
SIC: 2086 Bottled and canned soft drinks

(G-2)
BUILDERS FRSTSRCE - STHAST GRO
Also Called: Pbc of Aberdeen
900 Pinehurst Dr (28315)
P.O. Box 8 (28315-0008)
PHONE..................910 944-2516
Paul Portfilio, *Genl Mgr*
EMP: 84
SALES (corp-wide): 17.1B **Publicly Held**
Web: www.bldr.com
SIC: 5211 2431 Lumber products; Doors, wood
HQ: Builders Firstsource - Southeast Group, Llc
6031 Connection Dr # 400
Irving TX 75039
844 487-8625

(G-3)
CALCO ENTERPRISES INC (PA)
Also Called: Calco Sheet Metal Works
240 Crestline Ln (28315-7797)
P.O. Box 142 (28315-0142)
PHONE..................910 695-0089
Mark Francis, *Pr*
Joel Francis, *Treas*
Jonathon Francis, *Sec*
Timothy Buie, *VP*
EMP: 15 **EST:** 1991
SQ FT: 12,000
SALES (est): 1.62MM **Privately Held**
Web: www.francis-steel.com
SIC: 3545 3444 Machine tool accessories; Sheet metalwork

(G-4)
ERICO INTERNATIONAL CORP
188 Carolina Rd (28315-4754)
PHONE..................910 944-3355
Jarvis Daniel, *Mgr*
EMP: 5
Web: www.nvent.com
SIC: 3643 Current-carrying wiring services
HQ: Erico International Corporation
1665 Utica Ave S Ste 700
Saint Louis Park MN 55416
440 349-2630

(G-5)
GREAT PRODUCTS INC
Us Hwy 15 501 (28315)
P.O. Box 546 (28315-0546)
PHONE..................910 944-2020
William Marts, *Pr*
Sandy Marts, *VP*
Bruce Medlin, *Stockholder*
◆ **EMP:** 7 **EST:** 1989
SQ FT: 7,500
SALES (est): 477.09K **Privately Held**
SIC: 3589 5085 Coffee brewing equipment; Filters, industrial

(G-6)
HAMPTON CAPITAL PARTNERS LLC
Also Called: Gullistan Carpet
3140 Nc Highway 5 (28315)
P.O. Box 1059 (24151-8059)
▲ **EMP:** 700
SIC: 2273 Carpets and rugs

(G-7)
INDUSTRIAL METAL PRODUCTS OF
Also Called: Wire Form
461 Carolina Rd (28315-4733)
PHONE..................910 944-8110
Samuel Kenworthy, *Pr*
Barbara Kenworthy, *Sec*
EMP: 15 **EST:** 1988
SQ FT: 15,000
SALES (est): 4.52MM **Privately Held**
SIC: 3441 3429 3559 3599 Building components, structural steel; Hardware, nec ; Brick making machinery; Machine and other job shop work

(G-8)
INTERNTNAL TRAY PADS PACKG INC
3299 Nc Highway 5 (28315)
P.O. Box 307 (28315-0307)

Aberdeen - Moore County (G-9)   GEOGRAPHIC SECTION

PHONE..........................910 944-1800
Robert J Knorr, *Pr*
Shaen Kirkpatrick, *
Wilma Hogan, *Stockholder**
▲ **EMP:** 36 **EST:** 1988
SQ FT: 100,000
SALES (est): 2.36MM **Publicly Held**
Web: www.traypads.com
SIC: 2671 5199 Paper; coated and laminated packaging; Packaging materials
HQ: Pactiv Llc
1900 W Field Ct
Lake Forest IL 60045
847 482-2000

(G-9)
J SIGNS AND GRAPHICS LLC
1345 N Sandhills Blvd Ste 1 (28315)
PHONE..........................910 315-2657
Jeremy White, *Owner*
▲ **EMP:** 4 **EST:** 2005
SALES (est): 262.38K **Privately Held**
Web: www.jsignsandgraphics.com
SIC: 3993 Signs, not made in custom sign painting shops

(G-10)
KOLCRAFT ENTERPRISES INC
10832 Nc 211 Hwy (28315-4722)
PHONE..........................910 944-9345
Dave Schuchard, *Mgr*
EMP: 169
SALES (corp-wide): 44.43MM **Privately Held**
Web: www.kolcraft.com
SIC: 2512 2511 Juvenile furniture: upholstered on wood frames; Wood household furniture
PA: Kolcraft Enterprises, Inc.
1100 W Monroe St Ste 200
Chicago IL 60607
312 361-6315

(G-11)
MCMURRAY FABRICS INC (PA)
105 Vann Pl (Sandhills Industrial Park) (28315-8612)
PHONE..........................910 944-2128
Brian L Mcmurray, *Pr*
Connie Mcmurray, *VP*
▲ **EMP:** 150 **EST:** 1968
SALES (est): 77.47MM
SALES (corp-wide): 77.47MM **Privately Held**
Web: www.mcmurrayfabrics.com
SIC: 2257 Weft knit fabric mills

(G-12)
MERIDIAN ZERO DEGREES LLC (PA)
Also Called: Meridian Kiosks
312 S Pine St (28315-2608)
PHONE..........................866 454-6757
Christopher Gilder, *Pr*
◆ **EMP:** 43 **EST:** 2005
SQ FT: 63,000
SALES (est): 22.54MM
SALES (corp-wide): 22.54MM **Privately Held**
Web: www.meridiankiosks.com
SIC: 2851 7373 Coating, air curing; Computer systems analysis and design

(G-13)
METAL & MATERIALS PROC LLC
3250 Nc Highway 5 (28315-8618)
PHONE..........................260 438-8901
Markus Novosel Dirdof, *Operations*
EMP: 6
SALES (corp-wide): 970.68K **Privately Held**
SIC: 2899 3356 Anti-glare material; Nickel
PA: Metal & Materials Processing, L.L.C.
1513 W Dallas St Ste 200
Houston TX 77019
713 664-0050

(G-14)
METCHEM INC
106 Jordan Pl (28315-8613)
P.O. Box 3879 (28374-3879)
PHONE..........................910 944-1405
Thomas V Cirigliano, *CEO*
Robert Morris, *CFO*
Elizabeth Cirigliano, *Sec*
▲ **EMP:** 6 **EST:** 1990
SALES (est): 1.75MM **Privately Held**
Web: www.cobalt-nickel.com
SIC: 3339 Cobalt refining (primary)

(G-15)
MFI PRODUCTS INC (HQ)
105 Vann Pl (28315-8612)
P.O. Box 950 (28315-0950)
PHONE..........................910 944-2128
Brian Mcmurray, *Pr*
▼ **EMP:** 15 **EST:** 1999
SQ FT: 20,000
SALES (est): 77.47MM
SALES (corp-wide): 77.47MM **Privately Held**
SIC: 5013 2211 Automotive hardware; Apparel and outerwear fabrics, cotton
PA: Mcmurray Fabrics, Inc.
105 Vann Pl
Aberdeen NC 28315
910 944-2128

(G-16)
MORGAN TOOL & DIE LLC
911 Rose Ridge Rd (28315-4510)
PHONE..........................910 281-0201
Steven Edward Emorgan, *Admn*
EMP: 7 **EST:** 2016
SALES (est): 165.33K **Privately Held**
Web: www.morgantoolanddie.com
SIC: 3599 Machine shop, jobbing and repair

(G-17)
NAFSHI ENTERPRISES LLC ✪
14796 Us Highway 15 501 (28315)
PHONE..........................910 986-9888
EMP: 9 **EST:** 2023
SALES (est): 356.22K **Privately Held**
SIC: 2099 7389 Food preparations, nec; Business Activities at Non-Commercial Site

(G-18)
NEON ROOSTER LLC
114 Knight St (28315-2804)
PHONE..........................330 806-7291
EMP: 4 **EST:** 2021
SALES (est): 76.29K **Privately Held**
Web: www.theneonrooster.com
SIC: 2813 Neon

(G-19)
OLIVE PINEHURST OIL CO
124 Newington Way (28315-2229)
PHONE..........................910 315-9923
EMP: 5 **EST:** 2014
SALES (est): 160K **Privately Held**
Web: www.thepinehurstoliveoilco.com
SIC: 2079 Olive oil

(G-20)
PACTIV LLC
3299 Nc Hwy 5 (28315)
P.O. Box 307 (28315-0307)
PHONE..........................910 944-1800
EMP: 5
Web: www.pactivevergreen.com
SIC: 2657 5199 Folding paperboard boxes; Packaging materials
HQ: Pactiv Llc
1900 W Field Ct
Lake Forest IL 60045
847 482-2000

(G-21)
PINNACLE FURNISHINGS INC
10570 Nc Highway 211 E Ste G (28315-4813)
PHONE..........................910 944-0908
Jack Berggren, *Pr*
▲ **EMP:** 38 **EST:** 1996
SQ FT: 45,000
SALES (est): 2.18MM **Privately Held**
Web: www.pinnaclefurnishings.com
SIC: 2599 Bar, restaurant and cafeteria furniture

(G-22)
PREMIER KIT & CABINETRY DESIGN
1705 Crest Dr (28315-3219)
PHONE..........................910 224-5018
EMP: 5 **EST:** 2019
SALES (est): 194.76K **Privately Held**
Web: www.premierkitchencabinetry.com
SIC: 2434 Wood kitchen cabinets

(G-23)
QUANTICO TACTICAL INCORPORATED
9796 Aberdeen Rd (28315-7742)
PHONE..........................910 944-5800
David Hensley, *CEO*
EMP: 30 **EST:** 2017
SALES (est): 2.23MM **Privately Held**
Web: www.quanticotactical.com
SIC: 2499 Picture and mirror frames, wood

(G-24)
RALEIGH SCREEN PRINT INC
307 Fields Dr (28315-8611)
PHONE..........................919 662-0358
Logan H King, *Pr*
EMP: 5 **EST:** 2018
SALES (est): 217.6K **Privately Held**
Web: www.raleighscreenprint.com
SIC: 2752 Commercial printing, lithographic

(G-25)
ROBS BACKHOE SERVICE
1215 Foxfire Rd (28315-5657)
PHONE..........................910 295-3317
EMP: 4 **EST:** 2017
SALES (est): 97.14K **Privately Held**
SIC: 3531 Backhoes

(G-26)
ROSITAS TORTILLAS INC
1317 N Sandhills Blvd (28315-2211)
PHONE..........................910 944-0577
Aguirre A Jessie, *Prin*
EMP: 6 **EST:** 2013
SALES (est): 224.39K **Privately Held**
Web: www.aberdeengrocerystore.com
SIC: 2099 Tortillas, fresh or refrigerated

(G-27)
ROSTRA PRECISION CONTROLS INC
Also Called: Marmon Powertrain Controls
3056 Nc Hwy 5 (28315-8673)
PHONE..........................910 291-2502
Jim Pineau, *CEO*
Pete Kallgren, *
▲ **EMP:** 100 **EST:** 1987
SQ FT: 80,000
SALES (est): 22.82MM
SALES (corp-wide): 24.47MM **Privately Held**
Web: www.rostra.com
SIC: 3714 3679 Acceleration equipment, motor vehicle; Solenoids for electronic applications
PA: Aftermarket Controls Corp.
2519 Dana Dr
Laurinburg NC 28352
910 291-2500

(G-28)
SANDHILLS SENTINEL INC
624 Longleaf Rd (28315-2126)
PHONE..........................910 944-0992
Bj Goodridge, *Prin*
EMP: 7 **EST:** 2017
SALES (est): 94.19K **Privately Held**
Web: www.sandhillssentinel.com
SIC: 2711 Newspapers, publishing and printing

(G-29)
SOUTHEASTERN TOOL & DIE INC
105 Taylor St (28315-2026)
PHONE..........................910 944-7677
Jimmy Thompson, *Pr*
Lynne C Thompson, *
Samuel Watson, *
Darlene Roberts, *
Peggy Kumm, *
◆ **EMP:** 85 **EST:** 1984
SQ FT: 105,000
SALES (est): 14.15MM **Privately Held**
Web: www.setoolinc.com
SIC: 3441 3544 3599 Fabricated structural metal; Special dies, tools, jigs, and fixtures; Machine shop, jobbing and repair

(G-30)
SPIRITUS SYSTEMS COMPANY
Also Called: Spiritus Systems
112 Bud Pl (28315-8617)
PHONE..........................910 637-0196
Adam Holroyd, *Admn*
▼ **EMP:** 50 **EST:** 2015
SQ FT: 10,000
SALES (est): 4.98MM **Privately Held**
Web: www.spiritussystems.com
SIC: 2389 Uniforms and vestments

(G-31)
TFAM SOLUTIONS LLC
Also Called: Decorative Def Con Coatings
134 Aqua Shed Ct (28315-8685)
PHONE..........................910 637-0266
Judith Thompson, *CEO*
Timothy Thompson, *Pr*
EMP: 8 **EST:** 2014
SALES (est): 843K **Privately Held**
SIC: 5075 3444 3545 Compressors, air conditioning; Casings, sheet metal; Chucks: drill, lathe, or magnetic (machine tool accessories)

(G-32)
THERMAL METAL TREATING INC
9546 Hwy 211 East (28315)
P.O. Box 367 (28315-0367)
PHONE..........................910 944-3636
Jerry Ritter, *Pr*
Mark A Scott, *
EMP: 24 **EST:** 1988
SQ FT: 60,000
SALES (est): 4MM **Privately Held**
Web: www.thermalmetal.com
SIC: 3398 Metal heat treating

(G-33)
TRAVIS ALFREY WOODWORKING INC
9988 Aberdeen Rd (28315-7740)
PHONE..........................910 639-3553

GEOGRAPHIC SECTION

Travis Alfrey, *Pr*
EMP: 4 **EST:** 2008
SALES (est): 304.57K **Privately Held**
SIC: 2434 Wood kitchen cabinets

(G-34)
VA COMPOSITES INC
707 S Pinehurst St Ste D (28315)
PHONE.................................844 474-2387
Victor Afable, *Pr*
Heather Afable, *Prin*
EMP: 5 **EST:** 2016
SALES (est): 410.31K **Privately Held**
Web: www.vashafts.com
SIC: 3949 Shafts, golf club

(G-35)
VINYL WINDOWS & DOORS CORP
165 Taylor St (28315-2026)
PHONE.................................910 944-2100
Carol Barbera, *Pr*
Mike Barbera Senior, *Sec*
EMP: 14 **EST:** 1985
SQ FT: 62,000
SALES (est): 1.62MM **Privately Held**
Web: www.vwdcorp.com
SIC: 3442 5031 5033 1761 Storm doors or windows, metal; Windows; Siding, except wood; Siding contractor

(G-36)
ZOALLC
131 Ampersand Rd (28315-8937)
PHONE.................................910 215-0235
Lauren Harper, *Prin*
EMP: 5 **EST:** 2010
SALES (est): 74.41K **Privately Held**
SIC: 3221 Medicine bottles, glass

Advance
Davie County

(G-37)
ASHLEY FURNITURE INDS LLC
Also Called: Ashley Furniture
333 Ashley Furniture Way (27006-8005)
PHONE.................................336 998-1066
EMP: 79
SALES (corp-wide): 4.17B **Privately Held**
Web: www.ashleyfurniture.com
SIC: 4225 5021 2511 General warehousing and storage; Furniture; Bed frames, except water bed frames: wood
PA: Ashley Furniture Industries, Llc
   1 Ashley Way
   Arcadia WI 54612
   608 323-3377

(G-38)
BEAUFURN LLC
Also Called: Beaufurn
5269 Us Highway 158 (27006-6905)
P.O. Box 1795 (27012-1795)
PHONE.................................336 768-2544
◆ **EMP:** 24 **EST:** 1996
SALES (est): 8.54MM **Privately Held**
Web: www.beaufurn.com
SIC: 2599 2531 5021 Bar, restaurant and cafeteria furniture; Assembly hall furniture; Office and public building furniture

(G-39)
CARDINAL CREEK CNDLES GFTS LLC
119 Alexandria Ct (27006-7315)
PHONE.................................336 941-3158
Melinda Osborne, *Owner*
EMP: 5 **EST:** 2017
SALES (est): 62.81K **Privately Held**
SIC: 3999 Candles

(G-40)
DAVIE PROPERTY RESTORATION LLC
177 Sourwood Ln (27006-6733)
PHONE.................................336 923-4018
Nicole Blalock, *Managing Member*
Roger Blalock, *Managing Member*
EMP: 4 **EST:** 2019
SALES (est): 218.18K **Privately Held**
Web: www.daviepropertyrestoration.com
SIC: 7389 1389 Business Activities at Non-Commercial Site; Construction, repair, and dismantling services

(G-41)
DIAMOND APPAREL
100 Webb Way (27006-6927)
PHONE.................................866 578-9708
EMP: 5 **EST:** 2019
SALES (est): 129.25K **Privately Held**
Web: www.diamondgolfshirts.com
SIC: 2253 Knit outerwear mills

(G-42)
FRISBY TECHNOLOGIES INC (PA)
136 Medical Dr (27006-6651)
PHONE.................................336 998-6652
Duncan R Russell, *Pr*
Douglas J Mccrosson, *Sec*
Mark Gillis, *CRO*
EMP: 10 **EST:** 1989
SQ FT: 20,000
SALES (est): 1.56MM **Privately Held**
SIC: 3086 Plastics foam products

(G-43)
INDAUX USA INC
548 Nc Highway 801 N (27006-7949)
PHONE.................................336 861-0740
Mikel Arzallus, *Pr*
EMP: 8 **EST:** 2015
SALES (est): 471.95K **Privately Held**
SIC: 3599 Industrial machinery, nec

(G-44)
IQ BRANDS INC (HQ)
129 Nc Highway 801 S (27006-7645)
PHONE.................................336 751-0040
John Robinson, *CEO*
Jeff Arnold, *
James Clegg, *
Teresa Bridges, *
Tom Bowlds, *
▲ **EMP:** 10 **EST:** 1999
SQ FT: 6,340
SALES (est): 14.25MM
SALES (corp-wide): 142.75MM **Privately Held**
Web: www.iqbrands.net
SIC: 2252 Men's, boys', and girls' hosiery
PA: Huron Capital Partners Llc
   500 Griswold St Ste 2700
   Detroit MI 48226
   313 962-5800

(G-45)
JONES FAB LLC
897 Underpass Rd (27006-7527)
PHONE.................................336 940-2769
Zebulon L Jones, *Asst Sec*
EMP: 5 **EST:** 2017
SALES (est): 75.99K **Privately Held**
SIC: 7692 Welding repair

(G-46)
MARY KAY INC
685 Redland Rd (27006-6724)
PHONE.................................336 998-1663
Hellen Bennett, *Owner*
EMP: 4 **EST:** 2018
SALES (est): 176.09K **Privately Held**
Web: www.marykay.com
SIC: 3599 Industrial machinery, nec

(G-47)
N2 PUBLISHING
161 Shallowbrook Dr (27006-6731)
PHONE.................................336 293-3845
Leslie Mccraw, *Prin*
EMP: 5 **EST:** 2017
SALES (est): 102.69K **Privately Held**
Web: www.strollmag.com
SIC: 2741 Miscellaneous publishing

(G-48)
PRO TOOL COMPANY INC
1765 Peoples Creek Rd (27006-7453)
P.O. Box 2253 (27006-2253)
PHONE.................................336 998-9212
Andrew L Mossman, *Pr*
Jace Hougland, *VP*
EMP: 19 **EST:** 1998
SQ FT: 19,000
SALES (est): 4.55MM **Privately Held**
Web: www.protoolcompany.com
SIC: 3599 Machine shop, jobbing and repair

(G-49)
SALEM PROFESSIONAL ANESTHESIA
128 Peachtree Ln Ste B (27006-6783)
PHONE.................................336 998-3396
Jim Nitz, *Owner*
EMP: 7 **EST:** 2006
SALES (est): 484.02K **Privately Held**
Web: www.salemanesthesia.com
SIC: 3841 Anesthesia apparatus

(G-50)
SHADOW SPRINGS VINEYARD INC
264 James Way (27006-8517)
P.O. Box 2352 (27006-2352)
PHONE.................................336 998-6598
Charles Johnson, *Prin*
EMP: 5 **EST:** 2014
SALES (est): 227.28K **Privately Held**
Web: www.shadowspringsvineyard.com
SIC: 2084 Wines

(G-51)
SORNIG CSTM WDWRKS THMAS SRNIG
349 Covington Dr (27006-7892)
PHONE.................................734 925-3905
EMP: 4 **EST:** 2017
SALES (est): 109.61K **Privately Held**
SIC: 2431 Millwork

(G-52)
TWG INC
Also Called: Simply Stitching
652 Nc Highway 801 S (27006-7633)
PHONE.................................336 998-9731
Lori L Walker, *Pr*
EMP: 4 **EST:** 2000
SALES (est): 248.62K **Privately Held**
Web: www.simplystitching.com
SIC: 2395 Embroidery products, except Schiffli machine

(G-53)
WINDSOR RUN CELLARS INC
264 James Way (27006-8517)
P.O. Box 2352 (27006-2352)
PHONE.................................336 998-6598
Charles D Johnson, *Prin*
EMP: 6 **EST:** 2012
SALES (est): 67.11K **Privately Held**
Web: www.windsorrun.com
SIC: 2084 Wines

Ahoskie
Hertford County

(G-54)
ALBEMRLE ORTHOTICS PROSTHETICS (PA)
103 Nc Highway 42 W (27910-9725)
PHONE.................................252 332-4334
Scott Truesdale, *Pr*
Kim Williamson, *VP*
EMP: 4 **EST:** 1998
SALES (est): 937.23K
SALES (corp-wide): 937.23K **Privately Held**
Web: www.albemarleop.com
SIC: 3842 3845 Orthopedic appliances; Electromedical equipment

(G-55)
BERRY GLOBAL INC
Also Called: Berry Plastics
228 Johnny Mitchell Rd (27910-9461)
PHONE.................................252 332-7270
EMP: 27
Web: www.berryglobal.com
SIC: 3089 Plastics containers, except foam
HQ: Berry Global, Inc.
   101 Oakley St
   Evansville IN 47710

(G-56)
BOONE NEWSPAPERS INC
Also Called: Gates County Index Shopper
801 Parker Ave E Ste 803 (27910-3641)
P.O. Box 1325 (27910-1325)
PHONE.................................252 332-2123
David Sullens, *Brnch Mgr*
EMP: 25
SALES (corp-wide): 60.7MM **Privately Held**
Web: www.boonenewsmedia.com
SIC: 2711 Job printing and newspaper publishing combined
PA: Boone Newsmedia, Inc.
   3933 Rice Mine Rd Ne
   Tuscaloosa AL 35406
   205 330-4100

(G-57)
BRITTENHAMS REBUILDING SERVICE
2314 Us Hwy13 S (27910-9483)
P.O. Box 40 (27910-0040)
PHONE.................................252 332-3181
Thomas Earl Brittenham, *Pr*
Cumin Brittenham, *VP*
Lorraine Harrell, *Sec*
EMP: 14 **EST:** 1965
SQ FT: 10,000
SALES (est): 364.96K **Privately Held**
Web: www.brittenhams.com
SIC: 7694 Electric motor repair

(G-58)
COMMERCIAL READY MIX PDTS INC
Also Called: Crmp
100 Hayes St E (27910-3125)
PHONE.................................252 332-3590
Bill Ballance, *Mgr*
EMP: 7
SALES (corp-wide): 52.99MM **Privately Held**
Web: www.crmpinc.com
SIC: 1771 3273 Concrete work; Ready-mixed concrete
PA: Commercial Ready Mix Products, Inc.

Ahoskie - Hertford County (G-59)

115 Hwy 158 W
Winton NC 27986
252 358-5461

(G-59)
D T BRACY LOGGING INC
520 Kiwanis St (27910-3618)
PHONE..................................252 332-8332
Darrell Bracy, *Owner*
EMP: 5 **EST:** 1981
SALES (est): 331.17K **Privately Held**
SIC: 2411 Logging camps and contractors

(G-60)
DARRELL T BRACY
Also Called: Barcy, D T Logging
520 Kiwanis St (27910-3618)
PHONE..................................252 358-1432
Darrell T Bracy, *Owner*
EMP: 5 **EST:** 1983
SALES (est): 267.61K **Privately Held**
SIC: 2411 Logging camps and contractors

(G-61)
ELECTRIC MOTOR SVC AHOSKIE INC
2103 Us Highway 13 S (27910-9481)
P.O. Box 711 (27910-0711)
PHONE..................................252 332-4364
Ernest Venable, *Pr*
EMP: 9 **EST:** 2008
SALES (est): 832.89K **Privately Held**
Web: www.ahoskiecoc.com
SIC: 5063 7694 Motors, electric; Electric motor repair

(G-62)
ENC INDUSTRIAL SUPPLY ✪
423 Railroad St N (27910-2619)
PHONE..................................252 862-8300
EMP: 4 **EST:** 2023
SALES (est): 79.3K **Privately Held**
SIC: 2842 Disinfectants, household or industrial plant

(G-63)
H T JONES LUMBER COMPANY
Also Called: Down East Molding Company
204 Catherine Creek Rd N (27910-3404)
P.O. Box 608 (27910-0608)
PHONE..................................252 332-4135
M C Jones Iii, *Pr*
W Frank Jones, *VP*
W E Jones, *Sec*
EMP: 11 **EST:** 1966
SQ FT: 60,000
SALES (est): 416.97K **Privately Held**
SIC: 2431 2426 Moldings, wood: unfinished and prefinished; Hardwood dimension and flooring mills

(G-64)
PERDUE FARMS INC
Also Called: PERDUE FARMS INC.
2108 Us Highway 13 S (27910-9481)
PHONE..................................252 348-4287
Randy Mclawhorn, *Brnch Mgr*
EMP: 35
SALES (corp-wide): 1.24B **Privately Held**
Web: www.perdue.com
SIC: 2015 Chicken, processed: fresh
PA: Perdue Farms Incorporated
31149 Old Ocean City Rd
Salisbury MD 21804
800 473-7383

(G-65)
ROANOKE CHOWAN READY MIX INC
108 Williford Rd (27910-9646)
P.O. Box 146 (27967-0146)
PHONE..................................252 332-7995
Rhedda Waters, *Pr*
Gerald Waters, *Sec*
EMP: 5 **EST:** 2000
SQ FT: 192
SALES (est): 616.04K **Privately Held**
SIC: 3273 Ready-mixed concrete

(G-66)
STANLEY E DIXON JR INC
Also Called: Stitch Count
113 Rail Road St (27910-3331)
PHONE..................................252 332-5004
Stanley Dixon, *Pr*
Pat Dixon, *Sec*
EMP: 5 **EST:** 1988
SQ FT: 5,500
SALES (est): 286.11K **Privately Held**
SIC: 2395 Embroidery and art needlework

(G-67)
WOOD WORKS OF AHOSKIE LLC
117 Williford Rd (27910-9647)
PHONE..................................252 287-7396
David Calderado, *Prin*
EMP: 4
SALES (est): 110K **Privately Held**
SIC: 2431 Millwork

Alamance
Alamance County

(G-68)
CONTINENTAL TICKING CORP AMER (PA)
4101 South Nc 62 (27201)
P.O. Box 39 (27201-0039)
PHONE..................................336 570-0091
Rudolf Schriner, *Pr*
Ernie Farley, *
John Bauman, *
◆ **EMP:** 75 **EST:** 1995
SALES (est): 28.05MM
SALES (corp-wide): 28.05MM **Privately Held**
Web: www.ctnassau.com
SIC: 2241 5131 Narrow fabric mills; Piece goods and notions

(G-69)
CT-NASSAU TAPE LLC
Also Called: Nassau Tape
4101 S N Carolina Hwy 62 (27201)
P.O. Box 39 (27201-0039)
PHONE..................................336 570-0091
Rudolph Schreiner, *Managing Member*
Rudolph Schreiner, *Managing Member*
◆ **EMP:** 100 **EST:** 1959
SQ FT: 100,000
SALES (est): 19.82MM
SALES (corp-wide): 28.05MM **Privately Held**
Web: www.ctnassau.com
SIC: 2241 Narrow fabric mills
PA: Continental Ticking Corporation Of America
4101 S Nc 62
Alamance NC 27201
336 570-0091

Albemarle
Stanly County

(G-70)
ALBEMARLE GLASS COMPANY INC
Also Called: Albemarle Glass and Stone
1217 Pee Dee Ave (28001-5142)
PHONE..................................704 982-3323
Pat Banakes, *Pr*
Dean Banakes, *VP*
Phyllis Coley, *Sec*
EMP: 9 **EST:** 1974
SQ FT: 20,000
SALES (est): 494.46K **Privately Held**
Web: www.albemarleglassinc.com
SIC: 1793 3231 Glass and glazing work; Products of purchased glass

(G-71)
ALBEMARLE TIRE RETREADING INC
542 W Main St (28001-4644)
PHONE..................................704 982-4113
Kent Cook, *Pr*
Sandra Cook, *VP*
Wade Jones, *Mgr*
EMP: 6 **EST:** 1935
SQ FT: 7,500
SALES (est): 842.06K **Privately Held**
SIC: 5531 7534 Automotive tires; Rebuilding and retreading tires

(G-72)
ALBEMARLE WOOD PRSV PLANT INC
1509 Snuggs Park Rd (28001)
P.O. Box 181 (28002-0181)
PHONE..................................704 982-2516
Thomas S Griffin, *Pr*
Cirrie W Kendall, *Sec*
Stephen Griffin, *VP*
EMP: 4 **EST:** 1961
SQ FT: 1,300
SALES (est): 988.02K **Privately Held**
SIC: 2491 Structural lumber and timber, treated wood

(G-73)
AMERICAN FIBER & FINISHING INC (PA)
Also Called: AF&f
225 N Depot St (28001-3914)
PHONE..................................704 984-9256
Paul Robichaud, *Pr*
Marcus Weibel, *
▲ **EMP:** 28 **EST:** 1986
SQ FT: 450,000
SALES (est): 9.67MM
SALES (corp-wide): 9.67MM **Privately Held**
Web: www.rymplecothwipers.com
SIC: 3842 2844 2392 2211 Surgical appliances and supplies; Perfumes, cosmetics and other toilet preparations; Household furnishings, nec; Basket weave fabrics, cotton

(G-74)
AURIA ALBEMARLE LLC
313 Bethany Rd (28001-8520)
P.O. Box 580 (28002-0580)
PHONE..................................704 983-5166
EMP: 285
SIC: 3714 Motor vehicle parts and accessories
HQ: Auria Albemarle, Llc
26999 Centrl Pk Blvd # 30
Southfield MI 48076
248 728-8000

(G-75)
BROOMES POULTRY INC
24816 Austin Rd (28001-8385)
PHONE..................................704 983-0965
Randy Honeycutt, *Owner*
Randy Huneycutt, *Owner*
EMP: 4 **EST:** 1996
SALES (est): 356.82K **Privately Held**
SIC: 2015 Poultry slaughtering and processing

(G-76)
BROWNS WOODWORKING LLC
210 Charter St (28001-8702)
PHONE..................................704 983-5917
EMP: 5 **EST:** 2001
SALES (est): 347.89K **Privately Held**
SIC: 2431 5712 Woodwork, interior and ornamental, nec; Customized furniture and cabinets

(G-77)
CREATIVE DYEING & FINSHG LLC ✪
2035 Kingsley Dr (28001-4473)
PHONE..................................704 983-5555
EMP: 11 **EST:** 2022
SALES (est): 592.58K **Privately Held**
SIC: 2295 Coated fabrics, not rubberized

(G-78)
CTX BUILDERS SUPPLY
2100 Sterling Dr (28001-5390)
PHONE..................................704 983-6748
Chris Borrego, *Mgr*
Chris Borrego, *Prin*
EMP: 4 **EST:** 2004
SALES (est): 249.04K **Privately Held**
SIC: 3555 Printing trades machinery

(G-79)
CUSTOM DOORS INCORPORATED
800 Laton Rd (28001-8607)
PHONE..................................704 982-2885
Michael P Laton Senior, *Pr*
Michael P Laton Junior, *VP*
Brooke E Laton, *Sec*
▲ **EMP:** 10 **EST:** 1967
SQ FT: 15,200
SALES (est): 974.48K **Privately Held**
Web: www.customdoorsinc.com
SIC: 2431 7521 Garage doors, overhead, wood; Parking garage

(G-80)
D & M PACKING COMPANY
687 Morgan Rd (28001-5653)
PHONE..................................704 982-3716
Gary H Langford, *Owner*
EMP: 13 **EST:** 1962
SQ FT: 10,000
SALES (est): 900.81K **Privately Held**
SIC: 2011 Meat packing plants

(G-81)
DAILY VICTORIES INC
1006 Colonial Dr (28001-2917)
PHONE..................................704 982-1341
Benjamin Newport, *Prin*
EMP: 4 **EST:** 2017
SALES (est): 69.29K **Privately Held**
SIC: 2711 Newspapers, publishing and printing

(G-82)
DEAN S READY MIXED INC
517 Old Charlotte Rd (28001-5750)
PHONE..................................704 982-5520
Dusty West, *Pr*
Jessy Hayes, *VP*
Vicki Burleson, *Sec*
Wanda Hayes, *Stockholder*
EMP: 20 **EST:** 1951
SQ FT: 700
SALES (est): 2.61MM **Privately Held**
Web: www.atlanticairinc.com
SIC: 3273 Ready-mixed concrete

GEOGRAPHIC SECTION
Albemarle - Stanly County (G-109)

(G-83)
ENFORGE LLC
1600 Woodhurst Ln (28001-5374)
PHONE.....................704 983-4146
EMP: 49 **EST:** 2009
SQ FT: 100,000
SALES (est): 19.67MM **Privately Held**
Web: www.enforgellc.com
SIC: 3559 Automotive related machinery
HQ: Angstrom Usa Llc
  26980 Trolley Indus Dr
  Taylor MI 48180
  313 295-0100

(G-84)
FABRICATED SOLUTIONS LLC
1210 Poplar St (28001-3130)
P.O. Box 429 (28002-0429)
PHONE.....................704 982-7789
Danny Storm, *Managing Member*
EMP: 8 **EST:** 2006
SALES (est): 957.94K **Privately Held**
Web: www.fabsolutionsnc.com
SIC: 3441 Fabricated structural metal

(G-85)
FLEET FIXERS INC
927a Concord Rd (28001-8332)
P.O. Box 958 (28002-0958)
PHONE.....................704 986-0066
Henry Kiefer, *Pr*
Annette Kiefer, *Sec*
EMP: 4 **EST:** 2003
SALES (est): 447.62K **Privately Held**
Web: www.fleetfitters.net
SIC: 3537 Trucks, tractors, loaders, carriers, and similar equipment

(G-86)
GENTRY MILLS INC
2035 Kingsley Dr (28001-4473)
PHONE.....................704 983-5555
▲ **EMP:** 60 **EST:** 1992
SQ FT: 175,000
SALES (est): 10.63MM **Privately Held**
Web: www.gentrymills.com
SIC: 5131 3999 Textiles, woven, nec; Atomizers, toiletry

(G-87)
GMD LOGGING INC
44100 Dennis Rd (28001-7662)
PHONE.....................704 985-5460
Gregory Mark Dennis, *Pr*
EMP: 9 **EST:** 2016
SALES (est): 238.57K **Privately Held**
SIC: 2411 Logging

(G-88)
GRIFFIN MANUFACTURING LLC
210b Charter St (28001-8702)
PHONE.....................704 984-2070
EMP: 4 **EST:** 2019
SALES (est): 152.55K **Privately Held**
Web: www.griffincommercialflooring.com
SIC: 3999 Manufacturing industries, nec

(G-89)
HAMMOND ELECTRIC MOTOR COMPANY
811 Concord Rd (28001-8331)
PHONE.....................704 983-3178
Wayne Hoffman, *Pr*
Steven Hoffman, *VP*
EMP: 13 **EST:** 1960
SQ FT: 6,250
SALES (est): 901.23K **Privately Held**
Web: www.hammondelectricmotors.com
SIC: 7694 5063 Electric motor repair; Motors, electric

(G-90)
HUNTPACK INC
320 Anderson Rd (28001-8103)
PHONE.....................704 986-0684
Marc Hunt, *Pr*
Rick Armstrong, *VP*
Jennifer Michelle, *Sec*
EMP: 5 **EST:** 1997
SQ FT: 12,000
SALES (est): 362.27K **Privately Held**
Web: www.phoenixflexographic.com
SIC: 2752 2754 Tag, ticket, and schedule printing: lithographic; Labels: gravure printing

(G-91)
JENSEN ACTIVEWEAR
703 Concord Rd (28001-9301)
PHONE.....................704 982-3005
Theresa Blalock, *Mgr*
EMP: 4 **EST:** 2020
SALES (est): 142.57K **Privately Held**
Web: www.jensenapparel.com
SIC: 2321 Men's and boy's furnishings

(G-92)
KEEP STANLY BEAUTIFUL CORP
505 Muirfield Dr (28001-2843)
PHONE.....................704 982-2649
Sandra P Rogers, *Admn*
EMP: 5 **EST:** 2010
SALES (est): 82.68K **Privately Held**
SIC: 2434 Wood kitchen cabinets

(G-93)
KRAFTSMAN TACTICAL INC
1650 Woodhurst Ln (28001-5374)
PHONE.....................336 465-3576
Michael Kaufman, *Pr*
EMP: 5 **EST:** 2017
SALES (est): 292.81K **Privately Held**
Web: www.kraftsmantrailers.com
SIC: 2759 Promotional printing

(G-94)
LAMBERTS INDUSTRIES
1012 N 6th St (28001-3566)
PHONE.....................980 244-0898
Ellen Lambert, *Prin*
EMP: 4 **EST:** 2018
SALES (est): 60.43K **Privately Held**
SIC: 3999 Manufacturing industries, nec

(G-95)
LUCKY TUSK
1465 Us 52 North (28001-2601)
PHONE.....................704 985-1127
EMP: 5 **EST:** 2012
SALES (est): 132.54K **Privately Held**
Web: luckytusk.food-places.com
SIC: 2084 Wines

(G-96)
M & R FORESTRY SERVICE INC
24062 Sam Rd (28001-9032)
P.O. Box 2012 (28002-2012)
PHONE.....................980 439-1261
Lelis Mejia, *Pr*
Lelis Noel Mejia, *Owner*
EMP: 4 **EST:** 2011
SALES (est): 441.17K **Privately Held**
SIC: 0851 3448 Forestry services; Carports, prefabricated metal

(G-97)
MARTIN SPROCKET & GEAR INC
306 Bethany Rd (28001-8520)
PHONE.....................817 258-3000
Jimmy Mcswain, *Mgr*
EMP: 12
SALES (corp-wide): 292.47MM **Privately Held**
Web: www.martinsprocket.com
SIC: 3566 3568 Gears, power transmission, except auto; Power transmission equipment, nec
PA: Martin Sprocket & Gear, Inc.
  3100 Sprocket Dr
  Arlington TX 76015
  817 258-3000

(G-98)
NABELL USA CORPORATION
208 Charter St (28001-8702)
PHONE.....................704 986-2455
Don Stewart, *Pr*
EMP: 20 **EST:** 1998
SQ FT: 6,000
SALES (est): 3.11MM **Privately Held**
Web: www.nabell.com
SIC: 3599 3861 Bellows, industrial: metal; Sensitized film, cloth, and paper

(G-99)
PREFORMED LINE PRODUCTS CO
1700 Woodhurst Ln (28001-5376)
P.O. Box 818 (28002-0818)
PHONE.....................704 983-6161
John Ziebarth, *Mgr*
EMP: 168
SQ FT: 277,547
SALES (corp-wide): 669.68MM **Publicly Held**
Web: www.plp.com
SIC: 3644 3496 3229 3643 Pole line hardware; Miscellaneous fabricated wire products; Pressed and blown glass, nec; Current-carrying wiring services
PA: Preformed Line Products Company
  660 Beta Dr
  Mayfield Village OH 44143
  440 461-5200

(G-100)
QUALITY HOME FASHIONS INC
28569 Flint Ridge Rd (28001-8004)
PHONE.....................704 983-5906
Tony Hill, *Pr*
EMP: 5 **EST:** 1995
SQ FT: 50,000
SALES (est): 148.99K **Privately Held**
SIC: 2392 Sheets, fabric: made from purchased materials

(G-101)
R & S PRECISION CUSTOMS LLC
338 E Main St (28001-4922)
PHONE.....................704 984-3480
EMP: 4 **EST:** 2015
SALES (est): 77.71K **Privately Held**
SIC: 3482 Small arms ammunition

(G-102)
RAM INDUSTRIES INC
Also Called: Martin Industries
1135 Montgomery Ave (28001-4328)
P.O. Box 2252 (28002-2252)
PHONE.....................704 982-4015
Roger Martin, *Pr*
Gina Martin, *
▲ **EMP:** 10 **EST:** 1981
SQ FT: 95,000
SALES (est): 484.74K **Privately Held**
SIC: 3083 Plastics finished products, laminated

(G-103)
SAN KAWA LLC
403 W Main St (28001-4641)
PHONE.....................704 982-4527
Steve Morgan, *Owner*
EMP: 4 **EST:** 2020
SALES (est): 77.82K **Privately Held**
SIC: 3229 Pressed and blown glass, nec

(G-104)
SECURE CANOPY LLC
1215 Pineview St (28001-3048)
P.O. Box 833 (28002-0833)
PHONE.....................980 322-0590
EMP: 5 **EST:** 2013
SQ FT: 2,000
SALES (est): 302.28K **Privately Held**
Web: www.securecanopy.com
SIC: 3651 Video camera-audio recorders, household use

(G-105)
SMITH NOVELTY COMPANY INC
2120 W Main St (28001-5424)
PHONE.....................704 982-7413
Janet Swaringen, *Treas*
EMP: 7 **EST:** 1942
SQ FT: 20,000
SALES (est): 605.16K **Privately Held**
Web: www.smithnovelty.com
SIC: 2512 Chairs: upholstered on wood frames

(G-106)
SOUTH CENTRAL OIL AND PRPN INC
2121 W Main St (28001-5423)
PHONE.....................704 982-2173
Garrison J Banks, *Prin*
EMP: 7 **EST:** 2016
SALES (est): 2.64MM
SALES (corp-wide): 4.75MM **Privately Held**
Web: www.southcentraloil.com
SIC: 5172 1321 Petroleum products, nec; Propane (natural) production
PA: South Central Oil Co., Inc.
  2121 W Main St
  Albemarle NC 28001
  704 982-2173

(G-107)
SOUTHERN MARBLE CO LLC
2033 W Main St (28001-5421)
PHONE.....................704 982-4142
Donald Fincher, *Managing Member*
EMP: 6 **EST:** 1990
SQ FT: 12,000
SALES (est): 300K **Privately Held**
SIC: 3281 5719 5032 Marble, building: cut and shaped; Bath accessories; Marble building stone

(G-108)
SOUTHERN PIPE INC
445 N 4th St (28001-4021)
PHONE.....................704 550-5935
Bryan Mitchell, *Brnch Mgr*
EMP: 16
SALES (corp-wide): 14.87MM **Privately Held**
Web: www.southern-pipe.com
SIC: 3084 Plastics pipe
PA: Southern Pipe, Inc.
  135 Random Dr
  New London NC 28127
  704 463-5202

(G-109)
STONY GAP WHOLESALE CO INC
40616c Stony Gap Rd Ste C (28001-8151)

Albemarle - Stanly County (G-110)

P.O. Box 1016 (28002-1016)
PHONE...................................704 982-5360
John Lowder, *Pr*
Vicky Audy, *Mgr*
EMP: 7 **EST:** 1970
SALES (est): 307.46K **Privately Held**
SIC: 2099 5149 Cole slaw, in bulk; Groceries and related products, nec

(G-110)
SURE TRIP INC (PA)
703a Concord Rd (28001-9301)
PHONE...................................704 983-4651
Bill Penniston, *Pr*
Joel Henson, *VP*
EMP: 11 **EST:** 1996
SALES (est): 976.73K
SALES (corp-wide): 976.73K **Privately Held**
Web: www.suretrip.com
SIC: 3625 Industrial controls: push button, selector switches, pilot

(G-111)
TRITON GLASS LLC
232 S 1st St (28001-4809)
PHONE...................................704 982-4333
Hemant Patel, *Managing Member*
EMP: 6 **EST:** 2014
SALES (est): 775.32K **Privately Held**
Web: www.tritonglassllc.com
SIC: 3231 Tempered glass: made from purchased glass

(G-112)
WALTER PRINTING COMPANY INC
Also Called: Walter Tape & Label Co
130 Anderson Rd (28001-8114)
P.O. Box 10 (28002-0010)
PHONE...................................704 982-8899
Donald A Walter, *Pr*
Lillian Walter, *Sec*
EMP: 18 **EST:** 1957
SQ FT: 2,600
SALES (est): 698.78K **Privately Held**
Web: www.walterprinting.net
SIC: 2752 Offset printing

(G-113)
WENDYS EMBRDRED SPC SCREEN PRT
308 Concord Rd (28001-3606)
PHONE...................................704 982-5978
Wendy Lingerfelt, *Owner*
Randy Lingerfelt, *Pr*
EMP: 10 **EST:** 1991
SQ FT: 2,800
SALES (est): 653.71K **Privately Held**
Web: www.embroideredspecialties.com
SIC: 2395 Embroidery products, except Schiffli machine

Albertson
Duplin County

(G-114)
BAY VALLEY FOODS LLC
2953 N Nc 111 903 Hwy (28508-9635)
PHONE...................................715 366-4511
Dwight Jepson, *Brnch Mgr*
EMP: 100
SALES (corp-wide): 3.45B **Publicly Held**
Web: www.bayvalleyfoods.com
SIC: 2099 Food preparations, nec
HQ: Bay Valley Foods, Llc
3200 Riverside Dr Ste A
Green Bay WI 54301
800 558-4700

(G-115)
EAST COAST LOG & TIMBER INC
305 Kator Dunn Rd (28508-9629)
PHONE...................................252 568-4344
Nicholas Sholar, *Prin*
EMP: 9 **EST:** 2018
SALES (est): 416.62K **Privately Held**
SIC: 2411 Logging

(G-116)
TIMOTHY KORNEGAY
550 Woodland Church Rd (28508-9610)
PHONE...................................919 222-3184
Timothy Kornegay, *Prin*
EMP: 5 **EST:** 2005
SALES (est): 234.91K **Privately Held**
SIC: 2411 Logging

Alexander
Buncombe County

(G-117)
BLUE/GRAY BOOKS
804 Macedonia Rd (28701-0078)
PHONE...................................828 254-3972
EMP: 4 **EST:** 2019
SALES (est): 71.42K **Privately Held**
Web: www.blue-gray.com
SIC: 2731 Book publishing

(G-118)
G A LANKFORD CONSTRUCTION
Also Called: Hayfield Auto Sales
333 Old Nc 20 Hwy (28701)
PHONE...................................828 254-2467
Gary A Lankford, *Pr*
Diane Lankford, *Sec*
EMP: 4 **EST:** 1979
SALES (est): 393.3K **Privately Held**
SIC: 1521 2511 5521 New construction, single-family houses; Wood household furniture; Automobiles, used cars only

(G-119)
REECEWREATHANDCRAFTSETSYCOM
121 Old Nc 20 Hwy (28701)
PHONE...................................828 252-6228
Teresa Jarvis, *Prin*
EMP: 4 **EST:** 2017
SALES (est): 122.67K **Privately Held**
SIC: 3999 Wreaths, artificial

(G-120)
SOUTHERN CLASSIC STAIRS INC
24 Carl Roberts Rd (28701-9118)
PHONE...................................828 285-9828
Louis E Coker Junior, *Pr*
EMP: 8 **EST:** 1992
SQ FT: 3,500
SALES (est): 260.6K **Privately Held**
SIC: 2431 Staircases, stairs and railings

Alexis
Gaston County

(G-121)
ALLOY FABRICATORS INC
334 Alexis High Shoals Rd (28006)
P.O. Box 779 (28164-0779)
PHONE...................................704 263-2281
Jeffrey R Fisher, *Pr*
Donnie Fisher, *
Michael D Fisher, *
Donald K Fisher, *
EMP: 35 **EST:** 1966
SQ FT: 15,000
SALES (est): 8.57MM **Privately Held**
Web: www.alloyfab.net
SIC: 3443 7692 3444 3429 Metal parts; Welding repair; Sheet metalwork; Hardware, nec

Altamahaw
Alamance County

(G-122)
GLEN RAVEN INC
Also Called: Glen Touch Division
3726 Altamahaw Union Ridge Rd (27202)
P.O. Box 8 (27202-0008)
PHONE...................................336 227-6211
Charlie Edgerton, *Brnch Mgr*
EMP: 6
SALES (corp-wide): 878.83MM **Privately Held**
Web: www.glenraven.com
SIC: 2251 2282 Women's hosiery, except socks; Throwing and winding mills
PA: Glen Raven, Inc.
192 Glen Raven Rd
Burlington NC 27217
336 227-6211

Andrews
Cherokee County

(G-123)
ACCENT AWNINGS INC (PA)
91 Morgan Rd (28901-0739)
P.O. Box 1950 (28901-1950)
PHONE...................................828 321-4517
J A Rodeck, *Pr*
EMP: 10 **EST:** 1986
SQ FT: 8,000
SALES (est): 842.13K **Privately Held**
Web: www.accentawningsinc.com
SIC: 2394 1799 Awnings, fabric: made from purchased materials; Awning installation

(G-124)
ANDREWS TRUSS INC
47 Mcclelland Creek Rd (28901-7310)
P.O. Box 1429 (28901-1429)
PHONE...................................828 321-3105
Jonathan Chapman, *Pr*
Holly Chapman, *Sec*
EMP: 21 **EST:** 1990
SQ FT: 14,000
SALES (est): 4.74MM **Privately Held**
Web: www.andrewstruss.com
SIC: 2439 Trusses, wooden roof

(G-125)
CREATIVE PRINTERS & BRKS INC
Also Called: Creative Printers
980 Main St (28901-7087)
P.O. Box 757 (28901-0757)
PHONE...................................828 321-4663
William K Moore, *Pr*
Sherry Moore, *Sec*
Virginia Moore, *Treas*
Thomas Moore, *VP*
EMP: 6 **EST:** 1967
SALES (est): 491.29K **Privately Held**
Web: www.creativeprintersandbrokers.com
SIC: 2752 7389 Offset printing; Printing broker

(G-126)
INDUSTRIAL OPPORTUNITIES INC
Also Called: Elastic Products
2586 Business 19 (28901-8044)
P.O. Box 1649 (28901-1649)
PHONE...................................828 321-4754
EMP: 345 **EST:** 1974
SALES (est): 3.58MM **Privately Held**
Web: www.industrialopportunities.com
SIC: 2211 2395 8331 Elastic fabrics, cotton; Looping: for the trade; Job training and related services

(G-127)
JUNALUSKA MILL ENGINEERING
181 Gipp Creek Rd (28901-7200)
P.O. Box 2625 (28901-2625)
PHONE...................................828 321-3693
EMP: 5 **EST:** 1967
SQ FT: 5,000
SALES (est): 380K **Privately Held**
SIC: 3532 Mining machinery

(G-128)
TEAM INDUSTRIES INC
3750 Airport Rd (28901-7493)
PHONE...................................828 837-5377
David W Ricke, *Brnch Mgr*
EMP: 113
Web: www.team-ind.com
SIC: 8711 3599 Engineering services; Machine shop, jobbing and repair
HQ: Team Industries, Inc.
105 Park Ave Nw
Bagley MN 56621
218 694-3550

(G-129)
WILLIAMS SIGNS
1025 Main St (28901-5502)
P.O. Box 459 (28901-0459)
PHONE...................................828 321-2338
Dean Williams, *Owner*
EMP: 5 **EST:** 2001
SALES (est): 138.54K **Privately Held**
Web: www.williamssigns.com
SIC: 3993 Signs and advertising specialties

Angier
Harnett County

(G-130)
ADVANCE SIGNS & SERVICE INC
596 W Church St (27501-6052)
P.O. Box 1090 (27501-1090)
PHONE...................................919 639-4666
Scott Brown, *Pr*
Marcel Brown Junior, *VP*
EMP: 20 **EST:** 1990
SQ FT: 15,000
SALES (est): 2.38MM **Privately Held**
Web: www.advancesignservice.net
SIC: 1799 3993 Sign installation and maintenance; Signs and advertising specialties

(G-131)
ARS EXTREME CONSTRUCTION INC
175 Medical Dr (27501-6029)
P.O. Box 959 (27501-0959)
PHONE...................................919 331-8024
Sherry Harvey, *Pr*
Roger Harvey, *VP*
EMP: 23 **EST:** 2006
SALES (est): 445.75K **Privately Held**
Web: www.arsextreme.com
SIC: 1761 3441 Roofing contractor; Fabricated structural metal

(G-132)
BLACK RIVER WOODWORK LLC
574 N Broad St E (27501-8953)
PHONE...................................919 757-4559
Robert M Jusnes Senior, *Admn*

GEOGRAPHIC SECTION   Apex - Wake County (G-157)

EMP: 9 EST: 2013
SALES (est): 455.62K **Privately Held**
SIC: 2431 Millwork

(G-133)
BRICK & MORTAR GRILL
8 N Broad St E Ste 200 (27501-5638)
PHONE..........................919 639-9700
EMP: 4 EST: 2014
SALES (est): 126.2K **Privately Held**
Web: www.brickandmortargrill.com
SIC: 2024 5812 Ice cream and frozen deserts; Grills (eating places)

(G-134)
BULLDOG HOSE COMPANY LLC
141 Junny Rd (27501-8625)
PHONE..........................919 639-6151
EMP: 25 EST: 2018
SALES (est): 2.12MM **Privately Held**
Web: www.puck.com
SIC: 3492 Hose and tube couplings, hydraulic/pneumatic

(G-135)
C & D FABRICATIONS INC
199 Fabrication Ln (27501-7201)
P.O. Box 1778 (27501-1778)
PHONE..........................919 639-2489
Donny Hawley, *Pr*
Ricky Armentrout, *VP*
Sharon Broadwell, *Sec*
EMP: 13 EST: 1988
SQ FT: 5,600
SALES (est): 420.25K **Privately Held**
SIC: 3499 Machine bases, metal

(G-136)
CAROLINA SIGN SVC
174 Kinnis Creek Dr (27501-9591)
P.O. Box 127 (27501-0127)
PHONE..........................919 247-0927
Jaimie Parker, *Pr*
EMP: 6 EST: 2018
SALES (est): 245.11K **Privately Held**
Web: www.carolinasignandservice.com
SIC: 3993 Signs and advertising specialties

(G-137)
CHEROKEE INSTRUMENTS INC (PA)
Also Called: Amp-Cherokee Envmtl Solutions
100 Logan Ct (27501-8579)
PHONE..........................919 552-0554
EMP: 18 EST: 1995
SQ FT: 20,000
SALES (est): 6.42MM **Privately Held**
Web: www.ampcherokee.com
SIC: 7359 3829 7699 Equipment rental and leasing, nec; Measuring and controlling devices, nec; Scientific equipment repair service

(G-138)
CUSTOM SMILES INC
Also Called: Joy Dental Lab
123 Fish Dr Ste 101 (27501-9345)
PHONE..........................919 331-2090
Michael Creech, *Pr*
EMP: 17 EST: 2005
SQ FT: 6,200
SALES (est): 949.13K **Privately Held**
Web: www.customsmilesinc.com
SIC: 3843 Dental equipment and supplies

(G-139)
GREGORY VINEYARDS
275 Bowling Spring Dr (27501-9052)
PHONE..........................919 427-9409
EMP: 5 EST: 2018
SALES (est): 141.33K **Privately Held**
Web: www.gregoryvineyards.com
SIC: 2084 Wines

(G-140)
HEATMASTER LLC (PA)
3625 Benson Rd (27501-7380)
PHONE..........................919 639-4568
Scott Michaels, *Pr*
▲ EMP: 44 EST: 1974
SQ FT: 100,000
SALES (est): 6.06MM
SALES (corp-wide): 6.06MM **Privately Held**
Web: www.heatmaster.com
SIC: 3317 Conduit: welded, lock joint, or heavy riveted

(G-141)
INNOVATIVE DESIGN TECH LLC
Also Called: Rhinoshelf.com
475 S Raleigh St (27501-8256)
P.O. Box 2296 (27501-2296)
PHONE..........................919 331-0204
EMP: 7 EST: 2010
SALES (est): 824.64K **Privately Held**
Web: www.rhinoshelf.com
SIC: 5046 2542 Shelving, commercial and industrial; Shelving, office and store, except wood

(G-142)
J &D CONTRACTOR SERVICE INC
246 Scotts Ln (27501-7078)
PHONE..........................919 427-0218
Lee Johnson, *Pr*
Lee Scott Johnson, *Pr*
Dustin Lee Johnson, *VP*
Julie Bolton, *Sec*
EMP: 5 EST: 2017
SALES (est): 400.31K **Privately Held**
SIC: 7389 1521 1799 1389 Business Activities at Non-Commercial Site; Single-family housing construction; Construction site cleanup; Construction, repair, and dismantling services

(G-143)
L L C BATTERIES OF N C
101 Medical Dr (27501-6029)
P.O. Box 1969 (27546-1969)
PHONE..........................919 331-0241
Lonnie D Scott Junior, *Managing Member*
Ruth Scott, *Prin*
EMP: 5 EST: 2003
SALES (est): 2.45MM **Privately Held**
Web: www.batteriesofnc.com
SIC: 5063 5531 3692 Batteries; Auto and home supply stores; Primary batteries, dry and wet

(G-144)
LA ESTRELLA INC
61 W Williams St (27501-7277)
PHONE..........................919 639-6559
Fortino Rios, *Owner*
EMP: 4 EST: 1994
SALES (est): 243.91K **Privately Held**
Web: la-estrella.edan.io
SIC: 2051 Bread, cake, and related products

(G-145)
LEGACY DESIGNS & GRAPHX LLC
198 Windsor Dr (27501-8801)
PHONE..........................910 237-2916
Christina Kazakavage, *Prin*
EMP: 4 EST: 2017
SALES (est): 257.8K **Privately Held**
Web: www.legacydesignsgraphx.com
SIC: 3993 Signs and advertising specialties

(G-146)
LWS TOOLS INC
1139 Mabry Rd (27501-7685)
PHONE..........................919 247-1913
William Saddlemire, *Prin*
EMP: 6 EST: 2015
SALES (est): 206.94K **Privately Held**
SIC: 3599 Industrial machinery, nec

(G-147)
NATIONAL FOAM INC (PA)
Also Called: Angus Fire
141 Junny Rd (27501-8625)
PHONE..........................919 639-6100
Paul Williams, *CEO*
Hank Shaefer, *VP*
◆ EMP: 20 EST: 2013
SALES (est): 10.27MM
SALES (corp-wide): 10.27MM **Privately Held**
Web: www.nationalfoam.com
SIC: 3569 2899 5012 Firefighting and related equipment; Foam charge mixtures; Fire trucks

(G-148)
NATIONAL FOAM INC
Also Called: Angus Fire
141 Junny Rd (27501-8625)
PHONE..........................919 639-6151
Willy Brown, *Mgr*
EMP: 117
SALES (corp-wide): 10.27MM **Privately Held**
Web: www.nationalfoam.com
SIC: 5087 3052 3494 2241 Service establishment equipment; Rubber and plastics hose and beltings; Valves and pipe fittings, nec; Narrow fabric mills
PA: National Foam, Inc.
141 Junny Rd
Angier NC 27501
919 639-6100

(G-149)
R L LASATER PRINTING
32 E Depot St (27501-6017)
PHONE..........................919 639-6662
R L Lasater, *Prin*
EMP: 7 EST: 2004
SALES (est): 379.88K **Privately Held**
SIC: 2752 Commercial printing, lithographic

(G-150)
TRIMSTERS INC
150 West Rd (27501-6968)
PHONE..........................919 639-3126
Shawn Ogni, *Pr*
John F Ogni, *VP*
EMP: 17 EST: 1999
SQ FT: 5,000
SALES (est): 2.08MM **Privately Held**
Web: www.trimstersinc.com
SIC: 2431 Woodwork, interior and ornamental, nec

(G-151)
UNDER GODS AUTHORITY
108 High Standard Ln (27501-7293)
PHONE..........................910 891-1789
Mitchell K Williams, *Prin*
EMP: 9 EST: 2020
SALES (est): 852K **Privately Held**
SIC: 1389 Construction, repair, and dismantling services

Ansonville
Anson County

(G-152)
ANSONVILLE PIPING & FABG INC
122 Ansonville Polkton Rd (28007)
P.O. Box 394 (28007-0394)
PHONE..........................704 826-8403
Kenneth Wayne Pope, *Pr*
William Martin, *VP*
Brandon Pope, *VP*
EMP: 9 EST: 1975
SQ FT: 9,000
SALES (est): 229.4K **Privately Held**
SIC: 1711 7692 1791 Process piping contractor; Welding repair; Structural steel erection

(G-153)
NAT BLACK LOGGING INC
Mcbride Rd (28007)
P.O. Box 779 (28007-0779)
PHONE..........................704 826-8834
James Nathaniel Black, *Pr*
Carol P Black, *Sec*
Barry James, *VP*
EMP: 11 EST: 1976
SALES (est): 489.55K **Privately Held**
SIC: 2411 Logging camps and contractors

(G-154)
NICHOLSONS PALLET SERVICES INC
122 Ansonville Polkton Rd (28007)
P.O. Box 295 (28007-0295)
PHONE..........................704 826-8405
James Nicholson, *Pr*
Rasheda Nicholson, *VP*
Nakia Mcmendon, *Off Mgr*
EMP: 8 EST: 2015
SQ FT: 4,700
SALES (est): 67.51K **Privately Held**
SIC: 2448 Pallets, wood

(G-155)
PREMIERE FIBERS LLC
10056 Hwy 52 N (28007)
PHONE..........................704 826-8321
◆ EMP: 160 EST: 1999
SQ FT: 1,500
SALES (est): 24.96MM
SALES (corp-wide): 116.86MM **Privately Held**
Web: www.premierefibers.com
SIC: 2282 Throwing and winding mills
PA: Universal Fiber Systems, Llc
14401 Industrial Park Rd
Bristol VA 24202
276 669-1161

Apex
Wake County

(G-156)
ACCU-TOOL LLC
2490 Reliance Ave (27539-6331)
PHONE..........................919 363-2600
EMP: 15 EST: 1982
SQ FT: 12,000
SALES (est): 2.97MM **Privately Held**
Web: www.accutool.net
SIC: 3599 Machine shop, jobbing and repair

(G-157)
AIRCRAFT PARTS SOLUTIONS LLC
3378 Apex Peakway (27502-6310)
P.O. Box 3511 (29910-3511)

PHONE.................................843 300-1725
Todd Chambers, *Managing Member*
EMP: 4 **EST:** 2019
SALES (est): 484.89K **Privately Held**
Web: www.aps.parts
SIC: 3728 Aircraft parts and equipment, nec

(G-158)
ALTARAVISION INC
130 Salem Towne Ct (27502-2311)
PHONE.................................919 342-5778
Stuart Bradley, *CEO*
EMP: 4 **EST:** 2011
SALES (est): 471.23K **Privately Held**
Web: www.ndohd.com
SIC: 3845 Electromedical equipment

(G-159)
AMERICAN PHYSCL SEC GROUP LLC
1030 Goodworth Dr (27539-3869)
PHONE.................................919 363-1894
Kristen Mckenna, *Admn*
EMP: 8 **EST:** 2008
SQ FT: 10,000
SALES (est): 182.97K **Privately Held**
Web: www.americanpsg.com
SIC: 7382 3699 8712 Protective devices, security; Security control equipment and systems; Architectural engineering

(G-160)
APEX EMBROIDERY INC
996 Ambergate Sta (27502-2431)
PHONE.................................919 793-6083
EMP: 7 **EST:** 2009
SALES (est): 99.7K **Privately Held**
Web: www.apexembdesigns.com
SIC: 2395 Embroidery products, except Schiffli machine

(G-161)
APEX PRINTING COMPANY
514 E Williams St (27502-2183)
P.O. Box 1357 (27502-3357)
PHONE.................................919 362-9856
Hayden Woodard, *Owner*
EMP: 4 **EST:** 1977
SQ FT: 5,200
SALES (est): 234.15K **Privately Held**
Web: www.zebraprintsolutions.com
SIC: 2752 Offset printing

(G-162)
APEX SALSA COMPANY
912 N York Ct (27502-4647)
PHONE.................................919 363-1486
EMP: 4 **EST:** 2010
SALES (est): 195.67K **Privately Held**
Web: www.apexsalsa.com
SIC: 2099 Dips, except cheese and sour cream based

(G-163)
APEX SKIP-ITS LLC
1806 Keokuk Ct (27523-5108)
PHONE.................................919 270-1752
EMP: 5 **EST:** 2014
SALES (est): 132.91K **Privately Held**
Web: www.apexskipits.com
SIC: 2298 Cordage and twine

(G-164)
APEX TOOL GROUP LLC
Also Called: Apex Facility and Dist Ctr
1000 Lufkin Rd (27523-8160)
PHONE.................................919 387-0099
Mike Cox, *Ex Dir*
EMP: 128
SALES (corp-wide): 1.8MM **Privately Held**
Web: www.apextoolgroup.com
SIC: 3546 Power-driven handtools
HQ: Apex Tool Group, Llc
  910 Ridgebrook Rd Ste 200
  Sparks Glencoe MD 21152

(G-165)
ARISAKA LLC
Also Called: Arisaka
1600 Olive Chapel Rd Ste 260 (27502-6764)
PHONE.................................919 601-5625
EMP: 12 **EST:** 2014
SALES (est): 969.87K **Privately Held**
Web: www.arisakadefense.com
SIC: 3484 7389 Guns (firearms) or gun parts, 30 mm. and below; Business Activities at Non-Commercial Site

(G-166)
ASCO POWER TECHNOLOGIES LP
3412 Apex Peakway (27502-5756)
PHONE.................................919 460-5200
EMP: 112
SALES (corp-wide): 82.05K **Privately Held**
Web: www.ascopower.com
SIC: 3699 Electrical equipment and supplies, nec
HQ: Asco Power Technologies, L.P.
  160 Park Ave
  Florham Park NJ 07932

(G-167)
ATI INDUSTRIAL AUTOMATION INC (DH)
1031 Goodworth Dr (27539-3869)
PHONE.................................919 772-0115
Robert D Little, *Pr*
Keith A Morris, *
Dwayne M Perry, *
EMP: 122 **EST:** 1989
SQ FT: 8,000
SALES (est): 54.26MM **Publicly Held**
Web: www.ati-ia.com
SIC: 3823 3674 Process control instruments; Semiconductors and related devices
HQ: Novanta Corporation
  125 Middlesex Tpke
  Bedford MA 01730
  781 266-5700

(G-168)
AUTOSMART INC
510 Fairview Rd (27502-1306)
PHONE.................................919 210-7936
Thomas W Lewis, *Pr*
EMP: 6 **EST:** 2006
SQ FT: 5,500
SALES (est): 464.33K **Privately Held**
Web: www.driveautosmart.com
SIC: 7534 Tire repair shop

(G-169)
AXCCELLUS LLC
2501 Schieffelin Rd (27502-4431)
PHONE.................................919 589-9800
EMP: 10 **EST:** 2015
SALES (est): 2.1MM **Privately Held**
Web: www.axccellus.com
SIC: 3599 3444 Custom machinery; Machine guards, sheet metal

(G-170)
BARNES PRECISION MACHINE INC
1434 Farrington Rd Ste 300 (27523-5728)
PHONE.................................919 362-6805
EMP: 18 **EST:** 1992
SQ FT: 11,000
SALES (est): 1.24MM **Privately Held**
Web: www.usamade-ar15parts.com
SIC: 3599 Machine shop, jobbing and repair

(G-171)
BIORESOURCE INTERNATIONAL INC
Also Called: Apex Manufacturing Facility
2000 N Salem St (27523-8206)
PHONE.................................919 267-3758
EMP: 8 **EST:** 2017
SALES (est): 365.27K **Privately Held**
Web: www.briworldwide.com
SIC: 2834 Pharmaceutical preparations

(G-172)
BLUE GAS MARINE INC
2528 Schieffelin Rd (27502-7000)
PHONE.................................919 238-3427
Miguel Guerreiro, *CEO*
EMP: 10 **EST:** 2012
SALES (est): 2.04MM **Privately Held**
Web: www.bluegasmarine.com
SIC: 3519 4924 Internal combustion engines, nec; Natural gas distribution

(G-173)
BRUCATO POWER INC
122 N Salem St Ste 201 (27502-1564)
PHONE.................................919 234-1776
Kimberly Hudson, *Prin*
EMP: 6 **EST:** 2018
SALES (est): 223.07K **Privately Held**
Web: www.brucatopower.com
SIC: 3714 Motor vehicle parts and accessories

(G-174)
BUILDERS FRSTSRCE - RLEIGH LLC
23 Red Cedar Way (27523-8401)
PHONE.................................919 363-4956
Dennis Darling, *Mgr*
EMP: 55
SALES (corp-wide): 17.1B **Publicly Held**
Web: www.bldr.com
SIC: 2439 5211 Trusses, wooden roof; Lumber and other building materials
HQ: Builders Firstsource - Raleigh, Llc.
  401 Valley Forge Rd
  Hillsborough NC 27278
  919 644-1231

(G-175)
CABINET CONNECTION OF NC INC
1015 Tribayne Ct (27502-2425)
PHONE.................................919 653-1300
Eric Villeneuve, *Pr*
EMP: 4 **EST:** 2007
SALES (est): 404.13K **Privately Held**
Web: www.cabinetconnectionofnc.com
SIC: 2434 Wood kitchen cabinets

(G-176)
COMPUTATIONAL ENGRG INTL INC (HQ)
Also Called: C E I
2166 N Salem St Ste 101 (27523-6456)
PHONE.................................919 363-0883
Anders Grimsrud, *Pr*
EMP: 26 **EST:** 1994
SQ FT: 4,200
SALES (est): 5.5MM
SALES (corp-wide): 2.27B **Publicly Held**
Web: nexusdemo.ensight.com
SIC: 7372 7371 Prepackaged software; Computer software development and applications
PA: Ansys, Inc.
  2600 Ansys Dr
  Canonsburg PA 15317
  844 462-6797

(G-177)
CONMECH INDUSTRIES LLC
117 Beaver Creek Rd (27502-8011)
PHONE.................................919 306-6228
Jason Stephenson, *Prin*
EMP: 7 **EST:** 2016
SALES (est): 224.73K **Privately Held**
Web: www.conmechindustries.com
SIC: 3999 Manufacturing industries, nec

(G-178)
CREATIVEMARK CANVAS LLC
78 Old Grove Ln (27502-1894)
PHONE.................................919 267-4660
Peter Zeitler, *Prin*
EMP: 5 **EST:** 2018
SALES (est): 46.58K **Privately Held**
SIC: 2211 Canvas

(G-179)
DAMSEL IN DEFENSE
2821 Evans Rd (27502-9691)
PHONE.................................919 362-5972
EMP: 31 **EST:** 2014
SALES (est): 145.39K **Privately Held**
Web: www.damselindefense.net
SIC: 3812 Defense systems and equipment

(G-180)
DAVOSPHARMA
4009 Harriat Dr (27539-7634)
PHONE.................................919 662-8432
Marc Caddell, *Prin*
EMP: 6 **EST:** 2011
SALES (est): 232K **Privately Held**
SIC: 2834 Pharmaceutical preparations

(G-181)
DECARLO WOODWORKS
4917 Mashpee Ln (27539-4111)
PHONE.................................919 327-3647
Mike Decarlo, *Prin*
EMP: 4 **EST:** 2010
SALES (est): 55.62K **Privately Held**
Web: www.decarlowoodworks.com
SIC: 2431 Millwork

(G-182)
DIGITON CORP
4205 Holly Stream Ct (27539-7682)
PHONE.................................919 601-4826
Beth W Mullaney, *Prin*
EMP: 5 **EST:** 2011
SALES (est): 119.72K **Privately Held**
SIC: 3572 Computer storage devices

(G-183)
DOCENT PHARMA SERVICES LLC
1533 Armscroft Ln (27502-8608)
PHONE.................................229 310-0111
EMP: 4
SALES (est): 66.98K **Privately Held**
Web: www.docentpharma.com
SIC: 2834 Pharmaceutical preparations

(G-184)
DUMPSTER MATE LLC
2600 Hilltop Farms Rd (27502-6715)
PHONE.................................919 303-7402
EMP: 5 **EST:** 2016
SALES (est): 178.28K **Privately Held**
Web: www.dumpstermate.com
SIC: 3443 Dumpsters, garbage

(G-185)
DUTCHMAN CREEK SELF-STORAGE
8712 Holly Springs Rd (27539-9120)
PHONE.................................919 363-8878
Paul Brewer, *Pt*
Joe Thompson, *Pt*

GEOGRAPHIC SECTION
Apex - Wake County (G-213)

Webb White, *Pt*
Randy Miller, *Pt*
Laura Thompson, *Pt*
EMP: 5 **EST:** 2001
SALES (est): 203.27K **Privately Held**
Web: www.dcselfstorage.com
SIC: 7692 7513 Welding repair; Truck rental and leasing, no drivers

(G-186)
EAGLE ROCK CONCRETE LLC
Also Called: Apex Plant
500 Pristine Water Dr (27539-7206)
PHONE.................................919 596-7077
EMP: 44
SALES (corp-wide): 22.33MM **Privately Held**
Web: www.eaglerockconcrete.com
SIC: 3273 Ready-mixed concrete
PA: Eagle Rock Concrete Llc
8310 Bandford Way
Raleigh NC 27615
919 781-3744

(G-187)
ECODYST INC
Also Called: Ecodyst
1010 Goodworth Dr (27539-3869)
PHONE.................................919 599-4963
George Adjabeng, *Pr*
Kwabena Williams, *VP*
EMP: 6 **EST:** 2014
SALES (est): 1.09MM **Privately Held**
Web: www.ecodyst.com
SIC: 3821 Distilling apparatus, laboratory type

(G-188)
EJ USA INC
Also Called: Ej
1006 Investment Blvd (27502-1954)
P.O. Box 186 (27502-0186)
PHONE.................................919 362-7744
Gordon Wells, *Mgr*
EMP: 6
Web: www.ejco.com
SIC: 3321 Gray and ductile iron foundries
HQ: Ej Usa, Inc.
301 Spring St
East Jordan MI 49727
800 874-4100

(G-189)
ELLISMORRIS LLC
1908 Creekside Landing Dr (27502-3985)
PHONE.................................646 538-1870
Oding Ellis, *Managing Member*
EMP: 4 **EST:** 2021
SALES (est): 41.52K **Privately Held**
SIC: 2499 Food handling and processing products, wood

(G-190)
FARO10 LLC
105 Hasbrouck Dr (27523-3814)
PHONE.................................757 285-8069
EMP: 5 **EST:** 2016
SALES (est): 85.78K **Privately Held**
SIC: 7372 Prepackaged software

(G-191)
FERNEL THERAPEUTICS INC
408 Gablefield Ln (27521-1358)
PHONE.................................919 614-2375
Matthew Fraiser, *Pr*
EMP: 4 **EST:** 2021
SALES (est): 149.26K **Privately Held**
SIC: 3845 Electromedical apparatus

(G-192)
FORBES CUSTOM CABINETS LLC
Also Called: Forbes Fixtures
2025 Production Dr (27539-6349)
PHONE.................................919 362-4277
EMP: 28
SIC: 2542 Cabinets: show, display, or storage: except wood

(G-193)
FOUNDRY A PRINT CMMNCTIONS LLC
Also Called: Foundry, The
2725 Abruzzo Dr (27502-4742)
PHONE.................................703 329-3300
Michael Cialdella, *Pr*
EMP: 9 **EST:** 2006
SALES (est): 289.3K **Privately Held**
SIC: 2731 2711 7336 Book publishing; Commercial printing and newspaper publishing combined; Commercial art and graphic design

(G-194)
GEOTRAK INCORPORATED
2521 Schieffelin Rd Ste 136 (27502-4400)
PHONE.................................919 303-1467
Keith Lesage, *COO*
Donald Lesage, *CEO*
Judith Ann Lesage, *Pr*
Ann Evans, *Stockholder*
Margaret Schlereth, *Stockholder*
EMP: 12 **EST:** 1999
SALES (est): 912.95K **Privately Held**
Web: www.geotrakinc.com
SIC: 3679 Electronic circuits

(G-195)
GINGER SUPREME INC
4925 Lett Rd (27539-6629)
P.O. Box 1292 (27502-3292)
PHONE.................................919 812-8986
Randolph Duncan, *Pr*
Wendy Duncan, *Sec*
EMP: 4 **EST:** 2003
SALES (est): 310.65K **Privately Held**
Web: gingersupremedrinks.square.site
SIC: 2086 Soft drinks: packaged in cans, bottles, etc.

(G-196)
GOEMBEL INC
Also Called: The Design Center
7303 Vanclaybon Rd (27523-4110)
PHONE.................................919 303-0485
Patrick Goembel, *Pr*
Dina Goembel, *VP*
EMP: 10 **EST:** 1994
SQ FT: 3,000
SALES (est): 1.2MM **Privately Held**
SIC: 1521 2434 Single-family home remodeling, additions, and repairs; Wood kitchen cabinets

(G-197)
GRAPHIX SOLUTION INC
Also Called: Gxs Wraps
1094 Classic Rd (27539-4401)
PHONE.................................919 213-0371
EMP: 12 **EST:** 2018
SALES (est): 493.89K **Privately Held**
Web: www.graphixsolutionnc.com
SIC: 3993 Signs and advertising specialties

(G-198)
GRIFFIN MOTION LLC
1040 Classic Rd (27539-4401)
P.O. Box 1298 (27540-1298)
PHONE.................................919 577-6333
▲ **EMP:** 15 **EST:** 2005
SQ FT: 2,500
SALES (est): 2.2MM **Privately Held**
Web: www.griffinmotion.com
SIC: 3625 Motor controls and accessories

(G-199)
GRITS AND GRAVEL SERVICES LLC
251 Meadow Beauty Dr (27539-7623)
PHONE.................................919 758-8975
Daniel Walker Linville, *Owner*
EMP: 5 **EST:** 2017
SALES (est): 130.83K **Privately Held**
SIC: 1442 Construction sand and gravel

(G-200)
HARRISON FENCE INC
1680 E Williams St (27539-7703)
P.O. Box 828 (27502-0828)
PHONE.................................919 244-6908
Rob Harrison, *Pr*
Shauna Harrison, *CFO*
EMP: 8 **EST:** 2004
SQ FT: 1,000
SALES (est): 1.48MM **Privately Held**
Web: www.harrisonfence.com
SIC: 1799 3315 Fence construction; Chain link fencing

(G-201)
HBB GLOBAL LLC
8324 Covington Hill Way (27539-7939)
PHONE.................................615 306-1270
Hong Baker, *Prin*
EMP: 4 **EST:** 2014
SALES (est): 96.79K **Privately Held**
SIC: 2323 Men's and boy's neckwear

(G-202)
HIMCEN BATTERY INC
Also Called: Himcen Battery
2313 Blue Cedar Ct (27523-7155)
PHONE.................................408 828-8744
Soon Duck Kim, *CEO*
Chang Kyum Kim, *Pr*
EMP: 9 **EST:** 2019
SALES (est): 546.6K **Privately Held**
Web: www.himcenbattery.com
SIC: 3692 Dry cell batteries, single or multiple cell

(G-203)
IFANATIC LLC (PA)
105 Shalon Ct (27502-9019)
PHONE.................................919 387-6062
▲ **EMP:** 5 **EST:** 2006
SALES (est): 626.53K **Privately Held**
Web: www.i-fanatic.com
SIC: 3629 Electronic generation equipment

(G-204)
IMAGINATION FABRICATION
810 Center St (27502-1714)
PHONE.................................919 280-4430
Nicholas Spring, *Owner*
Nick String, *Owner*
▼ **EMP:** 6 **EST:** 2009
SALES (est): 524.8K **Privately Held**
Web: www.ncimaginationfabrication.com
SIC: 7692 Welding repair

(G-205)
INDUSTRIAL MOTIONS INC
1401 Boxwood Ln (27502-1505)
PHONE.................................734 284-8944
Frank Murray, *Owner*
EMP: 7 **EST:** 1961
SALES (est): 92.3K **Privately Held**
Web: www.industrial-motions.com
SIC: 2752 Commercial printing, lithographic

(G-206)
INNOVA-CON INCORPORATED
2521 Schieffelin Rd Ste 136 (27502-4400)
PHONE.................................919 303-1467
Keith Lesage, *Brnch Mgr*
EMP: 6
SALES (corp-wide): 626.53K **Privately Held**
SIC: 3679 Electronic circuits
PA: Innova-Con, Incorporated
8501 Potobac Shores Rd
Port Tobacco MD 20677
301 934-0481

(G-207)
INNOVATIVE MFG SOLUTIONS INC
675 Wooded Lake Dr (27523-6017)
PHONE.................................919 219-2424
EMP: 8 **EST:** 2017
SALES (est): 73.45K **Privately Held**
Web: www.imsigroup.com
SIC: 3469 Metal stampings, nec

(G-208)
JACK STEVENS INC
833 Us 64 Hwy W (27523-7188)
PHONE.................................919 363-8589
Daran Thomas, *Prin*
EMP: 6 **EST:** 2019
SALES (est): 121.84K **Privately Held**
Web: www.jackstevensinc.com
SIC: 2741 Miscellaneous publishing

(G-209)
JM WILLIAMS TIMBER COMPANY
4525 Green Level West Rd (27523-7301)
PHONE.................................919 362-1333
EMP: 4 **EST:** 1995
SALES (est): 466.39K **Privately Held**
SIC: 1629 2411 Timber removal; Timber, cut at logging camp

(G-210)
JUSTNEEM LLC
Also Called: Justneem Body Care
2416 Maxton Crest Dr (27539-7485)
PHONE.................................919 414-8826
◆ **EMP:** 5 **EST:** 2007
SALES (est): 336.17K **Privately Held**
Web: www.justneem.com
SIC: 3999 Chairs, hydraulic, barber and beauty shop

(G-211)
KLIERSOLUTIONS
4041 Brook Cross Dr (27539-8870)
PHONE.................................919 806-1287
Korey Klier, *Prin*
EMP: 6 **EST:** 2017
SALES (est): 134.68K **Privately Held**
Web: www.kleinertfamily.com
SIC: 3861 Photographic equipment and supplies

(G-212)
LARRY BISSETTE INC
8012 Dirt Rd (27529-6849)
P.O. Box 232 (27526-0232)
PHONE.................................919 773-2140
EMP: 12 **EST:** 1972
SALES (est): 659.79K **Privately Held**
SIC: 1761 3444 Roofing contractor; Sheet metalwork

(G-213)
LEARNING CRAFTSMEN INC
1000 Chedington Dr (27502-8881)
PHONE.................................813 321-5003
Jonathan Mckeown, *CEO*
Caitlin Mckeown, *Pr*

Apex - Wake County (G-214)   GEOGRAPHIC SECTION

Sara Healy, *VP*
EMP: 4 **EST:** 2015
SALES (est): 197.21K **Privately Held**
SIC: 5999 7372 7379 7389 Educational aids and electronic training materials; Educational computer software; Online services technology consultants

(G-214)
LIGHTHOUSE PRESS INC
5448 Apex Peakway (27502-3924)
PHONE....................919 371-8640
EMP: 5 **EST:** 2018
SALES (est): 46.57K **Privately Held**
Web: www.lighthouse-press.com
SIC: 2741 Miscellaneous publishing

(G-215)
MADERN USA INC
1010 Burma Dr (27539-5021)
PHONE....................919 363-4248
Jean H R Madern, *Pr*
▲ **EMP:** 40 **EST:** 1997
SQ FT: 45,000
SALES (est): 9.89MM **Privately Held**
Web: www.madern.com
SIC: 3544 Special dies and tools

(G-216)
MC PRECAST CONCRETE INC
520 Pristine Water Dr (27539-7206)
P.O. Box 189 (27502-0189)
PHONE....................919 367-3636
Raymond Duchaine, *Pr*
Chantale Duchaine, *
EMP: 55 **EST:** 1996
SQ FT: 30,000
SALES (est): 2.24MM **Privately Held**
SIC: 3272 Concrete products, precast, nec

(G-217)
MELLINEUM PRINTING
2015 Production Dr (27539-6349)
PHONE....................919 267-5752
Charles E Norton, *Pr*
Lorraine C Norton, *VP*
EMP: 10 **EST:** 1973
SQ FT: 5,000
SALES (est): 658.13K **Privately Held**
SIC: 2752 Offset printing

(G-218)
MERCURY SIGNS INC
Also Called: Custom Sgns - Dsign Mnfcture I
7306 Vanclaybon Rd (27523-4110)
PHONE....................919 808-1205
Hamid Lalani, *CEO*
EMP: 6 **EST:** 2019
SALES (est): 342.52K **Privately Held**
Web: www.mercurysignsinc.com
SIC: 3993 Signs and advertising specialties

(G-219)
MIL3 INC
500 Upchurch St (27502-1872)
PHONE....................919 362-1217
Pam Cleland, *Ex VP*
John Cleland, *Pr*
EMP: 10 **EST:** 1993
SQ FT: 3,200
SALES (est): 493.64K **Privately Held**
Web: www.pexcrimpusa.com
SIC: 3423 Plumbers' hand tools

(G-220)
MONO PLATE INC
2404 Pilsley Rd (27539-9048)
PHONE....................631 643-3100
Michael Bader, *Pr*
Harvey Bader, *VP*
EMP: 8 **EST:** 1965
SALES (est): 633.79K **Privately Held**
SIC: 3559 Rubber working machinery, including tires

(G-221)
OFM INC
1003 Investment Blvd Ste A (27502-0139)
PHONE....................919 303-6389
Coy Beamlett, *Admn*
EMP: 5 **EST:** 2016
SALES (est): 214.04K **Privately Held**
Web: www.ofminc.com
SIC: 2211 Furniture denim

(G-222)
ON-SITE HOSE INC
1001 Goodworth Dr (27539-3802)
P.O. Box 2216 (27502-2238)
PHONE....................919 303-3840
Andrew Brumsey, *Pr*
EMP: 5 **EST:** 2005
SALES (est): 912.27K **Privately Held**
Web: www.on-sitehose.com
SIC: 3492 Hose and tube couplings, hydraulic/pneumatic

(G-223)
OTTAWAY ASSOCIATES LLC
1300 Wimberly Rd (27523-6772)
PHONE....................919 467-9988
Danny Ottaway, *Managing Member*
EMP: 4 **EST:** 2017
SALES (est): 67.37K **Privately Held**
SIC: 2711 Newspapers

(G-224)
PACRIM INC
1041 Classic Rd (27539-4402)
P.O. Box 1839 (27502-2839)
PHONE....................919 363-7711
Tilak M Shah, *Pr*
Phil Robra, *Ex VP*
EMP: 20 **EST:** 1998
SQ FT: 14,000
SALES (est): 327.16K **Privately Held**
Web: www.pacrim-inc.com
SIC: 3081 Plastics film and sheet

(G-225)
PAPERWHITES PRESS
3134 Mantle Ridge Dr (27502-6616)
PHONE....................855 348-9848
Sarah Litty, *Prin*
EMP: 5 **EST:** 2010
SALES (est): 116.46K **Privately Held**
SIC: 2741 Miscellaneous publishing

(G-226)
PARHELION INCORPORATED
Also Called: Stripelight
126 N Salem St Ste 200 (27502-1476)
P.O. Box 5456 (27512-5456)
PHONE....................866 409-1839
James Redpath, *CEO*
Richard Redpath, *Pr*
Larry Switzer, *Dir*
EMP: 14 **EST:** 2010
SQ FT: 12,000
SALES (est): 1.65MM **Privately Held**
Web: www.parhelion.com
SIC: 3648 Lighting equipment, nec

(G-227)
PATRICIA SCHAEFER
5448 Apex Peakway (27502-3924)
PHONE....................919 302-2726
Patrick Seither, *Admn*
EMP: 5 **EST:** 2018
SALES (est): 137.93K **Privately Held**
SIC: 2741 Miscellaneous publishing

(G-228)
PEAK CITY CANDLES INC
916 Branch Line Ln (27502-2430)
PHONE....................919 601-8223
EMP: 5 **EST:** 2017
SALES (est): 62.54K **Privately Held**
Web: www.peakcity.church
SIC: 3999 Candles

(G-229)
PEAK STEEL LLC
1610 N Salem St (27523-9498)
PHONE....................919 362-5955
EMP: 17 **EST:** 2005
SALES (est): 2.54MM **Privately Held**
Web: www.peaksteel.com
SIC: 3441 Building components, structural steel

(G-230)
PERFECT MATCH CANDLES LLC
609 Culvert St (27502-1772)
PHONE....................919 482-6649
Stephanie Godwin, *Owner*
EMP: 5 **EST:** 2017
SALES (est): 70.16K **Privately Held**
Web: www.perfectmatchcandles.com
SIC: 3999 Candles

(G-231)
PIRATE PRESS LLC
104 Trackimire Ln (27539-9013)
PHONE....................919 720-2736
Daniel Smith, *Prin*
EMP: 5 **EST:** 2017
SALES (est): 60.26K **Privately Held**
SIC: 2741 Miscellaneous publishing

(G-232)
POLYZEN LLC
Also Called: Polyzen, Inc.
1041 Classic Rd (27539-4402)
P.O. Box 1299 (27502-3299)
PHONE....................919 319-9599
EMP: 65 **EST:** 1997
SQ FT: 32,000
SALES (est): 15.56MM
SALES (corp-wide): 64.21MM **Privately Held**
Web: www.polyzen.com
SIC: 3841 Diagnostic apparatus, medical
PA: The Secant Group Llc
   551 E Church Ave
   Telford PA 18969
   877 774-2835

(G-233)
PROGRESSIVE INDUSTRIES INC
1020 Goodworth Dr (27539-3869)
PHONE....................919 267-6948
EMP: 6 **EST:** 2018
SALES (est): 133.53K **Privately Held**
Web: www.progressiveindustries.net
SIC: 3999 Manufacturing industries, nec

(G-234)
PROPANE TRUCKS & TANKS INC (PA)
1600 E Williams St (27539-7703)
P.O. Box 340 (27502-0340)
PHONE....................919 362-5000
Paul Harris, *CEO*
Laura Kedzierzawski, *CFO*
John S Jay Wooten Iii, *Sec*
EMP: 12 **EST:** 1969
SQ FT: 5,000
SALES (est): 1.88MM
SALES (corp-wide): 1.88MM **Privately Held**
Web: www.propanetrucksandtanks.com
SIC: 3713 3711 3537 Truck bodies (motor vehicles); Motor vehicles and car bodies; Industrial trucks and tractors

(G-235)
PSNC ENERGY
2451 Schieffelin Rd (27502-6330)
PHONE....................919 367-2735
Gary Burney, *Mgr*
EMP: 9 **EST:** 2008
SALES (est): 341.86K **Privately Held**
Web: www.dominionenergy.com
SIC: 5722 5064 3639 Electric household appliances, major; Electrical appliances, major; Major kitchen appliances, except refrigerators and stoves

(G-236)
QUARRIES PETROLEUM
2540 Schieffelin Rd (27502-7000)
PHONE....................919 387-0986
EMP: 4 **EST:** 2007
SALES (est): 83.07K **Privately Held**
SIC: 1422 Crushed and broken limestone

(G-237)
QUILLSEDGE PRESS INC
365 Anterbury Dr (27502-4713)
PHONE....................410 207-0841
Jane Seitel, *Pr*
EMP: 5 **EST:** 2017
SALES (est): 75.28K **Privately Held**
SIC: 2741 Miscellaneous publishing

(G-238)
R & J MECHANICAL & WELDING LLC
Also Called: R&J Custom Exhaust
554 E Williams St (27502-2151)
PHONE....................919 362-6630
Robert Lowery, *Managing Member*
EMP: 7 **EST:** 1985
SQ FT: 3,200
SALES (est): 907.5K **Privately Held**
SIC: 7538 7692 General automotive repair shops; Welding repair

(G-239)
RENAISSANCE INNOVATIONS LLC (PA)
Also Called: Madame Gigi's Cottage
1322 Gloriosa St (27523-4105)
PHONE....................844 473-7246
James Corwin, *CEO*
EMP: 7 **EST:** 2016
SALES (est): 2.32MM
SALES (corp-wide): 2.32MM **Privately Held**
Web: www.retique.com
SIC: 2851 3991 5198 Paints and allied products; Paint and varnish brushes; Paints

(G-240)
S T WOOTEN CORPORATION
Also Called: Apex/Pittsboro Concrete Plant
51 Red Cedar Way (27523-8401)
PHONE....................919 363-3141
Scott Wooten, *Pr*
EMP: 22
SALES (corp-wide): 319.83MM **Privately Held**
Web: www.stwcorp.com
SIC: 3531 Concrete plants
PA: S. T. Wooten Corporation
   3801 Black Creek Rd Se
   Wilson NC 27893
   252 291-5165

GEOGRAPHIC SECTION

Archdale - Guilford County (G-269)

(G-241)
SAS SOLUTIONS INC
Also Called: Sitework Solutions
1449 Luther Rd (27523-3711)
PHONE..................919 369-4424
EMP: 8 **EST:** 2013
SALES (est): 348.96K Privately Held
SIC: 7372 Application computer software

(G-242)
SIGN SHOP OF THE TRIANGLE INC
4001 Midstream Ct (27539-6319)
PHONE..................919 363-3930
Nicole C Rowe, *Pr*
EMP: 5 **EST:** 2005
SALES (est): 283.19K Privately Held
Web: www.gosignshop.com
SIC: 3993 7389 Signs and advertising specialties; Business Activities at Non-Commercial Site

(G-243)
SPIDER PRESS INC
303 Hinton St (27502-1423)
PHONE..................919 302-2726
Patricia Schaefer, *Prin*
EMP: 6 **EST:** 2010
SALES (est): 75.08K Privately Held
SIC: 2741 Miscellaneous publishing

(G-244)
SPRANTO AMERICA INC
1870 Lazio Ln (27502-4753)
PHONE..................919 741-5095
Simon Horne, *Prin*
Xiaoke Chen, *Prin*
EMP: 5 **EST:** 2012
SALES (est): 219.84K Privately Held
Web: www.spranto.com
SIC: 7372 Application computer software

(G-245)
STEVENSON WOODWORKING
300 Hickory View Ln (27502-6599)
PHONE..................919 362-9121
Gregory Stevenson, *Prin*
EMP: 5 **EST:** 2005
SALES (est): 125.11K Privately Held
SIC: 2431 Millwork

(G-246)
SUNG INDUSTRIES INC
204 Kellyridge Dr (27502-9608)
PHONE..................919 387-8550
Ichael Edward Kilpatrick, *Prin*
EMP: 4 **EST:** 2018
SALES (est): 39.69K Privately Held
SIC: 3999 Manufacturing industries, nec

(G-247)
SWEETGRAN PRINTS
2410 Vetrina Way (27502-7747)
PHONE..................919 387-0711
Kathryn Nash, *Prin*
EMP: 5 **EST:** 2008
SALES (est): 196.38K Privately Held
SIC: 2752 Commercial printing, lithographic

(G-248)
TIGERSWAN LLC
3453 Apex Peakway (27502-5757)
PHONE..................919 439-7110
James Reese, *Ch*
Michael Biglin, *
Niki Taylor, *
Scott Cullather, *
Zachary Venegas, *
EMP: 120 **EST:** 2005
SALES (est): 20.42MM Privately Held
Web: www.tigerswan.com

SIC: 1542 3728 Nonresidential construction, nec; Military aircraft equipment and armament

(G-249)
TIPPER TIE INC (HQ)
2000 Lufkin Rd (27539-7068)
PHONE..................919 362-8811
Charlie Rogers, *VP*
◆ **EMP:** 179 **EST:** 1980
SQ FT: 130,000
SALES (est): 47.48MM Publicly Held
Web: www.jbtc.com
SIC: 3556 Meat processing machinery
PA: John Bean Technologies Corporation
70 W Madison St Ste 4400
Chicago IL 60602

(G-250)
TRAUMTIC DRECT TRNSFSION DVCS
1007 Woodbriar St (27502-1371)
PHONE..................423 364-5828
Michael Stout, *Mgr*
EMP: 4 **EST:** 2018
SALES (est): 103.91K Privately Held
SIC: 3841 Surgical and medical instruments

(G-251)
TRIANGLE CUSTOM CABINETS INC
807 Center St (27502-1713)
P.O. Box 1327 (27502-3327)
PHONE..................919 387-1133
Jack P Truelove, *Pr*
Mark Hearn, *VP*
EMP: 7 **EST:** 1989
SQ FT: 3,700
SALES (est): 792K Privately Held
SIC: 2541 Cabinets, lockers, and shelving

(G-252)
TRIANGLE INSTALLATION SVC INC
2445 Reliance Ave (27539-7012)
PHONE..................919 363-7637
John D Abood, *Pr*
Marilyn Abood, *Sec*
EMP: 8 **EST:** 1975
SQ FT: 7,000
SALES (est): 881.14K Privately Held
Web: www.carygutters.com
SIC: 3444 1761 Gutters, sheet metal; Gutter and downspout contractor

(G-253)
VINTAGE SOUTH INC
1100 Chimney Hill Dr (27502-8824)
P.O. Box 7 (27502-0007)
PHONE..................919 362-4079
Vic Lloyd, *Pr*
EMP: 5 **EST:** 1997
SALES (est): 560.69K Privately Held
SIC: 5149 2099 Condiments; Food preparations, nec

(G-254)
VISION TECHNOLOGIES INC
8509 Smith Rd (27539-8169)
PHONE..................919 387-7878
EMP: 10 **EST:** 1994
SALES (est): 993.35K Privately Held
Web: www.vision-technologies.com
SIC: 3643 Lightning arrestors and coils

(G-255)
VISITECH SYSTEMS INC
1012 Napa Pl (27502-7125)
PHONE..................919 387-0524
James P Rogers Iii, *Pr*
John Rogers, *VP*
EMP: 4 **EST:** 1994

SALES (est): 305.04K Privately Held
Web: www.visitechsystems.com
SIC: 3841 Surgical and medical instruments

(G-256)
VITTRO SIGN STUDIO
1106 Cameron Woods Dr (27523-3721)
PHONE..................917 698-1594
Sharon Munoz, *Prin*
EMP: 4 **EST:** 2014
SALES (est): 81.63K Privately Held
Web: www.vittroglass.com
SIC: 3993 Signs and advertising specialties

(G-257)
WALLWORX
200 N Bell Haven St (27539-7747)
PHONE..................919 422-8604
EMP: 4 **EST:** 2013
SALES (est): 66.92K Privately Held
SIC: 2679 Wallpaper

(G-258)
WE ORGANIZE YOU LLC
2031 Production Dr (27539-6349)
PHONE..................919 773-8990
EMP: 9 **EST:** 2018
SALES (est): 272.33K Privately Held
SIC: 2511 Wood household furniture

(G-259)
WHITEFIN VINEYARDS LLC
3400 Winding Way (27502-8744)
PHONE..................219 902-6647
Cotner Seth, *Prin*
EMP: 4 **EST:** 2018
SALES (est): 115.22K Privately Held
Web: www.whitefinvineyards.com
SIC: 2084 Wines

(G-260)
WOLFE PRODUCTS INC
Also Called: Eagle River
2617 Iveysprings Ct (27539-7937)
PHONE..................919 645-7573
Kimberlee L Longest, *Pr*
EMP: 5 **EST:** 2014
SALES (est): 176.96K Privately Held
SIC: 3949 Sporting and athletic goods, nec

(G-261)
XTRA LIGHT MANUFACTURING
1301 Davis Dr (27523-8229)
PHONE..................919 422-7281
Allen Kirk, *Prin*
EMP: 6 **EST:** 2011
SALES (est): 219.92K Privately Held
Web: www.xtralight.com
SIC: 3999 Manufacturing industries, nec

Arapahoe
Pamlico County

(G-262)
WILLIAMS SEAFOOD ARAPAHOE INC
2383 Don Lee Rd (28510-9534)
PHONE..................252 249-0594
Sherri Midyette, *Pr*
Jerry Midyette, *
EMP: 55 **EST:** 1980
SALES (est): 2.66MM Privately Held
SIC: 2092 Seafoods, fresh: prepared

Ararat
Surry County

(G-263)
C & B SALVAGE COMPANY INC
2882 Ararat Rd (27007-8324)
PHONE..................336 374-3946
Brent Simpson, *Pr*
EMP: 6 **EST:** 1976
SALES (est): 974.29K Privately Held
SIC: 5051 3599 Steel; Machine shop, jobbing and repair

(G-264)
CALVIN C MOONEY POULTRY
4167 Nc 268 (27007-8129)
PHONE..................336 374-6690
EMP: 5 **EST:** 2019
SALES (est): 84.29K Privately Held
SIC: 2015 Poultry slaughtering and processing

Archdale
Guilford County

(G-265)
ADVANTAGE FITNESS PRODUCTS LLC
Also Called: Advantage Fitness Products
3511 Garrell St (27263-2635)
P.O. Box 710 (29566-0710)
PHONE..................336 643-8810
Brent Johnson, *Pr*
EMP: 6 **EST:** 2015
SQ FT: 7,500
SALES (est): 235.82K Privately Held
Web: www.afpnorthamerica.com
SIC: 3841 5961 Muscle exercise apparatus, ophthalmic; Fitness and sporting goods, mail order

(G-266)
AMKO EXPRESS INC
10167 N Main St (27263-2905)
PHONE..................336 434-7192
Sam Seo, *Mgr*
EMP: 8 **EST:** 2005
SALES (est): 379.79K Privately Held
SIC: 5411 2741 Convenience stores; Miscellaneous publishing

(G-267)
ARCHDALE FURNITURE DISTRIBUTOR
112 Englewood Dr (27263-2814)
PHONE..................336 431-1081
John Hicks, *Owner*
EMP: 8 **EST:** 2003
SQ FT: 9,000
SALES (est): 247.48K Privately Held
SIC: 2512 Upholstered household furniture

(G-268)
ARCHDALE MILLWORKS INC
1204 Corporation Dr (27263-1649)
PHONE..................336 431-9019
John White, *Pr*
EMP: 6 **EST:** 2001
SALES (est): 605.9K Privately Held
Web: www.millworkin.com
SIC: 2499 2431 Decorative wood and woodwork; Millwork

(G-269)
BAYPOINTE PARTNERS LLC
Also Called: Paul Brayton Designs
403 Interstate Dr (27263-3162)

Archdale - Guilford County (G-270)   GEOGRAPHIC SECTION

PHONE................................336 882-5200
EMP: 9 EST: 2012
SALES (est): 267.7K **Privately Held**
SIC: **2599** 2521 2522 5023 Bar, restaurant and cafeteria furniture; Wood office furniture; Office furniture, except wood; Sheets, textile

(G-270)
BROOKLINE FURNITURE CO INC
Also Called: Brookline Furniture
4015 Cheyenne Dr (27263-3240)
PHONE................................336 841-8503
EMP: 85 EST: 1999
SQ FT: 79,000
SALES (est): 22.17MM **Privately Held**
Web: www.brooklinefurniture.com
SIC: **5021** 2512 Furniture; Chairs: upholstered on wood frames

(G-271)
BURROUGH FURNITURE
1302 Kersey Valley Rd (27263-9439)
PHONE................................336 841-3129
Stanton Edward Yarborough, *Owner*
EMP: 7 EST: 1981
SQ FT: 3,000
SALES (est): 351.24K **Privately Held**
SIC: **2512** 5712 Upholstered household furniture; Furniture stores

(G-272)
CAROLINA BUSINESS FURN INC
535 Archdale Blvd (27263-8590)
P.O. Box 4398 (27263-4398)
PHONE................................336 431-9400
Hank Menke, *Pr*
Ryan Menke, *General Vice President*
Robert H Menke Junior, *
Jeff Eckert, *
Michael Wagner, *
▲ EMP: 555 EST: 1999
SQ FT: 65,000
SALES (est): 2.3MM
SALES (corp-wide): 38.69MM **Privately Held**
Web: www.carolinabusinessfurniture.com
SIC: **2511** 2599 Wood household furniture; Hospital furniture, except beds
PA: Ofs Brands Inc.
1204 E 6th St
Huntingburg IN 47542
800 521-5381

(G-273)
CENTRAL MACHINE COMPANY
2509 Surrett Dr (27263-8500)
PHONE................................336 855-0022
Charles Harris, *Prin*
EMP: 10 EST: 2007
SALES (est): 450.2K **Privately Held**
Web: www.cmiperformance.com
SIC: **3599** Machine shop, jobbing and repair

(G-274)
CLARK SIGN CORPORATION
11530 N Main St (27263-2899)
PHONE................................336 431-4944
EMP: 4 EST: 1993
SALES (est): 346.95K **Privately Held**
Web: www.clarksigncorp.com
SIC: **3993** Signs, not made in custom sign painting shops

(G-275)
COVENANTMADE LLC
2509 Surrett Dr (27263-8500)
PHONE................................336 434-4725
EMP: 10 EST: 2012
SALES (est): 450.79K **Privately Held**
SIC: **2434** Wood kitchen cabinets

(G-276)
CRANFORD SILK SCREEN PRCESS IN
7066 Mendenhall Rd (27263-3909)
P.O. Box 7321 (27264-7321)
PHONE................................336 434-6544
Robert Leonard, *Pr*
Tanya Leonard, *VP*
EMP: 10 EST: 1976
SQ FT: 20,000
SALES (est): 674.21K **Privately Held**
Web: www.cranfordimaging.com
SIC: **2759** Screen printing

(G-277)
CUSTOM SAMPLE SERVICE INC
5415 Surrett Dr (27263-4047)
P.O. Box 209 (27370-0209)
PHONE................................336 861-2010
Steve Flynn, *Pr*
Sharon Jones, *Sec*
EMP: 7 EST: 1969
SALES (est): 225.87K **Privately Held**
SIC: **2789** 2782 Swatches and samples; Sample books

(G-278)
FAIRMONT METAL FINISHING INC
1301 Corporation Dr (27263-1652)
P.O. Box 7366 (27264-7366)
PHONE................................336 434-4188
Luther Moore, *Pr*
Paul Moore, *VP*
EMP: 8 EST: 1983
SQ FT: 9,600
SALES (est): 611.22K **Privately Held**
SIC: **3471** Electroplating of metals or formed products

(G-279)
FAST ARCH OF CAROLINAS INC
617 Eden Ter Ste B (27263-2698)
P.O. Box 577 (27370-0577)
PHONE................................336 431-2724
Mat Hawley, *Pr*
EMP: 5 EST: 2005
SALES (est): 330.56K **Privately Held**
SIC: **2439** Arches, laminated lumber

(G-280)
FIXXUS INDUS HOLDINGS CO LLC
6116 Old Mendenhall Rd (27263-3937)
PHONE................................336 674-3088
EMP: 40 EST: 2016
SALES (est): 2.96MM **Privately Held**
Web: www.gosuperior.com
SIC: **2851** Lacquers, varnishes, enamels, and other coatings

(G-281)
FUTURE FOAM INC
3803 Comanche Rd (27263-3167)
PHONE................................336 861-8095
John Cane, *Brnch Mgr*
EMP: 47
SALES (corp-wide): 495.02MM **Privately Held**
Web: www.futurefoam.com
SIC: **3086** Plastics foam products
PA: Future Foam, Inc.
1610 Avenue N
Council Bluffs IA 51501
712 323-9122

(G-282)
HARRIS HOUSE FURN INDS INC
104 Seminole Dr (27263-3253)
PHONE................................336 431-2802
Otis E Harris Senior, *Pr*
Otis E Harris Junior, *VP*
Kevin Harris, *
Amber Harris, *
EMP: 50 EST: 1981
SQ FT: 33,000
SALES (est): 4.33MM **Privately Held**
Web: www.habitat.org
SIC: **2531** 2521 Public building and related furniture; Wood office furniture

(G-283)
HUBBELL INDUSTRIAL CONTRLS INC (HQ)
Also Called: Femco Radio Controls
4301 Cheyenne Dr (27263-3246)
PHONE................................336 434-2800
Timothy H Powers, *Ch Bd*
David G Nord, *
James H Biggart Junior, *VP*
Gary N Amato, *
Gerben W Bakker, *
◆ EMP: 200 EST: 1985
SQ FT: 80,000
SALES (est): 98.28MM
SALES (corp-wide): 5.37B **Publicly Held**
Web: www.hubbell.com
SIC: **5063** 3625 Electrical apparatus and equipment; Motor controls, electric
PA: Hubbell Incorporated
40 Waterview Dr
Shelton CT 06484
800 626-0005

(G-284)
IE FURNITURE INC (PA)
1121 Corporation Dr (27263-1648)
P.O. Box 5861 (27262-5861)
PHONE................................336 475-5050
Tommy Mathena, *Pr*
Randy Woolard, *
EMP: 50 EST: 2014
SALES (est): 8.4MM
SALES (corp-wide): 8.4MM **Privately Held**
Web: www.iefurniture.com
SIC: **1799** 2521 5021 Office furniture installation; Wood office furniture; Office and public building furniture

(G-285)
INNOVATIVE CUSHIONS LLC
4010 Cheyenne Dr (27263-3239)
PHONE................................336 861-2060
Trela R Hendrix Junior, *Managing Member*
EMP: 10 EST: 2010
SALES (est): 217.4K **Privately Held**
SIC: **2392** Cushions and pillows

(G-286)
IV-S METAL STAMPING INC
2400 Shore St (27263-2514)
PHONE................................336 861-2100
Jerri Smith, *Pr*
Nelson Smith, *
David Willard, *
David Ernest, *
EMP: 35 EST: 1988
SQ FT: 100,000
SALES (est): 4.42MM **Privately Held**
Web: www.us-metalcrafters.com
SIC: **3469** 3499 2599 7692 Stamping metal for the trade; Strapping, metal; Hotel furniture; Welding repair

(G-287)
J & J MACHINE WORKS INC
1300 Corporation Dr (27263-1651)
P.O. Box 360 (27374-0360)
PHONE................................336 434-4081
Jerry Ledwell, *Pr*
EMP: 7 EST: 1974
SQ FT: 15,000
SALES (est): 673.27K **Privately Held**
Web: www.jjmachineworks.com
SIC: **3599** Machine shop, jobbing and repair

(G-288)
JOWAT CORPORATION
5637 Evelyn View Dr (27263-3863)
PHONE................................336 434-9356
EMP: 5
SALES (corp-wide): 451.27MM **Privately Held**
Web: www.jowat.com
SIC: **2891** Adhesives
HQ: Jowat Corporation
5608 Uwharrie Rd
Archdale NC 27263
336 434-9000

(G-289)
JOWAT CORPORATION (HQ)
Also Called: Jowat Adhesives
5608 Uwharrie Rd (27263-4167)
P.O. Box 1368 (27261-1368)
PHONE................................336 434-9000
Rainhard Kramme, *Pr*
Gerhard Haas, *
Jerry Crouse, *
◆ EMP: 82 EST: 1979
SQ FT: 120,000
SALES (est): 44.32MM
SALES (corp-wide): 451.27MM **Privately Held**
Web: www.jowat.com
SIC: **2891** 5169 Adhesives; Adhesives, chemical
PA: Jowat Se
Ernst-Hilker-Str. 10-14
Detmold NW 32758
52317490

(G-290)
JOWAT INTERNATIONAL CORP
5608 Uwharrie Rd (27263-4167)
P.O. Box 1368 (27261-1368)
PHONE................................336 434-9000
Rainhard Kramme, *Pr*
EMP: 28 EST: 1979
SALES (est): 460.4K
SALES (corp-wide): 451.27MM **Privately Held**
Web: www.jowat.com
SIC: **2891** 5169 Adhesives; Adhesives, chemical
PA: Jowat Se
Ernst-Hilker-Str. 10-14
Detmold NW 32758
52317490

(G-291)
JOWAT PROPERTIES CORP
5608 Uwharrie Rd (27263-4167)
P.O. Box 1368 (27261-1368)
PHONE................................336 434-9000
EMP: 13 EST: 2018
SALES (est): 294.13K
SALES (corp-wide): 451.27MM **Privately Held**
Web: www.jowat.com
SIC: **2891** Adhesives
PA: Jowat Se
Ernst-Hilker-Str. 10-14
Detmold NW 32758
52317490

(G-292)
LEITZ TOOLING SYSTEMS LP
Also Called: Leitz Tooling Demp's Div.
401 Interstate Dr (27263-3162)
P.O. Box 4129 (27263-4129)
PHONE................................336 861-3367

GEOGRAPHIC SECTION

Arden - Buncombe County (G-315)

Bill Johnsone, *Mgr*
EMP: 6
SQ FT: 25,660
SALES (corp-wide): 14.78MM **Privately Held**
Web: www.leitz.org
SIC: 3553 3546 3425 Woodworking machinery; Power-driven handtools; Saw blades and handsaws
HQ: Leitz Tooling Systems Lp
 4301 East Paris Ave Se
 Grand Rapids MI 49512
 800 253-6070

(G-293)
LOWDER STEEL INC
2450 Coltrane Mill Rd (27263-8907)
P.O. Box 4158 (27263-4158)
PHONE.................................336 431-9000
J Dean Lowder, *Pr*
EMP: 20 **EST:** 2015
SALES (est): 2.97MM **Privately Held**
Web: www.lowdersteel.net
SIC: 1521 3449 New construction, single-family houses; Bars, concrete reinforcing: fabricated steel

(G-294)
O HENRY HOUSE LTD
308 Greenoak Dr (27263-2344)
P.O. Box 7463 (27264-7463)
PHONE.................................336 431-5350
Richard Pulliam, *Pr*
John Sutton, *
EMP: 32 **EST:** 1988
SQ FT: 28,500
SALES (est): 2.27MM **Privately Held**
Web: www.ohenryhouseltd.com
SIC: 2512 5712 Upholstered household furniture; Furniture stores

(G-295)
ORNAMENTAL MOULDINGS LLC (DH)
Also Called: Ornamental
3804 Comanche Rd (27263-3166)
PHONE.................................336 431-9120
Dennis Berry, *Managing Member*
▲ **EMP:** 18 **EST:** 1993
SQ FT: 100,000
SALES (est): 11.49MM
SALES (corp-wide): 805.03MM **Privately Held**
Web: www.ornamental.com
SIC: 2431 5031 Moldings and baseboards, ornamental and trim; Molding, all materials
HQ: Fletcher Wood Solutions, Inc.
 200 Westgate Cir Ste 402
 Annapolis MD 21401

(G-296)
PROVISION CABINETRY
107 Sprucewood Ct (27263-3358)
P.O. Box 4416 (27263-4416)
PHONE.................................336 442-3537
Steve Alan Smith, *Owner*
EMP: 5 **EST:** 2010
SALES (est): 88.35K **Privately Held**
Web: www.provisioncabinetry.com
SIC: 2434 Wood kitchen cabinets

(G-297)
RELIABLE BEDDING COMPANY
7147 Mendenhall Rd (27263-3910)
PHONE.................................336 883-0648
Robert W Parris, *Pr*
Robert W Parris, *
Kember Parris, *
Dustin Rebert, *
EMP: 25 **EST:** 1967
SQ FT: 16,000
SALES (est): 1.81MM **Privately Held**
Web: www.reliablebeddingcompany.com
SIC: 2515 5712 Mattresses, innerspring or box spring; Mattresses

(G-298)
SALUTE INDUSTRIES INC
105 Apache Dr (27263-3153)
PHONE.................................844 937-2588
Malek Lahmar, *Pr*
EMP: 20 **EST:** 2013
SQ FT: 40,000
SALES (est): 492.98K **Privately Held**
Web: www.uniforms-4u.com
SIC: 2337 2311 2329 Women's and misses' suits and coats; Firemen's uniforms: made from purchased materials; Shirt and slack suits: men's, youths', and boys'

(G-299)
STEELCITY LLC (PA)
Also Called: Harts Striping
505 Aztec Dr (27263-3248)
PHONE.................................336 434-7000
EMP: 27 **EST:** 2018
SALES (est): 9.8MM
SALES (corp-wide): 9.8MM **Privately Held**
SIC: 2395 Quilting and quilting supplies

(G-300)
TECHO-BLOC
5135 Surrett Dr (27263-4030)
PHONE.................................336 431-4133
EMP: 8 **EST:** 2012
SALES (est): 133.68K **Privately Held**
Web: www.techo-bloc.com
SIC: 3272 Concrete products, nec

(G-301)
US METAL CRAFTERS LLC
Also Called: Raptor Attachments
2400 Shore St (27263-2514)
PHONE.................................336 861-2100
EMP: 50 **EST:** 2018
SALES (est): 5.1MM **Privately Held**
Web: www.us-metalcrafters.com
SIC: 3599 3444 3441 Machine and other job shop work; Sheet metalwork; Fabricated structural metal

(G-302)
VECOPLAN LLC
Also Called: Vecoplan
5708 Uwharrie Rd (27263-4168)
P.O. Box 7224 (27264-7224)
PHONE.................................336 861-6070
Werner Berens, *CEO*
Jeff Queen, *
Len Buesse, *
◆ **EMP:** 49 **EST:** 1969
SQ FT: 54,000
SALES (est): 19.7MM
SALES (corp-wide): 417.17MM **Privately Held**
Web: www.vecoplanllc.com
SIC: 3999 Grinding and pulverizing of materials, nec
HQ: Vecoplan Ag
 Vor Der Bitz 10
 Bad Marienberg (Westerwald) RP 56470
 266162670

(G-303)
VIC PANEL SALES DIVISION
5708 Uwharrie Rd (27263-4168)
PHONE.................................336 861-2899
EMP: 4 **EST:** 2014
SALES (est): 135.26K **Privately Held**
SIC: 3625 Relays and industrial controls

(G-304)
WAYNE INDUSTRIES INC
4107 Cheyenne Dr (27263-3242)
P.O. Box 4130 (27263-4130)
PHONE.................................336 434-5017
Wayne Smith, *Pr*
Doug Connor, *
▲ **EMP:** 27 **EST:** 1980
SQ FT: 36,000
SALES (est): 2.12MM **Privately Held**
SIC: 2392 Cushions and pillows

(G-305)
WESLEY LEBLANC RACING LLC
6815 Mendenhall Rd (27263-3907)
PHONE.................................336 560-7630
EMP: 4 **EST:** 2019
SALES (est): 226.49K **Privately Held**
SIC: 3714 Motor vehicle parts and accessories

Arden
Buncombe County

(G-306)
A-1 CONCRETE & CNSTR LLC
42 Avery Creek Rd (28704-8726)
PHONE.................................828 712-1160
EMP: 4 **EST:** 2010
SALES (est): 173.73K **Privately Held**
SIC: 3531 Finishers, concrete and bituminous: powered

(G-307)
ADVANTAGE PRINTING INC
1848 Brevard Rd (28704-9488)
PHONE.................................828 252-7667
Judy Montcastle, *Pr*
John P Montcastle, *VP*
EMP: 13 **EST:** 1981
SQ FT: 7,000
SALES (est): 2.54MM **Privately Held**
Web: www.buyadvantageprinting.com
SIC: 2752 Offset printing

(G-308)
ALTECH-ECO CORPORATION
101 Fair Oaks Rd (28704-9702)
PHONE.................................828 654-8300
Alexander Kovalchuk, *Pr*
Miles George, *VP*
EMP: 13 **EST:** 2006
SALES (est): 3.78MM **Privately Held**
Web: www.transecoenergy.com
SIC: 2869 Fuels

(G-309)
ANGELS PATH VENTURES INC
21 Commerce Way (28704-9712)
PHONE.................................828 654-9530
David Coates, *Pr*
Mellanie Coates, *Sec*
EMP: 8 **EST:** 1985
SQ FT: 5,000
SALES (est): 675.9K **Privately Held**
SIC: 3599 3451 Custom machinery; Screw machine products

(G-310)
ARCADIA BEVERAGE LLC (PA)
Also Called: Arcadia Beverage
34 Arcadia Farms Rd (28704-0015)
PHONE.................................828 684-3556
David Johnston, *CFO*
Dan Nifong, *VP Opers*
EMP: 6 **EST:** 2017
SALES (est): 7.06MM
SALES (corp-wide): 7.06MM **Privately Held**
Web: www.arcadiabev.com
SIC: 2033 Fruit juices: packaged in cans, jars, etc.

(G-311)
ARCADIA FARMS LLC
34 Arcadia Farms Rd (28704-0015)
PHONE.................................828 684-3556
Tom Moore, *Pr*
Steve Decorte, *
David Johnston, *
Dan Nifong, *
Michael Audet, *
EMP: 80 **EST:** 1940
SQ FT: 2,000
SALES (est): 18.6MM
SALES (corp-wide): 484.47MM **Privately Held**
Web: www.arcadiabev.com
SIC: 2033 Fruit juices: packaged in cans, jars, etc.
PA: Investors Management Corporation
 801 N West St
 Raleigh NC 27603
 919 653-7499

(G-312)
ASHEVILLE MAINTENANCE AND CONSTRUCTION INC
Also Called: AMC
150 Glenn Bridge Rd (28704-8502)
P.O. Box 1348 (28704-1348)
PHONE.................................828 687-8110
EMP: 50
Web: www.amcincorp.com
SIC: 1796 7349 3441 1791 Millwright; Building maintenance, except repairs; Building components, structural steel; Structural steel erection

(G-313)
BORGWARNER ARDEN LLC
1849 Brevard Rd (28704-9488)
PHONE.................................248 754-9200
Brady Ericson, *Pr*
EMP: 11 **EST:** 2018
SALES (est): 3.94MM
SALES (corp-wide): 3.5B **Publicly Held**
Web: www.phinia.com
SIC: 3714 Motor vehicle parts and accessories
PA: Phinia Inc.
 3000 University Dr
 Auburn Hills MI 48326
 248 732-1900

(G-314)
BORGWARNER INC
1849 Brevard Rd (28704-9488)
P.O. Box 15075 (28813-0509)
PHONE.................................828 684-4000
Nancy Payne, *Mgr*
EMP: 30
SALES (corp-wide): 14.2B **Publicly Held**
Web: www.borgwarner.com
SIC: 3714 Transmissions, motor vehicle
PA: Borgwarner Inc.
 3850 Hamlin Rd
 Auburn Hills MI 48326
 248 754-9200

(G-315)
BORGWARNER TURBO SYSTEMS LLC (DH)
1849 Brevard Rd (28704-9488)
P.O. Box 15075 (28813-0509)
PHONE.................................828 650-7515
Frederic Lissalde, *Pr*
▲ **EMP:** 89 **EST:** 1989
SALES (est): 161.65MM
SALES (corp-wide): 14.2B **Publicly Held**

Arden - Buncombe County (G-316) — GEOGRAPHIC SECTION

Web: www.borgwarner.com
SIC: 3089 3465 Automotive parts, plastic; Body parts, automobile: stamped metal
HQ: Bwa Turbo Systems Holding Llc
   3850 Hamlin Rd
   Auburn Hills MI

(G-316)
CAM CRAFT LLC
54 Atrium Trl (28704-9141)
PHONE..................828 681-5183
Charles Reichard, *CEO*
Harriett Reichard, *VP*
EMP: 4 **EST:** 2008
SALES (est): 310.04K **Privately Held**
Web: www.camcraftcams.com
SIC: 3714 5015 Camshafts, motor vehicle; Automotive supplies, used: wholesale and retail

(G-317)
CARING FOR BODY LLC
12 Whitleigh Ct (28704-6302)
PHONE..................706 897-9904
EMP: 4 **EST:** 2017
SALES (est): 113.3K **Privately Held**
Web: www.caringforthebody.org
SIC: 3999 Manufacturing industries, nec

(G-318)
CAT DADDY VENTURES LLC
62 Smokemont Dr (28704-7805)
PHONE..................252 229-8617
Michael Mahoney, *Prin*
EMP: 5 **EST:** 2018
SALES (est): 76.42K **Privately Held**
SIC: 3999 Candles

(G-319)
CCBCC OPERATIONS LLC
Also Called: Coca-Cola
36 Clayton Rd (28704-8707)
PHONE..................828 687-1300
EMP: 75
SALES (corp-wide): 6.65B **Publicly Held**
Web: www.coca-cola.com
SIC: 2086 Bottled and canned soft drinks
HQ: Ccbcc Operations, Llc
   4100 Coca Cola Plz
   Charlotte NC 28211
   704 364-8728

(G-320)
CELTIC OCEAN INTERNATIONAL INC
Also Called: Selina Naturally
4 Celtic Dr (28704-9157)
PHONE..................828 299-9005
▲ **EMP:** 31 **EST:** 1968
SQ FT: 19,000
SALES (est): 5.42MM **Privately Held**
Web: www.selinanaturally.com
SIC: 5961 2731 5153 5149 Catalog and mail-order houses; Books, publishing only; Grains; Natural and organic foods

(G-321)
CHEADLES AUTO ART & SIGN
6 Business Park Cir (28704-8587)
PHONE..................828 254-2600
EMP: 4 **EST:** 2019
SALES (est): 30.77K **Privately Held**
Web: www.cheadlesigns.com
SIC: 3993 Signs and advertising specialties

(G-322)
CONSOLIDATED METCO INC
90 Christ School Rd (28704-9556)
PHONE..................360 828-2689
EMP: 51
SALES (corp-wide): 3.96B **Privately Held**
Web: www.conmet.com
SIC: 3089 Injection molding of plastics
HQ: Consolidated Metco, Inc.
   5701 Se Columbia Way
   Vancouver WA 98661
   360 828-2599

(G-323)
CUSTOM PACKAGING INC
Also Called: Custom Packaging of Asheville
20 Beale Rd (28704-9235)
PHONE..................828 684-5060
Jeff West, *Genl Mgr*
EMP: 165 **EST:** 1970
SALES (est): 44.71MM
SALES (corp-wide): 44.71MM **Privately Held**
Web: www.hoodcontainer.com
SIC: 5113 2653 Corrugated and solid fiber boxes; Corrugated and solid fiber boxes
PA: Custom Packaging, Lp
   1315 W Baddour Pkwy
   Lebanon TN 37087
   615 444-6025

(G-324)
DG SOLUTIONS LLC
44 Buck Shoals Rd Ste F2 (28704-3386)
PHONE..................864 605-3223
Nancy Karen Martin, *Mgr*
EMP: 4 **EST:** 2019
SALES (est): 160.68K **Privately Held**
SIC: 2752 Offset printing

(G-325)
DIAMOND DOG TOOLS INC
Also Called: Stf Precision
75 Old Shoals Rd (28704-9401)
PHONE..................828 687-3686
Jason Ford, *Pr*
David Novak, *
◆ **EMP:** 52 **EST:** 1992
SQ FT: 15,000
SALES (est): 9.45MM **Privately Held**
Web: www.gwstoolgroup.com
SIC: 3545 5049 Precision tools, machinists'; Precision tools

(G-326)
EATON CORPORATION
221 Heywood Rd (28704-2655)
PHONE..................828 684-2381
Winston Stanton, *Mgr*
EMP: 500
SQ FT: 250,953
Web: www.dix-eaton.com
SIC: 3625 3613 3621 3612 Motor controls, electric; Switchgear and switchgear accessories, nec; Motors and generators; Transformers, except electric
HQ: Eaton Corporation
   1000 Eaton Blvd
   Cleveland OH 44122
   440 523-5000

(G-327)
ELEMENT TREE ESSENTIALS LLC
3873a Sweeten Creek Rd (28704-3135)
PHONE..................828 707-0407
Kasey Jackson, *Pr*
EMP: 7 **EST:** 2012
SALES (est): 1.45MM **Privately Held**
Web: www.elementtreeessentials.com
SIC: 3999 Candles

(G-328)
FILMON PROCESS CORP
100 Baldwin Rd (28704-8573)
P.O. Box 869 (28704-0869)
PHONE..................828 684-1360
Robert Ploeger, *Mgr*
Carl Ploeger, *Product Vice President*
EMP: 4 **EST:** 1961
SQ FT: 3,000
SALES (est): 477.14K **Privately Held**
Web: www.filmonploeger.com
SIC: 3955 Ribbons, inked: typewriter, adding machine, register, etc.

(G-329)
FISK TOOL COMPANY
24 Fisk Dr (28704-9469)
P.O. Box 1048 (28704-1048)
PHONE..................828 684-5454
Phillip B Fisk, *Pr*
Carol Fisk, *Govt*
Charles S Fisk, *Mgr*
EMP: 8 **EST:** 1938
SQ FT: 6,000
SALES (est): 735.77K **Privately Held**
SIC: 3544 3545 Special dies and tools; Comparators (machinists' precision tools)

(G-330)
FLINT GROUP INC (PA)
Also Called: Flint Group Flexographic Pdts
25 Old Shoals Rd (28704-9010)
PHONE..................828 687-4363
William B Miller, *Pr*
Paul R Carnarvon, *
Michelle A Domas, *
Peter M Schreck, *
EMP: 13 **EST:** 2016
SALES (est): 3.57MM
SALES (corp-wide): 3.57MM **Privately Held**
Web: www.flintgrp.com
SIC: 2893 Printing ink

(G-331)
FLINT GROUP US LLC
Also Called: Flint Group Print Media N Amer
95 Glenn Bridge Rd (28704-9414)
PHONE..................828 687-4309
EMP: 5
SALES (corp-wide): 1.91B **Privately Held**
Web: www.flintgrp.com
SIC: 2893 Printing ink
PA: Flint Group Us Llc
   17177 N Laurel Park Dr # 30
   Livonia MI 48152
   734 781-4600

(G-332)
FLINT GROUP US LLC
Also Called: Day International Prtg Pdts
95 Glenn Bridge Rd (28704-9414)
PHONE..................828 687-2485
John Hodges, *Brnch Mgr*
EMP: 9
SALES (corp-wide): 1.91B **Privately Held**
Web: www.flintgrp.com
SIC: 2759 3069 Commercial printing, nec; Molded rubber products
PA: Flint Group Us Llc
   17177 N Laurel Park Dr # 30
   Livonia MI 48152
   734 781-4600

(G-333)
FLINT GROUP US LLC
25 Old Shoals Rd (28704-9010)
PHONE..................828 687-4291
Amy Dill, *Brnch Mgr*
EMP: 5
SALES (corp-wide): 1.91B **Privately Held**
Web: www.flintgrp.com
SIC: 3552 Textile machinery
PA: Flint Group Us Llc
   17177 N Laurel Park Dr # 30
   Livonia MI 48152
   734 781-4600

(G-334)
GORMAC CUSTOM MFG INC
28 Wild Dogwood Trl (28704)
PHONE..................828 891-9984
Donald Gorgei, *Pr*
EMP: 6 **EST:** 1986
SALES (est): 219.32K **Privately Held**
SIC: 3599 Custom machinery

(G-335)
GRACE APPAREL COMPANY INC ✪
2 Business Park Cir (28704-8587)
PHONE..................828 242-8172
Shane Lee Lunsford, *CEO*
EMP: 5 **EST:** 2023
SALES (est): 251.75K **Privately Held**
SIC: 5621 2396 2395 Ready-to-wear apparel, women's; Screen printing on fabric articles; Embroidery and art needlework

(G-336)
GRACE-EVERETT PRESS
175 Carolina Bluebird Loop (28704-9108)
PHONE..................828 768-7366
Penny Williams, *Owner*
EMP: 4 **EST:** 2017
SALES (est): 84.93K **Privately Held**
Web: www.grace-everettpress.com
SIC: 2741 Miscellaneous publishing

(G-337)
HEALTH CHOICE PHARMACY
2690 Hendersonville Rd (28704-8576)
PHONE..................281 741-8358
EMP: 6 **EST:** 2010
SALES (est): 544.36K **Privately Held**
SIC: 2834 Pharmaceutical preparations

(G-338)
HIGH FALLS PUBLISHING
11 Flycatcher Way # 201 (28704-5531)
P.O. Box 22 (28768-0022)
PHONE..................904 234-0015
Rosemarie Knoll, *Owner*
EMP: 4 **EST:** 2017
SALES (est): 57.89K **Privately Held**
SIC: 2741 Miscellaneous publishing

(G-339)
HUBBELL INCORPORATED
Also Called: Hubbell Premise Wiring
20 Glenn Bridge Rd (28704-9450)
PHONE..................828 687-8505
Norman Vint, *Brnch Mgr*
EMP: 20
SALES (corp-wide): 5.37B **Publicly Held**
Web: www.hubbell.com
SIC: 3643 Current-carrying wiring services
PA: Hubbell Incorporated
   40 Waterview Dr
   Shelton CT 06484
   800 626-0005

(G-340)
INDUSTRIAL SHEET METAL WORKS
149 Old Shoals Rd (28704-5501)
PHONE..................828 654-9655
Perry Bartsch, *Prin*
EMP: 6 **EST:** 2015
SALES (est): 164.44K **Privately Held**
SIC: 3444 Sheet metalwork

(G-341)
INJECTION TECHNOLOGY CORPORATION
Also Called: Itech
199 Airport Rd (28704-8516)
P.O. Box 1107 (28704-1107)
PHONE..................828 684-1362
EMP: 105

▲ = Import ▼ = Export
◆ = Import/Export

GEOGRAPHIC SECTION

Arden - Buncombe County (G-366)

SIC: 3089 Injection molding of plastics

(G-342)
ISM INC
149 Old Shoals Rd (28704-5501)
EMP: 22 EST: 1977
SQ FT: 28,000
SALES (est): 5.14MM **Privately Held**
Web: www.ism-nc.com
SIC: 3444 3446 3499 3535 Sheet metalwork
; Architectural metalwork; Aerosol valves,
metal; Conveyors and conveying equipment

(G-343)
JABIL INC
100 Vista Blvd (28704-9457)
PHONE.................................828 684-3141
EMP: 23
SALES (corp-wide): 34.7B **Publicly Held**
Web: www.jabil.com
SIC: 3672 Printed circuit boards
PA: Jabil Inc.
  10800 Roosevelt Blvd N
  Saint Petersburg FL 33716
  727 577-9749

(G-344)
JAYSON CONCEPTS INC
115 Vista Blvd (28704-9457)
PHONE.................................828 654-8900
Jay Stingel, *Pr*
Janet Stingel, *
John Stingel, *
▲ EMP: 20 EST: 1981
SQ FT: 50,000
SALES (est): 606.42K **Privately Held**
Web: www.jaysonconcepts.com
SIC: 3535 Conveyors and conveying equipment

(G-345)
KHI LLC
Also Called: Kerrybeth Home Improvements
P.O. Box 1189 (28776-1189)
PHONE.................................828 654-9916
EMP: 5 EST: 2000
SALES (est): 477.17K **Privately Held**
SIC: 1521 2395 3553 General remodeling, single-family houses; Embroidery and art needlework; Furniture makers machinery, woodworking

(G-346)
LE BLEU CORPORATION
212 Baldwin Rd (28704-8568)
P.O. Box 8127 (28814-8127)
PHONE.................................828 254-5105
Andy Scotchie, *Brnch Mgr*
EMP: 5
Web: www.lebleu.com
SIC: 2086 Water, natural: packaged in cans, bottles, etc.
PA: Le Bleu Corporation
  3134 Cornatzer Rd
  Advance NC 27006

(G-347)
LEGACY AEROSPACE AND DEF LLC (PA)
Also Called: Legacy Aerospace & Defense
150 Glenn Bridge Rd (28704-8502)
PHONE.................................828 398-0981
Thomas Kane, *Ex Dir*
EMP: 4 EST: 2013
SQ FT: 10,000
SALES (est): 1.19MM
SALES (corp-wide): 1.19MM **Privately Held**
Web: www.legacy-aerospace.com

SIC: 3728 Aircraft parts and equipment, nec

(G-348)
LEGEND-TEES
37 Loop Rd (28704-8401)
PHONE.................................828 585-2066
EMP: 4 EST: 2019
SALES (est): 73.28K **Privately Held**
Web: www.legend-tees.com
SIC: 2759 Screen printing

(G-349)
LINAMAR NORTH CAROLINA INC
2169 Hendersonville Rd (28704-9742)
PHONE.................................828 348-5343
▲ EMP: 11 EST: 2011
SQ FT: 400,000
SALES (est): 15.21MM
SALES (corp-wide): 5.89B **Privately Held**
SIC: 3545 Precision measuring tools
HQ: Linamar Holding Nevada, Inc.
  32233 8 Mile Rd
  Livonia MI 48152
  248 477-6240

(G-350)
MEDICAL ACTION INDUSTRIES INC (HQ)
Also Called: Medical Action
25 Heywood Rd (28704-9302)
◆ EMP: 86 EST: 1987
SQ FT: 28,200
SALES (est): 140.75MM **Publicly Held**
Web: www.medical-action.com
SIC: 3842 Applicators, cotton tipped
PA: Owens & Minor, Inc.
  9120 Lockwood Blvd
  Mechanicsville VA 23116

(G-351)
MILLAR INDUSTRIES INC
20 Loop Rd (28704-8401)
P.O. Box 1259 (28704-1259)
PHONE.................................828 687-0639
Fred Millar, *CEO*
Brett Millar, *Pr*
Marilyn Millar, *Sec*
EMP: 21 EST: 1989
SQ FT: 27,000
SALES (est): 4.8MM **Privately Held**
Web: a-mtool-com.securec95biz.ezhostingserver.com
SIC: 3089 3544 Injection molding of plastics; Special dies, tools, jigs, and fixtures

(G-352)
MILLER GLASS
72 Bradley Branch Rd (28704-9303)
PHONE.................................828 681-8083
Cindy Miller, *Pr*
Jamie Zullo, *VP*
EMP: 12 EST: 2005
SALES (est): 545.69K **Privately Held**
Web: www.millerglass.biz
SIC: 3231 Products of purchased glass

(G-353)
MOUNTAIN LEISURE HOT TUBS LLC
40 Business Park Cir Ste 60 (28704-8649)
PHONE.................................828 649-7727
EMP: 10 EST: 2019
SALES (est): 460.14K **Privately Held**
Web: www.mountainleisurehottubs.com
SIC: 3999 Hot tubs

(G-354)
MRE-STAR
2099 Brevard Rd (28704-8900)
PHONE.................................407 403-3889

EMP: 8 EST: 2017
SALES (est): 176.15K **Privately Held**
Web: www.mrestar.com
SIC: 2099 Food preparations, nec

(G-355)
NEW PECO INC
10 Walden Dr (28704-3314)
PHONE.................................828 684-1234
Peter Cook, *Pr*
▲ EMP: 21 EST: 2009
SALES (est): 2.39MM **Privately Held**
Web: www.lawnvac.com
SIC: 3524 3444 Grass catchers, lawn mower; Sheet metal specialties, not stamped

(G-356)
NORTH CAROLINA DEPARTMENT OF A
Also Called: Western Anmal Dsase Dgnstc Lab
785 Airport Rd (28704)
P.O. Box 279 (28704-0279)
PHONE.................................828 684-8188
EMP: 6
Web: www.ncagr.gov
SIC: 2835 9512 Veterinary diagnostic substances; Land, mineral, and wildlife conservation, State government
HQ: North Carolina Department Of Agriculture & Consumer Services
  2 W Edenton St
  Raleigh NC 27601

(G-357)
NOVA ENTERPRISES INC (PA)
Also Called: Nova Kitchen & Bath
305 Airport Rd (28704-8402)
P.O. Box 1167 (28704-1167)
PHONE.................................828 687-8770
Bill Purdue, *Pr*
Renee Purdue, *
Ken Dinkins, *
EMP: 48 EST: 1969
SQ FT: 7,000
SALES (est): 9.79MM
SALES (corp-wide): 9.79MM **Privately Held**
Web: www.novakitchen.com
SIC: 5031 3281 1799 Kitchen cabinets; Table tops, marble; Kitchen and bathroom remodeling

(G-358)
NYPRO ASHEVILLE INC
Also Called: Nypro
100 Vista Blvd (28704-9457)
PHONE.................................828 684-3141
▲ EMP: 200
SIC: 3089 Injection molding of plastics

(G-359)
NYPRO OREGON INC
100 Vista Blvd (28704-9457)
PHONE.................................541 753-4700
Theodore E Lapres I, *Pr*
▲ EMP: 1389 EST: 1994
SQ FT: 94,000
SALES (est): 3.12MM
SALES (corp-wide): 34.7B **Publicly Held**
SIC: 3089 Molding primary plastics
HQ: Nypro Inc.
  101 Union St
  Clinton MA 01510
  978 365-9721

(G-360)
PARKWAY PRODUCTS LLC
Also Called: Parkway Asheville
199 Airport Rd (28704-8516)
PHONE.................................828 684-1362

EMP: 105
SALES (corp-wide): 101.06MM **Privately Held**
Web: www.parkwayproducts.com
SIC: 3089 Injection molding of plastics
PA: Parkway Products, Llc
  3 Research Dr Ste 135
  Greenville SC 29607
  864 484-8700

(G-361)
PARTS AND SYSTEMS COMPANY INC
Also Called: Pasco
44 Buck Shoals Rd Ste D2 (28704-3380)
P.O. Box 5468 (28813-5468)
PHONE.................................828 684-7070
John M Crook, *Pr*
Joy C Crook, *VP*
▲ EMP: 10 EST: 1987
SQ FT: 4,800
SALES (est): 983.36K **Privately Held**
Web: www.pascorolls.com
SIC: 3552 Textile machinery

(G-362)
PECO INC
Also Called: Peco
100 Airport Rd (28704-8516)
PHONE.................................828 684-1234
EMP: 22
SIC: 3524 3531 3553 3563 Blowers and vacuums, lawn; Chippers: brush, limb, and log; Woodworking machinery; Air and gas compressors

(G-363)
PERFECT SQUARE MUSIC INC
28 Fox Hollow Ct (28704-3004)
PHONE.................................478 718-5702
Love Henderson, *Prin*
EMP: 5 EST: 2016
SALES (est): 62.99K **Privately Held**
SIC: 2711 Newspapers, publishing and printing

(G-364)
POWDERTEK
6 Bagwell Mill Rd (28704-8553)
PHONE.................................828 225-3250
Bryan Street, *Prin*
EMP: 7 EST: 2009
SALES (est): 910.18K **Privately Held**
Web: www.powdertek.com
SIC: 3479 Coating of metals and formed products

(G-365)
PRECEPT MEDICAL PRODUCTS INC (DH)
Also Called: Precept
370 Airport Rd (28704-9202)
PHONE.................................828 681-0209
John Sopcisak, *CEO*
▲ EMP: 16 EST: 1960
SQ FT: 25,000
SALES (est): 9.85MM
SALES (corp-wide): 348.19MM **Privately Held**
SIC: 3842 2389 Clothing, fire resistant and protective; Disposable garments and accessories
HQ: Aspen Surgical Products, Inc.
  6945 Southbelt Dr Se
  Caledonia MI 49316
  888 364-7004

(G-366)
PRECISION PDTS ASHEVILLE INC (PA)

Arden - Buncombe County (G-367)

118 Glenn Bridge Rd (28704-8502)
P.O. Box 1047 (28704-1047)
PHONE..................................828 684-4207
Shannon Herren, *Pr*
Julie Herren, *VP*
EMP: 21 **EST:** 1962
SQ FT: 20,000
SALES (est): 7.03MM
SALES (corp-wide): 7.03MM **Privately Held**
Web: www.ppofa.com
SIC: 3599 Machine shop, jobbing and repair

(G-367)
PRECISION PDTS PRFMCE CTR INC
191 Airport Rd (28704-8516)
P.O. Box 1229 (28704-1229)
PHONE..................................828 684-8569
Leo Jackson, *Pr*
Debra Jackson, *Sec*
EMP: 37 **EST:** 1985
SQ FT: 30,000
SALES (est): 2.02MM **Privately Held**
Web: www.pppcenter.com
SIC: 3714 Motor vehicle parts and accessories

(G-368)
PRECISION TOOL DYE AND MOLD
69 Bagwell Mill Rd (28704-8553)
P.O. Box 727 (28704-0727)
PHONE..................................828 687-2990
EMP: 10 **EST:** 1995
SQ FT: 3,000
SALES (est): 952.99K **Privately Held**
SIC: 3544 3599 Special dies and tools; Machine shop, jobbing and repair

(G-369)
PRODUCTION WLDG FBRICATION INC
1791 Brevard Rd (28704-9659)
P.O. Box 726 (28728-0726)
PHONE..................................828 687-7466
Michael Philips, *Pr*
Elaine Phillips, *VP*
Michael Phillips, *Pr*
EMP: 25 **EST:** 1983
SQ FT: 6,000
SALES (est): 928.28K **Privately Held**
SIC: 3599 3441 Custom machinery; Fabricated structural metal

(G-370)
READY WHEN YOU ARE
7 Sabrina Dr (28704-9477)
PHONE..................................828 243-7514
Eric Glick, *Prin*
EMP: 6 **EST:** 2011
SALES (est): 84.14K **Privately Held**
SIC: 3273 Ready-mixed concrete

(G-371)
REICH LLC
140 Vista Blvd (28704-9457)
PHONE..................................828 651-9019
Andre Reich, *Managing Member*
◆ **EMP:** 120 **EST:** 2010
SQ FT: 40,000
SALES (est): 24.84MM **Privately Held**
Web: www.reich-llc.com
SIC: 3562 Ball bearings and parts

(G-372)
RGEES LLC
170 Bradley Branch Rd Ste 6&7 (28704-9216)
PHONE..................................828 708-7178
Harshul Gupta, *CEO*
▲ **EMP:** 6 **EST:** 2009
SALES (est): 529.37K **Privately Held**
Web: www.rgees.com
SIC: 2679 2671 2673 Crepe paper or crepe paper products; purchased material; Paper; coated and laminated packaging; Bags; plastic, laminated, and coated

(G-373)
ROTEC NORTH AMERICAN
95 Glenn Bridge Rd (28704-9414)
PHONE..................................828 681-0151
Gary Manson, *Prin*
▲ **EMP:** 5 **EST:** 2008
SALES (est): 226.43K **Privately Held**
SIC: 3555 Printing trades machinery

(G-374)
SARE GRANITE & TILE
Also Called: Sare Kitchen and Bed
128 Greene Rd (28704-9582)
PHONE..................................828 676-2666
Ray Koruk, *Pr*
EMP: 8 **EST:** 2012
SALES (est): 490.98K **Privately Held**
Web: www.saregranite.com
SIC: 1743 1799 2541 Tile installation, ceramic; Kitchen cabinet installation; Counter and sink tops

(G-375)
SIGN SOLUTIONS LLC
90 Old Shoals Rd Ste 105 (28704-9508)
PHONE..................................828 687-9789
EMP: 4 **EST:** 2018
SALES (est): 241.93K **Privately Held**
Web: www.signsolutionswnc.com
SIC: 3993 Signs and advertising specialties

(G-376)
SIMPLYHOME LLC
48 Fisk Dr (28704-9469)
P.O. Box 1155 (28704-1155)
PHONE..................................828 684-8441
Allen Ray, *Managing Member*
EMP: 19 **EST:** 2009
SQ FT: 2,000
SALES (est): 2.51MM **Privately Held**
Web: www.simply-home.com
SIC: 3669 Visual communication systems

(G-377)
SMITH & FOX INC
Also Called: Imagesmith
19 Walden Dr (28704-3314)
PHONE..................................828 684-4512
Mary Smith, *Pr*
David Smith, *Prin*
EMP: 10 **EST:** 1983
SQ FT: 21,000
SALES (est): 1.72MM **Privately Held**
Web: www.imagesmith.com
SIC: 2752 Offset printing

(G-378)
SOUTHERN CONCRETE MTLS INC
Hendersonville Rd (28704)
P.O. Box 5395 (28813-5395)
PHONE..................................828 684-3636
EMP: 20
SALES (corp-wide): 238.17MM **Privately Held**
Web: www.scmusa.com
SIC: 3273 Ready-mixed concrete
HQ: Southern Concrete Materials, Inc.
35 Meadow Rd
Asheville NC 28803
828 253-6421

(G-379)
SPECIALITY COX MFG LLC
25 Commerce Way (28704-9712)
PHONE..................................828 684-5762
Hoyt L Cox, *Managing Member*
EMP: 5 **EST:** 1986
SQ FT: 3,200
SALES (est): 362.35K **Privately Held**
SIC: 3544 Forms (molds), for foundry and plastics working machinery

(G-380)
SPEEDGRAPHICS SIGN DESIGN INC
35 Walden Dr (28704-3314)
PHONE..................................828 771-0322
Michael G Dickman, *Pr*
EMP: 6 **EST:** 2014
SALES (est): 229.63K **Privately Held**
Web: www.speedgraphics.net
SIC: 3993 Signs and advertising specialties

(G-381)
STONE MOUNTAIN CABINETARY
206 Vista Blvd (28704-6400)
PHONE..................................828 676-3600
EMP: 6 **EST:** 2017
SALES (est): 208.73K **Privately Held**
Web: www.stonemountaincabinetry.com
SIC: 2434 Wood kitchen cabinets

(G-382)
SUNSTAR NETWORK LLC
100 Thunderland Cir (28704-8775)
PHONE..................................828 684-3571
EMP: 4 **EST:** 2019
SALES (est): 154.73K **Privately Held**
SIC: 2834 Pharmaceutical preparations

(G-383)
THRILLS HAULING LLC
173 New Rockwood Rd (28704-9492)
PHONE..................................407 383-3483
EMP: 10 **EST:** 2021
SALES (est): 371.87K **Privately Held**
SIC: 1442 Construction sand and gravel

(G-384)
TRANSECO ENERGY CORPORATION
101 Fair Oaks Rd (28704-9702)
PHONE..................................828 684-6400
Alexander Kovalchuk, *CEO*
Miles George, *VP*
Mark Oleskiewicz, *CFO*
EMP: 7 **EST:** 2007
SALES (est): 888.4K **Privately Held**
Web: www.transecoenergy.com
SIC: 2869 Fuels

(G-385)
TREG TOOL INC
10 Summer Meadow Rd (28704-7601)
PHONE..................................828 676-0035
EMP: 5 **EST:** 2016
SALES (est): 81.71K **Privately Held**
SIC: 3089 Injection molding of plastics

(G-386)
TRIUMPH TOOL NC INC
44 Buck Shoals Rd Ste B3 (28704-3384)
PHONE..................................828 676-3677
John Duffy, *Pr*
Patrick Duffy,
EMP: 50 **EST:** 2011
SALES (est): 2.54MM **Privately Held**
Web: www.triumphtool.com
SIC: 3599 Machine shop, jobbing and repair

(G-387)
TUTCO INC
Farnam Custom Products
30 Legend Dr (28704-6203)
PHONE..................................828 654-1665
Neil Farnum, *Genl Mgr*
EMP: 54
SALES (corp-wide): 3.83B **Privately Held**
Web: www.tutco.com
SIC: 3567 Heating units and devices, industrial: electric
HQ: Tutco, Llc
500 Gould Dr
Cookeville TN 38506
931 432-4141

(G-388)
TUTCU-FARNAM CUSTOM PRODUCTS
30 Legend Dr (28704-6203)
PHONE..................................828 684-3766
EMP: 22 **EST:** 2011
SALES (est): 11.49MM **Privately Held**
Web: www.farnam-custom.com
SIC: 2819 Elements

(G-389)
VIKTORS GRAN MBL KIT CNTER TOP
28 Beale Rd (28704-9235)
PHONE..................................828 681-0713
Viktor Polishchuk, *Prin*
EMP: 15 **EST:** 2004
SALES (est): 503.83K **Privately Held**
Web: www.vgmwnc.com
SIC: 1799 3253 5032 5211 Kitchen and bathroom remodeling; Ceramic wall and floor tile; Ceramic wall and floor tile, nec; Counter tops

(G-390)
VISTA HORTICULTURAL GROUP INC
2099 Brevard Rd (28704-8900)
PHONE..................................828 633-6338
Sabine Randon, *Pr*
EMP: 17 **EST:** 2011
SALES (est): 1.01MM **Privately Held**
Web: www.edenbrothers.com
SIC: 2099 Food preparations, nec

(G-391)
WILLIAMS PLATING COMPANY INC
6 Industrial Dr (28704-7712)
P.O. Box 3042 (28802-3042)
PHONE..................................828 681-0301
Michael Williams, *Pr*
Deborah Williams, *Sec*
EMP: 16 **EST:** 1982
SQ FT: 10,000
SALES (est): 607.8K **Privately Held**
Web: www.williamsplating.com
SIC: 3471 Electroplating of metals or formed products

(G-392)
WPH VENTURES INC
Also Called: Hickman
4 Commerce Way (28704-9712)
P.O. Box 15005 (28813-0005)
PHONE..................................828 676-1700
▼ **EMP:** 28
SIC: 3444 Metal roofing and roof drainage equipment

(G-393)
XSYS NORTH AMERICA CORPORATION
Also Called: Xsys Global
95 Glenn Bridge Rd (28704-9414)
PHONE..................................828 654-6805
EMP: 32
SALES (corp-wide): 857.59K **Privately Held**
Web: www.xsysglobal.com
SIC: 2796 Platemaking services
HQ: Xsys North America Corporation

GEOGRAPHIC SECTION

Asheboro - Randolph County (G-417)

2915 Whthall Pk Dr Ste 60
Charlotte NC 28273
704 504-2626

(G-394)
XSYS NORTH AMERICA CORPORATION
25 Old Shoals Rd (28704-9010)
PHONE................................828 687-2485
Joe Bauer, *Mgr*
EMP: 32
SALES (corp-wide): 857.59K **Privately Held**
Web: www.xsysglobal.com
SIC: 2893 Printing ink
HQ: Xsys North America Corporation
2915 Whthall Pk Dr Ste 60
Charlotte NC 28273
704 504-2626

Ash
Brunswick County

(G-395)
JDS LOGGING LLC
6020 Ludlum Rd Nw (28420-3210)
PHONE................................910 713-5980
EMP: 5 EST: 2017
SALES (est): 157.15K **Privately Held**
SIC: 2411 Logging

(G-396)
SIMMONS LOGGING & TRUCKING INC
5923 Simmons Rd Nw (28420-3835)
PHONE................................910 287-6344
Lathion Simmons, *Pr*
Betty Simmons, *VP*
EMP: 11 EST: 1967
SALES (est): 469.8K **Privately Held**
SIC: 2411 Logging camps and contractors

Asheboro
Randolph County

(G-397)
3D PACKAGING LLC
451 Railroad St (27203-4322)
P.O. Box 18863 (27419-8863)
PHONE................................336 625-0652
EMP: 12 EST: 1990
SQ FT: 15,600
SALES (est): 289.61K **Privately Held**
Web: www.ceo3dpkg.com
SIC: 2653 5199 5113 Boxes, corrugated: made from purchased materials; Packaging materials; Corrugated and solid fiber boxes

(G-398)
ACME-MCCRARY CORPORATION
159 North St (27203-5411)
PHONE................................336 625-2161
Horace Luther, *Bmch Mgr*
EMP: 118
Web: www.acme-mccrary.com
SIC: 2251 Women's hosiery, except socks
HQ: Acme-Mccrary Corporation
162 N Cherry St
Asheboro NC 27203
336 625-2161

(G-399)
ACME-MCCRARY CORPORATION (DH)
162 N Cherry St (27203-5310)
PHONE................................336 625-2161
Charles W Mc Crary Junior, *Ch Bd*

John O H Toledano Senior, *V Ch Bd*
Neal Anderson, *
Donnie White, *
Bruce T Patram, *
◆ EMP: 350 EST: 1909
SQ FT: 200,000
SALES (est): 61.79MM **Privately Held**
Web: www.acme-mccrary.com
SIC: 2251 Panty hose
HQ: Mas Us Holdings, Inc.
162 N Cherry St
Asheboro NC 27203
336 625-2161

(G-400)
ALLEN MCH & FABRICATION LLC
420 Industrial Park Ave (27205-7330)
P.O. Box 309 (27204-0309)
PHONE................................336 521-4409
Todd Allen, *Pr*
EMP: 14 EST: 2016
SALES (est): 999.14K **Privately Held**
Web: www.allenmaf.com
SIC: 3599 Machine shop, jobbing and repair

(G-401)
AMERICAN PRINTING SERVICES
3048 Whippoorwill Dr (27205-2559)
PHONE................................336 465-0199
EMP: 4 EST: 2010
SALES (est): 66.81K **Privately Held**
SIC: 2752 Offset printing

(G-402)
ANTHOLOGY OF POETRY INC
307 E Salisbury St (27203-5545)
P.O. Box 698 (27204-0698)
PHONE................................336 626-7762
George Nickles, *Pr*
EMP: 10 EST: 1989
SQ FT: 21,000
SALES (est): 214.95K **Privately Held**
Web: www.anthologyofpoetry.com
SIC: 2731 Books, publishing only

(G-403)
ASHEBORO ELASTICS CORP (PA)
Also Called: AEC Narrow Fabrics
150 N Park St (27205-5455)
P.O. Box 1143 (27204-1143)
PHONE................................336 629-2626
Larry Himes, *CEO*
Robert B Lawson, *
John K Crisco Junior, *VP*
Jeff Crisco, *
Jane Crisco, *
◆ EMP: 60 EST: 1985
SQ FT: 60,000
SALES (est): 51.76MM
SALES (corp-wide): 51.76MM **Privately Held**
Web: www.aecnarrowfabrics.com
SIC: 2221 2241 Broadwoven fabric mills, manmade; Elastic narrow fabrics, woven or braided

(G-404)
ASHEBORO ELASTICS CORP
Also Called: AEC Narrow Fabrics
1947 N Fayetteville St (27205-3269)
PHONE................................336 629-2626
EMP: 4
SALES (corp-wide): 51.76MM **Privately Held**
SIC: 2241 2221 Elastic narrow fabrics, woven or braided; Broadwoven fabric mills, manmade
PA: Asheboro Elastics Corp.
150 N Park St
Asheboro NC 27203
336 629-2626

(G-405)
ASHEBORO MACHINE SHOP INC
3027 Us Business 220 S (27204)
P.O. Box 361 (27204-0361)
PHONE................................336 625-6322
Ronnie Hussey, *Pr*
Ricky Moore, *VP*
EMP: 8 EST: 1980
SQ FT: 7,425
SALES (est): 1.02MM **Privately Held**
SIC: 3599 Machine shop, jobbing and repair

(G-406)
ASHEBORO PIEDMONT PRINTING INC
Also Called: Piedmont Printing
2753 Us Highway 220 Bus S (27205-0820)
P.O. Box 430 (27204-0430)
PHONE................................336 899-7910
Larry Presnell, *Pr*
Betty Presnell, *
EMP: 12 EST: 1986
SQ FT: 6,000
SALES (est): 502.24K **Privately Held**
Web: www.piedmontprinting.com
SIC: 2752 2791 2789 Offset printing; Typesetting; Bookbinding and related work

(G-407)
ASHEBORO READY-MIX INC
524 W Bailey St (27203-3610)
P.O. Box 984 (27204-0984)
PHONE................................336 672-0957
Todd Richardson, *Pr*
EMP: 22 EST: 1979
SQ FT: 7,000
SALES (est): 1.36MM **Privately Held**
SIC: 3273 Ready-mixed concrete

(G-408)
BARGAINSTAIRPARTSCOM LLC
1525 Danny Bell Rd (27205-2026)
P.O. Box 1544 (27204-1544)
PHONE................................214 883-9524
Gerald Atkinson, *Managing Member*
EMP: 4 EST: 2018
SALES (est): 248.64K **Privately Held**
SIC: 3446 Stairs, staircases, stair treads: prefabricated metal

(G-409)
BEANE SIGNS INC
218 Vista Pkwy (27205-5064)
PHONE................................336 629-6748
William Beane, *Pr*
EMP: 4 EST: 1971
SQ FT: 600
SALES (est): 300K **Privately Held**
Web: www.beanesignsinc.com
SIC: 3993 Signs and advertising specialties

(G-410)
BOSSONG CORPORATION
840 W Salisbury St (27204-4327)
P.O. Box 789 (27204-0789)
PHONE................................336 625-2175
EMP: 7 EST: 2011
SQ FT: 140,000
SALES (est): 97.31K **Privately Held**
Web: www.bossonghosiery.com
SIC: 2251 Women's hosiery, except socks

(G-411)
BOSSONG HOSIERY MILLS INC (PA)
840 W Salisbury St (27204-4327)
P.O. Box 789 (27204-0789)
PHONE................................336 625-2175
Huntley Bossong, *CEO*
F Bossong, *
Charles J Bossong, *

Joseph C Bossong, *
▲ EMP: 220 EST: 1927
SQ FT: 140,000
SALES (est): 23.92MM
SALES (corp-wide): 23.92MM **Privately Held**
Web: www.bossonghosiery.com
SIC: 2252 Socks

(G-412)
CAROLINA PRECISION PLASTICS L (HQ)
Also Called: Cpp Global
405 Commerce Pl (27203-0553)
PHONE................................336 498-2654
◆ EMP: 99 EST: 1984
SQ FT: 95,000
SALES (est): 87.44MM
SALES (corp-wide): 480.33MM **Privately Held**
Web: www.cppglobal.com
SIC: 3089 Injection molding of plastics
PA: Westfall Technik, Inc.
3883 Howard Hughes Pkwy # 590
Las Vegas NV 89169
702 659-9898

(G-413)
CENTRAL CAROLINA PRINTING LLC
464 Cheshire Pl (27205-8229)
PHONE................................910 572-3344
Troy Danner, *Managing Member*
EMP: 9 EST: 2001
SALES (est): 821.47K **Privately Held**
Web: www.ccprintandmail.com
SIC: 2752 Offset printing

(G-414)
CHANDLER CONCRETE INC
Also Called: Central Concrete
205 W Academy St (27203-5650)
PHONE................................336 625-1070
Ronnie Faulkmer, *Bmch Mgr*
EMP: 10
Web: www.chandlerconcrete.com
SIC: 3273 Ready-mixed concrete
PA: Chandler Concrete Co., Inc.
1006 S Church St
Burlington NC 27215

(G-415)
CHRIS ISOM INC
Also Called: Carolina Frames
1228 Green Farm Rd (27205-2346)
PHONE................................336 629-0240
Chris Isom, *Prin*
EMP: 15 EST: 2001
SALES (est): 2.06MM **Privately Held**
SIC: 2511 2426 Wood household furniture; Hardwood dimension and flooring mills

(G-416)
CHROMA COLOR CORPORATION
Also Called: Plastics Color
1134 Nc Highway 49 S (27205-9584)
PHONE................................336 629-9184
Arely Palomino, *Prin*
EMP: 84
SALES (corp-wide): 117.78MM **Privately Held**
Web: www.chromacolors.com
SIC: 2821 Plastics materials and resins
PA: Chroma Color Corporation
3900 W Dayton St
Mchenry IL 60050
877 385-8777

(G-417)
COMM-KAB INC
1865 Spero Rd (27205-0501)
PHONE................................336 873-8787

(PA)=Parent Co (HQ)=Headquarters
✪ = New Business established in last 2 years

2024 Harris North Carolina Manufacturers Directory

Asheboro - Randolph County (G-418) — GEOGRAPHIC SECTION

Nelson Rowland, *Pr*
Kentie Rowland, *VP*
EMP: 11 **EST:** 1988
SALES (est): 825K **Privately Held**
SIC: 5712 1751 2521 2434 Cabinet work, custom; Cabinet and finish carpentry; Wood office furniture; Wood kitchen cabinets

(G-418)
CORNER STONE PLASTICS INC
1027 Luck Rd (27205-7864)
PHONE..................................336 629-1828
Virgil F Hill, *Pr*
Virgil F Hill, *Pr*
Gaye Hill, *VP*
EMP: 4 **EST:** 1983
SQ FT: 5,000
SALES (est): 455.7K **Privately Held**
SIC: 3089 Plastics hardware and building products

(G-419)
COX PRECISION SPRINGS INC
3162 Spoons Chapel Rd (27205-8129)
P.O. Box 1417 (27204-1417)
PHONE..................................336 629-8500
Gary Cox, *Pr*
Judy Cox, *Sec*
Todd Schwarz, *VP*
Jennifer Schwarz, *Treas*
▲ **EMP:** 10 **EST:** 2002
SQ FT: 6,000
SALES (est): 660K **Privately Held**
Web: www.coxprecisionspring.com
SIC: 3495 Precision springs

(G-420)
CUSTOM EXTRUSION INC
2971 Taylor Dr (27203-0554)
PHONE..................................336 495-7070
Gralen Cranford, *Mgr*
EMP: 7
SALES (corp-wide): 295.68MM **Privately Held**
Web: www.pexco.com
SIC: 3089 5162 Injection molding of plastics; Plastics sheets and rods
HQ: Custom Extrusion, Inc.
  34 Home Rd
  Sheffield MA 01257
  413 229-8748

(G-421)
DALIAH PLASTICS CORP
134 W Wainman Ave (27203-5639)
P.O. Box 27 (27204-0027)
PHONE..................................336 629-0551
Charles Gans, *Pr*
Daliah Gans, *
Al Holland, *
EMP: 50 **EST:** 1981
SQ FT: 25,000
SALES (est): 11.5MM **Privately Held**
Web: www.daliahplastics.com
SIC: 3081 Polyethylene film

(G-422)
DATAMARK GRAPHICS INC
603 W Bailey St (27203-3611)
PHONE..................................336 629-0267
Don Byers, *CEO*
Elizabeth Byers, *
Eric Mcpherson, *Genl Mgr*
EMP: 25 **EST:** 1984
SQ FT: 16,000
SALES (est): 2.04MM **Privately Held**
Web: www.datamarkgraphics.com
SIC: 2759 2672 2671 2241 Labels and seals: printing, nsk; Paper, coated and laminated, nec; Paper, coated and laminated packaging; Narrow fabric mills

(G-423)
DAUNTLESS MFG SOLUTIONS LLC
247 Sawyersville Rd (27205-2205)
PHONE..................................757 870-2173
Christopher Moss, *Owner*
EMP: 5 **EST:** 2018
SALES (est): 128.63K **Privately Held**
SIC: 3999 Manufacturing industries, nec

(G-424)
DONALD HENLEY & SONS SAWMILL
Also Called: Henley Sawmill
2351 Old Cedar Falls Rd (27203-8356)
PHONE..................................336 625-5665
EMP: 5
SALES (est): 478.54K **Privately Held**
SIC: 2421 Sawmills and planing mills, general

(G-425)
EDGEWELL PER CARE BRANDS LLC
2331 Carl Dr (27203)
P.O. Box 849 (27204-0849)
PHONE..................................336 672-4500
Jake Casper, *Brnch Mgr*
EMP: 21
SALES (corp-wide): 2.25B **Publicly Held**
Web: www.edgewell.com
SIC: 3421 Razor blades and razors
HQ: Edgewell Personal Care Brands, Llc
  6 Research Dr
  Shelton CT 06484
  203 944-5500

(G-426)
EDGEWELL PER CARE BRANDS LLC
800 Albemarle Rd (27203-6263)
PHONE..................................336 629-1581
Reggie Rodman, *Brnch Mgr*
EMP: 22
SALES (corp-wide): 2.25B **Publicly Held**
Web: www.edgewell.com
SIC: 3421 Razor blades and razors
HQ: Edgewell Personal Care Brands, Llc
  6 Research Dr
  Shelton CT 06484
  203 944-5500

(G-427)
EDGEWELL PER CARE BRANDS LLC
419 Art Bryan Dr (27203-3089)
PHONE..................................336 672-4500
Joe Tisone, *Brnch Mgr*
EMP: 9
SALES (corp-wide): 2.25B **Publicly Held**
Web: www.edgewell.com
SIC: 3421 3692 5063 Razor blades and razors; Primary batteries, dry and wet; Batteries, dry cell
HQ: Edgewell Personal Care Brands, Llc
  6 Research Dr
  Shelton CT 06484
  203 944-5500

(G-428)
EHS RETAIL LLC
Also Called: Everything Hemp Store, The
405 E Dixie Dr Ste A (27203-6827)
PHONE..................................336 629-4367
Bob Crumley, *Pr*
EMP: 10 **EST:** 2017
SALES (est): 224.3K **Privately Held**
SIC: 2833 5136 5137 Medicinals and botanicals; Men's and boys' outerwear; Women's and children's outerwear

(G-429)
ELASTIC THERAPY LLC
718 Industrial Park Ave (27205-7336)
P.O. Box 4068 (27204-4068)
PHONE..................................336 625-0529
◆ **EMP:** 52 **EST:** 1989
SQ FT: 125,000
SALES (est): 20.89MM
SALES (corp-wide): 1.71B **Publicly Held**
Web: www.elastictherapy.com
SIC: 3842 Elastic hosiery, orthopedic (support)
HQ: Djo, Llc
  2900 Lake Vista Dr # 200
  Lewisville TX 75067
  760 727-1283

(G-430)
ENERGIZER BATTERY MFG
419 Art Bryan Dr (27203-3089)
PHONE..................................336 736-7936
EMP: 9 **EST:** 2019
SALES (est): 730.57K **Privately Held**
SIC: 3999 Manufacturing industries, nec

(G-431)
ENERGIZER HOLDINGS INC
800 Albemarle Rd (27203-6263)
PHONE..................................336 672-3526
EMP: 24
SALES (corp-wide): 2.96B **Publicly Held**
Web: www.energizerholdings.com
SIC: 3691 3648 Storage batteries; Flashlights
PA: Energizer Holdings, Inc.
  533 Maryville Univ Dr
  Saint Louis MO 63141
  314 985-2000

(G-432)
EXLON EXTRUSION INC
2971 Taylor Dr (27203-0554)
PHONE..................................336 621-1295
Dennis Swink, *Pr*
Viola Fay Swink, *Sec*
EMP: 11 **EST:** 1984
SALES (est): 2.12MM
SALES (corp-wide): 295.68MM **Privately Held**
SIC: 3089 Injection molding of plastics
PA: Pexco Llc
  6470 E Johns Xing Ste 430
  Johns Creek GA 30097
  678 990-1523

(G-433)
FARR KNITTING COMPANY INC
171 Boyd Ave (27205-7405)
PHONE..................................336 625-5561
Billy Farr, *Pr*
Tim Farr, *VP*
EMP: 6 **EST:** 1991
SQ FT: 1,700
SALES (est): 476.14K **Privately Held**
SIC: 2252 Socks

(G-434)
FIBER CUSHIONING INC (PA)
4454 Us Highway 220 Bus S (27205-0837)
PHONE..................................336 629-8442
W E Mcgee, *Pr*
▲ **EMP:** 18 **EST:** 1988
SQ FT: 62,500
SALES (est): 3.1MM
SALES (corp-wide): 3.1MM **Privately Held**
Web: www.fibercushioning.com
SIC: 2392 Cushions and pillows

(G-435)
FINE LINE HOSIERY INC
2012 Sunny Ln (27205-7256)
P.O. Box 4606 (27204-4606)
PHONE..................................336 498-8022
◆ **EMP:** 14 **EST:** 1995
SQ FT: 20,000
SALES (est): 559.42K **Privately Held**
Web: www.finelinehosiery.com
SIC: 2251 5632 2843 Women's hosiery, except socks; Hosiery; Finishing agents

(G-436)
FOUNDERS HEMP LLC
1157 S Cox St # B (27205-6952)
PHONE..................................888 334-4367
EMP: 9 **EST:** 2014
SALES (est): 906.42K **Privately Held**
Web: www.foundershemp.com
SIC: 2833 0139 5999 Adrenal derivatives

(G-437)
FOX APPAREL INC
100 Industrial Park Ave (27205-7324)
PHONE..................................336 629-7641
Wallace Thompson, *Pr*
John Thompson, *
Dolores Thompson, *
EMP: 135 **EST:** 1966
SQ FT: 167,000
SALES (est): 23.82MM **Privately Held**
Web: www.foxapparel.net
SIC: 2325 2329 2337 2339 Jeans: men's, youths', and boys'; Jackets (suede, leatherette, etc.), sport: men's and boys'; Jackets and vests, except fur and leather: women's; Jeans: women's, misses', and juniors'

(G-438)
GALLIMORE FMLY INVESTMENTS INC
Also Called: Gallimore Body Shop
1431 E Salisbury St (27203-5053)
PHONE..................................336 625-5138
Kenneth Gallimore, *Pr*
Bridget Gallimore, *VP*
EMP: 18 **EST:** 2012
SALES (est): 941.85K **Privately Held**
Web: www.construction-products-maine.com
SIC: 3999 Atomizers, toiletry

(G-439)
GATEHOUSE MEDIA LLC
Also Called: Asheboro Courrier Tribune
500 Sunset Ave (27205-5330)
P.O. Box 340 (27204-0340)
PHONE..................................336 626-6103
Dave Renfro, *Mgr*
EMP: 17
SALES (corp-wide): 2.66B **Publicly Held**
Web: www.courier-tribune.com
SIC: 2711 7313 Newspapers: publishing only, not printed on site; Newspaper advertising representative
HQ: Gatehouse Media, Llc
  175 Sullys Trl Ste 203
  Pittsford NY 14534
  585 598-0030

(G-440)
GEORGIA-PACIFIC LLC
Also Called: Georgia-Pacific
200 Mcdowell Rd (27205-7357)
PHONE..................................336 629-2151
Beverly L Franks, *Brnch Mgr*
EMP: 105
SQ FT: 200,000
SALES (corp-wide): 36.93B **Privately Held**
Web: www.gp.com
SIC: 2653 5113 Boxes, corrugated: made from purchased materials; Corrugated and solid fiber boxes
HQ: Georgia-Pacific Llc
  133 Peachtree St Nw
  Atlanta GA 30303
  404 652-4000

▲ = Import ▼ = Export ◆ = Import/Export

GEOGRAPHIC SECTION

Asheboro - Randolph County (G-465)

(G-441)
HUNSUCKER PRINTING CO INC
522 N Fayetteville St (27203-4729)
P.O. Box 219 (27204-0219)
PHONE..................................336 629-9125
James T Russell Senior, *Pr*
Terry L Russell, *Sec*
Joe Russell, *VP*
EMP: 7 **EST:** 1946
SQ FT: 7,800
SALES (est): 505.68K **Privately Held**
Web: www.hunsuckerprinting.com
SIC: 2752 2759 Offset printing; Letterpress printing

(G-442)
INDIAN TFF-TANK GREENSBORO INC
2491 Mountain Lake Rd (27205-4433)
PHONE..................................336 625-2629
Mike Chewning Senior, *Pr*
Jackie Chewning, *Sec*
EMP: 8 **EST:** 1968
SQ FT: 10,000
SALES (est): 588.03K **Privately Held**
SIC: 3559 Chemical machinery and equipment

(G-443)
INDORAMA VENTURES USA INC (DH)
Also Called: Starpet
801 Pineview Rd (27203-3192)
PHONE..................................336 672-0101
Randall Brummett, *Contrlr*
Dk Agarwal, *Prin*
Sri Prakash Lohia, *Prin*
Aloke Lohia, *Prin*
Suchitra Lohia, *Prin*
◆ **EMP:** 113 **EST:** 2003
SQ FT: 80,000
SALES (est): 89.64MM **Privately Held**
Web: www.sptlab.com
SIC: 2821 Polyvinyl butyral resins
HQ: Indorama Polymers Public Company Limited
  75/102,103 Asok Road Soi Sukhumvit 19 (Vadhana)
  Vadhana 10110

(G-444)
INK N STITCHES LLC
2739 Us Highway 220 Bus S (27205-0820)
PHONE..................................336 633-3898
Penny York, *Pt*
Michael Wheless, *Pt*
Faye Wheless, *Pt*
EMP: 4 **EST:** 1999
SQ FT: 3,000
SALES (est): 352.97K **Privately Held**
Web: www.inknstitches.com
SIC: 2759 2395 5199 Screen printing; Embroidery and art needlework; Advertising specialties

(G-445)
INNOVATIVE BUSINESS GROWTH LLC
1157 S Cox St (27203-6952)
PHONE..................................888 334-4367
EMP: 22
SALES (est): 1.55MM **Privately Held**
SIC: 2068 Seeds: dried, dehydrated, salted or roasted

(G-446)
INTERRS-EXTERIORS ASHEBORO INC
Also Called: Carpet One
2013 S Fayetteville St (27205-7307)
PHONE..................................336 629-2148
Ken W Cornwell, *Pr*
Sally Cornwell, *Sec*
EMP: 15 **EST:** 1970
SQ FT: 18,000
SALES (est): 883.24K **Privately Held**
Web: www.carpetone.com
SIC: 5713 5211 2211 5719 Carpets; Lumber and other building materials; Draperies and drapery fabrics, cotton; Lighting fixtures

(G-447)
JAECO PRECISION INC
721 Jaeco Caudill Dr (27205-9678)
P.O. Box 726 (27204-0726)
PHONE..................................336 633-1025
Eric Lambeth, *Pr*
Jeff Callicutt, *Sec*
EMP: 6 **EST:** 1998
SQ FT: 4,000
SALES (est): 883.2K **Privately Held**
Web: www.jaecoprecision.com
SIC: 3599 Machine shop, jobbing and repair

(G-448)
KEANI FURNITURE INC
1546 N Fayetteville St (27203-3854)
PHONE..................................336 303-5484
Eric Racosta, *Pr*
EMP: 20 **EST:** 2013
SALES (est): 600K **Privately Held**
SIC: 2512 5712 2326 5047 Chairs: upholstered on wood frames; Furniture stores; Medical and hospital uniforms, men's; Medical equipment and supplies

(G-449)
KENNAMETAL INC
201 Yzex St (27203-3280)
PHONE..................................336 672-3313
Earl Leonard, *Mgr*
EMP: 61
SQ FT: 116,644
SALES (corp-wide): 2.08B **Publicly Held**
Web: www.kennametal.com
SIC: 3545 Cutting tools for machine tools
PA: Kennametal Inc.
  525 William Penn Pl # 3600
  Pittsburgh PA 15219
  412 248-8000

(G-450)
LABEL LINE LTD
5356 Nc Highway 49 S (27205-1974)
PHONE..................................336 857-3115
EMP: 95 **EST:** 1985
SALES (est): 9.2MM **Privately Held**
SIC: 2679 2672 2671 Labels, paper: made from purchased material; Labels (unprinted), gummed: made from purchased materials; Paper; coated and laminated packaging

(G-451)
LAMBETH DIMENSION INC
443 Mount Shepherd Road Ext (27205-2891)
PHONE..................................336 629-3838
Roger C Lambeth, *Pr*
Donna Lambeth, *VP*
▲ **EMP:** 15 **EST:** 1992
SALES (est): 1.54MM **Privately Held**
SIC: 2426 Frames for upholstered furniture, wood

(G-452)
LAMBETH FRAMES INC
443 Mount Shepherd Road Ext (27205-2891)
P.O. Box 2444 (27204-2444)
PHONE..................................336 953-9805
EMP: 6 **EST:** 2017
SALES (est): 154.25K **Privately Held**
SIC: 2426 2511 Frames for upholstered furniture, wood; Bed frames, except water bed frames: wood

(G-453)
LEONARD ELECTRIC MTR REPR INC
531 N Fayetteville St (27203-4728)
P.O. Box 292 (27204-0292)
PHONE..................................336 625-2375
Paul Comer, *Pr*
Ronnie Kinney, *VP*
EMP: 4 **EST:** 1952
SQ FT: 10,000
SALES (est): 248.13K **Privately Held**
SIC: 7694 Rewinding stators

(G-454)
LONGS MACHINE & TOOL INC
Also Called: G Force South
2224 S Fayetteville St (27205-7312)
PHONE..................................336 625-3844
Roger Chilton, *Brnch Mgr*
EMP: 25
Web: www.longsmachinetool.com
SIC: 3714 Air conditioner parts, motor vehicle
PA: Longs Machine & Tool Inc
  150 N Grant St
  Cleona PA 17042

(G-455)
LUNA METAL BUILDINGS AND CON
468 N Fayetteville St (27203-4727)
PHONE..................................336 628-0273
EMP: 4 **EST:** 2019
SALES (est): 179.48K **Privately Held**
Web: www.lunametalbuildings.com
SIC: 3441 Fabricated structural metal

(G-456)
MAS ACME USA
159 North St (27203-5411)
PHONE..................................336 625-2161
EMP: 8 **EST:** 2017
SALES (est): 265.19K **Privately Held**
Web: www.acme-mccrary.com
SIC: 2251 Women's hosiery, except socks

(G-457)
MATLAB INC (PA)
1112 Nc Highway 49 S (27205-9584)
P.O. Box 2046 (27204-2046)
PHONE..................................336 629-4161
Gayle F Peddycord Kurdian, *Pr*
Bill Kurdian, *VP*
William Kurdian, *Prin*
▲ **EMP:** 14 **EST:** 1979
SQ FT: 135,000
SALES (est): 18.58MM
SALES (corp-wide): 18.58MM **Privately Held**
Web: www.matlabinc.com
SIC: 2851 Paints and allied products

(G-458)
MID TOWN DIXIE EXPRESS FUEL
455 W Salisbury St (27205-5443)
PHONE..................................336 318-1200
EMP: 7 **EST:** 2010
SALES (est): 174.91K **Privately Held**
SIC: 2869 Fuels

(G-459)
OLIVER RUBBER COMPANY LLC
408 Telephone Ave (27205-6800)
PHONE..................................336 629-1436
Alan Blanton, *Mgr*
EMP: 394
SALES (corp-wide): 1.05B **Privately Held**
Web: www.oliverrubber.com
SIC: 3011 3061 Tires and inner tubes; Mechanical rubber goods
HQ: Oliver Rubber Company, Llc
  1 Parkway S
  Greenville SC 29615
  866 464-2580

(G-460)
PEMMCO MANUFACTURING INC
631 Veterans Loop Rd (27205-0818)
PHONE..................................336 625-1122
EMP: 51 **EST:** 1980
SALES (est): 9.89MM **Privately Held**
Web: www.pemmcomfg.com
SIC: 3599 Machine shop, jobbing and repair

(G-461)
PEXCO LLC
2971 Taylor Dr (27203-0554)
PHONE..................................336 493-7500
EMP: 51
SALES (corp-wide): 295.68MM **Privately Held**
Web: www.pexco.com
SIC: 3354 Aluminum extruded products
PA: Pexco Llc
  6470 E Johns Xing Ste 430
  Johns Creek GA 30097
  678 990-1523

(G-462)
PIEDMONT CUSTOM MEATS INC
430 Nc Highway 49 S (27205-9561)
PHONE..................................336 628-4949
Donna Moore, *Pr*
EMP: 35 **EST:** 2014
SQ FT: 20,000
SALES (est): 3.43MM **Privately Held**
Web: www.piedmontcustommeats.com
SIC: 2011 Meat packing plants

(G-463)
PIEDMONT ELC MTR REPR INC ASHB
4635 Us Highway 220 Bus N (27205-3331)
PHONE..................................336 495-0500
Thomas M Saunders, *Pr*
Sue W Saunders, *VP*
EMP: 12 **EST:** 1970
SQ FT: 26,000
SALES (est): 2.36MM **Privately Held**
Web: www.piedmontelectricmotor.com
SIC: 7694 5063 Rewinding services; Motors, electric

(G-464)
POST CONSUMER BRANDS LLC
Also Called: Asheboro Maltomeal
2525 Bank St (27203-3087)
PHONE..................................336 672-0124
Dale Ducommun, *Brnch Mgr*
EMP: 26
Web: www.postconsumerbrands.com
SIC: 2043 Oatmeal: prepared as cereal breakfast food
HQ: Post Consumer Brands, Llc
  20802 Kensington Blvd
  Lakeville MN 55044
  952 322-8000

(G-465)
POSTAL EXPRESS PLUS
2029 Woods Stream Ln (27205-8251)
PHONE..................................336 626-0162
Ronald Deese, *Owner*
EMP: 5 **EST:** 2005
SALES (est): 63.71K **Privately Held**
SIC: 2741 Miscellaneous publishing

Asheboro - Randolph County (G-466)

(G-466)
PREMIER POWDER COATING INC
1948 N Fayetteville St (27203-3270)
PHONE.................................336 672-3828
Jerry Raines, *Pr*
Karen Raines, *Sec*
EMP: 7 **EST:** 1994
SQ FT: 21,000
SALES (est): 945.05K **Privately Held**
Web: www.prempowdcoat.com
SIC: 3479 Coating of metals and formed products

(G-467)
PRESTIGE FABRICATORS INC
905 Nc Highway 49 S (27205-9566)
P.O. Box 816 (27204-0816)
PHONE.................................336 626-4595
Joseph R Wingfield, *Pr*
Hans Klaussner, *
J B Davis, *
Scott Kauffman, *
David O Bryant, *
EMP: 270 **EST:** 1993
SQ FT: 402,000
SALES (est): 43.43MM **Privately Held**
Web: www.vpcgroup.com
SIC: 3086 Insulation or cushioning material, foamed plastics

(G-468)
PRINTLOGIC INC
Also Called: Tiedmont Printing
2753 Us Highway 220 Bus S (27205-0820)
P.O. Box 430 (27204-0430)
PHONE.................................336 626-6680
EMP: 25 **EST:** 2011
SALES (est): 2.49MM **Privately Held**
Web: www.printlogicllc.com
SIC: 2752 Offset printing

(G-469)
QI SIGNS LLC
370 W Salisbury St (27203-5442)
PHONE.................................336 625-0938
Jeremy E Mcneill, *Prin*
EMP: 5 **EST:** 2018
SALES (est): 72.61K **Privately Held**
SIC: 3993 Signs and advertising specialties

(G-470)
RAMSEUR INTER-LOCK KNITTING CO
2409 Old Lexington Rd (27205-2578)
PHONE.................................336 824-2427
Samuel A Rankin Junior, *Pr*
Jane Rankin Slaughter, *Stockholder*
▲ **EMP:** 4 **EST:** 1946
SQ FT: 225,000
SALES (est): 297.29K **Privately Held**
SIC: 2257 2241 Weft knit fabric mills; Trimmings, textile

(G-471)
RANDOLPH MACHINE INC (PA)
1206 Uwharrie St (27203-7671)
P.O. Box 147 (27204-0147)
PHONE.................................336 625-0411
Steve Coleman, *Pr*
EMP: 5 **EST:** 1989
SQ FT: 3,200
SALES (est): 876.95K **Privately Held**
Web: www.randolphmachine.com
SIC: 3599 Machine shop, jobbing and repair

(G-472)
RANDOLPH PACKING COMPANY
403 W Balfour Ave (27203-3247)
PHONE.................................336 672-1470
C Donald Hamlet, *Pr*
Rebecca T Hamlet, *
D Craig Hamlet, *
Rex A Hamlet, *
EMP: 87 **EST:** 1947
SQ FT: 25,000
SALES (est): 4.61MM **Privately Held**
Web: www.randpacknc.com
SIC: 2011 Meat packing plants

(G-473)
RIM-TEC CASTINGS EASTERN LLC
421 Inwood Rd (27205-8879)
PHONE.................................336 302-0912
▲ **EMP:** 28
SALES (corp-wide): 509K **Privately Held**
Web: www.rimtec.us
SIC: 3325 Steel foundries, nec
PA: Rim-Tec Castings Eastern, L.L.C.
  16109 Halle Marie Cir # 3
  Davidson NC 28036
  336 302-0912

(G-474)
ROBBINS BEANE INC
621 Hazelwood St (27205-7075)
PHONE.................................336 953-5919
Joseph Beane, *Pr*
Robert Robbins, *Sec*
EMP: 6 **EST:** 2014
SALES (est): 112.26K **Privately Held**
Web: www.baghoop.com
SIC: 3089 Garbage containers, plastics

(G-475)
RODNEY TYLER
530 Albemarle Rd (27205-6257)
PHONE.................................336 629-0951
Rodney Tyler, *Prin*
EMP: 6 **EST:** 2017
SALES (est): 287.27K **Privately Held**
SIC: 2752 Commercial printing, lithographic

(G-476)
SAPONA MANUFACTURING CO INC
Also Called: Sapona Plastics
7039 Us Highway 220 S (27205-1581)
PHONE.................................336 873-8700
Dean Lail, *Mgr*
EMP: 205
SALES (corp-wide): 25.2MM **Privately Held**
Web: www.saponamfg.com
SIC: 2282 3089 Throwing and winding mills; Injection molding of plastics
PA: Sapona Manufacturing Company, Incorporated
  2478 Cedar Falls Rd
  Cedar Falls NC 27230
  336 625-2727

(G-477)
SAPONA MANUFACTURING CO INC
159 North St (27203-5411)
PHONE.................................336 625-2161
Kevin Flenniken, *Prin*
EMP: 8 **EST:** 2009
SALES (est): 34.49K **Privately Held**
SIC: 3999 Manufacturing industries, nec

(G-478)
SAPONA PLASTICS LLC
7039 Us Highway 220 S (27205-1581)
PHONE.................................336 873-8700
Jack Lail, *Managing Member*
▲ **EMP:** 72 **EST:** 2004
SQ FT: 52,000
SALES (est): 18.61MM **Privately Held**
Web: www.saponaplastics.com
SIC: 3089 Injection molding of plastics

(G-479)
SEDIA SYSTEMS INC
335 Commerce Pl (27203-0552)
PHONE.................................336 887-3818
Chris Mullins, *Brnch Mgr*
EMP: 10
Web: www.sediasystems.com
SIC: 2531 Public building and related furniture
PA: Sedia Systems, Inc.
  1820 W Hubbard St Ste 300
  Chicago IL 60622

(G-480)
SHEFFIBILT INC
1429 Cable Creek Rd (27205-2298)
PHONE.................................336 963-0086
James E Sheffield Junior, *Prin*
EMP: 6 **EST:** 2014
SALES (est): 232.33K **Privately Held**
Web: www.sheffibilt.com
SIC: 2836 Plasmas

(G-481)
SOULSHINE PUBLISHING CO LLC
344 Countryside Acres Dr (27205-0793)
PHONE.................................336 688-4612
A D Tilley, *Prin*
EMP: 5 **EST:** 2018
SALES (est): 69.45K **Privately Held**
SIC: 2741 Miscellaneous publishing

(G-482)
SOUTHCORR LLC
Also Called: Ds Smith Packaging
3021 Taylor Dr (27205-0555)
PHONE.................................336 498-1700
Jeff Mcneill, *Genl Mgr*
▲ **EMP:** 60 **EST:** 1994
SQ FT: 125,000
SALES (est): 24.72MM **Privately Held**
Web: www.southcorr.com
SIC: 2631 Corrugating medium

(G-483)
SOUTHERN ROOTS MILLWORK
466 Skycrest Country Rd (27205-0932)
PHONE.................................336 736-8812
Jason Gaines, *Prin*
EMP: 5 **EST:** 2019
SALES (est): 228.43K **Privately Held**
SIC: 2431 Millwork

(G-484)
SOUTHERN STATES COOP INC
Also Called: S S C 7516-7
504 E Dixie Dr (27203-7035)
PHONE.................................336 629-3977
Frank Thompson, *Mgr*
EMP: 9
SALES (corp-wide): 1.71B **Privately Held**
Web: www.southernstates.com
SIC: 5999 2048 Feed and farm supply; Prepared feeds, nec
PA: Southern States Cooperative, Incorporated
  6606 W Broad St Ste B
  Richmond VA 23230
  804 281-1000

(G-485)
STARPET INC
801 Pineview Rd (27203-3192)
PHONE.................................336 672-0101
Stephen C Edwards, *Pr*
Muthukumer Paramasivam, *
Hussam Awad, *
Yashwant Awasthi, *
Sachin Agarwalla, *
▲ **EMP:** 105 **EST:** 2000
SALES (est): 52.8MM **Privately Held**
SIC: 2821 Polyethylene resins
HQ: Indorama Ventures Public Company Limited
  75/102 Soi Sukhumvit 19 (Vadhana),
  Asok Road
  Vadhana 10110

(G-486)
STATE OF ART CUSTOM FRAMING
150 Sunset Ave (27203-5634)
PHONE.................................336 629-7377
EMP: 4 **EST:** 2017
SALES (est): 59.05K **Privately Held**
Web: www.stateoftheartframing.com
SIC: 2499 Picture frame molding, finished

(G-487)
STEEL SUPPLY AND ERECTION CO
1237 N Fayetteville St (27203-4563)
P.O. Box 607 (27204-0607)
PHONE.................................336 625-4830
Eric D Newton, *Pr*
Jonathan Newton, *Sec*
EMP: 18 **EST:** 1946
SQ FT: 6,400
SALES (est): 2.39MM **Privately Held**
Web: www.steelsupplycompany.com
SIC: 1791 7389 7692 Structural steel erection; Crane and aerial lift service; Welding repair

(G-488)
STICKLER WOODWORKING INC
458 Burney Rd (27205-1322)
PHONE.................................336 302-0683
David Stickler, *Prin*
EMP: 7 **EST:** 2008
SALES (est): 225.79K **Privately Held**
SIC: 2431 Millwork

(G-489)
SWATCH WORKS INC
453 Oakhurst Rd (27205-0996)
PHONE.................................336 626-9971
EMP: 7 **EST:** 2020
SALES (est): 553.97K **Privately Held**
Web: www.theswatchworks.com
SIC: 2211 Broadwoven fabric mills, cotton

(G-490)
SWATCHWORKS INC
730 Industrial Park Ave (27205-7336)
P.O. Box 369 (27204-0369)
PHONE.................................336 626-9971
James N Davis, *Pr*
EMP: 9 **EST:** 1989
SALES (est): 399.31K **Privately Held**
Web: www.theswatchworks.com
SIC: 2211 2782 Upholstery fabrics, cotton; Blankbooks and looseleaf binders

(G-491)
TECHNIMARK LLC
2536 Bank St (27203-3086)
P.O. Box 2068 (27204-2068)
PHONE.................................336 498-4171
Keith Mullin, *Brnch Mgr*
EMP: 5
SALES (corp-wide): 566.35MM **Privately Held**
Web: www.technimark.com
SIC: 3089 Injection molding of plastics
PA: Technimark Llc
  180 Commerce Pl
  Asheboro NC 27203
  336 498-4171

GEOGRAPHIC SECTION

Asheville - Buncombe County (G-515)

(G-492)
TECHNIMARK LLC
4509 Us Highway 220 Bus N (27203-3362)
P.O. Box 2068 (27204-2068)
PHONE..................................336 498-4171
Chris Clark, *Brnch Mgr*
EMP: 5
SALES (corp-wide): 566.35MM **Privately Held**
Web: www.technimark.com
SIC: 3089 Injection molding of plastics
PA: Technimark Llc
   180 Commerce Pl
   Asheboro NC 27203
   336 498-4171

(G-493)
TECHNIMARK LLC (PA)
180 Commerce Pl (27203-0515)
P.O. Box 2068 (27204-2068)
PHONE..................................336 498-4171
◆ **EMP:** 370 **EST:** 1983
SQ FT: 700,000
SALES (est): 566.35MM
SALES (corp-wide): 566.35MM **Privately Held**
Web: www.technimark.com
SIC: 3089 Injection molding of plastics

(G-494)
TECHNIMARK REYNOSA LLC
2510 Bank St (27203-3086)
PHONE..................................336 498-4171
EMP: 5
SALES (corp-wide): 566.35MM **Privately Held**
Web: www.technimark.com
SIC: 3089 Injection molding of plastics
HQ: Technimark Reynosa Llc
   180 Commerce Pl
   Asheboro NC 27203

(G-495)
TECHNIMARK REYNOSA LLC (HQ)
180 Commerce Pl (27203-0515)
P.O. Box 2068 (27204-2068)
PHONE..................................336 498-4171
Donald F Wellington, *Managing Member*
Robert Burkhart, *
▲ **EMP:** 475 **EST:** 2007
SQ FT: 67,000
SALES (est): 63.14MM
SALES (corp-wide): 566.35MM **Privately Held**
Web: www.technimark.com
SIC: 3089 Injection molding of plastics
PA: Technimark Llc
   180 Commerce Pl
   Asheboro NC 27203
   336 498-4171

(G-496)
TELEFLEX MEDICAL INCORPORATED
312 Commerce Pl (27203-0552)
PHONE..................................336 498-4153
Ryan Payne, *Brnch Mgr*
EMP: 7
SALES (corp-wide): 2.97B **Publicly Held**
Web: www.teleflex.com
SIC: 3841 Surgical and medical instruments
HQ: Teleflex Medical Incorporated
   3015 Carrington Mill Blvd # 100
   Morrisville NC 27560
   919 544-8000

(G-497)
THERMACO INCORPORATED
Also Called: Big Dipper
646 Greensboro St (27203-4739)
P.O. Box 2548 (27204-2548)
PHONE..................................336 629-4651
William C Batten, *Pr*
Susan Thomson Batten, *VP*
EMP: 9 **EST:** 1983
SQ FT: 15,000
SALES (est): 2.48MM **Privately Held**
Web: www.thermaco.com
SIC: 3823 Industrial process control instruments

(G-498)
THOMAS BROTHERS FOODS LLC
Also Called: Thomas Brothers Ham Company
1852 Gold Hill Rd (27203-4291)
PHONE..................................336 672-0337
EMP: 15 **EST:** 2009
SQ FT: 25,000
SALES (est): 8.98MM **Privately Held**
Web: www.thomasbrothersham.com
SIC: 5147 5142 2013 Meats, cured or smoked; Packaged frozen goods; Sausages and other prepared meats

(G-499)
TRIAD CORRUGATED METAL INC (PA)
208 Luck Rd (27205-7856)
P.O. Box 4907 (27204-4907)
PHONE..................................336 625-9727
Garrett Eugene Smith, *CEO*
Patrick Smith, *
Jeannie K Smith, *
EMP: 35 **EST:** 2000
SALES (est): 19.39MM
SALES (corp-wide): 19.39MM **Privately Held**
Web: www.triadcorrugatedmetal.com
SIC: 2952 5211 5033 5444 Roofing materials; Roofing material; Roofing and siding materials; Sheet metalwork

(G-500)
TRIAD CUTTING TOOLS INC
5527 Us Highway 220 S (27205-1568)
P.O. Box 60 (27341-0060)
PHONE..................................336 873-8708
James R Cain Junior, *Pr*
James R Cain Senior, *VP*
EMP: 6 **EST:** 1990
SQ FT: 6,000
SALES (est): 960.93K **Privately Held**
Web: www.tctoolz.com
SIC: 5251 7699 3541 Tools; Knife, saw and tool sharpening and repair; Machine tools, metal cutting type

(G-501)
TROTTERS SEWING COMPANY INC
321 Industrial Park Ave (27205-7327)
P.O. Box 1145 (27204-1145)
PHONE..................................336 629-4550
Barbara J Trotter, *Pr*
Jerry L Trotter, *
EMP: 55 **EST:** 1992
SQ FT: 47,000
SALES (est): 5.89MM **Privately Held**
Web: www.trotterssewing.com
SIC: 2311 Men's and boy's suits and coats

(G-502)
UNITED WOOD PRODUCTS INC
451 Railroad St (27203-4322)
P.O. Box 1083 (27204-1083)
PHONE..................................336 626-2281
David Smith, *Pr*
Roger C Chriscoe, *VP*
EMP: 8 **EST:** 1997
SQ FT: 10,000
SALES (est): 631.42K **Privately Held**
Web: www.unitedwoodproductsinc.com
SIC: 2431 Millwork

(G-503)
UNIVERSAL FIBERS INC
749 Pineview Rd (27203-3191)
P.O. Box 438 (28007-0438)
PHONE..................................336 672-2600
Deepak Khopkar, *Mgr*
EMP: 110
SQ FT: 166,584
SALES (corp-wide): 116.86MM **Privately Held**
Web: www.universalfibers.com
SIC: 2281 Polyester yarn, spun: made from purchased staple
HQ: Universal Fibers, Inc.
   14401 Industrial Park Rd
   Bristol VA 24202
   276 669-1161

(G-504)
UWHARRIE FRAMES MFG LLC
247 Leo Cranford Rd (27205-1060)
PHONE..................................336 626-6649
EMP: 30 **EST:** 2007
SALES (est): 2.34MM **Privately Held**
SIC: 2426 Frames for upholstered furniture, wood

(G-505)
VILLAGE PRINTING CO
530 Albemarle Rd (27203-6257)
PHONE..................................336 629-0951
Rodney Tyler, *Owner*
EMP: 16 **EST:** 1969
SQ FT: 10,000
SALES (est): 2.3MM **Privately Held**
Web: www.villageprinting.com
SIC: 2752 Offset printing

(G-506)
WAYNE TRADEMARK
5356 Nc Highway 49 S (27205-1974)
PHONE..................................336 887-3173
EMP: 9 **EST:** 2019
SALES (est): 906.12K **Privately Held**
Web: www.waynetrademark.com
SIC: 3999 Manufacturing industries, nec

(G-507)
WAYNE TRADEMARK PRTG PACKG LLC
Also Called: Wayne Trademark International
5346 Nc Highway 49 S (27205-1974)
P.O. Box 2683 (27261-2683)
PHONE..................................336 887-3173
EMP: 35 **EST:** 2007
SALES (est): 3.43MM **Privately Held**
Web: www.waynetrademark.com
SIC: 2752 Offset printing

(G-508)
WEATHERCRAFT OUTDOOR FURN INC
3524 Us Highway 220 Bus S (27205-0828)
P.O. Box 1042 (27204-1042)
PHONE..................................336 629-3939
William C Palmer, *Pr*
EMP: 7 **EST:** 1988
SQ FT: 10,000
SALES (est): 233.07K **Privately Held**
Web: www.weathercraftfurn.com
SIC: 2511 5712 Wood lawn and garden furniture; Furniture stores

(G-509)
WEB 4 HALF LLC
Also Called: Direct Promotional
720 Industrial Park Ave (27205-7336)
PHONE..................................855 762-4638
EMP: 50 **EST:** 2010
SQ FT: 15,000
SALES (est): 4.31MM **Privately Held**
Web: www.directpromotionals.com
SIC: 7371 3999 3993 Computer software development; Advertising display products; Signs and advertising specialties

(G-510)
WELLS HOSIERY MILLS INC (PA)
Also Called: Asheboro Activewear
1758 S Fayetteville St (27205-7356)
P.O. Box 1566 (27204-1566)
PHONE..................................336 633-4881
Theodore Cooley, *CEO*
Rodney Debusk, *
Janet L Nance, *
Paul Avato, *
◆ **EMP:** 200 **EST:** 1951
SALES (est): 45.47MM
SALES (corp-wide): 45.47MM **Privately Held**
Web: www.wellshosiery.com
SIC: 2252 Socks

(G-511)
WILLIAM BOSTIC
3854 Us Highway 64 E (27203-8462)
PHONE..................................336 629-5243
William Bostic, *Owner*
EMP: 5 **EST:** 2014
SALES (est): 186.98K **Privately Held**
SIC: 2899 Flares

Asheville
Buncombe County

(G-512)
8TH ELMENT CNDTNING PRFMCE LLC
Also Called: 8th Element
120 Elm Dr (28805-8767)
PHONE..................................828 298-1290
EMP: 6 **EST:** 2018
SALES (est): 434.58K **Privately Held**
Web: www.8thelementavl.com
SIC: 2819 Elements

(G-513)
A STITCH IN TIME
Also Called: A Balloon For You
1259 Sweeten Creek Rd 25a (28803-1865)
PHONE..................................828 274-5193
Elaine Mcpherson, *Owner*
EMP: 5 **EST:** 1962
SQ FT: 7,000
SALES (est): 199.77K **Privately Held**
Web: www.astitchintimenc.com
SIC: 7219 5947 3942 7389 Tailor shop, except custom or merchant tailor; Gift shop; Stuffed toys, including animals; Balloons, novelty and toy

(G-514)
ADAM DALTON DISTILLERY LLC
251 Biltmore Ave (28801-4158)
PHONE..................................828 785-1499
Joan Evans Dalton, *Prin*
EMP: 7 **EST:** 2011
SALES (est): 120.34K **Privately Held**
Web: www.dalton-distillery.com
SIC: 2082 Malt beverages

(G-515)
ADORATHERAPY INC
31 Mount Vernon Cir (28804-2440)
PHONE..................................917 297-8904
Laura Ramsey, *CEO*
Dorothy Winquist, *Pr*
EMP: 10 **EST:** 2013
SALES (est): 960.21K **Privately Held**

Asheville - Buncombe County (G-516) — GEOGRAPHIC SECTION

Web: www.adoratherapy.com
SIC: **2844** 7389 Perfumes, cosmetics and other toilet preparations; Business services, nec

(G-516)
AFFORDABLE BEDDING INC
996 Patton Ave Ste A (28806-3662)
PHONE.............................828 254-5555
Patrick Mcmahon, *Pr*
Rebecca Banner, *VP*
EMP: 5 **EST:** 2000
SQ FT: 3,000
SALES (est): 763.06K **Privately Held**
Web: www.affordablebedding.com
SIC: **5021** 2515 Mattresses; Mattresses and bedsprings

(G-517)
AMCOR TOB PACKG AMERICAS INC
3055 Sweeten Creek Rd (28803-2114)
PHONE.............................828 274-1611
Michael Schmitt, *Pr*
Eileen Burns Lerum, *VP*
Robert Mosesian, *VP*
♦ **EMP:** 562 **EST:** 2009
SALES (est): 8.31MM
SALES (corp-wide): 14.69B **Privately Held**
SIC: **3089** Molding primary plastics
HQ: Amcor Flexibles Llc
3 Parkway North Blvd # 300
Deerfield IL 60015
224 313-7000

(G-518)
ANDY-OXY CO INC (PA)
27 Heritage Dr (28806-1914)
P.O. Box 6389 (28816-6389)
PHONE.............................828 258-0271
EMP: 26 **EST:** 1975
SALES (est): 9.53MM
SALES (corp-wide): 9.53MM **Privately Held**
Web: www.andyoxy.com
SIC: **5084** 2813 Welding machinery and equipment; Acetylene

(G-519)
ANNALINE LLC
12 White Ash Dr (28803-2491)
PHONE.............................828 505-7115
Peter Christian Brewer, *Owner*
EMP: 5 **EST:** 2017
SALES (est): 92.36K **Privately Held**
SIC: **2741** Miscellaneous publishing

(G-520)
ANNETTE CAMERON
60 Holland St (28801-1811)
PHONE.............................828 505-0404
Annette Cameron, *Prin*
EMP: 5 **EST:** 2010
SALES (est): 82.98K **Privately Held**
SIC: **2711** Newspapers, publishing and printing

(G-521)
APPALACHIAN GETAWAYS
45 Pinedale Rd (28805-1529)
PHONE.............................828 243-3105
EMP: 5 **EST:** 2010
SALES (est): 84.51K **Privately Held**
Web: www.appalachiangetaways.com
SIC: **2421** Outdoor wood structural products

(G-522)
APPALACHIAN PUBG GROUP INC
183 Edgewood Rd (28804-3312)
P.O. Box 18192 (28814-0192)
PHONE.............................828 505-3643
Richard Corbitt, *Prin*
EMP: 5 **EST:** 2014
SALES (est): 54.76K **Privately Held**
SIC: **2741** Miscellaneous publishing

(G-523)
APPALACHIAN STRINGS INC
1 Page Ave Ste 126 (28801-2392)
PHONE.............................828 712-8721
Benjamin Aaron Williams, *Owner*
EMP: 5 **EST:** 2014
SALES (est): 50.37K **Privately Held**
Web: www.handcraftedmusicalinstruments.com
SIC: **3931** Musical instruments

(G-524)
APPALACHIAN TECHNOLOGY LLC
Also Called: Appalachian Technology
187 Elk Mountain Rd (28804-2045)
PHONE.............................828 210-8888
Astrid Schneider, *Pr*
Charles Billy Beck, *
Alfred Lewis Jackson Junior, *Treas*
Al Jackson, *
▲ **EMP:** 42 **EST:** 2001
SQ FT: 16,500
SALES (est): 5.54MM **Privately Held**
Web: www.appalachiantech.com
SIC: **3678** 3429 Electronic connectors; Locks or lock sets

(G-525)
APPALCHIAN STOVE FBRCATORS INC
Also Called: ASC Distribution
329 Emma Rd (28806-3809)
PHONE.............................828 253-0164
James S Rice, *Pr*
Thomas A Bryson, *
▲ **EMP:** 17 **EST:** 1976
SQ FT: 60,000
SALES (est): 791.19K **Privately Held**
Web: www.appalachianstove.com
SIC: **3433** 5023 5075 3429 Stoves, wood and coal burning; Fireplace equipment and accessories; Warm air heating equipment and supplies; Hardware, nec

(G-526)
APROTECH POWERTRAIN LLC
31 Adams Hill Rd (28806-3822)
PHONE.............................828 253-1350
Karyl Kyser, *Mgr*
EMP: 30
Web: www.aprotechgroup.com
SIC: **3612** Transformers, except electric
PA: Aprotech Powertrain, Llc
2150 Butterfield Dr
Troy MI 48084

(G-527)
AQUAPRO SOLUTIONS LLC
46 New Leicester Hwy Ste 102 (28806-2719)
P.O. Box 160 (28778-0160)
PHONE.............................828 255-0772
EMP: 6 **EST:** 2006
SQ FT: 2,500
SALES (est): 492.61K **Privately Held**
Web: www.aquaprosolutions.com
SIC: **3589** Water purification equipment, household type

(G-528)
ART ENTERPRISES INC
Also Called: Mountain Graphics
1156 Sweeten Creek Rd (28803-1728)
P.O. Box 9585 (28815-0585)
PHONE.............................828 277-1211
Alan Mojonnier, *Pr*
EMP: 5 **EST:** 1984
SQ FT: 5,200
SALES (est): 463.89K **Privately Held**
SIC: **2759** Screen printing

(G-529)
ASCEND ESSENCES LLC
Also Called: Ascend Fitness
6 N Kensington Rd (28804-1510)
PHONE.............................828 575-2502
EMP: 4 **EST:** 2017
SALES (est): 58.41K **Privately Held**
SIC: **2741** Miscellaneous publishing

(G-530)
ASHE HAMS INC
707 Merrimon Ave (28804-6628)
PHONE.............................828 259-9426
Carolyn Slider, *Mgr*
EMP: 5
SIC: **2013** 5421 Ham, smoked: from purchased meat; Meat and fish markets
PA: Ashe Hams Inc
78 Forest Rd
Asheville NC 28803

(G-531)
ASHEVILLE BIT & STEEL COMPANY
111 Edgewood Rd S (28803-1816)
P.O. Box 5913 (28813-5913)
PHONE.............................828 274-3766
James V Stafford, *Pr*
Vicki S Stafford, *VP*
▲ **EMP:** 13 **EST:** 1968
SQ FT: 12,500
SALES (est): 2.54MM **Privately Held**
Web: www.ashevillebit.com
SIC: **3423** 5051 Edge tools for woodworking: augers, bits, gimlets, etc.; Iron and steel (ferrous) products

(G-532)
ASHEVILLE CITIZEN-TIMES
Also Called: Tegna
14 Ohenry Ave (28803-9106)
P.O. Box 2090 (28802-0716)
PHONE.............................828 252-5611
Jeffrey P Green, *Pr*
Randy Hammer, *
Virgil L Smith, *
EMP: 7 **EST:** 1990
SALES (est): 10.44MM
SALES (corp-wide): 2.91B **Publicly Held**
Web: www.citizen-times.com
SIC: **2711** Newspapers, publishing and printing
PA: Tegna Inc.
8350 Broad St Ste 2000
Tysons VA 22102
703 873-6600

(G-533)
ASHEVILLE COLOR & IMAGING INC
611 Tunnel Rd Ste E (28805-1973)
PHONE.............................828 774-5040
Jeffrey Jones, *Pr*
EMP: 6 **EST:** 2013
SALES (est): 485.19K **Privately Held**
Web: www.goaciprint.com
SIC: **2759** 7389 Commercial printing, nec; Design services

(G-534)
ASHEVILLE CUSTOM CLOSETS
20 Stone River Dr (28804-4408)
PHONE.............................828 337-7539
Jimmy Commerford, *Prin*
EMP: 5 **EST:** 2008
SALES (est): 88.25K **Privately Held**
Web: www.dreamclosetsasheville.com
SIC: **2434** Wood kitchen cabinets

(G-535)
ASHEVILLE DISTILLING COMPANY
45 S French Broad Ave (28801-3364)
PHONE.............................828 575-2000
Albert L Sneed Junior, *Prin*
EMP: 14 **EST:** 2012
SALES (est): 422.55K **Privately Held**
Web: www.ashevilledistilling.com
SIC: **2085** Bourbon whiskey

(G-536)
ASHEVILLE GLOBAL REPORT
20 Battery Park Ave (28801-2720)
PHONE.............................828 236-3103
Shawn Gaynor, *Prin*
EMP: 9 **EST:** 2009
SALES (est): 120.75K **Privately Held**
SIC: **2711** Newspapers, publishing and printing

(G-537)
ASHEVILLE KOMBUCHA MAMAS LLC
54 Chestnut Ter (28803-9674)
PHONE.............................828 595-4340
EMP: 24
SALES (corp-wide): 11.02MM **Privately Held**
Web: www.drinkbuchi.com
SIC: **2086** Carbonated beverages, nonalcoholic: pkged. in cans, bottles
PA: Asheville Kombucha Mamas, Llc
242 Derringer Dr
Marshall NC 28753
828 394-2360

(G-538)
ASHEVILLE MEADERY LLC
Also Called: Fae Nectar
155 Johnston Blvd (28806-1820)
PHONE.............................828 454-6188
Tom Halladay Iii, *Pr*
EMP: 5 **EST:** 2020
SALES (est): 64.64K **Privately Held**
Web: www.faenectar.com
SIC: **2084** Wines

(G-539)
ASHEVILLE METAL FINISHING INC
178 Clingman Ave (28801-3240)
P.O. Box 16237 (28816-0237)
PHONE.............................828 253-1476
Thomas L Finger, *Pr*
Kay C Finger, *
EMP: 35 **EST:** 1988
SQ FT: 19,000
SALES (est): 4.56MM
SALES (corp-wide): 15.33MM **Privately Held**
Web: www.ashevillemetalfinishing.com
SIC: **3471** Electroplating of metals or formed products
PA: T L F Inc
280 Cane Creek Rd
Fletcher NC 28732
828 681-5343

(G-540)
ASHEVILLE PET SUPPLY
1451 Merrimon Ave (28804-1340)
PHONE.............................828 252-2054
EMP: 5 **EST:** 2020
SALES (est): 43.66K **Privately Held**
Web: www.ashevillepetsupply.com
SIC: **3999** Pet supplies

▲ = Import ▼ = Export
♦ = Import/Export

GEOGRAPHIC SECTION
Asheville - Buncombe County (G-568)

(G-541)
ASHEVILLE PRINT SHOP
740 Haywood Rd (28806-3136)
PHONE.................................828 214-5286
EMP: 7 EST: 2019
SALES (est): 94.55K **Privately Held**
Web: www.ashevillescreenprinting.com
SIC: 2752 Offset printing

(G-542)
ASHEVILLE PROMO LLC
202 Asheland Ave (28801-4016)
P.O. Box 18704 (28814-0704)
PHONE.................................828 575-2767
EMP: 6 EST: 2014
SALES (est): 406.04K **Privately Held**
Web: www.ashevillepromo.com
SIC: 2759 Screen printing

(G-543)
ASHEVILLE WOODWORKS
31 Panola St (28801-1017)
PHONE.................................828 734-0536
Merissa Walkenstein, *Prin*
EMP: 6 EST: 2010
SALES (est): 64.94K **Privately Held**
Web: www.ashevillehardware.com
SIC: 2431 Millwork

(G-544)
ASHEVLLE PRCSION MCH RBLDING I
51 Haywood Rd (28806-4521)
PHONE.................................828 254-0884
Jackie Queen, *Pr*
Hubert Queen, *VP*
Brenda Queen, *Sec*
EMP: 4 EST: 1997
SQ FT: 6,000
SALES (est): 238.3K **Privately Held**
Web: www.ppofa.com
SIC: 7699 7692 Industrial machinery and equipment repair; Welding repair

(G-545)
ASHVILLE POSTAGE EXPRESS
22 New Leicester Hwy Ste C (28806-2753)
PHONE.................................828 255-9250
Terry Simmons, *Owner*
EMP: 4 EST: 2005
SALES (est): 228.4K **Privately Held**
SIC: 2741 Miscellaneous publishing

(G-546)
ASHVILLE WRECKER SERVICE INC
80 Weaverville Rd (28804-1360)
PHONE.................................828 252-2388
Edward Peek, *Pr*
EMP: 9 EST: 1980
SQ FT: 1,287
SALES (est): 692.33K **Privately Held**
SIC: 3711 Wreckers (tow truck), assembly of

(G-547)
ASTRAL BUOYANCY COMPANY
Also Called: Astral Designs
347 Depot St # 201 (28801-4310)
P.O. Box 2 (28802-0002)
PHONE.................................828 255-2638
Philip G Curry, *Pr*
▲ EMP: 9 EST: 2002
SALES (est): 1.39MM **Privately Held**
Web: www.astralbuoyancy.com
SIC: 3842 Life preservers, except cork and inflatable

(G-548)
ATELIER MAISON AND CO LLC
121 Sweeten Creek Rd Ste 50 (28803-1526)
PHONE.................................828 277-7202
EMP: 15 EST: 2017
SALES (est): 1.28MM **Privately Held**
Web: www.ateliermaisonco.com
SIC: 2599 Furniture and fixtures, nec

(G-549)
ATHENS PUBLISHING COMPANY
70 Woodfin Pl (28801-2463)
PHONE.................................828 774-5270
EMP: 5 EST: 2017
SALES (est): 100.22K **Privately Held**
SIC: 2741 Miscellaneous publishing

(G-550)
AUTEN REPORTING
9 W Chestnut Ridge Ave (28804-3285)
PHONE.................................828 230-5035
EMP: 5 EST: 2010
SALES (est): 76.46K **Privately Held**
SIC: 2752 Commercial printing, lithographic

(G-551)
AVADIM HOLDINGS INC
600a Centrepark Dr (28805-1276)
PHONE.................................877 677-2723
EMP: 25
SALES (corp-wide): 12.03MM **Privately Held**
SIC: 2834 Pharmaceutical preparations
PA: Avadim Holdings, Inc.
   4 Old Patton Cove Rd
   Swannanoa NC 28778
   877 677-2723

(G-552)
AVL CUSTOM FABRICATION
250 Baird Cove Rd (28804-9706)
PHONE.................................828 713-0333
Coffey Robert Sean, *Owner*
EMP: 5 EST: 2014
SALES (est): 105.67K **Privately Held**
SIC: 3499 Novelties and giftware, including trophies

(G-553)
AVL TECHNOLOGIES INC
Also Called: Avl Technologies
15 N Merrimon Ave (28804-1367)
PHONE.................................828 250-9950
Jim Oliver, *Pr*
Esther O Cartwright, *
Jerry Ivester, *Chief Commercial Officer**
▲ EMP: 100 EST: 1994
SALES (est): 29.58MM **Privately Held**
Web: www.avltech.com
SIC: 3663 Space satellite communications equipment

(G-554)
AZALEA BINDERY LLC
1 Brookgreen Pl (28804-1812)
PHONE.................................828 545-6219
Mary Koester, *Prin*
EMP: 4 EST: 2011
SALES (est): 195.29K **Privately Held**
Web: www.azaleabindery.com
SIC: 2789 Binding only: books, pamphlets, magazines, etc.

(G-555)
B V HEDRICK GRAVEL & SAND CO
15 Yorkshire St (28803-7783)
PHONE.................................336 337-0706
EMP: 4
SALES (corp-wide): 332.33MM **Privately Held**
SIC: 1442 Construction sand and gravel
PA: B. V. Hedrick Gravel & Sand Company
   120 1/2 N Church St
   Salisbury NC 28144
   704 633-5982

(G-556)
BALL PHOTO SUPPLY INC
Also Called: Ball Photo
85 Tunnel Rd Ste 8 (28805-1232)
P.O. Box 1146 (28802-1146)
PHONE.................................828 252-2443
Laura Ball, *Pr*
Daniel Palmer, *Genl Mgr*
EMP: 6 EST: 1892
SQ FT: 18,000
SALES (est): 735.19K **Privately Held**
Web: www.ballphotosupply.com
SIC: 5946 3861 Cameras; Trays, photographic printing and processing

(G-557)
BAY TECH LABEL INC
36 Old Charlotte Hwy (28803-9404)
PHONE.................................828 296-8900
TOLL FREE: 800
Julie Goding, *Mgr*
EMP: 5
SALES (corp-wide): 9.38MM **Privately Held**
Web: www.baytechlabel.com
SIC: 2672 2679 Labels (unprinted), gummed: made from purchased materials; Labels, paper: made from purchased material
PA: Bay Tech Label, Inc.
   12177 28th St N
   Saint Petersburg FL 33716
   727 572-9311

(G-558)
BIANCAS STITCH WORKS LLC
122 Hudson St (28806-3308)
PHONE.................................828 505-0686
Bianca Schmidt, *Prin*
EMP: 5 EST: 2009
SALES (est): 80.58K **Privately Held**
Web: www.biancas-stitchworks.com
SIC: 2395 Embroidery and art needlework

(G-559)
BILTMORE EMBROIDERERS INC
448 Sondley Woods Pl (28805-1155)
PHONE.................................828 298-7403
Birchard C Snyder, *Prin*
EMP: 6 EST: 2010
SALES (est): 45.7K **Privately Held**
SIC: 2395 Embroidery and art needlework

(G-560)
BILTMORE ESTATE WINE CO LLC
1 N Pack Sq Ste 400 (28801-3409)
PHONE.................................828 225-6776
William A V Cecil Junior, *Pr*
Richard Pressley, *Sr VP*
Steve Miller, *Sr VP*
Mary Ryan, *VP*
John Stevens, *Sec*
▲ EMP: 120 EST: 1970
SQ FT: 95,000
SALES (est): 4.96MM **Privately Held**
Web: www.biltmore.com
SIC: 2084 Wines

(G-561)
BLACK OAK BOAT WORKS
23 Spring Cove Rd (28804-2716)
PHONE.................................828 252-4997
Laura Beeler, *Prin*
EMP: 5 EST: 2008
SALES (est): 112.15K **Privately Held**
SIC: 3732 Boatbuilding and repairing

(G-562)
BLACK WOLF CUSTOM WOODWORKS
48 Cris Ln (28806-0019)
PHONE.................................828 925-0399
Sarah Hess, *Prin*
EMP: 4 EST: 2017
SALES (est): 85.29K **Privately Held**
SIC: 2431 Millwork

(G-563)
BLUE RIDGE BRACKET CO
5 Creekside Ct (28803-2089)
PHONE.................................828 242-8577
Trent Van Dyke, *Prin*
EMP: 5 EST: 2010
SALES (est): 118.47K **Privately Held**
SIC: 3999 Manufacturing industries, nec

(G-564)
BLUE RIDGE ELC MTR REPR INC
Also Called: Wnc Starter
629 Emma Rd (28806-2839)
P.O. Box 16557 (28816-0557)
PHONE.................................828 258-0800
Rustin D Rice, *Pr*
Sharon Rice, *Sec*
EMP: 4 EST: 1987
SQ FT: 8,000
SALES (est): 491.89K **Privately Held**
SIC: 7694 5063 5999 Electric motor repair; Motors, electric; Motors, electric

(G-565)
BLUE RIDGE GLOBAL INC
128 Bingham Rd (28806-3884)
PHONE.................................828 252-5225
Alex Williams, *Pr*
EMP: 4 EST: 2005
SALES (est): 681.66K **Privately Held**
Web: www.blueridge.tech
SIC: 3429 Motor vehicle hardware

(G-566)
BLUE RIDGE PRINTING CO INC
544 Haywood Rd (28806-3556)
PHONE.................................828 254-1000
Bruce Fowler, *Pr*
EMP: 67 EST: 1974
SQ FT: 14,000
SALES (est): 4.38MM **Privately Held**
Web: www.blueridgeprinting.com
SIC: 2752 Offset printing

(G-567)
BLUE-HEN INC
Also Called: Fireproof Office Files
60 N Market St Ste C200 (28801-8124)
PHONE.................................407 322-2262
Henry Dieckhaus, *Pr*
Edith Dieckhaus, *Sec*
EMP: 8 EST: 1923
SQ FT: 7,000
SALES (est): 972.06K **Privately Held**
Web: www.bluehen.com
SIC: 2522 5712 Office cabinets and filing drawers, except wood; Office furniture

(G-568)
BOB CALLAHAN LLC
104 Lakeshore Dr (28804-2302)
PHONE.................................828 620-9730
Robert B Callahan Ii, *Mgr*
EMP: 9 EST: 2015
SALES (est): 417.9K **Privately Held**
SIC: 2431 Millwork

Asheville - Buncombe County (G-569)

(G-569)
BOGGS COLLECTIVE INC
239 Amboy Rd (28806-4331)
PHONE..................828 398-9701
▲ **EMP:** 4 **EST:** 2010
SALES (est): 320.53K **Privately Held**
Web: www.brianboggschairmakers.com
SIC: 2511 Wood household furniture

(G-570)
BP SOLUTIONS GROUP INC
24 Wilmington St (28806-4227)
P.O. Box 6250 (28816-6250)
PHONE..................828 252-4476
Robert W Williams, *Pr*
Barry Kempson, *
Scott Cotten, *
Carl Connelly, *
EMP: 40 **EST:** 1931
SQ FT: 40,000
SALES (est): 4.58MM **Privately Held**
Web: www.bpsg.us
SIC: 2752 2791 2789 Offset printing; Typesetting; Bookbinding and related work

(G-571)
BRAIFORM ENTERPRISES INC
Also Called: Plasti-Form
12 Gerber Rd Ste B (28803-2497)
PHONE..................828 277-6420
◆ **EMP:** 220
SIC: 3089 Clothes hangers, plastics

(G-572)
BRETT SALTER
9 Webb Cove Rd (28804-1926)
PHONE..................828 252-4311
Brett Salter, *Prin*
EMP: 4 **EST:** 2011
SALES (est): 59.23K **Privately Held**
SIC: 3999 Framed artwork

(G-573)
BRIGHT ANGLE LLC
207 Coxe Ave (28801-4006)
PHONE..................828 771-6966
Nick Moen, *Managing Member*
EMP: 5 **EST:** 2016
SALES (est): 508.81K **Privately Held**
Web: www.thebrightangle.com
SIC: 5032 5945 3229 Ceramic wall and floor tile, nec; Ceramics supplies; Tableware, glass or glass ceramic

(G-574)
BROOKSHIRE WOODWORKING INC (PA)
Also Called: Brookshire Buiulders
355 Haywood Rd (28806-4231)
PHONE..................828 779-2119
Jeremy Brookshire, *Prin*
EMP: 6 **EST:** 2007
SALES (est): 298.37K
SALES (corp-wide): 298.37K **Privately Held**
SIC: 2431 Millwork

(G-575)
BURCO INTERNATIONAL INC
1900 Hendersonville Rd Ste 10 (28803)
PHONE..................828 252-4481
James Burleson, *Pr*
Leslie Burleson, *Sec*
EMP: 13 **EST:** 1972
SQ FT: 36,000
SALES (est): 463.16K **Privately Held**
Web: www.goburco.com
SIC: 2752 Offset printing

(G-576)
BURCO PROMOTIONAL PRINTING INC
3106 Sweeten Creek Rd Ste B (28803-8106)
PHONE..................864 546-3443
EMP: 6 **EST:** 2018
SALES (est): 89.64K **Privately Held**
Web: www.1000words.com
SIC: 2752 Offset printing

(G-577)
C & C CHEMICAL COMPANY INC
119 Haywood Rd (28806-4523)
P.O. Box 6634 (28816-6634)
PHONE..................828 255-7639
William D Creasman, *Pr*
Joan Creasman, *Sec*
John W Creasman, *VP*
Nikki Herron, *Off Mgr*
EMP: 11 **EST:** 1972
SQ FT: 15,000
SALES (est): 552.93K **Privately Held**
SIC: 2841 Soap and other detergents

(G-578)
CALDWELLS WATER CONDITIONING
22 Country Spring Dr (28804-9710)
P.O. Box 6937 (28816-6937)
PHONE..................828 253-6605
EMP: 6 **EST:** 1981
SALES (est): 201.59K **Privately Held**
Web: www.caldwellsh2o.com
SIC: 3589 Swimming pool filter and water conditioning systems

(G-579)
CANNON & DAUGHTERS INC
2000 Riverside Dr Ste 9 (28804-2061)
PHONE..................828 254-9236
Becky Cannon, *Pr*
Memi Kubota, *
▲ **EMP:** 55 **EST:** 1982
SQ FT: 45,000
SALES (est): 12.65MM **Privately Held**
Web: www.greensprouts.com
SIC: 3944 2361 5641 Games, toys, and children's vehicles; Girl's and children's dresses, blouses; Children's and infants' wear stores

(G-580)
CARBON MARKET EXCHANGE LLC
28 Schenck Pkwy Ste 200 (28803-5088)
PHONE..................828 545-0140
Shenna Fortner, *Managing Member*
EMP: 5 **EST:** 2021
SALES (est): 177.63K **Privately Held**
SIC: 2299 Carbonizing of wool, mohair, and similar fibers

(G-581)
CAROLINA CUSTOM EXTERIORS INC
211 Amboy Rd (28806-4331)
PHONE..................828 232-0402
Mike Presley, *Owner*
EMP: 17 **EST:** 1995
SQ FT: 12,000
SALES (est): 998.78K **Privately Held**
Web: www.carolinacustomexteriorsinc.com
SIC: 1761 2439 Roofing contractor; Trusses, wooden roof

(G-582)
CAROLINA METALS INC
1398 Brevard Rd (28806-8511)
PHONE..................828 667-0876
Alan Wagner, *CEO*
Steve Cathcart, *
Tonya Bush, *
EMP: 21 **EST:** 1985
SQ FT: 23,000
SALES (est): 2.42MM **Privately Held**
Web: www.carolinametals.com
SIC: 3728 3769 3677 3469 Aircraft parts and equipment, nec; Space vehicle equipment, nec; Electronic coils and transformers; Metal stampings, nec

(G-583)
CAROLINA SOLAR STRUCTURES INC
1007 Tunnel Rd (28805-2013)
P.O. Box 905 (28704-0905)
PHONE..................828 684-9900
TOLL FREE: 800
Robert A Thompson, *Pr*
EMP: 24 **EST:** 1967
SQ FT: 13,575
SALES (est): 849.48K **Privately Held**
Web: www.carolinasolar.com
SIC: 3448 1799 Screen enclosures; Swimming pool construction

(G-584)
CAROLINA TRACTOR & EQP CO
Also Called: CAROLINA TRACTOR & EQUIPMENT COMPANY
40 Interstate Blvd (28806-2261)
PHONE..................828 251-2500
EMP: 6
SALES (corp-wide): 638.71MM **Privately Held**
Web: www.carolinacat.com
SIC: 7692 Welding repair
HQ: Carolina 1926 Llc
  9000 Statesville Rd
  Charlotte NC 28269
  704 596-6700

(G-585)
CASE GREEN CABINETRY
104 Lakeshore Dr (28804-2302)
PHONE..................828 620-9730
EMP: 5 **EST:** 2015
SALES (est): 86.59K **Privately Held**
Web: www.casegreen.com
SIC: 2434 Wood kitchen cabinets

(G-586)
CECO PUBLISHING INC (PA)
Also Called: Ceco Publishing
208 Elk Park Dr (28804-2063)
P.O. Box 1380 (28787-1380)
PHONE..................828 253-2047
EMP: 8 **EST:** 1985
SALES (est): 800K **Privately Held**
Web: www.expiredwixdomain.com
SIC: 2721 Magazines: publishing only, not printed on site

(G-587)
CFS PRESS SLIM RAY
8 Pelham Rd (28803-2550)
PHONE..................828 505-1030
Fred Ray, *Prin*
EMP: 6 **EST:** 2011
SALES (est): 142.47K **Privately Held**
Web: www.cfspress.com
SIC: 2741 Miscellaneous publishing

(G-588)
CHAOTIC TERRAIN PRESS
62 Wolf Rd (28805-9781)
PHONE..................828 575-7300
EMP: 4 **EST:** 2018
SALES (est): 75.48K **Privately Held**
Web: chaoticterrainpress.blogspot.com
SIC: 2741 Miscellaneous publishing

(G-589)
CHEMIST
151 Coxe Ave (28801-4025)
PHONE..................828 505-8778
Debra Werd, *Pr*
EMP: 5 **EST:** 2018
SALES (est): 58.73K **Privately Held**
Web: www.chemistspirits.com
SIC: 2085 Distilled and blended liquors

(G-590)
CHESTNUT LAND COMPANY
Also Called: Auntie Anne's
3 S Tunnel Rd Ste B-8 (28805-2558)
PHONE..................828 299-9108
Jennifer Irizarry, *Mgr*
EMP: 7
Web: www.auntieannes.com
SIC: 5461 2052 Pretzels; Pretzels
PA: Chestnut Land Company
  100 Debartolo Pl Ste 300
  Youngstown OH 44512

(G-591)
CHIRON PUBLICATIONS LLC
451 Beaucatcher Rd (28805-1710)
PHONE..................828 285-0838
Steven Buser, *Prin*
EMP: 7 **EST:** 2020
SALES (est): 65.16K **Privately Held**
Web: www.chironpublications.com
SIC: 2741 Miscellaneous publishing

(G-592)
CHOCOLATE FETISH LLC
36 Haywood St (28801-2832)
PHONE..................828 258-2353
EMP: 5 **EST:** 1986
SQ FT: 800
SALES (est): 515.97K **Privately Held**
Web: www.chocolatefetish.com
SIC: 2066 5441 5149 2064 Chocolate candy, solid; Confectionery produced for direct sale on the premises; Chocolate; Candy and other confectionery products

(G-593)
CINTOMS INC
3080 Sweeten Creek Rd (28803-2114)
PHONE..................828 684-1317
Thomas Barkei, *Pr*
Sandra Barkei, *Treas*
EMP: 8 **EST:** 2002
SQ FT: 2,458
SALES (est): 699.46K **Privately Held**
SIC: 2024 5812 Ice cream and frozen deserts ; Eating places

(G-594)
CLARKS PRINTING SERVICE INC
Also Called: Clark Communications
2 Westside Dr (28806-2845)
PHONE..................828 254-1432
Thomas A Clark, *Pr*
David E Diehn, *
Rebecca L Clark, *
Jane Altizer, *
Mary K Clark, *
EMP: 35 **EST:** 1973
SQ FT: 8,000
SALES (est): 5.07MM **Privately Held**
Web: www.oneclearchoice.com
SIC: 2752 7311 Offset printing; Advertising agencies

(G-595)
CLASSICAL ELEMENTS
9 Sweeten Creek Xing (28803-2543)

GEOGRAPHIC SECTION
Asheville - Buncombe County (G-619)

PHONE..................828 575-9145
Sean Catinella, *Prin*
EMP: 7 **EST:** 2016
SALES (est): 31.84K **Privately Held**
Web: www.classicalelements.com
SIC: 5736 5131 2221 Musical instrument stores; Upholstery fabrics, woven; Manmade and synthetic broadwoven fabrics

(G-596)
COLD MOUNTAIN CAPITAL LLC (PA)
2 Town Square Blvd (28803-5022)
PHONE..................828 210-8129
Horace Jennings, *Mgr*
Bernard Stanek Junior, *Mgr*
Anthony Bergen, *CFO*
EMP: 12 **EST:** 2011
SALES (est): 10.86MM
SALES (corp-wide): 10.86MM **Privately Held**
SIC: 3324 3792 Aerospace investment castings, ferrous; Tent-type camping trailers

(G-597)
CREASMANS WELDING
43 Sand Hill Ln (28806-1553)
PHONE..................828 667-1875
Evan Tcreasman, *Prin*
EMP: 6 **EST:** 2012
SALES (est): 72.25K **Privately Held**
SIC: 7692 Welding repair

(G-598)
CRIS BIFARO WOODWORKS INC
37 Langwell Ave (28806-3352)
PHONE..................828 776-2453
Cris Bifaro, *Owner*
EMP: 6 **EST:** 2010
SALES (est): 154.32K **Privately Held**
SIC: 2431 Millwork

(G-599)
CROSS CANVAS COMPANY INC
63 Glendale Ave (28803-1438)
P.O. Box 15024 (28813-0024)
PHONE..................828 252-0440
Glenn Russell, *Pr*
Paul Wayne Heflin, *VP*
EMP: 20 **EST:** 1986
SQ FT: 20,000
SALES (est): 2.49MM **Privately Held**
Web: www.crosscanvas.com
SIC: 2393 3161 2394 Duffle bags, canvas: made from purchased materials; Luggage; Canvas and related products

(G-600)
CSIT GROUP
205 Newstock Rd (28804-8749)
PHONE..................828 233-5750
Chuck Salerno, *Owner*
EMP: 4 **EST:** 2014
SALES (est): 108.21K **Privately Held**
SIC: 7372 Prepackaged software

(G-601)
D C CRSMAN MFR FINE JWLY INC
Also Called: Creasman D C Mfrs Fine Jewe
269 Tunnel Rd (28805-1832)
PHONE..................828 252-9891
David Creasman, *Pr*
Ramona Creasman, *Sec*
EMP: 7 **EST:** 1979
SQ FT: 1,500
SALES (est): 417.36K **Privately Held**
Web: www.dccreasmanjewelers.com
SIC: 3911 5944 7631 Jewel settings and mountings, precious metal; Jewelry, precious stones and precious metals; Jewelry repair services

(G-602)
DANIELS BUSINESS SERVICES INC (PA)
Also Called: Daniels Graphics
131 Sweeten Creek Rd 25a (28803-1526)
P.O. Box 40 (28802-0040)
PHONE..................828 277-8250
James W Daniels, *Pr*
Tim Bryant, *
James Cannon, *
Jeff Howell, *
Jami Daniels, *
EMP: 42 **EST:** 1948
SQ FT: 60,000
SALES (est): 8.7MM
SALES (corp-wide): 8.7MM **Privately Held**
Web: www.allegramarketingprint.com
SIC: 2752 7389 2759 Offset printing; Telephone answering service; Commercial printing, nec

(G-603)
DAVE STEEL COMPANY INC
76 Roberts Rd (28803-8613)
PHONE..................828 252-2771
EMP: 10
SALES (corp-wide): 47.72MM **Privately Held**
Web: www.davesteel.com
SIC: 3441 3449 5051 Fabricated structural metal; Miscellaneous metalwork; Steel
PA: Dave Steel Company, Inc.
  40 Meadow Rd
  Asheville NC 28803
  828 252-2771

(G-604)
DAVE STEEL COMPANY INC (PA)
40 Meadow Rd (28803-2652)
P.O. Box 2630 (28802-2630)
PHONE..................828 252-2771
Jeffrey Dave, *Pr*
Timothy Heffner, *
Babette Freund, *
Mark Buff, *
Chris Crosby, *
EMP: 54 **EST:** 1929
SQ FT: 90,000
SALES (est): 47.72MM
SALES (corp-wide): 47.72MM **Privately Held**
Web: www.davesteel.com
SIC: 5051 3449 3441 3471 Steel; Miscellaneous metalwork; Fabricated structural metal; Plating and polishing

(G-605)
DEA SASSO LIGHT OF DAY
117 Morningside Dr (28806-2908)
PHONE..................828 258-0141
L Sasso, *Prin*
EMP: 4 **EST:** 2010
SALES (est): 92.48K **Privately Held**
Web: www.deasasso.com
SIC: 2789 Binding only: books, pamphlets, magazines, etc.

(G-606)
DELKOTE MACHINE FINISHING INC
69 Bingham Rd (28806-3824)
PHONE..................828 253-1023
David Gutierrez, *Mgr*
EMP: 5 **EST:** 2005
SALES (est): 400K **Privately Held**
Web: www.deltechomes.com
SIC: 1742 3822 Insulation, buildings; Building services monitoring controls, automatic

(G-607)
DELTEC HOMES INC (PA)
69 Bingham Rd (28806-3824)
PHONE..................828 253-0483
▼ **EMP:** 42 **EST:** 1955
SQ FT: 110,000
SALES (est): 13.22MM **Privately Held**
Web: www.deltechomes.com
SIC: 5271 2452 Mobile home dealers; Prefabricated wood buildings

(G-608)
DEVERGER SYSTEMS INC
Also Called: DSI Blackpages
87 Downing St (28806-3523)
PHONE..................828 253-2255
Derrick A Deverger, *Pr*
Cynthia A Deverger, *VP*
EMP: 5 **EST:** 1986
SALES (est): 437.77K **Privately Held**
Web: www.dsiblackpages.com
SIC: 7371 2741 Custom computer programming services; Directories, nec: publishing and printing

(G-609)
DISSONANT SKATEBOARDS
147 Edgewood Rd Apt 1 (28804-3345)
PHONE..................607 793-8210
Anthony David Flis, *Owner*
EMP: 4 **EST:** 2016
SALES (est): 61.86K **Privately Held**
SIC: 3949 Skateboards

(G-610)
DJS PICKLES LLC
570 Brevard Rd Ste 16 (28806-2324)
PHONE..................828 647-0357
Donald Paleno, *Managing Member*
EMP: 6 **EST:** 2021
SALES (est): 71.76K **Privately Held**
Web: www.djspickles.com
SIC: 2035 Pickles, sauces, and salad dressings

(G-611)
DOREL ECOMMERCE INC
37 Haywood St Ste 300 (28801-2708)
PHONE..................828 378-0092
Martin Schwartz, *Pr*
Jeffrey Schwartz, *Ex VP*
EMP: 16 **EST:** 2007
SALES (est): 204.16K
SALES (corp-wide): 1.57B **Privately Held**
SIC: 2514 Household furniture: upholstered on metal frames
PA: Les Industries Dorel Inc
  1255 Av Greene Bureau 300
  Westmount QC H3Z 2
  514 934-3034

(G-612)
DOTSON METAL FINISHING INC
Also Called: Asheville Paint & Powder Coat
16 Old Charlotte Hwy (28803-9404)
P.O. Box 5814 (28813-5814)
PHONE..................828 298-9844
Thomas L Finger, *Pr*
Kay C Finger, *Sec*
EMP: 19 **EST:** 1975
SQ FT: 12,500
SALES (est): 3.04MM
SALES (corp-wide): 15.33MM **Privately Held**
Web: www.ashevillepowdercoat.com
SIC: 3479 Coating of metals and formed products
PA: T L F Inc
  280 Cane Creek Rd
  Fletcher NC 28732
  828 681-5343

(G-613)
EAST COAST OXYGEN INC
310 Elk Park Dr (28804-2066)
P.O. Box 18727 (28814-0727)
PHONE..................828 252-7770
EMP: 8 **EST:** 2010
SALES (est): 888.07K **Privately Held**
SIC: 2813 Industrial gases

(G-614)
EAST FORK POTTERY LLC
144 Caribou Rd Ste 70 (28803-1522)
PHONE..................828 237-7200
EMP: 7
SALES (corp-wide): 5.07MM **Privately Held**
Web: www.eastfork.com
SIC: 3269 Stoneware pottery products
PA: East Fork Pottery, Llc
  531 Short Mcdowell St
  Asheville NC 28803
  828 237-7200

(G-615)
EAST FORK POTTERY LLC (PA)
Also Called: East Fork
531 Short Mcdowell St (28803-2612)
PHONE..................828 237-7200
Alex Matisse, *CEO*
EMP: 10 **EST:** 2017
SALES (est): 5.07MM
SALES (corp-wide): 5.07MM **Privately Held**
Web: www.eastfork.com
SIC: 3269 Stoneware pottery products

(G-616)
EAST FORK POTTERY LLC
15 W Walnut St # A (28801-8102)
PHONE..................828 575-2150
Alex Matisse, *CEO*
EMP: 8
SALES (corp-wide): 5.07MM **Privately Held**
Web: www.eastfork.com
SIC: 3271 Concrete block and brick
PA: East Fork Pottery, Llc
  531 Short Mcdowell St
  Asheville NC 28803
  828 237-7200

(G-617)
ENPLAS LIFE TECH INC
230 Sardis Rd (28806-8504)
PHONE..................828 633-2250
EMP: 8 **EST:** 1995
SQ FT: 45,000
SALES (est): 1.83MM **Privately Held**
Web: en.enplas.com
SIC: 3544 3559 Forms (molds), for foundry and plastics working machinery; Plastics working machinery

(G-618)
EURISKO BEER COMPANY
255 Short Coxe Ave (28801-4143)
PHONE..................828 774-5055
Zac Harris, *CEO*
EMP: 7 **EST:** 2018
SALES (est): 331.76K **Privately Held**
SIC: 2082 Beer (alcoholic beverage)

(G-619)
EXPRESS CARPORT LLC
875 New Leicester Hwy (28806-1049)
PHONE..................888 389-2485
EMP: 4 **EST:** 2016
SALES (est): 262.16K **Privately Held**
Web: www.expresscarport.com

Asheville - Buncombe County (G-620)

(G-620)
FIBERLINK INC
122 Deerlake Dr (28803-3171)
PHONE..................828 274-5629
Andrew T Piatek, *Pr*
Stephanie F Cooper, *Sr VP*
Joseph C Harrison, *Genl Mgr*
EMP: 5 **EST:** 1999
SQ FT: 200
SALES (est): 521.73K **Privately Held**
SIC: 3661 Fiber optics communications equipment

(G-621)
FIRST COAST ENERGY LLP
301 Smokey Park Hwy (28806-1026)
PHONE..................828 667-0625
EMP: 8
Web: www.firstcoastenergy.com
SIC: 1311 Crude petroleum and natural gas
PA: First Coast Energy, L.L.P.
  6867 Southpoint Dr N # 101
  Jacksonville FL 32216

(G-622)
FIRSTREPORT SOFTWARE INC
369 London Rd (28803-2805)
PHONE..................828 441-0404
John Gellman, *Pr*
John Gallman, *Pr*
EMP: 4 **EST:** 1996
SALES (est): 264.33K **Privately Held**
Web: www.firstrecords.com
SIC: 7372 7371 Business oriented computer software; Custom computer programming services

(G-623)
FISHER SCIENTIFIC COMPANY LLC
275 Aiken Rd (28804-8740)
PHONE..................800 252-7100
Robert Hundley, *VP*
EMP: 63
SALES (corp-wide): 44.91B **Publicly Held**
Web: www.fishersci.com
SIC: 3821 5049 3829 3826 Clinical laboratory instruments, except medical and dental; Scientific instruments; Measuring and controlling devices, nec; Analytical instruments
HQ: Fisher Scientific Company Llc
  300 Industry Dr
  Pittsburgh PA 15275
  855 471-2255

(G-624)
FOREST MILLWORK INC
93 Thompson St (28803-2330)
PHONE..................828 251-5264
EMP: 16 **EST:** 1991
SALES (est): 1.48MM **Privately Held**
Web: www.forestmillwork.com
SIC: 2431 Millwork

(G-625)
FOUNDATION WOODWORKS LLC
17 Foundy St Ste 10 (28801-0146)
PHONE..................828 713-9665
Kean Werner, *Prin*
EMP: 5 **EST:** 2018
SALES (est): 54.13K **Privately Held**
Web: www.foundationwoodworks.com
SIC: 2431 Millwork

(G-626)
FOUR CORNERS HOME INC (PA)
1 Page Ave Ste 112l (28801-2389)
PHONE..................828 398-4187
William Griffin, *Pr*
Melissa Ness, *Prin*
Taylor Brandt, *Prin*
Joe Pawlus, *Prin*
EMP: 5 **EST:** 2008
SALES (est): 847.69K
SALES (corp-wide): 847.69K **Privately Held**
Web: www.fourcornershome.com
SIC: 2514 Household furniture: upholstered on metal frames

(G-627)
FOX FACTORY INC
1240 Brevard Rd (28806-9547)
PHONE..................828 633-6840
EMP: 12 **EST:** 2016
SALES (est): 190.35K **Privately Held**
SIC: 3714 Shock absorbers, motor vehicle

(G-628)
FRENCH BROAD BOATWORKS
211 Amboy Rd Ste D (28806-4331)
PHONE..................828 230-6600
EMP: 4 **EST:** 2017
SALES (est): 89.09K **Privately Held**
SIC: 3732 Boatbuilding and repairing

(G-629)
FRENCH BROAD CHOCOLATES LLC
821 Riverside Dr (28801-0281)
PHONE..................828 252-4181
Daniel Rattigan, *Managing Member*
EMP: 7 **EST:** 2006
SALES (est): 1.38MM **Privately Held**
Web: www.frenchbroadchocolates.com
SIC: 5441 2064 Candy; Candy bars, including chocolate covered bars

(G-630)
GALLO LEA ORGANICS LLC
Also Called: Gallolea Pizza Kits
9 Inglewood Rd (28804-1633)
PHONE..................828 337-1037
EMP: 6 **EST:** 2010
SALES (est): 245.29K **Privately Held**
Web: www.gallolea.com
SIC: 2099 Food preparations, nec

(G-631)
GE AVIATION SYSTEMS LLC
Also Called: GE Aviation
502 Sweeten Creek Industrial Park (28803-1730)
PHONE..................828 210-5076
EMP: 137
SALES (corp-wide): 67.95B **Publicly Held**
Web: www.geaerospace.com
SIC: 3728 Aircraft parts and equipment, nec
HQ: Ge Aviation Systems Llc
  1 Aviation Way
  Cincinnati OH 45215
  937 898-9600

(G-632)
GENELECT SERVICES INC
Also Called: Generac Distributors
50 Glendale Ave (28803-1463)
P.O. Box 3155 (28802-3155)
PHONE..................828 255-7999
EMP: 10 **EST:** 1994
SALES (est): 815.44K **Privately Held**
Web: www.genelectservices.com
SIC: 3621 7629 Motors and generators; Generator repair

(G-633)
GENERAL PAINTING & WOODWORK
16 Willow Creek Dr (28803-9696)
PHONE..................828 318-1252
Antonio Talamantes, *Prin*
EMP: 5 **EST:** 2018
SALES (est): 112.59K **Privately Held**
SIC: 2431 Millwork

(G-634)
GINGERS REVENGE LLC
829 Riverside Dr Ste 100 (28801-0228)
PHONE..................828 505-2462
EMP: 11 **EST:** 2015
SALES (est): 2.84MM **Privately Held**
Web: www.gingersrevenge.com
SIC: 2082 Beer (alcoholic beverage)

(G-635)
GINKGO PRINT STUDIO LLC
1 Grace Ave (28804-2503)
PHONE..................828 275-6300
Whitney Ponder, *Prin*
EMP: 4 **EST:** 2010
SALES (est): 180.88K **Privately Held**
Web: www.ginkgoprintstudio.com
SIC: 2752 Commercial printing, lithographic

(G-636)
GOLD LEAF LITERARY SVCS LLC
308 Cumberland Ave (28801-1716)
PHONE..................864 915-0226
Caroline Christopoulos, *Prin*
EMP: 5 **EST:** 2017
SALES (est): 56.29K **Privately Held**
Web: www.goldleafliterary.com
SIC: 2741 Miscellaneous publishing

(G-637)
GOLF ASSOCIATES ADVERTISING CO
Also Called: Golf Associates Score Card Co
91 Westside Dr (28806-2846)
P.O. Box 6917 (28816-6917)
PHONE..................828 252-6544
Edward S Pinkston Senior, *Pr*
Edward S Pinkston Junior, *VP*
Faye Pinkston, *
◆ **EMP:** 35 **EST:** 1972
SQ FT: 18,000
SALES (est): 6.11MM **Privately Held**
Web: www.golfassociates.com
SIC: 2752 7311 2761 2759 Offset printing; Advertising consultant; Manifold business forms; Commercial printing, nec

(G-638)
GRACE & GLORY GOODS LLC
402 Elk Park Dr (28804-2067)
PHONE..................828 575-2166
Nadine Mccowan, *Managing Member*
▲ **EMP:** 6 **EST:** 2013
SALES (est): 235.54K **Privately Held**
SIC: 3171 5621 Handbags, women's; Boutiques

(G-639)
GRATEFUL STEPS FOUNDATION
119 Buffalo Trl (28805-9761)
PHONE..................828 277-0998
Nicke Cavennes, *CEO*
Micki Cabaniss, *Ex Dir*
Jon Elliston, *Ch Bd*
EMP: 5 **EST:** 2011
SQ FT: 1,400
SALES (est): 194.34K **Privately Held**
Web: www.gratefulsteps.org
SIC: 5942 2731 Book stores; Book publishing

(G-640)
GRATEFUL UNION FAMILY INC (PA)
Also Called: Earth Guild
33 Haywood St (28801-2835)
PHONE..................828 622-3258
Marshall B Crawford, *Pr*
B J Crawford, *VP*
Barbara Hernden Field, *Sec*
Esther Holsen, *Treas*
EMP: 12 **EST:** 1976
SQ FT: 34,000
SALES (est): 2.06MM
SALES (corp-wide): 2.06MM **Privately Held**
Web: www.earthguild.com
SIC: 2331 5961 5945 5092 Women's and misses' blouses and shirts; Mail order house, nec; Arts and crafts supplies; Arts and crafts equipment and supplies

(G-641)
GRATZ INDUSTRIES
6 Vance Place Dr (28801-0241)
PHONE..................828 467-6380
Alan Gratz, *Prin*
EMP: 4 **EST:** 2018
SALES (est): 42.83K **Privately Held**
Web: www.alangratz.com
SIC: 3999 Manufacturing industries, nec

(G-642)
GREAT EASTERN SUN TRDG CO INC
Also Called: Great Eastern Sun
92 Mcintosh Rd (28806-1406)
PHONE..................828 665-7790
Barry E Evans, *CEO*
Janet Paige, *Pr*
Yoshihiro Kato, *VP*
Leila Bakkum, *VP*
Kenny Green, *Sec*
▲ **EMP:** 18 **EST:** 1982
SQ FT: 11,000
SALES (est): 12.02MM **Privately Held**
Web: www.great-eastern-sun.com
SIC: 2099 5149 2087 Food preparations, nec; Health foods; Flavoring extracts and syrups, nec

(G-643)
GREEN LINE MEDIA INC
Also Called: Mountain Xpress
2 Wall St Ste 214 (28801-2756)
P.O. Box 144 (28802-0144)
PHONE..................828 251-1333
Jeff Fobes, *Owner*
EMP: 22 **EST:** 1994
SALES (est): 1.83MM **Privately Held**
Web: www.mountainx.com
SIC: 2741 2711 Newsletter publishing; Newspapers

(G-644)
GREYBEARD PRINTING INC
Also Called: American Speedy Printing
1304c Patton Ave Ste C (28806-2604)
PHONE..................828 252-3082
Peter Boggs, *Pr*
EMP: 6 **EST:** 1979
SQ FT: 3,000
SALES (est): 402.47K **Privately Held**
Web: www.americanspeedy.com
SIC: 2752 Offset printing

(G-645)
GRIMME SERVICES LLC
26 Pelzer St (28804-2158)
PHONE..................828 490-6366
Tiffany N Grimme, *Prin*
EMP: 6 **EST:** 2018
SALES (est): 293.02K **Privately Held**
SIC: 3714 Motor vehicle parts and accessories

GEOGRAPHIC SECTION Asheville - Buncombe County (G-675)

(G-646)
H&H DISTILLERY LLC
Also Called: Cultivated Cocktails
204 Charlotte Hwy Ste D (28803-8681)
PHONE..................................828 338-9779
EMP: 7 **EST:** 2012
SALES (est): 252.63K **Privately Held**
Web: www.cultivated-cocktails.com
SIC: 2085 Distilled and blended liquors

(G-647)
HAMILTON INDUS GRINDING INC
Also Called: Carolina Knife Company
224 Mulvaney St (28803-1403)
PHONE..................................828 253-6796
Walter Ashbrook, *Mgr*
EMP: 21
SQ FT: 8,160
SALES (corp-wide): 4.63MM **Privately Held**
Web: www.carolinaknife.com
SIC: 5085 7699 3541 3423 Knives, industrial ; Knife, saw and tool sharpening and repair; Machine tools, metal cutting type; Hand and edge tools, nec
PA: Hamilton Industrial Grinding, Inc.
  240 N B St
  Hamilton OH 45013
  513 863-1221

(G-648)
HARRINS SAND & GRAVEL INC
195 Amboy Rd (28806-4330)
PHONE..................................828 254-2744
Danny Rice, *Pr*
Jeff Rice, *VP*
EMP: 4 **EST:** 1966
SQ FT: 6,000
SALES (est): 561.83K **Privately Held**
Web: www.harrinssandgravel.com
SIC: 1442 Construction sand and gravel

(G-649)
HELMET HALO
2 Williams St (28803-2454)
PHONE..................................828 407-3742
EMP: 4 **EST:** 2017
SALES (est): 102.03K **Privately Held**
Web: www.helmethalo.com
SIC: 3949 Sporting and athletic goods, nec

(G-650)
HENCO NORTH
1445 Merrimon Ave (28804-1340)
PHONE..................................828 552-3671
EMP: 5 **EST:** 2019
SALES (est): 127.65K **Privately Held**
Web: www.henconorth.com
SIC: 2752 Offset printing

(G-651)
HIGH NOON COFFEE ROASTERS LLC
191 Charlotte St Ste 101 (28801-1990)
PHONE..................................770 851-7004
EMP: 5 **EST:** 2017
SALES (est): 65.66K **Privately Held**
Web: www.highnooncoffee.com
SIC: 2095 Roasted coffee

(G-652)
HIGHLAND BREWING COMPANY INC
Also Called: Highland
12 Old Charlotte Hwy Ste H (28803-9419)
PHONE..................................828 299-3370
Oscar Wong, *Pr*
John M Lyda, *VP*
▲ **EMP:** 18 **EST:** 1994
SALES (est): 8.42MM **Privately Held**
Web: www.highlandbrewing.com

SIC: 2082 5813 Ale (alcoholic beverage); Bars and lounges

(G-653)
HIS GLASSWORKS INC
2000 Riverside Dr Ste 19 (28804-2099)
PHONE..................................828 254-2559
Robert W Stephan, *Pr*
Margaret Stephan, *VP*
Mark Bolick, *COO*
▼ **EMP:** 6 **EST:** 1980
SQ FT: 3,100
SALES (est): 2.07MM **Privately Held**
Web: www.hisglassworks.com
SIC: 5084 3291 3541 Industrial machinery and equipment; Abrasive stones, except grinding stones: ground or whole; Buffing and polishing machines

(G-654)
HK PUBLISHING INC
2 Sunset Dr (28804-3867)
PHONE..................................727 459-7724
Hope Koppelman, *Prin*
EMP: 4 **EST:** 2019
SALES (est): 59.23K **Privately Held**
SIC: 2741 Miscellaneous publishing

(G-655)
HOWLING MOON DISTILLERY INC
42 Old Elk Mountain Rd (28804-2070)
P.O. Box 18724 (28814-0724)
PHONE..................................828 208-1469
EMP: 5 **EST:** 2019
SALES (est): 186.09K **Privately Held**
Web: www.howlingmoonshine.com
SIC: 2085 Distilled and blended liquors

(G-656)
HYDRAULICS EXPRESS
40 Interstate Blvd (28806-2261)
P.O. Box 5637 (28813-5637)
PHONE..................................828 251-2500
Robert Bugg, *Prin*
EMP: 7 **EST:** 2016
SALES (est): 202.31K **Privately Held**
Web: www.hydraulicsexpress.com
SIC: 3599 Machine shop, jobbing and repair

(G-657)
ICON SIGN SYSTEMS INC
23 Villemagne Dr (28804-6109)
PHONE..................................828 253-4266
Scott Villemagne, *Pr*
Craig Garrett, *VP*
EMP: 4 **EST:** 1999
SALES (est): 267.65K **Privately Held**
Web: www.signsystemsnc.com
SIC: 3993 Signs and advertising specialties

(G-658)
ILUMIVU INC
1200 Ridgefield Blvd Ste 170 (28806)
PHONE..................................410 570-8846
Susan Steinmann, *Contrlr*
EMP: 7 **EST:** 2021
SALES (est): 188.76K **Privately Held**
Web: www.ilumivu.com
SIC: 7372 Prepackaged software

(G-659)
IMAGE 420 SCREENPRINTING INC
Also Called: Image 420 Screen Printing
420 Haywood Rd (28806-4260)
PHONE..................................828 253-9420
EMP: 8 **EST:** 1994
SALES (est): 381.55K **Privately Held**
Web: www.image420.com
SIC: 2759 2752 Screen printing; Commercial printing, lithographic

(G-660)
IN BLUE HANDMADE INC
20 Westside Dr (28806-2845)
PHONE..................................828 774-5094
EMP: 6 **EST:** 2015
SALES (est): 260.48K **Privately Held**
Web: www.inbluehandmade.com
SIC: 3199 Leather goods, nec

(G-661)
INDUSTRY NINE LLC
21 Old County Home Rd (28806-9713)
P.O. Box 16309 (28816-0309)
PHONE..................................828 210-5113
▲ **EMP:** 7 **EST:** 2008
SALES (est): 1.02MM **Privately Held**
Web: www.industrynine.com
SIC: 3751 Bicycles and related parts

(G-662)
INGRAM MACHINE & BALANCING
Also Called: Ingram Racing Engines
48 Ben Lippen Rd (28806-2028)
PHONE..................................828 254-3420
EMP: 6 **EST:** 1964
SQ FT: 10,000
SALES (est): 358.68K **Privately Held**
Web: ingram-machine-balancing.usautos.repair
SIC: 3599 Machine shop, jobbing and repair

(G-663)
INTERNATIONAL PAPER COM
35 Martindale Rd (28804-1427)
PHONE..................................828 200-9284
EMP: 5 **EST:** 2017
SALES (est): 86.83K **Privately Held**
SIC: 2621 Paper mills

(G-664)
ITS A SNAP
66 Asheland Ave (28801-3246)
PHONE..................................828 254-3456
Mike Rangel, *Prin*
EMP: 8 **EST:** 2009
SALES (est): 124.61K **Privately Held**
SIC: 3544 Special dies and tools

(G-665)
IWANNA
31 College Pl Ste B100 (28801-2400)
PHONE..................................828 505-7319
EMP: 5 **EST:** 2016
SALES (est): 58.19K **Privately Held**
SIC: 7313 2759 2711 Newspaper advertising representative; Commercial printing, nec; Newspapers, publishing and printing

(G-666)
J & K TOOLS LLC
490 Upper Grassy Br Rd (28805-9233)
PHONE..................................828 299-0589
Joseph Higdon, *Prin*
EMP: 6 **EST:** 2016
SALES (est): 98.61K **Privately Held**
SIC: 3599 Industrial machinery, nec

(G-667)
JACQUELINE COLE
676 Fairview Rd (28803-1343)
PHONE..................................828 277-3566
Jacqueline Cole, *Prin*
EMP: 5 **EST:** 2010
SALES (est): 60.8K **Privately Held**
SIC: 3299 Architectural sculptures: gypsum, clay, papier mache, etc.

(G-668)
JAG GRAPHICS INC
Also Called: Sir Speedy
231 Biltmore Ave (28801-4107)
PHONE..................................828 259-9020
Gary Forbes, *Pr*
EMP: 5 **EST:** 1994
SQ FT: 2,500
SALES (est): 510.76K **Privately Held**
Web: www.sirspeedy.com
SIC: 2752 2791 2789 Commercial printing, lithographic; Typesetting; Bookbinding and related work

(G-669)
JARRETT SHANE DBA JARRETT STUC
19 Broadview Dr (28803-1044)
PHONE..................................828 768-8385
EMP: 6 **EST:** 2009
SALES (est): 89.8K **Privately Held**
SIC: 3299 Stucco

(G-670)
JERSEYBINCOM
61 N Merrimon Ave # 407 (28804-1378)
PHONE..................................828 545-0445
Robin Kortus, *Owner*
EMP: 4 **EST:** 2010
SALES (est): 172.58K **Privately Held**
SIC: 2671 Wrapping paper, waterproof or coated

(G-671)
JEWELRY SPOKEN HERE
86 Lanvale Ave (28806-2641)
PHONE..................................828 225-8464
Gregory Alexander, *Prin*
EMP: 5 **EST:** 2003
SALES (est): 153.29K **Privately Held**
SIC: 3911 Jewelry, precious metal

(G-672)
JO MANGUM
60 Linden Ave (28801-1352)
PHONE..................................919 271-8822
Jo Mangum, *Owner*
EMP: 5 **EST:** 2017
SALES (est): 73.16K **Privately Held**
SIC: 2721 Periodicals

(G-673)
JOHNSON CONTROLS INC
Also Called: Johnson Controls
905 Riverside Dr (28804-3114)
PHONE..................................828 225-3200
John Ogden, *Mgr*
EMP: 19
Web: www.johnsoncontrols.com
SIC: 2531 Seats, automobile
HQ: Johnson Controls, Inc.
  5757 N Green Bay Ave
  Milwaukee WI 53209
  920 245-6409

(G-674)
KING BIO INC
150 Westside Dr (28806-2847)
PHONE..................................828 398-6058
EMP: 49
Web: www.drkings.com
SIC: 3221 Medicine bottles, glass
PA: King Bio, Inc.
  3 Westside Dr
  Asheville NC 28806

(G-675)
KING BIO INC (PA)
Also Called: Safe Care Rx
3 Westside Dr (28806-2846)

Asheville - Buncombe County (G-676) — GEOGRAPHIC SECTION

PHONE..............................828 255-0201
Frank J King Junior, *Pr*
Suzie King, *
EMP: 51 EST: 1989
SQ FT: 150,000
SALES (est): 21.84MM **Privately Held**
Web: www.drkings.com
SIC: 5912 2834 5122 Proprietary (non-prescription medicine) stores; Pharmaceutical preparations; Pharmaceuticals

(G-676)
KITCHEN CABINETS AND DESIGN
60 N Merrimon Ave Unit 107 (28804-1391)
PHONE..............................828 779-4453
EMP: 5 EST: 2019
SALES (est): 27.98K **Privately Held**
Web: www.kitchensunlimitednc.com
SIC: 2434 Wood kitchen cabinets

(G-677)
KKB BILTMORE INC
479 Hendersonville Rd (28803-2750)
P.O. Box 3243 (28717-3243)
PHONE..............................828 274-6711
Paul Bradham, *Prin*
EMP: 7 EST: 2011
SALES (est): 234.98K **Privately Held**
Web: www.keystonekb.com
SIC: 2434 Wood kitchen cabinets

(G-678)
L F T INC
123 Lyman St (28801-4371)
PHONE..............................828 253-6830
Tom Finger, *Prin*
EMP: 7
SALES (est): 192.1K **Privately Held**
Web: www.t-fab.com
SIC: 3471 Electroplating of metals or formed products

(G-679)
LAND OF SKY MOBILE CANNING LLC
26 Magnolia Ave (28801-1724)
PHONE..............................303 880-1297
EMP: 5 EST: 2013
SALES (est): 91.29K **Privately Held**
SIC: 3565 5921 Canning machinery, food; Beer (packaged)

(G-680)
LAURA COOKE CERAMICS
1 Brucemont Cir Apt 3 (28806-3453)
PHONE..............................336 580-4308
Laura O Cooke, *Owner*
EMP: 5 EST: 2013
SALES (est): 111.55K **Privately Held**
Web: www.cookeceramics.com
SIC: 3269 Pottery products, nec

(G-681)
LAUREL OF ASHEVILLE LLC
Also Called: Laurel of Asheville, The
110 Executive Park (28801-2426)
P.O. Box 2059 (28802-2059)
PHONE..............................828 670-7503
EMP: 16 EST: 2006
SALES (est): 6.81MM **Privately Held**
Web: www.thelaurelofasheville.com
SIC: 2759 Publication printing

(G-682)
LEGALIZE POT BELLY PIGS CO LLC
40 Old Elk Mountain Rd (28804-2070)
PHONE..............................828 505-7053
Tim Robinson, *Prin*
EMP: 5 EST: 2015
SALES (est): 60.65K **Privately Held**
SIC: 2299 Textile goods, nec

(G-683)
LEVI STRAUSS INTERNATIONAL
800 Brevard Rd (28806-2251)
PHONE..............................828 665-2417
EMP: 5
SALES (corp-wide): 6.17B **Publicly Held**
Web: www.levistrauss.com
SIC: 2329 2339 Men's and boys' sportswear and athletic clothing; Women's and misses' outerwear, nec
HQ: Levi Strauss International
    1155 Battery St
    San Francisco CA 94111
    415 501-6000

(G-684)
LIFESTORY PUBLISHING LLC
48 Greenwood Rd (28803-1110)
PHONE..............................601 594-0018
EMP: 5 EST: 2015
SALES (est): 78.84K **Privately Held**
SIC: 2741 Miscellaneous publishing

(G-685)
LIGHTFORM INC
403 Shelwood Cir Apt H (28804-8238)
PHONE..............................908 281-9098
Jeremy Lerner, *Pr*
EMP: 4 EST: 1996
SALES (est): 339.15K **Privately Held**
Web: www.nanoparticleanalysis.com
SIC: 3827 Optical instruments and apparatus

(G-686)
LIGHTNING BOLT INK LLC
100 N Lexington Ave (28801-2815)
PHONE..............................828 281-1274
EMP: 7 EST: 2019
SALES (est): 482.62K **Privately Held**
Web: www.lightningboltink.com
SIC: 3452 Bolts, nuts, rivets, and washers

(G-687)
LINTER NORTH AMERICA CORP (DH)
48 Patton Ave (28801-3321)
PHONE..............................828 645-4261
Alberto Moratiel, *Pr*
C Roy Mendenhall, *VP*
Ramon Noblejas, *Sec*
EMP: 8 EST: 2009
SQ FT: 127,000
SALES (est): 26.2MM **Privately Held**
Web: www.balcrank.com
SIC: 3569 Lubricating equipment
HQ: Linter Investments SI
    Calle Gandia, 8 - Local 13
    Madrid M 28007

(G-688)
LITTLE LEAPS PRESS INC
2 Lynwood Rd (28804-2603)
PHONE..............................404 664-1842
Bill Treasurer, *Pr*
EMP: 4 EST: 2018
SALES (est): 64.32K **Privately Held**
SIC: 2741 Newsletter publishing

(G-689)
LUCKY MAN INC (HQ)
160 Broadway St (28801-2305)
PHONE..............................828 251-0090
▲ EMP: 49 EST: 1978
SALES (est): 11.91MM
SALES (corp-wide): 93.76MM **Privately Held**
Web: www.moogmusic.com
SIC: 3931 Musical instruments
PA: Inmusic Brands, Inc.
    200 Scenic View Dr # 201
    Cumberland RI 02864
    401 658-3131

(G-690)
LUCY V DIERKS CERAMICS INC
105 Kimberly Knoll Rd (28804-3521)
PHONE..............................757 692-5145
Lucy V Dierks, *Prin*
EMP: 5 EST: 2016
SALES (est): 68.72K **Privately Held**
Web: www.lucyvdierks.com
SIC: 3269 Pottery products, nec

(G-691)
LUSTAR DYEING AND FINSHG INC
144 Caribou Rd (28803-1521)
PHONE..............................828 274-2440
Gerald Lubin, *Prin*
EMP: 8 EST: 2007
SQ FT: 121,140
SALES (est): 260K **Privately Held**
SIC: 2231 Broadwoven fabric mills, wool

(G-692)
LUSTY MONK LLC
29 Canoe Ln (28804-8612)
PHONE..............................828 645-5056
Kelly Davis, *Pt*
EMP: 4 EST: 2008
SALES (est): 312.65K **Privately Held**
Web: www.lustymonk.com
SIC: 2035 Mustard, prepared (wet)

(G-693)
MAIL MANAGEMENT SERVICES LLC
Also Called: Allegra Marketing
88 Roberts St (28803-3149)
P.O. Box 7557 (28802-7557)
PHONE..............................828 236-0076
David Campbell, *Managing Member*
EMP: 19 EST: 1998
SQ FT: 10,000
SALES (est): 4.99MM **Privately Held**
Web: www.allegramarketingprint.com
SIC: 2752 Offset printing

(G-694)
MAKE SOLUTIONS INC
23 Tacoma St (28801-1621)
PHONE..............................623 444-0098
Patti Marshall, *CEO*
Brian Kottenstette, *CFO*
Paul Marshall, *Sec*
EMP: 15 EST: 2012
SALES (est): 676.7K **Privately Held**
Web: www.makesolutionsinc.com
SIC: 7372 8742 7389 Prepackaged software ; Management consulting services; Business Activities at Non-Commercial Site

(G-695)
MARINE SYSTEMS INC
7 Westside Dr (28806-2846)
PHONE..............................828 254-5354
Edward Riester, *Pr*
Sylvia Riester, *Sec*
EMP: 16 EST: 1977
SQ FT: 24,250
SALES (est): 849.86K **Privately Held**
Web: www.airmsi.com
SIC: 3446 3544 Grillwork, ornamental metal; Forms (molds), for foundry and plastics working machinery

(G-696)
MATHIS ELEC SLS & SVC INC
Also Called: Mathis Electronics
102a Caribou Rd (28803-1523)
P.O. Box 5871 (28813-5871)
PHONE..............................828 274-5925
Edmond Mathis, *Pr*
EMP: 14 EST: 1980
SQ FT: 5,000
SALES (est): 2.35MM **Privately Held**
Web: www.mathiselectronics.com
SIC: 3672 Circuit boards, television and radio printed

(G-697)
MB MARKETING & MFG INC
Also Called: Mbm
27 Mulvaney St (28803-1457)
P.O. Box 2296 (28802-2296)
PHONE..............................828 285-0882
John Mc Leod, *Pr*
▲ EMP: 7 EST: 1984
SALES (est): 1.35MM **Privately Held**
Web: www.mbmbrakes.com
SIC: 3714 Motor vehicle parts and accessories

(G-698)
MEERKAT PRESS LLC
216 Patton Mountain Rd (28804-2848)
PHONE..............................678 984-5489
Tricia Reeks, *Prin*
EMP: 6 EST: 2018
SALES (est): 148.05K **Privately Held**
Web: www.meerkatpress.com
SIC: 2741 Miscellaneous publishing

(G-699)
MEN WITH WINGS PRESS
17 Shelby Dr (28803-9547)
PHONE..............................828 989-6124
Frank Thompson, *Prin*
EMP: 4 EST: 2017
SALES (est): 62.78K **Privately Held**
Web: www.menwithwingspress.com
SIC: 2741 Miscellaneous publishing

(G-700)
METROMONT MATERIALS CORP
190 Meadow Rd (28803-2615)
PHONE..............................828 253-9383
Jeff Hartig, *Owner*
EMP: 8 EST: 2013
SALES (est): 416.18K **Privately Held**
SIC: 3272 Concrete products, nec

(G-701)
MH LIBMAN WOODTURNING
191 Lyman St (28801-4371)
PHONE..............................828 360-5530
M H Libman, *Prin*
EMP: 6 EST: 2012
SALES (est): 175.1K **Privately Held**
Web: www.marlowelfrey.com
SIC: 2431 Millwork

(G-702)
MILKCO INC
Also Called: Milkco
220 Deaverview Rd (28806-1710)
P.O. Box 16160 (28816-0160)
PHONE..............................828 254-8428
Keith Collins, *Pr*
EMP: 265 EST: 1982
SQ FT: 120,000
SALES (est): 49.59MM
SALES (corp-wide): 5.89B **Publicly Held**
Web: www.milkco.com
SIC: 2026 2037 2086 Milk processing (pasteurizing, homogenizing, bottling); Fruit juices; Mineral water, carbonated: packaged in cans, bottles, etc.
PA: Ingles Markets, Incorporated
    2913 Us Highway 70

GEOGRAPHIC SECTION

Asheville - Buncombe County (G-730)

Black Mountain NC 28711
828 669-2941

(G-703)
MILLS MANUFACTURING CORP (PA)
22 Mills Pl (28804-1216)
P.O. Box 8100 (28814-8100)
PHONE.....................828 645-3061
James W Turner, *CEO*
Pamela M Turner, *
John Oswald, *
EMP: 149 **EST:** 1934
SQ FT: 172,000
SALES (est): 9.84MM
SALES (corp-wide): 9.84MM **Privately Held**
Web: www.millsmanufacturing.com
SIC: 2399 2298 Parachutes; Twine, cord and cordage

(G-704)
MONOGRAM ASHEVILLE
Also Called: Celesta's
800 Brevard Rd Ste 812 (28806-2297)
PHONE.....................828 707-8110
EMP: 6 **EST:** 2018
SALES (est): 86.22K **Privately Held**
Web: www.monogramasheville.com
SIC: 2395 Embroidery and art needlework

(G-705)
MORRISON MILL WORK
51 Thompson St (28803-2367)
PHONE.....................828 774-5415
EMP: 5 **EST:** 2013
SALES (est): 91.72K **Privately Held**
Web: www.morrisonmillwork.com
SIC: 2431 Millwork

(G-706)
MOSS SIGN COMPANY INC
526 Swannanoa River Rd (28805-2429)
P.O. Box 5099 (28813-5099)
PHONE.....................828 299-7766
EMP: 11 **EST:** 1996
SALES (est): 858.38K **Privately Held**
Web: www.mosssigncompany.com
SIC: 3993 1731 Electric signs; Electrical work

(G-707)
MOUNTAIN AREA INFO NETWRK
Also Called: M A I N
34 Wall St Ste 407 (28801-2713)
PHONE.....................828 255-0182
EMP: 10 **EST:** 1995
SALES (est): 789.91K **Privately Held**
Web: www.main.nc.us
SIC: 4813 2711 Internet host services; Newspapers

(G-708)
MOUNTAIN INTAGLIO LLC
180 Skycliff Dr (28804-8107)
P.O. Box 8664 (28814-8664)
PHONE.....................713 725-7926
EMP: 4 **EST:** 2018
SALES (est): 92.36K **Privately Held**
Web: www.mountain-intaglio.com
SIC: 2741 Miscellaneous publishing

(G-709)
NACHOS & BEER LLC
230 Charlotte Hwy (28803-8628)
PHONE.....................828 298-2280
Merle Butterick, *Prin*
EMP: 6 **EST:** 2009
SALES (est): 177.51K **Privately Held**
SIC: 2082 Beer (alcoholic beverage)

(G-710)
NATURES PHARMACY INC
752 Biltmore Ave (28803-2558)
PHONE.....................828 251-0094
Mike Rogers, *Pr*
Bill Cheek, *VP*
EMP: 5 **EST:** 1996
SQ FT: 2,000
SALES (est): 497.95K **Privately Held**
SIC: 2834 5912 5499 Druggists' preparations (pharmaceuticals); Drug stores ; Spices and herbs

(G-711)
NEURAMETRIX INC
18 Lookout Rd (28804-3238)
PHONE.....................408 507-2366
Jan Samzelius, *CEO*
Christian Olsson, *VP*
EMP: 4 **EST:** 2016
SALES (est): 306.16K **Privately Held**
Web: www.neurametrix.com
SIC: 8731 8071 7372 7389 Biotechnical research, commercial; Neurological laboratory; Application computer software; Business services, nec

(G-712)
NEXT GENERATION BEER CO
21 Westside Dr (28806-2846)
PHONE.....................828 989-7662
Danielle Wimpy, *Mgr*
EMP: 7 **EST:** 2005
SALES (est): 178.71K **Privately Held**
Web: www.nextgenerationbeer.com
SIC: 2082 Beer (alcoholic beverage)

(G-713)
OAK & GRIST DISTILLING CO LLC
40 West St (28801-1124)
PHONE.....................914 450-0589
EMP: 5
SALES (est): 64.7K **Privately Held**
Web: www.oakandgrist.com
SIC: 2085 Distilled and blended liquors

(G-714)
OCEAN 10 SECURITY LLC
329 Gashes Creek Rd (28803-9405)
PHONE.....................828 484-1481
EMP: 14 **EST:** 2015
SALES (est): 2.46MM **Privately Held**
Web: www.ocean10security.com
SIC: 3651 Video camera-audio recorders, household use

(G-715)
OCEANS FLAVOR
123 Cloverleaf Ln (28803-3164)
PHONE.....................828 277-7564
EMP: 4 **EST:** 2019
SALES (est): 66.08K **Privately Held**
SIC: 1499 Miscellaneous nonmetallic minerals, except fuels

(G-716)
ON THE INSIDE LLC
244 Bear Creek Rd (28806-1682)
PHONE.....................828 606-8483
EMP: 4 **EST:** 2018
SALES (est): 184.16K **Privately Held**
Web: www.ontheinsidelingerie.com
SIC: 2323 Men's and boy's neckwear

(G-717)
ORTHOPEDIC APPLIANCE COMPANY
75 Victoria Rd (28801-4487)
PHONE.....................828 254-6305
TOLL FREE: 800

William R Aycock Senior, *Pr*
William R Aycock Junior, *VP*
Owen E Aycock, *Sec*
EMP: 26 **EST:** 1960
SQ FT: 8,000
SALES (est): 7.31MM **Privately Held**
Web: www.orthopedicapplianceco.com
SIC: 3842 Orthopedic appliances

(G-718)
OTIS ELEVATOR COMPANY
203 Elk Park Dr (28804-2063)
PHONE.....................828 251-1248
Mary Green, *Mgr*
EMP: 6
SALES (corp-wide): 13.69B **Publicly Held**
Web: www.otis.com
SIC: 5084 1796 3534 Elevators; Installing building equipment; Dumbwaiters
HQ: Otis Elevator Company
1 Carrier Pl
Farmington CT 06032
860 674-3000

(G-719)
PALLET WORLD USA INC
124 Sondley Pkwy (28805-1149)
PHONE.....................828 298-7270
Robert Jolly, *Prin*
EMP: 6 **EST:** 2016
SALES (est): 162.55K **Privately Held**
SIC: 2448 Pallets, wood

(G-720)
PALMER INSTRUMENTS INC
Also Called: Palmer Wahl Instrmnttion Group
234 Old Weaverville Rd (28804-1260)
PHONE.....................828 658-3131
Stephen J Santangelo, *Pr*
Jack J Santangelo, *
Richard J Santangelo, *
Sky Tilly, *
▲ **EMP:** 50 **EST:** 1918
SQ FT: 50,000
SALES (est): 9.35MM **Privately Held**
Web: www.palmerinstruments.com
SIC: 3823 3829 3825 Differential pressure instruments, industrial process type; Measuring and controlling devices, nec; Instruments to measure electricity

(G-721)
PALMER WAHL INSTRUMENTS INC
Also Called: Palmer Wahl Instrmnttion Group
234 Old Weaverville Rd (28804-1260)
PHONE.....................828 658-3131
Stephen J Santangelo, *Pr*
Richard J Santangelo, *
▲ **EMP:** 35 **EST:** 1953
SQ FT: 20,000
SALES (est): 11.14MM **Privately Held**
Web: www.palmerwahl.com
SIC: 5084 3823 Industrial machinery and equipment; Temperature instruments: industrial process type

(G-722)
PARKER OIL INC
290 Depot St (28801-3998)
PHONE.....................828 253-7265
Tom Nuckolls, *Pr*
EMP: 4 **EST:** 2007
SALES (est): 168.89K **Privately Held**
SIC: 1389 Oil and gas field services, nec

(G-723)
PAYMENT COLLECT LLC
70 Charlotte St (28801-2434)
PHONE.....................828 214-5550
EMP: 9 **EST:** 2011
SALES (est): 129.68K **Privately Held**

Web: www.paymentcollect.com
SIC: 7372 Business oriented computer software

(G-724)
PBF LLC
19 Fieldcrest Cir (28806-9754)
PHONE.....................828 252-1742
Michael J Lawrence, *Prin*
EMP: 6 **EST:** 2019
SALES (est): 58.13K **Privately Held**
Web: www.pbfenergy.com
SIC: 2911 Petroleum refining

(G-725)
PEABERRY PRESS LLC
Also Called: Peaberry
802 Fairview Rd Ste 800 (28803-7773)
PHONE.....................828 773-1489
Brittony Miller, *Prin*
EMP: 4 **EST:** 2014
SALES (est): 215.02K **Privately Held**
Web: www.peaberrypress.com
SIC: 2741 Miscellaneous publishing

(G-726)
PERFECTION GEAR INC (DH)
9 N Bear Creek Rd (28806-1731)
PHONE.....................828 253-0000
Randy Gredly, *CEO*
Robert Sirak, *
▲ **EMP:** 60 **EST:** 1982
SQ FT: 65,000
SALES (est): 20.94MM
SALES (corp-wide): 241.4MM **Privately Held**
Web: www.perfectiongear.com
SIC: 3566 Reduction gears and gear units for turbines, except auto
HQ: Peerless-Winsmith, Inc.
5200 Upper Metro Pl # 11
Dublin OH 43017
614 526-7000

(G-727)
PHARMACEUTICAL EQUIPMENT SVCS
15 Magnolia Hill Ct (28806-8485)
PHONE.....................239 699-9120
Barbara Hosack, *Prin*
EMP: 4 **EST:** 2014
SALES (est): 91.1K **Privately Held**
SIC: 5084 2834 Industrial machinery and equipment; Pharmaceutical preparations

(G-728)
PHOENIX RISING PRESS LLC
157 Starling Pass (28804-0017)
PHONE.....................480 284-1250
Lynn Ames, *Prin*
EMP: 4 **EST:** 2019
SALES (est): 41.35K **Privately Held**
Web: www.lynnames.com
SIC: 2741 Miscellaneous publishing

(G-729)
PHOTON ENERGY CORP
1095 Hendersonville Rd (28803-1891)
PHONE.....................888 336-8128
Craig Sherman, *CFO*
Ashley Campbell, *Mgr*
EMP: 6 **EST:** 2017
SALES (est): 474.84K **Privately Held**
Web: www.photonenergy.com
SIC: 3661 Fiber optics communications equipment

(G-730)
PIEDMONT MEDIAWORKS INC
Also Called: Sign-A-Rama

(PA)=Parent Co (HQ)=Headquarters
✪ = New Business established in last 2 years

Asheville - Buncombe County (G-731)

5a Hedgerose Ct (28805-1986)
PHONE..................828 575-2250
Arlene Sullivan, *Pr*
Edward Sullivan, *Pr*
Graham Mew, *Prin*
EMP: 12 **EST:** 2011
SALES (est): 737.14K **Privately Held**
Web: www.signarama.com
SIC: 3993 Signs and advertising specialties

(G-731)
PIEDMONT TRUCK TIRES INC
125 Sweeten Creek Rd (28803-1526)
PHONE..................828 277-1549
EMP: 13
SALES (corp-wide): 339.82MM **Privately Held**
Web: www.piedmonttrucktires.com
SIC: 5014 5531 7534 Truck tires and tubes; Auto and home supply stores; Rebuilding and retreading tires
HQ: Piedmont Truck Tires, Inc.
312 S Regional Rd
Greensboro NC 27409
336 668-0091

(G-732)
PINKSTON PROPERTIES LLC
Also Called: Golf Associates
91 Westside Dr (28806-2846)
P.O. Box 6917 (28816-6917)
PHONE..................828 252-9867
EMP: 17 **EST:** 1995
SALES (est): 4.47MM **Privately Held**
Web: www.golfassociates.com
SIC: 6733 2759 Private estate, personal investment and vacation fund trusts; Card printing and engraving, except greeting

(G-733)
PINNIX DISTILLERY INC
101 Fairview Rd (28803-4300)
PHONE..................828 412-5441
EMP: 8 **EST:** 2016
SALES (est): 571.92K **Privately Held**
SIC: 2085 Distilled and blended liquors

(G-734)
PLASTICARD PRODUCTS INC
99 Pond Rd (28806-2250)
PHONE..................828 665-7774
Mark Goldberg, *Prin*
EMP: 8 **EST:** 2006
SALES (est): 198.76K **Privately Held**
Web: www.plicards.com
SIC: 2759 Commercial printing, nec

(G-735)
PLAYRACE INC
Also Called: Fastsigns
1202 Patton Ave (28806-2708)
PHONE..................828 251-2211
Ric Davenport, *Pr*
Carla Heatherly, *VP*
EMP: 20 **EST:** 2007
SQ FT: 4,940
SALES (est): 2.35MM **Privately Held**
Web: www.fastsigns.com
SIC: 3993 Signs and advertising specialties

(G-736)
PLEB URBAN WINERY
289 Lyman St (28801-4741)
PHONE..................828 767-6445
EMP: 5 **EST:** 2019
SALES (est): 135.25K **Privately Held**
Web: www.pleburbanwinery.com
SIC: 2084 Wines

(G-737)
PLUM PRINT INC
45 S French Broad Ave Ste 100 (28801-0187)
PHONE..................828 633-5535
EMP: 16 **EST:** 2015
SALES (est): 480.02K **Privately Held**
Web: www.plumprint.com
SIC: 2752 Commercial printing, lithographic

(G-738)
POPE PRINTING & DESIGN INC
Also Called: Kwik Kopy Printing
485 Hendersonville Rd Ste 7 (28803-2765)
PHONE..................828 274-5945
Larry Pope, *Pr*
Brad Pope, *VP*
EMP: 4 **EST:** 1983
SQ FT: 1,540
SALES (est): 321.33K **Privately Held**
SIC: 2752 Offset printing

(G-739)
POWELL INK INC
Also Called: Allegra Print & Imaging
191 Charlotte St (28801-1989)
PHONE..................828 253-6886
Mike Powell, *Pr*
Debbie Powell, *VP*
EMP: 10 **EST:** 1986
SQ FT: 2,400
SALES (est): 1.51MM **Privately Held**
Web: www.allegramarketingprint.com
SIC: 2752 2789 2791 Offset printing; Bookbinding and related work; Typesetting

(G-740)
PRATT & WHITNEY ENG SVCS INC
330 Pratt And Whitney Blvd (28806-0490)
PHONE..................860 565-4321
EMP: 6
SALES (corp-wide): 68.92B **Publicly Held**
Web: www.prattwhitney.com
SIC: 3724 Airfoils, aircraft engine
HQ: Pratt & Whitney Engine Services, Inc.
1525 Midway Park Rd
Bridgeport WV 26330
304 842-5421

(G-741)
PRESLEY GROUP LTD (DH)
Also Called: Hayes & Lunsford Elec Contrs
739 Dogwood Rd (28806-0366)
P.O. Box 973 (28802-0973)
PHONE..................828 254-9971
TOLL FREE: 800
Eugene L Presley, *Pr*
Richard H Presley, *
Ralph P Presley, *
Eugene L Presley, *Stockholder*
EMP: 100 **EST:** 1926
SQ FT: 40,000
SALES (est): 25.67MM
SALES (corp-wide): 5.21B **Publicly Held**
SIC: 1731 7694 7629 General electrical contractor; Electric motor repair; Electrical repair shops
HQ: Starr Electric Company Incorporated
6 Battleground Ct
Greensboro NC 27408
336 275-0241

(G-742)
PRINTING
1328 Patton Ave Ste B (28806-2649)
PHONE..................770 815-7367
EMP: 4 **EST:** 2017
SALES (est): 84.53K **Privately Held**
SIC: 2752 Commercial printing, lithographic

(G-743)
PRINTING PRESS
16 Pleasant Ridge Dr (28805-2623)
PHONE..................828 299-1234
Sandra Lawrence, *Pr*
George Lawrence, *VP*
EMP: 4 **EST:** 1985
SALES (est): 254.14K **Privately Held**
Web: www.blueridgeprinting.com
SIC: 2752 5943 5112 2782 Offset printing; Office forms and supplies; Envelopes; Checkbooks

(G-744)
PRINTVILLE
1 Page Ave Ste 107 (28801-2383)
PHONE..................828 225-3777
Jesse Maybin, *Mgr*
EMP: 6 **EST:** 2017
SALES (est): 101.53K **Privately Held**
Web: www.printville.net
SIC: 2752 Offset printing

(G-745)
PROCESS AUTOMATION TECH INC
3113 Sweeten Creek Rd (28803-2115)
PHONE..................828 298-1055
Bruce J Campbell, *Pr*
Bruce Campbell, *Pr*
EMP: 10 **EST:** 2001
SQ FT: 30,000
SALES (est): 470.94K **Privately Held**
SIC: 3535 Conveyors and conveying equipment

(G-746)
PROTECT ADOPTABLE LABS
23 Timber Ln (28806-2174)
PHONE..................253 383-2733
Elliot Weiner, *Prin*
EMP: 4 **EST:** 2009
SALES (est): 114.36K **Privately Held**
SIC: 3999 Pet supplies

(G-747)
PRS DUNN LLC
56 Rex Dr (28806-2938)
PHONE..................828 736-4907
Christopher Meyer, *Owner*
EMP: 5 **EST:** 2017
SALES (est): 41.35K **Privately Held**
SIC: 2741 Miscellaneous publishing

(G-748)
QUADALUPE INDUSTRIES INC
74 Saint Dunstans Cir (28803-2618)
PHONE..................786 241-0315
William Eilers, *Prin*
EMP: 4 **EST:** 2017
SALES (est): 78.99K **Privately Held**
SIC: 3999 Manufacturing industries, nec

(G-749)
QUINN PUBLISHING COMPANY
P.O. Box 278 (28762-0278)
PHONE..................828 668-4622
Jane Sutton, *Prin*
EMP: 5 **EST:** 2009
SALES (est): 59.71K **Privately Held**
SIC: 2741 Miscellaneous publishing

(G-750)
R & B PARTNERSHIP
Also Called: Stuart Nye Hand Wrought Jwly
940 Tunnel Rd (28805-2025)
P.O. Box 9068 (28815-0068)
PHONE..................828 298-7988
Ralph D Morris Junior, *Pt*
Betty F Morris, *Pt*
EMP: 7 **EST:** 1933
SQ FT: 2,000
SALES (est): 249.2K **Privately Held**
Web: www.stuartnye.com
SIC: 3911 5944 Jewelry, precious metal; Jewelry stores

(G-751)
R&H MACHINING FABRICATION INC
329 Emma Rd (28806-3809)
PHONE..................828 253-8930
Sean Gould, *Pr*
EMP: 5 **EST:** 2000
SQ FT: 640
SALES (est): 502.71K **Privately Held**
SIC: 3599 Machine shop, jobbing and repair

(G-752)
RAVEN SINCLAIRE LLC
177 Woodland Rd (28804-3839)
PHONE..................828 423-3819
EMP: 5 **EST:** 2015
SALES (est): 103.91K **Privately Held**
Web: www.ravensinclaire.com
SIC: 2741 Miscellaneous publishing

(G-753)
RCLGH INC
Also Called: Logangate Homes Timber Homes
69 Bingham Rd (28806-3824)
P.O. Box 1922 (28730-1922)
PHONE..................828 707-4383
Robert Cole, *Pr*
Carissa Cole, *Sec*
EMP: 5 **EST:** 1958
SQ FT: 30,000
SALES (est): 492.23K **Privately Held**
Web: www.deltechomes.com
SIC: 2452 Modular homes, prefabricated, wood

(G-754)
RED SKY SHELTERS LLC
2002 Riverside Dr Ste 42h (28804-2052)
PHONE..................828 258-8417
Peter Belt, *Owner*
EMP: 4 **EST:** 1995
SALES (est): 244.88K **Privately Held**
Web: www.redskyshelters.com
SIC: 2394 Tents: made from purchased materials

(G-755)
RHINO NETWORKS LLC
1025 Brevard Rd Ste 8 (28806-8563)
PHONE..................855 462-9434
Todd Carriker, *Mgr*
EMP: 23 **EST:** 2013
SALES (est): 10.19MM **Privately Held**
Web: www.rhinonetworks.com
SIC: 3674 Integrated circuits, semiconductor networks, etc.

(G-756)
RM LIQUIDATION INC (PA)
81 Thompson St (28803-2329)
PHONE..................828 274-7996
Charlie Owen Iii, *Ch*
David Fann, *Pr*
Scott Pasquith, *Sec*
EMP: 64 **EST:** 2015
SALES (est): 11.94MM
SALES (corp-wide): 11.94MM **Privately Held**
Web: www.relioninc.com
SIC: 3841 5047 5999 Surgical and medical instruments; Medical equipment and supplies; Medical apparatus and supplies

GEOGRAPHIC SECTION

Asheville - Buncombe County (G-783)

(G-757)
ROARING LION PUBLISHING
47 Stone River Dr (28804-4408)
PHONE....................828 350-1454
Tony Balistreri, *Prin*
EMP: 5 **EST:** 2006
SALES (est): 241.79K **Privately Held**
Web: www.roaringlionpublishing.com
SIC: 2741 Miscellaneous publishing

(G-758)
ROBERT WIGGINS WOOD WORK LLC
2 Lornelle Pl (28804-2200)
PHONE....................828 254-5644
Robert W Wiggins Iii, *Prin*
EMP: 5 **EST:** 2016
SALES (est): 59.54K **Privately Held**
SIC: 2431 Millwork

(G-759)
ROWLETT PUBLISHING LLC
225 Lovely Ln (28803-1371)
PHONE....................828 285-2351
Martha Rowlett, *Prin*
EMP: 5 **EST:** 2013
SALES (est): 76.51K **Privately Held**
SIC: 2741 Miscellaneous publishing

(G-760)
RUG & HOME INC
Also Called: Rug & Home
5 Rocky Ridge Rd (28806-2263)
PHONE....................828 785-4480
EMP: 9 **EST:** 2009
SALES (est): 384.98K **Privately Held**
Web: www.rugandhome.com
SIC: 2273 Floor coverings, textile fiber

(G-761)
RUSTIC GRAPE LLC
28 Greenwood Fields Dr (28804-0099)
PHONE....................828 319-7939
Patricia Mandaro, *Prin*
EMP: 5 **EST:** 2016
SALES (est): 115.4K **Privately Held**
Web: www.rusticgrapeavl.com
SIC: 2084 Wines

(G-762)
S M COMPANY INC
170 Broadway St (28801-2305)
PHONE....................828 274-0827
Daniel B Sellers, *Pr*
Sandy Sellers, *Sec*
EMP: 15 **EST:** 1966
SQ FT: 32,000
SALES (est): 1.13MM **Privately Held**
SIC: 3672 Printed circuit boards

(G-763)
SAUNDRA D HALL
Also Called: Liberty Street Baggage
237 S Liberty St (28801-2334)
PHONE....................828 251-9859
Saundra D Hall, *Owner*
EMP: 7 **EST:** 1991
SALES (est): 490.81K **Privately Held**
SIC: 3161 Luggage

(G-764)
SBFI-NORTH AMERICA INC (DH)
123 Lyman St (28801-4371)
P.O. Box 5677 (28813-5677)
PHONE....................828 236-3993
Tom Finger, *Pr*
▲ **EMP:** 17 **EST:** 2005
SQ FT: 80,000
SALES (est): 13.13MM
SALES (corp-wide): 22.85MM **Privately Held**
Web: www.sbfi-na.com
SIC: 2521 2522 Wood office furniture; Office furniture, except wood
HQ: Sbfi Group Limited
International House
London E1W 1

(G-765)
SCOTT MEEK WOODWORKS
261 Bear Creek Rd (28806-1608)
PHONE....................828 283-0796
EMP: 4 **EST:** 2017
SALES (est): 54.13K **Privately Held**
Web: www.scottmeekwoodworks.com
SIC: 2431 Millwork

(G-766)
SCOTT WOODWORKING
55 Memory Ln (28805-1510)
PHONE....................828 550-4742
David Scott, *Owner*
EMP: 4 **EST:** 2009
SALES (est): 61.03K **Privately Held**
Web: www.scottwoodworking.com
SIC: 2431 Millwork

(G-767)
SDV OFFICE SYSTEMS LLC (PA)
Also Called: SDV MEDICAL SERVICES
26 Macallan Ln (28805-1246)
P.O. Box 2427 (28776-2427)
PHONE....................844 968-9500
EMP: 6 **EST:** 2010
SQ FT: 1,400
SALES (est): 78.56MM **Privately Held**
Web: www.sdvosystems.com
SIC: 2522 5112 2521 5047 Office cabinets and filing drawers, except wood; Office filing supplies; Wood office furniture; Medical equipment and supplies

(G-768)
SHENK INDUSTRIES INC
18 Cedar Hill Dr (28803-3043)
PHONE....................828 808-3327
EMP: 4 **EST:** 2015
SALES (est): 49.66K **Privately Held**
SIC: 3999 Manufacturing industries, nec

(G-769)
SHEP BERRYHILL WOODWORKING
197 Deaverview Rd (28806-1707)
PHONE....................828 242-3227
Shep Berryhill, *Prin*
EMP: 8 **EST:** 2001
SALES (est): 129.09K **Privately Held**
SIC: 2431 Millwork

(G-770)
SIGN SYSTEMS INC
301 College St (28801-2449)
PHONE....................828 785-1722
EMP: 4 **EST:** 2017
SALES (est): 117.11K **Privately Held**
Web: www.signsystemsnc.com
SIC: 3993 Signs and advertising specialties

(G-771)
SILVER-LINE PLASTICS LLC (DH)
900 Riverside Dr (28804-3115)
PHONE....................828 252-8755
Ricky C Silver, *Pr*
William H Beard, *
Treena Cooper, *
◆ **EMP:** 121 **EST:** 1962
SQ FT: 98,000
SALES (est): 107.62MM
SALES (corp-wide): 87.53MM **Privately Held**
Web: www.slpipe.com
SIC: 3084 Plastics pipe
HQ: Ipex Usa Llc
10100 Rodney St
Pineville NC 28134

(G-772)
SIMPLESHOT INC
2000 Riverside Dr Ste 5a (28804-2061)
PHONE....................888 202-7475
Nathan Masters, *CEO*
Nathan Wade Masters, *Pr*
EMP: 6 **EST:** 2012
SQ FT: 1,800
SALES (est): 440.63K **Privately Held**
Web: www.simple-shot.com
SIC: 3949 Archery equipment, general

(G-773)
SJR INCORPORATED
Also Called: Kitchens Unlimited Asheville
120 New Leicester Hwy (28806-1918)
PHONE....................828 254-8966
James C Ramsey, *Pr*
Joy J Ramsey, *VP*
EMP: 20 **EST:** 1977
SQ FT: 6,000
SALES (est): 1.69MM **Privately Held**
Web: www.kitchensunlimitednc.com
SIC: 2434 Wood kitchen cabinets

(G-774)
SMITHS AEROSPACE COMPONENTS
401 Sweeten Way (28803-4610)
PHONE....................828 274-4540
Jon Bellows, *Contrlr*
EMP: 5 **EST:** 2019
SALES (est): 226.46K **Privately Held**
SIC: 3724 Aircraft engines and engine parts

(G-775)
SMOKEY MOUNTAIN LUMBER INC (PA)
19 Lower Grassy Branch Rd (28805-1618)
P.O. Box 9207 (28815-0207)
PHONE....................828 298-3958
Lynn L Fidler, *Pr*
Lynn C Fidler, *VP*
EMP: 9 **EST:** 1987
SQ FT: 10,000
SALES (est): 862.6K
SALES (corp-wide): 862.6K **Privately Held**
Web: www.smokeymountainlumberinc.com
SIC: 2431 5211 2439 Moldings, wood: unfinished and prefinished; Millwork and lumber; Structural wood members, nec

(G-776)
SMOKY MOUNTAIN MACHINING INC
80 Mcintosh Rd (28806-1406)
P.O. Box 6173 (28816-6173)
PHONE....................828 665-1193
Paul Mckinney, *CEO*
Bryan Mckinney, *Pr*
Phil Skidmore, *
EMP: 65 **EST:** 1978
SQ FT: 30,000
SALES (est): 8.48MM **Privately Held**
Web: www.smmasheville.com
SIC: 3599 5571 Machine shop, jobbing and repair; Motorcycle parts and accessories

(G-777)
SMOKY MOUNTAIN TIMBERWRIGHTS
904 Old Fairview Rd (28803-8307)
PHONE....................828 252-4205
Chad Leatherwood, *Prin*
EMP: 11 **EST:** 2008
SALES (est): 131.4K **Privately Held**
SIC: 2439 Timbers, structural: laminated lumber

(G-778)
SNYDER PAPER CORPORATION
85 Thompson St (28803-2329)
PHONE....................800 222-8562
Craig Faircloth, *Brnch Mgr*
EMP: 6
SALES (corp-wide): 75.1MM **Privately Held**
Web: www.snydersolutions.com
SIC: 2621 Text paper
PA: Snyder Paper Corporation
250 26th Street Dr Se
Hickory NC 28602
828 328-2501

(G-779)
SOCK BASKET LLC
99 Edgewood Rd Apt A (28804-3576)
PHONE....................828 251-7072
EMP: 6 **EST:** 2013
SALES (est): 66.59K **Privately Held**
Web: www.thesockbasket.com
SIC: 2252 Socks

(G-780)
SOULKU LLC (PA)
45 S French Broad Ave Ste 180 (28801-0188)
PHONE....................828 273-4278
EMP: 16 **EST:** 2011
SALES (est): 2.47MM
SALES (corp-wide): 2.47MM **Privately Held**
Web: www.soulku.com
SIC: 3911 5094 Jewelry, precious metal; Jewelry

(G-781)
SOUP MAVEN LLC
Also Called: 18 Chestnuts
117 Longspur Lane Ext (28804-0154)
PHONE....................727 919-5242
Ilona Kossoff, *Pr*
EMP: 6 **EST:** 2021
SALES (est): 262.74K **Privately Held**
SIC: 2032 Soups and broths, canned, jarred, etc.

(G-782)
SOUTHBRIDGE INC
Also Called: Artful Shelter
2000 Riverside Dr Ste 5 (28804-2061)
P.O. Box 19539 (28815-1539)
PHONE....................828 350-9112
Roger Roundtree, *Pr*
▲ **EMP:** 4 **EST:** 1990
SALES (est): 229.24K **Privately Held**
Web: www.artfulshelter.com
SIC: 2394 Tents: made from purchased materials

(G-783)
SOUTHERN CONCRETE MATERIALS INC (HQ)
35 Meadow Rd (28803-2651)
P.O. Box 5395 (28813-5395)
PHONE....................828 253-6421
EMP: 120 **EST:** 1958
SALES (est): 83.49MM
SALES (corp-wide): 238.17MM **Privately Held**
Web: www.scmusa.com
SIC: 3273 5211 Ready-mixed concrete; Electrical construction materials
PA: B. V. Hedrick Gravel & Sand Company
120 1/2 N Church St
Salisbury NC 28144
704 633-5982

Asheville - Buncombe County (G-784)   GEOGRAPHIC SECTION

(G-784)
SOUTHERN CONCRETE MTLS INC
80 Pond Rd (28806-2221)
P.O. Box 2569 (28802-2569)
PHONE..................................828 670-6450
Matt Parrett, *Mgr*
EMP: 20
SALES (corp-wide): 238.17MM **Privately Held**
Web: www.scmusa.com
SIC: 3273 Ready-mixed concrete
HQ: Southern Concrete Materials, Inc.
35 Meadow Rd
Asheville NC 28803
828 253-6421

(G-785)
SPARKS MILL WORKS LLC
6 Von Ruck Ct (28801-2026)
PHONE..................................512 779-5837
Rick Sparks, *Prin*
EMP: 5 **EST:** 2018
SALES (est): 230.98K **Privately Held**
Web: www.sparksmillworks.com
SIC: 2431 Millwork

(G-786)
SQUARE ONE WOODWORKING
33 Dorchester Ave (28806-3515)
PHONE..................................828 277-5164
EMP: 4 **EST:** 2017
SALES (est): 54.13K **Privately Held**
SIC: 2431 Millwork

(G-787)
SQUARE PEG CONSTRUCTION INC
28 London Rd (28803-2706)
PHONE..................................828 277-5164
Leslie Humphrey, *Pr*
EMP: 4 **EST:** 1999
SALES (est): 471.57K **Privately Held**
Web: www.squarepeginc.net
SIC: 2499 Decorative wood and woodwork

(G-788)
STANSELL INDUSTRIES LLC
118 Bradley St (28806-4408)
PHONE..................................864 371-2425
Paul J Stansell, *Prin*
▲ **EMP:** 5 **EST:** 2014
SALES (est): 240.63K **Privately Held**
SIC: 3999 Manufacturing industries, nec

(G-789)
SUGARCANE STUDIOS LLC
1550 Hendersonville Rd (28803-3245)
PHONE..................................828 785-3167
Tara Hawks Nyanga, *Prin*
EMP: 6 **EST:** 2018
SALES (est): 270.97K **Privately Held**
Web: www.sugarcanestudios.com
SIC: 2381 Fabric dress and work gloves

(G-790)
SUNJUNE LTRARY CLLBORATIVE LLC
19 Northview St (28801-1119)
PHONE..................................502 767-2867
Lorraine Brown, *Prin*
EMP: 5 **EST:** 2018
SALES (est): 92.11K **Privately Held**
SIC: 2741 Miscellaneous publishing

(G-791)
SUNRISE SAWMILL INC
68 W Chapel Rd (28803-9694)
PHONE..................................828 277-0120
Don Shuford, *Pr*
Michelle Shuford, *Sec*
EMP: 4 **EST:** 1980
SQ FT: 2,720
SALES (est): 388.59K **Privately Held**
Web: www.sunrisesawmill.com
SIC: 2421 Lumber: rough, sawed, or planed

(G-792)
SUSAN STRAZZELLA
8 Town Square Blvd # 407 (28803-5044)
PHONE..................................828 676-1162
Susan Strazzella, *Prin*
EMP: 4 **EST:** 2011
SALES (est): 101.47K **Privately Held**
Web: www.suestrazzella.com
SIC: 3999 Framed artwork

(G-793)
T PRECISION MACHINING INC
Also Called: T-Fab Precision Machining
123 Lyman St (28801-4371)
PHONE..................................828 250-0993
Tom Finger, *Pr*
▲ **EMP:** 20 **EST:** 1998
SALES (est): 636.51K **Privately Held**
Web: www.t-fab.com
SIC: 3599 Machine shop, jobbing and repair

(G-794)
TA LOST PINES WOODWORK
24 Rose Hill Rd (28803-9586)
PHONE..................................828 367-7517
Micah Goldfarb, *Owner*
EMP: 6 **EST:** 2015
SALES (est): 79.37K **Privately Held**
SIC: 2431 Millwork

(G-795)
TALKING DEVICES COMPANY
21 Prairie Path (28805-7903)
PHONE..................................828 658-0660
Lad E Ottofy, *Owner*
EMP: 8 **EST:** 1918
SALES (est): 128.13K **Privately Held**
Web: www.talkingdevicescompany.com
SIC: 3652 3993 3695 Master records or tapes, preparation of; Signs and advertising specialties; Magnetic and optical recording media

(G-796)
TENPENNY PRESS
3 Mulvaney St (28803-1403)
PHONE..................................828 423-0799
EMP: 6 **EST:** 2019
SALES (est): 86.98K **Privately Held**
SIC: 2741 Miscellaneous publishing

(G-797)
THERMO ELCTRON SCNTFIC INSTRS
Also Called: Thermo Electron
501 Elk Park Dr (28804-2065)
PHONE..................................828 281-2651
EMP: 5
SALES (corp-wide): 44.91B **Publicly Held**
SIC: 3826 Analytical instruments
HQ: Thermo Electron Scientific Instruments Llc
5225 Verona Rd
Fitchburg WI 53711
608 276-6100

(G-798)
THERMO FSHER SCNTFIC ASHVLLE L (HQ)
Also Called: Thermo Fisher Scientific
275 Aiken Rd (28804-8740)
PHONE..................................828 658-2711
Bill Mcmahon, *Pr*
▲ **EMP:** 260 **EST:** 1996
SALES (est): 386.75MM
SALES (corp-wide): 44.91B **Publicly Held**
Web: www.thermofisher.com
SIC: 3826 3821 3829 Analytical instruments; Laboratory apparatus and furniture; Measuring and controlling devices, nec
PA: Thermo Fisher Scientific Inc.
168 3rd Ave
Waltham MA 02451
781 622-1000

(G-799)
THROWIN STONES LLC
825c Merrimon Ave Ste 123 (28804-2404)
PHONE..................................828 280-7870
Rusty James, *Mgr*
EMP: 5 **EST:** 2015
SALES (est): 501.35K **Privately Held**
Web: www.throwinstones.com
SIC: 1499 Semiprecious stones mining, nec

(G-800)
TIARA INC
Also Called: Babeegreens
2002 Riverside Dr Ste 42k (28804-2052)
PHONE..................................828 484-8236
EMP: 5 **EST:** 2010
SALES (est): 399.14K **Privately Held**
Web: www.babeegreens.com
SIC: 2361 5137 Girl's and children's dresses, blouses; Infants' wear

(G-801)
TIMBER NINJA OUTDOORS LLC
1415 Patton Ave (28806-1721)
PHONE..................................828 380-1664
EMP: 5 **EST:** 2020
SALES (est): 98.83K **Privately Held**
Web: www.timberninjaoutdoors.com
SIC: 3949 Sporting and athletic goods, nec

(G-802)
TOMPKINS INDUSTRIES INC
Also Called: Philip Products
150 Westside Dr (28806-2847)
PHONE..................................828 254-2351
Dan Dippel, *Mgr*
EMP: 150
SALES (corp-wide): 55.84MM **Privately Held**
Web: www.tompkinsind.com
SIC: 5031 3442 Windows; Metal doors, sash, and trim
PA: Tompkins Industries, Inc.
1651 E Kansas City Rd
Olathe KS 66061
913 764-8088

(G-803)
TOURIST BASEBALL INC
Also Called: Asheville Tourist Baseball
30 Buchanan Pl (28801-4243)
PHONE..................................828 258-0428
Shawn Henry, *Pr*
Mike Bower, *Ex Dir*
EMP: 32 **EST:** 1976
SALES (est): 1.86MM **Privately Held**
Web: www.theashevilletourists.com
SIC: 7941 2721 Baseball club, professional and semi-professional; Periodicals

(G-804)
TRACYS GOURMET LLC
Also Called: Tracy's Gourmet
315 Old Haw Creek Rd (28805-1401)
PHONE..................................919 672-1731
EMP: 5 **EST:** 2013
SALES (est): 305.55K **Privately Held**
Web: www.tracysgourmet.com
SIC: 5149 2035 Salad dressing; Pickles, sauces, and salad dressings

(G-805)
TRANE US INC
Also Called: Trane
168 Sweeten Creek Rd (28803-1526)
PHONE..................................828 277-8664
Marianne Mace, *Mgr*
EMP: 7
Web: www.trane.com
SIC: 3585 Refrigeration and heating equipment
HQ: Trane U.S. Inc.
800 Beaty St Ste E
Davidson NC 28036
704 655-4000

(G-806)
TRIBUNE PAPERS INC
P.O. Box 5005 (28813-5005)
PHONE..................................828 606-5050
Rich C Bradham Iii, *Pr*
EMP: 5 **EST:** 2019
SALES (est): 113.33K **Privately Held**
Web: www.tribpapers.com
SIC: 2711 Newspapers, publishing and printing

(G-807)
TURNAMICS INC
25 Old County Home Rd (28806-9713)
PHONE..................................828 254-1059
Harvey Spiegel, *Pr*
Clint Spiegel, *
EMP: 42 **EST:** 1969
SALES (est): 6.85MM **Privately Held**
Web: www.turnamics.com
SIC: 3599 Custom machinery

(G-808)
UNISON ENGINE COMPONENTS INC
401 Sweeten Creek Industrial Park (28803-1729)
PHONE..................................828 274-4540
◆ **EMP:** 380 **EST:** 1981
SQ FT: 20,000
SALES (est): 97.9MM
SALES (corp-wide): 67.95B **Publicly Held**
SIC: 3728 Aircraft parts and equipment, nec
PA: General Electric Company
1 Financial Ctr Ste 3700
Boston MA 02111
617 443-3000

(G-809)
UNITED WRITERS PRESS
17 Willow Tree Run (28803-9535)
PHONE..................................828 505-1037
Vally Sharpe, *Prin*
EMP: 4 **EST:** 2019
SALES (est): 78.09K **Privately Held**
Web: www.uwpnew.com
SIC: 2741 Miscellaneous publishing

(G-810)
URBAN NEWS
959 Merrimon Ave Ste C (28804-2353)
PHONE..................................828 253-5585
EMP: 9 **EST:** 2017
SALES (est): 72.91K **Privately Held**
Web: www.theurbannews.com
SIC: 2711 Newspapers, publishing and printing

(G-811)
URBAN ORCHARD CIDER COMPANY
24 Buxton Ave (28801-4020)
PHONE..................................252 904-5135
Thomas Hilliard Miller, *Pr*
EMP: 10 **EST:** 2021
SALES (est): 613.06K **Privately Held**
Web: www.urbanorchardcider.com

SIC: 2084 Wines, brandy, and brandy spirits

(G-812)
US FILTER
1129 Sweeten Creek Rd (28803-1728)
PHONE..................................828 274-8282
Maurice Shuford, *Prin*
EMP: 7 **EST:** 1999
SALES (est): 149.59K **Privately Held**
SIC: 3569 Filters

(G-813)
VARIFORM INC
12 Gerber Rd Ste A (28803-2497)
PHONE..................................828 277-6420
EMP: 85
SALES (corp-wide): 5.58B **Privately Held**
SIC: 3089 Siding, plastics
HQ: Variform, Inc.
303 W Major St
Kearney MO 64060
919 677-3900

(G-814)
VENTURE PRODUCTS INTL INC
Also Called: Venture Products
27 Mulvaney St (28803-1457)
P.O. Box 1687 (28802-1687)
PHONE..................................828 285-0495
Stephen Mcleod, *Pr*
John W Mcleod Junior, *Pr*
▲ **EMP:** 9 **EST:** 1989
SQ FT: 43,000
SALES (est): 933.2K **Privately Held**
Web: www.ventureproducts.com
SIC: 3321 5013 Gray iron castings, nec; Truck parts and accessories

(G-815)
VICKI VERMONT AIRCRAFT SALE
23 Rolling View Dr (28805-1223)
PHONE..................................828 225-6517
Victoria Scoones, *Prin*
EMP: 7 **EST:** 2005
SALES (est): 220.45K **Privately Held**
Web: www.vickivt.com
SIC: 3721 Aircraft

(G-816)
WEARS INDUSTRIES INC
113 Spivey Mountain Rd (28806-9419)
PHONE..................................828 575-9466
Patrick Wears, *Pr*
EMP: 5 **EST:** 2016
SALES (est): 166.58K **Privately Held**
SIC: 3999 Manufacturing industries, nec

(G-817)
WEDGE BREWING CO
125b Roberts St (28801-3128)
PHONE..................................828 505-2792
Timothy Paul Schaller, *Prin*
EMP: 11 **EST:** 2008
SALES (est): 352.38K **Privately Held**
Web: www.wedgebrewing.com
SIC: 2082 Beer (alcoholic beverage)

(G-818)
WELLCO TWO INC
1835 Old Haywood Rd (28806-1129)
PHONE..................................828 667-4662
Timothy J Wells, *Prin*
EMP: 6 **EST:** 2005
SALES (est): 86.73K **Privately Held**
SIC: 2822 Synthetic rubber

(G-819)
WHEEL CITY WHOLESALE INC
200 Smokey Park Hwy (28806-1141)
PHONE..................................828 665-2442

Kenneth Dewayne Stephens, *Prin*
EMP: 11 **EST:** 2010
SALES (est): 679.43K **Privately Held**
SIC: 3312 Wheels

(G-820)
WHITE KNGHT ENGNEERED PDTS INC
Also Called: White Knight Engineered Products, Inc.
9 Sw Pack Sq Ste 201 (28801-3526)
PHONE..................................828 687-0940
EMP: 43
SALES (corp-wide): 443.7MM **Privately Held**
Web: www.criticoreinc.com
SIC: 2326 Service apparel (baker, barber, lab, etc.), washable: men's
HQ: Criticore, Inc.
9525 Monroe Rd Ste 150
Charlotte NC 28270
704 542-6876

(G-821)
WHITENER SALES COMPANY
91 Carter Cove Rd (28804-1743)
PHONE..................................828 253-0518
EMP: 4 **EST:** 1990
SALES (est): 289.25K **Privately Held**
SIC: 2411 Mine timbers, hewn

(G-822)
WILDWOOD STUDIOS INC
2163 Riceville Rd (28805-8709)
PHONE..................................828 299-8696
Carl Giesenschlag, *Pr*
Virginia Giesenschlag, *Sec*
EMP: 5 **EST:** 1984
SQ FT: 4,000
SALES (est): 484.24K **Privately Held**
Web: www.wildwdstudios.com
SIC: 2541 1751 5712 Cabinets, lockers, and shelving; Carpentry work; Customized furniture and cabinets

(G-823)
WNC CRAFT BEER EXPORT LLC
159 Burton St (28806-3544)
PHONE..................................828 407-9444
Virginia Gil Coss, *Prin*
EMP: 7 **EST:** 2017
SALES (est): 52.74K **Privately Held**
SIC: 2082 Beer (alcoholic beverage)

(G-824)
ZACK NOBLE METALWORKS LLC
4 Blackberry Ln (28804-1807)
PHONE..................................828 688-3468
Zachary Noble, *Mgr*
EMP: 5 **EST:** 2014
SALES (est): 125.88K **Privately Held**
Web: www.zacknoble.com
SIC: 3446 Architectural metalwork

(G-825)
ZEAL INDUSTRIES LLC
101 Bee Ridge Rd (28803-9423)
PHONE..................................828 575-9894
EMP: 5 **EST:** 2013
SALES (est): 109.48K **Privately Held**
SIC: 3999 Manufacturing industries, nec

Atkinson
Pender County

(G-826)
BLACK RVER WLDG FBRICATION LLC
127 Big Eagle Rd (28421-9383)

PHONE..................................910 471-7434
Matthew Edwards, *Prin*
EMP: 5 **EST:** 2018
SALES (est): 103.24K **Privately Held**
SIC: 7692 Welding repair

Atlantic
Carteret County

(G-827)
NORTHROP GRUMMAN SYSTEMS CORP
Also Called: Northrop Grmman Technical Svcs
Bldg 7029 (28511)
P.O. Box 99 (28511-0099)
PHONE..................................252 225-0911
Duke Savage, *Brnch Mgr*
EMP: 43
Web: www.northropgrumman.com
SIC: 3812 7374 7378 Search and navigation equipment; Computer processing services; Computer maintenance and repair
HQ: Northrop Grumman Systems Corporation
2980 Fairview Park Dr
Falls Church VA 22042
703 280-2900

Atlantic Beach
Carteret County

(G-828)
CARTERET CANVAS COMPANY
122 Old Causeway Rd (28512-7320)
PHONE..................................252 247-9588
EMP: 4 **EST:** 2019
SALES (est): 46.58K **Privately Held**
Web: www.carteretcanvas.com
SIC: 2394 Canvas and related products

(G-829)
EASTERN OFFSET PRINTING CO
410 W Fort Macon Rd (28512)
P.O. Box 1091 (28512-1091)
PHONE..................................252 247-6791
Rebecca Mcmillan, *Owner*
EMP: 4 **EST:** 1984
SQ FT: 2,500
SALES (est): 219.41K **Privately Held**
Web: easternoffset.blogspot.com
SIC: 2752 Offset printing

Aulander
Bertie County

(G-830)
HOG SLAT INCORPORATED
440 Nc Highway 561 W (27805-9219)
PHONE..................................252 209-0092
Bridget Askew, *Mgr*
EMP: 20
SALES (corp-wide): 538.94MM **Privately Held**
Web: www.hogslat.com
SIC: 3523 Farm machinery and equipment
PA: Hog Slat, Incorporated
206 Fayetteville St
Newton Grove NC 28366
800 949-4647

Aurora
Beaufort County

(G-831)
AURORA PACKING CO INC
655 Second St (27806)
P.O. Box 354 (27806-0354)
PHONE..................................252 322-5232
Glenn Williamson, *Pr*
EMP: 9 **EST:** 1945
SQ FT: 6,200
SALES (est): 456.25K **Privately Held**
SIC: 2092 Crab meat, fresh: packaged in nonsealed containers

(G-832)
BAY CITY CRAB INC
1131 Main Street Ext (27806-9502)
P.O. Box 608 (27806-0608)
PHONE..................................252 322-5291
Chris Fulcher, *Pr*
Debbie Fulcher, *
EMP: 9 **EST:** 1986
SQ FT: 9,000
SALES (est): 469.17K **Privately Held**
Web: www.bluecrabusa.net
SIC: 2091 2092 Crabmeat: packaged in cans, jars, etc.; Crab meat, fresh: packaged in nonsealed containers

(G-833)
CAROLINA SEAFOOD COMPANY INC
161 Muddy Creek Rd (27806-9618)
P.O. Box 428 (27806-0428)
PHONE..................................252 322-5455
Etles A Henries Junior, *Pr*
Vance Henries, *
Cathy Henries, *
EMP: 6 **EST:** 1964
SQ FT: 3,000
SALES (est): 697.9K **Privately Held**
SIC: 5146 2092 2091 Seafoods; Fresh or frozen packaged fish; Canned and cured fish and seafoods

(G-834)
FRANKLIN INDUSTRIAL CONTRS INC
Also Called: Franklin Industrial Contrs
8501 Nc Highway 306 S (27806-9186)
PHONE..................................252 670-6682
Dru Edward Franklin, *Prin*
EMP: 5 **EST:** 2018
SALES (est): 163.63K **Privately Held**
SIC: 7692 Welding repair

(G-835)
GLADSONS LOGGING LLC
8902 Nc Highway 306 S (27806-9184)
PHONE..................................252 670-8813
Gilbert A Gladson, *Prin*
EMP: 12 **EST:** 2014
SALES (est): 995.88K **Privately Held**
SIC: 2411 Logging camps and contractors

(G-836)
M F C INC
Hwy 33 (27806)
P.O. Box 309 (27806-0309)
PHONE..................................252 322-5004
John C Hooker Junior, *Pr*
John C Hooker Senior, *VP*
EMP: 48 **EST:** 1979
SQ FT: 16,000
SALES (est): 10.07MM **Privately Held**
SIC: 1542 3441 Commercial and office building, new construction; Fabricated structural metal

Aurora - Beaufort County (G-837)

GEOGRAPHIC SECTION

(G-837)
NUTRIEN AG SOLUTIONS INC
Also Called: Nutrien Phosphate
1530 Nc Highway 306 S (27806-9245)
PHONE..................252 322-4111
William Ponton, *Brnch Mgr*
EMP: 950
SALES (corp-wide): 27.71B **Privately Held**
Web: www.nutrienagsolutions.com
SIC: 2873 Fertilizers: natural (organic), except compost
HQ: Nutrien Ag Solutions, Inc.
3005 Rocky Mountain Ave
Loveland CO 80538
970 685-3300

(G-838)
PCS PHOSPHATE COMPANY INC
P.O. Box 48 (27806-0048)
PHONE..................252 322-4111
EMP: 36
SALES (corp-wide): 27.71B **Privately Held**
SIC: 1475 1474 2874 2819 Phosphate rock; Potash mining; Phosphatic fertilizers; Phosphates, except fertilizers: defluorinated and ammoniated
HQ: Pcs Phosphate Company, Inc.
1101 Skokie Blvd Ste 400
Northbrook IL 60062
847 849-4200

(G-839)
POTASH CORP SASKATCHEWAN INC
1530 Hwy 306 S (27806)
PHONE..................252 322-4111
Mark Johnson, *Genl Mgr*
EMP: 51
SALES (corp-wide): 27.71B **Privately Held**
Web: www.nutrien.com
SIC: 2874 Phosphates
HQ: Potash Corporation Of Saskatchewan Inc.
211 19 St E Suite 1700
Saskatoon SK S7K 5
306 933-8500

Autryville
Sampson County

(G-840)
C & R BUILDING SUPPLY INC
2300 Ernest Williams Rd (28318-7954)
PHONE..................910 567-6293
Charlie D Williams Junior, *Pr*
Regina Williams, *
EMP: 23 **EST:** 1970
SQ FT: 6,000
SALES (est): 943.35K **Privately Held**
SIC: 2439 5211 Trusses, wooden roof; Lumber and other building materials

(G-841)
HONEYCUTT CUSTOM CABINETS INC
1068 Baptist Chapel Rd (28318-8220)
PHONE..................910 567-6766
Joe Honeycutt, *Pt*
Greg Honeycutt, *Pt*
EMP: 22 **EST:** 1995
SALES (est): 1.84MM **Privately Held**
SIC: 2434 Wood kitchen cabinets

(G-842)
MAC GRADING CO
971 Leroy Autry Rd (28318-7053)
P.O. Box 376 (28318-0376)
PHONE..................910 531-4642
Melissa Amos, *Pr*

Christopher Hales, *
EMP: 13 **EST:** 1998
SALES (est): 846.95K **Privately Held**
SIC: 5031 7699 2448 Pallets, wood; Pallet repair; Pallets, wood

Avon
Dare County

(G-843)
AVON SEAFOOD
Harbor Rd (27915)
P.O. Box 251 (27915-0251)
PHONE..................252 995-4553
Tillman Gray, *Owner*
EMP: 6 **EST:** 1989
SALES (est): 426.82K **Privately Held**
Web: www.sunriseseafood.net
SIC: 2091 Fish, canned and cured

(G-844)
CLAY KINNAKEET INC
40462 N End Rd (27915-1313)
PHONE..................252 995-0101
EMP: 4 **EST:** 2018
SALES (est): 86.81K **Privately Held**
Web: www.kinnakeetclay.com
SIC: 3269 Pottery products, nec

(G-845)
NORTH SPORTS INC
Also Called: Windsurfing Hatteras
Waterside Shops Hwy 45 (27915)
PHONE..................252 995-4970
Brian Klouser, *Mgr*
EMP: 7
Web: www.oceanairsports.com
SIC: 3949 Windsurfing boards (sailboards) and equipment
PA: North Sports, Inc.
1345 Nw Wall St Ste 100
Bend OR 97703

(G-846)
ONE MORE CAST
40075 N End Rd (27915-1311)
PHONE..................252 995-6026
Joseph Moore, *Owner*
EMP: 5 **EST:** 2005
SALES (est): 104.83K **Privately Held**
SIC: 2411 Stumping for turpentine or powder manufacturing

Ayden
Pitt County

(G-847)
ANDERSON TRUSS COMPANY INC
4825 Anderson Truss Rd (28513-8635)
PHONE..................252 746-7726
Greg Anderson, *Pr*
EMP: 15 **EST:** 1995
SALES (est): 2.26MM **Privately Held**
Web: www.andersontrussnc.com
SIC: 2439 Trusses, wooden roof

(G-848)
BABCO INC
639 Sumrell Rd (28513-8717)
PHONE..................888 376-5083
David Orren Babcock, *Pr*
EMP: 9 **EST:** 2003
SALES (est): 825.32K **Privately Held**
SIC: 3499 Welding tips, heat resistant: metal

(G-849)
CLASSIC SEAFOOD GROUP INC
7178 Nc 11 S (28513-8404)
P.O. Box 10 (28513-0010)
PHONE..................252 746-2818
Robert A Mayo, *Pr*
◆ **EMP:** 120 **EST:** 1985
SQ FT: 11,500
SALES (est): 23.79MM **Privately Held**
Web: www.cccatfish.com
SIC: 5146 2091 Seafoods; Fish, filleted (boneless)

(G-850)
CMI PLASTICS INC
222 Pepsi Way (28513-7609)
PHONE..................252 746-2171
Steven Hasselbach, *CEO*
EMP: 26 **EST:** 2007
SALES (est): 5.75MM **Privately Held**
Web: www.cmiplastics.com
SIC: 3089 Injection molding of plastics

(G-851)
CONSOLIDATED MODELS INC
Also Called: CMI Plastics
222 Pepsi Way (28513-7609)
PHONE..................252 746-2171
Stephen D Hasselbach, *CEO*
Steven A Hasselbach, *
Mark D Hasselbach, *
EMP: 50 **EST:** 1939
SQ FT: 70,000
SALES (est): 9.07MM **Privately Held**
Web: www.cmiplastics.com
SIC: 3089 Injection molding of plastics

(G-852)
FREE WILL BPTST PRESS FNDTION (PA)
Also Called: CROSS & CROWN
3928 Lee St (28513-3026)
P.O. Box 159 (28513-0159)
PHONE..................252 746-6128
Rick Watson, *Pr*
Mike Scott, *Ch Bd*
Darren Davenport, *VP*
Mellinda Edwards, *Sec*
EMP: 10 **EST:** 1876
SQ FT: 20,000
SALES (est): 471.36K
SALES (corp-wide): 471.36K **Privately Held**
Web: www.cross-crown.org
SIC: 5999 2741 5942 2791 Religious goods; Miscellaneous publishing; Book stores; Typesetting

(G-853)
QUILT LIZZY
4260 Lee St (28513-7178)
PHONE..................252 257-3800
Susan Harris, *Prin*
EMP: 7 **EST:** 2011
SALES (est): 470.72K **Privately Held**
Web: www.quiltlizzy.com
SIC: 2395 Quilting and quilting supplies

(G-854)
READY MIXED CONCRETE
Also Called: Southern Equipment Company
3928 Jolly Rd (28513-8767)
P.O. Box 877 (27835-0877)
PHONE..................252 758-1181
George C Turner, *S*
EMP: 7 **EST:** 2002
SQ FT: 1,200
SALES (est): 558.68K **Privately Held**
Web: www.dpdconcrete.com

SIC: 3273 Ready-mixed concrete

(G-855)
SIEBER INDUSTRIAL INC
221 Pepsi Way (28513-7609)
PHONE..................252 746-2003
EMP: 10 **EST:** 2006
SQ FT: 17,000
SALES (est): 1.78MM **Privately Held**
Web: www.sieberindustrial.com
SIC: 3441 Fabricated structural metal

(G-856)
SIGNATURE SEASONINGS LLC
3254 Nc 102 E (28513-8566)
P.O. Box 56438 (23456-9438)
PHONE..................252 746-1001
Chris Anderson, *Managing Member*
EMP: 8 **EST:** 2006
SQ FT: 9,500
SALES (est): 771.5K **Privately Held**
Web: www.signatureseasonings.com
SIC: 2099 Seasonings and spices

(G-857)
SIMPLE & SENTIMENTAL LLC
6248 Nc 11 S (28513-8801)
PHONE..................252 320-9458
Taylor Walden, *Managing Member*
EMP: 8 **EST:** 2017
SALES (est): 595.21K **Privately Held**
Web: www.simplesentimental.com
SIC: 2396 2752 5961 5947 Fabric printing and stamping; Commercial printing, lithographic; Electronic shopping; Gifts and novelties

(G-858)
SIMPLY NATURAL CREAMERY LLC
1265 Carson Edwards Rd (28513-2173)
PHONE..................252 746-3334
Robert N Moye, *Mgr*
EMP: 10 **EST:** 2014
SALES (est): 2.32MM **Privately Held**
Web: www.simplynaturalcreamery.com
SIC: 2024 Ice cream and ice milk

(G-859)
SPM MACHINE WORKS INC
4721 Old Nc 11 (28513-8400)
P.O. Box 778 (28513-0778)
PHONE..................252 321-2134
Yan Lin, *Prin*
Clint Sanders, *Prin*
EMP: 5 **EST:** 2006
SALES (est): 456.42K **Privately Held**
Web: www.spmmachineworks.com
SIC: 3599 Machine shop, jobbing and repair

(G-860)
TODDLER TABLES
3779 Lee St (28513-3043)
PHONE..................919 772-4765
Tom Vaughan, *Owner*
EMP: 6 **EST:** 2020
SALES (est): 91.35K **Privately Held**
Web: www.toddlertables.com
SIC: 2531 Public building and related furniture

Aydlett
Currituck County

(G-861)
SALT LIFE CANVAS LLC
128 Tabernacle Ln (27916-9602)
PHONE..................252 722-2314
April Dennison, *Owner*
EMP: 5 **EST:** 2017

GEOGRAPHIC SECTION — Bakersville - Mitchell County (G-889)

SALES (est): 85.77K **Privately Held**
SIC: 2211 Canvas

Badin
Stanly County

(G-862)
ALCOA POWER GENERATING INC
Also Called: Alcoa Badin Works
293 Nc Hwy 740 (28009)
P.O. Box 576 (28009-0576)
PHONE...................704 422-5691
Larry E Tate, *Brnch Mgr*
EMP: 35
SALES (corp-wide): 10.55B **Publicly Held**
Web: www.alcoa.com
SIC: 3334 Primary aluminum
HQ: Alcoa Power Generating Inc.
   201 Isabella St Ste 500
   Pittsburgh PA 15212
   412 553-4545

Bahama
Durham County

(G-863)
HOOK PUBLICATIONS
11124 S Lowell Rd (27503-8798)
PHONE...................219 808-3989
EMP: 5 EST: 2010
SALES (est): 50.5K **Privately Held**
SIC: 2741 Miscellaneous publishing

(G-864)
LOCAL PRINT
14 Rountree Ln (27503-9692)
PHONE...................919 620-9050
EMP: 4 EST: 2017
SALES (est): 83.91K **Privately Held**
Web: local.fedex.com
SIC: 2752 Commercial printing, lithographic

(G-865)
LOUD LEMON BEVERAGE LLC
8512 Meadow View Ln (27503-8402)
PHONE...................919 949-7649
William Jeffrey Outlaw, *Managing Member*
EMP: 4 EST: 2019
SALES (est): 223.57K **Privately Held**
Web: www.loudlemon.com
SIC: 2085 Cocktails, alcoholic

(G-866)
MURRAH WOODCRAFT LLC
5 Pearse Wynd Rd (27503-8768)
PHONE...................919 302-3661
EMP: 5 EST: 2011
SALES (est): 71.65K **Privately Held**
SIC: 2511 Wood household furniture

(G-867)
TERRY LOGGING COMPANY
7917 S Lowell Rd (27503-8746)
PHONE...................919 477-9170
Davis Terry, *Owner*
EMP: 6 EST: 2000
SALES (est): 473.69K **Privately Held**
SIC: 2411 Logging camps and contractors

Bailey
Nash County

(G-868)
B & Y MACHINING CO INC
4495 Us Highway 264a (27807-9192)
PHONE...................252 235-2180
Teresa Renfrow, *Pr*
Michael Renfrow, *Sec*
EMP: 4 EST: 1976
SQ FT: 10,000
SALES (est): 311.08K **Privately Held**
SIC: 3451 Screw machine products

(G-869)
CUSTOM BOATWORKS INC
8957 Pace Rd (27807-8665)
PHONE...................252 235-2461
EMP: 4 EST: 2019
SALES (est): 86.08K **Privately Held**
Web: www.chawkboats.com
SIC: 3732 Boatbuilding and repairing

(G-870)
CUSTOM FIBERGLASS PRODUCTS
8957 Pace Rd (27807-8665)
PHONE...................252 235-2461
Bradford Grubbs, *Pr*
EMP: 6 EST: 2009
SALES (est): 246.32K **Privately Held**
Web: www.mitziskiffs.com
SIC: 3732 Non-motorized boat, building and repairing

(G-871)
DEAN ST PROCESSING LLC
5645 Deans St (27807-8642)
PHONE...................252 235-0401
Barrett Twitty, *Pr*
EMP: 7 EST: 2014
SALES (est): 456.39K **Privately Held**
Web: www.deanstreetprocessing.com
SIC: 3556 Meat processing machinery

(G-872)
GARCIA BROTHERS WELDING LLC
7154 Us Highway 264a (27807-9252)
PHONE...................919 207-8190
Santos D H Garcia-madrid, *Owner*
EMP: 5 EST: 2018
SALES (est): 100.91K **Privately Held**
Web: www.garciabrotherswelding.com
SIC: 7692 Welding repair

(G-873)
GARLAND LANGLEY SAND AND GRAV
5312 Roseheath Rd (27807-7827)
PHONE...................252 235-2812
James Brie, *Prin*
EMP: 6 EST: 2015
SALES (est): 72.95K **Privately Held**
Web: www.garlandlangleysandandgravel.com
SIC: 1442 Construction sand and gravel

(G-874)
HEIDELBERG MTLS STHAST AGG LLC
P.O. Box 458 (27807-0458)
PHONE...................252 235-4162
Chris White, *Mgr*
EMP: 10
SALES (corp-wide): 21.19B **Privately Held**
Web: www.hansonbiz.com
SIC: 1429 Trap rock, crushed and broken-quarrying
HQ: Heidelberg Materials Southeast Agg Llc
   3237 Satellite Blvd # 30
   Duluth GA 30096
   770 491-2756

(G-875)
IMAGE DESIGNS INK LLC
12687 Sanford St (27807-9623)
P.O. Box 277 (27807-0277)
PHONE...................252 235-1964
Amy Pearson, *Managing Member*
EMP: 9 EST: 2013
SALES (est): 503.64K **Privately Held**
Web: www.imagedesignsink.com
SIC: 2759 Screen printing

(G-876)
NUTRIEN AG SOLUTIONS INC
9702 Global Rd (27807)
P.O. Box 577 (27807-0577)
PHONE...................252 235-4161
Larry Boyant, *Mgr*
EMP: 4
SALES (corp-wide): 27.71B **Privately Held**
Web: www.nutrienagsolutions.com
SIC: 2873 Nitrogenous fertilizers
HQ: Nutrien Ag Solutions, Inc.
   3005 Rocky Mountain Ave
   Loveland CO 80538
   970 685-3300

(G-877)
PAMMYTS MONOGRAM GIFTS
4942 Strickland Rd (27807-9083)
PHONE...................252 363-6331
Pam Thorne, *Prin*
EMP: 4 EST: 2017
SALES (est): 50.23K **Privately Held**
SIC: 2395 Embroidery and art needlework

(G-878)
PBS VENTURES INC
5469 Us Highway 264a (27807)
PHONE...................252 235-2001
EMP: 5
SALES (corp-wide): 887.66K **Privately Held**
SIC: 3089 Injection molding of plastics
PA: Pbs Ventures, Inc.
   131 Johnston Pkwy
   Kenly NC 27542
   919 284-9001

(G-879)
WOODWORKING UNLIMITED
6378 Vance St (27807-9609)
PHONE...................252 235-5285
Isaac Glenn Perry, *Owner*
EMP: 4 EST: 1985
SALES (est): 208.03K **Privately Held**
Web: www.expiredwixdomain.com
SIC: 2434 Wood kitchen cabinets

Bakersville
Mitchell County

(G-880)
BETTER PUBLISHING INC
467 Byrd Rd (28705-7854)
PHONE...................828 688-9188
Doug Harrell, *CEO*
EMP: 8 EST: 2004
SALES (est): 184.36K **Privately Held**
SIC: 2741 Miscellaneous publishing

(G-881)
COURTNEY MARTINS KILN
3224 Snow Creek Rd (28705-7028)
PHONE...................828 467-1414
Courtney Martin, *Ofcr*
EMP: 6 EST: 2005
SALES (est): 92.55K **Privately Held**
SIC: 3559 Kilns

(G-882)
COVIA HOLDINGS CORPORATION
Also Called: COVIA HOLDINGS CORPORATION
2241 Nc 197 (28705)
PHONE...................828 688-2169
EMP: 5
SALES (corp-wide): 1.6B **Privately Held**
Web: www.coviacorp.com
SIC: 1446 Industrial sand
PA: Covia Holdings Llc
   3 Summit Park Dr Ste 700
   Independence OH 44131
   800 255-7263

(G-883)
COVIA HOLDINGS LLC
Red Hill Iota Plant (28705)
PHONE...................828 688-2169
EMP: 7
SALES (corp-wide): 1.6B **Privately Held**
Web: www.coviacorp.com
SIC: 1446 Industrial sand
PA: Covia Holdings Llc
   3 Summit Park Dr Ste 700
   Independence OH 44131
   800 255-7263

(G-884)
JAMES W MCMANUS INC
Also Called: McManus Microwave
2419 Beans Creek Rd (28705-7747)
PHONE...................828 688-2560
James W Mcmanus, *Pr*
EMP: 9 EST: 1981
SALES (est): 1.09MM **Privately Held**
Web: www.mcmanusmicrowave.com
SIC: 3679 3812 Microwave components; Search and navigation equipment

(G-885)
LEDGER HARDWARE INC
Also Called: Ace Hardware
5489 S 226 Hwy (28705-7329)
PHONE...................828 688-4798
James P Webb, *Pr*
Charles S Webb, *Sec*
EMP: 8 EST: 1987
SQ FT: 12,000
SALES (est): 928.42K **Privately Held**
Web: www.acehardware.com
SIC: 5251 5231 5084 3546 Hardware stores; Paint; Engines, gasoline; Saws and sawing equipment

(G-886)
PERKINS FABRICATIONS INC
5632 Nc 261 (28705-7709)
PHONE...................828 688-3157
Kay Perkins, *Prin*
EMP: 4 EST: 2010
SALES (est): 91.37K **Privately Held**
SIC: 7692 Welding repair

(G-887)
PIONEER CABINETS INC
102 Alfred Woody Dr (28705-8708)
PHONE...................828 688-2642
Christopher M Young, *Prin*
EMP: 5 EST: 2007
SALES (est): 236.63K **Privately Held**
SIC: 2434 Wood kitchen cabinets

(G-888)
ROCK CREEK WELDING INC
58 Wildscreek Rd (28705-7444)
PHONE...................828 385-1554
Andrew Marvin Hensley, *Admn*
EMP: 5 EST: 2017
SALES (est): 54.38K **Privately Held**
SIC: 7692 Welding repair

(G-889)
SOUTHEAST WLDG FABRICATION LLC

Bakersville - Mitchell County (G-890)

24 Reidy Rd (28705-8918)
PHONE.................................828 385-1380
EMP: 5 **EST:** 2017
SALES (est): 46.27K **Privately Held**
SIC: 7692 Welding repair

(G-890)
TOE RIVER SERVICE STATION LLC
4928 S 226 Hwy (28705-7256)
PHONE.................................828 688-6385
Daniel Pitman, *Owner*
Daniel Pitman, *Managing Member*
EMP: 4 **EST:** 1999
SALES (est): 223.1K **Privately Held**
SIC: 7534 Tire repair shop

Balsam Grove
Transylvania County

(G-891)
GEM PUBLISHING LLC
1950 Indian Creek Rd (28708-4503)
PHONE.................................828 885-5272
Gary Bullock, *Prin*
EMP: 5 **EST:** 2016
SALES (est): 90.56K **Privately Held**
SIC: 2741 Miscellaneous publishing

Banner Elk
Avery County

(G-892)
BANNER ELK WINERY INC
Also Called: Winery At The Blueberry Farm
135 Deer Run Ln (28604-6529)
PHONE.................................828 898-9090
Richard Arlen Wolfe, *Brnch Mgr*
EMP: 4
SALES (corp-wide): 294.92K **Privately Held**
Web: www.bannerelkwinery.com
SIC: 2084 Wines
PA: Banner Elk Winery Inc
  60 Deer Run Ln
  Banner Elk NC 28604
  828 260-1790

(G-893)
BANNER ELK WINERY INC (PA)
Also Called: Banner Elk Winery & Villa
60 Deer Run Ln (28604-6138)
P.O. Box 1274 (28604-1274)
PHONE.................................828 260-1790
John M Wright, *Prin*
EMP: 5 **EST:** 2004
SALES (est): 294.92K
SALES (corp-wide): 294.92K **Privately Held**
Web: www.bannerelkwinery.com
SIC: 2084 Wines

(G-894)
BLUE MOUNTAIN METALWORKS INC
567 Main St E (28604-8974)
P.O. Box 1805 (28604-1805)
PHONE.................................828 898-8582
Dirk Brown, *Owner*
EMP: 9 **EST:** 2006
SALES (est): 356.17K **Privately Held**
Web: www.bluemountainmetalworks.com
SIC: 3449 1799 3499 Miscellaneous metalwork; Ornamental metal work; Aerosol valves, metal

(G-895)
DARK MOON DISTILERIES LLC
60 Deer Run, Banner Elk (28604)
P.O. Box 30 (28168-0030)
PHONE.................................704 222-8063
Anthony Pruitt, *Managing Member*
EMP: 9 **EST:** 2021
SALES (est): 241.56K **Privately Held**
SIC: 2085 Distilled and blended liquors

(G-896)
DEWOOLFSON DOWN INTL INC (PA)
Also Called: Dewoolfson Down
9452 Nc Highway 105 S (28604-8646)
PHONE.................................828 963-2750
Richard B Schaffer, *Pr*
Marsha Turner, *Sec*
▲ **EMP:** 7 **EST:** 1983
SQ FT: 3,300
SALES (est): 1.45MM
SALES (corp-wide): 1.45MM **Privately Held**
Web: www.dewoolfsonlinens.com
SIC: 2392 5719 Comforters and quilts: made from purchased materials; Beddings and linens

(G-897)
FASTZONE DSL & INTERNET SERVIC
157 Seven Devils Rd (28604-9457)
PHONE.................................828 963-1350
John Dixon, *Prin*
EMP: 5 **EST:** 2007
SALES (est): 62.83K **Privately Held**
SIC: 4813 7372 7389 Internet connectivity services; Prepackaged software; Telephone services

(G-898)
GRANDFATHER VINYRD WINERY LLC
225 Vineyard Ln (28604-8053)
PHONE.................................828 963-2400
Dylan Tatum, *Mgr*
EMP: 7 **EST:** 2017
SALES (est): 463.68K **Privately Held**
Web: www.grandfathervineyard.com
SIC: 2084 Wines

(G-899)
GRIGGS CUSTOM WOODWORK
114 S Slope Cir (28604-6789)
PHONE.................................828 719-1503
Ben Griggs, *Prin*
EMP: 4 **EST:** 2017
SALES (est): 49.47K **Privately Held**
SIC: 2431 Millwork

(G-900)
JERKY OUTPOST
2107 Broadstone Rd (28604-9039)
PHONE.................................828 260-6221
EMP: 5 **EST:** 2017
SALES (est): 59.63K **Privately Held**
Web: www.jerkyoutpost.net
SIC: 2013 Sausages and other prepared meats

(G-901)
LANDSMAN FOREST LAWN GUARD
174 Maple Dr (28604-7884)
PHONE.................................828 898-3433
Joel Owen, *Owner*
Joel Ownes, *Owner*
EMP: 9 **EST:** 2004
SALES (est): 200.98K **Privately Held**
SIC: 3271 Blocks, concrete: landscape or retaining wall

(G-902)
M & M ENTPS BANNER ELK INC
318 Outback Ln (28604-7213)
PHONE.................................828 898-2401
EMP: 5 **EST:** 2019
SALES (est): 40.95K **Privately Held**
Web: www.bannerelk.com
SIC: 2399 Fabricated textile products, nec

(G-903)
MITERS TOUCH INC
Also Called: Miters Touch
591 Old Hartley Rd (28604-9142)
PHONE.................................828 963-4445
Denise R Grohs, *Pr*
Marshall J Stein, *VP*
EMP: 5 **EST:** 1982
SALES (est): 417.89K **Privately Held**
SIC: 2431 5712 2434 Woodwork, interior and ornamental, nec; Furniture stores; Wood kitchen cabinets

(G-904)
TATUM GALLERIES INC
5320 Nc Highway 105 S (28604-8726)
PHONE.................................828 963-6466
Stephen Tatum, *Pr*
Sally Tatum, *Sec*
EMP: 8 **EST:** 1983
SQ FT: 8,000
SALES (est): 1.52MM **Privately Held**
Web: www.tatumgalleries.com
SIC: 5712 2511 7389 Furniture stores; Wood household furniture; Interior design services

(G-905)
VAUGHN WOODWORKING INC
442 Aldridge Rd (28604-9002)
PHONE.................................828 963-6858
Henry Vaughn, *Pr*
EMP: 6 **EST:** 1981
SALES (est): 235.88K **Privately Held**
Web: www.vaughnwoodworking.com
SIC: 1751 2499 Cabinet and finish carpentry; Carved and turned wood

Barnardsville
Buncombe County

(G-906)
BROOKSHIRE WOODWORKING INC
99 Dodd Rd (28709-9733)
PHONE.................................828 779-2119
Jeremy Brookshire, *Brnch Mgr*
EMP: 52
SALES (corp-wide): 298.37K **Privately Held**
SIC: 2431 Millwork
PA: Brookshire Woodworking, Inc.
  355 Haywood Rd
  Asheville NC 28806
  828 779-2119

(G-907)
CYNTHIA DREW
154 Horseshoe Trl (28709-8723)
PHONE.................................828 301-8697
Cynthia Drew, *Prin*
EMP: 5 **EST:** 2011
SALES (est): 209.27K **Privately Held**
SIC: 2711 Newspapers, publishing and printing

(G-908)
DOMCO TECHNOLOGY LLC
1342 Barnardsville Hwy Ste A (28709-9709)
PHONE.................................888 834-8541
Quincey Brock, *Managing Member*
EMP: 4 **EST:** 2013
SALES (est): 80.38K **Privately Held**
Web: www.domco.us
SIC: 2741 Internet publishing and broadcasting

(G-909)
ELLIE INDUSTRIES INC
93 Buena Vista Dr (28709-6105)
PHONE.................................828 626-3935
Eloise Goldstein, *Prin*
EMP: 5 **EST:** 2008
SALES (est): 130K **Privately Held**
SIC: 3999 Manufacturing industries, nec

(G-910)
FOLKWEAR
1679 Barnardsville Hwy (28709-9715)
P.O. Box 732 (28730-0732)
PHONE.................................828 626-3100
Kate Mathews, *Owner*
EMP: 7 **EST:** 2006
SALES (est): 248.94K **Privately Held**
Web: www.folkwear.com
SIC: 7372 Publisher's computer software

(G-911)
HARLEY S WOODWORKS INC
917 N Fork Rd (28709-9760)
PHONE.................................828 776-0120
Harley Stewart, *Prin*
EMP: 6 **EST:** 2008
SALES (est): 119.51K **Privately Held**
Web: www.washluberepair.com
SIC: 2431 Millwork

(G-912)
OHIO ELECTRIC MOTORS INC
30 Paint Fork Rd (28709-9711)
P.O. Box 168 (28709-0168)
PHONE.................................828 626-2901
Randy L Greely, *Prin*
Mark R Dyll, *
Michael T Clancey, *
Robert A Sirak, *
◆ **EMP:** 63 **EST:** 1979
SQ FT: 80,000
SALES (est): 9.56MM
SALES (corp-wide): 241.4MM **Privately Held**
Web: www.ohioelectricmotors.com
SIC: 3621 Motors, electric
HQ: Peerless-Winsmith, Inc.
  5200 Upper Metro Pl # 11
  Dublin OH 43017
  614 526-7000

(G-913)
SMILING HARA LLC
Also Called: Smiling Hara Tempeh
735 N Fork Rd (28709-8711)
P.O. Box 570 (28709-0570)
PHONE.................................828 545-4150
EMP: 4 **EST:** 2011
SALES (est): 373.38K **Privately Held**
Web: www.eathempeh.com
SIC: 2099 Food preparations, nec

Bath
Beaufort County

(G-914)
BROOKS BOATWORKS INC
403 Handy Ln (27808-9791)
P.O. Box 1345 (27889-1345)
PHONE.................................252 974-1005
Roger Brooks, *VP*
Lisa Brooks, *Pr*
EMP: 6 **EST:** 2004

GEOGRAPHIC SECTION

SQ FT: 75,000
SALES (est): 139.72K **Privately Held**
Web: www.brooksboatworks.com
SIC: 3732 Boats, fiberglass: building and repairing

(G-915)
DERICK CORDON LOGGING INC
9040 Nc 99 Hwy South (27808)
PHONE..................................252 964-2009
EMP: 10 EST: 2002
SALES (est): 465.57K **Privately Held**
SIC: 2411 Logging camps and contractors

(G-916)
S & K SAND LLC
380 Mill Creek Ln (27808-9163)
PHONE..................................252 964-3144
Eric Slade, *Prin*
EMP: 5 EST: 2016
SALES (est): 90.59K **Privately Held**
SIC: 1442 Construction sand and gravel

(G-917)
SULLIVAN MOTORSPORTS INC
471 Creek Rd (27808-9358)
PHONE..................................252 923-2257
Lester Sullivan, *Owner*
EMP: 6 EST: 2015
SALES (est): 178.05K **Privately Held**
SIC: 7538 3732 General automotive repair shops; Non-motorized boat, building and repairing

Battleboro
Edgecombe County

(G-918)
BERRY GLOBAL INC
6941 Corporation Pkwy (27809-9274)
PHONE..................................252 984-4100
EMP: 9
Web: www.berryglobal.com
SIC: 3089 Plastics containers, except foam
HQ: Berry Global, Inc.
    101 Oakley St
    Evansville IN 47710

(G-919)
DELIZZA LLC
6610 Corporation Pkwy (27809-9804)
PHONE..................................252 442-0270
Raymond Laruelle, *CEO*
Frans Castelein, *Pr*
Delizza Pattiserie, *Sec*
Brian Hill, *VP*
▲ EMP: 10 EST: 1999
SQ FT: 6,000
SALES (est): 930K **Privately Held**
Web: www.delizza.us
SIC: 2024 Dairy based frozen desserts

(G-920)
FLOW X RAY CORPORATION
Also Called: Flow Dental
133 Wolf Rd (27809-7502)
PHONE..................................631 242-9729
Carolyn Camiola, *CEO*
Martin B Wolf, *
Howard Wolf, *
Arlene Wolf, *
Carolyn Price, *
▲ EMP: 72 EST: 1974
SALES (est): 4.86MM **Privately Held**
Web: www.flowdental.com
SIC: 3844 X-ray apparatus and tubes

(G-921)
HANOR CO INC
6717 Nc 97 W (27809-8956)
PHONE..................................252 977-0035
EMP: 75 EST: 1993
SALES (est): 3MM **Privately Held**
Web: www.hanorcompany.com
SIC: 2099 Food preparations, nec

(G-922)
HOSPIRA INC
6551 N Us Highway 301 (27809-9778)
PHONE..................................252 977-5111
Terry Chavis, *Prin*
EMP: 28
SALES (corp-wide): 100.33B **Publicly Held**
Web: www.pfizerhospitalus.com
SIC: 2834 Pharmaceutical preparations
HQ: Hospira, Inc.
    275 N Field Dr
    Lake Forest IL 60045
    224 212-2000

(G-923)
LANE LAND & TIMBER INC
5631 Hart Farm Rd (27809-9171)
PHONE..................................252 443-1151
Ralph H Lane, *Pr*
Ray Jordan, *Sec*
EMP: 5 EST: 1968
SALES (est): 506.28K **Privately Held**
SIC: 2411 0811 Logging camps and contractors; Timber tracts

(G-924)
LOG CABIN HOMES LTD
7677 N Halifax Rd (27809-9601)
PHONE..................................252 454-1548
EMP: 8
SALES (corp-wide): 9.77MM **Privately Held**
Web: www.logcabinhomes.com
SIC: 2452 Log cabins, prefabricated, wood
PA: Log Cabin Homes Ltd.
    513 Keen St 515
    Rocky Mount NC 27804
    252 454-1500

(G-925)
MONSANTO COMPANY
Also Called: MONSANTO COMPANY
5746 Pearsall St (27809-9184)
PHONE..................................252 212-5421
EMP: 6
SALES (corp-wide): 51.78B **Privately Held**
Web: www.monsanto.com
SIC: 2879 Agricultural chemicals, nec
HQ: Monsanto Technology Llc.
    800 N Lindbergh Blvd
    Saint Louis MO 63167
    314 694-1000

(G-926)
NUTKAO USA INC
7044 Nc 48 (27809-9561)
PHONE..................................252 595-1000
Luca Benedetto, *CEO*
Davide Braida, *
◆ EMP: 42 EST: 2013
SQ FT: 100,000
SALES (est): 9.81MM **Privately Held**
Web: www.nutkao.com
SIC: 2066 Chocolate
HQ: Nutkao Srl
    Via Alcide De Gasperi 2/Rstu
    Govone CN 12040
    017 362-1211

(G-927)
OSSID LLC (DH)
4000 College Rd (27809-8500)
P.O. Box 1968 (27802-1968)
PHONE..................................252 446-6177
Bud Lane, *Managing Member*
Kim Brewer, *
Jimmy Hemric, *
▲ EMP: 78 EST: 1981
SQ FT: 80,000
SALES (est): 24.34MM **Privately Held**
Web: www.ossid.com
SIC: 3565 Packaging machinery
HQ: Pro Mach, Inc.
    50 E Rvrcnter Blvd Ste 18
    Covington KY 41011
    513 831-8778

(G-928)
PFIZER INC
6563 N Us Highway 301 (27809-9778)
PHONE..................................252 382-3309
EMP: 5
SALES (corp-wide): 100.33B **Publicly Held**
Web: www.pfizer.com
SIC: 2834 Pharmaceutical preparations
PA: Pfizer Inc.
    66 Hudson Blvd E
    New York NY 10001
    800 879-3477

(G-929)
PHOENIX ASSEMBLY NC LLC
7101 N Us Highway 301 (27809-9651)
PHONE..................................252 801-4250
Brian Cousins, *Mgr*
EMP: 8 EST: 2010
SALES (est): 2.16MM **Privately Held**
SIC: 3569 4225 4731 8741 Assembly machines, non-metalworking; General warehousing; Freight transportation arrangement; Industrial management
HQ: Phoenix Assembly, Llc
    164 S Park Blvd
    Greenwood IN 46143
    317 884-3600

(G-930)
POPPIES INTERNATIONAL I INC
6610 Corporation Pkwy (27809-9804)
PHONE..................................252 442-4016
Frans Castelein, *Pr*
Raymond Laruelle, *
Bobby Davis, *
Anthony Popelier, *
▲ EMP: 70 EST: 1999
SALES (est): 22.21MM
SALES (corp-wide): 5.98MM **Privately Held**
Web: www.poppiesbakeries.com
SIC: 2038 Frozen specialties, nec
HQ: Poppies Bakeries
    Kasteelstraat 29
    Zonnebeke 8980
    57460200

(G-931)
WAKE STONE CORP
7379 N Halifax Rd (27809-9569)
PHONE..................................252 985-4411
Chris Puns, *Superintnt*
EMP: 16 EST: 1990
SALES (est): 224.97K **Privately Held**
Web: www.wakestonecorp.com
SIC: 1429 1423 Grits mining (crushed stone); Crushed and broken granite

(G-932)
WARD BACKHOE BULLDOZER SVC LLC
8029 Nc 4 (27809-9528)
P.O. Box 703 (27809-0703)
PHONE..................................252 446-5878
Steven Ward, *Admn*
EMP: 5 EST: 2014
SALES (est): 228.25K **Privately Held**
SIC: 3531 Backhoes

(G-933)
WEBB S MAINT & PIPING INC
217 Daniels Ave (27809-7509)
P.O. Box 928 (27809-0928)
PHONE..................................252 972-2616
James Dustin Webb, *Pr*
Ramsey Webb, *Sec*
EMP: 18 EST: 1991
SQ FT: 15,000
SALES (est): 2.19MM **Privately Held**
SIC: 7692 Welding repair

(G-934)
WOLF X-RAY CORPORATION
133 Wolf Rd (27809-7502)
PHONE..................................631 242-9729
Carolyn Camiola, *CEO*
Martin Wolf, *
▲ EMP: 60 EST: 1931
SALES (est): 8.24MM **Privately Held**
Web: www.wolfxray.com
SIC: 3844 X-ray apparatus and tubes

Bayboro
Pamlico County

(G-935)
HARDISON TIRE CO INC
13504 Nc Highway 55 (28515-9106)
PHONE..................................252 745-4561
Elmo Hardison, *Pr*
Barry Hardison, *VP*
EMP: 10 EST: 1974
SALES (est): 484.88K **Privately Held**
Web: www.hardisontire.com
SIC: 7534 5541 Tire repair shop; Gasoline service stations

Bear Creek
Chatham County

(G-936)
BEAR CREEK FABRICATION LLC
1930 Campbell Rd (27207-9484)
PHONE..................................919 837-2444
Allen Johnson, *CEO*
EMP: 13 EST: 2008
SALES (est): 1.61MM **Privately Held**
Web: www.bearcreekfabrication.com
SIC: 3441 Fabricated structural metal

(G-937)
CENTRAL CAROLINA BTLG CO INC
1506 Mays Chapel Rd (27207-8219)
PHONE..................................919 542-3226
Staffany Smith, *Pr*
EMP: 5 EST: 1998
SALES (est): 191.65K **Privately Held**
Web: www.grandsprings.com
SIC: 2086 Carbonated soft drinks, bottled and canned

(G-938)
GARY TUCKER
Also Called: Tucker Welding
12988 Nc 902 Hwy (27207-9293)

Bear Creek - Chatham County (G-939)

(G-939)
LILAS TRUNK
145 Cc Routh Rd (27207-9120)
PHONE.................................919 548-0784
Shelly Joyce, *Prin*
EMP: 5 **EST:** 2011
SALES (est): 148.98K **Privately Held**
SIC: 3161 Trunks

(G-940)
MOORE S WELDING SERVICE INC
142 Elmer Moore Rd (27207-9341)
PHONE.................................919 837-5769
Lewis D Moore Senior, *Pr*
Lewis D Moore Junior, *VP*
Ann Moore, *Sec*
EMP: 7 **EST:** 1970
SQ FT: 12,250
SALES (est): 806.5K **Privately Held**
Web: www.mooreswelidingandcraneservice.com
SIC: 7692 3452 7389 Welding repair; Bolts, metal; Crane and aerial lift service

(G-941)
MOORES MCH CO FAYETTEVILLE INC (PA)
13120 Nc 902 Hwy (27207-9295)
PHONE.................................919 837-5354
E Eugene Moore, *Pr*
Ruby Moore, *
▲ **EMP:** 100 **EST:** 1971
SQ FT: 22,500
SALES (est): 9.34MM
SALES (corp-wide): 9.34MM **Privately Held**
SIC: 3542 3469 7692 3714 Rebuilt machine tools, metal forming types; Machine parts, stamped or pressed metal; Welding repair; Motor vehicle parts and accessories

(G-942)
SCOTTS & ASSOCIATES INC
Also Called: Southern Supreme Fruit Cakes
1699 Hoyt Scott Rd (27207-8727)
PHONE.................................336 581-3141
Hoyt Scott, *Pt*
Berta Scott, *Pt*
Lisa Scott, *Pt*
Belinda Jordan, *Pt*
Wayne Jordan, *Pt*
▲ **EMP:** 12 **EST:** 1985
SQ FT: 7,400
SALES (est): 2.37MM **Privately Held**
Web: www.southernsupreme.com
SIC: 2051 2052 2099 Cakes, bakery; except frozen; Cookies; Food preparations, nec

Beaufort
Carteret County

(G-943)
ATLANTIC VENEER COMPANY LLC (HQ)
Also Called: Moehring-Group
2457 Lennoxville Rd (28516-7899)
P.O. Box 660 (28516-0660)
PHONE.................................252 728-3169
▼ **EMP:** 145 **EST:** 1964
SQ FT: 750,000
SALES (est): 23.89MM
SALES (corp-wide): 24.77MM **Privately Held**
PHONE.................................919 837-5724
Gary Tucker, *Owner*
EMP: 4 **EST:** 1977
SQ FT: 1,600
SALES (est): 235.76K **Privately Held**
SIC: 7692 Welding repair

Web: www.moehring-group.com
SIC: 2435 Plywood, hardwood or hardwood faced
PA: Moehring Group Holding, Llc
2457 Lennoxville Rd
Beaufort NC 28516
252 728-3169

(G-944)
BARBOUR S MARINE SUPPLY CO INC
410 Hedrick St (28516-2019)
P.O. Box 248 (28516-0248)
PHONE.................................252 728-2136
Nelson B Gillikin Ii, *Pr*
Harold Booth Iii, *VP*
EMP: 11 **EST:** 1919
SQ FT: 5,000
SALES (est): 1.75MM **Privately Held**
Web: www.barboursmarina.com
SIC: 5088 5551 3599 Marine supplies; Marine supplies, nec; Machine shop, jobbing and repair

(G-945)
BEACH HOUSE PUBLICATIONS LLC
2475 Hwy 70 Beaufort (28516-7877)
P.O. Box 1148 (28516-1148)
PHONE.................................252 504-2344
EMP: 4 **EST:** 2019
SALES (est): 215K **Privately Held**
SIC: 2759 Publication printing

(G-946)
BEAUFORT COMPOSITE TECH INC
Also Called: Composites.com
111 Safrit Dr (28516-9017)
PHONE.................................252 728-1547
EMP: 9 **EST:** 1995
SQ FT: 11,000
SALES (est): 887.6K **Privately Held**
Web: www.composites.com
SIC: 3089 Molding primary plastics

(G-947)
BRASWELL WELDING
502 Perkins Rd (28516-7870)
PHONE.................................252 838-0089
Eric Braswell, *Owner*
EMP: 6 **EST:** 2016
SALES (est): 52.65K **Privately Held**
SIC: 7692 Welding repair

(G-948)
CALYPSO COTTAGE LLC (PA)
324 Orange St (28516-1821)
PHONE.................................252 728-4299
Stacie Meislohn, *Managing Member*
EMP: 5 **EST:** 2007
SALES (est): 131.2K **Privately Held**
Web: www.calypsocottage.co
SIC: 3911 Jewelry apparel

(G-949)
CCBS & SIGN SHOP INC
1626 Live Oak St (28516-1532)
PHONE.................................252 728-4866
Kimberly Beasley, *Pr*
Joseph Beasley, *VP*
EMP: 7 **EST:** 2007
SQ FT: 4,500
SALES (est): 608.34K **Privately Held**
Web: www.ccbsandsignshop.com
SIC: 3993 Signs and advertising specialties

(G-950)
COASTAL CANVAS MFG INC
Also Called: Coastal Canvas
1403 Harkers Island Rd (28516-7226)
PHONE.................................252 728-4946

Michael Sasser, *Pr*
Joyce Sasser, *Off Mgr*
EMP: 9 **EST:** 1985
SQ FT: 2,000
SALES (est): 353.43K **Privately Held**
Web: www.coastalcanvasmfg.com
SIC: 2394 Awnings, fabric: made from purchased materials

(G-951)
CONWAY ENTPS CARTERET CNTY LLC
313 Laurel Rd (28516-6553)
PHONE.................................252 504-3518
Bruce Conway, *Prin*
EMP: 4 **EST:** 2011
SALES (est): 203.76K **Privately Held**
Web: www.conway-enterprises.com
SIC: 2451 Mobile buildings: for commercial use

(G-952)
CRYSTAL COAST BOATWORKS
1145 Sensation Weigh (28516-7766)
PHONE.................................252 723-9370
EMP: 5 **EST:** 2018
SALES (est): 68.67K **Privately Held**
Web: www.trueworldmarine.com
SIC: 3732 Boatbuilding and repairing

(G-953)
CRYSTAL COAST COMPOSITES INC
2630 Highway 101 (28516-7753)
PHONE.................................252 838-0025
William Brown Coulter, *Brnch Mgr*
EMP: 14
SALES (corp-wide): 240.14K **Privately Held**
Web: www.crystalcoastnc.org
SIC: 3732 Boatbuilding and repairing
PA: Crystal Coast Composites, Inc.
1707 River Dr
Morehead City NC 28557
252 838-0025

(G-954)
CURRIER WOODWORKS INC
1622 Live Oak St (28516-1532)
PHONE.................................252 725-4233
Donald H Currier, *Pr*
Judith Currier, *Treas*
EMP: 4 **EST:** 1993
SALES (est): 440.79K **Privately Held**
Web: www.currierwoodworks.com
SIC: 2431 Millwork

(G-955)
DOWN EAST SCREEN PRINTING LLC
208 Straits Haven Rd (28516-7228)
PHONE.................................252 808-7742
EMP: 4 **EST:** 2018
SALES (est): 83.91K **Privately Held**
Web: www.downeastscreenprinting.com
SIC: 2752 Commercial printing, lithographic

(G-956)
FISHERMAN CREATIONS INC
1175 Hwy 70 Otway (28516)
P.O. Box 118 (28512-0118)
PHONE.................................252 725-0138
Donald Acree, *Pr*
George Brearey, *VP*
Loretta Acree, *Sec*
EMP: 20 **EST:** 2009
SQ FT: 2,400
SALES (est): 1.43MM **Privately Held**
Web: www.crabpottrees.com
SIC: 3999 5093 Christmas trees, artificial; Scrap and waste materials

(G-957)
FRONT STREET VLG MSTR ASSN INC
2450 Lennoxville Rd (28516-7898)
PHONE.................................252 838-1524
Oliver Charles Ii, *Prin*
EMP: 5 **EST:** 2010
SALES (est): 397.77K **Privately Held**
Web: www.boathousemarinanc.com
SIC: 2335 Wedding gowns and dresses

(G-958)
GILLIKIN MARINE RAILWAYS INC
Also Called: Morgan Creek Seafood
195 Morgan St (28516-8656)
P.O. Box 533 (28516-0533)
PHONE.................................252 726-7284
James Gillikin, *Pr*
Jeannette Josey, *Sec*
EMP: 9 **EST:** 1971
SQ FT: 9,120
SALES (est): 631.38K **Privately Held**
SIC: 3732 5146 Boatbuilding and repairing; Seafoods

(G-959)
HANCOCK & GRANDSON INC
971 Harkers Island Rd (28516-7290)
PHONE.................................252 728-2416
EMP: 5 **EST:** 1989
SALES (est): 491.96K **Privately Held**
SIC: 3599 7692 Machine shop, jobbing and repair; Welding repair

(G-960)
HARDING ENTERPRISE INC
Also Called: Carolina Yachts
1110 Spartina Dr (28516-7760)
PHONE.................................252 725-9785
William Harding, *Pr*
Tracy Harding, *VP*
EMP: 8 **EST:** 2011
SALES (est): 721.87K **Privately Held**
Web: www.carolinayachtsnc.com
SIC: 3732 Boatbuilding and repairing

(G-961)
MOORES MARINE YACHT CENTER INC
182 Lewistown Rd (28516-7812)
PHONE.................................252 504-7060
James Moores, *Pr*
EMP: 13 **EST:** 2007
SALES (est): 268K **Privately Held**
Web: www.woodenboatrepair.com
SIC: 3732 Boatbuilding and repairing

(G-962)
OLIVE BEAUFORT OIL COMPANY
300 Front St Ste 4 (28516-2147)
PHONE.................................252 504-2474
Merrell Clarke, *Prin*
EMP: 6 **EST:** 2014
SALES (est): 175.47K **Privately Held**
Web: www.beaufortoliveoil.com
SIC: 2079 Olive oil

(G-963)
ONE HUNDRED TEN PERCENT SCREEN
150 Lake Rd (28516-7546)
PHONE.................................252 728-3848
EMP: 4 **EST:** 1991
SALES (est): 161.48K **Privately Held**
SIC: 2261 Screen printing of cotton broadwoven fabrics

GEOGRAPHIC SECTION   Belmont - Gaston County (G-988)

(G-964)
PARKER MARINE ENTERPRISES INC
2570 Nc Highway 101 (28516-7751)
P.O. Box 2129 (28516-5129)
PHONE..................................252 728-5621
E Linwood Parker Iii, *Pr*
Trudy G Parker, *
▼ **EMP:** 62 **EST:** 1960
SQ FT: 100,000
SALES (est): 10.15MM **Privately Held**
Web: www.parkerboats.com
SIC: 3732 Boats, fiberglass: building and repairing

(G-965)
PILOTHOUSE MARINE SERVICES LLC
277 Tosto Rd (28516-6682)
PHONE..................................252 732-6427
EMP: 5 **EST:** 2018
SALES (est): 252K **Privately Held**
Web: www.pilothousemarineservices.com
SIC: 3731 Shipbuilding and repairing

(G-966)
SHM JARRETT BAY TRS LLC
530 Sensation Weigh (28516-7672)
PHONE..................................972 488-1314
Gavin Mcclintock, *Prin*
David Glass, *Prin*
EMP: 5 **EST:** 2021
SALES (est): 288.87K **Privately Held**
Web: www.jarrettbay.com
SIC: 3732 Boatbuilding and repairing

(G-967)
SOL-REX MINIATURE LAMP WORKS
802 Mulberry St (28516-1936)
PHONE..................................845 292-1510
Charles Perrenod Junior, *Owner*
EMP: 4 **EST:** 1931
SALES (est): 232.25K **Privately Held**
SIC: 3641 Lamps, incandescent filament, electric

(G-968)
STARFLITE COMPANIES INC (PA)
530 Sensation Weigh (28516-7672)
PHONE..................................252 728-2690
▼ **EMP:** 123 **EST:** 1986
SALES (est): 20.66MM **Privately Held**
Web: www.jarrettbay.com
SIC: 3732 5983 5947 Boatbuilding and repairing; Fuel oil dealers; Gift shop

(G-969)
TRITON MARINE SERVICES INC
1050 Sensation Weigh (28516-7759)
P.O. Box 486 (28516-0486)
PHONE..................................252 728-9958
Angela Mcmahon, *Pr*
Croy Mcmahon, *VP*
EMP: 5 **EST:** 2001
SQ FT: 60,000
SALES (est): 787.9K **Privately Held**
Web: www.triton-marine.net
SIC: 1629 3663 7699 Marine construction; Marine radio communications equipment; Marine engine repair

(G-970)
TRUE WORLD MARINE LLC
1145 Sensation Weigh (28516-7766)
PHONE..................................252 728-2541
EMP: 6 **EST:** 2006
SALES (est): 405.82K **Privately Held**
Web: www.trueworldmarine.com
SIC: 3732 Fishing boats: lobster, crab, oyster, etc.: small

(G-971)
WOOD SURGEON
1403 Lennoxville Rd (28516-9023)
PHONE..................................252 728-5767
Kemp Guthrie, *Owner*
EMP: 7 **EST:** 1989
SALES (est): 391.96K **Privately Held**
SIC: 2431 Millwork

Beech Mountain
Avery County

(G-972)
MORETZ SIGNS INC
Also Called: Signs By Tomorrow
125 Staghorn Hollow Rd (28604-8218)
PHONE..................................828 387-4600
Dorothy Moretz, *Pr*
Michael Moretz, *VP*
EMP: 6 **EST:** 1997
SQ FT: 1,660
SALES (est): 447.93K **Privately Held**
Web: www.signsbytomorrow.com
SIC: 3993 Signs and advertising specialties

Belews Creek
Forsyth County

(G-973)
TITAN AMERICA LLC
3193 Pine Hall Rd (27009-9157)
PHONE..................................336 754-0143
Eric Poitras, *Pr*
EMP: 6
SALES (corp-wide): 8.01MM **Privately Held**
Web: www.titanamerica.com
SIC: 3273 Ready-mixed concrete
HQ: Titan America Llc
    5700 Lake Wright Dr # 300
    Norfolk VA 23502
    757 858-6500

Belmont
Gaston County

(G-974)
ALAMO DISTRIBUTION LLC (DH)
Also Called: Alamo Iron Works
2100 Oaks Pkwy (28012-5141)
PHONE..................................704 398-5600
Frances Shey, *Pr*
James C Melton, *
▼ **EMP:** 113 **EST:** 2010
SALES (est): 45.53MM **Privately Held**
SIC: 5051 3441 3443 3444 Steel; Fabricated structural metal; Fabricated plate work (boiler shop); Sheet metalwork
HQ: Vallen Distribution, Inc.
    2100 The Oaks Pkwy
    Belmont NC 28012

(G-975)
AVANTI HEARTH PRODUCTS LLC
110 Dorie Dr (28012-9557)
P.O. Box 403 (28012-0403)
PHONE..................................704 866-4342
▲ **EMP:** 6 **EST:** 2004
SALES (est): 152.28K **Privately Held**
SIC: 3429 5023 Fireplace equipment, hardware: andirons, grates, screens; Fireplace equipment and accessories

(G-976)
BUSBIN CABINETRY
180 Berkshire Ave (28012-3887)
PHONE..................................704 560-4485
John Busbin, *Prin*
EMP: 4 **EST:** 2017
SALES (est): 89.89K **Privately Held**
SIC: 2434 Wood kitchen cabinets

(G-977)
CARUS LLC
Also Called: CARUS LLC
181 Woodlawn St (28012-2149)
PHONE..................................704 822-1441
Craig Mazzucca, *Bmch Mgr*
EMP: 24
SALES (corp-wide): 117.4MM **Privately Held**
Web: www.carusllc.com
SIC: 2819 Industrial inorganic chemicals, nec
HQ: Carus Corporation
    315 5th St
    Peru IL 61354
    815 223-1500

(G-978)
CERTIFIED LAWNMOWER INC
124 Hubbard St (28012-2951)
PHONE..................................704 527-2765
Carlos Romeros, *Pr*
Graciela Romeros, *Sec*
EMP: 7 **EST:** 1977
SALES (est): 491.46K **Privately Held**
Web: www.certifiedlawnmowers.com
SIC: 7699 3524 5261 Lawn mower repair shop; Lawn and garden equipment; Garden tractors and tillers

(G-979)
CHAMPIONX LLC
2000 Oaks Pkwy (28012-5133)
PHONE..................................704 506-4830
EMP: 5
SALES (corp-wide): 3.76B **Publicly Held**
Web: www.championx.com
SIC: 2899 Chemical preparations, nec
HQ: Championx Llc
    2445 Tech Frest Blvd Bldg
    The Woodlands TX 77381
    281 632-6500

(G-980)
CHEM-TECH SOLUTIONS INC
427 Brook St (28012-3435)
PHONE..................................704 829-9202
Tony Phillips, *Pr*
EMP: 29 **EST:** 1999
SALES (est): 3.03MM **Privately Held**
Web: www.chemtechsolutions.com
SIC: 2842 2899 Polishes and sanitation goods; Acid resist for etching

(G-981)
CUSTOM INDUSTRIES INC
Also Called: Contract Manufacturing Div
111 Hubbard St (28012-2947)
P.O. Box 785 (28012-0785)
PHONE..................................704 825-3346
Paul Heffner, *Mgr*
EMP: 13
SALES (corp-wide): 4.87MM **Privately Held**
Web: www.customindustries.com
SIC: 3552 3599 Textile machinery; Machine and other job shop work
PA: Custom Industries, Inc.
    215 Aloe Rd
    Greensboro NC 27409
    336 299-2885

(G-982)
DELLINGER ENTERPRISES LTD
759 Cason St (28012-2219)
P.O. Box 627 (28012-0627)
PHONE..................................704 825-9687
Gregory Dellinger, *Pr*
Larry D Dellinger, *
EMP: 28 **EST:** 1979
SQ FT: 24,000
SALES (est): 9MM **Privately Held**
Web: www.dellingerenterprises.com
SIC: 3569 3599 Assembly machines, non-metalworking; Machine shop, jobbing and repair

(G-983)
DEPALO FOODS INC
2010 Oaks Pkwy (28012-5133)
PHONE..................................704 827-0245
Enrico Diraino, *Pr*
Enrico Piraino, *
Gianni Piraino, *
EMP: 35 **EST:** 2003
SALES (est): 5.61MM **Privately Held**
Web: www.depalofoods.com
SIC: 2051 Bakery: wholesale or wholesale/retail combined

(G-984)
DIABETIC SOCK CLUB
6325 Wilkinson Blvd Ste 103 (28012-3966)
PHONE..................................800 214-0218
Samantha Ledford, *Owner*
EMP: 5 **EST:** 2020
SALES (est): 180.72K **Privately Held**
Web: www.diabeticsockclub.com
SIC: 2252 Socks

(G-985)
DISPLAY OPTIONS WOODWORK INC
205 Colonial Dr (28012-9531)
PHONE..................................704 599-6525
EMP: 4 **EST:** 1995
SALES (est): 446.58K **Privately Held**
SIC: 2541 Display fixtures, wood

(G-986)
DIVERSIFIED SPECIALTIES INC
10 Airline Ave (28012-3854)
P.O. Box 1003 (28012-1003)
PHONE..................................704 825-3671
Douglas B Phifer, *Pr*
William J Phifer, *
Dorothy Phifer, *
EMP: 38 **EST:** 1974
SQ FT: 40,000
SALES (est): 6.01MM **Privately Held**
Web: www.div-spec.com
SIC: 3599 Machine shop, jobbing and repair

(G-987)
EQUIPMENT PARTS INC (PA)
Also Called: Carolina Machine Works
795 Cason St (28012-2219)
P.O. Box 1156 (28012-1156)
PHONE..................................704 827-7545
William L Jarchow, *Pr*
Karen S Jarchow, *
EMP: 35 **EST:** 1956
SQ FT: 25,000
SALES (est): 4.41MM
SALES (corp-wide): 4.41MM **Privately Held**
Web: www.mfgsolutionsinc.com
SIC: 3599 Machine shop, jobbing and repair

(G-988)
FEINBERG ENTERPRISES INC
3 Caldwell Dr (28012-2750)
PHONE..................................704 822-2400
▲ **EMP:** 12 **EST:** 1996
SQ FT: 42,500
SALES (est): 3.58MM **Privately Held**
Web: www.textum.com

Belmont - Gaston County (G-989)

SIC: 2221 Glass and fiberglass broadwoven fabrics

(G-989)
FERGUSON DESIGN INC
236 Hawthorne Park Ave (28012-4152)
PHONE..............................704 394-0120
Mike Ferguson, *Pr*
Suzanne Ferguson, *Sec*
EMP: 20 EST: 1998
SALES (est): 2.33MM **Privately Held**
Web: www.fergusondesign.com
SIC: 3993 Signs and advertising specialties

(G-990)
FIREHOUSE CABINETS
715 Brook Forest Dr (28012-9656)
PHONE..............................704 689-5243
Al Briggs, *Prin*
EMP: 5 EST: 2010
SALES (est): 164K **Privately Held**
Web: www.firehousecabinets.com
SIC: 2434 Wood kitchen cabinets

(G-991)
GASTON PRINTING AND SIGNS LLC
7204 W Wilkinson Blvd (28012-6212)
PHONE..............................702 267-5633
EMP: 9 EST: 2018
SALES (est): 709.28K **Privately Held**
Web: www.gastonprintingandsigns.com
SIC: 2752 Offset printing

(G-992)
GLOBAL SENSORS LLC
63 Mcadenville Rd (28012)
P.O. Box 750 (28012-0750)
PHONE..............................704 827-4331
David K Caskey, *Pr*
◆ EMP: 6 EST: 2004
SALES (est): 799.74K **Privately Held**
Web: www.global-sensors.com
SIC: 3823 Process control instruments

(G-993)
JO-MAR GROUP LLC
Also Called: Jo-Mar Spinning
701 Plum St (28012-3423)
EMP: 38 EST: 2010
SALES (est): 1.69MM **Privately Held**
SIC: 3523 Balers: farm: hay, straw, cotton, etc.

(G-994)
KURT WIDENHOUSE VIOLINS
318 Mellon Rd (28012-8614)
PHONE..............................704 825-3289
EMP: 4 EST: 2017
SALES (est): 69.88K **Privately Held**
Web: www.widenhouseviolins.com
SIC: 3931 Violins and parts

(G-995)
MUDDY RIVER DISTILLERY LLC
1500 River Dr Ste 100 (28012-3587)
PHONE..............................336 516-4190
Robert Jeffrey Delaney, *Prin*
EMP: 4 EST: 2011
SALES (est): 245.88K **Privately Held**
Web: www.muddyriverdistillery.com
SIC: 2085 Distilled and blended liquors

(G-996)
NC FILTRATION OF FLORIDA LLC
Also Called: Ssnc LLC Pba NC Filtration
1 Miller St (28012-2162)
PHONE..............................704 822-4444
Eli Kershaw, *Managing Member*
Jeffrey Kershaw, *
EMP: 85 EST: 2010
SQ FT: 2,000
SALES (est): 17.09MM **Privately Held**
Web: www.ncfiltration.com
SIC: 3585 Air conditioning equipment, complete

(G-997)
NUNN PROBST INSTALLATIONS INC
6428 W Wilkinson Blvd (28012-2858)
P.O. Box 549 (28098-0549)
PHONE..............................704 822-9443
Jason L Nunn, *Pr*
EMP: 9 EST: 2000
SALES (est): 940.19K **Privately Held**
SIC: 3535 Conveyors and conveying equipment

(G-998)
PARKDALE MILLS INCORPORATED
Also Called: Plant 15
103 E Woodrow Ave (28012-3164)
PHONE..............................704 825-5324
Bernard Harvey, *Mgr*
EMP: 45
SALES (corp-wide): 1.44B **Privately Held**
Web: www.parkdalemills.com
SIC: 2281 Cotton yarn, spun
HQ: Parkdale Mills, Incorporated
     531 Cotton Blossom Cir
     Gastonia NC 28054
     704 874-5000

(G-999)
PARKDALE MILLS INCORPORATED
Also Called: Plant 17
1000 Parkdale Dr (28012-3574)
P.O. Box 856 (28012-0856)
PHONE..............................704 913-3917
EMP: 66
SALES (corp-wide): 1.44B **Privately Held**
Web: www.parkdalemills.com
SIC: 2281 Cotton yarn, spun
HQ: Parkdale Mills, Incorporated
     531 Cotton Blossom Cir
     Gastonia NC 28054
     704 874-5000

(G-1000)
PARKDALE MILLS INCORPORATED
501 10th St (28012)
PHONE..............................704 825-2529
Danny Huntley, *Brnch Mgr*
EMP: 14
SALES (corp-wide): 1.44B **Privately Held**
Web: www.parkdalemills.com
SIC: 4225 2282 2281 4953 General warehousing and storage; Throwing and winding mills; Yarn spinning mills; Refuse systems
HQ: Parkdale Mills, Incorporated
     531 Cotton Blossom Cir
     Gastonia NC 28054
     704 874-5000

(G-1001)
PIEDMONT DIRECTIONAL SIGNS INC
4004 Beechwood Spring Ln (28012-6531)
PHONE..............................704 607-6809
Scott Rothenber, *Prin*
EMP: 5 EST: 2018
SALES (est): 197.12K **Privately Held**
Web: www.piedmontdirectionalsigns.com
SIC: 3993 Signs and advertising specialties

(G-1002)
PIEDMONT LITHIUM CAROLINAS INC (HQ)
42 E Catawba St (28012-3349)
PHONE..............................434 664-7643
Keith Phillips, *Pr*
Jeff Armstrong, *Ch Bd*
EMP: 18 EST: 2019
Web: www.piedmontlithium.com
SIC: 2819 Industrial inorganic chemicals, nec
PA: Piedmont Lithium Inc.
     42 E Catawba St
     Belmont NC 28012
     704 461-8000

(G-1003)
PIEDMONT LITHIUM INC (PA)
42 E Catawba St (28012-3349)
PHONE..............................704 461-8000
Keith Phillips, *Pr*
Jeff Armstrong, *Ch Bd*
Patrick Brindle, *Ex VP*
Michael White, *Ex VP*
Austin Devaney, *CCO*
EMP: 7 EST: 1983
SIC: 1479 Lithium mineral mining

(G-1004)
PREMIX NORTH CAROLINA LLC ◯
52a Ervin St (28012-3327)
PHONE..............................704 412-7922
Jari-matti Mehto, *Managing Member*
EMP: 5 EST: 2022
SALES (est): 2.48MM
SALES (corp-wide): 48.63MM **Privately Held**
Web: www.premixgroup.com
SIC: 3087 Custom compound purchased resins
HQ: Premix, Inc.
     52a Ervin St
     Belmont NC 28012
     704 412-7922

(G-1005)
RAMSEY INDUSTRIES INC
Also Called: Carolina Custom Windows
816 Woodlawn St (28012-2134)
PHONE..............................704 827-3560
Charles W Ramsey, *Pr*
Lavon Ramsey, *Sec*
EMP: 35 EST: 1980
SQ FT: 8,500
SALES (est): 1.9MM **Privately Held**
Web: www.ramseyindustries.com
SIC: 3089 6162 1761 3442 Windows, plastics ; Mortgage brokers, using own money; Roofing, siding, and sheetmetal work; Storm doors or windows, metal

(G-1006)
RAMSEY PRODUCTS CORPORATION
135 Performance Dr (28012-2446)
P.O. Box 668827 (28266-8827)
PHONE..............................704 394-0322
Mark Taylor, *CEO*
David Holcomb, *
Grier N Killough, *
◆ EMP: 84 EST: 1923
SQ FT: 80,000
SALES (est): 10.34MM
SALES (corp-wide): 167.14K **Privately Held**
Web: www.ramseychain.com
SIC: 3499 Ice cream freezers, household, nonelectric: metal
PA: Rondot International
     9 Rue Jean Elysee Dupuy
     Champagne Au Mont D Or

(G-1007)
SHORT RUN PRO LLC
710 E Catawba St Ste A (28012-3504)
PHONE..............................704 825-1599
Bruce Toal, *Prin*
Victoria Breeedlove, *Opers*
▼ EMP: 12 EST: 2006
SALES (est): 1.84MM **Privately Held**
Web: www.shortrunpro.com
SIC: 3471 Plating of metals or formed products

(G-1008)
SOLVERE LLC
69 Mcadenville Rd (28012-2434)
PHONE..............................704 829-1015
Barry Stringer, *Managing Member*
EMP: 27 EST: 2003
SQ FT: 12,000
SALES (est): 7.65MM **Privately Held**
Web: www.solvere.net
SIC: 3625 Relays and industrial controls

(G-1009)
SPARTAN DYERS INC
217 Sterling St (28012-3218)
P.O. Box 790 (28012-0790)
PHONE..............................704 829-0467
Alphonse G Kelada, *Prin*
George Kelada, *
Nabila R Kelada, *
▲ EMP: 53 EST: 1988
SQ FT: 150,000
SALES (est): 10.14MM **Privately Held**
Web: www.spartandyers.com
SIC: 2269 Dyeing: raw stock, yarn, and narrow fabrics

(G-1010)
STEEL SPECIALTY CO BELMONT INC (PA)
Also Called: Ssi
5907 W Wilkinson Blvd (28012-4802)
P.O. Box 985 (28012-0985)
PHONE..............................704 825-4745
Farrell W Mauldin, *CEO*
Jason S Mauldin, *
Jason Mauldin, *Prin*
Victor Scott, *
Edward H Reese, *
EMP: 45 EST: 1971
SQ FT: 60,000
SALES (est): 12.52MM
SALES (corp-wide): 12.52MM **Privately Held**
Web: www.steel-specialty.com
SIC: 3441 3446 Building components, structural steel; Stairs, staircases, stair treads: prefabricated metal

(G-1011)
STEP IN SOCK
208 Glenway St (28012-3182)
PHONE..............................704 508-9966
EMP: 7 EST: 2018
SALES (est): 98.65K **Privately Held**
Web: www.stepinshield.com
SIC: 2252 Socks

(G-1012)
SYNCOT PLASTICS INC
350 Eastwood Dr (28012-3754)
P.O. Box 1350 (28012-1350)
PHONE..............................704 967-0010
▲ EMP: 75 EST: 1995
SALES (est): 24.04MM **Privately Held**
Web: www.syncot.com
SIC: 2821 Plastics materials and resins

(G-1013)
T T S D PRODUCTIONS LLC
Also Called: T Toppers
27 E Woodrow Ave (28012-3142)
PHONE..............................704 829-6666
EMP: 7 EST: 1997
SALES (est): 429.4K **Privately Held**

GEOGRAPHIC SECTION

Benson - Johnston County (G-1038)

SIC: 2759 2396 Screen printing; Automotive and apparel trimmings

(G-1014)
TASTEBUDS LLC
Also Called: Tastebuds Popcorn
208 N Main St (28012-3125)
PHONE.....................704 461-8755
EMP: 7 **EST:** 2011
SQ FT: 1,000
SALES (est): 429.12K **Privately Held**
Web: www.tastebudspopcorn.com
SIC: 5441 2064 5145 Popcorn, including caramel corn; Popcorn balls or other treated popcorn products; Popcorn and supplies

(G-1015)
TECWORKS INC
4041 S Cove Ln (28012-9586)
PHONE.....................704 829-9700
P Craig Helton, *Prin*
EMP: 5 **EST:** 2006
SALES (est): 470.18K **Privately Held**
SIC: 3679 Antennas, receiving

(G-1016)
TEXTUM OPCO LLC
3 Caldwell Dr (28012-2750)
PHONE.....................704 822-2400
Aaron Feinberg, *Managing Member*
Kerstin Hunicke, *Acctg Mgr*
Chris Maynard, *Dir Opers*
EMP: 36 **EST:** 2020
SALES (est): 4.82MM **Privately Held**
Web: www.textum.com
SIC: 2211 Broadwoven fabric mills, cotton

(G-1017)
USA DRONES
240 Long Leaf Dr Unit 2b (28012-4200)
PHONE.....................937 830-1856
Wendy Leathely, *Prin*
EMP: 5 **EST:** 2017
SALES (est): 76.12K **Privately Held**
SIC: 3721 Motorized aircraft

(G-1018)
WILBERT INC (HQ)
Also Called: Wilbert Plastic Services
100 N Main St Ste 200 (28012-3104)
PHONE.....................704 247-3850
Greg Botner, *Pr*
▲ **EMP:** 20 **EST:** 2012
SALES (est): 218.2MM
SALES (corp-wide): 218.2MM **Privately Held**
Web: www.wilbertplastics.com
SIC: 3089 Injection molding of plastics
PA: Piedmont Manufacturing Group, Llc
   1411 Broadway Fl 34
   New York NY 10018
   212 752-1356

(G-1019)
WILBERT PLASTIC SERVICES INC
100 N Main St Ste 200 (28012-3104)
PHONE.....................866 273-1810
EMP: 11 **EST:** 2006
SALES (est): 180.65K **Privately Held**
Web: www.wilbertplastics.com
SIC: 3089 Injection molding of plastics

(G-1020)
WILBERT PLSTIC SVCS ACQSTION L (DH)
Also Called: Wilbert Plastic Services
1000 Oaks Pkwy (28012-5139)
PHONE.....................704 822-1423
▲ **EMP:** 103 **EST:** 2010

SALES (est): 50.76MM
SALES (corp-wide): 218.2MM **Privately Held**
SIC: 3089 Injection molding of plastics
HQ: Wilbert, Inc.
   100 N Main St Ste 200
   Belmont NC 28012
   704 247-3850

Belvidere
Perquimans County

(G-1021)
CJ STALLINGS LOGGING INC
1307 Acorn Hill Rd (27919-9802)
PHONE.....................252 297-2272
EMP: 10 **EST:** 1990
SALES (est): 597.04K **Privately Held**
SIC: 2411 Logging camps and contractors

(G-1022)
JOHN R BELL
112 Ridge Rd (27919-9512)
PHONE.....................252 297-2499
John R Bell Junior, *Prin*
EMP: 6 **EST:** 2012
SALES (est): 247.59K **Privately Held**
SIC: 3519 Marine engines

Belville
Brunswick County

(G-1023)
CURTI USA CORPORATION
161 Poole Rd (28451-9962)
PHONE.....................910 769-1977
EMP: 6 **EST:** 2020
SALES (est): 561.44K
SALES (corp-wide): 103.62MM **Privately Held**
Web: www.curti.com
SIC: 3599 Custom machinery
PA: Curti Costruzioni Meccaniche Spa
   Via Emilia Ponente 750
   Castel Bolognese RA 48014
   054 665-5911

(G-1024)
PSA INCORPORATED
150 Backhoe Rd Ne (28451-8506)
PHONE.....................910 371-1115
Bert Moody, *Pr*
EMP: 10 **EST:** 1998
SALES (est): 151.86K **Privately Held**
SIC: 2891 Adhesives

(G-1025)
QUALITY BEVERAGE LLC
157 Poole Rd (28451-9508)
PHONE.....................910 371-3596
Danny Curtis, *Genl Mgr*
EMP: 21
SALES (corp-wide): 10.39MM **Privately Held**
Web: www.cheerwine.com
SIC: 2086 Soft drinks: packaged in cans, bottles, etc.
PA: Quality Beverage, L.L.C.
   1413 Jake Anlxander Blvd S
   Salisbury NC 28146
   704 637-5881

(G-1026)
TECHNICAL COATING INTL INC
150 Backhoe Rd Ne (28451-8506)
PHONE.....................910 371-0860
Burt E Moody, *CEO*
Sean E Moody, *Pr*

David Stanbury, *VP*
◆ **EMP:** 44 **EST:** 1992
SQ FT: 65,000
SALES (est): 8.08MM **Privately Held**
Web: www.tciinc.com
SIC: 2672 2679 3089 Paper; coated and laminated, nec; Building, insulating, and packaging paper; Plastics containers, except foam

Bennett
Chatham County

(G-1027)
PHILIP BRADY
Also Called: Airloom Furnishing
185 Charlie Garner Rd (27208-9374)
PHONE.....................336 581-3999
Philip Brady, *Owner*
EMP: 5 **EST:** 1993
SQ FT: 30,120
SALES (est): 191.68K **Privately Held**
SIC: 2511 2517 Wood bedroom furniture; Home entertainment unit cabinets, wood

(G-1028)
TOZA TRUSS LLC
6633 Carl Cox Rd (27208-8053)
PHONE.....................336 301-6338
EMP: 5 **EST:** 2018
SALES (est): 474.55K **Privately Held**
Web: www.tozatruss.com
SIC: 3448 Trusses and framing, prefabricated metal

Benson
Johnston County

(G-1029)
ACME GENERAL DESIGN GROUP LLC
101 N Market St (27504-1514)
PHONE.....................843 466-6000
EMP: 4 **EST:** 2019
SALES (est): 139.88K **Privately Held**
SIC: 3911 Jewelry, precious metal

(G-1030)
AMWARE PALLET SERVICES LLC
1700 Chicopee Rd (27504-2147)
PHONE.....................919 207-2403
Jaime Loney, *Mgr*
EMP: 12
SALES (corp-wide): 8.36MM **Privately Held**
SIC: 2448 Pallets, wood
PA: Amware Pallet Services, Llc
   216 Main St Unit 100
   Edwards CO 81632
   970 337-7070

(G-1031)
BERRY GLOBAL INC
1203 Chicopee Rd (27504-2121)
PHONE.....................919 207-3202
EMP: 24
Web: www.berryglobal.com
SIC: 3089 Bottle caps, molded plastics
HQ: Berry Global, Inc.
   101 Oakley St
   Evansville IN 47710

(G-1032)
CHICOPEE INC
Also Called: Polymer Group
1203 Chicopee Rd (27504-2121)
P.O. Box 308 (27504-0308)

PHONE.....................919 894-4111
EMP: 4
Web: www.chicopee.com
SIC: 7389 2297 Personal service agents, brokers, and bureaus; Nonwoven fabrics
HQ: Chicopee, Inc.
   9335 Hrris Crners Pkwy St
   Charlotte NC 28269

(G-1033)
COUNTY PRESS INC
Also Called: Four Oks/Benson News In Review
113 S Market St (27504-1520)
P.O. Box 9 (27504-0009)
PHONE.....................919 894-2112
Norman Delano, *Pr*
EMP: 8 **EST:** 1951
SQ FT: 5,000
SALES (est): 587.57K **Privately Held**
Web: www.bensonfouroaksnews.com
SIC: 2711 Newspapers, publishing and printing

(G-1034)
DAVIS PUBLISHING GROUP IN
611 Chicopee Rd (27504-1943)
P.O. Box 130 (27504-0130)
PHONE.....................919 894-4170
Colon Davis, *Prin*
EMP: 6 **EST:** 2008
SALES (est): 103.4K **Privately Held**
Web: www.bnprinting.com
SIC: 2741 Miscellaneous publishing

(G-1035)
GRAPHIC PRODUCTS INC
Also Called: Benton Card
105 S Wall St (27504-1327)
P.O. Box 369 (27504-0369)
PHONE.....................919 894-3661
Suzanne Benton Cook, *Pr*
EMP: 6 **EST:** 1980
SQ FT: 12,000
SALES (est): 690.65K **Privately Held**
Web: www.bentonprint.com
SIC: 2752 Offset printing

(G-1036)
HAMLIN SHEET METAL COMPANY INC
200 N Walton Ave (27504-6697)
P.O. Box 249 (27504-0249)
PHONE.....................919 894-2224
Paul Turner, *Mgr*
EMP: 100
SALES (corp-wide): 13.19MM **Privately Held**
Web: www.hamlincos.com
SIC: 3444 Awnings and canopies
PA: Hamlin Sheet Metal Company, Incorporated
   1411 W Garner Rd
   Garner NC 27529
   919 772-8780

(G-1037)
HARRIS REBAR INC
803 S Market St (27504-2111)
PHONE.....................919 528-8333
Harris Rebar, *Owner*
EMP: 11 **EST:** 2015
SALES (est): 349.87K **Privately Held**
Web: www.harrisrebar.com
SIC: 5051 3325 3441 Steel; Steel foundries, nec; Fabricated structural metal

(G-1038)
JPS CUPCAKERY LLC
111 S Railroad St (27504-1325)
PHONE.....................919 894-5000

Joseph Parker, *Admn*
EMP: 16 **EST:** 2014
SALES (est): 852.88K **Privately Held**
Web: www.jpspastry.com
SIC: 2051 Bread, cake, and related products

(G-1039)
MARTIN MARIETTA MATERIALS INC
Also Called: Martin Marietta Aggregates
13661 Raleigh Rd (27504-6819)
P.O. Box 365 (27504-0365)
PHONE.................................919 894-2003
EMP: 7
Web: www.martinmarietta.com
SIC: 1422 Crushed and broken limestone
PA: Martin Marietta Materials Inc
 4123 Parklake Ave
 Raleigh NC 27612

(G-1040)
NEWS AND OBSERVER PUBG CO
Gold Leaf Publishers
611 Chicopee Rd (27504-1943)
P.O. Box 130 (27504-0130)
PHONE.................................919 894-4170
Colen Davis, *Brnch Mgr*
EMP: 10
SALES (corp-wide): 709.52MM **Privately Held**
SIC: 2711 Newspapers, publishing and printing
HQ: The News And Observer Publishing Company
 421 Fayetteville St # 104
 Raleigh NC 27601
 919 829-4500

(G-1041)
PRECISION METALS LLC
589 Old Roberts Rd (27504-6903)
PHONE.................................919 762-7481
EMP: 9 **EST:** 2017
SALES (est): 927.18K **Privately Held**
SIC: 3724 Aircraft engines and engine parts

(G-1042)
ROADRUNNER POWDER COATING
12900 Raleigh Rd (27504-6812)
PHONE.................................919 749-5290
EMP: 5 **EST:** 2015
SALES (est): 97.58K **Privately Held**
SIC: 3479 Coating of metals and formed products

(G-1043)
TAYLOR MADE CASES INC
107 Last Cast Dr (27504-8043)
PHONE.................................919 209-0555
Diane Perry, *Pr*
Greg Perry, *VP*
Jason Miles, *Sec*
EMP: 18 **EST:** 2003
SQ FT: 4,000
SALES (est): 2.24MM **Privately Held**
Web: www.taylormadecases.com
SIC: 3199 Holsters, leather

(G-1044)
TWIN TROLLER BOATS INC
Also Called: Carolina Electric Boats
501 S Wall St Ste A (27504-1856)
PHONE.................................919 207-2622
Frank Jones, *Pr*
EMP: 5 **EST:** 2005
SQ FT: 20,000
SALES (est): 414.4K **Privately Held**
Web: www.freedomelectricmarine.com
SIC: 3732 Tenders (small motor craft), building and repairing

(G-1045)
ULTRATECH INDUSTRIES INC
200 Hamlin Rd (27504)
P.O. Box 465 (27529-0465)
PHONE.................................919 779-2004
William F Hamlin Junior, *Pr*
Christine H Hamlin, *Sec*
EMP: 7 **EST:** 1980
SQ FT: 2,000
SALES (est): 852.8K **Privately Held**
SIC: 3822 Pneumatic relays, air-conditioning type

(G-1046)
WOODS CABINET COMPANY INC
1302 N Johnson St (27504-6602)
PHONE.................................919 207-1663
EMP: 8 **EST:** 2019
SALES (est): 319.09K **Privately Held**
Web: www.woodcabinetsinc.com
SIC: 2434 Wood kitchen cabinets

(G-1047)
XTREME POSTCARD PROFITS SYSTEM
22 Boardwalk Ave (27504-7848)
PHONE.................................919 894-8886
Emerson Jordan, *Prin*
EMP: 6 **EST:** 2016
SALES (est): 165.95K **Privately Held**
SIC: 2752 Commercial printing, lithographic

Bessemer City
Gaston County

(G-1048)
ACORN PRINTING
4122 Kings Mountain Hwy (28016-7525)
P.O. Box 244 (28016-0244)
PHONE.................................704 868-4522
EMP: 5 **EST:** 2008
SALES (est): 89.04K **Privately Held**
Web: www.acornprints.com
SIC: 5699 2759 Miscellaneous apparel and accessory stores; Screen printing

(G-1049)
ADVANCED DRAINAGE SYSTEMS
333 Southridge Pkwy (28016-7805)
PHONE.................................704 629-4151
EMP: 17
SALES (est): 3.18MM **Privately Held**
SIC: 3089 Plastics products, nec

(G-1050)
ADVANCED DRAINAGE SYSTEMS INC
Also Called: ADS
333 Southridge Pkwy (28016-7805)
P.O. Box 9 (28016-0009)
PHONE.................................704 629-4151
Doug Attit, *Rgnl Mgr*
EMP: 48
SALES (corp-wide): 3.07B **Publicly Held**
Web: www.adspipe.com
SIC: 3084 5051 Plastics pipe; Pipe and tubing, steel
PA: Advanced Drainage Systems, Inc.
 4640 Trueman Blvd
 Hilliard OH 43026
 614 658-0050

(G-1051)
ALCO METAL FABRICATO
1111 Oates Rd (28016-7574)
PHONE.................................704 739-1168
EMP: 9 **EST:** 2019
SALES (est): 726.52K **Privately Held**
Web: www.alcometalfabricatorsinc.com

SIC: 3499 Fabricated metal products, nec

(G-1052)
ARC STEEL FABRICATION LLC
649 Bess Town Rd (28016-7544)
P.O. Box 545 (28021-0545)
PHONE.................................980 533-8302
Ira Brewster Senior, *Pr*
EMP: 10 **EST:** 2015
SALES (est): 681.05K **Privately Held**
Web: www.arcsteelfab.com
SIC: 3499 Metal household articles

(G-1053)
BESSEMER CITY MACHINE SHOP INC
Also Called: Bessember City Machinery Sales
524 Bess Town Rd (28016-7543)
P.O. Box 305 (28016-0305)
PHONE.................................704 629-4111
Steven E Bowen, *Pr*
Janet Haynes, *Sec*
▲ **EMP:** 20 **EST:** 1963
SQ FT: 16,000
SALES (est): 3.19MM **Privately Held**
Web: www.bessemercity.com
SIC: 5051 3312 3599 Steel; Blast furnaces and steel mills; Machine shop, jobbing and repair

(G-1054)
C & B WELDING & FAB INC
2070 Mauney Rd (28016-9643)
PHONE.................................704 435-6942
Thomas J Carpender, *Pr*
EMP: 6 **EST:** 2008
SQ FT: 21,000
SALES (est): 239.94K **Privately Held**
SIC: 7692 Welding repair

(G-1055)
CARO-POLYMERS INC (PA)
611 Bess Town Rd (28016-7544)
P.O. Box 755 (28016-0755)
PHONE.................................704 629-5319
Todd Boyter, *Pr*
W Curtis Boyter, *VP*
Myrna Boyter, *Sec*
EMP: 10 **EST:** 1984
SQ FT: 24,500
SALES (est): 1.6MM
SALES (corp-wide): 1.6MM **Privately Held**
SIC: 3089 Plastics hardware and building products

(G-1056)
CONNER BROTHERS MACHINE CO INC
Also Called: Cbm
3200 Bessemer City Rd (28016-9774)
PHONE.................................704 864-6084
Bobby Conner, *Pr*
Cathy Conner, *
EMP: 95 **EST:** 1990
SQ FT: 200,000
SALES (est): 20.99MM **Privately Held**
Web: www.cbmprecisionparts.com
SIC: 3599 3451 Machine shop, jobbing and repair; Screw machine products

(G-1057)
CRC MACHINE & FABRICATION INC
4375 Dallas Cherryville Hwy (28016-7729)
P.O. Box 1001 (28016-1001)
PHONE.................................980 522-1361
David Halk, *Prin*
Kelly Halk, *Pr*
EMP: 16 **EST:** 2013
SALES (est): 1.94MM **Privately Held**
Web: www.crc-incorp.com

SIC: 3599 Machine shop, jobbing and repair

(G-1058)
CREATIVE DOCUMENTS
704 S Skyland Dr (28016-6524)
PHONE.................................704 674-5230
Patricia Clay, *Prin*
EMP: 5 **EST:** 2008
SALES (est): 75.76K **Privately Held**
Web: www.psalms6811.com
SIC: 2741 Miscellaneous publishing

(G-1059)
CUSTOM MACHINE COMPANY INC
221 White Jenkins Rd (28016-9559)
P.O. Box 625 (28016-0625)
PHONE.................................704 629-5326
Thomas M Jones, *Pr*
EMP: 15 **EST:** 1980
SQ FT: 7,300
SALES (est): 280.67K **Privately Held**
Web: www.cmtco.com
SIC: 3599 5084 7692 Machine shop, jobbing and repair; Textile machinery and equipment ; Welding repair

(G-1060)
DALLAS FABRICATION
1346 Ramseur Rd (28016-7636)
PHONE.................................704 629-4000
EMP: 9 **EST:** 2015
SALES (est): 90.89K **Privately Held**
Web: www.spgear.com
SIC: 3312 Ammonia and liquor, from chemical recovery coke ovens

(G-1061)
DALLAS MACHINE AND
Also Called: Dallas Machine Company
1326 Ramseur Rd (28016-7636)
P.O. Box 1340 (28016-1340)
PHONE.................................704 629-5611
Richard Easler, *Off Mgr*
EMP: 5 **EST:** 2010
SALES (est): 455.49K **Privately Held**
SIC: 3599 Machine shop, jobbing and repair

(G-1062)
DAWN PROCESSING COMPANY INC
205 E Alabama Ave (28016-2604)
P.O. Box 368 (28016-0368)
PHONE.................................704 629-5321
Henry P Moore, *Pr*
Don Curtis Moore, *VP*
Brenda Duckworth, *Sec*
EMP: 6 **EST:** 1961
SQ FT: 60,000
SALES (est): 235.63K **Privately Held**
SIC: 2269 2261 2281 Dyeing: raw stock, yarn, and narrow fabrics; Dyeing cotton broadwoven fabrics; Yarn spinning mills

(G-1063)
DHOLLANDIA US LLC (HQ)
270 Southridge Pkwy (28016-7801)
P.O. Box 310794 (92331-0794)
PHONE.................................909 251-7979
Jan Dhollander, *Managing Member*
Nancy Dhollander, *Managing Member*
Melissa Cash, *Managing Member*
Lieve Dehertogh, *Managing Member*
EMP: 6 **EST:** 2014
SALES (est): 4.58MM
SALES (corp-wide): 41.3MM **Privately Held**
Web: www.dhollandia.com
SIC: 3714 Motor vehicle parts and accessories
PA: Dhollandia Service
 Zoomstraat 9
 Lokeren 9160
 93490692

GEOGRAPHIC SECTION
Bessemer City - Gaston County (G-1087)

(G-1064)
FARMER MACHINE GROUP LLC
308 White Jenkins Rd (28016-7753)
P.O. Box 711 (28016-0711)
PHONE..............................704 629-5133
EMP: 10 **EST:** 1996
SQ FT: 10,000
SALES (est): 998.16K Privately Held
SIC: 3599 Machine shop, jobbing and repair

(G-1065)
FARRIS FAB & MACHINE INC
1941 Bess Town Rd (28016-6813)
PHONE..............................704 629-4879
Greg Farris, VP
EMP: 9
SALES (corp-wide): 46.34MM Privately Held
Web: www.farrisgrp.com
SIC: 3441 3599 Fabricated structural metal; Machine shop, jobbing and repair
PA: Farris Fab. & Machine, Inc.
1006 W Academy St
Cherryville NC 28021
704 629-4879

(G-1066)
FARRIS FAB & MACHINE INC
522 Bess Town Rd (28016-7543)
PHONE..............................704 629-4879
Kevin Wheeler, Brnch Mgr
EMP: 137
SALES (corp-wide): 46.34MM Privately Held
Web: www.farrisgrp.com
SIC: 3441 3599 Fabricated structural metal; Machine shop, jobbing and repair
PA: Farris Fab. & Machine, Inc.
1006 W Academy St
Cherryville NC 28021
704 629-4879

(G-1067)
FMC CORPORATION
F M C Lithium Division
161 Kings Mtn Hwy (28016)
P.O. Box 795 (28016-0795)
PHONE..............................704 868-5300
Robert Haire, Brnch Mgr
EMP: 34
SALES (corp-wide): 4.49B Publicly Held
Web: www.fmc.com
SIC: 2819 2899 Lithium compounds, inorganic; Chemical preparations, nec
PA: Fmc Corporation
2929 Walnut St
Philadelphia PA 19104
215 299-6000

(G-1068)
FMC CORPORATION
Also Called: FMC Lithium Division
1115 Bessemer City Kings Mtn Hwy (28016)
PHONE..............................704 426-5336
EMP: 272
SALES (corp-wide): 4.49B Publicly Held
Web: www.fmc.com
SIC: 2819 2899 Lithium compounds, inorganic; Chemical preparations, nec
PA: Fmc Corporation
2929 Walnut St
Philadelphia PA 19104
215 299-6000

(G-1069)
GASTON INDUS MACHINING LLC
125 Robinsons Park Dr (28016-7792)
P.O. Box 785 (28012-0785)
PHONE..............................704 825-3346
EMP: 7 **EST:** 2018
SALES (est): 190.82K Privately Held
Web:
www.gastonindustrialmachining.com
SIC: 3599 Machine shop, jobbing and repair

(G-1070)
HEART ELECTRIC MOTOR SERVICE
Also Called: Heart Electric
Costner School Rd Rr 1 (28016)
PHONE..............................704 922-4720
Thomas R Doss, Owner
EMP: 6 **EST:** 1991
SQ FT: 10,000
SALES (est): 299.74K Privately Held
SIC: 7694 5999 Rewinding services; Motors, electric

(G-1071)
IMPERIAL MACHINE COMPANY INC
Also Called: Imperial Machine Co
4429 Kings Mountain Hwy (28016-7528)
P.O. Box 12506 (28052-0021)
PHONE..............................704 739-8038
Tommy A Russell, Pr
EMP: 35 **EST:** 1958
SALES (est): 2.66MM Privately Held
Web: www.imperialmachineco.com
SIC: 3599 3552 Machine shop, jobbing and repair; Textile machinery

(G-1072)
JOE AND KITTY BROWN INC
1312 Ramseur Rd (28016-7636)
P.O. Box 15 (28053-0015)
PHONE..............................704 629-4327
Tim Carter, Pr
EMP: 23 **EST:** 1954
SQ FT: 25,500
SALES (est): 1.32MM Privately Held
Web: www.spgear.com
SIC: 3566 Speed changers, drives, and gears

(G-1073)
M S I PRECISION MACHINE INC
725 E Maine Ave (28016-2186)
PHONE..............................704 629-9375
Kenneth M Kirby, Pr
EMP: 4 **EST:** 2003
SALES (est): 387.34K Privately Held
SIC: 3599 Machine shop, jobbing and repair

(G-1074)
MANUFACTURING SERVICES INC
Also Called: MSI
725 E Maine Ave (28016-2186)
PHONE..............................704 629-4163
Ron Grenier, Pr
William Blalock Junior, VP
Kenneth Kirby, *
EMP: 45 **EST:** 1970
SQ FT: 31,700
SALES (est): 8.45MM Privately Held
Web: www.msicarolina.com
SIC: 3089 3451 3599 Plastics hardware and building products; Screw machine products; Machine and other job shop work

(G-1075)
METSO OUTOTEC USA INC
Also Called: METSO OUTOTEC USA INC.
3200 Bessemer City Rd (28016-9774)
PHONE..............................877 677-2005
EMP: 49
SIC: 3554 Paper industries machinery
HQ: Metso Usa Inc.
275 N Corporate Dr
Brookfield WI 53045

(G-1076)
OLD MILL PRECISION GUN WORKS &
323 Old Mill Rd (28016-7686)
PHONE..............................704 284-2832
EMP: 4 **EST:** 2013
SALES (est): 100K Privately Held
SIC: 2431 Millwork

(G-1077)
PATRICIA HALL
Also Called: Hull's Wall Covering
128 Terrace Dr (28016-2855)
PHONE..............................704 729-6133
Michael Hull, Owner
EMP: 4 **EST:** 2010
SALES (est): 149.78K Privately Held
SIC: 1721 2221 Wallcovering contractors; Wall covering fabrics, manmade fiber and silk

(G-1078)
PLASTIC PRODUCTS INC (PA)
1413 Bessemer City Kings Mtn Hwy (28016)
P.O. Box 69 (28086-0069)
PHONE..............................704 739-7463
Jay Raxter, Pr
Karen Fore, *
EMP: 24 **EST:** 1968
SQ FT: 20,000
SALES (est): 8.58MM
SALES (corp-wide): 8.58MM Privately Held
Web: www.plastic-products.com
SIC: 2821 Plastics materials and resins

(G-1079)
PRECISION DRIVE SYSTEMS LLC (PA)
4367 Dallas Cherryville Hwy (28016-7729)
P.O. Box 461 (28034-0461)
PHONE..............................704 922-1206
Robert Turk, Pr
▲ **EMP:** 9 **EST:** 1997
SQ FT: 10,000
SALES (est): 4.96MM
SALES (corp-wide): 4.96MM Privately Held
Web: www.spindlerepair.com
SIC: 3699 Electrical equipment and supplies, nec

(G-1080)
ROBINSON MCH & CUTTER GRINDING
1346 Ramseur Rd (28016-7636)
P.O. Box 1340 (28016-1340)
PHONE..............................704 629-5591
Elaine Robinson, Pr
Richard Easler, VP
James Robinson, Sec
Cindy Easler, Treas
EMP: 9 **EST:** 1973
SQ FT: 13,000
SALES (est): 223.66K Privately Held
SIC: 3599 3469 7692 3444 Machine shop, jobbing and repair; Machine parts, stamped or pressed metal; Welding repair; Sheet metalwork

(G-1081)
ROSS WOODWORKING INC
Also Called: Pallets & Such
125 L E Perry Rd (28016-9705)
PHONE..............................704 629-4551
EMP: 8
SALES (corp-wide): 615.23K Privately Held
SIC: 2448 Pallets, wood and wood with metal
PA: Ross Woodworking Inc
1004 Dameron Rd
Bessemer City NC 28016
704 629-4551

(G-1082)
ROSS WOODWORKING INC (PA)
Also Called: Pallets & Such
1004 Dameron Rd (28016-8793)
PHONE..............................704 629-4551
EMP: 8
SALES (est): 615.23K
SALES (corp-wide): 615.23K Privately Held
Web: www.rosswoodworking.com
SIC: 2448 Pallets, wood and wood with metal

(G-1083)
SEWING PLUS LLC
120 Pilots Ridge Dr (28016-6725)
PHONE..............................704 616-1750
Laura Wilkinson, Owner
EMP: 5 **EST:** 2007
SALES (est): 160.09K Privately Held
SIC: 2759 Screen printing

(G-1084)
STINE GEAR & MACHINE COMPANY
2015 Hephzibah Church Rd (28016-7673)
P.O. Box 1157 (28034-1157)
PHONE..............................704 445-1245
Brian Harper, Pr
Martha Harker, VP
EMP: 11 **EST:** 1970
SQ FT: 3,200
SALES (est): 1.03MM Privately Held
Web: www.stinegear.com
SIC: 3599 Machine shop, jobbing and repair

(G-1085)
TIM CONNER ENTERPRISES INC
Also Called: Spencer-Pettus Machine Co
1312 Ramseur Rd (28016-7636)
PHONE..............................704 629-4327
Timothy Dean Conner, Pr
◆ **EMP:** 20 **EST:** 2004
SALES (est): 2.54MM Privately Held
Web: www.spgear.com
SIC: 3462 Gears, forged steel

(G-1086)
TOSAF INC
132 W Virginia Ave (28016-2373)
P.O. Box 758 (28016-0758)
PHONE..............................704 396-7097
EMP: 9
SALES (corp-wide): 4.58K Privately Held
SIC: 2821 Plastics materials and resins
HQ: Tosaf, Inc.
330 Southridge Pkwy
Bessemer City NC 28016
980 533-3000

(G-1087)
TOSAF INC (DH)
330 Southridge Pkwy (28016-7805)
PHONE..............................980 533-3000
Amos Megides, Pr
Eldad Tveria, CFO
◆ **EMP:** 19 **EST:** 2014
SALES (est): 49.75MM Privately Held
Web: www.tosaf.com
SIC: 2821 2891 3089 Plasticizer/additive based plastic materials; Sealing compounds, synthetic rubber or plastic; Coloring and finishing of plastics products
HQ: Tosaf Compounds Ltd.
Tnuvot Industrial Zone
Kfar Yona

(G-1088)
TOSAF AW INC ✪
330 Southridge Pkwy (28016-7805)
PHONE.............................980 533-3000
EMP: 75 EST: 2022
SALES (est): 735.76K **Privately Held**
SIC: **2295** Resin or plastic coated fabrics
HQ: Tosaf, Inc.
   330 Southridge Pkwy
   Bessemer City NC 28016
   980 533-3000

Bethel
Pitt County

(G-1089)
BLOUNT PRECISION MACHINING INC
155 Railroad St W (27812-9303)
P.O. Box 201 (27812-0201)
PHONE.............................252 825-3701
Jordan Blount, *Pr*
EMP: 4 EST: 2009
SALES (est): 456.78K **Privately Held**
Web: www.blountprecisionmachining.com
SIC: **3599** Machine shop, jobbing and repair

(G-1090)
PACKAGE CRAFT LLC (DH)
146 Package Craft Rd (27812-9541)
P.O. Box 430 (27812-0430)
PHONE.............................252 825-0111
Craig Roberts, *Managing Member*
EMP: 28 EST: 1960
SQ FT: 54,000
SALES (est): 10.11MM
SALES (corp-wide): 573.33MM **Privately Held**
Web: www.packagecraft.com
SIC: **2653** Boxes, corrugated: made from purchased materials
HQ: Schwarz Partners Packaging, Llc
   10 W Carmel Dr Ste 300
   Carmel IN 46032
   317 290-1140

Beulaville
Duplin County

(G-1091)
BEULAVILLE WSTN AUTO VALUE INC
516 W Main St (28518-8672)
P.O. Box 328 (28518-0328)
PHONE.............................910 298-4246
Kenneth Jones, *Mgr*
EMP: 10 EST: 2016
SALES (est): 468.65K **Privately Held**
Web: beulavillewesternautovalveinc-beulaville-nc.brandsdirect.com
SIC: **3714** Motor vehicle parts and accessories

(G-1092)
CEDAR FORK WOODWORKS LLC
1362 Fountaintown Rd (28518-7566)
PHONE.............................910 340-0821
EMP: 4 EST: 2019
SALES (est): 99.49K **Privately Held**
SIC: **2431** Millwork

(G-1093)
DAPHNE LAWSON ESPINO
Also Called: East Cast Emrgncy Response Svc
413 N Railroad Ave (28518-8742)
PHONE.............................910 290-2762
EMP: 5
SALES (est): 252.41K **Privately Held**
SIC: **3524** Lawn and garden equipment

(G-1094)
ENSALES ELECTRICAL ASSOC INC
140 E Park Dr Unit B (28518-6925)
PHONE.............................910 298-3305
Barry Jones, *Pr*
Fred Murray, *CEO*
EMP: 10 EST: 1994
SALES (est): 1.53MM **Privately Held**
Web: www.ensales.com
SIC: **3629** Rectifiers (electrical apparatus)

(G-1095)
MAGNUM MOBILE WELDING WRAP UP
171 Reedy Ln (28518-9594)
PHONE.............................910 372-3380
EMP: 5 EST: 2014
SALES (est): 45.23K **Privately Held**
SIC: **7692** Welding repair

(G-1096)
MILLER S UTILITY MGT INC
163 Jackson Store Rd (28518-6801)
PHONE.............................910 298-3847
Stanley Miller, *Pr*
Thad Miller, *VP*
Angie Miller, *Sec*
EMP: 4 EST: 1994
SALES (est): 245.48K **Privately Held**
SIC: **3589** Water treatment equipment, industrial

(G-1097)
NATIONAL SPINNING CO INC
326 Lyman Rd (28518-7618)
P.O. Box 191 (27889-0191)
PHONE.............................910 298-3131
Jesse Sumner, *Brnch Mgr*
EMP: 109
SALES (corp-wide): 102.19MM **Privately Held**
Web: www.natspin.com
SIC: **2282** 2231 2281 Wool yarn: twisting, winding, or spooling; Wool broadwoven fabrics; Yarn spinning mills
PA: National Spinning Co., Inc.
   1481 W 2nd St Ste 103
   Washington NC 27889
   252 975-7111

(G-1098)
S DUFF FABRICATING INC
228 N Nc 41 Hwy (28518-8632)
PHONE.............................910 298-3060
Sheral Murphy, *Pr*
Sonya Hall, *Sec*
EMP: 6 EST: 1988
SQ FT: 6,000
SALES (est): 473.39K **Privately Held**
SIC: **3462** 3524 3444 3423 Anchors, forged; Lawn and garden equipment; Sheet metalwork; Hand and edge tools, nec

(G-1099)
WOODLAND LOGGING INC
596 Hallsville Rd (28518-6600)
PHONE.............................910 298-3350
Tracey Kornegay, *Pr*
EMP: 7 EST: 2007
SALES (est): 194.09K **Privately Held**
SIC: **5039** 3531 Prefabricated structures; Subgraders (construction equipment)

Biltmore Lake
Buncombe County

(G-1100)
INNSPECTOR SOFTWARE LLC
65 Gray Duster Cir (28715-9534)
PHONE.............................828 712-7127
R Scott Brown, *Owner*
EMP: 6 EST: 2016
SALES (est): 87.54K **Privately Held**
SIC: **7372** Prepackaged software

(G-1101)
MOUNTAINEER ENTERPRISE
83 Lake Dr (28715-7245)
PHONE.............................828 670-5425
Jonathan Key, *Owner*
EMP: 5 EST: 2005
SALES (est): 65.96K **Privately Held**
SIC: **2711** Newspapers, publishing and printing

(G-1102)
TRUEFLIES LLC
815 Quill Gordon Ct (28715-8927)
PHONE.............................828 337-9716
▲ EMP: 4 EST: 2015
SALES (est): 67.94K **Privately Held**
Web: www.trueflies.com
SIC: **2323** Men's and boy's neckwear

Biscoe
Montgomery County

(G-1103)
ARAUCO - NA
157 Atc Dr (27209-9669)
PHONE.............................910 569-7020
Pamela Daggett, *Prin*
EMP: 8 EST: 2015
SALES (est): 954.01K **Privately Held**
Web: na.arauco.com
SIC: **2493** 2411 2611 2621 Particleboard products; Timber, cut at logging camp; Pulp mills; Paper mills

(G-1104)
BELEVATION LLC
207 Shady Oak Dr (27209-9574)
P.O. Box 1554 (27209-1554)
PHONE.............................803 517-9030
Thomas Miles, *CEO*
EMP: 10 EST: 2008
SALES (est): 621.35K **Privately Held**
Web: www.belevation.com
SIC: **2253** 5621 Basque shirts, knit; Maternity wear

(G-1105)
CAROLINA DAIRY LLC
116 Industrial Park (27209-8096)
PHONE.............................910 569-7070
EMP: 10 EST: 2019
SALES (est): 2.67MM
SALES (corp-wide): 11.8B **Privately Held**
SIC: **2026** Yogurt
PA: Saputo Inc
   6869 Boul Metropolitain E
   Saint-Leonard QC H3B 4
   514 328-3869

(G-1106)
CENTRAL CAROLINA HOSIERY INC (PA)
211 Shady Oak Dr (27209-9574)
P.O. Box 99 (27209-0099)
PHONE.............................910 428-9688
Serge Babayan, *Pr*
▲ EMP: 48 EST: 1997
SALES (est): 4.81MM
SALES (corp-wide): 4.81MM **Privately Held**
Web: www.cchosiery.com
SIC: **2251** 2252 Women's hosiery, except socks; Tights, except women's

(G-1107)
CHANDLER CONCRETE CO INC
Also Called: Chandler Concrete
1517 Us Highway 220 Alt S (27209)
P.O. Box 460 (27209-0460)
PHONE.............................910 974-4744
Tom Dunn, *Mgr*
EMP: 5
Web: www.chandlerconcrete.com
SIC: **3273** Ready-mixed concrete
PA: Chandler Concrete Co., Inc.
   1006 S Church St
   Burlington NC 27215

(G-1108)
COMFORT TECH INC
Also Called: Comfort Seals
Hgwy 2427 (27209)
P.O. Box 768 (27209-0768)
PHONE.............................910 428-1779
Randy Deese, *Pr*
Ray Phillips, *VP*
EMP: 17 EST: 1996
SQ FT: 20,000
SALES (est): 740.58K **Privately Held**
Web: www.comforttechdocks.com
SIC: **3069** Weather strip, sponge rubber

(G-1109)
FLAKEBOARD AMERICA LIMITED
157 Atc Dr (27209-9669)
PHONE.............................910 569-7010
▲ EMP: 7 EST: 2015
SALES (est): 215K **Privately Held**
SIC: **2493** Flakeboard

(G-1110)
GREDE II LLC
Also Called: Biscoe Foundry
530 E Main St (27209-9779)
PHONE.............................910 428-2111
Ed Buker, *Brnch Mgr*
EMP: 430
SALES (corp-wide): 686.19MM **Privately Held**
Web: www.grede.com
SIC: **3714** Motor vehicle parts and accessories
HQ: Grede Ii Llc
   20750 Civic Center Dr # 100
   Southfield MI 48076
   248 440-9500

(G-1111)
HOME CITY LTD (PA)
2086 Hwy 2427 W (27209)
P.O. Box 99 (27356-0099)
PHONE.............................910 428-2196
Mike Allen, *Owner*
EMP: 6 EST: 1956
SALES (est): 1.42MM
SALES (corp-wide): 1.42MM **Privately Held**
SIC: **2451** 5271 Mobile homes; Mobile home dealers

(G-1112)
JIMMIE A HOGAN
392 Cedar Creek Rd (27209-9677)
PHONE.............................910 428-2535
Jimmie A Hogan, *Prin*
EMP: 5 EST: 2010

SALES (est): 191.49K **Privately Held**
SIC: 2411 Logging

(G-1113)
JORDAN INNVTIVE FBRICATION LLC
275 Sedberry Rd (27209-9688)
PHONE..................910 428-2368
EMP: 29 EST: 2021
SALES (est): 3.14MM **Privately Held**
SIC: 3441 Fabricated structural metal for bridges

(G-1114)
K-M MACHINE COMPANY INC
275 Sedberry Rd (27209-9688)
PHONE..................910 428-2368
Leslie Kellam, *Pr*
Kelly Kellam, *
Robert Kellam, *
Bobby Kellam, *
Dale Newman, *
▲ EMP: 72 EST: 1969
SQ FT: 37,450
SALES (est): 9.32MM **Privately Held**
Web: www.kmmachineco.com
SIC: 3599 7389 Machine shop, jobbing and repair; Crane and aerial lift service

(G-1115)
SAPUTO CHEESE USA INC
116 Industrial Park (27209-8096)
PHONE..................910 569-7070
Lino A Saputo Junior, *Brnch Mgr*
EMP: 10
SALES (corp-wide): 3.79B **Privately Held**
Web: www.saputousafoodservice.com
SIC: 2026 Yogurt
HQ: Saputo Cheese Usa Inc.
   10700 W Res Dr Ste 400
   Milwaukee WI 53226

(G-1116)
SELECT FRAME SHOP INC
138 Coggins Rd (27209-9699)
P.O. Box 216 (27247-0216)
PHONE..................910 428-1225
EMP: 56 EST: 1994
SQ FT: 75,000
SALES (est): 6.35MM **Privately Held**
Web: www.select-frames.com
SIC: 2426 Furniture stock and parts, hardwood

(G-1117)
UFP BISCOE LLC
402 Capel St (27209-8054)
PHONE..................910 294-8179
EMP: 10 EST: 2017
SALES (est): 2.07MM
SALES (corp-wide): 9.63B **Publicly Held**
SIC: 2491 Millwork, treated wood
PA: Ufp Industries, Inc.
   2801 E Beltline Ave Ne
   Grand Rapids MI 49525
   616 364-6161

Black Mountain
Buncombe County

(G-1118)
A E NESBITT WOODWORK
40 Bald Mountain Church Rd (28711-9592)
P.O. Box 276 (28710-0276)
PHONE..................828 625-2428
Arnold E Nesbitt, *Owner*
EMP: 4 EST: 1982
SALES (est): 173.13K **Privately Held**
SIC: 2511 Wood household furniture

(G-1119)
ASHLEYS KIT BATH DSIGN STDIO L
2950 Us 70 Hwy (28711-9103)
PHONE..................828 669-5281
Ashley Mcelreath, *Owner*
EMP: 10 EST: 2011
SALES (est): 987.77K **Privately Held**
Web: www.ashleyskb.com
SIC: 2434 Wood kitchen cabinets

(G-1120)
BLACK MOUNTAIN NEWS INC
111 Richardson Blvd (28711-3526)
PHONE..................828 669-8727
Jennifer Fitzgerald, *Genl Mgr*
EMP: 8 EST: 1986
SALES (est): 1.7MM
SALES (corp-wide): 2.66B **Publicly Held**
Web: www.blackmountainnews.com
SIC: 2711 Newspapers, publishing and printing
HQ: Gannett Media Corp.
   7950 Jones Branch Dr Fl 8
   Mc Lean VA 22102
   703 854-6000

(G-1121)
BLACK MTN MCH FABRICATION INC
Also Called: Black Mountain Machine & Tool
2988 Us 70 Hwy (28711-9103)
P.O. Box 1106 (28711-1106)
PHONE..................828 669-9557
James F Tolley, *Pr*
Samuel C Tolley, *
EMP: 30 EST: 1985
SQ FT: 10,500
SALES (est): 5.3MM **Privately Held**
Web: www.blackmtnmachine.com
SIC: 3451 3599 3499 Screw machine products; Machine and other job shop work; Machine bases, metal

(G-1122)
CELCORE INC
3148 Us Highway 70 W (28711-5526)
PHONE..................828 669-4875
Matt Hilton, *Mgr*
EMP: 5
SALES (corp-wide): 1.04MM **Privately Held**
Web: www.celcoreinc.com
SIC: 2899 Foam charge mixtures
PA: Celcore Inc
   7850 Freeway Cir Ste 100
   Cleveland OH 44130
   440 234-7888

(G-1123)
DARK CITY DEFENSE
178 Cragmont Rd (28711-3304)
P.O. Box 1102 (28711-1102)
PHONE..................805 729-8800
EMP: 4 EST: 2015
SALES (est): 73.06K **Privately Held**
SIC: 3812 Defense systems and equipment

(G-1124)
EYE GLASS LADY LLC
Also Called: Pack Your Wings
411 Tomahawk Ave (28711-2848)
PHONE..................828 669-2154
Kimberly Barber, *CEO*
EMP: 15 EST: 2013
SALES (est): 665.96K **Privately Held**
SIC: 3841 3851 Eye examining instruments and apparatus; Frames, lenses, and parts, eyeglass and spectacle

(G-1125)
IMAGINE THAT CREATIONS LLC
104 Eastside Dr (28711-8208)
PHONE..................480 528-6775
T Paige Jackson, *Prin*
EMP: 11 EST: 2008
SALES (est): 1.12MM **Privately Held**
SIC: 3272 Concrete products, nec

(G-1126)
INNERER KLANG LETTER PRESS
5 Balsam Rd (28711-8212)
PHONE..................828 253-3711
Mark W Olson, *Prin*
EMP: 5 EST: 2004
SALES (est): 81.46K **Privately Held**
SIC: 2741 Miscellaneous publishing

(G-1127)
KEARFOTT CORPORATION
2858 Us 70 Hwy (28711-9111)
PHONE..................828 350-5300
Mac Mccormic, *Genl Mgr*
EMP: 405
SALES (corp-wide): 471.74MM **Privately Held**
Web: www.kearfott.com
SIC: 3728 3812 3769 3643 Aircraft parts and equipment, nec; Search and navigation equipment; Space vehicle equipment, nec; Current-carrying wiring services
HQ: Kearfott Corporation
   19 Chapin Rd Bldg C
   Pine Brook NJ 07058
   973 785-6000

(G-1128)
KUDZU PRINTING COMPANY INC
111 Black Mountain Ave (28711-3402)
PHONE..................828 330-4887
EMP: 5 EST: 2013
SALES (est): 71.86K **Privately Held**
SIC: 2752 Offset printing

(G-1129)
MAX WOODWORKS INC
151 Nc 9 Hwy (28711-3456)
PHONE..................786 286-2668
EMP: 6 EST: 2015
SALES (est): 79.25K **Privately Held**
SIC: 2431 Woodwork, interior and ornamental, nec

(G-1130)
MELTON BACKHOE SERVICE INC
103 Chestnut Hill Rd (28711)
PHONE..................828 779-6728
EMP: 5 EST: 2008
SALES (est): 138.43K **Privately Held**
SIC: 3531 Backhoes

(G-1131)
OAK & GRIST DISTILLING CO LLC
1556 Grovestone Rd (28711-8722)
PHONE..................828 357-5750
Russell Dodson, *Pr*
EMP: 11 EST: 2017
SALES (est): 295.89K **Privately Held**
Web: www.oakandgrist.com
SIC: 2085 Distilled and blended liquors

(G-1132)
OUTDOOR PATHS LLC
7 Amys Way (28711-9589)
PHONE..................828 669-1526
Larry Odoski, *Prin*
EMP: 5 EST: 2013
SALES (est): 122.3K **Privately Held**
Web: www.oppmaps.com

SIC: 2741 Miscellaneous publishing

(G-1133)
PARAMETER GENERATION CTRL INC
1054 Old Us Hwy 70 W (28711-2518)
P.O. Box 129 (28711-0129)
PHONE..................828 669-8717
Clay Hile, *Pr*
Randy Wilson, *
Ross Hile, *
▼ EMP: 49 EST: 1977
SQ FT: 13,000
SALES (est): 6.6MM **Privately Held**
Web: www.humiditycontrol.com
SIC: 3822 3821 3585 Humidity controls, air-conditioning types; Laboratory apparatus and furniture; Refrigeration and heating equipment

(G-1134)
PAULS CUSTOM WOODWORKING INC
190 Eastside Dr (28711-8208)
PHONE..................828 712-6234
Paul Schmidtz, *Owner*
EMP: 6 EST: 2009
SALES (est): 70.99K **Privately Held**
Web: www.paulswoodworking.net
SIC: 2431 Millwork

(G-1135)
PILKINGTON
207 Ruby Ave (28711-3644)
PHONE..................828 357-8043
EMP: 4 EST: 2010
SALES (est): 47.11K **Privately Held**
Web: www.pilkington.com
SIC: 3211 Flat glass

(G-1136)
POPPY HANDCRAFTED POPCORN INC (PA)
127 Old Us Hwy 70 E (28711-3600)
P.O. Box 18448 (28814-0448)
PHONE..................828 552-3149
Ginger Frank, *Managing Member*
EMP: 10 EST: 2014
SALES (est): 2.68MM
SALES (corp-wide): 2.68MM **Privately Held**
Web: www.poppyhandcraftedpopcorn.com
SIC: 2099 Food preparations, nec

(G-1137)
ROSE PUBLISHING
12 W Cotton Ave (28711-3072)
PHONE..................828 669-1629
P Rose, *Prin*
EMP: 5 EST: 2008
SALES (est): 130.74K **Privately Held**
SIC: 2741 Miscellaneous publishing

(G-1138)
SAWMILL OPRATION SOLUTIONS LLC
99 Glasgow Trl (28711-8688)
PHONE..................828 442-5907
Michel Maurice Lariviere, *Prin*
EMP: 5 EST: 2010
SALES (est): 104.91K **Privately Held**
Web: www.sawmilloperationsolutions.com
SIC: 2421 Sawmills and planing mills, general

(G-1139)
SONG OF WOOD LTD
203 W State St (28711-3408)

Black Mountain – Buncombe County (G-1140)

P.O. Box 19112 (28815-1112)
PHONE.................................828 669-7675
Jerry R Smith, *Owner*
Jo Ann Smith, *Sec*
EMP: 6 EST: 1975
SQ FT: 1,000
SALES (est): 438.58K **Privately Held**
Web: www.songofthewood.com
SIC: **3931** 5736 5735 5099 String instruments and parts; String instruments; Audio tapes, prerecorded; Tapes and cassettes, prerecorded

(G-1140)
TURTLE DOVE PUBLICATIONS
1106 Montreat Rd (28711-3232)
PHONE.................................828 337-4057
Chazen Lois, *Prin*
EMP: 4 EST: 2019
SALES (est): 83.14K **Privately Held**
SIC: **2741** Miscellaneous publishing

(G-1141)
WESTERN CRLINA CSTM CSWORK INC
2952 Us 70 Hwy (28711-9103)
P.O. Box 1281 (28711-1281)
PHONE.................................828 669-0459
Allen Burpeau, *Owner*
EMP: 10 EST: 2010
SALES (est): 977.49K **Privately Held**
SIC: **2431** Millwork

(G-1142)
YOUR FIRE SOURCE INC
201 Black Mountain Ave (28711-3404)
P.O. Box 7106 (34101-7106)
PHONE.................................828 669-9000
Al Roe, *Pr*
EMP: 13 EST: 2008
SALES (est): 328.54K **Privately Held**
SIC: **3711** Fire department vehicles (motor vehicles), assembly of

Bladenboro
Bladen County

(G-1143)
AUTHENTIC IRON LLC
17838 Nc 131 Hwy (28320-6008)
PHONE.................................910 648-6989
Kelly Barnhill, *Owner*
EMP: 6 EST: 1995
SALES (est): 410.08K **Privately Held**
SIC: **3462** 5211 Iron and steel forgings; Lumber and other building materials

(G-1144)
BLADEN FABRICATORS LLC
2646 Old Hwy 41 (28320-7880)
PHONE.................................910 866-5225
EMP: 5 EST: 2009
SALES (est): 498.09K **Privately Held**
SIC: **7692** Welding repair

(G-1145)
CARROL POULTRY LLC
414 Industrial Dr (28320-6419)
PHONE.................................347 203-9637
Kashif Saeed, *Pr*
Awais Khan, *VP*
EMP: 6 EST: 2014
SQ FT: 4,000
SALES (est): 327.45K **Privately Held**
SIC: **2015** Poultry slaughtering and processing

(G-1146)
COLUMBUS INDUSTRIES LLC (PA)
Also Called: Gene Franklin Brisson
941 Cabbage Rd (28320-9055)
P.O. Box 65 (28320-0065)
PHONE.................................910 872-1625
EMP: 33 EST: 2008
SALES (est): 2.48MM **Privately Held**
SIC: **3589** 3441 Water purification equipment, household type; Fabricated structural metal

(G-1147)
DANNYS SANDBLASTING
119 Freeman St (28320-7093)
PHONE.................................910 876-4596
Danny Freeman, *Owner*
EMP: 5 EST: 2015
SALES (est): 62.79K **Privately Held**
SIC: **3479** Metal coating and allied services

(G-1148)
DYMETROL COMPANY INC (PA)
1305 W Seaboard St (28320)
P.O. Box 250 (28320-0250)
PHONE.................................866 964-8632
◆ EMP: 11 EST: 1993
SALES (est): 2.33MM **Privately Held**
Web: www.dymetrol.com
SIC: **3081** 3559 Packing materials, plastics sheet; Plastics working machinery

(G-1149)
INTEGRA FOODS LLC
476 Industrial Dr (28320-6419)
PHONE.................................910 984-2007
EMP: 15 EST: 2019
SALES (est): 1.9MM **Privately Held**
Web: www.integrafoods.net
SIC: **2015** Poultry, processed: cooked

(G-1150)
K L BUTLER LOGGING INC
12237 Nc 41 Hwy W (28320-7831)
PHONE.................................910 648-6016
Kirby Lee Butler, *Pr*
Tolmy Butler, *Sec*
EMP: 8 EST: 1972
SQ FT: 1,700
SALES (est): 300.2K **Privately Held**
SIC: **2411** Logging camps and contractors

Blanch
Caswell County

(G-1151)
COTTAGE HOUSE WREATHS
7213 Nc Highway 62 N (27212-9253)
PHONE.................................336 234-7079
April Oldham, *Prin*
EMP: 4 EST: 2018
SALES (est): 67.28K **Privately Held**
SIC: **3999** Wreaths, artificial

(G-1152)
LEA STREET PRESS LLC
37 Clear Springs Cir (27212-8400)
PHONE.................................336 514-2351
Derwood C Matkins, *Owner*
EMP: 4 EST: 2018
SALES (est): 88.7K **Privately Held**
Web: www.leastreetpress.com
SIC: **2741** Miscellaneous publishing

(G-1153)
WATER-REVOLUTION LLC
2246 Nc Highway 62 N (27212-9203)
PHONE.................................336 525-1015
▲ EMP: 9 EST: 2014
SALES (est): 2.4MM **Privately Held**
Web: www.water-revolution.com
SIC: **3589** Water filters and softeners, household type

Blowing Rock
Watauga County

(G-1154)
BILCAT INC (PA)
1103 Main St (28605-8280)
P.O. Box 682 (28605-0682)
PHONE.................................828 295-3088
Bill Williamson, *Pr*
Catherine Williamson, *
EMP: 30 EST: 1990
SALES (est): 2.33MM **Privately Held**
SIC: **2064** 2024 5812 5441 Candy and other confectionery products; Ice cream and frozen deserts; Ice cream stands or dairy bars; Candy

(G-1155)
CCO HOLDINGS LLC
278 Shoppes On The Parkway Rd (28605-8340)
PHONE.................................828 414-4238
EMP: 107
SALES (corp-wide): 54.61B **Publicly Held**
SIC: **4841** 3663 3651 Cable television services; Radio and t.v. communications equipment; Household audio and video equipment
HQ: Cco Holdings, Llc
400 Atlantic St
Stamford CT 06901
203 905-7801

(G-1156)
RHODDIE BICYCLE OUTFITTERS INC
257 Sunset Dr (28605-7206)
PHONE.................................828 414-9800
EMP: 6 EST: 2018
SALES (est): 240.84K **Privately Held**
Web: www.rhoddiebicycleoutfitters.com
SIC: **3751** Bicycles and related parts

(G-1157)
WILDFLWERS BTQ OF BLOWING ROCK
Also Called: High Country Candles
Old Martin House On Main Street (28605)
P.O. Box 374 (28605-0374)
PHONE.................................828 295-9655
EMP: 6 EST: 1992
SALES (est): 277.49K **Privately Held**
Web: www.highcountrycandles.net
SIC: **3999** 5999 Candles; Candle shops

Boiling Springs
Cleveland County

(G-1158)
BT AMERICA INC
415 S Main St (28017)
P.O. Box 818 (28017-0818)
PHONE.................................704 434-8072
Atacushi Deyaman, *Pr*
▲ EMP: 5 EST: 1996
SALES (est): 475.41K **Privately Held**
SIC: **3714** Motor vehicle parts and accessories

(G-1159)
GLENN LUMBER COMPANY INC
145 Rockford Rd (28017)
P.O. Box 756 (28017-0756)
PHONE.................................704 434-9661
John Glenn, *Pr*
Miriam Glenn, *
EMP: 25 EST: 1949
SQ FT: 13,100
SALES (est): 643.3K **Privately Held**
Web: www.glennlumber.com
SIC: **2421** 2448 Sawmills and planing mills, general; Pallets, wood

(G-1160)
HAMRICK FENCE COMPANY
407 E College Ave (28017)
P.O. Box 1195 (28017-1195)
PHONE.................................704 434-5011
Wesley Hamrick, *Owner*
EMP: 10 EST: 1985
SQ FT: 400
SALES (est): 1.16MM **Privately Held**
SIC: **1799** 3699 1521 Fence construction; Security devices; Single-family home remodeling, additions, and repairs

(G-1161)
INGLES MARKETS INCORPORATED
Also Called: Ingles
214 N Main St (28017)
P.O. Box 878 (28017-0878)
PHONE.................................704 434-0096
EMP: 88
SALES (corp-wide): 5.89B **Publicly Held**
Web: www.ingles-markets.com
SIC: **5411** 5461 2051 Supermarkets, chain; Retail bakeries; Bread, cake, and related products
PA: Ingles Markets, Incorporated
2913 Us Highway 70
Black Mountain NC 28711
828 669-2941

Bolivia
Brunswick County

(G-1162)
BEAVER TOOTH MILLING INC
209 Midway Rd Se (28422-7572)
PHONE.................................910 262-4438
Ted Williams, *Prin*
EMP: 4 EST: 2019
SALES (est): 92.36K **Privately Held**
SIC: **2041** Flour and other grain mill products

(G-1163)
COASTAL WOODWORKING
816 Folly Dr Se (28422-7726)
PHONE.................................910 477-1330
Kevin Artzner, *Prin*
EMP: 4 EST: 2017
SALES (est): 190.11K **Privately Held**
SIC: **5551** 2431 Kayaks; Millwork

(G-1164)
INTERIOR WOOD WORKS LLC
325 Colonial Landing Rd Se (28422-8888)
PHONE.................................910 754-3987
Jeremy Garcia, *Prin*
EMP: 5 EST: 2015
SALES (est): 74.6K **Privately Held**
Web: www.woodworks.org
SIC: **2431** Millwork

(G-1165)
MUD DUCK OPERATIONS
Also Called: Mud Duck Construction
1470 Old Lennon Rd Se (28422-8285)
P.O. Box 192 (28462-0192)
PHONE.................................910 253-7669
L Dean Hewitt, *Owner*

GEOGRAPHIC SECTION

Boone - Watauga County (G-1189)

EMP: 8 **EST:** 1972
SALES (est): 448.8K Privately Held
Web: www.customspecialist.com
SIC: 2411 Logging camps and contractors

(G-1166)
SEASIDE WOODWORKS
1620 Goley Hewett Rd Se Unit 307 (28422-8252)
PHONE.............................910 523-1377
David Smith, *Prin*
EMP: 5 **EST:** 2017
SALES (est): 54.13K Privately Held
SIC: 2431 Millwork

Bolton
Columbus County

(G-1167)
APPLIED PLASTIC SERVICES INC
5932 Old Lake Rd (28423-8914)
P.O. Box 99 (28423-0099)
PHONE.............................910 655-2156
Stefan M Jacobs, *Pr*
EMP: 22 **EST:** 2004
SALES (est): 2.18MM Privately Held
Web: www.appliedplasticservices.com
SIC: 3089 Injection molding of plastics

(G-1168)
T CS SERVICES INC
286 Jacobs Rd (28423-8936)
PHONE.............................910 655-2796
Travis Jacobs, *Pr*
EMP: 6 **EST:** 2014
SALES (est): 232.3K Privately Held
SIC: 3441 Fabricated structural metal

Boomer
Wilkes County

(G-1169)
EDMISTON HYDRLIC SWMILL EQP IN
8540 W Nc Highway 268 (28606-9236)
P.O. Box 428 (28624-0428)
PHONE.............................336 921-2304
William H Edmiston, *Pr*
Johnny J Edmiston, *Sec*
EMP: 25 **EST:** 1969
SQ FT: 11,000
SALES (est): 436.05K Privately Held
SIC: 3553 Sawmill machines

(G-1170)
GREEN PASTURES LAWN CARE
5920 Hollow Springs Cir (28606-9651)
PHONE.............................828 758-9265
EMP: 6 **EST:** 2011
SALES (est): 237.33K Privately Held
SIC: 3524 Lawn and garden equipment

(G-1171)
HARTLEY BROTHERS SAWMILL INC
8507 West North Carolina Hwy 268 (28606-9236)
P.O. Box 992 (28697-0992)
PHONE.............................336 921-2955
Gene Hartley, *Pr*
James Hartley, *Treas*
EMP: 9
SALES (est): 884.88K Privately Held
SIC: 2421 Sawmills and planing mills, general

Boone
Watauga County

(G-1172)
ADVERTISING DESIGN SYSTEMS INC
Also Called: ADS Graphic Design
269 Grand Blvd (28607-3617)
PHONE.............................828 264-8060
Dana Willett, *Pr*
EMP: 6 **EST:** 1975
SQ FT: 2,500
SALES (est): 406.3K Privately Held
SIC: 7335 7336 2791 7311 Photographic studio, commercial; Graphic arts and related design; Typesetting; Advertising agencies

(G-1173)
ALUMINUM BARGES COM LLC
154 Lilac Ln (28607-5401)
P.O. Box 2002 (28605-2002)
PHONE.............................239 272-4857
Joseph Wierback, *Prin*
EMP: 5 **EST:** 2017
SALES (est): 117.13K Privately Held
SIC: 7692 Welding repair

(G-1174)
APPALACHIAN STATE UNIVERSITY
Also Called: Office of Printing
169 Air Ln (28608-0001)
PHONE.............................828 262-2047
Joyce Mahaffay, *Dir*
EMP: 10
SALES (corp-wide): 4.81B Privately Held
Web: www.appstate.edu
SIC: 2741 2791 2789 2759 Miscellaneous publishing; Typesetting; Bookbinding and related work; Commercial printing, nec
HQ: Appalachian State University Inc
  438 Academy St Rm 340
  Boone NC 28608
  828 262-2000

(G-1175)
APPALACHIAN STATE UNIVERSITY
Also Called: The Physics Teacher Magazine
525 Rivers St Rm 221 (28608-0001)
P.O. Box 32142 (28608-2142)
PHONE.............................828 262-7497
Karl Mamola, *Editor*
EMP: 5
SALES (corp-wide): 4.81B Privately Held
Web: www.appstate.edu
SIC: 2754 8221 Magazines: gravure printing, not published on site; University
HQ: Appalachian State University Inc
  438 Academy St Rm 340
  Boone NC 28608
  828 262-2000

(G-1176)
BETTYS DRAPERY DESIGN WORKROOM
Also Called: Custom Win Trtments Dctr Items
3207 Nc Highway 105 S (28607-7310)
PHONE.............................828 264-2392
Betty S Hayes, *Owner*
Rebekah Hayes, *Asstg*
EMP: 7 **EST:** 1979
SALES (est): 397.65K Privately Held
SIC: 2221 5714 Draperies and drapery fabrics, manmade fiber and silk; Draperies

(G-1177)
BLUE RIDGE SILVER INC
173 Marsh Lndg (28607-7583)
PHONE.............................828 729-8610

Steven Griffin, *Pr*
EMP: 4 **EST:** 2013
SALES (est): 269.57K Privately Held
Web: www.blueridgesilver.com
SIC: 2023 Dietary supplements, dairy and non-dairy based

(G-1178)
BOLES HOLDING INC
2165 Highway 105 (28607-7812)
PHONE.............................828 264-4200
Todd Bingahn, *Mgr*
EMP: 7
SALES (corp-wide): 2.62MM Privately Held
SIC: 3585 5075 Air conditioning equipment, complete; Air conditioning equipment, except room units, nec
PA: Boles Holding, Inc.
  2748 Swan Creek Rd
  Jonesville NC 28642
  910 424-0319

(G-1179)
BOONE IRON WORKS INC
Also Called: Boone Ironworks
253 Ray Brown Rd (28607-9023)
P.O. Box 449 (28607-0449)
PHONE.............................828 264-5284
John Councill Junior, *Pr*
John Councill Senior, *VP*
EMP: 4 **EST:** 1980
SALES (est): 417.39K Privately Held
SIC: 3599 Machine shop, jobbing and repair

(G-1180)
BOONESHINE BREWING CO INC
465 Industrial Park Dr (28607-3942)
PHONE.............................828 263-4305
Tim Herdjlotb, *Pr*
EMP: 5 **EST:** 2015
SALES (est): 500.2K Privately Held
Web: www.booneshine.beer
SIC: 5813 3556 5812 Bars and lounges; Brewers' and maltsters' machinery; American restaurant

(G-1181)
BP OIL CORP DISTRIBUTORS
Also Called: Tarheel Oil
585 E King St (28607-4177)
P.O. Box 428 (28607-0428)
PHONE.............................828 264-8516
Ted Hall, *Pr*
Arthur Lankford, *Mgr*
EMP: 6 **EST:** 2001
SALES (est): 234.19K Privately Held
SIC: 1382 Oil and gas exploration services

(G-1182)
BREW CANDLE COMPANY
115b Corby Ct (28607-6757)
PHONE.............................980 275-9355
Anthony Carter, *Owner*
EMP: 4 **EST:** 2016
SALES (est): 66.92K Privately Held
SIC: 3999 Candles

(G-1183)
CANVAS BEAUTY BAR LLC
181 Meadowview Dr (28607-5213)
PHONE.............................828 355-9688
Romiah Zimmerman, *Admn*
EMP: 11 **EST:** 2014
SALES (est): 760.91K Privately Held
Web: www.canvasboone.com
SIC: 2211 Canvas

(G-1184)
CARROLL COMPANIES INC (PA)
1640 Old 421 S (28607-6291)
P.O. Box 1549 (28607-1549)
PHONE.............................828 264-2521
Sterling C Carroll, *Pr*
Royce A Carroll, *VP*
Jo Evelyn Miller, *Sec*
◆ **EMP:** 50 **EST:** 1950
SQ FT: 36,500
SALES (est): 43.23MM
SALES (corp-wide): 43.23MM Privately Held
Web: www.clgco.com
SIC: 5199 3199 Leather goods, except footwear, gloves, luggage, belting; Equestrian related leather articles

(G-1185)
CCBCC OPERATIONS LLC
Also Called: Coca-Cola
795 Nc Highway 105 Byp (28607-7605)
PHONE.............................828 297-2141
Allen Shelton, *Brnch Mgr*
EMP: 71
SALES (corp-wide): 6.65B Publicly Held
Web: www.coca-cola.com
SIC: 2086 Bottled and canned soft drinks
HQ: Ccbcc Operations, Llc
  4100 Coca Cola Plz
  Charlotte NC 28211
  704 364-8728

(G-1186)
CCO HOLDINGS LLC
531 W King St (28607-3536)
PHONE.............................828 355-4149
EMP: 107
SALES (corp-wide): 54.61B Publicly Held
SIC: 4841 3663 3651 Cable television services; Radio and t.v. communications equipment; Household audio and video equipment
HQ: Cco Holdings, Llc
  400 Atlantic St
  Stamford CT 06901
  203 905-7801

(G-1187)
CHANDLER CONCRETE HIGH CO
805 State Farm Rd Ste 203 (28607-4914)
PHONE.............................828 264-8694
Ted Greene, *Prin*
EMP: 13 **EST:** 2009
SALES (est): 845.88K Privately Held
Web: www.chandlerconcrete.com
SIC: 3273 Ready-mixed concrete

(G-1188)
CRAFT BREW ALLIANCE INC
Also Called: Appalachian Mountain Brewery
163 Boone Creek Dr (28607-7911)
PHONE.............................828 263-1111
EMP: 9
SALES (corp-wide): 627.12MM Privately Held
Web: www.amb.beer
SIC: 2082 Beer (alcoholic beverage)
HQ: Craft Brew Alliance, Inc.
  929 N Russell St
  Portland OR 97227
  503 331-7270

(G-1189)
CREATIVE PRINTING INC
1738 Nc Highway 105 Byp (28607-7613)
P.O. Box 2202 (28607-2202)
PHONE.............................828 265-2800
Mark Curry, *Pr*
Lee Q Mcmillian, *Pr*
Donna Carter, *VP*

Boone - Watauga County (G-1190)

EMP: 7 EST: 1993
SALES (est): 754.24K **Privately Held**
Web: www.creative-printing.com
SIC: **2791** 3555 Typesetting; Printing trades machinery

(G-1190)
CREATIVE PRTG INTRNET SVCS LLC
✪
1738 Nc Highway 105 Byp (28607-7613)
PHONE.................................828 265-2800
EMP: 4 EST: 2022
SALES (est): 76.29K **Privately Held**
Web: www.creative-printing.com
SIC: **2752** Offset printing

(G-1191)
CUSTOM CABINETS & RMDLG INC
699 Green Briar Rd (28607-8762)
PHONE.................................828 264-1806
Joseph A Tarbox, *Prin*
EMP: 4 EST: 2016
SALES (est): 90.99K **Privately Held**
SIC: **2434** Wood kitchen cabinets

(G-1192)
DANIEL WINKLER KNIFEMAKER LLC
Also Called: Winkler Knives
141 Leigh Ln (28607-9484)
P.O. Box 2166 (28605-2166)
PHONE.................................828 262-3691
Daniel Winkler, *Managing Member*
EMP: 9 EST: 1994
SALES (est): 948.84K **Privately Held**
Web: www.winklerknives.com
SIC: **3421** Knife blades and blanks

(G-1193)
DARREN MORETZ BACKHOE SER
225 Tom Jackson Rd (28607-9001)
PHONE.................................828 964-1006
EMP: 6 EST: 2010
SALES (est): 508.63K **Privately Held**
SIC: **3531** Backhoes

(G-1194)
DIVERSIFIED ENERGY LLC
148 Highway 105 Ext Ste 202 (28607)
P.O. Box 130 (28692-0130)
PHONE.................................828 266-9800
Kirk Bailey, *Brnch Mgr*
EMP: 5
SALES (corp-wide): 9.41MM **Privately Held**
Web: www.sharpenergy.com
SIC: **1321** 5084 Propane (natural) production; Propane conversion equipment
PA: Diversified Energy, Llc
   148 Highway 105 Ext # 202
   Boone NC 28607
   480 507-0297

(G-1195)
ECOATM LLC
200 Village Dr (28607)
PHONE.................................858 324-4111
EMP: 24
SALES (corp-wide): 32.64B **Publicly Held**
Web: www.ecoatm.com
SIC: **3671** Electron tubes
HQ: Ecoatm, Llc
   10121 Barnes Canyon Rd
   San Diego CA 92121

(G-1196)
ECR SOFTWARE CORPORATION (PA)
Also Called: Ecrs
277 Howard St (28607-4011)
PHONE.................................828 265-2907
◆ EMP: 50 EST: 1989
SALES (est): 11.05MM **Privately Held**
Web: www.ecrs.com
SIC: **7372** Prepackaged software

(G-1197)
EDCO PRODUCTS INC
643 Greenway Rd Ste J5 (28607-5304)
P.O. Box 2028 (28607-2028)
PHONE.................................828 264-1490
John Edmisten, *Pr*
EMP: 9 EST: 2008
SALES (est): 197.86K **Privately Held**
Web: www.edcoproducts.com
SIC: **3433** Heating equipment, except electric

(G-1198)
FASCOE REALTY
133 Echota Pkwy (28607-8386)
PHONE.................................828 963-7600
Mark Harrill, *Owner*
EMP: 5 EST: 2001
SALES (est): 182.45K **Privately Held**
SIC: **6531** 2452 Real estate brokers and agents; Log cabins, prefabricated, wood

(G-1199)
GEORGE F WLSON WLDG FBRICATION
1777 Nc Highway 194 N (28607-7702)
PHONE.................................828 262-1668
Grayson Gordon, *Prin*
EMP: 6 EST: 2009
SALES (est): 129.12K **Privately Held**
SIC: **7692** Welding repair

(G-1200)
GO POSTAL IN BOONE INC
207 New Market Ctr (28607-3993)
PHONE.................................828 262-0027
Christy Gottfried, *Pr*
EMP: 11 EST: 2008
SALES (est): 1.26MM **Privately Held**
Web: www.gopostalprinting.com
SIC: **4215** 2759 Package delivery, vehicular; Commercial printing, nec

(G-1201)
GOODNIGHT BROTHERS PROD CO INC (PA)
Also Called: Watauga County Country Hams
372 Industrial Park Dr (28607-3977)
P.O. Box 287 (28607-0287)
PHONE.................................828 264-8892
Bill Goodnight, *Pr*
James C Goodnight Junior, *Sec*
EMP: 26 EST: 1933
SALES (est): 15.36MM
SALES (corp-wide): 15.36MM **Privately Held**
Web: www.goodnightbrothers.com
SIC: **5147** 5191 2013 Meats, cured or smoked; Seeds: field, garden, and flower; Sausages and other prepared meats

(G-1202)
GREENE PRECISION PRODUCTS INC
4016 Nc Highway 194 N (28607-7293)
PHONE.................................828 262-0116
John F Greene Junior, *Pr*
John Greene Iii, *Mgr*
EMP: 4 EST: 1987
SQ FT: 4,800
SALES (est): 348.09K **Privately Held**
Web: www.greenemachinearchery.com
SIC: **3312** 3949 Tool and die steel and alloys; Sporting and athletic goods, nec

(G-1203)
H & T CHAIR CO INC
1598 Meat Camp Rd (28607-7259)
PHONE.................................828 264-7742
Richard Todd Junior, *CEO*
Mary Jane Todd, *Sec*
EMP: 7 EST: 1968
SQ FT: 10,000
SALES (est): 508K **Privately Held**
SIC: **2531** Chairs, portable folding

(G-1204)
HIGH CNTRY TMBRFRAME GLLERY WD
689 George Wilson Rd (28607-8613)
P.O. Box 1858 (28607-1858)
PHONE.................................828 264-8971
Tom M Owens, *Pr*
EMP: 8 EST: 1997
SALES (est): 1.6MM **Privately Held**
Web: www.highcountrytimberframe.com
SIC: **1521** 2439 New construction, single-family houses; Arches, laminated lumber

(G-1205)
HIGH COUNTRY NEWS INC
1600 Highway 105 (28607-8731)
P.O. Box 152 (28607-0152)
PHONE.................................828 264-2262
Ken Ketchie, *Pr*
EMP: 15 EST: 2005
SALES (est): 481.52K **Privately Held**
Web: www.hcpress.com
SIC: **2711** Commercial printing and newspaper publishing combined

(G-1206)
HIGHLAND INTERNATIONAL
160b Den-Mac Dr (28607-6543)
PHONE.................................828 265-2513
EMP: 6 EST: 2020
SALES (est): 497.43K **Privately Held**
Web: www.highland-international.com
SIC: **2819** Industrial inorganic chemicals, nec

(G-1207)
HIGHLAND INTERNATIONAL LLC
465 Industrial Park Dr (28607-3942)
P.O. Box 3564 (28607-0864)
PHONE.................................828 265-2513
EMP: 10
Web: www.highland-international.com
SIC: **5198** 2851 Paints; Paints and paint additives

(G-1208)
HOSPITALITY MINTS LLC
996 George Wilson Rd (28607-8616)
PHONE.................................828 262-0950
William Wacaster, *Brnch Mgr*
EMP: 40
SALES (corp-wide): 269.24MM **Privately Held**
Web: www.hospitalitymints.com
SIC: **2064** Candy and other confectionery products
HQ: Hospitality Mints Llc
   1800 Northwestern Dr
   El Paso TX 79912
   828 264-3045

(G-1209)
INOVATIVE VAPES OF BOONE
244 Shadowline Dr (28607-4921)
PHONE.................................828 386-1041
EMP: 5
SALES (est): 103.34K **Privately Held**
SIC: **3999** Cigar and cigarette holders

(G-1210)
JARED MUNDAY ELECTRIC INC
123 Tarheel Ln (28607-5489)
P.O. Box 2077 (28607-2077)
PHONE.................................828 355-9024
Jared Munday, *Owner*
EMP: 4 EST: 2010
SALES (est): 514.17K **Privately Held**
Web: www.mundayelectric.com
SIC: **3699** 1731 Electrical equipment and supplies, nec; Electrical work

(G-1211)
JOEL MORETZ
209 Blairmont Dr (28607-8713)
PHONE.................................828 355-9936
Joel Moretz, *Prin*
EMP: 5 EST: 2009
SALES (est): 89.72K **Privately Held**
Web: www.jmoretzwoodworking.com
SIC: **2431** Millwork

(G-1212)
JONES MEDIA
Also Called: Blowing Rocket
474 Industrial Park Dr (28607-3937)
PHONE.................................828 264-3612
EMP: 19 EST: 1994
SALES (est): 866.58K **Privately Held**
Web: www.wataugademocrat.com
SIC: **2711** 2752 2796 2791 Newspapers, publishing and printing; Commercial printing, lithographic; Platemaking services; Typesetting

(G-1213)
LEGACY VULCAN LLC
Mideast Division
3869 Hwy 105 S (28607)
P.O. Box 2995 (28607-2995)
PHONE.................................828 963-7100
Ronnie Godman, *Mgr*
EMP: 4
Web: www.vulcanmaterials.com
SIC: **3273** Ready-mixed concrete
HQ: Legacy Vulcan, Llc
   1200 Urban Center Dr
   Vestavia AL 35242
   205 298-3000

(G-1214)
LEIST STUDIOS INC
381 Tarleton Cir (28607-7067)
PHONE.................................828 262-5912
Nathanael Leist, *Prin*
EMP: 4 EST: 2009
SALES (est): 122.33K **Privately Held**
Web: www.leiststudios.com
SIC: **2499** Decorative wood and woodwork

(G-1215)
LOVEN READY MIX LLC
1996 Us Highway 421 N (28607-7646)
PHONE.................................828 265-4671
Richard Greer, *Mgr*
EMP: 8
SALES (corp-wide): 45.79MM **Privately Held**
Web: www.lovenreadymix.com
SIC: **3273** Ready-mixed concrete
HQ: Loven Ready Mix, Llc
   1995 Roan Creek Rd
   Mountain City TN 37683
   423 727-2000

(G-1216)
M-PRINTS INC
713 W King St (28607-3423)
P.O. Box 506 (28607-0506)
PHONE.................................828 265-4929

Stuart Mangum, *Pr*
Kim Havelos, *Sec*
EMP: 9 **EST:** 1992
SQ FT: 7,500
SALES (est): 451.37K **Privately Held**
Web: www.mprintsinc.com
SIC: 2396 2759 2395 Screen printing on fabric articles; Commercial printing, nec; Embroidery products, except Schiffli machine

(G-1217)
MANUFACTURING STRUCTURES LLC
355 Industrial Park Dr (28607-3978)
PHONE...................................828 264-6198
Heather Greene, *Prin*
EMP: 6 **EST:** 2012
SALES (est): 201.86K **Privately Held**
SIC: 3448 Buildings, portable: prefabricated metal

(G-1218)
MAST GENERAL STORE INC
Also Called: Mast General Store CPC
996 George Wilson Rd (28607-8616)
PHONE...................................423 895-1632
David Cliett, *Pr*
EMP: 9
SALES (corp-wide): 56.7MM **Privately Held**
Web: www.mastgeneralstore.com
SIC: 2064 Candy and other confectionery products
PA: The Mast General Store Inc
  Hwy 194
  Valle Crucis NC 28691
  828 963-6511

(G-1219)
MAX B SMITH JR
Also Called: Red Gremlin Design Studio
1055 Blowing Rock Rd (28607-6132)
PHONE...................................828 434-0238
Max Smith Junior, *Owner*
EMP: 4 **EST:** 2014
SALES (est): 150K **Privately Held**
SIC: 2759 7336 Screen printing; Chart and graph design

(G-1220)
MILL CAMP WINES & CIDERS LLC (PA)
Also Called: Mill Camp
1624 Tom Jackson Rd (28607-9009)
PHONE...................................810 923-7339
Mark Jolley, *Prin*
EMP: 8 **EST:** 2021
SALES (est): 266.57K
SALES (corp-wide): 266.57K **Privately Held**
SIC: 2084 Wines, brandy, and brandy spirits

(G-1221)
MILL CAMP WINES & CIDERS LLC
187 Rivers Crest Rd (28607-8193)
PHONE...................................810 923-7339
Mark Jolley, *Mgr*
EMP: 9
SALES (corp-wide): 266.57K **Privately Held**
SIC: 2084 Wines, brandy, and brandy spirits
PA: Mill Camp Wines & Ciders, Llc
  1624 Tom Jackson Rd
  Boone NC 28607
  810 923-7339

(G-1222)
MILLENNIUM MFG STRUCTURES LLC
353 Industrial Park Dr (28607-3978)
PHONE...................................828 265-3737
▼ **EMP:** 15 **EST:** 1987
SQ FT: 2,500
SALES (est): 953.22K **Privately Held**
SIC: 1541 3448 3441 Steel building construction; Prefabricated metal buildings and components; Fabricated structural metal

(G-1223)
MOLECULAR TOXICOLOGY INC
Also Called: Moltox
157 Industrial Park Dr (28607-3974)
P.O. Box 1189 (28607-1189)
PHONE...................................828 264-9099
Ray Cameron, *Pr*
Heather R Cameron, *VP*
Raymond S Cameron, *VP*
EMP: 10 **EST:** 1987
SQ FT: 6,000
SALES (est): 1.53MM **Privately Held**
Web: www.moltox.com
SIC: 2836 2899 2835 Biological products, except diagnostic; Chemical preparations, nec; Diagnostic substances

(G-1224)
MOOL LAW FIRM LLC ✪
163 Farm Valley Ln (28607-6793)
PHONE...................................217 496-3355
Robert Mool, *Mgr*
EMP: 6 **EST:** 2023
SALES (est): 76.29K **Privately Held**
SIC: 3842 Surgical appliances and supplies

(G-1225)
MR TIRE INC
Also Called: Clark Tire & Auto Service
1563 Blowing Rock Rd (28607-6143)
PHONE...................................828 262-3555
Travis Reese, *Brnch Mgr*
EMP: 6
SALES (corp-wide): 1.33B **Publicly Held**
Web: mrtireinc.business.site
SIC: 5941 5531 7538 7534 Bicycle and bicycle parts; Automotive tires; General automotive repair shops; Tire recapping
HQ: Mr. Tire Inc.
  2078 New York Ave Unit 2
  Huntington Station NY 11746
  631 499-3700

(G-1226)
OMEGA TEES + SCREEN PRTG LLC
115 Apple Rd (28607-8620)
PHONE...................................828 268-0600
EMP: 5 **EST:** 2015
SALES (est): 73.28K **Privately Held**
Web: www.omegascreenprinting.com
SIC: 2759 Screen printing

(G-1227)
PACE SCIENTIFIC INC
112 Paul Critcher Dr (28607-7932)
P.O. Box 2263 (28607-2263)
PHONE...................................704 799-0688
Joseph Dobson, *Pr*
Gayle Dobson, *Sec*
EMP: 8 **EST:** 1990
SQ FT: 2,000
SALES (est): 843.64K **Privately Held**
Web: www.pace-sci.com
SIC: 3829 Measuring and controlling devices, nec

(G-1228)
PRECISION CABINETS INC
1324 Old 421 S (28607-6288)
PHONE...................................828 262-5080
Ken Murray, *Pr*
EMP: 7 **EST:** 1980
SQ FT: 5,000
SALES (est): 576.83K **Privately Held**
Web: www.precisioncabinetinc.com
SIC: 2434 5211 Wood kitchen cabinets; Cabinets, kitchen

(G-1229)
QUALITY STEEL STRUCTURE LLC
375 Highway 105 Ext Apt 203 (28607)
PHONE...................................910 975-3409
David Mcbride, *Prin*
EMP: 4 **EST:** 2018
SALES (est): 73.47K **Privately Held**
SIC: 3441 Fabricated structural metal

(G-1230)
QUILT SHOP
251 Katie Way (28607-6537)
PHONE...................................828 263-8691
Kurk Prescott, *Sec*
EMP: 5 **EST:** 2005
SALES (est): 200.46K **Privately Held**
Web: www.thequiltshopinc.com
SIC: 3599 5949 7299 7692 Machine shop, jobbing and repair; Fabric stores piece goods; Quilting for individuals; Welding repair

(G-1231)
RADFORD QUARRIES INC (PA)
5605 Bamboo Rd (28607-9678)
P.O. Box 2071 (28607-2071)
PHONE...................................828 264-7008
EMP: 19 **EST:** 1992
SQ FT: 1,300
SALES (est): 4.59MM **Privately Held**
SIC: 1422 5032 Crushed and broken limestone; Stone, crushed or broken

(G-1232)
RADON CONTROL INC
P.O. Box 2873 (28607-2873)
PHONE...................................828 265-9534
EMP: 5 **EST:** 2001
SALES (est): 158.87K **Privately Held**
Web: www.focusbusinesssolutions.com
SIC: 3825 Radar testing instruments, electric

(G-1233)
RAYSWEATHERCOM INC
240 Shadowline Dr Ste L (28607-5088)
PHONE...................................828 264-2030
EMP: 7 **EST:** 2008
SALES (est): 247.9K **Privately Held**
Web: www.raysweather.com
SIC: 2711 Newspapers, publishing and printing

(G-1234)
RIBBON ENTERPRISES INC
1640 Old 421 S (28607-6291)
PHONE...................................828 264-6444
Thurman Johnson, *Owner*
EMP: 8 **EST:** 2001
SALES (est): 102.77K **Privately Held**
SIC: 2211 Broadwoven fabric mills, cotton

(G-1235)
RUPPARDS WELDING SERVICE LLC
816 Millers Pond Ln (28607-9356)
PHONE...................................828 386-8191
Joshua Ruppard, *CEO*
EMP: 6 **EST:** 2019
SALES (est): 66.1K **Privately Held**
SIC: 7692 Welding repair

(G-1236)
SOHA HOLDINGS LLC
Also Called: Harmony Timberworks
645 Roby Greene Rd (28607-9152)
PHONE...................................828 264-2314
EMP: 25 **EST:** 2009
SALES (est): 2.61MM **Privately Held**
Web: www.harmonytimberworks.com
SIC: 2491 Structural lumber and timber, treated wood

(G-1237)
SOS PRINTING INC
869 Highway 105 Ext Ste 3 (28607-5365)
PHONE...................................828 264-4262
Linda Steele, *Pr*
Kevin Conway, *VP*
EMP: 10 **EST:** 1973
SALES (est): 226.69K **Privately Held**
SIC: 2752 7334 2759 Offset printing; Photocopying and duplicating services; Commercial printing, nec

(G-1238)
SOUTHERN AG INSECTICIDES INC
Also Called: Southern AG Insecticides
395 Brook Hollow Rd (28607-8528)
P.O. Box 85 (28607-0085)
PHONE...................................828 264-8843
Mike Presnell, *Mgr*
EMP: 25
SALES (corp-wide): 50.49MM **Privately Held**
Web: www.southernag.com
SIC: 5191 2879 Insecticides; Agricultural chemicals, nec
PA: Southern Agricultural Insecticides Inc.
  7500 Bayshore Rd
  Palmetto FL 34221
  941 722-3285

(G-1239)
STACKHOUSE PUBLISHING INC
299 Blackberry Rd (28607-7023)
PHONE...................................203 699-6571
Timothy Prickett-morgan, *Ch*
EMP: 8 **EST:** 2017
SALES (est): 208.29K **Privately Held**
Web: www.nextplatform.com
SIC: 2741 Miscellaneous publishing

(G-1240)
SUNDOWN TIMES INC
Also Called: Mountain Times
474 Industrial Park Dr (28607-3937)
P.O. Box 1815 (28607-1815)
PHONE...................................828 264-1881
Kenneth Ketchie, *Pr*
Homer Ketchie, *VP*
Chuck Ketchie, *Sec*
EMP: 18 **EST:** 1978
SALES (est): 154.44K **Privately Held**
Web: www.wataugademocrat.com
SIC: 2711 Newspapers: publishing only, not printed on site

(G-1241)
SURELIFT INC
151 H O Aldridge Rd Unit B (28607-7825)
P.O. Box 3442 (28607-0742)
PHONE...................................828 963-6899
William Miller, *Pr*
EMP: 5 **EST:** 2013
SALES (est): 373.44K **Privately Held**
Web: www.sureliftinc.com
SIC: 4785 3569 Highway bridge operation; Bridge or gate machinery, hydraulic

(G-1242)
TRESCO
Also Called: I R C
736 Greenway Rd (28607-4830)
P.O. Box 1860 (28607-1860)
PHONE...................................361 985-3154

Boone - Watauga County (G-1243)

▲ **EMP**: 200 **EST**: 2005
SALES (est): 8.57MM **Privately Held**
SIC: 3679 Electronic circuits

(G-1243)
TRIPLETT & COFFEY INC
204 Jefferson Rd (28607-8811)
P.O. Box 1640 (28607-1640)
PHONE..........................828 263-0561
Bill Triplett, *Pr*
Kent W Coffey, *VP*
EMP: 10 **EST**: 1976
SQ FT: 6,000
SALES (est): 914.24K **Privately Held**
Web: www.triplettandcoffey.com
SIC: 3599 7692 Machine shop, jobbing and repair; Welding repair

(G-1244)
TY BROWN
Also Called: Homes & Land Mag of High S
126 Iris Ln Apt 4 (28607-3664)
PHONE..........................828 264-6865
Ty Brown, *Owner*
Ty Brown, *Pr*
EMP: 4 **EST**: 1992
SALES (est): 160K **Privately Held**
SIC: 2721 Magazines: publishing only, not printed on site

(G-1245)
US BUILDINGS LLC (PA)
Also Called: Millennium Mfg or US Chem
355 Industrial Park Dr (28607-3978)
PHONE..........................828 264-6198
▼ **EMP**: 99 **EST**: 1987
SALES (est): 8.49MM
SALES (corp-wide): 8.49MM **Privately Held**
Web: www.usbuildingsdirect.com
SIC: 3441 Fabricated structural metal

(G-1246)
VULCAN MATERIALS COMPANY
3869 Nc Highway 105 S (28607-3326)
PHONE..........................828 963-7100
Brad Allison, *Brnch Mgr*
EMP: 4
Web: www.vulcanmaterials.com
SIC: 3273 Ready-mixed concrete
PA: Vulcan Materials Company
    1200 Urban Center Dr
    Vestavia AL 35242

(G-1247)
WATAUGA OPPORTUNITIES INC (PA)
642 Greenway Rd (28607-4812)
P.O. Box 2330 (28607-2330)
PHONE..........................828 264-5009
Michael Maybee, *Pr*
EMP: 32 **EST**: 1974
SQ FT: 22,000
SALES (est): 5.86MM
SALES (corp-wide): 5.86MM **Privately Held**
Web: www.woiworks.org
SIC: 3086 8331 8361 Packaging and shipping materials, foamed plastics; Vocational rehabilitation agency; Mentally handicapped home

(G-1248)
WATAUGA READY MIXED
525 George Wilson Rd (28607-8612)
PHONE..........................336 246-6441
David Hardin, *Prin*
EMP: 7 **EST**: 1984
SALES (est): 193.55K **Privately Held**
SIC: 3273 Ready-mixed concrete

(G-1249)
WELDING - FBRCATION - REPR INC
178 Riley Rd (28607-7831)
P.O. Box 2557 (28607-2557)
PHONE..........................828 963-9372
EMP: 7 **EST**: 2015
SALES (est): 449.3K **Privately Held**
Web: www.weldingfabricationboone.com
SIC: 7699 7692 Repair services, nec; Welding repair

(G-1250)
WINDOW MOTOR WORLD INC
779 Ball Branch Rd (28607-8209)
PHONE..........................800 252-2649
Ernest Bonham, *Owner*
EMP: 7 **EST**: 2005
SALES (est): 705.97K **Privately Held**
Web: www.windowmotorworld.net
SIC: 3694 5511 Voltage regulators, automotive; New and used car dealers

(G-1251)
XP CLIMATE CONTROL LLC
643 Greenway Rd Ste P (28607-4840)
P.O. Box 432 (28605-0432)
PHONE..........................828 266-2006
Will Knight, *Managing Member*
EMP: 8 **EST**: 2012
SQ FT: 6,000
SALES (est): 2.45MM **Privately Held**
Web: www.xpclimate.com
SIC: 3585 Heating and air conditioning combination units

Boonville
Yadkin County

(G-1252)
A PLUS CARPORTS
6833 Us Highway 601 (27011-7944)
P.O. Box 1448 (27041-1448)
PHONE..........................336 367-1261
Chelsa Adkins, *Prin*
EMP: 5 **EST**: 2013
SALES (est): 78.27K **Privately Held**
Web: www.aplussuperstore.com
SIC: 3448 3444 Carports, prefabricated metal; Bins, prefabricated sheet metal

(G-1253)
BOONVILLE FLOUR FEED MILL INC
203 S Caralino Ave (27011-9065)
P.O. Box 337 (27011-0337)
PHONE..........................336 367-7541
Eugene Phillips, *Pr*
Marcus E Phillips, *VP*
Donna Phillips, *Sec*
EMP: 8 **EST**: 1898
SQ FT: 5,000
SALES (est): 773.13K **Privately Held**
Web: www.boonvillemill.com
SIC: 2048 5999 2041 Prepared feeds, nec; Feed and farm supply; Pizza dough, prepared

(G-1254)
DAVID MILLER LOGGING LLC
2541 Spencer Rd (27011-9105)
PHONE..........................336 831-4052
Christy Miller, *Owner*
EMP: 8 **EST**: 2018
SALES (est): 226.59K **Privately Held**
SIC: 2411 Logging camps and contractors

(G-1255)
OVERKILL FABRICATION
1700 Nebo Rd (27011-8218)
PHONE..........................336 480-1787

Douglas Brown, *Ofcr*
EMP: 6 **EST**: 2008
SALES (est): 189.56K **Privately Held**
SIC: 3089 Plastics products, nec

(G-1256)
SANDERS RIDGE INC (PA)
Also Called: Sanders Ridge Vinyrd & Winery
3200 Round Hill Rd (27011-8444)
PHONE..........................336 677-1700
Neil Shore, *Pr*
EMP: 4 **EST**: 2007
SALES (est): 654.03K
SALES (corp-wide): 654.03K **Privately Held**
Web: www.sandersridge.com
SIC: 2084 5921 0762 Wines; Wine; Vineyard management and maintenance services

(G-1257)
TC MACHINE &REPAIR
2517 Campbell Rd (27011-8187)
PHONE..........................336 468-4792
EMP: 5 **EST**: 2010
SALES (est): 91K **Privately Held**
SIC: 3599 Machine shop, jobbing and repair

(G-1258)
VIKING STEEL STRUCTURES LLC
113 W Main St, Nc (27011-9125)
PHONE..........................877 623-7549
Alberto Ochoa, *Prin*
EMP: 7 **EST**: 2017
SALES (est): 132.05K **Privately Held**
Web: www.vikingsteelstructures.com
SIC: 3448 Prefabricated metal buildings and components

Bostic
Rutherford County

(G-1259)
AMERICAN COIL INC
157 N Main St (28018-6744)
PHONE..........................310 515-1215
Jeff Aiello, *CEO*
▲ **EMP**: 10 **EST**: 2013
SQ FT: 23,000
SALES (est): 946.78K **Privately Held**
Web: www.american-coil.com
SIC: 3585 Heating and air conditioning combination units

(G-1260)
BLUE RIDGE DISTILLING CO INC
228 Redbud Ln (28018-6611)
PHONE..........................828 245-2041
Tim Serris, *Pr*
EMP: 5 **EST**: 2011
SALES (est): 488.53K **Privately Held**
Web: www.defiantwhisky.com
SIC: 2085 Distiller's dried grains and solubles, and alcohol

(G-1261)
BLUE SEAS LLC
228 Redbud Ln (28018-6611)
PHONE..........................828 245-2041
Timothy W Ferris, *Prin*
EMP: 5 **EST**: 2018
SALES (est): 87.14K **Privately Held**
SIC: 2085 Distilled and blended liquors

(G-1262)
ERIC MARTIN JERMEY
Also Called: Martin Logging
1815 Salem Church Rd (28018-7569)
PHONE..........................704 692-0389
Jeremy Eric Martin, *Prin*

EMP: 6 **EST**: 2012
SALES (est): 165.42K **Privately Held**
SIC: 2411 Logging

(G-1263)
MALCOLMS METAL & MORE
356 Winnies Rd (28018-6818)
PHONE..........................828 286-1419
Daniel Malcolm, *Owner*
EMP: 6 **EST**: 2017
SALES (est): 71.39K **Privately Held**
SIC: 3471 Plating and polishing

(G-1264)
MARK W MCKENZIE
182 Isham Dr (28018-9602)
PHONE..........................860 529-2476
Mark W Mckenzie, *Prin*
EMP: 5 **EST**: 2005
SALES (est): 210.16K **Privately Held**
SIC: 3441 Fabricated structural metal

(G-1265)
MILLIKEN & COMPANY
Also Called: Golden Valley Mfg Plant Div
2080 Nc Highway 226 (28018-7659)
PHONE..........................828 247-4300
EMP: 21
SALES (corp-wide): 1.69B **Privately Held**
Web: www.milliken.com
SIC: 2231 2211 2281 Broadwoven fabric mills, wool; Broadwoven fabric mills, cotton; Yarn spinning mills
PA: Milliken & Company
    920 Milliken Rd
    Spartanburg SC 29303
    864 503-2020

Brasstown
Clay County

(G-1266)
KELHORN CORPORATION
Also Called: Kelishek Workshop
199 Waldroup Rd (28902-8114)
PHONE..........................828 837-5833
Michael Kelischek, *Pr*
George Kelischek, *Prin*
Rose Marie Kelischek, *Sec*
EMP: 7 **EST**: 1960
SQ FT: 5,000
SALES (est): 438.75K **Privately Held**
Web: www.susato.com
SIC: 3931 5736 Guitars and parts, electric and nonelectric; Musical instrument stores

(G-1267)
LONG BRANCH PARTNERS LLC
1960 Brasstown Rd (28902-8002)
PHONE..........................828 837-1400
EMP: 6 **EST**: 2008
SALES (est): 253.46K **Privately Held**
SIC: 1442 Construction sand and gravel

(G-1268)
PEACHTREE LUMBER COMPANY INC
Also Called: Buckhorn Lumber and Wood Pdts
6926 Highway 64 W (28902-8081)
P.O. Box 100 (28902-0100)
PHONE..........................828 837-0118
Brian T Smith, *Pr*
EMP: 20 **EST**: 1993
SQ FT: 12,000
SALES (est): 3MM **Privately Held**
Web: www.peachtreelumber.com
SIC: 2421 Sawmills and planing mills, general

Brevard
Transylvania County

(G-1269)
ALLENS ENVIRONMENTAL CNSTR LLC
84 Greenfield Cir (28712-0149)
PHONE..................................407 774-7100
EMP: 8 **EST:** 2004
SALES (est): 486.45K **Privately Held**
Web: www.allensenvironmental.com
SIC: 3589 1799 Sewage and water treatment equipment; Protective lining installation, underground (sewage, etc.)

(G-1270)
BLUE RIDGE QUICK PRINT INC
Also Called: Quick Print
82 E French Broad St (28712-4751)
PHONE..................................828 883-2420
Carol L Mathews, *Pr*
EMP: 5 **EST:** 1978
SALES (est): 450.28K **Privately Held**
Web: www.blueridgequickprintinc.com
SIC: 2752 8742 7389 5999 Offset printing; Marketing consulting services; Finishing services; Banners, flags, decals, and posters

(G-1271)
BOBBOS STUFF LLC
550 Park Ave (28712-3993)
PHONE..................................828 883-8545
Robert S Sargent Junior, *Mgr*
EMP: 5 **EST:** 2009
SALES (est): 126.06K **Privately Held**
Web: www.bobbosstuff.com
SIC: 2033 Chili sauce, tomato: packaged in cans, jars, etc.

(G-1272)
BREVARD BUSINESS CTR
9 Encompass Plz E (28712-7949)
PHONE..................................828 883-4363
Pat Ream, *Owner*
EMP: 5 **EST:** 2017
SALES (est): 61.85K **Privately Held**
Web: www.brevardmusic.org
SIC: 2752 Commercial printing, lithographic

(G-1273)
DMARCIAN (PA)
43 S Broad St Ste 203 (28712-3985)
P.O. Box 1007 (28712-1007)
PHONE..................................828 767-7588
Shannon Draegen, *CEO*
EMP: 27 **EST:** 2016
SALES (est): 3.79MM
SALES (corp-wide): 3.79MM **Privately Held**
Web: www.dmarcian.com
SIC: 3861 Photographic equipment and supplies

(G-1274)
GREY HOLDINGS INC
Also Called: Genie Products
283 Old Rosman Hwy (28712-8329)
P.O. Box 1028 (28772-1028)
PHONE..................................828 862-4772
▼ **EMP:** 21
SIC: 3542 Plasma jet spray metal forming machines

(G-1275)
HEAVEN & EARTH WORKS
102 College Station Dr (28712-3194)
PHONE..................................845 797-0902
Teresa Cox, *Prin*

EMP: 6 **EST:** 2015
SALES (est): 109.32K **Privately Held**
Web: www.terahcox.com
SIC: 2741 Miscellaneous publishing

(G-1276)
HERBS GAIA INC (PA)
101 Gaia Herbs Rd (28712-8930)
PHONE..................................828 884-4242
Ric Scalzo, *CEO*
Etson Brandenburg, *
Angela Mcelwee, *Pr*
▲ **EMP:** 89 **EST:** 1992
SQ FT: 30,000
SALES (est): 40.49MM **Privately Held**
Web: www.gaiaherbs.com
SIC: 2079 8011 2833 Edible oil products, except corn oil; Offices and clinics of medical doctors; Medicinals and botanicals

(G-1277)
JACKSON WINE
183 King St (28712-3376)
P.O. Box 1649 (28712-1649)
PHONE..................................828 508-9292
Jackson Wine, *Admn*
EMP: 5 **EST:** 2019
SALES (est): 95.69K **Privately Held**
SIC: 2084 Wines

(G-1278)
LINDE ADVANCED MTL TECH INC
Praxair
283 Old Rosman Hwy (28712-8329)
P.O. Box B1028 (28772)
PHONE..................................828 862-4772
Brad Walsh, *Mgr*
EMP: 94
Web: www.linde-amt.com
SIC: 3542 Plasma jet spray metal forming machines
HQ: Linde Advanced Material Technologies Inc.
    1500 Polco St
    Indianapolis IN 46222
    317 240-2500

(G-1279)
MATTHEWS WELDING SERVICE
169 Cherryfield Loop (28712-7238)
PHONE..................................828 862-4510
Oren E Matthews Ii, *Prin*
EMP: 6 **EST:** 1984
SALES (est): 191.03K **Privately Held**
SIC: 7692 Welding repair

(G-1280)
MONSTER BREWING COMPANY LLC
342 Mountain Industrial Dr (28712-5122)
PHONE..................................828 883-2337
EMP: 88
SALES (corp-wide): 7.14B **Publicly Held**
Web: www.oskarblues.com
SIC: 2082 Beer (alcoholic beverage)
HQ: Monster Brewing Company Llc
    1800 Pike Rd Unit B
    Longmont CO 80501
    303 776-1914

(G-1281)
MOUNTAIN CABINETRY CLOSETS LLC
309 S Country Club Rd (28712-7822)
PHONE..................................828 966-9000
Robert Grieves, *Pr*
Cindy Grieves, *VP*
EMP: 6 **EST:** 2020
SALES (est): 790.8K **Privately Held**
SIC: 2434 Wood kitchen cabinets

(G-1282)
MOUNTAIN INTERNATIONAL LLC
1345 Old Hendersonville Hwy (28712-9359)
P.O. Box 394 (28787-0394)
PHONE..................................828 606-0194
Jerry Gaddy, *Managing Member*
Bruce W Rau, *
EMP: 25 **EST:** 2004
SALES (est): 1.94MM **Privately Held**
Web: www.mountainintl.com
SIC: 2393 2297 Textile bags; Nonwoven fabrics

(G-1283)
NATURAL ELEMENTS BATH AND BODY
60 W Main St (28712-3647)
PHONE..................................828 226-0853
EMP: 4 **EST:** 2019
SALES (est): 130.67K **Privately Held**
SIC: 2819 Elements

(G-1284)
PHARMAGRA HOLDING COMPANY LLC
158 Mclean Rd (28712-9432)
PHONE..................................828 884-8656
Peter Newsome, *Pr*
EMP: 23 **EST:** 1998
SALES (est): 1.76MM **Privately Held**
Web: www.raybow.com
SIC: 2834 8731 Druggists' preparations (pharmaceuticals); Commercial physical research
HQ: Zhejiang Raybow Pharmaceutical Co., Ltd.
    No. 18, Nanyangsan Road, Linhai, Taizhou ZJ 31701

(G-1285)
PISGAH IT COMPANY LLC
577 Island Ford Rd (28712-9735)
PHONE..................................828 884-5290
Robert Brown, *Prin*
EMP: 5 **EST:** 2018
SALES (est): 82.21K **Privately Held**
Web: www.pisgahmapcompany.com
SIC: 2741 Miscellaneous publishing

(G-1286)
RAYBOW USA INC
158 Mclean Rd (28712-9432)
PHONE..................................828 884-8656
Peter Newsome, *Pr*
EMP: 12 **EST:** 1999
SQ FT: 11,400
SALES (est): 4.75MM **Privately Held**
Web: www.raybow.com
SIC: 2834 8731 Druggists' preparations (pharmaceuticals); Commercial physical research
HQ: Zhejiang Raybow Pharmaceutical Co., Ltd.
    No. 18, Nanyangsan Road, Linhai, Taizhou ZJ 31701

(G-1287)
RITEWAY EXPRESS INC OF NC
1106 Rosman Hwy (28712-4173)
PHONE..................................828 966-4822
Larry E Morgan, *Prin*
EMP: 9 **EST:** 2006
SALES (est): 231.29K **Privately Held**
SIC: 2741 Miscellaneous publishing

(G-1288)
ROTATING MACHINERY ANALYS
66 Quanv Ct (28712-8412)
PHONE..................................512 743-1248

Brian Murphy, *Pr*
EMP: 8 **EST:** 1993
SALES (est): 149.57K **Privately Held**
SIC: 3569 Centrifuges, industrial

(G-1289)
SMITH SYSTEMS INC
Also Called: S S I
6 Mill Creek Ctr (28712-0236)
P.O. Box 667 (28712-0667)
PHONE..................................828 884-3490
Claire Smith, *Pr*
William Smith, *
EMP: 40 **EST:** 1982
SQ FT: 6,500
SALES (est): 8.34MM **Privately Held**
Web: www.smith-systems-inc.com
SIC: 3679 Transducers, electrical

(G-1290)
STARFANGLED PRESS
30 Stratford Ave (28712-4030)
PHONE..................................804 338-9972
EMP: 4 **EST:** 2015
SALES (est): 62.3K **Privately Held**
Web: www.starfangledpress.com
SIC: 2741 Miscellaneous publishing

(G-1291)
TRANSYLVNIA VCATIONAL SVCS INC (PA)
Also Called: T V S
11 Mountain Industrial Dr (28712-6723)
PHONE..................................828 884-3195
Jamie Brandenburg, *CEO*
Nancy Stricker, *
Rilla Hughart, *
EMP: 125 **EST:** 1967
SQ FT: 60,000
SALES (est): 35.16MM
SALES (corp-wide): 35.16MM **Privately Held**
Web: www.tvsinc.org
SIC: 8093 8331 2652 Rehabilitation center, outpatient treatment; Job training and related services; Setup paperboard boxes

(G-1292)
WELLS WOODWORKS GARY WELLS
2121 Big Branch Rd (28712-0296)
PHONE..................................828 553-0177
EMP: 4 **EST:** 2017
SALES (est): 81.7K **Privately Held**
SIC: 2431 Millwork

(G-1293)
WHEELHOUSE BUILDERS LLC
71 Trailcreek Ln (28712-0029)
PHONE..................................828 553-7519
EMP: 6 **EST:** 2013
SALES (est): 228.77K **Privately Held**
SIC: 2431 Millwork

Bridgeton
Craven County

(G-1294)
FRIT CAR INC
Hwy 17 N Ste 2012 (28519)
P.O. Box 569 (28519-0569)
PHONE..................................252 638-2675
Gary Barnes, *Mgr*
EMP: 25
Web: www.fritcar.com
SIC: 3743 Railroad equipment
HQ: Frit Car, Inc.
    1965 South Blvd
    Brewton AL 36426
    251 867-7752

Bridgeton - Craven County (G-1295)

(G-1295)
PHILLIPS PLATING CO INC
1617 Hwy 17 N Ste 1617 (28519)
P.O. Box 336 (28519-0336)
PHONE.................................252 637-2695
George E Phillips, *Pr*
Mark Phillips, *VP*
EMP: 6 **EST:** 1956
SALES (est): 445.04K **Privately Held**
Web: www.phillipselectroplating.com
SIC: 3471 Electroplating of metals or formed products

Broadway
Lee County

(G-1296)
FOO MACHINE & TOOL PRECISION
311 W Harrington Ave (27505-9543)
PHONE.................................919 258-5099
Steve Cran, *Owner*
EMP: 10 **EST:** 1997
SALES (est): 462.39K **Privately Held**
Web: www.foosprecision.com
SIC: 3599 Machine shop, jobbing and repair

(G-1297)
SOUTHERN CONCRETE INCORPORATED
3560 Mcarthur Rd (27505-9210)
P.O. Box 875 (27505-0875)
PHONE.................................919 906-4069
Steve Thomas, *Pr*
EMP: 18 **EST:** 1994
SALES (est): 2.46MM **Privately Held**
SIC: 3273 Ready-mixed concrete

Browns Summit
Guilford County

(G-1298)
ABCO AUTOMATION INC
6202 Technology Dr (27214-9702)
PHONE.................................336 375-6400
W Graham Ricks, *Ch Bd*
Brad Kemmerer, *
EMP: 155 **EST:** 1977
SQ FT: 135,000
SALES (est): 34.9MM **Privately Held**
Web: www.goabco.com
SIC: 3569 3599 8711 3625 Liquid automation machinery and equipment; Machine shop, jobbing and repair; Consulting engineer; Relays and industrial controls

(G-1299)
AIM INDUSTRIES INC
391 Brann Rd (27214)
PHONE.................................336 656-9990
Duval Dumas, *Prin*
EMP: 8 **EST:** 2014
SALES (est): 260.08K **Privately Held**
SIC: 3999 Manufacturing industries, nec

(G-1300)
BANKNOTE CORP AMERICA INC
6109 Corporate Park Dr (27214-9700)
PHONE.................................336 375-1134
Sandra Lane, *Pr*
▲ **EMP:** 150 **EST:** 1989
SQ FT: 9,000
SALES: 39.78MM
SALES (corp-wide): 4.75B **Privately Held**
Web: www.banknote.com
SIC: 2759 Bank notes: engraved
PA: Ccl Industries Inc.
  111 Gordon Baker Rd Suite 801
  Toronto ON M2H 3
  416 756-8500

(G-1301)
BONSET AMERICA CORPORATION (PA)
6107 Corporate Park Dr (27214-8301)
PHONE.................................336 375-0234
Shinji Takahashi, *CEO*
◆ **EMP:** 106 **EST:** 1989
SQ FT: 148,000
SALES (est): 21.58MM **Privately Held**
Web: www.bonset.com
SIC: 3081 Packing materials, plastics sheet

(G-1302)
FMP EQUIPMENT CORP
6204 Technology Dr (27214-9702)
PHONE.................................336 621-2882
Jennifer Friedrich, *Pr*
Laura Bargebuhr, *VP*
Robert Friedrich, *Treas*
EMP: 10 **EST:** 1985
SQ FT: 30,000
SALES (est): 140.94K **Privately Held**
SIC: 3556 Food products machinery

(G-1303)
FRIEDRICH METAL PDTS CO INC
6204 Technology Dr (27214-9702)
PHONE.................................336 375-3067
Laura Friedrich-bargebuhr, *Owner*
Jennifer Friedrich, *VP*
Robert Friedrich, *Asst VP*
▼ **EMP:** 20 **EST:** 1950
SQ FT: 30,000
SALES (est): 4.7MM **Privately Held**
Web: www.friedrichproducts.com
SIC: 3443 2542 3469 3556 Tanks, lined: metal plate; Cabinets: show, display, or storage: except wood; Electronic enclosures, stamped or pressed metal; Smokers, food processing equipment

(G-1304)
FUJI FOODS INC
6205 Corporate Park Dr (27214-9745)
PHONE.................................336 897-3373
Joshua Walker, *Mgr*
EMP: 20
Web: www.fujifoodsusa.com
SIC: 2087 Extracts, flavoring
HQ: Fuji Foods Inc.
  6206 Corporate Park Dr
  Browns Summit NC 27214
  336 375-3111

(G-1305)
FUJI FOODS INC (DH)
6206 Corporate Park Dr (27214-8302)
PHONE.................................336 375-3111
Hiroaki Nagatomi, *Pr*
Yasushi Muranaka, *
▲ **EMP:** 35 **EST:** 1982
SQ FT: 20,000
SALES (est): 24.45MM **Privately Held**
Web: www.fujifoodsusa.com
SIC: 2087 2099 Extracts, flavoring; Food preparations, nec
HQ: Fuji Foods Corporation
  94, Mamedocho, Kohoku-Ku
  Yokohama KNG 222-0

(G-1306)
GOLD REFINERY
2177 Scott Rd (27214-9608)
PHONE.................................336 501-2977
Donna Beasley, *Prin*
EMP: 5 **EST:** 2010
SALES (est): 65.87K **Privately Held**

SIC: 3559 Refinery, chemical processing, and similar machinery

(G-1307)
H T WADE ENTERPRISES INC
5838 Rudd Station Rd (27214-9708)
P.O. Box 13644 (27415-3644)
PHONE.................................336 375-8900
Harold T Wade, *Pr*
Harold T Wade, *Pr*
Gretchen Carden, *Sec*
EMP: 12 **EST:** 1992
SALES (est): 1.83MM **Privately Held**
SIC: 3441 Building components, structural steel

(G-1308)
HOPKINS POULTRY COMPANY
7741 Doggett Rd (27214-9875)
P.O. Box 595 (27214-0595)
PHONE.................................336 656-3361
Jerry R Hopkins, *Pr*
Jeff Hopkins Senior, *VP*
Phyllis Pascal, *Treas*
EMP: 10 **EST:** 1932
SQ FT: 1,800
SALES (est): 1.06MM **Privately Held**
Web: www.hopkinspoultry.com
SIC: 2015 Chicken slaughtering and processing

(G-1309)
JAMES MOORE & SON LOGGING
7435 Friendship Church Rd (27214-9756)
PHONE.................................336 656-9858
James Moore, *Pr*
EMP: 6 **EST:** 1974
SALES (est): 302.94K **Privately Held**
SIC: 2411 Logging camps and contractors

(G-1310)
JLY INVSTMNTS INC FKA NWMAN MC (HQ)
Also Called: Newman-Whitney
2949 Lees Chapel Rd (27214-9765)
P.O. Box 5467 (27435-0467)
PHONE.................................336 273-8261
Frank W York, *CEO*
James Laster, *Ex VP*
Jane L Stadler, *Sec*
◆ **EMP:** 45 **EST:** 1837
SQ FT: 150,000
SALES (est): 10.3MM
SALES (corp-wide): 35.91MM **Privately Held**
Web: www.newmanmachine.com
SIC: 3553 7699 Woodworking machinery; Industrial equipment services
PA: Incompass, Inc.
  3500 Viking Ln N Ste 174
  Minneapolis MN 55447
  651 379-1200

(G-1311)
JOHN JENKINS COMPANY
5949 Summit Ave (27214-9704)
P.O. Box 346 (27214-0346)
PHONE.................................336 375-3717
John M Jenkins Junior, *Pr*
Kelly Jenkins, *Ch Bd*
Perry Jenkins, *VP*
Carolyn Jenkins, *VP*
Terrie Boyd, *Sec*
EMP: 20 **EST:** 1962
SQ FT: 24,080
SALES (est): 2.39MM **Privately Held**
SIC: 3713 3441 3444 Truck beds; Fabricated structural metal; Sheet metalwork

(G-1312)
MDSI INC
3505 Lake Herman Dr Bldg A (27214-9746)
PHONE.................................919 783-8730
Milton R Peele, *CEO*
Milton Peele, *CEO*
Derrick Caul, *Pr*
Matt Roughgarden, *Treas*
Jim Schlosser, *VP*
EMP: 5 **EST:** 1992
SQ FT: 3,200
SALES (est): 901.39K **Privately Held**
Web: www.mdsi-mfg.net
SIC: 5162 3559 Plastics products, nec; Plastics working machinery

(G-1313)
PRECAST SOLUTIONS INC
7121 Choctaw Ct (27214-6000)
P.O. Box 127 (27214-0127)
PHONE.................................336 656-7991
▲ **EMP:** 15 **EST:** 2008
SALES (est): 2.99MM **Privately Held**
Web: www.precast-solutions.com
SIC: 3272 Concrete products, nec

(G-1314)
PROCTER & GAMBLE MFG CO
Also Called: Procter & Gamble
6200 Bryan Park Rd (27214-9755)
PHONE.................................336 954-0000
A R Hilton, *Brnch Mgr*
EMP: 559
SQ FT: 20,000
SALES (corp-wide): 82.01B **Publicly Held**
Web: us.pg.com
SIC: 2844 Hair preparations, including shampoos
HQ: The Procter & Gamble Manufacturing Company
  1 Procter And Gamble Plz
  Cincinnati OH 45202
  513 983-1100

(G-1315)
SENNETT SECURITY PRODUCTS LLC
Also Called: Banknote Corporation America
6109 Corporate Park Dr (27214-9700)
PHONE.................................336 375-1134
David Canon, *Brnch Mgr*
EMP: 60
SALES (corp-wide): 4.11MM **Privately Held**
SIC: 2752 Commercial printing, lithographic
PA: Sennett Security Products Llc
  15623 Jillians Forest Way
  Centreville VA 20120
  703 803-8880

(G-1316)
SOLACURE LLC
6208 Technology Dr (27214-9702)
PHONE.................................336 601-2868
Ricky Pierce, *Prin*
EMP: 5 **EST:** 2014
SALES (est): 305.2K **Privately Held**
Web: www.solacure.com
SIC: 3648 Lighting equipment, nec

(G-1317)
T SIMMONS BACKHOE
7507 Doggett Rd (27214-9699)
PHONE.................................336 295-3100
Theodore Simmons, *Prin*
EMP: 6 **EST:** 2010
SALES (est): 246.24K **Privately Held**
Web: www.applied-is.com
SIC: 3531 Backhoes

GEOGRAPHIC SECTION

Burgaw - Pender County (G-1342)

(G-1318)
TREFENA WELDS
8408 Exmoor Trce (27214-9879)
PHONE..........................203 551-1370
EMP: 4 **EST:** 2018
SALES (est): 25.09K **Privately Held**
SIC: 7692 Welding repair

Bryson City
Swain County

(G-1319)
B & B WOOD SHOP & BLDG CONTRS
Also Called: B&B Wood Shop Showroom
4829 Highway 19 W (28713-8575)
PHONE..........................828 488-2078
Thurmond Breedlove, *Owner*
EMP: 8 **EST:** 1979
SQ FT: 7,500
SALES (est): 821.92K **Privately Held**
SIC: 5712 2431 Cabinet work, custom; Doors, wood

(G-1320)
BEASLEY FLOORING PRODUCTS INC
77 Industrial Park Rd (28713)
PHONE..........................828 524-3248
EMP: 35
SALES (corp-wide): 115.61MM **Privately Held**
SIC: 2421 Flooring (dressed lumber), softwood
HQ: Beasley Flooring Products, Inc.
770 Uvalda Hwy
Hazlehurst GA 31539

(G-1321)
CCBCC OPERATIONS LLC
Also Called: Coca-Cola
441 Industrial Park Rd (28713-9424)
PHONE..........................828 488-2874
Gary Gray, *Brnch Mgr*
EMP: 43
SALES (corp-wide): 6.65B **Publicly Held**
Web: www.coca-cola.com
SIC: 2086 Bottled and canned soft drinks
HQ: Ccbcc Operations, Llc
4100 Coca Cola Plz
Charlotte NC 28211
704 364-8728

(G-1322)
CONSOLIDATED METCO INC
1821 Hwy 19 (28713-6533)
P.O. Box 1457 (28713-1457)
PHONE..........................828 488-5126
EMP: 96
SALES (corp-wide): 3.96B **Privately Held**
Web: www.conmet.com
SIC: 3714 Motor vehicle parts and accessories
HQ: Consolidated Metco, Inc.
5701 Se Columbia Way
Vancouver WA 98661
360 828-2599

(G-1323)
DEEP CREEK WINERY
380 Jonathan Walk (28713-8041)
P.O. Box 2029 (28713-5029)
PHONE..........................828 341-0592
Amanda Lesser, *Prin*
EMP: 5 **EST:** 2017
SALES (est): 97.21K **Privately Held**
Web: www.deepcreekwinery.com
SIC: 2084 Wines

(G-1324)
NOVASEARCH CONS & PUBG LLC
336 Berry Ln (28713-9104)
PHONE..........................828 788-2332
Brian Hannum, *Prin*
EMP: 5 **EST:** 2016
SALES (est): 137.19K **Privately Held**
SIC: 2741 Miscellaneous publishing

(G-1325)
SMOKY MOUNTAIN JET BOATS LLC
414 Black Hill Rd (28713-9722)
PHONE..........................828 488-0522
Bryan Nicholas Williams, *Managing Member*
EMP: 12 **EST:** 2002
SQ FT: 2,000
SALES (est): 952.73K **Privately Held**
Web: www.smokymountainjetboats.com
SIC: 3732 Motorboats, inboard or outboard: building and repairing

Bullock
Granville County

(G-1326)
ACTION GRAPHICS AND SIGNS INC
8694b Us Hwy 15 (27507-9618)
P.O. Box 277 (27507-0277)
PHONE..........................919 690-1260
Kenny Forbes, *Owner*
EMP: 4 **EST:** 1997
SALES (est): 279.88K **Privately Held**
SIC: 3993 Signs and advertising specialties

Bunn
Franklin County

(G-1327)
AROUND HOUSE IMPROVEMENT LLC
75 Gus Mcghee Rd (27508-7683)
PHONE..........................919 496-7029
EMP: 6 **EST:** 2003
SALES (est): 331.65K **Privately Held**
SIC: 2431 1521 Doors and door parts and trim, wood; General remodeling, single-family houses

(G-1328)
INTERNATIONAL INSTRUMENTATION
382 N Carolina 98 Hwy W (27508-7218)
PHONE..........................919 496-4208
Thomas Lancaster, *Genl Mgr*
EMP: 4 **EST:** 2001
SALES (est): 260K **Privately Held**
SIC: 3825 Measuring instruments and meters, electric

Bunnlevel
Harnett County

(G-1329)
B & B BUILDING MAINTENANCE LLC
5318 Hwy 210 S (28323)
PHONE..........................910 494-2715
Bennie Bryant, *Pr*
EMP: 4 **EST:** 2012
SALES (est): 228.97K **Privately Held**
SIC: 3432 Plastic plumbing fixture fittings, assembly

(G-1330)
HEIDELBERG MTLS STHAST AGG LLC
3155 Nc 210 S (28323-8993)
PHONE..........................910 893-8308
Chris Ward, *Mgr*
EMP: 35
SALES (corp-wide): 21.19B **Privately Held**
Web: www.hansonbiz.com
SIC: 3281 5032 1423 Slate products; Stone, crushed or broken; Crushed and broken granite
HQ: Heidelberg Materials Southeast Agg Llc
3237 Satellite Blvd # 30
Duluth GA 30096
770 491-2756

(G-1331)
STRICKLAND BACKHOE
3216 Nc 210 S (28323-8994)
PHONE..........................910 893-5274
Sarah Strickland, *Prin*
EMP: 4 **EST:** 2017
SALES (est): 72.86K **Privately Held**
SIC: 3531 Backhoes

Burgaw
Pender County

(G-1332)
AMERICAN SKIN FOOD GROUP LLC
140 Industrial Dr (28425-5081)
PHONE..........................910 259-2232
Neil Blake, *Managing Member*
EMP: 26 **EST:** 2005
SALES (est): 12.12MM **Privately Held**
Web: www.asfg.com
SIC: 2013 2096 Sausages and other prepared meats; Pork rinds
HQ: Smithfield Foods, Inc.
200 Commerce St
Smithfield VA 23430
757 365-3000

(G-1333)
ATLANTIC CORP WILMINGTON INC
Also Called: Prestige Label
151 Industrial Dr (28425-5080)
PHONE..........................910 259-3600
Tim Kegan, *Manager*
EMP: 50
SALES (corp-wide): 448MM **Privately Held**
Web: www.atlanticpkg.com
SIC: 5113 2621 2679 Industrial and personal service paper; Paper mills; Paper products, converted, nec
PA: Atlantic Corporation Of Wilmington Inc.
806 N 23rd St
Wilmington NC 28405
910 343-0624

(G-1334)
CARDINAL FOODS LLC
201 Progress Dr (28425-4619)
P.O. Box 990 (28425-0990)
PHONE..........................910 259-9407
David Ross, *Pr*
Cory Barnhill, *Prin*
EMP: 25 **EST:** 2021
SALES (est): 9.97MM **Privately Held**
Web: www.cardinalfoodsllc.com
SIC: 5411 2033 Grocery stores; Apple sauce: packaged in cans, jars, etc.

(G-1335)
CARDINAL METALWORKS LLC
1090 E Wilmington Street Ext (28425-3800)
P.O. Box 580 (28425-0580)
PHONE..........................910 259-9990
Max Valentine, *Pr*
Larry Isaacson, *General Vice President**
Thomas Rankin, **
▲ **EMP:** 65 **EST:** 2002
SQ FT: 27,000
SALES (est): 13.31MM **Privately Held**
Web: www.cardinalmetalworks.com
SIC: 3441 Fabricated structural metal

(G-1336)
COSTIN WELDING AND FABRICATION
310 Long Branch Ln (28425-3093)
PHONE..........................910 789-7961
EMP: 4 **EST:** 2017
SALES (est): 47.94K **Privately Held**
SIC: 7692 Welding repair

(G-1337)
DOWNSOUTH WOOD WORKING LLC
12766 Ashton Rd (28425-2942)
PHONE..........................910 259-4617
Dwayne K Moore, *Prin*
EMP: 4 **EST:** 2019
SALES (est): 63.67K **Privately Held**
SIC: 2431 Millwork

(G-1338)
EAST COAST HURRICANE SHUTTERS
4133 Highsmith Rd (28425-2905)
PHONE..........................910 352-5717
EMP: 4 **EST:** 2017
SALES (est): 79.59K **Privately Held**
SIC: 3442 Shutters, door or window: metal

(G-1339)
EDGE-WORKS MANUFACTURING CO
Also Called: Edgeworks
272 W Stag Park Service Rd (28425-4437)
PHONE..........................910 455-9834
EMP: 9 **EST:** 1992
SQ FT: 4,500
SALES (est): 1.31MM **Privately Held**
Web: www.tacticalholsters.com
SIC: 3421 Cutlery

(G-1340)
HARE ASIAN TRADING COMPANY LLC
49 International Rd (28425-4434)
PHONE..........................910 524-4667
Tiong Chen, *Pr*
EMP: 28 **EST:** 2021
SALES (est): 2.36MM **Privately Held**
SIC: 2092 5149 Fresh or frozen fish or seafood chowders, soups, and stews; Canned goods: fruit, vegetables, seafood, meats, etc.

(G-1341)
INTERNATIONAL PAPER COMPANY
Also Called: International Paper
3870 Highsmith Rd (28425-4736)
P.O. Box 710 (28456-0710)
PHONE..........................910 259-1723
Gary Beacher, *Brnch Mgr*
EMP: 5
SALES (corp-wide): 18.92B **Publicly Held**
Web: www.internationalpaper.com
SIC: 2621 Paper mills
PA: International Paper Company
6400 Poplar Ave
Memphis TN 38197
901 419-7000

(G-1342)
JOFRA GRAPHICS INC
Also Called: Bee Line Printing
401 Us Highway 117 S (28425-7742)
PHONE..........................910 259-1717
John Rau, *Pr*
EMP: 4 **EST:** 1970

SQ FT: 3,000
SALES (est): 294.46K **Privately Held**
SIC: **2752** 5943 Offset printing; Office forms and supplies

(G-1343)
KILN-DIRECTCOM
200a Progress Dr (28425-4618)
P.O. Box 159 (28425-0159)
PHONE.................................910 259-9794
EMP: **6 EST:** 2016
SALES (est): 254.63K **Privately Held**
Web: www.kiln-direct.com
SIC: **2421** Sawmills and planing mills, general

(G-1344)
LITTLE REDS ENGRAVING LLC
304 Lake Dr (28425-4448)
PHONE.................................910 599-7747
Bryon Macdonald, *Managing Member*
EMP: 5
SALES (est): 79.3K **Privately Held**
SIC: **3699** 7389 Laser systems and equipment; Business services, nec

(G-1345)
M&S ENTERPRISES INC
784 New Rd (28425-3128)
PHONE.................................910 259-1763
Mattie Boston, *Pr*
Mack Smith, *Ch Bd*
EMP: **9 EST:** 1994
SALES (est): 126.63K **Privately Held**
SIC: **1389** Construction, repair, and dismantling services

(G-1346)
NIELS JORGENSEN COMPANY INC
200 Progress Dr (28425-4618)
P.O. Box 159 (28425-0159)
PHONE.................................910 259-1624
EMP: **5 EST:** 1994
SQ FT: 5,000
SALES (est): 1.12MM **Privately Held**
Web: www.njc-usa.com
SIC: **3535** Conveyors and conveying equipment

(G-1347)
POST VOICE LLC
201 E Fremont St (28425-5092)
PHONE.................................910 259-9111
EMP: **6 EST:** 2013
SALES (est): 90.84K **Privately Held**
Web: www.postvoiceonline.com
SIC: **2711** Newspapers, publishing and printing

(G-1348)
RETRO MEADERY LLC
580 Meadow Ln (28425-3047)
PHONE.................................910 622-7098
EMP: **5 EST:** 2020
SALES (est): 74.17K **Privately Held**
Web: www.retromeadery.com
SIC: **2084** Wines

(G-1349)
ROGERS MANUFACTURING COMPANY (PA)
Also Called: Rogers Portable Buildings
505 W Wilmington St (28425-5577)
P.O. Box 1403 (28425-1403)
PHONE.................................910 259-9898
Aubrey A Rogers Iii, *Pr*
Joy C Rogers, *Sec*
EMP: **6 EST:** 1975
SQ FT: 6,000
SALES (est): 709.95K

SALES (corp-wide): 709.95K **Privately Held**
SIC: **3448** 1521 Buildings, portable: prefabricated metal; Patio and deck construction and repair

(G-1350)
SKIN BOYS LLC
Also Called: American Skin
140 Industrial Dr (28425-5081)
PHONE.................................910 259-2232
Neil Blake, *Managing Member*
EMP: **24 EST:** 1998
SQ FT: 40,000
SALES (est): 2.1MM **Privately Held**
SIC: **2096** 2013 Pork rinds; Sausages and other prepared meats

(G-1351)
SOLO FOODS LLC
201w Progress Dr (28425-4619)
P.O. Box 990 (28425-0990)
PHONE.................................910 259-9407
Willie R Moore, *Managing Member*
EMP: **10 EST:** 2001
SQ FT: 30,000
SALES (est): 365.83K **Privately Held**
Web: www.solofoods.com
SIC: **2099** Food preparations, nec

(G-1352)
SOUTHERN PRINTING COMPANY INC
203 S Dudley St (28425-5542)
P.O. Box 833 (28425-0833)
PHONE.................................910 259-4807
Benjamin R Pusey, *Pr*
Benjamin J Pusey, *Pr*
Matt Pusey, *VP*
EMP: **4 EST:** 1962
SQ FT: 3,000
SALES (est): 441.51K **Privately Held**
Web: southernprinting.webs.com
SIC: **5731** 2752 5943 Radio, television, and electronic stores; Offset printing; Office forms and supplies

(G-1353)
TEHAN COMPANY INC
Also Called: Tehan Distributing
2620 Stag Park Rd (28425-3360)
PHONE.................................800 283-7290
Harry Tehan, *CEO*
Colleen Bannerman, *Treas*
Tom Cox, *Svc Ex*
EMP: **5 EST:** 1957
SALES (est): 383.71K **Privately Held**
SIC: **3861** Photographic equipment and supplies

(G-1354)
VACS AMERICA INC
3490 Stag Park Rd (28425-3370)
PHONE.................................910 259-9854
EMP: **7 EST:** 1995
SQ FT: 2,900
SALES (est): 639.08K **Privately Held**
SIC: **3589** 8731 Vacuum cleaners and sweepers, electric: industrial; Commercial physical research

(G-1355)
W R RAYSON EXPORT LTD
720 S Dickerson St (28425-4904)
PHONE.................................910 686-5802
Michael Di Martino, *Pr*
Jean Swanson, *
▲ EMP: **23 EST:** 1978
SALES (est): 984.57K **Privately Held**
Web: www.wrraysonexport.com
SIC: **2679** Paper products, converted, nec

(G-1356)
WALKER PALLET COMPANY INC
3802 New Savannah Rd (28425-4126)
PHONE.................................910 259-2235
Harold Walker, *Pr*
EMP: **14 EST:** 1987
SQ FT: 10,000
SALES (est): 1.2MM **Privately Held**
SIC: **2448** Pallets, wood

(G-1357)
WELLS PORK AND BEEF PDTS INC
750 Croomsbridge Rd (28425-7964)
PHONE.................................910 259-2523
Teresa Swinson, *Pr*
EMP: **12 EST:** 2008
SALES (est): 867.68K **Privately Held**
Web: www.wellspork.com
SIC: **2011** Pork products, from pork slaughtered on site

(G-1358)
WILMINGTON BOX COMPANY
101 Industrial Dr (28425-5080)
P.O. Box 2106 (28402-2106)
PHONE.................................910 259-0402
EMP: **23 EST:** 1986
SQ FT: 29,000
SALES (est): 4.22MM **Privately Held**
Web: www.hoodcontainer.com
SIC: **2653** Boxes, corrugated: made from purchased materials

(G-1359)
WINDSOR FIBERGLASS INC
301 Progress Dr (28425-3280)
P.O. Box 597 (28425-0597)
PHONE.................................910 259-0057
Robert I Handler, *Pr*
Curtis Howard, *VP*
David Riebe, *VP*
EMP: **13 EST:** 1990
SALES (est): 511.99K **Privately Held**
Web: www.windsorfiberglass.com
SIC: **2221** Fiberglass fabrics

Burlington
Alamance County

(G-1360)
A SQUARED PRO SERVICES LLC
3441 Brookstone Dr (27215-9099)
PHONE.................................336 675-3546
Jeremy Ashley, *Owner*
EMP: **6 EST:** 2017
SALES (est): 100.09K **Privately Held**
Web: www.asquaredproservices.com
SIC: **3732** Boatbuilding and repairing

(G-1361)
ABEE CUSTOM SIGNS INC
544 Chapel Hill Rd (27215-6449)
P.O. Box 2514 (27216-2514)
PHONE.................................336 229-1554
Kyle Abee, *Pr*
EMP: **7 EST:** 1997
SALES (est): 494.12K **Privately Held**
Web: www.abeecustomsigns.com
SIC: **3993** Signs, not made in custom sign painting shops

(G-1362)
ALAMANCE FOODS INC (PA)
Also Called: Triton Water
840 Plantation Dr (27215-6711)
PHONE.................................336 226-6392
William C Scott Senior, *Ch*
Bill Scott, *
▼ EMP: **160 EST:** 1959

SQ FT: 40,000
SALES (est): 71.4MM
SALES (corp-wide): 71.4MM **Privately Held**
SIC: **2026** 2899 2024 2086 Milk and cream, except fermented, cultured, and flavored; Distilled water; Ice cream and frozen desserts; Fruit drinks (less than 100% juice): packaged in cans, etc.

(G-1363)
ALAMANCE KAFFEE WERKS LLC
3105 Midland Ct (27215-9148)
PHONE.................................662 617-4573
Daniel Krenzer, *Managing Member*
EMP: **19 EST:** 2016
SALES (est): 457.41K **Privately Held**
SIC: **5812** 2095 Coffee shop; Roasted coffee

(G-1364)
AMERICAN MULTIMEDIA INC (PA)
Also Called: American Media International
2609 Tucker St (27215-8857)
PHONE.................................336 229-7101
Bill B Brit, *Pr*
Richard Clark, *Pr*
Peggy Britt, *Sec*
Jay Jones, *CFO*
Dave Embler, *Sr VP*
EMP: **85 EST:** 1978
SQ FT: 180,000
SALES (est): 4.93MM
SALES (corp-wide): 4.93MM **Privately Held**
SIC: **7819** 2752 3652 2791 Video tape or disk reproduction; Offset printing; Magnetic tape (audio): prerecorded; Typesetting

(G-1365)
AMERICAN YARN LLC
1305 Graham St (27217-6148)
P.O. Box 1410 (27253-1410)
PHONE.................................919 614-1542
Pierre Willy Simmen, *Admn*
EMP: **13 EST:** 2006
SQ FT: 200,000
SALES (est): 459.85K **Privately Held**
Web: www.american-yarn.com
SIC: **2221** Textile warping, on a contract basis

(G-1366)
APOLLO CHEMICAL CORP
2001 Willow Spring Ln (27215-8854)
P.O. Box 2176 (27216-2176)
PHONE.................................336 226-1161
Dexter R Barbee Senior, *Ch Bd*
Rocky Butler, *CEO*
James Brown, *CFO*
◆ EMP: **89 EST:** 1977
SQ FT: 50,000
SALES (est): 17.25MM
SALES (corp-wide): 441.56MM **Privately Held**
Web: www.apollochemical.com
SIC: **2819** Industrial inorganic chemicals, nec
PA: Mount Vernon Mills, Inc.
503 S Main St
Mauldin SC 29662
864 688-7100

(G-1367)
ARMEN STONE LLC ✪
322 Fonville St (27217-2626)
PHONE.................................743 228-3901
EMP: **8 EST:** 2022
SALES (est): 426.38K **Privately Held**
SIC: **3281** Household articles, except furniture: cut stone

GEOGRAPHIC SECTION

Burlington - Alamance County (G-1392)

(G-1368)
ATLANTIC COAST SCREEN PRTG LLC
2312 Airpark Rd (27215-8818)
PHONE..................910 200-0818
Brian Brevard Harris, *Admn*
EMP: 5 EST: 2016
SALES (est): 204.37K Privately Held
Web: www.atlanticcoastscreenprinting.com
SIC: 2759 Screen printing

(G-1369)
ATLANTIC SIGN MEDIA INC
111 Trail One Ste 101 (27215-5672)
P.O. Box 4205 (27215-0902)
PHONE..................336 584-1375
Richard Orcutt, *VP*
EMP: 12 EST: 2001
SALES (est): 441.3K Privately Held
Web: www.atlanticsignmedia.com
SIC: 3993 Signs, not made in custom sign painting shops

(G-1370)
ATLAS LIGHTING PRODUCTS INC
Also Called: Atlas American Lighting
1406 S Mebane St (27215-6443)
PHONE..................336 222-9258
James Clark, *CEO*
James Galeese, *Treas*
◆ EMP: 137 EST: 1992
SQ FT: 300,000
SALES (est): 44.21MM
SALES (corp-wide): 496.98MM Publicly Held
Web: www.atlaslightingproducts.com
SIC: 3645 3646 Residential lighting fixtures; Commercial lighting fixtures
PA: Lsi Industries Inc.
10000 Alliance Rd
Blue Ash OH 45242
513 793-3200

(G-1371)
AUNT TEE LLC ✪
1327 N Beaumont Ct Apt B (27217-1785)
PHONE..................336 269-9466
EMP: 4 EST: 2022
SALES (est): 73.28K Privately Held
SIC: 2759 Screen printing

(G-1372)
AUTO TRIM DESIGN
614 Chapel Hill Rd (27215-6451)
PHONE..................336 747-3309
EMP: 4 EST: 2019
SALES (est): 110.16K Privately Held
Web: www.autotrimgraphics.com
SIC: 3993 Signs and advertising specialties

(G-1373)
AUTOSOUND 2000 INC
2557 Faucette Ln (27217-8913)
PHONE..................336 227-3434
Richard Clark, *Pr*
Dave Navone, *VP*
Wanda Hicks, *Off Mgr*
EMP: 4 EST: 1991
SALES (est): 275.64K Privately Held
Web: www.autosound2000.com
SIC: 2741 Newsletter publishing

(G-1374)
B&S SHINGLE SAVERS INC
Also Called: B & S Exterior Cleaning
4459 Bellemont Mount Hermon Rd (27215-8932)
PHONE..................336 264-3898
EMP: 4 EST: 2019
SALES (est): 75.42K Privately Held
SIC: 3732 Boatbuilding and repairing

(G-1375)
BARNHILL CONTRACTING COMPANY
APAC
1858 Huffman Mill Rd (27215-8898)
P.O. Box 1782 (27216-1782)
PHONE..................336 584-1306
Leonard Conway, *Mgr*
EMP: 11
SQ FT: 700
SALES (corp-wide): 389.14MM Privately Held
Web: www.barnhillcontracting.com
SIC: 2951 1771 Asphalt and asphaltic paving mixtures (not from refineries); Blacktop (asphalt) work
PA: Barnhill Contracting Company Inc
800 Tiffany Blvd Ste 200
Rocky Mount NC 27804
252 823-1021

(G-1376)
BNC NUTRITION LLC
1452a Industry Dr (27215-8951)
PHONE..................336 567-0104
EMP: 5 EST: 2011
SALES (est): 286.13K Privately Held
SIC: 2023 Dietary supplements, dairy and non-dairy based

(G-1377)
BNNANO INC
2119 W Webb Ave (27217-1065)
PHONE..................844 926-6266
Steve Wilcenski, *CEO*
EMP: 12 EST: 2016
SALES (est): 1.17MM Privately Held
Web: www.bnnano.com
SIC: 2899 Chemical preparations, nec

(G-1378)
BONAVENTURE CO LLC
Also Called: Peaches 'n Cream
1147 Saint Marks Church Rd Ste G (27215-9825)
PHONE..................336 584-7530
EMP: 15 EST: 1998
SQ FT: 2,700
SALES (est): 2.17MM Privately Held
Web: www.properprincess.com
SIC: 2369 Children's snowsuits, coats, and jackets

(G-1379)
BROOKS MFG SOLUTIONS INC
418 N Main St (27217-3908)
PHONE..................336 438-1280
Troy Brooks, *CEO*
Nancy Brooks, *Prin*
EMP: 15 EST: 2010
SALES (est): 1.03MM Privately Held
SIC: 3613 Control panels, electric

(G-1380)
BROTHERS METAL FAB INC
330 Holly Hill Ln (27215-5690)
PHONE..................336 270-3761
Michael D Brothers, *Owner*
EMP: 10 EST: 2016
SALES (est): 830.3K Privately Held
SIC: 3312 Blast furnaces and steel mills

(G-1381)
BURLINGTON MACHINE SERVICE
632 Chapel Hill Rd (27215-6664)
P.O. Box 1374 (27216-1374)
PHONE..................336 228-6758
R Mike Bryan, *Owner*
EMP: 5 EST: 1970
SQ FT: 1,800
SALES (est): 404.53K Privately Held
SIC: 3599 Custom machinery

(G-1382)
C S AMERICA INC (HQ)
1305 Graham St (27217-6148)
◆ EMP: 45 EST: 1997
SALES (est): 18.41MM Privately Held
SIC: 2282 Throwing and winding mills
PA: Chil Sung Textiles Co., Ltd.
80 Busong 1-Gil, Jiksan-Eup, Seobuk-Gu
Cheonan 31038

(G-1383)
CARAUSTAR BRLNGTON RGID BOX IN
Also Called: Burlington Rigid Box Plant
322 Fonville St (27217-2626)
P.O. Box 240 (27216-0240)
PHONE..................336 226-1616
Peggy Tew, *Sec*
Johnny Coffee, *
EMP: 48 EST: 1908
SQ FT: 125,000
SALES (est): 2.45MM
SALES (corp-wide): 5.22B Publicly Held
SIC: 2657 2653 2631 Folding paperboard boxes; Corrugated and solid fiber boxes; Paperboard mills
HQ: Caraustar Industries, Inc.
5000 Astell Pwdr Sprng Rd
Austell GA 30106
770 948-3101

(G-1384)
CAROLINA BIOLOGICAL SUPPLY COMPANY (PA)
Also Called: Carolina Biological Supply Co
2700 York Rd (27215-3387)
PHONE..................336 584-0381
◆ EMP: 220 EST: 1927
SALES (est): 82.68MM
SALES (corp-wide): 82.68MM Privately Held
Web: www.carolina.com
SIC: 5049 2836 3829 3826 Laboratory equipment, except medical or dental; Biological products, except diagnostic; Measuring and controlling devices, nec; Analytical instruments

(G-1385)
CAROLINA DYEING AND FINSHG LLC
220 Elmira St (27217-1322)
PHONE..................336 227-2770
Ashok Dhingra, *Executive President*
EMP: 50 EST: 2015
SALES (est): 167.84K Privately Held
SIC: 2269 Linen fabrics: dyeing, finishing, and printing
PA: Stanek Netting Co. Inc.
111 Orange St
Bloomfield NJ 07003

(G-1386)
CAROLINA HOSIERY MILLS INC
710 Koury Dr (27215-6721)
PHONE..................336 226-5581
EMP: 7
SALES (corp-wide): 22.87MM Privately Held
Web: www.carolinahosiery.com
SIC: 2252 Hosiery, nec
PA: Carolina Hosiery Mills, Inc.
2316 Tucker St
Burlington NC 27215
336 570-2129

(G-1387)
CAROLINA HOSIERY MILLS INC
735 Koury Dr (27215-6720)
P.O. Box 850 (27216-0850)
PHONE..................336 226-5581
Drew Dunn, *Brnch Mgr*
EMP: 7
SALES (corp-wide): 22.87MM Privately Held
Web: www.carolinahosiery.com
SIC: 2252 Hosiery, nec
PA: Carolina Hosiery Mills, Inc.
2316 Tucker St
Burlington NC 27215
336 570-2129

(G-1388)
CAROLINA HOSIERY MILLS INC (PA)
2316 Tucker St. Extension (27215-6741)
P.O. Box 850 (27216-0850)
PHONE..................336 570-2129
Maurice J Koury, *Pr*
Ernest A Koury Senior, *VP*
Ernest A Koury Junior, *VP*
Miltom E Petty, *
▲ EMP: 40 EST: 1946
SQ FT: 90,000
SALES (est): 22.87MM
SALES (corp-wide): 22.87MM Privately Held
Web: www.carolinahosiery.com
SIC: 2252 Hosiery, nec

(G-1389)
CARY KEISLER INC
1372 Tiki Ln (27215-8241)
PHONE..................336 586-9333
Cary Keisler, *Mgr*
EMP: 6 EST: 2016
SALES (est): 143.73K Privately Held
SIC: 2099 Food preparations, nec

(G-1390)
CDP INC
4014 Forbes Way (27215-9439)
PHONE..................336 270-6151
EMP: 8 EST: 2011
SALES (est): 98.39K Privately Held
Web: www.cdp-inc.com
SIC: 7372 Prepackaged software

(G-1391)
CEDARLANE LABORATORIES USA
Also Called: Cedarlane
1210 Turrentine St (27215-6836)
PHONE..................336 513-5135
Cindy Greer, *Pr*
John Course, *VP*
EMP: 23 EST: 2005
SALES (est): 8.04MM Privately Held
Web: www.cedarlanelabs.com
SIC: 2836 8731 Biological products, except diagnostic; Biotechnical research, commercial

(G-1392)
CENTRAL CAROLINA PRODUCTS INC
2804 Troxler Rd (27215-8534)
PHONE..................336 226-1449
Diego Diaz, *Brnch Mgr*
EMP: 110
Web: www.centralcarolinaproducts.com
SIC: 3089 Automotive parts, plastic
PA: Central Carolina Products, Inc.
250 W Old Glencoe Rd
Burlington NC 27217

Burlington - Alamance County (G-1393)   GEOGRAPHIC SECTION

(G-1393)
CENTRAL CAROLINA PRODUCTS INC (PA)
250 W Old Glencoe Rd (27217-8293)
PHONE................................336 226-0005
Carlos Diaz, *Pr*
EMP: 60 **EST:** 1993
SQ FT: 112,000
SALES (est): 27.92MM **Privately Held**
Web: www.centralcarolinaproducts.com
SIC: 3089 3599 Automotive parts, plastic; Machine and other job shop work

(G-1394)
CHANDLER CON PDTS OF CHRSTNBER
1006 S Church St (27215-5046)
P.O. Box 131 (27216-0131)
PHONE................................336 226-1181
EMP: 7
SALES (corp-wide): 9.34MM **Privately Held**
Web: www.chandlerconcrete.com
SIC: 3273 Ready-mixed concrete
PA: Chandler Concrete Products Of Christianberg Inc
700 Block Ln
Christiansburg VA 24073
540 382-1734

(G-1395)
CHANDLER CONCRETE CO INC (PA)
Also Called: Blue Stone Block Supermarket
1006 S Church St (27215-5046)
P.O. Box 131 (27216-0131)
PHONE................................336 272-6127
Ted Chandler, *Pr*
Thomas Chandler, *
Robert Chandler, *
Madeline Chandler, *
EMP: 75 **EST:** 1974
SALES (est): 153.25MM **Privately Held**
Web: www.chandlerconcrete.com
SIC: 3273 Ready-mixed concrete

(G-1396)
COBB SIGN COMPANY INCORPORATED
528 Elmira St (27217-1328)
P.O. Box 5030 (27216-5030)
PHONE................................336 227-0181
Kenneth Speagle, *Pr*
EMP: 15 **EST:** 1924
SQ FT: 35,000
SALES (est): 499.68K **Privately Held**
Web: www.cobbsign.com
SIC: 3993 Signs and advertising specialties

(G-1397)
COMMERCIAL METALS COMPANY
Park Road (27216)
PHONE................................336 584-0333
EMP: 8
SALES (corp-wide): 8.8B **Publicly Held**
Web: www.cmc.com
SIC: 3312 Blast furnaces and steel mills
PA: Commercial Metals Company
6565 N Macarthur Blvd # 800
Irving TX 75039
214 689-4300

(G-1398)
COMMERCIAL SPCLTY TRCK HLDNGS
1425 Brittney Ln (27215-9155)
PHONE................................859 234-1100
EMP: 196
SALES (corp-wide): 52.72MM **Privately Held**
Web: www.ezpacktrucks.com
SIC: 3273 Ready-mixed concrete
PA: Commercial Specialty Truck Holdings, Llc
200 Ladish Rd
Cynthiana KY 41031
859 234-1100

(G-1399)
COPLAND FABRICS INC
Also Called: Copland
1714 Carolina Mill Rd (27217-7837)
P.O. Box 1208 (27216-1208)
PHONE................................336 226-0272
EMP: 300
Web: www.coplandfabrics.com
SIC: 2221 Manmade and synthetic broadwoven fabrics

(G-1400)
COPLAND INDUSTRIES INC
1714 Carolina Mill Rd (27217-7837)
P.O. Box 1208 (27216-1208)
PHONE................................336 226-0272
◆ **EMP:** 355
SIC: 5131 2221 2211 Piece goods and other fabrics; Broadwoven fabric mills, manmade; Pocketing twill, cotton

(G-1401)
CROSS MANUFACTURING LLC
2505 Parrish St (27215-4423)
PHONE................................336 269-6542
John Agner, *Owner*
EMP: 6 **EST:** 2016
SALES (est): 247.75K **Privately Held**
SIC: 3999 Manufacturing industries, nec

(G-1402)
CS CAROLINA INC
1305 Graham St (27217-6148)
PHONE................................336 578-0110
Intae Joo, *Pr*
◆ **EMP:** 5 **EST:** 2008
SALES (est): 1.95MM **Privately Held**
SIC: 2281 Yarn spinning mills
HQ: C S America, Inc.
1305 Graham St
Burlington NC 27217

(G-1403)
CT-NASSAU TICKING LLC
1504 Anthony Rd (27215-8978)
P.O. Box 160 (27201-0160)
PHONE................................336 570-0091
Ernie Farley, *
Carl Carpenter, *
John Bauman, *
◆ **EMP:** 27 **EST:** 2000
SQ FT: 45,400
SALES (est): 8.22MM
SALES (corp-wide): 28.05MM **Privately Held**
Web: www.ctnassau.com
SIC: 2221 2211 Broadwoven fabric mills, manmade; Tickings
PA: Continental Ticking Corporation Of America
4101 S Nc 62
Alamance NC 27201
336 570-0091

(G-1404)
CULP INC
Also Called: Culp of Mississippi
2742 Tucker St # A (27215-8860)
PHONE................................662 844-7144
Tanya Scott, *Mgr*
EMP: 35
SALES (corp-wide): 234.93MM **Publicly Held**
Web: www.culp.com
SIC: 2211 5131 Upholstery fabrics, cotton; Piece goods and notions
PA: Culp, Inc.
1823 Eastchester Dr
High Point NC 27265
336 889-5161

(G-1405)
CUSTOM ENTERPRISES INC
129 E Ruffin St (27217-3959)
P.O. Box 1406 (27217-1406)
PHONE................................336 226-8296
Brian J Kelly, *Pr*
Sarah Sykes, *Sec*
▲ **EMP:** 7 **EST:** 1978
SQ FT: 40,000
SALES (est): 992.57K **Privately Held**
Web: www.customenterprisesinc.com
SIC: 3552 3441 3498 7692 Textile machinery; Fabricated structural metal; Tube fabricating (contract bending and shaping); Welding repair

(G-1406)
DICKSON ELBERTON MILL INC
1831 N Park Ave (27217-1137)
PHONE................................336 226-3556
Allen E Gant, *Pr*
Allen Gant, *Pr*
Carl Wallace, *VP*
EMP: 6 **EST:** 2005
SALES (est): 107.22K **Privately Held**
SIC: 2399 Military insignia, textile

(G-1407)
DISRUPTIVE ENTERPRISES LLC (PA)
Also Called: Primaforce
1452 Industry Dr (27215-8951)
PHONE................................336 567-0104
EMP: 10 **EST:** 2017
SALES (est): 2.42MM
SALES (corp-wide): 2.42MM **Privately Held**
Web: www.disruptive-enterprises.com
SIC: 2023 Dietary supplements, dairy and non-dairy based

(G-1408)
DODSON DEFENSE LLC
4756 Blanchard Rd (27215-6741)
PHONE................................336 421-9649
EMP: 5 **EST:** 2017
SALES (est): 92.84K **Privately Held**
SIC: 3812 Defense systems and equipment

(G-1409)
ELDER HOSIERY MILLS INC
139 Homewood Ave (27217-2835)
P.O. Box 2377 (27216-2377)
PHONE................................336 226-0673
Delos M Elder, *Pr*
John F Elder, *
EMP: 10 **EST:** 1931
SQ FT: 50,000
SALES (est): 246.31K **Privately Held**
Web: www.elderhosiery.com
SIC: 2252 Socks

(G-1410)
ELEVATE TEXTILES INC
906 N Anthony St (27217-6663)
PHONE................................336 379-6220
Brandon Crawley, *Brnch Mgr*
EMP: 5
SALES (corp-wide): 1.98B **Privately Held**
Web: www.elevatetextiles.com
SIC: 5023 2221 Homefurnishings; Broadwoven fabric mills, manmade
HQ: Elevate Textiles, Inc.
121 W Trade St Ste 1700
Charlotte NC 28202

(G-1411)
ENGINEERED CONTROLS INTL LLC
Also Called: Rego
3181 Lear Dr (27215-8817)
P.O. Box 247 (27244-0247)
PHONE................................336 226-3244
EMP: 229
SALES (corp-wide): 8.44B **Publicly Held**
Web: www.regoproducts.com
SIC: 3491 3494 Industrial valves; Valves and pipe fittings, nec
HQ: Engineered Controls International, Llc
100 Rego Dr
Elon NC 27244

(G-1412)
ERICS CHEESECAKES LLC
2439 Morningside Drive (27217-3147)
PHONE................................336 264-4303
Eric Hurdle, *Prin*
EMP: 5 **EST:** 2011
SALES (est): 70.64K **Privately Held**
Web: www.ericscheesecakes.com
SIC: 2591 Window blinds

(G-1413)
FALCON INDUSTRIES LLC
2834 Bedford St (27215-4673)
PHONE................................336 229-1048
EMP: 5 **EST:** 2019
SALES (est): 77.49K **Privately Held**
SIC: 3599 Machine shop, jobbing and repair

(G-1414)
FLYNT/AMTEX INC (PA)
Also Called: Tex Care Medical
2908 Alamance Rd (27215-5462)
PHONE................................336 226-0621
Ray Baynard, *CEO*
Robert Gibb, *
Jim Adams, *
Captain Ross Bryson, *Prin*
Chuck Flynt, *
◆ **EMP:** 49 **EST:** 1990
SQ FT: 120,000
SALES (est): 9.71MM
SALES (corp-wide): 9.71MM **Privately Held**
Web: www.carriff.com
SIC: 2221 Manmade and synthetic broadwoven fabrics

(G-1415)
FOTO GRAFIX
341 S Main St (27215-5836)
PHONE................................336 570-1885
Mary Williams, *Ch*
EMP: 6 **EST:** 1991
SALES (est): 75.4K **Privately Held**
Web: www.displayguys.com
SIC: 3993 Signs and advertising specialties

(G-1416)
FUJI FOODS INC
363 W Old Glencoe Rd (27217-8294)
PHONE................................336 226-8817
Maria Keating, *Pr*
EMP: 5
SQ FT: 10,394
Web: www.fujifoodsusa.com
SIC: 2087 2099 Flavoring extracts and syrups, nec; Food preparations, nec
HQ: Fuji Foods Inc.
6206 Corporate Park Dr
Browns Summit NC 27214
336 375-3111

GEOGRAPHIC SECTION
Burlington - Alamance County (G-1441)

(G-1417)
FULLER SPECIALTY COMPANY INC
Also Called: Clay Creek Athletics
804 Bradley St (27215-6806)
P.O. Box 947 (27216-0947)
PHONE...................................336 226-3446
Mark Fuller, *Pr*
Steve Wall, *VP*
Debbie Fuller, *Sec*
EMP: 19 **EST**: 1944
SQ FT: 10,000
SALES (est): 829.24K **Privately Held**
Web: www.claycreek.com
SIC: **3496** 2393 Miscellaneous fabricated wire products; Textile bags

(G-1418)
G S MATERIALS INC
1521 Huffman Mill Rd (27215-8815)
P.O. Box 1335 (27216-1335)
PHONE...................................336 584-1745
Ronald Kirkpatrick Senior, *Pr*
Karen Hilliard, *
EMP: 33 **EST**: 1984
SQ FT: 2,500
SALES (est): 5.02MM **Privately Held**
SIC: **1442** Sand mining

(G-1419)
GENERAL MCH WLDG OF BURLINGTON
3304 Maple Ave (27215-7005)
PHONE...................................336 227-5400
Thomas P Gathings, *Pr*
Lynda Gathings, *Sec*
EMP: 8 **EST**: 1971
SQ FT: 10,000
SALES (est): 667.32K **Privately Held**
Web: www.e-gmw.com
SIC: **3599** 7692 Machine shop, jobbing and repair; Welding repair

(G-1420)
GERRINGER ENTERPRISES
180 Spoon Dr (27217-3279)
PHONE...................................336 227-6535
Glenn R Gerringer, *Owner*
EMP: 4 **EST**: 1988
SALES (est): 180.77K **Privately Held**
SIC: **3549** Metalworking machinery, nec

(G-1421)
GFM INDUSTRIES LLC
3948 Clapp Mill Rd (27215-9289)
PHONE...................................614 439-5349
EMP: 4 **EST**: 2016
SALES (est): 93.13K **Privately Held**
SIC: **3999** Manufacturing industries, nec

(G-1422)
GIBSON ACCUMULATOR LLC
2208 Airpark Rd (27215-8824)
P.O. Box 44 (27249-0044)
PHONE...................................336 449-4753
EMP: 17 **EST**: 2004
SALES (est): 2.71MM **Privately Held**
SIC: **3569** Assembly machines, non-metalworking

(G-1423)
GLEN RAVEN INC (PA)
Also Called: Glenraven.com
192 Glen Raven Rd (27217-1085)
PHONE...................................336 227-6211
◆ **EMP**: 150 **EST**: 1880
SALES (est): 878.83MM
SALES (corp-wide): 878.83MM **Privately Held**
Web: www.glenraven.com
SIC: **2221** 2281 2261 2211 Manmade and synthetic broadwoven fabrics; Manmade and synthetic fiber yarns, spun; Finishing plants, cotton; Broadwoven fabric mills, cotton

(G-1424)
GLEN RVEN TCHNICAL FABRICS LLC (HQ)
Also Called: Glenraven.com
1831 N Park Ave (27217-1137)
PHONE...................................336 227-6211
Harold W Hill Junior, *Pr*
EMP: 39 **EST**: 1999
SALES (est): 95.39MM
SALES (corp-wide): 878.83MM **Privately Held**
Web: www.glenraven.com
SIC: **2221** Broadwoven fabric mills, manmade
PA: Glen Raven, Inc.
    192 Glen Raven Rd
    Burlington NC 27217
    336 227-6211

(G-1425)
GLEN RVEN TCHNICAL FABRICS LLC
Also Called: Park Ave Division
1821 N Park Ave (27217-1137)
PHONE...................................336 229-5576
Ricky Michael, *Brnch Mgr*
EMP: 111
SALES (corp-wide): 878.83MM **Privately Held**
Web: www.glenraven.com
SIC: **2281** 2221 2269 2261 Manmade and synthetic fiber yarns, spun; Manmade and synthetic broadwoven fabrics; Finishing plants, nec; Finishing plants, cotton
HQ: Glen Raven Technical Fabrics Llc
    1831 N Park Ave
    Burlington NC 27217
    336 227-6211

(G-1426)
GRAHAM DYEING & FINISHING INC
240 Hawkins St (27217-3926)
P.O. Box 2857 (27216-2857)
PHONE...................................336 228-9981
Greg Gravitte, *Pr*
Angela Gravitte, *
◆ **EMP**: 75 **EST**: 1987
SQ FT: 40,000
SALES (est): 4.92MM **Privately Held**
SIC: **2252** Socks

(G-1427)
HAAND
Also Called: Haand Hospitality
413 Tucker St (27215-5961)
PHONE...................................336 350-7597
Christopher Pence, *Pr*
Christopher Pence, *Prin*
Mark Warren, *Prin*
EMP: 16 **EST**: 2013
SALES (est): 947.75K **Privately Held**
Web: www.haand.us
SIC: **3269** Cookware: stoneware, coarse earthenware, and pottery

(G-1428)
HOLT HOSIERY MILLS INC
733 Koury Dr (27215-6720)
P.O. Box 1757 (27216-1757)
PHONE...................................336 227-1431
◆ **EMP**: 200
Web: www.holthosiery.com
SIC: **2252** Hosiery, nec

(G-1429)
HOLT SUBLIMATION PRTG PDTS INC (PA)
2208 Airpark Rd (27215-8824)
P.O. Box 2017 (27216-2017)
PHONE...................................336 222-3600
Frank Holt Iii, *CEO*
◆ **EMP**: 152 **EST**: 1947
SQ FT: 100,000
SALES (est): 9.36MM
SALES (corp-wide): 9.36MM **Privately Held**
Web: www.holtsublimation.com
SIC: **2261** 2262 2789 Printing of cotton broadwoven fabrics; Printing, manmade fiber and silk broadwoven fabrics; Bookbinding and related work

(G-1430)
HONDA AERO INC (HQ)
2989 Tucker Street Ext (27215-8904)
PHONE...................................336 226-2376
Atsukuni Waragai, *Pr*
EMP: 100 **EST**: 2004
SQ FT: 130,000
SALES (est): 45.17MM **Privately Held**
Web: www.honda.com
SIC: **3724** Aircraft engines and engine parts
PA: Honda Motor Co., Ltd.
    2-1-1, Minamiaoyama
    Minato-Ku TKY 107-0

(G-1431)
HUFFMAN SALES AND SERVICE LLC
326 Macarthur Ln (27217-8739)
PHONE...................................828 234-0693
EMP: 6 **EST**: 2009
SALES (est): 499.54K **Privately Held**
SIC: **2011** Meat by-products, from meat slaughtered on site

(G-1432)
HUMMINGBIRD 3D SOLUTIONS LLC
256 W Trade St (27217-2658)
PHONE...................................336 792-6637
Brian Isley, *Pr*
EMP: 5 **EST**: 2018
SALES (est): 333.28K **Privately Held**
SIC: **3569** Assembly machines, non-metalworking

(G-1433)
HYDRO EXTRUSION USA LLC
1512 Industry Dr (27215-8910)
PHONE...................................336 227-8826
Jerry Nies, *VP*
EMP: 63
SIC: **3354** 3644 Aluminum extruded products; Noncurrent-carrying wiring devices
HQ: Hydro Extrusion Usa, Llc
    6250 N River Rd Ste 5000
    Rosemont IL 60018

(G-1434)
IMPACT FULFILLMENT SVCS LLC (PA)
Also Called: Ifs
1601 Anthony Rd (27215-8979)
P.O. Box 2628 (27216-2628)
PHONE...................................336 227-1130
Ray Garcia, *CEO*
Kayleen Haberkorn, *
▲ **EMP**: 145 **EST**: 1998
SQ FT: 650,000
SALES (est): 113.86MM
SALES (corp-wide): 113.86MM **Privately Held**
Web: www.impactfs.com
SIC: **3999** 8748 Advertising curtains; Business consulting, nec

(G-1435)
INDIE SERVICES
205 E Davis St (27215-5987)
PHONE...................................336 524-6966
EMP: 5 **EST**: 2016
SALES (est): 101.67K **Privately Held**
SIC: **2741** Miscellaneous publishing

(G-1436)
INDUSTRIAL PANEL COMPANY LLC (PA)
121 E Market St (27217-3911)
PHONE...................................866 736-1290
Michael L Griggs, *Pr*
EMP: 7 **EST**: 2021
SALES (est): 1.07MM
SALES (corp-wide): 1.07MM **Privately Held**
Web: www.industrialpanelcompany.com
SIC: **3613** Control panels, electric

(G-1437)
INDUSTRIAL PANEL COMPANY LLC
147 N Main St (27217-3901)
PHONE...................................866 736-1290
EMP: 20
SALES (corp-wide): 1.07MM **Privately Held**
Web: www.industrialpanelcompany.com
SIC: **3613** Control panels, electric
PA: Industrial Panel Company, Llc
    121 E Market St
    Burlington NC 27217
    866 736-1290

(G-1438)
INNOVATIVE KNITTING LLC
3720 S Church St (27215-9107)
P.O. Box 2717 (27216-2717)
PHONE...................................336 350-8122
William Bo Foster Iii, *Managing Member*
EMP: 25 **EST**: 2017
SALES (est): 2.06MM **Privately Held**
SIC: **2257** Weft knit fabric mills

(G-1439)
JB II PRINTING LLC
Also Called: PIP Printing
825 S Main St (27215-5740)
PHONE...................................336 222-0717
Jimmy Brumley, *CEO*
Jimmy Brumley, *Managing Member*
EMP: 22 **EST**: 1983
SALES (est): 4.25MM **Privately Held**
Web: www.pip.com
SIC: **2752** 3993 7311 Offset printing; Signs and advertising specialties; Advertising agencies

(G-1440)
JEFFERIES SOCKS LLC
2203 Tucker St (27215-6738)
P.O. Box 850 (27216-0850)
PHONE...................................336 226-7316
▲ **EMP**: 25 **EST**: 1937
SQ FT: 28,000
SALES (est): 4.87MM **Privately Held**
Web: www.jefferiessocks.com
SIC: **2252** Socks

(G-1441)
JOE AND LA INC
326 Mcarthur Ln (27217-8739)
P.O. Box 1516 (27216-1516)
PHONE...................................336 585-0313
John R Michael, *Ch Bd*
Joseph R Michael, *Pr*

Burlington - Alamance County (G-1442)

EMP: 18 **EST:** 1963
SQ FT: 24,800
SALES (est): 2.38MM **Privately Held**
Web: www.dexcoinc.com
SIC: 3599 3444 3549 Machine shop, jobbing and repair; Sheet metalwork; Metalworking machinery, nec

(G-1442)
JON MITCHELL CABINETS
1413 Mccuiston Dr (27215-3345)
PHONE..................336 229-6261
Jonathan Mitchell, *Prin*
EMP: 5 **EST:** 2011
SALES (est): 67.83K **Privately Held**
SIC: 2434 Wood kitchen cabinets

(G-1443)
KCK HOLDING CORP
Also Called: TEC Tran Brake
2215 Airpark Rd (27215-8824)
PHONE..................336 513-0002
▲ **EMP:** 23
Web: www.wabteccorp.com
SIC: 5088 3714 3743 Railroad equipment and supplies; Motor vehicle parts and accessories; Brakes, air and vacuum: railway

(G-1444)
KNIT-WEAR FABRICS INC (PA)
145 N Cobb Ave (27217-2824)
P.O. Box 790 (27216-0790)
PHONE..................336 226-4342
Flavius D Hornaday Iii, *Pr*
David Hornaday, *VP*
EMP: 12 **EST:** 1967
SQ FT: 13,000
SALES (est): 2.28MM
SALES (corp-wide): 2.28MM **Privately Held**
SIC: 2258 2257 Lace and warp knit fabric mills; Weft knit fabric mills

(G-1445)
L & B MONOGRAMS PLUS
413 Maryland Ave (27217-4150)
PHONE..................336 229-0152
Phil Laughlin, *Owner*
EMP: 5 **EST:** 2005
SALES (est): 203.25K **Privately Held**
SIC: 2759 5949 Screen printing; Sewing and needlework

(G-1446)
L & K MACHINING INC
Also Called: Machine Shop, Job Shop
1312 Whitsett St (27215-6977)
P.O. Box 1312 (27253-1312)
PHONE..................336 222-9444
Ronnie Miles, *Pr*
EMP: 10 **EST:** 1997
SQ FT: 11,000
SALES (est): 993.08K **Privately Held**
Web: www.landkmachining.com
SIC: 3599 Machine shop, jobbing and repair

(G-1447)
LABELS TAGS & INSERTS INC
2302 Airpark Rd (27215-8818)
P.O. Box 2137 (27216-2137)
PHONE..................336 227-8485
EMP: 18 **EST:** 1996
SQ FT: 17,000
SALES (est): 4.44MM **Privately Held**
Web: www.labelstagsandinserts.com
SIC: 2759 Commercial printing, nec

(G-1448)
LAKESIDE DYEING & FINSHG INC
423 Lakeside Ave (27217-2329)
PHONE..................336 229-0064
Hooper Harris, *Pr*
EMP: 9 **EST:** 1983
SQ FT: 5,000
SALES (est): 185.16K **Privately Held**
SIC: 2252 2269 2261 Dyeing and finishing hosiery; Finishing plants, nec; Finishing plants, cotton

(G-1449)
LED INTEGRATIONS
415 Trail One (27215-5537)
PHONE..................336 257-9935
Casey Mcintyre, *Prin*
EMP: 4 **EST:** 2017
SALES (est): 230.64K **Privately Held**
Web: www.led-integrations.com
SIC: 3648 Lighting equipment, nec

(G-1450)
LEONARD ALUM UTLTY BLDNGS INC
Also Called: Leonard Building and Truck ACC
2602 Alamance Rd (27215-6256)
PHONE..................336 226-9410
Johanathon Hobbs, *Brnch Mgr*
EMP: 4
SALES (corp-wide): 98.91MM **Privately Held**
Web: www.leonardusa.com
SIC: 5531 3448 Truck equipment and parts; Prefabricated metal buildings
PA: Leonard Aluminum Utility Buildings, Inc.
630 W Indpndnce Blvd
Mount Airy NC 27030
336 789-5018

(G-1451)
LIGNA MACHINERY INC
315 Macarthur Ln (27217-8739)
PHONE..................336 584-0030
H E Wilson Junior, *Pr*
H Ed Wilson Iii, *Sec*
▲ **EMP:** 20 **EST:** 1986
SQ FT: 5,000
SALES (est): 809.93K **Privately Held**
SIC: 3553 5084 Sawmill machines; Industrial machinery and equipment

(G-1452)
LONG J E & SONS GRADING INC (PA)
Also Called: Long, J E Sand & Stone
3218 Foy Jane Trl (27217-7125)
PHONE..................336 228-9706
Anthony E Long, *Pr*
William S Long, *Treas*
EMP: 14 **EST:** 1971
SQ FT: 500
SALES (est): 2.23MM
SALES (corp-wide): 2.23MM **Privately Held**
SIC: 1442 Construction sand and gravel

(G-1453)
MAIN STREET VINYL LLC
321 S Main St (27215-5836)
PHONE..................336 585-3089
Joshua Garrett, *Prin*
EMP: 5 **EST:** 2016
SALES (est): 154.59K **Privately Held**
Web: www.mainstreetvinyl.com
SIC: 3993 Signs and advertising specialties

(G-1454)
MARKELL PUBLISHING COMPANY INC
Also Called: Markell Printing and Prom Pdts
718 E Davis St (27215-5924)
P.O. Box 668 (27216-0668)
PHONE..................336 226-7148
Robert A Forrester, *Pr*
Mark Forrester, *VP*
EMP: 4 **EST:** 1964
SALES (est): 364.97K **Privately Held**
Web: www.markellprinting.com
SIC: 2752 5199 Offset printing; Advertising specialties

(G-1455)
MARTIN MARIETTA MATERIALS INC
Also Called: Martin Marietta Aggregates
1671 Huffman Mill Rd (27215-9211)
PHONE..................336 584-8875
Tommy Jenkins, *Owner*
EMP: 7
Web: www.martinmarietta.com
SIC: 1422 1423 Crushed and broken limestone; Crushed and broken granite
PA: Martin Marietta Materials Inc
4123 Parklake Ave
Raleigh NC 27612

(G-1456)
MARVEL-SCHBLER ARCFT CRBRTORS
2208 Airpark Rd (27215-8824)
P.O. Box 44 (27249-0044)
PHONE..................336 446-0002
EMP: 11 **EST:** 2008
SALES (est): 889.32K **Privately Held**
Web: www.msacarbs.com
SIC: 3592 Carburetors

(G-1457)
MASSEY READY-MIX CONCRETE INC
1421 Railroad St (27217-7054)
P.O. Box 1983 (27216-1983)
PHONE..................336 221-8100
Randy Massey, *Pr*
EMP: 8 **EST:** 1998
SALES (est): 2.03MM **Privately Held**
SIC: 3273 Ready-mixed concrete

(G-1458)
MCCOMB INDUSTRIES LLLP
Also Called: Alexander Fabrics
1311 Industry Dr (27215-8950)
P.O. Box 147 (27216-0147)
PHONE..................336 229-9139
Todd Whitley, *Pt*
▼ **EMP:** 80 **EST:** 2002
SQ FT: 100,000
SALES (est): 9.11MM **Privately Held**
Web: www.mccombind.com
SIC: 2258 Dyeing and finishing lace goods and warp knit fabric

(G-1459)
MCMICHAEL MILLS INC
2050 Willow Spring Ln (27215-8854)
PHONE..................336 584-0134
Dalton L Mcmichael Junior, *Brnch Mgr*
EMP: 40
Web: www.mcmichaelmills.com
SIC: 2241 Rubber and elastic yarns and fabrics
PA: Mcmichael Mills, Inc.
130 Shakey Rd
Mayodan NC 27027

(G-1460)
MEREDITH - WEBB PRTG CO INC
334 N Main St (27217-3906)
P.O. Box 2196 (27216-2196)
PHONE..................336 228-8378
Travers G Webb, *Pr*
George T Webb Ii, *Ch*
Betty N Webb, *
H Cooper Walker, *Stockholder**
EMP: 96 **EST:** 1952
SQ FT: 40,000
SALES (est): 23.1MM **Privately Held**
Web: www.meredithwebb.com
SIC: 7331 2752 Direct mail advertising services; Commercial printing, lithographic

(G-1461)
MIDWAY BLIND & AWNING CO INC
1836 E Webb Ave (27217-7418)
P.O. Box 1761 (27216-1761)
PHONE..................336 226-4532
Randy Minor, *Pr*
Ricky Minor, *VP*
Hazel Minor, *Sec*
EMP: 4 **EST:** 1951
SQ FT: 4,000
SALES (est): 405.31K **Privately Held**
SIC: 1761 1521 3444 Siding contractor; General remodeling, single-family houses; Awnings, sheet metal

(G-1462)
MONGOOSE LLC
Also Called: Noa Living
423 Lakeside Ave (27217-2329)
PHONE..................919 400-0772
Sam Mehme, *CEO*
Sam Mehme, *Managing Member*
EMP: 12 **EST:** 2018
SALES (est): 1.79MM **Privately Held**
Web: www.noaliving.com
SIC: 5023 5021 5713 3281 Rugs; Household furniture; Rugs; Altars, cut stone

(G-1463)
MOUNT VERNON CHEMICALS LLC
Apollo Chemical
2001 Willow Spring Ln (27215-8854)
PHONE..................336 226-1161
EMP: 98
SALES (corp-wide): 441.56MM **Privately Held**
Web: www.apollochemical.com
SIC: 2819 Industrial inorganic chemicals, nec
HQ: Mount Vernon Chemicals Llc
2001 Willow Spring Ln
Burlington NC 27215

(G-1464)
MOUNT VERNON MILLS INC
Apollo Chemical Div
2001 Willow Spring Ln (27215-8854)
PHONE..................336 226-1161
Ed Fish, *Div Pres*
EMP: 411
SALES (corp-wide): 441.56MM **Privately Held**
Web: www.mvmills.com
SIC: 2819 Industrial inorganic chemicals, nec
PA: Mount Vernon Mills, Inc.
503 S Main St
Mauldin SC 29662
864 688-7100

(G-1465)
MTS HOLDINGS CORP INC
2900 Tucker St (27215-9575)
PHONE..................336 227-0151
Michael L Scoggins, *Pr*
Tommy G Scoggins, *
Michael Paul Spierer, *
▲ **EMP:** 35 **EST:** 1965
SQ FT: 60,000
SALES (est): 2.24MM **Privately Held**

GEOGRAPHIC SECTION

Burlington - Alamance County (G-1491)

Web: www.psmachine.com
SIC: 7692 3444 3441 Welding repair; Sheet metalwork; Fabricated structural metal

(G-1466)
NATEL INC
Also Called: Sir Speedy
1257 S Church St (27215-5049)
PHONE....................................336 227-1227
Deva Reece, *Pr*
Tim Clark, *VP*
EMP: 5 EST: 2010
SALES (est): 488.12K **Privately Held**
Web: www.sirspeedy.com
SIC: 2752 Commercial printing, lithographic

(G-1467)
NATIONAL SPINNING CO INC
226 Glen Raven Rd (27217-1026)
PHONE....................................336 226-0141
Ed Atkins, *Mgr*
EMP: 118
SALES (corp-wide): 102.19MM **Privately Held**
Web: www.natspin.com
SIC: 2281 Wool yarn, spun
PA: National Spinning Co., Inc.
    1481 W 2nd St Ste 103
    Washington NC 27889
    252 975-7111

(G-1468)
NC MOTOR VHCL LCNSE PLATE AGCY
Also Called: N C Mtor Vhcl Lcnse Plate Agcy
2668 Ramada Rd (27215-5469)
PHONE....................................336 228-7152
EMP: 7 EST: 1950
SALES (est): 511.36K **Privately Held**
SIC: 3469 Automobile license tags, stamped metal

(G-1469)
OVERMAN CABINET & SUPPLY LLC
Also Called: Overman Building Supply
1168 Saint Marks Church Rd (27215-9796)
PHONE....................................336 584-1349
Kendall Overman, *Managing Member*
Kendall Overman Presmbr, *Mgr*
EMP: 12 EST: 1952
SQ FT: 46,200
SALES (est): 923.25K **Privately Held**
Web: overmanbuildingsupply.blogspot.com
SIC: 5031 2431 Lumber, plywood, and millwork; Millwork

(G-1470)
P&S MACHINING FABRICATION LLC ✪
2900 Tucker St (27215-9575)
PHONE....................................336 227-0151
Michael Paul Spierer, *Managing Member*
EMP: 45 EST: 2022
SALES (est): 3.34MM **Privately Held**
SIC: 3444 Sheet metalwork

(G-1471)
PARADISE PRINTERS
3651 Alamance Rd (27215-9130)
PHONE....................................336 570-2922
Jeffrey Baldwin, *Pr*
Georgia Baldwin, *VP*
EMP: 4 EST: 1981
SQ FT: 3,000
SALES (est): 366.96K **Privately Held**
Web: www.paradiseprinters.com
SIC: 2759 Screen printing

(G-1472)
PICKETT HOSIERY MILLS INC
733 Koury Dr (27215-6720)
P.O. Box 877 (27216-0877)
PHONE....................................336 227-2716
Larry Small, *CEO*
J Nimrod Harris Junior, *Pr*
Amy Harris Deal, *
Christine Harris, *
EMP: 50 EST: 1927
SQ FT: 86,000
SALES (est): 4.55MM **Privately Held**
Web: www.picketthosiery.com
SIC: 2252 Socks

(G-1473)
PIEDMONT METALS BURLINGTON INC
215 Macarthur Ln (27215-8738)
PHONE....................................336 584-7742
Jeremy Troxler, *Pr*
EMP: 23
SALES (est): 1.19MM **Privately Held**
SIC: 3441 Fabricated structural metal

(G-1474)
PINE TREE POETRY
3529 Elk St (27215-8127)
PHONE....................................336 584-0631
Jane Thomas, *Prin*
EMP: 5 EST: 2006
SALES (est): 99.76K **Privately Held**
Web: www.pinetreepoetry.com
SIC: 2741 Miscellaneous publishing

(G-1475)
PIP PRINTING & DOCUMENT SERVIC
Also Called: PIP Printing
717 Chapel Hill Rd (27215-6452)
PHONE....................................336 222-0717
Judy Brumley, *Prin*
EMP: 9 EST: 2008
SALES (est): 19.86K **Privately Held**
Web: www.pip.com
SIC: 2752 Offset printing

(G-1476)
POP PRODUCTS LLC
532 Circle Dr (27215-5012)
PHONE....................................336 263-1884
Ronald L Shive, *Prin*
EMP: 4 EST: 2021
SALES (est): 69.32K **Privately Held**
SIC: 7822 2035 Motion picture and tape distribution; Dressings, salad: raw and cooked (except dry mixes)

(G-1477)
POSTAL INSTANT PRESS
Also Called: PIP Printing
825 S Main St (27215-5740)
PHONE....................................336 222-0717
Jimmy Burmley, *Owner*
EMP: 18 EST: 1983
SALES (est): 542.73K **Privately Held**
Web: www.pip.com
SIC: 2752 2789 Offset printing; Bookbinding and related work

(G-1478)
PRESS
215 Benjamin Ct (27215-8121)
PHONE....................................336 516-6074
Brett Devries, *Prin*
EMP: 4 EST: 2017
SALES (est): 64.2K **Privately Held**
SIC: 2741 Miscellaneous publishing

(G-1479)
PROWL PRECISION AND POWER LLC
3022 Forestdale Dr (27215-4649)
PHONE....................................336 580-1558
Chris Whitlow, *Prin*
EMP: 5 EST: 2017
SALES (est): 64.41K **Privately Held**
SIC: 3599 Machine shop, jobbing and repair

(G-1480)
QUALITY MECHANICAL CONTRS LLC
3032a Rock Hill Rd (27215-8623)
PHONE....................................336 228-0638
Barbara Newsome, *
EMP: 75 EST: 1985
SQ FT: 3,500
SALES (est): 15.8MM **Privately Held**
Web: www.qualitymechanicalcontractors.com
SIC: 3312 Stainless steel

(G-1481)
RACE TECH RACE CARS CMPNNTS IN
403 Macarthur Ln (27217-8740)
PHONE....................................336 538-4941
Russ Farmer, *Pr*
Donna Farmer Srec, *Treas*
EMP: 9 EST: 1988
SQ FT: 25,000
SALES (est): 889.69K **Privately Held**
Web: www.racetechracecars.com
SIC: 3711 Automobile assembly, including specialty automobiles

(G-1482)
RAVENOX ROPE
2824 Anthony Rd (27215-8985)
PHONE....................................336 226-5260
Genevieve Brownlee, *Prin*
EMP: 8 EST: 2018
SALES (est): 351.31K **Privately Held**
Web: www.ravenox.com
SIC: 5085 2298 Industrial supplies; Binder and baler twine

(G-1483)
RC INVESTMENT COMPANY
2727 Tucker St Extension (27215-8859)
PHONE....................................336 226-5511
▲ EMP: 36 EST: 1986
SALES (est): 5.5MM **Privately Held**
Web: www.leesona.com
SIC: 3469 Machine parts, stamped or pressed metal

(G-1484)
RG CONVERGENCE TECH LLC
Also Called: Convergence Technologies
1325 N Church St B (27217-2803)
P.O. Box 1490 (27302-1490)
PHONE....................................336 953-2796
EMP: 5 EST: 2006
SQ FT: 10,000
SALES (est): 550.38K **Privately Held**
Web: www.convergenceusa.com
SIC: 3829 Measuring and controlling devices, nec

(G-1485)
RIDDLE & COMPANY LLC
Also Called: Riddle Home & Gift
1214 Turrentine St (27215-6836)
PHONE....................................336 229-1856
▼ EMP: 24 EST: 1991
SQ FT: 68,600
SALES (est): 758.52K **Privately Held**
Web: www.rciwoven.com

SIC: 2211 2392 Blankets and blanketings, cotton; Household furnishings, nec

(G-1486)
RIVERVIEW CABINET & SUPPLY INC
1111 N Riverview Dr (27217-8735)
PHONE....................................336 228-1486
Tommy Murray, *Pr*
Harold Fogleman, *VP*
Barney Jordan, *Sec*
EMP: 4 EST: 1979
SQ FT: 3,000
SALES (est): 333.33K **Privately Held**
Web: www.riverviewcabinet.com
SIC: 2511 2434 Novelty furniture: wood; Vanities, bathroom: wood

(G-1487)
ROSE REPROGRAPHICS
2030 S Church St (27215-5326)
PHONE....................................336 222-0727
Todd Rose, *Pr*
EMP: 8 EST: 2006
SALES (est): 348.56K **Privately Held**
SIC: 2732 Book printing

(G-1488)
ROTO-PLATE INC
2025 Cesnna Dr (27215-8447)
P.O. Box 1559 (27216-1559)
PHONE....................................336 226-4965
James Freeman Junior, *Pr*
James W Freeman Junior, *Pr*
Alison Mary Freeman, *VP Mktg*
Tracy Alcorn, *CFO*
EMP: 13 EST: 1974
SQ FT: 15,000
SALES (est): 938.95K **Privately Held**
Web: www.roto-plate.com
SIC: 2796 Platemaking services

(G-1489)
RUSSELL PRINTING INC
2589 Deep Creek Church Rd (27217-7814)
PHONE....................................404 366-0552
Douglas Russell, *Pr*
Jeff Lindler, *VP*
EMP: 5 EST: 1977
SALES (est): 418.22K **Privately Held**
Web: www.russellprinting.com
SIC: 2752 2759 Offset printing; Visiting cards (including business): printing, nsk

(G-1490)
S AND D PUBLISHING CORPORATION
2409 Blanche Dr (27215-5453)
PHONE....................................301 642-6425
Sylvester Thompkins, *Prin*
EMP: 4 EST: 2019
SALES (est): 55.25K **Privately Held**
SIC: 2741 Miscellaneous publishing

(G-1491)
SAUERESSIG NORTH AMERICA INC
2056 Willow Spring Ln (27215-8854)
PHONE....................................336 395-6200
Robert L Frost, *Pr*
Carla Frost, *VP*
▲ EMP: 20 EST: 2004
SQ FT: 300
SALES (est): 6.99MM
SALES (corp-wide): 1.88B **Publicly Held**
Web: www.saueressig.com
SIC: 3366 Bronze foundry, nec
PA: Matthews International Corporation
    2 N Shore Ctr Ste 200
    Pittsburgh PA 15212
    412 442-8200

Burlington - Alamance County (G-1492)   GEOGRAPHIC SECTION

(G-1492)
SGB13 LLC
Also Called: Ravenox
2824 Anthony Rd (27215-8985)
P.O. Box 3588 (98273-0378)
PHONE..................844 627-5381
Sean Brownlee, *CEO*
EMP: 15 **EST:** 2017
SALES (est): 1.94MM **Privately Held**
Web: www.ravenox.com
SIC: 2298 Cordage and twine

(G-1493)
SHAWMUT CORPORATION
Also Called: Shawmut Corporation
1821 N Park Ave (27217-1137)
PHONE..................336 229-5576
EMP: 11
SALES (corp-wide): 96.2MM **Privately Held**
SIC: 2295 Coated fabrics, not rubberized
PA: Shawmut Llc
208 Manley St
West Bridgewater MA 02379
508 588-3300

(G-1494)
SHOFFNER INDUSTRIES INC
5631 S Nc Highway 62 (27215-9025)
PHONE..................336 226-9356
Butch Matthews, *Prin*
EMP: 5 **EST:** 2009
SALES (est): 157.83K **Privately Held**
Web: www.ufpi.com
SIC: 3999 Manufacturing industries, nec

(G-1495)
SIGN WORXPRESS
2529 S Church St (27215-5203)
P.O. Box 4038 (27215-0901)
PHONE..................336 437-9889
FAX: 336 437-1229
EMP: 4
SALES (est): 250.23K **Privately Held**
SIC: 3993 Signs and advertising specialties

(G-1496)
SMITH DRAPERIES INC
Also Called: Stevenso Vestal
2347 W Hanford Rd (27215-6765)
PHONE..................336 226-2183
David Stevenson, *Pr*
William Vestel, *Sec*
EMP: 22 **EST:** 1962
SQ FT: 30,000
SALES (est): 3.84MM **Privately Held**
Web: www.stevensonvestal.com
SIC: 2391 2392 Draperies, plastic and textile: from purchased materials; Bedspreads and bed sets: made from purchased materials

(G-1497)
SOUTHERN WOODWORKING INC
418 Hawthorne Ln (27215-2050)
PHONE..................336 693-5892
EMP: 4 **EST:** 2018
SALES (est): 72.62K **Privately Held**
SIC: 2431 Millwork

(G-1498)
SOUTHLAND ELECTRICAL SUP LLC
147 N Main St (27217-3901)
P.O. Box 1329 (27216-1329)
PHONE..................336 227-1486
James H Griggs, *Pr*
Michael Griggs, *
Virginia Griggs, *
▲ **EMP:** 115 **EST:** 1983
SQ FT: 100,000
SALES (est): 31.29MM **Privately Held**
Web: www.southlandelectrical.com
SIC: 5211 5063 3678 Electrical construction materials; Electrical supplies, nec; Electronic connectors

(G-1499)
SPECIAL T HOSIERY MILLS INC
1102 N Anthony St (27215-7013)
P.O. Box 1439 (27216-1439)
PHONE..................336 227-2858
Jerry Richardson, *Pr*
Jody Richardson, *
Wendy Davis, *
EMP: 9 **EST:** 1977
SQ FT: 50,000
SALES (est): 316.19K **Privately Held**
SIC: 2252 2251 Socks; Women's hosiery, except socks

(G-1500)
STANS QUALITY FOODS INC
1503 N Graham Hopedale Rd (27217-1819)
P.O. Box 477 (27216-0477)
PHONE..................336 570-2572
Sherriee Tapp, *Owner*
EMP: 5 **EST:** 1952
SQ FT: 4,000
SALES (est): 370.88K **Privately Held**
SIC: 2022 Cheese; natural and processed

(G-1501)
STAR FOOD PRODUCTS INC (PA)
727 S Spring St (27215-5870)
PHONE..................336 227-4079
George Bradford, *CEO*
Norman Mabry, *
▼ **EMP:** 57 **EST:** 1953
SQ FT: 15,000
SALES (est): 34.97MM
SALES (corp-wide): 34.97MM **Privately Held**
Web: www.starfoodproducts.com
SIC: 5147 2099 Meats and meat products; Ready-to-eat meals, salads, and sandwiches

(G-1502)
STILLWOOD AMMUN SYSTEMS LLC
Also Called: Stillwood
642 E Webb Ave (27217-5970)
PHONE..................919 721-9096
Joshua Kratky, *Managing Member*
▲ **EMP:** 7 **EST:** 2012
SQ FT: 30,000
SALES (est): 822.33K **Privately Held**
Web: www.stillwoodammo.com
SIC: 3331 3482 Refined primary copper products; Small arms ammunition

(G-1503)
SYNTECH OF BURLINGTON INC
1825 Frank Holt Dr (27215-8946)
P.O. Box 545 (27201-0545)
PHONE..................336 570-2035
EMP: 24 **EST:** 1992
SQ FT: 20,000
SALES (est): 3.89MM **Privately Held**
Web: www.syntechsigns.com
SIC: 3993 3949 Signs, not made in custom sign painting shops; Racket sports equipment

(G-1504)
T S DESIGNS INCORPORATED
2053 Willow Spring Ln (27215-8854)
PHONE..................336 226-5694
Thomas G Sineath, *CEO*
Eric Henry, *
EMP: 45 **EST:** 1977
SQ FT: 20,000
SALES (est): 4.98MM **Privately Held**
Web: www.tsdesigns.com
SIC: 2759 Screen printing

(G-1505)
TEMPEST AERO GROUP
2208 Airpark Rd (27215-8824)
PHONE..................336 449-5054
EMP: 13 **EST:** 2018
SALES (est): 985.08K **Privately Held**
Web: www.aeroaccessories.com
SIC: 3728 Aircraft parts and equipment, nec

(G-1506)
TIMES NEWS PUBLISHING COMPANY
Also Called: Times-News
707 S Main St (27215-5844)
P.O. Box 481 (27216-0481)
PHONE..................336 226-4414
Jonathan Segal, *Pr*
▲ **EMP:** 23 **EST:** 2008
SALES (est): 766.32K **Privately Held**
Web: www.thetimesnews.com
SIC: 2711 Commercial printing and newspaper publishing combined

(G-1507)
TRIAD ENGINES PARTS & SVCS INC
3439 S Aviation Dr (27215-9241)
PHONE..................800 334-6437
Bonnie Blough Managing, *Prin*
Janet Moore, *Prin*
EMP: 5 **EST:** 2014
SALES (est): 364.63K **Privately Held**
Web: www.hhtriad.com
SIC: 3724 Research and development on aircraft engines and parts

(G-1508)
TRINITY SOCK GROUP LLC
240 Hawkins St (27217-3926)
P.O. Box 2720 (27216-2720)
PHONE..................336 226-0237
Callum W Brown, *Managing Member*
EMP: 10 **EST:** 2014
SALES (est): 602.35K **Privately Held**
SIC: 2252 Socks

(G-1509)
TRIPATH IMAGING INC (HQ)
Also Called: Bd Diagnostics Tripath
780 Plantation Dr (27215-6723)
PHONE..................336 222-9707
◆ **EMP:** 100 **EST:** 1996
SQ FT: 70,000
SALES (est): 70.81MM
SALES (corp-wide): 19.37B **Publicly Held**
SIC: 2835 3841 5047 Diagnostic substances ; Diagnostic apparatus, medical; Diagnostic equipment, medical
PA: Becton, Dickinson And Company
1 Becton Dr
Franklin Lakes NJ 07417
201 847-6800

(G-1510)
TRIVANTAGE LLC (HQ)
1831 N Park Ave (27217-1137)
PHONE..................800 786-1876
Steve Ellington, *Pr*
Gary Smith, *
Derek Steed, *
◆ **EMP:** 90 **EST:** 1876
SQ FT: 100,000
SALES (est): 108.61MM
SALES (corp-wide): 878.83MM **Privately Held**
Web: www.trivantage.com
SIC: 5199 5088 5099 5091 Canvas products ; Marine supplies; Signs, except electric; Camping equipment and supplies
PA: Glen Raven, Inc.
192 Glen Raven Rd
Burlington NC 27217
336 227-6211

(G-1511)
TWO BROTHERS NC LLC
1601 Anthony Rd (27215-8979)
PHONE..................336 516-5181
John Porterfield, *Prin*
EMP: 7 **EST:** 2012
SALES (est): 151.8K **Privately Held**
SIC: 2451 Mobile homes, industrial or commercial use

(G-1512)
VANCE INDUSTRIAL ELEC INC
1208 Belmont St (27215-6933)
P.O. Box 1150 (27253-1150)
PHONE..................336 570-1992
EMP: 9 **EST:** 1994
SQ FT: 6,000
SALES (est): 1.35MM **Privately Held**
Web: www.vanceelectronics.com
SIC: 3625 Relays and industrial controls

(G-1513)
VINTAGE VACUUM TUBES LLC
404 Shadowbrook Dr (27215-4775)
PHONE..................336 688-7443
Stephen Glahn, *Owner*
EMP: 5 **EST:** 2017
SALES (est): 137.22K **Privately Held**
SIC: 3671 Vacuum tubes

(G-1514)
VISION DIRECTIONAL DRILLING
3462 Nc Highway 62 E (27215-9216)
P.O. Box 514 (27201-0514)
PHONE..................336 570-4621
Mark Hall, *Pr*
Gale Fernandes, *Acctg Mgr*
EMP: 9 **EST:** 2006
SALES (est): 1.6MM **Privately Held**
Web: www.visiondirectionaldrilling.com
SIC: 1381 1623 Directional drilling oil and gas wells; Telephone and communication line construction

(G-1515)
VITAFLEX LLC
Also Called: Vitaflex USA
1305 Graham St (27217-6148)
P.O. Box 585 (27216-0585)
PHONE..................888 616-8848
De-sheng Tsai, *Mgr*
Charles A Blalock, *CEO*
▲ **EMP:** 10 **EST:** 2009
SQ FT: 20,000
SALES (est): 1.2MM **Privately Held**
Web: www.vitaflexusastore.com
SIC: 2297 Nonwoven fabrics

(G-1516)
WEAPON WORKS LLC
1833 Anthony Rd Ste A (27215-9191)
PHONE..................800 556-9498
David Z Harward, *Owner*
EMP: 6 **EST:** 2017
SALES (est): 506.66K **Privately Held**
Web: www.weaponworksllc.com
SIC: 3479 3484 Painting of metal products; Small arms

(G-1517)
WELCOME INDUSTRIAL CORP
717 N Park Ave (27217-2343)

PHONE..................................336 329-9640
Anthony Lin, CEO
EMP: 71
SALES (corp-wide): 4.66MM **Privately Held**
Web: www.welcomeind.com
SIC: **1799** 3261 5021 Window treatment installation; Bathroom accessories/fittings, vitreous china or earthenware; Beds and bedding
PA: Welcome Industrial Corp.
261 5th Ave Rm 410
New York NY 10016
212 481-7112

(G-1518)
WILSON BROWN INC
Also Called: Pro Feet
2220 Anthony Rd (27215-8982)
P.O. Box 2720 (27216-2720)
PHONE..................................336 226-0237
Taylor L Wilson, Pr
W Callum Brown, VP
Russell R Wilson, Sec
▲ EMP: 15 EST: 1979
SQ FT: 45,000
SALES (est): 2.49MM **Privately Held**
Web: www.profeet.com
SIC: **2252** Socks

(G-1519)
WOODS AT GROVE PARK
2702 Monticello Ct (27215-6067)
PHONE..................................336 226-6171
EMP: 4 EST: 2016
SALES (est): 70.71K **Privately Held**
SIC: **2499** Wood products, nec

(G-1520)
YO ZONE
309 Huffman Mill Rd (27215-5150)
PHONE..................................336 270-5262
Jim Wood, Owner
EMP: 7 EST: 2011
SALES (est): 191.81K **Privately Held**
Web: yozonefrozenyogurt.5302309.attractionsbook.com
SIC: **2024** Ice cream, bulk

Burnsville
Yancey County

(G-1521)
ALTEC INDUSTRIES INC
150 Altec Rd (28714)
PHONE..................................828 678-5500
Jeff Mooney, Brnch Mgr
EMP: 58
SALES (corp-wide): 1.21B **Privately Held**
Web: www.altec.com
SIC: **3531** Construction machinery
HQ: Altec Industries, Inc.
210 Inverness Center Dr
Birmingham AL 35242
205 991-7733

(G-1522)
AMY SMITH
Also Called: Embroidery Authority
100 Club Dr Ste 270 (28714-3112)
PHONE..................................828 352-1001
Amy Smith, Owner
Thomas M Smith, Owner
EMP: 5 EST: 2004
SALES (est): 270.97K **Privately Held**
Web: www.embroideryauthority.com

SIC: **2395** 7389 2396 Embroidery and art needlework; Advertising, promotional, and trade show services; Screen printing on fabric articles

(G-1523)
ARTISAN AROMATICS
517 Jim Creek Rd (28714-6100)
PHONE..................................800 456-6675
EMP: 4
SALES (est): 114.03K **Privately Held**
Web: www.artisanaromatics.com
SIC: **2844** Perfumes, cosmetics and other toilet preparations

(G-1524)
B&V STUCCO LLC
37 Harmony Rdg (28714-9360)
PHONE..................................828 682-9700
EMP: 5 EST: 2010
SALES (est): 41K **Privately Held**
SIC: **3299** Stucco

(G-1525)
BWI ETN LLC
Also Called: Blue Wtr Indstries-Yancey Quar
19 Crushing Rd (28714-7084)
PHONE..................................828 682-2645
Jeff Ferrell, Brnch Mgr
EMP: 5
SALES (corp-wide): 99.56MM **Privately Held**
Web: www.bluewaterindustries.com
SIC: **1422** Crushed and broken limestone
HQ: Bwi Etn Llc
9509 Diggs Gap Rd
Heiskell TN 37754
865 573-7625

(G-1526)
GLEN RAVEN CUSTOM FABRICS LLC
Also Called: Filament Fabrics
73 E Us Highway 19e (28714-0087)
P.O. Box 100 (28714-0100)
PHONE..................................828 682-2142
Randy Blackston, Brnch Mgr
EMP: 150
SALES (corp-wide): 878.83MM **Privately Held**
Web: www.glenraven.com
SIC: **2221** 5961 Polyester broadwoven fabrics; Catalog and mail-order houses
HQ: Glen Raven Material Solutions, Llc
1831 N Park Ave
Burlington NC 27217
336 227-6211

(G-1527)
GOUGE LOGGING
360 Rock Creek Rd (28714-6509)
PHONE..................................828 675-9216
Rex Gouge, Owner
EMP: 6 EST: 1978
SALES (est): 269.78K **Privately Held**
SIC: **2411** Logging camps and contractors

(G-1528)
IENTERTAINMENT NETWORK INC (PA)
100 Club Dr Ste 203 (28714-3178)
P.O. Box 3897 (27519-3897)
PHONE..................................919 238-4090
EMP: 5 EST: 1994
SALES (est): 955.95K **Publicly Held**
Web: www.corporate-ient.com
SIC: **7372** Home entertainment computer software

(G-1529)
MINI SEMI LOGGING
346 Hunter St (28714-7137)
PHONE..................................828 284-1360
EMP: 4 EST: 2016
SALES (est): 81.72K **Privately Held**
SIC: **2411** Logging

(G-1530)
PHIL S TIRE SERVICE INC
617 W Main St (28714-2737)
PHONE..................................828 682-2421
Phillip C Harris, Pr
Mildred Harris, Sec
EMP: 4 EST: 1952
SQ FT: 5,000
SALES (est): 622.6K **Privately Held**
Web: www.philstireservice.com
SIC: **5531** 7534 Automotive tires; Tire recapping

(G-1531)
PK WOODWORKS
480 Fruit Tree Ln (28714-5519)
PHONE..................................828 284-4570
Patrick Halpin, Prin
EMP: 5 EST: 2010
SALES (est): 60.03K **Privately Held**
SIC: **2431** Millwork

(G-1532)
RIPTIDE PUBLISHING LLC
128 Academy St (28714-2904)
PHONE..................................908 295-4517
Rachel Haimowitz, Prin
EMP: 4 EST: 2011
SALES (est): 236.36K **Privately Held**
Web: www.riptidepublishing.com
SIC: **2741** Miscellaneous publishing

(G-1533)
SOUTHERN CONCRETE MTLS INC
129 Depot St (28714-3401)
PHONE..................................828 682-2298
Kevin Martin, Mgr
EMP: 8
SQ FT: 2,000
SALES (corp-wide): 238.17MM **Privately Held**
Web: www.scmusa.com
SIC: **3273** Ready-mixed concrete
HQ: Southern Concrete Materials, Inc.
35 Meadow Rd
Asheville NC 28803
828 253-6421

(G-1534)
STONE SUPPLY INC
159 Depot St (28714-3401)
PHONE..................................828 678-9966
Greg Bryant, Prin
EMP: 8 EST: 2005
SALES (est): 620K **Privately Held**
Web: www.bodyharmony.me
SIC: **3532** 4212 1611 3531 Rock crushing machinery, stationary; Local trucking, without storage; General contractor, highway and street construction; Graders, road (construction machinery)

(G-1535)
TIMES JOURNAL INC
Also Called: Yancey Common Times Journal
22 N Main St (28714-2925)
P.O. Box 280 (28714-0280)
PHONE..................................828 682-4067
Bob Tribble, Pr
EMP: 6 EST: 1971
SALES (est): 411.17K **Privately Held**
Web: www.yanceytimesjournal.com

SIC: **2711** Newspapers, publishing and printing

(G-1536)
WOOD-N-BOATS ETC INC
500 Hawk Branch Rd (28714-6056)
PHONE..................................828 682-7470
Leo Peters, Prin
EMP: 7 EST: 2008
SALES (est): 78.09K **Privately Held**
SIC: **2491** Wood products, creosoted

(G-1537)
YANCEY STONE INC
19 Crushing Rd (28714-7084)
PHONE..................................828 682-2645
William M Mccrary, Pr
Charles Patrick Mccrary, VP
Sally Young, Sec
EMP: 10 EST: 1956
SQ FT: 480
SALES (est): 475.79K **Privately Held**
SIC: **1429** Igneus rock, crushed and broken-quarrying

(G-1538)
YANCY COMMON TIMES JOURNAL
Also Called: Yancy County Common Times
22 N Main St (28714-2925)
P.O. Box 280 (28714-0280)
PHONE..................................828 682-2120
EMP: 5 EST: 1994
SALES (est): 297.99K **Privately Held**
Web: www.yanceytimesjournal.com
SIC: **2711** Newspapers, publishing and printing

(G-1539)
YOUNG & MCQUEEN GRADING CO INC
25 Crest View Rd (28714-8400)
PHONE..................................828 682-7714
Sam Young, Pr
Kim Young, Sec
Earl Tipton, VP
Jim Mcqueen Shkhldr, Prin
Earl Young Shkhldr, Prin
EMP: 100 EST: 1986
SQ FT: 9,000
SALES (est): 22.76MM **Privately Held**
Web: www.youngmcqueen.com
SIC: **1794** 1611 8711 1771 Excavation and grading, building construction; Highway and street paving contractor; Construction and civil engineering; Concrete work

---

Butner
Granville County

(G-1540)
ATHOL MANUFACTURING CORP
100 22nd St (27509-2441)
P.O. Box 105 (27509-0105)
PHONE..................................919 575-6523
John Givens, Ch Bd
▲ EMP: 17 EST: 1915
SQ FT: 210,000
SALES (est): 246.92K **Privately Held**
SIC: **2295** Coated fabrics, not rubberized

(G-1541)
AXIS CORRUGATED CONTAINER LLC (HQ)
201 Industrial Dr (27509-2511)
P.O. Box 299 (27509-0299)
PHONE..................................919 575-0500
EMP: 19 EST: 2008
SQ FT: 74,000
SALES (est): 5.18MM

Butner - Granville County (G-1542)

GEOGRAPHIC SECTION

SALES (corp-wide): 43.04MM **Privately Held**
Web: www.accbox.com
SIC: **2653** Boxes, corrugated: made from purchased materials
PA: Southern Lithoplate Inc.
105 Jeffrey Way
Youngsville NC 27596
919 556-9400

(G-1542)
BFS INDUSTRIES LLC
200 Industrial Dr (27509-2500)
PHONE.................................919 575-6711
Thomas Garbarino, *Managing Member*
◆ EMP: 30 EST: 1945
SQ FT: 25,000
SALES (est): 4.43MM **Privately Held**
Web: www.bfs-ind.com
SIC: **3561** 3443 Pumps and pumping equipment; Fabricated plate work (boiler shop)

(G-1543)
CAROLINA SUNROCK LLC (HQ)
1001 W B St (27509-1821)
P.O. Box 25 (27509-0025)
PHONE.................................919 575-4502
▲ EMP: 50 EST: 1984
SQ FT: 3,600
SALES (est): 54.53MM
SALES (corp-wide): 68.06MM **Privately Held**
Web: www.thesunrockgroup.com
SIC: **1429** 3273 2951 1411 Trap rock, crushed and broken-quarrying; Ready-mixed concrete; Asphalt paving mixtures and blocks; Dimension stone
PA: Sunrock Group Holdings Corporation
200 Horizon Dr Ste 100
Raleigh NC 27615
919 747-6400

(G-1544)
FCC BUTNER
P.O. Box 1600 (27509-4600)
PHONE.................................919 575-3900
Greg Jaenicke, *Prin*
EMP: 9 EST: 2010
SALES (est): 378.26K **Privately Held**
SIC: **2869** Industrial organic chemicals, nec

(G-1545)
MASONITE INTERNATIONAL CORP
1712 E D St (27509-2543)
PHONE.................................919 575-3700
Don Greene, *Brnch Mgr*
EMP: 30
SALES (corp-wide): 2.83B **Publicly Held**
Web: www.masonite.com
SIC: **2431** Doors, wood
PA: Masonite International Corporation
1242 E 5th Ave
Tampa FL 33605
813 877-2726

(G-1546)
NEWTON INSTRUMENT COMPANY (PA)
111 E A St (27509-2426)
P.O. Box 536915 (30353-6915)
PHONE.................................919 575-6426
▲ EMP: 140 EST: 1949
SALES (est): 24.73MM
SALES (corp-wide): 24.73MM **Privately Held**
Web: www.enewton.com
SIC: **3661** Telephone and telegraph apparatus

(G-1547)
PALLETONE NORTH CAROLINA INC
10 26th St (27509-2556)
PHONE.................................919 575-6491
Tony Fogleman, *Brnch Mgr*
EMP: 87
SALES (corp-wide): 7.22B **Publicly Held**
Web: www.palletone.com
SIC: **2448** Pallets, wood
HQ: Palletone Of North Carolina, Inc.
2340 Ike Brooks Rd
Siler City NC 27344
704 462-1882

(G-1548)
PREFERRED COMMUNICATION INC
410 Central Ave (27509-1916)
PHONE.................................919 575-4600
Bob Meeker, *CEO*
EMP: 6 EST: 2014
SALES (est): 98.99K **Privately Held**
Web: www.satstar.com
SIC: **3669** Communications equipment, nec

(G-1549)
RICEWRAP FOODS CORPORATION
300 Business Park Dr (27509-2477)
PHONE.................................919 614-1179
Richard Cronk, *Pr*
Kyle Cronk, *Sec*
EMP: 13 EST: 2011
SALES (est): 2.95MM **Privately Held**
Web: www.ricewrapsushi.com
SIC: **2092** 2038 Seafoods, frozen: prepared; Ethnic foods, nec, frozen

(G-1550)
TRIANGLE STAINLESS INC
200 20th St (27509-2443)
PHONE.................................919 596-1335
Mel Phillips, *Pr*
EMP: 5 EST: 1999
SALES (est): 798.33K **Privately Held**
Web: www.trianglestainless.com
SIC: **3444** Sheet metal specialties, not stamped

(G-1551)
UNITED LUMBER INC
10 26th St (27509-2556)
P.O. Box 510 (27509-0510)
PHONE.................................919 575-6491
Anthony C Fogleman, *Prin*
EMP: 4 EST: 2010
SALES (est): 434.69K **Privately Held**
SIC: **2448** Pallets, wood

Calabash
Brunswick County

(G-1552)
CAROLINA SHIRT COMPANY INC
262 Koolabrew Dr Nw (28467-1938)
PHONE.................................910 575-4447
EMP: 5 EST: 2014
SALES (est): 77.69K **Privately Held**
Web: www.carolinashirtcompany.com
SIC: **5699** 2329 Customized clothing and apparel; Athletic clothing, except uniforms: men's, youths' and boys'

(G-1553)
COLONIAL CABINETS LLC
259 Koolabrew Dr Nw (28467-1937)
P.O. Box 1747 (29566-1747)
PHONE.................................910 579-2954
EMP: 4 EST: 2011
SALES (est): 323.76K **Privately Held**
SIC: **2434** Wood kitchen cabinets

(G-1554)
TRADITION SURFBOARDS LLC
568 Boundary Loop Rd Nw (28467-1881)
PHONE.................................404 229-4223
Thomas Allen, *Prin*
EMP: 4 EST: 2018
SALES (est): 74.03K **Privately Held**
Web: www.traditionsurfboards.com
SIC: **3949** Surfboards

Camden
Camden County

(G-1555)
AMBROSE SIGNS INC
123 Sawyers Creek Rd (27921-7507)
P.O. Box 56 (27921-0056)
PHONE.................................252 338-8522
Roger Ambrose, *Pr*
Gary Ambrose, *VP*
EMP: 8 EST: 1945
SALES (est): 763.95K **Privately Held**
Web: www.ambrosesigns.com
SIC: **2759** Commercial printing, nec

(G-1556)
CAROLINA COMPOST
191 Lambs Rd (27921-7517)
PHONE.................................252 202-6602
Olaf Osmundson, *Prin*
EMP: 5 EST: 1999
SALES (est): 207.43K **Privately Held**
Web: www.carolinacompost.net
SIC: **2875** Compost

(G-1557)
DUNAVANTS WELDING & STEEL INC
207 Us Highway 158 E (27921-7524)
P.O. Box 28 (27921-0028)
PHONE.................................252 338-6533
EMP: 8 EST: 1988
SQ FT: 2,400
SALES (est): 939.65K **Privately Held**
SIC: **3441** 5051 7692 3444 Fabricated structural metal; Steel; Welding repair; Sheet metalwork

(G-1558)
PAULS CSTM FBRICATION MCH LLC
166 Us Highway 158 W (27921-9020)
PHONE.................................757 746-2743
Paul Justin Cohen, *Owner*
EMP: 6 EST: 2016
SALES (est): 48.49K **Privately Held**
SIC: **3499** Novelties and giftware, including trophies

(G-1559)
TARHEEL MATS INC
654 Nc Highway 343 N (27921-8311)
PHONE.................................252 325-1903
Gary Sawyer, *Pt*
EMP: 4 EST: 2004
SALES (est): 251.63K **Privately Held**
SIC: **3996** Hard surface floor coverings, nec

Cameron
Harnett County

(G-1560)
BRISK TRANSPORT 910 LLC
232 Old Montague Way (28326-4403)
PHONE.................................910 527-7398
Andre Dawkins, *Pr*
EMP: 4 EST: 2020

SALES (est): 80K **Privately Held**
SIC: **3799** Transportation equipment, nec

(G-1561)
HOPPERNCLEVE DESIGNS LLC
423 Crutchfield Dr (28326-5510)
PHONE.................................919 721-4406
EMP: 4 EST: 2021
SALES (est): 39.69K **Privately Held**
SIC: **3999** Candles

(G-1562)
PROTEK SERVICES LLC
905 Cranes Creek Rd (28326-8117)
PHONE.................................910 556-4121
Jonathan Floyd, *Managing Member*
EMP: 4 EST: 2019
SALES (est): 304.8K **Privately Held**
Web: www.protek-svcs.com
SIC: **4959** 2899 Environmental cleanup services; Acid resist for etching

(G-1563)
STAINLESS STEEL COUNTERTOPS NC
79 Bishops Ct (28326-6572)
PHONE.................................919 935-0835
EMP: 4 EST: 2016
SALES (est): 139.44K **Privately Held**
SIC: **3312** Stainless steel

(G-1564)
TRACEYMACK PRODUCTS
179 Highmeadow Dr (28326-7524)
PHONE.................................919 499-8459
EMP: 4 EST: 2015
SALES (est): 68.24K **Privately Held**
SIC: **2844** Perfumes, cosmetics and other toilet preparations

(G-1565)
XL PAWS WOODWORKING LLC
221 Arlington Dr (28326-6561)
PHONE.................................336 309-1173
Kevin Osborne, *Prin*
EMP: 5 EST: 2017
SALES (est): 72.39K **Privately Held**
SIC: **2431** Millwork

Candler
Buncombe County

(G-1566)
ADVANCED MFG SOLUTIONS NC INC
53 Rutherford Rd (28715-9204)
P.O. Box 1390 (28715-1390)
PHONE.................................828 633-2633
Bjorn Robert Johannessen, *Pr*
Carolyn Johannessen, *
EMP: 26 EST: 2010
SALES (est): 3.2MM **Privately Held**
Web: www.amsncinc.com
SIC: **3444** 7373 Sheet metal specialties, not stamped; Computer-aided manufacturing (CAM) systems service

(G-1567)
ASHEVILLE CONTRACTING CO INC
Also Called: Asheville Fence
1270 Smoky Park Hwy (28715-9248)
P.O. Box 1540 (28715-1540)
PHONE.................................828 665-8900
Carla H Maddux, *Pr*
Michael Maddux, *
EMP: 32 EST: 1993
SQ FT: 6,000
SALES (est): 4.51MM **Privately Held**
Web: www.ashevillefence.com

GEOGRAPHIC SECTION

Candor - Montgomery County (G-1593)

SIC: 1799 1611 5039 2411 Fence construction; Highway signs and guardrails; Wire fence, gates, and accessories; Rails, fence: round or split

(G-1568)
ASHEVILLE VAULT SERVICE INC
(PA)
Also Called: Asheville Wilbert Vault Svc
2239 Smoky Park Hwy (28715-9717)
PHONE.................................828 665-6799
Taylor Sword, *Pr*
Sally Sword, *
EMP: 31 **EST:** 1950
SQ FT: 38,000
SALES (est): 2.59MM
SALES (corp-wide): 2.59MM **Privately Held**
Web: www.ashevillewilbert.com
SIC: 3272 5087 Burial vaults, concrete or precast terrazzo; Caskets

(G-1569)
ASHLEY TAYLOR
809 Case Cove Rd (28715-9284)
PHONE.................................828 230-2953
Ashley Taylor, *Prin*
EMP: 4 **EST:** 2010
SALES (est): 127.68K **Privately Held**
SIC: 1442 Construction sand and gravel

(G-1570)
BALL S MACHINE & MFG CO INC
Also Called: Ball S Machine
2120 Smoky Park Hwy (28715-9702)
P.O. Box 267 (28715-0267)
PHONE.................................828 667-0411
FAX: 828 665-4764
EMP: 15
SQ FT: 18,150
SALES (est): 2.66MM **Privately Held**
Web: www.ballsmachine.com
SIC: 3599 Machine shop, jobbing and repair

(G-1571)
BIRDS EYE VIEW AERIAL DRONE
19 Westfield Way (28715-9561)
PHONE.................................828 691-1550
Jeffery Soto, *Prin*
EMP: 5 **EST:** 2016
SALES (est): 240.56K **Privately Held**
SIC: 3721 Motorized aircraft

(G-1572)
BRUCE TRULL SAWING MILL
26 Doyce Dr (28715-9720)
PHONE.................................828 667-1148
Bruce Trull, *Prin*
EMP: 5 **EST:** 2010
SALES (est): 79.92K **Privately Held**
SIC: 2421 Sawmills and planing mills, general

(G-1573)
CHARLES HILL ENTERPRISES
Also Called: Trugreen Chemlawn
145 Brooks Cove Rd (28715-9485)
P.O. Box 566 (28728-0566)
PHONE.................................828 665-2116
Charles Hill, *Pr*
Tammy Smith, *Mgr*
EMP: 10 **EST:** 1982
SQ FT: 5,000
SALES (est): 990.3K **Privately Held**
SIC: 2875 Fertilizers, mixing only

(G-1574)
CHARMING POT CANDLE CO LLC
427 Luther Rd (28715-9587)
PHONE.................................828 768-4827
Chrystal Parker, *Owner*
EMP: 4 **EST:** 2016
SALES (est): 65.94K **Privately Held**
SIC: 3999 Candles

(G-1575)
CLAYTON HOMES INC
651 Smoky Park Hwy (28715-9638)
PHONE.................................828 667-8701
Ken Meyers, *Mgr*
EMP: 9
SALES (corp-wide): 364.48B **Publicly Held**
Web: www.claytonhomes.com
SIC: 2451 Mobile homes
HQ: Clayton Homes, Inc.
    5000 Clayton Rd
    Maryville TN 37804
    865 380-3000

(G-1576)
CS SYSTEMS COMPANY INC
Also Called: Milspec Plastics
1465 Sand Hill Rd Ste 2050 (28715-8980)
P.O. Box 367 (28728-0367)
PHONE.................................800 525-9878
Robert Harrington, *Pr*
EMP: 11 **EST:** 1999
SALES (est): 1.11MM **Privately Held**
Web: www.milspecplastics.com
SIC: 2821 Plastics materials and resins

(G-1577)
DIVERSFIED MCHNING CNCEPTS INC
5 Sagefield Dr (28715-9477)
P.O. Box 2349 (28715-2349)
PHONE.................................828 665-2465
Jim Clontz, *Pr*
Kenneth Pike, *VP*
Dennis Edwards, *Treas*
EMP: 5 **EST:** 1995
SQ FT: 7,000
SALES (est): 663.1K **Privately Held**
SIC: 3599 Chemical milling job shop

(G-1578)
ELEMENTS IMAGING LLC
74 Suddreth Ln (28715-8841)
PHONE.................................504 258-3317
Alan Myer, *Brnch Mgr*
EMP: 11
SALES (corp-wide): 922.01K **Privately Held**
SIC: 2819 Elements
PA: Elements Imaging Llc
    76 Marlowe Dr
    Asheville NC

(G-1579)
FREUDENBERG PRFMCE MTLS LP
1301 Sand Hill Rd (28715-4508)
PHONE.................................828 665-5000
Bruce Olson, *CEO*
EMP: 226
SALES (corp-wide): 12.23B **Privately Held**
SIC: 5199 3296 2899 2297 Yarns, nec; Mineral wool; Chemical preparations, nec; Nonwoven fabrics
HQ: Freudenberg Performance Materials L.P.
    3500 Industrial Dr
    Durham NC 27704
    919 479-7443

(G-1580)
GLATFELTER INDS ASHEVILLE INC
1265 Sand Hill Rd (28715-6907)
PHONE.................................828 670-0041
Poul M Mikkelsen, *Ch*
Charles Holton, *
Stephen R Landon, *
Martin Mikkelsen, *
▲ **EMP:** 89 **EST:** 2004
SQ FT: 200,000
SALES (est): 44.85MM
SALES (corp-wide): 1.49B **Publicly Held**
Web: www.glatfelter.com
SIC: 2297 Bonded-fiber fabrics, except felt
HQ: Glatfelter Denmark A/S
    Alexandriagade 8
    Nordhavn
    59258500

(G-1581)
GOODSON ENTERPRISES INC
99 High Meadows Dr (28715-9495)
PHONE.................................410 303-5053
EMP: 4 **EST:** 2016
SALES (est): 55.79K **Privately Held**
Web: www.inevolvmentbaltimore.com
SIC: 2511 Wood household furniture

(G-1582)
HERBAL SPECTACLE INC
1 Mosers Pl (28715-8941)
PHONE.................................540 270-7543
Katherine Lauver, *Prin*
EMP: 5 **EST:** 2015
SALES (est): 64.36K **Privately Held**
SIC: 3851 Spectacles

(G-1583)
INFINITY LEARNING SOLUTIONS
1463 Sand Hill Rd Ste 324 (28715-8988)
PHONE.................................828 665-8292
Troy Tolle, *CEO*
EMP: 5 **EST:** 2017
SALES (est): 56.54K **Privately Held**
SIC: 7372 Prepackaged software

(G-1584)
INVISIBLE FENCING OF MTN REG
176 Pete Luther Rd (28715-9499)
PHONE.................................828 667-8847
EMP: 4 **EST:** 1989
SALES (est): 448.12K **Privately Held**
Web: www.theusi.com
SIC: 3676 1799 Electronic resistors; Fence construction

(G-1585)
KAYNE & SON CUSTOM HDWR INC
Also Called: Kayne & Son Hardware
100 Daniel Ridge Rd (28715-5557)
PHONE.................................828 665-1988
Shirley Kayne, *Pr*
David Kayne, *VP*
▲ **EMP:** 4 **EST:** 1957
SQ FT: 7,000
SALES (est): 499.52K **Privately Held**
Web: www.blacksmithsdepot.com
SIC: 7699 3366 3471 Blacksmith shop; Castings (except die), nec, bronze; Finishing, metals or formed products

(G-1586)
LENNOX INTERNATIONAL INC
Also Called: Lennox Store Asheville
1251 Sand Hill Rd (28715-6907)
PHONE.................................828 633-4805
EMP: 37
SALES (corp-wide): 4.98B **Publicly Held**
Web: www.lennox.com
SIC: 3621 3585 Coils, for electric motors or generators; Furnaces, warm air: electric
PA: Lennox International Inc.
    2140 Lake Park Blvd
    Richardson TX 75080
    972 497-5000

(G-1587)
METALCRAFT SPECIALTIES INC
64 Old Josh Creek Dr (28715-8112)
P.O. Box 808 (28715-0808)
PHONE.................................828 779-2523
Jamie Sexton, *Prin*
EMP: 6 **EST:** 2019
SALES (est): 100.19K **Privately Held**
SIC: 3599 Machine shop, jobbing and repair

(G-1588)
ROAD KING TRAILERS INC
2240 Smoky Park Hwy (28715-9717)
PHONE.................................828 670-8012
Larry Hamm, *Pr*
Steve Soule, *
Phyllis Hamm, *
EMP: 50 **EST:** 2002
SQ FT: 15,000
SALES (est): 8.88MM **Privately Held**
Web: www.roadkingtrailers.com
SIC: 5599 3715 Utility trailers; Bus trailers, tractor type

(G-1589)
SOUTHERN ORGAN SERVICES LTD
Also Called: Phil Parkey & Associates
3 English Pl (28715-9632)
PHONE.................................828 667-8230
Philip Parkey, *Pt*
EMP: 9 **EST:** 1987
SALES (est): 373.6K **Privately Held**
SIC: 3931 Blowers, pipe organ

(G-1590)
TGR ENTERPRISES INCORPORATED
26 Charity Ln (28715-8545)
P.O. Box 1030 (28715-1030)
PHONE.................................828 665-4427
Terry Rutherford, *Pr*
Brian Rutherford, *VP*
Jerrie Rutherford, *Sec*
EMP: 4 **EST:** 1989
SQ FT: 5,000
SALES (est): 498.31K **Privately Held**
Web: www.tgrenterprises.com
SIC: 3544 Special dies and tools

(G-1591)
W N C PALLET FOREST PDTS INC
1414 Smoky Park Hwy (28715-8237)
PHONE.................................828 667-5426
Dale Tharsh, *Pr*
Gary L Robinson, *
Thomas B Orr, *
EMP: 39 **EST:** 1959
SQ FT: 9,360
SALES (est): 1.77MM **Privately Held**
SIC: 2448 5031 2421 Pallets, wood; Lumber: rough, dressed, and finished; Sawmills and planing mills, general

(G-1592)
WALFLOR INDUSTRIES INC
1301 Sand Hill Rd (28715-4508)
P.O. Box 1057 (28715-1057)
PHONE.................................360 899-8060
EMP: 5 **EST:** 2016
SALES (est): 96.34K **Privately Held**
SIC: 3999 Manufacturing industries, nec

Candor
Montgomery County

(G-1593)
JL HOSIERY LLC
130 S Main St (27229-9092)
P.O. Box 725 (27229-0725)

Candor - Montgomery County (G-1594)

PHONE..................910 974-7156
John Lamonds, *Pr*
▲ **EMP:** 14 **EST:** 1982
SALES (est): 841.2K **Privately Held**
SIC: 2252 Socks

(G-1594)
KING CHARLES INDUSTRIES LLC
520 E Main St (27229-9111)
PHONE..................910 974-4114
EMP: 4 **EST:** 2017
SALES (est): 53.07K **Privately Held**
SIC: 3999 Manufacturing industries, nec

(G-1595)
LONGWORTH INDUSTRIES INC
480 E Main St (27229-9095)
P.O. Box 520 (27229-0520)
PHONE..................910 974-3068
Mittie Longworth, *Brnch Mgr*
EMP: 100
SALES (corp-wide): 99.5MM **Privately Held**
Web: www.proxgo.com
SIC: 2341 2322 Women's and children's undergarments; Underwear, men's and boys': made from purchased materials
HQ: Longworth Industries, Inc.
565 Air Tool Dr Ste K
Southern Pines NC 28387

(G-1596)
MOUNTAIRE FARMS LLC
Also Called: Mountaire Farms North Carolina
203 Morris Farm Rd (27229-8090)
P.O. Box 129 (27229-0129)
PHONE..................910 974-3232
Carol Tucker, *Mgr*
EMP: 255
SALES (corp-wide): 2.07B **Privately Held**
Web: www.mountaire.com
SIC: 2048 5191 Chicken feeds, prepared; Animal feeds
HQ: Mountaire Farms Inc.
1901 Napa Valley Dr
Little Rock AR 72212
501 372-6524

(G-1597)
PERDUE FARMS INC
Also Called: Perdue Farms
Hwy 211 S (27229)
P.O. Box 657 (27229-0657)
PHONE..................910 673-4148
Ronald Mcfayden, *Mgr*
EMP: 82
SALES (corp-wide): 1.24B **Privately Held**
Web: www.perdue.com
SIC: 2015 Poultry slaughtering and processing
PA: Perdue Farms Incorporated
31149 Old Ocean City Rd
Salisbury MD 21804
800 473-7383

(G-1598)
RUSS KNITS INC
520 E Main St (27229-9111)
PHONE..................910 974-4114
John B Martin, *Pr*
David Martin, *
EMP: 18 **EST:** 1971
SQ FT: 97,000
SALES (est): 230.53K **Privately Held**
Web: www.russknits.com
SIC: 2257 Pile fabrics, circular knit

Canton
Haywood County

(G-1599)
BEARWATERS BREWING COMPANY
101 Park St (28716-5013)
PHONE..................828 237-4200
Kevin Sandefur, *CEO*
Arthur Oneil, *COO*
Melanie Sandefur, *Treas*
Josphine Heart, *Dir*
EMP: 16 **EST:** 2011
SALES (est): 918.15K **Privately Held**
Web: www.bearwatersbrewing.com
SIC: 5813 2082 Bars and lounges; Malt beverages

(G-1600)
BLUE RIDGE PAPER PRODUCTS INC
Also Called: BLUE RIDGE PAPER PRODUCTS INC.
175 Main St (28716-4401)
P.O. Box 4000 (28716-4000)
PHONE..................828 646-2000
George Henson, *Mgr*
EMP: 1400
Web: www.pactiveevergreen.com
SIC: 2621 2678 2677 2631 Papeteries; Stationery products; Envelopes; Paperboard mills
HQ: Blue Ridge Paper Products Llc
41 Main St
Canton NC 28716
828 454-0676

(G-1601)
BLUE RIDGE PAPER PRODUCTS LLC (DH)
Also Called: Evergreen Packaging
41 Main St (28716-4331)
PHONE..................828 454-0676
John Rooney, *Pr*
John Wadsworth, *
Phillip Bowen, *
Terry Huskey, *
Robert Shanahan, *
◆ **EMP:** 80 **EST:** 1999
SALES (est): 479.16MM **Publicly Held**
Web: www.pactiveevergreen.com
SIC: 2621 Fine paper
HQ: Evergreen Packaging Llc
5350 Poplar Ave Ste 400
Memphis TN 38119

(G-1602)
BLUE RIDGE PAPER PRODUCTS LLC
Also Called: Evergreen Packaging
119 Park St (28716-4319)
PHONE..................828 235-3023
Albert Darlington, *Brnch Mgr*
EMP: 128
Web: www.pactiveevergreen.com
SIC: 2621 Fine paper
HQ: Blue Ridge Paper Products Llc
41 Main St
Canton NC 28716
828 454-0676

(G-1603)
BRIGMAN ELECTRIC MOTORS INC
6110 Old Clyde Rd (28716-3256)
P.O. Box 1047 (28716-1047)
PHONE..................828 492-0568
Jack Guinn, *Pr*
Kathleen Guinn, *VP*
EMP: 7 **EST:** 1949
SQ FT: 8,000
SALES (est): 472.76K **Privately Held**
SIC: 7694 5999 Electric motor repair; Motors, electric

(G-1604)
C AND L CABINETS LLC
390 Pressley Rd (28716-5062)
PHONE..................828 550-9820
Calvin Holcombe, *Prin*
EMP: 5 **EST:** 2016
SALES (est): 135.28K **Privately Held**
Web: www.candlcabinets.net
SIC: 2434 Wood kitchen cabinets

(G-1605)
CAMCRAFT PERFORMANCE CAMS
442 Phillipsville Loop (28716-2116)
PHONE..................828 492-0950
EMP: 5 **EST:** 2019
SALES (est): 172.22K **Privately Held**
Web: www.camcraftcams.com
SIC: 3714 Motor vehicle parts and accessories

(G-1606)
CANTON DRY KILNS LLC
649 Champion Dr (28716-6031)
P.O. Box 1463 (28716-1463)
PHONE..................828 492-0715
EMP: 5 **EST:** 2013
SALES (est): 247.22K **Privately Held**
Web: www.cantonsawmill.com
SIC: 2421 Sawmills and planing mills, general

(G-1607)
CANTON HARDWOOD COMPANY
5373 Thickety Rd (28716-8702)
PHONE..................828 492-0715
James T Powell Junior, *Pr*
James T Powell Iii, *VP*
J N Sam Powell Junior, *Sec*
EMP: 22 **EST:** 1950
SQ FT: 15,000
SALES (est): 1.54MM **Privately Held**
Web: www.cantonsawmill.com
SIC: 2421 Sawmills and planing mills, general

(G-1608)
CAROLINA CONVEYING INC
162 Great Oak Dr (28716-8715)
PHONE..................828 235-1005
Liam Mccauley, *Pr*
▲ **EMP:** 5 **EST:** 1999
SALES (est): 868.82K **Privately Held**
Web: www.carolinaconveying.com
SIC: 3491 Industrial valves

(G-1609)
CINDYS SOUTHER SCENTS
191 Miller Cove Rd (28716-9065)
PHONE..................828 492-0562
Cindy Bolden, *Owner*
EMP: 5 **EST:** 2015
SALES (est): 86.3K **Privately Held**
SIC: 2844 Perfumes, cosmetics and other toilet preparations

(G-1610)
COAST LAMP MANUFACTURING INC
Also Called: Lam Factory, The
35 Church St (28716-4431)
P.O. Box 887 (28716-0887)
PHONE..................828 648-7876
K Marshall Gann, *Pr*
Candy Smith, *Sec*
◆ **EMP:** 25 **EST:** 1955
SQ FT: 22,000
SALES (est): 404.46K **Privately Held**
Web: www.coastlampmfg.com

SIC: 3645 Table lamps

(G-1611)
CONSOLIDATED METCO INC
Also Called: Con Met
171 Great Oak Dr (28716-8715)
PHONE..................828 488-5114
Scott Yeager, *Brnch Mgr*
EMP: 200
SALES (corp-wide): 3.96B **Privately Held**
Web: www.conmet.com
SIC: 3714 Motor vehicle parts and accessories
HQ: Consolidated Metco, Inc.
5701 Se Columbia Way
Vancouver WA 98661
360 828-2599

(G-1612)
D & M LOGGING OF WNC LLC
1936 Beaverdam Rd (28716-7095)
P.O. Box 233 (28716-0233)
PHONE..................828 648-4366
Daniel Worley, *Prin*
EMP: 6 **EST:** 2016
SALES (est): 218.15K **Privately Held**
SIC: 2411 Logging camps and contractors

(G-1613)
DESMOND OFFICE FURNITURE INC
Also Called: Dof Office Seating
865 Beaverdam Rd (28716-8736)
PHONE..................828 235-9400
Desmond Suarez, *Pr*
R Kent Johnson, *Sec*
EMP: 11 **EST:** 1982
SQ FT: 14,000
SALES (est): 352.92K **Privately Held**
SIC: 2522 Office furniture, except wood

(G-1614)
DYNAMIC DEFENSE TACTICS II LLC
166 Mount Laurel Pl (28716-5915)
PHONE..................703 850-1103
EMP: 4 **EST:** 2013
SALES (est): 150.06K **Privately Held**
SIC: 3812 Defense systems and equipment

(G-1615)
EVERGREEN PACKAGING LLC
Also Called: Canton Mill
175 Main St (28716-4401)
PHONE..................828 454-0676
Larry Shutzberg, *Brnch Mgr*
EMP: 375
Web: www.pactiveevergreen.com
SIC: 2621 Absorbent paper
HQ: Evergreen Packaging Llc
5350 Poplar Ave Ste 400
Memphis TN 38119

(G-1616)
FORT BRAGG SURPLUS
13774 Cruso Rd (28716-9626)
PHONE..................828 351-4195
EMP: 4 **EST:** 2020
SALES (est): 225.61K **Privately Held**
Web: www.fortbraggsurplus.us
SIC: 3069 Fabricated rubber products, nec

(G-1617)
FRED WINFIELD LUMBER CO INC
Dutch Cove Rd (28716)
P.O. Box 1258 (28716-1258)
PHONE..................828 648-3414
John Plemmons, *Pr*
EMP: 10 **EST:** 1940
SQ FT: 500
SALES (est): 718.82K **Privately Held**

GEOGRAPHIC SECTION   **Carrboro - Orange County (G-1644)**

SIC: 2421 Sawmills and planing mills, general

(G-1618)
IMERYS CLAYS INC
125 N Main St (28716-4292)
P.O. Box 1008 (28716-1008)
PHONE....................828 648-2668
Peter O'rouke, *Mgr*
EMP: 9
SALES (corp-wide): 3.28MM **Privately Held**
SIC: 3295 Minerals, ground or treated
HQ: Imerys Clays, Inc.
   100 Mansell Ct E Ste 300
   Roswell GA 30076
   770 594-0660

(G-1619)
J & B HARDWOOD INC
592 Beaverdam Rd (28716-8778)
P.O. Box 1333 (28716-1333)
PHONE....................828 226-2326
Jeffrey Powell, *Prin*
EMP: 7 **EST:** 1999
SALES (est): 221.31K **Privately Held**
SIC: 2426 Flooring, hardwood

(G-1620)
LINTONS GAS PIPING & SERVICE
1549 Kims Cove Rd (28716-9125)
PHONE....................828 734-6259
Linton Wheeler, *Pr*
EMP: 11 **EST:** 2004
SALES (est): 558.4K **Privately Held**
Web: lintonsgaspiping.wordpress.com
SIC: 3533 Oil and gas drilling rigs and equipment

(G-1621)
PATTI BOO INC
1659 N Canton Rd (28716-3180)
P.O. Box 269 (28716-0269)
PHONE....................828 648-6495
Kevin Drury, *Pr*
Thomas L Drury, *VP*
EMP: 9 **EST:** 1979
SQ FT: 12,231
SALES (est): 676.66K **Privately Held**
Web: www.pattibooinc.com
SIC: 2331 2335 2339 7389 T-shirts and tops, women's: made from purchased materials; Women's, junior's, and misses' dresses; Women's and misses' outerwear, nec; Embroidery advertising

(G-1622)
PATTI BOO DESIGNS INC
1659 N Canton Rd (28716-3180)
P.O. Box 269 (28716-0269)
PHONE....................828 648-6495
David Mejia, *Pr*
EMP: 6 **EST:** 2008
SALES (est): 511.71K **Privately Held**
Web: www.pattiboodesigns.com
SIC: 2759 7389 Screen printing; Embroidery advertising

(G-1623)
PIGEON RVER CSTM MTALWORKS LLC
177 Academy St (28716-1218)
PHONE....................828 619-0559
EMP: 5 **EST:** 2019
SALES (est): 169.8K **Privately Held**
Web: www.prcmetalworks.com
SIC: 3449 Miscellaneous metalwork

(G-1624)
RAPID RIVER MAGAZINE
85 N Main St (28716-4286)
PHONE....................828 646-0071
Mary Beth Ray, *Prin*
EMP: 5 **EST:** 2005
SALES (est): 136.69K **Privately Held**
Web: www.rapidrivermagazine.com
SIC: 2721 Periodicals

(G-1625)
ROGERS EXPRESS LUBE LLC
167 Pisgah Dr (28716-1456)
PHONE....................828 648-7772
EMP: 4 **EST:** 2005
SALES (est): 358.54K **Privately Held**
Web: www.rogersexpresslubeandtire.com
SIC: 2741 Miscellaneous publishing

(G-1626)
SONOCO PRODUCTS COMPANY
6175 Pigeon Rd (28716-6511)
PHONE....................828 648-1987
EMP: 5
SALES (corp-wide): 6.78B **Publicly Held**
Web: www.sonoco.com
SIC: 2631 Paperboard mills
PA: Sonoco Products Company
   1 N 2nd St
   Hartsville SC 29550
   843 383-7000

(G-1627)
SUSAN LINK WOODWORKS LLC
29 Star Ridge Rd (28716-4122)
PHONE....................828 492-8026
Susan Link, *Prin*
EMP: 5 **EST:** 2019
SALES (est): 54.13K **Privately Held**
Web: www.linkwoodworks.com
SIC: 2431 Millwork

(G-1628)
WEBB OF WNC LLC
5717 Dutch Cove Rd (28716-9109)
PHONE....................828 648-2670
Sharon Webb, *Prin*
EMP: 8 **EST:** 2017
SALES (est): 69.17K **Privately Held**
SIC: 3993 Signs and advertising specialties

(G-1629)
WICKED FAB-WORX LLC
2962 Asheville Hwy (28716-8494)
PHONE....................828 492-0112
Terry E Williams, *Prin*
EMP: 6 **EST:** 2016
SALES (est): 108.99K **Privately Held**
Web: www.wickedfabworx.com
SIC: 3441 Fabricated structural metal

Cape Carteret
Onslow County

(G-1630)
CERTIFIED FIBERGLASS INC
1063 Hwy 58 (28584-8301)
P.O. Box 4281 (28594-4281)
PHONE....................252 241-9641
EMP: 9 **EST:** 1986
SALES (est): 575.54K **Privately Held**
SIC: 3732 Boatbuilding and repairing

Carolina Beach
New Hanover County

(G-1631)
ALLISON SAILS AND CANVAS LLC
915 Lake Park Blvd N Ste G (28428-4851)
PHONE....................910 515-1381
Rodney Allison, *Prin*
EMP: 4 **EST:** 2017
SALES (est): 60.28K **Privately Held**
Web: www.allisonsailsandcanvas.com
SIC: 2394 Canvas and related products

(G-1632)
CANVAS GICLEE PRINTING
1018 Lake Park Blvd N Ste 19 (28428-4162)
PHONE....................910 458-4229
EMP: 5 **EST:** 2019
SALES (est): 235.01K **Privately Held**
Web: www.canvasgicleeprinting.com
SIC: 2752 Commercial printing, lithographic

(G-1633)
CAPE FEAR PRESS
610 Atlanta Ave (28428-4407)
PHONE....................910 458-4647
Jennifer Page, *Prin*
EMP: 4 **EST:** 2008
SALES (est): 88K **Privately Held**
Web: www.capefearpress.com
SIC: 2741 Miscellaneous publishing

(G-1634)
CAROLINA COAST VINEYARD
1328 Lake Park Blvd N (28428-3935)
PHONE....................910 707-1777
EMP: 5 **EST:** 2016
SALES (est): 72.95K **Privately Held**
Web: www.carolinacoast-vc.org
SIC: 2084 Wines

(G-1635)
CISCO SYSTEMS INC
Also Called: Cisco Systems
1004 North Carolina Ave (28428-5631)
PHONE....................910 707-1052
EMP: 5
SALES (corp-wide): 57B **Publicly Held**
Web: www.cisco.com
SIC: 3577 Data conversion equipment, media-to-media: computer
PA: Cisco Systems, Inc.
   170 W Tasman Dr
   San Jose CA 95134
   408 526-4000

(G-1636)
CMS TOOL AND DIE INC
1331 Bridge Barrier Rd (28428-3996)
P.O. Box 819 (28428-0819)
PHONE....................910 458-3322
Nick Chambliss, *Pr*
Lynne Willis, *Sec*
EMP: 11 **EST:** 1988
SQ FT: 5,000
SALES (est): 1.6MM **Privately Held**
Web: www.cmsmachineshop.com
SIC: 3599 3469 Machine shop, jobbing and repair; Machine parts, stamped or pressed metal

(G-1637)
FOUR HOUNDS DISTILLING LLC
1117 Lake Park Blvd N (28428-4130)
PHONE....................757 717-9393
Joseph Stellaccio, *Bd of Dir*
EMP: 5 **EST:** 2020
SALES (est): 133.3K **Privately Held**
SIC: 2085 Distilled and blended liquors

(G-1638)
FUDGEBOAT INC
920 Riptide Ln (28428-4643)
PHONE....................910 617-9793
EMP: 4 **EST:** 2018
SALES (est): 80.38K **Privately Held**
Web: www.fudgeboat.com
SIC: 2064 Fudge (candy)

(G-1639)
LIGHT-BEAMS PUBLISHING
111 Island Palms Dr (28428-4331)
PHONE....................603 659-1300
▲ **EMP:** 10 **EST:** 1997
SALES (est): 292.63K **Privately Held**
Web: www.fairyhouses.com
SIC: 2731 Books, publishing only

(G-1640)
PROMOGRAPHIX INC
Also Called: Proforma Promographix
406 Fayetteville Ave (28428-5009)
PHONE....................919 846-1379
▲ **EMP:** 10 **EST:** 1996
SALES (est): 2.2MM **Privately Held**
Web: www.promographixinc.com
SIC: 7389 2752 3993 Advertising, promotional, and trade show services; Commercial printing, lithographic; Advertising novelties

(G-1641)
SEASIDE PRESS CO INC
Also Called: Island Gazette Newspaper, The
1003 Bennet Ln Ste F (28428-5770)
P.O. Box 183 (28428-0183)
PHONE....................910 458-8156
Roger Mckee, *Pr*
Beattie Mckee, *VP*
EMP: 7 **EST:** 1975
SALES (est): 975.5K **Privately Held**
SIC: 2752 2711 Offset printing; Newspapers, publishing and printing

(G-1642)
WINGS STORE 765
Also Called: L&L Wings
1014 Lake Park Blvd N (28428-4127)
PHONE....................910 458-0278
Shaul Levy, *Pr*
EMP: 4 **EST:** 1996
SALES (est): 69.02K **Privately Held**
SIC: 2253 5947 5632 Bathing suits and swimwear, knit; Gift, novelty, and souvenir shop; Women's accessory and specialty stores

(G-1643)
WIX BY MEL
110 Sugarloaf Ct (28428-3832)
PHONE....................973 479-0795
Allen Lombardi, *Owner*
EMP: 5 **EST:** 2017
SALES (est): 82.18K **Privately Held**
SIC: 3999 Candles

Carrboro
Orange County

(G-1644)
ARGOS USA LLC
219 Guthrie Ave (27510)
PHONE....................919 942-0381
James Walters, *Mgr*
EMP: 7
Web: www.argos-us.com

Carrboro - Orange County (G-1645)

GEOGRAPHIC SECTION

SIC: 3241 Cement, hydraulic
HQ: Argos Usa Llc
3015 Windward Plz Ste 300
Alpharetta GA 30005
678 368-4300

(G-1645)
BACKSTREETS PUBLISHING
200 N Greensboro St Ste D (27510-1838)
PHONE..................................919 968-9466
Christopher Phillips, Owner
EMP: 4 EST: 2005
SALES (est): 221.36K **Privately Held**
Web: www.backstreets.com
SIC: 2741 Miscellaneous publishing

(G-1646)
CORTICAL METRICS LLC
209 Lloyd St Ste 360 (27510-1858)
PHONE..................................919 903-9943
EMP: 5 EST: 2019
SALES (est): 155.54K **Privately Held**
Web: www.corticalmetrics.com
SIC: 3699 Electrical equipment and supplies, nec

(G-1647)
DALLAS L PRIDGEN INC
Also Called: Dallas L Pridgen Jewelry
104 Morningside Dr (27510-1253)
PHONE..................................919 732-4422
EMP: 4 EST: 1989
SQ FT: 800
SALES (est): 382.85K **Privately Held**
Web: www.dallaspridgenjewelry.com
SIC: 5961 3911 Jewelry, mail order; Jewelry, precious metal

(G-1648)
HTX TECHNOLOGIES LLC
Also Called: Htx Imaging
610 Jones Ferry Rd Ste 207 (27510-6113)
P.O. Box 16007 (27516-6007)
PHONE..................................919 928-5688
EMP: 10 EST: 2010
SALES (est): 899.69K **Privately Held**
Web: www.htximaging.com
SIC: 3826 Analytical instruments

(G-1649)
MANUFACTURING ANALYSIS INC
106 Amber Ct (27510-4110)
PHONE..................................919 434-3005
Janice Owens, VP
EMP: 4 EST: 2014
SALES (est): 121.14K **Privately Held**
Web: www.mfganalysis.com
SIC: 3999 Manufacturing industries, nec

(G-1650)
MERCH INC
101 Lloyd St (27510-1819)
PHONE..................................919 933-6037
EMP: 6 EST: 2019
SALES (est): 129.83K **Privately Held**
Web: www.themerch.net
SIC: 2759 Screen printing

(G-1651)
MIDDLE OF NOWHERE MUSIC LLC
112 Nc 54 Apt B8 (27510-1567)
PHONE..................................301 237-7290
EMP: 5 EST: 2018
SALES (est): 48K **Privately Held**
SIC: 2741 Miscellaneous publishing

(G-1652)
ONE BLACK SOCK LLC
203 Oak Ave (27510-1743)
PHONE..................................919 967-6855
John Nestor, Prin
EMP: 5 EST: 2017
SALES (est): 91.87K **Privately Held**
SIC: 2252 Socks

(G-1653)
PRESS FLEX LLC
101 Lloyd St (27510-1819)
PHONE..................................919 636-4551
EMP: 7 EST: 2009
SALES (est): 155.23K **Privately Held**
SIC: 2741 Miscellaneous publishing

(G-1654)
RAPP PRODUCTIONS INC
Also Called: Furniture Lab
103 W Weaver St (27510-6003)
PHONE..................................919 913-0270
EMP: 13 EST: 1988
SQ FT: 5,000
SALES (est): 3.34MM **Privately Held**
Web: www.furniturelab.com
SIC: 2599 7336 Restaurant furniture, wood or metal; Silk screen design

(G-1655)
RICE S GLASS COMPANY INC
107 Lloyd St (27510-1819)
P.O. Box 40 (27510-0040)
PHONE..................................919 967-9214
Alton Rice, Pr
Sara Rice, *
EMP: 32 EST: 1973
SQ FT: 25,000
SALES (est): 4.83MM **Privately Held**
Web: www.ricesglasscompany.com
SIC: 1793 7536 3442 Glass and glazing work; Automotive glass replacement shops; Metal doors, sash, and trim

(G-1656)
RINGS TRUE LLC
200 N Greensboro St Ste B9 (27510-1867)
PHONE..................................919 265-7600
EMP: 6 EST: 2016
SALES (est): 275.3K **Privately Held**
Web: www.thisringstrue.com
SIC: 3732 Boatbuilding and repairing

(G-1657)
TECHNICA EDITORIAL SERVICES
205 W Main St Ste 206 (27510-2087)
PHONE..................................919 918-3991
Jack Nestor, Pt
Arlene Furnon, Pt
EMP: 4 EST: 1990
SALES (est): 506.92K **Privately Held**
Web: www.technicaeditorial.com
SIC: 2731 Books, publishing only

(G-1658)
TOMS ROBINSON SEAFOOD INC
Also Called: Tom Robinsons Carolina Seafood
207 Roberson St (27510-2349)
PHONE..................................919 942-1221
Tom Robinson, Pr
EMP: 4 EST: 1977
SALES (est): 271.77K **Privately Held**
Web: www.tomrobinsonseafood.com
SIC: 2092 5812 Fresh or frozen packaged fish; Seafood restaurants

Carthage
Moore County

(G-1659)
ASHWORTH LOGGING
249 Hunter Ridge Ln (28327-7415)
PHONE..................................910 464-2136
Kester Ashworth, Owner
EMP: 7 EST: 1992
SALES (est): 440.27K **Privately Held**
SIC: 2411 Logging camps and contractors

(G-1660)
BIG VAC
551 Priest Hill Rd (28327-7823)
PHONE..................................910 947-3654
J R Cardona, Owner
Kathy Cardona, Owner
EMP: 5 EST: 1987
SALES (est): 249.76K **Privately Held**
SIC: 4959 3639 Sweeping service: road, airport, parking lot, etc.; Major kitchen appliances, except refrigerators and stoves

(G-1661)
BLACK ROCK LANDSCAPING LLC
6652 Us 15 501 Hwy (28327-9154)
PHONE..................................910 295-4470
Ronnie Swilliams, Admn
EMP: 5 EST: 2007
SALES (est): 407.78K **Privately Held**
SIC: 2084 Wines

(G-1662)
BLACK ROCK WINERY LLC
6652 Us 15 501 Hwy (28327-9154)
PHONE..................................910 295-9511
EMP: 6 EST: 2019
SALES (est): 240.3K **Privately Held**
SIC: 2084 Wines

(G-1663)
MACHINE SHOP
203 Country Ridge Ln (28327-9536)
PHONE..................................910 246-0720
Sandra Rochelle, Prin
EMP: 6 EST: 2009
SALES (est): 74.86K **Privately Held**
Web: www.kentechinc.com
SIC: 3599 Machine shop, jobbing and repair

(G-1664)
PUZZLE PIECE LLC
2287 Underwood Rd (28327-8819)
PHONE..................................910 688-7119
Brian Garton, Owner
EMP: 4 EST: 2011
SALES (est): 203.24K **Privately Held**
Web: www.thepuzzlepieceshop.com
SIC: 3944 Puzzles

(G-1665)
REEL SOLUTIONS INC
1341 Red Branch Rd (28327-9780)
P.O. Box 128 (28394-0128)
PHONE..................................910 947-3117
Mike Wilson, CEO
EMP: 6 EST: 1997
SQ FT: 22,500
SALES (est): 484.54K **Privately Held**
SIC: 2499 Spools, reels, and pulleys: wood

(G-1666)
SPEER CONCRETE INC
4221 Highway 15 501 (28327)
P.O. Box 280 (28327-0280)
PHONE..................................910 947-3144
Clayton Speer, Pr
Jeanette Speer, Sec
Mike Gatti, VP
EMP: 22 EST: 1978
SQ FT: 540
SALES (est): 3.44MM **Privately Held**
SIC: 5032 3273 3272 Concrete mixtures; Ready-mixed concrete; Concrete products, nec

(G-1667)
SPEER OIL COMPANY LLC
3790 Us 15-501 Hwy (28327-9785)
P.O. Box 415 (28327-0415)
PHONE..................................910 947-5494
EMP: 4 EST: 2011
SALES (est): 81.96K **Privately Held**
SIC: 1382 Oil and gas exploration services

(G-1668)
STEVENS LIGHTING INC (PA)
Also Called: Nolarec
488 Bibey Rd (28327-7230)
PHONE..................................910 944-7187
Charles H Stevens, Pr
EMP: 12 EST: 1973
SQ FT: 40,000
SALES (est): 1.7MM
SALES (corp-wide): 1.7MM **Privately Held**
SIC: 3645 3646 Residential lighting fixtures; Commercial lighting fixtures

Cary
Wake County

(G-1669)
2 WISHES TEES LLC
109 Tavernelle Pl (27519-6359)
PHONE..................................919 621-1401
Tami S Cunningham, Prin
EMP: 5 EST: 2018
SALES (est): 80.61K **Privately Held**
SIC: 2759 Screen printing

(G-1670)
360 BALLISTICS LLC
Also Called: Amidon Ballistic Concrete
206 High House Rd Ste 102 (27513-8496)
PHONE..................................919 883-8338
Mark Buchmann, Managing Member
EMP: 5 EST: 2010
SALES (est): 365.28K **Privately Held**
SIC: 3272 Concrete products, nec

(G-1671)
A GREETING ON GREEN LLC
3912 Overcup Oak Ln (27519-6543)
PHONE..................................919 607-0966
Emily Ferguson, Prin
EMP: 4 EST: 2015
SALES (est): 65.25K **Privately Held**
Web: www.agreetingonthegreen.com
SIC: 3993 Signs and advertising specialties

(G-1672)
A4 HEALTH SYSTEMS INC
5501 Dillard Dr (27518-9233)
PHONE..................................919 851-6177
Lee A Shapiro, Pr
David Bond, *
EMP: 400 EST: 1970
SQ FT: 55,000
SALES (est): 40.85MM
SALES (corp-wide): 1.5B **Publicly Held**
Web: www.a4healthsys.com
SIC: 7372 7379 Prepackaged software; Computer related consulting services
PA: Veradigm Inc.
222 Merchandise Mart Plz
Chicago IL 60654
800 334-8534

(G-1673)
ABB HOLDINGS INC (DH)
305 Gregson Dr (27511-6496)
PHONE..................................919 856-2360
Enrique Santacana, Pr
David Onuscheck, Sr VP
John Brett, VP

GEOGRAPHIC SECTION
Cary - Wake County (G-1696)

Michael Gray Senior, *Tax Vice President*
Daniel Hagmann, *Sr VP*
▲ **EMP:** 92 **EST:** 1998
SALES (est): 2.81B **Privately Held**
Web: www.abb.com
SIC: 3612 Transformers, except electric
HQ: Abb Asea Brown Boveri Ltd
Affolternstrasse 44
ZUrich ZH 8050

(G-1674)
ABB INC (DH)
305 Gregson Dr (27511-6496)
P.O. Box 90502 (27675-0502)
PHONE 919 856-2360
Michael Gray, *Prin*
Greg Scheu, *Pr*
Jan Allde, *CFO*
John Brett, *Sr VP*
Roger Bailey, *AUTOMATION TEC*
◆ **EMP:** 200 **EST:** 1980
SQ FT: 10,000
SALES (est): 1.74B **Privately Held**
Web: www.abb.com
SIC: 8711 3612 3511 5063 Engineering services; Transformers, except electric; Steam turbine generator set units, complete; Electrical apparatus and equipment
HQ: Abb Holdings Inc.
305 Gregson Dr
Cary NC 27511
919 856-2360

(G-1675)
ADMISSIONPROS LLC
800 Pinner Weald Way Ste 101 (27513-2607)
P.O. Box 1492 (27512-1492)
PHONE 919 256-3889
Jeffrey Hilts, *Pr*
EMP: 14 **EST:** 2004
SALES (est): 1.74MM **Privately Held**
Web: www.admissionpros.com
SIC: 7372 Prepackaged software

(G-1676)
AG CHEMICAL
140 Towerview Ct (27513-3595)
PHONE 561 886-0919
Jim Bolding, *Owner*
EMP: 5 **EST:** 2013
SALES (est): 113.98K **Privately Held**
Web: www.agchemical.com
SIC: 2879 Pesticides, agricultural or household

(G-1677)
AGILE MICROWAVE TECHNOLOGY INC
Also Called: Agile Mwt
701 Cascade Pointe Ln Ste 101 (27513-5799)
PHONE 984 228-8001
EMP: 6 **EST:** 2011
SQ FT: 5,000
SALES (est): 624.26K **Privately Held**
Web: www.agilemwt.com
SIC: 3674 Integrated circuits, semiconductor networks, etc.

(G-1678)
ALCO CUSTOM CABINETS INC
103 Stagville Ct (27519-9413)
PHONE 919 363-9480
EMP: 5 **EST:** 2013
SALES (est): 143.31K **Privately Held**
SIC: 2434 Wood kitchen cabinets

(G-1679)
ALL ELEMENTS INCORPORATED
2010 Roland Glen Rd (27519-8755)
PHONE 919 641-9576
Mutuk Karpakakunjaram, *Prin*
EMP: 5 **EST:** 2010
SALES (est): 121.39K **Privately Held**
Web: www.allelements.com
SIC: 2819 Industrial inorganic chemicals, nec

(G-1680)
AMETHYST PENCIL LLC
254 Northlands Dr (27519-8673)
PHONE 919 280-9025
EMP: 5 **EST:** 2018
SALES (est): 93.34K **Privately Held**
SIC: 2741 Miscellaneous publishing

(G-1681)
AMIKA LLC
5000 Centre Green Way (27513-5817)
PHONE 984 664-9804
Randall Canady, *Managing Member*
EMP: 4 **EST:** 2014
SALES (est): 1.04MM
SALES (corp-wide): 145.59MM **Privately Held**
Web: www.loveamika.com
SIC: 2879 Insecticides, agricultural or household
PA: Manna Pro Products, Llc
707 Spirit 40 Park Dr # 150
Chesterfield MO 63005
636 681-1700

(G-1682)
ANDERS NATURAL SOAP CO INC
1943 Evans Rd (27513-2041)
PHONE 919 678-9393
Michael Anderson, *Pr*
Patricia Anderson, *VP*
Jennifer Holmes, *Sec*
Jon Anderson, *Treas*
EMP: 4 **EST:** 1999
SQ FT: 1,600
SALES (est): 423.34K **Privately Held**
Web: www.andersnaturalsoap.com
SIC: 2841 Soap: granulated, liquid, cake, flaked, or chip

(G-1683)
ANTHONY DEMARIA LABS INC
122 Windbyrne Dr (27513-2830)
PHONE 845 255-4695
Anthony Demaria, *Pr*
EMP: 15 **EST:** 1989
SALES (est): 1MM **Privately Held**
SIC: 3651 Household audio and video equipment

(G-1684)
APEX WAVES LLC
1624 Old Apex Rd (27513-5719)
PHONE 919 809-5227
EMP: 4 **EST:** 2016
SALES (est): 614.03K **Privately Held**
Web: www.apexwaves.com
SIC: 3826 5961 Analytical instruments; Computers and peripheral equipment, mail order

(G-1685)
APPLE INC
Also Called: Apple
301 Metlife Way (27513-2294)
PHONE 516 318-6744
Andrea Toto Facility, *Superintnt*
EMP: 11
SALES (corp-wide): 383.29B **Publicly Held**
SIC: 3663 3571 3575 3577 Radio and t.v. communications equipment; Electronic computers; Computer terminals; Computer peripheral equipment, nec
PA: Apple Inc.
1 Apple Park Way
Cupertino CA 95014
408 996-1010

(G-1686)
APPSENSE INCORPORATED
Also Called: Appsense
1100 Crescent Green Ste 206 (27518-8110)
PHONE 919 666-0080
EMP: 120
SIC: 7372 Application computer software

(G-1687)
ARISTOS PHARMACEUTICALS INC
1255 Crescent Green Ste 250 (27518-8123)
PHONE 919 678-6592
Craig Collard, *CEO*
Steve Lutz, *Pr*
John Fogg, *Sec*
EMP: 10 **EST:** 2008
SALES (est): 231.07K **Privately Held**
Web: www.aristospharm.com
SIC: 2834 Pharmaceutical preparations

(G-1688)
ARKEMA INC
Also Called: Arkema Coating Resins
410 Gregson Dr (27511-6445)
PHONE 919 469-6700
EMP: 79
SALES (corp-wide): 125.67MM **Privately Held**
Web: www.arkema.com
SIC: 2819 Industrial inorganic chemicals, nec
HQ: Arkema Inc.
900 1st Ave
King Of Prussia PA 19406
610 205-7000

(G-1689)
ARTIBIS CORPORATION
2474 Walnut St Ste 203 (27518-9212)
PHONE 919 592-4794
Hanabel Khaing, *Pr*
EMP: 4 **EST:** 2014
SALES (est): 77.62K **Privately Held**
Web: www.artibis.com
SIC: 3571 7371 Personal computers (microcomputers); Computer software development and applications

(G-1690)
ARYSTA LIFESCIENCE INC
15401 Weston Pkwy Ste 150 (27513-8640)
P.O. Box 12219 (27709-2219)
PHONE 919 678-4900
Mark Gibbens, *Treas*
EMP: 72 **EST:** 2001
SALES (est): 20.74MM **Privately Held**
Web: www.arystalifescience.com
SIC: 2879 Agricultural chemicals, nec
HQ: Upl Corporation Limited
Harbour Front Building President John Kennedy Street
Port Louis 11324

(G-1691)
ARYSTA LIFESCIENCE N AMER LLC (HQ)
15401 Weston Pkwy Ste 150 (27513-8640)
P.O. Box 12219 (27709-2219)
PHONE 919 678-4900
Rico Christensen, *Pr*
Stuart Kippelman, *
Flavio Prezzi, *
Tom Smith, *
Diego Lopez Casanello, *
▲ **EMP:** 50 **EST:** 1995
SALES (est): 53.3MM **Privately Held**
SIC: 2879 Agricultural chemicals, nec
PA: Upl Limited
Upl House, 610 B/2, Bandra Village,
Mumbai MH 40005

(G-1692)
ASCO LP
111 Corning Rd Ste 120 (27518-9236)
PHONE 919 460-5200
Matt Rogers, *Mgr*
EMP: 7
SALES (corp-wide): 15.16B **Publicly Held**
Web: www.asco.com
SIC: 3491 Industrial valves
HQ: Asco, L.P.
160 Park Ave
Florham Park NJ 07932
800 972-2726

(G-1693)
ATMOSPHRIC PLSMA SOLUTIONS INC
Also Called: AP Solutions
11301 Penny Rd Ste D (27518-2433)
PHONE 919 341-8325
Peter Yancey, *Pr*
Jerome Cuomo, *VP*
EMP: 4 **EST:** 2005
SALES (est): 1.39MM **Privately Held**
Web: www.apsplasma.com
SIC: 3559 Electronic component making machinery

(G-1694)
ATTICUS LLC
940 Nw Cary Pkwy Ste 200 (27513-2792)
PHONE 984 465-4754
Randy Canady, *CEO*
EMP: 25 **EST:** 2014
SQ FT: 6,900
SALES (est): 9.09MM
SALES (corp-wide): 16.75MM **Privately Held**
Web: www.atticusllc.com
SIC: 2879 6719 Agricultural chemicals, nec; Investment holding companies, except banks
PA: Cse Life Science Holdings, Llc
5000 Centre Green Way # 10
Cary NC 27513
984 465-4754

(G-1695)
AURUM CAPITAL VENTURES INC
Also Called: Miningstore
270 Cornerstone Dr Ste 101c (27519-8400)
PHONE 877 467-7780
Jp Baric, *Prin*
EMP: 12 **EST:** 2018
SALES (est): 272.72K **Privately Held**
SIC: 1241 Mining services, nec: anthracite

(G-1696)
AVCON INC
101 Triangle Trade Dr Ste 101 (27513-3184)
P.O. Box 4793 (27519-4793)
PHONE 919 388-0203
Frank B Yarborough, *Pr*
Nick Senert, *
EMP: 27 **EST:** 1997
SQ FT: 4,500
SALES (est): 8.2MM **Privately Held**
Web: www.avconusa.com
SIC: 7812 3646 Audio-visual program production; Commercial lighting fixtures

Cary - Wake County (G-1697)

(G-1697)
AVIOR INC
Also Called: Avior Bio
221 James Jackson Ave (27513-3166)
PHONE..................................919 234-0068
Niraj Vasisht, *CEO*
Mani Vasisht, *Pr*
Samarth Vasisht, *VP*
Siddharth Vasisht, *Sec*
EMP: 4 **EST:** 2017
SQ FT: 500
SALES (est): 423.39K **Privately Held**
Web: www.aviorbio.com
SIC: 2834 Proprietary drug products

(G-1698)
AWC HOLDING COMPANY
5020 Weston Pkwy Ste 400 (27513-2322)
PHONE..................................919 677-3900
EMP: 15 **EST:** 2010
SALES (est): 3.43MM
SALES (corp-wide): 5.58B **Privately Held**
SIC: 3089 Plastics products, nec
HQ: Ply Gem Holdings, Inc.
5020 Weston Pkwy Ste 400
Cary NC 27513
919 677-3900

(G-1699)
BE PHARMACEUTICALS INC
203 New Edition Ct (27511-4452)
PHONE..................................704 560-1444
William Hill, *Pr*
▲ **EMP:** 4 **EST:** 2018
SQ FT: 2,200
SALES (est): 5MM **Privately Held**
Web: www.be-pharmaceuticals.com
SIC: 2834 Pharmaceutical preparations

(G-1700)
BEACH CRAFT WOODWORKING LLC
Also Called: Howard & Sons
100 Parkbow Ct (27519-6663)
PHONE..................................919 624-4463
EMP: 5 **EST:** 2016
SALES (est): 120.41K **Privately Held**
SIC: 2431 Millwork

(G-1701)
BELVEDERE CABINETS INC
103 Parkspring Ct (27519-7534)
PHONE..................................919 949-2005
EMP: 4 **EST:** 2017
SALES (est): 100.36K **Privately Held**
Web: www.belvederehomes.biz
SIC: 2434 Wood kitchen cabinets

(G-1702)
BG WOODWORKS
204 Lawrence Rd (27511-5957)
PHONE..................................919 656-2529
Brian Grzybowski, *Prin*
EMP: 4 **EST:** 2017
SALES (est): 69.35K **Privately Held**
Web: www.bg-woodworks.com
SIC: 2431 Millwork

(G-1703)
BIOLOGIX OF THE TRIANGLE INC
103 Hidden Rock Ct (27513-8309)
PHONE..................................919 696-4544
Van Kloempken, *Pr*
Gretel Kloempken, *VP*
EMP: 6 **EST:** 2000
SALES (est): 320K **Privately Held**
SIC: 2836 Biological products, except diagnostic

(G-1704)
BIOMONTR LABS ◯
15200 Weston Pkwy Ste 106 (27513-8620)
PHONE..................................919 650-1185
EMP: 7 **EST:** 2022
SALES (est): 79.3K **Privately Held**
Web: www.biomontr.com
SIC: 2834 Pharmaceutical preparations

(G-1705)
BIORAD
202 Preston Arbor Ln (27513-8402)
PHONE..................................919 463-7866
EMP: 6 **EST:** 2018
SALES (est): 48.5K **Privately Held**
Web: www.bio-rad.com
SIC: 3826 Analytical instruments

(G-1706)
BIRDDOG OUTDOOR CO INC
406 Crickentree Dr (27518-9164)
PHONE..................................919 604-8134
Thomas Padden, *Pr*
EMP: 4 **EST:** 2017
SALES (est): 69.14K **Privately Held**
Web: www.birddogoutdoorco.com
SIC: 3161 Clothing and apparel carrying cases

(G-1707)
BLACQUELADI STYLES LLC ◯
5000 Centre Green Way Ste 500 (27513)
PHONE..................................877 977-7798
Lula Jackson, *CEO*
EMP: 5 **EST:** 2022
SALES (est): 223.34K **Privately Held**
Web: blacqueladi-styles.myshopify.com
SIC: 3911 2339 3171 Jewelry apparel; Women's and misses' accessories; Women's handbags and purses

(G-1708)
BLOOM AI INC
101 S Devimy Ct (27511-6389)
PHONE..................................704 620-2886
Amit Shanker, *Pr*
EMP: 8 **EST:** 2021
SALES (est): 298.5K **Privately Held**
SIC: 7372 7389 Business oriented computer software; Business services, nec

(G-1709)
BLUE STONE INDUSTRIES LTD
10030 Green Level Church Rd (27519-8194)
PHONE..................................919 379-3986
Scott Olive, *Pr*
EMP: 6 **EST:** 1996
SALES (est): 1.03MM **Privately Held**
Web: www.bluestoneind.com
SIC: 5199 2448 3086 Packaging materials; Cargo containers, wood; Packaging and shipping materials, foamed plastics

(G-1710)
BLUESKY POLYMERS LLC
100 Woodsage Way (27518-8996)
PHONE..................................919 522-4374
EMP: 5 **EST:** 2020
SALES (est): 435.1K **Privately Held**
SIC: 2821 Plastics materials and resins

(G-1711)
BLUR DEVELOPMENT GROUP LLC
Also Called: Blur Product Development
170 Weston Oaks Ct (27513-2256)
PHONE..................................919 701-4213
EMP: 23 **EST:** 2019
SALES (est): 5.11MM **Privately Held**
Web: www.blurpd.com
SIC: 3999 Advertising curtains

(G-1712)
BMG LABTECH INC
13000 Weston Pkwy Ste 109 (27513-2250)
PHONE..................................919 678-1633
Ronald Earp, *Prin*
EMP: 10 **EST:** 1995
SQ FT: 3,500
SALES (est): 2.81MM
SALES (corp-wide): 50.82MM **Privately Held**
Web: www.bmglabtech.com
SIC: 3826 Analytical instruments
PA: Bmg Labtech Gmbh
Allmendgrun 8
Ortenberg BW 77799
781969680

(G-1713)
BRICK CITY GAMING INC ◯
80 Hamilton Hedge Pl (27519-9102)
PHONE..................................919 297-2081
Michael Robinson, *CEO*
EMP: 11 **EST:** 2022
SALES (est): 449.1K **Privately Held**
Web: www.brickcitygaming.net
SIC: 7372 Educational computer software

(G-1714)
BRIGHTLY SOFTWARE INC (PA)
Also Called: Schooldude
11000 Regency Pkwy Ste 110 (27518-8518)
P.O. Box 200236 (15251-0236)
PHONE..................................919 816-8237
Kevin Kemmerer, *CEO*
Lee Prevost, *
Dan Graham, *
Kent Norton, *
Erikka Buracchio, *
EMP: 154 **EST:** 1999
SQ FT: 50,000
SALES (est): 90.43MM
SALES (corp-wide): 90.43MM **Privately Held**
Web: www.brightlysoftware.com
SIC: 8748 7372 Educational consultant; Prepackaged software

(G-1715)
BUFFINGTONS COMMERCIAL TRIM
211 Shotts Ct (27511-5781)
P.O. Box 1487 (27545-1487)
PHONE..................................919 244-8848
Doran Buffington, *Owner*
EMP: 5 **EST:** 1986
SALES (est): 223.27K **Privately Held**
Web: www.buffingtoncommercialtrim.com
SIC: 2431 Millwork

(G-1716)
BUHLER INC
100 Aeroglide Dr (27511-6900)
PHONE..................................800 722-7483
Andreas Kratzer, *Mgr*
EMP: 208
Web: www.buhlergroup.com
SIC: 3556 3585 3567 Food products machinery; Refrigeration and heating equipment; Industrial furnaces and ovens
HQ: Buhler Inc.
13105 12th Ave N
Plymouth MN 55441
763 847-9900

(G-1717)
BURDETTS CUSTOM WOODWORKS INC
317 Hemlock St (27513-4313)
PHONE..................................919 592-9903
EMP: 4 **EST:** 2019
SALES (est): 75.92K **Privately Held**
Web: www.burdettscustomwoodworks.com
SIC: 2431 Millwork

(G-1718)
BURLINGTON COAT FCTRY WHSE COR
Also Called: Burlington Coat Factory
1741 Walnut St (27511-5930)
PHONE..................................919 468-9312
EMP: 39
SALES (corp-wide): 8.7B **Publicly Held**
Web: www.burlington.com
SIC: 5311 5137 5136 2389 Department stores; Women's and children's clothing; Men's and boy's clothing; Apparel for handicapped
HQ: Burlington Coat Factory Warehouse Corporation
1830 N Route 130
Burlington NJ 08016
609 387-7800

(G-1719)
C W LAWLEY INCORPORATED
Also Called: Transit & Level Clinic
201 Towerview Ct (27513-3592)
PHONE..................................919 467-7782
Charles Lawley, *Pr*
EMP: 6 **EST:** 1988
SALES (est): 1.71MM **Privately Held**
Web: www.transitandlevel.com
SIC: 3829 Measuring and controlling devices, nec

(G-1720)
CADENCE DESIGN SYSTEMS INC
11000 Regency Pkwy Ste 401 (27518-8518)
PHONE..................................919 380-3900
Rick Cole, *Mgr*
EMP: 8
SALES (corp-wide): 4.09B **Publicly Held**
Web: www.cadence.com
SIC: 7372 Application computer software
PA: Cadence Design Systems, Inc.
2655 Seely Ave Bldg 5
San Jose CA 95134
408 943-1234

(G-1721)
CAMELOT RTURN INTRMDATE HLDNGS (PA) ◯
5020 Weston Pkwy Ste 400 (27513-2322)
PHONE..................................866 419-0042
Rose Lee, *Pr*
EMP: 87 **EST:** 2022
SALES (est): 5.58B
SALES (corp-wide): 5.58B **Privately Held**
SIC: 3448 Buildings, portable: prefabricated metal

(G-1722)
CAROLINA
8204 Tryon Woods Dr (27518-7163)
PHONE..................................919 851-0906
Qing Lin, *Prin*
EMP: 18 **EST:** 2015
SALES (est): 880.72K **Privately Held**
Web: www.visitraleigh.com
SIC: 7539 3599 Automotive repair shops, nec ; Machine shop, jobbing and repair

(G-1723)
CAROLINA AD GROUP
116 Springfork Dr (27513-4956)
PHONE..................................919 628-0549
Anthony Mcqueen, *Mgr*

GEOGRAPHIC SECTION
Cary - Wake County (G-1750)

EMP: 4 EST: 2014
SALES (est): 57.29K **Privately Held**
Web: www.gmbmarketingsolutions.com
SIC: 2741 Miscellaneous publishing

(G-1724)
CAROLINA CAB SPECIALIST LLC
311 Ashville Ave Ste K (27518-6668)
PHONE.....................919 818-4375
EMP: 5 EST: 2014
SALES (est): 59.16K **Privately Held**
Web: www.carolinacabinetspecialist.com
SIC: 2434 5211 2541 Wood kitchen cabinets; Cabinets, kitchen; Cabinets, lockers, and shelving

(G-1725)
CAROLINA PRINT MILL
527 E Chatham St (27511-6933)
PHONE.....................919 607-9452
EMP: 5 EST: 2010
SALES (est): 106.61K **Privately Held**
Web: www.carolinaprintmill.com
SIC: 2752 Offset printing

(G-1726)
CELPLOR LLC
115 Centrewest Ct Ste B (27513-2015)
PHONE.....................919 961-1961
Simon Cooper, *Bd of Dir*
EMP: 5 EST: 2010
SALES (est): 192.04K **Privately Held**
Web: www.celplor.com
SIC: 2835 Microbiology and virology diagnostic products

(G-1727)
CENERX BIOPHARMA INC
270 Cornerstone Dr Ste 103 (27519-8400)
PHONE.....................919 234-4072
Daniel Burch, *Chief Medical Officer*
Paola Pagano, *Dir*
EMP: 6 EST: 2006
SALES (est): 491.19K **Privately Held**
Web: www.cenerx.com
SIC: 2834 Pharmaceutical preparations

(G-1728)
CHEROKEE PUBLISHING CO INC
Also Called: Smith & Associates
301 Cascade Pointe Ln (27513-5778)
PHONE.....................919 674-6020
Ronald H Smith, *Pr*
EMP: 22 EST: 1990
SQ FT: 1,500
SALES (est): 1.7MM **Privately Held**
Web: www.sacommunications.com
SIC: 2721 Magazines: publishing only, not printed on site

(G-1729)
CHOCOLATE SMILES VILLAGE LLC
312 W Chatham St Ste 101 (27511-3291)
PHONE.....................919 469-5282
Sandra Horton, *Managing Member*
EMP: 6 EST: 1982
SQ FT: 2,000
SALES (est): 483.39K **Privately Held**
Web: www.chocolatesmiles.com
SIC: 2066 5441 5149 Chocolate candy, solid; Candy; Chocolate

(G-1730)
CICERO INC (PA)
2500 Regency Pkwy (27518-8549)
PHONE.....................919 380-5000
John Broderick, *CEO*
John L Steffens, *Ch Bd*
Todd Sherin, *CRO*
EMP: 7 EST: 1988

SALES (est): 1.54MM **Privately Held**
Web: www.ciceroinc.com
SIC: 7373 7372 Computer integrated systems design; Prepackaged software

(G-1731)
CIVENTICHEM USA LLC
329 Matilda Pl (27513-9677)
PHONE.....................919 672-8865
Bhaskar Venepalli, *Prin*
EMP: 5 EST: 2019
SALES (est): 76.38K **Privately Held**
Web: www.civentichem.com
SIC: 2834 Pharmaceutical preparations

(G-1732)
CONNEXION TECHNOLOGIES
111 Corning Rd Ste 250 (27518-9238)
PHONE.....................919 674-0036
Peter Ley, *Prin*
EMP: 16 EST: 2013
SALES (est): 606.46K **Privately Held**
SIC: 3229 Fiber optics strands

(G-1733)
CONTAINER GRAPHICS CORP (PA)
Also Called: C G C
114 Edinburgh South Dr Ste 104 (27511)
PHONE.....................919 481-4200
▲ EMP: 16 EST: 1975
SALES (est): 4MM
SALES (corp-wide): 4MM **Privately Held**
Web: www.containergraphics.com
SIC: 3544 3555 5084 Special dies and tools; Printing plates; Printing trades machinery, equipment, and supplies

(G-1734)
CONVERSANT PRODUCTS INC
120 Preston Executive Dr Ste 200 (27513-8445)
PHONE.....................919 465-3456
Mike Sullivan, *Pr*
Robert Scherle, *VP*
◆ EMP: 10 EST: 2003
SALES (est): 459.87K **Privately Held**
Web: www.conversantproducts.com
SIC: 3661 7629 Telephone and telegraph apparatus; Telephone set repair

(G-1735)
CORNERSTONE BIOPHARMA INC
175 Regency Woods Pl Ste 600 (27518-6001)
PHONE.....................919 678-6507
Craig Collard, *CEO*
Alastair Mcewan, *CFO*
EMP: 19 EST: 2004
SALES (est): 4.34MM **Privately Held**
Web: www.chiesiusa.com
SIC: 2834 Proprietary drug products

(G-1736)
CORNERSTONE BLDG BRANDS INC (HQ)
Also Called: Cornerstone Building Brands
5020 Weston Pkwy (27513-2321)
PHONE.....................281 897-7788
Rose Lee, *Pr*
Jeffrey S Lee, *Ex VP*
Katy K Theroux, *Chief Human Resources Officer*
James F Keppler, *Ofcr*
Alena S Brenner, *Corporate Secretary*
▲ EMP: 400 EST: 1991
SALES (est): 5.4B
SALES (corp-wide): 5.58B **Privately Held**
Web: www.cornerstonebuildingbrands.com

SIC: 3448 3444 3442 1542 Buildings, portable: prefabricated metal; Metal roofing and roof drainage equipment; Rolling doors for industrial buildings or warehouses, metal; Nonresidential construction, nec
PA: Camelot Return Intermediate Holdings, Llc
5020 Weston Pkwy Ste 400
Cary NC 27513
866 419-0042

(G-1737)
COSYNC INC (PA)
106d Fountain Brook Cir Ste D (27511)
PHONE.....................919 523-8336
Richard Krueger, *CEO*
EMP: 7 EST: 2018
SALES (est): 71.56K
SALES (corp-wide): 71.56K **Privately Held**
Web: www.cosync.io
SIC: 7372 Application computer software

(G-1738)
COUNTYNC NEWS LLC
235 Rosenberry Hills Dr (27513-2782)
PHONE.....................919 650-2767
EMP: 5 EST: 2019
SALES (est): 75.75K **Privately Held**
SIC: 2741 Miscellaneous publishing

(G-1739)
CREATIVE IMAGES INC
226 E Chatham St (27511-3459)
PHONE.....................919 467-2188
Adita J Marshall, *Pr*
Paul G Marshall, *VP*
Chack J Cooke, *Sec*
EMP: 5 EST: 1983
SALES (est): 311.65K **Privately Held**
Web: www.creativeimagesnc.com
SIC: 3993 Signs and advertising specialties

(G-1740)
CREATIVE SCREENING
303 E Durham Rd Ste C (27513-4047)
PHONE.....................919 467-5081
Bing M Creasy, *Owner*
EMP: 6 EST: 1977
SQ FT: 8,000
SALES (est): 322.85K **Privately Held**
Web: www.creativescreening.com
SIC: 2759 Screen printing

(G-1741)
CRM A LLC
8000 Weston Pkwy Ste 100 (27513-2123)
PHONE.....................888 600-7567
Mathew B Rank, *Managing Member*
EMP: 9 EST: 2018
SALES (est): 495.79K **Privately Held**
Web: www.crma.com
SIC: 7372 Application computer software

(G-1742)
CROWDGUARD INC
12218 Bradford Green Sq Ste 151 (27519-9228)
PHONE.....................919 605-1948
Herbert Ubbens, *Pr*
EMP: 4
SALES (est): 343.2K **Privately Held**
Web: www.crowdguard.co.uk
SIC: 3699 Security devices

(G-1743)
CURLEE MACHINERY COMPANY
412 Field St (27513-4129)
P.O. Box 552 (27512-0552)
PHONE.....................919 467-9311
Greg Duke, *Pr*

EMP: 9 EST: 1947
SQ FT: 7,200
SALES (est): 973.97K **Privately Held**
Web: www.curleemachinery.com
SIC: 3648 Street lighting fixtures

(G-1744)
CYMBAL LLC
2500 Regency Pkwy (27518-8549)
PHONE.....................877 365-9622
Nathan Brinson, *CEO*
EMP: 7 EST: 2021
SALES (est): 506.12K **Privately Held**
SIC: 4789 7349 1799 5039 Transportation services, nec; Janitorial service, contract basis; Construction site cleanup; Construction materials, nec

(G-1745)
DECICCO WOODSHOP LLC
207 Penchant Ct (27513-4058)
PHONE.....................914 213-8553
Raig Decicco, *Prin*
EMP: 5 EST: 2018
SALES (est): 231.4K **Privately Held**
Web: www.deciccowoodshop.com
SIC: 2431 Millwork

(G-1746)
DEFINITIVE MEDIA CORP (PA)
Also Called: Thread
2000 Centre Green Way Ste 300 (27513-5756)
PHONE.....................714 730-4958
Jeff Fazier, *CEO*
EMP: 12 EST: 2008
SALES (est): 5.2MM
SALES (corp-wide): 5.2MM **Privately Held**
Web: www.threadresearch.com
SIC: 7372 Business oriented computer software

(G-1747)
DELTA MSRMENT CMBSTN CNTRLS LL
207 Kettlebridge Dr (27511-6344)
PHONE.....................919 623-7133
Richard A Nowak, *Pr*
EMP: 30 EST: 2017
SALES (est): 4.08MM **Privately Held**
Web: www.deltameasurement.com
SIC: 3823 3825 Combustion control instruments; Internal combustion engine analyzers, to test electronics
PA: Environmental Energy Services, Inc.
5 Turnberry Ln
Sandy Hook CT 06482

(G-1748)
DELZER CONSTRUCTION
632 Northwoods Dr (27513-3818)
PHONE.....................919 625-0755
Jeff Delzer, *Admn*
EMP: 6 EST: 1993
SALES (est): 313.39K **Privately Held**
SIC: 2421 Siding (dressed lumber)

(G-1749)
DEWILL INC
951 High House Rd (27513-3510)
PHONE.....................919 426-9550
EMP: 7 EST: 2014
SALES (est): 270.26K **Privately Held**
SIC: 2842 Laundry cleaning preparations

(G-1750)
DEX MEDIA EAST LLC
1001 Winstead Dr Ste 1 (27513-2154)
PHONE.....................919 297-1600
Brenda Davis, *Prin*

Cary - Wake County (G-1751) GEOGRAPHIC SECTION

EMP: 83 EST: 2003
SALES (est): 4.63MM
SALES (corp-wide): 916.96MM **Publicly Held**
SIC: 2731 Book publishing
HQ: Thryv, Inc.
2200 W Airfield Dr
Dfw Airport TX 75261
972 453-7000

(G-1751)
DEX ONE CORPORATION
1001 Winstead Dr (27513-2117)
PHONE......................919 297-1600
EMP: 2300
SIC: 2741 8732 Directories, telephone: publishing only, not printed on site; Market analysis or research

(G-1752)
DISTRIBUTECH
114 Crosswind Dr (27513-4710)
PHONE......................800 742-0141
EMP: 4 EST: 2014
SALES (est): 70.25K **Privately Held**
Web: www.distributech.com
SIC: 2752 Commercial printing, lithographic

(G-1753)
E&C MEDICAL INTELLIGENCE INC
Also Called: Perigen
100 Regency Forest Dr Ste 200 (27518-8597)
PHONE......................609 228-7898
Matthew Sappern, *CEO*
John Coats, *
Thomas J Garite, *CCO*
Rebecca Cypher, *
EMP: 38 EST: 1999
SQ FT: 7,800
SALES (est): 2.59MM **Privately Held**
SIC: 7372 Prepackaged software

(G-1754)
EAST COAST DIGITAL PRTG INC
800 Bell Arbor Ct (27519-6991)
PHONE......................919 465-3799
EMP: 5 EST: 2011
SALES (est): 72.68K **Privately Held**
SIC: 2752 Commercial printing, lithographic

(G-1755)
EDUCATED DESIGN & DEVELOPMENT INCORPORATED
Also Called: ED&d
901 Sheldon Dr (27513-2014)
PHONE......................919 469-9434
EMP: 30 EST: 1988
SALES (est): 4.02MM **Privately Held**
Web: www.productsafet.com
SIC: 3825 8734 3829 Instruments to measure electricity; Product testing laboratory, safety or performance; Measuring and controlling devices, nec

(G-1756)
ELEMENTS IN FOCUS LLC
104 Rozelle Valley Ln (27519-9307)
PHONE......................561 289-8641
Jill R Denbow, *Admn*
EMP: 5 EST: 2015
SALES (est): 236.57K **Privately Held**
Web: www.elementsinfocus.com
SIC: 2819 Industrial inorganic chemicals, nec

(G-1757)
EMATH360 LLC
302 Parish House Rd (27513-1676)
PHONE......................919 744-4944
Jawahar Lal, *Pr*

Raj Marota, *Dir*
EMP: 10 EST: 2010
SALES (est): 199.07K **Privately Held**
Web: www.emath360.com
SIC: 8299 8748 7372 8742 Tutoring school; Testing service, educational or personnel; Educational computer software; Business planning and organizing services

(G-1758)
EMPLOYUS INC
122 E Chatham St Ste 300 (27511-3360)
PHONE......................919 706-4008
Ryan O'donnell, *CEO*
Francis Stocks, *Ch Bd*
EMP: 10 EST: 2014
SALES (est): 971.87K **Privately Held**
Web: www.hireology.com
SIC: 7372 Business oriented computer software

(G-1759)
ENVIRONMENTAL SCIENCE US LLC (HQ)
Also Called: Bayer Cropscience
5000 Centre Green Way Ste 400 (27513)
PHONE......................800 331-2867
▲ EMP: 18 EST: 1995
SQ FT: 28,000
SALES (est): 106.88MM
SALES (corp-wide): 244.34MM **Privately Held**
Web: us.envu.com
SIC: 2834 Pharmaceutical preparations
PA: Cinven Limited
21 St. James's Square
London SW1Y
207 661-3333

(G-1760)
EPOCH TIMES NC INC
115 Joseph Pond Ln (27519-5538)
PHONE......................919 649-6014
Ming Cheng, *Owner*
EMP: 5 EST: 2017
SALES (est): 59.35K **Privately Held**
SIC: 2711 Newspapers, publishing and printing

(G-1761)
ERLECLAIR INC
Also Called: AlphaGraphics
301 Ashville Ave Ste 121 (27518-6131)
PHONE......................919 233-7710
Edwrad Erleclair, *Pr*
Carol Leclair, *VP*
EMP: 22 EST: 2007
SQ FT: 6,500
SALES (est): 2.48MM **Privately Held**
Web: www.alphagraphics.com
SIC: 2752 Commercial printing, lithographic

(G-1762)
ETHICON INC
Also Called: Ethicon Endo - Surgery
125 Edinburgh South Dr Ste 201 (27511-6484)
PHONE......................919 234-2124
Greg Casale, *Mgr*
EMP: 6
SALES (corp-wide): 85.16B **Publicly Held**
SIC: 3842 Surgical appliances and supplies
HQ: Ethicon Inc.
1000 Route 202
Raritan NJ 08869
800 384-4266

(G-1763)
EXPERSIS SOFTWARE INC
1060 Kennicott Ave (27513-8450)
PHONE......................919 874-0608

Manoj Patwardhan, *Pr*
EMP: 7 EST: 2010
SALES (est): 119K **Privately Held**
Web: www.expersis.com
SIC: 7372 Prepackaged software

(G-1764)
EZBREW INC
1006 Sw Maynard Rd (27511-4385)
PHONE......................833 233-2739
Andrew Baker, *Prin*
EMP: 7 EST: 2019
SALES (est): 218.55K **Privately Held**
Web: www.ezbrew.beer
SIC: 3556 Brewers' and maltsters' machinery

(G-1765)
FABCO INDUSTRIES
312 N Dixon Ave (27513-4427)
PHONE......................919 481-3010
Marty Garmon, *Owner*
EMP: 5 EST: 1985
SQ FT: 3,200
SALES (est): 399.29K **Privately Held**
Web: www.fabco-industries.com
SIC: 3441 Fabricated structural metal

(G-1766)
FACILITYDUDECOM INC
11000 Regency Pkwy Ste 200 (27518-8518)
PHONE......................919 459-6430
Kent Hudson, *Ch Bd*
Tom Knox, *
Brian Bell, *Strategy Vice President**
Joan Maddox, *Client Services Vice President**
EMP: 17 EST: 2006
SALES (est): 118.2K **Privately Held**
Web: www.brightlysoftware.com
SIC: 7372 Business oriented computer software

(G-1767)
FAIR PRODUCTS INC
806 Reedy Creek Rd (27513-3307)
P.O. Box 386 (27512-0386)
PHONE......................919 467-1599
H Frank Grainger, *Pr*
EMP: 7 EST: 1978
SALES (est): 983.55K **Privately Held**
Web: www.fairproductsinc.com
SIC: 2879 Agricultural chemicals, nec

(G-1768)
FAIRBANKS NIJHUIS
400 Regency Forest Dr (27518-7702)
PHONE......................262 728-7449
EMP: 5 EST: 2019
SALES (est): 247.69K **Privately Held**
SIC: 3561 Pumps and pumping equipment

(G-1769)
FATHOM HOLDINGS INC (PA)
2000 Regency Pkwy Ste 300 (27518-8506)
PHONE......................888 455-6040
Joshua Harley, *Ch Bd*
Marco Fregenal, *Pr*
Samantha Giuggio, *BROKERAGE*
EMP: 38 EST: 2010
SQ FT: 12,000
SALES (est): 412.96MM
SALES (corp-wide): 412.96MM **Publicly Held**
Web: www.fathomrealty.com
SIC: 6531 7372 Real estate listing services; Prepackaged software

(G-1770)
GALVIX INC
1036 Canyon Shadows Ct (27519-1003)
PHONE......................925 434-6243
Piyush Agrawal, *CEO*
EMP: 6
SALES (est): 180.32K **Privately Held**
SIC: 7389 7372 Business Activities at Non-Commercial Site; Prepackaged software

(G-1771)
GARMIN INTERNATIONAL INC
100 Regency Forest Dr (27518-8597)
PHONE......................919 337-0116
EMP: 493
Web: www.garmin.com
SIC: 3812 Navigational systems and instruments
HQ: Garmin International, Inc.
1200 E 151st St
Olathe KS 66062

(G-1772)
GEM ASSET ACQUISITION LLC
Also Called: Gemseal Pvments Pdts - Raleigh
200 Travis Park (27511-6908)
PHONE......................919 851-0799
EMP: 22
SALES (corp-wide): 17.13MM **Privately Held**
SIC: 2951 Asphalt paving mixtures and blocks
PA: Gem Asset Acquisition Llc
1855 Lindbergh St Ste 500
Charlotte NC 28208
704 225-3321

(G-1773)
GENOTECH INC
413 Legault Dr (27513-8333)
PHONE......................919 369-4947
Joe Toong, *Prin*
EMP: 5 EST: 2010
SALES (est): 228.15K **Privately Held**
Web: www.genotech.com
SIC: 2836 Biological products, except diagnostic

(G-1774)
GLOBAL FORMING TECH LTD
801 Cascade Pointe Ln Ste 102 (27513-5823)
PHONE......................919 234-1384
Erich Dominik, *Managing Member*
▲ EMP: 4 EST: 2001
SALES (est): 251.58K **Privately Held**
SIC: 3317 Tubing, mechanical or hypodermic sizes: cold drawn stainless

(G-1775)
GLOVES-ONLINE INC
Also Called: Go Gloves
231 E Johnson St Ste K (27513-4010)
P.O. Box 4468 (27519-4468)
PHONE......................919 468-4244
Joseph Mcgarry, *Pr*
▲ EMP: 6 EST: 1998
SALES (est): 785.45K **Privately Held**
Web: www.gloves-online.com
SIC: 2259 3089 3151 3842 Work gloves, knit ; Work gloves, plastics; Welders' gloves; Gloves, safety

(G-1776)
GOSHEN HOUSE & TRADING LLC
744 E Chatham St Ste G (27511-6913)
PHONE......................832 407-8153
EMP: 6 EST: 2014
SALES (est): 74.38K **Privately Held**

GEOGRAPHIC SECTION
Cary - Wake County (G-1803)

SIC: **2033** Canned fruits and specialties

(G-1777)
GREAT-R GOOD PUBLISHING INC
410 Highfield Ave (27519-6173)
PHONE......................................919 812-1555
EMP: 6 EST: 2012
SALES (est): 37.59K **Privately Held**
SIC: **2741** Miscellaneous publishing

(G-1778)
GREEN APPLE STUDIO
590 E Chatham St (27511-6955)
PHONE......................................919 377-2239
Jing Wang, *Admn*
EMP: 8 EST: 2015
SALES (est): 127.11K **Privately Held**
Web: green-apple-studio.hub.biz
SIC: **3571** Electronic computers

(G-1779)
GREENLIGHTS LLC
1211 Walnut St (27511-4730)
PHONE......................................919 766-8900
Alan D King, *Brnch Mgr*
EMP: 20
SALES (corp-wide): 49.6K **Privately Held**
SIC: **3641** Electric lamps
PA: Greenlights Llc
   221 Brook Manor Ct
   Cary NC

(G-1780)
HDH PHARMA INC
421 Charleville Ct (27519-6494)
PHONE......................................919 462-1494
Goverdhan Vavilala, *Prin*
Goverdhan Vavilala, *CEO*
Shobha Kasireddy, *Admn*
Kavitha Karakala, *Asst Tr*
EMP: 7 EST: 2011
SALES (est): 214.11K **Privately Held**
Web: www.hdhpharma.com
SIC: **2834** Pharmaceutical preparations

(G-1781)
HEALEY PUBLISHING
207 Queensferry Rd (27511-6313)
PHONE......................................919 614-6685
EMP: 4 EST: 2017
SALES (est): 59.88K **Privately Held**
Web: www.healey.work
SIC: **2741** Miscellaneous publishing

(G-1782)
HEAVY METAL SUPPLY LLC
141 Spring Cove Dr (27511-7219)
PHONE......................................919 625-3508
EMP: 9 EST: 2010
SALES (est): 559.99K **Privately Held**
SIC: **3441** Fabricated structural metal

(G-1783)
HELIUM BRANDS LLC
109 Granby Ct (27511-6702)
PHONE......................................561 350-1328
EMP: 11
SALES (corp-wide): 230.65K **Privately Held**
SIC: **2813** Helium
PA: Helium Brands Llc
   3201 Edwards Mill Rd # 1
   Raleigh NC

(G-1784)
HILL-ROM INC
1225 Crescent Green Ste 300 (27518-8119)
PHONE......................................919 854-3600
Mark Hesner, *Mgr*
EMP: 353
SALES (corp-wide): 14.81B **Publicly Held**
Web: www.hillrom.com
SIC: **2515** Sleep furniture
HQ: Hill-Rom, Inc.
   1069 State Route 46 E
   Batesville IN 47006
   812 934-7777

(G-1785)
HYPER ANALYTICAL SOFTWARE LLC
822 Blackmar St (27519-9420)
PHONE......................................919 267-4897
Derek Justice, *Prin*
EMP: 5 EST: 2011
SALES (est): 143.87K **Privately Held**
Web: www.hyperanalytical.com
SIC: **7372** Business oriented computer software

(G-1786)
IN PINK
112 Swiss Stone Ct (27513-4753)
PHONE......................................919 380-1487
Linda Pink, *Prin*
EMP: 6 EST: 2006
SALES (est): 121.55K **Privately Held**
Web: www.prettyinpinkfoundation.org
SIC: **2342** Bras, girdles, and allied garments

(G-1787)
INDUSTRIAL CNNCTONS SLTONS LLC (DH)
305 Gregson Dr (27511-6496)
PHONE......................................203 229-3932
Michael D Gray, *Managing Member*
Michael Plaster, *Managing Member**
Bridget Smith, *Managing Member**
EMP: 34 EST: 2017
SALES (est): 25.94MM **Privately Held**
SIC: **3613** Control panels, electric
HQ: Abb Inc.
   305 Gregson Dr
   Cary NC 27511

(G-1788)
INEO USA INC
120 James Jackson Ave Unit 16 (27513-3163)
PHONE......................................919 467-2199
EMP: 6 EST: 2019
SALES (est): 146.35K **Privately Held**
Web: www.ineos.com
SIC: **2821** Plastics materials and resins

(G-1789)
INFORMTION RTRVAL CMPANIES INC
Also Called: Irc
3500 Regency Pkwy Ste 140 (27518-8519)
PHONE......................................919 460-7447
Tony Colle, *Brnch Mgr*
EMP: 35
SALES (corp-wide): 2.55MM **Privately Held**
SIC: **7372** 7379 Application computer software; Computer related consulting services
PA: Information Retrieval Companies, Inc.
   225 W Wacker Dr Ste 2200
   Chicago IL 60606
   312 726-7587

(G-1790)
INN-FLOW INC
Also Called: Inn-Flow Hotel Software
5640 Dillard Rd Ste 300 (27518-7174)
PHONE......................................919 277-9027
John Erhart, *Pr*
EMP: 17 EST: 2012
SQ FT: 2,000
SALES (est): 587.9K **Privately Held**
Web: www.inn-flow.com
SIC: **7372** Application computer software

(G-1791)
INTERNATIONAL BUS CONNECTION
1148 Kildaire Farm Rd (27511-4583)
PHONE......................................251 391-1158
EMP: 4 EST: 2019
SALES (est): 94.73K **Privately Held**
SIC: **3731** Shipbuilding and repairing

(G-1792)
INTERNATIONAL PTNRSHP FOR VACC
114 Burgwin Wright Way (27519-2824)
PHONE......................................919 367-0379
Brandon J Price, *Prin*
EMP: 7 EST: 2010
SALES (est): 90.72K **Privately Held**
SIC: **2836** Vaccines

(G-1793)
INVESTORCOOKBOOKSCOM
301 Crickentree Dr (27518-9163)
PHONE......................................919 280-8600
Roger Elmer Junior, *Prin*
EMP: 5 EST: 2011
SALES (est): 135.27K **Privately Held**
SIC: **2741** Miscellaneous publishing

(G-1794)
INVITATION DUCK LLC
111 James Jackson Ave Ste 209 (27513-3598)
PHONE......................................919 341-3739
Lanny Scott, *Prin*
EMP: 5 EST: 2013
SALES (est): 94.59K **Privately Held**
SIC: **2759** Invitation and stationery printing and engraving

(G-1795)
J & S PARKSIDE LLC
7169 Okelly Chapel Rd (27519-6849)
PHONE......................................919 434-1293
EMP: 6 EST: 2014
SALES (est): 204.29K **Privately Held**
SIC: **2024** Ice cream and frozen deserts

(G-1796)
JMP STATISTICAL DISCOVERY LLC
100 Matrix Dr 8000 (27513-2089)
PHONE......................................877 594-6567
EMP: 51 EST: 2021
SALES (est): 7.39MM
SALES (corp-wide): 3.19B **Privately Held**
Web: www.jmp.com
SIC: **7372** Prepackaged software
PA: Sas Institute Inc.
   100 Sas Campus Dr
   Cary NC 27513
   919 677-8000

(G-1797)
JOBS MAGAZINE LLC
1240 Se Maynard Rd Ste 104 (27511-6929)
PHONE......................................919 319-6816
EMP: 7 EST: 1995
SALES (est): 243.69K **Privately Held**
SIC: **2721** Periodicals
PA: Prism Publishing, Inc.
   1240 Se Maynard Rd # 104
   Cary NC 27511

(G-1798)
JOHN DEERE CONSUMER PDTS INC (HQ)
Also Called: John Deere
2000 John Deere Run (27513-2789)
P.O. Box 8808 (61266-8808)
PHONE......................................919 804-2000
EMP: 170 EST: 1987
SALES (est): 174.23MM
SALES (corp-wide): 61.25B **Publicly Held**
Web: www.deere.com
SIC: **3546** 8711 3524 Chain saws, portable; Engineering services; Lawn and garden equipment
PA: Deere & Company
   1 John Deere Pl
   Moline IL 61265
   309 765-8000

(G-1799)
JOURNAL DOCTORS INC
1209 Chalk Maple Dr (27519-7416)
PHONE......................................919 469-1438
Dale Karlson, *Prin*
EMP: 5 EST: 2010
SALES (est): 152.41K **Privately Held**
SIC: **2711** Newspapers, publishing and printing

(G-1800)
JOURNAL VACUUM SCIENCE & TECH
Also Called: Jvst
51 Kilmayne Dr Ste 104 (27519-7719)
P.O. Box 13994 (27709-3994)
PHONE......................................919 361-2787
Yvonne Towse, *Dir*
EMP: 5 EST: 1990
SALES (est): 280.07K **Privately Held**
SIC: **2711** Newspapers, publishing and printing

(G-1801)
JUSTI LLC
109 Oxyard Way (27519-7327)
PHONE......................................919 434-5002
Selva Mohan, *CEO*
EMP: 11 EST: 2017
SALES (est): 479.49K **Privately Held**
SIC: **7372** Utility computer software

(G-1802)
KILDAIRE REGENCY PUBLISHING
100 Crestview Ct (27518-8602)
PHONE......................................919 469-5851
Janet C Mclaughlin, *Owner*
EMP: 4 EST: 2014
SALES (est): 66.01K **Privately Held**
SIC: **2741** Miscellaneous publishing

(G-1803)
KING PHRMCEUTICALS RES DEV LLC
Also Called: King Pharmaceutical R & D
4000 Centre Green Way Ste 300 (27513)
P.O. Box 13886 (27709-3886)
PHONE......................................919 653-7001
Bryan Markinson, *Pr*
King Jolly, *Ex VP*
EMP: 473 EST: 1978
SQ FT: 11,900
SALES (est): 2.12MM
SALES (corp-wide): 100.33B **Publicly Held**
SIC: **8733** 8731 2834 Medical research; Commercial physical research; Pharmaceutical preparations
HQ: King Pharmaceuticals Llc
   501 5th St
   Bristol TN 37620

Cary - Wake County (G-1804)

(G-1804)
KORBER MEDIPAK SYSTEMS NA INC
Also Called: Korber Medipak Systems Na Inc.
8000 Regency Pkwy Ste 403 (27518-8514)
PHONE..................................727 538-4644
Kerry Fillmore, *Brnch Mgr*
EMP: 37
SALES (corp-wide): 2.09MM **Privately Held**
Web: www.koerber-pharma.com
SIC: 3565 Packaging machinery
HQ: Korber Pharma, Inc.
969 34th St N
Fargo ND 58102
701 232-1780

(G-1805)
LA FARM INC
Also Called: La Farm Bakery
4248 Nw Cary Pkwy (27513-8478)
PHONE..................................919 657-0657
Elisabeth Vatinet, *Pr*
Lionel Vatinet, *Sec*
EMP: 20 **EST:** 1999
SALES (est): 1.58MM **Privately Held**
Web: www.lafarmbakery.com
SIC: 2051 Bread, cake, and related products

(G-1806)
LADDER CARRY LLC
401 Harlon Dr (27511-4829)
PHONE..................................704 245-2359
EMP: 5 **EST:** 2020
SALES (est): 79.26K **Privately Held**
Web: www.laddercarry.com
SIC: 3999 Manufacturing industries, nec

(G-1807)
LARRY SHACKELFORD
309 Dunhagan Pl (27511-5611)
PHONE..................................919 467-8817
Larry Shackelford, *Prin*
EMP: 4 **EST:** 2001
SALES (est): 239.8K **Privately Held**
SIC: 3674 Semiconductors and related devices

(G-1808)
LASER RECHARGE CAROLINA INC
Also Called: Lrc
2474 Walnut St (27518-9212)
PHONE..................................919 467-5902
Sam Robinson, *Pr*
Robert Wood, *VP*
EMP: 10 **EST:** 1989
SQ FT: 2,500
SALES (est): 1.6MM **Privately Held**
Web: www.go-lrc.com
SIC: 3861 7372 5112 Toners, prepared photographic (not made in chemical plants); Business oriented computer software; Laser printer supplies

(G-1809)
LIFERAY INC
7151 Okelly Chapel Rd (27519-6849)
PHONE..................................703 957-8542
EMP: 4 **EST:** 2019
SALES (est): 64.01K **Privately Held**
Web: www.liferay.com
SIC: 7372 Prepackaged software

(G-1810)
LIGHTHOUSE PRESS INC
102 Eagle Meadow Ct (27519-5070)
PHONE..................................919 371-8640
Scott C Wagner, *Prin*
EMP: 7 **EST:** 2005
SALES (est): 126.67K **Privately Held**
SIC: 2741 Miscellaneous publishing

(G-1811)
LINDE GAS & EQUIPMENT INC
Also Called: Linde Gas North America
1120 W Chatham St (27511-6230)
PHONE..................................919 380-7411
Robert Farrell, *Mgr*
EMP: 13
Web: www.lindedirect.com
SIC: 2813 Nitrogen
HQ: Linde Gas & Equipment Inc.
10 Riverview Dr
Danbury CT 06810
844 445-4633

(G-1812)
LIQUIDEHR INC
1939 High House Rd Ste 107 (27519-8452)
PHONE..................................866 618-1531
Gabie Lambrechtse, *Prin*
EMP: 25 **EST:** 2013
SALES (est): 974.29K **Privately Held**
Web: www.liquidehr.com
SIC: 7372 Prepackaged software

(G-1813)
LIVING INTNTIONALLY FOR EXCELL
Also Called: Life
200 Commonwealth Ct Ste 200 (27511-2431)
PHONE..................................810 600-3425
Robert Hallstrand, *Mng Pt*
Rob Hallstrand, *Mng Pt*
EMP: 33 **EST:** 2011
SALES (est): 1.69MM **Privately Held**
SIC: 2759 Publication printing

(G-1814)
LOPAREX LLC (DH)
Also Called: Easy Mask
1255 Crescent Green Ste 400 (27518-8132)
PHONE..................................919 678-7700
Michael Apperson,
Jack Taylor,
◆ **EMP:** 96 **EST:** 2001
SQ FT: 24,000
SALES (est): 260.34MM **Privately Held**
Web: www.loparex.com
SIC: 2672 Coated paper, except photographic, carbon, or abrasive
HQ: Loparex Holding B.V.
Laan Van Westenenk 45
Apeldoorn GE
555276999

(G-1815)
LORD CORPORATION
200 Lord Dr (27511-7924)
PHONE..................................877 275-5673
EMP: 7 **EST:** 1981
SALES (est): 70.85K **Privately Held**
Web: www.lord.com
SIC: 3829 Measuring and controlling devices, nec

(G-1816)
LORD CORPORATION
Also Called: Materials Division
406 Gregson Dr (27511-6445)
PHONE..................................919 342-3380
Gerald Estes, *VP*
EMP: 98
SQ FT: 35,835
SALES (corp-wide): 19.07B **Publicly Held**
Web: www.parker.com
SIC: 3593 2992 3714 2899 Fluid power actuators, hydraulic or pneumatic; Brake fluid (hydraulic): made from purchased materials; Shock absorbers, motor vehicle; Magnetic inspection oil or powder
HQ: Lord Corporation
111 Lord Dr
Cary NC 27511
919 468-5979

(G-1817)
LORD CORPORATION (HQ)
Also Called: Parker-Lord
111 Lord Dr (27511-7923)
P.O. Box 8012 (27512-8012)
PHONE..................................919 468-5979
◆ **EMP:** 391 **EST:** 1940
SALES (est): 794.78MM
SALES (corp-wide): 19.07B **Publicly Held**
Web: www.lord.com
SIC: 2891 3724 3728 2851 Adhesives; Engine mount parts, aircraft; Aircraft parts and equipment, nec; Polyurethane coatings
PA: Parker-Hannifin Corporation
6035 Parkland Blvd
Cleveland OH 44124
216 896-3000

(G-1818)
LORD CORPORATION
Stellar Technology
110 Lord Dr (27511-7917)
PHONE..................................919 469-2500
David G Thomas, *Brnch Mgr*
EMP: 80
SALES (corp-wide): 19.07B **Publicly Held**
Web: www.parker.com
SIC: 2891 8731 Adhesives; Commercial physical research
HQ: Lord Corporation
111 Lord Dr
Cary NC 27511
919 468-5979

(G-1819)
LORD FAR EAST INC
111 Lord Dr (27511-7923)
PHONE..................................919 468-5979
EMP: 32 **EST:** 1969
SALES (est): 988.74K
SALES (corp-wide): 19.07B **Publicly Held**
SIC: 2891 3724 3728 2851 Adhesives; Engine mount parts, aircraft; Aircraft parts and equipment, nec; Polyurethane coatings
HQ: Lord Corporation
111 Lord Dr
Cary NC 27511
919 468-5979

(G-1820)
LUCERNO DYNAMICS LLC
140 Towerview Ct (27513-3595)
PHONE..................................317 294-1395
EMP: 5 **EST:** 2011
SALES (est): 954.12K **Privately Held**
Web: www.lucerno.com
SIC: 3841 7389 Surgical and medical instruments; Business services, nec

(G-1821)
MATTRESS WAREHOUSE
5028 Arco St (27519-6012)
PHONE..................................919 463-0329
EMP: 5 **EST:** 2017
SALES (est): 72.92K **Privately Held**
Web: stores.sleephappens.com
SIC: 2515 Mattresses and foundations

(G-1822)
MCGILL CORPORATION
1220 Se Maynard Rd (27511-6944)
PHONE..................................919 467-1993
Todd Stine, *Brnch Mgr*
EMP: 8
SALES (corp-wide): 126.17MM **Privately Held**
Web: www.unitedmcgill.com
SIC: 3444 Ducts, sheet metal
PA: The Mcgill Corporation
1 Mission Park
Groveport OH 43125
614 829-1200

(G-1823)
MEDTRNIC SOFAMOR DANEK USA INC
Also Called: Medtronic
2000 Regency Pkwy Ste 270 (27518-8509)
PHONE..................................919 457-9982
EMP: 8
Web: www.medtronic.com
SIC: 5047 3842 Hospital equipment and furniture; Implants, surgical
HQ: Medtronic Sofamor Danek Usa, Inc.
4340 Swinnea Rd
Memphis TN 38118
901 396-3133

(G-1824)
MIDNIGHT PUBLISHING GROUP INC
107 Hawks Nest Ct (27513-4804)
PHONE..................................919 809-4277
Melanie Stewart, *CEO*
Lanont Cooper, *Ex Dir*
EMP: 6 **EST:** 2009
SALES (est): 106.36K **Privately Held**
SIC: 2741 Miscellaneous publishing

(G-1825)
MILTON GORHAM
120 Wee Loch Dr Ste 101 (27511-3866)
PHONE..................................919 816-8348
Milton Gorham, *Prin*
EMP: 5 **EST:** 2015
SALES (est): 52.8K **Privately Held**
Web: www.lindagorham.com
SIC: 2741 Miscellaneous publishing

(G-1826)
MOON AUDIO
1157 Executive Cir Ste 101 (27511-4665)
PHONE..................................919 649-5018
Drew Baird, *Owner*
EMP: 5 **EST:** 2008
SALES (est): 1.27MM **Privately Held**
Web: www.moon-audio.com
SIC: 5999 3651 2298 Audio-visual equipment and supplies; Audio electronic systems; Ropes and fiber cables

(G-1827)
MTS SYSTEMS CORPORATION
Also Called: MTS Sensors Division
3001 Sheldon Dr (27513-2006)
PHONE..................................919 677-2352
Joachim Hellwig, *Mgr*
EMP: 200
SQ FT: 55,835
SALES (corp-wide): 15.93B **Publicly Held**
Web: www.mts.com
SIC: 3679 3825 3823 Transducers, electrical; Test equipment for electronic and electric measurement; Process control instruments
HQ: Mts Systems Corporation
14000 Technology Dr
Eden Prairie MN 55344
952 937-4000

GEOGRAPHIC SECTION　　　　　　　　　　　　　　　　　　　　　　　　　　　　　　　Cary - Wake County (G-1853)

(G-1828)
MUDDY DOG LLC
Also Called: Muddy Dog Roasting Co
511 Edgemore Ave (27519-6218)
PHONE..................................919 371-2818
EMP: 5 **EST:** 2006
SALES (est): 380.56K **Privately Held**
Web: www.coffeedans.com
SIC: 2095 Coffee extracts

(G-1829)
N2 PUBLISHING
139 Dove Cottage Ln (27519-1874)
PHONE..................................828 337-9380
EMP: 4
SALES (est): 72.59K **Privately Held**
Web: www.strollmag.com
SIC: 2741 Miscellaneous publishing

(G-1830)
NCR VOYIX CORPORATION
Also Called: NCR
115 Centrewest Ct (27513-2015)
PHONE..................................937 445-5000
Bo Holmgreen, *Brnch Mgr*
EMP: 5
SALES (corp-wide): 7.84B **Publicly Held**
Web: www.ncr.com
SIC: 3575 3578 3577 7379 Computer terminals; Point-of-sale devices; Magnetic ink and optical scanning devices; Computer related maintenance services
PA: Ncr Voyix Corporation
　　864 Spring St Nw
　　Atlanta GA 30308
　　937 445-1936

(G-1831)
NIRAS INC
1000 Centre Green Way Ste 200 (27513)
PHONE..................................919 439-4562
Henrik Linnemann, *Pr*
EMP: 4 **EST:** 2016
SALES (est): 449.06K **Privately Held**
Web: www.niras.com
SIC: 2834 Druggists' preparations (pharmaceuticals)

(G-1832)
NKT INC
Also Called: Nkt Cables
1255 Crescent Green (27518-8123)
PHONE..................................919 601-1970
Andreas Berthou, *Pr*
Mikael Wenneberg, *VP*
EMP: 5 **EST:** 2017
SALES (est): 4.92MM
SALES (corp-wide): 2.16B **Privately Held**
SIC: 1731 3355 Fiber optic cable installation; Aluminum wire and cable
PA: Nkt A/S
　　Vibeholms Alle 20
　　Brondby
　　43482000

(G-1833)
NORTHWEST AG PRODUCT
1001 Winstead Dr Ste 480 (27513-2117)
PHONE..................................509 547-8234
David Bergevin, *Pr*
EMP: 9 **EST:** 2015
SALES (est): 193.59K **Privately Held**
SIC: 2875 Fertilizers, mixing only

(G-1834)
NXP USA INC
Also Called: Philips Semiconductors
113 Fieldbrook Ct (27519-7914)
PHONE..................................919 468-3251
Bradley Loisel, *Brnch Mgr*
EMP: 7
SALES (corp-wide): 13.21B **Privately Held**
Web: www.nxp.com
SIC: 3674 Semiconductors and related devices
HQ: Nxp Usa, Inc.
　　6501 W William Cannon Dr
　　Austin TX 78735
　　512 933-8214

(G-1835)
OAK & AXE CUSTOM WOODWORKING
1105 Highland Trl (27511-5162)
PHONE..................................919 434-1939
James Brown, *Prin*
EMP: 5 **EST:** 2017
SALES (est): 54.13K **Privately Held**
SIC: 2431 Millwork

(G-1836)
OAK CITY WOODSHOP LLC
103 Fox Ct (27513-4920)
PHONE..................................937 830-0808
Jacob Hogue, *Prin*
EMP: 4 **EST:** 2019
SALES (est): 69.67K **Privately Held**
Web: www.oakcitywoodshop.com
SIC: 2431 Millwork

(G-1837)
OASYS MOBILE INC
Also Called: Summus
8000 Regency Pkwy Ste 285 (27518-0004)
P.O. Box 519 (27540-0519)
PHONE..................................919 807-5600
Douglas B Dyer, *CEO*
Tracy T Jackson, *CFO*
Donald T Locke, *Executive Corporate Development Vice President*
EMP: 17 **EST:** 1984
SQ FT: 7,339
SALES (est): 791.03K **Privately Held**
Web: www.oasysmobile.com
SIC: 7372 Application computer software

(G-1838)
OPTIMUM SIGN AGE
106 Okehampton Ct (27518-2429)
PHONE..................................919 372-8018
Richard Drolet, *Prin*
EMP: 4 **EST:** 2015
SALES (est): 78.56K **Privately Held**
SIC: 3993 Signs and advertising specialties

(G-1839)
OUTLET MARINE ENGINES INC
120 Centrewest Ct Ste 695 (27513-2015)
PHONE..................................919 279-3338
EMP: 4 **EST:** 2010
SALES (est): 54.57K **Privately Held**
SIC: 3519 Marine engines

(G-1840)
OXFORD UNIVERSITY PRESS LLC
Also Called: Customer Service Department
4000 Centre Green Way (27513-5758)
PHONE..................................919 677-0977
TOLL FREE: 800
Thomas Mccarty, *Mgr*
EMP: 300
SALES (corp-wide): 3.69B **Privately Held**
Web: corp.oup.com
SIC: 8721 5192 2741 Accounting services, except auditing; Books, periodicals, and newspapers; Miscellaneous publishing
HQ: Oxford University Press, Llc
　　198 Madison Ave Fl 8
　　New York NY 10016
　　212 726-6000

(G-1841)
PARATA SYSTEMS LLC
205 Serence Ct (27518-9187)
PHONE..................................919 363-2454
EMP: 16
SALES (corp-wide): 19.37B **Publicly Held**
Web: www.parata.com
SIC: 3826 Automatic chemical analyzers
HQ: Parata Systems, Llc
　　106 Roche Dr
　　Durham NC 27703
　　888 727-2821

(G-1842)
PASSPORT HEALTH TRIANGLE
8450 Chapel Hill Rd Ste 205 (27513-4577)
PHONE..................................919 781-0053
Melissa Wagers, *Pr*
EMP: 10 **EST:** 2007
SALES (est): 1.66MM **Privately Held**
Web: www.passporthealthusa.com
SIC: 2836 Vaccines and other immunizing products

(G-1843)
PAW PHARMA SERVICES LLC
304 Kettlebridge Dr (27511-6358)
PHONE..................................919 367-0413
Julie Ross, *Prin*
EMP: 5 **EST:** 2012
SALES (est): 213.94K **Privately Held**
SIC: 2834 Pharmaceutical preparations

(G-1844)
PAYLOAD MEDIA INC
129 Parkcrest Dr (27519-6609)
PHONE..................................919 367-2969
Neil Smyth, *CEO*
EMP: 5 **EST:** 2016
SALES (est): 269.27K **Privately Held**
SIC: 5734 2731 Software, business and non-game; Books, publishing only

(G-1845)
PCI OF NORTH CAROLINA LLC
Also Called: Syracuse Plastics
100 Falcone Pkwy (27511-6712)
P.O. Box 1067 (27512-1067)
PHONE..................................919 467-5151
EMP: 50 **EST:** 2019
SALES (est): 9.39MM **Privately Held**
Web: www.syrplas.com
SIC: 3089 Injection molding of plastics

(G-1846)
PEAK LEVEL MEDIA SOLUTIONS LLC
17104 Musselburgh Dr (27518-6974)
PHONE..................................919 917-8002
EMP: 4
SALES (est): 128.13K **Privately Held**
SIC: 3999 7389 Cigarette and cigar products and accessories; Business services, nec

(G-1847)
PEFORMANCE CHASSIS
214 Hillsboro St (27513-4567)
PHONE..................................919 319-3484
Mark E Cooper, *Prin*
EMP: 5 **EST:** 2010
SALES (est): 479.79K **Privately Held**
Web: www.performance-chassis.com
SIC: 3569 Liquid automation machinery and equipment

(G-1848)
PENTAIR WATER POOL AND SPA INC
400 Regency Forest Dr Ste 300 (27518-7702)
PHONE..................................919 463-4640
EMP: 15
Web: www.pentair.com
SIC: 3589 3561 3569 3648 Swimming pool filter and water conditioning systems; Pumps, domestic: water or sump; Heaters, swimming pool: electric; Underwater lighting fixtures
HQ: Pentair Water Pool And Spa, Inc.
　　1620 Hawkins Ave
　　Sanford NC 27330
　　919 566-8000

(G-1849)
PEPSI BOTTLING VENTURES LLC
Also Called: Call Center
500 Gregson Dr (27511-6461)
PHONE..................................800 879-8884
EMP: 44
Web: www.pepsico.com
SIC: 2086 Carbonated soft drinks, bottled and canned
HQ: Pepsi Bottling Ventures Llc
　　4141 Parklake Ave Ste 600
　　Raleigh NC 27612
　　919 865-2300

(G-1850)
PERFECT 10 BRANDS LLC
129 Glenmore Rd (27519-6152)
PHONE..................................702 738-0183
Rajeev Prasad, *Pr*
EMP: 4 **EST:** 2017
SALES (est): 245.91K **Privately Held**
Web: www.p10mm.com
SIC: 2844 Shampoos, rinses, conditioners: hair

(G-1851)
PHOENIX ST CLAIRE PUBG LLC
Also Called: Cornell Lab Publishing Gropu
321 Glen Echo Ln Apt C (27518-9676)
PHONE..................................919 303-3223
Brian Scott Sockin, *CEO*
EMP: 4 **EST:** 2013
SALES (est): 190.93K **Privately Held**
SIC: 2731 Books, publishing only

(G-1852)
PLY GEM HOLDINGS INC (DH)
Also Called: Ply Gem
5020 Weston Pkwy Ste 400 (27513-2322)
PHONE..................................919 677-3900
Gary E Robinette, *Pr*
Shawn K Poe, *
John C Wayne, *
Bryan Boyle, *Chief Accounting Officer**
EMP: 55 **EST:** 2004
SQ FT: 38,000
SALES (est): 2.06B
SALES (corp-wide): 5.58B **Privately Held**
Web: www.plygem.com
SIC: 2431 2952 Millwork; Siding materials
HQ: Ply Gem Midco, Llc
　　5020 Weston Pkwy Ste 400
　　Cary NC 27513
　　919 677-3900

(G-1853)
PLY GEM INDUSTRIES INC (DH)
Also Called: Ply Gem Industries
5020 Weston Pkwy Ste 400 (27513-2322)
PHONE..................................919 677-3900
Gary E Robinette, *Pr*
Shawn K Poe, *
EMP: 100 **EST:** 1987
SALES (est): 1.98B
SALES (corp-wide): 5.58B **Privately Held**
Web: www.plygem.com
SIC: 2431 Windows, wood
HQ: Ply Gem Holdings, Inc.
　　5020 Weston Pkwy Ste 400

Cary - Wake County (G-1854)

Cary NC 27513
919 677-3900

(G-1854)
POLYZEN INC
115 Woodwinds Industrial Ct (27511-6240)
PHONE..................................919 319-9599
Lisa Bozinovic, *CFO*
EMP: 17 **EST:** 2010
SALES (est): 326.5K **Privately Held**
Web: www.polyzen.com
SIC: 3841 Surgical and medical instruments

(G-1855)
PORTABLE DISPLAYS LLC
Also Called: Godfrey Group
5640 Dillard Dr Ste 301 (27518-7199)
P.O. Box 788 (44087-0788)
PHONE..................................919 544-6504
◆ **EMP:** 48
SIC: 2522 8742 3993 Panel systems and partitions, office: except wood; Marketing consulting services; Signs and advertising specialties

(G-1856)
POWERMOLEKUL INC (PA)
Also Called: Powerserv International
205 Coltsgate Dr Ste 100 (27518-8316)
PHONE..................................919 264-8487
Ali Imece, *Pr*
EMP: 6 **EST:** 2001
SALES (est): 243.99K
SALES (corp-wide): 243.99K **Privately Held**
Web: www.power-serv.com
SIC: 3511 7389 Turbines and turbine generator sets and parts; Business services, nec

(G-1857)
PPG INDUSTRIES INC
Also Called: PPG 4650
210 Nottingham Dr (27511-4915)
PHONE..................................919 319-0113
Ronald Pegeus, *Mgr*
EMP: 4
SALES (corp-wide): 17.65B **Publicly Held**
Web: www.ppgpaints.com
SIC: 2851 Paints and allied products
PA: Ppg Industries, Inc.
1 Ppg Pl
Pittsburgh PA 15272
412 434-3131

(G-1858)
PRAMANA LLC
709 Dennison Ln (27519-8854)
PHONE..................................910 233-5118
Robert Corey Patton, *Managing Member*
EMP: 4 **EST:** 2018
SALES (est): 1MM **Privately Held**
SIC: 7372 7389 Application computer software; Business services, nec

(G-1859)
PRISM PRINTING & DESIGN INC
109 Loch Haven Ln (27518-8409)
PHONE..................................919 706-5977
William F Metcalfe, *Pr*
EMP: 5 **EST:** 1986
SQ FT: 3,200
SALES (est): 311.27K **Privately Held**
SIC: 2752 Offset printing

(G-1860)
PRISM PUBLISHING INC (PA)
Also Called: Job Finder USA
1240 Se Maynard Rd Ste 104 (27511-6946)
P.O. Box 4844 (27519-4844)
PHONE..................................919 319-6816
EMP: 10 **EST:** 1995
SQ FT: 2,000
SALES (est): 2.42MM **Privately Held**
SIC: 2721 7336 Periodicals, publishing and printing; Commercial art and graphic design

(G-1861)
PROFESSIONAL LAMINATING LLC
107 Turnberry Ln (27518-9772)
PHONE..................................919 465-0400
EMP: 5
SALES (est): 144.83K **Privately Held**
Web: www.prorecognition.com
SIC: 2752 Commercial printing, lithographic

(G-1862)
PROFESSIONAL LAMINATING LLC
Also Called: Professional Laminating
233 E Johnson St Ste M (27513-4046)
PHONE..................................919 465-0400
EMP: 7 **EST:** 2007
SALES (est): 997.96K **Privately Held**
Web: www.prolamsolutions.com
SIC: 3999 2759 3479 7331 Plaques, picture, laminated; Invitation and stationery printing and engraving; Etching and engraving; Direct mail advertising services

(G-1863)
PROPHYSICS INNOVATIONS INC
1911 Evans Rd (27513-2041)
PHONE..................................919 245-0406
William Deforest, *Owner*
William Defrost, *Owner*
Lani De Forest, *Point of Contact*
EMP: 17 **EST:** 1997
SALES (est): 983.26K
SALES (corp-wide): 6.07MM **Publicly Held**
Web: www.landauer.com
SIC: 3842 8999 Radiation shielding aprons, gloves, sheeting, etc.; Scientific consulting
PA: Fortive Corporation
6920 Seaway Blvd
Everett WA 98203
425 446-5000

(G-1864)
QC LLC (DH)
1001 Winstead Dr Ste 480 (27513-2117)
PHONE..................................800 883-0010
Jason Gordon, *Pr*
Eric Hyatt, *COO*
◆ **EMP:** 37 **EST:** 1981
SALES (est): 26.32MM
SALES (corp-wide): 4.71B **Privately Held**
SIC: 2819 Iron (ferric/ferrous) compounds or salts
HQ: Verdesian Life Sciences, Llc
1001 Winstead Dr Ste 480
Cary NC 27513
919 825-1901

(G-1865)
RAPIDFORM INC
1001 Winstead Dr Ste 400 (27513-2117)
PHONE..................................408 856-6200
Calvin Hur, *CEO*
Martin Chader, *VP*
Thomas Charron, *COO*
EMP: 7 **EST:** 2005
SQ FT: 3,000
SALES (est): 102.28K **Privately Held**
SIC: 7372 Prepackaged software

(G-1866)
RBW LLC
105 Graywick Way (27513-1610)
PHONE..................................919 319-1289
Patricia W Wheeley, *Prin*
EMP: 5 **EST:** 2018
SALES (est): 86.96K **Privately Held**
SIC: 3599 Machine shop, jobbing and repair

(G-1867)
REESES BALLOON ART
114 Seymour Creek Dr (27519-5870)
PHONE..................................919 303-2147
Reese Wing, *Prin*
EMP: 4 **EST:** 2010
SALES (est): 69.42K **Privately Held**
SIC: 3999 Framed artwork

(G-1868)
RENNASENTIENT INC
Also Called: AlphaGraphics
301 Ashville Ave (27518-6131)
PHONE..................................919 233-7710
Eric J Webb, *Prin*
Eric James Webb, *Prin*
EMP: 12 **EST:** 2017
SALES (est): 1.81MM **Privately Held**
Web: www.alphagraphics.com
SIC: 8742 2711 Marketing consulting services; Commercial printing and newspaper publishing combined

(G-1869)
RESEARCH TRIANGLE SOFTWARE INC
109 Lochview Dr (27518-9619)
PHONE..................................919 233-8796
Jeffrey W Lerose, *Prin*
EMP: 6 **EST:** 2011
SALES (est): 94.15K **Privately Held**
SIC: 2741 Miscellaneous publishing

(G-1870)
RHD SERVICE LLC
1001 Winstead Dr Ste 1 (27513-2154)
PHONE..................................919 297-1600
EMP: 28
SALES (est): 775.11K **Privately Held**
SIC: 2741 Directories, telephone: publishing only, not printed on site

(G-1871)
RITAS ONE INC
208 Dowington Ln (27519-6382)
PHONE..................................919 650-2415
EMP: 5 **EST:** 2009
SALES (est): 193.35K **Privately Held**
SIC: 2032 Canned specialties

(G-1872)
ROCKWELL AUTOMATION INC
113 Edinburgh South Dr Ste 200 (27511-6456)
PHONE..................................919 804-0200
Bill Feuerstein, *Mgr*
EMP: 6
Web: www.rockwellautomation.com
SIC: 3625 Control equipment, electric
PA: Rockwell Automation, Inc.
1201 S 2nd St
Milwaukee WI 53204

(G-1873)
RONAK LLC
2302 Skye Ln (27518-9334)
PHONE..................................781 589-1973
Raghav K Iyengar, *Prin*
EMP: 5 **EST:** 2012
SALES (est): 143.17K **Privately Held**
SIC: 7372 Prepackaged software

(G-1874)
RTP MACHINE INC
120 Centrewest Ct Ste 111 (27513-2015)
PHONE..................................919 279-3338
Edric Culbreth, *Prin*
EMP: 6 **EST:** 2016
SALES (est): 98.61K **Privately Held**
Web: www.rtpmachinesinc.com
SIC: 3599 Industrial machinery, nec

(G-1875)
RUCKUS WIRELESS INC
Also Called: Telewire Supply
101 Stamford Dr (27513-9503)
PHONE..................................919 677-0571
EMP: 345
Web: www.commscope.com
SIC: 3663 Radio and t.v. communications equipment
HQ: Ruckus Wireless Llc
350 W Java Dr
Sunnyvale CA 94089

(G-1876)
S & A CHEROKEE LLC
Also Called: S & A Cherokee Publishing
301 Cascade Pointe Ln Ste 101 (27513-5778)
PHONE..................................919 674-6020
EMP: 40 **EST:** 2004
SALES (est): 5MM **Privately Held**
Web: www.sacommunications.com
SIC: 2741 7374 8741 8743 Miscellaneous publishing; Computer graphics service; Management services; Public relations services

(G-1877)
S C I A INC
Also Called: Security Ultraviolet
204 Dundalk Way (27511-5056)
PHONE..................................919 387-7000
EMP: 5 **EST:** 1969
SQ FT: 3,000
SALES (est): 121.7K **Privately Held**
SIC: 7373 7389 3648 7371 Computer integrated systems design; Fund raising organizations; Lighting equipment, nec; Computer software development

(G-1878)
SAKUN INC ✪
Also Called: Gini's Beverages
114 Doric Ct (27519-5038)
PHONE..................................919 255-2994
Manoj Patel, *Pr*
EMP: 7 **EST:** 2022
SALES (est): 79.3K **Privately Held**
SIC: 2087 7389 Flavoring extracts and syrups, nec; Business Activities at Non-Commercial Site

(G-1879)
SAMSUNG SEMICONDUCTOR INC
8000 Regency Pkwy Ste 585 (27518-8589)
PHONE..................................919 380-8483
Matthew Allen, *Mgr*
EMP: 6
Web: www.samsung.com
SIC: 3674 Semiconductors and related devices
HQ: Samsung Semiconductor, Inc.
3655 N 1st St
San Jose CA 95134
408 544-4000

(G-1880)
SAS FEDERAL LLC
100 Sas Campus Dr (27513-8617)
PHONE..................................919 531-7505
EMP: 9 **EST:** 2009
SALES (est): 393.9K **Privately Held**
SIC: 7372 Application computer software

GEOGRAPHIC SECTION
Cary - Wake County (G-1904)

(G-1881)
SAS INSTITUTE INC
940 Nw Cary Pkwy (27513-2792)
PHONE.................954 494-8189
Marcelo Gavazzi, *Brnch Mgr*
EMP: 4
SALES (corp-wide): 3.19B **Privately Held**
Web: www.sas.com
SIC: 7372 Application computer software
PA: Sas Institute Inc.
  100 Sas Campus Dr
  Cary NC 27513
  919 677-8000

(G-1882)
SAS INSTITUTE INC
P.O. Box 610 (27512-0610)
PHONE.................919 677-8000
EMP: 6
SALES (corp-wide): 3.19B **Privately Held**
Web: www.sas.com
SIC: 7372 Application computer software
PA: Sas Institute Inc.
  100 Sas Campus Dr
  Cary NC 27513
  919 677-8000

(G-1883)
SAS INSTITUTE INC
820 Sas Campus Dr # C (27513-2086)
PHONE.................919 531-4153
Ethan Ekkens, *Brnch Mgr*
EMP: 7
SALES (corp-wide): 3.19B **Privately Held**
Web: www.sas.com
SIC: 7372 Application computer software
PA: Sas Institute Inc.
  100 Sas Campus Dr
  Cary NC 27513
  919 677-8000

(G-1884)
SAS INSTITUTE INC (PA)
100 Sas Campus Dr (27513-8617)
PHONE.................919 677-8000
▲ **EMP:** 1170 **EST:** 1976
SALES (est): 3.19B
SALES (corp-wide): 3.19B **Privately Held**
Web: www.sas.com
SIC: 7372 7371 Application computer software; Custom computer programming services

(G-1885)
SENSUS
113 Gorecki Pl (27513-9619)
PHONE.................919 376-2617
Carolina Cely, *Prin*
EMP: 11 **EST:** 2018
SALES (est): 79.92K **Privately Held**
Web: www.sensus.com
SIC: 3824 Fluid meters and counting devices

(G-1886)
SIEMENS CORPORATION
3333 Regency Pkwy (27518-7705)
PHONE.................919 465-1287
EMP: 8
SALES (corp-wide): 84.48B **Privately Held**
Web: www.siemens.com
SIC: 3661 Telephone and telegraph apparatus
HQ: Siemens Corporation
  300 New Jersey Ave Nw # 100
  Washington DC 20001
  202 434-2800

(G-1887)
SIEMENS MED SOLUTIONS USA INC
Also Called: Clinical Workflow Consulting
221 Gregson Dr (27511-6495)
PHONE.................919 468-7400
EMP: 34
SALES (corp-wide): 84.48B **Privately Held**
Web: new.siemens.com
SIC: 3621 Armatures, industrial
HQ: Siemens Medical Solutions Usa, Inc.
  40 Liberty Blvd
  Malvern PA 19355
  888 826-9702

(G-1888)
SIEMENS POWER TRANSMISSION & DISTRIBUTION INC
110 Macalyson Ct (27511-7912)
PHONE.................919 463-8702
▲ **EMP:** 2100
SIC: 3613 3625 Switches, electric power except snap, push button, etc.; Relays and industrial controls

(G-1889)
SIGNALSCAPE INC
200 Regency Forest Dr Ste 310 (27518-8695)
PHONE.................919 859-4565
Jhan Vannatta, *CEO*
Jhan Vannatta, *Pr*
Ed Allen, *
Barbara Mcnamara, *Dir*
Robert Kinney, *
EMP: 45 **EST:** 2000
SQ FT: 56,506
SALES (est): 6.21MM **Privately Held**
Web: www.signalscape.com
SIC: 8731 7371 3823 Commercial physical research; Custom computer programming services; Process control instruments

(G-1890)
SIMONTON WINDOWS & DOORS INC
5020 Weston Pkwy Ste 300 (27513-2322)
PHONE.................919 677-3938
EMP: 93 **EST:** 1946
SALES (est): 4.26MM
SALES (corp-wide): 5.58B **Privately Held**
Web: www.simonton.com
SIC: 3448 Buildings, portable: prefabricated metal
HQ: Cornerstone Building Brands, Inc.
  5020 Weston Pkwy
  Cary NC 27513
  281 897-7788

(G-1891)
SIMPLECERTIFIEDMAILCOM LLC
111 Commonwealth Ct Ste 103 (27511-4447)
PHONE.................888 462-1750
Charles W Crutchfield, *Prin*
EMP: 5 **EST:** 2012
SALES (est): 240.83K **Privately Held**
Web: www.simplecertifiedmail.com
SIC: 7372 Prepackaged software

(G-1892)
SIMPLICTI SFTWR SOLUTIONS INC
Also Called: Simplicti
1255 Crescent Green Ste 145 (27518-8123)
PHONE.................919 858-8898
Wen-kai Ho, *CEO*
Bruce Calhoon, *
EMP: 17 **EST:** 1997
SQ FT: 14,000
SALES (est): 348.67K **Privately Held**
SIC: 7372 Prepackaged software

(G-1893)
SIZE STREAM LLC
Also Called: Formcut 3d
223 Commonwealth Ct (27511-4474)
PHONE.................919 355-5708
David Bruner, *Managing Member*
EMP: 9 **EST:** 2012
SQ FT: 5,000
SALES (est): 1.34MM **Privately Held**
Web: www.sizestream.com
SIC: 3845 Ultrasonic scanning devices, medical

(G-1894)
SLICKEDIT INC
408 Bathgate Ln (27513-5582)
P.O. Box 1953 (27528-1953)
PHONE.................919 473-0070
Jill L Maurer, *Ch*
Donald L Reppert, *
William F Denman Junior, *Prin*
Joseph Clark Maurer, *
Howard H Lewis, *
EMP: 25 **EST:** 1988
SALES (est): 3.58MM **Privately Held**
Web: www.slickedit.com
SIC: 7372 Business oriented computer software

(G-1895)
SMALLHD LLC (DH)
301 Gregson Dr (27511-6496)
PHONE.................919 439-2166
Wes Phillips, *CEO*
▲ **EMP:** 42 **EST:** 2014
SQ FT: 5,400
SALES (est): 21.11MM
SALES (corp-wide): 543.23MM **Privately Held**
Web: www.smallhd.com
SIC: 3679 3861 Liquid crystal displays (LCD); Lens shades, camera
HQ: Videndum Production Solutions Inc.
  14 Progress Dr
  Shelton CT 06484
  203 929-1100

(G-1896)
SMARTLINK MOBILE SYSTEMS LLC
1000 Centre Green Way Ste 250 (27513)
PHONE.................919 674-8400
Alex Tse, *Chief Medical Officer*
EMP: 14 **EST:** 2015
SALES (est): 2.18MM **Privately Held**
Web: www.smartlinkhealth.com
SIC: 7372 Application computer software

(G-1897)
SMARTWARE GROUP INC
11000 Regency Pkwy Ste 110 (27518-8518)
PHONE.................866 858-7800
Paul Lachance, *CEO*
Marc Bromberg, *VP*
David Peelstrom, *CFO*
EMP: 11 **EST:** 2002
SALES (est): 213.68K **Privately Held**
SIC: 7372 Business oriented computer software

(G-1898)
SOCKS VTERINARY HSE CALLS PLLC
116 Benedum Pl (27518-8835)
PHONE.................919 244-2826
EMP: 5 **EST:** 2017
SALES (est): 88.63K **Privately Held**
Web: www.socksandcomobilevet.com
SIC: 2252 Socks

(G-1899)
SPATIAL LIGHT LLC
1017 Pueblo Ridge Pl (27519-0832)
P.O. Box 12658 (27709-2658)
PHONE.................617 213-0314
Willie Johnpadilla, *CEO*
Willie Padilla, *CEO*
EMP: 4 **EST:** 2015
SALES (est): 206K **Privately Held**
SIC: 3812 Infrared object detection equipment

(G-1900)
SPECTRASITE COMMUNICATIONS LLC (HQ)
400 Regency Forest Dr Ste 300 (27518-7702)
PHONE.................919 468-0112
Stephen Clark, *Pr*
David Tomick, *
Dan Hunt, *
Richard Byrne, *WIRELESS TOWER GROUP*
Timothy Biltz, *
▲ **EMP:** 35 **EST:** 1997
SQ FT: 150,000
SALES (est): 75.6MM **Publicly Held**
Web: www.spectrasite.com
SIC: 8748 1623 3661 4813 Business consulting, nec; Transmitting tower (telecommunication) construction; Telephone and telegraph apparatus; Telephone communication, except radio
PA: American Tower Corporation
  116 Huntington Ave # 1100
  Boston MA 02116

(G-1901)
SPECTRUM SCREEN PRTG SVC INC
214 Hillsboro St Ste 101 (27513-4567)
PHONE.................919 481-9905
Harry Gould, *Pr*
Donna Gould, *Sec*
EMP: 10 **EST:** 1986
SQ FT: 4,100
SALES (est): 735.73K **Privately Held**
Web: www.spectrumscreen.com
SIC: 2759 Screen printing

(G-1902)
SPNC ASSOCIATES INC
100 Falcone Pkwy (27511-6712)
P.O. Box 1067 (27512-1067)
PHONE.................919 467-5151
Thomas R Falcone, *CEO*
▲ **EMP:** 54 **EST:** 1981
SQ FT: 35,000
SALES (est): 24.66MM **Privately Held**
SIC: 3089 3544 Injection molding of plastics; Special dies, tools, jigs, and fixtures
PA: Plastic Components, Inc.
  N116w18271 Morse Dr
  Germantown WI 53022

(G-1903)
STELLAR TECHNOLOGY
111 Lord Dr (27511-7923)
PHONE.................716 250-1900
EMP: 6 **EST:** 2019
SALES (est): 70.82K **Privately Held**
Web: www.stellartech.com
SIC: 3829 Measuring and controlling devices, nec

(G-1904)
STERLING PHARMA USA LLC
Also Called: Sterling Pharma USA
1001 Sheldon Dr Ste 101 (27513-2079)
P.O. Box 12041 (27709-2041)
PHONE.................919 678-0702
Mathew Minardi, *Managing Member*

Tushar Bahadur,
EMP: 36 **EST:** 2019
SQ FT: 6,000
SALES (est): 6.21MM **Privately Held**
Web: www.sterlingpharmasolutions.com
SIC: 2834 Pharmaceutical preparations
HQ: Sterling Pharma Solutions Limited
Sterling Place, Dudley
Cramlington NORTHD NE23
191 250-0471

(G-1905)
STONEHAVEN JEWELRY GALLERY LTD
111 Adams St (27513-4527)
PHONE.................................919 462-8888
Billy Webster, *Pr*
Ron Lodholz, *VP*
EMP: 5 **EST:** 1996
SALES (est): 434.42K **Privately Held**
Web: www.stonehavenjewelry.com
SIC: 3915 7631 Jewelers' materials and lapidary work; Jewelry repair services

(G-1906)
SURFACE BUFF LLC
1140 Kildaire Farm Rd # 303-3 (27511-4562)
P.O. Box 857 (27529-0857)
PHONE.................................919 341-2873
Georgia Rivera, *Managing Member*
EMP: 5 **EST:** 2008
SALES (est): 484.06K **Privately Held**
Web: www.surfacebuff.com
SIC: 5032 1389 7349 3531 Stone, crushed or broken; Construction, repair, and dismantling services; Janitorial service, contract basis; Surfacers, concrete grinding

(G-1907)
TEMPOSONICS LLC
3001 Sheldon Dr (27513-2006)
PHONE.................................470 380-5103
David Hore, *Pr*
Michael Ivas, *VP*
Craig Lampo, *CFO*
Lance D'amico, *Sec*
EMP: 5 **EST:** 2021
SALES (est): 2.62MM
SALES (corp-wide): 12.55B **Publicly Held**
Web: www.temposonics.com
SIC: 3823 Primary elements for process flow measurement
PA: Amphenol Corporation
358 Hall Ave
Wallingford CT 06492
203 265-8900

(G-1908)
THINKING MAPS INC (PA)
401 Cascade Pointe Ln (27513-5780)
PHONE.................................919 678-8778
Shirwin Suddreth, *Pr*
EMP: 5 **EST:** 1990
SALES (est): 2.09MM
SALES (corp-wide): 2.09MM **Privately Held**
Web: www.thinkingmaps.com
SIC: 8748 2741 Educational consultant; Miscellaneous publishing

(G-1909)
THORCO LLC
301 Birdwood Ct (27519-9719)
PHONE.................................919 363-6234
Richard C Stephenson, *Managing Member*
EMP: 10 **EST:** 2012
SALES (est): 851.99K **Privately Held**
SIC: 7379 7372 Computer related services, nec; Utility computer software

(G-1910)
TOTAL SONO LLC
100 Conway Ct (27513-9400)
PHONE.................................908 349-8610
EMP: 5 **EST:** 2012
SALES (est): 152.28K **Privately Held**
SIC: 3829 Medical diagnostic systems, nuclear

(G-1911)
TOWERCO LLC
5000 Valleystone Dr Ste 200 (27519-8434)
PHONE.................................919 653-5700
Daniel Hunt, *CFO*
EMP: 18 **EST:** 2004
SQ FT: 2,500
SALES (est): 5.09MM **Privately Held**
Web: www.towerco.com
SIC: 3441 Tower sections, radio and television transmission

(G-1912)
TRIANGLE SOLUTIONS INC
Also Called: PIP Printing
1074 W Chatham St (27511-6201)
PHONE.................................919 481-1235
Dave Callaghan, *Pr*
Charles Wolff, *VP*
EMP: 5 **EST:** 1990
SQ FT: 2,700
SALES (est): 485.5K **Privately Held**
Web: www.pip.com
SIC: 2752 7334 7336 3993 Offset printing; Photocopying and duplicating services; Commercial art and graphic design; Signs and advertising specialties

(G-1913)
TRIGGERMESH INC
109 Harmony Hill Ln (27513-8306)
PHONE.................................919 228-8049
Mark Hinkle, *Owner*
EMP: 10 **EST:** 2020
SALES (est): 447.22K **Privately Held**
Web: www.triggermesh.com
SIC: 7372 Prepackaged software

(G-1914)
TRIMECH SOLUTIONS LLC
Also Called: Tri Mech Services
206 High House Rd Ste 104 (27513-8496)
PHONE.................................919 535-5662
Gretchen Bazeley, *Mgr*
EMP: 4
SALES (corp-wide): 24.06MM **Privately Held**
Web: www.trimech.com
SIC: 7372 Prepackaged software
PA: Trimech Solutions, Llc
4991 Lake Brook Dr # 300
Glen Allen VA 23060
804 257-9965

(G-1915)
TRUSS BUILDINGS LLC
1512 Wackena Rd (27519-9547)
PHONE.................................919 377-0217
John Ottaway, *Prin*
EMP: 9 **EST:** 2015
SALES (est): 807.46K **Privately Held**
Web: www.tbllcnc.com
SIC: 2439 Trusses, wooden roof

(G-1916)
VALUE PRINTING INC
604 E Chatham St Ste D (27511-6926)
PHONE.................................919 380-9883
Margaret Kehoe, *Pr*
Steven Kehoe, *Sec*
EMP: 8 **EST:** 2009
SQ FT: 1,200
SALES (est): 974.85K **Privately Held**
Web: www.value-printing.com
SIC: 2752 Offset printing

(G-1917)
VANILLA PRINT INC
2301 Cameron Pond Dr (27519-8686)
PHONE.................................919 637-0745
Julie Schaffroth, *Prin*
EMP: 6 **EST:** 2011
SALES (est): 116.22K **Privately Held**
SIC: 2752 Commercial printing, lithographic

(G-1918)
VENCEDOR SOFTWARE GROUP INC
Also Called: Vencedor
5000 Centre Green Way Ste 500 (27513)
PHONE.................................978 390-1187
Manoj Kathrani, *Prin*
EMP: 8 **EST:** 2010
SALES (est): 237.17K **Privately Held**
SIC: 7372 Prepackaged software

(G-1919)
VERDESIAN LIFE SCIENCE US LLC (DH)
Also Called: Verdesian Life Sciences
1001 Winstead Dr Ste 480 (27513-2117)
PHONE.................................919 825-1901
Francis Pirozzi, *Governor*
EMP: 37 **EST:** 2014
SALES (est): 29.95MM
SALES (corp-wide): 4.71B **Privately Held**
SIC: 1479 Fertilizer mineral mining
HQ: Verdesian Life Sciences, Llc
1001 Winstead Dr Ste 480
Cary NC 27513
919 825-1901

(G-1920)
VIDENDUM PROD SOLUTIONS INC
215 Trimble Ave (27511-6209)
PHONE.................................919 244-0760
Dale Backus, *Brnch Mgr*
EMP: 5
SALES (corp-wide): 543.23MM **Privately Held**
Web: www.antonbauer.com
SIC: 3861 Lens shades, camera
HQ: Videndum Production Solutions Inc.
14 Progress Dr
Shelton CT 06484
203 929-1100

(G-1921)
VIRSCIDIAN INC
104 Ludlow Ct (27513-5106)
PHONE.................................919 809-7651
Joseph Simpkins, *Pr*
EMP: 5 **EST:** 2020
SALES (est): 236.38K **Privately Held**
Web: www.virscidian.com
SIC: 3652 Prerecorded records and tapes

(G-1922)
VIRTUS ENTERTAINMENT INC
114 Mackenan Dr Ste 100 (27511-7920)
PHONE.................................919 467-9700
Mark Baric, *Ch Bd*
David A Smith, *
James H Hayne, *CFO*
EMP: 41 **EST:** 1990
SQ FT: 16,000
SALES (est): 3.19MM **Privately Held**
SIC: 7372 Prepackaged software

(G-1923)
WAKE STONE CORPORATION
Also Called: Triangel Quarry
222 Star Ln (27513-2114)
PHONE.................................919 677-0050
Paul Pierce, *Mgr*
EMP: 26
SQ FT: 9,129
SALES (corp-wide): 24.15MM **Privately Held**
Web: www.wakestonecorp.com
SIC: 3281 Stone, quarrying and processing of own stone products
PA: Wake Stone Corporation
6821 Knightdale Blvd
Knightdale NC 27545
919 266-1100

(G-1924)
WATERBOXER INC
120 Centrewest Ct Unit 695 (27513-2015)
PHONE.................................919 279-3338
EMP: 5 **EST:** 2011
SALES (est): 220K **Privately Held**
SIC: 3519 Engines, diesel and semi-diesel or dual-fuel

(G-1925)
WELDERS LOG
108 Craven Hill Ct (27518-2226)
PHONE.................................919 473-3045
EMP: 5 **EST:** 2016
SALES (est): 69.16K **Privately Held**
Web: www.welderslog.com
SIC: 7692 Welding repair

(G-1926)
WESTSTAR PRECISION INC
Also Called: Weststar
101 Fern Bluff Way (27518-8973)
PHONE.................................919 557-2820
▲ **EMP:** 24
Web: www.weststarprecision.com
SIC: 3728 R and D by manuf., aircraft parts and auxiliary equipment

(G-1927)
WINERY ASSOC SOUTHEAST INC
120 Trinity Grove Dr (27513-6272)
PHONE.................................919 219-1929
EMP: 5 **EST:** 2006
SALES (est): 59.36K **Privately Held**
SIC: 2084 Wines

(G-1928)
WISDOM FOR HEART
2703 Jones Franklin Rd Ste 105 (27518-7172)
P.O. Box 37297 (27627-7297)
PHONE.................................866 482-4253
Stephen Davey, *Pr*
Pastor Stephen Davey, *Prin*
Scott Wsylie, *Ex Dir*
EMP: 10 **EST:** 2005
SALES (est): 1.57MM **Privately Held**
Web: www.wisdomonline.org
SIC: 2731 Books, publishing only

(G-1929)
WISPRY INC
4001 Weston Pkwy St 200 (27513-2311)
PHONE.................................919 854-7500
EMP: 7 **EST:** 2002
SALES (est): 2.25MM
SALES (corp-wide): 17.43B **Publicly Held**
Web: www.wispry.com
SIC: 7372 3559 Prepackaged software; Electronic component making machinery
HQ: Coventor, Inc.
4650 Cushing Pkwy
Fremont CA 94538

GEOGRAPHIC SECTION

Castle Hayne - New Hanover County (G-1953)

(G-1930)
WIT & WHISTLE
929 Manchester Dr (27511-4716)
PHONE.................................919 609-5309
EMP: 4 **EST:** 2015
SALES (est): 111.62K **Privately Held**
SIC: 2771 5112 5947 Greeting cards; Social stationery and greeting cards; Greeting cards

(G-1931)
WORKCOM INC
1001 Winstead Dr (27513-2155)
PHONE.................................310 586-4000
Mark W Hianik, *Sr VP*
EMP: 43 **EST:** 2009
SALES (est): 700.8K **Privately Held**
SIC: 2741 Directories, telephone: publishing only, not printed on site

(G-1932)
XEROX CORPORATION
11000 Weston Pkwy (27513-2261)
PHONE.................................919 428-9718
EMP: 22
SALES (corp-wide): 6.89B **Publicly Held**
Web: www.xerox.com
SIC: 3577 Computer peripheral equipment, nec
HQ: Xerox Corporation
   201 Merritt 7 Ste 1
   Norwalk CT 06851
   203 849-5216

Casar
Cleveland County

(G-1933)
FISH GETTER LURE CO LLC
254 Hull Rd (28020-8757)
PHONE.................................704 538-9863
EMP: 5 **EST:** 1969
SALES (est): 194.93K **Privately Held**
SIC: 3949 Lures, fishing: artificial

(G-1934)
M O DEVINEY LUMBER CO INC (PA)
Also Called: Deviney Lumber & Salvage
838 Moriah School Rd (28020-7701)
PHONE.................................704 538-9071
James Deviney, *Pr*
James O Deviney, *Pr*
Robert M Deviney, *VP*
Max D Deviney, *Sec*
EMP: 5 **EST:** 1936
SQ FT: 10,000
SALES (est): 4.56MM
SALES (corp-wide): 4.56MM **Privately Held**
Web: www.beckercustomseating.com
SIC: 5031 5211 2449 Lumber, plywood, and millwork; Lumber and other building materials; Rectangular boxes and crates, wood

Cashiers
Jackson County

(G-1935)
COMMUNITY NEWSPAPERS INC
Also Called: Cashiers Crossroads Chronicles
426 Nc 107 S (28717)
P.O. Box 1040 (28717-1040)
PHONE.................................828 743-5101
Michael Henry, *Mgr*
EMP: 6
SALES (corp-wide): 49.22MM **Privately Held**

Web: www.cninewspapers.com
SIC: 2711 Newspapers, publishing and printing
PA: Community Newspapers, Inc.
   2365 Prince Ave A
   Athens GA 30606
   706 548-0010

(G-1936)
LIFE STYLE PUBLISHING INC
P.O. Box 3283 (28717-3283)
PHONE.................................828 507-2209
Bryan Stoker, *Prin*
EMP: 4 **EST:** 2008
SALES (est): 70.34K **Privately Held**
Web: www.lifestylepubs.com
SIC: 2741 Miscellaneous publishing

(G-1937)
STICK CANDLES
372 Valley Rd (28717-5507)
P.O. Box 806 (28741-0806)
PHONE.................................315 369-0011
Doug Collum, *Prin*
EMP: 4 **EST:** 2018
SALES (est): 226K **Privately Held**
Web: www.stickcandles.com
SIC: 3999 Candles

(G-1938)
TOXAWAY CONCRETE INC
Hwy 64 E (28717)
P.O. Box 40 (28774-0040)
PHONE.................................828 966-4270
Randy Dillard, *Mgr*
EMP: 10
SALES (corp-wide): 1.39MM **Privately Held**
Web: www.mcneelycompanies.com
SIC: 3273 Ready-mixed concrete
PA: Toxaway Concrete Inc
   Off Hwy 281 N Hwy 64 E
   Lake Toxaway NC 28747
   828 966-4270

Castalia
Nash County

(G-1939)
EAGLE ASSEMBLY UNLIMITED INC
8928 Main St (27816-9262)
PHONE.................................252 462-0408
EMP: 8 **EST:** 2000
SALES (est): 180.14K **Privately Held**
SIC: 3492 Hose and tube fittings and assemblies, hydraulic/pneumatic

(G-1940)
MYERS LOGGING LLC
602 T Model Jones Rd (27816-9163)
PHONE.................................919 496-0379
EMP: 6 **EST:** 2016
SALES (est): 221.17K **Privately Held**
SIC: 2411 Logging

Castle Hayne
New Hanover County

(G-1941)
AC VALOR REYES LLC
Also Called: Glam Gal
4610 College Rd N (28429-5664)
P.O. Box 11237 (28404-1237)
PHONE.................................910 431-3256
EMP: 7 **EST:** 2005
SQ FT: 3,000
SALES (est): 262.3K **Privately Held**

SIC: 2759 5137 3199 Screen printing; Women's and children's accessories; Dog furnishings: collars, leashes, muzzles, etc.: leather

(G-1942)
AMERICAN CHROME & CHEM NA INC
5408 Holly Shelter Rd (28429-6350)
PHONE.................................910 675-7200
EMP: 4
Web: www.elementis.com
SIC: 5169 2899 Chemicals and allied products, nec; Chemical preparations, nec
HQ: American Chrome & Chemicals N.A. Inc.
   3800 Buddy Lawrence Dr
   Corpus Christi TX
   361 883-6421

(G-1943)
ARGOS USA LLC
Also Called: Redi-Mix Concrete
5225 Holly Shelter Rd (28429-6358)
PHONE.................................910 675-1262
EMP: 34
Web: www.argos-us.com
SIC: 3273 Ready-mixed concrete
HQ: Argos Usa Llc
   3015 Windward Plz Ste 300
   Alpharetta GA 30005
   678 368-4300

(G-1944)
BURTON STEEL COMPANY (PA)
102b Ritter Dr (28429-5449)
P.O. Box 265 (28402-0265)
PHONE.................................910 675-9241
Paul Burton, *Pr*
Robert W Johnson, *Sec*
EMP: 18 **EST:** 1975
SQ FT: 35,000
SALES (est): 2.11MM
SALES (corp-wide): 2.11MM **Privately Held**
SIC: 1791 3441 Structural steel erection; Fabricated structural metal

(G-1945)
CASTLE HAYNE HARDWARE LLC
Also Called: Hudson's Hardware
6301 Castle Hayne Rd (28429-5013)
PHONE.................................910 675-9205
Doug Reeves, *Managing Member*
EMP: 10 **EST:** 2009
SQ FT: 16,000
SALES (est): 751.37K **Privately Held**
Web: www.hudsonsdoitbest.com
SIC: 5251 2329 Builders' hardware; Athletic clothing, except uniforms: men's, youths' and boys'

(G-1946)
EXLEY CUSTOM WOODWORK INC
2921 Castle Hayne Rd (28429-5430)
PHONE.................................910 763-5445
Michael Exley, *Pr*
Marsha Exley, *Sec*
EMP: 4 **EST:** 1990
SQ FT: 3,825
SALES (est): 324.62K **Privately Held**
Web: www.ceotnc.org
SIC: 2431 Interior and ornamental woodwork and trim

(G-1947)
FORGED CSTM MET FBRICATION LLC
6804 Holly Shelter Rd (28429-6374)
PHONE.................................910 274-8300

Pete Pucella, *Prin*
EMP: 9 **EST:** 2018
SALES (est): 665.71K **Privately Held**
Web: www.forgedcustommetal.com
SIC: 3499 Fabricated metal products, nec

(G-1948)
GE-HITCHI NCLEAR ENRGY AMRCAS (HQ)
3901 Castle Hayne Rd (28429-6546)
P.O. Box 780 (28402-0780)
PHONE.................................910 819-5073
Jay Wileman, *Managing Member*
Angela Thornhill, *
Mike Ford, *
◆ **EMP:** 2000 **EST:** 2007
SALES (est): 1.4B
SALES (corp-wide): 67.95B **Publicly Held**
Web: nuclear.gepower.com
SIC: 2819 Nuclear fuel and cores, inorganic
PA: General Electric Company
   1 Financial Ctr Ste 3700
   Boston MA 02111
   617 443-3000

(G-1949)
GLOBAL LASER ENRICHMENT LLC
3901 Castle Hayne Rd (28429-6546)
P.O. Box 5117 (12301-5117)
PHONE.................................910 819-7255
Stephen Long, *CEO*
EMP: 37 **EST:** 2007
SALES (est): 9.49MM **Privately Held**
SIC: 2819 Nuclear fuel and cores, inorganic

(G-1950)
GLOBAL NUCLEAR FUEL-AMERICAS LLC (HQ)
3901 Castle Hayne Rd (28429-6546)
P.O. Box 780 (28402-0780)
PHONE.................................910 819-5950
◆ **EMP:** 28 **EST:** 1999
SALES (est): 408.2MM
SALES (corp-wide): 67.95B **Publicly Held**
SIC: 2819 Nuclear fuel and cores, inorganic
PA: General Electric Company
   1 Financial Ctr Ste 3700
   Boston MA 02111
   617 443-3000

(G-1951)
HOLLINGSWORTH CUSTOM SHOP
2915 Castle Hayne Rd (28429-5430)
PHONE.................................910 251-8849
EMP: 5 **EST:** 2019
SALES (est): 58.05K **Privately Held**
Web: www.hollingsworthcabinetry.com
SIC: 2434 Wood kitchen cabinets

(G-1952)
HOLLINGSWRTH CBNETS INTRORS LL
2913 Castle Hayne Rd (28429-5430)
PHONE.................................910 251-1490
Robert M Hollingsworth, *Pr*
EMP: 12 **EST:** 1994
SQ FT: 6,000
SALES (est): 2.55MM **Privately Held**
Web: www.hollingsworthcabinetry.com
SIC: 2541 2511 2434 Cabinets, except refrigerated: show, display, etc.: wood; Wood household furniture; Wood kitchen cabinets

(G-1953)
MARTIN MARIETTA MATERIALS INC
Also Called: Martin Marietta Aggregates
5408 Holly Shelter Rd (28429-6350)
P.O. Box 398 (28429-0398)
PHONE.................................910 675-2283

Castle Hayne - New Hanover County (G-1954)

Butch Barnhardt, *Brnch Mgr*
EMP: 6
Web: www.martinmarietta.com
SIC: 1422 Crushed and broken limestone
PA: Martin Marietta Materials Inc
4123 Parklake Ave
Raleigh NC 27612

(G-1954)
MARTIN MARIETTA MATERIALS INC
Also Called: Castle Hayne Yard
5635 Holly Shelter Rd (28429-6362)
PHONE....................910 602-6058
Marietta Martin, *Mgr*
EMP: 4
Web: www.martinmarietta.com
SIC: 3273 Ready-mixed concrete
PA: Martin Marietta Materials Inc
4123 Parklake Ave
Raleigh NC 27612

(G-1955)
MASTER MACHINING INC
410 Hermitage Rd (28429-5832)
PHONE....................910 675-3660
James Carter, *Pr*
Marilyn Carter, *Sec*
Jonathan Carter, *VP*
EMP: 20 **EST:** 1982
SQ FT: 6,000
SALES (est): 4.75MM **Privately Held**
Web: www.mastermachininginc.com
SIC: 3599 Machine shop, jobbing and repair

(G-1956)
N2 PUBLISHING
3721 Stormy Gale Pl (28429-6234)
PHONE....................910 363-6919
EMP: 4
SALES (est): 74.89K **Privately Held**
Web: www.strollmag.com
SIC: 2741 Miscellaneous publishing

(G-1957)
NORCEP INDUSTRIES
2921 Blue Clay Rd (28429-6203)
PHONE....................910 762-5933
EMP: 4 **EST:** 2017
SALES (est): 73.91K **Privately Held**
SIC: 3999 Manufacturing industries, nec

(G-1958)
OCCIDENTAL CHEMICAL CORP
5408 Holly Shelter Rd (28429-6350)
P.O. Box 368 (28429-0368)
PHONE....................910 675-7200
Robert E Running, *Prin*
EMP: 6
SALES (corp-wide): 28.92B **Publicly Held**
SIC: 2812 Alkalies and chlorine
HQ: Occidental Chemical Corporation
14555 Dallas Pkwy Ste 400
Dallas TX 75254
972 404-3800

(G-1959)
PORT CITY ELEVATOR INC (PA)
5704 Nixon Ln (28429-5652)
PHONE....................910 790-9300
Robert Page, *Pr*
Seth Newman, *VP*
EMP: 25 **EST:** 2012
SALES (est): 2.4MM
SALES (corp-wide): 2.4MM **Privately Held**
Web: www.portcityelevator.com
SIC: 5084 3534 3537 Elevators; Dumbwaiters; Lift trucks, industrial: fork, platform, straddle, etc.

(G-1960)
VIDEO OPTIMIZE LLC
3135 Rustic Ln (28429-5470)
PHONE....................818 421-1489
EMP: 4 **EST:** 2018
SALES (est): 130.13K **Privately Held**
SIC: 2741 Internet publishing and broadcasting

(G-1961)
VISIONAIR INC
5601 Barbados Blvd (28429-5655)
PHONE....................910 675-9117
Mike Lyons, *Pr*
Gary Bunyard, *
Samuel T Hensley, *
Scott Macdonald, *CPO**
EMP: 560 **EST:** 1989
SQ FT: 22,500
SALES (est): 979.58K
SALES (corp-wide): 272.32MM **Privately Held**
Web: www.visionair.com
SIC: 7372 Application computer software
HQ: Tritech Software Systems, Inc.
1000 Business Center Dr
Lake Mary FL 32746
858 799-7000

(G-1962)
WOODS END LLC
4917 Indian Corn Trl (28429-5157)
PHONE....................910 470-0389
Jason Marella, *Prin*
EMP: 5 **EST:** 2019
SALES (est): 89.57K **Privately Held**
SIC: 2434 Wood kitchen cabinets

Catawba
Catawba County

(G-1963)
COMMUNICATIONS & PWR INDS LLC
1472 Joe Johnson Rd (28609-8387)
PHONE....................828 241-5735
EMP: 6 **EST:** 2021
SALES (est): 99.36K **Privately Held**
Web: www.cpii.com
SIC: 3663 Radio and t.v. communications equipment

(G-1964)
DAGENHART PALLET INC
2088 Mathis Church Rd (28609-7936)
PHONE....................828 241-2374
Wayne Dagenhart, *Pr*
G Michael Dagenhart, *
EMP: 18 **EST:** 1952
SQ FT: 7,200
SALES (est): 1.45MM **Privately Held**
SIC: 1629 2421 2448 Land clearing contractor; Sawmills and planing mills, general; Pallets, wood

(G-1965)
JENKINS SERVICES GROUP LLC
5577 Little Mountain Rd (28609-8220)
PHONE....................704 881-3210
Marya Jenkins, *Pr*
EMP: 7 **EST:** 2014
SALES (est): 572.58K **Privately Held**
SIC: 1711 3585 7389 Heating and air conditioning contractors; Heating equipment, complete; Business services, nec

(G-1966)
LEE ROYS FRAME CO INC
2221 Buffalo Shoals Rd (28609-8032)
P.O. Box 130 (28610-0130)
PHONE....................828 241-2513
Lee Roy Chandler, *Pr*
Alice Chandler, *VP*
Rhonda Chandler Smith, *Sec*
EMP: 16 **EST:** 1975
SALES (est): 699.43K **Privately Held**
Web: www.leeroysframecoinc.com
SIC: 2426 Frames for upholstered furniture, wood

(G-1967)
ROWES
7546 Long Island Rd (28609-8923)
PHONE....................828 241-2609
EMP: 4 **EST:** 1996
SALES (est): 157.29K **Privately Held**
SIC: 2512 Upholstered household furniture

(G-1968)
SMITH SETZER AND SONS INC
4708 E Nc 10 Hwy (28609-8115)
P.O. Box 250 (28609-0250)
PHONE....................828 241-3161
Jerry Setzer, *Pr*
Michael N Setzer, *
Mitchell Setzer, *
EMP: 48 **EST:** 1949
SQ FT: 15,000
SALES (est): 5.8MM **Privately Held**
SIC: 3545 Boring machine attachments (machine tool accessories)

Cedar Falls
Randolph County

(G-1969)
SAPONA MANUFACTURING CO INC (PA)
2478 Cedar Falls Rd (27230)
PHONE....................336 625-2727
Steele Redding, *Pr*
John O Toledano Senior, *Sec*
C W Mc Crary Junior, *Ch Bd*
Bruce Patram, *
William H Redding Junior, *Treas*
◆ **EMP:** 50 **EST:** 1916
SQ FT: 4,000
SALES (est): 25.2MM
SALES (corp-wide): 25.2MM **Privately Held**
Web: www.saponamfg.com
SIC: 2282 Throwing and winding mills

Cedar Grove
Orange County

(G-1970)
BOTANIST AND BARREL
105 Persimmon Hill Ln (27231-8807)
PHONE....................919 644-7777
EMP: 7 **EST:** 2019
SALES (est): 389.3K **Privately Held**
Web: www.botanistandbarrel.com
SIC: 2084 Wines

(G-1971)
JAMES COTTER IRONWORKS
5102 Eno Cemetery Rd (27231-9756)
PHONE....................919 644-2664
James Cotter, *Owner*
EMP: 10 **EST:** 1990
SALES (est): 498.89K **Privately Held**

SIC: 3446 Architectural metalwork

(G-1972)
STUDIO 180
606 Hamecon Pl (27231-8803)
P.O. Box 67 (27231-0067)
PHONE....................570 998-8746
Deb Tucker's, *Prin*
EMP: 6 **EST:** 2016
SALES (est): 116.5K **Privately Held**
Web: deb-tuckers-studio-180-design.myshopify.com
SIC: 2515 Studio couches

(G-1973)
TIN CAN VENTURES LLC
Also Called: Boxcarr Handmade Cheese
2207 Carr Store Rd (27231-9214)
PHONE....................919 732-9078
Austin Genke, *Prin*
Samantha Genke, *Prin*
EMP: 6 **EST:** 2013
SQ FT: 2,900
SALES (est): 823.13K **Privately Held**
Web: www.boxcarrhandmadecheese.com
SIC: 3411 2022 Tin cans; Cheese; natural and processed

Chadbourn
Columbus County

(G-1974)
BARTLEYS BACKHOE SERVICE
5751 Peacock Rd (28431-8192)
PHONE....................910 918-1384
Jarrett Bartley, *Prin*
EMP: 5 **EST:** 2012
SALES (est): 232.65K **Privately Held**
SIC: 3531 Backhoes

(G-1975)
FRANCES MACHINE SHOP
8421 Joe Brown Hwy S (28431-9082)
PHONE....................910 653-3477
Carol Duncan, *Prin*
EMP: 5 **EST:** 2008
SALES (est): 69.25K **Privately Held**
SIC: 3599 Machine shop, jobbing and repair

(G-1976)
FULL THROTTLE FABRICATION LLC
1047 Old Cribbtown Rd (28431-9319)
PHONE....................910 770-1180
Ryan Stephens, *Prin*
EMP: 6 **EST:** 2015
SALES (est): 75.95K **Privately Held**
Web: www.fullthrottlefabrication.com
SIC: 7692 Welding repair

(G-1977)
KATHYS SIGNS FOR LESS
1145 Bird Cage Rd (28431-7171)
PHONE....................910 840-1447
Michael A Barnes, *Prin*
EMP: 4 **EST:** 2016
SALES (est): 46.08K **Privately Held**
SIC: 3993 Signs and advertising specialties

Chapel Hill
Orange County

(G-1978)
/N SOFTWARE INC (PA)
101 Europa Dr Ste 150 (27517-2380)
PHONE....................919 544-7070
Gent Hito, *CEO*
EMP: 14 **EST:** 1994

SALES (est): 3.03MM
SALES (corp-wide): 3.03MM **Privately Held**
Web: www.nsoftware.com
SIC: 7372 Prepackaged software

(G-1979)
2U NC
1210 Environ Way (27517-4426)
PHONE..................919 525-5075
EMP: 9 EST: 2019
SALES (est): 93.26K **Privately Held**
Web: www.2u.com
SIC: 7372 Prepackaged software

(G-1980)
3 HUNGRY GUYS LLC
220 Lake Manor Rd (27516-4321)
PHONE..................408 644-3119
Thu D.o.s., *Prin*
EMP: 6 EST: 2015
SALES (est): 86.25K **Privately Held**
SIC: 2741 Internet publishing and broadcasting

(G-1981)
ABCOR SUPPLY INC (PA)
Also Called: Carolina Coating Solutions
811 Oxfordshire Ln (27517-6218)
PHONE..................919 468-0856
Jeanna Mccraw, *Pr*
Kenneth Mccraw, *VP*
EMP: 16 EST: 1999
SALES (est): 2.19MM
SALES (corp-wide): 2.19MM **Privately Held**
Web: www.carolinacoatingsolutions.com
SIC: 3479 Coating of metals and formed products

(G-1982)
ALLOTROPICA TECHNOLOGIES INC
601 W Rosemary St Unit 503 (27516-2353)
PHONE..................919 522-4374
Edward Samulski, *CEO*
EMP: 6 EST: 2008
SALES (est): 242.69K **Privately Held**
SIC: 8082 2821 Home health care services; Plastics materials and resins

(G-1983)
AMERICAN STONE COMPANY
1807 Nc Highway 54 W (27516-8801)
P.O. Box 1288 (27510-3288)
PHONE..................919 929-7131
Bill Allgood, *Prin*
EMP: 52 EST: 1969
SALES (est): 454.92K **Publicly Held**
Web: www.rockquarryfarm.com
SIC: 3281 Stone, quarrying and processing of own stone products
PA: Martin Marietta Materials Inc
4123 Parklake Ave
Raleigh NC 27612

(G-1984)
ANELLEO INC
519 Dairy Glen Rd (27516-4386)
PHONE..................919 448-4008
Rahima Benhabbour, *Ex Dir*
EMP: 4
SALES (est): 257.52K **Privately Held**
Web: www.anelleo.com
SIC: 2834 Proprietary drug products

(G-1985)
ARETEIA THERAPEUTICS INC ✪
101 Glen Lennox Dr (27517-4086)
PHONE..................973 985-0597
Frank Bosley, *Prin*

EMP: 16 EST: 2022
SALES (est): 5.99MM **Privately Held**
Web: www.areteiatx.com
SIC: 2834 Pharmaceutical preparations

(G-1986)
ARMACELL LLC (HQ)
55 Vilcom Center Dr Ste 200 (27514-1690)
PHONE..................919 913-0555
Patrick Mathieu, *CEO*
Max Padberg, *
Thomas Himmel, *
Karl Paetz-lauter, *VP*
Roberto Mengoli, *
◆ EMP: 195 EST: 1999
SALES (est): 139.59MM **Privately Held**
Web: www.armacell.us
SIC: 3086 Plastics foam products
PA: Insulation United States Holdings, Llc
7600 Oakwood Street Ext
Mebane NC 27302

(G-1987)
ARTESIAN FUTURE TECHNOLOGY LLC
Also Called: Artesian Builds
5801 Cascade Dr (27514-9692)
PHONE..................919 904-4940
Noah Katz, *Managing Member*
EMP: 10 EST: 2018
SALES (est): 497.61K **Privately Held**
Web: www.artesianfuturetechnology.com
SIC: 2752 7378 Commercial printing, lithographic; Computer and data processing equipment repair/maintenance

(G-1988)
AUGUST PRECISION
1712 Farrington Point Rd (27517-8197)
PHONE..................919 830-6616
EMP: 5 EST: 2015
SALES (est): 107.63K **Privately Held**
Web: www.augustprecision.com
SIC: 3599 Industrial machinery, nec

(G-1989)
BEER STUDY
504 W Franklin St (27516-2317)
PHONE..................919 240-5423
EMP: 6 EST: 2014
SALES (est): 245.84K **Privately Held**
Web: www.beerstudy.com
SIC: 2082 Malt beverages

(G-1990)
BIG BUNDTS
500 Market St (27516-4034)
PHONE..................919 448-4184
Kristen Benkendorfer, *Prin*
EMP: 5 EST: 2010
SALES (est): 64.28K **Privately Held**
SIC: 2053 Cakes, bakery; frozen

(G-1991)
BLAIR
421 Westwood Dr (27516-2805)
PHONE..................919 682-0555
EMP: 5 EST: 2018
SALES (est): 69.92K **Privately Held**
Web: www.blairpub.com
SIC: 2741 Miscellaneous publishing

(G-1992)
BLIND NAIL AND COMPANY INC
Also Called: Alf Sjoberg
3027 Blueberry Ln (27516-5711)
P.O. Box 157 (27510-0157)
PHONE..................919 967-0388
Alf Sjoberg, *Pr*
EMP: 4 EST: 1980

SALES (est): 296.86K **Privately Held**
SIC: 2499 Decorative wood and woodwork

(G-1993)
BLUE CRAB SOFTWARE LLC
325 Bayberry Dr (27517-9116)
PHONE..................301 585-8187
EMP: 4 EST: 2011
SALES (est): 110K **Privately Held**
SIC: 7372 Prepackaged software

(G-1994)
BONAP INC
9319 Bracken Ln (27516-7569)
PHONE..................919 967-6240
John Kartesz Data, *Mgr*
EMP: 5 EST: 2020
SALES (est): 80.05K **Privately Held**
Web: www.bonap.org
SIC: 2836 Biological products, except diagnostic

(G-1995)
BREAD & BUTTER CUSTOM SCRN PRT
Also Called: Bread N Butter Screenprinting
1201 Raleigh Rd Ste 100 (27514-4047)
PHONE..................919 942-3198
Melanie Wall, *Pr*
Anne Page-watson, *Treas*
EMP: 4 EST: 1977
SQ FT: 1,000
SALES (est): 328.57K **Privately Held**
Web: www.bread-butter.com
SIC: 2261 Screen printing of cotton broadwoven fabrics

(G-1996)
CARBON CONVERSION SYSTEMS LLC
95 Wood Laurel Ln (27517-7471)
PHONE..................919 883-4238
EMP: 5 EST: 2015
SALES (est): 338.91K **Privately Held**
SIC: 2869 High purity grade chemicals, organic

(G-1997)
CARDIOXYL PHARMACEUTICALS INC
1450 Raleigh Rd Ste 212 (27517-8833)
PHONE..................919 869-8586
Christopher A Kroeger, *Pr*
Doug Cowart, *Ex VP*
EMP: 7 EST: 2005
SALES (est): 1.58MM
SALES (corp-wide): 45.01B **Publicly Held**
SIC: 2834 Druggists' preparations (pharmaceuticals)
PA: Bristol-Myers Squibb Company
430 E 29th St Fl 14
New York NY 10016
212 546-4000

(G-1998)
CAROLINA WOMAN INC
1506 E Franklin St Ste 103 (27514-2825)
P.O. Box 1233 (03821-1233)
PHONE..................919 869-8200
Debra Simon, *Pr*
EMP: 5 EST: 1993
SALES (est): 428.85K **Privately Held**
Web: www.carolinawoman.com
SIC: 2721 Magazines: publishing and printing

(G-1999)
CDATA SOFTWARE INC (PA)
101 Europa Dr Ste 110 (27517-2380)
PHONE..................919 928-5214
Amit Sharma, *CEO*

Will Davis, *CMO**
EMP: 29 EST: 2014
SALES (est): 4.29MM
SALES (corp-wide): 4.29MM **Privately Held**
Web: www.cdata.com
SIC: 7372 Application computer software

(G-2000)
CEM-102 PHARMACEUTICALS INC
6320 Quadrangle Dr Ste 360 (27517-7815)
PHONE..................919 576-2306
EMP: 8 EST: 2010
SALES (est): 2.08MM
SALES (corp-wide): 30.6MM **Privately Held**
SIC: 2834 Pharmaceutical preparations
PA: Melinta Therapeutics, Llc
389 Interpace Pkwy Ste 45
Parsippany NJ 07054
908 617-1300

(G-2001)
CEMPRA PHARMACEUTICALS INC
6320 Quadrangle Dr Ste 360 (27517-7815)
PHONE..................919 803-6882
Mark W Hahn, *Ex VP*
Kong Garheng, *Ch Bd*
Carl T Foster, *VP*
EMP: 15 EST: 2005
SQ FT: 6,300
SALES (est): 4.87MM
SALES (corp-wide): 30.6MM **Privately Held**
SIC: 2834 Pharmaceutical preparations
PA: Melinta Therapeutics, Llc
389 Interpace Pkwy Ste 45
Parsippany NJ 07054
908 617-1300

(G-2002)
CENTER FOR ECOZOIC STUDIES
2516 Winningham Rd (27516-0518)
PHONE..................919 929-4116
Herman F Greene, *Prin*
EMP: 4 EST: 2010
SALES (est): 131.57K **Privately Held**
Web: www.ecozoicsocieties.org
SIC: 2759 Publication printing

(G-2003)
CLEAN PRESS 4 LESS
11312 Us 15 501 N (27517-6375)
PHONE..................919 942-4141
EMP: 5 EST: 2013
SALES (est): 105.6K **Privately Held**
Web: www.cleanpress4less.com
SIC: 2741 Miscellaneous publishing

(G-2004)
CLOUD SOFTWARE GROUP INC
200 W Franklin St Ste 250 (27516-2559)
PHONE..................919 969-6500
Naresh Bala, *Brnch Mgr*
EMP: 4
SALES (corp-wide): 4.38B **Privately Held**
Web: www.tibco.com
SIC: 7372 Prepackaged software
HQ: Cloud Software Group, Inc.
851 W Cypress Creek Rd
Fort Lauderdale FL 33309

(G-2005)
CONSERVATION STATION INC
Also Called: C S I
60 Sun Forest Way (27517-9105)
PHONE..................919 932-9201
Doreen Michaud, *Pr*
EMP: 5 EST: 1994
SQ FT: 1,800
SALES (est): 817.61K **Privately Held**

Web: www.conservationstation.net
SIC: 5063 3646 Lighting fixtures; Commercial lighting fixtures

(G-2006)
COOKE COMPANIES INTL
Also Called: Cooke Training
105 York Pl (27517-6521)
P.O. Box 810 (27514-0810)
PHONE.....................919 968-0848
William Cooke, Owner
EMP: 10 EST: 1972
SALES (est): 490.95K Privately Held
SIC: 3826 3822 Environmental testing equipment; Environmental controls

(G-2007)
DESIGNCRAFT
106 Berry Patch Ln (27514-1807)
PHONE.....................919 903-5711
Dennis Uhlir, Prin
EMP: 5 EST: 2017
SALES (est): 52.95K Privately Held
Web: www.designcraft.com
SIC: 3599 Machine shop, jobbing and repair

(G-2008)
DILLON L COLTER L C
513 North St (27514-3729)
PHONE.....................828 242-7750
EMP: 5 EST: 2021
SALES (est): 75.11K Privately Held
Web: www.colterdillon.com
SIC: 2759 Screen printing

(G-2009)
DIOMORPH PHARMACEUTICALS LP
6340 Quadrangle Dr Ste 120 (27517-8077)
PHONE.....................919 354-6233
Crist Frangakis, Prin
EMP: 5 EST: 2012
SQ FT: 720
SALES (est): 176.44K Privately Held
SIC: 2834 Pharmaceutical preparations

(G-2010)
DTH PUBLISHING INC
Also Called: Daily Tarheel
151 E Rosemary St Ste 101 (27514-3539)
P.O. Box 3257 (27515-3257)
PHONE.....................919 962-1163
Kevin Scawarz, Mgr
EMP: 180 EST: 1893
SQ FT: 5,500
SALES (est): 2.12MM Privately Held
Web: www.dailytarheel.com
SIC: 2711 Commercial printing and newspaper publishing combined

(G-2011)
EATCLUB INC
114 Saint Ayers Way (27517-2362)
PHONE.....................609 578-7942
EMP: 5 EST: 2018
SALES (est): 263.16K Privately Held
SIC: 7372 7389 Application computer software; Business Activities at Non-Commercial Site

(G-2012)
EDWARDS MOUNTAIN WOODWORKS LLC
57 Woodside Trl (27517-6077)
PHONE.....................919 932-6050
EMP: 4 EST: 2009
SALES (est): 71K Privately Held
Web: www.edwardsmountainwoodworks.com
SIC: 2431 Millwork

(G-2013)
ENERGY AND ENTROPY INC
301 Palafox Dr (27516-1181)
PHONE.....................919 933-1365
Weitao Yang, Prin
EMP: 7 EST: 2008
SALES (est): 219.32K Privately Held
SIC: 1382 Oil and gas exploration services

(G-2014)
ENG SOLUTIONS INC
1109 Pinehurst Dr (27517-5662)
PHONE.....................919 831-1830
Mark Enyedi, Pr
Martin Gentil, Sec
Michael Nativi, Treas
Julie Sandford, Prin
EMP: 19 EST: 1999
SALES (est): 801.18K Privately Held
SIC: 3823 Industrial process control instruments

(G-2015)
ENGINE WELLNESS INC
1067 Canterbury Ln (27517-5613)
PHONE.....................503 231-0495
EMP: 4 EST: 2016
SALES (est): 48.55K Privately Held
SIC: 3931 Musical instruments

(G-2016)
ENTEX TECHNOLOGIES INC
1340 Environ Way (27517-4430)
PHONE.....................919 933-1380
Wayne Flournoy, Pr
Richard Pehrson, VP
Robert Freudenberg, VP
D Ick Pehrson, Ex VP
◆ EMP: 12 EST: 2004
SALES (est): 2.27MM Privately Held
Web: www.entexinc.com
SIC: 3589 Water treatment equipment, industrial

(G-2017)
EPPIN PHARMA INC
3909 Windy Hill Rd (27514-9611)
PHONE.....................919 608-2984
Michael O'rand, Pr
EMP: 6 EST: 2014
SALES (est): 110.56K Privately Held
Web: www.eppinpharmainc.com
SIC: 2834 Pills, pharmaceutical

(G-2018)
FINES AND CARRIEL INC
Also Called: Signs Now
1322 Fordham Blvd Ste 5 (27514-5879)
PHONE.....................919 929-0702
Wayne Fines, Pr
Elizabeth Carriel, VP
EMP: 4 EST: 1980
SQ FT: 2,700
SALES (est): 363.01K Privately Held
Web: www.signsnow.com
SIC: 3993 7389 5999 2395 Signs and advertising specialties; Engraving service; Rubber stamps; Embroidery products, except Schiffli machine

(G-2019)
FIX-A-LATCH USA LLC (PA)
Also Called: Fix-A-Latch
133 1/2 E Franklin St Ste 104 (27514-3627)
P.O. Box 28 (27514-0028)
PHONE.....................435 901-4146
David Migee, Managing Member
EMP: 8 EST: 2015
SQ FT: 400
SALES (est): 342.74K

SALES (corp-wide): 342.74K Privately Held
Web: www.fixalatch.com
SIC: 3429 Builders' hardware

(G-2020)
FIX-A-LATCH USA LLC
122 Marin Dr (27516-8018)
PHONE.....................435 901-4146
David B Magee, Pr
EMP: 23
SALES (corp-wide): 342.74K Privately Held
Web: www.fixalatch.com
SIC: 3429 Builders' hardware
PA: Fix-A-Latch Usa, Llc
    133 1/2 E Franklin St # 104
    Chapel Hill NC 27514
    435 901-4146

(G-2021)
GIDDY LLC
326 Azalea Dr (27517-8105)
PHONE.....................813 767-1344
Tyler S Ward, Prin
EMP: 5 EST: 2014
SALES (est): 91.44K Privately Held
Web: www.getgiddy.com
SIC: 2844 Perfumes, cosmetics and other toilet preparations

(G-2022)
GOLD BOY MUSIC PUBLICATIO
108 Highland Trl (27516-8625)
PHONE.....................919 500-3023
EMP: 4 EST: 2018
SALES (est): 87.76K Privately Held
Web: www.musicgoldboy.com
SIC: 2741 Miscellaneous publishing

(G-2023)
GREEN BEAN COUNTERS LLC
587 Old Farrington Rd (27517-8724)
P.O. Box 1852 (27312-1852)
PHONE.....................919 545-2324
Tracy Kondracki, Prin
EMP: 7 EST: 2012
SALES (est): 284.1K Privately Held
SIC: 3131 Counters

(G-2024)
HOPE RENOVATIONS
3 Bolin Hts (27514-5739)
PHONE.....................919 960-1957
Nora Spencer, CEO
EMP: 10 EST: 2017
SALES (est): 1.02MM Privately Held
Web: www.hoperenovations.org
SIC: 2452 8331 1521 8249 Chicken coops, prefabricated, wood; Vocational training agency; General remodeling, single-family houses; Trade school

(G-2025)
INDAPHARMA LLC
512 Booth Rd (27516-9648)
PHONE.....................919 968-4500
Laurene Wang-smith, Prin
EMP: 6 EST: 2010
SALES (est): 157.78K Privately Held
SIC: 2834 Pharmaceutical preparations

(G-2026)
INFINITE CONTROLS INC
P.O. Box 16369 (27516-6369)
PHONE.....................919 623-4818
EMP: 6 EST: 2008
SALES (est): 170.53K Privately Held
Web: www.infinitecontrolsinc.com

SIC: 3699 Electrical equipment and supplies, nec

(G-2027)
JONATHAN HOLT LLC
1115 Old School Rd (27516-0529)
PHONE.....................919 391-7062
Jonathan Holt, Prin
EMP: 5 EST: 2017
SALES (est): 52.6K Privately Held
Web: www.jonathanholtwrites.com
SIC: 2741 Miscellaneous publishing

(G-2028)
JOURNALISTIC INC
Also Called: Dine America
101 Europa Dr Ste 150 (27517-2380)
PHONE.....................919 945-0700
Webb C Howell Iii, Pr
EMP: 23 EST: 1992
SQ FT: 2,000
SALES (est): 3.4MM Privately Held
Web: www.finebooksmagazine.com
SIC: 2741 Miscellaneous publishing

(G-2029)
KINTOR PHARMACEUTICALS INC
1011 S Hamilton Rd (27517-4409)
PHONE.....................984 208-1255
EMP: 7
SALES (est): 318.28K Privately Held
SIC: 2834 Pharmaceutical preparations

(G-2030)
KRENITSKY PHARMACEUTICALS INC
2516 Homestead Rd (27516-9086)
PHONE.....................919 493-4631
EMP: 6 EST: 1996
SQ FT: 800
SALES (est): 482.02K Privately Held
Web: www.kpi-pharma.com
SIC: 2834 Pharmaceutical preparations

(G-2031)
LEO GAEV METALWORKS INC
616 Nc Highway 54 W (27516-7911)
PHONE.....................919 883-4666
Leo Gaev, Prin
EMP: 12 EST: 2009
SALES (est): 394.01K Privately Held
Web: www.leogaevmetalworks.com
SIC: 3446 Acoustical suspension systems, metal

(G-2032)
LEONS WELDING & DECKING LLC
104 Crestwood Cir Lot 18 (27516-9452)
PHONE.....................919 923-7327
Sandra Polanco, Prin
EMP: 5 EST: 2014
SALES (est): 159.85K Privately Held
SIC: 7692 Welding repair

(G-2033)
LONGLEAF SERVICES INC
116 S Boundary St (27514-3808)
PHONE.....................800 848-6224
Jami Clay, Dir
▼ EMP: 10 EST: 2005
SALES (est): 4.13MM Privately Held
Web: www.longleafservices.org
SIC: 2731 Book publishing

(G-2034)
LOWMAN PUBLISHING
104 Chesley Ln (27514-1459)
PHONE.....................919 929-7829
EMP: 4 EST: 2020
SALES (est): 88.31K Privately Held

SIC: 2741 Miscellaneous publishing

(G-2035)
LUDLAM FAMILY FOODS LLC (PA)
Also Called: Obx Granola
9 Saint James Pl (27514-4218)
PHONE..................919 805-6061
Thomas J Ludlam, *Managing Member*
EMP: 6 **EST:** 2019
SALES (est): 227.72K
SALES (corp-wide): 227.72K **Privately Held**
SIC: 5499 2099 Gourmet food stores; Food preparations, nec

(G-2036)
MARTIN MARIETTA MATERIALS INC
Martin Marietta Aggregates
1807 Hwy 54 W (27516)
P.O. Box 1288 (27510-3288)
PHONE..................919 929-7131
Roger Ramey, *Mgr*
EMP: 5
Web: www.martinmarietta.com
SIC: 3273 Ready-mixed concrete
PA: Martin Marietta Materials Inc
4123 Parklake Ave
Raleigh NC 27612

(G-2037)
MARVIN SALTZMAN
717 Emory Dr (27517-3011)
PHONE..................919 942-7091
Marvin Saltzman, *Prin*
EMP: 5 **EST:** 2010
SALES (est): 82.71K **Privately Held**
Web: www.marvinsaltzman.com
SIC: 3999 Framed artwork

(G-2038)
MEI TAI BABY LLC
103 Wrenn Pl (27516-9700)
PHONE..................919 260-4022
Elisabeth Allore, *Prin*
EMP: 4 **EST:** 2009
SALES (est): 112.11K **Privately Held**
Web: www.catbirdbaby.com
SIC: 2323 Men's and boy's neckwear

(G-2039)
MELINTA THERAPEUTICS INC
Also Called: Melinta Therapeutics, Inc.
6340 Quadrangle Dr Ste 100 (27517-7841)
PHONE..................919 313-6601
EMP: 9
SALES (corp-wide): 30.6MM **Privately Held**
Web: www.melinta.com
SIC: 2834 Pharmaceutical preparations
PA: Melinta Therapeutics, Llc
389 Interpace Pkwy Ste 45
Parsippany NJ 07054
908 617-1300

(G-2040)
MERCK
214 Towne Ridge Ln (27516-4355)
PHONE..................919 423-4328
EMP: 5 **EST:** 2019
SALES (est): 107.28K **Privately Held**
Web: jobs.merck.com
SIC: 2834 Pharmaceutical preparations

(G-2041)
MERGE MEDIA LTD
Also Called: Merge Records
104 S Christopher Rd (27514-4466)
P.O. Box 1235 (27514-1235)
PHONE..................919 688-9969
EMP: 15 **EST:** 1989

SQ FT: 2,500
SALES (est): 777.41K **Privately Held**
Web: www.merge-records.com
SIC: 3652 Master records or tapes, preparation of

(G-2042)
MESURIO INC
1210 Holly Creek Ln (27516-5522)
PHONE..................919 633-8773
Michael Prorock, *Pr*
EMP: 6 **EST:** 2016
SALES (est): 461.61K **Privately Held**
Web: www.mesur.io
SIC: 2741 Internet publishing and broadcasting

(G-2043)
MEY CORPORATION (PA)
121 S Estes Dr Ste 101 (27514-2868)
PHONE..................919 932-5800
Antoine A Puech, *CEO*
Larry Hodges, *Dir*
Kathy Martyn, *VP Fin*
◆ **EMP:** 6 **EST:** 1993
SALES (est): 1.75MM
SALES (corp-wide): 1.75MM **Privately Held**
Web: www.meycorp.com
SIC: 2879 Insecticides, agricultural or household

(G-2044)
MINIPRO LLC
1289 Fordham Blvd Ste 263 (27514-6110)
PHONE..................844 517-4776
Jose M Mendez, *Prin*
EMP: 5 **EST:** 2017
SALES (est): 245.3K **Privately Held**
Web: www.minipro.com
SIC: 3825 Test equipment for electronic and electric measurement

(G-2045)
MYSTERY CIRCUITS LLC
3804 Moonlight Dr (27516-5538)
PHONE..................919 942-4992
Michael David Walters, *Prin*
EMP: 5 **EST:** 2015
SALES (est): 98.67K **Privately Held**
Web: www.mysterycircuits.com
SIC: 3679 Electronic circuits

(G-2046)
NEFF TOOL AND MACHINE LLC
104 Dixie Dr (27514-6615)
PHONE..................507 226-1708
EMP: 4 **EST:** 2020
SALES (est): 74.4K **Privately Held**
SIC: 3599 Machine shop, jobbing and repair

(G-2047)
NEW PARADIGM THERAPEUTICS INC
8024 Burnette Womack 100 (27599-0001)
PHONE..................919 259-0026
David Clemmons, *CEO*
EMP: 5
SQ FT: 400
SALES (est): 247.45K **Privately Held**
SIC: 2834 Druggists' preparations (pharmaceuticals)

(G-2048)
NOBSCOT CONSTRUCTION CO INC
Also Called: Hill Country Woodworks
2113 Old Greensboro Rd (27516-0515)
PHONE..................919 929-2075
Robert Bacon, *Pr*
EMP: 7 **EST:** 1976

SQ FT: 2,000
SALES (est): 402.12K **Privately Held**
Web: www.hillcountrywoodworks.com
SIC: 5712 2511 2512 1521 Customized furniture and cabinets; Wood household furniture; Upholstered household furniture; New construction, single-family houses

(G-2049)
OCUTECH INC
105 Conner Dr Ste 2105 (27514-7126)
PHONE..................919 967-6460
Henry Greene, *Pr*
◆ **EMP:** 8 **EST:** 1984
SQ FT: 700
SALES (est): 939.63K **Privately Held**
Web: www.ocutech.com
SIC: 3851 Ophthalmic goods

(G-2050)
ORTHORX INC
Also Called: Carolina Brace Systems
400 Meadowmont Village Cir # 425 (27517-7505)
PHONE..................919 929-5550
Tammy Wood, *Prin*
EMP: 5
SIC: 3842 Orthopedic appliances
HQ: Orthorx, Inc.
5204 Tennyson Pkwy # 100
Plano TX 75024
214 501-0180

(G-2051)
PAINTBOX PRESS LLC
208 Glandon Dr (27514-3816)
PHONE..................919 969-7512
EMP: 6 **EST:** 2020
SALES (est): 120.64K **Privately Held**
Web: www.paintboxpress.com
SIC: 2741 Miscellaneous publishing

(G-2052)
PENDERGAST INDUSTRIES LLC
203 Glenview Pl (27514-1950)
PHONE..................919 636-1621
Marc Pendergast, *Prin*
EMP: 5 **EST:** 2016
SALES (est): 75.97K **Privately Held**
SIC: 3999 Manufacturing industries, nec

(G-2053)
PINBALL LITERARY
15 S Circle Dr (27516-3104)
PHONE..................919 240-4012
Lucas Church, *Prin*
EMP: 4 **EST:** 2015
SALES (est): 53.63K **Privately Held**
SIC: 2711 Newspapers

(G-2054)
PRECISION ARBATICS USA PTY LTD
310 Dragonfly Trl (27517-9507)
PHONE..................770 292-9122
Shaun Vanunu, *CEO*
EMP: 5 **EST:** 2016
SALES (est): 72.66K **Privately Held**
SIC: 3721 Nonmotorized and lighter-than-air aircraft

(G-2055)
PRECISION OPTICS LLC
1015 Wave Rd (27517-8047)
PHONE..................919 619-4468
Charles S Christensen, *Admn*
EMP: 8 **EST:** 2017
SALES (est): 94.65K **Privately Held**
Web: www.precisionoptical.com
SIC: 3827 Optical instruments and lenses

(G-2056)
PREGNANCY SUPPORT SERVICES
1777 Fordham Blvd Ste 203 (27514-5885)
P.O. Box 52599 (27717-2599)
PHONE..................919 490-0203
Ruby Peters, *Ex Dir*
EMP: 7 **EST:** 1984
SALES (est): 349K **Privately Held**
Web: www.pregnancysupportservices.org
SIC: 8699 2835 8071 Charitable organization ; Pregnancy test kits; Ultrasound laboratory

(G-2057)
PRIVATE LABEL DIGITAL PRTG LLC
630 Arlington St (27514-6700)
PHONE..................919 929-6053
Christopher Stewart, *Prin*
EMP: 5 **EST:** 2018
SALES (est): 83.91K **Privately Held**
SIC: 2752 Commercial printing, lithographic

(G-2058)
QATCH TECHNOLOGIES LLC
Also Called: Qatch Techologies
551 Dairy Glen Rd (27516-4386)
PHONE..................678 908-3112
Zehra Parlak, *Pr*
EMP: 5 **EST:** 2016
SALES (est): 312.56K **Privately Held**
Web: www.qatchtech.com
SIC: 8731 3841 Commercial physical research; Diagnostic apparatus, medical

(G-2059)
QUANTUM USA LLP
15 Grey Squirrel Ct (27517-7605)
PHONE..................919 704-8266
Ovidiu Martin, *Prin*
EMP: 8 **EST:** 2014
SALES (est): 495.33K **Privately Held**
SIC: 3572 Computer storage devices

(G-2060)
QUICK COLOR SOLUTIONS INC
Also Called: Cooper Thomas & Benton
1801 E Franklin St Ste 208b (27514-5855)
P.O. Box 2515 (27515-2515)
PHONE..................336 282-3900
S Glenn Benton Junior, *Pr*
Mary Glenn Benton, *VP*
EMP: 9 **EST:** 1998
SQ FT: 1,000
SALES (est): 393.41K **Privately Held**
Web: www.quickcolorsolutions.com
SIC: 2752 Color lithography

(G-2061)
QUINSITE LLC FKA MILE 5 ANLYTI
1818 Martin Luther King Jr Blvd Pmb 185 (27514-7415)
PHONE..................317 313-5152
Jeff Maze, *CEO*
EMP: 10 **EST:** 2017
SALES (est): 649.07K **Privately Held**
Web: www.quinsite.com
SIC: 7374 7375 7372 Data processing service; Data base information retrieval; Business oriented computer software

(G-2062)
RASA MALAYSIA
410 Market St (27516-4061)
PHONE..................919 601-1765
EMP: 6 **EST:** 2016
SALES (est): 485.73K **Privately Held**
Web: www.rasamalaysiach.com
SIC: 3589 Commercial cooking and foodwarming equipment

Chapel Hill - Orange County (G-2063)   GEOGRAPHIC SECTION

(G-2063)
RETROJECT INC
1125 Pinehurst Dr (27517-5662)
PHONE 919 619-3042
Molly Walsh, *CEO*
Stuart Mckinnon, *Pr*
David Epstein, *Sec*
EMP: 4 EST: 2012
SALES (est): 200.43K **Privately Held**
SIC: **3841** 7389 Surgical and medical instruments; Business services, nec

(G-2064)
ROBAR RPP LLC
700 Durant St Apt 102 (27517-7361)
PHONE 860 480-6498
Robert Pazdziorko, *Owner*
EMP: 4 EST: 2017
SALES (est): 92.36K **Privately Held**
SIC: **2741** Miscellaneous publishing

(G-2065)
RSSBUS INC
490 Sun Forest Way (27517-7717)
PHONE 919 969-7675
Gent Hito, *Pr*
EMP: 17 EST: 2010
SALES (est): 531.84K **Privately Held**
Web: arc.cdata.com
SIC: **7372** Prepackaged software

(G-2066)
RUTLAND FIRE CLAY COMPANY
1430 Environ Way (27517-4433)
PHONE 802 775-5519
EMP: 8 EST: 2013
SALES (est): 1.18MM **Privately Held**
Web: www.rutland.com
SIC: **2891** Adhesives

(G-2067)
SAPPHIRE INNVTIVE THRAPIES LLC
Also Called: Nutraheal
510 Meadowmont Village Cir (27517-7584)
PHONE 877 402-4325
John Borrelli, *Managing Member*
EMP: 4 EST: 2021
SALES (est): 75K **Privately Held**
SIC: **2023** Dietary supplements, dairy and non-dairy based

(G-2068)
SEAC BANCHE USA INC
1202 Raleigh Rd (27517-4417)
PHONE 919 360-6442
EMP: 6 EST: 2019
SALES (est): 99.25K **Privately Held**
Web: www.bancor.it
SIC: **3429** Hardware, nec

(G-2069)
SEWERKOTE
150 Providence Rd (27514-2208)
PHONE 919 598-1974
Michael G Kinnaird, *Prin*
EMP: 6 EST: 2005
SALES (est): 291.52K **Privately Held**
Web: www.sewerkote.com
SIC: **3999** Manufacturing industries, nec

(G-2070)
SHANNON MEDIA INC
212 Village Gate Dr (27514-5891)
PHONE 919 933-1551
EMP: 7 EST: 2011
SALES (est): 192.31K **Privately Held**
SIC: **2759** Publication printing

(G-2071)
SHANNON MEDIA INC
Also Called: Chapel Hill Magazine
1777 Fordham Blvd Ste 105 (27514-5810)
PHONE 919 933-1551
Daniel Shannon, *Prin*
EMP: 11 EST: 2010
SALES (est): 2.09MM **Privately Held**
Web: www.chapelhillmagazine.com
SIC: **2721** 7311 Magazines: publishing and printing; Advertising agencies

(G-2072)
SIGNSATIONS LTD
104 Concord Dr (27516-3216)
PHONE 571 340-3330
Judith L Birchfield, *Prin*
EMP: 6 EST: 2010
SALES (est): 117.03K **Privately Held**
Web: www.signsationsrc.com
SIC: **3993** Signs and advertising specialties

(G-2073)
SITZER & SPURIA INC
Also Called: Sitzer Spuria Studios
601 W Rosemary St Unit 111 (27516-2353)
PHONE 919 929-0299
Cindy Spuria, *Pr*
Joseph Spuria, *VP*
EMP: 8 EST: 1987
SQ FT: 750
SALES (est): 993.51K **Privately Held**
Web: www.sitzerspuria.com
SIC: **8711** 3993 7389 Industrial engineers; Displays and cutouts, window and lobby; Design, commercial and industrial

(G-2074)
STORYBOOK FARM METAL SHOP INC
Also Called: Storybook Metal Shop
231 Storybook Farm Ln (27516-9160)
PHONE 919 967-9491
George W Barrett Junior, *Pr*
Kathleen Andrews, *VP*
EMP: 4 EST: 1980
SQ FT: 3,500
SALES (est): 206.68K **Privately Held**
Web: www.storybookmetals.com
SIC: **7699** 7692 Blacksmith shop; Welding repair

(G-2075)
SUN PUBLISHING COMPANY
107 N Roberson St (27516-2332)
PHONE 919 942-5282
Sy Safransky, *Pr*
EMP: 16 EST: 1974
SQ FT: 1,500
SALES (est): 2.79MM **Privately Held**
Web: www.thesunmagazine.org
SIC: **2741** Miscellaneous publishing

(G-2076)
SURGICAL GUIDE SYSTEMS LLC
658 The Preserve Trl (27517-9031)
PHONE 919 244-4463
EMP: 4 EST: 2020
SALES (est): 77.45K **Privately Held**
SIC: **3061** Medical and surgical rubber tubing (extruded and lathe-cut)

(G-2077)
SYNERECA PHARMACEUTICALS INC
Also Called: Synereca
39519 Glenn Glade (27517-8584)
PHONE 919 966-3929
Scott Singleton, *Prin*
Elaine Hamm, *Dir*
EMP: 4 EST: 2009
SALES (est): 324.17K **Privately Held**
Web: www.synereca.com
SIC: **2834** Pharmaceutical preparations

(G-2078)
T RENEE SEVERT LLC
101 Conner Dr Ste 401 (27514-7038)
PHONE 248 540-3741
EMP: 6 EST: 2019
SALES (est): 117.59K **Privately Held**
Web: www.severtsmiles.com
SIC: **3086** Plastics foam products

(G-2079)
TIN SHED LLC
30062 Benbury (27517-8494)
PHONE 919 928-0600
Jens C Hoeg, *Prin*
EMP: 7 EST: 2011
SALES (est): 222.14K **Privately Held**
SIC: **3356** Tin

(G-2080)
TODRIN FINE WOODWORK LLC
2900 Carl Durham Rd (27516-8855)
PHONE 413 478-2818
Michael Todrin, *Owner*
EMP: 4 EST: 2017
SALES (est): 247.54K **Privately Held**
Web: www.todrinfinewoodwork.com
SIC: **2431** Millwork

(G-2081)
TOMBOGANCRAFTSMAN COM
9622 Greenfield Rd (27516-7527)
PHONE 919 932-9878
Janet Bogan, *Prin*
EMP: 6 EST: 2010
SALES (est): 73.24K **Privately Held**
Web: www.tombogancraftsman.com
SIC: **2434** Wood kitchen cabinets

(G-2082)
TRIANGLE CHEMICAL COMPANY
7100 Old Greensboro Rd (27516-8539)
PHONE 919 942-3237
Thomas E Braxton, *Owner*
EMP: 4 EST: 1976
SQ FT: 3,000
SALES (est): 470.79K **Privately Held**
Web: www.trianglecc.com
SIC: **2869** Industrial organic chemicals, nec

(G-2083)
TRIANGLE POINTER INC
Also Called: Triangle Pointer Magazine
88 Vilcom Center Dr (27514-1660)
PHONE 919 968-4801
Sue Chen Reeder, *Publisher*
EMP: 8 EST: 1997
SALES (est): 673.71K **Privately Held**
SIC: **2741** Atlas, map, and guide publishing
PA: The Stamford Capital Group Inc
1266 E Main St
Stamford CT 06902

(G-2084)
TRIANGLE SYSTEMS INC (PA)
882 Pinehurst Dr (27517-6532)
P.O. Box 3260 (27515-3260)
PHONE 919 544-0090
James W Ott, *Pr*
Sara Virginia Ott, *Sec*
EMP: 6 EST: 1981
SALES (est): 970.62K
SALES (corp-wide): 970.62K **Privately Held**
Web: www.triangle-systems.com
SIC: **7372** Educational computer software

(G-2085)
TURNSMITH LLC
710 Market St (27516-9358)
PHONE 919 667-9804
EMP: 7 EST: 2019
SALES (est): 308.4K **Privately Held**
Web: www.turnsmith.com
SIC: **3652** Prerecorded records and tapes

(G-2086)
ULTRALOOP TECHNOLOGIES INC
1289 Fordham Blvd (27514-6110)
PHONE 919 636-2842
Aditya Bhatt, *Ch*
Tom Morioka, *Ofcr*
Jared Porter, *COO*
EMP: 4 EST: 2021
SALES (est): 304.43K **Privately Held**
SIC: **3559** Special industry machinery, nec

(G-2087)
UNC CAMPUS HEALTH SERVICES
320 Emergency Room Dr (27599-5035)
PHONE 919 966-2281
Kim Pittman, *Ex Dir*
Kim Pittman, *Dir*
EMP: 90 EST: 1980
SALES (est): 2.56MM **Privately Held**
Web: www.unc.edu
SIC: **8742** 7372 Hospital and health services consultant; Application computer software

(G-2088)
UNDERGROUND PRINTING
133 E Franklin St (27514-3620)
PHONE 919 525-2029
EMP: 6 EST: 2019
SALES (est): 91.56K **Privately Held**
Web: www.undergroundshirts.com
SIC: **2759** Screen printing

(G-2089)
UNIVERSITY NC AT CHAPEL HL
Also Called: University NC Press
116 S Boundary St (27514-3808)
P.O. Box 2288 (27515-2288)
PHONE 919 962-0369
Kate Torrey, *Dir*
EMP: 8
SALES (corp-wide): 4.81B **Privately Held**
Web: www.unc.edu
SIC: **2731** 8221 Book publishing; University
HQ: University Of North Carolina At Chapel Hill
104 Airport Dr
Chapel Hill NC 27599
919 962-1370

(G-2090)
UNIVERSITY NC PRESS INC
Also Called: UNIVERSITY OF NORTH CAROLINA P
116 S Boundary St (27514-3808)
PHONE 919 966-3561
Jami Clay, *Dir*
John Sherer, *
Vicky Wells, *
Joanna Ruth Marsland, *
▲ EMP: 50 EST: 1922
SALES (est): 5.68MM **Privately Held**
Web: uncpress.unc.edu
SIC: **2731** Book publishing

(G-2091)
USAT LLC
Also Called: U S A T
605 Eastowne Dr (27514-2211)
P.O. Box 9334 (27515-9334)

GEOGRAPHIC SECTION
Charlotte - Mecklenburg County (G-2121)

PHONE.................................919 942-4214
EMP: 50 **EST:** 1992
SQ FT: 5,500
SALES (est): 23.94MM **Privately Held**
Web: www.usatcorp.com
SIC: 7372 7379 3829 3812 Prepackaged software; Computer related consulting services; Measuring and controlling devices, nec; Search and navigation equipment

(G-2092)
VASCULAR PHARMACEUTICALS INC
116 Manning Dr (27599-6117)
PHONE.................................919 345-7933
Kenneth E Eheman, *Prin*
EMP: 8 **EST:** 2013
SALES (est): 263.72K **Privately Held**
Web: www.vascularpharma.com
SIC: 2834 Pharmaceutical preparations

(G-2093)
VIIV HEALTHCARE COMPANY
Also Called: Genetic Medicine Building
120 Mason Farm Rd (27514-4617)
PHONE.................................919 445-2770
EMP: 7
SALES (est): 415.67K **Privately Held**
Web: www.viivhealthcare.com
SIC: 2834 Pharmaceutical preparations

(G-2094)
VILLAGE INSTANT PRINTING INC
Also Called: VIP Printing and Signs Express
2204 Damascus Church Rd (27516-8035)
PHONE.................................919 968-0000
Kenneth Cash, *Pr*
Kenneth Cash, *Prin*
Donna Cash, *Treas*
EMP: 4 **EST:** 1980
SQ FT: 3,000
SALES (est): 285.2K **Privately Held**
SIC: 2752 7334 Offset printing; Photocopying and duplicating services

(G-2095)
VIP PRINT AND SIGNS
2208 Damascus Church Rd (27516-8035)
PHONE.................................919 968-0000
EMP: 4 **EST:** 2020
SALES (est): 50.69K **Privately Held**
Web: www.vipgraphicsnc.com
SIC: 2752 Offset printing

(G-2096)
VOLTAGE LLC
1450 Raleigh Rd Ste 208 (27517-8833)
PHONE.................................919 391-9405
EMP: 13 **EST:** 2016
SALES (est): 12.33MM **Privately Held**
Web: www.voltage-llc.com
SIC: 3496 3199 Cable, uninsulated wire; made from purchased wire; Harness or harness parts

(G-2097)
WILLIAM TRAVIS JEWELRY LTD
201 S Estes Dr Ste 400d (27514-7043)
PHONE.................................919 968-0011
William Kukovich, *Prin*
EMP: 4 **EST:** 2006
SALES (est): 415.32K **Privately Held**
Web: www.williamtravisjewelry.com
SIC: 3911 5944 Jewelry, precious metal; Jewelry stores

(G-2098)
WISDOM HOUSE BOOKS INC
209 Kousa Trl (27516-4669)
PHONE.................................919 883-4669
Ted Ruybal, *Prin*
EMP: 5 **EST:** 2016
SALES (est): 226.25K **Privately Held**
Web: www.wisdomhousebooks.com
SIC: 5192 2731 Books; Books, publishing only

(G-2099)
WOOD DONE RIGHT INC
525 Colony Woods Dr (27517-7906)
PHONE.................................919 623-4557
EMP: 7 **EST:** 2011
SALES (est): 129.31K **Privately Held**
Web: wooddoneright.houzzsite.com
SIC: 2434 Wood kitchen cabinets

(G-2100)
WORKMAN PUBLISHING CO INC
Also Called: Algonquin Books of Chapel Hill
400 Silver Cedar Ct Ste 300 (27514-1585)
P.O. Box 2225 (27515-2225)
PHONE.................................919 967-0108
Ina Stern, *Mgr*
EMP: 7
Web: www.hachettebookgroup.com
SIC: 2731 Books, publishing only
HQ: Workman Publishing Co. Inc.
1290 Ave Of The Americas
New York NY 10104
212 254-5900

(G-2101)
XINRAY SYSTEMS INC
312 Silver Creek Trl (27514-1840)
PHONE.................................919 701-4100
Moritz Beckmann, *CEO*
Michael Poe, *CFO*
EMP: 11 **EST:** 2007
SALES (est): 2.18MM **Privately Held**
SIC: 3844 X-ray apparatus and tubes

(G-2102)
XINTEK INC
312 Silver Creek Trl (27514-1840)
PHONE.................................919 449-5799
Otto Zhou, *Ch*
Doctor Shan Bai, *CEO*
EMP: 11 **EST:** 2001
SALES (est): 434.45K **Privately Held**
Web: www.xintek.com
SIC: 3671 Cathode ray tubes, including rebuilt

(G-2103)
YACKETY YACK PUBLISHING INC
P.O. Box 958 (27514-0958)
PHONE.................................919 843-5092
EMP: 5
SALES (est): 65.12K **Privately Held**
Web: heellife.unc.edu
SIC: 2741 Miscellaneous publishing

(G-2104)
ZENGERLE INDUSTRIES INC
705 Wellington Dr (27514-6723)
PHONE.................................919 240-5415
Jason Zengerle, *Owner*
EMP: 4 **EST:** 2018
SALES (est): 47.38K **Privately Held**
SIC: 3999 Manufacturing industries, nec

(G-2105)
ZYSENSE LLC
6701 Glen Forrest Dr (27517-8647)
PHONE.................................215 485-1955
Jeffrey Garwood, *Mgr*
Jeff Garwood, *Managing Member*
EMP: 4 **EST:** 2016
SALES (est): 211.74K **Privately Held**
Web: www.zysense.com

SIC: 3826 7389 Infrared analytical instruments; Business Activities at Non-Commercial Site

Charlotte
Mecklenburg County

(G-2106)
2TOPIA CYCLES INC
1512 Southwood Ave (28203-4445)
PHONE.................................704 778-7849
EMP: 5 **EST:** 2012
SALES (est): 56.33K **Privately Held**
Web: www.2topiacycles.com
SIC: 3732 Boatbuilding and repairing

(G-2107)
310 SIGN COMPANY
4335 Taggart Creek Rd Ste C (28208-5411)
PHONE.................................704 910-2242
Amy Nannini, *Prin*
EMP: 5 **EST:** 2010
SALES (est): 172.1K **Privately Held**
Web: www.310signs.com
SIC: 3993 Signs and advertising specialties

(G-2108)
3D QUALITY LLC
8021 Meadowdale Ln (28212-4855)
PHONE.................................201 580-0913
EMP: 6 **EST:** 2020
SALES (est): 462.6K **Privately Held**
SIC: 3599 Machine shop, jobbing and repair

(G-2109)
3RD PHAZE BDY OILS URBAN LNKS
3300 N Graham St (28206-1934)
PHONE.................................704 344-1138
Gary Gray, *CEO*
▲ **EMP:** 5 **EST:** 2005
SALES (est): 485.09K **Privately Held**
Web: www.3rdphazebodyoils.com
SIC: 2844 Face creams or lotions

(G-2110)
6 BROTHERS LLC
2628 Tanbridge Rd (28226-6781)
PHONE.................................706 662-2232
EMP: 6 **EST:** 2020
SALES (est): 179.81K **Privately Held**
SIC: 2082 Beer (alcoholic beverage)

(G-2111)
6EHOUSEPRODXIONS LLC
1300 Baxter St Ste 100b (28204-3806)
PHONE.................................704 334-7741
Melinda Morris Zanoni, *Owner*
EMP: 6 **EST:** 2016
SALES (est): 88.08K **Privately Held**
SIC: 2741 Miscellaneous publishing

(G-2112)
A & A FINANCIAL SERVICES LLC
9716 Rea Rd Ste B538 (28277-6789)
PHONE.................................800 572-6684
EMP: 4 **EST:** 2017
SALES (est): 56.54K **Privately Held**
SIC: 7372 Educational computer software

(G-2113)
A & W ELECTRIC INC
127 W 28th St (28206-2652)
P.O. Box 561898 (28256-1898)
PHONE.................................704 333-4986
Holly Hebert, *Pr*
Tim Hebert, *
EMP: 30 **EST:** 1987
SQ FT: 4,000

SALES (est): 7.29MM **Privately Held**
Web: www.aandwelectric.com
SIC: 7694 7629 Electric motor repair; Electrical repair shops

(G-2114)
A CREATE CARD INC
6409 Providence Farm Ln Apt 7401 (28277-7244)
PHONE.................................631 584-2273
EMP: 5 **EST:** 2020
SALES (est): 158.94K **Privately Held**
Web: www.createacardinc.com
SIC: 2759 Commercial printing, nec

(G-2115)
A HARTNESS INC
1143 Eastview Dr (28211-1562)
PHONE.................................704 351-2323
EMP: 4 **EST:** 2016
SALES (est): 42.61K **Privately Held**
Web: www.hartness.com
SIC: 3565 Packaging machinery

(G-2116)
A MATTER OF SCENTS
5329 Providence Rd (28226-5855)
PHONE.................................980 939-3285
James Moralez, *Prin*
EMP: 5 **EST:** 2010
SALES (est): 65.09K **Privately Held**
SIC: 2844 Perfumes, cosmetics and other toilet preparations

(G-2117)
A N E SERVICES LLC
1716 Garette Rd (28218)
PHONE.................................704 882-1117
EMP: 6 **EST:** 2002
SALES (est): 354.33K **Privately Held**
SIC: 2519 Lawn and garden furniture, except wood and metal

(G-2118)
A O SMITH WATER PRODUCTS CO
4302 Raleigh St (28213-6904)
PHONE.................................704 597-8910
Violet Carter Per, *Ofcr*
EMP: 18 **EST:** 2017
SALES (est): 1.51MM **Privately Held**
Web: www.hotwater.com
SIC: 3443 Fabricated plate work (boiler shop)

(G-2119)
A+ PRO TRANSPORT INC
6201 Fairview Rd (28210-3297)
PHONE.................................980 215-8694
Michael Daniel, *Pr*
EMP: 5 **EST:** 2019
SALES (est): 525.09K **Privately Held**
SIC: 3537 Trucks, tractors, loaders, carriers, and similar equipment

(G-2120)
A1 POWDER COATING LLC
8612 Wilkinson Blvd (28214-8059)
PHONE.................................704 394-0705
Neil Patel, *Prin*
EMP: 7 **EST:** 2008
SALES (est): 196.18K **Privately Held**
Web: www.a1-powdercoating.com
SIC: 3479 Coating of metals and formed products

(G-2121)
AALBERTS INTEGRATED PIPING SYSTEMS AMERICAS INC (HQ)
Also Called: Apollo Valves
10715 Sikes Pl Ste 200 (28277-8173)
P.O. Box 247 (28106-0247)

Charlotte - Mecklenburg County (G-2122) GEOGRAPHIC SECTION

PHONE..................704 841-6000
◆ **EMP:** 48 **EST:** 1982
SALES (est): 465.94MM
SALES (corp-wide): 3.35B **Privately Held**
Web: www.aalberts-ips.us
SIC: 3625 3494 Actuators, industrial; Valves and pipe fittings, nec
PA: Aalberts N.V.
   Stadsplateau 18
   Utrecht UT
   303079300

(G-2122)
ABB INC
Also Called: Abb, Inc.
12037 Goodrich Dr (28273-6511)
PHONE..................704 587-1362
Andrew Headley, *Brnch Mgr*
EMP: 24
Web: new.abb.com
SIC: 3625 5063 3612 3613 Relays and industrial controls; Electrical apparatus and equipment; Transformers, except electric; Switchgear and switchboard apparatus
HQ: Abb Inc.
   305 Gregson Dr
   Cary NC 27511

(G-2123)
ABCO CONTROLS AND EQP INC
4110 Monroe Rd (28205-7708)
P.O. Box 221918 (28222-1918)
PHONE..................704 394-2424
William Simmons, *Pr*
Derek Mulder, *VP*
EMP: 4 **EST:** 1998
SALES (est): 361.62K **Privately Held**
SIC: 3625 Control equipment, electric

(G-2124)
ABLE METAL FABRICATORS INC
3441 Reno Ave (28216-4111)
PHONE..................704 394-8972
Horace Strickland, *Pr*
Shelly Ford, *Sec*
EMP: 20 **EST:** 1981
SQ FT: 22,000
SALES (est): 1.45MM **Privately Held**
SIC: 3444 Sheet metal specialties, not stamped

(G-2125)
ABUNDANT POWER SOLUTIONS LLC
222 S Church St Ste 401 (28202-3247)
PHONE..................704 271-9890
Shannon Smith, *CEO*
Francis Pinckney, *COO*
Greg Montgomery, *CFO*
Dank Pinckney, *COO*
EMP: 10 **EST:** 2009
SALES (est): 589.9K **Privately Held**
Web: www.abundantpower.com
SIC: 3612 Voltage regulating transformers, electric power

(G-2126)
ABX INNVTIVE PCKG SLUTIONS LLC (PA)
3525 Whitehall Park Dr Ste 300 (28273)
PHONE..................980 443-1100
Larry Goldstein, *CEO*
Jeff Godsey, *COO*
EMP: 99 **EST:** 2020
SALES (est): 121.96MM
SALES (corp-wide): 121.96MM **Privately Held**
Web: www.abxpackaging.com
SIC: 3081 2671 2679 Plastics film and sheet; Paper; coated and laminated packaging; Tags and labels, paper

(G-2127)
ACE PLASTICS INC
Also Called: Ace Plastics
5130 Hovis Rd Ste A (28208-1208)
PHONE..................704 527-5752
Ray Dlugos, *Pr*
Mary Dlugos, *Sec*
Nikki Smalls, *Off Mgr*
▲ **EMP:** 5 **EST:** 1994
SALES (est): 4.91MM **Privately Held**
Web: www.aceframes.com
SIC: 5162 3089 Plastics materials and basic shapes; Air mattresses, plastics

(G-2128)
ACEYUS INC
11111 Carmel Commons Blvd Ste 210 (28226-4075)
PHONE..................704 443-7900
Mike Ary, *Pr*
EMP: 41 **EST:** 2002
SALES (est): 6.52MM **Privately Held**
Web: www.aceyus.com
SIC: 7372 8748 Business oriented computer software; Systems engineering consultant, ex. computer or professional

(G-2129)
ACME AEROFAB LLC
1907 Scott Futrell Dr (28208-2704)
PHONE..................704 806-3582
Matthew Mcswain, *COO*
Matthew Mcswain, *Pr*
Eric Robinson, *COO*
EMP: 8 **EST:** 2013
SALES (est): 545.55K **Privately Held**
SIC: 3469 3728 Appliance parts, porcelain enameled; Aircraft parts and equipment, nec

(G-2130)
ACQUIONICS INC
4215 Stuart Andrew Blvd Ste E (28217-4616)
PHONE..................980 256-5700
EMP: 12 **EST:** 2018
SALES (est): 389.01K
SALES (corp-wide): 2.23B **Privately Held**
SIC: 3641 Ultraviolet lamps
PA: Halma Public Limited Company
   Misbourne Court Rectory Way
   Amersham BUCKS HP7 0
   149 472-1111

(G-2131)
ACSM INC
113 Freeland Ln (28217-1617)
PHONE..................704 910-0243
Glen Nocik, *Pr*
EMP: 7 **EST:** 2012
SALES (est): 885.4K **Privately Held**
Web: www.acsminc.com
SIC: 3993 Signs and advertising specialties

(G-2132)
ACUMENT GLOBAL TECHNOLOGIES
3000 Crosspoint Center Ln Ste F (28269)
PHONE..................704 598-3539
EMP: 5 **EST:** 2019
SALES (est): 73.45K **Privately Held**
SIC: 3452 Bolts, nuts, rivets, and washers

(G-2133)
AD-ART SIGNS INC
2613 Lucena St (28206-2109)
PHONE..................704 377-5369
Coleman M Hambley, *Pr*
Mary Sullivan, *Sec*
EMP: 4 **EST:** 1973
SQ FT: 3,775
SALES (est): 492.04K **Privately Held**
SIC: 3993 Electric signs

(G-2134)
ADAMS BEVERAGES NC LLC (PA)
7505 Statesville Rd (28269-3704)
PHONE..................704 509-3000
Clay Adams, *Pr*
EMP: 18 **EST:** 2012
SALES (est): 11.91MM
SALES (corp-wide): 11.91MM **Privately Held**
Web: www.adamsbeverages.net
SIC: 2084 Wine coolers (beverages)

(G-2135)
ADAMS OLDCASTLE
9968 Metromont Industrial Blvd (28269-7608)
PHONE..................980 229-7678
EMP: 6 **EST:** 2019
SALES (est): 268.03K **Privately Held**
Web: www.adamsproducts.com
SIC: 3273 Ready-mixed concrete

(G-2136)
ADDITIVE PRTG & ROBOTICS INC
4601 Park Rd Ste 620 (28209-8800)
PHONE..................704 375-6788
Dale Morrison, *Prin*
EMP: 5 **EST:** 2014
SALES (est): 78.48K **Privately Held**
SIC: 2752 Commercial printing, lithographic

(G-2137)
ADEMCO INC
Also Called: ADI Global Distribution
800 Clanton Rd Ste F (28217-1324)
PHONE..................704 525-8899
Dan Denton, *Mgr*
EMP: 7
SALES (corp-wide): 6.24B **Publicly Held**
Web: www.adiglobaldistribution.us
SIC: 5063 3669 Electrical apparatus and equipment; Emergency alarms
HQ: Ademco Inc.
   275 Broadhollow Rd # 400
   Melville NY 11747
   631 692-1000

(G-2138)
ADVANCED POINT SL SYSTEMS INC
2800 Heathstead Pl (28210-7173)
PHONE..................877 381-6100
EMP: 6 **EST:** 2010
SALES (est): 40.94K **Privately Held**
Web: www.harbortouchpossoftware.com
SIC: 3578 Point-of-sale devices

(G-2139)
ADVANCED TEO CORP
5707 Hornet Dr (28216-2309)
P.O. Box 961330 (33296-1330)
PHONE..................305 278-4474
Walter Rodriguez, *Prin*
EMP: 6 **EST:** 2013
SALES (est): 341.62K **Privately Held**
SIC: 2752 Offset printing

(G-2140)
AEL SERVICES LLC
Also Called: United Printing Company
8200 Arrowridge Blvd Ste A (28273-5673)
PHONE..................704 525-3710
Daniel Marshall, *Pr*
EMP: 20 **EST:** 1996
SALES (est): 1.02MM **Privately Held**
Web: www.unitedprintingnc.com
SIC: 2752 2754 2759 Commercial printing, lithographic; Business form and card printing, gravure; Commercial printing, nec

(G-2141)
AES AMERICA INC
4508b Westinghouse Blvd Ste B (28273-9602)
PHONE..................847 879-1146
Ismet Toktas, *Pr*
EMP: 6 **EST:** 2020
SALES (est): 106.71K **Privately Held**
SIC: 3599 Machine shop, jobbing and repair

(G-2142)
AFSC LLC
Also Called: American Fence & Supply
3605 S Tryon St (28217-1629)
PHONE..................704 523-4936
EMP: 54 **EST:** 1968
SALES (est): 4.86MM
SALES (corp-wide): 24.02MM **Privately Held**
SIC: 3446 2411 5039 1799 Fences, gates, posts, and flagpoles; Rails, fence: round or split; Wire fence, gates, and accessories; Fence construction
PA: Oxco, Inc.
   547 Kings Ridge Dr Ste H
   Fort Mill SC 29708
   704 333-7514

(G-2143)
AGAINST GRAIN WOODWORKING INC
1015 Seigle Ave (28205-2746)
PHONE..................704 309-5750
Ian Ratcliffe, *Pr*
EMP: 4 **EST:** 2018
SALES (est): 119.25K **Privately Held**
Web: www.againstthegrainnc.com
SIC: 2431 Millwork

(G-2144)
AIM LLC
4910 Lakeview Rd (28216-2026)
PHONE..................980 333-0008
Connie Barnes, *CEO*
EMP: 5 **EST:** 2019
SALES (est): 72.06K **Privately Held**
SIC: 3089 Injection molding of plastics

(G-2145)
AIM MOLDING & DOOR LLC
5431 Starflower Dr (28215-7574)
PHONE..................704 913-7211
Michael Archie, *Prin*
EMP: 6 **EST:** 2013
SALES (est): 230.1K **Privately Held**
SIC: 3089 Molding primary plastics

(G-2146)
AIR & GAS SOLUTIONS LLC
Also Called: Nano-Purification Solutions
5509 David Cox Rd (28269-0324)
PHONE..................704 897-2182
EMP: 50 **EST:** 2020
SALES (est): 7.14MM
SALES (corp-wide): 13.47B **Privately Held**
Web: www.nano-purification.com
SIC: 3563 5169 Air and gas compressors; Industrial gases
PA: Atlas Copco Ab
   Sickla Industrivag 19
   Nacka 131 5
   87438000

(G-2147)
AIRGAS USA LLC
Also Called: Airgas National Carbonation
3101 Stafford Dr (28208-3572)
PHONE..................704 394-1420
Russell Jewett, *Brnch Mgr*
EMP: 11

GEOGRAPHIC SECTION

Charlotte - Mecklenburg County (G-2171)

SALES (corp-wide): 101.26MM **Privately Held**
Web: www.airgas.com
SIC: **5169** 5084 5085 2813 Industrial gases; Welding machinery and equipment; Welding supplies; Industrial gases
HQ: Airgas Usa, Llc
  259 N Radnor Chester Rd
  Radnor PA 19087
  216 642-6600

(G-2148)
AIRGAS USA LLC
5311 77 Center Dr (28217-2724)
PHONE...............................704 333-5475
EMP: 17
SALES (corp-wide): 101.26MM **Privately Held**
Web: www.airgas.com
SIC: **2813** 5084 Acetylene; Welding machinery and equipment
HQ: Airgas Usa, Llc
  259 N Radnor Chester Rd
  Radnor PA 19087
  216 642-6600

(G-2149)
AJ & RAINE SCRUBS & MORE LLC
Also Called: Upshinemedical
657 Fielding Rd (28214-1230)
PHONE...............................646 374-5198
Sydell Chewitt, *Managing Member*
EMP: 5 EST: 2020
SALES (est): 444.77K **Privately Held**
SIC: **5047** 2326 7389 Medical equipment and supplies; Medical and hospital uniforms, men's; Business Activities at Non-Commercial Site

(G-2150)
AKZO NOBEL COATINGS INC
7506 E Independence Blvd (28227-9471)
PHONE...............................704 366-8435
Ton Buchner, *CEO*
EMP: 16
SALES (corp-wide): 11.26B **Privately Held**
SIC: **2851** Paints: oil or alkyd vehicle or water thinned
HQ: Akzo Nobel Coatings Inc.
  535 Marriott Dr Ste 500
  Nashville TN 37214
  440 297-5100

(G-2151)
ALAN R WILLIAMS INC (HQ)
Also Called: Electro-Motion Agency
2318 Arty Ave (28208-5104)
P.O. Box 34549 (28234-4549)
PHONE...............................704 372-8281
EMP: 26 EST: 1954
SALES (est): 17.11MM
SALES (corp-wide): 21.46MM **Privately Held**
SIC: **5085** 3625 Power transmission equipment and apparatus; Relays and industrial controls
PA: Motor City Fasteners Llc
  1600 E 10 Mile Rd
  Hazel Park MI 48030
  248 399-2830

(G-2152)
ALBEMARLE CORPORATION (PA)
Also Called: Albemarle
4250 Congress St Ste 900 (28209-0044)
PHONE...............................980 299-5700
J Kent Masters Junior, *Ch Bd*
Neal Sheorey, *Ex VP*
Kristin M Coleman, *Corporate Secretary*
Melissa Anderson, *Chief Human Resources Officer*
John C Barichivich Iii, *CAO*
▼ EMP: 530 EST: 1993
SALES (est): 9.62B **Publicly Held**
Web: www.albemarle.com
SIC: **2821** 2834 2819 2899 Plastics materials and resins; Pharmaceutical preparations; Bromine, elemental; Fire retardant chemicals

(G-2153)
ALEX AND ANI LLC
4400 Sharon Rd Ste 201 (28211-3608)
PHONE...............................704 366-6029
EMP: 5
SALES (corp-wide): 91.95MM **Privately Held**
Web: www.alexandani.com
SIC: **3915** 3911 Jewelers' materials and lapidary work; Jewelry, precious metal
HQ: Alex And Ani, Llc
  10 Briggs Dr
  East Greenwich RI 02818

(G-2154)
ALL AMERICAN PUMPKIN PATCH LLC
4456 Central Ave (28205-5702)
PHONE...............................980 201-9104
EMP: 5 EST: 2018
SALES (est): 100.98K **Privately Held**
SIC: **2741** Miscellaneous publishing

(G-2155)
ALL OF F-WORDS
7007 Gardner Pond Ct (28270-2800)
PHONE...............................561 232-5824
Lauren Merola, *Prin*
EMP: 5 EST: 2018
SALES (est): 41.18K **Privately Held**
Web: www.laurenmerola.com
SIC: **2741** Miscellaneous publishing

(G-2156)
ALL SOURCE SECURITY CONT CAL
1500 Continental Blvd Ste K (28273-6376)
PHONE...............................704 504-9908
Martha Busch, *Pr*
▼ EMP: 13 EST: 2007
SALES (est): 495.68K **Privately Held**
SIC: **3089** Garbage containers, plastics

(G-2157)
ALL-STATE INDUSTRIES INC
Also Called: All State Belting
1400 Westinghouse Blvd Ste 100 (28273-6325)
PHONE...............................704 588-4081
Jay Mcneary, *Mgr*
EMP: 9
SQ FT: 3,500
SALES (corp-wide): 99.48MM **Privately Held**
Web: www.all-stateind.com
SIC: **2399** Belting and belt products
HQ: All-State Industries, Inc.
  500 S 18th St
  West Des Moines IA 50265
  515 223-5843

(G-2158)
ALLBIRDS INC
Also Called: ALLBIRDS, INC.
100 W Worthington Ave (28203-6813)
PHONE...............................980 296-0006
EMP: 19
SALES (corp-wide): 297.77MM **Publicly Held**
Web: www.allbirds.com
SIC: **3143** Men's footwear, except athletic
PA: Allbirds Inc.
  730 Montgomery St
  San Francisco CA 94111
  628 225-4848

(G-2159)
ALLIED METAL FINISHING INC
2525 Lucena St (28206-2107)
PHONE...............................704 347-1477
Steve Turner, *Pr*
Hilda Turner, *VP*
Bruce Turner, *Sec*
EMP: 26 EST: 1986
SQ FT: 25,000
SALES (est): 960.17K **Privately Held**
Web: www.alliedmetalfinishing.com
SIC: **3471** Electroplating of metals or formed products

(G-2160)
ALLIED PLATING FINISHING LLC
2525 Lucena St (28206-2107)
PHONE...............................704 347-1477
EMP: 5 EST: 2021
SALES (est): 241K **Privately Held**
Web: www.alliedplatingllc.com
SIC: **3471** Electroplating of metals or formed products

(G-2161)
ALLIED SHEET METAL WORKS INC
612 Charles Ave (28205-1040)
PHONE...............................704 376-8469
Michael D Herndon, *Pr*
EMP: 10 EST: 1952
SQ FT: 28,000
SALES (est): 994.57K **Privately Held**
Web: www.alliedsheetmetalworks.com
SIC: **3444** Sheet metal specialties, not stamped

(G-2162)
ALLISON GLOBL MNUFACTURING INC
3900 Sam Wilson Rd (28214-9599)
PHONE...............................704 392-7883
James Allison, *Pr*
EMP: 11 EST: 2004
SQ FT: 2,503
SALES (est): 177.46K **Privately Held**
SIC: **3792** Trailer coaches, automobile

(G-2163)
ALLTECH SIGN SERVICE LLC
8334 Arrowridge Blvd Ste C (28273-5611)
PHONE...............................803 548-9787
EMP: 5 EST: 2019
SALES (est): 349.5K **Privately Held**
Web: www.alltechsignservice.com
SIC: **3993** Signs and advertising specialties

(G-2164)
ALPEK POLYESTER MISS INC (DH)
7621 Little Ave Ste 500 (28226-8370)
PHONE...............................228 533-4000
Jorge Young, *Pr*
EMP: 160 EST: 1996
SALES (est): 44.53MM **Privately Held**
SIC: **2821** Plastics materials and resins
HQ: Alpek, S.A.B. De C.V.
  Av. Gomez Morin No. 1111 Sur
  San Pedro Garza Garcia NLE 66254

(G-2165)
ALPEK POLYESTER USA LLC (DH)
7621 Little Ave Ste 500 (28226-8370)
P.O. Box 470408 (28247-0408)
PHONE...............................704 940-7500
Jorge Young, *Pr*
Eammon Simmons, *VP*
Thomas Sherlock, *VP*
Jonathan Mcnaull, *VP*
Alejandro Gutierrez, *
◆ EMP: 60 EST: 2001
SALES (est): 653.81MM **Privately Held**
Web: www.alpekpolyester.com
SIC: **2821** Thermoplastic materials
HQ: Alpek, S.A.B. De C.V.
  Av. Gomez Morin No. 1111 Sur
  San Pedro Garza Garcia NLE 66254

(G-2166)
ALPHA 3D LLC
1141 Homestead Glen Blvd (28214-8710)
P.O. Box 1278 (28012-1278)
PHONE...............................704 277-6300
Harry Ellingwood, *Managing Member*
EMP: 4 EST: 2014
SALES (est): 387.3K **Privately Held**
SIC: **1796** 3599 Machinery installation; Machine shop, jobbing and repair

(G-2167)
ALPHA CANVAS AND AWNING CO INC
411 E 13th St (28206-3310)
PHONE...............................704 333-1581
Eric Riggins, *Pr*
Brian Regans, *VP*
Angie Riggins, *Sec*
EMP: 15 EST: 1983
SQ FT: 2,800
SALES (est): 988.85K **Privately Held**
Web: www.alphacanvas.com
SIC: **2394** Awnings, fabric: made from purchased materials

(G-2168)
ALPHA THEORY LLC
3537 Keithcastle Ct (28210-7008)
PHONE...............................212 235-2180
Cameron Hight, *Managing Member*
EMP: 4
Web: www.alphatheory.com
SIC: **7372** 8748 Prepackaged software; Business consulting, nec
PA: Alpha Theory, Llc
  5701 Westpark Dr Ste 105
  Charlotte NC 28217

(G-2169)
ALPHA THEORY LLC (PA)
5701 Westpark Dr Ste 105 (28217-3525)
PHONE...............................212 235-2180
Cameron Hight, *CEO*
EMP: 8 EST: 2005
SALES (est): 4.15MM **Privately Held**
Web: www.alphatheory.com
SIC: **7372** 8748 Prepackaged software; Business consulting, nec

(G-2170)
ALPHA THEORY LLC
2201 Coronation Blvd Ste 140 (28227-7764)
PHONE...............................704 844-1018
EMP: 4
Web: www.alphatheory.com
SIC: **7372** Prepackaged software
PA: Alpha Theory, Llc
  5701 Westpark Dr Ste 105
  Charlotte NC 28217

(G-2171)
ALPHAGRAPHICS
13850 Ballantyne Corporate Pl Ste 500 (28277-2829)
PHONE...............................704 887-3430
EMP: 6 EST: 2018
SALES (est): 83.91K **Privately Held**
Web: www.alphagraphics.com

Charlotte - Mecklenburg County (G-2172)

SIC: 2752 Commercial printing, lithographic

(G-2172)
ALPHAGRAPHICS PINEVILLE
Also Called: AlphaGraphics
10100 Park Cedar Dr Ste 178 (28210-8932)
PHONE..................................704 541-3678
Mike Brown, *Owner*
EMP: 15 **EST:** 2006
SALES (est): 241.4K **Privately Held**
Web: www.alphagraphics.com
SIC: 2752 7389 Commercial printing, lithographic; Lettering and sign painting services

(G-2173)
ALTRA INDUSTRIAL MOTION CORP
Boston Gear
701 N I-85 Service Rd (28216)
PHONE..................................704 588-5610
Ed Novotny, *Brnch Mgr*
EMP: 76
SALES (corp-wide): 6.25B **Publicly Held**
Web: www.altramotion.com
SIC: 3714 3462 Power transmission equipment, motor vehicle; Iron and steel forgings
HQ: Altra Industrial Motion Corp.
300 Granite St Ste 201
Braintree MA 02184
781 917-0600

(G-2174)
ALTRA INDUSTRIAL MOTION CORP
Also Called: Boston Gear
701 Carrier Dr (28216-3445)
PHONE..................................704 588-5610
EMP: 5
SALES (corp-wide): 6.25B **Publicly Held**
Web: www.altramotion.com
SIC: 3568 5085 Power transmission equipment, nec; Power transmission equipment and apparatus
HQ: Altra Industrial Motion Corp.
300 Granite St Ste 201
Braintree MA 02184
781 917-0600

(G-2175)
ALVEOLUS INC
9013 Perimeter Woods Dr Ste B (28216-0042)
P.O. Box 31247 (28231-1247)
PHONE..................................704 921-2215
Eric Mangiardi, *Pr*
Tony Alexander, *
EMP: 30 **EST:** 2001
SQ FT: 3,000
SALES (est): 4.15MM
SALES (corp-wide): 1.26B **Publicly Held**
Web: www.merit.com
SIC: 3841 Surgical and medical instruments
PA: Merit Medical Systems, Inc.
1600 W Merit Pkwy
South Jordan UT 84095
801 253-1600

(G-2176)
AMANN GIRRBACH NORTH AMER LP
Also Called: Amann Girrbach North America
13900 S Lakes Dr Ste D (28273-7119)
PHONE..................................704 837-1404
Kathleen Dunham, *Dir*
Carol Smith, *Mgr*
◆ **EMP:** 12 **EST:** 2012
SALES (est): 6.46MM
SALES (corp-wide): 2.67MM **Privately Held**
Web: www.amanngirrbach.com

SIC: 3843 Dental equipment and supplies
HQ: Amann Girrbach Ag
Herrschaftswiesen 1
Koblach 6842
552 362-3330

(G-2177)
AMANO PIONEER ECLIPSE CORP
9013 Perimeter Woods Dr Ste A (28216-1862)
PHONE..................................704 900-1352
EMP: 37
Web: www.pioneereclipse.com
SIC: 3589 Floor washing and polishing machines, commercial
HQ: Amano Pioneer Eclipse Corporation
1 Eclipse Rd
Sparta NC 28675
336 372-8080

(G-2178)
AMARR COMPANY
Also Called: Amarr Garage Doors
2801 Hutchison Mcdonald Rd (28269-4203)
PHONE..................................704 599-5858
Trey Varn, *Mgr*
EMP: 6
SALES (corp-wide): 11.51B **Privately Held**
Web: www.amarr.com
SIC: 2431 3442 Garage doors, overhead, wood; Garage doors, overhead: metal
HQ: Amarr Company
165 Carriage Ct
Winston Salem NC 27105
336 744-5100

(G-2179)
AMBRA LE ROY LLC
Also Called: Ambra Leroy Medical Products
8541 Crown Crescent Ct (28227-7733)
PHONE..................................704 392-7080
▲ **EMP:** 4 **EST:** 2001
SALES (est): 350.89K **Privately Held**
Web: www.ambraleroy.com
SIC: 3842 5122 Bandages and dressings; Bandages

(G-2180)
AMERICAN CIRCUITS INC
10100 Sardis Crossing Dr (28270-2412)
PHONE..................................704 376-2800
Vic Gondha, *Pr*
Jayant D Gondha, *
EMP: 25 **EST:** 1990
SALES (est): 6.24MM **Privately Held**
Web: www.americancircuits.com
SIC: 3672 Circuit boards, television and radio printed

(G-2181)
AMERICAN CITY BUS JOURNALS INC (HQ)
Also Called: South Florida Business Journal
120 W Morehead St Ste 400 (28202-1874)
PHONE..................................704 973-1000
Whitney R Shaw, *Pr*
Mike Olivieri, *
George B Guthinger, *
S I Newhouse Junior, *VP*
▲ **EMP:** 267 **EST:** 1985
SQ FT: 77,000
SALES (est): 226.41MM
SALES (corp-wide): 2.88B **Privately Held**
Web: www.acbj.com
SIC: 2711 2721 Newspapers: publishing only, not printed on site; Magazines: publishing only, not printed on site
PA: Advance Publications, Inc.
1 World Trade Ctr Fl 43
New York NY 10007
718 981-1234

(G-2182)
AMERICAN CITY BUS JOURNALS INC
Also Called: Charlotte Business Journal
550 S Caldwell St Ste 910 (28202-2881)
PHONE..................................704 973-1100
EMP: 5
SALES (corp-wide): 2.88B **Privately Held**
Web: www.acbj.com
SIC: 2721 Periodicals
HQ: American City Business Journals, Inc.
120 W Morehead St Ste 400
Charlotte NC 28202
704 973-1000

(G-2183)
AMERICAN RIPENER LLC
803 Pressley Rd Ste 106 (28217-0971)
PHONE..................................704 527-8813
Ann H Wilson, *Sec*
▼ **EMP:** 4 **EST:** 1987
SQ FT: 5,000
SALES (est): 778.23K **Privately Held**
Web: www.ripening.com
SIC: 2819 Catalysts, chemical

(G-2184)
AMERICAN SCALE COMPANY LLC
7231 Covecreek Dr (28215-1854)
PHONE..................................704 921-4556
C Hartman, *Managing Member*
EMP: 19 **EST:** 2018
SALES (est): 2.5MM **Privately Held**
Web: www.americanscaleus.com
SIC: 3596 Truck (motor vehicle) scales

(G-2185)
AMERICAN SIGN SHOP INC
Also Called: American Sign Shop
2440 Whitehall Park Dr Ste 100 (28273)
PHONE..................................704 527-6100
Walton Aldrend, *Pr*
EMP: 4 **EST:** 1985
SQ FT: 1,280
SALES (est): 249.77K **Privately Held**
Web: www.theamericansignshop.com
SIC: 3993 Signs and advertising specialties

(G-2186)
AMERICAN TRUTZSCHLER INC
5315 Heavy Equipment School Rd (28214-9497)
PHONE..................................704 399-4521
Pamela Harrelson, *Prin*
EMP: 20
SALES (corp-wide): 12.57MM **Privately Held**
Web: www.am-truetzschler.com
SIC: 3441 Fabricated structural metal
PA: American Trutzschler, Inc.
12300 Moores Chapel Rd
Charlotte NC 28214
704 399-4521

(G-2187)
AMERICAN TRUTZSCHLER INC (PA)
Also Called: American Truetzschler
12300 Moores Chapel Rd (28214-8928)
P.O. Box 669228 (28266-9228)
PHONE..................................704 399-4521
Kurt Scholler, *CEO*
Detlef Jaekel, *
Stefan Engel, *
James R Short, *
Michael Schuerenkramer, *
▲ **EMP:** 60 **EST:** 1969
SQ FT: 140,000
SALES (est): 12.57MM
SALES (corp-wide): 12.57MM **Privately Held**
Web: www.am-truetzschler.com

SIC: 3552 5084 Textile machinery; Textile machinery and equipment

(G-2188)
AMERICH CORPORATION
10700 John Price Rd (28273-4529)
PHONE..................................704 588-3075
Dino Pacifi, *Brnch Mgr*
EMP: 80
SALES (corp-wide): 23.68MM **Privately Held**
Web: www.americh.com
SIC: 3431 Bathtubs: enameled iron, cast iron, or pressed metal
PA: Americh Corporation
13222 Saticoy St
North Hollywood CA 91605
818 982-1711

(G-2189)
AMPLATE INC
7820 Tyner St (28262-3329)
PHONE..................................704 607-0191
David French, *Pr*
Kim Payseur, *CFO*
EMP: 21 **EST:** 1972
SQ FT: 17,000
SALES (est): 1.26MM **Privately Held**
Web: www.pro-phx.com
SIC: 3471 Electroplating and plating

(G-2190)
AMR SYSTEMS LLC
13850 Balntyn Corp Pl # 500 (28277-2829)
PHONE..................................704 980-9072
EMP: 4
SALES (est): 950K **Privately Held**
SIC: 3822 Environmental controls

(G-2191)
AMREP INC (DH)
6525 Morrison Blvd Ste 300 (28211-3561)
PHONE..................................909 923-0430
Gabriel Ghibaudo, *CEO*
Eric Mattson, *VP*
Vivian Ford, *Sec*
EMP: 47 **EST:** 1976
SQ FT: 40,000
SALES (est): 49.78MM **Privately Held**
Web: www.amrepproducts.com
SIC: 3713 Truck bodies (motor vehicles)
HQ: Wastequip, Llc
6525 Carnegie Blvd # 300
Charlotte NC 28211

(G-2192)
AMT DATASOUTH CORP
5033 Sirona Dr Ste 800 (28273-3960)
P.O. Box 240947 (28224-0947)
PHONE..................................704 523-8500
Chris Biggers, *Genl Mgr*
EMP: 20
SALES (corp-wide): 9.91MM **Privately Held**
Web: www.amtdatasouth.com
SIC: 3577 5045 Printers, computer; Printers, computer
PA: Amt Datasouth Corp.
3222 Corte Malpaso
Camarillo CA 93012
805 388-5799

(G-2193)
ANAV YOFI INC
1501 Majestic Meadow Dr (28216-9920)
PHONE..................................828 217-7746
Amanda Linder, *Prin*
EMP: 4 **EST:** 2019
SALES (est): 83.91K **Privately Held**
SIC: 2752 Commercial printing, lithographic

(G-2194)
ANHEUSER-BUSCH LLC
Also Called: Anheuser-Busch
11325 N Community House Rd
(28277-1978)
PHONE..................704 321-9319
Pat Harrison, *Mgr*
EMP: 13
SALES (corp-wide): 1.31B **Privately Held**
Web: www.anheuser-busch.com
SIC: 2082 Beer (alcoholic beverage)
HQ: Anheuser-Busch, Llc
1 Busch Pl
Saint Louis MO 63118
800 342-5283

(G-2195)
ANILOX ROLL COMPANY INC (PA)
Also Called: ARC West
10955 Withers Cove Park Dr (28278-0020)
PHONE..................704 588-1809
Michael Foran, *Pr*
Robert Perfetto, *Sec*
▲ EMP: 5 EST: 1984
SQ FT: 65,000
SALES (est): 7.07MM **Privately Held**
Web: www.arcinternational.com
SIC: 2759 3555 Engraving, nec; Printing trades machinery

(G-2196)
ANSGAR INDUSTRIAL LLC (PA)
6000 Fairview Rd Ste 1200 (28210-2252)
PHONE..................704 962-5249
Michael Edward Faulkner, *Pr*
Greg Boben, *Dir*
EMP: 1784 EST: 2016
SALES (est): 164.89MM
SALES (corp-wide): 164.89MM **Privately Held**
Web: www.ansgarindustrial.com
SIC: 1541 3498 Industrial buildings, new construction, nec; Pipe sections, fabricated from purchased pipe

(G-2197)
ANTHONY ALEXANDER PRINTS INC
834 Harrier Rd (28216-2763)
P.O. Box 667412 (28266-7412)
PHONE..................704 870-7213
Kimberly Douglas, *Prin*
EMP: 5 EST: 2014
SALES (est): 63.13K **Privately Held**
SIC: 2752 Commercial printing, lithographic

(G-2198)
AO SMITH CHATLOTTE
4302 Raleigh St (28213-6904)
PHONE..................704 597-8910
EMP: 9 EST: 2011
SALES (est): 1.56MM **Privately Held**
Web: www.hotwater.com
SIC: 3621 Motors and generators

(G-2199)
APB WRECKER SERVICE LLC
114 E 28th St (28206-2718)
PHONE..................704 400-0857
Alan Brown, *Managing Member*
EMP: 4 EST: 2012
SALES (est): 399.08K **Privately Held**
Web: www.selljunkcarcharlottenc.com
SIC: 3559 7549 Recycling machinery; Towing services

(G-2200)
APEX PACKAGING CORPORATION LLC
Also Called: United Packaging
15105 John J Delaney Dr (28277-2847)
PHONE..................704 847-7274
▲ EMP: 25
Web: sell.sawbrokers.com
SIC: 5085 3086 Packing, industrial; Packaging and shipping materials, foamed plastics

(G-2201)
APLIX INC (DH)
12300 Steele Creek Rd (28273-3738)
P.O. Box 7505 (28241-7505)
PHONE..................704 588-1920
Sandrine Billarant, *CEO*
Wes Barnes, *Pr*
Richard Little, *VP*
John Rinaldi, *Treas*
Quresh Sachee, *VP*
◆ EMP: 292 EST: 1978
SQ FT: 127,000
SALES (est): 56.24MM **Privately Held**
Web: www.aplix.com
SIC: 3965 Fasteners, hooks and eyes
HQ: Sa Aplix
Rd 723 Za
Le Cellier 44850
228220000

(G-2202)
APPALACHIAN PIPE DISTRS LLC
Also Called: APD
828 East Blvd (28203-5116)
P.O. Box 5217 (25361-0217)
PHONE..................704 688-5703
Michael Fox, *Managing Member*
EMP: 17 EST: 2013
SALES (est): 1.77MM **Privately Held**
Web: www.apdpipe.com
SIC: 3317 3494 7389 Steel pipe and tubes; Pipe fittings; Pipeline and power line inspection service

(G-2203)
APPERSON INC
2908 Stewart Creek Blvd (28216-3592)
P.O. Box 480309 (28269-5338)
PHONE..................704 399-2571
Paul Apperson, *Brnch Mgr*
EMP: 50
SQ FT: 600
SALES (corp-wide): 20.25MM **Privately Held**
Web: www.apperson.com
SIC: 2761 Manifold business forms
PA: Apperson, Inc.
17315 Studebaker Rd # 211
Cerritos CA 90703
562 356-3333

(G-2204)
APPLIED DRIVES INC
11016 Tara Oaks Dr (28227-5489)
P.O. Box 690245 (28227-7004)
PHONE..................704 573-2324
Dennis Hayes, *Pr*
Julie Hayes, *Sec*
EMP: 6 EST: 2001
SQ FT: 2,000
SALES (est): 577.49K **Privately Held**
Web: www.applieddrives.com
SIC: 3679 5999 7629 Electronic switches; Electronic parts and equipment; Electronic equipment repair

(G-2205)
APPLIED STRATEGIES INC
1515 Mockingbird Ln Ste 700 (28209-3236)
PHONE..................704 525-4478
James F Matthews, *Pr*
EMP: 5 EST: 1992
SALES (est): 488.92K **Privately Held**
Web: www.appstratinc.com
SIC: 7372 7371 8243 Prepackaged software; Computer software systems analysis and design, custom; Data processing schools

(G-2206)
APT INDUSTRIES INC
601 E Sugar Creek Rd (28213-6916)
P.O. Box 7486 (28241-7486)
PHONE..................704 598-9100
Roger D Blackwell, *Pr*
Greg Blackwell, *Sec*
EMP: 10 EST: 1979
SQ FT: 27,000
SALES (est): 2.33MM **Privately Held**
Web: www.aptair.com
SIC: 3444 Ducts, sheet metal

(G-2207)
AQUAHUT
600 Morris St (28202-1318)
PHONE..................704 335-8554
John Adams, *Owner*
EMP: 5 EST: 2002
SALES (est): 144.19K **Privately Held**
Web: www.myaquahut.com
SIC: 3466 Closures, stamped metal

(G-2208)
ARBA LLC
525 N Tryon St Ste 1600 (28202-0213)
PHONE..................302 946-0079
Verda Nazli Karan, *Prin*
EMP: 6 EST: 2020
SALES (est): 79.3K **Privately Held**
SIC: 2079 Olive oil

(G-2209)
ARBON EQUIPMENT CORPORATION
14100 S Lakes Dr (28273-7110)
PHONE..................414 355-2600
Tom Burrill, *Mgr*
EMP: 15
SALES (corp-wide): 798.11MM **Privately Held**
Web: arbon.ritehite.com
SIC: 3537 5084 5031 Loading docks, portable, adjustable, and hydraulic; Industrial machinery and equipment; Lumber, plywood, and millwork
HQ: Arbon Equipment Corporation
8900 N Arbon Dr
Milwaukee WI 53223
414 355-2600

(G-2210)
ARCHER-DANIELS-MIDLAND COMPANY
Also Called: ADM
620 W 10th St (28202-1430)
P.O. Box 31155 (28231-1155)
PHONE..................704 332-3165
Dennis Tucker, *Brnch Mgr*
EMP: 26
SALES (corp-wide): 101.56B **Publicly Held**
Web: www.adm.com
SIC: 2041 Flour and other grain mill products
PA: Archer-Daniels-Midland Company
77 W Wacker Dr Ste 4600
Chicago IL 60601
312 634-8100

(G-2211)
ARCHROMA US INC (DH)
Also Called: Archroma
5435 77 Center Dr Ste 10 (28217-0750)
P.O. Box 696523 (78269-6523)
PHONE..................704 353-4100
Bryan Dill, *Pr*
Roland Waibel, *
Robin Mccann, *Sec*
Bas Coolen, *
Mark Delevie, *
◆ EMP: 50 EST: 2013
SALES (est): 106.29MM
SALES (corp-wide): 2.67MM **Privately Held**
Web: www.archroma.com
SIC: 2819 Industrial inorganic chemicals, nec
HQ: Archroma Paper Gmbh
Hardstrasse 1
Pratteln BL 4133

(G-2212)
ARCUS MEDICAL LLC
2401 Distribution St Ste B (28203)
PHONE..................704 332-3424
EMP: 5 EST: 2002
SALES (est): 412.96K **Privately Held**
Web: www.arcusmedical.com
SIC: 3841 Diagnostic apparatus, medical

(G-2213)
ARDEN ENGRAVING US INC
100 Forsyth Hall Dr (28273-5727)
PHONE..................704 547-4581
Andrew Hall, *CFO*
EMP: 4 EST: 2013
SALES (est): 106.24K **Privately Held**
SIC: 2759 Engraving, nec

(G-2214)
ARGOS USA LLC
325 E Hebron St (28273-5974)
PHONE..................704 679-9431
Willie Hyes, *Mgr*
EMP: 5
Web: www.argos-us.com
SIC: 3273 Ready-mixed concrete
HQ: Argos Usa Llc
3015 Windward Plz Ste 300
Alpharetta GA 30005
678 368-4300

(G-2215)
ARGUS FIRE CONTROL-PF&S INC
Also Called: Argus Fire Control
2723 Interstate St (28208-3603)
PHONE..................704 372-1228
Bob Duncan, *Pr*
Frances K Duncan, *
▲ EMP: 26 EST: 1982
SQ FT: 5,300
SALES (est): 4.97MM **Privately Held**
Web: www.argusfirecontrol.com
SIC: 3669 Fire detection systems, electric

(G-2216)
ARIBEX INC
11727 Fruehauf Dr (28273-6507)
P.O. Box 7800 (28241-7800)
PHONE..................866 340-5522
EMP: 48
SIC: 3843 Ultrasonic dental equipment

(G-2217)
ARRIVAL AUTOMOTIVE USA INC (DH)
330 W Tremont Ave (28203-4946)
P.O. Box 37180 (29732-0519)
PHONE..................415 439-2002
Michael Ableson, *CEO*
EMP: 16 EST: 2018
SALES (est): 24.08MM
SALES (corp-wide): 2.67MM **Privately Held**
Web: www.arrival.com
SIC: 3714 Motor vehicle electrical equipment
HQ: Arrival Luxembourg Sarl
Rue Des Bruyeres 60a
Hesperange 1274

Charlotte - Mecklenburg County (G-2218)   GEOGRAPHIC SECTION

(G-2218)
ARROW EQUIPMENT LLC (PA)
Also Called: Caterpillar Authorized Dealer
9000 Statesville Rd (28269-7680)
PHONE..................................803 765-2040
Kevin Franklin, Prin
EMP: 5 EST: 2004
SALES (est): 643.2K Privately Held
Web: www.caterpillar.com
SIC: 3531 Construction machinery

(G-2219)
ARROW GLAZING FABRICATION INC
6161 Mcdaniel Ln (28213-6308)
PHONE..................................704 926-1509
Walter Baucom, Prin
EMP: 7 EST: 2018
SALES (est): 240.49K Privately Held
SIC: 7692 Welding repair

(G-2220)
ARTIFEX INC
3037 Silver Birch Dr (28269-9750)
PHONE..................................704 773-6942
Sara Ward, Prin
EMP: 9 EST: 2015
SALES (est): 41.8K Privately Held
Web: www.artifexnc.com
SIC: 7372 Prepackaged software

(G-2221)
ARTISTIC IMAGES INC
Also Called: Gallery G
900 Remount Rd 920 (28203-5553)
P.O. Box 470043 (28247-0043)
PHONE..................................704 332-6225
Charles G Williams, Pr
EMP: 9 EST: 1985
SALES (est): 319.32K Privately Held
Web: www.artisticimages.net
SIC: 3993 Signs and advertising specialties

(G-2222)
ARTISTIC SOUTHERN INC
Also Called: Southern Staircase
1108 Continental Blvd (28273-6385)
PHONE..................................919 861-4695
Caleb Stewart, Brnch Mgr
EMP: 90
SALES (corp-wide): 2.43MM Privately Held
Web: www.artisticstairs-us.com
SIC: 1751 2431 Carpentry work; Staircases, stairs and railings
PA: Artistic Southern, Inc.
    6025 Shiloh Rd Ste E
    Alpharetta GA 30005
    770 888-7233

(G-2223)
ARVA LLC
Also Called: Hylite Led
9410 D Ducks Ln (28273-4636)
PHONE..................................803 336-2230
▲ EMP: 5 EST: 2010
SALES (est): 421.16K Privately Held
Web: www.hyliteledlighting.com
SIC: 3641 3674 3646 Electric lamps and parts for generalized applications; Semiconductors and related devices; Commercial lighting fixtures

(G-2224)
ARZBERGER ENGRAVERS INC
2518 Dunavant St (28203-5034)
PHONE..................................704 376-1151
Luther Dudley, Pr
EMP: 20 EST: 1953
SQ FT: 6,000
SALES (est): 2.47MM Privately Held
SIC: 2754 2789 2759 2752 Commercial printing, gravure; Bookbinding and related work; Commercial printing, nec; Commercial printing, lithographic

(G-2225)
AS AMERICA INC
4500 Morris Field Dr (28208-5837)
PHONE..................................704 398-4602
Michael Tran, Mgr
EMP: 22
Web: www.americanstandard-us.com
SIC: 3261 Vitreous plumbing fixtures
HQ: As America, Inc.
    30 Knightsbridge Rd # 301
    Piscataway NJ 08854

(G-2226)
ASHLEY SLING INC
Also Called: ASHLEY SLING, INC.
2401 N Graham St (28206-2507)
PHONE..................................704 347-0071
EMP: 42
Web: www.ashleysling.com
SIC: 3496 Mesh, made from purchased wire
PA: Ashley Sling, Llc
    7929 Troon Cir Sw
    Austell GA 30168

(G-2227)
ASIAN (KOREAN) HERALD INC
1300 Baxter St Ste 155 (28204-0064)
PHONE..................................704 332-5656
Ki-hyun Chun, Owner
EMP: 6 EST: 2001
SALES (est): 209.7K Privately Held
Web: www.asianlibrary.org
SIC: 2711 Commercial printing and newspaper publishing combined

(G-2228)
ASSEMBLY TECHNOLOGIES INC
Also Called: ATI
6716 Orr Rd (28213-6439)
P.O. Box 560623 (28256-0623)
PHONE..................................704 596-3903
Rohit Savani, Pr
▲ EMP: 16 EST: 1990
SQ FT: 12,000
SALES (est): 5.66MM Privately Held
Web: www.assemblytechinc.com
SIC: 3672 Printed circuit boards

(G-2229)
AT YOUR SERVICE EXPRESS LLC
101 N Tryon St Ste 112 (28246-0104)
PHONE..................................704 270-9918
EMP: 27 EST: 2019
SALES (est): 1.31MM Privately Held
SIC: 3537 4789 5088 Trucks, tractors, loaders, carriers, and similar equipment; Transportation services, nec; Transportation equipment and supplies

(G-2230)
ATCOM INC
Also Called: Atcom Bus Telecom Solutions
3330 Oak Lake Blvd (28208-7707)
P.O. Box 13476 (27709-3476)
PHONE..................................704 357-7900
Rhonda Morgan, Brnch Mgr
EMP: 15
SALES (corp-wide): 13.11MM Privately Held
Web: www.atcombts.com
SIC: 3661 1731 Telephones and telephone apparatus; Computer installation
PA: Atcom Inc.
    4920 S Alston Ave
    Durham NC 27713
    919 544-5751

(G-2231)
ATLANTIC COMMERCIAL CASEWORKS
4700 Rozzelles Ferry Rd (28216-3341)
P.O. Box 35067 (28235-5067)
PHONE..................................704 393-9500
Nathaniel Gatewood, Owner
EMP: 4 EST: 2011
SALES (est): 908.17K Privately Held
Web: www.atlanticcaseworks.com
SIC: 3553 Cabinet makers' machinery

(G-2232)
ATLANTIC PNSTRIPING GREENSBORO
5072 Ashford Crest Ln (28226-3529)
PHONE..................................910 880-3717
EMP: 4 EST: 2019
SALES (est): 158.86K Privately Held
Web: www.stripeco.com
SIC: 3993 Signs and advertising specialties

(G-2233)
ATLANTIC TRADING LLC
307 Ridgewood Ave (28209-1633)
PHONE..................................
EMP: 10 EST: 2004
SALES (est): 952.76K Privately Held
Web: www.onelittlebox.com
SIC: 5331 2211 2389 Variety stores; Alpacas, cotton; Academic vestments (caps and gowns)

(G-2234)
ATLANTIC WINDOW COVERINGS INC
Also Called: AWC
6150 Brookshire Blvd Ste D (28216-2444)
PHONE..................................704 392-0043
Rob Mitchell, Pr
Margaret Mitchell, VP
EMP: 20 EST: 1963
SQ FT: 8,000
SALES (est): 4.7MM Privately Held
Web: www.awcproducts.com
SIC: 5023 2391 Window covering parts and accessories; Draperies, plastic and textile: from purchased materials

(G-2235)
ATLANTIC WOOD & TIMBER LLC
2200 Border Dr (28208-4061)
PHONE..................................704 390-7479
EMP: 10 EST: 2014
SALES (est): 6.47MM Privately Held
Web: www.atlanticwt.com
SIC: 2491 Wood preserving

(G-2236)
ATLAS COPCO COMPRESSORS LLC
Also Called: Woodward Compressor Sales
2101 Westinghouse Blvd # D (28273-6310)
PHONE..................................704 525-0124
EMP: 15
SALES (corp-wide): 13.47B Privately Held
Web: www.atlascopco.us
SIC: 3563 Air and gas compressors
HQ: Atlas Copco Compressors Llc
    300 Technology Center Way # 550
    Rock Hill SC 29730
    866 472-1015

(G-2237)
ATMOX INC
10612d Providence Rd Ste 229 (28277-0459)
PHONE..................................704 248-2858
Myriam Breedlove, Pr
EMP: 11 EST: 2008
SALES (est): 866.54K Privately Held
Web: www.atmox.com
SIC: 1389 Oil consultants

(G-2238)
ATTUS TECHNOLOGIES INC
13860 Ballantyne Corporate Pl Ste 200 (28277-2467)
PHONE..................................704 341-5750
Trey Sullivan, Pr
EMP: 20 EST: 1998
SALES (est): 2.48MM
SALES (corp-wide): 316.65MM Privately Held
SIC: 7372 Prepackaged software
PA: Computer Services, Inc.
    3901 Technology Dr
    Paducah KY 42001
    800 545-4274

(G-2239)
AURIGA POLYMERS INC (DH)
4235 Southstream Blvd Ste 450 (28217-4588)
PHONE..................................864 579-5570
Tom Brekovsky, Pr
Avnish Madan, VP
Hitendra Mathur, VP
Hunter Stamey, Sec
◆ EMP: 200 EST: 2010
SALES (est): 91.7MM Privately Held
SIC: 2821 2824 Plastics materials and resins ; Polyester fibers
HQ: Indorama Ventures Public Company Limited
    75/102 Soi Sukhumvit 19 (Vadhana), Asok Road
    Vadhana 10110

(G-2240)
AUTOM8 LLC
2925 Silverthorn Dr (28273-9622)
PHONE..................................704 252-3425
EMP: 5 EST: 2018
SALES (est): 236.06K Privately Held
Web: www.autom8.com
SIC: 3826 Analytical instruments

(G-2241)
AUTOPARK LOGISTICS LLC
2703 Madison Oaks Ct (28226-7672)
PHONE..................................704 365-3544
Peter Anderes, Managing Member
▲ EMP: 4 EST: 2013
SALES (est): 354.16K Privately Held
SIC: 3559 Parking facility equipment and supplies

(G-2242)
AUTRY CON PDTS & BLDRS SUP CO
Also Called: Autry Con Pdts & Septic Svcs
8918 Byrum Dr (28217-2368)
PHONE..................................704 504-8830
Steve Autry, Pr
Carol Autry, Sec
EMP: 6 EST: 1929
SQ FT: 4,000
SALES (est): 724.45K Privately Held
SIC: 3272 7699 Pipe, concrete or lined with concrete; Septic tank cleaning service

(G-2243)
AVA ALIZA CANDLE CO LLC
9814 Park Springs Ct (28210-7919)
PHONE..................................704 906-4328
Sarah Hudak, Prin
EMP: 5 EST: 2018
SALES (est): 39.69K Privately Held
SIC: 3999 Candles

(G-2244)
AVADIM HOLDINGS INC
4944 Parkway Plaza Blvd Ste 480 (28217-1972)

PHONE..............................877 677-2723
EMP: 25
SALES (corp-wide): 12.03MM Privately Held
SIC: 2834 Pharmaceutical preparations
PA: Avadim Holdings, Inc.
 4 Old Patton Cove Rd
 Swannanoa NC 28778
 877 677-2723

(G-2245)
AVAGO TECHNOLOGY
9815 David Taylor Dr (28262-2357)
PHONE..............................704 887-7735
EMP: 8 EST: 2016
SALES (est): 443.35K Privately Held
SIC: 3674 Semiconductors and related devices

(G-2246)
AVIATION METALS NC INC
Also Called: AVIATION METALS
1810 W Pointe Dr Ste D (28214-9293)
PHONE..............................704 264-1647
James Contes, CEO
Charles F Contes, Pr
Ames Contes, Sec
▲ EMP: 15 EST: 1976
SQ FT: 30,000
SALES (est): 11.44MM Privately Held
Web: www.aviationmetals.com
SIC: 5051 3354 3353 3356 Steel; Aluminum extruded products; Aluminum sheet, plate, and foil; Nickel and nickel alloy pipe, plates, sheets, etc.

(G-2247)
AVIDXCHANGE HOLDINGS INC (PA)
Also Called: AVIDXCHANGE
1210 Avid Xchange Ln (28206-3560)
PHONE..............................800 560-9305
Michael Praeger, Ch Bd
Joel Wilhite, Sr VP
Daniel Drees, CGO
Angelic Gibson, CIO
Todd Cunningham, CPO
EMP: 34 EST: 2000
SQ FT: 201,000
SALES (est): 380.72MM
SALES (corp-wide): 380.72MM Publicly Held
Web: www.avidxchange.com
SIC: 7372 Prepackaged software

(G-2248)
AVIENT COLORANTS USA LLC
Reedspectrum Division
4000 Monroe Rd (28205-7706)
PHONE..............................704 331-7000
Phil Strassle, Managing Member
EMP: 99
SQ FT: 63,320
Web: www.avient.com
SIC: 3087 2816 Custom compound purchased resins; Inorganic pigments
HQ: Avient Colorants Usa Llc
 85 Industrial Dr
 Holden MA 01520
 877 546-2885

(G-2249)
AVINTIV INC (HQ)
9335 Harris Corners Pkwy Ste 300 (28269)
PHONE..............................704 697-5100
J Joel Hackney Junior, Pr
◆ EMP: 164 EST: 2010
SALES (est): 1.76B Publicly Held
SIC: 2297 Nonwoven fabrics
PA: Berry Global Group, Inc.
 101 Oakley St
 Evansville IN 47710

(G-2250)
AVINTIV SPECIALTY MTLS INC (HQ)
9335 Harris Corners Pkwy Ste 300 (28269)
PHONE..............................704 697-5100
J Joel Hackney Junior, Pr
Dennis Norman, *
Daniel L Rikard, *
Daniel Guerrero Senior, Strategy Vice President
Mary Tomasello Senior, Vice-President Global Human Resources
◆ EMP: 2000 EST: 1994
SALES (est): 450.25MM Publicly Held
Web: www.berryglobal.com
SIC: 2297 2392 Nonwoven fabrics; Towels, dishcloths and dust cloths
PA: Berry Global Group, Inc.
 101 Oakley St
 Evansville IN 47710

(G-2251)
AZURE SKYE BEVERAGES INC
5253 Old Dowd Rd Unit 3 (28208-2162)
P.O. Box 668132 (28266-8132)
PHONE..............................704 909-7394
◆ EMP: 4 EST: 2010
SQ FT: 1,300
SALES (est): 236.9K Privately Held
Web: www.myazureskye.com
SIC: 2085 5149 Rum (alcoholic beverage); Flavorings and fragrances

(G-2252)
B & B LEATHER CO INC
5518 Nevin Rd (28269-7359)
PHONE..............................704 598-9080
Alan Blaentine, Pr
Rebecca Balentine, Treas
Robert H Balentine, Sec
EMP: 10 EST: 1961
SQ FT: 6,000
SALES (est): 494.72K Privately Held
Web: www.bbleather.com
SIC: 3199 5199 Harness or harness parts; Pet supplies

(G-2253)
B ROBERTS FOODS LLC
Also Called: B. Robert's Prepared Foods
2700 Westinghouse Blvd Ste A (28273-0114)
PHONE..............................704 522-1977
EMP: 40
Web: www.brobertsfoods.com
SIC: 2038 Frozen specialties, nec

(G-2254)
B S R-HESS RACE CARS INC
7701 N Tryon St (28262-3498)
PHONE..............................704 547-0901
Harold Stevens, Pr
EMP: 20 EST: 1986
SALES (est): 1.47MM Privately Held
SIC: 3711 7539 Automobile assembly, including specialty automobiles; Automotive repair shops, nec

(G-2255)
B&A WELDING MISCELLANEOUS LLC
8628 Catfish Dr (28214-3401)
PHONE..............................980 287-9187
Cristhian Alvarado, Owner
EMP: 5 EST: 2017
SALES (est): 71.67K Privately Held
SIC: 7692 Welding repair

(G-2256)
B&M DONNELLY INC
1230 W Morehead St Ste 108 (28208-5205)
PHONE..............................704 358-9229
EMP: 5 EST: 2017
SALES (est): 90.58K Privately Held
SIC: 3646 Commercial lighting fixtures

(G-2257)
BAAC BUSINESS SOLUTIONS INC
Also Called: Sign-A-Rama
1701 South Blvd (28203-4727)
PHONE..............................704 333-4321
William Cruz, Dir
EMP: 9 EST: 2016
SALES (est): 1.43MM Privately Held
Web: www.signarama.com
SIC: 3993 Signs and advertising specialties

(G-2258)
BABCOCK WLCOX EQITY INVSTMNTS
13024 Ballantyne Corporate Pl Ste 700 (28277-2113)
PHONE..............................704 625-4900
EMP: 23 EST: 2018
SALES (est): 9.14MM
SALES (corp-wide): 889.82MM Publicly Held
Web: www.babcock.com
SIC: 3511 Turbines and turbine generator sets
PA: Babcock & Wilcox Enterprises, Inc.
 1200 E Market St Ste 650
 Akron OH 44305
 330 753-4511

(G-2259)
BABCOCK WLCOX INTL SLS SVC COR
13024 Ballantyne Corporate Pl Ste 700 (28277-2113)
PHONE..............................704 625-4900
EMP: 10 EST: 2017
SALES (est): 3.97MM
SALES (corp-wide): 889.82MM Publicly Held
Web: www.babcock.com
SIC: 3511 Turbines and turbine generator sets
PA: Babcock & Wilcox Enterprises, Inc.
 1200 E Market St Ste 650
 Akron OH 44305
 330 753-4511

(G-2260)
BABUSCI CRTIVE PRTG IMGING LLC
Also Called: Minuteman Press
4115 Rose Lake Dr Ste A (28217-2870)
PHONE..............................704 423-9864
EMP: 4 EST: 2011
SALES (est): 387.14K Privately Held
Web: airport.intlminutepress.com
SIC: 2752 Commercial printing, lithographic

(G-2261)
BACCI AMERICA INC
1704 East Blvd Ste 101 (28203-5888)
PHONE..............................704 375-5044
Claudio Carpano, Pr
▲ EMP: 10 EST: 2014
SALES (est): 1.11MM Privately Held
Web: www.bacci.com
SIC: 3553 Bandsaws, woodworking

(G-2262)
BACE LLC
322 W 32nd St (28206-4256)
PHONE..............................704 394-2230
Fred Waite, CEO
Drew Sigmund Junior, Sr VP
Gregory J Leon, Sr VP
Randy Sossamon, Sr VP
EMP: 15 EST: 2006
SQ FT: 90,000
SALES (est): 9.81MM
SALES (corp-wide): 103.74MM Privately Held
Web: www.bacecorp.com
SIC: 3599 Machine and other job shop work
PA: Komar Industries, Llc
 4425 Marketing Pl
 Groveport OH 43125
 614 836-2368

(G-2263)
BAE SYSTEMS INC
11215 Rushmore Dr (28277-3439)
PHONE..............................855 223-8363
Robert Eggleston, Brnch Mgr
EMP: 72
SALES (corp-wide): 25.59B Privately Held
Web: www.baesystems.com
SIC: 3812 Search and navigation equipment
HQ: Bae Systems, Inc.
 2941 Frview Pk Dr Ste 100
 Falls Church VA 22042

(G-2264)
BAHAKEL COMMUNICATIONS LTD LLC
Also Called: Wcc Television
701 Television Pl (28205-1061)
P.O. Box 32488 (28232-2488)
PHONE..............................704 372-4434
Beverly Poston, Owner
EMP: 350 EST: 1992
SALES (est): 21.93MM Privately Held
Web: www.bahakelsports.com
SIC: 3663 Television broadcasting and communications equipment

(G-2265)
BAIKOWSKI INTERNATIONAL CORP (HQ)
6601 Northpark Blvd Ste H (28216-0092)
PHONE..............................704 587-7100
Claude Djololian, Pr
▲ EMP: 10 EST: 1979
SQ FT: 19,335
SALES (est): 10.9MM
SALES (corp-wide): 47.17MM Privately Held
Web: www.baikowski.com
SIC: 2819 Industrial inorganic chemicals, nec
PA: Baikowski
 1046 Route De Chaumontet
 Poisy 74330
 450226902

(G-2266)
BAILY ENTERPRISES LLC
Also Called: Special Service Plastic
12016 Steele Creek Rd (28273-3734)
PHONE..............................704 587-0109
Richard Baily, Pr
EMP: 12 EST: 2018
SALES (est): 3.93MM Privately Held
Web: www.specialserviceplastic.com
SIC: 3089 Injection molding of plastics

(G-2267)
BAKER TAYLOR INVESTMENTS I LLC
2810 Clseum Cntre Dr 30 # 300 (28217)
PHONE..............................704 998-3100
EMP: 15 EST: 2007
SALES (est): 183.3K Privately Held
SIC: 2731 Book publishing

(G-2268)
BAKESHOT PRTG & GRAPHICS LLC
121 Greenwich Rd Ste 101 (28211-2343)
PHONE..............................704 532-9326

Charlotte - Mecklenburg County (G-2269)

EMP: 4 **EST:** 2004
SALES (est): 233.79K **Privately Held**
Web: www.bakeshotprinting.com
SIC: 2752 Offset printing

(G-2269)
BAKKAVOR FOODS USA INC
10220 Western Ridge Rd Ste P (28273)
PHONE..................704 522-1977
EMP: 297
SALES (corp-wide): 2.58B **Privately Held**
SIC: 2051 Breads, rolls, and buns
HQ: Bakkavor Foods Usa, Inc.
2700 Westinghouse Blvd
Charlotte NC 28273
704 522-1977

(G-2270)
BAKKAVOR FOODS USA INC (DH)
2700 Westinghouse Blvd (28273-0113)
PHONE..................704 522-1977
Mike Edwards, *CEO*
Ben Waldron, *Chief Financial Officer USA*
▲ **EMP:** 150 **EST:** 1985
SQ FT: 97,000
SALES (est): 313.83MM
SALES (corp-wide): 2.58B **Privately Held**
Web: www.bakkavor.com
SIC: 2051 2013 2092 Bread, all types (white, wheat, rye, etc); fresh or frozen; Spreads, sandwich: meat, from purchased rown; Fresh or frozen fish or seafood chowders, soups, and stews
HQ: Bakkavor Usa Limited
5th Floor
London
177 566-3800

(G-2271)
BALANCED HEALTH PLUS LLC
7804 Fairview Rd Box 275 (28226-4998)
PHONE..................704 604-9524
Ronald Hunt, *Pr*
Richard Rauh, *Treas*
EMP: 10 **EST:** 2014
SALES (est): 618.01K **Privately Held**
Web: www.aromaidclips.com
SIC: 2911 Aromatic chemical products

(G-2272)
BALLANTYNE ONE
15720 Brixham Hill Ave Ste 300 (28277-4651)
PHONE..................704 926-7009
EMP: 6 **EST:** 2018
SALES (est): 207.7K **Privately Held**
Web: www.goballantyne.com
SIC: 2752 Commercial printing, lithographic

(G-2273)
BAMAL CORPORATION (HQ)
Also Called: Bamal Fastener
13725 S Point Blvd (28273-7715)
P.O. Box 7809 (28241-7809)
PHONE..................980 225-7700
Mikel D Miller, *Pr*
Kevin Miller, *Sr VP*
Kyle Miller, *Ofcr*
Marilyn Goodrich, *CFO*
▲ **EMP:** 15 **EST:** 1953
SQ FT: 20,000
SALES (est): 16.29MM **Privately Held**
Web: www.bamal.com
SIC: 5072 3565 7389 Bolts; Bottling machinery: filling, capping, labeling; Labeling bottles, cans, cartons, etc.
PA: Pacific Components De Mexico, S. De R.L. De C.V.
Juarez No. 1102 Oficina 3204
Monterrey NLE 64000

(G-2274)
BANDERA US LLC
2120 Airport Flex Dr (28208-6454)
PHONE..................224 250-6559
EMP: 6 **EST:** 2020
SALES (est): 72.96K **Privately Held**
SIC: 3089 Plastics products, nec

(G-2275)
BANNER SIGNS TODAY INC
2526 S Tryon St (28203-4966)
PHONE..................704 525-2241
Ronald A Oxford, *Pr*
Sarah M Oxford, *Sec*
Robin D Oxford-cobb, *VP*
Jeniffer D Oxford-suthrerland, *VP*
EMP: 5 **EST:** 1983
SQ FT: 1,680
SALES (est): 478.54K **Privately Held**
Web: www.allegramarketingprint.com
SIC: 3993 7389 5999 Signs, not made in custom sign painting shops; Design services; Banners

(G-2276)
BAR ARGON
4544 South Blvd Ste H (28209-2862)
PHONE..................704 574-9486
EMP: 5 **EST:** 2017
SALES (est): 170.08K **Privately Held**
Web: www.barargon.com
SIC: 2813 Argon

(G-2277)
BARBARAS CANINE CATERING INC
Also Called: Canine Cafe
1447 S Tryon St Ste 101 (28203-4259)
PHONE..................704 588-3647
Barbara Burg, *Pr*
EMP: 6 **EST:** 1995
SQ FT: 1,000
SALES (est): 523.16K **Privately Held**
SIC: 2047 Dog food

(G-2278)
BARCOVISION LLC
4420 Taggart Creek Rd (28208-5412)
PHONE..................704 392-9371
Steve Altman, *VP*
EMP: 10 **EST:** 2010
SALES (est): 249.22K **Privately Held**
Web: www.bmsvision.com
SIC: 3823 Process control instruments

(G-2279)
BARCOVVSION LLC (PA)
4420 Taggart Creek Rd Ste 110 (28208-5412)
PHONE..................704 392-9371
Steve Altman, *VP*
Steve Mccullough, *Sec*
Ann Watkins, *Asst Tr*
EMP: 16 **EST:** 2000
SALES (est): 2.45MM **Privately Held**
SIC: 2221 3571 Textile mills, broadwoven: silk and manmade, also glass; Electronic computers

(G-2280)
BARIATRIC PARTNERS INC
7401 Carmel Executive Park Dr (28226-8275)
P.O. Box 470176 (28247-0176)
PHONE..................704 542-2256
Edmund C Bujalski, *Pr*
Stephen R Puckett, *Ch Bd*
EMP: 11 **EST:** 2005
SALES (est): 372.42K **Privately Held**
SIC: 3841 Surgical and medical instruments

(G-2281)
BARKER INDUSTRIES INC (PA)
220 Crompton St (28273-6204)
PHONE..................704 391-1023
Robert F Settin, *Pr*
Marc F Settin, *Ex VP*
▲ **EMP:** 8 **EST:** 1973
SQ FT: 115,000
SALES (est): 2.23MM
SALES (corp-wide): 2.23MM **Privately Held**
Web: www.barkerind.com
SIC: 2899 Salt

(G-2282)
BARNHARDT MANUFACTURING CO
1300 Hawthorne Ln (28205-2922)
PHONE..................704 331-0657
Mark Dobbins, *Mgr*
EMP: 200
SALES (corp-wide): 268.75MM **Privately Held**
Web: www.barnhardt.net
SIC: 3086 0131 Plastics foam products; Cotton
PA: Barnhardt Manufacturing Company
1100 Hawthorne Ln
Charlotte NC 28205
800 277-0377

(G-2283)
BARNHARDT MANUFACTURING COMPANY (PA)
Also Called: Richmond Dental and Medical
1100 Hawthorne Ln (28205-2918)
P.O. Box 34276 (28234-4276)
PHONE..................800 277-0377
◆ **EMP:** 200 **EST:** 1900
SALES (est): 268.75MM
SALES (corp-wide): 268.75MM **Privately Held**
Web: www.barnhardt.net
SIC: 3086 2299 2211 Plastics foam products; Quilt fillings: curled hair, cotton waste, moss, hemp tow; Sheets, bedding and table cloths: cotton

(G-2284)
BARRDAY CORP (HQ)
Also Called: Barrday Protective Solutions
1450 W Pointe Dr Ste C (28214-9291)
PHONE..................704 395-0311
▲ **EMP:** 9 **EST:** 2000
SALES (est): 52.63MM
SALES (corp-wide): 18.34MM **Privately Held**
Web: www.barrday.com
SIC: 2231 Broadwoven fabric mills, wool
PA: Barrday, Inc
201e-181 Groh Ave
Cambridge ON N3C 1
519 621-3620

(G-2285)
BARRON LEGACY MGMT GROUP LLC
1737 Arbor Vista Dr (28262-2531)
PHONE..................301 367-4735
Keith Barron, *Managing Member*
EMP: 4 **EST:** 2019
SALES (est): 119.33K **Privately Held**
SIC: 2261 7336 8742 Screen printing of cotton broadwoven fabrics; Commercial art and graphic design; Marketing consulting services

(G-2286)
BASF CORPORATION
Also Called: B A S F Colors & Colorants
11501 Steele Creek Rd (28273-3730)
PHONE..................704 588-5280
EMP: 240
SQ FT: 43,252
SALES (corp-wide): 74.89B **Privately Held**
Web: www.basf.com
SIC: 2869 Industrial organic chemicals, nec
HQ: Basf Corporation
100 Park Ave
Florham Park NJ 07932
800 962-7831

(G-2287)
BASOFIL FIBERS LLC
4824 Parkway Plaza Blvd Ste 250 (28217-1970)
P.O. Box 1238 (28728-1238)
PHONE..................828 304-2307
Bogdan Ewendt, *Managing Member*
▼ **EMP:** 24 **EST:** 1995
SALES (est): 1.72MM **Privately Held**
Web: www.basofil.com
SIC: 2824 Organic fibers, noncellulosic

(G-2288)
BAYER CORP
2332 Croydon Rd (28207-2704)
PHONE..................704 373-0991
Shanna Simpson, *Marketing Executive*
EMP: 42 **EST:** 2017
SALES (est): 169.27K **Privately Held**
SIC: 2834 Pharmaceutical preparations

(G-2289)
BCP EAST LAND LLC
13860 Balntyn Corp Pl (28277-2467)
PHONE..................704 248-2000
EMP: 6 **EST:** 2012
SALES (est): 811.45K **Privately Held**
SIC: 1389 Construction, repair, and dismantling services

(G-2290)
BEACON INDUSTRIAL MFG LLC
4404a Chesapeake Dr (28216-3413)
PHONE..................704 399-7441
▼ **EMP:** 1242 **EST:** 2000
SALES (est): 2.14MM **Privately Held**
SIC: 3569 Filters, general line: industrial
HQ: Environmental Filtration Technologies Llc
4404a Chesapeake Dr
Charlotte NC 28216
704 399-7441

(G-2291)
BEACON ROOFING SUPPLY INC
Also Called: Lyf-Tym Building Products
1836 Equitable Pl (28213-6500)
PHONE..................704 886-1555
EMP: 4
SALES (corp-wide): 9.12B **Publicly Held**
Web: www.lyftym.com
SIC: 5031 3444 3089 Lumber, plywood, and millwork; Gutters, sheet metal; Windows, plastics
PA: Beacon Roofing Supply, Inc.
505 Huntmar Park Dr # 300
Herndon VA 20170
571 323-3939

(G-2292)
BEARDOWADAMS INC
3034 Horseshoe Ln (28208-6435)
PHONE..................704 359-8443
Bob Adams, *Ch*
Thomas Semans, *Pr*
Mark Rowland, *Dir*
Nick Beardow, *Dir*
▲ **EMP:** 12 **EST:** 2012
SALES (est): 10.78MM
SALES (corp-wide): 3.51B **Publicly Held**

GEOGRAPHIC SECTION

Charlotte - Mecklenburg County (G-2319)

Web: www.beardowadams.com
SIC: 2891 Adhesives
HQ: Beardow And Adams (Adhesives) Limited
32 Blundells Road
Milton Keynes BUCKS MK13
190 857-4000

(G-2293)
BEATY CORPORATION
Also Called: Fastsigns
7407 N Tryon St (28262-5051)
PHONE.................................704 599-4949
EMP: 6 EST: 2020
SALES (est): 662.36K Privately Held
Web: www.fastsigns.com
SIC: 3993 Signs and advertising specialties

(G-2294)
BEAUTY 4 LOVE LLC
1819 Sardis Rd N Ste 350 (28270-2471)
PHONE.................................704 802-2844
EMP: 4
SALES (est): 182.43K Privately Held
SIC: 2844 Depilatories (cosmetic)

(G-2295)
BECO HOLDING COMPANY INC (PA)
Also Called: Brooks Equipment
10926 David Taylor Dr Ste 300 (28262-1293)
P.O. Box 481888 (28269-5317)
PHONE.................................800 826-3473
Eric Smith, Pr
Richard Fairclough, Sec
EMP: 115 EST: 1998
SQ FT: 30,000
SALES (est): 128.16MM Privately Held
SIC: 5099 5087 3569 Fire extinguishers; Firefighting equipment; Firefighting and related equipment

(G-2296)
BEELINE GLOBAL LLC
5560 Holyoke Ln (28226-6897)
PHONE.................................704 562-8221
EMP: 5 EST: 2015
SALES (est): 134.38K Privately Held
SIC: 7372 Business oriented computer software

(G-2297)
BELHAM MANAGEMENT IND LLC
9307 Monroe Rd Ste A (28270-1484)
PHONE.................................704 815-4246
Ben Green, Mgr
EMP: 8 EST: 1980
SQ FT: 2,100
SALES (est): 891.69K Privately Held
SIC: 8711 1731 3822 Energy conservation engineering; Energy management controls; Air conditioning and refrigeration controls

(G-2298)
BELK DEPARTMENT STORES LP
2801 W Tyvola Rd (28217-4525)
PHONE.................................704 357-4000
Belk Mckay, Mng Pt
William R Langley, Pt
EMP: 231 EST: 2002
SALES (est): 4.94MM Publicly Held
SIC: 2211 5311 Dress fabrics, cotton; Department stores
HQ: Belk, Inc.
2801 W Tyvola Rd
Charlotte NC 28217
704 357-1000

(G-2299)
BELLAIRE DYNAMIK LLC
4714 Stockholm Ct (28273-5900)
PHONE.................................704 779-3755
Sergio Koppany, Managing Member
▲ EMP: 4 EST: 2012
SALES (est): 492.04K Privately Held
Web: www.b-dynamik.com
SIC: 2273 Carpets and rugs

(G-2300)
BENDEL TANK HEAT EXCHANGER LLC
4823 N Graham St (28269-4822)
PHONE.................................704 596-5112
Bill Beaver, Pr
Mark Oleskiewicz, CFO
EMP: 13 EST: 2020
SALES (est): 178.69K Privately Held
SIC: 3443 Tanks, standard or custom fabricated: metal plate

(G-2301)
BERMLORD LLC
8912 Windygap Rd (28278-8035)
PHONE.................................704 631-4304
Amalie Elaine Jahn, Owner
EMP: 5 EST: 2015
SALES (est): 47.93K Privately Held
SIC: 2741 Miscellaneous publishing

(G-2302)
BERRY GLOBAL INC
Also Called: Berry Plastics
9335 Harris Corners Pkwy Ste 300 (28269-3818)
PHONE.................................704 697-5100
EMP: 560
Web: www.berryglobal.com
SIC: 2297 2392 Spunbonded fabrics; Slip covers and pads
HQ: Berry Global, Inc.
101 Oakley St
Evansville IN 47710

(G-2303)
BETEK TOOLS INC
8325 Arrowridge Blvd Ste A (28273-5603)
PHONE.................................980 498-2523
Hannes Redman, CEO
▲ EMP: 13 EST: 2015
SALES (est): 2.67MM
SALES (corp-wide): 1.87B Privately Held
Web: www.betek.de
SIC: 3541 3313 Electrolytic metal cutting machine tools; Tungsten carbide powder
HQ: Betek GmbH & Co. Kg
Sulgener Str. 21-23
Aichhalden BW 78733
74225650

(G-2304)
BETTER BURGER GROUP LLC
4310 Sharon Rd Ste X05 (28211-4193)
PHONE.................................704 662-9152
Alan Springate, Prin
EMP: 5 EST: 2008
SALES (est): 127.39K Privately Held
SIC: 3131 Counters

(G-2305)
BEVS & BITES LLC
Also Called: Bruce Julian Heritage Foods
2913 Selwyn Ave (28209-1734)
PHONE.................................704 247-7573
Bruce Julian, Managing Member
EMP: 10 EST: 2014
SALES (est): 571.89K Privately Held
SIC: 2033 2035 Tomato cocktails: packaged in cans, jars, etc.; Vegetables, pickled

(G-2306)
BEYOND NORMAL MEDIA LLC
13656 Meade Glen Ct (28273-4897)
PHONE.................................980 263-9921
EMP: 4
SALES (est): 47.85K Privately Held
SIC: 2741 7389 Internet publishing and broadcasting; Business services, nec

(G-2307)
BI COUNTY GAS PRODUCERS LLC
10600 Nations Ford Rd (28273-5762)
PHONE.................................704 844-8990
William Brinker, Owner
EMP: 7 EST: 2009
SALES (est): 302.45K Privately Held
Web: www.landfillgroup.com
SIC: 1321 Natural gas liquids

(G-2308)
BIC CORPORATION
5900 Long Creek Park Dr (28269-3737)
PHONE.................................704 598-7700
Tod Adams, Mgr
EMP: 51
SALES (corp-wide): 800.85MM Privately Held
Web: corporate.bic.com
SIC: 3951 3421 5091 5112 Pens and mechanical pencils; Cutlery; Sporting and recreation goods; Stationery and office supplies
HQ: Bic Corporation
1 Bic Way Ste 1 # 1
Shelton CT 06484
203 783-2000

(G-2309)
BIESSE AMERICA INC
Intermac Glass and Stone Div
4110 Meadow Oak Dr (28208-7721)
PHONE.................................704 357-3131
EMP: 8
SQ FT: 36,000
Web: www.biesse.com
SIC: 3559 Glass making machinery: blowing, molding, forming, etc.
HQ: Biesse America, Inc.
4110 Meadow Oak Dr
Charlotte NC 28208

(G-2310)
BILGE MASTERS INC
6239 River Cabin Ln (28278-6574)
PHONE.................................704 995-4293
EMP: 6
SALES (est): 105.86K Privately Held
Web: www.clippinslawncare.com
SIC: 3732 Boatbuilding and repairing

(G-2311)
BILL TRUITT WOOD WORKS INC
3124 W Trade St # B (28208-3386)
PHONE.................................704 398-8499
Bill Truitt, Pr
EMP: 6 EST: 1974
SQ FT: 6,500
SALES (est): 509.37K Privately Held
Web: www.btwoodworks.com
SIC: 2434 Wood kitchen cabinets

(G-2312)
BINDERS INCORPORATED
1303 Upper Asbury Ave (28206-1527)
PHONE.................................704 377-9704
TOLL FREE: 800
Ronald Lee, Pr
EMP: 13 EST: 1981
SQ FT: 14,000
SALES (est): 2.46MM Privately Held
Web: www.bindersinc.com
SIC: 2782 Looseleaf binders and devices

(G-2313)
BINDERS OF JHC LLC
Also Called: Visual Products
3322 Leamington Ln (28226-6657)
PHONE.................................980 875-9274
Michael A Jones, Mgr
EMP: 6 EST: 2017
SALES (est): 102.99K Privately Held
Web: www.bindersinc.com
SIC: 2752 Offset printing

(G-2314)
BIO-TEC ENVIRONMENTAL LLC
Also Called: Biotec
8910 Pioneer Ave (28273-6389)
PHONE.................................505 629-1777
EMP: 4 EST: 2018
SALES (est): 74.42K Privately Held
SIC: 2821 Plastics materials and resins

(G-2315)
BIOSELECT INC
4740 Dwight Evans Rd (28217-0982)
P.O. Box 221216 (28222-1216)
PHONE.................................704 521-8585
Kathi Levine, Pr
▲ EMP: 6 EST: 2008
SALES (est): 620.33K Privately Held
Web: www.bioselect.com
SIC: 2673 3089 Food storage and frozen food bags, plastic; Cups, plastics, except foam

(G-2316)
BIOTAGE LLC (HQ)
10430 Harris Oak Blvd Ste C (28269-7518)
PHONE.................................704 654-4900
Torben Jorgensen, CEO
Ed Connell, Treas
▲ EMP: 90 EST: 2001
SQ FT: 51,000
SALES (est): 56.43MM Privately Held
Web: www.biotage.com
SIC: 3829 Chronometers, electronic
PA: Biotage Ab
Uppsala 751 0

(G-2317)
BIOVIND LLC
2219 Vail Ave (28207-1529)
PHONE.................................512 217-3077
Ehinomen Iyoha-nwani, CEO
EMP: 4 EST: 2021
SALES (est): 95.66K Privately Held
SIC: 3821 Laboratory apparatus, except heating and measuring

(G-2318)
BJMF INC
8200 South Blvd (28273-6916)
PHONE.................................704 554-6333
EMP: 40
SIC: 2515 5712 Mattresses and bedsprings; Mattresses

(G-2319)
BLACK & DECKER CORPORATION
Also Called: Black & Decker
15040 Choate Cir (28273-6947)
PHONE.................................803 396-3700
John Petza, Brnch Mgr
EMP: 6
SALES (corp-wide): 15.78B Publicly Held
Web: www.blackanddecker.com

Charlotte - Mecklenburg County (G-2320)   GEOGRAPHIC SECTION

SIC: **3546** Power-driven handtools
HQ: The Black & Decker Corporation
701 E Joppa Rd
Towson MD 21286
410 716-3900

(G-2320)
BLAZING FOODS LLC
1520 West Blvd (28208-7070)
PHONE..................................336 865-2933
David Foy, *Managing Member*
EMP: 6 **EST:** 2018
SALES (est): 415.34K **Privately Held**
Web: www.blazingfoods2.com
SIC: **5499** 2096 Gourmet food stores; Potato chips and similar snacks

(G-2321)
BLUE HORSESHOE
13024 Ballantyne Corporate Pl (28277-0784)
PHONE..................................980 312-8202
EMP: 7 **EST:** 2016
SALES (est): 176.59K **Privately Held**
SIC: **3462** Horseshoes

(G-2322)
BLUE UNICORN LLC
2724 Highworth Ln (28214-5438)
PHONE..................................704 748-4832
Christopher Crawford, *Managing Member*
EMP: 5 **EST:** 2016
SALES (est): 47.15K **Privately Held**
SIC: **2741** Miscellaneous publishing

(G-2323)
BLUEJAY ENTERPRISES GROUP INC
3721 Atmore St (28205-1301)
PHONE..................................866 670-8811
Raul Gonzalez, *Ch Bd*
EMP: 8 **EST:** 2014
SALES (est): 475.63K **Privately Held**
Web: www.bluejayeg.com
SIC: **3661** Telegraph or telephone carrier and repeater equipment

(G-2324)
BLUMENTHAL HOLDINGS LLC (PA)
1355 Greenwood Clfs Ste 200 (28204-2982)
PHONE..................................704 688-2302
Alan Blumenthal, *Managing Member*
EMP: 6 **EST:** 2010
SALES (est): 5.28MM
SALES (corp-wide): 5.28MM **Privately Held**
Web: www.gunk.com
SIC: **2992** Lubricating oils and greases

(G-2325)
BLYTHE CONSTRUCTION INC (DH)
2911 N Graham St (28206-3535)
P.O. Box 31635 (28231-1635)
PHONE..................................704 375-8474
Bill Carphardt, *Pr*
Alan Cahill, *
J Mcbryde, *VP*
Fred Odea, *
▲ **EMP:** 300 **EST:** 1949
SQ FT: 18,500
SALES (est): 159.07MM
SALES (corp-wide): 37.11MM **Privately Held**
Web: www.blytheconstruction.com
SIC: **1611** 1622 2951 Highway and street paving contractor; Bridge construction; Asphalt and asphaltic paving mixtures (not from refineries)
HQ: The Hubbard Group Inc
1936 Lee Rd Ste 101
Winter Park FL 32789
407 645-5500

(G-2326)
BMA AMERICA INC
2020 Starita Rd Ste E (28206-1298)
PHONE..................................970 353-3770
Dennis Brice, *Pr*
◆ **EMP:** 15 **EST:** 1926
SALES (est): 8.93MM
SALES (corp-wide): 105.86MM **Privately Held**
Web: www.bma-worldwide.com
SIC: **3441** 3443 Fabricated structural metal; Fabricated plate work (boiler shop)
HQ: Bma Braunschweigische Maschinenbauanstalt Gmbh
Am Alten Bahnhof 5
Braunschweig NI 38122
5318040

(G-2327)
BMC SOLUTIONS LLC
3119 Misty Creek Dr (28269-4057)
PHONE..................................704 386-0194
Gervin Bonilla Carcamo, *Prin*
EMP: 5 **EST:** 2020
SALES (est): 232.5K **Privately Held**
Web: www.bmc.com
SIC: **7372** Prepackaged software

(G-2328)
BOB TRAILERS INC
13501 S Ridge Dr (28273-6741)
PHONE..................................208 375-5171
EMP: 25
SIC: **3799** Trailers and trailer equipment

(G-2329)
BODY BUTTER BLENDS LLC
10419 Hyndman Ct (28214-9270)
PHONE..................................704 307-9200
Nickol Crews, *Prin*
EMP: 5 **EST:** 2016
SALES (est): 81.68K **Privately Held**
Web: www.bodybutterblends.com
SIC: **2844** Perfumes, cosmetics and other toilet preparations

(G-2330)
BOEING COMPANY
Also Called: Boeing
4930 Minuteman Way (28208-3866)
PHONE..................................704 572-8280
EMP: 8 **EST:** 2018
SALES (est): 217.79K **Privately Held**
SIC: **3721** Aircraft

(G-2331)
BOINGO GRAPHICS INC
656 Michael Wylie Dr (28217-1545)
PHONE..................................704 527-4963
Edward Nowokunski, *Ch*
Scott Nowokunski, *
Carolyn Nowokunski, *
Linda Kirby, *
EMP: 37 **EST:** 1979
SQ FT: 24,000
SALES (est): 8.46MM **Privately Held**
Web: www.boingographics.com
SIC: **2752** 2791 2789 2675 Offset printing; Typesetting; Bookbinding and related work; Die-cut paper and board

(G-2332)
BONDING MATERIALS LLC
809 Westmere Ave Ste C (28208-5343)
PHONE..................................704 277-6697
Koray Sanli, *Owner*
EMP: 6 **EST:** 2018
SALES (est): 358.99K **Privately Held**
SIC: **2891** Adhesives and sealants

(G-2333)
BONOMI NORTH AMERICA INC
306 Forsyth Hall Dr (28273-5817)
PHONE..................................704 412-9031
Aldo Bonomi, *Pr*
Alberto Malaguti, *Genl Mgr*
▲ **EMP:** 17 **EST:** 2005
SALES (est): 10.65MM
SALES (corp-wide): 312.4MM **Privately Held**
Web: www.bonominorthamerica.com
SIC: **5085** 3593 3491 3494 Valves and fittings; Fluid power actuators, hydraulic or pneumatic; Industrial valves; Plumbing and heating valves
PA: Bonomi Group Spa
Via Massimo Bonomi 1
Gussago BS 25064
030 825-0011

(G-2334)
BONSAL AMERICAN INC (DH)
625 Griffith Rd Ste 100 (28217-3576)
PHONE..................................704 525-1621
David J Maske, *Pr*
Robert D Quinn, *
Barry Hirsch, *
Marsha Lewis, *
Gil Seco, *
◆ **EMP:** 60 **EST:** 1895
SQ FT: 20,000
SALES (est): 117.68MM
SALES (corp-wide): 32.72B **Privately Held**
SIC: **3272** 1442 3253 2899 Dry mixture concrete; Construction sand and gravel; Ceramic wall and floor tile; Chemical preparations, nec
HQ: Crh Americas, Inc.
900 Ashwood Pkwy Ste 600
Atlanta GA 30338
770 804-3363

(G-2335)
BORDER CONCEPTS INC (PA)
Also Called: B C I
15720 Brixham Hill Ave (28277-4651)
PHONE..................................704 541-5509
Neil R Miller, *Pr*
Tony Ferguson, *VP*
Anthony J Fergusonf, *VP*
David Larr, *Dir*
Sandy Peterson, *Contrlr*
◆ **EMP:** 7 **EST:** 1990
SALES (est): 21.99MM **Privately Held**
Web: www.borderconcepts.com
SIC: **3317** 3446 3269 Steel pipe and tubes; Architectural metalwork; Art and ornamental ware, pottery

(G-2336)
BOSCH REXROTH CORPORATION (DH)
Also Called: Indramat Div
14001 S Lakes Dr South Point Business Park (28273)
P.O. Box 3264 (48333-3264)
PHONE..................................704 583-4338
Paul Cooke, *Pr*
Ken Hank, *
Steve Roberts, *
▲ **EMP:** 40 **EST:** 1967
SALES (est): 564.89MM
SALES (corp-wide): 230.19MM **Privately Held**
Web: www.boschrexroth-us.com
SIC: **5084** 3714 Hydraulic systems equipment and supplies; Acceleration equipment, motor vehicle
HQ: Bosch Rexroth Ag
Zum EisengieBer 1
Lohr A. Main BY 97816
9352180

(G-2337)
BOSTON GEAR LLC
701 Carrier Dr (28216-3445)
PHONE..................................704 588-5610
EMP: 270 **EST:** 2004
SALES (est): 98.54MM
SALES (corp-wide): 6.25B **Publicly Held**
Web: www.bostongear.com
SIC: **3568** 5085 Power transmission equipment, nec; Power transmission equipment and apparatus
HQ: Altra Industrial Motion Corp.
300 Granite St Ste 201
Braintree MA 02184
781 917-0600

(G-2338)
BOSTROM SEATING INC
3000 Crosspoint Center Ln Ste P (28269-4204)
PHONE..................................704 596-0040
EMP: 639
Web: www.bostromseating.com
SIC: **3714** Motor vehicle parts and accessories
HQ: Bostrom Seating, Inc.
50 Nances Creek Indus Blv
Piedmont AL 36272
256 447-9051

(G-2339)
BOTTOMLINE MEDICAL
5200 Milford Rd (28210-2846)
P.O. Box 12214 (28220-2214)
PHONE..................................704 527-0919
EMP: 8 **EST:** 2006
SALES (est): 160K **Privately Held**
SIC: **7372** Business oriented computer software

(G-2340)
BOUGIEJONES
5212 Galway Dr (28215-3131)
PHONE..................................704 492-3029
Cassandra Jones, *CEO*
EMP: 4 **EST:** 2021
SALES (est): 41.02K **Privately Held**
SIC: **3944** Craft and hobby kits and sets

(G-2341)
BOWMAN-HOLLIS MANUFACTURING CO (PA)
2925 Old Steele Creek Rd (28208-6726)
P.O. Box 19249 (28219-9249)
PHONE..................................704 374-1500
Tom Bowman, *Pr*
Russ Bowman, *
Debbie Price, *
Ann Bowman, *
▲ **EMP:** 35 **EST:** 1956
SQ FT: 20,000
SALES (est): 9.08MM
SALES (corp-wide): 9.08MM **Privately Held**
Web: www.bowmanhollis.com
SIC: **3552** 7699 Textile machinery; Industrial machinery and equipment repair

(G-2342)
BOXMAN STUDIOS LLC
12140 Vance Davis Dr (28269-7697)
PHONE..................................704 333-3733
David Campbell, *Managing Member*
EMP: 6 **EST:** 2009
SALES (est): 7.48MM **Privately Held**
Web: www.boxmanstudios.com
SIC: **5085** 3448 Commercial containers; Buildings, portable: prefabricated metal

▲ = Import   ▼ = Export
◆ = Import/Export

GEOGRAPHIC SECTION — Charlotte - Mecklenburg County

(G-2343)
BOY SCOUT TROOP
3000 Wamath Dr (28210-4888)
PHONE...................704 643-8955
Chip Morgan, *COO*
EMP: 5 EST: 2016
SALES (est): 74.57K Privately Held
Web: www.troop116.org
SIC: 3572 Computer storage devices

(G-2344)
BP SIGNS INC
4845 E Independence Blvd Unit B (28212-5407)
PHONE...................704 531-8000
Jim Lee, *Mgr*
EMP: 5 EST: 2009
SALES (est): 149.01K Privately Held
SIC: 3993 Signs and advertising specialties

(G-2345)
BRAND NEW LIFE CLOTHING LLC
1914 J N Pease Pl (28262-4504)
PHONE...................980 266-4788
EMP: 6
SALES (est): 79.3K Privately Held
SIC: 2329 Men's and boys' sportswear and athletic clothing

(G-2346)
BRANDEL LLC
2909 Rockbrook Dr (28211-2641)
PHONE...................704 525-4548
Prescott Little, *Prin*
EMP: 7 EST: 2011
SALES (est): 63.5K Privately Held
SIC: 3841 Surgical and medical instruments

(G-2347)
BRANDRPM LLC
Also Called: Brandrpm
9555 Monroe Rd (28270-1446)
PHONE...................704 225-1800
Vivienne Anderson, *Managing Member*
Vivienne S Anderson, *Managing Member*
EMP: 96 EST: 1998
SQ FT: 40,000
SALES (est): 18.42MM Privately Held
Web: www.brandrpm.com
SIC: 2396 5941 Screen printing on fabric articles; Team sports equipment

(G-2348)
BRANDS FASHION US INC
2600 Mcdonald Rd (28269)
PHONE...................704 953-8246
Doctor Ulrich Hofmann, *CEO*
EMP: 6 EST: 2017
SALES (est): 140.2K Privately Held
Web: www.brands-fashion.com
SIC: 7389 5699 2326 Textile and apparel services; Customized clothing and apparel; Work uniforms

(G-2349)
BRATZ PLAYGROUND LLC
9501 Lucy Jane Ln Apt 310 (28270-2586)
PHONE...................704 858-1934
EMP: 10 EST: 2020
SALES (est): 394.35K Privately Held
SIC: 3161 Clothing and apparel carrying cases

(G-2350)
BREEZEPLAY LLC
8045 Corporate Center Dr (28226-4555)
PHONE...................980 297-0885
Rick Sabath, *CEO*
EMP: 18 EST: 2008
SQ FT: 2,500
SALES (est): 1.43MM Privately Held
SIC: 3825 Energy measuring equipment, electrical

(G-2351)
BREEZER HOLDINGS LLC
Also Called: Breezer Mobile Cooling
4835 Sirona Dr Ste 400 (28273-3245)
PHONE...................844 233-5673
◆ EMP: 85 EST: 2010
SALES (est): 24.68MM Privately Held
Web: www.powerbreezer.com
SIC: 3564 Blowers and fans

(G-2352)
BREW PUBLIK INCORPORATED
312 W Park Ave (28203-4441)
PHONE...................704 231-2703
Charles Vincent Mulligan, *Prin*
EMP: 6 EST: 2015
SALES (est): 203.15K Privately Held
Web: www.brewpublik.beer
SIC: 2082 Malt beverages

(G-2353)
BREWITT & DREENKUPP INC
Also Called: Tea Rex Teahouse
4321 Stuart Andrew Blvd Ste I (28217-4625)
PHONE...................704 525-3366
Wayne Powers, *Prin*
EMP: 4 EST: 1997
SALES (est): 176.08K Privately Held
Web: www.tearex.com
SIC: 2086 5812 Tea, iced: packaged in cans, bottles, etc.; Coffee shop

(G-2354)
BRICK MASON MASONRY
1122 Goodman Rd (28214-1602)
PHONE...................704 502-4907
Steve Reese, *Prin*
EMP: 5 EST: 2018
SALES (est): 86.39K Privately Held
SIC: 2024 Yogurt desserts, frozen

(G-2355)
BRICKFIELDS INCORPORATED
6109 Hickory Forest Dr (28277-2325)
PHONE...................704 351-1524
EMP: 5 EST: 2010
SALES (est): 51.65K Privately Held
SIC: 2752 Commercial printing, lithographic

(G-2356)
BRILLIANT POS LLC
15210 Pangborn Pl (28278-7276)
PHONE...................704 315-2352
Matthew Hoerr, *Prin*
EMP: 9 EST: 2015
SALES (est): 106.3K Privately Held
SIC: 7372 Prepackaged software

(G-2357)
BRISTOL-MYERS SQUIBB COMPANY
Also Called: Bristol-Myers Squibb
P.O. Box 751095 (28275)
PHONE...................800 321-1335
EMP: 4
SALES (corp-wide): 45.01B Publicly Held
Web: www.bms.com
SIC: 2834 Pharmaceutical preparations
PA: Bristol-Myers Squibb Company
    430 E 29th St Fl 14
    New York NY 10016
    212 546-4000

(G-2358)
BROWN LADY PUBLISHING LLC
9137 Austin Ridge Ln (28214-9277)
PHONE...................980 833-0398
Gabrielle Brown, *Admn*
EMP: 4 EST: 2019
SALES (est): 76.29K Privately Held
SIC: 2741 Miscellaneous publishing

(G-2359)
BROWN MITCHELL HODGES LLC
Also Called: Playerz Haul
4111 Rose Lake Dr Ste E Pmb 678 (28217-2864)
PHONE...................800 477-8982
Latonya Brown, *Managing Member*
Kathy Brown, *Prin*
Dana Brown, *Prin*
Tracey Brown, *Prin*
Linda Fleet, *Prin*
EMP: 5 EST: 2020
SALES (est): 90.11K Privately Held
Web: www.playerzhaul.com
SIC: 7929 7993 3711 Entertainment service; Video game arcade; Mobile lounges (motor vehicle), assembly of

(G-2360)
BROWN PRINTING INC
Also Called: AlphaGraphics
9129 Monroe Rd Ste 160 (28270-2431)
P.O. Box 279 (28106-0279)
PHONE...................704 849-9292
Kedar Brown, *Pr*
EMP: 9 EST: 2009
SALES (est): 264.28K Privately Held
Web: www.alphagraphics.com
SIC: 2752 Commercial printing, lithographic

(G-2361)
BSN MEDICAL INC (DH)
5825 Carnegie Blvd (28209-4633)
PHONE...................704 554-9933
Darrell Jenkins, *Pr*
Steve Brown, *
Shawn Fry, *
◆ EMP: 110 EST: 2000
SQ FT: 12,000
SALES (est): 93.03MM
SALES (corp-wide): 14.89B Privately Held
Web: medical.essityusa.com
SIC: 3842 Orthopedic appliances
HQ: Bsn Medical Gmbh
    Schutzenstr. 1-3
    Hamburg HH 22761
    40593612100

(G-2362)
BTHEC INC (PA)
4823 N Graham St (28269-4822)
PHONE...................704 596-5112
EMP: 35 EST: 1983
SALES (est): 15.7MM
SALES (corp-wide): 15.7MM Privately Held
Web: www.bendelcorp.com
SIC: 3443 Tanks, standard or custom fabricated: metal plate

(G-2363)
BUCKEYE INTERNATIONAL INC
Also Called: Buckeye Cleaning Center
4123 Barringer Dr Ste A (28217-1521)
PHONE...................704 523-9400
Brian Morabito, *Brnch Mgr*
EMP: 5
SALES (corp-wide): 158.42MM Privately Held
Web: www.buckeyeinternational.com
SIC: 2842 2841 2899 2812 Specialty cleaning; Detergents, synthetic organic or inorganic alkaline; Chemical preparations, nec; Alkalies and chlorine
PA: Buckeye International, Inc.
    2700 Wagner Pl
    Maryland Heights MO 63043
    314 291-1900

(G-2364)
BULL ENGINEERED PRODUCTS INC
Also Called: Bull
12001 Steele Creek Rd (28273-3734)
P.O. Box 39170 (28278-1020)
PHONE...................704 504-0300
Gary Dickison, *Pr*
▲ EMP: 60 EST: 2001
SALES (est): 10.29MM Privately Held
Web: www.bullep.com
SIC: 3089 Molding primary plastics

(G-2365)
BUSINESS JOURNALS (DH)
120 W Morehead St Ste 420 (28202-1874)
PHONE...................704 371-3248
Mike Olivieri, *Pr*
Tina Carusillo, *
EMP: 54 EST: 1986
SALES (est): 23.65MM
SALES (corp-wide): 2.88B Privately Held
Web: advertise.bizjournals.com
SIC: 2711 Newspapers, publishing and printing
HQ: American City Business Journals, Inc.
    120 W Morehead St Ste 400
    Charlotte NC 28202
    704 973-1000

(G-2366)
BUSINESS SYSTEMS OF AMERICA
3020 Prosperity Church Rd (28269-7197)
PHONE...................704 766-2755
Eric S Martin, *Prin*
EMP: 5 EST: 2015
SALES (est): 63.41K Privately Held
Web: www.ordersplus.com
SIC: 7372 Prepackaged software

(G-2367)
BUSINESS WISE INC
615 S College St Ste 810 (28202-3355)
PHONE...................704 554-4112
Lee Martin, *Brnch Mgr*
EMP: 5
SALES (corp-wide): 2.63MM Privately Held
Web: www.businesswise.com
SIC: 2754 Commercial printing, gravure
PA: Business Wise Inc
    5641 Bahia Mar Cir
    Stone Mountain GA 30087
    770 956-1955

(G-2368)
BWX TECHNOLOGIES INC
11525 N Community House Rd Ste 600 (28277)
PHONE...................980 365-4000
Peyton S Baker, *Brnch Mgr*
EMP: 92
Web: www.bwxt.com
SIC: 3621 Power generators
PA: Bwx Technologies, Inc.
    800 Main St Ste 4
    Lynchburg VA 24504

(G-2369)
BWXT INVESTMENT COMPANY (HQ)
Also Called: B&W
13024 Ballantyne Corporate Pl Ste 700 (28277-2113)
PHONE...................704 625-4900
Peyton Baker, *Pr*
EMP: 21 EST: 1990
SALES (est): 1.36B Publicly Held
Web: www.babcock.com

Charlotte - Mecklenburg County (G-2370)

SIC: **3511** 3564 1629 1541 Turbines and turbine generator set units, complete; Purification and dust collection equipment; Industrial plant construction; Industrial buildings, new construction, nec
PA: Bwx Technologies, Inc.
800 Main St Ste 4
Lynchburg VA 24504

(G-2370)
BWXT MPOWER INC
11525 N Community House Rd Ste 600 (28277-3609)
PHONE..................................980 365-4000
William Fox, *Pr*
Jason Kerr, *
David Black, *
EMP: 21 **EST:** 2012
SALES (est): 4.14MM **Publicly Held**
Web: www.bwxt.com
SIC: 3443 Fabricated plate work (boiler shop)
PA: Bwx Technologies, Inc.
800 Main St Ste 4
Lynchburg VA 24504

(G-2371)
BYMONETCROCHET
8536 Caden Lee Way Apt 2208 (28273-8026)
PHONE..................................443 613-1736
Monae Terrell, *Prin*
EMP: 4 **EST:** 2016
SALES (est): 106.7K **Privately Held**
Web: www.bymonetcrochet.com
SIC: 2399 Hand woven and crocheted products

(G-2372)
C D STAMPLEY ENTERPRISES INC
6100 Orr Rd (28213-6326)
P.O. Box 33172 (28233-3172)
PHONE..................................704 333-6631
Crews Walden, *Pr*
Sam C Walden, *VP*
Zella Stampley, *VP*
◆ **EMP:** 10 **EST:** 1940
SQ FT: 13,082
SALES (est): 880.13K **Privately Held**
Web: www.stampley.com
SIC: 2731 Books, publishing only

(G-2373)
CABINETS PLUS INC
8431 Old Statesville Rd (28269-1852)
PHONE..................................718 213-3300
EMP: 5 **EST:** 2012
SALES (est): 134.82K **Privately Held**
SIC: 2434 Wood kitchen cabinets

(G-2374)
CABINETWORKS GROUP MICH LLC
1200 Westinghouse Blvd Ste O (28273-6313)
PHONE..................................803 984-2285
Ken Spangler, *Brnch Mgr*
EMP: 20
SALES (corp-wide): 1.6B **Privately Held**
Web: www.cabinetworksgroup.com
SIC: 2434 Wood kitchen cabinets
PA: Cabinetworks Group Michigan, Llc
20000 Victor Pkwy Ste 100
Livonia MI 48152
734 205-4600

(G-2375)
CABLE DEVICES INCORPORATED
10736 Nations Ford Rd (28273-5773)
PHONE..................................704 588-0859
Joseph R Hynes, *Brnch Mgr*
EMP: 10

SIC: 3663 Radio and t.v. communications equipment
HQ: Cable Devices Incorporated
1100 Commscope Pl Se
Hickory NC 28602
714 554-4370

(G-2376)
CAESARSTONE TECH USA INC (HQ)
1401 W Morehead St Ste 100 (28208-5260)
PHONE..................................818 779-0999
Yos Shiran, *Pr*
Alexios Vorissis, *CFO*
▲ **EMP:** 7 **EST:** 2012
SQ FT: 23,800
SALES (est): 7.32MM **Privately Held**
Web: www.caesarstoneus.com
SIC: 3281 Marble, building: cut and shaped
PA: Caesarstone Ltd
Kibbutz
Sdot Yam 37804

(G-2377)
CALSAK PLASTICS INC
3000 Crosspoint Center Ln Ste A (28269)
PHONE..................................704 597-8555
Gaston Penaba, *CFO*
EMP: 6 **EST:** 1975
SALES (est): 876.24K **Privately Held**
SIC: 2821 Thermoplastic materials

(G-2378)
CAMELOT COMPUTERS INC
Also Called: Camelot Software Consulting
10020 Park Cedar Dr Ste 205 (28210-8912)
PHONE..................................704 554-1670
Randy Stephenson, *Pr*
EMP: 10 **EST:** 1985
SQ FT: 2,204
SALES (est): 1.32MM **Privately Held**
Web: www.3plsoftware.com
SIC: 7371 7372 Computer software systems analysis and design, custom; Prepackaged software

(G-2379)
CAMERINS PIXEL FLARE
4066 Glenlea Commons Dr (28216-9515)
PHONE..................................704 502-6922
Crystal Westbrook, *Prin*
EMP: 4 **EST:** 2016
SALES (est): 74.42K **Privately Held**
SIC: 2899 Flares

(G-2380)
CAMSTAR SYSTEMS INC
13024 Ballantyne Corporate Pl (28277-2113)
PHONE..................................704 227-6600
EMP: 110
SIC: 7372 8748 8742 8243 Educational computer software; Systems engineering consultant, ex. computer or professional; Training and development consultant; Software training, computer

(G-2381)
CAN-AM CUSTOM TRUCKS INC
1734 University Commercial Pl (28213-6444)
PHONE..................................704 334-0322
Terry Potts, *Pr*
Tammy Potts-mcelreath, *VP*
EMP: 8 **EST:** 1998
SALES (est): 1.02MM **Privately Held**
Web: www.canamcustomtrucks.com
SIC: 3711 3713 3714 Truck and tractor truck assembly; Truck bodies and parts; Motor vehicle body components and frame

(G-2382)
CANDIES ITALIAN ICEE LLC
3428 Nevin Brook Rd Ste 101 (28269-2917)
PHONE..................................980 475-7429
EMP: 5 **EST:** 2020
SALES (est): 252.47K **Privately Held**
SIC: 2656 Frozen food and ice cream containers

(G-2383)
CANDLE BAR
1800 Camden Rd (28203-4690)
PHONE..................................704 497-6099
EMP: 4 **EST:** 2019
SALES (est): 39.69K **Privately Held**
Web: www.thecandlebar.co
SIC: 3999 Candles

(G-2384)
CANVAS SX LLC (HQ)
6325 Ardrey Kell Rd Ste 400 (28277-4966)
PHONE..................................980 474-3700
Eugene J Lowe Iii, *Pr*
Patrick J O'leary, *Ch Bd*
Mark A Carano, *VP*
Natausha H White, *Chief Human Resources Officer*
John W Nurkin, *VP*
◆ **EMP:** 200 **EST:** 1912
SALES (est): 1.22B
SALES (corp-wide): 1.74B **Publicly Held**
Web: www.spx.com
SIC: 3829 3443 3599 3559 Measuring and controlling devices, nec; Heat exchangers, condensers, and components; Air intake filters, internal combustion engine, except auto; Automotive related machinery
PA: Spx Technologies, Inc.
6325 Ardrey Kell Rd Ste 4
Charlotte NC 28277
980 474-3700

(G-2385)
CARAUSTAR INDUSTRIES INC
Also Called: Charlotte Recycling Plant
4915 Hovis Rd (28208-1512)
PHONE..................................704 333-5488
Joe Ciplletti, *Genl Mgr*
EMP: 16
SALES (corp-wide): 5.22B **Publicly Held**
Web: www.greif.com
SIC: 2631 Paperboard mills
HQ: Caraustar Industries, Inc.
5000 Astell Pwdr Sprng Rd
Austell GA 30106
770 948-3101

(G-2386)
CARAUSTAR INDUSTRIES INC
Also Called: Carolina Carton Plant
8800 Crump Rd (28273-7243)
P.O. Box 32816 (28232-2816)
PHONE..................................704 554-5796
Jimmy Hendrix, *Mgr*
EMP: 19
SQ FT: 112,570
SALES (corp-wide): 5.22B **Publicly Held**
Web: www.greif.com
SIC: 2631 Paperboard mills
HQ: Caraustar Industries, Inc.
5000 Astell Pwdr Sprng Rd
Austell GA 30106
770 948-3101

(G-2387)
CARDINAL HEALTH 414 LLC
Also Called: Cardinal Health 414
3845 Shopton Rd Ste 18a (28217-3027)
PHONE..................................704 644-7989
EMP: 9

SALES (corp-wide): 205.01B **Publicly Held**
SIC: 2834 2835 Pharmaceutical preparations; Radioactive diagnostic substances
HQ: Cardinal Health 414, Llc
7000 Cardinal Pl
Dublin OH 43017
614 757-5000

(G-2388)
CARGILL INCORPORATED
Also Called: Cargill
5000 South Blvd (28217-2700)
PHONE..................................704 523-0414
Jerry Zajecek, *BD*
EMP: 123
SALES (corp-wide): 176.74B **Privately Held**
Web: www.cargill.com
SIC: 2048 Prepared feeds, nec
PA: Cargill, Incorporated
15407 Mcginty Rd W
Wayzata MN 55391
800 227-4455

(G-2389)
CARGOMOVEMENT INTERNATIONAL
2111 Lawry Run Dr (28273-3498)
PHONE..................................704 688-9720
▲ **EMP:** 5 **EST:** 2008
SALES (est): 174.88K **Privately Held**
SIC: 2448 Cargo containers, wood and wood with metal

(G-2390)
CARLISLE CORPORATION (HQ)
Also Called: Carlisle Syntec Systems A Div
11605 N Community House Rd (28277-4797)
PHONE..................................704 501-1100
Stephen P Munn, *CEO*
David A Roberts, *Ch Bd*
Dennis J Hall, *Vice Chairman*
John S Barsanti, *VP*
Steven J Ford, *Secretary General*
◆ **EMP:** 5 **EST:** 1968
SQ FT: 15,500
SALES (est): 576.89MM
SALES (corp-wide): 4.59B **Publicly Held**
Web: www.carlisle.com
SIC: 2952 2899 3011 2295 Roofing materials; Waterproofing compounds; Industrial tires, pneumatic; Tape, varnished: plastic, and other coated (except magnetic)
PA: Carlisle Companies Incorporated
16430 N Scottsdale Rd
Scottsdale AZ 85254
480 781-5000

(G-2391)
CAROCRAFT CABINETS INC
1932 Statesville Ave (28206-3059)
P.O. Box 11739 (28220-1739)
PHONE..................................704 376-0022
Larry Stroud, *Pr*
Michael L Stroud, *
EMP: 37 **EST:** 1976
SQ FT: 30,000
SALES (est): 2.49MM **Privately Held**
Web: www.carocraftcabinets.com
SIC: 2434 Wood kitchen cabinets

(G-2392)
CAROLINA CARTRIDGE SYSTEMS INC
Also Called: Carolina Cartridge
516 E Hebron St (28273-5989)
P.O. Box 7304 (28241-7304)
PHONE..................................704 347-2447
Sharon Summers, *CEO*
Jim Gammill, *VP*

John E Summers, *Dir*
Mark Summers, *Sec*
EMP: 20 **EST:** 1991
SQ FT: 20,000
SALES (est): 2.49MM **Privately Held**
Web: www.ccsinside.com
SIC: 3861 7378 Toners, prepared photographic (not made in chemical plants); Computer maintenance and repair

(G-2393)
CAROLINA CONCRETE INC
11509 Reames Rd (28269-7676)
PHONE..................................704 596-6511
Danny Mcclain, *Mgr*
EMP: 15
SALES (corp-wide): 2.9MM **Privately Held**
SIC: 3273 Ready-mixed concrete
PA: Carolina Concrete, Inc.
   1316 Waxhaw Rd
   Matthews NC 28105
   704 821-7645

(G-2394)
CAROLINA DATA RECOVERY LLC
7512 E Independence Blvd Ste 100 (28227-9412)
PHONE..................................704 536-1717
EMP: 6 **EST:** 2018
SALES (est): 429.04K **Privately Held**
Web: www.carolinadatarecovery.com
SIC: 3572 Computer storage devices

(G-2395)
CAROLINA FOODS LLC
1807 S Tryon St (28203-4471)
P.O. Box 36816 (28236-6816)
PHONE..................................704 333-9812
Paul R Scarborough, *Pr*
Sallie Scarborough, *VP*
Kathryn Scarborough, *CFO*
▲ **EMP:** 350 **EST:** 1934
SQ FT: 250,000
SALES (est): 96.41MM **Privately Held**
Web: www.carolinafoodsinc.com
SIC: 2051 Pastries, e.g. danish: except frozen

(G-2396)
CAROLINA FOUNDRY INC
228 W Tremont Ave (28204-4944)
PHONE..................................704 376-3145
James L Griffin, *Pr*
EMP: 17 **EST:** 1946
SALES (est): 193.34K **Privately Held**
SIC: 3363 3364 Aluminum die-castings; Brass and bronze die-castings

(G-2397)
CAROLINA GOLFCO INC
209 E Exmore St (28217-1803)
PHONE..................................704 525-7846
Ellen Dooley, *Pr*
William Dooley, *VP*
EMP: 5 **EST:** 1992
SQ FT: 3,000
SALES (est): 432.68K **Privately Held**
SIC: 2999 3523 0711 Waxes, petroleum: not produced in petroleum refineries; Turf and grounds equipment; Soil preparation services

(G-2398)
CAROLINA LAWNSCAPE INC
Also Called: Landscape Design & Lawn Maint
13105 Greencreek Dr (28273-6972)
PHONE..................................803 230-5570
Octavius Watkins, *Pr*
EMP: 7 **EST:** 1993
SALES (est): 494.52K **Privately Held**
SIC: 0782 0781 3271 Lawn care services; Landscape services; Blocks, concrete: landscape or retaining wall

(G-2399)
CAROLINA MARBLE & GRANITE
1924 Dilworth Rd W (28203-5730)
PHONE..................................704 523-2112
Terrell Fridell, *Pt*
EMP: 6 **EST:** 1907
SQ FT: 1,203
SALES (est): 524.79K **Privately Held**
Web: www.integrativehealth.com
SIC: 3281 1799 Monuments, cut stone (not finishing or lettering only); Sandblasting of building exteriors

(G-2400)
CAROLINA MOLDINGS INC
4601 Macie St (28217-1834)
P.O. Box 11324 (28220-1324)
PHONE..................................704 523-7471
Jack S Crouch Senior, *Pr*
EMP: 10 **EST:** 1975
SQ FT: 15,000
SALES (est): 1.28MM **Privately Held**
Web: www.carolinamoldings.com
SIC: 3089 5084 Injection molding of plastics; Meters, consumption registering

(G-2401)
CAROLINA PAPER GUYS LLC
5800 Brookshire Blvd (28216-3384)
P.O. Box 31543 (28231-1543)
PHONE..................................704 980-3112
Freddy Grodino, *CEO*
Matthew Gragop, *Pr*
EMP: 4 **EST:** 2012
SALES (est): 330.57K **Privately Held**
Web: www.carolinapaperguys.com
SIC: 2621 Towels, tissues and napkins; paper and stock

(G-2402)
CAROLINA PARENTING INC (PA)
Also Called: Charlotte Parent
214 W Tremont Ave Ste 302 (28203-5161)
PHONE..................................704 344-1980
Mark Ethridge, *Pr*
Mary Kate Cline, *Mgr*
EMP: 15 **EST:** 1990
SALES (est): 2.04MM **Privately Held**
Web: www.charlotteparent.com
SIC: 2721 Magazines: publishing only, not printed on site

(G-2403)
CAROLINA PRODUCTS INC
Also Called: Honeywell Authorized Dealer
1132 Pro Am Dr (28211-1100)
PHONE..................................704 364-9029
John G Blackmon, *Pr*
William S Blackmon, *
EMP: 36 **EST:** 1969
SALES (est): 8.44MM **Privately Held**
Web: www.cpipanels.com
SIC: 3613 3644 3585 3443 Switchgear and switchboard apparatus; Electric outlet, switch, and fuse boxes; Refrigeration and heating equipment; Fabricated plate work (boiler shop)

(G-2404)
CAROLINA SIGN CO INC
2925 Beatties Ford Rd (28216-3713)
PHONE..................................704 399-3995
Ruth Singleton, *Pr*
Bob Singleton, *VP*
EMP: 5 **EST:** 1984
SALES (est): 402.13K **Privately Held**
Web: www.carolinarealtysigns.com
SIC: 3993 Signs and advertising specialties

(G-2405)
CAROLINA SIGNS AND WONDERS INC
Also Called: Provizion Led
1700 University Commercial Pl (28213-6444)
PHONE..................................704 286-1343
Jacquelyn M Golbus, *CEO*
Jacquelyn M Golbus, *Pr*
Todd A Golbus, *COO*
EMP: 12 **EST:** 2020
SALES (est): 1.07MM **Privately Held**
Web: www.carolinasignage.com
SIC: 3993 Signs and advertising specialties

(G-2406)
CAROLINA SPECIALTIES INC
4230 Barringer Dr (28217-1512)
PHONE..................................704 525-9599
Richard Ealy, *Dir*
EMP: 4
Web: www.carospec.com
SIC: 3299 Stucco
PA: Carolina Specialties, Inc.
   4706 Kirk Rd
   Winston Salem NC 27103

(G-2407)
CAROLINA SPRAL DUCT FBRCTION L
11524 Wilmar Blvd (28273-6448)
PHONE..................................704 395-3289
EMP: 10 **EST:** 2016
SALES (est): 988.52K **Privately Held**
SIC: 3444 Sheet metalwork

(G-2408)
CAROLINA STICKERS & SIGNS LLC
422 E 22nd St Ste 3 (28206-3424)
PHONE..................................704 649-7318
EMP: 4 **EST:** 2017
SALES (est): 50.69K **Privately Held**
Web: www.carolinastickers.com
SIC: 3993 Signs and advertising specialties

(G-2409)
CAROLINA TIME EQUIPMENT CO INC (PA)
Also Called: Carolina Time
1801 Norland Rd (28205-5707)
P.O. Box 18158 (28218-0158)
PHONE..................................704 536-2700
Henry Allen, *Pr*
Debra Jones, *
Alfred Tate, *
EMP: 24 **EST:** 1962
SQ FT: 26,000
SALES (est): 5.13MM
SALES (corp-wide): 5.13MM **Privately Held**
Web: www.carolinatime.net
SIC: 3446 1731 3579 5063 Fences, gates, posts, and flagpoles; Access control systems specialization; Time clocks and time recording devices; Service entrance equipment, electrical

(G-2410)
CAROLINA TRAFFIC DEVICES INC
11900 Goodrich Dr (28273-4506)
P.O. Box 38220 (28278-1003)
PHONE..................................704 588-7055
William Curtin, *Pr*
EMP: 10 **EST:** 2002
SQ FT: 2,000
SALES (est): 2.47MM **Privately Held**
Web: www.carolinatraffic.com
SIC: 5082 3272 Road construction equipment; Concrete products used to facilitate drainage

(G-2411)
CAROLINA WEEKLY NEWSPAPER GROU
10100 Park Cedar Dr Ste 150 (28210-8932)
PHONE..................................704 849-2261
Alain Lillie, *Prin*
EMP: 10 **EST:** 2010
SALES (est): 240.4K **Privately Held**
Web: www.thecharlotteweekly.com
SIC: 2711 Newspapers: publishing only, not printed on site

(G-2412)
CAROLINA WOODWORK & STAIR INC
309 E Morehead St Apt 918 (28202-2324)
PHONE..................................704 363-5114
Eric H Blythe, *Prin*
EMP: 5 **EST:** 2010
SALES (est): 248.41K **Privately Held**
SIC: 2431 Millwork

(G-2413)
CAROLINA YORK LLC
1235 East Blvd Ste E Pmb 248 (28203-5876)
PHONE..................................704 237-0873
EMP: 10 **EST:** 2016
SALES (est): 348.17K **Privately Held**
Web: www.carolinayork.com
SIC: 3229 Candlesticks, glass

(G-2414)
CAROLINAS TOP SHELF CUST CABN
Also Called: Carolinas Top Shelf Custom CA
519 Armour Dr (28206-3055)
PHONE..................................704 376-5844
EMP: 7 **EST:** 2014
SALES (est): 573.02K **Privately Held**
Web: www.ctscustom.com
SIC: 2434 2541 Wood kitchen cabinets; Cabinets, lockers, and shelving

(G-2415)
CARRIER CORPORATION
Also Called: Carrier Chiller Op
9701 Old Statesville Rd (28269-7630)
PHONE..................................704 921-3800
Mike Mckee, *Mgr*
EMP: 200
SQ FT: 260,794
SALES (corp-wide): 22.1B **Publicly Held**
Web: www.carrier.com
SIC: 3585 Air conditioning equipment, complete
HQ: Carrier Corporation
   13995 Pasteur Blvd
   Palm Beach Gardens FL 33418
   561 365-2000

(G-2416)
CARY MANUFACTURING CORPORATION
10815 John Price Rd Ste E (28273-4633)
PHONE..................................704 527-4402
Jim Kehoe, *Pr*
Lisa Kehoe, *Treas*
▲ **EMP:** 6 **EST:** 1978
SALES (est): 890.78K **Privately Held**
Web: www.carymfg.com
SIC: 3589 3555 Vacuum cleaners and sweepers, electric: industrial; Printing trades machinery

Charlotte - Mecklenburg County (G-2417) GEOGRAPHIC SECTION

(G-2417)
CASE & BEAR GREAT HOMES LLC
6535 Greenway Bend Dr (28226-5561)
PHONE..................................704 595-3832
Theodore Hammeke, *Prin*
EMP: 5 **EST:** 2016
SALES (est): 108.6K **Privately Held**
SIC: 3523 Farm machinery and equipment

(G-2418)
CATAMOUNT ENERGY CORPORATION (DH)
550 S Tryon St (28202-4200)
PHONE..................................802 773-6684
James J Moore Junior, *CEO*
Joseph E Cofelice, *Pr*
Robert H Young, *Ch Bd*
Robert J Charlebois, *Sr VP*
EMP: 18 **EST:** 1986
SQ FT: 2,500
SALES (est): 21.7MM
SALES (corp-wide): 180.97MM **Publicly Held**
SIC: 3569 Generators: steam, liquid oxygen, or nitrogen
HQ: Degs Wind I, Llc
2801 Via Fortuna Ste 100
Austin TX 78746

(G-2419)
CATES MECHANICAL CORPORATION
3901 Corporation Cir (28216-3420)
P.O. Box 550488 (28055-0488)
PHONE..................................704 458-5163
John Cates, *Pr*
John T Cates, *Pr*
EMP: 4 **EST:** 1969
SQ FT: 18,000
SALES (est): 407.93K **Privately Held**
Web: www.catesmechanical.com
SIC: 3565 3556 Packaging machinery; Food products machinery

(G-2420)
CATHOLIC NEWS AND HERALD
Also Called: Cathedral Publishing
1123 S Church St (28203-4003)
PHONE..................................704 370-3333
Kevin Murray, *Supervisor*
EMP: 5 **EST:** 2000
SALES (est): 267.38K **Privately Held**
Web: www.catholicnewsherald.com
SIC: 2711 Newspapers, publishing and printing

(G-2421)
CAUSA LLC
9303 Monroe Rd (28270-1472)
PHONE..................................866 695-7022
William Cameron, *Managing Member*
J Hayward Morgan, *Managing Member*
▲ **EMP:** 6 **EST:** 2011
SQ FT: 1,500
SALES (est): 783.45K **Privately Held**
Web: www.causadirect.com
SIC: 2326 Work apparel, except uniforms

(G-2422)
CBDMD INC (PA)
Also Called: Cbdmd
8845 Red Oak Blvd (28217-5593)
PHONE..................................704 445-3060
Scott G Stephen, *Ch Bd*
Kevin Macdermott, *Pr*
T Ronan Kennedy, *CFO*
Sibyl Swift, *FOR SCIENTIFIC Regulatory Affairs*
EMP: 19 **EST:** 2015
SQ FT: 50,000
SALES (est): 24.16MM
SALES (corp-wide): 24.16MM **Publicly Held**
Web: www.cbdmd.com
SIC: 2833 5961 Medicinals and botanicals; Catalog and mail-order houses

(G-2423)
CBG DRAFT SERVICES LC LLC
1720 Toal St (28206-1524)
PHONE..................................704 727-3300
EMP: 6 **EST:** 2020
SALES (est): 500.86K **Privately Held**
Web: www.cbgdraftservices.com
SIC: 3585 Refrigeration and heating equipment

(G-2424)
CBS RADIO HOLDINGS INC
Also Called: W F N Z Radio Station
1520 South Blvd Ste 300 (28203-3701)
PHONE..................................704 319-9369
Bill Schoening, *Genl Mgr*
EMP: 40 **EST:** 2001
SALES (est): 2.29MM **Privately Held**
Web: www.audacyinc.com
SIC: 7389 3663 Radio broadcasting music checkers; Radio broadcasting and communications equipment

(G-2425)
CCBCC INC
4115 Coca Cola Plz (28211-3400)
PHONE..................................704 557-4000
Hank W Flint, *Pr*
Umesh M Kasbekar, *
Clifford M Deal Iii, *VP*
EMP: 853 **EST:** 1994
SALES (est): 2.78MM
SALES (corp-wide): 6.65B **Publicly Held**
SIC: 2086 Bottled and canned soft drinks
PA: Coca-Cola Consolidated, Inc.
4100 Coca Cola Plz # 100
Charlotte NC 28211
704 557-4400

(G-2426)
CCBCC OPERATIONS LLC
Also Called: Coca-Cola
4115 Coca Cola Plz (28211-3400)
P.O. Box 31487 (28231-1487)
PHONE..................................704 557-4038
R Jack Hawkins, *Brnch Mgr*
EMP: 43
SALES (corp-wide): 6.65B **Publicly Held**
Web: www.cokeconsolidated.com
SIC: 2086 Bottled and canned soft drinks
HQ: Ccbcc Operations, Llc
4100 Coca Cola Plz
Charlotte NC 28211
704 364-8728

(G-2427)
CCBCC OPERATIONS LLC
Also Called: Coca-Cola
4690 First Flight Dr (28208-5770)
PHONE..................................704 359-5600
EMP: 10
SALES (corp-wide): 6.65B **Publicly Held**
Web: www.coca-cola.com
SIC: 2086 Bottled and canned soft drinks
HQ: Ccbcc Operations, Llc
4100 Coca Cola Plz
Charlotte NC 28211
704 364-8728

(G-2428)
CCBCC OPERATIONS LLC (HQ)
Also Called: Coca-Cola
4100 Coca Cola Plz (28211-3588)
P.O. Box 31487 (28231-1487)
PHONE..................................704 364-8728
EMP: 40 **EST:** 2003
SALES (est): 992.43MM
SALES (corp-wide): 6.65B **Publicly Held**
Web: www.cokeconsolidated.com
SIC: 2086 Bottled and canned soft drinks
PA: Coca-Cola Consolidated, Inc.
4100 Coca Cola Plz # 100
Charlotte NC 28211
704 557-4400

(G-2429)
CCBCC OPERATIONS LLC
Also Called: Coca-Cola
801 Black Satchel Rd (28216-3453)
PHONE..................................704 399-6043
Guy Tarrance, *Mgr*
EMP: 49
SALES (corp-wide): 6.65B **Publicly Held**
Web: www.coca-cola.com
SIC: 2086 Bottled and canned soft drinks
HQ: Ccbcc Operations, Llc
4100 Coca Cola Plz
Charlotte NC 28211
704 364-8728

(G-2430)
CCBCC OPERATIONS LLC
Also Called: Coca-Cola
4901a Chesapeake Dr (28216-2905)
PHONE..................................980 321-3226
Jon Dickson, *Brnch Mgr*
EMP: 163
SALES (corp-wide): 6.65B **Publicly Held**
Web: www.coca-cola.com
SIC: 2086 Bottled and canned soft drinks
HQ: Ccbcc Operations, Llc
4100 Coca Cola Plz
Charlotte NC 28211
704 364-8728

(G-2431)
CCL LABEL INC
Also Called: Robbinsville Plant
4000 Westinghouse Blvd (28273-4518)
PHONE..................................704 714-4800
Geoff Martin, *Pr*
EMP: 146
SALES (corp-wide): 4.75B **Privately Held**
Web: www.cclind.com
SIC: 2759 Labels and seals: printing, nsk
HQ: Ccl Label, Inc.
161 Worcester Rd Ste 403
Framingham MA 01701
508 872-4511

(G-2432)
CCM PRESS LLC
305 Fieldbrook Pl (28209-2245)
PHONE..................................704 825-9995
Matthew Matinata, *Prin*
EMP: 6 **EST:** 2014
SALES (est): 107.76K **Privately Held**
SIC: 2741 Miscellaneous publishing

(G-2433)
CD DICKIE & ASSOCIATES INC
Also Called: Fastsigns
3400 S Tryon St Ste D (28217-1326)
PHONE..................................704 527-9102
Barbara Dickie, *Pr*
EMP: 19 **EST:** 1999
SALES (est): 450.39K **Privately Held**
Web: www.fastsigns.com
SIC: 7389 7336 3993 Lettering and sign painting services; Commercial art and graphic design; Signs and advertising specialties

(G-2434)
CDA INC
8500 S Tryon St (28273-3312)
▲ **EMP:** 186 **EST:** 2000
SQ FT: 60,000
SALES (est): 39.18MM **Privately Held**
Web: www.cdaenvironmental.com
SIC: 5099 3652 Compact discs; Prerecorded records and tapes

(G-2435)
CEAST USA INC
4816 Sirus Ln (28208-6391)
PHONE..................................704 423-0081
Mario Grosso, *Prin*
EMP: 7 **EST:** 2016
SALES (est): 118.67K **Privately Held**
SIC: 3829 Measuring and controlling devices, nec

(G-2436)
CEFLA DENTAL GROUP AMERICA
6125 Harris Technology Blvd (28269-3731)
PHONE..................................704 731-5293
Vittorio Belus, *VP*
▲ **EMP:** 12 **EST:** 2010
SALES (est): 237.99K **Privately Held**
Web: www.ceflamedicalna.com
SIC: 3843 Dental equipment and supplies

(G-2437)
CEFLA NORTH AMERICA INC
6125 Harris Technology Blvd (28269-3731)
PHONE..................................704 598-0020
Recardo Quattrini, *Pr*
Walter Favruzzo, *
Vittorio Belluz, *
▲ **EMP:** 39 **EST:** 1987
SQ FT: 8,500
SALES (est): 25.65MM
SALES (corp-wide): 672.07MM **Privately Held**
Web: www.ceflamedicalna.com
SIC: 5084 3553 Woodworking machinery; Furniture makers machinery, woodworking
PA: Cefla Soc Coop
Via Bicocca 14/C
Imola BO 40026
054 265-4344

(G-2438)
CELEROS FLOW TECHNOLOGY LLC (PA)
14045 Ballantyne Corporate Pl Ste 300 (28277-0099)
PHONE..................................704 752-3100
Jose Larios, *Managing Member*
EMP: 87 **EST:** 2019
SALES (est): 122.35MM
SALES (corp-wide): 122.35MM **Privately Held**
Web: www.celerosft.com
SIC: 3491 Industrial valves

(G-2439)
CELGARD LLC
13800 S Lakes Dr (28273-6738)
PHONE..................................704 588-5310
Lei Shi, *Pr*
EMP: 90
Web: www.celgard.com
SIC: 2821 Plastics materials and resins
HQ: Celgard, Llc
11430 N Cmnity Hse Rd
Charlotte NC 28277
800 235-4273

(G-2440)
CELGARD LLC (HQ)
11430 N Community House Rd Ste 350 (28277-1591)

PHONE..................800 235-4273
Lie Shi, *Pr*
◆ **EMP:** 109 **EST:** 1999
SALES (est): 98.86MM **Privately Held**
Web: www.celgard.com
SIC: 2821 3081 Plastics materials and resins; Unsupported plastics film and sheet
PA: Asahi Kasei Corporation
1-1-2, Yurakucho
Chiyoda-Ku TKY 100-0

(G-2441)
CEMCO ELECTRIC INC
Also Called: Cemco Systems
10913 Office Park Dr (28273-6549)
P.O. Box 38100 (28278-1001)
PHONE..................704 504-0294
Cliff Morgan, *Pr*
Cheryl Morgan, *VP*
EMP: 10 **EST:** 1984
SQ FT: 800
SALES (est): 1.81MM **Privately Held**
Web: www.cemcosystemsinc.com
SIC: 1731 5063 3569 General electrical contractor; Generators; Firefighting and related equipment

(G-2442)
CENTOR INC
Also Called: Vibration Solutions
5900 Harris Technology Blvd Ste G (28269-3808)
PHONE..................704 896-7535
Michael Dickinson, *Owner*
▲ **EMP:** 11 **EST:** 2013
SALES (est): 213.79K **Privately Held**
Web: www.centor.com
SIC: 3559 Automotive maintenance equipment

(G-2443)
CENTURY PLACE II LLC
Also Called: Century Place Apparel
10220 Western Ridge Rd Ste A (28273)
P.O. Box 668 (28145-0668)
PHONE..................704 790-0970
Jeffrey Smith, *Pr*
Mike Carter, *
Tom Pepper, *
Juan Sanchez, *
◆ **EMP:** 48 **EST:** 2000
SQ FT: 45,000
SALES (est): 4.91MM **Privately Held**
Web: www.centuryplace.com
SIC: 2321 Polo shirts, men's and boys': made from purchased materials

(G-2444)
CERAMCO INCORPORATED
Also Called: Printech
11009 Carpet St (28273-6232)
P.O. Box 7265 (28241-7265)
PHONE..................704 588-4814
Terry Link, *Pr*
Jan Link, *
Steve Luther, *
◆ **EMP:** 40 **EST:** 1971
SQ FT: 20,000
SALES (est): 4.57MM **Privately Held**
Web: www.ceramcoprintech.com
SIC: 3469 Machine parts, stamped or pressed metal

(G-2445)
CHAMPION LLC
Also Called: Champion
8844 Mount Holly Rd (28214-8350)
PHONE..................704 392-1038
EMP: 15 **EST:** 1983
SQ FT: 11,600
SALES (est): 2.72MM **Privately Held**

Web: www.championcu.com
SIC: 3531 Graders, road (construction machinery)

(G-2446)
CHAMPION WIN CO OF CHARLOTTE
Also Called: Champion Wndows Sding Ptio Rom
9100 Perimeter Woods Dr Ste C (28216-2262)
PHONE..................704 398-0085
TOLL FREE: 800
Robert Fleischer, *Pr*
EMP: 19 **EST:** 1999
SALES (est): 1.46MM **Privately Held**
Web: www.championwindow.com
SIC: 3442 3444 Storm doors or windows, metal; Awnings, sheet metal

(G-2447)
CHARAH LLC
4235 Southstream Blvd Ste 180 (28217-0142)
PHONE..................704 731-2300
EMP: 138
SALES (corp-wide): 293.17MM **Publicly Held**
Web: www.charah.com
SIC: 1081 Metal mining exploration and development services
HQ: Charah, Llc
12601 Plantside Dr
Louisville KY 40299

(G-2448)
CHARGE ONSITE LLC
1015 East Blvd (28203-5713)
PHONE..................888 343-2688
Jim Swain, *Managing Member*
EMP: 5
SALES (est): 211.82K **Privately Held**
SIC: 7372 Application computer software

(G-2449)
CHARLOTTE AARROW LLC
401 Hawthorne Ln Ste 110-256 (28204-2484)
PHONE..................704 909-7692
EMP: 4 **EST:** 2013
SALES (est): 128.45K **Privately Held**
SIC: 3993 Signs and advertising specialties

(G-2450)
CHARLOTTE BLOCK INC
Also Called: Southern Concrete Materials
5125 Rozzelles Ferry Rd (28216-3397)
PHONE..................704 399-4526
Jim Combest, *Pr*
EMP: 8 **EST:** 1963
SQ FT: 500
SALES (est): 3.45MM **Privately Held**
SIC: 3273 Ready-mixed concrete
HQ: Giant Resource Recovery, Inc.
1504 Santa Rosa Rd Rm 200
Richmond VA

(G-2451)
CHARLOTTE COMPRESSOR LLC
338 S Sharon Amity Rd Ste 201 (28211)
PHONE..................704 399-9993
Morty Hodge, *CEO*
EMP: 10 **EST:** 2018
SALES (est): 540.76K **Privately Held**
Web: www.charlottecompressor.com
SIC: 3053 Packing: steam engines, pipe joints, air compressors, etc.

(G-2452)
CHARLOTTE INSTYLE INC
801 Pressley Rd Ste 1071 (28217-0981)

PHONE..................704 665-8880
Lennart Wiktorin, *Pr*
▲ **EMP:** 30 **EST:** 1995
SQ FT: 40,000
SALES (est): 2.35MM **Privately Held**
Web: www.instylecharlotte.com
SIC: 1423 Crushed and broken granite

(G-2453)
CHARLOTTE OBSERVER
550 S Caldwell St Ste 1010 (28202-2633)
PHONE..................704 358-5000
EMP: 34 **EST:** 2014
SALES (est): 970.08K **Privately Held**
Web: www.charlotteobserver.com
SIC: 2711 Newspapers, publishing and printing

(G-2454)
CHARLOTTE OBSERVER PUBG CO
9140 Research Dr Ste C1 (28262-8544)
P.O. Box Cornelius (28031)
PHONE..................704 987-3660
Bill Hutters, *Mgr*
EMP: 38
SALES (corp-wide): 709.52MM **Privately Held**
SIC: 2711 Newspapers, publishing and printing
HQ: The Charlotte Observer Publishing Company
550 S Caldwell St Fl 10
Charlotte NC 28202
704 358-5000

(G-2455)
CHARLOTTE OBSERVER PUBG CO
Also Called: Charlotte Observer
3100 Yorkmont Rd (28208-7303)
PHONE..................704 572-0747
Al Shelley, *Genl Mgr*
EMP: 38
SALES (corp-wide): 709.52MM **Privately Held**
SIC: 2711 Newspapers, publishing and printing
HQ: The Charlotte Observer Publishing Company
550 S Caldwell St Fl 10
Charlotte NC 28202
704 358-5000

(G-2456)
CHARLOTTE OBSERVER PUBG CO (DH)
Also Called: Charlotte Observer
550 S Caldwell St Ste 1010 (28202-2633)
PHONE..................704 358-5000
TOLL FREE: 800
Ann Coulkins, *Pr*
Victor Fields, *
Jim Lamm, *
Kelly Mirt, *
Ken Riddick, *
EMP: 600 **EST:** 1955
SALES (est): 202.72MM
SALES (corp-wide): 709.52MM **Privately Held**
SIC: 2711 4813 Commercial printing and newspaper publishing combined; Internet connectivity services
HQ: Jck Legacy Company
1601 Alhambra Blvd # 100
Sacramento CA 95816
916 321-1844

(G-2457)
CHARLOTTE PIPE AND FOUNDRY CO (PA)
2109 Randolph Rd (28207-1521)
P.O. Box 35430 (28235-5430)

PHONE..................704 372-5030
W Frank Dowd Iv, *CEO*
Roddey Dowd Junior, *Pr*
J Alan Biggers, *
Mark E Black, *
William R Hutaff Iii, *VP Fin*
◆ **EMP:** 110 **EST:** 1901
SQ FT: 27,000
SALES (est): 841.88MM
SALES (corp-wide): 841.88MM **Privately Held**
Web: www.charlottepipe.com
SIC: 3084 3089 3321 Plastics pipe; Fittings for pipe, plastics; Soil pipe and fittings: cast iron

(G-2458)
CHARLOTTE PIPE AND FOUNDRY CO
Also Called: Cast Iron Division
1335 S Clarkson St (28208-5315)
PHONE..................704 348-5416
Marshall Coble, *Mgr*
EMP: 450
SALES (corp-wide): 841.88MM **Privately Held**
Web: www.charlottepipe.com
SIC: 3084 3498 3312 Plastics pipe; Fabricated pipe and fittings; Blast furnaces and steel mills
PA: Charlotte Pipe And Foundry Company
2109 Randolph Rd
Charlotte NC 28207
704 372-5030

(G-2459)
CHARLOTTE PIPE AND FOUNDRY COM
2109 Randolph Rd (28207-1521)
PHONE..................704 379-0700
EMP: 18
SALES (est): 2.1MM **Privately Held**
Web: www.charlottepipe.com
SIC: 3084 Plastics pipe

(G-2460)
CHARLOTTE PLATING INC
8421 Kirchenbaum Dr (28210-5856)
PHONE..................704 552-2100
W Todd Osmolski, *Pr*
David H Osmolski, *Treas*
Susan Osmolski, *VP*
EMP: 8 **EST:** 1989
SALES (est): 842.83K **Privately Held**
Web: www.charlotteplating.com
SIC: 3471 Electroplating of metals or formed products

(G-2461)
CHARLOTTE POST PUBG CO INC
Also Called: Charlotte Post
5118 Princess St (28269-4861)
P.O. Box 30144 (28230-0144)
PHONE..................704 376-0496
Gerald Johnson, *Pr*
Robert Johnson, *VP*
EMP: 15 **EST:** 1971
SQ FT: 4,500
SALES (est): 1.87MM **Privately Held**
Web: www.thecharlottepost.com
SIC: 2711 Newspapers, publishing and printing

(G-2462)
CHARLOTTE PUBLISHING COMPANY
9140 Research Dr (28262-8544)
PHONE..................704 547-0900
EMP: 39
SALES (corp-wide): 79.3K **Privately Held**
Web: www.mcclatchy.com

Charlotte - Mecklenburg County (G-2463)

GEOGRAPHIC SECTION

SIC: 2711 Newspapers, publishing and printing
PA: Charlotte Publishing Company
   211 Worth St
   Asheboro NC

(G-2463)
CHARLOTTE SOCK BASKET
9200 Harris Corners Pkwy Ste B (28269-3717)
PHONE..............................704 910-2388
EMP: 4 EST: 2019
SALES (est): 107.16K **Privately Held**
Web: www.thesockbasket.com
SIC: 2252 Socks

(G-2464)
CHARLOTTE SPRINGFREE TRMPOLINE
9848 Rea Rd Ste E (28277-0460)
PHONE..............................704 312-1212
EMP: 5 EST: 2017
SALES (est): 196.22K **Privately Held**
Web: www.springfreetrampoline.com
SIC: 3949 Sporting and athletic goods, nec

(G-2465)
CHARLOTTE TRIMMING COMPANY INC (PA)
900 Pressley Rd (28217-0974)
PHONE..............................704 529-8427
Antonio Lopez Ibanez Junior, *Pr*
Antonio Lopez Ibanez Junior, *Pr*
Juan Lopez Ibanez, *Treas*
Raul Lopez Ibanez, *Sec*
◆ EMP: 86 EST: 1961
SQ FT: 75,000
SALES (est): 3.68MM
SALES (corp-wide): 3.68MM **Privately Held**
SIC: 2253 2396 Collar and cuff sets, knit; Trimming, fabric, nsk

(G-2466)
CHARLOTTE WEEKLY
9506 Monroe Rd Ste A (28270-1596)
PHONE..............................704 849-2261
Charlotte Weekly, *Prin*
EMP: 7 EST: 2018
SALES (est): 121.01K **Privately Held**
Web: www.thecharlotteweekly.com
SIC: 2711 Newspapers, publishing and printing

(G-2467)
CHARLTTE MCKLNBURG DREAM CTR I
129 W Trade St (28202-2143)
P.O. Box 30877 (28230-0877)
PHONE..............................704 421-4440
Kim Shaftner, *Admn*
EMP: 8 EST: 2017
SALES (est): 195.88K **Privately Held**
Web: www.charlotteballet.org
SIC: 2711 Newspapers

(G-2468)
CHARTER JET TRANSPORT INC
5400 Airport Dr (28208-5734)
P.O. Box 19333 (28219-9333)
PHONE..............................704 359-8833
Harold Singleton, *Pr*
Richard Keffer, *CEO*
EMP: 6 EST: 1997
SQ FT: 250
SALES (est): 1.04MM **Privately Held**
Web: www.flycjt.com
SIC: 4512 3721 Air passenger carrier, scheduled; Airplanes, fixed or rotary wing

(G-2469)
CHELSEA THERAPEUTICS INTERNATIONAL LTD
3530 Toringdon Way Ste 200 (28277-3431)
PHONE..............................704 341-1516
EMP: 18
Web: www.chelsearx.com
SIC: 2836 Biological products, except diagnostic

(G-2470)
CHEMRING SNSORS ELCTRNIC SYSTE
Also Called: Chemring Detection Systems
4205 Westinghouse Commons Dr (28273)
PHONE..............................980 235-2200
EMP: 6
SALES (corp-wide): 573MM **Privately Held**
Web: www.chemringds.com
SIC: 3812 Search and detection systems and instruments
HQ: Chemring Sensors And Electronic Systems, Inc.
   14401 Penrose Pl Ste 130
   Chantilly VA 20151

(G-2471)
CHEMTRADE LOGISTICS (US) INC (HQ)
814 Tyvola Rd Ste 126 (28217-3539)
PHONE..............................773 646-2500
Mark Davis, *Pr*
EMP: 44 EST: 2001
SALES (est): 18.47MM
SALES (corp-wide): 1.34B **Privately Held**
SIC: 2819 Industrial inorganic chemicals, nec
PA: Chemtrade Logistics Income Fund
   300-155 Gordon Baker Rd
   North York ON M2H 3
   416 496-5856

(G-2472)
CHEP RECYCLED PALLET SOLU
5808 Long Creek Park Dr (28269-5744)
PHONE..............................704 718-8199
EMP: 6 EST: 2019
SALES (est): 300.5K **Privately Held**
SIC: 2448 Pallets, wood

(G-2473)
CHF INDUSTRIES INC
Also Called: Cameo Curtains Div
9741 Southern Pine Blvd Ste A (28273-5541)
PHONE..............................212 951-7800
Frank Foley, *Brnch Mgr*
EMP: 31
SALES (corp-wide): 88.25MM **Privately Held**
Web: www.chfindustries.com
SIC: 5023 2511 2392 2391 Curtains; Wood household furniture; Household furnishings, nec; Curtains and draperies
PA: Chf Industries, Inc.
   1 Bridge St Ste 130
   Irvington NY 10533
   212 951-7800

(G-2474)
CHICADOO
8040 Providence Rd Ste 100 (28277-8738)
PHONE..............................704 562-8796
Nancy Hall, *Prin*
EMP: 4 EST: 2010
SALES (est): 71.73K **Privately Held**
Web: www.chicadoo.com
SIC: 3949 Sporting and athletic goods, nec

(G-2475)
CHICAGO PNEUMATIC TOOL CO LLC
11313 Steele Creek Rd (28273-3713)
PHONE..............................704 504-6937
John Cleveland, *Brnch Mgr*
EMP: 17
SALES (corp-wide): 13.47B **Privately Held**
Web: tools.cp.com
SIC: 3546 Power-driven handtools
HQ: Chicago Pneumatic Tool Company Llc
   1815 Clubhouse Dr
   Rock Hill SC 29730
   803 817-7100

(G-2476)
CHICOPEE INC (DH)
Also Called: Pgi Nonwovens
9335 Harris Corners Pkwy Ste 300 (28269)
PHONE..............................704 697-5100
◆ EMP: 20 EST: 1995
SQ FT: 8,000
SALES (est): 182.58MM **Publicly Held**
Web: www.chicopee.com
SIC: 2297 Spunbonded fabrics
HQ: Avintiv Specialty Materials Inc.
   9335 Hrris Crners Pkwy St
   Charlotte NC 28269

(G-2477)
CHIEF CORPORATION
10926 David Taylor Dr Ste 300 (28262-1293)
PHONE..............................704 916-4521
Jeff Tousa, *Pr*
EMP: 10 EST: 2005
SALES (est): 234.94K **Privately Held**
SIC: 2741 Catalogs: publishing and printing

(G-2478)
CHIRON AMERICA INC (DH)
10950 Withers Cove Park Dr (28278-0020)
PHONE..............................704 587-9526
Steve Morris, *Pr*
Morsey Tsiukes, *
▲ EMP: 60 EST: 1993
SQ FT: 76,000
SALES (est): 43.56MM
SALES (corp-wide): 804.13MM **Privately Held**
Web: www.chiron-group.com
SIC: 5084 7539 3599 Machine tools and accessories; Machine shop, automotive; Machine and other job shop work
HQ: Chiron Group Se
   Kreuzstr. 75
   Tuttlingen BW 78532
   74619400

(G-2479)
CHROME BUBBLES BY MAURICE
7233 Point Lake Dr # 108 (28227-0990)
PHONE..............................704 224-8866
EMP: 5 EST: 2007
SALES (est): 69.78K **Privately Held**
SIC: 2842 Automobile polish

(G-2480)
CHROMED OUT FRAME COVERS INC
7900 Waterford Tide Loop Apt 3121 (28226-8622)
PHONE..............................704 813-8811
Danny Long, *Prin*
EMP: 5 EST: 2010
SALES (est): 64.52K **Privately Held**
Web: www.chromefx.net
SIC: 3714 Windshield frames, motor vehicle

(G-2481)
CHT R BEITLICH CORPORATION
5046 Old Pineville Rd (28217-3032)
P.O. Box 240497 (28224-0497)
PHONE..............................704 523-4242
Theodore Dickson, *CEO*
◆ EMP: 34 EST: 1971
SQ FT: 65,000
SALES (est): 8.24MM
SALES (corp-wide): 144.19K **Privately Held**
Web: www.cht.com
SIC: 2843 Surface active agents
HQ: Cht Germany Gmbh
   Bismarckstr. 102
   Tubingen BW 72072
   70711540

(G-2482)
CISCO SYSTEMS INC
Also Called: Cisco Systems
1900 South Blvd Ste 200 (28203-0067)
P.O. Box 2063 (48090-2063)
PHONE..............................704 338-7350
EMP: 5
SALES (corp-wide): 57B **Publicly Held**
Web: www.cisco.com
SIC: 3577 Data conversion equipment, media-to-media: computer
PA: Cisco Systems, Inc.
   170 W Tasman Dr
   San Jose CA 95134
   408 526-4000

(G-2483)
CITILIFT COMPANY
Also Called: Elevators & Conveyors
4732 West Blvd Ste D (28208-6398)
PHONE..............................704 241-6477
EMP: 5 EST: 2010
SQ FT: 2,000
SALES (est): 419.15K **Privately Held**
Web: www.citilift.com
SIC: 3534 Elevators and moving stairways

(G-2484)
CITY COMPRESSOR REBUILDERS (PA)
9750 Twin Lakes Pkwy (28269-7650)
PHONE..............................704 947-1811
Dwayne Moreland, *Pr*
Sandra Moreland, *Sec*
EMP: 20 EST: 1938
SQ FT: 40,000
SALES (est): 3.19MM
SALES (corp-wide): 3.19MM **Privately Held**
Web: www.citycompressor.com
SIC: 3585 Refrigeration and heating equipment

(G-2485)
CITY COMPRESSOR REBUILDERS
9750 Twin Lakes Pkwy (28269-7650)
PHONE..............................704 947-1811
Dwayne Moreland, *Mgr*
EMP: 8
SALES (corp-wide): 3.19MM **Privately Held**
Web: www.citycompressor.com
SIC: 3585 Compressors for refrigeration and air conditioning equipment
PA: City Compressor Rebuilders Inc
   9750 Twin Lakes Pkwy
   Charlotte NC 28269
   704 947-1811

(G-2486)
CITY GRAPHICS INC
3139 Westinghouse Blvd Ste C (28273-6537)
P.O. Box 410746 (28241-0746)
PHONE..............................704 529-6448
Joe Washam, *Pr*

GEOGRAPHIC SECTION
Charlotte - Mecklenburg County (G-2512)

EMP: 8 EST: 1980
SQ FT: 6,200
SALES (est): 260.23K Privately Held
Web: www.citygraphics.biz
SIC: 2752 Offset printing

(G-2487)
CITY OF CHARLOTTE-ATANDO
1031 Atando Ave (28206-2252)
PHONE.................................704 336-2722
Gene White, *Owner*
EMP: 16 EST: 2018
SALES (est): 345.46K Privately Held
SIC: 3714 Motor vehicle parts and accessories

(G-2488)
CKKE PUBLISHING
6415 Yateswood Dr (28212-1827)
PHONE.................................704 236-5981
EMP: 4 EST: 2015
SALES (est): 59.32K Privately Held
Web: www.drugdealerthenovel.com
SIC: 2741 Miscellaneous publishing

(G-2489)
CLARIANT CORPORATION
4331 Chesapeake Dr (28216-3410)
PHONE.................................704 331-7000
John Schofield, *Mgr*
EMP: 58
SQ FT: 51,364
Web: www.clariant.com
SIC: 2865 2899 Dyes and pigments; Chemical preparations, nec
HQ: Clariant Corporation
    500 E Morehead St Ste 400
    Charlotte NC 28202
    704 331-7000

(G-2490)
CLARIANT CORPORATION
Also Called: Mt Holly Plant
11701 Mount Holly Rd (28214-9329)
PHONE.................................704 371-3272
Nick Altman, *Mgr*
EMP: 83
Web: www.clariant.com
SIC: 2869 Industrial organic chemicals, nec
HQ: Clariant Corporation
    500 E Morehead St Ste 400
    Charlotte NC 28202
    704 331-7000

(G-2491)
CLARIANT CORPORATION (HQ)
Also Called: Clariant
500 E Morehead St Ste 400 (28202-2744)
PHONE.................................704 331-7000
Gene Mueller, *Pr*
Scott Wood, *VP*
Akin Butuner, *CFO*
◆ EMP: 55 EST: 1983
SQ FT: 240,000
SALES (est): 1.01B Privately Held
Web: www.clariant.com
SIC: 2819 2869 Catalysts, chemical; High purity grade chemicals, organic
PA: Clariant Ag
    Rothausstrasse 61
    Muttenz BL 4132

(G-2492)
CLARIOS LLC
Also Called: Controls Group
9844 Southern Pine Blvd (28273-5502)
P.O. Box 905240 (28290-5240)
PHONE.................................866 589-8883
Jim Beam, *Mgr*
EMP: 39
SALES (corp-wide): 4.48B Privately Held
Web: www.clarios.com
SIC: 2531 Seats, automobile
HQ: Clarios, Llc
    5757 N Green Bay Ave
    Milwaukee WI 53209

(G-2493)
CLAUSEN CRAFTWORKS LLC
900 Pressley Rd Ste C (28217-0974)
PHONE.................................704 252-5048
EMP: 5
SALES (est): 309.06K Privately Held
SIC: 2499 Wood products, nec

(G-2494)
CLEAN CATCH FISH MARKET LLC
2820 Selwyn Ave Ste 150 (28209-1786)
PHONE.................................704 333-1212
EMP: 7 EST: 2009
SALES (est): 857.2K Privately Held
Web: www.cleancatchfish.com
SIC: 2099 5411 5421 Food preparations, nec; Grocery stores; Fish markets

(G-2495)
CLEAN SOLUTIONS LLC
6525 Providence Farm Ln Apt 5115 (28277-7226)
PHONE.................................919 391-8047
Radhames Ortiz, *Managing Member*
EMP: 4 EST: 2019
SALES (est): 156.69K Privately Held
SIC: 2899 Chemical preparations, nec

(G-2496)
CLINE PRINTING INC
3445 Carolina Ave Ste A (28208-5896)
PHONE.................................704 394-8144
Ben Cline Junior, *Pr*
Danny Lanier, *VP*
EMP: 4 EST: 1968
SQ FT: 5,000
SALES (est): 35.64K Privately Held
SIC: 2752 2721 Offset printing; Periodicals, publishing and printing

(G-2497)
CLINICIANS ADVOCACY GROUP INC
1433 Emerywood Dr Ste A (28210-4591)
PHONE.................................704 751-9515
Steven Crawford, *Pr*
EMP: 7 EST: 2020
SALES (est): 317.38K Privately Held
SIC: 3821 Clinical laboratory instruments, except medical and dental

(G-2498)
CLOSETS BY DESIGN
1108 Continental Blvd Ste A (28273-6385)
PHONE.................................704 361-6424
Laura Vansickle, *Owner*
EMP: 72 EST: 2008
SALES (est): 13MM Privately Held
Web: www.closetsbydesign.com
SIC: 1799 2511 Closet organizers, installation and design; Bed frames, except water bed frames: wood

(G-2499)
CLOUD9 COATINGS LLC
11219 Stony Path Dr (28214-9287)
PHONE.................................704 252-0287
Allison Williams, *Prin*
EMP: 4 EST: 2019
SALES (est): 103.91K Privately Held
Web: www.cloud9coatings.com
SIC: 3479 Coating of metals and formed products

(G-2500)
CLOUDGENERA INC
1824 Statesville Ave Ste 103 (28206)
PHONE.................................980 332-4040
Brian Kelly, *CEO*
EMP: 20 EST: 2012
SALES (est): 2.1MM Privately Held
Web: go.cloudgenera.com
SIC: 7372 Application computer software

(G-2501)
CLT 2016 INC
1836 Equitable Pl (28213-6500)
PHONE.................................704 886-1555
EMP: 59
SIC: 5031 3444 3089 Lumber, plywood, and millwork; Gutters, sheet metal; Windows, plastics

(G-2502)
CLT MACHINE LLC
14604 Arlandes Dr (28278-7271)
PHONE.................................704 778-8305
Andrew Kuszczak, *Prin*
EMP: 5 EST: 2020
SALES (est): 101.04K Privately Held
Web: www.cltmachine.com
SIC: 3599 Machine shop, jobbing and repair

(G-2503)
CLYDE UNION (US) INC (HQ)
Also Called: Clydeunion Pumps
14045 Ballantyne Corporate Pl Ste 300 (28277-0099)
PHONE.................................704 808-3000
◆ EMP: 225 EST: 2008
SALES (est): 95.51MM
SALES (corp-wide): 122.35MM Privately Held
Web: www.clydeunion.com
SIC: 3561 5084 Industrial pumps and parts; Pumps and pumping equipment, nec
PA: Celeros Flow Technology, Llc
    14045 Balntyn Corp Pl
    Charlotte NC 28277
    704 752-3100

(G-2504)
CLYDEUNION PUMPS INC
Also Called: SPX
13320 Ballantyne Corporate Pl (28277-3607)
PHONE.................................704 808-3848
Jeremy Smeltser, *Pr*
EMP: 35 EST: 2009
SALES (est): 10.12MM
SALES (corp-wide): 1.53B Privately Held
Web: www.celerosft.com
SIC: 3561 Pumps and pumping equipment
HQ: Spx Flow, Inc.
    13320 Balntyn Corp Pl
    Charlotte NC 28277
    704 752-4400

(G-2505)
CMISOLUTIONS INC
7520 E Independence Blvd Ste 400 (28227-9441)
PHONE.................................704 759-9950
EMP: 41 EST: 1995
SQ FT: 8,128
SALES (est): 3.8MM Privately Held
Web: www.cmisolutions.com
SIC: 7371 7372 Computer software development; Prepackaged software

(G-2506)
CMM QUARTERLY INC
13720 Woody Point Rd (28278-6948)
PHONE.................................704 995-3007
Nancy Boucher, *Prin*
EMP: 4 EST: 2016
SALES (est): 65.78K Privately Held
Web: www.cmmquarterly.com
SIC: 2721 Periodicals

(G-2507)
CMW MFG LLC
9821 Longstone Ln (28277-5740)
PHONE.................................330 283-5551
EMP: 4 EST: 2015
SALES (est): 57.23K Privately Held
SIC: 3999 Manufacturing industries, nec

(G-2508)
CNC PERFORMANCE ENG LLC
11125 Metromont Pkwy (28269-7510)
P.O. Box 3025 (28070-3025)
PHONE.................................704 599-2555
Chris Nachtmann, *Pr*
EMP: 8 EST: 2010
SALES (est): 781.8K Privately Held
Web: www.cncpe.com
SIC: 8711 3599 Consulting engineer; Machine shop, jobbing and repair

(G-2509)
CNC-KE INC
1340 Amble Dr (28206-1308)
P.O. Box 625 (37148-0625)
PHONE.................................704 333-0145
Ken Best Junior, *Pr*
Vince Haynes, *
EMP: 90 EST: 1969
SQ FT: 25,000
SALES (est): 10.07MM
SALES (corp-wide): 27.64MM Privately Held
Web: www.cncke.com
SIC: 3679 Electronic circuits
PA: Kentucky Electronics, Inc.
    222 Riggs Ave
    Portland TN 37148
    615 325-4127

(G-2510)
COALOGIX INC
11707 Steele Creek Rd (28273-3718)
PHONE.................................704 827-8933
EMP: 133
SIC: 8711 2819 Pollution control engineering; Catalysts, chemical

(G-2511)
COATING CONCEPTS INC
8154 Westbourne Dr (28216-1141)
PHONE.................................704 391-0499
EMP: 5 EST: 1995
SALES (est): 492.71K Privately Held
SIC: 3479 Coating of metals with plastic or resins

(G-2512)
COATS & CLARK INC (HQ)
Also Called: Coats N Amer De Rpblica Dmncan
13850 Ballantyne Corporate Pl Ste 250 (28277-3299)
PHONE.................................704 542-5959
Maxwell Perks, *Pr*
Donna L Armstrong, *VP*
Ryan Newell, *Sec*
◆ EMP: 65 EST: 1937
SALES (est): 96.07MM
SALES (corp-wide): 973.96K Privately Held
Web: www.makeitcoats.com
SIC: 2284 2281 3364 3089 Cotton thread; Cotton yarn, spun; Zinc and zinc-base alloy die-castings; Molding primary plastics
PA: Spinrite Inc

320 Livingstone Ave S
Listowel ON N4W 3
519 929-4146

(G-2513)
COATS AMERICAN INC (HQ)
Also Called: Coats North America
14120 Ballantyne Corporate Pl Ste 300
(28277-3169)
P.O. Box 1847 (28086-1847)
PHONE..................800 242-8095
Soundar Rajan, *Pr*
Michael Schofer, *
Rajiv Sharma, *
Simon Boddie, *
Ronan Cox, *
▲ **EMP:** 200 **EST:** 1898
SALES (est): 157.16MM
SALES (corp-wide): 1.58B **Privately Held**
SIC: 2284 Cotton thread
PA: Coats Group Plc
4th Floor
London EC2V
208 210-5086

(G-2514)
COATS HP INC (DH)
14120 Ballantyne Corporate Pl Ste 300
(28277-3169)
PHONE..................704 329-5800
Rajiv Sharma, *CEO*
EMP: 27 **EST:** 2019
SALES (est): 29.41MM
SALES (corp-wide): 1.58B **Privately Held**
SIC: 2281 2282 2824 Manmade and synthetic fiber yarns, spun; Manmade and synthetic fiber yarns, twisting, winding, etc.; Acrylic fibers
HQ: Coats American, Inc.
14120 Blntyn Corp Pl # 300
Charlotte NC 28277
800 242-8095

(G-2515)
COATS N AMER DE RPBLICA DMNCAN (HQ)
14120 Ballantyne Corporate Pl Ste 300
(28277-2858)
PHONE..................800 242-8095
Soundar Jan, *Pr*
Shawna Blomkvist, *
Julian Urquidi, *
▲ **EMP:** 175 **EST:** 1981
SQ FT: 34,000
SALES (est): 487.28MM
SALES (corp-wide): 1.58B **Privately Held**
SIC: 3089 2284 2281 3364 Molding primary plastics; Cotton thread; Cotton yarn, spun; Zinc and zinc-base alloy die-castings
PA: Coats Group Plc
4th Floor
London EC2V
208 210-5086

(G-2516)
COCA COLA BOTTLING CO ✪
5020 W W T Harris Blvd (28269-1861)
PHONE..................704 509-1812
EMP: 7 **EST:** 2022
SALES (est): 1.3MM **Privately Held**
Web: www.coca-cola.com
SIC: 5149 2086 Cooking oils and shortenings; Bottled and canned soft drinks

(G-2517)
COCA-COLA CONSOLIDATED INC
Also Called: Coca-Cola
801 Black Satchel Rd (28216-3453)
PHONE..................704 398-2252
Guy Tarrance, *Mgr*
EMP: 5
SALES (corp-wide): 6.65B **Publicly Held**
Web: www.cokeconsolidated.com
SIC: 2086 Bottled and canned soft drinks
PA: Coca-Cola Consolidated, Inc.
4100 Coca Cola Plz # 100
Charlotte NC 28211
704 557-4400

(G-2518)
COCA-COLA CONSOLIDATED INC
Also Called: Coca-Cola
5001 Chesapeake Dr (28216-2936)
PHONE..................980 321-3001
Dave Hopkins, *Genl Mgr*
EMP: 72
SALES (corp-wide): 6.65B **Publicly Held**
Web: www.cokeconsolidated.com
SIC: 2086 Bottled and canned soft drinks
PA: Coca-Cola Consolidated, Inc.
4100 Coca Cola Plz # 100
Charlotte NC 28211
704 557-4400

(G-2519)
COCA-COLA CONSOLIDATED INC (PA)
Also Called: Coca-Cola
4100 Coca Cola Plz Ste 100 (28211-3481)
P.O. Box 31487 (28231-1487)
PHONE..................704 557-4400
J Frank Harrison Iii, *Ch Bd*
Morgan H Everett, *
Umesh M Kasbekar, *Non-Executive Vice Chairman of the Board*
David M Katz, *
F Scott Anthony, *Ex VP*
▲ **EMP:** 554 **EST:** 1902
SQ FT: 172,000
SALES (est): 6.65B
SALES (corp-wide): 6.65B **Publicly Held**
Web: www.cokeconsolidated.com
SIC: 2086 Bottled and canned soft drinks

(G-2520)
COCO LUMBER COMPANY LLC
2101 Sardis Rd N Ste 201 (28227-6785)
PHONE..................336 906-3754
◆ **EMP:** 4 **EST:** 2007
SALES (est): 478.37K **Privately Held**
Web: www.cocolumber.com
SIC: 2421 Sawmills and planing mills, general

(G-2521)
CODER FOUNDRY
8430 University Exec Park Dr (28262-1350)
PHONE..................704 910-3077
EMP: 48 **EST:** 2015
SALES (est): 656.44K **Privately Held**
Web: www.coderfoundry.com
SIC: 3325 Steel foundries, nec

(G-2522)
COG IN GAMES LLP
10144 Elizabeth Crest Ln (28277-3831)
PHONE..................704 763-4609
Thomas Coggin, *Pr*
Thomas Coggin, *Mng Pt*
EMP: 4 **EST:** 2017
SALES (est): 139.88K **Privately Held**
SIC: 3944 Board games, children's and adults'

(G-2523)
COLEFIELDS PUBLISHING INC
Also Called: Real Estate Book, The
2626 Hampton Ave (28207-2522)
PHONE..................704 661-1599
William F Medearis Iii, *Pr*
Bill Medearis, *Pr*
Polly Medearis, *Sec*
EMP: 8 **EST:** 1991
SALES (est): 422.98K **Privately Held**
Web: www.realestatebook.net
SIC: 2721 Magazines: publishing only, not printed on site

(G-2524)
COLLINS AEROSPACE
2730 W Tyvola Rd (28217-4527)
PHONE..................704 423-7000
EMP: 11 **EST:** 2020
SALES (est): 5.07MM **Privately Held**
Web: www.collinsaerospace.com
SIC: 3728 8711 Bodies, aircraft; Aviation and/or aeronautical engineering

(G-2525)
COLQUIMICA ADHESIVES INC
2205 Beltway Blvd Ste 200 (28214-8153)
PHONE..................704 318-4750
Joao Pedro Koehler, *Ch*
Joao Pedro Koehler, *Ch*
Sofia Koehler, *
Pedro Goncalves, *COO*
EMP: 42 **EST:** 2019
SALES (est): 9.17MM **Privately Held**
Web: www.colquimica.com
SIC: 2891 Adhesives
HQ: Colquimica - IndUstria Nacional De Colas, S.A.
Rua Das Lousas, 885
Valongo 4440-

(G-2526)
COLSENKEANE LEATHER LLC
1707 E 7th St (28204-2413)
PHONE..................704 750-9887
EMP: 7 **EST:** 2017
SALES (est): 201.18K **Privately Held**
Web: www.colsenkeane.com
SIC: 3199 Leather goods, nec

(G-2527)
COLTEC INDUSTRIES INC
Also Called: Garlock Bearings
5605 Carnegie Blvd Ste 500 (28209-4642)
PHONE..................704 731-1500
▲ **EMP:** 1700
SIC: 3053 3519 3089 Gaskets and sealing devices; Engines, diesel and semi-diesel or dual-fuel; Plastics containers, except foam

(G-2528)
COMMERCIAL METALS COMPANY
419 Atando Ave (28206-1909)
PHONE..................704 375-5937
Trevor Bokor, *Manager*
EMP: 22
SALES (corp-wide): 8.8B **Publicly Held**
Web: www.cmc.com
SIC: 3441 Fabricated structural metal
PA: Commercial Metals Company
6565 N Macarthur Blvd # 800
Irving TX 75039
214 689-4300

(G-2529)
COMMERCIAL METALS COMPANY
Ameristeel Chrltte Fab Rnfrcin
301 Black Satchel Rd (28216-2941)
PHONE..................704 399-9020
Van Taylor, *Mgr*
EMP: 32
SALES (corp-wide): 8.8B **Publicly Held**
Web: www.cmc.com
SIC: 3441 Fabricated structural metal
PA: Commercial Metals Company
6565 N Macarthur Blvd # 800
Irving TX 75039
214 689-4300

(G-2530)
COMMON SCENTS
6812 Malagant Ln (28213-4926)
PHONE..................704 780-2230
Elenita Mcmullen, *Prin*
EMP: 5 **EST:** 2010
SALES (est): 61.73K **Privately Held**
SIC: 2844 Perfumes, cosmetics and other toilet preparations

(G-2531)
COMPASS COLOR & COATING LLC
3825 Corporation Cir (28216-3418)
PHONE..................704 393-6745
EMP: 6 **EST:** 2017
SALES (est): 712.09K **Privately Held**
SIC: 2851 Undercoatings, paint

(G-2532)
COMPASS GROUP USA INC
Canteen Vending Services
3112 Horseshoe Ln (28208-6457)
P.O. Box 698 (28002-0698)
PHONE..................704 398-6515
Bob Mangiafico, *Owner*
EMP: 1043
SALES (corp-wide): 39.16B **Privately Held**
Web: www.canteen.com
SIC: 5962 2099 Merchandising machine operators; Food preparations, nec
HQ: Compass Group Usa, Inc.
2400 Yorkmont Rd
Charlotte NC 28217

(G-2533)
COMPASS PRECISION LLC (PA)
4600 Westinghouse Blvd (28273-9619)
PHONE..................704 790-6764
Gary Holcomb, *Pr*
Paul Wilhelm, *VP*
Jim Miller, *VP Sls*
EMP: 10 **EST:** 2019
SALES (est): 13.5MM
SALES (corp-wide): 13.5MM **Privately Held**
Web: www.compassprecision.com
SIC: 3599 Machine shop, jobbing and repair

(G-2534)
COMPONENT SOURCING INTL LLC
Also Called: Csi
1301 Westinghouse Blvd Ste 1 (28273-6393)
PHONE..................704 843-9292
John Hornberger, *CEO*
Eric Llorey, *VP Fin*
EMP: 20 **EST:** 1995
SALES (est): 4.5MM
SALES (corp-wide): 7.7MM **Privately Held**
Web: www.componentsourcing.com
SIC: 3448 1629 5051 3469 Prefabricated metal components; Dams, waterways, docks, and other marine construction; Castings, rough: iron or steel; Stamping metal for the trade
PA: Cpc Llc
1511 Baltimore Ave # 500
Kansas City MO 64108
816 756-2225

(G-2535)
COMPONENT TECHNOLOGY INTL INC
1000 Upper Asbury Ave (28206-1509)
PHONE..................704 331-0888
Chad Mcellee, *Brnch Mgr*
EMP: 5
SIC: 3599 3568 Machine shop, jobbing and repair; Power transmission equipment, nec

GEOGRAPHIC SECTION
Charlotte - Mecklenburg County (G-2559)

PA: Component Technology International, Inc.
2229 S 54th St
Milwaukee WI 53219

(G-2536)
CONCIERGE TRANSIT LLC
Also Called: Concierge Consulting - Itsm
1623 Swan Dr (28216)
PHONE.................................704 778-0755
EMP: 5 **EST:** 2016
SQ FT: 500
SALES (est): 464.84K Privately Held
Web: www.conciergetransit.com
SIC: 4111 3499 4513 Local and suburban transit; Stabilizing bars (cargo), metal; Air courier services

(G-2537)
CONCRETE SUPPLY CO LLC (HQ)
3823 Raleigh St (28206-2042)
P.O. Box 5247 (28299-5247)
PHONE.................................864 517-4055
EMP: 6 **EST:** 2013
SALES (est): 19.02MM
SALES (corp-wide): 149.62MM Privately Held
Web: www.concretesupplyco.com
SIC: 3273 Ready-mixed concrete
PA: Concrete Supply Holdings, Inc.
3823 Raleigh St
Charlotte NC 28206
704 372-2930

(G-2538)
CONCRETE SUPPLY HOLDINGS INC (PA)
3823 Raleigh St (28206-2042)
P.O. Box 5247 (28299-5247)
PHONE.................................704 372-2930
EMP: 352 **EST:** 1958
SALES (est): 149.62MM
SALES (corp-wide): 149.62MM Privately Held
Web: www.concretesupplyco.com
SIC: 3273 Ready-mixed concrete

(G-2539)
CONFAB MANUFACTURING CO LLC
6525 Morrison Blvd Ste 300 (28211-3561)
PHONE.................................704 366-7140
EMP: 25 **EST:** 2019
SALES (est): 5.19MM Privately Held
Web: www.con-fab.com
SIC: 3441 Fabricated structural metal
HQ: Wastequip, Llc
6525 Carnegie Blvd # 300
Charlotte NC 28211

(G-2540)
CONJET INC
3400 International Airport Dr Ste 100 (28208-4784)
PHONE.................................636 485-4724
Stephen Sistrunk, *CEO*
EMP: 4
SALES (est): 512.37K Privately Held
Web: www.conjet.com
SIC: 3531 Construction machinery

(G-2541)
CONSOLIDATED PRESS INC
Also Called: Consolidated Press Charlotte
3900 Greensboro St (28206-2036)
PHONE.................................704 372-6785
Tim Mullaney, *Pr*
▼ **EMP:** 8 **EST:** 1966
SQ FT: 10,500
SALES (est): 968.7K Privately Held
Web: www.consolidatedpress.net

SIC: 2752 5112 Offset printing; Business forms

(G-2542)
CONSULTANTS IN DATA PROC INC
Also Called: Cdp
6911 Shannon Willow Rd Ste 100 (28226-1346)
P.O. Box 472046 (28247-2046)
PHONE.................................704 542-6339
Paul Riefenberg, *Pr*
EMP: 5 **EST:** 1981
SALES (est): 1.12MM Privately Held
Web: www.cdp-inc.com
SIC: 7372 7374 7379 Prepackaged software; Data processing service; Computer related consulting services

(G-2543)
CONTAGIOUS GRAPHICS INC
5901 Orr Rd (28213-6321)
P.O. Box 560825 (28256-0825)
PHONE.................................704 529-5600
William Vasil, *Pr*
Steve Munsell, *
EMP: 38 **EST:** 1995
SQ FT: 15,000
SALES (est): 2.48MM Privately Held
Web: www.contagiousgraphics.com
SIC: 2759 3993 2396 Screen printing; Signs and advertising specialties; Automotive and apparel trimmings

(G-2544)
CONTEC LLC
Also Called: CONTEC LLC
6800 Steele Creek Rd (28217-5324)
PHONE.................................408 389-7206
Michael Whitehead, *Brnch Mgr*
EMP: 28
SALES (corp-wide): 221.89MM Privately Held
Web: www.gocontec.com
SIC: 7372 Prepackaged software
PA: Contec, Llc
1011 State St
Schenectady NY 12307
518 382-8000

(G-2545)
CONTECH ENGNERED SOLUTIONS LLC
4242 Raleigh St (28213-6902)
PHONE.................................704 596-4226
Aaron Johnson, *Mgr*
EMP: 23
SQ FT: 25,355
Web: www.conteches.com
SIC: 3443 Fabricated plate work (boiler shop)
HQ: Contech Engineered Solutions Llc
9025 Centre Pointe Dr # 400
West Chester OH 45069
513 645-7000

(G-2546)
CONTROLLED PRODUCTS SYSTEMS G
1859 Lindbergh St Ste 300 (28208-3775)
PHONE.................................704 392-2859
EMP: 5
SALES (corp-wide): 44.38MM Privately Held
Web: www.controlledproducts.com
SIC: 3699 Door opening and closing devices, electrical
PA: Controlled Products Systems Group, Inc.
5000 Osage St Ste 500
Denver CO 80221
303 333-1141

(G-2547)
CONVERGENT INTEGRATION INC
10205 Foxhall Dr (28210-7848)
PHONE.................................704 516-5922
Trevor D Petruk, *Prin*
EMP: 7 **EST:** 2008
SALES (est): 156.99K Privately Held
SIC: 3674 Semiconductors and related devices

(G-2548)
CONXIT TECHNOLOGY GROUP INC
9101 Southern Pine Blvd # 250 (28273-5529)
PHONE.................................877 998-4227
Shawn Glenn Miller, *CEO*
EMP: 6 **EST:** 2007
SALES (est): 467.56K Privately Held
SIC: 7372 Educational computer software

(G-2549)
COOPER B-LINE INC
3810 Ayscough Rd (28211-3206)
PHONE.................................704 522-6272
EMP: 105
Web: www.eaton.com
SIC: 3441 Fabricated structural metal
HQ: Cooper B-Line, Inc.
509 Monroe St
Highland IL 62249
618 654-2184

(G-2550)
COPY CAT INSTANT PRTG CHRLTTE
4612 South Blvd Ste B (28209-2864)
PHONE.................................704 529-6606
Diane Gilbert, *Pr*
EMP: 5 **EST:** 1987
SALES (est): 328.59K Privately Held
Web: www.copycatsouth.com
SIC: 2752 Offset printing

(G-2551)
COPY EXPRESS CHARLOTTE INC
4004 South Blvd Ste A (28209-2054)
PHONE.................................704 527-1750
Bennett Z Travis, *Pr*
Sandy Travis, *VP*
EMP: 7 **EST:** 1986
SQ FT: 4,000
SALES (est): 949.71K Privately Held
Web: www.mycopyexpress.com
SIC: 2752 Offset printing

(G-2552)
COPY THAT BUSINESS SERVICES
2130 Ayrsley Town Blvd Ste B (28273-3527)
PHONE.................................980 297-7088
Atilla Molnar, *Owner*
EMP: 5 **EST:** 2005
SALES (est): 443.81K Privately Held
Web: www.copythatcharlotte.com
SIC: 2752 Offset printing

(G-2553)
CORDEX INSTRUMENTS INC
5309 Monroe Rd (28205-7829)
PHONE.................................877 836-0764
Gary Copeland, *Prin*
EMP: 9 **EST:** 2010
SALES (est): 225.33K Privately Held
SIC: 3823 Process control instruments

(G-2554)
CORMETECH INC (HQ)
11707 Steele Creek Rd (28273-3718)
PHONE.................................919 620-3000
Mike Mattes, *Pr*
◆ **EMP:** 176 **EST:** 1989

SQ FT: 90,000
SALES (est): 99.92MM
SALES (corp-wide): 99.92MM Privately Held
Web: www.cormetech.com
SIC: 3295 Filtering clays, treated
PA: Steag Scr-Tech, Inc.
11707 Steele Creek Rd
Charlotte NC 28273
704 827-8933

(G-2555)
CORNERSTONE WOODWORKS LLC
1782 Forest Side Ln (28213-2104)
PHONE.................................908 343-3708
Daniela Aloise, *Prin*
EMP: 4 **EST:** 2017
SALES (est): 54.13K Privately Held
SIC: 2431 Millwork

(G-2556)
CORNING OPTCAL CMMNCATIONS LLC (HQ)
4200 Corning Pl (28216-1298)
PHONE.................................828 901-5000
Giovanni Cortazzo, *Mgr*
◆ **EMP:** 510 **EST:** 1977
SALES (est): 581.2MM
SALES (corp-wide): 12.59B Publicly Held
Web: www.corning.com
SIC: 3661 Telephone and telegraph apparatus
PA: Corning Incorporated
1 Riverfront Plz
Corning NY 14831
607 974-9000

(G-2557)
CORNING OPTCAL CMMNCATIONS LLC
Also Called: Corning
4200 Corning Pl (28216-1298)
PHONE.................................828 901-5000
EMP: 201
SALES (corp-wide): 12.59B Publicly Held
Web: www.corning.com
SIC: 3661 Fiber optics communications equipment
HQ: Corning Optical Communications Llc
4200 Corning Pl
Charlotte NC 28216
828 901-5000

(G-2558)
COROB NORTH AMERICA INC
Also Called: Cpscolor
4901 Gibbon Rd A (28269-8531)
PHONE.................................704 588-8408
◆ **EMP:** 17 **EST:** 1994
SALES (est): 8.29MM
SALES (corp-wide): 2.67MM Privately Held
SIC: 3559 Paint making machinery
HQ: Corob Spa
Via Dell'agricoltura 103
San Felice Sul Panaro MO 41038

(G-2559)
CORPORATE PLACE LLC
13320 Ballantyne Corporate Pl (28277-3607)
PHONE.................................704 808-3848
Marc Michael, *Pr*
David Kowalski, *Global Manufacturing Operations President*
EMP: 28 **EST:** 2015
SALES (est): 4.2MM
SALES (corp-wide): 1.53B Privately Held
Web: www.goballantyne.com
SIC: 3556 3559 Dairy and milk machinery; Pharmaceutical machinery

Charlotte - Mecklenburg County (G-2560) GEOGRAPHIC SECTION

HQ: Spx Flow, Inc.
13320 Balntyn Corp Pl
Charlotte NC 28277
704 752-4400

(G-2560)
COSMOPROS
1001 E W T Harris Blvd (28213-4104)
PHONE.................................704 717-7420
Lisa Oldham, *Mgr*
EMP: 4 **EST:** 2007
SALES (est): 200.96K **Privately Held**
SIC: 3999 5087 Barber and beauty shop equipment; Beauty salon and barber shop equipment and supplies

(G-2561)
COTTONWOOD MANUFACTURING INC (PA)
14328 Arbor Ridge Dr (28273-8880)
PHONE.................................704 504-0374
Earl S Douglass, *Pr*
Vicky L Carr, *Sec*
EMP: 7 **EST:** 2003
SQ FT: 500
SALES (est): 609.08K
SALES (corp-wide): 609.08K **Privately Held**
Web: www.cottonwoodinc.com
SIC: 2493 Insulation board, cellular fiber

(G-2562)
COUNTRY LOTUS SOAPS LLC
2313 Ginger Ln Apt H (28213-6567)
PHONE.................................786 384-4174
Iris Gutierrez, *CEO*
EMP: 4 **EST:** 2020
SALES (est): 126.85K **Privately Held**
SIC: 2841 Soap and other detergents

(G-2563)
COURTESY OF KAMDYN LLC
5406 Strive St Apt 104 (28262-7023)
PHONE.................................706 831-5395
EMP: 4 **EST:** 2017
SALES (est): 72.08K **Privately Held**
SIC: 2211 Apparel and outerwear fabrics, cotton

(G-2564)
CP INDUSTRIES INC
660 Westinghouse Blvd Ste 107 (28273-6382)
PHONE.................................704 816-0580
EMP: 6 **EST:** 2018
SALES (est): 50.55K **Privately Held**
Web: www.cp-industries.com
SIC: 3999 Manufacturing industries, nec

(G-2565)
CP LIQUIDATION INC
5104 N Graham St (28269-4829)
PHONE.................................704 921-1100
EMP: 85
SIC: 2448 Pallets, wood

(G-2566)
CR APPRAISAL FIRM LLC
704 East Blvd Apt 1 (28203-5155)
PHONE.................................704 344-0909
Lynn Barwick, *Admn*
EMP: 5 **EST:** 2014
SALES (est): 86.46K **Privately Held**
SIC: 3999 Manufacturing industries, nec

(G-2567)
CRACKLE HOLDINGS LP
1800 Continental Blvd Ste 200c (28273)
PHONE.................................704 927-7620
John Heyman, *CEO*

EMP: 1302 **EST:** 2017
SQ FT: 69,953
SALES (est): 22.35MM **Privately Held**
SIC: 3679 Electronic circuits

(G-2568)
CRAFT REVOLUTION LLC (PA)
Also Called: Artisanal Brewing Ventures
4001 Yancey Rd Ste A (28217-1772)
PHONE.................................347 924-7540
EMP: 10 **EST:** 2016
SALES (est): 5.3MM
SALES (corp-wide): 5.3MM **Privately Held**
SIC: 2082 Malt beverage products

(G-2569)
CREST PUBLICATIONS
12701 Netherhall Dr (28269-8405)
P.O. Box 481022 (28269-5309)
PHONE.................................704 277-7194
Sarah Bolme, *Prin*
EMP: 9 **EST:** 2008
SALES (est): 154.56K **Privately Held**
Web: www.christianpublishers.net
SIC: 2741 Miscellaneous publishing

(G-2570)
CRITICORE INC (DH)
9525 Monroe Rd Ste 150 (28270-2451)
PHONE.................................704 542-6876
Scott Banks, *Pr*
Greg Winn, *VP*
▲ **EMP:** 10 **EST:** 1998
SALES (est): 23.35MM
SALES (corp-wide): 443.7MM **Privately Held**
Web: www.wkep.com
SIC: 2326 Service apparel (baker, barber, lab, etc.), washable: men's
HQ: Zb Holdings, Llc
4838 Jenkins Ave
North Charleston SC 29405

(G-2571)
CROFT PRECISION TOOLS INC
4424 Taggart Creek Rd Ste 108 (28208-5494)
PHONE.................................704 399-4124
Derek T Goring, *Pr*
EMP: 6 **EST:** 1982
SALES (est): 483.48K **Privately Held**
Web: www.crofttools.com
SIC: 3545 Diamond cutting tools for turning, boring, burnishing, etc.

(G-2572)
CROWN CASE CO
801 Atando Ave Ste C (28206-1949)
PHONE.................................704 453-1542
Fred Floye, *Pr*
EMP: 6 **EST:** 2010
SALES (est): 157.35K **Privately Held**
SIC: 3443 Containers, shipping (bombs, etc.): metal plate

(G-2573)
CROWN TOWN COMPOST LLC
1801 Merriman Ave (28203-4611)
PHONE.................................704 654-5689
Kristopher Steele, *Prin*
EMP: 8 **EST:** 2014
SALES (est): 974.2K **Privately Held**
Web: www.crowntowncompost.com
SIC: 2875 Compost

(G-2574)
CROWNTOWN TINKER LLC
6227 Hermsley Rd (28278-7452)
PHONE.................................843 614-9566
EMP: 5 **EST:** 2017

SALES (est): 48.34K **Privately Held**
Web: www.riftwoodwork.com
SIC: 2431 Millwork

(G-2575)
CRT INC
7515 Valleybrook Rd (28270-6550)
PHONE.................................704 905-9748
EMP: 4
SALES (corp-wide): 55.3K **Privately Held**
SIC: 2335 Women's, junior's, and misses' dresses
PA: Crt, Inc.
234 Locust Grove Rd
Weaverville NC

(G-2576)
CRYOVAC LLC (HQ)
2415 Cascade Pointe Blvd (28208-6899)
PHONE.................................980 430-7000
▲ **EMP:** 600 **EST:** 1981
SALES (est): 1.92B
SALES (corp-wide): 5.49B **Publicly Held**
Web: www.sealedair.com
SIC: 3086 Packaging and shipping materials, foamed plastics
PA: Sealed Air Corporation
2415 Cascade Pointe Blvd
Charlotte NC 28208
980 221-3235

(G-2577)
CRYOVAC INTL HOLDINGS INC (HQ)
2415 Cascade Pointe Blvd (28208-6899)
PHONE.................................980 430-7000
EMP: 50 **EST:** 1997
SALES (est): 370.16MM
SALES (corp-wide): 5.49B **Publicly Held**
Web: www.sealedair.com
SIC: 3086 Packaging and shipping materials, foamed plastics
PA: Sealed Air Corporation
2415 Cascade Pointe Blvd
Charlotte NC 28208
980 221-3235

(G-2578)
CRYOVAC LEASING CORPORATION
2415 Cascade Pointe Blvd (28208-6899)
PHONE.................................980 430-7000
EMP: 28 **EST:** 2001
SALES (est): 2MM
SALES (corp-wide): 5.49B **Publicly Held**
SIC: 2673 Bags: plastic, laminated, and coated
PA: Sealed Air Corporation
2415 Cascade Pointe Blvd
Charlotte NC 28208
980 221-3235

(G-2579)
CRYSTAL CLEAR IMAGES INC
8203 White Horse Ln (28270-1092)
PHONE.................................704 708-5420
EMP: 4 **EST:** 2016
SALES (est): 70.91K **Privately Held**
Web: www.cci-tees.com
SIC: 2759 Screen printing

(G-2580)
CS MANUFACTURING CS MFG
4525 Reagan Dr # A (28206-3192)
PHONE.................................704 837-1701
EMP: 4 **EST:** 2016
SALES (est): 240.55K **Privately Held**
SIC: 3999 Manufacturing industries, nec

(G-2581)
CSM LOGISTICS LLC
4835 Sirona Dr Ste 300 (28273-3965)

PHONE.................................980 800-2621
EMP: 4 **EST:** 2018
SALES (est): 216.55K **Privately Held**
SIC: 3537 Containers (metal), air cargo

(G-2582)
CTS CUSTOM CABINETS
519 Armour Dr (28206-3055)
PHONE.................................704 376-5844
Anthony Benneth, *Prin*
EMP: 7 **EST:** 2015
SALES (est): 143.81K **Privately Held**
Web: www.ctscustom.com
SIC: 2434 Wood kitchen cabinets

(G-2583)
CULTURE CUISINE LLC
801 E Morehead St (28202-2729)
PHONE.................................347 278-3210
EMP: 4
SALES (est): 116.15K **Privately Held**
SIC: 2099 Food preparations, nec

(G-2584)
CUMMINS ATLANTIC LLC
Also Called: Cummins
3700 Jeff Adams Dr (28206-1288)
PHONE.................................704 596-7690
Jeff Johnson, *Mgr*
EMP: 44
SALES (corp-wide): 34.06B **Publicly Held**
SIC: 5063 7538 5084 3519 Generators; Diesel engine repair: automotive; Industrial machinery and equipment; Internal combustion engines, nec
HQ: Cummins Atlantic Llc
11101 Nations Ford Rd
Charlotte NC 28273

(G-2585)
CUMMINS ATLANTIC LLC (HQ)
Also Called: Cummins
11101 Nations Ford Rd (28273)
P.O. Box 7787 (28241-7787)
PHONE.................................704 588-1240
Steven H Jordan, *CEO*
▲ **EMP:** 50 **EST:** 1970
SALES (est): 52.47MM
SALES (corp-wide): 34.06B **Publicly Held**
SIC: 7538 5084 5063 5999 Diesel engine repair: automotive; Engines and parts, diesel; Generators; Engine and motor equipment and supplies
PA: Cummins Inc.
500 Jackson St
Columbus IN 47201
812 377-5000

(G-2586)
CUMULUS FIBRES INC
1101 Tar Heel Rd (28208-1524)
P.O. Box 669609 (28266-9609)
PHONE.................................704 394-2111
Darrell C Steagall, *Pr*
EMP: 440 **EST:** 1981
SQ FT: 59,276
SALES (est): 471.68K
SALES (corp-wide): 48.16MM **Privately Held**
Web: www.cumulusfibres.com
SIC: 2297 2299 Nonwoven fabrics; Apparel filling: cotton waste, kapok, and related material
PA: Empire Investment Holdings, Llc
1220 Malaga Ave
Coral Gables FL 33134
305 403-1111

GEOGRAPHIC SECTION
Charlotte - Mecklenburg County (G-2612)

(G-2587)
CURTISS-WRIGHT CONTROLS INC (HQ)
15801 Brixham Hill Ave Ste 200 (28277-4792)
PHONE..................704 869-4600
Tom Quinly, *Pr*
Brian Freeman, *
Allan E Symonds, *
▲ **EMP:** 24 **EST:** 1945
SQ FT: 1,260
SALES (est): 793.61MM
SALES (corp-wide): 2.85B **Publicly Held**
Web: www.curtisswright.com
SIC: 3728 Aircraft assemblies, subassemblies, and parts, nec
PA: Curtiss-Wright Corporation
130 Harbour Place Dr # 300
Davidson NC 28036
704 869-4600

(G-2588)
CUSTOM CHROME & COATINGS INC
8208 Lawyers Rd (28227-5014)
PHONE..................704 226-6808
Christopher Louis Yelton, *Admn*
EMP: 6 **EST:** 2015
SALES (est): 87.32K **Privately Held**
SIC: 3479 Metal coating and allied services

(G-2589)
CUSTOM CORRUGATED CNTRS INC
5024 Westinghouse Blvd (28273-9641)
P.O. Box 38899 (28278-1015)
PHONE..................704 588-0371
W Wayne Forbis, *Pr*
Dean Forbis, *
EMP: 38 **EST:** 1972
SQ FT: 65,000
SALES (est): 4.7MM **Privately Held**
Web: www.customcorr.com
SIC: 2653 Boxes, corrugated: made from purchased materials

(G-2590)
CUSTOM GLASS WORKS INC
2000 W Morehead St Ste F (28208-5175)
PHONE..................704 597-0290
Georgia Droppelman, *Pr*
EMP: 9 **EST:** 1988
SQ FT: 5,000
SALES (est): 960K **Privately Held**
Web: www.customglassofnc.com
SIC: 3231 Leaded glass

(G-2591)
CUSTOM INK
530 Brandywine Rd Ste C (28209-2171)
PHONE..................704 935-5604
EMP: 45 **EST:** 2020
SALES (est): 110.83K **Privately Held**
Web: locations.customink.com
SIC: 2389 2331 2321 Apparel and accessories, nec; Women's and misses' blouses and shirts; Men's and boy's furnishings

(G-2592)
CUSTOM NEON & GRAPHICS INC
1722 Toal St (28206-1524)
PHONE..................704 344-1715
Cynthia Wilcox, *Pr*
Mike Wilcox, *Sec*
EMP: 6 **EST:** 1997
SQ FT: 10,000
SALES (est): 844.53K **Privately Held**
SIC: 5046 3993 Neon signs; Neon signs

(G-2593)
CUSTOM POLYMERS INC (PA)
Also Called: Custom Polymers
831 E Morehead St Ste 840 (28202-2726)
PHONE..................704 332-6070
◆ **EMP:** 10 **EST:** 1996
SQ FT: 42,000
SALES (est): 24.04MM **Privately Held**
Web: www.custompolymers.com
SIC: 4953 2821 2822 Recycling, waste materials; Plastics materials and resins; Ethylene-propylene rubbers, EPDM polymers

(G-2594)
CUSTOM POLYMERS PET LLC (PA)
831 E Morehead St Ste 840 (28202-2726)
PHONE..................866 717-0716
Byron Geiger, *Pr*
▲ **EMP:** 25 **EST:** 2008
SALES (est): 7.05MM **Privately Held**
Web: www.custompolymerspet.com
SIC: 2821 Plastics materials and resins

(G-2595)
CUSTOM SIGNAGE COMPANY
10423 Dickson Ln (28262-6415)
PHONE..................909 215-2404
Atiq Qureshi, *Prin*
EMP: 4 **EST:** 2019
SALES (est): 109.59K **Privately Held**
Web: www.qcsignscharlotte.com
SIC: 3993 Signs and advertising specialties

(G-2596)
CUSTOM TEES LAB
5121 Vanhoy Ln (28269-2903)
PHONE..................704 804-8706
Cherniqua Strayhorn, *Prin*
EMP: 4 **EST:** 2016
SALES (est): 124.08K **Privately Held**
SIC: 2759 Screen printing

(G-2597)
D&E FREIGHT LLC
Also Called: Freight Company
4427 Knollcrest Dr (28208-1424)
PHONE..................704 977-4847
Eric Mitchell, *Managing Member*
EMP: 10 **EST:** 2021
SALES (est): 507.24K **Privately Held**
Web: www.dandefreight.com
SIC: 4789 3537 Transportation services, nec ; Trucks: freight, baggage, etc.: industrial, except mining

(G-2598)
DAIKIN APPLIED AMERICAS INC
13504 S Point Blvd Ste G (28273-6763)
PHONE..................704 588-0087
Dimitris Alexand, *Mgr*
EMP: 8
Web: www.daikinapplied.com
SIC: 3585 7623 Air conditioning units, complete: domestic or industrial; Refrigeration service and repair
HQ: Daikin Applied Americas Inc.
13600 Industrial Pk Blvd
Minneapolis MN 55441
763 553-5330

(G-2599)
DAILY LIVING SOLUTIONS INC
9711 Stewart Spring Ln (28216-1857)
PHONE..................704 614-0977
Wilson Ford, *Prin*
EMP: 7 **EST:** 2010
SALES (est): 245.75K **Privately Held**
SIC: 2711 Newspapers, publishing and printing

(G-2600)
DAISY PINK CO
10335 Worsley Ln (28269-8163)
PHONE..................704 907-3526
Sutrina Benge, *Prin*
EMP: 6 **EST:** 2013
SALES (est): 87.88K **Privately Held**
Web: www.thepinkdaisy.com
SIC: 3999 Candles

(G-2601)
DALE REYNOLDS CABINETS INC
301 Kimmswick Rd (28214-1247)
PHONE..................704 890-5962
EMP: 5 **EST:** 2017
SALES (est): 222.85K **Privately Held**
SIC: 3999 2541 Manufacturing industries, nec; Cabinets, lockers, and shelving

(G-2602)
DAMBACH LAGERSYSTEME INC
121 W Trade St Ste 2850 (28202-2293)
PHONE..................704 421-6425
Thomas Himmel, *Prin*
EMP: 6 **EST:** 2019
SALES (est): 212.79K **Privately Held**
SIC: 3714 Motor vehicle parts and accessories

(G-2603)
DARAMIC LLC (DH)
11430 N Community House Rd Ste 350 (28277-0454)
PHONE..................704 587-8599
◆ **EMP:** 100 **EST:** 1994
SALES (est): 121.7MM **Privately Held**
Web: www.daramic.com
SIC: 3069 2499 3269 Roofing, membrane rubber; Battery separators, wood; Filtering media, pottery
HQ: Polypore International, Lp
11430 N Cmnity Hse Rd # 350
Charlotte NC 28277
704 587-8409

(G-2604)
DAVID YURMAN ENTERPRISES LLC
4400 Sharon Rd Ste 177 (28211-3612)
PHONE..................704 366-7259
Glen T Senk, *CEO*
EMP: 9
SALES (corp-wide): 187.43MM **Privately Held**
Web: www.davidyurman.com
SIC: 3911 Jewelry, precious metal
PA: David Yurman Enterprises Llc
24 Vestry St
New York NY 10013
212 896-1550

(G-2605)
DAVIS CONVEYOR COMPONENTS
1400 Sharon Rd W (28210-5699)
PHONE..................704 557-1742
Patrick Davis, *Owner*
EMP: 5 **EST:** 2007
SALES (est): 156.07K **Privately Held**
SIC: 3535 Conveyors and conveying equipment

(G-2606)
DAVIS EQUIPMENT HANDLERS INC
3860 Abiliene Rd (28205)
PHONE..................704 792-9176
Jonathan Davis, *Pr*
Laura Davis, *Sec*
EMP: 4 **EST:** 1991
SALES (est): 463.4K **Privately Held**
SIC: 3312 Stainless steel

(G-2607)
DAVIS VOGLER ENTERPRISES LLC
5316 Camilla Dr (28226-6769)
PHONE..................402 257-7188
Scott P Vgler, *Prin*
EMP: 6 **EST:** 2016
SALES (est): 30.77K **Privately Held**
Web: vogler-davis-enterprises.hub.biz
SIC: 2759 Screen printing

(G-2608)
DE LUXE PACKAGING CORP
3436 Toringdon Way Ste 100 (28277-2450)
PHONE..................800 845-6051
Richard Goulet, *Pr*
EMP: 50 **EST:** 2003
SALES (est): 17.08MM
SALES (corp-wide): 32.64B **Publicly Held**
SIC: 3497 2671 Foil containers for bakery goods and frozen foods; Paper, coated or laminated for packaging
HQ: Novolex Holdings, Llc
101 E Carolina Ave
Hartsville SC 29550
800 845-6051

(G-2609)
DEBMED USA LLC
2815 Coliseum Centre Dr # 6 (28217-1452)
PHONE..................704 263-4240
Dawn Huston, *Mktg Mgr*
EMP: 11 **EST:** 2013
SALES (est): 4.44MM
SALES (corp-wide): 1.11B **Privately Held**
Web: www.scjp.com
SIC: 2834 Medicines, capsuled or ampuled
PA: S. C. Johnson & Son, Inc.
1525 Howe St
Racine WI 53403
262 260-2000

(G-2610)
DECIMA CORPORATION LLC
529 W Summit Ave Ste 1c (28203-4400)
PHONE..................734 516-1535
Arto Diamond, *CEO*
EMP: 30 **EST:** 2019
SALES (est): 1.65MM **Privately Held**
SIC: 2434 5099 Wood kitchen cabinets; Wood and wood by-products

(G-2611)
DECOLUX USA
6024 Shining Oak Ln (28269-0001)
PHONE..................704 340-3532
Monica Vasquez, *Admn*
EMP: 5
SALES (est): 266.79K **Privately Held**
SIC: 2591 7389 Blinds vertical; Business services, nec

(G-2612)
DELANEY HOLDINGS CO
13320 Ballantyne Corporate Pl (28277-3607)
PHONE..................704 808-3848
Marc Michael, *Pr*
David Kowalski, *Global Manufacturing Operations President*
EMP: 27 **EST:** 2011
SALES (est): 2.59MM
SALES (corp-wide): 1.53B **Privately Held**
SIC: 3556 3559 Dairy and milk machinery; Pharmaceutical machinery
HQ: Spx Flow, Inc.
13320 Balntyn Corp Pl
Charlotte NC 28277
704 752-4400

Charlotte - Mecklenburg County (G-2613)

GEOGRAPHIC SECTION

(G-2613)
DELISH CAKERY CO
3425 Back Creek Church Rd (28213-5200)
PHONE.................................704 724-7743
Aryn Keogh, *Pr*
EMP: 4 **EST:** 2011
SALES (est): 85.98K **Privately Held**
Web: www.delishcakery.com
SIC: 2051 Cakes, bakery: except frozen

(G-2614)
DELLNER INC
Also Called: Dellner Brakes
4016 Shutterfly Rd Ste 100 (28217-3078)
PHONE.................................704 527-2121
Jeron Cain, *Pr*
David Pagels, *
Tom Sharp, *
▲ **EMP:** 37 **EST:** 1960
SQ FT: 10,000
SALES (est): 12.59MM
SALES (corp-wide): 185.39MM **Privately Held**
Web: www.dellner.com
SIC: 3743 Railroad locomotives and parts, electric or nonelectric
HQ: Dellner Couplers Ab
    Vikavagen 144
    Falun 791 9
    23765407

(G-2615)
DELTA MOLD INC
9415 Stockport Pl (28273-4564)
PHONE.................................704 588-6600
Eric Mozer, *CEO*
Jim Quinn, *
◆ **EMP:** 90 **EST:** 1978
SQ FT: 50,000
SALES (est): 21.45MM **Privately Held**
Web: www.deltamold.com
SIC: 3089 Injection molding of plastics

(G-2616)
DELUXE CORP
6125 Lakeview Rd (28269-2613)
PHONE.................................704 969-5200
EMP: 4 **EST:** 2019
SALES (est): 51.07K **Privately Held**
SIC: 2782 Checkbooks

(G-2617)
DENTAL EQUIPMENT LLC
Also Called: Marus Dental
11727 Fruehauf Dr (28273-6507)
P.O. Box 7800 (28241-7800)
PHONE.................................704 588-2126
John Regan, *Pr*
Vicente Reynal, *
▲ **EMP:** 500 **EST:** 2005
SQ FT: 137,438
SALES (est): 111.05MM
SALES (corp-wide): 31.47B **Publicly Held**
Web: www.peltonandcrane.com
SIC: 3843 Dental equipment and supplies
PA: Danaher Corporation
    2200 Penn Ave Nw Ste 800w
    Washington DC 20037
    202 828-0850

(G-2618)
DENTSPLY SIRONA INC (PA)
Also Called: DENTSPLY SIRONA
13320 Ballantyne Corporate Pl
(28273-3607)
PHONE.................................844 848-0137
Donald M Casey Junior, *CEO*
Eric K Brandt, *Non-Executive Chairman of the Board*
Jorge M Gomez, *Ex VP*
Cheree H Johnson, *CLO*
Ranjit S Chadha, *CAO*
◆ **EMP:** 600 **EST:** 1899
SALES (est): 3.96B
SALES (corp-wide): 3.96B **Publicly Held**
Web: www.dentsplysirona.com
SIC: 3843 Dental equipment and supplies

(G-2619)
DENVER GLOBAL PRODUCTS INC
6420 Rea Rd Ste A1 (28277-0771)
PHONE.................................704 665-1800
◆ **EMP:** 110 **EST:** 2010
SQ FT: 5,500
SALES (est): 9.29MM **Privately Held**
SIC: 3546 Power-driven handtools
PA: Chongqing Runtong Holding (Group) Co., Ltd.
    No.99, Jiujiang Ave, Area B, Shuangfu Industrial Park, Jiangjin
    Chongqing CQ 40224

(G-2620)
DERITA PRECISION MCH CO INC
605 Toddville Rd (28214-1835)
P.O. Box 645 (28130-0645)
PHONE.................................704 392-7285
Dennis L Butts Senior, *Pr*
Dennis L Butts Junior, *VP*
EMP: 10 **EST:** 1955
SQ FT: 12,000
SALES (est): 987.86K **Privately Held**
Web: www.derita.com
SIC: 3469 3452 Machine parts, stamped or pressed metal; Bolts, metal

(G-2621)
DESIGNLINE CORPORATION
Also Called: Designline Intl Holdings
2309 Nevada Blvd (28273-6430)
PHONE.................................704 494-7800
▲ **EMP:** 250
Web: www.transteq.com
SIC: 3711 Buses, all types, assembly of

(G-2622)
DESIGNLINE USA LLC
2309 Nevada Blvd (28273-6430)
P.O. Box 7405 (28241-7405)
PHONE.................................704 494-7800
G Michael Floyd, *Ex VP*
Joshua Anderson, *Ex VP*
Andy Maunder, *CFO*
Michael Floyd, *Ex VP*
EMP: 44 **EST:** 2008
SQ FT: 172,039
SALES (est): 1.42MM **Privately Held**
Web: www.designlineusa.com
SIC: 3711 3713 Bus and other large specialty vehicle assembly; Truck and bus bodies

(G-2623)
DEUROTECH AMERICA INC
4526 Westinghouse Blvd Ste A
(28273-9602)
PHONE.................................980 272-6827
EMP: 11 **EST:** 2016
SALES (est): 1.04MM **Privately Held**
Web: america.deurotechgroup.com
SIC: 3569 5084 General industrial machinery, nec; Industrial machinery and equipment

(G-2624)
DEVAN US INC
6525 Morrison Blvd Ste 516 (28211-3561)
PHONE.................................704 365-7111
▲ **EMP:** 6 **EST:** 2010
SALES (est): 72.63K **Privately Held**
Web: www.devan.net
SIC: 3999 Manufacturing industries, nec

(G-2625)
DFA DAIRY BRANDS FLUID LLC
3540 Toringdon Way Ste 200 (28277-3867)
PHONE.................................704 341-2794
EMP: 8
SALES (corp-wide): 24.52B **Privately Held**
Web: www.dfamilk.com
SIC: 2033 2097 5143 5149 Fruit juices: packaged in cans, jars, etc.; Manufactured ice; Ice cream and ices; Coffee, green or roasted
HQ: Dfa Dairy Brands Fluid, Llc
    1405 N 98th St
    Kansas City KS 66111
    816 801-6455

(G-2626)
DH SCREEN PRINT PLUS
10917 Wyndham Pointe Dr (28213-4127)
PHONE.................................704 609-4823
Dwight D Hailstock, *Owner*
EMP: 4 **EST:** 2018
SALES (est): 55.61K **Privately Held**
SIC: 2752 Commercial printing, lithographic

(G-2627)
DIAGNOSTIC DEVICES
2701 Hutchison Mcdonald Rd Ste A
(28269-4217)
PHONE.................................704 599-5908
Stephanie Cranford, *Mgr*
EMP: 8 **EST:** 2018
SALES (est): 162.5K **Privately Held**
SIC: 2834 Pharmaceutical preparations

(G-2628)
DIAMOND POWER INTL LLC
13024 Ballantyne Corporate Pl Ste 700
(28277-2113)
PHONE.................................704 625-4900
EMP: 11 **EST:** 2018
SALES (est): 4.37MM
SALES (corp-wide): 889.82MM **Publicly Held**
Web: www.babcock.com
SIC: 3511 Turbines and turbine generator sets
PA: Babcock & Wilcox Enterprises, Inc.
    1200 E Market St Ste 650
    Akron OH 44305
    330 753-4511

(G-2629)
DIAMOND PWR ASTRLIA HLDNGS INC
13024 Ballantyne Corporate Pl Ste 700
(28277-2113)
PHONE.................................704 625-4900
EMP: 9 **EST:** 2018
SALES (est): 3.58MM
SALES (corp-wide): 889.82MM **Publicly Held**
SIC: 3511 Turbines and turbine generator sets
PA: Babcock & Wilcox Enterprises, Inc.
    1200 E Market St Ste 650
    Akron OH 44305
    330 753-4511

(G-2630)
DIAMOND PWR EQITY INVSTMNTS IN
13024 Ballantyne Corporate Pl Ste 700
(28277-2113)
PHONE.................................704 625-4900
EMP: 7 **EST:** 2017
SALES (est): 2.78MM
SALES (corp-wide): 889.82MM **Publicly Held**
SIC: 3511 Turbines and turbine generator sets
PA: Babcock & Wilcox Enterprises, Inc.
    1200 E Market St Ste 650
    Akron OH 44305
    330 753-4511

(G-2631)
DICKERSON GROUP INC (PA)
1111 Metropolitan Ave Ste 1090 (28204)
P.O. Box 5011 (28111-5011)
PHONE.................................704 289-3111
John Joyner, *Pr*
EMP: 5 **EST:** 1945
SALES (est): 50.19MM
SALES (corp-wide): 50.19MM **Privately Held**
SIC: 1611 2951 Highway and street paving contractor; Asphalt paving mixtures and blocks

(G-2632)
DIEBOLD NIXDORF INCORPORATED
5900 Northwoods Business Pkwy Ste K
(28269)
PHONE.................................704 599-3100
Bud Hancock, *Mgr*
EMP: 19
SALES (corp-wide): 3.46B **Publicly Held**
Web: www.diebolnixdorf.com
SIC: 5049 1731 7382 7381 Bank equipment and supplies; Banking machine installation and service; Security systems services; Detective and armored car services
PA: Diebold Nixdorf, Incorporated
    50 Executive Pkwy
    Hudson OH 44236
    330 490-4000

(G-2633)
DIGITAL AP PRTG DBA F4MILY MTT
3623 Latrobe Dr (28211-4864)
PHONE.................................980 939-8066
Samir Hamid, *CEO*
EMP: 5 **EST:** 2012
SALES (est): 474.14K **Privately Held**
Web: www.f4milymatters.com
SIC: 2752 Commercial printing, lithographic

(G-2634)
DIGITAL DESIGNS INC
3540 Toringdon Way Ste 200 (28277-4650)
P.O. Box 5011 (28111-5011)
PHONE.................................704 790-7100
John C Queen, *Pr*
Sue Ratliff, *
Jeff Buckner, *
EMP: 25 **EST:** 1980
SALES (est): 4.15MM **Privately Held**
Web: www.ddilink.com
SIC: 7371 7379 7372 Custom computer programming services; Computer related consulting services; Prepackaged software

(G-2635)
DIGITAL INK TECHNOLOGY INC ✪
8107 Arrowridge Blvd (28273-6179)
PHONE.................................603 707-7843
EMP: 6 **EST:** 2022
SALES (est): 69.88K **Privately Held**
Web: www.digitalcolorink.com
SIC: 2752 Offset printing

(G-2636)
DIGITAL PRINTING SYSTEMS INC (PA)
Also Called: Visual Impressions
606 E Hebron St (28273-5991)
P.O. Box 470666 (28247-0666)
PHONE.................................704 525-0190
John Forgach, *Pr*

GEOGRAPHIC SECTION
Charlotte - Mecklenburg County (G-2659)

Brian Mckenna, *VP*
Roger Cox, *Contrlr*
EMP: 20 **EST:** 1994
SQ FT: 25,000
SALES (est): 6.45MM **Privately Held**
Web: www.visualimpressions.net
SIC: 3993 5712 7372 2759 Signs and advertising specialties; Cabinet work, custom; Application computer software; Posters, including billboards: printing, nsk

(G-2637)
DILWORTH CUSTOM FRAMING
125 Remount Rd Ste C2 (28203-6459)
PHONE.................................704 370-7660
EMP: 4 **EST:** 2017
SALES (est): 90.53K **Privately Held**
Web: www.dilworthcustomframing.com
SIC: 2499 Picture frame molding, finished

(G-2638)
DILWORTH MATTRESS COMPANY INC (PA)
211 W Worthington Ave (28203-4419)
PHONE.................................704 333-6564
Alan Hirsch, *Pr*
Deborah Hirsch, *Sec*
EMP: 4 **EST:** 1931
SQ FT: 15,000
SALES (est): 624.26K
SALES (corp-wide): 624.26K **Privately Held**
Web: www.dilworthmattressfactory.com
SIC: 2515 5712 Mattresses, innerspring or box spring; Mattresses

(G-2639)
DIRECT CHASSISLINK INC (PA)
Also Called: Dcli
3525 Whitehall Park Dr Ste 400 (28273)
PHONE.................................704 594-3800
Bill Shea, *CEO*
Lee Newitt, *Pr*
◆ **EMP:** 25 **EST:** 1974
SQ FT: 147,000
SALES (est): 116.43MM
SALES (corp-wide): 116.43MM **Privately Held**
Web: www.dcli.com
SIC: 3711 Chassis, motor vehicle

(G-2640)
DIRECT DIGITAL LLC (PA)
Also Called: Adaptive Health
615 S College St Ste 1300 (28202-0144)
PHONE.................................704 557-0987
John Kim, *Managing Member*
EMP: 21 **EST:** 2009
SALES (est): 68.47MM **Privately Held**
Web: www.adaptivehealth.com
SIC: 2833 Medicinals and botanicals

(G-2641)
DISCOUNT PRINTING INC
2914 Crosby Rd (28211-2815)
PHONE.................................704 365-3665
Paul Snyder, *Pr*
Connie Snyder, *Sec*
EMP: 5 **EST:** 1983
SQ FT: 2,000
SALES (est): 310.38K **Privately Held**
SIC: 2752 Offset printing

(G-2642)
DISTINCTIVE CABINETS INC
319 Old Hebron Rd Ste A (28273-5709)
PHONE.................................704 529-6243
EMP: 14 **EST:** 1995
SQ FT: 12,500
SALES (est): 550.81K **Privately Held**
Web: www.distinctivecabinets.com

SIC: 1751 2517 2434 Cabinet building and installation; Wood television and radio cabinets; Wood kitchen cabinets

(G-2643)
DISTINCTIVE SOUL CREATIONS LLC
214 Oakton Glen Ct (28262-1756)
PHONE.................................704 299-3269
Tameeka Ford, *Managing Member*
EMP: 5 **EST:** 2020
SALES (est): 150K **Privately Held**
Web: www.dsccatering.com
SIC: 2599 Food wagons, restaurant

(G-2644)
DIVERSFIED PRTG TECHNIQUES INC
Also Called: Franklin Investments
13336 S Ridge Dr (28273-4738)
P.O. Box 411409 (28241-1409)
PHONE.................................704 583-9433
Tony F Chaney Senior, *Pr*
Judy W Chaney, *Sec*
Tony F Chaney Junior, *VP*
▲ **EMP:** 20 **EST:** 1983
SQ FT: 8,694
SALES (est): 4.86MM **Privately Held**
Web: www.diverprint.com
SIC: 5084 3555 Printing trades machinery, equipment, and supplies; Printing trades machinery

(G-2645)
DIVERSIFIED SIGNS & GRAPHICS
Also Called: DIVERSIFIED SIGNS & GRAPHICS INC
5245 Old Dowd Rd (28208-2163)
PHONE.................................704 392-8165
EMP: 9
SALES (corp-wide): 3.32MM **Privately Held**
Web: www.diversified-signs.com
SIC: 3993 Signs and advertising specialties
PA: Diversified Signs & Graphics Inc.
 1123 James Harvey Rd
 York SC 29745
 803 628-1121

(G-2646)
DIXIE ELECTRO MECH SVCS INC
2115 Freedom Dr (28208-5153)
P.O. Box 668944 (28266-8944)
PHONE.................................704 332-1116
Peggy Hunnicutt, *Pr*
Daryl Hunnicutt, *VP*
EMP: 16 **EST:** 1958
SQ FT: 35,000
SALES (est): 2.52MM **Privately Held**
Web: www.dixieemsi.com
SIC: 7694 5063 5999 Electric motor repair; Motors, electric; Motors, electric

(G-2647)
DLM SALES INC
Also Called: Charlotte Tent & Awning Co
5901 N Hill Cir (28213-6237)
PHONE.................................704 399-2776
Travis Jenkins, *CEO*
EMP: 14 **EST:** 1994
SALES (est): 2.32MM **Privately Held**
Web: www.charlottetentandawning.com
SIC: 5999 2394 Awnings; Canvas and related products

(G-2648)
DMA INC
3123 May St (28217-1337)
PHONE.................................704 527-0992
Richard M Shanklin, *Pr*
Edward M Shanklin, *CEO*
Ronald Tucker, *VP*
EMP: 16 **EST:** 1972

SQ FT: 10,900
SALES (est): 384.3K **Privately Held**
Web: www.dmainc.net
SIC: 3599 Machine shop, jobbing and repair

(G-2649)
DMV COMMISSIONERS OFFICE
201 W Arrowood Rd (28217-4054)
PHONE.................................704 679-3914
EMP: 5 **EST:** 2016
SALES (est): 116.14K **Privately Held**
SIC: 3469 Automobile license tags, stamped metal

(G-2650)
DOLE FOOD COMPANY INC (DH)
Also Called: Dole Food
200 S Tyron St Ste 600 (28202-0065)
P.O. Box 5700 (91359-5700)
PHONE.................................818 874-4000
David Murdock, *CEO*
Johan Linden, *
Charlene Mims, * *
Yoon Hugh, *
Jay Esban, *
◆ **EMP:** 26 **EST:** 1851
SALES (est): 1.01B **Privately Held**
Web: www.dole.com
SIC: 5148 2033 0175 0161 Fruits; Fruit juices: fresh; Deciduous tree fruits; Lettuce farm
HQ: Total Produce Limited
 1 Beresford Street
 Dublin D07 T

(G-2651)
DONALD HAACK DIAMONDS INC
Also Called: Donald Hack Diamonds Fine Gems
3900 Colony Rd Ste E (28211-5022)
PHONE.................................704 365-4400
Julie Haack, *Pr*
Janet Haack, *Sec*
EMP: 9 **EST:** 1980
SQ FT: 2,200
SALES (est): 944.27K **Privately Held**
Web: www.donaldhaack.com
SIC: 7631 3911 6411 5944 Jewelry repair services; Jewel settings and mountings, precious metal; Loss prevention services, insurance; Jewelry, precious stones and precious metals

(G-2652)
DOT BLUE READI-MIX LLC
1022 Exchange St (28208-1220)
PHONE.................................704 391-3000
Donnie Presson, *Manager*
EMP: 27
SALES (corp-wide): 45.71MM **Privately Held**
Web: www.bluedotreadimix.com
SIC: 3273 Ready-mixed concrete
PA: Blue Dot Readi-Mix, Llc
 11330 Bain School Rd
 Mint Hill NC 28227
 704 971-7676

(G-2653)
DOT BLUE SERVICES INC
Also Called: Envirnmental Svcs of Charlotte
11819 Reames Rd (28269-7639)
PHONE.................................704 342-2970
James Brannen, *VP*
EMP: 12 **EST:** 1985
SALES (est): 200.86K **Privately Held**
SIC: 3444 Sheet metalwork

(G-2654)
DRIVECO INC
13519 Norlington Ct (28273-6784)
PHONE.................................704 615-2111
Tomeka Lynch-purcel, *CEO*
Tomeka Purcell, *Prin*
EMP: 4 **EST:** 2020
SALES (est): 322.13K **Privately Held**
SIC: 3537 Trucks, tractors, loaders, carriers, and similar equipment

(G-2655)
DRONESCAPE PLLC
9716 Rea Rd Ste B (28277-6790)
PHONE.................................704 953-3798
EMP: 5 **EST:** 2015
SQ FT: 2,000
SALES (est): 481.23K **Privately Held**
Web: www.dronescape.com
SIC: 3728 7389 8711 Target drones; Pipeline and power line inspection service; Engineering services

(G-2656)
DUFF-NORTON COMPANY INC (HQ)
Also Called: Yale Industrial Products, Inc.
9415 Pioneer Ave (28273-6318)
P.O. Box 7010 (28241-7010)
PHONE.................................704 588-0510
David J Wilson, *Pr*
Appal Chintapalli, *VP*
Yan Wei, *Dir Fin*
◆ **EMP:** 4 **EST:** 1983
SALES (est): 53.31MM
SALES (corp-wide): 936.24MM **Publicly Held**
Web: www.cmco.com
SIC: 3569 3625 3536 3593 Jack screws; Actuators, industrial; Hoists; Fluid power cylinders and actuators
PA: Columbus Mckinnon Corporation
 205 Crosspoint Pkwy
 Getzville NY 14068
 716 689-5400

(G-2657)
DUNSTONE COMPANY INC
15050 Choate Cir Ste B (28273-7342)
PHONE.................................704 841-1380
John P Kryder, *Pr*
Keith Puckett, *VP*
EMP: 10 **EST:** 1956
SQ FT: 6,450
SALES (est): 921.23K **Privately Held**
Web: www.shrinktape.com
SIC: 3089 Plastics processing

(G-2658)
DURABLE WOOD PRESERVERS INC
7901 Pence Rd (28215-4325)
P.O. Box 25825 (28229-5825)
PHONE.................................704 537-3113
Beverly E Barksdale Iii, *Pr*
B D Barksdale, *Sec*
EMP: 7 **EST:** 1939
SQ FT: 8,000
SALES (est): 999.46K **Privately Held**
Web: www.durablewood.com
SIC: 2491 5031 Wood preserving; Lumber, plywood, and millwork

(G-2659)
DURAMAX HOLDINGS LLC
Also Called: Otto Environmental Systems
12700 General Dr (28273-6415)
PHONE.................................704 588-9191
Bryan Coll, *Managing Member*
EMP: 215 **EST:** 2021
SALES (est): 17.93MM
SALES (corp-wide): 31.48MM **Privately Held**

Web: www.otto-usa.com
SIC: **4953** 3089 Recycling, waste materials; Garbage containers, plastics
PA: Duramax Solutions Llc
1660 W 2nd St Ste 1100
Cleveland OH 44113
704 588-9191

(G-2660)
DUTCH MILLER CHARLOTTE INC
Also Called: Dutch Miller Auto Group
7725 South Blvd (28273-5941)
PHONE.................................704 522-8422
Chris Miller, *Pr*
Matt Miller, *
Sam Miller, *
EMP: 21 **EST:** 2016
SALES (est): 2.16MM **Privately Held**
Web: www.dutchmillerclt.com
SIC: **5511** 3465 Automobiles, new and used; Body parts, automobile: stamped metal

(G-2661)
DWM INTERNATIONAL INC
Also Called: Society Awards
2151 Hawkins St Ste 1225 (28203-4981)
PHONE.................................646 290-7448
◆ **EMP:** 44 **EST:** 2007
SQ FT: 3,000
SALES (est): 4.71MM **Privately Held**
Web: www.societyawards.com
SIC: **3914** 7336 Trophies, nsk; Art design services

(G-2662)
DYNACAST LLC (DH)
Also Called: Dynacast
11325 N Community House Rd Ste 300 (28277-1978)
PHONE.................................704 927-2790
Simon Newman, *Pr*
Adrian Murphy, *
David J Angell, *
Josef Ungerhofer, *
Sheriff Babu, *
▲ **EMP:** 28 **EST:** 1988
SQ FT: 75,000
SALES (est): 92.29MM **Privately Held**
Web: www.dynacast.com
SIC: **3364** 3363 3089 3365 Nonferrous die-castings except aluminum; Aluminum die-castings; Molding primary plastics; Aluminum foundries
HQ: Dynacast Us Holdings, Inc.
14045 Balntyn Corp Pl
Charlotte NC 28277
704 927-2790

(G-2663)
DYNACAST INTERNATIONAL LLC (DH)
14045 Ballantyne Corporate Pl (28277-0099)
PHONE.................................704 927-2790
EMP: 7 **EST:** 2011
SALES (est): 108.12MM **Privately Held**
Web: www.dynacast.com
SIC: **3369** 3364 3363 White metal castings (lead, tin, antimony), except die; Nonferrous die-castings except aluminum; Aluminum die-castings
HQ: Form Technologies, Inc.
11325 N Cmnity Hse Rd # 300
Charlotte NC 28277
704 927-2790

(G-2664)
DYNACAST US HOLDINGS INC
Dynacast Indus Prdcts-Fsteners
14045 Ballantyne Corporate Pl Ste 300 (28277-0099)
PHONE.................................704 927-2786
Simon Newman, *Brnch Mgr*
EMP: 33
Web: www.dynacast.com
SIC: **3364** Nonferrous die-castings except aluminum
HQ: Dynacast Us Holdings, Inc.
14045 Balntyn Corp Pl
Charlotte NC 28277
704 927-2790

(G-2665)
DYNACAST US HOLDINGS INC (DH)
Also Called: Dynacast
14045 Ballantyne Corporate Pl Ste 400 (28277-0099)
PHONE.................................704 927-2790
Simon Newman, *CEO*
Adrian Murphy, *CFO*
David Angell, *Prin*
Josef Ungerhofer, *Ex VP*
Herv Mallet, *Ex VP*
▲ **EMP:** 9 **EST:** 1999
SALES (est): 92.29MM **Privately Held**
Web: www.dynacast.com
SIC: **3544** Dies and die holders for metal cutting, forming, die casting
HQ: Dynacast International Llc
14045 Balntyn Corp Pl
Charlotte NC 28277

(G-2666)
DYSTAR AMERICAS HOLDING CORP (PA)
9844 Southern Pine Blvd Ste A (28273-5502)
PHONE.................................704 561-3000
EMP: 9 **EST:** 2004
SALES (est): 22.66MM **Privately Held**
SIC: **2865** Dyes: azine, azo, azoic

(G-2667)
DYSTAR CAROLINA CHEMICAL CORP
8309 Wilkinson Blvd (28214-9052)
PHONE.................................704 391-6322
Ron Tedemonte, *CEO*
EMP: 100 **EST:** 2006
SALES (est): 22.66MM **Privately Held**
SIC: **2865** Dyes: azine, azo, azoic
PA: Dystar Americas Holding Corporation
9844 Southern Pine Blvd A
Charlotte NC 28273

(G-2668)
DYSTAR LP (DH)
9844 Southern Pine Blvd Ste A (28273-5503)
PHONE.................................704 561-3000
Ron Pedemonte, *Pr*
Steve Hennen, *CFO*
◆ **EMP:** 25 **EST:** 1995
SQ FT: 40,000
SALES (est): 169.25MM **Privately Held**
Web: www.dystar.com
SIC: **2819** 2869 2865 Industrial inorganic chemicals, nec; Industrial organic chemicals, nec; Cyclic crudes and intermediates
HQ: Dystar Global Holdings (Singapore) Pte. Ltd.
1a International Business Park
Singapore 60993

(G-2669)
E AND J PUBLISHING LLC ✪
3502 Lukes Dr (28216-7665)
PHONE.................................877 882-2138
Latravis E Blanton, *CEO*
EMP: 5 **EST:** 2022
SALES (est): 130.5K **Privately Held**
SIC: **2741** Miscellaneous publishing

(G-2670)
E CACHE & CO LLC
6316 Old Sugar Creek Rd Ste E (28269-7010)
PHONE.................................919 590-0779
EMP: 10 **EST:** 2019
SALES (est): 569.42K **Privately Held**
Web: www.ecacheco.com
SIC: **3999** Hair and hair-based products

(G-2671)
E R W PRINTING
1801 N Tryon St Ste 607 (28206-2781)
PHONE.................................704 201-5642
EMP: 6 **EST:** 2016
SALES (est): 107.29K **Privately Held**
SIC: **2759** Business forms: printing, nsk

(G-2672)
E2M KITCHEN LLC
1907 Gateway Blvd (28208-2748)
PHONE.................................704 985-5903
James Barbee, *Managing Member*
EMP: 49
SALES (est): 2.82MM **Privately Held**
SIC: **2099** Ready-to-eat meals, salads, and sandwiches

(G-2673)
EASTERN PLASTICS COMPANY
10724 Carmel Commons Blvd Ste 580 (28226-0919)
P.O. Box 470115 (28247-0115)
PHONE.................................704 542-7786
Andrew R Ball, *Pr*
Stephen S Ball, *VP*
Joann Ball, *Sec*
▲ **EMP:** 5 **EST:** 1976
SQ FT: 600
SALES (est): 1.3MM **Privately Held**
SIC: **2821** Plastics materials and resins

(G-2674)
EASTERN SUN COMMUNICATIONS INC
4019 Sheridan Dr (28205-5651)
PHONE.................................704 408-7668
Ryan Knick, *Pr*
Michelle Faulkenberry, *Sec*
EMP: 5 **EST:** 2004
SALES (est): 297.87K **Privately Held**
Web: www.easternsuncom.com
SIC: **3651** Audio electronic systems

(G-2675)
EASTONSWEB MULTIMEDIA
4111 Nicole Eileen Ln (28216-6750)
PHONE.................................704 607-0941
EMP: 4 **EST:** 2017
SALES (est): 69.74K **Privately Held**
Web: www.eastonsweb.com
SIC: **2741** Miscellaneous publishing

(G-2676)
EASY LIGHT LLC
715 N Church St (28202-2294)
PHONE.................................972 313-5474
EMP: 8 **EST:** 2012
SALES (est): 349.67K **Privately Held**
SIC: **3841** Surgical and medical instruments

(G-2677)
EASY STONES CORP
1440 Westinghouse Blvd Ste A (28273-6421)
PHONE.................................980 201-9506
Sreekanth Manam, *CEO*
EMP: 5 **EST:** 2018
SALES (est): 993.05K **Privately Held**
Web: www.easystones.com
SIC: **3272** Floor slabs and tiles, precast concrete

(G-2678)
EASYKEYSCOM INC
Also Called: Quickshipkeys
11407 Granite St (28273-6678)
PHONE.................................877 839-5397
Robert Maczka, *CEO*
Greg Martisauski, *Pr*
Cindy Cox, *VP*
EMP: 11 **EST:** 2008
SQ FT: 2,500
SALES (est): 1.94MM **Privately Held**
Web: www.easykeys.com
SIC: **3429** Keys and key blanks

(G-2679)
EATON-SCHULTZ INC
3800 Woodpark Blvd Ste I (28206-4247)
P.O. Box 30874 (28230-0874)
PHONE.................................704 331-8004
Phil Eaton, *Pr*
David Schultz, *VP*
Christopher Price, *Prin*
EMP: 10 **EST:** 1998
SALES (est): 1.26MM **Privately Held**
Web: www.steeltechus.com
SIC: **3446** Architectural metalwork

(G-2680)
EB5 CORPORATION
201 Rampart St (28203-4931)
PHONE.................................503 230-8008
Robert D Heldfond, *Pr*
Robert D Heldfond, *CEO*
Jim Keller, *CFO*
EMP: 7 **EST:** 1980
SQ FT: 5,000
SALES (est): 831.1K **Privately Held**
Web: www.eb5.com
SIC: **2844** 5961 Cosmetic preparations; Cosmetics and perfumes, mail order

(G-2681)
EBHC LLC
Also Called: Bubble
210 E Trade St (28202-2404)
PHONE.................................704 733-9427
Paul Borde, *Mgr*
EMP: 6 **EST:** 2012
SALES (est): 170.43K **Privately Held**
SIC: **2084** 5813 Wines, brandy, and brandy spirits; Cocktail lounge

(G-2682)
ECHO INDUSTRIES INC
11421 Reames Rd (28269-7675)
PHONE.................................704 921-2293
Carl Keller, *CEO*
EMP: 5 **EST:** 2005
SALES (est): 81.05K **Privately Held**
SIC: **3999** Manufacturing industries, nec

(G-2683)
ECOLAB INC
9335 Harris Corners Pkwy Ste 100 (28269)
PHONE.................................704 527-5912
Wayne Landerth, *Brnch Mgr*
EMP: 4
SALES (corp-wide): 15.32B **Publicly Held**
Web: www.ecolab.com
SIC: **2842** Polishes and sanitation goods
PA: Ecolab Inc.
1 Ecolab Pl
Saint Paul MN 55102
800 232-6552

GEOGRAPHIC SECTION — Charlotte - Mecklenburg County

(G-2684)
ECONOMY GRINDING STRAIGHTENING
Also Called: Economy Grinding
432 Springbrook Rd (28217-2145)
P.O. Box 3634 (28117-3634)
PHONE..................704 400-2500
David Rembowski, *Pr*
Marc Stankovich, *VP*
EMP: 23 **EST:** 1987
SQ FT: 30,000
SALES (est): 459.58K Privately Held
Web: www.economygrinding.com
SIC: 3599 Machine shop, jobbing and repair

(G-2685)
ECOVEHICLE ENTERPRISES INC
15022 Bllntyne Cntry Clb (28277-2719)
PHONE..................704 544-9907
John Dabels, *Pr*
EMP: 6 **EST:** 2004
SALES (est): 376.38K Privately Held
SIC: 3715 3711 Truck trailer chassis; Motor vehicles and car bodies

(G-2686)
EFCO USA INC
11600 Goodrich Dr (28273-6510)
P.O. Box 38839 (28278-1014)
PHONE..................800 332-6872
Thomas Wiget, *CEO*
▲ **EMP:** 6 **EST:** 2009
SALES (est): 971.24K Privately Held
Web: www.efcousa.com
SIC: 3546 3549 3541 3829 Power-driven handtools; Metalworking machinery, nec; Flange facing machines; Physical property testing equipment

(G-2687)
EGI ASSOCIATES INC
417 Minuet Ln Ste A (28217-2702)
P.O. Box 240993 (28224-0993)
PHONE..................704 561-3337
EMP: 13 **EST:** 2007
SALES (est): 1.42MM Privately Held
Web: www.teamlighting.com
SIC: 3645 5063 Residential lighting fixtures; Lighting fixtures

(G-2688)
EKOS BREWMASTER LLC
800 W Hill St Ste 101 (28208-5361)
PHONE..................704 973-5640
EMP: 8 **EST:** 2016
SALES (est): 234.44K Privately Held
Web: www.goekos.com
SIC: 2082 Malt beverages

(G-2689)
ELAN TRADING INC
Also Called: Southern Resources
3826 Raleigh St (28206-2043)
P.O. Box 3247 (28106-3247)
PHONE..................704 342-1696
Mark Clackum, *CEO*
Samuel Waldman, *
Elisa Clackum, *
◆ **EMP:** 28 **EST:** 1992
SQ FT: 40,000
SALES (est): 6.04MM Privately Held
Web: www.southernresources.com
SIC: 5093 4953 3341 Ferrous metal scrap and waste; Recycling, waste materials; Secondary nonferrous metals

(G-2690)
ELECTRONIC IMAGING SVCS INC
Also Called: Vestcom Retail Solutions
1500 Continental Blvd (28273-6376)
PHONE..................704 587-3323
Claudia Wallace, *Mgr*
EMP: 11
SALES (corp-wide): 8.36B Publicly Held
SIC: 8742 2759 Marketing consulting services; Commercial printing, nec
HQ: Electronic Imaging Services, Inc.
2800 Cantrell Rd Ste 400
Little Rock AR 72202
501 663-0100

(G-2691)
ELEMENT DESIGNS INC
Also Called: Element Designs
235 Crompton St (28273-6204)
P.O. Box 10 (29716-0010)
PHONE..................704 332-3114
Heinz Uerbersax, *Pr*
Nelson Wills, *
R N Wills Junior, *VP*
Kevin Creedon, *
Beata Klecha, *
▲ **EMP:** 58 **EST:** 2002
SQ FT: 65,000
SALES (est): 10.91MM Privately Held
Web: www.element-designs.com
SIC: 2521 Cabinets, office: wood

(G-2692)
ELEMENTS BRANDS LLC
Also Called: Elements Brands
1515 Mockingbird Ln (28209-3236)
PHONE..................503 230-8008
William Dalessandero, *CEO*
EMP: 10
SALES (corp-wide): 5.47MM Privately Held
Web: www.elementsbrands.com
SIC: 2819 Industrial inorganic chemicals, nec
PA: Elements Brands, Llc
2202 Hawkins St
Charlotte NC 28203
704 661-2244

(G-2693)
ELEVATE TEXTILES INC (HQ)
121 W Trade St Ste 1700 (28202-1154)
P.O. Box 26540 (27415-6540)
PHONE..................336 379-6220
Per-olof Loof, *Pr*
Gail A Kuczkowski, *Ex VP*
Neil W Koonce, *VP*
Craig J Hart, *VP*
Robert E Garren, *Chief Human Resources Officer*
◆ **EMP:** 10 **EST:** 1994
SALES (est): 1.61B
SALES (corp-wide): 1.98B Privately Held
Web: www.elevatetextiles.com
SIC: 2211 2231 2221 2273 Denims; Worsted fabrics, broadwoven; Polyester broadwoven fabrics; Carpets and rugs
PA: Elevate Textiles Holding Corporation
121 W Trade St Ste 1700
Charlotte NC 28202
336 379-6220

(G-2694)
ELEVATE TEXTILES HOLDING CORP (PA)
121 W Trade St Ste 1700 (28202-1154)
PHONE..................336 379-6220
Per-olof Loof, *Pr*
EMP: 61 **EST:** 2016
SALES (est): 1.98B
SALES (corp-wide): 1.98B Privately Held
SIC: 2211 2231 2221 2273 Denims; Worsted fabrics, broadwoven; Polyester broadwoven fabrics; Carpets and rugs

(G-2695)
ELGI COMPRESSORS USA INC (HQ)
4610 Entrance Dr Ste A (28273-4389)
PHONE..................704 943-7966
Jairam Varadaraj, *Pr*
John Patton, *
▲ **EMP:** 8 **EST:** 2012
SALES (est): 57.88MM Privately Held
Web: www.elgi.com
SIC: 3563 Air and gas compressors including vacuum pumps
PA: Elgi Equipments Limited
Elgi Industrial Complex Iii,
Coimbatore TN 64100

(G-2696)
ELITE FORESTRY SOLUTIONS LLC
9805 Statesville Rd Ste 6058 (28269)
PHONE..................757 777-2729
EMP: 4 **EST:** 2018
SALES (est): 222.25K Privately Held
SIC: 3537 Trucks, tractors, loaders, carriers, and similar equipment

(G-2697)
ELLA B CANDLES LLC
9517 Monroe Rd Ste C (28270-1489)
PHONE..................980 339-8898
Christopher Tassy, *Prin*
Julie Tassy, *Prin*
EMP: 22 **EST:** 2016
SALES (est): 1.38MM Privately Held
Web: www.ellabcandles.com
SIC: 3999 Candles

(G-2698)
ELLISON COMPANY INC
Specialty Mfg
13501 S Ridge Dr (28273-6741)
P.O. Box 240122 (28224-0122)
PHONE..................704 889-7518
John Peace, *VP Sls*
EMP: 120
SALES (corp-wide): 8.74MM Privately Held
SIC: 3199 Safety belts, leather
PA: The Ellison Company Inc
706 Green Valley Rd # 504
Greensboro NC 27408
336 275-8565

(G-2699)
ELLISON TECHNOLOGIES INC
9724 Southern Pine Blvd (28273-5539)
PHONE..................704 545-7362
Robert Johnson, *Mgr*
EMP: 60
Web: www.ellisontechnologies.com
SIC: 3451 5084 Screw machine products; Metalworking machinery
HQ: Ellison Technologies, Inc.
9828 Arlee Ave
Santa Fe Springs CA 90670
562 949-8311

(G-2700)
ELSTER AMERICAN METER COMPANY LLC (HQ)
855 S Mint St (28202-1517)
PHONE..................402 873-8200
◆ **EMP:** 15 **EST:** 1836
SALES (est): 198.19MM
SALES (corp-wide): 36.66B Publicly Held
Web: automation.honeywell.com
SIC: 3824 3613 Gasmeters, domestic and large capacity: industrial; Regulators, power
PA: Honeywell International Inc.
855 S Mint St
Charlotte NC 28202
704 627-6200

(G-2701)
ELXSI CORPORATION
6325 Ardrey Kell Rd Ste 400 (28277-4966)
PHONE..................407 849-1090
Alexander Milley, *Pr*
Farrokh K Kavarana, *
Denis M O'donnell, *Dir*
EMP: 317 **EST:** 1986
SALES (est): 117.15MM
SALES (corp-wide): 1.74B Publicly Held
SIC: 5812 3569 5046 Restaurant, family: chain; Filters and strainers, pipeline; Restaurant equipment and supplies, nec
HQ: Canvas Sx, Llc
6325 Ardrey Kell Rd Ste 4
Charlotte NC 28277
980 474-3700

(G-2702)
ELY TORTILLERIA LLC
6301 N Tryon St Ste 112 (28213-8069)
PHONE..................704 886-8501
Erasmo A Valenzuela, *Owner*
EMP: 6 **EST:** 2013
SALES (est): 211.46K Privately Held
SIC: 2099 Tortillas, fresh or refrigerated

(G-2703)
EMAGE MEDICAL LLC
15720 Brixham Hill Ave Ste 300 (28277-4651)
PHONE..................704 904-1873
Lonnie Roy Wallace, *Managing Member*
EMP: 5 **EST:** 2008
SALES (est): 2.5MM Privately Held
Web: www.emagemedical.com
SIC: 2844 Cosmetic preparations

(G-2704)
EMBROID IT
16324 York Rd (28278-5824)
PHONE..................704 617-0357
EMP: 5 **EST:** 2015
SALES (est): 44.49K Privately Held
Web: www.embroidit.net
SIC: 2395 Embroidery and art needlework

(G-2705)
EMC CORPORATION
10815 David Taylor Dr Ste 200 (28262-1047)
PHONE..................720 341-3274
Steven Elliott, *Mgr*
EMP: 7
Web: www.emc.com
SIC: 3572 7372 5045 Computer storage devices; Prepackaged software; Computers, peripherals, and software
HQ: Emc Corporation
176 South St
Hopkinton MA 01748
508 435-1000

(G-2706)
EMERALD CAROLINA CHEMICAL LLC
8309 Wilkinson Blvd (28214-9052)
PHONE..................704 393-0089
Sean Stack, *
EMP: 54 **EST:** 2001
SALES (est): 5.54MM Privately Held
SIC: 2899 Chemical preparations, nec
HQ: Dystar L.P.
9844 Southern Pine Blvd A
Charlotte NC 28273

(G-2707)
EMERGENT TECH SOLUTIONS INC
17004 Turtle Point Rd (28278-8429)
PHONE..................704 777-1909

(PA)=Parent Co (HQ)=Headquarters
✿ = New Business established in last 2 years

Charlotte - Mecklenburg County (G-2708)

GEOGRAPHIC SECTION

Shannon Slowik, *Pr*
EMP: 4 **EST:** 2021
SALES (est): 253.91K **Privately Held**
Web: www.emergentit.tech
SIC: 3572 Computer storage devices

(G-2708)
EMERSON PROCESS MANAGEMENT
6135 Lakeview Rd (28269-2615)
PHONE.................704 357-0294
Thomas Smith, *Brnch Mgr*
EMP: 15
SALES (corp-wide): 15.16B **Publicly Held**
Web: www.emerson.com
SIC: 3823 Process control instruments
HQ: Emerson Process Management Power & Water Solutions, Inc.
200 Beta Dr
Pittsburgh PA 15238
412 963-4000

(G-2709)
EMPIRE CARPET & BLINDS INC
10500 Mcmullen Creek Pkwy (28226-1632)
PHONE.................704 541-3988
EMP: 10 **EST:** 1996
SALES (est): 287.01K **Privately Held**
Web: www.empirecarpetandblinds.com
SIC: 2591 Window blinds

(G-2710)
END CAMP NORTH
300 Camp Rd (28206-4005)
PHONE.................980 337-4600
EMP: 8 **EST:** 2017
SALES (est): 193.87K **Privately Held**
Web: www.camp.nc
SIC: 3761 Guided missiles and space vehicles

(G-2711)
ENDGRAIN WOODWORKS LLC
301 Queens Rd Apt 302 (28204-3288)
PHONE.................980 237-2612
EMP: 4 **EST:** 2018
SALES (est): 74.98K **Privately Held**
SIC: 2431 Millwork

(G-2712)
ENGINEERED RECYCLING COMPANY LLC
Also Called: ERC
1011 Woodward Ave 1101 (28206-2461)
P.O. Box 790973 (28206-7915)
PHONE.................704 358-6700
▲ **EMP:** 35
SIC: 2295 Resin or plastic coated fabrics

(G-2713)
ENPRO INDUSTRIES INC (PA)
Also Called: Enpro
5605 Carnegie Blvd Ste 500 (28209-4674)
PHONE.................704 731-1500
Eric A Vaillancourt, *Pr*
David L Hauser, *
J Milton Childress Ii, *Ex VP*
Robert S Mclean, *Ex VP*
Steven R Bower, *CAO*
◆ **EMP:** 217 **EST:** 2002
SALES (est): 1.06B
SALES (corp-wide): 1.06B **Publicly Held**
Web: www.enproindustries.com
SIC: 3053 3519 3089 Gaskets and sealing devices; Engines, diesel and semi-diesel or dual-fuel; Bearings, plastics

(G-2714)
ENRG BRAND LLC
125 Remount Rd Ste C12168 (28203-6458)
PHONE.................980 298-8519
EMP: 5 **EST:** 2021
SALES (est): 90K **Privately Held**
SIC: 1389 Construction, repair, and dismantling services

(G-2715)
ENRICHED ABUNDANCE ENTP LLC
15316 Trickling Water Ct (28273)
PHONE.................704 369-6363
EMP: 10 **EST:** 2021
SALES (est): 450.69K **Privately Held**
SIC: 2621 Book paper

(G-2716)
ENTROPY SOLAR INTEGRATORS LLC
13950 Ballantyne (28277)
PHONE.................704 936-5018
Erik Lensch, *CEO*
EMP: 7 **EST:** 2014
SALES (est): 62.22K **Privately Held**
SIC: 1711 3433 3674 8711 Solar energy contractor; Solar heaters and collectors; Solar cells; Engineering services

(G-2717)
ENVIRNMENTAL WIN SOLUTIONS LLC
Also Called: Climate Seal
1401 Morningside Dr (28205-5328)
PHONE.................704 200-2001
EMP: 4 **EST:** 2008
SALES (est): 246.34K **Privately Held**
Web: www.climateseal.com
SIC: 3442 Storm doors or windows, metal

(G-2718)
ENVIRNMNTAL SYSTEMS RES INST I
Also Called: Esri
3325 Springbank Ln Ste 200 (28226-3365)
PHONE.................704 541-9810
Christian Carlson, *Prin*
EMP: 38
SALES (corp-wide): 490.13MM **Privately Held**
Web: www.esri.com
SIC: 5045 7372 Computer software; Prepackaged software
PA: Environmental Systems Research Institute, Inc.
380 New York St
Redlands CA 92373
909 793-2853

(G-2719)
ENVIROTEK WORLDWIDE LLC
Also Called: Sterimed
2701 Hutchison Mcdonald Rd Ste A (28269-4276)
PHONE.................704 285-6400
Richard Admani, *CEO*
EMP: 10 **EST:** 2015
SALES (est): 551.42K **Privately Held**
SIC: 3559 Chemical machinery and equipment

(G-2720)
EP NISBET COMPANY
1818 Baxter St (28204-3118)
P.O. Box 35367 (28235-5367)
PHONE.................704 332-7755
Heather Stroupe, *Prin*
EMP: 11 **EST:** 2003
SALES (est): 614.44K **Privately Held**
Web: www.nisbetoil.com
SIC: 1382 Oil and gas exploration services

(G-2721)
EPI CENTRE SUNDRIES
210 E Trade St (28202-2404)
PHONE.................704 650-9575
Keum Kim, *Prin*
EMP: 8 **EST:** 2008
SALES (est): 462.77K **Privately Held**
Web: www.epicentrenc.com
SIC: 3931 Musical instruments

(G-2722)
EPIC APPAREL
8118 Statesville Rd (28269-3829)
PHONE.................980 335-0463
Christopher Pham, *Prin*
EMP: 7 **EST:** 2013
SALES (est): 97.68K **Privately Held**
Web: www.4brandedproducts.com
SIC: 2759 Screen printing

(G-2723)
EPV CORPORATION
11435 Granite St Ste M (28273-6446)
PHONE.................704 494-7800
Damian Attwood, *Brnch Mgr*
EMP: 5
SALES (corp-wide): 2.61MM **Privately Held**
SIC: 3711 3713 Motor buses, except trackless trollies, assembly of; Truck and bus bodies
PA: Epv Corporation
2309 Nevada Blvd
Charlotte NC 28273
704 494-7800

(G-2724)
EPV CORPORATION (PA)
2309 Nevada Blvd (28273-6430)
PHONE.................704 494-7800
Tony Luo, *Pr*
Marla Teague, *VP*
Joshua Anderson, *VP*
Ruowen Chen, *Prin*
EMP: 46 **EST:** 2014
SQ FT: 100,000
SALES (est): 2.61MM
SALES (corp-wide): 2.61MM **Privately Held**
SIC: 3711 3713 Motor buses, except trackless trollies, assembly of; Truck and bus bodies

(G-2725)
EQUINOM ENTERPRISES LLC
16310 Magnolia Woods Ln (28277-3400)
PHONE.................704 817-8489
EMP: 5 **EST:** 2019
SALES (est): 30.77K **Privately Held**
Web: www.equi-nom.com
SIC: 2099 Food preparations, nec

(G-2726)
ERDLE PERFORATING HOLDINGS INC
Erdle Perforating Carolina Div
1100 Culp Rd # A (28241)
P.O. Box 411292 (28241-1292)
PHONE.................704 588-4380
Lou Ely, *Prin*
EMP: 15
SALES (corp-wide): 1.38B **Publicly Held**
Web: www.erdle.com
SIC: 3469 3569 3444 3498 Perforated metal, stamped; Filters, general line: industrial; Sheet metalwork; Fabricated pipe and fittings
HQ: Erdle Perforating Holdings, Inc.
100 Pixley Indus Pkwy
Rochester NY 14624
585 247-4700

(G-2727)
ERICO
9305 Whitethorn Dr (28277-9048)
PHONE.................704 846-5743
Andy Nobles, *Prs Mgr*
EMP: 4 **EST:** 2018
SALES (est): 67.07K **Privately Held**
Web: www.nvent.com
SIC: 3644 Noncurrent-carrying wiring devices

(G-2728)
ESSENCE NOIRE LLC
6840 Carradale Way (28278-7767)
PHONE.................704 351-8322
Tiffanie Moreland-travis, *Owner*
EMP: 4 **EST:** 2018
SALES (est): 55.32K **Privately Held**
SIC: 3999 Candles

(G-2729)
ESSENTIAL SOAP CO
4100 Barmettler Dr (28211-1444)
PHONE.................704 737-2385
Phyllis Rollins, *Prin*
EMP: 4 **EST:** 2016
SALES (est): 69.15K **Privately Held**
Web: www.essentialsoapcompany.com
SIC: 2841 Soap and other detergents

(G-2730)
ESSEX GROUP INC
3300 Woodpark Blvd (28206-4213)
PHONE.................704 921-9605
EMP: 5
SALES (corp-wide): 70.43MM **Privately Held**
SIC: 3357 3644 3496 3351 Building wire and cable, nonferrous; Insulators and insulation materials, electrical; Miscellaneous fabricated wire products; Copper rolling and drawing
HQ: Essex Group, Inc.
1601 Wall St
Fort Wayne IN 30327
260 461-4000

(G-2731)
ESTA EXTRACTION USA LP
301 Mccullough Dr Ste 400 (28262-1336)
PHONE.................704 942-8844
EMP: 5 **EST:** 2017
SALES (est): 183.55K **Privately Held**
Web: www.esta.com
SIC: 3714 Motor vehicle parts and accessories

(G-2732)
ETIMEX USA INC
9405 D Ducks Ln Ste A (28273-4513)
PHONE.................704 583-0002
Marc Vogt, *Pr*
H Ross, *
▲ **EMP:** 53 **EST:** 1997
SQ FT: 38,000
SALES (est): 14.22MM
SALES (corp-wide): 81.01K **Privately Held**
Web: www.etimex.global
SIC: 3089 Injection molding of plastics
HQ: Etimex Technical Components Gmbh
Ehinger Str. 30
Rottenacker BW 89616
7393520

(G-2733)
EUCLID INNOVATIONS INC (PA)
101 S Tryon St Ste 2410 (28280-0006)
PHONE.................877 382-5431
Satyavani Rayankula, *Pr*
Suresh Karusala, *VP*
EMP: 16 **EST:** 2009

▲ = Import ▼ = Export
◆ = Import/Export

GEOGRAPHIC SECTION
Charlotte - Mecklenburg County (G-2758)

SALES (est): 3.58MM
SALES (corp-wide): 3.58MM **Privately Held**
Web: www.euclidinnovations.com
SIC: 7372 Business oriented computer software

(G-2734)
EV FLEET INC
11701 Mount Holly Rd Bldg 32 (28214-9229)
PHONE 704 425-6272
EMP: 7 **EST:** 2014
SQ FT: 3,600
SALES (est): 116.81K **Privately Held**
Web: www.brooksagnew.blog
SIC: 3711 Cars, electric, assembly of

(G-2735)
EVOLUTION OF STYLE LLC
2901 N Davidson St Unit 170 (28205-1078)
PHONE 914 329-3078
EMP: 4 **EST:** 2017
SALES (est): 80.32K **Privately Held**
SIC: 7389 2329 Design services; Athletic clothing, except uniforms: men's, youths' and boys'

(G-2736)
EW2 ENVIRONMENTAL INC (PA)
7245 Pineville Matthews Rd Ste 100 (28226-6164)
P.O. Box 470503 (28247-0503)
PHONE 704 542-2444
Lewis D Eckley, *Pr*
Gail Kellar, *Sec*
EMP: 6 **EST:** 1991
SQ FT: 2,000
SALES (est): 888.77K **Privately Held**
Web: www.ew2.net
SIC: 3589 Water treatment equipment, industrial

(G-2737)
EXIDE
3308 Oak Lake Blvd Ste A (28208-7701)
PHONE 704 357-9845
EMP: 5 **EST:** 2011
SALES (est): 434.92K **Privately Held**
Web: www.exide.com
SIC: 3691 Storage batteries

(G-2738)
EXIDE TECHNOLOGIES LLC
Also Called: Exide Battery
648 Griffith Rd Ste G (28217-3573)
PHONE 704 521-8016
EMP: 5
SALES (corp-wide): 2.06B **Privately Held**
Web: www.exide.com
SIC: 5063 3629 Electrical apparatus and equipment; Battery chargers, rectifying or nonrotating
PA: Exide Technologies, Llc
   13000 Drfeld Pkwy Bldg 20
   Milton GA 30004
   678 566-9000

(G-2739)
EXPRESS WIRE SERVICES INC
2947 Interstate St (28208-3607)
PHONE 704 393-5156
Nick Huzzlla, *Pr*
Scott Ramsey, *VP*
Wayne Searcy, *VP*
EMP: 4 **EST:** 2000
SQ FT: 14,000
SALES (est): 1.07MM **Privately Held**
Web: www.expresswireservices.com
SIC: 3496 Miscellaneous fabricated wire products

(G-2740)
EYE DIALOGUE
412 N Crigler St (28216-3914)
PHONE 704 567-7789
Jack Kelly, *Prin*
EMP: 10 **EST:** 2010
SALES (est): 842.74K **Privately Held**
Web: www.eyedialogue.com
SIC: 3648 Stage lighting equipment

(G-2741)
F & C REPAIR AND SALES LLC
Also Called: A Foodtruckqueen
4720 Brookshire Blvd (28216-3818)
PHONE 704 907-2461
Charlene Steele, *Managing Member*
EMP: 12 **EST:** 2017
SALES (est): 611.84K **Privately Held**
SIC: 7538 3715 General automotive repair shops; Truck trailers

(G-2742)
FABRICATION ASSOCIATES INC
7950 Pence Rd (28215-4326)
P.O. Box 25326 (28229-5326)
PHONE 704 535-8050
EMP: 52 **EST:** 1996
SALES (est): 8.95MM **Privately Held**
Web: www.fai6.com
SIC: 3443 7692 3444 3441 Fabricated plate work (boiler shop); Welding repair; Sheet metalwork; Fabricated structural metal

(G-2743)
FABRIX INC
231 Foster Ave Ste A (28203-5462)
P.O. Box 33686 (28233-3686)
PHONE 704 953-1239
Scott Donovan, *Pr*
EMP: 4 **EST:** 2002
SQ FT: 5,850
SALES (est): 251.91K **Privately Held**
Web: www.fabrixdigital.com
SIC: 2759 Commercial printing, nec

(G-2744)
FAGUS GRECON INC
648 Griffith Rd Ste A (28217-3573)
PHONE 503 641-7731
Eric Peterson, *CEO*
EMP: 15 **EST:** 2017
SALES (est): 5.5MM **Privately Held**
Web: www.fagus-grecon.com
SIC: 3569 Firefighting and related equipment

(G-2745)
FAIRFAX DIGITAL LLC
7804 Fairview Rd (28226-4998)
PHONE 407 822-2918
EMP: 10 **EST:** 2015
SALES (est): 643.79K **Privately Held**
SIC: 2711 Newspapers, publishing and printing

(G-2746)
FAIRFIELD PRO AV INC
Also Called: Carolina Event Labor
17540 Westmill Ln (28277-3531)
PHONE 214 375-8570
EMP: 4 **EST:** 2020
SALES (est): 130.56K **Privately Held**
Web: www.fairfieldproav.com
SIC: 3651 Household audio and video equipment

(G-2747)
FAR FROM A MAID LLC
9716 Rea Rd Ste B (28277-6789)
PHONE 803 610-1727
Shainequa Franklin, *Managing Member*
EMP: 5
SALES (est): 79.3K **Privately Held**
SIC: 3471 Cleaning, polishing, and finishing

(G-2748)
FARRIS BELT & SAW COMPANY
235 Foster Ave (28203-5421)
PHONE 704 527-6166
Bill Garris, *Pr*
▲ **EMP:** 13 **EST:** 1942
SQ FT: 14,000
SALES (est): 1.65MM **Privately Held**
Web: www.farrisbelt.com
SIC: 3291 3553 Abrasive products; Bandsaws, woodworking

(G-2749)
FASTLIFE TRANSPORT LLC (PA)
7710 Holliswood Ct (28217-3098)
PHONE 484 350-6754
EMP: 5 **EST:** 2018
SALES (est): 502.6K
SALES (corp-wide): 502.6K **Privately Held**
SIC: 3537 Trucks, tractors, loaders, carriers, and similar equipment

(G-2750)
FE26 LLC
3150 Rozzelles Ferry Rd (28205)
P.O. Box 2316 (28053-2316)
PHONE 980 875-0170
Tuan Le, *Managing Member*
EMP: 6 **EST:** 2013
SQ FT: 2,200
SALES (est): 191.68K **Privately Held**
SIC: 3441 7389 Fabricated structural metal; Design, commercial and industrial

(G-2751)
FEREBEE CORPORATION (HQ)
Also Called: Ferebee Asphalt
10045 Metromont Industrial Blvd (28269-7611)
P.O. Box 480066 (28269-5300)
PHONE 704 509-2586
James Ferebee, *Pr*
James C Ferebee, *
Joseph B Ferebee, *
David Ferebee, *
Tiffany Ferebee, *
EMP: 117 **EST:** 1985
SQ FT: 13,000
SALES (est): 58.19MM
SALES (corp-wide): 1.56B **Publicly Held**
Web: www.ferebee.com
SIC: 1611 1623 1771 3531 General contractor, highway and street construction; Water, sewer, and utility lines; Blacktop (asphalt) work; Asphalt plant, including gravel-mix type
PA: Construction Partners, Inc.
   290 Healthwest Dr Ste 2
   Dothan AL 36303
   334 673-9763

(G-2752)
FERGUSON & COMPANY LLC
201 S Tryon St (28202-3212)
PHONE 704 332-4396
Ian Ferguson, *Prin*
EMP: 8 **EST:** 2010
SALES (est): 131.17K **Privately Held**
Web: www.fergusonbox.com
SIC: 2653 Boxes, corrugated: made from purchased materials

(G-2753)
FERGUSON BOX
10820 Quality Dr (28278-7702)
PHONE 704 597-0310
Pat Garvey, *Pr*
EMP: 41 **EST:** 2017
SALES (est): 5.08MM **Privately Held**
Web: www.fergusonbox.com
SIC: 2653 Boxes, corrugated: made from purchased materials

(G-2754)
FERGUSON SUPPLY AND BOX MFG CO (PA)
10820 Quality Dr (28278-7702)
PHONE 704 597-0310
Paige F Burgess, *Pr*
Charles L Ferguson Junior, *Ex VP*
Chip Ferguson, *
Janice Rappleyea, *
EMP: 85 **EST:** 1959
SQ FT: 60,000
SALES (est): 19.75MM
SALES (corp-wide): 19.75MM **Privately Held**
Web: www.fergusonbox.com
SIC: 2653 5113 Boxes, corrugated: made from purchased materials; Corrugated and solid fiber boxes

(G-2755)
FFI HOLDINGS III CORP (PA)
Also Called: Flow Control Group
3915 Shopton Rd (28217-3047)
PHONE 800 690-3650
David Patterson, *CEO*
Hans Van Der Meulen, *CFO*
EMP: 25 **EST:** 2015
SALES (est): 496.49MM
SALES (corp-wide): 496.49MM **Privately Held**
Web: www.flowcontrolgroup.com
SIC: 3564 3569 5075 5074 Air purification equipment; Filters; Air filters; Water purification equipment

(G-2756)
FG GROUP HOLDINGS INC (PA)
5960 Fairview Rd Ste 275 (28210-3102)
PHONE 704 994-8279
Mark D Roberson, *CEO*
D Kyle Cerminara, *
Todd R Major, *CFO*
▲ **EMP:** 48 **EST:** 1932
SALES (est): 41.24MM
SALES (corp-wide): 41.24MM **Privately Held**
Web: www.fundamentalglobal.com
SIC: 3861 3648 Motion picture apparatus and equipment; Stage lighting equipment

(G-2757)
FIBER TRANSPORT SYSTEMS INC
13000 S Tryon St Ste F-121 (28278-7652)
PHONE 704 905-3549
Ike Mowry, *Pr*
EMP: 4 **EST:** 2018
SALES (est): 39.69K **Privately Held**
SIC: 3999 Manufacturing industries, nec

(G-2758)
FIBRIX LLC
Also Called: Cumulus Fibres - Charlotte
1101 Tar Heel Rd (28208-1524)
PHONE 704 394-2111
Garry Furr, *Brnch Mgr*
EMP: 22
SALES (corp-wide): 47.37MM **Privately Held**
Web: www.fibrix.com
SIC: 2299 2297 Batting, wadding, padding and fillings; Nonwoven fabrics
HQ: Fibrix, Llc
   1820 Evans St Ne
   Conover NC 28613

Charlotte - Mecklenburg County (G-2759)   GEOGRAPHIC SECTION

(G-2759)
FICS AMERICA INC
2815 Coliseum Centre Dr Ste 300
(28217-1452)
PHONE.....................704 329-7391
EMP: 53 **EST:** 1996
SALES (est): 453.03K **Publicly Held**
SIC: 7372 7371 Prepackaged software; Custom computer programming services
HQ: S1 Corporation
    705 Westech Dr
    Norcross GA 30092
    678 966-9499

(G-2760)
FIELDS INDUSTRIES LLC
14624 Provence Ln (28277-2690)
PHONE.....................704 264-3872
David Fields, *Prin*
EMP: 4 **EST:** 2017
SALES (est): 56.68K **Privately Held**
SIC: 3999 Manufacturing industries, nec

(G-2761)
FILTER SRVCNG OF CHRLTTE 135
6608 Woodmont Pl (28211-5647)
PHONE.....................704 619-3768
Steven D Akins, *Admn*
EMP: 6 **EST:** 2014
SALES (est): 369.87K **Privately Held**
SIC: 1389 Roustabout service

(G-2762)
FINISHING PARTNERS INC
1301 Westinghouse Blvd Ste E
(28273-6475)
P.O. Box 410347 (28241-0347)
PHONE.....................704 583-7322
▲ **EMP:** 5 **EST:** 1998
SALES (est): 431.68K **Privately Held**
Web: www.finishingpartners.com
SIC: 2231 Fabric finishing: wool, mohair, or similar fibers

(G-2763)
FIRM ASCEND LLC
Also Called: Truventure Logistics
224 Westinghouse Blvd Ste 602
(28273-6228)
PHONE.....................704 464-3024
Bianca Payne, *Managing Member*
EMP: 5 **EST:** 2018
SALES (est): 229K **Privately Held**
SIC: 4213 7389 2621 Trucking, except local; Notary publics; Printing paper

(G-2764)
FIRST ALANCE LOGISTICS MGT LLC
14120 Ballantyne Corporate Pl
(28277-2858)
PHONE.....................704 522-0233
Glenn Merritt, *Pt*
Glenn Merritt, *CEO*
EMP: 10 **EST:** 1995
SALES (est): 2.72MM **Privately Held**
Web: www.falm.com
SIC: 2448 Pallets, wood

(G-2765)
FIRST IMPRESSIONS LTD
8500 Monroe Rd (28212-7514)
PHONE.....................704 536-3622
Treva Mason, *Pr*
Keith Mason, *Sec*
EMP: 15 **EST:** 1981
SQ FT: 11,500
SALES (est): 1.93MM **Privately Held**
Web: www.firstimpressionsltd.com
SIC: 2759 Screen printing

(G-2766)
FIRST NOODLE CO INC
333 Oakdale Rd (28216-2959)
PHONE.....................704 393-3238
Ying Yu Kan, *Pr*
Derren L Kan, *Treas*
Dennis V Leong, *Sec*
▲ **EMP:** 9 **EST:** 1988
SQ FT: 10,000
SALES (est): 441.26K **Privately Held**
Web: www.firstnoodleco.com
SIC: 2098 Noodles (e.g. egg, plain, and water), dry

(G-2767)
FIRSTSOURCE DISTRIBUTORS LLC
710 Peninsula Ln Ste E (28273-5981)
P.O. Box 242694 (28224-2694)
PHONE.....................704 553-8510
EMP: 5 **EST:** 2005
SALES (est): 251.2K **Privately Held**
Web: www.periscopedashboard.com
SIC: 3585 Heating and air conditioning combination units

(G-2768)
FLA ORTHOPEDICS INC (DH)
5825 Carnegie Blvd (28209-4633)
PHONE.....................800 327-4110
Rex Niles, *Pr*
George Blews, *
Carl Partridge, *
Rhonda Newman, *
EMP: 100 **EST:** 1975
SALES (est): 52.29MM
SALES (corp-wide): 14.89B **Privately Held**
SIC: 3842 5047 Supports: abdominal, ankle, arch, kneecap, etc.; Medical and hospital equipment
HQ: Bsn Medical, Inc.
    5825 Carnegie Blvd
    Charlotte NC 28209
    704 554-9533

(G-2769)
FLASH PRINTING COMPANY INC
Also Called: Metrographics Printing
1003 Louise Ave Ste A (28205-2726)
P.O. Box 18427 (28218-0427)
PHONE.....................704 375-2474
Jason Almes, *Pr*
Dana Almes, *VP*
EMP: 22 **EST:** 1970
SQ FT: 18,000
SALES (est): 5.37MM **Privately Held**
Web: www.metrographicsprinters.com
SIC: 2752 2791 2789 Offset printing; Typesetting; Bookbinding and related work

(G-2770)
FLASH TECHNOLOGY LLC ◊
6325 Ardrey Kell Rd Ste 400 (28277-4966)
PHONE.....................980 474-3700
EMP: 10 **EST:** 2022
SALES (est): 3.7MM
SALES (corp-wide): 1.74B **Publicly Held**
Web: www.flashtechnology.com
SIC: 3569 General industrial machinery, nec
HQ: Canvas Sx, Llc
    6325 Ardrey Kell Rd Ste 4
    Charlotte NC 28277
    980 474-3700

(G-2771)
FLAT WATER CORP
800 Clanton Rd Ste R (28217-1373)
PHONE.....................704 584-7764
Jason Otte, *Pr*
EMP: 4
SALES (est): 240.78K **Privately Held**

SIC: 3669 Visual communication systems

(G-2772)
FLAVOR SEED LLC
1419 Cavendish Ct (28211-3939)
PHONE.....................704 401-9319
EMP: 8 **EST:** 2017
SALES (est): 188.95K **Privately Held**
Web: www.flavorseed.com
SIC: 2099 Food preparations, nec

(G-2773)
FLEX FINISHING INC
4811 Worth Pl (28216-3321)
PHONE.....................704 342-3600
Craig J Hobbs, *Pr*
J Craig Hobbs, *Pr*
EMP: 9 **EST:** 1999
SQ FT: 7,000
SALES (est): 670.22K **Privately Held**
SIC: 2789 Binding only: books, pamphlets, magazines, etc.

(G-2774)
FLEXI NORTH AMERICA LLC
2405 Center Park Dr (28217-3257)
PHONE.....................704 588-0785
Dennis Dubblemen, *VP Sls*
EMP: 4 **EST:** 2013
SALES (est): 1.84MM
SALES (corp-wide): 6.51MM **Privately Held**
Web: www.flexi-northamerica.com
SIC: 2399 Pet collars, leashes, etc.: non-leather
PA: Flexi-Bogdahn International Gmbh & Co. Kg
    Carl-Benz-Weg 13
    Bargteheide SH 22941
    453240440

(G-2775)
FLEXO FACTOR
2814 Yorkview Ct (28270-1102)
PHONE.....................704 962-5404
EMP: 4 **EST:** 2019
SALES (est): 118.33K **Privately Held**
Web: www.theflexofactor.com
SIC: 2759 Commercial printing, nec

(G-2776)
FLEXTRONICS CORPORATION
6800 Solectron Dr (28262-2492)
PHONE.....................704 598-3300
EMP: 7
SALES (corp-wide): 24.42B **Privately Held**
SIC: 3672 Printed circuit boards
HQ: Flextronics Corporation
    6201 America Center Dr
    Alviso CA 95002
    803 936-5200

(G-2777)
FLEXTRONICS INTL USA INC
6800 Solectron Dr (28262-2492)
P.O. Box 562148 (28256-2148)
PHONE.....................704 509-8700
Richard Haywood, *Brnch Mgr*
EMP: 333
Web: www.flex.com
SIC: 3672 Printed circuit boards
HQ: Flextronics International Usa, Inc.
    6201 America Center Dr
    San Jose CA 95002

(G-2778)
FLEXVIEW SYSTEMS LLC
7751 Ballantyne C Ste 101 (28277)
PHONE.....................704 644-3079
EMP: 4 **EST:** 2003

SALES (est): 210.91K **Privately Held**
SIC: 3663 Television monitors

(G-2779)
FLINT GROUP US LLC
2915 Whitehall Park Dr Ste 600 (28273)
PHONE.....................704 504-2626
EMP: 7
SALES (corp-wide): 1.91B **Privately Held**
Web: www.flintgrp.com
SIC: 2893 Printing ink
PA: Flint Group Us Llc
    17177 N Laurel Park Dr # 30
    Livonia MI 48152
    734 781-4600

(G-2780)
FLOW FABRICATION
4110 Monroe Rd (28205-7708)
PHONE.....................704 376-8555
David Jones, *Ofcr*
EMP: 6 **EST:** 2005
SALES (est): 99.38K **Privately Held**
Web: www.flowfab.net
SIC: 3999 Manufacturing industries, nec

(G-2781)
FLOW RHYTHM INC
1520 Mockingbird Ln (28209-0063)
PHONE.....................704 737-2178
Adetutu Jacobs, *CEO*
EMP: 8
SALES (est): 330.92K **Privately Held**
SIC: 7372 Prepackaged software

(G-2782)
FLOWSERVE CORPORATION
Flowserve
2801 Hutchison Mcdonald Rd Ste T
(28269)
PHONE.....................704 494-0497
Christopher Robinson, *Off Mgr*
EMP: 27
SALES (corp-wide): 4.32B **Publicly Held**
Web: www.flowserve.com
SIC: 3561 Pumps and pumping equipment
PA: Flowserve Corporation
    5215 N Ocnnor Blvd Ste 70 Connor
    Irving TX 75039
    972 443-6500

(G-2783)
FONTAINE MODIFICATION COMPANY (DH)
9827 Mount Holly Rd (28214-9214)
P.O. Box 565 (28120-0565)
PHONE.....................704 392-8502
EMP: 17 **EST:** 1985
SALES (est): 32.2MM
SALES (corp-wide): 364.48B **Publicly Held**
Web: www.fontainemodification.com
SIC: 3713 5013 Truck bodies and parts; Truck parts and accessories
HQ: Marmon Group Llc
    181 W Madison St Ste 3900
    Chicago IL 60602
    312 372-9500

(G-2784)
FONTEM US INC
Also Called: Blu Ecigs
1100 S Tyron Ste 300 (28203-4297)
PHONE.....................888 207-4588
Murray Kessler, *CEO*
Jim Raport, *Pr*
▲ **EMP:** 7 **EST:** 2012
SALES (est): 8.66MM **Privately Held**
Web: us.blu.com

GEOGRAPHIC SECTION
Charlotte - Mecklenburg County (G-2810)

SIC: **2111** 5993 Cigarettes; Cigarette store
HQ: Itg Brands, Llc
    714 Green Valley Rd
    Greensboro NC 27408
    336 335-7000

(G-2785)
FOOT TO DIE FOR
2545 Valleyview Dr (28212-8306)
PHONE.....................704 577-2822
Melissa Myer, *Pr*
EMP: 6 **EST:** 2010
SALES (est): 104.59K **Privately Held**
SIC: 3544 Special dies and tools

(G-2786)
FORBO MOVEMENT SYSTEMS
Also Called: Transtex Belting
10125 S Tryon St (28273-6509)
PHONE.....................704 334-5353
This E Schneider, *Ch Bd*
This E Schneider, *Ch Bd*
◆ **EMP:** 47 **EST:** 2008
SALES (est): 4.57MM **Privately Held**
Web: www.forbo.com
SIC: 3496 3535 Conveyor belts; Conveyors and conveying equipment

(G-2787)
FORM TECH CONCRETE FORMS INC
Also Called: Charlotte Branch
1000 Thomasboro Dr (28208-2312)
PHONE.....................704 395-9910
Jim Upton, *Mgr*
EMP: 14
SALES (corp-wide): 7.35B **Privately Held**
Web: www.formtechinc.com
SIC: 7359 3444 Rental store, general; Concrete forms, sheet metal
HQ: Form Tech Concrete Forms, Inc.
    975 Ladd Rd
    Walled Lake MI 48390
    248 344-8260

(G-2788)
FORM TECHNOLOGIES INC (DH)
Also Called: Form Technologies
11325 N Community House Rd Ste 300 (28277-0524)
PHONE.....................704 927-2790
Keith Weidman, *CEO*
Tom Kerscher, *CSO**
Frank Lannielli, ***
EMP: 27 **EST:** 2011
SALES (est): 1.08B **Privately Held**
Web: www.formtechnologies.com
SIC: 3364 Zinc and zinc-base alloy die-castings
HQ: Partners Group Ag
    Zugerstrasse 57
    Baar ZG 6341

(G-2789)
FORMARK CORPORATION
Also Called: Prn Uniforms
7537 Hawkstand Ln (28210-6706)
P.O. Box 665 (28016-0665)
PHONE.....................704 922-9516
Mark W Cheetham, *Pr*
EMP: 10 **EST:** 1978
SALES (est): 211.66K **Privately Held**
Web: www.prnuniforms.biz
SIC: 2337 2339 Uniforms, except athletic: women's, misses', and juniors'; Women's and misses' outerwear, nec

(G-2790)
FORTECH INC
2124 Wilkinson Blvd (28208-5642)
PHONE.....................704 333-0621
Jon R Forrest, *Pr*
Nancy Forrest, *VP*
EMP: 10 **EST:** 1984
SQ FT: 6,500
SALES (est): 1.77MM **Privately Held**
Web: www.fortech.us
SIC: 3625 Control equipment, electric

(G-2791)
FORTERRA BRICK LLC
Also Called: Hanson Brick
7400 Carmel Executive Park Dr Ste 200 (28226-8400)
P.O. Box 842481 (75284-2481)
PHONE.....................704 341-8750
▲ **EMP:** 234
SIC: 3251 Structural brick and blocks

(G-2792)
FOUNDRY COMMERCIAL
101 N Tryon St Ste 1000 (28246-0108)
PHONE.....................704 348-6875
EMP: 10 **EST:** 2018
SALES (est): 476.51K **Privately Held**
Web: www.foundrycommercial.com
SIC: 3366 Copper foundries

(G-2793)
FRANKEN SIGNS
3100 South Blvd (28209-1807)
PHONE.....................704 339-0059
Norma Smith, *Prin*
EMP: 4 **EST:** 2016
SALES (est): 88.32K **Privately Held**
SIC: 3993 Signs and advertising specialties

(G-2794)
FREEDOM METALS INC
2014 Vanderbilt Rd (28206-2416)
P.O. Box 26397 (28221-6397)
PHONE.....................704 333-1214
TOLL FREE: 800
Bobby L Reitzel, *Pr*
Betty Reitzel, *VP*
EMP: 12 **EST:** 1982
SQ FT: 100,000
SALES (est): 3.22MM **Privately Held**
Web: www.freedommetalsinc.com
SIC: 5051 3441 Steel; Fabricated structural metal

(G-2795)
FREEMAN SCREEN PRINTERS INC
4442 South Blvd Ste B (28209-2739)
PHONE.....................704 521-9148
Joseph F Joe Freeman, *Pr*
Leroy F Roy Freeman, *VP*
Carol Freeman, *Sec*
EMP: 8 **EST:** 1989
SQ FT: 11,000
SALES (est): 458.41K **Privately Held**
Web: www.freemanscreenprinters.com
SIC: 2396 2395 Screen printing on fabric articles; Pleating and stitching

(G-2796)
FREIGHTPAL INC
201 Mccullough Dr Ste 300 (28262-1367)
PHONE.....................704 971-8183
EMP: 8 **EST:** 2013
SALES (est): 499.19K **Privately Held**
Web: www.freightpal.com
SIC: 3743 Train cars and equipment, freight or passenger

(G-2797)
FRESH-N-MOBILE LLC
8640 University City Blvd Ste 135 (28213-3501)
PHONE.....................704 251-4643
Madison Anderson, *Mng Pt*
EMP: 6 **EST:** 2021
SALES (est): 125.33K **Privately Held**
Web: www.freshnmobile.com
SIC: 2842 4212 Laundry cleaning preparations; Delivery service, vehicular

(G-2798)
FRITO-LAY NORTH AMERICA INC
Also Called: Frito-Lay
2911 Nevada Blvd (28273-6434)
PHONE.....................704 588-4150
Tony Mattie, *Mgr*
EMP: 113
SALES (corp-wide): 86.39B **Publicly Held**
Web: www.fritolay.com
SIC: 2096 2099 Corn chips and other corn-based snacks; Food preparations, nec
HQ: Frito-Lay North America, Inc.
    7701 Legacy Dr
    Plano TX 75024

(G-2799)
FSC THERAPEUTICS LLC
6100 Fairview Rd Ste 300 (28210-4262)
PHONE.....................704 941-2500
EMP: 15
SQ FT: 5,000
SALES (est): 1.1MM **Privately Held**
SIC: 2834 Solutions, pharmaceutical

(G-2800)
FUJI AMERICA INC
10817 Southern Loop Blvd (28273)
PHONE.....................704 527-3854
Seth J Perkinson Iii, *Pr*
EMP: 9 **EST:** 1978
SQ FT: 12,000
SALES (est): 313.85K **Privately Held**
Web: www.fujiamerica.com
SIC: 3569 Filters, general line: industrial

(G-2801)
FUTURE PRINTS INC
12517 Preservation Pointe Dr (28216-6735)
PHONE.....................704 241-4164
Reinhard Hecht, *Prin*
EMP: 6 **EST:** 2005
SALES (est): 125.02K **Privately Held**
SIC: 2752 Commercial printing, lithographic

(G-2802)
G & E INVESTMENTS INC
Also Called: Diamond Finish Car Wash
601 S Kings Dr (28204-3089)
PHONE.....................704 395-2155
George Rhyne, *Pr*
EMP: 10 **EST:** 1997
SALES (est): 919.44K **Privately Held**
Web: www.diamondclt.com
SIC: 3559 Automotive maintenance equipment

(G-2803)
GALAXY ELECTRONICS INC
4233 Trailer Dr (28269-4731)
PHONE.....................704 343-9881
EMP: 10 **EST:** 1993
SALES (est): 2.04MM **Privately Held**
Web: www.galaxyelectronicsinc.com
SIC: 3672 3674 Printed circuit boards; Integrated circuits, semiconductor networks, etc.

(G-2804)
GALE PACIFIC USA INC (HQ)
Also Called: Gale Pacific
5311 77 Center Dr Ste 150 (28217-2724)
PHONE.....................407 772-7900
▲ **EMP:** 11 **EST:** 1998
SQ FT: 25,000
SALES (est): 35.41MM **Privately Held**
Web: www.galepacific.com
SIC: 2221 Polypropylene broadwoven fabrics
PA: Gale Pacific Limited
    145 Woodlands Dr
    Braeside VIC 3195

(G-2805)
GALLOREECOM
6211 Moss Bank Ct (28262-4230)
PHONE.....................704 644-0978
EMP: 5 **EST:** 2017
SALES (est): 156.25K **Privately Held**
Web: www.galloree.com
SIC: 2759 Screen printing

(G-2806)
GAMBLE ASSOCIATES INC
Also Called: Gamble Pallet & Whse Eqp Co
701 Johnson Rd (28206-1634)
P.O. Box 217034 (28221-0034)
PHONE.....................704 375-9301
Cheryl A Gamble, *Pr*
John F Gamble Junior, *Sec*
EMP: 16 **EST:** 1980
SQ FT: 20,000
SALES (est): 625.8K **Privately Held**
SIC: 7699 2448 Pallet repair; Pallets, wood

(G-2807)
GARAGE GUYS
4820 N Graham St (28269-4823)
PHONE.....................704 494-8841
Vin Bang, *Prin*
EMP: 10 **EST:** 2007
SALES (est): 446.84K **Privately Held**
Web: www.autoinspectioncharlottenc.com
SIC: 3312 Blast furnaces and steel mills

(G-2808)
GARDNER MACHINERY CORPORATION
700 N Summit Ave (28216-5561)
P.O. Box 33818 (28233-3818)
PHONE.....................704 372-3890
Richard W Gardner, *Pr*
Ramona T Gardner, *Corporate Secretary*
EMP: 13 **EST:** 1947
SQ FT: 40,000
SALES (est): 2.19MM **Privately Held**
Web: www.gardnermachinery.com
SIC: 3535 5087 3559 Conveyors and conveying equipment; Laundry equipment and supplies; Petroleum refinery equipment

(G-2809)
GAS-FIRED PRODUCTS INC (PA)
Also Called: Space-Ray
1700 Parker Dr (28208-6236)
P.O. Box 36485 (28236-6485)
PHONE.....................704 372-3485
◆ **EMP:** 41 **EST:** 1949
SALES (est): 18.94MM
SALES (corp-wide): 18.94MM **Privately Held**
Web: www.gasfiredproducts.com
SIC: 3523 3433 Tobacco curers; Heating equipment, except electric

(G-2810)
GASTON SCREEN PRINTING INC
8620 Wilkinson Blvd (28214-8059)
P.O. Box 227 (28012-0227)
PHONE.....................704 399-0459
Kurt R Rawald, *Pr*
James C Poag Junior, *VP*
Larry L Martin Junior, *Sec*
EMP: 16 **EST:** 1975
SALES (est): 1.84MM **Privately Held**

Charlotte - Mecklenburg County (G-2811)   GEOGRAPHIC SECTION

Web: www.gastonprint.com
SIC: **2262** 2261 2396 2395 Screen printing: manmade fiber and silk broadwoven fabrics ; Screen printing of cotton broadwoven fabrics; Automotive and apparel trimmings; Pleating and stitching

(G-2811)
GBC DISTRIBUTION LLC
10123 Park Rd (28210-7826)
PHONE..................................704 341-8473
Michael Griffin, *Prin*
EMP: 8 EST: 2014
SALES (est): 585.54K **Privately Held**
SIC: **2653** Corrugated and solid fiber boxes

(G-2812)
GE VERNOVA INTERNATIONAL LLC
Also Called: GE
12037 Goodrich Dr (28273-6511)
PHONE..................................704 587-1300
Andrew Headley, *Brnch Mgr*
EMP: 13
SQ FT: 37,960
SALES (corp-wide): 67.95B **Publicly Held**
SIC: **7699** 7694 7629 3621 Industrial equipment services; Armature rewinding shops; Electrical repair shops; Motors and generators
HQ: Ge Vernova International Llc
58 Charles St
Cambridge MA 02141
617 443-3000

(G-2813)
GEFRAN INC
4209 Stuart Andrew Blvd Ste C (28217-4623)
PHONE..................................501 442-1521
Bob Vivier, *Brnch Mgr*
EMP: 10
SALES (corp-wide): 137.6MM **Privately Held**
Web: www.gefran.com
SIC: **3566** Speed changers, drives, and gears
HQ: Gefran, Inc.
400 Willow St
North Andover MA 01845
781 729-5249

(G-2814)
GEM ASSET ACQUISITION LLC (PA)
Also Called: Gemseal
1855 Lindbergh St Ste 500 (28208-3769)
PHONE..................................704 225-3321
Jeff Lax, *Managing Member*
EMP: 7 EST: 2015
SALES (est): 17.13MM
SALES (corp-wide): 17.13MM **Privately Held**
SIC: **2951** Asphalt paving mixtures and blocks

(G-2815)
GEM ASSET ACQUISITION LLC
Also Called: Gemseal Pvmnts Pdts - Chrlotte
1955 Scott Futrell Dr (28208-2704)
PHONE..................................704 697-9577
EMP: 28
SALES (corp-wide): 17.13MM **Privately Held**
SIC: **2951** Asphalt paving mixtures and blocks
PA: Gem Asset Acquisition Llc
1855 Lindbergh St Ste 500
Charlotte NC 28208
704 225-3321

(G-2816)
GENERAL CONTROL EQUIPMENT CO
Also Called: Gc Valves
456 Crompton St (28273-6215)
P.O. Box 7066 (28241-7066)
PHONE..................................704 588-0484
William B Young Junior, *Pr*
Beth Young, *Sec*
▲ EMP: 10 EST: 1964
SQ FT: 7,000
SALES (est): 1.62MM **Privately Held**
Web: www.gcvalves.com
SIC: **3491** Industrial valves

(G-2817)
GENERAL ELECTRIC COMPANY
Also Called: GE
4601 Park Rd Ste 400 (28209-3239)
PHONE..................................704 561-5700
Annet Davis, *Mgr*
EMP: 4
SALES (corp-wide): 67.95B **Publicly Held**
Web: www.ge.com
SIC: **3613** Switchgear and switchboard apparatus
PA: General Electric Company
1 Financial Ctr Ste 3700
Boston MA 02111
617 443-3000

(G-2818)
GENERAL STEEL DRUM LLC (PA)
4500 South Blvd (28209-2841)
P.O. Box 513840 (90051-3840)
PHONE..................................704 525-7160
Kyle Stavig, *Managing Member*
Christian Stavig, *
Cody Stavig, *
EMP: 11 EST: 2010
SALES (est): 33.9MM
SALES (corp-wide): 33.9MM **Privately Held**
Web: www.northcoastcontainer.com
SIC: **3412** Drums, shipping: metal

(G-2819)
GENERICS BIDCO II LLC
Also Called: Prinston Laboratories
3700 Woodpark Blvd Ste A (28026-4251)
PHONE..................................980 389-2501
EMP: 110
SQ FT: 16,000
SIC: **2834** Cough medicines
HQ: Generics Bidco Ii, Llc
3241 Woodpark Blvd
Charlotte NC 28206
704 612-8830

(G-2820)
GENERICS BIDCO II LLC (DH)
Also Called: Prinston Laboratories
3241 Woodpark Blvd (28206-4212)
PHONE..................................704 612-8830
◆ EMP: 45 EST: 1985
SALES (est): 60.89MM **Privately Held**
SIC: **2834** Cough medicines
HQ: Prinston Pharmaceutical Inc.
700 Atrium Dr
Somerset NJ 08873

(G-2821)
GENESIS WATER TECHNOLOGIES INC
10130 Perimeter Pkwy Ste 200 (28216-2447)
PHONE..................................704 360-5165
Nick Nicholas, *Brnch Mgr*
EMP: 40
Web: www.genesiswatertech.com
SIC: **5074** 3569 Plumbing and hydronic heating supplies; Assembly machines, non-metalworking
PA: Genesis Water Technologies, Inc.
555 Winderley Pl Ste 300
Maitland FL 32751

(G-2822)
GENPAK LLC
1001 Westinghouse Blvd (28273-6323)
P.O. Box 7846 (28241-7846)
PHONE..................................704 588-6202
Bruce Eveans, *Mgr*
EMP: 100
SQ FT: 22,428
Web: www.genpak.com
SIC: **5113** 2821 Sanitary food containers; Plastics materials and resins
HQ: Genpak Llc
10601 Westlake Dr
Charlotte NC 28273
800 626-6695

(G-2823)
GENPAK LLC (DH)
Also Called: Genpak
10601 Westlake Dr (28273-3930)
PHONE..................................800 626-6695
Jeff Hebert, *Pr*
◆ EMP: 45 EST: 1969
SQ FT: 30,000
SALES (est): 83.65MM **Privately Held**
Web: www.genpak.com
SIC: **3089** Plastics containers, except foam
HQ: C. P. Converters, Inc.
15 Grumbacher Rd
York PA 17406
717 764-1193

(G-2824)
GENT OF SCENT
15137 Taylor Ridge Ln (28273-7091)
PHONE..................................980 505-9903
W Douglas Wall, *Prin*
EMP: 5 EST: 2018
SALES (est): 91.76K **Privately Held**
Web: www.gentofscent.com
SIC: **2844** Perfumes, cosmetics and other toilet preparations

(G-2825)
GEOGRAPHICS SCREENPRINTING INC
3622 Green Park Cir (28217-2866)
PHONE..................................704 357-3300
James Mcnally, *Pr*
Josephine Mcnally, *Pr*
Susan Workley, *VP*
EMP: 7 EST: 1970
SQ FT: 5,815
SALES (est): 592.37K **Privately Held**
Web: www.geographicsprinting.com
SIC: **2759** Screen printing

(G-2826)
GEOMETRY WORKBOOK
3722 Providence Plan Ln (28270-3773)
PHONE..................................252 714-3327
Rachel Servia, *Prin*
EMP: 5 EST: 2017
SALES (est): 64.61K **Privately Held**
SIC: **3861** Photographic equipment and supplies

(G-2827)
GERDAU AMERISTEEL US INC
Ameristeel Chrltte Stl Mill Di
6601 Lakeview Rd (28269-2604)
P.O. Box 481980 (28269-5331)
PHONE..................................704 596-0361
Anthony Read, *Mgr*
EMP: 165
Web: gerdau.com
SIC: **3312** Blast furnaces and steel mills
HQ: Gerdau Ameristeel Us Inc.
4221 W Boy Scout Blvd # 600
Tampa FL 33607
813 286-8383

(G-2828)
GIANT CEMENT CO
10910 Texland Blvd (28273-6216)
PHONE..................................704 583-1568
Keith Wentzel, *Mgr*
EMP: 5 EST: 2018
SALES (est): 180.47K **Privately Held**
SIC: **3241** Cement, hydraulic

(G-2829)
GINGRAS SLEEP MEDICINE PA
6207 Park South Dr Ste 101 (28210-3653)
PHONE..................................704 944-0562
Jeannine Louise Gingras Md, *Prin*
EMP: 6 EST: 2010
SALES (est): 280.61K **Privately Held**
Web: www.gingrassleepmedicine.com
SIC: **2834** Medicines, capsuled or ampuled

(G-2830)
GINKGO STONE LLC
5340 Camilla Dr (28226-6769)
PHONE..................................704 451-8678
Collin Ladue, *Pr*
EMP: 8 EST: 2018
SALES (est): 92.92K **Privately Held**
SIC: **3281** Cut stone and stone products

(G-2831)
GLATFELTER CORPORATION (PA)
Also Called: Glatfelter
4350 Congress St Ste 600 (28209-4953)
PHONE..................................704 885-2555
Thomas Fahnemann, *Pr*
Kevin M Fogarty, *Non-Executive Chairman of the Board**
Samuel L Hillard, *Sr VP*
Christopher W Astley, *CCO*
David C Elder, *CAO*
EMP: 1100 EST: 1864
SALES (est): 1.49B
SALES (corp-wide): 1.49B **Publicly Held**
Web: www.glatfelter.com
SIC: **2621** Book paper

(G-2832)
GLATFLTER SNTARA OLD HCKRY INC (DH)
4350 Congress St Ste 600 (28209-4953)
PHONE..................................615 526-2100
Martin Mikkelsen, *CEO*
EMP: 14 EST: 2014
SALES (est): 28.11MM
SALES (corp-wide): 1.49B **Publicly Held**
Web: www.sontara.com
SIC: **2297** Nonwoven fabrics
HQ: Glatfelter Holding (Switzerland) Ag
Aeschenvorstadt 67
Basel BS 4051

(G-2833)
GLOBAL PLASMA SOLUTIONS INC
3101 Yorkmont Rd Ste 400 (28208-0034)
PHONE..................................980 279-5622
Glenn Brinckman, *CEO*
▲ EMP: 20 EST: 2018
SALES (est): 3.33MM **Privately Held**
Web: www.gpsair.com
SIC: **3564** Air purification equipment

GEOGRAPHIC SECTION   Charlotte - Mecklenburg County (G-2859)

(G-2834)
GLOBAL PRODUCTS & MFG SVCS INC
Also Called: Gpms
6000 Fairview Rd Ste 1200 (28210-2252)
PHONE..................................360 870-9876
Cynthea Williams, *Pr*
EMP: 6 **EST:** 2007
SALES (est): 390.7K **Privately Held**
SIC: 2299 8711 5699 5734 Textile goods, nec ; Engineering services; Customized clothing and apparel; Computer peripheral equipment

(G-2835)
GLOSSY WICKS LLC
7419 Quail Wood Dr Apt D (28226-7135)
PHONE..................................980 349-5908
Minya Brown, *Owner*
EMP: 4 **EST:** 2020
SALES (est): 39.69K **Privately Held**
SIC: 3999 Candles

(G-2836)
GLS PRODUCTS LLC
Also Called: Power Adhesives
1209 Lilac Rd (28209-1418)
PHONE..................................704 334-2345
Lee Stegall, *Pr*
EMP: 6 **EST:** 2004
SQ FT: 3,000
SALES (est): 920.75K **Privately Held**
Web: www.glsproducts.com
SIC: 2891 Adhesives

(G-2837)
GNB VENTURES LLC
Also Called: Sisco Safety
1800 Associates Ln (28217-2801)
PHONE..................................704 488-4468
Naomi Reale, *CEO*
EMP: 18 **EST:** 2003
SALES (est): 4.96MM **Privately Held**
Web: www.siscosafety.com
SIC: 5099 3999 5047 5999 Fire extinguishers ; Fire extinguishers, portable; Industrial safety devices: first aid kits and masks; Fire extinguishers

(G-2838)
GNH PHARMACEUTICALS USA LLC
125 Remount Rd Ste C1 (28203-6459)
PHONE..................................919 820-3077
EMP: 4 **EST:** 2019
SALES (est): 173.79K **Privately Held**
Web: www.gnhindia.com
SIC: 2834 Pharmaceutical preparations

(G-2839)
GO EV AND GO GREEN CORP ✪
9711 David Taylor Dr Apt 106 (28262-2366)
PHONE..................................704 327-9040
Edwin D Daniel, *CEO*
Edwin D Daniel, *Ex Dir*
Chandell Daniel, *COO*
EMP: 4 **EST:** 2023
SALES (est): 133.5K **Privately Held**
SIC: 3647 4911 7534 Vehicular lighting equipment; Tire repair shop

(G-2840)
GO FOR GREEN FLEET SVCS LLC ✪
1911 Greymouth Rd Apt 305 (28262-8233)
PHONE..................................803 306-3683
Michael Green, *Managing Member*
EMP: 4 **EST:** 2022
SALES (est): 222.87K **Privately Held**

SIC: 3537 7389 Trucks: freight, baggage, etc.: industrial, except mining; Business Activities at Non-Commercial Site

(G-2841)
GODGLAMIT LLC
620 N Church St Apt 2216 (28202-3311)
PHONE..................................336 558-1097
EMP: 5 **EST:** 2020
SALES (est): 73.17K **Privately Held**
SIC: 2678 Stationery products

(G-2842)
GOFFSTAR INC
Also Called: Lake Printing & Design
5015 W W T Harris Blvd Ste F (28269-3756)
PHONE..................................704 895-3878
Timothy Goff, *Pr*
EMP: 7 **EST:** 2006
SQ FT: 3,000
SALES (est): 980.44K **Privately Held**
Web: www.lakeprinting.biz
SIC: 2752 Offset printing

(G-2843)
GOLD BOND BUILDING PDTS LLC (HQ)
Also Called: National Gypsum
2001 Rexford Rd (28211-3415)
PHONE..................................704 365-7300
Thomas Nelson, *Managing Member*
EMP: 5 **EST:** 2020
SALES (est): 96.43MM
SALES (corp-wide): 96.43MM **Privately Held**
Web: www.nationalgypsum.com
SIC: 2621 Building and roofing paper, felts and insulation siding
PA: Ng Operations, Llc
      2001 Rexford Rd
      Charlotte NC 28211
      704 365-7300

(G-2844)
GOLDEN POP SHOP LLC ✪
9805 Statesville Rd Ste 6012 (28269-7647)
PHONE..................................704 236-9455
EMP: 5 **EST:** 2023
SALES (est): 222.74K **Privately Held**
SIC: 2096 Potato chips and other potato-based snacks

(G-2845)
GOLDMINE SOFTWARE
Also Called: Willis Consulting
10130 Mallard Creek Rd Ste 300 (28262-6000)
PHONE..................................704 944-3579
Greg Willis, *Pr*
EMP: 5 **EST:** 2001
SALES (est): 488.29K **Privately Held**
SIC: 7372 7371 Prepackaged software; Custom computer programming services

(G-2846)
GOM AMERICAS INC
9319 Robert D Snyder Rd 442 & 445 (28223-0001)
PHONE..................................704 912-1600
Dirk Behring, *Pr*
EMP: 5 **EST:** 2019
SALES (est): 193.19K **Privately Held**
SIC: 3829 Measuring and controlling devices, nec

(G-2847)
GOODRICH CORPORATION (HQ)
Also Called: Collins Aerospace
2730 W Tyvola Rd (28217-4527)

PHONE..................................704 423-7000
David Gitlin, *Pr*
Jennifer Pollino, *Sr VP*
Christopher T Calio, *Sec*
Richard S Caswell, *Treas*
Scott E Kuechle, *CFO*
◆ **EMP:** 120 **EST:** 1912
SQ FT: 120,000
SALES (est): 1.93B
SALES (corp-wide): 68.92B **Publicly Held**
Web: www.collinsaerospace.com
SIC: 7372 3724 3728 Prepackaged software ; Aircraft engines and engine parts; Aircraft parts and equipment, nec
PA: Rtx Corporation
      1000 Wilson Blvd
      Arlington VA 22209
      781 522-3000

(G-2848)
GOUGH ECON INC
9400 N Lakebrook Rd (28214-9008)
PHONE..................................704 399-4501
David P Risley, *Pr*
Don Calvert Junior, *VP*
▲ **EMP:** 38 **EST:** 1974
SQ FT: 42,000
SALES (est): 8.69MM **Privately Held**
Web: www.goughecon.com
SIC: 3535 Conveyors and conveying equipment

(G-2849)
GRACE COMMUNION INTERNATIONAL (PA)
3120 Whitehall Park Dr (28273-3335)
PHONE..................................626 650-2300
Joseph Tkach, *Pr*
Michael Feazell, *
Mathew Morgan, *
EMP: 32 **EST:** 1947
SQ FT: 54,000
SALES (est): 5.5MM
SALES (corp-wide): 5.5MM **Privately Held**
Web: www.gci.org
SIC: 2721 8661 Magazines: publishing only, not printed on site; Church of God

(G-2850)
GRACE PRESS LLC
1235 East Blvd Ste E (28203-5876)
PHONE..................................704 277-4007
EMP: 4 **EST:** 2016
SALES (est): 116.77K **Privately Held**
SIC: 2741 Miscellaneous publishing

(G-2851)
GRACEFULLY BROKEN LLC
14129 Perugia Way Apt 102 (28273-7215)
PHONE..................................980 474-0309
EMP: 5 **EST:** 2020
SALES (est): 102.36K **Privately Held**
SIC: 7389 2211 7929 Business Activities at Non-Commercial Site; Apparel and outerwear fabrics, cotton; Entertainment service

(G-2852)
GRANCREATIONS INC
3400 N Graham St (28206-1936)
P.O. Box 562880 (28256-2880)
PHONE..................................704 332-7625
Augusto P Septimio, *Pr*
Cristina Septimio, *Sec*
▲ **EMP:** 7 **EST:** 2007
SALES (est): 727.24K **Privately Held**
Web: www.grancreations.com
SIC: 1743 1799 5722 3281 Terrazzo, tile, marble and mosaic work; Counter top installation: Kitchens, complete (sinks, cabinets, etc.); Curbing, granite or stone

(G-2853)
GRAND COULEE CONSORTIUM
10735 David Taylor Dr # 5 (28262-1060)
PHONE..................................704 943-4343
Stephen M Schmidt, *Owner*
Thomas Murphy, *Prin*
EMP: 4 **EST:** 2009
SALES (est): 95.11K **Privately Held**
SIC: 3511 Turbines and turbine generator sets

(G-2854)
GRAND ENCORE CHARLOTTE LLC
Also Called: Encore Label & Packaging
3700 Rose Lake Dr (28217-2814)
PHONE..................................513 482-7500
Travis Potter, *Managing Member*
EMP: 25 **EST:** 2020
SALES (est): 1.02MM **Privately Held**
Web: www.encorelp.com
SIC: 2679 Labels, paper: made from purchased material

(G-2855)
GRAPHIC IMPRESSIONS INC
7910 District Dr (28213-6557)
PHONE..................................704 596-4921
W L Galloway Junior, *Pr*
W L Galloway Iii, *VP*
Kevin L Galloway, *
Bill Gallowa, *
EMP: 27 **EST:** 1975
SQ FT: 22,000
SALES (est): 4.7MM **Privately Held**
Web: www.giprinters.com
SIC: 2752 Offset printing

(G-2856)
GRAPHIC PACKAGING INTL LLC
800 Westinghouse Blvd (28273-6305)
P.O. Box 411288 (28241-1288)
PHONE..................................704 588-1750
Jim Seel, *Brnch Mgr*
EMP: 217
SQ FT: 118,462
Web: www.graphicpkg.com
SIC: 2657 2631 2671 Folding paperboard boxes; Paperboard mills; Paper; coated and laminated packaging
HQ: Graphic Packaging International, Llc
      1500 Riveredge Pkwy # 100
      Atlanta GA 30328

(G-2857)
GRAVEOKE INC
Also Called: National Textile Engravers
1814 Bradenton Dr (28206)
PHONE..................................704 534-3480
Andrew Graven, *Pr*
Philip Okey, *
EMP: 25 **EST:** 1972
SQ FT: 15,000
SALES (est): 1.55MM **Privately Held**
SIC: 2759 Textile printing rolls: engraving

(G-2858)
GRAY MANUFACTURING CO
8548 Highland Glen Dr (28269-6112)
P.O. Box 90363 (37209-0363)
PHONE..................................615 841-3066
William Gray, *Owner*
EMP: 10 **EST:** 1958
SQ FT: 2,500
SALES (est): 23.49K **Privately Held**
Web: www.grayusa.com
SIC: 3499 Metal household articles

(G-2859)
GREAT PACIFIC ENTPS US INC (DH)
Also Called: Genpak

Charlotte - Mecklenburg County (G-2860)   GEOGRAPHIC SECTION

10601 Westlake Dr (28273-3930)
PHONE..................980 256-7729
James Pattison, Ch Bd
Michael Korenberg, CEO
Nick Geer, VP
James Reilly, Ch
▲ EMP: 23 EST: 1978
SQ FT: 36,000
SALES (est): 54.52MM
SALES (corp-wide): 10.42B Privately Held
Web: www.genpak.com
SIC: 3089 Plastics containers, except foam
HQ: Great Pacific Enterprises Inc
1800-1067 Cordova St W
Vancouver BC V6C 1
604 278-4841

(G-2860)
GREAT WAGON ROAD DISTLG CO LLC
4150 Yancey Rd (28217-1738)
PHONE..................704 246-8740
Oliver Mulligan, Mgr
EMP: 5 EST: 2017
SALES (est): 104.33K Privately Held
Web: www.gwrdistilling.com
SIC: 2085 Distilled and blended liquors

(G-2861)
GREAT WAGON ROAD DISTLG CO LLC
227 Southside Dr Ste B (28217-1727)
PHONE..................704 469-9330
John Marrino, Pr
EMP: 6 EST: 2017
SALES (est): 240.16K Privately Held
Web: www.gwrdistilling.com
SIC: 2085 Distilled and blended liquors

(G-2862)
GRECON INC (HQ)
648 Griffith Rd Ste A (28217-3573)
PHONE..................503 641-7731
Hermann Staats, Ex VP
Cary Jentzsch, Treas
▲ EMP: 18 EST: 1989
SQ FT: 10,000
SALES (est): 5.1MM
SALES (corp-wide): 90.86MM Privately Held
Web: www.fagus-grecon.com
SIC: 5084 3825 3613 Instruments and control equipment; Instruments to measure electricity; Switchgear and switchboard apparatus
PA: Fagus-Grecon Greten Gmbh Und Co Kg
Hannoversche Str. 58
Alfeld (Leine) NI 31061
518179475

(G-2863)
GREEN POWER PRODUCERS
10600 Nations Ford Rd # 150 (28273-5762)
PHONE..................704 844-8990
William Brinker, Prin
EMP: 6 EST: 2009
SALES (est): 679.14K Privately Held
SIC: 1321 Natural gas liquids

(G-2864)
GREEN WASTE MANAGEMENT LLC
101 N Tryon St Ste 112 (28246-0104)
PHONE..................704 289-0720
EMP: 6 EST: 2018
SALES (est): 38.97K Privately Held
SIC: 7349 6531 3589 Janitorial service, contract basis; Real estate brokers and agents; Commercial cleaning equipment

(G-2865)
GREENLINE
3412 Monroe Rd (28205-7730)
PHONE..................704 333-3377
Patterson Dm, Prin
EMP: 5 EST: 2010
SALES (est): 243.72K Privately Held
Web: www.greenlineconveyor.com
SIC: 3567 Industrial furnaces and ovens

(G-2866)
GREENLINE CORPORATION
200 Forsyth Hall Dr Ste E (28273-5815)
PHONE..................704 333-3377
Donald Patterson, Prin
EMP: 9 EST: 2007
SALES (est): 188.38K Privately Held
Web: www.greenlineconveyor.com
SIC: 3535 Conveyors and conveying equipment

(G-2867)
GREIF INC
900 Westinghouse Blvd (28273-6306)
P.O. Box 7026 (28241-7026)
PHONE..................704 588-3895
Khalias Rahman, Mgr
EMP: 71
SALES (corp-wide): 5.22B Publicly Held
Web: www.greif.com
SIC: 2655 3412 Drums, fiber: made from purchased material; Metal barrels, drums, and pails
PA: Greif, Inc.
425 Winter Rd
Delaware OH 43015
740 549-6000

(G-2868)
GRICE SHOWCASE DISPLAY MFG INC
5001 White Oak Rd (28210-2326)
PHONE..................704 423-8888
Keely A Grice Iii, Pr
Keely Grice Iii, Pr
EMP: 8 EST: 1984
SALES (est): 721.76K Privately Held
Web: www.griceshowcase.com
SIC: 2541 2542 Display fixtures, wood; Office and store showcases and display fixtures

(G-2869)
GRINDING & METALS INC
1200 Westinghouse Blvd (28273-6474)
PHONE..................704 588-5999
EMP: 4 EST: 2018
SALES (est): 71.94K Privately Held
SIC: 3999 Grinding and pulverizing of materials, nec

(G-2870)
GRIZZLY COOKWARE LLC
2030 S Tryon St Ste 3g (28203-4956)
PHONE..................704 322-3521
Kyle A Caniglia, Admn
EMP: 4 EST: 2015
SALES (est): 341.63K Privately Held
Web: www.grizzlycookware.com
SIC: 3634 Housewares, excluding cooking appliances and utensils

(G-2871)
GRONINGER USA LLC
14045 S Lakes Dr (28273-6791)
PHONE..................704 588-3873
Horst Groeninger, Pr
Juergen Riedel, Managing Member*
Ana Pryor, *
EMP: 37 EST: 1996

SQ FT: 2,800
SALES (est): 11.91MM
SALES (corp-wide): 2.14MM Privately Held
Web: www.groningerusa.com
SIC: 3565 Packaging machinery
PA: Groninger Gmbh &Co. Kg
Alte Str. 9
Aichtal BW 72631
712750495

(G-2872)
GSAM RESIDUALS LLC
2901 Coltsgate Rd (28211-3571)
PHONE..................704 200-2634
Thomas Ricks, Prin
EMP: 5 EST: 2011
SALES (est): 468.18K Privately Held
SIC: 2911 Residues

(G-2873)
GSE DISPENSING
2625 Rustic Ridge Ct (28270-0704)
PHONE..................704 509-2651
Sjoerd Vollebregt, Prin
▲ EMP: 7 EST: 2006
SALES (est): 986.22K Privately Held
Web: www.gsedispensing.com
SIC: 2893 Printing ink

(G-2874)
H & B TOOL & DIE SUPPLY CO
5005 W Wt Harris Blvd Ste A (28269)
PHONE..................704 376-8531
David Black, Pr
EMP: 9 EST: 1963
SQ FT: 3,500
SALES (est): 1.4MM Privately Held
Web: www.handbtool.com
SIC: 3599 Machine shop, jobbing and repair

(G-2875)
H & C ERECTORS AND WELDING LLC
6505 Nevin Glen Dr (28269-6403)
PHONE..................704 615-9849
EMP: 6 EST: 2019
SALES (est): 65.38K Privately Held
SIC: 7692 Welding repair

(G-2876)
H & H POLISHING INC
4256 Golf Acres Dr (28208-5863)
PHONE..................704 393-8728
Don G Hurst, Pr
Myrna Hurst, Sec
EMP: 20 EST: 1987
SQ FT: 24,000
SALES (est): 938.47K Privately Held
Web: www.hhpolishinginc.com
SIC: 3471 Plating of metals or formed products

(G-2877)
H & H REPRESENTATIVES INC
Also Called: H & H REPRESENTATIVES, INC
University Parkway (28229)
PHONE..................704 596-6950
Scott Sansberry, Brnch Mgr
EMP: 4
SALES (corp-wide): 2.26MM Privately Held
Web: www.hhreps.com
SIC: 3432 Plastic plumbing fixture fittings, assembly
PA: H & H Representatives, Inc.
1708 University Coml Pl
Charlotte NC 28213
704 596-6950

(G-2878)
H + M USA MANAGEMENT CO INC
Also Called: Hinderer & Muehlich
2020 Starita Rd Ste I (28206-1298)
PHONE..................704 599-9325
Faust Muehlich, Pr
▲ EMP: 21 EST: 1997
SQ FT: 5,000
SALES (est): 757.74K Privately Held
SIC: 3544 Special dies and tools

(G-2879)
H-T-L PERMA USA LTD PARTNR (PA)
10333 Westlake Dr (28273-3785)
PHONE..................704 377-3100
Kevin Keating, Pt
▲ EMP: 20 EST: 1964
SQ FT: 1,000
SALES (est): 10.02MM
SALES (corp-wide): 10.02MM Privately Held
Web: www.permausa.com
SIC: 5085 3949 Industrial supplies; Ammunition belts, sporting type

(G-2880)
HAIS KOOKIES & MORE
600 Hartford Ave (28209-1931)
PHONE..................980 819-8256
EMP: 7
SALES (est): 631.97K Privately Held
SIC: 2053 Cakes, bakery: frozen

(G-2881)
HALOGEN SOFTWARE US INC
15801 Brixham Hill Ave Ste 430 (28277-4795)
PHONE..................866 566-7778
EMP: 5 EST: 2018
SALES (est): 68.41K Privately Held
Web: www.halogentv.com
SIC: 7372 Application computer software

(G-2882)
HAMILTON SUNDSTRAND CORP
Also Called: UTC Aerospace Systems
2730 W Tyvola Rd (28217-4527)
PHONE..................860 654-6000
EMP: 387
SALES (corp-wide): 68.92B Publicly Held
Web: www.rtx.com
SIC: 3714 Motor vehicle parts and accessories
HQ: Hamilton Sundstrand Corporation
1 Hamilton Rd
Windsor Locks CT 06096
619 714-9442

(G-2883)
HAMMOCK PHARMACEUTICALS INC
Also Called: Hammock Consumer
11922 General Dr Unit C (28273-7176)
PHONE..................704 727-7926
William Maichle, CEO
Terence Novak, COO
Frank Stokes, CFO
EMP: 5 EST: 2016
SALES (est): 472.04K Privately Held
SIC: 2834 Pharmaceutical preparations

(G-2884)
HANS KRUG
4310 Sharon Rd Ste U01 (28211-0033)
PHONE..................704 370-0809
Hans Krug, Prin
EMP: 20 EST: 2016
SALES (est): 273.99K Privately Held
Web: www.hanskrug.com

GEOGRAPHIC SECTION
Charlotte - Mecklenburg County (G-2907)

SIC: 2434 Wood kitchen cabinets

(G-2885)
HAPPITEESCOM
1060 Tara Ln (28213-8030)
PHONE..............................704 965-2507
Tasha Campbell, *Prin*
EMP: 4 **EST:** 2012
SALES (est): 77.53K **Privately Held**
SIC: 2759 Screen printing

(G-2886)
HAPPY SIGN SURPRISE LLC
10931 Chamberlain Hall Ct (28277-1769)
PHONE..............................704 341-3359
Jaime Volturno, *Prin*
EMP: 4 **EST:** 2011
SALES (est): 174.81K **Privately Held**
Web: www.happysignsurprise.com
SIC: 3993 Signs and advertising specialties

(G-2887)
HARBISONWALKER INTL INC
6600 Northpark Blvd Ste E (28216-0083)
PHONE..............................704 599-6540
Carol Jackson, *CEO*
EMP: 4
SALES (corp-wide): 183.75K **Privately Held**
Web: www.thinkhwi.com
SIC: 3255 5085 Clay refractories; Refractory material
HQ: Harbisonwalker International, Inc.
1305 Cherrington Pkwy # 1
Moon Township PA 15108

(G-2888)
HARDWOOD PUBLISHING CO INC
Also Called: Hardwood Review Export
6400 Bannington Rd (28226-1327)
PHONE..............................704 543-4408
George Barrett, *Pr*
Mike Barrett, *VP*
EMP: 9 **EST:** 1985
SALES (est): 621.74K **Privately Held**
Web: www.hardwoodreview.com
SIC: 2741 Newsletter publishing

(G-2889)
HARPER COMPANIES INTL INC
11625 Steele Creek Rd (28273-3731)
PHONE..............................800 438-3111
Ronald H Harper, *Pr*
EMP: 8 **EST:** 2017
SALES (est): 176.96K **Privately Held**
Web: www.harperimage.com
SIC: 3555 Printing trades machinery

(G-2890)
HARPER CORPORATION OF AMERICA (PA)
11625 Steele Creek Rd (28273-3731)
P.O. Box 38490 (28278-1008)
PHONE..............................704 588-3371
Margaret Harper Kluttz, *Pr*
Ronald H Kluttz, *
Katherine Harper, *
Ronald James Harper, *
Eckehard Mecklenburg, *
◆ **EMP:** 125 **EST:** 1971
SQ FT: 12,000
SALES (est): 21.46MM
SALES (corp-wide): 21.46MM **Privately Held**
Web: www.harperimage.com
SIC: 3555 2842 Printing trades machinery; Cleaning or polishing preparations, nec

(G-2891)
HARPER-LOVE ADHESIVES CORP (HQ)
11101 Westlake Dr (28273-3783)
P.O. Box 410408 (28241-0408)
PHONE..............................704 588-4395
Allan Clark, *CEO*
Thomas Evans, *
◆ **EMP:** 70 **EST:** 1978
SQ FT: 86,000
SALES (est): 24.56MM
SALES (corp-wide): 559.81MM **Privately Held**
Web: www.harperlove.com
SIC: 2891 Glue
PA: Hbm Holdings Company
101 S Hanley Rd Ste 1050
Saint Louis MO 63105
314 376-2522

(G-2892)
HARSCO METRO RAIL LLC
3440 Toringdon Way Ste 100 (28277-3191)
PHONE..............................980 960-2624
EMP: 4 **EST:** 2016
SALES (est): 1.2MM
SALES (corp-wide): 2.07B **Publicly Held**
SIC: 3531 Railroad related equipment
PA: Enviri Corporation
100 120 N 18th St 17
Philadelphia PA 19103
267 857-8715

(G-2893)
HARSCO RAIL LLC (HQ)
3440 Toringdon Way Ste 100 (28277-3191)
PHONE..............................980 960-2624
Nicholas Grasberger Iii, *Managing Member*
EMP: 4 **EST:** 2016
SALES (est): 8.85MM
SALES (corp-wide): 2.07B **Publicly Held**
Web: www.harscorail.com
SIC: 3531 5088 1629 4789 Railway track equipment; Railroad equipment and supplies; Railroad and railway roadbed construction; Railroad maintenance and repair services
PA: Enviri Corporation
100 120 N 18th St 17
Philadelphia PA 19103
267 857-8715

(G-2894)
HAYWARD INDUSTRIES INC (HQ)
Also Called: Haywood Pool Products
1415 Vantage Park Dr Pmb 400 (28203-4073)
PHONE..............................908 351-5400
Kevin Holleran, *CEO*
Oscar Davis, *
Eifion Jones, *
◆ **EMP:** 350 **EST:** 1925
SALES (est): 752.64MM
SALES (corp-wide): 992.45MM **Publicly Held**
Web: www.hayward.com
SIC: 3589 3561 3423 3494 Swimming pool filter and water conditioning systems; Pumps and pumping equipment; Leaf skimmers or swimming pool rakes; Valves and pipe fittings, nec
PA: Hayward Holdings, Inc.
400 Connell Dr Ste 6100
Berkeley Heights NJ 07922
908 351-5400

(G-2895)
HC FORKLIFT AMERICA CORP
Also Called: Hangcha America
1338 Hundred Oaks Dr Ste Dd (28217-3920)
PHONE..............................980 888-8335
Ning Zhang, *CEO*
Jimmy Zhang, *VP Opers*
EMP: 15 **EST:** 2017
SALES (est): 11.46MM **Privately Held**
Web: www.hcforkliftamerica.com
SIC: 3537 Forklift trucks

(G-2896)
HEALTH AT HOME INC
1321 Cavendish Ct (28211-3937)
PHONE..............................850 543-4482
Robert Murray, *CEO*
EMP: 10 **EST:** 2010
SALES (est): 582.65K **Privately Held**
Web: www.healthathomeinc.com
SIC: 8099 3999 Health and allied services, nec; Manufacturing industries, nec

(G-2897)
HEALTHY EATON LLC
9016 Griers Pasture Dr (28278-0050)
PHONE..............................980 207-3887
Samantha Eaton, *Prin*
EMP: 5 **EST:** 2016
SALES (est): 221.34K **Privately Held**
Web: www.healthyeaton.com
SIC: 3625 Relays and industrial controls

(G-2898)
HEARST CORPORATION
Also Called: Hearst Service Center
3540 Toringdon Way Ste 700 # 7 (28277-4969)
PHONE..............................704 348-8000
EMP: 10
SALES (corp-wide): 4.29B **Privately Held**
Web: www.hearst.com
SIC: 2721 Magazines: publishing only, not printed on site
PA: The Hearst Corporation
300 W 57th St Fl 42
New York NY 10019
212 649-2000

(G-2899)
HEARST CORPORATION
Also Called: King Features Syndicate
3540 Toringdon Way Ste 700 # 7 (28277-4969)
PHONE..............................704 348-8000
Teri Walding, *Asst Cont*
EMP: 17
SALES (corp-wide): 4.29B **Privately Held**
Web: www.hearst.com
SIC: 2721 Comic books: publishing and printing
PA: The Hearst Corporation
300 W 57th St Fl 42
New York NY 10019
212 649-2000

(G-2900)
HEIST BREWING COMPANY LLC
Also Called: Heist Brewery
525 Oakland Ave Apt 1 (28204-2355)
PHONE..............................603 969-8012
Kurt Hogan, *Managing Member*
EMP: 6 **EST:** 2011
SQ FT: 6,500
SALES (est): 273.16K **Privately Held**
SIC: 2082 Ale (alcoholic beverage)

(G-2901)
HELLO SIGNS LLC
4724 Old Pineville Rd Ste H (28217)
PHONE..............................704 572-4853
EMP: 4 **EST:** 2020
SALES (est): 46.08K **Privately Held**
Web: www.hellosignsusa.com
SIC: 3993 Signs and advertising specialties

(G-2902)
HERFF JONES LLC
Also Called: Herff Jones
14931 Santa Lucia Dr (28273-3382)
P.O. Box 568 (28173-1000)
PHONE..............................704 962-1483
Deborah Forrest, *Brnch Mgr*
EMP: 4
SALES (corp-wide): 2.02B **Privately Held**
Web: www.yearbookdiscoveries.com
SIC: 3911 Rings, finger: precious metal
HQ: Herff Jones, Llc
4501 W 62nd St
Indianapolis IN 46268
317 297-3741

(G-2903)
HERFF JONES LLC
9525 Monroe Rd Ste 150 (28270-2451)
PHONE..............................704 845-3355
Tom Reef, *Brnch Mgr*
EMP: 5
SQ FT: 160,152
SALES (corp-wide): 2.02B **Privately Held**
Web: www.herffjones.com
SIC: 2741 2732 Yearbooks: publishing and printing; Book printing
HQ: Herff Jones, Llc
4501 W 62nd St
Indianapolis IN 46268
317 297-3741

(G-2904)
HERITAGE CUSTOM SIGNS & DISP
2731 Interstate St (28208-3603)
PHONE..............................704 655-1465
EMP: 16 **EST:** 2017
SALES (est): 95.77K **Privately Held**
Web: www.heritagecustomsigns.com
SIC: 3993 Signs and advertising specialties

(G-2905)
HERITAGE PRTG & GRAPHICS INC
2739 Interstate St (28208-3603)
PHONE..............................704 551-0700
Joseph Gass, *Pr*
EMP: 9
SQ FT: 6,300
SALES (corp-wide): 8.6MM **Privately Held**
Web: www.heritageprintingcharlotte.com
SIC: 2752 5131 5199 5999 Offset printing; Flags and banners; Posters and decals; Banners, flags, decals, and posters
PA: Heritage Printing & Graphics, Inc.
2854 Old Washington Rd
Waldorf MD 20601
301 843-1997

(G-2906)
HERRIN BROS COAL & ICE CO
315 E 36th St (28206-2021)
P.O. Box 5291 (28299-5291)
PHONE..............................704 332-2193
Marshall L Herrin, *Pr*
Marshall L Herrin, *Pr*
Merl Lee Herrin, *General Vice President*
EMP: 9 **EST:** 1929
SQ FT: 700
SALES (est): 412.96K **Privately Held**
Web: www.herrinice.com
SIC: 5983 5172 2097 5989 Fuel oil dealers; Gasoline; Manufactured ice; Coal

(G-2907)
HERTZ KOMPRESSOREN USA INC
3320 Service St (28206-1518)
Rural Route 3320 Service St (28206)
PHONE..............................704 579-5900
EMP: 9 **EST:** 2016

Charlotte - Mecklenburg County (G-2908)   GEOGRAPHIC SECTION

SALES (est): 1.26MM **Privately Held**
Web: www.hertz-kompressoren.com
SIC: 3563 Air and gas compressors

(G-2908)
HEUBACH COLORANTS USA LLC
5500 77 Center Dr (28217-3072)
PHONE..............................408 686-2935
Alex Baron, *Managing Member*
EMP: 30 **EST:** 2019
SALES (est): 6.75MM **Privately Held**
SIC: 2865 Color pigments, organic

(G-2909)
HIATUS INC
1515 Mockingbird Ln (28209-3298)
PHONE..............................844 572-6185
EMP: 15 **EST:** 2019
SALES (est): 645.33K **Privately Held**
Web: www.hiatusapp.com
SIC: 7372 Prepackaged software

(G-2910)
HIGH GROUND INCORPORATED
2209 Park Rd Ste 1 (28203-6096)
PHONE..............................704 372-6620
Stephen Hofstatter, *Dir*
EMP: 4 **EST:** 2010
SALES (est): 270.51K **Privately Held**
Web: www.nspworldwide.com
SIC: 2326 Men's and boy's work clothing

(G-2911)
HILL-PUBLICATIONS LLC
2018 Mt Holly Huntersville Rd (28214-9311)
PHONE..............................704 399-7002
Larry Hill, *Prin*
EMP: 4 **EST:** 2016
SALES (est): 71.58K **Privately Held**
SIC: 2741 Miscellaneous publishing

(G-2912)
HKB ENTERPRISES LLC
Also Called: Elan Model Management
4936 Osage Cir (28269-4674)
PHONE..............................704 831-0402
Harriett Washington, *Prin*
EMP: 7 **EST:** 2019
SALES (est): 67.88K **Privately Held**
Web: www.hkbenterprises.com
SIC: 3599 Machine shop, jobbing and repair

(G-2913)
HODGE INDUSTRIES INC
1804 Dearmon Dr (28205-3711)
PHONE..............................704 491-0104
EMP: 5 **EST:** 2017
SALES (est): 158.62K **Privately Held**
SIC: 3999 Manufacturing industries, nec

(G-2914)
HOLMAN & MOODY INC
9119 Forsyth Park Dr (28273-3882)
PHONE..............................704 394-4141
Lee F Holman, *Pr*
Zona Holman, *Ch*
Tomoo Furusaka, *VP*
Jolana Holman, *Sec*
▲ **EMP:** 6 **EST:** 1955
SQ FT: 74,000
SALES (est): 578.35K **Privately Held**
Web: www.holmanmoody.com
SIC: 3714 3599 3519 Motor vehicle parts and accessories; Machine and other job shop work; Internal combustion engines, nec

(G-2915)
HOLMAN AUTOMOTIVE INC
9119 Forsyth Park Dr (28273-3882)
P.O. Box 669351 (28266-9351)
PHONE..............................704 583-2888
Lee Holman, *Pr*
Libby Holman, *Sec*
EMP: 4 **EST:** 1983
SQ FT: 8,500
SALES (est): 420.35K **Privately Held**
Web: www.holmanmoody.com
SIC: 3714 3519 3711 Motor vehicle engines and parts; Gas engine rebuilding; Motor vehicles and car bodies

(G-2916)
HOLY COW PUBLICATIONS LLC
811 Queens Rd Apt 1 (28207-1639)
PHONE..............................704 900-5779
Charles Bennett, *Prin*
EMP: 5 **EST:** 2011
SALES (est): 89.64K **Privately Held**
SIC: 2741 Miscellaneous publishing

(G-2917)
HOME T LLC
652 Griffith Rd Ste I (28217-3563)
PHONE..............................646 797-4768
Ryan Shell, *CEO*
EMP: 10 **EST:** 2012
SQ FT: 500
SALES (est): 1.13MM **Privately Held**
Web: www.thehomet.com
SIC: 5136 2326 Sweaters, men's and boys'; Men's and boy's work clothing

(G-2918)
HONEYWELL
Also Called: Honeywell
13509 S Point Blvd Ste 150 (28273-6897)
PHONE..............................734 942-5823
EMP: 33 **EST:** 2019
SALES (est): 4.24MM **Privately Held**
Web: www.honeywell.com
SIC: 3724 Aircraft engines and engine parts

(G-2919)
HONEYWELL INTERNATIONAL INC (PA)
Also Called: Honeywell
855 S Mint St (28202-1517)
PHONE..............................704 627-6200
Vimal Kapur, *CEO*
Darius Adamczyk, *
Gregory P Lewis, *Sr VP*
Anne T Madden, *Sr VP*
Karen Mattimore, *Chief Human Resource Officer*
♦ **EMP:** 3237 **EST:** 1920
SALES (est): 36.66B
SALES (corp-wide): 36.66B **Publicly Held**
Web: www.honeywell.com
SIC: 3724 Aircraft engines and engine parts

(G-2920)
HOOK-IT-UP
3837 Bon Rea Dr (28226-3151)
PHONE..............................980 253-4542
EMP: 4 **EST:** 2014
SALES (est): 51.33K **Privately Held**
SIC: 2399 Fabricated textile products, nec

(G-2921)
HOOKS INC CHRIS
6500 Tall Oaks Trl (28210-6129)
PHONE..............................704 516-1529
Christopher B Hooks, *Pr*
EMP: 5 **EST:** 2017
SALES (est): 80.22K **Privately Held**
SIC: 3599 Machine shop, jobbing and repair

(G-2922)
HORMEL FOODS CORP SVCS LLC
Also Called: Hormel
3420 Toringdon Way (28277-4433)
PHONE..............................704 527-1535
Clyde Maddux, *Prin*
EMP: 18
SALES (corp-wide): 12.11B **Publicly Held**
Web: www.hormelfoods.com
SIC: 2013 Sausages and other prepared meats
HQ: Hormel Foods Corporate Services, Llc
    1 Hormel Pl
    Austin MN 55912

(G-2923)
HOSPIRA INC
2815 Coliseum Centre Dr Ste 250 (28217)
PHONE..............................704 335-1300
EMP: 12
SALES (corp-wide): 100.33B **Publicly Held**
Web: www.pfizerhospitalus.com
SIC: 2834 Druggists' preparations (pharmaceuticals)
HQ: Hospira, Inc.
    275 N Field Dr
    Lake Forest IL 60045
    224 212-2000

(G-2924)
HOT BOX POWER COATING INC
1033 Berryhill Rd (28208-4117)
PHONE..............................704 398-8224
Sean Boudreaux, *Pr*
EMP: 4 **EST:** 2006
SALES (est): 468.05K **Privately Held**
Web: www.hotboxusa.com
SIC: 3479 Coating of metals and formed products

(G-2925)
HOWARD STEEL INC
3528 N Graham St (28206-1625)
PHONE..............................704 376-9631
James Howard, *Pr*
EMP: 12 **EST:** 1982
SQ FT: 25,000
SALES (est): 6.02MM **Privately Held**
Web: www.howardsteelinc.com
SIC: 5051 3441 Steel; Fabricated structural metal

(G-2926)
HOWMET AEROSPACE INC
Also Called: Howmet Aerospace Inc
301 N Smith St (28202)
PHONE..............................704 334-7276
EMP: 135
SALES (corp-wide): 6.64B **Publicly Held**
Web: www.howmet.com
SIC: 3353 Aluminum sheet and strip
PA: Howmet Aerospace Inc.
    201 Isabella St Ste 200
    Pittsburgh PA 15212
    412 553-1950

(G-2927)
HP INC
Also Called: HP
4035 South Blvd (28209-2616)
PHONE..............................704 523-3548
Bruce Chandler, *Mgr*
EMP: 5
SALES (corp-wide): 53.72B **Publicly Held**
Web: www.hp.com
SIC: 3571 Personal computers (microcomputers)
PA: Hp Inc.
    1501 Page Mill Rd
    Palo Alto CA 94304
    650 857-1501

(G-2928)
HUBER + SUHNER INC (DH)
8530 Steele Creek Place Dr Ste H (28273-3226)
PHONE..............................704 790-7300
Andy Hollywood, *Pr*
Yvonne Barney, *
Sean Thomas, *
▲ **EMP:** 40 **EST:** 1986
SQ FT: 35,000
SALES (est): 45.24MM **Privately Held**
Web: www.hubersuhner.com
SIC: 3679 3678 3357 5065 Microwave components; Electronic connectors; Nonferrous wiredrawing and insulating; Electronic parts and equipment, nec
HQ: Huber + Suhner (North America) Corporation
    8530 Steele Creek Pl
    Charlotte NC 28273

(G-2929)
HUBER + SUHNER NORTH AMER CORP (HQ)
Also Called: Huber Suhner USA Corporation
8530 Steele Creek Place Dr Ste H (28273-4276)
PHONE..............................704 790-7300
Ian Shergold, *Pr*
Drew Nixon, *VP*
Guy Petignat, *COO*
▲ **EMP:** 98 **EST:** 1988
SQ FT: 190,000
SALES (est): 122.4MM **Privately Held**
SIC: 3357 5065 Nonferrous wiredrawing and insulating; Electronic parts
PA: Huber+Suhner Ag
    Degersheimerstrasse 14
    Herisau AR 9100

(G-2930)
HUBER ENGINEERED WOODS LLC (HQ)
10925 David Taylor Dr Ste 300 (28262-1040)
PHONE..............................800 933-9220
Brian Carlson, *Pr*
Kirk Blanchette, *
Charles Lewis, *
Andrew Verrinder, *
♦ **EMP:** 50 **EST:** 2003
SQ FT: 21,000
SALES (est): 140.77MM
SALES (corp-wide): 1.24B **Privately Held**
Web: www.huberwood.com
SIC: 2493 Reconstituted wood products
PA: J.M. Huber Corporation
    3100 Cumberland Blvd Se # 600
    Atlanta GA 30339
    678 247-7300

(G-2931)
HUMBLE TREE NATURALS
4544 Randolph Rd Apt 70 (28211-2962)
PHONE..............................704 770-1007
Monique Sweeting, *Prin*
EMP: 5 **EST:** 2016
SALES (est): 50.66K **Privately Held**
Web: www.humbletreenaturals.com
SIC: 2844 Perfumes, cosmetics and other toilet preparations

(G-2932)
HUMILITY BRACELETS
5516 Challis View Ln (28226-2682)
PHONE..............................704 277-5896
EMP: 4 **EST:** 2016
SALES (est): 44.28K **Privately Held**
SIC: 3961 Bracelets, except precious metal

GEOGRAPHIC SECTION
Charlotte - Mecklenburg County (G-2956)

(G-2933)
HUNTSMAN CORPORATION
3400 Westinghouse Blvd (28273-4541)
PHONE.....................706 272-4020
Kay Moore, *Brnch Mgr*
EMP: 10
SALES (corp-wide): 6.11B **Publicly Held**
Web: www.huntsman.com
SIC: 2821 Polystyrene resins
PA: Huntsman Corporation
   10003 Woodloch Forest Dr # 260
   The Woodlands TX 77380
   281 719-6000

(G-2934)
HUNTSMAN INTERNATIONAL LLC
3400 Westinghouse Blvd (28273-4541)
PHONE.....................704 588-6082
Monte Edlund, *Mgr*
EMP: 29
SALES (corp-wide): 6.11B **Publicly Held**
Web: www.huntsman.com
SIC: 2821 Polystyrene resins
HQ: Huntsman International Llc
   10003 Woodloch Forest Dr # 260
   The Woodlands TX 77380
   281 719-6000

(G-2935)
HUNTSMAN TEXTILE EFFECTS
3400 Westinghouse Blvd (28273-4541)
PHONE.....................704 587-5000
Carol Walker, *Prin*
▲ **EMP:** 30 **EST:** 2009
SALES (est): 4.21MM **Privately Held**
Web: www.huntsman.com
SIC: 2821 Plastics materials and resins

(G-2936)
HUSQVRNA CNSMR OTDOOR PDTS NA (HQ)
Also Called: Husqvarna Forest & Garden
9335 Harris Corners Pkwy Ste 500 (28269)
PHONE.....................704 597-5000
Henric Andersson, *CEO*
Jill Jacobson, *
◆ **EMP:** 95 **EST:** 2005
SQ FT: 37,000
SALES (est): 2B
SALES (corp-wide): 5.15B **Privately Held**
SIC: 3524 Lawn and garden equipment
PA: Husqvarna Ab
   Drottninggatan 2
   Huskvarna 561 3
   36146500

(G-2937)
HUSQVRNA CNSMR OTDOOR PDTS NA
Also Called: Husqvarna Prof Outdoor Pdts
7349 Statesville Rd (28269-3702)
PHONE.....................704 597-5000
David Heinz, *Crdt Mgr*
EMP: 1096
SALES (corp-wide): 5.15B **Privately Held**
SIC: 3524 Lawn and garden equipment
HQ: Husqvarna Consumer Outdoor
   Products N.A., Inc.
   9335 Hrris Crners Pkwy St
   Charlotte NC 28269

(G-2938)
HUSQVRNA CNSMR OTDOOR PDTS NA
8825 Statesville Rd (28269-7638)
PHONE.....................704 494-4810
EMP: 834
SALES (corp-wide): 5.15B **Privately Held**
SIC: 3524 Lawn and garden tractors and equipment

HQ: Husqvarna Consumer Outdoor
   Products N.A., Inc.
   9335 Hrris Crners Pkwy St
   Charlotte NC 28269

(G-2939)
HYDE PARK PARTNERS INC (PA)
Also Called: Livingston & Haven
11529 Wilmar Blvd (28273-6448)
P.O. Box 7207 (28241-7207)
PHONE.....................704 587-4819
Anne Q Woody Prea, *Treas*
Anne Q Woody, *Pr*
Clifton B Vann Iii, *Ch*
Clifton B Vann Iv, *Pr*
James T Skinner Iii, *Sec*
▲ **EMP:** 95 **EST:** 1947
SQ FT: 50,000
SALES (est): 98.44MM
SALES (corp-wide): 98.44MM **Privately Held**
Web: www.hydeparkpartners.us
SIC: 5084 3594 Hydraulic systems equipment and supplies; Fluid power pumps and motors

(G-2940)
HYDRALIC ENGNERED PDTS SVC INC
Also Called: Hepsco
803 Pressley Rd Ste 101 (28217-0771)
P.O. Box 1528 (28070-1528)
PHONE.....................704 374-1306
Kenneth Jahns Senior, *CEO*
Kenneth Jahns Junior, *Pr*
Terry Treadwell, *Sec*
EMP: 4 **EST:** 1991
SQ FT: 5,000
SALES (est): 867.12K **Privately Held**
Web: www.hepsco.com
SIC: 5084 3594 Hydraulic systems equipment and supplies; Fluid power pumps and motors

(G-2941)
HYDRECO INC
1500 Continental Blvd Ste Z (28273-6376)
PHONE.....................704 295-7575
James Hill, *Prin*
EMP: 15 **EST:** 2008
SALES (est): 218.78K **Privately Held**
Web: www.hydreco.com
SIC: 3566 Speed changers, drives, and gears

(G-2942)
HYOSUNG HOLDINGS USA INC (HQ)
15801 Brixham Hill Ave Ste 575 (28277-0749)
PHONE.....................704 790-6134
Terry Swanner, *Pr*
Hyeong Seob Jeong, *CFO*
▲ **EMP:** 8 **EST:** 2008
SALES (est): 472.09MM **Privately Held**
Web: www.hyosungusa.com
SIC: 2221 2296 5199 Broadwoven fabric mills, manmade; Cord for reinforcing rubber tires; Fabrics, yarns, and knit goods
PA: Hyosung Corporation
   119 Mapo-Daero, Mapo-Gu
   Seoul 04144

(G-2943)
HYOSUNG USA INC (DH)
15801 Brixham Hill Ave Ste 575 (28277-0749)
PHONE.....................704 790-6100
Terry Swanner, *Pr*
Bong Kwan Choi, *
◆ **EMP:** 30 **EST:** 1993
SALES (est): 472.09MM **Privately Held**

Web: www.hyosungusa.com
SIC: 2221 2296 5199 Broadwoven fabric mills, manmade; Cord for reinforcing rubber tires; Fabrics, yarns, and knit goods
HQ: Hyosung Holdings Usa, Inc.
   15801 Brixham Hill Ave # 575
   Charlotte NC 28277
   704 790-6134

(G-2944)
HYPERNOVA INC
Also Called: Hypernova Solutions
1228 Archdale Dr Apt E (28217)
PHONE.....................704 360-0096
Matthew Cauthen, *Pr*
EMP: 8 **EST:** 2018
SALES (est): 548.15K **Privately Held**
SIC: 3571 Electronic computers

(G-2945)
IBENY EMBROIDERING LLC
4800 Express Dr (28208-6354)
PHONE.....................347 286-1299
EMP: 4 **EST:** 2017
SALES (est): 100.78K **Privately Held**
SIC: 2395 Embroidery and art needlework

(G-2946)
ICEE COMPANY
1901 Associates Ln Ste A (28217-2874)
PHONE.....................704 357-6865
Kurt Ritzel, *Prin*
EMP: 4
SALES (corp-wide): 1.56B **Publicly Held**
Web: www.icee.com
SIC: 2086 Bottled and canned soft drinks
HQ: The Icee Company
   265 Mason Rd
   La Vergne TN 37086
   800 426-4233

(G-2947)
ICT/DATA ON CD INC
9123 Monroe Rd Ste 145 (28270-2434)
PHONE.....................704 841-8404
Steward Scher, *Prin*
EMP: 6 **EST:** 2010
SALES (est): 195.17K **Privately Held**
SIC: 3572 Computer storage devices

(G-2948)
ID IMAGES LLC
2311 Distribution Center Dr Ste A (28269)
PHONE.....................704 494-0444
Robert Miller, *Pr*
EMP: 5 **EST:** 2016
SALES (est): 224.81K **Privately Held**
Web: www.idimages.com
SIC: 2759 Commercial printing, nec

(G-2949)
IGH ENTERPRISES INC
Also Called: Mitchum Quality Snack
2001 W Morehead St (28208-5139)
PHONE.....................704 372-6744
John Wilson, *Pr*
Bonnie Tirvette, *
Cheri Shipley, *
Henry D Pully, *
▲ **EMP:** 31 **EST:** 2004
SQ FT: 170,000
SALES (est): 1.79MM **Privately Held**
SIC: 2096 2099 Potato chips and other potato-based snacks; Food preparations, nec

(G-2950)
IGM RESINS USA INC (DH)
Also Called: I G M
3300 Westinghouse Blvd (28273-6521)

PHONE.....................704 588-2500
◆ **EMP:** 59 **EST:** 2010
SALES (est): 45.49MM **Privately Held**
Web: www.igmresins.com
SIC: 2851 Coating, air curing
HQ: Igm Specialties Holding, Inc.
   3300 Westinghouse Blvd
   Charlotte NC 28273
   704 945-8702

(G-2951)
IGM SPECIALTIES HOLDING INC (DH)
3300 Westinghouse Blvd (28273-6521)
PHONE.....................704 945-8702
Gerald Walker, *Prin*
Hohn Huiberts, *Prin*
EMP: 12 **EST:** 2012
SALES (est): 55.75MM **Privately Held**
Web: www.igmresins.com
SIC: 6799 2851 Investors, nec; Coating, air curing
HQ: I.G.M. Resins B.V.
   Gompenstraat 49
   Waalwijk NB 5145

(G-2952)
ILSEMANN CORP
2555 Westinghouse Blvd (28273-7509)
PHONE.....................610 323-4143
Stephan Ilsemann, *Pr*
▲ **EMP:** 4 **EST:** 2013
SALES (est): 452.81K **Privately Held**
Web: www.ilsemann.com
SIC: 3559 Robots, molding and forming plastics

(G-2953)
IMPERIAL FALCON GROUP INC
3440 Toringdon Way Ste 205 (28277-3190)
PHONE.....................646 717-1128
Wael Elias, *CEO*
EMP: 5 **EST:** 2014
SALES (est): 1.8MM **Privately Held**
SIC: 2052 3944 2869 7389 Biscuits, dry; Automobiles and trucks, toy; Industrial organic chemicals, nec; Business Activities at Non-Commercial Site

(G-2954)
IMPERIAL USA LTD
Also Called: Global Door Controls
1535 Elizabeth Ave Ste 201 (28204-2502)
PHONE.....................704 596-2444
Antoune E Battah Junior, *Pr*
◆ **EMP:** 30 **EST:** 1994
SALES (est): 8.04MM **Privately Held**
Web: www.impusa.com
SIC: 3429 5072 Furniture hardware; Hardware

(G-2955)
IMPRINT PUBLISHING LLC
3403 Arsenal Ct Apt 311 (28273-7202)
PHONE.....................678 650-1140
Shantel Tatem, *Prin*
EMP: 5 **EST:** 2012
SALES (est): 96.33K **Privately Held**
Web: www.petewardtravel.com
SIC: 2741 Miscellaneous publishing

(G-2956)
IMPRINTING SYSTEMS SPCALTY INC
803 Pressley Rd Ste 104 (28217-0971)
PHONE.....................704 527-4545
Glenn Randolph, *Pr*
Lois Randolph, *VP*
Mark Kessler, *VP*
Cindy Kessler, *Sec*
EMP: 6 **EST:** 1979
SQ FT: 8,000

Charlotte - Mecklenburg County (G-2957)

GEOGRAPHIC SECTION

SALES (est): 755.21K **Privately Held**
Web: www.imprintinginc.com
SIC: 2759 Labels and seals: printing, nsk

(G-2957)
INCANTARE ART BY MARILYN LLC
15701 Pedlar Mills Rd (28278-7686)
PHONE..................................704 713-8846
Marilyn Marte, *CEO*
EMP: 12 **EST:** 2020
SALES (est): 127.72K **Privately Held**
SIC: 8999 3229 Artist; Art, decorative and novelty glassware

(G-2958)
INDEPENDENCE HOLDINGS INC
1001 Westinghouse Blvd (28273-6323)
P.O. Box 220283 (28222-0283)
PHONE..................................704 588-6202
EMP: 5 **EST:** 2015
SALES (est): 81.2K **Privately Held**
SIC: 3086 Plastics foam products

(G-2959)
INDEPENDENT BEVERAGE CO LLC (PA)
3936 Corporation Cir (28216-3421)
PHONE..................................704 399-2504
Jeff Rogers, *Pr*
David Barker, *Sec*
◆ **EMP:** 10 **EST:** 1992
SQ FT: 105,000
SALES (est): 37.46MM **Privately Held**
Web: www.independentbeverage.com
SIC: 2086 Bottled and canned soft drinks

(G-2960)
INDESTRUCTIBLE LLC
525 N Tryon St Ste 1600 (28202-0202)
PHONE..................................804 601-4097
EMP: 4
SALES (est): 79.3K **Privately Held**
SIC: 2759 Fashion plates: printing, nsk

(G-2961)
INDIAN HEAD INDUSTRIES INC (PA)
Also Called: MGM Brakes
6200 Harris Technology Blvd (28269-3732)
PHONE..................................704 547-7411
Ron Parker, *CEO*
Jeffrey Parker, *
Susan Pfeiffr, *
◆ **EMP:** 45 **EST:** 1984
SQ FT: 15,000
SALES (est): 52.66MM
SALES (corp-wide): 52.66MM **Privately Held**
Web: www.mgmbrakes.com
SIC: 3593 3714 Fluid power cylinders and actuators; Motor vehicle brake systems and parts

(G-2962)
INDUSTRIAL MECHATRONICS INC
117 Freeland Ln (28217-1617)
P.O. Box 620457 (28262-0107)
PHONE..................................704 900-2407
David Lewis, *Pr*
EMP: 5 **EST:** 2005
SALES (est): 472.11K **Privately Held**
SIC: 3441 Fabricated structural metal

(G-2963)
INDUSTRIAL MGMT OF MATERIALS
647 Michael Wylie Dr (28217-1546)
PHONE..................................704 359-9928
Jason Ellis, *Brnch Mgr*
EMP: 10
SALES (corp-wide): 55.97MM **Privately Held**

Web: www.americanstainlessandsupply.com
SIC: 3494 Pipe fittings
PA: Industrial Management Of Materials Of The Carolinas, Llc
815 State Rd
Cheraw SC 29520
843 537-5231

(G-2964)
INDUSTRIAL PIPING INC
212 S Tryon St Ste 1050 (28281-0003)
P.O. Box Po Box 518 (28281)
PHONE..................................704 588-1100
▲ **EMP:** 650
Web: www.goipi.com
SIC: 3599 3569 Machine shop, jobbing and repair; Sprinkler systems, fire: automatic

(G-2965)
INDUSTRIAL SIGN & GRAPHICS INC (PA)
4227 N Graham St (28206-1214)
P.O. Box 35565 (28235-5565)
PHONE..................................704 371-4985
Larry M Lee, *Pr*
Alan Pressley, *VP*
▲ **EMP:** 21 **EST:** 1990
SQ FT: 20,000
SALES (est): 4.53MM **Privately Held**
Web: www.industrialsign.com
SIC: 3993 2752 Signs and advertising specialties; Commercial printing, lithographic

(G-2966)
INDUSTRIAL TIMBER LLC (PA)
6441 Hendry Rd Ste A (28269-3848)
PHONE..................................704 919-1215
Michael Ruch, *Mgr*
▲ **EMP:** 75 **EST:** 2017
SALES (est): 86.38MM
SALES (corp-wide): 86.38MM **Privately Held**
Web: www.thesmartplay.com
SIC: 2493 5031 Reconstituted wood products; Lumber, plywood, and millwork

(G-2967)
INFINITE SOFTWARE RESORCES LLC (PA)
3020 Prosperity Church Rd 1 (28269)
PHONE..................................704 509-0031
EMP: 9 **EST:** 1998
SQ FT: 1,500
SALES (est): 1.84MM
SALES (corp-wide): 1.84MM **Privately Held**
SIC: 8748 7372 Systems analysis and engineering consulting services; Prepackaged software

(G-2968)
INFINITY S END INC (PA)
Also Called: Infinity Signs and Screen Prtg
7804 Fairview Rd Ste C (28226-4999)
PHONE..................................704 900-8355
Frank Pietras, *Pr*
John Pietras, *Sec*
Patricia Ann Manning, *Prin*
EMP: 11 **EST:** 1970
SQ FT: 5,500
SALES (est): 3.07MM
SALES (corp-wide): 3.07MM **Privately Held**
Web: www.infinitysend.com
SIC: 5331 5999 2759 3993 Variety stores; Art and architectural supplies; Screen printing; Signs and advertising specialties

(G-2969)
INFISOFT SOFTWARE
7422 Carmel Executive Park Dr (28226-8273)
PHONE..................................704 307-2619
Jeff Barefoot, *Prin*
EMP: 8 **EST:** 2009
SALES (est): 153.37K **Privately Held**
SIC: 7372 7371 5734 Prepackaged software; Computer software development; Computer software and accessories

(G-2970)
INFO-GEL LLC (PA)
2311 Distribution Center Dr Ste F (28269)
PHONE..................................704 599-5770
Quint Barefoot, *Managing Member*
James Olesinski, *Owner*
▲ **EMP:** 7 **EST:** 2007
SQ FT: 1,000
SALES (est): 2.47MM **Privately Held**
Web: www.info-gel.com
SIC: 2899 Gelatin: edible, technical, photographic, or pharmaceutical

(G-2971)
INFOBELT LLC (PA)
4100 Beresford Rd (28211-3810)
PHONE..................................980 223-4000
Srinivas Mannava, *Managing Member*
EMP: 16 **EST:** 2011
SQ FT: 2,500
SALES (est): 1.47MM
SALES (corp-wide): 1.47MM **Privately Held**
Web: www.infobelt.com
SIC: 7373 7374 7372 7376 Computer integrated systems design; Data processing service; Business oriented computer software; Computer facilities management

(G-2972)
INFORMATION AGE PUBLISHING INC
11600 N Community House Rd # R (28277-1887)
P.O. Box 79049 (28271-7047)
PHONE..................................704 752-9125
George Johnson, *Prin*
EMP: 9 **EST:** 2007
SALES (est): 946.27K **Privately Held**
Web: www.infoagepub.com
SIC: 2741 Miscellaneous publishing

(G-2973)
INGERSOLL RAND INC
6000 General Commerce Dr (28213-6394)
PHONE..................................704 774-4290
EMP: 50
SALES (corp-wide): 6.88B **Publicly Held**
Web: www.irco.com
SIC: 3563 Air and gas compressors
PA: Ingersoll Rand Inc.
525 Harbour Place Dr # 600
Davidson NC 28036
704 896-4000

(G-2974)
INGERSOLL-RAND COMPANY
Also Called: Ingersoll-Rand
10000 Twin Lakes Pkwy (28269-7653)
PHONE..................................704 655-4836
EMP: 84
SIC: 3561 Pumps and pumping equipment
HQ: Ingersoll-Rand Company
800 Beaty St Ste B
Davidson NC 28036
704 655-4000

(G-2975)
INNAIT INC
Also Called: Innait
5524 Joyce Dr (28215-2417)
PHONE..................................406 241-5245
Roger Mukai, *CEO*
Roger Mukai, *Prin*
Jonathon Robin, *Prin*
Alan Anderson, *Prin*
Lee Speers, *Prin*
EMP: 6 **EST:** 2020
SALES (est): 240.74K **Privately Held**
SIC: 7371 7378 7372 7374 Software programming applications; Computer and data processing equipment repair/maintenance; Operating systems computer software; Data processing service

(G-2976)
INPLAC NORTH AMERICA INC
10926 S Tryon St Ste F (28273-4154)
PHONE..................................704 587-1151
Fernando Marcondes, *Pr*
▲ **EMP:** 4 **EST:** 2003
SALES (est): 488.56K **Privately Held**
Web: www.inplacna.com
SIC: 3089 5113 Plastics processing; Bags, paper and disposable plastic

(G-2977)
INSTA COPY SHOP LTD
Also Called: ICI Copy Forms & Printing
4311 South Blvd Ste D (28209-2624)
PHONE..................................704 376-1350
Don Lloyd, *Pr*
Rick Lloyd, *VP*
EMP: 14 **EST:** 1982
SQ FT: 6,000
SALES (est): 998.67K **Privately Held**
Web: www.iciprint.com
SIC: 2752 Offset printing

(G-2978)
INTEGRATED PRINT SERVICES INC
8534 Dennington Grove Ln (28277-0277)
PHONE..................................704 307-4495
Bipin Amin, *Prin*
EMP: 5 **EST:** 2018
SALES (est): 121.99K **Privately Held**
SIC: 2752 Commercial printing, lithographic

(G-2979)
INTEPLAST GROUP CORPORATION
10701 S Commerce Blvd Ste A (28273-5300)
PHONE..................................704 504-3200
Kim Knapik, *Off Mgr*
EMP: 24
Web: www.inteplast.com
SIC: 3081 Polyethylene film
PA: Inteplast Group Corporation
9 Peach Tree Hill Rd
Livingston NJ 07039

(G-2980)
INTER-CONTINENTAL GEAR & BRAKE (PA)
6431 Reames Rd (28216-5280)
PHONE..................................704 599-3420
Dave Morgan, *Mgr*
▲ **EMP:** 8 **EST:** 2007
SALES (est): 3.87MM
SALES (corp-wide): 3.87MM **Privately Held**
Web: www.icgb.ca
SIC: 3714 Motor vehicle parts and accessories

GEOGRAPHIC SECTION

Charlotte - Mecklenburg County (G-3005)

(G-2981)
INTERIOR TRIM CREATIONS INC
11912 Erwin Ridge Ave (28213-2137)
PHONE..................704 821-1470
EMP: 6 EST: 1986
SALES (est): 125.26K **Privately Held**
SIC: **1751** 2431 Finish and trim carpentry; Millwork

(G-2982)
INTERNATIONAL FOAM PDTS INC (PA)
10530 Westlake Dr (28273-3788)
PHONE..................704 588-0080
Steve Sklow, *Pr*
EMP: 5 EST: 1963
SQ FT: 65,000
SALES (est): 3.8MM
SALES (corp-wide): 3.8MM **Privately Held**
Web: www.internationalfoam.com
SIC: **2396** 5199 Bindings, bias: made from purchased materials; Foam rubber

(G-2983)
INTERNATIONAL PAPER COMPANY
Also Called: International Paper
11020 David Taylor Dr (28262-1101)
PHONE..................704 393-8210
EMP: 5
SALES (corp-wide): 18.92B **Publicly Held**
Web: www.internationalpaper.com
SIC: **2621** Paper mills
PA: International Paper Company
6400 Poplar Ave
Memphis TN 38197
901 419-7000

(G-2984)
INTERNATIONAL PAPER COMPANY
International Paper
10601 Westlake Dr (28273-3930)
PHONE..................704 588-8522
Keith Miller, *Brnch Mgr*
EMP: 7
SALES (corp-wide): 18.92B **Publicly Held**
Web: www.internationalpaper.com
SIC: **2621** Paper mills
PA: International Paper Company
6400 Poplar Ave
Memphis TN 38197
901 419-7000

(G-2985)
INTERNATIONAL PAPER COMPANY
Also Called: International Paper
5419 Hovis Rd (28208-1241)
PHONE..................704 398-8354
Jim Atkins, *Brnch Mgr*
EMP: 150
SALES (corp-wide): 18.92B **Publicly Held**
Web: www.internationalpaper.com
SIC: **2621** Paper mills
PA: International Paper Company
6400 Poplar Ave
Memphis TN 38197
901 419-7000

(G-2986)
INTERNATIONAL PAPER COMPANY
Also Called: International Paper
201 E 28th St (28206-2720)
PHONE..................704 334-5222
Jack Docell, *Mgr*
EMP: 6
SQ FT: 62,950
SALES (corp-wide): 18.92B **Publicly Held**
Web: www.internationalpaper.com
SIC: **2621** 2611 Paper mills; Pulp manufactured from waste or recycled paper
PA: International Paper Company
6400 Poplar Ave
Memphis TN 38197
901 419-7000

(G-2987)
INTERNATIONAL PAPER COMPANY
Also Called: International Paper
3700 Display Dr (28273-4133)
PHONE..................704 588-8522
EMP: 5
SALES (corp-wide): 18.92B **Publicly Held**
Web: www.internationalpaper.com
SIC: **2653** Boxes, corrugated: made from purchased materials
PA: International Paper Company
6400 Poplar Ave
Memphis TN 38197
901 419-7000

(G-2988)
INTERNATIONAL THERMODYNE INC
3120 Latrobe Dr Ste 110 (28211-2190)
PHONE..................704 579-8218
Greg Hackworth, *Admn*
EMP: 4 EST: 2013
SQ FT: 500
SALES (est): 469.59K **Privately Held**
Web: www.opal.us
SIC: **3699** Electrical equipment and supplies, nec

(G-2989)
INVENTIVE GRAPHICS INC
Also Called: AlphaGraphics
9129 Monroe Rd Ste 160 (28270-2431)
P.O. Box 279 (28106-0279)
PHONE..................704 814-4900
Gary Grefrath, *Prin*
EMP: 6 EST: 2005
SALES (est): 516.42K **Privately Held**
Web: www.alphagraphics.com
SIC: **2752** Commercial printing, lithographic

(G-2990)
INX INTERNATIONAL INK CO
Also Called: INX International
10820 Withers Cove Park Dr (28278-6928)
PHONE..................704 372-2080
Al Baird, *Mgr*
EMP: 16
Web: www.inxinternational.com
SIC: **2893** Printing ink
HQ: Inx International Ink Co.
150 N Martingale Rd # 700
Schaumburg IL 60173
630 382-1800

(G-2991)
IODINE POETRY JOURNAL
1543 Rumstone Ln (28262-4219)
P.O. Box 18548 (28218-0548)
PHONE..................704 595-9526
Jonathan Rice, *Owner*
EMP: 5 EST: 2001
SALES (est): 74.43K **Privately Held**
Web: www.iodinepoetryjournal.com
SIC: **2711** Newspapers, publishing and printing

(G-2992)
IPD CO
505 White Water Falls Dr Apt 716 (28217-5258)
PHONE..................704 999-4484
EMP: 10 EST: 2014
SALES (est): 195.98K **Privately Held**
Web: www.ipdcompany.com
SIC: **3441** Fabricated structural metal

(G-2993)
IPERIONX LIMITED
129 W Trade St Ste 1405 (28202-2143)
PHONE..................704 578-3217
Anastasios Arima, *CEO*
Todd W Hannigan, *Ex Ch Bd*
Gregory D Swan, *VP*
Dominic Allen, *CCO*
Jeanne Mcmullin, *CLO*
EMP: 20 EST: 2017
SALES (est): 3MM **Privately Held**
SIC: **1099** 3295 Titanium and zirconium ores mining; Minerals, ground or treated

(G-2994)
IPERIONX TECHNOLOGY LLC
129 W Trade St Ste 1405 (28202-2143)
PHONE..................704 578-3217
Kayla Luther, *
EMP: 5 EST: 2021
SALES (est): 381.65K **Privately Held**
SIC: **1081** Metal mining exploration and development services

(G-2995)
IPEX USA LLC
7125 Logistics Center Dr (28273-4638)
PHONE..................704 889-2431
EMP: 11
SALES (corp-wide): 87.53MM **Privately Held**
SIC: **3498** Piping systems for pulp, paper, and chemical industries
HQ: Ipex Usa Llc
10100 Rodney St
Pineville NC 28134

(G-2996)
IPI ACQUISITION LLC
13504 S Point Blvd Ste M (28273-6763)
P.O. Box 518 (28134-0518)
PHONE..................704 588-1100
Michael L Jones, *Pr*
Blair A Swogger, *
EMP: 650 EST: 2008
SIC: **6719** 3599 3569 Investment holding companies, except banks; Machine shop, jobbing and repair; Sprinkler systems, fire: automatic

(G-2997)
ISANA LLC
611 Cricketwood Ln (28215-2165)
PHONE..................704 439-6761
Alfredo Jr Camacho, *VP*
Alfredo Jr Camacho, *VP*
Nayan Kathwadia, *Prin*
EMP: 4 EST: 2016
SALES (est): 148.98K **Privately Held**
SIC: **2842** 7349 1799 Specialty cleaning; Cleaning service, industrial or commercial; Cleaning new buildings after construction

(G-2998)
ITLAQ TECHNOLOGIES
11420 Delores Ferguson Ln (28277-2131)
PHONE..................305 549-8561
Rafeef Sabri, *Owner*
EMP: 5 EST: 2017
SALES (est): 106.5K **Privately Held**
Web: www.itlaq.com
SIC: **7372** Prepackaged software

(G-2999)
ITT LLC
4828 Parkway Plaza Blvd # 200 (28217-1957)
PHONE..................704 716-7000
Jim Dartez, *Brnch Mgr*
EMP: 10
SALES (corp-wide): 3.28B **Publicly Held**
Web: www.itt.com
SIC: **3625** Control equipment, electric
HQ: Itt Llc
1133 Westchester Ave N-100
White Plains NY 10604
914 641-2000

(G-3000)
IVM CHEMICALS INC
Also Called: Milesi Wood Coatings
301 Mccullough Dr Fl 4 (28262-3310)
PHONE..................407 506-4913
Jeffrey Takac, *Pr*
EMP: 50 EST: 2015
SALES (est): 3.44MM **Privately Held**
Web: www.ivmchemicals.com
SIC: **2899** Chemical preparations, nec

(G-3001)
IVY BRAND LLC
106 Foster Ave (28203-5420)
PHONE..................980 225-7866
Lisa M Thompson, *CEO*
EMP: 4 EST: 2014
SALES (est): 235.42K **Privately Held**
SIC: **2231** 2211 2221 Apparel and outerwear broadwoven fabrics; Apparel and outerwear fabrics, cotton; Apparel and outerwear fabric, manmade fiber or silk

(G-3002)
J & D WELDING & FABG CORP
6120 Brookshire Blvd (28216-3323)
PHONE..................704 393-9115
EMP: 5 EST: 2020
SALES (est): 204.6K **Privately Held**
Web: j-d-welding-fabricating-corporation.business.site
SIC: **7692** Welding repair

(G-3003)
J & W STEEL INC
9601 Parkridge Dr (28214-9067)
PHONE..................980 579-0452
EMP: 11 EST: 2017
SALES (est): 589.15K **Privately Held**
Web: www.jwsteelinc.com
SIC: **3441** Fabricated structural metal

(G-3004)
J L SMITH & CO INC (PA)
901 Blairhill Rd Ste 400 (28217-1578)
PHONE..................704 521-1088
Jeff L Smith, *Pr*
Cathy Phillips, *Dir*
EMP: 15 EST: 1990
SQ FT: 8,575
SALES (est): 4.59MM **Privately Held**
Web: www.jlsmithco.com
SIC: **5736** 3931 5099 Musical instrument stores; Musical instruments; Musical instruments

(G-3005)
J R COLE INDUSTRIES INC
Labeltec
10708 Granite St (28273-6379)
PHONE..................704 523-6622
Ken Thunder, *Brnch Mgr*
EMP: 90
SALES (corp-wide): 24.59MM **Privately Held**
Web: www.jrcole.com
SIC: **7389** 2679 Packaging and labeling services; Labels, paper: made from purchased material
PA: J. R. Cole Industries, Inc.
435 Minuet Ln
Charlotte NC 28217
704 523-6622

Charlotte - Mecklenburg County (G-3006)   GEOGRAPHIC SECTION

(G-3006)
J R COLE INDUSTRIES INC (PA)
435 Minuet Ln (28217-2718)
PHONE.................................704 523-6622
Joseph Robert Cole Senior, *Ch Bd*
Donald W Griffin, *VP*
EMP: 19 **EST:** 1984
SQ FT: 8,500
SALES (est): 24.59MM
SALES (corp-wide): 24.59MM **Privately Held**
Web: www.jrcole.com
SIC: 2752 Commercial printing, lithographic

(G-3007)
J&C WELDING AND FABRICATION
3550 Briarthorne Dr (28269-1255)
PHONE.................................704 654-8253
Cory Justice, *Prin*
EMP: 5 **EST:** 2017
SALES (est): 47.55K **Privately Held**
SIC: 7692 Welding repair

(G-3008)
JALILUD EMBROIDERY LLC ✪
9419 Silverdale Ln (28269-3472)
PHONE.................................704 425-3492
EMP: 4 **EST:** 2022
SALES (est): 64.64K **Privately Held**
SIC: 2395 Embroidery and art needlework

(G-3009)
JASMINE WADE CO LLC
15120 Kellington Ct (28273-3455)
PHONE.................................704 345-8301
EMP: 5 **EST:** 2021
SALES (est): 67.2K **Privately Held**
Web: www.jasminewade.com
SIC: 3999 Candles

(G-3010)
JBS ORDNANCE INC
9036 Bremerton Ct (28227-3201)
PHONE.................................980 722-3659
EMP: 4 **EST:** 2016
SALES (est): 65.81K **Privately Held**
SIC: 3489 Ordnance and accessories, nec

(G-3011)
JC SIGNS INC
2336 Kenmore Ave Unit F (28204-4349)
PHONE.................................704 995-0988
Jeff Clayton, *Prin*
EMP: 4 **EST:** 2012
SALES (est): 233.7K **Privately Held**
Web: www.jcsignscharlotte.com
SIC: 3993 Electric signs

(G-3012)
JC SIGNS CHARLOTTE
9700 Research Dr (28262-8552)
PHONE.................................704 370-2725
Jeff Clayton, *Admn*
EMP: 5 **EST:** 2016
SALES (est): 233.94K **Privately Held**
Web: www.jcsignscharlotte.com
SIC: 3993 Signs and advertising specialties

(G-3013)
JC WICKS LLC
1220 Ballina Way (28214-7157)
PHONE.................................828 514-9788
EMP: 4 **EST:** 2021
SALES (est): 70.59K **Privately Held**
Web: www.jcwicks.com
SIC: 3999 Candles

(G-3014)
JCI JONES CHEMICALS INC
1500 Tar Heel Rd (28208-1533)
PHONE.................................704 392-9767
Lynn Martin, *Mgr*
EMP: 28
SALES (corp-wide): 196.9MM **Privately Held**
Web: www.jcichem.com
SIC: 2812 5169 2899 2842 Chlorine, compressed or liquefied; Chemicals and allied products, nec; Chemical preparations, nec; Polishes and sanitation goods
PA: Jci Jones Chemicals, Inc.
   1765 Ringling Blvd
   Sarasota FL 34236
   941 330-1537

(G-3015)
JCTM LLC
Also Called: Jctm
16710 Tulloch Rd (28278-8905)
PHONE.................................252 571-8678
Audie Cooper, *Mgr*
EMP: 60 **EST:** 2015
SALES (est): 8.28MM **Privately Held**
Web: www.jctm.us
SIC: 7371 7372 Computer software systems analysis and design, custom; Application computer software

(G-3016)
JDH CAPITAL LLC (PA)
3735 Beam Rd Unit B (28217-8800)
PHONE.................................704 357-1220
Gary J Davies, *Managing Member*
David P Hill, *Managing Member*
EMP: 13 **EST:** 1999
SALES (est): 187.63MM
SALES (corp-wide): 187.63MM **Privately Held**
SIC: 6531 2011 Real estate agents and managers; Meat packing plants

(G-3017)
JEANS PRINTSHOP LLC
4221 W Sugar Creek Rd (28269-1918)
PHONE.................................704 564-4348
EMP: 5 **EST:** 2009
SALES (est): 171.63K **Privately Held**
SIC: 2752 Commercial printing, lithographic

(G-3018)
JELD-WEN INC (HQ)
Also Called: Jeld Wen International Supply
2645 Silver Crescent Dr (28273-3566)
PHONE.................................800 535-3936
Kevin C Lilly, *CEO*
L Brooks Mallard, *
Krish Mani, *CIO**
Scott Vining, *CAO**
John A Dinger, *
◆ **EMP:** 266 **EST:** 1960
SQ FT: 12,000
SALES (est): 1.76B **Publicly Held**
Web: www.jeld-wen.com
SIC: 3442 5031 2421 Shutters, door or window: metal; Doors, combination, screen-storm; Building and structural materials, wood
PA: Jeld-Wen Holding, Inc.
   2645 Silver Crescent Dr
   Charlotte NC 28273

(G-3019)
JELD-WEN HOLDING INC (PA)
Also Called: Jeld-Wen
2645 Silver Crescent Dr (28273-3566)
PHONE.................................704 378-5700
William Christensen, *CEO*
David G Nord, *Ch Bd*
Kevin C Lilly, *Interim Chief Executive Officer*
Roderick C Wendt, *V Ch Bd*
John R Linker, *Ex VP*
▲ **EMP:** 388 **EST:** 1960
SALES (est): 4.3B **Publicly Held**
Web: www.jeld-wen.com
SIC: 2431 3442 Millwork; Metal doors, sash, and trim

(G-3020)
JENKINS ELECTRIC COMPANY
Also Called: Jenkins
5933 Brookshire Blvd (28216-3386)
P.O. Box 32127 (28232-2127)
PHONE.................................800 438-3003
Iain Jenkins, *Pr*
Edward Jenkins Junior, *Ch*
Wayne L Hall, *
◆ **EMP:** 74 **EST:** 1907
SQ FT: 50,000
SALES (est): 21.47MM **Privately Held**
Web: www.jenkinselectric.com
SIC: 3699 7694 5063 Electrical equipment and supplies, nec; Electric motor repair; Electrical apparatus and equipment

(G-3021)
JHONNY DELGADO
Also Called: Delgado's Fuego
7321 William Reynolds Dr (28215-2346)
PHONE.................................704 218-9424
Jhonny Delgado, *Owner*
EMP: 4 **EST:** 2019
SALES (est): 58.17K **Privately Held**
Web: www.delgadosfuego.com
SIC: 2035 Dressings, salad: raw and cooked (except dry mixes)

(G-3022)
JIM MYERS & SONS INC
5120 Westinghouse Blvd (28273-9637)
P.O. Box 38778 (28278-1013)
PHONE.................................704 554-8397
David L Myers, *Pr*
James B Myers Iii, *VP*
EMP: 55 **EST:** 1962
SQ FT: 50,000
SALES (est): 23.25MM **Privately Held**
Web: www.jmsequipment.com
SIC: 3589 Water treatment equipment, industrial

(G-3023)
JJ LED SOLUTION INC
5413 Stowe Derby Dr (28278-7379)
PHONE.................................704 261-4279
Jae Y Chung, *Prin*
EMP: 5 **EST:** 2017
SALES (est): 85.72K **Privately Held**
SIC: 3993 Signs and advertising specialties

(G-3024)
JM GRAPHICS INC
3400 International Airport Dr Ste 950 (28208-4787)
PHONE.................................704 375-1147
James Marek, *Pr*
EMP: 7 **EST:** 1974
SALES (est): 539K **Privately Held**
Web: www.jmgraphics.org
SIC: 2752 Offset printing

(G-3025)
JM INNOVATIONS LLC
7222 Lillian Way (28226-3027)
PHONE.................................704 495-4841
EMP: 4 **EST:** 2019
SALES (est): 162.72K **Privately Held**
SIC: 3523 Farm machinery and equipment

(G-3026)
JOANNA DIVISION CH F INDS
8701 Red Oak Blvd Ste 400 (28217-2960)
PHONE.................................704 522-5000
Mel Cohen, *Prin*
EMP: 5 **EST:** 2006
SALES (est): 58.58K **Privately Held**
SIC: 3999 Manufacturing industries, nec

(G-3027)
JOERNS HEALTHCARE PARENT LLC (PA)
2430 Whitehall Park Dr Ste 100 (28273-3948)
PHONE.................................800 966-6662
EMP: 275 **EST:** 2006
SALES (est): 152.39MM
SALES (corp-wide): 152.39MM **Privately Held**
Web: www.joerns.com
SIC: 5047 2512 Medical equipment and supplies; Recliners: upholstered on wood frames

(G-3028)
JOHN J MORTON COMPANY INC (PA)
2211 W Morehead St (28208-5143)
P.O. Box 32773 (28232-2773)
PHONE.................................704 332-6633
William R Standish Ii, *Pr*
Frank Morfit, *VP*
William R Standish, *Stockholder*
Betty E Standish, *Stockholder*
EMP: 17 **EST:** 1920
SQ FT: 29,000
SALES (est): 1.77MM
SALES (corp-wide): 1.77MM **Privately Held**
SIC: 3281 1741 Cut stone and stone products; Marble masonry, exterior construction

(G-3029)
JOHNSON CONTROLS
9826 Southern Pine Blvd (28273-5561)
PHONE.................................704 501-0500
Barry Wells, *Brnch Mgr*
EMP: 200
SIC: 3669 Emergency alarms
HQ: Johnson Controls Fire Protection Lp
   6600 Congress Ave
   Boca Raton FL 33487
   561 988-7200

(G-3030)
JOHNSON CONTROLS INC
Also Called: Johnson Controls
9844 Southern Pine Blvd Ste B (28273-5502)
PHONE.................................704 521-8889
Ernest Ray Thompson, *Genl Mgr*
EMP: 43
Web: www.johnsoncontrols.com
SIC: 3822 5075 5074 5063 Thermostats, except built-in; Warm air heating and air conditioning; Plumbing and hydronic heating supplies; Electrical apparatus and equipment
HQ: Johnson Controls, Inc.
   5757 N Green Bay Ave
   Milwaukee WI 53209
   920 245-6409

(G-3031)
JOHNSON CONTROLS INC
Also Called: Johnson Controls
9844 Southern Pine Blvd (28273-5502)
PHONE.................................704 521-8889
EMP: 20
Web: www.johnsoncontrols.com

GEOGRAPHIC SECTION

Charlotte - Mecklenburg County (G-3058)

SIC: 2531 Seats, automobile
HQ: Johnson Controls, Inc.
5757 N Green Bay Ave
Milwaukee WI 53209
920 245-6409

(G-3032)
JOHNSON GLOBAL CMPLNCE CONTRLS
13950 Ballantyne Corporate Pl (28277-3159)
PHONE................................704 552-1119
James Burke, CEO
EMP: 4 **EST:** 2011
SALES (est): 1.75MM
SALES (corp-wide): 1.65B **Privately Held**
Web: www.navex.com
SIC: 3822 Appliance regulators
PA: Vista Equity Partners Management, Llc
401 Congress Ave Ste 3100
Austin TX 78701
512 730-2400

(G-3033)
JOKEN PUBLICATIONS
3712 Charterhall Ln (28215-7800)
PHONE................................704 957-7030
Kenitra Jordan, Prin
EMP: 4 **EST:** 2015
SALES (est): 57.5K **Privately Held**
SIC: 2741 Miscellaneous publishing

(G-3034)
JORDAN GROUP CORPORATION
7007 Berolina Ln Apt 1613 (28226-8687)
PHONE................................803 309-9988
Robert Jordan, Pr
EMP: 4 **EST:** 2006
SALES (est): 259.65K **Privately Held**
SIC: 2499 Wood products, nec

(G-3035)
JOSEPH F DECKER
Also Called: Decker Advanced Fabrication
341 Dalton Ave (28206-3117)
PHONE................................704 335-0021
EMP: 8 **EST:** 1996
SQ FT: 13,000
SALES (est): 1.01MM **Privately Held**
SIC: 3446 3444 Architectural metalwork; Sheet metalwork

(G-3036)
JRG TECHNOLOGIES CORP
9300 Harris Corners Pkwy Ste 450 (28269)
PHONE................................850 362-4310
Joseph R Gregory, Prin
David Haadsma, Prin
William E Loran Iii, Prin
Andrew K Stull, Prin
EMP: 12 **EST:** 2007
SALES (est): 933.03K **Privately Held**
SIC: 7372 Application computer software
HQ: Avg Technologies Usa, Inc.
2100 Powell St
Emeryville CA 94608

(G-3037)
JRS CUSTOM FRAMING
7604 Waterford Lakes Dr (28210-6491)
P.O. Box 5202 (28299-5202)
PHONE................................704 449-2830
EMP: 4 **EST:** 2018
SALES (est): 46.85K **Privately Held**
Web: www.dilworthcustomframing.com
SIC: 2499 Picture frame molding, finished

(G-3038)
JS ROYAL HOME USA INC
13451 S Point Blvd (28273-2701)
PHONE................................704 542-2304
Kathy O Dayvault, CEO
Kathy O Dayvault, Pr
Lei Huang, *
▲ **EMP:** 45 **EST:** 2007
SQ FT: 80,000
SALES (est): 65.61MM **Privately Held**
Web: www.jsroyalhome.com
SIC: 5023 2392 Homefurnishings; Blankets, comforters and beddings

(G-3039)
JUST N TYME TRUCKING LLC
6015 Lake Forest Rd E (28227-0910)
PHONE................................704 804-9519
Enola Murchison-ottley, Managing Member
EMP: 4
SALES (est): 176.59K **Privately Held**
SIC: 3537 7389 Trucks, tractors, loaders, carriers, and similar equipment; Business services, nec

(G-3040)
K&K HOLDINGS INC
Also Called: Signs Now
1310 S Church St (28203-4112)
PHONE................................704 341-5567
Cathy Habluetzel, CEO
Randy Habluetzel, VP
Cathy Habluetzel, Pr
EMP: 8 **EST:** 2003
SALES (est): 677.95K **Privately Held**
Web: www.signsnow.com
SIC: 3993 7389 6719 Signs and advertising specialties; Lettering and sign painting services; Investment holding companies, except banks

(G-3041)
K2 SCIENTIFIC LLC
3029 Horseshoe Ln Ste D (28208-6434)
PHONE................................800 218-7613
Thomas Baugh, Managing Member
Dee Jetton, COO
Art Henson, Dir
Venitra White-dean, Contrlr
William Papathanassiou, Mgr
EMP: 10 **EST:** 2016
SALES (est): 1.79MM **Privately Held**
Web: www.k2sci.com
SIC: 3632 Household refrigerators and freezers

(G-3042)
KA-EX LLC ✪
125 Remount Rd Ste C1 Pmb 2002 (28203-6459)
PHONE................................704 343-5143
Pedro Schmidt, Managing Member
EMP: 8 **EST:** 2022
SALES (est): 510.73K **Privately Held**
SIC: 2023 Dietary supplements, dairy and non-dairy based

(G-3043)
KASK AMERICA INC
301 W Summit Ave (28203-4452)
PHONE................................704 960-4851
Kask Angelo Gotti, CEO
EMP: 31 **EST:** 2010
SALES (est): 3.67MM **Privately Held**
Web: www.kask.com
SIC: 3949 Helmets, athletic

(G-3044)
KAUFFMAN & CO
1420 S Mint St (28203-4145)
PHONE................................716 969-2005
Jon Kauffman, Prin
EMP: 6 **EST:** 2019
SALES (est): 155.66K **Privately Held**
Web: www.kauffmanandco.com
SIC: 2431 Millwork

(G-3045)
KAVO KERR GROUP
11727 Fruehauf Dr (28273-6507)
PHONE................................704 927-0617
EMP: 17 **EST:** 2016
SALES (est): 865.36K **Privately Held**
SIC: 3843 Dental equipment and supplies

(G-3046)
KDR VISUALITY LLC
Also Called: Kdr Visuality
9922 Nations Ford Rd (28273-5749)
PHONE................................704 451-1290
EMP: 4 **EST:** 2020
SALES (est): 74.42K **Privately Held**
SIC: 2836 Culture media

(G-3047)
KEE AUTO TOP MANUFACTURING CO
3018 Stewart Creek Blvd (28216-3594)
PHONE................................704 332-8213
Erman J Evans, Pr
EMP: 40 **EST:** 1964
SQ FT: 21,000
SALES (est): 4.86MM **Privately Held**
Web: www.keeautotop.com
SIC: 3714 Tops, motor vehicle

(G-3048)
KEIM MINERAL COATINGS AMER INC
3935 Perimeter W Dr Ste 100 (28214-0110)
PHONE................................704 588-4811
John C Bogert, CEO
◆ **EMP:** 10 **EST:** 2006
SALES (est): 2.35MM **Privately Held**
Web: www.keim.com
SIC: 2851 5198 Paints and paint additives; Paints, varnishes, and supplies

(G-3049)
KEM-WOVE INC (PA)
Also Called: K W
10530 Westlake Dr (28273-3788)
P.O. Box 3871 (08756-3871)
PHONE................................704 588-0080
Steven Sklow, Pr
Jennifer Sklow, *
EMP: 20 **EST:** 1962
SQ FT: 55,000
SALES (est): 3.31MM
SALES (corp-wide): 3.31MM **Privately Held**
Web: www.kemwove.com
SIC: 2299 2297 Batts and batting: cotton mill waste and related material; Nonwoven fabrics

(G-3050)
KENNAMETAL INC
8910 Lenox Pointe Dr Ste F (28273-3431)
PHONE................................704 588-4777
Suzanne Gillenwater, Prin
EMP: 7
SALES (corp-wide): 2.08B **Publicly Held**
Web: www.kennametal.com
SIC: 3545 Cutting tools for machine tools
PA: Kennametal Inc.
525 William Penn Pl # 3300
Pittsburgh PA 15219
412 248-8000

(G-3051)
KESSEL DEVELOPMENT LLC
Also Called: Embroid ME
16131 Lancaster Hwy Ste 6 (28277-3884)
PHONE................................704 752-4282
EMP: 5 **EST:** 2002
SALES (est): 346.37K **Privately Held**
SIC: 5949 2759 Sewing, needlework, and piece goods; Screen printing

(G-3052)
KEYMAC USA LLC
8301 Arrowridge Blvd Ste I (28273-5772)
PHONE................................704 877-5137
Michael C A Bradley, Mgr
▲ **EMP:** 11 **EST:** 2010
SALES (est): 1.13MM **Privately Held**
Web: www.keymac.co.uk
SIC: 3565 Packaging machinery

(G-3053)
KIDS PLAYHOUSE LLC ✪
10823 John Price Rd (28273-4510)
PHONE................................704 299-4449
Roxie S Carter, Prin
EMP: 4 **EST:** 2022
SQ FT: 1,300
SALES (est): 104.14K **Privately Held**
Web: www.kidsplayhousellc.com
SIC: 7359 2299 Party supplies rental services; Bagging, jute

(G-3054)
KIMBERLY GORDON STUDIOS INC
525 N Tryon St (28202-0202)
PHONE................................980 287-6420
Kimberly Mix, CEO
EMP: 22
SALES (est): 939.17K **Privately Held**
SIC: 2678 Stationery products

(G-3055)
KINCOL INDUSTRIES INCORPORATED
Also Called: Kci
1721 Toal St (28206-1523)
P.O. Box 26614 (28221-6614)
PHONE................................704 372-8435
Robert Collins, Pr
James S King, Ch Bd
▲ **EMP:** 9 **EST:** 1981
SQ FT: 10,000
SALES (est): 2.39MM **Privately Held**
Web: www.kciincorporated.com
SIC: 5169 3548 Chemicals, industrial and heavy; Gas welding equipment

(G-3056)
KING STONE INNOVATION LLC
7313 Mossborough Ct (28227-1244)
PHONE................................704 352-1134
Sergio Gonzalez Rios, Pr
EMP: 5 **EST:** 2017
SALES (est): 497.47K **Privately Held**
SIC: 3281 1791 1799 Granite, cut and shaped; Structural steel erection; Welding on site

(G-3057)
KLAZZY MAGAZINE INC
Also Called: Klazzy.com The Magazine
100 N Tryon St Ste B220-127 (28202-4000)
PHONE................................704 293-8321
Bobby Bowden, CEO
Stacy Moye, Pr
EMP: 8 **EST:** 2004
SQ FT: 1,500
SALES (est): 431.16K **Privately Held**
SIC: 2741 Art copy and poster publishing

(G-3058)
KNA
Also Called: Charlotte T Shirt Authority
9535 Monroe Rd Ste 150 (28270-2452)

Charlotte - Mecklenburg County (G-3059)

PHONE..................704 847-4280
Keith Abrams, *Pr*
EMP: 12 **EST:** 2002
SALES (est): 451.27K **Privately Held**
Web: www.tshirtauthority.com
SIC: 2759 Screen printing

(G-3059)
KOI FISH PUBLISHING HOUSE LLC
10705 Sapona Ct (28277-5101)
PHONE..................704 540-8805
Kristen Leake, *Prin*
EMP: 5 **EST:** 2018
SALES (est): 72.58K **Privately Held**
SIC: 2741 Miscellaneous publishing

(G-3060)
KRAFT HEINZ FOODS COMPANY
Also Called: Kraft Foods
2815 Coliseum Centre Dr Ste 100 (28217)
PHONE..................704 565-5500
Joe Polite, *Brnch Mgr*
EMP: 4
SALES (corp-wide): 26.64B **Publicly Held**
Web: www.kraftheinzcompany.com
SIC: 2033 Canned fruits and specialties
HQ: Kraft Heinz Foods Company
  1 Ppg Pl Ste 3400
  Pittsburgh PA 15222
  412 456-5700

(G-3061)
KRIEG CORP
8501 Castlebay Dr (28277-1880)
PHONE..................704 361-1223
EMP: 4 **EST:** 2018
SALES (est): 54.52K **Privately Held**
SIC: 7692 Welding repair

(G-3062)
KRISPY KREME DOUGHNUT CORP (DH)
2116 Hawkins St Ste 102 (28203-4477)
P.O. Box 83 (27102-0083)
PHONE..................980 270-7117
J Paul Breitbach, *Ex VP*
John Mc Aleer, *Ex VP*
John Tate, *CSO*
James Morgan, *Ch Bd*
Kenneth May, *Pr*
◆ **EMP:** 150 **EST:** 1933
SALES (est): 463.39MM
SALES (corp-wide): 1.69B **Publicly Held**
Web: www.krispykreme.com
SIC: 5461 2051 Doughnuts; Doughnuts, except frozen
HQ: Krispy Kreme Doughnuts, Inc.
  370 Knollwood St
  Winston Salem NC 27103
  336 725-2981

(G-3063)
KRISTEN SCREEN PRINTING & EMB
4115 Bloomdale Dr Apt 10 (28211-5107)
PHONE..................980 256-4561
Kristen Cornelius, *Prin*
EMP: 5 **EST:** 2017
SALES (est): 65.01K **Privately Held**
SIC: 2752 Commercial printing, lithographic

(G-3064)
KUEBLER INC
10430 Harris Oak Blvd Ste J (28269-7521)
PHONE..................704 705-4711
John Stanczuk, *VP*
EMP: 12 **EST:** 2013
SALES (est): 3.89MM **Privately Held**
Web: www.kuebler.com
SIC: 5065 3699 Electronic parts; Electrical equipment and supplies, nec

(G-3065)
L & S AUTOMOTIVE INC
Also Called: L & S Custom Trailer Service
1214 Caldwell Williams Rd (28216-2414)
PHONE..................704 391-7657
Lawrence Martin, *Pr*
Sandra M Martin, *VP*
EMP: 6 **EST:** 1986
SQ FT: 6,000
SALES (est): 623.65K **Privately Held**
Web: www.ls-automotive.com
SIC: 3715 7538 Truck trailers; General automotive repair shops

(G-3066)
L3HARRIS TECHNOLOGIES INC
Also Called: Harris Repair Service
8406 Mcalpine Dr (28217-5330)
PHONE..................704 588-7126
Douglas Harris, *Pr*
EMP: 6
SALES (corp-wide): 17.06B **Publicly Held**
Web: www.l3harris.com
SIC: 3699 Electrical equipment and supplies, nec
PA: L3harris Technologies, Inc.
  1025 W Nasa Blvd
  Melbourne FL 32919
  321 727-9100

(G-3067)
L6 REALTY LLC
2744 Yorkmont Rd (28208-7324)
PHONE..................704 654-3000
Michael Pratt, *Genl Mgr*
EMP: 9 **EST:** 2009
SALES (est): 222.64K **Privately Held**
Web: www.nascent.com
SIC: 6531 3444 Real estate brokers and agents; Booths, spray: prefabricated sheet metal

(G-3068)
LABEL SOUTHEAST LLC
227 W 4th St Ste 112 (28202-1545)
PHONE..................518 796-6320
Andy Cochran, *Prin*
EMP: 5 **EST:** 2015
SALES (est): 165.52K **Privately Held**
SIC: 2759 Commercial printing, nec

(G-3069)
LADDER & THINGS
7316 Rockwood Forest Ln (28212-6464)
PHONE..................704 779-7211
Jose A Pagan, *Prin*
EMP: 6 **EST:** 2015
SALES (est): 175.95K **Privately Held**
SIC: 3446 Ladders, for permanent installation: metal

(G-3070)
LAIRD PLASTICS INC
Also Called: Laird Plastics, Inc.
6100 Harris Technology Blvd Ste F (28269-5745)
PHONE..................704 597-8555
John Harmath, *Mgr*
EMP: 4
Web: www.lairdplastics.com
SIC: 3089 Air mattresses, plastics
HQ: Plastics Family Holdings Inc
  5800 Campus Circle Dr E # 1
  Irving TX 75063
  469 299-7000

(G-3071)
LAKOU LLC
10104 Bellhaven Blvd (28214-8714)
PHONE..................704 780-5129
EMP: 5
SALES (est): 222.74K **Privately Held**
SIC: 2599 Bar, restaurant and cafeteria furniture

(G-3072)
LANDFILL GAS PRODUCERS
10600 Nations Ford Rd # 150 (28273-5762)
PHONE..................704 844-8990
William Brinker, *Prin*
Peter Kamel, *Mgr*
EMP: 11 **EST:** 2009
SALES (est): 1.11MM **Privately Held**
Web: www.landfillgroup.com
SIC: 1321 Natural gas liquids

(G-3073)
LATINO COMMUNICATIONS INC
Also Called: Que Pasa Charlotte
7508 E Independence Blvd Ste 109 (28227-9473)
PHONE..................704 319-5044
Julio Suarez, *Brnch Mgr*
EMP: 10
SALES (corp-wide): 4.65MM **Privately Held**
Web: www.quepasamedia.com
SIC: 4832 2711 Radio broadcasting stations; Newspapers
PA: Latino Communications, Inc.
  3067 Waughtown St
  Winston Salem NC 27107
  336 714-2823

(G-3074)
LAWING ADVG MKTG & PUBG LLC
5210 Lincrest Pl (28211-4111)
PHONE..................704 364-8649
Christopher Lawing, *Prin*
EMP: 4 **EST:** 2017
SALES (est): 41.35K **Privately Held**
SIC: 2741 Miscellaneous publishing

(G-3075)
LCI CORPORATION INTERNATIONAL
4404b Chesapeake Dr (28216-3413)
PHONE..................704 399-7441
EMP: 8 **EST:** 1992
SALES (est): 57.58K **Privately Held**
Web: www.lcicorp.com
SIC: 3559 Special industry machinery, nec

(G-3076)
LCI CORPORATION INTERNATIONAL
Also Called: LCI
4433 Chesapeake Dr (28216-3412)
P.O. Box 16348 (28297-6348)
PHONE..................704 399-7441
Tomas Hagstrom, *CEO*
John Fields, *VP*
◆ **EMP:** 20 **EST:** 1992
SQ FT: 12,000
SALES (est): 8.76MM **Privately Held**
Web: www.lcicorp.com
SIC: 3559 5084 2899 2099 Refinery, chemical processing, and similar machinery; Chemical process equipment; Chemical preparations, nec; Food preparations, nec
HQ: Nederman Corporation
  4404a Chesapeake Dr
  Charlotte NC 28216
  704 399-7441

(G-3077)
LEAPFROG DOCUMENT SERVICES INC
4651 Charlotte Park Dr Ste 230 (28217-1956)
PHONE..................704 372-1078
Amy L Parris, *Pr*
Debbie Laflamme, *VP*
EMP: 15 **EST:** 2001
SALES (est): 1.75MM **Privately Held**
Web: www.leapfrogllc.com
SIC: 2621 5943 Parchment, securities, and bank note papers; Notary and corporate seals

(G-3078)
LEAR ENTERPRISES INC
8145 Ardrey Kell Rd (28277-5720)
PHONE..................704 321-0027
EMP: 8 **EST:** 2018
SALES (est): 236.79K **Privately Held**
SIC: 3714 Motor vehicle parts and accessories

(G-3079)
LEARNINGSTATIONCOM INC (PA)
8022 Providence Rd Ste 500 (28277-9719)
PHONE..................704 926-5400
James Kirchner, *Pr*
Bart Temperville, *Treas*
Steven Kirchner, *VP*
EMP: 12 **EST:** 1997
SQ FT: 2,548
SALES (est): 2.89MM
SALES (corp-wide): 2.89MM **Privately Held**
Web: www.learningstation.com
SIC: 7372 Application computer software

(G-3080)
LEGACY COMMERCIAL SERVICE LLC
13921 Allison Forest Trl (28278-7758)
PHONE..................757 831-5291
EMP: 4 **EST:** 2019
SALES (est): 175.11K **Privately Held**
SIC: 3589 Commercial cleaning equipment

(G-3081)
LEGACY RIVER COMPANY
935 Iberville St (28270-9500)
PHONE..................704 618-7260
Otto Caudell, *Pr*
EMP: 4 **EST:** 2004
SALES (est): 346.97K **Privately Held**
SIC: 5199 3999 Pet supplies; Pet supplies

(G-3082)
LEIGHDEUX LLC
355 Eastover Rd (28207-2349)
PHONE..................704 965-4889
Leigh Goodwyn, *Managing Member*
EMP: 6 **EST:** 2015
SALES (est): 237.8K **Privately Held**
Web: www.leighdeux.com
SIC: 2299 5719 Linen fabrics; Beddings and linens

(G-3083)
LEVEL TEN FACILITIES SVCS LLC
1213 W Morehead St # 500 (28208-5576)
PHONE..................704 759-6799
Natasha Winston, *CEO*
Natasha Winston, *Managing Member*
EMP: 5 **EST:** 2021
SALES (est): 235.98K **Privately Held**
SIC: 4789 3589 Cargo loading and unloading services; Commercial cleaning equipment

(G-3084)
LICK ER LIPS LIP BALM LLC
11512 Ridge Oak Dr (28273-4761)
PHONE..................702 355-5433
EMP: 6 **EST:** 2015
SALES (est): 248.54K **Privately Held**
SIC: 2834 Lip balms

GEOGRAPHIC SECTION
Charlotte - Mecklenburg County (G-3109)

(G-3085)
LIFE STORIES AND BEYOND
4001 Wilson Dr (28270-2603)
PHONE.................................704 579-7161
Lisa Kunkleman, *Prin*
EMP: 5 **EST:** 2019
SALES (est): 115.3K **Privately Held**
SIC: 2741 Miscellaneous publishing

(G-3086)
LIFESPAN INCORPORATED (PA)
1511 Shopton Rd Ste A (28217-3240)
PHONE.................................704 944-5100
Davan Claniger, *CEO*
Ralph Adams, *Treas*
Holly Newinski, *Corporate Secretary*
EMP: 20 **EST:** 1973
SQ FT: 75,000
SALES (est): 19.26MM
SALES (corp-wide): 19.26MM **Privately Held**
Web: www.lifespanservices.org
SIC: 8211 8361 3842 School for retarded, nec; Self-help group home; Surgical appliances and supplies

(G-3087)
LIGHT SOURCE USA INC
3935 Westinghouse Blvd (28273-4517)
PHONE.................................704 504-8399
Eric V Fange, *Pr*
Joy Von Fange, *
EMP: 35 **EST:** 2007
SQ FT: 67,000
SALES (est): 7.05MM **Privately Held**
Web: www.thelightsource.com
SIC: 3648 Decorative area lighting fixtures

(G-3088)
LIGHTNING X PRODUCTS INC
Also Called: Fire & Safety Outfitters
2365 Tipton Dr (28206-1060)
PHONE.................................704 295-0299
EMP: 7 **EST:** 2006
SALES (est): 1.94MM **Privately Held**
Web: www.gearbags.com
SIC: 5087 3569 Firefighting equipment; Firefighting and related equipment

(G-3089)
LIKEABLE PRESS LLC
227 W 4th St (28202-1545)
PHONE.................................844 882-8340
EMP: 4 **EST:** 2018
SALES (est): 135.75K **Privately Held**
SIC: 2741 Miscellaneous publishing

(G-3090)
LINDE GAS & EQUIPMENT INC
Also Called: Linde Gas North America
3810 Shutterfly Rd Ste 100 (28217-3070)
PHONE.................................704 587-7096
Mark Kimel, *Brnch Mgr*
EMP: 10
Web: www.lindeus.com
SIC: 2813 Nitrogen
HQ: Linde Gas & Equipment Inc.
10 Riverview Dr
Danbury CT 06810
844 445-4633

(G-3091)
LIONS SERVICES INC
4600 N Tryon St Ste A (28213-7058)
PHONE.................................704 921-1527
Jim Cranford, *CEO*
Philip Murph, *
EMP: 302 **EST:** 1935
SQ FT: 58,000
SALES (est): 15.97MM **Privately Held**
Web: www.lionsservices.org
SIC: 2392 7389 8331 Mops, floor and dust; Packaging and labeling services; Job training and related services

(G-3092)
LIQUI-BOX CORPORATION (HQ)
2415 Cascade Pointe Blvd (28208-6899)
PHONE.................................804 325-1400
Ken Swanson, *Pr*
Lou Marmo, *
Diana Smith, *
Andrew Mcleland, *COO*
◆ **EMP:** 65 **EST:** 1963
SALES (est): 370.16MM
SALES (corp-wide): 5.49B **Publicly Held**
Web: www.liquibox.com
SIC: 2673 3585 3089 3081 Plastic bags: made from purchased materials; Soda fountain and beverage dispensing equipment and parts; Plastics containers, except foam; Plastics film and sheet
PA: Sealed Air Corporation
2415 Cascade Pointe Blvd
Charlotte NC 28208
980 221-3235

(G-3093)
LITBYWHIT LLC
2810 Chalgrove Ln (28216-9619)
PHONE.................................704 293-5743
EMP: 4 **EST:** 2020
SALES (est): 45.87K **Privately Held**
SIC: 3999 Candles

(G-3094)
LITTON SYSTEMS INC
1201 Continental Blvd (28273-6320)
PHONE.................................704 588-2340
EMP: 4 **EST:** 2019
SALES (est): 93.23K **Privately Held**
SIC: 3571 Electronic computers

(G-3095)
LIVE IT BOUTIQUE LLC
Also Called: Retail
509 Old Vine Ct (28214-0032)
PHONE.................................704 492-2402
Oleta Harris, *CEO*
EMP: 5 **EST:** 2021
SALES (est): 117.24K **Privately Held**
SIC: 5621 2339 Women's clothing stores; Women's and misses' accessories

(G-3096)
LIVINGSTON & HAVEN LLC (HQ)
Also Called: AEG International
11529 Wilmar Blvd (28273-6448)
P.O. Box 7207 (28241-7207)
PHONE.................................704 588-3670
Clifton B Vann Iii, *Ch*
Clifton B Vann Iv, *Pr*
James T Skinner Iii, *Sec*
Anne Q Woody, *
Bruce Mckay, *Dir*
EMP: 140 **EST:** 1947
SQ FT: 50,000
SALES (est): 44.34MM
SALES (corp-wide): 98.44MM **Privately Held**
Web: www.livhaven.com
SIC: 5084 3594 4911 7389 Hydraulic systems equipment and supplies; Fluid power pumps and motors; Business services, nec
PA: Park Hyde Partners Inc
11529 Wilmar Blvd
Charlotte NC 28273
704 587-4819

(G-3097)
LLC DIAMOND BELL
6420 Rea Rd Ste A1 # 25 (28277-3612)
PHONE.................................704 806-4705
EMP: 4 **EST:** 2017
SALES (est): 227.07K **Privately Held**
SIC: 3675 Electronic capacitors

(G-3098)
LMB CORP
Also Called: Dairy Queen
3020 Prosperity Church Rd Ste D (28269-8100)
PHONE.................................704 547-8886
Lisa Battaglia, *Pr*
Stephanie Wicherstoon, *Mgr*
EMP: 8 **EST:** 2010
SALES (est): 491.36K **Privately Held**
Web: www.dairyqueen.com
SIC: 5812 2013 Ice cream stands or dairy bars; Sausages and other prepared meats

(G-3099)
LOCKWOOD IDENTITY INC
Also Called: Sign Art
6225 Old Concord Rd (28213-6311)
P.O. Box 560648 (28256-0648)
PHONE.................................704 597-9801
EMP: 104 **EST:** 2002
SALES (est): 14.28MM **Privately Held**
Web: www.signartsign.com
SIC: 3993 1799 Electric signs; Sign installation and maintenance

(G-3100)
LOFTIN & COMPANY INC
Also Called: Loftin & Company Printers
1908 Gateway Blvd (28208-2746)
P.O. Box 669407 (28266-9407)
PHONE.................................704 393-9393
William E Loftin Junior, *Pr*
EMP: 25 **EST:** 1898
SQ FT: 20,000
SALES (est): 4.29MM **Privately Held**
Web: www.loftinco.com
SIC: 2752 2789 2791 Offset printing; Bookbinding and related work; Typesetting

(G-3101)
LONDON LUXURY LLC ✪
3540 Toringdon Way Ste 200 (28277-3867)
PHONE.................................980 819-1966
EMP: 7 **EST:** 2023
SALES (est): 281.39K **Privately Held**
SIC: 7372 Prepackaged software

(G-3102)
LONE STAR CONTAINER SALES CORP
Also Called: Dixie Reel & Box Co
10901 Carpet St (28273-6206)
P.O. Box 7791 (28241-7791)
PHONE.................................704 588-1737
William Harkey, *Brnch Mgr*
EMP: 56
SALES (corp-wide): 12.83MM **Privately Held**
Web: www.lonestarcontainer.com
SIC: 2653 Boxes, corrugated: made from purchased materials
PA: Lone Star Container Sales Corporation
700 N Wildwood Dr
Irving TX 75061
972 579-1551

(G-3103)
LOOKWHATQMADE LLC
101 N Tryon St Ste 112 (28246-0100)
PHONE.................................980 330-1995
EMP: 5
SALES (est): 170.89K **Privately Held**
SIC: 2741 Internet publishing and broadcasting

(G-3104)
LOS VIENTOS WINDPOWER IB LLC
526 S Church St (28202-1802)
PHONE.................................704 594-6200
B Keith Trent, *CEO*
EMP: 22 **EST:** 2011
SALES (est): 56.1K
SALES (corp-wide): 29.06B **Publicly Held**
SIC: 3829 Wind direction indicators
PA: Duke Energy Corporation
526 S Church St
Charlotte NC 28202
704 382-3853

(G-3105)
LTD INDUSTRIES LLC (PA)
5509 David Cox Rd (28269-0324)
P.O. Box 481930 (28269-5319)
PHONE.................................704 897-2182
David Peters, *Managing Member*
Todd Allison, *
Anthony Hergert, *
Charles Herrig, *
David N Herrig, *
▲ **EMP:** 48 **EST:** 2011
SALES (est): 9.24MM **Privately Held**
Web: www.nano-purification.com
SIC: 3569 5085 Filters; Filters, industrial

(G-3106)
LUCAS CONCRETE PRODUCTS INC
401 Rountree Rd (28217-2130)
PHONE.................................704 525-9622
John R L Johnson Iii, *Pr*
Evelyn Johnson, *
EMP: 33 **EST:** 1971
SQ FT: 8,140
SALES (est): 4.9MM **Privately Held**
Web: www.lucasconcrete.com
SIC: 3272 Concrete products, precast, nec

(G-3107)
LUCKY LANDPORTS
Also Called: C Y Yard
6510 Rozzelles Ferry Rd (28214-1881)
PHONE.................................704 399-9880
Dim Feimster, *Owner*
EMP: 4 **EST:** 2000
SALES (est): 192.14K **Privately Held**
SIC: 2448 Cargo containers, wood and wood with metal

(G-3108)
LULLICOIN LLC
3540 Toringdon Way (28277-3867)
PHONE.................................336 955-1159
EMP: 5 **EST:** 2021
SALES (est): 472.06K **Privately Held**
SIC: 3674 Diodes, solid state (germanium, silicon, etc.)

(G-3109)
LUNAR INTERNATIONAL TECH LLC
338 S Sharon Amity Rd (28211-2806)
PHONE.................................800 975-7153
Omer Ford, *Pr*
Omer Ford, *Managing Member*
EMP: 12 **EST:** 2020
SALES (est): 697.93K **Privately Held**
Web: www.lunarinternationaltech.com
SIC: 4214 7382 1711 3663 Local trucking with storage; Security systems services; Solar energy contractor; Satellites, communications

Charlotte - Mecklenburg County (G-3110)

(G-3110)
LUTZE INC
13330 S Ridge Dr (28273-4738)
PHONE..................704 504-0222
Friedrich Lutze, *Sec*
Udo Lutze, *
▲ **EMP:** 26 **EST:** 1989
SQ FT: 24,000
SALES (est): 10.47MM
SALES (corp-wide): 92.57MM **Privately Held**
Web: www.lutze.com
SIC: 5063 5065 3679 Electronic wire and cable; Electronic parts and equipment, nec; Harness assemblies, for electronic use: wire or cable
HQ: Friedrich Lutze Gmbh
   Bruckwiesenstr. 17-19
   Weinstadt BW 71384
   71516053352

(G-3111)
LYNN LADDER SCAFFOLDING CO INC
3801 Corporation Cir (28216-3418)
PHONE..................301 336-4700
TOLL FREE: 800
Eric Yates, *Mgr*
EMP: 4
SALES (corp-wide): 47.21MM **Privately Held**
Web: www.lynnladderandscaffolding.com
SIC: 5082 2499 7359 Ladders; Ladders, wood; Equipment rental and leasing, nec
HQ: Lynn Ladder And Scaffolding Co., Inc.
   20 Boston St 24
   Lynn MA 01904
   781 598-6010

(G-3112)
M & A EQUIPMENT INC (PA)
Also Called: Quantum Machinery Group
7110 Expo Dr Ste D (28269-3844)
PHONE..................704 703-9400
Michael Bucciero, *Pr*
Alberto Solano, *VP*
▲ **EMP:** 4 **EST:** 2002
SALES (est): 2.28MM
SALES (corp-wide): 2.28MM **Privately Held**
Web: www.quantummachinerygroup.com
SIC: 3542 Presses: hydraulic and pneumatic, mechanical and manual

(G-3113)
M & W INDUSTRIES INC (PA)
Also Called: Mw Components
3426 Toringdon Way Ste 100 (28277-3496)
PHONE..................704 837-0331
Simon Newman, *CEO*
Tim Brasher, *CFO*
Janelle Weyers, *CIO*
Shelley Garrity, *Chief Human Resources Officer*
Nina Snelling, *Chief Digital Officer*
EMP: 27 **EST:** 1975
SQ FT: 40,000
SALES (est): 175.45MM
SALES (corp-wide): 175.45MM **Privately Held**
SIC: 3451 3444 Screw machine products; Sheet metalwork

(G-3114)
M AND R INC
Also Called: Eden Dry Cleaners
820 E 7th St Ste C (28202-3050)
PHONE..................704 332-5999
Inhonthi Lee, *Pr*
EMP: 4 **EST:** 2015
SALES (est): 239.34K **Privately Held**
SIC: 2842 Laundry cleaning preparations

(G-3115)
MAAG REDUCTION INC (HQ)
9401 Southern Pine Blvd Ste Q (28273-5598)
PHONE..................704 716-9000
▲ **EMP:** 48 **EST:** 1991
SALES (est): 22.27MM
SALES (corp-wide): 8.44B **Publicly Held**
Web: www.maag.com
SIC: 3561 5084 Pumps and pumping equipment; Pumps and pumping equipment, nec
PA: Dover Corporation
   3005 Highland Pkwy # 200
   Downers Grove IL 60515
   630 541-1540

(G-3116)
MACLEOD CONSTRUCTION INC (PA)
Also Called: Concrete Pumping By Macleod
4304 Northpointe Industrial Blvd (28216)
P.O. Box 320 (28037-0320)
PHONE..................704 483-3580
Robert Macleod, *Pr*
Lorne Macleod, *
Judith Macleod, *
EMP: 101 **EST:** 1987
SALES (est): 24.57MM **Privately Held**
Web: www.macleodnc.com
SIC: 3273 1611 Ready-mixed concrete; Grading

(G-3117)
MADE BY CUSTOM LLC
3206 N Davidson St (28205-1034)
PHONE..................704 980-9840
EMP: 4 **EST:** 2013
SALES (est): 395.12K **Privately Held**
Web: www.customjewelrylab.com
SIC: 3479 5094 5944 7631 Engraving jewelry, silverware, or metal; Jewelry and precious stones; Jewelry stores; Jewelry repair services

(G-3118)
MADISON WOODWORKING
10015 Metromont Indstrl (28269-6603)
PHONE..................704 634-1143
EMP: 4 **EST:** 2017
SALES (est): 54.13K **Privately Held**
SIC: 2431 Millwork

(G-3119)
MALLARD CREEK POLYMERS LLC
2800 Morehead Rd (28262-0430)
PHONE..................877 240-0171
EMP: 9
Web: www.mcpolymers.com
SIC: 2821 Elastomers, nonvulcanizable (plastics)
PA: Mallard Creek Polymers, Llc
   8901 Research Dr
   Charlotte NC 28262

(G-3120)
MALLARD CREEK POLYMERS LLC
14800 Mallard Creek Rd (28262-0430)
PHONE..................704 547-0622
EMP: 8
Web: www.mcpolymers.com
SIC: 2821 Plastics materials and resins
PA: Mallard Creek Polymers, Llc
   8901 Research Dr
   Charlotte NC 28262

(G-3121)
MALLARD CREEK POLYMERS LLC (PA)
Also Called: Mallard Creek Polymers
8901 Research Dr (28262-8541)
PHONE..................704 547-0622
◆ **EMP:** 20 **EST:** 1994
SALES (est): 40.52MM **Privately Held**
Web: www.mcpolymers.com
SIC: 2821 Plastics materials and resins

(G-3122)
MANTISSA CORPORATION
Also Called: Mantissa Material Handling
616 Pressley Rd (28217-4610)
PHONE..................704 525-1749
J David Fortenbery, *Pr*
Megan Mccormick, *VP*
▲ **EMP:** 42 **EST:** 1973
SQ FT: 28,300
SALES (est): 13.56MM **Privately Held**
Web: www.mantissacorporation.com
SIC: 1796 3535 Machinery installation; Conveyors and conveying equipment

(G-3123)
MAP SHOP LLC
3421 St Vardell Ln Ste H (28217-0086)
PHONE..................704 332-5557
Anthony Rodono, *Mgr*
EMP: 9 **EST:** 2016
SALES (est): 861.09K **Privately Held**
Web: www.mapshop.com
SIC: 2741 Miscellaneous publishing

(G-3124)
MARBACH AMERICA INC
100 Forsyth Hall Dr Ste B (28273-5726)
P.O. Box 935 (28134-0935)
PHONE..................704 644-4900
Jan Brunner, *Pr*
Fernando Tires, *
▲ **EMP:** 25 **EST:** 2011
SALES (est): 14.2MM
SALES (corp-wide): 154.74MM **Privately Held**
Web: www.marbach.com
SIC: 3423 Cutting dies, except metal cutting
PA: Karl Marbach Gmbh & Co. Kg
   Karl-Marbach-Str. 1
   Heilbronn BW 74080
   71319180

(G-3125)
MARIETTA MARTIN MATERIALS INC
Also Called: Martin Marietta Aggregates
8701 Red Oak Blvd Ste 540 (28217-2960)
P.O. Box 30013 (27622-0013)
PHONE..................704 525-7740
James Thompson, *VP*
EMP: 51
Web: www.martinmarietta.com
SIC: 1422 Crushed and broken limestone
PA: Martin Marietta Materials Inc
   4123 Parklake Ave
   Raleigh NC 27612

(G-3126)
MARKETING ONE SPORTSWEAR INC
3101 Yorkmont Rd Ste 1100 (28208-7375)
PHONE..................704 334-9333
EMP: 5 **EST:** 1992
SALES (est): 487.6K **Privately Held**
SIC: 7389 2396 5136 5137 Embroidery advertising; Screen printing on fabric articles ; Sportswear, men's and boys'; Sportswear, women's and children's

(G-3127)
MARLATEX CORPORATION
8425 Winged Bourne (28210-5930)
PHONE..................704 829-7797
Barnabas Martonffy, *Pr*
▲ **EMP:** 25 **EST:** 1982
SALES (est): 2.34MM **Privately Held**
Web: www.perfectdomain.com
SIC: 2211 Upholstery fabrics, cotton

(G-3128)
MARLEY COMPANY LLC (DH)
Also Called: S P X
13515 Ballantyne Corporate Pl (28277-2706)
PHONE..................704 752-4400
Steve Zeller, *CEO*
Christopher J Kearney, *
Patrick J O'leary, *VP Fin*
Robert B Foreman, *
▲ **EMP:** 200 **EST:** 1922
SALES (est): 960.82MM
SALES (corp-wide): 1.74B **Publicly Held**
SIC: 3443 3433 3586 3561 Cooling towers, metal plate; Heating equipment, except electric; Measuring and dispensing pumps; Pumps and pumping equipment
HQ: Canvas Sx, Llc
   6325 Ardrey Kell Rd Ste 4
   Charlotte NC 28277
   980 474-3700

(G-3129)
MARSHALL AIR SYSTEMS INC
419 Peachtree Dr S (28217-2098)
PHONE..................704 525-6230
Deborah B Stuck, *CEO*
Robert M Stuck, *
Ron B Reynders, *
▼ **EMP:** 100 **EST:** 1976
SQ FT: 85,000
SALES (est): 15.6MM **Privately Held**
Web: www.marshallair.com
SIC: 3589 Commercial cooking and foodwarming equipment

(G-3130)
MARTIN MARIETTA MATERIALS INC
Also Called: Martin Marietta Aggregates
4551 Beatties Ford Rd (28216-2849)
P.O. Box 680698 (28216-0012)
PHONE..................704 392-1333
Jerry Moss, *Brnch Mgr*
EMP: 5
Web: www.martinmarietta.com
SIC: 3273 Ready-mixed concrete
PA: Martin Marietta Materials Inc
   4123 Parklake Ave
   Raleigh NC 27612

(G-3131)
MARTIN MARIETTA MATERIALS INC
Also Called: Martin Marietta Aggregates
575 E Mallard Creek Church Rd (28262-0809)
P.O. Box 621238 (28262-0120)
PHONE..................704 547-9775
John Sherrill, *Mgr*
EMP: 5
Web: www.martinmarietta.com
SIC: 1422 Crushed and broken limestone
PA: Martin Marietta Materials Inc
   4123 Parklake Ave
   Raleigh NC 27612

(G-3132)
MARTIN MARIETTA MATERIALS INC
Also Called: Martin Marietta Aggregates
11325 Texland Blvd (28273)
P.O. Box 7121 (28241-7121)
PHONE..................704 588-1471

John Smith, *Mgr*
EMP: 7
Web: www.martinmarietta.com
SIC: 1422 Crushed and broken limestone
PA: Martin Marietta Materials Inc
4123 Parklake Ave
Raleigh NC 27612

(G-3133)
MARTIN SPROCKET & GEAR INC
3901 Scott Futrell Dr (28208-3548)
PHONE................................704 394-9111
David Sills, *Mgr*
EMP: 16
SALES (corp-wide): 292.47MM **Privately Held**
Web: www.martinsprocket.com
SIC: 3566 Gears, power transmission, except auto
PA: Martin Sprocket & Gear, Inc.
3100 Sprocket Dr
Arlington TX 76015
817 258-3000

(G-3134)
MARTINS FMOUS PSTRY SHOPPE INC
1933 Scott Futrell Dr (28208-2704)
PHONE................................800 548-1200
EMP: 5
SALES (corp-wide): 149.7MM **Privately Held**
Web: www.potatorolls.com
SIC: 2051 Bread, cake, and related products
PA: Martin's Famous Pastry Shoppe, Inc.
1000 Potato Roll Ln
Chambersburg PA 17202
800 548-1200

(G-3135)
MARVICA MCLENDON LLC
5906 Old Coach Rd (28215-1544)
PHONE................................704 965-9408
EMP: 6 **EST:** 2021
SALES (est): 214.47K **Privately Held**
SIC: 3999 7389 Hair and hair-based products; Business services, nec

(G-3136)
MAS DEFENSE LLC
8334 Pineville Matthews Rd Ste 103 (28226-3774)
PHONE................................980 265-1005
Mas Defense, *Prin*
EMP: 6 **EST:** 2013
SALES (est): 460.81K **Privately Held**
Web: www.masdefense.com
SIC: 3812 Defense systems and equipment

(G-3137)
MASON INTERNATIONAL
1525 E Worthington Ave (28203-6051)
PHONE................................704 921-3407
EMP: 6 **EST:** 2016
SALES (est): 472.55K **Privately Held**
Web: www.orchidstogo.com
SIC: 3571 Electronic computers

(G-3138)
MASONITE CORPORATION
7300 Reames Rd (28216-2228)
PHONE................................704 599-0235
Steve Stafstrom, *Brnch Mgr*
EMP: 430
Web: www.masonite.com
SIC: 3423 3546 3429 3315 Hand and edge tools, nec; Power-driven handtools; Builders' hardware; Nails, steel: wire or cut
HQ: Masonite Corporation
1242 E 5th Ave
Tampa FL 33605
813 877-2726

(G-3139)
MASONRY REINFORCING CORP AMER (PA)
Also Called: Wire-Bond
400 Rountree Rd (28217-2131)
P.O. Box 240988 (28224-0988)
PHONE................................704 525-5554
Ralph O Johnson Junior, *Ch Bd*
Ralph O Johnson Iii, *Pr*
Gary Tyler, *
Kathryn J Tyler, *
Mark Mcclure, *CFO*
▲ **EMP:** 130 **EST:** 1975
SQ FT: 111,200
SALES (est): 44.98MM
SALES (corp-wide): 44.98MM **Privately Held**
Web: www.wirebond.com
SIC: 3496 Concrete reinforcing mesh and wire

(G-3140)
MASTERWORK USA INC
3700 Rose Lake Dr (28217-2814)
PHONE................................704 288-9506
Li Li, *Pr*
Carol Jiang, *VP*
▲ **EMP:** 7 **EST:** 2012
SALES (est): 239.92K **Privately Held**
Web: www.masterworkusa.com
SIC: 3554 Die cutting and stamping machinery, paper converting

(G-3141)
MATHISEN VENTURES INC
Also Called: Cruise Industry News
17343 Meadow Bottom Rd (28277-6588)
PHONE................................212 986-1025
Oivind Mathisen, *Pr*
EMP: 6 **EST:** 1978
SALES (est): 948.9K **Privately Held**
Web: www.cruiseindustrynews.com
SIC: 2731 2721 2741 Book publishing; Periodicals, publishing only; Newsletter publishing

(G-3142)
MATSUSADA PRECISION INC
5960 Fairview Rd Ste 400 (28210-3119)
PHONE................................704 496-2644
Sadayoshi Matsuda, *Pr*
▲ **EMP:** 6 **EST:** 2004
SALES (est): 707.74K **Privately Held**
Web: www.matsusada.com
SIC: 3679 Power supplies, all types: static

(G-3143)
MATTHEW WARREN INC (DH)
Also Called: Paragon Medical - Southington
3426 Torringdon Way Ste 100 (28277-3497)
PHONE................................704 837-0331
Simon Newman, *CEO*
Kyle O'meara, *CFO*
EMP: 30 **EST:** 1995
SALES (est): 339.07MM
SALES (corp-wide): 1.05B **Privately Held**
Web: www.mwcomponents.com
SIC: 3493 Coiled flat springs
HQ: Mw Industries, Inc.
2400 Farrell Rd
Houston TX 77073
800 875-3510

(G-3144)
MAUSER USA LLC
1209 Tar Heel Rd (28208-1526)
PHONE................................704 398-2325
EMP: 42
Web: www.mauserpackaging.com
SIC: 3412 Metal barrels, drums, and pails
HQ: Mauser Usa, Llc
1515 W 22nd St Ste 1100
Oak Brook IL 60523

(G-3145)
MAUSER USA LLC
701 Lawton Rd (28216-3438)
PHONE................................704 625-0737
EMP: 151
Web: www.mauserpackaging.com
SIC: 3412 2655 Barrels, shipping: metal; Fiber cans, drums, and containers
HQ: Mauser Usa, Llc
1515 W 22nd St Ste 1100
Oak Brook IL 60523

(G-3146)
MAXIME KNITTING INTERNATIONAL
4925 Sirona Dr Ste 200 (28273-4201)
PHONE................................803 627-2768
Denis Th Riault, *CEO*
▲ **EMP:** 8 **EST:** 2015
SALES (est): 1MM **Privately Held**
Web: www.bekaertdeslee.com
SIC: 3069 Mattresses, pneumatic: fabric coated with rubber

(G-3147)
MAXTRONIC TECHNOLOGIES LLC
9545 Greyson Ridge Dr (28277-0659)
PHONE................................704 756-5354
EMP: 7 **EST:** 2004
SALES (est): 867.11K **Privately Held**
Web: www.maxtronictech.com
SIC: 3674 Solid state electronic devices, nec

(G-3148)
MC CULLOUGH AUTO ELC & ASSOC
3219 N Davidson St (28205-1033)
PHONE................................704 376-5388
George W Mc Cullough Iii, *Owner*
EMP: 7 **EST:** 1970
SQ FT: 4,500
SALES (est): 857K **Privately Held**
Web: auto-electrical-repair-services.cmac.ws
SIC: 5013 3694 7539 Automotive supplies and parts; Automotive electrical equipment, nec; Electrical services

(G-3149)
MCDONALD SERVICES INC
1734 University Commercial Pl (28213-6444)
P.O. Box 561238 (28256-1238)
PHONE................................704 597-0590
James Mcdold, *Mgr*
EMP: 30
SALES (corp-wide): 4.54MM **Privately Held**
Web: www.msibalers.com
SIC: 3559 Recycling machinery
PA: Mcdonald Services, Inc.
7427 Price Tucker Rd
Monroe NC 28110
704 753-9669

(G-3150)
MCGILL ADVSORY PBLICATIONS INC
8816 Red Oak Blvd Ste 240 (28217-5516)
PHONE................................866 727-6100
Brian Mcgillicuddy, *Dir*
EMP: 11 **EST:** 2019
SALES (est): 327.26K **Privately Held**
Web: www.corient.com
SIC: 2741 Miscellaneous publishing

(G-3151)
MCGRANN PAPER CORPORATION (PA)
Also Called: McGrann Digital Imaging
13400 Sage Thrasher Ln (28278-6861)
PHONE................................800 240-9455
Adam Mcgrann, *Pr*
Karl Mcgrann, *Pr*
◆ **EMP:** 40 **EST:** 1974
SALES (est): 9.68MM
SALES (corp-wide): 9.68MM **Privately Held**
Web: www.mcgrann.com
SIC: 5111 2752 Fine paper; Advertising posters, lithographed

(G-3152)
MCKELVEY FULKS
1432 Center Park Dr (28217-2909)
PHONE................................704 357-1550
EMP: 5 **EST:** 2005
SALES (est): 330.23K **Privately Held**
SIC: 3571 5045 Electronic computers; Computers, peripherals, and software

(G-3153)
MCLAMB GROUP INC
1003-B Louise Ave (28205-3257)
P.O. Box 36369 (28236-6369)
PHONE................................704 333-1171
Ed Mclamb, *Pr*
Steve Langdon, *Sec*
EMP: 7 **EST:** 2000
SQ FT: 14,000
SALES (est): 861.39K **Privately Held**
Web: www.themclambgroup.com
SIC: 2759 Promotional printing

(G-3154)
MCSHAN INC
Also Called: Wireless Communications NC
16607 Riverstone Way # 200 (28277-5749)
PHONE................................980 355-9790
Anthony Mcshan, *Pr*
EMP: 4 **EST:** 1999
SALES (est): 338.25K **Privately Held**
SIC: 3663 4812 Satellites, communications: Paging services

(G-3155)
MDB INVESTORS LLC
Also Called: Bilt USA Manufacturing
4000 Sam Wilson Rd (28214-8996)
P.O. Box 2905 (28070-2905)
PHONE................................704 507-6850
Richard Mikels, *Mng Pt*
EMP: 10 **EST:** 2011
SALES (est): 637.08K **Privately Held**
SIC: 3713 Truck and bus bodies

(G-3156)
MDKSCRUBS LLC
8401 Parkland Cir Apt 102 (28227-2203)
PHONE................................980 250-4708
Mary Mackins, *Managing Member*
EMP: 7 **EST:** 2021
SALES (est): 273.35K **Privately Held**
SIC: 2211 7389 Scrub cloths; Business services, nec

(G-3157)
MEASUREMENT CONTROLS INC
6131 Old Concord Rd (28213-6309)
P.O. Box 562775 (28256-2775)
PHONE................................704 921-1101
Paresh Patel, *Pr*
Ila Patel, *VP*
▲ **EMP:** 10 **EST:** 1977
SQ FT: 20,000
SALES (est): 790.42K **Privately Held**

Charlotte - Mecklenburg County (G-3158)
GEOGRAPHIC SECTION

Web: www.measurementcontrolsllc.com
SIC: **7699** 5085 3824 Professional instrument repair services; Gas equipment, parts and supplies; Fluid meters and counting devices

(G-3158)
MEDICAL DEVICE BUS SVCS INC
900 Center Park Dr Ste Bc (28217-2961)
PHONE..................................704 423-0033
Mark Hawkins, *Brnch Mgr*
EMP: 15
SALES (corp-wide): 85.16B **Publicly Held**
SIC: **3842** Surgical appliances and supplies
HQ: Medical Device Business Services, Inc.
    700 Orthopaedic Dr
    Warsaw IN 46582

(G-3159)
MEDICOR IMAGING INC
1927 S Tryon St Ste 200 (28203-4688)
PHONE..................................704 332-5532
Richard G Little, *Pr*
EMP: 21 **EST:** 2009
SALES (est): 244.01K **Privately Held**
Web: www.medicorimaging.com
SIC: **5045** 7371 7372 7373 Computer software; Computer software systems analysis and design, custom; Prepackaged software; Systems software development services

(G-3160)
MEGTEC INDIA HOLDINGS LLC
13024 Ballantyne Corporate Pl Ste 700 (28277-2113)
PHONE..................................704 625-4900
EMP: 7 **EST:** 2017
SALES (est): 2.78MM
SALES (corp-wide): 889.82MM **Publicly Held**
SIC: **3511** Turbines and turbine generator sets
PA: Babcock & Wilcox Enterprises, Inc.
    1200 E Market St Ste 650
    Akron OH 44305
    330 753-4511

(G-3161)
MEGTEC TURBOSONIC TECH INC
13024 Ballantyne Corporate Pl Ste 700 (28277-2113)
PHONE..................................704 625-4900
EMP: 11 **EST:** 2017
SALES (est): 4.37MM
SALES (corp-wide): 889.82MM **Publicly Held**
SIC: **3511** Turbines and turbine generator sets
PA: Babcock & Wilcox Enterprises, Inc.
    1200 E Market St Ste 650
    Akron OH 44305
    330 753-4511

(G-3162)
MELATEX INCORPORATED
3818 Northmore St (28205-1308)
P.O. Box 5127 (28299-5127)
PHONE..................................704 332-5046
▲ **EMP:** 10 **EST:** 1995
SQ FT: 21,000
SALES (est): 2.15MM **Privately Held**
Web: www.melatex.com
SIC: **2865** 5169 Cyclic crudes and intermediates; Dyestuffs

(G-3163)
MEMERE PUBLISHING
6247 Half Dome Dr (28269-1548)
PHONE..................................704 597-9160
Jean Smith-andrews, *CEO*

EMP: 5 **EST:** 2013
SALES (est): 80.17K **Privately Held**
SIC: **2741** Miscellaneous publishing

(G-3164)
MEMORYC INC
Also Called: Memoryc
8008 Corp Ctr Dr Ste 200 (28226-4489)
PHONE..................................980 224-2875
EMP: 9 **EST:** 2014
SALES (est): 105.64K **Privately Held**
Web: www.memoryc.com
SIC: **3674** 3572 Random access memory (RAM); Computer tape drives and components

(G-3165)
MERCHANTS METALS INC
Also Called: Meadow Burke Products
3401 Woodpark Blvd Ste A (28206-4249)
PHONE..................................704 921-9192
Baxter Ellis, *Mgr*
EMP: 4
SALES (corp-wide): 1.06B **Privately Held**
Web: www.merchantsmetals.com
SIC: **5032** 3272 Concrete building products; Concrete products, nec
HQ: Merchants Metals Llc
    3 Ravinia Dr Ste 1750
    Atlanta GA 30346
    770 741-0300

(G-3166)
MERCK & CO INC
Also Called: Merck
10301 David Taylor Dr (28262-2334)
PHONE..................................908 423-3000
John Canan, *Pr*
EMP: 47
SALES (corp-wide): 60.12B **Publicly Held**
Web: www.merck.com
SIC: **2834** Pharmaceutical preparations
PA: Merck & Co., Inc.
    126 E Lincoln Ave
    Rahway NJ 07065
    908 740-4000

(G-3167)
MESSER LLC
2820 Nevada Blvd (28273-6433)
PHONE..................................704 583-0313
Jay Navel, *Brnch Mgr*
EMP: 26
SALES (corp-wide): 1.63B **Privately Held**
Web: www.messeramericas.com
SIC: **2813** Oxygen, compressed or liquefied
HQ: Messer Llc
    200 Smrst Corp Blvd # 7000
    Bridgewater NJ 08807
    800 755-9277

(G-3168)
METAL IMPROVEMENT COMPANY LLC
500 Springbrook Rd (28217-2147)
PHONE..................................704 525-3818
EMP: 88
SALES (corp-wide): 2.85B **Publicly Held**
Web: www.imrtest.com
SIC: **3398** Shot peening (treating steel to reduce fatigue)
HQ: Metal Improvement Company, Llc
    80 E Rte 4 Ste 310
    Paramus NJ 07652
    201 843-7800

(G-3169)
METRO WOODCRAFTER OF NC INC
Also Called: Metro Woodcrafter
3710 Performance Rd (28214-8095)
P.O. Box 669488 (28266-9488)

PHONE..................................704 394-9622
Barry Rigby, *Pr*
Nicole Filion-ashline, *CFO*
EMP: 24 **EST:** 2015
SQ FT: 18,000
SALES (est): 5.33MM **Privately Held**
Web: www.metrowoodcrafter.com
SIC: **2434** Wood kitchen cabinets

(G-3170)
METROLINA SIGN CO
801 Atando Ave Ste D (28206-1949)
P.O. Box 5308 (28299-5308)
PHONE..................................704 343-0885
Wade Mcclure, *Prin*
EMP: 5 **EST:** 2010
SALES (est): 236.72K **Privately Held**
Web: www.metrolinasignsupply.com
SIC: **3993** Signs and advertising specialties

(G-3171)
METROLINA SIGN SUPPLY LLC
801 Atando Ave Ste D (28206-1949)
PHONE..................................704 343-0885
EMP: 6 **EST:** 2004
SALES (est): 85.72K **Privately Held**
Web: www.metrolinasignsupply.com
SIC: **3993** Signs and advertising specialties

(G-3172)
MIAHNA MOON LLC
5409 Prosperity Ridge Rd Apt 102 (28269-2583)
PHONE..................................704 449-9495
EMP: 4 **EST:** 2021
SALES (est): 182.76K **Privately Held**
Web: www.miahnamoon.com
SIC: **3999** Candles

(G-3173)
MIAS INC
Also Called: Mias Group
14240 S Lakes Dr (28273-6793)
PHONE..................................704 665-1098
Manfred Klug, *CEO*
Albert E Guarnieri, *Prin*
Nils Fleig, *CFO*
Doctor Cornelius Uhl, *Dir Opers*
Tracey Robins, *Off Mgr*
▲ **EMP:** 5 **EST:** 2006
SALES (est): 2.25MM
SALES (corp-wide): 4.95B **Privately Held**
Web: www.mias-group.com
SIC: **3536** Hoists, cranes, and monorails
HQ: Mias Gmbh
    Dieselstr. 12
    Eching BY 85386
    816570310

(G-3174)
MICHAEL EDITS
401 Michelle Linnea Dr Apt 11 (28262-8851)
PHONE..................................704 737-5220
EMP: 5 **EST:** 2016
SALES (est): 83.65K **Privately Held**
Web: www.michaeledits.com
SIC: **2741** Miscellaneous publishing

(G-3175)
MICROSOFT CORPORATION
Also Called: Microsoft
8055 Microsoft Way (28273-8106)
PHONE..................................704 527-2987
Keith Schifferli, *Brnch Mgr*
EMP: 2000
SALES (corp-wide): 211.91B **Publicly Held**
Web: www.microsoft.com
SIC: **7372** Application computer software
PA: Microsoft Corporation

1 Microsoft Way
Redmond WA 98052
425 882-8080

(G-3176)
MIDWOOD BARKERY LLC
3100 Monroe Rd (28205-7538)
PHONE..................................980 395-0498
Derrick Waynevidas, *CEO*
EMP: 5 **EST:** 2015
SALES (est): 66.87K **Privately Held**
Web: www.midwoodbarkery.com
SIC: **2499** Wood products, nec

(G-3177)
MIGN INC
301 Camp Rd Ste 105 (28206-3577)
PHONE..................................609 304-1617
Lisa Tweardy, *CEO*
Fredrik Meyer, *Prin*
Marcus Engman, *Prin*
EMP: 9 **EST:** 2019
SALES (est): 536.11K **Privately Held**
Web: www.mign.design
SIC: **3842** Surgical appliances and supplies

(G-3178)
MIKROPOR AMERICA INC
10512 Kilmory Ter (28210-8350)
◆ **EMP:** 10 **EST:** 2005
SALES (est): 980K **Privately Held**
Web: www.mikroporamerica.com
SIC: **3564** 3589 Air purification equipment; Water purification equipment, household type

(G-3179)
MIKROPUL LLC
4500 Chesapeake Dr (28216-3415)
PHONE..................................704 998-2600
Richard Bearse, *Managing Member*
EMP: 9 **EST:** 2014
SALES (est): 197.81K **Privately Held**
Web: www.nedermanmikropul.com
SIC: **3564** Purification and dust collection equipment

(G-3180)
MILLENNIUM PHARMACEUTICALS INC
10430 Harris Oak Blvd Ste 1 (28269-7521)
PHONE..................................866 466-7779
Zack Freese, *Brnch Mgr*
EMP: 55
Web: www.takedaoncology.com
SIC: **2834** Pharmaceutical preparations
HQ: Millennium Pharmaceuticals, Inc.
    40 Landsdowne St
    Cambridge MA 02139

(G-3181)
MILLER DUMPSTER SERVICE LLC
16450 Shallow Pond Rd (28278-8722)
PHONE..................................704 504-9300
Shannon Miller, *Prin*
EMP: 9 **EST:** 2017
SALES (est): 989.72K **Privately Held**
Web: www.millercarolina.com
SIC: **3443** Dumpsters, garbage

(G-3182)
MILLER PRODUCTS INC
Also Called: M P I Lable Systems Carolina
4100 Turtle Creek Ln (28273-3742)
PHONE..................................704 587-1870
Stephen Offits, *Mgr*
EMP: 34
SALES (corp-wide): 70.41MM **Privately Held**
Web: www.mpilabels.com

GEOGRAPHIC SECTION
Charlotte - Mecklenburg County (G-3207)

SIC: 2759 Labels and seals: printing, nsk
PA: Miller Products, Inc.
450 Courtney Rd
Sebring OH 44672
330 938-2134

(G-3183)
MILLWOOD INC
Also Called: Millwood
5950 Fairview Rd Ste 250 (28210-0093)
PHONE.................704 817-7541
EMP: 30
Web: www.millwoodinc.com
SIC: 2448 Pallets, wood
PA: Millwood, Inc.
3708 International Blvd
Vienna OH 44473

(G-3184)
MINNEWAWA INC
10612 Providence Rd Ste D (28277-9561)
PHONE.................865 522-8103
EMP: 7 **EST:** 2020
SALES (est): 200.02K **Privately Held**
Web: www.minnewawa.com
SIC: 3999 Manufacturing industries, nec

(G-3185)
MINOR PRESS
2715 W Sugar Creek Rd (28262-7304)
PHONE.................919 628-3044
EMP: 6 **EST:** 2016
SALES (est): 79.09K **Privately Held**
Web: www.minorxpress.com
SIC: 2741 Miscellaneous publishing

(G-3186)
MINT MACHINING A NORTH CAR
4321 Sawmill Trace Dr (28213-4875)
PHONE.................440 479-9074
EMP: 4 **EST:** 2017
SALES (est): 132.59K **Privately Held**
Web: www.mintmachining.com
SIC: 3599 Machine shop, jobbing and repair

(G-3187)
MIRRORMATE LLC
9317 Monroe Rd Ste A (28270-1476)
PHONE.................704 390-7377
EMP: 16 **EST:** 2003
SALES (est): 1.97MM **Privately Held**
Web: www.mirrormate.com
SIC: 5999 2499 Picture frames, ready made; Picture and mirror frames, wood

(G-3188)
MITSUBISHI CHEMICAL AMER INC (DH)
Also Called: Mitsubishi Chem Methacrylates
9115 Harris Corners Pkwy Ste 300 (28269-3810)
PHONE.................980 580-2839
Jean-marc Gilson, *CEO*
Randy Queen, *
◆ **EMP:** 53 **EST:** 1981
SALES (est): 1.28B **Privately Held**
Web: www.mitsubishichemicalholdings.com
SIC: 3355 3444 3443 2893 Aluminum rolling and drawing, nec; Sheet metalwork; Fabricated plate work (boiler shop); Printing ink
HQ: Mitsubishi Chemical Corporation
1-1-1, Marunouchi
Chiyoda-Ku TKY 100-8

(G-3189)
MJT US INC
Also Called: Dataforce
6801 Northpark Blvd Ste A (28216-0080)
P.O. Box 680490 (28216-0009)
PHONE.................704 826-7828
Mechelle Timmons, *Pr*
Daniel Hoover, *Sec*
John Timmons, *Dir Opers*
EMP: 7 **EST:** 2017
SQ FT: 25,000
SALES (est): 766.33K **Privately Held**
Web: www.dataforceresearch.com
SIC: 7389 7374 2752 7331 Printing broker; Data processing and preparation; Commercial printing, lithographic; Mailing service

(G-3190)
MK GLOBAL HOLDINGS LLC (DH)
Also Called: Mountain Khakis
5101 Terminal St (28208-1247)
PHONE.................704 334-1904
Ross Saldarini, *Managing Member*
EMP: 20 **EST:** 2003
SALES (est): 5.39MM
SALES (corp-wide): 101.34MM **Privately Held**
SIC: 2329 7999 2339 Men's and boys' sportswear and athletic clothing; Agricultural fair; Sportswear, women's
HQ: Mk Acquisition Llc
5101 Terminal St
Charlotte NC 28208
866 686-7778

(G-3191)
MMB ONE INC (PA)
4629 Dwight Evans Rd (28217-0907)
P.O. Box 30636 (28230-0636)
PHONE.................704 523-8163
Marvin Bruce Junior, *Pr*
Thomas Walker, *VP*
▲ **EMP:** 17 **EST:** 1963
SQ FT: 25,000
SALES (est): 5.32MM
SALES (corp-wide): 5.32MM **Privately Held**
Web: www.catawbarubber.com
SIC: 3052 5085 Automobile hose, rubber; Rubber goods, mechanical

(G-3192)
MOBIUS IMAGING LLC
Also Called: Mobius Imaging
1723 Beverly Dr (28207-2513)
PHONE.................704 773-7652
EMP: 30
SIC: 3845 CAT scanner (computerized axial tomography) apparatus

(G-3193)
MOMENTIVE PERFORMANCE MTLS INC
9129 Southern Pine Blvd (28273-5548)
PHONE.................704 805-6252
EMP: 167
Web: www.momentive.com
SIC: 2869 Silicones
HQ: Momentive Performance Materials Inc.
2750 Balltown Rd
Niskayuna NY 12309

(G-3194)
MOMMAMADE SCENTS LLC
13626 Riding Hill Ave (28213-4255)
PHONE.................704 458-5901
EMP: 4 **EST:** 2021
SALES (est): 84.64K **Privately Held**
SIC: 3999 Candles

(G-3195)
MOMMI & ME KOZMETICZ LLC
1822 Mcdonald St (28216-4455)
PHONE.................704 620-0082
EMP: 4 **EST:** 2021
SALES (est): 74.42K **Privately Held**
SIC: 2844 Cosmetic preparations

(G-3196)
MONARCH COLOR CORPORATION (PA)
5327 Brookshire Blvd (28216-3374)
PHONE.................704 394-4626
Gregory S West, *Pr*
Ian West, *
Ralph Petros, *
◆ **EMP:** 50 **EST:** 1977
SQ FT: 30,000
SALES (est): 9.79MM
SALES (corp-wide): 9.79MM **Privately Held**
Web: www.monarchcolor.com
SIC: 2893 Letterpress or offset ink

(G-3197)
MONARCH MEDICAL TECH LLC
112 S Tryon St Ste 800 (28284-2106)
PHONE.................704 335-1300
Bruce Lisanti, *Pr*
Stuart Long, *CEO*
Sharai Lavoie, *CFO*
Laurel Fuqua, *CCO*
EMP: 11 **EST:** 2012
SALES (est): 1.4MM **Privately Held**
Web: www.monarchmedtech.com
SIC: 7372 Application computer software

(G-3198)
MONARCH PRINTERS
3900 Greensboro St (28206-2036)
PHONE.................704 376-1533
Ira Kennedy, *Prin*
EMP: 6 **EST:** 2010
SALES (est): 100.51K **Privately Held**
SIC: 2752 Offset printing

(G-3199)
MONEY 4 LYFE
6426 Covecreek Dr (28215-1651)
PHONE.................704 606-8671
Michael Foster, *Pr*
EMP: 5 **EST:** 2000
SALES (est): 40.39K **Privately Held**
Web: www.moneyforlifechallenge.org
SIC: 2741 Music, sheet: publishing only, not printed on site

(G-3200)
MONOGRAM FOOD SOLUTIONS LLC (PA)
2330 E 5th St (28204-4337)
PHONE.................901 685-7167
Karl Schledwitz, *
Ches Jackson, *
David Dunavant, *
Don Brunson, *
▲ **EMP:** 35 **EST:** 2004
SALES (est): 819.37MM **Privately Held**
Web: www.monogramfoods.com
SIC: 2013 5142 5147 Pigs' feet, cooked and pickled: from purchased meat; Packaged frozen goods; Meats and meat products

(G-3201)
MONSTED MIX INC
3323 Holt St (28205-1660)
PHONE.................704 979-6911
Anne Monsted, *Prin*
EMP: 6 **EST:** 2010
SALES (est): 100.31K **Privately Held**
SIC: 3273 Ready-mixed concrete

(G-3202)
MOON N SEA NC LLC
Also Called: Kgi Trading NC
12810 Virkler Dr (28273-4253)
PHONE.................704 588-1963
EMP: 8 **EST:** 2018
SALES (est): 674.88K **Privately Held**
SIC: 3537 Trucks, tractors, loaders, carriers, and similar equipment

(G-3203)
MORRIS FAMILY THEATRICAL INC (PA)
Also Called: Morris East
6900 Morris Estate Dr (28262-4259)
PHONE.................704 332-3304
Scott Morris, *Pr*
Teri Bate, *VP*
Philip Morris Smith, *Sec*
Amy Morris Smith, *Treas*
▲ **EMP:** 20 **EST:** 1967
SQ FT: 300,000
SALES (est): 7.14MM
SALES (corp-wide): 7.14MM **Privately Held**
Web: www.morriscostumes.com
SIC: 2389 5632 5699 Costumes; Dancewear ; Costumes, masquerade or theatrical

(G-3204)
MORRIS SOUTH LLC
Also Called: Morris South M T S
12428 Sam Neely Rd Ste A (28278-7756)
PHONE.................704 523-6008
Rich Hussey, *Pr*
EMP: 81 **EST:** 1980
SQ FT: 16,000
SALES (est): 5.29MM **Privately Held**
Web: www.gotomorris.com
SIC: 3599 Machine shop, jobbing and repair

(G-3205)
MOSS SUPPLY COMPANY (PA)
Also Called: Old Dominion Win Door Hanover
5001 N Graham St (28269-4826)
P.O. Box 26338 (28221-6338)
PHONE.................704 596-8717
Robert Moss Senior, *CEO*
Robert Moss Junior, *VP*
Cassandra Nott, *
Juanita Moss, *Stockholder*
Gregory Smith, *
EMP: 250 **EST:** 1961
SQ FT: 225,000
SALES (est): 43.87MM
SALES (corp-wide): 43.87MM **Privately Held**
Web: www.mosssupply.com
SIC: 3442 Storm doors or windows, metal

(G-3206)
MOTION CONTROL INTEGRATION
9611 Brookdale Dr Ste 100 (28215-8776)
PHONE.................704 608-1279
Chris Ashworth, *Mgr*
EMP: 5 **EST:** 2008
SALES (est): 219.91K **Privately Held**
SIC: 3541 Machine tool replacement & repair parts, metal cutting types

(G-3207)
MOULDING MILLWORK LLC
11445 Granite St Unit C (28273-7174)
PHONE.................704 504-9880
Robert Wright, *Prin*
▲ **EMP:** 8 **EST:** 2005
SALES (est): 194.09K **Privately Held**
SIC: 2431 Millwork

Charlotte - Mecklenburg County (G-3208)

(G-3208)
MOUNT HOPE MACHINERY CO
2000 Donald Ross Rd (28208-6123)
P.O. Box 250 (22645-0250)
▲ **EMP:** 11 **EST:** 1954
SALES (est): 1.97MM **Privately Held**
Web: www.andritz.com
SIC: 3552 3312 3069 5084 Textile machinery ; Blast furnaces and steel mills; Medical and laboratory rubber sundries and related products; Plastic products machinery

(G-3209)
MOVERS AND SHAKERS LLC ✪
Also Called: Pink Zebra Moving Charlotte NC
1016 W Craighead Rd (28206-1613)
PHONE.................................980 771-0505
EMP: 7 **EST:** 2022
SALES (est): 281.39K **Privately Held**
SIC: 7372 Prepackaged software

(G-3210)
MRO STOP LLC (HQ)
11616 Wilmar Blvd (28273-6409)
PHONE.................................704 587-5429
John Colbert, *Managing Member*
EMP: 11 **EST:** 2013
SALES (est): 2.04MM
SALES (corp-wide): 98.44MM **Privately Held**
Web: www.mrostop.com
SIC: 5084 3594 Hydraulic systems equipment and supplies; Fluid power pumps and motors
PA: Park Hyde Partners Inc
    11529 Wilmar Blvd
    Charlotte NC 28273
    704 587-4819

(G-3211)
MRS GS TEES
2108 Double Oaks Rd (28206-1404)
PHONE.................................704 372-0610
Nadia Harris, *Prin*
EMP: 4 **EST:** 2014
SALES (est): 66.11K **Privately Held**
SIC: 2759 Screen printing

(G-3212)
MUDGEAR LLC
2522 Handley Pl (28226-4946)
PHONE.................................347 674-9102
Alex Thrasher, *Prin*
EMP: 6 **EST:** 2017
SALES (est): 227.48K **Privately Held**
Web: www.mudgear.com
SIC: 2323 Men's and boy's neckwear

(G-3213)
MUELLER DIE CUT SOLUTIONS INC (HQ)
10415 Westlake Dr (28273-3784)
P.O. Box 7503 (28241-7503)
PHONE.................................704 588-3900
Ken Stober, *Pr*
Donald Stober, *
Brian Stober, *
Carl Stober, *
James Brazas, *
◆ **EMP:** 25 **EST:** 1940
SQ FT: 44,000
SALES (est): 39.41MM
SALES (corp-wide): 115.03MM **Privately Held**
Web: www.muellercustomcut.com
SIC: 3053 5084 2675 Gaskets, all materials; Conveyor systems; Die-cut paper and board
PA: Sur-Seal, Llc
    6156 Wesselman Rd
    Cincinnati OH 45248
    513 574-8500

(G-3214)
MULLEN PUBLICATIONS INC
9301 Forsyth Park Dr Ste A (28273-3957)
P.O. Box 7746 (28241-7746)
PHONE.................................704 527-5111
Mason W Smith Iii, *Pr*
EMP: 15 **EST:** 1945
SALES (est): 1.8MM **Privately Held**
Web: www.mullenpublications.com
SIC: 2711 Newspapers, publishing and printing

(G-3215)
MULTI-SHIFTER INC
11110 Park Charlotte Blvd (28273-8859)
P.O. Box 38310 (28278-1005)
PHONE.................................704 588-9611
Dale Williams, *Pr*
Kelly Minchener, *CFO*
▼ **EMP:** 15 **EST:** 1983
SQ FT: 24,000
SALES (est): 3.89MM **Privately Held**
Web: www.multi-shifter.com
SIC: 3537 Lift trucks, industrial: fork, platform, straddle, etc.

(G-3216)
MULTISITE LED LLC
6715 Fairview Rd (28210-3355)
PHONE.................................650 823-7247
EMP: 4
SALES (corp-wide): 861.22K **Privately Held**
SIC: 3674 Light emitting diodes
PA: Multisite Led, Llc
    540 University Ave # 300
    Palo Alto CA 94301
    650 823-7247

(G-3217)
MULTITRODE INC
14125 S Bridge Cir (28273-6747)
PHONE.................................561 994-8090
▲ **EMP:** 31 **EST:** 1986
SQ FT: 7,700
SALES (est): 3.18MM **Publicly Held**
Web: www.xylem.com
SIC: 3825 Instruments to measure electricity
PA: Xylem Inc.
    301 Water St Se Ste 201
    Washington DC 20003

(G-3218)
MUNDO UNIFORMES LLC
10806 Reames Rd Ste W (28269-3766)
PHONE.................................704 287-1527
Juan Pablo Rojas, *Managing Member*
EMP: 5 **EST:** 2010
SALES (est): 340.97K **Privately Held**
Web: www.mundotees.com
SIC: 2759 Screen printing

(G-3219)
MURATA MACHINERY USA INC (DH)
Also Called: Muratec
2120 Queen City Dr (28208-2709)
P.O. Box 667609 (28266-7609)
PHONE.................................704 875-9280
Masahiko Hattori, *Pr*
Dale R Mitchell, *
Dan Luithle, *
◆ **EMP:** 120 **EST:** 1989
SQ FT: 97,000
SALES (est): 99.02MM **Privately Held**
Web: www.muratec-usa.com
SIC: 5084 5085 3542 Textile and leather machinery; Clean room supplies; Punching and shearing machines
HQ: Murata Machinery Usa Holdings, Inc.
    2120 Queen City Dr
    Charlotte NC 28208
    704 394-8331

(G-3220)
MURATA MCHY USA HOLDINGS INC (HQ)
Also Called: Muratatec
2120 Queen City Dr (28208-2709)
P.O. Box 667609 (28266-7609)
PHONE.................................704 394-8331
Masazumi Fukushima, *Pr*
Chris Cobb, *
◆ **EMP:** 15 **EST:** 2002
SQ FT: 100,000
SALES (est): 101.17MM **Privately Held**
Web: www.muratec-usa.com
SIC: 3542 3552 5065 Punching and shearing machines; Textile machinery; Facsimile equipment
PA: Murata Machinery, Ltd.
    136, Takedamukaishirocho, Fushimi-Ku
    Kyoto KYO 612-8

(G-3221)
MURRAY INC
4508 Westinghouse Blvd Ste B (28273-9602)
PHONE.................................704 329-0400
Tanner Hargens, *Prin*
EMP: 27
Web: www.medicalmurray.com
SIC: 3841 Surgical and medical instruments
PA: Murray, Inc.
    400 N Rand Rd
    North Barrington IL 60010

(G-3222)
MURRAY INC
Also Called: Medical Murray
8531 Steele Creek Place Dr Unit D (28273-4270)
PHONE.................................847 620-7990
EMP: 28
Web: www.medicalmurray.com
SIC: 3841 Surgical and medical instruments
PA: Murray, Inc.
    400 N Rand Rd
    North Barrington IL 60010

(G-3223)
MUSA GOLD LLC
8425 Cleve Brown Rd (28269-0969)
PHONE.................................704 579-7894
Alinda Mitchell, *CEO*
EMP: 10 **EST:** 2021
SALES (est): 521.67K **Privately Held**
SIC: 2834 Pharmaceutical preparations

(G-3224)
MVA LEATHERWOOD LLC
4530 Park Rd (28209-3716)
PHONE.................................704 519-4200
Lat W Purser Iii, *Admn*
EMP: 6 **EST:** 2005
SALES (est): 56.8K **Privately Held**
SIC: 3199 Leather goods, nec

(G-3225)
N2 PUBLISHING
2555 Stockbridge Dr Apt B (28210-5869)
PHONE.................................704 492-7206
EMP: 4
SALES (est): 74.89K **Privately Held**
Web: www.strollmag.com
SIC: 2741 Miscellaneous publishing

(G-3226)
N2 PUBLISHING
6322 Adobe Rd (28277-3680)
PHONE.................................704 497-7087
EMP: 4
SALES (est): 74.89K **Privately Held**
Web: www.strollmag.com
SIC: 2741 Miscellaneous publishing

(G-3227)
N3XT INC ✪
2708 Oakmeade Dr (28270-9730)
PHONE.................................704 905-2209
Jeffrey Wallis, *CEO*
Jeffrey Wallis, *Pr*
Scott Chay, *Ch*
EMP: 5 **EST:** 2023
SALES (est): 211.82K **Privately Held**
SIC: 7372 7389 Prepackaged software; Business Activities at Non-Commercial Site

(G-3228)
NAARVA
614 Chipley Ave (28205-7002)
PHONE.................................704 333-3070
Elbert Smith, *Prin*
EMP: 4 **EST:** 2007
SALES (est): 340.72K **Privately Held**
Web: www.naarva.com
SIC: 3799 Recreational vehicles

(G-3229)
NAKOS PAPER PRODUCTS INC
Also Called: Blp Paper
2020 Starita Rd Ste G (28206-1298)
P.O. Box 77181 (28271-7004)
PHONE.................................704 238-0717
Chris Nakos, *Pr*
Nick Nakos, *VP*
EMP: 7 **EST:** 2003
SALES (est): 673.95K **Privately Held**
SIC: 2621 Napkin stock, paper

(G-3230)
NAPOLEON JAMES
Also Called: Tshirtskings
7125 Spring Morning Ln (28227-8790)
PHONE.................................413 331-9560
Napoleon James, *Owner*
EMP: 4 **EST:** 2021
SALES (est): 130.28K **Privately Held**
SIC: 2759 Commercial printing, nec

(G-3231)
NASASPACEFLIGHT LLC
10926 Quality Dr Unit 39442 (28278-8931)
PHONE.................................980 430-9535
EMP: 5 **EST:** 2019
SALES (est): 64.67K **Privately Held**
SIC: 2711 Newspapers

(G-3232)
NASCENT TECHNOLOGY LLC
Also Called: Nascent
2744 Yorkmont Rd (28208-7324)
PHONE.................................704 654-3035
Ray West, *Pr*
Michael Bratt, *CFO*
Julie Corrado Ctrl, *Prin*
▲ **EMP:** 17 **EST:** 1996
SQ FT: 2,000
SALES (est): 6.2MM
SALES (corp-wide): 24.1MM **Privately Held**
Web: www.nascent.com
SIC: 3822 Building services monitoring controls, automatic
PA: System Development Resources Inc.
    1 International Blvd
    Mahwah NJ 07495
    201 995-9060

(G-3233)
NATIONAL CONTAINER GROUP LLC
1209c Tar Heel Rd (28208-1526)
PHONE.................................704 393-9050
Eric Perez, *Mgr*

GEOGRAPHIC SECTION

Charlotte - Mecklenburg County (G-3256)

EMP: 5
Web: www.mauserpackaging.com
SIC: 7699 5085 3999 4953 Plastics products repair; Drums, new or reconditioned; Grinding and pulverizing of materials, nec; Refuse collection and disposal services
PA: National Container Group, Llc
3620 W 38th St
Chicago IL 60632

(G-3234)
NATIONAL CONVEYORS COMPANY INC
4404a Chesapeake Dr (28216-3413)
P.O. Box 530176 (30353-0176)
PHONE.................860 325-4011
Tomas Hagstrom, *CEO*
Arnold Serenkin, *Pr*
Melissa Garrity, *Sec*
Brian Smith, *VP Engg*
James Dumaine-savage, *FOR ELCTL AND FIELD SERVICE*
▲ **EMP:** 4 **EST:** 1933
SQ FT: 17,500
SALES (est): 2.28MM **Privately Held**
Web: www.nationalconveyors.com
SIC: 3535 Conveyors and conveying equipment
HQ: Nederman Corporation
4404a Chesapeake Dr
Charlotte NC 28216
704 399-7441

(G-3235)
NATIONAL GYPS RECEIVABLES LLC
Also Called: Ngc Receivables
2001 Rexford Rd (28211-3498)
PHONE.................704 365-7300
Thomas C Nelson, *Pr*
EMP: 22 **EST:** 2015
SALES (est): 4.74MM
SALES (corp-wide): 795.88MM **Privately Held**
Web: www.nationalgypsum.com
SIC: 2679 Wallboard, decorated: made from purchased material
HQ: Proform Finishing Products, Llc
2001 Rexford Rd
Charlotte NC 28211

(G-3236)
NATIONAL GYPSUM SERVICES CO
2001 Rexford Rd (28211-3498)
PHONE.................704 365-7300
Tom Nelson, *Pr*
Cd Spangler Junior, *Pr*
EMP: 16 **EST:** 2003
SQ FT: 20,448
SALES (est): 8.82MM
SALES (corp-wide): 795.88MM **Privately Held**
Web: www.nationalgypsum.com
SIC: 1499 Gypsum and calcite mining
HQ: Proform Finishing Products, Llc
2001 Rexford Rd
Charlotte NC 28211

(G-3237)
NATIONAL TANK MONITOR INC
9801 Ferguson Rd (28227-6497)
PHONE.................704 335-8265
Rick Hardy, *Pr*
EMP: 10 **EST:** 1996
SALES (est): 736.56K **Privately Held**
SIC: 1389 Testing, measuring, surveying, and analysis services

(G-3238)
NAVEX GLOBAL INC
13950 Ballantyne Corporate Pl Ste 300
(28277-3193)
P.O. Box 60941 (28260-0941)
PHONE.................866 297-0224
EMP: 15
SALES (corp-wide): 1.65B **Privately Held**
Web: www.navex.com
SIC: 7372 Prepackaged software
HQ: Navex Global, Inc.
5500 Meadows Rd Ste 500
Lake Oswego OR 97035
971 250-4100

(G-3239)
NAVISTAR INC
Navistar
3325 Rotary Dr (28269-4494)
PHONE.................704 596-3860
Rebecca Jordan, *Owner*
EMP: 7
SALES (corp-wide): 350.31B **Privately Held**
Web: www.navistar.com
SIC: 3711 Motor vehicles and car bodies
HQ: Navistar, Inc.
2701 Navistar Dr
Lisle IL 60532
331 332-5000

(G-3240)
NC SATURN PARTS LLC
6603 Reafield Dr Apt 1 (28226-4565)
PHONE.................704 802-5277
Edward During, *Mgr*
EMP: 5 **EST:** 2018
SALES (est): 95.59K **Privately Held**
Web: www.ncsaturnpartsllc.com
SIC: 3714 Motor vehicle parts and accessories

(G-3241)
ND SOUTHEASTERN FASTENER
2220 Center Park Dr Ste C (28217-2994)
PHONE.................704 329-0033
EMP: 6 **EST:** 2019
SALES (est): 64.65K **Privately Held**
Web: www.ndindustries.com
SIC: 3965 Fasteners

(G-3242)
NEAL S PALLET COMPANY INC
8808 Wilkinson Blvd (28214-8061)
P.O. Box 992 (28012-0992)
PHONE.................704 393-8568
Phillip Neal Sparrow, *Pr*
William Hawley, *
EMP: 42 **EST:** 1981
SQ FT: 11,250
SALES (est): 4.3MM **Privately Held**
Web: www.nealspalletcompany.com
SIC: 2448 7699 Pallets, wood; Pallet repair

(G-3243)
NEALS PALLET CO INC NO 2
5100 Terminal St (28208-1248)
PHONE.................704 393-0308
Neil Starrow, *Pr*
EMP: 5 **EST:** 2005
SALES (est): 80.98K **Privately Held**
Web: www.nealspalletcompany.com
SIC: 2448 Pallets, wood

(G-3244)
NEDERMAN CORPORATION (HQ)
4404a Chesapeake Dr (28216-3413)
P.O. Box 16348 (28297-6348)
PHONE.................704 399-7441
▲ **EMP:** 14 **EST:** 1946
SALES (est): 45.47MM **Privately Held**
Web: www.nedermanmikropul.com
SIC: 3564 3469 3444 5084 Ventilating fans: industrial or commercial; Electronic enclosures, stamped or pressed metal; Sheet metalwork; Chemical process equipment
PA: Nederman Holding Ab
Sydhamnsgatan 2
Helsingborg 252 2

(G-3245)
NEDERMAN MANUFACTURING
4500 Chesapeake Dr (28216-3415)
PHONE.................704 898-7945
EMP: 18 **EST:** 2016
SALES (est): 899.13K **Privately Held**
Web: www.nederman.com
SIC: 3999 Barber and beauty shop equipment

(G-3246)
NEDERMAN MIKROPUL LLC (DH)
4404a Chesapeake Dr (28216-3413)
PHONE.................704 998-2600
Lacy Hayes Iii, *Pr*
Jonas Fogelberg, *CFO*
EMP: 6 **EST:** 2013
SALES (est): 23.93MM **Privately Held**
Web: www.nedermanmikropul.com
SIC: 5075 3564 Air filters; Air cleaning systems
HQ: Nederman Mikropul Holding Inc.
4404a Chesapeake Dr
Charlotte NC 28216
701 399-7441

(G-3247)
NEDERMAN MIKROPUL CANADA INC (DH)
4404a Chesapeake Dr (28216-3413)
P.O. Box 16348 (28297-6348)
PHONE.................704 998-2606
Lacy Hayes Iii, *Pr*
Sam Lavin, *VP*
◆ **EMP:** 7 **EST:** 1999
SALES (est): 9.41MM **Privately Held**
Web: www.nedermanmikropul.com
SIC: 3677 Filtration devices, electronic
HQ: Nederman Mikropul, Llc
4404a Chesapeake Dr
Charlotte NC 28216
704 998-2600

(G-3248)
NEW BEGINNINGS TRNSP LLC
5904 Johnnette Dr (28212-2365)
PHONE.................704 293-0493
EMP: 5
SALES (est): 229.6K **Privately Held**
SIC: 3799 Transportation equipment, nec

(G-3249)
NEW DIRECTIONS ENTERPRISES INC
2809 Mayfair Ave (28208-6026)
PHONE.................980 428-1866
Brandon Staton, *Prin*
EMP: 5 **EST:** 2016
SALES (est): 60.95K **Privately Held**
SIC: 2759 Screen printing

(G-3250)
NEW DRECTIONS SCREEN PRTRS INC
241 I K Beatty St (28214-1646)
PHONE.................704 393-1769
Wanda P Mauch, *Pr*
Curtis Phillips, *VP*
Harvey F Phillips, *Sec*
EMP: 4 **EST:** 1977
SQ FT: 2,000
SALES (est): 375.53K **Privately Held**
Web: www.newdirectionsco.com
SIC: 2759 Screen printing

(G-3251)
NEW ELEMENT
1021 Polk St (28206-2933)
PHONE.................704 890-7292
William Himes, *Prin*
EMP: 7 **EST:** 2010
SALES (est): 17.03K **Privately Held**
SIC: 2819 Elements

(G-3252)
NEW VISION MOMENTUM ENTP LLC
4456 The Plaza Ste E (28215-2176)
PHONE.................800 575-1244
EMP: 6 **EST:** 2019
SALES (est): 477.31K **Privately Held**
SIC: 3537 Trucks, tractors, loaders, carriers, and similar equipment

(G-3253)
NEWS 14 CAROLINA
316 E Morehead St Ste 316 (28202-2308)
PHONE.................704 973-5700
Ronald Miller, *Prin*
EMP: 10 **EST:** 2008
SALES (est): 355.16K **Privately Held**
Web: www.news14.com
SIC: 4833 2711 Television broadcasting stations; Newspapers, publishing and printing

(G-3254)
NEWTON MACHINE CO INC
1120 N Hoskins Rd (28216-3599)
PHONE.................704 394-2099
James E Newton Iii, *Pr*
William A Newton, *VP*
▲ **EMP:** 15 **EST:** 1948
SQ FT: 35,000
SALES (est): 1.55MM **Privately Held**
Web: www.newtonmachine.com
SIC: 3599 Machine shop, jobbing and repair

(G-3255)
NEXJEN SYSTEMS LLC
5933 Brookshire Blvd (28216-3386)
P.O. Box 29622 (27626-0622)
PHONE.................704 969-7070
Darren Lingafeldt, *Pr*
EMP: 22 **EST:** 2006
SQ FT: 10,850
SALES (est): 6.05MM
SALES (corp-wide): 14.42MM **Privately Held**
Web: www.thenexjen.com
SIC: 3823 3625 3825 Process control instruments; Relays and industrial controls; Instruments to measure electricity
PA: Averna Technologies Inc
87 Rue Prince Bureau 510
Montreal QC H3C 2
514 842-7577

(G-3256)
NEXXT LEVEL TRUCKING LLC
627 Minuet Ln (28217-2768)
PHONE.................980 205-4425
Aaron Simmons, *CEO*
Aaron C Simmons, *Prin*
EMP: 5 **EST:** 2008
SALES (est): 301.66K **Privately Held**
SIC: 8742 3537 Transportation consultant; Trucks: freight, baggage, etc.: industrial, except mining

Charlotte - Mecklenburg County (G-3257)

(G-3257)
NEXXUS LIGHTING INC
124 Floyd Smith Office Park Dr Ste 300 (28262-1684)
PHONE..................................407 857-9900
Michael Bauer, *Pr*
Gary Langford, *Treas*
EMP: 20 **EST:** 2014
SALES (est): 443.59K **Privately Held**
SIC: 3648 Lighting equipment, nec

(G-3258)
NEXXUSSOFT CORPORATION
6511 Bells Mill Dr (28269-9117)
PHONE..................................561 352-5232
Thomas P Pope, *CEO*
EMP: 5 **EST:** 2010
SALES (est): 60.72K **Privately Held**
Web: www.nexxussoft.com
SIC: 7372 Prepackaged software

(G-3259)
NG CORPORATE LLC
2001 Rexford Rd (28211-3415)
PHONE..................................704 365-7300
EMP: 12
SALES (est): 2.52MM **Privately Held**
SIC: 2679 Wallboard, decorated: made from purchased material

(G-3260)
NG OPERATIONS LLC (PA)
2001 Rexford Rd (28211-3415)
PHONE..................................704 365-7300
EMP: 6 **EST:** 2020
SALES (est): 96.43MM
SALES (corp-wide): 96.43MM **Privately Held**
SIC: 2679 Wallboard, decorated: made from purchased material

(G-3261)
NG OPERATIONS LLC
Also Called: NG OPERATIONS, LLC
5901 Carnegie Blvd (28209-4635)
P.O. Box 221799 (28222-1799)
PHONE..................................704 916-2082
EMP: 92
SALES (corp-wide): 795.88MM **Privately Held**
Web: www.nationalgypsum.com
SIC: 3275 Gypsum products
HQ: Proform Finishing Products, Llc
    2001 Rexford Rd
    Charlotte NC 28211

(G-3262)
NIC NAC WELDING CO
550 W 32nd St (28206-2215)
PHONE..................................704 502-5178
Marc Maddox, *Prin*
EMP: 8 **EST:** 2012
SALES (est): 467.85K **Privately Held**
SIC: 7692 Welding repair

(G-3263)
NITE CRAWLERS LLC
3626 Latrobe Dr (28211-1388)
PHONE..................................910 309-0543
EMP: 5
SALES (est): 75K **Privately Held**
SIC: 7372 Prepackaged software

(G-3264)
NN INC (PA)
6210 Ardrey Kell Rd Ste 600 (28277-4865)
PHONE..................................980 264-4300
Warren Veltman, *Pr*
Jeri J Harman, *Non-Executive Chairman of the Board*
John R Buchan, *Ex VP*
Michael C Felcher, *Sr VP*
Verlin Bush, *CCO*
▲ **EMP:** 6 **EST:** 1980
SALES (est): 489.27MM
SALES (corp-wide): 489.27MM **Publicly Held**
Web: www.nninc.com
SIC: 3562 Ball bearings and parts

(G-3265)
NONWOVEN MEDICAL TECH LLC
Also Called: Safetek Medical
635 Atando Ave Ste I (28206-1901)
PHONE..................................888 978-6199
Shawn B Padron, *Managing Member*
EMP: 4 **EST:** 2020
SALES (est): 149.26K **Privately Held**
SIC: 3842 Surgical appliances and supplies

(G-3266)
NORD GEAR CORPORATION
300 Forsyth Hall Dr (28273-5842)
PHONE..................................888 314-6673
Mike Vouchon, *Mgr*
EMP: 8
SALES (corp-wide): 1.12MM **Privately Held**
Web: www.nord.com
SIC: 3566 Gears, power transmission, except auto
HQ: Nord Gear Corporation
    800 Nord Dr
    Waunakee WI 53597
    608 849-7300

(G-3267)
NORDFAB DUCTING
4404 Chesapeake Dr (28216-3413)
P.O. Box 16348 (28297-6348)
PHONE..................................336 821-0840
EMP: 9 **EST:** 2015
SALES (est): 1.1MM **Privately Held**
Web: www.nordfab.com
SIC: 3444 Sheet metalwork

(G-3268)
NORSAN MEDIA LLC
4801 E Independence Blvd Ste 800 (28212-5400)
PHONE..................................704 494-7181
EMP: 25 **EST:** 2012
SALES (est): 2.48MM **Privately Held**
Web: www.norsanmedia.com
SIC: 2741 Internet publishing and broadcasting

(G-3269)
NORTH STAR FBRICATION REPR INC
124 Carothers St (28216-3820)
P.O. Box 742 (28130-0742)
PHONE..................................704 393-5243
Chris Kashino, *Pr*
Susan Kashino, *Sec*
EMP: 5 **EST:** 1984
SQ FT: 20,000
SALES (est): 390.75K **Privately Held**
SIC: 3499 3498 Fire- or burglary-resistive products; Tube fabricating (contract bending and shaping)

(G-3270)
NORTHROP GRMMAN GDNCE ELEC INC
Northrop Grumman Synoptics
1201 Continental Blvd (28273-6320)
PHONE..................................704 588-2340
Scott Griffin, *Mgr*
EMP: 30
Web: www.northropgrumman.com
SIC: 3812 3674 Search and navigation equipment; Infrared sensors, solid state
HQ: Northrop Grumman Guidance And Electronics Company, Inc.
    2980 Fairview Park Dr
    Falls Church VA 22042

(G-3271)
NOTEPAD ENTERPRISES LLC
Also Called: International
901 N Tryon St Ste G (28206-3294)
PHONE..................................704 377-3467
EMP: 5 **EST:** 2018
SALES (est): 700K **Privately Held**
SIC: 2752 Commercial printing, lithographic

(G-3272)
NOVA MOBILITY SYSTEMS INC
8604 Cliff Cameron Dr Ste 152 (28269)
PHONE..................................800 797-9861
George Ecker, *CEO*
EMP: 6 **EST:** 2012
SALES (est): 311.87K **Privately Held**
SIC: 3429 Hardware, nec

(G-3273)
NOVAERUS US INC (PA)
3540 Toringdon Way Ste 200 (28277-4650)
PHONE..................................813 304-2468
Kevin Maughan, *Pr*
Eric Murphy, *Sec*
EMP: 4 **EST:** 2013
SALES (est): 4.88MM
SALES (corp-wide): 4.88MM **Privately Held**
Web: www.novaerus.com
SIC: 3564 Air cleaning systems

(G-3274)
NOVANT HEALTH APPEL
1901 Brunswick Ave Ste 200 (28207-2809)
PHONE..................................704 316-5025
EMP: 8 **EST:** 2019
SALES (est): 256.69K **Privately Held**
Web: www.nhappelplasticsurgery.org
SIC: 8011 3571 Plastic surgeon; Personal computers (microcomputers)

(G-3275)
NOVAS BAKERY INC (PA)
1800 Odessa Ln (28216-1440)
PHONE..................................704 333-5566
Vlado Novakovic, *Pr*
Sladjana Novakovic, *
EMP: 15 **EST:** 1996
SALES (est): 6.3MM
SALES (corp-wide): 6.3MM **Privately Held**
Web: www.novasbakery.com
SIC: 5149 5461 2051 Bakery products; Retail bakeries; Bread, cake, and related products

(G-3276)
NOVEM INDUSTRIES INC
1801 Cottonwood St (28206-1280)
P.O. Box 1272 (28031-1272)
PHONE..................................704 660-6460
Allen Reyen, *Prin*
EMP: 6 **EST:** 2008
SALES (est): 451.78K **Privately Held**
Web: www.novemindustries.com
SIC: 3999 Manufacturing industries, nec

(G-3277)
NOVOLEX HOLDINGS LLC
3436 Toringdon Way Ste 100 (28277-2449)
PHONE..................................980 498-4082
EMP: 73
SALES (corp-wide): 32.64B **Publicly Held**
Web: www.novolex.com
SIC: 2673 2674 Plastic bags: made from purchased materials; Paper bags: made from purchased materials
HQ: Novolex Holdings, Llc
    101 E Carolina Ave
    Hartsville SC 29550
    800 845-6051

(G-3278)
NRS PRINTING & DISPLAYS LLC
1516 Wandering Way Dr (28226-5732)
P.O. Box 11174 (28220-1174)
PHONE..................................704 907-2887
EMP: 5 **EST:** 2015
SALES (est): 111.98K **Privately Held**
SIC: 2752 Commercial printing, lithographic

(G-3279)
NUCON WELDING INC
3706 Kilmarsh Ct (28262-2504)
PHONE..................................980 253-9369
EMP: 5 **EST:** 2012
SALES (est): 56K **Privately Held**
SIC: 7692 Welding repair

(G-3280)
NUCOR CASTRIP ARKANSAS LLC
1915 Rexford Rd (28211-3465)
PHONE..................................704 366-7000
Scott Andrews, *Pr*
EMP: 9 **EST:** 2014
SALES (est): 541.29K
SALES (corp-wide): 34.71B **Publicly Held**
Web: www.nucor.com
SIC: 3312 Blast furnaces and steel mills
PA: Nucor Corporation
    1915 Rexford Rd Ste 400
    Charlotte NC 28211
    704 366-7000

(G-3281)
NUCOR CORPORATION (PA)
Also Called: Nucor
1915 Rexford Rd Ste 400 (28211-3888)
PHONE..................................704 366-7000
Leon J Topalian, *Ch Bd*
David A Sumoski, *COO*
Stephen D Laxton, *Ex VP*
Douglas J Jellison, *Executive Strategy Vice President*
Gregory J Murphy, *Ex VP*
◆ **EMP:** 200 **EST:** 1905
SALES (est): 34.71B
SALES (corp-wide): 34.71B **Publicly Held**
Web: www.nucor.com
SIC: 3312 3441 3448 Blast furnaces and steel mills; Building components, structural steel; Prefabricated metal buildings

(G-3282)
NUCOR ENERGY HOLDINGS INC
1915 Rexford Rd (28211-3465)
PHONE..................................704 366-7000
EMP: 19 **EST:** 2012
SALES (est): 2.23MM
SALES (corp-wide): 34.71B **Publicly Held**
Web: www.nucor.com
SIC: 3312 Blast furnaces and steel mills
PA: Nucor Corporation
    1915 Rexford Rd Ste 400
    Charlotte NC 28211
    704 366-7000

(G-3283)
NUCOR STEEL SALES CORPORATION
1915 Rexford Rd (28211-3465)
PHONE..................................302 622-4066
Mark Ferucci, *Pr*
EMP: 10 **EST:** 1997
SALES (est): 5.24MM

GEOGRAPHIC SECTION
Charlotte - Mecklenburg County (G-3308)

SALES (corp-wide): 34.71B **Publicly Held**
Web: www.nucor.com
SIC: 3312 Blast furnaces and steel mills
PA: Nucor Corporation
1915 Rexford Rd Ste 400
Charlotte NC 28211
704 366-7000

(G-3284)
NUFABRX LLC ✪
1515 Mockingbird Ln Ste 400 (28209-3236)
PHONE..................................888 683-2279
Glenn Normoyle Junior, *CEO*
Glenn Normoyle Junior, *Managing Member*
EMP: 9 EST: 2023
SALES (est): 356.22K **Privately Held**
SIC: 3842 Surgical appliances and supplies

(G-3285)
NUTROTONIC LLC
5031 W W T Harris Blvd Ste H (28269-3761)
PHONE..................................855 948-0008
Hamed Khalili, *CEO*
Hamed Kahlili, *Managing Member*
EMP: 10 EST: 2021
SALES (est): 2.1MM **Privately Held**
SIC: 2048 5961 7389 5499 Feed supplements; Electronic shopping; Business services, nec; Health and dietetic food stores

(G-3286)
NZURI ACCESSORIES & CO LLC
6201 Fairview Rd Ste 200 (28210-3297)
PHONE..................................980 333-9530
EMP: 4 EST: 2021
SALES (est): 282.01K **Privately Held**
SIC: 3911 Jewelry apparel

(G-3287)
OASIS DENISTRY
2711 Randolph Rd (28207-2034)
PHONE..................................704 332-8188
Shawnda Coleman, *Off Mgr*
EMP: 5 EST: 2012
SALES (est): 100K **Privately Held**
Web: www.oasisdentistrync.com
SIC: 3843 Enamels, dentists'

(G-3288)
ODIN TECHNOLOGIES LLC
4810 Ashley Park Ln Unit C1-1307 (28210-3835)
PHONE..................................408 309-1925
EMP: 4 EST: 2018
SALES (est): 202.23K **Privately Held**
Web: www.odinhealthtech.com
SIC: 3845 3841 Electromedical equipment; Diagnostic apparatus, medical

(G-3289)
OKAYA SHINNICHI CORP AMERICA
Also Called: Osa
300 Crompton St (28273-6214)
P.O. Box 7027 (28241-7027)
PHONE..................................704 588-3131
Yoshio Kinoshita, *Pr*
Mikiya Nakamura, *
Akio Ichikawa, *
Masahide Yamazaki, *
Harry Kato, *
▲ EMP: 40 EST: 1990
SQ FT: 25,100
SALES (est): 9.66MM **Privately Held**
Web: www.osa-usa.com
SIC: 3312 Pipes, iron and steel
PA: Okaya & Co.,Ltd.
2-4-18, Sakae, Naka-Ku
Nagoya AIC 460-0

(G-3290)
OKUMA AMERICA CORPORATION (HQ)
11900 Westhall Dr (28278-7127)
P.O. Box 7866 (28241-7866)
PHONE..................................704 588-7000
▲ EMP: 145 EST: 1978
SALES (est): 41.61MM **Privately Held**
Web: www.okuma.com
SIC: 5084 3541 Machine tools and accessories; Machine tools, metal cutting type
PA: Okuma Corporation
5-25-1, Shimooguchi, Oguchicho
Niwa-Gun AIC 480-0

(G-3291)
OLDCASTLE BUILDINGENVELOPE INC
10405 Granite St Ste M (28273-6478)
PHONE..................................704 504-0345
Jess Busbin, *Brnch Mgr*
EMP: 15
SALES (corp-wide): 1.5B **Privately Held**
Web: www.obe.com
SIC: 3446 Ornamental metalwork
PA: Oldcastle Buildingenvelope, Inc.
5005 Lyndon B Johnson Fwy
Dallas TX 75244
214 273-3400

(G-3292)
OLDCASTLE RETAIL INC (DH)
625 Griffith Rd Ste 100 (28217-3576)
PHONE..................................704 525-1621
David Maske, *Pr*
◆ EMP: 17 EST: 2006
SALES (est): 61.36MM
SALES (corp-wide): 32.72B **Privately Held**
SIC: 3272 Concrete products, precast, nec
HQ: Bonsal American, Inc.
625 Griffith Rd Ste 100
Charlotte NC 28217
704 525-1621

(G-3293)
OLE MEXICAN FOODS INC
Also Called: Ole-Charlotte Distribution Ctr
11001a S Commerce Blvd (28273-6354)
PHONE..................................704 587-1763
Eduardo Moreno, *Pr*
EMP: 7
Web: www.olemex.com
SIC: 2099 Tortillas, fresh or refrigerated
PA: Ole' Mexican Foods, Inc.
6585 Crescent Dr
Norcross GA 30071

(G-3294)
OMEGA MANUFACTURING CORP
1800 Industrial Center Cir (28213-4301)
P.O. Box 560338 (28256-0338)
PHONE..................................704 597-0418
Ron C Hunte, *Pr*
▲ EMP: 12 EST: 1997
SQ FT: 5,000
SALES (est): 2.31MM **Privately Held**
Web: www.omega-mfg.com
SIC: 3599 Machine shop, jobbing and repair

(G-3295)
ON FOOT INNOVATIONS LLC
1820 Harris Houston Rd Unit 620242 (28262-9253)
PHONE..................................336 301-3732
Sarilla Saez, *Managing Member*
EMP: 5 EST: 2018
SALES (est): 208.61K **Privately Held**
SIC: 2252 Socks

(G-3296)
ON POINT MOBILE DETAILING LLC
10906 Featherbrook Rd (28262-7757)
PHONE..................................404 593-8882
EMP: 5
SALES (est): 210.25K **Privately Held**
SIC: 3714 7389 Cleaners, air, motor vehicle; Business services, nec

(G-3297)
ON THE SPOT GRILLING LLC
2814 Royal Fern Ln (28215-2881)
PHONE..................................704 963-4105
Adaryll Murray, *CEO*
EMP: 4 EST: 2020
SALES (est): 57.89K **Privately Held**
SIC: 2599 Food wagons, restaurant

(G-3298)
ONE LIBRARY AT A TIME INC
4107 Crossgate Rd (28226-7010)
PHONE..................................704 578-1812
EMP: 4 EST: 2018
SALES (est): 38.54K **Privately Held**
Web: www.onelibraryatatime.com
SIC: 2731 Book publishing

(G-3299)
ONE VALLEY STUDIOS LLC
1933 Pegram St (28205-2345)
PHONE..................................980 938-0465
Sly Ambroise, *Prin*
EMP: 4 EST: 2019
SALES (est): 74.76K **Privately Held**
SIC: 2741 Miscellaneous publishing

(G-3300)
ONEAKA DANCE COMPANY
4430 The Plaza # 13 (28215-2034)
PHONE..................................704 299-7432
Oneaka Mack, *Prin*
EMP: 5 EST: 2013
SALES (est): 177.34K **Privately Held**
SIC: 7922 8322 3931 7929 Performing arts center production; Child guidance agency; Drums, parts, and accessories (musical instruments); Popular music groups or artists

(G-3301)
ONSIGHT INC
2725 Westinghouse Blvd Ste 200 (28273-6534)
PHONE..................................704 747-4168
EMP: 6 EST: 2016
SALES (est): 211.31K **Privately Held**
Web: www.onsightcustomsigns.com
SIC: 3993 Signs and advertising specialties

(G-3302)
ONSITE WOODWORK CORPORATION
645 Pressley Rd Ste E (28217-4600)
PHONE..................................704 523-1380
Richard Greene, *Brnch Mgr*
EMP: 10
SALES (corp-wide): 20.83MM **Privately Held**
Web: www.osw.io
SIC: 2431 Woodwork, interior and ornamental, nec
PA: Onsite Woodwork Corporation
4100 Rock Valley Pkwy
Loves Park IL 61111
815 633-6400

(G-3303)
ONTARIO SPCIALTY COATINGS CORP
Also Called: Oscc
2905 Westinghouse Blvd (28273-6491)
PHONE..................................980 207-3944
EMP: 7 EST: 2017
SALES (est): 121.64K **Privately Held**
SIC: 3479 Metal coating and allied services

(G-3304)
ONWARD ENERGY HOLDINGS LLC
7621 Little Ave Ste 350 (28226-8109)
PHONE..................................980 294-0204
Steve Doyon, *CEO*
EMP: 6 EST: 2020
SALES (est): 69.5K **Privately Held**
SIC: 1382 Oil and gas exploration services

(G-3305)
OSPREA LOGISTICS USA LLC
Also Called: Osprea Logistics USA
11108 Quality Dr (28273-7714)
PHONE..................................704 504-1677
Michael Chamberlain, *
Raynard Mack, *
EMP: 40 EST: 2015
SQ FT: 1,000
SALES (est): 11.22MM
SALES (corp-wide): 14.85MM **Privately Held**
Web: www.osprea.com
SIC: 3713 Truck bodies and parts
HQ: Osprea Logistics Sa (Pty) Ltd
2 Warblers Rd
Cape Town WC 7806

(G-3306)
OTIS ELEVATOR COMPANY
9625 Southern Pine Blvd Ste G (28273-5506)
PHONE..................................704 519-0100
Jeff Duggan, *Rgnl Mgr*
EMP: 190
SALES (corp-wide): 13.69B **Publicly Held**
Web: www.otis.com
SIC: 3534 1796 5084 Elevators and equipment; Installing building equipment; Elevators
HQ: Otis Elevator Company
1 Carrier Pl
Farmington CT 06032
860 674-3000

(G-3307)
OVER RAINBOW INC
Also Called: Uptown Catering Company, The
1431 Bryant St (28208-5201)
PHONE..................................704 332-5521
Mike Ingersoll, *
EMP: 12 EST: 2003
SALES (est): 519.52K **Privately Held**
Web: www.uptowncateringco.com
SIC: 5812 5963 2099 Caterers; Food services, direct sales; Food preparations, nec

(G-3308)
PAI SERVICES LLC
Also Called: Sage Payroll Services
11215 N Community House Rd Ste 800 (28277-4961)
PHONE..................................856 231-4667
EMP: 7
SALES (corp-wide): 2.76B **Privately Held**
SIC: 7371 7372 Computer software development; Business oriented computer software
HQ: Pai Services, Llc
11215 N Cmnity Hse Rd # 800
Charlotte NC 28277
856 231-0195

Charlotte - Mecklenburg County (G-3309)

(G-3309)
PALMER SENN
Also Called: Mvi Productions
3113 Airlie St (28205-3244)
PHONE..............................704 451-3971
Palmer Senn, *Owner*
EMP: 5 **EST:** 1999
SALES (est): 236.8K **Privately Held**
SIC: 3544 7812 3651 Special dies and tools; Video tape production; Household audio and video equipment

(G-3310)
PANENERGY CORP (DH)
526 S Church St (28202-1802)
P.O. Box 1642 (77251-1642)
PHONE..............................704 594-6200
James E Rogers, *CEO*
EMP: 15 **EST:** 1997
SALES (est): 684.43MM
SALES (corp-wide): 29.06B **Publicly Held**
SIC: 4922 1321 2813 5172 Pipelines, natural gas; Natural gas liquids production; Helium; Gases
HQ: Duke Energy Registration Services, Inc.
526 S Church St
Charlotte NC 28202
704 594-6200

(G-3311)
PAPERWORKS
3040 Parker Green Trl (28269-1490)
PHONE..............................704 548-9057
EMP: 6 **EST:** 2010
SALES (est): 150.94K **Privately Held**
Web: www.onepaperworks.com
SIC: 2679 Wallpaper

(G-3312)
PARKER ATHLETIC PRODUCTS LLC
2401 Distribution St (28203-5377)
PHONE..............................704 370-0400
Bruce Parker, *Managing Member*
EMP: 8 **EST:** 1986
SQ FT: 7,500
SALES (est): 555.57K **Privately Held**
SIC: 3949 Team sports equipment

(G-3313)
PARKER MEDICAL ASSOCIATES LLC
2400 Distribution St (28203-5026)
PHONE..............................704 344-9998
▲ **EMP:** 11 **EST:** 1986
SQ FT: 5,000
SALES (est): 749.61K **Privately Held**
Web: www.parkermedicalassociates.com
SIC: 3949 2295 Protective sporting equipment; Varnished glass and coated fiberglass fabrics

(G-3314)
PARKER MEDICAL ASSOCIATES LLC (PA)
Also Called: Ultrascope
2400 Distribution St (28203-5026)
PHONE..............................704 344-9998
Bruce Parker, *CEO*
▲ **EMP:** 19 **EST:** 1981
SQ FT: 5,000
SALES (est): 2.65MM
SALES (corp-wide): 2.65MM **Privately Held**
Web: www.parkermedicalassociates.com
SIC: 3841 Stethoscopes and stethographs

(G-3315)
PARKER-HANNIFIN CORPORATION
Ssd Drives Division
9225 Forsyth Park Dr (28273-3884)
PHONE..............................704 588-3246
Jim Budnar, *Brnch Mgr*
EMP: 29
SALES (corp-wide): 19.07B **Publicly Held**
Web: www.parker.com
SIC: 3679 3566 Electronic loads and power supplies; Speed changers, drives, and gears
PA: Parker-Hannifin Corporation
6035 Parkland Blvd
Cleveland OH 44124
216 896-3000

(G-3316)
PARMER INTERNATIONAL INC
Also Called: Fluid Power Technology
1225 Graphic Ct Ste D (28206-1526)
PHONE..............................704 374-0066
Carl L Parmer, *Pr*
Dolores Parmer, *Sec*
EMP: 6 **EST:** 1983
SQ FT: 7,950
SALES (est): 793.33K **Privately Held**
Web: www.fluidpowertech.com
SIC: 3593 Fluid power actuators, hydraulic or pneumatic

(G-3317)
PARRISH TIRE COMPANY
300 E 36th St (28206-2022)
PHONE..............................704 372-2013
TOLL FREE: 800
EMP: 27
SALES (corp-wide): 378.88MM **Privately Held**
Web: www.parrishtire.com
SIC: 5014 5531 7534 Truck tires and tubes; Automotive tires; Tire retreading and repair shops
PA: Parrish Tire Company
5130 Indiana Ave
Winston Salem NC 27106
800 849-8473

(G-3318)
PATTERN BOX
8325 Nathanael Greene Ln (28227-0659)
PHONE..............................704 535-8743
EMP: 5 **EST:** 2008
SALES (est): 113.14K **Privately Held**
SIC: 3543 Industrial patterns

(G-3319)
PATTONS MEDICAL LLC
Also Called: Pattons Medical
4610 Entrance Dr Ste H (28273-4389)
PHONE..............................704 529-5442
▲ **EMP:** 26 **EST:** 2008
SALES (est): 5.29MM **Privately Held**
Web: www.pattonsmedical.com
SIC: 3563 3841 Air and gas compressors; Surgical and medical instruments
HQ: Patton's Inc.
3201 South Blvd
Charlotte NC 28209
704 523-4122

(G-3320)
PAUL NORMAN COMPANY INC
8700 Wilkinson Blvd (28214-8060)
P.O. Box 25118 (28229-5118)
PHONE..............................704 399-4221
Suzanne Norman, *Pr*
Jean Norman, *Treas*
EMP: 7 **EST:** 1965
SQ FT: 18,000
SALES (est): 582.28K **Privately Held**
SIC: 3599 Custom machinery

(G-3321)
PAVCO INC
9401 Nations Ford Rd (28273-5739)
PHONE..............................704 496-6800
▲ **EMP:** 49 **EST:** 1953
SALES (est): 10.54MM **Privately Held**
Web: www.pavco.com
SIC: 5084 5169 5051 2899 Industrial machinery and equipment; Chemicals and allied products, nec; Metals service centers and offices; Chemical preparations, nec

(G-3322)
PBI PERFORMANCE PRODUCTS INC (PA)
Also Called: Celanese Advanced Materials
9800 Southern Pine Blvd Ste D (28273-5527)
PHONE..............................704 554-3378
Bill Lawson, *Pr*
◆ **EMP:** 70 **EST:** 2002
SALES (est): 11.59MM
SALES (corp-wide): 11.59MM **Privately Held**
Web: www.pbipolymer.com
SIC: 3624 2824 Carbon and graphite products; Organic fibers, noncellulosic

(G-3323)
PCAI INC
Also Called: Cummins
11101 Nations Ford Rd (28206)
PHONE..............................704 588-1240
Mike Grace, *Ch Bd*
Steve Jordan, *VP*
EMP: 75 **EST:** 1970
SQ FT: 42,000
SALES (est): 18.82MM
SALES (corp-wide): 28.07B **Publicly Held**
SIC: 5084 5063 3519 Engines and parts, diesel; Generators; Internal combustion engines, nec
PA: Cummins Inc.
500 Jackson St
Columbus IN 47201
812 377-3842

(G-3324)
PEANUT BUTTER PROJECT
14720 Asheton Creek Dr (28273-3449)
PHONE..............................704 654-0212
Karen Lacey Barnes, *Prin*
EMP: 7 **EST:** 2019
SALES (est): 62.38K **Privately Held**
Web: www.projectpeanutbutter.org
SIC: 2099 Peanut butter

(G-3325)
PEGASUS ART AND SIGNS LLC
11908 Tanton Ln (28273-6734)
PHONE..............................704 588-4948
Janice Crook, *Owner*
EMP: 5 **EST:** 2017
SALES (est): 46.08K **Privately Held**
SIC: 3993 Signs and advertising specialties

(G-3326)
PELTON & CRANE COMPANY
11727 Fruehauf Dr (28273-6507)
PHONE..............................704 588-2126
Donald W Lochman, *Pr*
▲ **EMP:** 350 **EST:** 1900
SQ FT: 1,611,719
SALES (est): 31.67MM
SALES (corp-wide): 31.47B **Publicly Held**
Web: www.peltonandcrane.com
SIC: 3843 3841 Dental equipment; Surgical instruments and apparatus
PA: Danaher Corporation
2200 Penn Ave Nw Ste 800w
Washington DC 20037
202 828-0850

(G-3327)
PENDULUM INC
6128 Brookshire Blvd Ste A (28216-2423)
PHONE..............................704 491-6320
Willam Krause, *Pr*
EMP: 4 **EST:** 1996
SQ FT: 2,000
SALES (est): 311.96K **Privately Held**
SIC: 3577 Data conversion equipment, media-to-media: computer

(G-3328)
PEPSI COLA CO
Also Called: Pepsico
3530 Toringdon Way Ste 400 (28777-3431)
PHONE..............................704 357-9166
Tom Tansey, *Prin*
EMP: 8 **EST:** 2008
SALES (est): 335.04K **Privately Held**
Web: www.pepsistore.com
SIC: 2086 Carbonated soft drinks, bottled and canned

(G-3329)
PEPSI-COLA METRO BTLG CO INC
Also Called: Pepsico
2820 South Blvd (28209-1802)
PHONE..............................980 581-1099
Barksdale Halton, *Brnch Mgr*
EMP: 9
SALES (corp-wide): 86.39B **Publicly Held**
Web: www.pepsico.com
SIC: 2086 Carbonated soft drinks, bottled and canned
HQ: Pepsi-Cola Metropolitan Bottling Company, Inc.
700 Anderson Hill Rd
Purchase NY 10577
914 767-6000

(G-3330)
PERFECT FIT INDUSTRIES LLC
8501 Tower Point Dr Ste C (28227-7868)
PHONE..............................800 864-7618
▲ **EMP:** 125
SIC: 2392 2211 5712 Cushions and pillows; Yarn-dyed fabrics, cotton; Beds and accessories

(G-3331)
PERFORMANCE ORTHOTICS
2024 Randolph Rd # B (28207-1216)
PHONE..............................704 945-7790
Grace Turner, *Off Mgr*
EMP: 4 **EST:** 2010
SALES (est): 242.88K **Privately Held**
Web: www.charlotteorthotics.com
SIC: 3842 Orthopedic appliances

(G-3332)
PERLMAN INC
Also Called: Action Graphics
5312 Wingedfoot Rd (28226-7966)
PHONE..............................704 332-1164
Jackie J Perlman, *Pr*
David H Perlman, *VP*
EMP: 13 **EST:** 1982
SALES (est): 1.61MM **Privately Held**
SIC: 2752 Offset printing

(G-3333)
PF2 EIS LLC
10735 David Taylor Dr Ste 100 (28262-1060)
PHONE..............................704 549-6931
Annette Morris, *Asstg*
EMP: 154
SALES (corp-wide): 1.5B **Publicly Held**
SIC: 7372 Prepackaged software
HQ: Pf2 Eis Llc

5995 Windward Pkwy Fl 3
Alpharetta GA 30005
404 338-6000

(G-3334)
PFAFF MOLDS LTD PARTNERSHIP
11825 Westhall Dr (28278-7119)
PHONE.....................704 423-9484
Werkzeug Formenbau, *Mng Pt*
Michael Birkle, *Pt*
▲ **EMP:** 17 **EST:** 1998
SQ FT: 38,000
SALES (est): 5.53MM **Privately Held**
Web: www.pfaff-mold.de
SIC: 5013 3053 Automotive supplies and parts; Gaskets and sealing devices

(G-3335)
PFC GROUP LLC
Also Called: Plastex Fabricators
5900 Old Mount Holly Rd (28208-1131)
PHONE.....................704 393-4040
John Thompson, *Managing Member*
James Michael Lippard, *
Y Put Mloduondu, *
Hayes Lutz, *
Donald E Crumpton, *
EMP: 65 **EST:** 1968
SQ FT: 56,000
SALES (est): 8.37MM **Privately Held**
Web: www.plastexfab.com
SIC: 3993 Electric signs

(G-3336)
PGI POLYMER INC
Also Called: Chicopee
9335 Harris Corners Pkwy Ste 300 (28269-3818)
PHONE.....................704 697-5100
◆ **EMP:** 560
SIC: 2297 2392 Spunbonded fabrics; Slip covers and pads

(G-3337)
PHILPOTT MOTORS LTD
5401 E Independence Blvd (28212-0503)
PHONE.....................704 566-2400
Linda Rew, *Prin*
EMP: 19 **EST:** 2013
SALES (est): 650.62K **Privately Held**
Web: www.philpottmotors.net
SIC: 3612 Transformers, except electric

(G-3338)
PHOENIX TAPES USA LLC
10900 S Commerce Blvd (28273-6672)
PHONE.....................704 588-3090
◆ **EMP:** 4 **EST:** 2010
SALES (est): 1.03MM **Privately Held**
Web: www.phoenixtapes.com
SIC: 2891 Adhesives

(G-3339)
PIEDMONT COCA-COLA BTLG PARTNR (HQ)
Also Called: Coca-Cola
4115 Coca Cola Plz (28211-3400)
PHONE.....................704 551-4400
Frank Harrison, *CEO*
Scott Anthony, *
EMP: 30 **EST:** 2004
SALES (est): 100.02MM
SALES (corp-wide): 6.65B **Publicly Held**
Web: www.cokeconsolidated.com
SIC: 2086 Bottled and canned soft drinks
PA: Coca-Cola Consolidated, Inc.
4100 Coca Cola Plz # 100
Charlotte NC 28211
704 557-4400

(G-3340)
PIEDMONT PLASTICS INC (PA)
5010 W W T Harris Blvd (28269-1861)
P.O. Box 26006 (28221-6006)
PHONE.....................704 597-8200
Owen H Whitfield Junior, *Pr*
Tyler Booth, *
Greg Young, *
William Barth, *CSO*
Marc Klinger, *CIO*
◆ **EMP:** 100 **EST:** 1968
SQ FT: 73,000
SALES (est): 201.65MM
SALES (corp-wide): 201.65MM **Privately Held**
Web: www.piedmontplastics.com
SIC: 3081 3082 5162 Plastics film and sheet; Rods, unsupported plastics; Plastics sheets and rods

(G-3341)
PIEDMONT STAIRWORKS LLC (PA)
2246 Old Steele Creek Rd (28208-6031)
PHONE.....................704 697-0259
Jack Watson, *Prin*
Jack Watson, *Managing Member*
EMP: 8 **EST:** 2009
SALES (est): 2.14MM
SALES (corp-wide): 2.14MM **Privately Held**
Web: www.piedmontstairworks.com
SIC: 2431 Railings, stair: wood

(G-3342)
PIEDMONT TECHNICAL SERVICES
9127 Arbor Glen Ln (28210-7988)
PHONE.....................770 530-8313
Robert Stone, *Pr*
EMP: 5 **EST:** 2018
SALES (est): 115.78K **Privately Held**
Web: www.ptecserve.com
SIC: 3599 Industrial machinery, nec

(G-3343)
PILGRIM LLC
6428 Long Meadow Rd (28210-4732)
PHONE.....................980 224-9567
Lucas Weber, *Pr*
EMP: 5 **EST:** 2018
SALES (est): 99.3K **Privately Held**
Web: www.pilgrims.com
SIC: 2015 Poultry slaughtering and processing

(G-3344)
PIRANHA INDUSTRIES INC
2515 Allen Rd S (28269-4603)
PHONE.....................704 248-7843
Richard J Kuehler, *Prin*
EMP: 5 **EST:** 1995
SALES (est): 397.48K **Privately Held**
Web: www.piranhapackaging.com
SIC: 7389 7336 3993 3086 Packaging and labeling services; Package design; Displays and cutouts, window and lobby; Packaging and shipping materials, foamed plastics

(G-3345)
PITCH & BURL LLC
4215 Hiddenbrook Dr (28205-7235)
PHONE.....................512 653-9413
Adam Jochim, *Prin*
EMP: 5 **EST:** 2015
SALES (est): 88.69K **Privately Held**
SIC: 2431 Millwork

(G-3346)
PL&E SALES INC
11925 Sam Roper Dr Ste B (28269-7519)
PHONE.....................704 561-9650
EMP: 8 **EST:** 2010
SALES (est): 398.85K **Privately Held**
Web: www.plesales.com
SIC: 3999 Manufacturing industries, nec

(G-3347)
PLASKOLITE LLC
Also Called: Plazit-Polygal
1100 Bond St (28208-1212)
PHONE.....................704 588-3800
Ryan Schroeder, *CEO*
EMP: 129
SALES (corp-wide): 443.48MM **Privately Held**
Web: www.plaskolite.com
SIC: 2821 Plastics materials and resins
PA: Plaskolite, Llc
400 W Nationwide Blvd # 400
Columbus OH 43215
614 294-3281

(G-3348)
PLASMA WEB SERVICES INC
14129 Perugia Way Apt 102 (28273-7215)
PHONE.....................561 703-0485
David B Mann, *Owner*
EMP: 5 **EST:** 2013
SALES (est): 89.16K **Privately Held**
SIC: 2836 Plasmas

(G-3349)
PLAYER MADE LLC
1413 Russell Ave (28216-5141)
PHONE.....................704 303-6626
James W Blackmon Iii, *Managing Member*
EMP: 4 **EST:** 2020
SALES (est): 42.55K **Privately Held**
SIC: 2389 Apparel and accessories, nec

(G-3350)
PMA INDUSTRIES INC
Also Called: Fairway Insurance and Risk MGT
3834 Stokes Ave (28210-4750)
PHONE.....................704 575-6200
Michael David Carey, *Pr*
EMP: 5 **EST:** 2016
SALES (est): 68.38K **Privately Held**
SIC: 3999 Manufacturing industries, nec

(G-3351)
POLYGAL INC (HQ)
1100 Bond St (28208-1212)
PHONE.....................704 588-3800
Chai Tzadaka, *CEO*
Tamir Lavi, *Pr*
◆ **EMP:** 12 **EST:** 2003
SQ FT: 36,000
SALES (est): 19.33MM **Privately Held**
Web: www.plaskolite.com
SIC: 2821 Plastics materials and resins
PA: Polygal Plastics Industries Ltd
Kibbutz
Gazit

(G-3352)
POLYPORE INC
11430 N Community House Rd Ste 350 (28277-0454)
PHONE.....................704 587-8409
Robert B Toth, *CEO*
EMP: 59 **EST:** 2009
SALES (est): 1.21MM **Privately Held**
Web: www.polypore.com
SIC: 3999 Manufacturing industries, nec

(G-3353)
POLYPORE INTERNATIONAL LP (HQ)
11430 N Community House Rd Ste 350 (28277-0454)
PHONE.....................704 587-8409
Shgeki Takayama, *Pr*
Hiroyoshi Matsuyama, *
EMP: 99 **EST:** 2004
SALES (est): 331.16MM **Privately Held**
Web: www.polypore.net
SIC: 3691 Lead acid batteries (storage batteries)
PA: Asahi Kasei Corporation
1-1-2, Yurakucho
Chiyoda-Ku TKY 100-0

(G-3354)
POLYPRINT USA INC
1704 East Blvd (28203-5888)
PHONE.....................888 389-8618
EMP: 7 **EST:** 2010
SALES (est): 369.49K **Privately Held**
Web: www.polyprintdtg.com
SIC: 2752 Commercial printing, lithographic

(G-3355)
POLYSPINTEX INC
1301 Townes Rd (28209-4114)
PHONE.....................704 523-4382
Udo Schweizer, *Owner*
▲ **EMP:** 7 **EST:** 2000
SALES (est): 215.4K **Privately Held**
Web: www.polyspintex.com
SIC: 3552 2282 2299 Spinning machines, textile; Textured yarn; Broadwoven fabrics: linen, jute, hemp, and ramie

(G-3356)
POOL TABLES PLUS (PA)
4445 E Independence Blvd (28205-7403)
PHONE.....................704 535-8002
Cindy Kempisty, *Owner*
EMP: 6 **EST:** 1990
SQ FT: 20,000
SALES (est): 225.96K
SALES (corp-wide): 225.96K **Privately Held**
Web: www.carolinapooltablesplus.com
SIC: 3949 Sporting and athletic goods, nec

(G-3357)
POTEET PRINTING SYSTEMS LLC
9103 Forsyth Park Dr (28273-3882)
PHONE.....................704 588-0005
Carey Cannon, *
EMP: 60 **EST:** 1998
SQ FT: 36,000
SALES (est): 13.02MM
SALES (corp-wide): 1.91B **Privately Held**
Web: www.poteetsystems.com
SIC: 2759 Screen printing
PA: Flint Group Us Llc
17177 N Laurel Park Dr # 30
Livonia MI 48152
734 781-4600

(G-3358)
POWER ADHESIVES LTD
1209 Lilac Rd (28209-1418)
PHONE.....................704 578-9984
Lee Stegall, *Pr*
EMP: 4
SQ FT: 6,000
SALES (corp-wide): 18.71MM **Privately Held**
Web: www.poweradhesives.com
SIC: 2891 Adhesives
HQ: Power Adhesives Limited
1 Lords Way
Basildon SS13
126 888-5800

Charlotte - Mecklenburg County (G-3359)

GEOGRAPHIC SECTION

(G-3359)
POWER AND CTRL SOLUTIONS LLC
6205 Boykin Spaniel Rd (28277-8744)
PHONE..................................704 609-9623
James Keane Busker, *Pr*
EMP: 5 **EST:** 2009
SALES (est): 467.02K Privately Held
Web: www.pcssupply.com
SIC: 3699 7389 Electrical equipment and supplies, nec; Business Activities at Non-Commercial Site

(G-3360)
POWER COMPONENTS INC
10837 Coachman Cir (28277-9148)
P.O. Box 472221 (28247-2221)
PHONE..................................704 321-9481
Rick Mc Daniel, *Pr*
EMP: 6 **EST:** 1985
SALES (est): 416.35K Privately Held
Web: www.powercomponentsusa.com
SIC: 3559 Semiconductor manufacturing machinery

(G-3361)
POWER-UTILITY PRODUCTS COMPANY (PA)
Also Called: Pupco
8710 Air Park West Dr Ste 100 (28214-8686)
PHONE..................................704 375-0776
George C Todd Iii, *CEO*
EMP: 16 **EST:** 1973
SALES (est): 6.48MM
SALES (corp-wide): 6.48MM Privately Held
Web: www.pupco.com
SIC: 5063 3446 Electrical supplies, nec; Channels, furring

(G-3362)
POWERSNDS PPELINE PARTNERS LLC
129 W Trade St Ste 1405 (28202-2143)
PHONE..................................980 237-8900
EMP: 5 **EST:** 2019
SALES (est): 198.88K Privately Held
SIC: 1481 Nonmetallic mineral services

(G-3363)
POWERTEC INDUSTRIAL MOTORS INC
13509 S Point Blvd Ste 190 (28273-6897)
PHONE..................................704 227-1580
Cecil Thomas, *Pr*
Robert Lordo, *VP*
▲ **EMP:** 18 **EST:** 2000
SALES (est): 9.63MM
SALES (corp-wide): 241.4MM Privately Held
Web: www.powertecmotors.com
SIC: 3621 Motors, electric
HQ: Peerless-Winsmith, Inc.
5200 Upper Metro Pl # 11
Dublin OH 43017
614 526-7000

(G-3364)
PPG INDUSTRIES INC
Also Called: PPG 4670
10701 Park Rd (28210-8492)
PHONE..................................704 542-8880
Joe Corbin, *Mgr*
EMP: 4
SALES (corp-wide): 17.65B Publicly Held
Web: www.ppg.com
SIC: 2851 Paints and allied products
PA: Ppg Industries, Inc.
1 Ppg Pl
Pittsburgh PA 15272
412 434-3131

(G-3365)
PPG INDUSTRIES INC
Also Called: PPG 4668
3022 Griffith St (28203-5432)
PHONE..................................704 523-0888
David Mcmillan, *Brnch Mgr*
EMP: 4
SALES (corp-wide): 17.65B Publicly Held
Web: www.ppgpaints.com
SIC: 2851 Paints and allied products
PA: Ppg Industries, Inc.
1 Ppg Pl
Pittsburgh PA 15272
412 434-3131

(G-3366)
PRACTICEPRO SFTWR SYSTEMS INC
Also Called: Quick Practice
14225 Plantation Pk Blvd (28277-2275)
P.O. Box 620220 (28262-0103)
PHONE..................................212 244-2100
Gary Balsamo, *CEO*
EMP: 5 **EST:** 2010
SALES (est): 210.47K Privately Held
SIC: 7372 Prepackaged software

(G-3367)
PRECISE MOBILE WELDING
7713 Harrington Woods Rd (28269-0777)
P.O. Box 414 (28697-0414)
PHONE..................................980 785-7085
Sonya Freeman, *Prin*
EMP: 5 **EST:** 2016
SALES (est): 46.97K Privately Held
SIC: 7692 Welding repair

(G-3368)
PRECISE TECHNOLOGY INC
4201 Congress St Ste 340 (28209-4640)
PHONE..................................704 576-9527
Dave Outlaw, *Brnch Mgr*
EMP: 8
SALES (corp-wide): 14.03B Publicly Held
Web: www.ball.com
SIC: 3089 3082 Injection molded finished plastics products, nec; Unsupported plastics profile shapes
HQ: Rexam Limited
100 Capability Green
Luton BEDS LU1 3

(G-3369)
PRECISION PARTNERS LLC
Also Called: Stampsource
1830 Statesville Ave (28206-3229)
PHONE..................................704 560-6442
Stephen Taggart, *Mgr*
EMP: 7
SALES (corp-wide): 1.13MM Privately Held
SIC: 3499 Chair frames, metal
PA: Precision Partners, L.L.C.
400 Kellys Creek Rd # 10
Rabun Gap GA 30568
706 746-4012

(G-3370)
PRECISION PARTNERS LLC
Also Called: Stampsource
1830 Statesville Ave Ste C (28206-3229)
P.O. Box 32333 (28232-2333)
PHONE..................................800 545-3121
Luke Faulstick, *Managing Member*
Steve Hollis, *
Jim Murray, *
EMP: 40 **EST:** 2013
SQ FT: 18,000
SALES (est): 11.26MM Privately Held
SIC: 3469 3544 3599 Stamping metal for the trade; Special dies and tools; Machine shop, jobbing and repair
PA: Phoenix Stamping Group, Llc
6100 Emmanuel Dr Sw
Atlanta GA 30336

(G-3371)
PRECISION WLDG MCH CHARLOTTE
4701 Beam Rd (28217-9421)
PHONE..................................704 357-1288
Russell R Furr, *Owner*
EMP: 7 **EST:** 1969
SQ FT: 6,000
SALES (est): 512.25K Privately Held
Web: www.carolinaprecisioncontractors.com
SIC: 3599 Machine shop, jobbing and repair

(G-3372)
PRECOCIOUS PEN LLC
12427 Toscana Way (28273-4413)
PHONE..................................706 338-0010
Joylita Anderson, *Owner*
EMP: 5 **EST:** 2017
SALES (est): 50.18K Privately Held
SIC: 2741 Miscellaneous publishing

(G-3373)
PREM CORP
Also Called: Austin Tarp & Cargo Control
2901 Stewart Creek Blvd (28216-3593)
PHONE..................................704 921-1799
David Jacobson, *Pr*
Bellita Winger, *
Josh Albertson, *
▲ **EMP:** 33 **EST:** 1981
SALES (est): 8.04MM Privately Held
Web: www.austincanvas.com
SIC: 7699 5999 2394 5531 Miscellaneous automotive repair services; Canvas products; Canvas and related products; Auto and truck equipment and parts

(G-3374)
PRESS GANEY ASSOCIATES INC
700 E Morehead St Ste 100 (28202-2789)
PHONE..................................800 232-8032
EMP: 22 **EST:** 2019
SALES (est): 456.06K Privately Held
Web: www.pressganey.com
SIC: 2741 Miscellaneous publishing

(G-3375)
PRESTIGE CLEANING INCORPORATED
13903 Ballantyne Meadows Dr (28277-3727)
PHONE..................................704 752-7747
Margo Young, *Pr*
EMP: 10 **EST:** 2008
SALES (est): 525.25K Privately Held
Web: www.prestigecleaning-inc.com
SIC: 7349 1389 1711 Janitorial service, contract basis; Construction, repair, and dismantling services; Plumbing contractors

(G-3376)
PRESTRESS OF CAROLINAS LLC
11630 Texland Blvd (28273-6220)
P.O. Box 339 (28134-0339)
PHONE..................................704 587-4273
Bob Alger, *Managing Member*
EMP: 14 **EST:** 1998
SALES (est): 760.79K Privately Held
SIC: 3272 Concrete products, precast, nec

(G-3377)
PRETORIA TRANSIT INTERIORS INC
Also Called: Specialty Manufacturing
13501 S Ridge Dr (28273-6741)
PHONE..................................615 867-8515
▲ **EMP:** 39 **EST:** 1995
SALES (est): 4.14MM Privately Held
SIC: 3829 Transits, surveyors'
HQ: Specialty Manufacturing, Inc.
13501 S Ridge Dr
Charlotte NC 28273
704 247-9300

(G-3378)
PRETTY HONEST LLC
8232 Meadowdale Ln (28227-5982)
PHONE..................................804 837-1038
Andrea Bertrand, *Prin*
EMP: 5 **EST:** 2017
SALES (est): 98.1K Privately Held
SIC: 3999 Candles

(G-3379)
PRIDE COMMUNICATIONS INC
Also Called: Pride Magazine
8401 University Exec Park Dr Ste 122 (28262-4357)
P.O. Box 30113 (28230-0113)
PHONE..................................704 375-9553
Dee Dixon, *Pr*
EMP: 5 **EST:** 2000
SALES (est): 967.43K Privately Held
Web: www.pridemagazineonline.com
SIC: 2721 Magazines: publishing only, not printed on site

(G-3380)
PRIDE PUBLISHING & TYPSG INC
920 Central Ave (28204-2028)
P.O. Box 221841 (28222-1841)
PHONE..................................704 531-9988
James Yarbrough, *Pr*
EMP: 5 **EST:** 1984
SQ FT: 2,200
SALES (est): 407.71K Privately Held
SIC: 2711 Newspapers, publishing and printing

(G-3381)
PRIMAX USA INC
Also Called: Primax Pumps
11000 S Commerce Blvd Ste A (28273-6373)
PHONE..................................704 587-3377
Doug Bartholomew, *Pr*
▲ **EMP:** 9 **EST:** 2009
SQ FT: 5,500
SALES (est): 2.06MM Privately Held
Web: www.primaxproperties.com
SIC: 3561 Industrial pumps and parts

(G-3382)
PRINCETON INFORMATION
201 S College St (28244-0002)
PHONE..................................980 224-7114
EMP: 4 **EST:** 2018
SALES (est): 83.96K Privately Held
SIC: 2741 Miscellaneous publishing

(G-3383)
PRINT CHARLOTTE INC
5727 N Sharon Amity Rd Ste C (28215)
PHONE..................................704 488-5896
EMP: 6 **EST:** 2017
SALES (est): 174.63K Privately Held
Web: print-charlotte-inc-pci.business.site
SIC: 2752 Offset printing

(G-3384)
PRINT MAGIC TRANSFERS LLC ◊
6040 Sycamore Gardens Ln Apt 1404 (28273-4460)
PHONE..................................848 250-9906

Aijah Jacobs, *CEO*
EMP: 6 **EST:** 2023
SALES (est): 79.3K **Privately Held**
SIC: 2752 7389 Commercial printing, lithographic; Business services, nec

(G-3385)
PRINT MANAGEMENT GROUP LLC
425 E Arrowhead Dr (28213-6378)
PHONE..............................704 821-0114
Matthew Wilson, *Managing Member*
EMP: 15 **EST:** 2001
SALES (est): 4.2MM **Privately Held**
Web: www.printmgt.biz
SIC: 2752 3993 5943 5084 Offset printing; Signs and advertising specialties; Office forms and supplies; Printing trades machinery, equipment, and supplies

(G-3386)
PRINT MEDIA ASSOCIATES INC
Also Called: South City Print
834 Tyvola Rd Ste 110 (28217-3542)
PHONE..............................704 529-0555
Lee Clement Huffman, *Pr*
Jacquelyn Huffman, *VP*
EMP: 8 **EST:** 1988
SQ FT: 5,100
SALES (est): 806.68K **Privately Held**
Web: www.southcityprint.com
SIC: 2752 Offset printing

(G-3387)
PRINT ZILLA LLC
624 Tyvola Rd Ste 103 (28217-3585)
PHONE..............................800 340-6120
EMP: 8 **EST:** 2021
SALES (est): 278.02K **Privately Held**
SIC: 2759 Screen printing

(G-3388)
PRINTFUL INC (PA)
Also Called: Behappy.me
11025 Westlake Dr (28273-3782)
PHONE..............................818 351-7181
Alexander C Saltonstall, *CEO*
Baiba Orbidane, *
Lauris Liberts, *
EMP: 15 **EST:** 2013
SQ FT: 85,767
SALES (est): 32.24MM
SALES (corp-wide): 32.24MM **Privately Held**
Web: www.printful.com
SIC: 2759 Commercial printing, nec

(G-3389)
PRIORITY PRTG CHARLOTTE INC
3126 Milton Rd Ste E (28215-3774)
PHONE..............................802 374-8360
EMP: 5 **EST:** 2021
SALES (est): 83.91K **Privately Held**
Web: www.priorityprintingcharlotte.com
SIC: 2752 Offset printing

(G-3390)
PRODUCTION TOOL AND DIE CO INC
Also Called: PT&D
537 Scholtz Rd (28217-2138)
P.O. Box 11034 (28220-1034)
PHONE..............................704 525-0498
FAX: 704 525-3596
EMP: 10 **EST:** 1959
SQ FT: 12,000
SALES (est): 1MM **Privately Held**
Web: www.productiontool-die.com
SIC: 3545 Machine tool attachments and accessories

(G-3391)
PROFESSIONAL BUS SYSTEMS INC
201 E Cama St (28217-1701)
PHONE..............................704 333-2444
W T Hopkins, *Pr*
EMP: 4 **EST:** 1985
SALES (est): 330.43K **Privately Held**
Web: www.2pbsinc.com
SIC: 3993 2752 Signs and advertising specialties; Commercial printing, lithographic

(G-3392)
PROFORM FINISHING PRODUCTS LLC (DH)
Also Called: National Gypsum Company
2001 Rexford Rd (28211-3415)
P.O. Box 221799 (28222-1799)
PHONE..............................704 365-7300
Thomas C Nelson, *Pr*
John Mixson, *VP*
Craig Robertson, *VP*
Dennis Merriam, *VP*
Laura Budzichowski, *Sec*
◆ **EMP:** 275 **EST:** 1993
SQ FT: 40,000
SALES (est): 780.04MM
SALES (corp-wide): 795.88MM **Privately Held**
Web: www.nationalgypsum.com
SIC: 2679 3275 Wallboard, decorated: made from purchased material; Gypsum products
HQ: Delcor, Incorporated
834 Rivit St
Greenville NC 27834

(G-3393)
PSI CONTROL SOLUTIONS LLC (PA)
Also Called: PSI Power & Controls
9900 Twin Lakes Pkwy (28269-7614)
P.O. Box 2247 (28031-2247)
PHONE..............................704 596-5617
Mark Todd, *Pr*
Natalie Phillips, *
EMP: 35 **EST:** 1993
SQ FT: 10,000
SALES (est): 13.43MM
SALES (corp-wide): 13.43MM **Privately Held**
Web: www.psicontrolsolutions.com
SIC: 3613 Control panels, electric

(G-3394)
PSI GLOBAL USA
2725 Westinghouse Blvd Ste 100 (28273-6534)
PHONE..............................704 544-1893
Gary Yoho, *Pr*
EMP: 7 **EST:** 2014
SALES (est): 119.84K **Privately Held**
Web: www.psiglobal.co.uk
SIC: 3677 Filtration devices, electronic

(G-3395)
PTERIS GLOBAL (USA) INC
2401 Whitehall Park Dr Ste 1000 (28273)
PHONE..............................980 253-3267
David Haddaway, *Mktg Dir*
David Haddaway, *OF MKRT*
Scott Gordon, *Corporate Secretary*
▲ **EMP:** 10 **EST:** 2012
SQ FT: 4,800
SALES (est): 1.74MM **Privately Held**
Web: www.pterisglobal.com
SIC: 3535 Conveyors and conveying equipment

(G-3396)
PUBLISHING YOUR STORY LLC
2317 Kingsmill Ter (28270-9731)
PHONE..............................704 543-6555
EMP: 5 **EST:** 2015
SALES (est): 71.79K **Privately Held**
SIC: 2741 Miscellaneous publishing

(G-3397)
PUMPKIN PACIFIC LLC
10206 Pineshadow Dr Apt 107 (28262-1180)
PHONE..............................704 226-4176
Kevin Perkins, *Managing Member*
EMP: 8 **EST:** 2021
SALES (est): 150K **Privately Held**
Web: www.pumpkinpacific.com
SIC: 7549 7539 7534 Towing services; Automotive repair shops, nec; Tire repair shop

(G-3398)
QASIOUN LLC
Also Called: Fastsigns
4845 E Independence Blvd Unit B (28212-5407)
PHONE............../..............704 531-8000
EMP: 6 **EST:** 2018
SALES (est): 261.56K **Privately Held**
Web: www.fastsigns.com
SIC: 3993 Signs and advertising specialties

(G-3399)
QUAD/GRAPHICS INC
Also Called: QUAD/GRAPHICS INC.
10911 Granite St (28273-6316)
PHONE..............................706 648-5456
Tom Palmer, *Mgr*
EMP: 36
SALES (corp-wide): 2.96B **Publicly Held**
Web: www.quad.com
SIC: 2752 Offset printing
PA: Quad/Graphics, Inc.
N61w23044 Harrys Way
Sussex WI 53089
414 566-6000

(G-3400)
QUADSAW USA LLC
6739 Fairway Row Ln (28277-4190)
PHONE..............................980 339-8554
EMP: 4 **EST:** 2019
SALES (est): 69.17K **Privately Held**
Web: www.quadsaw.com
SIC: 3999 Manufacturing industries, nec

(G-3401)
QUAIL DRY CLEANING
5818 Prosperity Church Rd (28269-2298)
PHONE..............................704 947-7335
EMP: 6
SALES (corp-wide): 763.2K **Privately Held**
SIC: 2842 Laundry cleaning preparations
PA: Quail Dry Cleaning
6420 Rea Rd
Charlotte NC 28277
704 541-6199

(G-3402)
QUALISEAL TECHNOLOGY LLC
5605 Carnegie Blvd Ste 500 (28209-4642)
PHONE..............................704 731-1522
EMP: 6
SALES (est): 2MM
SALES (corp-wide): 1.06B **Publicly Held**
SIC: 3053 Gaskets; packing and sealing devices
PA: Enpro Industries, Inc.
5605 Carnegie Blvd # 500
Charlotte NC 28209
704 731-1500

(G-3403)
QUALITROL COMPANY LLC
3030 Whitehall Park Dr (28273-3334)
PHONE..............................704 587-9267
Roy Pelkey, *Brnch Mgr*
EMP: 7
SALES (corp-wide): 6.07MM **Publicly Held**
Web: www.qualitrolcorp.com
SIC: 3829 Measuring and controlling devices, nec
HQ: Qualitrol Company Llc
1385 Fairport Rd
Fairport NY 14450
585 586-1515

(G-3404)
QUEEN CITY EVENT MGMT CNSLTNG
1700 Lumarka Dr (28212-7669)
PHONE..............................704 780-7811
Angela Sherrill Simcox, *Admn*
EMP: 6 **EST:** 2013
SALES (est): 223.37K **Privately Held**
SIC: 3572 Computer storage devices

(G-3405)
R J YELLER DISTRIBUTION INC
Also Called: Biz On Wheels
1835 Lindbergh St (28208-3768)
PHONE..............................800 944-2589
Ron Yeller, *Pr*
EMP: 4 **EST:** 2007
SALES (est): 705.18K **Privately Held**
Web: www.foodtrucks4sale.com
SIC: 3713 Beverage truck bodies

(G-3406)
R T BARBEE COMPANY INC
724 Montana Dr Ste F (28216-3997)
P.O. Box 37246 (28237-7246)
PHONE..............................704 375-4421
David Schrum, *Managing Member*
John L Schrum Iii, *Pr*
Ramsy Schrum, *VP*
EMP: 14 **EST:** 1932
SQ FT: 5,000
SALES (est): 2.2MM **Privately Held**
Web: www.barbeetickets.com
SIC: 2752 2672 Forms, business: lithographed; Paper; coated and laminated, nec

(G-3407)
RA PRINTING & SIGN LLC
8524 Walden Ridge Dr (28216-1790)
PHONE..............................704 393-0264
EMP: 5 **EST:** 2018
SALES (est): 184.82K **Privately Held**
SIC: 3993 Signs and advertising specialties

(G-3408)
RANDALL-REILLY LLC
Also Called: Real Time Content
1509 Orchard Lake Dr Ste E (28270-1473)
PHONE..............................704 814-1390
David Schwartz, *Brnch Mgr*
EMP: 125
Web: www.randallreilly.com
SIC: 2721 7331 Magazines: publishing and printing; Mailing list compilers
HQ: Randall-Reilly, Llc
3200 Rice Mine Rd Ne
Tuscaloosa AL 35406
205 349-2990

(G-3409)
RAPID RESPONSE INC
Also Called: Label Store, The
218 Westinghouse Blvd (28273-6242)

Charlotte - Mecklenburg County (G-3410) — GEOGRAPHIC SECTION

PHONE..................................704 588-8890
Harris E Clark Junior, *Pr*
Carolyn Clark, *VP*
EMP: 4 **EST:** 1988
SALES (est): 771.33K **Privately Held**
Web: www.rapidresponselabels.com
SIC: 2679 5084 Labels, paper: made from purchased material; Printing trades machinery, equipment, and supplies

(G-3410)
RAPID RUN TRANSPORT LLC
12430 Clackwyck Ln (28262-1628)
PHONE..................................704 615-3458
Jonathon Lilley, *CEO*
Ankh Alli, *Managing Member*
EMP: 10 **EST:** 2018
SALES (est): 671.58K **Privately Held**
Web: www.rapidruntransportllc.com
SIC: 4215 4731 3537 Courier services, except by air; Freight forwarding; Trucks, tractors, loaders, carriers, and similar equipment

(G-3411)
RATED BEST OF CHARLOTTE
16151 Lancaster Hwy Ste A (28277-3881)
PHONE..................................704 309-3810
EMP: 5 **EST:** 2016
SALES (est): 96.03K **Privately Held**
Web: www.charlottemagazine.com
SIC: 2721 Magazines: publishing only, not printed on site

(G-3412)
RAW EARTH ENERGY CORPORATION
Also Called: Alternative Energy Products
5004 Wilkinson Blvd (28208-5446)
PHONE..................................704 492-0793
Gary W Mccullough Senior, *Pr*
EMP: 6 **EST:** 2011
SALES (est): 77.39K **Privately Held**
SIC: 3699 High-energy particle physics equipment

(G-3413)
RAW ELEMENTS
8538 Carolina Lily Ln (28262-6428)
PHONE..................................704 307-8025
Michelle Treadwell, *Prin*
EMP: 6 **EST:** 2015
SALES (est): 51.85K **Privately Held**
Web: www.rawelementsusa.com
SIC: 2844 Perfumes, cosmetics and other toilet preparations

(G-3414)
RAY ROOFING COMPANY INC
2921 N Tryon St (28206-2762)
P.O. Box 19150 (28219-9150)
PHONE..................................704 372-0100
Michael W Wilkinson, *Pr*
John W Wilkinson, *
James R Bradley, *
EMP: 24 **EST:** 1904
SQ FT: 20,000
SALES (est): 4.31MM **Privately Held**
Web: www.raycompany.com
SIC: 3444 1761 Sheet metalwork; Roofing contractor

(G-3415)
RAZOR MOTORSPORTS
3410 Country Club Dr (28205-3206)
PHONE..................................704 517-0649
EMP: 5 **EST:** 2009
SALES (est): 69.68K **Privately Held**
SIC: 3714 Motor vehicle parts and accessories

(G-3416)
RCR WELDING LLC
6011 Delta Crossing Ln Apt A (28212)
PHONE..................................704 200-8527
Roberto Castilleja Reyes, *Prin*
EMP: 5 **EST:** 2019
SALES (est): 97.6K **Privately Held**
SIC: 7692 Welding repair

(G-3417)
RE SHADS GROUP LLC
5819 Creola Rd (28270-5223)
PHONE..................................704 299-8972
EMP: 4 **EST:** 2019
SALES (est): 60K **Privately Held**
SIC: 1389 Construction, repair, and dismantling services

(G-3418)
REACT INNOVATIONS LLC
1809 Browning Ave (28205-3549)
PHONE..................................704 773-1276
EMP: 8 **EST:** 2015
SALES (est): 229.38K **Privately Held**
Web: www.reactinnovations.com
SIC: 3841 Surgical and medical instruments

(G-3419)
REC PLUS INC
1101 Central Ave (28204-2198)
PHONE..................................704 375-9098
Roy L Smith, *Ch*
Linda M Smith, *
Leigh Ann Neely, *
Jamie Neely, *
EMP: 42 **EST:** 1984
SQ FT: 20,000
SALES (est): 5.04MM **Privately Held**
Web: www.recognitionplus.net
SIC: 5999 3993 5699 Trophies and plaques; Signs and advertising specialties; Sports apparel

(G-3420)
RECOUPL INC
16430 Redstone Mtn Ln (28277-2994)
PHONE..................................704 544-0202
Richard L Smith, *Pr*
Rl Smith, *Pr*
Barbara Smith, *VP*
Barbara Smith, *Prin*
EMP: 5 **EST:** 1996
SALES (est): 400K **Privately Held**
SIC: 3569 Firehose equipment: driers, rack, and reels

(G-3421)
RED CLAY CIDERWORKS
245 Clanton Rd (28217-1303)
PHONE..................................980 498-0676
EMP: 8 **EST:** 2019
SALES (est): 248.09K **Privately Held**
Web: www.redclayciderworks.com
SIC: 2099 Cider, nonalcoholic

(G-3422)
RED HAND MEDIA LLC (PA)
Also Called: Business North Carolina
1230 W Morehead St Ste 308
(28208-5205)
PHONE..................................704 523-6987
David Kinney, *Managing Member*
EMP: 13 **EST:** 1981
SQ FT: 5,000
SALES (est): 1.45MM
SALES (corp-wide): 1.45MM **Privately Held**
Web: www.businessnc.com
SIC: 2721 Magazines: publishing and printing

(G-3423)
REDI-MIX LP
Also Called: Ready Mix
11509 Reames Rd (28269-7676)
PHONE..................................704 596-6511
Dan Montgomony, *Bmch Mgr*
EMP: 35
SIC: 3531 Construction machinery
HQ: Redi-Mix Lp
  1445 Mac Arthur Dr Ste 13
  Carrollton TX 75007
  972 242-4550

(G-3424)
REEDY INTERNATIONAL CORP (PA)
Also Called: Reedy Chem Foam Spclty Addtves
9301 Forsyth Park Dr Ste A (28273-3957)
P.O. Box 38486 (28278-1008)
PHONE..................................980 819-6930
Peter Schroeck, *Pr*
Elena Miller, *Ex VP*
Anne Marie Reedy, *CFO*
Kristen Reedy, *VP*
▼ **EMP:** 11 **EST:** 1989
SALES (est): 2.26MM **Privately Held**
Web: www.reedyintl.com
SIC: 3086 5169 Carpet and rug cushions, foamed plastics; Chemicals and allied products, nec

(G-3425)
REEL-SCOUT INC
1900 Abbott St Ste 100 (28203-4497)
PHONE..................................704 348-1484
Ed Henegar, *Pr*
EMP: 9 **EST:** 2001
SALES (est): 442.01K **Privately Held**
Web: www.reel-scout.com
SIC: 3652 Prerecorded records and tapes

(G-3426)
REGAL REXNORD CORPORATION
701 Carrier Dr (28216-3445)
PHONE..................................800 825-6544
EMP: 13
SALES (corp-wide): 6.25B **Publicly Held**
SIC: 3621 3566 Motors and generators; Speed changers, drives, and gears
PA: Regal Rexnord Corporation
  111 W Michigan St
  Milwaukee WI 53203
  608 364-8800

(G-3427)
REGINALD DWAYNE DILLARD ◆
Also Called: Global Dominion Enterprise
13026 Planters Row Dr (28278-0010)
PHONE..................................980 254-5505
Reginald D'wayne Dillard, *Owner*
EMP: 5 **EST:** 2022
SALES (est): 311.62K **Privately Held**
SIC: 3537 Trucks, tractors, loaders, carriers, and similar equipment

(G-3428)
REMAN TECHNOLOGIES INC
11421 Reames Rd (28269-7675)
PHONE..................................704 921-2293
Carl Keller, *Pr*
▲ **EMP:** 26 **EST:** 2004
SALES (est): 1.98MM **Privately Held**
Web: remantechnologies.lbu.com
SIC: 3694 Engine electrical equipment

(G-3429)
REMEDIOS LLC
Also Called: Component Sourcing Intl
1301 Westinghouse Blvd Ste I
(28273-6475)
PHONE..................................203 453-6000
▲ **EMP:** 5 **EST:** 2003
SALES (est): 412.97K **Privately Held**
SIC: 3448 Prefabricated metal components

(G-3430)
REMINGTON 1816 FOUNDATION
Also Called: 1816
1435 W Morehead St Ste 120
(28208-5208)
P.O. Box 700 (27025-0700)
PHONE..................................866 686-7778
Jason Watson, *Prin*
EMP: 5 **EST:** 2008
SALES (est): 99.5K **Privately Held**
SIC: 2342 2389 Corset accessories: clasps, stays, etc.; Uniforms and vestments

(G-3431)
REMODEEZ LLC
1920 Abbott St Ste 303 (28203-5194)
P.O. Box 301 (28106-0301)
PHONE..................................704 428-9050
Jason Jacobs, *CEO*
EMP: 10 **EST:** 2014
SQ FT: 1,700
SALES (est): 501.25K **Privately Held**
Web: www.remodeez.com
SIC: 2842 Deodorants, nonpersonal

(G-3432)
RENA SALES
3120 Latrobe Dr Ste 230 (28211-2183)
PHONE..................................704 364-3006
EMP: 4 **EST:** 2017
SALES (est): 124.07K **Privately Held**
Web: www.renaaquaticsupply.com
SIC: 3993 Signs and advertising specialties

(G-3433)
RENEWABLE POWER PRODUCERS LLC
10600 Nations Ford Rd # 150 (28273-5762)
PHONE..................................704 844-8990
EMP: 8 **EST:** 2009
SALES (est): 2.1MM **Privately Held**
Web: www.landfillgroup.com
SIC: 1321 Natural gas liquids

(G-3434)
RENEWBLE ENRGY INTGRTION GROUP
9115 Old Statesville Rd Ste A (28269-6605)
PHONE..................................704 596-6186
EMP: 8 **EST:** 2016
SQ FT: 3,500
SALES (est): 1.35MM **Privately Held**
Web: www.reig-us.com
SIC: 3825 Instruments to measure electricity

(G-3435)
RENNER USA CORP
651 Michael Wylie Dr (28217-1546)
P.O. Box 7172 (27264-7172)
PHONE..................................704 527-9261
Marcelo Cenacchi, *Pr*
Leo Migoto, *Dir*
▲ **EMP:** 5 **EST:** 2003
SALES (est): 4.48MM **Privately Held**
Web: rennerwoodcoatings.a2web1.srv.br
SIC: 2499 Decorative wood and woodwork
HQ: Renner Sayerlack S/A
  Av. Jordano Mendes 1500
  Cajamar SP 07776

(G-3436)
RENNER WOOD COMPANIES
651 Michael Wylie Dr (28217-1546)
PHONE..................................704 527-9261
EMP: 11 **EST:** 2020

GEOGRAPHIC SECTION
Charlotte - Mecklenburg County (G-3461)

SALES (est): 433.75K **Privately Held**
Web: rennerwoodcoatings.a2web1.srv.br
SIC: 2851 Epoxy coatings

(G-3437)
RESERVOIR GROUP LLC
9219 Heritage Woods Pl (28269-0300)
PHONE.................................610 764-0269
EMP: 5 **EST:** 2017
SALES (est): 104.73K **Privately Held**
Web: www.reservoirgroup.com
SIC: 1389 Oil field services, nec

(G-3438)
RESIDENT CULTURE BREWING LLC
2101 Central Ave (28205-5203)
P.O. Box 36369 (28236-6369)
PHONE.................................704 333-1862
Phillip Mclamb, CEO
EMP: 22 **EST:** 2016
SALES (est): 1.32MM **Privately Held**
Web: www.residentculturebrewing.com
SIC: 5813 2082 Bars and lounges; Beer (alcoholic beverage)

(G-3439)
REVLOC RECLAMATION SERVICE INC
13024 Ballantyne Corporate Pl Ste 700 (28277-2113)
PHONE.................................704 625-4900
EMP: 7 **EST:** 2017
SALES (est): 2.78MM
SALES (corp-wide): 889.82MM **Publicly Held**
SIC: 3511 Turbines and turbine generator sets
PA: Babcock & Wilcox Enterprises, Inc.
  1200 E Market St Ste 650
  Akron OH 44305
  330 753-4511

(G-3440)
REVMAX PERFORMANCE LLC
4400 Westinghouse Blvd 2 (28273-9620)
PHONE.................................877 780-4334
EMP: 10 **EST:** 2017
SALES (est): 1.74MM **Privately Held**
Web: www.revmaxconverters.com
SIC: 3465 Body parts, automobile: stamped metal

(G-3441)
REVOLUTION SCREEN PRINTING LLC
337 Dalton Ave (28206-3117)
PHONE.................................704 340-4406
Douglas Seamans, Prin
EMP: 6 **EST:** 2019
SALES (est): 332.66K **Privately Held**
Web: www.revolutionscreenprinting.com
SIC: 2752 Commercial printing, lithographic

(G-3442)
REXAM BEAUTY AND CLOSURES INC
Also Called: Rexam Cosmetic Packaging
4201 Congress St Ste 340 (28209-4640)
PHONE.................................704 551-1500
▲ **EMP:** 540
SIC: 3089 Injection molding of plastics

(G-3443)
REYNAERS INC
9347 D Ducks Ln (28273-4553)
PHONE.................................480 272-9688
EMP: 25
SALES (corp-wide): 409.31MM **Privately Held**
Web: www.reynaers.us

SIC: 3442 Metal doors, sash, and trim
HQ: Reynaers Inc.
  21430 N 15th Ln Ste 100
  Phoenix AZ 85027
  480 272-9688

(G-3444)
REYNOLDS ADVANCED MTLS INC
10725a John Price Rd (28273-4529)
PHONE.................................704 357-0600
Fal Bianco, Brnch Mgr
EMP: 42
SALES (corp-wide): 6.82MM **Privately Held**
Web: www.reynoldsam.com
SIC: 3442 5051 Molding, trim, and stripping; Castings, rough: iron or steel
PA: Reynolds Advanced Materials, Inc.
  13700 Diplomat Dr
  Farmers Branch TX 75234
  800 421-4378

(G-3445)
REYNOLDS AND REYNOLDS COMPANY
Also Called: Reynolds & Reynolds
6000 Monroe Rd Ste 340 (28212-6178)
PHONE.................................321 287-3939
Jim Riggs, Mgr
EMP: 6
SALES (corp-wide): 1.54B **Privately Held**
Web: www.reyrey.com
SIC: 2761 5045 7372 Manifold business forms; Computers, nec; Application computer service
HQ: The Reynolds And Reynolds Company
  1 Reynolds Way
  Kettering OH 45430
  937 485-2000

(G-3446)
RF DAS SYSTEMS INC
Also Called: Emergency Responder Systems
8230 Trail View Dr (28226-4672)
P.O. Box 471309 (28247-1309)
PHONE.................................980 279-2388
John Bone, Prin
EMP: 9 **EST:** 2018
SALES (est): 605.65K **Privately Held**
Web: www.rfdassystems.com
SIC: 3663 Antennas, transmitting and communications

(G-3447)
RGA ENTERPRISES INC (PA)
4001 Performance Rd (28214-8090)
PHONE.................................704 398-0487
Will Fidler, CEO
Julie Miller, *
EMP: 100 **EST:** 1977
SQ FT: 67,000
SALES (est): 24.09MM
SALES (corp-wide): 24.09MM **Privately Held**
Web: www.rgaenterprises.com
SIC: 2842 Specialty cleaning

(G-3448)
RICHA INC
231 E Tremont Ave (28203-5021)
PHONE.................................704 944-0230
Katherine Gerbanni, Mgr
EMP: 4
SALES (corp-wide): 243.66K **Privately Held**
Web: www.richa.com
SIC: 7374 7334 5199 2752 Computer graphics service; Blueprinting service; Architects' supplies (non-durable); Offset printing
PA: Richa, Inc.

  800 N College St
  Charlotte NC 28206
  704 331-9744

(G-3449)
RICHA INC (PA)
Also Called: RICHA GRAPHICS
800 N College St (28206-3227)
PHONE.................................704 331-9744
Rita Vyas, Pr
Suresh Vyas, VP
EMP: 14 **EST:** 1985
SQ FT: 11,500
SALES (est): 243.66K
SALES (corp-wide): 243.66K **Privately Held**
Web: www.richa.com
SIC: 7374 7334 5199 2752 Computer graphics service; Blueprinting service; Architects' supplies (non-durable); Offset printing

(G-3450)
RICHARD E PAGE
8500 Andrew Carnegie Blvd (28262-8500)
PHONE.................................704 988-7090
Richard Page, Owner
EMP: 4 **EST:** 2017
SALES (est): 129.64K **Privately Held**
SIC: 2261 Finishing plants, cotton

(G-3451)
RINGNECK AND LURE LLC
661 Hempstead Pl (28207-2319)
PHONE.................................704 377-8581
Roy Park, Prin
EMP: 4 **EST:** 2018
SALES (est): 47.08K **Privately Held**
SIC: 3949 Sporting and athletic goods, nec

(G-3452)
RIPARI AUTOMOTIVE LLC
2910 Patishall Ln (28214-5610)
PHONE.................................585 267-0228
Sabina Dixon, Managing Member
EMP: 7 **EST:** 2020
SALES (est): 467.01K **Privately Held**
SIC: 3714 Motor vehicle parts and accessories

(G-3453)
RNS INTERNATIONAL INC
5001 Sirus Ln (28208-6397)
P.O. Box 19867 (28219-0867)
PHONE.................................704 329-0444
Hans Nocher, Pr
EMP: 33 **EST:** 1983
SQ FT: 5,664
SALES (est): 4.35MM **Privately Held**
Web: www.rns-usa.com
SIC: 5013 3829 3825 Testing equipment, engine; Measuring and controlling devices, nec; Instruments to measure electricity

(G-3454)
ROADACTIVE SUSPENSION INC
330 E Hebron St Ste D (28273-5970)
PHONE.................................704 523-2646
Clive Schewitz, Pr
Andrea Schewitz, VP
▲ **EMP:** 8 **EST:** 1997
SQ FT: 5,000
SALES (est): 1.2MM **Privately Held**
Web: www.activesuspension.com
SIC: 3714 Motor vehicle parts and accessories

(G-3455)
ROBERTS POLYPRO INC
5416 Wyoming Ave (28273-8861)

PHONE.................................704 588-1794
John W Paxton, CEO
Allan Sutherland, *
Jack H Aguero, *
◆ **EMP:** 41 **EST:** 1978
SQ FT: 80,000
SALES (est): 10.66MM **Privately Held**
Web: www.robertspolypro.com
SIC: 3565 Packaging machinery
HQ: Pro Mach, Inc.
  50 E Rvrcnter Blvd Ste 18
  Covington KY 41011
  513 831-8778

(G-3456)
ROCKWELL AUTOMATION INC
9401 Southern Pine Blvd Ste E (28273-5596)
PHONE.................................704 665-6000
Michael Carbone, Mgr
EMP: 53
Web: www.rockwellautomation.com
SIC: 3625 Control equipment, electric
PA: Rockwell Automation, Inc.
  1201 S 2nd St
  Milwaukee WI 53204

(G-3457)
RODRIGUEZ WELDING LLC
4051 Walkers Cove Trl (28214-3476)
PHONE.................................980 299-9449
Avid O Rodriguez, Prin
EMP: 5 **EST:** 2018
SALES (est): 32.68K **Privately Held**
SIC: 7692 Welding repair

(G-3458)
ROI SALES SOLUTIONS INC
3313 Thaxton Pl (28226-3012)
PHONE.................................704 564-9748
Dean D Unumb, Pr
EMP: 5 **EST:** 2017
SALES (est): 114.3K **Privately Held**
SIC: 2752 Commercial printing, lithographic

(G-3459)
ROLF KOERNER LLC
Also Called: Rolf Koerner
514 Springbrook Rd Ste B (28217-2170)
PHONE.................................704 714-8866
Philip Lail, Managing Member
◆ **EMP:** 5 **EST:** 2005
SALES (est): 690.81K **Privately Held**
Web: www.rolfkoerner.com
SIC: 3496 Miscellaneous fabricated wire products

(G-3460)
ROSE OF CITY PRINTS
15120 Arbor Trail Ct Apt 1015 (28277-3368)
PHONE.................................980 201-9133
Jennifer Smith, Prin
EMP: 4 **EST:** 2017
SALES (est): 83.43K **Privately Held**
SIC: 2752 Commercial printing, lithographic

(G-3461)
ROYAL BATHS MANUFACTURING CO
Also Called: Royal Manufacturing
4525 Reagan Dr # A (28206-3192)
PHONE.................................704 837-1701
EMP: 48
SALES (corp-wide): 91.47MM **Privately Held**
Web: www.royal-mfg.com
SIC: 3842 3949 3432 3281 Whirlpool baths, hydrotherapy equipment; Sporting and athletic goods, nec; Plumbing fixture fittings and trim; Cut stone and stone products
PA: Royal Baths Manufacturing Company

Charlotte - Mecklenburg County (G-3462)
GEOGRAPHIC SECTION

14635 Chrisman Rd
Houston TX 77039
281 442-3400

(G-3462)
ROYAL BRASS & HOSE
3731 Woodpark Blvd Ste A (28206-4525)
PHONE..................704 847-2156
EMP: 10 **EST:** 2019
SALES (est): 493.51K **Privately Held**
Web: www.royalbrassandhose.com
SIC: 3429 Hardware, nec

(G-3463)
ROYAL CUP INC
3010 Hutchison Mcdonald Rd Ste F
(28269-4280)
PHONE..................704 597-5756
Scottie Kimble, Mgr
EMP: 10
SALES (corp-wide): 243.1MM **Privately Held**
Web: www.royalcupcoffee.com
SIC: 2095 5149 Roasted coffee; Coffee, green or roasted
PA: Royal Cup Inc.
160 Cleage Dr
Birmingham AL 35217
205 849-5836

(G-3464)
ROYAL MAPLE LLC (PA) ✪
Also Called: L&C Cabinetry
2908 Stewart Creek Blvd (28216-3592)
PHONE..................704 900-5086
EMP: 6 **EST:** 2023
SALES (est): 282.48K
SALES (corp-wide): 282.48K **Privately Held**
SIC: 2434 Wood kitchen cabinets

(G-3465)
ROYAL TEXTILE PRODUCTS SW LLC
2918 Caldwell Ridge Pkwy (28213-5888)
PHONE..................602 276-4598
Julie Henkel, Mgr
Kristian Henkel, Mgr
EMP: 5 **EST:** 2017
SALES (est): 382.81K **Privately Held**
Web: www.royaltextileproductssw.com
SIC: 2591 5023 7389 Window blinds; Window covering parts and accessories; Business services, nec

(G-3466)
ROYAL WIRE PRODUCTS INC
7500 Grier Rd (28213-6536)
PHONE..................704 596-2110
Rudy Maschke Junior, Mgr
EMP: 20
SQ FT: 17,520
SALES (corp-wide): 18.79MM **Privately Held**
Web: www.royalwire.com
SIC: 3496 Miscellaneous fabricated wire products
PA: Royal Wire Products, Inc.
13450 York Delta Dr
North Royalton OH 44133
440 237-8787

(G-3467)
RSC BIO SOLUTIONS LLC (HQ)
Also Called: Terresolve
2318 Arty Ave (28208-5104)
PHONE..................800 661-3558
EMP: 5 **EST:** 1996
SALES (est): 4.82MM
SALES (corp-wide): 5.28MM **Privately Held**
Web: www.rscbio.com
SIC: 2899 Chemical preparations, nec
PA: Blumenthal Holdings, Llc
1355 Greenwood Clfs # 200
Charlotte NC 28204
704 688-2302

(G-3468)
RSI LEASING INC NS TBT
2820 Nevada Blvd (28273-6433)
PHONE..................704 587-9300
James Davis, Prin
EMP: 5 **EST:** 2012
SALES (est): 116.19K **Privately Held**
SIC: 4213 3535 3537 Trucking, except local; Bulk handling conveyor systems; Trucks, tractors, loaders, carriers, and similar equipment

(G-3469)
RSTACK SOLUTIONS LLC
3540 Toringdon Way Ste 200 (28277-3867)
PHONE..................980 337-1295
EMP: 10
SALES (est): 372.02K **Privately Held**
SIC: 7372 Prepackaged software

(G-3470)
RTC VENTURES LLC
4520 Westinghouse Blvd Ste B
(28273-9625)
PHONE..................704 247-9781
EMP: 7 **EST:** 2011
SALES (est): 213.52K **Privately Held**
SIC: 3714 Motor vehicle parts and accessories

(G-3471)
RUCKER INTRGRTED LOGISTICS LLC
15519 Rathangan Dr (28273-7012)
PHONE..................704 352-2018
EMP: 4 **EST:** 2021
SALES (est): 232.02K **Privately Held**
SIC: 3537 7389 Trucks: freight, baggage, etc.: industrial, except mining; Business services, nec

(G-3472)
RUDDICK OPERATING COMPANY LLC
301 S Tryon St Ste 1800 (28282-1905)
PHONE..................704 372-5404
EMP: 20000
SIC: 5411 2284 Supermarkets, chain; Cotton thread

(G-3473)
RUSSELL T BUNDY ASSOCIATES INC
Also Called: Pan Glo, Charlotte
3400 Pelton St (28217-1320)
PHONE..................704 523-6132
Robert Sloan, Mgr
EMP: 10
SALES (corp-wide): 50.03MM **Privately Held**
Web: www.bundybakingsolutions.com
SIC: 3479 Pan glazing
PA: Russell T. Bundy Associates, Inc.
417 E Water St Ste 1
Urbana OH 43078
937 652-2151

(G-3474)
RUTLAND GROUP INC
13827 Carowinds Blvd Ste A (28273-4999)
PHONE..................704 553-0046
Jimmy Reed, Brnch Mgr
EMP: 5

Web: www.avientspecialtyinks.com
SIC: 2893 Printing ink
HQ: Rutland Group, Inc.
10021 Rodney St
Pineville NC 28134

(G-3475)
RYMON COMPANY INC
2015 Ayrsley Town Blvd Ste 202
(28273-4067)
PHONE..................704 519-5310
EMP: 5 **EST:** 2013
SALES (est): 214.9K **Privately Held**
Web: www.rymonco.com
SIC: 3545 Machine tool accessories

(G-3476)
S & S SCREENPRINTERS LLC
4135 Beauvista Dr (28269-1093)
PHONE..................704 707-5497
Brad D Sarchett, Prin
EMP: 5 **EST:** 2016
SALES (est): 107.17K **Privately Held**
Web: www.ssscreenprinters.com
SIC: 2759 Screen printing

(G-3477)
S TRI INC
Also Called: Hi-Tech Signs
10110 Johnston Rd Ste 12 (28210-9202)
PHONE..................704 542-8186
Art Sullivan, Pr
Tommie Sullivan, Mgr
EMP: 6 **EST:** 1988
SQ FT: 1,200
SALES (est): 395.66K **Privately Held**
SIC: 3993 Signs, not made in custom sign painting shops

(G-3478)
S&A MARKETING INC
Also Called: M & M Graphics
2526 S Tyron St (28203-4966)
P.O. Box 36633 (28236-6633)
PHONE..................704 376-0938
Matthre Christopher Kinser, Pr
EMP: 4 **EST:** 2018
SALES (est): 340.42K **Privately Held**
Web: www.mm4printing.com
SIC: 2752 Offset printing

(G-3479)
S&R INVESTMENTS LLC
13001 General Dr (28273-6444)
PHONE..................408 597-7007
EMP: 6 **EST:** 2018
SALES (est): 127.13K **Privately Held**
Web: www.solarcrest.com
SIC: 2731 Book publishing

(G-3480)
S-L SNACKS NATIONAL LLC (DH)
13024 Balntyn Corp Pl (28277-2113)
P.O. Box 32368 (28232-2368)
PHONE..................704 554-1421
▼ **EMP:** 31 **EST:** 2010
SALES (est): 357.68MM
SALES (corp-wide): 8.56B **Publicly Held**
Web: www.lance.com
SIC: 2052 Cookies
HQ: Snyder's-Lance, Inc.
13515 Balntyn Corp Pl
Charlotte NC 28277
704 554-1421

(G-3481)
S-L SNACKS PA LLC
13024 Balntyn Corp Pl (28277-2113)
P.O. Box 32368 (28232-2368)
PHONE..................704 554-1421

EMP: 123 **EST:** 2011
SQ FT: 357,193
SALES (est): 9.15MM
SALES (corp-wide): 8.56B **Publicly Held**
SIC: 2052 2096 Cookies and crackers; Potato chips and similar snacks
HQ: S-L Snacks National, Llc
13024 Balntyn Corp Pl
Charlotte NC 28277

(G-3482)
SAINT BENEDICT PRESS LLC
13315 Carowinds Blvd Ste 2 (28273-7700)
P.O. Box 269 (28053-0269)
PHONE..................704 731-0651
Conor Galgher, Managing Member
▲ **EMP:** 30 **EST:** 2009
SALES (est): 3.34MM
SALES (corp-wide): 29.7MM **Privately Held**
Web: www.tanbooks.com
SIC: 2741 Miscellaneous publishing
PA: Good Will Publishers, Inc.
1520 S York Rd
Gastonia NC 28052
704 853-3237

(G-3483)
SALICE AMERICA INC (DH)
Also Called: Salice
2123 Crown Centre Dr (28227-7701)
PHONE..................704 841-7810
Luciano Salice, CEO
Matteo Fregosi, *
Massimo Salice, *
Sergio Salice, *
Lori Miller, *
◆ **EMP:** 23 **EST:** 1989
SQ FT: 100,000
SALES (est): 14.62MM
SALES (corp-wide): 2.67MM **Privately Held**
Web: www.salice.com
SIC: 5072 3822 3545 Furniture hardware, nec; Damper operators: pneumatic, thermostatic, electric; Machine tool accessories
HQ: Arturo Salice Spa
Via Provinciale Novedratese 10
Novedrate CO 22060
031791508

(G-3484)
SALONEXCLUSIVE BEAUTY LLC ✪
3015 Kraus Glen Dr (28214-8918)
PHONE..................704 488-3909
EMP: 8 **EST:** 2022
SALES (est): 351.29K **Privately Held**
SIC: 2844 7389 Hair preparations, including shampoos; Business services, nec

(G-3485)
SALUD LLC
Also Called: Brewpub
3306 N Davidson St (28205-1036)
PHONE..................980 495-6612
Jason Scott Glunt, Mgr
EMP: 24 **EST:** 2012
SALES (est): 1.7MM **Privately Held**
Web: www.saludbeershop.com
SIC: 2082 Beer (alcoholic beverage)

(G-3486)
SALVIN DENTAL SPECIALTIES LLC
3450 Latrobe Dr (28211-4847)
PHONE..................704 442-5400
Robert H Salvin, CEO
William Simmons, Pr
Greg Slayton, VP
◆ **EMP:** 60 **EST:** 1981
SQ FT: 12,500

GEOGRAPHIC SECTION
Charlotte - Mecklenburg County (G-3510)

SALES (est): 9.96MM **Privately Held**
Web: www.salvin.com
SIC: 3843 Dental equipment and supplies

(G-3487)
SAM M BUTLER INC
Also Called: Service Thread Co
447 S Sharon Amity Rd Ste 125 (28211)
P.O. Box 673 (28353-0673)
PHONE.................................704 364-8647
Jim Myers, *Mgr*
EMP: 45
SALES (corp-wide): 10.06MM **Privately Held**
Web: www.servicethread.com
SIC: 5131 2284 2282 Piece goods and notions; Thread mills; Throwing and winding mills
PA: Sam M. Butler, Inc.
 17900 Dana Dr
 Laurinburg NC 28352
 910 277-7456

(G-3488)
SANHER STUCCO & LATHER INC
1101 Tyvola Rd Ste 110 (28217-3515)
PHONE.................................704 241-8517
Carlos Desantiago, *Pr*
EMP: 10 **EST:** 2008
SALES (est): 515.25K **Privately Held**
SIC: 3299 Stucco

(G-3489)
SAS INSTITUTE INC
2200 Interstate North Dr (28280)
PHONE.................................704 831-5595
EMP: 4
SALES (corp-wide): 3.19B **Privately Held**
Web: www.sas.com
SIC: 7372 Application computer software
PA: Sas Institute Inc.
 100 Sas Campus Dr
 Cary NC 27513
 919 677-8000

(G-3490)
SAS INSTITUTE INC
525 N Tryon St Ste 1600 (28202-0213)
PHONE.................................704 331-3956
Marcus Hassen, *Brnch Mgr*
EMP: 6
SALES (corp-wide): 3.19B **Privately Held**
Web: www.sas.com
SIC: 7372 Application computer software
PA: Sas Institute Inc.
 100 Sas Campus Dr
 Cary NC 27513
 919 677-8000

(G-3491)
SAS OF CAROLINAS LLC
5426 Old Pineville Rd (28217-2733)
PHONE.................................704 332-7165
Fadel J Shaheen, *Prin*
EMP: 5 **EST:** 2014
SALES (est): 81.61K **Privately Held**
SIC: 7372 Application computer software

(G-3492)
SAS R & D SERVICES INC
13929 Ballantyne Meadows Dr (28277-3727)
PHONE.................................954 432-2345
EMP: 4 **EST:** 1993
SALES (est): 96.16K **Privately Held**
SIC: 7372 Application computer software

(G-3493)
SATO AMERICA LLC (HQ)
Also Called: Sato America
14125 S Bridge Cir (28273-6747)
PHONE.................................704 644-1650
Goro Yumiba, *CEO*
Tim Cook, *
Rick Rumler, *
▲ **EMP:** 150 **EST:** 2002
SALES (est): 46.94MM **Privately Held**
Web: www.satoamerica.com
SIC: 5045 7372 Printers, computer; Prepackaged software
PA: Sato Holdings Corporation
 3-1-1, Shibaura
 Minato-Ku TKY 108-0

(G-3494)
SATO GLOBAL SOLUTIONS INC
10350 Nations Ford Rd Ste A (28273-5824)
PHONE.................................954 261-3279
Yumiba Goro, *CEO*
EMP: 14 **EST:** 2014
SALES (est): 316.9K **Privately Held**
SIC: 3577 7373 7371 3955 Bar code (magnetic ink) printers; Computer-aided manufacturing (CAM) systems service; Software programming applications; Print cartridges for laser and other computer printers
PA: Sato Holdings Corporation
 3-1-1, Shibaura
 Minato-Ku TKY 108-0

(G-3495)
SAVE-A-LOAD INC
327 W Tremont Ave Ste A (28203-4980)
PHONE.................................704 650-4947
EMP: 9 **EST:** 2018
SALES (est): 577.56K **Privately Held**
Web: hd.tramec.com
SIC: 3714 Motor vehicle parts and accessories

(G-3496)
SC JOHNSON PROF USA INC (DH)
2815 Coliseum Centre Dr Ste 600 (28217)
PHONE.................................443 521-1606
Michael Slagg, *Pr*
Stephen Havala, *
◆ **EMP:** 114 **EST:** 1989
SQ FT: 75,000
SALES (est): 88.01MM **Privately Held**
Web: www.scjp.com
SIC: 2844 Face creams or lotions
HQ: Sc Johnson Professional Group Limited
 Denby Hall Way
 Ripley DE5 8

(G-3497)
SCALTROL INC
2010 Sterling Rd (28209-1612)
P.O. Box 3288 (30024-0990)
PHONE.................................678 990-0858
Chris Hansen, *Pr*
EMP: 6 **EST:** 1994
SALES (est): 477.11K **Privately Held**
Web: www.scaltrolinc.com
SIC: 3589 5074 5999 Water purification equipment, household type; Water purification equipment; Water purification equipment

(G-3498)
SCENTAIR TECHNOLOGIES LLC (PA)
3810 Shutterfly Rd Ste 900 (28217-3070)
PHONE.................................704 504-2320
Andrew Kindfuller, *CEO*
Brian Edwards, *CRO**
Daniel Behrendt, *
▲ **EMP:** 84 **EST:** 2004
SQ FT: 33,000
SALES (est): 43.73MM
SALES (corp-wide): 43.73MM **Privately Held**
Web: www.scentair.com
SIC: 8731 2844 2821 Commercial physical research; Perfumes, natural or synthetic; Plastics materials and resins

(G-3499)
SCHAEFER SYSTEMS INTERNATIONAL INC (HQ)
Also Called: S S I
10021 Westlake Dr (28273-3787)
P.O. Box 7009 (28241-7009)
PHONE.................................704 944-4500
◆ **EMP:** 250 **EST:** 1968
SALES (est): 208.08MM
SALES (corp-wide): 2.16B **Privately Held**
Web: www.ssi-schaefer.com
SIC: 5084 7372 5046 5099 Industrial machinery and equipment; Business oriented computer software; Shelving, commercial and industrial; Containers: glass, metal or plastic
PA: Fritz Schafer Gmbh & Co Kg,
 Einrichtungssysteme
 Fritz-Schafer-Str. 20
 Neunkirchen NW 57290
 2735701

(G-3500)
SCHAEFER SYSTEMS INTL INC
Also Called: Schaefer Shelving
10125 Westlake Dr Bldg 3 (28273-3786)
PHONE.................................704 944-4500
EMP: 6
SALES (corp-wide): 2.16B **Privately Held**
Web: www.schaefershelving.com
SIC: 3089 Garbage containers, plastics
HQ: Schaefer Systems International, Inc.
 10021 Westlake Dr
 Charlotte NC 28273
 704 944-4500

(G-3501)
SCHAEFER SYSTEMS INTL INC
10124 Westlake Dr (28273-3739)
PHONE.................................704 944-4550
Arnold J Heuzen, *Brnch Mgr*
EMP: 5
SALES (corp-wide): 2.16B **Privately Held**
Web: www.ssi-schaefer.com
SIC: 3089 5046 5099 5084 Garbage containers, plastics; Shelving, commercial and industrial; Containers: glass, metal or plastic; Industrial machinery and equipment
HQ: Schaefer Systems International, Inc.
 10021 Westlake Dr
 Charlotte NC 28273
 704 944-4500

(G-3502)
SCHLEICH USA INC
10000 Twin Lakes Pkwy Ste A (28269)
PHONE.................................704 659-7997
▲ **EMP:** 9 **EST:** 2009
SALES (est): 13.93MM **Privately Held**
Web: us.schleich-s.com
SIC: 3944 Games, toys, and children's vehicles
HQ: Schleich Gmbh
 Am Limes 69
 Schwabisch Gmund BW 73527
 717180010

(G-3503)
SCHLETTER NA INC
11529 Wilmar Blvd (28273-6448)
PHONE.................................704 595-4200
Adrian Noronho, *Pr*
EMP: 13 **EST:** 2018
SALES (est): 853.6K **Privately Held**
Web: www.schletter-group.com
SIC: 3564 Air purification equipment

(G-3504)
SCHNITZER GROUP USA INC
121 W Trade St Ste 2900 (28202-1024)
PHONE.................................347 982-6880
EMP: 8 **EST:** 2015
SALES (est): 75.45K **Privately Held**
Web: www.schnitzer-group.com
SIC: 3714 Motor vehicle parts and accessories

(G-3505)
SCHOOL DIRECTOREASE LLC
1213 W Morehead St (28208-5581)
PHONE.................................240 206-6273
EMP: 4 **EST:** 2009
SALES (est): 244.65K **Privately Held**
Web: www.atozconnect.com
SIC: 2741 7371 Telephone and other directory publishing; Software programming applications

(G-3506)
SCHOOL OF ROCK CHARLOTTE
1105 Greenwood Clfs (28204-2820)
PHONE.................................704 842-3172
EMP: 7 **EST:** 2008
SALES (est): 63.57K **Privately Held**
Web: charlotte-sor.pike13.com
SIC: 8299 7929 3931 Music school; Entertainers and entertainment groups; Musical instruments

(G-3507)
SCHOOL TEAM SOCKS
4413 Mickleton Rd (28226-5549)
PHONE.................................704 500-1738
EMP: 5 **EST:** 2014
SALES (est): 80.74K **Privately Held**
SIC: 2252 Socks

(G-3508)
SCHOTT VENTURES LLC ✪
Also Called: Schott Sauce
4416 Monroe Rd Ste D1 (28205-7723)
PHONE.................................252 813-9660
Ahmir Scott, *Managing Member*
EMP: 6 **EST:** 2023
SALES (est): 63.22K **Privately Held**
SIC: 2035 Pickles, sauces, and salad dressings

(G-3509)
SCHUBERT PACKAGING SYSTEMS LLC
8848 Red Oak Blvd Ste H (28217-5518)
PHONE.................................941 757-8380
EMP: 7 **EST:** 2015
SALES (est): 170.47K **Privately Held**
Web: www.schubert.group
SIC: 2631 Container, packaging, and boxboard

(G-3510)
SCIENTIGO INC (PA)
6701 Carmel Rd Ste 205 (28226-0210)
PHONE.................................704 837-0500
Stuart J Yarbrough, *Ch Bd*
Harry Pettit, *CEO*
Paul Odom Senior, *Software Vice President*
Clifford A Clark, *CFO*
EMP: 6 **EST:** 1995
SQ FT: 5,000
SALES (est): 2.4MM
SALES (corp-wide): 2.4MM **Privately Held**
SIC: 7372 Business oriented computer software

Charlotte - Mecklenburg County (G-3511) — GEOGRAPHIC SECTION

(G-3511)
SCORPIO ACQUISITION CORP
9335 Harris Corners Pkwy Ste 300 (28269)
PHONE..................................704 697-5100
◆ **EMP:** 21 **EST:** 2010
SALES (est): 1.64MM **Publicly Held**
SIC: 2297 Nonwoven fabrics
HQ: Avintiv Inc.
    9335 Hrris Crners Pkwy St
    Charlotte NC 28269
    704 697-5100

(G-3512)
SCOTT SYSTEMS INTL INC (DH)
Also Called: Scott Automation
2205 Beltway Blvd Ste 100 (28214-8152)
P.O. Box 760 (44833-0760)
PHONE..................................704 362-1115
Stacey Mcgill, *Prin*
Greg Chiles, *
EMP: 17 **EST:** 2014
SALES (est): 24.45MM **Publicly Held**
SIC: 3549 8742 Assembly machines, including robotic; Automation and robotics consultant
HQ: Scott Technology Limited
    630 Kaikorai Valley Rd
    Dunedin OTA 9011

(G-3513)
SCR-TECH LLC
11707 Steele Creek Rd (28273-3718)
PHONE..................................704 504-0191
EMP: 131
Web: www.cormetech.com
SIC: 3564 8734 7389 Air purification equipment; Testing laboratories; Industrial and commercial equipment inspection service

(G-3514)
SE CO-BRAND VENTURES LLC
Also Called: Auntie Anne's
6801 Northlake Mall Dr Ste 188 (28216-0711)
PHONE..................................704 598-9322
Rick Belcher, *Brnch Mgr*
EMP: 8
SALES (corp-wide): 1.47MM **Privately Held**
Web: www.auntieannes.com
SIC: 5461 2052 Pretzels; Pretzels
PA: Se Co-Brand Ventures Llc
    12 Deer Moss Ct
    Pawleys Island SC

(G-3515)
SEACON CORP
525 N Tryon St Ste 1600 (28202-0213)
PHONE..................................704 331-3920
EMP: 9 **EST:** 2018
SALES (est): 296.21K **Privately Held**
Web: www.seaconcorp.com
SIC: 2869 Industrial organic chemicals, nec

(G-3516)
SEACON CORPORATION (PA)
1917 John Crosland Jr Dr (28208-5554)
PHONE..................................704 333-6000
Sean E Condren, *Pr*
▲ **EMP:** 14 **EST:** 2002
SQ FT: 22,000
SALES (est): 5.95MM
SALES (corp-wide): 5.95MM **Privately Held**
Web: www.seaconcorp.com
SIC: 2899 Chemical preparations, nec

(G-3517)
SEALED AIR CORPORATION (PA)
Also Called: Sealed Air
2415 Cascade Pointe Blvd (28208-6899)
PHONE..................................980 221-3235
Emile Chammas, *COO*
Jerry R Whitaker, *
Emile Z Chammas, *COO*
Dustin Semach, *CFO*
Angel S Willis, *VP*
EMP: 1500 **EST:** 1960
SALES (est): 5.49B
SALES (corp-wide): 5.49B **Publicly Held**
Web: www.sealedair.com
SIC: 2821 Plastics materials and resins

(G-3518)
SEALED AIR CORPORATION (US)
2415 Cascade Pointe Blvd (28208-6899)
PHONE..................................201 791-7600
Jerome Peribere, *Pr*
David H Kelsey, *
Robert A Pesci, *
H Katherine White, *
Tod Christie, *
EMP: 7500 **EST:** 1969
SALES (est): 1.02B
SALES (corp-wide): 5.49B **Publicly Held**
Web: www.sealedair.com
SIC: 2673 2671 3087 3086 Plastic and pliofilm bags; Paper; coated and laminated packaging; Custom compound purchased resins; Plastics foam products
PA: Sealed Air Corporation
    2415 Cascade Pointe Blvd
    Charlotte NC 28208
    980 221-3235

(G-3519)
SEALED AIR INTL HOLDINGS LLC
2415 Cascade Pointe Blvd (28208-6899)
PHONE..................................980 221-3235
EMP: 249 **EST:** 2017
SALES (est): 47.65MM
SALES (corp-wide): 5.49B **Publicly Held**
Web: www.sealedair.com
SIC: 3086 Packaging and shipping materials, foamed plastics
PA: Sealed Air Corporation
    2415 Cascade Pointe Blvd
    Charlotte NC 28208
    980 221-3235

(G-3520)
SEALED AIR LLC ◐
2415 Cascade Pointe Blvd (28208-6899)
PHONE..................................980 430-7000
EMP: 14 **EST:** 2023
SALES (est): 3.65MM
SALES (corp-wide): 5.49B **Publicly Held**
Web: www.sealedair.com
SIC: 2673 Plastic and pliofilm bags
PA: Sealed Air Corporation
    2415 Cascade Pointe Blvd
    Charlotte NC 28208
    980 221-3235

(G-3521)
SEANS TRANSPORTATION LLC
Also Called: Shawn Trucking and Towing
6826 Centerline Dr (28278-7398)
PHONE..................................646 603-8128
Travis Forde, *CEO*
EMP: 4 **EST:** 2019
SALES (est): 100K **Privately Held**
SIC: 3799 Transportation equipment, nec

(G-3522)
SECURITY CONSULT INC
1318 Beechdale Dr (28212-6804)
P.O. Box 12611 (28220-2611)
PHONE..................................704 531-8399
Julius L Ulanday, *Ofcr*
EMP: 5 **EST:** 2010
SALES (est): 242.03K **Privately Held**
Web: www.securityconsult411.com
SIC: 8748 3699 7382 Business consulting, nec; Security control equipment and systems; Security systems services

(G-3523)
SEEMINGLY OVERZEALOUS LLC ◐
2205 Remount Rd (28208-5052)
PHONE..................................770 634-7653
EMP: 5 **EST:** 2022
SALES (est): 79.3K **Privately Held**
SIC: 2024 Sorbets, non-dairy based

(G-3524)
SELECT STAINLESS PRODUCTS LLC
7621 Little Ave Ste 212 (28226-8402)
PHONE..................................888 843-2345
▲ **EMP:** 21 **EST:** 2012
SALES (est): 500.2K **Privately Held**
Web: www.selectstainless.com
SIC: 3431 3469 5078 2431 Metal sanitary ware; Kitchen fixtures and equipment: metal, except cast aluminum; Refrigerators, commercial (reach-in and walk-in); Millwork

(G-3525)
SELECTIVE ENTERPRISES INC (PA)
Also Called: United Supply Company
10701 Texland Blvd (28273-6202)
P.O. Box 410149 (28241-0149)
PHONE..................................704 588-3310
John J Hawkins Junior, *Pr*
◆ **EMP:** 103 **EST:** 1962
SQ FT: 65,000
SALES (est): 22.94MM
SALES (corp-wide): 22.94MM **Privately Held**
Web: www.unitedsupplyco.com
SIC: 5131 5023 2591 Drapery material, woven; Window covering parts and accessories; Window blinds

(G-3526)
SENOX CORPORATION
3500 Woodpark Blvd (28206-4243)
PHONE..................................704 371-5043
Patrick Wiley, *Mgr*
EMP: 9
SALES (corp-wide): 55.6MM **Privately Held**
Web: www.senox.com
SIC: 3089 Gutters (glass fiber reinforced), fiberglass or plastics
PA: Senox Corporation
    15409 Long Vista Dr
    Austin TX 78728
    512 251-3333

(G-3527)
SENSATIONAL SIGNS
2100 N Davidson St (28205-1828)
P.O. Box 142 (28037-0142)
PHONE..................................704 358-1099
Sharlene Green, *Owner*
EMP: 4 **EST:** 2000
SALES (est): 239.86K **Privately Held**
Web: www.yoursignneeds.com
SIC: 3993 Electric signs

(G-3528)
SENTINEL DOOR CONTROLS LLC
3020 Hutchison Mcdonald Rd Ste D (28269-4289)
PHONE..................................704 921-4627
David Maroon, *Managing Member*
▲ **EMP:** 12 **EST:** 1997
SALES (est): 2.98MM **Privately Held**
Web: www.sentineldoor.com
SIC: 5072 3429 3699 Builders' hardware, nec; Door opening and closing devices, except electrical; Door opening and closing devices, electrical

(G-3529)
SERRA WIRELESS INC ◐
2431 Tallet Trce (28216-1309)
PHONE..................................980 318-0873
Fahaad Sayed, *CEO*
EMP: 6 **EST:** 2022
SALES (est): 8.59MM **Privately Held**
SIC: 5065 3663 5731 3571 Mobile telephone equipment; Cellular radio telephone; Consumer electronic equipment, nec; Electronic computers

(G-3530)
SERVING OUR CMNTY KIDS SCKS SC
11203 Sir Francis Drake Dr (28277-8862)
PHONE..................................704 814-4704
Timothy Delea, *Prin*
EMP: 4 **EST:** 2018
SALES (est): 77.53K **Privately Held**
SIC: 2252 Socks

(G-3531)
SESMFG LLC
8404 Woodford Bridge Dr (28216-9679)
PHONE..................................803 917-3248
EMP: 6 **EST:** 2018
SALES (est): 228.06K **Privately Held**
Web: www.sesmfg.com
SIC: 3999 Manufacturing industries, nec

(G-3532)
SEVEN CAST
901 N Church St (28206-3220)
PHONE..................................704 335-0692
EMP: 8 **EST:** 1997
SALES (est): 91.88K **Privately Held**
SIC: 3325 Steel foundries, nec

(G-3533)
SGL CARBON LLC (DH)
10715 David Taylor Dr Ste 460 (28262-1283)
PHONE..................................704 593-5100
◆ **EMP:** 42 **EST:** 1939
SALES (est): 308.86MM
SALES (corp-wide): 1.18B **Privately Held**
Web: www.sglcarbon.com
SIC: 3624 Carbon and graphite products
HQ: Sgl Carbon Beteiligung Gmbh
    Sohnleinstr. 8
    Wiesbaden HE 65201
    61160290

(G-3534)
SGL COMPOSITES INC
10715 David Taylor Dr Ste 460 (28262-1283)
PHONE..................................704 593-5100
EMP: 13 **EST:** 2018
SALES (est): 2.69MM **Privately Held**
Web: www.sglcarbon.com
SIC: 3624 Carbon and graphite products

(G-3535)
SGL TECHNOLOGIES LLC
10715 David Taylor Dr Ste 460 (28262-1283)
PHONE..................................704 593-5100
Andreas Wuellner, *Pr*
Steve Swanson, *VP Opers*
Benoit Labelle, *VP Fin*
Jeffrey Schade, *VP Sls*

GEOGRAPHIC SECTION

Charlotte - Mecklenburg County (G-3559)

Anna Blackwelder, *Sec*
EMP: 5 **EST:** 1992
SALES (est): 1.54MM
SALES (corp-wide): 1.18B **Privately Held**
Web: www.sglcarbon.com
SIC: 3624 Fibers, carbon and graphite
HQ: Sgl Carbon, Llc
10715 David Taylor Dr # 4
Charlotte NC 28262
704 593-5100

(G-3536)
SHAW INDUSTRIES GROUP INC
Carpet Plant Division 25
10901 Texland Blvd (28273-6237)
PHONE...................877 996-5942
Robert Belden, *Mgr*
EMP: 49
SQ FT: 102,203
SALES (corp-wide): 364.48B **Publicly Held**
Web: www.shawfloors.com
SIC: 3086 2273 Carpet and rug cushions, foamed plastics; Carpets and rugs
HQ: Shaw Industries Group, Inc.
616 E Walnut Ave
Dalton GA 30721
706 278-3812

(G-3537)
SHAW INDUSTRIES GROUP INC
Also Called: Salem Carpet Mills
10901 Texland Blvd (28273-6237)
PHONE...................877 996-5942
David Moore, *Mgr*
EMP: 4
SALES (corp-wide): 364.48B **Publicly Held**
Web: www.shawfloors.com
SIC: 2273 Carpets and rugs
HQ: Shaw Industries Group, Inc.
616 E Walnut Ave
Dalton GA 30721
706 278-3812

(G-3538)
SHED BRAND INC (PA)
216 Iverson Way Ste A (28203-5617)
PHONE...................704 523-0096
Marvin Knight, *Pr*
Ellie Knight, *VP*
EMP: 9 **EST:** 1966
SQ FT: 2,250
SALES (est): 938.19K
SALES (corp-wide): 938.19K **Privately Held**
Web: www.shedbrandstudios.com
SIC: 3231 3269 Stained glass: made from purchased glass; Art and ornamental ware, pottery

(G-3539)
SHED BRAND STUDIOS LLC
216 Iverson Way Ste A (28203-5617)
PHONE...................704 523-0096
EMP: 6 **EST:** 2013
SALES (est): 69.59K **Privately Held**
Web: www.shedbrandstudios.com
SIC: 3231 Stained glass: made from purchased glass

(G-3540)
SHELFGENIE
4111 Kronos Pl (28210-1310)
PHONE...................704 705-0005
EMP: 6 **EST:** 2011
SALES (est): 78.43K **Privately Held**
Web: www.shelfgenie.com
SIC: 2511 Wood household furniture

(G-3541)
SHERWIN-WILLIAMS COMPANY
Also Called: Sherwin-Williams
10300 Claude Freeman Dr (28262-2339)
PHONE...................704 548-2820
John Mccracken, *Bmch Mgr*
EMP: 75
SALES (corp-wide): 22.15B **Publicly Held**
Web: www.sherwin-williams.com
SIC: 2851 Paints and paint additives
PA: The Sherwin-Williams Company
101 W Prospect Ave # 1020
Cleveland OH 44115
216 566-2000

(G-3542)
SHOWER ME WITH LOVE LLC
4845 Ashley Park Ln Ste H (28210-3341)
PHONE...................704 302-1555
Emily Shallal, *Managing Member*
EMP: 10 **EST:** 2006
SALES (est): 2MM **Privately Held**
Web: www.showermewithlove.com
SIC: 2676 Infant and baby paper products

(G-3543)
SHURTAPE TECHNOLOGIES LLC
4725 Piedmont Row Dr Ste 210 (28210-4279)
PHONE...................704 553-9441
EMP: 5
SALES (corp-wide): 787.56MM **Privately Held**
Web: www.shurtape.com
SIC: 2672 Tape, pressure sensitive: made from purchased materials
HQ: Shurtape Technologies, Llc
1712 8th Street Dr Se
Hickory NC 28602

(G-3544)
SHUTTERHUTCH
5416 Midvale Ter (28215-8600)
P.O. Box 911 (28075-0911)
PHONE...................704 918-7852
Jaime Lapish, *Prin*
EMP: 5 **EST:** 2017
SALES (est): 72.51K **Privately Held**
Web: www.shutterhutchphotoboothsandfilms.com
SIC: 3442 Shutters, door or window: metal

(G-3545)
SIEBENWURST US INC
112 S Tryon St Ste 1130 (28284-2109)
PHONE...................704 333-7790
Christian Walter, *Pr*
EMP: 6 **EST:** 2015
SALES (est): 187.55K **Privately Held**
Web: www.siebenwurst-us.com
SIC: 3714 Motor vehicle parts and accessories

(G-3546)
SIEMENS AIRPORT
5601 Wilkinson Blvd (28208-3557)
PHONE...................704 359-5551
EMP: 35 **EST:** 2018
SALES (est): 1.13MM **Privately Held**
Web: www.cltairport.com
SIC: 3661 Telephones and telephone apparatus

(G-3547)
SIEMENS ENERGY INC
5101 Westinghouse Blvd (28273-9601)
P.O. Box 4356 (97208-4356)
PHONE...................704 551-5100
Len Sharpe, *Mgr*
EMP: 200
SALES (corp-wide): 33.81B **Privately Held**
Web: new.siemens.com
SIC: 3511 Turbines and turbine generator sets
HQ: Siemens Energy, Inc.
4400 N Alafaya Trl
Orlando FL 32826
407 736-2000

(G-3548)
SIEMENS INDUSTRY SOFTWARE INC
Also Called: Siemens PLM Software
13024 Ballantyne Corporate Pl (28277-2113)
PHONE...................704 227-6600
EMP: 13
SALES (corp-wide): 84.48B **Privately Held**
Web: www.siemens.com
SIC: 7372 Prepackaged software
HQ: Siemens Industry Software Inc.
5800 Granite Pkwy Ste 600
Plano TX 75024
972 987-3000

(G-3549)
SIGHTTECH LLC
9421 Perimeter Station Dr Apt 101 (28216-4425)
PHONE...................855 997-4448
EMP: 6 **EST:** 2011
SALES (est): 213.68K **Privately Held**
Web: www.sighttech.us
SIC: 8331 8732 7379 5045 Job training and related services; Commercial sociological and educational research; Computer related maintenance services; Computers, peripherals, and software

(G-3550)
SIGN WORLD INC
200 Foster Ave (28203-5422)
P.O. Box 2784 (28070-2784)
PHONE...................704 529-4440
Jerry L Mc Kenzie, *Pr*
Debra Henson, *Mgr*
Debra Mckenzie, *Sec*
EMP: 13 **EST:** 1975
SQ FT: 6,000
SALES (est): 327.9K **Privately Held**
Web: www.signworldnc.com
SIC: 3993 1799 Electric signs; Sign installation and maintenance

(G-3551)
SIGNAGE INNOVATIONS GROUP LLC
5245 Old Dowd Rd Unit 4 (28208-2164)
PHONE...................704 392-8165
Ritchie Hogue, *Prin*
EMP: 7 **EST:** 2013
SALES (est): 85.26K **Privately Held**
SIC: 3993 Signs and advertising specialties

(G-3552)
SIGNS BY TOMORROW
2440 Whitehall Park Dr Ste 100 (28273-3552)
PHONE...................704 527-6100
EMP: 6 **EST:** 2015
SALES (est): 83.08K **Privately Held**
Web: www.signsbytomorrow.com
SIC: 3993 Signs and advertising specialties

(G-3553)
SIGNS ETC OF CHARLOTTE (PA)
4941 Chastain Ave (28217-2115)
PHONE...................704 522-8860
Spencer Brower, *Prin*
EMP: 15 **EST:** 2010
SALES (est): 2.24MM
SALES (corp-wide): 2.24MM **Privately Held**
Web: www.signsetcofcharlotte.com
SIC: 3993 Electric signs

(G-3554)
SIGNS ETC OF CHARLOTTE
Also Called: Signs Etc
4044 South Blvd (28209-2746)
PHONE...................704 522-8860
Spencer Brower, *Bmch Mgr*
EMP: 35
SALES (corp-wide): 2.24MM **Privately Held**
Web: www.signsetcofcharlotte.com
SIC: 3993 Signs, not made in custom sign painting shops
PA: Signs Etc Of Charlotte
4941 Chastain Ave
Charlotte NC 28217
704 522-8860

(G-3555)
SIMPLE BAKING
617 W Arrowood Rd (28217-5012)
PHONE...................704 523-4962
Tammy Gray, *Prin*
EMP: 5 **EST:** 2013
SALES (est): 214.71K **Privately Held**
SIC: 2051 Bread, cake, and related products

(G-3556)
SINGLE TEMPERATURE CONTRLS INC
14201 S Lakes Dr Ste B (28273-7708)
PHONE...................704 504-4800
Fred Hatberg, *VP*
Michael Bloomhuff, *Pr*
▲ **EMP:** 6 **EST:** 2008
SALES (est): 4.31MM **Privately Held**
SIC: 3559 Plastics working machinery
HQ: Single Temperiertechnik Gmbh
Ostring 17-19
Hochdorf BW 73269
715330090

(G-3557)
SISTAS 4 LIFE FOOD SVCS LLC
Also Called: City Biscuit Bus
5115 Speyside Ct (28215-2063)
PHONE...................704 957-6437
Janett Mcclain, *Pr*
Sharon Hampton, *COO*
Janett Mcclain, *CEO*
EMP: 5 **EST:** 2016
SALES (est): 181.72K **Privately Held**
SIC: 5812 5149 2099 American restaurant; Crackers, cookies, and bakery products; Ready-to-eat meals, salads, and sandwiches

(G-3558)
SIZZLEWICH LLC
3607 Whitehall Park Dr Ste 1200 (28273)
PHONE...................980 299-1389
EMP: 4 **EST:** 2019
SALES (est): 232.45K **Privately Held**
Web: www.thesizzlewich.com
SIC: 2099 Food preparations, nec

(G-3559)
SKAMOL AMERICAS INC
P.O. Box 470947 (28247-0947)
PHONE...................704 544-1015
Sam Loresta, *VP*
▲ **EMP:** 5 **EST:** 1992
SQ FT: 2,300
SALES (est): 1.78MM
SALES (corp-wide): 60.78K **Privately Held**
SIC: 3297 Brick refractories
HQ: Skamol A/S
Hasselager Centervej 1
Viby J 8260
97721533

Charlotte - Mecklenburg County (G-3560)

GEOGRAPHIC SECTION

(G-3560)
SKIN SO SOFT SPA INC
4456 The Plaza Ste 5e (28215-2175)
PHONE..................................800 674-7554
Sheleana Brown, *Prin*
EMP: 6 **EST:** 2021
SALES (est): 316.01K **Privately Held**
SIC: 2844 Perfumes, cosmetics and other toilet preparations

(G-3561)
SKYSPY LLC
3208 Eastover Ridge Dr Unit 633 (28211-1452)
PHONE..................................703 472-4639
Leonardo Adams, *Prin*
EMP: 5 **EST:** 2016
SALES (est): 82.64K **Privately Held**
SIC: 3699 Electrical equipment and supplies, nec

(G-3562)
SKYVIEW COMMERCIAL CLEANING ✧
Also Called: Building Stars of Charlotte
5725 Carnegie Blvd (28209-4867)
PHONE..................................704 858-0134
Antonio Norman, *CEO*
EMP: 8 **EST:** 2022
SALES (est): 364.19K **Privately Held**
SIC: 3589 7389 Commercial cleaning equipment; Business services, nec

(G-3563)
SL - LASER SYSTEMS LLC
2406 Dunavant St (28203-5032)
PHONE..................................704 561-9990
EMP: 6 **EST:** 2019
SALES (est): 259.01K **Privately Held**
Web: www.sl-laser.com
SIC: 3559 Special industry machinery, nec

(G-3564)
SLS BAKING COMPANY
15720 Brixham Hill Ave (28277-4651)
PHONE..................................704 421-2763
EMP: 5 **EST:** 2015
SALES (est): 189.87K **Privately Held**
SIC: 2051 Bread, cake, and related products

(G-3565)
SLUM DOG HEAD GEAR LLC
9912 Jeanette Cir (28213-2129)
PHONE..................................704 713-8125
EMP: 10 **EST:** 2020
SALES (est): 339.83K **Privately Held**
SIC: 2253 Hats and headwear, knit

(G-3566)
SMARTWAY OF CAROLINAS LLC
Also Called: Smart Way
3304 Eastway Dr (28205-5649)
PHONE..................................704 900-7877
Benjamin Bost, *Pr*
EMP: 12 **EST:** 2012
SALES (est): 2.43MM **Privately Held**
Web: www.gosmartwaync.net
SIC: 5712 3639 5045 Furniture stores; Major kitchen appliances, except refrigerators and stoves; Computers, nec

(G-3567)
SMITH PRINTING COMPANY LLC
3812 Coopersdale Rd (28273-3746)
P.O. Box 38527 (28278-1009)
PHONE..................................704 575-9235
Gary Douglassmith, *CEO*
EMP: 4 **EST:** 2014
SALES (est): 227.69K **Privately Held**
Web: www.thesmithprinting.com
SIC: 2752 Offset printing

(G-3568)
SMOOTHIESORG INC
416 Queens Rd Apt 14 (28207-1434)
PHONE..................................704 906-4121
EMP: 4 **EST:** 2009
SALES (est): 173.78K **Privately Held**
SIC: 2037 Frozen fruits and vegetables

(G-3569)
SNAP ONE LLC (HQ)
Also Called: Snapav
1800 Continental Blvd Ste 200 (28273-6388)
PHONE..................................704 927-7620
John Heyman, *CEO*
Craig Craze, *
Adam Levy, *
Brad Redmond, *
Carlos Catalahana, *
▲ **EMP:** 350 **EST:** 2000
SQ FT: 69,953
SALES (est): 449.36MM
SALES (corp-wide): 1.06B **Publicly Held**
Web: www.snapav.com
SIC: 3679 Electronic circuits
PA: Snap One Holdings Corp.
1800 Continental Blvd # 200
Charlotte NC 28273
704 927-7620

(G-3570)
SNAP ONE HOLDINGS CORP (PA)
Also Called: Snap One
1800 Continental Blvd Ste 200 (28273-6388)
PHONE..................................704 927-7620
John Heyman, *CEO*
Erik Ragatz, *Ch Bd*
Michael Carlet, *CFO*
Jefferson Dungan, *COO*
Jeffrey Hindman, *CRO*
EMP: 83 **EST:** 2017
SQ FT: 69,953
SALES (est): 1.06B
SALES (corp-wide): 1.06B **Publicly Held**
SIC: 3679 Electronic circuits

(G-3571)
SNIDER TIRE INC
900 Atando Ave (28206-1507)
PHONE..................................704 373-2910
Matt Creswell, *Mgr*
EMP: 59
SALES (corp-wide): 436.36MM **Privately Held**
Web: www.sniderfleet.com
SIC: 5531 7534 Automotive tires; Tire recapping
PA: Snider Tire, Inc.
1081 Red Ventures Dr
Fort Mill SC 29707
336 691-5480

(G-3572)
SNIFF TO REMEMBER LLC
1400 Cedarwood Ln (28212-4410)
PHONE..................................210 373-2115
EMP: 5 **EST:** 2020
SALES (est): 75.15K **Privately Held**
SIC: 3999 Candles

(G-3573)
SNYDERS-LANCE INC
1900 Continental Blvd (28273-6390)
PHONE..................................704 557-8013
◆ **EMP:** 5
SALES (corp-wide): 9.36B **Publicly Held**
Web: www.campbellsoupcompany.com
SIC: 2052 Cookies
HQ: Snyder's-Lance, Inc.
13515 Balntyn Corp Pl
Charlotte NC 28277
704 554-1421

(G-3574)
SNYDERS-LANCE INC (HQ)
Also Called: Snyder's-Lance
13515 Ballantyne Corporate Pl (28277-2706)
P.O. Box 32368 (28232-2368)
PHONE..................................704 554-1421
Christopher D Foley, *Pr*
John T Maples, *CCO**
Margaret E Wicklund, *
EMP: 1470 **EST:** 1926
SALES (est): 2.2B
SALES (corp-wide): 9.36B **Publicly Held**
Web: www.campbellsoupcompany.com
SIC: 2052 2064 2068 2096 Cookies; Candy bars, including chocolate covered bars; Nuts: dried, dehydrated, salted or roasted; Potato chips and other potato-based snacks
PA: Campbell Soup Company
1 Campbell Pl
Camden NJ 08103
856 342-4800

(G-3575)
SOCIALTOPIAS LLC
1415 S Church St Ste C (28203-4158)
PHONE..................................704 910-1713
Timothy Gruber, *CEO*
EMP: 10 **EST:** 2015
SALES (est): 227.22K **Privately Held**
Web: www.socialtopias.com
SIC: 7372 Application computer software

(G-3576)
SOCK INC
1908 Belvedere Ave (28205-3010)
PHONE..................................561 254-2223
Steven Heinecke, *Pr*
EMP: 5 **EST:** 2013
SALES (est): 109.44K **Privately Held**
Web: www.customsocklab.com
SIC: 2252 Socks

(G-3577)
SOCKS AND OTHER THINGS LLC
4413 Mickleton Rd (28226-5549)
PHONE..................................704 904-2472
EMP: 6 **EST:** 2017
SALES (est): 224.71K **Privately Held**
Web: www.socksthings.com
SIC: 2252 Socks

(G-3578)
SOLID HOLDINGS LLC
3820 Rose Lake Dr (28217-2833)
PHONE..................................704 423-0260
Phil Calabritto, *Pr*
EMP: 19 **EST:** 2014
SALES (est): 1MM **Privately Held**
Web: www.solidcare.com
SIC: 8712 2952 1771 Architectural services; Roofing felts, cements, or coatings, nec; Stucco, gunite, and grouting contractors

(G-3579)
SOMA INTIMATES LLC
Also Called: Soma
4400 Sharon Rd Ste G07 (28211-3531)
PHONE..................................704 365-1153
EMP: 6
SALES (corp-wide): 2.14B **Privately Held**
Web: www.soma.com
SIC: 2329 Bathing suits and swimwear: men's and boys'
HQ: Soma Intimates, Llc
11215 Metro Pkwy
Fort Myers FL 33966
239 277-6200

(G-3580)
SONABLATE CORP (PA)
10130 Perimeter Pkwy Ste 410 (28216-2447)
PHONE..................................888 874-4384
Richard Yang, *CEO*
Richard Yang, *Pr*
Stephen R Puckett, *
EMP: 19 **EST:** 2004
SALES (est): 24.87MM **Privately Held**
Web: www.sonablate.com
SIC: 3841 Surgical and medical instruments

(G-3581)
SONOCO PRODUCTS COMPANY
12000 Vance Davis Dr (28269-7696)
PHONE..................................704 875-2685
EMP: 23
SALES (corp-wide): 6.78B **Publicly Held**
Web: www.sonoco.com
SIC: 2653 Corrugated and solid fiber boxes
PA: Sonoco Products Company
1 N 2nd St
Hartsville SC 29550
843 383-7000

(G-3582)
SOTO INDUSTRIES LLC
6201 Fairview Rd Ste 200 (28210-3297)
PHONE..................................706 643-5011
EMP: 21 **EST:** 1991
SALES (est): 2.33MM **Privately Held**
SIC: 2861 2899 Gum and wood chemicals; Chemical preparations, nec

(G-3583)
SOUL DEFENSE LLC
1839 S Wendover Rd (28211-2155)
PHONE..................................704 726-7898
Skye Klink, *Prin*
EMP: 5 **EST:** 2016
SALES (est): 200.97K **Privately Held**
SIC: 3812 Defense systems and equipment

(G-3584)
SOUTH BOULEVARD ASSOCIATES INC
186 Cherokee Rd (28207-1904)
PHONE..................................704 525-7160
EMP: 90 **EST:** 1985
SALES (est): 5.79MM **Privately Held**
SIC: 3412 Metal barrels, drums, and pails

(G-3585)
SOUTH EAST WELDING
10935 Winds Crossing Dr Ste 10 (28273)
PHONE..................................980 428-0742
EMP: 4 **EST:** 2016
SALES (est): 107.66K **Privately Held**
SIC: 7692 Welding repair

(G-3586)
SOUTH POINT HOSPITALITY INC
13451 S Point Blvd (28273-2701)
PHONE..................................704 542-2304
Kathy Dayvault, *CEO*
EMP: 10 **EST:** 2020
SALES (est): 200K **Privately Held**
Web: www.southpointhospitality.com
SIC: 2299 Textile goods, nec

(G-3587)
SOUTHEAST AIR CONTROL INC (PA)
Also Called: Sac
7700 Frosch Rd (28278-9743)
PHONE..................................704 392-0149
Hernan Atencio, *Pr*

◆ **EMP:** 44 **EST:** 1971
SQ FT: 31,000
SALES (est): 2.89MM
SALES (corp-wide): 2.89MM **Privately Held**
SIC: 3585 Air conditioning, motor vehicle

(G-3588)
SOUTHEASTERN CORRUGATED LLC (PA)
10901 Carpet St (28273-6206)
PHONE..................980 224-9551
James Tolbert, *Managing Member*
EMP: 9 **EST:** 2019
SALES (est): 4.3MM
SALES (corp-wide): 4.3MM **Privately Held**
Web: www.southeasterncorrugated.com
SIC: 2631 Container, packaging, and boxboard

(G-3589)
SOUTHEASTERN ENTERPRISES (HQ)
3545 Asbury Ave (28206-1505)
PHONE..................704 373-1750
Fred Miltz, *Pr*
Eric Miltz, *VP*
EMP: 15 **EST:** 1997
SALES (est): 4.5MM
SALES (corp-wide): 18.69MM **Privately Held**
SIC: 3599 Machine shop, jobbing and repair
PA: Container Products Corporation
112 N College Rd
Wilmington NC 28405
910 392-6100

(G-3590)
SOUTHERN CAST INC
901 N Church St (28206-3220)
P.O. Box 9427 (28299-9427)
PHONE..................704 335-0692
William Ruettgers, *Pr*
Cheryl Ruettgers, *
William J Ruettgers, *
David P Ruettgers, *
EMP: 25 **EST:** 1983
SQ FT: 55,000
SALES (est): 4.81MM **Privately Held**
Web: www.southerncastinc.com
SIC: 3321 Gray iron castings, nec

(G-3591)
SOUTHERN CONCRETE MTLS INC
11609 Texland Blvd (28273-6221)
PHONE..................704 394-2346
Tom Hawthorne, *VP*
EMP: 18
SALES (corp-wide): 238.17MM **Privately Held**
Web: www.scmusa.com
SIC: 3273 Ready-mixed concrete
HQ: Southern Concrete Materials, Inc.
35 Meadow Rd
Asheville NC 28803
828 253-6421

(G-3592)
SOUTHERN CONCRETE MTLS INC
715 State St (28208-4147)
P.O. Box 33038 (28233-3038)
PHONE..................704 394-2344
Tom Hawthorne, *Brnch Mgr*
EMP: 44
SQ FT: 14,040
SALES (corp-wide): 238.17MM **Privately Held**
Web: www.scmusa.com
SIC: 3273 Ready-mixed concrete
HQ: Southern Concrete Materials, Inc.
35 Meadow Rd
Asheville NC 28803
828 253-6421

(G-3593)
SOUTHERN ELECTRICAL EQP CO INC (PA)
4045 Hargrove Ave (28208-5503)
P.O. Box 668547 (28266-8547)
PHONE..................704 392-1396
Barry Thomas, *Pr*
Craig Thomas, *
Andrew Panto, *
◆ **EMP:** 41 **EST:** 1920
SQ FT: 20,000
SALES (est): 9.89MM
SALES (corp-wide): 9.89MM **Privately Held**
Web: www.seecoswitch.com
SIC: 3625 Relays and industrial controls

(G-3594)
SOUTHERN METALS COMPANY
2200 Donald Ross Rd (28208-6127)
P.O. Box 668923 (28266-8923)
PHONE..................704 394-3161
Robert I Helbein, *Pr*
Marc Helbein, *
Michael Helbein, *
Mary Anne Davis, *
EMP: 50 **EST:** 1938
SQ FT: 55,000
SALES (est): 8.97MM **Privately Held**
Web: www.southernmetalscompany.com
SIC: 3356 3316 Nonferrous rolling and drawing, nec; Cold finishing of steel shapes

(G-3595)
SOUTHERN PRECISION SPRING INC
2200 Old Steele Creek Rd (28208-6031)
P.O. Box 668186 (28266-8186)
PHONE..................704 392-4393
Hugh M Duncan Junior, *Pr*
Thomas T Duncan, *
▲ **EMP:** 29 **EST:** 1956
SQ FT: 55,000
SALES (est): 9.2MM **Privately Held**
Web: www.spspring.com
SIC: 3495 Wire springs

(G-3596)
SOUTHERN STAIRCASE INC
1108 Continental Blvd Ste O (28273-6485)
PHONE..................704 363-2123
Billy Baker, *Off Mgr*
EMP: 5
SALES (corp-wide): 47.09MM **Privately Held**
Web: www.artisticstairs-us.com
SIC: 2431 Staircases and stairs, wood
PA: Southern Staircase, Inc.
6025 Shiloh Rd Ste E
Alpharetta GA 30005
770 888-7333

(G-3597)
SOUTHERN STAIRCASE INC
Also Called: Southern Staircase
1108 Continental Blvd Ste O (28273-6485)
PHONE..................704 357-1221
Diane Newport, *Mgr*
EMP: 81
SALES (corp-wide): 47.09MM **Privately Held**
Web: www.southernstaircase.com
SIC: 5031 3446 2431 Building materials, interior; Architectural metalwork; Millwork
PA: Southern Staircase, Inc.
6025 Shiloh Rd Ste E
Alpharetta GA 30005
770 888-7333

(G-3598)
SPECIALTY MANUFACTURING INC (HQ)
Also Called: SMI
13501 S Ridge Dr (28273-6741)
PHONE..................704 247-9300
Joseph Uebbing, *CEO*
Richard Ayre, *
◆ **EMP:** 121 **EST:** 1965
SQ FT: 90,000
SALES (est): 46.04MM **Privately Held**
Web: www.safefleet.net
SIC: 3648 3641 3444 3441 Lighting equipment, nec; Electric lamps; Sheet metalwork; Building components, structural steel
PA: The Sterling Group L P
9 Greenway Plz Ste 2400
Houston TX 77046

(G-3599)
SPECTRUM BRANDS INC
15040 Choate Cir (28273-6947)
PHONE..................800 854-3151
EMP: 4
SALES (corp-wide): 2.92B **Publicly Held**
Web: www.spectrumbrands.com
SIC: 3692 Primary batteries, dry and wet
HQ: Spectrum Brands, Inc.
3001 Deming Way
Middleton WI 53562
608 275-3340

(G-3600)
SPEEDCAL GRAPHICS INC
4327 Carlotta St (28208-5867)
PHONE..................704 412-3321
EMP: 4 **EST:** 2019
SALES (est): 184.53K **Privately Held**
Web: www.speedcalinc.com
SIC: 3993 Signs and advertising specialties

(G-3601)
SPEEDEE PRINTS LLC
4610 Sharon View Rd (28226-5008)
PHONE..................704 366-1405
Chris Economides Junior, *Pr*
EMP: 4 **EST:** 1971
SQ FT: 7,500
SALES (est): 208.19K **Privately Held**
SIC: 2752 Offset printing

(G-3602)
SPEEDPRO IMAGING
2301 Crownpoint Executive Dr (28227-7824)
PHONE..................704 321-1200
David Amo, *Prin*
EMP: 9 **EST:** 2011
SALES (est): 300.44K **Privately Held**
Web: www.speedpro.com
SIC: 3993 Signs and advertising specialties

(G-3603)
SPGPRINTS AMERICA INC (DH)
Also Called: Spg Prints
2121 Distribution Center Dr Ste E (28269)
P.O. Box 26458 (28221-6458)
PHONE..................704 598-7171
▲ **EMP:** 60 **EST:** 1968
SALES (est): 7.81MM **Privately Held**
Web: www.spgprints.com
SIC: 3552 3555 Printing machinery, textile; Printing trades machinery
HQ: Spgprints B.V.
Raamstraat 3
Boxmeer NB 5831
485599555

(G-3604)
SPOTLESS INDUSTRIES LLC
9739 Kings Parade Blvd Unit 318 (28273-5686)
PHONE..................980 430-1560
Victor Ramirez, *Prin*
EMP: 5 **EST:** 2016
SALES (est): 78.91K **Privately Held**
SIC: 3999 Manufacturing industries, nec

(G-3605)
SPRAYING SYSTEMS CO
5727 Westpark Dr Ste 204 (28217-3651)
PHONE..................704 357-6499
John Weir, *Owner*
EMP: 4
SALES (corp-wide): 434.45MM **Privately Held**
Web: www.spray.com
SIC: 3499 Nozzles, spray: aerosol, paint, or insecticide
PA: Spraying Systems Co.
200 W North Ave
Glendale Heights IL 60139
630 665-5000

(G-3606)
SPX COOLING TECH LLC
Also Called: SPX Cooling Tech, LLC
13515 Ballantyne Corporate Pl (28277-2706)
PHONE..................630 881-9777
Michael Reilly, *Brnch Mgr*
EMP: 21
SALES (corp-wide): 495.11MM **Privately Held**
Web: www.spxcooling.com
SIC: 3443 Cooling towers, metal plate
HQ: Canvas Ct, Llc
7401 W 129th St
Overland Park KS 66213
913 664-7400

(G-3607)
SPX FLOW INC (HQ)
Also Called: SPX Flow
13320 Ballantyne Corporate Pl (28277-3607)
PHONE..................704 752-4400
Marcus G Michael, *Pr*
Robert F Hull Junior, *Non-Executive Chairman of the Board*
Jaime M Easley, *VP*
Kevin J Eamigh, *CIO*
Tyrone Jeffers V, *President Global Manufacturing*
EMP: 127 **EST:** 2015
SALES (est): 1.53B
SALES (corp-wide): 1.53B **Privately Held**
Web: www.spxflow.com
SIC: 3556 3561 3491 Food products machinery; Pumps and pumping equipment; Industrial valves
PA: Lsf11 Redwood Acquisitions, Llc
2711 N Haskell Ave # 170
Dallas TX 75204
214 754-8300

(G-3608)
SPX FLOW HOLDINGS INC
13320 Ballantyne Corporate Pl (28277-3607)
PHONE..................704 808-3848
Marc Michael, *Pr*
David Kowalski, *Global Manufacturing Operations President*
EMP: 44 **EST:** 1997
SALES (est): 5.47MM
SALES (corp-wide): 1.53B **Privately Held**
Web: www.spxflow.com

Charlotte - Mecklenburg County (G-3609)

SIC: 3556 3559 Dairy and milk machinery; Pharmaceutical machinery
HQ: Spx Flow, Inc.
13320 Balntyn Corp Pl
Charlotte NC 28277
704 752-4400

(G-3609)
SPX FLOW TECH SYSTEMS INC
13320 Ballantyne Corporate Pl (28277-3607)
PHONE..................704 752-4400
EMP: 920
SALES (corp-wide): 1.53B Privately Held
Web: www.spxflow.com
SIC: 3556 Food products machinery
HQ: Spx Flow Technology Systems, Inc.
105 Crosspoint Pkwy
Getzville NY 14068
716 692-3000

(G-3610)
SPX FLOW TECHNOLOGY USA INC (DH)
13320 Ballantyne Corporate Pl (28277-3607)
PHONE..................704 808-3848
Marc Michael, *Pr*
David Kowalski, *Global Manufacturing Operations President*
EMP: 62 EST: 1992
SALES (est): 87.83MM
SALES (corp-wide): 1.53B Privately Held
Web: www.spx.com
SIC: 3556 3559 Dairy and milk machinery; Pharmaceutical machinery
HQ: Spx Flow, Inc.
13320 Balntyn Corp Pl
Charlotte NC 28277
704 752-4400

(G-3611)
SPX LATIN AMERICA CORPORATION (DH)
13320 Ballantyne Corporate Pl (28277-3607)
PHONE..................704 808-3848
Marc Michael, *Pr*
David Kowalski, *Global Manufacturing Operations President*
EMP: 30 EST: 2007
SALES (est): 9.61MM
SALES (corp-wide): 1.53B Privately Held
Web: www.spx.com
SIC: 3556 3559 Dairy and milk machinery; Pharmaceutical machinery
HQ: Spx Flow, Inc.
13320 Balntyn Corp Pl
Charlotte NC 28277
704 752-4400

(G-3612)
SRI GEAR LLC
2125 S Tryon St (28203-4957)
PHONE..................704 910-2751
EMP: 4 EST: 2014
SALES (est): 70.22K Privately Held
SIC: 3482 Small arms ammunition

(G-3613)
SRNG-LIBERTY LLC
1447 S Tryon St Ste 301 (28203-4259)
PHONE..................248 212-7209
Rick Wilcox, *CEO*
Don Yochum, *Business Development*
EMP: 4 EST: 2021
SALES (est): 270.03K Privately Held
SIC: 1311 Natural gas production

(G-3614)
SRNG-T&W LLC
Also Called: Sustain Rng
1447 S Tryon St Ste 301 (28203-4259)
PHONE..................704 271-9889
Rick Wilcox, *Managing Member*
EMP: 4 EST: 2020
SALES (est): 274.01K Privately Held
SIC: 1311 Natural gas production

(G-3615)
SSB MANUFACTURING COMPANY
Also Called: Simmons
5100r Wt Harris Blvd (28269-2157)
PHONE..................704 596-4935
Bill Wagner, *Brnch Mgr*
EMP: 85
Web: www.sertasimmons.com
SIC: 2515 Mattresses, innerspring or box spring
HQ: Ssb Manufacturing Company
2451 Industry Ave
Doraville GA 30360
404 534-5000

(G-3616)
SSD DESIGNS LLC (PA)
9935d Rea Rd # 433 (28277-6710)
PHONE..................980 245-2988
Sara Samuelson, *Pr*
Sara Samuelson, *Managing Member*
EMP: 18 EST: 2017
SQ FT: 5,000
SALES (est): 2.08MM
SALES (corp-wide): 2.08MM Privately Held
Web: www.ssd-designs.com
SIC: 2821 Plastics materials and resins

(G-3617)
SSPC INC
12016 Steele Creek Rd (28273-3734)
P.O. Box 38040 (28278-1000)
▲ EMP: 24 EST: 1992
SQ FT: 24,000
SALES (est): 2.8MM Privately Held
Web: www.sspc.org
SIC: 3089 Injection molding of plastics

(G-3618)
ST INVESTORS INC
Also Called: Source Technolgies Holdings
4064 Colony Rd Ste 150 (28211-5033)
PHONE..................704 969-7500
Miles T Busby, *Pr*
John R Spencer Junior, *Ex VP*
Gordon W Friedrich, *Finance Treasurer*
Rodger M Morrison, *
Michael E Bailey, *
EMP: 87 EST: 1986
SQ FT: 58,000
SALES (est): 5.45MM Privately Held
SIC: 3577 7373 5045 7378 Printers, computer; Computer integrated systems design; Printers, computer; Computer peripheral equipment repair and maintenance

(G-3619)
STAINLESS & NICKEL ALLOYS LLC
1700 W Pointe Dr Ste E (28214-7901)
P.O. Box 12446 (28220-2446)
PHONE..................704 201-2898
Tom Lockhart, *Managing Member*
▲ EMP: 4 EST: 2010
SQ FT: 1,000
SALES (est): 499.15K Privately Held
SIC: 3356 Nickel

(G-3620)
STAN BUNN 1856 PUBG CO LLC
2540 Radrick Ln (28262-4443)
PHONE..................980 613-0633
Mazie Sowell, *Prin*
EMP: 5 EST: 2016
SALES (est): 64.7K Privately Held
SIC: 2741 Miscellaneous publishing

(G-3621)
STANLEY BLACK & DECKER INC
9115 Old Statesville Rd Ste E (28269-6605)
PHONE..................704 509-0844
Dick Verwyane, *Brnch Mgr*
EMP: 7
SALES (corp-wide): 15.78B Publicly Held
Web: www.stanleyblackanddecker.com
SIC: 3429 Builders' hardware
PA: Stanley Black & Decker, Inc.
1000 Stanley Dr
New Britain CT 06053
860 225-5111

(G-3622)
STANZA MACHINERY INC
6801 Northpark Blvd Ste B (28216-0080)
PHONE..................704 599-0623
James L Desarno, *Pr*
▲ EMP: 50 EST: 2005
SALES (est): 9.55MM Privately Held
Web: www.stanzamachinery.com
SIC: 5084 3556 Machine tools and accessories; Bakery machinery

(G-3623)
STARCKE ABRASIVES USA INC
Also Called: Abrasive Resource
9109 Forsyth Park Dr (28273-3882)
PHONE..................704 583-3338
Robert Steve Kelly, *Pr*
Paul W Burzynski, *
▲ EMP: 30 EST: 2003
SQ FT: 10,000
SALES (est): 4.79MM
SALES (corp-wide): 63.3MM Privately Held
Web: www.starckeusa.com
SIC: 3291 Abrasive products
PA: Starcke Gmbh & Co. Kg
Markt 10
Melle NI 49324
54229660

(G-3624)
STARNES PALLET SERVICE INC (PA)
4000 Jeff Adams Dr (28206-1237)
P.O. Box 5484 (28299-5484)
PHONE..................704 596-9006
Tommy Starnes Junior, *Pr*
Tommy Starnes Senior, *VP*
EMP: 36 EST: 1994
SQ FT: 7,500
SALES (est): 5.28MM Privately Held
Web: www.starnespalletservice.com
SIC: 2448 Pallets, wood

(G-3625)
STATE INDUSTRIES INC
STATE INDUSTRIES, INC.
4302 Raleigh St (28213-6927)
PHONE..................704 597-8910
Roy Jones, *Brnch Mgr*
EMP: 8
SQ FT: 93,014
SALES (corp-wide): 3.85B Publicly Held
Web: www.statewaterheaters.com
SIC: 3639 Hot water heaters, household
HQ: State Industries, Llc
500 Tennessee Waltz Pkwy
Ashland City TN 37015
615 244-7040

(G-3626)
STEAG SCR-TECH INC (PA)
Also Called: Cormetech
11707 Steele Creek Rd (28273-3718)
PHONE..................704 827-8933
Mike Mattes, *CEO*
Dave Morris, *
Thies Hoffmann, *
EMP: 30 EST: 2016
SALES (est): 99.92MM
SALES (corp-wide): 99.92MM Privately Held
Web: www.cormetech.com
SIC: 2819 Fuel propellants, solid: inorganic

(G-3627)
STEELFAB INC (PA)
3025 Westport Rd (28208-3688)
P.O. Box 19289 (28219-9289)
PHONE..................704 394-5376
EMP: 365 EST: 1955
SALES (est): 327.38MM
SALES (corp-wide): 327.38MM Privately Held
Web: www.steelfab-inc.com
SIC: 3441 3449 Building components, structural steel; Miscellaneous metalwork

(G-3628)
STEFANO FOODS INC
4825 Hovis Rd (28208-1510)
PHONE..................704 399-3935
▼ EMP: 150
Web: www.stefanofoods.com
SIC: 2099 2053 2038 Ready-to-eat meals, salads, and sandwiches; Frozen bakery products, except bread; Frozen specialties, nec

(G-3629)
STEIN FIBERS LTD
Also Called: Stein Fibers, Ltd.
10130 Mallard Creek Rd (28262-6000)
PHONE..................704 599-2804
Marcus Dellinger, *Of Development*
EMP: 24
SALES (corp-wide): 98.42MM Privately Held
Web: www.steinfibers.com
SIC: 2824 Polyester fibers
PA: Stein Fibers, Llc
4 Computer Dr W Ste 200
Albany NY 12205
518 489-5700

(G-3630)
STEPHANIES MATTRESS LLC
5920 N Tryon St (28213-7811)
PHONE..................704 763-0705
Ramon A Mercedes, *CEO*
EMP: 5 EST: 2017
SALES (est): 528.81K Privately Held
Web: www.stephaniesmattressclt.com
SIC: 5712 2519 Mattresses; Furniture, household: glass, fiberglass, and plastic

(G-3631)
STI TURF EQUIPMENT LLC
4355 Golf Acres Dr (28208-5874)
PHONE..................704 393-8873
Wayne Smith, *Prin*
EMP: 98 EST: 2001
SALES (est): 4.71MM
SALES (corp-wide): 83.7MM Privately Held
SIC: 3523 Turf equipment, commercial
PA: Smith Turf & Irrigation Llc
4355 Golf Acres Dr
Charlotte NC 28208
704 393-8873

GEOGRAPHIC SECTION
Charlotte - Mecklenburg County (G-3658)

(G-3632)
STICKER FARM LLC
3516 Keithcastle Ct (28210-7008)
PHONE..............................919 332-1342
Alyssa Minshall, *CEO*
EMP: 6 **EST:** 2011
SALES (est): 100.11K **Privately Held**
SIC: 2731 Books, publishing and printing

(G-3633)
STILL THERE
12115 Creek Turn Dr (28278-0036)
PHONE..............................704 728-1888
David Joseph Bettendorf, *Prin*
EMP: 5 **EST:** 2014
SALES (est): 98.23K **Privately Held**
Web: www.stillthereshinesauce.com
SIC: 2099 Food preparations, nec

(G-3634)
STITCH X STITCH LLC
9805 Statesville Rd (28269-7647)
PHONE..............................704 970-0667
EMP: 5 **EST:** 2020
SALES (est): 75K **Privately Held**
SIC: 2395 Art goods for embroidering, stamped: purchased materials

(G-3635)
STITCHES OF THREAD
7300 Sheffingdell Dr (28226-3125)
PHONE..............................704 840-7215
Patricia Mihalko, *Prin*
EMP: 4 **EST:** 2017
SALES (est): 44.8K **Privately Held**
SIC: 2395 Embroidery and art needlework

(G-3636)
STITCHINWRIGHT
12235 Winget Rd (28278-7232)
PHONE..............................704 219-0697
Jennifer Barnes, *Prin*
EMP: 5 **EST:** 2016
SALES (est): 52.13K **Privately Held**
SIC: 2395 Embroidery and art needlework

(G-3637)
STOCKHOLM CORPORATION
4729 Stockholm Ct (28273-5995)
P.O. Box 240360 (28224-0360)
PHONE..............................704 552-9314
Charles H Wunner, *Pr*
Barbara J Wunner, *
▲ **EMP:** 28 **EST:** 1982
SQ FT: 10,000
SALES (est): 5.13MM **Privately Held**
Web: www.vooner.com
SIC: 3561 Industrial pumps and parts

(G-3638)
STONEMASTER INC
15105 John J Delaney Dr Ste D (28277-2847)
PHONE..............................704 333-0353
Zbigniew Habas, *Pr*
▼ **EMP:** 10 **EST:** 2006
SALES (est): 890.78K **Privately Held**
Web: www.stonemasterhome.com
SIC: 1741 3281 Masonry and other stonework; Stone, quarrying and processing of own stone products

(G-3639)
STORK UNITED CORPORATION
3201 Rotary Dr (28269-4493)
P.O. Box 26458 (28221-6458)
PHONE..............................704 598-7171
▲ **EMP:** 713

(G-3640)
STRONG GLOBAL ENTRMT INC
5960 Fairview Rd Ste 275 (28210-3102)
PHONE..............................704 471-6784
Mark D Roberson, *CEO*
D Kyle Cerminara, *
Ray F Boegner, *Pr*
Todd R Major, *CFO*
EMP: 175 **EST:** 2021
SALES (est): 11.29MM **Privately Held**
SIC: 3861 Photographic equipment and supplies

(G-3641)
STROUP MACHINE & MFG INC
2019 W Laporte Dr (28216-6114)
PHONE..............................704 394-0023
EMP: 7 **EST:** 2010
SQ FT: 6,600
SALES (est): 563.07K **Privately Held**
SIC: 3469 Machine parts, stamped or pressed metal

(G-3642)
STS PACKAGING CHARLOTTE LLC ✿
1201 Westinghouse Blvd (28273-6489)
PHONE..............................980 259-2290
Lauren Mikos, *Pr*
EMP: 82 **EST:** 2022
SALES (est): 8.12MM **Privately Held**
SIC: 2621 Paper mills

(G-3643)
STUMP AND GRIND LLC
7420 Ponders End Ln (28213-5752)
PHONE..............................704 488-2271
T Tillman, *Owner*
EMP: 4 **EST:** 2013
SALES (est): 140.03K **Privately Held**
Web: www.charlottestumpgrinding.com
SIC: 3599 Grinding castings for the trade

(G-3644)
SUAREZ BAKERY INC
4245 Park Rd (28209-2231)
PHONE..............................704 525-0145
Carlos A Suarez, *Pr*
EMP: 10 **EST:** 1962
SQ FT: 3,000
SALES (est): 939.95K **Privately Held**
Web: www.suarezbakery.com
SIC: 2051 Bakery: wholesale or wholesale/retail combined

(G-3645)
SUBARU FOLGER AUTOMOTIVE
Also Called: Daewoo-Folger Automotive
5701 E Independence Blvd (28212-0513)
PHONE..............................704 531-8888
Ward Williams, *Pr*
Glenn Moore, *
EMP: 23 **EST:** 1937
SQ FT: 70,000
SALES (est): 2.37MM **Privately Held**
Web: www.williamssubaru.com
SIC: 5511 7539 3711 Automobiles, new and used; Machine shop, automotive; Motor vehicles and car bodies

(G-3646)
SUGAR CREEK BREWING CO LLC
215 Southside Dr (28217-1727)
PHONE..............................704 521-3333
Joseph Vogelbacher, *Managing Member*
EMP: 22 **EST:** 2014
SQ FT: 30,000
SALES (est): 3.31MM **Privately Held**
Web: www.sugarcreekbrewing.com
SIC: 2082 5813 5812 Beer (alcoholic beverage); Beer garden (drinking places); Cafe

(G-3647)
SULLIVAN WORKSHOP LLC
1150 Laurel Park Ln (28270-9785)
PHONE..............................704 560-9900
EMP: 4 **EST:** 2017
SALES (est): 90.61K **Privately Held**
SIC: 2511 Wood household furniture

(G-3648)
SUMMIT SELTZER COMPANY LLC
Also Called: Summit Seltzer
2215 Thrift Rd (28208-4446)
PHONE..............................980 819-6416
Kristin Cagney, *Genl Mgr*
EMP: 8 **EST:** 2019
SALES (est): 1.12MM **Privately Held**
Web: www.summitseltzer.com
SIC: 2086 Bottled and canned soft drinks

(G-3649)
SUMPTERS JWLY & COLLECTIBLES
3501 Wilkinson Blvd (28208-5536)
PHONE..............................704 399-5348
Hal R Sumpter, *Pr*
EMP: 8 **EST:** 1991
SQ FT: 10,000
SALES (est): 213.81K **Privately Held**
Web: www.sumptersjewelry.com
SIC: 3911 5094 7631 5932 Jewelry, precious metal; Precious stones and metals; Jewelry repair services; Pawnshop

(G-3650)
SUN CHEMICAL CORPORATION
General Printing Ink Division
1701 Westinghouse Blvd (28273-6383)
P.O. Box 7087 (28241-7087)
PHONE..............................704 587-4531
Scott Smith, *Brnch Mgr*
EMP: 50
SQ FT: 81,744
Web: www.sunchemical.com
SIC: 2893 Printing ink
HQ: Sun Chemical Corporation
35 Waterview Blvd Ste 104
Parsippany NJ 07054
973 404-6000

(G-3651)
SUNCO POWDER SYSTEMS INC
3230 Valentine Ln (28270-0685)
PHONE..............................704 545-3922
Ivan Wilson, *Pr*
EMP: 20 **EST:** 1982
SALES (est): 1.86MM **Privately Held**
Web: www.suncoblowers.com
SIC: 3535 3564 Pneumatic tube conveyor systems; Filters, air: furnaces, air conditioning equipment, etc.

(G-3652)
SUNDYNE CORP
5509 Crosshill Ct (28277-0553)
PHONE..............................303 249-5350
Robert Wilson, *Area Sales Manager*
EMP: 12 **EST:** 1970
SALES (est): 141.28K **Privately Held**
Web: www.sundyne.com
SIC: 3561 Pumps and pumping equipment

(G-3653)
SUNNEX INC
Also Called: Sunnex
8001 Tower Point Dr (28227-7726)
PHONE..............................800 445-7869
John Herbert, *Pr*
Lena Melton, *VP*
◆ **EMP:** 11 **EST:** 1974
SQ FT: 58,300
SALES (est): 6.55MM
SALES (corp-wide): 226.86K **Privately Held**
Web: www.sunnex.com
SIC: 3648 3641 3645 Lighting equipment, nec; Electric lamps; Table lamps
HQ: Sunnex Equipment Ab
Korkarlsvagen 4
Karlstad 653 4
54555160

(G-3654)
SUNSTAR HEATING PRODUCTS INC
305 Doggett St (28203-4923)
P.O. Box 36485 (28236-6485)
PHONE..............................704 372-3486
Frank L Horne, *Pr*
EMP: 22 **EST:** 1987
SALES (est): 2.44MM
SALES (corp-wide): 18.94MM **Privately Held**
Web: www.sunstarheaters.com
SIC: 3433 Gas infrared heating units
PA: Gas-Fired Products, Inc.
1700 Parker Dr
Charlotte NC 28208
704 372-3485

(G-3655)
SUNSTEAD BREWING LLC
Also Called: Toucan Louie's Gold District
1200 S Graham St (28203-4118)
PHONE..............................980 949-6200
EMP: 6 **EST:** 2018
SALES (est): 142.04K **Privately Held**
SIC: 2082 Beer (alcoholic beverage)

(G-3656)
SUPPLIERS TO WHOLESALERS INC
1816 W Pointe Dr Ste A (28214-0100)
PHONE..............................704 375-7406
C N Witherspoon, *Pr*
Marcus E Yandle, *
Mike Eppley, *
Lois Yandle, *
EMP: 17 **EST:** 1963
SALES (est): 676.77K **Privately Held**
SIC: 3444 Ducts, sheet metal

(G-3657)
SUPREME SWEEPERS LLC
6135 Park South Dr Ste 510 (28210-3272)
PHONE..............................888 698-9996
EMP: 4 **EST:** 2011
SALES (est): 493.97K **Privately Held**
SIC: 3589 3569 Commercial cleaning equipment; Blast cleaning equipment, dustless

(G-3658)
SWEATNET LLC
310 Arlington Ave Unit 229 (28203-4289)
PHONE..............................847 331-7287
EMP: 6 **EST:** 2017
SALES (est): 346.44K **Privately Held**
Web: www.sweatnet.com
SIC: 7372 7312 Application computer software; Outdoor advertising services

Charlotte - Mecklenburg County (G-3659)

(G-3659)
SWEET SSSFRAS PUBLICATIONS INC
5828 Swanston Dr (28269-9143)
PHONE..................................704 340-3862
Nettie Lark, *Prin*
EMP: 6 **EST:** 2011
SALES (est): 108.47K **Privately Held**
SIC: 2741 Miscellaneous publishing

(G-3660)
SWEETS SYRUP LLC (PA)
6100 Creola Rd (28270-5230)
PHONE..................................704 989-2156
EMP: 7 **EST:** 2019
SALES (est): 229.8K
SALES (corp-wide): 229.8K **Privately Held**
Web: www.sweetselderberry.com
SIC: 2099 Syrups

(G-3661)
SWING KURVE LOGISTIC TRCKG LLC ✪
2428 Freedom Dr (28208-4045)
PHONE..................................704 506-7371
EMP: 4 **EST:** 2022
SALES (est): 176.59K **Privately Held**
SIC: 3537 Trucks: freight, baggage, etc.: industrial, except mining

(G-3662)
SWIRL OAKHURST LLC
Also Called: Cakes
1640 Oakhurst Commons Dr Ste 103 (28205-6299)
PHONE..................................704 258-1209
Curtis Stone, *CEO*
EMP: 7 **EST:** 2019
SALES (est): 284.32K **Privately Held**
Web: www.swirldessertbar.com
SIC: 2051 5812 5461 Cakes, pies, and pastries; Ice cream, soft drink and soda fountain stands; Cookies

(G-3663)
SWISS MADE BRANDS USA INC
Also Called: Swiss Diamond
200 Forsyth Hall Dr Ste H (28273-5815)
PHONE..................................704 900-6622
Amir Alon, *Pr*
▲ **EMP:** 11 **EST:** 2012
SALES (est): 801.17K **Privately Held**
Web: www.swissdiamond.com
SIC: 3263 Cookware, fine earthenware

(G-3664)
SYCAMORE BREWING LLC
401 W 24th St (28206-2664)
PHONE..................................704 910-3821
Sarah T Brigham, *Owner*
EMP: 27 **EST:** 2013
SALES (est): 5.46MM **Privately Held**
Web: www.sycamorebrew.com
SIC: 2082 5813 Beer (alcoholic beverage); Beer garden (drinking places)

(G-3665)
SYNQ MARKETING GROUP LLC
338 S Sharon Amity Rd (28211-2806)
PHONE..................................800 380-6360
John W Keith, *Mgr*
Mark M Williams, *Mgr*
EMP: 10 **EST:** 2018
SALES (est): 753.14K **Privately Held**
Web: www.gosynq.com
SIC: 2782 Account books

(G-3666)
SYNTECH ABRASIVES INC
8325 Arrowridge Blvd Ste H (28273-6128)
PHONE..................................704 525-8030
Fred Rodgers, *Pr*
William Tonuci, *Contrlr*
EMP: 10 **EST:** 1986
SQ FT: 8,500
SALES (est): 1.16MM
SALES (corp-wide): 11.94MM **Privately Held**
SIC: 3291 Abrasive products
HQ: Jassco Corp.
    9400 State Rd
    Philadelphia PA 19114
    215 824-0401

(G-3667)
T - SQUARE ENTERPRISES INC
8318 Pineville Matthews Rd (28226-4753)
PHONE..................................704 846-8233
Thomas G Duffy, *Pr*
▲ **EMP:** 5 **EST:** 1995
SQ FT: 4,000
SALES (est): 1.4MM **Privately Held**
SIC: 5169 2672 Industrial chemicals; Adhesive papers, labels, or tapes: from purchased material

(G-3668)
T AIR INC (PA)
Also Called: Airt
11020 David Taylor Dr Ste 350 (28262-1103)
PHONE..................................980 595-2840
Nicholas Swenson, *Ch Bd*
Brian Ochocki, *CAO*
EMP: 70 **EST:** 1980
SQ FT: 4,900
SALES (est): 247.32MM
SALES (corp-wide): 247.32MM **Publicly Held**
Web: www.airt.net
SIC: 4513 4512 3728 7699 Air courier services; Air cargo carrier, scheduled; Aircraft parts and equipment, nec; Aircraft flight instrument repair

(G-3669)
T-METRICS INC
4430 Stuart Andrew Blvd (28217-1543)
PHONE..................................704 523-9583
Ronald Kahn, *Pr*
Roger Pohl, *
EMP: 27 **EST:** 1989
SQ FT: 850
SALES (est): 5.2MM **Privately Held**
Web: www.tmetrics.com
SIC: 3663 Radio broadcasting and communications equipment

(G-3670)
TAFFORD UNIFORMS LLC
Also Called: Tafford
2121 Distribution Center Dr Ste E (28269-4228)
PHONE..................................888 823-3673
EMP: 60
Web: www.uniformadvantage.com
SIC: 2326 5632 Medical and hospital uniforms, men's; Apparel accessories

(G-3671)
TAILORED DESIGNS LLC
11700 Worstel Ln (28277-6607)
PHONE..................................919 605-6349
Jonathan Scott, *Prin*
EMP: 7 **EST:** 2021
SALES (est): 269.19K **Privately Held**
Web: www.tailoreddesigns.com
SIC: 2311 Tailored suits and formal jackets

(G-3672)
TAN BOOKS AND PUBLISHERS INC (PA)
13315 Carowinds Blvd Ste Q (28273-7700)
P.O. Box 269 (28053-0269)
PHONE..................................704 731-0651
Thomas A Nelson, *Pr*
Mary F Lester, *Sec*
▲ **EMP:** 8 **EST:** 1967
SQ FT: 354,000
SALES (est): 1.93MM
SALES (corp-wide): 1.93MM **Privately Held**
Web: www.tanbooks.com
SIC: 2731 2732 Books, publishing and printing; Books, printing and binding

(G-3673)
TAWNICO LLC
11612 James Jack Ln (28277-3747)
PHONE..................................704 606-2345
Tawanna Turner, *Managing Member*
EMP: 5 **EST:** 2021
SALES (est): 233.43K **Privately Held**
SIC: 3553 7389 Furniture makers machinery, woodworking; Business services, nec

(G-3674)
TAYLOR INTERIORS LLC
2818 Queen City Dr (28208-3682)
P.O. Box 561035 (28256-1035)
PHONE..................................980 207-3160
Tarris Arnold, *Managing Member*
EMP: 18 **EST:** 2007
SALES (est): 2.15MM **Privately Held**
Web: www.taylorinteriorsllc.com
SIC: 7389 1742 2295 Interior design services ; Insulation, buildings; Waterproofing fabrics, except rubberizing

(G-3675)
TB WOODS INCORPORATED
Also Called: Boston Gear
701 Carrier Dr (28216-3445)
PHONE..................................704 588-5610
EMP: 51
SALES (corp-wide): 6.25B **Publicly Held**
Web: www.tbwoods.com
SIC: 3568 Power transmission equipment, nec
HQ: Tb Wood's Incorporated
    440 5th Ave
    Chambersburg PA 17201
    717 264-7161

(G-3676)
TEC COAT
14030 S Lakes Dr (28273-6791)
PHONE..................................412 215-0152
David Kelley, *Managing Member*
▲ **EMP:** 35 **EST:** 2012
SALES (est): 1.89MM **Privately Held**
Web: www.teccoat-usa.com
SIC: 3479 Coating of metals and formed products

(G-3677)
TECHNOLOGY PARTNERS LLC (PA)
Also Called: Imaginesoftware
8757 Red Oak Blvd 2f (28217-3983)
PHONE..................................704 553-1004
Sam Khashman, *Pr*
Charles Kauffman, *
EMP: 100 **EST:** 2000
SQ FT: 8,000
SALES (est): 40MM
SALES (corp-wide): 40MM **Privately Held**
Web: www.imagineteam.com
SIC: 7372 3577 Application computer software; Computer peripheral equipment, nec

(G-3678)
TEGUAR CORPORATION
Also Called: Teguar Computers
2920 Whitehall Park Dr (28273-3333)
PHONE..................................704 960-1761
Jonathan Staub, *Pr*
▲ **EMP:** 40 **EST:** 2010
SQ FT: 5,000
SALES (est): 9.74MM **Privately Held**
Web: www.teguar.com
SIC: 3571 5045 Electronic computers; Computers, peripherals, and software

(G-3679)
TEKTRONIX INC
Also Called: Tektronix
4400 Stuart Andrew Blvd Ste O (28217-4626)
PHONE..................................704 527-5000
Beverly Peters, *Admn*
EMP: 5
SALES (corp-wide): 6.07MM **Publicly Held**
Web: www.tek.com
SIC: 3825 Instruments to measure electricity
HQ: Tektronix, Inc.
    14150 Sw Karl Braun Dr
    Beaverton OR 97005
    800 833-9200

(G-3680)
TELOS GROUP LLC
11518 Wheat Ridge Rd (28277-3632)
PHONE..................................704 904-0599
EMP: 4 **EST:** 2018
SALES (est): 75.47K **Privately Held**
Web: www.telosgroup.org
SIC: 7372 Prepackaged software

(G-3681)
TENNESSEE NEDGRAPHICS INC
1809 Cross Beam Dr Ste E (28217-2891)
PHONE..................................704 414-4224
Robbert Ausems, *Dir*
EMP: 10
Web: www.nedgraphics.com
SIC: 2759 Commercial printing, nec
HQ: Nedgraphics Of Tennessee, Inc.
    855 Abutment Rd Ste 6
    Dalton GA 30721

(G-3682)
TESA TAPE INC (DH)
5825 Carnegie Blvd (28209-4633)
PHONE..................................704 554-0707
Daniel Germain, *Pr*
Manosh Mukerji, *CFO*
◆ **EMP:** 70 **EST:** 1989
SQ FT: 27,000
SALES (est): 139.6MM
SALES (corp-wide): 12.51B **Privately Held**
Web: www.tesa.com
SIC: 5199 2672 Packaging materials; Paper; coated and laminated, nec
HQ: Tesa Se
    Hugo-Kirchberg-Str. 1
    Norderstedt SH 22848
    40888990

(G-3683)
TEXTILE PRINTING INC
2431 Thornridge Rd (28226-6450)
P.O. Box 337 (28042-0337)
PHONE..................................704 521-8099
Robert Dale Dixon, *Pr*
Jane Dixon, *
▲ **EMP:** 8 **EST:** 1987

GEOGRAPHIC SECTION

Charlotte - Mecklenburg County (G-3711)

SALES (est): 471.81K **Privately Held**
Web: www.marketamericagear.com
SIC: 2396 Screen printing on fabric articles

(G-3684)
TEXTRAM INC
801 Clanton Rd Ste 103 (28217-1365)
PHONE..................................704 527-7557
Norman Jameson, *Owner*
EMP: 8 EST: 2008
SALES (est): 117.24K **Privately Held**
SIC: 2426 Textile machinery accessories, hardwood

(G-3685)
TFS MANAGEMENT GROUP LLC
Also Called: New Wave Acrylics
4331 Chesapeake Dr (28216-3410)
PHONE..................................704 399-3999
EMP: 8 EST: 2005
SALES (est): 779.79K **Privately Held**
Web: www.newwaveacrylics.com
SIC: 3089 Injection molding of plastics

(G-3686)
THINK WELDING
3541 Durham Ln (28269-4115)
PHONE..................................980 230-2842
EMP: 5 EST: 2019
SALES (est): 63.84K **Privately Held**
SIC: 7692 Welding repair

(G-3687)
THOMAS B BRUGH MFG REP
6020 Aynrand Ct (28269-7162)
PHONE..................................858 385-8987
Thomas Brugh, *Prin*
EMP: 5 EST: 2007
SALES (est): 106.96K **Privately Held**
SIC: 3999 Manufacturing industries, nec

(G-3688)
THOMAS CONCRETE CAROLINA INC
3701 N Graham St (28206-1628)
P.O. Box 790105 (28206-7901)
PHONE..................................704 333-0390
Donny Senter, *Brnch Mgr*
EMP: 10
SALES (corp-wide): 1.01B **Privately Held**
Web: www.thomasconcrete.com
SIC: 3273 Ready-mixed concrete
HQ: Thomas Concrete Of Carolina, Inc.
1131 N West St
Raleigh NC 27603
919 832-0451

(G-3689)
THOMAS GOLF INC
9716 Rea Rd Ste B # 170 (28277-6663)
PHONE..................................704 461-1342
Thomas Sacco, *CEO*
EMP: 6 EST: 1995
SALES (est): 488.49K **Privately Held**
Web: www.thomasgolf.com
SIC: 3949 5091 Shafts, golf club; Golf equipment

(G-3690)
THOMAS M BROWN INC
Also Called: Tmb Cranes
1311 Amble Dr (28206-1307)
P.O. Box 26612 (28221-6612)
PHONE..................................704 597-0246
EMP: 15 EST: 1970
SALES (est): 2.03MM **Privately Held**
Web: www.tmbcranes.com
SIC: 3536 5084 1796 Hoists, cranes, and monorails; Cranes, industrial; Installing building equipment

(G-3691)
THREE LADIES AND A MALE LLC
3515 Arsenal Ct Apt 103 (28273-3997)
PHONE..................................704 287-1584
EMP: 5 EST: 2021
SALES (est): 240.47K **Privately Held**
SIC: 3537 7389 Trucks: freight, baggage, etc.: industrial, except mining; Business Activities at Non-Commercial Site

(G-3692)
THREE TREES BINDERY
1600 Burtonwood Cir (28212-7019)
PHONE..................................704 724-9409
Michelle Skiba-smith, *Owner*
EMP: 5 EST: 2015
SALES (est): 113.04K **Privately Held**
SIC: 2789 Bookbinding and related work

(G-3693)
THURSTON GENOMICS LLC
7806 Springs Village Ln (28226-3350)
PHONE..................................980 237-7547
Virginia Thurston, *Prin*
EMP: 5 EST: 2017
SALES (est): 97.34K **Privately Held**
SIC: 2835 Microbiology and virology diagnostic products

(G-3694)
TIMBER WOLF WOOD CREATIONS INC
2008 Starbrook Dr (28210-6007)
PHONE..................................704 309-5118
Ken Nahas, *Ofcr*
EMP: 4 EST: 2001
SALES (est): 274.95K **Privately Held**
SIC: 2431 Millwork

(G-3695)
TIMEPLANNER CALENDARS INC
Also Called: Journalbooks
1010 Timeplanner Dr (28206-1951)
P.O. Box 536400 (30353-6400)
PHONE..................................704 377-0024
▲ EMP: 110 EST: 1971
SALES (est): 27.1MM **Privately Held**
Web: www.journalbooks.com
SIC: 2759 Calendars: printing, nsk
HQ: Polyconcept North America, Inc.
400 Hunt Valley Rd
New Kensington PA 15068

(G-3696)
TITAN LAND GROUP LLC
8405 Dianthus Ct Unit 104 (28277-3982)
PHONE..................................704 400-1842
EMP: 5 EST: 2010
SALES (est): 58.93K **Privately Held**
SIC: 3999 Pet supplies

(G-3697)
TITEFLEX CORPORATION
P.O. Box 905743 (28290-5743)
PHONE..................................647 638-1600
EMP: 5
SALES (corp-wide): 3.83B **Privately Held**
Web: www.titeflex.com
SIC: 3052 3599 Plastic hose; Hose, flexible metallic
HQ: Titeflex Corporation
603 Hendee St
Springfield MA 01104
413 739-5631

(G-3698)
TLV CORPORATION
Also Called: T L V
13901 S Lakes Dr (28273-6790)
PHONE..................................704 597-9070

James Risko, *Pr*
Trevor Dubroff, *
▲ EMP: 30 EST: 1985
SQ FT: 25,000
SALES (est): 6.44MM **Privately Held**
SIC: 3494 Steam fittings and specialties

(G-3699)
TM15 PRINTING SERVICES
1906 Delaware Dr Apt F (28215-2442)
PHONE..................................704 606-0112
Michael Spearman, *Prin*
EMP: 4 EST: 2016
SALES (est): 58.06K **Privately Held**
SIC: 2752 Commercial printing, lithographic

(G-3700)
TMS INTERNATIONAL LLC
6601 Lakeview Rd (28269-2604)
PHONE..................................704 604-0287
EMP: 11
SIC: 3312 Blast furnaces and steel mills
HQ: Tms International, Llc
Southside Wrks Bldg 1 3f
Pittsburgh PA 15203
412 678-6141

(G-3701)
TO KNIT AND STITCH
7309 Kinsmore Ln (28269-8936)
PHONE..................................704 493-2523
Cornelia Dumitru, *Prin*
EMP: 4 EST: 2017
SALES (est): 43.11K **Privately Held**
Web: www.knitonestitchtoo.com
SIC: 2395 Embroidery and art needlework

(G-3702)
TOBACCO OUTLET PRODUCTS LLC
Also Called: Tobacco Outlet Products
6401 Carmel Rd Ste 204 (28226-8299)
PHONE..................................704 341-9388
Jennifer Lown, *Mgr*
Paul Walsh, *Prin*
EMP: 5 EST: 1997
SQ FT: 1,800
SALES (est): 339.68K **Privately Held**
Web: www.smokeodorsolution.com
SIC: 3999 5199 Candles; Candles

(G-3703)
TODAYS CHARLOTTE WOMAN
5200 Park Rd Ste 126 (28209-3675)
PHONE..................................704 521-6872
Cama Mcnamara, *Owner*
EMP: 6 EST: 2004
SALES (est): 294.9K **Privately Held**
Web: www.todayscharlottewoman.com
SIC: 2721 Magazines: publishing and printing

(G-3704)
TODAYTEC LLC
6701 Northpark Blvd Ste K (28216-0081)
PHONE..................................704 790-2440
Paggy Zhou, *Pr*
Jack Liu, *VP*
Keith Furr, *VP*
▲ EMP: 32 EST: 2010
SQ FT: 12,160
SALES (est): 5.5MM
SALES (corp-wide): 82.59MM **Privately Held**
Web: www.todaytecllc.com
SIC: 3825 Analog-digital converters, electronic instrumentation type
PA: Hangzhou Todaytec Digital Co., Ltd.
No.600, Kangxin Road, Qianjiang Economic Development Zone, Linpi Hangzhou ZJ 31110
57186358910

(G-3705)
TOKAI CARBON GE LLC (DH)
6210 Ardrey Kell Rd Ste 270 (28277-4864)
PHONE..................................980 260-1130
Scott Carlton, *Pr*
EMP: 21 EST: 2015
SQ FT: 10,000
SALES (est): 50.13MM **Privately Held**
Web: www.tokaicarbonusa.com
SIC: 3624 Carbon and graphite products
HQ: Tokai Carbon Ge Holding Llc
6210 Ardrey Kell Rd Ste 2
Charlotte NC 28277
704 593-5100

(G-3706)
TOM ROCHESTER & ASSOCIATES INC (PA)
Also Called: Southsern Archtctural Systems
9325 Forsyth Park Dr (28273-3885)
PHONE..................................704 896-5805
Tom Rochester, *Pr*
Cindy Rochester, *Treas*
EMP: 4 EST: 1989
SALES (est): 2.46MM **Privately Held**
Web: www.seas-tr.com
SIC: 3531 Construction machinery

(G-3707)
TOMORROW CELL LLC
5401 South Blvd (28217-4410)
PHONE..................................704 378-8555
Jong Park, *Admn*
EMP: 5 EST: 2016
SALES (est): 350.07K **Privately Held**
SIC: 3993 Signs and advertising specialties

(G-3708)
TONYAS CROCHETED CREATIONS
7535 Marlbrook Dr (28212-4769)
PHONE..................................704 421-2143
Guatonya Reese, *Prin*
EMP: 4 EST: 2011
SALES (est): 104.44K **Privately Held**
SIC: 2399 Hand woven and crocheted products

(G-3709)
TOPGOLF
8024 Savoy Corporate Dr (28273-6267)
PHONE..................................704 612-4745
EMP: 40 EST: 2017
SALES (est): 2.19MM **Privately Held**
Web: www.topgolf.com
SIC: 3949 Sporting and athletic goods, nec

(G-3710)
TOQUE INDUSTRIES LLC
5326 Twin Ln (28269-4634)
PHONE..................................704 640-6232
Thomas Brown, *Prin*
EMP: 4 EST: 2018
SALES (est): 42.83K **Privately Held**
SIC: 3999 Manufacturing industries, nec

(G-3711)
TOTER LLC
6525 Morrison Blvd Ste 300 (28211-3561)
PHONE..................................704 936-5610
EMP: 41
Web: www.toter.com
SIC: 3089 Garbage containers, plastics
HQ: Toter, Llc
841 Meacham Rd
Statesville NC 28677
800 424-0422

Charlotte - Mecklenburg County (G-3712)

(G-3712)
TRAFAG INC
8848 Red Oak Blvd Ste I (28217-5517)
PHONE..................................704 343-6339
Robert Kinkopf, *Mgr*
EMP: 5 **EST:** 2013
SQ FT: 2,357
SALES (est): 2.41MM **Privately Held**
Web: www.trafag.com
SIC: 3829 5049 3823 Thermometers and temperature sensors; Precision tools; Pressure measurement instruments, industrial
HQ: Trafag Ag
   Industriestrasse 11
   Bubikon ZH 8608

(G-3713)
TRANE COMPANY (DH)
4500 Morris Field Dr (28208-5837)
PHONE..................................704 398-4600
Michael Truan, *Prin*
▲ **EMP:** 36 **EST:** 1973
SALES (est): 97.81MM **Privately Held**
Web: www.trane.com
SIC: 3585 Air conditioning equipment, complete
HQ: Trane Technologies International Limited
   Units 170/175 Lake View Drive
   Swords K67 E

(G-3714)
TRANE US INC
Also Called: Trane
4501 S Tryon St (28217-1843)
P.O. Box 240605 (28224-0605)
PHONE..................................704 525-9600
Mark Cresitello, *Prin*
EMP: 94
Web: www.trane.com
SIC: 3585 Refrigeration and heating equipment
HQ: Trane U.S. Inc.
   800 Beaty St Ste E
   Davidson NC 28036
   704 655-4000

(G-3715)
TRANE US INC
Also Called: Trane
8610 Air Park West Dr Ste C (28214)
PHONE..................................704 697-9006
Jon White, *Brnch Mgr*
EMP: 11
Web: www.trane.com
SIC: 3585 1711 Refrigeration and heating equipment; Septic system construction
HQ: Trane U.S. Inc.
   800 Beaty St Ste E
   Davidson NC 28036
   704 655-4000

(G-3716)
TRANSBOTICS CORPORATION
3400 Latrobe Dr (28211-4847)
PHONE..................................704 362-1115
▲ **EMP:** 30
Web: www.scottautomation.com
SIC: 3535 7372 Conveyors and conveying equipment; Prepackaged software

(G-3717)
TRANSCENDENT TECHNOLOGIES LLC
2330 E 5th St (28204-4337)
PHONE..................................704 334-1258
James Rink, *Prin*
EMP: 8 **EST:** 2010
SALES (est): 430.08K **Privately Held**

SIC: 3357 Nonferrous wiredrawing and insulating

(G-3718)
TRANSTEX BELTING
10125 S Tryon St (28273-6509)
PHONE..................................704 334-5353
Peter Nikolich, *Mgr*
EMP: 8 **EST:** 2010
SALES (est): 277.67K **Privately Held**
Web: www.forbo.com
SIC: 3052 Rubber and plastics hose and beltings

(G-3719)
TRAXON TECHNOLOGIES LLC
2915 Whitehall Park Dr (28273-3383)
PHONE..................................201 508-1570
Terry H Oneal, *Pr*
EMP: 20 **EST:** 2016
SALES (est): 921.35K **Privately Held**
Web: www.traxon-ecue.com
SIC: 3641 Electric lamps

(G-3720)
TRESATA INC (PA)
1616 Candem Rd Ste 300 (28203)
PHONE..................................980 224-2097
Abhishek Mehta, *CEO*
Richard Morris, *
Elizabeth Sterling, *
Michael Dulin, *CMO*
EMP: 22 **EST:** 2011
SQ FT: 10,000
SALES (est): 4.51MM
SALES (corp-wide): 4.51MM **Privately Held**
Web: www.tresata.ai
SIC: 7372 Application computer software

(G-3721)
TREVA MASON LLC
8500 Monroe Rd (28212-7509)
PHONE..................................704 566-7973
EMP: 4
SALES (est): 72.7K **Privately Held**
Web: www.firstimpressionsltd.com
SIC: 2752 Offset printing

(G-3722)
TREVIRA NORTH AMERICA LLC
5206 Leonardslee Ct (28226-5552)
PHONE..................................704 910-0970
Reinhard Vonhennigs, *Admn*
EMP: 4
SALES (est): 241.98K **Privately Held**
Web: www.trevira.de
SIC: 3714 Motor vehicle parts and accessories

(G-3723)
TRI-CITY CONCRETE LLC
3823 Raleigh St (28206-2042)
PHONE..................................704 372-2930
Michael J Wenig, *Prin*
EMP: 8 **EST:** 2011
SALES (est): 124.97K **Privately Held**
SIC: 3273 Ready-mixed concrete

(G-3724)
TRI-TEC IND INC
200 Peachtree Dr S (28217-2066)
PHONE..................................704 424-5995
Michael Davidson, *Pr*
Raymond Motley, *Sec*
Richard Loyd, *Sec*
EMP: 15 **EST:** 1997
SQ FT: 6,000
SALES (est): 465.49K **Privately Held**
Web: www.tritecindustries.com

SIC: 3599 Machine shop, jobbing and repair

(G-3725)
TRIANGLE INDUS SUP HLDINGS LLC (PA)
228 Westinghouse Blvd Ste 104 (28273-6230)
PHONE..................................704 395-0600
EMP: 5 **EST:** 2001
SALES (est): 2.1MM **Privately Held**
Web: www.hughesindustrial.com
SIC: 5085 3052 5072 Industrial supplies; Rubber and plastics hose and beltings; Hardware

(G-3726)
TRICK TANK INC
2250 Toomey Ave (28203-4635)
PHONE..................................980 406-3200
Bob Gilbertson, *Pr*
▲ **EMP:** 6 **EST:** 2000
SALES (est): 555.69K **Privately Held**
Web: www.tricktank.com
SIC: 3634 Air purifiers, portable

(G-3727)
TRIMECH SOLUTIONS LLC
201 Mccullough Dr Ste 300 (28262-1367)
PHONE..................................704 503-6644
Mike Voll, *Mgr*
EMP: 6
SALES (corp-wide): 24.06MM **Privately Held**
Web: www.trimech.com
SIC: 7372 7373 Prepackaged software; Value-added resellers, computer systems
PA: Trimech Solutions, Llc
   4991 Lake Brook Dr # 300
   Glen Allen VA 23060
   804 257-9965

(G-3728)
TRINICOR TECHNOLOGY INCORPORAT
1300 S Tryon St Ste F227 (28203-4248)
PHONE..................................866 848-1232
EMP: 4 **EST:** 2015
SALES (est): 54.49K **Privately Held**
Web: www.trinicor.com
SIC: 2711 Newspapers

(G-3729)
TRIPLE C BREWING COMPANY LLC
Also Called: Triple C Brewing Co
2900 Griffith St (28203-5430)
PHONE..................................704 372-3212
Christopher J Harker, *Managing Member*
▲ **EMP:** 17 **EST:** 2011
SALES (est): 1.1MM **Privately Held**
Web: www.triplecbrewing.com
SIC: 5813 2082 Bars and lounges; Beer (alcoholic beverage)

(G-3730)
TRIPLE CROWN INTERNATIONAL LLC
Also Called: T C I
12205 Parks Farm Ln (28277-5621)
P.O. Box 79313 (28271-7063)
PHONE..................................704 846-4983
Thomas J Mcalpine Senior, *Managing Member*
◆ **EMP:** 5 **EST:** 2008
SALES (est): 312.97K **Privately Held**
SIC: 3554 8742 7389 Paper industries machinery; Distribution channels consultant; Business services, nec

(G-3731)
TROPICAL NUT & FRUIT CO (PA)
1100 Continental Blvd (28273-6380)
P.O. Box 7507 (28241-7507)
PHONE..................................800 438-4470
TOLL FREE: 800
John R Bauer, *Pr*
John Bauer, *
Carolyn Y Bennett, *
Angela Bauer, *
Michael R P York, *
◆ **EMP:** 101 **EST:** 1977
SALES (est): 100.82MM
SALES (corp-wide): 100.82MM **Privately Held**
Web: www.trulygoodfoods.com
SIC: 5149 5145 2099 2068 Specialty food items; Nuts, salted or roasted; Food preparations, nec; Salted and roasted nuts and seeds

(G-3732)
TRUCK PARTS INC
707 Kennedy St (28206-1939)
PHONE..................................704 332-7909
Robert K Sims, *Pr*
EMP: 12 **EST:** 1966
SQ FT: 14,750
SALES (est): 2.97MM **Privately Held**
Web: www.truckpartsinc.com
SIC: 5013 3714 Truck parts and accessories; Rebuilding engines and transmissions, factory basis

(G-3733)
TSG2 INC
1235 East Blvd Ste E (28203-5876)
PHONE..................................704 347-4484
Deborah Starne, *CEO*
Beborah Starne, *CEO*
EMP: 4 **EST:** 2009
SALES (est): 404.92K **Privately Held**
SIC: 2674 Shipping and shopping bags or sacks

(G-3734)
TSHIRTS MADE BY U
7925 N Tryon St Ste 201 (28262-3409)
PHONE..................................980 309-9749
EMP: 4 **EST:** 2019
SALES (est): 76.67K **Privately Held**
Web: www.undergroundshirts.com
SIC: 2759 Screen printing

(G-3735)
TTI FLOOR CARE NORTH AMER INC
Also Called: Techtronic Industries
8405 Ibm Dr (28262-4331)
PHONE..................................440 996-2000
EMP: 100
Web: www.ttifloorcare.com
SIC: 5722 3634 Vacuum cleaners; Air purifiers, portable
HQ: Tti Floor Care North America, Inc.
   8405 Ibm Dr
   Charlotte NC 28262

(G-3736)
TTI FLOOR CARE NORTH AMER INC (DH)
Also Called: Royal Appliance Manufacturing
8405 Ibm Dr (28262-4331)
PHONE..................................440 996-2000
Chris Gurreri, *Pr*
◆ **EMP:** 350 **EST:** 2007
SQ FT: 450,000
SALES (est): 137.26MM **Privately Held**
Web: www.ttifloorcare.com

GEOGRAPHIC SECTION

Charlotte - Mecklenburg County (G-3762)

SIC: **3825** 5072 Power measuring equipment, electrical; Power tools and accessories
HQ: Royal Appliance Mfg. Co.
  8405 Ibm Dr
  Charlotte NC 28262
  440 996-2000

(G-3737)
TUCKERS FARM INC
201 W 31st St (28206-2205)
P.O. Box 790008 (28206-7900)
PHONE....................704 375-8199
Mike Kelly, *Pr*
EMP: 7 **EST:** 1995
SQ FT: 9,000
SALES (est): 841.16K **Privately Held**
Web: www.millworkon31st.com
SIC: **2431** Millwork

(G-3738)
TUMI STORE - CHRLTTE DGLAS INT
5501 Josh Birmingham Pkwy Unit 21a (28208-5750)
PHONE....................704 359-8771
EMP: 39 **EST:** 2018
SALES (est): 309.81K
SALES (corp-wide): 8.01MM **Privately Held**
Web: www.cltairport.com
SIC: **3161** Luggage
PA: Samsonite International S.A.
  Avenue De La Liberte 13-15
  Luxembourg 1931

(G-3739)
TURMAR MARBLE INC
Also Called: Turmar
914 Richland Dr (28211-1250)
PHONE....................704 391-1800
Aydin Yoruk, *Pr*
▲ **EMP:** 14 **EST:** 2006
SALES (est): 389.88K **Privately Held**
Web: www.turmar.com
SIC: **3281** Marble, building: cut and shaped

(G-3740)
TURNING PGES PCTRIAL HEIRLOOMS
1113 Northwood Dr (28216-3108)
PHONE....................704 634-2911
Wornitha Mcilwain, *Mgr*
EMP: 5 **EST:** 2013
SALES (est): 72.18K **Privately Held**
Web: www.turningpagespictorialheirlooms.com
SIC: **2511** Wood household furniture

(G-3741)
TWO BROTHERS WLDG MISCELLANE
2660 Barringer Dr (28208-7007)
PHONE....................704 488-9845
S Abimael Landa Hernandez, *Owner*
EMP: 5 **EST:** 2016
SALES (est): 106.44K **Privately Held**
SIC: **7692** Welding repair

(G-3742)
TWO OF A KIND PUBLISHING LLC
8239 Romana Red Ln (28213-5328)
PHONE....................704 497-2879
Al Bogur, *COO*
EMP: 7 **EST:** 2003
SALES (est): 230.67K **Privately Held**
SIC: **2731** Books, publishing and printing

(G-3743)
TWORK TECHNOLOGY INC
3536 N Davidson St (28205-1125)
PHONE....................704 218-9675
EMP: 15 **EST:** 2002
SALES (est): 456.75K **Privately Held**
Web: www.tworktechnology.com
SIC: **7372** 7373 7379 7371 Business oriented computer software; Systems software development services; Online services technology consultants; Computer software systems analysis and design, custom

(G-3744)
U S BOTTLERS MCHY CO INC
11911 Steele Creek Rd (28273-3773)
P.O. Box 7203 (28241-7203)
PHONE....................704 588-4750
Tom Risser, *Pr*
Anthony J Triana, *
L Cameron Caudle, *
▲ **EMP:** 75 **EST:** 1912
SQ FT: 61,000
SALES (est): 24.6MM **Privately Held**
Web: www.usbottlers.com
SIC: **3565** 5084 Bottling machinery: filling, capping, labeling; Recapping machinery, for tires

(G-3745)
U TECH CNC SE LLC
10234 Rougemont Ln (28277-2359)
PHONE....................980 500-8263
Mike Hessney, *Pr*
EMP: 5 **EST:** 2020
SALES (est): 68.05K **Privately Held**
SIC: **3541** Lathes, metal cutting and polishing

(G-3746)
UKG KRONOS SYSTEMS LLC
8801 J M Keynes Dr Ste 240 (28262-8436)
PHONE....................800 225-1561
Janet Mcguirt, *Mgr*
EMP: 8
SALES (corp-wide): 1.85B **Privately Held**
Web: www.ukg.com
SIC: **7372** Business oriented computer software
HQ: Ukg Kronos Systems, Llc
  900 Chelmsford St
  Lowell MA 01851
  978 250-9800

(G-3747)
ULLMAN GROUP LLC
10925 Westlake Dr (28273-3740)
P.O. Box 430 (28173-1047)
PHONE....................704 246-7333
Luke Ullman, *Prin*
EMP: 17 **EST:** 2010
SQ FT: 10,000
SALES (est): 2.79MM **Privately Held**
Web: www.theullmangroup.com
SIC: **1751** 2541 Cabinet and finish carpentry ; Wood partitions and fixtures

(G-3748)
ULTIMATE FLOOR CLEANING
9625 Commons East Dr Apt L (28277-1717)
PHONE....................704 912-8978
Eric Chisholm, *VP*
Anthony Ceasar, *VP*
EMP: 4 **EST:** 2014
SALES (est): 302.63K **Privately Held**
SIC: **3645** 7359 7699 7389 Floor lamps; Floor maintenance equipment rental; Cleaning services; Business services, nec

(G-3749)
UNIQUE PRINTER SOLUTIONS LLC
9636 Cotton Stand Rd (28277-6702)
PHONE....................704 544-4822
Rodger B Morrison, *Admn*
EMP: 6 **EST:** 2015
SALES (est): 104.75K **Privately Held**
Web: www.uniqueprintersolutions.com
SIC: **2752** Offset printing

(G-3750)
UNITED AIR FILTER COMPANY CORP
Also Called: Clear-Flo Air Filters
1000 W Palmer St (28208-5344)
P.O. Box 34215 (28234-4215)
PHONE....................704 334-5311
William Kinney Iii, *Pr*
E Allen Miller, *
EMP: 25 **EST:** 1968
SQ FT: 40,000
SALES (est): 4.44MM **Privately Held**
Web: www.unitedairfilter.com
SIC: **3564** 3585 Filters, air: furnaces, air conditioning equipment, etc.; Refrigeration and heating equipment

(G-3751)
UNITED PALLETS & TRUCKIN
3435 Northerly Rd (28206-1036)
PHONE....................704 493-1636
John Stokes, *Owner*
EMP: 5 **EST:** 2006
SALES (est): 64.71K **Privately Held**
SIC: **2448** Pallets, wood

(G-3752)
UNITED SERVICES GROUP LLC (PA)
2505 Hutchison Mcdonald Rd (28269-4254)
PHONE....................980 237-1335
Joshua Armstrong, *CEO*
Stephen Gillman, *COO*
EMP: 5 **EST:** 2013
SQ FT: 5,000
SALES (est): 6.08MM
SALES (corp-wide): 6.08MM **Privately Held**
Web: www.united-services.com
SIC: **7692** Automotive welding

(G-3753)
UNITED TECHNICAL SERVICES LLC
2505 Hutchison Mcdonald Rd (28269-4254)
PHONE....................980 237-1335
Joshua Armstrong, *CEO*
Stephen Gillman, *COO*
Kerrie Holden, *Off Mgr*
EMP: 10 **EST:** 2013
SALES (est): 922.68K
SALES (corp-wide): 6.04MM **Privately Held**
Web: www.united-services.com
SIC: **7692** 3599 Welding repair; Machine shop, jobbing and repair
PA: United Services Group, Llc
  2505 Htchison Mcdonald Rd
  Charlotte NC 28269
  980 237-1335

(G-3754)
UNITY HLTHCARE LAB BILLING LLP
Also Called: Health Services
7508 E Independence Blvd Ste 109 (28227-9473)
PHONE....................980 209-0402
Tanya Diaz, *Pt*
EMP: 7 **EST:** 2007
SALES (est): 235K **Privately Held**
SIC: **8099** 8093 8734 3999 Health screening service; Mental health clinic, outpatient; Testing laboratories

(G-3755)
UNIVERSAL AIR PRODUCTS CORP
4715 Stockholm Ct (28273-5995)
PHONE....................704 374-0600
John Haslam, *Brnch Mgr*
EMP: 6
SALES (corp-wide): 9.08MM **Privately Held**
Web: www.uapc.com
SIC: **3563** 3564 Air and gas compressors; Blowers and fans
PA: Universal Air Products Corporation
  1140 Kingwood Ave
  Norfolk VA 23502
  757 461-0077

(G-3756)
UNPLUGGED INCORPORATED
402 W Trade St Ste 104 (28202-1673)
PHONE....................704 726-0614
EMP: 5 **EST:** 2013
SALES (est): 186.94K **Privately Held**
SIC: **3144** Women's footwear, except athletic

(G-3757)
UPCHURCH MACHINE CO INC
11633 Fruehauf Dr (28273-5510)
P.O. Box 7792 (28241-7792)
PHONE....................704 588-2895
Fred D Upchurch, *Pr*
Martha Upchurch, *Sec*
EMP: 21 **EST:** 1974
SQ FT: 16,000
SALES (est): 539.7K **Privately Held**
Web: www.upchurchmachine.com
SIC: **3599** Machine shop, jobbing and repair

(G-3758)
UPTOWN PUBLISHING INC
8037 Corporate Center Dr (28226-4545)
PHONE....................704 543-0690
Todd C Brockmann, *Prin*
EMP: 4 **EST:** 2008
SALES (est): 213.42K **Privately Held**
SIC: **2741** Miscellaneous publishing

(G-3759)
URBAN SPICED LLC
15720 Brixham Hill Ave Ste 300 (28277-4651)
PHONE....................704 741-1174
EMP: 5 **EST:** 2020
SALES (est): 254.23K **Privately Held**
SIC: **2099** Spices, including grinding

(G-3760)
US ONE DOT COM INC
13508 Norlington Ct (28273-6784)
PHONE....................704 587-0678
Fred Elhami, *Pr*
EMP: 8 **EST:** 1998
SALES (est): 83.03K **Privately Held**
SIC: **3089** Identification cards, plastics

(G-3761)
USA BLIND INC
6039 Charing Pl (28211-4322)
PHONE....................704 309-5171
EMP: 5 **EST:** 2019
SALES (est): 79.81K **Privately Held**
SIC: **2591** Window blinds

(G-3762)
VALD GROUP INC
2108 South Blvd Ste 115 (28203-5098)
PHONE....................704 345-5145
Christopher Rowe, *Pr*
EMP: 7 **EST:** 2018
SALES (est): 953.79K **Privately Held**
Web: www.valdperformance.com
SIC: **3845** Electromedical apparatus

Charlotte - Mecklenburg County (G-3763)   GEOGRAPHIC SECTION

(G-3763)
VALMET INC
Also Called: Metso Power USA
3430 Toringdon Way (28277-2446)
PHONE.................................704 541-1453
Calderone Vito, *Brnch Mgr*
EMP: 219
SALES (corp-wide): 5.27B **Privately Held**
Web: www.valmet.com
SIC: 3544 Special dies, tools, jigs, and fixtures
HQ: Valmet, Inc.
3720 Davinci Ct Ste 300
Norcross GA 30092
770 263-7863

(G-3764)
VALMET INC
3440 Toringdon Way Ste 300 (28277-3190)
PHONE.................................803 289-4900
Jim Longwith, *Mgr*
EMP: 6
SALES (corp-wide): 5.27B **Privately Held**
Web: www.valmet.com
SIC: 3554 Pulp mill machinery
HQ: Valmet, Inc.
3720 Davinci Ct Ste 300
Norcross GA 30092
770 263-7863

(G-3765)
VANDILAY INDUSTRIES LLC
11758 James Richard Dr (28277-4031)
PHONE.................................704 962-5140
Charles F Miller, *Prin*
EMP: 5 **EST:** 2015
SALES (est): 152.53K **Privately Held**
SIC: 3999 Manufacturing industries, nec

(G-3766)
VANS INC
4400 Sharon Rd Ste 159 (28211-3674)
PHONE.................................704 364-3811
Christine Quimby, *Brnch Mgr*
EMP: 6
SALES (corp-wide): 11.61B **Publicly Held**
Web: www.vans.com
SIC: 3021 Canvas shoes, rubber soled
HQ: Vans, Inc.
1588 S Coast Dr
Costa Mesa CA 92626
714 755-4000

(G-3767)
VAV PLASTICS NC LLC
8710 Air Park West Dr Ste 200 (28214-8686)
PHONE.................................704 325-9332
EMP: 8 **EST:** 2020
SALES (est): 635.53K **Privately Held**
SIC: 3085 Plastics bottles

(G-3768)
VELOCITOR SOLUTIONS
202 E Woodlawn Rd Ste 146 (28217-2343)
PHONE.................................704 635-4293
Holly Ong, *Ofcr*
EMP: 8 **EST:** 2010
SALES (est): 56.54K **Privately Held**
Web: www.velsol.com
SIC: 7372 Prepackaged software

(G-3769)
VERBATIM AMERICAS LLC
7300 Reames Rd (28216-2228)
PHONE.................................704 547-6551
EMP: 5
Web: www.verbatim.com
SIC: 3572 Computer storage devices
PA: Verbatim Americas Llc
8210 Univ Exec Pk Dr Ste
Charlotte NC 28262

(G-3770)
VERBATIM AMERICAS LLC (PA)
8210 University Exec Park Dr Ste 300 (28262-3368)
PHONE.................................704 547-6500
▲ **EMP:** 91 **EST:** 2007
SALES (est): 23.91MM **Privately Held**
Web: www.verbatim.com
SIC: 3572 Computer storage devices

(G-3771)
VERBATIM CORPORATION
8210 University Exec Park Dr Ste 300 (28262-3368)
PHONE.................................704 547-6500
◆ **EMP:** 62
Web: www.verbatim.com.sg
SIC: 3572 Computer storage devices

(G-3772)
VERMEER MANUFACTURING COMPANY
10900 Carpet St (28273-6205)
PHONE.................................410 285-0200
EMP: 10
SALES (corp-wide): 885.68MM **Privately Held**
Web: www.vermeer.com
SIC: 3531 Construction machinery
PA: Vermeer Manufacturing Company
1210 E Vermeer Rd
Pella IA 50219
641 628-3141

(G-3773)
VERONA CABINETS & SURFACES LLC
6700 South Blvd (28217-4379)
PHONE.................................704 755-5259
EMP: 4 **EST:** 2017
SALES (est): 94.34K **Privately Held**
SIC: 2434 Wood kitchen cabinets

(G-3774)
VESUVIUS PENN CORPORATION (HQ)
5510 77 Center Dr Ste 100 (28217-3108)
PHONE.................................724 535-4374
Cedric Woindrich, *Pr*
EMP: 15 **EST:** 2021
SALES (est): 23.72MM
SALES (corp-wide): 2.47B **Privately Held**
SIC: 3255 Castable refractories: clay
PA: Vesuvius Plc
165 Fleet Street
London EC4A
207 822-0000

(G-3775)
VESUVIUS USA CORPORATION
5510 77 Center Dr # 100 (28217-2729)
PHONE.................................412 429-1800
Glenn Cowie, *Pr*
Luis Alberto Ordaz, *
Steven Delcotto, *
Glenn Cowie, *Treas*
◆ **EMP:** 75 **EST:** 1989
SALES (est): 22.07MM
SALES (corp-wide): 2.47B **Privately Held**
SIC: 3297 Nonclay refractories
PA: Vesuvius Plc
165 Fleet Street
London EC4A
207 822-0000

(G-3776)
VIBRATION SOLUTIONS LLC
5900 Harris Technology Blvd Ste G (28269-3808)
PHONE.................................704 896-7535
Allan Hansen, *Managing Member*
EMP: 8 **EST:** 2003
SQ FT: 20,000
SALES (est): 1.19MM **Privately Held**
Web: www.vibration-solutions.com
SIC: 3465 Automotive stampings

(G-3777)
VIGOR LLC
1209 S College St Apt 1130 (28203-4368)
PHONE.................................980 474-1124
EMP: 7 **EST:** 2016
SALES (est): 101.1K **Privately Held**
SIC: 3731 Shipbuilding and repairing

(G-3778)
VINEYARD BLUFFTON LLC
1001 Morehead Square Dr Ste 320 (28203-4253)
PHONE.................................704 307-2737
Sean Pesek, *Owner*
EMP: 7 **EST:** 2018
SALES (est): 361.03K **Privately Held**
Web: www.vineyardseniorliving.com
SIC: 2084 Wines

(G-3779)
VISION ENVELOPE INC
Also Called: Vision Print Solutions
2451 Executive St (28208-3635)
PHONE.................................704 392-9090
Susan Zerona, *CEO*
Mark Zerona, *Pr*
EMP: 16 **EST:** 1990
SQ FT: 16,400
SALES (est): 3.05MM **Privately Held**
Web: www.visionenvelope.com
SIC: 2759 Envelopes: printing, nsk

(G-3780)
VMOD FIBER LLC
811 Pressley Rd (28217-0970)
PHONE.................................704 525-6851
William Younts, *Pr*
Michael Alexander, *CFO*
◆ **EMP:** 10 **EST:** 2004
SALES (est): 1.04MM
SALES (corp-wide): 14.43MM **Privately Held**
SIC: 2299 5023 Fibers, textile: recovery from textile mill waste and rags; Sheets, textile
PA: Rsm Co.
811 Pressley Rd
Charlotte NC 28217
704 525-6851

(G-3781)
VOCOLLECT INC
855 S Mint St (28202-1517)
PHONE.................................980 279-4119
EMP: 25
SALES (corp-wide): 36.66B **Publicly Held**
SIC: 3577 Encoders, computer peripheral equipment
HQ: Vocollect, Inc.
2555 Smallman St Ste 200
Pittsburgh PA 15222
412 829-8145

(G-3782)
VOLVO MOTOR GRADERS INC
8844 Mount Holly Rd (28214-8350)
PHONE.................................704 609-3604
Andres Larsson, *Pr*
Patrick Olnery, *
EMP: 56 **EST:** 1993
SQ FT: 14,562
SALES (est): 2.47MM
SALES (corp-wide): 45.13B **Privately Held**
SIC: 3462 Construction or mining equipment forgings, ferrous
HQ: Vna Holding Inc.
7825 National Service Rd
Greensboro NC 27409
336 393-4890

(G-3783)
VOONER FLOGARD LLC ✪
4729 Stockholm Ct (28273-5995)
PHONE.................................980 225-3277
Chuck Wunner, *Pr*
EMP: 11 **EST:** 2022
SALES (est): 251.05K
SALES (corp-wide): 539.04MM **Privately Held**
SIC: 3561 Industrial pumps and parts
HQ: Aerzen Usa Corp.
108 Independence Way
Coatesville PA 19320
610 380-0244

(G-3784)
VULCAN MATERIALS COMPANY
11435 Brooks Mill Rd (28227-8005)
PHONE.................................704 545-5687
EMP: 4
Web: www.vulcanmaterials.com
SIC: 3273 2951 Ready-mixed concrete; Asphalt paving mixtures and blocks
PA: Vulcan Materials Company
1200 Urban Center Dr
Vestavia AL 35242

(G-3785)
VULCAN MATERIALS COMPANY
11020 David Taylor Dr Ste 105 (28262-1101)
PHONE.................................704 549-1540
Dave Ford, *Mgr*
EMP: 4
Web: www.vulcanmaterials.com
SIC: 3273 Ready-mixed concrete
PA: Vulcan Materials Company
1200 Urban Center Dr
Vestavia AL 35242

(G-3786)
VULCRAFT CARRIER CORP
2100 Rexford Rd (28211-3589)
PHONE.................................704 367-8674
EMP: 12 **EST:** 2014
SALES (est): 692.82K **Privately Held**
Web: www.vulcraft.com
SIC: 3312 Blast furnaces and steel mills

(G-3787)
W B MASON CO INC
10800 Withers Cove Park Dr (28278-6928)
PHONE.................................888 926-2766
EMP: 34
SALES (corp-wide): 1.01B **Privately Held**
Web: www.wbmason.com
SIC: 5943 5712 2752 Office forms and supplies; Office furniture; Commercial printing, lithographic
PA: W. B. Mason Co., Inc.
59 Centre Street
Brockton MA 02301
508 586-3434

(G-3788)
W H RGERS SHTMTL IR WRKS INC
837 Toddville Rd (28214-1839)
PHONE.................................704 394-2191
Robert Canipe, *Pr*
Wendell Canipe, *

GEOGRAPHIC SECTION — Charlotte - Mecklenburg County (G-3813)

EMP: 23 EST: 1963
SQ FT: 46,000
SALES (est): 4.98MM Privately Held
Web: www.whrogers.com
SIC: 3599 3444 Machine shop, jobbing and repair; Sheet metalwork

(G-3789)
W M PLASTICS INC
Also Called: National Textile Supply
5301 Terminal St (28208-1254)
PHONE...................704 599-0511
William Mackinnon, Pr
Joyce Brown, Sec
▲ EMP: 16 EST: 1983
SQ FT: 30,000
SALES (est): 4.95MM Privately Held
Web: www.wmplasticsinc.com
SIC: 2821 Polyvinyl chloride resins, PVC

(G-3790)
WALDENWOOD GROUP INC
Also Called: Steel Tech
3800 Woodpark Blvd Ste I (28206-4247)
PHONE...................704 313-8004
EMP: 10 EST: 1998
SALES (est): 768.41K Privately Held
Web: www.steeltechus.com
SIC: 3441 1799 Bridge sections, prefabricated, railway; Welding on site

(G-3791)
WALDENWOOD GROUP LLC
Also Called: Steel Tech
3800 Woodpark Blvd Ste I (28206-4247)
PHONE...................704 331-8004
EMP: 10 EST: 2020
SALES (est): 520.67K Privately Held
SIC: 3441 Fabricated structural metal

(G-3792)
WALGREEN CO
Also Called: Walgreens
2215 W Arrowood Rd (28217-7939)
PHONE...................704 525-2628
EMP: 11
SALES (corp-wide): 139.08B Publicly Held
Web: www.wallgreensbootsalliance.com
SIC: 5912 5999 2771 2759 Drug stores; Alarm and safety equipment stores; Greeting cards; Commercial printing, nec
HQ: Walgreen Co.
    200 Wilmot Rd
    Deerfield IL 60015
    800 925-4733

(G-3793)
WALLETS FOR WATER
4228 Wanamassa Dr (28269-1640)
PHONE...................704 564-0763
James Mitchell, Prin
EMP: 5 EST: 2016
SALES (est): 65.07K Privately Held
SIC: 3172 Wallets

(G-3794)
WAMBAM FENCE INC
6935 Reames Rd Ste K (28216-2408)
PHONE...................877 778-5373
Linda Lachance, Pr
EMP: 10 EST: 2009
SALES (est): 2.49MM Privately Held
Web: www.wambamfence.com
SIC: 3089 Fences, gates, and accessories: plastics

(G-3795)
WARD VESSEL AND EXCHANGER CORP (PA)
Also Called: Equipment Enterprises Division
6835 E W T Harris Blvd (28215-4141)
P.O. Box 44568 (28215-0046)
PHONE...................704 568-3001
Jon Ward, Prin
Bob Besh, *
Tim Ramsey, *
▲ EMP: 60 EST: 1982
SALES (est): 25.4MM
SALES (corp-wide): 25.4MM Privately Held
Web: www.wardvesselandexchanger.com
SIC: 3443 Tanks, standard or custom fabricated: metal plate

(G-3796)
WASTEQUIP LLC (DH)
Also Called: Wastequip
6525 Carnegie Blvd Ste 300 (28211-0500)
PHONE...................704 366-7140
Marty Bryant, CEO
Steven Klueg, CFO
Mike Marchetti, CIO
Nick Wiseman, Chief Human Resource Officer
◆ EMP: 18 EST: 1988
SQ FT: 1,000
SALES (est): 1.22B Privately Held
Web: www.wastequip.com
SIC: 3443 3537 Dumpsters, garbage; Industrial trucks and tractors
HQ: H.I.G. Capital, L.L.C.
    1450 Brickell Ave Fl 31
    Miami FL 33131
    305 379-2322

(G-3797)
WASTEQUIP MANUFACTURING CO LLC (DH)
6525 Morrison Blvd Ste 300 (28211-3561)
PHONE...................704 504-7597
Robert Rasmussen, Pr
◆ EMP: 5 EST: 1992
SQ FT: 2,500
SALES (est): 408.58MM Privately Held
Web: www.wastequip.com
SIC: 3443 Dumpsters, garbage
HQ: Wastequip, Llc
    6525 Carnegie Blvd # 300
    Charlotte NC 28211

(G-3798)
WAXHAW CANDLE COMPANY LLC
9830 Rea Rd Ste G (28277-0793)
PHONE...................980 245-2827
Rebecca Walter, Pr
EMP: 5 EST: 2015
SALES (est): 225.8K Privately Held
Web: www.waxhawcandlecompany.com
SIC: 3999 Candles

(G-3799)
WE GLOWED UP LLC
6805 Walnut Branch Ln (28277-8942)
PHONE...................856 266-5000
EMP: 4 EST: 2019
SALES (est): 56.54K Privately Held
SIC: 7372 Application computer software

(G-3800)
WEB-DON INCORPORATED (PA)
Also Called: Web-Don
1400 Ameron Dr (28206-1604)
P.O. Box 26367 (28221-6367)
PHONE...................800 532-0434
▲ EMP: 30 EST: 1972
SALES (est): 23.71MM
SALES (corp-wide): 23.71MM Privately Held
Web: www.web-don.com

SIC: 2891 5722 2452 3281 Adhesives; Kitchens, complete (sinks, cabinets, etc.); Panels and sections, prefabricated, wood; Table tops, marble

(G-3801)
WEDDINGS TO REMEMBER
9319 Carrot Patch Dr (28216-7104)
PHONE...................704 608-1181
Tamie Wright, Prin
EMP: 5 EST: 2010
SALES (est): 71.42K Privately Held
SIC: 2335 Wedding gowns and dresses

(G-3802)
WEDECO UV TECHNOLOGIES INC
Also Called: Xylem
4828 Parkway Plaza Blvd Ste 200 (28217-1038)
PHONE...................704 716-7600
John Marrino, Pr
Jesse Rodriguez, *
▲ EMP: 79 EST: 1975
SALES (est): 24.44MM Publicly Held
SIC: 3589 Water treatment equipment, industrial
PA: Xylem Inc.
    301 Water St Se Ste 201
    Washington DC 20003

(G-3803)
WELL DOCTOR LLC
9607 Autumn Applause Dr (28277-1696)
P.O. Box 1420 (28124-1420)
PHONE...................704 909-9258
EMP: 4 EST: 2017
SALES (est): 366.65K Privately Held
Web: www.welldoctor.biz
SIC: 1389 Pumping of oil and gas wells

(G-3804)
WENKER INC (PA)
112 S Tryon St Ste 1130 (28284-2109)
PHONE...................704 333-7790
EMP: 8 EST: 2016
SALES (est): 5.98MM
SALES (corp-wide): 5.98MM Privately Held
Web: www.wenker.de
SIC: 3714 Motor vehicle parts and accessories

(G-3805)
WEST POINTE PRINTING
3924 Bearwood Ave (28205-1330)
PHONE...................704 806-3670
EMP: 4 EST: 2018
SALES (est): 83.91K Privately Held
SIC: 2752 Offset printing

(G-3806)
WESTROCK - GRAPHICS INC (DH)
9731 Southern Pine Blvd Ste E (28273-5543)
PHONE...................610 392-0416
Steven C Voorhees, Pr
Ward Dickson, *
Kevin Maxwell, *
John Stakel, *
▲ EMP: 18 EST: 1973
SALES (est): 4.14MM
SALES (corp-wide): 20.31B Publicly Held
SIC: 2752 Commercial printing, lithographic
HQ: Westrock Converting, Llc
    1000 Abernathy Rd Ste 125
    Atlanta GA 30328
    770 448-2193

(G-3807)
WEWOKA GAS PRODUCERS LLC
10600 Nations Ford Rd (28273-5762)
PHONE...................704 844-8990
Robin Keziah, Prin
EMP: 8 EST: 2010
SALES (est): 349.71K Privately Held
Web: www.landfillgroup.com
SIC: 1389 Building oil and gas well foundations on site

(G-3808)
WEYERHAEUSER COMPANY
10601 Westlake Dr (28273-3930)
PHONE...................253 924-2345
David Bowen, Branch
EMP: 9
SALES (corp-wide): 7.67B Publicly Held
Web: www.weyerhaeuser.com
SIC: 2653 Boxes, corrugated: made from purchased materials
PA: Weyerhaeuser Company
    220 Occidental Ave S
    Seattle WA 98104
    206 539-3000

(G-3809)
WHALEY FOODSERVICE LLC
8334 Arrowridge Blvd Ste K (28273-5611)
PHONE...................704 529-6242
Woody Adkins, Brnch Mgr
EMP: 77
SALES (corp-wide): 1.1B Privately Held
Web: www.whaleyfoodservice.com
SIC: 3631 7699 Household cooking equipment; Restaurant equipment repair
HQ: Whaley Foodservice, Llc
    137 Cedar Rd
    Lexington SC 29073
    803 996-9900

(G-3810)
WHITE CAP LP
5900 W Wt Harris Blvd (28269)
PHONE...................704 921-4420
Paul Harris, Brnch Mgr
EMP: 6
SALES (corp-wide): 7.35B Privately Held
Web: www.hdsupply.com
SIC: 3273 Ready-mixed concrete
HQ: White Cap, L.P.
    6250 Brook Hollow Pkwy # 100
    Norcross GA 30071
    800 944-8322

(G-3811)
WICHARD INC
3901 Pine Grove Cir (28206-1385)
PHONE...................704 597-1502
◆ EMP: 8 EST: 1995
SALES (est): 1.84MM Privately Held
Web: www.wichardamerica.com
SIC: 5023 2591 Stainless steel flatware; Drapery hardware and window blinds and shades

(G-3812)
WICKED WELDS LLC
4017 Hartley St (28206-1230)
PHONE...................704 907-5531
R Cheves, Prin
EMP: 5 EST: 2015
SALES (est): 143.64K Privately Held
SIC: 7692 Welding repair

(G-3813)
WIKOFF COLOR CORPORATION
Also Called: Wikoff Color
2828 Interstate St (28208-3606)
PHONE...................704 392-4657

Charlotte - Mecklenburg County (G-3814) — GEOGRAPHIC SECTION

Check Walters, *Mgr*
EMP: 40
SALES (corp-wide): 156.45MM **Privately Held**
Web: www.wikoff.com
SIC: 2893 Printing ink
PA: Wikoff Color Corporation
1886 Merritt Rd
Fort Mill SC 29715
803 548-2210

(G-3814)
WILBERT YATES VAULT CO INC
2839 Rosemont St (28208-5512)
P.O. Box 669343 (28266-9343)
PHONE.................704 399-8453
Dan G Yates Junior, *Pr*
Robert Yates, *
EMP: 19 **EST**: 1952
SQ FT: 29,900
SALES (est): 4.88MM **Privately Held**
Web: www.yateswilbert.com
SIC: 3272 Burial vaults, concrete or precast terrazzo

(G-3815)
WILLOWCROFT
15301 Marvin Rd (28277-1928)
PHONE.................704 540-0367
Kevin J Hall, *Prin*
EMP: 10 **EST**: 2008
SALES (est): 334.83K **Privately Held**
SIC: 2084 Wines

(G-3816)
WINE AND CANVAS STUDIO
8320 Pineville Matthews Rd Ste 602 (28226-4780)
PHONE.................251 591-7219
EMP: 4 **EST**: 2018
SALES (est): 46.58K **Privately Held**
Web: www.wineandcanvas.com
SIC: 2211 Canvas

(G-3817)
WINSO DSGNS SCREENPRINTING LLC
7027 Orr Rd Ste F (28213-6460)
PHONE.................704 967-5776
EMP: 4 **EST**: 2019
SALES (est): 83.72K **Privately Held**
SIC: 2759 Screen printing

(G-3818)
WINTON PRODUCTS COMPANY
2500 West Blvd Ste B (28208-6759)
P.O. Box 36332 (28236-6332)
PHONE.................704 399-5151
Jack Mc Creary, *Pr*
W Michael Mc Creary, *VP*
EMP: 10 **EST**: 1950
SQ FT: 15,000
SALES (est): 1.03MM **Privately Held**
Web: www.wintonproducts.com
SIC: 2899 Chemical preparations, nec

(G-3819)
WOODIES SUN EXPRESS
923 S Kings Dr (28204-3051)
PHONE.................704 332-7262
Glenda Brooks, *Mgr*
EMP: 7 **EST**: 2005
SALES (est): 85.4K **Privately Held**
SIC: 2741 Miscellaneous publishing

(G-3820)
WOODTECH/INTERIORS INC
2228 N Brevard St (28206-3454)
PHONE.................704 332-7215
Bob Binner, *Pr*
EMP: 8 **EST**: 1983
SQ FT: 7,500
SALES (est): 650K **Privately Held**
SIC: 2431 Millwork

(G-3821)
WORK CUSTOM LLC
5700 Copper Creek Ct Apt 11 (28227)
P.O. Box 31732 (28231-1732)
PHONE.................704 488-3113
Martel Robinson, *Prin*
EMP: 5 **EST**: 2013
SALES (est): 74.54K **Privately Held**
SIC: 2431 Millwork

(G-3822)
WORKING WIDGET TECHNOLOGY LLC
7920 Alexander Rd (28270-0860)
PHONE.................704 684-6277
Matt Bradford, *Owner*
EMP: 5 **EST**: 2012
SALES (est): 99.68K **Privately Held**
SIC: 2499 Wood products, nec

(G-3823)
WORLD CAM LLC
8000 Tower Point Dr (28227-7726)
PHONE.................704 655-1018
▲ **EMP**: 8 **EST**: 2010
SALES (est): 573.39K **Privately Held**
Web: www.worldcamlive.com
SIC: 7372 Application computer software

(G-3824)
WORLD NEWSPAPER PUBLISHING
Also Called: Charlotte World, The
8701 Mallard Creek Rd (28262-6006)
PHONE.................704 548-1737
Warren Smith, *Pr*
▲ **EMP**: 5 **EST**: 1993
SQ FT: 2,000
SALES (est): 127.98K **Privately Held**
Web: www.thecharlotteworld.com
SIC: 2711 Newspapers, publishing and printing

(G-3825)
WORLD STONE FABRICATORS INC
4908 Hovis Rd (28208-1513)
PHONE.................704 372-9968
EMP: 35 **EST**: 1996
SALES (est): 3.89MM **Privately Held**
Web: www.worldstonefabricators.com
SIC: 3281 Cut stone and stone products

(G-3826)
WORLDWIDE ENTRMT MLTIMEDIA LLC
11511 Sidney Crest Ave (28213-4873)
PHONE.................704 208-6113
EMP: 5 **EST**: 2021
SALES (est): 100K **Privately Held**
SIC: 3651 Music distribution apparatus

(G-3827)
WORSHAM SPRINKLER CO INC
3109 Westinghouse Blvd (28273-6519)
PHONE.................704 805-9700
EMP: 4 **EST**: 2019
SALES (est): 113.31K **Privately Held**
SIC: 3999 Manufacturing industries, nec

(G-3828)
WORTHYWARE DSGNS BY D MCHLLE L
891 Seigle Point Dr # 101 (28204-2259)
PHONE.................803 565-0615
EMP: 4 **EST**: 2020
SALES (est): 123.81K **Privately Held**
SIC: 2499 Decorative wood and woodwork

(G-3829)
WR ALLEN LLC
4100 Carmel Rd (28226-6150)
PHONE.................704 390-4032
Allen Woodard, *Prin*
EMP: 5 **EST**: 2012
SALES (est): 109.55K **Privately Held**
Web: www.swensonminerals.com
SIC: 1382 Oil and gas exploration services

(G-3830)
WRITE GOOD STUFF LLC
7237 Cormwell Ln (28217-7949)
PHONE.................704 522-8242
Nathan Jones, *Prin*
EMP: 5 **EST**: 2014
SALES (est): 70.52K **Privately Held**
Web: www.writegoodstuff.org
SIC: 2741 Miscellaneous publishing

(G-3831)
WTO INC
13900 S Lakes Dr Ste F (28273-7119)
PHONE.................704 714-7765
Sascha Tschiggfrei, *Pr*
EMP: 12 **EST**: 1993
SALES (est): 4.02MM
SALES (corp-wide): 60.87MM **Privately Held**
Web: www.wto-tools.com
SIC: 3546 Drills and drilling tools
PA: Wto Werkzeug - Einrichtungen Gmbh
Neuer Hohdammweg 1
Ohlsbach BW 77797
780393920

(G-3832)
XARM PUBLISHING INC
324 Ramona St (28208-3139)
PHONE.................888 717-3591
Marx C Dublin, *Admn*
EMP: 6 **EST**: 2015
SALES (est): 52.01K **Privately Held**
SIC: 2741 Miscellaneous publishing

(G-3833)
XELERA INC
10806 Reames Rd Ste Y (28269-3766)
PHONE.................855 493-5372
Rafael Gonzalez, *Pr*
Rafael Gonzalez Junior, *VP*
Cheri T Gonzalez, *Sec*
Kirsten Y Swanson, *Treas*
EMP: 4 **EST**: 1998
SALES (est): 250.45K **Privately Held**
SIC: 2899 Water treating compounds

(G-3834)
XENIAL INC (DH)
Also Called: Xenial
3420 Toringdon Way Ste 400 (28277-2439)
PHONE.................800 253-8664
David Green, *Pr*
EMP: 48 **EST**: 2011
SALES (est): 58.9MM
SALES (corp-wide): 9.65B **Publicly Held**
Web: www.xenial.com
SIC: 8741 7372 Restaurant management; Business oriented computer software
HQ: Heartland Payment Systems, Llc
3550 Lenox Rd Ne Ste 3000
Atlanta GA 30326
877 729-2968

(G-3835)
XEROXDATA CENTER
1400 Cross Beam Dr (28217-2803)
PHONE.................704 329-7245
EMP: 5 **EST**: 2013
SALES (est): 129.03K **Privately Held**
SIC: 3577 Computer peripheral equipment, nec

(G-3836)
XSPORT GLOBAL INC
1800 Camden Rd # 107-196 (28203-4690)
PHONE.................212 541-6222
Ray Mariorenzi, *Pr*
Maurice E Durschlag, *Ch Bd*
EMP: 13 **EST**: 2012
SALES (est): 367.62K **Privately Held**
Web: www.xsportglobal.com
SIC: 7371 7372 Computer software systems analysis and design, custom; Application computer software

(G-3837)
XSYS NORTH AMERICA CORPORATION (DH)
2915 Whitehall Park Dr Ste 600 (28273)
PHONE.................704 504-2626
Dagmar Schmidt, *CEO*
EMP: 17 **EST**: 2020
SALES (est): 13.13MM
SALES (corp-wide): 857.59K **Privately Held**
Web: www.xsysglobal.com
SIC: 2796 Platemaking services
HQ: Xsys Germany Gmbh
Industriestr. 1
Willstatt BW 77731
78529340

(G-3838)
XTINGUISH LLC
3021 N Myers St (28205-1558)
PHONE.................704 868-9500
Wim Debaudringhein, *Pr*
Dirk Duymelinck, *
Peter Duymelinck, *
▲ **EMP**: 16 **EST**: 2004
SQ FT: 30,000
SALES (est): 724.61K **Privately Held**
SIC: 2253 2261 2231 Knit outerwear mills; Finishing plants, cotton; Broadwoven fabric mills, wool

(G-3839)
XYLEM LNC (DH)
Also Called: Ultra Violet Systems Division
4828 Parkway Plaza Blvd # 200 (28217-1038)
P.O. Box 7107 (28241-7107)
PHONE.................704 409-9700
Ronald Port, *Pr*
Scott Miller, *VP*
Werner Klink, *
William Carr, *Treas*
James Anderson, *Sec*
▲ **EMP**: 26 **EST**: 1969
SALES (est): 31.57MM
SALES (corp-wide): 3.28B **Publicly Held**
SIC: 3621 3613 3674 3511 Power generators; Control panels, electric; Semiconductors and related devices; Turbines and turbine generator sets
HQ: Itt Llc
1133 Westchester Ave N-100
White Plains NY 10604
914 641-2000

(G-3840)
XYLEM WATER SOLUTIONS USA INC (HQ)
4828 Parkway Plaza Blvd Ste 200 (28217-1038)
PHONE.................704 409-9700
▲ **EMP**: 75 **EST**: 2011
SALES (est): 49.65MM **Publicly Held**

GEOGRAPHIC SECTION

Web: www.xylem.com
SIC: 3561 Pumps and pumping equipment
PA: Xylem Inc.
   301 Water St Se Ste 201
   Washington DC 20003

(G-3841)
XYLEM WATER SOLUTIONS USA INC
Also Called: Wedeco
14125 S Bridge Cir (28273-6747)
PHONE..............................704 409-9700
EMP: 42
Web: www.xylem.com
SIC: 2899 Water treating compounds
HQ: Xylem Water Solutions U.S.A., Inc.
   4828 Parkway Plaza Blvd # 200
   Charlotte NC 28217

(G-3842)
YANG MING AMERICA CORPORATION
Also Called: Yang Mine Lines
11124 Ascoli Pl (28277-4121)
PHONE..............................704 357-3817
EMP: 5
SIC: 3731 Cargo vessels, building and repairing
HQ: Ming Yang America Corporation
   1085 Raymond Blvd Fl 9
   Newark NJ 07102
   201 222-8899

(G-3843)
YATES WILBERT VAULT LLC
2839 Rosemont St (28208-5512)
P.O. Box 669343 (28266-9343)
PHONE..............................704 399-8453
EMP: 5
SALES (est): 248.73K Privately Held
Web: www.yateswilbert.com
SIC: 3272 Burial vaults, concrete or precast terrazzo

(G-3844)
YG-1 AMERICA INC
11001 Park Charlotte Blvd (28273-8860)
PHONE..............................980 318-5348
Don Hun Ham, *Pr*
✦ EMP: 25 EST: 2014
SQ FT: 60,000
SALES (est): 5.48MM Privately Held
SIC: 3545 Diamond cutting tools for turning, boring, burnishing, etc.
PA: Yg-1 Co., Ltd.
   13-40 Songdogwahak-Ro 16beon-Gil, Yeonsu-Gu
   Incheon 21984

(G-3845)
YOUNG WOOD WORKS LLC
6109 King George Dr (28213-6425)
PHONE..............................704 654-1722
Micah Joel Young, *Prin*
EMP: 5 EST: 2016
SALES (est): 67.68K Privately Held
SIC: 2431 Millwork

(G-3846)
YOUR SOURCE FOR PRINTING
8116 S Tryon St (28273-4300)
PHONE..............................704 957-5922
EMP: 4 EST: 2017
SALES (est): 114.77K Privately Held
Web: www.heritageprintingcharlotte.com
SIC: 2752 Commercial printing, lithographic

(G-3847)
YP ADVRTISING PUBG LLC NOT LLC
Also Called: BellSouth
9144 Arrowpoint Blvd Ste 150 (28273)
PHONE..............................704 522-5500
Jerry Furr, *Mgr*
EMP: 150
SALES (corp-wide): 916.96MM Publicly Held
SIC: 2741 7311 7331 7313 Directories, telephone: publishing only, not printed on site; Advertising agencies; Direct mail advertising services; Radio, television, publisher representatives
HQ: Yp Advertising & Publishing Llc (Not Llc)
   2247 Northlake Pkwy
   Tucker GA 30084

(G-3848)
ZARGES INC
1440 Center Park Dr (28217-2909)
P.O. Box 19768 (28219-9768)
PHONE..............................704 357-6285
✦ EMP: 10 EST: 2007
SQ FT: 10,000
SALES (est): 4.95MM
SALES (corp-wide): 479.35K Privately Held
Web: www.zargesusa.com
SIC: 3441 Fabricated structural metal
PA: Zarges Gmbh
   Markt 16-18
   Frankfurt Am Main HE 69299030

(G-3849)
ZEBRA TECHNOLOGIES CORPORATION
Also Called: Zebra Technologies
9075 Meadowmont View Dr (28269-6194)
PHONE..............................704 517-5271
EMP: 5
SALES (corp-wide): 4.58B Publicly Held
Web: www.zebra.com
SIC: 3577 Bar code (magnetic ink) printers
PA: Zebra Technologies Corporation
   3 Overlook Pt
   Lincolnshire IL 60069
   847 634-6700

(G-3850)
ZELAYA BROS LLC
3525 Ritch Ave (28206-2013)
PHONE..............................980 833-0099
EMP: 5 EST: 2020
SALES (est): 69.29K Privately Held
SIC: 3571 7389 Electronic computers; Business Activities at Non-Commercial Site

(G-3851)
ZINGERLE GROUP USA INC
Also Called: Mastertent
6965 Northpark Blvd (28216-2321)
PHONE..............................704 312-1600
Justin Russell, *Prin*
Russell Justin, *CEO*
EMP: 9 EST: 2018
SALES (est): 656.99K Privately Held
Web: www.mastertent.com
SIC: 3714 Motor vehicle parts and accessories

(G-3852)
ZIPPY ICE INC (PA)
5701 N Graham St (28269-4838)
PHONE..............................980 355-9851
Christine Mackie, *Pr*
EMP: 25 EST: 2006
SALES (est): 4.08MM Privately Held
Web: www.zippyicecompany.com
SIC: 2097 Block ice

Cherokee
Swain County

(G-3853)
C B C PRINTING
149 Childrens Home Rd (28719-8605)
P.O. Box 507 (28719-0507)
PHONE..............................828 497-5510
Skooter Maccoy, *Genl Mgr*
Ray Kinsland, *Mgr*
EMP: 6 EST: 1984
SALES (est): 145.32K Privately Held
Web: www.cherokeeboysclub.com
SIC: 2752 Commercial printing, lithographic

(G-3854)
CHEROKEE PUBLICATIONS
Also Called: Native Amercn Collections Xii
66 Luftee Lake Rd (28719)
P.O. Box 430 (28719-0430)
PHONE..............................828 627-2424
Ed Sharpe, *Owner*
EMP: 5 EST: 1970
SQ FT: 2,000
SALES (est): 609.21K Privately Held
SIC: 5192 2731 5961 Books; Pamphlets: publishing only, not printed on site; Book club, mail order

(G-3855)
CHEROKEE TRANSFER STATION
Aloveit Church Rdd (28719)
PHONE..............................828 497-4519
Bill Reid, *Mgr*
EMP: 5 EST: 2001
SALES (est): 289.32K Privately Held
SIC: 3443 Trash racks, metal plate

(G-3856)
EASTERN BAND CHEROKEE INDIANS
Also Called: Waste Water Treatment Plant
2000 Old #4 Rd (28719)
P.O. Box 547 (28719-0547)
PHONE..............................828 497-6824
Larry Hornbuckle, *Mgr*
EMP: 41
Web: www.cherokeegamingcommission.com
SIC: 3231 Products of purchased glass
PA: Eastern Band Of Cherokee Indians
   88 Council House Loop
   Cherokee NC 28719
   828 497-2771

Cherry Point
Craven County

(G-3857)
NORTHROP GRUMMAN SYSTEMS CORP
Bldg 4280 (28533)
PHONE..............................252 447-7557
EMP: 57
Web: www.northropgrumman.com
SIC: 3812 Search and navigation equipment
HQ: Northrop Grumman Systems Corporation
   2980 Fairview Park Dr
   Falls Church VA 22042
   703 280-2900

(G-3858)
UNITED STATES DEPT OF NAVY
Also Called: Fleet Readiness Center East
Cunningham Bldg 159 (28533)
PHONE..............................252 466-4415
Kathy Rogers, *Brnch Mgr*
EMP: 30
Web: www.navy.mil
SIC: 3728 Aircraft parts and equipment, nec
HQ: United States Department Of The Navy
   1200 Navy Pentagon
   Washington DC 20350

(G-3859)
UNITED STATES DEPT OF NAVY
Also Called: Naval Air Warfare
Av 8b Psc Box 8019 (28533)
PHONE..............................252 466-4514
EMP: 5
Web: www.navy.mil
SIC: 3812 9711 Aircraft/aerospace flight instruments and guidance systems; Navy
HQ: United States Department Of The Navy
   1200 Navy Pentagon
   Washington DC 20350

(G-3860)
UNITED STATES DEPT OF NAVY
Also Called: Air Force Fleet Readiness Ctr
Bldg 137 A St (28533)
PHONE..............................252 464-7228
Mary Beth Fennell, *Brnch Mgr*
EMP: 5
Web: www.navy.mil
SIC: 3721 9711 Aircraft; Navy
HQ: United States Department Of The Navy
   1200 Navy Pentagon
   Washington DC 20350

Cherryville
Gaston County

(G-3861)
1ST CHOICE SERVICE INC
3661 Eaker Rd (28021-9692)
PHONE..............................704 913-7685
Jonathan Watts, *Owner*
EMP: 12 EST: 2009
SALES (est): 2.18MM Privately Held
Web: www.stanleyenviro.com
SIC: 5039 1623 3561 Septic tanks; Sewer line construction; Industrial pumps and parts

(G-3862)
BRADINGTON-YOUNG LLC
Bradington-Young
941 Tot Dellinger Rd (28021-9246)
P.O. Box 9080 (28603-9080)
PHONE..............................276 656-3335
Ding Sconce, *Brnch Mgr*
EMP: 200
SALES (corp-wide): 583.1MM Publicly Held
Web: www.bradington-young.com
SIC: 2512 2511 Upholstered household furniture; Wood household furniture
HQ: Bradington-Young Llc
   4040 10th Avenue Dr Sw
   Hickory NC 28602
   704 435-5881

(G-3863)
CHERRYVILLE DISTRG CO INC
322 E Main St (28021-3411)
P.O. Box 250 (28021-0250)
PHONE..............................704 435-9692
Matthew H Dellinger, *Pr*
Linn Bowen, *Sec*
EMP: 6 EST: 1955
SQ FT: 60,000
SALES (est): 1.02MM Privately Held
Web: www.cherryvilledistributing.com
SIC: 5087 2842 Janitors' supplies; Cleaning or polishing preparations, nec

Cherryville - Gaston County (G-3864)   GEOGRAPHIC SECTION

(G-3864)
CLAR-MAR INC
3912 Tryon Courthouse Rd (28021-8973)
P.O. Box 123 (28021-0123)
PHONE.................704 435-9776
Jim Mc Quaige, *Pr*
Linda Mc Quaige, *
Shannon Henley, *
EMP: 76 **EST:** 1980
SQ FT: 15,000
SALES (est): 1.2MM **Privately Held**
SIC: 2339 Sportswear, women's

(G-3865)
CUSTOM HYDRAULICS & DESIGN (PA)
Also Called: Chd
242 Dick Beam Rd (28021-8943)
PHONE.................704 347-0023
Kelly D Watkins, *Pr*
Kelly D Watkins, *CEO*
Adam Watkins, *
Sherry Watkins, *
▲ **EMP:** 12 **EST:** 1981
SQ FT: 5,500
SALES (est): 10.4MM
SALES (corp-wide): 10.4MM **Privately Held**
Web: www.customhydraulicsdesign.com
SIC: 5084 5085 3492 Hydraulic systems equipment and supplies; Industrial supplies; Hose and tube fittings and assemblies, hydraulic/pneumatic

(G-3866)
CUSTOM METAL FINISHING
617 E Main St B (28021-3416)
PHONE.................704 445-1710
Rick Mullinax, *Owner*
EMP: 4 **EST:** 1992
SALES (est): 208.04K **Privately Held**
SIC: 3471 Electroplating of metals or formed products

(G-3867)
CVC EQUIPMENT COMPANY
Also Called: Cvc & Equipment
316 Old Stubbs Rd Ste 1 (28021-9395)
PHONE.................704 300-6242
EMP: 6 **EST:** 1989
SALES (est): 534.42K **Privately Held**
SIC: 3559 7389 Chemical machinery and equipment; Crane and aerial lift service

(G-3868)
FARRIS FAB & MACHINE INC (PA)
1006 W Academy St (28021-3004)
PHONE.................704 629-4879
Bryan Farris, *Pr*
Greg Farris, *
Corwin E Farris, *Stockholder*
▲ **EMP:** 78 **EST:** 1979
SQ FT: 110,000
SALES (est): 46.34MM
SALES (corp-wide): 46.34MM **Privately Held**
Web: www.farrisfab.com
SIC: 3441 3599 Fabricated structural metal; Machine shop, jobbing and repair

(G-3869)
FREEDOM STEEL WELDING LLC
206 W 4th St (28021-2412)
P.O. Box 1164 (28012-1164)
PHONE.................704 884-1277
EMP: 5 **EST:** 2017
SALES (est): 27.6K **Privately Held**
SIC: 7692 Welding repair

(G-3870)
KEYSTONE POWDERED METAL CO
100 Commerce Dr (28021-8905)
P.O. Box 189 (28021-0189)
PHONE.................704 435-4036
Randy Dacanal, *Mgr*
EMP: 44
SQ FT: 35,000
Web: www.keystonepm.com
SIC: 3399 3568 Paste, metal; Power transmission equipment, nec
HQ: Keystone Powdered Metal Co
251 State St
Saint Marys PA 15857
814 781-1591

(G-3871)
LNS TURBO NORTH AMERICA
242 Dick Beam Rd (28021-8943)
PHONE.................704 435-6376
Terry Dunn, *Pr*
EMP: 5 **EST:** 2015
SALES (est): 139.97K **Privately Held**
SIC: 3545 Machine tool accessories

(G-3872)
MODERN POLYMERS INC
875 W Academy St (28021-3143)
PHONE.................704 435-5825
EMP: 7 **EST:** 1970
SALES (est): 74.88K **Privately Held**
Web: www.modernpolymers.com
SIC: 2821 Plastics materials and resins

(G-3873)
MODERN POLYMERS INC
901 W Academy St (28021-3045)
P.O. Box 398 (28021-0398)
PHONE.................704 435-5825
W Richard Hilliard Senior, *Pr*
Ann Hilliard, *
Jon E Hilliard, *
W R Hilliard Ii, *VP*
Joyce Paysour, *
▼ **EMP:** 35 **EST:** 1970
SQ FT: 67,000
SALES (est): 7.8MM **Privately Held**
Web: www.modernpolymers.com
SIC: 2821 Plastics materials and resins

(G-3874)
PEPSI-COLA METRO BTLG CO INC
Also Called: Pepsi-Cola
152 Commerce Dr (28021-8905)
PHONE.................704 736-2640
Ernest Pharr, *Mgr*
EMP: 50
SQ FT: 44,216
SALES (corp-wide): 86.39B **Publicly Held**
Web: www.pepsico.com
SIC: 2086 Carbonated beverages, nonalcoholic: pkged. in cans, bottles
HQ: Pepsi-Cola Metropolitan Bottling Company, Inc.
700 Anderson Hill Rd
Purchase NY 10577
914 767-6000

(G-3875)
POCONO COATED PRODUCTS LLC
100 Sweetree St (28021-3066)
P.O. Box 303 (08867-0303)
PHONE.................704 445-7891
Susan Myer, *Managing Member*
▼ **EMP:** 6 **EST:** 2004
SQ FT: 15,000
SALES (est): 1.15MM **Privately Held**
Web: www.poconoctd.com
SIC: 2672 Adhesive backed films, foams and foils

(G-3876)
SHEALY DESIGNED WOOD PDTS LLC
101 Cricket Creek Dr (28021-8303)
PHONE.................704 308-9435
EMP: 4 **EST:** 2018
SALES (est): 124.83K **Privately Held**
SIC: 3999 Manufacturing industries, nec

(G-3877)
TAR HEEL CUISINE INC
1009 N Mountain St (28021-2020)
PHONE.................704 435-6979
EMP: 6 **EST:** 2008
SALES (est): 155.31K **Privately Held**
SIC: 2865 Tar

(G-3878)
WRIGHT ELECTRIC INC
3114 Tryon Courthouse Rd (28021-8934)
P.O. Box 815 (28016-0815)
PHONE.................704 435-6988
Jerry Wright, *Pr*
Brandon Wright, *VP*
Deanna Walker, *Sec*
EMP: 5 **EST:** 1974
SALES (est): 465.33K **Privately Held**
Web: www.weflywright.com
SIC: 3643 Current-carrying wiring services

Chimney Rock
Rutherford County

(G-3879)
DOUG BOWMAN GALLERIES
188 Hwy 64-74 (28720)
PHONE.................704 662-5620
Doug Bowman, *CEO*
EMP: 5 **EST:** 2013
SALES (est): 38.07K **Privately Held**
Web: www.therusticlamp.com
SIC: 8412 3645 Art gallery; Boudoir lamps

China Grove
Rowan County

(G-3880)
BOB PEAK ENTERPRISES INC
3550 Patterson Rd (28023-7736)
PHONE.................704 564-0711
EMP: 5 **EST:** 2014
SALES (est): 51.8K **Privately Held**
Web: www.prematech.net
SIC: 3599 Machine shop, jobbing and repair

(G-3881)
CAROLINA SITEWORKS INC
300 Wade Dr (28023-8464)
P.O. Box 280 (28023-0280)
PHONE.................704 855-7483
John D Shell, *Pr*
John J Reilly, *
EMP: 25 **EST:** 1999
SQ FT: 1,000
SALES (est): 4.78MM **Privately Held**
Web: www.carolinasiteworksinc.com
SIC: 1389 Construction, repair, and dismantling services

(G-3882)
DNJ ENGINE COMPONENTS
1450 N Main St (28023-6433)
PHONE.................704 855-5505
EMP: 4 **EST:** 2015
SALES (est): 96.82K **Privately Held**
SIC: 3714 Motor vehicle parts and accessories

(G-3883)
HARWOOD SIGNS
112 Chippewa Trl (28023-9700)
PHONE.................704 857-6203
N Harwood, *Prin*
EMP: 4 **EST:** 2008
SALES (est): 121.99K **Privately Held**
SIC: 3993 Signs, not made in custom sign painting shops

(G-3884)
HITACHI METALS NC LTD
1 Hitachi Metals Dr (28023-9461)
PHONE.................704 855-2800
Luke Koizumi, *Pr*
Mark Stockwell, *Sec*
◆ **EMP:** 150 **EST:** 1989
SQ FT: 480,000
SALES (est): 18.49MM **Privately Held**
SIC: 3264 Magnets, permanent: ceramic or ferrite
HQ: Proterial America, Ltd.
2 Manhattanville Rd # 301
Purchase NY 10577
914 694-9200

(G-3885)
MARTIN MARIETTA MATERIALS INC
Also Called: Martin Marietta Aggregates
2270 China Grove Rd (28023-6629)
PHONE.................704 932-4377
Ronald Borum, *Brnch Mgr*
EMP: 5
Web: www.martinmarietta.com
SIC: 1422 Crushed and broken limestone
PA: Martin Marietta Materials Inc
4123 Parklake Ave
Raleigh NC 27612

(G-3886)
OLD TOWN SOAP CO
104 S Main St (28023-2448)
PHONE.................704 796-8775
Brent Engelhardt, *Managing Member*
EMP: 16 **EST:** 2010
SALES (est): 2.51MM **Privately Held**
Web: www.oldtownsoapco.com
SIC: 5122 2841 Toilet soap; Detergents, synthetic organic or inorganic alkaline

(G-3887)
RITCHIE WOODWORKS
114 S Main St (28023-2448)
PHONE.................980 322-7779
Rusty Ritchie, *Prin*
EMP: 5 **EST:** 2017
SALES (est): 80.45K **Privately Held**
SIC: 2431 Millwork

(G-3888)
ROWAN CUSTOM CABINETS INC
2515 S Us 29 Hwy (28023-9644)
PHONE.................704 855-4778
Jacob C Speck, *Pr*
Judy Speck, *Sec*
Darrell Esrid, *VP*
EMP: 6 **EST:** 2002
SALES (est): 423.04K **Privately Held**
Web: www.rowancustomcabinets.com
SIC: 2434 Wood kitchen cabinets

(G-3889)
RPJ HONEYCUTT MBL DETAIL PRESS
895 Corriher Springs Rd (28023-8772)
PHONE.................704 640-5987
Jerry Honeycutt, *Prin*
EMP: 5 **EST:** 2015
SALES (est): 44.98K **Privately Held**

SIC: 2741 Miscellaneous publishing

(G-3890)
STITCHES IN GROVE
304 Keller St (28023-2481)
PHONE..................704 791-2402
Pauletta Harrington, Prin
EMP: 5 EST: 2017
SALES (est): 74.45K Privately Held
Web: stitches-in-the-grove.business.site
SIC: 2395 Embroidery and art needlework

Chinquapin
Duplin County

(G-3891)
A3-USA INC
1674 Fountaintown Rd (28521-8700)
PHONE..................724 871-7170
Jens Sonntag, VP
EMP: 4 EST: 2009
SALES (est): 436.89K Privately Held
Web: www.a3-usa.com
SIC: 3589 Water treatment equipment, industrial

(G-3892)
DONALDS WELDING INC
1806 S Nc 111 Hwy (28521-8554)
PHONE..................910 298-5234
Donald G Chase, Pr
Brenda Chase, Sec
EMP: 16 EST: 1980
SALES (est): 441.33K Privately Held
SIC: 7692 Welding repair

(G-3893)
RGPACK CONCRETE LLC
1255 Lyman Rd (28521-8607)
PHONE..................919 561-0855
EMP: 5 EST: 2019
SALES (est): 93.77K Privately Held
Web: www.rgpackseal.com
SIC: 2952 Asphalt felts and coatings

Chocowinity
Beaufort County

(G-3894)
ECO MODERN HOMES LLC
509 Bay Lake Dr (27817-9094)
PHONE..................252 833-4335
EMP: 5 EST: 2011
SALES (est): 103.54K Privately Held
Web: www.ecomodernhomes.com
SIC: 2451 Mobile homes

(G-3895)
ICONIC MARINE GROUP LLC (PA)
1653 Whichards Beach Rd (27817-9076)
P.O. Box 457 (27889-0457)
PHONE..................252 975-2000
Tom Klontz, CFO
Jeff Harris, *
EMP: 100 EST: 2016
SQ FT: 248,000
SALES (est): 62.66MM
SALES (corp-wide): 62.66MM Privately Held
Web: www.fountainpowerboats.com
SIC: 3732 5091 Boatbuilding and repairing; Boat accessories and parts

(G-3896)
OBI MACHINE & TOOL INC
411 Patrick Ln (27817)
P.O. Box 326 (27817-0326)
PHONE..................252 946-1580
J C Jenkins, Owner
EMP: 9 EST: 2000
SALES (est): 603.66K Privately Held
SIC: 3549 Metalworking machinery, nec

(G-3897)
SCOTT FORESMAN PUBLISHERS
108 Connecticut Dr (27817-8846)
PHONE..................252 946-7488
Ray Peede, Prin
EMP: 5 EST: 2010
SALES (est): 108.01K Privately Held
SIC: 2741 Miscellaneous publishing

(G-3898)
TAYLOR TIMBER TRANSPORT INC
1977 Old New Bern Rd (27817-8393)
PHONE..................252 943-1550
Barbara Taylor, Pr
James G Taylor, VP
EMP: 9 EST: 1977
SQ FT: 2,400
SALES (est): 1.04MM Privately Held
SIC: 1446 Industrial sand

Claremont
Catawba County

(G-3899)
A KLEIN & CO INC
1 Heart Dr (28610)
P.O. Box 670 (28610-0670)
PHONE..................828 459-9261
FAX: 828 459-9608
EMP: 145
SQ FT: 180,000
SALES (est): 16.97MM Privately Held
SIC: 2652 2657 Setup paperboard boxes; Folding paperboard boxes

(G-3900)
ADVANCEPIERRE FOODS INC
Also Called: Pierre Foods
3437 E Main St (28610-8672)
P.O. Box 399 (28610-0399)
PHONE..................828 459-7626
Ted Karre, Brnch Mgr
EMP: 1527
SALES (corp-wide): 52.88B Publicly Held
Web: www.tysonfoodservice.com
SIC: 2011 2013 2015 2099 Meat packing plants; Frozen meats, from purchased meat; Poultry, processed: frozen; Sandwiches, assembled and packaged: for wholesale market
HQ: Advancepierre Foods, Inc.
9990 Prnceton Glendale Rd
West Chester OH 45246
513 874-8741

(G-3901)
AMERICAN OLYMPUS FIBRGLS CORP
3054 Kelly Blvd (28610-7453)
P.O. Box 953 (28610-0953)
PHONE..................828 459-0444
Michael Douglas Griffin, Pr
Francis Griffin, VP
EMP: 6 EST: 1983
SQ FT: 15,160
SALES (est): 212.98K Privately Held
Web: www.aofcovers.net
SIC: 2221 Fiberglass fabrics

(G-3902)
ARTISTIC WOODWORKS INC
3748 Dericas Ct (28610-8591)
PHONE..................828 459-0178
Gabriel Mladin, Prin
EMP: 6 EST: 2005
SALES (est): 191.82K Privately Held
SIC: 2431 Millwork

(G-3903)
CAROLINA HOUSE FURNITURE INC (PA)
Also Called: Riverbend Frameworks
5485 Herman Rd (28610-9485)
PHONE..................828 459-7400
Dennis Abernathy, Pr
Donna Abernathy, *
▲ EMP: 24 EST: 1975
SQ FT: 22,000
SALES (est): 3.6MM
SALES (corp-wide): 3.6MM Privately Held
Web: www.carolinahousefurniture.com
SIC: 2521 Chairs, office: padded, upholstered, or plain: wood

(G-3904)
CATAWBA FRAMES INC
4827 S Depot St (28610-8549)
P.O. Box 302 (28610-0302)
PHONE..................828 459-7717
John A Bolick, Pr
Mark Bolick, VP
Shirley Bolick, Sec
EMP: 5 EST: 1968
SQ FT: 12,000
SALES (est): 503.9K Privately Held
SIC: 2426 Frames for upholstered furniture, wood

(G-3905)
CENTRO INC
2725 Kelly Blvd (28610-7451)
PHONE..................319 626-3200
Brian Olesen, Brnch Mgr
EMP: 27
SALES (corp-wide): 234.75MM Privately Held
Web: www.centroinc.com
SIC: 3089 Molding primary plastics
PA: Centro, Inc.
1 Centro Way
North Liberty IA 52317
319 626-3200

(G-3906)
CERTAINTEED LLC
2651 Penny Rd (28610-8635)
P.O. Box 760 (28610-0760)
PHONE..................828 459-0556
Denny Riffel, Brnch Mgr
EMP: 101
SALES (corp-wide): 397.78MM Privately Held
Web: www.certainteed.com
SIC: 3089 Siding, plastics
HQ: Certainteed Llc
20 Moores Rd
Malvern PA 19355
610 893-5000

(G-3907)
CLAREMONT PRODUCTS LLC
2932 Bethany Church Rd (28610-9220)
P.O. Box 1270 (28610-1270)
PHONE..................704 325-3580
Joseph Abernethy Junior, Admn
EMP: 5 EST: 2015
SALES (est): 134.21K Privately Held
SIC: 3999 Manufacturing industries, nec

(G-3908)
COMMSCOPE INC NORTH CAROLINA
3565 Centennial Blvd (28610)
PHONE..................828 459-5001
EMP: 9
Web: www.commscope.com
SIC: 3663 Microwave communication equipment
HQ: Commscope, Inc. Of North Carolina
3642 E Us Highway 70
Claremont NC 28610
828 324-2200

(G-3909)
COMMSCOPE INC NORTH CAROLINA (DH)
Also Called: Commscope
3642 E Us Highway 70 (28610-8583)
P.O. Box 1729 (28603-1729)
PHONE..................828 324-2200
Charles L Treadway, Pr
Mark Olson, Ex VP
Randall Crenshaw, Ex VP
Robert Suffern, Sr VP
Morgan Kurk, Sr VP
◆ EMP: 85 EST: 1977
SQ FT: 84,000
SALES (est): 3.92B Publicly Held
Web: www.commscope.com
SIC: 3663 3357 3679 3812 Microwave communication equipment; Communication wire; Waveguides and fittings; Search and navigation equipment
HQ: Commscope, Llc
3642 E Us Highway 70
Claremont NC 28610
828 324-2200

(G-3910)
COMMSCOPE INC NORTH CAROLINA
Also Called: Comm Scope Network
3642 E Us Highway 70 (28610-8583)
PHONE..................828 459-5000
Mike Kelley, Prin
EMP: 800
Web: www.commscope.com
SIC: 3357 1731 Communication wire; Cable television installation
HQ: Commscope, Inc. Of North Carolina
3642 E Us Highway 70
Claremont NC 28610
828 324-2200

(G-3911)
COMMSCOPE LLC (HQ)
Also Called: Commscope, Inc.
3642 E Us Highway 70 (28610-8583)
PHONE..................828 324-2200
Charles L Treadway, Pr
EMP: 129 EST: 1997
SALES (est): 3.92B Publicly Held
Web: www.commscope.com
SIC: 3663 4899 Radio and t.v. communications equipment; Communication signal enhancement network services
PA: Commscope Holding Company, Inc.
3642 E Us Highway 70
Claremont NC 28610

(G-3912)
COMMSCOPE CONNECTIVITY LLC (HQ)
3642 E Us Highway 70 (28610-8583)
PHONE..................828 324-2200
Marvin S Edwards Junior, CEO
Michael D Coppin, *
EMP: 50 EST: 1953
SALES (est): 450.03MM Publicly Held
Web: www.commscope.com
SIC: 3663 Radio and t.v. communications equipment
PA: Commscope Holding Company, Inc.

Claremont - Catawba County (G-3913) — GEOGRAPHIC SECTION

3642 E Us Highway 70
Claremont NC 28610

(G-3913)
COMMSCOPE HOLDING COMPANY INC (PA)
Also Called: COMMSCOPE
3642 E Us Highway 70 (28610-8583)
PHONE.................................828 459-5000
EMP: 770 **EST:** 1976
SALES (est): 5.79B **Publicly Held**
Web: www.commscope.com
SIC: 3663 4899 Radio and t.v. communications equipment; Communication signal enhancement network services

(G-3914)
COMMSCOPE INTL HOLDINGS LLC
3642 E Us Highway 70 (28610-8583)
PHONE.................................828 324-2200
EMP: 44 **EST:** 2010
SALES (est): 22.95MM **Publicly Held**
Web: www.commscope.com
SIC: 3663 Radio and t.v. communications equipment
HQ: Commscope, Inc. Of North Carolina
3642 E Us Highway 70
Claremont NC 28610
828 324-2200

(G-3915)
COMMSCOPE TECHNOLOGIES FIN LLC
3642 E Us Highway 70 (28610-8583)
PHONE.................................828 323-4970
EMP: 15 **EST:** 2015
SALES (est): 470.98K **Privately Held**
Web: www.commscope.com
SIC: 3663 Radio and t.v. communications equipment

(G-3916)
COMMSCOPE TECHNOLOGIES LLC
3642 E Us Highway 70 (28610-8583)
PHONE.................................828 324-2200
EMP: 1500
Web: www.commscope.com
SIC: 3661 3357 3643 8999 Telephones and telephone apparatus; Communication wire; Connectors and terminals for electrical devices; Communication services
HQ: Commscope Technologies Llc
4 Westbrook Corp Ctr
Westchester IL 60154
800 366-3891

(G-3917)
CRWW SPECIALTY COMPOSITES INC
2678 Heart Dr Bldg B (28610-8715)
P.O. Box 1087 (28610-1087)
PHONE.................................828 548-5002
Craig Girdwood, *Pr*
EMP: 15 **EST:** 2018
SQ FT: 20,000
SALES (est): 1.92MM **Privately Held**
Web: www.crwwassociates.com
SIC: 3357 Fiber optic cable (insulated)

(G-3918)
D & S FRAMES INC
1309 Shiloh Rd (28610-9236)
PHONE.................................828 241-5962
EMP: 5 **EST:** 1991
SALES (est): 217.66K **Privately Held**
SIC: 2426 Furniture stock and parts, hardwood

(G-3919)
DEXTER INC
Also Called: Livin' Rooms
5718 Oxford School Rd (28610-9437)
PHONE.................................828 459-7904
Gene Setzer, *Mgr*
EMP: 5
SALES (corp-wide): 1.1MM **Privately Held**
Web: www.dexterfurniture.com
SIC: 2512 Upholstered household furniture
PA: Dexter, Inc.
8411 Glenwood Ave Ste 101
Raleigh NC 27612
919 510-5050

(G-3920)
DIMENSION WOOD PRODUCTS INC
2885 Kelly Blvd (28610-7473)
P.O. Box 70 (28610-0070)
PHONE.................................828 459-9891
David Wayne-reinhardt, *Pr*
David Wayne Reinhardt, *
Karen Reinhardt, *
EMP: 12 **EST:** 1981
SQ FT: 20,000
SALES (est): 949.43K **Privately Held**
Web: www.dimensionwoodproducts.com
SIC: 2426 Carvings, furniture: wood

(G-3921)
DRAKA COMMUNICATIONS AMERICAS INC
Also Called: Draka Communication
2512 Penny Rd (28610-8634)
P.O. Box 39 (28610-0039)
PHONE.................................828 459-8456
▲ **EMP:** 500
SIC: 3357 Coaxial cable, nonferrous

(G-3922)
DRAKA HOLDINGS USA INC
Also Called: Prysmian Cables & Systems USA
2512 Penny Rd (28610-8634)
PHONE.................................828 383-0020
▲ **EMP:** 1130
SIC: 3357 Communication wire

(G-3923)
DRAKA TRANSPORT USA LLC
2512 Penny Rd (28610-8634)
PHONE.................................828 459-8895
EMP: 4 **EST:** 2007
SALES (est): 1.19MM **Privately Held**
SIC: 3357 Automotive wire and cable, except ignition sets: nonferrous
HQ: Prysmian Cables And Systems Usa, Llc
4 Tesseneer Dr
Highland Heights KY 41076
859 572-8000

(G-3924)
DRAKA USA INC
2512 Penny Rd (28610-8634)
PHONE.................................828 459-9787
EMP: 13 **EST:** 2011
SALES (est): 418.5K **Privately Held**
SIC: 3357 Nonferrous wiredrawing and insulating

(G-3925)
DYNAMIC AIR ENGINEERING INC
Also Called: Dae Systems
2421 Bga Dr (28610-9253)
PHONE.................................714 540-1000
Sharon C Morrison, *CEO*
Jeremy I Morrison, *
EMP: 43 **EST:** 1942
SQ FT: 45,000
SALES (est): 8.34MM **Privately Held**
Web: www.dynamic-air.co.uk
SIC: 3564 3585 Blowers and fans; Air conditioning units, complete: domestic or industrial

(G-3926)
EZ FABRICATION INC
5882 Crescent Dr (28610-9499)
PHONE.................................828 674-0661
Christopher Edward Hinds, *Prin*
EMP: 5 **EST:** 2019
SALES (est): 61.33K **Privately Held**
SIC: 7692 Welding repair

(G-3927)
FROSTIE BOTTOM TREE STAND LLC
Also Called: Frostie Bottom At Doors
3280 Yount Rd (28610-9524)
PHONE.................................828 466-1708
Shon Kale, *CEO*
Kisha Morrison, *Pr*
EMP: 7 **EST:** 2012
SALES (est): 396.35K **Privately Held**
Web: www.frostiebottom.com
SIC: 3949 7389 Hunting equipment; Business Activities at Non-Commercial Site

(G-3928)
GRAM FURNITURE
4513 Nc Highway 10 E (28610-8241)
PHONE.................................828 241-2836
EMP: 8
SALES (est): 90K **Privately Held**
SIC: 2531 2511 Church furniture; Wood bedroom furniture

(G-3929)
HARRISON MARTHA PRINT STUDIO
4010 Carlton Dr (28610-9649)
PHONE.................................949 290-8630
Martha Harrison, *Prin*
EMP: 5 **EST:** 2011
SALES (est): 75.08K **Privately Held**
SIC: 2752 Commercial printing, lithographic

(G-3930)
IREDELL HOLDING LLC
3724 Bunker Hill School Rd (28610-9454)
PHONE.................................828 506-2555
Charles Robert Bridges, *Prin*
EMP: 5 **EST:** 2019
SALES (est): 151.86K **Privately Held**
SIC: 2711 Newspapers, publishing and printing

(G-3931)
MCKINLEY LEATHER HICKORY INC
3131 W Main St (28610-9609)
P.O. Box 1030 (28610-1030)
PHONE.................................828 459-2884
Lewis Mitchell, *Pr*
Denise Mitchell, *
Lori M Shadowski, *
◆ **EMP:** 24 **EST:** 1989
SQ FT: 38,785
SALES (est): 2.85MM **Privately Held**
Web: www.mckinleyleatherfurniture.com
SIC: 3172 2512 Personal leather goods, nec ; Upholstered household furniture

(G-3932)
POPPELMANN PLASTICS USA
4436 Old Catawba Rd (28610)
PHONE.................................828 466-9500
EMP: 6 **EST:** 2019
SALES (est): 140K **Privately Held**
Web: www.poeppelmann.com

SIC: 3714 Motor vehicle parts and accessories

(G-3933)
POPPELMANN PLASTICS USA LLC
2180 Heart Dr (28610-8708)
P.O. Box 459 (28610-0459)
PHONE.................................828 466-9500
Jack Dempsey Shelton, *Managing Member*
Thomas Orr, *
◆ **EMP:** 35 **EST:** 2004
SALES (est): 14.61MM
SALES (corp-wide): 355.83K **Privately Held**
Web: www.poeppelmann.com
SIC: 2821 Plastics materials and resins
HQ: Poppelmann Gmbh & Co. Kg
Kunststoffwerk-Werkzeugbau
Bakumer Str. 73
Lohne (Oldenburg) NI 49393
44429820

(G-3934)
POPPELMANN PROPERTIES USA LLC
2180 Heart Dr (28610-8708)
PHONE.................................828 466-9500
Guido Schmidt, *Managing Member*
▲ **EMP:** 8 **EST:** 2004
SALES (est): 146.66K **Privately Held**
SIC: 3089 Air mattresses, plastics

(G-3935)
PROGRESSIVE FURNITURE INC
2555 Penny Rd (28610-8634)
P.O. Box 729 (28610-0729)
PHONE.................................828 459-2151
Ban Kendrick, *Prin*
EMP: 175
SALES (corp-wide): 489.89MM **Privately Held**
Web: www.progressivefurniture.com
SIC: 2511 Tables, household: wood
HQ: Progressive Furniture, Inc.
502 Middle St
Archbold OH 43502
419 446-4500

(G-3936)
REGENCY FIBERS LLC
2788 S Oxford St (28610)
PHONE.................................828 459-7645
James Julius Bush Junior, *Managing Member*
EMP: 36 **EST:** 2019
SALES (est): 2.6MM **Privately Held**
Web: www.regencyfibers.com
SIC: 2299 Batting, wadding, padding and fillings

(G-3937)
RESTAURANT FURNITURE INC
2688 E Us Highway 70 (28610-8674)
PHONE.................................828 459-9992
Ernest Baldwin, *Pr*
EMP: 10 **EST:** 1994
SQ FT: 20,000
SALES (est): 721.63K **Privately Held**
Web: www.restaurantfurnitureindustries.com
SIC: 2599 5046 2512 Restaurant furniture, wood or metal; Commercial cooking and food service equipment; Upholstered household furniture

(G-3938)
ROSENDAHL NEXTROM USA INC
4260 Nc Highway 10 E (28610-8325)
PHONE.................................828 464-2543
Mickey R Reynolds, *Pr*
Jouni Heinonen, *Ch*

GEOGRAPHIC SECTION
Clayton - Johnston County (G-3962)

Robert Perry, Contrlr
▲ **EMP:** 12 **EST:** 1975
SALES (est): 3.7MM
SALES (corp-wide): 168.46MM **Privately Held**
Web: www.rosendahlnextrom.com
SIC: 3549 Metalworking machinery, nec
HQ: Rosendahl Nextrom Oy
Ensimmainen Savu 2
Vantaa 01510

(G-3939)
SUBSTANCE INCORPORATED
3000 Frazier Dr (28610-8631)
PHONE................800 985-9485
EMP: 10 **EST:** 2012
SALES (est): 424.92K **Privately Held**
Web: www.substance.com
SIC: 2759 Commercial printing, nec

(G-3940)
SUTTER STREET MANUFACTURING
Also Called: Sutter Street
2973 Kelly Blvd (28610-7454)
PHONE................828 459-5598
Eric Fulcher, VP
Hank Engert, *
▲ **EMP:** 120 **EST:** 2007
SQ FT: 152,000
SALES (est): 24.53MM
SALES (corp-wide): 8.67B **Publicly Held**
SIC: 2511 Wood household furniture
PA: Williams-Sonoma, Inc.
3250 Van Ness Ave
San Francisco CA 94109
415 421-7900

(G-3941)
UNIVERSAL FURNITURE INTL INC
Also Called: Catawba Plant
4436 Old Catawba Rd (28610)
P.O. Box 160 (28610-0160)
PHONE................828 241-3191
Ron Young, Mgr
EMP: 5
Web: www.universalfurniture.com
SIC: 2511 2512 Wood household furniture; Upholstered household furniture
HQ: Universal Furniture International Inc.
2575 Penny Rd
High Point NC 27265
336 822-8425

(G-3942)
VEXTRA TECHNOLOGIES LLC
3642 E Us Highway 70 (28610-8530)
P.O. Box 520 (28610-0520)
PHONE................828 464-4419
Dale Sherrill, Pr
EMP: 6 **EST:** 2010
SALES (est): 215.64K **Privately Held**
Web: www.vextratech.com
SIC: 3663 Radio and t.v. communications equipment

(G-3943)
WESTROCK COMPANY
2690 Kelly Blvd (28610-7427)
PHONE................470 484-1183
EMP: 5
SALES (corp-wide): 20.31B **Publicly Held**
Web: www.westrock.com
SIC: 2653 Boxes, corrugated: made from purchased materials
PA: Westrock Company
1000 Abernathy Rd
Atlanta GA 30328
770 448-2193

(G-3944)
WESTROCK RKT LLC
2690 Kelly Blvd (28610-7427)
PHONE................828 459-8006
Martin Szalay, Mgr
EMP: 121
SALES (corp-wide): 20.31B **Publicly Held**
Web: www.westrock.com
SIC: 2657 2652 Folding paperboard boxes; Setup paperboard boxes
HQ: Westrock Rkt, Llc
1000 Abernathy Rd Ste 125
Atlanta GA 30328
770 448-2193

(G-3945)
WHITESIDE MCH & REPR CO INC
Also Called: Whiteside Machine Co
4506 Shook Rd (28610-8612)
PHONE................828 459-2141
William Whiteside, Pr
Mike Whiteside, *
Lark Whiteside, *
Barbara Whiteside, *
Lori W Garrett, *
▼ **EMP:** 45 **EST:** 1970
SQ FT: 44,000
SALES (est): 5.53MM **Privately Held**
Web: www.whitesiderouterbits.com
SIC: 3541 Machine tools, metal cutting type

Clarendon
Columbus County

(G-3946)
GTG ENGINEERING INC
768 Furnie Hammond Rd (28432-9017)
PHONE................877 569-8572
EMP: 5 **EST:** 2002
SALES (est): 50.32K **Privately Held**
Web: www.gtgengineering.com
SIC: 2899 Chemical preparations, nec

(G-3947)
GTG ENGINEERING INC (PA)
Also Called: Gtg Engineering
766 Furnie Hammond Rd (28432-9017)
P.O. Box 11182 (28461-1182)
PHONE................877 569-8572
Michael Leblanc, Pr
◆ **EMP:** 5 **EST:** 2001
SALES (est): 1.41MM
SALES (corp-wide): 1.41MM **Privately Held**
Web: www.gtgengineering.com
SIC: 2899 Insulating compounds

Clarkton
Bladen County

(G-3948)
SACHS PEANUTS LLC
9323 Hwy 70 (28433)
P.O. Box 7 (28433-0007)
PHONE................910 647-4711
EMP: 19 **EST:** 2010
SALES (est): 1.73MM **Privately Held**
Web: www.sachspeanuts.com
SIC: 5441 2068 Nuts; Nuts: dried, dehydrated, salted or roasted

Clayton
Johnston County

(G-3949)
316 PRINT COMPANY LLC
121 Palmer Dr (27527-7540)
PHONE................919 454-6906
Margarito Fernandez, Prin
EMP: 4 **EST:** 2018
SALES (est): 107.71K **Privately Held**
Web: www.316printco.com
SIC: 2323 Men's and boy's neckwear

(G-3950)
A PLUS FIVE STAR TRNSP LLC
301 Mccarthy Dr (27527-5795)
PHONE................919 771-4820
Charles Burroughs, Pr
EMP: 6 **EST:** 2015
SALES (est): 243.41K **Privately Held**
SIC: 3999 4212 Manufacturing industries, nec; Dump truck haulage

(G-3951)
AA WELDING AND FABRICATIO
1012 Ridge Dr (27520-9667)
PHONE................919 272-5433
EMP: 4 **EST:** 2019
SALES (est): 25.09K **Privately Held**
SIC: 7692 Welding repair

(G-3952)
ADC INDUSTRIES INC
Also Called: Automated Entrances
106 N Lombard St (27520-2544)
PHONE................919 550-9515
Ken Fisher, Mgr
EMP: 6
SALES (corp-wide): 4.97MM **Privately Held**
Web: www.airlockdoor.com
SIC: 3491 Valves, automatic control
PA: Adc Industries Inc.
181a E Jamaica Ave
Valley Stream NY 11580
516 596-1304

(G-3953)
ANGLERS MARINE NC
13578 Us 70 Business Hwy W (27520-2142)
PHONE................919 585-7900
EMP: 5 **EST:** 2019
SALES (est): 77.36K **Privately Held**
Web: www.anglersmarinenc.com
SIC: 7539 5551 3732 Automotive repair shops, nec; Boat dealers; Boatbuilding and repairing

(G-3954)
AP GRANITE INSTALLATION LLC
2213 Stephanie Ln (27520-8407)
PHONE................919 215-1795
Abel Salas Perea, Pr
EMP: 8 **EST:** 2016
SALES (est): 329.44K **Privately Held**
SIC: 1799 2541 Counter top installation; Counter and sink tops

(G-3955)
ARBOLES NC INCORPORATED
Also Called: Appalachian Truss
228 Sicily Dr (27527-9229)
PHONE................828 675-4882
Kevin Birkmayer, Pr
EMP: 13 **EST:** 2019
SALES (est): 795.16K **Privately Held**
Web: www.appalachiantruss.com
SIC: 3448 Trusses and framing, prefabricated metal

(G-3956)
ASHBRAN LLC
700 Parkridge Dr (27527-5304)
PHONE................919 215-3567
▲ **EMP:** 5 **EST:** 2009
SALES (est): 256.84K **Privately Held**
Web: www.ashbran.com
SIC: 3679 3621 Commutators, electronic; Sliprings, for motors or generators

(G-3957)
BAKER THERMAL SOLUTIONS LLC
Also Called: Turkington
8182 Us 70 Bus Hwy W (27520-9463)
PHONE................919 674-3750
Clive Tolson, Pr
John Rollins, VP Fin
▲ **EMP:** 50 **EST:** 2012
SALES (est): 17.5MM
SALES (corp-wide): 4.04B **Publicly Held**
Web: www.bakerthermal.com
SIC: 3556 Bakery machinery
PA: The Middleby Corporation
1400 Toastmaster Dr
Elgin IL 60120
847 741-3300

(G-3958)
BATISTA GRADING INC
710 E Main St (27520-2626)
PHONE................919 359-3449
Carlos Batista Junior, Pr
Carlos Batista, *
Connie Batista, Sec
EMP: 15 **EST:** 2001
SALES (est): 2.09MM **Privately Held**
Web: www.bgsus.com
SIC: 1611 1795 3532 1623 Surfacing and paving; Demolition, buildings and other structures; Crushing, pulverizing, and screening equipment; Underground utilities contractor

(G-3959)
BLACKLEYS PRINTING CO
Also Called: Blackleys Printing & Sign Shop
229 E Main St (27520-2449)
PHONE................919 553-6813
Joyce Blackley, Owner
EMP: 5 **EST:** 1974
SALES (est): 423.76K **Privately Held**
Web: www.blackleysprinting.com
SIC: 2752 Offset printing

(G-3960)
BLF PRESS LLC
370 Sugarberry Ln (27527-9409)
PHONE................706 442-1154
EMP: 4 **EST:** 2016
SALES (est): 50.03K **Privately Held**
SIC: 2741 Miscellaneous publishing

(G-3961)
CAROLINA WOODCRAFT LLC
325 Old York Cir (27527-4294)
PHONE................919 585-2563
Michael J Smith, Prin
EMP: 7 **EST:** 2016
SALES (est): 105K **Privately Held**
Web: www.woodcraft.com
SIC: 2511 Wood household furniture

(G-3962)
CARPATHIAN WOODWORKS INC
46 Albemarle Dr (27527-4210)
PHONE................919 669-7546
Paul Mcdonald, Owner

Clayton - Johnston County (G-3963) GEOGRAPHIC SECTION

EMP: 5 EST: 2011
SALES (est): 231.69K **Privately Held**
Web: www.carpathianwoodworks.com
SIC: 2431 Millwork

(G-3963)
CATERPILLAR INC
Also Called: Caterpillar
954 Nc Highway 42 E (27527-8078)
PHONE...........................919 550-1100
John Carpenter, *Brnch Mgr*
EMP: 59
SALES (corp-wide): 67.06B **Publicly Held**
Web: www.caterpillar.com
SIC: 3531 3594 3553 Loaders, shovel: self-propelled; Fluid power pumps and motors; Woodworking machinery
PA: Caterpillar Inc.
 5205 N Ocnnor Blvd Ste 10
 Irving TX 75039
 972 891-7700

(G-3964)
CCBCC OPERATIONS LLC
Also Called: Coca-Cola
977 Shotwell Rd Ste 104 (27520-5126)
PHONE...........................919 359-2966
Tim Kelley, *Mgr*
EMP: 68
SQ FT: 62,500
SALES (corp-wide): 6.65B **Publicly Held**
Web: www.coca-cola.com
SIC: 2086 Bottled and canned soft drinks
HQ: Ccbcc Operations, Llc
 4100 Coca Cola Plz
 Charlotte NC 28211
 704 364-8728

(G-3965)
CENTER FOR ORTHOTIC & PROSTHET
166 Springbrook Ave Ste 203 (27520-8520)
PHONE...........................919 585-4173
Donald Dixon, *CEO*
EMP: 70
SALES (corp-wide): 1.12B **Privately Held**
Web: www.hangerclinic.com
SIC: 3842 Limbs, artificial
HQ: Center For Orthotic & Prosthetic Care
 Of North Carolina, Inc.
 4702 Creekstone Dr
 Durham NC 27703
 919 797-1230

(G-3966)
CHAINED DRAGON LLC
70 Plott Hound Dr (27520-7387)
P.O. Box 1706 (27528-1706)
PHONE...........................919 243-0974
Lorelei J Logsdon, *Mgr*
EMP: 7 EST: 2018
SALES (est): 244.08K **Privately Held**
SIC: 2741 Miscellaneous publishing

(G-3967)
CITGO QUIK LUBE OF CLAYTON
11133 Us 70 Business Hwy W
(27520-2369)
PHONE...........................919 550-0935
Tim Matthews, *Pr*
EMP: 9 EST: 1996
SALES (est): 838.89K **Privately Held**
SIC: 2992 Lubricating oils

(G-3968)
COCA-COLA CONSOLIDATED INC
Also Called: Coca-Cola
977 Shotwell Rd Ste 104 (27520-5126)
PHONE...........................919 550-0611
Cola Coca, *Brnch Mgr*
EMP: 103

SALES (corp-wide): 6.65B **Publicly Held**
Web: www.cokeconsolidated.com
SIC: 5962 5149 2086 Merchandising machine operators; Beverages, except coffee and tea; Bottled and canned soft drinks
PA: Coca-Cola Consolidated, Inc.
 4100 Coca Cola Plz # 100
 Charlotte NC 28211
 704 557-4400

(G-3969)
CORNERSTONE CUSTOM PRINTI
149 Claire Dr (27520-5539)
PHONE...........................919 524-7420
Brian Light, *Pr*
EMP: 8 EST: 2014
SALES (est): 890.11K **Privately Held**
Web: www.cornerstonecustomprinting.com
SIC: 2752 Offset printing

(G-3970)
CRAIGSCABINET
107 Holder Cir (27527-6678)
PHONE...........................919 219-3970
Christopher Jovino, *Prin*
EMP: 5 EST: 2010
SALES (est): 101.19K **Privately Held**
SIC: 2434 Wood kitchen cabinets

(G-3971)
D M F INCORPORATED
Also Called: Davidson Machine Fabrication
5335 Us 70 Bus Hwy W (27520-6812)
PHONE...........................919 553-5191
William F Davidson, *Pr*
Doris Davidson, *Sec*
EMP: 6 EST: 1975
SQ FT: 5,500
SALES (est): 537.44K **Privately Held**
SIC: 3441 Fabricated structural metal

(G-3972)
DAMSEL IN DEFENSE
109 Lake Point Dr (27527-5217)
PHONE...........................919 744-8776
EMP: 14 EST: 2014
SALES (est): 138.88K **Privately Held**
Web: www.damselindefense.net
SIC: 3812 Defense systems and equipment

(G-3973)
DAYCO MANUFACTURING INC
6116 Us 70 W (27520-6312)
PHONE...........................919 989-1820
Mitch Day, *Prin*
EMP: 14 EST: 2007
SALES (est): 2.2MM **Privately Held**
Web: www.daycomanufacturing.com
SIC: 3599 Machine shop, jobbing and repair

(G-3974)
DEW GROUP ENTERPRISES INC
Also Called: C G P
501 Atkinson St (27520-2155)
P.O. Box 129 (27528-0129)
PHONE...........................919 585-0100
▼ EMP: 25 EST: 1988
SALES (est): 7.61MM **Privately Held**
Web: www.cgplabels.com
SIC: 2752 Offset printing
HQ: Sml (Hong Kong) Limited
 6/F C-Bons Intl Ctr
 Kwun Tong KLN

(G-3975)
EDGE PROMO TEAM LLC
7868 Us 70 Bus Hwy W Ste B
(27520-5008)

PHONE...........................919 946-4218
Theodore Ormsby, *Admn*
EMP: 16 EST: 2014
SALES (est): 3.42MM **Privately Held**
Web: www.edgepromoteam.com
SIC: 2759 Screen printing

(G-3976)
EDWARDS ELECTRONIC SYSTEMS INC (DH)
3821 Powhatan Rd (27520-9235)
P.O. Box 39 (27528-0039)
PHONE...........................919 359-2239
Jim Devries, *CEO*
EMP: 30 EST: 1997
SQ FT: 6,500
SALES (est): 14.55MM
SALES (corp-wide): 4.98B **Publicly Held**
Web: www.everonsolutions.com
SIC: 1731 1711 5065 5063 Sound equipment specialization; Fire sprinkler system installation; Security control equipment and systems; Fire alarm systems
HQ: Adt Commercial Llc
 1501 W Yamato Rd
 Boca Raton FL 33431
 877 387-0188

(G-3977)
EXIDE TECHNOLOGIES LLC
104 N Tech Dr (27520-5002)
PHONE...........................919 553-3578
Kim Parrish, *Mgr*
EMP: 5
SALES (corp-wide): 2.06B **Privately Held**
Web: www.exide.com
SIC: 5063 3629 Batteries; Battery chargers, rectifying or nonrotating
PA: Exide Technologies, Llc
 13000 Drfeld Pkwy Bldg 20
 Milton GA 30004
 678 566-9000

(G-3978)
FRAZIER HOLDINGS LLC
2009 Pope Ct (27520-8217)
PHONE...........................919 868-8651
EMP: 4 EST: 2008
SQ FT: 2,000
SALES (est): 499.63K **Privately Held**
SIC: 2522 Office furniture, except wood

(G-3979)
FULL CIRCLE GRINDING LLC
209 Clearwater Ct (27520-7832)
PHONE...........................919 879-9529
Brent Coor, *Prin*
EMP: 4 EST: 2018
SALES (est): 44.79K **Privately Held**
Web: www.fullcirclegrinding.com
SIC: 3999 Grinding and pulverizing of materials, nec

(G-3980)
GENERAL PRECISION SVC
321 E Main St (27520-2463)
P.O. Box 746 (27528-0746)
PHONE...........................919 553-2604
Larry E Belvin, *Owner*
Judy Belvin, *Mgr*
EMP: 4 EST: 1980
SQ FT: 6,000
SALES (est): 285.48K **Privately Held**
SIC: 3599 Machine shop, jobbing and repair

(G-3981)
GENIE TRCKING SLTONS LBELS LLC
111 Neuse Ridge Dr (27527-6604)
PHONE...........................919 201-2600
Amanda Dew, *Pr*
EMP: 5 EST: 2016

SALES (est): 356.77K **Privately Held**
SIC: 2679 Tags and labels, paper

(G-3982)
GRACE CONSTRUCTION & GLASS
671 Jack Rd (27520-6120)
PHONE...........................919 805-8380
EMP: 4 EST: 2017
SALES (est): 39.74K **Privately Held**
SIC: 3211 Construction glass

(G-3983)
GRIFOLS INC
8368 Us 70 Bus Hwy W (27520-9464)
PHONE...........................919 553-5011
Gregory Gene Rich, *CEO*
David Bell, *
EMP: 72 EST: 2003
SALES (est): 15.59MM **Privately Held**
Web: www.grifols.com
SIC: 2834 Pharmaceutical preparations

(G-3984)
GRIFOLS THERAPEUTICS LLC
Also Called: Grifols
9257 Us 70 Bus Hwy W Ste B-302
(27520-9461)
PHONE...........................919 359-7069
Gregory Rich, *Managing Member*
EMP: 99
Web: www.grifols.com
SIC: 2834 Pharmaceutical preparations
HQ: Grifols Therapeutics Llc
 79 Tw Alexander Dr
 Durham NC 27709

(G-3985)
GRIFOLS THERAPEUTICS LLC
8368 Us 70 Bus Hwy W (27520-9464)
PHONE...........................919 553-0172
Rich Gregory, *Brnch Mgr*
EMP: 155
Web: www.discovertheplasma.com
SIC: 2834 Pharmaceutical preparations
HQ: Grifols Therapeutics Llc
 79 Tw Alexander Dr
 Durham NC 27709

(G-3986)
HARDWARE VENTURES INC
213 Ryans Ln (27520-5544)
PHONE...........................919 818-9039
EMP: 6 EST: 2019
SALES (est): 226.81K **Privately Held**
Web: www.hardwareventures.com
SIC: 3429 Hardware, nec

(G-3987)
HEALTH EDUCATOR PUBLICATIONS
476 Shotwell Rd Ste 102 (27520-3506)
PHONE...........................919 243-1299
Dana F Oakes, *Prin*
EMP: 7 EST: 2016
SALES (est): 109.62K **Privately Held**
SIC: 2741 Miscellaneous publishing

(G-3988)
HOSPIRA INC
8484 Us 70 Bus Hwy W (27520-9465)
PHONE...........................919 553-3831
Tom Ludke, *Mgr*
EMP: 331
SALES (corp-wide): 100.33B **Publicly Held**
Web: www.pfizerhospitalus.com
SIC: 2869 2899 2834 Amines, acids, salts, esters; Chemical products, nec; Pharmaceutical preparations
HQ: Hospira, Inc.
 275 N Field Dr

GEOGRAPHIC SECTION
Clayton - Johnston County (G-4015)

Lake Forest IL 60045
224 212-2000

(G-3989)
IF TEES COULD TALK LLC
549 E Main St (27520-2621)
PHONE..................................919 938-8031
Jon Owens, *Mgr*
EMP: 4 **EST:** 2017
SALES (est): 91.04K **Privately Held**
Web: www.teestalk2u.com
SIC: 2759 Screen printing

(G-3990)
J & D THORPE ENTERPRISES INC
Also Called: Sign-A-Rama
116 Shady Meadow Ln (27520-6404)
PHONE..................................919 553-0918
James L Thorpe, *Pr*
Dolores A Thorpe, *VP*
EMP: 5 **EST:** 2011
SQ FT: 2,600
SALES (est): 366.87K **Privately Held**
Web: www.signarama.com
SIC: 3993 5999 Signs and advertising specialties; Banners, flags, decals, and posters

(G-3991)
KARWIN TECHNOLOGIES INC
2012 Briarwood Cir (27520-9141)
PHONE..................................919 612-3974
Raymond Chan, *VP*
EMP: 4 **EST:** 2019
SALES (est): 108.1K **Privately Held**
SIC: 3571 Electronic computers

(G-3992)
LASH OUT INC
117 Georgetowne Dr (27520-1846)
PHONE..................................919 342-0221
Amy Lynn Rhoden, *Prin*
EMP: 5 **EST:** 2012
SALES (est): 65.48K **Privately Held**
Web: www.lashoutpro.com
SIC: 2844 Face creams or lotions

(G-3993)
LEWIS BROTHERS TIRE & ALGNMT
451 E Main St (27520-2528)
PHONE..................................919 359-9050
Michael Lewis, *Owner*
EMP: 6 **EST:** 2004
SALES (est): 423.02K **Privately Held**
SIC: 7538 7534 General automotive repair shops; Tire repair shop

(G-3994)
M D PREVATT INC
338 Winding Oak Way (27520-8025)
PHONE..................................919 796-4944
Michael Prevatt, *Pr*
EMP: 10 **EST:** 2000
SALES (est): 757.38K **Privately Held**
SIC: 1389 Construction, repair, and dismantling services

(G-3995)
MAGNEVOLT INC
5335 Us 70 Bus Hwy W (27520-6812)
P.O. Box 58099 (27658-8099)
PHONE..................................919 553-2202
William Davidson, *Ch Bd*
EMP: 10 **EST:** 1985
SQ FT: 5,600
SALES (est): 887.1K **Privately Held**
Web: www.magnevolt.com
SIC: 3691 Storage batteries

(G-3996)
MINNIE ME MONOGRAMS INC
104 Hibiscus Dr (27527-8714)
PHONE..................................919 243-8367
Jeremy Hopkins, *Owner*
EMP: 5 **EST:** 2017
SALES (est): 85.33K **Privately Held**
SIC: 2395 Embroidery and art needlework

(G-3997)
MM CLAYTON LLC
Also Called: 3c Packaging LLC
1000 Ccc Dr (27520-8015)
PHONE..................................919 553-4113
John Cullen, *Pr*
Sparky Cullen, *
William Karstenson, *
EMP: 324 **EST:** 1979
SQ FT: 70,000
SALES (est): 62.1MM
SALES (corp-wide): 4.86B **Privately Held**
Web: www.3cpackaging.com
SIC: 5199 2655 Packaging materials; Ammunition cans or tubes, board laminated with metal foil
HQ: Mm Packaging Us Inc.
2 Westbrook Corp Ctr
Westchester IL 60154

(G-3998)
MONARCH EDUCATIONAL SVCS LLC
309 Collinsworth Dr (27527-3936)
PHONE..................................910 785-4087
Jennifer Lowry, *Owner*
EMP: 5 **EST:** 2018
SALES (est): 99.17K **Privately Held**
Web: www.monarcheducationalservices.com
SIC: 2741 Miscellaneous publishing

(G-3999)
MRSCHIS STICKER N TEES
2690 Polenta Rd (27520-9782)
PHONE..................................919 606-1940
Rikki Chiofalo, *Prin*
EMP: 4 **EST:** 2017
SALES (est): 98.74K **Privately Held**
SIC: 2759 Screen printing

(G-4000)
MULTI TECHNICAL SERVICES INC
Also Called: MTS Communication Products
950 Nc Highway 42 W (27520-7434)
PHONE..................................919 553-2995
Lnywood A Williams, *Pr*
Lynwood A Williams, *Pr*
▲ **EMP:** 7 **EST:** 1988
SQ FT: 15,000
SALES (est): 544.35K **Privately Held**
SIC: 3663 8711 3823 3651 Radio and t.v. communications equipment; Engineering services; Process control instruments; Household audio and video equipment

(G-4001)
NOBLE WHOLESALERS INC
Also Called: Youshirt
356 Trenburg Pl (27520-9241)
PHONE..................................409 739-3803
Ugur Soylu, *Pr*
EMP: 6 **EST:** 2013
SALES (est): 56.36K **Privately Held**
SIC: 2253 T-shirts and tops, knit

(G-4002)
NORTHEAST FOODS INC
68 Harvest Mill Ln (27520-4849)
PHONE..................................919 585-5178
EMP: 12 **EST:** 2010
SALES (est): 268.42K **Privately Held**

Web: www.nefoods.com
SIC: 2051 Bakery: wholesale or wholesale/retail combined

(G-4003)
NOVO NORDISK PHRM INDS LP
3611 Powhatan Rd (27527-6058)
PHONE..................................919 820-9985
Elliot Zieglmeier, *Prin*
EMP: 87 **EST:** 2020
SALES (est): 9.94MM **Privately Held**
SIC: 2834 Pharmaceutical preparations

(G-4004)
NOVO NORDISK PHRM INDS LP
646 Glp Oneway (27527)
PHONE..................................919 820-9985
EMP: 347
SALES (corp-wide): 24.71B **Privately Held**
Web: www.novonordisk-clayton.com
SIC: 2834 Pharmaceutical preparations
HQ: Novo Nordisk Pharmaceutical Industries, Lp
3612 Powhatan Rd
Clayton NC 27527

(G-4005)
PAINTING BY COLORS LLC
562 Rock Pillar Rd (27520-6876)
PHONE..................................919 963-2300
EMP: 5 **EST:** 2013
SALES (est): 277.04K **Privately Held**
SIC: 1721 3589 Residential painting; High pressure cleaning equipment

(G-4006)
RAY HOUSES MACHINE SHOP
110 N Tech Dr (27520-5002)
P.O. Box 1104 (27528-1104)
PHONE..................................919 553-1249
EMP: 7
SQ FT: 6,250
SALES (est): 586.87K **Privately Held**
SIC: 3599 Machine shop, jobbing and repair

(G-4007)
RENEW RECYCLING LLC
440 S Tech Park Ln (27520-5016)
PHONE..................................919 550-8012
Gary Taylor, *Pr*
EMP: 65 **EST:** 2020
SALES (est): 4.75MM **Privately Held**
Web: www.renewrecycling.com
SIC: 5093 3341 Ferrous metal scrap and waste; Recovery and refining of nonferrous metals

(G-4008)
SHIPWRECK RUM INC
2308 High Chaparral Dr (27527-9169)
PHONE..................................215 896-6172
John Kile, *Prin*
EMP: 4 **EST:** 2017
SALES (est): 47.54K **Privately Held**
Web: www.brinleygoldshipwreck.com
SIC: 2085 Distilled and blended liquors

(G-4009)
SMISSONS INC
425 Swann Trl (27527-6506)
PHONE..................................660 537-3219
Ramani Morales, *CEO*
Benino Morales, *Ch Bd*
EMP: 5 **EST:** 2020
SALES (est): 156.72K **Privately Held**
SIC: 7389 6221 5047 2326 Business Activities at Non-Commercial Site; Commodity contracts brokers, dealers; Medical laboratory equipment; Medical and hospital uniforms, men's

(G-4010)
SML RALEIGH LLC
501 Atkinson St (27520-2155)
P.O. Box 129 (27528-0129)
PHONE..................................919 585-0100
Tommy Dew, *Pr*
Beverly Dew, *VP*
EMP: 5 **EST:** 2012
SALES (est): 1.13MM **Privately Held**
Web: www.sml.com
SIC: 2741 2759 5131 Miscellaneous publishing; Commercial printing, nec; Labels
PA: Sml Usa Inc.
1 Harmon Plz Fl 6
Secaucus NJ 07094

(G-4011)
SOY CLEVER CANDLE CO LLC
62 Standing Oaks Ln (27527-9675)
PHONE..................................919 869-5360
Tressa Sutphin, *Mgr*
EMP: 4 **EST:** 2017
SALES (est): 69.48K **Privately Held**
SIC: 3999 Candles

(G-4012)
SPRING VALLEY CARVING SVCS LLC
2024 Spring Valley Dr (27520-9342)
PHONE..................................919 553-7906
Brian Henley, *Admn*
EMP: 4 **EST:** 2019
SALES (est): 67.24K **Privately Held**
SIC: 2431 Millwork

(G-4013)
STRUCTURAL STEEL PRODUCTS CORP
8029 Us 70 Bus Hwy W (27520-4807)
PHONE..................................919 359-2811
Trudy Hales, *Pr*
Ray Hales, *
Rick Brown, *
EMP: 80 **EST:** 1981
SQ FT: 53,000
SALES (est): 22.79MM **Privately Held**
Web: www.structuralcoatingsinc.com
SIC: 3441 Building components, structural steel

(G-4014)
STUDIO TK LLC
3940 Us 70 Hwy Business (27520)
P.O. Box 1529 (27528-1529)
PHONE..................................919 464-2920
Charlie Bell, *Pr*
▲ **EMP:** 45 **EST:** 2012
SQ FT: 75,000
SALES (est): 9.97MM
SALES (corp-wide): 109.98MM **Privately Held**
Web: www.studiotk.com
SIC: 2522 Office furniture, except wood
HQ: Teknion Limited
1150 Flint Rd
North York ON M3J 2
416 661-1577

(G-4015)
SWEET TEA GIRLS PATTERNS
137 Watsons Mill Ln (27527-5390)
PHONE..................................843 907-2727
Margaret Pate, *Prin*
EMP: 4 **EST:** 2015
SALES (est): 110.59K **Privately Held**
Web: www.thesweetteagirls.com
SIC: 3543 Industrial patterns

Clayton - Johnston County (G-4016)

(G-4016)
TARHEEL PUBLISHING CO
120 N Tech Dr Ste 102 (27520-5084)
PHONE.................................919 553-9042
Hayes Jeff, *Owner*
EMP: 16 EST: 1998
SQ FT: 4,000
SALES (est): 1.36MM **Privately Held**
Web: www.tmsdigi.com
SIC: 2741 Telephone and other directory publishing

(G-4017)
TEKNI-PLEX INC
Also Called: Natvar
8720 Us 70 Bus Hwy W (27520-4808)
P.O. Box 658 (27528-0658)
PHONE.................................919 553-4151
George Coggins, *Mgr*
EMP: 61
SQ FT: 50,000
SALES (corp-wide): 996.3MM **Privately Held**
Web: www.tekni-plex.com
SIC: 5999 3069 3083 Medical apparatus and supplies; Tubing, rubber; Laminated plastics plate and sheet
PA: Tekni-Plex, Inc.
460 E Swedesford Rd # 300
Wayne PA 19087
484 690-1520

(G-4018)
THAT MAKE SCENTS LLC
121 Rowan Dr (27520-2981)
PHONE.................................919 283-0237
W Chavis, *Prin*
EMP: 6 EST: 2014
SALES (est): 53.47K **Privately Held**
SIC: 2844 Perfumes, cosmetics and other toilet preparations

(G-4019)
TRUE BLUE WDCRFTING LSER ETCHI
408 Fontana Dr (27527-7305)
PHONE.................................609 784-2431
Michael Pincus, *Prin*
EMP: 5 EST: 2018
SALES (est): 54.13K **Privately Held**
SIC: 2431 Millwork

(G-4020)
TURNER & REEVES FENCE CO LLC
2016 Pope Ct (27520-8813)
PHONE.................................910 671-8851
EMP: 4 EST: 2012
SALES (est): 243.61K **Privately Held**
SIC: 3315 Chain link fencing

(G-4021)
WICKED CALM CANDLES LLC
595 Lockwood Dr (27527-5078)
PHONE.................................856 343-2499
Mary Morace, *Prin*
EMP: 4 EST: 2017
SALES (est): 39.69K **Privately Held**
SIC: 3999 Candles

(G-4022)
WRITE WAY PUBLISHING CO LLC
322 Fox Hollow Dr (27527-6643)
PHONE.................................919 606-2681
Lee Heinrich Radford, *Admn*
EMP: 5 EST: 2017
SALES (est): 38.8K **Privately Held**
SIC: 2741 Miscellaneous publishing

Clemmons
Forsyth County

(G-4023)
1ST TIME CONTRACTING
104 Western Villa Dr (27012-8277)
PHONE.................................774 289-3321
EMP: 4 EST: 2020
SALES (est): 151.96K **Privately Held**
SIC: 2499 Fencing, docks, and other outdoor wood structural products

(G-4024)
A&R PRINTING LLC
3551 Glenfield Ln (27012-7916)
PHONE.................................336 971-7677
Andre Bvan Staden, *Pr*
EMP: 5 EST: 2017
SALES (est): 111.68K **Privately Held**
SIC: 2752 Offset printing

(G-4025)
ALPHA AND OMEGA PRINTING INC
2554 Lewisville Clemmons Rd (27012-8110)
PHONE.................................336 778-1400
EMP: 4 EST: 2018
SALES (est): 158.2K **Privately Held**
SIC: 2752 Offset printing

(G-4026)
ARMAMENT CHIMERA
6332 Cephis Dr (27012-9230)
PHONE.................................336 893-5639
EMP: 4 EST: 2015
SALES (est): 102.84K **Privately Held**
SIC: 3489 Ordnance and accessories, nec

(G-4027)
ATLANTIS FOODS INC
Also Called: Atlantis Food Service
4525 Hampton Rd (27012-9456)
PHONE.................................336 768-6101
Vasileios Tsiaras, *Pr*
EMP: 30 EST: 1999
SQ FT: 125,000
SALES (est): 13.26MM **Privately Held**
Web: www.atlantisfoodsinc.com
SIC: 5146 2032 Fish and seafoods; Italian foods, nec: packaged in cans, jars, etc.

(G-4028)
AWNING INNOVATIONS
6325 Clementine Dr (27012-9481)
PHONE.................................336 831-8996
Brett Hodges, *Owner*
EMP: 5 EST: 2015
SALES (est): 224.97K **Privately Held**
Web: www.awninginnovations.com
SIC: 3993 Advertising artwork

(G-4029)
BAHNSON HOLDINGS INC (HQ)
4731 Commercial Park Ct (27012-8700)
PHONE.................................336 760-3111
Timothy J Whitener, *Pr*
James P Hutcherson, *Sec*
Lisa J Cunningham, *Treas*
EMP: 79 EST: 1915
SALES (est): 147.91MM
SALES (corp-wide): 12.58B **Publicly Held**
Web: www.bahnson.com
SIC: 8711 1711 3585 3564 Heating and ventilation engineering; Warm air heating and air conditioning contractor; Heating equipment, complete; Blowers and fans
PA: Emcor Group, Inc.
301 Merritt 7 Fl 6
Norwalk CT 06851
203 849-7800

(G-4030)
BATTERY WATERING SYSTEMS LLC
6645 Holder Rd (27012-9287)
PHONE.................................336 714-0448
Scott D Elliott, *Managing Member*
EMP: 6 EST: 2010
SALES (est): 982.98K **Privately Held**
Web: www.batterywatering.com
SIC: 2834 Chlorination tablets and kits (water purification)

(G-4031)
BELL BOOK & CANDLE LLC
1801 Curraghmore Rd (27012-8852)
PHONE.................................336 480-1422
Amanda Swiderski, *Prin*
EMP: 5 EST: 2016
SALES (est): 48.02K **Privately Held**
SIC: 3999 Candles

(G-4032)
BENT CREEK STUDIO LLC
162 Washington Dr (27012-7256)
PHONE.................................336 692-6477
Brett A Boger, *Admn*
EMP: 4 EST: 2015
SALES (est): 66.91K **Privately Held**
SIC: 2431 Millwork

(G-4033)
BUCKS WOODWORKS LLC
145 Saint Johns Ct (27012-9551)
PHONE.................................336 764-3979
Kevin S Buchanan, *Prin*
EMP: 4 EST: 2019
SALES (est): 71.1K **Privately Held**
SIC: 2431 Millwork

(G-4034)
CLEMMONS PALLET SKID WORKS INC
3449 Hwy 158 E (27012)
P.O. Box 745 (27012-0745)
PHONE.................................336 766-5462
Dewey B Edwards, *Pr*
Frances D Edwards, *VP*
EMP: 20 EST: 1971
SQ FT: 7,500
SALES (est): 2.45MM **Privately Held**
Web: www.clemmonspallet.com
SIC: 2448 2441 Pallets, wood; Nailed wood boxes and shook

(G-4035)
DONS FINE JEWELRY INC
2503 Lewisville Clemmons Rd (27012-8712)
P.O. Box 1544 (27012-1544)
PHONE.................................336 724-7826
Don Pope, *Pr*
Chris Pope, *VP*
Danny Wingo, *Mgr*
EMP: 6 EST: 1984
SALES (est): 802.56K **Privately Held**
Web: www.wingosfinejewelry.com
SIC: 5944 7631 3911 Jewelry, precious stones and precious metals; Jewelry repair services; Jewelry, precious metal

(G-4036)
DYNAMIC MACHINE WORKS LLC
2655 Knob Hill Dr (27012-8831)
PHONE.................................336 462-7370
Michael Kruth, *Prin*
EMP: 10 EST: 2015
SALES (est): 459.77K **Privately Held**
SIC: 3599 Amusement park equipment

(G-4037)
EDIT PLUS
900 Leonard Courtyard Blvd (27012-7089)
PHONE.................................336 775-2764
Joyce Cieszewski, *Owner*
EMP: 5 EST: 2017
SALES (est): 60.96K **Privately Held**
SIC: 2741 Miscellaneous publishing

(G-4038)
FORSYTH FAMILY MAGAZINE INC
6255 Towncenter Dr (27012-9376)
PHONE.................................336 782-0331
Kim Beane, *Prin*
EMP: 11 EST: 2010
SALES (est): 448.24K **Privately Held**
Web: www.forsythfamilymagazine.com
SIC: 2721 Magazines: publishing only, not printed on site

(G-4039)
FOURSHARE LLC
Also Called: Battery Watering Technology
6645 Holder Rd (27012-9287)
PHONE.................................336 714-0448
Scott Elliott, *Pr*
EMP: 17 EST: 2011
SQ FT: 9,300
SALES (est): 4.82MM **Privately Held**
Web: www.batterywatering.com
SIC: 3089 Battery cases, plastics or plastics combination

(G-4040)
FRISBY AEROSPACE INC
4520 Hampton Rd (27012-9456)
PHONE.................................336 712-8004
Michael Rife, *Engr*
EMP: 6 EST: 2017
SALES (est): 210.66K **Privately Held**
Web: www.frisbyaerospace.com
SIC: 3728 Aircraft parts and equipment, nec

(G-4041)
G & G ENTERPRISES
210 Industrial Dr Ste 2 (27012-6872)
PHONE.................................336 764-2493
Ann Beeson, *Owner*
EMP: 4 EST: 1983
SQ FT: 4,000
SALES (est): 261.23K **Privately Held**
SIC: 2396 5621 Screen printing on fabric articles; Women's sportswear

(G-4042)
GROUPE LACASSE LLC
Also Called: Neocase
2235 Lewisville Clemmons Rd Ste D (27012)
P.O. Box 129 (27012-0129)
PHONE.................................336 778-2098
Sylvain Garneau, *Pr*
Rene Frechette, *
Guy Lacasse, *
Robin Lacasse, *
Benjamin Wagenmaker, *
EMP: 20 EST: 2015
SALES (est): 622.95K **Privately Held**
Web: www.groupelacasse.com
SIC: 2521 Desks, office: wood

(G-4043)
HAYWARD INDUSTRIES INC
1 Hayward Industrial Dr (27012-9737)
P.O. Box 5100 (27012-5100)
PHONE.................................336 712-9900
Terry Payne, *Brnch Mgr*
EMP: 228
SALES (corp-wide): 992.45MM **Publicly Held**

GEOGRAPHIC SECTION

Cleveland - Rowan County (G-4068)

Web: www.hayward.com
SIC: 3589 3561 3423 3494 Swimming pool filter and water conditioning systems; Pumps and pumping equipment; Leaf skimmers or swimming pool rakes; Valves and pipe fittings, nec
HQ: Hayward Industries, Inc.
1415 Vantage Park Dr
Charlotte NC 28203
908 351-5400

(G-4044)
HAYWARD INDUSTRIES INC
Hayward Pool Products
1 Hayward Industrial Dr (27012-9737)
P.O. Box 5100 (27012-5100)
PHONE..............................336 712-9900
EMP: 700
SALES (corp-wide): 992.45MM Publicly Held
Web: www.hayward.com
SIC: 3589 3561 3563 Swimming pool filter and water conditioning systems; Pumps and pumping equipment; Air and gas compressors
HQ: Hayward Industries, Inc.
1415 Vantage Park Dr
Charlotte NC 28203
908 351-5400

(G-4045)
HERMIT FEATHERS PRESS LLC
3520 Saint Leonards Ct (27012-9049)
PHONE..............................336 404-8229
Angell Caudill, Prin
EMP: 4 EST: 2019
SALES (est): 40.66K Privately Held
Web: www.hermitfeatherspress.com
SIC: 2741 Miscellaneous publishing

(G-4046)
HORIZON HOME IMPORTS INC
6211 Clementine Dr (27012-9477)
P.O. Box 11742 (28220-1742)
PHONE..............................704 859-5133
Nash Smith, Managing Member
EMP: 8
SIC: 2273 Carpets and rugs
PA: Horizon Home Imports Inc.
4943 Park Rd Unit 506
Charlotte NC 28209

(G-4047)
IMAGE MATTERS INC
1808 Ramhurst Dr (27012-9201)
PHONE..............................336 940-3000
Roger K Laudy, Pr
Diane Laudy, Sec
EMP: 5 EST: 1991
SQ FT: 60,000
SALES (est): 479.38K Privately Held
Web: www.imagemattersinc.com
SIC: 3993 2392 2796 Advertising novelties; Pads and padding, table: except asbestos, felt, or rattan; Platemaking services

(G-4048)
INTELLIGENT ENDOSCOPY LLC
4740 Commercial Park Ct Ste 1 (27012)
PHONE..............................336 608-4375
EMP: 20 EST: 2014
SALES (est): 2.43MM Privately Held
SIC: 3841 Surgical and medical instruments

(G-4049)
J R CRAVER & ASSOCIATES INC
Also Called: Salem Collection, The
265 Ashbourne Lake Ct (27012-7907)
PHONE..............................336 769-3330
J Richard Craver, Pr
EMP: 23 EST: 1983

SQ FT: 88,000
SALES (est): 643.89K Privately Held
SIC: 2493 5199 3993 Reconstituted wood products; Christmas trees, including artificial; Signs and advertising specialties

(G-4050)
JRM INC
8491 N Nc Hwy 150 (27012-6843)
PHONE..............................888 576-7007
EMP: 49 EST: 1992
SQ FT: 10,000
SALES (est): 9.03MM Privately Held
Web: www.jrmonline.com
SIC: 3524 Lawn and garden mowers and accessories

(G-4051)
K9 INSTALLS INC ✪
6255 Towncenter Dr Ste 875 (27012-9376)
PHONE..............................743 207-1507
Staceyn Linster, CEO
EMP: 5 EST: 2022
SALES (est): 123.77K Privately Held
SIC: 1389 Construction, repair, and dismantling services

(G-4052)
KALAJDZIC INC
Also Called: My Kolors
1415 River Ridge Dr (27012-8355)
PHONE..............................855 465-4225
Dragoslav Kalajdzic, Pr
▲ EMP: 10 EST: 2008
SQ FT: 300,000
SALES (est): 961.96K Privately Held
Web: www.mykolors.com
SIC: 2759 Business forms: printing, nsk

(G-4053)
MUSCADINE NATURALS INC
6332 Cephis Dr (27012-9230)
PHONE..............................888 628-5898
Robert Dalton, Pr
Linn Davis, CFO
EMP: 6 EST: 2001
SALES (est): 540K Privately Held
Web: www.muscadinenaturals.com
SIC: 2023 Dietary supplements, dairy and non-dairy based

(G-4054)
PAINT COMPANY OF NC
Also Called: Johnson's Industrial Coatings
10436 N Nc Hwy 150 (27012-6863)
PHONE..............................336 764-1648
Jay Mehta, Pr
Jennifer Kinosh, Off Mgr
EMP: 7 EST: 1989
SQ FT: 14,000
SALES (est): 834.13K Privately Held
Web: www.johnsoncoating.com
SIC: 2851 Paints and paint additives

(G-4055)
PRINT EXPRESS ENTERPRISES INC
Also Called: Nu Expression
6255 Towncenter Dr (27012-9376)
PHONE..............................336 765-5505
Jan Allison, Pr
Brian Leimone, VP
Craig Phillips, Sec
EMP: 6 EST: 2008
SALES (est): 1MM Privately Held
Web: www.nuagency.com
SIC: 2752 Offset printing

(G-4056)
QUALCOMM INCORPORATED
Also Called: Qualcomm

6209 Ramada Dr Ste A (27012-9733)
PHONE..............................336 323-3300
Mark Dole, Dir
EMP: 8
SALES (corp-wide): 35.82B Publicly Held
Web: www.qualcomm.com
SIC: 3663 Space satellite communications equipment
PA: Qualcomm Incorporated
5775 Morehouse Dr
San Diego CA 92121
858 587-1121

(G-4057)
QUANTICO WATER & SEWER LLC
260 Fern Cliff Ln (27012-6887)
PHONE..............................336 528-9299
EMP: 8 EST: 2005
SALES (est): 902.31K Privately Held
SIC: 4952 3824 1623 4941 Sewerage systems; Water meters; Water, sewer, and utility lines; Water supply

(G-4058)
QUARTER TURN LLC
8340 Holler Farm Rd (27012-8084)
PHONE..............................336 712-0811
Grace C Jones, Prin
EMP: 4 EST: 2008
SALES (est): 148.22K Privately Held
SIC: 3131 Footwear cut stock

(G-4059)
ROADRNNER MTRCYCLE TURING TRVL
2245 Lewisville Clemmons Rd Ste D (27012)
PHONE..............................336 765-7780
Christa Neuheuser, Pr
▲ EMP: 4 EST: 2005
SALES (est): 439.95K Privately Held
Web: www.roadrunner.travel
SIC: 2741 Miscellaneous publishing

(G-4060)
STANFORD MANUFACTURING LLC
3720 Stanford Way (27012-8842)
PHONE..............................336 999-8799
Scott D Elliott, Managing Member
EMP: 10 EST: 2016
SALES (est): 660.41K Privately Held
Web: www.stanfordmanufacturing.com
SIC: 3089 Injection molding of plastics

(G-4061)
TEESHIZZLE PRINTING
106 Windsong Dr (27012-7095)
PHONE..............................336 715-1113
Gregory L Black, Prin
EMP: 4 EST: 2019
SALES (est): 67.69K Privately Held
SIC: 2752 Commercial printing, lithographic

(G-4062)
TOPSIDER BUILDING SYSTEMS INC
3710 Dillon Industrial Dr (27012-8571)
P.O. Box 1490 (27012-1490)
PHONE..............................336 766-9300
Sheldon J Storer, Pr
J Joseph Kruse, *
Peter F Anthony, *
▼ EMP: 40 EST: 1968
SQ FT: 105,000
SALES (est): 8.29MM Privately Held
Web: www.topsiderhomes.com
SIC: 2452 Modular homes, prefabricated, wood

(G-4063)
TRIAD WELDING CONTRACTORS INC
146 Silkwind Ct (27012-7271)
PHONE..............................336 882-3902
Daryl Hartsell, Owner
EMP: 4 EST: 1997
SALES (est): 383.92K Privately Held
SIC: 3444 Booths, spray: prefabricated sheet metal

(G-4064)
TRIUMPH ACTUATION SYSTEMS LLC (HQ)
Also Called: Triumph Acttion Systms-Clmmons
4520 Hampton Rd (27012-9456)
PHONE..............................336 766-9036
John B Wright Ii, Mgr
M David Kornblatt, *
Richard Reed, *
▲ EMP: 220 EST: 2003
SALES (est): 46.61MM Publicly Held
Web: www.triumphactuationsystems.com
SIC: 3593 3728 Fluid power cylinders and actuators; Aircraft parts and equipment, nec
PA: Triumph Group, Inc.
555 E Lancaster Ave # 400
Radnor PA 19087

(G-4065)
UNITED MOBILE IMAGING INC
2554 Lewisville Clemmons Rd Ste 201 (27012-8749)
P.O. Box 11 (27012-0011)
PHONE..............................800 983-9840
Paul Smith Junior, CEO
EMP: 5 EST: 2006
SALES (est): 490.9K Privately Held
SIC: 5047 5999 3845 Medical equipment and supplies; Medical apparatus and supplies; Electromedical equipment

(G-4066)
VELOCITA INC
383 Grant Rd (27012-7049)
PHONE..............................336 764-8513
Bradley Smith, Pr
EMP: 7 EST: 2015
SALES (est): 286.03K Privately Held
Web: www.velocita-usa.com
SIC: 3999 Manufacturing industries, nec

Cleveland
Rowan County

(G-4067)
ATLAS AEROSPACE INC
1536 Triplett Rd (27013-8737)
PHONE..............................704 528-3356
David A Wiles, Prin
EMP: 6 EST: 2012
SALES (est): 130.2K Privately Held
SIC: 3721 Aircraft

(G-4068)
BARBER FURNITURE & SUPPLY
590 Mountain Rd (27013-9707)
PHONE..............................704 278-9367
Charles P Barber, Owner
EMP: 10 EST: 1976
SQ FT: 4,600
SALES (est): 664.32K Privately Held
Web: www.barberwood.com
SIC: 2511 2434 2431 5211 Wood household furniture; Wood kitchen cabinets; Doors and door parts and trim, wood; Lumber and other building materials

Cleveland - Rowan County (G-4069)

(G-4069)
CARGILL INCORPORATED
Also Called: Cargill
9150 Statesville Blvd (27013-9022)
PHONE.....................704 278-2941
Mark Whitaker, *Mgr*
EMP: 9
SALES (corp-wide): 176.74B **Privately Held**
Web: www.cargill.com
SIC: 2048 Prepared feeds, nec
PA: Cargill, Incorporated
15407 Mcginty Rd W
Wayzata MN 55391
800 227-4455

(G-4070)
CLEVELAND FREIGHTLINER TRUCK
11550 Statesville Blvd (27013-8114)
P.O. Box 399 (27013-0399)
PHONE.....................704 645-5000
John Stevenson, *Mgr*
▲ **EMP:** 23 **EST:** 2002
SALES (est): 1.29MM **Privately Held**
Web: northamerica.daimlertruck.com
SIC: 3711 Truck and tractor truck assembly

(G-4071)
DAIMLER TRUCK NORTH AMER LLC
Also Called: Chrysler Freight Liner
11550 Statesville Blvd (27013-8114)
P.O. Box 399 (27013-0399)
PHONE.....................704 645-5000
Mike Mccurry, *Mgr*
EMP: 1200
SALES (corp-wide): 60.75B **Privately Held**
Web: northamerica.daimlertruck.com
SIC: 5511 3715 3711 3537 Automobiles, new and used; Truck trailers; Motor vehicles and car bodies; Industrial trucks and tractors
HQ: Daimler Truck North America Llc
4555 N Channel Ave
Portland OR 97217
503 745-8000

(G-4072)
GTW WOODWORKS
174 Brawley Rd (27013-8700)
PHONE.....................704 640-5402
Taylor Wyatt, *Prin*
EMP: 4 **EST:** 2018
SALES (est): 72.89K **Privately Held**
SIC: 2431 Millwork

(G-4073)
HERSEY METERS CO LLC
10210 Statesville Blvd (27013-8103)
PHONE.....................704 278-2221
EMP: 29 **EST:** 2006
SALES (est): 2.07MM
SALES (corp-wide): 1.28B **Publicly Held**
Web: www.muellersystems.com
SIC: 3491 Industrial valves
PA: Mueller Water Products, Inc.
1200 Abernathy Rd # 1200
Atlanta GA 30328
770 206-4200

(G-4074)
JIM FAB OF NORTH CAROLINA INC
10230 Statesville Blvd (27013-8103)
PHONE.....................704 278-1000
Robert Moss, *Pr*
EMP: 50 **EST:** 2010
SALES (est): 9.67MM **Privately Held**
SIC: 3498 5074 5993 Fabricated pipe and fittings; Pipes and fittings, plastic; Pipe store
PA: Miles Moss Of New York, Inc.
586 Commercial Ave
Garden City NY 11530

(G-4075)
MCCOY MOTORSPORTS
999 Triplett Rd (27013-8731)
PHONE.....................704 929-8802
EMP: 5 **EST:** 2017
SALES (est): 185.41K **Privately Held**
Web: www.mccoymotorsportsinc.com
SIC: 3714 Motor vehicle engines and parts

(G-4076)
MUELLER SYSTEMS LLC
Also Called: Hersey Meters Division
10210 Statesville Blvd (27013-8103)
P.O. Box 128 (27013-0128)
PHONE.....................704 278-2221
Hassan Ali, *
Thomas Butler, *
Tom Cullinan, *
Lowell Rust, *
▲ **EMP:** 156 **EST:** 1999
SALES (est): 45.06MM
SALES (corp-wide): 1.28B **Publicly Held**
Web: www.muellersystems.com
SIC: 3824 Water meters
PA: Mueller Water Products, Inc.
1200 Abernathy Rd # 1200
Atlanta GA 30328
770 206-4200

(G-4077)
MYERS FOREST PRODUCTS INC
Also Called: C & M Sawmill
355 Barber Junction Rd (27013-9775)
P.O. Box 38 (27013-0038)
PHONE.....................704 278-4532
Craig Myers, *Pr*
Gilbert Myers Senior, *VP*
Gilbert Myers Junior, *Treas*
Leanna Myers, *
EMP: 31 **EST:** 1981
SQ FT: 7,500
SALES (est): 1.02MM **Privately Held**
SIC: 2421 2448 Sawmills and planing mills, general; Pallets, wood

(G-4078)
PERDUE FARMS INC
Also Called: Perdue Grain Market
9150 Statesville Blvd (27013-9022)
PHONE.....................704 278-2228
Frank Perdue, *Pr*
EMP: 35
SALES (corp-wide): 1.24B **Privately Held**
Web: www.perdue.com
SIC: 2015 Poultry slaughtering and processing
PA: Perdue Farms Incorporated
31149 Old Ocean City Rd
Salisbury MD 21804
800 473-7383

(G-4079)
PHELPS WOOD PRODUCTS LLC
12010 Statesville Blvd (27013-9422)
PHONE.....................336 284-2149
James W Phelps, *Pr*
EMP: 15 **EST:** 2001
SALES (est): 469.85K **Privately Held**
SIC: 2499 Fencing, docks, and other outdoor wood structural products

(G-4080)
SHAVER WOOD PRODUCTS INC
14440 Statesville Blvd (27013-8791)
PHONE.....................704 278-1482
Richard Shaver, *Pr*
Chad Shaver, *
EMP: 60 **EST:** 1973
SQ FT: 15,600
SALES (est): 8.77MM **Privately Held**
Web: www.lilshavers.com
SIC: 2426 2421 Hardwood dimension and flooring mills; Chipper mill

(G-4081)
SOUTHERN ROOTS MONOGRAMMING
148 Cotton Wood Rd (27013-8938)
PHONE.....................706 599-5383
Erika Scott, *Prin*
EMP: 5 **EST:** 2018
SALES (est): 76.27K **Privately Held**
SIC: 2395 Embroidery and art needlework

(G-4082)
TAR HEEL MATERIALS & HDLG LLC
725 Kesler Rd (27013-9459)
PHONE.....................704 659-5143
Tim Ladowski, *Prin*
EMP: 8 **EST:** 2017
SALES (est): 481.18K **Privately Held**
Web: www.tarheelmaterials.com
SIC: 2865 Cyclic crudes and intermediates

(G-4083)
VISUAL IMPACT PRFMCE SYSTEMS L
2720 Amity Hill Rd (27013-9251)
PHONE.....................704 278-3552
EMP: 5 **EST:** 2010
SALES (est): 243.34K **Privately Held**
Web: www.visualimpactperformancesystems.com
SIC: 3714 Motor vehicle parts and accessories

Cliffside
Rutherford County

(G-4084)
CROSS-LINK INC
4734 Us 221a Hwy (28024)
P.O. Box 249 (29702-0249)
PHONE.....................828 657-4477
Kyle Bullock, *Pr*
EMP: 7 **EST:** 1991
SQ FT: 12,000
SALES (est): 841.08K **Privately Held**
Web: www.crosslinkgroup.com
SIC: 2843 Textile finishing agents

(G-4085)
CRYPTON MILLS LLC
3400 Hwy 221a (28024)
PHONE.....................828 202-5875
John G Regan, *CEO*
EMP: 23 **EST:** 2019
SALES (est): 2.22MM
SALES (corp-wide): 12.14B **Publicly Held**
Web: www.cryptonmills.com
SIC: 7389 2221 Textile and apparel services; Acetate broadwoven fabrics
PA: W. R. Berkley Corporation
475 Steamboat Rd Fl 1
Greenwich CT 06830
203 629-3000

Climax
Guilford County

(G-4086)
INDUSTRIAL WOOD PRODUCTS INC (PA)
9205 Hwy 22 S (27233)
P.O. Box 206 (27233-0206)
PHONE.....................336 333-5959
Johnny Hall, *CEO*
Ryan Hilsinger, *
Wendy Showalter, *
▲ **EMP:** 57 **EST:** 1979
SQ FT: 1,000
SALES (est): 23.43MM
SALES (corp-wide): 23.43MM **Privately Held**
Web: www.industrialwood.com
SIC: 2421 Lumber: rough, sawed, or planed

(G-4087)
MECHANICAL MAINTENANCE INC
6028 Liberty Rd (27233-8009)
PHONE.....................336 676-7133
Valarie Webb, *Pr*
Robert Webb, *VP*
EMP: 13 **EST:** 2003
SQ FT: 17,000
SALES (est): 2.28MM **Privately Held**
Web: www.mechanicalmaintenanceinc.com
SIC: 1711 7692 1799 Mechanical contractor; Welding repair; Welding on site

Clinton
Sampson County

(G-4088)
ARGOS USA LLC
Also Called: Ready Mixed Concrete
3095 Turkey Hwy (28328-0742)
PHONE.....................910 299-5046
EMP: 25
Web: www.argos-us.com
SIC: 3273 Ready-mixed concrete
HQ: Argos Usa Llc
3015 Windward Plz Ste 300
Alpharetta GA 30005
678 368-4300

(G-4089)
CAMOTECK LLC
1318 Lisbon St (28328-4612)
P.O. Box 54 (28329-0054)
PHONE.....................910 590-3213
Brian Demay, *Managing Member*
Salay Demay, *Sec*
EMP: 5 **EST:** 1985
SQ FT: 10,000
SALES (est): 492.69K **Privately Held**
Web: www.camoteckllc.com
SIC: 2394 2393 Canvas and related products; Canvas bags

(G-4090)
CCL METAL SCIENCE LLC
520 E Railroad St (28328-4304)
PHONE.....................910 299-0911
▲ **EMP:** 58 **EST:** 2014
SALES (est): 20.57MM
SALES (corp-wide): 4.75B **Privately Held**
SIC: 3354 Aluminum extruded products
PA: Ccl Industries Inc.
111 Gordon Baker Rd Suite 801
Toronto ON M2H 3
416 756-8500

(G-4091)
COMMERCIAL ENTERPRISES NC INC
Also Called: International Minute Press
103 E Morisey Blvd (28328-4122)
PHONE.....................910 592-8163
Windy Schulte, *Pr*
David Schulte, *Pr*
EMP: 5 **EST:** 2005
SQ FT: 6,000
SALES (est): 435.51K **Privately Held**
Web: www.impclinton.com
SIC: 2752 Offset printing

GEOGRAPHIC SECTION — Clinton - Sampson County

(G-4092)
COMMERCIAL PRTG CO OF CLINTON
Also Called: Minuteman Press
103 E Morisey Blvd (28328-4122)
P.O. Box 878 (28329-0878)
PHONE.................910 592-8163
Lynwood Daughtry, *Pr*
EMP: 8 **EST:** 1949
SQ FT: 6,000
SALES (est): 578.72K **Privately Held**
Web: www.minuteman.com
SIC: 2752 Commercial printing, lithographic

(G-4093)
CONCRETE SERVICE COMPANY
3095 Turkey Hwy (28328-0742)
PHONE.................910 590-0035
EMP: 4 **EST:** 2018
SALES (est): 90.92K **Privately Held**
SIC: 5211 5032 3273 1771 Cement; Concrete and cinder building products; Ready-mixed concrete; Concrete work

(G-4094)
DUBOSE STRAPPING INC (PA)
Also Called: Guardian Strapping
906 Industrial Dr (28328-8068)
P.O. Box 819 (28329-0819)
PHONE.................910 590-1020
Charles Dubose Junior, *Pr*
Paul Ruddock, *
Charles Dubose Iii, *VP*
Larry Johansen, *
◆ **EMP:** 80 **EST:** 1990
SQ FT: 13,000
SALES (est): 67.86MM **Privately Held**
Web: www.dubosestrapping.com
SIC: 2671 3499 Paper; coated and laminated packaging; Strapping, metal

(G-4095)
F L TURLINGTON LUMBER CO INC
229 E Railroad St (28328-4134)
P.O. Box 288 (28329-0288)
PHONE.................910 592-7197
William Turlington, *Pr*
Thomas E Turlington Junior, *VP*
Jean Turlington, *
Lyenette Willaims, *
EMP: 34 **EST:** 1918
SQ FT: 15,000
SALES (est): 2.8MM **Privately Held**
Web: www.turlingtonlbr.com
SIC: 2421 2426 Sawmills and planing mills, general; Hardwood dimension and flooring mills

(G-4096)
HEARTLAND PUBLICATIONS
303 W Elizabeth St (28328-4426)
P.O. Box 89 (28329-0089)
PHONE.................910 592-8137
EMP: 5 **EST:** 2019
SALES (est): 135.8K **Privately Held**
Web: www.heartland.org
SIC: 2741 Miscellaneous publishing

(G-4097)
MARY MACKS INC
Also Called: Hawaiian Shaved Ice
214 Armory Dr (28328-9731)
P.O. Box 10 (28366-0010)
PHONE.................770 234-6333
Gary Herring, *Managing Member*
Gary Mac Herring Junior, *Managing Member*
Carli Herring, *Sec*
▲ **EMP:** 4 **EST:** 1995
SQ FT: 3,000
SALES (est): 1.93MM **Privately Held**
Web: www.marymacks.com
SIC: 2087 Flavoring extracts and syrups, nec

(G-4098)
MILLER CTRL MFG INC CLINTON NC
1008 Southwest Blvd (28328-4624)
P.O. Box 1065 (28329-1065)
PHONE.................910 592-5112
William L Miller Junior, *Pr*
EMP: 6 **EST:** 1986
SQ FT: 13,000
SALES (est): 865.2K **Privately Held**
SIC: 3564 3625 3613 3822 Ventilating fans: industrial or commercial; Relays and industrial controls; Switchgear and switchboard apparatus; Environmental controls

(G-4099)
MOORE MACHINE PRODUCTS INC
919 Rowan Rd (28328-0872)
PHONE.................910 592-2718
Terry Moore, *Pr*
EMP: 6 **EST:** 1994
SQ FT: 5,000
SALES (est): 489.71K **Privately Held**
Web: www.mooremachine.com
SIC: 3599 Machine shop, jobbing and repair

(G-4100)
PARKER BROTHERS INCORPORATED
825 Kitty Fork Rd (28328-8211)
P.O. Box 1045 (28329-1045)
PHONE.................910 564-4132
Richard Wynn Parker, *Pr*
EMP: 8 **EST:** 1940
SALES (est): 853.33K **Privately Held**
SIC: 2542 Partitions and fixtures, except wood

(G-4101)
PARKER GAS COMPANY INC (PA)
Also Called: Rapid Exchange
1504 Sunset Ave (28328-3828)
P.O. Box 159 (28366-0159)
PHONE.................800 354-7250
Ethel Parker, *Pr*
Daren Parker, *Treas*
David Parker, *Sec*
▲ **EMP:** 10 **EST:** 1959
SQ FT: 1,500
SALES (est): 39.76MM
SALES (corp-wide): 39.76MM **Privately Held**
Web: www.parkergas.com
SIC: 5984 5983 2911 3714 Propane gas, bottled; Fuel oil dealers; Liquefied petroleum gases, LPG; Propane conversion equipment, motor vehicle

(G-4102)
PRECISION TOOL & STAMPING INC
800 Warsaw Rd (28328-3716)
P.O. Box 615 (28329-0615)
PHONE.................910 592-0174
Tart Lee, *Pr*
Sue Lee, *
EMP: 45 **EST:** 1980
SQ FT: 55,000
SALES (est): 9.16MM **Privately Held**
Web: www.precisiontool.com
SIC: 3469 3544 Metal stampings, nec; Special dies and tools

(G-4103)
ROBINSON & SON MACHINE INC
446 Faison Hwy (28328-3645)
PHONE.................910 592-4779
Walter T Robinson, *Pr*
Doris Robinson, *Treas*
Patricia Hering, *Sec*
Ellen R Jones, *VP*
EMP: 20 **EST:** 1975
SQ FT: 7,200
SALES (est): 457.47K **Privately Held**
SIC: 3599 Machine shop, jobbing and repair

(G-4104)
S & W READY MIX CON CO LLC (DH)
217 Lisbon St (28328-4116)
P.O. Box 872 (28329-0872)
PHONE.................910 592-1733
Bill West, *VP*
Earl Wells, *Pr*
EMP: 16 **EST:** 1986
SQ FT: 10,000
SALES (est): 63.4MM
SALES (corp-wide): 8.01MM **Privately Held**
SIC: 3273 Ready-mixed concrete
HQ: Titan America Llc
5700 Lake Wright Dr # 300
Norfolk VA 23502
757 858-6500

(G-4105)
S & W READY MIX CON CO LLC
1395 Turkey Hwy (28328-3731)
PHONE.................910 592-2191
Danny Bordeaux, *VP*
EMP: 19
SALES (corp-wide): 8.01MM **Privately Held**
Web: www.snwreadymix.com
SIC: 3273 Ready-mixed concrete
HQ: S & W Ready Mix Concrete Company Llc
217 Lisbon St
Clinton NC 28328
910 592-1733

(G-4106)
S KIVETT INC
711 Southwest Blvd (28328-4636)
P.O. Box 590 (28329-0590)
PHONE.................910 592-0161
R Jerol Kivett, *Pr*
Christine Kivett, *
John Weaks, *
◆ **EMP:** 27 **EST:** 1958
SQ FT: 55,000
SALES (est): 2.73MM **Privately Held**
Web: www.kivetts.com
SIC: 1799 2531 7641 5031 Fiberglass work; Public building and related furniture; Reupholstery and furniture repair; Lumber, plywood, and millwork

(G-4107)
SAFE TIRE & AUTOS LLC
Also Called: Safe Tire & Auto Services
1308 Hobbton Hwy (28328-1958)
PHONE.................910 590-3101
Patricia Martines, *Pr*
Sipriano Batista, *VP*
Chris Sherbert, *Executive Manager*
EMP: 6 **EST:** 2017
SALES (est): 224.69K **Privately Held**
SIC: 7534 Tire repair shop

(G-4108)
SAMPSON WEEKLY INC
414b Northeast Blvd (28328-2402)
P.O. Box 1915 (28329-1915)
PHONE.................910 590-2102
Melvin Henderson, *Prin*
EMP: 6 **EST:** 2010
SALES (est): 192.54K **Privately Held**
Web: www.thesampsonweekly.com
SIC: 2711 Newspapers: publishing only, not printed on site

(G-4109)
SCHINDLER ELEVATOR CORPORATION
Also Called: Schindler 9749
821 Industrial Dr (28328-9749)
PHONE.................910 590-5590
Charles Spell, *Genl Mgr*
EMP: 14
Web: www.schindler.com
SIC: 7699 3534 Elevators: inspection, service, and repair; Automobile elevators
HQ: Schindler Elevator Corporation
20 Whippany Rd
Morristown NJ 07960
973 397-6500

(G-4110)
SMITHFIELD FOODS INC
424 E Railroad St (28328-4360)
P.O. Box 49 (28329-0049)
PHONE.................910 299-3009
John Allis, *Brnch Mgr*
EMP: 124
Web: www.smithfieldfoods.com
SIC: 2011 2013 Meat packing plants; Sausages and other prepared meats
HQ: Smithfield Foods, Inc.
200 Commerce St
Smithfield VA 23430
757 365-3000

(G-4111)
SMITHFIELD PACKING COMPANY INC
424 E Railroad St (28328-4360)
PHONE.................910 592-2104
EMP: 19 **EST:** 2017
SALES (est): 5.9MM **Privately Held**
Web: www.smithfieldfoods.com
SIC: 2011 Meat packing plants

(G-4112)
STEEL TECHNOLOGIES LLC
Also Called: Steel Technologies Carolinas
112 Sycamore St (28328-3948)
PHONE.................910 592-1266
EMP: 97 **EST:** 1989
SQ FT: 63,000
SALES (est): 9.44MM **Privately Held**
Web: www.steeltechnologies.com
SIC: 3312 Blast furnaces and steel mills
HQ: Steel Technologies Llc
700 N Hurstbourne Pkwy # 400
Louisville KY 40222
502 245-2110

(G-4113)
STILES MFG CO INC
102 Coharie Dr (28328-3008)
PHONE.................910 592-6344
John Stiles, *Pr*
Jack Martin, *Sec*
▲ **EMP:** 8 **EST:** 1969
SQ FT: 20,000
SALES (est): 234.64K **Privately Held**
SIC: 3446 3799 3523 3441 Architectural metalwork; Transportation equipment, nec; Farm machinery and equipment; Fabricated structural metal

(G-4114)
TIRES INCORPORATED OF CLINTON
317 Southeast Blvd (28328-3625)
PHONE.................910 592-4741
Boyd A Mattocks, *Pr*
Trixie Mattocks, *Sec*
Boyed A Mattocks, *Pr*
EMP: 24 **EST:** 1978
SQ FT: 9,000
SALES (est): 1.13MM **Privately Held**

Clinton - Sampson County (G-4115)

Web: www.tireincofclinton.com
SIC: 7534 5531 Tire recapping; Automotive tires

(G-4115)
TONYS CABINETS
Also Called: Tony's Custom Cabinets
671 Cartertown Rd (28328-7439)
PHONE...................................910 592-2028
Tony Rackley, *Owner*
EMP: 6 EST: 1984
SALES (est): 375.15K **Privately Held**
SIC: 2434 Wood kitchen cabinets

(G-4116)
TRI-W FARMS INC
4671 Faison Hwy (28328-6141)
PHONE...................................910 533-3596
Wayne Wilson, *Pr*
Anthony G Wilson, *VP*
Daniel A Wilson, *Cnslt*
EMP: 6 EST: 1952
SALES (est): 438.09K **Privately Held**
SIC: 3523 Planting, haying, harvesting, and processing machinery

(G-4117)
UFP SITE BUILT LLC
Also Called: Ufp Mid-Atlantic
254 Superior Dr (28328-1828)
PHONE...................................910 590-3220
Patrick Benton, *VP*
EMP: 16
SALES (corp-wide): 7.22B **Publicly Held**
Web: www.ufpi.com
SIC: 5211 2426 Lumber products; Blanks, wood: bowling pins, handles, etc.
HQ: Ufp Site Built, Llc
   2801 E Beltline Ave Ne
   Grand Rapids MI 49525
   616 634-6161

(G-4118)
WILLIAMSON GREENHOUSES INC
Also Called: BJ Williamson
1469 Beulah Rd (28328-9773)
PHONE...................................910 592-7072
Burl Williamson, *CEO*
Trip Williamson, *Genl Mgr*
▲ EMP: 16 EST: 2003
SALES (est): 1.03MM **Privately Held**
Web: www.williamsongreenhouses.com
SIC: 3448 Greenhouses, prefabricated metal

(G-4119)
WOOD N THINGS
139 Buckhorn Creek Ln (28328-7451)
PHONE...................................910 990-4448
EMP: 5 EST: 2013
SALES (est): 69.27K **Privately Held**
SIC: 2511 Wood household furniture

Clyde
Haywood County

(G-4120)
AISTHESIS PRODUCTS INC
70 Brigadoon Dr (28721-8751)
PHONE...........................828 627-6555
Finch Dudley, *CEO*
Heidi Haehlen, *Sec*
EMP: 8 EST: 2015
SALES (est): 350.47K **Privately Held**
Web: www.aisthesis-products.com
SIC: 3821 Laboratory measuring apparatus

(G-4121)
CHEROKEE PUBLICATIONS INC
186 Bobcat Trl (28721-9443)
PHONE...........................828 627-2424
Travis Crisp, *Owner*
EMP: 4 EST: 2010
SALES (est): 249.44K **Privately Held**
SIC: 2741 Miscellaneous publishing

(G-4122)
CUSTOM CNC LLC
6989 Carolina Blvd (28721-7085)
P.O. Box 622 (28716-0622)
PHONE...........................828 734-8293
EMP: 4 EST: 2012
SALES (est): 263.11K **Privately Held**
Web: www.customcnc622.com
SIC: 3499 Machine bases, metal

(G-4123)
DAYDREAM EDUCATION LLC
21 Listening Cv (28721-6471)
P.O. Box 639 (28715-0639)
PHONE...........................800 591-6150
▲ EMP: 4 EST: 2007
SALES (est): 233.3K **Privately Held**
Web: www.daydreameducation.com
SIC: 3999 Education aids, devices and supplies

(G-4124)
E Z STOP NUMBER TWO
8721 Carolina Blvd (28721-8025)
PHONE...........................828 627-9081
David Pace, *Owner*
EMP: 5 EST: 1994
SALES (est): 176.27K **Privately Held**
SIC: 5541 2411 Gasoline Stations with convenience stores; Poles, posts, and pilings: untreated wood

(G-4125)
LANNINGS FARMING AND LOGGING
108 Lanning Rd (28721-8812)
PHONE...........................828 246-8938
Kenny Berry Lanning, *Owner*
EMP: 6 EST: 2014
SALES (est): 83K **Privately Held**
SIC: 2411 Logging

(G-4126)
MARK T GALVIN
324 Upper Crabtree Rd (28721-7713)
PHONE...........................828 627-0823
Mark Galvin, *Prin*
EMP: 6 EST: 2008
SALES (est): 183.65K **Privately Held**
SIC: 2431 Millwork

(G-4127)
MUSICLAND EXPRESS
500 Jones Cove Rd (28721-6400)
PHONE...........................828 627-9431
Robert Dany, *Pr*
EMP: 6 EST: 2005
SQ FT: 7,200
SALES (est): 106.01K **Privately Held**
SIC: 2741 Miscellaneous publishing

(G-4128)
STAIRWAYS FROM HEAVEN INC
262 Maple Leaf Ln (28721-7502)
PHONE...........................828 627-3860
Joseph Chase, *Owner*
EMP: 6 EST: 2005
SALES (est): 71.45K **Privately Held**
SIC: 2431 Millwork

Coats
Harnett County

(G-4129)
ECONOMY CLRS LILLINGTON LLC
235 Skeet Range Rd (27521-9506)
PHONE...........................910 893-3927
EMP: 8 EST: 2021
SALES (est): 340K **Privately Held**
SIC: 2842 Drycleaning preparations

(G-4130)
GRAY FLEX SYSTEMS INC (PA)
232 N Ida St (27521-8626)
P.O. Box 1326 (27521-1326)
PHONE...........................910 897-3539
William R Gray, *Pr*
Carrie Gray, *
EMP: 81 EST: 1997
SQ FT: 195,000
SALES (est): 24.35MM **Privately Held**
Web: www.grayflex.com
SIC: 3444 Ducts, sheet metal

(G-4131)
JMK TOOL & DIE INC
3482 Nc Hwy 27 E (27521-8509)
P.O. Box 828 (27521-0828)
PHONE...........................910 897-6373
EMP: 5 EST: 1996
SQ FT: 4,000
SALES (est): 484.37K **Privately Held**
Web: www.jmktoolanddie.com
SIC: 3544 Special dies and tools

(G-4132)
LIGHTS-LIGHTS LLC
1206 Bill Avery Rd (27521-9209)
P.O. Box 547 (27521-0547)
PHONE...........................919 798-2317
EMP: 7 EST: 2018
SALES (est): 457.31K **Privately Held**
SIC: 3993 Signs and advertising specialties

(G-4133)
LOVE THY SKIN LLC
227 Remington Dr (27521-9650)
PHONE...........................910 703-2321
EMP: 4 EST: 2020
SALES (est): 11K **Privately Held**
SIC: 2844 Face creams or lotions

(G-4134)
SNAP RITE MANUFACTURING INC (PA)
232 N Ida St (27521-8626)
P.O. Box 577 (27521-0577)
PHONE...........................910 897-4080
William R Gray, *Prin*
EMP: 20 EST: 1998
SQ FT: 155,000
SALES (est): 8.58MM
SALES (corp-wide): 8.58MM **Privately Held**
Web: www.snaprite.com
SIC: 3433 3585 Heating equipment, except electric; Air conditioning equipment, complete

Cofield
Hertford County

(G-4135)
HYDRAULIC HOSE DEPOT INC
1520c River Rd (27922-9502)
PHONE...........................252 356-1862
Edmund M Waters, *Pr*

Merrill Waters, *Sec*
EMP: 5 EST: 2002
SQ FT: 5,400
SALES (est): 808.35K **Privately Held**
SIC: 3492 Hose and tube fittings and assemblies, hydraulic/pneumatic

(G-4136)
NUCOR CORPORATION
Nucor Plate Mill
1505 River Rd (27922-9502)
P.O. Box 279 (27986-0279)
PHONE...........................252 356-3700
Giffin Daughtridge, *Brnch Mgr*
EMP: 102
SALES (corp-wide): 34.71B **Publicly Held**
Web: www.nucor.com
SIC: 3325 3312 Steel foundries, nec; Blast furnaces and steel mills
PA: Nucor Corporation
   1915 Rexford Rd Ste 400
   Charlotte NC 28211
   704 366-7000

(G-4137)
PERDUE FARMS INC
Also Called: Perdue Agribusiness
242 Perdue Rd (27922-9505)
PHONE...........................252 358-8245
Bill Mizelle, *Mgr*
EMP: 494
SALES (corp-wide): 1.24B **Privately Held**
Web: www.perdue.com
SIC: 2015 Poultry slaughtering and processing
PA: Perdue Farms Incorporated
   31149 Old Ocean City Rd
   Salisbury MD 21804
   800 473-7383

(G-4138)
STRUCTRAL CATINGS HERTFORD LLC
930 River Rd (27922-9577)
PHONE...........................919 553-3034
Edwin Hales, *Managing Member*
Tamara Bryan, *CFO*
EMP: 12 EST: 2011
SALES (est): 471.14K **Privately Held**
Web: www.structuralcoatingshertford.net
SIC: 3479 Coating of metals and formed products

Colerain
Bertie County

(G-4139)
PDF AND ASSOCIATES
116 Luther Brown Rd (27924-9418)
PHONE...........................252 332-7749
Patricia Ferguson, *Pr*
Steven Ferguson, *Prin*
EMP: 5 EST: 2001
SQ FT: 12,000
SALES (est): 115.72K **Privately Held**
SIC: 8299 5651 2741 Public speaking school ; Family clothing stores; Miscellaneous publishing

(G-4140)
ROSS PHELPS LOGGING CO INC
1548 Wakelon Rd (27924-8987)
PHONE...........................252 356-2560
Ross Phelps, *Pr*
Sandra Phelps, *Treas*
Vonda Hardin, *VP*
Marcie Todd, *Sec*
EMP: 10 EST: 1988
SALES (est): 657.28K **Privately Held**

Colfax - Guilford County (G-4163)

SIC: **2411** 2426 2421 Logging camps and contractors; Hardwood dimension and flooring mills; Sawmills and planing mills, general

Colfax
Guilford County

(G-4141)
BALTEK INC (DH)
5240 National Center Dr (27235-9719)
P.O. Box 16148 (27261-6148)
PHONE.................................336 398-1900
Roman Thomassin, *CEO*
Georg Reif, *
◆ **EMP:** 174 **EST:** 1927
SQ FT: 85,000
SALES (est): 110.3MM **Privately Held**
Web: www.3acomposites.com
SIC: **2436** Softwood veneer and plywood
HQ: 3a Composites Usa Inc.
   3480 Taylorsville Hwy
   Statesville NC 28625
   704 872-8974

(G-4142)
BLUE RIDGE TOOL INC
505 Lakedale Rd (27235-9755)
PHONE.................................336 993-8111
EMP: 5 **EST:** 2020
SALES (est): 171.69K **Privately Held**
SIC: **3599** Machine shop, jobbing and repair

(G-4143)
BURCHETTE SIGN COMPANY INC
Also Called: A & B Signs
8705 Triad Dr (27235-9440)
P.O. Box 56 (27235-0056)
PHONE.................................336 996-6501
Tim Burchette, *Pr*
Wendy Burchette, *VP*
EMP: 13 **EST:** 1960
SQ FT: 2,880
SALES (est): 2.48MM **Privately Held**
Web: www.burchettesign.com
SIC: **1799** 3993 Sign installation and maintenance; Signs and advertising specialties

(G-4144)
COLFAX TRAILER & REPAIR LLC
8426a Norcross Rd (27235-9754)
P.O. Box 448 (27235-0448)
PHONE.................................336 993-8511
EMP: 8 **EST:** 2006
SALES (est): 839.38K **Privately Held**
Web: www.colfaxtrailer.com
SIC: **3799** 7539 Trailers and trailer equipment; Trailer repair

(G-4145)
CREATIVE METAL AND WOOD INC
8512 Blackstone Dr (27235-9774)
PHONE.................................336 475-9400
Sean Farrell, *Pr*
John S Farrell, *VP*
EMP: 10 **EST:** 1954
SALES (est): 469.13K **Privately Held**
Web: www.creativemetalwood.com
SIC: **2514** 2519 Metal household furniture; Household furniture, except wood or metal: upholstered

(G-4146)
CROWN EQUIPMENT CORPORATION
Also Called: Crown Lift Trucks
8220 Tyner Dr (27235-9763)
PHONE.................................336 291-2500
Ron Winner, *Brnch Mgr*
EMP: 49
SALES (corp-wide): 7.12B **Privately Held**
Web: www.crown.com
SIC: **3537** 5084 Lift trucks, industrial: fork, platform, straddle, etc.; Materials handling machinery
PA: Crown Equipment Corporation
   44 S Washington St
   New Bremen OH 45869
   419 629-2311

(G-4147)
CSC FAMILY HOLDINGS INC
9035 Us Hwy 421 (27235)
PHONE.................................336 993-2680
Ernie Duggins, *Brnch Mgr*
EMP: 7
SALES (corp-wide): 17.66MM **Privately Held**
SIC: **3441** 3429 Fabricated structural metal; Hardware, nec
PA: Csc Family Holdings, Inc.
   101 Centreport Dr Ste 400
   Greensboro NC 27409
   336 275-9711

(G-4148)
DIGITAL PRINTING
4142 Brynwood Dr (27235-9706)
PHONE.................................336 430-8011
Daniel Gustafson, *Prin*
EMP: 5 **EST:** 2013
SALES (est): 89.46K **Privately Held**
Web: www.alldigitalprint.com
SIC: **2752** Offset printing

(G-4149)
ENDURA PRODUCTS LLC (HQ)
8817 W Market St (27235-9419)
PHONE.................................336 668-2472
▲ **EMP:** 300 **EST:** 1954
SALES (est): 92.2MM
SALES (corp-wide): 2.83B **Publicly Held**
Web: www.enduraproducts.com
SIC: **3429** Builders' hardware
PA: Masonite International Corporation
   1242 E 5th Ave
   Tampa FL 33605
   813 877-2726

(G-4150)
FIBEX LLC (PA)
5280 National Center Dr (27235-9719)
PHONE.................................336 605-9002
Jeff Bruner, *Prin*
▲ **EMP:** 6 **EST:** 2010
SALES (est): 816.63K
SALES (corp-wide): 816.63K **Privately Held**
SIC: **2822** 5169 5199 Synthetic rubber; Synthetic resins, rubber, and plastic materials; Industrial yarns

(G-4151)
HORIZON FOREST PRODUCTS CO LP
9050 W Market St (27235-9705)
PHONE.................................336 993-9663
Jd Ziegelhoser, *Prin*
EMP: 7
SALES (corp-wide): 595.03MM **Privately Held**
Web: www.horizonforest.com
SIC: **5031** 2426 Lumber: rough, dressed, and finished; Flooring, hardwood
HQ: Horizon Forest Products Company, L.P.
   4115 Commodity Pkwy
   Raleigh NC 27610

(G-4152)
ITT LLC
8511 Norcross Rd (27235-8703)
PHONE.................................336 662-0113
Al Bader, *Brnch Mgr*
EMP: 8
SALES (corp-wide): 3.28B **Publicly Held**
Web: www.itt.com
SIC: **3625** Control equipment, electric
HQ: Itt Llc
   1133 Westchester Ave N-100
   White Plains NY 10604
   914 641-2000

(G-4153)
LC AMERICA INC
8221 Tyner Rd (27235-9763)
PHONE.................................336 676-5129
Cristoforo Riva, *Pr*
▲ **EMP:** 13 **EST:** 2011
SALES (est): 14.03MM
SALES (corp-wide): 15.12MM **Privately Held**
Web: www.lcamerica.com
SIC: **5145** 2096 Snack foods; Cheese curls and puffs
PA: Le Caselle Spa
   Via Enrico Mattei 2
   Pontevico BS 25026
   030 930-6400

(G-4154)
M&N CONSTRUCTION SUPPLY INC
Also Called: M & N Equipment Rental
8431 Norcross Rd (27235-9754)
PHONE.................................336 996-7740
Ghris Greiner, *Brnch Mgr*
EMP: 6
SALES (corp-wide): 5.05MM **Privately Held**
Web: www.mnconstructionsupply.com
SIC: **7359** 5082 3444 Tool rental; Contractor's materials; Concrete forms, sheet metal
PA: M&N Construction Supply, Inc.
   323 Eastwood Rd
   Wilmington NC 28403
   910 791-0908

(G-4155)
NATIONAL PIPE & PLASTICS INC
9609 W Market St (27235-9615)
PHONE.................................336 996-2711
Robert Nappier, *Brnch Mgr*
EMP: 110
SALES (corp-wide): 32.72B **Privately Held**
Web: www.nationalpipe.com
SIC: **3084** Plastics pipe
HQ: National Pipe & Plastics, Inc.
   1 N Page Ave
   Endicott NY 13760

(G-4156)
OLDCASTLE ADAMS
3415 Sandy Ridge Rd (27235-9610)
PHONE.................................336 310-0542
EMP: 10 **EST:** 2013
SALES (est): 502.25K **Privately Held**
Web: www.adamsproducts.com
SIC: **3271** Concrete block and brick

(G-4157)
PHILLIPS CORPORATION
Also Called: Jeffreys Division
8500 Triad Dr (27235)
PHONE.................................336 665-1080
Brooks Barwick, *Pr*
Larry Hubbard, *
Kim Debruhl, *
EMP: 25 **EST:** 2000
SALES (est): 9.87MM **Privately Held**
Web: www.phillipscorp.com
SIC: **5084** 3999 Machine tools and accessories; Atomizers, toiletry

(G-4158)
PIEDMONT CHEERWINE BOTTLING CO
Also Called: Piedmont Cheerwine Bottling
2913 Sandy Ridge Rd (27235-9691)
PHONE.................................336 993-7733
EMP: 83
SALES (corp-wide): 28.79MM **Privately Held**
Web: www.cheerwine.com
SIC: **2086** Bottled and canned soft drinks
PA: Piedmont Cheerwine Bottling Co Inc
   1413 Jake Alxander Blvd S
   Salisbury NC
   704 636-2191

(G-4159)
QUANTUM MATERIALS LLC (HQ)
5280 National Center Dr (27235-9719)
PHONE.................................336 605-9002
Robert R Benko, *Pr*
Barbara Page, *
▲ **EMP:** 15 **EST:** 1985
SQ FT: 143,000
SALES (est): 23.14MM
SALES (corp-wide): 64.05MM **Privately Held**
Web: www.quantum5280.com
SIC: **2221** Broadwoven fabric mills, manmade
PA: Twitchell Technical Products, Llc
   4031 Ross Clark Cir
   Dothan AL 36303
   334 792-0002

(G-4160)
SECOND GREEN HOLDINGS INC
9501 W Market St (27235-9616)
P.O. Box 549 (27235-0549)
PHONE.................................336 996-6073
EMP: 18 **EST:** 1987
SALES (est): 2.41MM **Privately Held**
Web: www.ramcofabricators.com
SIC: **3443** Fabricated plate work (boiler shop)

(G-4161)
TENN-TEX PLASTICS INC
8011 National Service Rd (27235-9762)
P.O. Box 550 (27235-0550)
PHONE.................................336 931-1100
Richard Marsh, *Pr*
Robert Hightower, *
EMP: 27 **EST:** 1986
SQ FT: 40,000
SALES (est): 8.67MM **Privately Held**
Web: www.tenntex.com
SIC: **3089** Plastics hardware and building products

(G-4162)
VISIGRAPHIX INC
8911 Cedar Spring Dr (27235-9605)
PHONE.................................336 882-1935
Tom Livengood, *Pr*
Jean S Livengood, *Sec*
EMP: 5 **EST:** 1988
SQ FT: 4,500
SALES (est): 325.4K **Privately Held**
Web: www.visigraphix.com
SIC: **2262** 2759 Screen printing: manmade fiber and silk broadwoven fabrics; Commercial printing, nec

(G-4163)
W & F MANUFACTURING LLC
8817 W Market St (27235-9419)
PHONE.................................336 665-4023

Gregory A Piersanti, *Prin*
EMP: 6 **EST:** 2016
SALES (est): 67.14K **Privately Held**
Web: www.enduraproducts.com
SIC: 3999 Manufacturing industries, nec

(G-4164)
W&W-AFCO STEEL LLC
Also Called: 079948726
9035 W Market St (27235-9620)
PHONE.................................336 993-2680
EMP: 77
SALES (corp-wide): 364.48B **Publicly Held**
Web: www.wwafcosteel.com
SIC: 3441 Fabricated structural metal
HQ: W&W-Afco Steel Llc
   1730 W Reno Ave
   Oklahoma City OK 73106
   405 235-3621

Columbia
Tyrrell County

(G-4165)
CAPT CHARLIES SEAFOOD INC
Also Called: Captain Charlie's Seafood
508 N Road St (27925-8949)
PHONE.................................252 796-7278
Phillip Carawan, *Pr*
Melony Carawan, *
EMP: 41 **EST:** 1998
SQ FT: 12,000
SALES (est): 3.64MM **Privately Held**
Web: www.captcharliesdaughter.com
SIC: 5146 2092 Seafoods; Fresh or frozen packaged fish

(G-4166)
CAPT NEILLS SEAFOOD INC
508 N Road St (27925-8949)
P.O. Box 164 (27925-0164)
PHONE.................................252 796-0795
Phillip R Carawan, *Pr*
Melony S Carawan, *VP*
EMP: 138 **EST:** 1982
SALES (est): 16.2MM **Privately Held**
SIC: 2092 2091 Crab meat, fresh: packaged in nonsealed containers; Canned and cured fish and seafoods

(G-4167)
ROSE WELDING & CRANE SERVICE I
1060 S Gum Neck Rd (27925-9491)
PHONE.................................252 796-9171
Hank Rose, *Pr*
Sue Rose, *VP*
EMP: 5 **EST:** 2004
SALES (est): 686.61K **Privately Held**
SIC: 5084 7692 Cranes, industrial; Welding repair

(G-4168)
STILETTO MANUFACTURING INC
107 S Water St (27925)
PHONE.................................252 564-4877
Jay Phillips, *CEO*
Margaret Phillips, *VP*
EMP: 8 **EST:** 2015
SALES (est): 436.16K **Privately Held**
Web: www.sailstiletto.com
SIC: 3999 Boat models, except toy

(G-4169)
TYRRELL READY MIX INC
1280 Hwy 94 North (27925)
P.O. Box 300 (27925-0300)
PHONE.................................252 796-0265
Roger Hudson, *Pr*

Connie Hudson, *VP*
EMP: 5 **EST:** 1977
SQ FT: 5,000
SALES (est): 450.35K **Privately Held**
SIC: 3273 Ready-mixed concrete

(G-4170)
VINEYARDS ON SCUPPERNONG LLC
1894 Nc Highway 94 N (27925-9611)
PHONE.................................252 796-4727
EMP: 7 **EST:** 2008
SALES (est): 439.58K **Privately Held**
Web: www.vineyardsonthescuppernong.com
SIC: 2084 Wines

(G-4171)
WLDG HONEYCUTT & FABRICATION
1991 Sound Side Rd (27925-8657)
PHONE.................................252 413-8754
Brandon Honeycutt, *Prin*
EMP: 5 **EST:** 2019
SALES (est): 90.39K **Privately Held**
SIC: 7692 Welding repair

Columbus
Polk County

(G-4172)
BUFFER ZONE CERAMICS
655 John Weaver Rd (28722-9610)
PHONE.................................828 863-2000
Charlotte Morris Costa, *Owner*
EMP: 5 **EST:** 2009
SALES (est): 78.61K **Privately Held**
Web: www.bufferzoneceramics.com
SIC: 3269 Pottery products, nec

(G-4173)
ENERGY MANAGEMENT INSULATION
Also Called: EMI
P.O. Box 125 (28722-0125)
PHONE.................................828 894-3635
Joyce Hart, *Pr*
Johnathan Hart, *VP*
EMP: 10 **EST:** 1984
SQ FT: 9,000
SALES (est): 480.77K **Privately Held**
SIC: 2298 Insulator pads, cordage

(G-4174)
GREEN CREEK WINERY LLC
413 Gilbert Rd (28722-6494)
P.O. Box 309 (28722-0309)
PHONE.................................828 863-4136
Alvin Pack, *Owner*
EMP: 4 **EST:** 2005
SALES (est): 180.38K **Privately Held**
Web: www.greencreekwinery.com
SIC: 2084 Wines

(G-4175)
JEFF WEAVER LOGGING
617 John Weaver Rd (28722-9610)
PHONE.................................864 909-1758
Jeff Weaver, *Owner*
EMP: 5 **EST:** 2012
SALES (est): 197.39K **Privately Held**
SIC: 2411 Logging camps and contractors

(G-4176)
KINGDOM PRINTS LLC
190 Hatley Dr (28722-8789)
PHONE.................................828 894-8851
Jeremy Michael, *Owner*
EMP: 5 **EST:** 2017
SALES (est): 82.32K **Privately Held**

SIC: 2752 Commercial printing, lithographic

(G-4177)
LOOKING GLASS CREAMERY LLC
115 Harmon Dairy Ln (28722-8505)
PHONE.................................828 458-0088
▲ **EMP:** 7 **EST:** 2007
SALES (est): 777.39K **Privately Held**
Web: www.lookingglasscreamery.com
SIC: 2022 Natural cheese

(G-4178)
METALLUS INC
205 Industrial Park Dr (28722-7740)
PHONE.................................330 471-6293
EMP: 99
SALES (corp-wide): 1.36B **Publicly Held**
Web: www.metallus.com
SIC: 3312 Blast furnaces and steel mills
PA: Metallus Inc.
   1835 Dueber Ave Sw
   Canton OH 44706
   330 471-7000

(G-4179)
RONNIE GARRETT LOGGING
4625 Landrum Rd (28722-6460)
PHONE.................................828 894-8413
Ronnie M Garrett, *Owner*
Ronnie Garrett, *Owner*
EMP: 6 **EST:** 1970
SALES (est): 402.13K **Privately Held**
SIC: 2411 Logging camps and contractors

(G-4180)
RUSSIAN CHAPEL HILLS WINERY
2662 Green Creek Dr (28722-9685)
PHONE.................................828 863-0541
EMP: 4 **EST:** 2017
SALES (est): 95.98K **Privately Held**
Web: www.russianchapelhills.com
SIC: 2084 Wines

(G-4181)
TRYON EQUINE COMPOST LLC
3661 Nc 108 Hwy E (28722-7717)
PHONE.................................914 774-7486
Corbett W Stone, *Admn*
EMP: 6 **EST:** 2015
SALES (est): 247.72K **Privately Held**
SIC: 2875 Compost

(G-4182)
WOODLANE ENVMTL TECH INC
Also Called: Condar Company
111 Kangaroo Dr (28722-6828)
P.O. Box 250 (28722-0250)
PHONE.................................828 894-8383
Michael Mccue, *Pr*
Timothy R Pope, *VP*
◆ **EMP:** 22 **EST:** 1975
SQ FT: 17,000
SALES (est): 2.35MM **Privately Held**
Web: www.condar.com
SIC: 3823 3429 Resistance thermometers and bulbs, industrial process type; Fireplace equipment, hardware: andirons, grates, screens

Como
Hertford County

(G-4183)
COUNTRY ROADS LOGGING LLC
1130b Boones Bridge Rd (27818-9593)
PHONE.................................252 398-4770
EMP: 4 **EST:** 2017
SALES (est): 81.72K **Privately Held**
SIC: 2411 Logging

Concord
Cabarrus County

(G-4184)
26 INDUSTRIES INC
337 Sunnyside Dr Se (28025-3638)
P.O. Box 912 (28026-0912)
PHONE.................................704 839-3218
Ron Peterson, *Owner*
EMP: 7 **EST:** 2015
SALES (est): 248.6K **Privately Held**
SIC: 3999 Manufacturing industries, nec

(G-4185)
A A LOGO GEAR
310 Church St N (28025-4515)
PHONE.................................704 795-7100
Alex Mills, *Prin*
EMP: 6 **EST:** 2011
SALES (est): 185.65K **Privately Held**
SIC: 2759 Screen printing

(G-4186)
ABL ELECTRONICS SUPPLY INC
1032 Central Dr Nw Ste A (28027-4344)
PHONE.................................704 784-4225
Robert Diorio, *Pr*
Dena Diorio, *Sec*
EMP: 5 **EST:** 1975
SQ FT: 8,500
SALES (est): 884.33K **Privately Held**
Web: www.ablewire.com
SIC: 5063 3357 Wire and cable; Building wire and cable, nonferrous

(G-4187)
ACN OPPORTUNITY DELAWARE LLC
1000 Progress Pl (28025-2449)
PHONE.................................704 260-3000
EMP: 5 **EST:** 2018
SALES (est): 88.38K **Privately Held**
SIC: 3669 Communications equipment, nec

(G-4188)
ADVERTISING FOR YOU NOW INC
298 Church St N (28025-4571)
P.O. Box 2126 (28026-2126)
PHONE.................................704 706-9423
EMP: 5 **EST:** 2017
SALES (est): 105.9K **Privately Held**
SIC: 2711 Newspapers

(G-4189)
AIR SPEED STOCK CAR FABRICATIO
190b Pitts School Rd Nw (28027-0304)
PHONE.................................704 720-7245
EMP: 5 **EST:** 2003
SALES (est): 75.87K **Privately Held**
SIC: 3711 Automobile assembly, including specialty automobiles

(G-4190)
ALCATEL DUNKERMOTOREN
5850 Potomac Dr Nw (28027-8816)
PHONE.................................704 782-0691
Bob Ransom, *Prin*
EMP: 6 **EST:** 2004
SALES (est): 225.17K **Privately Held**
SIC: 3661 Telephone and telegraph apparatus

(G-4191)
ALLEGION ACCESS TECH LLC
Stanley Block and Decker
1000 Stanley Dr (28027-7679)
PHONE.................................704 789-7000
Bruce Watson, *Mgr*

GEOGRAPHIC SECTION

Concord - Cabarrus County (G-4216)

EMP: 32
Web: www.stanleyaccess.com
SIC: 3423 5072 Hand and edge tools, nec; Hardware
HQ: Allegion Access Technologies Llc
65 Scott Swamp Rd
Farmington CT 06032

(G-4192)
ALLIED/CARTER MACHINING INC
540 Lake Lynn Rd (28025-9648)
PHONE..................704 784-1253
Jeff Carter, *Pr*
Teresa Carter, *Sec*
EMP: 5 **EST:** 2006
SQ FT: 2,500
SALES (est): 344.07K **Privately Held**
SIC: 3561 Industrial pumps and parts

(G-4193)
AMERICAN MADE INDUSTRIES INC
4825 Chesney St Nw (28027-2863)
PHONE..................650 218-7608
Ken Parker, *Prin*
EMP: 6 **EST:** 2013
SALES (est): 113.37K **Privately Held**
SIC: 3999 Manufacturing industries, nec

(G-4194)
AMERICAN PROSTHETICS
P.O. Box 792 (28026-0792)
PHONE..................704 782-0908
Louise Price, *Owner*
EMP: 5 **EST:** 1997
SALES (est): 178.46K **Privately Held**
SIC: 3842 Surgical appliances and supplies

(G-4195)
AMERICHEM INC
723 Commerce Dr (28025-7746)
PHONE..................704 782-6411
James Cook, *Mgr*
EMP: 40
SALES (corp-wide): 188.64MM **Privately Held**
Web: www.americhem.com
SIC: 2865 2851 2816 Color pigments, organic; Paints and allied products; Inorganic pigments
PA: Americhem, Inc.
2000 Americhem Way
Cuyahoga Falls OH 44221
330 929-4213

(G-4196)
AMISH LIGHTS CANDLES
226 Kendra Dr Sw (28025-3723)
P.O. Box 111 (44493-0111)
PHONE..................330 546-3900
Tracy Oconnor, *Admn*
EMP: 5 **EST:** 2014
SALES (est): 220.86K **Privately Held**
SIC: 3999 Candles

(G-4197)
ANDREWS PRODUCTS INC
7168 Weddington Rd Nw (28027-3469)
PHONE..................704 785-9715
EMP: 8 **EST:** 2010
SALES (est): 66.92K **Privately Held**
Web: www.andrewsproducts.com
SIC: 3714 Motor vehicle parts and accessories

(G-4198)
ARTESIAS SWETS BNGED BY DIOR L
208 Church St Ne Ste 1 (28025-4766)
PHONE..................704 794-3792
EMP: 4
SALES (est): 116.15K **Privately Held**
SIC: 2051 Bakery, for home service delivery

(G-4199)
ARTISAN LLC
8620 Westmoreland Dr Nw (28027-7963)
PHONE..................855 582-3539
Robert Bender, *CEO*
EMP: 6 **EST:** 2021
SALES (est): 347.16K **Privately Held**
Web: www.venueflex.com
SIC: 2531 Stadium furniture

(G-4200)
ATLAS SIGN INDUSTRIES NC LLC
Also Called: Atlas Sign Industries
707 Commerce Dr (28025-7746)
PHONE..................704 788-3733
Jeffery Adinolfe, *Managing Member*
James Adinolfe, *
Jill Adinolfe, *
EMP: 50 **EST:** 2005
SALES (est): 5.09MM **Privately Held**
Web: www.atlasbtw.com
SIC: 3993 Signs, not made in custom sign painting shops

(G-4201)
ATWELL FABRICATION LLC
Also Called: Coalition Targets
4338 Motorsports Dr Sw (28027-8977)
P.O. Box 242 (28115-0242)
PHONE..................704 763-9792
Malinda Atwell, *Prin*
EMP: 4 **EST:** 2016
SALES (est): 382.68K **Privately Held**
SIC: 3441 Fabricated structural metal

(G-4202)
AXALTA COATING SYSTEMS LLC
5388 Stowe Ln (28027-6029)
PHONE..................855 629-2582
EMP: 12
SALES (corp-wide): 5.18B **Publicly Held**
SIC: 2851 Polyurethane coatings
HQ: Axalta Coating Systems, Llc
50 Applied Bank Blvd # 300
Glen Mills PA 19342
855 547-1461

(G-4203)
AXLE HOLDINGS LLC
Also Called: Rv One Superstores Charlotte
5051 Davidson Hwy (28027-8413)
PHONE..................800 895-3276
TOLL FREE: 800
▼ **EMP:** 42 **EST:** 1994
SALES (est): 21.12MM
SALES (corp-wide): 138.7MM **Privately Held**
Web: rvonecharlotte.rvone.com
SIC: 5511 5012 3714 Trucks, tractors, and trailers: new and used; Trailers for trucks, new and used; Acceleration equipment, motor vehicle
PA: Blue Compass Rv, Llc
301 E Las Olas Blvd Fl 7
Fort Lauderdale FL 33301
954 908-3645

(G-4204)
BARNHILL CONTRACTING COMPANY
Also Called: APAC
725 Derita Rd (28027-3343)
PHONE..................704 721-7500
John Taylor, *Brnch Mgr*
EMP: 6
SALES (corp-wide): 389.14MM **Privately Held**
Web: www.barnhillcontracting.com
SIC: 1611 2951 Highway and street paving contractor; Asphalt paving mixtures and blocks
PA: Barnhill Contracting Company Inc
800 Tiffany Blvd Ste 200
Rocky Mount NC 27804
252 823-1021

(G-4205)
BASSETT FURNITURE DIRECT INC
Also Called: Bassett Furniture Direct
7830 Lyles Ln Nw (28027-7193)
PHONE..................704 979-5700
Carla Voss, *Mgr*
EMP: 12
SALES (corp-wide): 17.96MM **Privately Held**
Web: www.bassettfurniture.com
SIC: 2511 Wood household furniture
PA: Bassett Furniture Direct, Inc.
15305 Katy Fwy
Houston TX 77094
281 616-5409

(G-4206)
BAYATRONICS LLC
7089 Weddington Rd Nw (28027-3411)
PHONE..................980 432-0438
Samir Patel, *Prin*
EMP: 13 **EST:** 2021
SALES (est): 3.55MM **Privately Held**
SIC: 3559 Semiconductor manufacturing machinery

(G-4207)
BELLE EMBROIDERY LLC
Also Called: Catamount 55
6744 Cress Rd (28025-7312)
PHONE..................704 436-6895
Alicia Cobb, *Prin*
EMP: 5 **EST:** 2019
SALES (est): 58.76K **Privately Held**
SIC: 2395 Embroidery and art needlework

(G-4208)
BEVERAGE INNOVATION CORP
1858 Kannapolis Pkwy (28027)
PHONE..................425 222-4900
Stephanie Meier, *Prin*
EMP: 10
SALES (corp-wide): 5.18MM **Privately Held**
SIC: 2082 Beer (alcoholic beverage)
PA: Beverage Innovation Corp.
30520 Se 84th St
Preston WA 98050
425 222-4900

(G-4209)
BLANKET AERO LLC
9300 Aviation Blvd Nw Ste A (28027)
PHONE..................704 591-2878
Donald Noarman, *Pr*
Donald Noarman, *Pr*
Tamara Noarman, *VP*
EMP: 10 **EST:** 2014
SALES (est): 914.92K **Privately Held**
SIC: 3728 Aircraft assemblies, subassemblies, and parts, nec

(G-4210)
BLUE HEAVEN WOODWORKS
5520 Old Monroe Cir (28025-0477)
PHONE..................704 743-6648
John Haynes, *Prin*
EMP: 5 **EST:** 2017
SALES (est): 63.66K **Privately Held**
SIC: 2431 Millwork

(G-4211)
BLYTHE CONSTRUCTION INC
Also Called: Blythe Construction
7450 Poplar Tent Rd (28027-7591)
PHONE..................704 788-9733
Allen Hendricks, *VP*
EMP: 6
SALES (corp-wide): 16.98MM **Privately Held**
Web: www.blytheconstruction.com
SIC: 2951 Asphalt paving mixtures and blocks
HQ: Blythe Construction, Inc.
2911 N Graham St
Charlotte NC 28206
704 375-8474

(G-4212)
BMRS MANAGEMENT SERVICES INC
4005 Dearborn Pl Nw (28027-4624)
PHONE..................704 793-4319
EMP: 4 **EST:** 2018
SALES (est): 99.09K **Privately Held**
Web: www.bmrs.net
SIC: 3492 Hose and tube fittings and assemblies, hydraulic/pneumatic

(G-4213)
BONITZ INC
4539 Enterprise Dr Nw (28027-6437)
PHONE..................803 799-0181
EMP: 41
SALES (corp-wide): 425MM **Privately Held**
Web: www.bonitz.com
SIC: 3448 Panels for prefabricated metal buildings
PA: Bonitz, Inc.
645 Rosewood Dr
Columbia SC 29201
803 799-0181

(G-4214)
BREMBO NORTH AMERICA INC
Also Called: Bremeo North America
7275 Westwinds Blvd Nw (28027-3310)
PHONE..................704 799-0530
Jim Contje, *Mgr*
EMP: 9
SALES (corp-wide): 3.77B **Privately Held**
Web: www.brembo.com
SIC: 3714 Motor vehicle parts and accessories
HQ: Brembo North America, Inc.
47765 Halyard Dr
Plymouth MI 48170

(G-4215)
BROOME SIGN COMPANY
348 Spring St Nw (28025-4542)
PHONE..................704 782-0422
Raymond Ned Blackwelder Junior, *Pr*
R Ned Blackwelder Junior, *Pr*
Leonard Franklin Turner Iii, *Sec*
EMP: 4 **EST:** 1927
SQ FT: 4,000
SALES (est): 395.25K **Privately Held**
Web: www.broomesignco.com
SIC: 7389 2396 Sign painting and lettering shop; Fabric printing and stamping

(G-4216)
CABARRUS BREWING COMPANY LLC
Also Called: Gibson Mill Ciderworks
329 Mcgill Ave Nw (28027-6149)
PHONE..................704 490-4487
EMP: 21 **EST:** 2016
SQ FT: 15,000

Concord - Cabarrus County (G-4217) — GEOGRAPHIC SECTION

SALES (est): 2.49MM **Privately Held**
Web: www.cabarrusbrewing.com
SIC: **2082** 5813 5812 Beer (alcoholic beverage); Beer garden (drinking places); Cafe

(G-4217)
CABARRUS CONCRETE CO (PA)
2807 Armentrout Dr (28025-5866)
PHONE.............................704 788-3000
Rusty Shealy Junior, *Pr*
William W Jory, *VP*
M L Williams, *Marketing*
Joanne Johnson, *Sec*
Jane Arnold, *Treas*
EMP: 18 EST: 1998
SQ FT: 3,200
SALES (est): 2.3MM
SALES (corp-wide): 2.3MM **Privately Held**
SIC: **3273** Ready-mixed concrete

(G-4218)
CABARRUS PLASTICS INC
2845 Armentrout Dr (28025-5866)
PHONE.............................704 784-2100
Ru Hayes, *Pr*
EMP: 200 EST: 1988
SQ FT: 150,000
SALES (est): 47.46MM
SALES (corp-wide): 994.68MM **Publicly Held**
Web: www.cvgrp.com
SIC: **3089** 3713 Injection molding of plastics; Truck bodies and parts
PA: Commercial Vehicle Group, Inc.
7800 Walton Pkwy
New Albany OH 43054
614 289-5360

(G-4219)
CABINETS TRIM AND MORE
46 Charing Pl Sw (28025-5876)
PHONE.............................704 680-7076
EMP: 5 EST: 2015
SALES (est): 121.63K **Privately Held**
SIC: **2434** Wood kitchen cabinets

(G-4220)
CABO WINERY LLC
37 Union St S (28025-5009)
PHONE.............................704 785-9463
Sue A Carter, *Prin*
EMP: 6 EST: 2014
SALES (est): 249.17K **Privately Held**
Web: www.cabowine.com
SIC: **2084** Wines

(G-4221)
CAKY-Q
1207 Janrose Ct Nw (28027-8235)
PHONE.............................215 287-9145
Eric Petty, *Prin*
EMP: 4 EST: 2019
SALES (est): 68.53K **Privately Held**
SIC: **2741** Miscellaneous publishing

(G-4222)
CALI METAL POLISH
2044 Wilshire Ct Sw (28025-6417)
PHONE.............................704 788-2466
Berto Barrida, *Owner*
EMP: 5 EST: 2011
SALES (est): 72.09K **Privately Held**
Web: www.calimetalpolish.com
SIC: **2842** Metal polish

(G-4223)
CAPNOSTICS LLC
9724 Colts Neck Ln (28027-2873)
PHONE.............................610 442-1363
EMP: 10 EST: 2017
SALES (est): 319.18K
SALES (corp-wide): 377K **Publicly Held**
Web: www.pavmed.com
SIC: **2834** Pharmaceutical preparations
PA: Pavmed Inc.
60 E 42nd St Rm 4600
New York NY 10165
212 949-4319

(G-4224)
CARBOTECH USA INC
4031 Dearborn Pl Nw (28027-4624)
P.O. Box 2907 (28151-2907)
PHONE.............................704 481-8500
Lawrence D Narcus, *Pr*
Deborah Narcus, *VP*
EMP: 6 EST: 2002
SALES (est): 909.54K **Privately Held**
Web: www.ctbrakes.com
SIC: **3714** Motor vehicle parts and accessories

(G-4225)
CAROLINA TARWHEELS WHLCHAIRBS
2404 Lynn Dr (28025-8904)
PHONE.............................704 791-5803
Donnie R Langford, *Prin*
EMP: 6 EST: 2009
SALES (est): 170.44K **Privately Held**
SIC: **3842** Wheelchairs

(G-4226)
CAROLINA VINYL SHACK LLC
7300 Flowes Store Rd (28025-9294)
PHONE.............................704 788-9493
Brandi A Roy, *Owner*
EMP: 8 EST: 2018
SALES (est): 232.49K **Privately Held**
Web: www.carolinavinylshack.com
SIC: **2759** Screen printing

(G-4227)
CARTERS MACHINE COMPANY INC
540 Lake Lynn Rd (28025-9648)
PHONE.............................704 784-3106
Jeff W Carter, *Pr*
EMP: 5 EST: 1985
SQ FT: 4,200
SALES (est): 509.65K **Privately Held**
SIC: **3599** Machine shop, jobbing and repair

(G-4228)
CASCO SIGNS INC
199 Wilshire Ave Sw (28025-5633)
PHONE.............................704 788-9055
Cheryl Crutchfield, *CEO*
Cheryl Trutthsield, *
EMP: 40 EST: 1998
SALES (est): 4.89MM **Privately Held**
Web: www.cascosigns.com
SIC: **3993** Signs and advertising specialties

(G-4229)
CELESTIAL PUBLISHING
208 Tournament Dr Sw (28025-5555)
PHONE.............................704 701-2027
Margaret Bell, *Prin*
EMP: 5 EST: 2018
SALES (est): 67.65K **Privately Held**
SIC: **2741** Miscellaneous publishing

(G-4230)
CELGARD LLC
390 Business Blvd Nw (28027-6597)
PHONE.............................704 720-5200
Michael S Swanson, *Prin*
EMP: 80
Web: www.celgard.com
SIC: **2821** Plastics materials and resins
HQ: Celgard, Llc
11430 N Cmnity Hse Rd
Charlotte NC 28277
800 235-4273

(G-4231)
CHARLOTTE PRINTING COMPANY INC (PA)
Also Called: Evangelistic Press
3751 Dakeita Cir (28025-9262)
PHONE.............................704 888-5181
James Martin, *Pr*
Greg Thorton, *VP*
Tommie S Burris, *Sec*
EMP: 13 EST: 1964
SQ FT: 15,000
SALES (est): 789.04K
SALES (corp-wide): 789.04K **Privately Held**
Web: www.charlotteprinting.com
SIC: **2752** Offset printing

(G-4232)
CHEM-TEX LABORATORIES INC
180 Gee Rd (28025)
P.O. Box 5228 (28027-1503)
PHONE.............................706 602-8600
Michael Smith, *Pr*
David Bilbro, *
▲ EMP: 26 EST: 1973
SQ FT: 1,000
SALES (est): 2.23MM **Privately Held**
Web: www.chemtexlaboratories.com
SIC: **2899** 5169 Chemical preparations, nec; Chemicals and allied products, nec

(G-4233)
CLEARWATER SERVICES LLC
563 Webb Rd (28025-9072)
PHONE.............................704 995-9260
Lisa Meador, *Prin*
Bill Meador, *Prin*
EMP: 4 EST: 2018
SALES (est): 81.58K **Privately Held**
SIC: **3432** Plumbing fixture fittings and trim

(G-4234)
CLIENT CARE WEB INC
Also Called: Ccw
4078 Morris Burn Dr Sw (28027-9411)
P.O. Box 503 (28075-0503)
PHONE.............................704 787-9901
William Copeland, *CEO*
EMP: 34 EST: 2004
SALES (est): 2.49MM **Privately Held**
Web: www.clientcareweb.com
SIC: **7372** Business oriented computer software

(G-4235)
COLEYS PRINTING
160 Warren C Coleman Blvd N 23 (28027-6786)
PHONE.............................704 785-8837
David Coley, *Prin*
EMP: 5 EST: 2010
SALES (est): 104.23K **Privately Held**
SIC: **2752** Commercial printing, lithographic

(G-4236)
COMFORT PUBLISHING SVCS LLC
Also Called: Cabarrus Business Magazine
8890 Brandon Cir (28025-8112)
P.O. Box 6265 (28027-1521)
PHONE.............................704 907-7848
EMP: 5 EST: 2000
SALES (est): 800K **Privately Held**
Web: www.comfortpublishing.com
SIC: **5192** 2731 Magazines; Book publishing

(G-4237)
COMMDOOR INC
5555 Yorke St Nw (28027-5333)
PHONE.............................800 565-1851
Larry Canipe, *Prin*
EMP: 9 EST: 2008
SALES (est): 109.33K **Privately Held**
Web: www.commdooraluminum.com
SIC: **3999** Manufacturing industries, nec

(G-4238)
COMMERCIAL VEHICLE GROUP INC
2845 Armentrout Dr (28025-5866)
PHONE.............................704 886-6407
EMP: 38
SALES (corp-wide): 994.68MM **Publicly Held**
Web: www.cvgrp.com
SIC: **3714** Motor vehicle parts and accessories
PA: Commercial Vehicle Group, Inc.
7800 Walton Pkwy
New Albany OH 43054
614 289-5360

(G-4239)
CONCORD CUSTOM CABINETS
4530 Cochran Farm Rd Sw (28027-9210)
PHONE.............................704 773-0081
EMP: 4 EST: 2011
SALES (est): 78.85K **Privately Held**
SIC: **2434** Wood kitchen cabinets

(G-4240)
CONCORD PRINTING COMPANY INC
660 Abington Dr Ne (28025-2568)
PHONE.............................704 786-3717
Ben Palmer, *Pr*
Pat Palmer, *
EMP: 10 EST: 1971
SALES (est): 427.69K **Privately Held**
Web: www.concordprint.com
SIC: **2752** 2759 Offset printing; Letterpress printing

(G-4241)
CONCORD TRADING INC
225 Wilshire Ave Sw (28025-5631)
PHONE.............................704 375-3333
Sam Kapland, *Pr*
Lake Elrod, *CNTR**
EMP: 27 EST: 2017
SQ FT: 70,000
SALES (est): 1.12MM **Privately Held**
SIC: **2251** 2252 Panty hose; Socks

(G-4242)
CONTAMINANT CONTROL
440 Action Dr Nw (28027-4128)
PHONE.............................704 886-0205
Mark Vestal, *Owner*
EMP: 7 EST: 2004
SALES (est): 101.21K **Privately Held**
SIC: **3292** Asbestos building materials, except asbestos paper

(G-4243)
CONTROLS INSTRUMENTATION INC
Also Called: CIC
272 International Dr Nw (28027-9406)
PHONE.............................704 786-1700
Joseph Krause, *Pr*
Bill Will, *VP*
EMP: 10 EST: 1985
SALES (est): 1.27MM **Privately Held**
Web: www.cicpro.com
SIC: **3825** Instruments to measure electricity

GEOGRAPHIC SECTION — Concord - Cabarrus County (G-4270)

(G-4244)
COSATRON
640 Church St N (28025-4320)
PHONE 704 785-8145
Eric Bratton, *Pr*
Doug Crooks, *Prin*
Larry Green, *Prin*
Hugh Bradley, *Prin*
EMP: 10 **EST:** 2014
SALES (est): 862.56K **Privately Held**
Web: www.cosatron.com
SIC: 3564   Air cleaning systems

(G-4245)
COUGAR RUN WINERY
215 Union St S (28025-5050)
PHONE 704 788-2746
John Boardson, *Bd of Dir*
EMP: 10 **EST:** 2012
SALES (est): 214.88K **Privately Held**
Web: www.cougarrunwinery.com
SIC: 2084   Wines

(G-4246)
CPM OF NC INC
4222 Barfield St (28027-9608)
PHONE 704 467-5819
EMP: 8 **EST:** 2011
SALES (est): 173.61K **Privately Held**
SIC: 1389 0721   Construction, repair, and dismantling services; Weed control services, after planting

(G-4247)
CROWN EQUIPMENT CORPORATION
Crown Lift Trucks
8401 Westmoreland Dr Nw (28027-7596)
PHONE 704 721-4000
Alan Rudolph, *Bmch Mgr*
EMP: 99
SALES (corp-wide): 7.12B **Privately Held**
Web: www.crown.com
SIC: 3537   Lift trucks, industrial: fork, platform, straddle, etc.
PA: Crown Equipment Corporation
   44 S Washington St
   New Bremen OH 45869
   419 629-2311

(G-4248)
CROWN TOWN INDUSTRIES LLC
813 Hydrangea Cir Nw (28027-7259)
PHONE 704 579-0387
Kenneth Baltes, *Managing Member*
EMP: 5 **EST:** 2015
SALES (est): 143.47K **Privately Held**
SIC: 3999   Manufacturing industries, nec

(G-4249)
CUSTOM ELECTRIC MFG LLC
Also Called: Kanthal
180 International Dr Nw (28027-9443)
PHONE 248 305-7700
Bob Edwards, *Pr*
EMP: 20 **EST:** 2018
SALES (est): 5.05MM
SALES (corp-wide): 1.75B **Privately Held**
Web: www.custom-electric.com
SIC: 3567   Heating units and devices, industrial: electric
HQ: Kanthal Ab
   Sorkvarnsvagen 3
   Hallstahammar 734 4
   22021101

(G-4250)
CZECHMATE ENTERPRISES LLC
6101 Zion Church Rd (28025-7058)
PHONE 704 784-6547
EMP: 5 **EST:** 1994
SQ FT: 1,000
SALES (est): 388.78K **Privately Held**
Web: www.czech-mate.com
SIC: 7371 3823   Software programming applications; Data loggers, industrial process type

(G-4251)
DARK HYDROGEN LLC
Also Called: Reapers Religous Secret Soc
2557 Fallbrook Pl Nw (28027-7708)
P.O. Box 7592 (28027-1544)
PHONE 530 360-8660
EMP: 4 **EST:** 2018
SALES (est): 118.52K **Privately Held**
SIC: 2813   Hydrogen

(G-4252)
DBW PRINT & PROMO
6012 Bayfield Pkwy (28027-7597)
PHONE 704 906-8551
Dianne Walker, *Prin*
EMP: 5 **EST:** 2013
SALES (est): 169.91K **Privately Held**
SIC: 2752   Commercial printing, lithographic

(G-4253)
DEB MANUFACTURING INC
4040 Dearborn Pl Nw (28027-4624)
PHONE 704 703-6618
Daniel Miller, *Pr*
Hollis Mueller, *Treas*
EMP: 8 **EST:** 1989
SALES (est): 998.1K **Privately Held**
Web: www.debmfg.com
SIC: 3544 3728   Industrial molds; Aircraft parts and equipment, nec

(G-4254)
DMC LLC
1319 Lily Green Ct Nw (28027-2304)
PHONE 980 352-9806
Airelle Mcneal, *CEO*
Airelle Dodson, *
EMP: 50 **EST:** 2019
SALES (est): 1.8MM **Privately Held**
SIC: 8742 3644 1731   Marketing consulting services; Scrubbers for CATV systems; Cable television installation

(G-4255)
DNP IMAGINGCOMM AMERICA CORP (DH)
Also Called: Dnp Photo Imaging
4524 Enterprise Dr Nw (28027-6437)
PHONE 704 784-8100
▲ **EMP:** 355 **EST:** 1994
SQ FT: 270,000
SALES (est): 143.7MM **Privately Held**
Web: www.dnpphoto.com
SIC: 3955   Ribbons, inked: typewriter, adding machine, register, etc.
HQ: Dnp Corporation Usa
   780 3rd Ave Rm 1000
   New York NY 10017

(G-4256)
DOUBLE O PLASTICS INC
981 Biscayne Dr (28027-8424)
PHONE 704 788-8517
EMP: 48 **EST:** 1990
SALES (est): 4.95MM **Privately Held**
Web: www.doubleoplastics.com
SIC: 3089   Injection molding of plastics

(G-4257)
DOUBLE R WELDING & FABRICATION
4441 Motorsports Dr Sw Ste 10 (28027-8933)
PHONE 704 340-5825
Richard Russell, *Owner*
EMP: 5 **EST:** 2013
SALES (est): 46.59K **Privately Held**
SIC: 7692   Welding repair

(G-4258)
DRAGONFLY STUDIOS
190 Pitts School Rd Nw (28027-0304)
PHONE 704 706-2910
EMP: 7 **EST:** 2011
SQ FT: 11,000
SALES (est): 485.21K **Privately Held**
Web: www.dragonflystudiosnc.com
SIC: 2431   Millwork

(G-4259)
EAST COAST DOOR & HARDWARE INC
464 Action Dr Nw (28027-4128)
PHONE 704 791-4128
Deanna Smith, *Pr*
EMP: 4 **EST:** 2016
SALES (est): 378.13K **Privately Held**
SIC: 2431   Doors and door parts and trim, wood

(G-4260)
ELOMI INC
Also Called: Piedmont Machine & Mfg
22 Carpenter Ct Nw (28027-4627)
PHONE 904 591-0095
Neil Lansing, *Pr*
EMP: 25 **EST:** 2016
SALES (est): 1.37MM **Privately Held**
Web: www.piedmontmachine.com
SIC: 3599   Machine shop, jobbing and repair

(G-4261)
FABRICATION AUTOMATION LLC
2772 Concord Pkwy S (28027-9046)
PHONE 704 785-2120
Randal Stewart, *Genl Mgr*
EMP: 5 **EST:** 1997
SALES (est): 2.06MM **Privately Held**
Web: www.fabricationautomation.com
SIC: 3441   Fabricated structural metal

(G-4262)
FABRICTED PARTS ASSEMBLIES LLC
5552 Yorke St Nw (28027-5333)
PHONE 704 784-3376
Alexander Nicholson, *Prin*
EMP: 4 **EST:** 2010
SALES (est): 76.07K **Privately Held**
SIC: 3441   Fabricated structural metal

(G-4263)
FAITH PRSTHTC-RTHOTIC SVCS INC (DH)
1025 Concord Pkwy N (28027-5923)
P.O. Box 792 (28026-0792)
PHONE 704 782-0908
Jim Price, *Pr*
Ida L Price, *Treas*
Steve Overcash, *VP*
Carol Lynn Price Rorie, *Sec*
EMP: 11 **EST:** 1960
SALES (est): 5.53MM
SALES (corp-wide): 1.12B **Privately Held**
Web: www.opiesoftware.com
SIC: 3842 5999   Limbs, artificial; Orthopedic and prosthesis applications
HQ: Hanger Prosthetics & Orthotics, Inc.
   10910 Domain Dr Ste 300
   Austin TX 78758
   512 777-3800

(G-4264)
FIBERON ✪
411 International Dr Nw (28027-9408)
PHONE 704 463-2955
EMP: 7 **EST:** 2022
SALES (est): 79.3K **Privately Held**
SIC: 2491   Wood preserving

(G-4265)
FINE SHEER INDUSTRIES INC
Also Called: Highland Mills
225 Wilshire Ave Sw (28025-5631)
P.O. Box 5043 (28027-1500)
PHONE 704 375-3333
EMP: 257
SALES (corp-wide): 9.59MM **Privately Held**
Web: www.finesheer.com
SIC: 2251 2252   Panty hose; Socks
PA: Fine Sheer Industries, Inc.
   350 5th Ave Ste 4710
   New York NY 10118
   212 594-4224

(G-4266)
FORTILINE LLC (DH)
Also Called: Fortiline Waterworks
7025 Northwinds Dr Nw (28027-3334)
P.O. Box 797507 (75379-7507)
PHONE 704 788-9800
Tim Tysinger, *Managing Member*
Mike Swedick, *
▼ **EMP:** 35 **EST:** 1988
SALES (est): 105.99MM **Privately Held**
Web: www.fortiline.com
SIC: 3317 5085   Steel pipe and tubes; Valves and fittings
HQ: Fortiline, Inc.
   7025 Northwinds Dr Nw
   Concord NC 28027

(G-4267)
FRANKLIN / KERR PRESS LLC
213 Franklin Ave Nw (28025-4908)
PHONE 828 216-3021
Jordon Greene, *Prin*
EMP: 6 **EST:** 2017
SALES (est): 39.14K **Privately Held**
Web: www.franklinkerr.com
SIC: 2741   Miscellaneous publishing

(G-4268)
FULLY INVOLVED PRINTING LLC
4008 Parkmont Rd (28025-1392)
PHONE 980 521-2670
Kenneth Good, *Prin*
EMP: 4 **EST:** 2020
SALES (est): 83.91K **Privately Held**
Web: www.fullyinvolvedprint.com
SIC: 2752   Commercial printing, lithographic

(G-4269)
FUN-TEES INC
2583 Armentrout Dr (28025-5864)
PHONE 704 788-3003
EMP: 5
SALES (corp-wide): 415.35MM **Publicly Held**
Web: www.campechesportswear.com
SIC: 2321   Men's and boy's furnishings
HQ: Fun-Tees, Inc.
   4735 Corp Dr Nw Ste 100
   Concord NC 28027
   704 788-3003

(G-4270)
FUN-TEES INC (HQ)
4735 Corporate Dr Nw Ste 100 (28027)
PHONE 704 788-3003
Will Mcghea, *Pr*

Concord - Cabarrus County (G-4271) — GEOGRAPHIC SECTION

Lewis Reid Junior, *Pr*
Chris Doughlas, *
Larry Martin Junior, *VP*
Marcus Weibel, *
◆ **EMP:** 78 **EST:** 1974
SQ FT: 72,000
SALES (est): 4.8MM
SALES (corp-wide): 415.35MM **Publicly Held**
Web: www.funtees.com
SIC: 2321 2361 2331 Men's and boy's furnishings; T-shirts and tops: girls', children's, and infants'; T-shirts and tops, women's: made from purchased materials
PA: Delta Apparel, Inc.
2750 Premiere Pkwy # 100
Duluth GA 30097
678 775-6900

(G-4271)
G60 CNC LLC
5817 Rocky Trace Ct Nw (28027-4609)
PHONE....................704 796-0478
Dennis Schoenfeldt, *Prin*
EMP: 5 **EST:** 2013
SALES (est): 80.63K **Privately Held**
SIC: 3599 Machine shop, jobbing and repair

(G-4272)
GENIXUS CORP
Also Called: Genixus
4715 Corporate Dr Nw Ste 100 (28027)
PHONE....................877 436-4987
EMP: 5
SALES (corp-wide): 2.66MM **Privately Held**
SIC: 2834 Pharmaceutical preparations
PA: Genixus, Corp.
150 N Research Campus Dr
Kannapolis NC 28081
877 436-4987

(G-4273)
GEONICS
4994 Aztec Dr (28025-8216)
PHONE....................704 956-7999
George W Cox, *Prin*
EMP: 6 **EST:** 2016
SALES (est): 46.2K **Privately Held**
Web: www.geonicsinc.com
SIC: 3599 Machine shop, jobbing and repair

(G-4274)
GIBBS PERFORMANCE SPC INC
7075 Aviation Blvd Nw Ste B (28027)
PHONE....................704 746-2225
EMP: 4 **EST:** 2020
SALES (est): 66.36K **Privately Held**
Web: www.gibbsperformancespecialties.com
SIC: 7692 Welding repair

(G-4275)
GM DEFENSE LLC
4540 Fortune Ave (28027-8788)
PHONE....................800 462-8782
EMP: 64
SIC: 3711 3714 Motor vehicles and car bodies; Motor vehicle parts and accessories
HQ: Gm Defense Llc
300 Renaissance Ctr Fl 24
Detroit MI 48243
313 462-8782

(G-4276)
GREY HOUSE PUBLISHING INC
Also Called: Grey House Publishing
624 Foxwood Dr Se (28027-2768)
PHONE....................704 784-0051
EMP: 4
SALES (corp-wide): 5.54MM **Privately Held**
SIC: 2741 Miscellaneous publishing
PA: Grey House Publishing, Inc.
4919 Route 22
Amenia NY 12501
518 789-8700

(G-4277)
HARRIS SOLAR INC
356 Belvedere Dr Nw (28027-9604)
PHONE....................704 490-8374
Rupert E Harris Junior, *Pr*
EMP: 5 **EST:** 2009
SALES (est): 292.05K **Privately Held**
SIC: 3674 Semiconductors and related devices

(G-4278)
HATLEYS SIGNS & SERVICE INC
4495 Motorsports Dr Sw Ste 110 # 1 (28028-8916)
PHONE....................704 723-4027
Danny Hatley, *Owner*
EMP: 5 **EST:** 2008
SALES (est): 326.8K **Privately Held**
Web: hatleysignservice.weebly.com
SIC: 3993 Signs and advertising specialties

(G-4279)
HIGH BRANCH BREWING CO LLC
325 Mcgill Ave Nw Ste 148 (28027-0011)
PHONE....................704 706-3807
EMP: 9 **EST:** 2015
SQ FT: 1,400
SALES (est): 366.42K **Privately Held**
Web: www.highbranchbrewing.com
SIC: 2082 5813 Beer (alcoholic beverage); Beer garden (drinking places)

(G-4280)
HIGHIQ LLC
261 Lincoln St Sw (28025-5424)
PHONE....................704 956-8716
EMP: 8 **EST:** 2020
SALES (est): 250K **Privately Held**
SIC: 3161 Clothing and apparel carrying cases

(G-4281)
HIGHLIGHT INDUSTRIES INC
537 Geary St Nw (28027-8210)
PHONE....................704 661-1734
Robert Hahn, *Prin*
EMP: 8 **EST:** 2008
SALES (est): 79.96K **Privately Held**
SIC: 3999 Manufacturing industries, nec

(G-4282)
HYDROMER INC (PA)
4715 Corporate Dr Nw Ste 200 (28027)
PHONE....................908 526-2828
Michael E Torti, *CEO*
Manfred F Dyck, *Ch Bd*
Robert Y Lee, *VP Fin*
Martin Von Dyck, *COO*
John Konar, *QA*
◆ **EMP:** 28 **EST:** 1980
SQ FT: 35,000
SALES (est): 10.57MM
SALES (corp-wide): 10.57MM **Publicly Held**
Web: www.hydromer.com
SIC: 8731 2261 Biotechnical research, commercial; Chemical coating or treating of cotton broadwoven fabrics

(G-4283)
ICS NORTH AMERICA CORP
Also Called: Reality Check Sports
323 Corban Ave Sw Ste 504 (28025-5176)
P.O. Box 1278 (28026-1278)
PHONE....................704 794-6620
Terry Fahmey, *Pr*
▲ **EMP:** 20 **EST:** 2003
SALES (est): 3.07MM **Privately Held**
Web: www.ramcolifestyles.com
SIC: 5136 5137 2329 2326 Men's and boys' sportswear and work clothing; Sportswear, women's and children's; Men's and boys' sportswear and athletic clothing; Medical and hospital uniforms, men's

(G-4284)
IMPACT TECHNOLOGIES LLC
4171 Deerfield Dr Nw (28027-4519)
PHONE....................704 400-5364
EMP: 7 **EST:** 2014
SALES (est): 510.03K **Privately Held**
Web: www.impactaudioandvideo.com
SIC: 2891 Sealants

(G-4285)
INGLE PROTECTIVE SYSTEMS INC
231 Pounds Ave Sw (28025-4700)
P.O. Box 586 (28026-0586)
PHONE....................704 788-3327
Dean Andrews, *Pr*
Mark Andrews, *VP*
Christopher Andrews, *Treas*
Gregory Andrews, *Sec*
EMP: 14 **EST:** 1997
SQ FT: 10,000
SALES (est): 466.06K **Privately Held**
Web: www.worldfibers.net
SIC: 3842 Gloves, safety

(G-4286)
INTELLIGENT TOOL CORP
1151 Biscayne Dr (28027-8403)
PHONE....................704 799-0449
Patrick Godwin, *Pr*
EMP: 15 **EST:** 1993
SALES (est): 1MM **Privately Held**
Web: www.intelligenttoolcorp.com
SIC: 3599 7389 Machine shop, jobbing and repair; Grinding, precision: commercial or industrial

(G-4287)
INTERNATIONAL EMBROIDERY
2890 Highway 49 N (28025-6203)
PHONE....................704 792-0641
Lori Jones, *Owner*
EMP: 4 **EST:** 1985
SQ FT: 11,000
SALES (est): 139.11K **Privately Held**
SIC: 2395 Embroidery products, except Schiffli machine

(G-4288)
INTERSTATE ALL BATTERIES CTR
8605 Concord Mills Blvd (28027-5400)
PHONE....................704 979-3430
Mike Rushing, *Mgr*
Mike Rushing, *Prin*
EMP: 4 **EST:** 2001
SALES (est): 485.97K **Privately Held**
Web: www.interstatebatteries.com
SIC: 5063 3613 Storage batteries, industrial; Distribution boards, electric

(G-4289)
IPS
338 Webb Rd (28025-9018)
PHONE....................704 788-3327
Dean Andrews, *Owner*
EMP: 8 **EST:** 2017
SALES (est): 46.43K **Privately Held**
Web: www.ips.us
SIC: 2791 Typesetting

(G-4290)
IRVAN-SMITH INC
1027 Central Dr Nw Frnt (28027-4201)
PHONE....................704 788-2554
Vic Irvan, *Pr*
Kevin Smith, *VP*
Jo Irvan, *Sec*
Tracy Smith, *Treas*
▲ **EMP:** 10 **EST:** 1982
SQ FT: 10,000
SALES (est): 1.48MM **Privately Held**
Web: www.irvansmith.com
SIC: 3465 5531 Body parts, automobile: stamped metal; Automotive parts

(G-4291)
ITEK GRAPHICS LLC
7075 Aviation Blvd Nw Ste B (28027)
PHONE....................704 357-6002
Rick Mitchell, *
Julli Goodwin, *
EMP: 40 **EST:** 2009
SQ FT: 90,000
SALES (est): 5.42MM **Privately Held**
Web: www.itekrocks.com
SIC: 2752 2789 Offset printing; Bookbinding and related work

(G-4292)
JASPER PENSKE ENGINES
Also Called: Power Tech Engines
4361 Motorsports Dr Sw (28027-8977)
PHONE....................704 788-8996
EMP: 12 **EST:** 1998
SALES (est): 896.62K **Privately Held**
Web: www.teampenske.com
SIC: 3519 3711 Engines, diesel and semi-diesel or dual-fuel; Motor vehicles and car bodies

(G-4293)
JFL ENTERPRISES INC
Also Called: Failure Free Reading
82 Spring St Sw (28025-5003)
P.O. Box 386 (28026-0386)
PHONE....................704 786-7838
Joseph F Lockavitch, *Pr*
Angela Lockavitch, *Sec*
EMP: 6 **EST:** 1988
SQ FT: 10,000
SALES (est): 825.54K **Privately Held**
Web: www.failurefree.com
SIC: 2731 7372 8299 Books, publishing only ; Publisher's computer software; Tutoring school

(G-4294)
JOHNSON CONCRETE COMPANY
Also Called: Johnson Concrete Products
106 Old Davidson Pl Nw (28027-4312)
PHONE....................704 786-4204
EMP: 34
SALES (corp-wide): 24.37MM **Privately Held**
Web: www.johnsonproductsusa.com
SIC: 3271 Blocks, concrete or cinder: standard
PA: Johnson Concrete Company
217 Klumac Rd
Salisbury NC 28144
704 636-5231

(G-4295)
JOIE OF SEATING INC
4537 Orphanage Rd (28027-9633)
PHONE....................704 795-7474
Randall Lajoie, *Pr*
Lisa Lajoie, *VP*
EMP: 17 **EST:** 1998
SALES (est): 1.78MM **Privately Held**
Web: www.thejoieofseating.com

GEOGRAPHIC SECTION

Concord - Cabarrus County (G-4321)

SIC: **2531 5947** Seats, automobile; Gift, novelty, and souvenir shop

(G-4296)
JR SIGNS LLC
Also Called: Fastsigns
147 Union St S (28025-5011)
PHONE.....................980 255-3083
EMP: 4 **EST:** 2020
SALES (est): 50.69K **Privately Held**
Web: www.fastsigns.com
SIC: **3993** Signs and advertising specialties

(G-4297)
K&H ACQUISITION COMPANY LLC
Also Called: D A Moore
36 Oak Dr Sw (28027-7107)
P.O. Box 1150 (28026-1150)
PHONE.....................704 788-1128
EMP: 9 **EST:** 1973
SQ FT: 25,000
SALES (est): 1.44MM **Privately Held**
Web: www.damoorecorp.com
SIC: **3444** Sheet metalwork

(G-4298)
KANTHAL THERMAL PROCESS INC
180 International Dr Nw Ste A (28027-9443)
PHONE.....................704 784-3001
James T Johnson, *CEO*
Frank Figoni, *Fin Mgr*
▲ **EMP:** 75 **EST:** 1981
SALES (est): 21.97MM
SALES (corp-wide): 11.77B **Privately Held**
SIC: **3559** Semiconductor manufacturing machinery
HQ: Sandvik, Inc.
  1483 Dogwood Way
  Mebane NC 27302
  919 563-5008

(G-4299)
KB SIGN SOLUTIONS LLC
4555 Mtrsprts Dr Sw Ste 1 (28027)
PHONE.....................217 474-5861
EMP: 4 **EST:** 2019
SALES (est): 158.28K **Privately Held**
SIC: **3993** Signs and advertising specialties

(G-4300)
KETCHIE-HOUSTON INC
Also Called: Ketchie-Houston
201 Winecoff School Rd (28027-4143)
PHONE.....................704 786-5101
Robert Ketchie, *Pr*
Edgar Ketchie, *Ch Bd*
Ann Ketchie, *Sec*
Courtney Ketchie, *VP*
Bobby Ketchie, *Prin*
▲ **EMP:** 20 **EST:** 1947
SQ FT: 25,000
SALES (est): 4.58MM **Privately Held**
Web: www.ketchiemeansquality.com
SIC: **3462 3562 3568 3429** Gears, forged steel; Ball bearings and parts; Power transmission equipment, nec; Hardware, nec

(G-4301)
LEGACY VULCAN LLC
Also Called: Mideast Division
7680 Poplar Tent Rd (28027-7593)
P.O. Box 3110 (28025)
PHONE.....................704 788-3833
EMP: 4
Web: www.vulcanmaterials.com
SIC: **3273 1423** Ready-mixed concrete; Crushed and broken granite
HQ: Legacy Vulcan, Llc
  1200 Urban Center Dr
  Vestavia AL 35242
  205 298-3000

(G-4302)
LEGENDS COUNTERTOPS LLC
138 Buffalo Ave Nw Unit 3 (28025-4622)
PHONE.....................980 230-4501
Jorge Guzman, *Managing Member*
EMP: 4
SALES (est): 184.13K **Privately Held**
SIC: **2499** Kitchen, bathroom, and household ware: wood

(G-4303)
LETS BUILD IT WOODWORKING
414 Arlee Cir Sw (28025-9204)
PHONE.....................704 352-7131
Thomas Empie, *Prin*
EMP: 5 **EST:** 2017
SALES (est): 61.97K **Privately Held**
SIC: **2431** Millwork

(G-4304)
LINDER INDUSTRIAL MACHINERY CO
5733 Davidson Hwy (28027-8482)
PHONE.....................980 777-8345
EMP: 7 **EST:** 2004
SALES (est): 714.12K **Privately Held**
SIC: **3531** Construction machinery

(G-4305)
LIONEL LLC (PA)
6301 Performance Dr Sw (28027-3426)
PHONE.....................704 454-4200
Howard Hitchcock, *CEO*
◆ **EMP:** 100 **EST:** 1986
SQ FT: 50,000
SALES (est): 25.57MM
SALES (corp-wide): 25.57MM **Privately Held**
Web: www.lionel.com
SIC: **3944** Trains and equipment, toy: electric and mechanical

(G-4306)
LOADING REPUBLIC INC
Also Called: Blackwater
191 Crowell Dr Nw (28025-4883)
PHONE.....................704 561-1077
Bradley Gresham, *CEO*
Caleb Clark, *COO*
EMP: 9 **EST:** 2014
SALES (est): 737.65K **Privately Held**
Web: www.loadingrepublicammo.com
SIC: **3489** Ordnance and accessories, nec

(G-4307)
LOMAR SPECIALTY ADVG INC
Also Called: Lsa
7148 Weddington Rd Nw Ste 110 (28027-3663)
PHONE.....................704 788-4380
Marlo Lee, *Pr*
Lorraine Lee, *CEO*
▲ **EMP:** 10 **EST:** 2001
SALES (est): 961.76K **Privately Held**
Web: www.lomarspecialtyad.com
SIC: **7311 2393 2399 2392** Advertising agencies; Textile bags; Sleeping bags; Laundry, garment and storage bags

(G-4308)
LYNN ELECTRONICS CORPORATION
5409 Shoreview Dr (28025-9417)
PHONE.....................704 369-0093
John Stuart Lynn, *Pr*
Jean Griswold, *VP*
EMP: 5 **EST:** 1985
SQ FT: 15,000
SALES (est): 445.89K **Privately Held**
Web: www.specialmachines.com
SIC: **3625 3577 3541** Relays and industrial controls; Encoders, computer peripheral equipment; Machine tools, metal cutting type

(G-4309)
MARTIN MARIETTA MATERIALS INC
Also Called: Martin Marietta Aggregates
7219 Weddington Rd Nw (28027-3468)
PHONE.....................704 786-8415
Ronald Borum, *Mgr*
EMP: 5
Web: www.martinmarietta.com
SIC: **1422** Crushed and broken limestone
PA: Martin Marietta Materials Inc
  4123 Parklake Ave
  Raleigh NC 27612

(G-4310)
MATEENBAR USA INC
2011 Highway 49 S (28027-8920)
PHONE.....................704 662-2005
Nick Crofts, *CEO*
EMP: 30 **EST:** 2020
SALES (est): 2.46MM **Privately Held**
Web: www.mateenbar.com
SIC: **3229** Glass fiber products

(G-4311)
MAX SOLUTIONS INC (PA)
Also Called: Max Solutions USA
700 Derita Rd Bldg B (28027-3343)
PHONE.....................203 683-8094
Richard Olear, *CEO*
Marc Shore, *Prin*
Dennis Kaltman, *Pr*
EMP: 24 **EST:** 2021
SALES (est): 9.22MM
SALES (corp-wide): 9.22MM **Privately Held**
Web: www.biggerthanpackaging.com
SIC: **2657** Folding paperboard boxes

(G-4312)
MELENDEZ SIGNS LLC
271 Crowell Dr Nw (28025-4819)
PHONE.....................980 298-4057
Silvia Melendez Escorza, *Prin*
EMP: 4 **EST:** 2016
SALES (est): 50.69K **Privately Held**
SIC: **3993** Signs and advertising specialties

(G-4313)
MICHAEL SIMMONS
Also Called: Fluid Sealing Supply
6012 Bayfield Pkwy Ste 302 (28027)
PHONE.....................704 298-1103
Michael Simmons, *Owner*
EMP: 4 **EST:** 2013
SALES (est): 221.72K **Privately Held**
Web: www.fluidsealingsupply.com
SIC: **3053** Gaskets, all materials

(G-4314)
MICHIGAN PACKAGING COMPANY
Also Called: Southeastern Packg Plant 2
2215 Mulberry Rd (28025-8951)
PHONE.....................704 455-4206
Todd Ross, *Mgr*
EMP: 25
SALES (corp-wide): 5.22B **Publicly Held**
SIC: **2653** Sheets, corrugated: made from purchased materials
HQ: Michigan Packaging Company Inc
  700 Eden Rd
  Mason MI 48854
  517 676-8700

(G-4315)
MIKES WELDING SERVICE OF CONC
643 Firecrest St Se (28025-9041)
PHONE.....................704 786-9795
Mike Herring, *Prin*
EMP: 5 **EST:** 2004
SALES (est): 78.73K **Privately Held**
SIC: **7692** Welding repair

(G-4316)
MINKA LIGHTING INC
Also Called: Madison Ave
435 Business Blvd Nw (28027-6556)
PHONE.....................704 785-9200
Dale Smith, *Mgr*
EMP: 83
SALES (corp-wide): 2.67MM **Privately Held**
Web: www.minkagroup.net
SIC: **3634 5063** Ceiling fans; Electrical apparatus and equipment
HQ: Minka Lighting, Llc
  1151 Bradford Cir
  Corona CA 92882
  951 735-9220

(G-4317)
MOBAY SPORTSWEAR EMBROIDERY
550 Cabarrus Ave W (28027-6259)
PHONE.....................704 262-7783
EMP: 4 **EST:** 2017
SALES (est): 54.01K **Privately Held**
SIC: **2395** Embroidery and art needlework

(G-4318)
MOORES CYLINDER HEADS LLC (PA)
Also Called: M C H
323 Corban Ave Sw Ste 515 (28025-5176)
P.O. Box 728 (28026-0728)
PHONE.....................704 786-8412
Larry Clark, *
▲ **EMP:** 30 **EST:** 1995
SQ FT: 35,000
SALES (est): 3.18MM **Privately Held**
SIC: **3714** Cylinder heads, motor vehicle

(G-4319)
MOROIL CORP
Also Called: Moroil Technologies
6867 Belt Rd (28027-2966)
P.O. Box 127 (28036-0127)
PHONE.....................704 795-9595
Ronald M Powell, *Pr*
▼ **EMP:** 11 **EST:** 1949
SQ FT: 15,000
SALES (est): 4.47MM **Privately Held**
Web: www.moroil.com
SIC: **5172 2992** Lubricating oils and greases; Brake fluid (hydraulic): made from purchased materials

(G-4320)
MUGO GRAVEL & GRADING INC (PA)
2600 Concord Pkwy S (28027-9045)
PHONE.....................704 782-3478
Karen Moore Christy, *Pr*
EMP: 40 **EST:** 2004
SALES (est): 10.25MM
SALES (corp-wide): 10.25MM **Privately Held**
Web: www.mugogravelgrading.com
SIC: **1442 1794** Construction sand and gravel; Excavation work

(G-4321)
MUSTANG REPRODUCTIONS INC
Also Called: Daniel Carpenter Mustang

Concord - Cabarrus County (G-4322)

4310 Concord Pkwy S (28027-4612)
PHONE..................704 786-0990
Daniel Carpenter, Pr
▲ EMP: 14 EST: 1982
SQ FT: 38,000
SALES (est): 1.87MM Privately Held
Web: www.dcmustang.com
SIC: 3069 Weather strip, sponge rubber

(G-4322)
MYSTIC LIFESTYLE INC
Also Called: Ibd Outdoor Rooms
184 Academy Ave Nw (28025-4829)
P.O. Box 2074 (28026-2074)
PHONE..................704 960-4530
Sheryl Isenhour, Pr
▲ EMP: 11 EST: 2002
SALES (est): 838.66K Privately Held
Web: www.ibdodr.com
SIC: 3271 Blocks, concrete: chimney or fireplace

(G-4323)
OFFICE SUP SVCS INC CHARLOTTE (PA)
Also Called: Office Supply Services
4490 Artdale Rd Sw (28027-0438)
PHONE..................704 786-4677
Linda Vreugdenhill, Pr
Garry G Vreugdenhill, *
Linda Vreugdenhill, *
EMP: 28 EST: 1985
SQ FT: 36,000
SALES (est): 2.31MM
SALES (corp-wide): 2.31MM Privately Held
Web: www.ossone.com
SIC: 2752 5021 5199 5943 Commercial printing, lithographic; Office furniture, nec; Advertising specialties; Office forms and supplies

(G-4324)
OILES AMERICA CORPORATION (HQ)
4510 Enterprise Dr Nw (28027-6437)
PHONE..................704 784-4500
Takahiko Uchida, Pr
Hiroshi Suda, Sec
Kazuhito Sato, Sec
Yasushi Honda, Sec
▲ EMP: 16 EST: 1998
SQ FT: 40,000
SALES (est): 42.91MM Privately Held
Web: www.oilesglobal.com
SIC: 3568 5085 Bearings, plain; Bearings
PA: Oiles Corporation
8, Kiriharacho
Fujisawa KNG 252-0

(G-4325)
OLD SOUTH MONOGRAMS & EMB LLC
2423 Christenbury Hall Dr Nw (28027-3312)
PHONE..................704 921-8115
Melissa Vacek, Prin
EMP: 4 EST: 2015
SALES (est): 57.47K Privately Held
SIC: 2395 Embroidery and art needlework

(G-4326)
OLDCASTLE INFRASTRUCTURE INC
4905 Stough Rd Sw (28027-8969)
PHONE..................704 788-4050
EMP: 24
SALES (corp-wide): 32.72B Privately Held
Web: www.oldcastleinfrastructure.com
SIC: 3272 Pipe, concrete or lined with concrete
HQ: Oldcastle Infrastructure, Inc.
7000 Central Pkwy Ste 800
Atlanta GA 30328
770 270-5000

(G-4327)
ON DEMAND SCREEN PRINTING LLC
2242 Roberta Rd (28027-5035)
PHONE..................704 661-0788
Bobby Joe Sturdivant Junior, Owner
EMP: 4 EST: 2016
SALES (est): 92.3K Privately Held
SIC: 2752 Commercial printing, lithographic

(G-4328)
OWENS CORNING GLASS METAL SVCS
4535 Enterprise Dr Nw (28027-6437)
PHONE..................704 721-2000
Jeff Smith, Prin
▲ EMP: 70 EST: 2003
SALES (est): 29.67MM Publicly Held
SIC: 3296 Fiberglass insulation
HQ: Owens Corning Sales, Llc
1 Owens Corning Pkwy
Toledo OH 43659
419 248-8000

(G-4329)
PASS & SEYMOUR INC
Also Called: Pass & Seymour Legrand
4515 Enterprise Dr Nw (28027-6437)
PHONE..................315 468-6211
Jim Todd, Brnch Mgr
EMP: 550
SQ FT: 331,666
Web: www.legrand.us
SIC: 3694 3643 Engine electrical equipment; Electric switches
HQ: Pass & Seymour, Inc.
50 Boyd Ave
Syracuse NY 13209
315 468-6211

(G-4330)
PATEL DEEPAL
Also Called: Power Clean Chem
4898 Aldridge Pl Nw (28027-3434)
PHONE..................704 634-5141
EMP: 5 EST: 2019
SALES (est): 101.56K Privately Held
SIC: 2842 7349 Disinfectants, household or industrial plant; Janitorial service, contract basis

(G-4331)
PERDUE FARMS INC
Perdue Farms
862 Harris St Nw (28025-4308)
PHONE..................704 789-2400
Karen Ray, Mgr
EMP: 1200
SQ FT: 126,708
SALES (corp-wide): 1.24B Privately Held
Web: www.perdue.com
SIC: 2015 Chicken, processed: fresh
PA: Perdue Farms Incorporated
31149 Old Ocean City Rd
Salisbury MD 21804
800 473-7383

(G-4332)
PIEDMONT WELD & PIPE INC
172 Buffalo Ave Nw (28025-4662)
P.O. Box 1314 (28026-1314)
PHONE..................704 782-7774
James Larry Templeton, Pr
EMP: 4 EST: 1983
SQ FT: 2,400
SALES (est): 456.52K Privately Held
SIC: 1799 7692 Welding on site; Welding repair

(G-4333)
PILGRIMS PRIDE CORPORATION
Also Called: Pilgrims Pride Chkn Oprtons Di
2925 Armentrout Dr (28025-5841)
PHONE..................704 721-3585
Douglas Jones, Mgr
EMP: 21
Web: www.pilgrims.com
SIC: 2015 Chicken, slaughtered and dressed
HQ: Pilgrim's Pride Corporation
1770 Promontory Cir
Greeley CO 80634
970 506-8000

(G-4334)
POWDER COATING BY 3 S X
4317 Triple Crown Dr Sw (28027-8978)
PHONE..................704 784-3724
Steve Burrows, Owner
EMP: 8 EST: 2006
SALES (est): 121.95K Privately Held
SIC: 3479 Metal coating and allied services

(G-4335)
PRECAST SUPPLY COMPANY INC
1201 Biscayne Dr (28027-9600)
P.O. Box 7589 (28027-1544)
PHONE..................704 784-2000
Mark Howard, Pr
EMP: 15 EST: 2005
SALES (est): 5.95MM Privately Held
Web: www.precastsupply.net
SIC: 3272 Precast terrazzo or concrete products

(G-4336)
PREGEL AMERICA INC (DH)
Also Called: Pregel America
4450 Fortune Ave Nw (28027-7901)
PHONE..................704 707-0300
Marco Casol, Pr
Russell Chapman, *
◆ EMP: 115 EST: 1967
SQ FT: 140,000
SALES (est): 17.43MM
SALES (corp-wide): 161.91MM Privately Held
Web: www.pregelamerica.com
SIC: 2099 Gelatin dessert preparations
HQ: Pre Gel Spa
Via Xi Settembre 2001 5/A
Scandiano RE 42019
052 239-4211

(G-4337)
PREZIOSO VENTURES LLC
Also Called: A-Line
5410 Powerhouse Ct (28027-5339)
PHONE..................704 793-1602
Charles Prezioso, Pr
Kristy Prezioso, Sec
EMP: 5 EST: 2015
SQ FT: 12,000
SALES (est): 492.47K Privately Held
SIC: 3499 3999 Machine bases, metal; Barber and beauty shop equipment

(G-4338)
PRIME BEVERAGE GROUP LLC (PA)
1858 Kannapolis Pkwy (28027-8550)
PHONE..................704 385-5450
Brian Hughs, Managing Member
EMP: 9 EST: 2019
SALES (est): 5.27MM
SALES (corp-wide): 5.27MM Privately Held
Web: www.primebev.com
SIC: 2087 Beverage bases

(G-4339)
PRIME BEVERAGE GROUP LLC
215 International Dr Nw Ste B (28027-6890)
PHONE..................704 385-5451
EMP: 138
SALES (corp-wide): 57MM Privately Held
SIC: 2087 Beverage bases
PA: Prime Beverage Group, Llc
12800 Jamesburg Dr
Huntersville NC 28027
704 385-5450

(G-4340)
PRO CAL PROF DECALS INC (PA)
4366 Triple Crown Dr Sw (28027-8978)
P.O. Box 2473 (29732-4473)
PHONE..................704 795-6090
Robert L Hogue, Pr
Charlotte Hogue, VP
EMP: 19 EST: 1981
SALES (est): 2.29MM
SALES (corp-wide): 2.29MM Privately Held
Web: www.procal1.com
SIC: 2759 2752 Decals: printing, nsk; Commercial printing, lithographic

(G-4341)
PRODUCT FINISHING SOLUTIONS CO
157 Softwind Ln (28025-9237)
PHONE..................704 785-8941
Paul Hurley, Pr
Sally Hurley, Sec
EMP: 4 EST: 2011
SALES (est): 269.83K Privately Held
SIC: 3089 3479 Coloring and finishing of plastics products; Painting, coating, and hot dipping

(G-4342)
PURPLE STAR GRAPHICS INC
32 Union St S (28025-5010)
PHONE..................704 723-4020
Corrella S Moran, Admn
EMP: 5 EST: 2016
SALES (est): 216.72K Privately Held
Web: www.purplestargraphics.com
SIC: 3993 Signs and advertising specialties

(G-4343)
PURSER CENTL REWINDING CO INC (PA)
865 Concord Pkwy N (28027-6039)
P.O. Box 1217 (28026-1217)
PHONE..................704 786-3131
Nicole Purser, Pr
Nancy H Purser, Sec
EMP: 12 EST: 1948
SQ FT: 6,000
SALES (est): 2.28MM
SALES (corp-wide): 2.28MM Privately Held
Web: www.pursercentral.com
SIC: 7694 5085 Electric motor repair; Industrial supplies

(G-4344)
QUEEN CITY ENGRG & DESIGN
369 Corban Ave Sw (28025-5160)
PHONE..................704 918-5851
EMP: 8 EST: 2020
SALES (est): 546.82K Privately Held
Web: www.queencityeng.com
SIC: 3449 Bars, concrete reinforcing: fabricated steel

(G-4345)
QUEEN WRIST BLING INC ✪
3066 Clover Rd Nw (28027-3810)
PHONE..................980 635-0287
Ayana Bramlett, *Prin*
EMP: 4 **EST:** 2022
SALES (est): 79.3K **Privately Held**
SIC: 3961 7389 Jewelry apparel, non-precious metals; Business Activities at Non-Commercial Site

(G-4346)
RACE TECHNOLOGIES CONCORD NC
7275 Westwinds Blvd Nw (28027-3310)
PHONE..................704 799-0530
EMP: 7 **EST:** 2018
SALES (est): 102.2K **Privately Held**
Web: www.racetechnologies.com
SIC: 3714 Motor vehicle parts and accessories

(G-4347)
RAMCO
323 Corban Ave Sw (28025-5173)
PHONE..................704 794-6620
EMP: 7 **EST:** 2013
SALES (est): 473.51K **Privately Held**
Web: wholesale.ramcolifestyles.com
SIC: 2329 Men's and boys' sportswear and athletic clothing

(G-4348)
RELIABLE WALLCOVERING LLC
7156 Weddington Rd Nw (28027-3476)
PHONE..................980 565-5224
Mike Coleman, *Brnch Mgr*
EMP: 7
SALES (corp-wide): 978.55K **Privately Held**
SIC: 2679 Wallpaper
PA: Reliable Wallcovering, Llc
   3439 Highway 411 Ne B
   White GA 30184
   770 428-7470

(G-4349)
RELIABLE WOODWORKS INC
Also Called: Reliable Hauling and Grading
2989 Old Salisbury Concord Rd (28025-7827)
PHONE..................704 785-9663
Josh W Airheart, *Pr*
Tamara Airheart, *VP*
EMP: 8 **EST:** 1991
SQ FT: 4,000
SALES (est): 1.23MM **Privately Held**
Web: www.reliablewoodworks.com
SIC: 2499 1611 Decorative wood and woodwork; General contractor, highway and street construction

(G-4350)
RICHARDSON RACING PRODUCTS INC
1028 Central Dr Nw Unit C (28027-4247)
PHONE..................704 784-2602
Steven Richardson, *Pr*
EMP: 7 **EST:** 1987
SALES (est): 600.05K **Privately Held**
Web: www.rrpinc.com
SIC: 3714 Motor vehicle parts and accessories

(G-4351)
ROBERT BLAKE
Also Called: Blake Enterprises
1522 La Forest Ln (28027-7508)
PHONE..................704 720-9341
Robert Blake, *Owner*
EMP: 5 **EST:** 1968
SQ FT: 7,500
SALES (est): 332.26K **Privately Held**
SIC: 3592 5013 Carburetors; Automotive supplies and parts

(G-4352)
ROMANOS PIZZA
Also Called: Romanos Pizza Italian Rest
349 Copperfield Blvd Ne Ste A (28025-2408)
PHONE..................704 782-5020
Salvatore Illiano, *Mgr*
EMP: 8 **EST:** 2000
SALES (est): 245.9K **Privately Held**
Web: romanospizzainc.a-zcompanies.com
SIC: 2041 Pizza dough, prepared

(G-4353)
RP MOTOR SPORTS INC
Also Called: Roush's Racing
4202 Roush Pl Nw (28027-7112)
PHONE..................704 720-4200
FAX: 704 720-4105
EMP: 32
SQ FT: 15,000
SALES (est): 1.87MM **Privately Held**
SIC: 7948 3714 3711 Auto race track operation; Motor vehicle parts and accessories; Motor vehicles and car bodies

(G-4354)
RQ INDUSTRIES INC
19 Franklin Ave Nw (28025-4703)
PHONE..................704 701-1071
Robert Nixon, *Owner*
EMP: 5 **EST:** 2016
SALES (est): 121.5K **Privately Held**
SIC: 3999 Manufacturing industries, nec

(G-4355)
S & D COFFEE INC (HQ)
Also Called: S & D Coffee and Tea
300 Concord Pkwy S (28027-6702)
P.O. Box 1628 (28026-1628)
PHONE..................704 782-3121
Jack Robinson, *Pr*
◆ **EMP:** 650 **EST:** 1927
SALES (est): 409.57MM **Publicly Held**
Web: www.westrockcoffee.com
SIC: 2095 5149 2086 Coffee roasting (except by wholesale grocers); Coffee, green or roasted; Tea, iced: packaged in cans, bottles, etc.
PA: Westrock Coffee Company
   4009 N Rodney Parham Rd
   Little Rock AR 72212

(G-4356)
SAFEWAZE LLC
225 Wilshire Ave Sw (28025-5631)
PHONE..................704 262-7893
Brian Colton, *CEO*
▲ **EMP:** 100 **EST:** 2016
SALES (est): 9.63MM **Privately Held**
Web: www.safewaze.com
SIC: 3842 Personal safety equipment

(G-4357)
SECURE BAG CUSTOM PRINTS
5225 Noble Dr Apt 201 (28027-0073)
PHONE..................856 834-9037
Atiya Williams, *Prin*
EMP: 4 **EST:** 2019
SALES (est): 76.29K **Privately Held**
SIC: 2752 Commercial printing, lithographic

(G-4358)
SIGN AND DOODLE
88 Church St Ne (28025-4757)
PHONE..................704 763-7501
EMP: 5 **EST:** 2014
SALES (est): 65.77K **Privately Held**
Web: www.signanddoodle.com
SIC: 3993 Signs and advertising specialties

(G-4359)
SIRIUS ENERGIES CORPORATION (PA)
545 Hamberton Ct Nw (28027-6513)
PHONE..................704 425-6272
Brooks Agnew, *Pr*
Robin H Lamb, *Sec*
▼ **EMP:** 5 **EST:** 2007
SALES (est): 793.7K **Privately Held**
SIC: 3621 Commutators, electric motor

(G-4360)
SMA ENTERPRISE LLC
4572 Kellybrook Dr (28025-7054)
PHONE..................980 616-0140
EMP: 4 **EST:** 2020
SALES (est): 186.56K **Privately Held**
SIC: 2051 Bakery: wholesale or wholesale/retail combined

(G-4361)
SNYDER PACKAGING INC
Also Called: Snyder Packaging
788 Harris St Nw (28025-4352)
PHONE..................704 786-3111
EMP: 86 **EST:** 1925
SALES (est): 13.02MM **Privately Held**
Web: www.snyderpkg.com
SIC: 2675 2657 Paperboard die-cutting; Folding paperboard boxes

(G-4362)
SONASPECTION INTERNATIONAL
6851 Belt Rd (28027-2966)
PHONE..................704 262-3384
Roy Duce, *Opers Mgr*
EMP: 11 **EST:** 1997
SQ FT: 1,750
SALES (est): 4.77MM
SALES (corp-wide): 34.57MM **Privately Held**
Web: www.sonaspection.com
SIC: 3699 Laser welding, drilling, and cutting equipment
HQ: Sonaspection International Limited
   10 Woodgate
   Morecambe LANCS LA3 3
   207 973-1264

(G-4363)
SOUTHERN CONCRETE MATERIALS
2807 Armentrout Dr (28025-5866)
PHONE..................704 641-9604
Aaron Barnes, *Prin*
EMP: 9 **EST:** 2017
SALES (est): 197.13K **Privately Held**
Web: www.scmusa.com
SIC: 3273 Ready-mixed concrete

(G-4364)
SPEED ENERGY DRINK LLC
7100 Weddington Rd Nw (28027-3412)
PHONE..................704 949-1255
EMP: 18 **EST:** 2010
SALES (est): 483.59K **Privately Held**
Web: www.speedenergy.com
SIC: 2087 Concentrates, drink

(G-4365)
SPEED UTV LLC
7100 Weddington Rd Nw (28027-3412)
PHONE..................704 949-1255
Robert W Gordon, *Managing Member*
EMP: 20 **EST:** 2019
SALES (est): 1.08MM **Privately Held**
Web: www.speedutv.com
SIC: 3799 5961 All terrain vehicles (ATV); Electronic shopping

(G-4366)
STANLEY CUSTOMER SUPPORT DIVIS
1000 Stanley Dr (28027-7679)
PHONE..................704 789-7000
Mike Gallagher, *Mgr*
EMP: 8 **EST:** 1996
SALES (est): 232.03K **Privately Held**
SIC: 3546 Power-driven handtools

(G-4367)
STAR AMERICA INC (PA)
190 Cabarrus Ave W (28025-5151)
P.O. Box 1501 (28026-1501)
PHONE..................704 788-4700
Harry D Hemphill Junior, *Pr*
Rebecca N Hemphill, *
▲ **EMP:** 150 **EST:** 1987
SQ FT: 210,000
SALES (est): 22.28MM
SALES (corp-wide): 22.28MM **Privately Held**
SIC: 2251 2252 Dyeing and finishing women's full- and knee-length hosiery; Tights, except women's

(G-4368)
SUNBELT ENTERPRISES INC
Also Called: Kennelpro
263 Litaker Ln (28025-8406)
PHONE..................704 788-4749
John Franklin, *Pr*
EMP: 11 **EST:** 1998
SALES (est): 479.49K **Privately Held**
SIC: 3496 Fencing, made from purchased wire

(G-4369)
TAMEKA BURROS
Also Called: Leanders
979 Ramsgate Dr Sw (28025-9222)
PHONE..................330 338-8941
Tameka Burros, *Owner*
EMP: 6 **EST:** 2019
SALES (est): 15.5K **Privately Held**
SIC: 2599 Food wagons, restaurant

(G-4370)
TARHEEL AIR & LUBE INC
195 Davidson Hwy (28027-4205)
P.O. Box 2061 (28026-2061)
PHONE..................704 469-1075
EMP: 10 **EST:** 2012
SALES (est): 721.2K **Privately Held**
Web: www.tarheelairandlube.com
SIC: 2865 Tar

(G-4371)
TARHEEL STATE RESTORATIONS
2140 Odell School Rd (28027-7452)
P.O. Box 5431 (28027-1507)
PHONE..................980 621-3196
William Mark, *Prin*
EMP: 5 **EST:** 2011
SALES (est): 91.11K **Privately Held**
Web: www.mytarheelstate.com
SIC: 2865 Tar

Concord - Cabarrus County (G-4372)

(G-4372)
TDC INTERNATIONAL LLC
Also Called: Technical Development
980 Derita Rd # B (28027-3680)
PHONE..............................704 875-1198
Keith Earhart, *Pr*
Kerry Earhart, *CFO*
▲ **EMP:** 7 **EST:** 1978
SALES (est): 1.12MM **Privately Held**
Web: www.technicaldevelopment.com
SIC: 3599 8711 Custom machinery; Mechanical engineering

(G-4373)
TECHNICON INDUSTRIES INC
Also Called: Technicon Acoustics
4412 Republic Ct Nw (28027-7722)
PHONE..............................704 788-1131
Tyler Keeley, *Pr*
Joan Benner, *
Mark Nye, *
John Gagliardi, *
EMP: 35 **EST:** 1980
SQ FT: 85,000
SALES (est): 8.84MM **Privately Held**
Web: www.techniconacoustics.com
SIC: 3086 Insulation or cushioning material, foamed plastics

(G-4374)
TECHNIQUE CHASSIS LLC
4101 Roush Pl Nw (28027-8196)
PHONE..............................517 819-3579
Ronald W Johncox, *Managing Member*
EMP: 38 **EST:** 2020
SALES (est): 875.82K **Privately Held**
Web: www.techniquejobs.com
SIC: 7692 Automotive welding
PA: Technique, Inc.
1500 Technology Dr
Jackson MI 49201

(G-4375)
TEF INC
Also Called: Profection Embroidery
3650 Zion Church Rd (28025-7036)
PHONE..............................704 786-9577
Tony Freeze, *Owner*
EMP: 4 **EST:** 1995
SALES (est): 274.29K **Privately Held**
SIC: 2759 Screen printing

(G-4376)
THERMAL CONTROL PRODUCTS INC
6324 Performance Dr Sw (28027-3426)
PHONE..............................704 454-7605
Colleen Matte, *Pr*
Paul Matte, *
EMP: 30 **EST:** 1996
SALES (est): 6.23MM **Privately Held**
Web: www.thermalcontrolproducts.com
SIC: 2261 Fire resistance finishing of cotton broadwoven fabrics

(G-4377)
TICO POLISHING
2044 Wilshire Ct Sw (28025-6417)
PHONE..............................704 788-2466
Berto Barrida, *Owner*
EMP: 5 **EST:** 2005
SALES (est): 281.07K **Privately Held**
SIC: 3471 Polishing, metals or formed products

(G-4378)
TOTAL LIMIT LURES
3950 Loblolly Ct Sw (28027-0405)
PHONE..............................910 330-5786
Tony Bush, *Prin*
EMP: 5 **EST:** 2012
SALES (est): 68.5K **Privately Held**
Web: www.totallimitlures.com
SIC: 3949 Lures, fishing; artificial

(G-4379)
TRU-CONTOUR INC
Also Called: Tru-Contour Precast Division
165 Brumley Ave Ne (28025-3460)
PHONE..............................704 455-8700
Jim Srackangast, *Pr*
Elaine Srackangast, *
EMP: 13 **EST:** 1982
SQ FT: 12,000
SALES (est): 901.07K **Privately Held**
Web: www.trucontourinc.com
SIC: 3087 3272 Custom compound purchased resins; Concrete products, nec

(G-4380)
TWISTED FIRE INDUSTIRES LLC
9150 Bethel Church Rd (28025-1251)
PHONE..............................704 652-8559
Joseph Yowler, *Prin*
EMP: 4 **EST:** 2018
SALES (est): 39.69K **Privately Held**
SIC: 3999 Manufacturing industries, nec

(G-4381)
UBORA DENS LLC
1114 Hanford Pl Nw (28027-8620)
PHONE..............................704 425-3560
William Stokes, *Pr*
EMP: 5 **EST:** 2015
SALES (est): 62.32K **Privately Held**
SIC: 3999 Barber and beauty shop equipment

(G-4382)
UNIQUE HOME THEATER INC
135 Scalybark Trl (28027-7550)
PHONE..............................704 787-3239
Viengkhone Saychay, *Pr*
EMP: 7 **EST:** 2019
SALES (est): 286.02K **Privately Held**
SIC: 3651 Home entertainment equipment, electronic, nec

(G-4383)
UNITED HOUSE PUBLISHING
4671 Garrison Inn Ct Nw (28027-8063)
PHONE..............................248 605-3787
Amber Olafsson, *Prin*
EMP: 5 **EST:** 2018
SALES (est): 78.79K **Privately Held**
SIC: 2741 Miscellaneous publishing

(G-4384)
UTILITY PRECAST INC
1420 Ivey Cline Rd (28027-9529)
PHONE..............................704 721-0106
Travis Overcash, *Pr*
Isaac Harris Iii, *Pr*
William K Foster, *
Larinda Buesch, *
EMP: 35 **EST:** 1972
SQ FT: 80,000
SALES (est): 4.92MM **Privately Held**
Web: www.utilityprecastinc.com
SIC: 3272 Concrete products, precast, nec

(G-4385)
VH INDUSTRIES INC
Also Called: Safe Waze
4451 Raceway Dr Sw (28027-8979)
PHONE..............................704 743-2400
Gary Warren, *Pr*
Darrell W Hagler, *
▲ **EMP:** 26 **EST:** 1994
SQ FT: 5,000
SALES (est): 1.69MM
SALES (corp-wide): 34.23B **Publicly Held**
Web: www.safewaze.com
SIC: 3199 5099 3842 Safety belts, leather; Safety equipment and supplies; Surgical appliances and supplies
HQ: Aearo Technologies Llc
7911 Zionsville Rd
Indianapolis IN 46268

(G-4386)
VISION MOTOR CARS INC (PA)
545 Hamberton Ct Nw (28027-6513)
PHONE..............................704 425-6271
Brooks Agnew, *CEO*
Tony Lanham, *Pr*
Robin Lamb, *Corporate Secretary*
EMP: 6 **EST:** 2009
SQ FT: 3,000
SALES (est): 840.02K
SALES (corp-wide): 840.02K **Privately Held**
Web: www.visionmotorcars.com
SIC: 3711 Motor vehicles and car bodies

(G-4387)
WALLINGFORD COFFEE MILLS INC (PA)
300 Concord Pkwy S (28027-6702)
PHONE..............................513 771-3131
Gary Weber Senior, *Pr*
▼ **EMP:** 80 **EST:** 1957
SALES (est): 4.92MM
SALES (corp-wide): 4.92MM **Privately Held**
Web: www.westrockcoffee.com
SIC: 2095 2099 Coffee roasting (except by wholesale grocers); Tea blending

(G-4388)
WHATEVER YOU NEED SCREEN PRINT
531 Brightleaf Pl Nw (28027-4542)
PHONE..............................704 287-8603
Gary Patterson, *Owner*
EMP: 5 **EST:** 2003
SALES (est): 139.38K **Privately Held**
SIC: 2752 Commercial printing, lithographic

(G-4389)
WHITAKER S TIRE SERVICE INC
Also Called: Whitakers Tire & Wheel Service
530 Concord Pkwy N (28027-6739)
PHONE..............................704 786-6174
Donald Whitaker, *Pr*
EMP: 18 **EST:** 1965
SQ FT: 4,000
SALES (est): 2.43MM **Privately Held**
Web: www.punchywhitaker.com
SIC: 5531 5014 5013 7539 Automotive tires; Automobile tires and tubes; Wheels, motor vehicle; Wheel alignment, automotive

(G-4390)
WIND SHEAR INC (PA)
1050 Ivey Cline Rd (28027-9525)
PHONE..............................704 788-9463
Gene Haas, *Pr*
Kurt Zierhut, *Sec*
Robert Murray, *Treas*
▼ **EMP:** 12 **EST:** 2006
SALES (est): 1.39MM **Privately Held**
Web: www.windshearinc.com
SIC: 3443 Wind tunnels

(G-4391)
WORLD ELASTIC CORPORATION (PA)
338 Webb Rd (28025-9018)
P.O. Box 463 (28026-0463)
PHONE..............................704 786-9508
Dean R Andrews, *Pr*
Chris Andrews, *VP*
Mark Andrews, *VP*
Greg Andrews, *Sec*
▲ **EMP:** 20 **EST:** 1973
SQ FT: 25,000
SALES (est): 4.62MM
SALES (corp-wide): 4.62MM **Privately Held**
Web: www.worldfibers.net
SIC: 2281 2241 Yarn spinning mills; Yarns, elastic: fabric covered

(G-4392)
WORLD FIBERS INC
231 Pounds Ave Sw (28025-4700)
PHONE..............................704 788-3017
EMP: 4
Web: www.worldfibers.net
SIC: 2281 Knitting yarn, spun
PA: World Fibers, Inc.
338 Webb Rd
Concord NC 28025

(G-4393)
WORLD FIBERS INC
340 Industrial Ct (28025-8016)
PHONE..............................704 788-3017
EMP: 4
Web: www.worldfibers.net
SIC: 2281 Knitting yarn, spun
PA: World Fibers, Inc.
338 Webb Rd
Concord NC 28025

(G-4394)
WORLD FIBERS INC (PA)
338 Webb Rd (28025-9018)
P.O. Box 586 (28026-0586)
PHONE..............................704 786-9508
Dean R Andrews, *Prin*
▲ **EMP:** 5 **EST:** 2006
SALES (est): 315.04K **Privately Held**
Web: www.worldfibers.net
SIC: 2299 Fibers, textile: recovery from textile mill waste and rags

(G-4395)
YEPZY INC
57 Union St S Pmb 1234 (28025-5009)
PHONE..............................855 461-2678
Christopher Dax Coan, *CEO*
EMP: 11 **EST:** 2021
SALES (est): 424.04K **Privately Held**
SIC: 7372 Prepackaged software

(G-4396)
ZEALOUSWEB
7404 Bosson St Sw (28025-8556)
PHONE..............................619 354-3216
Kandarp Bhatt, *Owner*
EMP: 4 **EST:** 2003
SALES (est): 64.03K **Privately Held**
Web: www.zealousweb.com
SIC: 7372 Business oriented computer software

Connelly Springs
Burke County

(G-4397)
BAKER INTERIORS FURNITURE CO (DH)
1 Baker Way (28612-7602)
PHONE..............................336 431-9115
Tsuan-chien Chang, *Pr*
Chen-kun Shih, *Sr VP*
Hau Ou-yang, *Sr VP*

GEOGRAPHIC SECTION   Conover - Catawba County (G-4423)

◆ **EMP:** 126 **EST:** 1966
SALES (est): 86.31MM **Privately Held**
SIC: 2511 Wood household furniture
HQ: Samson Investment Holding Co.
    2575 Penny Rd
    High Point NC 27265

(G-4398)
CHAPMAN BROTHERS LOGGING LLC
8849 Gus Peeler Rd (28612-8217)
PHONE....................828 437-6498
Harold U Chapman, *Pt*
Garland W Chapman, *Pt*
EMP: 5 **EST:** 1966
SALES (est): 468.19K **Privately Held**
SIC: 2411 Logging camps and contractors

(G-4399)
CIRCA 1801
1 Jacquard Dr (28612-7851)
PHONE....................828 397-7003
Mark Shelton, *Pr*
EMP: 24 **EST:** 1998
SQ FT: 167,000
SALES (est): 553.09K **Privately Held**
Web: www.valdeseweavers.com
SIC: 2211 2241 2231 Broadwoven fabric mills, cotton; Narrow fabric mills; Broadwoven fabric mills, wool

(G-4400)
ELK PRODUCTS INC
3266 Us Highway 70 (28612-7695)
P.O. Box 100 (28637-0100)
PHONE....................828 397-4200
Kirk Phillips, *CEO*
▲ **EMP:** 26 **EST:** 1989
SQ FT: 56,000
SALES (est): 9.68MM **Privately Held**
Web: www.elkproducts.com
SIC: 3669 Burglar alarm apparatus, electric

(G-4401)
GOLD CANYON CANDLES
2724 Knob Hill Dr (28612-7306)
PHONE....................828 358-5729
Carolyn Robinson, *Prin*
EMP: 4 **EST:** 2017
SALES (est): 39.69K **Privately Held**
Web: www.canyoncandles.com
SIC: 3999 Candles

(G-4402)
GRECON DIMTER INC
8658 Huffman Ave (28612-7689)
PHONE....................828 397-5139
Jeff Davidson, *Pr*
Jeff Davidson, *
Skip Weber, *
Manfred Witte, *
▲ **EMP:** 12 **EST:** 1997
SALES (est): 985.9K **Privately Held**
SIC: 5084 3553 Woodworking machinery; Woodworking machinery

(G-4403)
HIGH DEFINITION TOOL CORP
7600 Carolina Tool Dr (28612)
PHONE....................828 397-2467
Gary Dyer, *CEO*
EMP: 46 **EST:** 1983
SQ FT: 21,000
SALES (est): 6.43MM **Privately Held**
Web: www.carolinatools.com
SIC: 3549 Metalworking machinery, nec

(G-4404)
HYDROEYE MARINE GROUP LLC
8326 Mount Harmony Rd (28612-7641)
PHONE....................828 394-4406
Robert L Campbell Junior, *Prin*
EMP: 5 **EST:** 2020
SALES (est): 144.28K **Privately Held**
SIC: 3089 Plastics boats and other marine equipment

(G-4405)
JIMBUILT MACHINES INC
Also Called: Jimbuilt
2555 Israel Chapel Rd (28612-8002)
PHONE....................828 874-3530
James A Southerland, *Pr*
Judy Southerland, *VP*
EMP: 6 **EST:** 1970
SQ FT: 5,500
SALES (est): 463.69K **Privately Held**
SIC: 3599 Machine shop, jobbing and repair

(G-4406)
MR BS FUN FOODS INC (PA)
2616 Israel Chapel Rd (28612-8003)
P.O. Box 218 (28690-0218)
PHONE....................828 879-1901
Craig Pittman, *Pr*
Ann Benfield, *Sec*
EMP: 24 **EST:** 1933
SQ FT: 7,500
SALES (est): 2.36MM
SALES (corp-wide): 2.36MM **Privately Held**
Web: www.mrbsfunfoods.com
SIC: 2064 2096 Candy and other confectionery products; Popcorn, already popped (except candy covered)

(G-4407)
PARKER INDUSTRIES INC
4867 Rhoney Rd (28612-8142)
PHONE....................828 437-7779
Jeffrey Parker, *Pr*
EMP: 56 **EST:** 1959
SQ FT: 136,000
SALES (est): 10.13MM **Privately Held**
Web: www.parkerindustriesinc.com
SIC: 3469 3544 Stamping metal for the trade ; Die sets for metal stamping (presses)

(G-4408)
R EVANS HOSIERY LLC
Also Called: Evans Hosiery
8177 Grover Evans Sr Rd (28612-7798)
PHONE....................828 397-3715
EMP: 22 **EST:** 1985
SQ FT: 8,000
SALES (est): 1.73MM **Privately Held**
SIC: 2252 Socks

(G-4409)
SPARTACRAFT INC
7690 Sparta Craft Dr (28612-7221)
PHONE....................828 397-4630
▲ **EMP:** 45 **EST:** 1994
SQ FT: 80,000
SALES (est): 6.14MM **Privately Held**
Web: www.spartacraft.com
SIC: 2441 2541 2431 Nailed wood boxes and shook; Display fixtures, wood; Millwork

(G-4410)
US OPTICS
100 Beiersdorf Dr (28612-7544)
PHONE....................828 874-2242
EMP: 10 **EST:** 2019
SALES (est): 282.91K **Privately Held**
Web: www.usoptics.com
SIC: 3827 Optical instruments and lenses

(G-4411)
W M CRAMER LUMBER CO (PA)
3486 Texs Fish Camp Rd (28612-7635)
P.O. Box 2888 (28603-2888)
PHONE....................828 397-7481
Wendell M Cramer, *Pr*
Judith Cramer, *Stockholder**
Dave Peterson, *
Mark Vollinger, *
▲ **EMP:** 58 **EST:** 1969
SQ FT: 2,500
SALES (est): 9.19MM
SALES (corp-wide): 9.19MM **Privately Held**
Web: www.cramerlumber.com
SIC: 5031 2426 2421 Lumber: rough, dressed, and finished; Lumber, hardwood dimension; Sawmills and planing mills, general

Conover
Catawba County

(G-4412)
AB NEW BEGINNINGS INC
1211 Keisler Rd Se (28613-9336)
PHONE....................828 465-6953
▲ **EMP:** 85
SIC: 2512 Upholstered household furniture

(G-4413)
ACACIA HOME & GARDEN INC
101 N Mclin Creek Rd (28613-8900)
P.O. Box 426 (28613-0426)
PHONE....................828 465-1700
Alex U Te, *CEO*
Lorraine Te, *Dir*
▲ **EMP:** 10 **EST:** 1989
SQ FT: 87,000
SALES (est): 1.4MM **Privately Held**
Web: www.acaciahomeandgarden.com
SIC: 5712 2519 Outdoor and garden furniture ; Wicker and rattan furniture

(G-4414)
AMERICAN URNS
908 7th Ave Sw (28613-2828)
PHONE....................828 994-4239
EMP: 5 **EST:** 2015
SALES (est): 69.25K **Privately Held**
SIC: 3523 Farm machinery and equipment

(G-4415)
AMPHENOL ANTENNA SOLUTIONS
Also Called: Csa Wireless
1123 Industrial Dr Sw (28613-2754)
PHONE....................828 324-6971
Jim Hartman, *Pr*
▲ **EMP:** 32 **EST:** 2002
SQ FT: 15,000
SALES (est): 8.21MM
SALES (corp-wide): 12.55B **Publicly Held**
Web: www.amphenol-antennas.com
SIC: 3663 Airborne radio communications equipment
HQ: Jaybeam Limited
    Park Farm
    Wellingborough NORTHANTS NN8 6
    193 340-8408

(G-4416)
AMPHENOL PROCOM INC
1123 Industrial Dr Sw (28613-2754)
PHONE....................888 262-7542
Mette Brink, *Pr*
EMP: 99 **EST:** 2018
SALES (est): 24.88MM
SALES (corp-wide): 12.55B **Publicly Held**
Web: www.amphenolprocom.com
SIC: 3678 3643 3661 Electronic connectors; Connectors and terminals for electrical devices; Fiber optics communications equipment
PA: Amphenol Corporation
    358 Hall Ave
    Wallingford CT 06492
    203 265-8900

(G-4417)
ARMACELL LLC
1004 Keisler Rd Nw (28613)
PHONE....................828 464-5880
David Cox, *Mgr*
EMP: 71
Web: www.armacell.com
SIC: 3086 Plastics foam products
HQ: Armacell, Llc
    55 Vilcom Center Dr # 200
    Chapel Hill NC 27514

(G-4418)
AS IGNCO
1320 Fairgrove Church Rd Se (28613-8611)
PHONE....................828 466-1044
EMP: 5 **EST:** 2004
SALES (est): 69.99K **Privately Held**
Web: www.asignchickory.com
SIC: 3993 Signs, not made in custom sign painting shops

(G-4419)
ASPEN CABINETRY INC
908 Industrial Dr Sw (28613-2762)
PHONE....................828 466-0216
EMP: 6 **EST:** 1992
SQ FT: 3,500
SALES (est): 565.52K **Privately Held**
SIC: 2434 Wood kitchen cabinets

(G-4420)
AXJO AMERICA INC
221 S Mclin Creek Rd Ste A (28613-9025)
PHONE....................828 322-6046
Daniel Shelander, *Pr*
▲ **EMP:** 28 **EST:** 2011
SALES (est): 11.68MM
SALES (corp-wide): 50.31MM **Privately Held**
Web: www.axjoamerica.com
SIC: 2655 5113 Fiber spools, tubes, and cones; Fiber cans and drums
HQ: Axjo Plastic Ab
    Svarvargatan 6
    Gislaved 332 3
    371586730

(G-4421)
BEAUTIFUL BRAINS INC
508 4th Ave Ne (28613-1615)
PHONE....................828 244-5850
Jodi T Black, *Prin*
EMP: 5 **EST:** 2010
SALES (est): 145.18K **Privately Held**
Web: www.carolinagametables.com
SIC: 3949 Sporting and athletic goods, nec

(G-4422)
BENNETT BUILDINGS OF CONOVER
920 Conover Blvd W (28613-9603)
PHONE....................828 465-6117
EMP: 4 **EST:** 2019
SALES (est): 58.82K **Privately Held**
SIC: 3448 Prefabricated metal buildings and components

(G-4423)
BLUE INC USA LLC
Also Called: Drnc

Conover - Catawba County (G-4424) — GEOGRAPHIC SECTION

1808 Emmanuel Church Rd (28613-7328)
PHONE..................................828 346-8660
Cathy Nagel, *VP*
EMP: 45 **EST:** 2020
SALES (est): 5.1MM **Privately Held**
SIC: 3541 Machine tools, metal cutting type

(G-4424)
BLUE RIDGE
121 Fairgrove Church Rd Se (28613-8173)
PHONE..................................828 325-4705
EMP: 11 **EST:** 2013
SALES (est): 370.9K **Privately Held**
Web: www.blueridgemolding.com
SIC: 3089 Injection molding of plastics

(G-4425)
BLUE RIDGE MOLDING LLC
Also Called: Blue Ridge Plastic Molding
121a Fairgrove Church Rd Se
(28613-8173)
PHONE..................................828 485-2017
F Raymond Von Drehle Junior, *Managing Member*
Stephen P Von Drehle, *Managing Member*
EMP: 65 **EST:** 2012
SALES (est): 10.13MM
SALES (corp-wide): 467.08MM **Privately Held**
Web: www.blueridgemolding.com
SIC: 3089 Molding primary plastics
PA: Marcal Holdings Llc
   1 Market St
   Elmwood Park NJ 07407
   201 796-4000

(G-4426)
BLUE RIDGE TUBE & CORE LLC
1203 Farrington St Sw 2nd Fl (28613-8255)
P.O. Box 475 (28613-0475)
PHONE..................................704 530-4311
EMP: 7 **EST:** 2017
SQ FT: 21,000
SALES (est): 750K **Privately Held**
SIC: 2621 Paper mills

(G-4427)
C & S ANTENNAS INC
1123 Industrial Dr Sw (28613-2754)
PHONE..................................828 324-2454
Kirk Wentz, *Pr*
▲ **EMP:** 10 **EST:** 1985
SQ FT: 2,500
SALES (est): 2.43MM
SALES (corp-wide): 12.55B **Publicly Held**
Web: www.csantennas.com
SIC: 5731 3669 Antennas; Emergency alarms
HQ: Amphenol Antenna Solutions, Inc.
   1123 Industrial Dr Sw
   Conover NC 28613

(G-4428)
CABINET DOORS FOR LESS
908 Industrial Dr Sw (28613-2762)
PHONE..................................828 351-3510
EMP: 6 **EST:** 2017
SALES (est): 137.97K **Privately Held**
Web: www.cabinetdoorsforless.com
SIC: 2434 Wood kitchen cabinets

(G-4429)
CAMFIL USA INC
1008 1st St W (28613-9692)
PHONE..................................828 465-2880
EMP: 24
SALES (corp-wide): 1.18B **Privately Held**
Web: www.camfil.com
SIC: 3564 Blowers and fans
HQ: Camfil Usa, Inc.
   1 N Corporate Dr

Riverdale NJ 07457
973 616-7300

(G-4430)
CAROLINA CHAIR INC
1822 Brian Dr Ne (28613-8852)
P.O. Box 11367 (28603-4867)
PHONE..................................828 459-1330
Hubert D Fry Iii, *Pr*
EMP: 14 **EST:** 2000
SQ FT: 15,000
SALES (est): 485.49K **Privately Held**
Web: www.carolinachair.com
SIC: 2512 5712 Upholstered household furniture; Furniture stores

(G-4431)
CAROLINA CORE SOLUTIONS LLC
1605 Norfolk Pl Sw (28613-8220)
P.O. Box 1484 (28613-1484)
PHONE..................................704 900-4208
Michael E Young, *Prin*
EMP: 5 **EST:** 2019
SALES (est): 208.42K **Privately Held**
SIC: 2653 Corrugated and solid fiber boxes

(G-4432)
CAROLINA GLOVE COMPANY (PA)
Also Called: Carolina Gloves & Safety Co
116 S Mclin Creek Rd (28613-9024)
P.O. Box 999 (28613-0999)
PHONE..................................828 464-1132
▲ **EMP:** 30 **EST:** 1946
SALES (est): 28.29MM
SALES (corp-wide): 28.29MM **Privately Held**
Web: www.carolinaglove.com
SIC: 2381 Gloves, work: woven or knit, made from purchased materials

(G-4433)
CARPENTER CO
2009 Keisler Dairy Rd (28613-9138)
P.O. Box 879 (28613-0879)
PHONE..................................828 464-9470
Gary Gilliam, *Mgr*
EMP: 65
SALES (corp-wide): 1.85B **Privately Held**
Web: www.carpenter.com
SIC: 5999 2821 Foam and foam products; Plastics materials and resins
PA: Carpenter Co.
   5016 Monument Ave
   Richmond VA 23230
   804 359-0800

(G-4434)
CARROLL COMPANIES INC
Also Called: Carroll Leather
1226 Fedex Dr Sw (28613-7426)
PHONE..................................828 466-5489
Joe Franck, *Brnch Mgr*
EMP: 11
SQ FT: 27,621
SALES (corp-wide): 21.97MM **Privately Held**
Web: www.carrollleather.com
SIC: 5199 3111 Leather, leather goods, and furs; Leather tanning and finishing
PA: Carroll Companies, Inc.
   1640 Old 421 S
   Boone NC 28607
   828 264-2521

(G-4435)
CATAWBA VALLEY FABRICATION INC
1823 Brian Dr Ne (28613-8852)
PHONE..................................828 459-1191
William C Galliher, *Pr*
Darryl S Bost, *

Chad Stewart, *
EMP: 25 **EST:** 2003
SQ FT: 40,000
SALES (est): 1.96MM **Privately Held**
Web: www.lakemattress.biz
SIC: 3069 Foam rubber

(G-4436)
CLASSIC LEATHER INC (PA)
Also Called: St Timothy Chair Co Division
309 Simpson St Sw (28613-8208)
P.O. Box 2404 (28603-2404)
PHONE..................................828 328-2046
Thomas Shores Junior, *CEO*
Rachel Leclair, *
Guy Holbrook, *
▲ **EMP:** 400 **EST:** 1965
SQ FT: 750,000
SALES (est): 45.59MM
SALES (corp-wide): 45.59MM **Privately Held**
Web: www.centuryfurniture.com
SIC: 2512 2521 2511 Upholstered household furniture; Wood office furniture; Wood household furniture

(G-4437)
COMMUNICATIONS & PWR INDS LLC
1700 Cable Dr Ne (28613-8991)
PHONE..................................650 846-2900
EMP: 33
Web: www.cpii.com
SIC: 3671 3679 3699 Vacuum tubes; Microwave components; Electrical equipment and supplies, nec
HQ: Communications & Power Industries Llc
   811 Hansen Way
   Palo Alto CA 94304

(G-4438)
CONOVER LUMBER COMPANY INC
311 Conover Blvd E (28613-1926)
P.O. Box 484 (28613-0484)
PHONE..................................828 464-4591
O Kemit Lawing Junior, *Pr*
Tim Lawing, *VP*
Rodney Lawing, *Sec*
EMP: 18 **EST:** 1946
SQ FT: 30,000
SALES (est): 2.47MM **Privately Held**
Web: www.conoverlumber.net
SIC: 2421 5031 Planing mills, nec; Lumber: rough, dressed, and finished

(G-4439)
CONOVER METAL PRODUCTS INC
315 S Mclin Creek Rd (28613-9026)
P.O. Box 1147 (28613-1147)
PHONE..................................828 464-9414
Victor S Scott, *Pr*
Phillip Anthony, *Ex VP*
Gary Matthews, *Treas*
B E Matthews, *Sec*
EMP: 28 **EST:** 1971
SQ FT: 41,024
SALES (est): 2.11MM **Privately Held**
Web: www.conovermetalproducts.com
SIC: 3441 Fabricated structural metal

(G-4440)
CPI SATCOM & ANTENNA TECH INC
Also Called: Etc Division
1700 Cable Dr Ne (28613-8991)
P.O. Box 850 (28658-0850)
PHONE..................................704 462-7330
Robert Featherstone, *Brnch Mgr*
EMP: 211
Web: www.cpii.com
SIC: 3444 3663 Sheet metalwork; Antennas, transmitting and communications

HQ: Cpi Satcom & Antenna Technologies Inc.
   1700 Cable Dr Ne
   Conover NC 28613
   704 462-7330

(G-4441)
CPI SATCOM & ANTENNA TECH INC (DH)
1700 Cable Dr Ne (28613-8991)
P.O. Box 850 (28658-0850)
PHONE..................................704 462-7330
Christopher Marzilli, *Pr*
Mark Schalk, *
◆ **EMP:** 24 **EST:** 1994
SQ FT: 200,000
SALES (est): 444.87MM **Privately Held**
Web: www.cpii.com
SIC: 3663 Radio and t.v. communications equipment
HQ: Communications & Power Industries Llc
   811 Hansen Way
   Palo Alto CA 94304

(G-4442)
CREATIVE PROSTHETICS AND ORTHO
3305 16th Ave Se Ste 101 (28613-9213)
PHONE..................................828 994-4808
EMP: 4 **EST:** 2015
SALES (est): 247.03K **Privately Held**
Web: www.creativep-o.com
SIC: 3842 Prosthetic appliances

(G-4443)
CRYPTIC COATINGS
2684 Tiffany St (28613-9115)
PHONE..................................828 994-4474
Gary Huffman, *Prin*
EMP: 6 **EST:** 2014
SALES (est): 78.55K **Privately Held**
Web: www.crypticcoatings.com
SIC: 3479 Coating of metals and formed products

(G-4444)
DAL LEATHER INC
2139 St Johns Church Rd Ne (28613-8975)
PHONE..................................828 302-1667
Dwight J Gryder, *Pr*
EMP: 8 **EST:** 2005
SALES (est): 232.58K **Privately Held**
SIC: 2512 Wood upholstered chairs and couches

(G-4445)
DALCO GF TECHNOLOGIES LLC ✪
2050 Evergreen Dr Ne (28613-8166)
PHONE..................................828 459-2577
Joey Duncan, *CEO*
EMP: 79 **EST:** 2022
SALES (est): 1.99MM **Privately Held**
SIC: 2297 Nonwoven fabrics

(G-4446)
DALCO GFT NONWOVENS LLC
2050 Evergreen Dr Ne (28613-8166)
P.O. Box 1479 (28613-1479)
PHONE..................................828 459-2577
Joey Duncan, *CEO*
Anita Litten, *
▲ **EMP:** 79 **EST:** 2003
SALES (est): 8.92MM **Privately Held**
Web: www.dalcononwovens.com
SIC: 2297 Nonwoven fabrics

(G-4447)
DEETAG USA INC (DH)
1232 Fedex Dr Sw (28613-7426)

PHONE..................828 465-2644
Dean Gordon, *Pr*
Heather Nansy, *Sec*
▲ **EMP:** 6 **EST:** 2010
SQ FT: 4,000
SALES (est): 4.72MM
SALES (corp-wide): 484.16MM **Privately Held**
Web: www.deetag.com
SIC: 5084 3492 Hydraulic systems equipment and supplies; Hose and tube fittings and assemblies, hydraulic/pneumatic
HQ: Deetag Ltd
649 Third St
London ON N5V 2
519 659-4673

(G-4448)
DISTINCTION LEATHER COMPANY
210 Lap Rd Ne (28613-7618)
P.O. Box 397 (28613-0397)
EMP: 5 **EST:** 1982
SALES (est): 184.1K **Privately Held**
SIC: 3111 Upholstery leather

(G-4449)
EDWARD HEIL SCREW PRODUCTS
1114 1st St W (28613-9620)
PHONE....................828 345-6140
James G Heiligenthaler, *Pr*
EMP: 7 **EST:** 1938
SQ FT: 5,000
SALES (est): 893.39K **Privately Held**
Web: www.heilscrewproducts.com
SIC: 3451 Screw machine products

(G-4450)
ELITE COMFORT SOLUTIONS LLC
1115 Farrington St Sw Bldg 1 (28613-8251)
PHONE....................828 328-2201
Daniel Williams, *Mgr*
EMP: 120
SALES (corp-wide): 5.15B **Publicly Held**
Web: www.elitecomfortsolutions.com
SIC: 3069 Foam rubber
HQ: Elite Comfort Solutions Llc
24 Herring Rd
Newnan GA 30265
770 502-8577

(G-4451)
ENGINEERED CONTROLS INTL LLC
911 Industrial Dr Sw (28613-2761)
PHONE....................828 466-2153
Topper Andrade, *Mgr*
EMP: 193
SALES (corp-wide): 8.44B **Publicly Held**
Web: www.regoproducts.com
SIC: 3491 3494 3492 Regulators (steam fittings); Valves and pipe fittings, nec; Fluid power valves and hose fittings
HQ: Engineered Controls International, Llc
100 Rego Dr
Elon NC 27244

(G-4452)
EVERYTHING ATTACHMENTS
1506 Emmanuel Church Rd (28613-9017)
PHONE....................828 464-0161
Theodore H Corriher, *Prin*
EMP: 9 **EST:** 2016
SALES (est): 2.06MM **Privately Held**
Web: www.everythingattachments.com
SIC: 3531 Construction machinery

(G-4453)
FARLEYS CUSTOM CARVING INC
6653 St Peters Church Rd (28613-8754)
PHONE....................828 256-9124
Gary D Farley, *Owner*
EMP: 9 **EST:** 2004

SALES (est): 273.73K **Privately Held**
SIC: 2499 Carved and turned wood

(G-4454)
FIBRIX LLC (HQ)
Also Called: Cameo Fibers
1820 Evans St Ne (28613-9042)
P.O. Box 310 (28613-0310)
PHONE....................828 459-7064
Keith White, *CEO*
Dean Cobb, *
Darren White, *
◆ **EMP:** 50 **EST:** 2007
SQ FT: 130,000
SALES (est): 47.37MM
SALES (corp-wide): 47.37MM **Privately Held**
Web: www.fibrix.com
SIC: 2824 Polyester fibers
PA: Polycor Holdings, Inc.
1820 Evans St Ne
Conover NC 28613
828 459-7064

(G-4455)
FOOTHILLS DISTILLERY LLC
300 Thornburg Dr Se Unit A (28613-9429)
PHONE....................704 462-1055
Tim Weaver, *Prin*
EMP: 4 **EST:** 2013
SALES (est): 98.02K **Privately Held**
Web: www.seventeentwelvespirits.com
SIC: 2085 Distilled and blended liquors

(G-4456)
FORTRESS INTERNATIONAL CORP NC
Also Called: Fortress Forest International
1808 Emmanuel Church Rd (28613-7328)
PHONE....................336 645-9365
Michael Menz, *Pr*
Matthew Carsaro, *VP*
EMP: 8 **EST:** 2014
SQ FT: 53,000
SALES (est): 999.66K **Privately Held**
SIC: 3429 Furniture hardware

(G-4457)
FRAMEWRIGHT INC
1824 Brian Dr Ne (28613-8852)
P.O. Box 1390 (28613-1390)
PHONE....................828 459-2284
Clifford Spencer, *Pr*
Stanley Lail, *VP*
George Spencer, *Treas*
EMP: 10 **EST:** 1976
SALES (est): 448.14K **Privately Held**
SIC: 2512 2426 Couches, sofas, and davenports: upholstered on wood frames; Hardwood dimension and flooring mills

(G-4458)
GBC CONSTRUCTION GBC CONS
3482 Fredell Dr (28613-8623)
PHONE....................704 500-9232
EMP: 9 **EST:** 2019
SALES (est): 542.95K **Privately Held**
SIC: 2653 Corrugated and solid fiber boxes

(G-4459)
GKN SINTER METALS LLC
Also Called: Pennsylvania Press Metals
407 Thornburg Dr Se (28613-8845)
PHONE....................828 464-0642
Rick Rice, *Mgr*
EMP: 142
SALES (corp-wide): 9.07B **Privately Held**
Web: www.gknpm.com
SIC: 3312 Sinter, iron
HQ: Gkn Sinter Metals, Llc
1670 Opdyke Ct
Auburn Hills MI 48326
248 883-4500

(G-4460)
HANES COMPANIES INC
Also Called: Hanes Inds A Div Hnes Cmpanies
500 N Mclin Creek Rd (28613-8856)
P.O. Box 457 (28613-0457)
PHONE....................828 464-4673
Zach Cox, *Pr*
EMP: 312
SALES (corp-wide): 5.15B **Publicly Held**
Web: www.hanescompanies.com
SIC: 2221 Acetate broadwoven fabrics
HQ: Hanes Companies, Inc.
815 Buxton St
Winston Salem NC 27101
336 747-1600

(G-4461)
HAWORTH INC
Also Called: Haworth Conover Manufacturing
1610 Deborah Herman Rd Sw (28613-8218)
PHONE....................828 328-5600
Vyanna Reddiar, *Brnch Mgr*
EMP: 40
SALES (corp-wide): 1.87B **Privately Held**
Web: www.haworth.com
SIC: 2522 2521 Office furniture, except wood ; Wood office furniture
HQ: Haworth, Inc.
1 Haworth Ctr
Holland MI 49423
616 393-3000

(G-4462)
HAWORTH HEALTH ENVIRONMENTS LLC
1610 Deborah Herman Rd Sw (28613-8218)
P.O. Box 189 (28613-0189)
PHONE....................828 328-5600
EMP: 40
SIC: 2521 Wood office chairs, benches and stools

(G-4463)
HICKORY PRINTING GROUP INC H
725 Reese Dr Sw (28613-2935)
P.O. Box 69 (28603-0069)
PHONE....................828 465-3431
EMP: 18 **EST:** 2011
SALES (est): 310.74K **Privately Held**
Web: www.rrd.com
SIC: 2752 Commercial printing, lithographic

(G-4464)
HICKORY PRINTING SOLUTIONS LLC
725 Reese Dr Sw (28613-2935)
PHONE....................828 465-3431
EMP: 206 **EST:** 2010
SALES (est): 23.39MM
SALES (corp-wide): 15B **Privately Held**
Web: www.rrd.com
SIC: 2752 2759 2791 2789 Color lithography ; Labels and seals: printing, nsk; Typesetting ; Bookbinding and related work
HQ: Consolidated Graphics, Inc.
5858 Westheimer Rd # 200
Houston TX 77057

(G-4465)
HIGHLAND FOAM INC
1560 Deborah Herman Rd Sw (28613-8204)
P.O. Box 575 (28613-0575)
PHONE....................828 327-0400
Gary L Fox, *Pr*
EMP: 11 **EST:** 1986

SALES (est): 2.01MM **Privately Held**
Web: www.highlandfoam.net
SIC: 3069 Foam rubber

(G-4466)
IDEAITLIA CNTMPORARY FURN CORP
1902 Emmanuel Church Rd (28613-7301)
P.O. Box 1298 (28613-1298)
PHONE....................828 464-1000
Carlo Bargagli, *Pr*
▲ **EMP:** 140 **EST:** 2004
SQ FT: 300,000
SALES (est): 16.68MM **Privately Held**
Web: www.ideaitaliausa.com
SIC: 2426 5712 4226 Turnings, furniture: wood; Furniture stores; Household goods and furniture storage

(G-4467)
INNOVAKNITS LLC
350 5th Ave Se (28613-1941)
PHONE....................828 536-9348
Jason Wilkins, *Admn*
EMP: 7 **EST:** 2015
SALES (est): 798.72K **Privately Held**
Web: www.innovaknits.com
SIC: 5949 2257 2258 2253 Knitting goods and supplies; Weft knit fabric mills; Warp and flat knit products; Cold weather knit outerwear including ski wear

(G-4468)
INTERSTATE FOAM & SUPPLY INC
306 Comfort Dr Ne (28613-9297)
P.O. Box 338 (28613-0338)
PHONE....................828 459-9700
Mark A Webb, *Pr*
Lewis A Webb, *
▲ **EMP:** 215 **EST:** 1981
SQ FT: 240,000
SALES (est): 22.42MM **Privately Held**
Web: www.interstatefoamandsupply.com
SIC: 3069 Foam rubber

(G-4469)
J L FRAME SHOP INC
1310 Houston Mill Rd (28613-8503)
PHONE....................828 256-6290
Jerry Hollar, *Pr*
Lynda Hollar, *Treas*
EMP: 5 **EST:** 1985
SALES (est): 328.71K **Privately Held**
SIC: 2426 Frames for upholstered furniture, wood

(G-4470)
LEE INDUSTRIES LLC (PA)
210 4th St Sw (28613-2628)
PHONE....................828 464-8318
J Steve Shelor, *Prin*
Phyllis Starnes, *
J Steve Shelor, *Pr*
◆ **EMP:** 260 **EST:** 1969
SQ FT: 237,000
SALES (est): 87.21MM
SALES (corp-wide): 87.21MM **Privately Held**
Web: www.leeindustries.com
SIC: 2512 2599 Couches, sofas, and davenports: upholstered on wood frames; Hotel furniture

(G-4471)
LEGGETT & PLATT INCORPORATED
Also Called: L&P Dstribution Ctr Furn 8814
1401 Deborah Herman Rd Sw (28613-8247)
P.O. Box 609 (28613-0609)
PHONE....................828 322-6855
EMP: 54

Conover - Catawba County (G-4472) — GEOGRAPHIC SECTION

SALES (corp-wide): 5.15B **Publicly Held**
Web: www.leggett.com
SIC: 2515 Mattresses and bedsprings
PA: Leggett & Platt, Incorporated
1 Leggett Rd
Carthage MO 64836
417 358-8131

(G-4472)
MID-ATLANTIC DRAINAGE INC (PA)
105 Ge Plant Rd Sw (28613-8202)
P.O. Box 399 (28613-0399)
PHONE..................................828 324-0808
Howard Anderson, *Pr*
Laddie G Hiller, *Treas*
Ranny W Keys, *Sec*
EMP: 19 EST: 1984
SQ FT: 1,800
SALES (est): 5.06MM
SALES (corp-wide): 5.06MM **Privately Held**
Web: www.mid-atlanticdrainage.com
SIC: 5999 5074 3494 Plumbing and heating supplies; Plumbing and hydronic heating supplies; Plumbing and heating valves

(G-4473)
MOOSE CANDLE COMPANY
2548 Belshire Dr (28613-9100)
PHONE..................................828 244-1384
Jeremy Lail, *Prin*
EMP: 4 EST: 2019
SALES (est): 39.69K **Privately Held**
SIC: 3999 Candles

(G-4474)
NC CUSTOM LEATHER INC
Also Called: Carolina Custom Leather
1118 1st St W (28613-9620)
P.O. Box 9 (28613-0009)
PHONE..................................828 404-2973
Todd Strud, *Pr*
EMP: 11 EST: 2008
SALES (est): 991.42K **Privately Held**
Web: www.ccleather.com
SIC: 2512 Upholstered household furniture

(G-4475)
NEPTUNE HLTH WLLNESS INNVTION
408 S Mclin Creek Rd (28613-9500)
PHONE..................................888 664-9166
Michael Cammarata, *Pr*
Pritpal Thind, *
EMP: 226 EST: 2020
SALES (est): 18.48MM **Privately Held**
SIC: 3999 2834 2077 5999
; Vitamin preparations; Marine fats, oils, and meals

(G-4476)
OPTION 1 DISTRIBUTION LLC
103 N Mclin Creek Rd (28613-8900)
PHONE..................................704 325-3001
EMP: 7 EST: 2020
SALES (est): 236.65K **Privately Held**
Web: www.option1distribution.com
SIC: 2631 Container, packaging, and boxboard

(G-4477)
OYAMA CABINET INC
115 Ge Plant Rd Sw (28613-8202)
PHONE..................................828 327-2668
George C Ritchie, *Pr*
Donald R Lail, *VP*
Charlie M Ritchie, *Sec*
EMP: 7
SALES (est): 592.25K **Privately Held**
SIC: 2541 2431 2434 Store fixtures, wood; Millwork; Vanities, bathroom: wood

(G-4478)
PAN AMERICAN SCREW LLC
630 Reese Dr Sw (28613-2932)
PHONE..................................828 466-0060
Phil Lail, *Pr*
◆ EMP: 70 EST: 1982
SQ FT: 40,000
SALES (est): 9.69MM
SALES (corp-wide): 364.48B **Publicly Held**
Web: www.panamericanscrew.com
SIC: 3452 Screws, metal
PA: Berkshire Hathaway Inc.
3555 Farnam St Ste 1440
Omaha NE 68131
402 346-1400

(G-4479)
PATRIOT JERKY LLC
1297 Keri Pl (28613-7745)
PHONE..................................828 850-9160
Mark Minton, *Owner*
EMP: 5 EST: 2018
SALES (est): 189.34K **Privately Held**
Web: www.patriotjerky.net
SIC: 2013 Snack sticks, including jerky: from purchased meat

(G-4480)
PIEDMONT TRUCK TIRES INC
1317 Emmanuel Church Rd (28613-9015)
P.O. Box 625 (28613-0625)
PHONE..................................828 202-5337
Dan Rice, *Prin*
EMP: 10
SALES (corp-wide): 339.82MM **Privately Held**
Web: www.piedmonttrucktires.com
SIC: 7534 5531 Tire retreading and repair shops; Automotive tires
HQ: Piedmont Truck Tires, Inc.
312 S Regional Rd
Greensboro NC 27409
336 668-0091

(G-4481)
PLASTIC TECHNOLOGY INC
Also Called: P T I
1101 Farrington St Sw # 3 (28613-8251)
P.O. Box 819 (28603-0819)
PHONE..................................828 328-8570
EMP: 50
SALES (corp-wide): 898.03MM **Privately Held**
SIC: 3082 Unsupported plastics profile shapes
HQ: Plastic Technology, Inc.
235 2nd Ave Nw
Hickory NC 28601
828 328-2201

(G-4482)
PLASTICS MLDING DSIGN PLUS LLC
Also Called: Conover Plastics
1803 Conover Blvd E (28613-9696)
P.O. Box 1268 (28613-1268)
PHONE..................................828 459-7853
EMP: 14 EST: 1974
SQ FT: 24,000
SALES (est): 792.85K **Privately Held**
Web: www.conoverplastics.com
SIC: 3089 Injection molding of plastics

(G-4483)
POLYCOR HOLDINGS INC (PA)
1820 Evans St Ne (28613-9042)
PHONE..................................828 459-7064
Keith White, *Pr*
Darren White, *
Dean Cobb, *
▼ EMP: 52 EST: 2014
SQ FT: 130,000
SALES (est): 47.37MM
SALES (corp-wide): 47.37MM **Privately Held**
Web: www.fibrix.com
SIC: 2824 Polyester fibers

(G-4484)
POLYMASK CORPORATION
Also Called: 3M Polymask
500 Thornburg Dr Se (28613-9096)
P.O. Box 309 (28613-0309)
PHONE..................................828 465-3053
▲ EMP: 110 EST: 1991
SALES (est): 24.2MM
SALES (corp-wide): 810.75MM **Privately Held**
Web: www.pregis.com
SIC: 2672 Tape, pressure sensitive: made from purchased materials
HQ: Pregis Llc
2345 Waukegan Rd Ste 120
Bannockburn IL 60015

(G-4485)
PRECISION INDUSTRIES INC
305 N Mclin Creek Rd (28613-9093)
PHONE..................................828 465-3418
Conrad E Stewart, *Pr*
EMP: 12 EST: 1977
SQ FT: 25,000
SALES (est): 934.95K **Privately Held**
SIC: 3541 Screw machines, automatic

(G-4486)
PREGIS LLC
500 Thornburg Dr Se (28613-9096)
PHONE..................................828 465-9197
EMP: 20
SALES (corp-wide): 810.75MM **Privately Held**
Web: www.pregis.com
SIC: 2891 Adhesives
HQ: Pregis Llc
2345 Waukegan Rd Ste 120
Bannockburn IL 60015

(G-4487)
PREMIUM CUSHION INC
1009 1st St W (28613-9692)
P.O. Box 1125 (28613-1125)
PHONE..................................828 464-4783
Ronnie Wike, *Pr*
Patty Brendle, *
EMP: 49 EST: 1999
SALES (est): 4.03MM **Privately Held**
SIC: 2392 Pillows, bed: made from purchased materials

(G-4488)
PREMIUM FABRICATORS LLC
419 4th St Sw (28613-2630)
P.O. Box 227 (28613-0227)
PHONE..................................828 464-3818
EMP: 30 EST: 2011
SALES (est): 2.49MM **Privately Held**
SIC: 2396 Furniture trimmings, fabric

(G-4489)
PROFILE PRODUCTS LLC
219 Simpson St Sw (28613-8207)
PHONE..................................828 327-4165
Gary Bowers, *Brnch Mgr*
EMP: 23
SALES (corp-wide): 69.88MM **Privately Held**
Web: www.profileproducts.com
SIC: 2611 1459 2823 Pulp manufactured from waste or recycled paper; Fuller's earth mining; Cellulosic manmade fibers
PA: Profile Products Llc

750 W Lake Cook Rd # 440
Buffalo Grove IL 60089
847 215-1144

(G-4490)
PSI-POLYMER SYSTEMS INC
1703 Pineview St Se (28613-9339)
PHONE..................................828 468-2600
Glenn Woodcock, *Pr*
Glen Woodcock, *Pr*
Carla Woodcock, *VP*
▲ EMP: 23 EST: 1994
SQ FT: 55,000
SALES (est): 5.09MM **Privately Held**
Web: www.psi-polymersystems.com
SIC: 3559 5084 Plastics working machinery; Industrial machinery and equipment

(G-4491)
RICHARD SHEW
Also Called: Elite Cushion Company
6202 N Nc 16 Hwy (28613-7411)
P.O. Box 1341 (28613-1341)
PHONE..................................828 781-3294
Richard Shew, *Owner*
EMP: 15 EST: 2017
SALES (est): 622.65K **Privately Held**
SIC: 2392 2512 Pillows, bed: made from purchased materials; Upholstered household furniture

(G-4492)
RMG LEATHER USA LLC
1226 Fedex Dr Sw (28613-7426)
PHONE..................................828 466-5489
EMP: 10 EST: 2021
SALES (est): 2.2MM
SALES (corp-wide): 500.31K **Privately Held**
Web: www.carrollleather.com
SIC: 2386 Garments, leather
HQ: Rino Mastrotto Group Spa
Via Dell'artigianato 100
Trissino VI 36070
044 596-9696

(G-4493)
ROLLEASE ACMEDA INC
Also Called: Rollease Acmeda Dist Ctr
375 Workman St Sw (28613-8270)
PHONE..................................800 552-5100
EMP: 77
SALES (corp-wide): 1.49B **Privately Held**
Web: www.rolleaseacmeda.com
SIC: 2591 Window shade rollers and fittings
HQ: Rollease Acmeda, Inc.
750 E Main St Fl 7
Stamford CT 06902
203 964-1573

(G-4494)
RUBBER MILL INC
3109 15th Avenue Blvd Se (28613-9606)
PHONE..................................336 622-1680
Heidi Bradley, *CEO*
EMP: 6 EST: 1986
SALES (est): 132.32K **Privately Held**
SIC: 5085 3569 3069 3053 Rubber goods, mechanical; Filters; Molded rubber products; Gaskets; packing and sealing devices

(G-4495)
SCHENCK USA CORP
Also Called: Benz Tling A Bus Unit Schnck U
1232 Commerce St Sw (28613-8355)
PHONE..................................704 529-5300
Lars Kuenne, *Brnch Mgr*
EMP: 5
SALES (corp-wide): 4.48B **Privately Held**
Web: www.schenck-usa.com

GEOGRAPHIC SECTION

Cordova - Richmond County (G-4518)

SIC: 3541 Machine tools, metal cutting type
HQ: Schenck Usa Corp.
535 Acorn St
Deer Park NY 11729
631 242-4010

(G-4496)
SIGN GYPSIES HICKORY
2017 Conover Blvd E (28613-9664)
PHONE....................828 244-3085
Nathan Hure, *Prin*
EMP: 4 EST: 2019
SALES (est): 50.69K **Privately Held**
Web: www.signgypsieshky.com
SIC: 3993 Signs and advertising specialties

(G-4497)
SMART ELECTRIC NORTH AMER LLC
1550 Deborah Herman Rd Sw (28613-8204)
P.O. Box 697 (28613-0697)
PHONE....................828 323-1200
Jerry Yang, *Managing Member*
Kelvin Crisp, *Pr*
▲ EMP: 6 EST: 2012
SQ FT: 15,000
SALES (est): 689.41K **Privately Held**
Web: www.smartelectricoem.com
SIC: 3699 5063 Electrical equipment and supplies, nec; Electrical apparatus and equipment

(G-4498)
SOUTHLINE CONVERTING LLC
639 4th Street Pl Sw (28613-2646)
PHONE....................828 781-6414
Russell D Woy, *Managing Member*
EMP: 5 EST: 2005
SQ FT: 120,000
SALES (est): 499.49K **Privately Held**
Web: www.southlineconverting.com
SIC: 2221 Textile mills, broadwoven: silk and manmade, also glass

(G-4499)
SOUTHWOOD DOORS LLC
1222 Emmanuel Church Rd Ste 6 (28613-9386)
PHONE....................704 625-2578
Toni Dearstyne, *Managing Member*
EMP: 17 EST: 2017
SALES (est): 556.14K **Privately Held**
Web: www.southwooddoors.com
SIC: 2431 Doors, wood

(G-4500)
STAR SNAX LLC
103b Somerset Dr Nw (28613-9217)
PHONE....................828 261-0255
Bill Hood, *CEO*
Monica Consonery, *
Randall Wilson Ctrl, *Treas*
◆ EMP: 100 EST: 2002
SQ FT: 100,000
SALES (est): 25.35MM **Privately Held**
Web: www.starsnaxfoods.com
SIC: 2099 Food preparations, nec

(G-4501)
STATESMAN FURNITURE
1014 1st St W (28613-9692)
PHONE....................828 431-2146
David Welch, *Mgr*
EMP: 6 EST: 1990
SALES (est): 109.4K **Privately Held**
SIC: 2599 Furniture and fixtures, nec

(G-4502)
SUPREME ELASTIC CORPORATION
Also Called: U K I Supreme
325 Spencer Rd Ne (28613-8211)
P.O. Box 848 (28603-0848)
PHONE....................828 302-3836
Terry M Taylor, *Prin*
Nathaniel Kolmes, *
Wes Christopher, *
Mathew Kolmes, *
◆ EMP: 50 EST: 1964
SQ FT: 52,000
SALES (est): 8.01MM **Privately Held**
Web: www.supremecorporation.com
SIC: 2241 2284 2281 Rubber thread and yarns, fabric covered; Thread mills; Yarn spinning mills

(G-4503)
TB ARHAUS LLC
1211 Keisler Rd Se (28613-9336)
P.O. Box 1628 (28613-3003)
PHONE....................828 465-6953
Watkins Doug, *Genl Mgr*
Brenda Rodefeld Ctrl, *Prin*
EMP: 190 EST: 2015
SALES (est): 24.87MM
SALES (corp-wide): 130.15MM **Privately Held**
SIC: 2512 Upholstered household furniture
PA: Arhaus, Llc
51 E Hines Hill Rd
Hudson OH 44236
440 439-7700

(G-4504)
TEXTILE-BASED DELIVERY INC
Also Called: Texdel
350 5th Ave Se (28613-1941)
PHONE....................866 256-8420
Jordan Schindler, *CEO*
▲ EMP: 30 EST: 2013
SALES (est): 3MM **Privately Held**
Web: www.texdel.com
SIC: 2211 Dress fabrics, cotton

(G-4505)
TIMMERMAN MANUFACTURING INC
102 S Mclin Creek Rd (28613-9024)
P.O. Box 1148 (28613-1148)
PHONE....................828 464-1778
Dan Timmerman, *Pr*
Paula Timmerman, *Sec*
EMP: 15 EST: 1968
SQ FT: 36,000
SALES (est): 971.9K **Privately Held**
Web: www.timmermanmfg.com
SIC: 2514 3499 3446 Metal household furniture; Furniture parts, metal; Architectural metalwork

(G-4506)
TOP TIER PAPER PRODUCTS INC (PA)
409 Thornburg Dr Se (28613-8845)
PHONE....................828 994-2222
Rajiv Kaushal, *Pr*
Tracy High, *Sec*
Rob Williams, *VP*
Minakshi Kaushal, *Ch Bd*
EMP: 9 EST: 2015
SALES (est): 1MM
SALES (corp-wide): 1MM **Privately Held**
Web: www.toptierpaper.com
SIC: 2676 Towels, napkins, and tissue paper products

(G-4507)
UNITAPE (USA) INC
620 Reese Dr Sw (28613-2932)
PHONE....................828 464-5695
Kathy Weaber, *Acctnt*
▲ EMP: 16 EST: 2010
SALES (est): 791.86K **Privately Held**
Web: www.unitape.co.uk
SIC: 1731 3357 Fiber optic cable installation; Aircraft wire and cable, nonferrous

(G-4508)
UNITED MACHINE & METAL FAB INC
1220 Fedex Dr Sw (28613-7426)
P.O. Box 1234 (28613-1234)
PHONE....................828 464-5167
Amir Rashidi, *Prin*
Tony Johnson, *VP*
EMP: 22 EST: 1991
SQ FT: 14,500
SALES (est): 4.76MM **Privately Held**
Web: www.ummf.com
SIC: 3441 3545 Fabricated structural metal; Machine tool accessories

(G-4509)
UNIVERSAL FURNITURE INTL INC
1099 2nd Avenue Pl Se (28613-2165)
PHONE....................828 464-0311
Dale Smith, *Brnch Mgr*
EMP: 110
Web: www.universalfurniture.com
SIC: 2512 2511 Living room furniture: upholstered on wood frames; Tables, household: wood
HQ: Universal Furniture International Inc.
2575 Penny Rd
High Point NC 27265
336 822-8425

(G-4510)
VANGUARD FURNITURE CO INC (PA)
Also Called: Vanguard Furniture
109 Simpson St Sw (28613-8206)
P.O. Box 2187 (28603-2187)
PHONE....................828 328-5601
John N Bray, *CEO*
Dixon Mitchell, *
Jay Andrew Bray, *
Lauren Hoover, *
Charles Snipes, *
◆ EMP: 325 EST: 1968
SQ FT: 400,000
SALES (est): 46.13MM
SALES (corp-wide): 46.13MM **Privately Held**
Web: www.vanguardfurniture.com
SIC: 2512 Couches, sofas, and davenports: upholstered on wood frames

(G-4511)
VPC FOAM USA INC ✪
1820 Evans St Ne (28613-9042)
PHONE....................704 622-0552
Patricia Bohrer, *CFO*
EMP: 60 EST: 2023
SALES (est): 1.78MM **Privately Held**
SIC: 3086 Plastics foam products

(G-4512)
WESTROCK RKT LLC
214 Conover Blvd E (28613-1925)
P.O. Box 669 (28613-0669)
PHONE....................828 464-5560
Wayne A Noyes, *Mgr*
EMP: 132
SALES (corp-wide): 20.31B **Publicly Held**
Web: www.westrock.com
SIC: 2657 5113 Folding paperboard boxes; Bags, paper and disposable plastic
HQ: Westrock Rkt, Llc
1000 Abernathy Rd Ste 125
Atlanta GA 30328
770 448-2193

(G-4513)
WILLIS MANUFACTURING INC
Also Called: Willis Manufacturing
1924 Emmanuel Church Rd (28613-7301)
P.O. Box 335 (28613-0335)
PHONE....................828 244-0435
Brenda Willis Cayll, *Pr*
EMP: 10 EST: 1972
SALES (est): 610K **Privately Held**
SIC: 3541 Screw machines, automatic

(G-4514)
WINDAK INC
1661 4th St Sw (28613-9633)
P.O. Box 517 (28613-0517)
PHONE....................828 322-2292
Dan Shelander, *Pr*
Urban Bollo, *VP*
Staffan Edstrom, *Treas*
◆ EMP: 15 EST: 1997
SQ FT: 6,500
SALES (est): 2.35MM **Privately Held**
Web: www.windakgroup.com
SIC: 3565 Packaging machinery

(G-4515)
WOOD TECHNOLOGY INC (PA)
1317 Emmanuel Church Rd (28613-9015)
PHONE....................828 464-8049
Thomas Goff, *Pr*
Jeff Kaylor, *VP*
EMP: 20 EST: 1984
SQ FT: 14,000
SALES (est): 2.64MM **Privately Held**
Web: www.woodtechnology.com
SIC: 5021 2511 2517 2434 Racks; Stands, household, nec: wood; Wood television and radio cabinets; Wood kitchen cabinets

Conway
Northampton County

(G-4516)
NUTRIEN AG SOLUTIONS INC
Ampac Rd (27820)
PHONE....................252 585-0282
James Hatcher, *Mgr*
EMP: 7
SALES (corp-wide): 27.71B **Privately Held**
Web: www.nutrienagsolutions.com
SIC: 2875 5191 Fertilizers, mixing only; Fertilizer and fertilizer materials
HQ: Nutrien Ag Solutions, Inc.
3005 Rocky Mountain Ave
Loveland CO 80538
970 685-3300

Cordova
Richmond County

(G-4517)
ELEVATE TEXTILES INC
740 Old Cheraw Hwy (28330)
PHONE....................910 997-5001
Joseph Gorga, *Prin*
EMP: 6
SALES (corp-wide): 1.98B **Privately Held**
Web: www.elevatetextiles.com
SIC: 2211 Broadwoven fabric mills, cotton
HQ: Elevate Textiles, Inc.
121 W Trade St Ste 1700
Charlotte NC 28202

(G-4518)
LAUREL HILL PAPER CO
126 1st St (28330)
P.O. Box 159 (28330-0159)
PHONE....................910 997-4526

Kent Hogan, *Pr*
Phillip G Hogan, *
◆ **EMP:** 26 **EST:** 1974
SQ FT: 377,000
SALES (est): 1.92MM **Privately Held**
SIC: 2621 Tissue paper

Cornelius
Mecklenburg County

(G-4519)
A M P LABORATORIES LTD
20905 Torrence Chapel Rd Ste 204 (28031-4300)
PHONE.................................704 894-9721
Dean Victoria, *Pr*
EMP: 4 **EST:** 2000
SALES (est): 149.43K **Privately Held**
SIC: 2844 5122 Cosmetic preparations; Cosmetics

(G-4520)
ADVANCED PHOTONIC CRYSTALS LLC
19825 North Cove Rd # 216 (28031-6446)
PHONE.................................803 547-0881
John J Egan, *Managing Member*
EMP: 7 **EST:** 2002
SALES (est): 338.2K **Privately Held**
SIC: 3827 Optical instruments and apparatus

(G-4521)
APPLIED TECHNOLOGIES GROUP
19701 Bethel Church Rd Ste 103 (28031-4072)
PHONE.................................618 977-9872
Tom Tragesser, *Owner*
EMP: 5 **EST:** 2014
SALES (est): 174.84K **Privately Held**
Web: marshunicorn.business.site
SIC: 3861 Photographic equipment and supplies

(G-4522)
AQUA BLUE INC
9624 Bailey Rd Ste 270 (28031-6120)
PHONE.................................704 896-9007
EMP: 8 **EST:** 2004
SALES (est): 357.42K **Privately Held**
SIC: 3999 5091 Preparation of slides and exhibits; Water slides (recreation park)

(G-4523)
ARTISAN DIRECT LLC
18335 Old Statesville Rd Ste L (28031-9013)
PHONE.................................704 655-9100
EMP: 9 **EST:** 2019
SALES (est): 244.4K **Privately Held**
Web: www.artisandirect.us
SIC: 3993 Signs and advertising specialties

(G-4524)
ARTISAN SIGNS AND GRAPHICS INC
Also Called: Artisan Graphics
18335 Old Statesville Rd Ste L (28031-9014)
PHONE.................................704 655-9100
Scott Crosbie, *Pr*
▲ **EMP:** 18 **EST:** 2004
SQ FT: 12,500
SALES (est): 3.7MM **Privately Held**
Web: www.artisansignsandgraphics.com
SIC: 3993 Signs, not made in custom sign painting shops

(G-4525)
BALANCED PHARMA INCORPORATED
18204 Mainsail Pointe Dr (28031-5198)
PHONE.................................704 278-7054
EMP: 5 **EST:** 2020
SALES (est): 368.59K **Privately Held**
Web: www.balancedpharma.com
SIC: 2834 Pharmaceutical preparations

(G-4526)
BELEV EN U WATER MFG CO
19600 W Catawba Ave Ste 201 (28031-4024)
PHONE.................................704 620-0450
Norman Mundy, *CEO*
EMP: 5 **EST:** 2021
SALES (est): 39.69K **Privately Held**
SIC: 3999 Manufacturing industries, nec

(G-4527)
BLUE NANO INC
18946 Brigadoon Pl (28031-5500)
PHONE.................................888 508-6266
David Himebaugh, *Pr*
EMP: 10 **EST:** 2007
SALES (est): 646.16K **Privately Held**
Web: www.bluenanoinc.com
SIC: 2819 Industrial inorganic chemicals, nec

(G-4528)
BLUESTONE METALS & CHEM LLC
19720 Jetton Rd Ste 101 (28031-8263)
PHONE.................................704 662-8632
Wouter Vanloo, *Managing Member*
EMP: 4 **EST:** 2014
SQ FT: 80
SALES (est): 18.53MM **Privately Held**
Web: www.bluestonemc.com
SIC: 2819 Industrial inorganic chemicals, nec
HQ: Specialty Metals Resources
Tenbosstraat 42, Internal Postal Box A
Bruxelles 1050

(G-4529)
BLUESTONE SPECIALTY CHEM LLC
19720 Jetton Rd Ste 101 (28031-8263)
PHONE.................................704 662-8632
Wouter Van Loo, *Managing Member*
EMP: 17 **EST:** 2010
SALES (est): 7.59MM **Privately Held**
SIC: 2819 Industrial inorganic chemicals, nec
PA: Specialty Metals Resources Holding Limited
Rm 3602 36/F China Resources Bldg
Wan Chai HK

(G-4530)
BOKA INDUSTRIES LLC
19406 E Battery St (28031-6510)
PHONE.................................704 237-4692
Robert E Ward, *Prin*
EMP: 4 **EST:** 2018
SALES (est): 73.25K **Privately Held**
SIC: 3999 Manufacturing industries, nec

(G-4531)
BORDCHEK INDUSTRIES LLC
19701 Bethel Church Rd Ste 103-164 (28031-4072)
PHONE.................................864 363-2117
Steve Dyer, *Prin*
EMP: 4 **EST:** 2017
SALES (est): 68.63K **Privately Held**
SIC: 3999 Manufacturing industries, nec

(G-4532)
C6 MANUFACTURING
10515 Caldwell Depot Rd (28031-8178)
PHONE.................................704 896-3934
EMP: 4 **EST:** 2018
SALES (est): 77.18K **Privately Held**
SIC: 3999 Manufacturing industries, nec

(G-4533)
CAROLINA COPY SERVICES INC (PA)
21300 Blakely Shores Dr (28031-6610)
PHONE.................................704 375-9099
Perry Montgomery, *Pr*
EMP: 12 **EST:** 1998
SQ FT: 4,000
SALES (est): 1.32MM **Privately Held**
Web: www.carolinacopyservices.com
SIC: 7334 2752 Photocopying and duplicating services; Commercial printing, lithographic

(G-4534)
CAROLINA GYPS RECLAMATION LLC
19109 W Catawba Ave (28031-5611)
PHONE.................................704 895-4506
EMP: 8 **EST:** 2009
SALES (est): 479.55K **Privately Held**
SIC: 3999 Manufacturing industries, nec

(G-4535)
CHARLOTT CUSTOM WOODWORKS
20428 Willow Pond Rd (28031-9600)
PHONE.................................704 634-0863
Jeff Tracey, *Prin*
EMP: 5 **EST:** 2010
SALES (est): 107.93K **Privately Held**
Web: www.doctorcabinet.com
SIC: 2431 Millwork

(G-4536)
COASTAL CAROLINA WINERY
10301 Carriage Ct (28031-9249)
PHONE.................................843 443-9463
Gary Taylor, *Owner*
EMP: 7 **EST:** 2014
SALES (est): 341.58K **Privately Held**
Web: www.coastalcarolinawinery.com
SIC: 2084 Wines

(G-4537)
CORNHOLE STOP
19235 Dutch Iris Ln (28031-7868)
PHONE.................................704 728-1550
Sherrie Kowtko, *Prin*
EMP: 4 **EST:** 2017
SALES (est): 60K **Privately Held**
Web: www.cornholestop.com
SIC: 3993 Signs and advertising specialties

(G-4538)
DASH CABINET COMPANY LLC
19701 Bethel Church Rd Ste 201 (28031-4072)
PHONE.................................704 746-7382
EMP: 5 **EST:** 2018
SALES (est): 59.16K **Privately Held**
Web: www.dashcabinet.com
SIC: 2434 Wood kitchen cabinets

(G-4539)
DCE SOLAR SERVICE INC
19410 Jetton Rd Ste 220 (28031-4410)
PHONE.................................704 659-7474
EMP: 8 **EST:** 2009
SQ FT: 4,500
SALES (est): 2.4MM **Privately Held**
Web: www.dcesolar.com
SIC: 1711 3433 5074 Solar energy contractor ; Heating equipment, except electric; Heating equipment and panels, solar

(G-4540)
DEXIOS SERVICES LLC
10308 Bailey Rd Ste 430 (28031-9426)
PHONE.................................704 946-5101
EMP: 8
SALES (est): 351.29K **Privately Held**
SIC: 2844 Perfumes, cosmetics and other toilet preparations

(G-4541)
DURKEE EMBROIDERY INC
10620 Bailey Rd Ste G (28031-9364)
PHONE.................................980 689-2684
EMP: 5
SALES (est): 271.62K **Privately Held**
Web: www.durkeehoops.com
SIC: 2395 Embroidery and art needlework

(G-4542)
E BY DESIGN LLC
20823 N Main St, Ste 115 (28031-8206)
P.O. Box 2310 (28036-5310)
PHONE.................................980 231-5483
Heather Slosson Roberts, *CEO*
EMP: 4 **EST:** 2013
SQ FT: 1,000
SALES (est): 282.87K **Privately Held**
Web: www.ebydesign.net
SIC: 2299 Pillow fillings: curled hair, cotton waste, moss, hemp tow

(G-4543)
EMBROIDME LAKE NORMAN
19420 Jetton Rd Ste 104 (28031-4402)
PHONE.................................704 987-9630
EMP: 5 **EST:** 2020
SALES (est): 28.39K **Privately Held**
Web: www.fullypromoted.com
SIC: 7336 7311 3993 2759 Commercial art and graphic design; Advertising agencies; Signs and advertising specialties; Commercial printing, nec

(G-4544)
ETERNAL WRAPS
10603 Caldwell Depot Rd (28031-8183)
PHONE.................................704 756-1914
Michelle Bailey, *Prin*
EMP: 4 **EST:** 2015
SALES (est): 92.36K **Privately Held**
SIC: 3993 Signs and advertising specialties

(G-4545)
FAST PRO MEDIA LLC
Also Called: Speed Pro Imaging N Charlotte
10308 Bailey Rd Ste 422 (28031-9426)
PHONE.................................704 799-8040
EMP: 5 **EST:** 2017
SALES (est): 250K **Privately Held**
SIC: 2752 7389 7336 Commercial printing, lithographic; Printing broker; Graphic arts and related design

(G-4546)
FAST PRO MEDIA LLC
Also Called: Speed Pro Imaging N Charlotte
10308 Bailey Rd Ste 422 (28031-9426)
P.O. Box 1766 (28036-1766)
PHONE.................................704 799-8040
John Alan Casson, *Prin*
EMP: 5 **EST:** 2015
SALES (est): 22.34K **Privately Held**
SIC: 4899 2752 7389 7336 Communication services, nec; Commercial printing, lithographic; Business services, nec; Commercial art and graphic design

(G-4547)
FIRST RATE BLINDS
19701 Bethel Church Rd # 178 (28031-4072)

GEOGRAPHIC SECTION

Cornelius - Mecklenburg County (G-4575)

PHONE.....................800 655-1080
EMP: 5 **EST:** 2019
SALES (est): 72.97K **Privately Held**
Web: www.firstrateblinds.com
SIC: 2591 Window blinds

(G-4548)
FORKLIFT NETWORK
20802 Eastpoint Dr (28031-7064)
PHONE.....................877 327-7260
EMP: 6 **EST:** 2013
SALES (est): 150.07K **Privately Held**
Web: www.fork-lift-trucks.net
SIC: 3537 Forklift trucks

(G-4549)
GIRLIE JAMS
21200 Cold Spring Ln (28031-6439)
PHONE.....................704 575-5815
Linda Daley, *Prin*
EMP: 4 **EST:** 2017
SALES (est): 59.48K **Privately Held**
SIC: 2033 Jams, jellies, and preserves, packaged in cans, jars, etc.

(G-4550)
GLAXOSMITHKLINE LLC
8625 Covedale Crossings Cir (28031)
PHONE.....................704 962-5786
EMP: 6
SALES (corp-wide): 35.31B **Privately Held**
Web: us.gsk.com
SIC: 2834 Pharmaceutical preparations
HQ: Glaxosmithkline Llc
2929 Walnut St Ste 1700
Philadelphia PA 19104
888 825-5249

(G-4551)
GO GREEN MIRACLE BALM
17810 Half Moon Ln Apt A (28031-8007)
PHONE.....................630 209-0226
Kristina Lewandowski, *Prin*
EMP: 4 **EST:** 2019
SALES (est): 147.76K **Privately Held**
SIC: 2844 Perfumes, cosmetics and other toilet preparations

(G-4552)
GOURMET FOODS USA LLC
10415 Bailey Rd (28031-9442)
PHONE.....................704 248-1724
Calvin Glover, *Managing Member*
EMP: 5 **EST:** 2016
SALES (est): 241.38K **Privately Held**
SIC: 2099 5199 Popcorn, packaged: except already popped; General merchandise, non-durable

(G-4553)
GULFSTREAM PLANS & DESIGN INC
18725 The Commons Blvd (28031-7070)
PHONE.....................704 641-2544
Troy Smith, *Pr*
EMP: 4 **EST:** 2018
SALES (est): 27.98K **Privately Held**
SIC: 3721 Aircraft

(G-4554)
HARRAH ENTERPRISE LTD
10308 Bailey Rd Ste 416 (28031-9426)
PHONE.....................336 253-3963
Mark E Harrah, *Prin*
EMP: 9 **EST:** 2017
SALES (est): 829.69K **Privately Held**
Web: www.harrahenterprise.com
SIC: 3465 Body parts, automobile: stamped metal

(G-4555)
HIAB USA INC
Also Called: Hiab
18627 Starcreek Dr (28031-9328)
PHONE.....................704 896-9089
Jim Hunsuck, *Mgr*
EMP: 10
Web: www.hiab.com
SIC: 5084 3724 Cranes, industrial; Engine mount parts, aircraft
HQ: Hiab Usa Inc.
12233 Williams Rd
Perrysburg OH 43551
419 482-6000

(G-4556)
HOWELL & SONS CANVAS REPAIRS
29015 North Main St (28031)
P.O. Box 187 (28031-0187)
PHONE.....................704 892-7913
Nicholas Droffopoulous, *Pr*
EMP: 4 **EST:** 1972
SQ FT: 3,600
SALES (est): 167.29K **Privately Held**
Web: www.howellandsonscanvas.com
SIC: 2394 7219 Liners and covers, fabric: made from purchased materials; Accessory and non-garment cleaning and repair

(G-4557)
HUCK CYCLES CORPORATION
11020 Bailey Rd Ste D (28031-8102)
PHONE.....................704 275-1735
EMP: 6 **EST:** 2021
SALES (est): 295.39K **Privately Held**
Web: www.huckcycles.com
SIC: 3751 Bicycles and related parts

(G-4558)
HUNTER FAN COMPANY
20464 Chartwell Center Dr Ste H (28031-9629)
PHONE.....................704 896-9250
Jeff Newman, *Prin*
EMP: 4 **EST:** 2007
SALES (est): 371.79K **Privately Held**
SIC: 3564 5084 Blowers and fans; Fans, industrial

(G-4559)
IGNITE DIRT SPORTS LLC
19825 North Cove Rd Ste 171 (28031-6446)
PHONE.....................704 770-7806
EMP: 4 **EST:** 2017
SALES (est): 194.4K **Privately Held**
SIC: 3714 Motor vehicle parts and accessories

(G-4560)
IMPACT DIGITAL PRINTING INC
18605 Northline Dr Ste E11 (28031-9365)
PHONE.....................704 609-7638
EMP: 5 **EST:** 2013
SALES (est): 55.66K **Privately Held**
Web: www.idpwraps.com
SIC: 2752 Offset printing

(G-4561)
INNOVATIVE AWNGS & SCREENS LLC
19825 North Cove Rd Ste B (28031-0149)
PHONE.....................833 337-4233
Andrew Hoyt, *Managing Member*
EMP: 11 **EST:** 2017
SALES (est): 599.57K **Privately Held**
Web: www.innovativeawnings.com
SIC: 5999 5712 3448 Awnings; Outdoor and garden furniture; Screen enclosures

(G-4562)
INSOURCE SFTWR SOLUTIONS INC
19421 Liverpool Pkwy Ste A (28031-6283)
PHONE.....................704 895-1052
Bill Migirditch, *Brnch Mgr*
EMP: 6
SALES (corp-wide): 22.5MM **Privately Held**
Web: www.insource.solutions
SIC: 7372 Prepackaged software
PA: Insource Software Solutions, Inc.
10800 Midlothian Tpke # 2
North Chesterfield VA 23235
804 419-0674

(G-4563)
JALA WOODSHOP LLC
10301 Conistan Pl (28031-9212)
PHONE.....................704 439-6119
EMP: 5 **EST:** 2021
SALES (est): 63.22K **Privately Held**
Web: www.jalawoodshop.com
SIC: 2431 Millwork

(G-4564)
LAKE NORMAN EMB & MONOGRAMMING
21228 Catawba Ave (28031-8428)
PHONE.....................704 892-8450
Sandra Carrigan, *Owner*
EMP: 5 **EST:** 1990
SALES (est): 174.81K **Privately Held**
Web: www.lknemb.com
SIC: 2395 2759 Emblems, embroidered; Commercial printing, nec

(G-4565)
LAKE NORMAN INDUSTRIES LLC
19116 Statesville Rd (28031)
P.O. Box 2007 (28031-2007)
PHONE.....................704 987-9048
◆ **EMP:** 8 **EST:** 2010
SALES (est): 393.4K **Privately Held**
Web: www.businesstodaync.com
SIC: 2082 2085 2084 8748 Beer (alcoholic beverage); Distilled and blended liquors; Wines, brandy, and brandy spirits; Business consulting, nec

(G-4566)
LAKESIDE CSTM TEES & EMBROIDER
9216 Westmoreland Rd Ste B (28031-5675)
PHONE.....................704 274-3730
Shelly Hawley, *Prin*
EMP: 6 **EST:** 2017
SALES (est): 135.24K **Privately Held**
SIC: 2759 Screen printing

(G-4567)
LEBOS SHOE STORE INC
20605 Torrence Chapel Rd (28031-6878)
PHONE.....................704 987-6540
EMP: 10
SALES (corp-wide): 19.24MM **Privately Held**
Web: www.lebos.com
SIC: 5661 2389 Shoes, orthopedic; Men's miscellaneous accessories
PA: Lebo's Shoe Store, Inc.
2321 Crown Centre Dr
Charlotte NC 28227
704 321-5000

(G-4568)
LKN PERFORM LLC
11020 Bailey Rd Ste J (28031-8102)
PHONE.....................704 215-4900
EMP: 6

(G-4569)
LOGOTHREADS INC
20480 Chartwell Center Dr Ste H (28031-3400)
PHONE.....................704 892-9433
Jackson Reed, *Prin*
EMP: 6 **EST:** 2010
SALES (est): 59.68K **Privately Held**
SIC: 2323 Men's and boy's neckwear

(G-4570)
MP DIGITAL PRINT & SIGNS INC
20325 Sterling Bay Ln W (28031-4944)
PHONE.....................571 315-1562
Piirce Ajavon, *Mgr*
EMP: 4 **EST:** 2015
SALES (est): 93.2K **Privately Held**
SIC: 3993 Signs and advertising specialties

(G-4571)
OAKSTONE ASSOCIATES LLC
10308 Bailey Rd Ste 430 (28031-9426)
PHONE.....................704 946-5101
EMP: 14 **EST:** 2016
SALES (est): 1.05MM **Privately Held**
SIC: 2844 Depilatories (cosmetic)

(G-4572)
OLDCASTLE RETAIL INC
Also Called: Oldcastle Apg
18637 Northline Dr Ste S (28031-9322)
PHONE.....................704 799-8083
Randy Gottlieb, *Brnch Mgr*
EMP: 267
SALES (corp-wide): 32.72B **Privately Held**
SIC: 3273 3272 3271 3255 Ready-mixed concrete; Concrete products used to facilitate drainage; Concrete block and brick ; Clay refractories
HQ: Oldcastle Retail, Inc.
625 Griffith Rd Ste 100
Charlotte NC 28217
704 525-1621

(G-4573)
ORIGINAL NEW YORK SELTZER LLC (HQ)
19109 W Catawba Ave Ste 200 (28031-5614)
PHONE.....................323 500-0757
EMP: 20 **EST:** 2015
SALES (est): 484.96K
SALES (corp-wide): 1.29MM **Privately Held**
Web: www.newyorkseltzer.com
SIC: 2086 Bottled and canned soft drinks
PA: Entertainment Arts Research, Inc.
19109 W Catwba Ave # 200
Cornelius NC 28031
980 999-0270

(G-4574)
PEANUT BUTTER FINGERS LLC
17131 Green Dolphin Ln (28031-7692)
PHONE.....................704 997-5787
Julie B Fagan, *Prin*
EMP: 5 **EST:** 2012
SALES (est): 118K **Privately Held**
Web: www.pbfingers.com
SIC: 2099 Peanut butter

(G-4575)
PINCO USA INC
10620 Bailey Rd Ste A (28031-9364)
PHONE.....................704 895-5766
S Paul Whitaker, *Pr*
David T Culp, *CEO*

Cornelius - Mecklenburg County

Alistair H Deas, *VP Sls*
Frances W Smith, *Sec*
▲ **EMP:** 5 **EST:** 2005
SALES (est): 528.57K **Privately Held**
Web: www.allertex.com
SIC: 3552 Textile machinery
PA: Allertex Of America, Ltd.
  10620 Bailey Rd Ste A
  Cornelius NC 28031

(G-4576)
PING GPS INC
19825 North Cove Rd (28031-6446)
PHONE..................................704 806-7945
Josh Littener, *Pr*
EMP: 4 **EST:** 2018
SALES (est): 185.53K **Privately Held**
Web: www.pinggps.com
SIC: 3812 Search and navigation equipment

(G-4577)
PREMIER TOOL LLC
20409 Zion Ave (28031-8549)
PHONE..................................704 895-8223
Diane Hoskins, *CEO*
EMP: 5 **EST:** 1987
SQ FT: 5,000
SALES (est): 498.99K **Privately Held**
Web: www.premiertoolcorp.com
SIC: 3545 Cutting tools for machine tools

(G-4578)
PRIMO INC
Also Called: Primo Print
19009 Peninsula Point Dr (28031-7601)
PHONE..................................888 822-5815
Marc Levack, *Pr*
▼ **EMP:** 8 **EST:** 2009
SALES (est): 1.97MM **Privately Held**
Web: www.primoprint.com
SIC: 2752 Offset printing

(G-4579)
PROMOTHREADS INC
19824 W Catawba Ave Ste C (28031-4046)
PHONE..................................704 248-0942
William V Brisbin, *Prin*
EMP: 9 **EST:** 2013
SALES (est): 320.76K **Privately Held**
Web: www.promothreads.com
SIC: 2759 Screen printing

(G-4580)
RAWCO LLC
Also Called: Rawco Precision Manufacturing
18435 Train Station Dr (28031-8179)
P.O. Box 296 (07830-0296)
PHONE..................................908 832-7700
EMP: 8 **EST:** 2004
SALES (est): 940.23K **Privately Held**
Web: www.rawcoprecision.com
SIC: 3599 Machine shop, jobbing and repair

(G-4581)
RED 5 PRINTING LLC
18631 Northline Dr (28031-9357)
PHONE..................................704 996-3848
EMP: 5 **EST:** 2015
SALES (est): 265.18K **Privately Held**
Web: www.red5printing.com
SIC: 2752 Commercial printing, lithographic

(G-4582)
RESOLUTE FABRICATORS LLC
18708 W Catawba Ave (28031-5615)
PHONE..................................704 728-1249
EMP: 9 **EST:** 2017
SALES (est): 322.07K **Privately Held**
SIC: 3999 Manufacturing industries, nec

(G-4583)
RICKS CUSTOM MARINE CANVAS
20213 Middletown Rd (28031-6534)
PHONE..................................937 623-1672
Rick Berkey, *Prin*
EMP: 4 **EST:** 2014
SALES (est): 61.11K **Privately Held**
Web:
  www.rickscustommarinecanvas.com
SIC: 2394 Canvas and related products

(G-4584)
RPM INSTALLIONS INC
19843 Henderson Rd (28031-6879)
P.O. Box 1449 (28031-1449)
PHONE..................................704 907-0868
Christopher Mcauliffe, *CEO*
Edward Elacla, *Sec*
EMP: 4 **EST:** 1999
SALES (est): 301.63K **Privately Held**
SIC: 2541 Cabinets, lockers, and shelving

(G-4585)
SAFE HOME PRO INC
Also Called: Adams Line Striping
18635 Starcreek Dr Ste B (28031-9342)
P.O. Box 725 (28070-0725)
PHONE..................................704 662-2299
Nicole Lasarsky, *Pr*
Suzanne Roakes, *VP*
EMP: 16 **EST:** 2010
SQ FT: 4,000
SALES (est): 2.87MM **Privately Held**
Web: www.safehomepro.com
SIC: 1521 3842 Single-family housing construction; Surgical appliances and supplies

(G-4586)
SKC1 LLC
18802 Peninsula Club Dr (28031-5116)
PHONE..................................937 620-5187
EMP: 5 **EST:** 2019
SALES (est): 107.4K **Privately Held**
SIC: 2741 Miscellaneous publishing

(G-4587)
SPEEDPRO IMAGING
10308 Bailey Rd (28031-9425)
PHONE..................................704 799-8040
EMP: 4 **EST:** 2018
SALES (est): 61.11K **Privately Held**
Web: www.speedpro.com
SIC: 3993 Signs and advertising specialties

(G-4588)
STELLAR INNOVATIONS INC
21000 Torrence Chapel Rd Ste 104 (28031-6873)
PHONE..................................704 746-2886
Colby Stellhorn, *Prin*
EMP: 4 **EST:** 2010
SALES (est): 98.74K **Privately Held**
Web: www.stellar-innovations.com
SIC: 5999 2511 3999 Hot tub and spa chemicals, equipment, and supplies; Garden furniture: wood; Pet supplies

(G-4589)
SUNDANCE CSTM PAINTED CABINETS
20209 Church St (28031-8474)
PHONE..................................704 500-3732
EMP: 4 **EST:** 2017
SALES (est): 62.27K **Privately Held**
SIC: 2434 Wood kitchen cabinets

(G-4590)
SUNNINGHILL JILL BAKING CO LLC
16618 Flying Jib Rd (28031-7787)
PHONE..................................704 894-9901
Jill Dahan, *Prin*
EMP: 5 **EST:** 2009
SALES (est): 233.83K **Privately Held**
SIC: 2051 Bread, cake, and related products

(G-4591)
TARHEEL PAVEMENT CLG SVCS INC
18636 Starcreek Dr Ste G (28031-9330)
PHONE..................................704 895-8015
Randy Humphry, *Pr*
EMP: 19 **EST:** 1996
SALES (est): 655.74K **Privately Held**
SIC: 3991 Street sweeping brooms, hand or machine

(G-4592)
TIER 1 GRAPHICS LLC
18525 Statesville Rd Ste D10 (28031)
PHONE..................................704 625-6880
EMP: 5 **EST:** 2012
SALES (est): 492.61K **Privately Held**
Web: www.tieronegraphics.com
SIC: 3993 Signs, not made in custom sign painting shops

(G-4593)
VORTEX USA INC
Also Called: Vortex Aquatic Structures USA
11024 Bailey Rd Ste C (28031-8107)
PHONE..................................972 410-3619
Kevin Spence, *Mgr*
Jim Spence, *Sls Mgr*
Erica Montgomery, *Sls Mgr*
EMP: 19 **EST:** 1995
SALES (est): 1MM **Privately Held**
Web: www.vortex-intl.com
SIC: 3599 Amusement park equipment

(G-4594)
WHITE PICKET MEDIA INC
Also Called: Kitchens.com
21313 Island Forest Dr (28031-7131)
PHONE..................................773 769-8400
Steven Krengel, *Pr*
EMP: 9 **EST:** 2007
SALES (est): 238.16K **Privately Held**
Web: www.kitchens.com
SIC: 2741 Miscellaneous publishing

(G-4595)
YOURLOGOWEAR
18700 Statesville Rd (28031-6752)
PHONE..................................704 664-1290
Ken Brock, *Prin*
EMP: 6 **EST:** 2018
SALES (est): 173.08K **Privately Held**
Web: your-logo-wear.business.site
SIC: 2759 Screen printing

(G-4596)
ZETA PERFORMANCE VHCL TECH LLC
11148 Treynorth Dr Ste C (28031-8242)
PHONE..................................804 690-8979
Andrew May, *Prin*
EMP: 5 **EST:** 2019
SALES (est): 213.37K **Privately Held**
Web: www.zetapvt.com
SIC: 3714 Motor vehicle parts and accessories

Cove City
Craven County

(G-4597)
CAROLINA WOOD RESIDUALS LLC
1815 Asbury Rd (28523-9694)
PHONE..................................252 633-3374

Ashby Tippett, *Prin*
EMP: 6 **EST:** 2018
SALES (est): 90.74K **Privately Held**
SIC: 2911 Residues

(G-4598)
WARMACK LUMBER CO INC
321 E Sunset Blvd (28523-9638)
P.O. Box 127 (28523-0127)
PHONE..................................252 638-1435
W Guy Warmack Iii, *Pr*
Alan Warmack, *VP*
▼ **EMP:** 19 **EST:** 1956
SQ FT: 420
SALES (est): 471.25K **Privately Held**
SIC: 2421 Lumber: rough, sawed, or planed

(G-4599)
WORLD WOOD COMPANY
12045 Old Us Highway 70 (28523-9539)
PHONE..................................252 523-0021
Henry Dessauer, *Pr*
EMP: 65 **EST:** 1960
SQ FT: 2,000
SALES (est): 11.07MM
SALES (corp-wide): 595.03MM **Privately Held**
SIC: 5031 2421 Lumber: rough, dressed, and finished; Kiln drying of lumber
PA: Baillie Lumber Co., L.P.
  4002 Legion Dr
  Hamburg NY 14075
  800 950-2850

Cramerton
Gaston County

(G-4600)
BROOKLINE INC
112 Cramer Mountain Woods (28032-1624)
PHONE..................................704 824-1390
O'brien Brooks Junior, *Pr*
Debra Brooks, *VP*
EMP: 4 **EST:** 1981
SALES (est): 326.65K **Privately Held**
SIC: 2259 Convertors, knit goods

Creedmoor
Granville County

(G-4601)
AIRCRAFT BELTS INC (DH)
Also Called: A B I
1176 Telecom Dr (27522-8294)
PHONE..................................919 956-4395
Michael Donoho, *CEO*
Frank Mcknight, *Pr*
David Devine, *CEO*
▲ **EMP:** 20 **EST:** 1981
SQ FT: 7,500
SALES (est): 5.01MM
SALES (corp-wide): 450.6MM **Privately Held**
Web: www.aircraftbelts.com
SIC: 2399 7699 Seat belts, automobile and aircraft; Replating shop, except silverware
HQ: Firstmark Corp.
  2742 Live Oak Ln
  Midlothian VA 23113
  724 759-2850

(G-4602)
AISIN NORTH CAROLINA CORP
1187 Telecom Dr (27522-8262)
PHONE..................................919 529-0951
EMP: 200
Web: www.aisinnc.com

GEOGRAPHIC SECTION

Creston - Ashe County (G-4625)

SIC: 3714 Transmissions, motor vehicle
HQ: Aisin North Carolina Corporation
 4112 Old Oxford Rd
 Durham NC 27712
 919 479-6400

(G-4603)
ALTEC INDUSTRIES INC
1550 Aerial Ave (27522-8252)
PHONE.................................919 528-2535
Joe Gonenc, *Mgr*
EMP: 300
SALES (corp-wide): 1.21B **Privately Held**
Web: www.altec.com
SIC: 3531 3536 3713 3537 Derricks, except oil and gas field; Cranes, overhead traveling; Truck bodies (motor vehicles); Industrial trucks and tractors
HQ: Altec Industries, Inc.
 210 Inverness Center Dr
 Birmingham AL 35242
 205 991-7733

(G-4604)
ALTEC NORTHEAST LLC
1550 Aerial Ave (27522-8252)
PHONE.................................508 320-9041
▲ **EMP:** 85 EST: 2010
SALES (est): 4.37MM
SALES (corp-wide): 1.21B **Privately Held**
Web: www.altec.com
SIC: 3531 3536 3713 Derricks, except oil and gas field; Cranes, overhead traveling; Truck bodies (motor vehicles)
HQ: Altec Industries, Inc.
 210 Inverness Center Dr
 Birmingham AL 35242
 205 991-7733

(G-4605)
APPLIED MEDICAL TECH INC (PA)
Also Called: Airclean Systems
1506 Ivac Way (27522-8112)
PHONE.................................919 255-3220
Michael Kevin Mcgough, *Pr*
Stephen Mitchell Stott, *VP*
Susan F Dobbyn, *Treas*
William J Wickward Junior, *Corporate Secretary*
▲ **EMP:** 39 EST: 1992
SQ FT: 30,000
SALES (est): 9.93MM **Privately Held**
SIC: 3443 Hoods, industrial: metal plate

(G-4606)
BET-MAC WILSON STEEL INC
118 S Durham Ave (Hwy 15) (27522-8210)
P.O. Box 948 (27522-0948)
PHONE.................................919 528-1540
William A Mc Allister, *Pr*
EMP: 7 EST: 1982
SQ FT: 10,000
SALES (est): 919.62K **Privately Held**
Web: www.betmacwilson.com
SIC: 3441 Building components, structural steel

(G-4607)
BKC INDUSTRIES INC
2117 Will Suitt Rd (27522-8161)
P.O. Box 2446 (79105-2446)
PHONE.................................919 575-6699
Steve Aderholt, *Pr*
Helen Piehl, *Sec*
EMP: 9 EST: 1998
SALES (est): 836.91K **Privately Held**
Web: www.western.group
SIC: 3715 Trailer bodies

(G-4608)
CAREFUSION 303 INC
Also Called: Cardinal Alaris Products
1515 Ivac Way (27522-8113)
PHONE.................................919 528-5253
Tom Parker, *Pr*
EMP: 45 EST: 1996
SALES (est): 4.15MM
SALES (corp-wide): 19.37B **Publicly Held**
SIC: 3841 Surgical and medical instruments
HQ: Carefusion 303, Inc.
 10020 Pacific Mesa Blvd
 San Diego CA 92121
 858 617-2000

(G-4609)
CAROLINA SUNROCK LLC
3092 Rock Spring Church Rd (27522-8604)
PHONE.................................919 201-4201
Stuart Nanney, *Prin*
EMP: 4 EST: 2018
SALES (est): 51.16K **Privately Held**
Web: www.thesunrockgroup.com
SIC: 3273 Ready-mixed concrete

(G-4610)
CEDER CREEK GALLERY & POTTERY
Also Called: Cedar Creek Pot & Cft Gallery
1150 Fleming Rd (27522-9262)
PHONE.................................919 528-1041
Pat Oakley, *Pr*
EMP: 9 EST: 1969
SALES (est): 653.57K **Privately Held**
Web: www.cedarcreekgallery.com
SIC: 3269 5719 5947 Art and ornamental ware, pottery; Pottery; Artcraft and carvings

(G-4611)
CREEDMOOR FOREST PRODUCTS
2128 Hoerner Warldorf Rd (27522)
PHONE.................................919 529-1779
John Morgan, *Pr*
EMP: 32 EST: 2017
SALES (est): 3.6MM **Privately Held**
SIC: 2421 Building and structural materials, wood

(G-4612)
DANNIES LOGGING INC
2155 Tar River Rd (27522-8612)
PHONE.................................919 528-2370
Dannie Autrey, *Pr*
Brenda Autry, *Treas*
Brenda Autry, *Sec*
EMP: 8 EST: 1998
SALES (est): 787.01K **Privately Held**
SIC: 2411 Logging camps and contractors

(G-4613)
FIRSTMARK AEROSPACE CORP
Also Called: Firstmark Controls
1176 Telecom Dr (27522-8294)
PHONE.................................919 956-4200
Bill Coogan, *CEO*
Teresa Triddle, *
EMP: 55 EST: 1998
SQ FT: 102
SALES (est): 9.49MM
SALES (corp-wide): 450.6MM **Privately Held**
Web: www.firstmarkaerospace.com
SIC: 3812 3825 3769 Space vehicle guidance systems and equipment; Instruments to measure electricity; Space vehicle equipment, nec
HQ: Firstmark Corp.
 2742 Live Oak Ln
 Midlothian VA 23113
 724 759-2850

(G-4614)
GRANVILLE PUBLISHING CO INC
Also Called: Butner-Creedmoor News
418 N Main St (27522-8809)
P.O. Box 1919 (27588-1919)
PHONE.................................919 528-2393
Elizabeth Coleman, *Prin*
Harry R Coleman, *
Elizabeth Coleman, *Sec*
EMP: 9 EST: 1965
SALES (est): 206.53K **Privately Held**
SIC: 2711 Newspapers, publishing and printing

(G-4615)
J-M MANUFACTURING COMPANY INC
2602 W Lyon Station Rd (27522-7309)
PHONE.................................919 575-6515
James Song, *Mgr*
EMP: 52
SALES (corp-wide): 998.24MM **Privately Held**
Web: www.jmeagle.com
SIC: 2821 3084 Polyvinyl chloride resins, PVC; Plastics pipe
PA: J-M Manufacturing Company, Inc.
 5200 W Century Blvd
 Los Angeles CA 90045
 310 693-8200

(G-4616)
JHD ENTERPRISE LLC
Also Called: Trendy Nails
1102 Lake Ridge Dr (27522-7140)
PHONE.................................919 612-1787
EMP: 4 EST: 2021
SALES (est): 244.84K **Privately Held**
SIC: 3999 Fingernails, artificial

(G-4617)
JULIA LIPSCOMB
10408 Boyce Rd (27522-9200)
PHONE.................................919 528-1800
Julia Lipscomb, *Prin*
EMP: 4 EST: 2015
SALES (est): 84.3K **Privately Held**
SIC: 2741 Miscellaneous publishing

(G-4618)
MABLES HEADSTONE & MONU CO LLP (PA)
206 West Wilton Ave (27522)
P.O. Box 341 (27522-0341)
PHONE.................................919 724-8705
Robert James Harris, *Pt*
EMP: 4 EST: 1978
SQ FT: 400
SALES (est): 314.87K
SALES (corp-wide): 314.87K **Privately Held**
SIC: 3281 5999 Granite, cut and shaped; Monuments, finished to custom order

(G-4619)
ONTIC ENGINEERING AND MFG INC
1176 Telecom Dr (27522-8294)
PHONE.................................919 395-3908
Gareth Hall, *Prin*
EMP: 311
SALES (corp-wide): 450.6MM **Privately Held**
Web: www.ontic.com
SIC: 5088 3728 Aircraft equipment and supplies, nec; Accumulators, aircraft propeller
PA: Ontic Engineering And Manufacturing, Inc.
 20400 Plummer St
 Chatsworth CA 91311
 818 678-6555

(G-4620)
SOUTHERN STATES COOP INC
Also Called: West Jefferson Service
2089 Sam Moss Hayes Rd (27522-9331)
PHONE.................................336 246-3201
James D King, *Mgr*
EMP: 4
SALES (corp-wide): 1.71B **Privately Held**
Web: www.southernstates.com
SIC: 2048 2873 0181 2874 Prepared feeds, nec; Nitrogenous fertilizers; Bulbs and seeds; Phosphatic fertilizers
PA: Southern States Cooperative, Incorporated
 6606 W Broad St Ste B
 Richmond VA 23230
 804 281-1000

(G-4621)
SOUTHERN STATES COOP INC
Also Called: S S C 7579 7
301 N Main St (27522)
PHONE.................................919 528-1516
Paul Kelly, *Mgr*
EMP: 31
SALES (corp-wide): 1.71B **Privately Held**
Web: www.southernstates.com
SIC: 2048 5999 Prepared feeds, nec; Farm equipment and supplies
PA: Southern States Cooperative, Incorporated
 6606 W Broad St Ste B
 Richmond VA 23230
 804 281-1000

(G-4622)
STAY ONLINE LLC (PA)
1506 Ivac Way (27522-8112)
P.O. Box 52402 (27717-2402)
PHONE.................................888 346-4688
Bellinda Higgins, *Pr*
James Higgins, *
Guido Guidotti, *
Sarah Smits Filippini, *
▲ **EMP:** 47 EST: 1993
SQ FT: 24,000
SALES (est): 14.79MM **Privately Held**
Web: www.stayonline.com
SIC: 3643 3625 Connectors and terminals for electrical devices; Industrial electrical relays and switches

Creston
Ashe County

(G-4623)
MCCLELLAN PATRIC MICHAEL
Also Called: Mosse Quick Farm
219 Moose Creek Dr (28615-9589)
PHONE.................................336 385-1878
Patric Mcclellan, *Prin*
EMP: 5 EST: 2006
SALES (est): 77.2K **Privately Held**
SIC: 2434 0175 0171 Wood kitchen cabinets; Apple orchard; Raspberry farm

(G-4624)
NEW RIVER MILLS
2533 Ed Little Rd (28615-8636)
PHONE.................................336 385-1446
EMP: 4 EST: 2017
SALES (est): 69.58K **Privately Held**
SIC: 3999 Manufacturing industries, nec

(G-4625)
OSSIRIAND INC
Also Called: Potter's Lumber
106 Hidden Valley Rd (28615-9538)
P.O. Box 133 (28615-0133)

PHONE..............................336 385-1100
Jon Abrams, Pr
EMP: 26 EST: 2018
SALES (est): 4.24MM Privately Held
SIC: 2421 Sawmills and planing mills, general

Creswell
Washington County

(G-4626)
MAE RODGERS COLA
1703 Davenport Fork Rd (27928-9576)
PHONE..............................252 797-4253
Mae Rodgers, Prin
EMP: 5 EST: 2010
SALES (est): 92.84K Privately Held
SIC: 2086 Soft drinks: packaged in cans, bottles, etc.

Crouse
Lincoln County

(G-4627)
R-ANELL HOUSING GROUP LLC
235 Anthony Grove Rd (28033-8789)
P.O. Box 1143 (28021-1143)
PHONE..............................704 445-9610
Dennis Jones, Pr
Randy Cosby, *
Bill Mclucas, CFO
EMP: 51 EST: 2001
SQ FT: 237,000
SALES (est): 21.96MM
SALES (corp-wide): 2.14B Publicly Held
Web: www.r-anell.com
SIC: 2451 Mobile homes, except recreational
PA: Cavco Industries, Inc.
    3636 N Central Ave # 1200
    Phoenix AZ 85012
    602 256-6263

Crumpler
Ashe County

(G-4628)
CHANDLER CONCRETE INC
Also Called: Watauga Ready Mix
1992 Nc Highway 16 N (28617-9560)
PHONE..............................336 982-8760
Robbie Stevens, Brnch Mgr
EMP: 9
Web: www.chandlerconcrete.com
SIC: 3273 Ready-mixed concrete
PA: Chandler Concrete Co., Inc.
    1006 S Church St
    Burlington NC 27215

(G-4629)
NORTH FORK ELECTRIC INC
1309 Willie Brown Rd (28617-9374)
PHONE..............................336 982-4020
Andrew D Feimster, Pr
Kathryn Feimster, Sec
▲ EMP: 4 EST: 1989
SQ FT: 288
SALES (est): 412.07K Privately Held
Web: www.nfei.com
SIC: 3629 Electronic generation equipment

(G-4630)
R L ROTEN WOODWORKING LLC
1312 Howard Colvard Rd (28617-9540)
PHONE..............................336 982-3830
EMP: 5 EST: 2009
SALES (est): 202.2K Privately Held

Web: www.cabinetsbest.com
SIC: 2431 Millwork

Cullowhee
Jackson County

(G-4631)
DSD PRESS
245 Memorial Dr (28723-8911)
PHONE..............................919 606-9923
Daniel Decourt, Prin
EMP: 6 EST: 2010
SALES (est): 85.5K Privately Held
Web: www.dsdpress.com
SIC: 2741 Miscellaneous publishing

Currituck
Currituck County

(G-4632)
3 ALARM SMOKE DETECTOR SVCS
134 Laurel Woods Way (27929-9727)
PHONE..............................757 636-6773
Anthony Markun, Owner
EMP: 5 EST: 2014
SALES (est): 150.09K Privately Held
SIC: 3669 Smoke detectors

(G-4633)
CORRTRAC SYSTEMS CORPORATION
126 E Canvasback Dr (27929-9641)
P.O. Box 747 (27956-0747)
PHONE..............................252 232-3975
EMP: 4 EST: 1995
SALES (est): 478.91K Privately Held
SIC: 2819 Industrial inorganic chemicals, nec

Dallas
Gaston County

(G-4634)
ALERT METAL WORKS INC
105 Yates St (28034-9215)
P.O. Box 595 (28034-0595)
PHONE..............................704 922-3152
Fred Mcgee, Pr
Michael Mcgee, VP
EMP: 27 EST: 1951
SQ FT: 17,000
SALES (est): 868.47K Privately Held
SIC: 3444 Sheet metalwork

(G-4635)
BROOKS OF DALLAS INC
Also Called: Productive Tool
203 E Lay St (28034-1773)
P.O. Box 456 (28034-0456)
PHONE..............................704 922-5219
Chris Brooks, Pr
Amy Brooks Prince, *
Ted H Brooks, *
EMP: 27 EST: 1963
SALES (est): 2.51MM Privately Held
Web: www.productive-tool.com
SIC: 3544 Special dies and tools

(G-4636)
C & J MACHINE COMPANY INC
3519 Philadelphia Church Rd (28034-7560)
PHONE..............................704 922-5913
Carolyn Hensley, Pr
Amy Hunt, Sec
Jerry Hensley, VP
EMP: 6 EST: 1976
SQ FT: 2,460

SALES (est): 448.12K Privately Held
Web: www.cjmachinecompany.com
SIC: 3541 3552 Machine tools, metal cutting type; Dyeing machinery, textile

(G-4637)
DIXON VALVE & COUPLING CO LLC
Also Called: Dixon Quick Coupling
2925 Chief Ct (28034-9562)
PHONE..............................704 334-9175
Bob Grace, Pr
▲ EMP: 11
SALES (corp-wide): 439.82MM Privately Held
Web: www.dixonvalve.com
SIC: 3492 5085 Fluid power valves and hose fittings; Hose, belting, and packing
HQ: Dixon Valve & Coupling Company, Llc
    1 Dixon Sq
    Chestertown MD 21620

(G-4638)
ELLERRE TECH INC
107 E Robinson St (28034-2233)
PHONE..............................704 524-9096
Rafaele Falciai, Pr
EMP: 21 EST: 2010
SALES (est): 2.42MM Privately Held
SIC: 3552 Textile machinery

(G-4639)
ERECTO MCH & FABRICATION INC
Also Called: Emf Industries
3653 Dallas Cherryville Hwy (28034-8763)
P.O. Box 556 (28034-0556)
PHONE..............................704 922-8621
J Lamar Whisnant, Pr
EMP: 7 EST: 1973
SALES (est): 493.24K Privately Held
SIC: 3599 Custom machinery

(G-4640)
FAB-TEC INC
3626 Dallas Hgh Shls Hwy (28034-7721)
PHONE..............................704 864-6872
David Bolding, Pr
Dana Bolding, *
EMP: 64 EST: 1997
SQ FT: 56,000
SALES (est): 8.89MM Privately Held
Web: www.fab-tec.com
SIC: 3599 Machine shop, jobbing and repair

(G-4641)
FREEMAN CONTAINER COMPANY INC
Also Called: Freeman Corrugated Containers
121 Freeman Franklin Rd (28034-7812)
PHONE..............................704 922-7972
John H Freeman Junior, Pr
John H Ffreeman Junior, Pr
Paula Freeman, Sec
EMP: 6 EST: 1986
SQ FT: 14,100
SALES (est): 863.26K Privately Held
Web: www.freemancontainer.com
SIC: 2653 5113 Boxes, corrugated: made from purchased materials; Corrugated and solid fiber boxes

(G-4642)
GARDEN GATE ORNAMENTAL IRON IN
406 Miles Rd (28034-9725)
PHONE..............................704 922-1635
Linden Deaton, Owner
EMP: 6 EST: 2005
SALES (est): 279.32K Privately Held
Web: www.gardengatecompany.com

SIC: 3446 Fences or posts, ornamental iron or steel

(G-4643)
GNT USA LLC
One Exberry Dr (28034)
PHONE..............................914 524-0600
EMP: 40 EST: 2021
SALES (est): 5.18MM Privately Held
Web: www.exberry.com
SIC: 2087 Food colorings

(G-4644)
HOVIS METAL FABRICATING INC
842 Lower Dallas Hwy (28034-9368)
P.O. Box 515 (28034-0515)
PHONE..............................704 922-5293
Peggy Hovis Senior, Pr
Tim Hovis, Sec
EMP: 19 EST: 1986
SQ FT: 21,000
SALES (est): 1.17MM Privately Held
SIC: 3441 Fabricated structural metal

(G-4645)
ICONS AMERICA LLC ◆
1055 Gastonia Technology Pkwy (28034-6724)
PHONE..............................704 922-0041
Sue Nichols, CEO
EMP: 26 EST: 2023
SALES (est): 600.91K Privately Held
SIC: 3081 Film base, cellulose acetate or nitrocellulose plastics
PA: Icons Beauty Group Pte. Ltd.
    51 Marsiling Road
    Singapore 73911

(G-4646)
INDUSTRIAL MACHINE COMPANY
103 Nelda St (28034-9342)
P.O. Box 909 (28034-0909)
PHONE..............................704 922-9750
Harmon Rose, Pr
Jonathan Rose, VP
Melinda Rose, Treas
EMP: 10 EST: 1983
SQ FT: 2,750
SALES (est): 957.99K Privately Held
Web: www.industrialmachineco.com
SIC: 3599 Machine shop, jobbing and repair

(G-4647)
LANXESS CORPORATION
1225 Gastonia Technology Pkwy (28034-6720)
PHONE..............................704 923-0121
Flemming B Bjoernslev, Pr
EMP: 5
SALES (corp-wide): 7.3B Privately Held
Web: www.lanxess.com
SIC: 2821 Plastics materials and resins
HQ: Lanxess Corporation
    111 Ridc Park West Dr
    Pittsburgh PA 15275
    412 809-1000

(G-4648)
MUNDY MACHINE CO INC
Also Called: Mundy Machine & Fabricating Co
3934 Puetts Chapel Rd (28034-8734)
PHONE..............................704 922-8663
Corwin Farris, Pr
Greg Farris, VP
Bryan Farris, VP
Gloria Farris, Sec
EMP: 9 EST: 1969
SQ FT: 9,000
SALES (est): 222.68K Privately Held

SIC: 1799 3441 3599 Welding on site; Fabricated structural metal; Machine shop, jobbing and repair

(G-4649)
NEW SOUTH FABRICATOR LLC
930 Ashebrook Park Rd (28034-9599)
PHONE.................................704 922-2072
Charles C Millsaps, *Admn*
EMP: 9 **EST:** 2016
SALES (est): 845.46K **Privately Held**
Web: www.newsouthfabricators.com
SIC: 3441 Fabricated structural metal

(G-4650)
OWENS CRNING NN-WOVEN TECH LLC
Also Called: Owens Corning Gastonia Plant
1230 Gastonia Technology Pkwy (28034-6721)
PHONE.................................740 321-6131
Brad Lazorka, *Managing Member*
▲ **EMP:** 13 **EST:** 2012
SALES (est): 1.19MM **Publicly Held**
SIC: 1761 2282 Roofing contractor; Acetate filament yarn: throwing, twisting, winding, spooling
PA: Owens Corning
   1 Owens Corning Pkwy
   Toledo OH 43659

(G-4651)
PNEUMAX AUTOMATION LLC
128 Durkee Ln (28034-9793)
PHONE.................................704 215-6991
EMP: 4
SALES (est): 107.44K **Privately Held**
SIC: 3569 General industrial machinery, nec

(G-4652)
PRICE METAL SPINNING INC
3202 Puetts Chapel Rd (28034-8723)
P.O. Box 624 (28034-0624)
PHONE.................................704 922-3195
Helene Price, *Pr*
Tim Price, *VP*
EMP: 5 **EST:** 1984
SALES (est): 415.11K **Privately Held**
SIC: 3542 Spinning machines, metal

(G-4653)
R R POWDER COATING INC
190 Gibson Ct (28034-8764)
P.O. Box 476 (28034-0476)
PHONE.................................704 853-0727
Ray Jenkins, *Pr*
Charlotte M Jenkins, *VP*
EMP: 17 **EST:** 2000
SQ FT: 20,000
SALES (est): 2.49MM **Privately Held**
Web: www.rrpowdercoating.com
SIC: 3479 Coating of metals and formed products

(G-4654)
RICHARDSON ENTERPRISES NC INC
3201 Puetts Chapel Rd (28034-8722)
PHONE.................................704 675-8666
EMP: 6 **EST:** 2014
SALES (est): 82.59K **Privately Held**
SIC: 3599 Machine shop, jobbing and repair

(G-4655)
ROECHLING INDUS GASTONIA LP (DH)
Also Called: Rochling Engineering
903 Gastonia Technology Pkwy (28034-7791)
PHONE.................................704 922-7814
Timothy Brown, *Pr*
◆ **EMP:** 192 **EST:** 1987
SQ FT: 167,000
SALES (est): 76.64MM
SALES (corp-wide): 2.7B **Privately Held**
Web: www.roechling.com
SIC: 3081 3082 Unsupported plastics film and sheet; Unsupported plastics profile shapes
HQ: Rochling Industrial Se & Co. Kg
   Rochlingstr. 1
   Haren (Ems) NI 49733
   59347010

(G-4656)
ROMAC INDUSTRIES INC
Hays Fluid Control Division
400 E Fields St (28034-1723)
P.O. Box 580 (28034-0580)
PHONE.................................704 915-3317
Steve Williams, *Brnch Mgr*
EMP: 60
SALES (corp-wide): 94.76MM **Privately Held**
Web: www.romac.com
SIC: 3824 3494 3432 3492 Water meters; Valves and pipe fittings, nec; Plumbers' brass goods: drain cocks, faucets, spigots, etc.; Fluid power valves and hose fittings
PA: Romac Industries, Inc.
   21919 20th Ave Se Ste 100
   Bothell WA 98021
   425 951-6200

(G-4657)
SHERRILL CONTRACT MFG INC (PA)
110 Durkee Ln (28034-9793)
P.O. Box 478 (28034-0478)
PHONE.................................704 922-7871
Rick Hargis, *Pr*
EMP: 19 **EST:** 1956
SQ FT: 61,000
SALES (est): 5.31MM
SALES (corp-wide): 5.31MM **Privately Held**
Web: www.sherrillindustries.com
SIC: 3552 3535 5085 Looms, textile machinery; Conveyors and conveying equipment; Industrial supplies

(G-4658)
SLACK & PARR INTERNATIONAL (HQ)
Hwy 321 (28034)
PHONE.................................704 527-2975
Ted Hallsworth, *Ch Bd*
Ted Hallsworth, *Ch Bd*
A G Kellar, *Ex VP*
Lith Wingsile, *Mgr*
EMP: 5 **EST:** 1976
SALES (est): 8.17MM
SALES (corp-wide): 18.45MM **Privately Held**
SIC: 5084 3541 Pumps and pumping equipment, nec; Machine tools, metal cutting type
PA: Slack & Parr (Investments) Limited
   Long Lane
   Derby DE74
   150 967-2306

(G-4659)
SYCAMORE CABINETRY INC
644 Dallas Bessemer City Hwy (28034-9480)
PHONE.................................704 375-1617
Rodney Blackwell, *Prin*
Chuck Mcgee, *Pr*
EMP: 9 **EST:** 2000
SALES (est): 708.55K **Privately Held**
Web: www.sycamorecabinetry.com
SIC: 2517 Home entertainment unit cabinets, wood

(G-4660)
VENTURA SYSTEMS INC
160 Gibson Ct (28034-8764)
PHONE.................................704 712-8630
Sieto Ykema, *Prin*
EMP: 10 **EST:** 2017
SALES (est): 779.55K **Privately Held**
Web: www.venturasystems.com
SIC: 2431 Doors, wood

(G-4661)
WW&S CONSTRUCTION INC
817 Dallas Spencer Mtn Rd (28034-7609)
PHONE.................................217 620-4042
Eric Shively, *Pr*
Steve Wilson, *VP*
Jason Woodhead, *Opers Mgr*
EMP: 6 **EST:** 2021
SALES (est): 148.29K **Privately Held**
SIC: 1389 7389 Construction, repair, and dismantling services; Business Activities at Non-Commercial Site

Dana
Henderson County

(G-4662)
BLUE RIDGE BLDG COMPONENTS INC
208 Justice Hills Dr (28724)
P.O. Box 1038 (28724-1038)
PHONE.................................828 685-0452
Daniel J Hinkle Senior, *Pr*
Samuel Hinkle, *VP*
Rhonda Hinkle, *Sec*
EMP: 7 **EST:** 2002
SALES (est): 805.89K **Privately Held**
SIC: 2439 Trusses, wooden roof

Danbury
Stokes County

(G-4663)
RAYMOND BROWN WELL COMPANY INC
1109 N Main St (27016-7413)
P.O. Box 337 (27016-0337)
PHONE.................................336 374-4999
Raymond Brown, *Owner*
Ardina Fulp, *Sec*
EMP: 6 **EST:** 1985
SALES (est): 528.85K **Privately Held**
Web: www.raymondbrownwellco.com
SIC: 1781 3561 Servicing, water wells; Pumps and pumping equipment

Davidson
Mecklenburg County

(G-4664)
3A COMPOSITES HOLDING INC
721 Jetton St Ste 325 (28036-0359)
PHONE.................................704 658-3527
EMP: 38 **EST:** 2019
SALES (est): 3.55MM **Privately Held**
Web: www.3acompositesusa.com
SIC: 2821 Plastics materials and resins
PA: Schweiter Technologies Ag
   Hinterbergstrasse 20
   Steinhausen ZG 6312

(G-4665)
ACCUDYNE INDUSTRIES LLC (PA)
800 Beaty St Ste A (28036-6924)
PHONE.................................469 518-4777
Charles L Treadway, *CEO*
Kyle Lorentzen, *CFO*
EMP: 23 **EST:** 2012
SALES (est): 311.43MM
SALES (corp-wide): 311.43MM **Privately Held**
SIC: 3463 Pump, compressor, turbine, and engine forgings, except auto

(G-4666)
BLANDS WELDING
6764 Dare Dr (28036-8536)
PHONE.................................704 932-1864
Robert Bland, *Prin*
EMP: 5 **EST:** 2010
SALES (est): 52.42K **Privately Held**
SIC: 7692 Welding repair

(G-4667)
CAIRN STUDIO LTD (PA)
121 N Main St (28036-9402)
P.O. Box 400 (28036-0400)
PHONE.................................704 892-3581
Joe Poteat, *Pr*
▲ **EMP:** 4 **EST:** 1980
SALES (est): 1.75MM
SALES (corp-wide): 1.75MM **Privately Held**
Web: www.cairnstudio.com
SIC: 3299 Nonmetallic mineral statuary and other decorative products

(G-4668)
CRAZY PIG INC
402 S Main St (28036-8006)
PHONE.................................704 997-2320
Robert Mccrary, *Pr*
EMP: 6 **EST:** 2019
SALES (est): 75.77K **Privately Held**
Web: www.thecrazypigbbq.com
SIC: 2092 Fresh or frozen packaged fish

(G-4669)
CURTISS-WRIGHT CORPORATION (PA)
130 Harbour Place Dr Ste 300 (28036-7441)
PHONE.................................704 869-4600
Lynn M Bamford, *Ch Bd*
Kevin M Rayment, *VP*
K Christopher Farkas, *VP*
Gary A Ogilby, *Care Vice President*
Robert F Freda, *VP*
EMP: 338 **EST:** 1929
SALES (est): 2.85B
SALES (corp-wide): 2.85B **Publicly Held**
Web: www.curtisswright.com
• **SIC: 3491** 3621 3812 Industrial valves; Motors and generators; Aircraft control systems, electronic

(G-4670)
DAVIDSON HOUSE INC
Also Called: Contract Furniture Restoration
643 Portside Dr (28036-8927)
P.O. Box 2598 (28036-2598)
PHONE.................................704 791-0171
Shelia Kimball, *Pr*
Shelia Deal, *Pr*
EMP: 10 **EST:** 1995
SQ FT: 2,000
SALES (est): 449.81K **Privately Held**
Web: www.davidsonhouseinc.com
SIC: 7641 2522 Upholstery work; Office furniture, except wood

Davidson - Mecklenburg County (G-4671)

(G-4671)
DAVIDSON WINE CO LLC
10930 Zac Hill Rd (28036-0420)
PHONE..................614 738-0051
EMP: 6 EST: 2018
SALES (est): 334.5K Privately Held
Web: www.davidsonwineshop.com
SIC: 2084 Wines

(G-4672)
DIGITOME CORPORATION
210 Delburg St (28036-8655)
PHONE..................860 651-5560
Donald Twyman, Pr
EMP: 6 EST: 2000
SALES (est): 450.03K Privately Held
Web: www.digitomesite.com
SIC: 3844 7372 X-ray apparatus and tubes; Application computer software

(G-4673)
ELBORN HOLDINGS LLC
Also Called: Airdream.net
17408 Lynx Den Ct (28036-7834)
P.O. Box 354 (28166-0354)
PHONE..................919 917-1419
Don E Owens Iii, CFO
EMP: 7 EST: 2005
SALES (est): 78.71K Privately Held
SIC: 2515 Mattresses, containing felt, foam rubber, urethane, etc.

(G-4674)
ELEMENT STRATEGY LLC
13346 Robert Walker Dr (28036-6006)
PHONE..................704 997-5627
EMP: 5 EST: 2019
SALES (est): 81.87K Privately Held
SIC: 2819 Elements

(G-4675)
G DENVER AND CO LLC (HQ)
Also Called: Gardner Denver, Inc.
800 Beaty St (28036-9000)
PHONE..................704 896-4000
Vicente Reynal, CEO
Mark R Sweeney, *
Andrew Schiesl, *
Philip T Herndon, *
◆ EMP: 50 EST: 1993
SALES (est): 2.78B
SALES (corp-wide): 6.88B Publicly Held
Web: www.gardnerdenver.com
SIC: 3564 3561 3563 Blowers and fans; Industrial pumps and parts; Air and gas compressors including vacuum pumps
PA: Ingersoll Rand Inc.
525 Harbour Place Dr # 600
Davidson NC 28036
704 896-4000

(G-4676)
HAMILTON
400 Avinger Ln (28036-8800)
PHONE..................704 896-1427
Herman Hamilton, Prin
EMP: 5 EST: 2007
SALES (est): 143.89K Privately Held
SIC: 3826 Analytical instruments

(G-4677)
HEALTHLINE INFO SYSTEMS INC
705 Northeast Dr Ste 17 (28036-7431)
PHONE..................704 655-0447
Russ Lane, Pr
Chuck Lane, VP
EMP: 10 EST: 2000
SQ FT: 3,000
SALES (est): 710.65K Privately Held
Web: www.healthlineis.com

SIC: 7372 Application computer software

(G-4678)
INDEPENDENCE LUMBER INC
18900 Riverwind Ln (28036-7849)
PHONE..................276 773-3744
Eller Randall, Pr
Nelson D Weaver, *
Eller Damon Randell, *
Mike Bolling, *
Bolling Charles M, *
EMP: 100 EST: 1983
SALES (est): 20.37MM Privately Held
Web: www.independencelumberinc.com
SIC: 2421 Lumber: rough, sawed, or planed

(G-4679)
INGERSOLL RAND INC (PA)
525 Harbour Place Dr Ste 600 (28036-7444)
PHONE..................704 896-4000
Vicente Reynal, Ch Bd
Andrew Schiesl, CCO
Kathleen M Keene, Pers/VP
Michael A Weatherred, Sr VP
Enrique Minarro Viseras, Sr VP
EMP: 572 EST: 1859
SALES (est): 6.88B
SALES (corp-wide): 6.88B Publicly Held
Web: www.irco.com
SIC: 3561 3563 Pumps and pumping equipment; Air and gas compressors including vacuum pumps

(G-4680)
INGERSOLL-RAND INDUS US INC (HQ)
525 Harbour Place Dr Ste 600 (28036-7444)
PHONE..................704 896-4000
Reynal Vicente, Pr
Vikram Kini, *
Mark Siler, *
Herbert Jameson, *
Francisco De Barros, *
EMP: 64 EST: 2019
SALES (est): 372.02MM
SALES (corp-wide): 6.88B Publicly Held
SIC: 3561 3429 3546 3563 Pumps and pumping equipment; Furniture, builders' and other household hardware; Power-driven handtools; Air and gas compressors including vacuum pumps
PA: Ingersoll Rand Inc.
525 Harbour Place Dr # 600
Davidson NC 28036
704 896-4000

(G-4681)
INGERSOLL-RAND INTL HOLDG
800 Beaty St (28036-9000)
PHONE..................704 655-4000
Theodore Black, Ch Bd
James E Perrella, *
William G Mulligan, *
Thomas E Bennett, *
William J Armstrong, *
EMP: 300 EST: 1978
SALES (est): 136.46MM Privately Held
SIC: 3531 Construction machinery
HQ: Trane Technologies Company Llc
800 Beaty St Ste E
Davidson NC 28036
704 655-4000

(G-4682)
INGERSOLL-RAND US HOLDCO INC
800 Beaty St Ste E (28036-6924)
PHONE..................704 655-4000
EMP: 4
SALES (est): 122.91K Privately Held

SIC: 3569 General industrial machinery, nec

(G-4683)
JANELLCO PRODUCTS INC
400 Avinger Ln Apt 415 (28036-6701)
PHONE..................704 896-1415
Jane Elliott, Pr
EMP: 6 EST: 1995
SALES (est): 83.75K Privately Held
SIC: 3446 Architectural metalwork

(G-4684)
JE FREEZE LLC
Also Called: Whits Frozen Custard
20045 Verlaine Dr (28036-7770)
PHONE..................980 231-5365
EMP: 7 EST: 2016
SALES (est): 596.55K Privately Held
Web: www.whitsdavidson.com
SIC: 2024 Custard, frozen

(G-4685)
MIDAS SPRING WATER BTLG CO LLC
416 Armour St (28036-6905)
PHONE..................704 392-2150
EMP: 6 EST: 2002
SALES (est): 229.78K Privately Held
Web: www.midasspring.com
SIC: 2086 Bottled and canned soft drinks

(G-4686)
MOTORSPORT INNOVATIONS INC
19220 Callaway Hills Ln (28036-7710)
PHONE..................704 728-7837
David Holden, Pr
EMP: 8 EST: 1996
SQ FT: 1,200
SALES (est): 502.06K Privately Held
SIC: 8711 3714 Consulting engineer; Motor vehicle parts and accessories

(G-4687)
NINE-AI INC
359 Armour St (28036-6901)
PHONE..................781 825-3267
Joseph Zagrobelny, CEO
EMP: 10 EST: 2018
SALES (est): 508.12K Privately Held
Web: www.nine-ai.com
SIC: 3549 Assembly machines, including robotic

(G-4688)
NORMAN LAKE CABINET COMPANY
3342 Streamside Dr (28036-9503)
PHONE..................704 498-6647
Krysten Bule, Pr
EMP: 6 EST: 2017
SALES (est): 245.36K Privately Held
Web: www.thelakenormancabinetcompany.com
SIC: 2434 Wood kitchen cabinets

(G-4689)
ODD SOCK INC
610 Jetton St Ste 120-121 (28036-9318)
PHONE..................704 451-4298
EMP: 4 EST: 2015
SALES (est): 76.16K Privately Held
Web: www.theoddsock.org
SIC: 2252 Socks

(G-4690)
PERFORMNCE STRL CON SLTONS LLC
P.O. Box 2377 (28036-5377)
PHONE..................980 333-6414
EMP: 5 EST: 2014
SALES (est): 208.72K Privately Held

Web: www.pscs-llc.com
SIC: 3441 5032 Building components, structural steel; Brick, stone, and related material

(G-4691)
PRINTOLOGY SIGNS GRAPHICS LLC
10931 Zac Hill Rd (28036-0420)
PHONE..................843 473-4984
Mark Russell, Managing Member
Wendi Russell, Managing Member
EMP: 4 EST: 2015
SALES (est): 184.27K Privately Held
SIC: 3993 2262 Signs and advertising specialties; Printing, manmade fiber and silk broadwoven fabrics

(G-4692)
PROCTORFREE INC
210 Delburg St (28036-8655)
PHONE..................704 759-6569
Michael Murphy, CEO
Brad Davis, CEO
Velvet Nelson, Prin
Michael Murphy, Prin
EMP: 14 EST: 2014
SQ FT: 5,000
SALES (est): 1.76MM Privately Held
Web: www.proctorfree.com
SIC: 7371 7372 Computer software development and applications; Educational computer software

(G-4693)
READY SOLUTIONS INC
112 Eden St (28036-8131)
P.O. Box 1333 (28031-1333)
PHONE..................704 534-9221
Bob Confoy, Pr
Mike Geraghty, Treas
EMP: 6 EST: 2003
SALES (est): 483.46K Privately Held
Web: www.readysolutionsinc.com
SIC: 3081 Plastics film and sheet

(G-4694)
RETHINK TECHNOLOGIES INC
Also Called: Rethink Respironics
605 Jetton St (28036-9335)
PHONE..................980 250-4683
Richard Wenzel, CEO
Roger Webster Faulkner, Pr
EMP: 10 EST: 2019
SALES (est): 433.4K Privately Held
SIC: 3842 Abdominal supporters, braces, and trusses

(G-4695)
RIM-TEC CASTINGS EASTERN LLC (PA)
16109 Halle Marie Cir Ste 33 (28036-2319)
PHONE..................336 302-0912
EMP: 6 EST: 2008
SALES (est): 509K
SALES (corp-wide): 509K Privately Held
Web: www.rimtec.us
SIC: 3369 Nonferrous foundries, nec

(G-4696)
SINE WAVE TECHNOLOGIES INC
19232 Wildcat Trl (28036-7856)
PHONE..................704 765-9636
Lydia Watson, Prin
EMP: 6 EST: 2003
SALES (est): 125.94K Privately Held
Web: www.sinewavetechnologies.biz
SIC: 3699 Electrical equipment and supplies, nec

GEOGRAPHIC SECTION

(G-4697)
STRASSBERG CERAMICS
156 Anniston Way (28036-7790)
PHONE.....................704 315-2034
EMP: 4 **EST:** 2010
SALES (est): 67.1K **Privately Held**
Web: www.strassbergceramics.com
SIC: 3269 Pottery products, nec

(G-4698)
T & N MANUFACTURING CO INC
4345 Shiloh Church Rd (28036-9505)
PHONE.....................704 788-1418
Nancy Whipple, *Pr*
EMP: 8 **EST:** 1977
SQ FT: 4,600
SALES (est): 235.34K **Privately Held**
SIC: 3053 5013 3714 Gaskets, all materials; Automotive supplies and parts; Motor vehicle parts and accessories

(G-4699)
TELEPHYS INC
610 Jetton St Ste 120 (28036-9319)
PHONE.....................312 625-9128
Jan Pachon, *CEO*
EMP: 4 **EST:** 2018
SALES (est): 95.66K **Privately Held**
SIC: 7371 8011 3845 7299 Software programming applications; Radiologist; Magnetic resonance imaging device, nuclear; Information services, consumer

(G-4700)
THERMO KING CORPORATION
Also Called: Thermo King Svc
800 Beaty St (28036-9000)
PHONE.....................732 652-6774
EMP: 174
Web: www.thermoking.com
SIC: 3585 Refrigeration and heating equipment
HQ: Thermo King Llc
    314 W 90th St
    Bloomington MN 55420
    952 887-2200

(G-4701)
TRANE EXPORT LLC
800 Beaty St (28036-9000)
PHONE.....................608 788-0569
EMP: 28 **EST:** 1963
SALES (est): 1.02MM **Privately Held**
SIC: 3585 Refrigeration and heating equipment

(G-4702)
TRANE TECHNOLOGIES COMPANY LLC (HQ)
800 Beaty St Ste E (28036-6924)
PHONE.....................704 655-4000
Dave Regnery, *CEO*
Chris Kuehn, *Ex VP*
Maria Green, *Sr VP*
Marcia J Avedon, *Senior Vice President Human Resources*
Paul Camuti, *Sr VP*
◆ **EMP:** 575 **EST:** 1871
SALES (est): 685.76MM **Privately Held**
Web: www.tranetechnologies.com
SIC: 3564 3585 Filters, air; furnaces, air conditioning equipment, etc.; Air conditioning equipment, complete
PA: Trane Technologies Public Limited Company
    170/175 Lakeview Drive
    Swords K67 E

(G-4703)
TRANE TECHNOLOGIES MFG LLC ✪
800 Beaty St (28036-9000)
PHONE.....................704 655-4000
Dave Regnery, *CEO*
EMP: 12 **EST:** 2022
SALES (est): 1.49MM **Privately Held**
SIC: 3585 Air conditioning equipment, complete
PA: Trane Technologies Public Limited Company
    170/175 Lakeview Drive
    Swords K67 E

(G-4704)
TRANE US INC (DH)
Also Called: Trane
800 Beaty St Ste E (28036-6924)
P.O. Box 6820 (08855-6820)
PHONE.....................704 655-4000
Donald E Simmons, *Pr*
Chris Kuehn, *
◆ **EMP:** 638 **EST:** 1929
SALES (est): 2.11B **Privately Held**
Web: www.trane.com
SIC: 3585 3564 3822 3634 Air conditioning units, complete: domestic or industrial; Ventilating fans: industrial or commercial; Air conditioning and refrigeration controls; Dehumidifiers, electric: room
HQ: Trane Inc.
    1 Centennial Ave Ste 101
    Piscataway NJ 08854
    732 652-7100

(G-4705)
UNITED VISIONS CORP
Also Called: Visions Interior Designs
428 S Main St Ste B Pmb 135 (28036-7012)
P.O. Box 518 (28036-0518)
PHONE.....................704 953-4555
EMP: 6 **EST:** 1995
SALES (est): 910.87K **Privately Held**
SIC: 1522 1542 1389 2421 Residential construction, nec; Agricultural building contractors; Construction, repair, and dismantling services; Building and structural materials, wood

(G-4706)
VALSPAR CORPORATION
721 Jetton St (28036-7108)
PHONE.....................704 897-5700
EMP: 9 **EST:** 2015
SALES (est): 183.65K **Privately Held**
Web: www.valspar.com
SIC: 2851 Varnishes, nec

Davis
Carteret County

(G-4707)
HARVEY & SONS NET & TWINE
Also Called: Sound Trees
804 Hwy 70 Davis (28524)
P.O. Box 84 (28579-0084)
PHONE.....................252 729-1731
Neal L Harvey, *Owner*
EMP: 6 **EST:** 1981
SQ FT: 3,000
SALES (est): 249.93K **Privately Held**
SIC: 2399 Fishing nets

Deep Gap
Watauga County

(G-4708)
APPALACHIAN CABINET INC
7373 Old 421 S (28618-8900)
PHONE.....................828 265-0830
EMP: 4 **EST:** 1992
SQ FT: 3,800
SALES (est): 383.14K **Privately Held**
SIC: 2521 2541 2599 Cabinets, office: wood; Cabinets, lockers, and shelving; Factory furniture and fixtures

(G-4709)
JUSTIN MORETZ & GREG MORETZ DB
153 Monte Verde Rd (28618-9812)
PHONE.....................828 263-8668
EMP: 4 **EST:** 2017
SALES (est): 141.15K **Privately Held**
SIC: 2411 Logging

(G-4710)
NEW RIVER DISTILLING CO LLC
180 W Yuma Ln (28618-9811)
PHONE.....................732 673-4852
Danil Meehan, *Managing Member*
EMP: 6 **EST:** 2017
SALES (est): 502.29K **Privately Held**
Web: www.newriverdistilling.com
SIC: 2085 Distilled and blended liquors

(G-4711)
PEPSI BOTTLING VENTURES LLC
Also Called: Pepsi-Cola
7467 Old 421 S (28618-8928)
P.O. Box B (28618)
PHONE.....................828 264-7702
Stephen King, *Mgr*
EMP: 41
Web: www.pepsibottlingventures.com
SIC: 2086 Soft drinks: packaged in cans, bottles, etc.
HQ: Pepsi Bottling Ventures Llc
    4141 Parklake Ave Ste 600
    Raleigh NC 27612
    919 865-2300

(G-4712)
RANDY SMITH AND SONS LOGGING
826 Lawrence Greene Rd (28618-9605)
PHONE.....................828 263-0574
EMP: 4 **EST:** 2019
SALES (est): 81.72K **Privately Held**
SIC: 2411 Logging

(G-4713)
SMITH BROTHERS LOGGING
136 Clyde Ln (28618-9514)
PHONE.....................828 265-1506
Royce Smith, *Pt*
Richard Smith, *Pt*
Randy Smith, *Pt*
EMP: 4 **EST:** 1994
SALES (est): 416.5K **Privately Held**
SIC: 2411 Logging camps and contractors

(G-4714)
WANDA NICKEL
6764 Old 421 S (28618-8911)
PHONE.....................828 265-3246
Wanda Nickel, *Prin*
EMP: 6 **EST:** 2010
SALES (est): 230.25K **Privately Held**
SIC: 3356 Nickel

Deep Run
Lenoir County

(G-4715)
ALPHA LOGGING INC
3759 Live Oak Hog Co Road (28525-9577)
PHONE.....................252 568-2727
Mills Ethan, *Prin*
EMP: 6 **EST:** 2016
SALES (est): 89.89K **Privately Held**
SIC: 2411 Logging camps and contractors

(G-4716)
FUTRELL PRECASTING LLC
3430 Old Pink Hill Rd (28525-9446)
PHONE.....................252 568-3481
Odom M Futrell, *Pt*
EMP: 9 **EST:** 1962
SALES (est): 925.59K **Privately Held**
SIC: 3272 0213 Septic tanks, concrete; Hogs

(G-4717)
OUTLAW STEP CO
2491 Burncoat Rd (28525-9475)
PHONE.....................252 568-4384
Jimmie D Outlaw, *Owner*
EMP: 7 **EST:** 1980
SQ FT: 3,000
SALES (est): 382.83K **Privately Held**
SIC: 2452 5039 Prefabricated wood buildings ; Prefabricated structures

Delco
Columbus County

(G-4718)
BORDEAUX DYNOCAMS
P.O. Box 400 (28436-0400)
PHONE.....................910 655-9482
EMP: 6 **EST:** 2010
SALES (est): 237.62K **Privately Held**
Web: www.dynocams.com
SIC: 3714 Motor vehicle parts and accessories

(G-4719)
BRACEY BROS LOGGING LLC
418 Lennon Rd (28436-9394)
PHONE.....................910 231-9543
EMP: 8 **EST:** 2017
SALES (est): 834.26K **Privately Held**
SIC: 2411 Logging

(G-4720)
COLUMBUS PALLET COMPANY INC
813 Lennon Rd (28436-9591)
P.O. Box 70 (28436-0070)
PHONE.....................910 655-4513
Robert Lennon, *Pr*
Jeff Lennon, *Mgr*
Julia Blake, *VP*
Alisa Lennon, *Treas*
EMP: 8 **EST:** 1973
SQ FT: 5,000
SALES (est): 800K **Privately Held**
SIC: 2448 Pallets, wood

(G-4721)
J&J OUTDOOR ACCESSORIES
26955 Andrew Jackson Hwy E (28436-9819)
PHONE.....................910 742-1969
EMP: 4 **EST:** 2019
SALES (est): 129.95K **Privately Held**
Web: www.jandjoutdoorbuildings.com
SIC: 3448 Prefabricated metal buildings and components

Delco - Columbus County (G-4722)

(G-4722)
LR MANUFACTURING INC
60 Dream Ave (28436-8700)
PHONE..................910 399-1410
Melissa Lester, *Prin*
EMP: 6 EST: 2017
SALES (est): 284.24K **Privately Held**
SIC: 3999 Manufacturing industries, nec

(G-4723)
OBRIEN LOGGING CO
988 Livingston Chapel Rd (28436-9298)
PHONE..................910 655-3830
Richard O'brien, *Owner*
EMP: 4 EST: 1972
SALES (est): 243.25K **Privately Held**
SIC: 2411 Logging

(G-4724)
PREFERRED LOGGING
Also Called: Paul James O'Brian
969 Livingston Chapel Rd (28436-9299)
PHONE..................910 471-4011
Paul James O'brian, *Owner*
EMP: 6 EST: 2005
SQ FT: 2,000
SALES (est): 610.28K **Privately Held**
SIC: 2411 Logging

Denton
Davidson County

(G-4725)
AUSTIN POWDER COMPANY
Also Called: Austin Powder South East
372 Ernest Smith Rd (27239-6933)
PHONE..................828 645-4291
James Reese, *Mgr*
EMP: 19
SALES (corp-wide): 749.73MM **Privately Held**
Web: www.austinpowder.com
SIC: 2892 Explosives
HQ: Austin Powder Company
25800 Science Park Dr # 300
Cleveland OH 44122
216 464-2400

(G-4726)
BASELINE SCREEN PRINTING
7148 Charles Mountain Rd (27239-9004)
PHONE..................336 857-0101
EMP: 4 EST: 2015
SALES (est): 84.24K **Privately Held**
SIC: 2752 Commercial printing, lithographic

(G-4727)
CABINET MAN CABINETRY
9252 Nc Highway 49 S (27239-8370)
PHONE..................336 382-0879
EMP: 4 EST: 2013
SALES (est): 57.26K **Privately Held**
SIC: 2434 Wood kitchen cabinets

(G-4728)
CAGLE SAWMILL INC
7065 Charles Mountain Rd (27239-9003)
PHONE..................336 857-2274
Glen Cagle, *Pr*
Roger Cagle, *Sec*
EMP: 14 EST: 1976
SALES (est): 940.89K **Privately Held**
SIC: 2421 2426 Sawmills and planing mills, general; Hardwood dimension and flooring mills

(G-4729)
CENTURY HOSIERY INC (PA)
651 Garner Rd (27239-7542)
P.O. Box 1410 (27239-1410)
PHONE..................336 859-3806
Kathy Martin, *Pr*
Malcom Martin, *
EMP: 120 EST: 1990
SQ FT: 55,000
SALES (est): 9.69MM **Privately Held**
Web: www.centuryhosiery.com
SIC: 3143 3144 3149 Orthopedic shoes, men's; Orthopedic shoes, women's; Orthopedic shoes, children's

(G-4730)
CONTEMPORARY FURNISHINGS CORP
Carter Furniture Company
6550 Scarlet Oak Dr (27239-9079)
PHONE..................336 857-2988
Claud Wolfe, *Mgr*
EMP: 5
SALES (corp-wide): 4.35MM **Privately Held**
SIC: 2426 Furniture dimension stock, hardwood
PA: Contemporary Furnishings Corp
1000 N Long St
Salisbury NC 28144
704 633-8000

(G-4731)
COUNCILL COMPANY LLC
Also Called: Thomas & Gray
1156 N Main St (27239-7588)
P.O. Box 3444 (28603-3444)
PHONE..................336 859-2155
▲ EMP: 125
Web: www.kindelfurniture.com
SIC: 2512 2511 Upholstered household furniture; Wood household furniture

(G-4732)
DENTON ORATOR
26 N Main St (27239-6594)
P.O. Box 1546 (27239-1546)
PHONE..................336 859-3131
Stan Bingham, *Owner*
EMP: 4 EST: 1995
SALES (est): 207.07K **Privately Held**
Web: www.dentonorator.com
SIC: 2711 Newspapers, publishing and printing

(G-4733)
DIAMOND OUTDOOR ENTPS INC
9035 Nc Highway 49 S (27239-8368)
PHONE..................336 857-1450
Keith Chrismon, *Prin*
EMP: 6 EST: 2005
SQ FT: 1,744
SALES (est): 377.35K **Privately Held**
SIC: 3911 Medals, precious or semiprecious metal

(G-4734)
DIMENSION MILLING CO INC
12885 Nc Highway 47 (27239-7437)
P.O. Box 1306 (27239-1306)
PHONE..................336 983-2820
Alan Myers, *Pr*
Henry Mcmullin, *VP*
Jeff Kings, *Mgr*
EMP: 9 EST: 1962
SALES (est): 600K **Privately Held**
SIC: 2426 Hardwood dimension and flooring mills

(G-4735)
F-N-D MACHINERY SERVICES INC
1198 N Main St (27239-7588)
PHONE..................336 906-2817
Roger L Doyle, *Pr*
EMP: 6 EST: 2005
SALES (est): 160K **Privately Held**
SIC: 3569 Industrial shock absorbers

(G-4736)
HARDISTER LOGGING
5571 Sandalwood Dr (27239-9043)
PHONE..................336 857-2397
Donny Hardister, *Owner*
EMP: 5 EST: 1973
SALES (est): 380K **Privately Held**
SIC: 2411 Logging

(G-4737)
HARRIS LOGGING LLC
7508 Brantly Fords Rd (27239)
PHONE..................336 859-2786
David Harris, *Prin*
EMP: 6 EST: 2003
SALES (est): 480.17K **Privately Held**
SIC: 2411 Logging camps and contractors

(G-4738)
JACOBS CREEK STONE COMPANY INC
2081 W Slate Mine Rd (27239)
P.O. Box 608 (27239-0608)
PHONE..................336 857-2602
Robert J Mckinney, *Pr*
EMP: 10 EST: 1948
SQ FT: 3,000
SALES (est): 1.81MM **Privately Held**
Web: www.jacobscreekstone.com
SIC: 1411 3281 Flagstone mining; Flagstones

(G-4739)
JOHNNY DANIEL
Also Called: Daniel, Johnny Logging
230 Bringle Ferry Rd (27239-9137)
PHONE..................336 859-2480
Johnny Daniel, *Owner*
EMP: 6 EST: 2001
SALES (est): 300K **Privately Held**
SIC: 2411 Logging camps and contractors

(G-4740)
LANIERS SCREEN PRINTING
6271 Bombay School Rd (27239-8332)
PHONE..................336 857-2699
Arnold Lanier, *Owner*
EMP: 4 EST: 1988
SALES (est): 168.76K **Privately Held**
SIC: 2759 Screen printing

(G-4741)
LATHAM INC
6509 Scarlet Oak Dr (27239-9079)
PHONE..................336 857-3702
Rayford Latham, *Pr*
Bunny Latham, *VP*
EMP: 5 EST: 1994
SQ FT: 7,000
SALES (est): 329.14K **Privately Held**
Web: www.lathamcenters.org
SIC: 2426 Furniture stock and parts, hardwood

(G-4742)
LEGEND COMPRESSION WEAR
1450 Healing Springs Dr (27239-7275)
P.O. Box 1027 (27239-1027)
PHONE..................877 711-5343
Walter Kruger, *Prin*
EMP: 6 EST: 2020
SALES (est): 210.06K **Privately Held**
Web: www.legendcompressionwear.com
SIC: 5999 2252 Medical apparatus and supplies; Anklets (hosiery)

(G-4743)
LEONARD LOGGING CO
4057 Salem Church Rd (27239-9592)
PHONE..................336 857-2776
Ricky Leonard, *Prin*
EMP: 6 EST: 1999
SALES (est): 556.4K **Privately Held**
SIC: 2411 Logging camps and contractors

(G-4744)
LOFLIN FABRICATION LLC
Also Called: Loflin Fabrication
1382 Cranford Rd (27239-8952)
PHONE..................336 859-4333
Terry E Ferrell, *
▲ EMP: 35 EST: 1993
SQ FT: 69,000
SALES (est): 9.07MM **Privately Held**
Web: www.loflinfabrication.com
SIC: 3444 3531 Sheet metal specialties, not stamped; Construction machinery

(G-4745)
M & M FRAME COMPANY INC
Also Called: M-M Components
18847 S Nc Highway 109 (27239-7716)
P.O. Box 1337 (27239-1337)
PHONE..................336 859-8166
Clark Rogers Junior, *Pr*
EMP: 9 EST: 1990
SALES (est): 685.02K **Privately Held**
SIC: 3499 2426 2512 Furniture parts, metal; Frames for upholstered furniture, wood; Upholstered household furniture

(G-4746)
NOLAN MANUFACTURING LLC
18868 S Nc Highway 109 (27239-7716)
PHONE..................336 490-0086
Christopher Biesecker, *Managing Member*
EMP: 6 EST: 2020
SALES (est): 951.89K **Privately Held**
Web: www.nolanmanufacturing.com
SIC: 3537 Industrial trucks and tractors

(G-4747)
RUT MANUFACTURING INC
211 Bingham Industrial Dr (27239-7795)
P.O. Box 577 (27239-0577)
PHONE..................336 859-0328
EMP: 11 EST: 2015
SALES (est): 1.89MM **Privately Held**
Web: www.rutmfg.com
SIC: 3531 Construction machinery

(G-4748)
SOUTHERN LOGGING INC
250 Piedmont School Rd (27239-8921)
P.O. Box 1379 (27239-1379)
PHONE..................336 859-5057
Timothy D Hardister, *Prin*
EMP: 11 EST: 2008
SALES (est): 446.05K **Privately Held**
SIC: 2411 Logging camps and contractors

(G-4749)
STICKY FINGERS VINYL
705 Loflin Rd (27239-8735)
PHONE..................336 859-0262
EMP: 5 EST: 2019
SALES (est): 205.34K **Privately Held**
Web: www.stickyfingersvinyltransfers.com
SIC: 2759 Screen printing

GEOGRAPHIC SECTION

Denver - Lincoln County (G-4775)

(G-4750)
STONETREE SIGNS
5321 New Hope Rd (27239-9321)
PHONE.................336 625-0938
TOLL FREE: 866
Michele Bortree, *Owner*
EMP: 6 **EST:** 1996
SALES (est): 267.25K **Privately Held**
Web: www.stonetreesigns.com
SIC: 3993 Electric signs

(G-4751)
SURRATT HOSIERY MILL INC
22872 Nc Highway 8 (27239-8175)
PHONE.................336 859-4583
Irving A Surratt, *Pr*
Eric Surratt, *Sec*
EMP: 10 **EST:** 1965
SQ FT: 85,000
SALES (est): 489.97K **Privately Held**
Web: www.surratthosiery.com
SIC: 2251 2252 Women's hosiery, except socks; Socks

(G-4752)
THERMO PRODUCTS LLC (HQ)
92 W Fourth St (27239-7287)
P.O. Box 217 (46366-0217)
PHONE.................800 348-5130
Allen A Kuehl, *Pr*
EMP: 46 **EST:** 1946
SQ FT: 70,000
SALES (est): 20.36MM
SALES (corp-wide): 240.55MM **Publicly Held**
Web: www.thermopride.com
SIC: 3585 3433 Furnaces, warm air: electric; Heating equipment, except electric
PA: Burnham Holdings, Inc.
  1241 Harrisburg Ave
  Lancaster PA 17603
  717 390-7800

(G-4753)
TUCKER LOGGING
6957 Gravel Hill Rd (27239-8324)
PHONE.................336 857-2674
Jessie Tucker, *Owner*
EMP: 4 **EST:** 1990
SALES (est): 290.23K **Privately Held**
SIC: 2411 Logging camps and contractors

(G-4754)
ULTRA-MEK INC
487 Bombay Rd (27239-0130)
P.O. Box 518 (27239-0518)
PHONE.................336 859-4552
Steve Hoffman, *CEO*
Shane Hoffman, *
William S Bencini, *
◆ **EMP:** 100 **EST:** 1980
SQ FT: 75,000
SALES (est): 14.71MM **Privately Held**
Web: www.ultramek.com
SIC: 3429 Furniture hardware

(G-4755)
WALKER LOGGING
1157 Yates Rd (27239-7075)
PHONE.................336 964-1380
EMP: 4 **EST:** 2019
SALES (est): 77.94K **Privately Held**
SIC: 2411 Logging

(G-4756)
WST LOGGING LLC
7324 Checkmark Rd (27239-9025)
PHONE.................336 857-0147
William Stewart Tysinger, *Prin*
EMP: 6 **EST:** 2014
SALES (est): 125.37K **Privately Held**
SIC: 2411 Logging

Denver
Lincoln County

(G-4757)
3V PERFORMANCE LLC
7813 Commerce Dr (28037-9101)
PHONE.................980 222-7230
Wayne A Cassavaugh, *Prin*
EMP: 5 **EST:** 2020
SALES (est): 219.01K **Privately Held**
Web: www.3vperformance.com
SIC: 3599 Industrial machinery, nec

(G-4758)
ADMIRAL MARINE PDTS & SVCS INC
770 Crosspoint Dr (28037-7826)
PHONE.................704 489-8771
Michael Digh, *Pr*
Waco S Digh, *VP*
EMP: 5 **EST:** 1981
SALES (est): 388.68K **Privately Held**
Web: www.admiralmarine.biz
SIC: 7699 5999 2221 Boat repair; Fiberglass materials, except insulation; Fiberglass fabrics

(G-4759)
ADVANCED MCH & FABRICATION INC
7842 Commerce Dr (28037-9101)
P.O. Box 749 (28037-0749)
PHONE.................704 489-0096
Elizabeth Barr, *Pr*
Mike Barr, *VP*
EMP: 4 **EST:** 1999
SALES (est): 428.06K **Privately Held**
Web: www.advancemachinefab.com
SIC: 3599 Machine shop, jobbing and repair

(G-4760)
AMF-NC ENTERPRISE COMPANY LLC
3570 Denver Dr (28037-7217)
PHONE.................704 489-2206
Jerry Soots, *Genl Mgr*
EMP: 13 **EST:** 2013
SQ FT: 6,000
SALES (est): 2.29MM **Privately Held**
Web: www.gray-mfg.com
SIC: 3465 3728 Body parts, automobile: stamped metal; Aircraft body assemblies and parts

(G-4761)
ANATECH LTD (PA)
771 Crosspoint Dr (28037-7826)
PHONE.................704 489-1488
George Barr, *Pr*
Liliana Barr, *VP*
EMP: 19 **EST:** 2004
SQ FT: 5,000
SALES (est): 3.77MM
SALES (corp-wide): 3.77MM **Privately Held**
Web: www.industrialhardcarbon.com
SIC: 3479 2836 Coating of metals and formed products; Biological products, except diagnostic

(G-4762)
ANDY MAYLISH FABRICATION INC
5384 Stone Henge Dr (28037-8721)
PHONE.................704 785-1491
Andrew Maylish, *Prin*
EMP: 4 **EST:** 2016
SALES (est): 56.31K **Privately Held**
SIC: 3999 Manufacturing industries, nec

(G-4763)
ARGOS USA LLC
Also Called: Redi-Mix Concrete
4451 N Nc 16 Business Hwy (28037-6777)
PHONE.................704 483-4013
Tim Kinder, *Mgr*
EMP: 10
Web: www.argos-us.com
SIC: 3273 Ready-mixed concrete
HQ: Argos Usa Llc
  3015 Windward Plz Ste 300
  Alpharetta GA 30005
  678 368-4300

(G-4764)
BILL PERFECT INC
4207 Burnwood Trl (28037-6212)
PHONE.................954 889-6699
Michael Jlates Junior, *Pr*
EMP: 19 **EST:** 2015
SALES (est): 892.74K **Privately Held**
Web: www.timelybill.com
SIC: 7372 Prepackaged software

(G-4765)
BILL PINK CARBURETORS LLC
6137 Denver Industrial Park Rd Ste A (28037-7838)
PHONE.................704 575-1645
Bill Pink, *Prin*
EMP: 7 **EST:** 2017
SALES (est): 423.29K **Privately Held**
SIC: 3592 Carburetors

(G-4766)
C A ZIMMER INC
Also Called: Cornell Zimmer Organ Builders
731 Crosspoint Dr (28037-7826)
P.O. Box 2309 (28037-2309)
PHONE.................704 483-4560
Cornel A Zimmer, *Pr*
Ann Zimmer, *VP*
EMP: 8 **EST:** 1992
SQ FT: 9,000
SALES (est): 985.58K **Privately Held**
Web: www.zimmerorgans.com
SIC: 3931 Organs, all types: pipe, reed, hand, electronic, etc.

(G-4767)
CALICO TECHNOLOGIES INC (PA)
Also Called: Calico Coatings
5883 Balsom Ridge Rd (28037-9233)
P.O. Box 901 (28037-0901)
PHONE.................704 483-2202
Tracy Trotter, *Pr*
EMP: 23 **EST:** 1997
SQ FT: 20,000
SALES (est): 4.94MM
SALES (corp-wide): 4.94MM **Privately Held**
Web: www.calicocoatings.com
SIC: 3479 Coating of metals and formed products

(G-4768)
CRAWFORD COMPOSITES LLC
Also Called: High Performance Adaptive
3501 Denver Dr (28037-7217)
PHONE.................704 483-4175
Michael Joukowsky, *Managing Member*
Kathryn Becker, *Managing Member**
EMP: 47 **EST:** 2012
SALES (est): 5.47MM **Privately Held**
Web: www.crawfordcomposites.com
SIC: 3083 Thermoplastics laminates: rods, tubes, plates, and sheet

(G-4769)
CROWN DEFENSE LTD
2320 N Nc 16 Business Hwy (28037-8353)
PHONE.................202 800-8848
EMP: 8
SALES (corp-wide): 1.04MM **Privately Held**
Web: www.sosmil.org
SIC: 3799 3795 Off-road automobiles, except recreational vehicles; Amphibian tanks, military
PA: Crown Defense Ltd
  160 Taylor St
  Aberdeen NC 28315
  202 800-8848

(G-4770)
CRYPTIC COATINGS LTD
6515 Denver Industrial Park Rd (28037-9794)
PHONE.................704 966-1617
EMP: 9 **EST:** 2017
SALES (est): 510.29K **Privately Held**
Web: www.crypticcoatings.com
SIC: 3479 Coating of metals and formed products

(G-4771)
DELLINGER PRECAST INC
4531 N Nc 16 Business Hwy (28037-6215)
PHONE.................704 483-2868
Gary Dellinger, *Pr*
Virginia Dellinger, *VP*
EMP: 22 **EST:** 1973
SQ FT: 1,200
SALES (est): 8.82MM **Privately Held**
Web: www.dellingerprecast.com
SIC: 7699 3272 Septic tank cleaning service; Septic tanks, concrete

(G-4772)
DENVER WATERJET LLC
3865 N Nc 16 Business Hwy (28037-7906)
PHONE.................980 222-7447
EMP: 9 **EST:** 2019
SALES (est): 496.95K **Privately Held**
Web: www.denverwaterjet.com
SIC: 3599 Machine shop, jobbing and repair

(G-4773)
DISPLAY TECHS LLC
4251 Stormy Pointe Ct (28037-7311)
P.O. Box 32 (28037-0032)
PHONE.................704 966-0679
Mark Vandenberge, *Prin*
EMP: 5 **EST:** 2017
SALES (est): 108.79K **Privately Held**
SIC: 3993 Signs and advertising specialties

(G-4774)
DOIN IT RGHT CBNETRY MORE LLC
5248 King Wilkinson Rd (28037-6734)
PHONE.................980 297-3116
Randall Stertzbach, *Prin*
EMP: 4 **EST:** 2016
SALES (est): 188.58K **Privately Held**
Web: www.dircabinetryandmore.com
SIC: 2434 Wood kitchen cabinets

(G-4775)
EARTH MATTERS INC
4943 Looking Glass Trl (28037-9032)
P.O. Box 1589 (21041-1589)
PHONE.................410 747-4400
Michael P Wiley, *Pr*
Paul Van Doren, *VP*
EMP: 6 **EST:** 1998
SALES (est): 931.38K **Privately Held**
Web: www.earthmattersinc.com

Denver - Lincoln County (G-4776)

SIC: 1381 Drilling oil and gas wells

(G-4776)
FOUNDRY GROUP LLC
531 Brentwood Rd # 507 (28037-0269)
PHONE.................................412 973-9762
Bradley Robinson, *Mgr*
EMP: 9 EST: 2016
SALES (est): 430.46K **Privately Held**
Web: www.thefoundrygroupllc.com
SIC: 3599 Machine shop, jobbing and repair

(G-4777)
FURNACE REBUILDERS INC
915 Dove Ct (28037-9211)
P.O. Box 1067 (28037-1067)
PHONE.................................704 483-4025
John Murphy, *Pr*
EMP: 12 EST: 1995
SQ FT: 10,000
SALES (est): 2.31MM **Privately Held**
Web: www.furnacerebuilders.com
SIC: 3398 Metal heat treating

(G-4778)
GRAY MANUFACTURING TECH LLC
3570 Denver Dr (28037-7217)
PHONE.................................704 489-2206
Gary Holcomb, *Managing Member*
EMP: 17 EST: 2020
SALES (est): 1.04MM **Privately Held**
SIC: 3465 3728 Body parts, automobile: stamped metal; Aircraft body assemblies and parts

(G-4779)
GROUP 6 HOLDINGS INC
Also Called: American Power Products
1806 N Nc 16 Business Hwy (28037-8642)
PHONE.................................888 804-5008
Roger Leon, *CEO*
Keith Parker, *VP*
Larry Piercy, *CAO*
EMP: 10 EST: 2015
SALES (est): 882.39K **Privately Held**
Web: www.group6na.com
SIC: 3524 Lawnmowers, residential: hand or power

(G-4780)
HEADBANDS OF HOPE LLC
7498 Waterside Peak Dr (28037-7899)
PHONE.................................919 323-4140
Jess Ekstrom, *CEO*
Lauren Athey, *Pr*
EMP: 5 EST: 2015
SALES (est): 366.29K **Privately Held**
Web: www.headbandsofhope.com
SIC: 2339 Scarves, hoods, headbands, etc.: women's

(G-4781)
HIGH CONCEPTS LLC
7806 Creek Park Dr (28037-9111)
PHONE.................................704 377-3467
EMP: 5 EST: 2018
SALES (est): 242.45K **Privately Held**
SIC: 2752 Commercial printing, lithographic

(G-4782)
HUBER TECHNOLOGY INC (DH)
1009 Airlie Pkwy (28037-7705)
PHONE.................................704 949-1010
Henk-jan Van Ettekoven, *Pr*
Jennifer Covington, *
▲ EMP: 22 EST: 1999
SQ FT: 23,338
SALES (est): 33.81MM
SALES (corp-wide): 327.6MM **Privately Held**
Web: www.huber-technology.com
SIC: 5084 3491 Industrial machinery and equipment; Automatic regulating and control valves
HQ: Huber Se
Industriepark Erasbach A 1
Berching BY 92334
84622010

(G-4783)
HYDAC TECHNOLOGY CORP
Hydac International
1051 Airlie Pkwy (28037-7705)
PHONE.................................610 266-0100
Matthias Mueller, *Pr*
EMP: 85
SALES (corp-wide): 666.32MM **Privately Held**
Web: www.hydac-na.com
SIC: 3492 Fluid power valves and hose fittings
HQ: Hydac Technology Corp.
2260 City Line Rd
Bethlehem PA 18017
610 266-0100

(G-4784)
I-LUMENATE
2830 Hagers Ct (28037-8198)
PHONE.................................704 966-1910
EMP: 4 EST: 2017
SALES (est): 151.02K **Privately Held**
Web: www.nocqua.com
SIC: 3949 Sporting and athletic goods, nec

(G-4785)
INDUSTRIAL HARD CARBON LLC
771 Crosspoint Dr (28037-7826)
PHONE.................................704 489-1488
George Barr, *Pr*
◆ EMP: 23 EST: 2010
SALES (est): 3.65MM **Privately Held**
Web: www.industrialhardcarbon.com
SIC: 3674 Thin film circuits

(G-4786)
JD2 COMPANY LLC
3527 Governors Island Dr (28037-8442)
PHONE.................................800 811-6441
Jeff Sisterhen, *Managing Member*
EMP: 4 EST: 2021
SALES (est): 318.94K **Privately Held**
SIC: 2671 Plastic film, coated or laminated for packaging

(G-4787)
LEE PAVING SOLUTIONS LLC
688 N Nc 16 Business Hwy (28037)
PHONE.................................828 302-0415
EMP: 4 EST: 2018
SALES (est): 252.09K **Privately Held**
Web: www.leepavingsolutions.com
SIC: 3999 Manufacturing industries, nec

(G-4788)
LEONARD AUTOMATICS INC
Also Called: Leonard Frabrication & Design
5894 Balsom Ridge Rd (28037-9233)
P.O. Box 501 (28037-0501)
PHONE.................................704 483-9316
Jeffrey N Frushtick, *Pr*
Gwen B Frushtick, *Sec*
▼ EMP: 22 EST: 1969
SQ FT: 30,000
SALES (est): 8.56MM **Privately Held**
Web: www.leonardautomatics.com
SIC: 3582 Commercial laundry equipment

(G-4789)
MODACAM INCORPORATED
3762 Deer Run (28037-9157)
PHONE.................................704 489-8500
Bud Tschudin, *Pr*
Jonathan Elrod, *Prin*
EMP: 8 EST: 2001
SALES (est): 674.21K **Privately Held**
Web: www.modacam.com
SIC: 3321 Gray iron castings, nec

(G-4790)
MR TIRE INC
357 N Nc 16 Business Hwy (28037-8012)
PHONE.................................704 483-1500
Tim Mcgee, *Brnch Mgr*
EMP: 10
SALES (corp-wide): 1.33B **Publicly Held**
Web: mrtireinc.business.site
SIC: 5941 5531 5014 5722 Bicycle and bicycle parts; Automotive tires; Tires and tubes; Household appliance stores
HQ: Mr. Tire Inc.
2078 New York Ave Unit 2
Huntington Station NY 11746
631 499-3700

(G-4791)
OLD HICKORY LOG HOMES INC
4279 Burnwood Trl (28037-6212)
P.O. Box 2069 (28037-2069)
PHONE.................................704 489-8989
Paul Norman, *Pr*
EMP: 8 EST: 2002
SALES (est): 1.04MM **Privately Held**
Web: www.oldhickoryloghomes.com
SIC: 1521 2452 New construction, single-family houses; Log cabins, prefabricated, wood

(G-4792)
OSTEC INDUSTRIES CORP
4103 Sinclair St (28037-6207)
PHONE.................................704 488-3841
Richard Coste, *Pr*
EMP: 6 EST: 2000
SQ FT: 6,500
SALES (est): 946.89K **Privately Held**
Web: www.ostecindustries.com
SIC: 3599 Machine shop, jobbing and repair

(G-4793)
PIEDMONT PIPE MFG LLC
7871 Commerce Dr (28037-9101)
PHONE.................................704 489-0911
EMP: 9 EST: 2013
SALES (est): 1.39MM **Privately Held**
Web: www.piedmontpipe.com
SIC: 3317 Steel pipe and tubes

(G-4794)
PIEDMONT STAIRWORKS LLC
8135 Mallard Rd (28037-8633)
PHONE.................................704 483-3721
Jack Watson, *Brnch Mgr*
EMP: 20
SALES (corp-wide): 2.14MM **Privately Held**
Web: www.piedmontstairworks.com
SIC: 2431 Millwork
PA: Piedmont Stairworks Llc
2246 Old Steele Creek Rd
Charlotte NC 28208
704 697-0259

(G-4795)
POTTER LOGGING
2037 Cameron Heights Cir (28037-7818)
PHONE.................................704 483-2738
Clifford Potter, *Owner*
EMP: 4 EST: 2000
SALES (est): 320.81K **Privately Held**
SIC: 2411 Logging camps and contractors

(G-4796)
PRECISION MCH COMPONENTS INC
8075 Pine Lake Rd (28037-8810)
PHONE.................................704 201-8482
Brian Holder, *Pr*
▲ EMP: 8 EST: 2000
SQ FT: 6,000
SALES (est): 958.61K **Privately Held**
Web: www.precision-machine.net
SIC: 3599 Machine shop, jobbing and repair

(G-4797)
R-ANELL CUSTOM HOMES INC
3549 N Nc 16 Business Hwy (28037-8267)
P.O. Box 428 (28037-0428)
PHONE.................................704 483-5511
Dennis L Jones, *Pr*
Rollan L Jones, *
Randy Cosby, *
Steve Purdy, *
EMP: 21 EST: 1972
SQ FT: 88,000
SALES (est): 471.82K **Privately Held**
Web: www.r-anell.com
SIC: 2452 2451 Prefabricated buildings, wood; Mobile homes, except recreational

(G-4798)
RED OAK SALES COMPANY (PA)
7912 Commerce Dr (28037-9112)
PHONE.................................704 483-8464
Alex Barnette, *Pr*
Lillian Barnette, *Sec*
EMP: 6 EST: 1989
SQ FT: 7,000
SALES (est): 1.1MM **Privately Held**
Web: www.redoaksales.com
SIC: 2399 8742 Emblems, badges, and insignia; Management consulting services

(G-4799)
S & L SAWMILL INC
3044 N Nc 16 Business Hwy (28037-8262)
P.O. Box 526 (28037-0526)
PHONE.................................704 483-3264
Randy Miller, *Owner*
Ralph D Sherrill, *Owner*
EMP: 28 EST: 1973
SQ FT: 3,000
SALES (est): 1.9MM **Privately Held**
SIC: 2421 Lumber: rough, sawed, or planed

(G-4800)
SEYMOUR ADVANCED TECH LLC
3593 Denver Dr Unit 964 (28037-7269)
PHONE.................................704 709-9070
Robert Seymour Junior, *Managing Member*
EMP: 5 EST: 2019
SALES (est): 310.9K **Privately Held**
Web: www.seymouradvancedtechnologies.com
SIC: 3599 Industrial machinery, nec

(G-4801)
SIGN HERE OF LAKE NORMAN INC
Also Called: Sign Here
422 N Nc 16 Business Hwy (28037-8244)
P.O. Box 923 (28037-0923)
PHONE.................................704 483-6454
Jerry Allen Earnest, *Pr*
Jerry Earnest, *Pr*
June Earnest, *Sec*
EMP: 5 EST: 1994
SALES (est): 452.3K **Privately Held**
SIC: 3993 Electric signs

GEOGRAPHIC SECTION

Dobson - Surry County (G-4828)

(G-4802)
SOUTHSTERN PRCESS EQP CNTRLS I
Also Called: Spec
7558 Townsend Dr (28037-8904)
P.O. Box 746 (28037-0746)
PHONE..................704 483-1141
Marvin Mc Donald, *Pr*
Dickson Dorrier, *VP*
EMP: 12 **EST:** 1989
SQ FT: 12,000
SALES (est): 2.29MM **Privately Held**
Web: www.inkdispensingsystems.com
SIC: 3823 Industrial process measurement equipment

(G-4803)
STEELE RUBBER PRODUCTS INC
6180 Highway 150 E (28037-9650)
PHONE..................704 483-9343
Joanna Shere, *Pr*
Walter D Vaughan Junior, *VP*
Eric J Saltrick, *
Debra Lail, *
◆ **EMP:** 54 **EST:** 1956
SQ FT: 36,100
SALES (est): 9.11MM **Privately Held**
Web: www.steelerubber.com
SIC: 3052 Automobile hose, rubber

(G-4804)
SUSPENSIONS LLC
Also Called: Just Suspension
4723 Mountain Creek Ave (28037-6790)
PHONE..................704 809-1269
EMP: 16
SQ FT: 12,000
SALES (est): 3.5MM **Privately Held**
SIC: 3714 Ball joints, motor vehicle

(G-4805)
TABUR SERVICES
7845 Commerce Dr (28037-9109)
PHONE..................704 483-1650
EMP: 5
SALES (est): 381.24K **Privately Held**
Web: www.taburservices.com
SIC: 3663 Radio and t.v. communications equipment

(G-4806)
TEXTILE SALES INTL INC
Also Called: Tsi
8172 Malibu Pointe Ln (28037-8580)
PHONE..................704 483-7966
EMP: 5 **EST:** 1984
SQ FT: 20,000
SALES (est): 988.09K **Privately Held**
SIC: 3552 Bleaching machinery, textile

(G-4807)
THANET INC
3501 Denver Dr (28037-7217)
PHONE..................704 483-4175
Maxwell C Crawford, *Pr*
Janice G Crawford, *
▼ **EMP:** 36 **EST:** 1996
SQ FT: 24,000
SALES (est): 2.11MM **Privately Held**
Web: www.crawfordcomposites.com
SIC: 3089 3624 2823 Automotive parts, plastic; Carbon and graphite products; Cellulosic manmade fibers

(G-4808)
TORCHES DESIGN STUDIO INC
688 N Nc 16 Business Hwy Ste A (28037)
PHONE..................704 966-4000
Jeremy Lantz, *Pr*
EMP: 6 **EST:** 2013
SQ FT: 6,500
SALES (est): 214.99K **Privately Held**
Web: www.torchesdesignstudio.com
SIC: 2396 Screen printing on fabric articles

(G-4809)
TREE BRAND PACKAGING INC (PA)
7971 Graham Rd (28037-8602)
PHONE..................704 483-0719
Al Helms, *CEO*
Michael Helms, *
Chris Helms, *
EMP: 53 **EST:** 1991
SQ FT: 57,000
SALES (est): 11.4MM **Privately Held**
Web: www.treebrand.com
SIC: 2448 Pallets, wood

(G-4810)
TRI-STAR PLASTICS CORP
1387 N Nc 16 Business Hwy (28037-8637)
PHONE..................704 598-2800
Dan Gettis, *Brnch Mgr*
EMP: 50
SALES (corp-wide): 25.35MM **Privately Held**
Web: www.tstar.com
SIC: 5162 3089 Plastics products, nec; Air mattresses, plastics
PA: Tri-Star Plastics Corp
906 Boston Tpke
Shrewsbury MA 01545
508 845-1111

(G-4811)
TRIPLE C COMPANIES LLC
7911 Commerce Dr (28037-9112)
PHONE..................704 966-1999
Rachel Drake, *Managing Member*
EMP: 30 **EST:** 2020
SALES (est): 700K **Privately Held**
SIC: 2448 Wood pallets and skids

(G-4812)
UNIVERSAL RUBBER PRODUCTS INC
7780 Forest Oak Dr (28037-8830)
P.O. Box 546 (28037-0546)
PHONE..................704 483-1249
Robert Davis, *Pr*
Emily Davis, *VP*
▲ **EMP:** 7 **EST:** 1986
SQ FT: 6,000
SALES (est): 476.71K **Privately Held**
Web: www.universalrubberproducts.com
SIC: 3053 Gaskets, all materials

(G-4813)
WHISPERING WILLOW SOAP CO LLC
Also Called: Whispering Willow
5851 Balsom Ridge Rd Ste B (28037-9220)
PHONE..................828 455-0322
EMP: 4 **EST:** 2010
SALES (est): 455.39K **Privately Held**
Web: www.whisperingwillow.com
SIC: 2841 Soap and other detergents

(G-4814)
WHITE ROBERT CUSTOM WDWKG
7606 Townsend Dr (28037-9206)
PHONE..................704 489-2005
Robert White, *Prin*
EMP: 5 **EST:** 2009
SALES (est): 100.15K **Privately Held**
SIC: 2499 1751 Decorative wood and woodwork; Carpentry work

(G-4815)
WIREWAY/HUSKY CORP (PA)
Also Called: Husky Rack and Wire
6146 Denver Industrial Park Rd (28037-7805)
P.O. Box 645 (28037-0645)
PHONE..................704 483-1135
Ron Young, *Pr*
Reginald Young, *
Greg Young, *
Susan Meyers, *
▼ **EMP:** 155 **EST:** 1980
SQ FT: 264,400
SALES (est): 39.33MM
SALES (corp-wide): 39.33MM **Privately Held**
Web: www.huskyrackandwire.com
SIC: 3496 2542 3315 Grilles and grillework, woven wire; Pallet racks: except wood; Welded steel wire fabric

(G-4816)
XELERA INC
137 Cross Center Rd (28037-5009)
PHONE..................540 915-6181
EMP: 5
SALES (est): 853.99K **Privately Held**
Web: www.xelera.us
SIC: 2899 Chemical preparations, nec

Dillsboro
Jackson County

(G-4817)
MOUNTAIN BEAR & CO INC
28 Church St (28725)
P.O. Box 391 (28725-0391)
PHONE..................828 631-0156
Tonya Williams, *Pr*
Robert Williams, *VP*
Tammy Sessoms, *Sec*
EMP: 8 **EST:** 1998
SQ FT: 1,000
SALES (est): 644.86K **Privately Held**
Web: www.dillsborochocolate.com
SIC: 2066 Chocolate and cocoa products

Dobson
Surry County

(G-4818)
ALPACADABRA
125 Rock Lane Dr (27017-8205)
PHONE..................336 429-0124
Vivian Thompson, *Prin*
EMP: 4 **EST:** 2015
SALES (est): 69.56K **Privately Held**
Web: www.alpaca-dabra.com
SIC: 2231 Alpacas, mohair: woven

(G-4819)
BEAR CREEK RACEWAY INC
8736 Us 601 (27017-7309)
PHONE..................336 367-4264
Lorene Jones, *Prin*
EMP: 4 **EST:** 2008
SALES (est): 195.93K **Privately Held**
Web: www.bearcreekracing.com
SIC: 3644 Raceways

(G-4820)
BLUE ZEPHRY VINEYARD
6457 Haystack Rd (27017-6021)
PHONE..................336 366-5066
EMP: 4 **EST:** 2018
SALES (est): 106.06K **Privately Held**
SIC: 2084 Wines

(G-4821)
CAROLINA CARPORTS INC (PA)
187 Cardinal Ridge Ln (27017-8652)
P.O. Box 1263 (27017-1263)
PHONE..................336 367-6400
Adela Herrera, *Pr*
◆ **EMP:** 77 **EST:** 1997
SQ FT: 12,900
SALES (est): 24.51MM
SALES (corp-wide): 24.51MM **Privately Held**
Web: www.carolinacarportsinc.com
SIC: 3448 Carports, prefabricated metal

(G-4822)
CRAIG S PRINTING LLC
151 Royal Ln (27017-7631)
P.O. Box 985 (27017-0985)
PHONE..................336 786-2327
Cleve Hamlin, *Prin*
EMP: 5 **EST:** 2013
SALES (est): 235.4K **Privately Held**
SIC: 2752 Offset printing

(G-4823)
FANTASY SPORTS BREAKS LLC
302 Hodges Mill Rd (27017-7545)
PHONE..................276 233-5204
EMP: 5 **EST:** 2015
SALES (est): 178.33K **Privately Held**
SIC: 2759 Souvenir cards: printing, nsk

(G-4824)
HAZE GRAY VINEYARDS LLC
Also Called: Haze Gray Vineyards
765 Stony Knoll Rd (27017-8043)
PHONE..................610 247-9387
Deane Muhlenberg, *Prin*
EMP: 5 **EST:** 2017
SALES (est): 172.31K **Privately Held**
Web: www.hazegrayvineyards.com
SIC: 2084 Wines

(G-4825)
HODGES PRECISION MACHINE
116 Tobe Hudson Rd (27017-7636)
PHONE..................336 366-3024
David Hodges, *Owner*
EMP: 4 **EST:** 1989
SQ FT: 4,000
SALES (est): 218.92K **Privately Held**
SIC: 3599 Machine shop, jobbing and repair

(G-4826)
HOUSE OF STITCHES
2983 Simpson Mill Rd (27017-6417)
PHONE..................570 768-6930
Tina Parrish, *Prin*
EMP: 4 **EST:** 2017
SALES (est): 49.8K **Privately Held**
SIC: 2395 Embroidery and art needlework

(G-4827)
HUTTON VINEYARDS LLC
103 Buck Fork Rd (27017-7806)
PHONE..................336 374-2321
Malcolm Hutton, *Owner*
EMP: 6 **EST:** 2005
SALES (est): 277.82K **Privately Held**
Web: www.huttonvineyards.com
SIC: 2084 Wines

(G-4828)
LADYBUG VINEYARD LLC
607 Crossroad Church Rd (27017-7515)
PHONE..................336 366-4701
Judy H Haymore, *Admn*
EMP: 5 **EST:** 2010
SALES (est): 63.62K **Privately Held**
SIC: 2084 Wines

Dobson - Surry County (G-4829)

GEOGRAPHIC SECTION

(G-4829)
MILLENNIUM BUILDINGS INC
317 W Atkins St (27017-8711)
PHONE..................................866 216-8499
EMP: 6 **EST:** 2020
SALES (est): 128.5K **Privately Held**
Web: www.millenniumbuildings.com
SIC: 3448 Prefabricated metal buildings and components

(G-4830)
RUGGED METAL DESIGNS INC
1004 Red Hill Creek Rd (27017-7735)
PHONE..................................336 352-5150
Gary Wilmoth, *CEO*
Tony Stanley, *Pr*
Peggy Wilmoth, *Sec*
EMP: 9 **EST:** 2001
SQ FT: 30,000
SALES (est): 912.55K **Privately Held**
SIC: 3441 Fabricated structural metal

(G-4831)
SHELTON VINEYARDS INC
286 Cabernet Ln (27017-6322)
PHONE..................................336 366-4818
Charles Shelton, *Pr*
R Edwin Shelton, *
EMP: 28 **EST:** 1998
SALES (est): 5.79MM **Privately Held**
Web: www.sheltonvineyards.com
SIC: 2084 0172 Wines; Grapes

(G-4832)
USA METAL STRUCTURE LLP
507 W Kapp St (27017-8829)
PHONE..................................336 717-2884
Juan Lopez Cruz, *Pt*
Orlando Perez, *Pt*
EMP: 8 **EST:** 2021
SALES (est): 390.94K **Privately Held**
Web: www.usametalstructures.com
SIC: 3441 7371 Fabricated structural metal; Computer software development

(G-4833)
WAYNE FARMS LLC
Also Called: Wayne Farms
802 E Atkins St (27017-8707)
P.O. Box 383 (27017-0383)
PHONE..................................336 386-8151
Paul Norton, *Mgr*
EMP: 539
SALES (corp-wide): 405K **Privately Held**
Web: www.waynesandersonfarms.com
SIC: 2015 Poultry slaughtering and processing
HQ: Wayne Farms Llc
4110 Continental Dr
Oakwood GA 30566

Dover
Craven County

(G-4834)
CAROLINA STONE LLC
10600 Nc Highway 55 W (28526-8932)
P.O. Box 186 (28586-0186)
PHONE..................................252 208-1633
Andy Purifoy, *Genl Pt*
Allen Russell, *Genl Pt*
EMP: 10 **EST:** 2001
SALES (est): 856.52K **Privately Held**
Web: www.captkerry.com
SIC: 1442 Construction sand and gravel

(G-4835)
TRACTOR COUNTRY INC
5763 Hwy 70 (28526-8871)
PHONE..................................252 523-3007
Jonathan Care, *Prin*
EMP: 11 **EST:** 2016
SALES (est): 209.58K **Privately Held**
Web: www.tractorcountry.net
SIC: 5999 3523 7699 Farm equipment and supplies; Tractors, farm; Tractor repair

Drexel
Burke County

(G-4836)
POWELL WELDING INC
3156 Hwy 70 (28619)
P.O. Box 2655 (28619-2655)
PHONE..................................828 433-0831
Donnie Powell, *Pr*
Rodney Powell, *Sec*
Scott Powell, *Treas*
EMP: 4 **EST:** 1958
SQ FT: 3,600
SALES (est): 231.75K **Privately Held**
SIC: 7692 Welding repair

Dublin
Bladen County

(G-4837)
DUBLIN WOODWORK SHOP
N S Hwy 87 E (28332)
P.O. Box 52 (28332-0052)
PHONE..................................910 862-2289
David Hursey, *Owner*
EMP: 4 **EST:** 1945
SQ FT: 1,800
SALES (est): 211.9K **Privately Held**
SIC: 2434 Wood kitchen cabinets

(G-4838)
PEANUT PROCESSORS INC (PA)
Also Called: Peanut
7329 Albert St (28332-8901)
P.O. Box 160 (28332-0160)
PHONE..................................910 862-2136
Houston N Brisson Junior, *Ch Bd*
David S Cox, *
EMP: 10 **EST:** 1961
SQ FT: 50,000
SALES (corp-wide): 5.56MM
SALES (corp-wide): 5.56MM **Privately Held**
SIC: 2099 Peanut butter

(G-4839)
PEANUT PROCESSORS SHERMAN INC
7329 Albert St (28332-8901)
P.O. Box 160 (28332-0160)
PHONE..................................910 862-2136
Nile Brisson, *Pr*
David Cox, *VP*
EMP: 8 **EST:** 1992
SQ FT: 1,000
SALES (est): 307.24K **Privately Held**
SIC: 2099 Peanut butter

Dudley
Wayne County

(G-4840)
BEST MACHINE & FABRICATION INC
117 Sleepy Creek Rd (28333-6419)
P.O. Box 711 (28333-0711)
PHONE..................................919 731-7101
Ray Best, *Pr*
Phyliss Lewis, *Off Mgr*
EMP: 5
SALES (est): 552.9K **Privately Held**
SIC: 3089 Netting, plastics

(G-4841)
CASE FARMS LLC
330 Pecan Rd (28333-5369)
PHONE..................................919 735-5010
EMP: 97
Web: www.casefarms.com
SIC: 2015 8731 Poultry slaughtering and processing; Commercial physical research
PA: Case Farms, L.L.C.
385 Pilch Rd
Troutman NC 28166

(G-4842)
CLASSIC ADDRESS SIGNS
697 Sandhill Dr (28333-5352)
P.O. Box 924 (28333-0924)
PHONE..................................919 734-4482
Ela Nickerson, *Prin*
EMP: 5 **EST:** 2009
SALES (est): 66.97K **Privately Held**
Web: www.classicaddresssigns.com
SIC: 3993 Signs and advertising specialties

(G-4843)
GEORGIA-PACIFIC LLC
Also Called: Georgia-Pacific
139 Brewington Dr (28333-8197)
PHONE..................................919 580-1078
Charles Mclendon, *Mgr*
EMP: 62
SALES (corp-wide): 36.93B **Privately Held**
Web: www.gp.com
SIC: 2493 2436 2435 Particleboard, plastic laminated; Softwood veneer and plywood; Hardwood veneer and plywood
HQ: Georgia-Pacific Llc
133 Peachtree St Nw
Atlanta GA 30303
404 652-4000

(G-4844)
GEORGIA-PACIFIC LLC
Also Called: Georgia-Pacific
2457b Old Mt Olive Hwy (28333-8131)
PHONE..................................919 736-2722
William Collins, *Mgr*
EMP: 98
SALES (corp-wide): 36.93B **Privately Held**
Web: www.gp.com
SIC: 2621 Paper mills
HQ: Georgia-Pacific Llc
133 Peachtree St Nw
Atlanta GA 30303
404 652-4000

(G-4845)
NATIONAL SALVAGE & SVC CORP
430 Old Mt Olive Hwy (28333-5170)
PHONE..................................919 739-5633
Hugh Bray, *Brnch Mgr*
EMP: 21
SALES (corp-wide): 54.54MM **Privately Held**
Web: www.nssccorp.com
SIC: 2499 Applicators, wood
PA: National Salvage & Service Corporation
6755 S Old State Road 37
Bloomington IN 47401
812 339-8437

Dunn
Harnett County

(G-4846)
48FORTY SOLUTIONS LLC
2 Dinan Rd (28334-6753)
PHONE..................................910 891-1534
EMP: 630
SALES (corp-wide): 604.77MM **Privately Held**
Web: www.48forty.com
SIC: 2448 Pallets, wood
PA: 48forty Solutions, Llc
11740 Katy Fwy Ste 12
Houston TX 77079
678 722-3984

(G-4847)
A CLEANER TOMORROW DRY CLG LLC (PA)
Also Called: A Cleaner Tomorrow and Laundry
102 S Wilson Ave (28334-3200)
PHONE..................................919 639-6396
EMP: 8 **EST:** 2011
SALES (est): 1.63MM
SALES (corp-wide): 1.63MM **Privately Held**
Web: www.simplydivinenc.com
SIC: 3999 2842 7212 7216 Hosiery kits, sewing and mending; Laundry cleaning preparations; Retail agent, laundry and drycleaning; Drycleaning plants, except rugs

(G-4848)
ADA MARKETING INC
Also Called: Adams Handmade Soap
601 N Ashe Ave (28334-3611)
PHONE..................................910 221-2189
Anthony Adams, *Pr*
Maranatha Adams, *
Nathaniel Hinds, *
Kelby Mcclelland, *VP*
EMP: 40 **EST:** 2005
SALES (est): 3.58MM **Privately Held**
Web: www.naturalsoapwholesale.com
SIC: 2841 5169 Soap and other detergents; Detergents and soaps, except specialty cleaning

(G-4849)
ALLIED MOBILE SYSTEMS LLC
17665 Us 421 S (28334-6485)
PHONE..................................888 503-1501
James Godwin Junior, *Pr*
EMP: 7 **EST:** 2019
SALES (est): 491.09K **Privately Held**
Web: www.alliedmobilesystems.com
SIC: 3593 Fluid power actuators, hydraulic or pneumatic

(G-4850)
ALPHIN BROTHERS INC
2302 Us 301 S (28334-6165)
P.O. Box 1310 (28335-1310)
PHONE..................................910 892-8751
Jesse C Alphin Junior, *Pr*
▲ **EMP:** 26 **EST:** 1947
SQ FT: 80,000
SALES (est): 2.62MM **Privately Held**
Web: www.alphinbrothers.com
SIC: 2037 2092 Frozen fruits and vegetables; Seafoods, frozen: prepared

(G-4851)
ARC3 GASES INC (PA)
1600 Us-301 S (28334-6791)
P.O. Box 1708 (28335-1708)
PHONE..................................910 892-4016
Emmett Aldredge Iii, *Pr*

GEOGRAPHIC SECTION
Dunn - Harnett County (G-4875)

Emmett Aldredge Junior, *Ch*
Christopher Aldredge, *
EMP: 29 **EST:** 2014
SQ FT: 9,600
SALES (est): 204.15MM
SALES (corp-wide): 204.15MM **Privately Held**
Web: www.arc3gases.com
SIC: 2813 5084 5169 7359 Industrial gases; Industrial machinery and equipment; Chemicals and allied products, nec; Equipment rental and leasing, nec

(G-4852)
ARGOS USA LLC
Also Called: Ready Mixed Concrete Co
401 N Fayetteville Ave (28334-3913)
P.O. Box 1067 (28335-1067)
PHONE.................................910 892-3188
Bob Batts, *Mgr*
EMP: 9
Web: www.argos-us.com
SIC: 3273 Ready-mixed concrete
HQ: Argos Usa Llc
  3015 Windward Plz Ste 300
  Alpharetta GA 30005
  678 368-4300

(G-4853)
BEMCO SLEEP PRODUCTS INC
601 N Ashe Ave (28334-3611)
P.O. Box 697 (28335-0697)
PHONE.................................910 892-3107
Gene T Jernigan, *Pr*
Charlla M Jernigan, *
EMP: 25 **EST:** 1935
SQ FT: 36,000
SALES (est): 2.31MM **Privately Held**
Web: www.bemco.com
SIC: 2515 Mattresses, containing felt, foam rubber, urethane, etc.

(G-4854)
CAROLINA FIRE PROTECTION INC
4055 Hodges Chapel Rd (28334-8655)
P.O. Box 250 (28335-0250)
PHONE.................................910 892-1700
Jeffrey R Dunn, *Pr*
Terry L Parrish, *
EMP: 36 **EST:** 2002
SQ FT: 5,700
SALES (est): 6.01MM **Privately Held**
Web: www.carolinafireprotection.com
SIC: 3569 1711 Sprinkler systems, fire: automatic; Plumbing, heating, air-conditioning

(G-4855)
CAROLINA PRECAST CONCRETE
452 Webb Rd (28334-8742)
PHONE.................................910 230-0028
Robert Hill, *Prin*
EMP: 15 **EST:** 2007
SALES (est): 418.99K **Privately Held**
Web: www.concretepandp.com
SIC: 3272 Concrete products, precast, nec

(G-4856)
CARR PRECAST CONCRETE INC
7519 Plainview Hwy (28334-6883)
P.O. Box 1283 (28335-1283)
PHONE.................................910 892-1151
Robert B Carr, *Pr*
Loray F Carr, *Sec*
EMP: 20 **EST:** 1976
SQ FT: 15,000
SALES (est): 2.47MM **Privately Held**
Web: www.carrprecast.com
SIC: 3272 Concrete products, precast, nec

(G-4857)
CCO HOLDINGS LLC
102 W Divine St (28334-5202)
PHONE.................................910 292-4083
EMP: 107
SALES (corp-wide): 54.61B **Publicly Held**
SIC: 4841 3663 3651 Cable television services; Radio and t.v. communications equipment; Household audio and video equipment
HQ: Cco Holdings, Llc
  400 Atlantic St
  Stamford CT 06901
  203 905-7801

(G-4858)
CONCRETE PIPE & PRECAST LLC
452 Webb Rd (28334-8742)
PHONE.................................910 892-6411
Howard Tindal, *Brnch Mgr*
EMP: 32
SALES (corp-wide): 61.95MM **Privately Held**
Web: www.concretepandp.com
SIC: 3272 Precast terrazzo or concrete products
PA: Concrete Pipe & Precast, Llc
  11352 Virginia Precast Rd
  Ashland VA 23005
  804 798-6068

(G-4859)
CREATIVE CAPS INC
214 E Broad St (28334-4921)
P.O. Box 835 (27504-0835)
PHONE.................................919 701-1175
Eva Massengill, *Pr*
Brian Massengill, *VP*
EMP: 4 **EST:** 1990
SQ FT: 2,400
SALES (est): 488.87K **Privately Held**
Web: www.creativecaps.net
SIC: 2395 Embroidery products, except Schiffli machine

(G-4860)
DAVID BEASLEY
306 S Clinton Ave (28334-5344)
PHONE.................................910 891-2557
David Beasley, *Prin*
EMP: 5 **EST:** 2016
SALES (est): 84.05K **Privately Held**
SIC: 7692 Welding repair

(G-4861)
DEEP CREEK LURES INC
603 S Wilson Ave (28334-5832)
PHONE.................................910 892-1791
Gary D Ballard, *Pr*
EMP: 5 **EST:** 2013
SALES (est): 121.28K **Privately Held**
Web: www.deepcreeklures.com
SIC: 3949 Snow skiing equipment and supplies, except skis

(G-4862)
DISCOUNT PALLET SERVICES LLC
319 Ira B Tart Rd (28334-6093)
PHONE.................................910 892-3760
Sherwood Glenn Barefoot, *Prin*
EMP: 7 **EST:** 2011
SALES (est): 458.25K **Privately Held**
Web: www.discountpalletservices.com
SIC: 5251 3537 Hardware stores; Platforms, stands, tables, pallets, and similar equipment

(G-4863)
DUNBAR FOODS CORPORATION
1000 S Fayetteville Ave (28334-6213)
P.O. Box 519 (28335-0519)
PHONE.................................910 892-3175
Stanley K Dunbar, *Pr*
Christina M Dunbar, *
EMP: 68 **EST:** 1984
SALES (est): 2.7MM
SALES (corp-wide): 63.59MM **Privately Held**
SIC: 2033 Vegetables: packaged in cans, jars, etc.
PA: Moody Dunbar, Inc.
  2000 Waters Edge Dr # 21
  Johnson City TN 37604
  423 952-0100

(G-4864)
ENERGY CONVERSION SYSTE
10 Carlie Cs Dr (28334-3649)
PHONE.................................910 892-8081
N Farthing, *Admn*
EMP: 6 **EST:** 2014
SALES (est): 217.61K **Privately Held**
Web: www.ecs-global.net
SIC: 3624 Carbon and graphite products

(G-4865)
ENVIROSERVE CHEMICALS INC
603 S Wilson Ave (28334-5832)
PHONE.................................910 892-1791
Gary Ballard, *Pr*
EMP: 13 **EST:** 1996
SQ FT: 55,000
SALES (est): 2.42MM **Privately Held**
Web: www.enviroservechemicals.com
SIC: 2899 Chemical preparations, nec

(G-4866)
FAMOUS AMOS SIGNS
111 Averasboro Rd (28334-5401)
PHONE.................................919 820-2211
EMP: 5 **EST:** 2019
SALES (est): 160.67K **Privately Held**
Web: www.famousamossigns.com
SIC: 3993 Signs and advertising specialties

(G-4867)
FORTERRA PIPE & PRECAST LLC
452 Webb Rd (28334-8742)
PHONE.................................910 892-6411
Ray Rosser, *Brnch Mgr*
EMP: 9
Web: www.rinkerpipe.com
SIC: 3272 Precast terrazzo or concrete products
HQ: Forterra Pipe & Precast, Llc
  511 E John Carpenter Fwy
  Irving TX 75062
  469 458-7973

(G-4868)
FRANK PETERSON
285 Stonehenge Dr (28334-9705)
PHONE.................................910 892-6496
Frank Peterson, *Prin*
EMP: 4 **EST:** 2017
SALES (est): 56.72K **Privately Held**
SIC: 2741 Miscellaneous publishing

(G-4869)
FRAZEES TROPHIES
312 S Powell Ave (28334-4671)
PHONE.................................910 892-6722
Melinge Frazee, *CEO*
EMP: 6 **EST:** 2007
SALES (est): 254.44K **Privately Held**
Web: www.frazeestrophies.com
SIC: 3993 5099 5999 Signs and advertising specialties; Signs, except electric; Trophies and plaques

(G-4870)
GODWIN MANUFACTURING CO INC (PA)
17666 Us 421 S (28334-6484)
P.O. Box 1147 (28335-1147)
PHONE.................................910 897-4995
James P Godwin Senior, *Pr*
James P Godwin Junior, *VP*
Pam Faircloth, *
Mark Fentress, *
◆ **EMP:** 179 **EST:** 1966
SQ FT: 25,000
SALES (est): 46.63MM
SALES (corp-wide): 46.63MM **Privately Held**
Web: www.godwinmfg.com
SIC: 3713 3714 Truck bodies (motor vehicles); Dump truck lifting mechanism

(G-4871)
GRAVEL MONKEY GEODES LLC
106 Mar Joy Dr (28334-5292)
PHONE.................................224 848-0401
Stephen Clancy, *Prin*
EMP: 5 **EST:** 2017
SALES (est): 210K **Privately Held**
SIC: 1442 Construction sand and gravel

(G-4872)
GRAY METAL SOUTH INC (PA)
600 N Powell Ave (28334-4543)
P.O. Box 1126 (28335-1126)
PHONE.................................910 892-2119
Marguerite Gray, *Pr*
Joseph Gray, *
EMP: 117 **EST:** 1908
SQ FT: 135,000
SALES (est): 19.95MM **Privately Held**
Web: www.graymetalsouth.com
SIC: 3444 Sheet metal specialties, not stamped

(G-4873)
H & H PRODUCTS INCORPORATED (PA)
275 Carlie Cs Dr (28334-3651)
P.O. Box 366 (28335-0366)
PHONE.................................910 891-4276
Jerry Mel Hartman, *Pr*
Bob Holder, *VP*
EMP: 6 **EST:** 1982
SQ FT: 17,000
SALES (est): 1.33MM **Privately Held**
Web: www.hhprodinc.com
SIC: 2842 Specialty cleaning

(G-4874)
HALLS AUTO REPAIR
200 W Broad St (28334-4804)
PHONE.................................919 879-9946
EMP: 5 **EST:** 2020
SALES (est): 40.34K **Privately Held**
SIC: 7534 Tire repair shop

(G-4875)
HERITAGE CONCRETE SERVICE CORP
1300 N Mckay Ave (28334-3128)
PHONE.................................910 892-4445
Mike Haire, *Mgr*
EMP: 8
SALES (corp-wide): 3.24MM **Privately Held**
Web: www.heritageconcreteservice.com
SIC: 3273 Ready-mixed concrete
PA: Heritage Concrete Service Corporation
  140 Deep River Rd
  Sanford NC 27330
  919 775-5014

Dunn - Harnett County (G-4876)

(G-4876)
MIKE BEASLEY SERVICES INC
663 Ammons Rd 244 (28334-6234)
PHONE.....................910 892-6216
Mike Beasley, *Pr*
EMP: 5 **EST:** 1982
SALES (est): 246.77K **Privately Held**
SIC: 7692 Welding repair

(G-4877)
MORGAN ADVANCED MTLS TECH INC
MORGAN ADVANCED MATERIALS AND TECHNOLOGY, INC.
504 N Ashe Ave (28334-3610)
PHONE.....................910 892-9677
John Stang, *Brnch Mgr*
EMP: 141
SALES (corp-wide): 1.34B **Privately Held**
SIC: 3624 Carbon and graphite products
HQ: Pure Carbon Company, Inc.
441 Hall Ave
Saint Marys PA 15857

(G-4878)
PALLET WORLD
670 John Lee Rd (28334-8147)
PHONE.....................919 800-1113
Antwon Small, *Pr*
Shannon Lockamy, *CEO*
EMP: 5 **EST:** 2015
SALES (est): 232.15K **Privately Held**
SIC: 2448 Pallets, wood and wood with metal

(G-4879)
PATS MOBILE WELDING
2503 Erwin Rd (28334-6525)
PHONE.....................910 891-9581
Patrick Tew, *Prin*
EMP: 6 **EST:** 2019
SALES (est): 171.64K **Privately Held**
SIC: 7692 Welding repair

(G-4880)
RAVEN ROCK MANUFACTURING INC
803 E Broad St (28334-5103)
PHONE.....................910 308-8430
Veronica Livinggood, *Pr*
EMP: 7 **EST:** 2006
SALES (est): 247.9K **Privately Held**
SIC: 2591 Blinds vertical

(G-4881)
RECORD PUBLISHING COMPANY
Also Called: Daily Record The
99 W Broad St (28334-6031)
P.O. Box 1448 (28335-1448)
PHONE.....................910 230-1948
Bart S Adams, *Pr*
Hoover Adams, *Emeritus* ▲
Brenton D Adams, ▲
Mellicent Adams, ▲
EMP: 22 **EST:** 1950
SQ FT: 10,000
SALES (est): 750.19K **Privately Held**
Web: www.mydailyrecord.com
SIC: 2711 Newspapers, publishing and printing

(G-4882)
SALAZAR CUSTOM FRAMING LLC
111 Raynor Sands Dr (28334-8019)
PHONE.....................919 349-0830
Moises Salazar, *Prin*
EMP: 9 **EST:** 2016
SALES (est): 299.52K **Privately Held**
SIC: 2499 Picture frame molding, finished

(G-4883)
SIGN & AWNING SYSTEMS INC
2785 Us 301 N (28334-8383)
PHONE.....................919 892-5900
Jason Honeycutt, *CEO*
Michael R Godwin, ▲
Mickey Hodges, ▲
EMP: 13 **EST:** 1978
SQ FT: 40,000
SALES (est): 440.12K **Privately Held**
Web: www.signandawning.com
SIC: 2394 3993 1799 Canvas awnings and canopies; Electric signs; Awning installation

(G-4884)
SMITH WOODWORKS INC
1607 Clayhole Rd (28334-7067)
P.O. Box 365 (27521-0365)
PHONE.....................910 890-2923
Brandon E Smith, *Pr*
EMP: 8 **EST:** 2011
SALES (est): 445.81K **Privately Held**
SIC: 2431 Millwork

(G-4885)
SOLO WHEELS AND ACCESSORIES
100 N Moon Cir (28334-2700)
PHONE.....................919 333-2945
Wade Cole, *Prin*
EMP: 8 **EST:** 2019
SALES (est): 168.8K **Privately Held**
SIC: 3312 Blast furnaces and steel mills

(G-4886)
TORTILLERIA LA FAVORITA
1113 W Broad St (28334-4604)
PHONE.....................910 892-0302
EMP: 5 **EST:** 2011
SALES (est): 255.66K **Privately Held**
SIC: 2099 Tortillas, fresh or refrigerated

(G-4887)
TRANS EAST INC
Also Called: Southeastern Transformer Co
405 E Edgerton St (28334-4223)
P.O. Box 127 (28335-0127)
PHONE.....................910 892-1081
L Avery Corning Iv, *Pr*
EMP: 51 **EST:** 2001
SQ FT: 5,500
SALES (est): 9.28MM **Privately Held**
Web: www.setransformer.com
SIC: 7629 3612 Electrical equipment repair, high voltage; Power transformers, electric

(G-4888)
TWYFORD PRINTING COMPANY INC
200 E Canary St (28334-5812)
P.O. Box 728 (28335-0728)
PHONE.....................910 892-3271
William V Stephens, *Pr*
Virginia Stephens, *VP*
EMP: 6 **EST:** 1945
SQ FT: 9,800
SALES (est): 511.68K **Privately Held**
Web: www.twyfordprinting.com
SIC: 2752 2759 Offset printing; Letterpress printing

(G-4889)
UNIFIED PALLETS INC
2 Dinan Rd (28334-6753)
PHONE.....................910 891-2571
EMP: 6 **EST:** 2017
SALES (est): 594.56K **Privately Held**
SIC: 2448 Pallets, wood

(G-4890)
WARREN OIL COMPANY LLC (PA)
2340 Us 301 N (28334-8307)
P.O. Box 1507 (28335-1507)
PHONE.....................910 892-6456
William Irvin Warren, *Pr*
Larry Sanderson, ▲
▼ **EMP:** 86 **EST:** 1975
SQ FT: 125,000
SALES (est): 282.38MM
SALES (corp-wide): 282.38MM **Privately Held**
Web: www.warrenoil.com
SIC: 5171 3826 2911 5172 Petroleum bulk stations and terminals; Analytical instruments; Petroleum refining; Lubricating oils and greases

(G-4891)
WILLIAMS MECH & WLDG SVCS LLC
674 O W Ln (28334-1304)
PHONE.....................919 820-5287
Ricky Williams, *Prin*
EMP: 5 **EST:** 2017
SALES (est): 105.28K **Privately Held**
Web: www.williamsmechanicalandwelding.com
SIC: 7692 Welding repair

Durham
Durham County

(G-4892)
131 CANDLE CO
312 Wayne Cir (27707-3040)
PHONE.....................325 650-4903
Amanda Combass, *Prin*
EMP: 4 **EST:** 2017
SALES (est): 39.69K **Privately Held**
SIC: 3999 Candles

(G-4893)
410 MEDICAL INC
68 Tw Alexander Dr (27709-0151)
P.O. Box 110085 (27709-5085)
PHONE.....................919 241-7900
Kyle Chenet, *CEO*
Mark Piehl, *CMO*
Galen Robertson, *COO*
Jamie Baker, *Contrlr*
EMP: 14 **EST:** 2013
SQ FT: 800
SALES (est): 100K **Privately Held**
Web: www.410medical.com
SIC: 3842 Surgical appliances and supplies

(G-4894)
510NANO INC
5441 Lumley Rd Ste 101 (27703-7726)
P.O. Box 110401 (27709-5401)
PHONE.....................919 521-5982
EMP: 10 **EST:** 2011
SALES (est): 913.7K **Privately Held**
Web: www.510nano.com
SIC: 3674 5074 Solar cells; Heating equipment and panels, solar

(G-4895)
A & M PAPER AND PRINTING
4122 Bennett Memorial Road Ste 108 (27705-1209)
PHONE.....................919 813-7852
EMP: 5 **EST:** 2017
SALES (est): 87.41K **Privately Held**
Web: www.ampaperprinting.com
SIC: 2752 Commercial printing, lithographic

(G-4896)
A BETTER IMAGE PRINTING INC
4310 Garrett Rd (27707-3432)
PHONE.....................919 967-0319
Michael Celeste, *Managing Member*
Diana Minta, *Pr*
Steve Minta, *VP*
EMP: 12 **EST:** 1985
SQ FT: 1,600
SALES (est): 1.41MM **Privately Held**
Web: www.abetterimageprinting.com
SIC: 2752 Offset printing

(G-4897)
A&B INTEGRATORS LLC
Also Called: Security 101 Raleigh
2800 Meridian Pkwy (27713-5252)
PHONE.....................919 371-0750
EMP: 14 **EST:** 2014
SALES (est): 2.17MM **Privately Held**
SIC: 5065 3699 5072 7382 Security control equipment and systems; Security control equipment and systems; Security devices, locks; Burglar alarm maintenance and monitoring

(G-4898)
AC IMPORTS LLC
6211 Cabin Branch Dr (27712-9090)
PHONE.....................919 229-6650
Osvaldo Diaz, *Prin*
EMP: 5 **EST:** 2015
SALES (est): 188.3K **Privately Held**
SIC: 4731 2095 Freight transportation arrangement; Roasted coffee

(G-4899)
ACADEMY ASSOCIATION INC
Also Called: Eli Research It Journals
2222 Sedwick Rd Ste 101 (27713-2658)
PHONE.....................919 544-0835
Leslie Norins, *Brnch Mgr*
EMP: 17
SALES (corp-wide): 8.71MM **Privately Held**
SIC: 8243 8742 2721 Software training, computer; Management consulting services ; Periodicals
PA: Academy Association, Inc.
2222 Sedwick Rd
Durham NC 27713
919 544-0835

(G-4900)
ACERAGEN INC
15 Tw Alexander Dr 418 (27709-0152)
PHONE.....................919 271-1032
EMP: 10 **EST:** 2021
SALES (est): 27.98K **Publicly Held**
Web: www.aceragen.com
SIC: 2834 Pharmaceutical preparations
PA: Idera Pharmaceuticals, Inc.
505 Eagleview Blvd # 212
Exton PA 19341

(G-4901)
ACHELIOS THERAPEUTICS LLC
4364 S Alston Ave Ste 300 (27713-2565)
P.O. Box 13965 (27709-3965)
PHONE.....................919 354-6233
EMP: 5 **EST:** 2012
SALES (est): 493.7K **Privately Held**
Web: www.achelios.com
SIC: 2834 Pharmaceutical preparations

(G-4902)
AD SPICE MARKETING LLC
4310 Garrett Rd (27707-3432)
PHONE.....................919 286-7110
EMP: 5 **EST:** 2012
SQ FT: 2,000
SALES (est): 377.53K **Privately Held**
Web: adspicemarketing.espwebsite.com
SIC: 7389 2752 Advertising, promotional, and trade show services; Promotional printing, lithographic

GEOGRAPHIC SECTION

Durham - Durham County (G-4929)

(G-4903)
ADAMA US
4134 S Alston Ave (27713-1870)
PHONE.................919 817-7103
EMP: 4 **EST:** 2019
SALES (est): 65.44K **Privately Held**
SIC: 3577 Computer peripheral equipment, nec

(G-4904)
ADVANCED DIGITAL SYSTEMS INC
Also Called: Mi-
4601 Creekstone Dr Ste 180 (27703-8496)
P.O. Box 991 (24063-0991)
PHONE.................919 485-4819
Gregory J Clary, *Pr*
James Clary, *Ch*
Chris Dipierro, *Ofcr*
David Nakamura, *Ofcr*
Will Shook, *Ofcr*
EMP: 11 **EST:** 1999
SQ FT: 5,000
SALES (est): 2.67MM **Privately Held**
Web: www.mi-corporation.com
SIC: 7371 7372 Computer software development; Prepackaged software

(G-4905)
AERAMI THERAPEUTICS INC (PA)
600 Park Offices Dr (27709-1009)
PHONE.................650 773-5926
EMP: 12 **EST:** 2009
SALES (est): 4.74MM **Privately Held**
Web: www.aerami.com
SIC: 2834 Pharmaceutical preparations

(G-4906)
AERAMI THRPEUTICS HOLDINGS INC
2520 Meridian Pkwy Ste 400 (27713-4202)
PHONE.................919 589-7495
EMP: 6
SALES (est): 521.64K **Privately Held**
Web: www.aerami.com
SIC: 2834 Pharmaceutical preparations

(G-4907)
AERIE PHARMACEUTICALS INC (HQ)
4301 Emperor Blvd Ste 400 (27703-7615)
PHONE.................919 237-5300
EMP: 8 **EST:** 2005
SQ FT: 61,000
SALES (est): 194.13MM **Privately Held**
Web: www.alcon.com
SIC: 2834 Pharmaceutical preparations
PA: Alcon Ag
0
Freiburg FR 1701

(G-4908)
AIRGAS USA LLC
Also Called: Airgas
2810 S Miami Blvd (27703-9247)
PHONE.................919 544-1056
James Beasley, *Mgr*
EMP: 5
SALES (corp-wide): 101.26MM **Privately Held**
Web: www.airgas.com
SIC: 2813 5169 5999 Dry ice, carbon dioxide (solid); Dry ice; Ice
HQ: Airgas Usa, Llc
259 N Radnor Chester Rd
Radnor PA 19087
216 642-6600

(G-4909)
AIRGAS USA LLC
630 United Dr (27713-1407)
PHONE.................919 544-3773
Charlie Winston, *Brnch Mgr*
EMP: 6
SALES (corp-wide): 101.26MM **Privately Held**
Web: www.airgas.com
SIC: 5169 5084 5085 2813 Industrial gases; Welding machinery and equipment; Welding supplies; Industrial gases
HQ: Airgas Usa, Llc
259 N Radnor Chester Rd
Radnor PA 19087
216 642-6600

(G-4910)
AISIN NORTH CAROLINA CORP (DH)
4112 Old Oxford Rd (27712-9428)
P.O. Box 15970 (27704-0970)
PHONE.................919 479-6400
Shuji Oda, *CEO*
Shigeo Tsuzuki, *
Mitsuru Fukumoto, *
Takashi Kurauchi, *
◆ **EMP:** 1800 **EST:** 1998
SQ FT: 316,000
SALES (est): 486.95MM **Privately Held**
Web: www.aisinnc.com
SIC: 3714 Transmissions, motor vehicle
HQ: Aisin Holdings Of America, Inc.
1665 E 4th Street Rd
Seymour IN 47274
812 524-8144

(G-4911)
ALCAMI CAROLINAS CORPORATION
Also Called: Alcami
4620 Creekstone Dr Ste 200 (27703-0108)
PHONE.................919 957-5500
Stephan Kutzer, *Mgr*
EMP: 7
SALES (corp-wide): 418.48MM **Privately Held**
Web: www.alcami.com
SIC: 2834 Pharmaceutical preparations
HQ: Alcami Carolinas Corporation
2320 Scientific Park Dr
Wilmington NC 28405

(G-4912)
ALPHAMED COMPANY INC (PA)
Also Called: Alphamed Press
6100 Guess Rd (27712-9278)
P.O. Box 12723 (27709-2723)
PHONE.................919 680-0011
EMP: 7 **EST:** 1996
SALES (est): 1.31MM **Privately Held**
Web: www.alphamedpress.com
SIC: 2741 Miscellaneous publishing

(G-4913)
AMBCOPY LLC
214 Crisp Rd (27713-9669)
PHONE.................919 308-1033
EMP: 5 **EST:** 2018
SALES (est): 79.15K **Privately Held**
Web: www.ambcopy.com
SIC: 2741 Miscellaneous publishing

(G-4914)
AMBIENT NOISE CONTROL LLC
2903 Carver St (27705-2025)
PHONE.................919 477-6791
Tim Marbrey, *Prin*
EMP: 6 **EST:** 2012
SALES (est): 148.39K **Privately Held**
SIC: 3625 Noise control equipment

(G-4915)
AMERICAN INST CRTIF PUB ACCNTN (PA)
Also Called: American Institute of Cpas
220 Leigh Farm Rd (27707-8110)
P.O. Box 52383 (27717-2383)
PHONE.................919 402-0682
Barry C Melancon, *CPA*
Eric L Hansen, *
Tim Kristen, *
Gregory J Anton C.p.a., *Vice Chairman*
Richard Miller, *
▲ **EMP:** 450 **EST:** 1887
SQ FT: 105,000
SALES (est): 80.31MM
SALES (corp-wide): 80.31MM **Privately Held**
SIC: 8299 8621 2721 Educational service, nondegree granting: continuing educ.; Professional organizations; Periodicals, publishing only

(G-4916)
AMKOR TECHNOLOGY INC
3021 Cornwallis Rd (27709-0146)
PHONE.................919 248-1800
Wayne Machon, *Brnch Mgr*
EMP: 8
SALES (corp-wide): 6.5B **Publicly Held**
Web: www.amkor.com
SIC: 3674 Integrated circuits, semiconductor networks, etc.
PA: Amkor Technology, Inc.
2045 E Innovation Cir
Tempe AZ 85284
480 821-5000

(G-4917)
AMPAC MACHINERY LLC
319 Us 70 Service Rd (27703-4525)
P.O. Box 21077 (27703-1077)
PHONE.................919 596-5320
EMP: 10 **EST:** 2009
SALES (est): 2.15MM **Privately Held**
Web: www.ampacmachinery.com
SIC: 3531 Aggregate spreaders

(G-4918)
ANALOG DEVICES INC
4001 Nc Hwy 54 Ste 3100 (27709-0101)
PHONE.................336 202-6503
EMP: 8
SALES (corp-wide): 12.31B **Publicly Held**
SIC: 3674 Integrated circuits, semiconductor networks, etc.
PA: Analog Devices, Inc.
1 Analog Way
Wilmington MA 01887
781 935-5565

(G-4919)
ANDERSON DESIGNS
3406 Westover Rd (27707-5029)
PHONE.................919 489-1514
Mary Anderson, *Prin*
EMP: 4 **EST:** 2016
SALES (est): 94K **Privately Held**
SIC: 3993 Signs and advertising specialties

(G-4920)
APIDAE PRINTS
601 Ramseur St (27701-3735)
P.O. Box 2 (08542-0002)
PHONE.................413 320-3839
EMP: 4 **EST:** 2015
SALES (est): 93.41K **Privately Held**
SIC: 2752 Commercial printing, lithographic

(G-4921)
APOLLONIAS CANDLES THINGS LLC
2112 Broad St Apt E8 (27705-3430)
PHONE.................910 408-2508
Apollonia Fassett, *Owner*
EMP: 4 **EST:** 2016
SALES (est): 58.25K **Privately Held**
SIC: 3999 Candles

(G-4922)
AQUA ANALYTICA PRESS INC
1024 Laceflower Dr (27713-2568)
PHONE.................336 263-6612
EMP: 4 **EST:** 2019
SALES (est): 62.35K **Privately Held**
SIC: 2741 Miscellaneous publishing

(G-4923)
ARCHIVESOCIAL INC
Also Called: Archivesocial
212 W Main St Ste 500 (27701-3239)
P.O. Box 3330 (27702-3330)
PHONE.................888 558-6032
Anil Chawla, *Pr*
EMP: 41 **EST:** 2011
SALES (est): 4.53MM **Privately Held**
Web: www.archivesocial.com
SIC: 7372 Utility computer software

(G-4924)
ARMORRI COSMETICS LLC
5534 Sunlight Dr Apt 108 (27707-9062)
PHONE.................910 352-6209
Shanta Outlaw, *CEO*
Shanta Outlaw, *Prin*
Sareece Armwood, *Prin*
Demetrice Armwood, *Prin*
EMP: 4 **EST:** 2019
SALES (est): 95.24K **Privately Held**
SIC: 2844 Cosmetic preparations

(G-4925)
ART SIGN CO
209 S Goley St (27701-4203)
P.O. Box 11116 (27703-0116)
PHONE.................919 596-8681
EMP: 5 **EST:** 1954
SALES (est): 246.72K **Privately Held**
Web: www.artsignco.com
SIC: 3993 Signs and advertising specialties

(G-4926)
ARTHUR WOODWORKING
1805 Vale St (27703-4060)
PHONE.................919 381-0329
David Arthur, *Prin*
EMP: 5 **EST:** 2016
SALES (est): 59.54K **Privately Held**
SIC: 2431 Millwork

(G-4927)
ARTISTIC IRONWORKS LLC
700 E Club Blvd Ste B (27704-4506)
PHONE.................919 908-6888
EMP: 9 **EST:** 2015
SALES (est): 435.49K **Privately Held**
SIC: 3499 3462 Metal household articles; Iron and steel forgings

(G-4928)
ASENSUS SURGICAL INC (PA)
1 Tw Alexander Dr Ste 160 (27703-7035)
PHONE.................919 765-8400
EMP: 4 **EST:** 1988
SQ FT: 27,807
SALES (est): 7.09MM **Publicly Held**
Web: www.asensus.com
SIC: 3841 Surgical instruments and apparatus

(G-4929)
ASKBIO ✪
8 Davis Dr (27709-0003)
PHONE.................336 407-6217
EMP: 6 **EST:** 2022
SALES (est): 297.72K **Privately Held**
Web: www.askbio.com

Durham - Durham County (G-4930) *GEOGRAPHIC SECTION*

SIC: 2834 Pharmaceutical preparations

(G-4930)
ASSOCTION INTL CRTIF PROF ACCN (PA)
220 Leigh Farm Rd (27707-8110)
PHONE.................................919 402-4500
Barry Melancon, *CEO*
Michael J Buddendeck, *
EMP: 550 EST: 2016
SQ FT: 125,000
SALES (est): 44.43MM
SALES (corp-wide): 44.43MM **Privately Held**
Web: www.aicpa-cima.com
SIC: 8299 8621 2721 Educational service, nondegree granting; continuing educ.; Professional organizations; Periodicals, publishing only

(G-4931)
ASTRAZENECA PHARMACEUTICALS LP
4222 Emperor Blvd Ste 560 (27703-8466)
PHONE.................................919 647-4990
Charles J Bramlage, *Pr*
EMP: 63
SALES (corp-wide): 45.81B **Privately Held**
Web: www.astrazeneca.com
SIC: 2834 Pharmaceutical preparations
HQ: Astrazeneca Pharmaceuticals Lp
1800 Concord Pike
Wilmington DE 19850

(G-4932)
ATLANTIC PROSTHETICS ORTHTCS
6208 Fayetteville Rd # 101 (27713-6286)
PHONE.................................919 806-3260
Brandon Barham, *Pr*
EMP: 6 EST: 2017
SALES (est): 117.12K **Privately Held**
SIC: 3842 Prosthetic appliances

(G-4933)
ATLANTIS GRAPHICS INC (PA)
Also Called: Universal Printing & Pubg
2410 E Nc Highway 54 (27713-2254)
PHONE.................................919 361-5809
Robert Moura, *Pr*
Sandra Moura, *
EMP: 34 EST: 1979
SQ FT: 17,500
SALES (est): 4.67MM
SALES (corp-wide): 4.67MM **Privately Held**
Web: www.universalprinting.com
SIC: 2791 2752 2789 Typesetting; Offset printing; Bookbinding and related work

(G-4934)
ATLAS BOX AND CRATING CO INC
3829 S Miami Blvd Ste 100 (27703-5419)
PHONE.................................919 941-1023
EMP: 5 EST: 2018
SALES (est): 176.94K **Privately Held**
SIC: 2448 Pallets, wood

(G-4935)
ATSENA THERAPEUTICS INC
280 S Mangum St Ste 350 (27701-3681)
PHONE.................................352 273-9342
Patrick Ritschel, *CEO*
Kenji Fujita, *CMO*
Linda B Couto, *CSO*
EMP: 20 EST: 2019
SALES (est): 3.56MM **Privately Held**
Web: www.atsenatx.com
SIC: 2834 Pharmaceutical preparations

(G-4936)
AUROBINDO PHARMA USA INC
2929 Weck Dr (27709-0186)
P.O. Box 12167 (27709-2167)
PHONE.................................732 839-9400
EMP: 37 EST: 2015
SALES (est): 10.52MM **Privately Held**
Web: www.aurobindousa.com
SIC: 2834 Pharmaceutical preparations
PA: Aurobindo Pharma Limited
Galaxy, Floors 22-24, Plot No. 1, Survey No.83/1
Hyderabad TG 50003

(G-4937)
AUROLIFE PHARMA LLC
2929 Weck Dr (27709-0186)
PHONE.................................732 839-9408
Gangadhar Gorla, *VP Fin*
EMP: 40
Web: www.aurolifepharma.com
SIC: 2834 Pharmaceutical preparations
HQ: Aurolife Pharma Llc
2400 Us Highway 130
Dayton NJ 08810

(G-4938)
AVIOQ INC
76 Tw Alexander Dr (27709-0152)
P.O. Box 12808 (27709-2808)
PHONE.................................919 314-5535
Chamroen Chetty, *CEO*
X James Li, *Prin*
Zhiyuan Che, *
Xingxiang Li, *Bd of Dir*
Samuel Chetty, *
▲ EMP: 49 EST: 2008
SQ FT: 80,000
SALES (est): 13.5MM **Privately Held**
Web: www.avioq.com
SIC: 3841 Diagnostic apparatus, medical
PA: Shandong Oriental Ocean Sci-Tech Co.,Ltd.
No.18 Aokema St., Laishan Dist.
Yantai SD 26400

(G-4939)
AVISTA PHARMA SOLUTIONS INC (HQ)
Also Called: Cambrex
3501 Tricenter Blvd Ste C (27713-1868)
PHONE.................................919 544-8600
Patrick Walsh, *CEO*
Eric Evans, *
Cathy Butler, *
Ken Domagalski, *
EMP: 50 EST: 2011
SQ FT: 200,000
SALES (est): 48.92MM
SALES (corp-wide): 523.07MM **Privately Held**
Web: www.avistapharma.com
SIC: 8734 2834 Testing laboratories; Pharmaceutical preparations
PA: Cambrex Corporation
1 Meadowlands Plz # 1510
East Rutherford NJ 07073
201 804-3000

(G-4940)
B3 BIO INC
6 Davis Dr (27709-0003)
PHONE.................................919 226-3079
Robert Bonczek, *Pr*
EMP: 9 EST: 2008
SALES (est): 868.32K **Privately Held**
SIC: 2834 Pharmaceutical preparations

(G-4941)
BAE SYSTEMS INFO ELCTRNIC SYST
Also Called: BAE SYSTEMS INFORMATION AND ELECTRONIC SYSTEMS INTEGRATION INC.
4721 Emperor Blvd Ste 330 (27703-8580)
PHONE.................................919 323-5800
James Baxter, *II Technology Development*
EMP: 41
SALES (corp-wide): 25.59B **Privately Held**
Web: www.baesystems.com
SIC: 3663 7371 Global positioning systems (GPS) equipment; Computer software development and applications
HQ: Bae Systems Information And Electronic Systems Integration Inc.
65 Spit Brook Rd
Nashua NH 03060
603 885-4321

(G-4942)
BAEBIES INC
25 Alexandria Way (27709-0300)
P.O. Box 14403 (27709-4403)
PHONE.................................919 891-0432
Richard West, *CEO*
EMP: 85 EST: 2014
SQ FT: 30,000
SALES (est): 22.15MM **Privately Held**
Web: www.baebies.com
SIC: 2835 In vitro diagnostics

(G-4943)
BARRETTE WELCH MCFALL MS
3705 Saint Marks Rd (27707-5010)
PHONE.................................919 606-7537
Barrette Welch Mcfall, *Prin*
EMP: 5 EST: 2011
SALES (est): 117.84K **Privately Held**
SIC: 3999 Barrettes

(G-4944)
BASF CORPORATION
2 Tw Alexander Dr (27709-0144)
P.O. Box 13911 (27709-3911)
PHONE.................................919 433-6773
EMP: 83
SALES (corp-wide): 74.89B **Privately Held**
Web: www.basf.com
SIC: 2869 Industrial organic chemicals, nec
HQ: Basf Corporation
100 Park Ave
Florham Park NJ 07932
800 962-7831

(G-4945)
BASF CORPORATION
26 Davis Dr (27709-0003)
P.O. Box 13528 (27709-3528)
PHONE.................................919 547-2000
John Rabby, *Brnch Mgr*
EMP: 1200
SALES (corp-wide): 74.89B **Privately Held**
Web: www.basf.com
SIC: 2869 Industrial organic chemicals, nec
HQ: Basf Corporation
100 Park Ave
Florham Park NJ 07932
800 962-7831

(G-4946)
BASF PLANT SCIENCE LP
26 Davis Dr (27709-0003)
P.O. Box 13528 (27709-3528)
PHONE.................................919 547-2000
Peter Eckes, *CEO*
EMP: 100 EST: 1999
SALES (est): 26.74MM
SALES (corp-wide): 74.89B **Privately Held**
Web: www.basf.com

SIC: 2869 Industrial organic chemicals, nec
PA: Basf Se
Carl-Bosch-Str. 38
Ludwigshafen Am Rhein RP 67056
621600

(G-4947)
BATTLE FERMENTABLES LLC (PA) ◆
1604 Lathrop St (27703-2136)
PHONE.................................336 225-4585
EMP: 6 EST: 2022
SALES (est): 389.87K
SALES (corp-wide): 389.87K **Privately Held**
SIC: 2084 Wines, brandy, and brandy spirits

(G-4948)
BAUSCH HEALTH AMERICAS INC
406 Blackwell St Ste 410 (27701-3985)
PHONE.................................949 461-6000
EMP: 14
SALES (corp-wide): 8.05B **Privately Held**
Web: www.bauschhealth.com
SIC: 5912 2834 Drug stores and proprietary stores; Pharmaceutical preparations
HQ: Bausch Health Americas, Inc.
400 Somerset Corp Blvd
Bridgewater NJ 08807
908 927-1400

(G-4949)
BAYER CORPORATION
Also Called: Bayer Agriculture
2 Tw Alexander Dr (27709-0144)
PHONE.................................800 242-5897
James Kahl, *Dir*
EMP: 43
SALES (corp-wide): 51.78B **Privately Held**
Web: cropscience.bayer.com
SIC: 2834 Pills, pharmaceutical
HQ: Bayer Corporation
100 Bayer Blvd
Whippany NJ 07981
412 777-2000

(G-4950)
BAYER CROPSCIENCE INC
2400 Ellis Rd (27703-5543)
P.O. Box 526 (63166-0526)
PHONE.................................412 777-2000
◆ EMP: 68 EST: 2011
SALES (est): 46.65MM
SALES (corp-wide): 51.78B **Privately Held**
Web: cropscience.bayer.us
SIC: 2834 Pharmaceutical preparations
HQ: Bayer Corporation
100 Bayer Blvd
Whippany NJ 07981
412 777-2000

(G-4951)
BECKETT MEDIA LP
2222 Sedwick Rd Ste 102 (27713-2658)
PHONE.................................800 508-2582
Greg Lindberg, *Pt*
EMP: 15 EST: 2011
SALES (est): 411.65K **Privately Held**
Web: www.beckett.com
SIC: 2741 Newsletter publishing

(G-4952)
BECTON DICKINSON AND COMPANY
Also Called: Bd Medical Technology
21 Davis Dr (27709-0003)
PHONE.................................201 847-6800
EMP: 300
SALES (corp-wide): 19.37B **Publicly Held**
Web: www.bd.com

SIC: 3841 Hypodermic needles and syringes
PA: Becton, Dickinson And Company
1 Becton Dr
Franklin Lakes NJ 07417
201 847-6800

(G-4953)
BELL AND HOWELL LLC (PA)
3791 S Alston Ave (27713-1880)
PHONE.................................919 767-4401
▲ EMP: 1259 EST: 1907
SALES (est): 335.94MM Privately Held
Web: www.bellhowell.net
SIC: 3579 Envelope stuffing, sealing, and addressing machines

(G-4954)
BELL AND HOWELL LLC
Also Called: Bh Holdings
3791 S Alston Ave (27713-1880)
PHONE.................................919 767-6400
EMP: 20 EST: 2010
SALES (est): 841.87K Privately Held
Web: www.bellhowell.net
SIC: 3579 Mailing machines

(G-4955)
BENNETT & ASSOCIATES INC
Also Called: Sir Speedy
3312 Guess Rd (27705-2106)
PHONE.................................919 477-7362
Terry M Bennett, Pr
EMP: 8 EST: 1982
SQ FT: 2,400
SALES (est): 854.68K Privately Held
Web: www.sirspeedy.com
SIC: 2752 2791 2789 Commercial printing, lithographic; Typesetting; Bookbinding and related work

(G-4956)
BILL S IRON SHOP INC
Also Called: Bill's Ornamental Iron Shop
2243 Glover Rd (27703-6032)
P.O. Box 11487 (27703-0487)
PHONE.................................919 596-8360
Bill Emory, Pr
Larry Emory, VP
EMP: 4 EST: 1964
SQ FT: 8,000
SALES (est): 465.61K Privately Held
Web: www.billironshopinc.com
SIC: 3441 Fabricated structural metal

(G-4957)
BILLSOFT INC
Also Called: Eztax
512 S Mangum St Ste 100 (27701-3973)
PHONE.................................913 859-9674
Timothy J Lopatofsky, Pr
Maria Hoofer, *
Amanda Meglemre, *
Vicki J Klein, *
Staci K Grew, *
EMP: 28 EST: 1997
SALES (est): 2.77MM Privately Held
Web: www.avalara.com
SIC: 7373 7372 Systems software development services; Prepackaged software

(G-4958)
BIOCRYST PHARMACEUTICALS INC (PA)
Also Called: BIOCRYST
4505 Emperor Blvd Ste 200 (27703-8457)
PHONE.................................919 859-1302
Jon P Stonehouse, Pr
Robert A Ingram, *
Anthony J Doyle, CFO
Alane P Barnes, CLO

Charles K Gayer, CCO
▲ EMP: 431 EST: 1986
SQ FT: 24,500
SALES (est): 331.41MM Publicly Held
Web: www.biocryst.com
SIC: 2834 Pharmaceutical preparations

(G-4959)
BIOGEN MA INC
5000 Davis Dr (27709-0200)
P.O. Box 14627 (27709-4627)
PHONE.................................919 941-1100
Hal Price, Genl Mgr
EMP: 126
SALES (corp-wide): 9.84MM Publicly Held
Web: www.biogen.com
SIC: 2834 Pharmaceutical preparations
HQ: Biogen Ma Inc.
225 Binney St
Cambridge MA 02142
617 679-2000

(G-4960)
BIOMERIEUX INC (DH)
100 Rodolphe St (27712-9402)
PHONE.................................919 620-2000
Brian Armstrong, Pr
Gary Mills, *
▲ EMP: 500 EST: 1977
SALES (est): 473.35MM
SALES (corp-wide): 7.5MM Privately Held
Web: www.biomerieux-usa.com
SIC: 3845 8071 3841 3826 Automated blood and body fluid analyzers, except lab; Medical laboratories; Surgical and medical instruments; Analytical instruments
HQ: Biomerieux Sa
376 Chemin De L Orme
Marcy L Etoile 69280
478872000

(G-4961)
BIOTECH PRSTHTICS ORTHTICS DRH
314 Crutchfield St (27704-2725)
PHONE.................................919 471-4994
Michael Astilla, Pr
EMP: 8 EST: 2001
SALES (est): 2.81MM
SALES (corp-wide): 1.12B Privately Held
Web: www.biotechnc.com
SIC: 3842 Limbs, artificial
PA: Hanger, Inc.
10910 Domain Dr Ste 300
Austin TX 78758
512 777-3800

(G-4962)
BIOVENTUS INC (PA)
Also Called: BIOVENTUS
4721 Emperor Blvd Ste 100 (27703-7663)
PHONE.................................919 474-6700
Kenneth M Reali, CEO
William A Hawkins, Ch Bd
John E Nosenzo, CCO
Gregory O Anglum, Sr VP
Katrina Church, Chief Compliance Officer
EMP: 39 EST: 2012
SALES (est): 512.35MM
SALES (corp-wide): 512.35MM Publicly Held
Web: www.bioventus.com
SIC: 3841 3843 Surgical and medical instruments; Orthodontic appliances

(G-4963)
BIOVENTUS LLC (HQ)
4721 Emperor Blvd Ste 100 (27703-7663)
PHONE.................................800 396-4325
Ken Reali, CEO

Greg Anglum, *
John Nosenzo, *
Anthony D'adamio, Sr VP
▲ EMP: 100 EST: 2012
SALES (est): 99.53MM
SALES (corp-wide): 512.35MM Publicly Held
Web: www.bioventus.com
SIC: 3845 5122 Ultrasonic medical equipment, except cleaning; Pharmaceuticals
PA: Bioventus Inc.
4721 Emperor Blvd Ste 100
Durham NC 27703
919 474-6700

(G-4964)
BLACK TIRE SERVICE INC
1400 E Geer St (27704-5039)
PHONE.................................919 908-6347
Ricky Benton, Pr
▲ EMP: 7 EST: 2012
SALES (est): 233.43K Privately Held
Web: bts.tireweb.com
SIC: 3011 Tires and inner tubes

(G-4965)
BLU DISTILLING COMPANY LLC
Also Called: Liberty & Plenty Distillery
609 Foster St (27701-2108)
PHONE.................................919 999-6736
EMP: 22
SALES (corp-wide): 70.88K Privately Held
SIC: 2085 Distilled and blended liquors
PA: Blu Distilling Company Llc
3420 Landor Rd
Raleigh NC 27609
919 999-6736

(G-4966)
BLUE BAY DISTRIBUTING INC
3720 Appling Way (27703-9227)
P.O. Box 31807 (27622-1807)
PHONE.................................919 957-1300
Sharon Cronauer, Pr
Robert Cronauer, VP
EMP: 7 EST: 1995
SQ FT: 2,300
SALES (est): 540K Privately Held
Web: www.bluebaydist.com
SIC: 2253 T-shirts and tops, knit

(G-4967)
BLUE LZARD CSTM SCRNPRNTING IN
2305 Orangewood Dr Ste 108 (27705-2238)
PHONE.................................919 296-9041
Anthony W Holleman, Pr
EMP: 5 EST: 2015
SALES (est): 124.99K Privately Held
Web: www.bluelizardscreenprinting.com
SIC: 2759 Screen printing

(G-4968)
BMC STUDIOS
240 Erlwood Way Apt 204 (27704-5906)
PHONE.................................443 547-7319
Brittany Mcinnis, Prin
EMP: 4 EST: 2017
SALES (est): 95.25K Privately Held
SIC: 7372 Prepackaged software

(G-4969)
BODY BILLBOARDS INC
4905 S Alston Ave (27713-4424)
PHONE.................................919 544-4540
William R Drago, Pr
EMP: 9 EST: 1982
SQ FT: 8,000
SALES (est): 414.14K Privately Held

Web: www.bodybillboards.com
SIC: 7336 2759 2396 2395 Silk screen design; Screen printing; Automotive and apparel trimmings; Pleating and stitching

(G-4970)
BOLES INDUSTRIES LLC
112 Landsbury Dr (27707-2412)
PHONE.................................919 489-9254
Kathy Dutton, Prin
EMP: 4 EST: 2018
SALES (est): 65.01K Privately Held
SIC: 3999 Manufacturing industries, nec

(G-4971)
BOLTON INVESTORS INC
Also Called: Portable Outdoor Equipment
4914 N Roxboro St Ste 7 (27704-1464)
PHONE.................................919 471-1197
Melissa Bolton, Pr
EMP: 7 EST: 1990
SQ FT: 3,600
SALES (est): 684.04K Privately Held
Web: portableoutdoorequipmentdurham.stihldealer.net
SIC: 3546 5063 5251 Saws and sawing equipment; Generators; Tools, power

(G-4972)
BOOKCASE SHOP (PA)
Also Called: Durham Bookcases
301 S Duke St (27701-2820)
PHONE.................................919 683-1922
Elaine S Fletcher, Pr
Phillip S Fletcher, VP
EMP: 5 EST: 1992
SQ FT: 26,000
SALES (est): 984.53K Privately Held
Web: www.bookcaseshop.com
SIC: 2511 5021 Wood household furniture; Bookcases

(G-4973)
BORAMED INC
4800 Centerway Dr (27705-5482)
PHONE.................................919 419-9518
Andrew W Kennedy, Pr
EMP: 7 EST: 1997
SQ FT: 30,000
SALES (est): 99.06K Privately Held
SIC: 7389 3082 Personal service agents, brokers, and bureaus; Unsupported plastics profile shapes

(G-4974)
BOTTOM LINE TECHNOLOGIES INC
Also Called: Enviroclean Solutions
1000 Parliament Ct # 310 (27703-0088)
PHONE.................................919 472-0541
EMP: 10 EST: 2008
SALES (est): 505.31K Privately Held
SIC: 2841 Soap and other detergents

(G-4975)
BPL USA LLC
302 E Pettigrew St Ste C190 (27701-3712)
PHONE.................................919 354-8405
EMP: 10 EST: 2017
SALES (est): 410.03K Privately Held
Web: www.kedrion.us
SIC: 2834 Pharmaceutical preparations

(G-4976)
BRIAN ALLEN ARTISAN PRINTER
807 E Main St Ste 3141 (27701-4076)
P.O. Box 15884 (27704-0884)
PHONE.................................919 609-8992
Brian Allen, Owner
EMP: 4 EST: 2017

Durham - Durham County (G-4977) — GEOGRAPHIC SECTION

SALES (est): 79.56K **Privately Held**
Web: www.artisanprinter.com
SIC: 2752 Commercial printing, lithographic

(G-4977)
BRIDGESTONE RET OPERATIONS LLC
Also Called: Firestone
3809 N Duke St (27704-1727)
PHONE...............................919 471-4468
Colt Hunter, Mgr
EMP: 9
SQ FT: 5,176
Web: www.bridgestoneamericas.com
SIC: 5531 7534 Automotive tires; Rebuilding and retreading tires
HQ: Bridgestone Retail Operations, Llc
 333 E Lake St Ste 300
 Bloomingdale IL 60108
 630 259-9000

(G-4978)
BRIGHT VIEW TECHNOLOGIES CORP
4022 Stirrup Creek Dr Ste 301 (27703-8971)
PHONE...............................919 228-4370
Jennifer Aspell, CEO
Emily Friedman, CFO
EMP: 23 EST: 2002
SQ FT: 37,000
SALES (est): 9MM **Publicly Held**
Web: www.brightviewtechnologies.com
SIC: 3081 Plastics film and sheet
PA: Tredegar Corporation
 1100 Boulders Pkwy # 200
 North Chesterfield VA 23225

(G-4979)
BRIGHTFISH PRESS
2514 State St (27704-4442)
PHONE...............................919 452-5737
Jennifer Mcconnel, Owner
EMP: 5 EST: 2012
SALES (est): 105.19K **Privately Held**
SIC: 2741 Miscellaneous publishing

(G-4980)
BRII BIOSCIENCES INC
110 N Corcoran St Unit 5-130 (27701-5015)
PHONE...............................919 240-5605
Zhi Hong, CEO
EMP: 11 EST: 2018
SALES (est): 1.39MM **Privately Held**
Web: www.briibio.com
SIC: 2834 Pharmaceutical preparations

(G-4981)
BROADCOM CORPORATION
1030 Swabia Ct Ste 400 (27703-8070)
PHONE...............................919 865-2954
EMP: 51
SALES (corp-wide): 35.82B **Publicly Held**
Web: www.broadcom.com
SIC: 3674 Integrated circuits, semiconductor networks, etc.
HQ: Broadcom Corporation
 1320 Ridder Park Dr
 San Jose CA 95131

(G-4982)
BROMMA INC
4400 Ben Franklin Blvd Ste 200 (27704-2386)
PHONE...............................919 620-8039
Terry E Howell, Pr
Johnny Alvarsson, Ch Bd
Robert H Clark, VP
◆ EMP: 33 EST: 1982
SQ FT: 65,000
SALES (est): 2.35MM **Privately Held**
Web: www.bromma.com
SIC: 3531 3537 Aggregate spreaders; Industrial trucks and tractors

(G-4983)
BRONTO SOFTWARE LLC
324 Blackwell St Ste 410 (27701-3600)
PHONE...............................919 595-2500
Joe Colopy, CEO
Chaz Felix, *
EMP: 109 EST: 2002
SQ FT: 14,000
SALES (est): 29.82MM
SALES (corp-wide): 49.95B **Publicly Held**
SIC: 7372 Prepackaged software
HQ: Netsuite, Inc.
 2955 Campus Dr Ste 100
 San Mateo CA 94403
 650 627-1000

(G-4984)
BUDD-PIPER ROOFING COMPANY
506 Ramseur St (27701-4891)
P.O. Box 708 (27702-0708)
PHONE...............................919 682-2121
Charles A Budd, Pr
Joseph E King, VP
EMP: 16 EST: 1905
SQ FT: 20,000
SALES (est): 436.01K **Privately Held**
SIC: 1761 3444 Roofing contractor; Sheet metalwork

(G-4985)
BUFFALO CRUSHED STONE INC
Also Called: Carolina Sunrock
1503 Camden Ave (27704-4609)
PHONE...............................919 688-6881
EMP: 14
SALES (corp-wide): 1.15B **Privately Held**
Web: www.nesl.com
SIC: 1422 Crushed and broken limestone
HQ: Buffalo Crushed Stone, Inc.
 500 Como Park Blvd
 Buffalo NY 14227
 716 826-7310

(G-4986)
BULL CITY DESIGNS LLC
Also Called: B C D
1111 Neville St (27701-2681)
PHONE...............................919 908-6252
EMP: 24 EST: 2011
SALES (est): 2.95MM **Privately Held**
Web: www.bullcitydesigns.com
SIC: 2521 2514 2519 7389 Wood office furniture; Household furniture: upholstered on metal frames; Household furniture, except wood or metal: upholstered; Design, commercial and industrial

(G-4987)
BULL CITY PRESS LLC
1217 Odyssey Dr (27713-1772)
PHONE...............................919 883-5585
Ross White, Prin
EMP: 7 EST: 2010
SALES (est): 49K **Privately Held**
Web: www.bullcitypress.com
SIC: 2741 Miscellaneous publishing

(G-4988)
BULL CITY SHEET METAL LLC
4008 Comfort Ln (27705-6177)
PHONE...............................919 354-0993
EMP: 10 EST: 2019
SALES (est): 2.14MM **Privately Held**
Web: www.bullcitysheetmetal.com
SIC: 3444 Sheet metalwork

(G-4989)
BULL CY ARTS COLLABORATIVE LLC
401 Foster St Ste B1 (27701-2184)
PHONE...............................919 949-4847
Dave Wofford, Prin
EMP: 5 EST: 2010
SALES (est): 91.79K **Privately Held**
Web: www.wholesalejerseysnflforcheapest.com
SIC: 2752 Commercial printing, lithographic

(G-4990)
BULL DURHAM BEER CO LLC
409 Blackwell St (27701-3972)
PHONE...............................919 744-3568
Michael Goodman, Pr
EMP: 6 EST: 2016
SALES (est): 238.33K **Privately Held**
Web: www.bulldurhambeer.com
SIC: 2082 Beer (alcoholic beverage)

(G-4991)
BULLDURHAMFABRICATIONS COM
5004 Mandel Rd (27712-2519)
PHONE...............................919 479-1919
Robert Pickard, Mgr
EMP: 4 EST: 2014
SALES (est): 162.43K **Privately Held**
Web: www.bulldurhamfabrications.com
SIC: 3441 Fabricated structural metal

(G-4992)
BURCHETTE SERVICES CORPORATION
Also Called: Real Prprty Mngment Trstworthy
202 Long Crescent Dr (27712-1451)
PHONE...............................919 225-2890
EMP: 5 EST: 2021
SALES (est): 67.04K **Privately Held**
SIC: 3993 Signs and advertising specialties

(G-4993)
BURTS BEES INC (HQ)
210 W Pettigrew St (27701-3666)
P.O. Box 13489 (27709-3489)
PHONE...............................919 998-5200
John Replogle, CEO
M Beth Springer, *
Daniel J Heinrich, *
Angela Hilt, *
Charles R Conradi, *
◆ EMP: 130 EST: 1991
SQ FT: 108,000
SALES (est): 89.9MM
SALES (corp-wide): 7.39B **Publicly Held**
Web: www.burtsbees.com
SIC: 2844 5122 5087 Cosmetic preparations; Cosmetics, perfumes, and hair products; Beauty parlor equipment and supplies
PA: The Clorox Company
 1221 Broadway Ste 1300
 Oakland CA 94612
 510 271-7000

(G-4994)
BURTS BEES INC
701 Distribution Dr (27709)
PHONE...............................919 998-5200
EMP: 400
SALES (corp-wide): 7.39B **Publicly Held**
Web: www.burtsbees.com
SIC: 2844 5122 Bath salts; Cosmetics, perfumes, and hair products
HQ: Burt's Bees, Inc.
 210 W Pettigrew St
 Durham NC 27701

(G-4995)
CAMARGO PHRM SVCS LLC
800 Taylor St Ste 101 (27701-4893)
PHONE...............................513 618-0325
Stuart Byham, Prin
EMP: 4
SALES (corp-wide): 25.54MM **Privately Held**
Web: www.premierconsulting.com
SIC: 2834 Proprietary drug products
HQ: Camargo Pharmaceutical Services, Llc
 1 E 4th St Ste 1400
 Cincinnati OH 45202

(G-4996)
CAMPUS SAFETY PRODUCTS LLC
2530 Meridian Pkwy Ste 300 (27713-5272)
PHONE...............................919 321-1477
Ernest Johnson Iii, CEO
Surjeet Johnson, Pr
Lowell Oakley, CFO
EMP: 6 EST: 2014
SALES (est): 461.17K **Privately Held**
Web: www.campussafetyproducts.com
SIC: 7382 3699 Protective devices, security; Security devices

(G-4997)
CANCER DIAGNOSTICS INC (PA)
Also Called: Anatech
116 Page Point Cir (27703-9120)
P.O. Box 1205 (48012-1205)
PHONE...............................877 846-5393
Patrick O'neil, Pr
Michael Franskoviak, *
▲ EMP: 31 EST: 1998
SALES (est): 11.79MM
SALES (corp-wide): 11.79MM **Privately Held**
Web: www.cancerdiagnostics.com
SIC: 3841 Anesthesia apparatus

(G-4998)
CARGOTEC PORT SECURITY LLC (DH)
4400 Ben Franklin Blvd Ste 200a (27704-2385)
PHONE...............................919 620-1763
Troy A Thompson, Managing Member
▲ EMP: 6 EST: 2008
SQ FT: 5,000
SALES (est): 3.72MM **Privately Held**
SIC: 3699 5065 Security control equipment and systems; Security control equipment and systems
HQ: Kalmar Solutions Llc
 415 E Dundee St
 Ottawa KS 66067
 785 242-2200

(G-4999)
CAROLINA ACADEMIC PRESS LLC
700 Kent St (27701-3049)
PHONE...............................919 489-7486
EMP: 45 EST: 1976
SQ FT: 4,300
SALES (est): 6.7MM **Privately Held**
Web: www.cap-press.com
SIC: 2741 Miscellaneous publishing

(G-5000)
CAROLINA CERTIF MUS GROUP LLC
1128 Vermillion Dr (27713-8231)
PHONE...............................984 234-2073
Stephen Mcleod, Prin
EMP: 5 EST: 2019
SALES (est): 100K **Privately Held**
SIC: 3651 Music distribution apparatus

GEOGRAPHIC SECTION

Durham - Durham County (G-5025)

(G-5001)
CAROLINA COMPONENTS GROUP INC
Also Called: Carolina Components Group
1001 Hill Dr (27703-7092)
PHONE................................919 635-8438
John Cooling, *CEO*
Michael Walsh, *
EMP: 45 **EST:** 2020
SALES (est): 11.56MM **Privately Held**
Web: www.carolinaflow.com
SIC: 3492 3545 3053 Hose and tube fittings and assemblies, hydraulic/pneumatic; Gauges (machine tool accessories); Gaskets, all materials

(G-5002)
CAROLINA MECHANICAL SERVICES INC
5100 International Dr (27712-8947)
PHONE................................919 477-7100
EMP: 43 **EST:** 1994
SALES (est): 7.81MM **Privately Held**
Web: www.carolinamechanical.com
SIC: 3559 Pharmaceutical machinery

(G-5003)
CAROLINA ROAD MEDIA LLC
105 Settlers Mill Ln (27713-8541)
PHONE................................844 222-7069
Robert L Flora, *Prin*
EMP: 5 **EST:** 2009
SALES (est): 94.76K **Privately Held**
Web: www.jigsawaddict.com
SIC: 7372 Application computer software

(G-5004)
CAROLINA SGNS GRPHIC DSGNS INC
Also Called: Carolina Signs and Graphics,
3535 Hillsborough Rd (27705-2916)
PHONE................................919 383-3344
EMP: 4 **EST:** 1990
SQ FT: 2,000
SALES (est): 344.1K **Privately Held**
Web: www.carolinabanner.com
SIC: 3993 5999 2759 1799 Signs and advertising specialties; Banners; Screen printing; Sandblasting of building exteriors

(G-5005)
CAROLINA WREN PRESS INC
Also Called: BLAIR
811 9th St Ste 130-127 (27705-4149)
PHONE................................919 560-2738
Lynn York, *Pr*
Robin Miura, *VP*
EMP: 5 **EST:** 1999
SALES (est): 517.62K **Privately Held**
Web: www.carolinawrenpress.org
SIC: 2731 Books, publishing only

(G-5006)
CAROLINAS CORD BLOOD BANK
Also Called: Ccbb Affl With The Duke Univ S
2400 Pratt St Ste 1400 (27705-3976)
P.O. Box Dumc 3850 (27710-0001)
PHONE................................919 668-1102
Joanne Kurtzberg, *Dir*
Ana Valverde, *
Amanda Parrish, *
EMP: 9 **EST:** 1998
SQ FT: 5,600
SALES (est): 179.44K **Privately Held**
SIC: 2834 8731 Proprietary drug products; Biological research

(G-5007)
CASEIRO INTERNATIONAL LLC
105 Hood St Ste 7 (27701-3794)
PHONE................................919 530-8333
Roquel Siqueira, *Ofcr*
EMP: 5 **EST:** 2001
SQ FT: 4,400
SALES (est): 318.02K **Privately Held**
SIC: 2037 Frozen fruits and vegetables

(G-5008)
CATALENT PHARMA SOLUTIONS INC
160 N Pharma Dr (27703)
PHONE................................919 465-8206
Charlotte Carroll, *Brnch Mgr*
EMP: 10
Web: www.catalent.com
SIC: 2834 Pharmaceutical preparations
HQ: Catalent Pharma Solutions, Inc.
   14 Schoolhouse Rd
   Somerset NJ 08873

(G-5009)
CATAWAMPUS PRESS LLC
1616 S Mineral Springs Rd (27703-9568)
PHONE................................201 572-3990
EMP: 4 **EST:** 2018
SALES (est): 65.16K **Privately Held**
Web: www.catawampuspress.com
SIC: 2741 Miscellaneous publishing

(G-5010)
CELL MICROSYSTEMS INC
801 Capitola Dr Ste 10 (27713-4384)
P.O. Box 13169 (27709-3169)
PHONE................................919 608-2035
EMP: 6 **EST:** 2010
SALES (est): 1.48MM **Privately Held**
Web: www.cellmicrosystems.com
SIC: 2834 Adrenal pharmaceutical preparations

(G-5011)
CENTER FOR ORTHTIC PRSTHTIC CA (HQ)
Also Called: Center For Orthtic Prsthtic Ca
4702 Creekstone Dr (27703-8410)
PHONE................................919 797-1230
Don Dixon, *Pr*
Keith Senn, *
David Sickles, *
Michael Mattingly, *
Timothy Nutgrass, *
EMP: 28 **EST:** 2011
SALES (est): 10.44MM
SALES (corp-wide): 1.12B **Privately Held**
Web: www.centeropcare.com
SIC: 3842 Limbs, artificial
PA: Hanger, Inc.
   10910 Domain Dr Ste 300
   Austin TX 78758
   512 777-3800

(G-5012)
CHANDLER CONCRETE INC
Also Called: Ready Mix Concrete
2700 E Pettigrew St (27703-4410)
P.O. Box 131 (27016-0131)
PHONE................................919 598-1424
Bruce Oakley, *Mgr*
EMP: 14
SQ FT: 288
Web: www.chandlerconcrete.com
SIC: 3273 1611 Ready-mixed concrete; Surfacing and paving
PA: Chandler Concrete Co., Inc.
   1006 S Church St
   Burlington NC 27215

(G-5013)
CHATHAM STEEL CORPORATION
2702 Cheek Rd (27704-5263)
PHONE................................912 233-4182
Mike Young, *Owner*
EMP: 38
SALES (corp-wide): 14.81B **Publicly Held**
Web: www.chathamsteel.com
SIC: 5051 3462 Steel; Aircraft forgings, ferrous
HQ: Chatham Steel Corporation
   501 W Boundary St
   Savannah GA 31401
   912 233-4182

(G-5014)
CHECKFREE SERVICES CORPORATION
Also Called: Checkfree Mobius
4819 Emperor Blvd Ste 300 (27703-5420)
PHONE................................919 941-2640
Randy Stalings, *Brnch Mgr*
EMP: 323
SALES (corp-wide): 19.09B **Publicly Held**
Web: www.checkfreecsp.com
SIC: 7374 7372 Data processing service; Prepackaged software
HQ: Checkfree Services Corporation
   2900 Westside Pkwy
   Alpharetta GA 30004
   678 375-3000

(G-5015)
CHEMOGENICS BIOPHARMA LLC (PA)
3325 Durham Chapel Hill Blvd Ste 250 (27707-6235)
PHONE................................919 323-8133
EMP: 6 **EST:** 2009
SALES (est): 960.99K **Privately Held**
Web: www.chemogenicsbiopharma.com
SIC: 2834 Pharmaceutical preparations

(G-5016)
CHIMERIX INC (PA)
2505 Meridian Pkwy Ste 100 (27713-2288)
PHONE................................919 806-1074
Michael A Sherman, *Pr*
Martha J Demski, *
Michael T Andriole, *Chief Business Officer*
Allen Melemed, *CMO*
Michelle Laspaluto, *CFO*
EMP: 25 **EST:** 2000
SQ FT: 24,862
SALES (est): 324K
SALES (corp-wide): 324K **Publicly Held**
Web: www.chimerix.com
SIC: 2834 Pharmaceutical preparations

(G-5017)
CHINA FREE PRESS INC
4711 Hope Valley Rd 122 (27707-5651)
PHONE................................919 308-9826
Watson Meng, *Ex Dir*
EMP: 4 **EST:** 2007
SALES (est): 131.58K **Privately Held**
SIC: 2741 Miscellaneous publishing

(G-5018)
CHUDY GROUP LLC
Also Called: Tcgrx
106 Roche Dr (27703-0359)
PHONE................................262 279-5307
Neville Dowell, *
Matt Noffsinger, *
Mark Hoffmann, *CIO*
▲ **EMP:** 65 **EST:** 2007
SQ FT: 20,000
SALES (est): 13.58MM
SALES (corp-wide): 19.37B **Publicly Held**
SIC: 3565 Packaging machinery
PA: Becton, Dickinson And Company
   1 Becton Dr
   Franklin Lakes NJ 07417
   201 847-6800

(G-5019)
CLEAN AS A WHISTLE
706 Justice St (27704-1320)
PHONE................................919 949-7738
Leeshawn Deshazo, *Prin*
EMP: 5 **EST:** 2009
SALES (est): 75.16K **Privately Held**
Web: www.cleanasawhistlewnc.com
SIC: 3999 Whistles

(G-5020)
CLEAN GREEN INC
Also Called: Clean Green Environmental Svcs
928 Harvest Rd (27704-5216)
PHONE................................919 596-3500
Charles T Wilkinson, *Pr*
Kathie Wilkinson, *VP*
EMP: 9 **EST:** 1997
SQ FT: 10,000
SALES (est): 1.04MM **Privately Held**
Web: www.cleangreennc.com
SIC: 4953 3559 Recycling, waste materials; Automotive related machinery

(G-5021)
CLOUD PHARMACEUTICALS INC
6 Davis Dr (27709-0003)
P.O. Box 110081 (27709-5081)
PHONE................................919 558-1254
EMP: 6 **EST:** 2009
SALES (est): 880.27K **Privately Held**
Web: www.cloudpharmaceuticals.com
SIC: 2834 Pharmaceutical preparations

(G-5022)
CLUTCH INC
Also Called: Carpe
120 W Parrish St (27701-3321)
PHONE................................919 448-8654
David Spratte, *CEO*
EMP: 11 **EST:** 2014
SALES (est): 1.41MM **Privately Held**
Web: www.mycarpe.com
SIC: 2844 Face creams or lotions

(G-5023)
CODING INSTITUTE LLC
2222 Sedwick Rd Ste 1 (27713-2655)
PHONE................................239 280-2300
EMP: 46 **EST:** 2002
SALES (est): 759.97K **Privately Held**
Web: www.aapc.com
SIC: 2731 7389 Book publishing; Business services, nec

(G-5024)
COLLEGATE CLORS CHRISTN COLORS
Also Called: CC
4204 Destrier Dr (27703-3756)
PHONE................................919 536-8179
Tonya J Mcmannen, *Owner*
EMP: 4 **EST:** 2008
SALES (est): 196.09K **Privately Held**
SIC: 2397 Schiffli machine embroideries

(G-5025)
COLOWRAP LLC
3333 Durham Chapel Hill Blvd Ste A200 (27707-6238)
PHONE................................888 815-3376
EMP: 15 **EST:** 2012
SALES (est): 2.4MM **Privately Held**
Web: www.colowrap.com
SIC: 5047 3841 Medical and hospital equipment; Surgical and medical instruments

Durham - Durham County (G-5026)

(G-5026)
COMAN PUBLISHING CO INC (PA)
324 Blackwell St Ste 560 (27701-3600)
P.O. Box 2331 (27702-2331)
PHONE..............................919 688-0218
J Stuart Coman Junior, *Pr*
J S Coman Junior, *Pr*
Helena Coman, *VP*
Linda P Autry, *Sec*
EMP: 14 **EST:** 1980
SQ FT: 2,138
SALES (est): 1.35MM
SALES (corp-wide): 1.35MM **Privately Held**
Web: www.comanpub.com
SIC: 2711 2741 Newspapers: publishing only, not printed on site; Miscellaneous publishing

(G-5027)
COMFORT ENGINEERS INC (PA)
4008 Comfort Ln (27705-6177)
P.O. Box 2955 (27715-2955)
PHONE..............................919 383-0158
Alan Williams, *Pr*
Layne M Hessee, *
H Christopher Perry, *
Jerry W Overajer, *
Robert D Teer Junior, *Stockholder*
EMP: 40 **EST:** 1955
SQ FT: 20,000
SALES (est): 24.38MM
SALES (corp-wide): 24.38MM **Privately Held**
Web: www.comfortengineers.com
SIC: 1711 3441 3444 Warm air heating and air conditioning contractor; Fabricated structural metal; Sheet metalwork

(G-5028)
COMP ENVIRONMENTAL INC
5007 Southpark Dr Ste 200e (27713-7739)
PHONE..............................919 316-1321
Yanling Wang, *Brnch Mgr*
EMP: 10
SALES (corp-wide): 439.54K **Privately Held**
Web: www.compenviron.com
SIC: 8711 7371 3822 1731 Civil engineering; Custom computer programming services; Building services monitoring controls, automatic; Voice, data, and video wiring contractor
PA: Comp Environmental, Inc.
5615 Recker Hwy
Winter Haven FL 33880
407 416-9368

(G-5029)
COMTECH GROUP INC
Also Called: Geeks On Call
4819 Emperor Blvd Ste 400 (27703-5420)
P.O. Box 14443 (27709-4443)
PHONE..............................919 313-4800
Etner Hill, *Pr*
Etner Hill, *Pr*
Saron Hill, *VP*
EMP: 4 **EST:** 2003
SQ FT: 600
SALES (est): 444.17K **Privately Held**
Web: www.teamcomtech.com
SIC: 7379 3825 7378 Computer related consulting services; Network analyzers; Computer maintenance and repair

(G-5030)
CONSOLDTED ELCTRNIC RSRCES INC
2933 S Miami Blvd Ste 124 (27703-9041)
PHONE..............................919 321-0004
Julio Cordoba, *CEO*
EMP: 10 **EST:** 1997
SALES (est): 488.96K **Privately Held**
SIC: 3699 Electrical equipment and supplies, nec

(G-5031)
CONSOLDTED GRPHICS - PBM GRPHI
3700 S Miami Blvd (27703-9130)
PHONE..............................919 544-6222
EMP: 4 **EST:** 2019
SALES (est): 73.28K **Privately Held**
SIC: 2759 Screen printing

(G-5032)
CONTROL AND BARRICADE LLC
2025 October Dr (27703-7824)
PHONE..............................704 315-2138
Charles L Baxter, *Prin*
EMP: 5 **EST:** 2016
SALES (est): 153.91K **Privately Held**
SIC: 3499 Barricades, metal

(G-5033)
CORK TEE
3436 Rugby Rd (27707-5449)
PHONE..............................919 536-3200
EMP: 4 **EST:** 2018
SALES (est): 187.78K **Privately Held**
Web: www.corkandtee.com
SIC: 2759 Screen printing

(G-5034)
CORNING INCORPORATED
Also Called: Corning
1 Becton Cir (27712-9483)
PHONE..............................919 620-6200
EMP: 237
SALES (corp-wide): 12.59B **Publicly Held**
Web: www.corning.com
SIC: 3821 3841 Pipettes, hemocytometer; Surgical and medical instruments
PA: Corning Incorporated
1 Riverfront Plz
Corning NY 14831
607 974-9000

(G-5035)
CREELED INC
4400 Silicon Dr (27703-8013)
PHONE..............................919 313-5330
Jack Pacheco, *Pr*
EMP: 270 **EST:** 2020
SALES (est): 63.31MM
SALES (corp-wide): 1.44B **Publicly Held**
Web: www.cree-led.com
SIC: 3674 Light emitting diodes
PA: Smart Global Holdings, Inc.
1390 Mccarthy Blvd
Milpitas CA 95035
866 977-4446

(G-5036)
CRICKET FORGE LLC
2314 Operations Dr (27705-2336)
PHONE..............................919 680-3513
EMP: 5 **EST:** 2018
SALES (est): 458.1K **Privately Held**
Web: www.cricketforge.com
SIC: 3441 Fabricated structural metal

(G-5037)
CRIZAF INC
Also Called: Crizaf Srl
2, 1534 Cher Dr, (27713)
PHONE..............................919 251-7661
EMP: 4 **EST:** 2015
SALES (est): 525.28K
SALES (corp-wide): 6.03MM **Privately Held**
Web: www.crizaf.com
SIC: 5084 3639 4953 Food industry machinery; Major kitchen appliances, except refrigerators and stoves; Recycling, waste materials
PA: Crizaf Srl
Via Edvar Hagerup Grieg 15
Saronno VA 21047
029619951

(G-5038)
CSC SHEET METAL INC
1310 E Cornwallis Rd (27713-1423)
PHONE..............................919 544-8887
▲ **EMP:** 12
Web: www.kmsheetmetal.com
SIC: 3444 Sheet metalwork

(G-5039)
CUPCAKE BAR
315 Monmouth Ave (27701-1816)
PHONE..............................919 816-2905
Anna Branly, *Owner*
EMP: 8 **EST:** 2011
SALES (est): 238.27K **Privately Held**
Web: www.cupcakebarbakery.com
SIC: 5812 2051 Family restaurants; Bakery, for home service delivery

(G-5040)
CUSTOM LIGHT AND SOUND INC
Also Called: C L S
2506 Guess Rd (27705-3307)
PHONE..............................919 286-1122
Bob R Phelps, *Pr*
Stephen Brown, *VP*
EMP: 22 **EST:** 1977
SQ FT: 5,000
SALES (est): 2.01MM **Privately Held**
Web: www.customlightandsound.com
SIC: 1731 3699 5065 Voice, data, and video wiring contractor; Electric sound equipment; Paging and signaling equipment

(G-5041)
CUSTOM SHEETMETAL SERVICES INC
5109 Neal Rd (27705-2364)
PHONE..............................919 282-1088
Joseph M Lee Iii, *Pr*
EMP: 4 **EST:** 2007
SALES (est): 525.93K **Privately Held**
SIC: 3444 Sheet metalwork

(G-5042)
CUSTOM STEEL INCORPORATED
3161 Hillsborough Rd (27705-4336)
PHONE..............................919 383-9170
Wendy Walker, *Owner*
EMP: 5 **EST:** 2007
SALES (est): 965.18K **Privately Held**
Web: www.customsteel.org
SIC: 3441 Fabricated structural metal

(G-5043)
CYBERBIOTA INCORPORATED
405 Gresham Ave (27704-4213)
PHONE..............................919 308-3839
Peter Charles, *Pr*
◆ **EMP:** 8 **EST:** 2000
SQ FT: 1,500
SALES (est): 186.82K **Privately Held**
SIC: 3845 Ultrasonic scanning devices, medical

(G-5044)
CYTONET LLC
801 Capitola Dr Ste 8 (27713-4384)
EMP: 18 **EST:** 2007
SQ FT: 8,000
SALES (est): 563.65K **Privately Held**
Web: www.cytonet.llc
SIC: 2836 Biological products, except diagnostic

(G-5045)
DANIELS HOUSE PUBLICATIONS
201 Monticello Ave (27707-3910)
PHONE..............................919 328-0709
EMP: 4 **EST:** 2015
SALES (est): 65.16K **Privately Held**
SIC: 2741 Miscellaneous publishing

(G-5046)
DANTE CABINETS
2905 Sparger Rd (27705-1644)
PHONE..............................919 306-3261
EMP: 5 **EST:** 2013
SALES (est): 91.96K **Privately Held**
SIC: 2434 Wood kitchen cabinets

(G-5047)
DATA443 RISK MITIGATION INC
4000 Sancar Way Ste 400 (27709)
PHONE..............................919 858-6542
Jason Remillard, *Ch Bd*
Greg Mccraw, *CFO*
EMP: 26 **EST:** 1998
SQ FT: 5,000
SALES (est): 2.63MM **Privately Held**
Web: www.data443.com
SIC: 7372 Prepackaged software

(G-5048)
DATABASE INCORPORATED
3342 Rose Of Sharon Rd (27712-3302)
P.O. Box 3054 (27715-3054)
PHONE..............................202 684-6252
W E Hammond Ii, *Pr*
Kay Hammond, *VP*
EMP: 7 **EST:** 1981
SQ FT: 1,500
SALES (est): 712.25K **Privately Held**
SIC: 7372 5045 Prepackaged software; Computers, peripherals, and software

(G-5049)
DATANYZE LLC
2530 Meridian Pkwy Ste 300 (27713-5272)
PHONE..............................866 408-1633
Ilya Semin, *CEO*
Tatiana Semeniakin, *
EMP: 50 **EST:** 2014
SALES (est): 2.34MM
SALES (corp-wide): 1.24B **Publicly Held**
SIC: 2741 7379 Internet publishing and broadcasting; Online services technology consultants
HQ: Zoom Information, Llc
275 Wyman St Ste 120
Waltham MA 02451
781 693-7500

(G-5050)
DAVIE PAPER CO
5303 Grandhaven Dr (27713-6092)
PHONE..............................425 941-1994
Suzy Porterfield, *Prin*
EMP: 5 **EST:** 2015
SALES (est): 147.83K **Privately Held**
SIC: 2711 Newspapers

(G-5051)
DIGITAL TURBINE MEDIA INC (HQ)
410 Blackwell St (27701-3986)
PHONE..............................866 254-2453
Jud Bowman, *CEO*
Tim Oakley, *
Jamie Fellows, *Chief Product Officer**
Ken Hayes, *

GEOGRAPHIC SECTION — Durham - Durham County (G-5073)

EMP: 24 **EST:** 2008
SALES (est): 20.43MM **Publicly Held**
Web: www.digitalturbine.com
SIC: 7372 7371 Prepackaged software; Custom computer programming services
PA: Digital Turbine, Inc.
   110 San Antonio St # 160
   Austin TX 78701

(G-5052)
DIGNIFY THERAPEUTICS LLC
2 Davis Dr (27709-0003)
P.O. Box 13169 (27709-3169)
PHONE..................919 371-8138
EMP: 7 **EST:** 2013
SALES (est): 1.02MM **Privately Held**
Web: www.dignifytherapeutics.com
SIC: 2834 Pharmaceutical preparations

(G-5053)
DILISYM SERVICES INC
6 Davis Dr (27709-0003)
P.O. Box 12317 (27709-2317)
PHONE..................919 558-1323
Brett Howell, *CEO*
EMP: 8 **EST:** 2014
SALES (est): 1.35MM **Publicly Held**
Web: www.simulations-plus.com
SIC: 7372 Prepackaged software
PA: Simulations Plus, Inc.
   42505 10th St W Ste 103
   Lancaster CA 93534

(G-5054)
DITEX LLC
Also Called: Voyant Solutions, Carolinas
5112 Greyfield Blvd (27713-8140)
P.O. Box 14007 (27709-4007)
PHONE..................919 215-3773
EMP: 4 **EST:** 2008
SALES (est): 247.64K **Privately Held**
SIC: 3822 Environmental controls

(G-5055)
DOCSITE LLC (DH)
280 S Mangum St Ste 540 (27701-3678)
PHONE..................866 823-3958
John Haughton, *Chief Medical Officer*
EMP: 14 **EST:** 1996
SALES (est): 978.46K
SALES (corp-wide): 832.31MM **Privately Held**
Web: www.docsite.com
SIC: 7372 Prepackaged software
HQ: Covisint Corporation
   26533 Evergreen Rd # 500
   Southfield MI 48076

(G-5056)
DOE & INGALLS INVESTORS INC (HQ)
4813 Emperor Blvd Ste 300 (27703-8467)
PHONE..................919 598-1986
Thomas S Todd, *Pr*
EMP: 27 **EST:** 2005
SALES (est): 101.92MM
SALES (corp-wide): 44.91B **Publicly Held**
SIC: 3826 Analytical instruments
PA: Thermo Fisher Scientific Inc.
   168 3rd Ave
   Waltham MA 02451
   781 622-1000

(G-5057)
DOE & INGALLS MANAGEMENT LLC (DH)
4813 Emperor Blvd Ste 300 (27703-8467)
PHONE..................919 598-1986
EMP: 13 **EST:** 2005
SALES (est): 101.92MM
SALES (corp-wide): 44.91B **Publicly Held**
Web: www.thermofisher.com
SIC: 3826 Analytical instruments
HQ: Doe & Ingalls Investors, Inc.
   4813 Emperor Blvd Ste 300
   Durham NC 27703
   919 598-1986

(G-5058)
DOE & INGLLS NRTH CRLINA OPRTI
4063 Stirrup Creek Dr (27703-9001)
PHONE..................919 282-1792
John Hollenbach, *CEO*
Spencer Todd, *VP*
Henry Clark, *Dir*
Andrew Finn, *Dir*
Joe Frijia, *Dir*
▲ **EMP:** 21 **EST:** 2005
SALES (est): 21.19MM
SALES (corp-wide): 44.91B **Publicly Held**
SIC: 3826 Analytical instruments
HQ: Doe & Ingalls Management, Llc
   4813 Emperor Blvd Ste 300
   Durham NC 27703

(G-5059)
DOLLAR EDDIE REV
4420 Holloman Rd (27703-5834)
PHONE..................919 596-7564
Eddie Dollar, *Prin*
EMP: 5 **EST:** 2006
SALES (est): 105.19K **Privately Held**
SIC: 2389 Clergymen's vestments

(G-5060)
DOVA PHARMACEUTICALS INC (HQ)
Also Called: Dova Pharmaceuticals
240 Leigh Farm Rd Ste 245 (27707-8100)
PHONE..................919 748-5975
Duane Barnes, *Pr*
Guled Adam, *
Christine Belin, *
Mark W Hahn, *
Lee F Allen, *CMO**
EMP: 14 **EST:** 2016
SQ FT: 14,378
SALES (est): 7.02MM
SALES (corp-wide): 1.79B **Privately Held**
Web: www.sobi-northamerica.com
SIC: 2834 Pharmaceutical preparations
PA: Swedish Orphan Biovitrum Ab (Publ)
   Tomtebodavagen 23a
   Solna 171 6
   86972000

(G-5061)
DOYLES VINEYARD
8913 Nc Highway 751 (27713-6873)
PHONE..................919 544-6291
EMP: 5 **EST:** 2015
SALES (est): 137.36K **Privately Held**
Web: www.doylesvineyard.com
SIC: 2084 Wines

(G-5062)
DRAXLOR INDUSTRIES INC
228 S Riverdale Dr (27712-2502)
PHONE..................757 274-6771
Elliott Richter, *Prin*
EMP: 5 **EST:** 2016
SALES (est): 82.47K **Privately Held**
Web: www.draxlorindustries.com
SIC: 3999 Manufacturing industries, nec

(G-5063)
DRCH INC
Also Called: Dracor Water Systems
3518 Medford Rd (27705-2458)
P.O. Box 2993 (27715-2993)
PHONE..................919 383-9421
TOLL FREE: 800
Richard M Hall, *Pr*
Susan B Hall, *Sec*
EMP: 8 **EST:** 1954
SQ FT: 6,500
SALES (est): 1.04MM **Privately Held**
Web: www.dracorwatersystems.com
SIC: 5074 3589 Water purification equipment; Water treatment equipment, industrial

(G-5064)
DREAMFLYER PUBLICATIONS
1013 Gunston Ln (27703-3910)
PHONE..................919 596-1906
William Heitman, *Prin*
EMP: 5 **EST:** 2010
SALES (est): 53K **Privately Held**
SIC: 2741 Miscellaneous publishing

(G-5065)
DRINK A BULL LLC
Also Called: Waldensian Style Wines
921 Holloway St Ste 103 (27703-3856)
PHONE..................919 818-3321
Andrew Zimmerman, *Managing Member*
EMP: 5
SALES (corp-wide): 25K **Privately Held**
Web: www.drink-a-bull.com
SIC: 2084 5182 5921 Wines; Wine; Wine and beer
PA: Drink A Bull Llc
   3904 Sterling Ridge Ln
   Durham NC 27707
   984 219-1232

(G-5066)
DRUG SAFETY NAVIGATOR LLC
2605 Meridian Pkwy Ste 115 (27713-2294)
PHONE..................919 885-0549
Molly James, *Managing Member*
Lynda Spiker, *Prin*
EMP: 12 **EST:** 2011
SALES (est): 1.05MM **Privately Held**
Web: www.drugsafetynavigator.com
SIC: 7372 Business oriented computer software

(G-5067)
DUKE STUDENT PUBLISHING CO INC
Also Called: THE CHRONICLE
101 Union Dr (27708-9980)
P.O. Box 90858 (27708-0858)
PHONE..................919 684-3811
Jonathon Angier, *Genl Mgr*
Mary Weaver, *Opers Mgr*
EMP: 6 **EST:** 1993
SALES (est): 673.55K **Privately Held**
Web: www.dukechronicle.com
SIC: 2711 Commercial printing and newspaper publishing combined

(G-5068)
DUKE UNIVERSITY
Also Called: Duke University Press
905 W Main St Ste 19 (27701-2076)
PHONE..................919 687-3600
Steve Cohen, *Dir*
EMP: 54
SALES (corp-wide): 4.51MM **Privately Held**
Web: www.duke.edu
SIC: 2731 2721 Book publishing; Periodicals
PA: Duke University
   324 Blackwell St
   Durham NC 27701
   919 684-8111

(G-5069)
DUPONT ELECTRONIC POLYMERS L P (HQ)
14 Tw Alexander Dr (27709-0149)
PHONE..................919 248-5135
EMP: 13 **EST:** 2003
SALES (est): 9.36MM
SALES (corp-wide): 12.07B **Publicly Held**
Web: www.dupont.com
SIC: 2822 Ethylene-propylene rubbers, EPDM polymers
PA: Dupont De Nemours, Inc.
   974 Centre Rd Bldg 730
   Wilmington DE 19805
   302 774-3034

(G-5070)
DUPONT SPECIALTY PDTS USA LLC
Also Called: Dupont
4020 Stirrup Creek Dr (27703-9410)
P.O. Box 13999 (27709-3999)
PHONE..................919 248-5109
EMP: 50
SQ FT: 166,000
SALES (corp-wide): 12.07B **Publicly Held**
Web: www.dupont.com
SIC: 2819 5065 Industrial inorganic chemicals, nec; Electronic parts and equipment, nec
HQ: Dupont Specialty Products Usa, Llc
   974 Centre Rd
   Wilmington DE 19805
   302 992-2941

(G-5071)
DURHAM COCA-COLA BOTTLING COMPANY (PA)
3214 Hillsborough Rd (27705-3005)
P.O. Box 31487 (28231-1487)
PHONE..................919 383-1531
EMP: 150 **EST:** 1928
SALES (est): 45.47MM
SALES (corp-wide): 45.47MM **Privately Held**
Web: www.durhamcocacola.com
SIC: 2086 5962 Soft drinks: packaged in cans, bottles, etc.; Sandwich and hot food vending machines

(G-5072)
DURHAM DISTILLERY LLC
711 Washington St (27701-2147)
PHONE..................919 937-2121
Melissa Katrincic, *Managing Member*
Lee Katrincic, *Managing Member*
EMP: 8 **EST:** 2013
SALES (est): 2.57MM
SALES (corp-wide): 9.45B **Publicly Held**
Web: www.durhamdistillery.com
SIC: 2085 Distilled and blended liquors
PA: Constellation Brands, Inc.
   207 High Point Dr # 100
   Victor NY 14564
   585 678-7100

(G-5073)
DYNAMAC CORPORATION
1910 Sedwick Rd Ste 300a (27713-4367)
PHONE..................919 544-6428
Jay Early, *Brnch Mgr*
EMP: 38
SALES (corp-wide): 27.32MM **Privately Held**
Web: www.css-inc.com
SIC: 3822 7371 Environmental controls; Computer software systems analysis and design, custom
HQ: Dynamac Corporation
   10301 Democracy Ln # 300
   Fairfax VA 22030
   703 691-4612

Durham - Durham County (G-5074)

(G-5074)
E&G INDUSTRIES INC
202 Hillview Dr (27703-9614)
PHONE..................347 665-3039
George Singleton, *Prin*
EMP: 8 EST: 2016
SALES (est): 87.09K **Privately Held**
SIC: 3999 Manufacturing industries, nec

(G-5075)
EASY E ENTERPRISES LLC
2232 Page Rd Ste 104 (27703-7724)
PHONE..................704 763-7906
Samuel Morton, *Prin*
EMP: 6 EST: 2010
SALES (est): 101.72K **Privately Held**
SIC: 3482 Small arms ammunition

(G-5076)
ECLIPSE HEALTH OUTCOMES INC
35 Wilhelm Dr (27705-4923)
PHONE..................706 589-4086
EMP: 4 EST: 2018
SALES (est): 56.54K **Privately Held**
SIC: 7372 Application computer software

(G-5077)
EDWARD & LAMAR PUBLISHING
1418 Leon St (27705-3451)
PHONE..................919 433-6625
Michael Holmes, *Prin*
EMP: 4 EST: 2018
SALES (est): 72.48K **Privately Held**
SIC: 2741 Miscellaneous publishing

(G-5078)
ELI LILLY AND COMPANY
59 Moore Dr (27709-0009)
PHONE..................317 296-1226
Graciela Romero, *Mgr*
EMP: 12
SALES (corp-wide): 34.12B **Publicly Held**
Web: www.lilly.com
SIC: 2834 Pharmaceutical preparations
PA: Eli Lilly And Company
  Lilly Corporate Ctr
  Indianapolis IN 46285
  317 276-2000

(G-5079)
ELMORE WELDING INC
318 Nita Ln (27712-3434)
PHONE..................919 584-7460
Edel Rene Perez Hernandez, *Prin*
EMP: 5 EST: 2019
SALES (est): 109.78K **Privately Held**
SIC: 7692 Welding repair

(G-5080)
EMBREX LLC (HQ)
Also Called: Embrex, Inc.
1040 Swabia Ct (27703-8481)
P.O. Box 13989 (27709-3989)
PHONE..................919 941-5185
Clinton Lewis Junior, *Pr*
Don T Seaquist, *Corporate Secretary**
David M Baines, *Global Sales Vice President**
Joseph P Odowd, *Global Vice President**
Heidi Chen, *
▲ EMP: 114 EST: 1985
SQ FT: 60,000
SALES (est): 43.21MM
SALES (corp-wide): 8.08B **Publicly Held**
Web: www.poultryhealthtoday.com
SIC: 2836 3556 Vaccines and other immunizing products; Poultry processing machinery
PA: Zoetis Inc.
  10 Sylvan Way Ste 100
  Parsippany NJ 07054
  973 822-7000

(G-5081)
EMBROIDME
105 W Nc Highway 54 Ste 261 (27713-6646)
PHONE..................919 316-1538
Mike Ganesan, *Owner*
EMP: 4 EST: 2014
SALES (est): 155.35K **Privately Held**
Web: www.fullypromoted.com
SIC: 5949 3993 Sewing, needlework, and piece goods; Signs and advertising specialties

(G-5082)
EMC CORPORATION
4121 Surles Ct (27703-8055)
PHONE..................919 767-0641
EMP: 18
Web: www.emc.com
SIC: 3572 Computer tape drives and components
HQ: Emc Corporation
  176 South St
  Hopkinton MA 01748
  508 435-1000

(G-5083)
EMERGO THERAPEUTICS INC
6208 Fayetteville Rd Ste 104 (27713-6286)
PHONE..................919 649-5544
Robin Hyde-deruyscher, *Pr*
EMP: 15 EST: 2016
SALES (est): 830.71K **Privately Held**
Web: www.emergotherapeutics.com
SIC: 2833 Medicinals and botanicals

(G-5084)
EMRISE CORPORATION
2530 Meridian Pkwy (27713-5272)
PHONE..................408 200-3040
▲ EMP: 203
Web: www.emrise.com
SIC: 3679 3825 3661 3568 Electronic loads and power supplies; Instruments to measure electricity; Telephone and telegraph apparatus; Power transmission equipment, nec

(G-5085)
ENCUBE ETHICALS INC
200 Meredith Dr Ste 202 (27713-2287)
PHONE..................984 439-2761
EMP: 10 EST: 2019
SALES (est): 931.01K **Privately Held**
Web: www.encubeusa.com
SIC: 2834 Pharmaceutical preparations

(G-5086)
ENDEAVOUR FBRICATION GROUP INC
Also Called: Endeavor Fabrication Group
1534 Cher Dr (27713-5423)
P.O. Box 733 (27510-0733)
PHONE..................919 479-1453
Tom Schopler, *Pr*
Russell Shores, *VP*
EMP: 9 EST: 2005
SQ FT: 9,000
SALES (est): 992.23K **Privately Held**
SIC: 2541 Counter and sink tops

(G-5087)
ENGAGED MEDIA INC
3622 Lyckan Pkwy Ste 3003 (27707-2572)
PHONE..................239 280-4202
Greg Lindberg, *Ch*
EMP: 45 EST: 2015
SALES (est): 2.51MM **Privately Held**
Web: www.engagedmedia.store
SIC: 2836 Biological products, except diagnostic

(G-5088)
ENTTEC AMERICAS LLC
3874 S Alston Ave Ste 103 (27713-1883)
P.O. Box 13965 (27709-3965)
PHONE..................919 200-6468
EMP: 12 EST: 2016
SALES (est): 2.15MM **Privately Held**
Web: www.enttec.com
SIC: 3646 3648 Commercial lighting fixtures; Stage lighting equipment

(G-5089)
ENVIRONMENTAL SUPPLY CO INC
708 E Club Blvd (27704-4506)
PHONE..................919 956-9688
▲ EMP: 14 EST: 1995
SQ FT: 10,000
SALES (est): 2.43MM **Privately Held**
Web: www.environsupply.com
SIC: 3826 7389 8748 Analytical instruments; Air pollution measuring service; Business consulting, nec

(G-5090)
ENVISIA THERAPEUTICS INC
4301 Emperor Blvd Ste 200 (27703-7616)
P.O. Box 110065 (27709-5065)
PHONE..................919 973-1440
Benjamin Yerxa, *Pr*
Shawn Glidden, *
Rhett M Schiffman, *CMO**
Tomas Navratil, *
Eric Linsley, *
EMP: 24 EST: 2013
SALES (est): 2.81MM **Privately Held**
Web: www.envisiatherapeutics.com
SIC: 2834 Pharmaceutical preparations

(G-5091)
EPI GROUP LLC (PA)
Also Called: Post & Courier, The
4020 Stirrup Creek Dr (27703-9410)
PHONE..................843 577-7111
John P Barnwell, *CEO*
Pierre Manigault, *
Edward M Gilbreth, *
Daniel P Herres, *
Roger A Berardinis, *
▲ EMP: 350 EST: 1894
SALES (est): 233.03MM
SALES (corp-wide): 233.03MM **Privately Held**
Web: www.postandcourier.com
SIC: 2711 Newspapers, publishing and printing

(G-5092)
EPICYPHER INC
Also Called: Epicypher
6 Davis Dr (27709-0003)
P.O. Box 14453 (27709-4453)
PHONE..................855 374-2461
James Bone, *Pr*
EMP: 11 EST: 2012
SALES (est): 3.59MM **Privately Held**
Web: www.epicypher.com
SIC: 8731 2836 Biotechnical research, commercial; Veterinary biological products

(G-5093)
ESCAPIST
2530 Meridian Pkwy Ste 200 (27713-5272)
PHONE..................919 806-4448
EMP: 4 EST: 2019
SALES (est): 249.22K **Privately Held**
SIC: 2741 Miscellaneous publishing

(G-5094)
EVOQUA WATER TECHNOLOGIES LLC
1301 S Briggs Ave Ste 116 (27703-5070)
PHONE..................919 477-2161
Tom Bell, *Brnch Mgr*
EMP: 19
SQ FT: 2,400
Web: www.evoqua.com
SIC: 2834 5999 Chlorination tablets and kits (water purification); Water purification equipment
HQ: Evoqua Water Technologies Llc
  210 6th Ave Ste 3300
  Pittsburgh PA 15222
  724 772-0044

(G-5095)
FACTOR INC
1901 Sedwick Rd (27713-9424)
PHONE..................919 358-0004
John Newnam, *Prin*
EMP: 5 EST: 2015
SALES (est): 112.7K **Privately Held**
SIC: 2741 Miscellaneous publishing

(G-5096)
FINLEY ENTERPRISES LLC ◆
Also Called: Queercos.com
2826 Green Lane Dr (27712-2435)
PHONE..................910 747-6679
Valerie Lawson, *Prin*
EMP: 8 EST: 2022
SALES (est): 79.3K **Privately Held**
SIC: 2741 Internet publishing and broadcasting

(G-5097)
FIRST LEADS INC
Also Called: House Staffer
201 W Main St Ste 305 (27701-3228)
PHONE..................919 672-5329
Michael Schneider, *CEO*
EMP: 6 EST: 2014
SALES (est): 1.39MM
SALES (corp-wide): 325.67MM **Publicly Held**
Web: www.first.io
SIC: 7372 Prepackaged software
PA: Re/Max Holdings, Inc.
  5075 S Syracuse St
  Denver CO 80237
  303 770-5531

(G-5098)
FIRSTMARK AEROSPACE CORP
921 Holloway St (27701-3856)
PHONE..................919 956-4323
EMP: 5 EST: 2019
SALES (est): 226.19K **Privately Held**
Web: www.firstmarkaerospace.com
SIC: 3728 Aircraft parts and equipment, nec

(G-5099)
FISHER SIGNS MURALS & FRAMES
2606 Hillsborough Rd (27705-4081)
PHONE..................919 286-0591
EMP: 4 EST: 2019
SALES (est): 112.67K **Privately Held**
SIC: 3993 Signs and advertising specialties

(G-5100)
FLEXGEN POWER SYSTEMS INC
2175 Presidential Dr Ste 100 (27703-0960)
PHONE..................855 327-5674
EMP: 4
SALES (corp-wide): 26.29MM **Privately Held**

Web: www.flexgen.com
SIC: 4931 3674 Electric and other services combined; Semiconductors and related devices
PA: Flexgen Power Systems, Inc.
280 S Mangum St Ste 150
Durham NC 27701
855 327-5674

(G-5101)
FLEXGEN POWER SYSTEMS INC (PA)
280 S Mangum St Ste 150 (27701-3674)
PHONE................................855 327-5674
Kelcy Pegler, *CEO*
Yann Brandt, *CCO*
Diane Giacomozzi, *COO*
Gary Cristini, *CFO*
Aruna Chandra, *Ex VP*
EMP: 14 **EST:** 2015
SALES (est): 26.29MM
SALES (corp-wide): 26.29MM **Privately Held**
Web: www.flexgen.com
SIC: 4931 3674 Electric and other services combined; Semiconductors and related devices

(G-5102)
FORTREA HOLDINGS INC (PA)
8 Moore Dr (27709-0009)
PHONE................................877 495-0816
Thomas Pike, *Ch Bd*
Jill Mcconnell, *CFO*
Mark Morais, *COO*
Oren Cohen, *CMO*
Amanda Warren, *CAO*
EMP: 27 **EST:** 1971
SALES (est): 3.11B
SALES (corp-wide): 3.11B **Publicly Held**
SIC: 2834 Pharmaceutical preparations

(G-5103)
FREUDENBERG NONWOVENS LIMITED PARTNERSHIP
3500 Industrial Dr (27704-9309)
P.O. Box 15910 (27704-0910)
PHONE................................919 620-3900
▲ **EMP:** 691
SIC: 2297 5023 Nonwoven fabrics; Floor coverings

(G-5104)
FREUDENBERG PRFMCE MTLS LP (HQ)
Also Called: Freudenberg Nonwoven
3500 Industrial Dr (27704-9309)
P.O. Box 15910 (27704-0910)
PHONE................................919 479-7443
Bruce Olson, *CEO*
Edward Cann, *VP*
Stephan Liozu, *VP*
◆ **EMP:** 62 **EST:** 2013
SALES (est): 116.21MM
SALES (corp-wide): 12.23B **Privately Held**
Web: www.freudenberg-pm.com
SIC: 2297 5131 Nonwoven fabrics; Piece goods and other fabrics
PA: Freudenberg & Co. Kg
Hohneweg 2-4
Weinheim BW 69469
6201800

(G-5105)
FREUDENBERG PRFMCE MTLS LP
3440 Industrial Dr (27704-9429)
PHONE................................919 620-3900
Heiner Heng, *Mgr*
EMP: 10
SALES (corp-wide): 12.23B **Privately Held**
Web: www.freudenberg-pm.com
SIC: 2821 Plastics materials and resins
HQ: Freudenberg Performance Materials L.P.
3500 Industrial Dr
Durham NC 27704
919 479-7443

(G-5106)
FS LLC
Also Called: Ram Jack Foundation Repair
4122 Bennett Memorial Rd Ste 304 (27705-1209)
PHONE................................919 309-9727
Richard D Sykes, *Managing Member*
EMP: 40 **EST:** 1989
SQ FT: 25,000
SALES (est): 4.61MM **Privately Held**
Web: www.ramjack.com
SIC: 2295 Waterproofing fabrics, except rubberizing

(G-5107)
FUJIFILM DIOSYNTH BIOTECHNOLOG
6051 George Watts Hill Dr (27709-0218)
PHONE................................919 337-4400
Michael Baldauff, *Brnch Mgr*
EMP: 8
SQ FT: 121,200
Web: www.fujifilmdiosynth.com
SIC: 2834 Pharmaceutical preparations
HQ: Fujifilm Diosynth Biotechnologies U.S.A., Inc.
101 J Morris Comns Ln
Morrisville NC 27560

(G-5108)
FULLY PROMOTED DURHAM
Also Called: Fully Promoted
105 W Nc Highway 54 Ste 261 (27713-6646)
PHONE................................919 316-1538
EMP: 5 **EST:** 2019
SALES (est): 45.64K **Privately Held**
Web: www.fullypromoted.com
SIC: 2395 Embroidery and art needlework

(G-5109)
FUSION SPORT INC
122 E Parrish St (27701-3319)
PHONE................................720 987-4403
Markus Deutsch, *CEO*
Leslie Milne, *
EMP: 35 **EST:** 2011
SALES (est): 2.7MM **Privately Held**
Web: www.smartabase.com
SIC: 5941 7372 Sporting goods and bicycle shops; Publisher's computer software

(G-5110)
G1 THERAPEUTICS INC
Also Called: G1 Therapeutics
700 Park Offices Dr Ste 200 (27709)
P.O. Box 110341 (27709-5341)
PHONE................................919 213-9835
John E Bailey Junior, *Pr*
Garry A Nicholson, *
Terry L Murdock, *COO*
Jennifer K Moses, *CFO*
Rajesh K Malik, *CMO*
EMP: 122 **EST:** 2008
SQ FT: 60,000
SALES (est): 82.51MM **Privately Held**
Web: www.g1therapeutics.com
SIC: 2834 Pharmaceutical preparations

(G-5111)
GE AIRCRAFT ENGS HOLDINGS INC
Also Called: GE
3701 S Miami Blvd (27703-9131)
PHONE................................919 361-4400
▲ **EMP:** 525
SALES (corp-wide): 67.95B **Publicly Held**
SIC: 3724 7699 Air scoops, aircraft; Aircraft and heavy equipment repair services
HQ: Ge Aircraft Engines Holdings, Inc.
1 Aviation Way
Cincinnati OH 45215
888 999-5103

(G-5112)
GEA INTEC LLC
4319 S Alston Ave Ste 105 (27713-2488)
PHONE................................919 433-0131
▲ **EMP:** 26
Web: www.intecvrt.com
SIC: 3556 Food products machinery

(G-5113)
GENESYS CLOUD SERVICES INC
Also Called: Interactive Intelligence
4307 Emperor Blvd Ste 300 (27703-8080)
PHONE................................317 872-3000
EMP: 37
SALES (corp-wide): 220.02MM **Privately Held**
Web: www.genesys.com
SIC: 7372 Business oriented computer software
HQ: Genesys Cloud Services, Inc.
1302 El Cmino Real Ste 30
Menlo Park CA 94025

(G-5114)
GIGABEAM CORPORATION
4021 Stirrup Creek Dr Ste 400 (27703-9352)
P.O. Box 50266 (33074-0266)
PHONE................................919 206-4426
Louis Slaughter, *Ch*
EMP: 14 **EST:** 2004
SALES (est): 441.19K **Privately Held**
SIC: 3663 Radio and t.v. communications equipment

(G-5115)
GILERO LLC (HQ)
Also Called: Eg-Gilero
4319 S Alston Ave (27713-2487)
PHONE................................919 595-8220
Theodore Mosler, *CEO*
Todd Korogi, *
Kevin Miller, *
EMP: 148 **EST:** 2002
SALES (est): 51.41MM
SALES (corp-wide): 338.9MM **Privately Held**
Web: www.gilero.com
SIC: 3841 Surgical and medical instruments
PA: Ernie Green Industries, Inc.
1785 Big Hill Rd
Dayton OH 45439
614 219-1423

(G-5116)
GLASS JUG
5410 Nc Highway 55 Ste V (27713-7802)
PHONE................................919 818-6907
Chris Creech, *Managing Member*
Kathryn Creech, *Managing Member*
EMP: 15 **EST:** 2014
SALES (est): 1.79MM **Privately Held**
Web: www.glass-jug.com
SIC: 2082 5181 5921 5813 Beer (alcoholic beverage); Beer and ale; Wine and beer; Beer garden (drinking places)

(G-5117)
GLASS JUG LLC
5410 Nc Highway 55 Ste V (27713-7802)
PHONE................................919 813-0135
Chris Creech, *Managing Member*
Kathryn Creech, *Managing Member*
EMP: 15 **EST:** 2014
SALES (est): 1.7MM **Privately Held**
Web: www.glass-jug.com
SIC: 5921 2082 5181 5813 Wine and beer; Beer (alcoholic beverage); Beer and ale; Beer garden (drinking places)

(G-5118)
GLAXOSMITHKLINE 69 PHARMA
1 Moore Dr (27709-0009)
PHONE................................612 719-4438
EMP: 5 **EST:** 2010
SALES (est): 165.93K **Privately Held**
SIC: 2834 Pharmaceutical preparations

(G-5119)
GLAXOSMITHKLINE LLC
5 3313 Gsk Co (27713)
PHONE................................919 483-5302
EMP: 27
SQ FT: 8,556
SALES (corp-wide): 35.31B **Privately Held**
Web: us.gsk.com
SIC: 2834 Pharmaceutical preparations
HQ: Glaxosmithkline Llc
2929 Walnut St Ste 1700
Philadelphia PA 19104
888 825-5249

(G-5120)
GLAXOSMITHKLINE LLC
Also Called: Glaxosmithkline
410 Blackwell St (27701-3986)
P.O. Box 13398 (27709-3398)
PHONE................................919 483-2100
EMP: 27
SALES (corp-wide): 35.31B **Privately Held**
Web: us.gsk.com
SIC: 2834 Pharmaceutical preparations
HQ: Glaxosmithkline Llc
2929 Walnut St Ste 1700
Philadelphia PA 19104
888 825-5249

(G-5121)
GLAXOSMITHKLINE LLC
406 Blackwell St (27701-3983)
PHONE................................252 315-9774
EMP: 7
SALES (corp-wide): 35.31B **Privately Held**
SIC: 2834 5122 Pharmaceutical preparations ; Pharmaceuticals
HQ: Glaxosmithkline Llc
2929 Walnut St Ste 1700
Philadelphia PA 19104
888 825-5249

(G-5122)
GLAXOSMITHKLINE LLC
2512 S Tricenter Blvd (27713-1852)
PHONE................................919 483-2100
EMP: 10
SALES (corp-wide): 35.31B **Privately Held**
Web: us.gsk.com
SIC: 2834 5122 Pharmaceutical preparations ; Pharmaceuticals
HQ: Glaxosmithkline Llc
2929 Walnut St Ste 1700
Philadelphia PA 19104
888 825-5249

(G-5123)
GLAXOSMITHKLINE SERVICES INC
5 Moore Dr (27709-0143)
P.O. Box 13398 (27709-3398)
PHONE................................919 483-2100
Ryan Harris, *Prin*
EMP: 453 **EST:** 1998
SALES (est): 76.88MM
SALES (corp-wide): 35.31B **Privately Held**

Durham - Durham County (G-5124)

Web: www.gsk.com
SIC: 2834 Pharmaceutical preparations
PA: Gsk Plc
   G S K House
   Brentford MIDDX TW8 9
   208 047-5000

(G-5124)
GLENNSTONE FIELD OFFICE
4028 Lady Slipper Ln (27704-6418)
PHONE.................................919 680-8700
Bill Beard, Mgr
EMP: 5 EST: 2001
SALES (est): 86.73K Privately Held
SIC: 2452 Prefabricated wood buildings

(G-5125)
GRAEDON ENTERPRISES INC
Also Called: People's Pharmacy, The
5900 Beech Bluff Ln (27705-8114)
P.O. Box 52027 (27717-2027)
PHONE.................................919 493-0448
EMP: 8 EST: 1978
SALES (est): 686.1K Privately Held
SIC: 2731 Pamphlets: publishing only, not printed on site

(G-5126)
GRAYBEARD DISTILLERY INC
4625 Industry Ln (27713-1497)
PHONE.................................919 361-9980
EMP: 11 EST: 2016
SALES (est): 738.42K Privately Held
Web: www.bedlamvodka.com
SIC: 2085 Distilled and blended liquors

(G-5127)
GRIFOLS THERAPEUTICS LLC (DH)
79 Tw Alexander Dr (27709-0152)
P.O. Box 110526 (27709-5526)
PHONE.................................919 316-6300
David Bell, *
Max Debrouwer, *
▲ EMP: 300 EST: 2004
SALES (est): 549.53MM Privately Held
SIC: 2834 2836 Pharmaceutical preparations; Agar culture media
HQ: Grifols Shared Services North America, Inc.
   2410 Lillyvale Ave
   Los Angeles CA 90032
   323 225-2221

(G-5128)
GRIFOLS THERAPEUTICS LLC
79 Tw Alexander Dr (27709-0152)
PHONE.................................919 316-6668
Lawrence D Stern, Brnch Mgr
EMP: 79
SIC: 2834 Drugs acting on the central nervous system & sense organs
HQ: Grifols Therapeutics Llc
   79 Tw Alexander Dr
   Durham NC 27709

(G-5129)
GRIFOLS THERAPEUTICS LLC
85 Tw Alexander Dr (27709-0152)
PHONE.................................919 316-6214
Leslie Tremlett, Mgr
EMP: 10
SIC: 2836 Blood derivatives
HQ: Grifols Therapeutics Llc
   79 Tw Alexander Dr
   Durham NC 27709

(G-5130)
HAND 2 HAND SIGNS
17 Streamview Ct (27713-9337)
PHONE.................................919 401-2420
Leslie Stern, Prin
EMP: 5 EST: 2010
SALES (est): 121.14K Privately Held
SIC: 3993 Signs and advertising specialties

(G-5131)
HAPPY WAX
120 W Parrish St (27701-3321)
PHONE.................................888 400-3053
EMP: 5 EST: 2017
SALES (est): 243.95K Privately Held
Web: www.happywax.com
SIC: 3999 Candles

(G-5132)
HARRISON WOODWORKS INC
2322 Glendale Ave (27704-4168)
PHONE.................................919 632-3703
Tim Harrison, Prin
EMP: 4 EST: 2008
SALES (est): 489.54K Privately Held
Web: www.piedmontjoinery.com
SIC: 2431 Millwork

(G-5133)
HEATED BED PRINTING LLC
808 Advancement Ave Apt 202 (27703-6464)
PHONE.................................860 230-6142
Adam Becher, Prin
EMP: 4 EST: 2019
SALES (est): 92.3K Privately Held
SIC: 2752 Commercial printing, lithographic

(G-5134)
HEIDELBERG MTLS US CEM LLC
1031 Drew St (27701-2630)
PHONE.................................919 682-5791
Buddy Howell, Brnch Mgr
EMP: 4
SQ FT: 816
SALES (corp-wide): 21.9B Privately Held
Web: www.heidelbergmaterials.us
SIC: 3273 Ready-mixed concrete
HQ: Heidelberg Materials Us Cement Llc
   300 E John Carpenter Fwy
   Irving TX 75062
   877 534-4442

(G-5135)
HEMO BIOSCIENCE INC
4022 Stirrup Creek Dr Ste 311 (27703-8998)
PHONE.................................919 313-2888
Noel Brown, Pr
◆ EMP: 6 EST: 2003
SALES (est): 1.65MM Privately Held
Web: www.hemobioscience.com
SIC: 2819 Chemicals, reagent grade: refined from technical grade

(G-5136)
HEMOSONICS LLC
4020 Stirrup Creek Dr (27703-9410)
PHONE.................................800 280-5589
EMP: 49
SALES (corp-wide): 8.49MM Privately Held
Web: www.hemosonics.com
SIC: 3845 3829 Ultrasonic scanning devices, medical; Measuring and controlling devices, nec
PA: Hemosonics, Llc
   400 Preston Ave Ste 250
   Charlottesville VA 27703
   800 280-5589

(G-5137)
HEMOSONICS LLC
4020 Stirrup Creek Dr Ste 105 (27703-9410)
PHONE.................................800 280-5589
Timothy J Fischer, Pr
Steve Erwine, *
EMP: 96 EST: 2005
SALES (est): 11.43MM Privately Held
Web: www.hemosonics.com
SIC: 3845 3829 Ultrasonic scanning devices, medical; Measuring and controlling devices, nec

(G-5138)
HL JAMES LLC
1911 W Club Blvd (27705-3503)
PHONE.................................516 398-3311
SALES (est): 74.52K Privately Held
Web: www.hljames.com
SIC: 2323 Men's and boy's neckwear

(G-5139)
HONEYGIRL MEADERY LLC
105 Hood St Ste 6 (27701-3794)
PHONE.................................919 399-3056
EMP: 5 EST: 2012
SALES (est): 246.34K Privately Held
Web: www.honeygirlmeadery.com
SIC: 2084 Wines

(G-5140)
HOODOO HONEY LLC
3600 N Duke St Ste 1 (27704-1769)
PHONE.................................252 548-0697
Ebone Hinnant, Managing Member
EMP: 8 EST: 2020
SALES (est): 270.82K Privately Held
SIC: 3999 Magic equipment, supplies, and props

(G-5141)
HORTONWORKS INC
312 Blackwell St Ste 100 (27701-3669)
PHONE.................................855 846-7866
EMP: 4
SALES (corp-wide): 1.26B Privately Held
Web: www.cloudera.com
SIC: 7372 Prepackaged software
HQ: Hortonworks, Inc.
   5470 Great America Pkwy
   Santa Clara CA 95054

(G-5142)
HYDRO SERVICE & SUPPLIES INC (PA)
513 United Dr (27713-1477)
P.O. Box 12197 (27709-2197)
PHONE.................................919 544-3744
Dave Currin, Pr
Charles S Atwater, *
Paul Rigsbee, *
Charles S Atwater Junior, CFO
Charles Riley, *
▲ EMP: 30 EST: 1967
SQ FT: 14,000
SALES (est): 11.19MM
SALES (corp-wide): 11.19MM Privately Held
Web: www.hydroservice.com
SIC: 3589 7699 Water treatment equipment, industrial; Industrial equipment services

(G-5143)
HYPERBRANCH MEDICAL TECH INC
800 Capitola Dr Ste 12 (27713-4385)
PHONE.................................919 433-3325
Jeffrey Clark, CEO
EMP: 13 EST: 2003
SALES (est): 6.15MM
SALES (corp-wide): 20.5B Publicly Held
Web: cmf.stryker.com
SIC: 3842 3841 Surgical appliances and supplies; Surgical and medical instruments
PA: Stryker Corporation
   1941 Stryker Way
   Portage MI 49002
   269 385-2600

(G-5144)
ICAGEN LLC
1035 Swabia Ct Ste 110 (27703-0963)
PHONE.................................919 941-5206
Richard Cunningham, CEO
EMP: 84 EST: 2020
SALES (est): 9.17MM
SALES (corp-wide): 59.08MM Publicly Held
SIC: 2834 Pharmaceutical preparations
PA: Omniab, Inc.
   5980 Horton St Ste 600
   Emeryville CA 94608
   510 250-7800

(G-5145)
IDEABLOCK LLC
212 W Main St Ste 302 (27701-3239)
P.O. Box 29622 (27626-0622)
PHONE.................................919 551-5054
Eli M Sheets, Pr
EMP: 5 EST: 2018
SALES (est): 56.54K Privately Held
Web: www.ideablock.io
SIC: 7372 Business oriented computer software

(G-5146)
IDEAL PRECAST INC
7020 Mount Hermon Church Rd (27705-8067)
P.O. Box 61219 (27715-1219)
PHONE.................................919 801-8287
Mary Beth Johen, Prin
EMP: 11 EST: 2008
SALES (est): 2.34MM Privately Held
Web: www.idealprecast.com
SIC: 3272 Concrete products, precast, nec

(G-5147)
IFTA USA INC
4819 Emperor Blvd Ste 400 (27703-5420)
PHONE.................................919 659-8393
EMP: 6 EST: 2015
SALES (est): 248.13K Privately Held
Web: www.iftausa.com
SIC: 2048 Prepared feeds, nec
PA: Biovet Sa
   Calle De Luxemburg 25
   Constanti T 43120

(G-5148)
IGNITERATE LLC
600 Park Offices Dr Ste 300-137 (27709-1009)
PHONE.................................919 473-9560
EMP: 4 EST: 2020
SALES (est): 79.23K Privately Held
Web: www.igniterate.com
SIC: 7372 Prepackaged software

(G-5149)
IMAGINEOPTIX CORPORATION
20 Tw Alexander Dr Ste 100 (27709-0148)
PHONE.................................919 757-4945
Erin Clark, CEO
Jason Kekas, CFO
Jon Warren, Ex VP
EMP: 18 EST: 2004
SALES (est): 6.5MM
SALES (corp-wide): 134.9B Publicly Held
SIC: 3827 Optical instruments and lenses
PA: Meta Platforms, Inc.
   1 Meta Way

Menlo Park CA 94025
650 543-4800

(G-5150)
IMPLUS FOOTCARE LLC (DH)
Also Called: Airplus
2001 Tw Alexander Dr (27709-0184)
P.O. Box 13925 (27709-3925)
PHONE..................................800 446-7587
Michael Polk, *Managing Member*
Seth Richards, *
Todd Vore, *
Rodney Bullock, *
◆ **EMP:** 300 **EST:** 1988
SQ FT: 315,000
SALES (est): 166.21MM
SALES (corp-wide): 300MM **Privately Held**
Web: www.implus.com
SIC: 5139 3949 7389 Footwear, athletic; Sporting and athletic goods, nec; Business services, nec
HQ: Implus, Llc
2001 Tw Alexander Dr
Durham NC 27709
919 544-7900

(G-5151)
INDUSPAC USA
3829 S Miami Blvd (27703-5419)
PHONE..................................919 484-9484
EMP: 6 **EST:** 2018
SALES (est): 113.98K **Privately Held**
SIC: 2671 Paper; coated and laminated packaging

(G-5152)
INDUSTRIAL MTAL FLAME SPRYERS
419 Salem St (27703-4255)
PHONE..................................919 596-9381
Dwight Crabtree, *Pr*
Mark Wilson, *VP*
EMP: 9 **EST:** 1961
SQ FT: 5,510
SALES (est): 845.37K **Privately Held**
SIC: 3544 3599 Extrusion dies; Machine shop, jobbing and repair

(G-5153)
INFERENSYS INC
112 Dare Pines Way (27703-8349)
PHONE..................................910 398-1200
Edwin Addison, *CEO*
Don Joder, *VP*
EMP: 4
SQ FT: 150
SALES (est): 98.37K **Privately Held**
Web: www.inferensys.net
SIC: 7372 Prepackaged software

(G-5154)
INFINITY COMMUNICATIONS LLC (PA)
5201 International Dr (27712-8950)
P.O. Box 91751 (27675-1751)
PHONE..................................919 797-2334
Jeff Coffey, *Managing Member*
EMP: 23 **EST:** 2012
SALES (est): 10.33MM
SALES (corp-wide): 10.33MM **Privately Held**
Web: www.infinitycommgroup.net
SIC: 8748 8322 3825 4812 Telecommunications consultant; Disaster service; Network analyzers; Cellular telephone services

(G-5155)
INHALON BIOPHARMA INC
104 Tw Alexander Dr Rm 2021rtp (27709-0002)
PHONE..................................650 439-0110
Samuel Lai, *Pr*
EMP: 5 **EST:** 2018
SALES (est): 490.27K **Privately Held**
Web: www.inhalon.com
SIC: 2834 Pharmaceutical preparations

(G-5156)
INK WELL INC
Also Called: Ink Well
3112 N Roxboro St (27704-3252)
PHONE..................................919 682-8279
EMP: 6 **EST:** 2016
SALES (est): 94.24K **Privately Held**
Web: www.theinkwellusa.com
SIC: 2752 Commercial printing, lithographic

(G-5157)
INK WELL TATOO
2416 Lindmont Ave (27704-4734)
PHONE..................................919 682-8279
Shawn Corbet, *Mgr*
EMP: 5 **EST:** 2010
SALES (est): 166.79K **Privately Held**
SIC: 2752 Commercial printing, lithographic

(G-5158)
INNAVASC MEDICAL INC
110 Swift Ave (27705-4880)
PHONE..................................813 902-2228
Joseph Knight, *CEO*
EMP: 10 **EST:** 2013
SALES (est): 907.45K **Privately Held**
Web: www.innavasc.com
SIC: 3841 Surgical and medical instruments

(G-5159)
INPERNUM PHARMA SOLUTIONS LLC
3815 Saint Marks Rd (27707-5012)
PHONE..................................919 599-5501
Steven A Castillo, *Prin*
EMP: 4 **EST:** 2016
SALES (est): 239.31K **Privately Held**
SIC: 2834 Pharmaceutical preparations

(G-5160)
INSTROTEK INC (PA)
1 Triangle Dr (27709-0005)
P.O. Box 13944 (27709-3944)
PHONE..................................919 875-8371
Al Regimand, *Pr*
Lawrence James, *VP*
Maurice Arbelaez, *Dir*
▲ **EMP:** 23 **EST:** 1997
SQ FT: 23,000
SALES (est): 8.07MM
SALES (corp-wide): 8.07MM **Privately Held**
Web: www.instrotek.com
SIC: 3531 Construction machinery

(G-5161)
INTERNATIONAL BUS MCHS CORP
Also Called: IBM
3039 Cornwallis Rd (27709-0154)
P.O. Box 12195 (27709-2195)
PHONE..................................919 543-6919
Tina Wilson, *Brnch Mgr*
EMP: 464
SALES (corp-wide): 60.53B **Publicly Held**
Web: www.ibm.com
SIC: 7371 7373 3577 3571 Computer software systems analysis and design, custom; Computer systems analysis and design; Computer peripheral equipment, nec; Electronic computers
PA: International Business Machines Corporation
1 New Orchard Rd Ste 1 # 1
Armonk NY 10504
914 499-1900

(G-5162)
INTERNATIONAL SOCIETY AUTOMTN (PA)
Also Called: I S A
67 T W Alexander Dr (27709-0185)
P.O. Box 12277 (27709-2277)
PHONE..................................919 206-4176
Patrick Gouhin, *Ex Dir*
Leo Staples, *
James Keaveney, *
Mary Ramsey, *
EMP: 50 **EST:** 1945
SQ FT: 43,000
SALES (est): 14.87MM
SALES (corp-wide): 14.87MM **Privately Held**
Web: www.isa.org
SIC: 8621 2721 2731 Scientific membership association; Magazines: publishing only, not printed on site; Books, publishing and printing

(G-5163)
IPAS
4711 Hope Valley Rd (27707-5651)
P.O. Box 9990 (27515-1990)
PHONE..................................919 967-7052
John Herrington, *Pr*
Terrence Cominski, *
Barbara Crane, *
EMP: 110 **EST:** 1973
SALES (est): 44.92MM **Privately Held**
Web: www.ipas.org
SIC: 8399 3842 Fund raising organization, non-fee basis; Gynecological supplies and appliances
PA: Ips
Addis Ababa

(G-5164)
IPS CORPORATION
Scigrip Americas
600 Ellis Rd (27703-6015)
P.O. Box 12729 (27709-2729)
PHONE..................................919 598-2400
Kevin Connolly, *Brnch Mgr*
EMP: 25
SQ FT: 32,934
Web: www.ipscorp.com
SIC: 5085 2891 Industrial supplies; Adhesives
HQ: Ips Corporation
455 W Victoria St
Compton CA 90220
310 898-3300

(G-5165)
IPS STRUCTURAL ADHESIVES INC (DH)
600 Ellis Rd (27703-6015)
PHONE..................................919 598-2400
EMP: 24 **EST:** 2006
SALES (est): 9.23MM **Privately Held**
Web: www.ipscorp.com
SIC: 2891 Adhesives, plastic
HQ: Ips Corporation
455 W Victoria St
Compton CA 90220
310 898-3300

(G-5166)
IQVIA PHARMA INC (HQ)
Also Called: Quintiles Pharma, Inc.
4820 Emperor Blvd (27703-8426)
PHONE..................................919 998-2000
Pamela Long, *Ex Dir*
John Ratliff, *Pr*
R David Andrews, *Treas*
Kim L Rose, *Sec*
EMP: 55 **EST:** 2005
SALES (est): 42.52MM **Publicly Held**
SIC: 2834 Pharmaceutical preparations
PA: Iqvia Holdings Inc.
2400 Ellis Rd
Durham NC 27703

(G-5167)
ISA
67 Alexander Dr (27709-0185)
P.O. Box 12277 (27709-2277)
PHONE..................................919 549-8411
Jim Keabney, *Pr*
Tony Fragnito, *
EMP: 98 **EST:** 1985
SALES (est): 949.53K
SALES (corp-wide): 14.87MM **Privately Held**
Web: www.isa.org
SIC: 2721 2731 Magazines: publishing only, not printed on site; Book publishing
PA: International Society Of Automation
67 Tw Alexander Dr
Durham NC 27709
919 206-4176

(G-5168)
ISS
3108 Thistlecone Way (27703-3964)
PHONE..................................919 317-8314
Chris Kromm, *Prin*
EMP: 6 **EST:** 2010
SALES (est): 131.21K **Privately Held**
SIC: 3315 Steel wire and related products

(G-5169)
IXC DISCOVERY INC (PA)
4222 Emperor Blvd Ste 350 (27703-8030)
P.O. Box 14487 (27709-4487)
PHONE..................................919 941-5206
Richard Cunningham, *Pr*
Timothy C Tyson, *Non-Executive Chairman of the Board*
Mark Korb, *CFO*
Douglas Krafte, *CSO*
EMP: 29 **EST:** 2003
SALES (est): 23.49MM
SALES (corp-wide): 23.49MM **Privately Held**
SIC: 2834 Pharmaceutical preparations

(G-5170)
JAMES E LATTA
2725 Beck Rd (27704-3701)
PHONE..................................919 682-5793
James E Latta, *Owner*
EMP: 6 **EST:** 2001
SALES (est): 76.54K **Privately Held**
SIC: 3211 Construction glass

(G-5171)
JASON CASE CORP
4809 Hillsborough Rd (27705-2237)
PHONE..................................212 786-2288
Jason Comparetto, *CEO*
EMP: 10 **EST:** 2015
SALES (est): 570.85K **Privately Held**
Web: www.jasoncases.com
SIC: 3861 Photographic equipment and supplies

(G-5172)
JOHNSON CONTROLS INC
Also Called: Johnson Controls
5 Moore Dr (27709-0143)
P.O. Box 13398 (27709-3398)
PHONE..................................919 905-5745
Seth Haywood, *Mgr*
EMP: 19
Web: www.johnsoncontrols.com
SIC: 2531 Seats, automobile
HQ: Johnson Controls, Inc.
5757 N Green Bay Ave

Durham - Durham County (G-5173)   GEOGRAPHIC SECTION

Milwaukee WI 53209
920 245-6409

(G-5173)
JOYCE HEFLIN PRESIDENT
5015 Lazywood Ln (27712-9792)
PHONE..................................919 451-0003
Joyce Heflin, *Prin*
EMP: 5 **EST:** 2011
SALES (est): 88.84K **Privately Held**
SIC: 3825 Network analyzers

(G-5174)
JUSTENOUGH SOFTWARE CORP INC
1009 Slater Rd Ste 420 (27703-8327)
PHONE..................................800 949-3432
Malcolm Edward Buxton, *Brnch Mgr*
EMP: 4
SALES (corp-wide): 28.94MM **Privately Held**
Web: www.justenoughsoftware.com
SIC: 7372 Business oriented computer software
HQ: Justenough Software Corporation, Inc.
15440 Laguna Canyon Rd # 100
Irvine CA 92618

(G-5175)
K&M SHEET METAL LLC
1310 E Cornwallis Rd (27713-1423)
PHONE..................................919 544-8887
EMP: 17 **EST:** 2019
SALES (est): 4.25MM **Privately Held**
Web: www.kmsheetmetal.com
SIC: 3444 Sheet metalwork

(G-5176)
KASHIF MAZHAR
68 Tw Alexander Dr (27709-0151)
PHONE..................................919 314-2891
Kashif Mazhar, *Prin*
EMP: 5
SALES (est): 155.87K **Privately Held**
SIC: 3841 Surgical and medical instruments

(G-5177)
KBI BIOPHARMA INC (PA)
Also Called: K B I Biopharma
1101 Hamlin Rd (27704-9658)
P.O. Box 15579 (27704-0579)
PHONE..................................919 479-9898
J D Mowery, *CEO*
Timothy Kelly, *
Dan Povia, *
Dirk Lange, *
Marykay Marchigiani, *
EMP: 66 **EST:** 2001
SQ FT: 145,000
SALES (est): 430.83MM
SALES (corp-wide): 430.83MM **Privately Held**
Web: www.kbibiopharma.com
SIC: 2834 8733 Pharmaceutical preparations ; Biotechnical research, noncommercial

(G-5178)
KBI BIOPHARMA INC
2 Triangle Dr (27709-0005)
PHONE..................................919 479-9898
EMP: 6
SALES (corp-wide): 430.83MM **Privately Held**
Web: www.kbibiopharma.com
SIC: 2834 Pharmaceutical preparations
PA: Kbi Biopharma, Inc.
1101 Hamlin Rd
Durham NC 27704
919 479-9898

(G-5179)
KELLEY G CUPCAKES
2341 Huron St (27707-1913)
PHONE..................................314 368-5316
Kelley Gill, *Prin*
EMP: 5 **EST:** 2010
SALES (est): 157.55K **Privately Held**
SIC: 2051 Bread, cake, and related products

(G-5180)
KESTREL I ACQUISITION CORPORATION
1035 Swabia Ct (27703-8462)
P.O. Box 13582 (27709-3582)
PHONE..................................919 990-7500
EMP: 1567
SIC: 2822 2869 2899 2891 Butadiene-acrylonitrile, nitrile rubbers, NBR; Vinyl acetate; Rosin sizes; Adhesives

(G-5181)
KINETIC SYSTEMS INC
4900 Prospectus Dr Ste 500 (27713-4407)
PHONE..................................919 322-7200
James Wilber, *Opers Mgr*
EMP: 75
SALES (corp-wide): 395.55K **Privately Held**
Web: www.kinetics.net
SIC: 1711 3312 Mechanical contractor; Blast furnaces and steel mills
HQ: Kinetic Systems, Inc.
4309 Hacienda Dr Ste 450
Pleasanton CA 94588
510 683-6000

(G-5182)
KOLB BOYETTE & ASSOC INC
Also Called: Triangle Web Printing
514 United Dr Ste A (27713-1663)
P.O. Box 13345 (27709-3345)
PHONE..................................919 544-7839
Al Thorn, *Pr*
Willis Roberson, *
Eric Kolb, *
EMP: 35 **EST:** 1992
SQ FT: 9,000
SALES (est): 4.61MM **Privately Held**
Web: www.triwebprinting.com
SIC: 2752 Offset printing

(G-5183)
KWG MUSIC LLC
2211 Pear Tree Ln (27703-6286)
PHONE..................................773 771-2017
EMP: 5 **EST:** 2019
SALES (est): 72.25K **Privately Held**
SIC: 3599 Machine shop, jobbing and repair

(G-5184)
KYMERA INTERNATIONAL LLC (PA)
2601 Weck Dr (27709-1100)
PHONE..................................919 544-8090
Barton White, *CEO*
EMP: 10 **EST:** 2018
SALES (est): 26.44MM
SALES (corp-wide): 26.44MM **Privately Held**
SIC: 3334 5169 3399 Ingots (primary), aluminum; Industrial chemicals; Metal powders, pastes, and flakes

(G-5185)
L C INDUSTRIES INC (PA)
4500 Emperor Blvd (27703-8420)
P.O. Box 13629 (27709-3649)
PHONE..................................919 596-8277
Richard M Hudson, *Ch*
William L Hudson, *
Tom White, *
Susan Johnson, *
◆ **EMP:** 125 **EST:** 1938
SQ FT: 229,000
SALES (est): 7.49MM
SALES (corp-wide): 7.49MM **Privately Held**
Web: www.lcindustries.com
SIC: 5943 2675 2515 2253 Office forms and supplies; Folders, filing, die-cut: made from purchased materials; Mattresses and foundations; Shirts(outerwear), knit

(G-5186)
LASER INK CORPORATION
Also Called: Laser Image Printing & Mktg
4018 Patriot Dr Ste 200 (27703-8083)
PHONE..................................919 361-5822
Richard Smith, *Pr*
Kelly Clark, *
▲ **EMP:** 30 **EST:** 1987
SALES (est): 4.16MM **Privately Held**
Web: www.laserimagenc.com
SIC: 2759 2741 7331 2752 Laser printing; Miscellaneous publishing; Direct mail advertising services; Commercial printing, lithographic

(G-5187)
LEATHERBOUND BOOK WORKS
608 Starmont Dr (27705-2931)
PHONE..................................919 448-7847
Michael Greer, *Owner*
EMP: 4 **EST:** 2012
SALES (est): 167.03K **Privately Held**
Web: www.leatherboundbindery.com
SIC: 2789 Bookbinding and related work

(G-5188)
LEE MARKS (PA)
Also Called: Print Marks Screen Prtg & EMB
4304 Amesbury Ln (27707-5386)
PHONE..................................919 493-2208
EMP: 6 **EST:** 1988
SALES (est): 200K **Privately Held**
Web: www.localprintnc.com
SIC: 2395 2396 Embroidery products, except Schiffli machine; Screen printing on fabric articles

(G-5189)
LEXITAS PHARMA SERVICES INC
5425 Page Rd Ste 410 (27703-2059)
PHONE..................................919 205-0012
George Magrath, *CEO*
Jeanne Hecht, *
Chad Ice, *
EMP: 95 **EST:** 2011
SALES (est): 6.57MM **Privately Held**
Web: www.lexitas.com
SIC: 8731 2834 Commercial physical research; Pharmaceutical preparations

(G-5190)
LINDE GAS & EQUIPMENT INC
Also Called: Linde Gas North America
11 Triangle Dr (27709-0005)
P.O. Box 12338 (27709-2338)
PHONE..................................919 549-0633
Roger Wyett, *Mgr*
EMP: 59
Web: www.lindeus.com
SIC: 2813 8731 Oxygen, compressed or liquefied; Commercial physical research
HQ: Linde Gas & Equipment Inc.
10 Riverview Dr
Danbury CT 06810
844 445-4633

(G-5191)
LIQUIDATING REICHHOLD INC
Also Called: Reichhold Liquidation, Inc.
1035 Swabia Ct (27703-8462)
P.O. Box 13582 (27709-3582)
PHONE..................................919 990-7500
◆ **EMP:** 550
SIC: 2821 2822 2869 2899 Plastics materials and resins; Butadiene-acrylonitrile, nitrile rubbers, NBR; Vinyl acetate; Rosin sizes

(G-5192)
LMG HOLDINGS INC
4920 S Alston Ave (27713-4423)
PHONE..................................919 653-0910
Kathryn Claire Haertel, *Prin*
EMP: 19 **EST:** 1993
SALES (est): 1.8MM **Privately Held**
SIC: 3694 Ignition systems, high frequency

(G-5193)
LO & BEHOLD LLC
202 E Maynard Ave (27704-3238)
PHONE..................................336 988-0589
Gina Marie Wisotzky, *Admn*
EMP: 4 **EST:** 2014
SALES (est): 114.48K **Privately Held**
Web: www.loandbeholdnaturals.com
SIC: 2844 Perfumes, cosmetics and other toilet preparations

(G-5194)
LOGICBIT SOFTWARE LLC
Also Called: Houdiniesq
2530 Meridian Pkwy Ste 300 (27713-5272)
PHONE..................................888 366-2280
Francisco Rivera, *CEO*
Annie Zhang, *Sec*
Frank Rivera, *Managing Member*
EMP: 20 **EST:** 2008
SQ FT: 12,000
SALES (est): 914.36K **Privately Held**
Web: www.houdiniesq.com
SIC: 7371 7372 Computer software systems analysis and design, custom; Prepackaged software

(G-5195)
LOGO LABEL PRINTING COMPANY
4416 Bennett Memorial Rd Ste 101 (27705-2484)
PHONE..................................919 309-0007
Timothy Oats, *Pr*
Catherine Bacon, *VP*
EMP: 4 **EST:** 2006
SALES (est): 866.99K **Privately Held**
Web: www.logolabelprinting.com
SIC: 2759 Screen printing

(G-5196)
LRW HOLDINGS INC
Also Called: Little Red Wagon Granola
2310 Sparger Rd Ste B (27705-1208)
PHONE..................................919 609-4172
Venmathy Mcmahan, *Pr*
EMP: 7 **EST:** 2019
SALES (est): 602.21K **Privately Held**
SIC: 5145 2043 Snack foods; Cereal breakfast foods

(G-5197)
LUDLAM FAMILY FOODS LLC
1408 Christian Ave Ste 3 (27705-2909)
PHONE..................................919 805-6061
EMP: 6
SALES (corp-wide): 227.72K **Privately Held**
SIC: 2099 Food preparations, nec
PA: Ludlam Family Foods, Llc

GEOGRAPHIC SECTION

Durham - Durham County (G-5223)

9 Saint James Pl
Chapel Hill NC 27514
919 805-6061

(G-5198)
LULU PRESS INC
700 Park Offices Dr Ste 250 (27709)
P.O. Box 12018 (27709-2018)
PHONE..............................919 447-3290
Robert Young, *CEO*
Dale Pithers, *Finance**
Don Cvetko, *
EMP: 88 **EST:** 2003
SQ FT: 27,600
SALES (est): 10.32MM **Privately Held**
Web: www.lulujr.com
SIC: 2741 Miscellaneous publishing

(G-5199)
LUMEDICA INC
1312 Dollar Ave (27701-1120)
PHONE..............................919 886-1863
William Brown, *Pr*
EMP: 5 **EST:** 2014
SALES (est): 656.72K **Privately Held**
Web: www.lumedica.co
SIC: 3845 Retinoscopes, electromedical

(G-5200)
LUXOR HYDRATION LLC
3600 N Duke St (27704-1709)
PHONE..............................919 568-5047
Maya Peacock, *Managing Member*
EMP: 11 **EST:** 2020
SALES (est): 300K **Privately Held**
SIC: 3841 7389 IV transfusion apparatus; Business Activities at Non-Commercial Site

(G-5201)
MACHINE CONSULTING SVCS INC
Also Called: MCS
1545 Cooper St (27703-5082)
PHONE..............................919 596-3033
Mike Appel, *Pr*
EMP: 5 **EST:** 1998
SQ FT: 1,800
SALES (est): 841.13K **Privately Held**
SIC: 3599 Machine shop, jobbing and repair

(G-5202)
MAGNAREP INCORPORATED
1618 Crystal Creek Dr (27712-2484)
PHONE..............................919 949-5488
Michael T Hoekstra, *Pr*
EMP: 5 **EST:** 2005
SALES (est): 138.91K **Privately Held**
Web: www.magnarep.com
SIC: 3495 Wire springs

(G-5203)
MAGNET GUYS
100 Capitola Dr Ste 101 (27713-4497)
PHONE..............................816 259-5201
Blesson George, *Owner*
EMP: 5 **EST:** 2017
SALES (est): 230.04K **Privately Held**
Web: www.themagnetguys.com
SIC: 2759 Promotional printing

(G-5204)
MAN AROUND HOUSE
908 Grandview Dr (27703-2631)
PHONE..............................919 625-5933
Anthony Parrish, *Prin*
EMP: 6 **EST:** 2010
SALES (est): 181.34K **Privately Held**
SIC: 3585 Heating equipment, complete

(G-5205)
MANDA PANDAS LLC
109 Stinhurst Dr (27713-7531)
PHONE..............................919 452-7917
EMP: 5 **EST:** 2020
SALES (est): 64.64K **Privately Held**
SIC: 3999 Candles

(G-5206)
MANUFACTUR LLC
201 W Main St (27701-3228)
PHONE..............................919 937-2090
EMP: 5 **EST:** 2018
SALES (est): 186.74K **Privately Held**
SIC: 3999 Manufacturing industries, nec

(G-5207)
MAPJOY LLC
4501 Marena Pl (27707-9220)
PHONE..............................919 450-8360
Bryan Conner, *Prin*
EMP: 4 **EST:** 2014
SALES (est): 142.96K **Privately Held**
Web: www.mapjoync.com
SIC: 7372 Prepackaged software

(G-5208)
MARC STAPLES SCULPTURE
3801 Shoccoree Dr (27705-1802)
PHONE..............................919 475-9633
Mark Staples, *Admn*
EMP: 4 **EST:** 2016
SALES (est): 97.09K **Privately Held**
Web: www.marcstaples.com
SIC: 3499 3471 Fabricated metal products, nec; Decontaminating and cleaning of missile or satellite parts

(G-5209)
MARSH WELDING
1608 Sherron Rd (27703-8879)
PHONE..............................919 335-5332
EMP: 4 **EST:** 2017
SALES (est): 51.24K **Privately Held**
Web: www.marshwelding.com
SIC: 7692 Welding repair

(G-5210)
MAVERICK BIOFEULS
104 Tw Alexander Dr Bldg 4a (27709-0002)
P.O. Box 13108 (27709-3108)
PHONE..............................919 749-8717
David Bradin, *Prin*
EMP: 5 **EST:** 2008
SALES (est): 436.89K **Privately Held**
Web: www.mavericksynfuels.com
SIC: 2869 Industrial organic chemicals, nec

(G-5211)
MAVERICK BIOFUELS
104 Tw Alexander Dr (27709-0002)
P.O. Box 13108 (27709-3108)
PHONE..............................919 931-1434
Sam Yenne, *CEO*
EMP: 8 **EST:** 2011
SALES (est): 588.74K **Privately Held**
Web: www.mavericksynfuels.com
SIC: 1382 Oil and gas exploration services

(G-5212)
MCCORKLE SIGN COMPANY INC
1107 E Geer St (27704-5024)
P.O. Box 11384 (27703-0384)
PHONE..............................919 687-7080
Tommy J Mccorkle, *Pr*
EMP: 21 **EST:** 1983
SQ FT: 12,000
SALES (est): 2.43MM **Privately Held**
Web: www.signdesignandinstallation.com
SIC: 3993 1799 Electric signs; Sign installation and maintenance

(G-5213)
MEASUREMENT INCORPORATED (PA)
Also Called: M I
423 Morris St (27701-2128)
PHONE..............................919 683-2413
Henry H Scherich, *Pr*
Michael Bunch, *
Holly Baker, *
Kirk Ridge, *
Kendra Timberlake, *
EMP: 123 **EST:** 1980
SQ FT: 63,000
SALES (est): 90.64MM
SALES (corp-wide): 90.64MM **Privately Held**
Web: www.measurementinc.com
SIC: 2752 8748 2791 2789 Offset printing; Testing service, educational or personnel; Typesetting; Bookbinding and related work

(G-5214)
MED EXPRESS/MEDICAL SPC INC
4620 Industry Ln Ste A (27713-1657)
P.O. Box 13816 (27709-3816)
PHONE..............................919 572-2568
Curtis Beatty, *CEO*
Annette Beatty, *Sec*
EMP: 19 **EST:** 1996
SQ FT: 2,000
SALES (est): 2.39MM **Privately Held**
Web: www.specialtycma.com
SIC: 5047 3841 Medical equipment and supplies; Surgical and medical instruments

(G-5215)
MEDKOO INC
Also Called: Medkoo Biosciences
2224 Sedwick Rd Ste 102 (27713-2656)
PHONE..............................919 636-5577
Qingqi Chen, *Pr*
EMP: 6 **EST:** 2009
SQ FT: 1,900
SALES (est): 732.8K **Privately Held**
Web: www.medkoo.com
SIC: 2833 Medicinals and botanicals

(G-5216)
MEDLIO INC
Also Called: Medlio
3313 Old Chapel Hill Rd (27707-3611)
PHONE..............................919 599-4870
David Brooks, *CEO*
EMP: 5 **EST:** 2013
SALES (est): 290.25K **Privately Held**
Web: www.medl.io
SIC: 7372 Application computer software

(G-5217)
MEMSCAP INC (HQ)
3021 E Cornwallis Rd Research Triangle Pk (27709-0146)
P.O. Box 14486 (27709-4486)
PHONE..............................919 248-4102
Jean Michel Karam, *CEO*
Ron Wages, *
Jan Hallenstvedt, *
Yann Cousinet, *
Nicolas Bertsch, *
EMP: 45 **EST:** 1999
SQ FT: 14,000
SALES (est): 47.23MM **Privately Held**
Web: www.memscap.com
SIC: 3674 Microcircuits, integrated (semiconductor)
PA: Memscap
Parc Activillage
Bernin

(G-5218)
MEMSCAP INC
3026 Cornwallis Rd (27709-0007)
P.O. Box 13942 (27709-3942)
PHONE..............................919 248-1441
James Carter, *Opers Mgr*
EMP: 110
SQ FT: 112,000
Web: www.memscap.com
SIC: 3699 Electrical equipment and supplies, nec
HQ: Memscap, Inc.
3021 Cornwallis Rd
Durham NC 27709
919 248-4102

(G-5219)
MERCK SHARP & DOHME LLC
Also Called: Merck
5325 Old Oxford Rd (27712-8730)
PHONE..............................919 425-4000
John Wagner, *Mgr*
EMP: 120
SALES (corp-wide): 60.12B **Publicly Held**
Web: www.merck.com
SIC: 2834 Pharmaceutical preparations
HQ: Merck Sharp & Dohme Llc
126 E Lincoln Ave
Rahway NJ 07065
908 740-4000

(G-5220)
MERCK TEKNIKA LLC
100 Rodolphe St Bldg 1300 (27712-9402)
PHONE..............................919 620-7200
Rita Karachun, *Pr*
Caroline Litchfield, *
Jon Filderman, *
EMP: 35 **EST:** 2000
SALES (est): 9.67MM
SALES (corp-wide): 60.12B **Publicly Held**
SIC: 2834 Pharmaceutical preparations
PA: Merck & Co., Inc.
126 E Lincoln Ave
Rahway NJ 07065
908 740-4000

(G-5221)
MEREDITH MEDIA CO
Also Called: Fastsigns
4015 University Dr Ste 2d (27707-2548)
PHONE..............................919 748-4808
EMP: 12 **EST:** 2020
SALES (est): 268.38K **Privately Held**
Web: www.fastsigns.com
SIC: 3993 Signs and advertising specialties

(G-5222)
METALCRAFT FABRICATING COMPANY
1316 Old Oxford Rd (27704-9500)
P.O. Box 15238 (27704-0238)
PHONE..............................919 477-2117
James D Fletcher, *Pr*
EMP: 12 **EST:** 1956
SQ FT: 9,250
SALES (est): 997.67K **Privately Held**
Web: www.metalfabricating.com
SIC: 3441 Fabricated structural metal

(G-5223)
MICELL TECHNOLOGIES INC
801 Capitola Dr Ste 1 (27713-4384)
PHONE..............................919 313-2102
EMP: 47 **EST:** 1996
SQ FT: 12,000
SALES (est): 7.04MM **Privately Held**
Web: www.micell.com
SIC: 3841 Surgical and medical instruments

Durham - Durham County (G-5224) — GEOGRAPHIC SECTION

(G-5224)
MICROSS ADVNCED INTRCNNECT TEC
Also Called: Micross Components
3021 Cornwallis Rd (27709-0146)
P.O. Box 110283 (27709-5283)
PHONE..................919 248-1872
John Lannon, *Genl Mgr*
Anna Khlebnikova Ctrl, *Prin*
Michael Rooney, *CFO*
EMP: 30 **EST:** 1998
SQ FT: 95,000
SALES (est): 9.33MM
SALES (corp-wide): 340.38MM **Privately Held**
SIC: 3674 Microcircuits, integrated (semiconductor)
PA: Micross Inc.
225 Broadhollow Rd # 305
Melville NY 11747
407 298-7100

(G-5225)
MIKE DS BBQ LLC
455 S Driver St (27703-4201)
P.O. Box 11872 (27703-0872)
PHONE..................866 960-8652
Michael Delossantos, *Managing Member*
Michael De Los Santos, *Managing Member*
EMP: 5 **EST:** 2013
SALES (est): 206.73K **Privately Held**
Web: www.mikedsbbq.com
SIC: 5999 2033 5812 Miscellaneous retail stores, nec; Barbecue sauce: packaged in cans, jars, etc.; Restaurant, lunch counter

(G-5226)
MIKRON INDUSTRIES
2505 Meridian Pkwy # 250 (27713-1799)
PHONE..................253 398-1382
EMP: 8
SALES (est): 235.18K **Privately Held**
Web: www.mikron.com
SIC: 3999 Manufacturing industries, nec

(G-5227)
MIKRON INDUSTRIES INC (HQ)
2505 Meridian Pkwy Ste 250 (27713-1799)
PHONE..................713 961-4600
F Reese, *Pr*
Kevin Delaney, *VP*
William Griffiths, *VP*
Brent Korb, *VP*
Dewayne Williams, *VP*
EMP: 55 **EST:** 2005
SALES (est): 27.72MM **Publicly Held**
Web: www.quanex.com
SIC: 3081 3089 Vinyl film and sheet; Extruded finished plastics products, nec
PA: Quanex Building Products Corporation
945 Bunker Hill Rd # 900
Houston TX 77024

(G-5228)
MISS TORTILLAS INC
3801 Wake Forest Rd Ste 106 (27703)
PHONE..................919 598-8646
Marcelo Ocampo, *Pr*
▲ **EMP:** 6 **EST:** 2004
SALES (est): 381.63K **Privately Held**
SIC: 2099 Tortillas, fresh or refrigerated

(G-5229)
MITT S NITTS INC
1014 S Hoover Rd (27703-4338)
PHONE..................919 596-6793
Dennis Russell, *Pr*
EMP: 45 **EST:** 1977
SQ FT: 25,000
SALES (est): 4.24MM **Privately Held**
Web: www.mittsnitts.com
SIC: 2253 2259 2297 2381 Sweaters and sweater coats, knit; Gloves, knit, except dress and semidress gloves; Nonwoven fabrics; Fabric dress and work gloves

(G-5230)
MURANO CORPORATION
68 Tw Alexander Dr Ste 207 (27709-0151)
PHONE..................919 294-8233
Rajagopalan Sreekumar, *Prin*
EMP: 11 **EST:** 2010
SALES (est): 312.82K **Privately Held**
Web: www.muranocorp.com
SIC: 7372 Prepackaged software

(G-5231)
MURRAH WOODCRAFT
2112 Vintage Hill Dr (27712-9470)
PHONE..................919 302-3661
Cheri Murrah, *Prin*
EMP: 8 **EST:** 2011
SALES (est): 84.73K **Privately Held**
Web: www.murrahwoodcraft.com
SIC: 3553 Furniture makers machinery, woodworking

(G-5232)
MY FAVORITE CHEESECAKE
4801 Danube Ln (27704-1845)
PHONE..................919 824-0782
EMP: 8 **EST:** 2014
SALES (est): 142.56K **Privately Held**
Web: my-favorite-cheesecake.business.site
SIC: 2591 Window blinds

(G-5233)
MYSTIC FARM & DISTILLERY
1212 N Mineral Springs Rd (27703-2717)
PHONE..................336 409-0131
EMP: 5 **EST:** 2013
SALES (est): 175.66K **Privately Held**
Web: www.whatismystic.com
SIC: 0191 2085 General farms, primarily crop ; Applejack (alcoholic beverage)

(G-5234)
N2 PUBLISHING
5116 Greyfield Blvd (27713-8140)
PHONE..................919 795-6347
EMP: 4
SALES (est): 76.06K **Privately Held**
Web: www.strollmag.com
SIC: 2741 Miscellaneous publishing

(G-5235)
N2 PUBLISHING
1010 Beyer Pl (27703-6517)
PHONE..................919 280-9566
EMP: 4
SALES (est): 74.89K **Privately Held**
Web: www.strollmag.com
SIC: 2741 Miscellaneous publishing

(G-5236)
NACHO INDUSTRIES INC
8 Heath Pl (27705-5713)
PHONE..................919 937-9471
Jacob D Baldridge, *Pr*
EMP: 6 **EST:** 2012
SALES (est): 302.75K **Privately Held**
Web: www.nachoindustries.com
SIC: 3999 Manufacturing industries, nec

(G-5237)
NALA MEMBRANES INC
2 Davis Dr # 113 (27709-0003)
PHONE..................540 230-5606
Beverly Mecham, *Pr*
EMP: 6 **EST:** 2018
SALES (est): 667.64K **Privately Held**
Web: www.nalamembranes.com
SIC: 3589 Water treatment equipment, industrial

(G-5238)
NATURALLY ME BOUTIQUE INC
3231 Shannon Rd Apt 31c (27707-6306)
PHONE..................919 519-0783
Chaudra Smith, *Pr*
EMP: 4 **EST:** 2012
SALES (est): 162.48K **Privately Held**
SIC: 2844 2841 Face creams or lotions; Soap and other detergents

(G-5239)
NAUTILUS HOLDCO INC
4505 Emperor Blvd Ste 200 (27703-8457)
PHONE..................919 859-1302
EMP: 5 **EST:** 2018
SALES (est): 95.12K **Privately Held**
SIC: 2834 Pharmaceutical preparations

(G-5240)
NBN SPORTS INC
616 Clarion Dr (27705-1725)
P.O. Box 13292 (27709-3292)
PHONE..................919 824-5143
Reggie Parker, *Prin*
EMP: 6 **EST:** 2013
SALES (est): 118.28K **Privately Held**
Web: www.nbn-sports.com
SIC: 2311 Men's and boy's suits and coats

(G-5241)
NDSL INC
1000 Parliament Ct (27703-8456)
PHONE..................919 790-7877
Earl Philmon, *CEO*
Rob Willcock, *CFO*
▲ **EMP:** 14 **EST:** 1999
SALES (est): 12.22MM
SALES (corp-wide): 2.65MM **Privately Held**
Web: www.cellwatch.com
SIC: 3825 Electrical power measuring equipment
PA: Ndsl Group Limited
Gloucester House
Milton Keynes BUCKS MK9 2
190 830-3730

(G-5242)
NETAPP INC
7301 Kit Creek Rd (27709-0266)
PHONE..................919 476-4571
EMP: 38
Web: www.netapp.com
SIC: 3572 Computer storage devices
PA: Netapp, Inc.
3060 Olsen Dr
San Jose CA 95128

(G-5243)
NETQEM LLC
1012 Park Glen Pl (27713-8998)
PHONE..................919 544-4122
James Huan, *Dir Opers*
▲ **EMP:** 4 **EST:** 2005
SALES (est): 477.69K **Privately Held**
Web: www.netqem.us
SIC: 2819 Industrial inorganic chemicals, nec

(G-5244)
NEUROTRONIK INC
4021 Stirrup Creek Dr Ste 210 (27703-9352)
P.O. Box 98553 (27624-8553)
PHONE..................919 883-4155
Shawn Peterson, *Pr*
EMP: 14 **EST:** 2013
SALES (est): 941.84K **Privately Held**
SIC: 2834 Pharmaceutical preparations

(G-5245)
NEWS AND OBSERVER PUBG CO
Also Called: Herald-Sun, The
2530 Meridian Pkwy Ste 300 (27713-5272)
PHONE..................919 419-6500
EMP: 10
SALES (corp-wide): 709.52MM **Privately Held**
SIC: 2711 Newspapers, publishing and printing
HQ: The News And Observer Publishing Company
421 Fayetteville St # 104
Raleigh NC 27601
919 829-4500

(G-5246)
NEXPERIA USA INC (DH)
630 Davis Dr Ste 200 (27713)
PHONE..................919 740-6235
Conrad Rodriguez, *Pr*
EMP: 8 **EST:** 2016
SALES (est): 12.77MM **Privately Held**
SIC: 3674 Semiconductors and related devices
HQ: Nexperia B.V.
Jonkerbosplein 52
Nijmegen GE

(G-5247)
NOCTURNAL PRODUCT DEV LLC
8128 Renaissance Pkwy Ste 210 (27713-6695)
PHONE..................919 321-1331
Kenneth Armstrong, *Prin*
EMP: 12 **EST:** 2010
SALES (est): 1.91MM **Privately Held**
Web: www.nocturnalpd.com
SIC: 3841 Surgical and medical instruments

(G-5248)
NORTH DRHAM WTR RCLMTION FCLTY
1900 E Club Blvd (27704-3412)
PHONE..................919 560-4384
William Bell, *Mayor*
EMP: 7 **EST:** 2002
SALES (est): 189.18K **Privately Held**
Web: www.durhamnc.gov
SIC: 3589 Water treatment equipment, industrial

(G-5249)
NOTEMEAL INC
122 E Parrish St (27701-3319)
PHONE..................312 550-2049
James Coffos, *Pr*
EMP: 20 **EST:** 2019
SALES (est): 1.03MM **Privately Held**
Web: explore.teamworks.com
SIC: 7372 Prepackaged software

(G-5250)
NOVO NORDISK PHRM INDS LP
5235 International Dr (27712-8950)
PHONE..................919 550-2200
Dale Pulczinski, *Pt*
EMP: 40
SALES (corp-wide): 24.71B **Privately Held**
Web: www.novonordisk-clayton.com
SIC: 2834 Pharmaceutical preparations
HQ: Novo Nordisk Pharmaceutical Industries, Lp
3612 Powhatan Rd
Clayton NC 27527

GEOGRAPHIC SECTION

Durham - Durham County (G-5277)

(G-5251)
NUVOTRONICS INC (DH)
2305 Presidential Dr (27703-8039)
PHONE..................984 666-3543
Jean-marc Rollin, *Pr*
Scott Meller, *
Martin J Amen, *
EMP: 52 **EST:** 2008
SALES (est): 24.42MM
SALES (corp-wide): 1.48B **Privately Held**
Web: www.cubic.com
SIC: 8731 3679 Electronic research; Microwave components
HQ: Cubic Corporation
  9233 Balboa Ave
  San Diego CA 92123
  858 277-6780

(G-5252)
NVIDIA CORPORATION
2600 Meridian Pkwy (27713-2203)
PHONE..................408 486-2000
EMP: 11
Web: www.nvidia.com
SIC: 3674 Semiconductors and related devices
PA: Nvidia Corporation
  2788 San Tomas Expy
  Santa Clara CA 95051

(G-5253)
OIL AND VINEGAR MARKET INC
264 Crimson Oak Dr (27713-9503)
PHONE..................919 491-9225
Kacey Zucchino, *Prin*
EMP: 5 **EST:** 2010
SALES (est): 56K **Privately Held**
SIC: 2099 Vinegar

(G-5254)
OLA MARIMBA INC
3600 N Duke St Ste 29 (27704-1788)
PHONE..................919 479-9995
Juan Lopez, *Prin*
EMP: 5 **EST:** 2009
SALES (est): 104.21K **Privately Held**
SIC: 3931 Marimbas

(G-5255)
OLD CASTLE APG SOUTH INC
Also Called: Adams Products
106 S Lasalle St (27705-3017)
PHONE..................919 383-2521
Hank Hox, *Mgr*
EMP: 4
SQ FT: 3,806
SALES (corp-wide): 32.72B **Privately Held**
Web: www.adamsproducts.com
SIC: 3271 5032 3272 Blocks, concrete or cinder: standard; Concrete building products; Concrete products, precast, nec
HQ: Oldcastle Apg South, Inc.
  333 N Greene St Ste 500
  Greensboro NC 27401

(G-5256)
OLD-TIME MUSIC GROUP INC
Also Called: OLD-TIME HERALD
1109 Clarendon St (27705-3511)
P.O. Box 61679 (27715-1679)
PHONE..................919 286-2041
Sarah Bryan, *Ex Dir*
EMP: 7 **EST:** 2010
SALES (est): 70.9K **Privately Held**
Web: www.oldtimeherald.org
SIC: 2711 Newspapers, publishing and printing

(G-5257)
ONCOCEUTICS INC
2505 Meridian Pkwy Ste 100 (27713-2288)
PHONE..................678 897-0563
Wolfgang Oster, *CEO*
Joshua Allen, *VP*
Lee Schalop, *CFO*
EMP: 12 **EST:** 2009
SALES (est): 72K
SALES (corp-wide): 324K **Publicly Held**
Web: www.chimerix.com
SIC: 2834 Pharmaceutical preparations
PA: Chimerix, Inc.
  2505 Meridian Pkwy # 100
  Durham NC 27713
  919 806-1074

(G-5258)
ONLINE MEMORIAL SERVICES LLC
810 9th St Apt 340 (27705-4327)
PHONE..................914 471-6852
EMP: 4 **EST:** 2017
SALES (est): 42.75K **Privately Held**
SIC: 2741 Internet publishing and broadcasting

(G-5259)
OPPORTUNITY KNOCKS TWICE INC
1011 Glenrose Dr (27703-2646)
PHONE..................919 672-5374
Felicia A Farrar, *Brnch Mgr*
EMP: 26
SIC: 2741 Miscellaneous publishing
PA: Opportunity Knocks Twice, Inc.
  3404 Vireo Ct
  Raleigh NC

(G-5260)
ORGBOOK INC
4307 Emperor Blvd Ste 300 (27703-8080)
PHONE..................615 483-5410
EMP: 7 **EST:** 2012
SALES (est): 80.61K **Privately Held**
SIC: 7372 Business oriented computer software

(G-5261)
ORGSPAN INC
4307 Emperor Blvd Ste 300 (27703-8080)
PHONE..................855 674-7726
EMP: 5
SALES (est): 739.06K
SALES (corp-wide): 37.98MM **Privately Held**
SIC: 7372 Prepackaged software
HQ: Interactive Intelligence Group, Inc.
  7601 Interactive Way
  Indianapolis IN 46278
  317 872-3000

(G-5262)
ORI DIAGNOSTIC INSTRUMENTS LLC
3407 Middlebrook Dr (27705-7401)
PHONE..................919 864-8140
Zsolt Ori, *Prin*
EMP: 5 **EST:** 2015
SALES (est): 180.23K **Privately Held**
Web: www.oridiagnosticinstruments.com
SIC: 3845 Electromedical apparatus

(G-5263)
ORIEL THERAPEUTICS INC
630 Davis Dr Ste 120 (27713)
P.O. Box 14087 (27709-4087)
PHONE..................919 313-1290
Richard Fuller, *CEO*
Paul J Atkins, *Pr*
EMP: 48 **EST:** 2001
SALES (est): 1.82MM **Privately Held**
SIC: 2834 Pharmaceutical preparations
HQ: Sandoz Inc.
  100 College Rd W
  Princeton NJ 08540
  609 627-8500

(G-5264)
ORLANDOS CSTM DESIGN T-SHIRTS
2824 N Roxboro St (27704-3246)
PHONE..................919 220-5515
Orlando Clark, *Owner*
EMP: 6 **EST:** 1995
SALES (est): 395.9K **Privately Held**
Web: www.orlandoscdp.com
SIC: 2759 7389 Screen printing; Embroidery advertising

(G-5265)
OUR DAILY LIVING
102 E Murray Ave (27704-3242)
PHONE..................919 220-8160
Christopher C Onwuka, *Prin*
EMP: 5 **EST:** 2008
SALES (est): 157.14K **Privately Held**
SIC: 2711 Newspapers, publishing and printing

(G-5266)
OVERSTREET SIGN CONTRS INC
2210 Page Rd Ste 101 (27703-5949)
PHONE..................919 596-7300
Gregory L Overstreet, *Pr*
John E Couch Junior, *VP*
Martin J Horn, *Sec*
EMP: 7 **EST:** 1996
SQ FT: 3,750
SALES (est): 822.5K **Privately Held**
Web: www.overstreetsigns.com
SIC: 3993 Displays and cutouts, window and lobby

(G-5267)
PACIFIC CABINETS
312 S Miami Blvd (27703-4508)
PHONE..................919 695-3640
EMP: 4 **EST:** 2019
SALES (est): 109.53K **Privately Held**
Web: www.pacificcabinetsnc.com
SIC: 2434 Wood kitchen cabinets

(G-5268)
PALLET ALLIANCE INC
318 Blackwell St Ste 260 (27701-2884)
PHONE..................919 442-1400
Sandra Messinger, *Pr*
Paul Messinger, *Genl Mgr*
EMP: 13 **EST:** 1995
SALES (est): 3.26MM **Privately Held**
Web: www.tpai.com
SIC: 2448 Pallets, wood

(G-5269)
PANACEUTICS NUTRITION INC
6 Davis Dr (27709-0003)
PHONE..................919 797-9623
Adam Monroe, *CEO*
EMP: 13
SALES (est): 519.64K **Privately Held**
Web: www.panaceutics.com
SIC: 2099 7389 Food preparations, nec; Business services, nec

(G-5270)
PARATA SYSTEMS LLC (HQ)
Also Called: Tcgrx
106 Roche Dr (27709-0359)
PHONE..................888 727-2821
Rob Kill, *CEO*
Jason Buchwald, *General Vice President**
Mark Longley, *CCO**
Marcus Kennedy, *
Graham Schillmoller, *
EMP: 235 **EST:** 2001
SALES (est): 158.04MM
SALES (corp-wide): 19.37B **Publicly Held**
Web: www.parata.com
SIC: 3826 8733 Automatic chemical analyzers; Research institute
PA: Becton, Dickinson And Company
  1 Becton Dr
  Franklin Lakes NJ 07417
  201 847-6800

(G-5271)
PARKER EDITING LLC
108 Maybank Ct (27713-2515)
PHONE..................919 544-8557
Carol Parker, *Prin*
EMP: 5 **EST:** 2016
SALES (est): 68.45K **Privately Held**
SIC: 2741 Miscellaneous publishing

(G-5272)
PARTY TABLES LAND CO LLC
2455 S Alston Ave (27713-1301)
P.O. Box 13447 (27709-3447)
PHONE..................919 596-3521
EMP: 10 **EST:** 2019
SALES (est): 239.06K **Privately Held**
Web: www.partytables.com
SIC: 2392 Household furnishings, nec

(G-5273)
PATHEON INC
4815 Emperor Blvd Ste 100 (27703-8470)
PHONE..................919 226-3200
EMP: 4
SALES (corp-wide): 44.91B **Publicly Held**
Web: www.patheon.com
SIC: 2834 Pharmaceutical preparations
HQ: Patheon Inc
  2100 Syntex Crt
  Mississauga ON L5N 7
  905 821-4001

(G-5274)
PATHEON INC
4815 Emperor Blvd Ste 100 (27703-8470)
PHONE..................919 226-3200
EMP: 1200
SIC: 2834 Pharmaceutical preparations

(G-5275)
PAVE WELLNESS LLC
420 Glenview Ln (27703-9481)
PHONE..................919 335-3575
EMP: 4 **EST:** 2020
SALES (est): 39.59K **Privately Held**
SIC: 2023 Dietary supplements, dairy and non-dairy based

(G-5276)
PBM GRAPHICS INC
4102 S Miami Blvd (27703-9138)
P.O. Box 2665 (28221)
PHONE..................919 544-6222
Daniel Pink, *Prin*
EMP: 114
SALES (corp-wide): 15B **Privately Held**
Web: www.rrd.com
SIC: 2752 Offset printing
HQ: Pbm Graphics, Inc.
  3700 S Miami Blvd
  Durham NC 27703
  919 544-6222

(G-5277)
PBM GRAPHICS INC (DH)
Also Called: R. R. Donnelley & Sons
3700 S Miami Blvd (27703-9130)

Durham - Durham County (G-5278) — GEOGRAPHIC SECTION

P.O. Box 13603 (27709-3603)
PHONE..................919 544-6222
Rick Jones, *CEO*
Adam Geerts, *
Dave Mattingly, *
Greg Simpson, *
Johnny Mendoza, *
◆ **EMP:** 230 **EST:** 1983
SQ FT: 130,000
SALES (est): 171.53MM
SALES (corp-wide): 15B **Privately Held**
Web: www.pbmgraphics.com
SIC: 2752 Offset printing
HQ: Consolidated Graphics, Inc.
 5858 Westheimer Rd # 200
 Houston TX 77057

(G-5278)
PEACE OF MIND PUBLICATIONS
1321 Shiley Dr (27704-1495)
PHONE..................919 308-5137
Tonya Headen, *Prin*
EMP: 5 **EST:** 2013
SALES (est): 79.39K **Privately Held**
SIC: 2741 Miscellaneous publishing

(G-5279)
PEGASUS BUILDERS SUPPLY LLC
2228 Page Rd Ste 108 (27703-7933)
PHONE..................919 244-1586
EMP: 10 **EST:** 2007
SALES (est): 302.8K **Privately Held**
Web: www.pegasusbuilderssupply.com
SIC: 2431 Doors, wood

(G-5280)
PERFORMANCE PRINT SERVICES LLC
1 Tw Alexander Dr Ste 130 (27709-0152)
PHONE..................919 957-9995
EMP: 6 **EST:** 2017
SALES (est): 597.98K **Privately Held**
Web: www.performanceprintservices.com
SIC: 2752 Commercial printing, lithographic

(G-5281)
PERSEUS INTERMEDIATE INC
4721 Emperor Blvd Ste 100 (27703-7663)
PHONE..................919 474-6700
EMP: 34 **EST:** 2021
SALES (est): 1.43MM
SALES (corp-wide): 512.35MM **Publicly Held**
SIC: 3841 Surgical and medical instruments
HQ: Bioventus Llc
 4721 Emperor Blvd Ste 100
 Durham NC 27703
 800 396-4325

(G-5282)
PERSONAL XPRESSIONZ LLC
600 Park Offices Dr Ste 300 Pmb 103 (27709-1009)
PHONE..................919 587-7462
Latishia Duffie, *CEO*
EMP: 4 **EST:** 2020
SALES (est): 70.81K **Privately Held**
Web: www.facialxpressions.com
SIC: 3944 7389 Craft and hobby kits and sets ; Business Activities at Non-Commercial Site

(G-5283)
PETNET SOLUTIONS INC
2310 Presidential Dr Ste 108 (27703-8569)
PHONE..................919 572-5544
Susan Gridgers, *Prin*
EMP: 4
SALES (corp-wide): 84.48B **Privately Held**
Web: www.siemens.com
SIC: 2835 Radioactive diagnostic substances
HQ: Petnet Solutions, Inc.
 810 Innovation Dr
 Knoxville TN 37932
 865 218-2000

(G-5284)
PFIZER INC
Also Called: Pfizer
1040 Swabia Ct (27703-8481)
PHONE..................919 941-5185
Brian Hrudka, *Mgr*
EMP: 10
SALES (corp-wide): 100.33B **Publicly Held**
Web: www.pfizer.com
SIC: 2834 Pharmaceutical preparations
PA: Pfizer Inc.
 66 Hudson Blvd E
 New York NY 10001
 800 879-3477

(G-5285)
PHITONEX INC
701 W Main St Ste 200 (27701-5012)
PHONE..................855 874-4866
Mike Stadnisky, *CEO*
EMP: 13 **EST:** 2017
SALES (est): 2.4MM
SALES (corp-wide): 44.91B **Publicly Held**
Web: www.thermofisher.com
SIC: 3826 Analytical instruments
PA: Thermo Fisher Scientific Inc.
 168 3rd Ave
 Waltham MA 02451
 781 622-1000

(G-5286)
PHONONIC INC
800 Capitola Dr Ste 7 (27713-4385)
PHONE..................919 908-6300
Anthony Atti, *Pr*
Tom Werthan, *
Ron Tarter, *
Mick Wilcox, *CMO**
▲ **EMP:** 110 **EST:** 2008
SQ FT: 2,500
SALES (est): 36.47MM **Privately Held**
Web: www.phononic.com
SIC: 3674 7371 Semiconductors and related devices; Computer software development and applications

(G-5287)
PHOTONICARE INC
2800 Meridian Pkwy Ste 175 (27713-5257)
PHONE..................866 411-3277
Ryan Shelton, *CEO*
Stephen Boppart, *CMO*
Ryan Nolan, *VP*
EMP: 22 **EST:** 2013
SALES (est): 4.89MM **Privately Held**
Web: www.photoni.care
SIC: 3841 Surgical and medical instruments

(G-5288)
PIE PUSHERS
625 Hugo St (27704-4554)
PHONE..................919 901-0743
EMP: 6 **EST:** 2017
SALES (est): 96.71K **Privately Held**
Web: www.piepushers.com
SIC: 3545 Pushers

(G-5289)
PIECE OF PIE LLC
904 9th St (27705-4105)
PHONE..................919 286-7421
EMP: 13 **EST:** 2006
SALES (est): 476.52K **Privately Held**
Web: www.regencycleaner.com
SIC: 2842 Laundry cleaning preparations

(G-5290)
PINE RES INSTRUMENTATION INC
2741 Campus Walk Ave Bldg 100 (27705-8878)
PHONE..................919 782-8320
Joseph Hines, *Pr*
EMP: 16 **EST:** 2005
SQ FT: 5,000
SALES (est): 1.59MM **Privately Held**
Web: www.pineresearch.com
SIC: 3826 Protein analyzers, laboratory type

(G-5291)
PLANTATION HOUSE FOODS INC
3316 Stoneybrook Dr (27705-2423)
PHONE..................919 381-5495
Doug Sharpe, *Pr*
EMP: 6 **EST:** 1991
SALES (est): 381.63K **Privately Held**
SIC: 2032 Mexican foods, nec: packaged in cans, jars, etc.

(G-5292)
PMG-DH COMPANY
1530 N Gregson St Ste 2a (27701-1164)
PHONE..................919 419-6500
TOLL FREE: 888
David Paxton, *Pr*
EMP: 184 **EST:** 1896
SQ FT: 116,000
SALES (est): 2.08MM
SALES (corp-wide): 243.17MM **Privately Held**
SIC: 2711 Newspapers, publishing and printing
PA: Paxton Media Group, Llc
 100 Television Ln
 Paducah KY 42003
 270 575-8630

(G-5293)
POLAREAN INC
2500 Meridian Pkwy Ste 175 (27713-4214)
P.O. Box 14805 (27709-4805)
PHONE..................919 206-7900
Bastiaan Driehuys, *Pr*
Kenneth West, *Pr*
Charles Osborne Junior, *CFO*
EMP: 18 **EST:** 2011
SALES (est): 2.92MM **Privately Held**
Web: www.polarean.com
SIC: 3845 Respiratory analysis equipment, electromedical

(G-5294)
POMDEVICES LLC
178 Colvard Park Dr (27713-5815)
PHONE..................919 200-6538
EMP: 10 **EST:** 2011
SALES (est): 516.12K **Privately Held**
SIC: 3669 Communications equipment, nec

(G-5295)
PONYSAURUS BREWING LLC
219 Hood St (27701-3715)
PHONE..................919 455-3737
Nick Johnson, *Pr*
EMP: 26 **EST:** 2015
SALES (est): 842.76K **Privately Held**
Web: www.ponysaurusbrewing.com
SIC: 2082 Beer (alcoholic beverage)

(G-5296)
POSH INDUSTRIES LLC
604 Lindley Dr (27703-4712)
PHONE..................919 596-8434
Tamara Hayes, *Prin*
EMP: 4 **EST:** 2017
SALES (est): 85.97K **Privately Held**
SIC: 3999 Manufacturing industries, nec

(G-5297)
POSITIVE PRINTS PROF SVCS LLC
1821 Hillandale Rd Ste 1b Pmb 256 (27705-2659)
PHONE..................336 701-2330
EMP: 5 **EST:** 2011
SALES (est): 258.37K **Privately Held**
SIC: 8742 2731 Marketing consulting services; Books, publishing only

(G-5298)
POSTAL LIQUIDATION INC
3791 S Alston Ave (27713-1803)
EMP: 132
SIC: 3579 Mailing, letter handling, and addressing machines

(G-5299)
POWERSECURE SOLAR LLC
Also Called: Powersecure Solar
4068 Stirrup Creek Dr (27703-9000)
PHONE..................919 213-0798
Marty Meadows, *
Eric Dupont, *
EMP: 294 **EST:** 2012
SALES (est): 5.04MM
SALES (corp-wide): 25.25B **Publicly Held**
Web: www.powersecure.com
SIC: 3674 Diodes, solid state (germanium, silicon, etc.)
HQ: Powersecure, Inc.
 4068 Stirrup Creek Dr
 Durham NC 27703
 919 556-3056

(G-5300)
PPG INDUSTRIES INC
Also Called: PPG 4685
3161 Hillsborough Rd (27705-4336)
PHONE..................919 382-3100
Tommy Howard, *Mgr*
EMP: 4
SALES (corp-wide): 17.65B **Publicly Held**
Web: www.ppg.com
SIC: 2851 Paints and allied products
PA: Ppg Industries, Inc.
 1 Ppg Pl
 Pittsburgh PA 15272
 412 434-3131

(G-5301)
PRAETEGO INC
68 Tw Alexander Dr (27709-0151)
P.O. Box 13628 (27709-3628)
PHONE..................919 237-7969
Pepper Landson, *CEO*
John Mazur, *Prin*
J Wesley Fox, *Prin*
EMP: 6 **EST:** 2017
SALES (est): 414.63K **Privately Held**
Web: www.praetego.com
SIC: 8731 2834 Biotechnical research, commercial; Pharmaceutical preparations

(G-5302)
PRECISION FERMENTATIONS INC
2810 Meridian Pkwy (27713-5241)
PHONE..................919 717-3983
Jared Resnick, *CEO*
EMP: 11 **EST:** 2017
SALES (est): 1.02MM **Privately Held**
Web: www.precisionfermentation.com
SIC: 7372 Prepackaged software

(G-5303)
PRECISION PACKAGING SERVICES I
2910 Weck Dr (27709-0186)

GEOGRAPHIC SECTION

PHONE..................................919 806-8152
Robert Hofstadter, *Prin*
EMP: 11 **EST:** 2005
SALES (est): 217.51K **Privately Held**
SIC: 2631 Container, packaging, and boxboard

(G-5304)
PREMEX INC
Also Called: Iluma Alliance
1307 Person St (27703-5057)
PHONE..................................561 962-4128
Carlos Valencia, *Pr*
Alejandro Mesa, *Sec*
◆ **EMP:** 15 **EST:** 2002
SALES (est): 5.05MM **Privately Held**
Web: www.premex.co
SIC: 2834 5122 8099 Vitamin preparations; Vitamins and minerals; Nutrition services
PA: Premex S A S
Carrera 50 2 Sur 251 Autopista Sur
Medellin ANT

(G-5305)
PRODUCT IDENTIFICATION INC
1725 Carpenter Fletcher Rd Ste 201 (27713)
P.O. Box 13157 (27709-3157)
PHONE..................................919 544-4136
Kingsley D Maynard, *Pr*
EMP: 20 **EST:** 1995
SQ FT: 8,900
SALES (est): 2.52MM **Privately Held**
Web: www.prod-id.com
SIC: 2759 3479 Labels and seals: printing, nsk; Name plates: engraved, etched, etc.

(G-5306)
PROFORMA PRINT SOURCE
3600 N Duke St (27704-1709)
P.O. Box 16592 (27516-6592)
PHONE..................................919 383-2070
Vero Muzzillo, *CEO*
Michael Baucom, *Pr*
EMP: 6 **EST:** 2010
SALES (est): 399.69K **Privately Held**
SIC: 2752 Offset printing

(G-5307)
PROMETHERA BIOSCIENCES LLC
6 Davis Dr (27709-0003)
PHONE..................................919 354-1930
EMP: 60
SALES (corp-wide): 2MM **Privately Held**
Web: www.cellaion.com
SIC: 2834 Pharmaceutical preparations
PA: Promethera Biosciences Llc
4700 Falls Of Neuse Rd # 400
Raleigh NC 27609
919 354-1933

(G-5308)
PSI PHARMA SUPPORT AMERICA INC
10 Laboratory Dr (27709-0161)
PHONE..................................919 249-2660
EMP: 41
SIC: 2834 Pharmaceutical preparations
HQ: Psi Pharma Support America, Inc.
875 1st Ave
King Of Prussia PA 19406
267 464-2500

(G-5309)
PUMPS BLOWERS & ELC MTRS LLC
2712 Edmund St (27705-3909)
PHONE..................................919 286-4975
EMP: 4 **EST:** 2005
SQ FT: 1,269
SALES (est): 493.51K **Privately Held**
Web: www.pumpsblowers.com

SIC: 7694 Electric motor repair

(G-5310)
Q-EDGE CORPORATION
4018 Patriot Dr Ste 175 (27703-8104)
PHONE..................................919 935-8167
EMP: 5 **EST:** 2017
SALES (est): 93.8K **Privately Held**
SIC: 3571 Electronic computers

(G-5311)
QUALITY CLEANING SERVICES LLC
3639 Guess Rd (27705-6908)
PHONE..................................919 638-4969
EMP: 12 **EST:** 2018
SALES (est): 620.17K **Privately Held**
SIC: 3589 Commercial cleaning equipment

(G-5312)
QUALITY EQUIPMENT LLC
3821 Durham Chapel Hill Blvd (27707-2523)
PHONE..................................919 493-3545
Jason Jarrett, *Brnch Mgr*
EMP: 7
Web: www.qualityequip.com
SIC: 5261 5251 7699 5082 Lawnmowers and tractors; Chainsaws; Lawn mower repair shop; Contractor's materials
PA: Quality Equipment, Llc
2214 N Main St Ste 501
Fuquay Varina NC 27526

(G-5313)
QUALITY INSTANT PRINTING INC
1920 E Nc Highway 54 Ste 30 (27713-2293)
PHONE..................................919 544-1777
Lynn Tilley, *Pr*
Lynette Tilley, *Sec*
EMP: 11 **EST:** 1982
SQ FT: 4,000
SALES (est): 396.46K **Privately Held**
Web: www.qip1.com
SIC: 2752 7334 Offset printing; Photocopying and duplicating services

(G-5314)
QUEEN OF WINES LLC
122 Wright Hill Dr (27712-9093)
PHONE..................................919 348-6630
Laure Levesque, *Pr*
EMP: 10 **EST:** 2014
SALES (est): 428.81K **Privately Held**
Web: www.queenofwines.com
SIC: 2084 Wines

(G-5315)
R & A MASONRY LLC
1509 N Miami Blvd (27701-2739)
PHONE..................................919 672-6253
EMP: 4 **EST:** 2018
SALES (est): 97.25K **Privately Held**
SIC: 2024 Yogurt desserts, frozen

(G-5316)
R R DONNELLEY & SONS COMPANY
Also Called: RR Donnelley
1 Litho Way (27703-8929)
PHONE..................................919 596-8942
Michael Phelps, *Brnch Mgr*
EMP: 47
SALES (corp-wide): 15B **Privately Held**
Web: www.rrd.com
SIC: 2759 Commercial printing, nec
HQ: R. R. Donnelley & Sons Company
35 W Wacker Dr
Chicago IL 60601
800 782-4892

(G-5317)
R65 LABS INC
108.5 E Parrish St (27701)
PHONE..................................919 219-1983
Mark Williams, *Pr*
Nancy Owens, *Treas*
EMP: 5 **EST:** 2013
SALES (est): 278.03K **Privately Held**
Web: www.r65labs.com
SIC: 7372 Application computer software

(G-5318)
RADCON INC
1717 Southpoint Crossing Dr (27713-6612)
PHONE..................................919 806-5233
John A Goree, *Prin*
EMP: 5 **EST:** 2010
SALES (est): 197.34K **Privately Held**
SIC: 3567 Industrial furnaces and ovens

(G-5319)
RANDOM & KIND LLC
1348 Scholar Dr (27703-6565)
PHONE..................................919 249-8809
EMP: 7
SALES (est): 268.21K **Privately Held**
SIC: 7389 3161 Business Activities at Non-Commercial Site; Clothing and apparel carrying cases

(G-5320)
RCWS INC (PA)
421 W Corporation St (27701-2164)
PHONE..................................919 680-2655
Carlton Saul, *CEO*
Mona Saul, *Pr*
EMP: 17 **EST:** 1997
SQ FT: 50,000
SALES (est): 1.71MM **Privately Held**
SIC: 2521 Panel systems and partitions (free-standing), office: wood

(G-5321)
RDU PRINT STUDIO LLC
1509 Ward St (27707-1557)
PHONE..................................919 260-0173
Gonzalo E Arriagada, *Prin*
EMP: 5 **EST:** 2017
SALES (est): 100.43K **Privately Held**
Web: www.gonzocustomtees.com
SIC: 2759 Screen printing

(G-5322)
REALXPERIENCE LLC
5109 Sweet Clover Ct (27703-9108)
PHONE..................................512 775-4386
EMP: 5 **EST:** 2010
SALES (est): 258.38K **Privately Held**
Web: www.realxperience.com
SIC: 3822 Air flow controllers, air conditioning and refrigeration

(G-5323)
REICHHOLD HOLDINGS US INC
1035 Swabia Ct (27703-0962)
P.O. Box 13582 (27709-3582)
PHONE..................................919 990-7500
◆ **EMP:** 553
SIC: 2821 2822 2891 3089 Plastics materials and resins; Synthetic rubber; Adhesives and sealants; Bands, plastics

(G-5324)
RENAISSANCE INNOVATIONS LLC
2534 Whilden Dr (27713-1356)
PHONE..................................774 901-4642
James Corwin, *Prin*
EMP: 39
SALES (corp-wide): 2.32MM **Privately Held**

Web: www.retique.com
SIC: 2851 Paints and allied products
PA: Renaissance Innovations, Llc
1322 Gloriosa St
Apex NC 27523
844 473-7246

(G-5325)
RENEW LIFE FORMULAS LLC (HQ)
Also Called: Renew Life Cleansing Co
210 W Pettigrew St (27701-3666)
PHONE..................................727 450-1061
Ron Fugate, *CEO*
Don Pollo, *
EMP: 57 **EST:** 1997
SQ FT: 30,000
SALES (est): 21.68MM
SALES (corp-wide): 7.39B **Publicly Held**
SIC: 2074 Cottonseed oil mills
PA: The Clorox Company
1221 Broadway Ste 1300
Oakland CA 94612
510 271-7000

(G-5326)
REPLAR MFG INC
5 Beaufort Ct (27713-6197)
PHONE..................................919 622-5942
EMP: 4 **EST:** 2010
SALES (est): 195.56K **Privately Held**
SIC: 3999 Manufacturing industries, nec

(G-5327)
RESEARCH INSTRUMENTS INC
2618 Pleasant Green Rd (27705-7125)
PHONE..................................919 383-2775
Ronald Overaker, *Pr*
Charlotte Overaker, *Sec*
EMP: 5 **EST:** 1977
SQ FT: 1,100
SALES (est): 293.65K **Privately Held**
Web: fertility.coopersurgical.com
SIC: 3821 Laboratory apparatus and furniture

(G-5328)
RESEARCH TRNGLE EDTRIAL SLTONS
9 Amador Pl (27712-1461)
PHONE..................................919 808-2719
Julie Vo, *CEO*
EMP: 5 **EST:** 2019
SALES (est): 68.29K **Privately Held**
SIC: 2741 Miscellaneous publishing

(G-5329)
RESTORATION HARDWARE INC
8030 Renaissance Pkwy Ste 805 (27713-8278)
PHONE..................................919 544-4196
Shaydee Rivera, *CFO*
EMP: 10
SALES (corp-wide): 3.59B **Publicly Held**
Web: www.rh.com
SIC: 5072 3429 Hardware; Furniture hardware
HQ: Restoration Hardware, Inc.
15 Koch Rd Ste K
Corte Madera CA 94925
800 762-1005

(G-5330)
RIBA FAIRFIELD
4116 Colville Rd (27707-5086)
PHONE..................................919 294-4819
Joel Muse, *Prin*
EMP: 7 **EST:** 2010
SALES (est): 542.53K **Privately Held**
SIC: 2899 Chemical preparations, nec

Durham - Durham County (G-5331)   GEOGRAPHIC SECTION

(G-5331)
RIBOMETRIX
701 W Main St Ste 200 (27701-5012)
P.O. Box 12878 (27709-2878)
PHONE.....................................919 744-9634
Christina Davis, *Prin*
EMP: 8 **EST:** 2017
SALES (est): 937.08K **Privately Held**
Web: www.ribometrix.com
SIC: 3845 Electromedical equipment

(G-5332)
RIPSTOP BY ROLL LLC
2101 Tobacco Rd (27704-5065)
PHONE.....................................877 525-7210
Kyle Baker, *CEO*
Kyle Baker, *Managing Member*
EMP: 18 **EST:** 2014
SQ FT: 4,800
SALES (est): 2.78MM **Privately Held**
Web: www.ripstopbytheroll.com
SIC: 5131 2211 Piece goods and other fabrics; Sheets, bedding and table cloths: cotton

(G-5333)
RIVERBED TECHNOLOGY LLC
5425 Page Rd Ste 200 (27703-7009)
PHONE.....................................415 247-8800
EMP: 35
SALES (corp-wide): 912.58MM **Privately Held**
Web: www.riverbed.com
SIC: 3577 Computer peripheral equipment, nec
HQ: Riverbed Technology Llc
    680 Folsom St Ste 600
    San Francisco CA 94107
    415 247-8200

(G-5334)
ROCAS WELDING LLC
923 E Trinity Ave Ste F (27704-5076)
PHONE.....................................252 290-2233
Roberto Lopez, *Prin*
EMP: 6 **EST:** 2016
SALES (est): 284.62K **Privately Held**
Web: www.rocaswelding.com
SIC: 7692 Welding repair

(G-5335)
RTO SERVICES LLC
Also Called: Amish Barns
2805 E Us 70 Hwy (27703-8974)
PHONE.....................................919 596-5406
Charles T Floyd, *Managing Member*
EMP: 4
SALES (est): 80.44K **Privately Held**
SIC: 2499 Wood products, nec

(G-5336)
S & D MACHINE & TOOL INC
1404 Old Oxford Rd (27704-9505)
PHONE.....................................919 479-8433
Warren Daniels, *Pr*
Thomas Jones, *VP*
EMP: 21 **EST:** 1965
SQ FT: 30,000
SALES (est): 2.93MM **Privately Held**
Web: www.sdmachinetool.com
SIC: 3599 Machine shop, jobbing and repair

(G-5337)
SAPERE BIO INC
Also Called: Healthspan Dx
400 Park Offices Dr Ste 113 (27709)
P.O. Box 13075 (27709-3975)
PHONE.....................................919 260-2565
Claudia Black, *Mgr*
Natalia Mitin, *Pr*
EMP: 4 **EST:** 2013
SALES (est): 641.32K **Privately Held**
Web: www.saperebio.com
SIC: 2835 Diagnostic substances

(G-5338)
SARDA TECHNOLOGIES INC
100 Capitola Dr Ste 308 (27713-4497)
PHONE.....................................919 757-6825
Bob Conner, *CEO*
Larry Krauss, *Prin*
Brian Wong, *Prin*
John Cambier, *Prin*
Phil Anthony, *Prin*
EMP: 5 **EST:** 2011
SQ FT: 2,000
SALES (est): 402.44K **Privately Held**
Web: www.sardatech.com
SIC: 3674 Semiconductors and related devices

(G-5339)
SASSY QUEEN COLLECTION LLC
215 Cheryl Ave (27712-2303)
PHONE.....................................919 949-0085
Marsha Adams Rucker, *Managing Member*
EMP: 4 **EST:** 2021
SALES (est): 10K **Privately Held**
SIC: 3999 Hair and hair-based products

(G-5340)
SATCO TRUCK EQUIPMENT INC
2007 Cheek Rd (27704-5115)
P.O. Box 3182 (27715-3182)
PHONE.....................................919 383-5547
Michael Diruscio, *Pr*
EMP: 14 **EST:** 2010
SALES (est): 1.78MM **Privately Held**
Web: www.satcotruck.com
SIC: 5046 1799 3713 3714 Commercial equipment, nec; Hydraulic equipment, installation and service; Utility truck bodies; Dump truck lifting mechanism

(G-5341)
SATSUMA PHARMACEUTICALS INC
4819 Emperor Blvd Ste 340 (27703-5420)
PHONE.....................................650 410-3200
John Kollins, *Pr*
EMP: 9
Web: www.satsumarx.com
SIC: 2834 Pharmaceutical preparations
PA: Satsuma Pharmaceuticals, Inc.
    400 Oyster Point Blvd # 221
    South San Francisco CA 94080
    650 410-3200

(G-5342)
SCALAWAG
318 Blackwell St (27701-2883)
PHONE.....................................917 671-7240
EMP: 7 **EST:** 2019
SALES (est): 279.91K **Privately Held**
Web: www.scalawagmagazine.org
SIC: 2721 Periodicals

(G-5343)
SCIEPHARM LLC
Also Called: CRS Laboratories
5441 Lumley Rd Ste 103 (27703-7726)
PHONE.....................................907 352-9559
Estela Molini, *Managing Member*
EMP: 129
SALES (corp-wide): 10.4MM **Privately Held**
SIC: 2819 Industrial inorganic chemicals, nec
PA: Sciepharm Llc
    2201 Candun Dr
    Apex NC 27523
    307 352-9559

(G-5344)
SCIPHER MEDICINE CORPORATION
4134 S Alston Ave Ste 104 (27713-1870)
P.O. Box 110087 (27709-5087)
PHONE.....................................781 755-2063
EMP: 6
SALES (est): 312.23K **Privately Held**
Web: www.sciphermedicine.com
SIC: 2834 Pharmaceutical preparations

(G-5345)
SCM METAL PRODUCTS INC (HQ)
Also Called: Kymera International
2601 Weck Dr (27709-1100)
P.O. Box 12166 (27709-2166)
PHONE.....................................919 544-8090
◆ **EMP:** 46 **EST:** 2004
SALES (est): 51.31MM
SALES (corp-wide): 418.5MM **Privately Held**
Web: www.kymerainternational.com
SIC: 3399 Powder, metal
PA: Palladium Equity Partners, Llc
    1270 Avenue Of The Americ
    New York NY 10020
    212 218-5150

(G-5346)
SCRIPTORIUM PUBG SVCS INC
4220 Apex Hwy Ste 340 (27713-5295)
P.O. Box 12761 (27709-2761)
PHONE.....................................919 481-2701
Sarah O'keefe, *Pr*
Alan Pringle, *Sec*
EMP: 7 **EST:** 1993
SALES (est): 1.01MM **Privately Held**
Web: www.scriptorium.com
SIC: 2752 7371 Commercial printing, lithographic; Custom computer programming services

(G-5347)
SEAL SEASONS INC
4426 S Miami Blvd # 105 (27703-9144)
PHONE.....................................919 245-3535
Patrick Mateer, *CEO*
Dawn Paffenroth Ctrl, *Prin*
EMP: 15 **EST:** 2014
SALES (est): 1.33MM **Privately Held**
Web: www.sealtheseasons.com
SIC: 2037 Frozen fruits and vegetables

(G-5348)
SECURITY SELF STORAGE
1945 E Cornwallis Rd (27713-1493)
PHONE.....................................919 544-3969
Antoinette Caron, *Mgr*
EMP: 4 **EST:** 2005
SALES (est): 196.22K **Privately Held**
Web: www.selfstoragenc.com
SIC: 2741 7513 Miscellaneous publishing; Truck rental and leasing, no drivers

(G-5349)
SENECA DEVICES INC
2 Davis Dr (27709-0003)
PHONE.....................................301 412-3576
Samuel Fox, *CEO*
EMP: 7 **EST:** 2017
SALES (est): 294.47K **Privately Held**
Web: www.senecadevices.com
SIC: 3999 Manufacturing industries, nec

(G-5350)
SEWERKOTE LLC
3612 Courtland Dr (27704-1728)
PHONE.....................................919 602-8002
EMP: 7 **EST:** 2003
SALES (est): 83.5K **Privately Held**
Web: www.sewerkote.com

SIC: 3999 Atomizers, toiletry

(G-5351)
SHARKFLIGHT PUBLISHING LLC
2233 Tanners Mill Dr (27703-9524)
PHONE.....................................919 744-5997
Ian Thomas, *Prin*
EMP: 4 **EST:** 2017
SALES (est): 41.28K **Privately Held**
SIC: 2741 Miscellaneous publishing

(G-5352)
SHIMADZU SCIENTIFIC INSTRS INC
4022 Stirrup Creek Dr Ste 312 (27703-9411)
PHONE.....................................919 425-1010
Chris Gaylor, *Mgr*
EMP: 4
Web: ssi.shimadzu.com
SIC: 3826 Analytical instruments
HQ: Shimadzu Scientific Instruments Incorporated
    7102 Riverwood Dr
    Columbia MD 21046
    800 477-1227

(G-5353)
SHIPMAN TECHNOLOGIES INC
2933-122 South Miami Blvd (27703-9041)
PHONE.....................................919 294-8405
Douglas Shipman, *Pr*
EMP: 26 **EST:** 1986
SQ FT: 20,000
SALES (est): 898.46K **Privately Held**
Web: www.shipmantech.com
SIC: 3699 Electrical equipment and supplies, nec

(G-5354)
SHOPBOT TOOLS INC
3333b Industrial Dr (27704-9307)
PHONE.....................................919 680-4800
▲ **EMP:** 41 **EST:** 1996
SQ FT: 15,000
SALES (est): 10.11MM **Privately Held**
Web: www.shopbottools.com
SIC: 5251 3625 Tools; Actuators, industrial

(G-5355)
SIERRA NEVADA CORPORATION
1030 Swabia Ct Ste 100 (27703-8070)
PHONE.....................................919 595-8551
EMP: 62
SALES (corp-wide): 2.38B **Privately Held**
Web: www.sncorp.com
SIC: 3812 3728 Search and navigation equipment; Aircraft parts and equipment, nec
PA: Sierra Nevada Corporation
    444 Salomon Cir
    Sparks NV 89434
    775 331-0222

(G-5356)
SIGMA XI SCNTFIC RES HNOR SOC
3200 Chapel Hill Nelson Hwy Ste 300 (27709-0013)
P.O. Box 13975 (27709-3975)
PHONE.....................................919 549-4691
Jamie Vernon, *Ex Dir*
EMP: 26 **EST:** 1886
SQ FT: 52,000
SALES (est): 4.92MM **Privately Held**
Web: www.sigmaxi.org
SIC: 2721 8733 Magazines: publishing only, not printed on site; Scientific research agency

GEOGRAPHIC SECTION
Durham - Durham County (G-5383)

(G-5357)
SIGNS SEALED DELIVERED
6409 Fayetteville Rd (27713-6297)
PHONE.................................919 213-1280
K Shevon Skinner, *Owner*
EMP: 4 **EST:** 2017
SALES (est): 53.15K **Privately Held**
SIC: 3993 Signs and advertising specialties

(G-5358)
SIGNS UNLIMITED INC
6801 Mount Hermon Church Rd Unit C (27705-8318)
PHONE.................................919 596-7612
Gaston Ballbe, *Pr*
EMP: 16 **EST:** 1997
SALES (est): 2.43MM **Privately Held**
Web: www.signsunlimitedusa.com
SIC: 3993 Electric signs

(G-5359)
SMART WIRES INC (PA)
Also Called: S W G
1035 Swabia Ct Ste 130 (27703-0963)
P.O. Box 819 (27540-0819)
PHONE.................................919 294-3999
EMP: 65 **EST:** 2010
SALES (est): 15.44MM **Privately Held**
Web: www.smartwires.com
SIC: 3677 Electronic coils and transformers

(G-5360)
SNOWMAN SOFTWARE
3608 Shannon Rd Ste 200 (27707-6344)
PHONE.................................888 918-4384
EMP: 6 **EST:** 1996
SALES (est): 58.56K **Privately Held**
Web: www.snowmansoftware.com
SIC: 3652 Prerecorded records and tapes

(G-5361)
SNP INC
1301 S Briggs Ave Ste 110 (27703-5070)
PHONE.................................919 598-0400
Joseph D Kehoe, *Pr*
◆ **EMP:** 25 **EST:** 1961
SALES (est): 5.46MM **Privately Held**
Web: www.snpinc.com
SIC: 2824 Acrylic fibers

(G-5362)
SOBI INC
240 Leigh Farm Rd Ste 245 (27707-8100)
PHONE.................................844 506-3682
Mian M Ashraf, *Prin*
EMP: 4
SALES (corp-wide): 1.79B **Privately Held**
Web: www.sobi.com
SIC: 2834 Pharmaceutical preparations
HQ: Sobi, Inc
  77 4th Ave Fl 3
  Waltham MA 02451
  781 786-7370

(G-5363)
SOCIAL GRIND GOURMET COF LLC
4527 American Dr (27705-6420)
PHONE.................................919 937-9503
Jason Sholtz, *Prin*
EMP: 5 **EST:** 2017
SALES (est): 157.07K **Privately Held**
SIC: 3599 Grinding castings for the trade

(G-5364)
SOSTRAM CORPORATION
2525 Meridian Pkwy Ste 350 (27713-5348)
PHONE.................................919 226-1195
Lynn Brookhouser, *Pr*
Fred Hallemann, *Pr*
▲ **EMP:** 4 **EST:** 1999
SALES (est): 1.99MM
SALES (corp-wide): 750.34MM **Privately Held**
Web: www.sipcamagrousa.com
SIC: 2819 5169 7373 Industrial inorganic chemicals, nec; Industrial chemicals; Computer integrated systems design
HQ: Sipcam Agro Usa, Inc.
  2525 Meridian Pkwy # 100
  Durham NC 27713
  919 226-1195

(G-5365)
SOUTHERN ELECTRIC MOTOR CO
2121 Front St # 25 (27705-2518)
PHONE.................................919 688-7879
Martin E Rigsbee, *Pr*
Myra Rigsbee, *Sec*
EMP: 8 **EST:** 1961
SALES (est): 888K **Privately Held**
Web: www.southernelectricmotornc.com
SIC: 7694 5063 5999 Electric motor repair; Motors, electric; Motors, electric

(G-5366)
SPECTACULAR PUBLISHING INC
3333 Durham Chapel Hill Blvd Ste A101 (27707-6237)
PHONE.................................919 672-0289
Lawrence Davis Iii, *Prin*
EMP: 12 **EST:** 2017
SALES (est): 499.11K **Privately Held**
Web: www.spectacularmag.com
SIC: 2711 Newspapers, publishing and printing

(G-5367)
SPEE DEE QUE INSTANT PRTG INC
301 E Chapel Hill St (27701-3301)
P.O. Box 25243 (27702-5243)
PHONE.................................919 683-1307
H Thomas Driver, *Pr*
Gloria Driver, *Sec*
Mike Driver, *VP*
EMP: 6 **EST:** 1975
SQ FT: 2,000
SALES (est): 449.39K **Privately Held**
Web: www.speedeeque.com
SIC: 2752 Offset printing

(G-5368)
SPEEDPRO IMAGING DURHAM
1055 Stillwell Dr Unit 1141 (27707-6365)
PHONE.................................919 278-7964
EMP: 4 **EST:** 2018
SALES (est): 144.75K **Privately Held**
SIC: 3993 Signs and advertising specialties

(G-5369)
SPENCO MEDICAL CORPORATION
2001 Tw Alexander Dr (27709-0184)
PHONE.................................919 544-7900
Seth Richards, *CEO*
Todd Vore, *
Bill Alfano, *
Steve Head, *
▲ **EMP:** 23 **EST:** 1970
SQ FT: 160,000
SALES (est): 489.21K **Privately Held**
Web: www.implus.com
SIC: 3842 Orthopedic appliances

(G-5370)
SPOONFLOWER INC (DH)
Also Called: Spoonflower
3871 S Alston Ave (27713-1805)
PHONE.................................919 886-7885
Gart Davis, *CEO*
Michael Jones, *Pr*
Allison Polish, *Pr*
▲ **EMP:** 51 **EST:** 2008
SQ FT: 20,000
SALES (est): 28.68MM
SALES (corp-wide): 2.47B **Privately Held**
Web: www.spoonflower.com
SIC: 2262 Finishing plants, manmade
HQ: Shutterfly, Llc
  10 Almaden Blvd Ste 900
  San Jose CA 95113
  650 610-5200

(G-5371)
STARRLIGHT MEAD LLC
4606 Stillview Dr (27712-2750)
PHONE.................................919 672-1469
EMP: 5 **EST:** 2008
SALES (est): 206.47K **Privately Held**
Web: www.starrlightmead.com
SIC: 2084 Wines

(G-5372)
STAUNTON SAW SERVICE
1611 Milton Rd (27712-1528)
PHONE.................................919 471-3883
William Staunton, *Owner*
EMP: 5 **EST:** 2000
SALES (est): 149.76K **Privately Held**
SIC: 3541 Saws and sawing machines

(G-5373)
STEEL CITY SERVICES LLC
1129 E Geer St (27704-5024)
PHONE.................................919 698-2407
J D Mcqueen, *Pt*
EMP: 14 **EST:** 2010
SALES (est): 1.88MM **Privately Held**
Web: www.steelcityservices.com
SIC: 3312 1796 Rails, steel or iron; Installing building equipment

(G-5374)
STERLING CLEORA CORPORATION
3115 Buckingham Rd (27707-4505)
PHONE.................................919 563-5800
Chip Cappelletti, *Pr*
Rich Cappelletti, *
EMP: 21 **EST:** 1994
SALES (est): 4.98MM **Privately Held**
Web: www.csterling.com
SIC: 2541 8712 1542 Store fixtures, wood; Architectural services; Design and erection, combined: non-residential

(G-5375)
STIEFEL LABORATORIES INC (DH)
5 Moore Dr (27709-0143)
PHONE.................................888 784-3335
Charles W Stiefel, *Ch Bd*
William D Humphries, *
Gavin Corcoran, *
Michael T Cornelius, *
Simon Jose, *
EMP: 40 **EST:** 1944
SQ FT: 13,000
SALES (est): 227.46MM
SALES (corp-wide): 35.31B **Privately Held**
SIC: 5122 2834 Pharmaceuticals; Pharmaceutical preparations
HQ: Glaxosmithkline Sl Holdings, Inc.
  1500 Spring Garden St
  Philadelphia PA 19130

(G-5376)
STIEFEL LABORATORIES INC
410 Blackwell St (27701-3986)
PHONE.................................888 784-3335
EMP: 110
SALES (corp-wide): 35.31B **Privately Held**
Web: www.stiefel.com
SIC: 5122 2834 Pharmaceuticals; Pharmaceutical preparations
HQ: Stiefel Laboratories, Inc.
  5 Moore Dr
  Durham NC 27709
  888 784-3335

(G-5377)
STRAWBRIDGE STUDIOS INC (PA)
3616 Hillsborough Rd Ste D (27705-2900)
P.O. Box 3005 (27715-3005)
PHONE.................................919 286-9512
EMP: 90 **EST:** 1923
SALES (est): 11.62MM
SALES (corp-wide): 11.62MM **Privately Held**
Web: www.strawbridge.net
SIC: 7221 2741 School photographer; Directories, nec: publishing and printing

(G-5378)
STRYKER CORPORATION
Also Called: Hyperbranch
800 Capitola Dr Ste 12 (27713-4385)
PHONE.................................919 433-3325
EMP: 13
SALES (corp-wide): 20.5B **Publicly Held**
Web: www.stryker.com
SIC: 3842 3841 Surgical appliances and supplies; Surgical and medical instruments
PA: Stryker Corporation
  1941 Stryker Way
  Portage MI 49002
  269 385-2600

(G-5379)
SUMMIT AGRO USA LLC
240 Leigh Farm Rd Ste 415 (27707-8103)
PHONE.................................984 260-0407
William M Lewis, *Pr*
Ryan Mccue, *CFO*
▲ **EMP:** 7 **EST:** 2011
SALES (est): 2.56MM **Privately Held**
Web: www.summitagro-usa.com
SIC: 2879 Fungicides, herbicides
PA: Sumitomo Corporation
  2-3-2, Otemachi
  Chiyoda-Ku TKY 100-0

(G-5380)
SUNHS WAREHOUSE LLC
607 Ellis Rd Bldg 42a (27703-6014)
PHONE.................................919 908-1523
Arturo Leon, *Managing Member*
EMP: 4 **EST:** 2019
SALES (est): 264.88K **Privately Held**
Web: www.sunhswarehouse.com
SIC: 2434 Wood kitchen cabinets

(G-5381)
SUPER G PRINT LAB LLC
813 Onslow St (27705-4244)
PHONE.................................919 864-9351
William Fick, *Owner*
EMP: 5 **EST:** 2015
SALES (est): 88.78K **Privately Held**
SIC: 2752 Commercial printing, lithographic

(G-5382)
SWINER PUBLISHING COMPANY INC
2 Crawford Ct (27703-9475)
PHONE.................................919 599-3441
Carmelita Swiner, *Prin*
EMP: 6 **EST:** 2016
SALES (est): 82.07K **Privately Held**
Web: www.docswiner.blog
SIC: 2741 Miscellaneous publishing

(G-5383)
SWIR VISION SYSTEMS INC
3021 Cornwallis Rd (27709-0146)
P.O. Box 110373 (27709-5373)
PHONE.................................919 248-0032

Durham - Durham County (G-5384)

George Wildeman, *CEO*
Ethan Klem, *VP*
Allan Hilton, *VP*
Chris Gregory, *VP*
EMP: 21 **EST:** 2018
SALES (est): 1.04MM **Privately Held**
Web: www.swirvisionsystems.com
SIC: 3663 Cameras, television

(G-5384)
SYNNOVATOR INC
104 Tw Alexander Dr # 1 (27709-0002)
PHONE..................................919 360-0518
Xin Wang, *Brnch Mgr*
EMP: 5
SALES (corp-wide): 101.75K **Privately Held**
Web: www.thesynnovator.com
SIC: 2819 Chemicals, reagent grade: refined from technical grade
PA: Synnovator, Inc
  115 Centrewest Ct
  Cary NC 27513
  919 360-0518

(G-5385)
SYNTHON PHARMACEUTICALS INC
Also Called: Synthon
1007 Slater Rd Ste 150 (27703-8057)
P.O. Box 110487 (27709-5487)
PHONE..................................919 493-6006
Edwin De Rooij, *CEO*
Angelo Cornelissen, *
EMP: 42 **EST:** 1991
SQ FT: 1,429
SALES (est): 10.42MM **Privately Held**
Web: www.synthon.com
SIC: 2834 Pharmaceutical preparations
HQ: Synthon International Holding B.V.
  Microweg 22
  Nijmegen GE 6545
  243727700

(G-5386)
TAPPED TEES LLC
600 W Main St Apt 613 (27701-1796)
PHONE..................................919 943-9692
Benjamin Ingold, *Mgr*
EMP: 8 **EST:** 2017
SALES (est): 440K **Privately Held**
SIC: 2396 Screen printing on fabric articles

(G-5387)
TAVROS THERAPEUTICS INC
8 Davis Dr Ste 100 (27709-0003)
PHONE..................................919 602-2631
Eoin R Mcdonnell, *CEO*
Greg Mossinghoff, *Chief Business Officer*
EMP: 21 **EST:** 2019
SALES (est): 8.46MM **Privately Held**
Web: www.tavrostx.com
SIC: 2834 Druggists' preparations (pharmaceuticals)

(G-5388)
TELEFLEX INCORPORATED
Also Called: Teleflex
2917 Weck Dr Research Triangle Park (27709-0186)
PHONE..................................919 433-2575
EMP: 9
SALES (corp-wide): 2.97B **Publicly Held**
Web: www.teleflex.com
SIC: 3841 3842 Surgical and medical instruments; Surgical appliances and supplies
PA: Teleflex Incorporated
  550 E Swedesford Rd # 400
  Wayne PA 19087
  610 225-6800

(G-5389)
TELEFLEX INCORPORATED
Also Called: Teleflex
1805a Tw Alexander Dr (27703-8389)
PHONE..................................919 433-2575
Keri Brang, *Brnch Mgr*
EMP: 7
SALES (corp-wide): 2.97B **Publicly Held**
Web: www.teleflex.com
SIC: 3842 Surgical appliances and supplies
PA: Teleflex Incorporated
  550 E Swedesford Rd # 400
  Wayne PA 19087
  610 225-6800

(G-5390)
TELEFLEX MEDICAL INCORPORATED
4024 Stirrup Creek Dr Ste 270 (27703-9464)
PHONE..................................919 544-8000
EMP: 5
SALES (corp-wide): 2.97B **Publicly Held**
Web: www.teleflex.com
SIC: 3841 Surgical and medical instruments
HQ: Teleflex Medical Incorporated
  3015 Carrington Mill Blvd # 100
  Morrisville NC 27560
  919 544-8000

(G-5391)
TELIT WIRELESS SOLUTIONS INC (PA)
5425 Page Rd Ste 120 (27703-7009)
PHONE..................................919 439-7977
Roger Dewey, *Pr*
Michael Ueland, *
Yariv Dafna, *
Teemu Vasankari, *
Inbal Barak-etzion, *Treas*
EMP: 69 **EST:** 2006
SQ FT: 4,100
SALES (est): 22.08MM **Privately Held**
Web: www.telit.com
SIC: 3674 4813 Modules, solid state; Internet connectivity services

(G-5392)
TELLAD SUPPLY COMPANY
2320 Presidential Dr # 105 (27703-8077)
P.O. Box 15448 (27704-0448)
PHONE..................................919 572-6700
Darrell E White, *Pr*
Michael E White, *VP*
EMP: 5 **EST:** 1984
SQ FT: 10,000
SALES (est): 506.83K **Privately Held**
SIC: 5065 3661 Communication equipment; Telephones and telephone apparatus

(G-5393)
TEMPEST ENVIRONMENTAL CORP
7 Al Acqua Dr (27707-9211)
PHONE..................................919 973-1609
Tom Sparks, *COO*
Roddy Tempest, *CEO*
Tim Pate, *CFO*
EMP: 9 **EST:** 1985
SQ FT: 4,576
SALES (est): 303.91K **Privately Held**
Web: www.tempestenvironmental.com
SIC: 8999 4941 3589 8744 Scientific consulting; Water supply; Water treatment equipment, industrial; Environmental remediation

(G-5394)
TEMPEST ENVMTL SYSTEMS INC
Also Called: Tempest Environmental
7 Al Acqua Dr (27707-9211)
PHONE..................................919 973-1609
Roddy Tempest, *CEO*
Scott Jones, *Pr*
Connie Tempest, *VP*
Tom Sparks, *COO*
▼ **EMP:** 11 **EST:** 1985
SQ FT: 8,000
SALES (est): 822.13K **Privately Held**
Web: www.aquapura.com
SIC: 3589 Water purification equipment, household type

(G-5395)
TERARECON INC (PA)
4309 Emperor Blvd Ste 310 (27703-8069)
PHONE..................................650 372-1100
Dan Mcsweeney, *Pr*
Tiecheng Zhao, *Sr VP*
Dianne Oseto, *Corporate Secretary*
Martin Clanty, *CFO*
▲ **EMP:** 80 **EST:** 1997
SALES (est): 43.34MM
SALES (corp-wide): 43.34MM **Privately Held**
Web: www.terarecon.com
SIC: 3577 5734 Computer peripheral equipment, nec; Computer peripheral equipment

(G-5396)
TERGUS PHARMA LLC (PA)
4018 Stirrup Creek Dr (27703-9000)
P.O. Box 12012 (27709-2012)
PHONE..................................919 549-9700
EMP: 30 **EST:** 2012
SQ FT: 4,100
SALES (est): 26.59MM **Privately Held**
Web: www.terguspharma.com
SIC: 2834 8734 Pharmaceutical preparations; Testing laboratories

(G-5397)
THATCHER FOREST PUBLISHING
3524 Manford Dr (27707-5143)
P.O. Box 3358 (27702-3358)
PHONE..................................919 402-9245
Robert Kesler, *Prin*
EMP: 4 **EST:** 2018
SALES (est): 37.59K **Privately Held**
SIC: 2741 Miscellaneous publishing

(G-5398)
THERMO FISHER SCIENTIFIC INC
4063 Stirrup Creek Dr (27703-9001)
PHONE..................................800 955-6288
EMP: 7
SALES (corp-wide): 44.91B **Publicly Held**
Web: www.thermofisher.com
SIC: 3826 Analytical instruments
PA: Thermo Fisher Scientific Inc.
  168 3rd Ave
  Waltham MA 02451
  781 622-1000

(G-5399)
THERMOCHEM RECOVERY INTL
5201 International Dr (27712-8950)
PHONE..................................919 606-3282
EMP: 10 **EST:** 2017
SALES (est): 752K **Privately Held**
Web: www.tri-inc.net
SIC: 3312 Chemicals and other products derived from coking

(G-5400)
THIN LINE SADDLE PADS INC
2945 S Miami Blvd Ste 120-120 (27703-8024)
PHONE..................................919 680-6803
EMP: 7 **EST:** 2007
SALES (est): 376.87K **Privately Held**
Web: www.thinlineglobal.com
SIC: 3199 2399 Leather goods, nec; Fabricated textile products, nec

(G-5401)
THOMPSON JOINERY LLC
912 Burch Ave (27701-2816)
PHONE..................................919 672-2770
EMP: 5 **EST:** 2014
SALES (est): 187.45K **Privately Held**
SIC: 2431 Millwork

(G-5402)
THRIFTY TIRE
2903 N Roxboro St (27704-3247)
P.O. Box 1095 (27573-1095)
PHONE..................................919 220-7800
Rick Gamble, *Genl Mgr*
EMP: 6 **EST:** 2006
SALES (est): 536.32K **Privately Held**
Web: www.thriftytireonline.com
SIC: 5531 7534 Automotive tires; Tire retreading and repair shops

(G-5403)
TIMMONS FABRICATIONS INC
2818 Pervis Rd (27704-5334)
PHONE..................................919 688-8998
David Timmons, *Pr*
Marianna Timmons, *Sec*
EMP: 10 **EST:** 1989
SQ FT: 15,000
SALES (est): 947.5K **Privately Held**
SIC: 3441 Fabricated structural metal

(G-5404)
TOSHIBA GLOBL CMMRCE SLTONS IN (DH)
Also Called: Toshiba
3901 S Miami Blvd (27703-9135)
PHONE..................................984 444-2767
Rance M Poehler, *Pr*
Sam Craig, *
John Gaydac, *
Kenneth Hammer, *CLO*
Willis Lumpkin, *
EMP: 43 **EST:** 2012
SALES (est): 521.22MM **Privately Held**
Web: commerce.toshiba.com
SIC: 3577 Input/output equipment, computer
HQ: Toshiba Global Commerce Solutions Holdings Corporation
  2-17-2, Higashigotanda
  Shinagawa-Ku TKY 141-0

(G-5405)
TRIANGLE BIOSYSTEMS INC
Also Called: Triangle Biosystems Intl
2224 Page Rd Ste 108 (27703-8908)
PHONE..................................919 361-2663
James Morizio, *Pr*
EMP: 11 **EST:** 2001
SQ FT: 3,600
SALES (est): 478.4K **Publicly Held**
Web: www.trianglebiosystems.com
SIC: 8731 3429 Biotechnical research, commercial; Hardware, nec
PA: Harvard Bioscience, Inc.
  84 October Hill Rd Ste 10
  Holliston MA 01746

(G-5406)
TRIANGLE BRICK COMPANY (PA)
6523 Nc Highway 55 (27713-9436)
PHONE..................................919 544-1796
Scott D Mollenkopf, *Pr*
Wilhelm Roeben, *
Arch Lynch, *
▲ **EMP:** 25 **EST:** 1959
SQ FT: 10,000
SALES (est): 48.2MM

GEOGRAPHIC SECTION

Durham - Durham County (G-5431)

SALES (corp-wide): 48.2MM **Privately Held**
Web: www.trianglebrick.com
SIC: **3251** 5211 8741 Brick and structural clay tile; Brick; Management services

(G-5407)
TRIANGLE CONVERTING CORP
2021 S Briggs Ave (27703-6076)
P.O. Box 2244 (27702-2244)
PHONE..............................919 596-6656
James B Brame Junior, *Pr*
Anita W Brame, *
EMP: 30 **EST:** 1983
SQ FT: 20,000
SALES (est): 2.55MM **Privately Held**
Web: www.bramespecialty.com
SIC: **2679** 2675 2621 Paper products, converted, nec; Die-cut paper and board; Paper mills

(G-5408)
TRIANGLE GLASS SERVICE INC
1320 Old Oxford Rd Ste 12 (27704-2470)
P.O. Box 15429 (27704-0429)
PHONE..............................919 477-9508
John Beck, *Pr*
William James, *VP*
EMP: 5 **EST:** 1988
SQ FT: 2,400
SALES (est): 570.15K **Privately Held**
Web: www.triangleglassservice.com
SIC: **1793** 7699 5231 5084 Glass and glazing work; Door and window repair; Glass; Machine tools and accessories

(G-5409)
TRIANGLE PRCSION DGNOSTICS INC
2 Davis Dr Rm 203 (27709-0003)
PHONE..............................919 345-0110
Tong Zhou, *CEO*
Zhiyuan Hu, *VP*
Ping Zhang, *COO*
Jiechun Zhou, *CFO*
EMP: 4 **EST:** 2014
SALES (est): 235.8K **Privately Held**
SIC: **2835** 7389 In vivo diagnostics; Business Activities at Non-Commercial Site

(G-5410)
TRIANGLE SYSTEMS INC
4364 S Alston Ave (27713-2564)
PHONE..............................919 544-0090
Jim Ott, *Owner*
EMP: 8
SALES (corp-wide): 970.62K **Privately Held**
Web: www.triangle-systems.com
SIC: **7372** Educational computer software
PA: Triangle Systems, Inc.
    882 Pinehurst Dr
    Chapel Hill NC 27517
    919 544-0090

(G-5411)
TRIANGLE TRIBUNE
Also Called: Consuldated Media Group
115 Market St Ste 211 (27701-3241)
PHONE..............................704 376-0496
Gerald Johnson, *Pt*
EMP: 4 **EST:** 1998
SALES (est): 234.72K **Privately Held**
Web: www.triangletribune.com
SIC: **2711** Newspapers, publishing and printing

(G-5412)
TROXLER ELECTRONIC LABS INC (PA)
3008 Cornwallis Rd (27709-0007)
P.O. Box 12057 (27709-2057)
PHONE..............................919 549-8661
William F Troxler, *Pr*
James H Boylan Junior, *Sec*
▲ **EMP:** 85 **EST:** 1956
SQ FT: 64,000
SALES (est): 25.57MM
SALES (corp-wide): 25.57MM **Privately Held**
Web: www.troxlerlabs.com
SIC: **8731** 3823 3825 3829 Commercial research laboratory; Density and specific gravity instruments, industrial process; Test equipment for electronic and electric measurement; Measuring and controlling devices, nec

(G-5413)
TRUEFAB LLC
3401 Industrial Dr (27704-9430)
PHONE..............................919 620-8158
Lloyd Johnson, *Prin*
EMP: 15 **EST:** 2016
SALES (est): 2.15MM **Privately Held**
SIC: **3441** 3499 Fabricated structural metal; Fabricated metal products, nec

(G-5414)
TSENG INFORMATION SYSTEMS INC
813 Watts St (27701-1532)
PHONE..............................919 682-9197
Larry Tseng, *Pr*
Charles Ellertson, *VP*
EMP: 7 **EST:** 1980
SALES (est): 395.95K **Privately Held**
SIC: **2791** Typesetting

(G-5415)
TUMI STORE - STREETS SOUTH PT
6910 Fayetteville Rd Ste 168 (27713-9714)
PHONE..............................919 224-1028
EMP: 4 **EST:** 2018
SALES (est): 102.89K **Privately Held**
SIC: **3161** Luggage

(G-5416)
TWINVISION NORTH AMERICA INC
4018 Patriot Dr Ste 100 (27703-8083)
PHONE..............................919 361-2155
Dave L Turney, *Pr*
Dave Turney, *
▲ **EMP:** 226 **EST:** 1996
SQ FT: 18,000
SALES (est): 2.26MM
SALES (corp-wide): 169.16MM **Privately Held**
Web: www.twinvisionna.com
SIC: **3993** Signs and advertising specialties
HQ: Xdric, Inc.
    13760 Noel Rd Ste 830
    Dallas TX 75240
    214 378-8992

(G-5417)
TYRATA INC
101 W Chapel Hill St Ste 200 (27701-3255)
PHONE..............................919 210-8992
Jesko Windheim, *Pr*
Richard Scott, *VP*
Tracey Timothy, *Ch Bd*
EMP: 12 **EST:** 2017
SALES (est): 1.06MM **Privately Held**
Web: www.tyrata.com
SIC: **3011** Retreading materials, tire

(G-5418)
UAI TECHNOLOGY INC
68 Tw Alexander Dr (27709-0056)
PHONE..............................919 541-9339
Steven Maier, *Brnch Mgr*
EMP: 9
SALES (corp-wide): 4.85MM **Privately Held**
Web: www.phoenixhecht.com
SIC: **2741** Miscellaneous publishing
PA: Uai Technology, Inc.
    68 Tw Alexander Dr
    Durham NC 27709
    919 541-9339

(G-5419)
UNECOL ADHESIVES N AMER LLC
1408 Christian Ave (27705-2909)
P.O. Box 2535 (27715-2535)
PHONE..............................888 963-8879
Bryan John Dodd, *CEO*
EMP: 9 **EST:** 2016
SALES (est): 244.28K **Privately Held**
Web: www.unecol.com
SIC: **2891** Adhesives

(G-5420)
UNIFIED2 GLOBL PACKG GROUP LLC
3829 S Miami Blvd Ste 300 (27703-5419)
PHONE..............................774 696-3643
Arthur Mahassel, *Pr*
EMP: 200 **EST:** 2018
SALES (est): 23.96MM **Privately Held**
SIC: **5199** 3086 Packaging materials; Cups and plates, foamed plastics

(G-5421)
UNITED GROUP GRAPHICS INC
2608 Carver St (27705-2797)
PHONE..............................919 596-3932
EMP: 4 **EST:** 2016
SALES (est): 171.03K **Privately Held**
Web: www.unitedgroupgraphics.com
SIC: **3993** Signs and advertising specialties

(G-5422)
UNITED THERAPEUTICS CORP
2 Maughan Dr (27709)
PHONE..............................919 246-9389
EMP: 11 **EST:** 1977
SALES (est): 7.32MM **Privately Held**
Web: www.unither.com
SIC: **2834** Pharmaceutical preparations

(G-5423)
UNITED THERAPEUTICS CORP
Also Called: United Therapeatics
55 Tw Alexander Dr (27709-0152)
P.O. Box 14186 (27709-4186)
PHONE..............................919 361-6141
Roger Jess, *Brnch Mgr*
EMP: 90
Web: www.unither.com
SIC: **2834** Pharmaceutical preparations
PA: United Therapeutics Corporation
    1000 Spring St
    Silver Spring MD 20910

(G-5424)
UNIVERSITY DIRECTORIES LLC
Also Called: Around Campus Group, The
2520 Meridian Pkwy Ste 470 (27713-4202)
P.O. Box 364 (27302-0364)
PHONE..............................800 743-5556
EMP: 59 **EST:** 1996
SALES (est): 13.01MM **Privately Held**
Web: www.universitydirectories.com
SIC: **2741** Directories, telephone: publishing and printing

(G-5425)
UNSPECIFIED INC
65 Tw Alexander Dr Unit 110324 (27709)
PHONE..............................919 907-2726

EMP: 7 **EST:** 2018
SALES (est): 391.47K **Privately Held**
Web: www.unspecified.life
SIC: **7372** Prepackaged software

(G-5426)
UPL NA INC (HQ)
Also Called: Upi
5 Laboratory Dr Bldg 1 Ste 1100 (27709-0012)
PHONE..............................610 491-2800
David Elser, *CEO*
Kevin Meitzler, *
William Herbert, *
Joao Esteves, *
▲ **EMP:** 30 **EST:** 1996
SQ FT: 2,100
SALES (est): 91.15MM **Privately Held**
Web: www.upl-ltd.com
SIC: **5191** 2879 Chemicals, agricultural; Agricultural chemicals, nec
PA: Upl Limited
    Upl House, 610 B/2, Bandra Village,
    Mumbai MH 40005

(G-5427)
UPPER DECK COMPANY
1750 Tw Alexander Dr (27703-9241)
PHONE..............................760 496-9149
EMP: 9
SALES (est): 477.23K **Privately Held**
Web: www.upperdeck.com
SIC: **3131** Uppers

(G-5428)
UROVANT SCIENCES INC
324 Blackwell St Bay 11 (27701-3658)
PHONE..............................919 323-8528
EMP: 10
SALES (corp-wide): 24.69MM **Privately Held**
Web: www.urovant.com
SIC: **2834** Pharmaceutical preparations
HQ: Urovant Sciences, Inc.
    5281 California Ave # 100
    Irvine CA
    949 226-6029

(G-5429)
VALASSIS COMMUNICATIONS INC
Also Called: Valassis Durham Printing Div
4918 Prospectus Dr (27713-4407)
PHONE..............................919 544-4511
Blaine G Gerber, *Brnch Mgr*
EMP: 69
SQ FT: 10,000
Web: www.vericast.com
SIC: **2759** 2752 Promotional printing; Commercial printing, lithographic
HQ: Valassis Communications, Inc.
    19975 Victor Pkwy
    Livonia MI 48152

(G-5430)
VALASSIS COMMUNICATIONS INC
Also Called: Valassis Wichita Printing
4918 Prospectus Dr (27713-4407)
PHONE..............................919 361-7900
Michael A Wood, *Brnch Mgr*
EMP: 85
Web: www.vericast.com
SIC: **2759** 2752 Promotional printing; Commercial printing, lithographic
HQ: Valassis Communications, Inc.
    19975 Victor Pkwy
    Livonia MI 48152

(G-5431)
VALLEY RUN CANDLES LLC
2 Spreading Oak Ct (27713-6511)
PHONE..............................828 729-8652

Durham - Durham County (G-5432) — GEOGRAPHIC SECTION

Lyndsey Gibson, *Prin*
EMP: 4 **EST:** 2017
SALES (est): 39.69K **Privately Held**
SIC: 3999 Candles

(G-5432)
VESTARON CORPORATION
4025 Stirrup Creek Dr Ste 400 (27703-9398)
PHONE..................919 694-1022
Juan Estupinan, *Pr*
EMP: 91 **EST:** 2005
SALES (est): 14.97MM **Privately Held**
Web: www.vestaron.com
SIC: 2879 Insecticides and pesticides

(G-5433)
VIASIC INC
5015 Southpark Dr Ste 240 (27713-7736)
PHONE..................336 774-2150
Lynn Hayden, *Pr*
Denise Hummell, *Sec*
EMP: 6 **EST:** 1999
SQ FT: 2,100
SALES (est): 542.58K **Privately Held**
Web: www.viasic.com
SIC: 7372 Application computer software

(G-5434)
VIIV HEALTHCARE COMPANY
Also Called: Viiv Healthcare US
410 Blackwell St (27701-3986)
PHONE..................919 483-2100
Deborah Waterhouse, *CEO*
Jill Anderson, *
EMP: 1100 **EST:** 2009
SALES (est): 193.65MM
SALES (corp-wide): 35.31B **Privately Held**
Web: www.viivhealthcare.com
SIC: 2834 7389 Pharmaceutical preparations; Business Activities at Non-Commercial Site
HQ: Glaxosmithkline Llc
2929 Walnut St Ste 1700
Philadelphia PA 19104
888 825-5249

(G-5435)
VOGENX INC
3920 S Alston Ave (27713-1829)
PHONE..................919 659-5677
Steve Delmar, *CFO*
EMP: 5 **EST:** 2021
SALES (est): 561.72K **Privately Held**
Web: www.vogenx.com
SIC: 2834 Pharmaceutical preparations

(G-5436)
VOLUMETRICS MED SYSTEMS LLC
4711 Hope Valley Rd Ste 4f (27707-5651)
PHONE..................800 472-0900
Mark Foster, *Prin*
Olaf Von Ramm, *Prin*
Kent Moore, *Prin*
EMP: 4 **EST:** 2021
SALES (est): 279.18K **Privately Held**
SIC: 3845 Electromedical equipment

(G-5437)
WALKER DRAPERIES INC
Also Called: Walker's
2503 Broad St (27704-3007)
PHONE..................919 220-1424
W Barry Walker, *Pr*
Janet Walker, *Sec*
EMP: 12 **EST:** 1959
SQ FT: 8,500
SALES (est): 767.85K **Privately Held**
Web: www.walkersdraperies.com
SIC: 2391 5714 Draperies, plastic and textile: from purchased materials; Draperies

(G-5438)
WATSON PARTY TABLES INC (PA)
2455 S Alston Ave (27713-1301)
P.O. Box 13447 (27709-3447)
PHONE..................919 294-9153
Shawn Watson, *Pr*
Ronnie Watson, *VP*
Vicky Watson, *Sec*
▲ **EMP:** 12 **EST:** 1986
SQ FT: 12,000
SALES (est): 1.32MM **Privately Held**
Web: www.partytables.com
SIC: 2392 7359 Tablecloths: made from purchased materials; Dishes, silverware, tables, and banquet accessories rental

(G-5439)
WEAVEUP INC
4810 Hope Valley Rd Ste 210 (27707-6631)
PHONE..................443 540-4201
Flint Davis, *Pr*
Ann Aber, *Sec*
Renee Jefferson, *Treas*
EMP: 5 **EST:** 2018
SALES (est): 819.74K
SALES (corp-wide): 2.22B **Publicly Held**
Web: www.weaveup.com
SIC: 2262 2396 7389 Printing, manmade fiber and silk broadwoven fabrics; Fabric printing and stamping; Design services
PA: Joann Inc.
5555 Darrow Rd
Hudson OH 44236
330 656-2600

(G-5440)
WHIMSICAL PRINTS PAPER & GIFTS
5826 Fayetteville Rd Ste 105 (27713-8684)
PHONE..................919 544-8491
EMP: 5 **EST:** 2011
SALES (est): 201.18K **Privately Held**
Web: www.whimsicalprints.com
SIC: 2752 Commercial printing, lithographic

(G-5441)
WILLIAMS EASY HITCH INC
2310 Old Oxford Rd (27704-9583)
PHONE..................919 302-0062
EMP: 6 **EST:** 2010
SALES (est): 181.5K **Privately Held**
SIC: 3799 Transportation equipment, nec

(G-5442)
WINDLIFT INC
Also Called: Windlift
2445 S Alston Ave (27713-1301)
P.O. Box 3324 (27702-3324)
PHONE..................919 490-8575
Robert Creighton, *CEO*
EMP: 5 **EST:** 2020
SALES (est): 1.06MM **Privately Held**
Web: www.windlift.com
SIC: 3511 Turbines and turbine generator sets

(G-5443)
WOLFSPEED INC
Also Called: Lightcreed Labs
4601 Silicon Dr 3rd Fl (27703-8449)
PHONE..................919 407-5300
Billy Moon, *Mgr*
EMP: 6
SALES (corp-wide): 921.9MM **Publicly Held**
Web: www.wolfspeed.com
SIC: 3674 Semiconductors and related devices
PA: Wolfspeed, Inc.
4600 Silicon Dr
Durham NC 27703
919 407-5300

(G-5444)
WOLFSPEED INC (PA)
Also Called: Wolfspeed
4600 Silicon Dr (27703-8475)
PHONE..................919 407-5300
Gregg A Lowe, *Pr*
Thomas Werner, *
Neill P Reynolds, *Ex VP*
▲ **EMP:** 175 **EST:** 1987
SQ FT: 1,054,000
SALES (est): 921.9MM
SALES (corp-wide): 921.9MM **Publicly Held**
Web: www.wolfspeed.com
SIC: 3674 3672 Integrated circuits, semiconductor networks, etc.; Printed circuit boards

(G-5445)
WOLFSPEED EMPLOYEE SERVICES CO
4600 Silicon Dr (27703-8475)
PHONE..................919 313-5300
Michael E Mcdevitt, *Pr*
EMP: 12 **EST:** 2014
SALES (est): 353.73K **Privately Held**
Web: www.wolfspeed.com
SIC: 3674 Semiconductors and related devices

(G-5446)
WOODLAKE WOOD WORKS
2 Ontario Ct (27713-8822)
PHONE..................919 972-1000
David Wait, *Prin*
EMP: 4 **EST:** 2017
SALES (est): 63.52K **Privately Held**
SIC: 2431 Millwork

(G-5447)
WOODS AT LOWER RIVER LLC
125 Royal Sunset Dr (27713-7604)
PHONE..................919 544-8044
Kevin Howard, *Prin*
EMP: 5 **EST:** 2015
SALES (est): 43.99K **Privately Held**
SIC: 2499 Wood products, nec

(G-5448)
WRIGHT CHEMICALS LLC
4804 Page Creek Ln (27703-8582)
PHONE..................919 296-1771
EMP: 8
SALES (est): 351.29K **Privately Held**
SIC: 2869 Industrial organic chemicals, nec

(G-5449)
WRIT PRESS INC
1308 N Duke St (27701-1652)
PHONE..................815 988-7074
Adam Lewis, *Prin*
EMP: 6 **EST:** 2019
SALES (est): 65.16K **Privately Held**
Web: www.writpress.shop
SIC: 2741 Miscellaneous publishing

(G-5450)
WRITING PENN LLC
4400 Turnberry Cir (27712-9466)
PHONE..................301 529-5324
EMP: 5 **EST:** 2016
SALES (est): 103.91K **Privately Held**
SIC: 2741 Miscellaneous publishing

(G-5451)
WTVD TELEVISION LLC
Also Called: ABC 11
411 Liberty St (27701-3407)
PHONE..................919 683-1111
Ed O'connor, *Dir*
Caroline Welch, *Managing Member**
EMP: 150 **EST:** 2008
SQ FT: 40,000
SALES (est): 23.08MM
SALES (corp-wide): 88.9B **Publicly Held**
Web: www.abc11.com
SIC: 4833 4832 2711 Television broadcasting stations; News; Newspapers, publishing and printing
HQ: Abc, Inc.
77 W 66th St Rm 100
New York NY 10023
212 456-7777

(G-5452)
WUNDERKIND PRESS LLC
601 Watts St (27701-1723)
PHONE..................919 381-0713
Sanyin Siang, *Prin*
EMP: 6 **EST:** 2015
SALES (est): 100.53K **Privately Held**
SIC: 2741 Miscellaneous publishing

(G-5453)
X-CELEPRINT INC
3021 Cornwallis Rd Bldg 1 (27709-0146)
P.O. Box 13788 (27709-3788)
PHONE..................919 248-0020
Kyle Benkendorfer, *CEO*
EMP: 10 **EST:** 2019
SALES (est): 900.94K **Privately Held**
Web: www.x-celeprint.com
SIC: 3674 Hybrid integrated circuits

(G-5454)
XDRI INC
4018 Patriot Dr Ste 100 (27703-8083)
PHONE..................919 361-2155
David L Turney, *Pr*
David Turney, *Pr*
EMP: 8 **EST:** 1983
SALES (est): 326.74K **Privately Held**
SIC: 3652 Prerecorded records and tapes

(G-5455)
XO SIGNS
414 Currin Rd (27703-4806)
PHONE..................919 328-9110
Ariot Juarez, *Prin*
EMP: 5 **EST:** 2018
SALES (est): 163.11K **Privately Held**
Web: www.xo-signs.com
SIC: 3993 Signs and advertising specialties

(G-5456)
XONA MICROFLUIDICS INC
76 Tw Alexander Dr (27709-0152)
P.O. Box 14205 (27709-4205)
PHONE..................951 553-6400
Anne Taylor, *Ex Dir*
Anne Taylor, *Pr*
Brad Taylor, *CEO*
Joseph Harris, *Managing Member*
EMP: 5 **EST:** 2008
SQ FT: 1,400
SALES (est): 505.61K **Privately Held**
Web: www.xonamicrofluidics.com
SIC: 8999 2869 3821 Scientific consulting; Silicones; Laboratory apparatus, except heating and measuring

(G-5457)
YEEKA LLC
11 Yarmouth Pl (27707-5537)

PHONE..................................919 308-9826
Weican Meng, Pt
EMP: 5 EST: 2006
SALES (est): 92K Privately Held
Web: www.yeeka.com
SIC: 2741 Internet publishing and broadcasting

(G-5458)
YELLOW RUBBER BALL LLC
4100 Five Oaks Dr Unit 41 (27707-5256)
PHONE..................................919 357-6307
Katherine Benedetto, Admn
EMP: 4 EST: 2019
SALES (est): 101.77K Privately Held
Web: www.yellowrubberball.com
SIC: 3652 Prerecorded records and tapes

(G-5459)
YUKON MEDICAL LLC
4021 Stirrup Creek Dr Ste 200 (27703-9352)
PHONE..................................919 595-8250
EMP: 6 EST: 2008
SALES (est): 1.05MM Privately Held
Web: www.yukonmedical.com
SIC: 3841 5047 Physiotherapy equipment, electrical; Medical equipment and supplies

(G-5460)
ZOETIS INC
1040 Swabia Ct (27703-8481)
PHONE..................................919 941-5185
EMP: 220
SALES (corp-wide): 8.08B Publicly Held
Web: www.zoetis.com
SIC: 2834 Pharmaceutical preparations
PA: Zoetis Inc.
   10 Sylvan Way Ste 100
   Parsippany NJ 07054
   973 822-7000

Eagle Springs
Moore County

(G-5461)
T H BLUE INC
Also Called: T. H. Blue Mulch
226 Flowers Rd (27242-8172)
P.O. Box 97 (27242-0097)
PHONE..................................910 673-3033
Tommy Blue, CEO
T Harold Blue Senior, Pr
Thomas H Blue Junior, VP
EMP: 32 EST: 1965
SQ FT: 7,000
SALES (est): 3.39MM Privately Held
Web: www.thbluemulch.com
SIC: 2875 4212 4213 2421 Potting soil, mixed; Local trucking, without storage; Trucking, except local; Sawmills and planing mills, general

(G-5462)
WAR SPORT LLC
13117 Nc Highway 24 27 (27242-8072)
PHONE..................................910 948-2237
EMP: 8 EST: 2009
SALES (est): 236.29K Privately Held
SIC: 3483 Ammunition components

(G-5463)
WHITNEY SCREEN PRINTING
2244 Nc Highway 211 (27242-7950)
PHONE..................................910 673-0309
EMP: 4 EST: 2016
SALES (est): 71.57K Privately Held
SIC: 2752 Commercial printing, lithographic

East Bend
Yadkin County

(G-5464)
CELLAR 4201 LLC
4201 Apperson Rd (27018-7031)
PHONE..................................336 699-6030
Donna Carlyle Hutchins, Prin
EMP: 4 EST: 2007
SALES (est): 223.43K Privately Held
Web: www.cellar4201.com
SIC: 2084 Wines

(G-5465)
CROSS TECHNOLOGY INC (PA)
Also Called: Nu-Tech
305 Junia Ave (27018-8865)
PHONE..................................336 725-4700
James F Inman, Pr
EMP: 37 EST: 2000
SQ FT: 39,000
SALES (est): 10.46MM Privately Held
Web: www.crosstech.us
SIC: 3399 8711 3089 3545 Brads: aluminum, brass, or other nonferrous metal or wire; Engineering services; Injection molded finished plastics products, nec; Precision tools, machinists'

(G-5466)
DIVINE LLAMA VINEYARDS LLC
4179 Divine Llama Ln (27018-7498)
PHONE..................................336 699-2525
Patrick West, Brnch Mgr
EMP: 5
SALES (corp-wide): 363.57K Privately Held
Web: www.divinellamavineyards.com
SIC: 2084 Wines
PA: Divine Llama Vineyards, Llc
   3524 Yadkinville Rd
   Winston Salem NC 27106
   336 407-8413

(G-5467)
REYNOLDA MFG SOLUTIONS INC
1200 Flint Hill Rd (27018-8502)
P.O. Box 455 (27023-0455)
PHONE..................................336 699-4204
EMP: 12 EST: 2005
SALES (est): 442.51K Privately Held
Web: www.reynolda.com
SIC: 3599 Machine shop, jobbing and repair

(G-5468)
REYNOLDA MFG SOLUTIONS INC
1200 Flint Hill Rd (27018-8502)
P.O. Box 455 (27023-0455)
PHONE..................................336 699-4204
Scott Riddles, CEO
Richard Sechrist, *
EMP: 30 EST: 1994
SALES (est): 4.4MM Privately Held
Web: www.reynolda.com
SIC: 3599 Machine shop, jobbing and repair

(G-5469)
TERRYS TIRES & SERVICES LLC
7849 Nc 67 Hwy (27018-8053)
PHONE..................................336 251-7366
EMP: 4 EST: 2016
SALES (est): 148.53K Privately Held
SIC: 7534 Tire repair shop

(G-5470)
TWIN CARPORTS LLC
1014 Melrose Ct (27018-7279)
PHONE..................................336 790-8284
EMP: 17
SALES (corp-wide): 1.12MM Privately Held
Web: www.twincarports.com
SIC: 3448 Prefabricated metal buildings and components
PA: Twin Carports Llc
   202 Hamlin Dr
   Pilot Mountain NC 27041
   866 486-3924

(G-5471)
VERSATILE MACHINE FAB
2107 Iron Ridge Dr (27018-7474)
PHONE..................................336 699-8271
EMP: 4 EST: 2020
SALES (est): 119.31K Privately Held
SIC: 3441 Fabricated structural metal

East Flat Rock
Henderson County

(G-5472)
AGILE VENTURES LLC
Also Called: Cosaint Arms
2107 Spartanburg Hwy (28726-2134)
PHONE..................................202 716-7958
EMP: 6 EST: 2018
SALES (est): 393.97K Privately Held
Web: www.cosaintarms.com
SIC: 3489 Guns or gun parts, over 30 mm.

(G-5473)
DEMMEL INC
100 Old World Cir (28726-0277)
PHONE..................................828 585-6600
Cornel Broenner, Ex Dir
Cornel Broenner, Genl Mgr
Simone Diett, *
◆ EMP: 95 EST: 2016
SQ FT: 12,000
SALES (est): 10.36MM
SALES (corp-wide): 127.87MM Privately Held
Web: www.demmel-group.com
SIC: 3711 Automobile assembly, including specialty automobiles
PA: Demmel Ag
   Gruntenweg 14
   Scheidegg BY 88175
   838191900

(G-5474)
ELKAMET INC
201 Mills St (28726-2116)
P.O. Box 265 (28726-0265)
PHONE..................................828 233-4001
Eberhard Flammer, Pr
Michael Parsch, *
Carsten Erkel, *
Brent Coston, *
◆ EMP: 165 EST: 2006
SQ FT: 145,000
SALES (est): 31.14MM
SALES (corp-wide): 123.5MM Privately Held
Web: www.elkamet.com
SIC: 3089 Injection molding of plastics
PA: Elkamet Kunststofftechnik Gmbh
   Georg-Kramer-Str. 3
   Biedenkopf HE
   64619300

(G-5475)
GB INDUSTRIES
3005 Spartanburg Hwy (28726-2925)
PHONE..................................828 692-9163
Julia Staton, Pr
Alan Staton, VP
Mark Staton, Sec
EMP: 8 EST: 1995
SQ FT: 5,000
SALES (est): 682.03K Privately Held
SIC: 3441 Fabricated structural metal

(G-5476)
GREENLEAF CORPORATION
Technical Ceramics Div
761 Roper Rd (28726)
P.O. Box 756 (28726-0756)
PHONE..................................828 693-0461
Chuck Dziedzic, Mgr
EMP: 24
SALES (corp-wide): 63.67MM Privately Held
Web: www.greenleafcorporation.com
SIC: 3545 3264 Cutting tools for machine tools; Porcelain electrical supplies
PA: Greenleaf Corporation
   18695 Greenleaf Dr
   Saegertown PA 16433
   814 763-2915

(G-5477)
MINUTE-MAN PRODUCTS INC
305 W King St (28726-2318)
PHONE..................................828 692-0256
Martha G Moreno, Pr
Thomas W Hackney, *
Pat Hudpheth, Stockholder*
EMP: 35 EST: 1965
SQ FT: 45,000
SALES (est): 4.92MM Privately Held
Web: www.minutemanproducts.com
SIC: 3462 Anchors, forged

(G-5478)
MMA MANUFACTURING INC
Also Called: Minute Man Anchors
305 W King St (28726-2318)
PHONE..................................828 692-0256
Mark Vollan, Pr
William Hackney, *
EMP: 35 EST: 2019
SALES (est): 2.5MM Privately Held
Web: www.minutemanproducts.com
SIC: 3499 Fire- or burglary-resistive products

(G-5479)
VOCATNAL SLTONS HNDRSON CNTY I
Also Called: VOCATIONAL SOLUTONS
2110 Spartanburg Hwy (28726-2135)
PHONE..................................828 692-9626
Mike Horton, Ex Dir
EMP: 36 EST: 1967
SQ FT: 45,000
SALES (est): 1.56MM Privately Held
Web: www.vocsol.com
SIC: 8331 2396 2395 Vocational rehabilitation agency; Automotive and apparel trimmings; Pleating and stitching

(G-5480)
WRKCO INC
200 Tabor Rd (28726-2832)
PHONE..................................828 692-6254
EMP: 6
SALES (corp-wide): 20.31B Publicly Held
SIC: 2631 Paperboard mills
HQ: Wrkco Inc.
   1000 Abernathy Rd Ste 12
   Atlanta GA 30328
   770 448-2193

Eastover
Cumberland County

(G-5481)
J & L BCKH/NVRNMENTAL SVCS INC
3043 Tom Geddie Rd (28312-8143)
PHONE.................................910 237-7351
Debra M Davis, *Pr*
Loyde L Davis, *VP*
Maxine J Mclaurin, *Vice Chairman*
Jack G Mclaurin, *Stockholder*
EMP: 9 **EST:** 1999
SQ FT: 900
SALES (est): 221.27K **Privately Held**
SIC: 1794 3443 1795 4213 Excavation work; Dumpsters, garbage; Demolition, buildings and other structures; Contract haulers

(G-5482)
ROBERT WRREN MBL TV PRDUCTIONS
2121 Middle Rd (28312-9753)
PHONE.................................910 483-4777
Robert Warren, *Owner*
EMP: 8 **EST:** 1975
SALES (est): 381.04K **Privately Held**
SIC: 4833 7922 7819 6512 Television broadcasting stations; Television program, including commercial producers; Video tape or disk reproduction; Nonresidential building operators

(G-5483)
TYSON FOODS INC
Also Called: Tyson
3281 Baywood Rd (28312-9033)
PHONE.................................910 483-3282
Mitchell Sessoms, *Mgr*
EMP: 13
SQ FT: 7,000
SALES (corp-wide): 52.88B **Publicly Held**
Web: www.tysonfoods.com
SIC: 2015 Poultry slaughtering and processing
PA: Tyson Foods, Inc.
2200 W Don Tyson Pkwy
Springdale AR 72762
479 290-4000

Eden
Rockingham County

(G-5484)
A C FURNITURE COMPANY INC
724 Riverside Dr (27288-2634)
P.O. Box 40013 (24022-0013)
PHONE.................................336 623-3430
Lee Manick, *Brnch Mgr*
EMP: 325
SALES (corp-wide): 26.83MM **Privately Held**
Web: www.acfurniture.com
SIC: 2426 2531 2522 2521 Furniture stock and parts, hardwood; Public building and related furniture; Office furniture, except wood; Wood office furniture
PA: A. C. Furniture Company, Inc.
3872 Martin Dr
Axton VA 24054
276 650-3356

(G-5485)
ALADDIN MANUFACTURING CORP
712 Henry St (27288-6122)
P.O. Box 130 (27289-0130)
PHONE.................................336 623-6000
Phil C Raiford, *Brnch Mgr*
EMP: 1378
Web: www.mohawkind.com
SIC: 2273 Carpets: twisted paper, grass, reed, coir, sisal, jute, etc.
HQ: Aladdin Manufacturing Corporation
160 S Industrial Blvd
Calhoun GA 30701
706 629-7721

(G-5486)
ALLTECH INC
11761 Hwy 770 E (27288)
PHONE.................................336 635-5190
Jp Woodrum, *Brnch Mgr*
EMP: 20
SALES (corp-wide): 1.49B **Privately Held**
Web: www.alltech.com
SIC: 2869 Enzymes
PA: Alltech, Inc.
3031 Catnip Hill Rd
Nicholasville KY 40356
859 885-9613

(G-5487)
CAROLINA SHEDS LLC
131 N Van Buren Rd (27288-3333)
PHONE.................................336 623-7433
EMP: 5 **EST:** 2015
SALES (est): 114.3K **Privately Held**
SIC: 2431 Millwork

(G-5488)
CHANDLER CONCRETE INC
Also Called: CHANDLER CONCRETE INC
6354 Main St (27288)
PHONE.................................336 342-5771
Danny Manroind, *Dist Mgr*
EMP: 9
Web: www.chandlerconcrete.com
SIC: 3273 Ready-mixed concrete
PA: Chandler Concrete Co., Inc.
1006 S Church St
Burlington NC 27215

(G-5489)
CLASSIC CARBURETOR REBUILDERS
1909 Stovall St (27288-4337)
PHONE.................................336 613-5715
Tim Lancaster, *Prin*
EMP: 5 **EST:** 2016
SALES (est): 71.09K **Privately Held**
SIC: 3592 Carburetors

(G-5490)
FULLER DYNASTY BRAND LLC
719 Westwood Dr (27288-6431)
PHONE.................................336 847-3875
Christain Fuller, *Managing Member*
EMP: 4 **EST:** 2021
SALES (est): 95.58K **Privately Held**
SIC: 3537 Trucks, tractors, loaders, carriers, and similar equipment

(G-5491)
GILDAN ACTIVEWEAR (EDEN) INC
602 E Meadow Rd (27288-3426)
P.O. Box 1247 (27289-1247)
PHONE.................................336 623-9555
Glenn Chamandry, *Pr*
Laurence G Sellyn, *
◆ **EMP:** 160 **EST:** 1985
SQ FT: 400,000
SALES (est): 35.54MM
SALES (corp-wide): 3.24B **Privately Held**
Web: jobs.gildancorp.com
SIC: 5136 5311 2258 Men's and boy's clothing; Department stores; Lace and warp knit fabric mills
PA: Les Vetements De Sport Gildan Inc
600 Boul De Maisonneuve O 33eme Etage
Montreal QC H3A 3
514 735-2023

(G-5492)
INNOFA USA LLC
716 Commerce Dr (27288-3681)
PHONE.................................336 635-2900
Roger Droge, *Managing Member*
◆ **EMP:** 34 **EST:** 2003
SQ FT: 84,000
SALES (est): 9.23MM **Privately Held**
Web: www.innofa.com
SIC: 2257 2824 Pile fabrics, circular knit; Organic fibers, noncellulosic
HQ: Innofa Beheer B.V.
Minosstraat 20
Tilburg NB 5048
134634205

(G-5493)
KARASTAN
335 Summit Rd (27288-2829)
PHONE.................................336 627-7200
Richard Scales, *Pr*
EMP: 8 **EST:** 2013
SALES (est): 91.99K **Privately Held**
Web: www.karastan.com
SIC: 2273 Finishers of tufted carpets and rugs

(G-5494)
KDH DEFENSE SYSTEMS INC
Also Called: Kdh Defense Systems
750a W Fieldcrest Rd (27288-3631)
PHONE.................................336 635-4158
David E Herbener, *CEO*
EMP: 140 **EST:** 2003
SQ FT: 250,000
SALES (est): 36.55MM
SALES (corp-wide): 8.99MM **Privately Held**
Web: www.armorexpress.com
SIC: 3812 Defense systems and equipment
PA: Praesidium Spa
Via Della Giustizia 10/A
Milano MI 20125
023030971

(G-5495)
KINGS CHANDELIER COMPANY
1023 Friendly Rd (27288-2805)
P.O. Box 667 (27289-0667)
PHONE.................................336 623-6188
Nancy Daniel, *Pr*
Tim Lillard, *VP*
EMP: 7 **EST:** 1934
SALES (est): 985.63K **Privately Held**
Web: www.chandelier.com
SIC: 3645 3646 Chandeliers, residential; Chandeliers, commercial

(G-5496)
LOPAREX LLC
816 W Fieldcrest Rd (27288-3633)
PHONE.................................336 635-0192
Chip Sheeran, *Brnch Mgr*
EMP: 160
Web: www.loparex.com
SIC: 2672 5199 Adhesive backed films, foams and foils; Packaging materials
HQ: Loparex Llc
1255 Crescent Green # 400
Cary NC 27518
919 678-7700

(G-5497)
MARLEY-WYLAIN COMPANY
Weil-Mclain Assembly Facility
523 S New St (27288-3623)
PHONE.................................336 627-6000
Ed Lodics, *Brnch Mgr*
EMP: 224
SALES (corp-wide): 1.74B **Publicly Held**
Web: www.weil-mclain.com
SIC: 3433 Boilers, low-pressure heating: steam or hot water
HQ: The Marley-Wylain Company
500 Blaine St
Michigan City IN 46360
630 560-3703

(G-5498)
NESTLE PURINA PETCARE COMPANY
863 E Meadow Rd (27288-3636)
PHONE.................................314 982-1000
EMP: 30
SIC: 2047 Dog and cat food
HQ: Nestle Purina Petcare Company
800 Chouteau Ave
Saint Louis MO 63102
314 982-1000

(G-5499)
PIEDMONT SURFACES OF TRIAD LLC
615 Monroe St (27288-6110)
PHONE.................................336 627-7790
EMP: 20 **EST:** 2011
SALES (est): 1.02MM **Privately Held**
Web: www.piedmonttriadflemingrealtors.com
SIC: 3272 Slabs, crossing: concrete

(G-5500)
PRINT & PACK SENSE LLC
708 Meadowgreen Village Dr Apt 2a (27288-3672)
PHONE.................................336 394-6930
EMP: 4 **EST:** 2013
SALES (est): 65.09K **Privately Held**
SIC: 2752 Commercial printing, lithographic

(G-5501)
RONNIE BOYDS LOGGING LLC
153 Nance St (27288-3084)
PHONE.................................336 613-0229
Ronnie Boyd, *Prin*
EMP: 6 **EST:** 2010
SALES (est): 478.88K **Privately Held**
SIC: 2411 Logging camps and contractors

(G-5502)
SGRTEX LLC
335 Summit Rd (27288-2829)
PHONE.................................336 635-9420
Ramkumar Varadarajan, *Managing Member*
EMP: 84 **EST:** 2013
SQ FT: 180,000
SALES (est): 12.05MM **Privately Held**
SIC: 2281 Yarn spinning mills
PA: Shri Govindaraja Mills Private Limited
258, Thiruchuli Road
Aruppukottai TN 62610

(G-5503)
SPX CORPORATION
Also Called: SPX CORPORATION
523 S New St (27288-3623)
PHONE.................................336 627-6020
Dennis Chase, *Mgr*
EMP: 12
SALES (corp-wide): 1.74B **Publicly Held**
Web: www.spx.com
SIC: 3443 Cooling towers, metal plate
HQ: Canvas Sx, Llc
6325 Ardrey Kell Rd Ste 4
Charlotte NC 28277
980 474-3700

Edenton
Chowan County

(G-5504)
A&W WELDING INC
1106 Haughton Rd 37 (27932-9462)
PHONE.................252 482-3233
Wade Nixon, *Pr*
EMP: 6 **EST:** 1988
SALES (est): 277.98K **Privately Held**
SIC: 7692 Welding repair

(G-5505)
ALB BOATS
140 Midway Dr (27932-8908)
PHONE.................252 482-7600
J Scott Harrell Junior, *Prin*
J Scott Harrell Junior, *Prin*
Burch Perry, *
Carol Ricketts, *
▼ **EMP:** 200 **EST:** 1978
SQ FT: 100,000
SALES (est): 9.61MM **Privately Held**
Web: www.albemarleboats.com
SIC: 3732 Boats, fiberglass: building and repairing

(G-5506)
ALBEMARLE CORPORATION
140 Midway Dr (27932-8908)
PHONE.................252 482-7423
Carroll Bundy, *COO*
EMP: 7
Web: www.albemarle.com
SIC: 2821 Plastics materials and resins
PA: Albemarle Corporation
4250 Congress St Ste 900
Charlotte NC 28209

(G-5507)
ASHLEY WELDING & MACHINE CO
104 Tower Dr (27932-9762)
P.O. Box 383 (27932-0383)
PHONE.................252 482-3321
Mitchell Byrd, *Pr*
Mysi Fortenbery, *Off Mgr*
Steven Byrd, *VP*
EMP: 10 **EST:** 1947
SQ FT: 24,000
SALES (est): 1.16MM **Privately Held**
Web: www.ashleywelding.com
SIC: 3441 Fabricated structural metal

(G-5508)
BATEMAN LOGGING CO INC
1531 Virginia Rd (27932-9533)
PHONE.................252 482-8959
Cecil Ray Bateman, *Pr*
Teresa Bateman, *
EMP: 14 **EST:** 1978
SALES (est): 945.41K **Privately Held**
SIC: 2411 Logging camps and contractors

(G-5509)
CC BOATS INC
140 Midway Dr (27932-8908)
P.O. Box 968 (27932-0968)
PHONE.................252 482-3699
Mac Privott, *Pr*
Joan R Privott, *Sec*
▼ **EMP:** 15 **EST:** 1992
SQ FT: 27,000
SALES (est): 300.15K **Privately Held**
Web: www.carolinaclassicboats.com
SIC: 3732 Motorboats, inboard or outboard: building and repairing

(G-5510)
COX NRTH CRLINA PBLCATIONS INC
Also Called: Chowan Herald
421 S Broad St (27932-1935)
P.O. Box 207 (27932-0207)
PHONE.................252 482-4418
Robert S Piazza Iii, *Prin*
EMP: 9
SALES (corp-wide): 2.85B **Privately Held**
Web: www.reflector.com
SIC: 2711 Newspapers, publishing and printing
HQ: Cox North Carolina Publications, Inc.
1150 Sugg Pkwy
Greenville NC 27834
252 329-9643

(G-5511)
CUSTOM MARINE CANVAS
121 Montpelier Dr (27932-8909)
PHONE.................252 482-0675
Donald Gillis, *Owner*
EMP: 5 **EST:** 2017
SALES (est): 46.58K **Privately Held**
SIC: 2211 Canvas

(G-5512)
DAEDALUS COMPOSITES LLC
Also Called: Daedalus Yachts
109 Anchors Way Dr (27932-9746)
P.O. Box 428 (27932-0428)
PHONE.................252 368-9000
Michael Reardon, *Managing Member*
◆ **EMP:** 15 **EST:** 2016
SALES (est): 1.59MM **Privately Held**
Web: www.daedalusyachts.com
SIC: 3732 Yachts, building and repairing

(G-5513)
DWELLING NC INC
103 Brickells Glade (27932-9623)
PHONE.................252 619-0226
Donald E Herr, *Prin*
EMP: 7 **EST:** 2006
SALES (est): 97.13K **Privately Held**
SIC: 2431 Moldings, wood: unfinished and prefinished

(G-5514)
EDENTON BOATWORKS LLC
Also Called: Albemarle Boats
140 Midway Dr (27932-8908)
PHONE.................252 482-7600
Burch Perry, *Genl Mgr*
EMP: 30 **EST:** 2015
SALES (est): 4.24MM **Privately Held**
Web: www.albemarleboats.com
SIC: 3731 Barges, building and repairing

(G-5515)
HERMES MARINE LLC (PA)
109 Anchors Way Dr (27932-9746)
PHONE.................252 368-9000
EMP: 29 **EST:** 2021
SALES (est): 4.13MM
SALES (corp-wide): 4.13MM **Privately Held**
SIC: 3732 Boat kits, not models

(G-5516)
HOLLAND SIGN PLUS ENGRV SLTONS
1123 Macedonia Rd (27932-9591)
PHONE.................252 339-5389
Troy Holland, *Prin*
EMP: 4 **EST:** 2018
SALES (est): 66.01K **Privately Held**
SIC: 3993 Signs and advertising specialties

(G-5517)
INNOVTIVE MSRMENT SLUTIONS INC
1201 Arrowhead Trl (27932-9130)
PHONE.................757 560-0820
Phil Bartley, *CEO*
EMP: 6 **EST:** 1984
SALES (est): 70K **Privately Held**
SIC: 7372 Business oriented computer software

(G-5518)
LAYTONS CUSTOM BOATWORKS LLC
103 Anchors Way Dr (27932-9746)
P.O. Box 147 (27932-0147)
PHONE.................252 482-1504
Carlton Layton, *Managing Member*
Doug Layton, *Managing Member*
EMP: 9 **EST:** 1998
SALES (est): 992.45K **Privately Held**
Web: www.laytonscustomboatworks.com
SIC: 3732 Boatbuilding and repairing

(G-5519)
MORVEN PARTNERS LP
Also Called: Original Nuthouse Brand
185 Peanut Dr (27932-9604)
P.O. Box 465 (27932-0465)
PHONE.................252 482-2193
Paul Britton, *Mgr*
EMP: 28
SIC: 2099 Peanut butter
PA: Morven Partners, L.P.
11 Leigh Fisher Blvd
El Paso TX 79906

(G-5520)
NOBLE BROS CABINETS MLLWK LLC (PA)
107 Marine Dr (27932-9748)
PHONE.................252 482-9100
Scott Noble, *Managing Member*
EMP: 8 **EST:** 1985
SQ FT: 8,000
SALES (est): 2.05MM
SALES (corp-wide): 2.05MM **Privately Held**
Web: www.noblebroscabinets.com
SIC: 1521 2434 General remodeling, single-family houses; Wood kitchen cabinets

(G-5521)
REGULATOR MARINE INC
187 Peanut Dr (27932-9604)
P.O. Box 49 (27932-0049)
PHONE.................252 482-3837
▼ **EMP:** 65 **EST:** 1988
SALES (est): 15.94MM **Privately Held**
Web: www.regulatormarine.com
SIC: 3732 Fishing boats: lobster, crab, oyster, etc.: small

(G-5522)
UNIVERSAL BLANCHERS LLC
Also Called: Seabrook Ingredients
115 Peanut Dr (27932-9604)
P.O. Box 609 (27932-0609)
PHONE.................252 482-2112
Larry Hughs, *Mgr*
EMP: 75
SALES (corp-wide): 592.45MM **Privately Held**
SIC: 2099 2068 Peanut butter; Salted and roasted nuts and seeds
HQ: Universal Blanchers, L.L.C.
2077 Cnvntion Ctr Cncrse
Atlanta GA 30337
404 209-2600

(G-5523)
W E NIXONS WLDG & HDWR INC
3036 Rocky Hock Rd (27932-9556)
PHONE.................252 221-4348
William Thomas Nixon, *Pr*
Terry Nixon Britton, *Credit Officer*
Robin P Nixon, *Sec*
EMP: 7 **EST:** 1952
SQ FT: 30,000
SALES (est): 986.4K **Privately Held**
SIC: 7692 5251 5999 5661 Welding repair; Hardware stores; Farm equipment and supplies; Women's shoes

Efland
Orange County

(G-5524)
CHAPMAN WELDING LLC
Also Called: Cw Landscapes
4501 Gails Trl (27243-9237)
PHONE.................919 951-8131
EMP: 7 **EST:** 2019
SALES (est): 178.4K **Privately Held**
SIC: 7692 Welding repair

(G-5525)
CHEEKY LATHER LLC
4117 High Rock Rd (27243-9455)
PHONE.................919 672-8071
Julie C Perez, *Admn*
EMP: 5 **EST:** 2014
SALES (est): 73.05K **Privately Held**
SIC: 2844 Perfumes, cosmetics and other toilet preparations

(G-5526)
CONVEYOR TECHNOLOGIES INC
1218 Blacksmith Rd (27243-9760)
PHONE.................919 732-8291
Bryan M Wood, *Pr*
EMP: 6 **EST:** 1994
SALES (est): 486.02K **Privately Held**
Web: www.conveyor-technologies.com
SIC: 3535 Belt conveyor systems, general industrial use

(G-5527)
ERVIN WOODWORKS LLC
407 Chadwick Ln (27243-9562)
PHONE.................919 451-0652
EMP: 4 **EST:** 2019
SALES (est): 54.13K **Privately Held**
Web: www.ervinwoodworks.com
SIC: 2431 Millwork

(G-5528)
USA DUTCH INC (PA)
3604 Southern Dr (27243-9704)
P.O. Box 1299 (27253-1299)
PHONE.................919 732-6956
Ronald Keizer, *Pr*
EMP: 25 **EST:** 1989
SQ FT: 13,500
SALES (est): 12.93MM **Privately Held**
Web: www.usadutchinc.com
SIC: 3444 Sheet metal specialties, not stamped

Elizabeth City
Pasquotank County

(G-5529)
4D DIRECTIONAL BORING LLC
204 Ibis Way (27909-8739)
PHONE.................614 348-1339
Brian E Dalton, *Admn*

Elizabeth City - Pasquotank County (G-5530)

EMP: 6 EST: 2014
SALES (est): 425.84K **Privately Held**
SIC: 1381 Directional drilling oil and gas wells

(G-5530)
ACUCAL INC
108 Enterprise Dr (27909-6340)
PHONE..................252 337-9975
Thomas N Efaw, *Brnch Mgr*
EMP: 9
SALES (corp-wide): 2.25B **Privately Held**
Web: www.trescal.com
SIC: 3823 Industrial process control instruments
HQ: Acucal, Inc.
 11090 Industrial Rd
 Manassas VA 20109
 703 369-3090

(G-5531)
ALBEMRLE ORTHOTICS PROSTHETICS
Also Called: East Crlina Orthtics Prsthtics
106 Medical Dr (27909-3361)
P.O. Box 1471 (27906-1471)
PHONE..................252 338-3002
EMP: 33 EST: 1994
SALES (est): 2.39MM **Privately Held**
Web: www.albemarleop.com
SIC: 3842 5047 Limbs, artificial; Medical and hospital equipment

(G-5532)
C A PERRY & SON INC
683 Dry Ridge Rd (27909-7173)
PHONE..................252 330-2323
Daniel Birch, *Brnch Mgr*
EMP: 6
SALES (corp-wide): 14.75B **Publicly Held**
Web: www.caperryandson.com
SIC: 5159 5191 4221 5153 Peanuts (bulk), unroasted; Farm supplies; Farm product warehousing and storage; Grains
HQ: C. A. Perry & Son, Inc.
 4033 Virginia Rd
 Hobbsville NC 27946
 252 221-4463

(G-5533)
CERAMAWIRE
786 Pitts Chapel Rd (27909-7864)
PHONE..................252 335-7411
Edward Hamilton, *Owner*
EMP: 4 EST: 2001
SALES (est): 311.21K **Privately Held**
Web: www.ceramawire.com
SIC: 3496 Woven wire products, nec

(G-5534)
COASTAL OFFICE EQP & COMPUTERS
Also Called: Adica Enterprises
501 E Church St Ste A (27909-4879)
P.O. Box 321 (27907-0321)
PHONE..................252 335-9427
Jeff Meads, *Owner*
EMP: 5 EST: 1989
SQ FT: 2,500
SALES (est): 56.23K **Privately Held**
Web: coastalofficeequipment.web-guardian.technology
SIC: 7378 3577 5734 Computer maintenance and repair; Computer peripheral equipment, nec; Computer and software stores

(G-5535)
COCA-COLA CONSOLIDATED INC
Also Called: Coca-Cola
1210 George Wood Dr (27909-9600)
PHONE..................252 334-1820
Ron Verstat, *Mgr*
EMP: 59
SALES (corp-wide): 6.65B **Publicly Held**
Web: www.coca-cola.com
SIC: 2086 5149 Bottled and canned soft drinks; Groceries and related products, nec
PA: Coca-Cola Consolidated, Inc.
 4100 Coca Cola Plz # 100
 Charlotte NC 28211
 704 557-4400

(G-5536)
COMMERCIAL READY MIX PDTS INC
168 Knobbs Creek Dr (27909-7001)
PHONE..................252 335-9740
Steve Duncan, *Mgr*
EMP: 12
SALES (corp-wide): 52.99MM **Privately Held**
Web: www.crmpinc.com
SIC: 3273 Ready-mixed concrete
PA: Commercial Ready Mix Products, Inc.
 115 Hwy 158 W
 Winton NC 27986
 252 358-5461

(G-5537)
COURTESY FORD INC
Also Called: Courtesy Ford Lincoln-Mercury
1310 N Road St (27909-3338)
PHONE..................252 338-4783
Frank Bernard, *Pr*
EMP: 44 EST: 1984
SQ FT: 25,000
SALES (est): 2.08MM **Privately Held**
Web: www.lincoln.com
SIC: 5511 7538 7515 5531 Automobiles, new and used; General automotive repair shops; Passenger car leasing; Auto and home supply stores

(G-5538)
COX NRTH CRLINA PBLCATIONS INC
Daily Advance Newspaper
215 S Water St (27909-4844)
P.O. Box 588 (27907-0588)
PHONE..................252 335-0841
Tim Hobbs, *Publisher*
EMP: 110
SALES (corp-wide): 2.85B **Privately Held**
Web: www.dailyadvance.com
SIC: 2711 Newspapers, publishing and printing
HQ: Cox North Carolina Publications, Inc.
 1150 Sugg Pkwy
 Greenville NC 27834
 252 329-9643

(G-5539)
D & D INDUSTRIES
Also Called: Black Ops
2299 Delia Dr (27909-7727)
PHONE..................252 331-2528
Debra Edwards, *Owner*
EMP: 4 EST: 1998
SALES (est): 74.46K **Privately Held**
SIC: 3999 Military insignia

(G-5540)
DARLA WARD
1096 Commissary Rd (27909-7308)
PHONE..................252 340-1895
Darla Ward, *Prin*
EMP: 4 EST: 2018
SALES (est): 83.91K **Privately Held**

SIC: 2752 Commercial printing, lithographic

(G-5541)
DOUGLAS TEMPLE & SON INC
1273 Lynchs Corner Rd (27909-7515)
PHONE..................252 771-5676
Doug Temple, *Pr*
Linda Temple, *Sec*
EMP: 11 EST: 2001
SALES (est): 408.94K **Privately Held**
SIC: 2411 Logging

(G-5542)
EGADS PRINTING CO
1403 N Road St (27909-3241)
PHONE..................252 335-1554
EMP: 6 EST: 2019
SALES (est): 239.98K **Privately Held**
Web: www.egadsobx.com
SIC: 2759 Screen printing

(G-5543)
ELECTRIC MOTOR REWINDING INC
407 N Poindexter St (27909-4039)
PHONE..................252 338-8856
Robert D Lunsford, *Pr*
EMP: 6 EST: 1956
SQ FT: 5,000
SALES (est): 529K **Privately Held**
SIC: 7694 Electric motor repair

(G-5544)
EVENT EXTRAVAGANZA LLC
407 S Griffin St Ste E (27909-4693)
PHONE..................252 679-7004
De'mondrae Harris, *Managing Member*
EMP: 15 EST: 2021
SALES (est): 190K **Privately Held**
Web: www.eventextravaganza.org
SIC: 2051 Bread, cake, and related products

(G-5545)
F & H PRINT SIGN DESIGN LLC
1725 City Center Blvd Ste C (27909-8962)
PHONE..................252 335-0181
EMP: 5 EST: 2017
SQ FT: 5,000
SALES (est): 393.32K **Privately Held**
Web: www.fhprintsign.com
SIC: 2396 Fabric printing and stamping

(G-5546)
GALLISHAW ELITE RIGGING LLC
1409 Lambs Grove Rd (27909-7503)
PHONE..................757 240-8963
Kirro Gallishaw, *CEO*
EMP: 4 EST: 2019
SALES (est): 82K **Privately Held**
SIC: 3731 Shipbuilding and repairing

(G-5547)
HERTFORD PRINTING SIGNS
2713 Peartree Rd (27909-7119)
PHONE..................252 426-5505
EMP: 4 EST: 2019
SALES (est): 57.06K **Privately Held**
Web: www.hertfordprintingandsigns.com
SIC: 3993 Signs and advertising specialties

(G-5548)
HOCKMEYER EQUIPMENT CORP
Also Called: HOCKMEYER EQUIPMENT CORP.
6 Kitty Hawk Ln (27909-6726)
PHONE..................252 338-4705
Rick Vandesande, *Mgr*
EMP: 54
SQ FT: 37,500
SALES (corp-wide): 22.82MM **Privately Held**

Web: www.hockmeyer.com
SIC: 3559 3531 3443 3582 Anodizing equipment; Construction machinery; Fabricated plate work (boiler shop); Commercial laundry equipment
PA: Hockmeyer Equipment Corp
 610 Supor Blvd
 Harrison NJ 07029
 973 482-0225

(G-5549)
HOFFER CALIBRATION SVCS LLC
1100 W Ehringhaus St Ste C (27909-6943)
P.O. Box 583 (27907-0583)
PHONE..................252 338-6379
Nixon R William, *Prin*
EMP: 5 EST: 2016
SALES (est): 206.26K **Privately Held**
Web: www.hofferflow.com
SIC: 3823 Process control instruments

(G-5550)
HOFFER FLOW CONTROLS INC
107 Kitty Hawk Ln (27909-6756)
P.O. Box 2145 (27906-2145)
PHONE..................252 331-1997
Kenneth Hoffer, *CEO*
Bob Carrell, *
Sandee Kelly, *
▼ EMP: 80 EST: 1969
SQ FT: 32,000
SALES (est): 18.37MM **Privately Held**
Web: www.hofferflow.com
SIC: 3823 Flow instruments, industrial process type

(G-5551)
J W JONES LUMBER COMPANY INC (PA)
1443 Northside Rd (27909-8531)
PHONE..................252 771-2497
▼ EMP: 90 EST: 1939
SALES (est): 16.78MM
SALES (corp-wide): 16.78MM **Privately Held**
Web: www.jwjoneslumber.com
SIC: 2421 Lumber: rough, sawed, or planed

(G-5552)
KAYLA JONISE BERNHARDT CRUTCH
115 Carver St (27909-5833)
PHONE..................252 457-5367
K Jonise Bernhardt Crutch, *Owner*
EMP: 4 EST: 2020
SALES (est): 144.09K **Privately Held**
SIC: 2339 Women's and misses' athletic clothing and sportswear

(G-5553)
KWIK ELC MTR SLS & SVC INC (PA)
511 Witherspoon St (27909-5265)
P.O. Box 1602 (27906-1602)
PHONE..................252 335-2524
John T Cox, *Pr*
John Cox, *Pr*
Aubrey Snowden, *VP*
Elizabeth Snowden, *Sec*
EMP: 5 EST: 1973
SQ FT: 5,000
SALES (est): 681.98K
SALES (corp-wide): 681.98K **Privately Held**
SIC: 5999 3677 7694 Motors, electric; Coil windings, electronic; Rewinding services

(G-5554)
LEGACY VULCAN LLC
Also Called: Elizabeth City Yard
174 Knobbs Creek Dr (27909-7001)

PHONE.....................252 338-2201
Rene Salamone, *Mgr*
EMP: 4
Web: www.vulcanmaterials.com
SIC: 3273 Ready-mixed concrete
HQ: Legacy Vulcan, Llc
1200 Urban Center Dr
Vestavia AL 35242
205 298-3000

(G-5555)
MABLE MULLEN
111 Bayberry Dr (27909-3396)
PHONE.....................252 599-1181
Mable Brothers Mullen, *Owner*
EMP: 4 **EST:** 2020
SALES (est): 99.81K **Privately Held**
SIC: 2731 Books, publishing and printing

(G-5556)
MARVIN BAILEY SCREEN PRINTING
Also Called: E Gads Screen Printing & EMB
1403 N Road St (27909-3241)
PHONE.....................252 335-1554
Marvin Bailey, *Owner*
EMP: 5 **EST:** 1982
SQ FT: 3,600
SALES (est): 298.44K **Privately Held**
Web: www.egadsobx.com
SIC: 2261 2396 Finishing plants, cotton; Automotive and apparel trimmings

(G-5557)
MOTION SENSORS INC
786 Pitts Chapel Rd (27909-7864)
PHONE.....................252 335-7294
Arthur Bergman, *CEO*
Marcy Bergman, *
Patti Bergman, *
EMP: 35 **EST:** 1970
SQ FT: 6,200
SALES (est): 5.45MM **Privately Held**
Web: www.motionsensors.com
SIC: 3823 Process control instruments

(G-5558)
MOTOR VHCLES LCENSE PLATE AGCY
1545 N Road St Ste E (27909-4268)
PHONE.....................252 338-6965
Lynn Cartwright, *Pr*
EMP: 5 **EST:** 1994
SALES (est): 181.99K **Privately Held**
SIC: 2796 6411 Platemaking services; Insurance agents, brokers, and service

(G-5559)
NOBLE BROS CABINETS MLLWK LLC
505 E Church St Apt 2 (27909-4868)
PHONE.....................252 335-1213
EMP: 8
SALES (corp-wide): 2.05MM **Privately Held**
Web: www.noblebroscabinets.com
SIC: 1521 2434 General remodeling, single-family houses; Wood kitchen cabinets
PA: Noble Brothers Cabinets & Millwork, Llc
107 Marine Dr
Edenton NC 27932
252 482-9100

(G-5560)
NORTHEASTERN READY MIX
183 Knobbs Creek Dr (27909-7002)
P.O. Box 1731 (27906-1731)
PHONE.....................252 335-1931
James G Gaskins Junior, *Pr*
EMP: 7 **EST:** 1977
SALES (est): 898.34K **Privately Held**

Web: www.crmpinc.com
SIC: 3273 3272 Ready-mixed concrete; Septic tanks, concrete

(G-5561)
PEPSI BOTTLING VENTURES LLC
109 Corporate Dr (27909-7028)
PHONE.....................252 335-4355
EMP: 40
Web: www.pepsico.com
SIC: 2086 Bottled and canned soft drinks
HQ: Pepsi Bottling Ventures Llc
4141 Parklake Ave Ste 600
Raleigh NC 27612
919 680-2300

(G-5562)
PERDUE FARMS INC
Also Called: PERDUE FARMS INC.
1268 Us Highway 17 S (27909-7631)
PHONE.....................252 338-1543
EMP: 24
SALES (corp-wide): 1.24B **Privately Held**
Web: www.perdue.com
SIC: 2015 Poultry slaughtering and processing
PA: Perdue Farms Incorporated
31149 Old Ocean City Rd
Salisbury MD 21804
800 473-7383

(G-5563)
PITT ROAD LLC
Also Called: Pitt Road Ex Lube & Car Wash
711 N Hughes Blvd (27909-3532)
PHONE.....................252 331-5818
Jeanna Albertson, *Prin*
EMP: 5 **EST:** 1998
SALES (est): 492.13K **Privately Held**
SIC: 2911 Road oils

(G-5564)
PRECISION PRINTING
307 S Road St (27909-4759)
PHONE.....................252 338-2450
Jesse Carden, *Owner*
EMP: 4 **EST:** 1981
SQ FT: 5,000
SALES (est): 225.55K **Privately Held**
Web: www.precisionprint.com
SIC: 2752 Offset printing

(G-5565)
QUALITY FOODS FROM SEA INC
Also Called: Sea Food Express
173 Knobbs Creek Dr (27909-7002)
P.O. Box 1837 (27906-1837)
PHONE.....................252 338-5455
William E Barclift, *Pr*
William E Barclift Junior, *Pr*
Roy P Martin Iii, *VP*
Susan Martin, *
▲ **EMP:** 80 **EST:** 1986
SQ FT: 24,000
SALES (est): 9.19MM **Privately Held**
SIC: 2091 5146 Canned and cured fish and seafoods; Seafoods

(G-5566)
QUALITY SEAFOOD CO INC
177 Knobbs Creek Dr (27909-7002)
PHONE.....................252 338-2800
William E Barclift, *Pr*
Russell Barclift, *
EMP: 11 **EST:** 1983
SALES (est): 1.75MM **Privately Held**
Web: www.qualityseafoodco.com
SIC: 5146 2092 2091 Seafoods; Fresh or frozen packaged fish; Canned and cured fish and seafoods

(G-5567)
R O GIVENS SIGNS INC
Also Called: Atlantic Screen Print
1145 Parsonage St (27909-3303)
P.O. Box 9 (27907-0009)
PHONE.....................252 338-6578
Robert O Givens Junior, *Pr*
Scott Givens, *VP*
Mary G Lane, *Sec*
EMP: 9 **EST:** 1947
SALES (est): 238.58K **Privately Held**
Web: www.rogivenssigns.com
SIC: 3993 7359 Signs and advertising specialties; Sign rental

(G-5568)
ROBINSON MANUFACTURING COMPANY
Also Called: Elizabeth City Cotton Mills
451 N Hughes Blvd (27909-3507)
P.O. Box 186 (27907-0186)
PHONE.....................252 335-2985
C H Robinson, *Ch*
Harry J Robinson, *
T G Skinner, *
Katie Varnard, *
EMP: 33 **EST:** 1895
SQ FT: 31,700
SALES (est): 1.7MM **Privately Held**
SIC: 2281 Carded yarn, spun

(G-5569)
SANDERS COMPANY INC
410 N Poindexter St (27909-4040)
P.O. Box 324 (27907-0324)
PHONE.....................252 338-3995
H T Sanders, *Pr*
E Craig Sawyer, *VP*
Colleen Sanders, *Stockholder*
EMP: 23 **EST:** 1880
SQ FT: 12,000
SALES (est): 1.87MM **Privately Held**
SIC: 5085 3599 5051 Industrial supplies; Machine shop, jobbing and repair; Foundry products

(G-5570)
SAS INDUSTRIES INC
100 Corporate Dr (27909-7027)
P.O. Box 245 (11949-0245)
PHONE.....................631 727-1441
Steve Steckis, *Pr*
▲ **EMP:** 15 **EST:** 1973
SQ FT: 10,000
SALES (est): 1.88MM **Privately Held**
Web: www.sasindustries.com
SIC: 3053 5085 Gaskets, all materials; Industrial supplies

(G-5571)
STALLINGS CABINETS INC
508 N Hughes Blvd (27909-3529)
PHONE.....................252 338-6747
Don Stallings, *Prin*
EMP: 4 **EST:** 2010
SALES (est): 254.12K **Privately Held**
Web: www.stallingscabinets.com
SIC: 2434 Wood kitchen cabinets

(G-5572)
SUBSEA VIDEO SYSTEMS INC
611 Hull Dr (27909-6924)
P.O. Box 159 (27907-0159)
PHONE.....................252 338-1001
Fred Meyer, *Pr*
Walter Brunner, *Sec*
EMP: 8 **EST:** 1990
SQ FT: 10,000
SALES (est): 753.78K **Privately Held**

Web: subsea-video-systems-inc-in-elizabeth-city-nc.cityfos.com
SIC: 3861 8711 Cameras, still and motion picture (all types); Electrical or electronic engineering

(G-5573)
SWEETEASY LLC
507 E Main St Ste C (27909-4461)
PHONE.....................252 698-0109
EMP: 5 **EST:** 2019
SALES (est): 142.8K **Privately Held**
Web: www.thesweeteasync.com
SIC: 2099 Food preparations, nec

(G-5574)
TCE MANUFACTURING LLC
1287 Salem Church Rd (27909-7415)
PHONE.....................252 330-9919
EMP: 4 **EST:** 1999
SQ FT: 11,000
SALES (est): 427.23K **Privately Held**
Web: www.tcemfg.com
SIC: 3441 Fabricated structural metal

(G-5575)
TCOM LIMITED PARTNERSHIP
Also Called: TCOM, LIMITED PARTNERSHIP
190 T Com Dr (27909)
PHONE.....................252 330-5555
Charles Knauss, *Brnch Mgr*
EMP: 339
SQ FT: 10,000
SALES (corp-wide): 152.81MM **Privately Held**
Web: www.tcomlp.com
SIC: 3721 3829 3728 3537 Blimps; Measuring and controlling devices, nec; Aircraft parts and equipment, nec; Industrial trucks and tractors
HQ: Tcom, L.P.
7115 Thomas Edison Dr A
Columbia MD 21046
410 312-2300

(G-5576)
TCOM GROUND SYSTEMS LP
Also Called: Tcom
190 T Com Dr (27909-2942)
PHONE.....................252 338-3200
EMP: 10 **EST:** 1989
SALES (est): 2.5MM **Privately Held**
Web: www.tcomlp.com
SIC: 3531 Marine related equipment

(G-5577)
TELEPHONICS CORPORATION
1014 Consolidated Rd (27909-7835)
PHONE.....................631 755-7446
EMP: 8
SALES (corp-wide): 2.23B **Publicly Held**
Web: www.telephonics.com
SIC: 3669 Intercommunication systems, electric
HQ: Telephonics Corporation
815 Broadhollow Rd
Farmingdale NY 11735
631 755-7000

(G-5578)
TRANSFORMATIONAL BIBLE INST
714 Richardson St (27909-3816)
PHONE.....................702 218-3528
EMP: 5 **EST:** 2018
SALES (est): 67.66K **Privately Held**
SIC: 2759 Commercial printing, nec

Elizabeth City - Pasquotank County (G-5579)

(G-5579)
TRIPLE H HAULING LLC
390 Shadneck Rd (27909-7454)
PHONE.............................984 220-4676
EMP: 4 **EST:** 2017
SALES (est): 246.32K **Privately Held**
SIC: 4212 3537 Light haulage and cartage, local; Trucks: freight, baggage, etc.: industrial, except mining

(G-5580)
UNIVERSAL FOREST PRODUCTS INC
Also Called: Universal Forest Products
141 Knobbs Creek Dr (27909-7002)
PHONE.............................252 338-0319
EMP: 19
SALES (corp-wide): 7.22B **Publicly Held**
Web: www.ufpi.com
SIC: 2491 2439 2426 2499 Wood preserving; Structural wood members, nec; Dimension, hardwood; Fencing, docks, and other outdoor wood structural products
PA: Ufp Industries, Inc.
2801 E Beltline Ave Ne
Grand Rapids MI 49525
616 364-6161

(G-5581)
WARD & SON INC
920 Riverside Ave (27909-5342)
PHONE.............................252 338-6589
Jack Ward, *Pr*
EMP: 5 **EST:** 1946
SALES (est): 95.29K **Privately Held**
Web: www.wardandsoninc.com
SIC: 3441 Fabricated structural metal

(G-5582)
WHITE BROS PACKING CO LLC
2551 Peartree Rd (27909-7801)
PHONE.............................252 331-9253
Ronnie E White, *Admn*
EMP: 8 **EST:** 2012
SALES (est): 242.44K **Privately Held**
SIC: 2011 Meat packing plants

Elizabethtown
Bladen County

(G-5583)
ANTHEM DISPLAYS LLC
518 Ben Greene Industrial Park Rd (28337)
PHONE.............................910 746-8988
EMP: 10 **EST:** 2014
SALES (est): 2.49MM
SALES (corp-wide): 509.22MM **Privately Held**
Web: www.anthemdisplays.com
SIC: 3993 Electric signs
PA: Circle Graphics, Inc.
120 9th Ave
Longmont CO 80501
303 532-2370

(G-5584)
ANTHEM DISPLAYS LLC
113 W Broad St (28337-9311)
P.O. Box 1945 (28337-1945)
PHONE.............................910 862-3550
Evan Brooks, *Asst Sec*
EMP: 10 **EST:** 2018
SALES (est): 493.11K **Privately Held**
Web: www.anthemdisplays.com
SIC: 3993 Electric signs

(G-5585)
BAILEY SALES AND SERVICE LLC
1604 Suggs Taylor Rd (28337-5159)
PHONE.............................910 876-1103
Richard W Bailey Ii, *Managing Member*
EMP: 6 **EST:** 2021
SALES (est): 345.37K **Privately Held**
SIC: 1389 7389 Construction, repair, and dismantling services; Business services, nec

(G-5586)
BURNETT WELDING
870 Sweet Home Church Rd (28337-6760)
P.O. Box 2421 (28337-2421)
PHONE.............................803 360-7406
EMP: 4 **EST:** 2017
SALES (est): 44.6K **Privately Held**
SIC: 7692 Welding repair

(G-5587)
BURNEY SWEETS & MORE INC (PA)
Also Called: Burneys Sweets & More
106-B Martin Luther King Dr (28337)
PHONE.............................910 862-2099
EMP: 8 **EST:** 2011
SALES (est): 318.16K
SALES (corp-wide): 318.16K **Privately Held**
SIC: 2051 2052 Bread, cake, and related products; Cookies and crackers

(G-5588)
CAPE FEAR CHEMICALS INC
Also Called: Tiger Products
4271 Us Highway 701 N (28337-6627)
P.O. Box 695 (28337-0695)
PHONE.............................910 862-3139
Henry James Brice Iii, *Pr*
Phyllis Brice, *VP*
Melody Lane Brice, *Sec*
Henry James Brice Junior, *Stockholder*
EMP: 20 **EST:** 1950
SQ FT: 35,750
SALES (est): 544K **Privately Held**
SIC: 2879 Insecticides, agricultural or household

(G-5589)
CAPE FEAR VINEYARD WINERY LLC
195 Vineyard Dr (28337-5748)
PHONE.............................844 846-3386
Homer Munroe, *Prin*
EMP: 7 **EST:** 2016
SALES (est): 563.42K **Privately Held**
Web: www.capefearwinery.com
SIC: 2084 Wines

(G-5590)
CAPE FEAR VINYRD & WINERY LLC
218 Aviation Pkwy Ste C (28337-8401)
PHONE.............................910 645-4292
EMP: 8 **EST:** 2014
SALES (est): 544.38K **Privately Held**
Web: www.capefearwinery.com
SIC: 2084 Wines

(G-5591)
CAROLINA SURFACES LLC
242 Woodlief Dr (28337-9737)
PHONE.............................910 874-1335
EMP: 4
SALES (corp-wide): 997.81K **Privately Held**
SIC: 2434 Wood kitchen cabinets
PA: Carolina Surfaces Llc
414 Peanut Rd
Elizabethtown NC 28337
910 874-1335

(G-5592)
DANAHER INDUS SENSORS CONTRLS
2100 W Broad St (28337-8826)
PHONE.............................910 862-5426
EMP: 8 **EST:** 2019
SALES (est): 819.78K **Privately Held**
Web: www.specialtyproducttechnologies.com
SIC: 3824 Fluid meters and counting devices

(G-5593)
DELGADOS WELDING INC
1275 Willard Tatum Rd (28337-6451)
PHONE.............................910 588-4762
Alejandro Delgado, *Prin*
EMP: 4 **EST:** 2018
SALES (est): 40.91K **Privately Held**
SIC: 7692 Welding repair

(G-5594)
DVINE FOODS
1585 Hwy 107 South (28337)
P.O. Box 490 (28337-0490)
PHONE.............................910 862-2576
EMP: 8 **EST:** 2014
SALES (est): 479.79K **Privately Held**
Web: www.dvinefoods.com
SIC: 2033 Apple sauce: packaged in cans, jars, etc.

(G-5595)
DYNAPAR CORPORATION (HQ)
2100 W Broad St (28337-8826)
PHONE.............................800 873-8731
Joseph Alexander, *Pr*
Patrick K Murphy, *
Daniel B Kim, *
▲ **EMP:** 130 **EST:** 2016
SALES (est): 262.04MM
SALES (corp-wide): 6.07MM **Publicly Held**
Web: www.dynapar.com
SIC: 3824 Controls, revolution and timing instruments
PA: Fortive Corporation
6920 Seaway Blvd
Everett WA 98203
425 446-5000

(G-5596)
HOG SLAT INCORPORATED
2229 Us Highway 701 N (28337-6137)
PHONE.............................910 862-7081
Pat Klemme, *Brnch Mgr*
EMP: 4
SALES (corp-wide): 538.94MM **Privately Held**
Web: www.hogslat.com
SIC: 3523 Farm machinery and equipment
PA: Hog Slat, Incorporated
206 Fayetteville St
Newton Grove NC 28366
800 949-4647

(G-5597)
IMAGE DESIGN
113 W Broad St (28337-9311)
P.O. Box 835 (28337-0835)
PHONE.............................910 862-8988
▲ **EMP:** 10 **EST:** 1993
SQ FT: 10,000
SALES (est): 892.85K **Privately Held**
Web: www.imagedesign.us
SIC: 3993 Signs and advertising specialties

(G-5598)
MCKOYS LOGGING COMPANY INC
3006 W Broad St (28337-7000)
P.O. Box 460 (28337-0460)
PHONE.............................910 862-2706
Robert W Mccoy Junior, *Prin*
Mashonia Daniels, *Prin*
EMP: 5 **EST:** 2017
SALES (est): 231.09K **Privately Held**
SIC: 2411 Logging

(G-5599)
MERRITT LOGGING & CHIPPING CO
1109 W Swanzy St (28337-9069)
P.O. Box 1225 (28337-1225)
PHONE.............................910 862-4905
Kenneth Merritt, *Pr*
Robert Merritt, *VP*
Sheila Merritt, *Sec*
EMP: 15 **EST:** 1969
SQ FT: 5,000
SALES (est): 438.8K **Privately Held**
SIC: 2411 Logging camps and contractors

(G-5600)
MERRITTS POTTERY INC
3943 Us Highway 701 N (28337-6631)
PHONE.............................910 862-3774
Floyd Merritt, *Pr*
EMP: 14 **EST:** 1980
SQ FT: 10,000
SALES (est): 488.92K **Privately Held**
SIC: 3272 Concrete products, precast, nec

(G-5601)
OCEANIA HARDWOODS LLC
474 Sweet Home Church Rd (28337-6122)
P.O. Box 310 (28337-0310)
PHONE.............................910 862-4447
EMP: 6 **EST:** 2005
SALES (est): 204.3K **Privately Held**
SIC: 2426 Hardwood dimension and flooring mills

(G-5602)
PRISMAFLEX USA INC
113 E Broad St (28337-9005)
P.O. Box 1945 (28337-1945)
PHONE.............................910 862-3550
Pierre Bassouls, *Pr*
▲ **EMP:** 10 **EST:** 2001
SALES (est): 2.21MM **Privately Held**
Web: www.prismaflex.com
SIC: 3993 Electric signs
PA: Prismaflex International
Lieudit La Boury
Haute Rivoire 69610

(G-5603)
S & W READY MIX CON CO LLC
Also Called: S & W Ready Mix Concrete
1460 Mercer Mill Rd (28337-5620)
PHONE.............................910 645-6868
David Cook, *Brnch Mgr*
EMP: 5
SALES (corp-wide): 8.01MM **Privately Held**
SIC: 3273 Ready-mixed concrete
HQ: S & W Ready Mix Concrete Company Llc
217 Lisbon St
Clinton NC 28328
910 592-1733

(G-5604)
SIGNLOGIC INC
174 S Poplar St (28337-9066)
P.O. Box 340 (28337-0340)
PHONE.............................910 862-8965
Martha Walters, *Pr*
Scott Walters, *Pur Mgr*
Brant Allen, *VP*
EMP: 4 **EST:** 2004
SALES (est): 270.29K **Privately Held**
Web: www.signlogic.biz
SIC: 3993 Signs and advertising specialties

GEOGRAPHIC SECTION

(G-5605)
TAYLOR MANUFACTURING INC
1585 Us Hwy 701 S (28337)
P.O. Box 518 (28337-0518)
PHONE.................................910 862-2576
Ron Taylor, *Pr*
Denise Taylor Bridgers, *
Oren Taylor, *Stockholder**
Victoria Taylor, *Stockholder**
EMP: 50 **EST:** 1988
SQ FT: 22,400
SALES (est): 5.32MM **Privately Held**
Web: www.taylormfg.com
SIC: 3433 3732 3599 3523   Stoves, wood and coal burning; Boatbuilding and repairing; Machine shop, jobbing and repair; Cotton pickers and strippers

(G-5606)
TAYLOR PRODUCTS INC
1585 Us Hwy 701 S (28337)
P.O. Box 490 (28337-0490)
PHONE.................................910 862-2576
Denise T Bridgers, *Pr*
EMP: 5 **EST:** 1982
SALES (est): 407.39K **Privately Held**
SIC: 2097   Manufactured ice

(G-5607)
TURN BULL LUMBER COMPANY
474 Sweet Home Church Rd (28337-6122)
P.O. Box 310 (28337-0310)
PHONE.................................910 862-4447
Pembroke N Jenkins, *Pr*
◆ **EMP:** 43 **EST:** 1993
SQ FT: 980
SALES (est): 6.63MM **Privately Held**
Web: www.turnbulllumber.com
SIC: 2426 2499   Lumber, hardwood dimension; Mulch or sawdust products, wood

Elkin
Surry County

(G-5608)
ACC COATINGS LLC
620 E Main St (28621-3537)
PHONE.................................336 701-0080
David Steele, *Managing Member*
EMP: 10 **EST:** 2005
SQ FT: 20,000
SALES (est): 2.03MM **Privately Held**
Web: www.acc-coatings.com
SIC: 2851   Coating, air curing

(G-5609)
ADAGIO VINEYARDS
139 Benge Dr (28621-8722)
PHONE.................................336 258-2333
EMP: 5 **EST:** 2019
SALES (est): 20.84K **Privately Held**
Web: www.adagiovineyards.com
SIC: 2084   Wines

(G-5610)
BASALT SPECIALTY PRODUCTS INC
600 E Main St (28621-3537)
P.O. Box 457 (27018-0457)
PHONE.................................336 835-5153
Anthony Fanale, *Pr*
EMP: 6 **EST:** 2004
SQ FT: 22,500
SALES (est): 785.25K **Privately Held**
Web: www.bspmat.com
SIC: 3644   Insulators and insulation materials, electrical

(G-5611)
BEST CHOICE MET STRUCTURES LLC
370 Standard St (28621-3534)
PHONE.................................877 683-1168
Karina Juarez, *Managing Member*
EMP: 10 **EST:** 2018
SALES (est): 211.63K **Privately Held**
SIC: 3441   Fabricated structural metal

(G-5612)
CAROLINA CANDLE
430 Gentry Rd (28621-9241)
PHONE.................................336 835-6020
Charlie Leichtweis, *Prin*
EMP: 5 **EST:** 2008
SALES (est): 241.09K **Privately Held**
Web: www.carolinacandle.com
SIC: 3999   Candles

(G-5613)
CAROLINA HERITG VINYRD WINERY ✿
170 Heritage Vines Way (28621-8916)
PHONE.................................336 448-4781
EMP: 5 **EST:** 2022
SALES (est): 62.17K **Privately Held**
Web:
www.carolinaheritagevineyards.com
SIC: 2084   Wines

(G-5614)
CAVU PRINTING INC
339 Benham Church Rd (28621-8244)
PHONE.................................336 818-9790
EMP: 6 **EST:** 2009
SALES (est): 319.17K **Privately Held**
Web: www.cavuprinting.com
SIC: 2752   Commercial printing, lithographic

(G-5615)
CROCKERS INC
1821 Joe Layne Mill Rd (28621-8411)
P.O. Box 500 (28621-0500)
PHONE.................................336 366-2005
Patti Crocker, *Pr*
EMP: 10 **EST:** 1991
SQ FT: 4,000
SALES (est): 903.64K **Privately Held**
SIC: 3534   Elevators and equipment

(G-5616)
CROWN HERITAGE INC
296 Gentry Rd (28621-8511)
PHONE.................................336 835-1424
Wayne Carter, *Mgr*
EMP: 34
Web: www.crownheritage.com
SIC: 2431   Millwork
PA: Crown Heritage, Inc.
    1708 Industrial Dr
    Wilkesboro NC 28697

(G-5617)
ECMD INC
Arndt & Herman Lumber Co
541 Gentry Rd (28621-9318)
P.O. Box 349 (28621-0349)
PHONE.................................336 835-1182
Don Mclarry, *Mgr*
EMP: 149
SALES (corp-wide): 186.49MM **Privately Held**
Web: www.ecmd.com
SIC: 2431   Millwork
PA: Ecmd, Inc.
    2 Grandview St
    North Wilkesboro NC 28659
    336 667-5976

(G-5618)
ELKIN CREEK VINEYARD LLC
318 Elkin Creek Mill Rd (28621-8860)
PHONE.................................336 526-5119
Mark Greene, *Prin*
EMP: 4 **EST:** 2004
SALES (est): 317.79K **Privately Held**
Web: www.elkincreekvineyard.com
SIC: 2084   Wines

(G-5619)
INDEPENDENCE LUMBER
350 Elkin Wildlife Rd (28621-8728)
PHONE.................................336 366-3400
Mike Miller, *Mgr*
EMP: 5 **EST:** 2017
SALES (est): 181.01K **Privately Held**
Web: www.independencelumberinc.com
SIC: 2421   Sawmills and planing mills, general

(G-5620)
INTERFACE FABRICS GROUP
304 E Main St (28621-3514)
PHONE.................................336 526-0407
Raymond Ogden, *Pr*
EMP: 7 **EST:** 2015
SALES (est): 154.43K **Privately Held**
SIC: 2221   Broadwoven fabric mills, manmade

(G-5621)
JENNIFER NITEN LOGGING
823 Edwards Lakeview Dr (28621-8827)
PHONE.................................336 428-6245
EMP: 4 **EST:** 2019
SALES (est): 81.72K **Privately Held**
SIC: 2411   Logging

(G-5622)
KATHIE S MC DANIEL
Also Called: Graphic Printing
765 Oakland Dr (28621-2955)
PHONE.................................336 835-1544
Kathie S Mcdaniel, *Pr*
EMP: 5 **EST:** 1989
SALES (est): 351.06K **Privately Held**
Web: www.graphicsprintingelkin.com
SIC: 2752 7334 7336 2791   Offset printing; Photocopying and duplicating services; Graphic arts and related design; Typesetting

(G-5623)
KENS TRIM & STAIRS KEN SWAREY
506 W Main St (28621-3318)
PHONE.................................336 835-4298
Kenneth Swarey, *Prin*
EMP: 5 **EST:** 2010
SALES (est): 66.66K **Privately Held**
SIC: 3446   Stairs, staircases, stair treads: prefabricated metal

(G-5624)
LEGACY VULCAN LLC
Mideast Division
12362 Nc 268 (28621-7332)
P.O. Box 71 (28621-0071)
PHONE.................................336 835-1439
Tim Hendrix, *Mgr*
EMP: 6
Web: www.vulcanmaterials.com
SIC: 3273   Ready-mixed concrete
HQ: Legacy Vulcan, Llc
    1200 Urban Center Dr
    Vestavia AL 35242
    205 298-3000

(G-5625)
MID SOUTH MANAGEMENT NC INC
Also Called: Tribune, The
214 E Main St (28621-3545)
PHONE.................................336 835-1513
R Fletcher Good Iv, *Pr*
Phyllis Buchheit Delapp, *Ch Bd*
EMP: 46 **EST:** 1911
SQ FT: 10,000
SALES (est): 798.7K
SALES (corp-wide): 13.53MM **Privately Held**
Web: www.elkintribune.com
SIC: 2711   Newspapers, publishing and printing
PA: Mid-South Management Co Inc
    172 E Main St Ste 300
    Spartanburg SC 29306
    864 583-2907

(G-5626)
MILLER BROTHERS LUMBER CO INC
Also Called: Miller Brothers Lumber Co
350 Elkin Wildlife Rd (28621-8728)
PHONE.................................336 366-3400
Mike Miller, *Pr*
Ricky Miller, *
Brenda Miller, *
EMP: 30 **EST:** 1952
SQ FT: 10,000
SALES (est): 2.37MM **Privately Held**
SIC: 2421   Sawmills and planing mills, general

(G-5627)
MVP GROUP INTERNATIONAL INC (HQ)
Also Called: TLC
430 Gentry Rd (28621-9241)
PHONE.................................843 216-8380
Sean Peters, *CEO*
Gautham S Pai, *
Jayaraman Ramachandran, *
Karpe Laxminarayana Rao, *Dir*
Venkata Valiveti, *
◆ **EMP:** 40 **EST:** 1998
SALES (est): 95.76MM **Privately Held**
Web: www.mvpgroupint.com
SIC: 3999 5122   Candles; Perfumes
PA: Primacy Industries Private Limited
    Udayavani Building, Press Corner
    Udupi KA 57610

(G-5628)
PERDUE FARMS INC
Also Called: Perdue Farms
105 Greenwood Cir (28621-8391)
PHONE.................................336 366-2591
Spergie Blue, *Mgr*
EMP: 94
SALES (corp-wide): 1.24B **Privately Held**
Web: www.perdue.com
SIC: 2015   Chicken, processed: fresh
PA: Perdue Farms Incorporated
    31149 Old Ocean City Rd
    Salisbury MD 21804
    800 473-7383

(G-5629)
TAMPCO INC
316 Stainless Way (28621-3126)
PHONE.................................336 835-1895
Kenneth G Nicks Junior, *Pr*
Irving Miles, *
Ed Hagen, *
EMP: 70 **EST:** 1969
SQ FT: 32,000
SALES (est): 7.08MM **Privately Held**
Web: www.tampcoinc.com
SIC: 3446   Railings, banisters, guards, etc: made from metal pipe

Elkin - Surry County (G-5630)

(G-5630)
TRIPLETTE FENCING SUPPLY INC
Also Called: Triplette Competition Arms
331 Standard St (28621-3533)
PHONE..................................336 835-1205
Walter Triplette, *Pr*
▲ **EMP:** 5 **EST:** 1977
SALES (est): 410.5K **Privately Held**
Web: www.triplette.com
SIC: 3949 5091 5941 Sporting and athletic goods, nec; Sporting and recreation goods; Sporting goods and bicycle shops

(G-5631)
VAUGHAN-BASSETT FURN CO INC
Also Called: Elkin Furniture
4109 Poplar Springs Rd (28621-8461)
P.O. Box 230 (28621-0230)
PHONE..................................336 835-2670
Danny Arnold, *Mgr*
EMP: 503
SALES (corp-wide): 88.99MM **Privately Held**
Web: www.vaughanbassett.com
SIC: 2511 2515 2512 Wood household furniture; Mattresses and bedsprings; Upholstered household furniture
PA: Vaughan-Bassett Furniture Company, Incorporated
300 E Grayson St
Galax VA 24333
276 236-6161

(G-5632)
WAYNE FARMS LLC
Also Called: Wayne Farms
10949 Nc 268 (28621-8790)
PHONE..................................336 366-4413
Doug Hester, *Brnch Mgr*
EMP: 305
SALES (corp-wide): 405K **Privately Held**
Web: www.waynesandersonfarms.com
SIC: 2015 Chicken, processed, nsk
HQ: Wayne Farms Llc
4110 Continental Dr
Oakwood GA 30566

(G-5633)
WEYERHAEUSER COMPANY
Eastern Osb Business
184 Gentry Rd (28621-8489)
PHONE..................................336 835-5100
Ross Gardner, *Mgr*
EMP: 21
SALES (corp-wide): 7.67B **Publicly Held**
Web: www.weyerhaeuser.com
SIC: 2436 5031 2493 Softwood veneer and plywood; Plywood; Reconstituted wood products
PA: Weyerhaeuser Company
220 Occidental Ave S
Seattle WA 98104
206 539-3000

Ellenboro
Rutherford County

(G-5634)
CAMP S WELL AND PUMP CO INC
149 Ola Dr (28040-7690)
P.O. Box 429 (28040-0429)
PHONE..................................828 453-7322
David Camp, *Pr*
EMP: 6 **EST:** 1954
SALES (est): 775K **Privately Held**
Web: www.campswellandpump.com
SIC: 1781 3561 Servicing, water wells; Pumps, domestic: water or sump

(G-5635)
EDS PALLET WORLD INC
559 Race Path Church Rd (28040-8363)
P.O. Box 37 (28040-0037)
PHONE..................................828 453-8986
Ed Romney, *Pr*
Gurdy Angalin, *VP*
Aertia Angtail, *VP*
EMP: 15 **EST:** 1988
SQ FT: 2,600
SALES (est): 1.88MM **Privately Held**
Web: www.edspalletworld.com
SIC: 2448 Pallets, wood

(G-5636)
NEXT GENERATION PLASTICS INC
161 Bugger Hollow Rd (28040-9340)
PHONE..................................828 453-0221
John Lahrmer, *Pr*
EMP: 4 **EST:** 2008
SALES (est): 264.64K **Privately Held**
SIC: 1446 Molding sand mining

(G-5637)
PLASTIC SOLUTIONS INC
324 Tiney Rd (28040-7611)
PHONE..................................678 353-2100
Bradley B Morgan, *CEO*
Richard R Hughes Junior, *Sec*
EMP: 18 **EST:** 2002
SALES (est): 8.06MM **Privately Held**
Web: www.plasticsolutions.net
SIC: 2821 Plastics materials and resins

(G-5638)
R & D WEAVING INC
376 Pinehurst Rd (28040-7600)
PHONE..................................828 248-1910
Robert Martin, *Pr*
EMP: 10 **EST:** 1988
SQ FT: 15,250
SALES (est): 816.48K **Privately Held**
Web: www.rdweaving.com
SIC: 2512 2392 Upholstered household furniture; Blankets, comforters and beddings

(G-5639)
SHYTLE SIGN AND LTG SVCS LLC
567 Terry Rd (28040-8673)
PHONE..................................828 429-4120
EMP: 5 **EST:** 2020
SALES (est): 122.86K **Privately Held**
Web: www.shytlesigns.com
SIC: 3993 Signs and advertising specialties

(G-5640)
THIEMAN MANUFACTURING TECH LLC
Also Called: Thieman Technology
531 Webb Rd (28040-8396)
P.O. Box 39 (28040-0039)
PHONE..................................828 453-1866
Keith Jackson, *CEO*
Todd Meldrum, *Prin*
EMP: 17 **EST:** 1998
SALES (est): 4.25MM **Privately Held**
Web: www.tmtfab.com
SIC: 3441 3444 3443 Fabricated structural metal; Sheet metalwork; Fabricated plate work (boiler shop)
PA: Maverick Corporate Partners, Llc
301 W Prospect St
Smithville OH 44677

Ellerbe
Richmond County

(G-5641)
BOYLES LOGGING LLC
496 Pleasant Hill Church Rd (28338-9189)
PHONE..................................910 206-7086
Boyle Richard, *Prin*
EMP: 6 **EST:** 2015
SALES (est): 224.48K **Privately Held**
SIC: 2411 Logging

(G-5642)
MEACHAM LOGGING INC
1530 Grassy Island Rd (28338-9206)
PHONE..................................910 652-2794
Butch Meacham, *Pr*
Glenda Meacham, *Sec*
Jeff Meacham, *VP*
EMP: 6 **EST:** 1992
SALES (est): 510.51K **Privately Held**
SIC: 2411 Logging camps and contractors

(G-5643)
RICHMOND SPECIALTY YARNS LLC
Also Called: Filspecusa
1748 N Us Highway 220 (28338-9336)
PHONE..................................910 652-5554
Ronald Audet, *Pr*
Nicolas Fournier, *
Kenneth Goodman, *Managing Member**
▲ **EMP:** 120 **EST:** 1976
SQ FT: 150,000
SALES (est): 10.59MM
SALES (corp-wide): 330K **Privately Held**
Web: www.filspec.com
SIC: 2281 Yarn spinning mills
HQ: Filspec Inc
85 Rue De La Burlington
Sherbrooke QC J1L 1
819 573-8700

(G-5644)
ROCK INDUSTRIAL SERVICES INC
157 S Railroad St (28338)
P.O. Box 660 (28338-0660)
PHONE..................................910 652-6267
Carl Puckett, *Pr*
Carter Kelly, *VP*
EMP: 18 **EST:** 1983
SQ FT: 45,000
SALES (est): 865.48K **Privately Held**
SIC: 3599 Machine shop, jobbing and repair

(G-5645)
SUGG LOGGING LLC
207 Crawford Rd (28338-8503)
PHONE..................................910 995-5728
EMP: 7 **EST:** 2016
SALES (est): 428.12K **Privately Held**
SIC: 2411 Logging

Elm City
Wilson County

(G-5646)
BARNHILL METAL FABRICATION
6247 Webb Lake Rd (27822-8398)
PHONE..................................252 236-5114
EMP: 4 **EST:** 2016
SALES (est): 59.8K **Privately Held**
SIC: 3499 Fabricated metal products, nec

(G-5647)
BOONE LOGGING COMPANY INC
1996 Vaughan Rd (27822-7921)
PHONE..................................252 443-7641
Vincent H Boone, *Pr*
EMP: 6 **EST:** 1991
SALES (est): 626.3K **Privately Held**
SIC: 2411 Logging camps and contractors

(G-5648)
CJS WELDING
4946 Temperance Hall Rd (27822-9612)
PHONE..................................252 972-7511
EMP: 4 **EST:** 2018
SALES (est): 69.58K **Privately Held**
SIC: 7692 Welding repair

(G-5649)
EASTERN COMPOST LLC
8487 Bttleboro Leggett Rd (27822)
P.O. Box 460 (27809-0460)
PHONE..................................252 446-3636
Joel Boseman, *Prin*
EMP: 4 **EST:** 2005
SALES (est): 193.49K **Privately Held**
SIC: 2875 Compost

(G-5650)
IND FAB INC
8311 Vickers Rd (27822-9649)
PHONE..................................252 977-0811
Harry Truman Vickers, *Pr*
Sandi Vickers, *VP*
EMP: 10 **EST:** 1988
SALES (est): 484.31K **Privately Held**
SIC: 3443 Tanks, standard or custom fabricated: metal plate

(G-5651)
MACK INDUSTRIES
4879 Us 301 N (27822-9009)
PHONE..................................252 977-3733
EMP: 6 **EST:** 2006
SALES (est): 323.94K **Privately Held**
Web: www.mackconcrete.com
SIC: 3272 Concrete products, precast, nec

(G-5652)
QUALITY TRCK BODIES & REPR INC
5316 Rock Quarry Rd (27822-8728)
P.O. Box 1669 (27894-1669)
PHONE..................................252 245-5100
Michael D Gira, *Pr*
EMP: 30 **EST:** 1975
SQ FT: 54,000
SALES (est): 3.1MM **Privately Held**
SIC: 3713 7532 Truck bodies (motor vehicles); Body shop, trucks

(G-5653)
SENTRY VAULT SERVICE INC
6905 Shallingtons Mill Rd (27822-8903)
P.O. Box 904 (27822-0904)
PHONE..................................252 243-2241
John J Lee, *Pr*
Carrie Lee, *Sec*
EMP: 9 **EST:** 1966
SQ FT: 10,000
SALES (est): 726.38K **Privately Held**
SIC: 3272 Burial vaults, concrete or precast terrazzo

(G-5654)
VIVAS CUSTOM CABINETS LLC
515 Gray St (27822-4501)
PHONE..................................252 650-1103
Marisol Romero, *Prin*
EMP: 4 **EST:** 2018
SALES (est): 131.89K **Privately Held**
SIC: 2434 Wood kitchen cabinets

(G-5655)
WOODWRIGHT OF WILSON CO INC
Also Called: Woodwright Co

GEOGRAPHIC SECTION

Enfield - Halifax County (G-5680)

5753 Nc 58 (27822-9129)
PHONE.................252 243-9663
EMP: 4 **EST:** 1994
SQ FT: 3,500
SALES (est): 633.55K **Privately Held**
Web: www.thewoodwrightco.com
SIC: 5021 5712 2426 Household furniture; Furniture stores; Furniture stock and parts, hardwood

Elon
Alamance County

(G-5656)
ALAMANCE ELECTRIC & WLDG INC
3562 Stoney Creek Church Rd (27244-9597)
P.O. Box 1367 (27244-1367)
PHONE.................336 584-9339
Donald Moore, *Pr*
EMP: 6 **EST:** 2010
SALES (est): 109.47K **Privately Held**
SIC: 7692 Welding repair

(G-5657)
ENGINEERED CONTROLS INTL LLC (HQ)
100 Rego Dr (27244-9159)
P.O. Box 247 (27244-0247)
PHONE.................336 449-7707
▲ **EMP:** 210 **EST:** 2010
SQ FT: 100,000
SALES (est): 113.73MM
SALES (corp-wide): 8.44B **Publicly Held**
Web: www.regoproducts.com
SIC: 3491 Pressure valves and regulators, industrial
PA: Dover Corporation
    3005 Highland Pkwy # 200
    Downers Grove IL 60515
    630 541-1540

(G-5658)
GREGORY PALLET CO LLC
745 Underwood Rd (27244-8897)
PHONE.................336 342-3590
EMP: 6 **EST:** 2017
SALES (est): 130.56K **Privately Held**
SIC: 2448 Pallets, wood

(G-5659)
HEARSAY GUIDES LLC ✪
5005 Windsor Ct (27244-9410)
PHONE.................336 584-1440
EMP: 4 **EST:** 2022
SALES (est): 92.1K **Privately Held**
SIC: 2741 Internet publishing and broadcasting

(G-5660)
JACODY PUBLISHING
3065 Gwyn Rd (27244-9589)
PHONE.................336 438-1579
Timothy W Clapp, *Prin*
EMP: 5 **EST:** 2016
SALES (est): 73.67K **Privately Held**
SIC: 2741 Miscellaneous publishing

(G-5661)
TAK CNC LLC
1238 Jamestowne Dr Ste C (27244-8322)
PHONE.................336 506-7775
EMP: 5 **EST:** 2020
SALES (est): 93.12K **Privately Held**
SIC: 3599 Machine shop, jobbing and repair

(G-5662)
TEAMWORK INC
1000 Georgetowne Dr (27244-8335)
PHONE.................336 578-3456
Robert Weavil, *Pr*
EMP: 8 **EST:** 1985
SALES (est): 737.64K **Privately Held**
Web: www.teamwork.com
SIC: 2252 2251 Socks; Women's hosiery, except socks

(G-5663)
VILLAGE CREAMERY & CAF INC
7111 Summerdale Rd (27244-9612)
PHONE.................336 447-4726
Robert A Lough, *Prin*
EMP: 5 **EST:** 2010
SALES (est): 62.29K **Privately Held**
SIC: 2021 Creamery butter

Elon College
Alamance County

(G-5664)
CLAYTON ELECTRIC MTR REPR INC
1407 N Nc Highway 87 (27244-9712)
PHONE.................336 584-3756
Jay Clayton, *Pr*
J Wayne Clayton, *Pr*
James W Clayton, *VP*
Nelda Cook, *Sec*
EMP: 11 **EST:** 1980
SQ FT: 2,000
SALES (est): 892.75K **Privately Held**
Web: www.claytonelectricmotorrepair.com
SIC: 7694 5063 Electric motor repair; Motors, electric

(G-5665)
KNIT TECH INC
2448 Pitt Rd # A (27244-7662)
P.O. Box 627 (27244-0627)
PHONE.................336 584-8999
Alex Moser, *Pr*
Jeanette S Moser, *Sec*
EMP: 5 **EST:** 1990
SQ FT: 11,000
SALES (est): 233.82K **Privately Held**
SIC: 2252 Socks

(G-5666)
MABRY INDUSTRIES INC
2903 Gibsonville Ossipee Rd (27244-9706)
P.O. Box 277 (27244-0277)
PHONE.................336 584-1311
James B Mabry, *Pr*
James B Mabry Junior, *VP*
Linda D Mabry, *
▲ **EMP:** 28 **EST:** 1976
SQ FT: 25,000
SALES (est): 4.97MM **Privately Held**
Web: www.mabryind.com
SIC: 3599 Machine shop, jobbing and repair

(G-5667)
SONOCO PRODUCTS COMPANY
Also Called: Sonoco
212 Cook Rd (27244-9390)
P.O. Box 428 (27244-0428)
PHONE.................336 449-7731
Chip Goodman, *Mgr*
EMP: 28
SALES (corp-wide): 6.78B **Publicly Held**
Web: www.sonoco.com
SIC: 2655 Fiber cans, drums, and similar products
PA: Sonoco Products Company
    1 N 2nd St
    Hartsville SC 29550
    843 383-7000

(G-5668)
WILSON TIRE AND AUTOMOTIVE INC
1807 N Nc Highway 87 (27244-9735)
PHONE.................336 584-9638
Steven Moss, *Pr*
Susan Moss, *VP*
EMP: 7 **EST:** 1972
SQ FT: 3,300
SALES (est): 1.34MM **Privately Held**
Web: www.wilsontireandautomotive.com
SIC: 5531 7534 Automotive tires; Tire repair shop

Emerald Isle
Carteret County

(G-5669)
AVERCAST LLC
8921 Crew Dr (28594-1927)
PHONE.................208 538-5380
EMP: 24 **EST:** 2008
SALES (est): 728.1K **Privately Held**
Web: www.avercast.com
SIC: 7372 Prepackaged software

(G-5670)
NATIONAL MARBLE PRODUCTS INC
404 Channel Dr (28594-2009)
P.O. Box 33 (28584-0033)
PHONE.................910 326-3005
Mat Matheson, *Pr*
EMP: 9 **EST:** 1986
SALES (est): 1.08MM **Privately Held**
Web: www.nationalmarbleproducts.com
SIC: 3281 Marble, building: cut and shaped

(G-5671)
PROGRESSIVE ELC GREENVILLE LLC
8606 Canal Dr (28594-2503)
PHONE.................252 413-6957
EMP: 10 **EST:** 2006
SQ FT: 12,000
SALES (est): 453.75K **Privately Held**
SIC: 3559 Electronic component making machinery

(G-5672)
TEABAR PUBLISHING INC
201n James Dr (28594-3039)
PHONE.................252 764-2453
Elaine Teachey, *Prin*
EMP: 4 **EST:** 2016
SALES (est): 40.43K **Privately Held**
SIC: 2741 Miscellaneous publishing

Enfield
Halifax County

(G-5673)
A & B MILLING COMPANY
200 Halifax St (27823-1100)
P.O. Box 278 (27823-0278)
PHONE.................252 445-3161
Bob Allsbrook, *Owner*
EMP: 7 **EST:** 2005
SALES (est): 456.43K **Privately Held**
Web: www.auntrubyspeanuts.com
SIC: 2048 Prepared feeds, nec

(G-5674)
ALLSBROOK LOGGING LLC
173 Pro House Dr (27823-9094)
PHONE.................252 567-1085
Gary Allsbrook, *Admn*
EMP: 5 **EST:** 2016
SALES (est): 140.97K **Privately Held**
SIC: 2411 Logging

(G-5675)
AMERICAP CO INC
276 Daniels Bridge Rd (27823-8897)
PHONE.................252 445-2388
Carlton T Qualls Iii, *Pr*
Byron Ransdell, *
Carlton T Qualls Junior, *VP*
Craig Stephenson, *
Edwin Borden Junior, *Dir*
▲ **EMP:** 21 **EST:** 1989
SQ FT: 15,000
SALES (est): 944.83K **Privately Held**
Web: www.americap.com
SIC: 2353 Baseball caps

(G-5676)
BINDERHOLZ ENFIELD LLC
260 Piper Ln (27823-8974)
PHONE.................770 362-0558
EMP: 43 **EST:** 2020
SALES (est): 6.2M
SALES (corp-wide): 2.59B **Privately Held**
Web: www.binderholz.com
SIC: 2421 Sawmills and planing mills, general
HQ: Binderholz East Gmbh
    ZillertalstraBe 39
    FUgen 6263
    52886010

(G-5677)
ENFIELD TIRE SERVICE INC
301 N Mcdaniel St (27823-1241)
PHONE.................252 445-5016
Lillian Cofield, *Pr*
Vivian Spence, *Sec*
Nathaniel Cofield, *VP*
EMP: 5 **EST:** 1971
SQ FT: 1,200
SALES (est): 694.22K **Privately Held**
SIC: 5531 7534 Automotive tires; Tire recapping

(G-5678)
HALIFAX EMC
12867 Nc Highway 481 (27823-8204)
PHONE.................252 445-5111
EMP: 11 **EST:** 2014
SALES (est): 953.85K **Privately Held**
Web: www.ncelectriccooperatives.com
SIC: 3572 Computer storage devices

(G-5679)
HEWLIN BROTHERS LUMBER CO
18555 Nc Highway 48 (27823-9244)
PHONE.................252 586-6473
Rodward Hewlin, *Pt*
Tyrone Hewlin, *Pt*
EMP: 4 **EST:** 1965
SALES (est): 356.29K **Privately Held**
SIC: 2421 5211 Lumber: rough, sawed, or planed; Planing mill products and lumber

(G-5680)
NASH BRICK COMPANY
532 Nash Brick Rd (27823-9634)
P.O. Box 6579 (27628-6579)
PHONE.................252 443-4965
Thomas G Fisher, *Pr*
Donald R Bowden, *Sec*
EMP: 20 **EST:** 1902
SQ FT: 1,500
SALES (est): 782.87K **Privately Held**
Web: www.nashbrick.com
SIC: 3251 Brick clay: common face, glazed, vitrified, or hollow

(G-5681)
WELLS WELDING SVC
24488 Nc Highway 561 (27823-8661)
PHONE..................252 519-2808
Michael Wells, *Prin*
EMP: 8 **EST:** 2018
SALES (est): 459.8K **Privately Held**
SIC: 7692 Welding repair

(G-5682)
WILSON BROS LOGGING INC
72 Gennie Rd (27823-9666)
PHONE..................252 445-5317
Daniel Wilson, *Pr*
EMP: 10 **EST:** 2002
SALES (est): 485.87K **Privately Held**
SIC: 2411 Logging camps and contractors

Enka
Buncombe County

(G-5683)
LEGACY VULCAN LLC
Mideast Division
Hwy 19 & 23 S (28728)
P.O. Box 549 (28728-0549)
PHONE..................828 255-8561
Weldon Peek, *Mgr*
EMP: 4
Web: www.vulcanmaterials.com
SIC: 3273 1423 Ready-mixed concrete; Crushed and broken granite
HQ: Legacy Vulcan, Llc
1200 Urban Center Dr
Vestavia AL 35242
205 298-3000

(G-5684)
SOUTHEASTERN CONTAINER INC (PA)
1250 Sand Hill Rd (28728)
P.O. Box 909 (28728-0909)
PHONE..................828 350-7200
Doug Wehrkamp, *Pr*
Mike Ramos, *VP*
◆ **EMP:** 164 **EST:** 1982
SQ FT: 400,000
SALES (est): 319.93MM
SALES (corp-wide): 319.93MM **Privately Held**
Web: www.secontainer.com
SIC: 3085 Plastics bottles

Ennice
Alleghany County

(G-5685)
RONNIE L POOLE
14596 Nc Highway 18 N (28623-9409)
PHONE..................336 657-3956
Ronnie L Poole, *Prin*
EMP: 6 **EST:** 2009
SALES (est): 419.7K **Privately Held**
SIC: 2411 Logging

Ernul
Craven County

(G-5686)
COASTAL CAROLINA LOGGIN
250 Aurora Rd (28527-9601)
PHONE..................252 474-2165
Joseph Clydelockey Junior, *Mgr*
EMP: 8 **EST:** 2013
SALES (est): 251.15K **Privately Held**
SIC: 2411 Logging

Erwin
Harnett County

(G-5687)
MICHEAL LANGDON LOGGING INC
7249 Ross Rd (28339-8634)
PHONE..................910 890-5295
Michael Langdon, *Pr*
EMP: 6 **EST:** 2000
SALES (est): 386.58K **Privately Held**
SIC: 2411 Logging camps and contractors

(G-5688)
SPECIALTY PRODUCTS INTL LTD
820 N 14th St (28339-2613)
PHONE..................910 897-4706
Leigh Beadle, *Prin*
▲ **EMP:** 5 **EST:** 2010
SALES (est): 119.73K **Privately Held**
SIC: 2087 Extracts, flavoring

(G-5689)
VEGHERB LLC
Also Called: Scenery Solutions
200 N 13th St Ste 3b (28339-1746)
PHONE..................800 914-9835
▲ **EMP:** 11 **EST:** 1997
SALES (est): 1.78MM **Privately Held**
Web: www.frameitall.com
SIC: 3524 5261 Lawn and garden equipment; Retail nurseries and garden stores

Ether
Montgomery County

(G-5690)
BLACKSTONE FURNITURE INDS INC
Also Called: Little River Furniture
624 Hogan Farm Rd (27247)
P.O. Box 212 (27247-0212)
PHONE..................910 428-2833
Gary Mabe, *Pr*
Greg Mabe, *VP*
David Mcrae, *VP Fin*
Sandy Mcfarlane, *VP Opers*
EMP: 17 **EST:** 1992
SQ FT: 27,000
SALES (est): 982.98K **Privately Held**
SIC: 2512 Upholstered household furniture

Etowah
Henderson County

(G-5691)
BOONDOCK S MANUFACTURING INC
Also Called: B C M Company
6085 Brevard Rd (28729-9758)
PHONE..................828 891-4242
Mike Hodges, *Pr*
Ryan Hodges, *VP*
Greg Hodges, *Prin*
EMP: 6 **EST:** 1972
SQ FT: 8,643
SALES (est): 660.63K **Privately Held**
SIC: 3792 3448 5531 Campers, for mounting on trucks; Farm and utility buildings; Automotive accessories

(G-5692)
KILN DRYING SYSTEMS CMPNNTS IN
Also Called: K D S
234 Industrial Dr (28729)
PHONE..................828 891-8115
Rob Girardi, *Prin*
Charles Moniotte, *VP*
Mary Girardi, *Sec*
▲ **EMP:** 21 **EST:** 1992
SQ FT: 22,000
SALES (est): 10.33MM **Privately Held**
Web: www.kdskilns.com
SIC: 3559 Kilns, lumber

(G-5693)
SALTY LANDING
6577 Brevard Rd (28729-8739)
PHONE..................404 245-5699
EMP: 6 **EST:** 2019
SALES (est): 126.33K **Privately Held**
Web: www.thesaltylanding.com
SIC: 2092 Fresh or frozen packaged fish

(G-5694)
TINMAN CANDLES
205 Mckinney Rd 1 (28729-8725)
PHONE..................828 329-1140
Crystal Phillips, *Prin*
EMP: 4 **EST:** 2018
SALES (est): 62.54K **Privately Held**
SIC: 3999 Candles

Everetts
Martin County

(G-5695)
INTERTAPE POLYMER CORP
1622 Twin Bridges Rd (27825-8700)
PHONE..................252 792-2083
EMP: 83
SALES (corp-wide): 571.43MM **Privately Held**
Web: www.itape.com
SIC: 2821 Plastics materials and resins
HQ: Intertape Polymer Corp.
100 Paramount Dr Ste 300
Sarasota FL 34232
888 898-7834

Evergreen
Columbus County

(G-5696)
3 KIDS SCREEN PRINTING
10860 Old Lumberton Rd (28438-9302)
PHONE..................910 212-0672
Amanda West, *Prin*
EMP: 5 **EST:** 2015
SALES (est): 67.83K **Privately Held**
SIC: 2752 Commercial printing, lithographic

(G-5697)
EVERGREEN LOGGING LLC
686 Homer Nance Rd (28438-9516)
PHONE..................910 654-1662
Lennon Hinson, *Prin*
EMP: 10 **EST:** 2014
SALES (est): 470.8K **Privately Held**
SIC: 2411 Logging camps and contractors

(G-5698)
JK LOGGING LLC
3564 Paul Willoughby Rd (28438-9140)
PHONE..................910 648-5471
Joshua Rising, *Prin*
EMP: 6 **EST:** 2018
SALES (est): 150.35K **Privately Held**
SIC: 2411 Logging

Fair Bluff
Columbus County

(G-5699)
PIPELINE PLASTICS LLC
15159 Andrew Jackson Hwy Sw (28439-9663)
PHONE..................817 693-4100
Mike Leathers, *CEO*
EMP: 5
SALES (corp-wide): 17.54MM **Privately Held**
Web: www.pipe.us
SIC: 3089 1623 Fittings for pipe, plastics; Pipeline construction, nsk
PA: Pipeline Plastics, Llc
1453 Fm 2264
Decatur TX 76234
940 627-9100

Fairmont
Robeson County

(G-5700)
APPAREL USA INC
102 Trinity St (28340-1636)
PHONE..................212 869-5495
Sanjay Israni, *Brnch Mgr*
EMP: 25
SALES (corp-wide): 2MM **Privately Held**
SIC: 5136 5137 2389 2339 Men's and boy's clothing; Women's and children's clothing; Men's miscellaneous accessories; Women's and misses' accessories
PA: Apparel Usa Inc
57 W 38th St Fl 4
New York NY 10018
212 869-5495

(G-5701)
CLAYBOURN WALTERS LOG CO INC
16071 Nc Highway 130 E (28340-5571)
P.O. Box 26 (28375-0026)
PHONE..................910 628-7075
Claybourn Walters, *Pr*
Michael Walters, *
EMP: 19 **EST:** 1978
SALES (est): 873.37K **Privately Held**
Web: www.claybournwalters.com
SIC: 2411 Logging camps and contractors

(G-5702)
HERALD A PIERRE LLC
707 Church St (28340-1208)
PHONE..................919 730-2965
Pierre A Herald, *Prin*
EMP: 5 **EST:** 2010
SALES (est): 54.17K **Privately Held**
SIC: 2711 Newspapers, publishing and printing

(G-5703)
J & D WOOD INC
4940 Centerville Church Rd (28340-8439)
P.O. Box 271 (28340-0271)
PHONE..................910 628-9000
Johnie F Allen, *Pr*
Diane T Allen, *Treas*
EMP: 19 **EST:** 1987
SQ FT: 65,000
SALES (est): 2.29MM **Privately Held**
Web: www.qualitypinebedding.com
SIC: 2426 2421 Dimension, hardwood; Sawdust, shavings, and wood chips

GEOGRAPHIC SECTION

Fallston - Cleveland County (G-5729)

(G-5704)
MEATINTERNATIONAL LLC
266 Bethesda Church Rd (28340-9616)
PHONE...............910 628-8267
EMP: 5 **EST:** 2014
SALES (est): 97.83K **Privately Held**
SIC: 2011 Pork products, from pork slaughtered on site

(G-5705)
ROGERS SCREENPRINTING EMB INC (PA)
10306 Nc Highway 41 S (28340-5934)
PHONE...............910 628-1983
Missy Rogers, *Pr*
Keith Rogers, *VP*
Bonita Rogers, *Treas*
EMP: 9 **EST:** 1999
SQ FT: 12,000
SALES (est): 2.37MM
SALES (corp-wide): 2.37MM **Privately Held**
Web: www.rogersseinc.com
SIC: 2396 2395 Screen printing on fabric articles; Embroidery and art needlework

Fairview
Buncombe County

(G-5706)
ARTEX GROUP INC
1004 Charlotte Hwy (28730-8795)
PHONE...............866 845-1042
Richard Camuto, *Pr*
EMP: 6 **EST:** 2010
SALES (est): 282.74K **Privately Held**
Web: www.artexgroup.net
SIC: 2395 Embroidery products, except Schiffli machine

(G-5707)
ASHEVILLE GUIDEBOOK
18 Garren Mountain Ln (28730-7650)
PHONE...............828 779-1569
Lee Pantas, *Mgr*
EMP: 7 **EST:** 2007
SALES (est): 65.43K **Privately Held**
Web: www.ashevilleguidebook.com
SIC: 2731 Book publishing

(G-5708)
BARRY LOWE FABRICATION
1583 Charlotte Hwy (28730-9556)
PHONE...............828 776-7354
Barry Lowe, *Mgr*
EMP: 5 **EST:** 2014
SALES (est): 88.63K **Privately Held**
SIC: 3999 Manufacturing industries, nec

(G-5709)
BYRD DESIGNS INC
140 Lee Dotson Rd (28730-8642)
PHONE...............828 628-0151
Jaime Byrd, *Pr*
EMP: 7 **EST:** 1992
SQ FT: 2,376
SALES (est): 420K **Privately Held**
Web: www.byrddesigns.com
SIC: 3911 5944 3961 Jewelry, precious metal ; Jewelry stores; Costume jewelry

(G-5710)
FAIRVIEW TOWN CRIER
1185 Charlotte Hwy Ste G (28730-7783)
PHONE...............828 628-4547
EMP: 5 **EST:** 2018
SALES (est): 5.21K **Privately Held**
Web: www.fairviewtowncrier.com

SIC: 2711 Newspapers, publishing and printing

(G-5711)
GROVE CABINET LLC
6 Miller Rd (28730-9510)
PHONE...............828 575-4463
EMP: 4 **EST:** 2017
SALES (est): 99.18K **Privately Held**
Web: www.grovecabinet.com
SIC: 2434 Wood kitchen cabinets

(G-5712)
HENSLEY CORPORATION
9 Madelyn Ln (28730-8524)
PHONE...............828 230-9447
Jeff Hensley, *Admn*
EMP: 5 **EST:** 2016
SALES (est): 64.88K **Privately Held**
SIC: 3999 Manufacturing industries, nec

(G-5713)
HIGHLANDER UNMANNED DRONE
35 Kirkpatrick Ln (28730-8668)
PHONE...............828 776-6061
Patrick Nichols, *Owner*
EMP: 5 **EST:** 2017
SALES (est): 86.08K **Privately Held**
SIC: 3721 Motorized aircraft

(G-5714)
INDUSTRY CHOICE SOLUTIONS LLC
98 Bishop Cove Rd (28730-9799)
PHONE...............828 628-1991
Mark Puzerewski, *CEO*
EMP: 5 **EST:** 2005
SALES (est): 397.98K **Privately Held**
Web: www.icsolutions-hq.com
SIC: 3559 Semiconductor manufacturing machinery

(G-5715)
LAURA GASKIN
922 Garren Creek Rd (28730-8650)
PHONE...............828 628-5891
Laura Gaskin, *Prin*
EMP: 4 **EST:** 2011
SALES (est): 77K **Privately Held**
Web: www.lauragaskin.com
SIC: 3999 Framed artwork

(G-5716)
MONOGRAM ASHEVILLE LLC
19 E Owl Creek Ln (28730-8816)
PHONE...............828 545-5367
Victoria Edge, *Prin*
EMP: 6 **EST:** 2016
SALES (est): 110.14K **Privately Held**
SIC: 2395 Embroidery and art needlework

(G-5717)
POOLE COMPANY LLC
5 E Owl Creek Ln (28730-8816)
PHONE...............828 275-0460
EMP: 6 **EST:** 2016
SALES (est): 270.92K **Privately Held**
Web: www.poolecompany.com
SIC: 2821 Plastics materials and resins

(G-5718)
SMITHWAY INC
20 Smith Farm Rd (28730-9570)
PHONE...............828 628-1756
Rocky Smith, *VP*
EMP: 6 **EST:** 2015
SALES (est): 269.49K **Privately Held**
Web: www.smithwayinc.com
SIC: 3715 3713 3537 Truck trailers; Truck and bus bodies; Industrial trucks and tractors

(G-5719)
TE CONNECTIVITY CORPORATION
Also Called: Cii Technologies
1396 Charlotte Hwy (28730-1409)
PHONE...............828 338-1000
Bill Foley, *Brnch Mgr*
EMP: 281
Web: www.te.com
SIC: 3678 3643 Electronic connectors; Current-carrying wiring services
HQ: Te Connectivity Corporation
1050 Westlakes Dr
Berwyn PA 19312
610 893-9800

(G-5720)
TE CONNECTIVITY CORPORATION
Also Called: Agastat
1396 Charlotte Hwy (28730-1409)
PHONE...............828 338-1000
EMP: 9
Web: www.te.com
SIC: 3625 Industrial electrical relays and switches
HQ: Te Connectivity Corporation
1050 Westlakes Dr
Berwyn PA 19312
610 893-9800

Faison
Duplin County

(G-5721)
BAY VALLEY FOODS LLC
354 N Faison Ave (28341-7608)
PHONE...............910 267-4711
E Bailey, *Pr*
▲ **EMP:** 33 **EST:** 2011
SALES (est): 12.23MM
SALES (corp-wide): 3.43B **Publicly Held**
SIC: 2099 Vegetables, peeled for the trade
HQ: Bay Valley Foods, Llc
3200 Riverside Dr Ste A
Green Bay WI 54301
800 558-4700

(G-5722)
BERRY COLD LLC
2488 W Nc 403 Hwy (28341-8534)
PHONE...............910 267-4531
Ron E Cottle, *Pr*
EMP: 7 **EST:** 2018
SALES (est): 317.5K **Privately Held**
Web: www.berrycoldnc.net
SIC: 2034 Fruits, freeze-dried

(G-5723)
EUGENES TRUCKING INC
10422 Faison Hwy (28341-5878)
PHONE...............910 267-0555
Eugene Pearsall, *Pr*
EMP: 5 **EST:** 2006
SALES (est): 507.32K **Privately Held**
SIC: 3715 Truck trailers

(G-5724)
PICKLES MANUFACTURING LLC ✪
354 N Faison Ave (28341-7608)
PHONE...............910 267-4711
Steven Okland, *Managing Member*
EMP: 203 **EST:** 2022
SALES (est): 94.14MM
SALES (corp-wide): 3.43B **Publicly Held**
SIC: 2099 Food preparations, nec
PA: Treehouse Foods, Inc.
2021 Spring Rd Ste 600
Oak Brook IL 60523
708 483-1300

(G-5725)
R D JONES PACKING CO INC
192 N Nc Hwy 50 (28341)
PHONE...............910 267-2846
Taylor W Best, *Pr*
Joseph M Price, *Sec*
EMP: 8 **EST:** 1981
SQ FT: 1,782
SALES (est): 727.27K **Privately Held**
SIC: 2011 Beef products, from beef slaughtered on site

Faith
Rowan County

(G-5726)
WOOD PRODUCTS PACKG INTL INC
3725 Faith Rd (28041)
PHONE...............704 279-3011
Lloyd Pullen, *Pr*
EMP: 8 **EST:** 2003
SQ FT: 48,000
SALES (est): 938.25K **Privately Held**
SIC: 3086 Packaging and shipping materials, foamed plastics

Falcon
Cumberland County

(G-5727)
REUBEN JAMES AUTO ELECTRIC
7386 N West St (28342)
P.O. Box 126 (28342-0126)
PHONE...............910 980-1056
David James, *Owner*
EMP: 5 **EST:** 1981
SALES (est): 402.07K **Privately Held**
SIC: 3714 Motor vehicle parts and accessories

Fallston
Cleveland County

(G-5728)
BOGGS FARM CENTER INC
807 E Stagecoach Trl (28042)
P.O. Box 660 (28042-0660)
PHONE...............704 538-7176
A Max Boggs Junior, *Pr*
Mary Boggs, *VP*
EMP: 5 **EST:** 1930
SQ FT: 12,000
SALES (est): 468.16K **Privately Held**
SIC: 0724 5191 0191 0212 Cotton ginning; Fertilizer and fertilizer materials; General farms, primarily crop; Beef cattle, except feedlots

(G-5729)
FURNLITE INC
Also Called: Furnlite
344 Wilson Rd (28042)
P.O. Box 159 (28042-0159)
PHONE...............704 538-3193
Kieth Helms, *Genl Mgr*
▲ **EMP:** 23 **EST:** 1981
SQ FT: 4,400
SALES (est): 5.07MM
SALES (corp-wide): 4.41B **Publicly Held**
Web: www.furnlite.com
SIC: 3648 3645 Lighting equipment, nec; Residential lighting fixtures
PA: Graham Holdings Company
1300 17th St N Fl 17
Arlington VA 22209
703 345-6362

Fallston - Cleveland County (G-5730)   GEOGRAPHIC SECTION

(G-5730)
SPECIALTY LIGHTING LLC
4203 Fallston Rd (28042)
P.O. Box 780 (28042-0780)
PHONE.................................704 538-6522
Gregg Carpenter, *Managing Member*
▲ **EMP: 12 EST:** 2009
SALES (est): 2.42MM **Privately Held**
Web: www.specialtylighting.com
SIC: 3646 Commercial lighting fixtures

Farmville
Pitt County

(G-5731)
CAROLINA MARBLE PRODUCTS INC
3973 W Wilson St (27828-8549)
P.O. Box 302 (27828-0302)
PHONE.................................252 753-3020
Ronald H Williams, *Pr*
Hugh Williams, *Mgr*
EMP: 10 EST: 1997
SALES (est): 482.19K **Privately Held**
Web: www.carolinamarbleproducts.com
SIC: 3281 Marble, building: cut and shaped

(G-5732)
CMP PHARMA INC
8026 East Marlboro Rd (27828-9656)
P.O. Box 147 (27828-0147)
PHONE.................................252 753-7111
Gerald D Sakowski, *CEO*
Henry Smith, *
Tracey Smith, *
Kelly F Whitley, *
Peter Jerome, *
EMP: 30 EST: 1975
SALES (est): 13.21MM **Privately Held**
Web: www.cmppharma.com
SIC: 2834 Pharmaceutical preparations

(G-5733)
D R BURTON HEALTHCARE LLC
3936 South Fields St (27828-8570)
P.O. Box 229 (27828-0229)
PHONE.................................252 228-7038
Dennis Cook, *Managing Member*
EMP: 10 EST: 2016
SALES (est): 1.94MM **Privately Held**
Web: www.drburtonhpi.com
SIC: 3841 Surgical and medical instruments

(G-5734)
DUCK-RABBIT CRAFT BREWERY INC
4519 West Pine St (27828-8526)
PHONE.................................252 753-7745
Paul Philippon, *Pr*
EMP: 8 EST: 2004
SQ FT: 10,000
SALES (est): 921.75K **Privately Held**
Web: www.duckrabbitbrewery.com
SIC: 2082 Ale (alcoholic beverage)

(G-5735)
ESCO ELECTRONIC SERVICES INC
Also Called: Electronic Services
268 Hwy 121 And 264 Alternate (27828)
P.O. Box 732 (27828-0732)
PHONE.................................252 753-4433
Kenneth H Strickland, *Pr*
Pamela Jo Strickland, *VP*
▲ **EMP: 10 EST:** 1977
SQ FT: 15,000
SALES (est): 872.21K **Privately Held**
SIC: 7694 7629 Electric motor repair; Circuit board repair

(G-5736)
GARRIS GRADING AND PAVING INC
5950 Gay Rd (27828-8901)
PHONE.................................252 749-1101
Angela Garris, *Pr*
EMP: 15 EST: 2003
SALES (est): 2.34MM **Privately Held**
Web: www.asphaltgradingmillingpaving.com
SIC: 1611 1771 1794 2951 Surfacing and paving; Parking lot construction; Excavation and grading, building construction; Asphalt and asphaltic paving mixtures (not from refineries)

(G-5737)
GOLDSBORO MILLING COMPANY
Also Called: Farmville Service
3628 South Fields St (27828-2124)
PHONE.................................252 753-5371
Frank Bradley, *Mgr*
EMP: 157
SALES (corp-wide): 148.85MM **Privately Held**
Web: mail.goldsboromilling.com
SIC: 2048 Feed concentrates
PA: Goldsboro Milling Company
938 Millers Chapel Rd
Goldsboro NC 27534
919 778-3130

(G-5738)
HARVEY FERTILIZER AND GAS CO
Also Called: Morgan Fertilizer
4419 W Pine St (27828)
P.O. Box 649 (27828-0649)
PHONE.................................252 753-2063
Glenn Shirley, *Genl Mgr*
EMP: 24
SALES (corp-wide): 80.5MM **Privately Held**
Web: www.harveyfertilizerandgas.com
SIC: 5191 2879 Fertilizer and fertilizer materials; Agricultural chemicals, nec
PA: Harvey Fertilizer And Gas Co.
303 Bohannon Rd
Kinston NC 28501
252 526-4150

(G-5739)
LIMITLESS WLDG FABRICATION LLC
3543 South Fields St (27828-1983)
P.O. Box 134 (27828-0134)
PHONE.................................252 753-0660
Dustin Coffey, *CEO*
EMP: 5 EST: 2016
SALES (est): 420K **Privately Held**
Web: www.limitlesswelding.com
SIC: 7692 1799 3441 7699 Welding repair; Hydraulic equipment, installation and service; Fabricated structural metal; Industrial machinery and equipment repair

(G-5740)
MODLINS ANONIZED ALUMINUM WLDG
4551 Nc Highway 121 (27828-9363)
PHONE.................................252 753-7274
Keith Modlin, *Owner*
EMP: 4 EST: 2003
SALES (est): 217.88K **Privately Held**
Web: www.modlinswelding.com
SIC: 7692 3548 Welding repair; Welding and cutting apparatus and accessories, nec

(G-5741)
PACKAGING CORPORATION AMERICA
Also Called: PCA
9156 West Marlboro Rd (27828-8504)
PHONE.................................252 753-8450

Jason Tatum, *Brnch Mgr*
EMP: 5
SALES (corp-wide): 8.48B **Publicly Held**
Web: www.packagingcorp.com
SIC: 2653 Boxes, corrugated: made from purchased materials
PA: Packaging Corporation Of America
1 N Field Ct
Lake Forest IL 60045
847 482-3000

(G-5742)
PYXUS INTERNATIONAL INC
8958 West Marlboro Rd (27828-8571)
P.O. Box 166 (27828-0166)
PHONE.................................252 753-8000
William Loyd, *Brnch Mgr*
EMP: 150
SALES (corp-wide): 1.91B **Privately Held**
Web: www.aointl.com
SIC: 2141 5159 Tobacco stemming and redrying; Tobacco, leaf
PA: Pyxus International, Inc.
6001 Hospitality Ct # 100
Morrisville NC 27560
919 379-4300

(G-5743)
SAG HARBOR INDUSTRIES INC
3595 Mandarin Dr (27828-8580)
P.O. Box 269 (27828-0269)
PHONE.................................252 753-7175
Gene W Michelsen, *Manager*
EMP: 29
SALES (corp-wide): 24.73MM **Privately Held**
Web: www.sagharborind.com
SIC: 3621 Coils, for electric motors or generators
PA: Sag Harbor Industries, Inc.
1668 Bhmpton Sag Hbr Tpke
Sag Harbor NY 11963
631 725-0440

Fayetteville
Cumberland County

(G-5744)
21ST CENTURY TECH OF AMER
Also Called: 21st Century Technologies Amer
6316 Yadkin Rd (28303-2647)
PHONE.................................910 826-3676
William Mathes Iii, *Pr*
EMP: 18 EST: 1997
SQ FT: 18,000
SALES (est): 1.2MM **Privately Held**
SIC: 3545 Tools and accessories for machine tools

(G-5745)
222 DREAM CO LLC
627 Northampton Rd (28303-5704)
PHONE.................................919 803-9741
Sade Stubbs, *Managing Member*
EMP: 4 EST: 2020
SALES (est): 25K **Privately Held**
SIC: 3999 2841 Candles; Soap: granulated, liquid, cake, flaked, or chip

(G-5746)
4 LOVE AND ART
3701 Standard Dr (28306-8328)
PHONE.................................210 838-4288
Annette Rivers, *Prin*
EMP: 6 EST: 2015
SALES (est): 81.47K **Privately Held**
SIC: 2621 Art paper

(G-5747)
5 STAR SATELLITE INC
2537 Lull Water Dr (28306-4524)
PHONE.................................910 584-4354
Chris Lusardi, *Pr*
EMP: 6 EST: 2010
SALES (est): 147.72K **Privately Held**
SIC: 3663 Satellites, communications

(G-5748)
822TEES INC
2598 Raeford Rd (28305-5118)
PHONE.................................910 822-8337
Kurin S Keys, *Pr*
Sherin Keys, *Treas*
Ashley Brown, *Sec*
EMP: 7 EST: 2016
SQ FT: 2,500
SALES (est): 518.85K **Privately Held**
Web: www.822tees.com
SIC: 7311 8742 8743 2395 Advertising agencies; Marketing consulting services; Promotion service; Embroidery products, except Schiffli machine

(G-5749)
A2A INTEGRATED LOGISTICS INC
1830 Owen Dr Ste 102 (28304-3412)
PHONE.................................800 493-3736
▼ **EMP: 4 EST:** 2011
SALES (est): 929.73K **Privately Held**
Web: www.a2a-logistics.com
SIC: 2834 Pharmaceutical preparations

(G-5750)
ACENTO LATINO
458 Whitfield St (28306-1614)
PHONE.................................910 486-2760
Diana Lopez, *Prin*
EMP: 6 EST: 2010
SALES (est): 113.85K **Privately Held**
SIC: 2711 Newspapers, publishing and printing

(G-5751)
ADVANCED BRACE & LIMB INC
Also Called: Advanced Brace and Limb
4140 Ferncreek Dr Ste 803 (28314-2572)
PHONE.................................910 483-5737
Christopher Eney, *VP*
EMP: 8 EST: 2010
SALES (est): 552.27K **Privately Held**
Web: www.advancedbraceandlimb.com
SIC: 3842 Limbs, artificial

(G-5752)
ADVANCED COMPUTER LRNG CO LLC
Also Called: Aclc
208 Hay St Ste 2c (28301-5534)
PHONE.................................910 779-2254
Bradd Chi, *Managing Member*
EMP: 43 EST: 2003
SQ FT: 16,000
SALES (est): 4.98MM **Privately Held**
Web: www.goaclc.com
SIC: 7372 8299 7371 8711 Educational computer software; Educational services; Custom computer programming services; Engineering services

(G-5753)
ADVANTAGE NEWSPAPER
501 Executive Pl Ste B (28305-5391)
PHONE.................................910 323-0349
Timothy O Dellinger, *Prin*
EMP: 34 EST: 2011
SALES (est): 2.47MM **Privately Held**
Web: www.newspaperconsultants.com

GEOGRAPHIC SECTION

Fayetteville - Cumberland County (G-5779)

SIC: **2711** Newspapers, publishing and printing

(G-5754)
AEC CONSUMER PRODUCTS LLC
Also Called: AEC Consumer Products
3005 Bankhead Dr (28306-2683)
PHONE.....................704 904-0578
Richard Guy, *CEO*
Tammy Claussen, *COO*
EMP: 10 EST: 2012
SALES (est): 261.29K **Privately Held**
Web: www.bac-d.com
SIC: **7822** 2842 Motion picture and tape distribution; Sanitation preparations, disinfectants and deodorants

(G-5755)
AFA BILLING SERVICES
894 Elm St Ste D (28303-4384)
PHONE.....................910 868-8324
Cornelius Williams, *Mgr*
EMP: 7 EST: 2017
SALES (est): 149.27K **Privately Held**
Web: www.afap.com
SIC: **3669** Communications equipment, nec

(G-5756)
ALASKA STRUCTURES INC
Also Called: ALASKA STRUCTURES, INC.
2545 Ravenhill Dr Ste 101 (28303-5460)
P.O. Box 64577 (28306-0577)
PHONE.....................910 323-0562
Jimmy White, *Brnch Mgr*
EMP: 71
SALES (corp-wide): 48.99MM **Privately Held**
Web: www.alaskastructures.com
SIC: **3448** Buildings, portable: prefabricated metal
PA: Aks Industries, Inc.
6991 E Camelback Rd D21
Scottsdale AZ 85251
480 677-6088

(G-5757)
ALL SIGNS & GRAPHICS LLC
301 Hope Mills Rd (28304-3152)
PHONE.....................910 323-3115
EMP: 7 EST: 2011
SALES (est): 498.69K **Privately Held**
Web: www.allsignsnc.com
SIC: **3944** 3993 8721 Erector sets, toy; Electric signs; Accounting, auditing, and bookkeeping

(G-5758)
ALPEK POLYESTER USA LLC
Also Called: Dak Americas
3216 Cedar Creek Rd (28312-7955)
P.O. Box 1690 (28302-1690)
PHONE.....................910 433-8200
Cindy Jergensen, *Brnch Mgr*
EMP: 115
Web: www.alpekpolyester.com
SIC: **2821** Polytetrafluoroethylene resins, teflon
HQ: Alpek Polyester Usa, Llc
7621 Little Ave Ste 500
Charlotte NC 28226
704 940-7500

(G-5759)
AMERICAN EMBROIDERY LLC
424 Swan Island Ct (28311-8947)
PHONE.....................910 229-3837
EMP: 6 EST: 2019
SALES (est): 238.56K **Privately Held**
SIC: **2395** Embroidery and art needlework

(G-5760)
AMERICAN PHOENIX INC
318 Blount St (28301-5606)
PHONE.....................910 484-4007
Tommy Stewart, *Brnch Mgr*
EMP: 149
Web: www.apimix.net
SIC: **3069** 2899 Custom compounding of rubber materials; Chemical preparations, nec
PA: American Phoenix, Inc.
5500 Wayzata Blvd # 1010
Golden Valley MN 55416

(G-5761)
AMERICAN SIGNS BY TOMORROW
425 W Russell St (28301-5547)
PHONE.....................910 484-2313
EMP: 4 EST: 2018
SALES (est): 50.69K **Privately Held**
SIC: **3993** Signs and advertising specialties

(G-5762)
AMERICAN WDWRKERY BNJMIN HTCHI
3617 Clinton Rd (28312-9271)
PHONE.....................910 302-5678
EMP: 5 EST: 2019
SALES (est): 131.68K **Privately Held**
Web: www.uscustomwoodwork.com
SIC: **2431** Millwork

(G-5763)
AMERICAN WOODWORKERY INC
802 Bladen Cir (28312-9268)
PHONE.....................910 916-8098
EMP: 8 EST: 2015
SALES (est): 241.31K **Privately Held**
Web: www.uscustomwoodwork.com
SIC: **2431** Millwork

(G-5764)
ARNOLD S WELDING SERVICE INC (PA)
Also Called: A W S
1405 Waterless St (28306-1611)
PHONE.....................910 323-3822
Bill Arnold, *CEO*
EMP: 28 EST: 1970
SQ FT: 18,000
SALES: 4.65MM
SALES (corp-wide): 4.65MM **Privately Held**
SIC: **5084** 3542 3949 Industrial machinery and equipment; Machine tools, metal forming type; Golf equipment

(G-5765)
AUTO MACHINE SHOP INC
309 Winslow St (28301-5553)
PHONE.....................910 483-6016
Richard Butler Junior, *Pr*
EMP: 4 EST: 1949
SQ FT: 2,500
SALES (est): 287.41K **Privately Held**
Web: www.automachinefayetteville.com
SIC: **3599** 5013 Machine shop, jobbing and repair; Automotive supplies and parts

(G-5766)
AUTO PARTS FAYETTEVILLE LLC
Also Called: Auto Parts USA
929 Bragg Blvd Ste 2 (28301-4509)
PHONE.....................910 889-4026
EMP: 5 EST: 2019
SALES (est): 800K **Privately Held**
Web: www.devorecookeauto.com
SIC: **5015** 3089 2851 7699 Automotive parts and supplies, used; Automotive parts, plastic; Paints and paint additives; Hydraulic equipment repair

(G-5767)
AVERY MACHINE & WELDING CO
1312 Longleaf Dr (28305-5207)
P.O. Box 339 (28657-0339)
PHONE.....................828 733-4944
Todd Lecka, *Pr*
Steve Lecka, *VP*
EMP: 7 EST: 1984
SQ FT: 10,000
SALES (est): 805.77K **Privately Held**
SIC: **3599** 7692 1799 Machine shop, jobbing and repair; Welding repair; Welding on site

(G-5768)
BALLASH WOODWORKS LLC
701 Murray Hill Rd (28303-5148)
PHONE.....................910 709-0717
Kurt Ballash, *Prin*
EMP: 5 EST: 2019
SALES (est): 118.42K **Privately Held**
Web: www.ballashwoodworks.com
SIC: **2431** Millwork

(G-5769)
BARNHILL CONTRACTING COMPANY
1100 Robeson St (28305-5528)
P.O. Box 35376 (28303-0376)
PHONE.....................910 488-1319
Kermit Moser, *Brnch Mgr*
EMP: 74
SQ FT: 2,000
SALES (corp-wide): 389.14MM **Privately Held**
Web: www.barnhillcontracting.com
SIC: **1611** 1629 2951 1771 Grading; Drainage system construction; Asphalt paving mixtures and blocks; Concrete work
PA: Barnhill Contracting Company Inc
800 Tiffany Blvd Ste 200
Rocky Mount NC 27804
252 823-1021

(G-5770)
BIGNISHA RGRTS CHILL CREAM LLC ✪
Also Called: Glow Gorgeous
3547 Gainey Rd (28306-3378)
PHONE.....................910 528-8966
EMP: 4 EST: 2023
SALES (est): 79.3K **Privately Held**
SIC: **2024** Ice cream, packaged: molded, on sticks, etc.

(G-5771)
BLACKSAND METAL WORKS LLC
433 Delbert Dr (28306-8849)
P.O. Box 41627 (28309-1627)
PHONE.....................703 489-8282
EMP: 10 EST: 2015
SQ FT: 21,780
SALES (est): 144.09K **Privately Held**
SIC: **7692** 3317 3441 Welding repair; Welded pipe and tubes; Building components, structural steel

(G-5772)
BLASHFIELD SIGN COMPANY INC
303 Williams St (28301-5661)
PHONE.....................910 485-7200
Matt Blashfield, *Pr*
Stacey Blashfield, *VP*
EMP: 9 EST: 1989
SALES (est): 955.06K **Privately Held**
Web: www.bcsignage.com
SIC: **3993** Electric signs

(G-5773)
BLINDS PLUS INC
5137 Raeford Rd (28304-3145)
P.O. Box 41035 (28309-1035)
PHONE.....................910 487-5196
EMP: 7 EST: 2009
SALES (est): 85.53K **Privately Held**
SIC: **2431** 5719 7699 Blinds (shutters), wood; Window furnishings; Venetian blind repair shop

(G-5774)
BRANDY THOMPSON
Also Called: Spa and Salon
6712 Bone Creek Dr Apt A (28314-2931)
P.O. Box 1704 (28302-1704)
PHONE.....................321 252-2911
Brandy Thompson, *Prin*
Brandy Thompson, *Owner*
EMP: 10 EST: 2015
SALES (est): 60K **Privately Held**
SIC: **7231** 3999 7299 Cosmetologist; Barber and beauty shop equipment; Personal appearance services

(G-5775)
BRIDGESTONE RET OPERATIONS LLC
Also Called: Firestone
660 Cross Creek Mall (28303-7266)
PHONE.....................910 864-4106
Michael Diantonio, *Mgr*
EMP: 9
Web: www.bridgestoneamericas.com
SIC: **5531** 7534 Automotive tires; Rebuilding and retreading tires
HQ: Bridgestone Retail Operations, Llc
333 E Lake St Ste 300
Bloomingdale IL 60108
630 259-9000

(G-5776)
BUVIC LLC
6798 Weeping Water Run (28314-5148)
PHONE.....................910 302-7950
David Thompson, *Managing Member*
EMP: 6 EST: 2019
SALES (est): 484.31K **Privately Held**
SIC: **3578** Automatic teller machines (ATM)

(G-5777)
BUZZ SAW INC
Also Called: Sign-A-Rama
1015 Robeson St Ste 103 (28305-5635)
PHONE.....................910 321-7446
Robert M Degroff, *Pr*
Crystal A Degroff, *VP*
EMP: 5 EST: 2012
SALES (est): 386.47K **Privately Held**
Web: www.signarama.com
SIC: **3993** Signs and advertising specialties

(G-5778)
CAPE FEAR CABINET CO INC
2908 Fort Bragg Rd (28303-4725)
PHONE.....................910 703-8760
William Konen, *Pr*
EMP: 10 EST: 2016
SALES (est): 268.21K **Privately Held**
Web: www.capefearcabinets.com
SIC: **2434** Wood kitchen cabinets

(G-5779)
CAPE FEAR MUSIC CENTER LLC
150 Rowan St (28301-4920)
P.O. Box 195 (28302-0195)
PHONE.....................910 480-2362
Jeffrey Stone, *Prin*

Fayetteville - Cumberland County (G-5780) GEOGRAPHIC SECTION

EMP: 5 **EST:** 2007
SALES (est): 422.54K **Privately Held**
Web: www.capefearmusiccenter.com
SIC: 3931 Musical instruments

(G-5780)
CAPE FEAR ORTHTICS PRSTHTICS I
435 W Russell St (28301-5576)
P.O. Box 58611 (28305-8611)
PHONE..................................910 483-0933
Demetri Sleem, *Prin*
EMP: 8 **EST:** 1999
SALES (est): 946.96K **Privately Held**
Web: www.cfop.org
SIC: 5999 3842 8093 Orthopedic and prosthesis applications; Prosthetic appliances; Specialty outpatient clinics, nec

(G-5781)
CAPITOL BUMPER (PA)
126 Drake St (28301-4710)
PHONE..................................919 772-7330
Curtis Rogers, *Mgr*
EMP: 8 **EST:** 2003
SALES (est): 1.16MM
SALES (corp-wide): 1.16MM **Privately Held**
SIC: 3471 Rechroming auto bumpers

(G-5782)
CAPITOL BUMPER
Also Called: Capital Bumper
126 Drake St (28301-4710)
PHONE..................................919 772-7330
Curtis Rogers, *Mgr*
EMP: 7
SQ FT: 6,000
SALES (corp-wide): 1.16MM **Privately Held**
SIC: 3471 5013 Rechroming auto bumpers; Motor vehicle supplies and new parts
PA: Capitol Bumper
126 Drake St
Fayetteville NC 28301
919 772-7330

(G-5783)
CARGILL INCORPORATED
Cargill
1754 River Rd (28312-7362)
PHONE..................................800 227-4455
Walker Humpries, *Mgr*
EMP: 76
SQ FT: 17,778
SALES (corp-wide): 176.74B **Privately Held**
Web: www.cargill.com
SIC: 2075 2099 Soybean oil mills; Food preparations, nec
PA: Cargill, Incorporated
15407 Mcginty Rd W
Wayzata MN 55391
800 227-4455

(G-5784)
CAROLINA PWR SIGNALIZATION LLC
Also Called: Carolina Signals and Lightings
1416 Middle River Loop (28312-9182)
P.O. Box 53650 (28305-3650)
PHONE..................................910 323-5589
Garrett L Fulcher, *Pr*
Brian L Fulcher, *VP*
EMP: 22 **EST:** 2008
SQ FT: 1,100
SALES (est): 10.19MM
SALES (corp-wide): 20.88B **Publicly Held**
Web: www.carolinapowerandsignalization.com
SIC: 3669 Traffic signals, electric
PA: Quanta Services, Inc.
2727 North Loop W Ste 100
Houston TX 77008
713 629-7600

(G-5785)
CAROLINA TRADER
458 Whitfield St (28306-1614)
PHONE..................................910 433-2229
EMP: 4 **EST:** 2019
SALES (est): 67.53K **Privately Held**
Web: www.carolina-trader.com
SIC: 2711 Newspapers, publishing and printing

(G-5786)
CBA PRODUCTIONS INC
Also Called: Nomadic State of Mind
579 Baywood Rd (28312-8470)
PHONE..................................703 568-4758
Chris Anderson, *Pr*
▲ **EMP:** 6 **EST:** 2007
SALES (est): 485.63K **Privately Held**
Web: www.nomadicstateofmind.com
SIC: 3021 Sandals, rubber

(G-5787)
CCBCC OPERATIONS LLC
Also Called: Coca-Cola
800 Tom Starling Rd (28306-8100)
PHONE..................................910 483-6158
EMP: 75
SQ FT: 45,333
SALES (corp-wide): 6.65B **Publicly Held**
Web: www.coca-cola.com
SIC: 2086 Bottled and canned soft drinks
HQ: Ccbcc Operations, Llc
4100 Coca Cola Plz
Charlotte NC 28211
704 364-8728

(G-5788)
CHEMOURS COMPANY
22828 Nc Highway 87 W (28306-7332)
PHONE..................................910 483-4681
EMP: 33
SALES (corp-wide): 6.79B **Publicly Held**
Web: www.chemours.com
SIC: 2879 Agricultural chemicals, nec
PA: The Chemours Company
1007 Market St
Wilmington DE 19898
302 773-1000

(G-5789)
CHEMOURS COMPANY FC LLC
22828 Nc Highway 87 W (28306-7332)
PHONE..................................910 678-1314
EMP: 115
SALES (corp-wide): 6.79B **Publicly Held**
Web: www.chemours.com
SIC: 2879 Agricultural chemicals, nec
HQ: The Chemours Company Fc Llc
1007 Market St
Wilmington DE 19898
302 773-1000

(G-5790)
CITYVIEW PUBLISHING LLC
Also Called: Cityview Magazine
2533 Raeford Rd Ste A (28305-5094)
P.O. Box 53967 (28305-3967)
PHONE..................................910 423-6500
Marshal Waren, *Pr*
EMP: 11 **EST:** 2008
SALES (est): 1.17MM **Privately Held**
Web: www.cityviewnc.com
SIC: 2721 Magazines: publishing only, not printed on site

(G-5791)
CJK CUSTOM PRINTING AND D
2110 Murchison Rd Unit A (28301-3644)
PHONE..................................910 488-1288
EMP: 5 **EST:** 2018
SALES (est): 207.97K **Privately Held**
SIC: 2752 Commercial printing, lithographic

(G-5792)
CLEAR PATH RECYCLING LLC
3500 Cedar Creek Rd (28312-7981)
PHONE..................................877 387-3738
EMP: 7 **EST:** 2009
SALES (est): 82.58K **Privately Held**
SIC: 2611 Pulp mills, mechanical and recycling processing

(G-5793)
COLLIERS WELDING LLC
773 Mary Jordan Ln (28311-7076)
PHONE..................................910 818-5728
EMP: 4 **EST:** 2009
SALES (est): 130K **Privately Held**
SIC: 3441 Fabricated structural metal

(G-5794)
CONCRETE SERVICE CO INC (HQ)
130 Builders Blvd (28301-4703)
P.O. Box 1867 (28302-1867)
PHONE..................................910 483-0396
Richard R Allen Senior, *Pr*
Jerry King, *
Richard R Allen Junior, *VP*
EMP: 40 **EST:** 1965
SQ FT: 4,500
SALES: 15.02MM
SALES (corp-wide): 50.62MM **Privately Held**
Web: www.concreteservice.com
SIC: 3273 5032 Ready-mixed concrete; Aggregate
PA: D.R. Allen & Son, Inc.
130 Builders Blvd
Fayetteville NC 28301
910 323-8509

(G-5795)
CONNECTED 2K LLC
Also Called: Sign Manufacturing
1015 Robeson St Ste 103 (28305-5635)
PHONE..................................910 321-7446
EMP: 4 **EST:** 2017
SALES (est): 242.58K **Privately Held**
Web: www.signarama.com
SIC: 3993 7336 5999 1799 Signs and advertising specialties; Graphic arts and related design; Banners, flags, decals, and posters; Sign installation and maintenance

(G-5796)
COOPERS FAYETTEVILLE INC
1326 Sapona Rd (28312-6221)
PHONE..................................910 483-0606
Thomas E Cooper Junior, *Prin*
EMP: 10 **EST:** 2006
SALES (est): 166.01K **Privately Held**
SIC: 3465 Body parts, automobile: stamped metal

(G-5797)
COUNCIL TRNSP & LOGISTICS LLC
6217 Rhemish Dr (28304-4751)
PHONE..................................910 322-7588
EMP: 5
SALES (est): 222.74K **Privately Held**
SIC: 2519 7389 Household furniture, nec; Business Activities at Non-Commercial Site

(G-5798)
CRAZY INK STITCHES
2467 Powell St (28306-2970)
PHONE..................................910 964-2889
EMP: 4 **EST:** 2017
SALES (est): 48.09K **Privately Held**
SIC: 2395 Embroidery and art needlework

(G-5799)
CREATIVE STONE FYETTEVILLE INC (PA)
Also Called: Creative Stone
6253 Raeford Rd (28304-2425)
PHONE..................................910 491-1225
Richard Johnson, *CEO*
EMP: 12 **EST:** 2014
SQ FT: 10,000
SALES (est): 2.35MM
SALES (corp-wide): 2.35MM **Privately Held**
Web: www.creativestonenc.com
SIC: 5722 1752 7299 3281 Kitchens, complete (sinks, cabinets, etc.); Wood floor installation and refinishing; Home improvement and renovation contractor agency; Granite, cut and shaped

(G-5800)
CROWDER TRUCKING LLC
6776 Saint Julian Way (28314-5816)
PHONE..................................910 797-4163
Carlos D Crowder, *Pr*
EMP: 8 **EST:** 2005
SALES (est): 502.77K **Privately Held**
SIC: 4212 1611 1442 Local trucking, without storage; Highway and street construction; Construction sand and gravel

(G-5801)
CTS CLEANING SYSTEMS INC
2185 Angelia M St (28312-8398)
PHONE..................................910 483-5349
Fred R Adkins, *Pr*
Rodney Adkins, *Sec*
EMP: 6 **EST:** 1967
SALES (est): 1.64MM **Privately Held**
Web: www.ctsclean.com
SIC: 5087 5074 2841 Janitors' supplies; Water purification equipment; Soap and other detergents

(G-5802)
CUSTOM CREATIONS BY ELLEN
3210 Kentyre Dr (28303-5341)
PHONE..................................509 480-0263
EMP: 4 **EST:** 2015
SALES (est): 47.87K **Privately Held**
Web: www.custcreations.com
SIC: 2759 Screen printing

(G-5803)
CYBERMATRIX INC
1323 Carolee Ct (28314-6062)
PHONE..................................910 292-9370
Rick Boelke, *Prin*
EMP: 5 **EST:** 2017
SALES (est): 144.76K **Privately Held**
SIC: 3443 Fabricated plate work (boiler shop)

(G-5804)
DARLING INGREDIENTS INC
Cape Fear Feed Products Div
1309 Industrial Dr (28301-6323)
P.O. Box 1659 (28302-1659)
PHONE..................................910 483-0473
Reed Park, *Brnch Mgr*
EMP: 19
SALES (corp-wide): 6.53B **Publicly Held**
Web: www.darlingii.com

▲ = Import ▼ = Export
◆ = Import/Export

GEOGRAPHIC SECTION

Fayetteville - Cumberland County (G-5829)

SIC: 2048 2077 Feed concentrates; Tallow rendering, inedible
PA: Darling Ingredients Inc.
5601 N Macarthur Blvd
Irving TX 75038
972 717-0300

(G-5805)
DAY & NGHT CREAL BAR CLMBIA SC
2316 Foster Gwin Ln (28304-0488)
PHONE..................................719 323-8265
Danavon Morris, *Managing Member*
EMP: 10 **EST:** 2021
SALES (est): 400K **Privately Held**
SIC: 2024 Ice cream and frozen deserts

(G-5806)
DAY 3 LWNCARE LDSCPG PRFCTNIST
1637 Woodfield Rd (28303-3844)
PHONE..................................910 574-8422
Kenneth Haywood, *Pt*
Charles Peele, *Pt*
EMP: 8 **EST:** 2014
SALES (est): 484.23K **Privately Held**
SIC: 0782 3524 7389 Mowing services, lawn ; Edgers, lawn; Business Activities at Non-Commercial Site

(G-5807)
DAYTON METALS
P.O. Box 229 (28302-0229)
PHONE..................................937 615-9812
EMP: 5 **EST:** 2010
SALES (est): 183.12K **Privately Held**
SIC: 3444 Sheet metalwork

(G-5808)
DB NORTH CAROLINA HOLDINGS INC (HQ)
Also Called: Fayetteville Observer, The
458 Whitfield St (28316-1614)
P.O. Box 849 (28302-0849)
PHONE..................................910 323-4848
Robert Gruber, *Pr*
Jill Koonce, *VP*
EMP: 49 **EST:** 2015
SQ FT: 101,158
SALES (est): 119.59MM
SALES (corp-wide): 2.66B **Publicly Held**
Web: www.fayobserver.com
SIC: 2711 Newspapers, publishing and printing
PA: Gannett Co., Inc.
7950 Jones Branch Dr Fl 8
Mc Lean VA 22102
703 854-6000

(G-5809)
DEFENSE LOGISTICS SERVICES LLC
231 Meed Ct Ste 104 (28302-2076)
PHONE..................................703 449-1620
EMP: 238 **EST:** 2011
SALES (est): 423.48K **Publicly Held**
SIC: 3812 Search and navigation equipment
HQ: Lockheed Martin Integrated Systems, Llc
6801 Rockledge Dr
Bethesda MD 20817

(G-5810)
DELABY BRACE AND LIMB CO
405 Owen Dr (28304-3411)
P.O. Box 250 (28399-0250)
PHONE..................................910 484-2509
Joan Benner, *Pr*
Joan Benner, *Prin*
David Benner, *VP*
EMP: 5 **EST:** 2008

SALES (est): 263.69K **Privately Held**
SIC: 3842 Limbs, artificial

(G-5811)
DEM PARTY GURLS ENTRMT LLC
Also Called: D P G Entertainment
7582 Beverly Dr (28314-5998)
PHONE..................................910 964-3599
EMP: 4
SALES (est): 92.78K **Privately Held**
SIC: 3993 Signs and advertising specialties

(G-5812)
DIVERSE FLOORING SYSTEMS
2112 Birchcreft Dr (28304-0532)
PHONE..................................910 425-8915
Joseph Semprevivo, *Owner*
EMP: 6 **EST:** 1998
SQ FT: 5,000
SALES (est): 194.39K **Privately Held**
Web: www.mariotoscanoart.us
SIC: 3823 Flow instruments, industrial process type

(G-5813)
DUPONT TEIJIN FILMS
3216 Cedar Creek Rd (28312-7955)
PHONE..................................910 433-8200
Craig Leite, *Mgr*
EMP: 7 **EST:** 2018
SALES (est): 29.6K **Privately Held**
Web: www.dupontteijinfilms.com
SIC: 2821 Plastics materials and resins

(G-5814)
E-N-G MOBILE SYSTEMS LLC (HQ)
810 Tom Starling Rd (28306-8100)
PHONE..................................925 798-4060
EMP: 14 **EST:** 1977
SALES (est): 9.74MM
SALES (corp-wide): 12.27MM **Privately Held**
Web: www.e-n-g.com
SIC: 3711 Automobile assembly, including specialty automobiles
PA: Positiveid Corporation
1690 S Congress Ave # 201
Delray Beach FL 33445
561 805-8000

(G-5815)
EAST COAST BIOLOGICS
311 Wagoner Dr (28303-4646)
PHONE..................................717 919-9980
Rachael Buzzelli, *Prin*
EMP: 4 **EST:** 2017
SALES (est): 48.34K **Privately Held**
Web: www.eastcoastbiologics.com
SIC: 2834 Pharmaceutical preparations

(G-5816)
EAST COAST DESIGNS LLC
781 Tobermory Rd (28306-9447)
PHONE..................................910 865-1070
James Baker, *Owner*
EMP: 8 **EST:** 2007
SALES (est): 433.77K **Privately Held**
Web: www.eastcoastdesigns.org
SIC: 2759 Screen printing

(G-5817)
EATON CORPORATION
2900 Doc Bennett Rd (28306-9219)
PHONE..................................910 677-5375
John Stanpfel, *Mgr*
EMP: 370
Web: www.dix-eaton.com
SIC: 3625 Electric controls and control accessories, industrial
HQ: Eaton Corporation

1000 Eaton Blvd
Cleveland OH 44122
440 523-5000

(G-5818)
EDWIN REAVES
1630 Flintshire Rd (28304-4943)
PHONE..................................901 326-6382
Edwin Reaves, *Owner*
EMP: 8
SALES (est): 184.31K **Privately Held**
SIC: 1389 Construction, repair, and dismantling services

(G-5819)
EIDP INC
Also Called: Dupont
22828 Nc Highway 87 W (28306-7332)
PHONE..................................910 483-4681
Barry Hudson, *Brnch Mgr*
EMP: 99
SALES (corp-wide): 17.23B **Publicly Held**
Web: www.dupont.com
SIC: 2819 Industrial inorganic chemicals, nec
HQ: Eidp, Inc.
9330 Zionsville Rd
Indianapolis IN 46268
833 267-6382

(G-5820)
ELEVATE CLEANING SERVICE
2120 Fort Bragg Rd (28303-7030)
PHONE..................................347 928-4030
Misty Burch, *Owner*
EMP: 4 **EST:** 2021
SALES (est): 156.69K **Privately Held**
SIC: 2842 Cleaning or polishing preparations, nec

(G-5821)
ENERGETICS INC
Also Called: Electrotek
455 Hillsboro St (28301-4861)
P.O. Box 1864 (28302-1864)
PHONE..................................910 483-2581
David Phillips Junior, *Pr*
Dave K Phillips, *Sec*
EMP: 9 **EST:** 1973
SQ FT: 13,500
SALES (est): 980.02K **Privately Held**
Web: www.electrotek.biz
SIC: 7694 Electric motor repair

(G-5822)
F B PUBLICATIONS INC
909 S Mcpherson Church Rd (28303-5350)
P.O. Box 53461 (28305-3461)
PHONE..................................910 484-6200
Bill Bowman, *Pr*
EMP: 10 **EST:** 2000
SALES (est): 577.1K **Privately Held**
SIC: 2711 Newspapers

(G-5823)
FAYBLOCK MATERIALS INC
130 Builders Blvd (28301-4703)
P.O. Box 1867 (28302-1867)
PHONE..................................910 323-9198
Richard R Allen Junior, *Pr*
Larry Little, *
Jerry T King, *
Keith T Mcfadyen, *Sec*
▼ **EMP:** 100 **EST:** 1991
SALES (est): 17.65MM
SALES (corp-wide): 50.62MM **Privately Held**
Web: www.fayblock.com
SIC: 3272 4212 3271 Concrete products, nec ; Local trucking, without storage; Concrete block and brick
PA: D.R. Allen & Son, Inc.

130 Builders Blvd
Fayetteville NC 28301
910 323-8509

(G-5824)
FAYETTEVILLE PUBLISHING CO (DH)
Also Called: Fayetteville Observer, The
302 Worth St (28301-5632)
P.O. Box 1181 (27239-1181)
PHONE..................................910 323-4848
Charles W Broadwell, *Pr*
Virginia L Yarborough, *
▲ **EMP:** 52 **EST:** 1923
SALES (est): 37.23MM
SALES (corp-wide): 2.66B **Publicly Held**
Web: www.fayobserver.com
SIC: 2711 2791 2759 2752 Commercial printing and newspaper publishing combined; Typesetting; Commercial printing, nec; Commercial printing, lithographic
HQ: Db North Carolina Holdings, Inc.
458 Whitfield St
Fayetteville NC 28306
910 323-4848

(G-5825)
FIELDPROOF PRINTS LLC
439 Westwood Shopping Ctr Pmb 471 (28314-1532)
PHONE..................................270 313-8439
Anthony Kassinger, *Managing Member*
EMP: 5 **EST:** 2018
SALES (est): 83.91K **Privately Held**
SIC: 2752 Commercial printing, lithographic

(G-5826)
FORTEM GENUS INC
427 Franklin St (28301-6143)
P.O. Box 9159 (28311-9081)
PHONE..................................910 574-5214
Don Feeney, *CEO*
Donald Feeney, *Pr*
EMP: 9 **EST:** 2016
SALES (est): 265.25K **Privately Held**
Web: www.fortemgenus.com
SIC: 3711 Military motor vehicle assembly

(G-5827)
FOSTERSCAPE LLP
Also Called: Fosters Consulting
5694 Juneberry Ln (28304-4859)
PHONE..................................910 401-7638
Melissa Foster, *Pt*
Danny Foster, *Pt*
EMP: 7 **EST:** 2018
SALES (est): 287.74K **Privately Held**
SIC: 5149 0279 5999 0139 Honey; Apiary (bee and honey farm); Alarm and safety equipment stores

(G-5828)
FRANKEN WOODWORKING
7683 Wilkins Dr (28311-9260)
PHONE..................................910 488-6931
Dennis Franken, *Prin*
EMP: 5 **EST:** 2010
SALES (est): 149.75K **Privately Held**
SIC: 2431 Millwork

(G-5829)
FULCHER ELC FAYETTEVILLE INC
1744 Middle River Loop (28312-7366)
P.O. Box 2799 (28302-2799)
PHONE..................................910 483-7772
Frances Fulcher, *Pr*
EMP: 40 **EST:** 1993
SQ FT: 5,000
SALES (est): 4.65MM **Privately Held**
Web: www.fulcherelectric.com

Fayetteville - Cumberland County (G-5830) GEOGRAPHIC SECTION

SIC: 3669 Traffic signals, electric

(G-5830)
GOODYEAR TIRE & RUBBER COMPANY
Goodyear
6650 Ramsey St (28311-9318)
PHONE....................910 488-9295
James R Konneker, *Manager*
EMP: 87
SALES (corp-wide): 20.07MM **Publicly Held**
Web: www.goodyear.com
SIC: 3011 Agricultural inner tubes
PA: The Goodyear Tire & Rubber Company
200 E Innovation Way
Akron OH 44316
330 796-2121

(G-5831)
GRAHAMS TRANSPORTATION LLC ✪
Also Called: Trucking
6642 Keeler Dr (28303-2325)
PHONE....................910 627-6880
Peter Graham, *CEO*
EMP: 4 **EST:** 2022
SALES (est): 159.56K **Privately Held**
SIC: 3711 7389 Truck tractors for highway use, assembly of; Business services, nec

(G-5832)
H C PRODUCTION CO
218 Tolar St (28306-1534)
PHONE....................910 483-5267
Judy Hart, *Owner*
EMP: 7 **EST:** 2001
SALES (est): 470.04K **Privately Held**
SIC: 3549 3629 Assembly machines, including robotic; Electrical industrial apparatus, nec

(G-5833)
HAWTHORNE SERVICES
1 Fort Bragg (28307-5000)
PHONE....................910 436-9013
Dan Lawson, *Genl Mgr*
EMP: 10 **EST:** 2002
SALES (est): 187.12K **Privately Held**
SIC: 3721 Aircraft

(G-5834)
HEAT PRESS UNLIMITED LLC ✪
6595 Stillwater Dr (28304-4609)
PHONE....................910 273-6831
EMP: 5 **EST:** 2022
SALES (est): 76.29K **Privately Held**
Web: www.heatpressunlimited.shop
SIC: 2741 Miscellaneous publishing

(G-5835)
HECKLER BREWING COMPANY
5780 Ramsey St Ste 110 (28311-1414)
PHONE....................910 748-0085
Daniel Miller, *Pr*
EMP: 6 **EST:** 2020
SALES (est): 265.37K **Privately Held**
Web: www.hecklerbeer.com
SIC: 2082 Malt beverages

(G-5836)
HEFTY CONCRETE INC
309 Ivan Dr (28306-3308)
PHONE....................910 483-1598
Rafael Valdez, *Pr*
EMP: 8 **EST:** 2002
SALES (est): 126.7K **Privately Held**
SIC: 3271 Blocks, concrete or cinder: standard

(G-5837)
HERCULES STEEL COMPANY INC (PA)
950 Country Club Dr (28301-2904)
P.O. Box 35208 (28303-0208)
PHONE....................910 488-5110
Lewis Jourden, *Pr*
H C Bud Gore Junior, *VP*
Robert Petroski, *
EMP: 50 **EST:** 1954
SQ FT: 8,000
SALES (est): 9.02MM
SALES (corp-wide): 9.02MM **Privately Held**
Web: www.herculessteelco.com
SIC: 3441 5051 Building components, structural steel; Steel

(G-5838)
HEXION INC
Also Called: Borden
1411 Industrial Dr (28301-6325)
PHONE....................910 483-1311
EMP: 23
SQ FT: 2,926
SALES (corp-wide): 1.26B **Privately Held**
Web: www.hexion.com
SIC: 2899 2869 2821 Chemical preparations, nec; Industrial organic chemicals, nec; Plastics materials and resins
PA: Hexion Inc.
180 E Broad St
Columbus OH 43215
888 443-9466

(G-5839)
HIGHLAND PAVING CO LLC
1351 Wilmington Hwy (28306-3005)
P.O. Box 1843 (28302-1843)
PHONE....................910 482-0080
EMP: 95 **EST:** 2003
SALES (est): 26.15MM **Privately Held**
Web: www.highlandpaving.com
SIC: 1611 2951 Highway and street paving contractor; Asphalt and asphaltic paving mixtures (not from refineries)

(G-5840)
ICAN CLOTHES COMPANY
1617 Owen Dr (28304-3425)
P.O. Box 25433 (28314-5007)
PHONE....................910 670-1494
Shannon Battle, *CEO*
Kelsey Battle, *VP*
EMP: 12 **EST:** 2016
SQ FT: 5,000
SALES (est): 746.67K **Privately Held**
SIC: 2339 2329 2326 7218 Women's and misses' athletic clothing and sportswear; Athletic clothing, except uniforms: men's, youths' and boys'; Men's and boy's work clothing; Work clothing supply

(G-5841)
INDUSTRIAL POWER INC (PA)
703 Whitfield St (28306-1617)
PHONE....................910 483-4230
William Merritt, *Pr*
Mike Hillenbrand, *VP*
▼ **EMP:** 7 **EST:** 1997
SQ FT: 1,250
SALES (est): 4.79MM **Privately Held**
Web: www.industrialpowerinc.com
SIC: 3052 Rubber hose

(G-5842)
INDUSTRIAL WELDING &
5936 Tabor Church Rd (28312-7377)
PHONE....................910 309-8540
EMP: 4 **EST:** 2011

SALES (est): 46.38K **Privately Held**
SIC: 7692 Welding repair

(G-5843)
INKWELL
2823 Bragg Blvd (28303-4173)
PHONE....................919 433-7539
James Vinson, *Prin*
EMP: 5 **EST:** 2018
SALES (est): 88.26K **Privately Held**
Web: www.theinkwellusa.com
SIC: 2752 Offset printing

(G-5844)
J&R PRECISION HEATING AND AIR
1625 Cumberland Dr (28311-1283)
PHONE....................910 480-8322
Richard Ford, *Pr*
EMP: 4 **EST:** 2017
SALES (est): 190.46K **Privately Held**
SIC: 3585 Heating and air conditioning combination units

(G-5845)
JAMES KING
Also Called: Tactical Mobility Training
9998 Fayetteville Rd (28304-5969)
PHONE....................910 308-8818
James King, *Prin*
James King, *Owner*
EMP: 6 **EST:** 2000
SQ FT: 10,000
SALES (est): 312.86K **Privately Held**
Web: www.tacticalmobilitytraining.com
SIC: 8748 9711 3751 Safety training service; Military training schools; Frames, motorcycle and bicycle

(G-5846)
JASIE BLANKS LLC
Also Called: Wholesale
3725 Ramsey St Ste 103c (28311-7669)
PHONE....................910 485-0016
Sheri Fowler, *Pr*
▲ **EMP:** 16 **EST:** 2015
SALES (est): 1.51MM **Privately Held**
Web: www.jasieblanks.com
SIC: 7371 7389 3944 5111 Computer software development and applications; Business services, nec; Craft and hobby kits and sets; Printing paper

(G-5847)
JB-ISECURITY LLC
505 Toxaway Ct (28314-0956)
PHONE....................910 824-7601
Joseph Jenifer, *CEO*
EMP: 5 **EST:** 2021
SALES (est): 250K **Privately Held**
SIC: 3581 Automatic vending machines

(G-5848)
JEFF ANDERSON
3741 Butler Nursery Rd (28306-7925)
PHONE....................910 481-8923
Jeff Anderson, *Prin*
EMP: 4 **EST:** 2017
SALES (est): 87.26K **Privately Held**
SIC: 3711 Motor vehicles and car bodies

(G-5849)
JFK CONFERENCES LLC
322 Ridgeway Ct (28311-0370)
PHONE....................980 255-3336
EMP: 26 **EST:** 2020
SALES (est): 532.79K **Privately Held**
Web: www.jfkdallasconference.com
SIC: 7389 2731 Business services, nec; Books, publishing only

(G-5850)
JO-NATTA TRANSPORTATION LLC
348 Foothill Ln (28311-6317)
PHONE....................888 424-8789
EMP: 6 **EST:** 2011
SALES (est): 200K **Privately Held**
SIC: 3799 Transportation equipment, nec

(G-5851)
JUNK FOOD CLOTHING INC
1 Soffe Dr (28312-5262)
P.O. Box 2507 (28302-2507)
PHONE....................910 483-2500
James F Soffe, *CEO*
EMP: 125 **EST:** 2008
SALES (est): 1.56MM
SALES (corp-wide): 415.35MM **Publicly Held**
SIC: 2339 Athletic clothing: women's, misses', and juniors'
HQ: M. J. Soffe Co.
1 Soffe Dr
Fayetteville NC 28312
910 435-3138

(G-5852)
K & L RESOURCES
7809 Gallant Ridge Dr (28314-6219)
PHONE....................910 494-3736
Keith Howard, *Owner*
EMP: 9 **EST:** 2003
SALES (est): 177.95K **Privately Held**
SIC: 7349 3676 Janitorial service, contract basis; Resistor networks

(G-5853)
K FORMULA ENTERPRISES INC
829 Gillespie St Ste A (28306-1555)
PHONE....................910 323-3315
Ronald L Formulak, *Pr*
EMP: 5 **EST:** 1979
SQ FT: 1,500
SALES (est): 358.14K **Privately Held**
Web: www.faynet.com
SIC: 2261 5699 Screen printing of cotton broadwoven fabrics; T-shirts, custom printed

(G-5854)
KEYTUNE MUS PUBG WRLD WIDE LLC
505 Cypress Trace Dr (28314-1089)
PHONE....................910 286-7868
Roosevelt Harmon Junior, *Managing Member*
EMP: 4 **EST:** 2020
SALES (est): 63.91K **Privately Held**
SIC: 2741 Miscellaneous publishing

(G-5855)
KRAKEN-SKULLS
Also Called: Barber Shop AP Screen Prtg
822 Shannon Dr (28303-3950)
PHONE....................910 500-9100
Chadwick Mckeown, *Owner*
Chadwick Mckeown, *Managing Member*
EMP: 12 **EST:** 2019
SALES (est): 96.81K **Privately Held**
Web: www.kraken-skulls.com
SIC: 7241 2395 7299 2759 Barber shops; Embroidery and art needlework; Tattoo parlor; Screen printing

(G-5856)
KUNTRYS SOUL-FOOD & BBQ LLC
418 Minnow Ct (28312-6549)
PHONE....................910 797-0766
Monroe Junior, *Managing Member*
EMP: 6
SALES (est): 230.93K **Privately Held**

GEOGRAPHIC SECTION

Fayetteville - Cumberland County (G-5881)

SIC: 2599 Food wagons, restaurant

(G-5857)
L C INDUSTRIES INC
4525 Campground Rd (28314-1435)
PHONE..................................919 596-8277
Tina Watson, *Mgr*
EMP: 200
SALES (corp-wide): 7.49MM **Privately Held**
Web: www.lcindustries.com
SIC: 5943 2675 2515 Office forms and supplies; Folders, filing, die-cut: made from purchased materials; Mattresses and foundations
PA: L C Industries Inc.
   4500 Emperor Blvd
   Durham NC 27703
   919 596-8277

(G-5858)
LA SKY CREATIONS LLC ✪
3930 Bardstown Ct Apt 103 (28304-0815)
PHONE..................................516 996-1231
EMP: 4 EST: 2023
SALES (est): 79.3K **Privately Held**
SIC: 2389 Apparel and accessories, nec

(G-5859)
LARRY S SAUSAGE COMPANY
1624 Middle River Loop (28312-7365)
P.O. Box 4 (28302-0004)
PHONE..................................910 483-5148
Larry Godwin, *CEO*
Sheila Abe, *
EMP: 35 EST: 1952
SQ FT: 32,000
SALES (est): 4.26MM **Privately Held**
Web: www.larryssausage.com
SIC: 2013 Sausages, from purchased meat

(G-5860)
LET IT FLO LLC
3522 Harrisburg Dr (28306-4573)
PHONE..................................717 421-3754
Bradley K Lewis, *Owner*
EMP: 4 EST: 2018
SALES (est): 59.1K **Privately Held**
SIC: 3999 Hair and hair-based products

(G-5861)
LN WOODWORKS
3210 Kentyre Dr (28303-5341)
PHONE..................................509 480-0263
Ellen Newbauer, *Prin*
EMP: 5 EST: 2016
SALES (est): 54.13K **Privately Held**
SIC: 2431 Millwork

(G-5862)
LUXOTTICA OF AMERICA INC
Also Called: Lenscrafters
302 Cross Creek Mall (28303-7242)
PHONE..................................910 867-0200
Steven Earwood, *Brnch Mgr*
EMP: 4
SALES (corp-wide): 2.55MM **Privately Held**
Web: www.luxottica.com
SIC: 5995 3851 Eyeglasses, prescription; Ophthalmic goods
HQ: Luxottica Of America Inc.
   4000 Luxottica Pl
   Mason OH 45040

(G-5863)
M J SOFFE CO (HQ)
Also Called: Mj Soffe
1 Soffe Dr (28312-5262)
P.O. Box 2507 (28302-2507)
PHONE..................................910 435-3138
Steve Cochran, *Pr*
Tony Cimaglia, *
John Mabry, *
◆ EMP: 800 EST: 1946
SQ FT: 750,000
SALES (est): 146.62MM
SALES (corp-wide): 415.35MM **Publicly Held**
Web: www.soffe.com
SIC: 2339 2329 2369 2321 Athletic clothing: women's, misses', and juniors'; Athletic clothing, except uniforms: men's, youths' and boys'; Girl's and children's outerwear, nec; Men's and boy's furnishings
PA: Delta Apparel, Inc.
   2750 Premiere Pkwy # 100
   Duluth GA 30097
   678 775-6900

(G-5864)
MANN+HMMEL PRLATOR FILTERS LLC (DH)
Also Called: Oe Filters
3200 Natal St Ste 64069 (28306-2845)
P.O. Box 64069 (28306-0069)
PHONE..................................910 425-4181
Kurk Wilks, *Pr*
Marion Grill, *
Matt Cloninger, *
Joel Ihrig, *
◆ EMP: 21 EST: 2006
SQ FT: 680,000
SALES (est): 312.75MM
SALES (corp-wide): 5.01B **Privately Held**
SIC: 3714 Motor vehicle parts and accessories
HQ: Mann + Hummel Holding Gmbh
   Schwieberdinger Str. 126
   Ludwigsburg BW 71636
   7141980

(G-5865)
MANN+HMMEL PRLATOR FILTERS LLC
Facet Purolator
3200 Natal St (28306-2845)
P.O. Box 64069 (28306-0069)
PHONE..................................910 425-4181
Rob Malone, *Mgr*
EMP: 121
SALES (corp-wide): 5.01B **Privately Held**
SIC: 3714 Motor vehicle parts and accessories
HQ: Mann+Hummel Purolator Filters Llc
   3200 Natal St Ste 64069
   Fayetteville NC 28306

(G-5866)
MARK STODDARD
Also Called: Lava Cable
1935 Brawley Ave (28314-8491)
PHONE..................................910 797-7214
Mark Stoddard, *Owner*
EMP: 5 EST: 2009
SALES (est): 419.03K **Privately Held**
SIC: 3355 7389 Aluminum wire and cable; Business services, nec

(G-5867)
MARTINS FMOUS PSTRY SHOPPE INC
2320 Southern Ave (28306-2260)
PHONE..................................800 548-1200
EMP: 5
SALES (corp-wide): 149.7MM **Privately Held**
Web: www.potatorolls.com
SIC: 2051 Rolls, bread type: fresh or frozen
PA: Martin's Famous Pastry Shoppe, Inc.
   1000 Potato Roll Ln
   Chambersburg PA 17202
   800 548-1200

(G-5868)
MASS CONNECTION INC
Also Called: King Signs
2828 Enterprise Ave (28306-2005)
PHONE..................................910 424-0940
Dean Holzinger, *Pr*
EMP: 9 EST: 2003
SALES (est): 763.14K **Privately Held**
Web: www.kingsignsnc.com
SIC: 3953 1611 2759 Stationery embossers, personal; Highway signs and guardrails; Promotional printing

(G-5869)
MASTER TOW INC
783 Slocomb Rd (28311-9367)
PHONE..................................910 630-2000
John W Tart, *Pr*
Joi-anna Tart, *Sec*
▲ EMP: 30 EST: 1991
SQ FT: 14,000
SALES (est): 4.49MM **Privately Held**
Web: www.mastertow.com
SIC: 3715 3714 3537 Trailer bodies; Third axle attachments or six wheel units for motor vehicles; Industrial trucks and tractors

(G-5870)
MATTRESS FIRM
1920 Skibo Rd (28314-1514)
PHONE..................................910 868-0950
EMP: 6 EST: 2014
SALES (est): 76.08K **Privately Held**
Web: www.mattressfirm.com
SIC: 5712 5021 2515 Mattresses; Mattresses; Mattresses and bedsprings

(G-5871)
MCCUNE TECHNOLOGY INC
Also Called: Fayetteville Steel
4801 Research Dr (28306-8149)
P.O. Box 53834 (28305-3834)
PHONE..................................910 424-2978
David M Mccune Senior, *Pr*
David Mccune Junior, *VP*
EMP: 16 EST: 1976
SQ FT: 27,450
SALES (est): 2.38MM **Privately Held**
Web: www.mccune1.com
SIC: 3441 5051 3444 3443 Building components, structural steel; Steel; Sheet metalwork; Fabricated plate work (boiler shop)

(G-5872)
MERITOR INC
3200 Natal St (28306-2845)
PHONE..................................910 425-4181
Richard Pitt, *Brnch Mgr*
EMP: 13
SALES (corp-wide): 34.06B **Publicly Held**
Web: www.meritor.com
SIC: 3714 Filters: oil, fuel, and air, motor vehicle
HQ: Meritor, Inc.
   2135 W Maple Rd
   Troy MI 48084

(G-5873)
MICHAELS CREAMERY INC
439 Westwood Shopping Ctr Ste 148 (28314-1532)
PHONE..................................910 292-4172
EMP: 5 EST: 2011
SALES (est): 372.13K **Privately Held**
SIC: 2021 Creamery butter

(G-5874)
MIKES CORE & BATTERY INC
119 Drake St (28301-4709)
PHONE..................................910 920-4490
EMP: 7 EST: 2011
SALES (est): 423.82K **Privately Held**
SIC: 3621 Storage battery chargers, motor and engine generator type

(G-5875)
MIND FLOW PUBG & PROD LLC
1784 Inverness Dr (28304-4951)
PHONE..................................910 339-0005
Carlette Whitlock, *Prin*
EMP: 4 EST: 2018
SALES (est): 88.78K **Privately Held**
Web: www.mindflowpublishingproduction.com
SIC: 2741 Miscellaneous publishing

(G-5876)
MITER POINT LLC
6423 Greyfield Rd (28303-2120)
PHONE..................................910 864-3645
EMP: 5 EST: 2015
SALES (est): 80.59K **Privately Held**
SIC: 2431 Millwork

(G-5877)
MOFFITT MACHINE COMPANY INC
232 Winslow St (28301-5594)
PHONE..................................910 485-2159
John Marshall, *Pr*
Marie Marshall, *VP*
EMP: 5 EST: 1944
SQ FT: 5,700
SALES (est): 486.28K **Privately Held**
Web: www.moffittmachine.com
SIC: 3599 Machine shop, jobbing and repair

(G-5878)
MSE BEAUTYSHAPEWEAR LLC
511 N Reilly Rd Ste A-90 (28303-2440)
PHONE..................................910 500-0179
EMP: 5 EST: 2017
SALES (est): 186.2K **Privately Held**
SIC: 2339 Women's and misses' outerwear, nec

(G-5879)
MURIEL HARRIS INVESTMENTS INC
Also Called: M H Investments
3900 Murchison Rd (28311)
PHONE..................................800 932-3191
EMP: 10 EST: 2012
SALES (est): 760K **Privately Held**
SIC: 3334 1761 3312 3444 Primary aluminum; Architectural sheet metal work; Bars and bar shapes, steel, cold-finished: own hot-rolled; Pipe, sheet metal

(G-5880)
NBC ENTERPRISES INC
Also Called: NBC
2905 Bakers Mill Rd (28306-8273)
PHONE..................................910 705-5781
Nathan Pate, *Prin*
EMP: 10 EST: 2018
SALES (est): 641.51K **Privately Held**
Web: nbcenterprisesinc.business.site
SIC: 1623 1731 1629 1381 Telephone and communication line construction; Fiber optic cable installation; Trenching contractor; Directional drilling oil and gas wells

(G-5881)
NEED T-SHIRTS NOW
1830 Owen Dr (28304-1611)
PHONE..................................910 644-0455
EMP: 4 EST: 2018

Fayetteville - Cumberland County (G-5882)

SALES (est): 184.94K **Privately Held**
Web: www.needtshirtsnow.com
SIC: 2759 Screen printing

(G-5882)
NEXT MAGAZINE
458 Whitfield St (28306-1614)
PHONE..................910 609-0638
Charles Broadwell, *Pr*
EMP: 6 EST: 2005
SALES (est): 299.94K **Privately Held**
Web: www.next-magazine.com
SIC: 2711 Newspapers, publishing and printing

(G-5883)
NITTA GELATIN USA INC
4341 Production Dr (28306-9513)
PHONE..................910 484-0457
Raymond Merz, *Pr*
Tsuneo Sasaki, *
Hiroshi Takase, *
▲ EMP: 25 EST: 2004
SALES (est): 9.14MM **Privately Held**
Web: www.nitta-gelatin.com
SIC: 2899 Gelatin
PA: Nitta Gelatin Holdings, Inc.
  598 Airport Blvd Ste 900
  Morrisville NC 27560

(G-5884)
NORTH CRLINA LCENSE PLATE AGCY
815 Elm St (28303-4151)
PHONE..................910 485-1590
Marilyn Cullison, *Owner*
EMP: 5 EST: 2002
SALES (est): 305.81K **Privately Held**
SIC: 3469 Automobile license tags, stamped metal

(G-5885)
OFF ROAD ADDICTION
2090 Angelia M St (28312-9403)
PHONE..................910 620-4675
EMP: 5 EST: 2019
SALES (est): 94.28K **Privately Held**
SIC: 3465 Body parts, automobile: stamped metal

(G-5886)
OHERNS WELDING INC
5379 Butler Nursery Rd (28306-7696)
PHONE..................910 484-2087
Michael Lewis O'hern, *Pr*
EMP: 7 EST: 2004
SALES (est): 805.15K **Privately Held**
Web: www.ohernswelding.com
SIC: 7692 Welding repair

(G-5887)
OLDCASTLE INFRASTRUCTURE INC
3960 Cedar Creek Rd (28312-7965)
PHONE..................910 433-2931
EMP: 13
SALES (corp-wide): 32.72B **Privately Held**
Web: www.oldcastleinfrastructure.com
SIC: 3272 Concrete products, nec
HQ: Oldcastle Infrastructure, Inc.
  7000 Central Pkwy Ste 800
  Atlanta GA 30328
  770 270-5000

(G-5888)
ONE STOP SHIPG & PRTG ETC LLC
3308 Bragg Blvd Ste 108 (28303-3900)
PHONE..................910 745-9733
EMP: 5 EST: 2019
SALES (est): 127.47K **Privately Held**

SIC: 2752 Commercial printing, lithographic

(G-5889)
OPERATION WHEELCHAIR
538 Mayview St (28306-1750)
PHONE..................910 391-1945
George Butterfly, *Prin*
EMP: 5 EST: 2015
SALES (est): 104.88K **Privately Held**
SIC: 3842 Wheelchairs

(G-5890)
OS PRESS LLC
Also Called: International Minute Press
1005 Arsenal Ave (28305-5329)
PHONE..................910 485-7955
EMP: 5 EST: 2009
SALES (est): 501.01K **Privately Held**
Web: fayetteville.intlminutepress.com
SIC: 2752 Commercial printing, lithographic

(G-5891)
PACKIQ LLC
Also Called: Packiq
800 Technology Dr Ste 110 (28306-9417)
PHONE..................910 964-4331
Mark Beck, *CEO*
EMP: 29
Web: www.packiq.com
SIC: 3441 Fabricated structural metal
PA: Packiq, Llc
  1 American Way
  Anderson SC 29621

(G-5892)
PAINTED CANVAS
3809 Heartpine Dr (28306-7431)
PHONE..................770 331-2462
Keisha Clay, *Prin*
EMP: 4 EST: 2018
SALES (est): 46.58K **Privately Held**
SIC: 2211 Canvas

(G-5893)
PAPA PARUSOS FOODS INC
716 Whitfield St (28306-1618)
P.O. Box 1328 (28302-1328)
PHONE..................910 484-8801
EMP: 16 EST: 1989
SQ FT: 35,000
SIC: 2032 Italian foods, nec: packaged in cans, jars, etc.

(G-5894)
PARK SHIRT COMPANY
321 E Russell St (28301-5743)
PHONE..................931 879-5894
Rajan Shamdasani, *Prin*
▲ EMP: 13 EST: 2000
SQ FT: 20,000
SALES (est): 254.06K **Privately Held**
SIC: 2253 Knit outerwear mills

(G-5895)
PEACHES ENTERPRISES INC
Also Called: Painting By Bill
1014 Cain Rd (28303-4017)
P.O. Box 35636 (28303-0636)
PHONE..................910 868-5800
Kenneth Hardin, *Pr*
Catherine Wagner, *Sec*
EMP: 8 EST: 1977
SALES (est): 178.01K **Privately Held**
SIC: 1721 3993 Residential painting; Signs and advertising specialties

(G-5896)
PEDAL 2 METAL LLP
2069 Osceola Dr (28301-3831)
PHONE..................910 723-2289

Anthony Holmes, *Owner*
EMP: 4 EST: 2017
SALES (est): 51.63K **Privately Held**
SIC: 3499 Fabricated metal products, nec

(G-5897)
PETER J HAMANN
Also Called: Arcright Welding Service
337 Mcmillan St (28301-5503)
PHONE..................910 484-7877
Peter J Hamann, *Owner*
EMP: 8 EST: 2000
SALES (est): 643.78K **Privately Held**
SIC: 3356 7692 3444 Welding rods; Welding repair; Sheet metalwork

(G-5898)
PONDEROSA NEWS LLC
5338 Plateau Ct (28303-3311)
PHONE..................910 867-6571
Ivan Washington, *Prin*
EMP: 4 EST: 2015
SALES (est): 97.66K **Privately Held**
SIC: 2711 Newspapers: publishing only, not printed on site

(G-5899)
PPG ARCHITECTURAL FINISHES INC
Also Called: Glidden Professional Paint Ctr
894 Elm St Ste A (28303-4384)
PHONE..................910 484-5161
Tj Beasley, *Brnch Mgr*
EMP: 4
SALES (corp-wide): 17.65B **Publicly Held**
Web: www.ppg.com
SIC: 2851 Paints and allied products
HQ: Ppg Architectural Finishes, Inc.
  1 Ppg Pl
  Pittsburgh PA 15272
  412 434-3131

(G-5900)
PRIMA ELEMENTS LLC
124 Anderson St (28301-5014)
PHONE..................910 483-8406
Hilda Burgos, *Mgr*
EMP: 7 EST: 2012
SALES (est): 583.75K **Privately Held**
Web: www.primaelements.org
SIC: 3556 7999 8299 Juice extractors, fruit and vegetable: commercial type; Yoga instruction; Meditation therapy

(G-5901)
PRINT USA INC
505 S Eastern Blvd (28301-6313)
P.O. Box 43352 (28309-3352)
PHONE..................910 485-2254
Harriett Shooter, *Pr*
EMP: 5 EST: 2003
SQ FT: 20,000
SALES (est): 468.15K **Privately Held**
Web: www.printusa.com
SIC: 2752 Offset printing

(G-5902)
PRINT WORKS FAYETTEVILLE INC
Also Called: Allegra Print & Imaging
3724 Sycamore Dairy Rd Ste 100 (28303-3495)
PHONE..................910 864-8100
Bruce S Sykes, *Pr*
Kathy Sykes, *VP*
EMP: 7 EST: 1986
SQ FT: 2,400
SALES (est): 695.49K **Privately Held**
Web: www.allegramarketingprint.com
SIC: 2752 Offset printing

(G-5903)
QUALITY CONCRETE CO INC
1587 Wilmington Hwy (28306-3103)
P.O. Box 53413 (28305-3413)
PHONE..................910 483-7155
Marvin E Howell Junior, *Pr*
EMP: 16 EST: 1961
SQ FT: 1,200
SALES (est): 2.42MM **Privately Held**
Web: www.qualityconcreteco.com
SIC: 3273 Ready-mixed concrete

(G-5904)
R E MASON ENTERPRISES INC (PA)
Also Called: U-Teck
515 Person St (28301-5840)
P.O. Box 2484 (28302-2484)
PHONE..................910 483-5016
EMP: 9 EST: 1984
SALES (est): 4.73MM
SALES (corp-wide): 4.73MM **Privately Held**
SIC: 3661 5261 Telephone and telegraph apparatus; Lawn and garden equipment

(G-5905)
REID FOR READ PUBLISHING LLC
6402 Redcliff Dr (28311-2977)
PHONE..................910 263-8090
Aren M Reid, *Prin*
EMP: 4 EST: 2018
SALES (est): 70.24K **Privately Held**
Web: www.reidforread.com
SIC: 2741 Miscellaneous publishing

(G-5906)
RIVERSIDE MATTRESS CO INC
225 Dunn Rd (28312-5227)
PHONE..................910 483-0461
William T Allen, *Pr*
Nancy Allen, *
EMP: 35 EST: 1932
SQ FT: 60,000
SALES (est): 1.28MM **Privately Held**
Web: www.riversidemattressinc.com
SIC: 2515 Mattresses, innerspring or box spring

(G-5907)
RIZE LLC
1882 Spiralwood Dr (28304-0498)
PHONE..................910 487-9759
EMP: 4 EST: 2019
SALES (est): 71.52K **Privately Held**
SIC: 3429 Hardware, nec

(G-5908)
RK ENTERPRISES LLC
Also Called: James Ricks
121 N Racepath St (28301-5258)
P.O. Box 428 (28391-0428)
PHONE..................910 481-0777
Michael Sutton, *Prin*
Joshua Cain, *Prin*
James Ricks, *Prin*
▲ EMP: 4 EST: 2012
SALES (est): 134.24K **Privately Held**
SIC: 7699 3827 3083 Fire control (military) equipment repair; Optical instruments and apparatus; Laminated plastics plate and sheet

(G-5909)
ROBERT S CONCRETE SERVICE INC
508 Lamon St (28301-5158)
PHONE..................910 391-3973
Robert Mace Junior, *Owner*
EMP: 4 EST: 1966
SALES (est): 333.89K **Privately Held**

GEOGRAPHIC SECTION

Fayetteville - Cumberland County (G-5934)

SIC: 3273 Ready-mixed concrete

(G-5910)
RTD PRECISION LLC
7653 Spurge Dr (28311-9266)
PHONE.............................910 624-2624
Robert Timothy Davis, *Genl Mgr*
EMP: 4 EST: 2016
SALES (est): 151.92K **Privately Held**
SIC: 3489 Ordnance and accessories, nec

(G-5911)
S & W READY MIX CON CO LLC
1309 S Reilly Rd (28314-5513)
PHONE.............................910 864-0939
Earl Wells, *Brnch Mgr*
EMP: 19
SALES (corp-wide): 8.01MM **Privately Held**
Web: www.snwreadymix.com
SIC: 3273 Ready-mixed concrete
HQ: S & W Ready Mix Concrete Company Llc
217 Lisbon St
Clinton NC 28328
910 592-1733

(G-5912)
SCIENCE APPLICATIONS INTL CORP
4317 Ramsey St Ste 303 (28311-2161)
PHONE.............................910 822-2100
Karen Lounsberry, *Mgr*
EMP: 4
SALES (corp-wide): 7.7B **Publicly Held**
Web: www.saic.com
SIC: 7373 7372 Systems integration services; Prepackaged software
PA: Science Applications International Corporation
12010 Sunset Hills Rd
Reston VA 20190
703 676-4300

(G-5913)
SELECT MOLD SERVICE INC
419 Glidden St (28301-5621)
PHONE.............................910 323-1387
Mary F Blaylock, *CEO*
Richard Fisher Senior, *Ch*
▲ EMP: 14 EST: 1973
SQ FT: 8,000
SALES (est): 451.58K **Privately Held**
SIC: 3544 Industrial molds

(G-5914)
SELENIS NORTH AMERICA LLC ✪
3218 Cedar Creek Rd (28312-7955)
PHONE.............................210 380-2723
Duarte Matos Gil, *CEO*
EMP: 6 EST: 2022
SALES (est): 79.3K **Privately Held**
SIC: 2519 Fiberglass and plastic furniture

(G-5915)
SIERRA NEVADA CORPORATION
3139 Doc Bennett Rd (28306-8669)
PHONE.............................910 307-0362
Paul Zeisman, *Brnch Mgr*
EMP: 36
SALES (corp-wide): 2.38B **Privately Held**
Web: www.sncorp.com
SIC: 3663 3812 3699 Radio and t.v. communications equipment; Search and navigation equipment; Countermeasure simulators, electric
PA: Sierra Nevada Corporation
444 Salomon Cir
Sparks NV 89434
775 331-0222

(G-5916)
SIGNIFY IT INC
Also Called: Fastsigns
700 Ramsey St (28301-4738)
PHONE.............................910 678-8111
EMP: 10 EST: 1995
SALES (est): 903.68K **Privately Held**
Web: www.fastsigns.com
SIC: 3993 Signs and advertising specialties

(G-5917)
SIGNS NOW
Also Called: Signs Now
3724 Sycamore Dairy Rd Ste 100 (28303-3495)
PHONE.............................410 923-3534
EMP: 5 EST: 2019
SALES (est): 154.37K **Privately Held**
Web: www.signsnow.com
SIC: 3993 Signs and advertising specialties

(G-5918)
SINGER EQUIPMENT COMPANY INC
Also Called: Singer T&L
933 Robeson St (28305-5613)
PHONE.............................910 484-1128
Andrew O'quinn, *Pr*
EMP: 44
SQ FT: 20,000
SALES (corp-wide): 167.67MM **Privately Held**
Web: www.singerequipment.com
SIC: 3469 5046 Kitchen fixtures and equipment: metal, except cast aluminum; Restaurant equipment and supplies, nec
PA: Singer Equipment Company, Inc.
150 S Twin Valley Rd
Elverson PA 19520
610 387-6400

(G-5919)
SONARON LLC
7790 Cottonwood Ave (28314-6481)
PHONE.............................808 232-6168
Ronald Cogdell, *Pr*
Suniray Ballard, *CEO*
Anton Cogdell, *COO*
EMP: 8 EST: 2014
SALES (est): 812.06K **Privately Held**
SIC: 1541 7622 8742 3442 Industrial buildings and warehouses; Radio and television receiver installation; Management consulting services; Rolling doors for industrial buildings or warehouses, metal

(G-5920)
SOUTHERN SOFTWARE INC
7231 Cayman St (28306-5609)
P.O. Box 877 (28327-0877)
PHONE.............................910 638-8700
Christy C Seawell, *Prin*
EMP: 6 EST: 2011
SALES (est): 92.29K **Privately Held**
Web: www.southernsoftware.com
SIC: 7372 Prepackaged software

(G-5921)
SPEEDIPRINT INC
164 Westwood Shopping Ctr (28314-1521)
PHONE.............................910 483-2553
John Lynch, *Pr*
Wanda Lynch, *VP*
EMP: 12 EST: 1972
SALES (est): 848.14K **Privately Held**
Web: www.fayettevilleprintshop.com
SIC: 2752 Offset printing

(G-5922)
STAMP APPROVAL - ANITA WHITE
2949 Delaware Dr (28304-3703)
PHONE.............................910 433-2279
Edge Anita, *Ofcr*
EMP: 4 EST: 2018
SALES (est): 64.26K **Privately Held**
Web: www.stamp-of-approval.com
SIC: 3953 Marking devices

(G-5923)
STORK NEWS TM OF AMERICA (PA)
Also Called: Stork News
5075 Morganton Rd 12a (28314-1587)
PHONE.............................910 868-3065
Cheryl L Young, *Pr*
John M Young, *VP*
EMP: 11 EST: 1982
SQ FT: 1,600
SALES (est): 911.33K
SALES (corp-wide): 911.33K **Privately Held**
SIC: 2741 5641 Miscellaneous publishing; Infants' wear

(G-5924)
TACTICAL SUPPORT EQUIPMENT INC
Also Called: T S E
4039 Barefoot Rd (28306-8254)
PHONE.............................910 425-3360
Carl Beene, *Pr*
Wayne Dadetto, *CEO*
Richard Lovato, *VP*
EMP: 10 EST: 2002
SQ FT: 11,000
SALES (est): 2.03MM **Privately Held**
Web: www.tserecon.com
SIC: 3671 5065 Electronic tube parts, except glass blanks; Electronic parts and equipment, nec

(G-5925)
TALLADEGA MCHY & SUP CO NC (PA)
Also Called: Talladega Machinery & Supply
3510 Gillespie St (28306-9264)
PHONE.............................256 362-4124
Sam Yates, *Pr*
James W Heacock, *VP*
Gary M Heacock, *Sec*
EMP: 5 EST: 1986
SQ FT: 3,200
SALES (est): 2.45MM **Privately Held**
SIC: 5085 5084 3492 Mill supplies; Hydraulic systems equipment and supplies; Hose and tube fittings and assemblies, hydraulic/pneumatic

(G-5926)
TAR HEEL GRND CMMNDERY ORDER K
1940 Caviness St (28314-8485)
PHONE.............................910 867-6764
Daniel L Dt Thompson, *Owner*
EMP: 7 EST: 2011
SALES (est): 105.64K **Privately Held**
SIC: 2865 Tar

(G-5927)
TCE COFFEE LLC
408 Trespar Ln Apt 307 (28311-0051)
PHONE.............................910 336-3439
EMP: 4 EST: 2021
SALES (est): 62.38K **Privately Held**
SIC: 2095 Coffee roasting (except by wholesale grocers)

(G-5928)
TEAM 21ST
6316 Yadkin Rd (28303-2647)
PHONE.............................910 826-3676
Bill Mathes, *CEO*
Vickie Mathes, *Pr*
EMP: 14 EST: 1995
SQ FT: 9,600
SALES (est): 196.72K **Privately Held**
Web: www.21sttactical.com
SIC: 3469 Machine parts, stamped or pressed metal

(G-5929)
THOMPSON & LITTLE INC
933 Robeson St (28305-5613)
PHONE.............................910 484-1128
EMP: 20
Web: www.thompsonlittle.com
SIC: 3469 5046 Kitchen fixtures and equipment: metal, except cast aluminum; Restaurant equipment and supplies, nec

(G-5930)
TINT PLUS
2850 Owen Dr (28306-2937)
PHONE.............................910 229-5303
Charles Locklear, *Owner*
EMP: 6 EST: 2011
SALES (est): 256.1K **Privately Held**
SIC: 3211 1799 Window glass, clear and colored; Glass tinting, architectural or automotive

(G-5931)
TIRE SLS SVC INC FYTTEVILLE NC (PA)
400 Person St (28301-5738)
P.O. Box 104 (28302-0104)
PHONE.............................910 485-1121
Jimmy Crumpler, *Pr*
Wendell Keith Phillips,
EMP: 30 EST: 1972
SQ FT: 10,000
SALES (est): 4.99MM
SALES (corp-wide): 4.99MM **Privately Held**
Web: www.tiresalesandserviceinc.com
SIC: 5531 7534 Automotive tires; Rebuilding and retreading tires

(G-5932)
TRINKET TRUNK
599 Winding Creek Rd (28305-5293)
PHONE.............................910 483-2292
Barbara Ashley, *Prin*
EMP: 5 EST: 2008
SALES (est): 198.21K **Privately Held**
SIC: 3161 Trunks

(G-5933)
TRIPLE M CONSOLIDATED INC
716 Three Wood Dr (28312-8720)
PHONE.............................910 484-1303
Richard B Minges, *Pr*
Glenda M Minges, *VP*
EMP: 7 EST: 2004
SQ FT: 400
SALES (est): 235.5K **Privately Held**
Web: www.tripleconsolidated.com
SIC: 1442 0781 Construction sand and gravel; Landscape services

(G-5934)
TROPHY HOUSE INC (PA)
3006 Bragg Blvd (28303-4098)
P.O. Box 35691 (28303-0691)
PHONE.............................910 323-1791
Jimmy Keefe, *Pr*
▲ EMP: 10 EST: 1967
SQ FT: 35,000
SALES (est): 3.03MM
SALES (corp-wide): 3.03MM **Privately Held**
Web: www.thetrophyhouseinc.com

(PA)=Parent Co (HQ)=Headquarters
✪ = New Business established in last 2 years

Fayetteville - Cumberland County (G-5935)

SIC: **5999** 3953 5094 5961 Trophies and plaques; Screens, textile printing; Trophies; Catalog sales

(G-5935)
TROPICAL FRUIT JUICE BAR
419 Cross Creek Mall (28303-7238)
PHONE....................910 426-5842
EMP: 5 EST: 2016
SALES (est): 83.03K Privately Held
SIC: **2037** Fruit juices

(G-5936)
TURBOMED LLC
1830 Owen Dr Ste 9 (28304-1611)
PHONE....................973 527-5299
Anthony Bryant, CEO
EMP: 10 EST: 2016
SALES (est): 222.68K Privately Held
SIC: **7699** 3699 5049 2834 Life saving and survival equipment, non-medical: repair; Cleaning equipment, ultrasonic, except medical and dental; Laboratory equipment, except medical or dental; Barbituric acid pharmaceutical preparations

(G-5937)
UNION CORRUGATING COMPANY (DH)
Also Called: Orange Steel Roofing Products
701 S King St (28301-6351)
PHONE....................910 483-0479
Keith Medick, CEO
◆ EMP: 40 EST: 1934
SQ FT: 35,000
SALES (est): 188.69MM
SALES (corp-wide): 5.58B Privately Held
Web: www.unioncorrugating.com
SIC: **3444** 5033 Metal roofing and roof drainage equipment; Roofing and siding materials
HQ: Cornerstone Building Brands, Inc.
5020 Weston Pkwy
Cary NC 27513
281 897-7788

(G-5938)
UNIQUE BODY BLENDS INC
1108 Strathdon Ave (28304-0349)
PHONE....................910 302-5484
Regina Davis, Pr
EMP: 6 EST: 2012
SALES (est): 390.3K Privately Held
Web: www.uniquebodyblends.com
SIC: **2844** Perfumes, cosmetics and other toilet preparations

(G-5939)
UNITED TL & STAMPING CO NC INC
2817 Enterprise Ave (28306-2004)
PHONE....................910 323-8588
Bryant Van Vlaanderen, Pr
Marc Townsend, *
EMP: 72 EST: 1996
SQ FT: 90,000
SALES (est): 15.86MM Privately Held
Web: www.uts-nc.com
SIC: **3469** 7692 3398 3479 Stamping metal for the trade; Welding repair; Metal heat treating; Painting, coating, and hot dipping

(G-5940)
UNIVERSAL MANIA INC
1031 Robeson St Ste A (28305-5727)
PHONE....................866 903-0852
Kurt Krol, Prin
EMP: 9 EST: 2008
SALES (est): 236.73K Privately Held
SIC: **3663** Global positioning systems (GPS) equipment

(G-5941)
UP & COMING MAGAZINE
Also Called: F B Publications
208 Rowan St (28301-4922)
P.O. Box 53461 (28305-3461)
PHONE....................910 391-3859
William Bowman, Pt
EMP: 10 EST: 1996
SALES (est): 242.06K Privately Held
Web: www.kateymorrill.com
SIC: **2711** 2721 Newspapers, publishing and printing; Periodicals

(G-5942)
UP AND COMING WEEKLY
208 Rowan St (28301-4922)
P.O. Box 53461 (28305-3461)
PHONE....................910 484-6200
EMP: 24 EST: 2019
SALES (est): 313.49K Privately Held
Web: www.upandcomingweekly.com
SIC: **2711** Newspapers, publishing and printing

(G-5943)
US LBM OPERATING CO 2009 LLC
Comtech
1001 S Reilly Rd Ste 639 (28314-5560)
PHONE....................910 864-8787
EMP: 125
SALES (corp-wide): 141.88MM Privately Held
SIC: **2439** Trusses, wooden roof
HQ: Us Lbm Operating Co. 2009, Llc
2150 E Lake Cook Rd # 101
Buffalo Grove IL 60089
706 266-8856

(G-5944)
US LOGOWORKS LLC
Also Called: US Logoworks
4200 Morganton Rd Ste 105 (28314-1564)
PHONE....................910 307-0312
EMP: 10 EST: 2012
SALES (est): 1.34MM Privately Held
Web: www.uslogoworks.com
SIC: **7389** 3993 Embroidery advertising; Signs and advertising specialties

(G-5945)
USA WHOLESALE AND DISTRG INC
203 Blount St (28301-5603)
PHONE....................888 484-6872
Ali Abdo, Pr
◆ EMP: 11 EST: 2012
SQ FT: 15,000
SALES (est): 2.07MM Privately Held
Web: www.usawdistributing.com
SIC: **5141** 5947 3999 5812 Groceries, general line; Novelties; Cigarette and cigar products and accessories; Snack bar

(G-5946)
UTECK
159 Rock Hill Rd (28312-8276)
PHONE....................910 483-5016
EMP: 10 EST: 2013
SALES (est): 933.33K Privately Held
Web: www.uteck.com
SIC: **3661** Telephone and telegraph apparatus

(G-5947)
VANGUARD CULINARY GROUP LTD
716 Whitfield St (28306-1618)
P.O. Box 65029 (28306-1029)
PHONE....................910 484-8999
Charles Manis, Pr
Kenneth Reidy, *
EMP: 70 EST: 1998
SQ FT: 40,000
SALES (est): 22.67MM Privately Held
Web: www.vanguardculinary.com
SIC: **2099** Food preparations, nec

(G-5948)
VENTURE PUBLISHING
2729 Millmann Rd (28304-8917)
PHONE....................910 670-0552
Margaret M Brown, Owner
EMP: 6 EST: 2017
SALES (est): 76.16K Privately Held
SIC: **2741** Miscellaneous publishing

(G-5949)
WASTE CONTAINER REPAIR SVCS
2405 Wilmington Hwy (28306-3121)
PHONE....................910 257-4474
Jesus Benitez, Pr
EMP: 7 EST: 2015
SQ FT: 2,000
SALES (est): 353.86K Privately Held
Web: www.dumpsterrepairshop.com
SIC: **7692** 5084 3443 7699 Welding repair; Waste compactors; Dumpsters, garbage; Industrial equipment services

(G-5950)
WASTE CONTAINER SERVICES LLC
705 W Mountain Dr (28306-3230)
PHONE....................910 257-4474
Jesus Benitez, Mgr
EMP: 6
SALES (corp-wide): 733.04K Privately Held
Web: www.dumpsterrepairshop.com
SIC: **3411** 3412 3444 Metal cans; Metal barrels, drums, and pails; Sheet metalwork
PA: Waste Container Services, Llc
11 E Deer Ct
Midway GA 31320
912 980-5282

(G-5951)
WE PRINT T-SHIRTS INC
2598 Raeford Rd (28305-5118)
PHONE....................910 822-8337
EMP: 4 EST: 2011
SALES (est): 346.67K Privately Held
Web: www.822tees.com
SIC: **2759** Screen printing

(G-5952)
WELBUILT HOMES INC
Also Called: Whi Sand & Gravel
2311 Clinton Rd (28312-6113)
P.O. Box 1382 (28302-1382)
PHONE....................910 323-0098
Johnny Bullock, VP
Joyce Bullock, Sec
Greg Bullock, Asst Tr
EMP: 15 EST: 1973
SQ FT: 1,400
SALES (est): 842.06K Privately Held
Web: www.whisandandgravel.com
SIC: **1442** 5032 Construction sand mining; Sand, construction

(G-5953)
WIGAL WOOD WORKS
508 Anson Dr (28311-1530)
PHONE....................580 890-9723
EMP: 4 EST: 2011
SALES (est): 66.22K Privately Held
SIC: **2431** Millwork

(G-5954)
WILLIAMS SKIN CO
1812 Sapona Rd (28312-6536)
PHONE....................910 323-2628
Grace Hinton, Pr
Cybil Hinton, Sec
Michael Hinton, Treas
EMP: 13 EST: 1980
SQ FT: 4,000
SALES (est): 245.23K Privately Held
SIC: **2013** 2099 Prepared pork products, from purchased pork; Food preparations, nec

(G-5955)
YOUNGS WELDING & MACHINE SVCS
787 Mcarthur Rd (28311-1959)
PHONE....................910 488-1190
Michael B Young, Owner
EMP: 4 EST: 2009
SALES (est): 193.41K Privately Held
SIC: **7692** 3469 Welding repair; Machine parts, stamped or pressed metal

Ferguson
Wilkes County

(G-5956)
CALVIN LAWS JAY
2036 Kendell Town Rd (28624-9007)
PHONE....................336 973-4318
Tommy Laws, Prin
EMP: 8 EST: 2010
SALES (est): 193.14K Privately Held
SIC: **2411** Logging

(G-5957)
CLUTCH CLIMBING GEAR LLC
1215 Rom Eller Rd (28624-9092)
PHONE....................336 262-9719
Erik Mittet, Prin
EMP: 5 EST: 2018
SALES (est): 70.41K Privately Held
Web: www.clutchclimbinggear.com
SIC: **3949** Sporting and athletic goods, nec

(G-5958)
LAWS LOGGING
2036 Kendell Town Rd (28624-9007)
P.O. Box 335 (28606-0335)
PHONE....................336 973-4318
EMP: 4 EST: 2019
SALES (est): 81.72K Privately Held
SIC: **2411** Logging

Flat Rock
Henderson County

(G-5959)
AUTOMATED DESIGNS INC
105 Education Dr (28731-8572)
PHONE....................828 696-9625
Larry T Orr, Pr
Denise Orr, VP
EMP: 10 EST: 1979
SQ FT: 5,400
SALES (est): 1.15MM Privately Held
Web: www.adinc.net
SIC: **3531** 5085 8711 Construction machinery ; Industrial supplies; Industrial engineers

(G-5960)
BLUE RIDGE QUARRY
3675 Spartanburg Hwy (28731-7737)
PHONE....................828 693-0025
Ralph Shelton, Mgr
EMP: 5 EST: 2016
SALES (est): 93.36K Privately Held
SIC: **1442** Construction sand and gravel

(G-5961)
BRUNNER & LAY INC
90 Reeds Way (28731-0770)
PHONE..................828 274-2770
Connie Byrd, *Brnch Mgr*
EMP: 5
SQ FT: 20,264
SALES (corp-wide): 39.1MM **Privately Held**
Web: www.brunnerlay.com
SIC: 3532 Mining machinery
PA: Brunner & Lay, Inc.
  1510 N Old Missouri Rd
  Springdale AR 72764
  479 756-0880

(G-5962)
CARROLL-BACCARI INC (PA)
Also Called: Mavidon
110 Commercial Blvd (28731-7747)
PHONE..................561 585-2227
Timothy Carroll, *Pr*
EMP: 7 EST: 1993
SQ FT: 17,000
SALES (est): 1.19MM **Privately Held**
Web: www.mavidon.com
SIC: 2891 Adhesives and sealants

(G-5963)
COASTAL AGROBUSINESS INC
814 Mcmurray Rd (28731-5781)
P.O. Box 750 (28724-0750)
PHONE..................828 697-2220
EMP: 7
SALES (corp-wide): 61.99MM **Privately Held**
Web: www.coastalagro.com
SIC: 5191 3523 Chemicals, agricultural; Sprayers and spraying machines, agricultural
PA: Coastal Agrobusiness, Inc.
  112 Staton Rd
  Greenville NC 27834
  252 238-7391

(G-5964)
DURALINE IMAGING INC
580 Upward Rd Ste 1 (28731-9477)
P.O. Box 1763 (28731-1763)
PHONE..................828 692-1301
William Wick, *Pr*
Thomas P Dunn, *Pr*
Derek Bryan, *VP*
EMP: 4 EST: 1970
SALES (est): 474.24K **Privately Held**
Web: www.duralineimaging.com
SIC: 3955 Ribbons, inked: typewriter, adding machine, register, etc.

(G-5965)
FLAT ROCK SIGNS & GRAPHICS
578 Upward Rd Unit 8 (28731-9473)
PHONE..................828 693-0908
Jeff Clark, *Prin*
EMP: 6 EST: 2002
SALES (est): 140.96K **Privately Held**
SIC: 3993 Signs, not made in custom sign painting shops

(G-5966)
JUST SAYIN SOCKS LLC
225 Winding Meadows Dr (28731-9571)
PHONE..................828 513-1517
Daniel J Stubbs, *Prin*
EMP: 6 EST: 2018
SALES (est): 110.24K **Privately Held**
SIC: 2252 Socks

(G-5967)
LEISURE CRAFT HOLDINGS LLC
940 Upward Rd (28731-8799)
P.O. Box 1190 (28793-1190)
PHONE..................828 693-8241
Richard Herman, *Pr*
EMP: 65 EST: 2021
SALES (est): 10.52MM **Privately Held**
SIC: 2514 2542 3411 2531 Metal household furniture; Partitions and fixtures, except wood; Metal cans; Public building and related furniture
PA: Palmer Hamilton Llc
  143 S Jackson St Ste 1
  Elkhorn WI 53121

(G-5968)
LEISURE CRAFT INC
Also Called: USA Display
940 Upward Rd (28731-8799)
P.O. Box 1700 (28793-1700)
PHONE..................828 693-8241
EMP: 132 EST: 1979
SALES (est): 17.66MM **Privately Held**
Web: www.leisurecraftinc.com
SIC: 2514 2542 3411 2531 Metal household furniture; Partitions and fixtures, except wood; Metal cans; Public building and related furniture

(G-5969)
MAP SUPPLY INC
132 Poplar Loop Dr (28731-8583)
PHONE..................336 731-3230
Al Cleveland, *Pr*
Tim Carpenter, *
Carol Cleveland, *
EMP: 8 EST: 1977
SQ FT: 9,000
SALES (est): 478.62K **Privately Held**
Web: www.mapsupplyinc.com
SIC: 5199 2741 Maps and charts; Maps: publishing only, not printed on site

(G-5970)
NATIONAL VOCTNL TECH HONOR SOC
Also Called: Nv-Ths
1011 Airport Rd (28731-4725)
P.O. Box 1336 (28731-1336)
PHONE..................828 698-8011
Allen Powell, *Ex Dir*
EMP: 6 EST: 1984
SQ FT: 1,932
SALES (est): 477.06K **Privately Held**
Web: www.nths.org
SIC: 3999 8748 Education aids, devices and supplies; Educational consultant

(G-5971)
SALUDA MOUNTAIN PRODUCTS INC
561 S Allen Rd (28731-9447)
PHONE..................828 696-2296
Richard Canfield, *Pr*
EMP: 10 EST: 1992
SQ FT: 20,000
SALES (est): 1.17MM **Privately Held**
Web: www.wncguide.com
SIC: 2541 2499 Store and office display cases and fixtures; Decorative wood and woodwork

(G-5972)
THREE GS ENTERPRISES INC
Also Called: Elite Auto Lights, Inc.
100 Tabor Road Ext (28731-6744)
PHONE..................828 696-2060
Dustin Gosnell, *Pr*
EMP: 17 EST: 2009
SALES (est): 5.67MM **Privately Held**
Web: www.bbbind.com
SIC: 3647 Automotive lighting fixtures, nec
HQ: Bbb Industries, Llc
  29627 Renaissance Blvd
  Daphne AL 36526
  800 280-2737

(G-5973)
WALNUT WOODWORKS
83 Riley Ln (28731-5675)
PHONE..................828 290-6438
EMP: 4 EST: 2018
SALES (est): 54.13K **Privately Held**
SIC: 2431 Millwork

Fleetwood
Ashe County

(G-5974)
CRANBERRY WOOD WORKS INC
Also Called: Carolina Leatherwork
13830 Us Highway 221 S (28626-9827)
P.O. Box 31 (28618-0031)
PHONE..................336 877-8771
Pete Yates, *Pr*
Edward J Greene, *VP*
EMP: 4 EST: 1990
SALES (est): 349.55K **Privately Held**
Web: www.cranberrywoodworks.com
SIC: 2499 2511 Decorative wood and woodwork; Wood lawn and garden furniture

(G-5975)
GUM RIDGE MILLING COMPANY
650b Bear Ridge Trl (28626-9730)
PHONE..................336 877-8894
Raul Ocampo, *Prin*
EMP: 4 EST: 2001
SALES (est): 103.41K **Privately Held**
Web: www.gumridgemill.com
SIC: 2491 Flooring, treated wood block

(G-5976)
MORETZ BLDG & WOODWORKS LLC
13830 Us Highway 221 S Unit A (28626-9827)
PHONE..................828 406-4672
Joel Warren Moretz, *Prin*
EMP: 5 EST: 2015
SALES (est): 54.13K **Privately Held**
SIC: 2431 Millwork

(G-5977)
WEAVER FABRICATION
1478 Trojan Horse Cir (28626-9211)
PHONE..................336 877-3427
Gary W Weaver, *Prin*
EMP: 5 EST: 2007
SALES (est): 76.92K **Privately Held**
SIC: 3999 Manufacturing industries, nec

Fletcher
Henderson County

(G-5978)
A 1 TIRE SERVICE INC
24 Cane Creek Rd (28732-9707)
P.O. Box 1685 (28732-1685)
PHONE..................828 684-1860
Earl Youngblood, *Pr*
Patrica Youngblood, *Sec*
Gene Youngblood, *Stockholder*
EMP: 4 EST: 1987
SQ FT: 3,450
SALES (est): 494.97K **Privately Held**
SIC: 7534 7539 5531 Tire repair shop; Brake services; Automotive tires

(G-5979)
AAA PAVER CARE INC
124 Old Salem Ct (28732-9241)
PHONE..................828 687-1669
James M Smyth, *Prin*
EMP: 4
SALES (est): 200K **Privately Held**
SIC: 3531 Pavers

(G-5980)
ACCURATE TECHNOLOGY INC (PA)
270 Rutledge Rd (28732-9398)
PHONE..................828 654-7920
Ed Fiantaca, *Pr*
◆ EMP: 6 EST: 1989
SALES (est): 1.39MM **Privately Held**
Web: www.proscale.com
SIC: 3812 Distance measuring equipment

(G-5981)
ACME MACHINE LLC
101 Continuum Dr # 100 (28732-7459)
PHONE..................828 483-6440
EMP: 11 EST: 2019
SALES (est): 875.56K **Privately Held**
Web: www.acmemachinenc.com
SIC: 3599 Machine shop, jobbing and repair

(G-5982)
ADVANCE CABINETRY INC
15 Design Ave Unit 201 (28732-7826)
PHONE..................828 676-3550
EMP: 8 EST: 2019
SALES (est): 335.75K **Privately Held**
Web: www.advancecabinetry.com
SIC: 2434 Wood kitchen cabinets

(G-5983)
ALPHATECH INC
388 Cane Creek Rd (28732-9471)
P.O. Box 519 (28732-0519)
PHONE..................828 684-9709
Al Worley, *Pr*
EMP: 35 EST: 1999
SQ FT: 44,000
SALES (est): 6.65MM **Privately Held**
Web: www.atimfg.com
SIC: 3599 Machine shop, jobbing and repair

(G-5984)
ASHEVILLE QUICKPRINT
Also Called: Quick Print
8 Chanter Dr (28732-8566)
PHONE..................828 252-7667
Larry M Brady, *Owner*
EMP: 4 EST: 1981
SQ FT: 1,200
SALES (est): 176.59K **Privately Held**
SIC: 2752 7334 Offset printing; Photocopying and duplicating services

(G-5985)
ASHEVILLE THERMOFORM PLAS INC
200 Cane Creek Industrial Park Rd (28732-9753)
PHONE..................828 684-8440
William Trometer, *Pr*
EMP: 10 EST: 1998
SQ FT: 15,000
SALES (est): 2.01MM **Privately Held**
Web: www.ashevillethermoformplastics.com
SIC: 3089 Injection molding of plastics

(G-5986)
AURALITES INC
9a National Ave (28732-8655)
PHONE..................828 687-7990
Martien Vloet, *Prin*

Fletcher - Henderson County (G-5987) **GEOGRAPHIC SECTION**

EMP: 8 **EST:** 2010
SALES (est): 807.66K **Privately Held**
Web: www.auralites.com
SIC: 3999 Candles

(G-5987)
BETECH INC
190 Continuum Dr (28732-7459)
PHONE...............................828 687-9917
Ronald Brevard, *Pr*
Richard Brevard, *Sec*
Amy Rhinehart, *Prin*
EMP: 22 **EST:** 1991
SQ FT: 10,000
SALES (est): 839.99K **Privately Held**
Web: www.betechinc.net
SIC: 3599 Custom machinery

(G-5988)
BLUE RIDGE BRACKET INC
66 Fletcher Commercial Dr (28732-8628)
PHONE...............................828 808-3273
EMP: 8 **EST:** 2015
SALES (est): 224.53K **Privately Held**
Web: www.blueridgemetals.com
SIC: 3999 Manufacturing industries, nec

(G-5989)
BLUE RIDGE METALS CORPORATION
180 Mills Gap Rd (28732-8548)
P.O. Box 189 (28732-0189)
PHONE...............................828 687-2525
Kazumasa Yoshida, *Ch Bd*
Isao Yoshida, *
Shigero Goda, *
▲ **EMP:** 160 **EST:** 1988
SQ FT: 3,484,800
SALES (est): 41.61MM **Privately Held**
Web: www.blueridgemetals.com
SIC: 3399 3315 Aluminum atomized powder; Fencing made in wiredrawing plants
PA: Central Yoshida Corporation
   1-4-1, Mori
   Ama AIC 490-1

(G-5990)
BORG-WARNER AUTOMOTIVE INC
Cane Creek Ind Pk (28732)
PHONE...............................828 684-3501
EMP: 5 **EST:** 2011
SALES (est): 889.74K **Privately Held**
Web: www.borgwarner.com
SIC: 3714 Motor vehicle parts and accessories

(G-5991)
CANE CREEK CYCLING CMPNNTS INC
355 Cane Creek Rd (28732-7404)
P.O. Box 798 (28732-0798)
PHONE...............................828 684-3551
Brent Graves, *Pr*
▲ **EMP:** 35 **EST:** 1974
SQ FT: 28,035
SALES (est): 7.91MM **Privately Held**
Web: www.canecreek.com
SIC: 5941 3751 Bicycle and bicycle parts; Motorcycles, bicycles and parts

(G-5992)
CAROLINA WATER CONSULTANTS LLC
4 Vaughn Cir (28732-9372)
PHONE...............................828 251-2420
EMP: 7 **EST:** 1997
SALES (est): 738.73K **Privately Held**
Web: www.medwaterpros.com

SIC: 3589 5999 Water filters and softeners, household type; Water purification equipment

(G-5993)
CERTIFICATION SERVICES INTERNATIONAL LLC
510 La White Dr Bldg 12 (28732-9118)
P.O. Box 813 (28758-0813)
PHONE...............................828 458-1573
EMP: 8
SIC: 3714 Motor vehicle parts and accessories

(G-5994)
CLAYTON HOMES INC
Also Called: Oakwood Homes
5250 Hendersonville Rd (28732-6672)
PHONE...............................828 684-1550
Bryant Moss, *Brnch Mgr*
EMP: 6
SALES (corp-wide): 364.48B **Publicly Held**
Web: www.claytonhomes.com
SIC: 2451 Mobile homes
HQ: Clayton Homes, Inc.
   5000 Clayton Rd
   Maryville TN 37804
   865 380-3000

(G-5995)
COGENT DYNAMICS INC
33 Meadow Brook Dr (28732-9101)
PHONE...............................828 628-9025
Carl Tannenbum, *Pr*
EMP: 4 **EST:** 2005
SALES (est): 359.01K **Privately Held**
Web: www.motocd.com
SIC: 3555 0119 Printing trades machinery; Barley farm

(G-5996)
CONTINENTAL AUTO SYSTEMS INC
1 Quality Way (28732-9303)
PHONE...............................828 654-2000
John D'haenens, *Prin*
EMP: 400
SQ FT: 254,000
SALES (corp-wide): 40.93B **Privately Held**
Web: www.continental.com
SIC: 3465 3714 Body parts, automobile: stamped metal; Motor vehicle parts and accessories
HQ: Continental Automotive Systems, Inc.
   1 Continental Dr
   Auburn Hills MI 48326
   248 393-5300

(G-5997)
DAYSTAR MACHINING TECH INC
356 Cane Creek Rd (28732-7403)
P.O. Box 1377 (28732-1377)
PHONE...............................828 684-1316
James Lytle, *Pr*
Margaret Lytle, *
Anna Viands, *
James Lytle, *VP Opers*
◆ **EMP:** 40 **EST:** 1999
SQ FT: 25,000
SALES (est): 7.93MM **Privately Held**
Web: www.daystarmachining.com
SIC: 3599 Machine shop, jobbing and repair

(G-5998)
DIAMOND BRAND GEAR COMPANY
Also Called: Diamond Brand
145 Cane Creek Industrial Park Rd Ste 100 (28732-8306)
PHONE...............................828 684-9848
John Delaloye, *Pr*
▲ **EMP:** 24 **EST:** 2015

SQ FT: 85,000
SALES (est): 5.03MM **Privately Held**
Web: www.diamondbrandgear.com
SIC: 2394 Tarpaulins, fabric: made from purchased materials

(G-5999)
DREAMSEEDSCOM SEEDS OF LIGHT
41 Foxridge Dr (28732-9114)
PHONE...............................239 541-0501
Robert Buchanan, *Pr*
EMP: 7 **EST:** 2011
SALES (est): 182.21K **Privately Held**
Web: www.dreamseeds.com
SIC: 3911 Jewelry apparel

(G-6000)
EMTELLE USA INC ✪
101 Mills Gap Rd Unit A (28732-8548)
PHONE...............................828 707-9970
Tony Rodgers, *CEO*
Debra Davenport, *
EMP: 35 **EST:** 2022
SALES (est): 7.78MM
SALES (corp-wide): 355.83K **Privately Held**
Web: www.emtelle.com
SIC: 3357 Fiber optic cable (insulated)
HQ: Emtelle Uk Limited
   Haughhead
   Hawick TD9 8
   145 036-4000

(G-6001)
EQUILIBAR LLC
320 Rutledge Rd (28732-9328)
PHONE...............................828 650-6590
David Reed, *Pr*
Jeff Jennings, *
David Reed, *VP Opers*
EMP: 35 **EST:** 2007
SQ FT: 10,000
SALES (est): 5.89MM
SALES (corp-wide): 49.62MM **Privately Held**
Web: www.equilibar.com
SIC: 3491 Industrial valves
PA: Richards Industrials, Inc.
   3170 Wasson Rd
   Cincinnati OH 45209
   513 533-5600

(G-6002)
EXCELSIOR SEWING LLC
125 Brickton Dr (28732-0358)
PHONE...............................828 398-8056
Judith D Gross, *Managing Member*
EMP: 10 **EST:** 2012
SALES (est): 742.45K **Privately Held**
Web: excelsiorsewing.business.site
SIC: 2326 Aprons, work, except rubberized and plastic: men's

(G-6003)
EXPRESSIONS CABINETRY LLC
106 Lytle Rd (28732-9110)
PHONE...............................828 278-7999
Lane Pressley, *Prin*
Angela Pressley, *Prin*
EMP: 6 **EST:** 2019
SALES (est): 226.94K **Privately Held**
Web: www.expressionscabinetry.com
SIC: 2434 Wood kitchen cabinets

(G-6004)
FIELDCO MACHINING INC
5164 Old Haywood Rd (28732)
P.O. Box 1305 (28732-1305)
PHONE...............................828 891-4100
Steve Fields, *Pr*

Michael Fields, *VP*
Tammy Swayngim, *Sec*
EMP: 14 **EST:** 1989
SQ FT: 7,500
SALES (est): 403K **Privately Held**
SIC: 3599 Machine shop, jobbing and repair

(G-6005)
FLETCHER LIMESTONE COMPANY INC
639 Faning Bridge Rd (28732-8360)
P.O. Box 32626 (37930-2626)
PHONE...............................828 684-6701
Bob Stevens, *Pr*
John Brooks, *VP*
Barbara Stevens, *Sec*
Mark Stevens, *Asst VP*
EMP: 12 **EST:** 1948
SALES (est): 224.93K **Privately Held**
SIC: 3272 5032 Cast stone, concrete; Stone, crushed or broken

(G-6006)
FLETCHER PRINTVILLE
222 Old Airport Rd (28732-9273)
PHONE...............................828 348-5126
EMP: 4 **EST:** 2018
SALES (est): 186.29K **Privately Held**
Web: www.printville.net
SIC: 2752 Offset printing

(G-6007)
GASP INC
80 Emma Sharp Rd Ste 5 (28732)
PHONE...............................828 891-1628
Mark D Garrison, *Prin*
EMP: 5 **EST:** 2004
SALES (est): 821.09K **Privately Held**
Web: www.gaspinc.com
SIC: 3613 Power circuit breakers

(G-6008)
GREENS MACHINE & TOOL INC
8 Park Ridge Dr (28732-9339)
PHONE...............................828 654-0042
Donald C Green, *Pr*
Mary Green, *CEO*
Adam Green, *VP*
EMP: 11 **EST:** 1986
SQ FT: 1,344
SALES (est): 428.37K **Privately Held**
Web: www.gmtcnc.com
SIC: 3599 Machine shop, jobbing and repair

(G-6009)
HANSON SYSTEMS INC
Also Called: Hanson Welding
340 L.A. White Dr (28732)
PHONE...............................828 687-3701
Charles P Miller, *Pr*
EMP: 8 **EST:** 1993
SQ FT: 15,000
SALES (est): 205.73K **Privately Held**
SIC: 3699 3548 Welding machines and equipment, ultrasonic; Welding apparatus

(G-6010)
HASCO AMERICA INC
270 Rutledge Rd Unit B (28732-9399)
PHONE...............................828 650-2631
Marna Duckett, *Pr*
Sharon Chrisman, *Sec*
▲ **EMP:** 9 **EST:** 1999
SQ FT: 20,000
SALES (est): 2.55MM
SALES (corp-wide): 624.98MM **Privately Held**
Web: www.hasco.com
SIC: 3544 Industrial molds
HQ: Hasco Hasenclever Gmbh + Co Kg
   Romerweg 4

GEOGRAPHIC SECTION
Fletcher - Henderson County (G-6034)

Ludenscheid NW 58513
235 195-7466

(G-6011)
HENSEL PHELPS ✪
171 Wright Brothers Way (28732-7808)
PHONE..................................828 585-4689
Richard G Tucker, *VP*
EMP: 6 **EST:** 2023
SALES (est): 285.91K **Privately Held**
SIC: 1389 Construction, repair, and dismantling services

(G-6012)
HORIBA INSTRUMENTS INC
270 Rutledge Rd Unit D (28732-9399)
PHONE..................................828 676-2801
Jai Hakhu, *Ch Bd*
EMP: 15
Web: www.horiba.com
SIC: 3826 Analytical instruments
HQ: Horiba Instruments Incorporated
9755 Research Dr
Irvine CA 92618
949 250-4811

(G-6013)
INTERNATIONAL TELA-COM INC
103 Underwood Rd Unit C (28732-8661)
PHONE..................................828 651-9801
Edmund C Horgan Iii, *Pr*
Dennis Deranek, *VP*
EMP: 15 **EST:** 1969
SQ FT: 2,000
SALES (est): 406.58K **Privately Held**
Web: www.itcsolutions.us
SIC: 1731 1542 3643 Electronic controls installation; Commercial and office buildings, renovation and repair; Current-carrying wiring services

(G-6014)
JACOB HOLM INDUSTRIES AMER INC
145 Cane Creek Indus Park (28732-8306)
PHONE..................................828 490-6017
EMP: 4 **EST:** 2018
SALES (est): 114.46K **Privately Held**
SIC: 3999 Manufacturing industries, nec

(G-6015)
KATTERMANN VENTURES INC
282 Cane Creek Rd (28732-7402)
P.O. Box 550 (28732-0550)
PHONE..................................828 651-8737
David W Kattermann Junior, *Pr*
Robert Kattermann, *
▲ **EMP:** 34 **EST:** 1974
SQ FT: 78,000
SALES (est): 4MM **Privately Held**
Web: www.bromleyplastics.com
SIC: 2821 Plastics materials and resins

(G-6016)
KBB TOWERS LLC
75 Jackson Rd (28732-8523)
PHONE..................................828 243-1812
Richie Blackwell, *Owner*
EMP: 6 **EST:** 2017
SALES (est): 113.19K **Privately Held**
SIC: 3441 Fabricated structural metal

(G-6017)
LEGACY PADDLESPORTS LLC
210 Old Airport Rd (28732-9273)
PHONE..................................828 684-1933
◆ **EMP:** 110
Web: www.legacypaddlesports.com
SIC: 3732 Kayaks, building and repairing

(G-6018)
LEVI INNOVATIONS INC
122 Continuum Dr (28732-7459)
PHONE..................................828 684-6640
Michael K Levi, *Pr*
EMP: 11 **EST:** 2008
SALES (est): 494.66K **Privately Held**
Web: www.levitool.com
SIC: 3599 Machine shop, jobbing and repair

(G-6019)
LOW IMPACT TECH USA INC
269 Cane Creek Rd (28732-7401)
PHONE..................................828 428-6310
Nick Probert, *CEO*
Eddiebee Farrar, *Corporate Secretary*
Dale E Polk Junior, *Dir*
EMP: 7 **EST:** 2020
SALES (est): 1.08MM
SALES (corp-wide): 2.44MM **Privately Held**
SIC: 3433 Solar heaters and collectors
PA: D & D Manufacturing, Llc
2655 Cherrywood Ln
Titusville FL 32780
321 652-4509

(G-6020)
MAHLE MOTORSPORTS INC
270 Rutledge Rd Unit C (28732-9399)
PHONE..................................888 255-1942
Hans D Jehle, *Pr*
Lee Morse, *VP*
▲ **EMP:** 16 **EST:** 1999
SQ FT: 10,000
SALES (est): 5.13MM
SALES (corp-wide): 3.75MM **Privately Held**
Web: us.mahle.com
SIC: 3714 Motor vehicle parts and accessories
HQ: Mahle Engine Components Usa, Inc.
23030 Mahle Dr
Farmington MI 48335
248 305-8200

(G-6021)
MDT BROMLEY LLC ✪
Also Called: Bromley Plastics
282 Cane Creek Rd (28732-7402)
PHONE..................................828 651-8737
Terry Ingham, *Pr*
EMP: 34 **EST:** 2022
SALES (est): 7.17MM
SALES (corp-wide): 25.62MM **Privately Held**
Web: www.bromleyplastics.com
SIC: 2821 5162 Plastics materials and resins ; Plastics materials and basic shapes
PA: Material Difference Technologies Llc
1501 Sarasota Center Blvd
Sarasota FL 34240
888 818-1283

(G-6022)
MEDI MALL INC
Also Called: Medimassager.com
189 Continuum Dr (28732-7459)
PHONE..................................877 501-6334
Michael Terblanche, *Pr*
◆ **EMP:** 6 **EST:** 2009
SALES (est): 1.06MM **Privately Held**
Web: www.medmassager.com
SIC: 5047 5999 3845 3841 Medical equipment and supplies; Medical apparatus and supplies; Electromedical equipment; Physiotherapy equipment, electrical

(G-6023)
MERITOR INC
1000 Rockwell Dr (28732-9494)
P.O. Box Ckwell Dr (28732)
PHONE..................................828 687-2000
Mark Kanapeel, *Brnch Mgr*
EMP: 19
SALES (corp-wide): 34.06B **Publicly Held**
Web: www.meritor.com
SIC: 3714 Axles, motor vehicle
HQ: Meritor, Inc.
2135 W Maple Rd
Troy MI 48084

(G-6024)
MERITOR INC
Also Called: Arvinmeritor Hvy Vhcl Systems
1000 Rockwell Dr (28732-9494)
P.O. Box Ckwell Dr (28732)
PHONE..................................828 687-2000
William Keith, *Mgr*
EMP: 157
SALES (corp-wide): 34.06B **Publicly Held**
Web: www.meritor.com
SIC: 3714 Axles, motor vehicle
HQ: Meritor, Inc.
2135 W Maple Rd
Troy MI 48084

(G-6025)
MICRONICS TIG-WELDING
42 Willie Mae Way (28732-7477)
PHONE..................................828 691-0755
Brian Ritchie, *Prin*
EMP: 5 **EST:** 2010
SALES (est): 58.22K **Privately Held**
SIC: 7692 Welding repair

(G-6026)
MICROTECH DEFENSE INDS INC
15a National Ave (28732-8655)
PHONE..................................828 684-4355
Anthony Marfione, *Pr*
Susan Marfione, *Prin*
EMP: 9 **EST:** 2013
SALES (est): 206.49K **Privately Held**
Web: www.microtechdefense.com
SIC: 3484 Pistols or pistol parts, 30 mm. and below

(G-6027)
MOLD TRANS LLC
279 Hutch Mountain Rd (28732-8708)
PHONE..................................828 356-5181
Andrei Vladicescu, *Admn*
EMP: 5 **EST:** 2015
SALES (est): 151.49K **Privately Held**
SIC: 3544 Industrial molds

(G-6028)
MOTO GROUP LLC
Also Called: Trojan Defense
40 Cane Creek Industrial Park Rd (28732-7754)
PHONE..................................828 350-7653
EMP: 18 **EST:** 2010
SALES (est): 1.7MM **Privately Held**
SIC: 3751 Motorcycles and related parts

(G-6029)
MTI MEDICAL CABLES LLC
2133 Old Fanning Bridge Rd (28732)
PHONE..................................828 890-2888
EMP: 10 **EST:** 2015
SALES (est): 690.21K
SALES (corp-wide): 61.46MM **Privately Held**
Web: www.lifesync.com
SIC: 3841 Medical instruments and equipment, blood and bone work
HQ: American Biosurgical, Llc
1850 Beaver Ridge Cir B
Norcross GA 30071

(G-6030)
NORTH AMERICAN TRADE LLC
Also Called: Nat
388 Cane Creek Rd Ste 22 (28732-9471)
PHONE..................................828 712-3004
Neil Myers, *CEO*
EMP: 5 **EST:** 2013
SQ FT: 3,000
SALES (est): 511.01K **Privately Held**
Web: www.natrade.net
SIC: 7389 3482 5091 3483 Business Activities at Non-Commercial Site; Small arms ammunition; Firearms, sporting; Ammunition components

(G-6031)
PEPSI COLA BOTTLING CO
200 Fanning Field (28732)
P.O. Box 1207 (28732-1207)
PHONE..................................828 650-7800
Lee Teeter, *VP*
EMP: 190 **EST:** 1937
SALES (est): 1.28MM
SALES (corp-wide): 50.09MM **Privately Held**
Web: www.pepsico.com
SIC: 2086 Carbonated soft drinks, bottled and canned
PA: Pepsi-Cola Bottling Company Of Hickory, N.C., Inc.
2401 14th Avenue Cir Nw
Hickory NC 28601
828 322-8090

(G-6032)
PROMATIC AUTOMATION INC
9a National Ave (28732-8655)
PHONE..................................828 684-1700
EMP: 17 **EST:** 2000
SQ FT: 36,000
SALES (est): 3.89MM **Privately Held**
Web: www.promaticautomation.com
SIC: 3599 Machine shop, jobbing and repair

(G-6033)
PUTSCH & COMPANY INC (HQ)
Also Called: Putsch
352 Cane Creek Rd (28732-7403)
P.O. Box 5128 (28813-5128)
PHONE..................................828 684-0671
Carl Christian, *Pr*
Elisabeth Paumen Radinger, *VP*
Carol Eubank, *Sec*
Karl H Straus, *Sec*
▲ **EMP:** 23 **EST:** 1973
SQ FT: 16,000
SALES (est): 8.76MM
SALES (corp-wide): 9.23MM **Privately Held**
Web: www.putschusa.com
SIC: 3556 3541 3545 Sugar plant machinery ; Machine tools, metal cutting type; Machine tool accessories
PA: Putsch Gmbh & Co. Kg
Frankfurter Str. 5-21
Hagen NW 58095
23313990

(G-6034)
RESINART EAST INC
201 Old Airport Rd (28732-9273)
PHONE..................................828 687-0215
Thomas V Trombatore, *Pr*
EMP: 15 **EST:** 1992
SQ FT: 25,000
SALES (est): 5.3MM **Privately Held**
Web: www.resinart.com

Fletcher - Henderson County (G-6035) GEOGRAPHIC SECTION

SIC: 5031 3089 Molding, all materials; Injection molding of plastics

(G-6035)
RINEHART RACING INC
40 Cane Creek Industrial Park Rd (28732-7754)
PHONE.............................828 350-7653
Gerald Rinehart, *Pr*
Judd Hollifield, *CEO*
EMP: 29 EST: 1995
SALES (est): 11.44MM **Privately Held**
Web: www.rinehartracing.com
SIC: 3751 Bicycles and related parts

(G-6036)
SCITECK DIAGNOSTICS INC
317 Rutledge Rd (28732-9328)
P.O. Box 562 (28704-0562)
PHONE.............................828 650-0409
Kerstin Lanier, *CEO*
EMP: 4 EST: 1989
SQ FT: 15,000
SALES (est): 573.74K **Privately Held**
Web: www.sciteck.org
SIC: 2819 2835 3826 Industrial inorganic chemicals, nec; In vitro diagnostics; Automatic chemical analyzers

(G-6037)
SDV OFFICE SYSTEMS LLC
34 Redmond Dr Apt C (28732-9315)
PHONE.............................844 968-9500
EMP: 12
SIC: 5047 2521 2522 5112 Medical equipment and supplies; Wood office furniture; Office cabinets and filing drawers, except wood; Office filing supplies
PA: Sdv Office Systems, Llc
26 Macallan Ln
Asheville NC 28805

(G-6038)
SHADOWTRACK 247 LLC
Also Called: Shadowtrack 24/7
45 Park Ridge Dr (28732-9339)
PHONE.............................828 398-0980
Jeffrey Stingel, *Pr*
EMP: 10 EST: 2018
SQ FT: 10,000
SALES (est): 1.1MM **Privately Held**
Web: www.shadowtrack247.com
SIC: 3663 Global positioning systems (GPS) equipment

(G-6039)
SILVER MOON NUTRACEUTICALS LLC
111 Fletcher Commercial Dr Ste B (28732-8635)
PHONE.............................828 698-5795
Dennis Putnam, *Managing Member*
EMP: 6 EST: 2016
SALES (est): 475.08K **Privately Held**
Web: www.silvermoonnutra.com
SIC: 2899 Oils and essential oils

(G-6040)
SKYLAND PRSTHTICS ORTHTICS INC
3845 Hendersonville Rd (28732-8241)
P.O. Box 428 (28776-0428)
PHONE.............................828 684-1644
Pippa Dolen, *Pr*
Shaun Dolen, *VP*
EMP: 20 EST: 1979
SQ FT: 1,500
SALES (est): 2.46MM **Privately Held**
Web: www.skylandprosthetics.net
SIC: 3842 Limbs, artificial

(G-6041)
SMARTRAC TECH FLETCHER INC
267 Cane Creek Rd (28732-7401)
PHONE.............................828 651-6051
Christian Uhl, *CEO*
Mike Keen, *
◆ EMP: 217 EST: 2010
SQ FT: 50,000
SALES (est): 47.07MM **Privately Held**
SIC: 3612 Transformers, except electric
HQ: Smart Solutions Holdings B.V.
Eduard Van Beinumstraat 30
Amsterdam NH

(G-6042)
SOUTHER WILLIAMS VINEYARD LLC
655 Hoopers Creek Rd (28732-8592)
PHONE.............................828 651-8011
Kenneth T Parker, *Prin*
EMP: 4 EST: 2019
SALES (est): 81.22K **Privately Held**
Web: www.southerwilliams.com
SIC: 2084 Wines

(G-6043)
SOUTHERN CONCRETE MTLS INC
250 Old Hendersonville Rd (28732-9679)
PHONE.............................828 681-5178
Billy Jackson, *Genl Mgr*
EMP: 9
SQ FT: 1,424
SALES (corp-wide): 238.17MM **Privately Held**
Web: www.scmusa.com
SIC: 3273 5039 Ready-mixed concrete; Septic tanks
HQ: Southern Concrete Materials, Inc.
35 Meadow Rd
Asheville NC 28803
828 253-6421

(G-6044)
T D M CORPORATION
333 White Pine Dr (28732-9717)
EMP: 23 EST: 1969
SALES (est): 2.08MM **Privately Held**
Web: tdm-corporation-in-fletcher-nc.cityfos.com
SIC: 3599 3544 Machine shop, jobbing and repair; Industrial molds

(G-6045)
TRANSYLVNIA VCATIONAL SVCS INC
1 Quality Way (28732-9385)
PHONE.............................828 884-1548
John Safi, *Mgr*
EMP: 63
SALES (corp-wide): 35.16MM **Privately Held**
SIC: 8093 8331 2652 Rehabilitation center, outpatient treatment; Job training and related services; Setup paperboard boxes
PA: Transylvania Vocational Services, Inc.
11 Mountain Industrial Dr
Brevard NC 28712
828 884-3195

(G-6046)
TWO TREES DISTILLING CO LLC
17 Continuum Dr (28732-7445)
PHONE.............................803 767-1322
EMP: 7 EST: 2018
SALES (est): 364.08K **Privately Held**
Web: www.twotreesdistilling.com
SIC: 2085 Distilled and blended liquors

(G-6047)
UPM RAFLATAC INC
Also Called: Upm Raflatac At Fletcher Bus

535 Cane Creek Rd (28732-9703)
PHONE.............................828 335-3289
EMP: 16
Web: www.upmraflatac.com
SIC: 2672 Paper; coated and laminated, nec
HQ: Upm Raflatac, Inc.
400 Broadpointe Dr
Mills River NC 28759
828 651-4800

(G-6048)
UPM RAFLATAC INC
Also Called: Smartrac Technology
267 Cane Creek Rd (28732-7401)
PHONE.............................828 651-4800
Noel Mitchell, *Mgr*
EMP: 19
Web: www.upmraflatac.com
SIC: 2672 Paper; coated and laminated, nec
HQ: Upm Raflatac, Inc.
400 Broadpointe Dr
Mills River NC 28759
828 651-4800

(G-6049)
VINEYARD HILL DISTRIBUTING LLC
215 Vineyard Hill Dr (28732-7689)
PHONE.............................828 684-5113
Jeff Garren, *Prin*
EMP: 4 EST: 2016
SALES (est): 90.06K **Privately Held**
SIC: 2084 Wines

(G-6050)
WC&R INTERESTS LLC
Also Called: Diamond Brand Canvas Products
145 Cane Creek Industrial Park Rd Ste 100 (28732-8306)
PHONE.............................828 684-9848
▲ EMP: 150 EST: 1881
SALES (est): 7.4MM **Privately Held**
SIC: 2394 Canvas and related products

(G-6051)
WELDING SOLUTIONS LLC
Also Called: Metal Creations
3632 Butler Bridge Rd (28732)
PHONE.............................828 665-4363
Gina Newnam, *Managing Member*
EMP: 21 EST: 1995
SQ FT: 15,000
SALES (est): 2.4MM **Privately Held**
Web: www.weldingunl.com
SIC: 3441 7692 Fabricated structural metal; Welding repair

(G-6052)
WILSONART LLC
145 Cane Creek Industrial Park Rd (28732-8306)
PHONE.............................866 267-7360
EMP: 5
SALES (corp-wide): 979.84MM **Privately Held**
Web: www.wilsonart.com
SIC: 2541 Wood partitions and fixtures
HQ: Wilsonart Llc
2501 Wilsonart Dr
Temple TX 76504
254 207-7000

(G-6053)
WINFIELD WOODWORKS
20 American Way (28732-7739)
PHONE.............................828 808-9727
Winfield Aub, *Prin*
EMP: 4 EST: 2013
SALES (est): 66.25K **Privately Held**
Web: www.winfieldwoodworks.com
SIC: 2431 Millwork

(G-6054)
YANCEY STONE INC
5 Williams Rd (28732-9430)
PHONE.............................828 684-5522
William Michael Mccrary, *Pr*
EMP: 7 EST: 1993
SALES (est): 970.75K **Privately Held**
SIC: 1429 Igneus rock, crushed and broken-quarrying

(G-6055)
YOUNG BAT ENTERPRISES INC
360 Jackson Rd (28732-9556)
PHONE.............................828 376-3706
Christopher Young, *Prin*
EMP: 6 EST: 2018
SALES (est): 246.24K **Privately Held**
Web: www.youngbatcompany.com
SIC: 3949 Sporting and athletic goods, nec

Forest City
Rutherford County

(G-6056)
ABC TEES STUFF
289 Knollwood Dr (28043-9651)
PHONE.............................828 287-7843
EMP: 4 EST: 2018
SALES (est): 107.97K **Privately Held**
SIC: 2759 Screen printing

(G-6057)
AEROQUIP CORP
240 Daniel Rd (28043-9186)
PHONE.............................828 286-4157
Glenn Lean, *Prin*
▲ EMP: 7 EST: 2008
SALES (est): 203.6K **Privately Held**
SIC: 3634 Electric housewares and fans

(G-6058)
AMERICAN WATER GRAPHICS INC
317 Vance St (28043-7747)
P.O. Box 86 (28043-0086)
PHONE.............................828 247-0700
John Ruppe Junior, *Pr*
▲ EMP: 14 EST: 1988
SQ FT: 50,000
SALES (est): 734.1K **Privately Held**
Web: www.americanwatergraphics.com
SIC: 2893 Printing ink

(G-6059)
ANDERSON LIVING CENTER LLC
390 Hardin Rd (28043-3858)
PHONE.............................828 229-3243
EMP: 4 EST: 2017
SALES (est): 101.14K **Privately Held**
SIC: 5713 5113 5087 3589 Floor covering stores; Paper, wrapping or coarse, and products; Vacuum cleaning systems; Commercial cleaning equipment

(G-6060)
BIGANODES LLC
117 Westerly Hills Dr (28043-9690)
PHONE.............................828 245-1115
Paul Skelton, *CEO*
EMP: 7 EST: 2015
SALES (est): 460.44K **Privately Held**
Web: www.biganodes.com
SIC: 5051 5085 3999 Metals service centers and offices; Industrial supplies; Atomizers, toiletry

(G-6061)
BOYD WELDING AND MFG INC
Also Called: Boyd's Welding and Fabrication

GEOGRAPHIC SECTION

Forest City - Rutherford County (G-6086)

324 Pine St (28043-4505)
P.O. Box 414 (28043-0414)
PHONE..............................828 247-0630
▲ **EMP:** 12 **EST:** 1999
SQ FT: 16,000
SALES (est): 928.26K **Privately Held**
Web: www.bwmcompany.com
SIC: 7692 Welding repair

(G-6062)
BUILDINGS R US
242 S Church St (28043-3504)
PHONE..............................828 382-0167
Byron Jack Callahan, *Admn*
EMP: 5 **EST:** 2017
SALES (est): 242.54K **Privately Held**
Web: www.buildingsrusllc.com
SIC: 3448 Prefabricated metal buildings and components

(G-6063)
CAROLINA WHELCHAIR BASKTBAL CO
629 Hardin Rd (28043-3423)
PHONE..............................828 248-2055
Patrick Barnes, *Prin*
EMP: 5 **EST:** 2016
SALES (est): 86.67K **Privately Held**
SIC: 3842 Wheelchairs

(G-6064)
CMI ENTERPRISES
135 Pine St (28043-4590)
PHONE..............................305 685-9651
EMP: 5 **EST:** 2017
SALES (est): 225.41K **Privately Held**
SIC: 2295 Coated fabrics, not rubberized

(G-6065)
DIVERSE CORPORATE TECH INC
Also Called: Plastic Oddities
289 Shiloh Rd (28043-6958)
P.O. Box 1528 (28139-1528)
PHONE..............................828 245-3717
TOLL FREE: 800
Kent Covington, *Pr*
Martin Bryson, *
Russell Millwood, *
Diane Mckinny, *Prin*
Gregory Southerland, *
▲ **EMP:** 25 **EST:** 1996
SQ FT: 29,000
SALES (est): 4.01MM **Privately Held**
Web: www.plasticoddities.com
SIC: 3089 Injection molding of plastics

(G-6066)
EATON CORPORATION
240 Daniel Rd (28043-9186)
PHONE..............................828 286-4157
Robert Williams, *Mgr*
EMP: 75
Web: www.dix-eaton.com
SIC: 3492 3052 Hose and tube fittings and assemblies, hydraulic/pneumatic; Rubber and plastics hose and beltings
HQ: Eaton Corporation
1000 Eaton Blvd
Cleveland OH 44122
440 523-5000

(G-6067)
EVEREST TEXTILE USA LLC
1331 W Main St (28043-2525)
PHONE..............................828 245-2696
Henry Lian, *Managing Member*
Scott Chen, *
EMP: 50 **EST:** 2016
SQ FT: 375,904
SALES (est): 10.01MM **Privately Held**
Web: www.everest.com.tw

SIC: 2299 Fabrics: linen, jute, hemp, ramie
PA: Everest Textile Co., Ltd.
No. 256, Minghe Vil.
Tainan City 74300

(G-6068)
FILER MICRO WELDING
251 Terry Filer Rd (28043-7016)
PHONE..............................828 248-1813
Gary E Filer, *Owner*
Gary Filer, *Owner*
EMP: 5 **EST:** 1996
SALES (est): 345.09K **Privately Held**
Web: www.filermicrowelding.com
SIC: 7692 Welding repair

(G-6069)
GREG GOODWIN PA
1269 Us Highway 221a (28043-5921)
PHONE..............................828 657-5371
EMP: 5 **EST:** 2019
SALES (est): 86.67K **Privately Held**
SIC: 3841 Surgical and medical instruments

(G-6070)
HERITAGE CLASSIC WOVENS LLC
Also Called: Millstreet Design
155 Westerly Hills Dr (28043-9690)
PHONE..............................828 247-6010
Jeff Carpenter, *Managing Member*
EMP: 11 **EST:** 2004
SALES (est): 480.65K **Privately Held**
Web: www.hcwllc.com
SIC: 2211 Upholstery fabrics, cotton

(G-6071)
INTEGRITY PLASTICS
291 Shiloh Rd (28043-6958)
PHONE..............................828 247-8801
Marty Bryson, *Prin*
EMP: 8 **EST:** 1995
SALES (est): 119.93K **Privately Held**
SIC: 3089 Molding primary plastics

(G-6072)
JENESIS SOFTWARE INC
Also Called: Agency Management Soluitons
294 S Broadway St (28043-4082)
PHONE..............................828 245-1171
Eddie Price, *Prin*
Lisa Price, *VP*
EMP: 5 **EST:** 2000
SALES (est): 517.6K **Privately Held**
Web: www.jenesissoftware.com
SIC: 7372 Prepackaged software

(G-6073)
KCH SERVICES INC
Also Called: Kch Engineered Systems
144 Industrial Dr (28043-9675)
P.O. Box 1287 (28043-1287)
PHONE..............................828 245-9836
Ken Hankinson, *CEO*
Kyle Hankinson, *
Rick Hall, *
EMP: 40 **EST:** 1980
SQ FT: 35,000
SALES (est): 9.32MM **Privately Held**
Web: www.kchservices.com
SIC: 3564 Air purification equipment

(G-6074)
KUTE N KLASSY BY JEN LLC
285 Crowe Dairy Rd (28043-9187)
PHONE..............................828 755-5613
EMP: 4 **EST:** 2020
SALES (est): 77.45K **Privately Held**
SIC: 3161 Clothing and apparel carrying cases

(G-6075)
LIBERTY STREET LLC
Also Called: Heritage Clssic Wven Mllstreet
155 Westerly Hills Dr (28043-9690)
PHONE..............................828 247-6010
Alan Clark, *Managing Member*
EMP: 6 **EST:** 2015
SQ FT: 30,000
SALES (est): 181.08K **Privately Held**
SIC: 2221 Textile mills, broadwoven: silk and manmade, also glass

(G-6076)
MAYSE MANUFACTURING CO INC (PA)
2201 Us Highway 221 S (28043-7058)
PHONE..............................828 245-1891
Johnny L Mayse, *Pr*
Sandra Mayse, *VP*
EMP: 7 **EST:** 1972
SQ FT: 25,000
SALES (est): 948.85K
SALES (corp-wide): 948.85K **Privately Held**
Web: www.maysemfg.com
SIC: 3448 Buildings, portable: prefabricated metal

(G-6077)
MERITOR INC
160 Ash Dr (28043-7767)
PHONE..............................828 247-0440
Lucille Gartman, *Mgr*
EMP: 72
SALES (corp-wide): 34.06B **Publicly Held**
Web: www.meritor.com
SIC: 3714 Axles, motor vehicle
HQ: Meritor, Inc.
2135 W Maple Rd
Troy MI 48084

(G-6078)
MISTRETTA LASER ENGRAVING
272 Nursery Rd (28043-6164)
PHONE..............................704 418-5786
Kevin Mistretta, *Prin*
EMP: 4 **EST:** 2017
SALES (est): 53.97K **Privately Held**
SIC: 3993 Signs and advertising specialties

(G-6079)
PARKER-HANNIFIN CORPORATION
Also Called: Hydraulic Valve Division
203 Pine St (28043-4589)
PHONE..............................828 245-3233
Andy Ross, *Brnch Mgr*
EMP: 22
SALES (corp-wide): 19.07B **Publicly Held**
Web: www.parker.com
SIC: 5084 3491 Hydraulic systems equipment and supplies; Automatic regulating and control valves
PA: Parker-Hannifin Corporation
6035 Parkland Blvd
Cleveland OH 44124
216 896-3000

(G-6080)
ROCKTENN IN-STORE SOLUTIONS INC
376 Pine St (28043-4505)
P.O. Box 4098 (30091-4098)
PHONE..............................828 245-9871
EMP: 400
SIC: 2653 Display items, corrugated: made from purchased materials

(G-6081)
SONOCO HICKORY INC
681 Piney Ridge Rd (28043-9019)

PHONE..............................828 286-1356
EMP: 103
SALES (corp-wide): 6.78B **Publicly Held**
SIC: 2673 2671 Bags: plastic, laminated, and coated; Paper; coated and laminated packaging
HQ: Sonoco Hickory, Inc.
1246 Main Ave Se
Hickory NC 28602
828 328-2466

(G-6082)
SONOCO PRODUCTS COMPANY
Also Called: Sonoco
323 Pine St (28043-4504)
P.O. Box 749 (28043-0749)
PHONE..............................828 245-0118
Steve Trummont, *Mgr*
EMP: 92
SALES (corp-wide): 6.78B **Publicly Held**
Web: www.sonoco.com
SIC: 3089 Plastics containers, except foam
PA: Sonoco Products Company
1 N 2nd St
Hartsville SC 29550
843 383-7000

(G-6083)
SPECIALTY WELDING
737 Hardin Rd (28043-3425)
PHONE..............................828 248-6229
EMP: 4 **EST:** 2018
SALES (est): 28.12K **Privately Held**
SIC: 7692 Welding repair

(G-6084)
TRI CITY CONCRETE CO LLC
158 Withrow Rd (28043-9464)
P.O. Box 241 (28043-0241)
PHONE..............................828 245-2011
Steve Barnes, *Managing Member*
Bill Morris, *Managing Member*
EMP: 29 **EST:** 1949
SALES (est): 2.88MM **Privately Held**
SIC: 3273 Ready-mixed concrete

(G-6085)
UNITED SOUTHERN INDUSTRIES INC (DH)
486 Vance St (28043-2958)
PHONE..............................866 273-1810
Joe Y Bennett, *CEO*
Todd Bennett, *
▲ **EMP:** 100 **EST:** 1983
SQ FT: 90,000
SALES (est): 10.08MM
SALES (corp-wide): 218.2MM **Privately Held**
SIC: 3089 3524 3423 Injection molding of plastics; Lawn and garden equipment; Hand and edge tools, nec
HQ: Wilbert Plastic Services Acquisition Llc
1000 Oaks Pkwy
Belmont NC 28012

(G-6086)
WELLS JNKINS WELLS MT PROC INC
145 Rollins Rd (28043-9324)
PHONE..............................828 245-5544
Grady H Wells, *Pr*
Jeffrey Wells, *VP*
William R Wells, *Sec*
EMP: 6 **EST:** 1972
SQ FT: 4,000
SALES (est): 501.98K **Privately Held**
SIC: 5421 2011 Meat markets, including freezer provisioners; Beef products, from beef slaughtered on site

Forest City - Rutherford County (G-6087)

(G-6087)
WESTROCK COMPANY
376 Pine Street Ext (28043-5800)
PHONE.................828 248-4815
EMP: 5
SALES (corp-wide): 20.31B Publicly Held
Web: www.westrock.com
SIC: 2653 Boxes, corrugated: made from purchased materials
PA: Westrock Company
1000 Abernathy Rd
Atlanta GA 30328
770 448-2193

(G-6088)
WESTROCK CONVERTING LLC
376 Pine St (28043-4505)
PHONE.................828 245-9871
EMP: 400
SALES (corp-wide): 20.31B Publicly Held
Web: www.westrock.com
SIC: 2653 Boxes, corrugated: made from purchased materials
HQ: Westrock Converting, Llc
1000 Abernathy Rd Ste 125
Atlanta GA 30328
770 448-2193

Fort Bragg
Cumberland County

(G-6089)
GENERAL DYNMICS MSSION SYSTEMS
Also Called: General Dynamics Worldwide
6812 Butner Rd And Letterman St Bldg 8 (28310-0001)
P.O. Box 71158 (28307-1158)
PHONE.................910 497-7900
Mike Divittorio, Mgr
EMP: 10
SALES (corp-wide): 42.27B Publicly Held
Web: www.gdmissionsystems.com
SIC: 3571 Electronic computers
HQ: General Dynamics Mission Systems, Inc.
12450 Fair Lakes Cir
Fairfax VA 22033
877 449-0600

(G-6090)
HONEYWELL INTERNATIONAL INC
Also Called: Honeywell
1 Fort Bragg (28307-5000)
P.O. Box 73721 (28307-6721)
PHONE.................910 436-5144
EMP: 4
SALES (corp-wide): 36.66B Publicly Held
Web: www.honeywell.com
SIC: 3724 Aircraft engines and engine parts
PA: Honeywell International Inc.
855 S Mint St
Charlotte NC 28202
704 627-6200

(G-6091)
US PATRIOT LLC
Also Called: US PATRIOT LLC
Bldg Z 3252 - 1017 Canopy Lane (28307)
PHONE.................803 787-9398
Phillips N Dee, Brnch Mgr
EMP: 10
SALES (corp-wide): 732.04MM Privately Held
Web: www.uspatriottactical.com
SIC: 2311 Military uniforms, men's and youths': purchased materials
HQ: Us Patriot, Llc
1340 Russell Cave Rd
Lexington KY 40505
800 805-5294

Fountain
Pitt County

(G-6092)
AE WIRING LLC
5887 W Blount St (27829-8209)
PHONE.................252 749-0195
EMP: 10 EST: 2019
SALES (est): 1.43MM Privately Held
Web: www.aewiring.com
SIC: 3714 Automotive wiring harness sets

(G-6093)
EASY FRESH PRODUCTS
5403 Dilda Church Rd (27829-9384)
PHONE.................704 216-4111
Melinda Schwab, Prin
EMP: 6 EST: 2018
SALES (est): 57.45K Privately Held
SIC: 2842 Polishes and sanitation goods

(G-6094)
LAD WAYS OF PRINTING INC
3820 Nc Highway 222 (27829-9316)
PHONE.................252 814-9559
EMP: 5 EST: 2019
SALES (est): 92.3K Privately Held
SIC: 2752 Commercial printing, lithographic

(G-6095)
MARIETTA MARTIN MATERIALS INC
Also Called: Martin Marietta Aggregates
5368 Allen Gay Rd (27829-9506)
P.O. Box 187 (27829-0187)
PHONE.................252 749-2641
Ed Judy, Mgr
EMP: 11
Web: www.martinmarietta.com
SIC: 1422 Crushed and broken limestone
PA: Martin Marietta Materials Inc
4123 Parklake Ave
Raleigh NC 27612

(G-6096)
RA FOUNTAIN LLC
6754 E Wilson St (27829-9635)
P.O. Box 44 (27829-0044)
PHONE.................252 749-3228
EMP: 9 EST: 2005
SALES (est): 206.61K Privately Held
Web: www.rafountain.com
SIC: 2741 Miscellaneous publishing

(G-6097)
SEVEN PINES VINEYARD INC
544 Seven Pines Rd (27829-9311)
PHONE.................252 717-2283
Philip Guy, Owner
EMP: 4 EST: 2018
SALES (est): 54.9K Privately Held
SIC: 2084 Wines

(G-6098)
TAR RIVER MINING INC
1769 Seven Pines Rd (27829-9799)
P.O. Box 366 (27828-0366)
PHONE.................252 753-3447
David Vendemia, Pr
EMP: 5 EST: 2009
SALES (est): 87K Privately Held
SIC: 2865 Tar

Four Oaks
Johnston County

(G-6099)
ALLEN & SON S CABINET SHOP INC
5942 Us Highway 301 S (27524-9328)
P.O. Box 370 (27524-0370)
PHONE.................919 963-2196
Donald K Allen, Pr
EMP: 9 EST: 1972
SQ FT: 11,000
SALES (est): 456.15K Privately Held
Web: www.allenandsonscabinets.com
SIC: 2434 Vanities, bathroom: wood

(G-6100)
BECTON DICKINSON AND COMPANY
130 Four Oaks Pkwy (27524-7228)
PHONE.................919 963-1307
EMP: 34
SALES (corp-wide): 19.37B Publicly Held
Web: www.bd.com
SIC: 3841 Surgical and medical instruments
PA: Becton, Dickinson And Company
1 Becton Dr
Franklin Lakes NJ 07417
201 847-6800

(G-6101)
BOUNDLESS INC
102 S Main St (27524-8223)
P.O. Box 105 (27524-0105)
PHONE.................919 622-9051
David Faircloth, Pr
EMP: 6 EST: 2020
SALES (est): 35K Privately Held
Web: www.feelboundless.com
SIC: 7336 2752 Commercial art and graphic design; Commercial printing, lithographic

(G-6102)
D & W LOGGING INC
1771 Stricklands Crossroads Rd (27524-8710)
PHONE.................919 820-0826
Daniel Knight, Admn
EMP: 10 EST: 2021
SALES (est): 261.23K Privately Held
SIC: 2411 Logging

(G-6103)
ELITE MARINE LLC
Also Called: Savannah Boats
377 King Mill Rd (27524-8335)
PHONE.................919 495-6388
EMP: 37 EST: 2019
SALES (est): 2.78MM Privately Held
Web: www.savannahboats.com
SIC: 3732 Boatbuilding and repairing

(G-6104)
FIELDSWAY SOLUTIONS LLC ◊
177 Ridgemoore Ct (27524-7509)
PHONE.................984 920-7791
Arthur Fields, Managing Member
EMP: 4 EST: 2022
SALES (est): 63.22K Privately Held
SIC: 7372 1731 7373 7336 Application computer software; Computer installation; Systems engineering, computer related; Commercial art and graphic design

(G-6105)
GENCO
130 Four Oaks Pkwy (27524-7228)
PHONE.................919 963-4227
EMP: 5 EST: 2015
SALES (est): 95.88K Privately Held
SIC: 3841 Surgical and medical instruments

(G-6106)
GRADY & SON ATKINS LOGGING
1401 Devils Racetrack Rd (27524-9313)
PHONE.................919 934-7785
Grady Atkins, Pr
Gary Atkins, VP
Patricia Atkins, Sec
EMP: 9 EST: 1989
SALES (est): 965.58K Privately Held
SIC: 2411 Logging camps and contractors

(G-6107)
HOUSE-AUTRY MILLS INC (PA)
7000 Us Highway 301 S (27524-7628)
P.O. Box 460 (27524-0460)
PHONE.................919 963-6200
Roger F Mortenson, Pr
Robert T Depree, *
EMP: 46 EST: 1966
SQ FT: 50,000
SALES (est): 22.57MM
SALES (corp-wide): 22.57MM Privately Held
Web: www.house-autry.com
SIC: 2041 Corn meal

(G-6108)
LYNX DEFENSE CORPORATION
Also Called: Lynx Outdoor Gear
212 Ivey Rd (27524-7867)
P.O. Box 1041 (27504-1041)
PHONE.................919 701-9411
Michael D Savage, Admn
EMP: 5 EST: 2013
SALES (est): 225.22K Privately Held
Web: www.lynxdefense.com
SIC: 3812 Defense systems and equipment

(G-6109)
MAY-CRAFT FIBERGLASS PDTS INC
96 Hillsboro Rd (27524-8028)
P.O. Box 450 (27577-0450)
PHONE.................919 934-3000
Kenneth L May, Pr
Dianne May, Sec
▼ EMP: 21 EST: 1992
SQ FT: 44,000
SALES (est): 903.08K Privately Held
Web: www.maycraftboats.com
SIC: 3732 Boats, fiberglass: building and repairing

(G-6110)
OCEAN ROAD GRAPHICS SIGNS
914 Parkertown Rd (27524-8908)
PHONE.................919 404-1444
EMP: 4 EST: 2018
SALES (est): 89.79K Privately Held
SIC: 3993 Signs and advertising specialties

(G-6111)
ROY DUNN
Also Called: NAPA Auto Parts
101 Dunn St (27524-7105)
PHONE.................919 963-3700
Roy Dunn, Owner
EMP: 4 EST: 1987
SALES (est): 505.33K Privately Held
Web: www.napaonline.com
SIC: 5531 3599 Automotive parts; Machine shop, jobbing and repair

(G-6112)
SOUTHERN WOODS LUMBER INC
3872 Old School Rd (27524-8675)
PHONE.................919 963-2233
EMP: 12 EST: 2017
SALES (est): 789.3K Privately Held

SIC: 2421 Lumber: rough, sawed, or planed

(G-6113)
T E JOHNSON LUMBER CO INC
Also Called: T E Johnson Building and Rentl
3872 Old School Rd (27524-8675)
P.O. Box 341 (27504-0341)
PHONE..................919 963-2233
Thom E Johnson, *Pr*
Lana Massengill, *VP*
Heather Cliston, *Sec*
Thom Johnson Iii, *Stockholder*
EMP: 13 **EST:** 1946
SQ FT: 10,000
SALES (est): 383.39K **Privately Held**
Web: www.tejohnsonlumber.com
SIC: 2421 5211 Lumber: rough, sawed, or planed; Lumber and other building materials

Franklin
Macon County

(G-6114)
ALL STAR SIGN COMPANY
Also Called: All Star Marketing & Media Co
20 Coddies Ter (28734-8584)
PHONE..................214 862-6797
EMP: 5 **EST:** 2019
SALES (est): 70K **Privately Held**
Web: www.allstarsigncompany.com
SIC: 3993 Signs and advertising specialties

(G-6115)
ANDERS CUSTOM CABINETRY
540 Terrell Rd (28734-8708)
PHONE..................828 342-4222
Tim Anders, *Prin*
EMP: 6 **EST:** 2009
SALES (est): 124.12K **Privately Held**
Web: www.anderscustomcabinets.com
SIC: 2434 Wood kitchen cabinets

(G-6116)
BEASLEY FLOORING PRODUCTS INC
Also Called: Flooring Manufacturing
41 Hardwood Dr (28734-3012)
PHONE..................828 349-7000
EMP: 35
SALES (corp-wide): 115.61MM **Privately Held**
Web: www.beasleyflooring.com
SIC: 2426 Hardwood dimension and flooring mills
HQ: Beasley Flooring Products, Inc.
  770 Uvalda Hwy
  Hazlehurst GA 31539

(G-6117)
BRYANT GRANT MUTUAL BURIAL ASN
105 W Main St (28734-2916)
PHONE..................828 524-2411
EMP: 5 **EST:** 2011
SALES (est): 160.68K **Privately Held**
Web: www.bryantgrantfuneralhome.com
SIC: 3272 Burial vaults, concrete or precast terrazzo

(G-6118)
CANVASMASTERS LLC
78 Cabe Cove Rd (28734-5979)
PHONE..................828 369-0406
Gred Mcgaha, *Owner*
Greg Mcgaha, *Owner*
EMP: 4 **EST:** 1997
SALES (est): 188.7K **Privately Held**
Web: www.canvasmasterswnc.com

SIC: 2394 Canvas and related products

(G-6119)
CLUB THE NANTAHALA BICYCLE INC
Also Called: Nantahala Bicycle Shop
1863 Georgia Rd (28734-7323)
PHONE..................828 524-4900
Angelo Arduengo, *CEO*
EMP: 5 **EST:** 2020
SALES (est): 180.74K **Privately Held**
Web: www.nantahalabikes.com
SIC: 3751 Bicycles and related parts

(G-6120)
COATES DESIGNERS & CRAFTSMEN
57 Mill St (28734-2710)
P.O. Box 1273 (28744-1273)
PHONE..................828 349-9700
Alan F Coates, *Pr*
EMP: 8 **EST:** 1960
SQ FT: 8,000
SALES (est): 504.51K **Privately Held**
Web: www.coatesplaques.com
SIC: 3999 2821 3993 Plaques, picture, laminated; Polymethyl methacrylate resins, plexiglass; Signs and advertising specialties

(G-6121)
COMMUNITY NEWSPAPERS INC
Also Called: Cni Regional
690 Wayah St (28734-3390)
P.O. Box 530 (28744-0530)
PHONE..................828 369-3430
Judy Waldrop, *Mgr*
EMP: 4
SALES (corp-wide): 49.22MM **Privately Held**
Web: www.cninewspapers.com
SIC: 2711 Newspapers, publishing and printing
PA: Community Newspapers, Inc.
  2365 Prince Ave A
  Athens GA 30606
  706 548-0010

(G-6122)
COOK BROTHERS LUMBER CO INC
85 Peaceful Cove Rd (28734-8925)
P.O. Box 699 (28744-0699)
PHONE..................828 524-4857
Leneord Cook, *Pr*
Elizabeth Cook, *Sec*
EMP: 12 **EST:** 1968
SQ FT: 1,000
SALES (est): 577.39K **Privately Held**
SIC: 2421 Sawmills and planing mills, general

(G-6123)
COWEE MOUNTAIN RUBY MINE
6771 Sylva Rd (28734-2243)
PHONE..................828 369-5271
Sonja Eldridge, *Prin*
▲ **EMP:** 7 **EST:** 2002
SALES (est): 463.02K **Privately Held**
Web: www.coweemtnrubymine.com
SIC: 1241 Coal mining services

(G-6124)
DRAKE ENTERPRISES LTD
Also Called: Macon Printing
219 E Palmer St (28734-3049)
PHONE..................828 524-7045
Billy Banhook, *Mgr*
EMP: 5
SALES (corp-wide): 47.33MM **Privately Held**
Web: www.drakesoftware.com

SIC: 2752 Business form and card printing, lithographic
PA: Drake Enterprises, Ltd.
  235 E Palmer St
  Franklin NC 28734
  828 524-2922

(G-6125)
DRAKE SOFTWARE LLC
235 E Palmer St (28734-3049)
PHONE..................828 524-2922
Dominic Morea, *Pr*
Euan Menzies, *
Leslie Gibson, *
EMP: 295 **EST:** 2010
SALES (est): 23.81MM **Privately Held**
Web: www.drakesoftware.com
SIC: 7372 Business oriented computer software

(G-6126)
DUOTECH SERVICES INC
245 Industrial Park Rd (28734-7920)
PHONE..................828 369-5411
Daniel L Rogers, *Pr*
Cheryl Rogers, *VP*
EMP: 25 **EST:** 1983
SQ FT: 20,000
SALES (est): 10.02MM **Privately Held**
Web: www.duotechservices.com
SIC: 7629 3679 Electronic equipment repair; Electronic circuits

(G-6127)
DUSTY PALLET
52 E Main St (28734-3026)
PHONE..................828 524-5676
EMP: 4 **EST:** 2016
SALES (est): 142.28K **Privately Held**
Web: www.thedustypallet.com
SIC: 2448 Pallets, wood and wood with metal

(G-6128)
ELITE MOUNTAIN BUSINESS LLC
Also Called: Ridge Line Homes
21 Sanderstown Rd (28734-8622)
PHONE..................828 349-0403
Carey Lannon, *Managing Member*
Cynthia Truesdale, *Managing Member*
EMP: 4 **EST:** 2015
SALES (est): 240.3K **Privately Held**
SIC: 2451 Mobile homes

(G-6129)
FRANKLIN MACHINE COMPANY LLC
231 Depot St (28734-3001)
P.O. Box 1149 (28744-1149)
PHONE..................828 524-2313
Tommy Potts, *VP*
EMP: 11 **EST:** 1950
SALES (est): 485.52K **Privately Held**
Web: www.franklinmachineandsteel.com
SIC: 3599 Machine shop, jobbing and repair

(G-6130)
FRANKLIN SHEET METAL SHOP INC
Also Called: Franklin Sheet Metal
791 Ulco Dr Ste A (28734-3365)
PHONE..................828 524-2821
James T Mann Senior, *Pr*
Ed Cope, *Sec*
EMP: 17 **EST:** 1952
SALES (est): 794.97K **Privately Held**
SIC: 1711 3444 Warm air heating and air conditioning contractor; Sheet metalwork

(G-6131)
GOODER GRAFIX INC
1021 E Main St (28734-2676)
PHONE..................828 349-4097

Guy Gooder, *Pr*
Alicia Gooder, *VP*
EMP: 4 **EST:** 1982
SALES (est): 464.51K **Privately Held**
Web: www.goodergrafix.com
SIC: 3993 7261 Signs, not made in custom sign painting shops; Funeral service and crematories

(G-6132)
HARMONY HOUSE FOODS INC
277 Industrial Park Rd (28734-7920)
PHONE..................800 696-1395
John Seaman, *Pr*
Linda Seaman, *VP*
EMP: 8 **EST:** 2005
SALES (est): 858.83K **Privately Held**
Web: www.harmonyhousefoods.com
SIC: 2099 Food preparations, nec

(G-6133)
K & M PRODUCTS OF NC INC
3248 Patton Rd (28734-7896)
PHONE..................828 524-5905
Judy Kirkland, *Pr*
Ronald Lee Kirkland, *VP*
EMP: 10 **EST:** 1979
SALES (est): 838.89K **Privately Held**
Web: www.kmproductsofnc.com
SIC: 3829 Surveying and drafting equipment

(G-6134)
KISS MANUFACTURING CO INC
188 Falling Rock Rd (28734-7107)
P.O. Box 150 (28744-0150)
PHONE..................828 524-6293
Keller Newton, *Pr*
EMP: 7 **EST:** 1976
SALES (est): 202.99K **Privately Held**
Web: www.kissmfg.com
SIC: 3199 Dog furnishings: collars, leashes, muzzles, etc.: leather

(G-6135)
LIBASCI WOODWORKS INC
401 Dobson Mountain Rd R (28734-6157)
PHONE..................828 524-7073
Gary Libasci, *Prin*
EMP: 4 **EST:** 2008
SALES (est): 154.48K **Privately Held**
SIC: 2431 Millwork

(G-6136)
LIBERTY WOOD PRODUCTS INC
874 Iotla Church Rd (28734-0329)
PHONE..................828 524-7958
Tim Hubbs, *Pr*
Phil Drake, *Ch*
John Sapp, *Treas*
EMP: 14 **EST:** 1978
SQ FT: 5,000
SALES (est): 2.02MM **Privately Held**
Web: www.libertywoodproducts.net
SIC: 2431 Millwork

(G-6137)
MAJOR DISPLAY INC
131 Franklin Plaza Dr Ste 363 (28734-3249)
PHONE..................800 260-1067
Glen Whittaker, *Pr*
EMP: 9 **EST:** 2015
SALES (est): 492.21K **Privately Held**
Web: www.majordisplay.com
SIC: 3993 Scoreboards, electric

(G-6138)
MAMA NEDS SUBSCRIPTION BOX LLC
2880 Old Murphy Rd (28734-7211)

Franklin - Macon County (G-6139)

PHONE..................954 703-9308
Jennifer Collins, *Prin*
EMP: 5 **EST:** 2018
SALES (est): 79.09K **Privately Held**
Web: www.mamaneedsbox.com
SIC: 2741 Miscellaneous publishing

(G-6139)
MOONSHINE PRESS
162 Riverwood Dr (28734-1375)
PHONE..................828 371-8519
EMP: 4 **EST:** 2013
SALES (est): 60.52K **Privately Held**
SIC: 2741 Miscellaneous publishing

(G-6140)
MOTHER OF PEARL CO INC
86 Belden Terrace Ln (28734-8575)
P.O. Box 445 (28744-0445)
PHONE..................828 524-6842
Joseph Culpepper, *Prin*
EMP: 5 **EST:** 2016
SALES (est): 72.89K **Privately Held**
Web: www.motherofpearl.us
SIC: 3421 Cutlery

(G-6141)
PARRISH CONTRACTING LLC
3370 Bryson City Rd (28734-4315)
P.O. Box 1026 (28744-1026)
PHONE..................828 524-9100
Matthew Holland, *Pr*
Jim Parrish, *Owner*
EMP: 8 **EST:** 2019
SALES (est): 781.6K **Privately Held**
Web: www.desototrailrealty.com
SIC: 1721 1799 1442 Painting and paper hanging; Construction site cleanup; Construction sand and gravel

(G-6142)
SEAMLESS SATELLITE SOLUTIONS
591 Town Mountain Dr (28734-9714)
PHONE..................828 421-8988
EMP: 4 **EST:** 2010
SALES (est): 67.98K **Privately Held**
SIC: 3663 Space satellite communications equipment

(G-6143)
SHAW INDUSTRIES INC
301 Depot St (28734-3060)
PHONE..................828 369-1701
Tien Ellington, *Brnch Mgr*
EMP: 275
SALES (corp-wide): 364.48B **Publicly Held**
Web: www.shawinc.com
SIC: 2273 Carpets and rugs
HQ: Shaw Industries, Inc.
   616 E Walnut Ave
   Dalton GA 30721

(G-6144)
SOUTHERN CONCRETE MTLS INC
493 Wells Grove Rd (28734-7521)
PHONE..................828 524-3555
Eddie Evans, *Manager*
EMP: 17
SALES (corp-wide): 238.17MM **Privately Held**
Web: www.scmusa.com
SIC: 3273 1771 Ready-mixed concrete; Driveway contractor
HQ: Southern Concrete Materials, Inc.
   35 Meadow Rd
   Asheville NC 28803
   828 253-6421

(G-6145)
TEKTONE SOUND & SIGNAL MFG INC
324 Industrial Park Rd (28734-1006)
PHONE..................828 524-9967
Carlos Mira, *Pr*
Manuel S Mira, *
Maria Mira, *
Teresa Knippel, *
◆ **EMP:** 90 **EST:** 1973
SQ FT: 32,800
SALES (est): 22.08MM **Privately Held**
Web: www.tektone.com
SIC: 7382 3669 Security systems services; Burglar alarm apparatus, electric

(G-6146)
TRICORN USA INC
66 Van Raalte St (28734-2760)
PHONE..................828 369-6682
Michael Welburn, *Pr*
David Leakey, *
Phillip Lee, *
▲ **EMP:** 110 **EST:** 2013
SQ FT: 60,000
SALES (est): 34.54MM **Privately Held**
SIC: 3317 Steel pipe and tubes
PA: Tricorn Group Plc
   Spring Lane
   Malvern WORCS WR14

(G-6147)
WATAUGA CREEK LLC
25 Setser Branch Rd (28734-9215)
PHONE..................828 369-7881
Robert W Moyer, *Owner*
▲ **EMP:** 5 **EST:** 1982
SALES (est): 500.35K **Privately Held**
Web: www.wataugacreek.com
SIC: 5712 2512 5021 Mattresses; Upholstered household furniture; Furniture

(G-6148)
WATERWHEEL FACTORY
320 Arbor Ln (28734-6116)
PHONE..................828 369-5928
Robert Vitale, *Owner*
EMP: 4 **EST:** 1999
SALES (est): 231.06K **Privately Held**
Web: www.waterwheelfactory.com
SIC: 3511 Hydraulic turbine generator set units, complete

(G-6149)
ZICKGRAF ENTERPRISES INC
Franklin Machine
231 Depot St (28734-3001)
P.O. Box 1149 (28744-1149)
PHONE..................828 524-2313
Paul Thomas Potts, *VP*
EMP: 6
SQ FT: 2,000
SALES (corp-wide): 7.06MM **Privately Held**
Web: www.nantahalaflooring.com
SIC: 7699 7692 7538 Industrial machinery and equipment repair; Welding repair; General automotive repair shops
PA: Zickgraf Enterprises, Inc.
   301 Depot St
   Franklin NC 28734
   828 369-1200

(G-6150)
ZICKGRAF ENTERPRISES INC
301 Depot St (28734-3060)
PHONE..................704 369-1200
Bodenheimer Fp, *Sr*
EMP: 7 **EST:** 2009
SALES (est): 109.44K **Privately Held**

SIC: 2426 Hardwood dimension and flooring mills

Franklinton
Franklin County

(G-6151)
C-TRON INCORPORATED
22 N Main St (27525-1357)
PHONE..................919 494-7811
Donna Albright, *CEO*
Thomas Albright, *Pr*
EMP: 17 **EST:** 1991
SQ FT: 8,000
SALES (est): 729.13K **Privately Held**
Web: www.ctroninc.com
SIC: 3672 3643 Printed circuit boards; Current-carrying wiring services

(G-6152)
CARDEN FARMS SOAP INC
204 King Dr (27525-7285)
PHONE..................919 570-0745
Ann Johnston, *Prin*
EMP: 4 **EST:** 2001
SALES (est): 182.05K **Privately Held**
Web: www.cardenfarmsnc.com
SIC: 2841 Soap: granulated, liquid, cake, flaked, or chip

(G-6153)
CONTAINER SYSTEMS INCORPORATED
6863 N Carolina 56 Hwy E (27525-7379)
P.O. Box 519 (27525-0519)
PHONE..................919 496-6133
TOLL FREE: 800
EMP: 75
SIC: 2449 3565 2657 Shipping cases and drums, wood: wirebound and plywood; Packaging machinery; Folding paperboard boxes

(G-6154)
FRANKLIN VENEERS INC
5735 Nc Hwy 56 E (27525)
P.O. Box 70 (27525-0070)
PHONE..................919 494-2284
Richard H Morgan Junior, *Pr*
Richard H Morgan Iii, *VP*
Judy Morgan, *
EMP: 25 **EST:** 1937
SQ FT: 20,000
SALES (est): 1.1MM **Privately Held**
SIC: 2435 2426 Veneer stock, hardwood; Hardwood dimension and flooring mills

(G-6155)
INDULGENT ESSENTIAL SPICES LLC
Also Called: Indulgent Essential Spices
7 W Mason St Ste A (27525-1335)
PHONE..................919 973-3069
Queen Precious-jewel Zabriskie, *Prin*
Queen Precious-jewel Zabriskie, *Prin*
EMP: 4 **EST:** 2021
SALES (est): 75.25K **Privately Held**
Web: www.indulgentessentialspices.com
SIC: 2099 Seasonings and spices

(G-6156)
KATESVILLE PALLET MILL INC
7119 Nc 56 Hwy (27525-7249)
PHONE..................919 496-3162
David Kemp, *Pr*
EMP: 35 **EST:** 1971
SQ FT: 2,000
SALES (est): 2.17MM **Privately Held**
SIC: 2421 Sawmills and planing mills, general

(G-6157)
LINDSAY PRECAST INC
Also Called: LINDSAY PRECAST, INC.
2675 Us1 Hwy (27525-8499)
P.O. Box 580 (27525-0580)
PHONE..................919 494-7600
Matt Blind, *Genl Mgr*
EMP: 50
SALES (corp-wide): 98.36MM **Privately Held**
Web: www.lindsayprecast.com
SIC: 3272 Precast terrazzo or concrete products
PA: Lindsay Precast, Llc
   6845 Erie Ave Nw
   Canal Fulton OH 44614
   800 837-7788

(G-6158)
LUXURIOUSLY NATURAL PRODUCTS
4158 Winchester Ln (27525-7553)
PHONE..................919 345-9050
Sonya Evans, *Owner*
EMP: 5 **EST:** 2017
SALES (est): 82.16K **Privately Held**
Web: www.lnsoaps.com
SIC: 2844 Perfumes, cosmetics and other toilet preparations

(G-6159)
NOVOZYMES INC
77 Perrys Chapel Church Rd (27525-9677)
PHONE..................919 494-3950
EMP: 63
SALES (corp-wide): 2.45B **Privately Held**
Web: www.novozymes.com
SIC: 2869 Industrial organic chemicals, nec
HQ: Novozymes, Inc.
   1445 Drew Ave
   Davis CA 95618

(G-6160)
NOVOZYMES NORTH AMERICA INC (HQ)
Also Called: Novozymes
77 Perrys Chapel Church Rd (27525-9677)
P.O. Box 610 (27525-0610)
PHONE..................919 494-2014
Adam Monroe, *Ch Bd*
Steen Riisgaard, *
Thomas Nagy, *
Per Falholt, *
Kristian Merser, *
◆ **EMP:** 62 **EST:** 1969
SALES (est): 522.07MM
SALES (corp-wide): 2.45B **Privately Held**
Web: www.novozymes.com
SIC: 2869 Enzymes
PA: Novozymes A/S
   Krogshojvej 36
   Bagsvard 2880
   44460000

(G-6161)
OLYMPIAN WELDING
3660 Windsor Dr (27525-7617)
PHONE..................919 608-3829
Joshua Pfohl, *Prin*
EMP: 5 **EST:** 2017
SALES (est): 41.25K **Privately Held**
SIC: 7692 Welding repair

(G-6162)
PALLETS AND MORE
119 N Cheatham St (27525-1302)
PHONE..................919 815-6134
Joshua Roberson, *Prin*
EMP: 5 **EST:** 2016
SALES (est): 129.42K **Privately Held**

SIC: 2448 Wood pallets and skids

(G-6163)
S T WOOTEN CORPORATION
Also Called: Franklinton Concrete Plant
255 Material Rd (27525)
PHONE.....................919 562-1851
Scott Wooten, Pr
EMP: 22
SALES (corp-wide): 319.83MM **Privately Held**
Web: www.stwcorp.com
SIC: 3531 Concrete plants
PA: S. T. Wooten Corporation
3801 Black Creek Rd Se
Wilson NC 27893
252 291-5165

(G-6164)
STAY-RIGHT PRE-CAST CONCRETE INC
2675 Us1 Hwy (27525)
P.O. Box 580 (27525-0580)
PHONE.....................919 494-7600
EMP: 52
SIC: 3272 Concrete products, nec

(G-6165)
TETAC
135 Cedarhurst Ln (27525-8028)
PHONE.....................919 369-9106
Brandon Gayle, Prin
EMP: 5 EST: 2010
SALES (est): 129.56K **Privately Held**
SIC: 3523 Farm machinery and equipment

(G-6166)
THOMPSON TIMBER HARVEST LLC
350 W Green St (27525-9325)
PHONE.....................919 632-4326
William C Thompson, Prin
EMP: 5 EST: 2019
SALES (est): 103.91K **Privately Held**
SIC: 2411 Logging

Franklinville
Randolph County

(G-6167)
CAUSEKEEPERS INC
Also Called: 4 Your Cause
5068 Us Highway 64 E (27248-8656)
PHONE.....................336 824-2518
Donald Lafferty, Pr
Samuel Hicks, VP
◆ EMP: 20 EST: 2004
SQ FT: 120,000
SALES (est): 1.69MM **Privately Held**
Web: www.causekeepers.com
SIC: 2759 2752 5199 7336 Screen printing; Offset printing; Advertising specialties; Art design services

(G-6168)
DEEP RIVER FABRICATORS INC
240 E Main St (27248-8603)
P.O. Box 100 (27248-0100)
PHONE.....................336 824-8881
Roy Luckenbach, Pr
Eric Luckenbach, Pr
EMP: 24 EST: 1993
SQ FT: 30,000
SALES (est): 2.01MM **Privately Held**
SIC: 3086 2392 Plastics foam products; Household furnishings, nec

(G-6169)
KEN STALEY CO INC
4675 Us Highway 64 E Bldg 16 (27248-8611)
PHONE.....................336 685-4294
Ken Staley, Pr
Judi Mills, Sec
EMP: 7 EST: 1973
SALES (est): 496.04K **Privately Held**
Web: www.bleachers101.com
SIC: 2531 5941 1796 Stadium furniture; Sporting goods and bicycle shops; Installing building equipment

(G-6170)
SLEEPY BEE WORX LLC
3709 Arthurs Ct (27248-7901)
PHONE.....................336 824-6998
Christina Zink, Prin
EMP: 5 EST: 2019
SALES (est): 109.67K **Privately Held**
Web: www.sleepybeeworx.com
SIC: 2844 Perfumes, cosmetics and other toilet preparations

(G-6171)
UNIQUE TOOL AND MFG CO
2054 Bruce Pugh Rd (27248-8019)
P.O. Box 909 (27317-0909)
PHONE.....................336 498-2614
Jimmy Scott, Pr
Vincent Scott, *
Doris Scott, *
EMP: 46 EST: 1986
SQ FT: 30,000
SALES (est): 8.15MM **Privately Held**
Web: www.uniquetool.net
SIC: 3545 3724 3714 Precision tools, machinists'; Aircraft engines and engine parts; Motor vehicle transmissions, drive assemblies, and parts

Fremont
Wayne County

(G-6172)
BIG SHOW FOODS INC
588 Turner Swamp Rd (27830-9300)
P.O. Box 3182 (27830-3182)
PHONE.....................919 920-1888
Lynn Dan, Asstg
EMP: 10 EST: 2008
SALES (est): 223.16K **Privately Held**
Web: www.bigshowfoods.com
SIC: 2033 Barbecue sauce: packaged in cans, jars, etc.

(G-6173)
SANCTUARY SYSTEMS LLC
701 S Wilson St (27830-8649)
P.O. Box 692 (27830-0692)
PHONE.....................305 989-0953
Jason Shockley, *
Andy Parker, *
EMP: 61 EST: 2016
SALES (est): 114.7K **Privately Held**
Web: www.sanctuarysystem.com
SIC: 2821 Plastics materials and resins

(G-6174)
VENTURA INC
7061 Pennwright Rd (27830-9565)
PHONE.....................252 291-7125
Reece Daniels, Pr
EMP: 7 EST: 1991
SQ FT: 5,000
SALES (est): 989.28K **Privately Held**
SIC: 3553 Cabinet makers' machinery

(G-6175)
VENTURE CABINETS
7061 Pennwright Rd (27830-9565)
PHONE.....................252 299-0051
EMP: 4 EST: 2019
SALES (est): 106.06K **Privately Held**
SIC: 3553 Woodworking machinery

Frisco
Dare County

(G-6176)
CASHMAN INC
Also Called: All Decked Out
53392 Hwy 12 (27936)
P.O. Box 363 (27943-0363)
PHONE.....................252 995-4319
Dale Cashman, Pr
Betty Swanson, VP
EMP: 5 EST: 1984
SQ FT: 1,500
SALES (est): 373.84K **Privately Held**
SIC: 2511 Wood lawn and garden furniture

Fuquay Varina
Wake County

(G-6177)
648 WOODWORKS LLC
601 Sage Ct (27526-9573)
PHONE.....................910 603-6286
Matthew R Patterson, Owner
EMP: 5 EST: 2016
SALES (est): 105.35K **Privately Held**
SIC: 2431 Millwork

(G-6178)
AMERICAN NETTING CORP
Also Called: Super-Net
3209 Air Park Rd (27526-8516)
PHONE.....................919 567-3737
Glenn Passner, Pr
▲ EMP: 10 EST: 1978
SQ FT: 3,900
SALES (est): 827.67K **Privately Held**
Web: www.supernetsusa.com
SIC: 3949 Baseball equipment and supplies, general

(G-6179)
APEX INSTRUMENTS INCORPORATED
204 Technology Park Ln (27526-9310)
PHONE.....................919 557-7300
William H Howe, Pr
▲ EMP: 40 EST: 1988
SQ FT: 6,000
SALES (est): 7.36MM **Privately Held**
Web: www.apexinst.com
SIC: 8734 3829 Pollution testing; Measuring and controlling devices, nec

(G-6180)
ARGOS USA LLC
Also Called: Ready Mixed Concrete Co Fuquay
1506 Holland Rd (27526-7895)
PHONE.....................919 552-2294
James Holmes, Mgr
EMP: 9
Web: www.argos-us.com
SIC: 3273 Ready-mixed concrete
HQ: Argos Usa Llc
3015 Windward Plz Ste 300
Alpharetta GA 30005
678 368-4300

(G-6181)
ART HOUSE
3325 Air Park Rd (27526-8518)
PHONE.....................919 552-7327
Newton Prince Junior, Pr
EMP: 4 EST: 1984
SQ FT: 4,200
SALES (est): 470.37K **Privately Held**
Web: www.arthouseinks.com
SIC: 2759 Screen printing

(G-6182)
ATLANTIC MOLD INC
1000 N Main St Ste 221 (27526-2056)
PHONE.....................919 832-8151
Danyelle Holland, Pr
EMP: 6 EST: 2008
SALES (est): 466.31K **Privately Held**
Web: www.atlanticmoldexperts.com
SIC: 3544 Industrial molds

(G-6183)
BECWILL CORP
3209 Air Park Rd (27526-8516)
P.O. Box 2294 (27529-2294)
PHONE.....................919 552-8266
Laura Passner, Pr
EMP: 6 EST: 2001
SQ FT: 5,000
SALES (est): 475.5K **Privately Held**
SIC: 3949 Baseball equipment and supplies, general

(G-6184)
BOB BARKER COMPANY INC (PA)
7925 Purfoy Rd (27526-8937)
P.O. Box 429 (27526-0429)
PHONE.....................800 334-9880
Robert J Barker Senior, CEO
Robert Barker Junior, Pr
Patricia M Barker, *
Mark Bacon, CRO*
◆ EMP: 220 EST: 1972
SQ FT: 29,000
SALES (est): 1.5MM
SALES (corp-wide): 1.5MM **Privately Held**
Web: www.bobbarker.com
SIC: 5131 5122 2392 5136 Linen piece goods, woven; Toiletries; Household furnishings, nec; Uniforms, men's and boys'

(G-6185)
BOEHRINGER INGLHEIM ANMAL HLTH
Also Called: Manufacturing
3225 Air Park Rd (27526-8516)
PHONE.....................919 577-9020
Brittni Hathcock, Brnch Mgr
EMP: 73
SALES (corp-wide): 23.34B **Privately Held**
Web: www.boehringer-ingelheim.com
SIC: 2836 Biological products, except diagnostic
HQ: Boehringer Ingelheim Animal Health Usa Inc.
3239 Satellite Blvd
Duluth GA 30096
800 325-9167

(G-6186)
CAROLINA MONOGRAM COMPANY
208 Church St (27526-1906)
PHONE.....................919 285-3091
EMP: 6 EST: 2015
SALES (est): 82.6K **Privately Held**
Web: www.carolinamonogram.com
SIC: 2395 Embroidery and art needlework

Fuquay Varina - Wake County (G-6187)

(G-6187)
CLASSIC CAR METAL & PARTS LLC
3600 Knightcroft Pl (27526-8694)
PHONE.................................919 567-0693
Donald Kisley, *Prin*
EMP: 5 **EST:** 2013
SALES (est): 98.25K **Privately Held**
SIC: 3443 Metal parts

(G-6188)
CLEAN AND VAC
2013 Sterling Hill Dr (27526-5368)
PHONE.................................919 753-7951
Joseph Mussanlevy, *Owner*
EMP: 6 **EST:** 2011
SALES (est): 312.44K **Privately Held**
SIC: 3635 Household vacuum cleaners

(G-6189)
CLEAVER RETURNS INC
608 Bristlecone Pine Dr (27526-7674)
P.O. Box 910 (27526-0910)
PHONE.................................630 508-8062
Steven Usedom, *CIO*
EMP: 5 **EST:** 2018
SALES (est): 70.12K **Privately Held**
SIC: 3423 Hand and edge tools, nec

(G-6190)
COLT WELDING
404 Beaverdam Lake Dr (27526-0107)
PHONE.................................361 244-2513
Clint Rehak, *Prin*
EMP: 5 **EST:** 2015
SALES (est): 99.97K **Privately Held**
SIC: 7692 Welding repair

(G-6191)
COLUMN & POST INC
Also Called: Column & Post
8013 Purfoy Rd (27526-8939)
PHONE.................................919 255-1533
David Szilezy, *Pr*
Robert Koren, *VP*
Terry Slate, *Sec*
EMP: 20 **EST:** 2002
SALES (est): 1.3MM **Privately Held**
Web: www.columnpost.com
SIC: 3272 Columns, concrete

(G-6192)
CRANE COFFEE ROASTERS LLC
908 Cotten Farm Dr (27526-1718)
PHONE.................................443 960-0654
EMP: 4
SALES (est): 79.3K **Privately Held**
SIC: 2095 7389 Coffee roasting (except by wholesale grocers); Business services, nec

(G-6193)
CROMPTON INSTRUMENTS
8000 Purfoy Rd (27526-8938)
PHONE.................................919 557-8698
Scarlett Sears, *Dir*
EMP: 7 **EST:** 2014
SALES (est): 190.84K **Privately Held**
Web: www.crompton-instruments.com
SIC: 3678 Electronic connectors

(G-6194)
DAVID BENNETT
80 H H Mckoy Ln (27526-5609)
PHONE.................................919 798-3424
Bennett David, *Prin*
EMP: 10 **EST:** 2012
SALES (est): 414.66K **Privately Held**
SIC: 7692 Welding repair

(G-6195)
DEERE & COMPANY
Also Called: John Deere Turf Care
6501 S Nc 55 Hwy (27526-7834)
PHONE.................................919 567-6400
Greg Van Grinsvin, *Manager*
EMP: 400
SALES (corp-wide): 61.25B **Publicly Held**
Web: www.deere.com
SIC: 3523 3524 Turf and grounds equipment; Lawn and garden equipment
PA: Deere & Company
1 John Deere Pl
Moline IL 61265
309 765-8000

(G-6196)
DIGGER SPECIALTIES INC
8013 Purfoy Rd (27526-8939)
PHONE.................................919 255-2533
EMP: 11
SALES (corp-wide): 22.78MM **Privately Held**
SIC: 3089 Plastics hardware and building products
PA: Digger Specialties, Inc.
3446 Us Highway 6
Bremen IN 46506
574 546-5999

(G-6197)
E & M CONCRETE INC
Also Called: M.C. Exteriors
7505 Troy Stone Dr (27526-7111)
PHONE.................................919 235-7221
Micke Douglas, *Pr*
EMP: 24 **EST:** 2013
SALES (est): 1.16MM **Privately Held**
Web: www.emconcretenc.com
SIC: 1771 3273 Concrete work; Ready-mixed concrete

(G-6198)
EONCOAT LLC (PA)
3337 Air Park Rd Ste 6 (27526-7277)
PHONE.................................941 928-9401
Tony Collins, *CEO*
Merrick Albert, *Pr*
EMP: 7 **EST:** 2015
SALES (est): 2.56MM
SALES (corp-wide): 2.56MM **Privately Held**
Web: www.eoncoat.com
SIC: 2851 Lacquers, varnishes, enamels, and other coatings

(G-6199)
EXTREME TRACTOR PARTS LLC
1518 Miranda Woods Ln (27526-5843)
P.O. Box 712 (27526-0712)
PHONE.................................919 605-6040
Raymond R Castner, *Prin*
EMP: 6 **EST:** 2009
SALES (est): 121.98K **Privately Held**
Web: www.extremetractorparts.com
SIC: 3599 Machine shop, jobbing and repair

(G-6200)
FULLY PROMOTED FUQUAY-VARINA
Also Called: Fully Promoted
504 Broad St (27526-1708)
PHONE.................................919 346-8955
EMP: 4 **EST:** 2019
SALES (est): 51.74K **Privately Held**
Web: www.fullypromoted.com
SIC: 2395 Embroidery and art needlework

(G-6201)
FUQUAY-VARINA BAKING CO INC
127 S Main St (27526-2220)
P.O. Box 665 (27526-0665)
PHONE.................................919 557-2237
Katie Dies, *Owner*
EMP: 9 **EST:** 2011
SALES (est): 167.69K **Privately Held**
Web: www.fuquay-varina.org
SIC: 2051 Bread, cake, and related products

(G-6202)
GRANDWELL INDUSTRIES INC
6109 S Nc 55 Hwy (27526-7920)
P.O. Box 5722 (27512-5722)
PHONE.................................919 557-1221
Charles Lai, *CEO*
Mei-chieng Lai, *VP*
Roger Lai, *VP*
▲ **EMP:** 20 **EST:** 1989
SQ FT: 8,000
SALES (est): 1.85MM **Privately Held**
Web: www.grandwell.com
SIC: 3993 Electric signs

(G-6203)
IMPACT PRINTING AND DESIGN LLC
2908 N Main St Ste 112 (27526-5498)
PHONE.................................919 377-9747
EMP: 5 **EST:** 2020
SALES (est): 76.29K **Privately Held**
Web: www.ipd-nc.com
SIC: 2752 Offset printing

(G-6204)
INNOCRIN PHARMACEUTICALS INC
701 Wagstaff Rd (27526-8101)
PHONE.................................919 467-8539
Fred Eshelman, *CEO*
Andrew Von Eschenbach, *Prin*
James Rosen, *Prin*
Robert Schotzinger, *Prin*
Ed Torres, *Prin*
EMP: 6 **EST:** 2005
SALES (est): 812.14K **Privately Held**
Web: www.abcapotek.com
SIC: 2834 Pharmaceutical preparations

(G-6205)
INTERNATIONAL MINUTE PRESS
316 Angier Rd (27526-2209)
PHONE.................................919 762-0054
Dann Vander, *Mgr*
EMP: 6 **EST:** 2014
SALES (est): 234.44K **Privately Held**
Web: fv-nc.intlminutepress.com
SIC: 2752 Commercial printing, lithographic

(G-6206)
J&L MANUFACTURING INC
192 Jarco Dr (27526-5071)
PHONE.................................919 801-3219
Jim Thomas, *Pr*
Lee Revis, *VP*
EMP: 13 **EST:** 2021
SALES (est): 1.08MM **Privately Held**
SIC: 3625 Controls for adjustable speed drives

(G-6207)
JEFFREY ANCHETA
4817 Frankie Rd (27526-9429)
PHONE.................................919 552-0892
Jeffrey Ancheta, *Prin*
EMP: 5 **EST:** 2017
SALES (est): 85.33K **Privately Held**
SIC: 7372 Prepackaged software

(G-6208)
LEAR CORPORATION
200 Dickens Rd (27526-8303)
PHONE.................................919 552-5667
Byron Mccutchen, *Pr*
EMP: 30
SQ FT: 369,648
SALES (corp-wide): 23.47B **Publicly Held**
Web: www.lear.com
SIC: 3714 Motor vehicle parts and accessories
PA: Lear Corporation
21557 Telegraph Rd
Southfield MI 48033
248 447-1500

(G-6209)
LIN WGGINS MEM SCHLARSHIP FUND
5653 Soft Wind Dr (27526-9207)
PHONE.................................919 749-2340
Renee Wiggins Lawing, *Admn*
EMP: 7 **EST:** 2007
SALES (est): 66.08K **Privately Held**
Web: www.linwigginsscholarship.com
SIC: 2515 Mattresses and foundations

(G-6210)
LOVEGRASS KITCHEN INC
5305 Hilltop Needmore Rd (27526-9273)
PHONE.................................919 234-7541
Samson Kassa, *Ex Dir*
Meron Afework, *Owner*
EMP: 5 **EST:** 2017
SALES (est): 264.61K **Privately Held**
Web: www.lovegrasskitchen.com
SIC: 2045 2064 Pancake mixes, prepared: from purchased flour; Granola and muesli, bars and clusters

(G-6211)
MAC-VANN INC
4792 Rawls Church Rd (27526-6384)
P.O. Box 1030 (27526-1030)
PHONE.................................919 577-0746
Michele M Freeman, *VP*
John M Van Nest Senior, *Pr*
Michael Freeman, *VP*
EMP: 5 **EST:** 2005
SALES (est): 981.16K **Privately Held**
Web: www.mac-vann.com
SIC: 2426 Hardwood dimension and flooring mills

(G-6212)
MARSHALL MIDDLEBY INC
Southbend Division
1100 Old Honeycutt Rd (27526-9312)
PHONE.................................919 762-1000
John Peruccio, *Pr*
EMP: 75
SQ FT: 138,855
SALES (corp-wide): 4.04B **Publicly Held**
Web: www.middleby.com
SIC: 3589 3631 3556 Cooking equipment, commercial; Household cooking equipment; Food products machinery
HQ: Middleby Marshall Inc.
1100 Old Honeycutt Rd
Fuquay Varina NC 27526
919 762-1000

(G-6213)
MARTIN MARIETTA MATERIALS INC
Also Called: Martin Marietta Aggregates
7400 Buckhorn Duncan Road (27526)
P.O. Box 1957 (27526-2957)
PHONE.................................919 557-7412
Les Goshorn, *Mgr*
EMP: 10
Web: www.martinmarietta.com
SIC: 3273 Ready-mixed concrete
PA: Martin Marietta Materials Inc
4123 Parklake Ave
Raleigh NC 27612

(G-6214)
MECO INC
501 Community Dr (27526-7108)
PHONE..................919 557-7330
Don Batot, *Prin*
EMP: 7 **EST:** 2016
SALES (est): 56.72K **Privately Held**
Web: www.meco.com
SIC: 3589 Water treatment equipment, industrial

(G-6215)
MERGE SCIENTIFIC SOLUTIONS LLC
208 Technology Park Ln Ste 108 (27526-5875)
PHONE..................919 346-0999
EMP: 6 **EST:** 2022
SALES (est): 63.22K **Privately Held**
SIC: 3231 Aquariums and reflectors, glass

(G-6216)
MIDDLEBY MARSHALL INC (HQ)
Also Called: Southbend
1100 Old Honeycutt Rd (27526-9312)
PHONE..................919 762-1000
John Perruccio, *Pr*
◆ **EMP:** 200 **EST:** 1888
SQ FT: 210,000
SALES (est): 1.92B
SALES (corp-wide): 4.04B **Publicly Held**
Web: www.middleby.com
SIC: 3556 3585 3631 Ovens, bakery; Refrigeration equipment, complete; Household cooking equipment
PA: The Middleby Corporation
   1400 Toastmaster Dr
   Elgin IL 60120
   847 741-3300

(G-6217)
NOLES CABINETS INC
2290 N Grassland Dr (27526-6893)
PHONE..................919 552-4257
R Douglas Doug Noles, *Pr*
EMP: 11 **EST:** 1970
SQ FT: 10,000
SALES (est): 445.42K **Privately Held**
Web: www.nolescabinets.com
SIC: 2434 Wood kitchen cabinets

(G-6218)
NVENT THERMAL LLC
8000 Purfoy Rd (27526-8938)
PHONE..................919 552-3811
EMP: 879
Web: www.nvent.com
SIC: 3661 Telephone and telegraph apparatus
HQ: Nvent Thermal Llc
   899 Broadway St
   Redwood City CA 94063
   650 474-7414

(G-6219)
OLDCASTLE INFRASTRUCTURE INC
1431 Products Rd (27526-8614)
P.O. Box 548 (27526-0548)
PHONE..................919 552-2252
Gregory Levine, *Mgr*
EMP: 23
SQ FT: 5,500
SALES (corp-wide): 32.72B **Privately Held**
Web: www.oldcastleinfrastructure.com
SIC: 3272 Manhole covers or frames, concrete
HQ: Oldcastle Infrastructure, Inc.
   7000 Central Pkwy Ste 800
   Atlanta GA 30328
   770 270-5000

(G-6220)
OLDCASTLE INFRASTRUCTURE INC
1424 Products Rd (27526-8614)
PHONE..................919 552-5715
Greg Levine, *Mgr*
EMP: 6
SALES (corp-wide): 32.72B **Privately Held**
Web: www.oldcastleinfrastructure.com
SIC: 3272 Precast terrazzo or concrete products
HQ: Oldcastle Infrastructure, Inc.
   7000 Central Pkwy Ste 800
   Atlanta GA 30328
   770 270-5000

(G-6221)
P & C LOGGING LLC
305 Spence Mill Rd (27526-8061)
PHONE..................919 552-3420
Peggy Bryant, *Prin*
EMP: 5 **EST:** 2017
SALES (est): 118.12K **Privately Held**
SIC: 2411 Logging

(G-6222)
PRIORITY BACKGROUNDS LLC
118 N Johnson St (27526-1973)
P.O. Box 1589 (27526-1589)
PHONE..................919 557-3247
EMP: 8 **EST:** 2005
SALES (est): 452.75K **Privately Held**
Web: www.prioritybackgrounds.com
SIC: 7372 Prepackaged software

(G-6223)
RAVE NETWORX INC
1421 E Broad St Ste 408 (27526-1968)
PHONE..................910 808-9346
Kathy Sousa, *Prin*
EMP: 5 **EST:** 2017
SALES (est): 165.6K **Privately Held**
Web: www.ravenetworx.com
SIC: 3357 Communication wire

(G-6224)
RENT PATH INC
913 Old Baron Dr (27526-7000)
PHONE..................919 567-8166
Marty Mccallen, *Pr*
EMP: 5 **EST:** 2018
SALES (est): 101.06K **Privately Held**
SIC: 2741 Miscellaneous publishing

(G-6225)
RESCUED WOOD REHAB LLC
718 N Main St (27526-2029)
PHONE..................984 500-7904
EMP: 5 **EST:** 2019
SALES (est): 239.68K **Privately Held**
Web: www.rwrnc.com
SIC: 2431 Millwork

(G-6226)
REVELS TURF AND TRACTOR LLC (PA)
Also Called: John Deere
2217 N Main St (27526-8560)
PHONE..................919 552-5697
▲ **EMP:** 35 **EST:** 1961
SALES (est): 8.52MM
SALES (corp-wide): 8.52MM **Privately Held**
Web: www.revelstractor.com
SIC: 3949 Golf equipment

(G-6227)
S T WOOTEN CORPORATION
Also Called: Banks Rd Concrete Plant
3625 Banks Rd (27526)
PHONE..................919 772-7991
Scott Wooten, *Pr*
EMP: 22
SALES (corp-wide): 319.83MM **Privately Held**
Web: www.stwcorp.com
SIC: 3531 Concrete plants
PA: S. T. Wooten Corporation
   3801 Black Creek Rd Se
   Wilson NC 27893
   252 291-5165

(G-6228)
SCREEN AND EMBROIDERY
704 Broad St (27526-1712)
PHONE..................919 557-3151
Liberty Printing, *Prin*
EMP: 5 **EST:** 2018
SALES (est): 31.29K **Privately Held**
SIC: 2395 Embroidery and art needlework

(G-6229)
TE CONNECTIVITY CORPORATION
8000 Purfoy Rd (27526-8938)
PHONE..................919 552-3811
Barry Allen, *Prin*
EMP: 6
Web: www.te.com
SIC: 3678 Electronic connectors
HQ: Te Connectivity Corporation
   1050 Westlakes Dr
   Berwyn PA 19312
   610 893-9800

(G-6230)
TE CONNECTIVITY CORPORATION
8009 Purfoy Rd (27526-8939)
PHONE..................919 557-8425
Bob Fennel, *Brnch Mgr*
EMP: 5
Web: www.te.com
SIC: 3678 3643 Electronic connectors; Current-carrying wiring services
HQ: Te Connectivity Corporation
   1050 Westlakes Dr
   Berwyn PA 19312
   610 893-9800

(G-6231)
TE CONNECTIVITY CORPORATION
Tyco Electronics Energy Plant
8000 Purfoy Rd (27526-8938)
PHONE..................919 552-3811
Jim Robert, *Mgr*
EMP: 15
Web: www.te.com
SIC: 3678 3643 Electronic connectors; Current-carrying wiring services
HQ: Te Connectivity Corporation
   1050 Westlakes Dr
   Berwyn PA 19312
   610 893-9800

(G-6232)
TEC GRAPHICS INC
101 Technology Park Ln (27526-9363)
PHONE..................919 567-2077
Thomas Cherry, *Pr*
EMP: 10 **EST:** 1992
SQ FT: 10,000
SALES (est): 1.75MM **Privately Held**
Web: www.tecgraphics.com
SIC: 2759 3993 3643 2672 Screen printing; Signs and advertising specialties; Current-carrying wiring services; Paper; coated and laminated, nec

(G-6233)
THOMAS CONCRETE CAROLINA INC
140 Pamela Ct (27526-5662)
PHONE..................919 557-3144
John Holding, *VP*
EMP: 11
SALES (corp-wide): 1.01B **Privately Held**
Web: www.thomasconcrete.com
SIC: 3273 Ready-mixed concrete
HQ: Thomas Concrete Of Carolina, Inc.
   1131 N West St
   Raleigh NC 27603
   919 832-0451

(G-6234)
TRIANGLE CUSTOM WOODWORKS LLC (PA)
526 Victoria Hills Dr S (27526-5680)
PHONE..................919 637-8857
Melissa Myers, *Prin*
EMP: 7 **EST:** 2015
SALES (est): 245.51K
SALES (corp-wide): 245.51K **Privately Held**
Web: www.trianglecustomwoodworks.com
SIC: 2431 Millwork

(G-6235)
VERITY YACHT PUBLICATIONS
281 Kinsman Ct (27526-3705)
PHONE..................760 803-2550
EMP: 4 **EST:** 2019
SALES (est): 223.09K **Privately Held**
Web: www.verityyachtpubs.com
SIC: 2741 Miscellaneous publishing

(G-6236)
VICTORY SIGNS LLC
2908 N Main St (27526-5497)
PHONE..................919 642-3091
EMP: 4 **EST:** 2018
SALES (est): 88.2K **Privately Held**
SIC: 3993 Signs and advertising specialties

(G-6237)
WALKER STREET LLC
104 Birchland Dr (27526-6800)
PHONE..................919 880-3959
Carl D Phelan, *Prin*
EMP: 4 **EST:** 2008
SALES (est): 174.44K **Privately Held**
SIC: 3842 Walkers

(G-6238)
WEATHERS MACHINE MFG INC
9535 Us 401 N (27526-8071)
PHONE..................919 552-5945
Linda Weathers, *Pr*
Phillip Ray Weathers, *VP*
Gwen Weathers, *Sec*
EMP: 15 **EST:** 1973
SQ FT: 13,000
SALES (est): 4.67MM **Privately Held**
Web: www.weathersmfg.com
SIC: 5084 3599 Instruments and control equipment; Machine shop, jobbing and repair

(G-6239)
WYATT WOODWORKS
1317 Spence Mill Rd (27526-8051)
PHONE..................919 619-8593
Shane Wyatt, *Prin*
EMP: 5 **EST:** 2017
SALES (est): 54.13K **Privately Held**
SIC: 2431 Millwork

(G-6240)
YOUR CHOICE PREGNANCY CLINIC
607 N Ennis St (27526-2014)
PHONE..................919 577-9050
EMP: 4
SALES (corp-wide): 210.39K **Privately Held**

Web: www.yourchoicepregnancyclinic.com
SIC: 2835 Pregnancy test kits
PA: Your Choice Pregnancy Clinic
1701 Jones Franklin Rd
Raleigh NC 27606
919 758-8444

Garland
Sampson County

(G-6241)
CYPRESS CREEK HARVESTING INC
6993 Old Fayetteville Rd (28441-8933)
PHONE..................805 462-9412
EMP: 7 EST: 2017
SALES (est): 261.58K Privately Held
SIC: 2411 Logging camps and contractors

(G-6242)
FIRST MIRACLE VINE & WINE LLC
365 Johnson Rd (28441-8399)
PHONE..................910 990-5681
Stephanie Carter, *Managing Member*
EMP: 4 EST: 2016
SALES (est): 49.83K Privately Held
Web: www.visitsampsonnc.com
SIC: 2084 5921 Wines; Wine

(G-6243)
GARLAND APPAREL GROUP LLC
Also Called: Garland Heritage NC
120 S Church Ave (28441-1201)
PHONE..................646 647-2790
Kenneth Ragland, *Managing Member*
EMP: 40 EST: 2021
SALES (est): 2.54MM Privately Held
Web: www.garlandapparelgroup.com
SIC: 2326 Aprons, work, except rubberized and plastic: men's

(G-6244)
GARLAND FARM SUPPLY INC (PA)
Also Called: Clinton Grains
250 N Belgrade Ave (28441-8100)
P.O. Box 741 (28441-0741)
PHONE..................910 529-9731
Ernest Smith, *Pr*
Doris Smith, *VP*
Alfred Smith, *Sec*
Charles Smith, *Treas*
EMP: 15 EST: 1963
SQ FT: 15,000
SALES (corp-wide): 2.38MM
SALES (corp-wide): 2.38MM Privately Held
SIC: 0723 2048 Feed milling, custom services; Prepared feeds, nec

(G-6245)
H&R TRANSPORT LLC
1315 Bull St (28441-9171)
PHONE..................910 588-4410
EMP: 5 EST: 2011
SALES (est): 180K Privately Held
SIC: 2411 Logging

(G-6246)
ROBERT L RICH TMBER HRVSTG INC
360 Rich Rd (28441-9718)
P.O. Box 272 (28441-0272)
PHONE..................910 529-7321
Robert Rich, *Pr*
Daniel Rich, *VP*
Frances Rich, *Sec*
EMP: 8 EST: 1955
SALES (est): 787K Privately Held

(G-6247)
WAYNE LAMB LOGGING CO
1050 Lisbon Bridge Rd (28441-8420)
PHONE..................910 529-1115
Wayne H Lamb, *Prin*
EMP: 5 EST: 2000
SALES (est): 122.69K Privately Held
SIC: 2411 Logging camps and contractors

Garner
Wake County

(G-6248)
3-OCEANS MFG INC
3301 Jones Sausage Rd Ste 121 (27529-7281)
PHONE..................919 600-4500
Vinson Nguyen, *Prin*
EMP: 4 EST: 2016
SALES (est): 49.17K Privately Held
SIC: 3999 Manufacturing industries, nec

(G-6249)
A & G MACHINING LLC
333 Technical Ct Ste 33 (27529)
PHONE..................919 329-7207
Mark Paskovich, *Managing Member*
EMP: 5 EST: 2004
SALES (est): 389.18K Privately Held
Web: www.agmachinenc.com
SIC: 3599 Machine shop, jobbing and repair

(G-6250)
A BEAN COUNTER INC
176 Foxglove Dr (27529-7731)
PHONE..................919 359-9586
Wilson L Feick, *Prin*
EMP: 4 EST: 2009
SALES (est): 196.67K Privately Held
SIC: 3131 Counters

(G-6251)
ALCAMI CAROLINAS CORPORATION
Also Called: Alcami
5100 Jones Sausage Rd Ste 110 (27529-3578)
PHONE..................910 619-3952
EMP: 8
SALES (corp-wide): 418.48MM Privately Held
SIC: 2834 8734 8731 Drugs affecting neoplasms and endocrine systems; Product testing laboratories; Biological research
HQ: Alcami Carolinas Corporation
2320 Scientific Park Dr
Wilmington NC 28405

(G-6252)
ALPHAGRAPHICS DOWNTOWN RALEIGH
Also Called: AlphaGraphics
3731 Centurion Dr (27529-8581)
PHONE..................919 832-2828
EMP: 11 EST: 2019
SALES (est): 1.18MM Privately Held
Web: www.alphagraphics.com
SIC: 2752 Commercial printing, lithographic

(G-6253)
AMERICAN LABEL TECH INC
343 Technology Dr Ste 2106 (27529-6637)
PHONE..................984 269-5078
Darrin Schmitt, *Pr*
Gustavo Garcia, *VP*
EMP: 11 EST: 2017
SQ FT: 12,000
SALES (est): 1.36MM Privately Held
Web: www.americanlabeltech.com
SIC: 2759 Labels and seals: printing, nsk

(G-6254)
ANDREA HURST AND ASSOC LLC
1424 Cane Creek Dr (27529-5198)
PHONE..................916 743-1846
EMP: 4 EST: 2019
SALES (est): 123.75K Privately Held
Web: www.andreahurst.com
SIC: 2731 Book publishing

(G-6255)
ARGOS USA LLC
Also Called: Redi-Mix Concrete
1915 W Garner Rd (27529-2819)
PHONE..................919 772-4188
Kim Nielsen, *Mgr*
EMP: 34
SQ FT: 2,708
Web: www.argos-us.com
SIC: 3273 Ready-mixed concrete
HQ: Argos Usa Llc
3015 Windward Plz Ste 300
Alpharetta GA 30005
678 368-4300

(G-6256)
BENTLY NEVADA LLC
Also Called: GE Energy
1411 Kenbrook Dr (27529-4447)
PHONE..................919 772-5530
EMP: 5
SALES (corp-wide): 25.51B Publicly Held
Web: www.bently.com
SIC: 3829 Measuring and controlling devices, nec
HQ: Bently Nevada, Llc
1631 Bently Pkwy S
Minden NV 89423
775 782-3611

(G-6257)
BIGRED KRAFTS LLC
5100 Solemn Grove Rd (27529-7496)
PHONE..................919 480-2388
Heather L Heffner, *Admn*
EMP: 5 EST: 2014
SALES (est): 86.51K Privately Held
Web: www.bigredkrafts.com
SIC: 2323 Men's and boy's neckwear

(G-6258)
BUTTERBALL LLC (HQ)
Also Called: Gusto Packing Company
1 Butterball Ln (27529-5971)
P.O. Box 1547 (28086-1547)
PHONE..................919 255-7900
▼ EMP: 50 EST: 2006
SALES (est): 618.29MM
SALES (corp-wide): 11.24B Publicly Held
Web: www.butterballfoodservice.com
SIC: 2015 Turkey, processed, nsk
PA: Seaboard Corporation
9000 W 67th St
Merriam KS 66202
913 676-8800

(G-6259)
C E HICKS ENTERPRISES INC
Also Called: Auto Marine Boat Repairs
230 Us 70 Hwy E (27529-4050)
PHONE..................919 772-5131
EMP: 10 EST: 1967
SALES (est): 676.43K Privately Held
SIC: 3732 Boatbuilding and repairing

(G-6260)
CAPITAL OF GARNER
200 Waterfield Ridge Pl (27529-6990)
PHONE..................919 582-0202
EMP: 5 EST: 2019
SALES (est): 105.99K Privately Held
Web: www.garnernc.gov
SIC: 3544 Special dies, tools, jigs, and fixtures

(G-6261)
CARDINAL BUILDINGS LLC
1641 Us 70 Hwy E (27529-5505)
PHONE..................919 422-5670
Joel L Williams, *Prin*
EMP: 8 EST: 2008
SALES (est): 407.64K Privately Held
Web: www.cardinalbuildingsllc.com
SIC: 3448 Buildings, portable: prefabricated metal

(G-6262)
CARROLL CO
Also Called: East Carolina Trucks
5771 Nc Highway 42 W (27529-8445)
P.O. Box 18108 (27619-8108)
PHONE..................919 779-1900
Robert Carroll, *Pr*
Robert Carrol, *Pr*
EMP: 10 EST: 1996
SALES (est): 927.01K Privately Held
Web: www.gregorypoole.com
SIC: 3713 3462 Truck bodies and parts; Iron and steel forgings

(G-6263)
CBJ TRANSIT LLC
1220 Timber Dr E (27529-6917)
PHONE..................252 417-9972
EMP: 56
SALES (est): 2.76MM Privately Held
SIC: 3537 Trucks: freight, baggage, etc.: industrial, except mining

(G-6264)
COLUMBIA FLOORING
2000 Pergo Pkwy (27529-8553)
PHONE..................304 239-2633
EMP: 5 EST: 2018
SALES (est): 55.04K Privately Held
SIC: 2426 Hardwood dimension and flooring mills

(G-6265)
COMMERCIAL PRINTING COMPANY
3731 Centurion Dr (27529-8581)
PHONE..................919 832-2828
Ralph C Moore, *Pr*
Mory A Read, *VP*
Juliet B Moore, *Sec*
Linda Maxa, *Contrlr*
EMP: 20 EST: 1907
SALES (est): 5.15MM
SALES (corp-wide): 24.41MM Privately Held
Web: www.comprintco.com
SIC: 2752 Offset printing
HQ: Alphagraphics, Inc.
143 Union Blvd Ste 650
Lakewood CO 80228
800 955-6246

(G-6266)
COMMSCOPE TECHNOLOGIES LLC
Also Called: Grayson Wireless
620 N Greenfield Pkwy (27529-6947)
PHONE..................919 329-8700
Morgan Kurk, *Dir*
EMP: 11

GEOGRAPHIC SECTION
Garner - Wake County (G-6292)

SIC: **3663** 5065 Radio and t.v. communications equipment; Electronic parts and equipment, nec
HQ: Commscope Technologies Llc
4 Westbrook Corp Ctr
Westchester IL 60154
800 366-3891

(G-6267)
COMPASS GROUP USA INC
Also Called: Canteen Raleigh/Durham
3300 Waterfield Dr (27529-6318)
PHONE..................................919 381-9577
EMP: 363
SALES (corp-wide): 39.16B **Privately Held**
Web: www.compass-usa.com
SIC: **5962** 2099 Merchandising machine operators; Food preparations, nec
HQ: Compass Group Usa, Inc.
2400 Yorkmont Rd
Charlotte NC 28217

(G-6268)
CONTEMPORARY PRODUCTS INC
275 Hein Dr (27529-7221)
PHONE..................................919 779-4228
Joan Squillini, *Pr*
EMP: 7 EST: 1979
SQ FT: 24,000
SALES (est): 614.61K **Privately Held**
Web: www.ceocontemporaryproducts.com
SIC: **3499** 3423 Trophies, metal, except silver; Engravers' tools, hand

(G-6269)
CROWN EQUIPMENT CORPORATION
Also Called: Crown Lift Trucks
1000 N Greenfield Pkwy Ste 1090 (27529)
PHONE..................................919 773-4160
EMP: 42
SALES (corp-wide): 7.12B **Privately Held**
Web: www.crown.com
SIC: **3537** Lift trucks, industrial: fork, platform, straddle, etc.
PA: Crown Equipment Corporation
44 S Washington St
New Bremen OH 45869
419 629-2311

(G-6270)
CUSTOM CANVAS WORKS INC
Also Called: Awnings Etc
540 Dynamic Dr (27529-2508)
PHONE..................................919 662-4800
Donald K Kelly, *Pr*
EMP: 19 EST: 1976
SQ FT: 6,000
SALES (est): 899.04K **Privately Held**
Web: www.customcanvasworks.com
SIC: **2394** Awnings, fabric: made from purchased materials

(G-6271)
DOUGLAS DUANE SNIFFEN
Also Called: B W Woodworks
101 Oak Hollow Ct (27529-4658)
PHONE..................................919 924-8337
Douglas D Sniffen, *Owner*
EMP: 4 EST: 2019
SALES (est): 54.13K **Privately Held**
SIC: **2431** Millwork

(G-6272)
DYNO NOBEL EXPLOSIVE BLASTING
1201 Aversboro Rd Ste H101 (27529-5208)
PHONE..................................919 771-1522
EMP: 4 EST: 2018
SALES (est): 246.82K **Privately Held**
SIC: **2892** Explosives

(G-6273)
GENERAL REFRIGERATION COMPANY
96 Shipwash Dr (27529-6861)
PHONE..................................919 661-4727
Jim Thompson, *Pr*
EMP: 8
SALES (corp-wide): 14.19MM **Privately Held**
Web: www.generalrefrig.com
SIC: **1711** 3494 7692 Refrigeration contractor; Pipe fittings; Welding repair
PA: General Refrigeration Company
34971 Sussex Hwy
Delmar DE 19940
302 846-3073

(G-6274)
HAMLIN SHEET METAL COMPANY INCORPORATED (PA)
1411 W Garner Rd (27529-3029)
P.O. Box 465 (27529-0465)
PHONE..................................919 772-8780
◆ EMP: 25 EST: 1954
SALES (est): 13.19MM
SALES (corp-wide): 13.19MM **Privately Held**
SIC: **3444** Ducts, sheet metal

(G-6275)
HOWARD BROTHERS MFG LLC
1321 Bobbitt Dr (27529-3039)
PHONE..................................919 772-4800
Matthew G Howard, *Managing Member*
EMP: 6 EST: 2012
SALES (est): 210.73K **Privately Held**
SIC: **2421** Building and structural materials, wood

(G-6276)
HUDSON S HARDWARE INC (PA)
Also Called: Do It Best
305 Benson Rd (27529-3003)
PHONE..................................919 553-3030
Leigh S Hudson, *Pr*
Helen B Hudson, *Sec*
▲ EMP: 22 EST: 1958
SQ FT: 22,000
SALES (est): 8.1MM
SALES (corp-wide): 8.1MM **Privately Held**
Web: www.hudsonshardware.com
SIC: **5251** 3999 Hardware stores; Pet supplies

(G-6277)
IMPROVED NATURE LLC
101 Vandora Springs Rd (27529-5336)
PHONE..................................919 588-2299
Richard Hawkins, *Pr*
EMP: 51 EST: 2015
SALES (est): 4.97MM **Privately Held**
Web: www.improvednature.com
SIC: **2099** Food preparations, nec

(G-6278)
KONICA MNLTA HLTHCARE AMRCAS I
2217 Us 70 Hwy E (27529-9424)
PHONE..................................919 792-6420
EMP: 23
Web: www.konicaminolta.us
SIC: **8732** 3825 Business research service; Digital test equipment, electronic and electrical circuits
HQ: Konica Minolta Healthcare Americas, Inc.
411 Newark Pompton Tpke
Wayne NJ 07470
973 633-1500

(G-6279)
LA SIGNS INC
1140 Benson Rd Ste 107 (27529-4659)
PHONE..................................919 779-1185
Bonnie Henderson, *Admn*
EMP: 5 EST: 2019
SALES (est): 50.69K **Privately Held**
SIC: **3993** Signs and advertising specialties

(G-6280)
LANDMARK MUSIC GROUP INC
Also Called: A New Gnrtion Entrmt MGT Cnslt
412 Henry Dr (27529-2503)
PHONE..................................919 800-7277
Trenton Denning, *Prin*
EMP: 6 EST: 2015
SALES (est): 107.5K **Privately Held**
SIC: **2731** Book music: publishing and printing

(G-6281)
LEGACY GRAPHICS INC
191 Technology Dr (27529-9289)
P.O. Box 5279 (27512-5279)
PHONE..................................919 741-6262
Peter A Reckert, *Pr*
Robert Price, *VP*
EMP: 21 EST: 2007
SQ FT: 7,500
SALES (est): 389.45K **Privately Held**
Web: www.resourcelabel.com
SIC: **2752** Offset printing

(G-6282)
MANNING BUILDING PRODUCTS LLC
108 Professional Ct Ste A (27529-7975)
PHONE..................................919 662-9894
David Manning, *Managing Member*
EMP: 6 EST: 2010
SQ FT: 4,200
SALES (est): 505.01K **Privately Held**
Web: www.permaboot.co
SIC: **2452** Prefabricated buildings, wood

(G-6283)
MARIETTA MARTIN MATERIALS INC
Also Called: Martin Marietta
1111 E Garner Rd (27529-8746)
P.O. Box 37 (27529-0037)
PHONE..................................919 772-3563
Ben Brown, *Mgr*
EMP: 24
SQ FT: 12,039
Web: www.martinmarietta.com
SIC: **1422** Crushed and broken limestone
PA: Martin Marietta Materials Inc
4123 Parklake Ave
Raleigh NC 27612

(G-6284)
MARTIN WELDING INC
816 Old Crowder Dr (27529-9768)
PHONE..................................919 436-8805
Martin Montes Maldonado, *Pr*
EMP: 6 EST: 2017
SALES (est): 88.73K **Privately Held**
SIC: **7692** Welding repair

(G-6285)
MDN CABINETS INC
Also Called: M D N Cabinets
3411 Integrity Dr Ste 100 (27529-6226)
PHONE..................................919 662-1090
Justin Hanlon, *Pr*
EMP: 7 EST: 1987
SALES (est): 1.01MM **Privately Held**
Web: www.mdncabinets.com
SIC: **2434** Wood kitchen cabinets

(G-6286)
MEDLIT SOLUTIONS
191 Technology Dr (27529-9289)
PHONE..................................919 878-6789
EMP: 6
SALES (est): 79.3K **Privately Held**
Web: www.medlitsolutions.com
SIC: **2752** Commercial printing, lithographic

(G-6287)
MEDLIT SOLUTIONS LLC (HQ)
191 Technology Dr (27529-9289)
PHONE..................................919 878-6789
Kevin Grogan, *CEO*
▲ EMP: 58 EST: 1987
SQ FT: 7,500
SALES (est): 14.81MM **Privately Held**
Web: www.tcglegacy.com
SIC: **2791** 2752 2789 2759 Typesetting; Offset printing; Bookbinding and related work; Commercial printing, nec
PA: Resource Label Group, Llc
2550 Meridian Blvd # 370
Franklin TN 37067

(G-6288)
MODUSLINK CORPORATION
990 N Greenfield Pkwy (27529-6953)
PHONE..................................781 663-5000
Brenda Rice, *Brnch Mgr*
EMP: 24
SALES (corp-wide): 40.8MM **Publicly Held**
Web: www.moduslink.com
SIC: **7372** Prepackaged software
HQ: Moduslink Corporation
2000 Midway Ln
Smyrna TN 37167
615 267-6100

(G-6289)
MOHAWK INDUSTRIES INC
800 N Greenfield Pkwy (27529-6951)
PHONE..................................919 609-4759
EMP: 6
Web: www.mohawkind.com
SIC: **5735** 2273 Video discs and tapes, prerecorded; Carpets and rugs
PA: Mohawk Industries, Inc.
160 S Industrial Blvd
Calhoun GA 30701

(G-6290)
MOHAWK INDUSTRIES INC
Also Called: Mohawk Industries
2000 Pergo Pkwy (27529-8553)
PHONE..................................919 661-5590
EMP: 18
Web: www.mohawkind.com
SIC: **2273** Finishers of tufted carpets and rugs
PA: Mohawk Industries, Inc.
160 S Industrial Blvd
Calhoun GA 30701

(G-6291)
MONTYS WELDING & FABRICATION
157 Creek Commons Ave (27529-2881)
PHONE..................................919 337-7859
EMP: 5 EST: 2017
SALES (est): 50.04K **Privately Held**
Web: www.montyswelding.com
SIC: **7692** Welding repair

(G-6292)
MORRIS & ASSOCIATES INC
803 Morris Dr (27529-4037)
PHONE..................................919 582-9200
◆ EMP: 51 EST: 1949
SALES (est): 10.39MM **Privately Held**

Garner - Wake County (G-6293)

Web: www.morristhermal.com
SIC: **3585** Refrigeration and heating equipment

(G-6293)
MOTHER SAND FATHERS BLACK SONS
1413 Beichler Rd (27529-3503)
PHONE..........................919 301-8161
Wendolyn Cotten, *Prin*
EMP: 5 EST: 2015
SALES (est): 163.13K **Privately Held**
SIC: **1442** Construction sand and gravel

(G-6294)
MUSIC & ARTS
2566 Timber Dr (27529-2589)
PHONE..........................919 329-6069
EMP: 7 EST: 1952
SALES (est): 43.98K **Privately Held**
Web: stores.musicarts.com
SIC: **8299** 5736 3931 Schools and educational services, nec; Musical instrument stores; Musical instruments

(G-6295)
NEW LIFE MEDICALS INC ✪
146 Donmoor Ct (27529-2500)
PHONE..........................610 615-1483
EMP: 4 EST: 2022
SALES (est): 63.22K **Privately Held**
Web: www.newlifemedicals.com
SIC: **2834** Pharmaceutical preparations

(G-6296)
NEWS AND OBSERVER PUBG CO
Also Called: News & Observer Recycling Ctr
1402 Mechanical Blvd (27529-2539)
PHONE..........................919 829-8903
EMP: 10
SALES (corp-wide): 709.52MM **Privately Held**
SIC: **2711** Newspapers, publishing and printing
HQ: The News And Observer Publishing Company
421 Fayetteville St # 104
Raleigh NC 27601
919 829-4500

(G-6297)
NORFIELD LLC
264 Hein Dr (27529-7224)
PHONE..........................530 879-3121
EMP: 9 EST: 2017
SALES (est): 172.26K **Privately Held**
Web: www.norfield.com
SIC: **3999** Manufacturing industries, nec

(G-6298)
OLD SCHOOL CRUSHING CO INC
250 Old Mechanical Ct (27529-2596)
PHONE..........................919 661-0011
John Dillinger, *Pr*
EMP: 15 EST: 2012
SALES (est): 977K **Privately Held**
SIC: **2611** Pulp mills, mechanical and recycling processing

(G-6299)
OUTSIDE LINES
1408 Kenbrook Dr (27529-4448)
PHONE..........................919 327-3041
Jo Cicci, *Prin*
EMP: 5 EST: 2010
SALES (est): 133.37K **Privately Held**
SIC: **3993** Signs and advertising specialties

(G-6300)
PC SIGNS & GRAPHICS LLC
180 Hein Dr (27529-8546)
PHONE..........................919 661-5801
EMP: 9 EST: 1996
SALES (est): 530.77K **Privately Held**
Web: www.pcsigns.biz
SIC: **3993** 7389 Signs and advertising specialties; Business services, nec

(G-6301)
PEPSI BOTTLING VENTURES LLC
Also Called: Pepsi-Cola
1900 Pepsi Way Fl 1 (27529-7232)
PHONE..........................919 863-4000
Tom Wiza, *Mgr*
EMP: 221
Web: www.pepsibottlingventures.com
SIC: **2086** 5149 Carbonated soft drinks, bottled and canned; Groceries and related products, nec
HQ: Pepsi Bottling Ventures Llc
4141 Parklake Ave Ste 600
Raleigh NC 27612
919 865-2300

(G-6302)
PEPSI BOTTLING VENTURES LLC
1900 Treygan Rd (27529-3592)
PHONE..........................919 865-2388
Derek Hill, *CEO*
EMP: 90
SIC: **2086** Bottled and canned soft drinks
HQ: Pepsi Bottling Ventures Llc
4141 Parklake Ave Ste 600
Raleigh NC 27612
919 865-2300

(G-6303)
PLATIPUS ANCHORS LTD
1427 Mechanical Blvd (27529-2538)
PHONE..........................919 662-0900
▲ EMP: 4 EST: 2005
SALES (est): 58.6K **Privately Held**
Web: www.platipus.us
SIC: **2451** Mobile homes

(G-6304)
POWERSOLVE CORPORATION LLC
117b Pierce Rd (27529-7909)
PHONE..........................919 662-8515
EMP: 14 EST: 2017
SALES (est): 2.19MM **Privately Held**
Web: www.powersolve.com
SIC: **7372** Prepackaged software

(G-6305)
PRECISION SIGNS INC
5455 Raynor Rd (27529-9452)
PHONE..........................919 615-0979
Laurie Peach, *Pr*
Daniel Peach, *VP*
EMP: 4 EST: 2013
SQ FT: 2,100
SALES (est): 490.78K **Privately Held**
Web: www.precisionsignsnc.com
SIC: **3993** Signs, not made in custom sign painting shops

(G-6306)
R & H WELDING LLC
3020 Cornwallis Rd (27529-7617)
PHONE..........................919 763-7955
Ruben Hernandez-trejo, *Prin*
EMP: 7 EST: 2015
SALES (est): 241.16K **Privately Held**
Web: r-h-welding-llc.business.site
SIC: **7692** Welding repair

(G-6307)
RAIL-SCALE-MODELS
140 Tallowwood Dr (27529-5922)
PHONE..........................248 421-6276
R Stephen Milley, *Prin*
EMP: 4 EST: 2018
SALES (est): 74.28K **Privately Held**
Web: www.rail-scale-models.com
SIC: **3999** Manufacturing industries, nec

(G-6308)
RED ADEPT PUBLISHING LLC
104 Bugenfield Ct (27529-3790)
PHONE..........................919 798-7410
EMP: 5 EST: 2018
SALES (est): 109.38K **Privately Held**
Web: www.redadeptpublishing.com
SIC: **2741** Miscellaneous publishing

(G-6309)
RENT A GUY NOW LLC ✪
404 Butler Dr (27529-3628)
PHONE..........................919 637-1104
EMP: 4 EST: 2022
SALES (est): 63.22K **Privately Held**
Web: www.rentaguynow.com
SIC: **3732** Boatbuilding and repairing

(G-6310)
ROOFING SUPPLY
3609 Jones Sausage Rd (27529-9495)
PHONE..........................919 779-6223
Joan Pitcer, *Prin*
EMP: 6 EST: 2016
SALES (est): 66.08K **Privately Held**
SIC: **3531** Construction machinery

(G-6311)
RVB SYSTEMS GROUP INC
5504 Quails Call Ct (27529-7421)
P.O. Box 966 (27512-0966)
PHONE..........................919 362-5211
Robert Brown, *Pr*
EMP: 5 EST: 1997
SALES (est): 763.67K **Privately Held**
Web: www.barcode-solutions.com
SIC: **5084** 7372 7371 Industrial machinery and equipment; Business oriented computer software; Computer software development

(G-6312)
S T WOOTEN CORPORATION
Also Called: Newport/Morehead Cy Con Plant
12200 Cleveland Rd (27529-8181)
PHONE..........................252 393-2206
Seth Wooten, *Pr*
EMP: 22
SALES (corp-wide): 319.83MM **Privately Held**
Web: www.stwcorp.com
SIC: **3531** Concrete plants
PA: S. T. Wooten Corporation
3801 Black Creek Rd Se
Wilson NC 27893
252 291-5165

(G-6313)
S T WOOTEN CORPORATION
Also Called: Garner Concrete Plant
925 E Garner Rd (27529-3328)
PHONE..........................919 779-6089
Jeff Palmer, *Mgr*
EMP: 26
SALES (corp-wide): 319.83MM **Privately Held**
Web: www.stwcorp.com
SIC: **3531** Concrete plants
PA: S. T. Wooten Corporation
3801 Black Creek Rd Se
Wilson NC 27893
252 291-5165

(G-6314)
S T WOOTEN CORPORATION
Also Called: Garner Concrete Plant
12204 Cleveland Rd (27529-8181)
PHONE..........................919 779-7589
Reed Dawson, *Mgr*
EMP: 37
SALES (corp-wide): 319.83MM **Privately Held**
Web: www.stwcorp.com
SIC: **3531** Concrete plants
PA: S. T. Wooten Corporation
3801 Black Creek Rd Se
Wilson NC 27893
252 291-5165

(G-6315)
SIGMA ENGINEERED SOLUTIONS PC (PA)
120 Sigma Dr (27529-8542)
PHONE..........................919 773-0011
Viren Joshi, *Pr*
Niteen Inamdar, *
Neville Kharas, *
Umesh Joshi, *Executive Global Human Resources Vice-President**
Kirankumar Acharya, *Global Chief Financial Officer**
▲ EMP: 95 EST: 2008
SQ FT: 185,000
SALES (est): 93.78MM
SALES (corp-wide): 93.78MM **Privately Held**
Web: www.sigmaengineeringsolutions.com
SIC: **5063** 3644 Electrical fittings and construction materials; Noncurrent-carrying wiring devices

(G-6316)
STUDIO GRIFFIN LLC
105 Marianna Pl (27529-7683)
PHONE..........................919 661-9634
EMP: 4 EST: 2019
SALES (est): 75.53K **Privately Held**
SIC: **2741** Miscellaneous publishing

(G-6317)
T & R SIGNS
Also Called: T & R Signs & Screen Printing
110 E Main St (27529-3238)
PHONE..........................919 779-1185
Stan Powell, *Owner*
EMP: 5 EST: 1983
SQ FT: 4,000
SALES (est): 306.86K **Privately Held**
SIC: **3993** 2261 5199 2752 Signs, not made in custom sign painting shops; Screen printing of cotton broadwoven fabrics; Advertising specialties; Offset printing

(G-6318)
TRIANGLE STEEL SYSTEMS LLC
133 Us 70 Hwy W (27529-3942)
PHONE..........................919 615-0282
Kyle Reece, *Pr*
EMP: 6 EST: 2014
SALES (est): 763.02K **Privately Held**
Web: www.specifichouse.com
SIC: **3441** Fabricated structural metal

(G-6319)
TURN KEY TIRE SERVICE INC
Also Called: Turner Tire Service
1340 Bobbitt Dr (27529-3040)
P.O. Box 1145 (27529-1145)
PHONE..........................919 836-8473
Jerry Laffieter, *CEO*

GEOGRAPHIC SECTION

Gastonia - Gaston County (G-6344)

EMP: 6 EST: 2001
SALES (est): 383.85K Privately Held
SIC: 7534 5531 Tire retreading and repair shops; Automotive tires

(G-6320)
UNILIN NORTH AMERICA LLC
1001 Pergo Pkwy (27529-8552)
PHONE..................919 773-6000
EMP: 26
SIC: 3996 Hard surface floor coverings, nec
HQ: Unilin North America, Llc
 7834 C F Hawn Fwy
 Dallas TX 75217

(G-6321)
UNILIN NORTH AMERICA LLC
2000 Pergo Pkwy (27529-8553)
PHONE..................919 773-5900
EMP: 26
SIC: 3996 3083 Tile, floor: supported plastic; Laminated plastics plate and sheet
HQ: Unilin North America, Llc
 7834 C F Hawn Fwy
 Dallas TX 75217

(G-6322)
UNIQUE CONCEPTS
310 Shipwash Dr Ste 101 (27529-6893)
P.O. Box 1471 (27528-1471)
PHONE..................919 366-2001
Lonnie Sawyer Junior, *Owner*
EMP: 4 EST: 2005
SALES (est): 244.58K Privately Held
Web: www.uniqueconcepts.com
SIC: 3599 Machine shop, jobbing and repair

(G-6323)
USA DREAMSTONE LLC
Also Called: Dreamstone Gran MBL & Quartz
128 Yeargan Rd Ste C (27529-5504)
PHONE..................919 615-4329
Rafael Preto, *Owner*
EMP: 4 EST: 2015
SALES (est): 804.17K Privately Held
Web: www.usadreamstone.com
SIC: 3679 3281 Quartz crystals, for electronic application; Marble, building: cut and shaped

(G-6324)
VIZTEK LLC
2217 Us 70 Hwy E (27529-9424)
P.O. Box 122272 (75312-2272)
PHONE..................919 792-6420
EMP: 50
SIC: 8732 3825 Business research service; Digital test equipment, electronic and electrical circuits

(G-6325)
WEBBS LOGISTICS LLC
111 Saint Marys St (27529-3129)
PHONE..................919 591-4308
EMP: 10 EST: 2020
SALES (est): 674.45K Privately Held
SIC: 3537 Trucks, tractors, loaders, carriers, and similar equipment

(G-6326)
WILSONS PLANNING & CONSULTING
1402 Harth Dr (27529-4817)
PHONE..................919 592-0935
Wilson Latrice, *Prin*
EMP: 4 EST: 2017
SALES (est): 91.96K Privately Held
SIC: 2752 Commercial printing, lithographic

(G-6327)
WURTH REVCAR FASTENERS INC
800 N Greenfield Pkwy Ste 810 (27529)
PHONE..................919 772-9930
Ron Mcgaugh, *Brnch Mgr*
EMP: 28
SALES (corp-wide): 20.7B Privately Held
Web: www.wurthindustry.com
SIC: 3399 Metal fasteners
HQ: Wurth Revcar Fasteners, Inc.
 1 Avery Row
 Roanoke VA 24012
 540 561-6565

(G-6328)
XYLEM INC
1328 Bobbitt Dr (27529-3040)
PHONE..................919 772-4126
Stefan Van Staveren, *Pr*
Jamie Smith, *VP*
EMP: 7 EST: 1995
SALES (est): 500K Privately Held
Web: www.xylemonline.com
SIC: 2434 2521 2511 Wood kitchen cabinets; Wood office furniture; Wood household furniture

Garysburg
Northampton County

(G-6329)
PRIZE MANAGEMENT LLC
8287 Nc Hwy 46 (27831-9616)
PHONE..................252 532-1939
EMP: 7 EST: 2018
SALES (est): 510.49K Privately Held
SIC: 1442 Sand mining

Gaston
Northampton County

(G-6330)
CLARY LUMBER COMPANY
204 Mitchell St (27832-9787)
PHONE..................252 537-2558
John C Lucy Junior, *Ch Bd*
John C Lucy Iii, *Pr*
EMP: 68 EST: 1969
SQ FT: 1,800
SALES (est): 6.78MM Privately Held
Web: www.clarylumber.com
SIC: 2421 2448 2426 Lumber: rough, sawed, or planed; Wood pallets and skids; Hardwood dimension and flooring mills

(G-6331)
MICHAEL H BRANCH INC
Also Called: Branch Welding Greensville Co
1621 Old Emporia Rd (27832-9570)
PHONE..................252 532-0930
Michael Branch, *Owner*
EMP: 8 EST: 2008
SALES (est): 712.16K Privately Held
Web: www.branchwelding.com
SIC: 3842 Welders' hoods

(G-6332)
T E GARNER LOGGING
985 Nc Highway 48 (27832-9516)
PHONE..................252 678-3836
EMP: 5 EST: 2017
SALES (est): 81.72K Privately Held
SIC: 2411 Logging camps and contractors

Gastonia
Gaston County

(G-6333)
277 METAL INC
201 Davis Heights Dr (28052-6392)
PHONE..................704 372-4513
Jeremy Yaekel, *Prin*
EMP: 7 EST: 2017
SALES (est): 244.18K Privately Held
Web: www.277metal.com
SIC: 7692 Welding repair

(G-6334)
A B CARTER INC (PA)
Also Called: Carter Traveler Division
4801 York Hwy (28052-6808)
P.O. Box 518 (28053-0518)
PHONE..................704 865-1201
J Bynum Carter, *CEO*
J Bynum Carter, *Ch Bd*
T Henderson Wise, *Pr*
Louis Mitchell, *VP Fin*
▲ EMP: 62 EST: 1922
SQ FT: 140,000
SALES (est): 24.75MM
SALES (corp-wide): 24.75MM Privately Held
Web: www.abcarter.com
SIC: 3315 3552 Welded steel wire fabric; Textile machinery

(G-6335)
ACME DIE & MACHINE CORPORATION
202 Trakas Blvd (28052-9221)
P.O. Box 12507 (28052-0021)
PHONE..................704 864-8426
Richard Littlejohn, *Pr*
Stephen Littlejohn, *VP*
Helen Littlejohn, *Treas*
Sandra Wilson, *Sec*
EMP: 10 EST: 1965
SQ FT: 12,000
SALES (est): 800K Privately Held
SIC: 3599 3544 Machine shop, jobbing and repair; Special dies, tools, jigs, and fixtures

(G-6336)
ACTION SPECIALTIES LLC
1916 S York Rd (28052-6369)
PHONE..................704 865-6699
EMP: 4 EST: 2018
SALES (est): 154.87K Privately Held
Web: www.actionspecialties.com
SIC: 2759 Commercial printing, nec

(G-6337)
AEK INC
3705 Saint Regis Dr (28056-7542)
PHONE..................704 864-7968
Ann Edwards, *VP*
EMP: 6 EST: 2017
SALES (est): 195.09K Privately Held
SIC: 2084 Wines

(G-6338)
AGAINST THE GRAIN WOODWORKING
154 Superior Stainless Rd (28052-8744)
PHONE..................704 969-5837
EMP: 4 EST: 2011
SALES (est): 68K Privately Held
Web: www.againstthegrainnc.com
SIC: 2431 Millwork

(G-6339)
ALL AMERICAN BRAIDS INC
1613 Warren Ave (28054-7451)
P.O. Box 789 (28164-0789)
PHONE..................704 852-4380
John L Larson Junior, *Pr*
Robyn Ann Larson,
EMP: 30 EST: 1995
SALES (est): 1.94MM Privately Held
Web: www.allamericanbraids.com
SIC: 2241 2298 Braids, textile; Cordage and twine

(G-6340)
ALLIANCE MCH & FABRICATION LLC
3421 Fairview Dr (28052-7162)
P.O. Box 76 (28034-0076)
PHONE..................704 629-5677
EMP: 7 EST: 2011
SALES (est): 970.87K Privately Held
SIC: 3441 Fabricated structural metal

(G-6341)
ALTUS FINISHING LLC
1711 Sparta Ct (28052-9111)
P.O. Box 3736 (28054-0038)
PHONE..................704 861-1536
Ron Sytz, *Pr*
Janet Sytz Ctrl, *Prin*
EMP: 25 EST: 2018
SALES (est): 1.76MM
SALES (corp-wide): 23.38MM Privately Held
SIC: 2231 Bleaching, dying and specialty treating: wool, mohair, etc.
PA: Beverly Knits, Inc.
 1675 Garfield Dr
 Gastonia NC 28052
 704 861-1536

(G-6342)
AMBASSADOR SERVICES INC
Also Called: Beyond This Day
1520 S York Rd (28052-6138)
PHONE..................800 576-8627
EMP: 185 EST: 1998
SALES (est): 26.36MM
SALES (corp-wide): 29.7MM Privately Held
Web: www.milestonescompany.com
SIC: 2731 Books, publishing only
PA: Good Will Publishers, Inc.
 1520 S York Rd
 Gastonia NC 28052
 704 853-3237

(G-6343)
AMERICAN & EFIRD LLC
Also Called: American & Efird 56
3200 York Hwy (28056)
PHONE..................704 864-0977
Morris Dillenger, *Mgr*
EMP: 14
SALES (corp-wide): 1.98B Privately Held
Web: www.amefird.com
SIC: 2284 2281 Thread mills; Yarn spinning mills
HQ: American & Efird Llc
 24 American St
 Mount Holly NC 28120
 704 827-4311

(G-6344)
AMERICAN & EFIRD LLC
401 Grover St (28054-3231)
P.O. Box 507 (28120-0507)
PHONE..................704 867-3664
Brian Mull, *Brnch Mgr*
EMP: 19
SALES (corp-wide): 1.98B Privately Held
Web: www.amefird.com

Gastonia - Gaston County (G-6345)

SIC: **2284** Thread mills
HQ: American & Efird Llc
24 American St
Mount Holly NC 28120
704 827-4311

(G-6345)
AMERICAN FORMS MFG INC (PA)
170 Tarheel Dr (28056-8719)
PHONE.................................704 866-9139
Calvin Price, *Ch*
David Price, *
Karen P Carpenter, *Stockholder*
Ann R Daniels, *Stockholder*
▲ **EMP**: 26 **EST**: 1990
SQ FT: 35,000
SALES (est): 2.3MM **Privately Held**
Web: www.americanformsmfg.com
SIC: **5943** 2761 Office forms and supplies; Manifold business forms

(G-6346)
AMERICAN LINC CORPORATION
159 Wolfpack Rd (28056-9776)
PHONE.................................704 861-9242
D Lynn Hoover, *Pr*
Danny Lockman, *
◆ **EMP**: 30 **EST**: 1985
SQ FT: 20,000
SALES (est): 3.84MM **Privately Held**
Web: www.americanlinc.com
SIC: **3599** 5084 3552 Machine shop, jobbing and repair; Industrial machinery and equipment; Textile machinery

(G-6347)
AMERICAN METAL FABRICATORS INC
2608 Lowell Rd (28054-1428)
PHONE.................................704 824-8585
EMP: 35 **EST**: 1988
SALES (est): 2.4MM **Privately Held**
Web: www.americanmetalfabinc.com
SIC: **3443** Fabricated plate work (boiler shop)

(G-6348)
AMPED EVENTS LLC
401 S Marietta St (28052-4651)
PHONE.................................888 683-4386
EMP: 12 **EST**: 2008
SQ FT: 4,000
SALES (est): 988.38K **Privately Held**
SIC: **2759** Screen printing

(G-6349)
ATKINSON INTERNATIONAL INC
3800 Little Mountain Rd (28056-6875)
P.O. Box 6303 (28056-6020)
PHONE.................................704 865-7750
Claire Atkinson, *Pr*
Darin Atkinson, *
Connie Atkinson, *
▲ **EMP**: 55 **EST**: 2004
SQ FT: 196,000
SALES (est): 4.99MM **Privately Held**
SIC: **3714** Air brakes, motor vehicle

(G-6350)
AZUSA INTERNATIONAL INC
2510 N Chester St (28052-1808)
P.O. Box 550336 (28055-0336)
PHONE.................................704 879-4464
Zeshan Lakhani, *Pr*
▲ **EMP**: 5 **EST**: 2011
SALES (est): 477.43K **Privately Held**
SIC: **2299** Fabrics: linen, jute, hemp, ramie

(G-6351)
BARNYARD UTILITY BLDNGS-STRG/TL
Also Called: CSS
1990 E Franklin Blvd (28054-4742)
PHONE.................................704 867-4700
EMP: 4
SALES (corp-wide): 2.21MM **Privately Held**
Web: www.4barnyard.com
SIC: **3448** Prefabricated metal buildings and components
PA: Barnyard Utility Buildings-Storage/Utility, S.C. Corp.
707 N Main St
Clover SC 29710
803 831-9408

(G-6352)
BELT SHOP INC
1941 Chespark Dr (28052-9108)
PHONE.................................704 865-3636
Donna Badger, *Pr*
James Mull, *VP*
Gloria Mull, *CFO*
Mark Mull, *Sec*
EMP: 15 **EST**: 1988
SQ FT: 18,000
SALES (est): 4.08MM **Privately Held**
Web: www.industrialbeltshop.com
SIC: **3496** 3052 2387 2386 Conveyor belts; Transmission belting, rubber; Apparel belts; Leather and sheep-lined clothing

(G-6353)
BETTER BUSINESS PRINTING INC
Also Called: International Minute Press
495 E Long Ave (28054-2526)
PHONE.................................704 867-3366
Pamela Joles, *Pr*
Bill Joles, *Pr*
EMP: 9 **EST**: 1991
SQ FT: 6,000
SALES (est): 1.7MM **Privately Held**
Web: www.impressnc.com
SIC: **2752** 7334 Offset printing; Photocopying and duplicating services

(G-6354)
BEVERLY KNITS INC
1640 Federal St (28052-0502)
PHONE.................................704 964-0835
Ronald M Sytz, *Pr*
EMP: 9
SALES (corp-wide): 23.38MM **Privately Held**
Web: www.beverlyknits.com
SIC: **2211** Broadwoven fabric mills, cotton
PA: Beverly Knits, Inc.
1675 Garfield Dr
Gastonia NC 28052
704 861-1536

(G-6355)
BEVERLY KNITS INC (PA)
1675 Garfield Dr (28052-8403)
P.O. Box 3736 (28054-0038)
PHONE.................................704 861-1536
▲ **EMP**: 100 **EST**: 1980
SALES (est): 23.38MM
SALES (corp-wide): 23.38MM **Privately Held**
Web: www.beverlyknits.com
SIC: **2211** Broadwoven fabric mills, cotton

(G-6356)
BLUE STEEL INC
4905 Sparrow Dairy Rd (28056-8940)
PHONE.................................704 864-2583
EMP: 4 **EST**: 1994
SALES (est): 382.57K **Privately Held**
SIC: **3599** Machine shop, jobbing and repair

(G-6357)
BOWEN MACHINE COMPANY INC
3421 Fairview Dr (28052-7162)
PHONE.................................704 629-9111
Stuart Bowen Junior, *Pr*
Jonathan Bowen, *
EMP: 19 **EST**: 1979
SQ FT: 20,000
SALES (est): 477.74K **Privately Held**
Web: www.bowenmachine.com
SIC: **3599** Machine shop, jobbing and repair

(G-6358)
BP ASSOCIATES INC (PA)
2408 Forbes Rd (28056-6267)
P.O. Box 12885 (28052-0043)
PHONE.................................704 864-3032
◆ **EMP**: 138 **EST**: 1994
SQ FT: 167,000
SALES (est): 99.92MM **Privately Held**
Web: www.ifabrication.com
SIC: **3441** Fabricated structural metal

(G-6359)
BP ASSOCIATES INC
105 Wolfpack Rd (28056-9776)
PHONE.................................704 833-1494
EMP: 206
Web: www.ifabrication.com
SIC: **3441** Fabricated structural metal
PA: Bp Associates Inc.
2408 Forbes Rd
Gastonia NC 28056

(G-6360)
BRIDGESTONE RET OPERATIONS LLC
Also Called: Firestone
142 N New Hope Rd (28054-4755)
PHONE.................................704 861-8146
Davon Bryd, *Mgr*
EMP: 10
Web: www.bridgestoneamericas.com
SIC: **5531** 7534 Automotive tires; Rebuilding and retreading tires
HQ: Bridgestone Retail Operations, Llc
333 E Lake St Ste 300
Bloomingdale IL 60108
630 259-9000

(G-6361)
BULK SAK INTERNATIONAL INC
1302 Industrial Pike Rd (28052-8430)
PHONE.................................704 833-1361
EMP: 30
SALES (corp-wide): 109.59MM **Privately Held**
Web: www.sonoco.com
SIC: **2673** Bags: plastic, laminated, and coated
HQ: Bulk Sak International, Inc.
103 Industrial Dr
Malvern AR 72104

(G-6362)
BURLAN MANUFACTURING LLC (PA)
Also Called: Carolina Strapping Buckles Co
2740 W Franklin Blvd (28052-9480)
PHONE.................................704 349-0000
William Lee Cornwell, *Pr*
Suzanne M Landis, *
Kevin Wassil, *
David Devane, *
David Hinson, *
◆ **EMP**: 150 **EST**: 1971
SQ FT: 200,000
SALES (est): 45.26MM
SALES (corp-wide): 45.26MM **Privately Held**
Web: www.burlan.com
SIC: **2296** Fabric for reinforcing industrial belting

(G-6363)
BURNETT MACHINE COMPANY INC
924 Hanover St (28054-2452)
PHONE.................................704 867-7786
Robert D Burnett, *Pr*
Robert M Burnett, *Stockholder*
Tim Hickson, *VP*
EMP: 10 **EST**: 1976
SQ FT: 6,400
SALES (est): 916.38K **Privately Held**
Web: www.burnettmachine.com
SIC: **3552** 3599 Textile machinery; Machine and other job shop work

(G-6364)
C & R HARD CHROME SERVICE INC
940 Hanover St (28054-2452)
PHONE.................................704 861-8831
William A Cottingham, *Pr*
Charles Martin Reynolds, *VP*
Dora Cottingham, *Sec*
Jerri Reynolds, *Treas*
EMP: 7 **EST**: 1967
SQ FT: 5,000
SALES (est): 720.62K **Privately Held**
Web: www.cr-plating.com
SIC: **3471** Chromium plating of metals or formed products

(G-6365)
C L RABB INC
103 Wolfpack Rd (28056-9776)
P.O. Box 6009 (28056-6000)
PHONE.................................704 865-0295
EMP: 48 **EST**: 1986
SQ FT: 45,000
SALES (est): 24.56MM **Privately Held**
Web: www.clrabb.com
SIC: **5113** 2655 2653 Industrial and personal service paper; Ammunition cans or tubes, board laminated with metal foil; Corrugated boxes, partitions, display items, sheets, and pad

(G-6366)
CAROLINA BRUSH COMPANY
3093 Northwest Blvd (28052-1166)
P.O. Box 2469 (28053-2469)
PHONE.................................704 867-0286
Fred P Spach, *Pr*
Barbara Glenn, *CEO*
Gerrii Spach, *Ch Bd*
▲ **EMP**: 46 **EST**: 1919
SQ FT: 27,000
SALES (est): 8.88MM
SALES (corp-wide): 8.88MM **Privately Held**
Web: www.carolinabrush.com
SIC: **5085** 3991 Brushes, industrial; Brooms and brushes
PA: Carolina Brush Manufacturing Company Inc
3093 Northwest Blvd
Gastonia NC 28052
704 867-0286

(G-6367)
CAROLINA BRUSH MFG CO (PA)
3093 Northwest Blvd (28052-1166)
P.O. Box 2469 (28053-2469)
PHONE.................................704 867-0286
Fred Spach, *Pr*
Gerrii Spach, *Ch Bd*
Jonathan Hicks, *Treas*
▲ **EMP**: 43 **EST**: 1919
SQ FT: 27,000
SALES (est): 8.88MM

GEOGRAPHIC SECTION
Gastonia - Gaston County (G-6393)

SALES (corp-wide): 8.88MM **Privately Held**
Web: www.carolinabrush.com
SIC: 3991 Brushes, household or industrial

(G-6368)
CAROLINA CUSTOM TANK LLC
924 Dr Martin Luther King Jr Way (28054-7301)
PHONE.................980 406-3200
▲ EMP: 14 EST: 2012
SALES (est): 541.26K **Privately Held**
SIC: 3795 Tanks and tank components

(G-6369)
CAROLINA SIGNS
3319 Lincoln Ln (28056-8807)
PHONE.................704 622-1939
Erin A Hayes, *Prin*
EMP: 6 EST: 2013
SALES (est): 216.06K **Privately Held**
Web: www.carolinasignsnc.com
SIC: 3993 8748 Signs and advertising specialties; Lighting consultant

(G-6370)
CAROLINA WARP PRINTS INC
221 Meek Rd (28056-8122)
PHONE.................704 866-4763
Vincent N Murphy, *Pr*
Vincent N Nat Murphy, *Pr*
Tessia Steele, *VP*
▲ EMP: 10 EST: 1988
SQ FT: 9,200
SALES (est): 760.38K **Privately Held**
SIC: 2752 Poster and decal printing, lithographic

(G-6371)
CAROLINA WATER JETS
219 Superior Stainless Rd (28052-8747)
PHONE.................704 853-3663
Mark Cobb, *Ofcr*
EMP: 5 EST: 1999
SALES (est): 81.91K **Privately Held**
SIC: 3634 Electric housewares and fans

(G-6372)
CENTURION INDUSTRIES INC
1990 Industrial Pike Rd (28052-8436)
PHONE.................704 867-2304
EMP: 110
SALES (corp-wide): 242.37MM **Privately Held**
Web: www.centurionind.com
SIC: 3444 Canopies, sheet metal
PA: Centurion Industries, Inc.
    1107 N Taylor Rd
    Garrett IN 46738
    260 357-6665

(G-6373)
CENTURY TEXTILE MFG INC
803 N Oakland St (28054-7300)
PHONE.................704 869-6660
Alexander Gendelman, *Pr*
EMP: 14 EST: 2002
SQ FT: 100,000
SALES (est): 943.45K **Privately Held**
SIC: 2261 2257 Finishing plants, cotton; Dyeing and finishing circular knit fabrics

(G-6374)
CHAMPION POWDERCOATING INC
Also Called: Xpress Powder Coat
1220 Industrial Ave (28054-4629)
PHONE.................704 866-8148
EMP: 5 EST: 2002
SALES (est): 476.43K **Privately Held**
Web: www.championpowdercoat.com
SIC: 3479 Coating of metals and formed products

(G-6375)
CHAMPION THREAD COMPANY (PA)
Also Called: Ctc
165 Bluedevil Dr (28056-8610)
PHONE.................704 867-6611
Robert Poovey Iii, *CEO*
Robert Poovey, *Ch*
William Poovey, *Pr*
Pj Mccord, *VP*
Jim Lee, *VP*
▲ EMP: 5 EST: 1979
SALES (est): 4.79MM
SALES (corp-wide): 4.79MM **Privately Held**
Web: www.championthread.com
SIC: 5131 2211 7389 Thread; Elastic fabrics, cotton; Business Activities at Non-Commercial Site

(G-6376)
CHARLOTTE CABINETRY LLC
156 S South St Ste 201 (28052-4218)
PHONE.................704 966-2500
EMP: 5 EST: 2016
SALES (est): 160.64K **Privately Held**
SIC: 2434 Wood kitchen cabinets

(G-6377)
CHOICE USA BEVERAGE INC
809 E Franklin Blvd (28054-4254)
P.O. Box 40 (28098-0040)
PHONE.................704 861-1029
Jim Mccune, *Mgr*
EMP: 40
SALES (corp-wide): 30.99MM **Privately Held**
Web: www.choiceusabeverage.com
SIC: 2086 Soft drinks: packaged in cans, bottles, etc.
PA: Choice U.S.A. Beverage, Inc.
    603 Groves St
    Lowell NC 28098
    704 823-1651

(G-6378)
CHRONICLE MILL LAND LLC
3826 S New Hope Rd Ste 4 (28056-4401)
P.O. Box 810 (28012-0810)
PHONE.................704 527-3227
John Church, *Prin*
EMP: 8 EST: 2012
SALES (est): 222.84K **Privately Held**
SIC: 2711 Newspapers, publishing and printing

(G-6379)
CMC REBAR
2528 N Chester St (28052-1808)
P.O. Box 1928 (28053-1928)
PHONE.................704 865-8571
▲ EMP: 8 EST: 2010
SALES (est): 1.01MM **Privately Held**
Web: www.cmc.com
SIC: 3441 Fabricated structural metal

(G-6380)
COLLINS FABRICATION & WLDG LLC
1204 N Chester St (28052-1855)
PHONE.................704 861-9326
Mike Collins, *Prin*
EMP: 4 EST: 1985
SQ FT: 4,000
SALES (est): 362.09K **Privately Held**
SIC: 7692 1799 3444 3441 Welding repair; Welding on site; Sheet metalwork; Fabricated structural metal

(G-6381)
COMMERCIAL METALS COMPANY
Also Called: CMC Rebar
2528 N Chester St (28052-1808)
PHONE.................919 833-9737
EMP: 6
SALES (corp-wide): 8.8B **Publicly Held**
Web: www.cmc.com
SIC: 3312 Blast furnaces and steel mills
PA: Commercial Metals Company
    6565 N Macarthur Blvd # 800
    Irving TX 75039
    214 689-4300

(G-6382)
CONCEPT STEEL INC
1801 Bradbury Ct (28052-9107)
PHONE.................704 874-0414
Ryan Chapman, *Pr*
EMP: 25 EST: 1999
SQ FT: 2,000
SALES (est): 4.51MM **Privately Held**
Web: www.conceptsteel.com
SIC: 3449 3441 Miscellaneous metalwork; Fabricated structural metal

(G-6383)
CONFERENCE INC
259 W Main Ave (28052-4140)
PHONE.................704 349-0203
Souheil Anthony Tony Azar, *Pr*
EMP: 6 EST: 2013
SALES (est): 832.38K **Privately Held**
Web: www.conference-inc.com
SIC: 2819 Industrial inorganic chemicals, nec

(G-6384)
CONITEX SONOCO USA INC
1302 Industrial Pike Rd (28052-8430)
PHONE.................704 864-5406
Joseph Artiga, *Pr*
David Monteith, *
Carl Smith, *
Michael Schmidlin, *
Joaquin Vinas, *
◆ EMP: 140 EST: 1982
SQ FT: 103,000
SALES (est): 49.32MM
SALES (corp-wide): 6.78B **Publicly Held**
Web: www.sonoco.com
SIC: 5199 2655 Packaging materials; Ammunition cans or tubes, board laminated with metal foil
PA: Sonoco Products Company
    1 N 2nd St
    Hartsville SC 29550
    843 383-7000

(G-6385)
CONTEMPORARY CONCEPTS INC
2940 Audrey Dr (28054-7268)
P.O. Box 550910 (28055-0910)
PHONE.................704 864-9572
Doug Cullen, *Pr*
EMP: 30 EST: 1982
SQ FT: 3,800
SALES (est): 2.16MM **Privately Held**
Web: www.contemporaryconcepts.net
SIC: 2731 Books, publishing only

(G-6386)
CONTEMPORARY DESIGN CO LLC
Also Called: Carolina Custom Millwork
513 N Broad St (28054-2508)
PHONE.................704 375-6030
EMP: 19 EST: 2019
SALES (est): 1.35MM **Privately Held**
SIC: 2599 2431 Cabinets, factory; Millwork

(G-6387)
CREATIVE FABRIC SERVICES LLC
1675 Garfield Dr (28052-8403)
P.O. Box 3736 (28054-0038)
PHONE.................704 861-8383
Robert V Sytz, *Managing Member*
◆ EMP: 5 EST: 1997
SQ FT: 47,500
SALES (est): 2.39MM
SALES (corp-wide): 23.38MM **Privately Held**
Web: www.creativeticking.com
SIC: 2211 Broadwoven fabric mills, cotton
PA: Beverly Knits, Inc.
    1675 Garfield Dr
    Gastonia NC 28052
    704 861-1536

(G-6388)
CRISP PRINTERS INC
2022 E Ozark Ave (28054-3361)
PHONE.................704 867-6663
Monty Teague, *Pr*
Melody Teague, *Sec*
EMP: 6 EST: 1961
SQ FT: 1,900
SALES (est): 506.22K **Privately Held**
Web: www.crispprinters.com
SIC: 2752 Offset printing

(G-6389)
CS ALLOYS
2888 Colony Woods Dr (28054-7779)
PHONE.................704 675-5810
EMP: 5 EST: 2009
SALES (est): 406.04K **Privately Held**
Web: www.csalloys.com
SIC: 3363 Aluminum die-castings

(G-6390)
CTC HOLDINGS LLC (PA)
165 Bluedevil Dr (28056-8610)
P.O. Box 150 (29703-0150)
PHONE.................704 867-6611
EMP: 9 EST: 2005
SALES (est): 2.38MM **Privately Held**
SIC: 2284 Sewing thread

(G-6391)
CURTISS-WRIGHT CONTROLS INC
3120 Northwest Blvd (28052-1167)
PHONE.................704 869-2320
EMP: 16
SALES (corp-wide): 2.85B **Publicly Held**
Web: www.cwcontrols.com
SIC: 3728 Aircraft assemblies, subassemblies, and parts, nec
HQ: Curtiss-Wright Controls, Inc.
    15801 Brixham Hill Ave # 200
    Charlotte NC 28277
    704 869-4600

(G-6392)
CUSTOM MARKING & PRINTING INC
907 Bessemer City Rd (28052-1133)
P.O. Box 1772 (28053-1772)
PHONE.................704 866-8245
James G Silver, *Pr*
Laura A Silver, *Sec*
EMP: 6 EST: 1978
SQ FT: 5,000
SALES (est): 472.38K **Privately Held**
Web: www.petrolaenergy.com
SIC: 2752 3069 Offset printing; Stationer's rubber sundries

(G-6393)
D BLOCK METALS LLC (PA)
1111 Jenkins Rd (28052-1158)
PHONE.................704 705-5895

Gastonia - Gaston County (G-6394)

Craig Hefner, *Pr*
Cheryl Hefner, *CFO*
▲ **EMP:** 10 **EST:** 2011
SQ FT: 37,000
SALES (est): 2.13MM
SALES (corp-wide): 2.13MM **Privately Held**
Web: www.dblockmetals.com
SIC: 3399 Powder, metal

(G-6394)
DAIMLER TRUCK NORTH AMER LLC
Also Called: Freightliner Parts Plant
1400 Tulip Dr (28052-1873)
PHONE..................704 868-5700
Bob Pacillas, *Brnch Mgr*
EMP: 1300
SALES (corp-wide): 60.75B **Privately Held**
Web: northamerica.daimlertruck.com
SIC: 3714 3713 Motor vehicle parts and accessories; Truck and bus bodies
HQ: Daimler Truck North America Llc
4555 N Channel Ave
Portland OR 97217
503 745-8000

(G-6395)
DARLING INGREDIENTS INC
Carolina By Pdts Gastonia Div
5533 York Hwy (28052)
PHONE..................704 864-9941
Paul Humphries, *Brnch Mgr*
EMP: 15
SALES (corp-wide): 6.53B **Publicly Held**
Web: www.darlingii.com
SIC: 2048 2077 Prepared feeds, nec; Tallow rendering, inedible
PA: Darling Ingredients Inc.
5601 N Macarthur Blvd
Irving TX 75038
972 717-0300

(G-6396)
DAVIS MACHINE CO INC
158 Superior Stainless Rd (28052-8744)
P.O. Box 2183 (28053-2183)
PHONE..................704 865-2863
David B Davis, *Pr*
Robert M Davis, *Sr VP*
Sandra Davis, *VP*
D Allen Davis, *VP Mfg*
EMP: 6 **EST:** 1984
SQ FT: 7,700
SALES (est): 496.86K **Privately Held**
SIC: 3599 Machine shop, jobbing and repair

(G-6397)
DIAMOND ORTHOPEDIC LLC
1669 Federal St (28052-0504)
P.O. Box 1470 (28012-1470)
PHONE..................704 585-8258
Roy Bivens, *CEO*
Jonathan Crumpler, *CFO*
Jd Williams, *VP Sls*
EMP: 5 **EST:** 2017
SQ FT: 2,000
SALES (est): 488.42K **Privately Held**
Web: www.diamondortho.com
SIC: 3841 Surgical and medical instruments

(G-6398)
DRAMAR MACHINE DEVICES INC
108 Chickasaw Rd (28056-6235)
P.O. Box 635 (29703-0635)
PHONE..................704 866-0904
Howard Collmar, *Pr*
Danny Freeman, *VP*
EMP: 20 **EST:** 1994
SQ FT: 40,000
SALES (est): 2.11MM **Privately Held**
Web: www.dramarinc.com

SIC: 3599 Machine shop, jobbing and repair

(G-6399)
DYNAMIC STAMPINGS OF NC I
1412 Castle Ct (28052-1198)
PHONE..................704 864-1572
Gary Rauch, *Brnch Mgr*
EMP: 6 **EST:** 2006
SALES (est): 532.78K **Privately Held**
Web: www.dynamicstampings.com
SIC: 3469 Stamping metal for the trade

(G-6400)
ELECTRICAL APPARATUS & MCH CO
5619 Gallagher Dr (28052-8702)
P.O. Box 37432 (28237-7432)
PHONE..................704 333-2987
Douglas G James, *Pr*
Bess Thompson, *Sec*
Alan K James, *VP*
Donald C James, *VP*
▲ **EMP:** 10 **EST:** 1975
SALES (est): 987.34K **Privately Held**
Web: www.electricalapparatus.net
SIC: 3599 Machine shop, jobbing and repair

(G-6401)
EQUIPMENT DSIGN FBRICATION INC
201 Davis Heights Dr (28052-6392)
PHONE..................704 372-4513
Terry D Miller, *Pr*
▲ **EMP:** 9 **EST:** 1964
SALES (est): 751.06K **Privately Held**
Web: www.equipmentdesignandfab.com
SIC: 3441 Fabricated structural metal

(G-6402)
FIDELITY ASSOCIATES INC
Also Called: Family Traditions
2936 Rousseau Ct (28054-2102)
P.O. Box 550968 (28055-0968)
PHONE..................704 864-3766
Chris Cherry, *FAMILY TRADITIONS*
EMP: 31 **EST:** 1982
SQ FT: 5,000
SALES (est): 2.44MM **Privately Held**
Web: www.fidelityassociates.com
SIC: 2731 8021 Book publishing; Offices and clinics of dentists

(G-6403)
FRENCH APRON MANUFACTURING CO
1619 Madison St (28052-0846)
P.O. Box 2324 (28053-2324)
PHONE..................704 865-7666
Randy Beavers, *CEO*
Robert A Main Junior, *Pr*
William Main, *Ex VP*
Susan Main, *VP*
EMP: 9 **EST:** 1952
SQ FT: 10,000
SALES (est): 1.09MM
SALES (corp-wide): 31.25MM **Privately Held**
Web: www.french-apron.com
SIC: 3552 Textile machinery
PA: Main, Robert A & Sons Holding Company Inc
20-21 Wagaraw Rd
Fair Lawn NJ 07410
201 447-3700

(G-6404)
GASTEX LLC
3051 Aberdeen Blvd (28054-0622)
P.O. Box 3806 (28054-0039)
PHONE..................704 824-9861
EMP: 5 **EST:** 1974

SQ FT: 32,000
SALES (est): 493.15K **Privately Held**
SIC: 3552 7699 Textile machinery; Industrial machinery and equipment repair

(G-6405)
GASTON GAZETTE LLP
1893 Remount Rd (28054-7413)
P.O. Box 1538 (28053-1538)
PHONE..................704 869-1700
Marlene Smith, *Mgr*
EMP: 2557 **EST:** 1880
SQ FT: 89,000
SALES (est): 8.58MM
SALES (corp-wide): 2.66B **Publicly Held**
Web: www.gastongazette.com
SIC: 2711 Commercial printing and newspaper publishing combined
HQ: Halifax Media Group, Llc
2339 Beville Rd
Daytona Beach FL 32119
386 265-6700

(G-6406)
GASTONIA
860 Summit Crossing Pl (28054-2216)
PHONE..................704 377-3687
EMP: 9 **EST:** 2019
SALES (est): 140.88K **Privately Held**
Web: www.gastongazette.com
SIC: 2711 Newspapers, publishing and printing

(G-6407)
GENTRY PLASTICS INC
Also Called: Gpi
1808 Bradbury Ct (28052-9107)
PHONE..................704 864-4300
Michael Stephens, *Pr*
▲ **EMP:** 45 **EST:** 2000
SQ FT: 6,000
SALES (est): 7.17MM **Privately Held**
Web: www.gentryplastics.com
SIC: 3089 Injection molded finished plastics products, nec

(G-6408)
GOOD WILL PUBLISHERS INC (PA)
1520 S York Rd (28052-6138)
P.O. Box 269 (28053-0269)
PHONE..................704 853-3237
John Briody, *Pr*
Robert M Gallagher, *
Richard Hoefling, *
▲ **EMP:** 70 **EST:** 1949
SQ FT: 30,000
SALES (est): 29.7MM
SALES (corp-wide): 29.7MM **Privately Held**
Web: www.goodwillpublishers.com
SIC: 2731 5942 Books, publishing only; Book stores

(G-6409)
GRACEFUL STITCHING
1511 S New Hope Rd (28054-5835)
PHONE..................704 964-2121
Maria Stanley, *Prin*
EMP: 4 **EST:** 2018
SALES (est): 56.12K **Privately Held**
SIC: 2395 Embroidery and art needlework

(G-6410)
GRENADE MENTALITY PUBG CO
4217 Sunflower Ct (28052-9780)
PHONE..................704 865-7786
Bradford Marker, *Prin*
EMP: 5 **EST:** 2016
SALES (est): 68.72K **Privately Held**
SIC: 2741 Miscellaneous publishing

(G-6411)
HALIFAX MEDIA GROUP
1893 Remount Rd (28054-7413)
PHONE..................704 869-1700
EMP: 13 **EST:** 2014
SALES (est): 558.63K **Privately Held**
Web: www.gastongazette.com
SIC: 2711 Newspapers, publishing and printing

(G-6412)
HAM BROTHERS INC
205 Shamrock Rd (28056-7671)
P.O. Box 407 (28120-0407)
PHONE..................704 827-1303
Tod Ham, *Pr*
Joseph F Ham, *Pr*
Todd Ham, *Pr*
EMP: 15 **EST:** 1976
SALES (est): 4.33MM **Privately Held**
Web: www.hambrothers.com
SIC: 3441 Fabricated structural metal

(G-6413)
HANAK ENTERPRISES
2133 Rocky Falls Ln (28054-8505)
PHONE..................704 315-5249
Madison Smith, *Prin*
EMP: 4 **EST:** 2018
SALES (est): 165.33K **Privately Held**
SIC: 3714 Motor vehicle parts and accessories

(G-6414)
HAPPY SHACK SMOKE SHOP
4322 Wilkinson Blvd (28056-8676)
PHONE..................980 833-8053
EMP: 6 **EST:** 2014
SALES (est): 82.23K **Privately Held**
Web: happyshack.business.site
SIC: 2111 Cigarettes

(G-6415)
HERMAN REEVES TEX SHTMTL INC
Also Called: Herman Reeves Sheet Metal
1617 E Ozark Ave (28054-3513)
P.O. Box 249 (28098-0249)
PHONE..................704 865-2231
Michael W Clagg, *Pr*
Joshua Clagg, *
EMP: 42 **EST:** 1962
SQ FT: 7,000
SALES (est): 8.96MM **Privately Held**
Web: www.hermanreeves.com
SIC: 1761 3444 Sheet metal work, nec; Sheet metalwork

(G-6416)
HESTER ENTERPRISES INC
214 Superior Stainless Rd (28052-8747)
PHONE..................704 865-4480
Janet Hester, *Pr*
Tom Hester, *
EMP: 35 **EST:** 1993
SQ FT: 37,000
SALES (est): 1.99MM **Privately Held**
Web: www.hesterenterprises.com
SIC: 2512 5084 Upholstered household furniture; Sewing machines, industrial

(G-6417)
HOLLYWOOD FIT LLC
4491 Posterity Ct (28056-2401)
PHONE..................704 879-7426
EMP: 4 **EST:** 2015
SALES (est): 50.24K **Privately Held**
Web: www.hollywoodfit15.com
SIC: 2499 Wood products, nec

GEOGRAPHIC SECTION — Gastonia - Gaston County (G-6442)

(G-6418)
HOLSTERS FOR LIFE LLC
4531 Binwhe Ln (28052-8723)
PHONE..................704 862-0212
Elizabeth Jane Hamilton, *Prin*
EMP: 5 EST: 2015
SALES (est): 158.67K **Privately Held**
Web: www.holstersforlife.com
SIC: 3484 Machine guns and grenade launchers

(G-6419)
HOOVER BB INC
2129 Kingstree Cir (28054-5823)
PHONE..................615 872-4510
EMP: 5 EST: 2018
SALES (est): 84.77K **Privately Held**
SIC: 2741 Miscellaneous publishing

(G-6420)
HUBBARD IRON INC
4383 Mintwood Dr (28056-9307)
PHONE..................828 776-7168
Jeremy Hubbard, *Prin*
EMP: 9 EST: 2017
SALES (est): 265.71K **Privately Held**
Web: www.hubbardiron.com
SIC: 3441 Fabricated structural metal

(G-6421)
ID PROS LLC
Also Called: Software Publishers
2618 Crowders Creek Rd (28052-9208)
PHONE..................904 887-6210
Jason Donahoe, *Prin*
EMP: 4 EST: 2018
SALES (est): 62.19K **Privately Held**
SIC: 7372 7375 Business oriented computer software; Information retrieval services

(G-6422)
IFAB CORP ✪
2408 Forbes Rd (28056-6267)
PHONE..................704 864-3032
Hugo L Ochoa, *Pr*
Olga C Ochoa, *
Darien Ledford, *
EMP: 9 EST: 2023
SALES (est): 1.84MM
SALES (corp-wide): 29.08MM **Privately Held**
SIC: 3441 Fabricated structural metal
PA: South American Parts Corp.
5301 Nw 74th Ave Ste 200
Miami FL 33166
305 594-2844

(G-6423)
IMAGEMARK BUSINESS SVCS INC (PA)
Also Called: Imagemark
3145 Northwest Blvd (28052-1168)
PHONE..................704 865-4912
Walter Payne, *Pr*
David Walsh, *VP*
Greg Sellers, *CFO*
Karen Kaufman, *Ex VP*
EMP: 9 EST: 1931
SQ FT: 11,000
SALES (est): 5.21MM
SALES (corp-wide): 5.21MM **Privately Held**
Web: www.imagemarkonline.com
SIC: 2752 2759 Offset printing; Letterpress printing

(G-6424)
INDUSTRIAL ELCPLTG CO INC
Also Called: Warehouse Facility
1401 Gaston Ave (28052-2027)
P.O. Box 1537 (28053-1537)
PHONE..................704 867-4547
Walter Prescott, *CEO*
EMP: 4
SALES (corp-wide): 9.51MM **Privately Held**
Web: www.electroplate.biz
SIC: 3471 Electroplating of metals or formed products
PA: Industrial Electroplating Company, Inc.
307 Linwood Rd
Gastonia NC 28052
704 867-4547

(G-6425)
INDUSTRIAL ELCPLTG CO INC (PA)
307 Linwood Rd (28052-3720)
P.O. Box 1537 (28053-1537)
PHONE..................704 867-4547
Walter C Prescott, *Owner*
Terry Brooks, *
Kevin Prescott, *
Amelia Prescott, *
Anna S Clinton, *
EMP: 60 EST: 1971
SQ FT: 12,000
SALES (est): 9.51MM
SALES (corp-wide): 9.51MM **Privately Held**
Web: www.electroplate.biz
SIC: 3471 Plating of metals or formed products

(G-6426)
INDUSTRIAL GLASS TECH LLC
Also Called: Industrial Glass Technologies
112 Superior Stainless Rd (28054-8744)
PHONE..................704 853-2429
Carroll Barger, *Managing Member*
▲ EMP: 15 EST: 2005
SALES (est): 2.39MM **Privately Held**
Web: www.industrialglasstech.com
SIC: 5231 3211 Glass; Antique glass

(G-6427)
INDUSTRIAL METAL CRAFT INC
901 Tulip Dr (28052-1825)
PHONE..................704 864-3416
Max Clark Junior, *Pr*
Dan S Wise, *VP*
G Glen Adams, *Sec*
EMP: 16 EST: 1975
SQ FT: 23,000
SALES (est): 2.49MM
SALES (corp-wide): 5.31MM **Privately Held**
Web: www.industrialmetalcraft.com
SIC: 3444 Sheet metalwork
PA: Sherrill Contract Manufacturing, Inc.
110 Durkee Ln
Dallas NC 28034
704 922-7871

(G-6428)
INKA OUTDOOR LLC
1236 Industrial Ave # 107 (28054-4629)
P.O. Box 221641 (28222-1641)
PHONE..................828 539-0842
EMP: 6 EST: 2017
SALES (est): 377.08K **Privately Held**
SIC: 3792 Tent-type camping trailers

(G-6429)
INSTANT IMPRINTS
2258 Helen Dr (28054-1936)
PHONE..................704 864-1510
Gary Lutz, *Owner*
EMP: 4 EST: 2006
SALES (est): 228.71K **Privately Held**
Web: www.instantimprints.com
SIC: 2752 Commercial printing, lithographic

(G-6430)
INTRINSIC ADVANCED MTLS LLC
531 Cotton Blossom Cir (28054-5245)
PHONE..................704 874-5000
Steve Staley, *Managing Member*
EMP: 8 EST: 2018
SALES (est): 718.03K **Privately Held**
SIC: 2821 Polymethyl methacrylate resins, plexiglass

(G-6431)
J & P ENTRPRSES OF CRLINAS INC
5640 Gallagher Dr (28052-8702)
PHONE..................704 861-1867
C Lamar Greene, *Pr*
Jeffrey L Greene, *VP*
Paula Painter, *Sec*
▲ EMP: 20 EST: 1981
SQ FT: 25,000
SALES (est): 4.35MM **Privately Held**
SIC: 3552 5084 5199 Textile machinery; Industrial machinery and equipment; Fabrics, yarns, and knit goods

(G-6432)
J CHARLES SAUNDERS CO INC
Also Called: Saunders Thread Company
1004 E Long Ave (28054-3171)
P.O. Box 4016 (28054-0041)
PHONE..................704 866-9156
Charles J Sanders, *Pr*
Sarah W Saunders, *
Dean Queen, *
◆ EMP: 40 EST: 1968
SQ FT: 55,000
SALES (est): 4.14MM **Privately Held**
Web: www.saunders-thread.com
SIC: 2282 2284 Throwing yarn; Sewing thread

(G-6433)
J F HEAT TREATING INC
409 Airport Rd (28056-8804)
PHONE..................704 864-0998
TOLL FREE: 800
John Freeman Junior, *Pr*
Jimmy Freeman, *VP*
Emma Freeman, *Sec*
EMP: 7 EST: 1980
SQ FT: 10,000
SALES (est): 803.5K **Privately Held**
Web: www.jfheattreatinginc.com
SIC: 3398 Metal heat treating

(G-6434)
JAMES T WHITE COMPANY
4415 Little Mountain Rd (28056-6824)
PHONE..................704 865-9811
John White, *Pr*
Kay White, *VP*
EMP: 14 EST: 1953
SQ FT: 6,200
SALES (est): 344.38K **Privately Held**
Web: www.jtwhiteco.com
SIC: 3552 Textile machinery

(G-6435)
JIMMYS COATING UNLIMITED INC
420 N Morehead St (28054-2534)
PHONE..................704 915-2420
Jimmy Collins, *Prin*
EMP: 4 EST: 2016
SALES (est): 98.02K **Privately Held**
Web: www.jimmyscoatingsunlimitedinc.com
SIC: 3479 Metal coating and allied services

(G-6436)
JUST BLACK LLC
1124 Crowders Woods Dr (28052-5715)
PHONE..................252 204-5437
Tyson Mckinney, *Managing Member*
EMP: 4 EST: 2020
SALES (est): 171.59K **Privately Held**
SIC: 7372 7389 Application computer software; Business Activities at Non-Commercial Site

(G-6437)
KEDPLASMA
588 N New Hope Rd (28054-7409)
PHONE..................704 691-3287
EMP: 6 EST: 2018
SALES (est): 74.42K **Privately Held**
Web: www.kedplasma.us
SIC: 2836 Plasmas

(G-6438)
KEITHS KUSTOMZ LLC
1676 Lowell Bethesda Rd Apt B (28056-7347)
PHONE..................704 524-8684
Vanessa Ragland, *Prin*
EMP: 6 EST: 2016
SALES (est): 74.1K **Privately Held**
SIC: 2396 Screen printing on fabric articles

(G-6439)
KINDRED ROLLING DOORS LLC
Also Called: The Rolling Door Company
3420 Country Club Dr (28056-6680)
PHONE..................704 905-3806
EMP: 5 EST: 2016
SALES (est): 242.28K **Privately Held**
SIC: 3442 Baseboards, metal

(G-6440)
KRISPY KREME DOUGHNUT CORP
Also Called: Krispy Kreme
2990 E Franklin Sq (28056-7225)
PHONE..................919 669-6151
Chip Crump, *Mgr*
EMP: 31
SALES (corp-wide): 1.69B **Publicly Held**
Web: www.krispykreme.com
SIC: 5461 2051 Doughnuts; Doughnuts, except frozen
HQ: Krispy Kreme Doughnut Corp
2116 Hawkins St Ste 102
Charlotte NC 28203
980 270-7117

(G-6441)
L & R SPECIALTIES INC
2757 W Franklin Blvd (28052-9480)
P.O. Box 12805 (28052-0015)
PHONE..................704 853-3296
Chit Jones, *Pr*
EMP: 10 EST: 1992
SQ FT: 12,000
SALES (est): 1.01MM **Privately Held**
Web: www.landr-newbritain.com
SIC: 3541 Lathes

(G-6442)
L AND L MACHINE CO INC
158 Superior Stainless Rd (28052-8744)
P.O. Box 178 (29703-0178)
PHONE..................704 864-5521
Robert Lamm, *Pr*
EMP: 17 EST: 1976
SQ FT: 7,500
SALES (est): 465.76K **Privately Held**
SIC: 3599 Machine shop, jobbing and repair

Gastonia - Gaston County (G-6443)

(G-6443)
LANXESS CORPORATION
214 W Ruby Ave (28054-7507)
PHONE..................704 868-7200
Richard Lissende, *Brnch Mgr*
EMP: 18
SALES (corp-wide): 7.3B **Privately Held**
Web: www.lanxess.com
SIC: **2899** 2821 2822 2879 Chemical supplies for foundries; Plastics materials and resins; Synthetic rubber; Insecticides, agricultural or household
HQ: Lanxess Corporation
111 Ridc Park West Dr
Pittsburgh PA 15275
412 809-1000

(G-6444)
LPM INC
2703 Ashbourne Dr (28056-7564)
PHONE..................704 922-6137
Dana Bumgardner, *Pr*
Jeff Bumgardner, *VP*
EMP: 6 EST: 2000
SALES (est): 499.76K **Privately Held**
SIC: **2679** Labels, paper: made from purchased material

(G-6445)
LSRWM CORP
Also Called: Rwm Casters
1225 Isley Rd (28052-8106)
PHONE..................704 866-8533
EMP: 4 EST: 2020
SALES (est): 92.75K **Privately Held**
SIC: **3562** Casters

(G-6446)
LSRWM CORP
Also Called: Rwm Casters
1225 Isley Rd (28052-8106)
P.O. Box 668 (28053-0668)
PHONE..................704 866-8533
Peter D Comeau, *Pr*
◆ EMP: 49 EST: 1967
SQ FT: 87,000
SALES (est): 3.88MM **Privately Held**
SIC: **3562** Casters

(G-6447)
LUBRIZOL GLOBAL MANAGEMENT INC
207 Telegraph Dr (28056-1306)
PHONE..................704 865-7451
James Nelli, *Mgr*
EMP: 67
SALES (corp-wide): 364.48B **Publicly Held**
Web: www.lubrizol.com
SIC: **2899** 3087 2851 Chemical preparations, nec; Custom compound purchased resins; Paints and allied products
HQ: Lubrizol Global Management, Inc.
9911 Brecksville Rd
Cleveland OH 44141
216 447-5000

(G-6448)
M & M ELECTRIC SERVICE INC
Also Called: M & M Electric Service NC
1680 Garfield Dr (28052-8403)
P.O. Box 12847 (28052-0043)
PHONE..................704 867-0221
Marvin R Foy, *Pr*
Jeffrey Foy, *
Sheryll Foy, *
EMP: 40 EST: 1973
SQ FT: 17,000
SALES (est): 8.74MM **Privately Held**
Web: www.mme.com
SIC: **1731** 3643 General electrical contractor ; Bus bars (electrical conductors)

(G-6449)
MANN+HMMEL FLTRTION TECH GROUP (DH)
1 Wix Way (28054-6142)
PHONE..................704 869-3300
Keith Wilson, *CEO*
Jorge Schertel, *Pr*
Steven Klueg S, *VP*
▲ EMP: 4 EST: 2004
SQ FT: 24,000
SALES (est): 811.77MM
SALES (corp-wide): 5.01B **Privately Held**
SIC: **5013** 3714 Automotive supplies and parts; Motor vehicle brake systems and parts
HQ: Mann+Hummel Filtration Technology Intermediate Holdings Inc.
1 Wix Way
Gastonia NC 28054
704 869-3300

(G-6450)
MANN+HMMEL FLTRTION TECH INTRM (DH)
1 Wix Way (28054-6142)
PHONE..................704 869-3300
Keith A Wilson, *Pr*
Steven P Klueg, *Sr VP*
Karl J Westrick, *CIO*
Kay Teixeira, *Senior Vice President Human Resources*
David E Sturgess, *Sr VP*
▼ EMP: 28 EST: 2004
SALES (est): 899MM
SALES (corp-wide): 5.01B **Privately Held**
Web: www.wixfilters.com
SIC: **3714** Filters: oil, fuel, and air, motor vehicle
HQ: Mann + Hummel Usa, Inc.
6400 S Sprinkle Rd
Portage MI 49002
269 329-3900

(G-6451)
MANN+HMMEL FLTRTION TECH US LL
Wix Filtration Products Div
1 Wix Way (28054-6142)
P.O. Box 1902 (28053-1902)
PHONE..................704 869-3700
Keith Wilson, *Brnch Mgr*
EMP: 55
SQ FT: 36,000
SALES (corp-wide): 5.01B **Privately Held**
Web: www.wixfilters.com
SIC: **3714** Motor vehicle engines and parts
HQ: Mann+Hummel Filtration Technology Us Llc
1 Wix Way
Gastonia NC 28054
704 869-3300

(G-6452)
MANN+HMMEL FLTRTION TECH US LL (DH)
Also Called: Mannhmmel Fltration Tech Group
1 Wix Way (28054-6142)
P.O. Box 1967 (28053-1967)
PHONE..................704 869-3300
Kurk Wilks, *CEO*
Keith Wilson, *
◆ EMP: 120 EST: 2004
SALES (est): 195.01MM
SALES (corp-wide): 5.01B **Privately Held**
Web: www.wixfilters.com
SIC: **3569** 3677 3589 Filters, general line: industrial; Filtration devices, electronic; Sewage and water treatment equipment
HQ: Mann+Hummel Filtration Technology Group Inc.
1 Wix Way
Gastonia NC 28054
704 869-3300

(G-6453)
MANN+HMMEL PRLATOR FILTERS LLC
1 Wix Way (28054-6142)
PHONE..................704 869-3441
EMP: 121
SALES (corp-wide): 5.01B **Privately Held**
SIC: **3714** Motor vehicle parts and accessories
HQ: Mann+Hummel Purolator Filters Llc
3200 Natal St Ste 64069
Fayetteville NC 28306

(G-6454)
MANN+HUMMEL FILTRATION TECHNOL
2900 Northwest Blvd (28052-1162)
PHONE..................704 869-3500
David Palmer, *Brnch Mgr*
EMP: 96
SALES (corp-wide): 5.01B **Privately Held**
SIC: **3714** Motor vehicle parts and accessories
HQ: Mann+Hummel Filtration Technology Group Inc.
1 Wix Way
Gastonia NC 28054
704 869-3300

(G-6455)
MANN+HUMMEL FILTRATION TECHNOL
Also Called: Wix Filtration Products
1551 Mount Olive Church Rd (28052-9412)
PHONE..................704 869-3952
John Winters, *Brnch Mgr*
EMP: 7
SALES (corp-wide): 5.01B **Privately Held**
Web: www.wixfilters.com
SIC: **3714** 3569 Filters: oil, fuel, and air, motor vehicle; Filters
HQ: Mann+Hummel Filtration Technology Us Llc
1 Wix Way
Gastonia NC 28054
704 869-3300

(G-6456)
MANN+HUMMEL FILTRATION TECHNOL
Also Called: Wix Filters
2900 Northwest Blvd (28052-1162)
P.O. Box 1967 (28053-1967)
PHONE..................704 869-3501
Steve Renfrow, *Brnch Mgr*
EMP: 55
SALES (corp-wide): 5.01B **Privately Held**
Web: www.wixfilters.com
SIC: **3569** 3714 Filters, general line: industrial; Motor vehicle parts and accessories
HQ: Mann+Hummel Filtration Technology Us Llc
1 Wix Way
Gastonia NC 28054
704 869-3300

(G-6457)
MANN+HUMMEL FILTRATION TECHNOLOGY HOLDINGS INC
1 Wix Way (28054-6142)
PHONE..................704 869-3300
◆ EMP: 5615
SIC: **3714** Filters: oil, fuel, and air, motor vehicle

(G-6458)
MARC MACHINE WORKS INC
5042 York Hwy (28052-6818)
PHONE..................704 865-3625
Frank Hubbard, *Pr*
Frances Hubbard, *VP*
EMP: 12 EST: 1984
SQ FT: 1,188
SALES (est): 958.61K **Privately Held**
Web: www.marcmachine.com
SIC: **3599** 7692 Machine shop, jobbing and repair; Welding repair

(G-6459)
MAYSTEEL PORTERS LLC
469 Hospital Dr Ste A (28054-4778)
PHONE..................704 864-1313
Kevin Matkin, *CEO*
EMP: 300
SALES (corp-wide): 396.03MM **Privately Held**
Web: www.maysteel.com
SIC: **3441** 3317 Fabricated structural metal; Steel pipe and tubes
HQ: Maysteel Porters, Llc
6199 County Rd W
Allenton WI 53002
262 251-1632

(G-6460)
MERIDIAN INDUSTRIES INC
Also Called: Meridian Dyed Yarn Group
40 Rex Ave (28054-3026)
PHONE..................704 824-7880
Joel Goodrich, *Mgr*
EMP: 24
SALES (corp-wide): 331.16MM **Privately Held**
Web: www.meridiancompanies.com
SIC: **2281** Acrylic yarn, spun: made from purchased staple
PA: Meridian Industries, Inc.
735 N Water St Ste 630
Milwaukee WI 53202
414 224-0610

(G-6461)
METAL IMPROVEMENT COMPANY LLC
Also Called: Mic Equip Rebuild
1931 Jordache Ct (28052-5435)
PHONE..................414 536-1573
Steve Smtih, *Mgr*
EMP: 4
SALES (corp-wide): 2.85B **Publicly Held**
Web: www.imrtest.com
SIC: **3398** Shot peening (treating steel to reduce fatigue)
HQ: Metal Improvement Company, Llc
80 E Rte 4 Ste 310
Paramus NJ 07652
201 843-7800

(G-6462)
METRO FIRE LIFESAFETY LLC
2714 Forbes Rd (28056-6287)
PHONE..................704 529-7348
Pierre Zenie, *Pr*
EMP: 6 EST: 2004
SALES (est): 578.15K **Privately Held**
Web: www.metrolifesafety.com
SIC: **3569** Firefighting and related equipment

(G-6463)
METROPOLITAN WOODWORKS INC
2005 W Poplar St (28052-1416)
PHONE..................704 215-5018
EMP: 7 EST: 2016

GEOGRAPHIC SECTION

Gastonia - Gaston County (G-6486)

SALES (est): 479.55K **Privately Held**
Web: www.metropolitanwoodworks.com
SIC: **2431** Millwork

(G-6464)
METYX USA INC
2504 Lowell Rd (28054-3409)
PHONE................................704 824-1030
Besim Ugur Ustunel, *Pr*
EMP: 70 EST: 2017
SALES (est): 7.92MM **Privately Held**
Web: www.metyx.com
SIC: **2221** Textile mills, broadwoven: silk and manmade, also glass

(G-6465)
MIK ALL MACHINE CO INC (PA)
Also Called: Metal Treating Div
905 Hanover St (28054-2455)
PHONE................................704 866-4302
Charles Allen, *Prin*
Ruby Fail, *VP*
EMP: 13 EST: 1976
SQ FT: 4,500
SALES (est): 1.84MM
SALES (corp-wide): 1.84MM **Privately Held**
Web: www.mikall.com
SIC: **3599** Machine shop, jobbing and repair

(G-6466)
MINGES PRINTING & ADVG CO
Also Called: Minges Printing Company
323 S Chestnut St (28054-4542)
PHONE................................704 867-6791
Gene M Minges Senior, *Pr*
Gene M Minges Junior, *VP*
EMP: 6 EST: 1959
SQ FT: 2,700
SALES (est): 453.84K **Privately Held**
Web: www.mingesprinting.com
SIC: **2752** 7389 Offset printing; Lettering and sign painting services

(G-6467)
MINUTEMAN PRESS OF GASTONIA ✪
Also Called: Minuteman Press
495 E Long Ave (28054-2526)
PHONE................................704 867-3366
Toni Marder, *Owner*
EMP: 5 EST: 2023
SALES (est): 182.38K **Privately Held**
SIC: **2752** Commercial printing, lithographic

(G-6468)
MODENA SOUTHERN DYEING CORP
Also Called: Saunders Phrad
1010 E Ozark Ave (28054)
P.O. Box 4016 (28054-0041)
PHONE................................704 866-9156
J Charles Saunders, *Pr*
David Saunders, *Sec*
Wallace Ammons, *VP Mfg*
Kathryn V Saunders, *Stockholder*
Dorothy Z Saunders, *Stockholder*
EMP: 5 EST: 1983
SQ FT: 15,000
SALES (est): 430K **Privately Held**
SIC: **2211** Yarn-dyed fabrics, cotton

(G-6469)
MORNINGSTAR SIGNS AND BANNERS
307 E Franklin Blvd (28054-7134)
PHONE................................704 861-0020
Robert Claiborne, *Owner*
EMP: 4 EST: 2003
SALES (est): 270.21K **Privately Held**
SIC: **5999** 3993 Banners; Signs and advertising specialties

(G-6470)
MORRIS MACHINE COMPANY INC
Also Called: Morris Machine Sales
122 Stroupe Rd (28056-8499)
P.O. Box 550817 (28055-0817)
PHONE................................704 824-4242
William Morris Junior, *Pr*
William Morris, *Pr*
EMP: 5 EST: 1986
SQ FT: 4,000
SALES (est): 424.92K **Privately Held**
SIC: **3599** 5084 Machine shop, jobbing and repair; Industrial machinery and equipment

(G-6471)
MOTOR SHOP INC
5001 York Hwy (28052-6810)
P.O. Box 12885 (28052-0043)
PHONE................................704 867-8488
Ken Gordon, *Pr*
Sarah Gordon, *Sec*
EMP: 8 EST: 1989
SQ FT: 60,000
SALES (est): 974.82K **Privately Held**
SIC: **5063** 7694 7699 5999 Motors, electric; Electric motor repair; Pumps and pumping equipment repair; Motors, electric

(G-6472)
MOUNT OLIVE PICKLE COMPANY
1534 Union Rd Ste A (28054-2203)
PHONE................................704 867-5585
EMP: 7
SALES (est): 76.29K **Privately Held**
Web: www.mtolivepickles.com
SIC: **2035** Pickles, vinegar

(G-6473)
MOUNT OLIVE PICKLE COMPANY INC
1534 Union Rd Ste A (28054-2203)
PHONE................................704 867-5585
EMP: 14
SALES (corp-wide): 835.67K **Privately Held**
Web: www.mtolivepickles.com
SIC: **2035** Pickles, vinegar
PA: Mount Olive Pickle Company, Inc.
1 Cucumber Blvd
Mount Olive NC 28365
919 658-2535

(G-6474)
NAPA FILTERS
1 Wix Way (28054-6142)
P.O. Box 1892 (28053-1892)
PHONE................................704 864-6748
Keith Wilson, *Prin*
EMP: 4 EST: 2011
SALES (est): 306.21K **Privately Held**
Web: www.napaindustrialfilters.com
SIC: **3569** Filters

(G-6475)
NATIONAL ROLLER SUPPLY INC
811 Grover St (28054-3282)
P.O. Box 240321 (28224-0321)
PHONE................................704 853-1174
Mike Harris, *Pr*
Dennis Crowley, *Pr*
Cathy P Stout, *Sec*
Mike Harris, *Mgr*
EMP: 5 EST: 1980
SQ FT: 18,000
SALES (est): 453.1K **Privately Held**
SIC: **3555** Printing trades machinery

(G-6476)
NEW CAN COMPANY INC
121 Crowders Creek Rd (28052-9787)
PHONE................................704 853-3711
Rodney Huffstetler, *Mgr*
EMP: 4
SALES (corp-wide): 14.08MM **Privately Held**
Web: www.newcan.com
SIC: **3469** Metal stampings, nec
HQ: The New Can Company Inc
1 Mear Rd
Holbrook MA 02343
330 928-1191

(G-6477)
NEWCOMB SPRING CORP
Also Called: Newcomb Spring of Carolina
2633 Plastics Dr (28054-1419)
PHONE................................704 588-2043
Keith Porter Junior, *Mgr*
EMP: 21
SALES (corp-wide): 60.18MM **Privately Held**
Web: www.newcombspring.com
SIC: **3495** Wire springs
PA: Newcomb Spring Corp.
3155 North Point Pkwy G220
Alpharetta GA 30005
770 981-2803

(G-6478)
NEWELL BRANDS DISTRIBUTION LLC
3211 Aberdeen Blvd (28054-0669)
PHONE................................770 418-7000
Robert Westreich, *Pr*
EMP: 100
SALES (corp-wide): 8.13B **Publicly Held**
Web: www.newellbrands.com
SIC: **3089** Plastics kitchenware, tableware, and houseware
HQ: Newell Brands Distribution Llc
6655 Pachtree Dunwoody Rd
Atlanta GA 30328
770 418-7000

(G-6479)
NOLEN MACHINE CO INC
119 Bob Nolen Rd (28056-9296)
P.O. Box 455 (28053-0455)
PHONE................................704 867-7851
Bill Nolen, *Pr*
Herman E Nolen, *VP*
EMP: 4 EST: 1953
SQ FT: 4,000
SALES (est): 286.42K **Privately Held**
SIC: **3599** Machine shop, jobbing and repair

(G-6480)
NUSSBAUM AUTO SOLUTIONS LP
1932 Jorache Ct (28052)
PHONE................................704 864-2470
Kim Nivens, *Contrlr*
▲ EMP: 10 EST: 2012
SALES (est): 3.47MM **Privately Held**
Web: www.nussbaum-usa.com
SIC: **3534** Automobile elevators

(G-6481)
OSTEEL BUILDINGS INC (PA)
1180 Old Redbud Dr (28056)
P.O. Box 3667 (29582-0667)
PHONE................................704 824-6061
Beverly Lynn, *Pr*
Larry Lynn, *VP*
EMP: 15 EST: 1990
SQ FT: 5,000
SALES (est): 1.39MM **Privately Held**
Web: www.osteel.com
SIC: **3448** Prefabricated metal buildings and components

(G-6482)
PAKARAIMA FIBER OPTICS INC
1602 Backcreek Ln (28054-5871)
PHONE................................704 671-2229
Mahamood Ally, *Prin*
EMP: 6 EST: 2011
SALES (est): 113.39K **Privately Held**
SIC: **3661** Fiber optics communications equipment

(G-6483)
PARK MANUFACTURING COMPANY (PA)
Also Called: Park Elevator Co
3112 Northwest Blvd (28052-1167)
P.O. Box 12866 (28052-0043)
PHONE................................704 869-6128
Nilla Stevens, *Pr*
EMP: 19 EST: 1898
SQ FT: 10,000
SALES (est): 2.17MM
SALES (corp-wide): 2.17MM **Privately Held**
Web: www.parkelevators.com
SIC: **3534** 1796 Elevators and equipment; Elevator installation and conversion

(G-6484)
PARKDALE INCORPORATED (PA)
531 Cotton Blossom Cir (28054-5245)
P.O. Box 1787 (28053-1787)
PHONE................................704 874-5000
Charles Heilig, *Pr*
◆ EMP: 120 EST: 2013
SALES (est): 1.44B
SALES (corp-wide): 1.44B **Privately Held**
Web: www.parkdalemills.com
SIC: **2281** Polyester yarn, spun: made from purchased staple

(G-6485)
PARKDALE AMERICA LLC (HQ)
Also Called: Parkdale1
531 Cotton Blossom Cir (28054-5245)
P.O. Box 1787 (28053-1787)
PHONE................................704 874-5000
Anderson D Warlick, *Managing Member*
◆ EMP: 1004 EST: 1997
SALES (est): 422.19MM
SALES (corp-wide): 1.44B **Privately Held**
Web: www.uscotton.com
SIC: **2281** Polyester yarn, spun: made from purchased staple
PA: Parkdale, Incorporated
531 Cotton Blossom Cir
Gastonia NC 28054
704 874-5000

(G-6486)
PARKDALE MILLS INCORPORATED (HQ)
531 Cotton Blossom Cir (28054-5245)
P.O. Box 1787 (28053-1787)
PHONE................................704 874-5000
Anderson D Warlick, *CEO*
W Duke Kimbrell, *
Cecelia Meade, *
◆ EMP: 100 EST: 1916
SQ FT: 20,000
SALES (est): 888.46MM
SALES (corp-wide): 1.44B **Privately Held**
Web: www.parkdalemills.com
SIC: **2281** 2844 2241 Cotton yarn, spun; Perfumes, cosmetics and other toilet preparations; Cotton narrow fabrics
PA: Parkdale, Incorporated
531 Cotton Blossom Cir
Gastonia NC 28054
704 874-5000

Gastonia - Gaston County (G-6487)

(G-6487)
PAUL CHARLES ENGLERT
Also Called: Scrappy's Metal Recycling
1820 Spencer Mountain Rd (28054-9600)
PHONE....................................704 824-2102
EMP: 4 EST: 2011
SALES (est): 289.62K Privately Held
SIC: 3449 Miscellaneous metalwork

(G-6488)
PETTY MACHINE COMPANY INC
2403 E Forbes Rd (28056-6268)
P.O. Box 1888 (28053-1888)
PHONE....................................704 864-3254
Larry K Petty, CEO
Frank Hovis, Pr
Jane Griffin, Sec
EMP: 22 EST: 1936
SQ FT: 98,000
SALES (est): 4.86MM Privately Held
Web: www.pettymachinecompany.com
SIC: 3565 3559 3552 3621 Packaging machinery; Plastics working machinery; Card clothing, textile machinery; Motors, electric

(G-6489)
PIONEER MACHINE WORKS INC
1221 W 2nd Ave (28052-3749)
P.O. Box 12826 (28052-0017)
PHONE....................................704 864-5528
Hugh H Jones, Pr
Ray Jones, VP
EMP: 5 EST: 1970
SQ FT: 20,000
SALES (est): 470K Privately Held
Web: www.pioneermachineworks.com
SIC: 3599 Machine shop, jobbing and repair

(G-6490)
PORTERS GROUP LLC
Also Called: Porter's Fabrications
469 Hospital Dr Ste A (28054-4778)
PHONE....................................704 864-1313
▲ EMP: 300
SIC: 3441 3317 Fabricated structural metal; Steel pipe and tubes

(G-6491)
POWDER COATING SERVICES INC
Also Called: Pcsi
1260 Shannon Bradley Rd (28052-1076)
PHONE....................................704 349-4100
Daryn E Parnham, Pr
Robert Burford, *
Jose I Venegas, *
EMP: 33 EST: 1996
SQ FT: 50,000
SALES (est): 5.29MM Privately Held
Web: www.pcsi-nc.com
SIC: 3479 Coating of metals and formed products

(G-6492)
POWERHOUSE DUGOUT
246 N New Hope Rd 127 (28054-4977)
PHONE....................................704 215-6604
EMP: 5 EST: 2019
SALES (est): 73.93K Privately Held
Web: www.hipposportinggoods.com
SIC: 7999 2389 Amusement and recreation, nec; Apparel and accessories, nec

(G-6493)
PPG ARCHITECTURAL FINISHES INC
Also Called: Glidden Professional Paint Ctr
729 E Franklin Blvd (28054-7149)
PHONE....................................704 864-6783
Raymond Grahmn, Brnch Mgr
EMP: 5
SALES (corp-wide): 17.65B Publicly Held
Web: www.glidden.com
SIC: 2851 Paints and allied products
HQ: Ppg Architectural Finishes, Inc.
1 Ppg Pl
Pittsburgh PA 15272
412 434-3131

(G-6494)
PRATT INDUSTRIES
975 Tulip Dr (28052-1825)
PHONE....................................704 864-4022
EMP: 10 EST: 2018
SALES (est): 123.33K Privately Held
Web: www.prattindustries.com
SIC: 2653 Boxes, corrugated: made from purchased materials

(G-6495)
PRECISION COMB WORKS INC
2524 N Chester St (28052-1808)
P.O. Box 2167 (28053-2167)
PHONE....................................704 864-2761
Larry G Brown, Pr
Patricia Carter, VP
Joyce Swanson, Mgr
EMP: 6 EST: 1958
SQ FT: 3,500
SALES (est): 474.14K Privately Held
Web: www.precisioncombworks.com
SIC: 3552 Textile machinery

(G-6496)
PRECISION MACHINE PRODUCTS INC
2347 N Chester St (28052-1810)
P.O. Box 1576 (28053-1576)
PHONE....................................704 865-7490
Robert H Blalock Junior, Pr
Robert Blalock Iii, VP
Linda Bess, *
EMP: 70 EST: 1947
SQ FT: 40,000
SALES (est): 9.32MM Privately Held
Web: www.pmpgastonia.com
SIC: 3552 3444 Textile machinery; Sheet metalwork

(G-6497)
PREMIER BODY ARMOR LLC
1552 Union Rd Ste E (28054-5523)
P.O. Box 335 (28086-0335)
PHONE....................................704 750-3118
Frank Stewart, Managing Member
EMP: 10 EST: 2013
SALES (est): 1.01MM Privately Held
Web: www.premierbodyarmor.com
SIC: 3842 Bulletproof vests

(G-6498)
PROTOTYPE TOOLING CO
1811 W Franklin Blvd (28052-1426)
PHONE....................................704 864-7777
William Hall, Owner
EMP: 4 EST: 1990
SQ FT: 5,600
SALES (est): 223.58K Privately Held
SIC: 3544 Special dies and tools

(G-6499)
QUIKNIT CRAFTING INC
1916 S York Rd (28052-6369)
PHONE....................................704 861-1030
Charles Quick, Pr
Loretta Trammell, VP
EMP: 12 EST: 1986
SQ FT: 165,000
SALES (est): 470.45K Privately Held
Web: www.quiknit.com
SIC: 2241 5199 Fringes, woven; Knit goods

(G-6500)
R A SERAFINI INC
111 Lagrande St (28056-6317)
P.O. Box 6100 (28056-6022)
PHONE....................................704 864-6763
Robert A Serafini, Pr
▼ EMP: 29 EST: 1965
SALES (est): 2.41MM Privately Held
Web: www.raserafini.com
SIC: 3544 Industrial molds

(G-6501)
R R DONNELLEY & SONS COMPANY
Also Called: R R Donnelley
1205 Isley Rd (28052-8106)
P.O. Box 1577 (28053-1577)
PHONE....................................704 864-5717
Ann Payne, Mgr
EMP: 5
SALES (corp-wide): 15B Privately Held
Web: www.rrd.com
SIC: 2761 2752 Manifold business forms; Color lithography
HQ: R. R. Donnelley & Sons Company
35 W Wacker Dr
Chicago IL 60601
800 782-4892

(G-6502)
REDDY ICE GROUP INC
2306 Lowell Rd (28054-3407)
PHONE....................................704 824-4611
Bob Joyner, Mgr
EMP: 78
SALES (corp-wide): 1.22B Privately Held
Web: www.reddyice.com
SIC: 2097 Manufactured ice
HQ: Reddy Ice Group, Inc.
5710 Lyndon B Johnson Fwy
Dallas TX 75240

(G-6503)
REEL-TEX INC
4905 Sparrow Dairy Rd (28056-8940)
PHONE....................................704 868-4419
Jack C Barbee, Pr
Joyce Barbee, Sec
Dwain Barbee, VP
EMP: 10 EST: 1979
SQ FT: 3,400
SALES (est): 775.35K Privately Held
Web: www.reeltex.com
SIC: 3599 Machine shop, jobbing and repair

(G-6504)
ROOSEVELT TIRE SERVICE INC
191 E Franklin Blvd (28052-4147)
P.O. Box 146 (28053-0146)
PHONE....................................704 864-5464
Kenneth H Parks Junior, Pr
Douglas H Parks, VP
EMP: 19 EST: 1939
SQ FT: 17,000
SALES (est): 2.13MM Privately Held
Web: www.roosevelttirepros.com
SIC: 5531 7534 Automotive tires; Tire retreading and repair shops

(G-6505)
SANS TECHNICAL FIBERS LLC
Also Called: Sans
2020 Remount Rd (28054-7476)
PHONE....................................704 869-8311
John Nagle, Managing Member
◆ EMP: 21 EST: 2000
SALES (est): 2.5MM Privately Held
Web: www.sansfibers.com
SIC: 2284 Nylon thread
PA: Aeci Ltd
1st Floor Aeci Place, 24 The Woodlands Woodlands Dr Gauteng
Saxonwold GP 2196

(G-6506)
SCHWARTZ STEEL SERVICE INC
525 N Broad St (28054-2508)
P.O. Box 1055 (28053-1055)
PHONE....................................704 865-9576
EMP: 35
Web: www.pasteel.com
SIC: 5051 3444 Steel; Sheet metalwork

(G-6507)
SIGN CONNECTION INC
1660 Pacolet Dr (28052-9467)
PHONE....................................704 868-4500
Sidney W Chip Craig Junior, Pr
Sidney W Craig Senior, Treas
Brenda Craig, Sec
EMP: 34 EST: 1988
SQ FT: 8,500
SALES (est): 2.44MM Privately Held
Web: www.signcon.com
SIC: 1799 3993 Sign installation and maintenance; Electric signs

(G-6508)
SIGN WITH ANDERSON LLC
1820 Spencer Mountain Rd Ste 110-A (28054-9600)
PHONE....................................704 599-6977
Tammy Anderson, Prin
EMP: 5 EST: 2016
SALES (est): 210.12K Privately Held
SIC: 3993 Signs and advertising specialties

(G-6509)
SIGNZ INC
Also Called: Signs Now
3608 S New Hope Rd (28056-8325)
P.O. Box 550399 (28055-0399)
PHONE....................................704 824-7446
Lanny J Henderson, Pr
Susan Henderson, VP
EMP: 7 EST: 1956
SQ FT: 4,000
SALES (est): 634.06K Privately Held
Web: www.signsnow.com
SIC: 3993 Signs and advertising specialties

(G-6510)
SIKA CORPORATION (DH)
1909 Kyle Ct (28052-8420)
PHONE....................................704 810-0500
Tim A Smith, VP
Thomas Adolf, *
◆ EMP: 20 EST: 1999
SQ FT: 90,000
SALES (est): 51.31MM Privately Held
Web: automotive.sika.com
SIC: 5531 1742 2891 Automotive parts; Acoustical and insulation work; Adhesives
HQ: Sika Automotive Deutschland Gmbh
Flinschstr. 10-16
Frankfurt Am Main HE 60388
62413010

(G-6511)
SPECIALTY MACHINE CO INC
1669 Federal St (28052-0504)
P.O. Box 12634 (28052-0013)
PHONE....................................704 853-2102
James C Brooks, Pr
James Brooks, Pr
Bryan Brooks, Treas
EMP: 21 EST: 1977
SQ FT: 10,000
SALES (est): 885.01K Privately Held
SIC: 3544 Special dies and tools

GEOGRAPHIC SECTION
Gastonia - Gaston County (G-6535)

(G-6512)
SPEEDWELL MACHINE WORKS INC
Also Called: Smw
1301 Crowders Creek Rd (28052-8148)
PHONE..............................704 866-7418
Amos R Benefield, *Pr*
Udora S Benefield, *
EMP: 25 **EST:** 1975
SQ FT: 14,000
SALES (est): 4.46MM **Privately Held**
Web: www.speedwellmachineworks.com
SIC: 3599 3545 Machine shop, jobbing and repair; Machine tool accessories

(G-6513)
STABILUS INC (DH)
Also Called: Stabilus
1201 Tulip Dr (28052-1842)
PHONE..............................704 865-7444
Anthony Haba, *Pr*
Craig Pospiech, *
Tom Napoli, *
◆ **EMP:** 89 **EST:** 2001
SQ FT: 200,000
SALES (est): 153.32MM
SALES (corp-wide): 1.32B **Privately Held**
Web: www.stabilus.com
SIC: 3493 Steel springs, except wire
HQ: Stabilus Gmbh
    Wallersheimer Weg 100
    Koblenz RP 56070
    26189000

(G-6514)
STABLE HOLDCO INC
1201 Tulip Dr (28052-1842)
PHONE..............................704 866-7140
Ansgar Kroetz, *Pr*
EMP: 401 **EST:** 2008
SALES (est): 65.88MM
SALES (corp-wide): 1.32B **Privately Held**
SIC: 3493 Steel springs, except wire
HQ: Stable Beteiligungs Gmbh
    Wallersheimer Weg 100
    Koblenz RP 56070
    261 890-0226

(G-6515)
STAR WIPERS INC
2260 Raeford Ct (28052-8422)
PHONE..............................888 511-2656
EMP: 43
Web: www.starwipers.com
SIC: 2211 Scrub cloths
PA: Star Wipers, Inc.
    1125 E Main St
    Newark OH 43055

(G-6516)
STERLING RACK INC
176 Tarheel Dr (28056-8719)
PHONE..............................704 866-9131
Ron Dalrymple, *Pr*
EMP: 10 **EST:** 1981
SALES (est): 427.55K **Privately Held**
Web: www.sterlingrack.com
SIC: 2542 3537 3471 Racks, merchandise display or storage; except wood; Industrial trucks and tractors; Plating and polishing

(G-6517)
SUMMIT YARN LLC
531 Cotton Blossom Cir (28054-5245)
P.O. Box 1787 (28053-1787)
PHONE..............................704 874-5000
EMP: 1025 **EST:** 1998
SALES (est): 4.44MM
SALES (corp-wide): 1.44B **Privately Held**
SIC: 2281 Needle and handicraft yarns, spun
HQ: Parkdale America, Llc
    531 Cotton Blossom Cir
    Gastonia NC 28054
    704 874-5000

(G-6518)
SUPERIOR PLASTICS INC
533 N Broad St (28054-2508)
P.O. Box 1812 (28053-1812)
PHONE..............................704 864-5472
Thurman E Looper, *Pr*
Charles Looper, *VP*
Glenda Looper, *Sec*
▲ **EMP:** 10 **EST:** 1969
SALES (est): 934.41K **Privately Held**
Web: www.superiorplastics.com
SIC: 3089 Injection molding of plastics

(G-6519)
SUPERIOR POWDER COATING LLC
123 Shannon Bradley Rd (28052-9202)
P.O. Box 821 (28053-0821)
PHONE..............................704 869-0004
Antonia H Callahan, *Managing Member*
EMP: 8 **EST:** 2010
SQ FT: 16,000
SALES (est): 791.87K **Privately Held**
Web: www.superiorpowder.com
SIC: 3479 Coating of metals and formed products

(G-6520)
TCI MOBILITY INC
1720 Industrial Pike Rd (28052-8434)
P.O. Box 939 (28053-0939)
PHONE..............................704 867-8331
Hannes M Charen, *Pr*
▼ **EMP:** 16 **EST:** 1947
SQ FT: 18,000
SALES (est): 4.85MM **Privately Held**
Web: www.tcimobility.com
SIC: 5084 3552 3699 3537 Textile machinery and equipment; Textile machinery; Electrical equipment and supplies, nec; Industrial trucks and tractors

(G-6521)
TEES PRETTY THINGS
2833 Crawford Ave (28052-6424)
PHONE..............................704 674-0982
Tierra Barnett, *Prin*
EMP: 4 **EST:** 2018
SALES (est): 74.56K **Privately Held**
SIC: 2759 Screen printing

(G-6522)
TEXLON PLASTICS CORP
135 Wolfpack Rd (28053)
P.O. Box 1284 (28053-1284)
PHONE..............................704 866-8785
William Glover, *Pr*
Ellen Beam, *
EMP: 35 **EST:** 1976
SQ FT: 23,400
SALES (est): 3.32MM **Privately Held**
Web: www.texlonplastics.com
SIC: 3089 Injection molding of plastics

(G-6523)
TEXPACK USA INC
1302 Industrial Pike Rd (28052-8430)
PHONE..............................704 864-5406
Michael Schmidlin, *Pr*
EMP: 22 **EST:** 2000
SALES (est): 279.97K **Privately Held**
SIC: 2678 Stationery products

(G-6524)
TEXTILE PARTS AND MCH CO INC
Also Called: Stewart Gear Manufacturing
1502 W May Ave (28052-1410)
P.O. Box 12305 (28052-0020)
PHONE..............................704 865-5003
John G Stewart, *Pr*
David M Stewart Junior, *VP*
EMP: 11 **EST:** 1944
SQ FT: 25,000
SALES (est): 617.26K **Privately Held**
Web: www.stewartgear.com
SIC: 3569 Filters

(G-6525)
THE MCQUACKINS COMPANY LLC ✪
2335 Jenkins Dairy Rd (28052-7157)
PHONE..............................980 254-2309
Eve Lowry, *Managing Member*
EMP: 4 **EST:** 2022
SALES (est): 182.43K **Privately Held**
SIC: 2389 7389 Apparel and accessories, nec; Business services, nec

(G-6526)
THOMAS CONCRETE SC INC
Also Called: Thomas Concrete South Carolina
5614 Union Rd (28056-9578)
PHONE..............................704 868-4545
Earl Strickland, *Mgr*
EMP: 4
SALES (corp-wide): 1.01B **Privately Held**
Web: www.thomasconcrete.com
SIC: 5211 3273 Lumber and other building materials; Ready-mixed concrete
HQ: Thomas Concrete Of South Carolina, Inc.
    2500 Cumberland Pkwy Se # 200
    Atlanta GA 30339
    919 832-0451

(G-6527)
TOMS KNIT FABRICS
699 Carlton Dr Apt A (28054-5265)
PHONE..............................704 867-4236
Tommy B Atkinson, *Owner*
EMP: 6 **EST:** 1962
SQ FT: 8,000
SALES (est): 340.08K **Privately Held**
SIC: 2257 Pile fabrics, circular knit

(G-6528)
TONY S ICE CREAM COMPANY INC (PA)
604 E Franklin Blvd (28054-7111)
PHONE..............................704 867-7085
Robert Coletta, *Pr*
▲ **EMP:** 18 **EST:** 1915
SQ FT: 4,500
SALES (est): 1.37MM
SALES (corp-wide): 1.37MM **Privately Held**
Web: www.tonysicecream.com
SIC: 2024 5451 Ice cream and frozen deserts ; Ice cream (packaged)

(G-6529)
TONYS ICE CREAM CO INC
Also Called: TONY'S ICE CREAM CO INC
520 E Franklin Blvd (28054-7110)
PHONE..............................704 853-0018
Robert Coletta, *Pr*
EMP: 7
SALES (corp-wide): 1.37MM **Privately Held**
Web: www.tonysicecream.com
SIC: 5143 5812 2024 Ice cream and ices; Eating places; Ice cream and frozen deserts
PA: Tony S Ice Cream Company, Inc.
    604 E Franklin Blvd
    Gastonia NC 28054
    704 867-7085

(G-6530)
TOTAL TECHNOLOGIES LLC
4702 King Crowder Dr (28052-8766)
PHONE..............................336 259-5541
Adam Mendieta, *Admn*
EMP: 6 **EST:** 2013
SALES (est): 123.79K **Privately Held**
Web: www.total-technologies.com
SIC: 3699 5072 5065 Security devices; Security devices, locks; Security control equipment and systems

(G-6531)
TRAC PLASTICS INC
140 Superior Stainless Rd (28052-8744)
P.O. Box 12547 (28052-0035)
PHONE..............................704 864-9140
W D Turlington, *Pr*
Brenda Turlington, *Sec*
EMP: 10 **EST:** 1979
SQ FT: 20,000
SALES (est): 906.32K **Privately Held**
Web: www.tracplastics.com
SIC: 3089 Injection molding of plastics

(G-6532)
TRI STATE PLASTICS INC
507 E Davidson Ave (28054-2444)
PHONE..............................704 865-7431
Thomas A Hope Junior, *Pr*
Carol N Hope, *VP*
Cindy Lynn Hope, *Sec*
EMP: 5 **EST:** 1967
SQ FT: 15,000
SALES (est): 451.2K **Privately Held**
SIC: 3552 Textile machinery

(G-6533)
TWISTED METAL FABRICATION
3309 Linwood Rd (28052-5025)
PHONE..............................704 915-1023
Michael Clack, *Prin*
EMP: 6 **EST:** 2018
SALES (est): 144.08K **Privately Held**
SIC: 3499 Fabricated metal products, nec

(G-6534)
UNIVERSAL BLACK OXIDE INC
205 Oxford St (28054-5422)
P.O. Box 2041 (28053-2041)
PHONE..............................704 867-1772
Randy Lewallen, *Pr*
Kenneth Lewallen, *VP*
Daphene Lewallen, *Sec*
EMP: 5 **EST:** 1985
SQ FT: 3,600
SALES (est): 457.36K **Privately Held**
Web: www.universalblackoxide.com
SIC: 3479 3471 Coating of metals and formed products; Coloring and finishing of aluminum or formed products

(G-6535)
US COTTON LLC (DH)
531 Cotton Blossom Cir (28054-5245)
P.O. Box 1787 (28053-1787)
PHONE..............................216 676-6400
Anthony Thomas, *Ch Bd*
John B Nims, *
◆ **EMP:** 250 **EST:** 1983
SQ FT: 160,000
SALES (est): 220.67MM
SALES (corp-wide): 1.44B **Privately Held**
Web: www.uscotton.com
SIC: 2844 2241 Perfumes, cosmetics and other toilet preparations; Cotton narrow fabrics
HQ: Parkdale Mills, Incorporated
    531 Cotton Blossom Cir
    Gastonia NC 28054
    704 874-5000

Gastonia - Gaston County (G-6536)

GEOGRAPHIC SECTION

(G-6536)
VAL-U-KING GROUP INC
2312 Rufus Ratchford Rd (28056-8179)
PHONE..................980 306-5342
Valdez Tilton, *CEO*
Valdez Hilton, *CEO*
EMP: 5 **EST:** 2019
SALES (est): 150K **Privately Held**
SIC: 5311 2519 Department stores, discount ; Furniture, household: glass, fiberglass, and plastic

(G-6537)
W D LEE & COMPANY
212 Trakas Blvd (28052-9221)
P.O. Box 12157 (28052-0011)
PHONE..................704 864-0346
Dennis J Lee, *Pr*
Karen Rhyne, *Sec*
Selina Lee, *Treas*
EMP: 25 **EST:** 1954
SQ FT: 22,000
SALES (est): 497.65K **Privately Held**
Web: www.wdlee.com
SIC: 3599 7692 3545 Machine shop, jobbing and repair; Welding repair; Machine tool accessories

(G-6538)
WALLACE SPENCER
Also Called: Spencer Machine Company
4306 Derrydowne Ln (28056-9330)
PHONE..................704 865-1147
Wallace Spencer, *Prin*
EMP: 6 **EST:** 2002
SALES (est): 71.15K **Privately Held**
SIC: 3599 Machine and other job shop work

(G-6539)
WANGS AND THANGS LLC
2309 Penny Park Dr (28052-6068)
PHONE..................980 925-7010
EMP: 4
SALES (est): 234.87K **Privately Held**
SIC: 2599 Food wagons, restaurant

(G-6540)
WATSON-HEGNER CORPORATION
1006 Union Rd Ste C (28054-5591)
PHONE..................704 922-9660
EMP: 7 **EST:** 2019
SALES (est): 479.93K **Privately Held**
Web: www.watsonhegner.com
SIC: 3559 Special industry machinery, nec

(G-6541)
WILDER TACTICAL LLC
120 Wolfpack Rd (28056-9776)
P.O. Box 335 (28086-0335)
PHONE..................704 750-7141
EMP: 9 **EST:** 2017
SALES (est): 400.63K **Privately Held**
Web: www.wildertactical.com
SIC: 3949 Ammunition belts, sporting type

(G-6542)
WOOD CREATIONS NC INC
2223 Plastics Dr (28054-1415)
PHONE..................704 865-1822
Ronald Honeycutt, *Pr*
Ann Honeycutt, *
EMP: 14 **EST:** 1997
SQ FT: 48,000
SALES (est): 439.08K **Privately Held**
Web: www.woodcreations.com
SIC: 2431 Doors, wood

(G-6543)
WORK WELL HYDRTION SYSTEMS LLC
1680 Garfield Dr (28052-8403)
P.O. Box 551360 (28055-1360)
PHONE..................704 853-7788
Scott Foy, *Managing Member*
Marvin Foy, *Managing Member*
EMP: 8 **EST:** 2012
SALES (est): 969.83K **Privately Held**
Web: www.workwellhs.com
SIC: 5074 3585 Water purification equipment ; Ice making machinery

(G-6544)
WV HOLDINGS INC
Also Called: Witten Vent Company
404 E Long Ave (28054-2527)
PHONE..................704 853-8338
Erik H Witten, *Pr*
Alvin E Witten, *VP*
Susan Nichols, *Mgr*
EMP: 6 **EST:** 1969
SQ FT: 13,000
SALES (est): 855.79K **Privately Held**
Web: www.bestvents.com
SIC: 3564 3444 Blowers and fans; Metal ventilating equipment

Gates
Gates County

(G-6545)
SOUTHSIDE PROTECTIVE COATINGS
67 Green Acres (27937-9698)
PHONE..................757 938-9188
EMP: 5 **EST:** 2010
SALES (est): 119.33K **Privately Held**
SIC: 3479 Metal coating and allied services

Gatesville
Gates County

(G-6546)
ASHTON LEWIS LUMBER CO INC
96 Lewis Mill Rd (27938-8003)
P.O. Box 25 (27938-0025)
PHONE..................252 357-0050
James Rane, *CEO*
Steven Good, *
EMP: 100 **EST:** 2017
SALES (est): 9.29MM **Privately Held**
Web: www.ashton-lewis.com
SIC: 2421 Sawmills and planing mills, general

(G-6547)
BAUR LOGGING LLC
613 Court St (27938-9516)
PHONE..................757 535-5693
EMP: 4 **EST:** 2016
SALES (est): 127.79K **Privately Held**
SIC: 2411 Logging

(G-6548)
BUNDY LOGGING COMPANY INC
Also Called: Bundy Trucking
37 Main St (27938)
P.O. Box 597 (27938-0597)
PHONE..................252 357-0191
Claude Bundy, *Pr*
Jackie Bundy, *VP*
EMP: 11 **EST:** 1966
SALES (est): 463.02K **Privately Held**
SIC: 2411 4214 4213 Logging camps and contractors; Local trucking with storage; Trucking, except local

(G-6549)
GATES CUSTOM MILLING INC (PA)
681 Nc Hwy 37 S (27938-9628)
P.O. Box 405 (27938-0405)
PHONE..................252 357-0116
Mark Truck, *Pr*
Mark Tuck, *
Nancy Tuck, *
Caroline Martin, *Stockholder**
EMP: 39 **EST:** 1978
SQ FT: 24,900
SALES (est): 6.28MM
SALES (corp-wide): 6.28MM **Privately Held**
Web: www.gatesmilling.com
SIC: 2426 2431 2435 2421 Hardwood dimension and flooring mills; Millwork; Hardwood veneer and plywood; Planing mills, nec

Germanton
Stokes County

(G-6550)
ANGELL CRAFTED CABINETRY
1070 Reich Dr (27019-8219)
PHONE..................336 655-7735
Jodi Manuel, *Prin*
EMP: 4 **EST:** 2017
SALES (est): 59.16K **Privately Held**
SIC: 2434 Wood kitchen cabinets

(G-6551)
BOYLES SIGN SHOP INC
4050 Stafford Mill Rd (27019-9421)
PHONE..................336 782-1189
Robbie Boyles, *Pr*
Joyce Boyles, *VP*
EMP: 6 **EST:** 1985
SALES (est): 299.3K **Privately Held**
SIC: 3993 Signs and advertising specialties

(G-6552)
BUFFALO CREEK FARM & CRMRY LLC
Also Called: Buffalo Creek Farm
3241 Buffalo Creek Farm Rd (27019-9596)
PHONE..................336 969-5698
EMP: 4 **EST:** 1991
SALES (est): 218.91K **Privately Held**
Web: www.buffalocreekfarmandcreamery.com
SIC: 5451 0241 2022 Dairy products stores; Dairy farms; Cheese spreads, dips, pastes, and other cheese products

(G-6553)
BURNS WELDING SERVICES LLC
2443 Flat Shoals Rd (27019-8916)
PHONE..................336 908-5716
Jennifer Burns, *Prin*
EMP: 5 **EST:** 2017
SALES (est): 68.78K **Privately Held**
SIC: 7692 Welding repair

(G-6554)
KEVINS BACKHOE SERVICE
1108 Brook Crossing Rd (27019-8317)
PHONE..................336 591-7751
EMP: 4 **EST:** 2017
SALES (est): 60.08K **Privately Held**
SIC: 3531 Backhoes

Gibson
Scotland County

(G-6555)
OIL MILL SALVAGE RECYCLERS INC
13840 Oil Mill Rd (28343-8273)
PHONE..................910 268-2111
Daniel Junecampbell, *CEO*
EMP: 6 **EST:** 2015
SALES (est): 159.88K **Privately Held**
Web: oilmillsalvagerecyclers.business.site
SIC: 2074 Cottonseed oil mills

Gibsonville
Guilford County

(G-6556)
ASHTON LLC (PA)
309 Bethel St (27249-2081)
PHONE..................336 447-4951
Billy Whitehurst, *Managing Member*
EMP: 14 **EST:** 2011
SQ FT: 4,000
SALES (est): 2.14MM
SALES (corp-wide): 2.14MM **Privately Held**
Web: www.ashtonus.com
SIC: 2759 Screen printing

(G-6557)
CROSS MANUFACTURING LLC
138 Eugene St (27249-2411)
PHONE..................336 603-6926
EMP: 5 **EST:** 2017
SALES (est): 243.56K **Privately Held**
SIC: 3999 Manufacturing industries, nec

(G-6558)
D D LAWNCARE SERVICE
5304 N Nc Highway 87 (27249-9300)
PHONE..................336 895-3353
EMP: 4 **EST:** 2015
SALES (est): 82K **Privately Held**
SIC: 5083 3524 Cultivating machinery and equipment; Lawn and garden mowers and accessories

(G-6559)
GRACE SOUTHERN EMBROIDERY
4351 High Rock Rd (27249-9750)
PHONE..................336 254-5585
Lisa Goudy, *Prin*
EMP: 4 **EST:** 2017
SALES (est): 45.2K **Privately Held**
SIC: 2395 Embroidery and art needlework

(G-6560)
GRIFFIN TUBING COMPANY INC
906 Burlington Ave (27249-2952)
P.O. Box 228 (27249-0228)
PHONE..................336 449-4822
Richard W Griffin, *Pr*
Adele L Griffin, *VP*
EMP: 7 **EST:** 1950
SQ FT: 5,000
SALES (est): 485.9K **Privately Held**
SIC: 2259 Bags and bagging, knit

(G-6561)
HARDWOOD STORE OF NC INC
106v E Railroad Ave (27249-2300)
P.O. Box 15 (27249-0015)
PHONE..................336 449-9627
Hilton B Peel Junior, *Pr*
Hilton Peal Senior, *Treas*
▼ **EMP:** 12 **EST:** 1996

SQ FT: 43,000
SALES (est): 2.13MM **Privately Held**
Web: www.hardwoodstore.com
SIC: **2541** 5211 Wood partitions and fixtures; Lumber products

(G-6562)
HAW RIVER VALLEY ENTPS LLC ✪
Also Called: Grove Vineyards & Winery
1183 University Dr Ste 105-1044 (27249-9763)
PHONE..................336 584-4060
EMP: 5 EST: 2022
SALES (est): 63.22K **Privately Held**
Web: www.grovewinery.com
SIC: **2084** Wines

(G-6563)
J C CUSTOM SEWING INC
106 E Railroad Ave (27249-2300)
P.O. Box 213 (27249-0213)
PHONE..................336 449-4586
Josephine Feyrer, *Pr*
Christel Schappacher, *VP*
EMP: 9 EST: 1980
SQ FT: 16,000
SALES (est): 928.17K **Privately Held**
SIC: **2339** 2392 2393 Aprons, except rubber or plastic: women's, misses', juniors'; Bags, laundry: made from purchased materials; Textile bags

(G-6564)
KECK LOGGING & CHIPPING INC
576 Browns Chapel Rd (27249-9522)
PHONE..................336 538-6903
Charles Keck, *Prin*
EMP: 9 EST: 2016
SALES (est): 70.19K **Privately Held**
SIC: **2411** Logging camps and contractors

(G-6565)
KECK LOGGING COMPANY
576 Browns Chapel Rd (27249-9522)
PHONE..................336 538-6903
Charles Keck, *Owner*
EMP: 7 EST: 1972
SALES (est): 450.97K **Privately Held**
SIC: **2411** Logging camps and contractors

(G-6566)
LARRY D TROXLER
Also Called: L T Welding
6170 Nc Highway 87 N (27249-9323)
PHONE..................336 585-1141
EMP: 5 EST: 1996
SALES (est): 151.72K **Privately Held**
SIC: **7692** Welding repair

(G-6567)
LINDLEY LABORATORIES INC (PA)
106 E Railroad Ave (27249-2300)
P.O. Box 341 (27216-0341)
PHONE..................336 449-7521
J Thomas Lindley Senior, *Ch Bd*
William Clarke Lindley, *Pr*
▼ EMP: 10 EST: 1977
SQ FT: 200,000
SALES (est): 1.61MM
SALES (corp-wide): 1.61MM **Privately Held**
Web: www.lindleylabs.com
SIC: **2843** 6531 2869 Finishing agents; Real estate agents and managers; Industrial organic chemicals, nec

(G-6568)
NEW GENERATION YARN CORP
1248 Springwood Church Rd (27249-2646)
PHONE..................336 449-5607
Shartel Smith, *Pr*
EMP: 11 EST: 2006
SALES (est): 365.36K **Privately Held**
Web: www.newgenerationyarn.com
SIC: **2282** Nylon yarn: throwing, twisting, winding or spooling

(G-6569)
PERFECTLY THREADED LLC
6578 Bethel Church Rd (27249-8718)
PHONE..................336 229-0152
Frank Longest, *Mgr*
EMP: 7 EST: 2016
SALES (est): 59.58K **Privately Held**
Web: www.perfectlythreaded.com
SIC: **2397** Schiffli machine embroideries

(G-6570)
PUBLIC SAFETY UAS LLC
50 Falcon Ct (27249-8403)
PHONE..................336 601-7578
David Young, *Managing Member*
EMP: 5 EST: 2021
SALES (est): 79.3K **Privately Held**
SIC: **3699** Security devices

(G-6571)
TEMPEST AERO GROUP
Also Called: Tempest Plus Marketing Group
1240 Springwood Church Rd (27249-2646)
PHONE..................336 449-5054
Tim Henderson, *
Charles Henderson, *
EMP: 42 EST: 1984
SQ FT: 3,500
SALES (est): 9.73MM **Privately Held**
Web: www.aeroaccessories.com
SIC: **3728** 3812 Aircraft parts and equipment, nec; Search and navigation equipment

(G-6572)
TOMMYS TUBING & STOCKENETTES
628 Wood St (27249-2557)
PHONE..................336 449-6461
Thomas Tickle, *Pr*
Janice Tickle, *
EMP: 10 EST: 1969
SQ FT: 4,800
SALES (est): 217.09K **Privately Held**
SIC: **2259** 2257 Meat bagging, knit; Weft knit fabric mills

Glade Valley
Alleghany County

(G-6573)
WILLIAMSON MEAD & BREWING LLC ✪
Also Called: Williamson Mead and Brewing
3047 Shawtown Rd (28627-9172)
PHONE..................661 827-7290
Matthew Lee Williamson, *Pr*
EMP: 11 EST: 2022
SALES (est): 55.21K **Privately Held**
Web: www.williamsonbrewing.com
SIC: **5813** 2084 Bar (drinking places); Brandy

Gloucester
Carteret County

(G-6574)
BRYAN BLAKE JAMES
Also Called: Blake Boat Works
134 Shore Dr (28528-9000)
P.O. Box 91 (28528-0091)
PHONE..................252 729-8021
James Bryan Blake, *Owner*
EMP: 5 EST: 1977
SALES (est): 99.02K **Privately Held**
Web: www.blakeboatworks.com
SIC: **3732** Boats, fiberglass: building and repairing

Godwin
Sampson County

(G-6575)
BRANDT CONSOLIDATED INC
2126 Old Wrench School Rd (28344-9172)
PHONE..................910 567-2965
Gregory Jackson, *Rgnl Mgr*
EMP: 5 EST: 2017
SALES (est): 100.7K **Privately Held**
SIC: **2875** Fertilizers, mixing only

(G-6576)
BRITE SKY LLC ✪
6461 Sherrill Baggett Rd (28344-8200)
PHONE..................757 589-4676
Tracy Frith Carvalho, *Managing Member*
EMP: 6 EST: 2022
SALES (est): 227.41K **Privately Held**
SIC: **3999** 7389 Manufacturing industries, nec; Business services, nec

(G-6577)
COASTAL PROTEIN PRODUCTS INC
Also Called: Martin Meats
1600 Martin Rd (28344-9068)
PHONE..................910 567-6102
Carlton Martin, *Pr*
EMP: 4 EST: 1989
SQ FT: 40,000
SALES (est): 431.73K **Privately Held**
SIC: **2077** Animal and marine fats and oils

(G-6578)
KANSAS CITY SAUSAGE CO LLC
Also Called: Coastal Proteins
1600 Martin Rd (28344-9068)
PHONE..................910 567-5604
EMP: 5
SIC: **2013** Sausages and other prepared meats
HQ: Kansas City Sausage Company, Llc
8001 Nw 106th St
Kansas City MO 64153

(G-6579)
OLD HICKORY STAINLESS STL INC
8759 Fayetteville Hwy (28344-8905)
PHONE..................910 567-6751
R Wrench, *Pr*
Amelia Wrench, *Sec*
EMP: 4 EST: 1998
SALES (est): 315.45K **Privately Held**
Web: www.oldhickorystainless.com
SIC: **3312** Stainless steel

Gold Hill
Rowan County

(G-6580)
CAROLINA STALITE CO LTD PARTNR
16815 Old Beatty Ford Rd (28071)
PHONE..................704 279-2166
EMP: 21
SALES (corp-wide): 22.99MM **Privately Held**
Web: www.stalite.com
SIC: **3281** 0711 Slate products; Soil chemical treatment services
PA: Carolina Stalite Company Limited Partnership
205 Klumac Rd
Salisbury NC 28144
704 637-1515

(G-6581)
CAROLINA STALITE CO LTD PARTNR
17700 Old Beatty Ford Rd (28071-9655)
P.O. Box 1037 (28145-1037)
PHONE..................704 279-2166
Jessie Penley, *Brnch Mgr*
EMP: 23
SALES (corp-wide): 22.99MM **Privately Held**
Web: www.stalite.com
SIC: **3295** Clay for petroleum refining, chemically processed
PA: Carolina Stalite Company Limited Partnership
205 Klumac Rd
Salisbury NC 28144
704 637-1515

(G-6582)
HAMMILL CONSTRUCTION CO INC
5051 St Stephens Church Rd (28071-9427)
PHONE..................704 279-5309
Jerry Hammill, *Pr*
Jerry Hammill, *CEO*
Donna Hammill, *Pr*
Larry Hammill, *VP*
EMP: 14 EST: 1957
SQ FT: 3,000
SALES (est): 3.93MM **Privately Held**
Web: www.puppylovedscspa.com
SIC: **1446** 4212 Abrasive sand mining; Dump truck haulage

(G-6583)
LEGACY VULCAN LLC
Mideast Division
16745 Old Beatty Ford Rd (28071-9710)
P.O. Box 188 (28071-0188)
PHONE..................704 279-5566
Corey Viers, *Mgr*
EMP: 4
Web: www.vulcanmaterials.com
SIC: **3273** Ready-mixed concrete
HQ: Legacy Vulcan, Llc
1200 Urban Center Dr
Vestavia AL 35242
205 298-3000

(G-6584)
LYERLYS WLDG & FABRICATION INC
215 Woodson Rd (28071-9635)
PHONE..................704 680-2317
Wesley Lyerly, *Pr*
EMP: 9 EST: 2014
SALES (est): 225.85K **Privately Held**
SIC: **7692** 3441 Welding repair; Fabricated structural metal

(G-6585)
NC BACKYARD COOPS
154 Morgan Acres (28071-6709)
PHONE..................336 250-0838
EMP: 4 EST: 2017
SALES (est): 67.69K **Privately Held**
Web: www.ncbackyardcoops.com
SIC: **2449** Chicken coops (crates), wood: wirebound

(G-6586)
TRINITY WOODWORKS LLC
764 St Stephens Church Rd (28071-9413)
PHONE..................980 938-4765
EMP: 4 EST: 2018
SALES (est): 76.29K **Privately Held**
SIC: **2431** Millwork

Goldsboro
Wayne County

(G-6587)
AIRGAS USA LLC
109 Hinnant Rd (27530-7618)
PHONE..................................919 735-5276
EMP: 5
SALES (corp-wide): 101.26MM **Privately Held**
Web: www.airgas.com
SIC: 5169 5084 5085 2813 Industrial gases; Welding machinery and equipment; Welding supplies; Industrial gases
HQ: Airgas Usa, Llc
259 N Radnor Chester Rd
Radnor PA 19087
216 642-6600

(G-6588)
ALTA FOODS LLC
105 Industry Ct (27530-9124)
P.O. Box 1876 (27533-1876)
PHONE..................................919 734-0233
Donald Best Barnes Ii, *Managing Member*
EMP: 55 EST: 2007
SQ FT: 50,000
SALES (est): 19.32MM **Privately Held**
Web: www.altafoods.com
SIC: 5141 2099 Food brokers; Tortillas, fresh or refrigerated

(G-6589)
AMF AUTOMATION TECH LLC
2815 Carolina Commerce Dr (27530-5556)
PHONE..................................919 288-1523
EMP: 6
Web: www.amfbakery.com
SIC: 3556 Food products machinery
PA: Amf Automation Technologies, Llc
2115 W Laburnum Ave
Richmond VA 23227

(G-6590)
ANCHOR COUPLING INC
106 Industry Ct (27530-9124)
PHONE..................................919 739-8000
EMP: 308
SALES (corp-wide): 67.06B **Publicly Held**
Web: www.anchorcoupling.com
SIC: 3492 Hose and tube couplings, hydraulic/pneumatic
HQ: Anchor Coupling Inc.
5520 13th St
Menominee MI 49858
906 863-2672

(G-6591)
AP EMISSIONS TECHNOLOGIES LLC
Also Called: Airtek
300 Dixie Trl (27530-7119)
PHONE..................................919 580-2000
Rich Biel, *Pr*
◆ EMP: 688 EST: 2013
SQ FT: 900,000
SALES (est): 195.66MM
SALES (corp-wide): 364.48B **Publicly Held**
Web: www.apemissions.com
SIC: 3714 Mufflers (exhaust), motor vehicle
HQ: Marmon Holdings, Inc.
181 W Madison St Ste 3900
Chicago IL 60602
312 372-9500

(G-6592)
ARNOLD-WILBERT CORPORATION (PA)
1401 W Grantham St (27530-1115)
PHONE..................................919 735-5008
John Williams, *Pr*
Ron Turner, *
Stephen L Velker, *General Vice President**
EMP: 70 EST: 1953
SQ FT: 12,000
SALES (est): 8.18MM
SALES (corp-wide): 8.18MM **Privately Held**
Web: www.arnoldwilbert.com
SIC: 3272 Burial vaults, concrete or precast terrazzo

(G-6593)
BNB DESIGNS INC
601 N James St Ste A (27530-2700)
PHONE..................................919 587-9800
Stewart Bryan, *Prin*
EMP: 6 EST: 2005
SALES (est): 160.91K **Privately Held**
Web: www.swpromos.com
SIC: 2395 Embroidery products, except Schiffli machine

(G-6594)
BOEING AROSPC OPERATIONS INC
Also Called: Boeing
1950 Jabara Ave Bldg 4517 (27531-2520)
PHONE..................................919 722-4351
James Clue, *Mgr*
EMP: 14
SALES (corp-wide): 77.79B **Publicly Held**
SIC: 3721 8711 Aircraft; Engineering services
HQ: Boeing Aerospace Operations, Inc.
6001 S A Depo Blvd Ste E
Oklahoma City OK 73150
405 622-6000

(G-6595)
BORDEN MFG CO FUND INC
1506 E Ash St (27530-5204)
P.O. Box P (27533-9715)
PHONE..................................919 734-4301
Jack Kannan, *CEO*
EMP: 5 EST: 2001
SALES (est): 194.67K **Privately Held**
SIC: 3999 Manufacturing industries, nec

(G-6596)
BREW MASTERS OF GOLDSBORO
2402 E Ash St (27534-7511)
P.O. Box 10277 (27532-0277)
PHONE..................................919 288-2014
EMP: 9 EST: 2017
SALES (est): 511.1K **Privately Held**
Web: www.brewmastersnc.com
SIC: 2082 Malt beverages

(G-6597)
BRIDGESTONE RET OPERATIONS LLC
Also Called: Firestone
507 N Berkeley Blvd (27534-3442)
PHONE..................................919 778-0230
Terry Turnage Junior, *Mgr*
EMP: 5
Web: www.bridgestoneamericas.com
SIC: 5531 7534 Automotive tires; Rebuilding and retreading tires
HQ: Bridgestone Retail Operations, Llc
333 E Lake St Ste 300
Bloomingdale IL 60108
630 259-9000

(G-6598)
BUTTERBALL LLC
938 Millers Chapel Rd (27534-7772)
PHONE..................................919 658-6743
EMP: 56
SALES (corp-wide): 11.24B **Publicly Held**
Web: www.butterballfoodservice.com
SIC: 2015 Turkey, processed, nsk
HQ: Butterball, Llc
1 Butterball Ln
Garner NC 27529
919 255-7900

(G-6599)
CASE FARMS LLC
330 Westbrook Rd (27530-8476)
PHONE..................................919 658-2252
EMP: 44
Web: www.casefarms.com
SIC: 2015 8731 Poultry slaughtering and processing; Commercial physical research
PA: Case Farms, L.L.C.
385 Pilch Rd
Troutman NC 28166

(G-6600)
CASE FOODS INC
Also Called: Case Farms
259 Sandhill Dr (27530-0901)
PHONE..................................919 736-4498
Gene Short, *Mgr*
EMP: 209
SALES (corp-wide): 490.71MM **Privately Held**
Web: www.casefarms.com
SIC: 2015 Poultry slaughtering and processing
PA: Case Foods, Inc.
385 Pilch Rd
Troutman NC 28166
704 528-4501

(G-6601)
CLOTH BARN INC
Also Called: Home Fabrics
1701 E Ash St (27530-4042)
PHONE..................................919 735-3643
John M Bridgers, *Pr*
Elizabeth Bridgers, *VP*
Lillian O Bridgers, *Sec*
EMP: 15 EST: 1958
SQ FT: 16,000
SALES (est): 927.37K **Privately Held**
Web: www.theclothbarn.net
SIC: 5949 2211 5131 5714 Fabric stores piece goods; Draperies and drapery fabrics, cotton; Piece goods and other fabrics; Upholstery materials

(G-6602)
COKER FEED MILL INC
1439 Hood Swamp Rd (27534-8563)
PHONE..................................919 778-3491
R Brantley Coker, *Pr*
Mabel S Coker, *VP*
Gaye Coker, *Sec*
EMP: 19 EST: 1949
SQ FT: 15,000
SALES (est): 1.69MM **Privately Held**
Web: www.cokerfeedmill.com
SIC: 2048 5411 Prepared feeds, nec; Convenience stores

(G-6603)
CONETOE LAND & TIMBER LLC
3820 Stevens Mill Rd (27530-9705)
P.O. Box 160 (27819-0160)
PHONE..................................252 717-4648
G Forrest York, *Admn*
EMP: 10 EST: 2017
SALES (est): 472.26K **Privately Held**
SIC: 2411 Logging

(G-6604)
COOPER-STANDARD AUTOMOTIVE INC
Also Called: Cooper
308 Fedelon Trl (27530-9001)
PHONE..................................919 735-5394
Renzo Bulgarelli, *Brnch Mgr*
EMP: 82
SALES (corp-wide): 2.82B **Publicly Held**
Web: www.cooperstandard.com
SIC: 3714 Motor vehicle parts and accessories
HQ: Cooper-Standard Automotive Inc.
40300 Traditions Dr
Northville MI 48168
248 596-5900

(G-6605)
CV INDUSTRIES
105 Pinehaven Ct (27534-9464)
PHONE..................................919 778-7280
Zeb Jones, *Owner*
EMP: 5 EST: 2010
SALES (est): 91K **Privately Held**
SIC: 3999 Manufacturing industries, nec

(G-6606)
D&J SAND & GRAVEL
380 Claridge Nursery Rd (27530-7957)
PHONE..................................919 584-8267
EMP: 10 EST: 2018
SALES (est): 2.73MM **Privately Held**
Web: www.dandjsandandgravelnc.com
SIC: 1442 Construction sand and gravel

(G-6607)
DALY COMPANY INC
4043 Mclain St (27534-7118)
PHONE..................................919 751-3625
Jeff Daly, *Admn*
EMP: 7 EST: 2016
SALES (est): 214.62K **Privately Held**
Web: www.dalyhomes.net
SIC: 2451 1629 Mobile homes; Heavy construction, nec

(G-6608)
DAMSEL IN DEFENSE
1401 Cuyler Best Rd (27534-8244)
PHONE..................................919 901-9926
EMP: 4 EST: 2015
SALES (est): 132.12K **Privately Held**
Web: www.damselindefense.net
SIC: 3812 Defense systems and equipment

(G-6609)
DAYSTAR MATERIALS INC
200 W Dewey St (27530-1304)
P.O. Box 10561 (27532-0561)
PHONE..................................919 734-0460
Larry Davis, *Manager*
EMP: 20
SALES (corp-wide): 1.87MM **Privately Held**
SIC: 2891 5052 Epoxy adhesives; Coal and other minerals and ores
PA: Daystar Materials, Inc
1712 Stablersville Rd
White Hall MD
410 357-4761

(G-6610)
DOBBINS PRODUCTS
208 Earl Dr (27530-9032)
PHONE..................................919 580-0621
Paul Dobbin, *Owner*
EMP: 5 EST: 2011
SALES (est): 133.68K **Privately Held**
Web: www.trapperman.com
SIC: 3949 5941 5735 5942 Lures, fishing: artificial; Bait and tackle; Video discs, prerecorded; Book stores

GEOGRAPHIC SECTION — Goldsboro - Wayne County (G-6636)

(G-6611)
EASTERN MANUFACTURING LLC
300 Dixie Trl (27530-7119)
PHONE.................................919 580-2058
EMP: 4 **EST:** 2017
SALES (est): 116.42K **Privately Held**
SIC: 3999 Manufacturing industries, nec

(G-6612)
ELECTROPIN TECHNOLOGIES LLC
110 Centura Dr (27530-7745)
PHONE.................................919 288-1203
Keith Brenton, *Pr*
EMP: 8 **EST:** 2018
SALES (est): 893.99K **Privately Held**
Web: www.electropintech.com
SIC: 3671 Cathode ray tubes, including rebuilt

(G-6613)
EVERETTES INDUSTRIAL REPR SVC
117 Dobbs Pl (27534-7874)
PHONE.................................252 527-4269
Travis D Everette, *Owner*
EMP: 10 **EST:** 1989
SALES (est): 637.4K **Privately Held**
SIC: 3599 7692 3441 Machine shop, jobbing and repair; Welding repair; Fabricated structural metal

(G-6614)
FRANKLIN BAKING COMPANY LLC (HQ)
Also Called: Flowers Bakery
500 W Grantham St (27530-1928)
P.O. Box 228 (27533-0228)
PHONE.................................919 735-0344
▲ **EMP:** 350 **EST:** 1939
SQ FT: 200,000
SALES (est): 94.01MM
SALES (corp-wide): 5.09B **Publicly Held**
Web: franklin-co4goldsboro.edan.io
SIC: 2051 Bread, all types (white, wheat, rye, etc); fresh or frozen
PA: Flowers Foods, Inc.
  1919 Flowers Cir
  Thomasville GA 31757
  229 226-9110

(G-6615)
GENERAL INDUSTRIES INC
3048 Thoroughfare Rd (27534-7728)
P.O. Box 1279 (27533-1279)
PHONE.................................919 751-1791
John T Wiggins, *Pr*
Teresa Finley, *Stockholder*
EMP: 45 **EST:** 1951
SQ FT: 50,000
SALES (est): 6.04MM **Privately Held**
Web: www.gitank.com
SIC: 3443 Tanks, standard or custom fabricated: metal plate

(G-6616)
GLENOIT UNIVERSAL LTD (PA)
Also Called: Excell Home Fashions
One Excell Linde Dr (27533)
P.O. Box 1879 (27533-1879)
PHONE.................................919 735-7111
Barry Leonard, *CEO*
Cliff Campbell, *Treas*
Dan Martin, *Sec*
◆ **EMP:** 206 **EST:** 1994
SALES (est): 14.54MM **Privately Held**
SIC: 2273 2392 Rugs, tufted; Cushions and pillows

(G-6617)
GODWIN DOOR & HARDWARE INC
105 E Holly St (27530-2709)
P.O. Box 2025 (27533-2025)
PHONE.................................919 580-0543
David A Godwin, *Pr*
Judy Godwin, *Sec*
EMP: 24 **EST:** 1991
SALES (est): 701.38K **Privately Held**
SIC: 3442 5072 Window and door frames; Hardware

(G-6618)
GOLDSBORO MILLING COMPANY (PA)
Also Called: Goldsboro Mil & Grn Stor Co
938 Millers Chapel Rd (27534-7772)
PHONE.................................919 778-3130
J L Maxwell Junior, *Ch Bd*
Hugh Gordon Maxwell Iii, *Pr*
J W Pelletier Iii, *VP*
J L Maxwell Iii, *Sec*
Thomas Howell, *
EMP: 138 **EST:** 1916
SQ FT: 21,000
SALES (est): 148.85MM
SALES (corp-wide): 148.85MM **Privately Held**
Web: www.goldsboromilling.com
SIC: 2048 Poultry feeds

(G-6619)
GOLDSBORO NEON SIGN CO INC
712 N George St (27530-2428)
P.O. Box 1811 (27533-1811)
PHONE.................................919 735-2035
Donald Ray Westbrooke, *Pr*
Donald Ray Westbrooke, *Pr*
Carolyn Weaks, *Treas*
James Westbrook, *Owner*
EMP: 4 **EST:** 1950
SQ FT: 5,000
SALES (est): 251.5K **Privately Held**
Web: www.goldsboroneonsignco.com
SIC: 3993 7389 Electric signs; Sign painting and lettering shop

(G-6620)
GOLDSBORO STRTER ALTRNTOR SVC
105 E Oak St (27530-2740)
PHONE.................................919 735-6745
Edward L Underwood, *Pr*
Richard Burgess, *VP*
Dianne Underwood, *Sec*
EMP: 5 **EST:** 1965
SQ FT: 5,000
SALES (est): 552.14K **Privately Held**
SIC: 3694 3621 7539 Alternators, automotive; Starters, for motors; Electrical services

(G-6621)
GRAPHIXX SCREEN PRINTING INC
601 N James St Ste B (27530-2700)
P.O. Box 1318 (27533-1318)
PHONE.................................919 736-3995
David Gibson, *Pr*
Jimmy Bryan, *VP*
Richard Narron, *Sec*
EMP: 6 **EST:** 1990
SALES (est): 377.2K **Privately Held**
SIC: 2759 Screen printing

(G-6622)
GRUMA CORPORATION
Also Called: Mission Foods
401 Gateway Dr (27534-7058)
PHONE.................................919 778-5553
EMP: 20
Web: www.gruma.com
SIC: 2096 Tortilla chips
HQ: Gruma Corporation
  5601 Executive Dr Ste 800
  Irving TX 75038
  972 232-5000

(G-6623)
HAM WAYCO COMPANY
506 N William St (27530-2804)
P.O. Box 841 (27533-0841)
PHONE.................................919 735-3962
George A Worrell, *Pr*
Sallie B Worrell, *Sec*
EMP: 20 **EST:** 1947
SQ FT: 31,000
SALES (est): 1.99MM **Privately Held**
Web: www.waycohams.com
SIC: 2013 2011 Prepared pork products, from purchased pork; Meat packing plants

(G-6624)
HARVEY FERTILIZER AND GAS CO
Patetown-Dixie Fert & Gas
2937 N William St (27530-8009)
P.O. Box 1454 (27533-1454)
PHONE.................................919 731-2474
Bobby Finch, *Mgr*
EMP: 24
SALES (corp-wide): 80.5MM **Privately Held**
Web: www.harveyfertilizerandgas.com
SIC: 2873 2911 2875 Fertilizers: natural (organic), except compost; Petroleum refining; Fertilizers, mixing only
PA: Harvey Fertilizer And Gas Co.
  303 Bohannon Rd
  Kinston NC 28501
  252 526-4150

(G-6625)
HILL & FERENCZ ELC MTR CO INC
301 S George St (27530-4715)
PHONE.................................919 736-7373
June Hill, *Pr*
EMP: 5 **EST:** 1981
SQ FT: 4,225
SALES (est): 957.92K **Privately Held**
SIC: 5063 7694 Motors, electric; Electric motor repair

(G-6626)
IRON-CRETE DESIGNS
595 Dollard Town Rd (27534-9333)
PHONE.................................919 738-2803
EMP: 4 **EST:** 2019
SALES (est): 88.91K **Privately Held**
SIC: 3446 Architectural metalwork

(G-6627)
ISLAND TIMEZ
1206 N Berkeley Blvd (27534-3476)
PHONE.................................919 351-0346
Peggy Reese, *Owner*
EMP: 4 **EST:** 2018
SALES (est): 64.86K **Privately Held**
SIC: 2741 Miscellaneous publishing

(G-6628)
KDM ENTERPRISE LLC
1594 Us Highway 13 S (27530-8996)
PHONE.................................919 689-9720
Melissa Shaw, *Prin*
EMP: 5 **EST:** 2010
SALES (est): 138.23K **Privately Held**
SIC: 2759 Commercial printing, nec

(G-6629)
LEGACY BIOGAS LLC
Also Called: Legacy Biogas
107 Cassedale Dr (27534-9408)
PHONE.................................713 253-9013
Robert Hoffland, *Prin*
EMP: 5 **EST:** 2013
SALES (est): 363.59K **Privately Held**
SIC: 2813 Industrial gases

(G-6630)
LIGHTHOUSE OF WAYNE COUNTY INC
405 E Walnut St (27530-4838)
P.O. Box 227 (27533-0227)
PHONE.................................919 736-1313
EMP: 10 **EST:** 1980
SALES (est): 130.06K **Privately Held**
Web: www.waynegov.com
SIC: 3731 8322 Lighthouse tenders, building and repairing; Crisis intervention center

(G-6631)
LITTLE RIVER METALWORKS LLC
132 Blueberry Rd (27530-9502)
PHONE.................................919 920-0292
Casey Matthew Lee, *Asst Sec*
EMP: 5 **EST:** 2018
SALES (est): 97.16K **Privately Held**
Web: www.lrmetalworks.com
SIC: 3446 Architectural metalwork

(G-6632)
LUXOTTICA OF AMERICA INC
Also Called: Lenscrafters
611 N Berkeley Blvd Ste B (27534-3468)
PHONE.................................919 778-5692
Steven Earwood, *Brnch Mgr*
EMP: 4
SALES (corp-wide): 2.55MM **Privately Held**
Web: www.luxottica.com
SIC: 5995 3851 Eyeglasses, prescription; Ophthalmic goods
HQ: Luxottica Of America Inc.
  4000 Luxottica Pl
  Mason OH 45040

(G-6633)
MAJESTIC XPRESS HANDWASH INC
103 N John St Ste D (27530-3632)
PHONE.................................919 440-7611
Jomokenyatta Jones, *CEO*
EMP: 5 **EST:** 2019
SQ FT: 900
SALES (est): 325.56K **Privately Held**
SIC: 3589 Car washing machinery

(G-6634)
MEDIA PUBLISHING LLC
122 S Berkeley Blvd (27534-4508)
PHONE.................................919 273-0488
Danny Wroblewski, *Admn*
EMP: 6 **EST:** 2012
SALES (est): 69.61K **Privately Held**
Web: www.thebuzzaroundwaynecounty.com
SIC: 2741 Miscellaneous publishing

(G-6635)
METAL CRAFTERS OF GOLDSBORO NC
855 Nc 111 Hwy S (27534-6325)
P.O. Box 10008 (27532-0008)
PHONE.................................919 778-7200
C Brooks Marriner, *Pr*
Kenneth L Cox, *VP*
EMP: 16 **EST:** 1956
SQ FT: 7,200
SALES (est): 347.06K **Privately Held**
SIC: 2431 Staircases, stairs and railings

(G-6636)
METALCRAFT & MECH SVC INC
147 Aycock Dr (27530-9501)
PHONE.................................919 736-1029
Warren Woodard, *Pr*
Richard Woodard Senior, *Pr*
EMP: 6 **EST:** 1981
SQ FT: 2,500

Goldsboro - Wayne County (G-6637)

SALES (est): 458.27K **Privately Held**
Web: www.alldriveshafts.com
SIC: 3714 Motor vehicle parts and accessories

(G-6637)
MONK LEKEISHA
Also Called: Dukester Productions Entrmt Co
P.O. Box 405 (27533-0405)
PHONE..................910 385-0361
Lekeisha Monk, *Owner*
EMP: 6 **EST**: 1999
SQ FT: 1,000
SALES (est): 367.5K **Privately Held**
SIC: 7389 2752 Decoration service for special events; Commercial printing, lithographic

(G-6638)
NORTH CAROLINA MFG INC
Also Called: NCM
100 Industry Ct (27530-9124)
PHONE..................919 734-1115
Ray Mayo, *Pr*
Janice Mayo, *Sec*
EMP: 20 **EST**: 1990
SQ FT: 6,000
SALES (est): 2.82MM **Privately Held**
Web: www.ncmfginc.com
SIC: 3599 3545 Machine shop, jobbing and repair; Machine tool accessories

(G-6639)
NRFP LOGGING LLC
206 Connie Cir (27530-9309)
PHONE..................919 738-0989
Ason B Tew, *Prin*
EMP: 8 **EST**: 2018
SALES (est): 481.75K **Privately Held**
SIC: 2411 Logging camps and contractors

(G-6640)
NUWORKS
1208 N Berkeley Blvd (27534-3420)
PHONE..................919 223-2587
EMP: 4 **EST**: 2019
SALES (est): 83.36K **Privately Held**
Web: nuworks-remodeler.business.site
SIC: 2434 1521 Wood kitchen cabinets; Single-family housing construction

(G-6641)
OCCASIONS GROUP INC
Also Called: Taylor Prime Labels & Packg
305 N Spence Ave (27534-4346)
PHONE..................919 751-2400
Kevin Coakley, *Mgr*
EMP: 4
SALES (corp-wide): 3.81B **Privately Held**
Web: www.theoccasionsgroup.com
SIC: 7334 2752 Blueprinting service; Commercial printing, lithographic
HQ: The Occasions Group Inc
1750 Tower Blvd
North Mankato MN 56003

(G-6642)
PACKAGING CORPORATION AMERICA
Also Called: PCA
801 N William St (27530-2469)
PHONE..................336 434-0600
EMP: 5
SALES (corp-wide): 8.48B **Publicly Held**
Web: www.packagingcorp.com
SIC: 2653 Boxes, corrugated: made from purchased materials
PA: Packaging Corporation Of America
1 N Field Ct
Lake Forest IL 60045
847 482-3000

(G-6643)
PCORE
Also Called: Reuel
200 W Dewey St (27530-1304)
PHONE..................919 734-0460
EMP: 12 **EST**: 2017
SALES (est): 670.66K **Privately Held**
Web: www.hubbell.com
SIC: 3644 Noncurrent-carrying wiring devices

(G-6644)
PEPSI BOTTLING VENTURES LLC
Also Called: Pepsi-Cola
2707 N Park Dr (27534-7483)
PHONE..................919 778-8300
Rick Poillon, *Brnch Mgr*
EMP: 54
Web: www.pepsibottlingventures.com
SIC: 2086 Carbonated soft drinks, bottled and canned
HQ: Pepsi Bottling Ventures Llc
4141 Parklake Ave Ste 600
Raleigh NC 27612
919 865-2300

(G-6645)
PETRA PRECISION MACHINING
3413 Central Heights Rd (27534-7713)
PHONE..................919 751-3461
Ernest Richards, *Pr*
EMP: 7 **EST**: 2005
SALES (est): 202.04K **Privately Held**
SIC: 3599 Machine shop, jobbing and repair

(G-6646)
PROLEC-GE WAUKESHA INC
Also Called: Heavy Duty Electric
2701 Us Highway 117 S (27530-0915)
P.O. Box 268 (27533-0268)
PHONE..................919 734-8900
Mark Krueger, *Mgr*
EMP: 280
Web: www.waukeshatransformers.com
SIC: 3677 Electronic coils and transformers
HQ: Prolec-Ge Waukesha, Inc.
400 S Prairie Ave
Waukesha WI 53186
262 547-0121

(G-6647)
PROSIGN
504 Rosewood Rd (27530-7808)
PHONE..................919 222-6907
EMP: 4 **EST**: 2018
SALES (est): 103.38K **Privately Held**
SIC: 3993 Signs and advertising specialties

(G-6648)
QDE PRESS
104 W Raintree Ln (27534-7362)
PHONE..................256 390-4668
EMP: 5 **EST**: 2018
SALES (est): 122.04K **Privately Held**
Web: www.qdepress.com
SIC: 2741 Miscellaneous publishing

(G-6649)
REESE SIGN SERVICE INC
Also Called: Reese Sign Service
3271 Us Highway 117 N (27530-8837)
P.O. Box 10593 (27532-0593)
PHONE..................919 580-0705
EMP: 6 **EST**: 1990
SALES (est): 439.11K **Privately Held**
Web: www.reesesign.com
SIC: 3993 Electric signs

(G-6650)
REUEL INC
200 W Dewey St (27530-1304)
P.O. Box 10561 (27532-0561)
PHONE..................919 734-0460
▲ **EMP**: 40
SIC: 3264 3699 3675 3674 Insulators, electrical: porcelain; Electrical equipment and supplies, nec; Electronic capacitors; Semiconductors and related devices

(G-6651)
ROSE MEDIA INC
200 N Cottonwood Dr (27530-9177)
PHONE..................919 736-1154
Margaret Harrison, *Pr*
Ken Harrison, *Stockholder*
EMP: 10 **EST**: 1997
SQ FT: 1,800
SALES (est): 474.51K **Privately Held**
SIC: 2721 Magazines: publishing and printing

(G-6652)
RUSKIN LLC
166 Nc 581 Hwy S (27530-9404)
PHONE..................919 583-5444
Melissa Watson, *Managing Member*
EMP: 5 **EST**: 2017
SALES (est): 485.86K **Privately Held**
Web: www.ruskin.com
SIC: 3822 Environmental controls

(G-6653)
S & W READY MIX CON CO LLC
624 Powell Rd (27534-7852)
PHONE..................919 751-1796
Robbie Trice, *Mgr*
EMP: 19
SALES (corp-wide): 8.01MM **Privately Held**
SIC: 3273 Ready-mixed concrete
HQ: S & W Ready Mix Concrete Company Llc
217 Lisbon St
Clinton NC 28328
910 592-1733

(G-6654)
SCREEN IT
1907 E Ash St (27530-4046)
PHONE..................919 581-9981
EMP: 8 **EST**: 2005
SALES (est): 682.1K **Privately Held**
Web: www.goldsboroscreenprinting.com
SIC: 2759 Screen printing

(G-6655)
SDP IMPRESS ME
315 N Spence Ave (27534-4346)
PHONE..................919 947-1197
EMP: 4 **EST**: 2019
SALES (est): 114.22K **Privately Held**
Web: www.sdpimpressme.com
SIC: 2752 Offset printing

(G-6656)
SEPHORA INSIDE JCPENNEY
607 N Berkeley Blvd (27534-3443)
PHONE..................919 778-4800
EMP: 5 **EST**: 2019
SALES (est): 108.77K **Privately Held**
SIC: 2844 Perfumes, cosmetics and other toilet preparations

(G-6657)
SLEEPY CREEK TURKEYS LLC
Also Called: Sleepy Creek Turkeys, Inc.
938 Millers Chapel Rd (27534-7772)
PHONE..................919 778-3130
James L Maxwell Junior, *Pr*
H Gordon Maxwell Iii, *Sec*
EMP: 165 **EST**: 1979
SALES (est): 8.31MM
SALES (corp-wide): 148.85MM **Privately Held**
SIC: 0253 3523 Turkey farm; Feed grinders, crushers, and mixers
HQ: Sleepy Creek Farms, Inc.
938 Millers Chapel Rd
Goldsboro NC 27534
919 778-3130

(G-6658)
SOUTHERN HLDINGS GOLDSBORO INC
501 Patetown Rd Ste 4 (27530-5570)
PHONE..................919 920-6998
Stephanie Rhodes Myers, *Prin*
EMP: 13 **EST**: 2018
SALES (est): 1.2MM **Privately Held**
SIC: 3273 Ready-mixed concrete

(G-6659)
SOUTHERN READY MIX LLC ◆
501 Patetown Rd Ste 4 (27530-5570)
P.O. Box 2888 (27402-2888)
PHONE..................919 988-8448
Dustin Myers, *Pr*
EMP: 6 **EST**: 2022
SALES (est): 79.3K **Privately Held**
SIC: 3273 Ready-mixed concrete

(G-6660)
SPX FLOW US LLC
Also Called: APV Heat Exchanger PDT Group
2719 Graves Dr Ste 10 (27534-4536)
P.O. Box 1718 (27533-1718)
PHONE..................919 735-4570
Tim Taylor, *Brnch Mgr*
EMP: 200
SALES (corp-wide): 1.53B **Privately Held**
SIC: 3443 Fabricated plate work (boiler shop)
HQ: Spx Flow Us, Llc
135 Mount Read Blvd
Rochester NY 14611
585 436-5550

(G-6661)
STEVENS MILL WOODWORKS LLC
3048 Stevens Mill Rd (27530-9737)
PHONE..................919 440-8834
EMP: 5 **EST**: 2018
SALES (est): 59.54K **Privately Held**
SIC: 2431 Millwork

(G-6662)
STORMBERG FOODS LLC
1002b Sunburst Dr (27534-8667)
PHONE..................919 947-6011
Gary William Moorcroft, *Managing Member*
EMP: 50 **EST**: 2016
SALES (est): 3.49MM **Privately Held**
Web: www.stormbergfoods.com
SIC: 5499 2096 Gourmet food stores; Cheese curls and puffs
PA: Stormberg Certified Organic Farms (Pty) Ltd
15 Buick St
Gqeberha EC 6000

(G-6663)
SUPER RETREAD CENTER INC (PA)
Also Called: Hill's Tire & Auto
1213 S George St (27530-6803)
PHONE..................919 734-0073
Ila Hill, *Pr*
Janet Hill, *VP*
EMP: 19 **EST**: 1968
SQ FT: 20,000
SALES (est): 2.34MM
SALES (corp-wide): 2.34MM **Privately Held**
Web: www.hillstire.com

GEOGRAPHIC SECTION

SIC: 5531 7534 Automotive tires; Tire recapping

(G-6664)
SUPERIOR CUSTOM CABINETS LLC
170 Scott St (27534-8914)
PHONE.............................919 778-1845
Joseph P Rousay, *Owner*
EMP: 5 **EST:** 2016
SALES (est): 208.38K **Privately Held**
SIC: 2434 Wood kitchen cabinets

(G-6665)
TELAIR US LLC
Also Called: Telair US Cargo Systems
500a Gateway Dr (27534-7071)
PHONE.............................919 705-2400
Christopher Spagnoletti, *Pr*
EMP: 150 **EST:** 2015
SALES (est): 32.09MM
SALES (corp-wide): 6.58B **Publicly Held**
Web: www.uscargosystems.com
SIC: 3728 Aircraft parts and equipment, nec
HQ: Transdigm, Inc.
1301 E 9th St Ste 3000
Cleveland OH 44114

(G-6666)
TURNAGE BLIND CO
415 Sandhill Dr (27530-8486)
PHONE.............................919 736-1809
EMP: 5 **EST:** 2019
SALES (est): 74.35K **Privately Held**
SIC: 2591 Window blinds

(G-6667)
TURNER EQUIPMENT COMPANY INC
Also Called: Turner Greenhouses
1502 Us Highway 117 S (27530)
P.O. Box 1260 (27533-1260)
PHONE.............................919 734-8328
Gary Smithwick, *Pr*
Nancy Lilly Sales, *Prin*
Ashley Fleming Sales, *Prin*
David Ellis Cad Shipping, *Prin*
Rhonda Stokes Bookkeeping, *Accounting*
EMP: 30 **EST:** 1939
SQ FT: 17,000
SALES (est): 4.94MM **Privately Held**
Web: www.turnertanks.com
SIC: 3443 3448 Fabricated plate work (boiler shop); Prefabricated metal buildings and components

(G-6668)
UCHIYAMA MFG AMER LLC
494 Arrington Bridge Rd (27530-8538)
PHONE.............................919 731-2364
Taizo Uchiyama, *CEO*
Masatomo Sueki, *
Nick Gambella, *Managing Member**
Linda Jennings, *
▲ **EMP:** 300 **EST:** 1999
SQ FT: 89,000
SALES (est): 92.74MM **Privately Held**
Web: www.umc-net.co.jp
SIC: 5085 3714 Gaskets; Motor vehicle parts and accessories
PA: Uchiyama Manufacturing Corp.
338, Enami, Naka-Ku
Okayama OKA 702-8

(G-6669)
WAYNE PRINTING COMPANY INC
Also Called: Goldsboro News-Argus
310 N Berkeley Blvd (27534-4326)
P.O. Box 10629 (27532-0629)
PHONE.............................919 778-2211
Hal H Tanner Junior, *Pr*
Hal H Tanner Iii, *VP*
Barbara Sturm, *

▲ **EMP:** 36 **EST:** 1953
SQ FT: 21,000
SALES (est): 2.28MM **Privately Held**
Web: www.newsargus.com
SIC: 2711 Newspapers, publishing and printing

(G-6670)
WESTLIFT LLC
Also Called: Westlift
186 Belfast Rd (27530-8160)
PHONE.............................919 242-4379
E West, *Mgr*
Heather Ferris, *CFO*
EMP: 17 **EST:** 2009
SQ FT: 2,700
SALES (est): 2.45MM **Privately Held**
Web: www.westliftllc.com
SIC: 3537 7699 Forklift trucks; Industrial equipment services

(G-6671)
WILSON GRADING LLC
132 Blue Bird Ln (27534-8104)
PHONE.............................919 778-1580
Regis Wilson, *Pt*
Dennis Wilson, *Pt*
EMP: 10 **EST:** 1965
SALES (est): 776.43K **Privately Held**
SIC: 1411 Gneiss, dimension-quarrying

Goldston
Chatham County

(G-6672)
ALOTECH INC
751 S Church St (27252-9551)
PHONE.............................919 774-1297
William H Murphy, *Pr*
◆ **EMP:** 50 **EST:** 1991
SQ FT: 15,000
SALES (est): 8.82MM **Privately Held**
Web: www.alotechinc.com
SIC: 3599 3484 3565 Machine shop, jobbing and repair; Small arms; Packaging machinery

(G-6673)
ALOTECH NORTH
751 S Church St (27252-9551)
PHONE.............................919 774-1297
EMP: 7 **EST:** 2012
SALES (est): 170.77K **Privately Held**
Web: www.alotechinc.com
SIC: 3599 Machine shop, jobbing and repair

(G-6674)
CONVEYOR TECH LLC
Also Called: Conveyor Technologies
751 S Church St (27252-9551)
PHONE.............................919 776-7227
Gary Kabot, *CEO*
Thomas R Kirk Ii, *COO*
◆ **EMP:** 131 **EST:** 2017
SQ FT: 120,000
SALES (est): 21.64MM **Privately Held**
Web: www.conveyor-technologies.com
SIC: 3535 Conveyors and conveying equipment

(G-6675)
J T METALS LLC
3032 Nc Highway 42 (27252-9140)
PHONE.............................336 737-4189
EMP: 5 **EST:** 2021
SALES (est): 77.02K **Privately Held**

SIC: 1799 2851 1761 Coating of metal structures at construction site; Undercoatings, paint; Roofing and gutter work

(G-6676)
SANFORD STEEL CORPORATION
375 Claude Hash Rd (27252-9448)
PHONE.............................919 898-4799
Andy B Starling, *Pr*
B Andy Starling, *Pr*
Rhonda G Starling, *VP*
EMP: 10 **EST:** 1993
SQ FT: 26,000
SALES (est): 2.47MM **Privately Held**
Web: www.welcometosanford.com
SIC: 3441 Building components, structural steel

Graham
Alamance County

(G-6677)
ACUCOTE INC (DH)
Also Called: Acucote
910 E Elm St (27253-1908)
P.O. Box 538 (27253-0538)
PHONE.............................336 578-1800
John B Leath Junior, *Pr*
Brenda Seel, *
◆ **EMP:** 130 **EST:** 1987
SQ FT: 90,000
SALES (est): 56.21MM **Privately Held**
Web: www.acucote.com
SIC: 2672 2679 Adhesive backed films, foams and foils; Building paper, laminated: made from purchased material
HQ: Fedrigoni Spa
Via Enrico Fermi 13/F
Verona VR 37135

(G-6678)
ATLANTIC CUSTOM CONTAINER INC
327 E Elm St (27253-3023)
P.O. Box 1071 (27253-1071)
PHONE.............................336 437-9302
Edward O'brien, *Pr*
EMP: 7 **EST:** 2002
SQ FT: 30,000
SALES (est): 976.07K **Privately Held**
Web: www.atlanticcustomcontainers.com
SIC: 2655 Containers, laminated phenolic and vulcanized fiber

(G-6679)
BLUE ARC FABRICATION MECH LLC
2126 S Nc Highway 54 (27253-9067)
PHONE.............................336 693-7878
Dustin Love, *Prin*
EMP: 5 **EST:** 2018
SALES (est): 73.54K **Privately Held**
SIC: 7692 Welding repair

(G-6680)
BRAXTON SAWMILL INC
7519 Lindley Mill Rd Lot D (27253-8348)
PHONE.............................336 376-6798
Christopher Braxton, *Pr*
Wanda Braxton, *
EMP: 12 **EST:** 1978
SALES (est): 476.88K **Privately Held**
SIC: 2421 2426 Sawmills and planing mills, general; Hardwood dimension and flooring mills

(G-6681)
BROOKS MANUFACTURING SOLUTIONS

1017 Davis Ln (27253-4618)
P.O. Box 846 (27216-0846)
PHONE.............................336 438-1280
Troy Brooks, *Pr*
EMP: 16 **EST:** 2008
SALES (est): 1.86MM **Privately Held**
Web: www.bmscontrolpanels.com
SIC: 3613 3999 Control panels, electric; Manufacturing industries, nec

(G-6682)
BURLINGTON MSCLLNEOUS MTLS LLC
3406 William Newlin Dr (27253-9821)
PHONE.............................336 376-1264
Michael Workman, *Prin*
EMP: 11 **EST:** 2014
SALES (est): 2.34MM **Privately Held**
Web: www.burlingtonmiscmetals.website
SIC: 3446 Stairs, staircases, stair treads: prefabricated metal

(G-6683)
CHANDLER CONCRETE INC
Also Called: Truck Shop
301 W River St (27253-1755)
PHONE.............................336 222-9716
Thomas E Chandler, *Owner*
EMP: 5
Web: www.chandlerconcrete.com
SIC: 3273 Ready-mixed concrete
PA: Chandler Concrete Co., Inc.
1006 S Church St
Burlington NC 27215

(G-6684)
CITY OF GRAHAM
111 E Crescent Square Dr (27253-4013)
PHONE.............................336 570-6811
EMP: 11
Web: www.cityofgraham.com
SIC: 3469 Automobile license tags, stamped metal
PA: Graham, City Of (Inc)
201 S Main St
Graham NC 27253
336 570-6705

(G-6685)
CKS PACKAGING INC
943 Trollingwood Road (27253)
P.O. Box 478 (27253-0478)
PHONE.............................336 578-5800
Ken Pierce, *Brnch Mgr*
EMP: 75
SALES (corp-wide): 483.16MM **Privately Held**
Web: www.ckspackaging.com
SIC: 3089 3085 Plastics containers, except foam; Plastics bottles
PA: C.K.S. Packaging, Inc.
350 Great Sw Pkwy
Atlanta GA 30336
404 691-8900

(G-6686)
CSM MANUFACTURING INC
Also Called: CSM
913 Washington St (27253-1645)
PHONE.............................336 570-2282
Scott Cobb, *Pr*
Richard Shevlin, *VP*
EMP: 14 **EST:** 2001
SQ FT: 3,000
SALES (est): 2.47MM **Privately Held**
Web: www.csm-mfg.com
SIC: 3599 Machine shop, jobbing and repair

Graham - Alamance County (G-6687)

GEOGRAPHIC SECTION

(G-6687)
D & L CABINETS INC
1010 Rolling Oaks Dr (27253-9966)
PHONE..................336 376-6009
Phil Demarco, *Pr*
EMP: 15 EST: 2003
SALES (est): 1.16MM **Privately Held**
Web: www.dandlcabinets.com
SIC: **2434** Wood kitchen cabinets

(G-6688)
DOG BLACK SERVICES LLC
6261 Whitney Rd (27253-8105)
PHONE..................336 266-0778
William Wright, *Prin*
EMP: 4 EST: 2017
SALES (est): 57.88K **Privately Held**
SIC: **3826** Analytical instruments

(G-6689)
FARM SERVICES INC
125 E Elm St (27253-3019)
P.O. Box 872 (27253-0872)
PHONE..................336 226-7381
William Talley, *Pr*
Jennifer Talley, *VP*
EMP: 6 EST: 1955
SQ FT: 6,000
SALES (est): 600K **Privately Held**
Web: www.farmservicesgraham.com
SIC: **5261** 5999 5083 3546 Fertilizer; Feed and farm supply; Mowers, power; Chain saws, portable

(G-6690)
GONZALEZ WELDING INC
817 E Parker St (27253-1957)
PHONE..................336 270-8179
Gabriel Gonzalez, *CEO*
EMP: 7 EST: 2017
SALES (est): 279.14K **Privately Held**
Web: www.salemiindustries.com
SIC: **7692** Welding repair

(G-6691)
HESTER CABINETS
6662 S Nc Highway 87 (27253-9315)
PHONE..................336 376-0186
Robert Hester, *Prin*
EMP: 5 EST: 2008
SALES (est): 61.59K **Privately Held**
SIC: **2434** Wood kitchen cabinets

(G-6692)
INDULOR AMERICA LP
932 E Elm St (27253-1908)
PHONE..................336 578-6855
Sebastian Fengler, *Prin*
▲ EMP: 43 EST: 2008
SALES (est): 12.11MM **Privately Held**
Web: www.blankophor-oba.com
SIC: **2822** Ethylene-propylene rubbers, EPDM polymers

(G-6693)
IVARS SPORTSWEAR INC
408 W Interstate Service Rd (27253-3524)
P.O. Box 2449 (27216-2449)
PHONE..................336 227-9683
Corbin Sapp, *Pr*
Corbin I Sapp, *Pr*
Adelaide Raye Sapp, *Sec*
Bennett Sapp, *VP*
EMP: 8 EST: 1976
SQ FT: 12,000
SALES (est): 636.77K **Privately Held**
Web: www.ivars-sportswear.com
SIC: **2395** Embroidery products, except Schiffli machine

(G-6694)
JAMES FODS FRNCHISE CORP AMER
611 E Gilbreath St (27253-3747)
PHONE..................336 437-0393
Charles Timothy James, *Pr*
EMP: 8 EST: 2014
SQ FT: 39,000
SALES (est): 179.41K **Privately Held**
SIC: **2038** 5411 Frozen specialties, nec; Frozen food and freezer plans, except meat

(G-6695)
JAMES FOODS INC
611 E Gilbreath St (27253-3747)
PHONE..................336 437-0393
Charles T James, *Pr*
Charles Timothy James, *Pr*
Wanda Metzger, *
EMP: 40 EST: 2004
SQ FT: 40,000
SALES (est): 6.57MM **Privately Held**
Web: www.jamesfoods.com
SIC: **2099** Food preparations, nec

(G-6696)
KAYSER-ROTH HOSIERY INC
714 W Interstate Service Rd (27253-3527)
PHONE..................336 229-2269
▲ EMP: 31 EST: 1982
SALES (est): 6.36MM
SALES (corp-wide): 192.57MM **Privately Held**
Web: www.kayser-roth.com
SIC: **2252** Socks
HQ: Kayser-Roth Corporation
    102 Corporate Center Blvd
    Greensboro NC 27408
    336 852-2030

(G-6697)
LINDLEY MILLS INC
7763 Lindley Mill Rd (27253-8326)
PHONE..................336 376-6190
Joe J Lindley Senior, *Treas*
Joe J Lindley, *Junior Principal*
EMP: 16 EST: 1976
SALES (est): 938.43K **Privately Held**
Web: www.lindleymills.com
SIC: **2041** Flour

(G-6698)
LOWES WELDING AND CAMPER REPR
2417 S Nc Highway 87 (27253-9474)
PHONE..................336 214-9058
EMP: 4 EST: 2012
SALES (est): 65.34K **Privately Held**
Web: www.loweswelding.com
SIC: **7692** Welding repair

(G-6699)
LOY & LOY INC
205 Travora St (27253-2339)
PHONE..................919 942-6356
Michael W Loy, *Pr*
Joyce Loy, *Sec*
EMP: 4 EST: 1966
SALES (est): 419.18K **Privately Held**
SIC: **2899** Water treating compounds

(G-6700)
MARSH FURNITURE COMPANY
Also Called: Alamance Cabinets
605 W Harden St (27253-2106)
P.O. Box 1401 (27253-1401)
PHONE..................336 229-5122
Jon Lawson, *Brnch Mgr*
EMP: 10
SALES (corp-wide): 43.2MM **Privately Held**
Web: www.marshkb.com
SIC: **2434** Wood kitchen cabinets
PA: Marsh Furniture Company
    1001 S Centennial St
    High Point NC 27260
    336 884-7363

(G-6701)
MC STITCH & PRINT
864 Rivers Edge Dr (27253-8706)
PHONE..................336 263-3677
Nita Mckirgan, *Prin*
EMP: 5 EST: 2015
SALES (est): 101.53K **Privately Held**
SIC: **2752** Commercial printing, lithographic

(G-6702)
METAL IMPACT EAST LLC
Also Called: Luxfer
235 Riverbend Rd (27253-2621)
PHONE..................336 578-4515
Philip Kretekos, *Pr*
EMP: 110 EST: 2021
SALES (est): 45.13MM
SALES (corp-wide): 126.13MM **Privately Held**
SIC: **3354** Aluminum rod and bar
HQ: Metal Impact Llc
    1501 Oakton St
    Elk Grove Village IL 60007

(G-6703)
METAL IMPACT EAST LLC
Also Called: Thunderbird Metals East
1200 Jay Ln (27253-2614)
PHONE..................743 205-1900
Csr Seraphina Senior, *Brnch Mgr*
EMP: 31
SALES (corp-wide): 494.29K **Privately Held**
SIC: **3563** Air and gas compressors
PA: Metal Impact East Llc
    900 Commerce Dr Ste 150
    Oak Brook IL 60523
    743 205-1900

(G-6704)
MINUTEMAN PRESS
Also Called: Minuteman Press
236 Riverbend Rd (27253-2620)
PHONE..................336 270-4426
EMP: 8 EST: 2017
SALES (est): 154.63K **Privately Held**
Web: www.minutemanpress.com
SIC: **2752** Commercial printing, lithographic

(G-6705)
NEW SOUTH LUMBER COMPANY INC
4408 Mount Hermon Rock Crk Rd (27253-8909)
PHONE..................336 376-3130
Terry Bishop, *Mgr*
EMP: 135
SALES (corp-wide): 5.53B **Privately Held**
SIC: **2421** 5031 Lumber: rough, sawed, or planed; Lumber, plywood, and millwork
HQ: New South Lumber Company, Inc.
    3700 Claypond Rd Ste 6
    Myrtle Beach SC 29579
    843 236-9399

(G-6706)
PIEDMONT TRUCK TIRES INC
704 Myrtle Dr (27253-1955)
PHONE..................336 223-9412
Mitch Glover, *Brnch Mgr*
EMP: 13
SALES (corp-wide): 339.82MM **Privately Held**
Web: www.piedmonttrucktires.com
SIC: **5014** 5531 7534 Truck tires and tubes; Auto and home supply stores; Rebuilding and retreading tires
HQ: Piedmont Truck Tires, Inc.
    312 S Regional Rd
    Greensboro NC 27409
    336 668-0091

(G-6707)
PRECISION BOAT MFG
808 Carraway Dr (27253-4457)
PHONE..................336 395-8795
James Allen, *Prin*
EMP: 4 EST: 2017
SALES (est): 89.25K **Privately Held**
SIC: **3999** Manufacturing industries, nec

(G-6708)
PRESS COFFEE+CREPES
133 N Main St (27253-2848)
PHONE..................336 263-1180
EMP: 6 EST: 2017
SALES (est): 41.35K **Privately Held**
Web: www.pressccc.com
SIC: **2741** Miscellaneous publishing

(G-6709)
PURE FLOW INC (PA)
Also Called: Pfi
1241 Jay Ln (27253-2615)
PHONE..................336 532-0300
Daniel Johnson, *Pr*
Lucinda Johnson, *
Gary Allred, *
EMP: 83 EST: 1985
SQ FT: 65,847
SALES (est): 22.29MM
SALES (corp-wide): 22.29MM **Privately Held**
Web: www.pureflowinc.com
SIC: **3589** Water treatment equipment, industrial

(G-6710)
SOLA PUBLISHING
1074 W Main St (27253-8546)
PHONE..................336 226-8240
EMP: 10 EST: 2019
SALES (est): 406.01K **Privately Held**
Web: www.solapublishing.com
SIC: **2741** Miscellaneous publishing

(G-6711)
SOUTH ATLANTIC LLC
Also Called: South Atlantic Galvanizing
3025 Steelway Dr (27253)
P.O. Box 1380 (27253-1380)
PHONE..................336 376-0410
David Monroe, *Brnch Mgr*
EMP: 16
SALES (corp-wide): 336.48MM **Privately Held**
Web: www.southatlanticllc.com
SIC: **3479** 3547 Galvanizing of iron, steel, or end-formed products; Galvanizing lines (rolling mill equipment)
HQ: South Atlantic, Llc
    1907 S 17th St Ste 2
    Wilmington NC 28401
    910 332-1900

(G-6712)
TE WHEEL INC
207 Dakota Dr (27253-8252)
PHONE..................336 376-1364
EMP: 5 EST: 2010
SALES (est): 110K **Privately Held**
SIC: **3312** Wheels

GEOGRAPHIC SECTION

(G-6713)
USA DUTCH INC
778 Woody Dr (27253-3813)
P.O. Box 1299 (27253-1299)
PHONE..............................336 227-8600
Ronald Keizer, *Pr*
EMP: 40
Web: www.usadutchinc.com
SIC: 3444 Sheet metalwork
PA: Usa Dutch, Inc.
3604 Southern Dr
Efland NC 27243

(G-6714)
VAN WELDER LLC
219 Ward St (27253-2939)
PHONE..............................919 495-2902
Cort Van Wingerden, *Prin*
EMP: 6 **EST:** 2019
SALES (est): 517.86K **Privately Held**
Web: www.vanwelder.com
SIC: 3548 Arc welding generators, a.c. and d.c.

(G-6715)
VESUVIUS NC LLC
Also Called: Permatech, LLC
911 E Elm St (27253-1907)
PHONE..............................336 578-7328
Joseph D Trettel, *Pr*
John Schneider, *VP*
◆ **EMP:** 74 **EST:** 2003
SQ FT: 65,000
SALES (est): 10.56MM
SALES (corp-wide): 22.69MM **Privately Held**
Web: www.permatech.net
SIC: 3297 Alumina fused refractories
PA: Ccpi Inc.
838 Cherry St
Blanchester OH 45107
937 783-2476

(G-6716)
VINATORU ENTERPRISES INC
209 W Hanover Rd (27253-1723)
PHONE..............................336 227-4300
Mihai Vinatoru, *Pr*
EMP: 9 **EST:** 1980
SQ FT: 3,500
SALES (est): 966.81K **Privately Held**
Web: www.vinatoru.com
SIC: 3829 Accelerometers

(G-6717)
ZIMMERMANN - DYNAYARN USA LLC
327 E Elm St (27253-3023)
P.O. Box 811 (27253-0811)
PHONE..............................336 222-8129
John A Holt, *Managing Member*
Tommy Crowson, *
◆ **EMP:** 32 **EST:** 1999
SQ FT: 100,000
SALES (est): 4.39MM **Privately Held**
Web: www.zimdyn.com
SIC: 2241 2251 2281 Rubber thread and yarns, fabric covered; Women's hosiery, except socks; Yarn spinning mills

Grandy
Currituck County

(G-6718)
BETTS CONSTRUCTION UNITED INC
119 Edgewater Dr (27939-9628)
P.O. Box 2561 (27954-2561)
PHONE..............................252 203-2849
Eric Betts, *Pr*
EMP: 25 **EST:** 2019
SALES (est): 784.25K **Privately Held**
Web: betts-construction.ueniweb.com
SIC: 1389 Construction, repair, and dismantling services

(G-6719)
WEEPING RADISH FARM BREWRY LLC
6810 Caratoke Hwy (27939-9635)
P.O. Box 1471 (27954-1471)
PHONE..............................252 491-5205
Uli Bennewitz, *Managing Member*
EMP: 10 **EST:** 2007
SALES (est): 390.33K **Privately Held**
Web: www.weepingradish.com
SIC: 2082 Beer (alcoholic beverage)

Granite Falls
Caldwell County

(G-6720)
80 ACRES URBAN AGRICULTURE INC
4141 Yorkview Ct (28630-8771)
PHONE..............................704 437-6115
Tracy Canipe, *Brnch Mgr*
EMP: 8
SALES (corp-wide): 28.81MM **Privately Held**
Web: www.80acresfarms.com
SIC: 3532 Mining machinery
PA: 80 Acres Urban Agriculture, Inc.
345 High St Fl 7
Hamilton OH 45011
513 218-4387

(G-6721)
A MCGEE WOOD PRODUCTS INC
171 N Main St (28630-1329)
P.O. Box 1009 (28630-1009)
PHONE..............................828 212-1700
T Andrew Mcgee, *CEO*
EMP: 10 **EST:** 2019
SALES (est): 989.34K **Privately Held**
SIC: 2441 Ammunition boxes, wood

(G-6722)
ASSOCIATED HARDWOODS INC (PA)
650 N Main St (28630-8572)
P.O. Box 491 (28630-0491)
PHONE..............................828 396-3321
▲ **EMP:** 35 **EST:** 1978
SALES (est): 22.92MM
SALES (corp-wide): 22.92MM **Privately Held**
Web: www.associatedhardwoods.com
SIC: 2426 5031 Hardwood dimension and flooring mills; Lumber: rough, dressed, and finished

(G-6723)
AUTOMATED SOLUTIONS LLC (PA)
4101 Us Highway 321a (28630-9602)
PHONE..............................828 396-9900
◆ **EMP:** 11 **EST:** 1998
SQ FT: 75,000
SALES (est): 9.16MM
SALES (corp-wide): 9.16MM **Privately Held**
Web: www.automatedsolutionsllc.com
SIC: 2674 3496 2671 3111 Shipping bags or sacks, including multiwall and heavy duty; Conveyor belts; Plastic film, coated or laminated for packaging; Cutting of leather

(G-6724)
AUTUMN HOUSE INC
Also Called: Autumn Wood Products
1206 Premier Rd (28630-7400)
PHONE..............................828 728-1121
Howard L Pruitt, *CEO*
Howard L Pruitt, *Pr*
Ernest Rosenquist, *
▲ **EMP:** 65 **EST:** 1977
SQ FT: 90,000
SALES (est): 8.51MM **Privately Held**
Web: www.autumnhouse.com
SIC: 2435 Hardwood veneer and plywood

(G-6725)
CABINET MASTERS AND MORE LLC
239 River Bend Dr (28630-9388)
PHONE..............................828 396-1881
Lucas Shook, *Prin*
EMP: 5 **EST:** 2016
SALES (est): 124.12K **Privately Held**
SIC: 2434 Wood kitchen cabinets

(G-6726)
CAROLINA PRCSION CMPONENTS INC
4181 Us Highway 321a (28630-9602)
PHONE..............................828 496-1045
EMP: 38 **EST:** 1995
SQ FT: 52,000
SALES (est): 4.04MM **Privately Held**
Web: www.carpreco.com
SIC: 3599 Machine shop, jobbing and repair

(G-6727)
CARRINGTON COURT INC
2 Winchester Ave (28630-1110)
P.O. Box 600 (28603-0600)
PHONE..............................828 396-1049
Brad Haas, *Pr*
Rick Rand, *Ex Dir*
EMP: 8 **EST:** 1998
SALES (est): 217.07K **Privately Held**
SIC: 2426 5712 2511 2512 Carvings, furniture: wood; Custom made furniture, except cabinets; Wood household furniture; Upholstered household furniture

(G-6728)
CASE BASKET CREATIONS
4975 J M Craig Rd (28630-9295)
PHONE..............................828 381-4908
EMP: 5 **EST:** 2018
SALES (est): 101.34K **Privately Held**
SIC: 3523 Farm machinery and equipment

(G-6729)
CHASE CORPORATION
Also Called: Granite Falls Plant
3908 Hickory Blvd (28630-8373)
P.O. Box 800 (28630-0800)
PHONE..............................828 396-2121
EMP: 4
Web: www.chasecorp.com
SIC: 3644 Insulators and insulation materials, electrical
HQ: Chase Corporation
375 University Ave
Westwood MA 02090
781 332-0700

(G-6730)
CUSTOM CABINET WORKS
180 N Main St (28630-1332)
PHONE..............................828 396-6348
William Fisher, *Owner*
EMP: 8 **EST:** 1997
SALES (est): 548.34K **Privately Held**
Web: www.customcabinetworks.net
SIC: 2434 Wood kitchen cabinets

(G-6731)
DEOHGES WELDING SERVICE LLC
2800 Campground Rd (28630-8529)
PHONE..............................828 396-2770
EMP: 4 **EST:** 2019
SALES (est): 25.09K **Privately Held**
SIC: 7692 Welding repair

(G-6732)
EVERGREEN PALLETS LLC
3815 N Main St (28630-8516)
PHONE..............................828 313-0050
EMP: 11 **EST:** 2005
SALES (est): 778.8K **Privately Held**
SIC: 2448 Pallets, wood and wood with metal

(G-6733)
FUELTEC SYSTEMS LLC
3821 N Main St (28630-8516)
P.O. Box 14889 (34979-4889)
PHONE..............................828 212-1141
Ronald Lenz, *Pt*
Ronald Lenz, *Managing Member*
EMP: 6 **EST:** 2008
SALES (est): 481.35K **Privately Held**
Web: www.fueltecsystems.com
SIC: 3677 Filtration devices, electronic

(G-6734)
GRANITE FALLS FURNACES LLC
1230 Premier Rd (28630-7400)
PHONE..............................828 324-4394
David Duncan Junior, *Pr*
Matthew Duncan, *
EMP: 24 **EST:** 2002
SALES (est): 2.96MM **Privately Held**
Web: www.granitefallsfurnace.com
SIC: 3315 Steel wire and related products

(G-6735)
GRANITE TAPE CO
4 Cedar St (28630-1602)
P.O. Box 1012 (28630-1012)
PHONE..............................828 396-5614
Barton Potter, *Owner*
EMP: 6 **EST:** 1982
SQ FT: 18,000
SALES (est): 493.39K **Privately Held**
SIC: 2672 Tape, pressure sensitive: made from purchased materials

(G-6736)
HOFFMAN MATERIALS LLC
230 Timberbrook Ln (28630-1976)
PHONE..............................717 243-2011
Diana Rauchfuss, *CEO*
EMP: 16 **EST:** 2007
SALES (est): 2.5MM **Privately Held**
Web: www.hoffmanmaterials.com
SIC: 3674 Wafers (semiconductor devices)

(G-6737)
HOFFMAN MATERIALS INC
230 Timberbrook Ln (28630-1976)
PHONE..............................717 243-2011
Diana Rauchfuss, *Ch Bd*
Marci E Staudte, *Ch Bd*
Tom Hardy, *CEO*
Mark S Rauchfuss, *Pr*
EMP: 26 **EST:** 1938
SALES (est): 2.08MM **Privately Held**
Web: www.hoffmanmaterials.com
SIC: 3679 Quartz crystals, for electronic application

(G-6738)
HOFFMAN MATERIALS LLC
230 Timberbrook Ln (28630-1976)

Granite Falls - Caldwell County (G-6739)

PHONE.................................828 212-1669
EMP: 11 **EST:** 2018
SALES (est): 906.49K **Privately Held**
Web: www.hoffmanmaterials.com
SIC: 3674 Semiconductors and related devices

(G-6739)
HUFFMAN FINISHING COMPANY INC
4919 Hickory Blvd (28630-8390)
P.O. Box 170 (28630-0170)
PHONE.................................828 396-1741
A W Huffman Junior, *Pr*
A W Huffman Iii, *VP Sls*
Paul Marshall, *
Mildred Wike, *
▲ **EMP:** 125 **EST:** 1945
SQ FT: 25,000
SALES (est): 9.76MM **Privately Held**
SIC: 2252 2251 2262 2261 Dyeing and finishing hosiery; Women's hosiery, except socks; Finishing plants, manmade; Finishing plants, cotton

(G-6740)
JORDAN-HOLMAN LUMBER CO INC
650 N Main St (28630-8572)
P.O. Box 436 (28630-0436)
PHONE.................................828 396-3101
Rick Jordan, *Pr*
Jane T Jordan, *
EMP: 58 **EST:** 1981
SQ FT: 18,000
SALES (est): 5.76MM **Privately Held**
Web: www.associatedhardwoods.com
SIC: 2421 Kiln drying of lumber

(G-6741)
KNITWEAR AMERICA INC
5740 Rocky Mount Rd (28630-8308)
PHONE.................................704 396-1193
Edna Dunne, *Pr*
EMP: 7 **EST:** 1995
SALES (est): 620.4K **Privately Held**
SIC: 2253 Warm weather knit outerwear, including beachwear

(G-6742)
LUBRIMETAL CORPORATION
Also Called: Lm
2889 Countryside Dr (28630-1996)
PHONE.................................828 212-1083
Giorgio Corso, *Pr*
▲ **EMP:** 19 **EST:** 2012
SALES (est): 2.46MM **Privately Held**
Web: www.lubrimetal.com
SIC: 2992 Lubricating oils and greases

(G-6743)
MARX LLC
4276 Helena St (28630)
P.O. Box 826 (28630-0826)
PHONE.................................828 396-6700
EMP: 90 **EST:** 2018
SALES (est): 8.39MM **Privately Held**
Web: www.marxllc.net
SIC: 3086 Plastics foam products

(G-6744)
MATTHEW LAWS
Also Called: Signal Technologies
12 Falls Ave Ste 3 (28630-1510)
PHONE.................................828 313-2204
Matthew Laws, *Owner*
EMP: 5 **EST:** 2010
SALES (est): 71.32K **Privately Held**
SIC: 3679 Electronic components, nec

(G-6745)
METAL WORKS
116 Duke St (28630-1827)
P.O. Box 1805 (28604-1805)
PHONE.................................828 898-8582
EMP: 5 **EST:** 2009
SALES (est): 139.1K **Privately Held**
Web: www.bluemountainmetalworks.com
SIC: 3446 Architectural metalwork

(G-6746)
MINDA NORTH AMERICA LLC
10 N Summit Ave (28630-1333)
P.O. Box 425 (28630-0425)
PHONE.................................828 313-0092
Charles Martin, *CEO*
Todd Beal, *Managing Member*
EMP: 25 **EST:** 2012
SALES (est): 3.08MM **Privately Held**
Web: www.minda.com
SIC: 3441 Fabricated structural metal

(G-6747)
NEPTCO INCORPORATED
3908 Hickory Blvd (28630-8373)
P.O. Box 800 (28630-0800)
PHONE.................................828 313-0149
Randy Dula, *Mgr*
EMP: 230
SQ FT: 8,460
Web: www.chasecorp.com
SIC: 2672 2823 Tape, pressure sensitive: made from purchased materials; Cellulosic manmade fibers
HQ: Neptco Incorporated
295 University Ave
Westwood MA 02090
401 722-5500

(G-6748)
PACTIV LLC
3825 N Main St (28630-8516)
P.O. Box 750 (28630-0750)
PHONE.................................828 396-2373
Darren Green, *Manager*
EMP: 6
SQ FT: 50,000
Web: www.pactivevergreen.com
SIC: 3086 4225 Insulation or cushioning material, foamed plastics; General warehousing and storage
HQ: Pactiv Llc
1900 W Field Ct
Lake Forest IL 60045
847 482-2000

(G-6749)
PEPSI-COLA BTLG HICKRY NC INC
Also Called: Pepsi-Cola
47 Duke St (28630-1807)
PHONE.................................828 322-8090
France Teeter, *Mgr*
EMP: 9
SALES (corp-wide): 50.09MM **Privately Held**
Web: www.pepsico.com
SIC: 5149 2086 Soft drinks; Bottled and canned soft drinks
PA: Pepsi-Cola Bottling Company Of Hickory, N.C., Inc.
2401 14th Avenue Cir Nw
Hickory NC 28601
828 322-8090

(G-6750)
PLAT LLC
5740 Rocky Mount Rd (28630-8308)
P.O. Box 1303 (28603-1303)
PHONE.................................828 358-4564
Pamela Jean Payne, *Mng Pt*
Jerry Strickland, *Mng Pt*
EMP: 10 **EST:** 2016
SQ FT: 5,000
SALES (est): 611.2K **Privately Held**
SIC: 2512 Upholstered household furniture

(G-6751)
PREGIS INNOVATIVE PACKG LLC (DH)
3825 N Main St (28630-8516)
PHONE.................................847 597-2200
Kevin Baudhuin, *Pr*
Keith Lavanway, *CFO*
EMP: 45 **EST:** 1997
SALES (est): 9.75MM
SALES (corp-wide): 810.75MM **Privately Held**
Web: www.pregis.com
SIC: 2671 5199 Paper; coated and laminated packaging; Packaging materials
HQ: Pregis Llc
2345 Waukegan Rd Ste 120
Bannockburn IL 60015

(G-6752)
PREGIS LLC
3825 N Main St (28630-8516)
PHONE.................................828 396-2373
Tony Smith, *Mgr*
EMP: 53
SALES (corp-wide): 810.75MM **Privately Held**
Web: www.pregis.com
SIC: 5999 2621 Foam and foam products; Wrapping and packaging papers
HQ: Pregis Llc
2345 Waukegan Rd Ste 120
Bannockburn IL 60015

(G-6753)
RICHARDS WELDING AND REPR INC
3080 Dry Ponds Rd (28630-9653)
PHONE.................................828 396-8705
Richard Miller, *Pr*
Kendra Miller, *Sec*
EMP: 6 **EST:** 1995
SALES (est): 494.74K **Privately Held**
Web: www.richardsweldingandrepair.com
SIC: 7692 Automotive welding

(G-6754)
ROBLON US INC
3908 Hickory Blvd (28630-8373)
PHONE.................................828 396-2121
Lars Stergaard, *Pr*
EMP: 60 **EST:** 2017
SALES (est): 20.99MM
SALES (corp-wide): 49.06MM **Privately Held**
Web: www.roblon.com
SIC: 3229 Fiber optics strands
HQ: Roblon Aktieselskab
Fabriksvej 7
Frederikshavn 9900
96203300

(G-6755)
ROYAL HOSIERY COMPANY INC (PA)
10 N Summit Ave (28630-1333)
P.O. Box 1053 (28630-1053)
PHONE.................................828 496-2200
▲ **EMP:** 6 **EST:** 1988
SQ FT: 28,000
SALES (est): 1.33MM **Privately Held**
Web: royalhosiery.blogspot.com
SIC: 2252 2251 Men's, boys', and girls' hosiery; Women's hosiery, except socks

(G-6756)
SHADOW LINE VINEYARD LLC
2550 Shadow Line Ln (28630-8101)
PHONE.................................828 234-5773
Geba R Davenport, *Admn*
EMP: 4 **EST:** 2014
SALES (est): 89.18K **Privately Held**
Web: www.shadowlinevineyard.com
SIC: 2084 Wines

(G-6757)
SHUFORD YARNS LLC
5100 Burns Rd (28630-8247)
PHONE.................................828 396-2342
Mike Bradshaw, *Brnch Mgr*
EMP: 108
Web: www.shufordyarns.com
SIC: 2281 Manmade and synthetic fiber yarns, spun
PA: Shuford Yarns, Llc
1985 Tate Blvd Se Ste 54
Hickory NC 28602

(G-6758)
SPECTRUM ADHESIVES INC
3815 N Main St (28630-8516)
PHONE.................................828 396-4200
Angela Clark, *Mgr*
EMP: 5
SALES (corp-wide): 9.65MM **Privately Held**
Web: www.spectrumadhesives.com
SIC: 2891 Glue
PA: Spectrum Adhesives, Inc.
5611 Universal Dr
Memphis TN 38118
901 795-1943

(G-6759)
W & S FRAME COMPANY INC
4833 J M Craig Rd (28630-9294)
PHONE.................................828 728-6078
Mark Smith, *Pr*
Maxine Smith, *Treas*
Tracy Smith, *Sec*
EMP: 13 **EST:** 1976
SALES (est): 503.95K **Privately Held**
SIC: 2426 Frames for upholstered furniture, wood

Granite Quarry
Rowan County

(G-6760)
GRANITE KNITWEAR INC (PA)
Also Called: Cal-Cru
805 S Salisbury Ave (28072)
P.O. Box 498 (28072-0498)
PHONE.................................704 279-5526
Michael R Jones, *Pr*
Billy Jones, *
▼ **EMP:** 38 **EST:** 1968
SQ FT: 31,200
SALES (est): 4.34MM
SALES (corp-wide): 4.34MM **Privately Held**
Web: www.calcru.com
SIC: 2321 2339 2335 Polo shirts, men's and boys': made from purchased materials; Women's and misses' outerwear, nec; Women's, junior's, and misses' dresses

(G-6761)
ROWAN PRECISION MACHINING INC
707 N Salisbury Ave (28072)
P.O. Box 778 (28072-0778)
PHONE.................................704 279-6092
Reginald J Hall Junior, *Pr*
Doris Hall, *Sec*

GEOGRAPHIC SECTION
Greensboro - Guilford County (G-6784)

EMP: 8 EST: 1985
SALES (est): 607.12K **Privately Held**
SIC: 3599 Machine shop, jobbing and repair

(G-6762)
SOUTHERN ATL SPRING MFG SLS LL
127 Rowan St (28072)
P.O. Box 1165 (28072-1165)
PHONE..................704 279-1331
Tony Nielsen, *Manager*
EMP: 31 EST: 2007
SALES (est): 2.98MM **Privately Held**
SIC: 3493 Steel springs, except wire

Grantsboro
Pamlico County

(G-6763)
BOBBY CAHOON CONSTRUCTION INC
Also Called: Bobby Choon Mar Cnstr Land Dev
6003 Neuse Rd (28529-9530)
PHONE..................252 249-1617
Teresa Cahoon, *Pr*
EMP: 25 EST: 1999
SALES (est): 2.52MM **Privately Held**
Web: www.bobbycahoonconstruction.com
SIC: 1629 4212 1442 1794 Dams, waterways, docks, and other marine construction; Local trucking, without storage; Construction sand and gravel; Excavation work

(G-6764)
C & C CHIPPING INC
Also Called: Cahoon, Bobby Logging
6003 Neuse Rd (28529-9530)
PHONE..................252 249-1617
Bobby Cahoon, *Pr*
EMP: 17 EST: 1990
SQ FT: 10,000
SALES (est): 430.49K **Privately Held**
Web: www.bobbycahoonconstruction.com
SIC: 2421 2439 Chipper mill; Structural wood members, nec

(G-6765)
PAMLICO PACKING CO INC (PA)
66 Cross Rd S (28529-5805)
P.O. Box 336 (28529-0336)
PHONE..................252 745-3688
William Ed Cross, *Pr*
Douglas E Cross, *VP*
Don Cross, *Sec*
EMP: 10 EST: 1944
SQ FT: 1,400
SALES (est): 5.49MM
SALES (corp-wide): 5.49MM **Privately Held**
Web: www.bestseafood.com
SIC: 2092 2091 5146 Seafoods, fresh: prepared; Bouillon, clam: packaged in cans, jars, etc.; Fish and seafoods

Greensboro
Guilford County

(G-6766)
3D UPFITTERS LLC
Also Called: Historical Aviation Tshirts
1814 Swannanoa Dr (27410-3934)
PHONE..................336 355-8673
EMP: 5 EST: 2017
SALES (est): 105.61K **Privately Held**
SIC: 2752 Commercial printing, lithographic

(G-6767)
A M MOORE AND COMPANY INC (PA)
Also Called: McLean Lighting Works
1207 Park Ter (27403-1957)
P.O. Box 20345 (27420-0345)
PHONE..................336 294-6994
Alexander Moore, *Pr*
▲ EMP: 8 EST: 1977
SALES (est): 852.09K
SALES (corp-wide): 852.09K **Privately Held**
Web: www.mcleanlighting.com
SIC: 3645 2499 3646 Residential lighting fixtures; Decorative wood and woodwork; Commercial lighting fixtures

(G-6768)
A TASTE OF HEAVENLY SWEETNESS
4518 W Market St (27407-1542)
PHONE..................336 825-7321
EMP: 7 EST: 2011
SQ FT: 1,000
SALES (est): 75.15K **Privately Held**
SIC: 2051 Cakes, bakery: except frozen

(G-6769)
A W SPEARS RESEARCH CTR
420 N English St (27405-7310)
PHONE..................336 335-6724
William True, *Prin*
EMP: 6 EST: 2013
SALES (est): 152.68K **Privately Held**
SIC: 2111 Cigarettes

(G-6770)
A-1 SANDROCK INC (PA)
Also Called: A-1 Trucking
2606 Phoenix Dr Ste 518 (27406-6351)
PHONE..................336 855-8195
Ronald Eugene Petty, *Pr*
Betty Petty, *VP*
Ronald E Petty, *VP*
EMP: 24 EST: 1987
SQ FT: 3,000
SALES (est): 6.81MM
SALES (corp-wide): 6.81MM **Privately Held**
Web: www.a-1servicegroup.com
SIC: 1442 4953 1629 Sand mining; Recycling, waste materials; Waste disposal plant construction

(G-6771)
ABACON TELECOMMUNICATIONS LLC (PA)
4388 Federal Dr (27410-8172)
PHONE..................336 855-1179
EMP: 22 EST: 1985
SQ FT: 30,400
SALES (est): 3.02MM
SALES (corp-wide): 3.02MM **Privately Held**
SIC: 3661 5065 Telephone and telegraph apparatus; Telephone and telegraphic equipment

(G-6772)
ABB MOTORS AND MECHANICAL INC
Also Called: Baldor Motors & Drives
1220 Rotherwood Rd (27406-3826)
P.O. Box 16500 (27416-0500)
PHONE..................336 272-6104
David Cousins, *Brnch Mgr*
EMP: 7
Web: www.baldor.com
SIC: 3621 5063 Motors, electric; Motors, electric
HQ: Abb Motors And Mechanical Inc.
5711 Rs Boreham Jr St
Fort Smith AR 72901
479 646-4711

(G-6773)
ABE ENTERCOM HOLDINGS LLC
Also Called: Lincoln Financial
100 N Greene St Ste M (27401-2530)
PHONE..................336 691-4337
Mendol Hoover, *Mgr*
EMP: 41
SALES (corp-wide): 1.25B **Publicly Held**
Web: www.audacyinc.com
SIC: 2759 Commercial printing, nec
HQ: Abe Entercom Holdings Llc
401 E City Ave Ste 809
Bala Cynwyd PA 19004
404 239-7211

(G-6774)
ABOLDER IMAGE
205 Aloe Rd (27409-2105)
P.O. Box 8565 (27419-0565)
PHONE..................336 856-1300
John Sturm, *Prin*
Ruth Sturm, *Prin*
EMP: 6 EST: 2016
SALES (est): 208.47K **Privately Held**
Web: www.abolderimage.net
SIC: 2752 Offset printing

(G-6775)
AC CORPORATION (DH)
Also Called: AC Corporation North Carolina
301 Creek Ridge Rd (27406-4421)
P.O. Box 16367 (27416-0367)
PHONE..................336 273-4472
▲ EMP: 440 EST: 1935
SALES (est): 57.95MM
SALES (corp-wide): 216.28MM **Privately Held**
Web: www.accorporation.com
SIC: 1711 1731 3556 3823 Warm air heating and air conditioning contractor; Electrical work; Food products machinery; Industrial process control instruments
HQ: Crete Mechanical Group, Inc.
2701 N Rocky Point Dr # 660
Tampa FL 33607
833 273-8364

(G-6776)
ACCURIDE CORPORATION
7031 Albert Pick Rd Ste 305 (27409-9522)
PHONE..................336 393-0671
George Anderson, *Mgr*
EMP: 7
Web: www.accuridecorp.com
SIC: 3714 Wheels, motor vehicle
HQ: Accuride Corporation
38777 6 Mile Rd Ste 410
Livonia MI 48152
812 962-5000

(G-6777)
ACE CSTM KICKS N PRINTS LLC
5939 W Friendly Ave Apt 26l (27410-3330)
PHONE..................336 457-9059
Ariel Davies, *Managing Member*
EMP: 4 EST: 2021
SALES (est): 83.67K **Privately Held**
Web: a-c-e-customs.ueniweb.com
SIC: 2752 Commercial printing, lithographic

(G-6778)
ACTON CORPORATION
1451 S Elm Eugene St (27406-2200)
PHONE..................434 728-4491
Said Elfayar, *CEO*
EMP: 6 EST: 2013
SALES (est): 466.4K **Privately Held**
SIC: 2873 Fertilizers: natural (organic), except compost

(G-6779)
ADEMCO INC
Also Called: ADI Global Distribution
4500 Green Point Dr (27410-8125)
PHONE..................336 668-3644
Anna Ferguson, *Brnch Mgr*
EMP: 6
SALES (corp-wide): 6.24B **Publicly Held**
Web: www.adiglobaldistribution.us
SIC: 5063 3669 Electrical apparatus and equipment; Emergency alarms
HQ: Ademco Inc.
275 Broadhollow Rd # 400
Melville NY 11747
631 692-1000

(G-6780)
ADVANCE STORES COMPANY INC
Also Called: Advance Auto Parts
2514 Battleground Ave Ste A (27408-1938)
PHONE..................336 545-9091
West Gregory, *Mgr*
EMP: 10
SALES (corp-wide): 11.15B **Publicly Held**
Web: shop.advanceautoparts.com
SIC: 5531 7534 5063 Auto and truck equipment and parts; Tire retreading and repair shops; Storage batteries, industrial
HQ: Advance Stores Company Incorporated
5008 Airport Rd Nw
Roanoke VA 24012
540 362-4911

(G-6781)
ADVANCED SUBSTRATE
7860 Thorndike Rd (27409-9690)
PHONE..................336 285-5955
EMP: 10 EST: 2009
SALES (est): 978.75K **Privately Held**
Web: www.advancedsubstrate.com
SIC: 3679 Electronic circuits

(G-6782)
ADVANCED TECH SYSTEMS INC
2606 Phoenix Dr Ste 602 (27406-6355)
PHONE..................336 299-6695
Jeffery Bill, *Pr*
EMP: 15 EST: 2002
SALES (est): 2.33MM **Privately Held**
Web: www.atstriad.com
SIC: 3651 Household audio and video equipment

(G-6783)
ADVANCED TECHNOLOGY INC
Also Called: ATI Laminates
6106 W Market St (27409-2040)
PHONE..................336 668-0488
◆ EMP: 45 EST: 1979
SALES (est): 8.75MM **Privately Held**
Web: www.atilaminates.com
SIC: 3446 5162 Architectural metalwork; Plastics materials and basic shapes

(G-6784)
AEROSPACE FILTRATION DIVISION
8439 Triad Dr (27409-9018)
PHONE..................336 668-4444
EMP: 5 EST: 2019
SALES (est): 27.98K **Privately Held**
SIC: 3569 General industrial machinery, nec

Greensboro - Guilford County (G-6785)

(G-6785)
AFFORDABLE BEDS & FURNITURE
Also Called: ABF Store
4607 W Gate City Blvd (27407-2956)
P.O. Box 7496 (27417-0496)
PHONE..................................336 988-1520
EMP: 7 EST: 2016
SALES (est): 90.18K Privately Held
Web:
www.consignmentstoregreensboronc.com
SIC: 2511 Wood bedroom furniture

(G-6786)
AFFORDABLE WHEELCHAIR VANS LLC
1304 Quail Dr (27408-6116)
PHONE..................................910 443-6989
Ohn Bishop Byerly, Prin
EMP: 4 EST: 2018
SALES (est): 75.56K Privately Held
Web: www.amsvans.com
SIC: 3842 Wheelchairs

(G-6787)
AKZO NOBEL COATINGS INC
Also Called: Car RE Finish
4500 Green Point Dr Ste 104 (27410-8125)
PHONE..................................336 665-9897
EMP: 8
SALES (corp-wide): 11.26B Privately Held
SIC: 5198 2851 Paints; Paints: oil or alkyd vehicle or water thinned
HQ: Akzo Nobel Coatings Inc.
   535 Marriott Dr Ste 500
   Nashville TN 37214
   440 297-5100

(G-6788)
ALAMANCE IRON WORKS INC
3900 Patterson St (27407-3240)
PHONE..................................336 852-5940
Kurt Lents, Pr
EMP: 8 EST: 1970
SQ FT: 900
SALES (est): 621.15K Privately Held
Web: www.alamanceironworks.com
SIC: 1799 1521 3446 Ornamental metal work; General remodeling, single-family houses; Fences or posts, ornamental iron or steel

(G-6789)
ALAMEEN A HAQQ
4424 Gray Wolf Way (27406-8099)
PHONE..................................336 965-8339
Alameen A Haqq, Prin
EMP: 6 EST: 2007
SALES (est): 105.35K Privately Held
SIC: 2711 Newspapers, publishing and printing

(G-6790)
ALBERDINGK BOLEY INC
6008 W Gate City Blvd (27407-7009)
PHONE..................................336 454-5000
Thomas Baur, Pr
Frank Dreisoerner, *
Beth Foust, *
◆ EMP: 69 EST: 2000
SQ FT: 125,000
SALES (est): 28.36MM
SALES (corp-wide): 322.33MM Privately Held
Web: www.alberdingkusa.com
SIC: 2851 Coating, air curing
PA: Alberdingk Boley Gmbh
   Dusseldorfer Str. 53
   Krefeld NW 47829
   21515280

(G-6791)
ALLEN INDUSTRIES INC (PA)
6434 Burnt Poplar Rd (27409-9712)
PHONE..................................336 668-2791
Thomas L Allen, Pr
John Allen, General Vice President*
David W Allen, *
▼ EMP: 100 EST: 1931
SQ FT: 75,000
SALES (est): 76.87MM
SALES (corp-wide): 76.87MM Privately Held
Web: www.allenindustries.com
SIC: 3993 Electric signs

(G-6792)
ALLEN INDUSTRIES INC
4100 Sheraton Ct (27410-8120)
PHONE..................................336 294-4777
Tom Allen, Brnch Mgr
EMP: 103
SQ FT: 69,650
SALES (corp-wide): 76.87MM Privately Held
Web: www.allenindustries.com
SIC: 3993 Electric signs
PA: Allen Industries, Inc.
   6434 Burnt Poplar Rd
   Greensboro NC 27409
   336 668-2791

(G-6793)
ALLIANCE HOSE & TUBE WORKS INC
3012 S Elm Eugene Street Ste F (27406-4455)
PHONE..................................336 378-9736
Jeoff Ash, Owner
▲ EMP: 7 EST: 2007
SALES (est): 141.65K Privately Held
Web: www.alliancehtw.com
SIC: 3052 3317 Rubber hose; Tubes, seamless steel

(G-6794)
ALTERNATIVE INGREDIENTS INC
300 Dougherty St (27406-4306)
P.O. Box 16846 (27416-0846)
PHONE..................................336 378-5368
James A Murphy Junior, Ch
Robin W Conner, VP
Ashley Sutton, Sec
EMP: 7 EST: 2014
SALES (est): 217.07K Privately Held
SIC: 2087 Concentrates, flavoring (except drink)

(G-6795)
ALUMINUM SCREEN MANUFACTURING
4501 Green Point Dr Ste 104 (27410-8141)
PHONE..................................336 605-8080
Donny Rauschuber, Pr
EMP: 8 EST: 2006
SALES (est): 249.63K Privately Held
Web: www.nrmlaw.com
SIC: 3496 Screening, woven wire: made from purchased wire

(G-6796)
AMALFI SEMICONDUCTOR INC
7628 Thorndike Rd (27409-9421)
PHONE..................................336 664-1233
EMP: 8 EST: 2019
SALES (est): 2.5MM
SALES (corp-wide): 3.57B Publicly Held
Web: www.qorvo.com
SIC: 3674 Semiconductors and related devices
PA: Qorvo, Inc.

7628 Thorndike Rd
Greensboro NC 27409
336 664-1233

(G-6797)
AMERICAN CITY BUS JOURNALS INC
Also Called: Triad Business Journal
101 S Elm St Ste 100 (27401-2649)
PHONE..................................336 271-6539
Douglas Copeland, Publisher
EMP: 141
SALES (corp-wide): 2.88B Privately Held
Web: www.acbj.com
SIC: 2711 Newspapers: publishing only, not printed on site
HQ: American City Business Journals, Inc.
   120 W Morehead St Ste 400
   Charlotte NC 28202
   704 973-1000

(G-6798)
AMERICAN CLTVTION EXTRCTION SV
245 E Friendly Ave Ste 100 (27401-2986)
PHONE..................................336 544-1072
EMP: 8 EST: 2019
SALES (est): 462.06K Privately Held
SIC: 2079 Edible fats and oils

(G-6799)
AMERICAN EXTRUDED PLASTICS INC
938 Reynolds Pl (27403-2212)
P.O. Box 7422 (27417-0422)
PHONE..................................336 274-1131
EMP: 30 EST: 1983
SALES (est): 7.14MM
SALES (corp-wide): 295.68MM Privately Held
Web: www.aeplastics.com
SIC: 3082 Unsupported plastics profile shapes
PA: Pexco Llc
   6470 E Johns Xing Ste 430
   Johns Creek GA 30097
   678 990-1523

(G-6800)
AMERICAN INDIAN PRINTING INC
Also Called: Bulldog Printing
1310 Beaman Pl (27408-8704)
PHONE..................................336 230-1551
Robert Martin Bundy, Pr
EMP: 4 EST: 1994
SALES (est): 489.69K Privately Held
Web: www.ncbulldogprinting.com
SIC: 2752 Offset printing

(G-6801)
AMERICAN PRINTING CO INC
600c Edwardia Dr (27409-2806)
P.O. Box 18244 (27419-8244)
PHONE..................................336 852-9894
Daniel Wright, Pr
EMP: 6 EST: 1997
SALES (est): 366.2K Privately Held
SIC: 2752 Offset printing

(G-6802)
AMERICAN VALVE INC (PA)
Also Called: Accord Ventilation Products
4321 Piedmont Pkwy (27410-8114)
PHONE..................................336 668-0554
Seth Guterman, Pr
Seth Guterman, CEO
Jeff Shaver, *
Carolyn Hinterberger, *
Marcy Jane Crump, *
▲ EMP: 60 EST: 1994

SQ FT: 20,000
SALES (est): 8.78MM Privately Held
Web: www.americanvalve.com
SIC: 3494 5074 Plumbing and heating valves; Plumbing fittings and supplies

(G-6803)
AMERITEK INC
118 S Walnut Cir (27409-2625)
PHONE..................................336 292-1165
EMP: 22 EST: 1996
SALES (est): 3.5MM Privately Held
Web: www.ameritekinc.com
SIC: 3544 Special dies and tools

(G-6804)
AMERITEK INC
122 S Walnut Cir Ste B (27409-2625)
PHONE..................................336 292-1165
Bill Hicks, Prin
EMP: 19 EST: 2007
SALES (est): 1.44MM Privately Held
Web: www.ameritekinc.com
SIC: 3554 Paper industries machinery

(G-6805)
AMERITEK LASERCUT DIES INC
Also Called: Ameritek
122 S Walnut Cir Ste B (27409-2641)
PHONE..................................336 292-1165
Bill Hicks, Pr
EMP: 24 EST: 1960
SQ FT: 22,000
SALES (est): 912.77K Privately Held
Web: www.ameritekinc.com
SIC: 3544 Special dies and tools

(G-6806)
AMPLIFIED ELCTRONIC DESIGN INC
Also Called: Amped
7617 Boeing Dr (27409-9046)
P.O. Box 747 (27310-0747)
PHONE..................................336 223-4811
Sidney L Flake Iii, Pr
Robin Flake, Sec
EMP: 13 EST: 2012
SALES (est): 929.78K Privately Held
Web: www.ampedco.com
SIC: 1731 3669 8748 7382 Voice, data, and video wiring contractor; Intercommunication systems, electric; Communications consulting; Protective devices, security

(G-6807)
ANALOG DEVICES INC
7910 Triad Center Dr (27409-9758)
PHONE..................................336 668-9511
Gary Selders, Mgr
EMP: 30
SQ FT: 6,000
SALES (corp-wide): 12.31B Publicly Held
Web: www.analog.com
SIC: 3674 Integrated circuits, semiconductor networks, etc.
PA: Analog Devices, Inc.
   1 Analog Way
   Wilmington MA 01887
   781 935-5565

(G-6808)
ANGUNIQUE
6190 Pine Cove Ct (27410-9570)
PHONE..................................336 392-5866
Kenneth Henderson, Prin
EMP: 5 EST: 2010
SALES (est): 113.77K Privately Held
Web: www.angunique.com
SIC: 2323 Men's and boy's neckwear

GEOGRAPHIC SECTION
Greensboro - Guilford County (G-6834)

(G-6809)
ANNDORI OUTDOOR ART LLC
4001 Hickory Tree Ln (27405-9600)
PHONE..................................336 202-8400
Sandra Alexander, *Managing Member*
Rondal Alexander, *Sec*
EMP: 22 **EST:** 2012
SALES (est): 905.46K **Privately Held**
SIC: 3699 Christmas tree lighting sets, electric

(G-6810)
APEX ANALYTIX LLC (HQ)
1501 Highwoods Blvd Ste 200 (27410-2050)
PHONE..................................336 272-4669
Steve Yurko, *CEO*
John Roberts, *
EMP: 150 **EST:** 1988
SALES (est): 61.87MM
SALES (corp-wide): 61.87MM **Privately Held**
Web: www.apexanalytix.com
SIC: 8742 7389 7372 Management consulting services; Financial services; Prepackaged software
PA: Apex Analytix Holding Llc
1501 Highwoods Blvd # 200
Greensboro NC 27410
336 272-4669

(G-6811)
APPLE ROCK ADVG & PROM INC (PA)
Also Called: Apple Rock Displays
7602 Business Park Dr (27409-9696)
PHONE..................................336 232-4800
Eric Burg, *Pr*
Eric Burg, *CEO*
Terri Burg, *
Diane Rowell, *
Heidi Sanfilippo, *
EMP: 45 **EST:** 1988
SQ FT: 110,000
SALES (est): 22.46MM **Privately Held**
Web: www.applerock.com
SIC: 7319 8743 3993 Display advertising service; Promotion service; Signs and advertising specialties

(G-6812)
ARC3 GASES INC
810 Post St (27405-7261)
PHONE..................................336 275-3333
Danny Hollifield, *Mgr*
EMP: 10
SALES (corp-wide): 204.15MM **Privately Held**
Web: www.arc3gases.com
SIC: 2813 5169 7359 7692 Industrial gases; Chemicals and allied products, nec; Equipment rental and leasing, nec; Welding repair
PA: Arc3 Gases, Inc.
1600 Us 301 S
Dunn NC 28334
910 892-4016

(G-6813)
ARCHIE SUPPLY LLC (PA)
5939 W Friendly Ave Apt 51k (27410-3330)
PHONE..................................336 987-0895
Brent Archie, *CEO*
EMP: 5 **EST:** 2014
SALES (est): 729.27K
SALES (corp-wide): 729.27K **Privately Held**
Web: www.archiesupply.com
SIC: 0279 5712 5112 5111 Worm farms; Office furniture; Stationery and office supplies; Printing and writing paper

(G-6814)
ARK AVIATION INC
200 N Raleigh St (27401-4822)
PHONE..................................336 379-0900
Carl Rshew, *Pr*
EMP: 8 **EST:** 2021
SALES (est): 904.54K **Privately Held**
Web: www.arkaviation.aero
SIC: 3728 Aircraft parts and equipment, nec

(G-6815)
ARNOLD B COCHRANE INC
3 Kenbridge Ct (27410-6044)
PHONE..................................336 294-8038
David M Cochrane, *Pr*
EMP: 4 **EST:** 2000
SALES (est): 192.7K **Privately Held**
SIC: 2519 Household furniture, except wood or metal: upholstered

(G-6816)
ARROWHEAD GRAPHICS INC
508 Houston St (27401-2332)
PHONE..................................336 274-2419
Bill Revels, *Pr*
William Revels Junior, *Pr*
EMP: 4 **EST:** 1979
SQ FT: 3,100
SALES (est): 447.96K **Privately Held**
Web: www.arrowheadgraphics.com
SIC: 2752 2759 Offset printing; Letterpress printing

(G-6817)
ARTIST S NEEDLE INC
2611 Phoenix Dr (27406-6320)
PHONE..................................336 294-5884
Mike Warwick, *Pr*
EMP: 8 **EST:** 2002
SQ FT: 5,000
SALES (est): 425.14K **Privately Held**
Web: www.artistneedle.com
SIC: 5949 2395 Sewing supplies; Embroidery products, except Schiffli machine

(G-6818)
ASHDAN ENTERPRISES
608 Summit Ave Ste 201 (27405-7754)
P.O. Box 67 (27301-0067)
PHONE..................................336 375-9698
EMP: 4 **EST:** 1970
SALES (est): 226.85K **Privately Held**
SIC: 5719 3469 Kitchenware; Household cooking and kitchen utensils, metal

(G-6819)
ASI SIGNAGE INNOVATIONS
4204 Hobbs Rd (27410-3516)
PHONE..................................336 508-4668
Silas Bass, *VP*
EMP: 6 **EST:** 2014
SALES (est): 91.52K **Privately Held**
Web: www.asisignage.net
SIC: 3993 Signs and advertising specialties

(G-6820)
ASP DISTRIBUTION INC
100 Bonita Dr (27405-7602)
PHONE..................................336 375-5672
Michael Caviness, *Pr*
EMP: 10 **EST:** 2003
SALES (est): 990.42K **Privately Held**
SIC: 3281 Curbing, granite or stone

(G-6821)
ATLANTIC BANKCARD CENTER INC
Also Called: Cardservice of Carolinas
2920 Manufacturers Rd (27406-4606)
PHONE..................................336 855-9250
EMP: 8 **EST:** 1992
SQ FT: 1,500
SALES (est): 238.9K **Privately Held**
Web: www.posregister.com
SIC: 7389 3578 Credit card service; Cash registers

(G-6822)
AURORIUM LLC
Also Called: Aurorium
2110 W Gate City Blvd (27403-2642)
PHONE..................................336 292-1781
John Van Hulle, *CEO*
EMP: 100
SALES (corp-wide): 636.82MM **Privately Held**
Web: www.aurorium.com
SIC: 2869 Industrial organic chemicals, nec
HQ: Aurorium Llc
201 N Illinois St # 1800
Indianapolis IN 46204
317 247-8141

(G-6823)
AUTUMN CREEK VINEYARDS INC
2105 Lafayette Ave (27408-6303)
PHONE..................................336 548-9463
Timothy Quinton Haley, *Prin*
EMP: 7 **EST:** 2007
SALES (est): 547.73K **Privately Held**
Web: www.gioiadellamorecellars.com
SIC: 2084 Wines

(G-6824)
AVERY DENNISON CORPORATION
2100 Summit Ave (27405-5012)
PHONE..................................336 621-2570
Simon Coulson, *Genl Mgr*
EMP: 75
SALES (corp-wide): 8.36B **Publicly Held**
Web: www.averydennison.com
SIC: 2672 Paper; coated and laminated, nec
PA: Avery Dennison Corporation
8080 Norton Pkwy
Mentor OH 44060
440 534-6000

(G-6825)
AVERY DENNISON CORPORATION
620 Green Valley Rd Ste 306 (27408-7729)
PHONE..................................336 553-2436
Greg Knoll, *VP*
EMP: 5
SALES (corp-wide): 8.36B **Publicly Held**
Web: www.averydennison.com
SIC: 2672 Adhesive papers, labels, or tapes: from purchased material
PA: Avery Dennison Corporation
8080 Norton Pkwy
Mentor OH 44060
440 534-6000

(G-6826)
AVERY DENNISON CORPORATION
1100 Revolution Mill Dr # 11 (27405-5067)
PHONE..................................336 856-8235
EMP: 5
SALES (corp-wide): 8.36B **Publicly Held**
Web: www.averydennison.com
SIC: 2672 Adhesive backed films, foams and foils
PA: Avery Dennison Corporation
8080 Norton Pkwy
Mentor OH 44060
440 534-6000

(G-6827)
AVERY DENNISON CORPORATION
Avery Dennison
1100 Revolution Mill Dr # 11 (27405-5067)
PHONE..................................864 938-1400
Al Greene, *Brnch Mgr*
EMP: 5
SALES (corp-wide): 8.36B **Publicly Held**
Web: www.averydennison.com
SIC: 2672 Coated paper, except photographic, carbon, or abrasive
PA: Avery Dennison Corporation
8080 Norton Pkwy
Mentor OH 44060
440 534-6000

(G-6828)
AVERY DENNISON CORPORATION
200 Citation Ct (27409-9026)
PHONE..................................336 665-6481
David Bullard, *Mgr*
EMP: 11
SALES (corp-wide): 8.36B **Publicly Held**
Web: www.averydennison.com
SIC: 2672 Coated paper, except photographic, carbon, or abrasive
PA: Avery Dennison Corporation
8080 Norton Pkwy
Mentor OH 44060
440 534-6000

(G-6829)
AVERY DENNISON RFID COMPANY
1100 Revolution Mill Dr # 11 (27405-5067)
PHONE..................................626 304-2000
Starla Parrish, *Dir*
EMP: 11 **EST:** 2016
SALES (est): 459.42K **Privately Held**
SIC: 2672 Paper; coated and laminated, nec

(G-6830)
B & J TOOL INC
4515 Pleasant Garden Rd (27406-9241)
PHONE..................................336 265-8306
Bryan Welch, *Prin*
EMP: 5 **EST:** 2019
SALES (est): 80.08K **Privately Held**
SIC: 3599 Machine shop, jobbing and repair

(G-6831)
BARKER AND MARTIN INC
Also Called: Phil Barker's Refinishing
1316 Headquarters Dr (27405-7920)
PHONE..................................336 275-5056
Phil Barker, *Pr*
EMP: 4 **EST:** 1976
SQ FT: 2,500
SALES (est): 232.56K **Privately Held**
Web: www.philbarkerantiques.com
SIC: 7641 2511 5932 Furniture refinishing; Wood household furniture; Antiques

(G-6832)
BARRIER1 SYSTEMS INC
Also Called: Barrier1
8015 Thorndike Rd (27409-9412)
PHONE..................................336 617-8478
Michael J Lamore, *Pr*
EMP: 12 **EST:** 2006
SALES (est): 2.66MM **Privately Held**
Web: www.barrier1.com
SIC: 3499 Barricades, metal

(G-6833)
BEACHBUB USA
561 Pegg Rd (27409-9413)
PHONE..................................336 965-5941
EMP: 4 **EST:** 2018
SALES (est): 69.34K **Privately Held**
Web: www.beachbub.com
SIC: 3999 Manufacturing industries, nec

(G-6834)
BENGAL-PROTEA LTD
Also Called: Bengal Protea

Greensboro - Guilford County (G-6835)   GEOGRAPHIC SECTION

600 Green Valley Rd Ste 303 (27408-7731)
PHONE..............................336 299-0299
EMP: 4 **EST:** 1995
SALES (est): 204.96K **Privately Held**
SIC: 3915 5094 Diamond cutting and polishing; Diamonds (gems)

(G-6835)
BENNETT UNIFORM MFG INC (PA)
4377 Federal Dr (27410-8116)
PHONE..............................336 232-5772
Ervon R Bennett, *Pr*
Beatrice R Bennett, *Sec*
◆ **EMP:** 18 **EST:** 1972
SQ FT: 36,000
SALES (est): 2.13MM
SALES (corp-wide): 2.13MM **Privately Held**
Web: www.bennettuniform.com
SIC: 2337 2326 2339 Uniforms, except athletic: women's, misses', and juniors'; Work uniforms; Women's and misses' outerwear, nec

(G-6836)
BERCO OF AMERICA INC
615 Pegg Rd (27409-9414)
PHONE..............................336 931-1415
Marco Malsatti, *Brnch Mgr*
EMP: 28
SALES (corp-wide): 40.78B **Privately Held**
Web: www.thyssenkrupp-berco.com
SIC: 3531 5082 Construction machinery; General construction machinery and equipment
HQ: Berco Of America, Inc.
W229n1420 Westwood Dr
Waukesha WI 53186

(G-6837)
BEST PRICE APPLIANCE LLC
2101 Patterson St Ste A (27407-2547)
PHONE..............................336 662-3117
EMP: 4 **EST:** 2019
SALES (est): 82.1K **Privately Held**
Web: best-price-appliance.business.site
SIC: 5722 3639 Household appliance stores; Household appliances, nec

(G-6838)
BIBEY MACHINE COMPANY INC
642 S Spring St (27406-1252)
PHONE..............................336 275-9421
Ronald G Bibey, *Pr*
Ken Younger, *
Kathy Bibey, *
EMP: 45 **EST:** 1978
SQ FT: 25,000
SALES (est): 8.43MM **Privately Held**
Web: www.bibeymachine.com
SIC: 3599 Machine shop, jobbing and repair

(G-6839)
BIO-TECH PRSTHTICS ORTHTICS IN (HQ)
Also Called: Hanger Clinic
2301 N Church St (27405-4309)
PHONE..............................336 333-9081
EMP: 7 **EST:** 1995
SQ FT: 1,600
SALES (est): 5.81MM
SALES (corp-wide): 1.12B **Privately Held**
Web: www.hangerclinic.com
SIC: 3842 5999 5661 Prosthetic appliances; Orthopedic and prosthesis applications; Shoes, orthopedic
PA: Hanger, Inc.
10910 Domain Dr Ste 300
Austin TX 78758
512 777-3800

(G-6840)
BLACK & DECKER (US) INC
Also Called: Dewalt Industrial Tool
4621 W Gate City Blvd (27407-4239)
PHONE..............................336 852-1300
Chris Dennis, *Mgr*
EMP: 5
SALES (corp-wide): 15.78B **Publicly Held**
Web: www.blackanddecker.com
SIC: 3546 Power-driven handtools
HQ: Black & Decker (U.S.) Inc.
1000 Stanley Dr
New Britain CT 06053
860 225-5111

(G-6841)
BLACKTIP SOLUTIONS
3125 Kathleen Ave Ste 221 (27408-7819)
PHONE..............................336 303-1580
Kevin Walsh, *Admn*
EMP: 4 **EST:** 2019
SALES (est): 80K **Privately Held**
SIC: 7372 Application computer software

(G-6842)
BLUE SUN ENERGY INC
408 Gallimore Dairy Rd Ste C (27409-9526)
PHONE..............................336 218-6707
▲ **EMP:** 4 **EST:** 2009
SALES (est): 271.74K **Privately Held**
Web: www.bluesunenergy.com
SIC: 3648 5063 Lighting equipment, nec; Light bulbs and related supplies

(G-6843)
BLUESCOPE BUILDINGS N AMER INC
Also Called: Varco Pruden Buildings
7031 Albert Pick Rd Ste 200 (27409-9537)
PHONE..............................336 996-4801
Tim Mcneely, *Brnch Mgr*
EMP: 134
Web: www.bluescopeconstruction.com
SIC: 3448 Prefabricated metal buildings and components
HQ: Bluescope Buildings North America, Inc.
1540 Genessee St
Kansas City MO 64102

(G-6844)
BLUETICK INC
Also Called: Bluetick Services
1501 Highwoods Blvd Ste 104 (27410-2050)
PHONE..............................336 294-4102
Michael Mills, *Pr*
EMP: 16 **EST:** 2009
SALES (est): 2.12MM **Privately Held**
Web: www.bluetickinc.com
SIC: 7379 4899 7375 7371 Online services technology consultants; Data communication services; On-line data base information retrieval; Computer software development and applications

(G-6845)
BLYTHE CONSTRUCTION INC
2606 Phoenix Dr Ste 502 (27406-6351)
PHONE..............................336 854-9003
David Melton, *Mgr*
EMP: 42
SALES (corp-wide): 16.98MM **Privately Held**
Web: www.blytheconstruction.com
SIC: 1611 2951 Highway and street paving contractor; Asphalt paving mixtures and blocks
HQ: Blythe Construction, Inc.
2911 N Graham St
Charlotte NC 28206
704 375-8474

(G-6846)
BOB HARRINGTON ASSOC
3411 N Rockingham Rd (27407-7247)
PHONE..............................336 855-7252
Robert Harrington, *CEO*
EMP: 4 **EST:** 1996
SALES (est): 66.08K **Privately Held**
Web: www.bobharringtonassociates.com
SIC: 1442 Construction sand and gravel

(G-6847)
BONSAL AMERICAN INC
139 S Walnut Cir (27409-2624)
PHONE..............................336 854-8200
Robert Carter, *Brnch Mgr*
EMP: 5
SALES (corp-wide): 32.72B **Privately Held**
SIC: 3272 Concrete products, nec
HQ: Bonsal American, Inc.
625 Griffith Rd Ste 100
Charlotte NC 28217
704 525-1621

(G-6848)
BOOMERANG FOODS LLC
2602 Lamroc Rd (27407-6609)
PHONE..............................336 558-3798
Travis N Mcadoo, *Prin*
EMP: 4 **EST:** 2018
SALES (est): 47.08K **Privately Held**
SIC: 3949 Boomerangs

(G-6849)
BOX BOARD PRODUCTS INC
8313 Triad Dr (27409-9621)
P.O. Box 18863 (27419-8863)
PHONE..............................336 668-3347
TOLL FREE: 800
▲ **EMP:** 220 **EST:** 1968
SALES (est): 51.94MM
SALES (corp-wide): 5.22B **Publicly Held**
Web: www.boxboardproducts.com
SIC: 5113 2671 Corrugated and solid fiber boxes; Paper; coated and laminated packaging
PA: Greif, Inc.
425 Winter Rd
Delaware OH 43015
740 549-6000

(G-6850)
BRETAGNE LLC
814 Pebble Dr (27410-4534)
PHONE..............................336 299-8729
EMP: 4 **EST:** 2010
SALES (est): 173.09K **Privately Held**
SIC: 1311 Crude petroleum and natural gas

(G-6851)
BRICE MANUFACTURING CO INC
Also Called: Haeco Americas Cabin Solutions
8010 Piedmont Triad Pkwy (27409-9407)
PHONE..............................818 896-2938
Richard Kendall, *CEO*
Mark Peterman, *
Lee Fox, *
▲ **EMP:** 25 **EST:** 1968
SALES (est): 7.82MM
SALES (corp-wide): 17.24B **Privately Held**
Web: www.timco.aero
SIC: 3728 7641 Aircraft parts and equipment, nec; Furniture repair and maintenance
HQ: Haeco Americas, Llc
623 Radar Rd
Greensboro NC 27410

(G-6852)
BRIDGESTONE RET OPERATIONS LLC
Also Called: Firestone
3311 Battleground Ave (27410-2401)
PHONE..............................336 282-6646
Dylan Smith, *Mgr*
EMP: 8
Web: www.bridgestoneamericas.com
SIC: 5531 7534 Automotive tires; Rebuilding and retreading tires
HQ: Bridgestone Retail Operations, Llc
333 E Lake St Ste 300
Bloomingdale IL 60108
630 259-9000

(G-6853)
BRIDGESTONE RET OPERATIONS LLC
Also Called: Firestone
3937 W Gate City Blvd (27407-4611)
PHONE..............................336 852-8524
Noel Cecil, *Mgr*
EMP: 10
SQ FT: 6,349
Web: www.bridgestoneamericas.com
SIC: 5531 7534 7539 Automotive tires; Rebuilding and retreading tires; Brake services
HQ: Bridgestone Retail Operations, Llc
333 E Lake St Ste 300
Bloomingdale IL 60108
630 259-9000

(G-6854)
BRIDGETOWER MEDIA LLC (PA)
7025 Albert Pick Rd Ste 200 (27409-9539)
PHONE..............................612 317-9420
Hal Cohen, *CEO*
Tom Callahan, *CFO*
EMP: 26 **EST:** 2015
SALES (est): 11.2MM
SALES (corp-wide): 11.2MM **Privately Held**
Web: www.bridgetowermedia.com
SIC: 2711 Newspapers: publishing only, not printed on site

(G-6855)
BRILLIANT YOU LLC
1451 S Elm Eugene St Ste 1102 (27406-2200)
PHONE..............................336 343-5535
EMP: 7 **EST:** 2012
SALES (est): 493.65K **Privately Held**
Web: www.brilliantyoudenim.com
SIC: 2339 2325 Jeans: women's, misses', and juniors'; Men's and boys' jeans and dungarees

(G-6856)
BRISPA INVESTMENTS INC
4833 W Gate City Blvd (27407-5305)
P.O. Box 77634 (27417-7634)
PHONE..............................336 668-3636
Stephen K Bright, *Pr*
L Kirk Sparks, *
Joseph H Vest, *
Jo Anna Bright, *
▲ **EMP:** 105 **EST:** 1987
SQ FT: 115,000
SALES (est): 16.56MM **Privately Held**
Web: www.brightplastics.com
SIC: 3089 Injection molding of plastics

(G-6857)
BRISTOL-MYERS SQUIBB COMPANY
Bristol-Myers Squibb
211 American Ave (27409-1803)
PHONE..............................336 855-5500

GEOGRAPHIC SECTION

Greensboro - Guilford County (G-6883)

Michael Hession, *Brnch Mgr*
EMP: 400
SALES (corp-wide): 45.01B **Publicly Held**
Web: www.bms.com
SIC: 2834 Pharmaceutical preparations
PA: Bristol-Myers Squibb Company
430 E 29th St Fl 14
New York NY 10016
212 546-4000

(G-6858)
BRITTANY SMITH
Also Called: Glitzbybritt
2508 Glenhaven Dr (27406-4211)
PHONE..................912 313-0588
Brittany Smith, *Owner*
EMP: 8 **EST:** 2021
SALES (est): 245.56K **Privately Held**
SIC: 3999 Hair and hair-based products

(G-6859)
BRUSHY MOUNTAIN DRY KILNS LLC
10 Branch Ct (27408-6305)
PHONE..................336 379-8314
EMP: 5 **EST:** 2010
SALES (est): 150.32K **Privately Held**
SIC: 3559 Kilns

(G-6860)
BUILDERS FIRSTSOURCE INC
7601 Boeing Dr (27409-9046)
PHONE..................336 884-5454
Oza Humphrey, *Brnch Mgr*
EMP: 4
SALES (corp-wide): 17.1B **Publicly Held**
Web: www.bldr.com
SIC: 2421 5211 2431 Building and structural materials, wood; Lumber and other building materials; Doors and door parts and trim, wood
PA: Builders Firstsource, Inc.
6031 Connection Dr # 400
Irving TX 75039
214 880-3500

(G-6861)
BURLINGTON CHEMICAL CO LLC
8646 W Market St Ste 116 (27409-9447)
PHONE..................336 584-0111
Bret Holmes, *Managing Member*
Michael Matzinger, *Prin*
◆ **EMP:** 7 **EST:** 1954
SQ FT: 23,000
SALES (est): 4.38MM **Privately Held**
Web: www.burco.com
SIC: 5169 2899 2865 Dyestuffs; Chemical preparations, nec; Cyclic crudes and intermediates

(G-6862)
BURLINGTON DISTRIBUTING CO
Also Called: Old Master Cabinets
2232 Westbrook St (27407-2524)
P.O. Box 5486 (27435-0486)
PHONE..................336 292-1415
Joseph P Mitchell Senior, *Pr*
William S Mitchell, *VP*
Gerald R Mitchell, *VP*
EMP: 8 **EST:** 1958
SQ FT: 16,000
SALES (est): 251.7K **Privately Held**
SIC: 2434 Wood kitchen cabinets

(G-6863)
BURLINGTON HOUSE LLC
804 Green Valley Rd Ste 300 (27408-7013)
PHONE..................336 379-6220
Joe Gorga, *CEO*
EMP: 58 **EST:** 2004
SALES (est): 3.99MM
SALES (corp-wide): 1.98B **Privately Held**
SIC: 2211 Sheets, bedding and table cloths: cotton
HQ: Elevate Textiles, Inc.
121 W Trade St Ste 1700
Charlotte NC 28202

(G-6864)
BURLINGTON INDUSTRIES III LLC
3330 W Friendly Ave (27410-4806)
P.O. Box 21207 (27420-1207)
PHONE..................336 379-2000
EMP: 7 **EST:** 2001
SALES (est): 102.34K **Privately Held**
SIC: 2231 Worsted fabrics, broadwoven

(G-6865)
BURLINGTON INDUSTRIES LLC (DH)
804 Green Valley Rd Ste 300 (27408-7039)
PHONE..................336 379-6220
Joey Underwood, *Pr*
◆ **EMP:** 150 **EST:** 2003
SALES (est): 442.45MM
SALES (corp-wide): 1.98B **Privately Held**
Web: www.burlingtonfabrics.com
SIC: 2231 2211 2221 2273 Bleaching yarn and fabrics: wool or similar fibers; Denims; Polyester broadwoven fabrics; Carpets and rugs
HQ: Elevate Textiles, Inc.
121 W Trade St Ste 1700
Charlotte NC 28202

(G-6866)
BURLINGTON INTL SVCS CO (PA)
804 Green Valley Rd # 300 (27408-7039)
PHONE..................336 379-2000
Karyl Mcclusky, *Prin*
EMP: 5 **EST:** 2001
SALES (est): 607.78K
SALES (corp-wide): 607.78K **Privately Held**
SIC: 2231 Worsted fabrics, broadwoven

(G-6867)
BURLINGTON INVESTMENT II INC
3330 W Friendly Ave (27410-4806)
P.O. Box 21207 (27420-1207)
PHONE..................336 379-2000
EMP: 7 **EST:** 2001
SALES (est): 102.34K **Privately Held**
SIC: 2231 Worsted fabrics, broadwoven

(G-6868)
BURLINGTON WORSTEDS INC
3330 W Friendly Ave (27410-4806)
P.O. Box 21207 (27420-1207)
PHONE..................336 379-2000
EMP: 7 **EST:** 2001
SALES (est): 102.34K **Privately Held**
SIC: 2231 Worsted fabrics, broadwoven

(G-6869)
BURLOW PROMOTIONS INC
4802 Tamaron Dr (27410-7908)
P.O. Box 39176 (27438-9176)
PHONE..................336 856-0500
Bob Burlow, *Pr*
EMP: 5 **EST:** 1981
SALES (est): 532.44K **Privately Held**
Web: www.burlowpromotions.com
SIC: 5199 2759 Advertising specialties; Commercial printing, nec

(G-6870)
C ALAN PUBLICATIONS LLC
6 Oak Branch Dr Ste A (27407-2396)
PHONE..................336 272-3920
Cort Mcclaren, *Pr*
EMP: 4 **EST:** 2017
SALES (est): 125.72K **Privately Held**

SIC: 2711 Newspapers, publishing and printing

(G-6871)
C E SMITH CO INC
6396 Burnt Poplar Rd (27409-9710)
PHONE..................336 273-0166
Kellie Barricks, *Mgr*
EMP: 23
SALES (corp-wide): 9.93MM **Privately Held**
Web: www.cesmith.com
SIC: 3469 Metal stampings, nec
PA: C. E. Smith Co., Inc.
1001 Bitting St
Greensboro NC 27403
336 273-0166

(G-6872)
C E SMITH CO INC (PA)
1001 Bitting St (27403-2165)
P.O. Box 9948 (27429-0948)
PHONE..................336 273-0166
Carl E Smith, *Pr*
Robert Barricks, *
▲ **EMP:** 50 **EST:** 1966
SQ FT: 60,000
SALES (est): 9.93MM
SALES (corp-wide): 9.93MM **Privately Held**
Web: www.cesmith.com
SIC: 3469 3452 Metal stampings, nec; Screws, metal

(G-6873)
C P EAKES COMPANY
2012 Fairfax Rd (27403-3065)
PHONE..................336 574-1800
EMP: 16 **EST:** 1996
SQ FT: 40,000
SALES (est): 2.25MM **Privately Held**
Web: www.cpeakes.com
SIC: 3444 3446 Sheet metalwork; Architectural metalwork

(G-6874)
CABINET TRANSITIONS INC
5310 Solar Pl (27406-9144)
PHONE..................336 382-7154
EMP: 5 **EST:** 2019
SALES (est): 75.19K **Privately Held**
Web: www.cabinettransitions.com
SIC: 2434 Wood kitchen cabinets

(G-6875)
CALI STITCHES
204 S Westgate Dr (27407-1687)
PHONE..................336 895-4714
Stephen Farrell, *Pr*
EMP: 5 **EST:** 2016
SALES (est): 115.69K **Privately Held**
SIC: 2395 Embroidery and art needlework

(G-6876)
CAMCO MANUFACTURING LLC (PA)
121 Landmark Dr (27409-9626)
PHONE..................800 334-2004
Lisa C Cook, *Managing Member*
Donald R Caine, *
Dwayne Moore, *
Elizabeth B Tedder, *
Edward D Gorman, *
◆ **EMP:** 160 **EST:** 1966
SQ FT: 302,000
SALES (est): 100.88MM
SALES (corp-wide): 100.88MM **Privately Held**
Web: www.camco.net
SIC: 2899 Chemical preparations, nec

(G-6877)
CANGILOSI SPCIALTY SAUSAGE INC
115 Landmark Dr (27409-9603)
PHONE..................336 665-5775
Giacomo Cangialosi, *Pr*
EMP: 5 **EST:** 1991
SQ FT: 12,000
SALES (est): 466.45K **Privately Held**
Web: www.cangialosispecialtyinc.com
SIC: 2013 Sausages and other prepared meats

(G-6878)
CARDINAL MILLWORK & SUPPLY INC
7620 W Market St (27409-1848)
PHONE..................336 665-9811
Richie V Fahnestock, *CEO*
Chris Fahnestock, *
Dannie Fahnestock, *
Patti Byrd, *
EMP: 34 **EST:** 2003
SALES (est): 5.21MM **Privately Held**
Web: www.cardinalmillwork.com
SIC: 2431 Millwork

(G-6879)
CARDINAL PLASTICS SALES INC
2416 Old Towne Dr (27455-3438)
PHONE..................336 540-9013
EMP: 6 **EST:** 2016
SALES (est): 91.17K **Privately Held**
SIC: 3089 Injection molding of plastics

(G-6880)
CARLISLE FINISHING LLC
804 Green Valley Rd Ste 300 (27408-7039)
PHONE..................864 466-4173
James Payne, *Pr*
EMP: 54
SALES (corp-wide): 1.98B **Privately Held**
SIC: 2231 Broadwoven fabric mills, wool
HQ: Carlisle Finishing Llc
804 Green Valley Rd # 300
Greensboro NC 27408
336 379-6220

(G-6881)
CARMEL BY D3SIGN LLC
3408 Winchester Dr (27406-5838)
PHONE..................336 617-6383
Heather Carmel Pynes, *Prin*
EMP: 4 **EST:** 2018
SALES (est): 99.21K **Privately Held**
SIC: 3993 Signs and advertising specialties

(G-6882)
CAROLINA BY-PRODUCTS CO
2410 Randolph Ave (27406-2910)
PHONE..................336 333-3030
Mike Hooks, *Mgr*
EMP: 7 **EST:** 1985
SALES (est): 220.49K **Privately Held**
SIC: 8742 2077 2047 Management consulting services; Animal and marine fats and oils; Dog and cat food

(G-6883)
CAROLINA CSTM SIGNS & GRAPHICS
1023 Huffman St (27405-7209)
PHONE..................336 681-4337
EMP: 5 **EST:** 2017
SALES (est): 163.04K **Privately Held**
Web: www.greensborosigncompany.com
SIC: 3993 Signs and advertising specialties

Greensboro - Guilford County (G-6884)

(G-6884)
CAROLINA EXTRUDED PLASTICS INC
728 Utility St (27405-7224)
P.O. Box 14728 (27415-4728)
PHONE...................336 272-1191
◆ **EMP:** 24 **EST:** 1977
SALES (est): 4.46MM Privately Held
Web: www.carolinaextrudedplast.com
SIC: 3089 Extruded finished plastics products, nec

(G-6885)
CAROLINA GRAPHIC SERVICES LLC
4328 Federal Dr Ste 105 (27410-8115)
PHONE...................336 668-0871
EMP: 9
SIC: 2752 Offset printing

(G-6886)
CAROLINA LASER CUTTING INC
4400 S Holden Rd (27406-9508)
PHONE...................336 292-1474
Bruce Cromes, Pr
Shirley Massingill, Sec
EMP: 20 **EST:** 1986
SQ FT: 12,000
SALES (est): 4.78MM Privately Held
Web: www.carolinalasercutting.com
SIC: 3599 Machine shop, jobbing and repair

(G-6887)
CAROLINA LOOM REED COMPANY INC
3503 Holts Chapel Rd (27401-4526)
P.O. Box 22111 (27420-2111)
PHONE...................336 274-7631
Ernest J Mcfetters Junior, Pr
EMP: 10 **EST:** 1938
SQ FT: 30,000
SALES (est): 422.55K Privately Held
Web: www.loomreeds.com
SIC: 3552 Textile machinery

(G-6888)
CAROLINA LQUID CHMISTRIES CORP (PA)
313 Gallimore Dairy Rd (27409-9724)
PHONE...................336 722-8910
◆ **EMP:** 49 **EST:** 1994
SALES (est): 24.57MM Privately Held
Web: www.carolinachemistries.com
SIC: 3841 Anesthesia apparatus

(G-6889)
CAROLINA MATERIAL HANDLING INC
Also Called: Caster House
2209 Patterson Ct (27407-2541)
PHONE...................336 294-2346
TOLL FREE: 800
John Middleton, CEO
Mid Middleton, Pr
Jay Mitchell, VP
EMP: 18 **EST:** 1971
SQ FT: 4,000
SALES (est): 9.62MM Privately Held
Web: www.cmh-inc.com
SIC: 5084 3537 3496 Materials handling machinery; Cradles, drum; Cages, wire

(G-6890)
CAROLINA NEWSPAPERS INC
Also Called: Carolina Peacemaker
807 Summit Ave (27405-7833)
P.O. Box 20853 (27420-0853)
PHONE...................336 274-7829
John Marshall Kilimanjaro, Pr
Vickie Kilimanjaro, Prin
Afrique Kilimanjaro, Editor
EMP: 6 **EST:** 1967
SQ FT: 1,000
SALES (est): 475.92K Privately Held
Web: www.peacemakeronline.com
SIC: 2711 2752 Newspapers: publishing only, not printed on site; Commercial printing, lithographic

(G-6891)
CAROLINA UNPLUGGED
300 Meadowood St (27409-2306)
PHONE...................336 965-4443
Joseph Mcdowell, Pr
EMP: 5 **EST:** 2006
SALES (est): 151.81K Privately Held
SIC: 3663 Satellites, communications

(G-6892)
CARRIER CAROLINAS
7203 W Friendly Ave (27410-6237)
PHONE...................336 292-0909
Scott Ritchey, Mgr
EMP: 5 **EST:** 2016
SALES (est): 87.98K Privately Held
SIC: 3585 Refrigeration and heating equipment

(G-6893)
CARSON-DELLOSA PUBLISHING LLC (PA)
Also Called: Carson Dellosa Education
7027 Albert Pick Rd Ste 300 (27409-9828)
P.O. Box 35665 (27425-5665)
PHONE...................336 632-0084
Ira Hernowitz, CEO
Joshua Loew, CMO
◆ **EMP:** 100 **EST:** 2009
SALES (est): 62.33MM
SALES (corp-wide): 62.33MM Privately Held
Web: www.carsondellosa.com
SIC: 5943 2731 School supplies; Textbooks: publishing and printing

(G-6894)
CARSON-DELLOSA PUBLISHING LLC
Also Called: Carson Dellosa Education
657 Brigham Rd Ste A (27409-9098)
PHONE...................336 632-0084
EMP: 45
SALES (corp-wide): 48.3MM Privately Held
Web: www.carsondellosa.com
SIC: 2741 Miscellaneous publishing
PA: Carson-Dellosa Publishing, Llc
7027 Albert Pick Rd # 300
Greensboro NC 27409
336 632-0084

(G-6895)
CATLOW INC ✪
7300 W Friendly Ave (27410-6232)
PHONE...................336 894-3367
EMP: 6 **EST:** 2022
SALES (est): 79.3K Privately Held
SIC: 3714 Motor vehicle parts and accessories

(G-6896)
CCBCC OPERATIONS LLC
Also Called: Coca-Cola
8200 Capital Dr 067 (27409-9038)
PHONE...................336 664-1116
Mark Moore, Brnch Mgr
EMP: 54
SQ FT: 12,200
SALES (corp-wide): 6.65B Publicly Held
Web: www.coca-cola.com
SIC: 2086 Bottled and canned soft drinks
HQ: Ccbcc Operations, Llc
4100 Coca Cola Plz
Charlotte NC 28211
704 364-8728

(G-6897)
CED INCORPORATED
7910 Industrial Village Rd (27409-9691)
P.O. Box 2515 (28329-2515)
PHONE...................336 378-0044
George Carver, Prin
Calvin Edward Davis, Prin
EMP: 13 **EST:** 2010
SALES (est): 1.16MM Privately Held
SIC: 3612 Distribution transformers, electric

(G-6898)
CENTER FOR CREATIVE LEADERSHIP (PA)
1 Leadership Pl (27410-9427)
PHONE...................336 288-7210
Martin Schneider, Pr
Bradley E Shumaker, *
EMP: 400 **EST:** 1970
SQ FT: 180,000
SALES (est): 106.68MM
SALES (corp-wide): 106.68MM Privately Held
Web: www.ccl.org
SIC: 8299 2731 Educational services; Book publishing

(G-6899)
CENTRAL CAROLINA CONCRETE LLC (HQ)
296 Edwardia Dr (27409-2604)
P.O. Box 8308 (27419-0308)
PHONE...................336 315-0785
Ray Ledford, *
Henry Batten, *
EMP: 44 **EST:** 2000
SALES (est): 61.41MM
SALES (corp-wide): 149.62MM Privately Held
Web: www.centralcarolinaconcrete.com
SIC: 3273 4212 Ready-mixed concrete; Local trucking, without storage
PA: Concrete Supply Holdings, Inc.
3823 Raleigh St
Charlotte NC 28206
704 372-2930

(G-6900)
CENTRIC BRANDS LLC
620 S Elm St Ste 395 (27406-1399)
PHONE...................646 582-6000
Jason Rabin, CEO
Anurup Pruthi, CFO
Joe Favuzza, CSO
EMP: 161 **EST:** 1987
SALES (est): 1.93MM Privately Held
Web: www.centricbrands.com
SIC: 2339 2311 2325 2387 Women's and misses' accessories; Men's and boy's suits and coats; Men's and boy's trousers and slacks; Apparel belts
PA: Centric Brands Llc
350 5th Ave Fl 6
New York NY 10118

(G-6901)
CGR PRODUCTS INC (PA)
4655 Us Highway 29 N (27405-9446)
PHONE...................336 621-4568
Charles S Keeley Iii, Pr
Richard C Wilmoth, *
Thomas J Schultz, *
◆ **EMP:** 75 **EST:** 1963
SQ FT: 70,000
SALES: 20.76MM
SALES (corp-wide): 20.76MM Privately Held
Web: www.cgrproducts.com
SIC: 3053 Gaskets, all materials

(G-6902)
CHANDLER CONCRETE INC
Also Called: Chandler Concrete
300 S Swing Rd (27409-2010)
P.O. Box 9679 (27429-0679)
PHONE...................336 297-1179
Tom Chandler, Mgr
EMP: 14
Web: www.chandlerconcrete.com
SIC: 3273 Ready-mixed concrete
PA: Chandler Concrete Co., Inc.
1006 S Church St
Burlington NC 27215

(G-6903)
CHANDLER FOODS INC
2727 Immanuel Rd (27407-2515)
PHONE...................336 299-1934
Jerry Hendrix, Pr
Doctor John E Chandler Iii, VP
Martha Chandler, *
EMP: 35 **EST:** 1955
SQ FT: 45,000
SALES (est): 7.12MM Privately Held
Web: www.chandlerfoodsinc.com
SIC: 2013 2032 2099 2038 Prepared pork products, from purchased pork; Chili, with or without meat: packaged in cans, jars, etc.; Food preparations, nec; Frozen specialties, nec

(G-6904)
CHAOS WORLDWIDE LLC
208 Sandbar Cir Apt 2f (27406-9873)
PHONE...................336 558-5654
EMP: 5 **EST:** 2020
SALES (est): 50K Privately Held
SIC: 2211 Apparel and outerwear fabrics, cotton

(G-6905)
CHASE-LOGEMAN CORPORATION
303 Friendship Dr (27409-9332)
PHONE...................336 665-0754
Douglas Logeman, Pr
Jean Logeman, Sec
EMP: 19 **EST:** 1939
SQ FT: 18,000
SALES (est): 4.94MM Privately Held
Web: www.chaselogeman.com
SIC: 5084 3565 Packaging machinery and equipment; Packaging machinery

(G-6906)
CHEMOL COMPANY INC
2300 Randolph Ave (27406-2908)
P.O. Box 16286 (27416-0286)
PHONE...................336 333-3050
EMP: 30 **EST:** 1969
SQ FT: 15,000
SALES (est): 21.69MM
SALES (corp-wide): 50.99MM Privately Held
Web: www.seydel.com
SIC: 2869 2819 Industrial organic chemicals, nec; Industrial inorganic chemicals, nec
PA: The Seydel Companies
244 John B Brooks Rd
Pendergrass GA 30567
706 693-2266

(G-6907)
CHERRYRICH PUBLISHING LLC
2303 Phoenix Dr (27406-6314)
PHONE...................336 587-0805
EMP: 4 **EST:** 2013

SALES (est): 58.58K **Privately Held**
SIC: 2741 Miscellaneous publishing

(G-6908)
CHOPIN VODKA
4 Asheland Ridge Ct (27410-3544)
PHONE.............................336 707-8305
Kristy Kennedy, *Prin*
EMP: 5 EST: 2018
SALES (est): 61.71K **Privately Held**
SIC: 2085 Distilled and blended liquors

(G-6909)
CINTAS CORPORATION NO 2
Also Called: Cintas
4345 Federal Dr (27410-8116)
PHONE.............................336 632-4412
Jeff Wilt, *Genl Mgr*
EMP: 53
SALES (corp-wide): 8.82B **Publicly Held**
Web: www.cintas.com
SIC: 5084 2395 Safety equipment; Embroidery products, except Schiffli machine
HQ: Cintas Corporation No. 2
    6800 Cintas Blvd
    Mason OH 45040

(G-6910)
CITI ENERGY LLC
2309 W Cone Blvd Ste 200 (27408-4047)
P.O. Box 39599 (27438-9599)
PHONE.............................336 379-0800
Derrick Mcdow, *Pr*
EMP: 11 EST: 2010
SALES (est): 496.12K **Privately Held**
Web: www.citienergyllc.com
SIC: 1382 Oil and gas exploration services

(G-6911)
CITY OF GREENSBORO
Also Called: Mitchell Water/Filtering Plant
1041 Battleground Ave (27408-8322)
PHONE.............................336 373-5855
Steven Drew, *Mgr*
EMP: 39
SALES (corp-wide): 479.53MM **Privately Held**
Web: www.greensboro-nc.gov
SIC: 3589 5541 Water filters and softeners, household type; Gasoline service stations
PA: City Of Greensboro
    300 W Washington St
    Greensboro NC 27401
    336 373-2002

(G-6912)
CLAROLUX INC
2501 Greengate Dr (27406-5242)
P.O. Box 4554 (27404-4554)
PHONE.............................336 378-6800
Robert Groat, *Pr*
Brian Groat, *
▲ EMP: 25 EST: 2004
SALES (est): 5.33MM **Privately Held**
Web: www.clarolux.com
SIC: 5063 3645 Lighting fixtures; Boudoir lamps

(G-6913)
CLASSIC WOOD MANUFACTURING
1006 N Raleigh St (27405-7328)
PHONE.............................336 691-1344
Steve Cannon, *Owner*
EMP: 5 EST: 1985
SQ FT: 3,000
SALES (est): 484.65K **Privately Held**
Web: www.classicwoodproductsllc.com
SIC: 3714 Motor vehicle parts and accessories

(G-6914)
CLASSY DOLLS MASSAGE & BTQ LLC
1901 Ashwood Ct Ste E (27455-3039)
PHONE.............................336 209-3933
EMP: 5
SALES (est): 249.61K **Privately Held**
SIC: 3999 Massage machines, electric; barber and beauty shops

(G-6915)
CLEAN GREEN SUSTAINABLE LF LLC
610 N Elam Ave (27408-6810)
PHONE.............................855 946-8785
Vince Pinpin, *Managing Member*
EMP: 15
SALES (est): 591.41K **Privately Held**
SIC: 3999 Manufacturing industries, nec

(G-6916)
CLEAR DEFENSE LLC
2000 N Church St (27405-5634)
P.O. Box 41316 (27404-1316)
PHONE.............................336 370-1699
EMP: 22 EST: 2000
SQ FT: 1,200
SALES (est): 1.95MM **Privately Held**
SIC: 3081 3083 Unsupported plastics film and sheet; Laminated plastics plate and sheet

(G-6917)
CLINTON PRESS INC
2100 Tennyson Dr (27410-2234)
PHONE.............................336 275-8491
Walter C Jackson Iv, *Pr*
EMP: 10 EST: 1946
SALES (est): 857.58K **Privately Held**
Web: www.clintonpress.com
SIC: 2752 2741 Offset printing; Miscellaneous publishing

(G-6918)
CLONDALKIN PHARMA & HEALTHCARE
1072 Boulder Rd (27409-9106)
PHONE.............................336 292-4555
Peter Hunt, *CEO*
EMP: 10 EST: 2019
SALES (est): 961.22K **Privately Held**
SIC: 2752 Commercial printing, lithographic

(G-6919)
COLONIAL TIN WORKS INC
7609 Canoe Rd (27409-9002)
P.O. Box 49909 (27419-1909)
PHONE.............................336 668-4126
Tom La Rose, *Pr*
Charlie Lederer, *
▲ EMP: 25 EST: 1980
SQ FT: 60,000
SALES (est): 4.9MM **Privately Held**
Web: www.ctwhomecollection.com
SIC: 5947 3499 5023 Gift, novelty, and souvenir shop; Novelties and giftware, including trophies; Decorative home furnishings and supplies

(G-6920)
COLUMBIA FOREST PRODUCTS INC
Centruty Drive Ste 200 (27401)
PHONE.............................336 605-0429
EMP: 4
SALES (corp-wide): 494.11K **Privately Held**
Web: www.columbiaforestproducts.com
SIC: 5031 2426 2273 Lumber: rough, dressed, and finished; Hardwood dimension and flooring mills; Carpets and rugs
PA: Columbia Forest Products, Inc.
    7900 Mccloud Rd Ste 200
    Greensboro NC 27409
    336 605-0429

(G-6921)
COLUMBIA WEST VIRGINIA CORP (HQ)
7820 Thorndike Rd (27409-9690)
PHONE.............................336 605-0429
Harry L Demorest, *Pr*
Cliff Barry, *
▲ EMP: 38 EST: 1990
SALES (est): 56.92K
SALES (corp-wide): 494.11K **Privately Held**
SIC: 2411 Veneer logs
PA: Columbia Forest Products, Inc.
    7900 Mccloud Rd Ste 200
    Greensboro NC 27409
    336 605-0429

(G-6922)
COMBILIFT USA LLC
303 Concord St (27406-3635)
PHONE.............................336 378-8884
▲ EMP: 14 EST: 2005
SALES (est): 8.12MM **Privately Held**
Web: www.combilift.com
SIC: 3537 Forklift trucks
PA: Combilift Unlimited Company
    Annabagh
    Monaghan H18 Y

(G-6923)
COMEDYCD
400 Nottingham Rd (27408-7526)
PHONE.............................336 273-0077
Douglas Key, *Pt*
EMP: 5 EST: 2016
SALES (est): 73.28K **Privately Held**
SIC: 2759 Commercial printing, nec

(G-6924)
COMMERCIAL FLTER SVC OF TRIAD
107 Creek Ridge Rd Ste F (27406-4439)
PHONE.............................336 272-1443
Lacy Alton Cole Junior, *Pr*
Janice Cole, *VP*
EMP: 7 EST: 1989
SALES (est): 493.09K **Privately Held**
SIC: 1711 3564 Heating and air conditioning contractors; Filters, air: furnaces, air conditioning equipment, etc.

(G-6925)
COMMONWEALTH BRANDS INC
714 Green Valley Rd (27408-7018)
PHONE.............................336 634-4200
EMP: 230
Web: www.itgbrands.com
SIC: 2111 Cigarettes
HQ: Commonwealth Brands, Inc.
    5900 N Andrews Ave Ste 11
    Fort Lauderdale FL 33309

(G-6926)
COMMSCOPE TECHNOLOGIES LLC
Also Called: Te Connectivity
8420 Triad Dr (27409-9018)
PHONE.............................336 665-6000
Al Link, *Brnch Mgr*
EMP: 29
Web: www.commscope.com
SIC: 3663 Radio and t.v. communications equipment
HQ: Commscope Technologies Llc
    4 Westbrook Corp Ctr
    Westchester IL 60154
    800 366-3891

(G-6927)
COMPLETE TRNSP & DIST CTR INC
3211 Stonypointe Dr (27406-5421)
PHONE.............................336 457-6960
Donald Clapp, *CEO*
EMP: 5 EST: 2016
SALES (est): 93.33K **Privately Held**
SIC: 3799 Transportation equipment, nec

(G-6928)
CONE DENIM LLC (DH)
Also Called: Cone Denim Mills
804 Green Valley Rd Ste 300 (27408-7013)
PHONE.............................336 379-6165
Ken Kunberger, *CEO*
◆ EMP: 59 EST: 2004
SALES (est): 38.84MM
SALES (corp-wide): 1.98B **Privately Held**
Web: www.conedenim.com
SIC: 2211 Denims
HQ: Elevate Textiles, Inc.
    121 W Trade St Ste 1700
    Charlotte NC 28202

(G-6929)
CONE JACQUARDS LLC (DH)
804 Green Valley Rd Ste 300 (27408-7013)
PHONE.............................336 379-6220
Joe Gorga, *Managing Member*
▲ EMP: 30 EST: 2004
SALES (est): 3.76MM
SALES (corp-wide): 1.98B **Privately Held**
SIC: 2211 2221 Jacquard woven fabrics, cotton; Jacquard woven fabrics, manmade fiber and silk
HQ: Elevate Textiles, Inc.
    121 W Trade St Ste 1700
    Charlotte NC 28202

(G-6930)
CONSOLIDATED PIPE & SUP CO INC
Also Called: Store 72
2410 Binford St (27407-2502)
PHONE.............................336 294-8577
Jaret Ledermann, *Mgr*
EMP: 10
SALES (corp-wide): 808.75MM **Privately Held**
Web: www.consolidatedpipe.com
SIC: 5051 5085 3462 3084 Pipe and tubing, steel; Valves and fittings; Nuclear power plant forgings, ferrous; Plastics pipe
PA: Consolidated Pipe & Supply Company, Inc.
    1205 Hilltop Pkwy
    Birmingham AL 35204
    205 323-7261

(G-6931)
CONVATEC INC
7815 National Service Rd Ste 600 (27409-9403)
PHONE.............................336 855-5500
Steven Forden, *Mgr*
EMP: 200
SALES (corp-wide): 2.07B **Privately Held**
Web: www.convatec.com
SIC: 3841 Surgical and medical instruments
HQ: Convatec Inc.
    200 Crossing Blvd Ste 101
    Bridgewater NJ 08807

(G-6932)
CONVATEC INC
7815 National Service Rd Ste 600 (27409-9403)
PHONE.............................336 297-3021
Sharon Tate, *Brnch Mgr*
EMP: 239
SALES (corp-wide): 2.07B **Privately Held**
Web: www.convatec.com

Greensboro - Guilford County (G-6933) GEOGRAPHIC SECTION

SIC: 3841 Surgical and medical instruments
HQ: Convatec Inc.
200 Crossing Blvd Ste 101
Bridgewater NJ 08807

(G-6933)
CONVATEC PURCHASING DEPARTMENT
7900 Triad Center Dr Ste 400 (27409-9073)
PHONE...................336 297-3021
Paul Moraviec, CEO
Robert Steele, VP
John Oney, Fin Mgr
▲ EMP: 4 EST: 2008
SALES (est): 97.52K Privately Held
SIC: 3841 Surgical and medical instruments

(G-6934)
CONVERTING TECHNOLOGY INC
514 Teague St (27406-4314)
PHONE...................336 333-2386
Michael Keaton, Pr
John Norgard, VP
EMP: 6 EST: 2004
SALES (est): 607.82K Privately Held
Web: www.converting-technology.com
SIC: 3544 Special dies and tools

(G-6935)
COOPER INDUSTRIES LLC
3912 Battleground Ave (27410-8575)
PHONE...................304 545-1482
EMP: 4 EST: 2017
SALES (est): 217.03K Privately Held
SIC: 3999 Manufacturing industries, nec

(G-6936)
COPY KING INC (PA)
Also Called: Copy King Printing
611 W Gate City Blvd (27403-3034)
P.O. Box 1057 (27402-1057)
PHONE...................336 333-9900
Matthew N Hopman, Pr
Alana L Hopman, Mgr
Steven Hopman, VP
EMP: 8 EST: 1981
SQ FT: 2,400
SALES (est): 457.47K
SALES (corp-wide): 457.47K Privately Held
Web: www.copykinggso.com
SIC: 7334 2752 Blueprinting service; Offset printing

(G-6937)
CORE TECHNOLOGY MOLDING CORP
2911 E Gate City Blvd Ste 201 (27401-4922)
PHONE...................336 294-2018
Jeoff Foster, Pr
EMP: 25 EST: 2006
SALES (est): 3.51MM Privately Held
Web: www.coretechnologycorp.com
SIC: 8731 1799 3069 Commercial physical research; Fiberglass work; Floor coverings, rubber

(G-6938)
CRAIG HART
2007 Griffin Run Ct (27455-1294)
PHONE...................269 365-5568
EMP: 4 EST: 2016
SALES (est): 54.95K Privately Held
SIC: 3999 Candles

(G-6939)
CREST CAPITAL LLC
7800 Mccloud Rd (27409-9819)
PHONE...................336 664-2400
EMP: 11 EST: 2002
SALES (est): 117.28K Privately Held
Web: www.crestcapital.com
SIC: 2451 Mobile homes

(G-6940)
CREST ELECTRONICS INC
3703 Alliance Dr Ste A (27407-2385)
P.O. Box 8073 (27419-0073)
PHONE...................336 855-6422
Dennis Castelli, CEO
▲ EMP: 18 EST: 1974
SQ FT: 12,514
SALES (est): 457.76K Privately Held
Web: www.crestelectronics.com
SIC: 3663 7382 3861 5731 Television closed circuit equipment; Protective devices, security; Cameras and related equipment; Video cameras and accessories

(G-6941)
CRESTLINE SOFTWARE LLC
2733 Horse Pen Creek Rd Ste 101 (27410-8399)
PHONE...................336 217-1005
EMP: 7 EST: 2016
SALES (est): 262.12K Privately Held
SIC: 7372 Prepackaged software

(G-6942)
CROSS TECHNOLOGIES INC (HQ)
Also Called: Cross Precision Measurement
4400 Piedmont Pkwy (27410-8121)
P.O. Box 18508 (27419-8508)
PHONE...................800 327-7727
John King, CEO
Rock Able, *
Jerry Bohnsack, *
EMP: 50 EST: 1954
SQ FT: 67,000
SALES (est): 47.66MM
SALES (corp-wide): 50MM Privately Held
Web: www.crossco.com
SIC: 3492 5084 8734 3625 Hose and tube fittings and assemblies, hydraulic/pneumatic; Industrial machine parts; Calibration and certification; Electric controls and control accessories, industrial
PA: Cross Technology Inc
6541 Franz Warner Pkwy
Whitsett NC 27377
336 271-3759

(G-6943)
CROSS TECHNOLOGIES INC
Also Called: Cross Hose and Fitting
3012 S Elm Eugene St Ste A (27406-4455)
PHONE...................336 370-4673
EMP: 5
SALES (corp-wide): 50MM Privately Held
Web: www.crossco.com
SIC: 3492 5085 Hose and tube couplings, hydraulic/pneumatic; Hose, belting, and packing
HQ: Cross Technologies, Inc.
4400 Piedmont Pkwy
Greensboro NC 27410
800 327-7727

(G-6944)
CROWN TROPHY INC
Also Called: National Reconition
201 Pomona Dr Ste C (27407-1635)
PHONE...................336 851-1011
Norb W Burske, VP
Lana Burske, Pr
EMP: 4 EST: 1999
SALES (est): 399.3K Privately Held
Web: www.crowntrophy.com
SIC: 5999 5199 3479 Trophies and plaques; Badges; Engraving jewelry, silverware, or metal

(G-6945)
CSC FAMILY HOLDINGS INC (PA)
Also Called: Hirschfeld Industries
101 Centreport Dr Ste 400 (27409-9422)
P.O. Box 20888 (27420-0888)
PHONE...................336 275-9711
W H Reeves, Pr
EMP: 41 EST: 1919
SQ FT: 65,000
SALES (est): 17.66MM
SALES (corp-wide): 17.66MM Privately Held
SIC: 3441 Fabricated structural metal

(G-6946)
CUMMINS ATLANTIC LLC
Also Called: Cummins
512 Teague St (27406-4314)
PHONE...................336 275-4531
Charlie Townsend, Mgr
EMP: 59
SALES (corp-wide): 34.06B Publicly Held
SIC: 5084 5013 5531 3519 Engines and parts, diesel; Motor vehicle supplies and new parts; Auto and home supply stores; Internal combustion engines, nec
HQ: Cummins Atlantic Llc
11101 Nations Ford Rd
Charlotte NC 28273

(G-6947)
CURTIS PACKING COMPANY (PA)
2416 Randolph Ave (27406-2910)
P.O. Box 1470 (27402-1470)
PHONE...................336 275-7684
Douglas B Curtis, Pr
John R Curtis, *
EMP: 100 EST: 1946
SQ FT: 40,000
SALES (est): 5.48MM
SALES (corp-wide): 5.48MM Privately Held
Web: www.curtispackingcompany.com
SIC: 2011 Frankfurters, from meat slaughtered on site

(G-6948)
CUSTOM ARMOR GROUP INC
4270 Piedmont Pkwy Ste 102 (27410-8160)
PHONE...................336 617-4667
Todd M Dix, Pr
EMP: 4 EST: 2011
SALES (est): 488.5K Privately Held
Web: www.customarmorgroup.com
SIC: 3483 Ammunition, except for small arms, nec

(G-6949)
CUSTOM CNVERTING SOLUTIONS INC
Also Called: C C S
1207 Boston Rd (27407-2107)
PHONE...................336 292-2616
Matthew O'connell, Pr
Laura O'connell, VP
▲ EMP: 40 EST: 2001
SQ FT: 44,000
SALES (est): 7.82MM Privately Held
Web: www.customconvertingsolutions.com
SIC: 3711 3469 Automobile assembly, including specialty automobiles; Appliance parts, porcelain enameled

(G-6950)
CUSTOM INDUSTRIES INC (PA)
Also Called: Bio Air
215 Aloe Rd (27409-2105)
P.O. Box 18547 (27419-8547)
PHONE...................336 299-2885
James E Nagel, Pr
Wilbert Everett, *
▲ EMP: 30 EST: 1962
SQ FT: 85,000
SALES (est): 4.87MM
SALES (corp-wide): 4.87MM Privately Held
Web: www.customindustries.com
SIC: 3599 3444 5047 3429 Machine shop, jobbing and repair; Restaurant sheet metalwork; Medical equipment and supplies ; Marine hardware

(G-6951)
CUTTING EDGE INDUSTRIES
3502 Cloverdale Dr (27408-2904)
PHONE...................336 937-2129
Jeremy Pegram, Prin
EMP: 4 EST: 2019
SALES (est): 61.26K Privately Held
SIC: 3999 Manufacturing industries, nec

(G-6952)
CYBER DEFENSE ADVISORS
3336 Wall Rd (27407-9726)
PHONE...................336 899-6072
Kevin Fiscus, Prin
EMP: 5 EST: 2017
SALES (est): 204.11K Privately Held
SIC: 3812 Defense systems and equipment

(G-6953)
CYGANY INC
2712 Denise Dr (27407-6648)
PHONE...................773 293-2999
Patricia L C Henderson, Pr
▲ EMP: 5 EST: 1996
SALES (est): 418.66K Privately Held
SIC: 3911 Jewelry apparel

(G-6954)
CYRCO INC
120 N Chimney Rock Rd (27409-1854)
P.O. Box 7292 (27417-0292)
PHONE...................336 668-0977
Peter Couture, Pr
Paul Couture, *
Paula C Mcgee, Sec
▲ EMP: 26 EST: 1980
SQ FT: 9,000
SALES (est): 9.31MM Privately Held
Web: www.cyrco.com
SIC: 3499 1796 Aerosol valves, metal; Installing building equipment

(G-6955)
D & D ENTPS GREENSBORO INC
Also Called: D & D Precision Tool
1337 Burnetts Chapel Rd (27406-8815)
PHONE...................336 495-3407
Ralph Davis, Pr
Harold Davis, VP
EMP: 14 EST: 1976
SALES (est): 359.47K Privately Held
SIC: 3599 Machine shop, jobbing and repair

(G-6956)
D C THOMAS GROUP INC (PA)
Also Called: Thomas Foods
6540 W Market St (27409-1836)
P.O. Box 8822 (27419-0822)
PHONE...................336 299-6263
Dwight C Thomas Senior, Pr
Dwight C Thomas Junior, VP

GEOGRAPHIC SECTION   Greensboro - Guilford County (G-6981)

Becky Thomas, Sec
EMP: 6 **EST:** 1971
SALES (est): 2.47MM **Privately Held**
Web: www.thomasgourmetfoods.net
SIC: 2035 Pickles, sauces, and salad dressings

(G-6957)
DAILY N-GINE LLC
909 Thorncroft Rd (27406-8271)
PHONE...............................336 285-8042
Toby Williams, Prin
EMP: 4 **EST:** 2015
SALES (est): 163.18K **Privately Held**
SIC: 2711 Newspapers, publishing and printing

(G-6958)
DAVID CONRAD
212 Staunton Dr (27410-6065)
PHONE...............................336 253-6966
David Conrad, Pt
EMP: 5 **EST:** 2016
SALES (est): 103.66K **Privately Held**
SIC: 3491 Industrial valves

(G-6959)
DAVID ORECK CANDLE
3500 N Ohenry Blvd (27405-3814)
PHONE...............................336 375-8411
James Mccain, Prin
EMP: 12 **EST:** 2012
SALES (est): 492K **Privately Held**
Web: www.davidoreckcandles.com
SIC: 3999 Candles

(G-6960)
DAVID R WEBB COMPANY INC
300 Standard Dr (27409-9641)
PHONE...............................336 605-3355
Gary Cox, Mgr
EMP: 4
SALES (corp-wide): 73.29MM **Privately Held**
Web: www.danzer.com
SIC: 2435 2436 Veneer stock, hardwood; Veneer stock, softwood
HQ: David R. Webb Company, Inc.
   206 S Holland St
   Edinburgh IN 46124
   812 526-2601

(G-6961)
DBT COATINGS LLC
1908 Fairfax Rd Ste A (27407-4992)
P.O. Box 4121 (27404-4121)
PHONE...............................336 834-9700
Timothy Leeper, CEO
David Parker, VP
Daniel Sroka, VP
Thomas Mckenna, COO
David Leeper, CFO
EMP: 7 **EST:** 2011
SALES (est): 991.14K **Privately Held**
Web: www.polytexus.com
SIC: 2631 2759 2891 Container, packaging, and boxboard; Commercial printing, nec; Adhesives and sealants

(G-6962)
DDP SPCLTY ELCTRNIC MTLS US 9
Also Called: CSS
2914 Patterson St (27407-3337)
PHONE...............................336 547-7100
Darren W Cammin, Brnch Mgr
EMP: 65
SALES (corp-wide): 12.07B **Publicly Held**
SIC: 2821 2869 2891 3569 Plastics materials and resins; Industrial organic chemicals, nec; Adhesives and sealants; Filters

HQ: Ddp Specialty Electronic Materials Us 9, Llc
   974 Centre Rd
   Wilmington DE 19805
   302 774-1000

(G-6963)
DEDON INC (DH)
657 Brigham Rd Ste C (27409-9153)
PHONE...............................336 790-1070
Bobby Dekeyser, Ch Bd
David Kennedy, *
◆ **EMP:** 14 **EST:** 2009
SALES (est): 22.72MM
SALES (corp-wide): 355.83K **Privately Held**
Web: www.dedon.de
SIC: 2511 5712 Lawn furniture: wood; Outdoor and garden furniture
HQ: Dedon Gmbh
   Zeppelinstr. 22
   Luneburg NI
   413 122-4470

(G-6964)
DEEP RVER MLLS CTD FABRICS INC (PA)
Also Called: Deep River Printing
1904 Lendew St (27408-7007)
P.O. Box 66 (27259-0066)
PHONE...............................910 464-3135
Larry Booth, Pr
Vicky Booth, VP
▲ **EMP:** 10 **EST:** 1979
SQ FT: 55,000
SALES (est): 2.45MM
SALES (corp-wide): 2.45MM **Privately Held**
Web: www.deeprivermills.com
SIC: 2261 Chemical coating or treating of cotton broadwoven fabrics

(G-6965)
DELFORTGROUP PRINTING SERVICES
206 Bruce St (27403-2282)
P.O. Box 185 (23834-0185)
PHONE...............................336 272-9344
EMP: 5 **EST:** 2016
SALES (est): 92.3K **Privately Held**
Web: www.delfortgroup.com
SIC: 2752 Commercial printing, lithographic

(G-6966)
DELTA PHOENIX INC
Also Called: Wysong Parts and Service
4820 Us Hwy 29 N (27405)
P.O. Box 21168 (27420-1168)
PHONE...............................336 621-3960
Russell F Hall Iii, Pr
Suzanne C Hall, *
William F Herr Ii, VP
Billy R Carter, *
EMP: 26 **EST:** 2011
SALES (est): 4.31MM **Privately Held**
Web: www.wysong.us
SIC: 3541 3542 Machine tools, metal cutting type; Brakes, metal forming

(G-6967)
DELUXE CORPORATION
3703 Farmington Dr (27407-5616)
PHONE...............................336 851-4600
EMP: 19
SALES (corp-wide): 2.19B **Publicly Held**
Web: www.deluxe.com
SIC: 2782 Checkbooks
PA: Deluxe Corporation
   801 Marquette Ave
   Minneapolis MN 55402
   651 483-7111

(G-6968)
DELVE INTERIORS LLC
7820 Thorndike Rd (27409-9690)
PHONE...............................336 274-4661
▲ **EMP:** 113
SIC: 2521 5021 2426 1742 Wood office furniture; Office and public building furniture; Frames for upholstered furniture, wood; Acoustical and insulation work

(G-6969)
DEMOCRACY GREENSBORO
5214 Skylark Dr (27405-9439)
PHONE...............................336 635-7016
William Hurd, Owner
EMP: 9 **EST:** 2017
SALES (est): 58.7K **Privately Held**
Web: www.greensboro.com
SIC: 2711 Newspapers, publishing and printing

(G-6970)
DIGITAL PROGRESSIONS INC
5101 W Market St (27409-2613)
P.O. Box 16792 (27416-0792)
PHONE...............................336 676-6570
Thomas Wayman, Pr
Mark Woodall, VP
EMP: 13 **EST:** 1997
SQ FT: 3,000
SALES (est): 357.3K **Privately Held**
SIC: 3861 Printing equipment, photographic

(G-6971)
DIGNIFY INC
3907 N Elm St (27455-2594)
PHONE...............................336 500-8668
Zachary Tran, Prin
EMP: 5 **EST:** 2018
SALES (est): 137.97K **Privately Held**
Web: www.dignifytherapeutics.com
SIC: 2834 Pharmaceutical preparations

(G-6972)
DISSTON CO INC
7345 W Friendly Ave Ste G (27410-6252)
PHONE...............................336 547-6300
EMP: 6 **EST:** 2018
SALES (est): 85.25K **Privately Held**
SIC: 3545 Machine tool accessories

(G-6973)
DIVISION EIGHT INC
2206 N Church St (27405-4308)
P.O. Box 14985 (27415-4985)
PHONE...............................336 852-1275
Peter B Norton, Pr
EMP: 16 **EST:** 2004
SQ FT: 15,000
SALES (est): 2.08MM **Privately Held**
Web: www.divisioneightinc.com
SIC: 3429 3261 Furniture hardware; Bathroom accessories/fittings, vitreous china or earthenware

(G-6974)
DOGGIES R US
2940 E Market St (27405-7407)
PHONE...............................336 455-1113
William Goode, Owner
EMP: 4 **EST:** 2021
SALES (est): 154.77K **Privately Held**
SIC: 3199 Dog furnishings: collars, leashes, muzzles, etc.: leather

(G-6975)
DOKJA INC (PA)
Also Called: Sir Speedy
602 S Edwardia Dr (27409-2806)
PHONE...............................336 852-5190

EMP: 8 **EST:** 1993
SQ FT: 1,500
SALES (est): 975.14K **Privately Held**
Web: www.sirspeedy.com
SIC: 2752 2791 2789 Commercial printing, lithographic; Typesetting; Bookbinding and related work

(G-6976)
DOUBLE HUNG LLC
2801 Patterson St (27407-2318)
PHONE...............................888 235-8956
EMP: 47 **EST:** 2008
SALES (est): 5.02MM **Privately Held**
Web: www.double-hung.com
SIC: 2431 5031 Door frames, wood; Windows

(G-6977)
DOVE COMMUNICATIONS INC
7 Wendy Ct Ste B (27409-2248)
PHONE...............................336 855-5491
John Liner, Pr
E Gordon Liner, Sec
EMP: 8 **EST:** 1988
SQ FT: 6,800
SALES (est): 704.4K **Privately Held**
Web: www.dovecommunication.com
SIC: 2752 Offset printing

(G-6978)
DOW SILICONES CORPORATION
2914 Patterson St (27407-3337)
PHONE...............................336 547-7100
Jane Waldron, Mgr
EMP: 100
SALES (corp-wide): 44.62B **Publicly Held**
SIC: 2821 Plastics materials and resins
HQ: Dow Silicones Corporation
   2200 W Salzburg Rd
   Midland MI 48686
   989 496-4000

(G-6979)
DP SOLUTIONS INC (DH)
Also Called: Dpsi
1801 Stanley Rd Ste 301 (27407-2644)
P.O. Box 49003 (27419-1003)
PHONE...............................336 854-7700
Frederick M Riek, Ch Bd
Carol Owens, Pr
Eric Lynn Carriker, Ex VP
EMP: 12 **EST:** 1986
SQ FT: 13,464
SALES (est): 2.85MM
SALES (corp-wide): 300K **Privately Held**
Web: www.dpsi.com
SIC: 7372 Application computer software
HQ: Societe Valsoft Inc
   7405 Rte Transcanadienne Bureau 100
   Saint-Laurent QC H4T 1
   514 316-7647

(G-6980)
DS SMITH PACKAGING AND PAPER
4328 Federal Dr Ste 105 (27410-8115)
PHONE...............................336 668-0871
EMP: 7 **EST:** 2019
SALES (est): 662.72K **Privately Held**
SIC: 2621 Packaging paper

(G-6981)
DTBTLA INC
4301 Waterleaf Ct (27410-8106)
PHONE...............................336 769-0000
Al Hutchison, Pr
Allie Hutchison Senior, Ch Bd
Douglas S Flynn, *
Terry Preston, *
Carrie Stankwytch, *
▼ **EMP:** 49 **EST:** 1931

Greensboro - Guilford County (G-6982) GEOGRAPHIC SECTION

SQ FT: 37,000
SALES (est): 916.34K **Privately Held**
SIC: **2752** 2759 Offset printing; Commercial printing, nec

(G-6982)
DTP INC
1 Wendy Ct Ste E (27409-2247)
PHONE...................................336 272-5122
Steve Lacivita, *Pr*
EMP: 4 EST: 1987
SQ FT: 3,000
SALES (est): 320.8K **Privately Held**
SIC: **2796** 7338 7384 Color separations, for printing; Proofreading service; Photofinish laboratories

(G-6983)
DUCK HEAD LLC
816 S Elm St (27406-1332)
PHONE...................................855 457-1865
EMP: 12 EST: 2013
SALES (est): 104.04K **Privately Held**
Web: www.duckhead.com
SIC: **2389** Men's miscellaneous accessories

(G-6984)
DVD RULERS
6303 Muirfield Dr (27410-8270)
PHONE...................................336 270-9269
Andreas Lixl, *Prin*
EMP: 5 EST: 2013
SALES (est): 50.26K **Privately Held**
SIC: **2741** Miscellaneous publishing

(G-6985)
EAGLE COMPRESSORS INC (PA)
Also Called: Eagle Compressors
3003 Thurston Ave (27406-4516)
PHONE...................................336 370-4159
Anthony M Gonzalez, *Prin*
▲ EMP: 24 EST: 1999
SQ FT: 30,000
SALES (est): 4.7MM **Privately Held**
Web: www.eaglecompressors.com
SIC: **3563** Air and gas compressors

(G-6986)
EAGLEAIR INC
3003 Thurston Ave (27406-4516)
PHONE...................................336 398-8000
Kenneth Nielsen, *Pr*
Becky Dreier, *CFO*
Richard Yorke, *Sec*
EMP: 8 EST: 2015
SQ FT: 25,000
SALES (est): 178.29K **Privately Held**
Web: www.eaglecompressors.com
SIC: **3563** Air and gas compressors

(G-6987)
EASTH20 HOLDINGS LLC
Also Called: Miller Products Co
4224 Tudor Ln Ste 101 (27410-8145)
PHONE...................................919 313-2100
John Westland, *Brnch Mgr*
EMP: 9
SALES (corp-wide): 10MM **Privately Held**
SIC: **3069** 3061 3089 5085 Clothing, vulcanized rubber or rubberized fabric; Mechanical rubber goods; Blow molded finished plastics products, nec; Rubber goods, mechanical
PA: Easth20 Holdings, Llc.
15041 Bake Pkwy Ste F
Irvine CA 92618
714 533-2827

(G-6988)
EATUMUP LURE COMPANY INC
Also Called: Revi Technical Wear
116 S Walnut Cir (27409-2625)
PHONE...................................336 218-0896
James Murray, *Pr*
EMP: 9 EST: 1982
SQ FT: 6,000
SALES (est): 929.22K **Privately Held**
SIC: **2329** 2339 2759 Athletic clothing, except uniforms: men's, youths' and boys'; Athletic clothing: women's, misses', and juniors'; Commercial printing, nec

(G-6989)
ECOLAB INC
Also Called: Ecolab Kay Chemical Company
8300 Capital Dr (27409-9790)
PHONE...................................336 931-2289
Steve Mosh, *Brnch Mgr*
EMP: 38
SALES (corp-wide): 15.32B **Publicly Held**
Web: www.ecolab.com
SIC: **2842** Specialty cleaning
PA: Ecolab Inc.
1 Ecolab Pl
Saint Paul MN 55102
800 232-6522

(G-6990)
EFA INC
Also Called: Elastic Fabrics of America
3112 Pleasant Garden Rd (27406-4608)
P.O. Box 21986 (27420-1986)
PHONE...................................336 378-2603
James Robbins, *Pr*
Rick Bauer, *
Terry Murphy, *
▼ EMP: 230 EST: 2007
SALES (est): 52.51MM **Privately Held**
Web: www.elasticfabrics.com
SIC: **2221** Broadwoven fabric mills, manmade
HQ: Nueva Expresion Textil Sa.
Calle Isabel Colbrand, 10 - Loc 130 5 Plt
Madrid M 28050

(G-6991)
EFA INC (DH)
Also Called: Elastic Fabric of America
3112 Pleasant Garden Rd (27406-4608)
P.O. Box 21986 (27420-1986)
PHONE...................................336 275-9401
James Robbins, *Pr*
Sandra Jones, *
Terry Murphy, *
▼ EMP: 147 EST: 2007
SALES (est): 22.77MM **Privately Held**
Web: www.elasticfabrics.com
SIC: **2241** 2221 Rubber and elastic yarns and fabrics; Elastic fabrics, manmade fiber and silk
HQ: Nueva Expresion Textil Sa.
Calle Isabel Colbrand, 10 - Loc 130 5 Plt
Madrid M 28050

(G-6992)
ELANCO US INC
3200 Northline Ave Ste 300 (27408-7616)
PHONE...................................812 230-2745
Neel Ambani, *CFO*
EMP: 12 EST: 1996
SALES (est): 68.25K **Privately Held**
Web: www.elanco.com
SIC: **2834** Pharmaceutical preparations

(G-6993)
ELITE ACCESS INTERNATIONAL INC (PA)
3718 Alliance Dr Ste A (27407-2389)
PHONE...................................336 327-8096
Scott Sobkowski, *VP*
▲ EMP: 5 EST: 2013
SALES (est): 156,45K
SALES (corp-wide): 156.45K **Privately Held**
SIC: **2451** Mobile homes, industrial or commercial use

(G-6994)
ELLIS BACKHOE SERVICE INC
151 Burton Farm Rd (27455-8254)
PHONE...................................336 451-6265
John Ellis Ii, *Pr*
EMP: 5 EST: 2015
SALES (est): 101.36K **Privately Held**
SIC: **3531** Backhoes

(G-6995)
ELSAG NORTH AMERICA LLC (PA)
4221 Tudor Ln (27410-8105)
PHONE...................................336 379-7135
Mark Windover, *Managing Member*
EMP: 36 EST: 2004
SALES (est): 10.21MM
SALES (corp-wide): 10.21MM **Privately Held**
Web: www.leonardocompany-us.com
SIC: **3829** Photogrammetrical instruments

(G-6996)
EM2 MACHINE CORPORATION
1030 Boulder Rd (27409-9106)
PHONE...................................336 707-8409
Vince Simmons, *CEO*
EMP: 4 EST: 2006
SALES (est): 356.84K **Privately Held**
SIC: **3499** Friction material, made from powdered metal

(G-6997)
ENCERTEC INC
415 Pisgah Church Rd Ste 302 (27455-2590)
PHONE...................................336 288-7226
Don Denison, *Pr*
▲ EMP: 4 EST: 1992
SQ FT: 1,200
SALES (est): 483.91K **Privately Held**
Web: www.encertec.com
SIC: **3559** 5084 2621 Kilns; Industrial machinery and equipment; Absorbent paper

(G-6998)
ENDLESS PLASTICS LLC
3704 Alliance Dr Ste B (27407-2989)
PHONE...................................336 346-1839
Robert Long, *Managing Member*
EMP: 10 EST: 2002
SQ FT: 12,000
SALES (est): 2.25MM **Privately Held**
Web: www.endlessplastics.com
SIC: **5162** 3993 2542 Plastics sheets and rods; Displays and cutouts, window and lobby; Stands, merchandise display: except wood

(G-6999)
ENGINEERED SOFTWARE
615 Guilford Ave (27401-1975)
PHONE...................................336 299-4843
Bill L Stanley, *Pr*
Susan Stanley, *VP*
EMP: 6 EST: 2002
SALES (est): 318.2K **Privately Held**
Web: www.engsw.com

SIC: **7372** Prepackaged software

(G-7000)
ENNIS-FLINT INC (HQ)
4161 Piedmont Pkwy Ste 370 (27410-8176)
PHONE...................................800 331-8118
Edward Baiden, *Pr*
Laura Greer, *Sec*
Brice Hester, *VP*
John A Jankowski, *Treas*
◆ EMP: 14 EST: 1996
SALES (est): 110.85MM
SALES (corp-wide): 17.65B **Publicly Held**
Web: www.ennisflintamericas.com
SIC: **3953** 2851 Marking devices; Paints and allied products
PA: Ppg Industries, Inc.
1 Ppg Pl
Pittsburgh PA 15272
412 434-3131

(G-7001)
ENOCO LLC
112 Maxfield Rd (27405-8643)
P.O. Box 20461 (27420-0461)
PHONE...................................336 398-5650
William H Dubose, *Prin*
EMP: 7 EST: 1998
SALES (est): 154.99K **Privately Held**
SIC: **3999** Manufacturing industries, nec

(G-7002)
ENTRUST SERVICES LLC
130 S Walnut Cir (27409-2625)
P.O. Box 35228 (27425-5228)
PHONE...................................336 274-5175
EMP: 18 EST: 2005
SALES (est): 2.14MM **Privately Held**
SIC: **2842** 3463 Drain pipe solvents or cleaners; Plumbing fixture forgings, nonferrous

(G-7003)
EPSILON HOLDINGS LLC (PA)
Also Called: Box Drop Furniture Whl NC
2103 E Town Blvd Ste 105 (27455)
PHONE...................................336 763-6147
Frank Park, *Mng Pt*
EMP: 5 EST: 2015
SQ FT: 4,000
SALES (est): 106.81K
SALES (corp-wide): 106.81K **Privately Held**
SIC: **2599** Bar furniture

(G-7004)
ETHERNGTON CNSERVATION CTR INC
1010 Arnold St (27405-7102)
PHONE...................................336 665-1317
Donald G Etherington, *Pr*
EMP: 60 EST: 2001
SALES (est): 651.63K **Privately Held**
Web: www.hfgroup.com
SIC: **2789** 5932 Bookbinding and related work; Used merchandise stores
PA: Hf Group, Llc
400 Arora Cmmons Cir Unit
Aurora OH 44202

(G-7005)
EVOLUTION MOBILE WELDING LLC
3020 Stratford Dr (27408-2625)
PHONE...................................336 383-9277
EMP: 5 EST: 2019
SALES (est): 106.99K **Privately Held**
Web: www.evolutionwelding.com
SIC: **7692** Welding repair

Greensboro - Guilford County (G-7030)

(G-7006)
EVONIK CORPORATION
2401 Doyle St (27406-2911)
PHONE.............................336 333-3565
Reinhold Brand, *Brnch Mgr*
EMP: 61
SALES (corp-wide): 2.27B Privately Held
Web: corporate.evonik.com
SIC: 2869 Industrial organic chemicals, nec
HQ: Evonik Corporation
2 Turner Pl
Piscataway NJ 08854
732 982-5000

(G-7007)
EVONIK SUPERABSORBER LLC (DH)
2401 Doyle St (27406-2911)
PHONE.............................336 333-7540
Frank Lelek, *Pr*
Sonja Cauble, *VP*
EMP: 120 EST: 2021
SALES (est): 61.74MM
SALES (corp-wide): 2.27B Privately Held
Web: www.superabsorber.com
SIC: 2821 Acrylic resins
HQ: Evonik Corporation
2 Turner Pl
Piscataway NJ 08854
732 982-5000

(G-7008)
EXACT CUT INC
824 Winston St (27405-7236)
PHONE.............................336 207-4022
John Bradley, *Pr*
EMP: 10 EST: 2007
SALES (est): 939.94K Privately Held
Web: www.exactcut.net
SIC: 3541 Machine tools, metal cutting type

(G-7009)
EXQUISITE GRANITE AND MBL INC
6207 Tri Port Ct (27409-2013)
PHONE.............................336 851-8890
Jody Esque, *Owner*
EMP: 6 EST: 2013
SQ FT: 10,000
SALES (est): 602.51K Privately Held
Web: www.exquisitegranitestudio.com
SIC: 3281 Marble, building: cut and shaped

(G-7010)
FAINTING GOAT SPIRITS LLC
321 W Wendover Ave (27408-8401)
PHONE.............................336 273-6221
Shelley A Johnson, *Prin*
EMP: 5 EST: 2015
SALES (est): 349.21K Privately Held
Web: www.faintinggoatspirits.com
SIC: 2085 Distilled and blended liquors

(G-7011)
FEENEYS (PA)
1603 New Garden Rd (27410-2001)
PHONE.............................336 617-5874
Colleen Hodges, *Managing Member*
EMP: 5 EST: 2010
SALES (est): 99.92K Privately Held
Web: www.feeneyinc.com
SIC: 2026 Yogurt

(G-7012)
FIBEX LLC
7109 Cessna Dr (27409-9793)
PHONE.............................336 358-5014
Jeff Bruner, *Brnch Mgr*
EMP: 33
SALES (corp-wide): 816.63K Privately Held
SIC: 2822 Synthetic rubber
PA: Fibex Llc
5280 National Center Dr
Colfax NC 27235
336 605-9002

(G-7013)
FILTRATION TECHNOLOGY INC
Also Called: Filtration Technology
110 Pomona Dr (27407-1616)
P.O. Box 18168 (27419-8168)
PHONE.............................336 509-9960
Scott Mathews, *Pr*
EMP: 7
SALES (corp-wide): 1.57MM Privately Held
Web: www.filtrationtechnology.com
SIC: 3564 Filters, air: furnaces, air conditioning equipment, etc.
PA: Filtration Technology, Inc.
110 Pomona Dr
Greensboro NC 27407
336 294-5655

(G-7014)
FILTRATION TECHNOLOGY INC (PA)
110 Pomona Dr (27407-1616)
P.O. Box 18168 (27419-8168)
PHONE.............................336 294-5655
Richard A Matthews, *Ch Bd*
Scott Matthews, *Pr*
▼ EMP: 8 EST: 1971
SQ FT: 12,500
SALES (est): 1.57MM
SALES (corp-wide): 1.57MM Privately Held
Web: www.filtrationtechnology.com
SIC: 1799 5075 3564 Decontamination services; Air conditioning and ventilation equipment and supplies; Purification and dust collection equipment

(G-7015)
FILTRONA FILTERS INC
303 Gallimore Dairy Rd (27409-9724)
PHONE.............................336 362-1333
Robert Pye, *CEO*
EMP: 93
SALES (corp-wide): 1.03MM Privately Held
Web: www.essentra.com
SIC: 3999 2621 Cigarette filters; Cigarette paper
HQ: Filtrona Filters Inc
2 Westbrook Corp Ctr
Westchester IL 60154

(G-7016)
FISKARS BRANDS INC
Ginger
322 Edwardia Dr Ste D (27409-2636)
PHONE.............................336 292-6237
Anca Vladu, *Brnch Mgr*
EMP: 23
SALES (corp-wide): 1.3B Privately Held
Web: www.fiskars.com
SIC: 3423 Hand and edge tools, nec
HQ: Fiskars Brands, Inc.
7800 Discovery Dr
Middleton WI 53562
608 259-1649

(G-7017)
FLARE DICHIARO
3700 Madison Ave (27403-1034)
PHONE.............................336 500-5160
EMP: 4 EST: 2015
SALES (est): 75.42K Privately Held
SIC: 2899 Flares

(G-7018)
FLINT SPINNING LLC
7736 Mccloud Rd Ste 300 (27409-9324)
PHONE.............................336 665-3000
Authur C Wiener, *Ch Bd*
Authur C Wiener, *Pr*
EMP: 9 EST: 2001
SALES (est): 171.49K Privately Held
SIC: 2211 Broadwoven fabric mills, cotton

(G-7019)
FORVESON CORP
322 Edwardia Dr Ste D (27409-2636)
PHONE.............................336 292-6237
Mauro Lizzoli, *Pr*
Angelo Lizzoli, *Sec*
Giacomo Lizzoli, *Treas*
▲ EMP: 7 EST: 2012
SALES (est): 255.97K Privately Held
Web: www.gingher.com
SIC: 3421 Scissors, shears, clippers, snips, and similar tools

(G-7020)
FRAGRANT PASSAGE CANDLE CO LP
3500 N Ohenry Blvd (27405-3814)
PHONE.............................336 375-8411
David Oreck, *Ch Bd*
Carol Ritchie, *Acctnt*
Kathy Lavanier, *Genl Mgr*
▲ EMP: 25 EST: 2004
SQ FT: 20,000
SALES (est): 1.25MM Privately Held
Web: www.fragrantpassage.com
SIC: 3999 Candles

(G-7021)
FRED MARVIN AND ASSOCIATES INC
Also Called: Fred Marvin Associates
496 Gallimore Dairy Rd Ste D (27409-9202)
PHONE.............................330 784-9211
Jeff Mussay, *Pr*
▲ EMP: 6 EST: 1946
SALES (est): 875.02K Privately Held
Web: www.fredmarvin.com
SIC: 3421 Cutlery

(G-7022)
FREEDOM BEVERAGE COMPANY
4319 Waterleaf Ct Ste 101 (27410-8171)
PHONE.............................336 316-1260
Tim Booras, *Pr*
▲ EMP: 5 EST: 2013
SALES (est): 932.52K Privately Held
Web: www.freedombev.com
SIC: 2087 Beverage bases, concentrates, syrups, powders and mixes

(G-7023)
FRONT LINE EXPRESS LLC
4086 Clovelly Dr (27406-8563)
PHONE.............................800 260-1357
EMP: 7 EST: 2019
SALES (est): 343.26K Privately Held
SIC: 3799 Transportation equipment, nec

(G-7024)
FT MEDIA HOLDINGS LLC (HQ)
Also Called: Progressive Business Media
7025 Albert Pick Rd Ste 200 (27409-9539)
PHONE.............................336 605-0121
Catherine Silver, *Pr*
EMP: 10 EST: 2013
SALES (est): 11.2MM
SALES (corp-wide): 11.2MM Privately Held
Web: www.progressivebusinessmedia.com
SIC: 2741 2721 Business service newsletters: publishing and printing; Trade journals: publishing and printing
PA: Bridgetower Media, Llc
7025 Albert Pick Rd # 200
Greensboro NC 27409
612 317-9420

(G-7025)
FURNITURE TDAY MEDIA GROUP LLC
7025 Albert Pick Rd Ste 200 (27409-9539)
PHONE.............................336 605-0121
EMP: 65 EST: 2013
SALES (est): 447.98K
SALES (corp-wide): 11.2MM Privately Held
Web: www.furnituretoday.com
SIC: 2721 Magazines: publishing only, not printed on site
HQ: Ft Media Holdings Llc
7025 Albert Pick Rd Ste 2
Greensboro NC 27409
336 605-0121

(G-7026)
FYI PRESS INC
818 Walker Ave (27403-2528)
PHONE.............................336 254-3452
EMP: 4 EST: 2019
SALES (est): 65.16K Privately Held
SIC: 2741 Miscellaneous publishing

(G-7027)
G & G MANAGEMENT LLC
Also Called: AR Workshop Greensboro
1603 Battleground Ave Ste F (27408-8049)
PHONE.............................336 444-6271
Gabrielle W Gilllett, *Pr*
Lawrence C Gillett, *VP*
EMP: 12 EST: 2020
SALES (est): 989.07K Privately Held
Web: www.arworkshop.com
SIC: 2499 5999 Decorative wood and woodwork; Miscellaneous retail stores, nec

(G-7028)
G & J MACHINE SHOP INC (PA)
7800 Boeing Dr (27409-9706)
P.O. Box 941 (27261-0941)
PHONE.............................336 668-0996
Michael Jones, *Pr*
EMP: 20 EST: 1950
SQ FT: 15,000
SALES (est): 4.82MM Privately Held
Web: www.gandjmachineshop.com
SIC: 3599 Machine shop, jobbing and repair

(G-7029)
GAME BOX LLC (PA)
Also Called: Game Box Builders
143 Industrial Ave (27406-4504)
PHONE.............................866 241-1882
Benjamin Haskin, *Managing Member*
EMP: 4 EST: 2016
SALES (est): 651.41K
SALES (corp-wide): 651.41K Privately Held
Web: www.gameboxbuilders.com
SIC: 3944 Video game machines, except coin-operated

(G-7030)
GASBOY INTERNATIONAL INC
7300 W Friendly Ave (27410-6232)
PHONE.............................336 547-5000
David Kaehler, *Prin*
EMP: 9 EST: 2016
SALES (est): 450.2K Privately Held

Greensboro - Guilford County (G-7031)   GEOGRAPHIC SECTION

Web: www.gasboy.com
SIC: 3586 Measuring and dispensing pumps

(G-7031)
GATE CITY KITCHENS LLC
201 Creek Ridge Rd Ste D (27406-4437)
PHONE..................................336 378-0870
▲ **EMP:** 4 **EST:** 2004
SQ FT: 8,302
SALES (est): 468.27K **Privately Held**
Web: www.gatecitykitchens.com
SIC: 2434 Wood kitchen cabinets

(G-7032)
GB BIOSCIENCES LLC (DH)
410 S Swing Rd (27409-2012)
PHONE..................................336 632-6000
Robert Woods, *CEO*
▲ **EMP:** 90 **EST:** 1986
SQ FT: 300,000
SALES (est): 52.34MM **Privately Held**
SIC: 2879 2834 2899 Pesticides, agricultural or household; Pharmaceutical preparations; Chemical preparations, nec
HQ: Syngenta Corporation
    3411 Silverside Rd # 100
    Wilmington DE 19810
    302 425-2000

(G-7033)
GEM ASSET ACQUISITION LLC
139 S Walnut Cir (27409-2624)
PHONE..................................336 854-8200
Renee Gilbert, *Brnch Mgr*
EMP: 5
SALES (corp-wide): 17.13MM **Privately Held**
SIC: 2951 Asphalt paving mixtures and blocks
PA: Gem Asset Acquisition Llc
    1855 Lindbergh St Ste 500
    Charlotte NC 28208
    704 225-3321

(G-7034)
GENERAL DYNMICS MSSION SYSTEMS
Also Called: Gdais
3801 Boren Dr (27407-2046)
PHONE..................................336 323-9752
Alex Eksir, *Mgr*
EMP: 243
SALES (corp-wide): 42.27B **Publicly Held**
Web: www.gdmissionsystems.com
SIC: 3663 Radio and t.v. communications equipment
HQ: General Dynamics Mission Systems, Inc.
    12450 Fair Lakes Cir
    Fairfax VA 22033
    877 449-0600

(G-7035)
GENERAL FERTILIZER EQP INC
Also Called: Speedy Spread
429 Edwardia Dr (27409-2607)
P.O. Box 19409 (27419-9409)
PHONE..................................336 299-4711
Ben Coston, *Pr*
Hunter Dalton Iii, *Treas*
Marshall Pike, *Sec*
EMP: 13 **EST:** 1985
SQ FT: 13,000
SALES (est): 2.48MM **Privately Held**
Web: www.speedyspread.com
SIC: 5083 3523 3531 Agricultural machinery and equipment; Fertilizing machinery, farm; Construction machinery

(G-7036)
GENERAL MOTOR REPAIR & SVC INC
2206 Westbrook St (27407-2592)
PHONE..................................336 292-1715
David Ross, *Pr*
Donna M Ross, *VP*
EMP: 8 **EST:** 1956
SALES (est): 1.53MM **Privately Held**
Web: www.generalmotorrepair.com
SIC: 5063 7694 Motors, electric; Electric motor repair

(G-7037)
GENEVA SOFTWARE CO INC
445 Dolley Madison Rd Ste 402 (27410-5168)
PHONE..................................336 275-8887
Thomas Vincent, *Pr*
EMP: 5 **EST:** 1990
SALES (est): 472.89K **Privately Held**
Web: www.genevasoftware.com
SIC: 7372 Business oriented computer software

(G-7038)
GEORGE W DAHL COMPANY INC
8439 Triad Dr (27409-9018)
PHONE..................................336 668-4444
Lawrence Nicolette, *Pr*
Anthony Simone, *VP*
▼ **EMP:** 20 **EST:** 1991
SQ FT: 87,000
SALES (est): 2.16MM **Privately Held**
SIC: 3492 Fluid power valves and hose fittings

(G-7039)
GERBINGS LLC
Also Called: Gerbing's Heated Clothing
816 S Elm St Ste D (27406-1332)
PHONE..................................800 646-5916
Steve Wuebker, *CEO*
▲ **EMP:** 69 **EST:** 2012
SALES (est): 770.25K
SALES (corp-wide): 3.97MM **Privately Held**
Web: www.gerbing.com
SIC: 2386 2253 Coats and jackets, leather and sheep-lined; Blouses, shirts, pants, and suits
PA: Prospect Brands, Llc
    816 S Elm St
    Greensboro NC 27406
    336 790-0085

(G-7040)
GET STUCK INC
2710 N Church St (27405-3657)
P.O. Box 4160 (27263-4160)
PHONE..................................336 698-3277
EMP: 8 **EST:** 2013
SALES (est): 189.29K **Privately Held**
Web: www.gameprosports.us
SIC: 2759 Screen printing

(G-7041)
GGS TECHNICAL PUBLICATIONS
420 Gallimore Dairy Rd Ste A (27409-9524)
PHONE..................................336 256-9600
EMP: 6 **EST:** 2016
SALES (est): 95.01K **Privately Held**
Web: www.ggsinc.com
SIC: 2759 Publication printing

(G-7042)
GIBBS MACHINE COMPANY INCORPORATED
2012 Fairfax Rd (27407-3065)
PHONE..................................336 856-1907

EMP: 22
Web: www.gibbsmachineco.com
SIC: 3599 7692 3444 Machine shop, jobbing and repair; Welding repair; Sheet metalwork

(G-7043)
GILBARCO INC (HQ)
Also Called: Gilbarco Veeder-Root
7300 W Friendly Ave (27410-6200)
P.O. Box 22087 (27420-2087)
PHONE..................................336 547-5000
◆ **EMP:** 1500 **EST:** 1865
SALES (est): 545.88MM
SALES (corp-wide): 3.1B **Publicly Held**
Web: www.gilbarco.com
SIC: 3586 3578 2752 7372 Gasoline pumps, measuring or dispensing; Cash registers; Tag, ticket, and schedule printing: lithographic; Business oriented computer software
PA: Vontier Corporation
    5438 Wade Park Blvd # 601
    Raleigh NC 27607
    984 275-6000

(G-7044)
GLADIATOR ENTERPRISES INC
5505 Weslo Willow Dr (27409-1935)
PHONE..................................336 944-6932
Ivor Buffong, *CEO*
EMP: 6 **EST:** 2015
SALES (est): 129.15K **Privately Held**
SIC: 3559 8361 7991 3949 Semiconductor manufacturing machinery; Rehabilitation center, residential: health care incidental; Physical fitness facilities; Protective sporting equipment

(G-7045)
GLAXOSMITHKLINE LLC
3408 Old Barn Rd (27410-9606)
PHONE..................................336 392-3058
EMP: 6
SALES (corp-wide): 35.31B **Privately Held**
Web: us.gsk.com
SIC: 2834 Pharmaceutical preparations
HQ: Glaxosmithkline Llc
    2929 Walnut St Ste 1700
    Philadelphia PA 19104
    888 825-5249

(G-7046)
GLOBAL PRODUCTS LLC
Also Called: Wiper Technologies
144 Industrial Ave (27406-4505)
P.O. Box 2883 (46515-2883)
PHONE..................................336 227-7327
Douglas Diaab, *Prin*
EMP: 6 **EST:** 2011
SALES (est): 309.82K **Privately Held**
Web: www.globalproducts.llc
SIC: 3714 Motor vehicle parts and accessories

(G-7047)
GLOBAL STONE IMPEX LLC
5088 Bartholomews Ln (27407-2722)
PHONE..................................336 609-1113
Neeraj Bhadouria, *Managing Member*
EMP: 6 **EST:** 2016
SALES (est): 578.27K **Privately Held**
SIC: 3271 Blocks, concrete: landscape or retaining wall

(G-7048)
GO GREEN SERVICES LLC
Also Called: Go Green Plumbing
300 Pomona Dr (27407-1620)
PHONE..................................336 252-2999
EMP: 67 **EST:** 2015
SALES (est): 4.84MM **Privately Held**

Web: www.gogreenplumb.com
SIC: 1711 3585 Plumbing contractors; Heating and air conditioning combination units

(G-7049)
GOAERO LLC
7680 Airline Rd Ste C (27409-1897)
PHONE..................................815 713-1190
Greg Denning, *CEO*
Neil Sparkman, *Pr*
EMP: 4 **EST:** 2013
SALES (est): 496.03K **Privately Held**
Web: www.goaero.net
SIC: 3728 Aircraft parts and equipment, nec

(G-7050)
GOLD MEDAL NORTH CAROLINA II
410 Gallimore Dairy Rd Ste G (27409-9780)
PHONE..................................336 665-4997
Rob Morgan, *Genl Mgr*
EMP: 7 **EST:** 2014
SALES (est): 104.86K **Privately Held**
Web: www.gmpopcorn.com
SIC: 3469 Utensils, household: metal, except cast

(G-7051)
GOLD MEDAL PRODUCTS CO
Also Called: Gold Medal Products-Carolina
410 Gallimore Dairy Rd Ste G (27409-9782)
PHONE..................................336 665-4997
Jeff Kellner, *Mgr*
EMP: 7
SALES (corp-wide): 99.8MM **Privately Held**
Web: www.gmpopcorn.com
SIC: 5145 5113 5046 3589 Snack foods; Industrial and personal service paper; Commercial cooking and food service equipment; Popcorn machines, commercial
PA: Gold Medal Products Co.
    10700 Medallion Dr
    Cincinnati OH 45241
    513 769-7676

(G-7052)
GONZALEZ CAB INSTALLERS LLC
2404 New Orleans St (27406-4034)
PHONE..................................336 897-1046
EMP: 6 **EST:** 2017
SALES (est): 93.3K **Privately Held**
SIC: 2434 Wood kitchen cabinets

(G-7053)
GOOD GRIEF MARKETING LLC
2609 E Market St (27401-4839)
PHONE..................................336 989-1984
Kishon Francis, *CEO*
EMP: 5 **EST:** 2017
SALES (est): 193.87K **Privately Held**
SIC: 7319 5943 3537 Advertising, nec; Notary and corporate seals; Trucks, tractors, loaders, carriers, and similar equipment

(G-7054)
GORDON WLDG & FABRICATION LLC
5311 Bailey Rd (27406-8739)
PHONE..................................336 406-7471
David Gordon, *Prin*
EMP: 5 **EST:** 2018
SALES (est): 146.4K **Privately Held**
Web: www.gordonweldingandfabrication.com
SIC: 7692 Welding repair

GEOGRAPHIC SECTION
Greensboro - Guilford County (G-7079)

(G-7055)
GPX INTELLIGENCE INC
Also Called: Logistimatics
620a S Elm St (27406-1328)
PHONE.................888 260-0706
Gabriel Weeks, *CEO*
Matthew Oliver Hannam, *CIO**
Brendan Christopher Younger, *
EMP: 28 **EST:** 2021
SALES (est): 4.52MM **Privately Held**
Web: www.logistimatics.com
SIC: 4899 3663 Data communication services; Global positioning systems (GPS) equipment

(G-7056)
GRAHAM CRACKER LLC
514 Pisgah Church Rd (27455-2524)
PHONE.................336 288-4440
Grant Chilton, *Prin*
EMP: 10 **EST:** 2006
SALES (est): 499.66K **Privately Held**
SIC: 2052 Graham crackers

(G-7057)
GRAPHIC COMPONENTS LLC
2800 Patterson St (27407-2319)
PHONE.................336 542-2128
Vince Cvijanovic, *Prin*
EMP: 22 **EST:** 2012
SALES (est): 1.98MM **Privately Held**
Web: www.graphiccomponents.com
SIC: 7336 3993 Graphic arts and related design; Advertising artwork

(G-7058)
GRAPHIC FINSHG SOLUTIONS LLC
1207 Boston Rd (27407-2107)
PHONE.................336 255-7857
EMP: 5 **EST:** 2003
SQ FT: 6,000
SALES (est): 460.09K **Privately Held**
SIC: 2679 2752 Tags and labels, paper; Tag, ticket, and schedule printing: lithographic

(G-7059)
GRAPHIC SYSTEMS INTL INC
Also Called: G S I
7 Lockheed Ct (27409-9060)
P.O. Box 18345 (27419-8345)
PHONE.................336 662-8686
Robert Kisstoth, *Pr*
Lisa Elkins, *
Brian Cagle, *
Jason Carrol, *
▼ **EMP:** 25 **EST:** 1978
SQ FT: 17,000
SALES (est): 2.77MM **Privately Held**
Web: www.gsi-signage.com
SIC: 3993 Signs, not made in custom sign painting shops

(G-7060)
GREENGATE SKATEPARK LLC
2616 Greengate Dr (27406-5243)
PHONE.................336 333-5800
Daniel Skeel, *Prin*
EMP: 4 **EST:** 2012
SALES (est): 97.55K **Privately Held**
Web: www.aboveboardskate.com
SIC: 3949 Skateboards

(G-7061)
GREENHECK FAN CO
3816 Patterson St (27407-3238)
PHONE.................336 852-5788
Patrice Pergolski, *COO*
EMP: 10 **EST:** 2005
SALES (est): 214.94K **Privately Held**
Web: www.greenheck.com
SIC: 3564 Blowing fans: industrial or commercial

(G-7062)
GREENSBORO DISTILLING LLC
321 W Wendover Ave (27408-8401)
PHONE.................336 273-6221
Shelley A Johnson, *Admn*
EMP: 5 **EST:** 2016
SALES (est): 510.05K **Privately Held**
Web: www.faintinggoatspirits.com
SIC: 2085 Distilled and blended liquors

(G-7063)
GREENSBORO DRIFTERS INC
4311 King Arthur Pl (27405-6323)
PHONE.................336 375-6743
Yvonne J Johnson, *Prin*
EMP: 7 **EST:** 2018
SALES (est): 64.11K **Privately Held**
Web: www.greensboro.com
SIC: 2711 Newspapers, publishing and printing

(G-7064)
GREENSBORO NEWS & RECORD LLC
3001 S Elm Eugene St (27406-4448)
PHONE.................336 373-7000
Robin Saul, *Pr*
EMP: 600
SALES (est): 100.94MM
SALES (corp-wide): 691.14MM **Publicly Held**
Web: www.greensboro.com
SIC: 2711 2791 2796 2752 Newspapers, publishing and printing; Typesetting; Platemaking services; Commercial printing, lithographic
HQ: Bh Media Group, Inc.
1314 Douglas St Ste 1500
Omaha NE 68102
402 444-1154

(G-7065)
GREENSBORO PLATERS
725 Kenilworth St (27403-2417)
P.O. Box 4466 (27404-4466)
PHONE.................336 274-7654
EMP: 5 **EST:** 2011
SALES (est): 102.23K **Privately Held**
Web: www.gboroplaters.com
SIC: 3471 Plating of metals or formed products

(G-7066)
GREENSBORO TIRE & AUTO SERVICE
Also Called: Greensboro Tire 3
4615 W Market St Ste A (27407-2973)
PHONE.................336 294-9495
Dustin Allred, *Mgr*
EMP: 6
SALES (corp-wide): 2.67MM **Privately Held**
Web: www.greensborotireandauto.com
SIC: 7534 7538 5531 Tire recapping; General automotive repair shops; Automotive tires
PA: Greensboro Tire & Auto Service Center, Inc.
1901 E Bessemer Ave
Greensboro NC
336 273-6748

(G-7067)
GREENSBORO VOICE
407 E Washington St (27401-2930)
PHONE.................336 255-1006
Susan Thomas, *Prin*
EMP: 10 **EST:** 2015
SALES (est): 60.02K **Privately Held**
Web: www.greensboro.com
SIC: 2711 Newspapers, publishing and printing

(G-7068)
GRIFFIN MARKETING GROUP
4608 Knightbridge Rd (27455-1916)
PHONE.................336 558-5802
EMP: 6 **EST:** 2018
SALES (est): 118.86K **Privately Held**
Web: www.griffinreps.com
SIC: 3556 Food products machinery

(G-7069)
GSO PRINTING
317 S Westgate Dr Ste A (27407-1633)
PHONE.................336 292-1601
Mike Ealley, *Mng Pt*
Mary Ealley, *Pt*
EMP: 5 **EST:** 2008
SALES (est): 297.91K **Privately Held**
SIC: 2752 Offset printing

(G-7070)
GSO PRINTING INC
2 Hill Valley Ct (27410-9628)
PHONE.................336 288-5778
Darrell Ealley, *Pr*
EMP: 4 **EST:** 2003
SQ FT: 2,100
SALES (est): 233.76K **Privately Held**
SIC: 2752 Commercial printing, lithographic

(G-7071)
GUERRILLA RF INC
2000 Pisgah Church Rd (27455-3308)
PHONE.................336 510-7840
Ryan Pratt, *CEO*
Desiree Pratt, *
Jeff Broxson, *
John Berg, *
Alan Ake, *
EMP: 68 **EST:** 2013
SQ FT: 10,000
SALES (est): 11.6MM **Privately Held**
Web: www.guerrilla-rf.com
SIC: 3674 Monolithic integrated circuits (solid state)

(G-7072)
GUILFORD ORTHTIC PROTHETIC INC
405 Parkway St Ste G (27401-1693)
PHONE.................336 676-5394
Randy Johnson, *Owner*
EMP: 5 **EST:** 2014
SALES (est): 51.81K **Privately Held**
SIC: 3842 Limbs, artificial

(G-7073)
HAECO AMERICAS LLC (DH)
Also Called: Haeco Americas
623 Radar Rd (27410-6221)
PHONE.................336 668-4410
Richard Kendall, *Managing Member*
Doug Rasmussen, *Managing Member*
Bruce Patterson, *Managing Member*
Lee Fox, *Managing Member*
◆ **EMP:** 1000 **EST:** 1989
SQ FT: 190,000
SALES (est): 514.41MM
SALES (corp-wide): 17.24B **Privately Held**
Web: www.haeco.aero
SIC: 5088 4581 2396 Transportation equipment and supplies; Aircraft servicing and repairing; Automotive trimmings, fabric
HQ: Haeco Usa Holdings, Llc
623 Radar Rd
Greensboro NC 27410
336 668-4410

(G-7074)
HAECO CABIN SOLUTIONS LLC (DH)
Also Called: Haeco Americas Cabin Solutions
8010 Piedmont Triad Pkwy (27409-9407)
PHONE.................336 862-1418
EMP: 62 **EST:** 2006
SALES (est): 59.89MM
SALES (corp-wide): 17.24B **Privately Held**
Web: www.haeco.aero
SIC: 4581 2531 Aircraft maintenance and repair services; Seats, aircraft
HQ: Haeco Airframe Services, Llc
623 Radar Rd
Greensboro NC 27410
336 668-4410

(G-7075)
HALL TIRE AND BATTERY CO INC
2222 Martin Luther King Jr Dr (27406-3710)
PHONE.................336 275-3812
Frank I Hall, *Pr*
Mary Hall, *VP*
Gregory F Hall, *Sec*
EMP: 10 **EST:** 1960
SQ FT: 4,000
SALES (est): 1.62MM **Privately Held**
Web: www.halltire.com
SIC: 5531 7539 7534 Automotive tires; Wheel alignment, automotive; Tire repair shop

(G-7076)
HAMMER & SHAW WOODWORKS
910 Mccormick St (27403-2928)
PHONE.................336 339-4829
David Shaw, *Prin*
EMP: 4 **EST:** 2017
SALES (est): 57.28K **Privately Held**
Web: shawwdavid.wixsite.com
SIC: 2431 Millwork

(G-7077)
HARTLEY READY MIX CON MFG INC
1040 Boulder Rd (27409-9106)
P.O. Box 1719 (27374-1719)
PHONE.................336 294-5995
Scott Ball, *Brnch Mgr*
EMP: 7
SALES (corp-wide): 6.36MM **Privately Held**
Web: www.hartleyreadymix.com
SIC: 3273 Ready-mixed concrete
PA: Hartley Ready Mix Concrete Manufacturing, Inc.
3510 Rothrock St
Winston Salem NC 27107
336 788-3928

(G-7078)
HATRACK RIVER ENTERPRISES INC
401 Willoughby Blvd (27408-3135)
P.O. Box 18184 (27419-8184)
PHONE.................336 282-9848
Orson Scott Card, *Pr*
EMP: 7 **EST:** 1997
SALES (est): 490.85K **Privately Held**
Web: www.hatrack.com
SIC: 2731 Books, publishing only

(G-7079)
HB FULLER COMPANY
2302 W Meadowview Rd (27407-3721)
PHONE.................336 294-5939
Jamie Mittel, *Brnch Mgr*
EMP: 4
SALES (corp-wide): 3.51B **Publicly Held**
Web: www.hbfuller.com
SIC: 2891 Adhesives
PA: H.B. Fuller Company
1200 Willow Lake Blvd

Greensboro - Guilford County (G-7080)   GEOGRAPHIC SECTION

Saint Paul MN 55110
651 236-5900

(G-7080)
HDB INC
3901 Riverdale Dr (27406-7599)
PHONE..................800 403-2247
EMP: 8 **EST:** 1984
SALES (est): 81.13K **Privately Held**
SIC: 2393 Bags and containers, except sleeping bags: textile

(G-7081)
HEALING SPRINGS FARMACY
812 Stoney Hill Cir (27406-9187)
PHONE..................336 549-6159
Laylah Cooper Holman, *Pr*
Tinece Holman, *Ex Dir*
EMP: 4 **EST:** 2015
SALES (est): 466.29K **Privately Held**
Web: www.viyc.org
SIC: 2833 Medicinals and botanicals
PA: Volunteer In Your Community Inc.
805 Stoney Hill Cir
Greensboro NC 27406

(G-7082)
HEARTH & HOME TECHNOLOGIES LLC
Also Called: HEARTH & HOME TECHNOLOGIES, LLC
215 Industrial Ave Ste A (27406-4546)
PHONE..................336 274-1663
Jessica Schrader, *Mgr*
EMP: 118
SALES (corp-wide): 479.1MM **Publicly Held**
Web: www.fireside.com
SIC: 3259 3433 3429 Flue lining, clay; Heating equipment, except electric; Fireplace equipment, hardware: andirons, grates, screens
HQ: Hearth & Home Technologies, Llc
7571 215th St W
Lakeville MN 55044

(G-7083)
HEAT TRANSFER SALES LLC
Hoffman Hydronics Div
4321 Piedmont Pkwy (27410-8114)
PHONE..................800 842-3328
EMP: 29
SALES (corp-wide): 166.15MM **Privately Held**
Web: www.hoffmanhydronics.com
SIC: 3433 Heating equipment, except electric
HQ: Heat Transfer Sales, Llc
3816 Patterson St
Greensboro NC 27407
336 292-8777

(G-7084)
HEAT TRANSFER SALES LLC (HQ)
3816 Patterson St (27407-3238)
P.O. Box 8608 (27419-0608)
PHONE..................336 292-8777
Joseph Britt, *Pr*
Gardner Casey, *
EMP: 11 **EST:** 2019
SALES (est): 12.36MM
SALES (corp-wide): 166.15MM **Privately Held**
Web: www.hoffmanhydronics.com
SIC: 3433 3585 Heating equipment, except electric; Refrigeration and heating equipment
PA: Hoffman & Hoffman, Inc.
3816 Patterson St
Greensboro NC 27407
336 292-8777

(G-7085)
HEAT TRANSFER SALES OF THE CAROLINAS INC (PA)
4101 Beechwood Dr (27410-8118)
P.O. Box 8608 (27419-0608)
PHONE..................336 294-3838
EMP: 25 **EST:** 1971
SALES (est): 9.57MM
SALES (corp-wide): 9.57MM **Privately Held**
Web: www.heattransfersales.com
SIC: 5074 5075 7692 5084 Plumbing and hydronic heating supplies; Air conditioning equipment, except room units, nec; Welding repair; Industrial machinery and equipment

(G-7086)
HEMISPHERES MAGAZINE
1301 Carolina St (27401-1032)
PHONE..................336 255-0195
David Brown, *Prin*
EMP: 22 **EST:** 2008
SALES (est): 241.85K **Privately Held**
Web: www.paceco.com
SIC: 2721 Magazines: publishing only, not printed on site

(G-7087)
HERSHEY GROUP LLC
2010 New Garden Rd Ste A (27410-2528)
PHONE..................336 855-3888
Erik Hershey, *Managing Member*
EMP: 5 **EST:** 2018
SALES (est): 231.15K **Privately Held**
Web: www.thersheygroup.com
SIC: 3999 4783 Handbag and luggage frames and handles; Packing goods for shipping

(G-7088)
HF GROUP LLC
Also Called: Mid Atlantic Book Bindery
1010 Arnold St (27405-7102)
PHONE..................336 931-0800
Keith Roberts, *Brnch Mgr*
EMP: 48
Web: www.hfgroup.com
SIC: 2732 Books, printing and binding
PA: Hf Group, Llc
400 Arora Cmmons Cir Unit
Aurora OH 44202

(G-7089)
HIGHLAND COMPOSITES
416 Gallimore Dairy Rd Ste N (27409-9535)
PHONE..................704 924-3090
EMP: 9 **EST:** 2017
SALES (est): 242.19K **Privately Held**
SIC: 2211 Broadwoven fabric mills, cotton

(G-7090)
HIGHLAND INDUSTRIES INC
10 Northline Pl (27410-4842)
PHONE..................336 855-0625
Frank Roe, *Prin*
EMP: 43
SALES (corp-wide): 6.91B **Privately Held**
Web: www.highlandindustries.com
SIC: 2221 Automotive fabrics, manmade fiber
HQ: Highland Industries, Inc.
650 Chesterfield Hwy
Cheraw SC 29520
336 992-7500

(G-7091)
HIGHLAND INDUSTRIES INC
629 Green Valley Rd Ste 300 (27408-7726)
PHONE..................336 547-1600

EMP: 43
SALES (corp-wide): 6.91B **Privately Held**
Web: www.highlandindustries.com
SIC: 2221 Automotive fabrics, manmade fiber
HQ: Highland Industries, Inc.
650 Chesterfield Hwy
Cheraw SC 29520
336 992-7500

(G-7092)
HIGHLAND TANK NC INC
2700 Patterson St (27407-2317)
PHONE..................336 218-0801
Michael Vanlenten, *CEO*
John Jacob, *
Charles A Frey, *
EMP: 140 **EST:** 1994
SQ FT: 43,000
SALES (est): 23.22MM **Privately Held**
Web: www.highlandtank.com
SIC: 3443 Tanks, standard or custom fabricated: metal plate

(G-7093)
HIRSCHFELD INDUSTRIES BRDG LLC
Also Called: Hirschfeld Industries-Bridge
101 Centreport Dr Ste 400 (27409-9422)
P.O. Box 20888 (27420-0888)
PHONE..................336 271-8252
John O'quinn, *Ex VP*
Rodney L Goodwill, *
EMP: 717 **EST:** 1994
SQ FT: 885,000
SALES (est): 3.94MM **Privately Held**
Web: hirschfeld.wwafcosteel.com
SIC: 3441 Fabricated structural metal
PA: Hirschfeld Holdings Lp
112 W 29th St
San Angelo TX 76903

(G-7094)
HOFFMAN BUILDING TECH INC
Also Called: Thermatec
3816 Patterson St (27407-3238)
PHONE..................336 292-8777
William M Easterday, *Pr*
Louis Hoffman, *
EMP: 200 **EST:** 2016
SQ FT: 20,000
SALES (est): 17.81MM **Privately Held**
Web: www.hbtech.com
SIC: 3822 Temperature controls, automatic

(G-7095)
HOFFMAN STEINBERG
1806 Fairfax Rd Ste A (27407-4999)
PHONE..................336 292-5501
Rich Wright, *Owner*
EMP: 5 **EST:** 2017
SALES (est): 73.93K **Privately Held**
SIC: 2893 Printing ink

(G-7096)
HONDA AIRCRAFT COMPANY LLC
6423 Bryan Blvd Ste B (27409-9466)
P.O. Box 35805 (27425)
PHONE..................336 662-0849
Nori Furuichi, *Brnch Mgr*
EMP: 15
Web: www.hondajet.com
SIC: 3728 Aircraft parts and equipment, nec
HQ: Honda Aircraft Company, Llc
6430 Ballinger Rd
Greensboro NC 27410

(G-7097)
HONDA AIRCRAFT COMPANY LLC
Also Called: Honda Aircraft Co Service Ctr
6420 Ballinger Rd Bldg 400 (27410-9063)
PHONE..................336 662-0246

David Sunda, *Mgr*
EMP: 15
SIC: 3721 Aircraft
HQ: Honda Aircraft Company, Llc
6430 Ballinger Rd
Greensboro NC 27410

(G-7098)
HONDA AIRCRAFT COMPANY LLC
404 S Chimney Rock Rd (27409-9260)
PHONE..................336 662-0246
Timothy Peters, *Prin*
EMP: 15
SIC: 3721 Aircraft
HQ: Honda Aircraft Company, Llc
6430 Ballinger Rd
Greensboro NC 27410

(G-7099)
HONDA AIRCRAFT COMPANY LLC (HQ)
6430 Ballinger Rd (27410-9063)
PHONE..................336 662-0246
Michimasa Fujino, *Managing Member*
Tetsuo Iwamura, *
Hiroshi Soda, *
◆ **EMP:** 390 **EST:** 2011
SQ FT: 256,000
SALES (est): 257.52MM **Privately Held**
Web: www.hondajet.com
SIC: 3721 Aircraft
PA: Honda Motor Co., Ltd.
2-1-1, Minamiaoyama
Minato-Ku TKY 107-0

(G-7100)
HONES ENTERPRISES
1102 Briarcliff Rd (27408-7534)
PHONE..................336 378-9351
Deborah Hones, *Prin*
EMP: 6 **EST:** 2008
SALES (est): 163.81K **Privately Held**
SIC: 3291 Hones

(G-7101)
HORIZON TOOL INC
Also Called: Cal-Van
7918 Industrial Village Rd (27409-9691)
PHONE..................336 299-4182
Sean Kenny, *Pr*
▲ **EMP:** 111 **EST:** 1989
SQ FT: 35,000
SALES (est): 12.27MM **Privately Held**
Web: www.cal-vantools.com
SIC: 3423 Hand and edge tools, nec

(G-7102)
HPT HITOMS LLC
3008 Redford Dr (27408-3116)
PHONE..................336 541-8093
Greg Suire, *Owner*
EMP: 6 **EST:** 2017
SALES (est): 143.48K **Privately Held**
Web: www.hitoms.com
SIC: 2711 Newspapers, publishing and printing

(G-7103)
HUBERGROUP USA INC
651 Brigham Rd Ste C (27409-9078)
PHONE..................336 292-5501
EMP: 17
SALES (corp-wide): 242.12K **Privately Held**
Web: www.hubergroup.com
SIC: 2893 Printing ink
HQ: Hubergroup Usa, Inc.
1701 Golf Rd Ste 3-201
Rolling Meadows IL 60008
815 929-9293

(G-7104)
HUDSON OVERALL COMPANY INC
Also Called: Hudson's Hill
527 S Elm St (27406-1325)
PHONE..........................336 314-5024
William Clayton, *Pr*
Harold Clayton, *Sec*
Evan Morrison, *Prin*
EMP: 4 **EST:** 2014
SALES (est): 141.23K **Privately Held**
SIC: 5611 2329 Men's and boys' clothing stores; Athletic clothing, except uniforms: men's, youths' and boys'

(G-7105)
HUGHES METAL WORKS LLC
Also Called: Hughes Metal Works
1914 Fairfax Rd (27407-4145)
P.O. Box 7363 (27417-0363)
PHONE..........................336 297-0808
EMP: 23 **EST:** 1994
SQ FT: 11,000
SALES (est): 2.18MM **Privately Held**
Web: www.hughesmetalworks.com
SIC: 3441 Fabricated structural metal

(G-7106)
HUSH GREENSBORO
433 Spring Garden St (27401-2789)
PHONE..........................336 676-6133
EMP: 8 **EST:** 2019
SALES (est): 125.14K **Privately Held**
Web: www.greensboro.com
SIC: 2711 Newspapers, publishing and printing

(G-7107)
I & I SLING INC
3824 Patterson St (27407-3238)
PHONE..........................336 323-1532
Dennis St Germain Junior, *Mgr*
EMP: 9
SALES (corp-wide): 19.76MM **Privately Held**
Web: www.iandisling.com
SIC: 3496 Miscellaneous fabricated wire products
PA: I & I Sling, Inc.
205 Bridgewater Rd
Aston PA 19014
610 485-8500

(G-7108)
I PRINT TTEES LLC
241 E Market St (27401-2909)
PHONE..........................336 202-8148
Candra Morgan, *COO*
EMP: 4 **EST:** 2014
SALES (est): 197.51K **Privately Held**
Web: www.i-print-tees.com
SIC: 2759 Screen printing

(G-7109)
IBOLILI NATURAL FIBERS
Also Called: Ibolili Natural Home Furn
104 Leonard Dr (27410-4414)
PHONE..........................866 834-9857
John Stein, *Prin*
EMP: 5 **EST:** 2015
SALES (est): 98.82K **Privately Held**
Web: www.ibolili.com
SIC: 2511 5023 Wood household furniture; Homefurnishings

(G-7110)
ICON BOILER INC
2025 16th St (27405-5119)
PHONE..........................844 562-4266
Jim Brady, *Pr*
EMP: 23 **EST:** 2020
SALES (est): 1.59MM **Privately Held**
Web: www.iconboiler.com
SIC: 3443 Boiler and boiler shop work

(G-7111)
IDEACODE INC
11010 W Northwood St (27408)
PHONE..........................919 341-5170
Charles Bettini, *Pr*
John Acre, *VP*
EMP: 5 **EST:** 2000
SALES (est): 363.71K **Privately Held**
Web: www.ideacode.com
SIC: 7371 8243 5734 7372 Computer software development; Software training, computer; Software, computer games; Application computer software

(G-7112)
IDEXX PHARMACEUTICALS INC
7009 Albert Pick Rd (27409-9654)
PHONE..........................336 834-6500
Doug Hepler, *Ex VP*
Steve Capps, *VP Fin*
EMP: 37 **EST:** 1996
SALES (est): 2.86MM
SALES (corp-wide): 3.66B **Publicly Held**
Web: www.idexx.com
SIC: 2834 Pharmaceutical preparations
PA: Idexx Laboratories, Inc.
1 Idexx Dr
Westbrook ME 04092
207 556-0300

(G-7113)
INDUSTRIAL AIR INC ☉
428 Edwardia Dr (27409-2608)
P.O. Box 8769 (27419-0769)
PHONE..........................336 292-1030
EMP: 125 **EST:** 2023
SALES (est): 20.53MM
SALES (corp-wide): 516.35MM **Publicly Held**
Web: www.industrialairinc.com
SIC: 1711 3443 Warm air heating and air conditioning contractor; Tanks, standard or custom fabricated: metal plate
PA: Limbach Holdings, Inc.
1251 Waterfront Pl # 201
Pittsburgh PA 15222
412 359-2100

(G-7114)
INDUSTRIES OF BLIND INC (PA)
920 W Gate City Blvd (27403-2803)
PHONE..........................336 274-1591
David Thompson, *Prin*
David Thompson, *Prin*
EMP: 194 **EST:** 1932
SQ FT: 100,000
SALES (est): 1.58MM
SALES (corp-wide): 1.58MM **Privately Held**
Web: www.industriesoftheblind.com
SIC: 3951 Fountain pens and fountain pen desk sets

(G-7115)
INMYLIFE INC
900 Troublesome Creek Dr (27455-8319)
PHONE..........................336 644-8856
Anthony Maddalone, *Owner*
EMP: 5 **EST:** 2013
SALES (est): 224.7K **Privately Held**
SIC: 3572 Computer storage devices

(G-7116)
INNOBIOACTIVES LLC
7325 W Friendly Ave Ste H (27410-6211)
PHONE..........................336 235-0838
Chen Chen, *Managing Member*
▲ **EMP:** 8 **EST:** 2007
SALES (est): 947.91K **Privately Held**
SIC: 2834 Pharmaceutical preparations

(G-7117)
INNOVATIVE KITCHENS BATHS INC
2912 Manufacturers Rd (27406-4606)
PHONE..........................336 279-1188
Patrick Bunn, *Pr*
EMP: 7 **EST:** 2004
SQ FT: 9,200
SALES (est): 835.53K **Privately Held**
Web: www.ikbgreensboro.com
SIC: 2434 Wood kitchen cabinets

(G-7118)
INSECT SHIELD LLC (PA)
814 W Market St (27401-1813)
P.O. Box 10129 (27404-0129)
PHONE..........................336 272-4157
Haynes G Griffin, *Managing Member*
Richard Lane, *
▲ **EMP:** 38 **EST:** 2002
SALES (est): 10.14MM
SALES (corp-wide): 10.14MM **Privately Held**
Web: www.insectshield.com
SIC: 2269 Finishing plants, nec

(G-7119)
INTERNATIONAL MINUTE PRESS
2417 Spring Garden St (27403-2042)
P.O. Box 18424 (27419-8424)
PHONE..........................336 854-1589
Jim Gouge, *Owner*
EMP: 7 **EST:** 2010
SALES (est): 244.76K **Privately Held**
SIC: 2741 Miscellaneous publishing

(G-7120)
INTERTECH CORPORATION
Also Called: Funball
3240 N Ohenry Blvd (27405-3808)
P.O. Box 14690 (27415-4690)
PHONE..........................336 621-1891
TOLL FREE: 800
EMP: 65 **EST:** 1968
SALES (est): 12.01MM
SALES (corp-wide): 868.81MM **Privately Held**
SIC: 3089 3085 Blow molded finished plastics products, nec; Plastics bottles
PA: Pretium Packaging, L.L.C.
1555 Page Industrial Blvd
Saint Louis MO 63132
314 727-8200

(G-7121)
IQE NORTH CAROLINA LLC
494 Gallimore Dairy Rd (27409-9514)
PHONE..........................336 609-6270
Ken Baker, *Mgr*
EMP: 13 **EST:** 2012
SALES (est): 4.83MM **Privately Held**
Web: www.iqep.com
SIC: 5045 7371 3674 Computer software; Computer software systems analysis and design, custom; Computer logic modules

(G-7122)
IRONMEX FABRICATION INC
2001 Carpenter St (27403-3207)
PHONE..........................336 937-1045
EMP: 4 **EST:** 2020
SALES (est): 64.64K **Privately Held**
SIC: 3999 Manufacturing industries, nec

(G-7123)
IRONWORKS MOTORCYCLES
313 W Fisher Ave (27401-2038)
PHONE..........................336 542-7868
EMP: 5 **EST:** 2013
SALES (est): 86.3K **Privately Held**
SIC: 5012 7699 5571 3751 Motorcycles; Motorcycle repair service; Motorcycle dealers; Motorcycle accessories

(G-7124)
ITG BRANDS
420 N English St (27405-7310)
PHONE..........................336 335-6600
Martin Orlowsky, *Mgr*
EMP: 57
Web: www.itgbrands.com
SIC: 2111 Cigarettes
HQ: Itg Brands
714 Green Valley Rd
Greensboro NC 27408
336 335-7000

(G-7125)
ITG BRANDS LLC (HQ)
714 Green Valley Rd (27408-7018)
P.O. Box 21688 (27420-1688)
PHONE..........................336 335-7000
EMP: 79 **EST:** 2012
SALES (est): 648.07M **Privately Held**
Web: www.itgbrands.com
SIC: 2111 Cigarettes
PA: Imperial Brands Plc
121 Winterstoke Road
Bristol BS3 2

(G-7126)
ITG HOLDINGS INC
Also Called: I T G
804 Green Valley Rd Ste 300 (27408-7039)
PHONE..........................336 379-6220
◆ **EMP:** 4000
SIC: 2211 2231 2221 2273 Denims; Worsted fabrics, broadwoven; Polyester broadwoven fabrics; Carpets and rugs

(G-7127)
ITG HOLDINGS USA INC
714 Green Valley Rd (27408-7018)
PHONE..........................954 772-9000
Kevin Freudenchal, *Pr*
EMP: 39 **EST:** 2007
SALES (est): 2.27MM **Privately Held**
Web: www.itgbrands.com
SIC: 2131 Chewing and smoking tobacco
PA: Imperial Brands Plc
121 Winterstoke Road
Bristol BS3 2

(G-7128)
ITM LTD SOUTH
1903 Brassfield Rd (27410-2155)
PHONE..........................336 883-2400
Scott Vanderlinder, *Pr*
◆ **EMP:** 6 **EST:** 1959
SALES (est): 516.98K **Privately Held**
Web: www.itmsouth.com
SIC: 3552 Textile machinery

(G-7129)
IVEY LN INC
Also Called: Ivey Lane
103 Ward Rd (27405-9651)
P.O. Box 29185 (27429-9185)
PHONE..........................336 230-0062
EMP: 8 **EST:** 1992
SALES (est): 919.67K **Privately Held**
Web: www.iveylane.com
SIC: 5211 1799 3281 Counter tops; Counter top installation; Cut stone and stone products

Greensboro - Guilford County (G-7130) — GEOGRAPHIC SECTION

(G-7130)
J & M CABINET INSTALLERS LLC
2811 Bears Creek Rd (27406-5147)
PHONE.................336 500-7148
Aguilar Martell, *Prin*
EMP: 4 EST: 2015
SALES (est): 70.45K Privately Held
SIC: 2434 Wood kitchen cabinets

(G-7131)
J MORGAN SIGNS INC
4421 S Elm Eugene St (27406-8931)
PHONE.................336 274-6509
Jeff Morgan, *Pr*
EMP: 10 EST: 1972
SALES (est): 850.76K Privately Held
Web: jmorgansigns.wordpress.com
SIC: 3993 Signs and advertising specialties

(G-7132)
JACK M JARRETT
512 N Mendenhall St (27401-1755)
PHONE.................336 772-4108
Jack M Jarrett, *Prin*
EMP: 6 EST: 2011
SALES (est): 57.12K Privately Held
SIC: 2741 Miscellaneous publishing

(G-7133)
JAMES M PLEASANTS COMPANY INC (PA)
Also Called: Jpm
603 Diamond Hill Ct (27406-4617)
P.O. Box 16706 (27416-0706)
PHONE.................336 275-3152
TOLL FREE: 800
J Chris Edmonson, *Pr*
Jamie Edmondson, *
G David Pleasants, *
EMP: 50 EST: 1963
SQ FT: 26,000
SALES (est): 42.9MM
SALES (corp-wide): 42.9MM Privately Held
Web: www.jmpco.com
SIC: 5075 3585 3561 3494 Warm air heating and air conditioning; Refrigeration and heating equipment; Pumps and pumping equipment; Valves and pipe fittings, nec

(G-7134)
JAMES M PLEASANTS COMPANY INC
Hyfab
206 E Seneca Rd (27406-4533)
PHONE.................888 902-8324
EMP: 11
SALES (corp-wide): 42.9MM Privately Held
Web: www.hyfabco.com
SIC: 3494 Valves and pipe fittings, nec
PA: James M Pleasants Company Incorporated
603 Diamond Hill Ct
Greensboro NC 27406
336 275-3152

(G-7135)
JBT AEROTECH SERVICES
6035 Old Oak Ridge Rd (27410-9240)
PHONE.................336 740-3737
EMP: 7 EST: 2010
SALES (est): 280.73K Privately Held
SIC: 3556 Food products machinery

(G-7136)
JEWERS DOORS US INC
3714 Alliance Dr Ste 305 (27407-2060)
P.O. Box 16639 (27416-0639)
PHONE.................888 510-5331
Michael Peters, *CEO*
Michael L Peters, *
April H Peters, *
EMP: 50 EST: 2020
SALES (est): 2.75MM Privately Held
SIC: 3442 1751 Metal doors, sash, and trim; Window and door installation and erection

(G-7137)
JOCHUM INDUSTRIES
710 Freemasons Dr (27407-1862)
PHONE.................336 288-7975
Jim Jochum, *Prin*
EMP: 4 EST: 2008
SALES (est): 102.72K Privately Held
SIC: 3999 Manufacturing industries, nec

(G-7138)
JOE ARMSTRONG
Also Called: Arms & Hopie Dist & Sup
3205 Liberty Rd (27406-5405)
PHONE.................336 207-6503
Joe Armstrong, *Owner*
EMP: 4 EST: 2012
SALES (est): 69.45K Privately Held
SIC: 5251 5072 3564 7389 Tools, hand; Garden tools, hand; Filters, air: furnaces, air conditioning equipment, etc.; Business services, nec

(G-7139)
JONES FABRICARE INC (PA)
Also Called: Jones Furs
502 E Cornwallis Dr (27405-5680)
PHONE.................336 272-7261
Hugh N Jones, *Pr*
EMP: 7 EST: 1906
SQ FT: 20,000
SALES (est): 543.97K
SALES (corp-wide): 543.97K Privately Held
SIC: 7219 2371 5632 Fur garment cleaning, repairing, and storage; Fur coats and other fur apparel; Fur apparel

(G-7140)
JORLINK USA INC
Also Called: Jorlink.com
3714 Alliance Dr Ste 100 (27407-2060)
PHONE.................336 288-1613
Mackenzie J Quiros, *CEO*
EMP: 10 EST: 1988
SQ FT: 5,000
SALES (est): 2.38MM Privately Held
Web: www.jorlink.com
SIC: 5087 3564 Engraving equipment and supplies; Dust or fume collecting equipment, industrial

(G-7141)
JQ PRO DETAILING LLC
2524 Yow Rd (27407-5952)
PHONE.................336 543-0663
EMP: 5 EST: 2020
SALES (est): 161.86K Privately Held
SIC: 3589 Car washing machinery

(G-7142)
JUS DOORS INC
3714 Alliance Dr Ste 305 (27407-2060)
PHONE.................888 510-5331
Michael Peters, *CEO*
EMP: 10 EST: 2021
SALES (est): 5MM Privately Held
Web: www.jusdoors.us
SIC: 3442 Metal doors, sash, and trim

(G-7143)
K & C MACHINE CO INC
601 Industrial Ave (27406-4696)
PHONE.................336 373-0745
Barry Collins, *Ch Bd*
Jeff Collins, *Pr*
Anita Jones, *Sec*
EMP: 16 EST: 1975
SQ FT: 10,000
SALES (est): 371.32K Privately Held
Web: www.kcmachine.com
SIC: 3599 Machine shop, jobbing and repair

(G-7144)
KAY CHEMICAL COMPANY
Also Called: Ecolab
8300 Capital Dr (27409-9790)
PHONE.................336 668-7290
◆ EMP: 620
SIC: 2842 Specialty cleaning

(G-7145)
KAYSER-ROTH CORPORATION (DH)
Also Called: No Nonsense
102 Corporate Center Blvd (27408-3172)
P.O. Box 26530 (27415-6530)
PHONE.................336 852-2030
Nicola Galloti, *Ch Bd*
Kevin Toomey, *
◆ EMP: 120 EST: 1985
SALES (est): 348.67MM
SALES (corp-wide): 192.57MM Privately Held
Web: www.kayser-roth.com
SIC: 5961 2251 3842 8741 Women's apparel, mail order; Women's hosiery, except socks; Surgical appliances and supplies; Management services
HQ: Golden Lady Company Spa
Via Giacomo Leopardi 3/5
Castiglione Delle Stiviere MN 46043
037 694-1211

(G-7146)
KAYSER-ROTH HOSIERY INC
102 Corporate Center Blvd (27408-3172)
P.O. Box 26530 (27415-6530)
PHONE.................336 852-2030
EMP: 37 EST: 1955
SALES (est): 7.39MM Privately Held
Web: www.kayser-roth.com
SIC: 2389 2252 Men's miscellaneous accessories; Socks

(G-7147)
KCS IMPRV & CNSTR CO INC
Also Called: General Contractor
510 N Church St Ste C (27401-6097)
PHONE.................336 288-3865
R Crabtree, *Pr*
Keith Crabtree, *Pr*
EMP: 5 EST: 1982
SQ FT: 3,500
SALES (est): 848.6K Privately Held
Web: www.kcsimprovement.com
SIC: 1521 1389 General remodeling, single-family houses; Construction, repair, and dismantling services

(G-7148)
KELLER CRES U TO BE PHRMGRAPHI
1072 Boulder Rd (27409-9106)
PHONE.................336 851-1150
Bill Wentz, *CFO*
EMP: 10 EST: 2019
SALES (est): 447.98K Privately Held
SIC: 2752 Commercial printing, lithographic

(G-7149)
KILOP USA INC
3714 Alliance Dr Ste 401 (27407-2060)
PHONE.................336 297-4999
EMP: 4 EST: 2018
SALES (est): 78.5K Privately Held
Web: www.kilopusa.com
SIC: 2821 Plastics materials and resins

(G-7150)
KIMBEES INC
317 Martin Luthe (27406)
PHONE.................336 323-8773
EMP: 4
SALES (est): 314.34K Privately Held
SIC: 2099 Tea blending

(G-7151)
KINDERMUSIK INTERNATIONAL INC
Also Called: Kindermusik
237 Burgess Rd (27409-9787)
PHONE.................800 628-5687
Scott Kinsey, *CEO*
Judy L Harris, *
▲ EMP: 40 EST: 1980
SALES (est): 5.52MM Privately Held
Web: www.kindermusik.com
SIC: 8299 2741 Music school; Music, book: publishing and printing

(G-7152)
KIRK & BLUM MANUFACTURING CO
8735 W Market St (27409-9653)
P.O. Box 35423 (27425)
PHONE.................801 728-6533
Paul Gillespie, *Mgr*
EMP: 39
Web: www.cecoenviro.com
SIC: 3444 5075 3564 3443 Sheet metal specialties, not stamped; Dust collecting equipment; Blowers and fans; Fabricated plate work (boiler shop)
HQ: The Kirk & Blum Manufacturing Company
4625 Red Bank Rd Ste 200
Cincinnati OH 45227
513 458-2600

(G-7153)
KLB ENTERPRISES INCORPORATED
Also Called: Carolina Fine Snacks
209 Citation Ct (27409-9026)
PHONE.................336 605-0773
Phillip Kosak, *Pr*
Jim Buck, *VP*
▲ EMP: 10 EST: 1982
SQ FT: 30,000
SALES (est): 1.6MM Privately Held
SIC: 2096 2064 Corn chips and other corn-based snacks; Nuts, candy covered

(G-7154)
KLOUD HEMP CO
2701 S Elm Eugene St Ste E (27406-3634)
PHONE.................336 740-2528
Katrina Travis, *Pr*
EMP: 4 EST: 2019
SALES (est): 177.63K Privately Held
SIC: 2299 2099 5999 Hemp yarn, thread, roving, and textiles; Tea blending; Miscellaneous retail stores, nec

(G-7155)
KONTOOR BRANDS INC
Also Called: Vf
400 N Elm St (27401-2143)
P.O. Box 21407 (27420-1407)
PHONE.................336 332-3586
EMP: 77
SALES (corp-wide): 2.61B Publicly Held
Web: www.kontoorbrands.com
SIC: 2325 2331 Men's and boy's trousers and slacks; Shirts, women's and juniors': made from purchased materials
PA: Kontoor Brands, Inc.
400 N Elm St

GEOGRAPHIC SECTION   Greensboro - Guilford County (G-7179)

Greensboro NC 27401
336 332-3400

(G-7156)
KONTOOR BRANDS INC (PA)
Also Called: Kontoor Brands
400 N Elm St (27401-2143)
PHONE...........................336 332-3400
Scott H Baxter, *Ch Bd*
Rustin Welton, *Ex VP*
Thomas E Waldron, *Ex VP*
Christopher Waldeck, *Ex VP*
Thomas L Doerr Junior, *Corporate Secretary*
EMP: 166 EST: 2018
SQ FT: 140,000
SALES (est): 2.61B
SALES (corp-wide): 2.61B **Publicly Held**
Web: www.kontoorbrands.com
SIC: **2326** 2339 5699 Work apparel, except uniforms; Service apparel, washable: women's; Work clothing

(G-7157)
KONTOOR BRANDS INC
1421 S Elm Eugene St (27406-2237)
PHONE...........................336 332-3577
EMP: 79
SALES (corp-wide): 2.61B **Publicly Held**
Web: www.kontoorbrands.com
SIC: **2221** Acetate broadwoven fabrics
PA: Kontoor Brands, Inc.
    400 N Elm St
    Greensboro NC 27401
    336 332-3400

(G-7158)
KRISPY KREME DOUGHNUT CORP
Also Called: Krispy Kreme
3704 W Gate City Blvd (27407-4628)
PHONE...........................336 854-8275
Clifford Janes, *Brnch Mgr*
EMP: 26
SALES (corp-wide): 1.69B **Publicly Held**
Web: www.krispykreme.com
SIC: **5461** 2051 Doughnuts; Doughnuts, except frozen
HQ: Krispy Kreme Doughnut Corp
    2116 Hawkins St Ste 102
    Charlotte NC 28203
    980 270-7117

(G-7159)
L & R INSTALLATIONS INC
2303 Adams Farm Pkwy (27407-5406)
PHONE...........................336 547-8998
Lamar Coward Junior, *Pr*
Bobbiejo Coward, *Sec*
EMP: 4 EST: 1989
SALES (est): 210K **Privately Held**
SIC: **2531** Pews, church

(G-7160)
LA OAXAQUENA
2708 S Elm Eugene St (27406-3625)
PHONE...........................336 274-0173
Berenice Bravo, *Mgr*
EMP: 5 EST: 2018
SALES (est): 113.79K **Privately Held**
SIC: **3999** Manufacturing industries, nec

(G-7161)
LA T DA BTQ MONOGRAMMING
1 Brackenwood Ct (27407-5081)
PHONE...........................336 457-9831
Theresa West, *Mgr*
EMP: 5 EST: 2015
SALES (est): 56.29K **Privately Held**
SIC: **2395** Embroidery and art needlework

(G-7162)
LAKE SHORE RADIATOR INC
211c Creek Ridge Rd (27406-4419)
PHONE...........................336 271-2626
TOLL FREE: 800
Mark Dean, *Mgr*
EMP: 10
SALES (corp-wide): 3.93MM **Privately Held**
Web: www.getallparts.com
SIC: **5013** 3714 Automotive supplies and parts; Radiators and radiator shells and cores, motor vehicle
PA: Lake Shore Radiator, Inc.
    5355 Ramona Blvd
    Jacksonville FL 32205
    904 786-0954

(G-7163)
LEE APPAREL COMPANY INC (DH)
Also Called: Lee
400 N Elm St (27401-2143)
PHONE...........................336 332-3400
Scott Baxter, *Pr*
L R Pugh, *Dir*
G G Johnson, *Dir*
Mackey J Mcdonald, *Dir*
Frank C Pickard Iii, *Dir*
EMP: 450 EST: 1889
SQ FT: 147,000
SALES (est): 345.48MM
SALES (corp-wide): 2.61B **Publicly Held**
Web: www.lee.com
SIC: **2325** 2339 Jeans: men's, youths', and boys'; Jeans: women's, misses', and juniors'
HQ: Kontoor Us, Llc
    400 N Elm St
    Greensboro NC 27401

(G-7164)
LEE SPRING COMPANY
3013 S Elm Eugene St (27406-4405)
PHONE...........................336 275-3631
EMP: 5 EST: 2016
SALES (est): 133.09K **Privately Held**
Web: www.leespring.com
SIC: **3495** Wire springs

(G-7165)
LEE SPRING COMPANY LLC
104 Industrial Ave (27406-4505)
PHONE...........................336 275-3631
Jorge Cortes, *Brnch Mgr*
EMP: 20
SQ FT: 12,544
SALES (corp-wide): 46.66MM **Privately Held**
Web: www.leespring.com
SIC: **3495** 3493 5085 3315 Mechanical springs, precision; Steel springs, except wire; Springs; Wire and fabricated wire products
PA: Lee Spring Company Llc
    140 58th St Ste 3c
    Brooklyn NY 11220
    888 777-4647

(G-7166)
LEGGETT & PLATT INCORPORATED
Matrex
911 Northridge St (27403-2112)
P.O. Box 444 (27402-0444)
PHONE...........................336 379-7777
Roger Tornero, *Prin*
EMP: 125
SALES (corp-wide): 5.15B **Publicly Held**
Web: www.leggett.com
SIC: **2515** Mattresses and bedsprings
PA: Leggett & Platt, Incorporated
    1 Leggett Rd
    Carthage MO 64836
    417 358-8131

(G-7167)
LOGIKSAVVY SOLUTIONS LLC
2204 Flora Vista Ct (27406-8557)
P.O. Box 1572 (27402-1572)
PHONE...........................336 392-6149
EMP: 6 EST: 2013
SALES (est): 331.2K **Privately Held**
Web: www.logiksavvysolutions.com
SIC: **3841** 7371 7379 8742 Surgical and medical instruments; Custom computer programming services; Online services technology consultants; New business start-up consultant

(G-7168)
LONGWOOD INDUSTRIES INC (DH)
706 Green Valley Rd Ste 212 (27408-7023)
PHONE...........................336 272-3710
Kimberly L Rice, *Sr VP*
Joseph E Mihalick, *Sr VP*
James J Mcdonnell, *Ex VP*
Michael R Groves, *Dir*
▲ EMP: 10 EST: 1991
SALES (est): 93.95MM **Publicly Held**
SIC: **3069** 3081 Molded rubber products; Unsupported plastics film and sheet
HQ: Wabtec Components Llc
    30 Isabella St
    Pittsburgh PA 15212
    412 825-1000

(G-7169)
LORILLARD Q-TECH INC
714 Green Valley Rd (27408-7018)
P.O. Box 21688 (27420-1688)
PHONE...........................877 703-0386
EMP: 6 EST: 2014
SALES (est): 185.99K **Privately Held**
SIC: **2111** Cigarettes

(G-7170)
LORILLARD TOBACCO COMPANY LLC
714 Green Valley Rd (27408-7018)
P.O. Box 10529 (27404-0529)
PHONE...........................336 335-6600
◆ EMP: 2700
SIC: **2111** Cigarettes

(G-7171)
LOVE KNOT CANDLES
4603 Barn Owl Ct (27406-8065)
PHONE...........................336 456-1619
Sharon Bennett, *Prin*
EMP: 5 EST: 2016
SALES (est): 46.82K **Privately Held**
SIC: **3999** Candles

(G-7172)
M DAVIS AND ASSOCIATES LLC (PA)
Also Called: Wholesale Distributor
1918 Bradford St (27405-5614)
PHONE...........................336 337-7089
Melody Davis, *Managing Member*
EMP: 5 EST: 2014
SALES (est): 198.88K
SALES (corp-wide): 198.88K **Privately Held**
SIC: **5099** 5047 5087 2252 Durable goods, nec; Medical equipment and supplies; Janitors' supplies; Socks

(G-7173)
M G NEWELL CORPORATION (PA)
301 Citation Ct (27409-9027)
P.O. Box 18765 (27419-8765)
PHONE...........................336 393-0100
J Michael Sherrill, *Pr*
Grey Sherill, *
EMP: 60 EST: 1885
SQ FT: 32,000
SALES (est): 26.56MM
SALES (corp-wide): 26.56MM **Privately Held**
Web: www.mgnewell.com
SIC: **3556** Bakery machinery

(G-7174)
M PRESS INC
3400 W Wendover Ave (27407-1583)
PHONE...........................336 292-5005
EMP: 6 EST: 2018
SALES (est): 59.23K **Privately Held**
SIC: **2741** Miscellaneous publishing

(G-7175)
M&J OLDCO INC
Also Called: Mail Box Book Company, The
3515 W Market St Ste 200 (27403-4442)
P.O. Box 9753 (27429-0753)
PHONE...........................336 854-0309
▲ EMP: 70
SIC: **2721** Magazines: publishing and printing

(G-7176)
MACK TRUCKS INC
496 Gallimore Dairy Rd Ste D (27409-9795)
PHONE...........................336 291-9064
EMP: 8 EST: 2015
SALES (est): 182.5K **Privately Held**
Web: www.macktrucks.com
SIC: **3711** Motor trucks, except off-highway, assembly of

(G-7177)
MACK TRUCKS INC (HQ)
7900 National Service Rd (27409-9416)
P.O. Box 26259 (27402-6259)
PHONE...........................336 291-9001
Terry Mack, *CEO*
Stephen Roy, *
◆ EMP: 800 EST: 1974
SALES (est): 1.32B
SALES (corp-wide): 45.13B **Privately Held**
Web: www.macktrucks.com
SIC: **3711** 3714 5012 6141 Motor trucks, except off-highway, assembly of; Motor vehicle parts and accessories; Truck tractors; Financing: automobiles, furniture, etc., not a deposit bank
PA: Ab Volvo
    Amazonvagen 8
    GOteborg 418 7
    31660000

(G-7178)
MAGNUSSEN HOME FURNISHINGS INC (HQ)
Also Called: Magnussen
4523 Green Point Dr Ste 109 (27410-8167)
PHONE...........................336 841-4424
Nathan Cressman, *Pr*
Kent Macfarlane, *CFO*
EMP: 7 EST: 1931
SALES (est): 6.91MM
SALES (corp-wide): 57.54MM **Privately Held**
Web: www.magnussen.com
SIC: **2511** 5021 Wood household furniture; Household furniture
PA: Magnussen Home Furnishings Ltd
    94 Bridgeport Rd E Unit 2
    Waterloo ON N2J 2
    519 662-3040

(G-7179)
MANN MEDIA INC
Also Called: Our State Magazine
800 Green Valley Rd Ste 106 (27408-7027)

Greensboro - Guilford County (G-7180)   GEOGRAPHIC SECTION

P.O. Box 4552 (27404-4552)
PHONE..................................336 286-0600
Bernard Mann, *Pr*
Lynn Tutterow, *
Roberta Mann, *
EMP: 33 EST: 1978
SQ FT: 7,000
SALES (est): 4.91MM **Privately Held**
Web: www.ourstate.com
SIC: 2721 Magazines: publishing only, not printed on site

(G-7180)
MARIETTA MARTIN MATERIALS INC
Also Called: Martin Marietta Aggregates
413 S Chimney Rock Rd (27409-9260)
P.O. Box 30013 (27622-0013)
PHONE..................................336 668-3253
Dean Hardy, *Genl Mgr*
EMP: 12
Web: www.martinmarietta.com
SIC: 1422 Crushed and broken limestone
PA: Martin Marietta Materials Inc
4123 Parklake Ave
Raleigh NC 27612

(G-7181)
MARK/TRECE INC
Also Called: Mark Trece
902 Norwalk St (27407-2027)
PHONE..................................973 884-1005
EMP: 12
SALES (corp-wide): 24.32MM **Privately Held**
Web: www.marktrece.com
SIC: 3555 Printing trades machinery
PA: Mark/Trece, Inc.
2001 Stockton Rd
Joppa MD 21085
410 879-0060

(G-7182)
MARSH FURNITURE COMPANY
Also Called: Kitchen Art
2503 Greengate Dr (27406-5242)
PHONE..................................336 273-8196
David Gainey, *Brnch Mgr*
EMP: 10
SALES (corp-wide): 43.2MM **Privately Held**
Web: www.marshkb.com
SIC: 2434 5211 1799 1751 Wood kitchen cabinets; Cabinets, kitchen; Counter top installation; Cabinet and finish carpentry
PA: Marsh Furniture Company
1001 S Centennial St
High Point NC 27260
336 884-7363

(G-7183)
MARSHALL USA LLC
111 W Lewis St (27406-1343)
PHONE..................................301 481-1241
EMP: 4
SALES (est): 182.43K **Privately Held**
SIC: 3721 Airplanes, fixed or rotary wing

(G-7184)
MARTIN MARIETTA MATERIALS INC
Also Called: Martin Marietta Aggregates
5800 Eckerson Rd (27405-9466)
PHONE..................................336 375-7584
Terry Small, *Brnch Mgr*
EMP: 8
Web: www.martinmarietta.com
SIC: 1422 Crushed and broken limestone
PA: Martin Marietta Materials Inc
4123 Parklake Ave
Raleigh NC 27612

(G-7185)
MARTIN MARIETTA MATERIALS INC
Also Called: Martin Marietta Aggregates
3957 Liberty Rd (27406-6109)
P.O. Box 16867 (27416-0867)
PHONE..................................336 674-0836
David Thorn, *Brnch Mgr*
EMP: 6
Web: www.martinmarietta.com
SIC: 1422 5032 Crushed and broken limestone; Stone, crushed or broken
PA: Martin Marietta Materials Inc
4123 Parklake Ave
Raleigh NC 27612

(G-7186)
MARTIN MATERIALS INC
4801 Burlington Rd (27405-8615)
PHONE..................................336 697-1800
Roger D Martin, *Pr*
Amanda Hopkins, *VP*
EMP: 4 EST: 2009
SALES (est): 468.1K **Privately Held**
Web: www.martinmaterialsinc.com
SIC: 2611 Pulp mills, mechanical and recycling processing

(G-7187)
MARVIDA ACRES LLC
2011 Vanstory St (27403-3645)
PHONE..................................336 392-0414
EMP: 4 EST: 2019
SALES (est): 60.02K **Privately Held**
SIC: 2431 Millwork

(G-7188)
MATTHEWS MOBILE MEDIA LLC
6343 Burnt Poplar Rd (27409-9711)
PHONE..................................336 303-4982
Bradley J Matthews, *Managing Member*
EMP: 6 EST: 2019
SALES (est): 113.64K **Privately Held**
Web: www.matthewsmobile.com
SIC: 3993 Signs and advertising specialties

(G-7189)
MATTHEWS SPCIALTY VEHICLES INC
211 American Ave (27409-1803)
PHONE..................................336 297-9600
Bradley Mathews, *Pr*
Glenn Matthews, *
Kathy Drapeau, *
EMP: 55 EST: 1994
SALES (est): 14.74MM **Privately Held**
Web: www.msvehicles.com
SIC: 3711 3713 3716 Ambulances (motor vehicles), assembly of; Truck and bus bodies; Recreational van conversion (self-propelled), factory basis

(G-7190)
MAXSON & ASSOCIATES
Also Called: Maxson and Assoc Greensboro
2618 Battleground Ave (27408-1924)
PHONE..................................336 632-0524
William Maxson, *Owner*
EMP: 8 EST: 1976
SALES (est): 188.95K **Privately Held**
Web: www.maxsonassociates.com
SIC: 3537 7699 5211 5084 Loading docks: portable, adjustable, and hydraulic; Door and window repair; Door and window products; Materials handling machinery

(G-7191)
MAYNARD S FABRICATORS INC
2227 W Lee St Ste A (27403-2503)
PHONE..................................336 230-1048
John Maynard, *Pr*
Adrienne K Maynard, *Sec*
Ann Maynards, *Treas*
EMP: 4 EST: 1989
SALES (est): 206.69K **Privately Held**
Web: www.waterfordatgoldmarkapts.com
SIC: 7692 1799 Welding repair; Welding on site

(G-7192)
MB-F INC (PA)
620 Industrial Ave (27406-4619)
P.O. Box 22107 (27420-2107)
PHONE..................................336 379-9352
Bobby Christiansen, *Pr*
Fred Lyman, *
Dorie Crowe, *
EMP: 75 EST: 1967
SQ FT: 40,000
SALES (est): 5.24MM
SALES (corp-wide): 5.24MM **Privately Held**
Web: www.infodog.com
SIC: 7331 2721 7999 2759 Direct mail advertising services; Periodicals; Animal shows in circuses, fairs, and carnivals; Commercial printing, nec

(G-7193)
MCAD INC
Also Called: Carolina Custom Surfaces
100 Landmark Dr (27409-9602)
PHONE..................................336 299-3030
Joe Duszka, *Pr*
EMP: 50 EST: 1995
SQ FT: 2,500
SALES (est): 3.4MM **Privately Held**
SIC: 3281 2541 Bathroom fixtures, cut stone ; Table or counter tops, plastic laminated

(G-7194)
MCLEAN SBSRFACE UTLITY ENGRG L
Also Called: Engineering Consulting Svcs
3015 E Bessemer Ave (27405-7503)
PHONE..................................336 340-0024
Stacey Slaw, *CEO*
Stacey E Slaw, *Prin*
EMP: 10 EST: 2015
SALES (est): 413.96K **Privately Held**
SIC: 1389 8713 8711 1623 Testing, measuring, surveying, and analysis services ; Surveying services; Engineering services; Underground utilities contractor

(G-7195)
MECHANICAL SPECIALTY INC
1901 E Wendover Ave (27405-6899)
PHONE..................................336 272-5606
David Smith, *Pr*
EMP: 6 EST: 1948
SQ FT: 20,000
SALES (est): 964.36K **Privately Held**
Web: www.mechspecialty.com
SIC: 3599 Machine shop, jobbing and repair

(G-7196)
MEDALONI CELLARS LLC
811 Eula St Ste A (27403-4381)
P.O. Box 4486 (27404-4486)
PHONE..................................336 398-7818
EMP: 5 EST: 2012
SALES (est): 249.42K **Privately Held**
Web: www.medalonicellars.com
SIC: 2084 5921 Wines, brandy, and brandy spirits; Wine

(G-7197)
MEMIOS LLC
7609 Business Park Dr # B (27409-9696)
PHONE..................................336 664-5256
EMP: 80 EST: 2003
SALES (est): 5.28MM **Privately Held**
Web: www.memios.com
SIC: 3535 Conveyors and conveying equipment

(G-7198)
MERCH CONNECT STUDIOS INC
1724 Holbrook St (27403-2713)
PHONE..................................336 501-6722
EMP: 4 EST: 2021
SALES (est): 84.45K **Privately Held**
Web: www.merchconnect.com
SIC: 2759 Screen printing

(G-7199)
MERCHANT 1 MARKETING LLC
2900 Pacific Ave (27406-4513)
PHONE..................................888 853-9992
William B Turner Junior, *Managing Member*
EMP: 4 EST: 2009
SALES (est): 331.13K **Privately Held**
Web: www.m1equipment.com
SIC: 5013 3559 Automotive supplies and parts; Automotive maintenance equipment

(G-7200)
MERIDIAN POINT OF SALE INC
7343 W Friendly Ave Ste L (27410-6209)
PHONE..................................336 315-9800
EMP: 6 EST: 2010
SALES (est): 198.88K **Privately Held**
Web: www.meripos.com
SIC: 3578 Cash registers

(G-7201)
MIDSOUTH POWER EQP CO INC
518 Corliss St (27406-5216)
P.O. Box 16025 (27416-0025)
PHONE..................................336 389-0515
Roger Johnson, *Pr*
Cathy Johnson, *VP*
EMP: 12 EST: 1999
SQ FT: 15,000
SALES (est): 1.54MM **Privately Held**
Web: www.clyde-industries.com
SIC: 3589 Commercial cleaning equipment

(G-7202)
MISCHIEF MAKERS LOCAL 816 LLC
Also Called: Home State Apparel
1504 Rainbow Dr (27403-3158)
PHONE..................................336 763-2003
EMP: 25 EST: 2009
SALES (est): 1.31MM **Privately Held**
SIC: 2389 Men's miscellaneous accessories

(G-7203)
MODERN MARBLE & GLASS INC
107 Arrow Rd (27409-9655)
PHONE..................................336 668-4197
David Hoolbrook, *Prin*
EMP: 6 EST: 2017
SALES (est): 62.63K **Privately Held**
SIC: 3281 Cut stone and stone products

(G-7204)
MOORES PRINTING
Also Called: Moore, James R
4209 Princeton Ave (27407-1725)
PHONE..................................336 856-0540
Cathy Moore, *Prin*
EMP: 6 EST: 2006
SALES (est): 118.93K **Privately Held**
SIC: 2752 Commercial printing, lithographic

(G-7205)
MOTHER MURPHYS LABS INC
300 Dougherty St (27406-4306)
PHONE..................................336 273-1737
EMP: 41

GEOGRAPHIC SECTION
Greensboro - Guilford County (G-7228)

SALES (corp-wide): 105.82MM **Privately Held**
Web: www.mothermurphys.com
SIC: 2087 Extracts, flavoring
PA: Mother Murphy's Laboratories, Inc.
2826 S Elm Eugene St
Greensboro NC 27406
336 273-1737

(G-7206)
MOTHER MURPHYS LABS INC (PA)
2826 S Elm Eugene St (27406-4435)
P.O. Box 16846 (27416-0846)
PHONE..............................336 273-1737
Robert B Murphy, *Ch*
David Murphy, *
James A Murphy, *
Timothy Hansen, *
Janet Murphy, *
EMP: 79 EST: 1946
SQ FT: 39,000
SALES (est): 105.82MM
SALES (corp-wide): 105.82MM **Privately Held**
Web: www.mothermurphys.com
SIC: 2087 Extracts, flavoring

(G-7207)
MULTI PACKAGING SOLUTIONS
Also Called: MPS Greensboro
7915 Industrial Village Rd (27409-9691)
PHONE..............................336 855-7142
EMP: 962 EST: 1987
SQ FT: 57,000
SALES (est): 2.65MM
SALES (corp-wide): 20.31B **Publicly Held**
SIC: 2752 2759 7336 2671 Commercial printing, lithographic; Labels and seals: printing, nsk; Commercial art and graphic design; Paper; coated and laminated packaging
HQ: Lansing Mps Inc
5800 W Grand River Ave
Lansing MI 48906
517 323-9000

(G-7208)
MULTIGEN DIAGNOSTICS LLC
1100 Revolution Mill Dr Ste 1 (27405-5067)
PHONE..............................336 510-1120
Thuraiayah Moorthy, *Managing Member*
EMP: 6 EST: 2015
SALES (est): 95.34K **Privately Held**
SIC: 3841 2835 Diagnostic apparatus, medical; Cytology and histology diagnostic agents

(G-7209)
MUNIBILLING
3300 Battleground Ave Ste 402 (27410-2465)
PHONE..............................800 259-7020
John A Vergey, *Prin*
EMP: 57 EST: 2017
SALES (est): 707.96K **Privately Held**
Web: www.munibilling.com
SIC: 7372 Business oriented computer software

(G-7210)
MUSIC MATTERS INC
Also Called: Music Garden
507 Arlington St (27406-1407)
PHONE..............................336 272-5303
Lorna Heyge, *Pr*
Jeff Stickard, *VP*
▲ EMP: 7 EST: 1994
SALES (est): 767.76K **Privately Held**
Web: www.musikgarten.org
SIC: 2741 5736 Music, book: publishing and printing; Sheet music

(G-7211)
MYLAN PHARMACEUTICALS INC
Also Called: Lpmylan Specialty
2898 Manufacturers Rd (27406-4600)
PHONE..............................336 271-6571
Larry Salmon, *Mgr*
EMP: 40
SQ FT: 160,642
SALES (corp-wide): 15.43B **Publicly Held**
Web: www.viatris.com
SIC: 2834 Druggists' preparations (pharmaceuticals)
HQ: Mylan Pharmaceuticals Inc.
3711 Collins Ferry Rd
Morgantown WV 26505
304 599-2595

(G-7212)
NARRICOT INDUSTRIES LLC
804 Green Valley Rd Ste 300 (27408-7013)
PHONE..............................215 322-3908
EMP: 9 EST: 2000
SALES (est): 422.93K **Privately Held**
SIC: 3999 Manufacturing industries, nec

(G-7213)
NATIVE NATURALZ INC
805 Stoney Hill Cir (27406-8135)
PHONE..............................336 334-2984
Tinece Holman, *Pr*
EMP: 10 EST: 2013
SALES (est): 135.03K **Privately Held**
SIC: 8999 8748 5211 2911 Earth science services; Urban planning and consulting services; Insulation and energy conservation products; Mineral oils, natural

(G-7214)
NB CORPORATION
Also Called: Greensboro Industrial Platers
123 S Edwardia Dr (27409-2601)
P.O. Box 4466 (27404-4466)
PHONE..............................336 852-8786
Allison Davis, *Mgr*
EMP: 10
SALES (corp-wide): 2.45MM **Privately Held**
Web: www.gboroplaters.com
SIC: 3471 Electroplating of metals or formed products
PA: Nb Corporation
725 Kenilworth St
Greensboro NC 27403
336 274-7654

(G-7215)
NB CORPORATION (PA)
Also Called: Greensboro Industrial Platers
725 Kenilworth St (27403-2417)
P.O. Box 4466 (27404-4466)
PHONE..............................336 274-7654
Harold O'tuel, *Pr*
Allison Davis, *Pr*
EMP: 20 EST: 1933
SQ FT: 28,000
SALES (est): 2.45MM
SALES (corp-wide): 2.45MM **Privately Held**
Web: www.gboroplaters.com
SIC: 3471 Electroplating of metals or formed products

(G-7216)
NEW JOURNEY NOW
4413 W Market St (27407-1376)
PHONE..............................336 234-1534
Crystal Bray, *Pr*
Lynda Brown, *Dir*
Danielle Springs, *Dir*
EMP: 5 EST: 2021
SALES (est): 117.29K **Privately Held**
SIC: 2732 8661 Book printing; Religious organizations

(G-7217)
NEWS & RECORD COMMERCIAL PRTG
200 E Market St (27401-2910)
PHONE..............................336 373-7300
EMP: 21 EST: 1965
SALES (est): 478.15K **Privately Held**
SIC: 2759 2711 Commercial printing, nec; Newspapers

(G-7218)
NEWS FROM AN ANGEL
3010 Lacy Ave (27405-6126)
PHONE..............................336 456-5429
Willette Burton, *Owner*
EMP: 4 EST: 2015
SALES (est): 56.28K **Privately Held**
SIC: 2741 Miscellaneous publishing

(G-7219)
NICHOLS SPDMTR & INSTR CO INC
Also Called: Nichols Speedometer & Instr Co
1336 Oakland Ave (27403-2748)
P.O. Box 4281 (27404-4281)
PHONE..............................336 273-2881
Charles Nichols, *Pr*
Renee Nichols, *Sec*
EMP: 8 EST: 1962
SQ FT: 1,900
SALES (est): 819.12K **Privately Held**
Web: www.nsifleet.com
SIC: 7539 5013 3824 Automotive repair shops, nec; Motor vehicle supplies and new parts; Speedometers

(G-7220)
NICO SOLID MAPLE CABINETS LLC
2925 Battleground Ave (27408-1921)
PHONE..............................602 319-2758
Nicolas Kroll, *Pr*
EMP: 5 EST: 2018
SALES (est): 156.54K **Privately Held**
Web: www.nicosolidmaplecabinets.com
SIC: 2434 Wood kitchen cabinets

(G-7221)
NOMADIC DISPLAY LLC
7602 Business Park Dr (27409-9696)
PHONE..............................800 336-5019
Franklin Gaskins, *Prin*
EMP: 10 EST: 2016
SALES (est): 260.87K **Privately Held**
Web: www.nomadicdisplay.com
SIC: 3993 Signs and advertising specialties

(G-7222)
NOMADIC NORTH AMERICA LLC (HQ)
Also Called: Nomadic Display
7602 Business Park Dr (27409-9696)
PHONE..............................703 866-9200
▲ EMP: 44 EST: 1975
SALES (est): 5.03MM **Privately Held**
Web: www.nomadicdisplay.com
SIC: 3993 Displays and cutouts, window and lobby
PA: Apple Rock Advertising & Promotion, Inc.
7602 Business Park Dr
Greensboro NC 27409

(G-7223)
NOREGON SYSTEMS INC
7823 National Service Rd Ste 100 (27409-9464)
PHONE..............................336 615-8555
William Hathaway, *CEO*
EMP: 220 EST: 1993
SALES (est): 48.21MM **Privately Held**
Web: www.noregon.com
SIC: 7371 3578 Computer software development; Automatic teller machines (ATM)

(G-7224)
NOUVEAU VERRE HOLDINGS INC (DH)
3802 Robert Porcher Way (27410-2190)
PHONE..............................336 545-0011
Phillipe Porcher, *CEO*
James R Henderson, *Ofcr*
Philippe R Dorier, *CFO*
EMP: 15 EST: 2004
SALES (est): 275.37MM
SALES (corp-wide): 2.67MM **Privately Held**
SIC: 2221 3624 2241 2295 Glass broadwoven fabrics; Fibers, carbon and graphite; Glass narrow fabrics; Mats, varnished glass
HQ: Porcher Industries
2440 Rd 1085
Eclose Badinieres 38300
474431010

(G-7225)
NOVALENT LTD
2319 Joe Brown Dr (27405-3960)
PHONE..............................336 375-7555
Joseph E Mason, *Pr*
Babu Patel, *VP*
▼ EMP: 15 EST: 1981
SQ FT: 30,000
SALES (est): 4.82MM **Privately Held**
Web: www.novalent.com
SIC: 2819 2842 2899 Industrial inorganic chemicals, nec; Polishes and sanitation goods; Chemical preparations, nec

(G-7226)
NS PACKAGING LLC
Also Called: North State Packaging
2600 Phoenix Dr (27406-6321)
P.O. Box 240007 (28224-0007)
PHONE..............................800 688-7391
EMP: 17 EST: 1997
SALES (est): 146.3K **Privately Held**
SIC: 2671 Paper; coated and laminated packaging

(G-7227)
NUVASIVE INC
1250 Revolution Mill Dr (27405-5191)
PHONE..............................336 430-3169
EMP: 19 EST: 1998
SALES (est): 235.44K **Privately Held**
Web: www.nuvasive.com
SIC: 3841 Surgical and medical instruments

(G-7228)
NVH INC (DH)
3802 Robert Porcher Way (27410-2190)
PHONE..............................336 545-0011
Philippe Porcher, *CEO*
Philippe R Dorier, *CFO*
EMP: 7 EST: 2004
SALES (est): 247.83MM
SALES (corp-wide): 2.67MM **Privately Held**
SIC: 2221 3624 2241 2295 Glass broadwoven fabrics; Fibers, carbon and graphite; Glass narrow fabrics; Mats, varnished glass
HQ: Nouveau Verre Holdings, Inc.
3802 Robert Porcher Way
Greensboro NC 27410

Greensboro - Guilford County (G-7229)

(G-7229)
OAKHURST TEXTILES INC
Also Called: Logan Text Fabrics
203 Citation Ct (27409-9026)
P.O. Box 18744 (27419-8744)
PHONE................336 668-0733
Richard L Stark Junior, *CEO*
Richard Wotring, *
Matthew Brennan, *OK Vice President*
▲ **EMP:** 27 **EST:** 1975
SQ FT: 84,000
SALES (est): 4.97MM **Privately Held**
SIC: 5131 2299 Piece goods and notions; Fabrics: linen, jute, hemp, ramie

(G-7230)
OLYMPIC PRODUCTS LLC (PA)
4100 Pleasant Garden Rd (27406-7699)
PHONE................336 378-9620
Mike Cooke, *Pr*
Joe Cladey, *Managing Member*
EMP: 71 **EST:** 2006
SALES (est): 23.51MM **Privately Held**
Web: www.olympic-products.com
SIC: 2821 Plastics materials and resins

(G-7231)
OLYMPIC PRODUCTS LLC
Also Called: Vita Foam
4100 Pleasant Garden Rd (27406-7699)
PHONE................336 378-9620
Britt Keaton, *Genl Mgr*
EMP: 76
Web: www.witpfoam.com
SIC: 2821 5199 Plastics materials and resins; Foams and rubber
PA: Olympic Products Llc
4100 Pleasant Garden Rd
Greensboro NC 27406

(G-7232)
ONE FURNITURE GROUP CORP
6520 Arprt Ctr Dr Ste 204 (27409)
PHONE................336 235-0221
EMP: 4 **EST:** 2010
SALES (est): 34.01K **Privately Held**
SIC: 2511 Wood household furniture

(G-7233)
ONE SOURCE DOCUMENT SOLUTIONS
311 Pomona Dr Ste D (27407-1694)
PHONE................336 482-2360
John Kinney, *Owner*
EMP: 5 **EST:** 2018
SALES (est): 103.9K **Privately Held**
SIC: 2759 Commercial printing, nec

(G-7234)
ONE SRCE DCUMENT SOLUTIONS INC
4355 Federal Dr Ste 140 (27410-8143)
P.O. Box 8227 (27419-0227)
PHONE................800 401-9544
Kevin Smith, *Pr*
EMP: 35 **EST:** 1994
SALES (est): 2.38MM **Privately Held**
Web: www.osdsinc.com
SIC: 7372 8742 Prepackaged software; Management consulting services

(G-7235)
OPTICAL PLACE INC (PA)
Also Called: Optical Wholesale
2633 Randleman Rd (27406-5107)
P.O. Box 26092 (27420-6092)
PHONE................336 274-1300
William R Fonner, *Pr*
Jerry Burleson, *
Maurice P Johnson, *
EMP: 25 **EST:** 1976
SALES (est): 4.35MM
SALES (corp-wide): 4.35MM **Privately Held**
Web: www.opticalplacenc.com
SIC: 5995 5049 3851 Opticians; Optical goods; Ophthalmic goods

(G-7236)
OPTICS INC
Also Called: Layton Optics
1607 Westover Ter Ste B (27408-1997)
PHONE................336 288-9504
Bernie Dehoog, *Owner*
EMP: 5
SALES (corp-wide): 479.08K **Privately Held**
Web: www.optics-eyewear.com
SIC: 8042 3827 5995 Offices and clinics of optometrists; Optical instruments and lenses; Opticians
PA: Optics Inc
1105 N Lindsay St Side
High Point NC 27262
336 884-5677

(G-7237)
ORPAK USA INC
7300 W Friendly Ave (27410-6232)
PHONE................201 441-9820
Shlomo Slotwiner, *Pr*
Vito Cantatore, *Contrlr*
EMP: 63 **EST:** 1991
SQ FT: 4,000
SALES (est): 764.54K **Privately Held**
Web: www.gilbarco.com
SIC: 7549 3829 Fuel system conversion, automotive; Measuring and controlling devices, nec
PA: Orpak Systems Ltd
31 Lechi
Bnei Brak 51200

(G-7238)
P R SPARKS ENTERPRISES INC
Also Called: Perfection Products Co
1333 Headquarters Dr (27405-7919)
P.O. Box 14571 (27415-4571)
PHONE................336 272-7200
Paul Sparks, *Pr*
Patricia L Sparks, *Sec*
EMP: 5 **EST:** 1980
SQ FT: 11,000
SALES (est): 320.18K **Privately Held**
SIC: 2434 2511 2431 Wood kitchen cabinets; Whatnot shelves: wood; Doors, wood

(G-7239)
PACE COMMUNICATIONS INC (PA)
1301 Carolina St Ste 200 (27401-1022)
PHONE................336 378-6065
Bonnie Mcelveen-hunter, *CEO*
Leigh Ann Klee, *
Grodon Locke, *
Patricia M Mc Connell, *
▲ **EMP:** 225 **EST:** 1983
SQ FT: 22,000
SALES (est): 49.14MM
SALES (corp-wide): 49.14MM **Privately Held**
Web: www.paceco.com
SIC: 8742 2721 Marketing consulting services; Magazines: publishing only, not printed on site

(G-7240)
PACTIV LLC
520 Radar Rd (27410-6212)
PHONE................336 292-2796
Ernie Calahan, *Brnch Mgr*
EMP: 46
Web: www.pactivevergreen.com
SIC: 2679 5113 Book covers, paper; Containers, paper and disposable plastic
HQ: Pactiv Llc
1900 W Field Ct
Lake Forest IL 60045
847 482-2000

(G-7241)
PALLET RACK WORLD
6404 Birkdale Dr (27410-8279)
PHONE................336 253-8766
EMP: 5 **EST:** 2015
SALES (est): 160.33K **Privately Held**
Web: www.pallettrackworld.com
SIC: 2448 Pallets, wood and wood with metal

(G-7242)
PALMETTO AND ASSOCIATE LLC
223 S Elm St (27401-2602)
PHONE................336 382-7432
EMP: 8 **EST:** 2010
SALES (est): 499.73K **Privately Held**
SIC: 2099 Food preparations, nec

(G-7243)
PARAGON NAVIGATOR INC
2801 Lawndale Dr (27408-4119)
PHONE................336 316-1206
Qiang Zhou, *Pr*
▲ **EMP:** 7 **EST:** 2015
SALES (est): 279.81K **Privately Held**
Web: www.paragonwheels.com
SIC: 3471 Plating and polishing

(G-7244)
PARKER METAL FINISHING COMPANY
719 W Gate City Blvd Ste D (27403-3068)
P.O. Box 16084 (27416-0084)
PHONE................336 275-9657
Jack R Parker, *Pr*
Tracy Dickerson, *Sec*
Yvonne Parker, *VP*
EMP: 16 **EST:** 1981
SQ FT: 10,000
SALES (est): 655.61K **Privately Held**
Web: www.parkermetalfinishing.com
SIC: 3471 Electroplating of metals or formed products

(G-7245)
PARKER-HANNIFIN CORPORATION
Also Called: Hose Products Division
125 E Meadowview Rd (27410-4518)
PHONE................336 373-1761
Lonnie Gallup, *Brnch Mgr*
EMP: 15
SALES (corp-wide): 19.07B **Publicly Held**
Web: www.parker.com
SIC: 2241 5085 Hose fabric, tubular; Industrial supplies
PA: Parker-Hannifin Corporation
6035 Parkland Blvd
Cleveland OH 44124
216 896-3000

(G-7246)
PARRISH TIRE COMPANY
2809 Thurston Ave (27406-4514)
PHONE................336 334-9979
Tony George, *Brnch Mgr*
EMP: 17
SALES (corp-wide): 378.88MM **Privately Held**
Web: www.parrishtire.com
SIC: 7539 7537 7534 5531 Frame and front end repair services; Automotiv e transmission repair shops; Tire retreading and repair shops; Automotive tires
PA: Parrish Tire Company
5130 Indiana Ave
Winston Salem NC 27106
800 849-8473

(G-7247)
PATHEON SOFTGELS INC
Also Called: Federal Ridge
7902 Indlea Point Ste 112 (27409)
PHONE................336 812-8700
Michelle Stinson, *Mgr*
EMP: 10
SALES (corp-wide): 44.91B **Publicly Held**
Web: www.patheon.com
SIC: 2834 4225 Vitamin preparations; General warehousing and storage
HQ: Patheon Softgels Inc.
4125 Premier Dr
High Point NC 27265
336 812-8700

(G-7248)
PBM GRAPHICS INC
Also Called: Rrd Packaging Solutions
415 Westcliff Rd (27409-9786)
PHONE................336 664-5800
Steve Welch, *Mgr*
EMP: 114
SQ FT: 115,400
SALES (corp-wide): 15B **Privately Held**
Web: www.rrd.com
SIC: 2752 Offset printing
HQ: Pbm Graphics, Inc.
3700 S Miami Blvd
Durham NC 27703
919 544-6222

(G-7249)
PBRANDECOM
4842 Tower Rd Unit C (27410-5837)
PHONE................336 294-9771
Phillip Brande, *Prin*
EMP: 4 **EST:** 2018
SALES (est): 80.04K **Privately Held**
SIC: 2046 Wet corn milling

(G-7250)
PECULIAR ROOTS LLC
3709 Alliance Dr Ste A (27407-2059)
PHONE................845 379-4039
Tara Darnley, *CEO*
Detara Darnley, *CEO*
Carl Darnley, *CEO*
EMP: 5 **EST:** 2020
SALES (est): 243.35K **Privately Held**
Web: www.peculiarroots.com
SIC: 2844 Hair preparations, including shampoos

(G-7251)
PERFORMANCE ENTPS & PARTS INC
4104 Burlington Rd (27405-8629)
PHONE................336 621-6572
Alfred Williams, *Pr*
EMP: 5 **EST:** 1964
SALES (est): 489.91K **Privately Held**
Web: www.performance-enterprises.com
SIC: 7539 3465 Machine shop, automotive; Body parts, automobile: stamped metal

(G-7252)
PHARMACEUTICAL DIMENSIONS
7353 W Friendly Ave # A (27410-6233)
PHONE................336 297-4851
Michael P Deason, *Pr*
▲ **EMP:** 7 **EST:** 2004
SALES (est): 789.63K **Privately Held**
Web: www.phdreturns.com
SIC: 2834 Pharmaceutical preparations

Greensboro - Guilford County (G-7276)

(G-7253)
PHARMACUTICAL DIMENSION
7353 W Friendly Ave # A (27410-6233)
PHONE..................336 664-5287
Michael Deason, *Prin*
EMP: 7 **EST:** 2007
SALES (est): 190.27K **Privately Held**
SIC: 2834 5122 Pharmaceutical preparations; Pharmaceuticals

(G-7254)
PIEDMONT ANIMAL HEALTH INC
Also Called: Triad Specialty Products
204 Muirs Chapel Rd Ste 200 (27410-6173)
PHONE..................336 544-0320
Roland Johnson, *CEO*
Michael F Kelly, *CFO*
EMP: 20 **EST:** 2019
SALES (est): 2.39MM **Privately Held**
Web: www.piedmontanimalhealth.com
SIC: 2834 Pharmaceutical preparations

(G-7255)
PIEDMONT AVI CMPONENT SVCS LLC
Also Called: Tat Piedmont
7102 Cessna Dr (27409-9793)
PHONE..................336 423-5100
Dean Hall, *
Todd Schwarz, *
EMP: 108 **EST:** 1954
SQ FT: 65,000
SALES (est): 55.48MM **Privately Held**
SIC: 4581 3721 Aircraft maintenance and repair services; Aircraft
HQ: Limco Airepair Inc.
5304 S Lawton Ave
Tulsa OK 74107
918 445-4300

(G-7256)
PIEDMONT FABRICATION
116 Industrial Ave (27406-4505)
PHONE..................336 634-0096
Ronald G Bibey, *Owner*
EMP: 5 **EST:** 2004
SALES (est): 159.91K **Privately Held**
SIC: 3441 Fabricated structural metal

(G-7257)
PIEDMONT GRAPHICS INC
6903 International Dr (27409-9028)
P.O. Box 4509 (27404-4509)
PHONE..................336 230-0040
▲ **EMP:** 26 **EST:** 1993
SQ FT: 24,000
SALES (est): 6.27MM **Privately Held**
Web: www.source4greensboro.com
SIC: 2752 Offset printing

(G-7258)
PIEDMONT LMINATING COATING INC
1812 Sullivan St (27405-7216)
PHONE..................336 272-1600
Tom Snyder, *Pr*
Guy Pawson, *Genl Mgr*
EMP: 10 **EST:** 1991
SALES (est): 773.13K **Privately Held**
Web: www.piedmontlaminating.com
SIC: 3479 Coating of metals and formed products

(G-7259)
PIEDMONT PAPER STOCK LLC
Also Called: Record Stor Depot-Shred Depo
3909 Riverdale Dr (27406-7505)
P.O. Box 20146 (27420-0146)
PHONE..................336 285-8592
EMP: 16
SALES (corp-wide): 2.53MM **Privately Held**
Web: www.piedmontpaperstock.com
SIC: 5093 3589 Waste paper; Shredders, industrial and commercial
PA: Piedmont Paper Stock, Llc
2235 Cesnna Dr
Burlington NC 27215
336 437-8500

(G-7260)
PIEDMONT PLATING CORPORATION
3005 Holts Chapel Rd (27401-4454)
PHONE..................336 272-2311
Matthew T Marsh, *Pr*
Mitchell T Marsh, *VP*
David A Willox, *Treas*
EMP: 38 **EST:** 2007
SALES (est): 1.18MM
SALES (corp-wide): 24.79MM **Privately Held**
Web: www.piedmontplating.com
SIC: 3471 Electroplating of metals or formed products
PA: Marsh Plating Corporation
103 N Grove St
Ypsilanti MI 48198
734 483-5767

(G-7261)
PIEDMONT TRIAD PRINTING INC
6520 Airport Center Dr (27409-9029)
PHONE..................336 235-3080
EMP: 6 **EST:** 2000
SALES (est): 79.58K **Privately Held**
SIC: 2752 Offset printing

(G-7262)
PIEDMONT TRUCK TIRES INC (HQ)
312 S Regional Rd (27409-9674)
P.O. Box 18228 (27419-8228)
PHONE..................336 668-0091
Dan Rice, *Pr*
Mitch Glover, *
Greg Herring, *
EMP: 30 **EST:** 1978
SQ FT: 24,000
SALES (est): 41.24MM
SALES (corp-wide): 339.82MM **Privately Held**
Web: www.piedmonttrucktires.com
SIC: 5014 5531 7534 Truck tires and tubes; Auto and home supply stores; Rebuilding and retreading tires
PA: Mccarthy Tire Service Company Inc
340 Kidder St
City Of Wilkes Barre PA 18702
570 822-3151

(G-7263)
PIKE ELECTRIC LLC
Also Called: Pike Electric
3511 W Market St (27403-4443)
PHONE..................336 316-7068
EMP: 263
SALES (corp-wide): 1.08B **Privately Held**
Web: www.pike.com
SIC: 4911 3699 1731 Electric services; Electrical equipment and supplies, nec; Electrical work
HQ: Pike Electric, Llc
100 Pike Way
Mount Airy NC 27030
336 789-2171

(G-7264)
PILKINGTON GROUP INC
3307 Timberview Cir (27410-2123)
PHONE..................336 545-0425
Rosemary S Pilkington, *Admn*
EMP: 5 **EST:** 2015
SALES (est): 50.03K **Privately Held**
SIC: 3211 Flat glass

(G-7265)
PIRANHA NAIL AND STAPLE INC
Also Called: Piranha
901 Norwalk St Ste E (27407-2039)
PHONE..................336 852-8358
Mike Mitchell, *Pr*
EMP: 5 **EST:** 1999
SQ FT: 3,000
SALES (est): 1.42MM **Privately Held**
Web: www.piranhanail.com
SIC: 3399 5049 Metal fasteners; Precision tools

(G-7266)
PITNEY BOWES INC
Also Called: Pitney Bowes
4161 Piedmont Pkwy (27410-8175)
PHONE..................336 805-3320
EMP: 13
SALES (corp-wide): 3.27B **Publicly Held**
Web: www.pitneybowes.com
SIC: 3579 Postage meters
PA: Pitney Bowes Inc.
3001 Summer St
Stamford CT 06905
203 356-5000

(G-7267)
PLATESETTERSCOM
114 Industrial Ave (27406-4505)
PHONE..................888 380-7483
EMP: 8 **EST:** 2016
SALES (est): 381.24K **Privately Held**
Web: www.platesetters.com
SIC: 2752 Commercial printing, lithographic

(G-7268)
POSH PICKLE COMPANY LLC
4901 Hackamore Rd (27410-9387)
P.O. Box 8518 (27419-0518)
PHONE..................336 870-6712
Mark A Mcmasters, *Prin*
EMP: 6 **EST:** 2011
SALES (est): 126.56K **Privately Held**
Web: www.poshpickle.com
SIC: 2035 Pickled fruits and vegetables

(G-7269)
POWER INTEGRITY CORP
2109 Patterson St (27407-2531)
P.O. Box 9682 (27429-0682)
PHONE..................336 379-9773
James T Fesmire, *Pr*
Debbie Wilson, *VP*
EMP: 20 **EST:** 1980
SALES (est): 2.36MM **Privately Held**
Web: www.powerintegritycorp.com
SIC: 3629 3612 1731 Electronic generation equipment; Transformers, except electric; Electric power systems contractors

(G-7270)
POWERTAC USA INC
3702 Alliance Dr Ste C (27407-2052)
PHONE..................919 239-4470
James Rath, *Prin*
Bamrung Carroll, *Prin*
Jian Li, *Prin*
EMP: 7 **EST:** 2017
SALES (est): 916.08K **Privately Held**
Web: www.powertac.com
SIC: 3648 Lighting equipment, nec

(G-7271)
PPG ARCHITECTURAL FINISHES INC
Also Called: Glidden Professional Paint Ctr
5103 W Market St (27409-2644)
PHONE..................336 273-9761
Jim Fausett, *Genl Mgr*
EMP: 4
SALES (corp-wide): 17.65B **Publicly Held**
Web: www.glidden.com
SIC: 2851 Paints and allied products
HQ: Ppg Architectural Finishes, Inc.
1 Ppg Pl
Pittsburgh PA 15272
412 434-3131

(G-7272)
PPG INDUSTRIES INC
4347 Baylor St (27455-2563)
PHONE..................919 772-3093
EMP: 4
SALES (corp-wide): 17.65B **Publicly Held**
Web: www.ppg.com
SIC: 2851 3211 3231 3229 Paints and allied products; Flat glass; Strengthened or reinforced glass; Glass fiber products
PA: Ppg Industries, Inc.
1 Ppg Pl
Pittsburgh PA 15272
412 434-3131

(G-7273)
PPG INDUSTRIES INC
Also Called: Industrial Coatings
109 P P G Rd (27409-1801)
PHONE..................336 856-9280
Scott Mcmillen, *Mgr*
EMP: 201
SALES (corp-wide): 17.65B **Publicly Held**
Web: www.ppg.com
SIC: 2851 Coating, air curing
PA: Ppg Industries, Inc.
1 Ppg Pl
Pittsburgh PA 15272
412 434-3131

(G-7274)
PRECISION FABRICS GROUP INC (PA)
333 N Greene St (27401-2142)
PHONE..................336 281-3049
Lanty Smith, *Ch*
Pat Burns, *
Walter Jones, *CEO*
◆ **EMP:** 49 **EST:** 1988
SALES (est): 198.9MM
SALES (corp-wide): 198.9MM **Privately Held**
Web: www.precisionfabrics.com
SIC: 2262 2221 Decorative finishing of manmade broadwoven fabrics; Manmade and synthetic broadwoven fabrics

(G-7275)
PRECISION PRINTING
2832 Randleman Rd Ste D (27406-5158)
PHONE..................336 273-5794
Wayne Willard, *Owner*
EMP: 4 **EST:** 1988
SALES (est): 241.58K **Privately Held**
SIC: 2752 Offset printing

(G-7276)
PRECISION WALLS INC
7215 Cessna Dr (27409-9685)
PHONE..................336 852-7710
Bruce Wolfe, *Brnch Mgr*
EMP: 8
SALES (corp-wide): 102.56MM **Privately Held**
Web: www.precisionwalls.com
SIC: 1743 5046 3275 2631 Tile installation, ceramic; Partitions; Gypsum products; Paperboard mills
PA: Precision Walls, Inc.
1230 Ne Maynard Rd
Cary NC 27513
919 832-0380

Greensboro - Guilford County (G-7277)

(G-7277)
PRECOR INCORPORATED
1818 Youngs Mill Rd (27406-9060)
PHONE..................................336 603-1000
Chris Torgtler, *Brnch Mgr*
EMP: 36
SALES (corp-wide): 2.8B **Publicly Held**
Web: www.precor.com
SIC: 3949 Ammunition belts, sporting type
HQ: Precor Incorporated
   20031 142nd Ave Ne
   Woodinville WA 98072
   425 486-9292

(G-7278)
PREMEDIA GROUP LLC
7605 Business Park Dr Ste F (27409-9460)
PHONE..................................336 274-2421
EMP: 13 **EST:** 2005
SQ FT: 20,000
SALES (est): 2.42MM **Privately Held**
Web: www.premediagroup.com
SIC: 2782 Account books

(G-7279)
PRESS PLAY COUNSELING PLLC
5605 Clustermill Dr (27407-5414)
PHONE..................................336 223-4234
Shanta Brown, *General MEDICAL*
EMP: 5 **EST:** 2019
SALES (est): 76.29K **Privately Held**
Web: www.pressplaycounseling.com
SIC: 2741 Miscellaneous publishing

(G-7280)
PRETIUM PACKAGING LLC
Also Called: Pretium Packaging
3240 N Ohenry Blvd (27405-3808)
PHONE..................................336 621-1891
Jim Sitton, *Pr*
EMP: 50
SALES (corp-wide): 868.81MM **Privately Held**
Web: www.pretiumpkg.com
SIC: 5199 3089 Packaging materials; Air mattresses, plastics
PA: Pretium Packaging, L.L.C.
   1555 Page Industrial Blvd
   Saint Louis MO 63102
   314 727-8200

(G-7281)
PREVOST CAR (US) INC (DH)
Also Called: Novabus
7817 National Service Rd (27409-9451)
PHONE..................................908 222-7211
Gaetan Bolduc, *Pr*
▲ **EMP:** 35 **EST:** 1993
SALES (est): 154.16MM
SALES (corp-wide): 45.13B **Privately Held**
Web: www.prevostcar.com
SIC: 3711 5013 7539 3713 Buses, all types, assembly of; Motor vehicle supplies and new parts; Automotive repair shops, nec; Truck and bus bodies
HQ: Volvo Trucks North America, Inc.
   7900 National Service Rd
   Greensboro NC 27409
   336 393-2000

(G-7282)
PREYER BREWING COMPANY LLC
600 Battleground Ave (27401-2015)
PHONE..................................336 420-0902
N Preyer, *VP*
John Preyer, *Pr*
Nicole Preyer, *VP*
William Preyer, *VP*
Alice Preyer, *Prin*
EMP: 8 **EST:** 2014
SALES (est): 839.6K **Privately Held**
Web: www.preyerbrewing.com
SIC: 2082 Beer (alcoholic beverage)

(G-7283)
PRINT 4 ME INC
104 Meadowood St Ste G (27409-3276)
P.O. Box 18424 (27419-8424)
PHONE..................................336 854-1589
James Gouge, *Prin*
EMP: 5 **EST:** 2014
SALES (est): 110K **Privately Held**
SIC: 2752 Commercial printing, lithographic

(G-7284)
PRINTERY
2100 Fairfax Rd Ste 101a (27407-3010)
PHONE..................................336 852-9774
Galen Hill, *Owner*
EMP: 10 **EST:** 1985
SQ FT: 4,500
SALES (est): 936.1K **Privately Held**
Web: www.printeryweb.com
SIC: 2752 2791 Offset printing; Typesetting

(G-7285)
PRINTING SVCS GREENSBORO INC
Also Called: P S G
2206 N Church St (27405-4308)
PHONE..................................336 274-7663
Eddie Franklin Brame, *Pr*
Russ Brame, *Treas*
EMP: 10 **EST:** 1969
SQ FT: 29,000
SALES (est): 470.84K **Privately Held**
Web: www.phase3communications.com
SIC: 2752 7334 2791 2789 Offset printing; Photocopying and duplicating services; Typesetting; Bookbinding and related work

(G-7286)
PRO-FACE AMERICA LLC (HQ)
Also Called: Proface America
235 Burgess Rd Ste D (27409-9778)
PHONE..................................734 477-0600
Jeff Roberts, *Off Mgr*
▲ **EMP:** 48 **EST:** 1968
SALES (est): 10.16MM
SALES (corp-wide): 82.05K **Privately Held**
Web: www.profaceamerica.com
SIC: 3571 3575 3577 Minicomputers; Computer terminals; Computer peripheral equipment, nec
PA: Schneider Electric Se
   35 Rue Joseph Monier
   Rueil Malmaison
   146046982

(G-7287)
PROCTER & GAMBLE MFG CO
Also Called: Procter & Gamble
100 S Swing Rd (27409-2006)
P.O. Box 18647 (27419-8647)
PHONE..................................336 954-0000
Mary Jane Harris, *Brnch Mgr*
EMP: 91
SALES (corp-wide): 82.01B **Publicly Held**
Web: us.pg.com
SIC: 2844 2676 3421 2842 Deodorants, personal; Towels, napkins, and tissue paper products; Razor blades and razors; Specialty cleaning
HQ: The Procter & Gamble Manufacturing Company
   1 Procter And Gamble Plz
   Cincinnati OH 45202
   513 983-1100

(G-7288)
PROFESSIONAL IMAGE
4602 W Market St (27407-1232)
PHONE..................................336 294-6200
Tanya Dickens, *Owner*
EMP: 7 **EST:** 2015
SALES (est): 114.7K **Privately Held**
SIC: 2329 Men's and boy's clothing, nec

(G-7289)
PROGRESSIVE TOOL & MFG INC
245 Standard Dr (27409-9600)
PHONE..................................336 664-1130
Daniel Thompson, *Pr*
Richard Thompson, *VP*
EMP: 18 **EST:** 1984
SQ FT: 15,000
SALES (est): 2.14MM **Privately Held**
Web: www.progtool.net
SIC: 3544 Special dies and tools

(G-7290)
PROXIMITY FOODS CORPORATION
Also Called: Proximity Bakery
1117 W Cornwallis Dr (27408-6331)
PHONE..................................336 691-1700
Natalie Hyde, *Pr*
EMP: 4 **EST:** 2003
SALES (est): 250.56K **Privately Held**
SIC: 2041 Bread and bread-type roll mixes

(G-7291)
PUBLIC HEALTH CORPS INC
Also Called: Sanicap
3300 Battleground Ave Ste 270 (27410-2465)
P.O. Box 39253 (27438-9253)
PHONE..................................336 545-2999
EMP: 5 **EST:** 1993
SALES (est): 437.39K **Privately Held**
Web: www.sanicap.com
SIC: 2842 Industrial plant disinfectants or deodorants

(G-7292)
PURELY PALLETS
4701 Olde Forest Dr (27406-8747)
PHONE..................................336 676-7107
Zachary Spence, *Owner*
EMP: 5 **EST:** 2015
SALES (est): 57.7K **Privately Held**
SIC: 2448 Pallets, wood and wood with metal

(G-7293)
PUROLATOR FACET INC (HQ)
Also Called: Purolator Advanced Filtration
8439 Triad Dr (27409-9018)
PHONE..................................336 668-4444
Russell D Stellfox, *Pr*
Richard Wolfson, *
David Fallon, *
▲ **EMP:** 40 **EST:** 1999
SQ FT: 90,000
SALES (est): 38.6MM
SALES (corp-wide): 19.07B **Publicly Held**
Web: www.purolator-afg.com
SIC: 3677 5085 3728 3564 Filtration devices, electronic; Filters, industrial; Aircraft parts and equipment, nec; Blowers and fans
PA: Parker-Hannifin Corporation
   6035 Parkland Blvd
   Cleveland OH 44124
   216 896-3000

(G-7294)
QORVO INC
7908 Piedmont Triad Pkwy Bldg D (27409-9417)
PHONE..................................336 664-1233
Robert Bruggeworth, *CEO*
EMP: 269
SALES (corp-wide): 3.57B **Publicly Held**
Web: www.qorvo.com
SIC: 3674 Semiconductors and related devices
PA: Qorvo, Inc.
   7628 Thorndike Rd
   Greensboro NC 27409
   336 664-1233

(G-7295)
QORVO INC (PA)
Also Called: Qorvo
7628 Thorndike Rd (27409-9421)
PHONE..................................336 664-1233
Robert A Bruggeworth, *Pr*
Ralph G Quinsey, *
Grant A Brown, *Sr VP*
Philip J Chesley, *Sr VP*
Steven E Creviston, *Sr VP*
EMP: 1020 **EST:** 1981
SALES (est): 3.57B
SALES (corp-wide): 3.57B **Publicly Held**
Web: www.qorvo.com
SIC: 3674 3825 Semiconductors and related devices; Oscillators, audio and radio frequency (instrument types)

(G-7296)
QORVO INTERNATIONAL HOLDG INC (DH)
7628 Thorndike Rd (27409-9421)
PHONE..................................336 664-1233
Robert A Bruggeworth, *Pr*
EMP: 8 **EST:** 2000
SALES (est): 5.84MM
SALES (corp-wide): 3.57B **Publicly Held**
Web: www.qorvo.com
SIC: 3674 Semiconductors and related devices
HQ: Qorvo Us, Inc.
   2300 Ne Brookwood Pkwy
   Hillsboro OR 97124
   336 664-1233

(G-7297)
QORVO INTERNATIONAL SVCS INC
7628 Thorndike Rd (27409-9421)
PHONE..................................336 664-1233
Robert Bruggeworth, *CEO*
EMP: 29 **EST:** 2016
SALES (est): 3.38MM
SALES (corp-wide): 3.57B **Publicly Held**
Web: www.qorvo.com
SIC: 3674 Semiconductors and related devices
HQ: Qorvo Us, Inc.
   2300 Ne Brookwood Pkwy
   Hillsboro OR 97124
   336 664-1233

(G-7298)
QORVO US INC
7907 Piedmont Triad Pkwy (27409-9457)
PHONE..................................336 662-1150
Vic Steel, *Mgr*
EMP: 7
SQ FT: 147,705
SALES (corp-wide): 3.57B **Publicly Held**
Web: www.qorvo.com
SIC: 3674 Semiconductors and related devices
HQ: Qorvo Us, Inc.
   2300 Ne Brookwood Pkwy
   Hillsboro OR 97124
   336 664-1233

(G-7299)
QORVO US INC
7914 Piedmont Triad Pkwy (27409-9417)
PHONE..................................336 931-8298
EMP: 52
SALES (corp-wide): 3.57B **Publicly Held**
Web: www.qorvo.com

GEOGRAPHIC SECTION
Greensboro - Guilford County (G-7324)

SIC: 3674 Integrated circuits, semiconductor networks, etc.
HQ: Qorvo Us, Inc.
2300 Ne Brookwood Pkwy
Hillsboro OR 97124
336 664-1233

(G-7300)
QUALITY HOUSING CORPORATION
Also Called: Insul Kor
1400 Battleground Ave Ste 205 (27408-8042)
PHONE..............................336 274-2622
S Sanders Junior, *Pr*
Major S Sanders Junior, *Pr*
Kenneth Lenz, *Treas*
Chris Samuels, *Prin*
EMP: 11 **EST:** 2000
SALES (est): 933.49K **Privately Held**
SIC: 2452 Prefabricated wood buildings

(G-7301)
QUALITY PRTG CARTRIDGE FCTRY
Also Called: M C B Displays
6700 W Market St (27409-1890)
PHONE..............................336 852-2505
Bonnie Ferguson, *Pr*
Mary Beisner, *VP*
EMP: 6 **EST:** 1978
SQ FT: 5,800
SALES (est): 907.98K **Privately Held**
Web: www.qualityprinting.info
SIC: 2752 2791 2789 Offset printing; Typesetting; Bookbinding and related work

(G-7302)
RALPH LAUREN CORPORATION
4100 Beechwood Dr (27410-8117)
P.O. Box 35868 (27425-5868)
PHONE..............................336 632-5000
EMP: 4
SALES (corp-wide): 6.44B **Publicly Held**
SIC: 2325 Men's and boy's trousers and slacks
PA: Ralph Lauren Corporation
650 Madison Ave
New York NY 10022
212 318-7000

(G-7303)
RANDALL PRINTING INC
1029 Huffman St (27405-7209)
PHONE..............................336 272-3333
EMP: 8 **EST:** 1991
SQ FT: 4,598
SALES (est): 770.14K **Privately Held**
Web: www.randallprinting.com
SIC: 2752 7389 Offset printing; Printing broker

(G-7304)
RBI
7025 Albert Pick Rd Ste 200 (27409-9539)
PHONE..............................336 605-0121
Jenny York, *Sales & Marketing*
EMP: 5 **EST:** 2015
SALES (est): 146.41K **Privately Held**
Web: triadrbi.leagueapps.com
SIC: 2721 Magazines: publishing only, not printed on site

(G-7305)
RECAP INC
5201 Woodberry Forest Rd (27406-8038)
PHONE..............................336 299-8794
Jonathan Miller, *Prin*
EMP: 8 **EST:** 2013
SALES (est): 25.09K **Privately Held**
Web: www.recap.org
SIC: 7692 Welding repair

(G-7306)
RESCO PRODUCTS INC
3600 W Wendover Ave (27407-1508)
PHONE..............................336 299-1441
EMP: 18 **EST:** 2019
SALES (est): 1.07MM **Privately Held**
Web: www.rescoproducts.com
SIC: 3255 Clay refractories

(G-7307)
RESCO PRODUCTS INC
North State Prophyllite Div
3600 W Wendover Ave (27407-1508)
P.O. Box 7247 (27417-0247)
PHONE..............................336 299-1441
R B Arthur Junior, *VP*
EMP: 9
SQ FT: 5,000
SALES (corp-wide): 111.18MM **Privately Held**
Web: www.rescoproducts.com
SIC: 3255 3297 Ladle brick, clay; Cement: high temperature, refractory (nonclay)
PA: Resco Products, Inc.
1 Robinson Plz Ste 300
Pittsburgh PA 15205
412 494-4491

(G-7308)
RF MICRO DEVICES INC
Also Called: Rfmd
7628 Thorndike Rd (27409-9421)
PHONE..............................336 664-1233
▲ **EMP:** 3482
Web: www.qorvo.com
SIC: 3674 Semiconductors and related devices

(G-7309)
RFMD LLC
7628 Thorndike Rd (27409-9421)
PHONE..............................336 664-1233
EMP: 16 **EST:** 2019
SALES (est): 24.51MM
SALES (corp-wide): 3.57B **Publicly Held**
Web: www.qorvo.com
SIC: 3674 Semiconductors and related devices
PA: Qorvo, Inc.
7628 Thorndike Rd
Greensboro NC 27409
336 664-1233

(G-7310)
RHINOCEROS TIMES
Also Called: Hammer Publications
216 W Market St (27401-2504)
P.O. Box 9023 (27429-0023)
PHONE..............................336 763-4170
William Hammer, *Pt*
John Hammer, *Pt*
EMP: 14 **EST:** 1993
SQ FT: 4,500
SALES (est): 455.31K **Privately Held**
Web: www.rhinotimes.com
SIC: 2711 Newspapers, publishing and printing

(G-7311)
RILEY JARON
509 Houston St (27401-2458)
PHONE..............................929 462-8300
Jaron Riley, *Owner*
EMP: 5
SALES (est): 65.61K **Privately Held**
SIC: 2329 Men's and boy's clothing, nec

(G-7312)
RLM/UNIVERSAL PACKAGING INC
Also Called: Universal Packaging
8607 Cedar Hollow Rd (27455-8253)
PHONE..............................336 644-6161
EMP: 15 **EST:** 1996
SQ FT: 70,000
SALES (est): 709.29K **Privately Held**
SIC: 2653 5113 7319 5199 Corrugated and solid fiber boxes; Corrugated and solid fiber boxes; Display advertising service; Packaging materials

(G-7313)
ROBERT D STARR
Also Called: Starr's Party Ice
1211 Youngs Mill Rd (27405-9650)
PHONE..............................336 697-0286
Robert Starr, *Owner*
EMP: 5 **EST:** 1963
SALES (est): 338.15K **Privately Held**
SIC: 2097 Manufactured ice

(G-7314)
ROBIX AMERICA INC
7104 Cessna Dr (27409-9793)
PHONE..............................336 668-9555
▲ **EMP:** 210
SQ FT: 65,000
SALES (est): 15.7MM **Privately Held**
Web: www.canplast.com
SIC: 2891 2821 Adhesives; Polyvinyl chloride resins, PVC

(G-7315)
ROCK-WELD INDUSTRIES INC
3515 Associate Dr (27405-3879)
PHONE..............................336 375-6862
Chris Salter, *Pr*
Mike Salter, *VP*
EMP: 9 **EST:** 1946
SQ FT: 17,000
SALES (est): 772.25K **Privately Held**
SIC: 3545 5084 Diamond cutting tools for turning, boring, burnishing, etc.; Drilling bits

(G-7316)
ROEHRIG ENGINEERING INC
Also Called: MTS Systems Roehrig
603 Woodland Dr (27408-7416)
P.O. Box 728 (27299-0728)
PHONE..............................336 956-3800
Kurt Roehrig, *Pr*
Scott Treichler, *VP*
Carmella Roehrig, *Treas*
Kimberly Elliot, *Sec*
EMP: 20 **EST:** 1977
SQ FT: 2,500
SALES (est): 2.37MM
SALES (corp-wide): 15.93B **Publicly Held**
Web: www.roehrigengineering.com
SIC: 3829 8711 Physical property testing equipment; Consulting engineer
HQ: Mts Systems Corporation
14000 Technology Dr
Eden Prairie MN 55344
952 937-4000

(G-7317)
ROOBRIK INC
301 S Elm St Ste 421 (27401-2675)
PHONE..............................919 667-7750
Nate O'keefe, *CEO*
EMP: 5 **EST:** 2015
SALES (est): 532.9K **Privately Held**
Web: www.roobrik.com
SIC: 7372 Business oriented computer software

(G-7318)
ROUTH SIGN SERVICE
318 Creek Ridge Rd Ste B (27406-4459)
PHONE..............................336 272-0895
John Humble, *Owner*
EMP: 6 **EST:** 1984
SQ FT: 2,200
SALES (est): 426.9K **Privately Held**
Web: www.routhsigns.com
SIC: 3993 Signs and advertising specialties

(G-7319)
ROYAL IMPRESSIONS LLC
2603 W Woodlyn Way (27407-5027)
PHONE..............................910 340-5955
EMP: 4 **EST:** 2019
SALES (est): 99.81K **Privately Held**
SIC: 2431 Millwork

(G-7320)
RUSSELL STANDARD CORPORATION
1124 S Holden Rd (27407-2914)
PHONE..............................336 292-6875
EMP: 8
SALES (corp-wide): 121.53MM **Privately Held**
Web: www.russellstandard.com
SIC: 1611 2951 Highway and street paving contractor; Asphalt paving mixtures and blocks
PA: Russell Standard Corporation
285 Kappa Dr Ste 300
Pittsburgh PA 15238
412 449-0700

(G-7321)
RUSSELL STANDARD NC LLC
Also Called: Russell Standard
1124 S Holden Rd (27407-2914)
PHONE..............................336 292-6875
Matthew Wjohnson, *Mgr*
EMP: 117 **EST:** 2008
SALES (est): 3.65MM
SALES (corp-wide): 121.53MM **Privately Held**
SIC: 2951 Asphalt paving mixtures and blocks
PA: Russell Standard Corporation
285 Kappa Dr Ste 300
Pittsburgh PA 15238
412 449-0700

(G-7322)
SAFETY & SECURITY INTL INC
4270 Piedmont Pkwy Ste 102 (27410-8160)
PHONE..............................336 285-8673
EMP: 8 **EST:** 2009
SQ FT: 1,500
SALES (est): 5.02MM **Privately Held**
Web: www.safesecint.com
SIC: 3728 2311 Military aircraft equipment and armament; Military uniforms, men's and youths': purchased materials

(G-7323)
SAGE MULE
608 Battleground Ave (27401-2015)
PHONE..............................336 209-9183
EMP: 6 **EST:** 2019
SALES (est): 119.12K **Privately Held**
Web: www.thesagemule.com
SIC: 2099 Food preparations, nec

(G-7324)
SALSA GREENSBORO
512 S Elm St (27406-1326)
PHONE..............................781 648-4140
EMP: 4 **EST:** 2015
SALES (est): 82.7K **Privately Held**
SIC: 2099 Dips, except cheese and sour cream based

Greensboro - Guilford County (G-7325) — GEOGRAPHIC SECTION

(G-7325)
SARAHS SALSA INC
622 Myers Ln (27408-7522)
PHONE...........................336 508-3033
Sarah Ward, *Pr*
Susan Kennedy, *VP*
Katherine Meadows, *VP*
Wes Ward, *Sec*
Mike Kennedy, *CFO*
EMP: 5 **EST:** 2005
SALES (est): 286.09K **Privately Held**
SIC: 2099 Salads, fresh or refrigerated

(G-7326)
SC JOHNSON PROF USA INC
2408 Doyle St (27406-2912)
PHONE...........................704 263-4240
EMP: 51
Web: www.scjp.com
SIC: 2841 Textile soap
HQ: Sc Johnson Professional Usa, Inc.
2815 Clseum Cntre Dr Ste
Charlotte NC 28217

(G-7327)
SCHNADIG CORPORATION (HQ)
Also Called: International Furniture
1150 Pleasant Ridge Rd Ste A
(27409-9847)
PHONE...........................336 389-5200
Jeff Young, *Ch*
Howard Pan, *
◆ **EMP:** 40 **EST:** 1898
SALES (est): 49.55MM **Privately Held**
Web: www.caracole.com
SIC: 2512 5021 Living room furniture: upholstered on wood frames; Tables, occasional
PA: Markor International Home Furnishings Co., Ltd.
No.506, Beijing S. Road, Xinshi District
Urumqi XJ 83001

(G-7328)
SCULPTURAL ARTS COATING INC
2912 Baltic Ave (27406-4542)
P.O. Box 10546 (27404-0546)
PHONE...........................336 379-7651
EMP: 7 **EST:** 2000
SALES (est): 105.07K **Privately Held**
Web: www.sculpturalarts.com
SIC: 3634 Electric housewares and fans

(G-7329)
SECOND EARTH INC
3716 Alliance Dr Ste C (27407-2387)
PHONE...........................336 740-9333
Robert Haskin, *CEO*
Gary Slack, *CFO*
EMP: 5 **EST:** 2010
SALES (est): 377.93K **Privately Held**
SIC: 2899 5999 Water treating compounds; Water purification equipment

(G-7330)
SEE CLEARLY INC
Also Called: Sippin Snax Cft Beer Wine Snck
207 S Westgate Dr Ste B (27407)
PHONE...........................929 464-6887
Melissa Wallace, *CEO*
EMP: 4 **EST:** 2010
SALES (est): 150K **Privately Held**
SIC: 2068 Nuts: dried, dehydrated, salted or roasted

(G-7331)
SELEX ES LLC
4221 Tudor Ln (27410-8105)
PHONE...........................336 379-7135
EMP: 67
SALES (corp-wide): 15.28B **Publicly Held**
Web: www.leonardocompany-us.com
SIC: 3571 Electronic computers
HQ: Selex Es, Llc
11300 W 89th St
Overland Park KS 66214
800 765-0861

(G-7332)
SELPRO LLC
408 Gallimore Dairy Rd Ste C
(27409-9530)
PHONE...........................336 513-0550
▲ **EMP:** 10 **EST:** 2010
SALES (est): 669.1K **Privately Held**
Web: www.norbridgecabinets.com
SIC: 2434 Wood kitchen cabinets

(G-7333)
SENSORY ANALYTICS LLC
405b Pomona Dr (27407-1431)
PHONE...........................336 315-6090
Greg Frisby, *CEO*
EMP: 49 **EST:** 2004
SALES (est): 12.93MM **Privately Held**
Web: www.specmetrix.com
SIC: 3826 Analytical optical instruments

(G-7334)
SHAMROCK CORPORATION (PA)
Also Called: Innisbrook Wraps
422 N Chimney Rock Rd (27410-6249)
P.O. Box 19448 (27419-9448)
PHONE...........................336 574-4200
Alexander W Worth, *Pr*
David M Worth, *
Robert P Worth, *
◆ **EMP:** 125 **EST:** 1957
SQ FT: 253,000
SALES (est): 20.79MM
SALES (corp-wide): 20.79MM **Privately Held**
Web: www.shamrockwraps.com
SIC: 2754 Rotogravure printing

(G-7335)
SHERWIN-WILLIAMS COMPANY
Also Called: Sherwin-Williams
113 Stage Coach Trl (27409-1859)
PHONE...........................336 292-3000
Mark Hamilton, *Mgr*
EMP: 47
SQ FT: 20,048
SALES (corp-wide): 22.15B **Publicly Held**
Web: www.sherwin-williams.com
SIC: 5231 5198 2851 Paint; Paints; Coating, air curing
PA: The Sherwin-Williams Company
101 W Prospect Ave # 1020
Cleveland OH 44115
216 566-2000

(G-7336)
SHORT CIRCUIT AUDIO LLC
3501 Yanceyville St (27405-4063)
PHONE...........................908 868-7077
Steven Voytac, *Owner*
EMP: 4 **EST:** 2018
SALES (est): 223.52K **Privately Held**
SIC: 3613 Switchgear and switchboard apparatus

(G-7337)
SID JENKINS INC
Also Called: Tiffany Marble Company
3004 Harnett Dr (27407-6102)
PHONE...........................336 632-0707
Sid Jenkins, *Pr*
Jano Jenkins, *Sec*
▲ **EMP:** 5 **EST:** 1975
SQ FT: 5,000
SALES (est): 915.79K **Privately Held**
SIC: 5032 1793 3496 3281 Brick, stone, and related material; Glass and glazing work; Miscellaneous fabricated wire products; Cut stone and stone products

(G-7338)
SIERRA SOFTWARE LLC
Also Called: Acetrace
143 Industrial Ave (27406-4504)
PHONE...........................877 285-2867
Bradley Snyder, *Prin*
EMP: 10 **EST:** 2013
SALES (est): 476.81K **Privately Held**
Web: www.sierrasoftwarellc.com
SIC: 7372 Prepackaged software

(G-7339)
SIGGBEY INDUSTRIES LLC
717 Shelby Dr (27409-2252)
PHONE...........................336 483-6035
EMP: 4 **EST:** 2021
SALES (est): 63.22K **Privately Held**
SIC: 3999 Manufacturing industries, nec

(G-7340)
SIMONTIC COMPOSITE INC
2901 E Gate City Blvd Ste 2500
(27401-4898)
PHONE...........................336 897-9885
Simon Senibi, *CEO*
EMP: 20 **EST:** 2010
SALES (est): 1.03MM **Privately Held**
Web: simonticcomposite.comcastbiz.net
SIC: 3999 Advertising curtains

(G-7341)
SIMPLE SUPPLIES LLC
2945 Cottage Pl Apt G (27455-2321)
PHONE...........................336 358-7704
Delricho Moore, *Managing Member*
EMP: 4 **EST:** 2020
SALES (est): 25K **Privately Held**
SIC: 2051 Bakery: wholesale or wholesale/retail combined

(G-7342)
SINGLEY SPECIALTY CO INC
1025 Willowbrook Dr (27403-2059)
PHONE...........................336 852-8581
Charles P Kennedy, *Pr*
S B Kennedy, *Sec*
EMP: 6 **EST:** 1952
SQ FT: 2,000
SALES (est): 541.5K **Privately Held**
SIC: 3553 Sanding machines, except portable floor sanders: woodworking

(G-7343)
SKINNER COMPANY
414 E Montcastle Dr (27406-5387)
PHONE...........................336 580-4716
EMP: 4 **EST:** 2017
SALES (est): 54.38K **Privately Held**
Web: www.skinnerco.com
SIC: 3429 Hardware, nec

(G-7344)
SKYWORKS SOLUTIONS INC
406 Gallimore Dairy Rd (27409-9725)
PHONE...........................336 291-4200
EMP: 21
SALES (corp-wide): 4.77B **Publicly Held**
Web: www.skyworksinc.com
SIC: 3674 Semiconductors and related devices
PA: Skyworks Solutions, Inc.
5260 California Ave # 100
Irvine CA 92617
949 231-3000

(G-7345)
SMITH ARCHITECTURAL METALS LLC
4536 S Holden Rd (27406-9510)
P.O. Box 16303 (27416-0303)
PHONE...........................336 273-1970
EMP: 30 **EST:** 1997
SQ FT: 30,000
SALES (est): 5.41MM **Privately Held**
Web: www.smithmetals.net
SIC: 3441 Fabricated structural metal

(G-7346)
SNAP PUBLICATIONS LLC
Also Called: Rhino Times
216 W Market St Ste A (27401-2504)
P.O. Box 9846 (27429-0846)
PHONE...........................336 274-8531
Roy Carroll, *Managing Member*
EMP: 10 **EST:** 2013
SALES (est): 215.22K **Privately Held**
Web: www.rhinotimes.com
SIC: 2711 Newspapers, publishing and printing

(G-7347)
SNIDER TIRE INC
330 E Lindsay St (27401-2924)
PHONE...........................336 691-5480
EMP: 18
SALES (corp-wide): 436.36MM **Privately Held**
Web: www.sniderfleet.com
SIC: 5531 7534 7538 Automotive tires; Tire recapping; General automotive repair shops
PA: Snider Tire, Inc.
1081 Red Ventures Dr
Fort Mill SC 29707
336 691-5480

(G-7348)
SOLVEKTA LLC
2110 Rockglen Ln (27410-2481)
PHONE...........................336 944-4677
EMP: 4 **EST:** 2012
SALES (est): 174.2K **Privately Held**
Web: www.solvekta.com
SIC: 2834 Pharmaceutical preparations

(G-7349)
SONGS OF WATER LLC
Also Called: Brightbell Creative
3204 Wingrave Ter (27410-8310)
PHONE...........................336 337-4674
EMP: 4 **EST:** 2011
SALES (est): 56.54K **Privately Held**
SIC: 7372 Prepackaged software

(G-7350)
SOUTH / WIN LLC (DH)
112 Maxfield Rd (27405-8643)
P.O. Box 20461 (27420-0461)
PHONE...........................336 398-5650
William H Dubose, *Pr*
EMP: 57 **EST:** 1987
SALES (est): 25.06MM
SALES (corp-wide): 741.18MM **Privately Held**
Web: www.highlinewarren.com
SIC: 2841 5169 Detergents, synthetic organic or inorganic alkaline; Detergents
HQ: Highline Warren Llc
8700 W Trail Lake Dr # 30
Memphis TN 38125
800 986-2211

(G-7351)
SOUTHEASTER PLASTIC INC
Also Called: Southeastern Plastics
605 Diamond Hill Ct (27406-4617)

GEOGRAPHIC SECTION

Greensboro - Guilford County (G-7375)

P.O. Box 36256 (27416-6256)
PHONE.................336 275-6616
Al Faust, *Prin*
Al Faust, *Pr*
David Faust, *VP*
EMP: 10 **EST:** 1980
SQ FT: 4,500
SALES (est): 913.28K **Privately Held**
Web: www.seplastics.com
SIC: 3089 Injection molding of plastics

(G-7352)
SOUTHEASTERN DIE OF NC
510 Corliss St (27406-5272)
PHONE.................336 275-5212
Bert Ficquette, *Genl Mgr*
EMP: 9 **EST:** 2010
SALES (est): 175.94K **Privately Held**
SIC: 3544 Special dies and tools

(G-7353)
SOUTHERN DIGITAL WATCH REPAIR
4009 Groometown Rd (27407-7915)
PHONE.................336 299-6718
Betty Matthews, *Owner*
EMP: 5 **EST:** 1978
SALES (est): 429.79K **Privately Held**
SIC: 3873 7631 Clocks, except timeclocks; Watch repair

(G-7354)
SOUTHERN HOME SPA AND WTR PDTS
Also Called: Southern Home Spa & Water Pdts
105 Edwardia Dr (27409-2601)
PHONE.................336 286-3564
TOLL FREE: 800
John J Mathews, *Pr*
EMP: 4 **EST:** 1981
SQ FT: 4,700
SALES (est): 270K **Privately Held**
Web: www.southernhomespas.com
SIC: 3999 7991 Hot tubs; Spas

(G-7355)
SOUTHERN RUBBER COMPANY INC
2209 Patterson St (27407-2533)
PHONE.................336 299-2456
H Edward Bowman, *Pr*
David J Delman, *
Carol S Bowman, *
EMP: 29 **EST:** 1925
SQ FT: 30,000
SALES (est): 7.42MM **Privately Held**
Web: www.southernrubber.com
SIC: 3053 5085 Gaskets, all materials; Rubber goods, mechanical

(G-7356)
SOUTHERN TRADE PUBLICATIONS CO (PA)
6520 Airport Center Dr Ste 204 (27409)
P.O. Box 7344 (27417-0344)
PHONE.................336 454-3516
Emmet D Atkins Iii, *Pr*
EMP: 5 **EST:** 1957
SALES (est): 506.65K
SALES (corp-wide): 506.65K **Privately Held**
Web: www.southernphc.com
SIC: 2721 Trade journals: publishing only, not printed on site

(G-7357)
SPECIALIZED PACKAGING RADISSON LLC
Also Called: Specialized Packaging Flexo
600 Industrial Ave (27406-4604)
PHONE.................336 574-1513
EMP: 75
SIC: 2657 Folding paperboard boxes

(G-7358)
SPORTSEDGE INC
3425 Derby Pl (27405-3601)
P.O. Box 837 (28166-0837)
PHONE.................704 528-0188
Russell Petty, *Prin*
EMP: 13 **EST:** 1997
SALES (est): 471.65K **Privately Held**
Web: www.sportsedge.com
SIC: 3949 Sporting and athletic goods, nec

(G-7359)
SPRING AIR MATTRESS CORP
401 N Raleigh St (27401-4842)
P.O. Box 20028 (27420-0028)
PHONE.................336 272-1141
John R Grove Senior, *CEO*
Frank Grove Iii, *Ch Bd*
Mathew Grove, *
John R Grove Senior, *Pr*
EMP: 85 **EST:** 1926
SQ FT: 80,000
SALES (est): 13.73MM **Privately Held**
Web: www.mattressgrove.com
SIC: 2515 Mattresses, innerspring or box spring

(G-7360)
SPRING REPAIR SERVICE INC
Also Called: Olens B Enterprises
5800 W Gate City Blvd (27407-7097)
PHONE.................336 299-5660
Harry Owensby, *Pr*
Larry J Owensby, *Sec*
EMP: 14 **EST:** 1954
SQ FT: 5,000
SALES (est): 394.49K **Privately Held**
Web: www.angelakenbokphotography.com
SIC: 7699 7538 3715 7519 Welding equipment repair; General automotive repair shops; Truck trailers; Trailer rental

(G-7361)
SPRINGLIGHT CREATIVE LLC
1807 Swannanoa Dr (27410-3933)
PHONE.................336 383-8076
EMP: 4 **EST:** 2019
SALES (est): 41.35K **Privately Held**
SIC: 2741 Miscellaneous publishing

(G-7362)
ST JOHNS PACKAGING USA LLC
Also Called: North State Flexibles
2619 Phoenix Dr (27406-6320)
P.O. Box 5466 (27435-0466)
PHONE.................336 292-9911
T W Mages, *
Bill M Wentz, *
W Battle Wall, *
Tim Mages, *
▲ **EMP:** 190 **EST:** 1997
SQ FT: 122,000
SALES (est): 49.81MM
SALES (corp-wide): 419.36K **Privately Held**
Web: www.sjpack.com
SIC: 2671 7336 2759 Paper; coated and laminated packaging; Package design; Commercial printing, nec
HQ: Emballage St-Jean Ltee
80 Rue Moreau
Saint-Jean-Sur-Richelieu QC J2W 2
450 349-5871

(G-7363)
ST OF GREENSBORO LLC
6383 Burnt Poplar Rd (27409-9711)
P.O. Box 18928 (27419-8928)
PHONE.................336 851-1600
EMP: 8 **EST:** 2010
SALES (est): 72.31K **Privately Held**
Web: www.greensboro.com
SIC: 2711 Newspapers, publishing and printing

(G-7364)
STAGE DECORATION AND SUPS INC
Also Called: Stage Dec
3519 Associate Dr (27405-3879)
PHONE.................336 621-5454
Robert J Thurston, *Pr*
Eric Lowell, *Sec*
Melanie Baynes, *VP*
Beth Cole, *Treas*
▲ **EMP:** 10 **EST:** 1923
SQ FT: 13,500
SALES (est): 318.83K **Privately Held**
Web: www.stagedec.com
SIC: 3999 7922 2391 Stage hardware and equipment, except lighting; Equipment rental, theatrical; Curtains and draperies

(G-7365)
STAMPING & SCRAPBOOKING RM INC
2806 Randleman Rd (27406-5265)
PHONE.................336 389-9538
Eric Sarachik, *VP*
EMP: 7 **EST:** 2005
SALES (est): 65.17K **Privately Held**
SIC: 8299 2782 Arts and crafts schools; Scrapbooks, albums, and diaries

(G-7366)
STANDARD TOOLS AND EQP CO
Also Called: Tools USA
4810 Clover Rd (27405-9607)
PHONE.................336 697-7177
Kat Mendenhall, *CEO*
Robert G Shepley, *
◆ **EMP:** 28 **EST:** 1996
SQ FT: 67,000
SALES (est): 6MM **Privately Held**
Web: www.paint-booths.com
SIC: 3444 Booths, spray: prefabricated sheet metal

(G-7367)
STATE ELECTRIC SUPPLY COMPANY
2709 Patterson St (27407-2316)
PHONE.................336 855-8200
Rick Sheets, *Mgr*
EMP: 10
SALES (corp-wide): 657.57MM **Privately Held**
Web: www.stateelectric.com
SIC: 5063 3625 Electrical supplies, nec; Motor control accessories, including overload relays
HQ: State Electric Supply Company
2010 2nd Ave
Huntington WV 25703
304 523-7491

(G-7368)
STAUNTON CAPITAL INC (PA)
Also Called: Rwm Casters
3406 W Wendover Ave Ste E (27407-1527)
P.O. Box 668 (28053-0668)
PHONE.................704 866-8533
Peter D Comeau, *Pr*
EMP: 49 **EST:** 1948
SQ FT: 87,000
SALES (est): 9.32MM **Privately Held**
Web: www.rwmcasters.com
SIC: 3562 Casters

(G-7369)
STEEN INC
5306 Century Oaks Dr (27455-2187)
PHONE.................336 545-3328
Michael Steen, *Prin*
EMP: 7 **EST:** 2001
SALES (est): 129.71K **Privately Held**
SIC: 3554 Paper industries machinery

(G-7370)
STERLING PRODUCTS CORPORATION
Also Called: Sterling Sign
3924 S Holden Rd (27406-8962)
P.O. Box 7069 (27417-0069)
PHONE.................646 423-3175
Robert P Hilemn, *Pr*
EMP: 8 **EST:** 1986
SALES (est): 86.17K **Privately Held**
SIC: 3993 Signs and advertising specialties

(G-7371)
STEVENS PACKING INC
Also Called: Triad Meats
3023 Randleman Rd (27406-6610)
PHONE.................336 274-6033
Darren Keith Stevens, *Pr*
EMP: 8 **EST:** 2004
SALES (est): 308.26K **Privately Held**
Web: www.triadmeat.com
SIC: 5421 5411 5147 2013 Meat markets, including freezer provisioners; Grocery stores; Meats and meat products; Sausages and other prepared meats

(G-7372)
STITCH OF ROYALTY
721 Pine St (27401-4421)
PHONE.................336 457-1888
Betty Striblin, *Prin*
EMP: 5 **EST:** 2010
SALES (est): 40.66K **Privately Held**
SIC: 2395 Embroidery and art needlework

(G-7373)
STITCHMASTER LLC
Also Called: Stitchmaster
309 S Regional Rd (27409-9674)
PHONE.................336 852-6448
EMP: 9 **EST:** 1984
SQ FT: 1,000
SALES (est): 242.31K **Privately Held**
Web: www.stitchmaster.com
SIC: 7374 2395 3999 Computer graphics service; Embroidery and art needlework; Embroidery kits

(G-7374)
STRANDBERG ENGRG LABS INC
1302 N Ohenry Blvd (27405-6768)
PHONE.................336 274-3775
John A Strandberg, *Pr*
EMP: 10 **EST:** 1949
SQ FT: 31,000
SALES (est): 1.02MM **Privately Held**
Web: www.strandberg.com
SIC: 3823 3822 3625 Industrial process control instruments; Environmental controls; Relays and industrial controls

(G-7375)
STRIKE & FLAME CANDLES
3213 Pleasant Garden Rd Apt 2e (27406-4633)
PHONE.................336 207-4487
Tiffany L Phelps, *Prin*
EMP: 5 **EST:** 2018
SALES (est): 243.67K **Privately Held**

Greensboro - Guilford County (G-7376)

GEOGRAPHIC SECTION

Web: www.strikeflame.com
SIC: 3999 Candles

(G-7376)
STUART DISCHELL
611 Howard St (27403-2003)
PHONE..........................336 334-4695
Stuart Dischell, *Owner*
EMP: 5 EST: 2015
SALES (est): 93.91K **Privately Held**
Web: www.stuartdischellpoetry.com
SIC: 2741 Miscellaneous publishing

(G-7377)
STUDIO STITCH LLC
1616 Battleground Ave Ste D3
(27408-8035)
PHONE..........................336 288-9200
Emily B Fisher, *Prin*
EMP: 6 EST: 2012
SALES (est): 312.22K **Privately Held**
Web: www.studiostitchonline.com
SIC: 2395 Embroidery products, except Schiffli machine

(G-7378)
SUDANESE CMNTY SCHL GREENSBORO
604 Orourke Dr (27409-9671)
PHONE..........................336 763-7761
Taha Babiker, *Prin*
EMP: 8 EST: 2016
SALES (est): 45.34K **Privately Held**
Web: www.greensboro.com
SIC: 2711 Newspapers, publishing and printing

(G-7379)
SUMMIT AVIATION INC
243 Burgess Rd Ste A (27409-9314)
PHONE..........................302 834-5400
Ralph Kunz, *Pr*
EMP: 16
SALES (corp-wide): 241.62MM **Publicly Held**
Web: www.summit-aviation.com
SIC: 3721 4581 Aircraft; Airports, flying fields, and services
HQ: Summit Aviation, Inc.
4200 Summit Bridge Rd
Middletown DE 19709
302 834-5400

(G-7380)
SUPERSKINSYSTEMS INC
3329 N Rockingham Rd (27407-7270)
PHONE..........................336 601-6005
Stuart Smith, *Prin*
EMP: 7 EST: 2010
SALES (est): 149.91K **Privately Held**
SIC: 2821 Plastics materials and resins

(G-7381)
SURTECO USA INC
Also Called: Surteco SE
7104 Cessna Dr (27409-9793)
PHONE..........................336 668-9555
Friedhelm Pafgen, *Ch*
Tim Valters, *
Kenneth Seeto, *
▲ EMP: 50 EST: 2008
SQ FT: 65,000
SALES (est): 16.14MM
SALES (corp-wide): 246.55MM **Privately Held**
Web: www.surteco.com
SIC: 3089 Bands, plastics
HQ: Surteco Group Se
Johan-Viktor-Bausch-Str. 2
Buttenwiesen BY 86647
827499880

(G-7382)
SWK TECHNOLOGIES INC
2309 W Cone Blvd Ste 220 (27408-4047)
PHONE..........................336 230-0200
Christopher Oates, *Brnch Mgr*
EMP: 10
SALES (corp-wide): 44.99MM **Publicly Held**
Web: www.swktech.com
SIC: 7372 Business oriented computer software
HQ: Swk Technologies, Inc.
120 Eagle Rock Ave # 330
East Hanover NJ 07936

(G-7383)
SYD INC
Also Called: American Sign
5223c W Market St Ste C (27409-2629)
PHONE..........................336 294-8807
EMP: 7 EST: 1990
SQ FT: 1,300
SALES (est): 442.89K **Privately Held**
Web: www.theamericansignshop.com
SIC: 3993 Signs and advertising specialties

(G-7384)
SYRUP AND MORE LLC
3702 Kirby Dr (27403-1024)
PHONE..........................781 548-1346
Jennifer Zullo, *Prin*
EMP: 5 EST: 2017
SALES (est): 53.76K **Privately Held**
SIC: 2099 Maple syrup

(G-7385)
SYSTEL BUSINESS EQP CO INC
Also Called: Systel Office Automation
3517 W Wendover Ave (27407-1505)
PHONE..........................336 808-8000
Jeff Dalto, *Mgr*
EMP: 42
SALES (corp-wide): 50.23MM **Privately Held**
Web: www.systeloa.com
SIC: 5044 2752 Copying equipment; Publication printing, lithographic
PA: Systel Business Equipment Co., Inc.
2604 Fort Bragg Rd
Fayetteville NC 28303
910 483-7114

(G-7386)
T J S WOODWORKS
707 Shelby Dr (27409-2252)
PHONE..........................336 299-5913
EMP: 4 EST: 2008
SALES (est): 205.86K **Privately Held**
Web: www.tjswoodworks.com
SIC: 2431 Millwork

(G-7387)
TAG STRINGING SERVICE INC
7 Wendy Ct Ste E (27409-2248)
PHONE..........................336 294-9394
William Harding, *Prin*
EMP: 5 EST: 2017
SALES (est): 110.72K **Privately Held**
SIC: 3999 Manufacturing industries, nec

(G-7388)
TALLEY MACHINERY CORPORATION (HQ)
7009 Cessna Dr (27409-9792)
PHONE..........................336 664-0012
Randy Vansparrentak, *VP*
◆ EMP: 5 EST: 1902
SQ FT: 14,500
SALES (est): 4.52MM
SALES (corp-wide): 91.79MM **Privately Held**
Web: www.talleymachinery.com
SIC: 3582 5087 Commercial laundry equipment; Laundry equipment and supplies
PA: Tingue, Brown & Co.
535 N Midland Ave
Saddle Brook NJ 07663
201 796-4490

(G-7389)
TAPESTRIES LTD
Also Called: Debbing Inspirations
6 Westmount Ct (27410-2183)
PHONE..........................336 883-9864
Nancy Herman, *Pr*
Andrew Kane, *Sec*
▲ EMP: 6 EST: 1973
SQ FT: 2,300
SALES (est): 977.28K **Privately Held**
Web: www.heirloomtapestries.com
SIC: 5023 2221 Decorative home furnishings and supplies; Upholstery, tapestry, and wall covering fabrics

(G-7390)
TAR HEEL CREDIT COUNCILING
2223 N Church St (27405-4307)
PHONE..........................336 254-0348
Latonya Swift, *Pt*
EMP: 6 EST: 2011
SALES (est): 509.94K **Privately Held**
SIC: 2865 Tar

(G-7391)
TARHEEL WAVES LLC
3912 Battleground Ave Ste 112
(27410-8575)
PHONE..........................855 897-2327
Sandy Cox Strayer, *Owner*
EMP: 5 EST: 2017
SALES (est): 243.29K **Privately Held**
Web: www.tarheelwaves.com
SIC: 3823 Process control instruments

(G-7392)
TBC RETAIL GROUP INC
Also Called: Ntb
2514 Battleground Ave Ste B (27408-1938)
PHONE..........................336 540-8066
William Miller, *Brnch Mgr*
EMP: 8
SQ FT: 12,099
SALES (corp-wide): 1.8B **Privately Held**
Web: jobs.tbccorp.com
SIC: 7534 7539 Tire repair shop; Brake services
HQ: Tbc Retail Group, Inc.
4280 Prof Ctr Dr Ste 400
Palm Beach Gardens FL 33410
561 383-3000

(G-7393)
TE CONNECTIVITY CORPORATION
Also Called: Tyco Electronics
8000 Piedmont Triad Pkwy (27409-9407)
PHONE..........................336 664-7000
Randy Krull, *Brnch Mgr*
EMP: 48
Web: www.te.com
SIC: 3678 Electronic connectors
HQ: Te Connectivity Corporation
1050 Westlakes Dr
Berwyn PA 19312
610 893-9800

(G-7394)
TE CONNECTIVITY CORPORATION
719 Pegg Rd Bldg 253 (27409-9672)
PHONE..........................336 665-4400
John Cramfort, *Brnch Mgr*
EMP: 147
Web: www.te.com
SIC: 3678 3471 Electronic connectors; Plating and polishing
HQ: Te Connectivity Corporation
1050 Westlakes Dr
Berwyn PA 19312
610 893-9800

(G-7395)
TENCARVA MACHINERY COMPANY LLC
Essco
1800 Sullivan St (27405-7216)
PHONE..........................336 665-1435
EMP: 18
SALES (corp-wide): 235.69MM **Privately Held**
Web: www.tencarva.com
SIC: 5063 3613 7694 Motors, electric; Control panels, electric; Electric motor repair
HQ: Tencarva Machinery Company, Llc
1115 Pleasant Ridge Rd
Greensboro NC 27409
336 665-1435

(G-7396)
TEXINNOVATE INC
7109 Cessna Dr (27409-9793)
PHONE..........................336 279-7800
Jeffrey W Bruner, *Pr*
Robert Benko, *
Elaine Miller, *
EMP: 39 EST: 2017
SALES (est): 2.73MM **Privately Held**
Web: www.hempblack.com
SIC: 2221 Broadwoven fabric mills, manmade

(G-7397)
TEXTILE INTL ENTPS LLC
4008 Hazel Ln (27408-3190)
PHONE..........................336 545-0146
EMP: 4 EST: 2018
SALES (est): 46.58K **Privately Held**
SIC: 2299 Textile goods, nec

(G-7398)
TEXTRON AVIATION INC
Also Called: Cessna Grnsboro Cttion Svc Ctr
615 Service Center Rd (27410-6250)
PHONE..........................336 605-7000
Jack Blondeau, *Genl Mgr*
EMP: 145
SALES (corp-wide): 12.87B **Publicly Held**
Web: www.txtav.com
SIC: 3721 4581 Airplanes, fixed or rotary wing; Aircraft servicing and repairing
HQ: Textron Aviation Inc.
1 Cessna Blvd
Wichita KS 67215
316 517-6000

(G-7399)
THEM INTERNATIONAL INC
1005 N Eugene St (27401-1612)
PHONE..........................336 855-7880
Mike Stokes, *Pr*
Robert Darby, *VP*
▼ EMP: 6 EST: 1985
SALES (est): 520.96K **Privately Held**
Web: www.them-int.com
SIC: 3089 Plastics containers, except foam

(G-7400)
THEODORE ALEXANDER
3407 W Gate City Blvd Ste B (27407-4779)
PHONE..........................336 689-4178
EMP: 5
SALES (est): 79.3K **Privately Held**
SIC: 2512 Upholstered household furniture

▲ = Import ▼ = Export
◆ = Import/Export

GEOGRAPHIC SECTION
Greensboro - Guilford County (G-7425)

(G-7401)
THOMCO INC
2005 Boulevard St Ste F (27407-4557)
P.O. Box 130 (27868-0130)
PHONE...................336 292-3300
Stephen R Thompson, *Pr*
Jim Gibbons, *VP*
EMP: 5 **EST:** 1980
SQ FT: 2,200
SALES (est): 890.02K **Privately Held**
Web: www.thomcoincorporated.com
SIC: 3577 2759 5113 2657 Bar code (magnetic ink) printers; Labels and seals: printing, nsk; Containers, paper and disposable plastic; Folding paperboard boxes

(G-7402)
THOMPSON TRADERS INC
2024 E Market St (27401-3345)
P.O. Box 7404 (27417-0404)
PHONE...................336 272-3003
Cliff Thompson, *Pr*
Alexandria Thompson, *VP*
◆ **EMP:** 15 **EST:** 1995
SQ FT: 28,000
SALES (est): 3.62MM **Privately Held**
Web: www.thompsontraders.com
SIC: 3431 Sinks: enameled iron, cast iron, or pressed metal

(G-7403)
THUNDRBIRD MLDING GRNSBORO LLC ✪
4833 W Gate City Blvd (27407-5305)
PHONE...................336 668-3636
Kirk Sparks, *Pr*
Mackenzie Bone Ctrl, *Prin*
EMP: 64 **EST:** 2022
SALES (est): 10.32MM
SALES (corp-wide): 58.52MM **Privately Held**
Web: www.brightplastics.com
SIC: 3089 Injection molding of plastics
PA: Thunderbird Llc
    900 Commerce Dr Ste 105
    Oak Brook IL 60523
    847 718-9300

(G-7404)
TK ELEVATOR CORPORATION
22 Oak Branch Dr Ste C (27407-2448)
PHONE...................336 272-4563
Brian James, *Brnch Mgr*
EMP: 108
SALES (corp-wide): 2.67MM **Privately Held**
Web: www.thyssenkruppelevator.com
SIC: 5084 7699 3999 Elevators; Elevators: inspection, service, and repair; Wheelchair lifts
HQ: Tk Elevator Corporation
    788 Cir 75 Pkwy Se # 500
    Atlanta GA 30339
    678 319-3240

(G-7405)
TMCM SERVICES LLC
3 Long Cove Ct (27407-5843)
PHONE...................336 609-4378
EMP: 4 **EST:** 2020
SALES (est): 20K **Privately Held**
SIC: 3999 Hair and hair-based products

(G-7406)
TRANE US INC
Also Called: Trane
3101 S Elm Eugene St # 100 (27406-5201)
PHONE...................336 273-6353
John White, *Mgr*
EMP: 8
Web: www.trane.com
SIC: 3585 Refrigeration and heating equipment
HQ: Trane U.S. Inc.
    800 Beaty St Ste E
    Davidson NC 28036
    704 655-4000

(G-7407)
TRANE US INC
Also Called: Trane
1915 N Church St (27405-5631)
P.O. Box 13587 (27415-3587)
PHONE...................336 378-0670
Don Brady, *Brnch Mgr*
EMP: 10
Web: www.trane.com
SIC: 3585 Refrigeration and heating equipment
HQ: Trane U.S. Inc.
    800 Beaty St Ste E
    Davidson NC 28036
    704 655-4000

(G-7408)
TRANE US INC
Also Called: Trane
8408 Triad Dr (27409-9018)
PHONE...................336 387-1735
Baron Qualls, *Brnch Mgr*
EMP: 8
Web: www.trane.com
SIC: 3585 Heating equipment, complete
HQ: Trane U.S. Inc.
    800 Beaty St Ste E
    Davidson NC 28036
    704 655-4000

(G-7409)
TREEFORMS INC
Also Called: Treeforms Lockers
4242 Regency Dr (27410-8100)
PHONE...................336 292-8998
William B Richardson, *Pr*
Carol Bauer, *
Ellen Richardson, *
▼ **EMP:** 35 **EST:** 1973
SQ FT: 70,000
SALES (est): 3.31MM **Privately Held**
Web: www.treeforms.com
SIC: 2541 2511 2499 2542 Lockers, except refrigerated: wood; Wood household furniture; Decorative wood and woodwork; Partitions and fixtures, except wood

(G-7410)
TRI-CITY MECHANICAL CONTRS INC
706 Utility St (27405-7224)
P.O. Box 21546 (27420-1546)
PHONE...................336 272-9495
Richard G Nester, *Pr*
Claude E Holder, *
Dick Nester, *
Gene Holder, *
Claude Smith, *
EMP: 85 **EST:** 1983
SQ FT: 10,000
SALES (est): 22.34MM **Privately Held**
Web: www.tricitymech.com
SIC: 1711 3441 3663 5013 Mechanical contractor; Fabricated structural metal; Current-carrying wiring services; Exhaust systems (mufflers, tail pipes, etc.)

(G-7411)
TRIAC CORPORATION
611 Norwalk St (27407-1409)
PHONE...................336 297-1130
EMP: 10 **EST:** 1995
SQ FT: 3,500
SALES (est): 2.28MM **Privately Held**
Web: www.triaccorporation.com
SIC: 3625 Relays and industrial controls
PA: Portwest Corporation
    30 Larsen Way
    North Attleboro MA 02763
    508 809-5112

(G-7412)
TRIAD ANODIZING & PLATING INC
3502 Spring Garden St (27407-1830)
P.O. Box 154 (27235-0154)
PHONE...................336 292-7028
Patricia T Proco, *Pr*
Steve M Proco, *VP*
EMP: 5 **EST:** 1972
SQ FT: 1,500
SALES (est): 262.9K **Privately Held**
SIC: 3471 Electroplating of metals or formed products

(G-7413)
TRIAD BUSINESS CARD ASSOC
3201 Summit Ave (27405-3741)
PHONE...................336 706-2729
Donald Harnage, *Ofcr*
EMP: 6 **EST:** 2009
SALES (est): 229.69K **Privately Held**
SIC: 2752 Business form and card printing, lithographic

(G-7414)
TRIAD POWER & CONTROLS INC
215 Industrial Ave Ste G (27406-4546)
PHONE...................336 375-9780
Billy Parrish, *Pr*
Shayn Hayes, *Prin*
EMP: 9 **EST:** 2005
SALES (est): 2.92MM **Privately Held**
Web: www.triadpowerandcontrols.com
SIC: 3643 Power line cable

(G-7415)
TRIAD PREFINISH & LBR SLS INC
3514 Associate Dr (27405-3878)
P.O. Box 13496 (27415-3496)
PHONE...................336 375-4849
Ronald Cottelli, *Pr*
Donna Cottelli, *Sec*
EMP: 6 **EST:** 1989
SQ FT: 10,000
SALES (est): 1.06MM **Privately Held**
Web: www.triadprefinish.com
SIC: 5211 5031 2431 Millwork and lumber; Lumber: rough, dressed, and finished; Exterior and ornamental woodwork and trim

(G-7416)
TRIAD PRINTING NC INC
Also Called: Triad Printing NC
1306 E Wendover Ave (27405-6717)
PHONE...................336 422-8752
Alan E Martinez, *Admn*
EMP: 6 **EST:** 2015
SALES (est): 207.85K **Privately Held**
Web: www.triadprintingnc.com
SIC: 2759 Commercial printing, nec

(G-7417)
TRIAD SHEET METAL & MECH INC
300 Lowdermilk St (27401-4437)
PHONE...................336 379-9891
Harold Amick Junior, *Pr*
Dwayne Bingman, *VP*
EMP: 10 **EST:** 1990
SQ FT: 2,200
SALES (est): 2.57MM **Privately Held**
Web: www.triadsheetmetalhvac.com
SIC: 3444 5051 1711 Sheet metalwork; Copper products; Mechanical contractor

(G-7418)
TRIAD STAINLESS INC
4927 W Market St (27407-1879)
PHONE...................336 315-5515
R N Adams, *Pr*
EMP: 8 **EST:** 2012
SALES (est): 308.85K **Privately Held**
SIC: 3441 Fabricated structural metal

(G-7419)
TRIDENT FIBERS INC
7109 Cessna Dr (27409-9793)
PHONE...................336 605-9002
Jeffrey W Bruner, *Prin*
EMP: 8 **EST:** 2015
SALES (est): 156.13K **Privately Held**
SIC: 2655 Fiber cans, drums, and similar products

(G-7420)
TRU-CAST INC
1208 Rail St (27407-2199)
P.O. Box 18167 (27419-8167)
PHONE...................336 294-2370
S Wayne Gibbs, *Prin*
Paula Tuggle, *
EMP: 35 **EST:** 1978
SQ FT: 24,000
SALES (est): 4.35MM **Privately Held**
Web: www.trucastnc.com
SIC: 3369 3599 Nonferrous foundries, nec; Machine shop, jobbing and repair

(G-7421)
TWISTED PAPER PRODUCTS INC
7100 Cessna Dr (27409-9793)
PHONE...................336 393-0273
Massimo Fantechi, *Pr*
▲ **EMP:** 45 **EST:** 1976
SQ FT: 60,000
SALES (est): 4.59MM **Privately Held**
Web: www.twistedpaperproducts.com
SIC: 2621 Paper mills

(G-7422)
TWO LITTLE BIRDS SCREEN PTG
4810 Carolwood Dr (27407-2803)
PHONE...................336 988-7488
Eva Gantt, *Owner*
EMP: 4 **EST:** 2015
SALES (est): 88.67K **Privately Held**
SIC: 2759 Screen printing

(G-7423)
TYCO ELECTRONICS CORPORATION
8300 Triad Dr (27409-9621)
PHONE...................717 986-5311
EMP: 9 **EST:** 2015
SALES (est): 3.26MM **Privately Held**
SIC: 3357 Nonferrous wiredrawing and insulating

(G-7424)
TYCO ELECTRONICS CORPORATION
Also Called: Te Connectivity
719 Pegg Rd (27409-9672)
PHONE...................336 665-4562
EMP: 38 **EST:** 2016
SALES (est): 4.47MM **Privately Held**
SIC: 3678 Electronic connectors

(G-7425)
UKG KRONOS SYSTEMS LLC
Also Called: Kronos Carolinas
101 Centreport Dr Ste 340 (27409-9446)
PHONE...................800 225-1561
Jim Beacham, *Mgr*

Greensboro - Guilford County (G-7426) — GEOGRAPHIC SECTION

EMP: 8
SALES (corp-wide): 1.85B **Privately Held**
Web: www.ukg.com
SIC: 7372 Business oriented computer software
HQ: Ukg Kronos Systems, Llc
900 Chelmsford St
Lowell MA 01851
978 250-9800

(G-7426)
ULTIMIX RECORDS
Also Called: Carolina Custom Pressing
3404 W Wendover Ave Ste E (27407-1524)
PHONE 336 288-7566
John Deets, *Pr*
EMP: 5 **EST:** 1986
SQ FT: 17,000
SALES (est): 369.95K **Privately Held**
Web: www.ultimix.com
SIC: 5735 3652 Records, audio discs, and tapes; Phonograph record blanks

(G-7427)
UNIFI INC (PA)
Also Called: Unifi
7201 W Friendly Ave (27410-6237)
P.O. Box 19109 (27419-9109)
PHONE 336 294-4410
Edmund M Ingle, *CEO*
Albert P Carey, *
Hongjun Ning, *Ex VP*
Gregory K Sigmon, *Corporate Secretary*
Aj Eaker, *Ex VP*
◆ **EMP:** 100 **EST:** 1969
SQ FT: 121,000
SALES (est): 623.53MM
SALES (corp-wide): 623.53MM **Publicly Held**
Web: www.unifi.com
SIC: 2281 2282 2221 Nylon yarn, spinning of staple; Polyester filament yarn: throwing, twisting, winding, etc.; Spandex broadwoven fabrics

(G-7428)
UNIFI MANUFACTURING INC (HQ)
7201 W Friendly Ave (27410-6237)
P.O. Box 19109 (27419-9109)
PHONE 336 294-4410
William L Jasper, *CEO*
Brian D Moore, *Pr*
Sean D Goodman, *CFO*
Thomas H Caudle Junior, *VP*
W Randy Eaddy, *Sec*
◆ **EMP:** 119 **EST:** 1996
SALES (est): 373.49MM
SALES (corp-wide): 623.53MM **Publicly Held**
Web: www.unifi.com
SIC: 2281 Nylon yarn, spinning of staple
PA: Unifi, Inc.
7201 W Friendly Ave
Greensboro NC 27410
336 294-4410

(G-7429)
UNIQUE COLLATING & BINDERY SVC
Also Called: Carson Dellosa Publishing
237 Burgess Rd Ste A (27409-9787)
P.O. Box 35665 (27425-5665)
PHONE 336 664-0960
Ronnie Kennedy, *Pr*
Ronnie Kennedy, *Pr*
▲ **EMP:** 20 **EST:** 1987
SALES (est): 2.39MM
SALES (corp-wide): 2.39MM **Privately Held**
Web: www.carsondellosa.com
SIC: 2789 Binding only: books, pamphlets, magazines, etc.

PA: Cookie Jar Education Inc.
7027 Albert Pick Rd Fl 3
Greensboro NC 27409
336 362-0084

(G-7430)
UNIQUE OFFICE SOLUTIONS INC
408 Gallimore Dairy Rd Ste E (27409-9541)
PHONE 336 854-0900
Amy Lane, *Pr*
William Lane, *VP*
EMP: 16 **EST:** 1996
SQ FT: 12,000
SALES (est): 2.5MM **Privately Held**
Web: www.uosinc.com
SIC: 1799 5712 2522 5021 Office furniture installation; Office furniture; Office furniture, except wood; Office furniture, nec

(G-7431)
UNITED MTAL FNSHG INC GRNSBORO
Also Called: United Metal Finishing
133 Blue Bell Rd (27406-5301)
P.O. Box 16623 (27416-0623)
PHONE 336 272-8107
Claude Church, *Pr*
EMP: 26 **EST:** 1985
SQ FT: 1,000
SALES (est): 2.19MM **Privately Held**
Web: www.unitedmetalfinishing.us
SIC: 3471 Electroplating of metals or formed products

(G-7432)
UNITEX CHEMICAL CORP
520 Broome Rd (27406-3799)
P.O. Box 16344 (27416-0344)
PHONE 336 378-0965
◆ **EMP:** 35
Web: www.unitexchemical.com
SIC: 2899 Chemical preparations, nec

(G-7433)
US CUSTOM SOCKS CO LLC
2522 Brandt Forest Ct (27455-1983)
PHONE 336 549-1088
Dennis J Finnegan, *Prin*
EMP: 5 **EST:** 2012
SALES (est): 84.86K **Privately Held**
Web: www.uscustomsocks.com
SIC: 2252 Socks

(G-7434)
US LABEL CORPORATION
2118 Enterprise Rd (27408-7004)
PHONE 336 332-7000
John M Andrew, *Pr*
H Allen Andrew, *Ch Bd*
Clyde M Andrew, *
James N Grant, *
Edward Tidaback, *
EMP: 21 **EST:** 1960
SQ FT: 92,000
SALES (est): 400.2K **Privately Held**
SIC: 2241 2269 Fabric tapes; Labels, cotton: printed

(G-7435)
VALLEY PROTEINS (DE) INC
Also Called: Carolina By-Products
2410 Randolph Ave (27406-2910)
PHONE 336 333-3030
David Rosenstein, *Brnch Mgr*
EMP: 217
SALES (corp-wide): 6.53B **Publicly Held**
Web: www.darpro-solutions.com
SIC: 2048 7699 2077 Prepared feeds, nec; Waste cleaning services; Animal and marine fats and oils
HQ: Valley Proteins (De), Llc

151 Randall Stuewe Dr
Winchester VA 22603
540 877-2533

(G-7436)
VAN BLAKE DIXON
378 Air Harbor Rd (27455-9280)
PHONE 336 282-1861
Van Blake Dixon, *Owner*
EMP: 10 **EST:** 2011
SALES (est): 348.35K **Privately Held**
SIC: 3315 Welded steel wire fabric

(G-7437)
VERITIV OPERATING COMPANY
International Paper
3 Centerview Dr Ste 100 (27407-3727)
PHONE 336 834-3488
Harrison Stewart, *Mgr*
EMP: 46
SALES (corp-wide): 13.94B **Privately Held**
Web: www.veritiv.com
SIC: 2679 5113 Paper products, converted, nec; Industrial and personal service paper
HQ: Veritiv Operating Company
1000 Abernathy Rd Bldg 4
Atlanta GA 30328
770 391-8200

(G-7438)
VF CORPORATION
105 Corporate Center Blvd (27408-3194)
PHONE 336 424-6000
Steve Rendle, *Pr*
Scott A Roe, *Ex VP*
EMP: 9 **EST:** 1998
SALES (est): 176.53K **Privately Held**
Web: www.vfc.com
SIC: 5139 2211 Footwear; Apparel and outerwear fabrics, cotton

(G-7439)
VF CORPORATION
105 Corp Ctr Blvd (27408-3194)
PHONE 336 424-6000
EMP: 10
SALES (est): 73.4K **Privately Held**
Web: www.vfc.com
SIC: 2211 5139 Apparel and outerwear fabrics, cotton; Footwear

(G-7440)
VF CORPORATION
Also Called: Wrangler V K Jeans Wear
400 N Elm St (27401-2143)
PHONE 336 332-3400
EMP: 5
SALES (corp-wide): 11.61B **Publicly Held**
Web: www.vfc.com
SIC: 2325 Jeans: men's, youths', and boys'
PA: V.F. Corporation
1551 Wewatta St
Denver CO 80202
720 778-4000

(G-7441)
VF JEANSWEAR INC (PA)
105 Corporate Center Blvd (27408-3194)
P.O. Box 21647 (27420-1647)
PHONE 336 332-3400
EMP: 17 **EST:** 1986
SALES (est): 27.16MM
SALES (corp-wide): 27.16MM **Privately Held**
Web: www.vfc.com
SIC: 2323 Men's and boys' neckties and bow ties

(G-7442)
VF RECEIVABLES LP
105 Corporate Center Blvd (27408-3194)
PHONE 336 424-6000
EMP: 11 **EST:** 2014
SALES (est): 2.36MM
SALES (corp-wide): 11.61B **Publicly Held**
Web: www.vfc.com
SIC: 2325 Jeans: men's, youths', and boys'
PA: V.F. Corporation
1551 Wewatta St
Denver CO 80202
720 778-4000

(G-7443)
VIC INC
Also Called: Sign-A-Rama
3410 W Wendover Ave Ste C (27407-1585)
PHONE 336 545-1124
Vince V Cvijanovic, *Pr*
Mathew S Cvijanovic, *
Ivy J Cvijanovic, *
EMP: 22 **EST:** 2004
SQ FT: 23,500
SALES (est): 843.22K **Privately Held**
Web: www.signarama.com
SIC: 3993 Signs and advertising specialties

(G-7444)
VIVET INC
1150 Pleasant Ridge Rd Ste A (27409-9846)
P.O. Box 8905 (91701-0905)
PHONE 909 390-1039
Mark L Feng, *CEO*
Jing Chen, *CFO*
Howard Pan, *Sec*
EMP: 6 **EST:** 2017
SALES (est): 700.17K **Privately Held**
SIC: 2426 1771 Flooring, hardwood; Flooring contractor

(G-7445)
VNA HOLDING INC (HQ)
7825 National Service Rd (27409-9667)
PHONE 336 393-4890
Ava Persson, *CEO*
Eva Pesson, *
Donald W Shumaker, *
Therence Pickett, *
◆ **EMP:** 3700 **EST:** 1996
SALES (est): 3.74B
SALES (corp-wide): 45.13B **Privately Held**
SIC: 6159 3713 5012 5013 Equipment and vehicle finance leasing companies; Specialty motor vehicle bodies; Commercial vehicles; Motor vehicle supplies and new parts
PA: Ab Volvo
Amazonvagen 8
GOteborg 418 7
31660000

(G-7446)
VOLVO GROUP NORTH AMERICA LLC (DH)
Also Called: Volvo Trucks North America
7900 National Service Rd (27409-9416)
P.O. Box 26115 (27402-6115)
PHONE 336 393-2000
◆ **EMP:** 600 **EST:** 1998
SQ FT: 60,000
SALES (est): 1.77B
SALES (corp-wide): 45.13B **Privately Held**
Web: www.volvogroup.com
SIC: 3713 5012 5013 Specialty motor vehicle bodies; Commercial vehicles; Motor vehicle supplies and new parts
HQ: Vna Holding Inc.
7825 National Service Rd
Greensboro NC 27409
336 393-4890

Greensboro - Guilford County (G-7471)

(G-7447)
VOLVO GROUP NORTH AMERICA LLC
8203 Piedmont Triad Pkwy (27409-9454)
PHONE.................................336 393-2000
EMP: 4701
SALES (corp-wide): 45.13B Privately Held
Web: www.volvogroup.com
SIC: 3713 5012 5013 Specialty motor vehicle bodies; Commercial vehicles; Motor vehicle supplies and new parts
HQ: Volvo Group North America, Llc
  7900 National Service Rd
  Greensboro NC 27409

(G-7448)
VOLVO GROUP NORTH AMERICA LLC
7821 National Service Rd 1 (27409-9667)
PHONE.................................731 968-0151
EMP: 5033
SALES (corp-wide): 45.13B Privately Held
Web: www.volvogroup.com
SIC: 3429 Motor vehicle hardware
HQ: Volvo Group North America, Llc
  7900 National Service Rd
  Greensboro NC 27409

(G-7449)
VOLVO LOGISTICS NORTH AMERICA INC
7900 National Service Rd (27409-9416)
PHONE.................................336 393-4746
◆ EMP: 163
Web: www.volvotrucks.us
SIC: 3713 8741 Truck and bus bodies; Management services

(G-7450)
VOLVO TRUCKS NORTH AMERICA INC (DH)
7900 National Service Rd (27409-9416)
P.O. Box 26115 (27402-6115)
PHONE.................................336 393-2000
Peter Karlsten Pickett, Pr
Gary Mccartney, Sr VP
◆ EMP: 600 EST: 1986
SQ FT: 60,000
SALES (est): 1.16B
SALES (corp-wide): 45.13B Privately Held
Web: www.volvotrucks.us
SIC: 5511 5012 5013 3713 Automobiles, new and used; Commercial vehicles; Motor vehicle supplies and new parts; Truck bodies and parts
HQ: Vna Holding Inc.
  7825 National Service Rd
  Greensboro NC 27409
  336 393-4890

(G-7451)
VPM LIQUIDATING INC
2110 W Gate City Blvd (27403-2642)
PHONE.................................336 292-1781
◆ EMP: 10
SIC: 2869 2879 Plasticizers, organic: cyclic and acyclic; Agricultural chemicals, nec

(G-7452)
W W INDUSTRIES
2907 Saint Regis Rd (27408-4315)
PHONE.................................336 312-1806
William Weatherly, Prin
EMP: 5 EST: 2010
SALES (est): 70.72K Privately Held
SIC: 3999 Manufacturing industries, nec

(G-7453)
W&W-AFCO STEEL LLC
101 Centreport Dr Ste 400 (27409-9422)
PHONE.................................336 275-9711
Jenny Carter, Brnch Mgr
EMP: 50
SALES (corp-wide): 364.48B Publicly Held
Web: www.wwafcosteel.com
SIC: 3441 Fabricated structural metal
HQ: W&W-Afco Steel Llc
  1730 W Reno Ave
  Oklahoma City OK 73106
  405 235-3621

(G-7454)
WANT OF ADS OF GREENSBORO
Also Called: Thrifty Nickel of Greensboro
7715 Kenmont Rd (27409-9012)
P.O. Box 8529 (27419-0529)
PHONE.................................336 297-4300
EMP: 10 EST: 1998
SALES (est): 461.03K Privately Held
Web: www.greensboroamericanclassifieds.com
SIC: 2711 Newspapers, publishing and printing

(G-7455)
WELCHS RECYCLING INC
5103 Blakeshire Rd (27406-9714)
PHONE.................................336 638-9601
Sherry Welch, Owner
EMP: 5 EST: 2013
SALES (est): 96.73K Privately Held
SIC: 2033 Canned fruits and specialties

(G-7456)
WELSH CSTM SLTTING RWNDING LLC
200 Citation Ct (27409-9026)
PHONE.................................336 665-6481
▲ EMP: 31 EST: 2011
SQ FT: 105,000
SALES (est): 6.82MM Privately Held
Web: www.welshslitting.com
SIC: 2679 Paper products, converted, nec

(G-7457)
WESTERN ROTO ENGRAVERS INCORPORATED (PA)
Also Called: Wre/Colortech
533 Banner Ave (27401-4397)
PHONE.................................336 275-9821
EMP: 36 EST: 1951
SALES (est): 12.93MM
SALES (corp-wide): 12.93MM Privately Held
Web: www.wrecolor.com
SIC: 2759 Engraving, nec

(G-7458)
WET DOG GLASS LLC
938 Reynolds Pl (27403-2212)
PHONE.................................910 428-4111
EMP: 7 EST: 2008
SALES (est): 87.89K Privately Held
SIC: 3559 Special industry machinery, nec

(G-7459)
WHEEL PROS LLC
2606 Phoenix Dr Ste 804 (27406-6357)
PHONE.................................336 851-6705
Corey Kiesel, Mgr
EMP: 4
Web: www.wheelpros.com
SIC: 3312 Wheels
PA: Wheel Pros, Llc
  5347 S Valentia Way # 200
  Greenwood Village CO 80111

(G-7460)
WIKOFF COLOR CORPORATION
7212 Cessna Dr (27409-9685)
PHONE.................................336 668-3423
David Hall, Mgr
EMP: 22
SQ FT: 7,872
SALES (corp-wide): 156.45MM Privately Held
Web: www.wikoff.com
SIC: 2893 Printing ink
PA: Wikoff Color Corporation
  1886 Merritt Rd
  Fort Mill SC 29715
  803 548-2210

(G-7461)
WILBERT FUNERAL SERVICES INC
Also Called: Greensboro Wilbert
108 Buchanan Church Rd (27405-8631)
PHONE.................................800 828-5879
Tom Shank, Mgr
EMP: 30
SALES (corp-wide): 364.48B Publicly Held
Web: www.greensborowilbert.com
SIC: 3272 Burial vaults, concrete or precast terrazzo
HQ: Wilbert Funeral Services, Inc.
  10965 Granada Ln Ste 300
  Overland Park KS 66211
  913 345-2120

(G-7462)
WINDSORS CBNETRY FOR KIT BATHS
1816 Pembroke Rd Ste 2 (27408-7910)
PHONE.................................336 275-0190
Dale Windsor, Prin
EMP: 7 EST: 2011
SALES (est): 98.34K Privately Held
Web: www.windsorscabinetry.com
SIC: 2434 Wood kitchen cabinets

(G-7463)
WITH PURPOSE PRESSURE WSHG LLC
2702 Renee Dr (27407-5946)
PHONE.................................336 965-9473
EMP: 8 EST: 2019
SALES (est): 319.01K Privately Held
Web: www.martinspressurewashing.com
SIC: 1521 1389 1799 Patio and deck construction and repair; Construction, repair, and dismantling services; Cleaning building exteriors, nec

(G-7464)
WLC LLC
5509b W Friendly Ave Ste 201 (27410-4270)
PHONE.................................336 852-6422
EMP: 5 EST: 1997
SALES (est): 395.62K Privately Held
SIC: 2731 Books, publishing only

(G-7465)
WOMACK NEWSPAPER INC
Also Called: Yes Weekly
5500 Adams Farm Ln Ste 204 (27407-7059)
PHONE.................................336 316-1231
Charles Womack, Brnch Mgr
EMP: 4
SALES (corp-wide): 2.2MM Privately Held
Web: www.yesweekly.com
SIC: 2711 Newspapers, publishing and printing
PA: Womack Newspaper, Inc.
  30 N Main St
  Chatham VA 24531
  434 432-1654

(G-7466)
WOOD WORKS
722 Cannon Rd (27410-4315)
PHONE.................................336 580-4134
John Rose, Prin
EMP: 5 EST: 2018
SALES (est): 237.44K Privately Held
SIC: 2431 Millwork

(G-7467)
WORKWEAR OUTFITTERS LLC
Also Called: Vf
No Physical Location (27420)
P.O. Box 21647 (27420-1647)
PHONE.................................877 824-0613
EMP: 88
SALES (corp-wide): 2.07B Privately Held
Web: www.wwof.com
SIC: 2326 Men's and boy's work clothing
HQ: Workwear Outfitters, Llc
  545 Marriott Dr
  Nashville TN 37214
  800 733-5271

(G-7468)
WRANGLER APPAREL CORP
Also Called: Wrangler
400 N Elm St (27401-2143)
PHONE.................................336 332-3400
Scott Baxter, Pr
EMP: 500 EST: 1993
SALES (est): 49.87MM
SALES (corp-wide): 2.61B Publicly Held
Web: www.kontoorbrands.com
SIC: 2325 2321 2329 2339 Men's and boy's trousers and slacks; Sport shirts, men's and boys': from purchased materials; Jackets (suede, leatherette, etc.), sport: men's and boys'; Jeans: women's, misses', and juniors'
PA: Kontoor Brands, Inc.
  400 N Elm St
  Greensboro NC 27401
  336 332-3400

(G-7469)
WRIGHT ROLLER COMPANY
1800 Fairfax Rd Ste K (27407-4124)
P.O. Box 7753 (27417-0753)
PHONE.................................336 852-8393
Toni Wright, Pr
Rodney Dabbs, VP
Carrie Moyel, Off Mgr
EMP: 11 EST: 1988
SQ FT: 14,000
SALES (est): 1.34MM Privately Held
Web: www.wrightroller.com
SIC: 3069 Roll coverings, rubber

(G-7470)
WUKO INC
3505 Associate Dr (27405-3879)
PHONE.................................980 938-0512
Lucia Hakala, Pr
EMP: 5 EST: 2014
SALES (est): 455.46K Privately Held
Web: www.wukoinc.com
SIC: 3542 Machine tools, metal forming type

(G-7471)
WYSONG AND MILES COMPANY
Also Called: Wysong Parts & Service
4820 Us 29 N (27405)
PHONE.................................336 621-3960
Russell F Hall Iii, Pr
Thomas Adkisson, VP Opers
Suzanne Hall, Dir
Patricia Herr, Dir
Franz Herr, Dir

Greensboro - Guilford County (G-7472)

EMP: 20 EST: 1903
SQ FT: 104,000
SALES (est): 4.97MM **Privately Held**
Web: www.wysong.us
SIC: 3542 Machine tools, metal forming type

(G-7472)
YELLOW DOG DESIGN INC
112 Oconnor St (27406-2206)
PHONE.................................336 553-2172
Donald Brian Dempsey, Pr
▲ EMP: 15 EST: 2000
SQ FT: 15,000
SALES (est): 2.05MM **Privately Held**
Web: www.yellowdog-design.com
SIC: 2399 Pet collars, leashes, etc.: non-leather

(G-7473)
YESCO SIGN LIGHTING SERVICE
Also Called: Yesco
5710 W Gate City Blvd Ste K-190 (27407-7061)
PHONE.................................336 285-0795
EMP: 7 EST: 2014
SALES (est): 144.36K **Privately Held**
Web: www.yesco.com
SIC: 3993 Electric signs

(G-7474)
YKK AP AMERICA INC
4524 Green Point Dr Ste 106 (27410-8123)
PHONE.................................336 665-1963
Kim Law, Mgr
EMP: 16
Web: www.ykkap.com
SIC: 3442 Sash, door or window: metal
HQ: Ykk Ap America Inc.
    101 Marietta St Nw # 2700
    Atlanta GA 30303

(G-7475)
ZIEHL-ABEGG INC (DH)
719 N Regional Rd (27409-9016)
P.O. Box 19971 (27419-1971)
PHONE.................................336 834-9339
Jimmy Mitchell, *
▲ EMP: 24 EST: 2003
SQ FT: 240,000
SALES (est): 52.96MM
SALES (corp-wide): 688.71MM **Privately Held**
Web: www.ziehl-abegg.com
SIC: 3694 3443 3564 Engine electrical equipment; Fabricated plate work (boiler shop); Blowers and fans
HQ: Ziehl - Abegg Elektrizitats-Gmbh
    Heinz-Ziehl-Str.
    Kunzelsau BW 74653

(G-7476)
ZOETIS PRODUCTS LLC
620 S Elm St Ste 363 (27406-1398)
PHONE.................................336 333-9356
April Willis, Brnch Mgr
EMP: 9
SALES (corp-wide): 8.08B **Publicly Held**
Web: www.zoetis.com
SIC: 2834 Pharmaceutical preparations
HQ: Zoetis Products Llc
    100 Campus Dr Ste 3
    Florham Park NJ 07932
    973 660-5000

Greenville
Pitt County

(G-7477)
ABBOTT ENTERPRISES
3383 Prescott Ln (27858-8332)
PHONE.................................252 757-1298
Rickey Abbott, Prin
EMP: 8 EST: 2008
SALES (est): 117.25K **Privately Held**
SIC: 2834 Pharmaceutical preparations

(G-7478)
ALL STAR PRINTING
903 Dickinson Ave (27834-3184)
PHONE.................................252 689-6464
EMP: 5 EST: 2015
SALES (est): 148.65K **Privately Held**
SIC: 2752 Commercial printing, lithographic

(G-7479)
ALNAMER INC
Also Called: Dreams Tobacco Mart
501 S Memorial Dr (27834-2853)
PHONE.................................252 215-0323
Barrag Abdo Nasser, Prin
EMP: 6 EST: 2010
SALES (est): 161.81K **Privately Held**
SIC: 2131 Smoking tobacco

(G-7480)
AMERICAN BACKFLOW TECHNOLOGIES
5414 Nc Highway 33 E (27858-8758)
PHONE.................................252 714-8378
Amy Leggett, Prin
EMP: 7 EST: 2000
SALES (est): 99.9K **Privately Held**
Web: www.backflowparts.com
SIC: 3432 Plumbing fixture fittings and trim

(G-7481)
AMERICAN MATERIALS COMPANY LLC
2703 Nc Highway 222 (27834-7483)
PHONE.................................252 752-2124
Harry Shaw, Brnch Mgr
EMP: 6
SALES (corp-wide): 2.62B **Publicly Held**
Web: www.americanmaterialsco.com
SIC: 1442 Construction sand mining
HQ: American Materials Company, Llc
    1410 Commwl Dr Ste 201
    Wilmington NC 28403
    910 799-1411

(G-7482)
ANDREW BATES
3161 Mills Rd (27858-8263)
PHONE.................................252 413-6988
Andrew Bates, Owner
EMP: 4 EST: 2016
SALES (est): 56.14K **Privately Held**
SIC: 2431 Millwork

(G-7483)
ANGSTROM MEDICA INC
Also Called: Pioneer Srgical Orthobiologics
1800 N Greene St Ste A (27834-9013)
PHONE.................................781 933-6121
Paul Mraz, CEO
Edward Ahn, Pr
EMP: 10 EST: 2001
SQ FT: 6,500
SALES (est): 1.72MM
SALES (corp-wide): 81.98MM **Publicly Held**

SIC: 3841 Surgical and medical instruments
HQ: Pioneer Surgical Technology, Inc.
    7 Switchbud Pl Ste 192-18
    The Woodlands TX 77380

(G-7484)
APG/EAST LLC
1150 Sugg Pkwy (27834-9077)
P.O. Box 1967 (27835-1967)
PHONE.................................252 329-9500
EMP: 198 EST: 2016
SALES (est): 16MM
SALES (corp-wide): 333.51MM **Privately Held**
Web: www.reflector.com
SIC: 2711 Newspapers, publishing and printing
PA: Adams Publishing Group, Llc
    4095 Coon Rapids Blvd Nw
    Minneapolis MN 55433
    218 348-3391

(G-7485)
ARCHIE S STEEL SERVICE INC
4575 Us Highway 13 S (27834-0044)
PHONE.................................252 355-5007
Archie Oakley, Pr
Janie Oakley, VP
Archie Oakley Junior, Pr
EMP: 6 EST: 1985
SALES (est): 383.16K **Privately Held**
SIC: 7692 Welding repair

(G-7486)
ASMO GREENVILLE OF NORTH CAROLINA INC
Also Called: Asamo Co
1125 Sugg Pkwy (27834-9009)
PHONE.................................252 754-1000
▲ EMP: 463
SIC: 3594 Fluid power motors

(G-7487)
ASSOCIATED HYGIENIC PDTS LLC (PA)
Also Called: Associated Hygienic Products
1029 Old Creek Rd (27834-8178)
P.O. Box 1749 (30096-0031)
PHONE.................................770 497-9800
▲ EMP: 70 EST: 2000
SALES (est): 98.06MM
SALES (corp-wide): 98.06MM **Privately Held**
Web: www.attindas.com
SIC: 2676 Diapers, paper (disposable): made from purchased paper

(G-7488)
ATTENDS HEALTHCARE PDTS INC
1029 Old Creek Rd (27834-8178)
PHONE.................................252 752-1100
EMP: 7
SALES (corp-wide): 103.92MM **Privately Held**
Web: www.attends.com
SIC: 2676 Sanitary paper products
PA: Attends Healthcare Products Inc.
    8020 Arco Corp Dr Ste 200
    Raleigh NC 27617
    800 428-8363

(G-7489)
ATTINDAS HYGIENE PARTNERS INC
350 Industrial Blvd (27834-9014)
PHONE.................................252 752-1100
EMP: 95
SALES (corp-wide): 18.86MM **Privately Held**
Web: www.attindas.com
SIC: 2621 Paper mills

PA: Attindas Hygiene Partners Inc.
    8020 Arco Corp Dr Ste 200
    Raleigh NC 27617
    919 237-4000

(G-7490)
AVIENT PROTECTIVE MTLS LLC (HQ)
Also Called: DSM Hpf
5750 Martin Luther King Jr Hwy (27834-8624)
PHONE.................................252 707-2547
Scott Mcintyre, Pr
Avery Johnson, *
Robert K James, *
◆ EMP: 53 EST: 2001
SALES (est): 52.41MM **Publicly Held**
SIC: 2821 Plastics materials and resins
PA: Avient Corporation
    33587 Walker Rd
    Avon Lake OH 44012

(G-7491)
BAILEYS SAUCES INC
3765 Mills Rd (27858-8269)
PHONE.................................252 756-7179
Dale Bailey, Pr
Nikki Bailey, VP
EMP: 4 EST: 2002
SALES (est): 259.77K **Privately Held**
SIC: 2033 Barbecue sauce: packaged in cans, jars, etc.

(G-7492)
BANILLA GAMES INC
3506 Greenville Blvd Ne (27834-8980)
PHONE.................................252 329-7977
Garrett Blackwelder, Pr
EMP: 8 EST: 2014
SALES (est): 1.78MM **Privately Held**
Web: www.banillagames.com
SIC: 3944 Board games, children's and adults'

(G-7493)
BARNHILL CONTRACTING COMPANY
Also Called: APAC
562 Barrus Construction Rd (27834-7365)
P.O. Box 1467 (27835-1467)
PHONE.................................252 752-7608
Eddie Briley, Pr
EMP: 26
SALES (corp-wide): 389.14MM **Privately Held**
Web: www.barnhillcontracting.com
SIC: 1611 2951 Highway and street paving contractor; Asphalt paving mixtures and blocks
PA: Barnhill Contracting Company Inc
    800 Tiffany Blvd Ste 200
    Rocky Mount NC 27804
    252 823-1021

(G-7494)
BELVOIR MANUFACTURING CORP (PA)
4081 Nc Highway 33 W (27834-7349)
PHONE.................................252 746-1274
Robert Danzger, Pr
Joshua Danzger, *
Joanne Palmer, *
▲ EMP: 55 EST: 1981
SQ FT: 60,000
SALES (est): 4.69MM
SALES (corp-wide): 4.69MM **Privately Held**
SIC: 2389 2339 2326 Hospital gowns; Women's and misses' outerwear, nec; Men's and boy's work clothing

GEOGRAPHIC SECTION

Greenville - Pitt County (G-7519)

(G-7495)
CARDIAC WLLNESS SPPLEMENTS LLC
2459 Emerald Pl Ste 102 (27834-5739)
PHONE.............................252 757-3939
EMP: 11 EST: 2005
SALES (est): 403.11K Privately Held
SIC: 2834 Vitamin, nutrient, and hematinic preparations for human use

(G-7496)
CARGILL INCORPORATED
Also Called: Cargill
6 Miles East Farmville (27834)
P.O. Box 31a (27835-0031)
PHONE.............................252 752-1879
Michael Foster, *Brnch Mgr*
EMP: 25
SALES (corp-wide): 176.74B Privately Held
Web: www.cargill.com
SIC: 2048 Prepared feeds, nec
PA: Cargill, Incorporated
15407 Mcginty Rd W
Wayzata MN 55391
800 227-4455

(G-7497)
CARLINA SHOTWELL LLC
Also Called: ASAP Marketing
204 E Arlington Blvd Ste C-103 (27858-5022)
PHONE.............................252 417-8688
Carlina Shotwell, *CEO*
Carlina Whiting, *CEO*
EMP: 4 EST: 2016
SALES (est): 240.43K Privately Held
SIC: 2731 Book publishing

(G-7498)
CAROLINA BARGAIN TRADER INC
72 Howell St (27834-5316)
P.O. Box 879 (27817-0879)
PHONE.............................252 756-1500
Pamela Gray, *CEO*
Wayne Hardee, *
Ron Boyd, *
EMP: 8 EST: 1977
SALES (est): 474.15K Privately Held
Web: www.carolinabargaintrader.net
SIC: 2721 Magazines: publishing only, not printed on site

(G-7499)
CATALENT GREENVILLE INC
5440 Martin Luther King Jr Hwy (27834-8618)
PHONE.............................732 537-6200
EMP: 35
Web: www.catalent.com
SIC: 2834 Pharmaceutical preparations
HQ: Catalent Greenville, Inc.
1240 Sugg Pkwy
Greenville NC 27834
252 752-3800

(G-7500)
CATALENT GREENVILLE INC (DH) ✪
1240 Sugg Pkwy (27834-9006)
PHONE.............................252 752-3800
Alessandro Masseli, *Pr*
EMP: 65 EST: 2022
SALES (est): 25.67MM Publicly Held
Web: www.catalent.com
SIC: 2834 Pharmaceutical preparations
HQ: Catalent Pharma Solutions, Inc.
14 Schoolhouse Rd
Somerset NJ 08873

(G-7501)
CHESTER LEWIS NEWSOME
Also Called: Newsome Home Improvement
200 Lancaster Dr (27834-6414)
PHONE.............................919 605-4887
Chester L Newsome, *Owner*
EMP: 4
SALES (est): 80.39K Privately Held
SIC: 3423 Carpet layers' hand tools

(G-7502)
CNA TECHNOLOGY LLC
220 Indl Blvd (27834)
PHONE.............................954 312-1200
EMP: 6 EST: 2009
SALES (est): 301.9K Privately Held
Web: www.cnatechnology.com
SIC: 4813 Telephone cable service, land or submarine; Aircraft wire and cable, nonferrous

(G-7503)
COASTAL AGROBUSINESS INC (PA)
112 Staton Rd (27834-6549)
P.O. Box 856 (27835-0856)
PHONE.............................252 238-7391
James C Whitehurst Iii, *Pr*
James C Whitehurst Junior, *Ch Bd*
Mike Seymour, *VP*
Ann H Whitehurst, *Sec*
◆ EMP: 55 EST: 1953
SQ FT: 50,000
SALES (est): 61.99MM
SALES (corp-wide): 61.99MM Privately Held
Web: www.coastalagro.com
SIC: 5191 3523 Chemicals, agricultural; Sprayers and spraying machines, agricultural

(G-7504)
COLLINS BANKS INVESTMENTS INC
Also Called: Super Shred
311 Staton Rd (27834-9038)
P.O. Box 2725 (27836-0725)
PHONE.............................252 439-1200
Ruth Collins, *Pr*
EMP: 9 EST: 1999
SALES (est): 977.57K Privately Held
SIC: 2611 Pulp manufactured from waste or recycled paper

(G-7505)
CONWAY DEVELOPMENT INC (PA)
Also Called: Greenville Marble & Gran Works
2218 Dickinson Ave (27834-5104)
P.O. Box 103 (27835-0103)
PHONE.............................252 756-2168
John A Conway Iii, *Pr*
Pat Conway, *VP*
EMP: 15 EST: 1933
SALES (est): 2.67MM
SALES (corp-wide): 2.67MM Privately Held
SIC: 5099 5999 3281 Monuments and grave markers; Monuments and tombstones; Cut stone and stone products

(G-7506)
COOKE COMMUNICATIONS NC LLC
1150 Sugg Pkwy (27834-9077)
P.O. Box 1967 (27835-1967)
PHONE.............................252 329-9500
EMP: 14 EST: 2012
SALES (est): 235.48K Privately Held
Web: www.reflector.com
SIC: 2711 Commercial printing and newspaper publishing combined

(G-7507)
COPYMATIC UNITED CEREBRAL
Also Called: Copymatic of Greenville
200 W 4th St (27858-1816)
PHONE.............................252 695-6155
Mark Carter, *Ex Dir*
EMP: 10 EST: 2004
SALES (est): 700.03K Privately Held
Web: www.copymatic.ai
SIC: 2752 Cards, lithographed

(G-7508)
CORE GRIP LLC
2120 E Fire Tower Rd (27858-8013)
PHONE.............................252 341-7783
EMP: 5 EST: 2019
SALES (est): 96.26K Privately Held
Web: www.coregrip.com
SIC: 3999 Manufacturing industries, nec

(G-7509)
COTTON BELT INC
Also Called: Sleepworthy
310 Staton Rd (27834-9037)
P.O. Box 108 (27864-0108)
PHONE.............................252 689-6847
EMP: 100 EST: 1932
SALES (est): 13.39MM Privately Held
Web: www.edgecombe.com
SIC: 2515 2512 Box springs, assembled; Living room furniture: upholstered on wood frames

(G-7510)
COX NRTH CRLINA PBLCATIONS INC (DH)
Also Called: Daily Reflector , The
1150 Sugg Pkwy (27834-9077)
P.O. Box 1967 (27835-1967)
PHONE.............................252 329-9643
Jay Smith, *Pr*
Brian G Cooper, *
Andrew Merdek, *
EMP: 200 EST: 1882
SQ FT: 90,000
SALES (est): 21.5MM
SALES (corp-wide): 2.85B Privately Held
Web: www.reflector.com
SIC: 2711 Newspapers, publishing and printing
HQ: Cox Newspapers, Inc.
6205 Pchtree Dnwody Rd N
Atlanta GA 30328

(G-7511)
CUSTOM WOOD CREATIONS
901 Trolling Wood Ct (27858-8318)
PHONE.............................252 341-7923
Todd Olson, *Prin*
EMP: 4 EST: 2015
SALES (est): 75.09K Privately Held
SIC: 2431 Millwork

(G-7512)
CYPRESS MOUNTAIN COMPANY (HQ)
107 Staton Ct (27834-9016)
PHONE.............................252 758-2179
M Michael Richardson, *Pr*
Michael Richardson, *Pr*
Harry H Esbenshade Iii, *Sec*
Michael D Cain, *Treas*
Barry T Sugg, *VP*
EMP: 5 EST: 2000
SALES (est): 24.89MM
SALES (corp-wide): 109.23MM Privately Held
SIC: 3444 1761 Sheet metalwork; Roofing, siding, and sheetmetal work
PA: The Mountain Company

166 60th St
Parkersburg WV 26105
304 295-0036

(G-7513)
DENSO MANUFACTURING NC INC
Also Called: Dmnc Greenville Plant
1125 Sugg Pkwy (27834-9078)
PHONE.............................252 754-1000
EMP: 463
Web: www.denso.com
SIC: 3594 Fluid power motors
HQ: Denso Manufacturing North Carolina, Inc.
470 Crawford Rd
Statesville NC 28625

(G-7514)
DEXTERITY LLC
104 Azalea Dr (27858-5401)
PHONE.............................919 524-7732
EMP: 10 EST: 2012
SQ FT: 2,000
SALES (est): 889.67K Privately Held
Web: www.4dpick.co
SIC: 3089 3663 Cases, plastics; Mobile communication equipment

(G-7515)
DOMTAR PAPER COMPANY LLC
1029 Old Creek Rd (27834-8178)
PHONE.............................252 752-1100
EMP: 69
Web: www.domtar.com
SIC: 5099 2621 Pulpwood; Paper mills
HQ: Domtar Paper Company, Llc
234 Kingsley Park Dr
Fort Mill SC 29715

(G-7516)
DPI NEWCO LLC
Also Called: Newco
5900 Martin Luther King Jr Hwy (27834-8628)
PHONE.............................252 758-3436
Jim Mullen, *CEO*
EMP: 1200 EST: 2014
SALES (est): 189.13MM
SALES (corp-wide): 44.91B Publicly Held
SIC: 2834 Pharmaceutical preparations
HQ: Patheon Holdings I B.V.
Takkebijsters 1
Breda NB

(G-7517)
DSM
202 Crestline Blvd (27834-6816)
PHONE.............................408 582-2610
EMP: 7 EST: 2017
SALES (est): 151.2K Privately Held
Web: www.dsm.com
SIC: 2834 Pharmaceutical preparations

(G-7518)
DSM PHARMACEUTICALS INC
5900 Martin Luther King Jr Hwy (27834-8628)
P.O. Box 127 (27889-0127)
PHONE.............................252 758-3436
▲ EMP: 25 EST: 2011
SALES (est): 3.81MM Privately Held
Web: www.dsm.com
SIC: 2834 Pharmaceutical preparations

(G-7519)
DSM PHARMACEUTICALS INC
Also Called: Dpi
5900 Martin Luther King Jr Hwy (27834)
P.O. Box 2451 (30903-2451)
PHONE.............................252 758-3436

Greenville - Pitt County (G-7520) — GEOGRAPHIC SECTION

▲ EMP: 1200
SIC: 2834 Pharmaceutical preparations

(G-7520)
E C U UNIV PRTG & GRAPHICS
Also Called: Ecu Print Shop
2612 E 10th St (27858-3122)
PHONE..................252 737-1301
EMP: 16 EST: 1980
SALES (est): 170.12K **Privately Held**
Web: www.ecu.edu
SIC: 2752 Commercial printing, lithographic

(G-7521)
EASTERN CRLINA VCTONAL CTR INC (PA)
Also Called: ECVC
2100 N Greene St (27834-9024)
P.O. Box 1686 (27835-1686)
PHONE..................252 758-4188
Robert G Jones, *Pr*
Beth Davis, *
Daneel Le Roux, *
EMP: 62 EST: 1965
SQ FT: 145,000
SALES (est): 10.8MM
SALES (corp-wide): 10.8MM **Privately Held**
Web: www.ecvcinc.com
SIC: 8331 4953 3069 Vocational training agency; Refuse systems; Battery boxes, jars, or parts, hard rubber

(G-7522)
ELECTRIC MTR SLS SVC PITT CNTY
202 Hooker Rd (27834-5121)
P.O. Box 7044 (27835-7044)
PHONE..................252 752-3170
Bobby Bowen, *Pr*
Marshall Bowen, *VP*
EMP: 7 EST: 1977
SQ FT: 10,000
SALES (est): 2.01MM **Privately Held**
Web: www.electricmotorsalesgreenville.com
SIC: 5063 7694 Motors, electric; Electric motor repair

(G-7523)
ENERGY SVERS WINDOWS DOORS INC
Also Called: Home Security Bars
1806 Dickinson Ave (27834-3804)
PHONE..................252 758-8700
Charles H Hagan Junior, *Pr*
EMP: 4 EST: 1986
SALES (est): 468.99K **Privately Held**
SIC: 5211 3442 Windows, storm: wood or metal; Storm doors or windows, metal

(G-7524)
FASTSIGNS
2294a County Home Rd (27858-7932)
PHONE..................252 364-8745
EMP: 7 EST: 2019
SALES (est): 211.41K **Privately Held**
Web: www.fastsigns.com
SIC: 3993 Signs and advertising specialties

(G-7525)
FERVENT PHARMACEUTICALS LLC
740 Greenville Blvd Ste 400-151 (27834-6715)
PHONE..................252 558-9700
George E Royster Junior, *CEO*
EMP: 7 EST: 2011
SALES (est): 223.98K **Privately Held**
Web: www.ferventpharma.com
SIC: 2834 Pharmaceutical preparations

(G-7526)
FIXED-NC LLC
1830a Old Fire Tower Rd (27858-7985)
PHONE..................252 751-1911
EMP: 9 EST: 2018
SQ FT: 1,500
SALES (est): 803.34K **Privately Held**
Web: www.fixednc.com
SIC: 1389 1521 7299 8322 Construction, repair, and dismantling services; Repairing fire damage, single-family houses; Home improvement and renovation contractor agency; Disaster service

(G-7527)
FORWARD DSPTCHING LGISTICS LLC
3033 Clubway Dr Apt 124 (27834-8978)
PHONE..................252 907-9797
EMP: 4
SALES (est): 182.43K **Privately Held**
SIC: 3537 7389 Trucks: freight, baggage, etc.: industrial, except mining; Business Activities at Non-Commercial Site

(G-7528)
FOXFIRE PRINTING
300 W Arlington Blvd E (27834-5745)
PHONE..................252 329-8181
EMP: 4 EST: 2019
SALES (est): 88.48K **Privately Held**
SIC: 2752 Offset printing

(G-7529)
FRANKLIN BAKING COMPANY LLC
1107 Myrtle St (27834-3141)
PHONE..................252 752-4600
Billy Killian, *Brnch Mgr*
EMP: 13
SALES (corp-wide): 5.09B **Publicly Held**
Web: franklin-co4goldsboro.edan.io
SIC: 2051 Bread, cake, and related products
HQ: Franklin Baking Company, Llc
500 W Grantham St
Goldsboro NC 27530
919 735-0344

(G-7530)
FUJI SILYSIA CHEMICAL LTD
1215 Sugg Pkwy (27834-9008)
PHONE..................919 484-4158
EMP: 10
Web: www.fujisilysia.com
SIC: 8732 2819 Market analysis or research; Silica compounds
PA: Fuji Silysia Chemical Ltd.
2-1846, Kozojicho
Kasugai AIC 487-0

(G-7531)
FUJI SILYSIA CHEMICAL USA LTD
1215 Sugg Pkwy (27834-9008)
PHONE..................252 413-0003
Seiji Takahashi, *Pr*
Brian R Baymiller, *
Yasuo Ezaki, *
▲ EMP: 31 EST: 1998
SQ FT: 60,000
SALES (est): 18.11MM **Privately Held**
Web: www.fujisilysia.com
SIC: 2819 Industrial inorganic chemicals, nec
PA: Fuji Silysia Chemical Ltd.
2-1846, Kozojicho
Kasugai AIC 487-0

(G-7532)
GOODSTUFF JUICES LLC
803 Moye Blvd Ste A (27834-4141)
PHONE..................252 347-2341
EMP: 5 EST: 2015
SALES (est): 172.09K **Privately Held**
Web: www.goodstuffjuices.com
SIC: 2033 2037 5499 Fruit juices: fresh; Fruit juices; Juices, fruit or vegetable

(G-7533)
GRADY F SMITH & CO INC
Also Called: Scaffold Mart
1705 Evans St (27834-5717)
PHONE..................866 900-0983
Grady F Smith, *Pr*
◆ EMP: 15 EST: 1997
SQ FT: 122,000
SALES (est): 2.49MM **Privately Held**
Web: www.scaffoldmart.com
SIC: 3446 Scaffolds, mobile or stationary: metal

(G-7534)
GRADY-WHITE BOATS INC
5121 Martin Luther King Jr Hwy (27834-8613)
P.O. Box 1527 (27835-1527)
PHONE..................252 752-2111
▼ EMP: 200 EST: 1968
SALES (est): 38.67MM **Privately Held**
Web: www.gradywhite.com
SIC: 3732 Boats, fiberglass: building and repairing

(G-7535)
GREGORY POOLE EQUIPMENT CO
Also Called: Yale Material Handling
5200 Martin Luther King Jr Hwy (27834-8614)
PHONE..................252 931-5100
EMP: 7
SALES (corp-wide): 592.57MM **Privately Held**
Web: www.gregorypoole.com
SIC: 5084 3537 Materials handling machinery; Industrial trucks and tractors
HQ: Gregory Poole Equipment Company
4807 Beryl Rd
Raleigh NC 27606
919 828-0641

(G-7536)
GROVER GAMING INC (PA)
Also Called: New Market
3506 Greenville Blvd Ne (27834-3331)
PHONE..................252 329-7900
Garrett Blackwelder, *Pr*
EMP: 52 EST: 2013
SALES (est): 11.52MM
SALES (corp-wide): 11.52MM **Privately Held**
Web: www.grovergaming.com
SIC: 7993 5734 3823 Game machines; Software, computer games; Absorption analyzers: infrared, x-ray, etc.: industrial

(G-7537)
HATTERAS HAMMOCKS INC
Also Called: Hatteras Canvas Products
305 Industrial Blvd (27834-9015)
P.O. Box 1602 (27835-1602)
PHONE..................252 758-0641
◆ EMP: 125 EST: 1973
SALES (est): 21.88MM **Privately Held**
Web: www.hatterashammocks.com
SIC: 2399 2298 2394 Hammocks, fabric: made from purchased materials; Rope, except asbestos and wire; Canvas and related products

(G-7538)
HEATHS R&R TRANSPORT LLC
875 Spring Frest Rd Apt 1 (27834)
PHONE..................252 558-5215
EMP: 4 EST: 2021
SALES (est): 86.08K **Privately Held**
SIC: 3799 Transportation equipment, nec

(G-7539)
HERMES MEDICAL SOLUTIONS INC
710 Cromwell Dr Ste A (27858-5441)
PHONE..................252 355-4373
Jan Bertling, *CEO*
Guy Asterius, *Sec*
EMP: 7 EST: 2001
SALES (est): 2.85MM
SALES (corp-wide): 13.52MM **Privately Held**
Web: www.hermesmedical.com
SIC: 3577 Computer peripheral equipment, nec
HQ: Hermes Medical Solutions Limited
7-8 Henrietta Street Covent Garden
London
207 839-2513

(G-7540)
HYSTER-YALE GROUP INC
Yale Materials Handling
1400 Sullivan Dr (27834-9007)
PHONE..................252 931-5100
Chuck Pascarelli, *Pr*
EMP: 40
Web: www.hyster-yale.com
SIC: 3537 Aircraft engine cradles
HQ: Hyster-Yale Group, Inc.
1400 Sullivan Dr
Greenville NC 27834
252 931-5100

(G-7541)
HYSTER-YALE GROUP INC
5200 Martin Luther King Jr Hwy (27834-8614)
P.O. Box 12010 (27835-2010)
PHONE..................252 931-5100
Christopher Goodwin, *Engr*
EMP: 10
Web: www.hyster-yale.com
SIC: 3537 Forklift trucks
HQ: Hyster-Yale Group, Inc.
1400 Sullivan Dr
Greenville NC 27834
252 931-5100

(G-7542)
HYSTER-YALE GROUP INC (HQ)
Also Called: Yale Materials Handling
1400 Sullivan Dr (27834-9007)
P.O. Box 12010 (27835-2010)
PHONE..................252 931-5100
Alfred M Rankin, *Ch Bd*
Rajiv K Prasad, *
Charles A Bittenbender, *Senior Vice President Law*
Gregory J Breier, *Tax Vice President*
Brian K Frentzko, *
◆ EMP: 67 EST: 1993
SQ FT: 25,000
SALES (est): 1.41B **Publicly Held**
Web: www.hyster-yale.com
SIC: 3537 Forklift trucks
PA: Hyster-Yale Materials Handling, Inc.
5875 Landerbrook Dr # 300
Cleveland OH 44124

(G-7543)
INSTANT IMPRINTS GREENVILLE
1011 Charles Blvd (27858-3344)
PHONE..................252 364-3254
EMP: 5 EST: 2017
SALES (est): 98.1K **Privately Held**
SIC: 2752 Commercial printing, lithographic

GEOGRAPHIC SECTION
Greenville - Pitt County (G-7568)

(G-7544)
INSTITUTE FOR RESCH BIOTECNOLY
2905 S Memorial Dr (27834-6222)
PHONE.................252 689-2205
Farid Ahmed, *Dir*
EMP: 6
SALES (est): 473.94K **Privately Held**
SIC: 3826 Analytical instruments

(G-7545)
IOTO USA LLC
1997 N Greene St (27834-9021)
P.O. Box 1811 (27835-1811)
PHONE.................252 413-7343
▲ **EMP:** 10 **EST:** 2006
SALES (est): 1.53MM **Privately Held**
Web: www.iotointernational.com
SIC: 2131 2834 Chewing and smoking tobacco; Pharmaceutical preparations

(G-7546)
IT IS SEW
926 Thomas St (27834-9590)
PHONE.................252 531-7859
Joann Tyson, *Prin*
EMP: 5 **EST:** 2018
SALES (est): 103.29K **Privately Held**
SIC: 3566 Speed changers, drives, and gears

(G-7547)
J & P MACHINE WORKS INC
4291 Us Highway 264 E (27834-0707)
PHONE.................252 758-1719
John Mccoy, *Pr*
Barbara Mccoy, *VP*
EMP: 6 **EST:** 1989
SALES (est): 410.18K **Privately Held**
SIC: 3599 Machine shop, jobbing and repair

(G-7548)
JANUS DEVELOPMENT GROUP INC
308 W Arlington Blvd Ste 300 (27834-5736)
PHONE.................252 551-9042
Alan Newton, *Pr*
EMP: 10 **EST:** 2000
SALES (est): 935.81K **Privately Held**
Web: www.janusdevelopment.com
SIC: 3841 5047 Surgical and medical instruments; Medical and hospital equipment

(G-7549)
JEFFERSON GROUP INC
Transeast
225 Martin St (27834-1479)
P.O. Box 39 (27835-0039)
PHONE.................252 752-6195
Edward Glenn, *Sec*
EMP: 25
SQ FT: 60,000
SALES (corp-wide): 4.7MM **Privately Held**
Web: www.newgrowthdesigns.com
SIC: 5193 3999 Artificial flowers; Chairs, hydraulic, barber and beauty shop
PA: Jefferson Group, Inc.
310 W 9th St
Greenville NC 27834
252 355-5600

(G-7550)
JKL INC (PA)
Also Called: Jenni K Jewelry
727 Red Banks Rd (27858-5832)
PHONE.................252 355-6714
Jenni Kolczynski Landis, *Pr*
Gerald Landis Junior, *Sec*
Gerald Landis Senior, *VP*
Christine Kolczynski, *Treas*
EMP: 19 **EST:** 1987
SQ FT: 8,700
SALES (est): 2.3MM
SALES (corp-wide): 2.3MM **Privately Held**
Web: www.jennik.com
SIC: 3911 5944 7631 5921 Jewelry, precious metal; Jewelry stores; Watch, clock, and jewelry repair; Wine

(G-7551)
JOHNNYS TIRE SALES AND SVC INC
2400 S Memorial Dr Ste 3a (27834-5031)
PHONE.................252 353-8473
John Edmison, *Pr*
Johnny Joyner, *VP*
EMP: 11 **EST:** 2010
SQ FT: 10,000
SALES (est): 2.15MM **Privately Held**
Web: www.johnnystire.com
SIC: 5014 5531 7534 Automobile tires and tubes; Automotive tires; Tire repair shop

(G-7552)
KERDEA TECHNOLOGIES INC
1800 N Greene St (27834-9013)
PHONE.................971 900-1113
Douglas Carnes, *CEO*
Douglas Carnes Md Ph.d., *CEO*
Lloyd A Pearson, *CFO*
EMP: 12 **EST:** 2012
SALES (est): 1.07MM **Privately Held**
SIC: 5531 3999 Automotive parts; Atomizers, toiletry

(G-7553)
LBA GROUP INC (PA)
3400 Tupper Dr (27834-0781)
P.O. Box 8026 (27835-8026)
PHONE.................252 329-9243
EMP: 22 **EST:** 1985
SQ FT: 12,000
SALES (est): 6.35MM **Privately Held**
Web: www.lbagroup.com
SIC: 3663 3661 8711 Antennas, transmitting and communications; Telephones and telephone apparatus; Consulting engineer

(G-7554)
LBA TECHNOLOGY INC
3400 Tupper Dr (27834-0781)
P.O. Box 8026 (27835-8026)
PHONE.................252 757-0279
Lawrence V Behr, *CEO*
Wayne A Hildebrandt, *
Jerry Brown, *
◆ **EMP:** 25 **EST:** 1975
SQ FT: 10,000
SALES (est): 4.92MM **Privately Held**
Web: www.lbatechnology.com
SIC: 3663 3661 Antennas, transmitting and communications; Telephones and telephone apparatus
PA: Lba Group, Inc.
3400 Tupper Dr
Greenville NC 27834

(G-7555)
LDR DESIGNS
3113 Cleere Ct (27858-5570)
PHONE.................252 375-4484
Lakisha Randolph, *CEO*
Lakisha Randolph, *Owner*
EMP: 6 **EST:** 2008
SALES (est): 390.98K **Privately Held**
Web: www.ldr-designs.com
SIC: 2759 7389 7336 7379 Letterpress and screen printing; Apparel designers, commercial; Art design services; Online services technology consultants

(G-7556)
LIGHTHOUSE LED INC
3602 Huntington Rd (27858-6575)
P.O. Box 1086 (27835-1086)
PHONE.................252 916-0998
Walter Benton, *Prin*
EMP: 4 **EST:** 2016
SALES (est): 66.84K **Privately Held**
SIC: 3993 Signs and advertising specialties

(G-7557)
MAOLA MILK AND ICE CREAM CO
Also Called: MAOLA MILK AND ICE CREAM COMPANY
107 Hungate Dr (27858-8046)
PHONE.................252 756-3160
Harold Suber, *Brnch Mgr*
EMP: 46
SALES (corp-wide): 177.64MM **Privately Held**
SIC: 2026 2024 Fluid milk; Ice cream, bulk
HQ: Maola Milk And Ice Cream Company, Llc
5500 Chestnut Ave
Newport News VA 23605
252 638-1131

(G-7558)
MAPLIGHT THERAPEUTICS INC
1240 Sugg Pkwy (27834-9006)
PHONE.................603 553-9013
EMP: 6 **EST:** 2018
SALES (est): 72.66K **Privately Held**
SIC: 3841 Surgical and medical instruments

(G-7559)
METALLIX REFINING INC
251 Industrial Blvd (27834-9004)
PHONE.................252 413-0346
John Santos, *Brnch Mgr*
EMP: 34
SALES (corp-wide): 23.19MM **Privately Held**
Web: www.metallix.com
SIC: 3356 2819 3339 Solder: wire, bar, acid core, and rosin core; Industrial inorganic chemicals, nec; Precious metals
PA: Metallix Refining Inc.
59 Ave At The Cmmons Ste
Shrewsbury NJ 07702
732 945-4132

(G-7560)
METROHOSE INCORPORATED
2009 N Greene St (27834-9023)
PHONE.................252 329-9891
Mark Jozwicki, *Brnch Mgr*
EMP: 4
SIC: 3492 4225 Hose and tube fittings and assemblies, hydraulic/pneumatic; General warehousing and storage
PA: Metrohose, Incorporated
2211 W 3rd St
Farmville VA 23901

(G-7561)
MODERN LIGHTNING PROTECTION CO
Also Called: Ftp Co
302 Queen Annes Rd (27858-6303)
PHONE.................252 756-3006
Ben Gibbs, *Pr*
EMP: 16 **EST:** 1944
SALES (est): 546.58K **Privately Held**
Web: www.modernlightning.com
SIC: 7382 3643 Burglar alarm maintenance and monitoring; Current-carrying wiring services

(G-7562)
MOJO SPORTSWEAR INC
Also Called: Mojo Sportswear
1016 Myrtle St (27834-3140)
PHONE.................252 758-4176
Perry Swain, *Pr*
Kathy Swain, *Treas*
EMP: 6 **EST:** 1985
SQ FT: 3,000
SALES (est): 490.49K **Privately Held**
Web: www.mojosportswear.com
SIC: 2261 2395 Screen printing of cotton broadwoven fabrics; Emblems, embroidered

(G-7563)
NEW EAST CARTRIDGE INC
1809 Dickinson Ave (27834-3803)
PHONE.................252 329-0837
Mack Taha, *CEO*
EMP: 6 **EST:** 2002
SALES (est): 472.63K **Privately Held**
SIC: 3955 Print cartridges for laser and other computer printers

(G-7564)
NMHG
3953 Dunhagan Rd (27858-6628)
PHONE.................252 229-0071
EMP: 5 **EST:** 2018
SALES (est): 144.15K **Privately Held**
SIC: 3537 Industrial trucks and tractors

(G-7565)
NORTH STATE STEEL INC (PA)
1010 W Gum Rd (27834-1191)
P.O. Box 5003 (27835-5003)
PHONE.................252 830-8884
EMP: 30 **EST:** 1984
SALES (est): 10.24MM
SALES (corp-wide): 10.24MM **Privately Held**
Web: www.northstatesteel.com
SIC: 3441 Fabricated structural metal

(G-7566)
OCCASIONS GROUP INC
Also Called: Taylor Prime Labels & Packg
1055 Greenville Blvd Sw (27834-7021)
PHONE.................252 321-5805
Tom Obrien, *Brnch Mgr*
EMP: 20
SALES (corp-wide): 3.81B **Privately Held**
Web: www.theoccasionsgroup.com
SIC: 2752 7334 2789 7389 Photo-offset printing; Photocopying and duplicating services; Bookbinding and related work; Labeling bottles, cans, cartons, etc.
HQ: The Occasions Group Inc
1750 Tower Blvd
North Mankato MN 56003

(G-7567)
P A INDL FABRICATIONS
1413 Evans St Ste E (27834-4100)
PHONE.................252 329-8881
Claude Pruitt, *Pr*
EMP: 52 **EST:** 2017
SALES (est): 1.77MM **Privately Held**
Web: www.thepagroupllc.com
SIC: 3999 Manufacturing industries, nec

(G-7568)
PATHEON MANUFACTURING SVCS LLC
5900 Martin Luther King Jr Hwy (27834-8628)
PHONE.................252 758-3436
▲ **EMP:** 99 **EST:** 2014
SALES (est): 27.37MM
SALES (corp-wide): 44.91B **Publicly Held**

Greenville - Pitt County (G-7569)

Web: www.patheon.com
SIC: **2834** Druggists' preparations (pharmaceuticals)
PA: Thermo Fisher Scientific Inc.
168 3rd Ave
Waltham MA 02451
781 622-1000

(G-7569)
PEARL BLACK FASHION INC
652 E Arlington Blvd (27858-5837)
PHONE..................................252 689-6799
Shoumei Wang, *Admn*
EMP: 4 EST: 2017
SALES (est): 52.57K **Privately Held**
SIC: **2299** Jute and flax textile products

(G-7570)
PENCO PRODUCTS INC (DH)
1820 Stonehenge Dr (27858-5965)
PHONE..................................252 917-5287
TOLL FREE: 800
Greg Grogan, *Pr*
Charlie Mcbride, *VP*
Alan Kolody, *
Thomas Kulikawski, *
◆ EMP: 50 EST: 1979
SQ FT: 50,000
SALES (est): 100.3MM
SALES (corp-wide): 545.92MM **Privately Held**
Web: www.pencoproducts.com
SIC: **2599** 2542 Factory furniture and fixtures ; Lockers (not refrigerated): except wood
HQ: Industrial Manufacturing Company Llc
8223 Brecksville Rd # 100
Brecksville OH 44141
440 838-4700

(G-7571)
PERDUE FARMS INC
Also Called: Perdue Farms Warehouse
1623 N Greene St (27834-1285)
PHONE..................................252 758-2141
EMP: 6
SALES (corp-wide): 1.24B **Privately Held**
Web: www.perdue.com
SIC: **2015** Poultry slaughtering and processing
PA: Perdue Farms Incorporated
31149 Old Ocean City Rd
Salisbury MD 21804
800 473-7383

(G-7572)
PERFUSIO CORP
102a Hungate Dr (27858-8045)
P.O. Box 2611 (27602-2611)
PHONE..................................252 656-0404
Monte B Tucker, *CEO*
Jeffrey Basham, *Prin*
Phillip Hodges, *Prin*
Cheng Chen, *Prin*
Peter Geiger, *Prin*
EMP: 9 EST: 2014
SQ FT: 400
SALES (est): 962.45K **Privately Held**
Web: www.perfusio.com
SIC: **3841** Diagnostic apparatus, medical

(G-7573)
PHOENIX SOFTWARE SYSTEMS INC
111 Asbury Rd (27858-6320)
PHONE..................................252 756-6451
Phyllis P Hodges, *Prin*
EMP: 6 EST: 2002
SALES (est): 89.15K **Privately Held**
SIC: **7372** Prepackaged software

(G-7574)
PIEDMONT COCA-COLA BTLG PARTNR
Also Called: Coca-Cola
1051 Staton Rd (27834-9052)
PHONE..................................252 752-2446
Chuck Jenkins, *Mgr*
EMP: 178
SALES (corp-wide): 6.65B **Publicly Held**
Web: www.coca-cola.com
SIC: **2086** Bottled and canned soft drinks
HQ: Piedmont Coca-Cola Bottling Partnership
4115 Coca Cola Plz
Charlotte NC 28211
704 551-4400

(G-7575)
PIONEER SRGCAL ORTHBLOGICS INC (DH)
1800 N Greene St Ste A (27834-9013)
PHONE..................................252 355-4405
Anton Lewis Usala, *Ch Bd*
Mark Metzger, *Ex VP*
EMP: 14 EST: 1991
SALES (est): 2.06MM
SALES (corp-wide): 81.98MM **Publicly Held**
Web: www.rtix.com
SIC: **3841** Surgical and medical instruments
HQ: Pioneer Surgical Technology, Inc.
7 Switchbud Pl Ste 192-18
The Woodlands TX 77380

(G-7576)
PRESS AIR LLC
1303 Westpointe Dr Apt 7 (27834-8047)
PHONE..................................240 313-6832
Cameron Dixon, *Owner*
EMP: 5 EST: 2017
SALES (est): 44.72K **Privately Held**
SIC: **2741** Miscellaneous publishing

(G-7577)
PURILUM LLC
967 Woodridge Park Rd (27834-0055)
P.O. Box 1673 (27835-1673)
PHONE..................................252 931-8020
Bianca Iodice, *Pr*
EMP: 23 EST: 2013
SALES (est): 3.75MM **Privately Held**
Web: www.purilum.com
SIC: **3999** Cigarette and cigar products and accessories

(G-7578)
QUANTUM INSULATION INC
2554 Black Jack Grimesland Rd (27858-8384)
PHONE..................................252 752-7828
David Mills, *Prin*
EMP: 8 EST: 2013
SALES (est): 395.29K **Privately Held**
SIC: **3572** Computer storage devices

(G-7579)
RANDOM RUES BOTANICAL LLC
1290 E Arlington Blvd (27858-7854)
PHONE..................................252 214-2759
Christmas Smith, *Pr*
EMP: 8 EST: 2016
SALES (est): 369.1K **Privately Held**
SIC: **5499** 3842 5963 5122 Spices and herbs ; Cosmetic restorations; Cosmetic sales, house-to-house; Cosmetics, perfumes, and hair products

(G-7580)
ROBERT BOSCH TOOL CORPORATION
Also Called: Greenville Division
310 Staton Rd (27834-9037)
PHONE..................................252 551-7512
Gary W Utz, *Mgr*
EMP: 16
SALES (corp-wide): 230.19MM **Privately Held**
Web: www.boschtools.com
SIC: **3545** 3423 Drills (machine tool accessories); Hand and edge tools, nec
HQ: Robert Bosch Tool Corporation
1800 W Central Rd
Mount Prospect IL 60056

(G-7581)
SALT WOOD PRODUCTS INC (PA)
Also Called: Salt Wood Products 2.
3016 Jones Park Rd (27834-8361)
PHONE..................................252 830-8875
Gary Salt, *Pr*
Teresa Salt, *Sec*
Alger Salt, *Stockholder*
EMP: 6 EST: 1957
SQ FT: 12,000
SALES (est): 1.75MM
SALES (corp-wide): 1.75MM **Privately Held**
Web: www.saltwoodproducts.com
SIC: **2452** 5031 5211 Prefabricated buildings, wood; Lumber, plywood, and millwork; Lumber and other building materials

(G-7582)
SERVICE ROOFING AND SHTMTL CO
107 Staton Ct (27834-9016)
P.O. Box 1864 (27835-1864)
PHONE..................................252 758-2179
M Michael Richardson, *Pr*
Harry H Esbenshade Iii, *Ch Bd*
Max Michael Richardson, *Pr*
Barry Sugg, *VP*
Paul E Tyndall, *VP*
EMP: 86 EST: 1960
SQ FT: 6,000
SALES (est): 12.48MM
SALES (corp-wide): 109.23MM **Privately Held**
Web: www.tri-stateservicegroup.com
SIC: **3444** 1761 Sheet metalwork; Roofing, siding, and sheetmetal work
HQ: The Cypress Mountain Company
107 Staton Ct
Greenville NC 27834
252 758-2179

(G-7583)
SIGNS NOW 103 LLC
Also Called: Signs Now
118b Greenville Blvd Se (27834-5706)
PHONE..................................252 355-0768
EMP: 6 EST: 1989
SQ FT: 2,000
SALES (est): 416.75K **Privately Held**
Web: www.signsnow.com
SIC: **3993** Signs and advertising specialties

(G-7584)
SIGNSMITH CUSTOM SIGNS & AWNIN
1709 Evans St (27834-5772)
PHONE..................................252 752-4321
Leighton Blount, *Owner*
EMP: 11 EST: 2007
SALES (est): 968.72K **Privately Held**
Web: www.signsmithinc.com
SIC: **3993** Signs, not made in custom sign painting shops

(G-7585)
SIMPLY BTIFUL EVENTS DECOR LLC
1263 Windsong Dr (27858-9750)
PHONE..................................252 375-3839
EMP: 5 EST: 2021
SALES (est): 150K **Privately Held**
SIC: **2621** Printing paper

(G-7586)
SPHENODON TOOL CO INC
Also Called: STC Precision Cutting Tools
3530 Tupper Dr (27834-0755)
PHONE..................................252 757-3460
Jeffery A Dill, *Pr*
Amy Dill, *VP*
EMP: 6 EST: 1981
SQ FT: 6,500
SALES (est): 785.13K **Privately Held**
SIC: **3599** Machine shop, jobbing and repair

(G-7587)
STITCH BARN
1709 Eckerts Ln (27834-7564)
PHONE..................................252 717-1262
Alicia Eckert, *Prin*
EMP: 5 EST: 2017
SALES (est): 35.31K **Privately Held**
SIC: **2395** Embroidery and art needlework

(G-7588)
TEAM GSG LLC
Also Called: Greenville Seamless Gutters
851 Black Jack Simpson Rd (27858-8728)
PHONE..................................252 830-1032
EMP: 5 EST: 2010
SALES (est): 369.53K **Privately Held**
Web: www.greenvillegutters.com
SIC: **3089** Gutters (glass fiber reinforced), fiberglass or plastics

(G-7589)
THERMO FISHER SCIENTIFIC INC
5900 Martin Luther King Jr Hwy (27834-8628)
PHONE..................................252 707-7093
EMP: 11
SALES (corp-wide): 44.91B **Publicly Held**
Web: www.thermofisher.com
SIC: **3826** Analytical instruments
PA: Thermo Fisher Scientific Inc.
168 3rd Ave
Waltham MA 02451
781 622-1000

(G-7590)
THOMAS JEWELERS
714 Greenville Blvd Se (27858-5141)
PHONE..................................252 756-1641
EMP: 4 EST: 2016
SALES (est): 224.51K **Privately Held**
SIC: **5944** 3911 Jewelry, precious stones and precious metals; Jewelry, precious metal

(G-7591)
THURMAN TOLER
Also Called: Toler Welding & Repair
1229 Sheppard Mill Rd (27834-8271)
PHONE..................................252 758-4082
Thurman Toler, *Owner*
EMP: 6 EST: 1988
SALES (est): 247.13K **Privately Held**
Web: www.tolerswelding.com
SIC: **7692** Welding repair

(G-7592)
UNITED MACHINE WORKS INC
1716 Nc Highway 903 N (27834-6009)
PHONE..................................252 752-7434
Herbert Brown, *Pr*

GEOGRAPHIC SECTION

C Russell Brown, *
EMP: 44 **EST:** 1964
SQ FT: 23,750
SALES (est): 9.94MM **Privately Held**
Web: www.unitedmachineworksnc.com
SIC: 3599 Machine shop, jobbing and repair

(G-7593)
UNX INDUSTRIES INC
Also Called: Unx Industries, Inc.
1704 E Arlington Blvd Ste A (27858-7828)
PHONE.................252 355-8433
Joe Daxtor, *Supervisor*
EMP: 6
SALES (corp-wide): 13.41MM **Privately Held**
Web: www.unxchristeyns.com
SIC: 2842 2841 Automobile polish; Detergents, synthetic organic or inorganic alkaline
PA: Unx-Christeyns, Llc
  707 E Arlington Blvd
  Greenville NC 27858
  252 756-8616

(G-7594)
UNX INDUSTRIES INC
Also Called: Unx Industries, Inc.
201 W 9th St (27834-3245)
PHONE.................252 756-8616
Ben Wilson, *Brnch Mgr*
EMP: 51
SALES (corp-wide): 13.41MM **Privately Held**
Web: www.unxchristeyns.com
SIC: 2842 Bleaches, household: dry or liquid
PA: Unx-Christeyns, Llc
  707 E Arlington Blvd
  Greenville NC 27858
  252 756-8616

(G-7595)
UNX-CHRISTEYNS LLC (PA)
707 E Arlington Blvd (27858-5810)
P.O. Box 7206 (27835-7206)
PHONE.................252 756-8616
Joshua Clark, *Pr*
EMP: 22 **EST:** 2019
SALES (est): 13.41MM
SALES (corp-wide): 13.41MM **Privately Held**
Web: www.unxathletics.com
SIC: 2841 Soap and other detergents

(G-7596)
VA CLAIMS LLC
300 E 1st St (27858-1201)
PHONE.................305 984-0936
Matthew Richard Mccall, *Prin*
EMP: 8 **EST:** 2015
SALES (est): 59.14K **Privately Held**
SIC: 8299 7372 7379 8711 Tutoring school; Prepackaged software; Computer related maintenance services; Engineering services

(G-7597)
WATSON ELECTRICAL CNSTR CO LLC
3121 Bismarck St (27834-6807)
P.O. Box 1250 (27835-1250)
PHONE.................252 756-4550
Greg Phillign, *Mgr*
EMP: 61
SALES (corp-wide): 278.97MM **Privately Held**
Web: www.watsonelec.com
SIC: 1731 7694 General electrical contractor ; Electric motor repair
HQ: Watson Electrical Construction Co Llc
  1500 Charleston St Se
  Wilson NC 27893
  252 237-7511

(G-7598)
WELDING NEEDS
3151 Penny Hill Rd (27834-6634)
PHONE.................252 902-4082
EMP: 4 **EST:** 2016
SALES (est): 29.66K **Privately Held**
SIC: 7692 Welding repair

Grifton
Pitt County

(G-7599)
EIDP INC
Also Called: Dupont
4693 Highway 11 N (28530-0017)
P.O. Box 800 (28502-0800)
PHONE.................252 522-6111
Harold Thomas, *Mgr*
EMP: 70
SALES (corp-wide): 17.23B **Publicly Held**
Web: www.dupont.com
SIC: 2819 Industrial inorganic chemicals, nec
HQ: Eidp, Inc.
  9330 Zionsville Rd
  Indianapolis IN 46268
  833 267-8382

(G-7600)
ENGLISHS ALL WOOD HOMES INC
Also Called: Carolina Vinyl Products
608 Queen St (28530-7347)
P.O. Box 1137 (28530-1137)
PHONE.................252 524-5000
EMP: 18 **EST:** 1995
SQ FT: 12,000
SALES (est): 2.28MM **Privately Held**
Web: www.carolinavp.com
SIC: 1799 3089 Fence construction; Air mattresses, plastics

(G-7601)
MAGNUM ENTERPRIZE INC
Also Called: Magnum Telemetry
525 Country Acres Rd (28530-8909)
P.O. Box 1060 (28530-1060)
PHONE.................252 524-5391
Gary Tripp, *Pr*
Tracy Tripp, *Sec*
▲ **EMP:** 7 **EST:** 1997
SQ FT: 6,000
SALES (est): 521.92K **Privately Held**
Web: www.magnumtelemetry.com
SIC: 3699 Sound signaling devices, electrical

(G-7602)
ROADMSTER TRCK CONVERSIONS INC
Also Called: Roadmaster Truck Company
6482 N Highland Blvd (28530-8101)
PHONE.................252 412-3980
Ronald Lassiter, *Pr*
EMP: 5 **EST:** 2011
SQ FT: 800
SALES (est): 659.33K **Privately Held**
Web: www.roadmastertruck.com
SIC: 2515 Sleep furniture

(G-7603)
WEYERHAEUSER COMPANY
371 E Hanrahan Rd (28530-8717)
P.O. Box 280 (28513-0280)
PHONE.................252 746-7200
EMP: 12
SALES (corp-wide): 7.68B **Publicly Held**
Web: www.weyerhaeuser.com
SIC: 4226 2426 2421 Lumber terminal (storage for hire); Hardwood dimension and flooring mills; Sawmills and planing mills, general
PA: Weyerhaeuser Company
  220 Occidental Ave S
  Seattle WA 98104
  206 539-3000

Grimesland
Pitt County

(G-7604)
BEC-FAYE LLC
3393 Mobleys Bridge Rd (27837-8857)
PHONE.................252 714-8700
Overton V Parker, *Prin*
EMP: 6 **EST:** 2005
SALES (est): 163.62K **Privately Held**
SIC: 3721 Aircraft

Grover
Cleveland County

(G-7605)
A B C SCREENPRINTING AND EMB
106 Sprouse Ln (28073-9600)
P.O. Box 324 (28073-0324)
PHONE.................704 937-3452
Angie Richardson, *VP*
Angie Richardson, *Cnslt*
Donna Mabry, *Treas*
EMP: 6 **EST:** 1999
SALES (est): 295.54K **Privately Held**
SIC: 2759 Screen printing

(G-7606)
CELANESE INTL CORP
Also Called: Celanese
2523 Blacksburg Rd (28073-9641)
PHONE.................704 480-5798
EMP: 11 **EST:** 2016
SALES (est): 2.45MM **Privately Held**
SIC: 2821 Plastics materials and resins

(G-7607)
GENERAL SHALE BRICK INC
1622 Longbranch Rd (28073-8501)
PHONE.................704 937-7431
EMP: 19
SALES (corp-wide): 5.17B **Privately Held**
Web: www.generalshale.com
SIC: 3251 5211 Structural brick and blocks; Brick
HQ: General Shale Brick, Inc.
  3015 Bristol Hwy
  Johnson City TN 37601
  423 282-4661

(G-7608)
GROVER INDUSTRIES INC (PA)
219 Laurel Ave (28073-1207)
PHONE.................828 859-9125
James A Harry, *Pr*
O John Harry, *VP*
Ronald W Hewett, *VP Sls*
Gregory D Blalock, *Sec*
▲ **EMP:** 10 **EST:** 1962
SQ FT: 200,000
SALES (est): 9.57MM
SALES (corp-wide): 9.57MM **Privately Held**
SIC: 2269 Bleaching: raw stock, yarn, and narrow fabrics

(G-7609)
UNIQUETEX LLC
700 S Battleground Ave (28073-9541)
PHONE.................704 457-3003
Fang Wang, *Managing Member*
EMP: 50 **EST:** 2015
SALES (est): 7.31MM **Privately Held**
Web: www.uniquetex.com
SIC: 2221 Textile mills, broadwoven: silk and manmade, also glass

Halifax
Halifax County

(G-7610)
PERDUE FARMS INC
Also Called: Perdue Farms
1201 State Rd (27839)
P.O. Box 508 (27839-0508)
PHONE.................252 583-5731
Darrell Bryant, *Mgr*
EMP: 35
SALES (corp-wide): 1.24B **Privately Held**
Web: www.perdue.com
SIC: 2015 Poultry slaughtering and processing
PA: Perdue Farms Incorporated
  31149 Old Ocean City Rd
  Salisbury MD 21804
  800 473-7383

(G-7611)
PIEDMONT COCA-COLA BTLG PARTNR
Also Called: Coca-Cola
80 Industrial Dr (27839-9276)
PHONE.................252 536-3611
Dan Treadway, *Brnch Mgr*
EMP: 79
SALES (corp-wide): 6.65B **Publicly Held**
Web: www.coca-cola.com
SIC: 2086 Bottled and canned soft drinks
HQ: Piedmont Coca-Cola Bottling Partnership
  4115 Coca Cola Plz
  Charlotte NC 28211
  704 551-4400

(G-7612)
QUALITY CABINETS WOODWORKS
906 Poplar Ln (27839-8006)
PHONE.................252 536-0568
EMP: 4 **EST:** 2015
SALES (est): 121.27K **Privately Held**
Web: www.qualitycabinetsandwoodworks.com
SIC: 2434 Wood kitchen cabinets

Hamilton
Martin County

(G-7613)
COASTAL AGROBUSINESS INC
12011 Nc 125 (27840)
PHONE.................252 798-3481
Andy Tuer, *Mgr*
EMP: 7
SALES (corp-wide): 61.99MM **Privately Held**
Web: www.coastalagro.com
SIC: 5191 3523 Chemicals, agricultural; Sprayers and spraying machines, agricultural
PA: Coastal Agrobusiness, Inc.
  112 Staton Rd
  Greenville NC 27834
  252 238-7391

(G-7614)
PENCO PRODUCTS INC
1301 Penco Dr Hwy 125 (27840)
P.O. Box 400 (27840-0400)
PHONE.................252 798-4000
Bruce Woodword, *Brnch Mgr*
EMP: 200

SALES (corp-wide): 545.92MM **Privately Held**
Web: www.pencoproducts.com
SIC: **3499** 2599 5021 3444 Tablets, bronze or other metal; Factory furniture and fixtures; Lockers; Sheet metalwork
HQ: Penco Products, Inc.
1820 Stonehenge Dr
Greenville NC 27858

Hamlet
Richmond County

(G-7615)
AFFORDABLE SEPTIC TANK
315 Fox Trot Rd (28345-4345)
PHONE.....................910 417-9537
Joey Bostick, *Owner*
EMP: **7** EST: 2007
SALES (est): 115.37K **Privately Held**
Web: www.septic.com
SIC: **1711** 3272 4212 Septic system construction; Septic tanks, concrete; Dump truck haulage

(G-7616)
ASSOCIATED DISTRIBUTORS INC
120 Doe Loop (28345-9305)
PHONE.....................910 895-5800
Sheila Locklear, *Pr*
Wyatt Pegram, *Sec*
Mitchell Spivey, *VP*
EMP: **9** EST: 1992
SQ FT: 5,000
SALES (est): 957.27K **Privately Held**
Web: www.associateddistributors.ne
SIC: **2253** 5136 Shirts(outerwear), knit; Shirts, men's and boys'

(G-7617)
BOX COMPANY OF AMERICA LLC ⊘
12 Ev Hogan Dr (28345-8822)
PHONE.....................910 582-0100
EMP: **50** EST: 2022
SALES (est): 5.56MM **Privately Held**
SIC: **2631** 2679 5113 2675 Chip board; Corrugated paper: made from purchased material; Corrugated and solid fiber boxes; Die-cut paper and board

(G-7618)
CAVCO INDUSTRIES INC
Also Called: Cavco of North Carolina
106 Innovative Way (28345-4440)
PHONE.....................910 410-5050
EMP: **57**
SALES (corp-wide): 2.14B **Publicly Held**
Web: www.cavcoindustries.com
SIC: **2452** Modular homes, prefabricated, wood
PA: Cavco Industries, Inc.
3636 N Central Ave # 1200
Phoenix AZ 85012
602 256-6263

(G-7619)
CCBCC OPERATIONS LLC
Also Called: Coca-Cola
1662 E Us 74 Hwy (28345-8102)
P.O. Box 711 (28345-0711)
PHONE.....................910 582-3543
Wayne Andrews, *Brnch Mgr*
EMP: **33**
SALES (corp-wide): 6.65B **Publicly Held**
Web: www.coca-cola.com
SIC: **2086** Bottled and canned soft drinks
HQ: Ccbcc Operations, Llc
4100 Coca Cola Plz
Charlotte NC 28211
704 364-8728

(G-7620)
DR LOGGING LLC
506 Bauersfeld St (28345-2103)
PHONE.....................910 417-9643
EMP: **4** EST: 2011
SALES (est): 485.9K **Privately Held**
SIC: **2411** Logging camps and contractors

(G-7621)
FERROFAB INC
1416 Hylan Ave (28345-4743)
PHONE.....................910 557-5624
Willy Hauer, *Pr*
▲ EMP: **27** EST: 2012
SALES (est): 2.39MM **Privately Held**
Web: www.ferro-fab.com
SIC: **3441** Fabricated structural metal

(G-7622)
GLOBAL PACKAGING INC
106 Marks Creek Ln (28345-7273)
PHONE.....................610 666-1608
EMP: **82**
SALES (corp-wide): 78.16MM **Privately Held**
Web: www.glopkg.com
SIC: **5199** 3089 Packaging materials; Air mattresses, plastics
PA: Global Packaging, Inc.
209 Brower Ave
Oaks PA 19456
610 666-1608

(G-7623)
HOOD PACKAGING CORPORATION
Also Called: Hamlet Paper Packaging
740 Cheraw Rd (28345-7157)
PHONE.....................910 582-1842
Jimmy Dawkins, *Brnch Mgr*
EMP: **200**
Web: www.hoodpkg.com
SIC: **2674** 2673 Shipping bags or sacks, including multiwall and heavy duty; Bags: plastic, laminated, and coated
HQ: Hood Packaging Corporation
25 Woodgreen Pl
Madison MS 39110
601 853-7260

(G-7624)
IMPACT PLASTICS INC
1057 County Home Rd (28345-4390)
PHONE.....................910 205-1493
John Sousa, *Prin*
EMP: **10** EST: 2005
SALES (est): 202.32K **Privately Held**
Web: www.impactplastics.co
SIC: **3089** Injection molding of plastics

(G-7625)
KNIT-RITE INC
167 Marks Creek Ln (28345-7273)
P.O. Box 495 (28338-0495)
PHONE.....................910 557-5378
Mark W L Smith, *Pr*
EMP: **140**
SALES (corp-wide): 1.25MM **Privately Held**
Web: www.knitrite.com
SIC: **3842** Orthopedic appliances
HQ: Knit-Rite, Inc.
120 Osage Ave
Kansas City KS 66105
913 279-6310

(G-7626)
LATICRETE INTERNATIONAL INC
299 Industry Dr (28345-7324)
PHONE.....................910 582-2252
Ron Nunnerlyn, *Brnch Mgr*
EMP: **19**
SALES (corp-wide): 135.71MM **Privately Held**
Web: www.laticrete.com
SIC: **2891** 2899 Epoxy adhesives; Chemical preparations, nec
PA: Laticrete International, Inc.
1 Laticrete Park N
Bethany CT 06524
203 393-0010

(G-7627)
MCKENZIES TREE SERVICE & LOG
670 Boyd Lake Rd (28345-8137)
P.O. Box 706 (28338-0706)
PHONE.....................910 995-1576
Gene Mckenzie, *Prin*
EMP: **4** EST: 2018
SALES (est): 89.89K **Privately Held**
SIC: **2411** Logging camps and contractors

(G-7628)
P & P DISTRIBUTING COMPANY
Also Called: Page Plantation Shuttering Co
307 Industry Dr (28345-7323)
PHONE.....................910 582-1968
Willard Page, *Pr*
Judy Page, *Sec*
EMP: **10** EST: 1990
SQ FT: 21,000
SALES (est): 492.47K **Privately Held**
Web: www.pageplantationshutter.com
SIC: **2431** 5031 Louver doors: wood; Lumber, plywood, and millwork

(G-7629)
PLASTEK INDUSTRIES INC
Also Called: Plastek Group
1015 County Home Rd (28345-4390)
PHONE.....................814 878-4457
EMP: **114**
SALES (corp-wide): 166.12K **Privately Held**
Web: www.plastekgroup.com
SIC: **3089** Injection molding of plastics
PA: Plastek Industries, Inc.
2425 W 23rd St
Erie PA 16506
814 878-4400

(G-7630)
QUALICE LLC
Also Called: Qualice
11 Ev Hogan Dr (28345-8821)
P.O. Box 1169 (28345-1169)
PHONE.....................910 419-6589
EMP: **10** EST: 2012
SALES (est): 337.4K **Privately Held**
Web: www.qualicellc.com
SIC: **2911** 5169 Paraffin wax; Oil additives

(G-7631)
R R MICKEY LOGGING INC
1014 Boyd Lake Rd (28345-8146)
PHONE.....................910 205-0525
Richard R Mickey, *Pr*
Donna Reishel, *Sec*
EMP: **9** EST: 1980
SALES (est): 689.69K **Privately Held**
SIC: **2411** Logging camps and contractors

(G-7632)
SOUTHERN BAG CORPORATION LTD
740 Cheraw Rd (28345-7157)
PHONE.....................910 582-1842
Gene Schneck, *Prin*
EMP: **6** EST: 2008
SALES (est): 102.37K **Privately Held**
SIC: **2674** Bags: uncoated paper and multiwall

(G-7633)
TRINITY MANUFACTURING INC
11 Ev Hogan Dr (28345-8821)
P.O. Box 1519 (28345-1519)
PHONE.....................910 582-5650
Dean Storkan, *Pr*
◆ EMP: **68** EST: 1989
SQ FT: 7,000
SALES (est): 24.22MM **Privately Held**
Web: www.trinitymfg.com
SIC: **2879** 2869 Agricultural chemicals, nec; Industrial organic chemicals, nec

(G-7634)
VISTA PRODUCTS INC
10 Ev Hogan Dr (28345-8822)
PHONE.....................910 582-0130
Alen Courtwright, *Mgr*
EMP: **75**
Web: www.vistaproducts.com
SIC: **2591** 5072 Blinds vertical; Hardware
HQ: Vista Products, Inc.
8801 Corporate Square Ct
Jacksonville FL 32216
904 725-2242

Hampstead
Pender County

(G-7635)
AGGRESSIVE ADHESIVES INC
1971 Sloop Point Loop Rd (28443-8607)
PHONE.....................910 270-3282
Jason Leonard, *Prin*
EMP: **7** EST: 2009
SALES (est): 86.72K **Privately Held**
SIC: **2891** Adhesives

(G-7636)
ALLFUEL HST INC ⊘
109 W High Bluff Dr (28443-7133)
PHONE.....................919 868-9410
Joe Cochran, *CEO*
EMP: **10** EST: 2024
SALES (est): 336.84K **Privately Held**
SIC: **3259** 7389 Chimney pipe and tops, clay; Business Activities at Non-Commercial Site

(G-7637)
ALLIED MARINE CONTRACTORS LLC
92 Harold Ct (28443-8247)
PHONE.....................910 367-2159
EMP: **9** EST: 2007
SALES (est): 980.49K **Privately Held**
Web: www.alliedmarinecontractors.com
SIC: **3531** Marine related equipment

(G-7638)
ATLANTIC TOOL & DIE CO INC
2363 Nc Highway 210 W (28443-3455)
PHONE.....................910 270-2888
Hugh Hawthorne, *Pr*
Andy Hawkins, *VP*
EMP: **9** EST: 1987
SQ FT: 6,000
SALES (est): 758.82K **Privately Held**
Web: www.atlantictoolanddie.com
SIC: **3544** 3469 Special dies and tools; Metal stampings, nec

(G-7639)
BABINE LAKE CORPORATION (PA)
Also Called: Whisper Soft Mills
113 Dogwood Cir (28443-2596)
PHONE.....................910 285-7955
Nicholas Sokol, *Pr*
Richard F Tunner Junior, *Ex VP*

◆ EMP: 25 EST: 1973
SQ FT: 100,000
SALES (est): 1.52MM
SALES (corp-wide): 1.52MM **Privately Held**
SIC: 2392 Sheets, fabric: made from purchased materials

(G-7640)
BEACON THERMOGRAPHY INC
406 Adelaide Dr (28443-1017)
PHONE..................727 470-1694
EMP: 5 EST: 2018
SALES (est): 73.28K **Privately Held**
Web: www.beaconthermography.com
SIC: 2759 Thermography

(G-7641)
CAISON YACHTS INC
585 Lewis Rd (28443-8603)
P.O. Box 991 (28443-0991)
PHONE..................910 270-6394
Don Caison, *CEO*
EMP: 6 EST: 2007
SALES (est): 844.29K **Privately Held**
Web: www.caisonyachts.com
SIC: 3732 Yachts, building and repairing

(G-7642)
CAROLINA ENERGY CONCEPTS LLC
203 Cole Dr (28443-8681)
PHONE..................910 833-4203
Sara J Crawford, *Managing Member*
EMP: 6 EST: 2017
SALES (est): 244.67K **Privately Held**
Web: www.carolinaenergyconcepts.com
SIC: 3086 Insulation or cushioning material, foamed plastics

(G-7643)
COASTAL FISH PRINTS LLC
1675 Corcus Ferry Rd (28443-8276)
PHONE..................910 200-7005
Alec Webster, *Prin*
EMP: 5 EST: 2019
SALES (est): 92.1K **Privately Held**
Web: www.coastalfishprints.com
SIC: 2752 Commercial printing, lithographic

(G-7644)
CORBETT TIMBER COMPANY
105 Chuckanut Dr (28443-3753)
PHONE..................910 406-1129
EMP: 4 EST: 2016
SALES (est): 127.3K **Privately Held**
SIC: 2411 Logging camps and contractors

(G-7645)
CREATIVE WOODWORKS
109 Fox Run Dr (28443-3441)
PHONE..................910 233-3042
Simon Sanders, *Prin*
EMP: 5 EST: 2018
SALES (est): 122.66K **Privately Held**
SIC: 2431 Millwork

(G-7646)
ELAND INDUSTRIES INC
353 Washington Acres Rd (28443-3737)
PHONE..................910 304-5353
Tim Ennis, *Pr*
Kevin Ennis, *
EMP: 24 EST: 2017
SALES (est): 1.57MM **Privately Held**
SIC: 3449 Miscellaneous metalwork

(G-7647)
FOXSTER OPCO LLC
118 Circle Dr (28443-2108)
PHONE..................910 297-6996
Adam Fox, *Managing Member*
EMP: 22 EST: 2016
SALES (est): 1.43MM **Privately Held**
SIC: 5088 7372 Transportation equipment and supplies; Business oriented computer software

(G-7648)
GREG PRICE
Also Called: Wood and Anvil
107 Patton Ln (28443-7600)
PHONE..................847 778-4426
Greg Price, *Owner*
EMP: 9 EST: 2021
SALES (est): 278.78K **Privately Held**
SIC: 3479 2514 Coating of metals and formed products; Kitchen cabinets: metal

(G-7649)
INTRACOASTAL WOODWORKS LLC
390 Knollwood Dr (28443-8441)
PHONE..................910 270-5515
Darren L Rivenbark, *Admn*
EMP: 6 EST: 2010
SALES (est): 179.53K **Privately Held**
SIC: 2431 Millwork

(G-7650)
JOSEPH DECICCO
121 Topsail Lake Dr (28443-2790)
PHONE..................910 262-9701
Joseph Decicco, *Prin*
EMP: 4 EST: 2017
SALES (est): 87.99K **Privately Held**
SIC: 2731 Book publishing

(G-7651)
MONICAL ENTERPRISES INC
499 Lea Dr (28443-2281)
PHONE..................757 692-1345
EMP: 5 EST: 2020
SALES (est): 103.91K **Privately Held**
SIC: 7692 Welding repair

(G-7652)
OMNICELL
1705 Kings Landing Rd (28443-8375)
PHONE..................910 538-2141
Jeff Schlossnagle, *Prin*
EMP: 6 EST: 2018
SALES (est): 63.63K **Privately Held**
Web: www.omnicell.com
SIC: 3571 Electronic computers

(G-7653)
ONSLOW BAY BOATWORKS & MARINE
175 Sloop Point Loop Rd (28443-2616)
PHONE..................910 270-3703
EMP: 6
SALES (est): 1.05MM **Privately Held**
SIC: 3732 Boatbuilding and repairing

(G-7654)
RAYS CLASSIC VINYL REPAIR INC
440 Crooked Creek Rd (28443-7977)
PHONE..................910 520-1626
EMP: 5 EST: 2003
SALES (est): 420K **Privately Held**
Web: www.nbccbakersfield.com
SIC: 3081 Vinyl film and sheet

(G-7655)
SLOOP PT VLNTR FIRE DEPT INC
19470 Us Highway 17 (28443-3202)
PHONE..................910 270-3267
David Stancil, *Pr*
Scott Sills, *
EMP: 8 EST: 1988
SALES (est): 221.15K **Privately Held**
SIC: 3569 Firefighting and related equipment

(G-7656)
SOUTHERN SCENTS
274 Crystal Ct (28443-2798)
PHONE..................910 431-6492
Tina Coleman, *Prin*
EMP: 5 EST: 2010
SALES (est): 96.91K **Privately Held**
Web: www.southernscentssoap.com
SIC: 2844 Perfumes, cosmetics and other toilet preparations

(G-7657)
SWEET SANCTIONS LLC
48 Petrel Trce (28443-5702)
PHONE..................717 222-1859
Elizabeth Reddinger, *Prin*
EMP: 11 EST: 2012
SALES (est): 239.21K **Privately Held**
Web: www.sweetsanctions.com
SIC: 3421 Table and food cutlery, including butchers'

(G-7658)
TECH-TOOL INC
2561 Country Club Dr (28443-2528)
PHONE..................919 906-6229
EMP: 8 EST: 1993
SQ FT: 10,000
SALES (est): 500K **Privately Held**
SIC: 3599 Machine shop, jobbing and repair

(G-7659)
TEN NAILS CONSTRUCTION INC
449 Landsdowne Cir (28443-3912)
PHONE..................910 232-4883
Jon Ford, *Prin*
EMP: 8 EST: 2016
SALES (est): 240.2K **Privately Held**
SIC: 1389 1521 1542 Construction, repair, and dismantling services; New construction, single-family houses; Restaurant construction

(G-7660)
TOM MARSH JR DBA TM WOODWORKS
101 Sandtrail Ct (28443-2730)
PHONE..................910 376-2760
EMP: 5 EST: 2010
SALES (est): 72K **Privately Held**
SIC: 2431 Millwork

(G-7661)
TOPSAIL SPORTSWEAR INC
15530 Us Highway 17 (28443-3084)
P.O. Box 995 (28443-0995)
PHONE..................910 270-4903
Bill Lanier, *Pr*
Mitch Lanier, *VP*
EMP: 7 EST: 1986
SALES (est): 251.75K **Privately Held**
Web: www.topsailsportswear.com
SIC: 2395 Embroidery products, except Schiffli machine

(G-7662)
TOPSAIL VOICE LLC
Also Called: Hampstead Publishing
14886 Us Highway 17 (28443-3217)
P.O. Box 880 (28443-0880)
PHONE..................910 270-2944
Lockwood Phillips, *Pr*
EMP: 9 EST: 1991
SALES (est): 559.67K **Privately Held**
Web: www.topsailvoice.com
SIC: 2711 Newspapers, publishing and printing

(G-7663)
UTILITY METERING SOLUTIONS INC
Also Called: Carolina Meter and Supply
231 Sloop Point Loop Rd (28443-2618)
P.O. Box 12448 (28405-0119)
PHONE..................910 270-2885
Barry Hales, *CEO*
Nancy S Jones, *CFO*
EMP: 9 EST: 1999
SALES (est): 233.31K **Privately Held**
SIC: 3824 Water meters

(G-7664)
WATERS CORPORATION
15430 Us Highway 17 (28443-3549)
P.O. Box 998 (28443-0998)
PHONE..................910 270-3137
Lee Piver, *Brnch Mgr*
EMP: 4
Web: www.waters.com
SIC: 3826 Chromatographic equipment, laboratory type
PA: Waters Corporation
34 Maple St
Milford MA 01757

Hamptonville
Yadkin County

(G-7665)
ALBATROSS SUPPLY LLC
Also Called: Albatross Steel Buildings
2851 Rocky Branch Rd (27020-8379)
PHONE..................336 488-1128
Joshua Eicher, *Managing Member*
EMP: 7 EST: 2020
SALES (est): 476.21K **Privately Held**
SIC: 3677 5031 Coil windings, electronic; Building materials, exterior

(G-7666)
AMERICAN IMAGE PRESS
5043 Highland Grove Pl (27020-8190)
P.O. Box 42 (27020-0042)
PHONE..................336 468-2796
Vonda Blackburn, *Prin*
EMP: 4 EST: 2010
SALES (est): 165.02K **Privately Held**
Web: www.ifpo.net
SIC: 2741 Miscellaneous publishing

(G-7667)
BESANA-LOVATI INC (PA)
4112 W Old Us 421 Hwy (27020-8413)
PHONE..................336 768-6064
Angelo Lovati, *Pr*
Annibale Besana, *VP*
Stewart Walmsley, *Sec*
Lorendana Lovati, *Treas*
Darrell Green, *Sec*
▲ EMP: 11 EST: 1990
SALES (est): 1.02MM **Privately Held**
Web: www.besana-usa.com
SIC: 3559 Glass making machinery: blowing, molding, forming, etc.

(G-7668)
BLACK BARREL DEFENSE LLC
7541 Mayberry Mill Rd (27020-7944)
PHONE..................336 468-8102
Jonathan Mckaig, *Prin*
EMP: 4 EST: 2018
SALES (est): 98.52K **Privately Held**
Web: www.blackbarreldefense.com
SIC: 3812 Defense systems and equipment

Hamptonville - Yadkin County (G-7669)

(G-7669)
DUTCH KETTLE LLC
Also Called: Dutch Kettle, The
5016 Hunting Creek Church Rd (27020-7750)
PHONE..................336 468-8422
Paul Peachey, *Managing Member*
▲ EMP: 5 EST: 1986
SALES (est): 499.84K **Privately Held**
Web: www.dutchkettle.net
SIC: **2033** Jams, jellies, and preserves, packaged in cans, jars, etc.

(G-7670)
GOLD CREEK INC
3441 Lone Hickory Rd (27020-7201)
PHONE..................336 468-4495
Dale Wooten, *Pr*
EMP: 4 EST: 1982
SALES (est): 498.43K **Privately Held**
SIC: **2411** Logging camps and contractors

(G-7671)
HOSTETLER SAWMILL
5400 Saint Paul Church Rd (27020-7840)
PHONE..................336 468-1800
Dean Hostetler, *Prin*
EMP: 7 EST: 2000
SALES (est): 192.25K **Privately Held**
SIC: **2421** Sawmills and planing mills, general

(G-7672)
IFPO - IFMO/AMERICAN IMAGE INC
Also Called: Today's Photographer Magazine
5043 Highland Grove Pl (27020-8190)
P.O. Box 42 (27020-0042)
PHONE..................336 945-9867
Vonda Blackburn, *Pr*
Jack Gallimore, *Sec*
EMP: 4 EST: 1984
SQ FT: 4,500
SALES (est): 319.65K **Privately Held**
Web: www.ifpo.net
SIC: **2721** 7311 Magazines: publishing only, not printed on site; Advertising agencies

(G-7673)
LAUREL GRAY VINEYARDS INC
5726 W Old Us 421 Hwy (27020-8225)
PHONE..................336 468-9463
Kim Myers, *Pr*
EMP: 7 EST: 2004
SALES (est): 449.07K **Privately Held**
Web: www.laurelgray.com
SIC: **2084** Wines

(G-7674)
LYDALL INC
1241 Buck Shoals Rd (27020-7624)
PHONE..................336 468-8522
Joe Abbruzzi, *Brnch Mgr*
EMP: 4
Web: www.lydall.com
SIC: **2297** Nonwoven fabrics
HQ: Lydall, Inc.
1 Colonial Rd
Manchester CT 06042
860 646-1233

(G-7675)
LYDALL THERMAL/ACOUSTICAL INC (DH)
Also Called: Thermal Acoustical Group
1241 Buck Shoals Rd (27020-7624)
P.O. Box 109 (27020-0109)
PHONE..................336 468-8522
David Glenn, *Pr*
▲ EMP: 68 EST: 1977
SQ FT: 60,000
SALES (est): 104.24MM **Privately Held**
Web: www.lydallautomotive.com
SIC: **3441** Fabricated structural metal
HQ: Lydall, Inc.
1 Colonial Rd
Manchester CT 06042
860 646-1233

(G-7676)
LYDALL THERMAL/ACOUSTICAL INC
Fibers
1241 Buck Shoals Rd (27020-7624)
PHONE..................336 468-8522
William Hume, *Mgr*
EMP: 527
Web: www.lydallautomotive.com
SIC: **3441** Fabricated structural metal
HQ: Lydall Thermal/Acoustical, Inc.
1241 Buck Shoals Rd
Hamptonville NC 27020
336 468-8522

(G-7677)
MAST WOODWORKS
5328 Saint Paul Church Rd (27020-7839)
PHONE..................336 468-1194
Alvin Dale Mast, *Owner*
EMP: 10 EST: 2000
SALES (est): 750K **Privately Held**
Web: www.affordablebuildingsonline.com
SIC: **3448** 2452 Prefabricated metal buildings and components; Log cabins, prefabricated, wood

(G-7678)
STEELMAN LUMBER & PALLET LLC
4744 Us 21 Hwy (27020-7322)
PHONE..................336 468-2757
Spencer Steelman, *Managing Member*
EMP: 12 EST: 2015
SALES (est): 1.21MM **Privately Held**
Web: www.steelmanlumber.com
SIC: **4953** 2448 5031 Recycling, waste materials; Wood pallets and skids; Pallets, wood

(G-7679)
TARHEEL SAND & STONE INC
1108 Tuckda Way (27020-8398)
PHONE..................336 468-4003
Keith Adams, *Pr*
Terry Jester, *VP*
EMP: 4 EST: 1989
SALES (est): 452.69K **Privately Held**
SIC: **1411** 1442 Dimension stone; Construction sand and gravel

(G-7680)
VINYL STRUCTURES LLC
Also Called: Trupoint Backyards
4708 Hunting Creek Church Rd (27020-7747)
PHONE..................336 468-4311
Mark Schlabach, *Managing Member*
EMP: 5 EST: 1997
SQ FT: 12,000
SALES (est): 992.98K **Privately Held**
SIC: **3448** Buildings, portable: prefabricated metal

(G-7681)
YADKIN VALLEY HERBS INC
6324 Laurel Gray Ln (27020-8399)
PHONE..................336 468-4062
EMP: 4 EST: 2008
SALES (est): 155.66K **Privately Held**
SIC: **2084** Wines

(G-7682)
YADKIN VALLEY WINE COMPANY
6324 Laurel Gray Ln (27020-8399)
PHONE..................336 467-0257
EMP: 5 EST: 2019
SALES (est): 76.99K **Privately Held**
Web: www.yadkinvalleync.com
SIC: **2084** Wines

Harbinger
Currituck County

(G-7683)
GRAPHIC ATTACK INC
Harbinger Commercial Park Ste 34 (27941)
P.O. Box 38 (27941-0038)
PHONE..................252 491-2174
▼ EMP: 4 EST: 1987
SQ FT: 6,000
SALES (est): 320.46K **Privately Held**
Web: www.graphicattack.com
SIC: **2261** Screen printing of cotton broadwoven fabrics

(G-7684)
TRI-H MOLDING CO
135 W Side Ln (27941)
P.O. Box 159 (27941-0159)
PHONE..................252 491-8530
Stanley Hopkins, *Pr*
David S Hopkins, *Stockholder*
EMP: 4 EST: 1985
SQ FT: 7,500
SALES (est): 467.19K **Privately Held**
SIC: **2491** Structural lumber and timber, treated wood

Harmony
Iredell County

(G-7685)
ASSOCIATED METAL WORKS INC
137 E Memorial Hwy (28634-9131)
P.O. Box 449 (28634-0449)
PHONE..................704 546-7002
EMP: 36 EST: 1997
SQ FT: 30,000
SALES (est): 4.68MM **Privately Held**
Web: www.associatedmetalworks.com
SIC: **3564** Air purification equipment

(G-7686)
G & G LUMBER COMPANY INC
179 Lumber Dr (28634-9200)
PHONE..................704 539-5110
Cecil S Gregory, *Pr*
EMP: 32 EST: 1973
SQ FT: 4,000
SALES (est): 1.56MM **Privately Held**
Web: www.gandglumber.com
SIC: **2435** 2421 Hardwood plywood, prefinished; Sawmills and planing mills, general

(G-7687)
JAMES MICHAEL VINEYARDS LLC
440 Lake Mullis Rd (28634-9205)
PHONE..................704 539-4749
James Mullis, *Prin*
EMP: 4 EST: 2018
SALES (est): 75.98K **Privately Held**
Web: www.jamesmichaelvineyards.com
SIC: **2084** Wines

(G-7688)
ROCKY SPRINGS APPLICATOR
698 Rock Springs Rd (28634-9255)
PHONE..................704 546-7560
David Burgess, *Owner*
EMP: 5 EST: 1996
SALES (est): 200.48K **Privately Held**
SIC: **3531** Finishers and spreaders (construction equipment)

(G-7689)
SML TRANSPORTATION LLC
354 Mount Bethel Rd (28634-9001)
PHONE..................704 402-6744
Jennifer Wright, *Managing Member*
EMP: 4 EST: 2021
SALES (est): 248.83K **Privately Held**
SIC: **3537** 7389 Trucks: freight, baggage, etc.: industrial, except mining; Business Activities at Non-Commercial Site

(G-7690)
SOMERS LUMBER AND MFG INC
126 Oakleaf Rd (28634-9222)
P.O. Box 87 (28689-0087)
EMP: 11 EST: 1964
SQ FT: 21,000
SALES (est): 7.99MM **Privately Held**
Web: www.somerslumber.com
SIC: **5031** 2448 2421 Lumber: rough, dressed, and finished; Wood pallets and skids; Sawmills and planing mills, general

Harrells
Sampson County

(G-7691)
CUSTOM ENGINES LTD
2560 Wildcat Rd (28444-7838)
PHONE..................910 532-4114
Graham L Cole Junior, *Prin*
EMP: 6 EST: 2009
SALES (est): 235.79K **Privately Held**
SIC: **3519** Internal combustion engines, nec

(G-7692)
DNL SERVICES LLC
64 Blue Heron Dr (28444-8889)
PHONE..................910 689-8759
EMP: 8 EST: 2016
SALES (est): 439.19K **Privately Held**
SIC: **3271** Blocks, concrete: landscape or retaining wall

(G-7693)
LAKE CREEK LOGGING & TRCKG INC
3744 Nc Highway 210 E (28444-8919)
PHONE..................910 532-2041
Mark Long, *Pr*
Jill Long, *Sec*
EMP: 10 EST: 1991
SALES (est): 967.41K **Privately Held**
SIC: **2411** Logging camps and contractors

(G-7694)
LEES LOGGING COMPANY
201 Nc Highway 210 E (28444-8714)
PHONE..................910 385-7201
Jason Lee Cain, *Pr*
EMP: 13 EST: 2017
SALES (est): 474.3K **Privately Held**
Web: lees-logging-company-inc.business.site
SIC: **2411** Logging

(G-7695)
NORTH CAPE FEAR LOGGING LLC
125 Charlie Smith Dr (28444-8043)
PHONE..................910 876-3197
EMP: 5 EST: 2014
SALES (est): 135.92K **Privately Held**

SIC: 2411 Logging

(G-7696)
TAYLOR TIMBER CO LLC
113 Mote Fields Rd (28444-8838)
P.O. Box 2108 (28337-2108)
PHONE.................................910 588-6214
Greg Taylor, *Owner*
EMP: 5 EST: 2004
SALES (est): 292.33K **Privately Held**
SIC: 2411 Logging

(G-7697)
THOMAS TIMBER INC
3344 Nc Highway 210 E (28444-8924)
PHONE.................................910 532-4542
G Dean Thomas, *Pr*
Winnie Lewis, *Sec*
EMP: 12 EST: 1946
SALES (est): 938.45K **Privately Held**
SIC: 2411 2421 Logging camps and contractors; Chipper mill

Harrellsville
Hertford County

(G-7698)
SANDY LAND PEANUT COMPANY INC
229 Swains Mill Rd (27942-9779)
P.O. Box 38 (27924-0038)
PHONE.................................252 356-2679
EMP: 15 EST: 2007
SALES (est): 509.79K **Privately Held**
Web: www.sandylandpeanut.com
SIC: 0723 2068 Crop preparation services for market; Nuts: dried, dehydrated, salted or roasted

Harrisburg
Cabarrus County

(G-7699)
ACME WELDING CO
7200 Robinson Church Rd (28075-9353)
PHONE.................................770 841-4335
EMP: 5 EST: 2019
SALES (est): 48.7K **Privately Held**
SIC: 7692 Welding repair

(G-7700)
AMERICA SHEET METAL INC
5502 Roberta Rd (28075-0316)
PHONE.................................980 318-7749
Ysaura De Los S Garcia, *Pr*
EMP: 5 EST: 2016
SALES (est): 70.19K **Privately Held**
SIC: 3444 Sheet metalwork

(G-7701)
AMP AGENCY ✪
Also Called: Residential/Commercial Cnstr
6220 Hudspeth Rd (28075-5001)
PHONE.................................704 430-2313
Akeiamarie Saunders, *CEO*
EMP: 5 EST: 2022
SALES (est): 419.48K **Privately Held**
Web: www.ampagency.com
SIC: 1389 7389 Construction, repair, and dismantling services; Design, commercial and industrial

(G-7702)
ANGEL TREE PUBLISHING
8378 Pompano Rd (28075-9666)
PHONE.................................704 454-7604
Mary Ann Drummond, *Prin*
EMP: 5 EST: 2016
SALES (est): 40.43K **Privately Held**
Web: www.angeltreepublishing.com
SIC: 2741 Miscellaneous publishing

(G-7703)
CARBON-LESS INDUSTRIES INC
12059 University Cy Blvd (28075-8466)
PHONE.................................704 361-1231
John Meeks, *Prin*
EMP: 5 EST: 2016
SALES (est): 76.45K **Privately Held**
SIC: 3999 Manufacturing industries, nec

(G-7704)
CEMEX MATERIALS LLC
Also Called: Cemex
5601 Pharr Mill Rd (28075-0390)
PHONE.................................704 455-1100
Rick Santiago, *Mgr*
EMP: 110
SIC: 3273 Ready-mixed concrete
HQ: Cemex Materials Llc
  1720 Centrepark Dr E # 100
  West Palm Beach FL 33401
  561 833-5555

(G-7705)
CLOUD STREAM SYSTEMS LLC
415 Williams Rd (28075-9483)
P.O. Box 621162 (28262-0119)
PHONE.................................704 916-9664
EMP: 4 EST: 2015
SALES (est): 122.08K **Privately Held**
Web: www.cloudstreamsystems.com
SIC: 7372 Business oriented computer software

(G-7706)
COMBAT MEDICAL SYSTEMS LLC
Also Called: Safeguard America
5555 Harrisburg Ind Pk Dr (28075-7407)
PHONE.................................704 705-1222
Greg Keyes, *Dir*
Kim Salvi, *
EMP: 25 EST: 2008
SALES (est): 8.94MM
SALES (corp-wide): 8.94MM **Privately Held**
Web: www.combatmedical.com
SIC: 3845 5047 Arc lamp units, electrotherapeutic (except IR and UV); Medical equipment and supplies
PA: Safeguard Us Operating, Llc
  5555 Harrisburg Ind Pk Dr
  Harrisburg NC 28075
  855 428-6074

(G-7707)
DOT BLUE READI-MIX LLC
7406 Millbrook Rd (28075-7410)
PHONE.................................704 247-2778
Ken Hall, *Manager*
EMP: 27
SALES (corp-wide): 45.71MM **Privately Held**
Web: www.bluedotreadimix.com
SIC: 3273 Ready-mixed concrete
PA: Blue Dot Readi-Mix, Llc
  11330 Bain School Rd
  Mint Hill NC 28227
  704 971-7676

(G-7708)
FAB-CON MACHINERY DEV CORP
Also Called: Fab-Con
12145 University City Blvd (28075-7406)
P.O. Box 423 (28075-0423)
PHONE.................................516 883-3999
Christopher Snyder, *Mgr*
EMP: 21
SALES (corp-wide): 15.67MM **Privately Held**
Web: www.fab-con.com
SIC: 3552 Finishing machinery, textile
PA: Fab-Con Machinery Development Corp.
  201 E 10th St
  Oakboro NC 28129
  704 486-7120

(G-7709)
FLUTTERBY EMBROIDERY
8524 Indian Summer Trl (28075-9686)
PHONE.................................980 225-6053
EMP: 5 EST: 2015
SALES (est): 52.68K **Privately Held**
SIC: 2759 Screen printing

(G-7710)
FURR SIGNS
929 Patricia Ave (28075-8454)
PHONE.................................704 455-5849
Larry Furr, *Prin*
EMP: 5 EST: 1999
SALES (est): 75.15K **Privately Held**
SIC: 3993 Signs and advertising specialties

(G-7711)
GALVAN INDUSTRIES INC
7315 Galvan Way (28075-4300)
P.O. Box 369 (28075-0369)
PHONE.................................704 455-5102
Laurens Willard, *Pr*
Elizabeth Willard, *
Brad Wittensoldner, *
◆ EMP: 150 EST: 1960
SQ FT: 100,000
SALES (est): 33.41MM **Privately Held**
Web: www.galvan-ize.com
SIC: 3479 Coating of metals and formed products

(G-7712)
GARICK LLC
Also Called: Tar Heel Bark
8829 Rocky River Rd (28075-7636)
PHONE.................................704 455-6418
Shane Baucom, *Brnch Mgr*
EMP: 8
SALES (corp-wide): 20.43B **Publicly Held**
Web: www.garick.com
SIC: 2499 Mulch, wood and bark
HQ: Garick, Llc
  8400 Sweet Valley Dr # 408
  Cleveland OH 44125
  216 581-0100

(G-7713)
J F FABRICATORS LLC (PA)
7315 Millbrook Rd (28075-7489)
PHONE.................................704 454-7224
EMP: 5 EST: 2008
SQ FT: 20,000
SALES (est): 996.58K **Privately Held**
SIC: 3449 Fabricated bar joists and concrete reinforcing bars

(G-7714)
JG AGNEW HOLDINGS INC
Also Called: USA Insulation
2535 Red Maple Ln (28075-4506)
PHONE.................................704 594-0900
EMP: 4 EST: 2019
SALES (est): 147.54K **Privately Held**
SIC: 3732 Boatbuilding and repairing

(G-7715)
KABINET WERKS LLC
8501 Middleton Cir (28075-8332)
PHONE.................................704 359-7311
EMP: 5 EST: 2018
SALES (est): 103.91K **Privately Held**
SIC: 2431 Millwork

(G-7716)
MALLARD CREEK POLYMERS LLC
2388 Speedrail Dr (28075-0378)
PHONE.................................704 547-0622
EMP: 8
Web: www.mcpolymers.com
SIC: 2821 Plastics materials and resins
PA: Mallard Creek Polymers, Llc
  8901 Research Dr
  Charlotte NC 28262

(G-7717)
MARCON INTERNATIONAL INC
Also Called: Keyper Systems
5679 Harrisburg Ind Pk Dr (28075-7412)
P.O. Box 1540 (28075-1540)
PHONE.................................704 455-9400
Ric Stone, *CEO*
Walt Leaver, *
▲ EMP: 30 EST: 1993
SQ FT: 20,000
SALES (est): 5.35MM
SALES (corp-wide): 17.42MM **Privately Held**
Web: www.marcon.com
SIC: 7382 3429 Protective devices, security; Keys and key blanks
PA: Ucc-Kp Investment, Llc
  485 W Putnam Ave
  Greenwich CT 06830
  203 580-5740

(G-7718)
MAUSER USA LLC
Also Called: Berenfield Containers
12180 University Cy Blvd (28075-7406)
PHONE.................................704 455-2111
EMP: 60
SIC: 3412 Drums, shipping: metal
HQ: Mauser Usa, Llc
  2 Tower Center Blvd
  East Brunswick NJ 60523

(G-7719)
OMNINVEST LLC (PA)
4213 Abernathy Pl (28075-6694)
PHONE.................................336 623-1717
Hadi Sayess, *CEO*
EMP: 6 EST: 2015
SALES (est): 7.23MM
SALES (corp-wide): 7.23MM **Privately Held**
SIC: 7694 3599 Electric motor repair; Machine shop, jobbing and repair

(G-7720)
PEPSI BOTTLING VENTURES LLC
Also Called: Pepsi-Cola
22 Pepsi Way (28075-8416)
PHONE.................................704 455-0800
David Brown Michael Mills, *Brnch Mgr*
EMP: 250
Web: www.pepsibottlingventures.com
SIC: 2086 Carbonated soft drinks, bottled and canned
HQ: Pepsi Bottling Ventures Llc
  4141 Parklake Ave Ste 600
  Raleigh NC 27612
  919 865-2300

(G-7721)
PERFORMANCE GOODS LLC
4365 School House Cmns Ste 500 # 143 (28075-7565)
PHONE.................................704 361-8600
EMP: 6 EST: 2010
SALES (est): 391.13K **Privately Held**

Harrisburg - Cabarrus County (G-7722)

SIC: 2299 Insulating felts

(G-7722)
PICS AND PRINTS LLC
8473 Mossy Cup Trl (28075-5627)
PHONE.....................917 753-3542
Joseph F Souffrant Junior, *Prin*
EMP: 5 **EST:** 2018
SALES (est): 212.42K **Privately Held**
Web: www.itspicsandprints.com
SIC: 2752 Commercial printing, lithographic

(G-7723)
PROJECT BEAN LLC
Also Called: Water-Jel Technologies
5555 Harrisburg Ind Pk Dr (28075-7407)
PHONE.....................201 438-1598
James Hartnett, *Pr*
Mark Lait, *
▲ **EMP:** 70 **EST:** 1999
SALES (est): 10.29MM
SALES (corp-wide): 16.02MM **Privately Held**
Web: www.safeguardmedical.com
SIC: 3842 5199 First aid, snake bite, and burn kits; First aid supplies
PA: Safeguard Medical Alarms, Inc.
 5555 Harrisburg Ind Pk Dr
 Harrisburg NC 28075
 312 506-2900

(G-7724)
RINKER MATERIALS
2268 Speedrail Dr (28075-0390)
PHONE.....................704 455-1100
EMP: 10 **EST:** 2018
SALES (est): 860.42K **Privately Held**
SIC: 3273 Ready-mixed concrete

(G-7725)
S FOIL INCORPORATED
2283 Nc Highway 49 S (28075)
P.O. Box 296 (28075-0296)
PHONE.....................704 455-5134
Ralph M Torrence, *Pr*
EMP: 18 **EST:** 1947
SQ FT: 10,000
SALES (est): 1.65MM **Privately Held**
Web: www.foilsinc.com
SIC: 5093 3341 Metal scrap and waste materials; Secondary nonferrous metals

(G-7726)
SAFEGUARD MEDICAL ✪
5555 Harrisburg Ind Pk Dr (28075-7407)
PHONE.....................855 428-6074
EMP: 83 **EST:** 2022
SALES (est): 6.78MM **Privately Held**
Web: www.safeguardmedical.com
SIC: 3841 Surgical and medical instruments

(G-7727)
SAFEGUARD MEDICAL ALARMS INC (PA)
5555 Harrisburg Ind Pk Dr (28075-7407)
PHONE.....................312 506-2900
Adam Johnson, *CEO*
EMP: 11 **EST:** 2003
SALES (est): 16.02MM
SALES (corp-wide): 16.02MM **Privately Held**
Web: www.safeguardmedical.com
SIC: 3669 5999 Emergency alarms; Medical apparatus and supplies

(G-7728)
SKI TIME INDUSTRIES INC
6650 Kee Ln (28075-7470)
PHONE.....................704 455-3870
EMP: 5 **EST:** 2007
SALES (est): 120K **Privately Held**
SIC: 3999 Manufacturing industries, nec

(G-7729)
STRAIGHT EDGE WOODWORKS LLC
4800 Annelise Dr (28075-7649)
PHONE.....................704 456-7046
John Miller, *Prin*
EMP: 5 **EST:** 2016
SALES (est): 56.36K **Privately Held**
SIC: 2431 Millwork

(G-7730)
TCU INDUSTRIES INC ✪
5540 Morehead Rd Ste 2 (28075-3926)
PHONE.....................602 369-7270
Curtis Pyle, *CEO*
Cutis Pyle, *CEO*
EMP: 6 **EST:** 2023
SALES (est): 545.08K **Privately Held**
SIC: 2241 Webbing, woven

(G-7731)
THREE WISHES MONOGRAMMING
8200 Blackjack Oak Ct (28075-7612)
PHONE.....................980 298-2981
Anitra Simpson, *Prin*
EMP: 4 **EST:** 2017
SALES (est): 47.02K **Privately Held**
SIC: 2395 Embroidery and art needlework

(G-7732)
US LEGEND CARS INTL INC
Also Called: 600 Racing Service
5245 Nc Highway 49 S (28075-8476)
PHONE.....................704 455-3896
Bill Brooks, *Sec*
◆ **EMP:** 40 **EST:** 1992
SQ FT: 93,000
SALES (est): 5.49MM
SALES (corp-wide): 523.83MM **Privately Held**
Web: www.uslegendcars.com
SIC: 3944 5091 3714 3711 Go-carts, children's; Go-carts; Motor vehicle parts and accessories; Motor vehicles and car bodies
HQ: Speedway Motorsports, Llc
 5555 Concord Pkwy S
 Concord NC 28027

(G-7733)
VENATOR CHEMICALS LLC
Also Called: Mineral Research & Development
5910 Pharr Mill Rd (28075-8625)
P.O. Box 640 (28075-0640)
PHONE.....................704 454-4811
Jona Stein, *Brnch Mgr*
EMP: 100
SQ FT: 93,472
SALES (corp-wide): 2.21B **Privately Held**
Web: www.mrdc.com
SIC: 2819 8731 2899 Industrial inorganic chemicals, nec; Commercial physical research; Chemical preparations, nec
HQ: Venator Chemicals Llc
 10001 Woodloch Forest Dr # 600
 The Woodlands TX 77380
 704 455-4135

(G-7734)
VORTEX BOTTLE SHOP LLC
4469 School House Commons (28075-7558)
PHONE.....................980 258-0827
EMP: 10 **EST:** 2019
SALES (est): 151.21K **Privately Held**
Web: www.vortexbottleshop.com

SIC: 5812 2086 7371 American restaurant; Bottled and canned soft drinks; Computer software development and applications

(G-7735)
WILBERT PLSTIC SVCS ACQSTION L
7301 Caldwell Rd (28075-7413)
PHONE.....................704 455-5191
Tony Colson, *Brnch Mgr*
▲ **EMP:** 21
SALES (corp-wide): 218.2MM **Privately Held**
SIC: 5162 3089 Plastics products, nec; Thermoformed finished plastics products, nec
HQ: Wilbert Plastic Services Acquisition Llc
 1000 Oaks Pkwy
 Belmont NC 28012

(G-7736)
WOBO WALLET LLC
5445 Somerset Ln (28075-8325)
PHONE.....................704 604-6041
Brent Whichel, *Prin*
EMP: 5 **EST:** 2015
SALES (est): 93.71K **Privately Held**
Web: www.wobowallet.com
SIC: 3172 Wallets

Hatteras
Dare County

(G-7737)
JANET W WHITBECK INC
Also Called: Jeffrey's Seafood
57158 Altona Ln (27943)
P.O. Box 515 (27943-0515)
PHONE.....................252 986-2800
EMP: 9 **EST:** 1982
SALES (est): 472.24K **Privately Held**
SIC: 2092 5146 Fresh or frozen packaged fish; Fish and seafoods

Havelock
Craven County

(G-7738)
ABC SIGNS AND GRAPHICS LLC
160 Us Highway 70 W (28532-9506)
PHONE.....................252 652-6620
Dennis Baker, *Dir Opers*
EMP: 4 **EST:** 2015
SALES (est): 384.77K **Privately Held**
Web: www.abcsignsnc.com
SIC: 3993 Electric signs

(G-7739)
ADAMANTIUM AEROSPACE INC
412 Cherry Branch Dr (28532-9758)
PHONE.....................252 444-6265
Gregory T Sabin, *Pr*
EMP: 6 **EST:** 2011
SALES (est): 109.45K **Privately Held**
SIC: 3721 Aircraft

(G-7740)
BARDEN METAL FABRICATION LLC
116 Elizabeth St (28532-2308)
PHONE.....................252 772-5984
Daniel Barden, *Prin*
EMP: 4 **EST:** 2019
SALES (est): 134.82K **Privately Held**
Web: www.bardenmetalfabrication.com
SIC: 3499 Fabricated metal products, nec

(G-7741)
DARREN LEE DEPALO
Also Called: Mdcsat
108 Crocker Rd (28532-2226)
PHONE.....................252 259-4515
Darren Lee Depalo, *Owner*
EMP: 5 **EST:** 2009
SALES (est): 225.43K **Privately Held**
Web: www.mdcustomsigns.com
SIC: 5099 3993 Signs, except electric; Signs and advertising specialties

(G-7742)
EVIDENT FAB LLC
101 Poplar Rd (28532-2720)
PHONE.....................973 294-4507
EMP: 5 **EST:** 2019
SALES (est): 58.57K **Privately Held**
SIC: 7692 Welding repair

(G-7743)
MERCHANTS INC
Also Called: Merchants
174 Us Highway 70 W (28532-9506)
PHONE.....................252 447-2121
Orland Wolford, *Pr*
EMP: 9 **EST:** 1963
SQ FT: 16,000
SALES (est): 960.6K **Privately Held**
SIC: 5531 7534 Automotive tires; Tire recapping

(G-7744)
NORTHROP GRMMAN TCHNCAL SVCS I
4280 6th Ave Cherry Point Air Station (28532)
P.O. Box 2070 (28532-4070)
PHONE.....................252 447-7575
Armand Escobio, *Prin*
EMP: 22
SIC: 3812 Search and navigation equipment
HQ: Northrop Grumman Technical Services, Inc.
 7575 Colshire Dr
 Mc Lean VA 22102
 703 556-1144

(G-7745)
RED BULL DISTRIBUTION CO INC
95 Outer Banks Dr (28532-1603)
PHONE.....................910 500-1566
Jay Hutzler, *Brnch Mgr*
EMP: 15
SALES (corp-wide): 10.06B **Privately Held**
Web: www.redbulldistributioncompany.com
SIC: 2086 Carbonated soft drinks, bottled and canned
HQ: Red Bull Distribution Company, Inc.
 1740 Stewart St
 Santa Monica CA 90404

(G-7746)
ROCCO INC
1415 E Main St (28532-1822)
PHONE.....................252 634-1642
EMP: 4 **EST:** 2018
SALES (est): 93.18K **Privately Held**
SIC: 2099 Food preparations, nec

(G-7747)
SMYRNA READY MIX CONCRETE LLC
417 Miller Blvd (28532-2643)
PHONE.....................252 447-5356
Van Valkenburg, *Manager*
EMP: 8
SALES (corp-wide): 1.05B **Privately Held**
Web: www.argos-us.com

GEOGRAPHIC SECTION

SIC: 3273 Ready-mixed concrete
PA: Smyrna Ready Mix Concrete, Llc
1000 Hollingshead Cir
Murfreesboro TN 37129
615 355-1028

(G-7748)
TANDEMLOC INC
824 Nc Highway 101 Fontana Blvd (28532)
PHONE...................................252 447-7155
EMP: 56 **EST:** 1984
SALES (est): 11.6MM **Privately Held**
Web: www.tandemloc.com
SIC: 3531 Construction machinery

Haw River
Alamance County

(G-7749)
ANDERSEN ENERGY INC
3151 Caroline Dr (27258-9575)
PHONE...................................336 376-0107
H W Andersen, *Prin*
H W Andersen, *Pr*
EMP: 4 **EST:** 1980
SALES (est): 328.44K **Privately Held**
SIC: 3841 Surgical and medical instruments

(G-7750)
ANDERSEN PRODUCTS INC
3202 Caroline Dr (27258-9564)
PHONE...................................336 376-3000
Harold W Andersen, *Pr*
Shirley Andersen, *
▼ **EMP:** 50 **EST:** 1958
SQ FT: 24,000
SALES (est): 8.37MM **Privately Held**
Web: www.anpro.com
SIC: 8731 3841 3842 Commercial research laboratory; Surgical and medical instruments; Surgical appliances and supplies

(G-7751)
ANDERSEN STERILIZERS INC
Also Called: Andersen Products
3202 Caroline Dr (27258-9564)
PHONE...................................336 376-8622
EMP: 45 **EST:** 1995
SALES (est): 8.12MM **Privately Held**
Web: www.anpro.com
SIC: 3841 3842 Surgical and medical instruments; Surgical appliances and supplies

(G-7752)
H W ANDERSEN PRODUCTS INC
3202 Caroline Dr (27258-9564)
PHONE...................................336 376-3000
Harold W Anderson, *Pr*
William K Anderson, *
EMP: 8 **EST:** 1967
SQ FT: 2,646
SALES (est): 208.84K **Privately Held**
Web: www.sterility.com
SIC: 3841 Surgical and medical instruments

(G-7753)
INTERSTATE NARROW FABRICS INC
1101 Porter Ave (27258-9547)
P.O. Box 28 (27253-0028)
PHONE...................................336 578-1037
Tony Vailati, *Pr*
Marie Vailati, *
Anthony H Vailati, *
▲ **EMP:** 90 **EST:** 1985
SALES (est): 9.61MM **Privately Held**
Web: www.interstatenarrowfabrics.com

SIC: 2241 Elastic narrow fabrics, woven or braided

(G-7754)
JOCEPHUS ORIGINALS INC
1003 W Main St Ste A4 (27258-8930)
PHONE...................................336 229-9600
Joe Wade, *Pr*
Joe Wade, *Owner*
EMP: 10 **EST:** 1998
SALES (est): 871.04K **Privately Held**
Web: www.jocephusoriginals.com
SIC: 2384 Bathrobes, men's and women's: made from purchased materials

(G-7755)
NOVAFLEX HOSE INC
449 Trollingwood Rd (27258-8750)
PHONE...................................336 578-2161
Melinda Donnelly, *Pr*
Claire Howard, *
▲ **EMP:** 85 **EST:** 1986
SQ FT: 8,500
SALES (est): 37.92MM
SALES (corp-wide): 49.34MM **Privately Held**
Web: www.novaflex.com
SIC: 5085 3061 Hose, belting, and packing; Mechanical rubber goods
HQ: Z-Flex Realty, Inc.
20 Commerce Park North # 107
Bedford NH 03110

(G-7756)
QUALITY TURF HAULING LLC
325 Chris St (27258)
P.O. Box 848 (27258-0848)
PHONE...................................336 516-1156
EMP: 11 **EST:** 2009
SALES (est): 956.18K **Privately Held**
Web: www.qualityturftrucking.com
SIC: 0782 4212 3713 Turf installation services, except artificial; Dump truck haulage; Dump truck bodies

(G-7757)
SUE-LYNN TEXTILES INC (PA)
Also Called: 21st Century Hosiery
302 Roxboro St (27258-9673)
P.O. Box 939 (27258-0939)
PHONE...................................336 578-0871
Thurman B Oakley, *Pr*
Mary L Oakley, *
Randy Ector, *
Diane Ector, *
EMP: 112 **EST:** 1971
SQ FT: 70,000
SALES (est): 4.05MM
SALES (corp-wide): 4.05MM **Privately Held**
SIC: 2251 5137 Panty hose; Hosiery: women's, children's, and infants'

(G-7758)
UNICHEM IV LTD (PA)
916 W Main St (27258-9661)
P.O. Box 612 (27258-0612)
PHONE...................................336 578-5476
◆ **EMP:** 15 **EST:** 1981
SALES (est): 10.64MM
SALES (corp-wide): 10.64MM **Privately Held**
Web: www.unichem.com
SIC: 2819 Industrial inorganic chemicals, nec

Hayesville
Clay County

(G-7759)
ADVANCED DIGITAL CABLE INC (PA)
Also Called: ADC
94 Eagle Fork Rd (28904-5255)
P.O. Box 305 (30546-0305)
PHONE...................................828 389-1652
Steve Payne, *Pr*
Adam C Payne, *VP*
Mary Payne, *
▲ **EMP:** 49 **EST:** 1997
SQ FT: 105,000
SALES (est): 26.39MM
SALES (corp-wide): 26.39MM **Privately Held**
Web: www.adcable.com
SIC: 3671 Cathode ray tubes, including rebuilt

(G-7760)
APPALACHIAN ARMS INC
45 Davis Loop (28904-7377)
PHONE...................................828 332-1900
EMP: 2 **EST:** 2019
SALES (est): 79.51K **Privately Held**
SIC: 3489 Ordnance and accessories, nec

(G-7761)
CLAY COUNTY FOOD PANTRY INC
2278 Hinton Center Rd (28904-4884)
P.O. Box 853 (28904-0853)
PHONE...................................828 389-1657
Bert Wiley, *Pr*
EMP: 9 **EST:** 2005
SALES (est): 197.73K **Privately Held**
Web: www.claycountyfoodpantry.org
SIC: 8322 2099 5149 Meal delivery program; Ready-to-eat meals, salads, and sandwiches; Dried or canned foods

(G-7762)
COLEMAN CABLE LLC
Intercomp Wire & Cable
788 Tusquittee Rd (28904-7889)
P.O. Box 206 (28904-0206)
PHONE...................................828 389-8013
Lee Ferguson, *Mgr*
EMP: 50
SALES (corp-wide): 1.7B **Privately Held**
Web: www.colemancable.com
SIC: 3496 3678 3643 3357 Cable, uninsulated wire: made from purchased wire ; Electronic connectors; Current-carrying wiring services; Nonferrous wiredrawing and insulating
HQ: Coleman Cable, Llc
1 Overlook Pt Ste 265
Lincolnshire IL 60069
847 672-2300

(G-7763)
COMMUNITY NEWSPAPERS INC
Also Called: Clay County Progress
43 Main St (28904-5808)
P.O. Box 483 (28904-0483)
PHONE...................................828 389-8431
Becky Long, *Prin*
EMP: 9
SALES (corp-wide): 49.22MM **Privately Held**
Web: www.claycountyprogress.com
SIC: 2711 Newspapers, publishing and printing
PA: Community Newspapers, Inc.
2365 Prince Ave A
Athens GA 30606
706 548-0010

Hayesville - Clay County (G-7771)

(G-7764)
CORVAC INC
Also Called: Best Vacuum Cleaners
1654 Myers Chapel Rd (28904-7129)
PHONE...................................772 692-5514
Donna W Cormier, *Prin*
EMP: 7 **EST:** 2019
SALES (est): 241.95K **Privately Held**
Web: www.corvaccomposites.com
SIC: 3714 Motor vehicle parts and accessories

(G-7765)
CUTWORM SPECIALTIES INC
62 Church St (28904-7769)
P.O. Box 648 (28904-0648)
PHONE...................................828 389-1999
Jeb Greenstone, *Owner*
EMP: 9 **EST:** 2012
SALES (est): 168.49K **Privately Held**
Web: www.cutwormspecialties.com
SIC: 3441 Fabricated structural metal

(G-7766)
GOLDEN RCTANGLE ENTEPRISES INC
2966 Nc 69 (28904-7256)
P.O. Box 34 (28904-0034)
PHONE...................................828 389-3336
Cathy Jones, *Genl Mgr*
EMP: 4 **EST:** 2005
SALES (est): 166.93K **Privately Held**
SIC: 2512 Upholstered household furniture

(G-7767)
JUST STITCHIN QUILTS LLC
321 Hwy 64 W (28904-7071)
PHONE...................................828 644-3368
EMP: 5 **EST:** 2019
SALES (est): 245.77K **Privately Held**
Web: www.just-stitchin.com
SIC: 2395 Quilted fabrics or cloth

(G-7768)
LIDSEEN NORTH CAROLINA INC
6382 Old Hwy 64 W (28904)
PHONE...................................828 389-8082
Melvin Swanson, *Pr*
Edwin James, *Treas*
Mitchell Swanson, *VP*
Merinda Woody, *Sec*
EMP: 9 **EST:** 1901
SQ FT: 24,000
SALES (est): 452.43K **Privately Held**
Web: www.chicagopipebender.com
SIC: 3423 3469 Hand and edge tools, nec; Metal stampings, nec

(G-7769)
MORGAN & SON LOGGING
111 Sally Gap Trl (28904-5234)
P.O. Box 192 (28788-0192)
PHONE...................................828 389-9618
EMP: 4 **EST:** 2008
SALES (est): 73.87K **Privately Held**
SIC: 2411 Logging

(G-7770)
PRINTS PLUS
1124 Nc 69 Ste 105 (28904-7876)
PHONE...................................828 389-7190
Robert Seibert, *Prin*
EMP: 5 **EST:** 2017
SALES (est): 116.36K **Privately Held**
SIC: 2752 Commercial printing, lithographic

(G-7771)
SENTINEL NEWSPAPERS (PA)
Also Called: Union Sentinel
23 Riverwalk Cir (28904-7949)

PHONE..................828 389-8338
Frank Bradley, *Owner*
EMP: 16 **EST:** 1987
SQ FT: 3,000
SALES (est): 753.17K **Privately Held**
SIC: 2711 Newspapers: publishing only, not printed on site

(G-7772)
T SHIRT MORE
96 Sanderson St (28904-7371)
P.O. Box 296 (28904-0296)
PHONE..................828 389-3200
Monya Seibert, *Ofcr*
EMP: 5 **EST:** 2018
SALES (est): 78.34K **Privately Held**
SIC: 2759 Screen printing

Hays
Wilkes County

(G-7773)
C & L MANUFACTURING
1519 Oak Ridge Church Rd (28635)
P.O. Box 250 (28635-0250)
PHONE..................336 957-8359
Charles Farrington, *Owner*
EMP: 5 **EST:** 1976
SQ FT: 3,568
SALES (est): 231.78K **Privately Held**
SIC: 2253 Collar and cuff sets, knit

Henderson
Vance County

(G-7774)
A R PERRY CORPORATION
Also Called: Perry Glass Co
220 Old Epsom Rd (27536-5342)
P.O. Box 206 (27536-0206)
PHONE..................252 492-6181
Richard A Davis Iii, *Pr*
Richard A Davis Iv, *VP*
EMP: 12 **EST:** 1920
SQ FT: 25,000
SALES (est): 457.29K **Privately Held**
Web: www.arperryglass.com
SIC: 1793 7536 5085 3442 Glass and glazing work; Automotive glass replacement shops; Welding supplies; Metal doors, sash, and trim

(G-7775)
AIR CONTROL INC
237 Raleigh Rd (27536-4977)
P.O. Box 1738 (27536-1738)
PHONE..................252 492-2300
EMP: 25 **EST:** 1961
SALES (est): 3.57MM **Privately Held**
Web: www.aircontrol-inc.com
SIC: 3564 3821 3674 3561 Air purification equipment; Laboratory apparatus and furniture; Semiconductors and related devices; Pumps and pumping equipment

(G-7776)
CAROLINA COPACKING LLC
860 Commerce Dr (27537-7450)
PHONE..................252 433-0130
Sherri Matthews, *Off Mgr*
EMP: 22 **EST:** 2017
SQ FT: 80,000
SALES (est): 2.67MM **Privately Held**
Web: www.carolinacopacking.com
SIC: 3221 Bottles for packing, bottling, and canning: glass

(G-7777)
CAROLINA GIANT TIRES INC
389 Americal Rd (27537-3381)
P.O. Box 872 (27522-0872)
PHONE..................919 609-9077
Shawn Reaves, *Pr*
EMP: 13 **EST:** 2014
SQ FT: 6,400
SALES (est): 1.02MM **Privately Held**
Web: www.carolinagianttirellc.com
SIC: 7534 3011 Tire retreading and repair shops; Tires and inner tubes

(G-7778)
CAROLINA WOODWORKS TRIM OF NC
625 Parham Rd (27536-2624)
PHONE..................252 492-9259
Bill Atkinson, *Owner*
EMP: 8 **EST:** 2006
SALES (est): 203.79K **Privately Held**
SIC: 2431 Millwork

(G-7779)
COMMERCIAL SEAMING CO INC
501 Walnut St (27536)
P.O. Box 39 (27536-0039)
PHONE..................252 492-6178
Doug Capps, *Pr*
Faye Capps, *
◆ **EMP:** 13 **EST:** 1979
SQ FT: 43,000
SALES (est): 452.65K **Privately Held**
Web: www.commercialseaming.com
SIC: 2262 Finishing plants, manmade

(G-7780)
D C THOMAS GROUP INC
Also Called: Carolina Co Packaging LLC
860 Commerce Dr (27537-7450)
PHONE..................252 433-0132
Dwight C Thomas Senior, *Pr*
EMP: 30
Web: www.thomasgourmetfoods.net
SIC: 2035 Pickles, sauces, and salad dressings
PA: D. C. Thomas Group, Inc.
6540 W Market St
Greensboro NC 27409

(G-7781)
E T C OF HENDERSON N C INC (PA)
601 Wakefield Ave (27536-3153)
P.O. Box 948 (27536-0948)
PHONE..................252 492-4033
◆ **EMP:** 7 **EST:** 1978
SALES (est): 430.41K
SALES (corp-wide): 430.41K **Privately Held**
SIC: 2392 3291 Mops, floor and dust; Pads, scouring: soap impregnated

(G-7782)
EDWARDS UNLIMITED INC
Also Called: Metal Fabrication
3355 Raleigh Rd (27537-7461)
PHONE..................252 226-4583
Boyd C Edwards Iv, *Pr*
EMP: 9 **EST:** 2005
SALES (est): 1.18MM **Privately Held**
Web: www.edwardsunlimitednc.com
SIC: 3441 3599 Fabricated structural metal; Machine and other job shop work

(G-7783)
FLORIDA MARINE TANKS INC (HQ)
Also Called: Fmt
120 Peter Gill Rd (27537-4297)
PHONE..................305 620-9030
Rose Marie Fiori, *Pr*
Vince G Di Rosa, *VP*
Jennie Di Rosa, *VP*
James A Pearson, *Prin*
Steven A Lurus, *Prin*
◆ **EMP:** 12 **EST:** 1974
SQ FT: 54,000
SALES (est): 12.69MM
SALES (corp-wide): 3.47B **Publicly Held**
Web: www.floridamarinetanks.com
SIC: 3443 3231 Tanks, standard or custom fabricated: metal plate; Windshields, glass: made from purchased glass
PA: Patrick Industries, Inc.
107 W Franklin St
Elkhart IN 46516
574 294-7511

(G-7784)
FLOWERS BKG CO JAMESTOWN LLC
Also Called: FLOWERS BAKING CO. OF JAMESTOWN, LLC
875 S Beckford Dr (27536-5910)
PHONE..................252 492-1519
Johnny Moodiham, *Mgr*
EMP: 6
SALES (corp-wide): 5.09B **Publicly Held**
Web: www.flowersfoods.com
SIC: 2051 Bread, cake, and related products
HQ: Flowers Baking Co. Of Newton, Llc
801 W Main St
Jamestown NC 27282
336 841-8840

(G-7785)
GREYSTONE CONCRETE PDTS INC
2100 Us 1/158 Hwy (27537-8265)
P.O. Box 680 (27536-0680)
PHONE..................252 438-5144
John F Cannady Iii, *Pr*
Samuel Cannady, *
Ernestine C Cannady, *
John F Cannady Iv, *Ex VP*
Susan Martin, *Stockholder*
EMP: 27 **EST:** 1946
SQ FT: 3,000
SALES (est): 7.06MM **Privately Held**
Web: www.greystoneconcreteproducts.com
SIC: 3271 3273 3272 Blocks, concrete or cinder: standard; Ready-mixed concrete; Building materials, except block or brick: concrete

(G-7786)
HENDERSON NEWSPAPERS INC
Also Called: Daily Dispatch
420 S Garnett St (27536-4540)
PHONE..................252 436-2700
J Edward Publisher, *Prin*
Rick Bean, *Pr*
James Edwards, *Publisher*
EMP: 66 **EST:** 1994
SALES (est): 2.68MM
SALES (corp-wide): 243.17MM **Privately Held**
Web: www.hendersondispatch.com
SIC: 2711 Newspapers, publishing and printing
PA: Paxton Media Group, Llc
100 Television Ln
Paducah KY 42003
270 575-8630

(G-7787)
HIGH AND HIGH INC
268 Country Club Dr (27536-4711)
P.O. Box 201 (27586-0201)
PHONE..................252 257-2390
Robert High, *Pr*
EMP: 18

SALES (corp-wide): 2.3MM **Privately Held**
SIC: 2421 Sawmills and planing mills, general
PA: High And High Inc
2843 Triplet Rd
Lawrenceville VA
434 577-2372

(G-7788)
HOLLAND SUPPLY COMPANY
Also Called: Holland Industrial
518 W Montgomery St (27536-3318)
P.O. Box 987 (27536-0987)
PHONE..................252 492-7541
EMP: 35 **EST:** 1946
SALES (est): 12.76MM **Privately Held**
Web: www.hollandindustrial.com
SIC: 5085 5063 7694 Industrial supplies; Motors, electric; Rebuilding motors, except automotive

(G-7789)
IDAHO TIMBER NC LLC (HQ)
1431 Nicholas St (27536-5330)
P.O. Box 847 (27536-0847)
PHONE..................252 430-0030
EMP: 60 **EST:** 1998
SALES (est): 20.88MM
SALES (corp-wide): 308.2MM **Privately Held**
Web: www.idahotimber.com
SIC: 2421 5031 2439 Lumber: rough, sawed, or planed; Lumber: rough, dressed, and finished; Structural wood members, nec
PA: Hampton Investment Company
9600 Sw Barnes Rd Ste 200
Portland OR 97225
503 297-7691

(G-7790)
J & J LOGGING INC
255 J P Taylor Rd (27537-4290)
P.O. Box 785 (27536-0785)
PHONE..................252 430-1110
Joe Ross, *Pr*
EMP: 33 **EST:** 1976
SQ FT: 800
SALES (est): 2.25MM **Privately Held**
SIC: 2411 Logging camps and contractors

(G-7791)
KENNAMETAL INC
139 Warehouse Rd (27537-4214)
P.O. Box 159 (27536-0159)
PHONE..................252 492-4163
John V Lazar, *Mgr*
EMP: 76
SALES (corp-wide): 2.08B **Publicly Held**
Web: www.kennametal.com
SIC: 3545 Machine tool accessories
PA: Kennametal Inc.
525 William Penn Pl # 3300
Pittsburgh PA 15219
412 248-8000

(G-7792)
KERR LAKE CORNHOLE & PRINTING
335 N Chestnut St (27536-4217)
PHONE..................252 430-7144
▲ **EMP:** 4 **EST:** 2014
SALES (est): 81.43K **Privately Held**
SIC: 2759 Screen printing

(G-7793)
LAKE COUNTRY ALPACAS
1256 Twnsville Landing Rd (27537-6728)
P.O. Box 160 (27584-0160)
PHONE..................252 430-0963
EMP: 4 **EST:** 2017
SALES (est): 83.82K **Privately Held**

GEOGRAPHIC SECTION

Hendersonville - Henderson County (G-7819)

SIC: 2231 Alpacas, mohair: woven

(G-7794)
LEGACY VULCAN LLC
Mideast Division
696 Greystone Rd (27537-5513)
P.O. Box 470 (27536-0470)
PHONE......................252 438-3161
Billy Stevenson, Mgr
EMP: 4
Web: www.vulcanmaterials.com
SIC: 3273 Ready-mixed concrete
HQ: Legacy Vulcan, Llc
    1200 Urban Center Dr
    Vestavia AL 35242
    205 298-3000

(G-7795)
LIVING WATER FILTER CO INC
123 Horner St (27536-4126)
P.O. Box 58 (27536-0058)
PHONE......................252 438-6600
EMP: 4 EST: 2018
SALES (est): 58.3K Privately Held
SIC: 3589 Water treatment equipment, industrial

(G-7796)
LUMENFOCUS LLC
Also Called: Lumenfocus
880 Facet Rd (27537-5412)
PHONE......................252 430-6970
EMP: 10 EST: 2016
SQ FT: 90,000
SALES (est): 1.48MM Privately Held
Web: www.lumenfocus.com
SIC: 3646 Commercial lighting fixtures

(G-7797)
MARKHAM WOODWORKS LLC
82 Epsom Rocky Ford Rd (27537-9119)
PHONE......................252 492-5823
James Markham, Prin
EMP: 5 EST: 2012
SALES (est): 66.87K Privately Held
SIC: 2431 Millwork

(G-7798)
MARS PETCARE US INC
Also Called: IAMS
845 Commerce Dr (27537-7450)
PHONE......................252 438-1600
Pickson Pratt, Mgr
EMP: 84
SALES (corp-wide): 42.84B Privately Held
Web: www.marspetcare.com
SIC: 2047 Dog food
HQ: Mars Petcare Us, Inc.
    2013 Ovation Pkwy
    Franklin TN 37067
    615 807-4626

(G-7799)
NUNNERY-FREEMAN INC
Also Called: Nunnery-Freeman Mfg Co
2117 Coleman Pl (27536-3839)
P.O. Box 332 (27536-0332)
PHONE......................252 438-3149
Gary Freeman, Pr
Ann Freeman, Sec
EMP: 10 EST: 1949
SQ FT: 6,000
SALES (est): 426.29K Privately Held
SIC: 3589 5812 Cooking equipment, commercial; Barbecue restaurant

(G-7800)
OPTIMUM LIGHTING LLC
Also Called: Optimum Lighting
880 Facet Rd (27537-5412)
PHONE......................508 646-3324
EMP: 40
Web: www.signify.com
SIC: 3646 Fluorescent lighting fixtures, commercial

(G-7801)
PACIFIC COAST FEATHER LLC
Also Called: Southern Quilters
100 Comfort Dr (27537-5933)
PHONE......................252 492-0051
Richard Aldrich, Brnch Mgr
EMP: 4
SALES (corp-wide): 99.44MM Privately Held
Web: www.pacificcoast.com
SIC: 2392 2395 Bedspreads and bed sets: made from purchased materials; Pleating and stitching
PA: Pacific Coast Feather, Llc
    901 W Yamato Rd Ste 250
    Boca Raton FL 33431
    206 624-1057

(G-7802)
PITTMANBAC
1079 Eaves Rd (27537-9157)
PHONE......................252 430-4745
Ronald Pittman, Owner
EMP: 5 EST: 2010
SALES (est): 202.6K Privately Held
SIC: 3531 Backhoes

(G-7803)
PROFILFORM US INC
101 Eastern Minerals Rd (27537-4288)
PHONE......................252 430-0392
Thilo Hessler, Pr
Friedrizh Hessler, *
▲ EMP: 40 EST: 1998
SQ FT: 24,000
SALES (est): 8.18MM Privately Held
Web: www.versatrim.com
SIC: 2431 Moldings, wood: unfinished and prefinished

(G-7804)
QUALITY INSULATION COMPANY
132 Carey Chapel Rd (27537-8473)
P.O. Box 866 (27536-0866)
PHONE......................252 438-3711
Judith S Riley, Owner
EMP: 4 EST: 1983
SALES (est): 340.51K Privately Held
SIC: 2493 Insulation board, cellular fiber

(G-7805)
QUALITY INVESTMENTS INC
Also Called: V I P
1902 N Garnett St (27536-2723)
P.O. Box 1528 (27536-1528)
PHONE......................252 492-8777
Phillip White, Pr
EMP: 50 EST: 1972
SQ FT: 1,380
SALES (est): 4.45MM Privately Held
SIC: 5531 7534 7538 5521 Automotive tires; Tire repair shop; General automotive repair shops; Automobiles, used cars only

(G-7806)
RALEIGH ROAD BOX CORPORATION
Rr 9 Box 403 (27536)
PHONE......................252 438-7401
Charlie M Smith, Pr
Mary Smith, Sec
Ronnie Smith, VP
EMP: 6 EST: 1975
SALES (est): 427.07K Privately Held
SIC: 4212 2449 Lumber (log) trucking, local; Casks, wood: coopered

(G-7807)
ROBCO MANUFACTURING INC
Also Called: Alumadock Marine Structure
651 Bearpond Rd (27537-9616)
P.O. Box 2600 (27536-6600)
PHONE......................252 438-7399
M Thomas Roberson, Pr
Annette C Roberson, *
Michael T Roberson Junior, VP Sls
▲ EMP: 30 EST: 1983
SQ FT: 35,000
SALES (est): 8.55MM Privately Held
Web: www.alumadock.com
SIC: 3448 Docks, prefabricated metal

(G-7808)
ROY BRIDGMOHAN
596 Industry Dr (27537-8795)
PHONE......................804 426-9652
Roy Bridgmohan, Owner
EMP: 7 EST: 2001
SALES (est): 128.34K Privately Held
SIC: 3812 Search and navigation equipment

(G-7809)
SANFORD S ATV REPAIR LLC
887 Weldon Rd (27537-9152)
PHONE......................252 438-2730
Freddy Sanford, Owner
EMP: 4 EST: 1995
SALES (est): 250.48K Privately Held
SIC: 3799 All terrain vehicles (ATV)

(G-7810)
SCREEN MASTER
904 Buckhorn St (27536-3004)
PHONE......................252 492-8407
Eugene Watkins, Pt
Lorraine Watkins, Pt
EMP: 6 EST: 1976
SALES (est): 511.7K Privately Held
Web: www.screenmasterofhenderson.com
SIC: 5941 5699 2261 5999 Sporting goods and bicycle shops; T-shirts, custom printed; Screen printing of cotton broadwoven fabrics; Trophies and plaques

(G-7811)
SOUTHEASTERN MINERALS INC
Also Called: SOUTHEASTERN MINERALS, INC.
170 Eastern Minerals Rd (27537-4288)
P.O. Box 226 (27536-0226)
PHONE......................252 492-0831
Charles Gordon, Mgr
EMP: 22
SALES (corp-wide): 23MM Privately Held
Web: www.seminerals.com
SIC: 2048 3295 2879 Prepared feeds, nec; Minerals, ground or treated; Agricultural chemicals, nec
PA: Eastern Minerals, Inc.
    1100 Dothan Rd
    Bainbridge GA 39817
    229 246-3396

(G-7812)
T T BECKHAM BACKHOE SERVICE
1870 N Lynnbank Rd (27537-7335)
PHONE......................252 438-7620
T Beckham, Prin
EMP: 5 EST: 2008
SALES (est): 149.53K Privately Held
SIC: 3531 Backhoes

(G-7813)
TARHEEL WOODCRAFTERS INC
1570 Hicksboro Rd (27537-7762)
PHONE......................252 432-3035

John D Edwards, Pr
EMP: 5 EST: 1998
SALES (est): 337.43K Privately Held
SIC: 2434 Wood kitchen cabinets

(G-7814)
TIMBERLINE ACQUISITION LLC
Also Called: Timberline
235 Warehouse Rd (27537-4229)
P.O. Box 1457 (27537-1457)
PHONE......................252 492-6144
EMP: 25 EST: 1973
SQ FT: 90,000
SALES (est): 2.38MM Privately Held
Web: www.timberlinellc.com
SIC: 2448 2441 Pallets, wood; Nailed wood boxes and shook

(G-7815)
VENABLE
563 Thomas Rd (27537-8392)
PHONE......................252 430-6208
Carolyn Venable, Prin
EMP: 5 EST: 2010
SALES (est): 82.05K Privately Held
Web: www.venableinstruments.com
SIC: 3825 Instruments to measure electricity

(G-7816)
VESCOM AMERICA INC
2289 Ross Mill Rd (27537-5966)
P.O. Box 1698 (27536-1698)
PHONE......................252 431-6200
Joe Berasi, Pr
▲ EMP: 20 EST: 1969
SQ FT: 50,000
SALES (est): 5.15MM Privately Held
Web: www.vescom.com
SIC: 2295 Coated fabrics, not rubberized

Hendersonville
Henderson County

(G-7817)
ALLEGRA MARKETING PRINT MAIL
348 7th Ave E (28792-3706)
PHONE......................828 698-7622
EMP: 5 EST: 2016
SALES (est): 101.53K Privately Held
Web: www.allegramarketingprint.com
SIC: 2752 Offset printing

(G-7818)
AMERICAN PRIDE INC
135 Sugarloaf Rd (28792-9326)
PHONE......................828 697-8847
Joe Bright, Genl Mgr
Joe Bright, Genl Mgr
▲ EMP: 22 EST: 1984
SQ FT: 17,500
SALES (est): 2.7MM
SALES (corp-wide): 6.08MM Privately Held
Web: www.apcabinets.com
SIC: 2393 Textile bags
HQ: Zwd Products Corporation
    400 Lukens Dr
    Historic New Castle DE 19720
    302 326-8200

(G-7819)
ANDREANI USA INC ✪
137 E Central St (28792-0330)
PHONE......................828 435-0125
EMP: 6 EST: 2022
SALES (est): 80.44K Privately Held
SIC: 3714 Motor vehicle parts and accessories

Hendersonville - Henderson County (G-7820)

(G-7820)
APPLE VALLEY CABIN LLC
1609 Kanuga Rd (28739-6839)
PHONE..................828 513-1911
EMP: 4 EST: 2019
SALES (est): 93.15K **Privately Held**
SIC: 3571 Personal computers (microcomputers)

(G-7821)
ARROWOOD MECHANICAL DESIGN LLC
Also Called: Arrowood 3d Printing
104 Arrowood Ln (28791-8714)
PHONE..................828 989-1605
EMP: 5 EST: 2014
SALES (est): 210.45K **Privately Held**
Web: www.arrowood3d.com
SIC: 3545 Angle rings

(G-7822)
AVANTI COATINGS INC
26 P E M Dr (28792-8847)
PHONE..................908 723-4596
EMP: 8 EST: 2017
SALES (est): 340.74K **Privately Held**
Web: www.avanticoating.com
SIC: 2891 Adhesives

(G-7823)
BARRY CALLEBAUT USA LLC
Also Called: Mona Lisa Foods
51 Saint Pauls Rd (28792-1625)
PHONE..................828 685-2443
Peter Thom, *Mgr*
EMP: 63
Web: www.barry-callebaut.com
SIC: 2066 Chocolate
HQ: Barry Callebaut U.S.A. Llc
600 W Chicago Ave Ste 860
Chicago IL 60654

(G-7824)
BAY BREEZE SEAFOOD REST INC
Also Called: Bay Breeze Seafood
1830 Asheville Hwy (28791-2310)
PHONE..................828 697-7106
Bill Katsadouros, *CEO*
Jimmy Katsadouros, *Prin*
EMP: 22 EST: 2010
SALES (est): 7.84MM **Privately Held**
Web: www.baybreezeseafood.com
SIC: 5146 2091 Fish and seafoods; Canned and cured fish and seafoods

(G-7825)
BLOSSOM COTTON PRESS LLC
100 Springhead Trl (28739-5573)
PHONE..................828 407-0467
Macon York, *Admn*
EMP: 5 EST: 2016
SALES (est): 41.83K **Privately Held**
Web: www.maconyorkcustom.com
SIC: 2741 Miscellaneous publishing

(G-7826)
BLUE RIDGE JAMS
75 Lytle Rd (28792-6475)
P.O. Box 6 (28724-0006)
PHONE..................828 685-1783
Steve Pridmore, *Owner*
EMP: 5 EST: 1961
SALES (est): 249.22K **Privately Held**
Web: www.blueridgejam.com
SIC: 5499 2033 Gourmet food stores; Canned fruits and specialties

(G-7827)
BLUE RIDGE PLATING COMPANY
127 Foxwood Dr (28791-8504)
PHONE..................828 274-1795
Carolyn Benfield, *Pr*
Ken Schmidt, *Genl Mgr*
EMP: 4 EST: 1967
SQ FT: 10,000
SALES (est): 316.29K **Privately Held**
SIC: 3471 Electroplating of metals or formed products

(G-7828)
BOLD LIFE PUBLICATION
105 S Main St Ste A (28792-5028)
PHONE..................828 692-3230
Mary Diorio, *Owner*
EMP: 7 EST: 2008
SALES (est): 343.49K **Privately Held**
Web: www.boldlife.com
SIC: 2741 Miscellaneous publishing

(G-7829)
BON WORTH INC (PA)
Also Called: Bon Worth Factory Outlets
219 Commercial Hill Dr (28792-7089)
P.O. Box 2890 (28793-2890)
PHONE..................800 355-5131
Gurusankar Gurumoorthy, *COO*
Nick Dmytryszyn, *Prin*
▲ EMP: 25 EST: 1971
SALES (est): 45.79MM
SALES (corp-wide): 45.79MM **Privately Held**
Web: www.bonworth.com
SIC: 2331 2339 2335 2337 Blouses, women's and juniors': made from purchased material; Slacks: women's, misses', and juniors'; Dresses,paper, cut and sewn; Skirts, separate: women's, misses', and juniors'

(G-7830)
BURNTSHIRT VINEYARDS LLC
3737 Howard Gap Rd (28792-3174)
PHONE..................828 685-2402
Oates Lemuel, *Prin*
EMP: 15 EST: 2013
SALES (est): 1.21MM **Privately Held**
Web: www.burntshirtvineyards.com
SIC: 2084 Wines

(G-7831)
BYERS PRCISION FABRICATORS INC
675 Dana Rd (28792-3005)
P.O. Box 5127 (28793-5127)
PHONE..................828 693-4088
Roger Byers, *CEO*
Shirley Byers, *
Charlene Case, *
▲ EMP: 28 EST: 1943
SQ FT: 60,000
SALES (est): 9.69MM **Privately Held**
Web: www.byersprecision.com
SIC: 3444 Sheet metal specialties, not stamped

(G-7832)
CANIS LUPUS ENTERPRISES LLC
220 S Rugby Rd (28791-8453)
PHONE..................828 450-2074
EMP: 4 EST: 2016
SALES (est): 114.17K **Privately Held**
SIC: 3482 Small arms ammunition

(G-7833)
CARBO-CUT INC
3937 Chimney Rock Rd (28792-9385)
P.O. Box 674 (28793-0674)
PHONE..................828 685-7890
Ludwik Bochynek, *Pr*
William Synder, *VP*
EMP: 6 EST: 1992
SQ FT: 2,500
SALES (est): 530.64K **Privately Held**
SIC: 3545 Machine tool accessories

(G-7834)
CAROLINA BLIND OUTLET INC (PA)
225 Duncan Hill Rd (28792-2714)
PHONE..................828 697-8525
Joel Wayne Patterson Ii, *Pr*
Tony Edward Goodwin, *VP*
EMP: 4 EST: 1992
SQ FT: 1,870
SALES (est): 873.83K **Privately Held**
Web: www.carolinablinds.com
SIC: 5719 2591 Window furnishings; Blinds vertical

(G-7835)
CAROLINA HOME GARDEN
Also Called: Verve
105 S Main St (28792-5022)
PHONE..................828 692-3230
EMP: 5 EST: 2010
SALES (est): 135.46K **Privately Held**
Web: www.carolinahomegarden.com
SIC: 2721 Magazines: publishing only, not printed on site

(G-7836)
CHIMNEYROCK STORAGE
175 Fascination Dr (28792-7542)
PHONE..................828 685-2893
Jarrett D Mitchem, *Prin*
EMP: 6 EST: 2008
SALES (est): 153.09K **Privately Held**
Web: www.chimneyrockstorage.com
SIC: 3715 7513 Truck trailers; Truck rental and leasing, no drivers

(G-7837)
CJT MACHINE INC
Also Called: Cjt Machine
1172 Terrys Gap Rd (28792-0236)
PHONE..................828 376-3693
Christopher Hare, *Pr*
EMP: 5 EST: 2013
SALES (est): 454.61K **Privately Held**
Web: www.cjtmachine.com
SIC: 3599 Machine shop, jobbing and repair

(G-7838)
CLEMENT PAPPAS NC LLC
125 Industrial Park Rd (28792-9012)
PHONE..................856 455-1000
Mark Mcneil, *Pr*
Caroline Lemoine, *Sec*
Glenn Mckellar, *Treas*
EMP: 5
SALES (est): 123.72K **Privately Held**
SIC: 2033 Fruit juices: packaged in cans, jars, etc.

(G-7839)
CONTINENTAL TOOL WORKS INC
690 Shepherd St (28792-6470)
PHONE..................828 692-2578
EMP: 8 EST: 1992
SQ FT: 10,000
SALES (est): 868.04K **Privately Held**
SIC: 3544 Special dies and tools

(G-7840)
COPY WORKS
348 7th Ave E (28792-3706)
PHONE..................828 698-7622
Don Bowman, *Ex Dir*
EMP: 4 EST: 2008
SALES (est): 238.99K **Privately Held**
Web: www.copy-works.net
SIC: 2752 Offset printing

(G-7841)
CRAWFORDS FORGE
4160 Sugarloaf Rd (28792-8832)
PHONE..................828 280-2555
Randy Crawford, *Prin*
EMP: 6 EST: 2015
SALES (est): 60.6K **Privately Held**
Web: www.crawfordsforge.com
SIC: 7692 Welding repair

(G-7842)
DAMPP-CHASER ELECTRONICS CORP
Also Called: Dampp-Chaser
1410 Spartanburg Hwy (28792-6445)
P.O. Box 1610 (28793-1610)
PHONE..................828 692-8271
Gayle Mair, *Pr*
Roger Wheelock, *
▲ EMP: 25 EST: 1947
SQ FT: 6,000
SALES (est): 4.46MM **Privately Held**
Web: www.pianolifesaver.com
SIC: 3634 3822 Dehumidifiers, electric: room ; Humidistats: wall, duct, and skeleton

(G-7843)
DANA FANCY FOODS
101 Lytle Rd (28792-6476)
P.O. Box 192 (28724-0192)
PHONE..................828 685-2937
Robert Morris, *Owner*
EMP: 6 EST: 2012
SALES (est): 170K **Privately Held**
SIC: 2035 Pickles, vinegar

(G-7844)
DIGITAL AUDIO CORPORATION
Also Called: Salient Sciences
116 Brightwater Heights Dr (28791-9705)
PHONE..................919 572-6767
Donald Tunstall, *Pr*
Donald E Tunstall, *Pr*
Jason Williams, *VP*
Kelly K Smith, *Sec*
Peter Salas, *Ex Dir*
EMP: 10 EST: 1979
SALES (est): 1.7MM **Privately Held**
Web: www.salientsciences.com
SIC: 3571 7372 Electronic computers; Prepackaged software
PA: Dolphin Equity Partners, Lp
4924 Frst Cast Hwy Ste 12
Fernandina Beach FL 32034

(G-7845)
DISPLAY YOUR GRAPHICS LLC
140 Jaymar Park Dr (28792-7300)
PHONE..................828 489-2282
Kenneth Cowart, *CEO*
EMP: 6 EST: 2019
SALES (est): 231.8K **Privately Held**
Web: www.mydyg.com
SIC: 3993 Signs and advertising specialties

(G-7846)
EDDIE S MOUNTAIN MACHINE INC
Also Called: Mountain Machine
2011 Pilot Mountain Rd (28792-8806)
P.O. Box 331 (28727-0331)
PHONE..................828 685-0733
Eddie Merrell, *Pr*
Brian Merrell, *VP*
EMP: 4 EST: 1985
SALES (est): 305.96K **Privately Held**

GEOGRAPHIC SECTION

Hendersonville - Henderson County (G-7873)

SIC: 3599 Machine shop, jobbing and repair

(G-7847)
FIBERGLASS FABRICATION INC
14 Twin Willow Dr (28792-9709)
P.O. Box 339 (28727-0339)
PHONE..................828 685-0940
Tom Foie, *Owner*
EMP: 9 EST: 1982
SALES (est): 237.03K **Privately Held**
Web: www.fiberglassfabricationinc.com
SIC: 3089 3732 3443 3088 Plastics products, nec; Boatbuilding and repairing; Fabricated plate work (boiler shop); Plastics plumbing fixtures

(G-7848)
FIMIA INC
201 Arbutus Ln (28739-3903)
PHONE..................828 697-8447
John Brookshire, *Pr*
Betty Kay Brookshire, *VP*
EMP: 4 EST: 1990
SALES (est): 341.98K **Privately Held**
SIC: 2299 Broadwoven fabrics: linen, jute, hemp, and ramie

(G-7849)
FINELY FINISHED WDWKG LLC
662 Holiday Dr (28739-7353)
PHONE..................828 553-9549
Matthew D Dbelanger, *Pr*
EMP: 6 EST: 2008
SALES (est): 220.31K **Privately Held**
Web: www.finelyfinishedwoodworking.com
SIC: 2431 Millwork

(G-7850)
FLAME-TEC LLC
136 Hillview Blvd (28792-5333)
PHONE..................844 352-6383
EMP: 12 EST: 2016
SALES (est): 1.09MM **Privately Held**
Web: www.flame-tec.com
SIC: 3822 Air flow controllers, air conditioning and refrigeration

(G-7851)
FLANAGAN PRINTING COMPANY INC
127 3rd Ave W (28792-4313)
P.O. Box 1613 (28793-1613)
PHONE..................828 693-7380
Dennis Brooks, *Pr*
EMP: 4 EST: 1931
SQ FT: 3,750
SALES (est): 290.42K **Privately Held**
Web: www.flanaganprinting.com
SIC: 2752 Offset printing

(G-7852)
FLAT ROCK TOOL & MOLD INC
690 Shepherd St (28792-6470)
PHONE..................828 692-2578
Lewis Kuykendall, *Pr*
Anthony R Corn, *Sec*
EMP: 8 EST: 2010
SALES (est): 937.15K **Privately Held**
Web: www.flatrocktoolandmold.com
SIC: 3544 Special dies and tools

(G-7853)
FOGLE COMPUTING CORPORATION
131 Camellia Way (28739-9306)
P.O. Box 1045 (28793-1045)
PHONE..................828 697-9080
John B Fogle, *CEO*
Carolyn Fogle, *VP*
EMP: 7 EST: 1981
SALES (est): 700.25K **Privately Held**
Web: www.foglecomputing.com
SIC: 7372 Application computer software

(G-7854)
GALDE PRESS INC
110 Lloyd Barnwell Rd (28792-8897)
PHONE..................612 965-5515
EMP: 5 EST: 2017
SALES (est): 84.84K **Privately Held**
Web: www.galdepress.com
SIC: 2741 Miscellaneous publishing

(G-7855)
GARYS GARAGE
36 P E M Dr (28792-8847)
PHONE..................828 513-5055
EMP: 4 EST: 2019
SALES (est): 91.06K **Privately Held**
SIC: 3751 Motorcycles, bicycles and parts

(G-7856)
GOLDSMITH BY RUDI LTD
434 N Main St (28792-4901)
PHONE..................828 693-1030
Rudolf H Haug, *Pr*
Yvonne Hill, *Adm/Dir*
EMP: 8 EST: 1975
SALES (est): 483.36K **Privately Held**
Web: www.thegoldsmithbyrudi.com
SIC: 3911 Jewelry, precious metal

(G-7857)
HALIFAX MEDIA HOLDINGS LLC
1717 Four Seasons Blvd (28792-2859)
PHONE..................828 692-5763
EMP: 4
SALES (corp-wide): 295.49MM **Privately Held**
Web: www.news-journalonline.com
SIC: 2711 Commercial printing and newspaper publishing combined
PA: Halifax Media Holdings, Llc
    901 6th St
    Daytona Beach FL 32117
    386 681-2404

(G-7858)
HARDIN MANUFACTURING CO
Also Called: Hardin Company
1281 Ridge Rd (28792-7496)
P.O. Box 702 (28793-0702)
PHONE..................828 685-2008
Carolyn Hardin, *Pr*
Noah Hardin, *VP*
◆ EMP: 9 EST: 1977
SQ FT: 24,000
SALES (est): 246.22K **Privately Held**
Web: www.hardincompany.com
SIC: 2392 Pillows, bed: made from purchased materials

(G-7859)
HEARTLAND HARPS
172 Highlands Square Dr (28792-5852)
PHONE..................828 329-6477
EMP: 4 EST: 2019
SALES (est): 335.22K **Privately Held**
Web: www.heartlandharps.com
SIC: 3931 Musical instruments

(G-7860)
HEARTWOOD REFUGE
389 Courtland Blvd (28791-8545)
PHONE..................828 513-5016
EMP: 8 EST: 2016
SALES (est): 474.92K **Privately Held**
Web: www.heartwoodrefuge.org
SIC: 2499 Wood products, nec

(G-7861)
HELENA AGRI-ENTERPRISES LLC
3642 Chimney Rock Rd (28792-9382)
PHONE..................828 685-1182
Travis Nix, *Mgr*
EMP: 5
Web: www.helenaagri.com
SIC: 5191 2879 Chemicals, agricultural; Pesticides, agricultural or household
HQ: Helena Agri-Enterprises, Llc
    225 Schilling Blvd
    Collierville TN 38017
    901 761-0050

(G-7862)
HENDERSNVLLE AFFRDBL HSING COR
203 N Justice St (28739-4943)
P.O. Box 1106 (28793-1106)
PHONE..................828 692-6175
Diana Brow, *Prin*
Ronnie Pepper, *Prin*
Garry Sherill, *Prin*
Dan Williams, *Prin*
Mike Wagner, *Prin*
EMP: 13 EST: 2018
SALES (est): 3.37MM **Privately Held**
SIC: 2711 Newspapers, publishing and printing

(G-7863)
HENDERSONVILLE PHRM RES
709 5th Ave W (28739-4101)
PHONE..................828 696-2483
Lyn Moody, *Prin*
EMP: 7 EST: 2012
SALES (est): 131.38K **Privately Held**
SIC: 2834 Pharmaceutical preparations

(G-7864)
HIVIZ LED LIGHTING LLC
149 Twin Springs Rd (28792-9262)
P.O. Box 1553 (27546-1553)
PHONE..................703 662-3458
Sam Massa, *Managing Member*
EMP: 10 EST: 2011
SALES (est): 951.05K **Privately Held**
Web: www.hivizleds.com
SIC: 3674 Light emitting diodes

(G-7865)
HIVIZ LIGHTING INC
Also Called: Firetech
149 Twin Springs Rd (28792-9262)
P.O. Box 565 (28760-0565)
PHONE..................703 382-5675
Sam Massa, *Prin*
EMP: 8 EST: 2019
SALES (est): 307.86K **Privately Held**
Web: www.hivizleds.com
SIC: 3641 Electric lamps

(G-7866)
INTERNATIONAL CABINETRY INC
1437 Dana Rd (28792-3096)
PHONE..................828 393-7998
EMP: 6 EST: 2014
SALES (est): 303.15K **Privately Held**
Web: www.intlcabinetry.com
SIC: 2434 Wood kitchen cabinets

(G-7867)
JONES ORNAMENTAL CONCRETE
417 Pilot Mountain Rd (28792-8816)
PHONE..................828 685-3740
Gallileo Jones, *Mng Pt*
Cindy Jones, *Pt*
EMP: 11 EST: 1980
SALES (est): 197.57K **Privately Held**
SIC: 3272 5032 Dry mixture concrete; Concrete mixtures

(G-7868)
KELLY SIGNS
309 White St (28739-5239)
PHONE..................828 778-4146
EMP: 4 EST: 2019
SALES (est): 94.87K **Privately Held**
Web: www.kellysignswnc.com
SIC: 3993 Signs and advertising specialties

(G-7869)
KIMBERLY-CLARK CORPORATION
Kimberly-Clark
32 Smyth Ave (28792-8503)
PHONE..................828 698-5230
Stephen King, *Mgr*
EMP: 250
SALES (corp-wide): 20.43B **Publicly Held**
Web: www.kimberly-clark.com
SIC: 2621 2676 Sanitary tissue paper; Sanitary paper products
PA: Kimberly-Clark Corporation
    351 Phelps Dr
    Irving TX 75038
    972 281-1200

(G-7870)
KYOCERA PRECISION TOOLS INC (DH)
102 Industrial Park Rd (28792-9011)
Rural Route 102 Indtrl Park (28792)
PHONE..................800 823-7284
Koichi Nosaka, *Pr*
Jim Good, *VP*
▲ EMP: 7 EST: 2013
SALES (est): 27.95MM **Privately Held**
Web: www.kyoceraprecisiontools.com
SIC: 3545 3541 3845 3843 Machine tool accessories; Machine tools, metal cutting type; Endoscopic equipment, electromedical, nec; Cutting instruments, dental
HQ: Kyocera International, Inc.
    8611 Balboa Ave
    San Diego CA 92123
    858 492-1456

(G-7871)
L & B JANDREW ENTERPRISES
Also Called: Animal Supply House
1927 Spartanburg Hwy (28792-6528)
PHONE..................828 687-8927
Larry Jandrew, *Pr*
Barbara Jandrew, *VP*
EMP: 7 EST: 1999
SALES (est): 579.13K **Privately Held**
SIC: 3999 5999 Pet supplies; Pets

(G-7872)
LANTERN OF HENDERSONVILLE LLC
755 N Main St (28792-5079)
PHONE..................828 513-5033
John Bell, *VP*
EMP: 6 EST: 2015
SALES (est): 86.04K **Privately Held**
Web: www.thecharleston.net
SIC: 2711 Newspapers

(G-7873)
LEGACY VULCAN LLC
Mideast Division
2960 Clear Creek Rd (28792-8515)
P.O. Box 905 (28793-0905)
PHONE..................828 692-0254
Sammy Peak, *Mgr*
EMP: 5
Web: www.vulcanmaterials.com

Hendersonville - Henderson County (G-7874)

SIC: **3273** Ready-mixed concrete
HQ: Legacy Vulcan, Llc
1200 Urban Center Dr
Vestavia AL 35242
205 298-3000

(G-7874)
M T INDUSTRIES INC
1584 Airport Rd (28792-9155)
PHONE.................................828 697-2864
Gary D Salvaggio, *Pr*
Bart Salvaggio, *VP*
Dale Bradshaw, *VP*
EMP: 10 **EST:** 1985
SQ FT: 15,000
SALES (est): 975.82K **Privately Held**
SIC: **3861** Photographic equipment and supplies

(G-7875)
MANNA CORP NORTH CAROLINA (PA)
Also Called: Manna Designs
508 N Main St (28792-5070)
PHONE.................................828 696-3642
Charles Paskus, *Pr*
Kathleen Paskus, *VP*
EMP: 4 **EST:** 1993
SALES (est): 455.95K **Privately Held**
SIC: **2396** 2395 5699 Screen printing on fabric articles; Embroidery and art needlework; Customized clothing and apparel

(G-7876)
MANUAL WOODWORKERS WEAVERS INC (PA)
Also Called: Mww On Demand
3737 Howard Gap Rd (28792-3174)
PHONE.................................828 692-7333
Travis L Oates, *CEO*
Molly Oates Sherrill, *
James Clarke, *
Lemuel Oates, *Adviser**
Sandra T Oates, *
◆ **EMP:** 201 **EST:** 1932
SQ FT: 500,000
SALES (est): 56.07MM
SALES (corp-wide): 56.07MM **Privately Held**
Web: www.manualww.com
SIC: **2392** Household furnishings, nec

(G-7877)
MARATHON PUBLICATIONS INC
1068 Maplewood Ct (28791-3302)
PHONE.................................651 341-4202
Hale Meserow, *Prin*
EMP: 4 **EST:** 2015
SALES (est): 66.66K **Privately Held**
SIC: **2741** Miscellaneous publishing

(G-7878)
MCF OPERATING LLC
352 Jet St (28792-8004)
PHONE.................................828 685-8821
John Webber, *Mgr*
EMP: 42
Web: www.mrsclarks.com
SIC: **2033** 2099 Fruit juices: fresh; Food preparations, nec
PA: Mcf Operating, Llc
740 Se Dalbey Dr
Ankeny IA 50021

(G-7879)
MESA QUALITY FENESTRATION INC
Also Called: Mesa Quality
968 Crab Creek Rd (28739-8437)
P.O. Box 494 (28793-0494)
PHONE.................................828 393-0132
Warren Morris, *Pr*
EMP: 5 **EST:** 2016
SALES (est): 239.97K **Privately Held**
SIC: **2431** 5031 Millwork; Millwork

(G-7880)
MICHELSON ENTERPRISES INC
Also Called: Oriole Mill, The
701 Oriole Dr (28792-2642)
PHONE.................................828 693-5500
Stephan Michelson, *Pr*
EMP: 8 **EST:** 2010
SALES (est): 612.25K **Privately Held**
Web: www.theoriolemill.com
SIC: **2231** Weaving mill, broadwoven fabrics: wool or similar fabric

(G-7881)
MOUNTAIN SHOWCASE GROUP INC
Also Called: Mountain Showcase
211 Sugarloaf Rd (28792-9386)
PHONE.................................828 692-9494
EMP: 23 **EST:** 1997
SQ FT: 10,000
SALES (est): 2.93MM **Privately Held**
Web: www.mountainshowcase.com
SIC: **1751** 5211 2517 2434 Cabinet building and installation; Cabinets, kitchen; Wood television and radio cabinets; Wood kitchen cabinets

(G-7882)
MURPHY S CUSTOM CABINETRY INC
351 Hidden Woods Ln (28791-5500)
PHONE.................................828 891-3050
Paul Defoy Murphy, *Pr*
Jewell Irene Murphy, *Sec*
EMP: 4 **EST:** 1976
SQ FT: 4,000
SALES (est): 283.58K **Privately Held**
Web: www.murphyscustomcabinetry.com
SIC: **5712** 2434 5031 Cabinet work, custom; Wood kitchen cabinets; Kitchen cabinets

(G-7883)
MY WINE SAVER LLC
162 N Anvil Ave (28792-0087)
PHONE.................................828 595-2632
EMP: 4 **EST:** 2016
SALES (est): 62.38K **Privately Held**
SIC: **2084** Wines

(G-7884)
NATIVES REST CANDLES
2132 Gerton Hwy (28792-1094)
PHONE.................................828 774-9838
Heidi Ladlee, *Prin*
EMP: 4 **EST:** 2018
SALES (est): 39.69K **Privately Held**
Web: www.nativesrestcandles.com
SIC: **3999** Candles

(G-7885)
NC PRINTING LLC
1524 Haywood Rd (28791-2338)
PHONE.................................828 393-4615
EMP: 4 **EST:** 2010
SALES (est): 416.71K **Privately Held**
Web: www.ncprinting.com
SIC: **2752** Offset printing

(G-7886)
NORMAC INCORPORATED (PA)
Also Called: Normac
93 Industrial Dr (28739-7895)
P.O. Box 69 (28704-0069)
PHONE.................................828 209-9000
Raymond Bodie, *Pr*
Mark Kushigian, *
Patricia Hunnicutt, *
Emmanuel Gauzer, *
◆ **EMP:** 40 **EST:** 1967
SQ FT: 27,000
SALES (est): 9.87MM
SALES (corp-wide): 9.87MM **Privately Held**
Web: www.normac.com
SIC: **3541** Grinding machines, metalworking

(G-7887)
OHLINS USA INC
703 S Grove St (28792-5794)
PHONE.................................828 692-4525
Scott Macdonald, *Ex Dir*
▲ **EMP:** 36 **EST:** 1997
SALES (est): 25MM
SALES (corp-wide): 18.04B **Privately Held**
Web: www.ohlinsusa.com
SIC: **3714** Shock absorbers, motor vehicle
HQ: Ohlins Racing Ab
Instrumentvagen 8-10
Upplands VAsby 194 5
859002500

(G-7888)
OKLAWAHA BREWING COMPANY LLC
147 1st Ave E (28792-5191)
PHONE.................................828 595-9956
Joseph Dinan, *Prin*
Josep Dinan, *Owner*
EMP: 10 **EST:** 2015
SALES (est): 497.08K **Privately Held**
Web: www.oklawahabrewing.com
SIC: **5813** 2084 Bars and lounges; Wine cellars, bonded: engaged in blending wines

(G-7889)
OXLIFE OF NC LLC
110 Big Willow Rd (28739-0079)
PHONE.................................828 684-7353
▲ **EMP:** 7 **EST:** 1988
SALES (est): 247.28K **Privately Held**
Web: www.oxygensuperstore.com
SIC: **3842** 3845 3841 5169 Respirators; Electromedical equipment; Surgical and medical instruments; Oxygen

(G-7890)
PATTY CAKES
5 Star Ln (28791-9058)
PHONE.................................828 696-8240
Patricia Lowes, *Pr*
Charles Moore, *VP*
EMP: 4 **EST:** 1999
SALES (est): 175.26K **Privately Held**
SIC: **2051** Cakes, pies, and pastries

(G-7891)
PLANE DEFENSE LTD
175 N Mason Way (28792-1159)
P.O. Box 193 (28726-0193)
PHONE.................................828 254-6061
Stephen J Wilde, *Pr*
EMP: 5 **EST:** 2005
SALES (est): 301.81K **Privately Held**
SIC: **3812** Defense systems and equipment

(G-7892)
PRINTPACK INC
3510 Asheville Hwy (28791-0739)
PHONE.................................828 693-1723
Timothy Garrity, *Brnch Mgr*
EMP: 162
SALES (corp-wide): 1.3B **Privately Held**
Web: www.printpack.com
SIC: **2673** Bags: plastic, laminated, and coated
HQ: Printpack, Inc.
2800 Overlook Pkwy Ne
Atlanta GA 30339
404 460-7000

(G-7893)
QRMC LTD
11 S Egerton Rd (28792-1129)
P.O. Box 709 (28793-0709)
PHONE.................................828 696-2000
L A Lorenzo, *Ch Bd*
Bernard J Garcarz, *VP*
T J Hoyland, *VP*
Brian Lavell, *Sec*
▲ **EMP:** 43 **EST:** 1939
SQ FT: 72,000
SALES (est): 785.64K **Privately Held**
Web: www.qualityrubber.com
SIC: **3544** 3069 Extrusion dies; Molded rubber products

(G-7894)
RAMIREZSTUCCO COMPANY
62 Alverson Ln (28791-9005)
PHONE.................................828 458-8495
Jose Ramirez, *Owner*
EMP: 6 **EST:** 2010
SALES (est): 57.19K **Privately Held**
SIC: **3299** Stucco

(G-7895)
RC INDUSTRIES
931 Mid Allen Rd (28792-9141)
PHONE.................................828 693-1953
EMP: 4 **EST:** 2012
SALES (est): 69K **Privately Held**
SIC: **3999** Manufacturing industries, nec

(G-7896)
ROCK AGES WINERY & VINEYARD
2150 Charlie Long Rd (28739)
PHONE.................................336 364-7625
Kevin Moore, *Owner*
EMP: 6 **EST:** 2004
SALES (est): 179.6K **Privately Held**
Web: www.rockofageswinery.com
SIC: **2084** Wines

(G-7897)
SAINT PAUL MOUNTAIN VINEYARDS
588 Chestnut Gap Rd (28792-3256)
PHONE.................................828 685-4002
Alan Ward, *Owner*
EMP: 14 **EST:** 2013
SALES (est): 862.4K **Privately Held**
Web: www.saintpaulfarms.com
SIC: **2084** Wines

(G-7898)
SELEE CORPORATION (DH)
700 Shepherd St (28792-6400)
PHONE.................................828 693-0256
Mark Morse, *Pr*
Tim Kriegel, *
Watt Jackson, *
Daren Rogers, *
◆ **EMP:** 170 **EST:** 1992
SQ FT: 135,000
SALES (est): 50.37MM
SALES (corp-wide): 197.94MM **Privately Held**
Web: www.selee.com
SIC: **3269** Filtering media, pottery
HQ: Porvair Corporation
700 Shepherd St
Hendersonville NC 28792

GEOGRAPHIC SECTION

Hertford - Perquimans County (G-7925)

(G-7899)
SHAREWELL COFFEE COMPANY LLC
416 N Main St (28792-4901)
PHONE.................................828 290-8188
EMP: 5 **EST:** 2015
SALES (est): 115.29K **Privately Held**
Web: www.sharewellcoffee.com
SIC: 2095 Roasted coffee

(G-7900)
SOFWARE LLC
Also Called: Sofware
217 Covington Cove Ln (28739-5844)
PHONE.................................757 287-7409
EMP: 8 **EST:** 2011
SALES (est): 603.52K **Privately Held**
Web: www.sofwarellc.com
SIC: 7372 Application computer software

(G-7901)
SOLUTIONS IN WOOD
65 Lake Pointe Cir (28792-2842)
PHONE.................................828 696-2996
Donald Haynes, *Owner*
EMP: 4 **EST:** 2015
SALES (est): 161.19K **Privately Held**
Web: www.solutionsinwood.com
SIC: 2431 Millwork

(G-7902)
SOUTHERN AG INSECTICIDES INC
511 Maple St (28792-3752)
P.O. Box 429 (28793-0429)
PHONE.................................828 692-2233
Richard Baxter, *Mgr*
EMP: 25
SALES (corp-wide): 50.49MM **Privately Held**
Web: www.southernag.com
SIC: 5191 2879 2875 Insecticides; Agricultural chemicals, nec; Fertilizers, mixing only
PA: Southern Agricultural Insecticides Inc.
7500 Bayshore Rd
Palmetto FL 34221
941 722-3285

(G-7903)
SOUTHERN CONCRETE MTLS INC
715 Shepherd St (28792-6473)
PHONE.................................828 692-6517
John Holt, *Mgr*
EMP: 20
SQ FT: 6,311
SALES (corp-wide): 238.17MM **Privately Held**
Web: www.scmusa.com
SIC: 3273 5039 Ready-mixed concrete; Septic tanks
HQ: Southern Concrete Materials, Inc.
35 Meadow Rd
Asheville NC 28803
828 253-6421

(G-7904)
SPRING CREEK PRESS
159 Atwood Dr (28792-2403)
PHONE.................................828 337-8296
Cc Tillery, *Prin*
EMP: 5 **EST:** 2015
SALES (est): 57.8K **Privately Held**
SIC: 2741 Miscellaneous publishing

(G-7905)
STAMPING SCHOOL LLC
32 Loggers Run (28739-9313)
PHONE.................................407 435-3135
Linda Heller, *Pr*
EMP: 5 **EST:** 2017

SALES (est): 107.02K **Privately Held**
Web: www.lindastamps.com
SIC: 3469 Stamping metal for the trade

(G-7906)
STANDARD TYTAPE COMPANY INC
1495 N Main St (28792-2568)
P.O. Box 2270 (28793-2270)
PHONE.................................828 693-6594
Robert Herrmann, *Pr*
EMP: 11 **EST:** 1935
SQ FT: 35,000
SALES (est): 483.99K **Privately Held**
Web: www.tytape.com
SIC: 2396 2241 2298 Automotive and apparel trimmings; Braids, textile; Cordage and twine

(G-7907)
TINA M JONES
Also Called: Jones Salsa
101 Lytle Rd (28792-6476)
PHONE.................................828 685-2937
Tina M Jones, *Owner*
EMP: 4 **EST:** 2019
SALES (est): 76.48K **Privately Held**
SIC: 2033 Chili sauce, tomato: packaged in cans, jars, etc.

(G-7908)
TODDS RV & MARINE INC
130 Lyndale Rd (28739-6119)
PHONE.................................828 651-0007
Daniel Todd, *Pr*
Edwina Garrison, *VP*
Alineen Todd, *Sec*
EMP: 10 **EST:** 1956
SQ FT: 62,000
SALES (est): 498.35K **Privately Held**
Web: www.toddsrvandmarine.com
SIC: 5561 5551 7699 3732 Motor homes; Motor boat dealers; Recreational vehicle repair services; Motorized boat, building and repairing

(G-7909)
TRINKETS AND WHIMSEY
165 Haynes Blvd (28792-5586)
PHONE.................................919 368-6044
Christina Nelson, *Pr*
EMP: 5 **EST:** 2014
SALES (est): 83.8K **Privately Held**
SIC: 3914 Silverware and plated ware

(G-7910)
UNDERGROUND BAKING CO LLC
304 Yon Hill Rd (28792-2460)
PHONE.................................828 674-7494
Matthew N Hickman, *Prin*
EMP: 8 **EST:** 2010
SALES (est): 447.23K **Privately Held**
Web: www.undergroundbaking.com
SIC: 2051 Bakery: wholesale or wholesale/retail combined

(G-7911)
VILLAGE CERAMICS INC
320 Q P Ln (28792-5600)
PHONE.................................828 685-9491
Q P Anderson, *Pr*
Elaine Anderson, *Sec*
EMP: 9 **EST:** 1970
SALES (est): 236.24K **Privately Held**
SIC: 3843 3842 8072 Denture materials; Prosthetic appliances; Dental laboratories

(G-7912)
VULCAN MATERIALS COMPANY
2284 Clear Creek Rd (28792-9078)
PHONE.................................828 692-0039

EMP: 4
Web: www.vulcanmaterials.com
SIC: 3273 Ready-mixed concrete
PA: Vulcan Materials Company
1200 Urban Center Dr
Vestavia AL 35242

(G-7913)
WARM PRODUCTS INC
Also Called: Warm Industrial Nonwovens
581 Old Sunset Hill Rd (28792-8362)
PHONE.................................425 248-2424
EMP: 18
SALES (corp-wide): 9.31MM **Privately Held**
Web: www.warmindustrial.com
SIC: 5131 2297 Piece goods and notions; Nonwoven fabrics
PA: Warm Products, Inc.
5529 186th Pl Sw
Lynnwood WA 98037
425 248-2424

(G-7914)
WICKED ROOSTER SIGNS INC
204 Woods End Dr (28739-9362)
PHONE.................................828 844-0404
Thomas Gray, *Prin*
EMP: 5 **EST:** 2016
SALES (est): 125.87K **Privately Held**
SIC: 3993 Signs and advertising specialties

(G-7915)
WIRTZ WIRE EDM LLC
65a Commercial Hill Dr (28792-4563)
PHONE.................................828 696-0830
W Wirtz, *Managing Member*
Patrick Wirtz, *Pr*
EMP: 14 **EST:** 1993
SQ FT: 4,500
SALES (est): 2.45MM **Privately Held**
Web: www.wirtzwireedm.com
SIC: 3544 Special dies and tools

Hertford
Perquimans County

(G-7916)
BILLY HARRELL LOGGING INC
108 Ililda Dr (27944-9559)
PHONE.................................252 426-1362
Billy Harrell, *Prin*
EMP: 9 **EST:** 2016
SALES (est): 494.79K **Privately Held**
SIC: 2411 Logging camps and contractors

(G-7917)
CROSSROAD PRESS
141 Brayden Dr (27944-7926)
PHONE.................................252 340-3952
EMP: 6 **EST:** 2017
SALES (est): 80.56K **Privately Held**
Web: www.crossroadpress.com
SIC: 2741 Miscellaneous publishing

(G-7918)
CROSSROADS FUEL SERVICE INC
395 Ocean Hwy N (27944-8956)
P.O. Box 67 (27944-0067)
PHONE.................................252 426-5216
EMP: 26
SALES (corp-wide): 52.91MM **Privately Held**
Web: www.crossroadsfuel.com
SIC: 5172 2893 Fuel oil; Printing ink
PA: Crossroads Fuel Service, Inc.
1441 Fentress Rd
Chesapeake VA 23322
757 482-2179

(G-7919)
DAVID E MEIGGS
114 Calm Harbor St (27944-1564)
PHONE.................................252 340-1640
David Meiggs, *Prin*
EMP: 5 **EST:** 2004
SALES (est): 158.18K **Privately Held**
SIC: 2411 Logging

(G-7920)
EAST COAST STL FABRICATION INC
116 N Granby St (27944)
PHONE.................................757 351-2601
Cynthia Overman, *Prin*
Mark Overman, *
Mary Miller, *
▲ **EMP:** 37 **EST:** 2006
SALES (est): 4.32MM **Privately Held**
Web: www.ecsfi.com
SIC: 3441 3317 Fabricated structural metal; Boiler tubes (wrought)

(G-7921)
HERTFORD ABC BOARD
803 S Church St (27944-1210)
P.O. Box 23 (27944-0023)
PHONE.................................252 426-5290
Don Keaton, *Mgr*
EMP: 6 **EST:** 2010
SALES (est): 219.77K **Privately Held**
Web: www.townofhertfordnc.com
SIC: 2084 Wines, brandy, and brandy spirits

(G-7922)
JOHNIE GREGORY TRCK BODIES INC
337 Old Us Highway 17 (27944-9111)
PHONE.................................252 264-2626
Johnie M Gregory, *Pr*
William J Gregory, *VP*
Ashley Gregory, *Sec*
Tim Gregory, *Stockholder*
EMP: 6 **EST:** 1898
SQ FT: 6,000
SALES (est): 861.2K **Privately Held**
Web: www.johniegregorytruckbodies.com
SIC: 3713 Truck bodies (motor vehicles)

(G-7923)
R & S LOGGING INC
771 Lake Rd (27944-8752)
PHONE.................................252 426-5880
Janis Rhodes, *Pr*
James Rhodes, *Prin*
EMP: 7 **EST:** 1998
SALES (est): 1.44MM **Privately Held**
Web: www.insiteshred.com
SIC: 2411 Logging camps and contractors

(G-7924)
STARLIGHT MANUFACTURING INC
113 Starlight Dr (27944-1453)
P.O. Box 158 (27944-0158)
PHONE.................................252 426-7867
Edward L Walker Senior, *Pr*
Edward L Walker Junior, *VP*
Sally Walker, *Treas*
Tanya Walker, *Sec*
EMP: 9 **EST:** 1987
SQ FT: 1,800
SALES (est): 474.56K **Privately Held**
Web: www.starlightmfginc.com
SIC: 3843 Teeth, artificial (not made in dental laboratories)

(G-7925)
WHITEHAT SEED FARMS INC
102 Whitehat Rd (27944-9008)
PHONE.................................252 264-2427

Burt Eure, *Pr*
Karl M Eure, *Stockholder*
Betty Eure, *Treas*
Paige Eure, *Sec*
EMP: 7 **EST:** 1956
SQ FT: 55,000
SALES (est): 731.15K **Privately Held**
Web: www.whitehat.com.au
SIC: 2041 2083 2075 Oat flour; Barley malt; Soybean oil, cake or meal

Hickory
Catawba County

(G-7926)
057 TECHNOLOGY LLC
728 11th Street Pl Nw (28601-3441)
P.O. Box 2127 (28603-2127)
PHONE..................................855 557-7057
Jason Hughes, *Pr*
Jason David Hughes, *Managing Member*
EMP: 4 **EST:** 2018
SQ FT: 31,000
SALES (est): 456.98K **Privately Held**
Web: www.057tech.com
SIC: 3621 7373 Motors, electric; Computer integrated systems design

(G-7927)
A PLUS SERVICE INC
2233a Highland Ave Ne (28601-8162)
P.O. Box 1390 (28603-1390)
PHONE..................................828 324-4397
Bill Hasty, *Pr*
EMP: 8 **EST:** 2005
SQ FT: 60,000
SALES (est): 736.55K **Privately Held**
Web: www.aplusserviceinc.com
SIC: 3086 Plastics foam products

(G-7928)
ABB INSTALLATION PRODUCTS INC
415 19th Street Dr Se (28602-4446)
PHONE..................................828 322-1855
EMP: 22
Web: elis-secure.abb.com
SIC: 3643 3312 3567 Electric connectors; Structural shapes and pilings, steel; Heating units and devices, industrial: electric
HQ: Abb Installation Products Inc.
     860 Ridge Lake Blvd
     Memphis TN 38120
     901 252-5000

(G-7929)
AFFORDABLE WELDING SPECIALISTS
7460 Burke County Line Rd (28602-8642)
PHONE..................................828 446-4436
EMP: 4 **EST:** 2016
SALES (est): 47.07K **Privately Held**
SIC: 7692 Welding repair

(G-7930)
AIKEN-BLACK TIRE SERVICE INC
823 1st Ave Nw (28601-6064)
P.O. Box 1605 (28603-1605)
PHONE..................................828 322-3736
David Black, *Pr*
John Black, *
EMP: 40 **EST:** 1960
SQ FT: 20,500
SALES (est): 5.99MM **Privately Held**
Web: www.aikenblacktire.com
SIC: 5531 7534 7538 Automotive tires; Tire recapping; General automotive repair shops

(G-7931)
ALL GLASS INC
1125 S Center St (28602-3446)
P.O. Box 11002 (28603-4502)
PHONE..................................828 324-8609
Bob Inman, *Owner*
Ray Prewitt, *Pr*
Beth Prewitt, *VP*
EMP: 9 **EST:** 1993
SALES (est): 878.62K **Privately Held**
Web: www.allglasscompany.com
SIC: 5211 5999 3231 Screens, door and window; Alarm signal systems; Aquariums and reflectors, glass

(G-7932)
ALMORE INTERNATIONAL INC
441 19th St Se (28602-4232)
P.O. Box 25214 (97298-0214)
PHONE..................................503 643-6633
Davy Dupon, *Pr*
EMP: 9 **EST:** 1948
SALES (est): 697.4K **Privately Held**
Web: www.almore.com
SIC: 3843 Dental equipment

(G-7933)
AMERICAN PHARMACEUTICAL SVCS
1255 25th Street Pl Se (28602-9658)
PHONE..................................828 328-1816
Berta Leuhrs, *Prin*
EMP: 6 **EST:** 2005
SALES (est): 203.72K **Privately Held**
SIC: 2834 Pharmaceutical preparations

(G-7934)
AMERICAN SPEEDY PRINTING CTRS
Also Called: American Speedy Printing
337 Main Ave Ne (28601-5121)
PHONE..................................828 322-3981
Marcus Woodie, *Pr*
EMP: 5 **EST:** 2018
SALES (est): 99.15K **Privately Held**
Web: www.americanspeedy.com
SIC: 2752 Offset printing

(G-7935)
ANEW LOOK HOMES LLC
1717 Highland Ave Ne Ste 102 (28601-5305)
PHONE..................................800 796-5152
Melissa Hall, *Managing Member*
EMP: 12 **EST:** 2016
SALES (est): 591.88K **Privately Held**
Web: www.anewlookhomes.com
SIC: 8742 6531 1389 6798 Management consulting services; Real estate leasing and rentals; Construction, repair, and dismantling services; Real estate investment trusts

(G-7936)
APPLIED COMPONENTS MFG LLC
101 33rd Street Dr Se (28602-8375)
PHONE..................................828 323-8915
Hans Peterson, *Prin*
EMP: 7 **EST:** 2009
SALES (est): 250.28K **Privately Held**
Web: www.appliedcompmfg.com
SIC: 3999 Manufacturing industries, nec

(G-7937)
APPLIED COMPONENTS MFG LLC
415 19th St Sw (28602-2270)
PHONE..................................828 322-6535
Leslie Hudson, *Prin*
EMP: 4 **EST:** 2004
SALES (est): 96K **Privately Held**
SIC: 3999 Manufacturing industries, nec

(G-7938)
APS HICKORY
1257 25th Street Pl Se (28602-9658)
PHONE..................................828 323-1010
EMP: 5 **EST:** 2012
SALES (est): 140.33K **Privately Held**
SIC: 2711 Newspapers, publishing and printing

(G-7939)
AQUA PLASTICS INC
1474 17th St Ne (28601-2824)
PHONE..................................828 324-6284
Miguel Crouch, *Pr*
Ana Crouch, *VP*
◆ **EMP:** 44 **EST:** 2006
SALES (est): 969.93K **Privately Held**
Web: www.aquaplasticsusa.com
SIC: 2821 3089 3081 Thermoplastic materials; Molding primary plastics; Unsupported plastics film and sheet

(G-7940)
ARENAS TIRES
128 15th St Se (28602-1310)
PHONE..................................828 962-9422
EMP: 5 **EST:** 2017
SALES (est): 50.94K **Privately Held**
SIC: 7534 Tire repair shop

(G-7941)
ARGOS USA LLC
Also Called: Redi-Mix Concrete
2001 Main Ave Se (28602-1404)
P.O. Box 1847 (28603-1847)
PHONE..................................828 322-9325
Chet Miller, *Brnch Mgr*
EMP: 50
Web: www.argos-us.com
SIC: 3273 Ready-mixed concrete
HQ: Argos Usa Llc
     3015 Windward Plz Ste 300
     Alpharetta GA 30005
     678 368-4300

(G-7942)
ARRIS GLOBAL SERVICES INC
1100 Commscope Pl Se (28602-3619)
PHONE..................................215 323-1000
Charles L Treadway, *Pr*
Justin C Chasseur, *VP*
Justin C Choi, *Sec*
EMP: 33 **EST:** 1999
SALES (est): 4.41MM **Publicly Held**
Web: www.commscope.com
SIC: 3663 Radio broadcasting and communications equipment
PA: Commscope Holding Company, Inc.
     3642 E Us Highway 70
     Claremont NC 28610

(G-7943)
ARRIS SOLUTIONS LLC (DH)
Also Called: Arris Solutions, Inc.
1100 Commscope Pl Se (28602-3619)
PHONE..................................678 473-2000
Charles L Treadway, *CEO*
James Douglas Moore Junior, *CFO*
Patrick W Macken, *
◆ **EMP:** 600 **EST:** 2007
SALES (est): 703.8MM **Publicly Held**
Web: www.commscope.com
SIC: 3661 3663 3357 Telephone and telegraph apparatus; Radio and t.v. communications equipment; Fiber optic cable (insulated)
HQ: Ruckus Wireless Llc
     350 W Java Dr
     Sunnyvale CA 94089

(G-7944)
ARRIS TECHNOLOGY INC (DH)
1100 Commscope Pl Se (28602-3619)
PHONE..................................678 473-2907
Charles L Treadway, *CEO*
Kyle D Lorentzen, *CFO*
Justin C Choi, *Sec*
◆ **EMP:** 60 **EST:** 1997
SQ FT: 1,100,000
SALES (est): 393.01MM **Publicly Held**
Web: www.commscope.com
SIC: 7372 3825 Application computer software; Network analyzers
HQ: Arris Solutions Llc
     1100 Commscope Pl Se
     Hickory NC 28602

(G-7945)
ASPIRE WOODWORKS
4946 Alexander Pl Ne (28601-9702)
PHONE..................................828 855-6811
Harrison Spires, *Prin*
EMP: 5 **EST:** 2018
SALES (est): 54.13K **Privately Held**
SIC: 2431 Millwork

(G-7946)
B & M ELECTRIC MOTOR SERVICE
20 17th Street Pl Nw (28601-5819)
P.O. Box 2676 (28603-2676)
PHONE..................................828 267-0829
Shannon Mcdonald, *Pr*
Dee Dee Brittin, *Sec*
▲ **EMP:** 7 **EST:** 2001
SQ FT: 11,000
SALES (est): 717.74K **Privately Held**
Web: www.clearelectricinc.net
SIC: 7694 Electric motor repair

(G-7947)
B&P ENTERPRISE NC INC
4128 Icard Ridge Rd (28601-7656)
PHONE..................................727 669-6877
James Jackson, *Pr*
EMP: 9 **EST:** 1998
SALES (est): 608.64K **Privately Held**
SIC: 3993 7311 Electric signs; Advertising consultant

(G-7948)
BARRYS CUSTOM LURES LLC
3463 38th Street Dr Ne (28601-7728)
PHONE..................................828 256-1792
Barry Sullivan, *Brnch Mgr*
EMP: 9
SALES (corp-wide): 75.06K **Privately Held**
SIC: 3949 Lures, fishing: artificial
PA: Barry's Custom Lures, Llc
     933 Davis Cove Rd
     Taylorsville NC

(G-7949)
BETHLEHEM MANUFACTURING CO (PA)
Also Called: Molds of Bethlehem
36 Bethlehem Manufacturing Ln (28601-7831)
PHONE..................................828 495-7731
Latt Moretz, *Pr*
Ashley Moretz, *VP*
EMP: 13 **EST:** 1963
SQ FT: 2,400
SALES (est): 1.36MM
SALES (corp-wide): 1.36MM **Privately Held**
Web: www.moldsofbethlehem.com
SIC: 3544 3537 Industrial molds; Trucks, tractors, loaders, carriers, and similar equipment

GEOGRAPHIC SECTION
Hickory - Catawba County (G-7972)

(G-7950)
BLOSSMAN PROPANE GAS & APPL
2315 Catawba Valley Blvd Se (28602-4162)
PHONE..............................828 396-0144
Jimmy Daley, *Genl Mgr*
EMP: 12 **EST:** 1951
SALES (est): 822.46K **Privately Held**
Web: www.blossmangas.com
SIC: 5984 3634 Propane gas, bottled; Heating units, for electric appliances

(G-7951)
BLUE LAGOON INC
Also Called: TEC-Ops
1011 10th Street Blvd Nw (28601-3459)
P.O. Box 1890 (28603-1890)
PHONE..............................828 324-2333
Peter Menzies, *Pr*
EMP: 4 **EST:** 2008
SALES (est): 392.72K **Privately Held**
Web: www.covertthreads.com
SIC: 2253 Knit outerwear mills

(G-7952)
BLUE RIDGE PRODUCTS CO INC
3050 Main Ave Nw (28601-5663)
P.O. Box 2028 (28603-2028)
PHONE..............................828 322-7990
Charles Ingle, *Pr*
EMP: 20 **EST:** 1950
SQ FT: 125,000
SALES (est): 172.56K **Privately Held**
Web: www.blueridgeproducts.com
SIC: 2515 2426 2392 Spring cushions; Hardwood dimension and flooring mills; Household furnishings, nec

(G-7953)
BRADINGTON-YOUNG LLC (HQ)
4040 10th Avenue Dr Sw (28602-4535)
PHONE..............................704 435-5881
C Scott Young, *Managing Member*
▲ **EMP:** 200 **EST:** 1978
SALES (est): 43.85MM
SALES (corp-wide): 583.1MM **Publicly Held**
Web: www.bradington-young.com
SIC: 2512 Chairs: upholstered on wood frames
PA: Hooker Furnishings Corporation
   440 Commonwealth Blvd E
   Martinsville VA 24112
   276 632-2133

(G-7954)
BUD BAUMGARNER
Also Called: JB Cabinets
3551 28th St Ne (28601-8234)
PHONE..............................828 256-6230
Bud Baumgarner, *Owner*
EMP: 5 **EST:** 1999
SALES (est): 74.62K **Privately Held**
SIC: 2599 Cabinets, factory

(G-7955)
BURRIS MACHINE COMPANY INC (PA)
3155 Highland Ave Ne (28601-8106)
P.O. Box 2858 (28603-2858)
PHONE..............................828 322-6914
Jerry Sellers, *Pr*
EMP: 9 **EST:** 1976
SQ FT: 28,100
SALES (est): 1.1MM
SALES (corp-wide): 1.1MM **Privately Held**
Web: www.burrismachineco.com
SIC: 3545 5084 3469 Tool holders; Industrial machinery and equipment; Metal stampings, nec

(G-7956)
BURRIS MACHINE COMPANY INC
1631 Main Avenue Dr Nw (28601-5834)
PHONE..............................828 322-6914
Jerry Sellers, *Brnch Mgr*
EMP: 6
SALES (corp-wide): 1.1MM **Privately Held**
Web: www.burrismachineco.com
SIC: 3599 Machine shop, jobbing and repair
PA: Burris Machine Company Inc
   3155 Highland Ave Ne
   Hickory NC 28601
   828 322-6914

(G-7957)
C R LAINE FURNITURE CO INC
2829 Us Highway 70 Se (28602)
P.O. Box 2128 (28603-2128)
PHONE..............................828 328-1831
C E Roseman Junior, *Pr*
Warren L Frye, *
Lori Whisnant, *
▲ **EMP:** 155 **EST:** 1958
SQ FT: 130,000
SALES (est): 23.66MM **Privately Held**
Web: www.crlaine.com
SIC: 2512 Chairs: upholstered on wood frames

(G-7958)
CABINET DOOR WORLD LLC
1711 11th Ave Sw (28602-4909)
PHONE..............................877 929-2750
Richard Healey, *Prin*
EMP: 12 **EST:** 2012
SALES (est): 575.92K **Privately Held**
Web: www.cabinetdoorworld.com
SIC: 2434 Wood kitchen cabinets

(G-7959)
CABINET SOLUTIONS USA INC
1711 11th Ave Sw (28602-4909)
PHONE..............................828 358-2349
James Christopher Robinson, *Pr*
EMP: 24 **EST:** 2017
SALES (est): 2.24MM **Privately Held**
Web: www.usacabinetsolutions.com
SIC: 2434 3429 1751 1799 Wood kitchen cabinets; Cabinet hardware; Cabinet and finish carpentry; Kitchen cabinet installation

(G-7960)
CABLE DEVICES INCORPORATED (HQ)
Also Called: Cable Exchange
1100 Commscope Pl Se (28602-3619)
PHONE..............................714 554-4370
Marvin S Edwards, *Pr*
Charles L Treadway, *
Kyle D Lorentzen, *
Frank B Wyatt, *
▲ **EMP:** 150 **EST:** 1979
SQ FT: 24,516
SALES (est): 26MM **Publicly Held**
SIC: 3577 Computer peripheral equipment, nec
PA: Commscope Holding Company, Inc.
   3642 E Us Highway 70
   Claremont NC 28610

(G-7961)
CANIPE & LYNN ELC MTR REPR INC
1909 1st Ave Sw (28602-2224)
P.O. Box 1422 (28603-1422)
PHONE..............................828 322-9052
Sherry Lynn, *Pr*
Dock Lynn, *VP*
Ramona Lynn, *Sec*
EMP: 9 **EST:** 1959
SALES (est): 986.98K **Privately Held**
SIC: 5999 7694 Motors, electric; Electric motor repair

(G-7962)
CAROLINA CLTCH BRAKE RBLDRS IN
430 Us Highway 70 Se (28602-5122)
PHONE..............................828 327-9358
EMP: 6 **EST:** 2019
SALES (est): 137.63K **Privately Held**
Web: www.carolinaclutch.com
SIC: 3714 Motor vehicle parts and accessories

(G-7963)
CAROLINA CONTAINER LLC
Also Called: Digital High Point
61 30th St Nw (28601-5630)
P.O. Box 2166 (27261-2166)
PHONE..............................828 322-3380
Jack Pressley, *Mgr*
EMP: 18
SALES (corp-wide): 679.24MM **Privately Held**
Web: www.carolinacontainer.com
SIC: 2653 Boxes, corrugated: made from purchased materials
HQ: Carolina Container Company
   909 Prospect St
   High Point NC 27260
   336 883-7146

(G-7964)
CAROLINA PAVING HICKORY INC
Also Called: Carolina Asphalt
445 9th St Se (28602-4041)
PHONE..............................828 328-3909
Jim Taylor, *Mgr*
EMP: 4
SALES (corp-wide): 3.57MM **Privately Held**
Web: www.carolinapaving.com
SIC: 1611 3531 Grading; Asphalt plant, including gravel-mix type
PA: Carolina Paving Of Hickory, Inc.
   3203 Highland Ave Ne
   Hickory NC 28601
   828 322-1706

(G-7965)
CAROLINA PAVING HICKORY INC (PA)
3203 Highland Ave Ne (28601-9375)
PHONE..............................828 322-1706
Marie H Huffman, *Pr*
E Dane Huffman, *VP*
EMP: 17 **EST:** 1964
SQ FT: 2,000
SALES (est): 3.57MM
SALES (corp-wide): 3.57MM **Privately Held**
Web: www.carolinapaving.com
SIC: 1611 3531 Grading; Asphalt plant, including gravel-mix type

(G-7966)
CAROLINA SOLVENTS INC
Also Called: C S I
2274 1st St Se (28602-5338)
P.O. Box 9206 (28603-9206)
PHONE..............................828 322-1920
EMP: 24 **EST:** 1969
SALES (est): 3.89MM **Privately Held**
Web: www.carolinasolventsinc.com
SIC: 2952 2891 Asphalt felts and coatings; Sealants

(G-7967)
CAROLINA SWATCHING INC
725 14th Street Dr Sw (28602-3128)
P.O. Box 9255 (28603-9255)
PHONE..............................828 327-9499
David Robinson, *Pr*
Katherine Robinson, *Sec*
EMP: 15 **EST:** 1993
SQ FT: 10,000
SALES (est): 1.21MM **Privately Held**
Web: www.carolinaswatching.com
SIC: 2789 2782 Swatches and samples; Blankbooks and looseleaf binders

(G-7968)
CAROLINA TAPE & SUPPLY CORP
502 19th Street Pl Se (28602-4403)
P.O. Box 2488 (28603-2488)
PHONE..............................828 322-3991
TOLL FREE: 800
K Shawn Dagenhardt, *Pr*
D W Dagenhardt, *
Marcus B Dagenhardt, *
James Dagenhardt, *
◆ **EMP:** 29 **EST:** 1966
SQ FT: 30,000
SALES (est): 15.11MM **Privately Held**
Web: www.carolinatape.com
SIC: 5113 2512 Pressure sensitive tape; Upholstered household furniture

(G-7969)
CARPENTER CO
30 29th St Nw (28601-5650)
PHONE..............................828 322-6545
Randy Hefner, *Mgr*
EMP: 27
SALES (corp-wide): 1.85B **Privately Held**
Web: www.carpenter.com
SIC: 3086 2821 Insulation or cushioning material, foamed plastics; Plastics materials and resins
PA: Carpenter Co.
   5016 Monument Ave
   Richmond VA 23230
   804 359-0800

(G-7970)
CATAWBA VALLEY QUILTERS GUILD
1880 6th St Nw (28601-5248)
PHONE..............................828 322-4517
EMP: 4 **EST:** 2011
SALES (est): 42K **Privately Held**
Web: www.catawbavalleyquiltersguild.com
SIC: 2395 Quilting and quilting supplies

(G-7971)
CATAWBA VLY YOUTH SOCCER ASSOC
3404 6th Street Dr Nw (28601-9092)
P.O. Box 2246 (28603-2246)
PHONE..............................828 234-7082
James Knuckles, *Prin*
EMP: 5 **EST:** 2016
SALES (est): 298.35K **Privately Held**
Web: www.cvysa.org
SIC: 2711 Newspapers, publishing and printing

(G-7972)
CCBCC OPERATIONS LLC
Also Called: Coca-Cola
820 1st Ave Nw (28601-6063)
PHONE..............................828 322-5097
Phillip Davidson, *Mgr*
EMP: 73
SALES (corp-wide): 6.65B **Publicly Held**
Web: www.coca-cola.com
SIC: 2086 Bottled and canned soft drinks
HQ: Ccbcc Operations, Llc
   4100 Coca Cola Plz
   Charlotte NC 28211
   704 364-8728

Hickory - Catawba County (G-7973)

(G-7973)
CCO HOLDINGS LLC
483 Us Highway 70 Sw (28602-5019)
PHONE..................828 270-7016
EMP: 179
SALES (corp-wide): 54.61B **Publicly Held**
SIC: **4841** 3663 3651 Cable television services; Radio and t.v. communications equipment; Household audio and video equipment
HQ: Cco Holdings, Llc
400 Atlantic St
Stamford CT 06901
203 905-7801

(G-7974)
CENTRAL TOOL & MFG CO INC
1021 17th St Sw (28602-4925)
P.O. Box 2325 (28603-2325)
PHONE..................828 328-2383
Charles Threewitt, *Pr*
June Threewitt, *Sec*
EMP: 6 EST: 1967
SQ FT: 15,000
SALES (est): 472.87K **Privately Held**
SIC: **7699** 3545 3541 Precision instrument repair; Machine tool attachments and accessories; Machine tools, metal cutting type

(G-7975)
CENTURY FURNITURE LLC
Also Called: Century Furniture Uphl Plant
535 27th St Nw (28601-4551)
PHONE..................828 326-8410
Terry Jennings, *Mgr*
EMP: 60
SALES (corp-wide): 212.17MM **Privately Held**
Web: www.centuryfurniture.com
SIC: **2511** Wood household furniture
HQ: Century Furniture, Llc
401 11th St Nw
Hickory NC 28601
828 267-8739

(G-7976)
CENTURY FURNITURE LLC
Also Called: Century Case Goods Division
420 12th Street Dr Nw (28601-4741)
P.O. Box 608 (28603-0608)
PHONE..................828 326-8201
Wade Yount, *Div Mgr*
EMP: 121
SALES (corp-wide): 212.17MM **Privately Held**
Web: www.centuryfurniture.com
SIC: **2511** 2512 Wood household furniture; Upholstered household furniture
HQ: Century Furniture, Llc
401 11th St Nw
Hickory NC 28601
828 267-8739

(G-7977)
CENTURY FURNITURE LLC
Also Called: Technical Center
25 18th St Nw (28601-5822)
PHONE..................828 326-8535
Jim Conley, *Mgr*
EMP: 58
SALES (corp-wide): 212.17MM **Privately Held**
Web: www.centuryfurniture.com
SIC: **2511** 8711 Wood household furniture; Engineering services
HQ: Century Furniture, Llc
401 11th St Nw
Hickory NC 28601
828 267-8739

(G-7978)
CENTURY FURNITURE LLC
Chair
3086 Main Ave Nw (28601-5663)
P.O. Box 608 (28603-0608)
PHONE..................828 326-8458
Kevin Boyle, *Mgr*
EMP: 109
SQ FT: 390,000
SALES (corp-wide): 212.17MM **Privately Held**
Web: www.centuryfurniture.com
SIC: **2511** 2512 Chairs, household, except upholstered: wood; Chairs: upholstered on wood frames
HQ: Century Furniture, Llc
401 11th St Nw
Hickory NC 28601
828 267-8739

(G-7979)
CENTURY FURNITURE LLC
420 27th St Nw (28601-4550)
P.O. Box 608 (28603-0608)
PHONE..................828 326-8410
Terry Jennings, *Mgr*
EMP: 48
SALES (corp-wide): 212.17MM **Privately Held**
Web: www.centuryfurniture.com
SIC: **2512** Upholstered household furniture
HQ: Century Furniture, Llc
401 11th St Nw
Hickory NC 28601
828 267-8739

(G-7980)
CENTURY FURNITURE LLC
820 21st St Nw (28601-3354)
P.O. Box 608 (28603-0608)
PHONE..................828 326-8650
Norman Carson, *Brnch Mgr*
EMP: 48
SALES (corp-wide): 212.17MM **Privately Held**
Web: www.centuryfurniture.com
SIC: **2512** Upholstered household furniture
HQ: Century Furniture, Llc
401 11th St Nw
Hickory NC 28601
828 267-8739

(G-7981)
CENTURY FURNITURE LLC
Also Called: Highland House
401 11th St Nw (28601-4750)
P.O. Box 608 (28603-0608)
PHONE..................828 326-8300
Carrie Regan, *Mgr*
EMP: 4
SALES (corp-wide): 212.17MM **Privately Held**
Web: www.centuryfurniture.com
SIC: **2512** 2511 Upholstered household furniture; Wood household furniture
HQ: Century Furniture, Llc
401 11th St Nw
Hickory NC 28601
828 267-8739

(G-7982)
CENTURY FURNITURE LLC
126 33rd St Nw (28601-5676)
PHONE..................828 326-8495
EMP: 10
SALES (corp-wide): 212.17MM **Privately Held**
Web: www.centuryfurniture.com
SIC: **2512** Chairs: upholstered on wood frames
HQ: Century Furniture, Llc
401 11th St Nw
Hickory NC 28601
828 267-8739

(G-7983)
CENTURY FURNITURE LLC (HQ)
Also Called: Highland House
401 11th St Nw (28601-4750)
P.O. Box 608 (28603-0608)
PHONE..................828 267-8739
◆ EMP: 160 EST: 1946
SALES (est): 92.85MM
SALES (corp-wide): 212.17MM **Privately Held**
Web: www.centuryfurniture.com
SIC: **2521** 5023 6799 Wood office furniture; Decorative home furnishings and supplies; Investors, nec
PA: Rhf Investments, Inc.
401 11th St Nw
Hickory NC 28601
828 326-8350

(G-7984)
CHARLES STEWART CO
931 18th Street Pl Nw (28601-3347)
PHONE..................828 322-9464
Stewart Stoudemire, *Pr*
EMP: 115
SALES (corp-wide): 7.23MM **Privately Held**
Web: www.charlesstewartcompany.com
SIC: **2512** Upholstered household furniture
PA: The Charles Stewart Co
931 18th Street Pl Nw
Hickory NC
828 322-9464

(G-7985)
CHASE CORPORATION
1954 Main Ave Se (28602-1401)
PHONE..................828 855-9316
EMP: 4
Web: www.chasecorp.com
SIC: **2821** Plastics materials and resins
HQ: Chase Corporation
375 University Ave
Westwood MA 02090
781 332-0700

(G-7986)
CHASE CORPORATION
1527 7th Street Ln Se (28602-8690)
PHONE..................828 649-5578
EMP: 6 EST: 2021
SALES (est): 176.12K **Privately Held**
Web: www.chasecorp.com
SIC: **2821** Plastics materials and resins

(G-7987)
CODE LLC
Also Called: Coaxle Optical Device and Eqp
2013 1st St Se (28602-5353)
PHONE..................828 328-6004
Daryl Finger, *VP*
EMP: 20 EST: 2002
SALES (est): 2.38MM **Privately Held**
Web: www.code.org
SIC: **3661** 5063 8748 Telephone station equipment and parts, wire; Electrical apparatus and equipment; Telecommunications consultant

(G-7988)
COMFORT BAY HOME FASHIONS INC
Also Called: Dromma Bed
2200 Main Ave Se (28602-1407)
PHONE..................843 442-7477
EMP: 4
SIC: **2515** Bedsprings, assembled
PA: Comfort Bay Home Fashions, Inc.
428 Hudson River Rd
Waterford NY 12188

(G-7989)
COMMSCOPE INC NORTH CAROLINA
2908 2nd Ave Nw (28601-5648)
PHONE..................828 324-2200
Jeff Wossord, *Mgr*
EMP: 10
Web: www.commscope.com
SIC: **3663** Radio and t.v. communications equipment
HQ: Commscope, Inc. Of North Carolina
3642 E Us Highway 70
Claremont NC 28610
828 324-2200

(G-7990)
COMMSCOPE CNNCTVITY SLTONS LLC
1100 Commscope Pl Se (28602-3619)
P.O. Box 1729 (28603-1729)
PHONE..................828 324-2200
EMP: 10
SALES (est): 1.1MM **Privately Held**
Web: www.commscope.com
SIC: **3663** Microwave communication equipment

(G-7991)
COMMSCOPE DSL SYSTEMS LLC
1100 Commscope Pl Se (28602-3619)
P.O. Box 69035 (17106-9035)
PHONE..................828 324-2200
Suzan M Campbell, *VP*
EMP: 89 EST: 1988
SALES (est): 9.8MM **Publicly Held**
Web: www.commscope.com
SIC: **3663** Radio and t.v. communications equipment
HQ: Commscope Technologies Llc
4 Westbrook Corp Ctr
Westchester IL 60154
800 366-3891

(G-7992)
COMMSCOPE TECHNOLOGIES LLC
1100 Commscope Pl Se (28602-3619)
PHONE..................828 324-2200
EMP: 8
SIC: **3643** Power line cable
HQ: Commscope Technologies Llc
4 Westbrook Corp Ctr
Westchester IL 60154
800 366-3891

(G-7993)
CONOVER MACHINE AND DESIGN INC
231 33rd Street Dr Se (28602-8399)
P.O. Box 977 (28613-0977)
PHONE..................828 328-6737
Herman T Christenbury, *Pr*
Hal E Lail, *Sec*
EMP: 6 EST: 1985
SQ FT: 14,000
SALES (est): 476.69K **Privately Held**
SIC: **3599** Machine shop, jobbing and repair

(G-7994)
CONTRACT SEATING INC
796 20th St Ne 4 (28601-4316)
P.O. Box 3485 (28603-3485)
PHONE..................828 322-6662
Randy Stillwell, *Pr*
Ron Woody, *COO*
EMP: 7 EST: 1986

GEOGRAPHIC SECTION
Hickory - Catawba County (G-8021)

SQ FT: 22,000
SALES (est): 263.11K Privately Held
SIC: 2512 Upholstered household furniture

(G-7995)
COPYMASTERS PRINTING SVCS INC
818 1st Ave Sw (28602-2614)
P.O. Box 3738 (28603-3738)
PHONE.................................828 324-0532
Sandy Mangum, Pr
Jimmy Mangum, VP
EMP: 4 EST: 1987
SQ FT: 2,000
SALES (est): 387.1K Privately Held
Web: www.copymastersprinting.com
SIC: 2752 Offset printing

(G-7996)
CORNING OPTCAL CMMNCATIONS LLC
Also Called: Corning
1164 23rd St Se (28602-7320)
PHONE.................................828 327-5290
EMP: 1460
SALES (corp-wide): 12.59B Publicly Held
Web: www.corning.com
SIC: 3357 Communication wire
HQ: Corning Optical Communications Llc
  4200 Corning Pl
  Charlotte NC 28216
  828 901-5000

(G-7997)
COX MANUFACTURING COMPANY INC
220 10th St Sw (28602-2518)
PHONE.................................828 397-4123
Mark R Romeo, Pr
▲ EMP: 39 EST: 1932
SALES (est): 7.69MM Privately Held
Web: www.coxmfg.com
SIC: 2512 Upholstered household furniture

(G-7998)
CRAYMER MCELWEE HOLDINGS INC
6429 Hildebran Shelby Rd (28602-8748)
P.O. Box 1028 (28603-1028)
PHONE.................................828 326-6100
Carrie B Cramer, Pr
Nathan Mcelwee Junior, VP
EMP: 11 EST: 2000
SQ FT: 74,000
SALES (est): 943.17K Privately Held
Web: www.ourhousedesigns.com
SIC: 2512 Upholstered household furniture

(G-7999)
CREATIVE LABEL SOLUTIONS INC
1025 19th St Sw (28602-4812)
PHONE.................................828 320-5389
Allen Watson, Pr
EMP: 6 EST: 1999
SALES (est): 254.9K Privately Held
SIC: 2759 2269 Commercial printing, nec; Labels, cotton: printed

(G-8000)
CUSHION MANUFACTURING INC
1343 9th Ave Ne (28601-4101)
PHONE.................................828 324-9555
Sonny Lackey, Pr
EMP: 6 EST: 1988
SALES (est): 243.83K Privately Held
SIC: 2393 Cushions, except spring and carpet: purchased materials

(G-8001)
CV INDUSTRIES INC (PA)
Also Called: Century Furniture Industries
401 11th St Nw (28601-4750)
P.O. Box 608 (28603-0608)
PHONE.................................828 328-1851
A Alex Shuford Ii, Pr
Harley F Shuford Junior, Ch Bd
Nancy S Dowdy, VP
Brandon Hucks, CFO
Richard L Reese, Sec
◆ EMP: 6 EST: 1973
SQ FT: 700,000
SALES (est): 309.83MM Privately Held
Web: www.centuryfurniture.com
SIC: 2511 2512 2211 Wood household furniture; Upholstered household furniture; Upholstery fabrics, cotton

(G-8002)
DAVIS BROTHERS ROOFING
2404 N Center St Unit B (28601-1335)
PHONE.................................828 578-8561
Joshua Bellew, Prin
EMP: 5 EST: 2018
SALES (est): 54.36K Privately Held
Web: www.davisbrosroofing.com
SIC: 3499 Fabricated metal products, nec

(G-8003)
DB POWER SPORTS
2830 Springs Rd Ne (28601-9106)
PHONE.................................828 324-1500
EMP: 4 EST: 2009
SALES (est): 128.73K Privately Held
SIC: 3949 Sporting and athletic goods, nec

(G-8004)
DEERHUNTER TREE STANDS INC
5944 Leil Rd (28602-7199)
PHONE.................................704 462-1116
Kenneth Benfield, Pr
Bradley Scott Benfield, VP
Jody Vance Benfield, Sec
EMP: 4 EST: 1977
SALES (est): 470K Privately Held
SIC: 3949 Hunting equipment

(G-8005)
DEFY HICKORY
1843 Catawba Valley Blvd Se (28602-4144)
PHONE.................................828 222-4144
EMP: 6 EST: 2018
SALES (est): 146.06K Privately Held
Web: www.defyhickory.com
SIC: 2711 Newspapers, publishing and printing

(G-8006)
DEL-MARK INC
1225 Main Ave Sw (28602-2438)
P.O. Box 1988 (28603-1988)
PHONE.................................828 322-6180
J Wells Walker, Pr
Davis Walker, VP
Wells Walker, Pr
EMP: 10 EST: 1947
SQ FT: 30,000
SALES (est): 748.03K Privately Held
Web: www.delmarktransfers.com
SIC: 2752 Transfers, decalcomania or dry: lithographed

(G-8007)
DELUXE PRINTING CO INC
Also Called: Deluxe Printing Group
10 9th St Nw (28601-6025)
P.O. Box 9467 (28603-9467)
PHONE.................................828 322-1329
Tom K East Junior, Pr
Jeremy East, Genl Mgr
Chad East, Sls Mgr
EMP: 23 EST: 1974
SQ FT: 25,000
SALES (est): 2.28MM Privately Held
Web: www.deluxeprintinggroup.com
SIC: 2752 Offset printing

(G-8008)
DESIGNMASTER FURNITURE INC
1283 23rd St Se (28602-7333)
PHONE.................................828 324-7992
▲ EMP: 20 EST: 1989
SALES (est): 2.65MM Privately Held
Web: www.designmasterfurniture.com
SIC: 2511 5021 Dining room furniture: wood; Dining room furniture

(G-8009)
DIAMOND ENTERPRISES
Also Called: Diamond Research and Dev
5171 Icard Ridge Rd (28601-8968)
PHONE.................................828 495-4448
Darryl Diamond, Pr
Georgia Diamond, Sec
EMP: 5 EST: 1986
SQ FT: 20,000
SALES (est): 250K Privately Held
SIC: 3599 Machine shop, jobbing and repair

(G-8010)
DIPLY LLC
2425 N Center St Ste 247 (28601-1320)
PHONE.................................828 495-4352
▲ EMP: 5 EST: 2004
SQ FT: 10,000
SALES (est): 490.63K Privately Held
Web: www.diplyllc.com
SIC: 2435 Hardwood plywood, prefinished

(G-8011)
DMG MANUFACTURING LLC
719 Old Lenoir Rd (28601-3442)
PHONE.................................828 855-1997
EMP: 20 EST: 2020
SALES (est): 1.31MM Privately Held
SIC: 2326 Medical and hospital uniforms, men's

(G-8012)
DR PEPPER/SEVEN-UP BOTTLING
2401 14th Avenue Cir Nw (28601-7336)
P.O. Box 550 (28603-0550)
PHONE.................................828 322-8090
Lee Teeter, Prin
EMP: 12 EST: 1984
SALES (est): 201.75K Privately Held
Web: www.drpepper.com
SIC: 2086 Soft drinks: packaged in cans, bottles, etc.

(G-8013)
DYNISCO INSTRUMENTS LLC
Also Called: Dynisco Bearing
1291 19th Street Ln Nw (28601-4677)
PHONE.................................828 326-9888
EMP: 31
SALES (corp-wide): 223.55MM Privately Held
Web: www.dynisco.com
SIC: 3829 8734 3561 Aircraft and motor vehicle measurement equipment; Testing laboratories; Pumps and pumping equipment
HQ: Dynisco Instruments Llc
  38 Forge Pkwy
  Franklin MA 02038
  508 541-9400

(G-8014)
EAGLE SUPERABRASIVES INC
141 33rd Street Dr Se (28602-8375)
P.O. Box 3856 (28603-3856)
PHONE.................................828 261-7281
Robert Comer, Pr
EMP: 10 EST: 2009
SALES (est): 811.85K Privately Held
Web: www.eaglesuperabrasives.com
SIC: 3291 Abrasive products

(G-8015)
EARLY BIRD HOSIERY MILLS INC
1011 10th Street Blvd Nw (28601-3459)
P.O. Box 1890 (28603-1890)
PHONE.................................828 324-6745
Eljoe Mullins, Pr
Martha Mullins, Sec
EMP: 13 EST: 1948
SQ FT: 10,000
SALES (est): 353.02K Privately Held
SIC: 2257 Weft knit fabric mills

(G-8016)
EARTH EDGE LLC
940 23rd St Sw (28602-4861)
P.O. Box 849 (28603-0849)
PHONE.................................828 624-0252
EMP: 11 EST: 2010
SALES (est): 1.58MM Privately Held
Web: www.earthedgeproducts.com
SIC: 3069 Latex, foamed

(G-8017)
ENECO EAST INC
P.O. Box 2531 (28603-2531)
PHONE.................................828 322-6008
David Snyder, CEO
EMP: 4 EST: 1975
SALES (est): 217.05K Privately Held
SIC: 3585 Air conditioning equipment, complete

(G-8018)
EVENTIDE SOLUTIONS LLC
1126 10th Street Ln Nw (28601-3586)
PHONE.................................828 855-0448
Clare L Gray, Admn
EMP: 6 EST: 2013
SALES (est): 247.56K Privately Held
Web: www.eventidesolutions.com
SIC: 2741 Miscellaneous publishing

(G-8019)
EVERSHARP SAW & TOOL INC
1241 13th St Ne (28601-4135)
PHONE.................................828 345-1200
Art Chaffee, Pr
Diane Chaffee, VP
Christina Chaffee, Sec
EMP: 5 EST: 1992
SQ FT: 4,500
SALES (est): 247.82K Privately Held
Web: www.eversharpsawandtool.com
SIC: 7629 3545 Tool repair, electric; Machine tool attachments and accessories

(G-8020)
EVERYDAY FIX CYCLERY
4426 N Center St (28601-8024)
PHONE.................................828 855-9989
EMP: 5 EST: 2015
SALES (est): 56.88K Privately Held
Web: www.everydayfixcyclery.com
SIC: 4822 2611 Cablegram service; Pulp mills, mechanical and recycling processing

(G-8021)
FAIRGROVE FURNITURE CO INC
1350 21st Street Dr Se (28602-8386)
PHONE.................................828 322-8570
Melvin M Jones, Pt
Steve Jones, Pt
Adrian Jones, Pt
EMP: 7 EST: 1963

Hickory - Catawba County (G-8022)

SQ FT: 15,000
SALES (est): 492.15K **Privately Held**
SIC: 2426 Frames for upholstered furniture, wood

(G-8022)
FASTRACK PUBLISHING CO INC
1602 Corral Dr (28602-9786)
P.O. Box 1590 (28603-1590)
PHONE 828 294-0544
EMP: 5 **EST:** 2011
SALES (est): 57.74K **Privately Held**
SIC: 2741 Miscellaneous publishing

(G-8023)
FIBER-LINE LLC
280 Performance Dr Se (28602-4045)
PHONE 828 326-8700
Robert Stulpin, *Brnch Mgr*
EMP: 75
Web: www.fiber-line.com
SIC: 2295 2281 Coated fabrics, not rubberized; Manmade and synthetic fiber yarns, spun
HQ: Fiber-Line, Llc
3050 Campus Dr
Hatfield PA 19440
215 997-9181

(G-8024)
FILL PAC LLC
1140 Tate Blvd Se (28602-4025)
PHONE 828 322-1916
William F Hadley, *Managing Member*
▲ **EMP:** 15 **EST:** 2006
SALES (est): 410.36K **Privately Held**
Web: www.fill-pac.com
SIC: 3999 Pet supplies

(G-8025)
FIRST IN FLGHT SKATEBOARDS LLC
220 14th Ave Se Apt B (28602-5243)
PHONE 828 449-9150
Thadus D Jennings, *Prin*
EMP: 4 **EST:** 2018
SALES (est): 47.08K **Privately Held**
SIC: 3949 Skateboards

(G-8026)
FIXTURES & MORE
Also Called: Light Place, The
2220 Us Highway 70 Se Ste 384 (28602)
PHONE 828 855-9093
Anne Wetner, *Owner*
EMP: 5 **EST:** 2015
SALES (est): 213.45K **Privately Held**
Web: www.fixturesnmore.com
SIC: 4213 1731 3641 Building materials transport; Lighting contractor; Glow lamp bulbs

(G-8027)
FOOTHILLS FIRE DEFENSE LLC
63 George Baker Dr (28601-8331)
PHONE 828 381-3988
Wesley Baker, *Prin*
EMP: 4 **EST:** 2018
SALES (est): 111.1K **Privately Held**
Web: foothills-fire-defense-llc.business.site
SIC: 3812 Defense systems and equipment

(G-8028)
FOOTHILLS FIRE DEFENSE LLC
25 Heron Cove Loop (28601-7843)
PHONE 828 612-9575
Wesley Baker, *Owner*
EMP: 4 **EST:** 2018
SALES (est): 97.48K **Privately Held**
Web: foothills-fire-defense-llc.business.site
SIC: 3812 Defense systems and equipment

(G-8029)
FURNITURE CONCEPTS
909 10th St Ne (28601-4035)
PHONE 828 323-1590
Herman Fox, *Owner*
EMP: 15 **EST:** 1984
SALES (est): 875.04K **Privately Held**
Web: www.furnitureconcepts.com
SIC: 2512 2511 Chairs: upholstered on wood frames; Chairs, household, except upholstered: wood

(G-8030)
FUTURE ENDEAVORS HICKORY LLC
2608 Springs Rd Ne (28601-3170)
PHONE 828 256-5488
Douglas B Huffman, *Prin*
EMP: 8 **EST:** 2006
SALES (est): 127.75K **Privately Held**
SIC: 2711 Newspapers, publishing and printing

(G-8031)
GAINES MOTOR LINES INC (PA)
2349 13th Ave Sw (28602-4740)
P.O. Box 1549 (28603-1549)
PHONE 828 322-2000
Forest M Gaines, *CEO*
Timothy Gaines, *Prin*
Corey Gaines, *Prin*
Sara Gaines, *Prin*
EMP: 110 **EST:** 1940
SQ FT: 76,000
SALES (est): 14.84MM
SALES (corp-wide): 14.84MM **Privately Held**
Web: www.gainesml.com
SIC: 3715 4731 Truck trailers; Freight transportation arrangement

(G-8032)
GIFTED HANDS STYLING SALON
1316 Us Highway 70 Sw (28602-3133)
PHONE 828 781-2781
Gwendolyn Roseboro, *Owner*
EMP: 9 **EST:** 2014
SALES (est): 43.84K **Privately Held**
SIC: 7231 3999 Beauty shops; Hair and hair-based products

(G-8033)
GLASS WORKS OF HICKORY INC
1040 Old Lenoir Rd Ste B (28601-3473)
PHONE 828 322-2122
EMP: 4 **EST:** 1995
SQ FT: 3,000
SALES (est): 284.01K **Privately Held**
Web: www.glassworksofhickory.com
SIC: 3231 5719 Mirrored glass; Mirrors

(G-8034)
GRASCHE USA INC
Also Called: Grasche
240 Performance Dr Se (28602-4045)
P.O. Box 1348 (28603-1348)
PHONE 828 322-1226
Guenter Grass, *Pr*
Klaus Jensen, *
Guenter Grass, *Stockholder*
Astrid Grass, *Stockholder**
Michael Downing, *
▲ **EMP:** 26 **EST:** 1979
SQ FT: 30,000
SALES (est): 4.43MM **Privately Held**
Web: www.grasche.com
SIC: 3425 5085 Saws, hand: metalworking or woodworking; Knives, industrial

(G-8035)
GUEST INTERIORS
904 3rd Ave Nw (28601-4849)
PHONE 828 244-5738
EMP: 4 **EST:** 1993
SALES (est): 92.88K **Privately Held**
Web: www.guestinteriors.com
SIC: 5719 2391 1799 Miscellaneous homefurnishings; Curtains and draperies; Special trade contractors, nec

(G-8036)
GUNPOWDER CREEK DISTILLERS LLC
1260 25th Street Pl Se (28602-9657)
PHONE 828 851-0799
Christopher Lee Willis, *Owner*
EMP: 5 **EST:** 2016
SALES (est): 139.91K **Privately Held**
SIC: 2892 Gunpowder

(G-8037)
H W S COMPANY INC (HQ)
Also Called: Hickory White Company
856 7th Ave Se (28602-3938)
P.O. Box 189 (28603-0189)
PHONE 828 322-8624
▲ **EMP:** 300 **EST:** 1997
SQ FT: 479,200
SALES (est): 57.38MM
SALES (corp-wide): 104.33MM **Privately Held**
SIC: 2512 Couches, sofas, and davenports: upholstered on wood frames
PA: Sherrill Furniture Company Inc
2405 Highland Ave Ne
Hickory NC 28601
828 322-2640

(G-8038)
HARGENRADER CSTM WOODCRAFT LLC
2481 23rd St Ne (28601-9193)
PHONE 828 896-7182
Luke Hargenrader, *Prin*
EMP: 7 **EST:** 2014
SALES (est): 238.14K **Privately Held**
Web: www.hargenradercustomwoodcraft.com
SIC: 2434 Wood kitchen cabinets

(G-8039)
HDM FURNITURE INDUSTRIES INC
Hickory Chair Company
37 9th Street Pl Se (28602-1215)
P.O. Box 2147 (28603-2147)
PHONE 800 349-4579
EMP: 1770
SALES (corp-wide): 384.13MM **Privately Held**
SIC: 2512 2511 Chairs: upholstered on wood frames; Wood household furniture
PA: Hdm Furniture Industries Inc
1925 Eastchester Dr
High Point NC 27265
336 888-4800

(G-8040)
HDM FURNITURE INDUSTRIES INC
Also Called: Pearson Company
37 9th Street Pl Se (28602-1215)
PHONE 336 882-8135
EMP: 165
SALES (corp-wide): 384.13MM **Privately Held**
SIC: 2511 Wood household furniture
PA: Hdm Furniture Industries Inc
1925 Eastchester Dr
High Point NC 27265
336 888-4800

(G-8041)
HEICO FASTENERS INC (HQ)
2377 8th Ave Nw (28601-4511)
P.O. Box 2905 (28603-2905)
PHONE 828 261-0184
Stefan Waltermann, *Pr*
Michael Zeller, *Sec*
◆ **EMP:** 23 **EST:** 1996
SQ FT: 75,000
SALES (est): 5.57MM
SALES (corp-wide): 76.52MM **Privately Held**
Web: www.heicofasteners.com
SIC: 3965 Fasteners
PA: Theo Heimann Holding Gmbh & Co. Kg
Osterweg 21
Ense NW 59469
29388050

(G-8042)
HEICO MANUFACTURING INC
2377 8th Ave Nw (28601-4511)
PHONE 828 304-5499
EMP: 6 **EST:** 2019
SALES (est): 377.32K **Privately Held**
Web: www.heicofasteners.com
SIC: 3999 Manufacturing industries, nec

(G-8043)
HICKORY ADCHEM INC
123 23rd St Sw (28602-2154)
P.O. Box 1451 (28603-1451)
PHONE 828 327-0936
Robert G Hadley, *Pr*
Elaine Hadley, *VP*
EMP: 7 **EST:** 1968
SQ FT: 42,000
SALES (est): 992.23K **Privately Held**
SIC: 2891 Adhesives

(G-8044)
HICKORY BRANDS INC
429 27th St Nw (28601-4549)
PHONE 828 322-2600
Nisson Joseph, *Pr*
Julie Huffman, *
Catherine Pitts, *
◆ **EMP:** 91 **EST:** 1987
SQ FT: 80,000
SALES (est): 14.59MM **Privately Held**
Web: www.hickorybrands.com
SIC: 2241 2842 Shoe laces, except leather; Shoe polish or cleaner

(G-8045)
HICKORY BUSINESS FURNITURE LLC (HQ)
Also Called: Hbf Textiles
900 12th Street Dr Nw (28601-4763)
P.O. Box 8 (28603-0008)
PHONE 828 328-2064
Stan A Askren, *Ch*
Steven M Bradford, *VP*
Kurt A Tjaden, *CFO*
Don Mead, *Ex VP*
▲ **EMP:** 325 **EST:** 1979
SQ FT: 200,000
SALES (est): 105.59MM
SALES (corp-wide): 479.1MM **Publicly Held**
Web: www.hbf.com
SIC: 2521 2299 Wood office furniture; Batting, wadding, padding and fillings
PA: Hni Corporation
600 E 2nd St
Muscatine IA 52761
563 272-7400

GEOGRAPHIC SECTION
Hickory - Catawba County (G-8068)

(G-8046)
HICKORY CHAIR COMPANY
Also Called: Hickory Chair
37 9th Street Pl Se (28602-1215)
P.O. Box 2147 (28603-2147)
PHONE..................................800 225-0265
◆ **EMP:** 58
SIC: 2511 Wood household furniture

(G-8047)
HICKORY DYG & WINDING CO INC
Also Called: Hickory Yarns
1025 10th St Ne (28601-4037)
P.O. Box 1975 (28603-1975)
PHONE..................................828 322-1550
Robert Miller Junior, *Pr*
▲ **EMP:** 19 **EST:** 1938
SQ FT: 70,000
SALES (est): 2.15MM **Privately Held**
Web: www.hickoryyarns.com
SIC: 2282 2281 Throwing and winding mills; Yarn spinning mills

(G-8048)
HICKORY HERITAGE OF FALLING CREEK INC
3211b Falling Creek Rd (28601-9606)
EMP: 12 **EST:** 2010
SALES (est): 1.83MM **Privately Held**
SIC: 2221 Upholstery fabrics, manmade fiber and silk

(G-8049)
HICKORY PUBLISHING CO INC
Also Called: Hickory Daily Record
1100 Park Place 11th Ave Se (28601)
PHONE..................................828 322-4510
Suzanne G Millholland, *Pr*
Kenneth Millholland, *
John G Millholland, *
David K Millholland, *
EMP: 33 **EST:** 1915
SQ FT: 40,000
SALES (est): 1.58MM **Privately Held**
Web: www.hickoryrecord.com
SIC: 2711 Newspapers, publishing and printing

(G-8050)
HICKORY SAW & TOOL INC
406 9th St Se (28602-4040)
PHONE..................................828 324-5585
Mike L Pannell, *Pr*
J Robert Busbee, *
Barry Whisnant, *
Larry C Pannell, *
Don Jones, *Stockholder*
▲ **EMP:** 23 **EST:** 1983
SQ FT: 10,000
SALES (est): 4.49MM **Privately Held**
Web: www.hickorysawandtool.com
SIC: 3545 7699 Cutting tools for machine tools; Knife, saw and tool sharpening and repair

(G-8051)
HICKORY SPRINGS CALIFORNIA LLC
235 2nd Ave Nw (28601-4950)
P.O. Box 128 (28603-0128)
PHONE..................................828 328-2201
David Underdown, *Ch*
Parks C Underdown Junior, *Ch Bd*
J Donald Coleman, *
Lee Lunsford, *
▲ **EMP:** 607 **EST:** 1985
SQ FT: 30,000
SALES (est): 139.77MM
SALES (corp-wide): 430.3MM **Privately Held**
Web: www.hsmsolutions.com
SIC: 3429 3086 Furniture hardware; Plastics foam products
PA: Hickory Springs Manufacturing Company
235 2nd Ave Nw
Hickory NC 28601
828 328-2201

(G-8052)
HICKORY SPRINGS MANUFACTURING COMPANY (PA)
Also Called: Hsm Solutions
235 2nd Ave Nw (28601-4950)
P.O. Box 128 (28603-0128)
PHONE..................................828 328-2201
◆ **EMP:** 100 **EST:** 1944
SALES (est): 430.3MM
SALES (corp-wide): 430.3MM **Privately Held**
Web: www.hickorysprings.com
SIC: 3069 3495 2514 5072 Foam rubber; Furniture springs, unassembled; Frames for box springs or bedsprings: metal; Furniture hardware, nec

(G-8053)
HICKORY SPRINGS MFG CO
871 Highland Ave Ne (28601-4053)
PHONE..................................828 322-7994
Robert L Campbell Junior, *Brnch Mgr*
EMP: 7
SALES (corp-wide): 430.3MM **Privately Held**
Web: www.hsmsolutions.com
SIC: 3069 Foam rubber
PA: Hickory Springs Manufacturing Company
235 2nd Ave Nw
Hickory NC 28601
828 328-2201

(G-8054)
HICKORY SPRINGS MFG CO
2230 Main Ave Se (28601-1407)
P.O. Box 128 (28603-0128)
PHONE..................................828 328-2201
Jim Tate, *Mgr*
EMP: 62
SALES (corp-wide): 430.3MM **Privately Held**
Web: www.hsmsolutions.com
SIC: 3429 Furniture hardware
PA: Hickory Springs Manufacturing Company
235 2nd Ave Nw
Hickory NC 28601
828 328-2201

(G-8055)
HICKORY THROWING COMPANY
520 20th St Se (28602-4400)
PHONE..................................828 322-1158
William H Taylor Senior, *Ch Bd*
William H Taylor Junior, *Pr*
Nancy Pittman, *
◆ **EMP:** 45 **EST:** 1958
SQ FT: 48,500
SALES (est): 2.5MM **Privately Held**
Web: www.hickorythrowing.com
SIC: 2281 2282 Yarn spinning mills; Twisting yarn

(G-8056)
HICKORY WIRE INC
1711 11th Ave Sw (28602-4909)
P.O. Box 1229 (29585-1229)
PHONE..................................828 322-9473
Robert Moser, *Pr*
Sharon Moser, *Sec*
EMP: 10 **EST:** 1990
SQ FT: 66,000
SALES (est): 1.72MM **Privately Held**
SIC: 3351 Wire, copper and copper alloy

(G-8057)
HICKORY YOUTH SPORTS INC
425 44th Avenue Dr Nw (28601-9017)
PHONE..................................828 327-9550
Hubert Fry, *Prin*
EMP: 4 **EST:** 2018
SALES (est): 84K **Privately Held**
SIC: 2711 Newspapers, publishing and printing

(G-8058)
HM LIQUIDATION INC
Also Called: Cabot Wrenn
166 Hancock & Moore Ln (28601)
PHONE..................................828 495-8235
Jack Glasheen, *CEO*
Timothy Rogers, *Pr*
Jimmy Moore, *VP*
EMP: 4 **EST:** 1981
SQ FT: 150,000
SALES (est): 711.71K **Privately Held**
Web: www.hancockandmoore.com
SIC: 2512 2522 Couches, sofas, and davenports: upholstered on wood frames; Chairs, office: padded or plain: except wood

(G-8059)
HOME IMPRESSIONS INC
420 3rd Ave Nw (28601-4983)
P.O. Box 9181 (28603-9181)
PHONE..................................828 328-1142
Cliff Tucker, *Pr*
▲ **EMP:** 460 **EST:** 1994
SQ FT: 10,000
SALES (est): 2.08MM
SALES (corp-wide): 1.38B **Publicly Held**
Web: www.homeimpressions.com
SIC: 5099 3469 Containers: glass, metal or plastic; Metal stampings, nec
HQ: Solar Group, Inc.
107 Fellowship Rd
Taylorsville MS 39168
601 785-4711

(G-8060)
HUNTINGTON HOUSE INC (PA)
661 Rink Dam Rd (28601)
P.O. Box 6231 (28603-6231)
PHONE..................................828 495-4400
▲ **EMP:** 101 **EST:** 1985
SALES (est): 19.15MM
SALES (corp-wide): 19.15MM **Privately Held**
Web: www.huntingtonhouse.com
SIC: 2512 Upholstered household furniture

(G-8061)
IMAGINE ONE LLC
420 3rd Ave Nw (28601-4983)
P.O. Box 9349 (28603-9349)
PHONE..................................828 324-6454
EMP: 4 **EST:** 2001
SALES (est): 442.42K **Privately Held**
Web: www.imagine-one.com
SIC: 3589 Water filters and softeners, household type

(G-8062)
IMAGINE ONE RESOURCES LLC
420 3rd Ave Nw (28601-4983)
P.O. Box 9181 (28603-9181)
PHONE..................................828 328-1142
EMP: 8 **EST:** 2011
SALES (est): 4.46MM
SALES (corp-wide): 23.69MM **Privately Held**
Web: www.protectplus.com
SIC: 3589 Water treatment equipment, industrial
PA: Protect Plus Llc
420 3rd Ave Nw Ste A
Hickory NC 28601
828 328-1142

(G-8063)
IMMUNOTEK BIO CENTERS LLC
1040 2nd St Ne (28601-3844)
PHONE..................................828 569-6264
Matthew Lindstaedt, *Mgr*
EMP: 36
SALES (corp-wide): 140.79MM **Privately Held**
Web: www.immunotek.com
SIC: 2836 Blood derivatives
PA: Immunotek Bio Centers, L.L.C.
1430 E Southlake Blvd # 200
Southlake TX 76092
337 500-1175

(G-8064)
IMPLUS LLC
Balega
1279 19th Street Ln Nw (28601-4677)
PHONE..................................828 485-3318
EMP: 16
SALES (corp-wide): 300MM **Privately Held**
Web: www.implus.com
SIC: 2252 Socks
HQ: Implus, Llc
2001 Tw Alexander Dr
Durham NC 27709
919 544-7900

(G-8065)
ING SOURCE LLC
1340 14th Avenue Ct Sw (28602-4859)
PHONE..................................828 855-0481
David Higgins, *CEO*
David B Higgins, *CEO*
▲ **EMP:** 19 **EST:** 2008
SALES (est): 2.84MM **Privately Held**
Web: www.ingsource.com
SIC: 3842 Orthopedic appliances

(G-8066)
INOTEC AMD INC
1350 4th St Nw (28601-2444)
PHONE..................................888 354-9772
Jenifer Walter, *CEO*
EMP: 6 **EST:** 2018
SALES (est): 543.32K **Privately Held**
Web: www.natroxwoundcare.com
SIC: 3829 Thermometers, including digital: clinical

(G-8067)
INTERNTONAL SPECIALTY PDTS INC
1720 Tate Blvd Se (28602-4246)
P.O. Box 3826 (28603-3826)
PHONE..................................828 326-9053
Heather Gragg, *VP*
▲ **EMP:** 7 **EST:** 1993
SALES (est): 609.64K **Privately Held**
SIC: 3312 Wire products, steel or iron

(G-8068)
INVICTUS LIGHTING LLC
1401 Main Ave Sw (28602-2440)
P.O. Box 2708 (28603-2708)
PHONE..................................828 855-9324
Eric Mcmillan, *Managing Member*
Peter Lohr, *Mng Pt*
Erik Mcmillan, *Managing Member*
EMP: 9 **EST:** 2015
SQ FT: 2,250
SALES (est): 894.94K **Privately Held**
Web: www.invictuslighting.com

Hickory - Catawba County (G-8069)

SIC: **3646** 3641 Commercial lighting fixtures; Electric lamps and parts for generalized applications

(G-8069)
ISABELLAS OILS LLC
5152 Sulphur Springs Rd Ne (28601-9720)
PHONE.................................828 221-4274
Joanna Smith, *Prin*
EMP: 4 EST: 2017
SALES (est): 106.86K Privately Held
SIC: **3999** Candles

(G-8070)
JACOB HOLTZ COMPANY
Also Called: JACOB HOLTZ COMPANY
747 22nd Street Pl Se (28602-7316)
PHONE.................................828 328-1003
Buddy Burchan, *Mgr*
EMP: 22
SALES (corp-wide): 4.09MM Privately Held
Web: www.jacobholtz.com
SIC: **3429** 3469 Furniture hardware; Metal stampings, nec
PA: Jacob Holtz Company, Llc
10 Industrial Hwy Ste Ms6
Philadelphia PA 19113
215 423-2800

(G-8071)
JAMES OXYGEN AND SUPPLY CO (PA)
Also Called: James O 2
30 Us Highway 321 Nw (28601-6801)
P.O. Box 159 (28603-0159)
PHONE.................................704 322-5438
Vance T James Junior, *Pr*
Andrew C James, *
Margaret James, *
EMP: 31 EST: 1956
SQ FT: 14,000
SALES (est): 9.57MM
SALES (corp-wide): 9.57MM Privately Held
Web: www.jameso2.com
SIC: **5169** 5084 2813 Gases, compressed and liquefied; Welding machinery and equipment; Industrial gases

(G-8072)
JBS USA LLC
1207 25th Street Pl Se (28602-9658)
PHONE.................................828 855-9571
EMP: 10 EST: 2018
SALES (est): 1.01MM Privately Held
Web: www.jbsfoodsgroup.com
SIC: **2011** Meat packing plants

(G-8073)
KELLY HOSIERY MILL INC
6450 Applehill Dr (28602-8744)
PHONE.................................828 324-6456
Joe J Watts, *Pr*
Orlee Watts, *VP*
EMP: 6 EST: 1965
SALES (est): 482.77K Privately Held
Web: www.kellyhosiery.com
SIC: **2252** Socks

(G-8074)
KERRS HICKRY READY-MIXED CON (PA)
Also Called: Kerr's H R M Concrete
1126 1st Ave Sw (28602-2606)
P.O. Box 1924 (28603-1924)
PHONE.................................828 322-3157
Helen Kerr, *Pr*
James Kerr Junior, *VP*
Roger S Kerr, *
Donna Kerr, *
EMP: 45 EST: 1920
SQ FT: 3,000
SALES (est): 9.96MM
SALES (corp-wide): 9.96MM Privately Held
Web: www.kerrsconcrete.com
SIC: **3273** Ready-mixed concrete

(G-8075)
KING HICKORY FURNITURE COMPANY
728 Highland Ave Ne (28601-4028)
PHONE.................................828 324-0472
EMP: 7
SALES (corp-wide): 36.28MM Privately Held
Web: www.kinghickory.com
SIC: **2512** Couches, sofas, and davenports: upholstered on wood frames
PA: King Hickory Furniture Company
1820 Main Ave Se
Hickory NC 28602
828 322-6025

(G-8076)
KING HICKORY FURNITURE COMPANY (PA)
1820 Main Ave Se (28602-1340)
P.O. Box 1179 (28603-1179)
PHONE.................................828 322-6025
Robert E Palmer, *Ch*
▲ EMP: 180 EST: 1958
SQ FT: 30,000
SALES (est): 36.28MM
SALES (corp-wide): 36.28MM Privately Held
Web: www.kinghickory.com
SIC: **2512** Couches, sofas, and davenports: upholstered on wood frames

(G-8077)
KISHWA LEATHER LLC
4331 1st Street Dr Nw (28601-8185)
PHONE.................................828 234-4592
EMP: 5 EST: 2019
SALES (est): 96.26K Privately Held
SIC: **3199** Leather goods, nec

(G-8078)
KLINGSPOR ABRASIVES INC (HQ)
Also Called: Klingspor
2555 Tate Blvd Se (28602-1445)
P.O. Box 2367 (28603-2367)
PHONE.................................828 322-3030
Christoph Klingspor, *Pr*
Berthold Spatz, *
◆ EMP: 209 EST: 1979
SQ FT: 150,000
SALES (est): 54.55MM
SALES (corp-wide): 332.18MM Privately Held
Web: www.klingspor.com
SIC: **3291** Coated abrasive products
PA: Klingspor Ag
Huttenstr. 36
Haiger HE 35708
27739220

(G-8079)
KOHNLE CABINETRY
250 Rocky Acres Rd (28601-8354)
PHONE.................................828 640-2498
EMP: 4 EST: 2014
SALES (est): 137.49K Privately Held
SIC: **2434** Wood kitchen cabinets

(G-8080)
KONTANE LOGISTICS INC (PA)
3876 Martin Fish Pond St (28602-8445)
P.O. Box 1702 (28603-1702)
PHONE.................................828 397-5501
▲ EMP: 4 EST: 1975
SALES (est): 11.2MM
SALES (corp-wide): 11.2MM Privately Held
Web: www.kontanelogistics.com
SIC: **2441** 2449 Shipping cases, wood: nailed or lock corner; Wood containers, nec

(G-8081)
L & R KNITTING INC
6350 Claude Brittain Rd (28602-9571)
PHONE.................................828 874-2960
Ronnie Brittain, *Pr*
Loretta Brittain, *Sec*
EMP: 6 EST: 1972
SQ FT: 14,000
SALES (est): 243.05K Privately Held
SIC: **2252** Men's, boys', and girls' hosiery

(G-8082)
LADY C E CREWS LLC
2740 6th Street Ct Ne (28601-9263)
PHONE.................................703 565-3687
Charlie E Crews, *Prin*
EMP: 4 EST: 2019
SALES (est): 43.66K Privately Held
SIC: **3999** Manufacturing industries, nec

(G-8083)
LARLIN CUSHION COMPANY
1950 Fairgrove Church Rd (28602)
PHONE.................................828 465-5599
Lawrence Swaney, *Owner*
EMP: 10 EST: 1975
SQ FT: 15,000
SALES (est): 701.09K Privately Held
Web: www.larlincushion.com
SIC: **2515** Spring cushions

(G-8084)
LATHERS SKIN ESSENTIALS
1891 Plaza Dr (28602-8272)
PHONE.................................828 449-9244
Joseph Dixon, *Owner*
Jessa Dixon, *Owner*
EMP: 5 EST: 2014
SALES (est): 128.06K Privately Held
SIC: **2841** 5169 Soap: granulated, liquid, cake, flaked, or chip; Detergents and soaps, except specialty cleaning

(G-8085)
LCF ENTERPRISE (PA)
719 6th Ave Nw (28601-3509)
PHONE.................................208 415-4300
Lorna Finman, *Owner*
EMP: 9 EST: 1986
SALES (est): 863.14K
SALES (corp-wide): 863.14K Privately Held
SIC: **3663** Amplifiers, RF power and IF

(G-8086)
LEATHER MIRACLES LLC
3350 20th Ave Se (28602)
P.O. Box 2171 (28603-2171)
PHONE.................................828 464-7448
◆ EMP: 67 EST: 2000
SQ FT: 50,000
SALES (est): 13.7MM Privately Held
Web: www.leathermiracles.com
SIC: **5199** 3111 Leather and cut stock; Leather tanning and finishing

(G-8087)
LITTLE RIVER YACHTS LLC
1100 Commscope Pl Se (28602-3619)
P.O. Box 9212 (28603-9212)
PHONE.................................828 323-4955
Sandra O Walters, *Managing Member*
EMP: 4 EST: 2009
SALES (est): 119.05K Privately Held
Web: www.commscope.com
SIC: **3663** Radio and t.v. communications equipment

(G-8088)
LOVEKIN & YOUNG PC
110 N Center St (28601-6294)
P.O. Box 585 (10536-0585)
PHONE.................................828 322-5435
Gary F Young, *Prin*
EMP: 6 EST: 2014
SALES (est): 65.76K Privately Held
SIC: **2741** Miscellaneous publishing

(G-8089)
LTLB HOLDING COMPANY (PA)
Also Called: American Roller Bearing Co
1350 4th St Dr Nw (28601-2524)
PHONE.................................828 624-1460
Benjamin S Succop, *Pr*
Larry Succop, *CEO*
Marshall Kim Harkins, *CFO*
Lawrence N Succop, *Ch Bd*
Tim Hopkins, *CFO*
▲ EMP: 18 EST: 2007
SQ FT: 21,000
SALES (est): 45.63MM
SALES (corp-wide): 45.63MM Privately Held
Web: www.amroll.com
SIC: **3562** Ball and roller bearings

(G-8090)
MARCAL PAPER MILLS LLC
612 3rd Ave Ne (28601-5164)
PHONE.................................828 322-1805
EMP: 500
SALES (corp-wide): 467.08MM Privately Held
Web: www.marcalpaper.com
SIC: **2676** Towels, napkins, and tissue paper products
HQ: Marcal Paper Mills, Llc
1 Market St
Elmwood Park NJ 07407
828 322-1805

(G-8091)
MARIETTA MARTIN MATERIALS INC
Also Called: Martin Marietta Aggregates
1989 11th Ave Se (28602-4325)
PHONE.................................828 322-8386
Justin Nelson, *Brnch Mgr*
EMP: 6
Web: www.martinmarietta.com
SIC: **1422** Crushed and broken limestone
PA: Martin Marietta Materials Inc
4123 Parklake Ave
Raleigh NC 27612

(G-8092)
MAXIMIZER SYSTEMS INC
1010 21st Street Dr Se (28602-8320)
PHONE.................................828 345-6036
Richard Neville-dove, *Prin*
EMP: 13 EST: 2018
SALES (est): 972.61K Privately Held
Web: www.maximizersystems.com
SIC: **3999** Manufacturing industries, nec

(G-8093)
MCCRORIE GROUP LLC (PA)
Also Called: McCrorie Wood Products
330 19th St Se (28602-4229)
P.O. Box 9007 (28603-9007)
PHONE.................................828 328-4538
EMP: 21 EST: 1969

GEOGRAPHIC SECTION
Hickory - Catawba County (G-8117)

SQ FT: 100,000
SALES (est): 4.84MM
SALES (corp-wide): 4.84MM **Privately Held**
Web: www.mccroriewoodproducts.com
SIC: 2499 Carved and turned wood

(G-8094)
MILLENIA USA LLC
3211c Falling Creek Rd (28601-9606)
▲ EMP: 16 EST: 2006
SALES (est): 959.71K **Privately Held**
Web: www.millenia-furniture.com
SIC: 2519 Lawn and garden furniture, except wood and metal

(G-8095)
MINELLI USA LLC
1245 26th St Se (28602-7317)
PHONE..................828 578-6734
Alberto Tansi, *Prin*
EMP: 10 EST: 2017
SALES (est): 542.45K **Privately Held**
Web: www.minelligroup.com
SIC: 2499 Wood products, nec

(G-8096)
MODERN RECREATIONAL TECH
Valvtect Petroleum Products
2220 Us Highway 70 Se Ste 100 (28602-5192)
PHONE..................847 272-2278
Gerald H Nessenson, *Prin*
EMP: 49
SALES (corp-wide): 7.26B **Publicly Held**
Web: www.kop-coat.com
SIC: 2851 Paints and allied products
HQ: Kop-Coat, Inc.
3040 William Pitt Way
Pittsburgh PA 15238
412 227-2426

(G-8097)
MOORESVILLE TRIBUNE
1100 11th Avenue Blvd Se (28602-4351)
PHONE..................704 872-0148
EMP: 7 EST: 2017
SALES (est): 120.75K **Privately Held**
Web: www.mooresvilletribune.com
SIC: 2711 Newspapers, publishing and printing

(G-8098)
MORETZ & SIPE INC
3261 Highland Ave Ne (28601-9375)
PHONE..................828 327-8661
Pauline Moretz, *Pr*
EMP: 6 EST: 1951
SALES (est): 550K **Privately Held**
Web: www.toddstapley.com
SIC: 1611 3272 Highway and street paving contractor; Septic tanks, concrete

(G-8099)
MR TIRE INC
2105 N Center St (28601-1317)
PHONE..................828 322-8130
Baron Bobgarner, *Brnch Mgr*
EMP: 10
SALES (corp-wide): 1.33B **Publicly Held**
Web: mrtireinc.business.site
SIC: 3714 5531 7538 7534 Automotive wiring harness sets; Automotive tires; General automotive repair shops; Tire recapping
HQ: Mr. Tire Inc.
2078 New York Ave Unit 2
Huntington Station NY 11746
631 499-3700

(G-8100)
NELSON HOLDINGS NC INC
Also Called: Nelson Oil Company
5 20th St Sw (28602-2216)
P.O. Box 1472 (28603-1472)
PHONE..................828 322-9226
Andrew N Hines, *Pr*
Leslie Hines Iii, *VP*
EMP: 10 EST: 1925
SALES (est): 4.38MM **Privately Held**
Web: www.nelsonlubricants.com
SIC: 5172 3586 Petroleum products, nec; Measuring and dispensing pumps

(G-8101)
NETWORK INTEGRITY SYSTEMS INC
Also Called: Network Integrity Systems
1937 Tate Blvd Se (28602-1430)
PHONE..................828 322-2181
David Vokey, *Pr*
Joe Giovannini, *VP*
EMP: 5 EST: 2003
SQ FT: 5,767
SALES (est): 1.11MM **Privately Held**
Web: www.networkintegritysystems.com
SIC: 3825 Network analyzers

(G-8102)
NEXANS USA INC (DH)
39 2nd St Nw (28601-6104)
P.O. Box 900 (28603-0900)
PHONE..................828 323-2660
Stephen Hall, *Pr*
Yvon Raak, *
Kevin Stinson, *
Frank S Ryan, *
◆ EMP: 290 EST: 2000
SQ FT: 150,000
SALES (est): 92.91MM **Privately Held**
SIC: 3357 3661 3678 Communication wire; Telephones and telephone apparatus; Electronic connectors
HQ: Nexans Participations
4 Allee De L Arche
Courbevoie
147375869

(G-8103)
NORDSON CORPORATION
Also Called: Nordson Xaloy
1291 19th Street Ln Nw (28601-4677)
PHONE..................724 656-5600
EMP: 6
SALES (corp-wide): 2.63B **Publicly Held**
Web: www.nordson.com
SIC: 3563 Air and gas compressors
PA: Nordson Corporation
28601 Clemens Rd
Westlake OH 44145
440 892-1580

(G-8104)
NORTH CAROLINA SOCK INC
Also Called: N C Sock
5521 Suttlemyre Ln (28601-9426)
PHONE..................828 327-4664
EMP: 5 EST: 1994
SQ FT: 25,000
SALES (est): 100.92MM **Privately Held**
SIC: 2252 2251 Socks; Women's hosiery, except socks

(G-8105)
NOT JUST ARCHERY
2201 Moss Farm Rd (28602-8313)
PHONE..................828 294-7727
Ty Drum, *Owner*
EMP: 4 EST: 1993
SQ FT: 2,400
SALES (est): 182.94K **Privately Held**
SIC: 3949 7699 Sporting and athletic goods, nec; Gun services

(G-8106)
OMNI GROUP LLC
1140 Tate Blvd Se (28602-4025)
PHONE..................828 404-3104
Janet Anderson, *Prin*
EMP: 7 EST: 2008
SALES (est): 121.23K **Privately Held**
SIC: 3532 Screeners, stationary

(G-8107)
ONEH2 INC
620 23rd St Nw (28601-4526)
PHONE..................844 996-6342
Paul Dawson, *CEO*
EMP: 42 EST: 2015
SALES (est): 11.93MM **Privately Held**
Web: www.oneh2.com
SIC: 2819 Industrial inorganic chemicals, nec

(G-8108)
OPTICONCEPTS INC
925b Old Lenoir Rd (28601-3446)
P.O. Box 1170 (28690-1170)
PHONE..................828 320-0138
EMP: 5 EST: 2000
SQ FT: 3,000
SALES (est): 431.27K **Privately Held**
Web: www.opticoncepts.com
SIC: 3357 Fiber optic cable (insulated)

(G-8109)
ORTHOPEDIC APPLIANCE COMPANY
910 Tate Blvd Se (28602-4030)
PHONE..................828 348-1960
EMP: 8 EST: 2018
SALES (est): 240.68K **Privately Held**
Web: www.orthopedicapplianceco.com
SIC: 3842 Orthopedic appliances

(G-8110)
PEPSI-COLA BTLG HICKRY NC INC
Also Called: Pepsi-Cola
2640 Main Ave Nw (28601-5655)
PHONE..................828 322-8090
Frans Katherine, *Ex VP*
EMP: 24
SALES (corp-wide): 50.09MM **Privately Held**
Web: www.pepsico.com
SIC: 5149 2086 Soft drinks; Soft drinks: packaged in cans, bottles, etc.
PA: Pepsi-Cola Bottling Company Of Hickory, N.C., Inc.
2401 14th Avenue Cir Nw
Hickory NC 28601
828 322-8090

(G-8111)
PEPSI-COLA BTLG HICKRY NC INC (PA)
Also Called: Pepsi-Cola
2401 14th Avenue Cir Nw (28601-7336)
P.O. Box 550 (28603-0550)
PHONE..................828 322-8090
James Lee Teeter, *Pr*
Katherine Frans, *
Margaret Brady, *
Mary Teeter, *
John Teeter, *
EMP: 115 EST: 1926
SQ FT: 53,000
SALES (est): 50.09MM
SALES (corp-wide): 50.09MM **Privately Held**
Web: www.pepsico.com

SIC: 2086 5149 Carbonated soft drinks, bottled and canned; Soft drinks

(G-8112)
PERFECTION FABRICS INC
841a F Avenue Dr Se (28602-1123)
P.O. Box 2946 (28603-2946)
PHONE..................828 328-3322
George Lane, *Pr*
EMP: 8 EST: 1993
SQ FT: 12,500
SALES (est): 886.19K **Privately Held**
SIC: 3582 Washing machines, laundry: commercial, incl. coin-operated

(G-8113)
PFLAG HICKORY
3065 44th Avenue Dr Ne (28601-9762)
PHONE..................828 244-5578
Kathy Wood, *Prin*
EMP: 5 EST: 2016
SALES (est): 92.7K **Privately Held**
Web: www.pflaghickorync.com
SIC: 2711 Newspapers, publishing and printing

(G-8114)
PIEDMONT PRECISION PRODUCTS
347 Highland Ave Se (28602-3033)
P.O. Box 3171 (28603-3171)
PHONE..................828 304-0791
David Ridgeway, *Pr*
Eric Harwell, *VP*
EMP: 11 EST: 1997
SQ FT: 5,000
SALES (est): 338.67K **Privately Held**
Web: www.piedmontprecision.com
SIC: 3599 Machine shop, jobbing and repair

(G-8115)
PIEDMONT SPRINGS COMPANY INC
118 11th Street Pl Sw (28602-2608)
P.O. Box 335 (28603-0335)
PHONE..................828 322-5347
Robert A Gaston, *Pr*
Ed Henry, *Mgr*
Jo Henry, *VP*
EMP: 17 EST: 1956
SQ FT: 2,975
SALES (est): 476.5K **Privately Held**
SIC: 3495 Furniture springs, unassembled

(G-8116)
PLASTIC TECHNOLOGY INC (HQ)
Also Called: Pti
235 2nd Ave Nw (28601-4950)
P.O. Box 128 (28603-0128)
PHONE..................828 328-2201
J Donald Coleman, *Pr*
Parks C Underdown Junior, *Ch Bd*
Stephen W Ellif, *CFO*
C Hampton Queen, *Asst Tr*
David F Underdown, *Sec*
EMP: 15 EST: 1983
SQ FT: 44,000
SALES (est): 23.52MM
SALES (corp-wide): 430.3MM **Privately Held**
Web: www.ptifoam.com
SIC: 3082 Unsupported plastics profile shapes
PA: Hickory Springs Manufacturing Company
235 2nd Ave Nw
Hickory NC 28601
828 328-2201

(G-8117)
POPPE INC
Also Called: Resource Recovery Company
313 Main Ave Ne (28601-5121)

Hickory - Catawba County (G-8118) GEOGRAPHIC SECTION

PHONE..............................828 345-6036
Dean Poppe, *Pr*
Denise Johnson, *Off Mgr*
EMP: 10 **EST:** 2001
SQ FT: 6,500
SALES (est): 994.93K **Privately Held**
SIC: 3443 Heat exchangers, condensers, and components

(G-8118)
PPA INDUSTRIES INC (PA)
420 3rd Ave Nw (28601-4983)
PHONE..............................828 328-1142
Robert Lackey, *Pr*
Ronn Price, *COO*
Brian Davis, *CFO*
EMP: 21 **EST:** 2017
SALES (est): 49.2MM
SALES (corp-wide): 49.2MM **Privately Held**
SIC: 3585 5075 Heating and air conditioning combination units; Warm air heating and air conditioning

(G-8119)
PRECISION MTLS - BLUE RDGE LLC
3050 Main Ave Nw (28601-5663)
P.O. Box 848 (28681-0848)
PHONE..............................828 322-7990
Scott E Mchugh, *CEO*
D Richard Oliver Junior, *CFO*
EMP: 7 **EST:** 2021
SALES (est): 263.84K **Privately Held**
SIC: 2521 Wood office furniture

(G-8120)
PRECISION SPORTS PAINTBALL
4994 Hickory Blvd (28601-8919)
PHONE..............................828 212-0415
Michael Jacobs, *Pr*
EMP: 5 **EST:** 2008
SALES (est): 74.52K **Privately Held**
SIC: 3949 Fencing equipment (sporting goods)

(G-8121)
PRIME COATINGS
609 2nd St Ne (28601-3855)
PHONE..............................828 217-8287
EMP: 5 **EST:** 2014
SALES (est): 92.23K **Privately Held**
Web: www.ecustomcoatings.com
SIC: 3479 Coating of metals and formed products

(G-8122)
PRIME COATINGS LLC
442 Highland Ave Se (28602-1148)
P.O. Box 3874 (28603-3874)
PHONE..............................828 855-1136
EMP: 9 **EST:** 2007
SALES (est): 326.74K **Privately Held**
Web: www.ecustomcoatings.com
SIC: 3479 Metal coating and allied services

(G-8123)
PRINT PATH
926 Lenoir Rhyne Blvd Se (28602-4126)
PHONE..............................843 615-7882
EMP: 5 **EST:** 2018
SALES (est): 213.41K **Privately Held**
Web: www.printpathllc.com
SIC: 2752 Commercial printing, lithographic

(G-8124)
PRINT PATH LLC
1215 15th Street Dr Ne (28601-4269)
PHONE..............................828 855-9966
David Filmore Wooten Iii, *Prin*
EMP: 6 **EST:** 2010

SALES (est): 599.24K **Privately Held**
Web: www.printpathllc.com
SIC: 2752 Commercial printing, lithographic

(G-8125)
PRINTMARKETING LLC
320 19th St Se (28602-4229)
PHONE..............................828 261-0063
Gerald Wayne Miller, *Prin*
EMP: 6 **EST:** 2011
SALES (est): 516.36K **Privately Held**
Web: www.printmarketingnc.com
SIC: 2752 Offset printing

(G-8126)
PROTECT PLUS PRO LLC
420 3rd Ave Nw Ste A (28601-4984)
PHONE..............................828 328-1142
EMP: 6 **EST:** 2017
SALES (est): 705.83K **Privately Held**
Web: www.protectplus.com
SIC: 3589 Water treatment equipment, industrial

(G-8127)
PROTECTION PRODUCTS INC
1010 3rd Ave Nw (28601-4851)
PHONE..............................828 324-2173
Jeff Hale, *Pr*
▲ **EMP:** 25 **EST:** 2010
SALES (est): 5MM **Privately Held**
Web: www.p-p-i.com
SIC: 3842 5047 Personal safety equipment; Medical equipment and supplies

(G-8128)
PRYSMIAN CBLES SYSTEMS USA LLC
1711 11th Ave Sw (28602-4909)
PHONE..............................828 322-9473
Scott Bachman, *Mgr*
EMP: 25
Web: na.prysmian.com
SIC: 3496 Miscellaneous fabricated wire products
HQ: Prysmian Cables And Systems Usa, Llc
4 Tesseneer Dr
Highland Heights KY 41076
859 572-8000

(G-8129)
PURTHERMAL LLC
Also Called: Manufacturer
1720 Tate Blvd Se (28602-4246)
PHONE..............................828 855-0108
Todd Duckwitz, *CEO*
EMP: 5 **EST:** 2020
SALES (est): 577.33K **Privately Held**
Web: www.purthermal.com
SIC: 3443 3479 3498 Heat exchangers, condensers, and components; Painting, coating, and hot dipping; Tube fabricating (contract bending and shaping)

(G-8130)
QUANTUM SOLUTIONS
365 Main Ave Sw (28602-2928)
P.O. Box 141 (28613-0141)
PHONE..............................828 615-7500
Michael Mcneely, *Prin*
EMP: 10 **EST:** 2012
SALES (est): 984.18K **Privately Held**
SIC: 3572 Computer storage devices

(G-8131)
QUIKTRON INC
925 Old Lenoir Rd (28601-3446)
PHONE..............................828 327-6009
Steve Rockwell, *Pr*

▲ **EMP:** 16 **EST:** 2004
SALES (est): 647.9K **Privately Held**
Web: www.quiktron.com
SIC: 3643 Current-carrying wiring services

(G-8132)
R H BOLICK & COMPANY INC
1210 9th Ave Ne (28601-4108)
PHONE..............................828 322-7847
Richard H Bolick, *Pr*
Judy Bolick, *VP*
▲ **EMP:** 8 **EST:** 1970
SQ FT: 6,000
SALES (est): 946.86K **Privately Held**
Web: www.rhbolick.com
SIC: 3599 Machine shop, jobbing and repair

(G-8133)
R&D PLASTICS OF HICKORY LTD
345 26th Street Dr Se (28602-1459)
PHONE..............................828 431-4660
David Duncan, *Pr*
Robert Canterbury, *
▲ **EMP:** 27 **EST:** 1999
SQ FT: 40,000
SALES (est): 2.91MM **Privately Held**
Web: www.randdplastics.com
SIC: 3089 Injection molding of plastics

(G-8134)
REDI-FRAME INC
207 20th St Se (28602-1414)
PHONE..............................828 322-4227
Joseph Parris, *Pr*
EMP: 20 **EST:** 2001
SALES (est): 733.56K **Privately Held**
SIC: 2426 Frames for upholstered furniture, wood

(G-8135)
RHF INVESTMENTS INC (PA)
401 11th St Nw (28601-4750)
P.O. Box 608 (28603-0608)
PHONE..............................828 326-8350
Brandon M Hucks, *CEO*
A Alex Shuford Iii, *Pr*
A Shuford, *Pr*
EMP: 5 **EST:** 2013
SALES (est): 212.17MM
SALES (corp-wide): 212.17MM **Privately Held**
Web: www.centuryfurniture.com
SIC: 6799 5023 2512 Investors, nec; Decorative home furnishings and supplies; Upholstered household furniture

(G-8136)
RILEY DEFENSE INC
25 18th St Nw (28601-5822)
PHONE..............................704 507-9224
EMP: 6 **EST:** 2015
SALES (est): 505.01K **Privately Held**
Web: www.rileydefense.com
SIC: 3482 3484 Small arms ammunition; Small arms

(G-8137)
ROBERT ABBEY INC (PA)
3166 Main Ave Se (28602-8374)
PHONE..............................828 322-3480
Jerry Rose, *Pr*
Joseph Rose Junior, *VP*
Ken Wilkinson, *
◆ **EMP:** 249 **EST:** 1946
SQ FT: 350,000
SALES (est): 24.01MM
SALES (corp-wide): 24.01MM **Privately Held**
Web: www.robertabbey.biz
SIC: 3645 3641 Residential lighting fixtures; Electric lamps

(G-8138)
ROL-MOL INC
2205 Us Highway 70 Sw (28602-4827)
P.O. Box 1686 (28603-1686)
PHONE..............................828 328-1210
Steve Whisnant, *Pr*
Rush Whisnant, *Asst VP*
Connie Whisnant, *Sec*
EMP: 6 **EST:** 1966
SQ FT: 16,000
SALES (est): 510.73K **Privately Held**
Web: www.rolmol.com
SIC: 3531 Rollers, road: steam or other power

(G-8139)
ROLL-TECH MOLDING PRODUCTS LLC
Also Called: Roll-Tech
243 Performance Dr Se (28602-4046)
PHONE..............................828 431-4515
◆ **EMP:** 26 **EST:** 1995
SQ FT: 26,000
SALES (est): 7.5MM
SALES (corp-wide): 2.5MM **Privately Held**
Web: www.roll-tech.net
SIC: 3011 Tires and inner tubes
HQ: Roll-Gom
Zone Industrielle Est
Tilloy Les Mofflaines 62217
321249495

(G-8140)
RPM WOOD FINISHES GROUP INC (HQ)
Also Called: Finishworks
2220 Us Highway 70 Se Ste 100 (28602-5192)
PHONE..............................828 261-0325
Ronnie G Holman, *Pr*
Glenn R Hasman, *
Wesley Harris, *
▲ **EMP:** 338 **EST:** 1997
SALES (est): 205.9MM
SALES (corp-wide): 7.26B **Publicly Held**
Web: www.rpmwfg.com
SIC: 2851 Lacquers, varnishes, enamels, and other coatings
PA: Rpm International Inc.
2628 Pearl Rd
Medina OH 44256
330 273-5090

(G-8141)
RPM WOOD FINISHES GROUP INC
C C I Division
22 S Center St (28602-3028)
PHONE..............................828 261-0325
EMP: 100
SALES (corp-wide): 7.26B **Publicly Held**
Web: wfgpmt.rpmwfg.com
SIC: 2851 2893 3479 Lacquers, varnishes, enamels, and other coatings; Printing ink; Coating of metals and formed products
HQ: Rpm Wood Finishes Group, Inc.
2220 Us Highway 70 Se # 100
Hickory NC 28602
828 261-0325

(G-8142)
RPM WOOD FINISHES GROUP INC
Mohawk Finishing Products Div
22 S Center St (28602-3028)
PHONE..............................828 261-0325
EMP: 100
SALES (corp-wide): 7.26B **Publicly Held**
Web: wfgpmt.rpmwfg.com
SIC: 2851 5072 Stains: varnish, oil, or wax; Furniture hardware, nec
HQ: Rpm Wood Finishes Group, Inc.
2220 Us Highway 70 Se # 100

GEOGRAPHIC SECTION

Hickory NC 28602
828 261-0325

(G-8143)
RUSKIN INC
1189 27th Street Dr Se (28602-8394)
P.O. Box 9350 (28603-9350)
PHONE................................828 324-6500
Jay Rubino, *Pr*
Pedie King, *VP*
EMP: 10 **EST:** 1999
SQ FT: 21,500
SALES (est): 178.07K **Privately Held**
SIC: 2426 2511 Furniture stock and parts, hardwood; Wood household furniture

(G-8144)
RUST911 INC
925 3rd Ave Se Ste 102 (28602-3054)
PHONE................................607 425-2882
Howard Philips Junior, *Pr*
EMP: 4 **EST:** 2015
SALES (est): 188.66K **Privately Held**
Web: www.rust911.com
SIC: 2899 Chemical preparations, nec

(G-8145)
SAMPLE HOUSE INC
721 17th St Sw (28602-3141)
P.O. Box 1087 (28603-1087)
PHONE................................828 327-4786
William Y Rink Senior, *Ch Bd*
Betty Rink, *Pr*
William Y Rink Junior, *VP*
Janice Miller, *Sec*
EMP: 10 **EST:** 1967
SQ FT: 14,000
SALES (est): 235.36K **Privately Held**
Web: www.samplehousecatalog.com
SIC: 2782 Sample books

(G-8146)
SCHUELER INDUSTRIES INC
121 Pleasant Point Dr (28601-8817)
PHONE................................847 613-0673
EMP: 4 **EST:** 2017
SALES (est): 169.66K **Privately Held**
SIC: 3999 Manufacturing industries, nec

(G-8147)
SHERRILL FURNITURE COMPANY
Also Called: Hickory Mfg Division
856 7th Ave Se (28602-3938)
P.O. Box 998 (28603-0998)
PHONE................................828 322-8624
Chuck Auten, *Prin*
EMP: 8
SALES (corp-wide): 104.33MM **Privately Held**
Web: www.sherrillfurniture.com
SIC: 2512 Upholstered household furniture
PA: Sherrill Furniture Company Inc
2405 Highland Ave Ne
Hickory NC 28601
828 322-2640

(G-8148)
SHERRILL FURNITURE COMPANY
Also Called: Cth-Shrrill Occsional Furn Div
2425 Highland Ave Ne (28601-8164)
PHONE................................828 328-5241
Chuck Auten, *Brnch Mgr*
EMP: 16
SQ FT: 184,000
SALES (corp-wide): 104.33MM **Privately Held**
Web: www.sherrillfurniture.com
SIC: 2512 Upholstered household furniture
PA: Sherrill Furniture Company Inc
2405 Highland Ave Ne
Hickory NC 28601
828 322-2640

(G-8149)
SHERRILL FURNITURE COMPANY (PA)
Also Called: Sherrill Furniture
2405 Highland Ave Ne (28601-8164)
P.O. Box 189 (28603-0189)
PHONE................................828 322-2640
Harold W Sherrill, *Pr*
Michael E Powers, *Admn Execs*
Steve Cartee, *VP*
William Smith, *VP Engg*
Walter Bost, *VP*
◆ **EMP:** 460 **EST:** 1943
SQ FT: 265,000
SALES (est): 104.33MM
SALES (corp-wide): 104.33MM **Privately Held**
Web: www.sherrillfurniture.com
SIC: 2512 2511 Couches, sofas, and davenports: upholstered on wood frames; Wood household furniture

(G-8150)
SHUFORD MILLS LLC (HQ)
Also Called: Shuford Yarns
1985 Tate Blvd Se Ste 54 (28602-1433)
P.O. Box 1530 (28603-1530)
PHONE................................828 324-4265
Stephen Shuford, *Pr*
C Hunt Shuford Junior, *Sec*
Amy Hawn, *Contrlr*
Marvin Smith, *VP*
◆ **EMP:** 5 **EST:** 1926
SQ FT: 25,000
SALES (est): 11.41MM
SALES (corp-wide): 787.56MM **Privately Held**
Web: www.shufordyarns.com
SIC: 2221 Broadwoven fabric mills, manmade
PA: Stm Industries, Inc.
1712 8th Street Dr Se
Hickory NC 28602
828 322-2700

(G-8151)
SHUFORD YARNS LLC (PA)
1985 Tate Blvd Se Ste 54 (28602-1433)
PHONE................................828 324-4265
Marvin Smith, *CEO*
Khalid Majeed, *COO*
▲ **EMP:** 92 **EST:** 2006
SQ FT: 560,000
SALES (est): 24.01MM **Privately Held**
Web: www.shufordyarns.com
SIC: 2281 Yarn spinning mills

(G-8152)
SHUFORD YARNS MANAGEMENT INC
1985 Tate Blvd Se Ste 54 (28602-1433)
PHONE................................828 324-4265
EMP: 8 **EST:** 2018
SALES (est): 46.58K **Privately Held**
Web: www.shufordyarns.com
SIC: 2281 Yarn spinning mills

(G-8153)
SHURTAPE TECHNOLOGIES LLC
1985 Tate Blvd Se (28603)
PHONE................................828 304-8302
Steve Byrd, *Brnch Mgr*
EMP: 5
SALES (corp-wide): 787.56MM **Privately Held**
Web: www.shurtape.com
SIC: 2672 Tape, pressure sensitive: made from purchased materials
HQ: Shurtape Technologies, Llc
1712 8th Street Dr Se
Hickory NC 28602

(G-8154)
SHURTAPE TECHNOLOGIES LLC
1620 Highland Ave Ne (28601-5304)
PHONE................................828 322-2700
EMP: 5
SALES (corp-wide): 787.56MM **Privately Held**
Web: www.shurtape.com
SIC: 2672 Tape, pressure sensitive: made from purchased materials
HQ: Shurtape Technologies, Llc
1712 8th Street Dr Se
Hickory NC 28602

(G-8155)
SIGN SYSTEMS INC
315 9th St Se (28602-4039)
P.O. Box 3767 (28603-3767)
PHONE................................828 322-5622
Charles Hines, *CEO*
EMP: 12 **EST:** 1954
SQ FT: 9,000
SALES (est): 2.19MM **Privately Held**
Web: www.signsystemsnc.com
SIC: 1799 3993 Sign installation and maintenance; Signs, not made in custom sign painting shops

(G-8156)
SIGNATURE SEATING INC
1718 9th Ave Nw (28601-3328)
PHONE................................828 325-0174
Don Mcmullin, *Pr*
Jean Mcmullin, *Treas*
Leigh Ann Huffman, *
Michael J Huffman, *
EMP: 50 **EST:** 2001
SQ FT: 15,000
SALES (est): 4.93MM **Privately Held**
Web: corporate.lippert.com
SIC: 2392 Cushions and pillows

(G-8157)
SIMMONS HOSIERY MILL INC (PA)
3715 9th Street Cir Ne (28601-9630)
PHONE................................828 327-4890
Marion Roseman, *Pr*
EMP: 8 **EST:** 1981
SQ FT: 100,000
SALES (est): 2.13MM
SALES (corp-wide): 2.13MM **Privately Held**
SIC: 5136 5137 2252 2251 Hosiery, men's and boys'; Hosiery: women's, children's, and infants'; Hosiery, nec; Women's hosiery, except socks

(G-8158)
SIPES CARVING SHOP INC
1450 10th Ave Sw (28602-4902)
PHONE................................828 327-3077
Darrell Wilson, *Pr*
Teddy Wilson, *VP*
Christine Wilson, *Sec*
EMP: 8 **EST:** 1946
SALES (est): 946.94K **Privately Held**
SIC: 2426 Carvings, furniture: wood

(G-8159)
SMART START INC
216 10th St Nw Ste 1 (28601-4801)
PHONE................................828 328-2822
EMP: 5 **EST:** 2012
SALES (est): 70.85K **Privately Held**
Web: www.smartstart.org
SIC: 8322 3694 Individual and family services; Ignition apparatus and distributors

(G-8160)
SNIDER TIRE INC
1226 21st Street Dr Se (28602-8350)
PHONE................................828 324-9955
David Benfield, *Opers Mgr*
EMP: 5
SALES (corp-wide): 436.36MM **Privately Held**
Web: www.sniderfleet.com
SIC: 5531 7534 Automotive tires; Tire recapping
PA: Snider Tire, Inc.
1081 Red Ventures Dr
Fort Mill SC 29707
336 691-5480

(G-8161)
SOCK FACTORY INC
1371 13th St Sw (28602-4918)
P.O. Box 40 (28637-0040)
PHONE................................828 328-5207
Michael Banks Senior, *Pr*
Michael Banks Junior, *VP*
EMP: 30 **EST:** 1991
SQ FT: 22,000
SALES (est): 2.34MM **Privately Held**
SIC: 2252 Socks

(G-8162)
SOLOMON ENGINEERING INC
Also Called: SEI Technologies
340 9th St Se (28602-4038)
PHONE................................828 855-1652
Constantin Solomon, *Pr*
EMP: 20 **EST:** 1997
SQ FT: 6,000
SALES (est): 2.15MM **Privately Held**
Web: www.seitechnologies.com
SIC: 3599 Machine and other job shop work

(G-8163)
SONOCO HICKORY INC (HQ)
1246 Main Ave Se (28602-1238)
P.O. Box 2029 (28603-2029)
PHONE................................828 328-2466
Rodger D Fuller, *Pr*
Julie C Albrecht, *
R Howard Coker, *
Russell Grissett, *
Harold G Cummings Iii, *Treas*
◆ **EMP:** 89 **EST:** 1921
SQ FT: 185,000
SALES (est): 67.09MM
SALES (corp-wide): 6.78B **Publicly Held**
SIC: 5199 3089 Packaging materials; Injection molded finished plastics products, nec
PA: Sonoco Products Company
1 N 2nd St
Hartsville SC 29550
843 383-7000

(G-8164)
SONOCO PRODUCTS COMPANY
1214 Highland Ave Ne (28601-4146)
PHONE................................828 322-8844
David Tumey, *Brnch Mgr*
EMP: 18
SALES (corp-wide): 6.78B **Publicly Held**
Web: www.sonoco.com
SIC: 2655 Fiber cans, drums, and similar products
PA: Sonoco Products Company
1 N 2nd St
Hartsville SC 29550
843 383-7000

(G-8165)
SOUTHWOOD FURNITURE CORP (PA)
2860 Nathan St (28601)

Hickory - Catawba County (G-8166)

P.O. Box 1054 (27282-1054)
PHONE..................828 465-1776
Rocky Holscher, *Pr*
Lee Lyerly, *
Howard Pruitt, *Stockholder**
Joe Rowe, *Stockholder**
▲ **EMP:** 80 **EST:** 1973
SQ FT: 100,000
SALES (est): 4.9MM
SALES (corp-wide): 4.9MM **Privately Held**
Web: www.southwoodfurn.com
SIC: 2512 2511 2426 Couches, sofas, and davenports: upholstered on wood frames; Wood household furniture; Frames for upholstered furniture, wood

(G-8166)
SOVEREIGN TECHNOLOGIES LLC
1108 9th Ave Ne (28601-4032)
PHONE..................828 358-5355
EMP: 15 **EST:** 2012
SQ FT: 10,000
SALES (est): 4.71MM **Privately Held**
Web: www.sovereigntechinc.com
SIC: 2869 Industrial organic chemicals, nec

(G-8167)
SQUAREHEAD TECHNOLOGY LLC
200 1st Ave Nw (28601-6113)
PHONE..................571 299-4849
Stig Nyvold, *CEO*
EMP: 5 **EST:** 2015
SALES (est): 963.28K **Privately Held**
Web: www.sqhead.com
SIC: 5049 3669 8731 Law enforcement equipment and supplies; Emergency alarms ; Commercial physical research

(G-8168)
STEWART SUPERABSORBENTS LLC
1954 Main Ave Se (28602-1401)
PHONE..................828 855-9316
Kip Clyburn, *Managing Member*
▲ **EMP:** 6 **EST:** 1999
SQ FT: 22,000
SALES (est): 3.1MM **Publicly Held**
Web: www.chasecorp.com
SIC: 2869 Industrial organic chemicals, nec
HQ: Chase Corporation
375 University Ave
Westwood MA 02090
781 332-0700

(G-8169)
STITCHCRAFTERS INCORPORATED
7923 Houston Ave (28602-8616)
PHONE..................828 397-7656
Tommy Fraley, *Pr*
EMP: 7 **EST:** 1992
SQ FT: 7,700
SALES (est): 633.78K **Privately Held**
Web: www.stitchcraftersinc.com
SIC: 2395 2396 Embroidery products, except Schiffli machine; Automotive and apparel trimmings

(G-8170)
STM INDUSTRIES INC (PA)
Also Called: Shurtech Brands
1712 8th Street Dr Se (28602-9656)
P.O. Box 1530 (28603-1530)
PHONE..................828 322-2700
Stephen Sufford, *CEO*
James B Shuford, *Pr*
Don Pomeroy, *CFO*
Matt Raymer, *Contrlr*
◆ **EMP:** 50 **EST:** 1996
SQ FT: 25,000
SALES (est): 787.56MM
SALES (corp-wide): 787.56MM **Privately Held**
Web: www.shurtapetech.com
SIC: 2672 Tape, pressure sensitive: made from purchased materials

(G-8171)
STYLE UPHOLSTERING INC
33 23rd Ave Ne (28601-1499)
P.O. Box 1368 (28603-1368)
PHONE..................828 322-4882
Ralph F Bowman, *Pr*
Nathan Bowman, *
Sylvia Bowman, *
EMP: 7 **EST:** 1948
SQ FT: 35,000
SALES (est): 479.94K **Privately Held**
Web: www.styleupholstering.com
SIC: 2512 2511 2221 Chairs: upholstered on wood frames; Wood household furniture; Broadwoven fabric mills, manmade

(G-8172)
SURE WOOD PRODUCTS INC
980 3rd Ave Se (28602-4009)
P.O. Box 1507 (28658-4507)
PHONE..................828 261-0004
J L Murtagh, *Pr*
Gary Truesdale, *Sec*
EMP: 13 **EST:** 1988
SQ FT: 45,000
SALES (est): 462.34K **Privately Held**
SIC: 2426 Furniture stock and parts, hardwood

(G-8173)
TAILORED CHEMICAL PRODUCTS INC (PA)
Also Called: Tailored Chemical
700 12th Street Dr Nw Ste B (28601-4792)
P.O. Box 4186 (28603-4186)
PHONE..................828 322-6512
E J Temple Iii, *Pr*
E J Temple Junior, *Pr*
E J Temple Iii, *VP*
Mark Huckabee, *
William Pope, *
◆ **EMP:** 96 **EST:** 1977
SQ FT: 120,000
SALES: 36.41MM
SALES (corp-wide): 36.41MM **Privately Held**
Web: www.tailoredchemical.com
SIC: 2899 2891 2672 2821 Insulating compounds; Adhesives and sealants; Adhesive papers, labels, or tapes: from purchased material; Polyurethane resins

(G-8174)
TARASON LABEL INC
1640 5th St Nw (28601-5208)
PHONE..................828 464-4743
Ralph Hinson, *Pr*
Mary Caldwell, *Sec*
EMP: 7 **EST:** 1983
SQ FT: 16,000
SALES (est): 217.02K **Privately Held**
Web: www.tarason.com
SIC: 2396 2752 2679 2759 Screen printing on fabric articles; Offset printing; Labels, paper: made from purchased material; Commercial printing, nec

(G-8175)
TCS DESIGNS INC
1851 9th Ave Ne (28601-4209)
PHONE..................828 324-9944
Jobie Redmond, *Pr*
Susie Redmond, *Sec*
EMP: 10 **EST:** 1994
SQ FT: 30,000
SALES (est): 1.37MM **Privately Held**
Web: www.tcsdesignsfurniture.com
SIC: 2512 Upholstered household furniture

(G-8176)
TECHMET CARBIDES INC
Also Called: Techmet
730 21st Street Dr Se (28602-4443)
P.O. Box 1658 (28613-3003)
PHONE..................828 624-0222
James E Kuykendall, *CEO*
▲ **EMP:** 71 **EST:** 1998
SALES (est): 9.24MM **Privately Held**
Web: www.techmet-carbide.com
SIC: 3549 2819 Cutting and slitting machinery; Carbides

(G-8177)
TENDER CARE PRODUCTS INC
Also Called: Tcp
4151 1st Street Pl Nw (28601-8075)
PHONE..................828 726-8241
Jan Mcneal, *Pr*
Martha Mcneal, *VP*
EMP: 10 **EST:** 1988
SALES (est): 407.87K **Privately Held**
Web: www.tendercareproducts.com
SIC: 2515 Chair beds

(G-8178)
TENSOR FIBER OPTICS TECH
1075 13th St Se (28602-4165)
P.O. Box 1086 (28603-1086)
PHONE..................828 322-8224
EMP: 4 **EST:** 1996
SALES (est): 455.67K **Privately Held**
Web: www.tensormachinery.com
SIC: 3357 Fiber optic cable (insulated)

(G-8179)
THE WHEELCHAIR PLACE LLC
920 Tate Blvd Se Ste 104 (28602-4032)
PHONE..................828 855-9099
EMP: 5 **EST:** 2007
SALES (est): 519.98K **Privately Held**
Web: www.thewheelchairplace.com
SIC: 3842 Wheelchairs

(G-8180)
THOMASVILLE UPHOLSTERY INC
890 F Avenue Dr Se (28602-1122)
P.O. Box 500 (28603-0500)
PHONE..................828 345-6225
EMP: 120
SIC: 2512 2521 Couches, sofas, and davenports: upholstered on wood frames; Chairs, office: padded, upholstered, or plain: wood

(G-8181)
THUNDERBOLT TEES
1010 21st Street Dr Se (28602-8320)
PHONE..................828 855-1124
EMP: 5 **EST:** 2016
SALES (est): 114.06K **Privately Held**
SIC: 2759 Screen printing

(G-8182)
TIGRA USA INC
1106 8th Street Ct Se (28602-3403)
P.O. Box 9197 (28603-9197)
PHONE..................828 324-8227
Bernd Motzer, *CEO*
▲ **EMP:** 9 **EST:** 2000
SQ FT: 24,000
SALES (est): 2.61MM
SALES (corp-wide): 30.54MM **Privately Held**
Web: www.tigra.com
SIC: 3541 Machine tools, metal cutting type
PA: Tigra Gmbh
Gewerbering 2
Oberndorf A. Lech BY 86698
909 096-8001

(G-8183)
TILEWARE GLOBAL LLC
Also Called: Tileware
1021 16th St Ne (28601-4236)
P.O. Box 793 (28603-0793)
PHONE..................828 322-9273
David Scalise, *Managing Member*
▲ **EMP:** 4 **EST:** 2010
SQ FT: 6,000
SALES (est): 351.51K **Privately Held**
Web: www.tilewareproducts.com
SIC: 3261 Bathroom accessories/fittings, vitreous china or earthenware

(G-8184)
TRADITIONS WOOD CARVING & FRMS
120 11th St Nw (28601-5958)
P.O. Box 2388 (28603-2388)
PHONE..................828 322-5625
Catherine C Fuller, *Pr*
Joe Whitener, *
EMP: 5 **EST:** 1959
SQ FT: 90,000
SALES (est): 209.58K **Privately Held**
Web: www.carvingcraft.com
SIC: 2499 2426 Carved and turned wood; Turnings, furniture: wood

(G-8185)
TRUE CABINET LLC
2401 Us Highway 70 Sw (28602-4751)
PHONE..................828 855-9200
EMP: 10 **EST:** 2015
SALES (est): 360.86K **Privately Held**
Web: www.truecabinet.com
SIC: 2434 Wood kitchen cabinets

(G-8186)
TSG FINISHING LLC
Also Called: Synthetics Finishing
2246 Us Hwy 70 (28602-4827)
PHONE..................828 328-5522
EMP: 5
SALES (corp-wide): 22.27MM **Privately Held**
Web: www.tsgfinishing.com
SIC: 3552 Textile machinery
PA: Tsg Finishing, Llc
7 N Waterloo Rd
Devon PA 19333
215 628-2000

(G-8187)
TSG FINISHING LLC
Long View Machinary Co
515 23rd St Sw (28602-2106)
PHONE..................828 328-5541
Darr Grater, *VP*
EMP: 46
SALES (corp-wide): 22.27MM **Privately Held**
Web: www.tsgfinishing.com
SIC: 3552 Textile machinery
PA: Tsg Finishing, Llc
7 N Waterloo Rd
Devon PA 19333
215 628-2000

(G-8188)
TSG FINISHING LLC
Also Called: Synthetic Finishing
515 23rd St Sw (28602-2106)
P.O. Box 2141 (28603-2141)
PHONE..................828 328-5522
Rich Grecki, *Brnch Mgr*
EMP: 36
SQ FT: 31,001

GEOGRAPHIC SECTION
Hickory - Catawba County (G-8210)

SALES (corp-wide): 22.27MM **Privately Held**
Web: www.tsgfinishing.com
SIC: **3552** 2261 Textile machinery; Finishing plants, cotton
PA: Tsg Finishing, Llc
7 N Waterloo Rd
Devon PA 19333
215 628-2000

(G-8189)
TSG FINISHING LLC
Also Called: Synthetic Finishing Co
1006 19th St Ne (28601-4314)
P.O. Box 2141 (28603-2141)
PHONE.................................828 328-5535
David Poody, *Brnch Mgr*
EMP: 57
SALES (corp-wide): 22.27MM **Privately Held**
Web: www.tsgfinishing.com
SIC: **2269** 2261 Dyeing: raw stock, yarn, and narrow fabrics; Finishing plants, cotton
PA: Tsg Finishing, Llc
7 N Waterloo Rd
Devon PA 19333
215 628-2000

(G-8190)
TUCKER PRODUCTION INCORPORATED
Also Called: Focus Newspaper
264 1st Ave Nw (28601-6103)
P.O. Box 1721 (28603-1721)
PHONE.................................828 322-1036
Tammy Panther, *Pr*
Lynn Jenkins, *Sec*
Tammy Panther, *VP*
John Tucker, *Pr*
EMP: 4 EST: 1977
SQ FT: 3,400
SALES (est): 254K **Privately Held**
Web: www.focusnewspaper.com
SIC: **2711** Newspapers, publishing and printing

(G-8191)
TURBOCOATING CORP
Also Called: Lincotek Surface Solutions
1928 Main Ave Se (28602-1401)
PHONE.................................828 328-8726
▲ EMP: 33 EST: 2010
SALES (est): 9.87MM
SALES (corp-wide): 234.95MM **Privately Held**
Web: www.lincoteksurfacesolutions.com
SIC: **3479** Coating of metals and formed products
HQ: Lincotek Rubbiano Spa
Via Mistrali 7
Solignano PR 43046
052 530-5808

(G-8192)
TWO GREEN THUMBS AND MORE INC
1109 7th St Ne (28601-3911)
PHONE.................................704 614-8703
Amanda Pearce, *Owner*
EMP: 5 EST: 2017
SALES (est): 59.55K **Privately Held**
SIC: **2431** Millwork

(G-8193)
UNIFOUR FINISHERS INC (PA)
Also Called: Division One
120 21st St Nw (28601-4678)
P.O. Box 1965 (28603-1965)
PHONE.................................828 322-9435
Harold D Setzer, *CEO*
Richard Setzer, *

EMP: 32 EST: 1979
SQ FT: 23,000
SALES (est): 4.03MM
SALES (corp-wide): 4.03MM **Privately Held**
Web: www.unifourfinishers.com
SIC: **2257** 2261 Dyeing and finishing circular knit fabrics; Finishing plants, cotton

(G-8194)
UNIFOUR FINISHERS INC
Also Called: Division II
54 29th St Nw (28601-5650)
P.O. Box 1965 (28603-1965)
PHONE.................................828 322-9435
Rick Setzer, *Mgr*
EMP: 34
SALES (corp-wide): 4.03MM **Privately Held**
Web: www.unifourfinishers.com
SIC: **2257** 2261 Dyeing and finishing circular knit fabrics; Finishing plants, cotton
PA: Unifour Finishers, Inc.
120 21st St Nw
Hickory NC 28601
828 322-9435

(G-8195)
UNIGEL INC
1027 19th St Sw (28602-4812)
PHONE.................................828 228-2095
Jiry Robinson, *Pr*
◆ EMP: 4 EST: 2010
SQ FT: 35,000
SALES (est): 511.87K **Privately Held**
Web: www.unigel.co.uk
SIC: **2511** Wood household furniture

(G-8196)
UPHOLSTERY DESIGNS HICKORY INC
Also Called: Upholstery Design
1251 19th St Ne (28601-2833)
P.O. Box 2561 (28603-2561)
PHONE.................................828 324-2002
Henry Lail, *Pr*
Bob E Watts, *
Piero Caglies, *
EMP: 25 EST: 1984
SQ FT: 80,000
SALES (est): 888.1K
SALES (corp-wide): 103.81MM **Privately Held**
SIC: **2512** 2521 Upholstered household furniture; Wood office furniture
PA: Chateau D'ax Spa
Via Nazionale 159
Lentate Sul Seveso MB 20823
036 256-9068

(G-8197)
US CONEC LTD
830 21st Street Dr Se (28602-8376)
PHONE.................................828 323-8883
EMP: 5
Web: www.usconec.com
SIC: **3357** Fiber optic cable (insulated)
PA: Us Conec Ltd.
1138 25th St Se
Hickory NC 28602

(G-8198)
US CONEC LTD (PA)
1138 25th St Se (28602-7313)
P.O. Box 2306 (28603-2306)
PHONE.................................828 323-8883
Joe Graham, *Pr*
Russell Granger, *
David Kiel, *
Shannon Fichter, *
EMP: 92 EST: 1992

SQ FT: 6,200
SALES (est): 30.01MM **Privately Held**
Web: www.usconec.com
SIC: **3357** 3678 Fiber optic cable (insulated); Electronic connectors

(G-8199)
US DRAINAGE SYSTEMS LLC
26 5th St Se (28602-1112)
PHONE.................................828 855-1906
Travis Obermeyer, *Managing Member*
EMP: 6 EST: 2011
SQ FT: 60,000
SALES (est): 968.68K **Privately Held**
Web: www.usdrainage.co
SIC: **3089** Thermoformed finished plastics products, nec

(G-8200)
UTILITY SOLUTIONS INC
101 33rd S Dr Se (28602)
PHONE.................................828 323-8914
Hans Peterson, *CEO*
Bryan Lackey, *CFO*
Matt Nolte, *COO*
◆ EMP: 4 EST: 1990
SQ FT: 10,250
SALES (est): 2.69MM
SALES (corp-wide): 2.69MM **Privately Held**
Web: www.utilitysolutionsinc.com
SIC: **3679** 3699 Electronic loads and power supplies; Electrical equipment and supplies, nec
PA: Evolution Sustainability Group Llc
1 E Uwchlan Ave Ste 312
Exton PA 19341
877 280-4655

(G-8201)
VACUUM HANDLING NORTH AMER LLC
Also Called: Joulin
2551 Us Highway 70 Sw (28602-4744)
PHONE.................................828 327-2290
▲ EMP: 21 EST: 2007
SALES (est): 6.42MM **Privately Held**
Web: www.joulin.com
SIC: **3635** Household vacuum cleaners

(G-8202)
VELCO INC
130 11th St Nw (28601-5958)
P.O. Box 3523 (28603-3523)
PHONE.................................828 324-5440
George Farr, *Pr*
Gloria S Farr, *
EMP: 12 EST: 1987
SQ FT: 20,000
SALES (est): 220.81K **Privately Held**
SIC: **2392** Blankets, comforters and beddings

(G-8203)
VENOM STARS INC
6397 Hayden Dr (28601-7082)
PHONE.................................828 256-8621
Clayton P Buff, *Owner*
EMP: 6 EST: 2016
SALES (est): 90.45K **Privately Held**
SIC: **2836** Venoms

(G-8204)
VOLEX INC
915 Tate Blvd Se Ste 144 (28602-4042)
PHONE.................................828 485-4500
Martin May, *CEO*
EMP: 24
SQ FT: 8,000
SALES (corp-wide): 722.8MM **Privately Held**
Web: www.volex.com

SIC: **3089** Injection molded finished plastics products, nec
HQ: Volex Inc.
511 E San Ysidro Blvd
San Ysidro CA 92173
669 444-1740

(G-8205)
VOLEX INC
915 Tate Blvd Se (28602-4042)
PHONE.................................828 485-4500
EMP: 38
SALES (corp-wide): 722.8MM **Privately Held**
Web: www.volex.com
SIC: **3089** Injection molded finished plastics products, nec
HQ: Volex Inc.
511 E San Ysidro Blvd
San Ysidro CA 92173
669 444-1740

(G-8206)
WARD HOSIERY COMPANY INC
1410 13th St Sw (28602-4939)
P.O. Box 2442 (28603-2442)
PHONE.................................828 381-2346
Richard S Ward, *Pr*
Libby Chambers, *Sec*
◆ EMP: 7 EST: 1975
SQ FT: 21,000
SALES (est): 232.66K **Privately Held**
SIC: **2252** 2251 2261 Dyeing and finishing hosiery; Dyeing and finishing women's full- and knee-length hosiery; Finishing plants, cotton

(G-8207)
WB FRAMES INC
3771 Sandy Ford Rd (28602-8938)
PHONE.................................828 459-2147
Wayne Bollinger, *Pr*
Janie Bollinger, *VP*
Gary Bollinger, *Treas*
EMP: 7 EST: 2000
SALES (est): 245.18K **Privately Held**
SIC: **2511** Wood household furniture

(G-8208)
WEATHERVANE CREATIVE INC
2359 Us Highway 70 Se Ste 270 (28602)
PHONE.................................828 542-0136
Shane Bender, *Prin*
EMP: 7 EST: 2018
SALES (est): 170.45K **Privately Held**
Web: www.weathervanecreative.com
SIC: **2759** 7336 2752 Commercial printing, nec; Commercial art and graphic design; Commercial printing, lithographic

(G-8209)
WEN BRAY HEATING & AC
6034 Norcross Ln (28601-9007)
PHONE.................................828 267-0635
Joseph W Icard, *Pr*
Carol A Icard, *VP*
EMP: 4 EST: 1980
SALES (est): 295K **Privately Held**
SIC: **1711** 5722 7841 3585 Warm air heating and air conditioning contractor; Electric household appliances; Video disk/tape rental to the general public; Refrigeration and heating equipment

(G-8210)
WOOTEN JOHN
3763 1st Ave Sw (28602-1605)
P.O. Box 4095 (28603-4095)
PHONE.................................828 322-4031
John Wooten, *Owner*
EMP: 5 EST: 2000

Hickory - Catawba County (G-8211)

SALES (est): 347.61K **Privately Held**
SIC: 7538 3599 General automotive repair shops; Machine shop, jobbing and repair

(G-8211)
WRIGHT BUSINESS CONCEPTS INC
Also Called: A Sign Co
1320 Fairgrove Church Rd (28603)
P.O. Box 1709 (28603-1709)
PHONE.................................828 466-1044
EMP: 5 EST: 1995
SQ FT: 1,400
SALES (est): 401.34K **Privately Held**
Web: www.asigncohickory.com
SIC: 3993 Signs, not made in custom sign painting shops

(G-8212)
XALOY EXTRUSION LLC
Also Called: Nordson Xaloy
1291 19th Street Ln Nw (28601-4677)
PHONE.................................828 326-9888
◆ EMP: 48 EST: 2000
SQ FT: 40,000
SALES (est): 8.22MM **Privately Held**
SIC: 5084 3561 Plastic products machinery; Pumps and pumping equipment

Hiddenite
Alexander County

(G-8213)
AMERICAN ROLLER BEARING INC
1095 Mcclain Rd (28636-6202)
PHONE.................................828 624-1460
Michael J Connors, Pr
EMP: 200
SALES (corp-wide): 4.77B **Publicly Held**
SIC: 3562 Roller bearings and parts
HQ: American Roller Bearing Inc.
307 Burke Dr
Morganton NC 28655
828 624-1460

(G-8214)
CRAFTMASTER FURNITURE INC
(DH)
221 Craftmaster Rd (28636-9309)
P.O. Box 759 (28681-0759)
PHONE.................................828 632-9786
Alex Reeves, Pr
Anderson Shih, *
◆ EMP: 350 EST: 2006
SQ FT: 175,000
SALES (est): 285.11MM **Privately Held**
Web: www.cmfurniture.com
SIC: 2512 Couches, sofas, and davenports: upholstered on wood frames
HQ: Samson Investment Holding Co.
2575 Penny Rd
High Point NC 27265

(G-8215)
CRAFTMASTER FURNITURE INC
750 Sharpe Ln (28636-8389)
P.O. Box 759 (28681-0759)
PHONE.................................828 632-8127
Harold Bentley, Mgr
EMP: 693
Web: www.cmfurniture.com
SIC: 2512 2511 Couches, sofas, and davenports: upholstered on wood frames; Wood household furniture
HQ: Craftmaster Furniture, Inc.
221 Craftmaster Rd
Hiddenite NC 28636
828 632-9786

(G-8216)
FORTNER LUMBER INC
991 Liberty Church Rd (28636-9336)
P.O. Box 39 (28636-0039)
PHONE.................................704 585-2383
Ronald L Fortner, Pr
Justin Fortner, VP
Josh Fortner, Sec
EMP: 11 EST: 1961
SQ FT: 800
SALES (est): 240.14K **Privately Held**
SIC: 2426 Lumber, hardwood dimension

(G-8217)
HICKORY SPRINGS MFG CO
Sharpe Rd (28636)
P.O. Box 116 (28636-0116)
PHONE.................................828 632-9733
Candy Duffey, Mgr
EMP: 29
SALES (corp-wide): 430.3MM **Privately Held**
Web: www.hsmsolutions.com
SIC: 3086 Insulation or cushioning material, foamed plastics
PA: Hickory Springs Manufacturing Company
235 2nd Ave Nw
Hickory NC 28601
828 328-2201

(G-8218)
HIDDENITE CONFERENCE CTR LLC
Also Called: Parchment Press
471 Sulphur Springs Rd (28636-5141)
P.O. Box 100 (28636-0100)
PHONE.................................828 352-9200
David Burleigh, Managing Member
EMP: 10 EST: 2011
SALES (est): 196.61K **Privately Held**
Web: www.hiddenitearts.org
SIC: 2741 Miscellaneous publishing

(G-8219)
HIDDENITE GEMS INC
Also Called: Emerald Hollow Gems
484 Emerald Hollow Mine Dr (28636-7393)
PHONE.................................828 632-3394
Dorothy Watkins, Pr
EMP: 4 EST: 1986
SALES (est): 462.41K **Privately Held**
Web: www.emeraldhollowmine.com
SIC: 1499 Gem stones (natural) mining, nec

(G-8220)
INDUSTRIAL TIMBER LLC
330 White Plains Rd (28636-8767)
PHONE.................................704 919-1215
EMP: 82
SALES (corp-wide): 86.38MM **Privately Held**
Web: www.thesmartplay.com
SIC: 2493 5031 Reconstituted wood products; Lumber, plywood, and millwork
PA: Industrial Timber, Llc
6441 Hendry Rd Ste A
Charlotte NC 28269
704 919-1215

(G-8221)
J & R SALES INC
380 Old Mountain Rd (28636-8306)
P.O. Box 168 (28636-0168)
PHONE.................................828 632-7402
Johnny Gant, Pr
EMP: 5 EST: 1983
SQ FT: 2,100
SALES (est): 477.66K **Privately Held**
Web: www.j-nsales.com
SIC: 2449 Chicken coops (crates), wood: wirebound

(G-8222)
KDS FABRICATING AND MCH SP LLC
4838 Nc Highway 90 E (28636-9396)
P.O. Box 2868 (42002-2868)
PHONE.................................828 632-5091
Robert Petter Junior, Mgr
Olivia Petter, Prin
Meredith Petter, Prin
Bruce Wilcox, Mgr
EMP: 10 EST: 2017
SALES (est): 594.75K **Privately Held**
SIC: 3498 3549 Tube fabricating (contract bending and shaping); Wiredrawing and fabricating machinery and equipment, ex. die

(G-8223)
LTLB HOLDING COMPANY
1095 Mcclain Rd (28636-6202)
P.O. Box 117 (28636-0117)
PHONE.................................704 585-2908
Frank Dickson, Pr
EMP: 84
SALES (corp-wide): 45.63MM **Privately Held**
Web: www.amroll.com
SIC: 3562 Ball and roller bearings
PA: Ltlb Holding Company
1350 4th Street Dr Nw
Hickory NC 28601
828 624-1460

(G-8224)
ON TIME METAL LLC
31 Wayfound Church Rd (28636-7333)
PHONE.................................828 635-1001
EMP: 9 EST: 2016
SALES (est): 551.53K **Privately Held**
Web: www.ontimemetal.com
SIC: 1761 3444 Roofing contractor; Metal roofing and roof drainage equipment

(G-8225)
PALADIN INDUSTRIES INC
Also Called: Paladin Furniture
5270 Nc Highway 90 E (28636-8300)
P.O. Box 218 (28636-0218)
PHONE.................................828 635-0448
Timothy R Bolick, Pr
Elaine Bolick, *
◆ EMP: 100 EST: 2002
SQ FT: 120,000
SALES (est): 15MM **Privately Held**
Web: www.paladinfurniture.com
SIC: 2512 Upholstered household furniture

(G-8226)
PARCHMENT PRESS
140 Old Mountain Rd (28636-8304)
PHONE.................................931 347-2393
EMP: 4 EST: 2020
SALES (est): 123.96K **Privately Held**
Web: www.parchmentpress.net
SIC: 2741 Miscellaneous publishing

(G-8227)
STATESVILLE PALLET COMPANY INC
351 Old Mountain Rd (28636-8306)
P.O. Box 36 (28636-0036)
PHONE.................................828 632-0268
Eric Sloop, Pr
Regina Pierce, Sec
EMP: 11 EST: 1988
SQ FT: 35,000
SALES (est): 434K **Privately Held**
SIC: 2448 Pallets, wood

High Point
Guilford County

(G-8228)
615 ALTON PLACE LLC
615 Alton Pl (27263-2272)
PHONE.................................336 431-4487
Herbert R Bolick Junior, Prin
EMP: 7 EST: 2012
SALES (est): 113.45K **Privately Held**
Web: www.nimbusinc.com
SIC: 3672 Printed circuit boards

(G-8229)
A LAND OF FURNITURE INC
430 S Main St Ste 431 (27260-6635)
PHONE.................................336 882-3866
▲ EMP: 4 EST: 1990
SQ FT: 6,000
SALES (est): 177.17K **Privately Held**
SIC: 2299 Upholstery filling, textile

(G-8230)
ABBEY ROBERT INC
633 Huntington Dr (27262-4566)
PHONE.................................336 883-1078
EMP: 5 EST: 2010
SALES (est): 77.16K **Privately Held**
Web: www.robertabbey.biz
SIC: 2511 Wood household furniture

(G-8231)
ACME SAMPLE BOOKS INC
Also Called: Asb Graphics
603 Fraley Rd (27263-1762)
PHONE.................................336 883-4336
Steve Lambert, VP
EMP: 20
SQ FT: 17,765
SALES (corp-wide): 7.43MM **Privately Held**
Web: www.acmesample.com
SIC: 2752 Offset printing
PA: Acme Sample Books, Inc.
2410 Schirra Pl
High Point NC
336 883-4187

(G-8232)
ADAMS WOOD TURNING INC
Also Called: Sedgefield By Adams
216 Woodbine St (27260-8340)
P.O. Box 1113 (32778-1113)
PHONE.................................336 882-0196
Walter Blackburn, Pr
Terri Thomas, Sec
Sherri Mickey, VP
▲ EMP: 8 EST: 1958
SQ FT: 50,000
SALES (est): 262.99K **Privately Held**
Web: www.adamswoodturning.com
SIC: 2426 3645 3641 Turnings, furniture: wood; Table lamps; Electric lamps

(G-8233)
ADORA
1245 Hickory Chapel Rd (27260-7189)
PHONE.................................336 880-0342
EMP: 8 EST: 2017
SALES (est): 232.04K **Privately Held**
Web: www.balancedayspa.com
SIC: 2844 Perfumes, cosmetics and other toilet preparations

(G-8234)
ADVANCED METAL SUPPLY
5873 Parker St (27263-8502)
PHONE.................................336 883-7135
Bob Caviness, Pr

GEOGRAPHIC SECTION High Point - Guilford County (G-8259)

EMP: 5 **EST:** 2003
SALES (est): 86.89K **Privately Held**
Web: www.advancedmetalsupply.com
SIC: 3499 Fabricated metal products, nec

(G-8235)
ADWOOD CORPORATION
260 Durand Ave (27263-9761)
P.O. Box 1195 (27261-1195)
PHONE.................336 884-1846
Rudolf Stockinger, *Pr*
▲ **EMP:** 21 **EST:** 1981
SQ FT: 20,000
SALES (est): 9.2MM
SALES (corp-wide): 451.27MM **Privately Held**
Web: www.adwood.com
SIC: 5084 2435 Woodworking machinery; Hardwood veneer and plywood
PA: Jowat Se
   Ernst-Hilker-Str. 10-14
   Detmold NW 32758
   52317490

(G-8236)
AGM CAROLINA INC
1031 E Springfield Rd (27263-2157)
PHONE.................336 431-4100
Carman Parrente, *Pr*
Chad William, *VP*
▲ **EMP:** 8 **EST:** 2012
SQ FT: 2,000
SALES (est): 1.97MM **Privately Held**
Web: www.agmcarolina.com
SIC: 5072 5251 3334 Hardware; Hardware stores; Aluminum ingots and slabs

(G-8237)
AKZO NOBEL COATINGS INC
Also Called: Akzo Nobel Coatings
1431 Progress Ave (27260-8322)
PHONE.................336 841-5111
James Burray, *Brnch Mgr*
EMP: 30
SALES (corp-wide): 11.26B **Privately Held**
SIC: 2851 Paints and allied products
HQ: Akzo Nobel Coatings Inc.
   535 Marriott Dr Ste 500
   Nashville TN 37214
   440 297-5100

(G-8238)
ALAMANCE STEEL FABRICATORS
5926 Prospect St (27263-3970)
PHONE.................336 887-3015
Scott Troxler, *Pr*
EMP: 6 **EST:** 1974
SQ FT: 7,000
SALES (est): 716.21K **Privately Held**
Web: www.alamancesteel.com
SIC: 3446 3441 Railings, prefabricated metal ; Fabricated structural metal

(G-8239)
ALEXANDER PRESS INC
701 Greensboro Rd (27260-2651)
PHONE.................336 884-8063
Mary Fay Bodenheimer, *Owner*
Mary Fay Bodenheimer, *Prin*
EMP: 6 **EST:** 2010
SALES (est): 69.47K **Privately Held**
SIC: 2752 Commercial printing, lithographic

(G-8240)
ALI GROUP NORTH AMERICA CORP
Also Called: Carpigiani Corporation America
738 Gallimore Dairy Rd Ste 113 (27265-9721)
PHONE.................800 648-4389
EMP: 28
SALES (corp-wide): 2.67MM **Privately Held**

Web: www.aligroup.com
SIC: 3589 Cooking equipment, commercial
HQ: Ali Group North America Corporation
   101 Corporate Woods Pkwy
   Vernon Hills IL 60061
   847 215-6565

(G-8241)
ALL BAKED OUT COMPANY
629 Mcway Dr (27263-2059)
PHONE.................336 861-1212
EMP: 15 **EST:** 2010
SALES (est): 1.61MM **Privately Held**
Web: www.bigbossbaking.com
SIC: 2051 Bakery: wholesale or wholesale/retail combined

(G-8242)
ALLRED METAL STAMPING WORKS INC
1305 Old Thomasville Rd (27260)
P.O. Box 2566 (27261-2566)
PHONE.................336 886-5221
EMP: 35 **EST:** 1964
SALES (est): 4.79MM **Privately Held**
Web: www.allredmetal.com
SIC: 3469 Stamping metal for the trade

(G-8243)
AMADA AMERICA INC
109 Penny Rd (27260-2500)
PHONE.................877 262-3287
EMP: 6
Web: www.amada.com
SIC: 5084 3541 Metalworking machinery; Machine tools, metal cutting type
HQ: Amada America, Inc.
   7025 Firestone Blvd
   Buena Park CA 90621
   714 739-2111

(G-8244)
AMCASE INC
2214 Shore St (27263-2512)
PHONE.................336 784-5992
Lindy Mulford, *CEO*
Mike Mulford, *
EMP: 34 **EST:** 1984
SALES (est): 9.78MM **Privately Held**
Web: www.amcase.com
SIC: 2521 2542 2541 2531 Wood office furniture; Office and store showcases and display fixtures; Wood partitions and fixtures ; Public building and related furniture

(G-8245)
AMERICAN INDIAN PRINTING INC
710 Dorado Cir (27265-9502)
PHONE.................336 884-5442
Bundy R Martin, *Prin*
EMP: 4 **EST:** 2010
SALES (est): 51.53K **Privately Held**
SIC: 2752 Offset printing

(G-8246)
AMERICAN METALLURGY INC
Also Called: American Metal Treating
505 Garrison St (27260-7042)
P.O. Box 4912 (27263-4912)
PHONE.................336 889-3277
Michael Ram, *Pr*
EMP: 9 **EST:** 1990
SALES (est): 284.13K **Privately Held**
Web: www.americanmetaltreatinginc.com
SIC: 3398 Metal heat treating

(G-8247)
AMERICAN OF HIGH POINT INC
2224 Shore St (27263-2512)

P.O. Box 7103 (27264-7103)
PHONE.................336 431-1513
David Richardson, *Pr*
Bobbie Richardson, *
EMP: 33 **EST:** 1959
SQ FT: 83,000
SALES (est): 2.05MM **Privately Held**
Web: www.highpoint.edu
SIC: 2512 Upholstered household furniture

(G-8248)
AMERICAN SILK MILLS LLC (PA)
329 S Wrenn St Ste 101 (27260-6684)
PHONE.................570 822-7147
Cynthia Dluthit, *Pr*
♦ **EMP:** 14 **EST:** 1930
SQ FT: 3,700
SALES (est): 2.96MM
SALES (corp-wide): 2.96MM **Privately Held**
Web: www.americansilk.com
SIC: 2211 2221 Cotton broad woven goods; Broadwoven fabric mills, manmade

(G-8249)
AMERIFAB INTERNATIONAL INC
203 Feld Ave (27263-1929)
PHONE.................336 882-9010
Raj Mehta, *CEO*
Kajal Bhat, *
▲ **EMP:** 48 **EST:** 1994
SALES (est): 9.76MM **Privately Held**
Web: www.amerifabintl.com
SIC: 2211 Draperies and drapery fabrics, cotton

(G-8250)
APOLLO DESIGNS LLC (PA)
Also Called: Apollo Designs
2147 Brevard Rd (27263-1703)
PHONE.................336 886-0260
Nihar Upadhyaya, *CEO*
Janki Upadhyaya, *Pr*
▲ **EMP:** 25 **EST:** 2015
SALES (est): 4.28MM
SALES (corp-wide): 4.28MM **Privately Held**
Web: www.apollodesigns.net
SIC: 5021 3272 2511 2499 Furniture; Stone, cast concrete; Vanity dressers: wood; Kitchen, bathroom, and household ware: wood

(G-8251)
ARCHDALE PRINTING COMPANY INC
1316 Trinity Ave (27260-8358)
P.O. Box 433 (27370-0433)
PHONE.................336 884-5312
Ed Smith, *Pr*
EMP: 4 **EST:** 2006
SALES (est): 248.59K **Privately Held**
SIC: 2752 Offset printing

(G-8252)
ARE MANAGEMENT LLC
1420 Lorraine Ave (27263-2040)
PHONE.................336 855-7800
▲ **EMP:** 25 **EST:** 1993
SALES (est): 4.96MM **Privately Held**
Web: www.ancoeaglin.com
SIC: 3556 Food products machinery

(G-8253)
ARGOS USA LLC
406 Tomlinson St (27260-6639)
PHONE.................336 841-3379
Howard Hepler, *Brnch Mgr*
EMP: 25
Web: www.argos-us.com
SIC: 3273 Ready-mixed concrete
HQ: Argos Usa Llc

3015 Windward Plz Ste 300
Alpharetta GA 30005
678 368-4300

(G-8254)
ARISTON HOSPITALITY INC
Also Called: Motivo Furniture
1581 Prospect St (27260-8457)
PHONE.................626 458-8668
Tony Tsai, *CEO*
Tony Tsai, *Prin*
▲ **EMP:** 20 **EST:** 2006
SALES (est): 2.48MM **Privately Held**
Web: www.aristonhospitality.com
SIC: 2599 2426 Furniture and fixtures, nec; Furniture stock and parts, hardwood

(G-8255)
ARPER USA (PA)
660 Southwest St (27260-8107)
PHONE.................336 434-2376
Danielle Incati, *Genl Mgr*
▲ **EMP:** 5 **EST:** 2015
SALES (est): 505.37K
SALES (corp-wide): 505.37K **Privately Held**
SIC: 2599 Furniture and fixtures, nec

(G-8256)
ARTISANS GUILD INCORPORATED
639 Mcway Dr Ste 101 (27263-2492)
PHONE.................336 841-4140
Bruce Thomas, *Pr*
Cindy Thomas, *VP*
EMP: 5 **EST:** 1970
SQ FT: 5,000
SALES (est): 418.85K **Privately Held**
Web: www.artisansguild.biz
SIC: 2511 2392 5023 2531 Novelty furniture: wood; Household furnishings, nec; Floor cushion and padding; School furniture

(G-8257)
AXALTA COATING SYSTEMS LTD
1717 W English Rd (27262)
PHONE.................336 802-5701
EMP: 9
SALES (corp-wide): 5.18B **Publicly Held**
Web: www.axalta.com
SIC: 2851 Paints and allied products
PA: Axalta Coating Systems Ltd.
   50 Applied Bank Blvd # 300
   Glen Mills PA 19342
   855 547-1461

(G-8258)
AXALTA COATING SYSTEMS LTD
2137 Brevard Rd (27263-1703)
PHONE.................336 802-4392
Charlie Jacobs, *Mgr*
EMP: 36
SALES (corp-wide): 5.18B **Publicly Held**
Web: www.axalta.com
SIC: 2851 Paints and paint additives
PA: Axalta Coating Systems Ltd.
   50 Applied Bank Blvd # 300
   Glen Mills PA 19342
   855 547-1461

(G-8259)
AXALTA COATING SYSTEMS USA LLC
1717 W English Rd (27262-7205)
PHONE.................336 802-5701
EMP: 15 **EST:** 2017
SALES (est): 2.28MM
SALES (corp-wide): 5.18B **Publicly Held**
Web: www.axalta.com
SIC: 2952 Asphalt felts and coatings
HQ: Axalta Coating Systems, Llc
   50 Applied Bank Blvd # 300

High Point - Guilford County (G-8260)

(G-8260)
B&H MILLWORK AND FIXTURES INC
1130 Bedford St (27263-1604)
PHONE..................336 431-0068
EMP: 32
Web: www.bandhmillwork.com
SIC: 2542 2431 2521 Partitions and fixtures, except wood; Millwork; Cabinets, office: wood

(G-8261)
B/E AEROSPACE INC
2376 Hickswood Rd Ste 106 (27265-7918)
PHONE..................336 841-7698
John Gonzalez, *Brnch Mgr*
EMP: 6
SALES (corp-wide): 68.92B Publicly Held
Web: www.collinsaerospace.com
SIC: 3728 Aircraft parts and equipment, nec
HQ: B/E Aerospace, Inc.
150 Oak Plaza Blvd # 200
Winston Salem NC 27105
336 747-5000

(G-8262)
BAKEBOXX COMPANY ✪
Also Called: Big Boss Baking Company
629 Mcway Dr (27263-2059)
PHONE..................336 861-1212
Melissa Shenker, *Pr*
Edward Shenker, *VP*
EMP: 10 EST: 2023
SALES (est): 367.79K Privately Held
SIC: 5461 2064 2043 5149 Retail bakeries; Granola and muesli, bars and clusters; Cereal breakfast foods; Breakfast cereals

(G-8263)
BAKER INTERIORS FURNITURE CO
Also Called: Baker Furniture
2219 Shore St (27263-2511)
PHONE..................336 431-9115
William Simmons, *Mgr*
EMP: 8
SIC: 2511 2512 Wood household furniture; Upholstered household furniture
HQ: Baker Interiors Furniture Company
1 Baker Way
Connelly Springs NC 28612
336 431-9115

(G-8264)
BANNER LIFE SCIENCES LLC
3980 Premier Dr Ste 110 (27265-8409)
PHONE..................336 812-8700
Michael Lytton, *Pr*
Aqeel Fatmi, *
EMP: 50 EST: 2014
SALES (est): 9.07MM Privately Held
Web: www.bannerls.com
SIC: 2834 Vitamin preparations

(G-8265)
BARSINA PUBLISHING
3510 Pine Valley Rd (27265-2015)
PHONE..................336 869-2849
Cherl T Harrison, *Owner*
EMP: 4 EST: 2014
SALES (est): 41.35K Privately Held
SIC: 2741 Miscellaneous publishing

(G-8266)
BARUDAN AMERICA INC
9826 Us Highway 311 Ste 4 (27263-8844)
PHONE..................800 627-4776
Dave Davidson, *Brnch Mgr*
EMP: 7

Glen Mills PA 19342
855 547-1461

Web: www.barudanamerica.com
SIC: 3552 Embroidery machines
HQ: Barudan America, Inc.
30901 Carter St Frnt A
Solon OH 44139
440 248-8770

(G-8267)
BASIC AMERICAN FOODS
1560 N Main St Ste 101a (27262-2664)
PHONE..................336 887-3930
EMP: 6 EST: 2015
SALES (est): 153.03K Privately Held
Web: www.baffoodservice.com
SIC: 2015 Poultry slaughtering and processing

(G-8268)
BEAST CHAINS
733 Spinning Wheel Pt (27265-3452)
PHONE..................336 346-9081
EMP: 4 EST: 2017
SALES (est): 96.61K Privately Held
Web: www.beastchains.com
SIC: 3999 Manufacturing industries, nec

(G-8269)
BEDEX LLC
210 Swathmore Ave (27263-1932)
PHONE..................336 617-6755
EMP: 40 EST: 2012
SALES (est): 1.11MM Privately Held
Web: www.gobedex.com
SIC: 7641 2515 Reupholstery and furniture repair; Spring cushions

(G-8270)
BELWITH PRODUCTS LLC
1006 N Main St (27262-3166)
PHONE..................336 841-3899
Mark Smith, *Brnch Mgr*
EMP: 4
SQ FT: 3,666
Web: www.belwith-keeler.com
SIC: 3469 3465 3429 5072 Metal stampings, nec; Automotive stampings; Furniture hardware; Hardware
PA: Belwith Products, Llc
3100 Broadway Ave Sw
Grandville MI 49418

(G-8271)
BERKELEY HOME FURNITURE LLC
2228 Shore St (27263-2512)
P.O. Box 5023 (27262-5023)
PHONE..................336 882-0012
Thomas A Forrester Junior, *Managing Member*
EMP: 8 EST: 2017
SQ FT: 60,000
SALES (est): 604.93K Privately Held
SIC: 2512 Living room furniture: upholstered on wood frames

(G-8272)
BERRY GLOBAL INC
314 Mandustry St (27262-3199)
PHONE..................336 841-1723
EMP: 5
Web: www.berryglobal.com
SIC: 3089 3081 Bottle caps, molded plastics; Unsupported plastics film and sheet
HQ: Berry Global, Inc.
101 Oakley St
Evansville IN 47710

(G-8273)
BLUE RIDGE TOOL INC
2546 Willard Dairy Rd (27265-8117)
PHONE..................336 993-8111

Ronald Lamy, *Pr*
EMP: 5 EST: 1993
SQ FT: 3,000
SALES (est): 430.03K Privately Held
Web: www.blueridgetool.net
SIC: 3599 Machine shop, jobbing and repair

(G-8274)
BOOK LOVER SEARCH
P.O. Box 694 (27261-0694)
PHONE..................336 889-6127
Denise Jones, *Owner*
EMP: 5 EST: 2002
SALES (est): 294.1K Privately Held
SIC: 5192 2789 Books; Binding and repair of books, magazines, and pamphlets

(G-8275)
BOSS DESIGN US INC
2014 Chestnut Street Ext (27262-4408)
PHONE..................844 353-7834
Richard K Schell, *Prin*
EMP: 7 EST: 2014
SALES (est): 492.77K Privately Held
Web: www.bossdesign.com
SIC: 2521 Wood office furniture

(G-8276)
BRYAN AUSTIN
Also Called: UPS
1589 Skeet Club Rd Ste 102 (27265-8017)
PHONE..................336 841-6573
Bryan Austin, *Owner*
EMP: 10 EST: 2007
SALES (est): 233.7K Privately Held
Web: www.uscellphonedetective.com
SIC: 7389 2759 5044 Mailbox rental and related service; Commercial printing, nec; Office equipment

(G-8277)
BUILDING AUTOMATION SVCS LLC
1515 Bethel Dr (27260-8348)
PHONE..................336 884-4026
Robert Koonts, *Pr*
EMP: 10 EST: 2017
SALES (est): 1.05MM Privately Held
Web: www.basllco.com
SIC: 3822 Environmental controls

(G-8278)
BURCO WELDING & CUTNG PDTS INC
614 Old Thomasville Rd (27260-8433)
P.O. Box 2804 (27261-2804)
PHONE..................336 887-6100
▲ EMP: 7 EST: 1990
SQ FT: 25,000
SALES (est): 888.77K Privately Held
Web: www.burco.net
SIC: 5084 3548 Welding machinery and equipment; Welding apparatus

(G-8279)
BURROW FAMILY CORPORATION
Also Called: Wayne Trademark
660 Southwest St (27260-8107)
P.O. Box 2683 (27261-2683)
PHONE..................336 887-3173
Gary Burrow, *Pr*
Douglas Burrow, *
EMP: 80 EST: 1941
SQ FT: 100,000
SALES (est): 9.92MM Privately Held
SIC: 2752 Offset printing

(G-8280)
C R LAINE FURNITURE CO INC
310 N Hamilton St (27260-5034)
PHONE..................336 841-5337

EMP: 4 EST: 2019
SALES (est): 90.43K Privately Held
Web: www.crlaine.com
SIC: 2599 Furniture and fixtures, nec

(G-8281)
CAMBREX HIGH POINT INC
4180 Mendenhall Oaks Pkwy (27265-8017)
PHONE..................336 841-5250
Steven Klosk, *Pr*
EMP: 62 EST: 1999
SQ FT: 35,000
SALES (est): 37.5MM
SALES (corp-wide): 523.07MM Privately Held
Web: www.cambrex.com
SIC: 2834 Pharmaceutical preparations
PA: Cambrex Corporation
1 Meadowlands Plz # 1510
East Rutherford NJ 07073
201 804-3000

(G-8282)
CARBIDE SAWS INCORPORATED
701 Garrison St (27260-7098)
PHONE..................336 882-6835
Rogene Mc Guinn, *Pr*
Jane Goodman Burnette, *VP*
EMP: 11 EST: 1954
SQ FT: 1,600
SALES (est): 472.83K Privately Held
Web: www.carbidesawsinc.com
SIC: 7699 3553 Knife, saw and tool sharpening and repair; Woodworking machinery

(G-8283)
CARGILL & PENDLETON INC
Also Called: Cargill
330 N Hamilton St (27260-5034)
PHONE..................336 882-5510
EMP: 24
SIC: 2512 Upholstered household furniture
HQ: Cargill & Pendleton, Inc.
411 Tomlinson St
High Point NC 27260

(G-8284)
CAROLINA CONTAINER COMPANY (HQ)
Also Called: Digital High Point
909 Prospect St (27260-8273)
P.O. Box 2166 (27261-2166)
PHONE..................336 883-7146
Nicholas Smith, *CEO*
Ronald T Sessions, *
Randall L Black, *
◆ EMP: 100 EST: 1928
SQ FT: 9,200
SALES (est): 193.02MM
SALES (corp-wide): 679.24MM Privately Held
Web: www.carolinacontainer.com
SIC: 2653 2679 Boxes, corrugated: made from purchased materials; Corrugated paper: made from purchased material
PA: New-Indy Jv Corp.
3500 Porsche Way Ste 150
Ontario CA 91764
909 296-3400

(G-8285)
CAROLINA CUSTOM BOOTH CO LLC
Also Called: Carolina Custom Booth
901 W Market Center Dr (27260-8238)
P.O. Box 150 (27261-0150)
PHONE..................336 886-3127
Renee Surratt, *
Stephanie Roberts, *
Amy Blum Grady, *

GEOGRAPHIC SECTION

High Point - Guilford County (G-8307)

◆ **EMP:** 26 **EST:** 2010
SALES (est): 4.94MM **Privately Held**
Web: www.carolinacustombooth.com
SIC: 3444 Booths, spray: prefabricated sheet metal

(G-8286)
CARPENTER CO
1021 E Springfield Rd Ste 101 (27263)
PHONE..............................336 861-5730
Randy Wisner, *Genl Mgr*
EMP: 58
SQ FT: 127,616
SALES (corp-wide): 1.85B **Privately Held**
Web: www.carpenter.com
SIC: 3086 2821 Insulation or cushioning material, foamed plastics; Plastics materials and resins
PA: Carpenter Co.
  5016 Monument Ave
  Richmond VA 23230
  804 359-0800

(G-8287)
CARR MILL SUPPLIES INC
1015 Manley St (27260-7062)
P.O. Box 2766 (27261-2766)
PHONE..............................336 883-0135
Sara W Carr, *Pr*
Guy E Carr Junior, *VP*
Doctor Jennifer Savitz, *Sec*
EMP: 9 **EST:** 1952
SQ FT: 9,600
SALES (est): 576.32K **Privately Held**
SIC: 3599 5085 Machine shop, jobbing and repair; Industrial supplies

(G-8288)
CARTRIDGE WORLD
Also Called: Earnmoore
2640 Willard Dairy Rd Ste 114 (27265-8708)
PHONE..............................336 885-0989
James Steven Moore, *Owner*
Robert Wessman, *Prin*
EMP: 8 **EST:** 2004
SALES (est): 356.16K **Privately Held**
Web: www.cartridgeworld.com
SIC: 5112 3955 Office filing supplies; Print cartridges for laser and other computer printers

(G-8289)
CASCADE DIE CASTING GROUP INC
Also Called: Cascade Die Casting
1800 Albertson Rd (27260-8206)
P.O. Box 8045 (27264-8045)
PHONE..............................336 882-0186
Phil Torchio, *Brnch Mgr*
EMP: 230
SQ FT: 40,000
SALES (corp-wide): 97.08MM **Privately Held**
Web: www.cascade-cdc.com
SIC: 3364 3365 3363 Zinc and zinc-base alloy die-castings; Aluminum foundries; Aluminum die-castings
HQ: Cascade Die Casting Group Inc
  7441 Division Ave S A1
  Grand Rapids MI 49548
  616 281-1660

(G-8290)
CASCADE DIE CASTING GROUP INC
Also Called: Atlantic Division
501 Old Thomasville Rd (27260-8430)
PHONE..............................336 882-0186
Kent Nifong, *Prin*
EMP: 43
SALES (corp-wide): 97.08MM **Privately Held**
Web: www.cascade-cdc.com
SIC: 3544 Special dies and tools
HQ: Cascade Die Casting Group Inc
  7441 Division Ave S A1
  Grand Rapids MI 49548
  616 281-1660

(G-8291)
CECIL-JOHNSON MFG INC
1445 Jackson Lake Rd (27263-9764)
PHONE..............................336 431-5233
Richard Pokrivka, *Pr*
Katherine Johnson, *Treas*
Evon Pokrivka, *Sec*
EMP: 18 **EST:** 1979
SQ FT: 20,000
SALES (est): 1.79MM **Privately Held**
SIC: 2426 Frames for upholstered furniture, wood

(G-8292)
CENTURY FURNITURE LLC
Also Called: Highpoint Century Showroom
200 Steele St (27260-5153)
PHONE..............................336 889-8286
Sandra Royals, *Mgr*
EMP: 5
SALES (corp-wide): 212.17MM **Privately Held**
Web: www.centuryfurniture.com
SIC: 2511 Wood household furniture
HQ: Century Furniture, Llc
  401 11th St Nw
  Hickory NC 28601
  828 267-8739

(G-8293)
CH PUBLISHING
701 Shamrock Rd (27265-1346)
PHONE..............................336 886-1984
Scott Nicklow, *Prin*
EMP: 5 **EST:** 2010
SALES (est): 172.96K **Privately Held**
Web: www.chpublish.com
SIC: 2741 Miscellaneous publishing

(G-8294)
CHATEAU DAX USA LTD
1838 Eastchester Dr Ste 106 (27265)
PHONE..............................336 885-9777
Giulio Rainoldi, *CEO*
Walter Colombo, *Pr*
Amir Kalipour, *Sec*
Giolio Rainoldi, *CEO*
◆ **EMP:** 7 **EST:** 1985
SQ FT: 2,500
SALES (est): 1.02MM
SALES (corp-wide): 103.81MM **Privately Held**
SIC: 2512 5021 Upholstered household furniture; Chairs
PA: Chateau D'ax Spa
  Via Nazionale 159
  Lentate Sul Seveso MB 20823
  036 256-9068

(G-8295)
CHILDERS CONCRETE COMPANY
200 Wise Ave (27260-7646)
P.O. Box 777 (27261-0777)
PHONE..............................336 841-3111
Mitchel L Childers Junior, *Pr*
Kelly Vickers, *Sec*
EMP: 12 **EST:** 1946
SQ FT: 1,200
SALES (est): 2.1MM **Privately Held**
Web: www.childersconcrete.com
SIC: 3273 Ready-mixed concrete

(G-8296)
CLARIOS LLC
Also Called: Johnson Controls
211 S Hamilton St (27260-5232)
PHONE..............................336 884-5832
EMP: 32
SALES (corp-wide): 4.48B **Privately Held**
Web: www.clarios.com
SIC: 2531 Seats, automobile
HQ: Clarios, Llc
  5757 N Green Bay Ave
  Milwaukee WI 53209

(G-8297)
CLARKE HARLAND CORP
4475 Premier Dr (27265-8336)
PHONE..............................210 697-8888
Julie Kellman, *Prin*
EMP: 8
Web: www.harlandclarke.com
SIC: 2782 Bank checkbooks and passbooks
HQ: Harland Clarke Corp.
  15955 La Cantera Pkwy
  San Antonio TX 78256
  830 609-5500

(G-8298)
COAST TO COAST LEA & VINYL INC
Also Called: Southeast Leather
1022 Porter St (27263-1638)
PHONE..............................336 886-5050
Cicki Reez, *Mgr*
EMP: 4
SALES (corp-wide): 2.09MM **Privately Held**
Web: www.coast2coastleather.com
SIC: 3111 3199 Mechanical leather; Leather garments
PA: Coast To Coast Leather & Vinyl, Inc.
  1 Crossman Rd S
  Sayreville NJ 08872
  732 525-8877

(G-8299)
COLONIAL LLC
536 Townsend Ave (27263-2046)
P.O. Box 148 (27261-0148)
PHONE..............................336 434-5600
Mark Hobson, *Pr*
James R Keever, *Managing Member*
Jim Keever Senior, *Pr*
Wes Keever, *VP*
Jimmy Keever, *VP*
▲ **EMP:** 40 **EST:** 1982
SQ FT: 22,000
SALES (est): 6.93MM **Privately Held**
Web: www.colonialllc.com
SIC: 2395 Embroidery and art needlework

(G-8300)
COLUMBIA PANEL MFG CO INC
100 Giles St (27263-2108)
P.O. Box 7447 (27264-7447)
PHONE..............................336 861-4100
Todd Rush, *Pr*
Brenda Rush, *
EMP: 70 **EST:** 1920
SQ FT: 46,000
SALES (est): 8.65MM **Privately Held**
Web: www.columbiapanel.com
SIC: 2435 Hardwood veneer and plywood

(G-8301)
COMPETITION TOOLING INC
219 Dublin Ave (27260-8352)
P.O. Box 7203 (27264-7203)
PHONE..............................336 887-4414
Carl L Warrell, *Pr*
Johnnie Cox, *Sec*
EMP: 8 **EST:** 1968
SQ FT: 9,000
SALES (est): 745.86K **Privately Held**
Web: www.competitionengineering.net
SIC: 3312 Tool and die steel

(G-8302)
COMPUTERWAY FOOD SYSTEMS INC
2700 Westchester Dr (27262-8037)
PHONE..............................336 841-7289
Jeff Jackson, *CEO*
EMP: 25 **EST:** 2017
SALES (est): 4.17MM **Privately Held**
Web: www.mycfs.com
SIC: 7373 3596 Computer integrated systems design; Scales and balances, except laboratory

(G-8303)
CONCEPT PLASTICS INC (PA)
Also Called: Craft-Tex
1210 Hickory Chapel Rd (27260-7187)
P.O. Box 847 (27261-0847)
PHONE..............................336 889-2001
Paul Saperstein, *Pr*
Sara L Saperstein, *
EMP: 144 **EST:** 1970
SALES (est): 9.89MM
SALES (corp-wide): 9.89MM **Privately Held**
Web: www.cpico.com
SIC: 3089 Injection molding of plastics

(G-8304)
CRAFTWOOD VENEERS INC
822 Herman Ct (27263-2166)
PHONE..............................336 434-2158
Victor Furr, *Pr*
EMP: 7 **EST:** 2015
SALES (est): 226.84K **Privately Held**
Web: www.craftwoodproducts.com
SIC: 2449 Containers, plywood and veneer wood

(G-8305)
CRAVEN SIGN SERVICES INC
508 Old Thomasville Rd (27260-8431)
PHONE..............................336 883-7306
TOLL FREE: 800
Tony Craven, *Pr*
EMP: 4 **EST:** 1965
SQ FT: 1,200
SALES (est): 497.48K **Privately Held**
Web: www.cravensigns.com
SIC: 3993 Signs, not made in custom sign painting shops

(G-8306)
CRAWFORD INDUSTRIES INC
Also Called: Artistic Quilting
108 Lane Ave (27260-8719)
P.O. Box 5171 (27262-5171)
PHONE..............................336 884-8822
Kent Crawford, *Pr*
Lynn Crawford, *VP*
▼ **EMP:** 11 **EST:** 1985
SQ FT: 11,000
SALES (est): 551.79K **Privately Held**
Web: www.artisticquiltinginc.com
SIC: 2395 Quilting and quilting supplies

(G-8307)
CREATIVE SERVICES USA INC
1231 Montlieu Ave (27262-3560)
P.O. Box 2344 (27282-2344)
PHONE..............................336 887-1958
Michael West, *Pr*
EMP: 7 **EST:** 1970
SQ FT: 30,000
SALES (est): 387.73K **Privately Held**
Web: www.creativeservicesusa.com

High Point - Guilford County (G-8308)

SIC: 2789 Swatches and samples

(G-8308)
CROSS CO
608 Ashe St (27262-4629)
PHONE..................336 856-6110
Pete Cross, *CEO*
EMP: 5 EST: 2017
SALES (est): 171.53K **Privately Held**
SIC: 3559 Special industry machinery, nec

(G-8309)
CROWN FOAM PRODUCTS INC
921 Baker Rd Ste 3 (27263-2127)
P.O. Box 1224 (27261-1224)
PHONE..................336 434-4024
Steve Roach, *Pr*
Betty Roach, *Sec*
EMP: 12 EST: 1973
SQ FT: 20,000
SALES (est): 972.95K **Privately Held**
SIC: 3086 Plastics foam products

(G-8310)
CULP INC (PA)
1823 Eastchester Dr (27265-1558)
P.O. Box 2686 (27261-2686)
PHONE..................336 889-5161
Robert G Culp Iv, *Pr*
Franklin N Saxon, *
Kenneth R Bowling, *Ex VP*
Ashley C Durbin, *Corporate Secretary*
Teresa Huffman, *Chief Human Resource Officer*
EMP: 18 EST: 1972
SQ FT: 36,643
SALES (est): 234.93MM
SALES (corp-wide): 234.93MM **Publicly Held**
Web: www.culp.com
SIC: 2221 Upholstery fabrics, manmade fiber and silk

(G-8311)
CUSTOM AIR TRAYS INC (PA)
2112 S Elm St (27260-8811)
P.O. Box 7026 (27264-7026)
PHONE..................336 889-8729
Jim Hardy, *Genl Mgr*
▼ EMP: 10 EST: 1992
SALES (est): 2.34MM **Privately Held**
Web: www.customairtrays.com
SIC: 2449 7261 Shipping cases and drums, wood: wirebound and plywood; Funeral service and crematories

(G-8312)
CUSTOM CONTRACT FURN LLC
667 W Ward Ave (27260-1644)
P.O. Box 7264 (27264-7264)
PHONE..................336 882-8565
◆ EMP: 6 EST: 1997
SALES (est): 176.29K **Privately Held**
Web: www.customcontract.com
SIC: 7389 2512 Interior designer; Chairs: upholstered on wood frames

(G-8313)
CUSTOM FINISHERS INC (PA)
Also Called: Eagle Laser
2213 Shore St (27263-2511)
P.O. Box 7008 (27264-7008)
PHONE..................336 431-7141
Christopher Wayne Wilkins, *Pr*
Sylvia Hicks, *
EMP: 39 EST: 1972
SQ FT: 45,000
SALES (est): 5.96MM
SALES (corp-wide): 5.96MM **Privately Held**
Web: www.customfinishers.com

SIC: 2493 7389 Hardboard; Metal cutting services

(G-8314)
CUSTOM SIGNS
2724 Belmont Dr (27263-2254)
PHONE..................336 847-7700
Thang Nguyen, *Prin*
EMP: 5 EST: 2018
SALES (est): 98.32K **Privately Held**
SIC: 3993 Signs and advertising specialties

(G-8315)
D & B CONCEPTS INC
613 Prospect St (27260-1522)
PHONE..................336 885-8292
William Slate, *Pr*
Thomas Waterhouse, *VP*
EMP: 13 EST: 2004
SALES (est): 736.6K **Privately Held**
Web: www.dandbconcepts.com
SIC: 5031 2541 Lumber, plywood, and millwork; Bar fixtures, wood

(G-8316)
D3 SOFTWARE INC
277 Creekside Dr (27265-9254)
PHONE..................336 870-9138
EMP: 5 EST: 2016
SALES (est): 96.07K **Privately Held**
SIC: 7372 Prepackaged software

(G-8317)
DANI LEATHER USA INC
635 Southwest St Ste A (27260-8223)
PHONE..................973 598-0890
Silvano Fumei, *Prin*
▲ EMP: 6 EST: 2005
SALES (est): 935.63K
SALES (corp-wide): 169.4MM **Privately Held**
Web: www.gruppodani.com
SIC: 3111 Leather tanning and finishing
HQ: Dani Spa
  Via Concia 186
  Arzignano VI 36071
  044 445-4111

(G-8318)
DARRAN FURNITURE INDS INC
Also Called: Darran Furniture
2402 Shore St (27263-2514)
P.O. Box 7614 (27264-7614)
PHONE..................336 861-2400
Jennifer H Cushion, *Pr*
EMP: 135 EST: 1977
SQ FT: 225,000
SALES (est): 22.55MM
SALES (corp-wide): 22.55MM **Privately Held**
Web: www.darran.com
SIC: 2521 Wood office furniture

(G-8319)
DAVIS FURNITURE INDUSTRIES INC (PA)
2401 College Dr (27260-8816)
P.O. Box 2065 (27261-2065)
PHONE..................336 889-2009
Danny Davis, *Pr*
◆ EMP: 165 EST: 1942
SQ FT: 350,000
SALES (est): 55.12MM
SALES (corp-wide): 55.12MM **Privately Held**
Web: www.davisfurniture.com
SIC: 2521 2531 2522 2511 Chairs, office: padded, upholstered, or plain: wood; Public building and related furniture; Office furniture, except wood; Wood household furniture

(G-8320)
DERSHENG USA INC
2019 Brevard Rd (27263-1701)
P.O. Box 250 (27313-0250)
PHONE..................336 434-5055
Lane Yates, *Pr*
▲ EMP: 8 EST: 2007
SALES (est): 444.78K **Privately Held**
Web: www.dershengusa.com
SIC: 3562 Casters

(G-8321)
DESIGN CONCEPTS INCORPORATED
341 South Rd (27262-8198)
PHONE..................336 887-1932
Hal A Kennerly Junior, *Pr*
Kay Miller, *
EMP: 19 EST: 1968
SQ FT: 36,000
SALES (est): 1.43MM **Privately Held**
Web: www.designconceptslv.com
SIC: 2782 2221 Sample books; Broadwoven fabric mills, manmade

(G-8322)
DESIGN THEORY LLC
1020 Surrett Dr (27260-8821)
PHONE..................336 912-0155
Scott Kim, *Managing Member*
EMP: 11 EST: 2014
SALES (est): 2.66MM **Privately Held**
Web: www.designtheoryhp.com
SIC: 2512 Upholstered household furniture

(G-8323)
DFP INC (PA)
Also Called: Edward Ferrell Lewis Mittman
685 Southwest St (27260-8108)
PHONE..................336 841-3028
Ira Glazer, *Pr*
▲ EMP: 100 EST: 1972
SALES (est): 10.67MM
SALES (corp-wide): 10.67MM **Privately Held**
Web: www.ferrellmittman.com
SIC: 2512 2531 Upholstered household furniture; Public building and related furniture

(G-8324)
DIGITAL HIGHPOINT LLC
401 Model Farm Rd Ste 101 (27263-1827)
P.O. Box 2166 (27261-2166)
PHONE..................336 883-7146
Ronald T Sessions, *CEO*
EMP: 155 EST: 2004
SALES (est): 1.01MM
SALES (corp-wide): 679.24MM **Privately Held**
Web: www.highpoint.edu
SIC: 3555 3955 5084 Printing plates; Print cartridges for laser and other computer printers; Printing trades machinery, equipment, and supplies
HQ: Carolina Container Company
  909 Prospect St
  High Point NC 27260
  336 883-7146

(G-8325)
DISTINCTION HOSPITALITY INC
4100 Mendenhall Oaks Pkwy Ste 200 (27265-8074)
PHONE..................336 875-3043
Stanley Sapp, *Pr*
EMP: 10 EST: 2014
SALES (est): 957.39K **Privately Held**
Web: www.distinctionhospitality.com
SIC: 2599 Hotel furniture

(G-8326)
DIVERSIFIED WOODCRAFTS INC
923 Shamrock Rd (27265-1358)
PHONE..................336 688-3114
Kelly Brant, *Mgr*
EMP: 22 EST: 2013
SALES (est): 104.27K **Privately Held**
SIC: 3821 Laboratory apparatus and furniture

(G-8327)
DIX ENTERPRISES INC
2436 Lake Oak (27265-9256)
PHONE..................336 558-9512
EMP: 10 EST: 1992
SALES (est): 473.48K **Privately Held**
Web: www.dixgroupinc.com
SIC: 3949 7389 Sporting and athletic goods, nec; Fund raising organizations

(G-8328)
DLP PUBLISHING LLC
2530 Willard Rd (27265-8114)
PHONE..................336 803-2188
N Grant Swaim, *Owner*
EMP: 5 EST: 2018
SALES (est): 73.6K **Privately Held**
Web: www.divinelegacypublishing.com
SIC: 2741 Miscellaneous publishing

(G-8329)
DOMENICKS FURNITURE MFR LLC
1107 Tate St (27260-7846)
PHONE..................336 442-3348
EMP: 20 EST: 2017
SALES (est): 2.41MM **Privately Held**
Web: www.domenicksfurniture.com
SIC: 2512 Upholstered household furniture

(G-8330)
DRAKE S FRESH PASTA COMPANY
636 Southwest St (27260-8107)
P.O. Box 5072 (27262-5072)
PHONE..................336 861-5454
Richard Drake, *Ch*
Simone Drake, *
▲ EMP: 50 EST: 1985
SALES (est): 7.51MM **Privately Held**
Web: www.drakesfreshpasta.com
SIC: 2099 Food preparations, nec

(G-8331)
DREXEL HERITAGE HOME FURNSNGS
741 W Ward Ave (27260-1645)
PHONE..................336 812-4430
Bryon Milleson, *CFO*
EMP: 5 EST: 2016
SALES (est): 57.78K **Privately Held**
SIC: 2599 Furniture and fixtures, nec

(G-8332)
DRUM FILTER MEDIA INC
901 W Fairfield Rd (27263-1607)
PHONE..................336 434-4195
John C Hollinger Iii, *Pr*
EMP: 4 EST: 1992
SALES (est): 439.89K **Privately Held**
Web: www.dfmiusa.com
SIC: 3569 5084 Filters, general line: industrial; Industrial machinery and equipment

(G-8333)
E FEIBUSCH COMPANY INC
Also Called: Swatchcraft
516 Townsend Ave (27263-2046)
PHONE..................336 434-5095
Gerald Feibusch, *Pr*
▲ EMP: 48 EST: 1934
SALES (est): 6.42MM **Privately Held**

GEOGRAPHIC SECTION

High Point - Guilford County (G-8360)

Web: www.swatchcraft.com
SIC: 2782 2789 Blankbooks and looseleaf binders; Swatches and samples

(G-8334)
EAGLE PRODUCTS INC
1200 Surrett Dr (27260-8823)
P.O. Box 7387 (27264-7387)
PHONE..................................336 886-5688
EMP: 10 EST: 1981
SALES (est): 234.4K Privately Held
SIC: 2674 Bags: uncoated paper and multiwall

(G-8335)
EAGLESTONE TECHNOLOGY INC
1401 Kensington Dr (27262-7319)
PHONE..................................336 476-0244
Robert M Barnard, Pr
EMP: 10 EST: 1993
SALES (est): 989.48K Privately Held
SIC: 3599 Machine shop, jobbing and repair

(G-8336)
ED KEMP ASSOCIATES INC
Also Called: Ed Kemp Associates
3001 N Main St (27265-1938)
PHONE..................................336 869-2155
Jon Kemp, CEO
Tony Faucette, VP
EMP: 8 EST: 1961
SQ FT: 1,500
SALES (est): 636.67K Privately Held
Web: www.edkemp.com
SIC: 7311 2752 8743 Advertising consultant; Commercial printing, lithographic; Public relations and publicity

(G-8337)
EDM TECHNOLOGY INC
210 Old Thomasville Rd (27260-8187)
PHONE..................................336 882-8115
Clem Garvey, CEO
EMP: 23 EST: 2021
SALES (est): 3.82MM
SALES (corp-wide): 2.12MM Privately Held
SIC: 2752 2759 Business form and card printing, lithographic; Tickets: printing, nsk
HQ: Paragon Id
    Allee Des Aubepins
    Argent Sur Sauldre 18410

(G-8338)
ELECTRICAL PANEL & CONTRLS INC
645 Mcway Dr (27263-2398)
PHONE..................................336 434-4445
Martin Goodpasture, Pr
Paul Jones, VP
EMP: 15 EST: 2000
SQ FT: 15,000
SALES (est): 189.37K Privately Held
SIC: 3823 Process control instruments

(G-8339)
ELEMENTAL BEE
4115 Aberdare Dr (27265-9194)
PHONE..................................336 471-9085
Amy Honey, Prin
EMP: 4 EST: 2016
SALES (est): 46.35K Privately Held
SIC: 2819 Industrial inorganic chemicals, nec

(G-8340)
ELITE FURNITURE MFG INC
928 Millis St (27260-7257)
PHONE..................................336 882-0406
EMP: 9 EST: 1997
SQ FT: 158,000
SALES (est): 152.84K Privately Held
SIC: 2512 5021 Upholstered household furniture; Household furniture

(G-8341)
ELITE TEXTILES FABRICATION INC
1124 Roberts Ln (27260-7211)
PHONE..................................888 337-0977
Ryan West, CEO
EMP: 12 EST: 2018
SALES (est): 1.02MM Privately Held
Web: www.draperyfabrication.com
SIC: 2591 Window blinds

(G-8342)
EMB INC
4180 Mendenhall Oaks Pkwy Ste 100 (27265-8017)
PHONE..................................336 945-0759
EMP: 4 EST: 2010
SALES (est): 46.38K Privately Held
SIC: 2395 Embroidery products, except Schiffli machine

(G-8343)
ENDURA PRODUCTS LLC
210 E Commerce Ave (27260-6686)
PHONE..................................336 991-8818
EMP: 15
SALES (corp-wide): 2.83B Publicly Held
Web: www.enduraproducts.com
SIC: 3429 Hardware, nec
HQ: Endura Products, Llc
    8817 W Market St
    Colfax NC 27235
    336 668-2472

(G-8344)
ENGCON NORTH AMERICA
2827 Earlham Pl (27263-1948)
PHONE..................................203 691-5920
Krister Blomgren, Prin
EMP: 23 EST: 2017
SALES (est): 2.25MM Privately Held
SIC: 3531 Construction machinery

(G-8345)
ENGLAND INC
222 S Main St (27260-5208)
PHONE..................................336 861-5266
Otis Sawyer, Prin
EMP: 29
SALES (corp-wide): 2.35B Publicly Held
Web: www.englandfurniture.com
SIC: 2512 Upholstered household furniture
HQ: England, Inc.
    145 England Dr
    New Tazewell TN 37825
    423 626-5211

(G-8346)
ETHNICRAFT USA LLC
101 Prospect St (27260-7259)
PHONE..................................336 885-2055
Jack G Hendrix, Admn
EMP: 19 EST: 2016
SALES (est): 4.57MM Privately Held
SIC: 2022 Processed cheese

(G-8347)
EUROHANSA INC
1213 Dorris Ave (27260-1575)
P.O. Box 6416 (27262-6416)
PHONE..................................336 885-1010
Hans Zoellinger, Pr
Frank H Zoellinger, VP
▲ EMP: 9 EST: 1988
SQ FT: 15,000
SALES (est): 1.05MM Privately Held
Web: www.eurohansa.com

SIC: 3553 Woodworking machinery

(G-8348)
EXTREME SCENES INC
Also Called: Extreme Millwork
1525 Blandwood Dr (27260-8294)
PHONE..................................336 687-3369
Mark Quinn, Prin
EMP: 11 EST: 2005
SALES (est): 296.86K Privately Held
Web: www.extremescenesinc.com
SIC: 2431 Millwork

(G-8349)
F C C LLC
Also Called: Furniture City Color
4045 Premier Dr Ste 200 (27265-9431)
P.O. Box 35304 (27425-5304)
PHONE..................................336 883-7314
Tim Frye, Managing Member
Bill Franklin, Managing Member
EMP: 9 EST: 1969
SQ FT: 7,000
SALES (est): 279.11K Privately Held
Web: www.lastnamefirst.com
SIC: 2796 2759 2791 Lithographic plates, positives or negatives; Commercial printing, nec; Typesetting

(G-8350)
FACES SOUTH INC
1330 Lincoln Dr (27260-1515)
P.O. Box 1837 (27261-1837)
PHONE..................................336 883-0647
EMP: 14 EST: 1995
SALES (est): 1.88MM Privately Held
Web: www.ritchfaceveneer.com
SIC: 2436 Softwood veneer and plywood

(G-8351)
FFNC INC
Also Called: Future Foam
1300 Prospect St (27260-8329)
P.O. Box 1017 (68101-1017)
PHONE..................................336 885-4121
◆ EMP: 83
SIC: 3086 Plastics foam products

(G-8352)
FIBER CUSHIONING INC
113 Motsinger St (27260-8836)
P.O. Box 4877 (27263-4877)
PHONE..................................336 887-4782
Dob Mc Gee, Brnch Mgr
EMP: 14
SALES (corp-wide): 3.1MM Privately Held
Web: www.fibercushioning.com
SIC: 2392 Household furnishings, nec
PA: Fiber Cushioning, Inc.
    4454 Us Highway 220 Bus S
    Asheboro NC 27205
    336 629-8442

(G-8353)
FIBER DYNAMICS INC
Also Called: Fiber Dynamics
200 S West Point Ave (27260-7200)
P.O. Box 1910 (27261-1910)
PHONE..................................336 886-7111
James Heery, Pr
Ralph A Matergia, *
▲ EMP: 70 EST: 1983
SQ FT: 225,000
SALES (est): 9.04MM Privately Held
Web: www.fdinonwovens.com
SIC: 2297 Nonwoven fabrics

(G-8354)
FLINT ENNIS INC
4189 Eagle Hill Dr (27265-8315)

PHONE..................................800 331-8118
EMP: 4 EST: 2016
SALES (est): 48.57K Privately Held
Web: www.ennisflint.com
SIC: 2851 Paints and allied products

(G-8355)
FORRENTCOM
3708 Lexham Ct (27265-9299)
PHONE..................................336 420-9562
Shelbie Beato, Mgr
EMP: 6 EST: 2013
SALES (est): 225.47K Privately Held
Web: www.forrent.com
SIC: 2721 Periodicals

(G-8356)
FORTRESS WOOD PRODUCTS INC
3874 Bethel Drive Ext (27260-8465)
P.O. Box 4991 (24115-4991)
PHONE..................................336 854-5121
Brandt A Mitchell, Pr
N Dillard Jones, VP
Janet M Decker, Sec
EMP: 12 EST: 1986
SQ FT: 1,500
SALES (est): 4.79MM
SALES (corp-wide): 95.93MM Privately Held
Web: www.fortresswood.com
SIC: 2491 Wood preserving
PA: The Lester Group Inc
    101 Commonwealth Blvd E
    Martinsville VA 24112
    276 638-8834

(G-8357)
FOUNDING FATHERS DISTILLERY
6116 Hickory Creek Rd (27263-9773)
PHONE..................................336 434-0149
EMP: 5 EST: 2017
SALES (est): 111.31K Privately Held
Web: www.foundingfathersdistillery.com
SIC: 2085 Distilled and blended liquors

(G-8358)
FRENCH HERITAGE INC (PA)
1638 W English Rd (27262-7204)
P.O. Box 2054 (27285-2054)
PHONE..................................336 882-3565
Jacques Wayser, Pr
Hennessy Wayser, VP
▲ EMP: 16 EST: 1994
SALES (est): 4.53MM
SALES (corp-wide): 4.53MM Privately Held
Web: www.frenchheritage.com
SIC: 2519 5021 Household furniture, except wood or metal: upholstered; Household furniture

(G-8359)
FRESH AS A DAISY INC
Also Called: Fresh As A Daisy
3601 Huntingridge Dr (27265-1258)
PHONE..................................336 869-3002
Edythe Golden, Pr
James Golden, *
EMP: 9 EST: 1999
SALES (est): 363.12K Privately Held
Web: www.faadinc.com
SIC: 2842 Cleaning or polishing preparations, nec

(G-8360)
FREUD AMERICA INC
Also Called: Freud
218 Feld Ave (27263-1930)
P.O. Box 7187 (27264-7187)
PHONE..................................800 334-4107
Russell Kohl, Pr

High Point - Guilford County (G-8361) — GEOGRAPHIC SECTION

David Lewis, *
Russell Kohl, *Chief Executive Officer Freud US*
Jim Brewer, *
Gregory Thiess, *
◆ **EMP:** 120 **EST:** 1991
SQ FT: 50,000
SALES (est): 88.74MM
SALES (corp-wide): 230.19MM **Privately Held**
SIC: 5072 3546 3545 Cutlery; Power-driven handtools; Machine tool accessories
HQ: Bosch Rexroth Ag
Zum EisengieBer 1
Lohr A. Main BY 97816
9352180

(G-8361)
FUTURE FOAM INC
Also Called: Ffnc
1300 Prospect St (27260-8329)
P.O. Box 7185 (27264-7185)
PHONE.................................336 885-4121
Tim Akins, *Brnch Mgr*
EMP: 55
SALES (corp-wide): 495.02MM **Privately Held**
Web: www.futurefoam.com
SIC: 2821 3086 Plastics materials and resins; Insulation or cushioning material, foamed plastics
PA: Future Foam, Inc.
1610 Avenue N
Council Bluffs IA 51501
712 323-9122

(G-8362)
FXI INC
2222 Surrett Dr (27263-8508)
PHONE.................................336 431-1171
EMP: 90
Web: www.fxi.com
SIC: 3086 Carpet and rug cushions, foamed plastics
HQ: Fxi, Inc.
100 W Matsonford Rd
Radnor PA 19087

(G-8363)
GBF INC
Also Called: Guilford Business Forms
2427 Penny Rd (27265-8120)
P.O. Box 16128 (27261-6128)
PHONE.................................336 665-0205
Danny Bowman, *CEO*
Jason Bowman, *
Coy Shields, *
EMP: 72 **EST:** 1964
SQ FT: 240,000
SALES (est): 23.27MM **Privately Held**
Web: www.gbf-inc.com
SIC: 2835 2899 5112 Diagnostic substances; Drug testing kits, blood and urine; Business forms

(G-8364)
GENERAL ELASTIC CORPORATION
Also Called: General Elastic Sales
6086 Old Mendenhall Rd (27263-3936)
P.O. Box 75 (27261-0075)
PHONE.................................336 431-8714
James Kendall Senior, *Pr*
James Kendall Junior, *VP*
Carrie Butler, *Sec*
EMP: 10 **EST:** 1979
SQ FT: 9,000
SALES (est): 246.84K **Privately Held**
SIC: 2241 Yarns, elastic: fabric covered

(G-8365)
GERSAN INDUSTRIES INCORPORATED
607 Blake Ave (27260-8371)
P.O. Box 7043 (27264-7043)
PHONE.................................336 886-5455
Gerald Swanson, *Owner*
EMP: 4 **EST:** 1972
SQ FT: 8,000
SALES (est): 489.3K **Privately Held**
Web: www.gersanindustries.com
SIC: 2821 Plastics materials and resins

(G-8366)
GLASS UNLIMITED HIGH POINT INC
Also Called: Glass Unlimited
2149 Brevard Rd (27263-1703)
P.O. Box 528 (27261-0528)
PHONE.................................336 889-4551
Keith Eichhorn, *Pr*
Clint Field, *
▲ **EMP:** 55 **EST:** 1977
SQ FT: 75,000
SALES (est): 9.31MM **Privately Held**
Web: www.glass-unlimited.com
SIC: 3231 Products of purchased glass

(G-8367)
GLOBAL BIOPROTECT LLC
2714 Uwharrie Rd (27263-1680)
PHONE.................................336 861-0162
EMP: 10 **EST:** 2016
SALES (est): 1.02MM **Privately Held**
Web: www.globalbioprotect.com
SIC: 2899 Chemical preparations, nec

(G-8368)
GLOBAL VENEER SALES INC
112 Hodgin St (27262-7909)
P.O. Box 5829 (27262-5829)
PHONE.................................336 885-5061
Elwood S Cain Junior, *Pr*
Sandra Cain, *Sec*
David Hiatt, *VP*
▲ **EMP:** 6 **EST:** 1985
SQ FT: 20,000
SALES (est): 845.15K **Privately Held**
Web: www.globalveneer.com
SIC: 5031 7534 Veneer; Vulcanizing tires and tubes

(G-8369)
GOLD REFINERY
3954 Huttons Lake Ct (27265-1873)
PHONE.................................336 471-4817
Angela Tripp, *Prin*
EMP: 8 **EST:** 2010
SALES (est): 78.37K **Privately Held**
SIC: 3559 Refinery, chemical processing, and similar machinery

(G-8370)
GP FOAM FABRICATORS INC
220 Swathmore Ave (27263-1932)
P.O. Box 7483 (27264-7483)
PHONE.................................336 434-3600
Bob Pace, *Pr*
Elsie Pace, *
EMP: 21 **EST:** 1987
SQ FT: 20,000
SALES (est): 3.01MM **Privately Held**
SIC: 3069 Foam rubber

(G-8371)
GRAPHIK DIMENSIONS LIMITED
Also Called: Pictureframes.com
2103 Brentwood St (27263-1807)
PHONE.................................800 332-8884
Lauri Feinsod, *Pr*
Joan Feinsod, *
Dave Shelton, *
Mike Keyes, *
◆ **EMP:** 100 **EST:** 1966
SQ FT: 108,000
SALES (est): 18.44MM
SALES (corp-wide): 509.22MM **Privately Held**
Web: www.pictureframes.com
SIC: 3499 2499 7379 Picture frames, metal; Picture and mirror frames, wood; Computer related consulting services
PA: Circle Graphics, Inc.
120 9th Ave
Longmont CO 80501
303 532-2370

(G-8372)
GUILFORD FABRICATORS INC
5261 Glenola Industrial Dr (27263-8152)
P.O. Box 7245 (27264-7245)
PHONE.................................336 434-3163
Don Payne, *Pr*
Randy Rains, *VP*
Trudy Payne, *Sec*
▲ **EMP:** 10 **EST:** 1977
SQ FT: 28,000
SALES (est): 597.98K **Privately Held**
SIC: 5999 3086 Foam and foam products; Plastics foam products

(G-8373)
GUM DROP CASES LLC
1515 W Green Dr (27260-1657)
PHONE.................................206 805-0818
EMP: 7 **EST:** 2018
SALES (est): 354.49K **Privately Held**
SIC: 3523 Farm machinery and equipment

(G-8374)
H & H WOODWORKING INC
530 Gatewood Ave (27262-4720)
PHONE.................................336 884-5848
EMP: 8 **EST:** 1976
SQ FT: 13,000
SALES (est): 730K **Privately Held**
SIC: 1751 2431 Cabinet building and installation; Millwork

(G-8375)
HARRIS WELDING
809 Richland St (27260-6830)
PHONE.................................336 514-6640
EMP: 4 **EST:** 2016
SALES (est): 33.24K **Privately Held**
SIC: 7692 Welding repair

(G-8376)
HARRISS & COVINGTON HSY MILLS
1232 Hickory Chapel Rd (27260-7187)
PHONE.................................336 882-6811
EMP: 7 **EST:** 1920
SALES (est): 71.04K **Privately Held**
Web: www.harrissandcov.com
SIC: 2252 Socks

(G-8377)
HARRISS CVINGTON HSY MILLS INC
Also Called: Harriss & Covington Hosiery
1250 Hickory Chapel Rd (27260-7187)
P.O. Box 1909 (27261-1909)
PHONE.................................336 882-6811
Edward H Covington, *Pr*
Darrell Frye, *
Danny Mcnair, *VP*
Edward Covington, *Prin*
◆ **EMP:** 240 **EST:** 1920
SQ FT: 130,000
SALES (est): 33.94MM **Privately Held**
Web: www.harrissandcov.com
SIC: 2252 Socks

(G-8378)
HAWORTH INC
1673 W English Rd (27262-7203)
P.O. Box 189 (28613-0189)
PHONE.................................336 885-4021
Steve Snyder, *Mgr*
EMP: 7
SALES (corp-wide): 1.87B **Privately Held**
Web: www.haworth.com
SIC: 2521 2531 Wood office chairs, benches and stools; Public building and related furniture
HQ: Haworth, Inc.
1 Haworth Ctr
Holland MI 49423
616 393-3000

(G-8379)
HDM FURNITURE INDUSTRIES INC
741 W Ward Ave Plant37 (27260-1645)
PHONE.................................336 812-4434
EMP: 38
SALES (corp-wide): 384.13MM **Privately Held**
SIC: 2512 Upholstered household furniture
PA: Hdm Furniture Industries Inc
1925 Eastchester Dr
High Point NC 27265
336 888-4800

(G-8380)
HEALING CRAFTER
4435 Garden Club St (27265-1196)
PHONE.................................336 567-1620
Brandi Oliver, *Owner*
EMP: 4
SALES (est): 125.39K **Privately Held**
SIC: 2389 Apparel and accessories, nec

(G-8381)
HEDGECOCK RACING ENTPS INC
1520 Horneytown Rd (27265-9255)
PHONE.................................336 887-4221
Jay Hedgecock Junior, *Pr*
EMP: 10 **EST:** 1982
SQ FT: 16,700
SALES (est): 864.89K **Privately Held**
Web: www.hedgecockracing.com
SIC: 3711 Automobile assembly, including specialty automobiles

(G-8382)
HENDRIX BATTING COMPANY
2310 Surrett Dr (27263-8509)
P.O. Box 7408 (27264-7408)
PHONE.................................336 431-1181
Kenneth Hendrix Junior, *Pr*
Lesley Theirault, *
Angela Hendrix Bennett, *
▲ **EMP:** 150 **EST:** 1960
SQ FT: 125,000
SALES (est): 21.35MM **Privately Held**
Web: www.hendrixbatting.com
SIC: 2299 2297 Batting, wadding, padding and fillings; Nonwoven fabrics

(G-8383)
HENRY WILLIAMS JR (PA) ✪
Also Called: Henry The Great
455 S Main St (27260-6634)
PHONE.................................336 897-8714
Henry Williams Junior, *Owner*
EMP: 6 **EST:** 2022
SALES (est): 203.61K
SALES (corp-wide): 203.61K **Privately Held**
SIC: 3999 Hair clippers for human use, hand and electric

High Point - Guilford County

(G-8384)
HEXION INC
Also Called: Borden
1717 W Ward Ave (27260)
PHONE..................336 884-8918
EMP: 5
SALES (corp-wide): 1.26B Privately Held
Web: www.hexion.com
SIC: 2891 2821 Adhesives; Plastics materials and resins
PA: Hexion Inc.
  180 E Broad St
  Columbus OH 43215
  888 443-9466

(G-8385)
HICKORY SPRINGS MFG CO
Triad-Fabco Industries
1325 Baker Rd (27263-2031)
PHONE..................336 861-4195
Donald Leonard, VP Opers
EMP: 68
SALES (corp-wide): 430.3MM Privately Held
Web: www.hsmsolutions.com
SIC: 3086 2392 Insulation or cushioning material, foamed plastics; Cushions and pillows
PA: Hickory Springs Manufacturing Company
  235 2nd Ave Nw
  Hickory NC 28601
  828 328-2201

(G-8386)
HICKORY SPRINGS MFG CO
Also Called: Ultra Flex
1905 Alleghany St (27263-2027)
P.O. Box 4549 (27263-4549)
PHONE..................336 491-4131
Faye Glevins, Brnch Mgr
EMP: 12
SALES (corp-wide): 430.3MM Privately Held
Web: www.hsmsolutions.com
SIC: 2241 3714 Webbing, woven; Motor vehicle parts and accessories
PA: Hickory Springs Manufacturing Company
  235 2nd Ave Nw
  Hickory NC 28601
  828 328-2201

(G-8387)
HIGH POINT ENTERPRISE INC
Also Called: Archdale Trinity News
213 Woodbine St (27260-8339)
PHONE..................336 434-2716
Kathy Stuart, Brnch Mgr
EMP: 5
SALES (corp-wide): 7.91MM Privately Held
Web: www.hpenews.com
SIC: 2711 Newspapers, publishing and printing
PA: The High Point Enterprise Inc
  213 Woodbine St
  High Point NC 27260
  336 888-3500

(G-8388)
HIGH POINT ENTERPRISE INC
Also Called: Region 3 Tasc Services
712 W Lexington Ave (27262-2583)
PHONE..................336 883-2839
EMP: 12
SALES (corp-wide): 7.91MM Privately Held
Web: www.hpenews.com
SIC: 2711 Newspapers, publishing and printing

PA: The High Point Enterprise Inc
  213 Woodbine St
  High Point NC 27260
  336 888-3500

(G-8389)
HIGH POINT ENTERPRISE INC (PA)
Also Called: Thomasville Times
213 Woodbine St (27260-8339)
P.O. Box 1009 (27261-1009)
PHONE..................336 888-3500
Fred Paxton, Pr
David Paxton, *
Nick Maheras, *
John Mcclure, Dir
Nancy Baker, *
EMP: 160 EST: 1884
SALES (est): 7.91MM
SALES (corp-wide): 7.91MM Privately Held
Web: www.hpenews.com
SIC: 2711 Commercial printing and newspaper publishing combined

(G-8390)
HIGH POINT FIBERS INC
601 Old Thomasville Rd (27260-8432)
PHONE..................336 887-8771
John Hailey, Pr
Ronny Odell, *
Robert Hampton, *
▼ EMP: 30 EST: 1998
SQ FT: 31,496
SALES (est): 2.03MM Privately Held
Web: www.highpointfibers.com
SIC: 2299 Padding and wadding, textile

(G-8391)
HIGH POINT FURNITURE INDS INC (PA)
Also Called: Hpfi
1104 Bedford St (27263-1604)
P.O. Box 2063 (27261-2063)
PHONE..................336 431-7101
Spencer O'meara, CEO
Harry Samet, *
Jerry Samet, *
Joan Samet, *
Jon Goskolka, *
▲ EMP: 92 EST: 1958
SQ FT: 180,000
SALES (est): 25.41MM
SALES (corp-wide): 25.41MM Privately Held
Web: www.hpfi.com
SIC: 2521 Chairs, office: padded, upholstered, or plain: wood

(G-8392)
HIGH POINT PHARMACEUTICALS LLC
4170 Mendenhall Oaks Pkwy (27265-8345)
PHONE..................336 841-0300
Stephen L Holcombe, Pr
EMP: 12 EST: 2009
SALES (est): 200.75K Privately Held
Web: www.highpointctc.com
SIC: 2834 Pharmaceutical preparations

(G-8393)
HIGH POINT QUILTING INC
1601 Blandwood Dr (27260-8302)
P.O. Box 311 (27370-0311)
PHONE..................336 861-4180
Gary Weavil, CEO
Jerrine Mathis, Sec
▼ EMP: 14 EST: 1986
SQ FT: 125,000
SALES (est): 1.06MM Privately Held
Web: www.highpointquilting.com

SIC: 2395 Quilted fabrics or cloth

(G-8394)
HIGHTOWER GROUP LLC
211 Fraley Rd (27263-1711)
PHONE..................816 286-1051
Marty Peterson, Managing Member
Kristin Goodman, Prin
Casandra Sheyman, Prin
▲ EMP: 11 EST: 2006
SALES (est): 2.25MM Privately Held
Web: www.hightower.design
SIC: 2599 Factory furniture and fixtures

(G-8395)
HILL-PAK INC
5453 Lilly Flower Rd (27263-8002)
PHONE..................336 431-3833
Walter J Hill, Pr
EMP: 7
SALES (corp-wide): 660.1K Privately Held
SIC: 2679 Paper products, converted, nec
PA: Hill-Pak, Inc.
  5825 Edgar Rd
  High Point NC 27263
  336 431-3833

(G-8396)
HOFFMAN PLASTI-FORM COMPANY
Also Called: Hoffman Plasti
5432 Edgar Rd (27263-8102)
PHONE..................336 431-2934
Nancy Hoffman, Pr
EMP: 5 EST: 1972
SQ FT: 6,000
SALES (est): 450.07K Privately Held
SIC: 3089 Molding primary plastics

(G-8397)
HOHN WELDING SERVICES LLC
2132 Crssing Way Crt Apt (27262)
PHONE..................336 870-9617
Jacob Hohn, Prin
EMP: 5 EST: 2016
SALES (est): 75.39K Privately Held
SIC: 7692 Welding repair

(G-8398)
HOLT GROUP INC (PA)
Also Called: Holt Group
4198 Eagle Hill Dr Ste 105 (27265-8330)
PHONE..................336 668-2770
Mike Cirsculoo, Pr
EMP: 13 EST: 1975
SQ FT: 7,500
SALES (est): 5.29MM
SALES (corp-wide): 5.29MM Privately Held
Web: www.holtxp.com
SIC: 2541 Bar fixtures, wood

(G-8399)
HOME MERIDIAN GROUP LLC (HQ)
Also Called: Hmi USA
2485 Penny Rd (27265-8375)
PHONE..................336 819-7200
EMP: 66 EST: 2016
SQ FT: 40,000
SALES (est): 9.19MM
SALES (corp-wide): 583.1MM Publicly Held
SIC: 2511 Wood household furniture
PA: Hooker Furnishings Corporation
  440 Commonwealth Blvd E
  Martinsville VA 24112
  276 632-2133

(G-8400)
HOME MERIDIAN HOLDINGS INC
Also Called: Pulaski Furniture

2485 Penny Rd (27265-8375)
PHONE..................336 887-1985
▲ EMP: 200
SIC: 2511 Wood household furniture

(G-8401)
HOOKER FURNITURE CORPORATION
Home Meridian International
2485 Penny Rd Fl 2 (27265-8375)
PHONE..................336 819-7200
Lee Boone, Pr
EMP: 130
SALES (corp-wide): 583.1MM Publicly Held
Web: www.hookerfurnishings.com
SIC: 2511 Wood bedroom furniture
PA: Hooker Furnishings Corporation
  440 Commonwealth Blvd E
  Martinsville VA 24112
  276 632-2133

(G-8402)
HOPE TREE PUBLISHING LLC
916 Big Creek Ct (27265-3173)
PHONE..................336 858-5301
Paige Lyerly, Prin
EMP: 5 EST: 2016
SALES (est): 92.98K Privately Held
SIC: 2741 Miscellaneous publishing

(G-8403)
HUNTER FARMS
Also Called: Hunter Farms
1900 N Main St (27262-2132)
PHONE..................336 822-2300
Dwight Moore, VP
Chester Marsh, *
EMP: 130 EST: 1917
SALES (est): 24.7MM
SALES (corp-wide): 148.26B Publicly Held
SIC: 2024 Dairy based frozen desserts
HQ: Harris Teeter, Llc
  701 Crestdale Rd
  Matthews NC 28105
  704 844-3100

(G-8404)
I2E GROUP LLC
Also Called: NTI Systems
2108 S Elm St (27260-8811)
PHONE..................336 884-2014
EMP: 6 EST: 2013
SALES (est): 504.24K Privately Held
Web: www.innov2exec.com
SIC: 3571 3599 Computers, digital, analog or hybrid; Custom machinery

(G-8405)
IDENTITY CUSTOM SIGNAGE INC
324 Burton Ave (27262-8070)
PHONE..................336 882-7446
Matt Craven, Pr
EMP: 11 EST: 2007
SALES (est): 441.31K Privately Held
Web: www.identitycustomsignage.com
SIC: 3993 Signs and advertising specialties

(G-8406)
IMMUNOTEK BIO CENTERS LLC
1628 S Main St Ste 105 (27260-4498)
PHONE..................336 781-4901
Frank Perrotto, Mgr
EMP: 30
SALES (corp-wide): 140.79MM Privately Held
Web: www.immunotek.com
SIC: 2836 Blood derivatives
PA: Immunotek Bio Centers, L.L.C.
  1430 E Southlake Blvd # 200

High Point - Guilford County (G-8407)

Southlake TX 76092
337 500-1175

(G-8407)
INDIANA MILLS & MANUFACTURING
Also Called: Immi Safeguard
200 Swathmore Ave (27263-1932)
PHONE.................336 862-7519
Chad Blankenship, *Brnch Mgr*
EMP: 209
SALES (corp-wide): 241.71MM **Privately Held**
Web: www.imminet.com
SIC: 2531 Seats, automobile
PA: Indiana Mills & Manufacturing Inc
 18881 Immi Way
 Westfield IN 46074
 317 896-9531

(G-8408)
INDUSTRIAL CONTAINER CORP
Also Called: ICC
107 Motsinger St (27260-8836)
PHONE.................336 886-7031
Daniel Ross, *Pr*
Bernard Rosinsky, *Pr*
Daniel Ross, *VP*
Randy Chambers, *Genl Mgr*
EMP: 19 **EST:** 1965
SQ FT: 34,000
SALES (est): 2.36MM **Privately Held**
Web: www.iccpkg.com
SIC: 2653 Boxes, corrugated: made from purchased materials

(G-8409)
INDUSTRIAL CONTAINER INC
107 Motsinger St (27260-8836)
PHONE.................336 882-1310
Bernie Rosinski, *Pr*
Ron Horny, *Genl Mgr*
Dan Roth, *VP*
EMP: 10 **EST:** 1970
SQ FT: 85,000
SALES (est): 352.62K **Privately Held**
SIC: 6512 2653 Commercial and industrial building operation; Corrugated and solid fiber boxes

(G-8410)
INNOSPEC ACTIVE CHEMICALS LLC (HQ)
Also Called: Innospec
510 W Grimes Ave (27260-6545)
PHONE.................336 882-3308
Patrick Williams, *Managing Member*
Ian Clemison, *
David E Williams, *
▲ **EMP:** 60 **EST:** 2001
SQ FT: 86,000
SALES (est): 96.38MM
SALES (corp-wide): 1.95B **Publicly Held**
SIC: 2869 Industrial organic chemicals, nec
PA: Innospec Inc.
 8310 S Valley Hwy Ste 350
 Englewood CO 80112
 303 792-5554

(G-8411)
INTENSA INC
1810 S Elm St (27260-8703)
P.O. Box 5981 (27262-5981)
PHONE.................336 884-4096
Marty Cagle, *Pr*
Dwan Richardson, *VP*
William Gurney, *Sec*
EMP: 20 **EST:** 2002
SQ FT: 40,000
SALES (est): 2.64MM
SALES (corp-wide): 93.55MM **Privately Held**
Web: www.intensa.net
SIC: 3821 Laboratory apparatus and furniture
PA: Gf Health Products, Inc.
 1 Graham Field Way
 Atlanta GA 30340
 770 368-4700

(G-8412)
INTENSA INC
1810 S Elm St (27260-8703)
P.O. Box 5981 (27262-5981)
PHONE.................336 884-4003
Dwan Richardson, *Pr*
▲ **EMP:** 12 **EST:** 1998
SQ FT: 40,000
SALES (est): 506.25K **Privately Held**
SIC: 2512 2522 Upholstered household furniture; Office furniture, except wood

(G-8413)
INTERIOR WOOD SPECIALTIES INC
Also Called: I W S
1130 Bedford St (27263-1604)
PHONE.................336 431-0068
Huig Zuiderent, *Pr*
EMP: 35 **EST:** 1984
SQ FT: 40,000
SALES (est): 4.95MM **Privately Held**
Web: www.interiorwoodspecialties.com
SIC: 2531 School furniture

(G-8414)
JACK CARTWRIGHT INCORPORATED
2014 Chestnut Street Ext (27262-7160)
P.O. Box 2798 (27261-2798)
PHONE.................336 889-9400
Brian Murray, *Pr*
Steve Bannister, *
▲ **EMP:** 50 **EST:** 1963
SQ FT: 100,000
SALES (est): 8.86MM
SALES (corp-wide): 65.49MM **Privately Held**
Web: www.jackcartwright.com
SIC: 2512 Chairs: upholstered on wood frames
HQ: Boss Design Limited
 Boss Drive New Road
 Dudley W MIDLANDS DY2 8
 138 445-5570

(G-8415)
JAMES G GOUGE
Also Called: International Minute Press
1001 Phillips Ave (27262-7252)
P.O. Box 18424 (27419-8424)
PHONE.................336 854-1551
Jim Gouge, *Owner*
EMP: 6 **EST:** 2002
SALES (est): 403.97K **Privately Held**
Web: www.greensboroimp.com
SIC: 2752 Offset printing

(G-8416)
JESSICA CHARLES LLC
535 Townsend Ave (27263-2047)
P.O. Box 3444 (28603-3444)
PHONE.................336 434-2124
▲ **EMP:** 80
Web: www.jessicacharles.com
SIC: 2512 Chairs: upholstered on wood frames

(G-8417)
JONES FRAME INC
5456 Uwharrie Rd (27263-4165)
P.O. Box 153 (27370-0153)
PHONE.................336 434-2531
Molly Jones, *CEO*
Rick Hartley, *
Carolee Hartley, *
EMP: 30 **EST:** 1978
SQ FT: 60,000
SALES (est): 2.33MM **Privately Held**
SIC: 2511 2426 2515 Bed frames, except water bed frames: wood; Hardwood dimension and flooring mills; Mattresses and bedsprings

(G-8418)
K & S TOOL & MANUFACTURING CO
1247 Elon Pl (27263-9745)
P.O. Box 2037 (27282-2037)
PHONE.................336 410-7260
Kenneth Hughes, *Pr*
EMP: 19
SALES (corp-wide): 14.46MM **Privately Held**
Web: www.ks-tool.com
SIC: 3599 Machine shop, jobbing and repair
PA: K & S Tool & Manufacturing Company
 614 Hendrix St
 High Point NC 27260
 336 410-7260

(G-8419)
K & S TOOL & MANUFACTURING CO (PA)
614 Hendrix St (27260-4306)
P.O. Box 2037 (27282-2037)
PHONE.................336 410-7260
Kenneth Hughes, *Pr*
Joe Hughes, *
Sally Hughes, *
◆ **EMP:** 50 **EST:** 1974
SQ FT: 80,000
SALES (est): 14.46MM
SALES (corp-wide): 14.46MM **Privately Held**
Web: www.ks-tool.com
SIC: 3469 3441 Stamping metal for the trade ; Fabricated structural metal

(G-8420)
K&S RUSTIC WOODWORKS
3315 Pine Valley Rd (27265-2010)
PHONE.................336 504-6988
Andrew Key, *Prin*
EMP: 5 **EST:** 2017
SALES (est): 88.03K **Privately Held**
SIC: 2431 Millwork

(G-8421)
KAMP USA INC
Also Called: Keya USA
2321 E Martin Luther King Jr Dr (27260-6287)
PHONE.................336 668-1169
Abdul Khaleque Pathan, *Prin*
Bill Van Dolan, *VP Mktg*
Greg Brown, *Sr VP*
Chris Douglass, *Dir Fin*
Rose Timmons, *Contrlr*
◆ **EMP:** 10 **EST:** 2009
SQ FT: 60,000
SALES (est): 622.86K **Privately Held**
Web: www.keyagroupbd.com
SIC: 2253 T-shirts and tops, knit

(G-8422)
KAO SPECIALTIES AMERICAS LLC (HQ)
Also Called: KSA
243 Woodbine St (27260-8339)
P.O. Box 2316 (27261-2316)
PHONE.................336 884-2214
Yasuo Monoe, *Pr*
Terry Singleton, *
Gerald Sykes, *
Hisanori Hagi, *
Shinichiro Suda, *
◆ **EMP:** 160 **EST:** 1999
SQ FT: 3,049,200
SALES (est): 104.24MM **Privately Held**
Web: chemical.kao.com
SIC: 2869 Industrial organic chemicals, nec
PA: Kao Corporation
 1-14-10, Nihombashikayabacho
 Chuo-Ku TKY 103-0

(G-8423)
KENMAR INC
2531 Willard Dairy Rd (27265-8117)
PHONE.................336 884-8722
Jimmy Clegg, *Pr*
Marion Shoemaker, *VP*
EMP: 15 **EST:** 1963
SQ FT: 1,100
SALES (est): 1.59MM **Privately Held**
Web: www.kenmarprecision.com
SIC: 3569 3545 Firefighting apparatus; Precision tools, machinists'

(G-8424)
KING HICKORY FURNITURE COMPANY
Also Called: Showroom
2016 W Green Dr (27260-8709)
P.O. Box 1179 (28603-1179)
PHONE.................336 841-6140
EMP: 8
SALES (corp-wide): 36.28MM **Privately Held**
Web: www.kinghickory.com
SIC: 2512 Upholstered household furniture
PA: King Hickory Furniture Company
 1820 Main Ave Se
 Hickory NC 28602
 828 322-6025

(G-8425)
KREBER
Also Called: Kreber Enterprises
221 Swathmore Ave (27263-1931)
PHONE.................336 861-2700
EMP: 68 **EST:** 1967
SQ FT: 249,600
SALES (est): 2.44MM
SALES (corp-wide): 19.37MM **Privately Held**
Web: www.kreber.com
SIC: 7336 2752 2789 7335 Graphic arts and related design; Color lithography; Swatches and samples; Color separation, photographic and movie film
PA: Kreber Graphics, Inc.
 2580 Westbelt Dr
 Columbus OH 43228
 614 529-5701

(G-8426)
KRUEGER INTERNATIONAL INC
217 Feld Ave (27263-1929)
PHONE.................336 434-5011
Kenneth Neves, *Brnch Mgr*
EMP: 22
SALES (corp-wide): 682.99MM **Privately Held**
Web: www.ki.com
SIC: 2531 School furniture
PA: Krueger International, Inc.
 1330 Bellevue St
 Green Bay WI 54302
 920 468-8100

(G-8427)
LA BARGE INC
1925 Eastchester Dr (27265-1404)
PHONE.................336 812-2400
EMP: 10 **EST:** 2018
SALES (est): 208.05K **Privately Held**
Web: www.labargeinc.com

GEOGRAPHIC SECTION

High Point - Guilford County (G-8451)

SIC: 2426 Frames for upholstered furniture, wood

(G-8428)
LACQUER CRAFT HOSPITALITY INC (DH)
Also Called: Samson Marketing
2575 Penny Rd (27265-8334)
PHONE..................336 822-8086
◆ EMP: 105 EST: 2010
SALES (est): 13.63MM **Privately Held**
Web: lacquercraft.great-site.net
SIC: 2511 Wood household furniture
HQ: Samson Investment Holding Co.
  2575 Penny Rd
  High Point NC 27265

(G-8429)
LEGGETT & PLATT INCORPORATED
Also Called: High Point Spring 1506
1629 Blandwood Dr (27260-8302)
P.O. Box 7327 (27264-7327)
PHONE..................336 884-4306
Gerald Rigney, *Brnch Mgr*
EMP: 59
SALES (corp-wide): 5.15B **Publicly Held**
Web: www.leggett.com
SIC: 2515 Mattresses and bedsprings
PA: Leggett & Platt, Incorporated
  1 Leggett Rd
  Carthage MO 64836
  417 358-8131

(G-8430)
LEGGETT & PLATT INCORPORATED
Also Called: High Point Furniture 0n64
1430 Sherman Ct (27260-8200)
P.O. Box 7107 (27264-7107)
PHONE..................336 889-2600
Murray Catton, *Brnch Mgr*
EMP: 70
SQ FT: 213,652
SALES (corp-wide): 5.15B **Publicly Held**
Web: www.leggett.com
SIC: 2515 Mattresses and bedsprings
PA: Leggett & Platt, Incorporated
  1 Leggett Rd
  Carthage MO 64836
  417 358-8131

(G-8431)
LEGGETT & PLATT INCORPORATED
Leggett & Platt 0n64
1430 Sherman Ct (27260-8200)
PHONE..................336 889-2600
Murray Catton, *Mgr*
EMP: 51
SALES (corp-wide): 5.15B **Publicly Held**
Web: www.leggett.com
SIC: 3495 3496 Furniture springs, unassembled; Miscellaneous fabricated wire products
PA: Leggett & Platt, Incorporated
  1 Leggett Rd
  Carthage MO 64836
  417 358-8131

(G-8432)
LITTLE BLANK CANVAS LLC
3623 Single Leaf Ct (27265-9375)
PHONE..................336 887-6133
EMP: 4 EST: 2013
SALES (est): 116.35K **Privately Held**
Web: www.littleblankcanvas.com
SIC: 2211 Canvas

(G-8433)
LLOYDS CHATHAM LTD PARTNERSHIP
511 Dorado Dr (27265-8670)
PHONE..................919 742-4692
▲ EMP: 18 EST: 1996
SALES (est): 529.65K **Privately Held**
SIC: 2512 Upholstered household furniture

(G-8434)
M D C GRAPHICS LLC
Also Called: Motor Sports Designs Holding
2410 E Martin Luther King Jr Dr (27260-5916)
PHONE..................336 454-6467
EMP: 9 EST: 2001
SQ FT: 22,552
SALES (est): 165.48K **Privately Held**
SIC: 2759 Advertising literature: printing, nsk

(G-8435)
MAC PANEL COMPANY (PA)
Also Called: Mac Panel
551 W Fairfield Rd (27263-1741)
P.O. Box 7728 (27264-7728)
PHONE..................336 861-3100
Joseph L Craycroft Junior, *Ch*
Tom Craycroft, *
Anthony Sedberry, *
▲ EMP: 44 EST: 1971
SQ FT: 60,000
SALES (est): 10.8MM
SALES (corp-wide): 10.8MM **Privately Held**
Web: www.macpanel.com
SIC: 3823 3672 Computer interface equipment, for industrial process control; Printed circuit boards

(G-8436)
MACHINEX
716 Gallimore Dairy Rd (27265-9176)
PHONE..................336 665-5030
Pierre Stare, *Pr*
EMP: 6 EST: 2012
SALES (est): 502.36K **Privately Held**
SIC: 3599 5084 Machine shop, jobbing and repair; Industrial machinery and equipment

(G-8437)
MACHINEX TECHNOLOGIES INC
716 Gallimore Dairy Rd (27265-9176)
PHONE..................773 867-8801
EMP: 20 EST: 1996
SALES (est): 5.71MM **Privately Held**
Web: www.machinexrecycling.com
SIC: 5084 3535 Conveyor systems; Conveyors and conveying equipment

(G-8438)
MANNINGTON MILLS INC
Mannington Wood Floors Company
210 N Pendleton St (27260-5800)
PHONE..................336 884-5600
Douglas Brown, *VP*
EMP: 13
SALES (corp-wide): 686.34MM **Privately Held**
Web: www.mannington.com
SIC: 2426 2435 Flooring, hardwood; Veneer stock, hardwood
PA: Mannington Mills Inc.
  75 Mannington Mills Rd
  Salem NJ 08079
  800 356-6787

(G-8439)
MARINE TOOLING TECHNOLOGY INC
2100 E Martin Luther King Jr Dr Ste 106 (27260-5834)
P.O. Box 2564 (27261-2564)
PHONE..................336 887-9577
William D Burris, *Pr*
Regina Burris, *Sec*
EMP: 4 EST: 1999
SALES (est): 439.66K **Privately Held**
Web: www.marinetooling.com
SIC: 3429 3732 Marine hardware; Boats, fiberglass: building and repairing

(G-8440)
MARLOWE-VAN LOAN CORPORATION
Also Called: Marlowe Loans Sales
1224 W Ward Ave (27260-1534)
P.O. Box 1851 (27261-1851)
PHONE..................336 886-7126
Paul Tharp, *Pr*
EMP: 38 EST: 1933
SQ FT: 55,000
SALES (est): 4.78MM **Privately Held**
Web: marlowevanloan.lookchem.com
SIC: 2869 2865 2819 Industrial organic chemicals, nec; Cyclic crudes and intermediates; Industrial inorganic chemicals, nec

(G-8441)
MARLOWE-VAN LOAN SALES CO
Also Called: Hickory Color & Chemical Co
1224 W Ward Ave (27260-1534)
P.O. Box 1851 (27261-1851)
PHONE..................336 882-3351
Donald W Van Loan, *Pt*
Kathleen Poag Minchak, *Pt*
EMP: 11 EST: 1933
SQ FT: 15,000
SALES (est): 253.9K **Privately Held**
Web: marlowevanloan.lookchem.com
SIC: 5169 2899 Chemicals, industrial and heavy; Chemical preparations, nec

(G-8442)
MARQUIS CONTRACT CORPORATION (PA)
Also Called: Marquis Seating
231 South Rd (27262-8152)
P.O. Box 2208 (27261-2208)
PHONE..................336 884-8200
Gary M Lindenberg, *Pr*
Jana M Lindenberg, *Sec*
▲ EMP: 38 EST: 1992
SALES (est): 10.09MM **Privately Held**
Web: www.marquisseating.com
SIC: 2512 Upholstered household furniture

(G-8443)
MARSH FURNITURE COMPANY
Also Called: Marsh Kitchens of High Point
1015 S Centennial St (27260-7850)
P.O. Box 870 (27261-0870)
PHONE..................336 884-7393
Steve Schadt, *Brnch Mgr*
EMP: 10
SALES (corp-wide): 43.2MM **Privately Held**
Web: www.marshkb.com
SIC: 2434 Wood kitchen cabinets
PA: Marsh Furniture Company
  1001 S Centennial St
  High Point NC 27260
  336 884-7363

(G-8444)
MARSH FURNITURE COMPANY (PA)
Also Called: Marsh Kitchens
1001 S Centennial St (27260-8126)
P.O. Box 870 (27261-0870)
PHONE..................336 884-7363
▲ EMP: 484 EST: 1906
SALES (est): 43.2MM
SALES (corp-wide): 43.2MM **Privately Held**
Web: www.marshfurniture.com
SIC: 2434 5712 2421 Wood kitchen cabinets ; Cabinets, except custom made: kitchen; Lumber: rough, sawed, or planed

(G-8445)
MARSH-ARMFIELD INCORPORATED
1237 Hickory Chapel Rd (27260-7189)
P.O. Box 1407 (27261-1407)
PHONE..................336 882-4175
Ben Armfield, *Pr*
Sharee Mcarthur, *Sec*
Bonnie Black, *Off Mgr*
EMP: 37 EST: 1945
SQ FT: 75,000
SALES (est): 2.33MM **Privately Held**
Web: www.marsharmfield.com
SIC: 2672 Adhesive backed films, foams and foils

(G-8446)
MARTIES MINIATURES
392 Northbridge Dr (27265-3061)
PHONE..................336 869-5952
Martha Tyler, *Prin*
EMP: 5 EST: 2010
SALES (est): 73K **Privately Held**
SIC: 3999 Miniatures

(G-8447)
MARY BOGEST IMPRESSIONS
2913 Mossy Meadow Dr (27265-7962)
P.O. Box 5753 (27262-5753)
PHONE..................336 848-0910
EMP: 4 EST: 2019
SALES (est): 109.98K **Privately Held**
SIC: 2869 Industrial organic chemicals, nec

(G-8448)
MASTER DISPLAYS INC
Also Called: Design Master Displays
5657 Prospect St (27263-3967)
PHONE..................336 884-5575
◆ EMP: 90 EST: 1984
SALES (est): 10.92MM **Privately Held**
Web: www.masterdisplays.com
SIC: 2542 Office and store showcases and display fixtures

(G-8449)
MASTERCRAFT LAMP INTL FURN
156 S Main St (27260-5206)
PHONE..................336 882-1535
EMP: 4 EST: 2000
SALES (est): 69.02K **Privately Held**
Web: www.mastercraftlamps.com
SIC: 2512 Upholstered household furniture

(G-8450)
MATCHEM INC
1115 Clinton Ave (27260-1581)
P.O. Box 808 (27261-0808)
PHONE..................336 886-5000
Thomas Mattocks, *Pr*
Rebecca Mattocks, *VP*
EMP: 4 EST: 1983
SQ FT: 2,500
SALES (est): 99.92K **Privately Held**
SIC: 2899 Water treating compounds

(G-8451)
MAXIM LABEL PACKG HIGH PT INC (PA)
506 Townsend Ave (27263-2046)
PHONE..................336 861-1666
Roy J Johnston, *Pr*
Sam Chororos, *VP*
▲ EMP: 19 EST: 1985
SQ FT: 31,000
SALES (est): 5.52MM
SALES (corp-wide): 5.52MM **Privately Held**

High Point - Guilford County (G-8452)

Web: www.jcmfg.com
SIC: 2672 2759 2752 Labels (unprinted), gummed: made from purchased materials; Commercial printing, nec; Commercial printing, lithographic

(G-8452)
MEERA INDUSTRIES USA LLC
2020 W Green Dr (27260-8725)
PHONE..................................336 906-7570
Bijal Desai, *Prin*
EMP: 7 **EST:** 2016
SALES (est): 198.27K **Privately Held**
Web: www.meeraind.com
SIC: 3999 Manufacturing industries, nec

(G-8453)
METAL WORKS HIGH POINT INC
918 W Kivett Dr (27262-6814)
P.O. Box 2002 (27261-2002)
PHONE..................................336 886-4612
J Campbell Hall Iii, *Pr*
Margaret Ann Hall, *
EMP: 56 **EST:** 1969
SQ FT: 39,000
SALES (est): 9.57MM **Privately Held**
Web: www.metalworkshp.com
SIC: 3499 3469 Aerosol valves, metal; Metal stampings, nec

(G-8454)
MICKEY TRUCK BODIES INC
1425 Bethel Dr (27260-8307)
PHONE..................................336 882-6806
EMP: 4
SALES (corp-wide): 213.06K **Privately Held**
Web: www.mickeybody.com
SIC: 3713 Truck and bus bodies
PA: Mickey Truck Bodies Inc.
    1305 Trinity Ave
    High Point NC 27260
    336 882-6806

(G-8455)
MICKEY TRUCK BODIES INC (PA)
1305 Trinity Ave (27260-8357)
P.O. Box 2044 (27261-2044)
PHONE..................................336 882-6806
Matt Sink, *CEO*
Tom Arland, *
Carl F Mickey Junior, *Ex VP*
Kent Lapp, *
Carolyn Sink, *
▼ **EMP:** 275 **EST:** 1904
SQ FT: 108,000
SALES (est): 213.06K
SALES (corp-wide): 213.06K **Privately Held**
Web: www.mickeybody.com
SIC: 3713 7532 3711 3715 Beverage truck bodies; Body shop, trucks; Motor vehicles and car bodies; Truck trailers

(G-8456)
MICROTRONIC US LLC
401 Dorado Dr (27265-8669)
PHONE..................................336 869-0429
EMP: 10 **EST:** 2010
SALES (est): 182.07K **Privately Held**
Web: www.microtronicus.com
SIC: 5932 3581 Used merchandise stores; Automatic vending machines

(G-8457)
MLG TRNSCNDENT TRCKG TRNSP SVC
3495 Hickswood Forest Dr (27265-7925)
PHONE..................................336 905-1192
Melvin Green Li, *CEO*
EMP: 6 **EST:** 2019

SALES (est): 150K **Privately Held**
SIC: 3537 Trucks: freight, baggage, etc.: industrial, except mining

(G-8458)
MORBERN LLC
401 Fraley Rd (27263-1715)
PHONE..................................336 883-4332
EMP: 22 **EST:** 2019
SALES (est): 2.54MM **Privately Held**
Web: www.morbern.com
SIC: 2824 Vinyl fibers

(G-8459)
MORBERN USA INC (HQ)
401 Fraley Rd (27263-1715)
P.O. Box 7404 (27264-7404)
PHONE..................................336 883-4332
David Bloomfield, *CEO*
Mark Bloomfield, *
Tom Mccuddy, *VP*
Richard Fox, *
Mike Leap, *
▲ **EMP:** 25 **EST:** 1995
SQ FT: 42,000
SALES (est): 9.88MM
SALES (corp-wide): 94.6MM **Privately Held**
Web: www.morbern.com
SIC: 2295 5131 Buckram: varnished, waxed, and impregnated; Coated fabrics
PA: Morbern Inc
    80 Boundary Rd
    Cornwall ON
    613 932-8811

(G-8460)
MOTORSPORTS DESIGNS INC
300 Old Thomasville Rd (27260-8189)
PHONE..................................336 454-1181
John Mc Kenzie, *CEO*
Mark Sexton, *
EMP: 30 **EST:** 1982
SQ FT: 13,172
SALES (est): 1.63MM **Privately Held**
SIC: 2759 3993 2752 2396 Screen printing; Signs and advertising specialties; Commercial printing, lithographic; Automotive and apparel trimmings

(G-8461)
N STYLE LIVING INC
265 Eastchester Dr (27262)
PHONE..................................336 938-4014
Shyam Suthar, *CEO*
P R Suthar, *Pr*
EMP: 6 **EST:** 2017
SALES (est): 242.61K **Privately Held**
Web: www.stylenliving.com
SIC: 2512 Couches, sofas, and davenports: upholstered on wood frames

(G-8462)
NC LICENSE PLATE
1701 Westchester Dr # 220 (27262-7008)
PHONE..................................336 889-8247
Mary Knight, *Pr*
EMP: 5 **EST:** 2013
SALES (est): 77.5K **Privately Held**
SIC: 3469 Automobile license tags, stamped metal

(G-8463)
NC METAL CRAFTERS INC
1505 Penny Rd (27265-9160)
PHONE..................................336 425-9727
James E Carlson, *Prin*
EMP: 7 **EST:** 2015
SALES (est): 165.24K **Privately Held**
SIC: 3444 Sheet metalwork

(G-8464)
NC PATCHES
1225 W Market Center Dr (27260-8235)
PHONE..................................703 314-3428
EMP: 5 **EST:** 2018
SALES (est): 302.16K **Privately Held**
Web: www.ncpatches.com
SIC: 2395 Embroidery products, except Schiffli machine

(G-8465)
NEIL ALLEN INDUSTRIES INC
2101 E Martin Luther King Jr Dr (27260-5819)
PHONE..................................336 887-6500
Neil Aberman, *Pr*
Debbi Aberman, *Sec*
EMP: 8 **EST:** 1986
SQ FT: 30,000
SALES (est): 985.39K **Privately Held**
Web: www.neilallenindustries.com
SIC: 2599 5712 Hotel furniture; Furniture stores

(G-8466)
NEWELL BRANDS INC
4110 Premier Dr (27265-8343)
PHONE..................................336 812-8181
EMP: 6
SALES (corp-wide): 8.13B **Publicly Held**
Web: www.newellbrands.com
SIC: 2591 Window blinds
PA: Newell Brands Inc.
    6655 Pachtree Dunwoody Rd
    Atlanta GA 30328
    770 418-7000

(G-8467)
NO1 CAN DO IT BETTA TRCKG LLC
1418 Bragg Ave (27265-3306)
PHONE..................................336 858-7693
Jayden Coleman, *Mgr*
EMP: 4 **EST:** 2021
SALES (est): 95.58K **Privately Held**
SIC: 3537 Trucks: freight, baggage, etc.: industrial, except mining

(G-8468)
OAKHURST COMPANY INC (PA)
Also Called: Clayton & Co
2016 Van Buren St # 101 (27260-1564)
P.O. Box 433 (27261-0433)
PHONE..................................336 474-4600
Walter J Haarsgaard, *Pr*
Margaret Haarsgaard, *Sec*
▲ **EMP:** 9 **EST:** 1991
SALES (est): 1.04MM **Privately Held**
Web: www.claytoncolamps.com
SIC: 3645 Residential lighting fixtures

(G-8469)
OBX BOATWORKS LLC
2100 E Martin Luther King Jr Dr Ste 121 (27260-5834)
P.O. Box 5181 (27262-5181)
PHONE..................................336 878-9490
EMP: 6 **EST:** 2009
SALES (est): 744.72K **Privately Held**
Web: www.obx-boatworks.com
SIC: 3732 Boatbuilding and repairing

(G-8470)
OFS BRANDS INC
Also Called: High Point Showroom
1264 Jackson Lake Rd (27263-9731)
PHONE..................................800 763-0212
Donna Dill, *Brnch Mgr*
EMP: 18
SALES (corp-wide): 38.69MM **Privately Held**

Web: www.ofs.com
SIC: 2511 Wood household furniture
PA: Ofs Brands Inc.
    1204 E 6th St
    Huntingburg IN 47542
    800 521-5381

(G-8471)
OPTICS INC (PA)
1105 N Lindsay St Side Side (27262-3935)
PHONE..................................336 884-5677
Harry Allen, *Pr*
EMP: 5 **EST:** 1947
SQ FT: 2,120
SALES (est): 479.08K
SALES (corp-wide): 479.08K **Privately Held**
Web: www.optics-eyewear.com
SIC: 3827 8042 Optical instruments and lenses; Offices and clinics of optometrists

(G-8472)
OTTO AND MOORE INC
Also Called: Otto & Moore Furn Designers
701 Eastchester Dr (27262-7637)
P.O. Box 5627 (27262-5627)
PHONE..................................336 887-0017
William Dudley Moore, *CEO*
William Dudley Moore Junior, *Pr*
EMP: 12 **EST:** 1960
SQ FT: 2,700
SALES (est): 1.03MM **Privately Held**
SIC: 2519 7641 Lawn and garden furniture, except wood and metal; Furniture repair and maintenance

(G-8473)
PACKAGE CRAFTERS INCORPORATED
1040 E Springfield Rd (27263-2158)
P.O. Box 2563 (27261-2563)
PHONE..................................336 431-9700
Gary Brewer, *Pr*
Wayne Brewer, *
EMP: 51 **EST:** 2003
SQ FT: 72,500
SALES (est): 8.69MM **Privately Held**
Web: www.packagecrafters.com
SIC: 2653 Boxes, corrugated: made from purchased materials

(G-8474)
PAG ASB LLC
Also Called: Acme Sample Books
2410 Schirra Pl (27263-1730)
PHONE..................................336 883-4187
EMP: 8 **EST:** 2019
SALES (est): 706.23K **Privately Held**
SIC: 3999 Manufacturing industries, nec

(G-8475)
PATHEON PHARMACEUTICALS INC
4125 Premier Dr (27265-8144)
PHONE..................................866 728-4366
Michelle Stinson, *Brnch Mgr*
EMP: 1797
SALES (corp-wide): 44.91B **Publicly Held**
Web: www.patheon.com
SIC: 2834 Pharmaceutical preparations
HQ: Patheon Pharmaceuticals Inc.
    3900 Paramount Pkwy
    Morrisville NC 27560
    919 226-3200

(G-8476)
PATHEON SOFTGELS INC (DH)
4125 Premier Dr (27265-8144)
PHONE..................................336 812-8700
Michelle Stinson, *Genl Mgr*
◆ **EMP:** 51 **EST:** 1971
SQ FT: 21,920

SALES (est): 105.1MM
SALES (corp-wide): 44.91B **Publicly Held**
Web: www.patheon.com
SIC: 2834 Vitamin preparations
HQ: Patheon U.S. Holdings Inc.
  4815 Emperor Blvd Ste 110
  Durham NC 27703

(G-8477)
PAULS WATER TREATMENT LLC
1224 W Ward Ave (27260-1534)
P.O. Box 567 (27261-0567)
PHONE..................336 886-5600
Paul Thaurp, *Owner*
▲ EMP: 8 EST: 2003
SALES (est): 1.16MM **Privately Held**
SIC: 3589 Water treatment equipment, industrial

(G-8478)
PAWS AND CLAWS PUBLISHING LLC
1589 Skeet Club Rd Ste 102-175 (27265-8817)
PHONE..................336 541-3997
EMP: 4 EST: 2019
SALES (est): 38.8K **Privately Held**
Web: www.pawsandclawspublishing.com
SIC: 2741 Miscellaneous publishing

(G-8479)
PENINSULA POLYMERS
1709 Blandwood Dr (27260-8313)
PHONE..................336 885-8185
EMP: 6 EST: 2019
SALES (est): 243.06K **Privately Held**
Web: www.penpoly.com
SIC: 2821 Plastics materials and resins

(G-8480)
PHOENIX HOME FURNISHINGS INC
2485 Penny Rd (27265-8375)
◆ EMP: 113
SIC: 2511 Wood household furniture

(G-8481)
PIEDMONT CHEMICAL INDS I LLC
331 Burton Ave (27262-8071)
P.O. Box 2728 (27261-2728)
PHONE..................336 885-5131
Ray Soyars, *Prin*
▼ EMP: 68 EST: 1996
SALES (est): 29.48MM
SALES (corp-wide): 111.75MM **Privately Held**
Web: www.piedmontchemical.com
SIC: 2869 Industrial organic chemicals, nec
PA: Syntha Group, Inc.
  331 Burton Ave
  High Point NC 27262
  336 885-5131

(G-8482)
PIEDMONT PACKAGING INC (PA)
1141 Foust Ave (27260-8706)
P.O. Box 7025 (27264-7025)
PHONE..................336 886-5043
Edward L Lee, *Pr*
EMP: 5 EST: 1973
SQ FT: 50,000
SALES (est): 4.58MM
SALES (corp-wide): 4.58MM **Privately Held**
Web: www.ppihp.com
SIC: 2653 Boxes, corrugated: made from purchased materials

(G-8483)
PIEDMONT STEEL COMPANY LLC
1838 Eastchester Dr Ste 108 (27265)
PHONE..................336 875-5133

EMP: 12 EST: 2019
SALES (est): 181.94K **Privately Held**
Web: www.piedmontsteelco.com
SIC: 3441 Fabricated structural metal

(G-8484)
PILOT VIEW WOOD WORKS INC
Also Called: Pilot View Wood Works
412 Berkley St (27260-8458)
PHONE..................336 883-2511
Rickie Garner, *Pr*
Nolan S Garner, *
Norma Smith, *
Brent Garner, *
Pauline B Garner, *
EMP: 10 EST: 1960
SQ FT: 6,800
SALES (est): 370.22K **Privately Held**
SIC: 2426 Furniture stock and parts, hardwood

(G-8485)
PIONEER SQUARE BRANDS INC (PA)
Also Called: Brenthaven
1515 W Green Dr (27260-1657)
PHONE..................360 733-5608
Michael Ferren, *CEO*
EMP: 4 EST: 2017
SALES (est): 4.95MM
SALES (corp-wide): 4.95MM **Privately Held**
SIC: 3172 Card cases

(G-8486)
PLAN NINE PUBLISHING INC
1237 Elon Pl (27263-9745)
PHONE..................336 454-7766
David Allen, *Pr*
EMP: 5 EST: 1996
SALES (est): 295.03K **Privately Held**
Web: www.plan9publishing.com
SIC: 2731 Books, publishing only

(G-8487)
PLUSH COMFORTS
508 Ashe St (27262-4628)
PHONE..................336 882-9185
Jonathan Connor, *Prin*
EMP: 4 EST: 2006
SALES (est): 122.69K **Privately Held**
SIC: 2221 Plushes, manmade fiber and silk

(G-8488)
PNB MANUFACTURING
2315 E Martin Luther King Jr Dr Ste A (27260-6292)
PHONE..................336 883-0021
EMP: 6 EST: 2014
SALES (est): 210.71K **Privately Held**
SIC: 3999 Manufacturing industries, nec

(G-8489)
POLY PACKAGING SYSTEMS INC
2150 Brevard Rd (27263-1704)
P.O. Box 4506 (27263-4506)
PHONE..................336 889-8334
▼ EMP: 80
SIC: 2621 2671 3086 5199 Towels, tissues and napkins; paper and stock; Paper; coated and laminated packaging; Plastics foam products; Packaging materials

(G-8490)
POWDER SYSTEMS INC
Also Called: P S I
1018 Roberts Ln Ste C (27260-7100)
PHONE..................336 885-1352
Bobby G Kale, *Pr*
EMP: 15 EST: 2002

SALES (est): 102.44K **Privately Held**
Web: www.productionsystems-usa.com
SIC: 3479 Coating of metals and formed products

(G-8491)
PRECISION DESIGN MACHINERY
Also Called: ADI/PDM Trade Group
1509 Bethel Dr (27260-8348)
PHONE..................336 889-8157
Chad Butler, *Pr*
Joseph White, *VP*
EMP: 7 EST: 1998
SALES (est): 924.89K **Privately Held**
Web: www.arcdoyle.com
SIC: 3599 Machine shop, jobbing and repair

(G-8492)
PRECISION FABRICATION INC
2000 Nuggett Rd (27263-2009)
PHONE..................336 885-6091
Allen Henkel, *Pr*
Leann Henkel, *VP*
EMP: 15 EST: 1993
SQ FT: 15,720
SALES (est): 2.05MM **Privately Held**
Web: www.precisionfabricationinc.com
SIC: 3441 Fabricated structural metal

(G-8493)
PRECISION PRODUCTS INC
1219 Dorris Ave Apt A (27260-1675)
P.O. Box 7444 (27264-7444)
PHONE..................336 688-0298
John Lyon, *Prin*
EMP: 8
SALES (est): 242.37K **Privately Held**
Web: www.precisionpocketdoors.com
SIC: 3599 Machine shop, jobbing and repair

(G-8494)
PRECISION TEXTILES LLC
Also Called: Precision Textiles
5522 Uwharrie Rd (27263-4166)
PHONE..................336 861-0168
EMP: 178
SALES (corp-wide): 79.21MM **Privately Held**
Web: www.precisiontextiles-usa.com
SIC: 2295 Coated fabrics, not rubberized
PA: Precision Textiles Llc
  90 New Dutch Ln
  Fairfield NJ 07004
  973 890-3873

(G-8495)
PREFERRED DATA CORPORATION
3910 Tinsley Dr Ste 105 (27265-3678)
P.O. Box 16102 (27261-6103)
PHONE..................336 886-3282
Wade Wellborn, *Pr*
EMP: 5 EST: 1987
SQ FT: 3,200
SALES (est): 799.63K **Privately Held**
Web: www.pdcsoftware.com
SIC: 5734 7371 7372 Computer peripheral equipment; Custom computer programming services; Prepackaged software

(G-8496)
PREVOST CAR (US) INC
1951 Eastchester Dr Unit E (27265)
PHONE..................336 812-3504
Dann Wiltgen, *Brnch Mgr*
EMP: 16
SALES (corp-wide): 45.13B **Privately Held**
Web: www.prevostcar.com
SIC: 3711 Motor vehicles and car bodies
HQ: Prevost Car (Us) Inc.
  7817 National Service Rd
  Greensboro NC 27409
  908 222-7211

(G-8497)
PRICELY INC
7210 Suits Rd (27263-4019)
P.O. Box 7626 (27264-7626)
PHONE..................336 431-2055
EMP: 30 EST: 1993
SQ FT: 30,000
SALES (est): 2.46MM **Privately Held**
Web: www.uwharriechair.com
SIC: 2511 Wood lawn and garden furniture

(G-8498)
PRIME MILL LLC
Also Called: Sparta Plastics
1946 W Green Dr (27260-1666)
PHONE..................336 819-4300
EMP: 15 EST: 2007
SQ FT: 3,000
SALES (est): 498.89K **Privately Held**
Web: www.primemill.com
SIC: 3089 5021 Thermoformed finished plastics products, nec; Furniture

(G-8499)
PRODUCTION SYSTEMS INC
1500 Trinity Ave (27260-8362)
P.O. Box 5373 (27262-5373)
PHONE..................336 886-7161
William A Ball, *Pr*
Brian T Ball, *
Alice F Ball, *
William A Ball Junior, *Stockholder*
Alyssa Ball, *Stockholder**
▲ EMP: 37 EST: 1973
SQ FT: 25,000
SALES (est): 9MM **Privately Held**
Web: www.productionsystems-usa.com
SIC: 3444 3563 3567 3535 Booths, spray: prefabricated sheet metal; Spraying and dusting equipment; Paint baking and drying ovens; Conveyors and conveying equipment

(G-8500)
PROFESSINAL SALES ASSOCIATES
2783 Nc Highway 68 S # 116 (27265-8324)
PHONE..................336 210-2756
EMP: 11 EST: 2007
SALES (est): 83.01K **Privately Held**
SIC: 2521 5021 Wood office furniture; Office furniture, nec

(G-8501)
PROFORMA HANSON BRANDING
4257 Wallburg High Point Rd (27265-7619)
PHONE..................210 437-3061
EMP: 7 EST: 2008
SALES (est): 258.63K **Privately Held**
Web: proformahansonbranding.proforma.com
SIC: 2759 Commercial printing, nec

(G-8502)
QUALITY PACKAGING CORP (PA)
255 Swathmore Ave (27263-1931)
PHONE..................336 881-5300
Jerry Hill, *CEO*
Dewey Hill, *Pr*
Joey Hill, *VP*
Tommy Hill, *Sec*
EMP: 7 EST: 1977
SALES (est): 16MM
SALES (corp-wide): 16MM **Privately Held**
Web: www.qualitypackagingcorp.com
SIC: 2679 2671 Corrugated paper: made from purchased material; Paper; coated and laminated packaging

(G-8503)
QUALITY SAW SHOP INC
1208 Elon Pl (27263-9745)

High Point - Guilford County (G-8504)

PHONE..................336 882-1722
Tony Taylor, Pr
Jeremy Taylor, Sec
EMP: 5 **EST:** 1955
SQ FT: 2,500
SALES (est): 367.57K **Privately Held**
SIC: 3425 Saw blades and handsaws

(G-8504)
RALPH LAUREN CORPORATION
4190 Eagle Hill Dr (27265-8237)
P.O. Box 35868 (27425-5868)
PHONE..................336 632-5000
EMP: 4
SALES (corp-wide): 6.44B **Publicly Held**
Web: www.ralphlauren.com
SIC: 5651 2329 Family clothing stores; Athletic clothing, except uniforms: men's, youths' and boys'
PA: Ralph Lauren Corporation
650 Madison Ave
New York NY 10022
212 318-7000

(G-8505)
RALPH S FRAME WORKS INC
2231 Shore St (27263-2511)
P.O. Box 7192 (27264-7192)
PHONE..................336 431-2168
Ralph Thomas Rice Junior, Pr
Lennis Ashe, *
EMP: 100 **EST:** 1950
SQ FT: 60,000
SALES (est): 10.39MM **Privately Held**
Web: www.ralphsframe.com
SIC: 2426 Frames for upholstered furniture, wood

(G-8506)
RBC INC
Also Called: Ashley Interiors
310 S Elm St (27260-6617)
PHONE..................336 889-7573
Bob Holt, Mgr
EMP: 5
SALES (corp-wide): 23.83MM **Privately Held**
Web: www.braxtonculler.com
SIC: 2512 Upholstered household furniture
PA: Rbc, Inc.
7310 Us Highway 311
Sophia NC 27350
336 861-5800

(G-8507)
RELENTLESS WLDG & FABRICATION
903 Londonderry Dr (27265-2792)
PHONE..................336 402-3749
EMP: 4 **EST:** 2018
SALES (est): 48.86K **Privately Held**
Web: www.mandmweldingnc.com
SIC: 7692 Welding repair

(G-8508)
RELIABLE BEDDING COMPANY
Also Called: Reliable Quilting
414 South Rd (27262-8155)
PHONE..................336 886-7036
Tommy Thompson, Managing Member
EMP: 7
SALES (est): 79.3K **Privately Held**
SIC: 2515 Mattresses and bedsprings

(G-8509)
RELIABLE QUILTING COMPANY
414 South Rd (27262-8155)
PHONE..................336 886-7036
Robert Parris, Pr
EMP: 7 **EST:** 2016
SALES (est): 290.37K **Privately Held**

SIC: 2515 Mattresses and bedsprings

(G-8510)
RICKETY BRIDGE WINERY INC USA
518 N Hamilton St (27262-4057)
P.O. Box 665 (27285-0665)
PHONE..................336 781-0645
Andrew Woolgar, CEO
EMP: 6 **EST:** 2016
SALES (est): 243.99K **Privately Held**
Web: www.ricketybridge.com
SIC: 2084 Wines

(G-8511)
RIFLED AIR CONDITIONING INC
2810 Earlham Pl (27263-1949)
PHONE..................800 627-1707
EMP: 35 **EST:** 1997
SQ FT: 55,000
SALES (est): 4.8MM **Privately Held**
Web: www.rifledair.com
SIC: 3585 Air conditioning units, complete: domestic or industrial

(G-8512)
RITCH FACE VENEER COMPANY
1330 Lincoln Dr (27260-1515)
P.O. Box 1837 (27261-1837)
PHONE..................336 883-4184
John Michael Ritch, Pr
Donna Ritch, *
EMP: 23 **EST:** 1941
SQ FT: 45,000
SALES (est): 2.13MM **Privately Held**
Web: www.ritchfaceveneer.com
SIC: 2435 2426 Veneer stock, hardwood; Hardwood dimension and flooring mills

(G-8513)
ROADSAFE TRAFFIC SYSTEMS INC
913 Finch Ave (27263-1623)
PHONE..................919 772-9401
Rick Dean, Brnch Mgr
EMP: 5
Web: www.roadsafetraffic.com
SIC: 3531 Construction machinery
PA: Roadsafe Traffic Systems, Inc.
8750 W Bryn Mawr Ave
Chicago IL 60631

(G-8514)
ROBERTSONS WOODWORKING
6967 Weant Rd (27263-4290)
PHONE..................336 841-7221
Donald Robertson, Owner
EMP: 5 **EST:** 1991
SALES (est): 386.07K **Privately Held**
SIC: 2426 Frames for upholstered furniture, wood

(G-8515)
ROUTER BIT SERVICE COMPANY INC
7018 Tomball Rd (27263-9754)
PHONE..................336 431-5535
Buren Scott Andrews, Pr
EMP: 21 **EST:** 1972
SQ FT: 2,000
SALES (est): 957.22K **Privately Held**
Web: www.routerbitservice.com
SIC: 3553 7699 Saws, power: bench and table, except portable: woodworking; Knife, saw and tool sharpening and repair

(G-8516)
ROWLAND WOODWORKING INC
111 E Market Center Dr (27260-7865)
P.O. Box 1510 (27261-1510)
PHONE..................336 887-0700
Jeffrey S Cox, Pr

Marion Rowland Junior, VP
Kristine M Cox, *
EMP: 25 **EST:** 1992
SQ FT: 20,000
SALES (est): 4.01MM **Privately Held**
Web: www.rowlandwoodworking.com
SIC: 2541 2431 Cabinets, except refrigerated: show, display, etc.: wood; Millwork

(G-8517)
ROYALL DEVELOPMENT CO INC
325 Kettering Rd (27263-1719)
P.O. Box 519 (38879-0519)
PHONE..................336 889-2569
Mickey James, Pr
Joseph Lanham, *
EMP: 215 **EST:** 1990
SALES (est): 21.89MM **Privately Held**
SIC: 3443 Metal parts

(G-8518)
S E BOARD INC
1102 Dorris Ave (27260-1544)
PHONE..................336 885-7230
EMP: 5 **EST:** 2014
SALES (est): 162.58K **Privately Held**
SIC: 2426 Hardwood dimension and flooring mills

(G-8519)
SAMPLETECH INC
2101 W Green Dr (27260-8710)
PHONE..................336 882-1717
Eric Doss, Pr
▲ **EMP:** 10 **EST:** 1997
SALES (est): 705.25K **Privately Held**
SIC: 2789 Swatches and samples

(G-8520)
SEALED AIR CORPORATION
Also Called: Jiffy Division
2150 Brevard Rd (27263-1704)
P.O. Box 2083 (27261-2083)
PHONE..................336 883-9184
Roger Jackson, Brnch Mgr
EMP: 49
SQ FT: 2,500
SALES (corp-wide): 5.49B **Publicly Held**
Web: www.sealedair.com
SIC: 3086 Packaging and shipping materials, foamed plastics
PA: Sealed Air Corporation
2415 Cascade Pointe Blvd
Charlotte NC 28208
980 221-3235

(G-8521)
SEAM-CRAFT INC
702 Prospect St (27260-8230)
P.O. Box 7045 (27264-7045)
PHONE..................336 861-4156
Greg Parlier, Pr
EMP: 16 **EST:** 1972
SALES (est): 372.27K **Privately Held**
SIC: 2512 Upholstered household furniture

(G-8522)
SELECT FURNITURE COMPANY INC
408 South Rd (27262-8155)
P.O. Box 817 (27261-0817)
PHONE..................336 886-3572
Lloyd Graves, Pr
EMP: 17 **EST:** 1981
SQ FT: 20,000
SALES (est): 2.16MM **Privately Held**
Web: www.selectfurniturecompany.com
SIC: 2512 Living room furniture: upholstered on wood frames

(G-8523)
SHERRILL FURNITURE COMPANY
Also Called: Precedent Furniture
301 Steele St Ste 4 (27260-5100)
P.O. Box 730 (28658-0730)
PHONE..................336 884-0974
Buddy Sherrill, Mgr
EMP: 8
SALES (corp-wide): 104.33MM **Privately Held**
Web: www.sherrillfurniture.com
SIC: 2512 Upholstered household furniture
PA: Sherrill Furniture Company Inc
2405 Highland Ave Ne
Hickory NC 28601
828 322-2640

(G-8524)
SIDES FURNITURE INC
Also Called: Sides Custom Furniture
1812 Horneytown Rd (27265-9279)
PHONE..................336 869-5509
Judy Sides, Pr
EMP: 7 **EST:** 1981
SQ FT: 796
SALES (est): 442.44K **Privately Held**
SIC: 2512 5712 Upholstered household furniture; Furniture stores

(G-8525)
SIGMA PLASTICS GROUP
Also Called: Southern Film Extruders
2319 W English Rd (27262-8055)
PHONE..................336 885-8091
EMP: 21 **EST:** 2014
SALES (est): 9.77MM **Privately Held**
Web: www.sigmaplasticsgroup.com
SIC: 3089 Injection molding of plastics

(G-8526)
SIGN MINE INC
2211 Eastchester Dr (27265-1456)
PHONE..................336 884-5780
Michael Hague, Pr
Mary Hague, VP
EMP: 4 **EST:** 2004
SALES (est): 298.05K **Privately Held**
Web: www.signmineinc.com
SIC: 3993 Signs, not made in custom sign painting shops

(G-8527)
SIGN TECHNOLOGY INC
311 Berkley St (27260-8103)
P.O. Box 866 (30549-0866)
PHONE..................336 887-3211
Lonnie Poole, Pr
Debra Poole, VP
EMP: 5 **EST:** 1989
SQ FT: 5,000
SALES (est): 410.63K **Privately Held**
SIC: 3993 Signs and advertising specialties

(G-8528)
SIGNATURE SIGNS INC
211 Berkley St (27260-8101)
PHONE..................336 431-2072
Jeffrey A Curtis, Pr
Julie A Curtis, Sec
Matt Craven, VP
EMP: 7 **EST:** 1988
SQ FT: 15,000
SALES (est): 977.44K **Privately Held**
Web: www.signaturesignage.com
SIC: 3993 5046 5099 Electric signs; Neon signs; Signs, except electric

(G-8529)
SILICONES INC
211 Woodbine St (27260-8339)

GEOGRAPHIC SECTION

High Point - Guilford County (G-8556)

P.O. Box 363 (27261-0363)
PHONE..............336 886-5018
Gerald Swanson, Pr
Richie Ashburn, VP
▲ EMP: 17 EST: 1974
SQ FT: 72,000
SALES (est): 4.96MM Privately Held
Web: www.silicones-inc.com
SIC: 2869 Industrial organic chemicals, nec

(G-8530)
SILICONES INC
1828 Blandwood Dr (27260-8314)
PHONE..............336 886-5018
EMP: 5 EST: 2017
SALES (est): 183.85K Privately Held
Web: www.silicones-inc.com
SIC: 2869 Silicones

(G-8531)
SIMPLICITY SOFAS INC
414 Grayson St (27260-7302)
PHONE..............800 813-2889
Jeff Frank, Pr
Ann Sankevitsch, VP
EMP: 6 EST: 2018
SALES (est): 191.49K Privately Held
Web: www.simplicitysofas.com
SIC: 2512 5021 5714 Upholstered household furniture; Furniture; Drapery and upholstery stores

(G-8532)
SIMPSON STRONG-TIE COMPANY INC
4485 Premier Dr Ste 101 (27265-8389)
PHONE..............336 841-1338
EMP: 27
SALES (corp-wide): 2.21B Publicly Held
Web: www.strongtie.com
SIC: 3449 Joists, fabricated bar
HQ: Simpson Strong-Tie Company Inc.
5956 W Las Positas Blvd
Pleasanton CA 94588
925 560-9000

(G-8533)
SINGSA
2401 Penny Rd (27265-8162)
PHONE..............336 882-9160
Singha Srikumfun, Owner
EMP: 4 EST: 2010
SALES (est): 178.22K Privately Held
SIC: 3421 Table and food cutlery, including butchers'

(G-8534)
SK PUBLISHING LLC
4112 Saint Johns St (27265-1297)
PHONE..............336 885-3637
Nancy Kattenfeld, Prin
EMP: 5 EST: 2015
SALES (est): 83.84K Privately Held
SIC: 2711 Newspapers: publishing only, not printed on site

(G-8535)
SKEEN DECORATIVE FABRICS INC
1220 W Market Center Dr (27260-8236)
P.O. Box 329 (27370-0329)
PHONE..............336 884-4044
Brian M Skeen, Pr
Karmen Skeen, Dir
EMP: 14 EST: 2015
SALES (est): 510.28K Privately Held
SIC: 2211 Broadwoven fabric mills, cotton

(G-8536)
SKEEN TEXTILES INC
1900 S Elm St (27260-8807)
P.O. Box 2283 (27261-2283)
PHONE..............336 884-4044
◆ EMP: 11
Web: www.skeentextiles.com
SIC: 2299 Fabrics: linen, jute, hemp, ramie

(G-8537)
SKEEN TXTILES AUTO FABRICS INC
1900 S Elm St (27260-8807)
PHONE..............336 884-4044
Stephen Skeen, Prin
EMP: 9 EST: 2015
SALES (est): 419.84K Privately Held
SIC: 2299 Fabrics: linen, jute, hemp, ramie

(G-8538)
SLANE HOSIERY MILLS INC
313 S Centennial St (27260-6753)
P.O. Box 2486 (27261-2486)
PHONE..............336 883-4136
Jim Cobb, CEO
Gloria White, *
◆ EMP: 219 EST: 1915
SQ FT: 180,000
SALES (est): 24.58MM Privately Held
Web: www.slanehosiery.com
SIC: 2251 2252 Women's hosiery, except socks; Men's, boys', and girls' hosiery

(G-8539)
SNYDER PAPER CORPORATION
Also Called: Chushion Division
1104 W Ward Ave (27260-1533)
PHONE..............336 884-1172
Robert Dutnell, Mgr
EMP: 11
SALES (corp-wide): 75.1MM Privately Held
Web: www.snydersolutions.com
SIC: 2392 Cushions and pillows
PA: Snyder Paper Corporation
250 26th Street Dr Se
Hickory NC 28602
828 328-2501

(G-8540)
SOLACE HEALTHCARE FURN LLC ✪
314 Mandustry St Ste 5 (27262-8265)
PHONE..............336 884-0046
Geovanny Brown, Managing Member
EMP: 12 EST: 2022
SALES (est): 592.07K Privately Held
SIC: 2599 Furniture and fixtures, nec

(G-8541)
SOLID FRAMES INC
Also Called: Hale's Sample Shop
501 Garrison St (27260-7042)
PHONE..............336 882-5082
Jerry Walker, Pr
EMP: 7 EST: 1988
SQ FT: 12,000
SALES (est): 587.98K Privately Held
SIC: 2426 Frames for upholstered furniture, wood

(G-8542)
SONY MUSIC HOLDINGS INC
921 Eastchester Dr (27262-7646)
PHONE..............336 886-1807
John Cannon, Pr
EMP: 8
Web: www.sonymusic.com
SIC: 3652 5099 Prerecorded records and tapes; Phonograph records
HQ: Sony Music Holdings Inc.
25 Madison Ave Fl 26
New York NY 10010
212 833-8000

(G-8543)
SOUTHANDENGLISH LLC
1314 Starr Dr (27260-8204)
PHONE..............336 888-8333
David Ebbetts, CEO
David Ebbetts, Managing Member
Palmer Smith, Managing Member
Kathy Wilson, Opers Mgr
EMP: 4 EST: 2019
SALES (est): 126.46K Privately Held
Web: www.southandenglish.com
SIC: 2512 5021 Upholstered household furniture; Household furniture

(G-8544)
SOUTHERN ENGRAVING COMPANY
3008 Windchase Ct (27265-3015)
PHONE..............336 656-0084
G Jordan Clapp Junior, Pr
Carole W Clapp, Sec
Charles K Williams, VP
EMP: 5 EST: 1921
SALES (est): 449.45K Privately Held
Web: www.southernengraving.com
SIC: 2759 Invitation and stationery printing and engraving

(G-8545)
SOUTHERN FILM EXTRUDERS INC
2319 W English Rd (27262-8055)
P.O. Box 2104 (27261-2104)
PHONE..............336 885-8091
EMP: 145
SIC: 3081 Polyethylene film

(G-8546)
SOUTHFIELD LTD
Also Called: Southfield Upholstered Furn
2224 Shore St (27263-2512)
P.O. Box 2064 (27261-2064)
PHONE..............336 434-6220
Mike Gulledge, Pr
EMP: 12 EST: 1997
SQ FT: 100,000
SALES (est): 4.23MM Privately Held
Web: www.southfieldfurniture.net
SIC: 2512 Wood upholstered chairs and couches

(G-8547)
SOUTHLAND INDUSTRIES
129 Hartley Dr Apt D (27265-2863)
PHONE..............336 989-0944
EMP: 7 EST: 2017
SALES (est): 77.07K Privately Held
SIC: 3999 Manufacturing industries, nec

(G-8548)
SPECIALTY NAILS COMPANY
5050 Prospect St (27263-3961)
P.O. Box 1213 (27261-1213)
PHONE..............336 883-0135
Guy E Carr Junior, Owner
EMP: 6 EST: 1981
SQ FT: 22,000
SALES (est): 490.58K Privately Held
SIC: 3315 Nails, steel: wire or cut

(G-8549)
STANFAST
4191 Mendenhall Oaks Pkwy Ste 101 (27265-8373)
PHONE..............336 841-7700
Eric Brown, Mgr
EMP: 5 EST: 2018
SALES (est): 79.65K Privately Held
SIC: 2752 Commercial printing, lithographic

(G-8550)
STANLEY FURNITURE COMPANY LLC
200 N Hamilton St No 200 (27260-5032)
PHONE..............336 884-7700
Richard Ledger, CEO
EMP: 101 EST: 2017
SALES (est): 7.9MM Privately Held
SIC: 2511 Wood household furniture

(G-8551)
STEPHEN J MCCUSKER
1705 Heathgate Pt (27262-7462)
PHONE..............336 884-1916
Stephen Mccusker, Owner
EMP: 7 EST: 1979
SALES (est): 338.9K Privately Held
SIC: 2741 Technical manual and paper publishing

(G-8552)
STERI-AIR LLC
2109 Brevard Rd (27263-1703)
PHONE..............336 434-1166
EMP: 4
SALES (est): 118.6K Privately Held
SIC: 3999 Manufacturing industries, nec

(G-8553)
STEWART SCREEN PRINTING INC
1318 Starr Dr (27260-8204)
PHONE..............336 451-9636
Glen Brooks, Prin
EMP: 4 EST: 2017
SALES (est): 73.08K Privately Held
Web: www.stewartscreenprinting.com
SIC: 2752 Commercial printing, lithographic

(G-8554)
STONE RESOURCE INC
2101 E Martin Luther King Jr Dr (27260-5819)
PHONE..............336 889-7800
Neil Aberman, Pr
◆ EMP: 30 EST: 1989
SQ FT: 30,000
SALES (est): 3.94MM Privately Held
Web: www.thestoneresource.com
SIC: 3281 Furniture, cut stone

(G-8555)
STOWED LLC
Also Called: Stowed Home
1100 W Ward Ave (27260-1533)
PHONE..............203 346-5687
Elissia Sigalow, Managing Member
EMP: 14
SALES (corp-wide): 78.03K Privately Held
SIC: 2511 Bed frames, except water bed frames: wood
PA: Stowed, Llc
12 Elm St
Westport CT 06880
203 346-5687

(G-8556)
SUN FABRICATORS INC
701 W Ward Ave (27260-1645)
P.O. Box 2898 (27361-2898)
PHONE..............336 885-0095
Betty Easley, Pr
EMP: 40 EST: 1997
SQ FT: 57,000
SALES (est): 4.8MM Privately Held
Web: www.sunfabricators.com
SIC: 3069 Latex, foamed

High Point - Guilford County (G-8557) — GEOGRAPHIC SECTION

(G-8557)
SUNBELT ABRASIVES INC
1507 Bethel Dr (27260-8348)
PHONE..................336 882-6837
Betty Goodman, VP
EMP: 6 EST: 1984
SQ FT: 10,000
SALES (est): 420.92K Privately Held
Web: www.sunbeltabrasives.com
SIC: 3291 Abrasive products

(G-8558)
SUPERIOR SIGN COMPANY INC
506 Overbrook Dr (27262-2444)
P.O. Box 1082 (27282-1082)
PHONE..................336 454-2226
William C Cox, Pr
EMP: 6 EST: 1947
SALES (est): 640.51K Privately Held
Web: www.superiorsigncorp.com
SIC: 3993 Neon signs

(G-8559)
SWAIM INC (PA)
Also Called: Classics
1801 S University Pkwy (27260-7860)
P.O. Box 4189 (27263-4189)
PHONE..................336 885-6131
Richard A Swaim, Pr
Glenn E Swaim Junior, Ch Bd
Andy Swaim, *
Rhonda S Warren, *
Zachary A Swaim, *
◆ EMP: 185 EST: 1945
SQ FT: 178,587
SALES (est): 19.95MM
SALES (corp-wide): 19.95MM Privately Held
Web: www.swaim-inc.com
SIC: 2514 2512 Tables, household: metal; Living room furniture: upholstered on wood frames

(G-8560)
SWEET ROOM LLC
4435 Garden Club St (27265-1196)
PHONE..................336 567-1620
EMP: 4 EST: 2015
SALES (est): 249.5K Privately Held
SIC: 5813 2051 5812 5632 Bars and lounges ; Cakes, bakery: except frozen; Caterers; Apparel accessories

(G-8561)
SYNTEC INC
200 Swathmore Ave (27263-1932)
PHONE..................336 861-9023
◆ EMP: 78
SIC: 2531 8742 Seats, miscellaneous public conveyances; Marketing consulting services

(G-8562)
SYNTHA GROUP INC (PA)
331 Burton Ave (27262-8071)
P.O. Box 2728 (27261-2728)
PHONE..................336 885-5131
Fred Wilson Junior, Pr
Fred Wilson Iii, VP
Bill Goodman, *
Lloyd Roghelia, *
Ray Soyars, *
◆ EMP: 100 EST: 1958
SQ FT: 500,000
SALES (est): 111.75MM
SALES (corp-wide): 111.75MM Privately Held
Web: www.piedmontchemical.com
SIC: 2841 2843 Textile soap; Surface active agents

(G-8563)
TASMAN INDUSTRIES INC
1011 Porter St Ste 103 (27263-1637)
PHONE..................502 587-0701
EMP: 9
SALES (corp-wide): 43.78MM Privately Held
Web: www.tasmanusa.com
SIC: 3111 Accessory products, leather
PA: Tasman Industries, Inc.
930 Geiger St
Louisville KY 40206
502 785-7477

(G-8564)
TAYLOR COMMUNICATIONS INC
4189 Eagle Hill Dr Ste 101 (27265-8315)
PHONE..................336 841-7700
Eric Brown, Mgr
EMP: 13
SALES (corp-wide): 3.81B Privately Held
Web: www.taylor.com
SIC: 2761 Manifold business forms
HQ: Taylor Communications, Inc.
1725 Roe Crest Dr
North Mankato MN 56003
866 541-0937

(G-8565)
TEMPO PRODUCTS LLC
2130 Brevard Rd (27263-1704)
P.O. Box 2005 (27261-2005)
PHONE..................336 434-8649
Martha Kennedy Romer, Managing Member
▲ EMP: 22 EST: 2004
SQ FT: 20,000
SALES (est): 2.44MM Privately Held
Web: www.tempohomeproducts.com
SIC: 2392 Pillows, bed: made from purchased materials

(G-8566)
THAYER COGGIN INC
Also Called: Thayer Coggin
230 South Rd (27262-8153)
PHONE..................336 841-6000
Royale Wiggin, COO
Doris Coggin, *
Clarence Coggin, *
◆ EMP: 55 EST: 1956
SQ FT: 200,000
SALES (est): 7.96MM Privately Held
Web: www.thayercoggin.com
SIC: 2511 Wood household furniture

(G-8567)
THAYER COGGIN FURNITURE
230 South Rd (27262-8153)
PHONE..................336 841-6000
Thayer Coggin, Prin
EMP: 6 EST: 2016
SALES (est): 103.14K Privately Held
Web: www.thayercoggin.com
SIC: 2511 Wood household furniture

(G-8568)
THERMO FISHER SCIENTIFIC INC
4125 Premier Dr (27265-8144)
PHONE..................800 955-6288
EMP: 4
SALES (corp-wide): 44.91B Publicly Held
Web: www.thermofisher.com
SIC: 3826 Analytical instruments
PA: Thermo Fisher Scientific Inc.
168 3rd Ave
Waltham MA 02451
781 622-1000

(G-8569)
THOMAS BUILT BUSES INC (DH)
Also Called: Thomas Buses
1408 Courtesy Rd (27260-7248)
P.O. Box 2450 (27261-2450)
PHONE..................336 889-4871
EMP: 1749 EST: 1916
SALES (est): 215.51MM
SALES (corp-wide): 60.75B Privately Held
Web: www.thomasbuiltbuses.com
SIC: 3713 3711 Bus bodies (motor vehicles); Chassis, motor vehicle
HQ: Daimler Truck North America Llc
4555 N Channel Ave
Portland OR 97217
503 745-8000

(G-8570)
THOMAS OF HIGH POINT
1408 Courtesy Rd (27260-7248)
PHONE..................336 889-4871
EMP: 4 EST: 2019
SALES (est): 87.26K Privately Held
SIC: 3711 Motor vehicles and car bodies

(G-8571)
THOMASVILLE-DEXEL INCORPORATED
Also Called: Td Fiber
2041 Brevard Rd (27263-1701)
P.O. Box 2278 (27261-2278)
PHONE..................336 819-5550
Doris P Deal, Pr
Plair Whitworth, *
Raymond L Deal Junior, Prin
EMP: 50 EST: 1925
SALES (est): 5.3MM Privately Held
Web: www.tdfiber.com
SIC: 2655 Fiber cans, drums, and similar products

(G-8572)
TOM KLEEBERG
1148 Nc Highway 62 W (27263-9752)
PHONE..................336 516-2363
Thomas Kleeberg, Mgr
EMP: 6 EST: 2011
SALES (est): 155.24K Privately Held
SIC: 2491 Structural lumber and timber, treated wood

(G-8573)
TOTAL PRINT SOLUTIONS
320 Habersham Rd Ste 105 (27260-6300)
PHONE..................336 841-5292
Michael Prillaman, Ofcr
EMP: 5 EST: 2018
SALES (est): 87.65K Privately Held
Web: www.proformatps.com
SIC: 2752 Offset printing

(G-8574)
TRANSARCTIC NORTH CAROLINA INC
Also Called: Transarctic
5270 Glenola Industrial Dr (27263-8152)
P.O. Box 98 (27361-0098)
PHONE..................336 861-6116
Michael Marlin, Pr
Dale Mason, *
James Stewart, *
EMP: 25 EST: 2002
SQ FT: 1,000
SALES (est): 2.3MM Privately Held
Web: www.transarctic.com
SIC: 3585 Air conditioning equipment, complete

(G-8575)
TRANSTECH PHARMA LLC (PA)
Also Called: Vtv Therapeutics
3980 Premier Dr Ste 310 (27265-8409)
PHONE..................336 841-0300
Stephen Holcombe, Pr
Stephen L Holcombe, Pr
EMP: 119 EST: 1999
SALES (est): 22.08MM
SALES (corp-wide): 22.08MM Privately Held
Web: www.ttpharma.com
SIC: 2834 Pharmaceutical preparations

(G-8576)
TRIANGLE CABINET COMPANY
809 Aberdeen Rd (27265-1306)
PHONE..................336 869-6401
Daniel Adams, Owner
EMP: 6 EST: 1980
SALES (est): 411.51K Privately Held
SIC: 2434 Wood kitchen cabinets

(G-8577)
TRISTATE WELDING & FABRICATION
704 Ferndale Blvd (27262-4712)
P.O. Box 2186 (27006-2186)
PHONE..................336 899-5206
EMP: 4 EST: 2017
SALES (est): 36.56K Privately Held
Web: www.tristatefabricators.com
SIC: 7692 Welding repair

(G-8578)
TRIUNE BUSINESS FURNITURE INC
1101 Roberts Ln (27260-7196)
P.O. Box 1270 (27261-1270)
PHONE..................336 884-8341
Charles Baker, Pr
Charley Stephens, VP
EMP: 8 EST: 1993
SQ FT: 10,000
SALES (est): 881.24K Privately Held
Web: www.triuneseating.com
SIC: 2521 Wood office furniture

(G-8579)
TRUE PORTION INC
Also Called: Millennium Landscaping
5220 High Point Rd (27265-1146)
PHONE..................336 362-6326
Richard V Knowles, Pr
Brenda S Knowles, Treas
EMP: 14 EST: 1992
SQ FT: 5,500
SALES (est): 733.45K Privately Held
SIC: 3596 5046 Weighing machines and apparatus; Scales, except laboratory

(G-8580)
TUBS-USA LLC ✪
322 Fraley Rd (27263-1714)
PHONE..................336 884-5737
Hp Mccoy, Managing Member
EMP: 12 EST: 2022
SALES (est): 1.02MM Privately Held
SIC: 3431 Shower stalls, metal

(G-8581)
TWE NONWOVENS US INC (HQ)
Also Called: Vita Nonwovens
2215 Shore St (27263-2511)
PHONE..................336 431-7187
Kevin Womble, Pr
Dave Kame, *
Jason Johnson, *
◆ EMP: 25 EST: 2012
SQ FT: 339,000
SALES (est): 98.52MM
SALES (corp-wide): 393.89MM Privately Held

Web: www.twenonwovensus.com
SIC: 2297 Nonwoven fabrics
PA: Twe Group Gmbh
Hollefeldstr. 46
Emsdetten NW 48282
25722050

(G-8582)
U S CABINETS EXPRESS LLC
2505 N Main St (27262-8216)
PHONE..................336 875-4011
EMP: 6 EST: 2019
SALES (est): 290.42K Privately Held
Web: www.uscabinetsexpress.net
SIC: 2434 Wood kitchen cabinets

(G-8583)
ULLMANIQUE INC
323 Old Thomasville Rd (27260-8190)
P.O. Box 1636 (27261-1636)
PHONE..................336 885-5111
Thomas L Ullman, Pr
William L Ullman, VP
Carol M Young, Sec
EMP: 8 EST: 1992
SQ FT: 7,000
SALES (est): 970.94K Privately Held
SIC: 2521 Tables, office: wood

(G-8584)
ULTRA COATINGS INCORPORATED
3509 Jamac Rd (27260-7179)
P.O. Box 57 (27261-0057)
PHONE..................336 883-8853
Floyd Zeno Moore, Pr
Michael Moore, *
Bonnie Moore, *
EMP: 20 EST: 1964
SQ FT: 40,000
SALES (est): 2.32MM Privately Held
Web: www.ultracoatings.com
SIC: 3479 2816 Painting of metal products; Inorganic pigments

(G-8585)
UNITED FINISHERS INTL INC
1950 W Green Dr (27260-1666)
P.O. Box 5462 (27262-5462)
PHONE..................336 883-3901
▲ EMP: 8 EST: 1993
SALES (est): 2.4MM Privately Held
Web: www.unitedfinishers.com
SIC: 5031 2431 2426 Kitchen cabinets; Millwork; Hardwood dimension and flooring mills

(G-8586)
UNIVERSAL FURNITURE LIMITED (PA)
Also Called: Universal Bedroom Furniture
2575 Penny Rd (27265-8334)
PHONE..................336 822-8888
Ronald J Hoffman, Pr
Larry Lilan, *
Tom Lyons, CTRL*
Catherine T Mcgee, VP
Peggy R Cook, *
◆ EMP: 70 EST: 1973
SQ FT: 150,000
SALES (est): 153.72MM
SALES (corp-wide): 153.72MM Privately Held
Web: www.universalfurniture.com
SIC: 2511 2512 Dining room furniture: wood; Upholstered household furniture

(G-8587)
UWHARRIE CHAIR COMPANY LLC
5873 Parker St (27263-8502)
PHONE..................336 431-2055
Erica Lloyd, Managing Member
EMP: 6 EST: 2015
SALES (est): 389.78K Privately Held
Web: www.uwharriechair.com
SIC: 2511 Wood household furniture

(G-8588)
V AND E COMPONENTS INC (PA)
720 W Fairfield Rd (27263-1746)
P.O. Box 7352 (27264-7352)
PHONE..................336 884-0088
Bill Vest, Pr
Woody Vest, Sec
Karen Hamilton, VP
▲ EMP: 17 EST: 1976
SQ FT: 50,000
SALES (est): 9.7MM
SALES (corp-wide): 9.7MM Privately Held
SIC: 3089 Injection molding of plastics

(G-8589)
VAUGHAN-BASSETT FURN CO INC
210 E Commerce Ave (27260-6686)
PHONE..................336 889-9111
Candace Hicks, Mgr
EMP: 504
SALES (corp-wide): 88.99MM Privately Held
Web: www.vaughanbassett.com
SIC: 2511 Wood household furniture
PA: Vaughan-Bassett Furniture Company, Incorporated
300 E Grayson St
Galax VA 24333
276 236-6161

(G-8590)
VAULT LLC
Also Called: Vault Enclosures
1515 W Green Dr (27260-1657)
PHONE..................336 698-3796
EMP: 13 EST: 2013
SQ FT: 40,000
SALES (est): 4.95MM
SALES (corp-wide): 4.95MM Privately Held
Web: www.byvault.com
SIC: 3089 Plastics containers, except foam
PA: Pioneer Square Brands, Inc.
1515 W Green Dr
High Point NC 27260
360 733-5608

(G-8591)
VEN-PLY INCORPORATED
5250 High Point Rd Ste K1 (27265-1654)
P.O. Box 5962 (27262-5962)
PHONE..................336 841-4858
Alton L Slay, Pr
EMP: 11 EST: 1986
SQ FT: 28,700
SALES (est): 539.75K Privately Held
SIC: 2436 Softwood veneer and plywood

(G-8592)
VERELLEN INC
5297 Prospect St (27263-3963)
P.O. Box 1018 (27261-1018)
PHONE..................336 889-7379
Tom Verellen, Prin
◆ EMP: 52 EST: 2007
SALES (est): 10.02MM Privately Held
Web: www.verellen.biz
SIC: 5712 2512 Furniture stores; Chairs: upholstered on wood frames

(G-8593)
VERENA DESIGNS INC (PA)
812 W Green Dr (27260-7336)
P.O. Box 869 (27261-0869)
PHONE..................336 869-8235
Verena Houghtaling, Pr
EMP: 25 EST: 1990
SQ FT: 11,000
SALES (est): 2.34MM
SALES (corp-wide): 2.34MM Privately Held
Web: www.verenadesigns.com
SIC: 2254 2341 Shorts, shirts, slips, and panties (underwear): knit; Women's and children's underwear

(G-8594)
VIOLINO USA LTD
123 S Hamilton St (27260-5230)
PHONE..................336 889-6623
EMP: 20 EST: 2015
SALES (est): 1.3MM Privately Held
Web: www.violino.us
SIC: 2512 Living room furniture: upholstered on wood frames

(G-8595)
VISION CONTRACT MFG LLC
1327 Lincoln Dr (27260-1514)
PHONE..................336 405-8784
Chris Morris, Prin
Woon Lee, *
EMP: 30 EST: 2021
SALES (est): 2.38MM Privately Held
SIC: 3999 Manufacturing industries, nec

(G-8596)
VISUAL PRODUCTS INC
1019 Porter St (27263-1637)
PHONE..................336 883-0156
TOLL FREE: 800
Gail Wright, Pr
Sylvia J Breed, Sec
Marsha Talton, VP
Angela Osborne, VP
EMP: 12 EST: 1967
SQ FT: 20,000
SALES (est): 851.46K Privately Held
Web: www.visualproductsinc.com
SIC: 2782 Blankbooks and looseleaf binders

(G-8597)
VRUSH INDUSTRIES INC
Also Called: Rushfurnitiure.com
118 N Wrenn St (27260-5020)
PHONE..................336 886-7700
Vicky L Rush, Pr
Mike Rush, Ex VP
◆ EMP: 10 EST: 2009
SALES (est): 198.26K Privately Held
Web: www.vrushinc.com
SIC: 5045 5021 7379 3469 Computer peripheral equipment; Furniture; Computer related consulting services; Furniture components, porcelain enameled

(G-8598)
VTV THERAPEUTICS INC (PA)
3980 Premier Dr Ste 310 (27265-8409)
PHONE..................336 841-0300
Rich Nelson, Pr
Jeffrey B Kindler, Ex Ch Bd
Steven Tuch, CFO
Thomas Strack, Chief Medical Officer
EMP: 25 EST: 2015
SQ FT: 12,786
SALES (est): 2.02MM
SALES (corp-wide): 2.02MM Publicly Held
Web: www.vtvtherapeutics.com
SIC: 2834 Pharmaceutical preparations

(G-8599)
VTV THERAPEUTICS LLC
3980 Premier Dr Ste 310 (27265-8409)
PHONE..................336 841-0300
EMP: 27 EST: 2015
SALES (est): 569.65K
SALES (corp-wide): 2.02MM Publicly Held
Web: www.vtvtherapeutics.com
SIC: 2834 Pharmaceutical preparations
PA: Vtv Therapeutics Inc.
3980 Premier Dr Ste 310
High Point NC 27265
336 841-0300

(G-8600)
W V DOYLE ENTERPRISES INC
Also Called: Doyle Enterprises
1816 Belmar St (27260-8401)
PHONE..................336 885-2035
Randy Doyle, Pr
Roger Doyle, VP
Walter Doyle Junior, Treas
Carolyn Doyle Cobler, Sec
EMP: 8 EST: 1981
SQ FT: 56,000
SALES (est): 683.69K Privately Held
SIC: 3554 Box making machines, paper

(G-8601)
WARRIOR BOATS
2100 E Martin Luther King Jr Dr (27260-5834)
PHONE..................336 885-2628
Brian Kilgariff, Owner
EMP: 4 EST: 1992
SALES (est): 255.09K Privately Held
Web: www.thewarriorboat.com
SIC: 3732 Boatbuilding and repairing

(G-8602)
WEBER & WEBER INC
Also Called: Sir Speedy
117 W Lexington Ave (27262-2531)
PHONE..................336 889-6322
Dwight Shaw, Genl Mgr
EMP: 8
SALES (corp-wide): 4.56MM Privately Held
Web: www.sirspeedy.com
SIC: 2752 Commercial printing, lithographic
PA: Weber And Weber, Inc.
1011 Burke St
Winston Salem NC 27101
336 722-4109

(G-8603)
WHITEWOOD CONTRACTS LLC
Also Called: Sedgewick Industries
667 W Ward Ave (27260-1644)
PHONE..................336 885-9300
Kim Crossman, Brnch Mgr
EMP: 44
SALES (corp-wide): 20.02MM Privately Held
Web: www.customcontract.com
SIC: 2512 2389 Chairs: upholstered on wood frames; Hospital gowns
HQ: Whitewood Contracts, Llc
100 Liberty Dr
Thomasville NC 27360
336 882-8565

(G-8604)
WILLOW CREEK FURNITURE INC
1949 W Green Dr (27260-1686)
PHONE..................336 889-0076
Steve Shumate, Pr
EMP: 5 EST: 1989
SQ FT: 12,000
SALES (est): 444.96K Privately Held
Web: www.willowcreekfurniture.com
SIC: 2511 Wood household furniture

High Point - Guilford County (G-8605)   **GEOGRAPHIC SECTION**

(G-8605)
WINTER BELL COMPANY (PA)
2018 Brevard Rd (27263-1702)
P.O. Box 48 (27261-0048)
PHONE..................................336 887-2651
Richard Lewis, *Pr*
Gurney L Stroud Ii, *VP*
Glenda Kemp, *Sec*
▼ **EMP:** 5 **EST:** 1960
SQ FT: 70,000
SALES (est): 4.38MM
SALES (corp-wide): 4.38MM **Privately Held**
Web: www.winterbell.com
SIC: 2679 Paper products, converted, nec

(G-8606)
WISE LIVING INC
Also Called: Living Wise
216 Woodbine St (27260-8340)
PHONE..................................336 991-5346
EMP: 19
SALES (corp-wide): 2.44MM **Privately Held**
Web: www.wiselivinginc.com
SIC: 2512 2511 Wood upholstered chairs and couches; Wood household furniture
PA: Wise Living, Inc.
  2001 W 60th St
  Los Angeles CA 90047
  323 541-0410

(G-8607)
WOODMARK ORIGINALS INC
1920 Jarrell St (27260-8812)
PHONE..................................336 841-6409
▲ **EMP:** 105 **EST:** 1964
SQ FT: 90,000
SALES (est): 254.45K
SALES (corp-wide): 1.21MM **Privately Held**
SIC: 2512 Upholstered household furniture
PA: Howard Miller Company
  860 E Main Ave
  Zeeland MI 49464
  616 772-9131

(G-8608)
WOOLFOAM CORPORATION
Also Called: Wool Novelty
107 Whittier Ave (27262-8042)
PHONE..................................336 886-4964
Bernard Lodzyski, *Brnch Mgr*
EMP: 6
SQ FT: 25,000
SALES (corp-wide): 5.7MM **Privately Held**
SIC: 3552 Loopers, textile machinery
HQ: The Woolfoam Corporation
  3000 Hempstead Tpke # 302
  Levittown NY
  516 731-5380

(G-8609)
YORKSHIRE HOUSE INC
1904 Alleghany St (27263-2028)
P.O. Box 5872 (27262-5872)
PHONE..................................336 869-9714
Michael Beaver, *Pr*
Thomas J Beaver, *CEO*
▲ **EMP:** 5 **EST:** 1990
SQ FT: 1,100
SALES (est): 494.36K **Privately Held**
Web: www.modernhistoryhome.com
SIC: 2511 Wood household furniture

(G-8610)
ZAGROS SADJADI SOFTWARE
2968 Shady View Dr (27265-8230)
PHONE..................................336 848-8171
Zagros Sadjadi, *Prin*
EMP: 4 **EST:** 2011
SALES (est): 100.37K **Privately Held**
Web: www.zagros.com
SIC: 7372 Prepackaged software

Highlands
Macon County

(G-8611)
ALLAN DRTH SONS GNRTOR SLS SVC
Also Called: Allan Dearth and Sons
11259 Buck Creek Rd (28741-8918)
P.O. Box 2768 (28741-2768)
PHONE..................................828 526-9325
EMP: 4 **EST:** 2007
SALES (est): 865.11K **Privately Held**
Web: www.adsemergencypower.com
SIC: 3621 7629 Motors and generators; Generator repair

(G-8612)
BLACK ROCK GRANITE & CABINETRY
2543 Cashiers Rd (28741-0089)
PHONE..................................828 787-1100
Kevin J Bradle, *Prin*
EMP: 6 **EST:** 2010
SALES (est): 552.66K **Privately Held**
Web: www.blackrockgraniteandcabinetry.com
SIC: 2434 Wood kitchen cabinets

(G-8613)
CASHIERS PRINTING INC
Also Called: Cashiers Printing & Graphics
68 Highlands Walk (28741-8375)
P.O. Box 39 (28741-0039)
PHONE..................................828 787-1324
Russel Majors, *Pr*
EMP: 5 **EST:** 1983
SQ FT: 3,000
SALES (est): 684.29K **Privately Held**
Web: www.cashiersareachamber.com
SIC: 2752 Offset printing

(G-8614)
CHOCOLATE HEAVEN COMPANY
2254 Dillard Rd (28741-6679)
PHONE..................................828 421-2042
Krysti Henderson, *Managing Member*
EMP: 6 **EST:** 2017
SALES (est): 211.15K **Privately Held**
Web: www.lovechocolateheaven.com
SIC: 2066 Baking chocolate

(G-8615)
DIVINE SOUTH BAKING CO LLC ◆
2254 Dillard Rd (28741-6679)
PHONE..................................828 421-2042
Krysti Henderson, *Managing Member*
EMP: 6 **EST:** 2022
SALES (est): 500K **Privately Held**
Web: www.lovechocolateheaven.com
SIC: 2052 Bakery products, dry

(G-8616)
NEW MEDIA GOLF INC
Also Called: Advantage Golf School
381 Main St (28741-8606)
P.O. Box 804 (28741-0804)
PHONE..................................828 533-9954
Vance Wood, *CEO*
EMP: 10 **EST:** 2007
SQ FT: 1,800
SALES (est): 447.38K **Privately Held**
Web: www.elenagolf.com
SIC: 3161 5699 7999 Luggage; Sports apparel; Instruction schools, camps, and services

(G-8617)
SOUTHERN STEELWORKS LLC
2251 N 4th St (28741-9321)
PHONE..................................828 548-3660
EMP: 5 **EST:** 2019
SALES (est): 465.65K **Privately Held**
Web: southern-steel-works.business.site
SIC: 3441 Fabricated structural metal

(G-8618)
TIGER MOUNTAIN WOODWORKS INC
Also Called: The Summer House
2089 Dillard Rd (28741-6677)
P.O. Box 1088 (28741-1088)
PHONE..................................828 526-5577
Paula Jones, *Pr*
Barry Jones, *
▲ **EMP:** 32 **EST:** 1988
SQ FT: 3,000
SALES (est): 1.1MM **Privately Held**
Web: www.summerhousehighlands.com
SIC: 5712 2511 2431 Customized furniture and cabinets; Wood household furniture; Millwork

Hildebran
Burke County

(G-8619)
AMERICAN TOPS INC
8968 Dietz Ave (28637)
P.O. Box 382 (28637-0382)
PHONE..................................828 397-4910
Brian Walker, *Mgr*
Brian Walker, *Mgr*
EMP: 4 **EST:** 2002
SALES (est): 267.9K **Privately Held**
SIC: 2517 Sewing machine cabinets and cases, wood

(G-8620)
CONTOUR ENTERPRISES LLC
3345 Clarence Towery Cir (28637-8231)
P.O. Box 945 (28637-0945)
PHONE..................................828 328-1550
David L Baird, *Mgr*
EMP: 75 **EST:** 2003
SALES (est): 5.16MM **Privately Held**
SIC: 3069 Rubberized fabrics

(G-8621)
DE FEET INTERNATIONAL INC
Also Called: De Feet
371 I40 Access Rd (28637-8041)
PHONE..................................828 397-7025
Shane Cooper, *Pr*
EMP: 22 **EST:** 1993
SQ FT: 30,000
SALES (est): 1.27MM **Privately Held**
Web: www.defeet.com
SIC: 2251 2252 Women's hosiery, except socks; Socks

(G-8622)
FABRIC SERVICES HICKORY INC
130 Kline Industrial Park 3rd St Ne (28637)
P.O. Box 2102 (28603-2102)
PHONE..................................828 397-7331
Stanley Knox, *Pr*
▲ **EMP:** 10 **EST:** 1969
SQ FT: 2,000
SALES (est): 252.98K **Privately Held**
Web: www.allenrussellchase.com
SIC: 2395 Quilted fabrics or cloth

(G-8623)
GEIGER INTERNATIONAL INC
218 Cline Park Dr (28637-8115)
P.O. Box 22 (53551-0022)
PHONE..................................828 324-6500
Michael Glassford, *Mgr*
EMP: 12
SALES (corp-wide): 4.09B **Publicly Held**
Web: www.geigerfurniture.com
SIC: 2521 2512 Wood office furniture; Upholstered household furniture
HQ: Geiger International, Inc.
  6095 Fulton Indus Blvd Sw
  Atlanta GA 30336
  404 344-1100

(G-8624)
HUITT MILLS INC (PA)
115 10th St Ne (28637-8102)
P.O. Box 640 (28637-0640)
PHONE..................................828 322-8628
Kevin Huitt, *Pr*
Susan Huitt, *
Kenneth Huitt, *
Norine Huitt, *
EMP: 26 **EST:** 1946
SQ FT: 20,000
SALES (est): 2.01MM
SALES (corp-wide): 2.01MM **Privately Held**
Web: www.huitt.com
SIC: 2252 Socks

(G-8625)
INDUSTRIAL MECHANICAL SERVICES
2354 Us Hwy 70 (28637)
P.O. Box 580 (28637-0580)
PHONE..................................828 397-3231
Johnny R Williams, *Pr*
Pat Honeycutt, *
EMP: 9 **EST:** 1971
SALES (est): 208.18K **Privately Held**
SIC: 3441 1711 Fabricated structural metal; Mechanical contractor

(G-8626)
LYON ROOFING INC
Also Called: Lyon Metal & Supply
323 S Center St (28637-8306)
PHONE..................................828 397-2301
Brett Lyon, *Brnch Mgr*
EMP: 10
Web: www.lyonmetalroofing.com
SIC: 3444 Sheet metalwork
PA: Lyon Roofing, Inc.
  485 Industrial Park Rd
  Piney Flats TN 37686

(G-8627)
MARVES INDUSTRIES INC
205 Cline Park Dr (28637-8114)
P.O. Box 946 (28637-0946)
PHONE..................................828 397-4400
Elias Gomez, *Pr*
EMP: 68 **EST:** 2009
SALES (est): 14MM **Privately Held**
Web: www.marvesindustries.com
SIC: 3086 Insulation or cushioning material, foamed plastics

(G-8628)
TAB STEEL & FABRICATING INC
3345 Clarence Towery Cir (28637-8231)
P.O. Box 9516 (28603-9516)
PHONE..................................828 323-8300
Tripp Burns, *Pr*
Jamie Burns, *Sec*
EMP: 22 **EST:** 2000
SQ FT: 8,000
SALES (est): 864.86K **Privately Held**

GEOGRAPHIC SECTION

Hillsborough - Orange County (G-8657)

SIC: 3441 Fabricated structural metal

(G-8629)
ZION INDUSTRIES INC
9480 Neuville Ave (28637-8374)
PHONE.................828 397-2701
Mark Shoemaker, *Brnch Mgr*
EMP: 18
SALES (corp-wide): 11.08MM **Privately Held**
Web: www.zioninduction.com
SIC: 3398 Brazing (hardening) of metal
PA: Zion Industries, Inc.
 6229 Grafton Rd
 Valley City OH 44280
 330 225-3246

Hillsborough
Orange County

(G-8630)
3PETER LLC (PA)
1621 Rosebriar Pl (27278-6880)
PHONE.................919 475-2334
EMP: 7 **EST:** 2019
SALES (est): 113.76K
SALES (corp-wide): 113.76K **Privately Held**
SIC: 2035 Pickles, sauces, and salad dressings

(G-8631)
3PETER LLC
500 Valley Forge Rd (27278-9502)
PHONE.................919 475-2334
Jon Peter, *Pr*
EMP: 13
SALES (corp-wide): 113.76K **Privately Held**
SIC: 2035 Pickles, sauces, and salad dressings
PA: 3peter Llc
 1621 Rosebriar Pl
 Hillsborough NC 27278
 919 475-2334

(G-8632)
ACCIDENTAL BAKER
115 Boone Square St (27278-2561)
PHONE.................919 732-6777
EMP: 5 **EST:** 2011
SALES (est): 144.74K **Privately Held**
Web: www.theaccidentalbakernc.com
SIC: 2051 Bread, cake, and related products

(G-8633)
AIRSPEED LLC
980 Corporate Dr Ste 200 (27278-8655)
PHONE.................919 644-1222
▲ **EMP:** 31 **EST:** 1996
SQ FT: 5,500
SALES (est): 4.03MM **Privately Held**
Web: www.airspeedllc.com
SIC: 3399 5051 3442 8711 Nails: aluminum, brass, or other nonferrous metal or wire; Castings, rough: iron or steel; Moldings and trim, except automobile: metal; Mechanical engineering

(G-8634)
ARGOS USA LLC
Also Called: Union Concrete
411 Valley Forge Rd (27278-8544)
PHONE.................919 732-7509
Marcus William, *Brnch Mgr*
EMP: 4
Web: www.argos-us.com
SIC: 3273 Ready-mixed concrete
HQ: Argos Usa Llc
 3015 Windward Plz Ste 300
 Alpharetta GA 30005
 678 368-4300

(G-8635)
ARTIFICIAL FUNHOUSE
101 Cheshire Dr (27278-2620)
PHONE.................919 423-4103
EMP: 4 **EST:** 2017
SALES (est): 207.27K **Privately Held**
SIC: 3842 Braces, orthopedic

(G-8636)
ATHOL ARBOR CORPORATION
Also Called: Hardwood Designs
511 Valley Forge Rd (27278-9502)
PHONE.................919 643-1100
EMP: 17
SIC: 2431 1751 Millwork; Carpentry work

(G-8637)
AVIARY PUBLISHERS INC
221 Crawford Rd (27278-9493)
PHONE.................919 331-0003
EMP: 4 **EST:** 2008
SALES (est): 99.61K **Privately Held**
SIC: 2741 Miscellaneous publishing

(G-8638)
BIG SPOON ROASTERS LLC
500 Meadowlands Dr (27278-8504)
PHONE.................919 309-9100
Mark Overbay, *Prin*
▼ **EMP:** 10 **EST:** 2011
SALES (est): 953.29K **Privately Held**
Web: www.bigspoonroasters.com
SIC: 2068 Salted and roasted nuts and seeds

(G-8639)
BIODOT INC
2211 Leah Dr (27278-9010)
PHONE.................949 440-3685
EMP: 5 **EST:** 2021
SALES (est): 142.55K **Privately Held**
SIC: 3823 Process control instruments

(G-8640)
BRIAN MCGREGOR ENTERPRISE
2207 Leah Dr (27278-9010)
PHONE.................919 732-2317
Brian Mcgregor, *Owner*
EMP: 8 **EST:** 2005
SALES (est): 492.54K **Privately Held**
Web: www.videogaming.com
SIC: 3999 Coin-operated amusement machines

(G-8641)
CABINETS 4 U LLC
1108 Crown Ct (27278-7638)
PHONE.................919 291-4617
Ronald L Gammon, *Prin*
EMP: 4 **EST:** 2010
SALES (est): 161.13K **Privately Held**
SIC: 2434 Wood kitchen cabinets

(G-8642)
CAROLINA GYM SUPPLY CORP
575 Dimmocks Mill Rd (27278-2352)
PHONE.................919 732-6999
Benjamin S Edkins, *Pr*
▲ **EMP:** 6 **EST:** 1978
SALES (est): 963.45K **Privately Held**
Web: www.carolinagym.com
SIC: 5941 3949 Gymnasium equipment, nec ; Gymnasium equipment

(G-8643)
CBA SOFTWARE INC
512 Grand Oak Dr (27278-8851)
PHONE.................919 289-9820
EMP: 10 **EST:** 2010
SALES (est): 89.69K **Privately Held**
Web: www.cbasoftware.com
SIC: 7372 Prepackaged software

(G-8644)
CHANDLER CONCRETE INC
Also Called: CHANDLER CONCRETE INC
1501 Old North Carolina Hwy 10 (27278-9510)
P.O. Box 131 (27216-0131)
PHONE.................919 644-1058
Marvin Thrasher, *Mgr*
EMP: 32
Web: www.chandlerconcrete.com
SIC: 3273 Ready-mixed concrete
PA: Chandler Concrete Co., Inc.
 1006 S Church St
 Burlington NC 27215

(G-8645)
CMA SIGNS LLC
610 Meadowlands Dr (27278-8561)
PHONE.................919 245-8339
Smyrna Robinson, *Managing Member*
EMP: 12 **EST:** 2020
SALES (est): 545.41K **Privately Held**
SIC: 3993 Signs and advertising specialties

(G-8646)
COMPETITION CAGES
522 East Dr (27278-2371)
PHONE.................919 644-1334
EMP: 4 **EST:** 2017
SALES (est): 59.97K **Privately Held**
SIC: 3949 Sporting and athletic goods, nec

(G-8647)
CREDLE WOODWORKS LLC
3810 Marklyn Pl (27278-7664)
PHONE.................919 353-4298
Ameron Credle, *Prin*
EMP: 5 **EST:** 2018
SALES (est): 59.54K **Privately Held**
Web: www.credlewoodworks.com
SIC: 2431 Millwork

(G-8648)
DT AEROSPACE INC
1220 E Hardscrabble Dr (27278-9645)
PHONE.................919 417-1895
EMP: 6 **EST:** 2013
SALES (est): 88.7K **Privately Held**
Web: www.dtaerospace.com
SIC: 3728 Aircraft parts and equipment, nec

(G-8649)
ENO MT CABINETS JAMES RAY
506 Eno Mountain Rd (27278-9651)
PHONE.................919 644-1981
Donna Ray, *Prin*
EMP: 7 **EST:** 2008
SALES (est): 209.97K **Privately Held**
Web: enomountaincustomcabinets.yolasite.com
SIC: 2434 Wood kitchen cabinets

(G-8650)
ENO SCIENTIFIC LLC
1606 Faucette Mill Rd (27278-7556)
P.O. Box 1586 (27278-1586)
PHONE.................910 778-2660
▲ **EMP:** 5 **EST:** 2009
SQ FT: 2,000
SALES (est): 940.14K **Privately Held**
Web: www.enoscientific.com
SIC: 3823 Pressure measurement instruments, industrial

(G-8651)
HARTFORD PRODUCTS INC
6224 Acorn Ridge Trl (27278-8890)
PHONE.................919 471-5937
EMP: 4 **EST:** 1997
SALES (est): 208.41K **Privately Held**
SIC: 3944 Trains and equipment, toy: electric and mechanical

(G-8652)
HELLO PHD LLC
1519 Rutoni Dr (27278-8305)
PHONE.................919 414-3215
Daniel Arneman, *Prin*
EMP: 5 **EST:** 2018
SALES (est): 93.64K **Privately Held**
Web: www.hellophd.com
SIC: 2741 Miscellaneous publishing

(G-8653)
HIGH CREEK WOODWORKS
2921 Miller Rd (27278-8488)
PHONE.................919 418-1210
Kenton Althiser, *Prin*
EMP: 5 **EST:** 2011
SALES (est): 93.7K **Privately Held**
SIC: 2431 Millwork

(G-8654)
HOMETOWN CABINETS INC
903 Apple Ln (27278-9466)
PHONE.................919 245-3554
Mark Robinson, *Prin*
EMP: 5 **EST:** 2018
SALES (est): 97.64K **Privately Held**
Web: www.hometowncabinets.com
SIC: 2434 Wood kitchen cabinets

(G-8655)
HOMETOWN SPORTS INC
Also Called: Hometown Sports Embroidery
3301 St Marys Rd (27278-9726)
PHONE.................919 732-7090
Robert R Castona Junior, *Pr*
Linda Castona, *Sec*
Susan Billat, *International Marketing Director*
Bill Berard, *Dir*
George Horton, *Dir*
EMP: 5 **EST:** 1994
SALES (est): 171.33K **Privately Held**
SIC: 2395 5961 Embroidery products, except Schiffli machine; Novelty merchandise, mail order

(G-8656)
INNEROPTIC TECHNOLOGY INC
3421 Carriage Trl (27278-9512)
PHONE.................919 732-2090
Kurtis Keller, *Ch Bd*
EMP: 6 **EST:** 2002
SALES (est): 491.46K **Privately Held**
Web: www.inneroptic.com
SIC: 2833 7371 3845 Endocrine products; Software programming applications; Ultrasonic medical equipment, except cleaning

(G-8657)
KAYE PRODUCTS INC
535 Dimmocks Mill Rd (27278-2352)
PHONE.................919 732-6444
◆ **EMP:** 35 **EST:** 1976
SALES (est): 4.78MM **Privately Held**
Web: www.kayeproducts.com
SIC: 3842 Orthopedic appliances

Hillsborough - Orange County (G-8658)

(G-8658)
KORU NATURALS LLC
218 S Churton St (27278-2699)
P.O. Box 1252 (27278-1252)
PHONE...........................800 253-7011
EMP: 5 EST: 2018
SALES (est): 104.21K **Privately Held**
Web: www.korunaturals.com
SIC: **2844** Perfumes, cosmetics and other toilet preparations

(G-8659)
KOTEK HOLDINGS INC
Also Called: HARDWOOD DESIGNS
511 Valley Forge Rd (27278-9502)
PHONE...........................919 643-1100
Michael Kaisersatt, *CEO*
EMP: 25 EST: 2016
SALES (est): 2.89MM **Privately Held**
Web: www.hardwooddesigns.com
SIC: **2431** Door sashes, wood

(G-8660)
LUTHIERS WORKSHOP LLC
Also Called: Pre - War Guitars Co.
2207 Leah Dr Ste 102 (27278-9010)
PHONE...........................919 241-4578
EMP: 8 EST: 2015
SALES (est): 331.46K **Privately Held**
SIC: **3931** Musical instruments

(G-8661)
MAPLE VIEW ICE CREAM
6900 Rocky Ridge Rd (27278-7952)
PHONE...........................919 960-5535
Muffin Brosig, *Owner*
EMP: 10 EST: 2001
SALES (est): 878.5K **Privately Held**
Web: www.mapleviewfarm.com
SIC: **2024** Ice cream and frozen deserts

(G-8662)
MDM MFG LLC
206 Stockbridge Pl (27278-9773)
PHONE...........................919 908-6574
EMP: 6 EST: 2019
SALES (est): 290.52K **Privately Held**
SIC: **3999** Manufacturing industries, nec

(G-8663)
NORTH CRLINA SOC FOR RSPRTORY
732 Phelps Rd (27278-8955)
PHONE...........................919 619-4206
EMP: 5 EST: 2018
SALES (est): 103.3K **Privately Held**
Web: www.ncsrc.org
SIC: **3842** Respirators

(G-8664)
NORTHSIDE MILLWORK INC
301 Millstone Dr (27278-8777)
PHONE...........................919 732-6100
Peter Singer, *Pr*
Debra Singer, *
EMP: 35 EST: 1982
SQ FT: 25,000
SALES (est): 5.71MM **Privately Held**
Web: www.northsidemillwork.com
SIC: **2431** Millwork

(G-8665)
PICASSOMOESLLC ⊙
513 Patriots Pointe Dr (27278-9030)
PHONE...........................216 703-4547
Maurice Morrison, *CEO*
EMP: 5 EST: 2023
SALES (est): 97.55K **Privately Held**

SIC: **7299 3161 5999 2051** Tattoo parlor; Clothing and apparel carrying cases; Miscellaneous retail stores, nec; Bakery: wholesale or wholesale/retail combined

(G-8666)
REDUX BEVERAGES LLC
2318 Oakhurst Trl (27278-6639)
PHONE...........................951 304-1144
James Kirby, *Managing Member*
EMP: 5 EST: 2006
SALES (est): 361.85K **Privately Held**
Web: www.reduxdirect.com
SIC: **2086** Soft drinks: packaged in cans, bottles, etc.

(G-8667)
SHEET METAL DUCT SUPPLIERS LLC
214 Millstone Dr (27278-8776)
PHONE...........................919 732-4362
Larry F Warren, *Prin*
EMP: 6 EST: 2009
SALES (est): 235.14K **Privately Held**
Web: www.sheetmetalductsuppliers.com
SIC: **3444** Sheet metalwork

(G-8668)
SOMMERVILLE ENTERPRISES LLC
Also Called: Open South Imports
202 Holiday Park Rd (27278-8603)
PHONE...........................919 924-1594
Steve Sommerville, *Pr*
EMP: 11 EST: 2018
SALES (est): 655.13K **Privately Held**
SIC: **2084** Wines

(G-8669)
TINAS FABULOUS FUDGE LLC
4720 Schley Rd (27278-6846)
PHONE...........................919 606-2616
Euthena Smith, *Owner*
EMP: 4 EST: 2018
SALES (est): 93.86K **Privately Held**
SIC: **2064** Fudge (candy)

(G-8670)
TOUCHAMERICA INC
437 Dimmocks Mill Rd (27278-2300)
P.O. Box 1304 (27278-1304)
PHONE...........................919 732-6968
◆ EMP: 12 EST: 1985
SALES (est): 428.61K **Privately Held**
Web: www.touchamerica.com
SIC: **3841** Surgical and medical instruments

(G-8671)
TRACKX TECHNOLOGY LLC
437 Dimmocks Mill Rd Ste 28 (27278-2379)
PHONE...........................888 787-2259
Robert Isaacs, *CEO*
EMP: 15 EST: 2016
SALES (est): 1.72MM **Privately Held**
Web: www.trackx.tech
SIC: **3845** Ultrasonic scanning devices, medical

(G-8672)
WILMORE ELECTRONICS COMPANY INC (PA)
Also Called: Wilmore Electronics
607 Us Highway 70a E (27278-8526)
P.O. Box 1329 (27278-1329)
PHONE...........................919 732-9351
EMP: 55 EST: 1963
SALES (est): 9.48MM
SALES (corp-wide): 9.48MM **Privately Held**
Web: www.wilmoreelectronics.com

SIC: **3699** Electrical equipment and supplies, nec

(G-8673)
WOMACK PUBLISHING CO INC
Also Called: News of Orange County
109 E King St (27278-2570)
P.O. Box 580 (27278-0580)
PHONE...........................919 732-2171
Keith Coleman, *Genl Mgr*
EMP: 4
SALES (corp-wide): 21.7MM **Privately Held**
Web: www.newsoforange.com
SIC: **2711** Newspapers: publishing only, not printed on site
PA: Womack Publishing Company, Inc.
28 N Main St
Chatham VA 24531
434 432-2791

Hobbsville
Gates County

(G-8674)
BASS FABRICATIONS LLC
36 Keys Cross Rd (27946-9759)
PHONE...........................252 312-8937
EMP: 4 EST: 2017
SALES (est): 130.24K **Privately Held**
SIC: **3999** Manufacturing industries, nec

(G-8675)
C A PERRY & SON INC (DH)
4033 Virginia Rd (27946-9508)
PHONE...........................252 221-4463
Sidney L Perry, *Owner*
Sydney Kopland, *
EMP: 33 EST: 1950
SQ FT: 100,000
SALES (est): 36.2MM
SALES (corp-wide): 14.75B **Publicly Held**
Web: www.caperryandson.com
SIC: **5159 5191 4221 5153** Peanuts (bulk), unroasted; Farm supplies; Farm product warehousing and storage; Grains
HQ: Lansing Trade Group, Llc
10975 Benson Dr Ste 400
Overland Park KS 66210
913 748-3000

Hoffman
Richmond County

(G-8676)
SOUTHERN PRODUCTS COMPANY INC
4303 Us Hwy 1 N (28347)
P.O. Box 189 (28347-0189)
PHONE...........................910 281-3189
TOLL FREE: 800
Marshall B Gilchrist, *Pr*
Peter Gilchrist Iii, *Sec*
EMP: 25 EST: 1970
SQ FT: 12,000
SALES (est): 2.31MM **Privately Held**
Web: www.sandandgravel.net
SIC: **3295 3569** Minerals, ground or treated; Filters

Hollister
Halifax County

(G-8677)
TAILORED VISIONZ & DREAMZ LLC
1406 Lynch Rd Ste B (27844-9488)

PHONE...........................919 340-3613
EMP: 5 EST: 2021
SALES (est): 222.86K **Privately Held**
SIC: **2431 7389** Woodwork, interior and ornamental, nec; Business Activities at Non-Commercial Site

Holly Ridge
Onslow County

(G-8678)
ABOVE TOPSAIL LLC
301 Us Highway 17 S (28445-8788)
PHONE...........................910 803-1759
Jeffery Wenzel, *Managing Member*
EMP: 4 EST: 2017
SALES (est): 477.77K **Privately Held**
Web: www.abovetopsail.com
SIC: **7335 3861** Commercial photography; Printing frames, photographic

(G-8679)
AMERICAN ARTWORKS
714 E Ocean Rd (28445-8712)
PHONE...........................910 803-2525
EMP: 4 EST: 2017
SALES (est): 53.24K **Privately Held**
SIC: **3544** Special dies and tools

(G-8680)
BULK TRANSPORT SERVICE INC
169 Preston Wells Rd (28445-8543)
PHONE...........................910 329-0555
Kendall R Moore, *Pr*
EMP: 7 EST: 1994
SQ FT: 500
SALES (est): 637.66K **Privately Held**
SIC: **1442** Common sand mining

(G-8681)
DEAN COMPANY OF NORTH CAROLINA
Also Called: Coastal Carolina Cutng Boards
301 Us Highway 17 S Ste 9 (28445-8785)
PHONE...........................910 622-1012
EMP: 10 EST: 2015
SALES (est): 376.75K **Privately Held**
Web: www.cccboards.com
SIC: **2499** Decorative wood and woodwork

(G-8682)
JAXONSIGNS
874 E Ocean Hwy (28445-8714)
PHONE...........................910 467-3409
Cathy Jackson, *Mgr*
EMP: 4 EST: 2015
SALES (est): 162.25K **Privately Held**
Web: www.jaxonsigns.com
SIC: **3993** Signs and advertising specialties

(G-8683)
JOHNNY SLICKS INC
624 Us Highway 17 S Unit 1 (28445-8660)
PHONE...........................910 803-2159
Johnny Raushi, *Prin*
EMP: 7 EST: 2019
SALES (est): 508.81K **Privately Held**
Web: www.johnnyslicks.com
SIC: **5999 5087 3999 2844** Miscellaneous retail stores, nec; Beauty parlor equipment and supplies; Hair and hair-based products; Lotions, shaving

(G-8684)
KINETIC SLTONS FABRICATION LLC
405 Salvo Ct (28445-8609)
PHONE...........................607 749-0946
Joseph Freeman, *Prin*
EMP: 5 EST: 2019

GEOGRAPHIC SECTION
Holly Springs - Wake County (G-8710)

SALES (est): 74.11K **Privately Held**
SIC: 7692 Welding repair

(G-8685)
S & W READY MIX CON CO LLC
Also Called: S & W Ready Mix Concrete
307 W Ocean Rd (28445-7871)
PHONE.............................910 329-1201
EMP: 19
SALES (corp-wide): 8.01MM **Privately Held**
Web: www.snwreadymix.com
SIC: 3273 Ready-mixed concrete
HQ: S & W Ready Mix Concrete Company Llc
  217 Lisbon St
  Clinton NC 28328
  910 592-1733

Holly Springs
Wake County

(G-8686)
ASI SIGNAGE NORTH CAROLINA
600 Irving Pkwy (27540-8445)
P.O. Box 819 (27540-0819)
PHONE.............................919 362-9669
EMP: 17 EST: 2019
SALES (est): 1.01MM **Privately Held**
Web: www.asisignage.net
SIC: 3993 Signs and advertising specialties

(G-8687)
AVIATOR BREWING COMPANY INC
5504 Caleb Knolls Dr (27540-7611)
PHONE.............................919 601-5497
Mark D Doble, *Pr*
EMP: 9 EST: 2008
SQ FT: 2,500
SALES (est): 602.76K **Privately Held**
Web: www.aviatorbrew.com
SIC: 2082 5182 5921 Beer (alcoholic beverage); Wine and distilled beverages; Beer (packaged)

(G-8688)
BEAZER EAST INC
7000 Cass Holt Rd (27540-9781)
PHONE.............................919 567-9512
Jim Hilton, *Mgr*
EMP: 10
SQ FT: 4,672
SALES (corp-wide): 21.19B **Privately Held**
SIC: 3241 1442 Natural cement; Construction sand and gravel
HQ: Beazer East, Inc.
  600 River Ave Ste 200
  Pittsburgh PA 15212
  412 428-9407

(G-8689)
BEC
4908 Linksland Dr (27540-7325)
PHONE.............................919 244-0831
Brian Egler, *Prin*
EMP: 6 EST: 2010
SALES (est): 237.65K **Privately Held**
SIC: 3672 Circuit boards, television and radio printed

(G-8690)
BIOLOGIC SOLUTIONS LLC
5004 Sadelia Pl (27540-9377)
PHONE.............................919 770-8266
Paula Keith, *Prin*
EMP: 5 EST: 2016
SALES (est): 180.31K **Privately Held**
SIC: 3842 Braces, orthopedic

(G-8691)
BOMBSHELL BEER COMPANY LLC
120 Quantum St (27540-8861)
PHONE.............................919 823-1933
Ellen Joyner, *Pr*
EMP: 11 EST: 2012
SALES (est): 1MM **Privately Held**
Web: www.bombshellbeer.com
SIC: 2082 5813 Beer (alcoholic beverage); Drinking places

(G-8692)
BRICKSTONE PUBLISHING
133 Clay Ridge Way Ste 200 (27540-8527)
PHONE.............................919 522-4052
Lori Verni Fogarsi, *Owner*
EMP: 5 EST: 2011
SALES (est): 58.18K **Privately Held**
Web: www.loritheauthor.com
SIC: 2741 Miscellaneous publishing

(G-8693)
C & J WELDING INC
136 Acorn Ridge Ln (27540-7337)
P.O. Box 1299 (27526-1299)
PHONE.............................919 552-0275
Chuck Wombles, *Prin*
EMP: 9 EST: 2003
SALES (est): 256.74K **Privately Held**
SIC: 7692 Welding repair

(G-8694)
CHENTECH CORP
524 Texanna Way (27540-7352)
PHONE.............................919 749-8765
Richard Chen, *Admn*
EMP: 4 EST: 2015
SALES (est): 247.27K **Privately Held**
SIC: 3851 Contact lenses

(G-8695)
CITRIX SYSTEM
1304 Dexter Ridge Dr (27540-6993)
PHONE.............................919 607-9973
EMP: 4 EST: 2019
SALES (est): 49.23K **Privately Held**
SIC: 7372 Prepackaged software

(G-8696)
DS SMITH PLC
301 Thomas Mill Rd (27540-8447)
PHONE.............................919 557-3148
EMP: 25
SALES (corp-wide): 10.12B **Privately Held**
Web: www.dssmith.com
SIC: 2653 2542 2671 Boxes, corrugated: made from purchased materials; Partitions and fixtures, except wood; Paper; coated and laminated packaging
PA: Ds Smith Plc
  3 Level
  London W2 1D
  754 542-9001

(G-8697)
DYNAGRAPHICS SCREENPRINTNG
125 Quantum St (27540-8862)
PHONE.............................919 212-2898
Steve Knight, *Pr*
Shelley L Knight, *VP*
EMP: 5 EST: 1997
SQ FT: 2,500
SALES (est): 486.46K **Privately Held**
Web: www.tshirtsraleigh.com
SIC: 2759 Screen printing

(G-8698)
EW JACKSON TRANSPORTATION LLC
113 Gingerlilly Ct (27540-7868)
PHONE.............................919 586-2514
Vinson Jackson, *Prin*
EMP: 7 EST: 2016
SALES (est): 330.17K **Privately Held**
SIC: 3547 Primary rolling mill equipment

(G-8699)
FIVE STAR COFFEE ROASTERS LLC
108 Thomas Mill Rd Ste 101 (27540-9253)
PHONE.............................919 671-0645
Nelson Amador, *Pr*
EMP: 8 EST: 2016
SALES (est): 199.09K **Privately Held**
Web: www.5starcoffeeroasters.com
SIC: 2095 Coffee roasting (except by wholesale grocers)

(G-8700)
GOODYEAR TIRE & RUBBER COMPANY
Also Called: Goodyear
932 N Main St (27540-8782)
PHONE.............................919 552-9340
Mike Correll, *Mgr*
EMP: 7
SALES (corp-wide): 20.07MM **Publicly Held**
Web: www.goodyear.com
SIC: 5531 3714 3011 Automotive tires; Motor vehicle wheels and parts; Tires and inner tubes
PA: The Goodyear Tire & Rubber Company
  200 E Innovation Way
  Akron OH 44316
  330 796-2121

(G-8701)
JACKWAY SOFTWARE LLC
552 Wanderview Ln (27540-6257)
PHONE.............................919 747-1190
Robert Jackness, *CEO*
EMP: 5 EST: 2015
SALES (est): 116.25K **Privately Held**
SIC: 7372 Prepackaged software

(G-8702)
JEBCO INC
121 Thomas Mill Rd (27540-9320)
PHONE.............................919 557-2001
EMP: 37
SALES (corp-wide): 17.29MM **Privately Held**
SIC: 3631 5812 8741 Barbecues, grills, and braziers (outdoor cooking); Eating places; Management services
PA: Jebco, Inc.
  7798 Ga Highway 88 E
  Keysville GA 30816
  706 465-3378

(G-8703)
KARESS KRAFTERS
P.O. Box 521 (27540-0521)
PHONE.............................919 961-5575
EMP: 4 EST: 2011
SALES (est): 68.99K **Privately Held**
Web: www.rdrewnaturals.com
SIC: 2844 Perfumes, cosmetics and other toilet preparations

(G-8704)
KENNETH PERKINS
225 Marsh Landing Dr (27540-5509)
PHONE.............................919 267-9396
Kenneth Perkins, *Prin*
EMP: 6 EST: 2005
SALES (est): 185.58K **Privately Held**
SIC: 2411 Logging

(G-8705)
LAFAUCI
5001 Sunset Forest Cir (27540-7817)
PHONE.............................919 244-5912
EMP: 4 EST: 2018
SALES (est): 73.16K **Privately Held**
SIC: 2721 Periodicals

(G-8706)
LIPSTICK CHATTER LLC
149 Smith Rock Dr (27540-6961)
PHONE.............................919 285-3439
Chauntele Holley, *Prin*
EMP: 5 EST: 2015
SALES (est): 80.28K **Privately Held**
Web: www.lipstickchatter.com
SIC: 2844 Lipsticks

(G-8707)
MAKE AN IMPRESSION INC
202 Premier Dr (27540-8413)
PHONE.............................919 557-7400
Dawn Joseph, *Pr*
Joann Randall, *VP*
James R Randall, *Treas*
James L Joseph, *Sec*
EMP: 7 EST: 2001
SQ FT: 3,012
SALES (est): 636.41K **Privately Held**
Web: www.makeanimpressioninc.com
SIC: 2759 7334 Screen printing; Photocopying and duplicating services

(G-8708)
NOVARTIS VCCNES DAGNOSTICS INC (HQ)
475 Green Oaks Pkwy (27540-7976)
PHONE.............................617 871-7000
Joerg Reinhardt, *CEO*
▲ EMP: 500 EST: 1986
SQ FT: 119,600
SALES (est): 384.78MM
SALES (corp-wide): 35.31B **Privately Held**
SIC: 2835 2836 2834 Diagnostic substances; Vaccines and other immunizing products; Drugs affecting parasitic and infective diseases
PA: Gsk Plc
  G S K House
  Brentford MIDDX TW8 9
  208 047-5000

(G-8709)
OFM LLC
Also Called: Office Furniture Marketing
161 Tradition Trl (27540-7045)
PHONE.............................919 303-6389
▲ EMP: 91 EST: 1995
SQ FT: 124,000
SALES (est): 22.21MM
SALES (corp-wide): 479.1MM **Publicly Held**
Web: www.ofminc.com
SIC: 2521 Wood office furniture
PA: Hni Corporation
  600 E 2nd St
  Muscatine IA 52761
  563 272-7400

(G-8710)
PEAK TRUSS BUILDERS LLC
1220 N Main St (27540-9396)
P.O. Box 639 (27540-0639)
PHONE.............................919 552-5933
Le Greene, *Managing Member*
EMP: 9 EST: 2011
SQ FT: 8,000
SALES (est): 1MM **Privately Held**
Web: www.peaktruss.com

Holly Springs - Wake County (G-8711)

SIC: 2439 Trusses, wooden roof

(G-8711)
RALEIGH SIGN DESIGN
5316 Shadow Valley Rd (27540-8943)
PHONE..................919 244-1802
EMP: 4 EST: 2019
SALES (est): 130.87K Privately Held
Web: www.raleighsigndesign.com
SIC: 3993 Signs and advertising specialties

(G-8712)
RODNEY S CSTM CUT SIGN CO INC
Also Called: Rodney's Sign Company
600 Irving Pkwy (27540-8445)
P.O. Box 819 (27540-0819)
PHONE..................919 362-9669
Tayler Dalpe, Pr
John Dalpe Junior, COO
EMP: 27 EST: 1983
SQ FT: 45,000
SALES (est): 2.19MM Privately Held
Web: www.asisignage.com
SIC: 3993 2499 Signs, not made in custom sign painting shops; Handles, poles, dowels and stakes: wood

(G-8713)
ROMEO SIX LLC
260 Premier Dr (27540-5303)
PHONE..................919 589-7150
David Mannheim, Admn
W David Mannheim, Prin
EMP: 10 EST: 2015
SALES (est): 1.14MM Privately Held
Web: www.romeosix.com
SIC: 7373 7379 3669 Local area network (LAN) systems integrator; Computer related consulting services; Emergency alarms

(G-8714)
S&F PRODUCTS
6112 N Deer Ridge Dr (27540-7809)
PHONE..................714 412-1298
Fred Brown, Owner
◆ EMP: 4 EST: 2002
SALES (est): 209.53K Privately Held
SIC: 2851 Paints and allied products

(G-8715)
SEQIRUS INC (DH)
475 Green Oaks Pkwy (27540-7976)
PHONE..................919 577-5000
Dave Sehgal, Pr
EMP: 18 EST: 2015
SALES (est): 400.22MM Privately Held
Web: www.csl.com
SIC: 2836 Vaccines and other immunizing products
HQ: Seqirus Uk Limited
Point
Maidenhead BERKS SL6 8
162 864-1500

(G-8716)
SIGN WITH EASE INC
132 Trevor Ridge Dr (27540-7587)
PHONE..................919 285-3224
Harvey Goodman, Prin
EMP: 4 EST: 2016
SALES (est): 60.72K Privately Held
SIC: 3993 Signs and advertising specialties

(G-8717)
SOFTWARE GOLDSMITH INC
5305 Lake Edge Dr (27540-9340)
PHONE..................919 346-0403
Swapna Gangopadhyay, Pr
EMP: 8 EST: 2001
SALES (est): 178.7K Privately Held

Web: www.softsmithinc.com
SIC: 7372 Prepackaged software

(G-8718)
SPLENDIDCRM SOFTWARE INC
705 Laurel Bay Ln (27540-8741)
PHONE..................919 604-1258
Paul Rony, Prin
EMP: 5 EST: 2005
SALES (est): 491.83K Privately Held
Web: www.splendidcrm.com
SIC: 7372 7371 Prepackaged software; Software programming applications

(G-8719)
SUPER STITCHY LLC
216 Abbeville Ln (27540-4401)
PHONE..................919 762-0626
Barbara Sanders, Owner
EMP: 4 EST: 2017
SALES (est): 164.6K Privately Held
Web: www.superstitchy.com
SIC: 2395 Embroidery and art needlework

(G-8720)
SWORD CONSERVATORY INC
112 Tonks Trl (27540-8280)
PHONE..................919 557-4465
Stephenson Lindbeck, Prin
EMP: 5 EST: 2016
SALES (est): 132.49K Privately Held
SIC: 3421 Cutlery

(G-8721)
TIMOTHY W GILLESPIE
5028 Salem Ridge Rd (27540-7800)
PHONE..................919 567-2687
Timothy W Gillespie, Prin
EMP: 8 EST: 2005
SALES (est): 128.72K Privately Held
SIC: 3399 Powder, metal

(G-8722)
TOPLINE CABINET CO INC
608 Hollymont Dr (27540-5969)
PHONE..................919 762-0045
Brad Chaffee, Pr
EMP: 4 EST: 2015
SALES (est): 228.89K Privately Held
SIC: 2434 Wood kitchen cabinets

(G-8723)
TRIAXIS GAMES LLC
808 Chambord Way (27540-9426)
PHONE..................919 720-7804
EMP: 4 EST: 2015
SALES (est): 86.23K Privately Held
Web: www.triaxis.games
SIC: 7372 Prepackaged software

(G-8724)
VERTICAL SOLUTIONS OF NC INC
5040 Kinderston Dr (27540-9165)
P.O. Box 451 (27540-0451)
PHONE..................919 285-2251
Michael L Lassiter, Prin
EMP: 10 EST: 2010
SALES (est): 551.2K Privately Held
SIC: 2591 Blinds vertical

(G-8725)
W G OF SOUTHWEST RALEIGH INC
413 Redhill Rd (27540-6272)
P.O. Box 1151 (27540-1151)
PHONE..................919 629-7327
Micheal Boone, Pr
EMP: 4 EST: 2012
SALES (est): 115.99K Privately Held
SIC: 7349 2842 Window cleaning; Specialty cleaning

(G-8726)
WARP TECHNOLOGIES INC
601 Irving Pkwy (27540-8446)
P.O. Box 500 (27540-0500)
PHONE..................919 552-2311
Shartel Smith, Pr
EMP: 130 EST: 1988
SQ FT: 150,000
SALES (est): 10.68MM Privately Held
SIC: 2824 2258 Polyester fibers; Lace and warp knit fabric mills

(G-8727)
WINDRIDGE SENSORS LLC
209 Sunset Grove Dr (27540-6808)
PHONE..................919 272-8714
John Duff, Brnch Mgr
EMP: 14
SALES (corp-wide): 124.5K Privately Held
Web: www.windridgesensors.com
SIC: 3829 Thermometers and temperature sensors
PA: Windridge Sensors, Llc
4826 Whitner Dr
Wilmington NC

Hookerton
Greene County

(G-8728)
AMERICAN MADE PRODUCTS INC
606 5th St (28538)
P.O. Box 176 (62626-0176)
PHONE..................252 747-2010
EMP: 10
SALES (corp-wide): 2.33MM Privately Held
SIC: 2381 Gloves, work: woven or knit, made from purchased materials
PA: American Made Products Inc.
1155 Morgan St
Carlinville IL
217 854-4496

(G-8729)
PHOENIX EPOXY SYSTEMS LLC
123 Main St (28538-9663)
PHONE..................252 747-3735
Charles Albritton, Managing Member
EMP: 8 EST: 2009
SALES (est): 808.44K Privately Held
Web: www.phoenixepoxysystems.com
SIC: 3087 Custom compound purchased resins

Hope Mills
Cumberland County

(G-8730)
AEC IMAGING & GRAPHICS LLC (PA)
5755 Dove Dr (28348-1707)
PHONE..................910 693-1034
EMP: 4 EST: 1998
SALES (est): 497.09K
SALES (corp-wide): 497.09K Privately Held
Web: www.aecimaging.com
SIC: 7334 5049 2752 Blueprinting service; Drafting supplies; Commercial printing, lithographic

(G-8731)
AFFORDABLE SIGNS & AWNINGS
3959 Stone St (28348-2359)
PHONE..................910 237-1323
James Lawless, Prin
EMP: 4 EST: 2017
SALES (est): 54.18K Privately Held

SIC: 3993 Signs and advertising specialties

(G-8732)
BAD MONKEY LURES LLC
835 Jack Pine St (28348-9474)
PHONE..................910 433-5617
James H Strickland Junior, Owner
EMP: 4 EST: 2017
SALES (est): 47.08K Privately Held
SIC: 3949 Golf equipment

(G-8733)
C & F CUSTOM CABINETS INC
140 Sanders St (28348-8985)
PHONE..................910 424-7475
Frank Carter, Pr
Steve Ford, VP
EMP: 20 EST: 1987
SQ FT: 16,000
SALES (est): 2.37MM Privately Held
Web: www.cfcustomcabinets.com
SIC: 2434 Wood kitchen cabinets

(G-8734)
CAROLINA MCH FAYETTEVILLE INC
3465 Black And Decker Rd (28348-9332)
P.O. Box 632 (28348-0632)
PHONE..................910 425-9115
James Dietzen, Pr
Elek Torok, VP
Cnythia Torok, Prin
EMP: 16 EST: 1973
SQ FT: 7,000
SALES (est): 331.74K Privately Held
SIC: 3599 Machine shop, jobbing and repair

(G-8735)
CCI HAIR BOUTIQUE LLC
3059 N Main St (28348-2798)
PHONE..................407 216-9213
EMP: 15 EST: 2018
SALES (est): 579.85K Privately Held
SIC: 3999 Hair and hair-based products

(G-8736)
COMSET MANAGEMENT GROUP
3926 Gaithersburg Ln (28348-2092)
PHONE..................910 574-6007
Darrell Williams, Owner
EMP: 5 EST: 2000
SALES (est): 234.21K Privately Held
SIC: 1499 Gemstone and industrial diamond mining

(G-8737)
FRANKLIN BAKING COMPANY LLC
Also Called: Branch 0457
217 Woodington Rd (28348-8551)
PHONE..................910 425-5090
Joseph Mulligan, Brnch Mgr
EMP: 10
SALES (corp-wide): 5.09B Publicly Held
Web: franklin-co4goldsboro.edan.io
SIC: 2051 Bread, cake, and related products
HQ: Franklin Baking Company, Llc
500 W Grantham St
Goldsboro NC 27530
919 735-0344

(G-8738)
WILLIAM GEORGE PRINTING LLC
Also Called: Relyus
3469 Black And Decker Rd (28348-9332)
PHONE..................910 221-2700
Marshall Waren, Pr
▲ EMP: 46 EST: 2004
SQ FT: 95,000
SALES (est): 9.57MM Privately Held
Web: www.relyus.com

GEOGRAPHIC SECTION   Hudson - Caldwell County (G-8764)

SIC: **2752** 7331 Offset printing; Direct mail advertising services

Horse Shoe
Henderson County

(G-8739)
COLD MTN CABINETRY
40 Meadow Dr (28742-9621)
PHONE.................................828 577-8582
Brenda James, *Prin*
EMP: 4 **EST:** 2017
SALES (est): 49.38K **Privately Held**
SIC: 2434 Wood kitchen cabinets

(G-8740)
LIBERTY HSE UTILITY BUILDINGS
65 Dalton Rd (28742-9759)
PHONE.................................828 209-3390
Phillip C Whitaker, *Pr*
Rhonda Whitaker, *Sec*
EMP: 4 **EST:** 2004
SALES (est): 483.36K **Privately Held**
SIC: 2511 Storage chests, household: wood

(G-8741)
MICHAELIAN & KOHLBERG INC (PA)
5216 Brevard Rd (28742-9664)
P.O. Box 398 (28742-0398)
PHONE.................................828 891-8511
William T Sumner, *Ch Bd*
Sandra Lemke, *VP*
▲ **EMP:** 5 **EST:** 1920
SQ FT: 2,600
SALES (est): 4.84MM
SALES (corp-wide): 4.84MM **Privately Held**
Web: www.michaelian.com
SIC: 5023 2273 Rugs; Carpets and rugs

(G-8742)
MODERN WORKBENCH LLC
31 Amber Dr (28742-9766)
PHONE.................................828 845-4466
EMP: 5 **EST:** 2021
SALES (est): 63.22K **Privately Held**
SIC: 2431 Millwork

(G-8743)
ZUMCO INC
199 Forest Knolls Pl (28742-4767)
PHONE.................................828 891-3300
Daniel Zumstein, *Pr*
Virginia Zumstein, *VP*
EMP: 12 **EST:** 1974
SQ FT: 15,000
SALES (est): 323.42K **Privately Held**
SIC: 3599 Machine shop, jobbing and repair

Hot Springs
Madison County

(G-8744)
BLUFF MOUNTAIN OUTFITTERS INC
152 Bridge St (28743-9231)
P.O. Box 114 (28743-0114)
PHONE.................................828 622-7162
Wayne Crosby, *Pr*
Daniel Gallagher, *VP*
EMP: 7 **EST:** 1997
SQ FT: 4,800
SALES (est): 491.47K **Privately Held**
SIC: 3949 5945 5411 Sporting and athletic goods, nec; Hobby, toy, and game shops; Grocery stores, independent

(G-8745)
MADISON MANUFACTURING COMPANY
Also Called: Peerless Blowers
172 S Andrews Ave (28743-9213)
P.O. Box 187 (28743-0187)
PHONE.................................828 622-7500
Craig Neuhardt, *Pr*
Margaret Mcinnis, *Sec*
▲ **EMP:** 91 **EST:** 1991
SALES (est): 21.01MM **Privately Held**
Web: www.peerlessblowers.com
SIC: 3634 Electric housewares and fans

(G-8746)
RONNY D PHELPS
12 E Lawson Rd (28743-7780)
PHONE.................................828 206-6339
Ronny D Phelps, *Prin*
EMP: 6 **EST:** 2005
SALES (est): 157.39K **Privately Held**
SIC: 3531 Backhoes

Hubert
Onslow County

(G-8747)
AIRFIELD SOLUTIONS LLC
142 Leslie Ct (28539-3743)
PHONE.................................844 478-6929
Erica Rogers, *Brnch Mgr*
EMP: 5
SALES (corp-wide): 226.03K **Privately Held**
Web: www.airfield-solutions.com
SIC: 3812 Search and navigation equipment
PA: Airfield Solutions Llc
   825 Gum Branch Rd Ste 102
   Jacksonville NC 28540
   919 348-4271

(G-8748)
GENE LEATHER MEAN
333 Highway 172 (28539-3556)
PHONE.................................910 325-7098
EMP: 4 **EST:** 2018
SALES (est): 167.86K **Privately Held**
Web: www.meangeneleather.com
SIC: 3199 Leather goods, nec

(G-8749)
INK PALLETS & STITCHES LLC
118 Villa Park Dr (28539-3400)
PHONE.................................239 826-4772
Julianne Froncek, *Prin*
EMP: 5 **EST:** 2016
SALES (est): 80.09K **Privately Held**
SIC: 2395 Embroidery and art needlework

(G-8750)
KEVS WOODWORKING LLC
219 Toucan Way (28539-4655)
PHONE.................................850 559-3228
Kevin Lachat, *Pr*
EMP: 4 **EST:** 2017
SALES (est): 54.13K **Privately Held**
SIC: 2431 Millwork

(G-8751)
MEDALS TO HONOR INC
176 Oyster Ln (28539-3759)
P.O. Box 96 (28539-0096)
PHONE.................................910 326-4275
Michelle Holmquist, *Pr*
Karen Golden, *Sec*
EMP: 4 **EST:** 1999
SALES (est): 477.11K **Privately Held**
Web: www.medalstohonor.com

SIC: 2541 Store and office display cases and fixtures

(G-8752)
QUEENS CREEK SEAFOOD
105 Huffman Ln (28539)
PHONE.................................910 326-4801
EMP: 5 **EST:** 2010
SALES (est): 179.31K **Privately Held**
SIC: 2091 Clams: packaged in cans, jars, etc.

(G-8753)
U V REPTILE LABS INC
107 Craig Dr (28539-3863)
PHONE.................................252 241-4584
Bob Maccargar, *CEO*
EMP: 6 **EST:** 2011
SALES (est): 70.52K **Privately Held**
SIC: 3641 Ultraviolet lamps

(G-8754)
UDIO COMMERCIAL LLC
Also Called: Udio Commercial
101 Gillcrest Ln (28539-4305)
PHONE.................................609 977-2700
EMP: 6 **EST:** 2018
SALES (est): 66.18K **Privately Held**
SIC: 7372 Prepackaged software

(G-8755)
UPULL LLC
101 Gillcrest Ln (28539-4305)
PHONE.................................609 977-2700
Juliette Kemp, *Bd of Dir*
EMP: 4 **EST:** 2018
SALES (est): 56.54K **Privately Held**
SIC: 7372 Prepackaged software

(G-8756)
WATERLINE SYSTEMS INC
270 Hogans Rd (28539-4508)
PHONE.................................910 708-1000
Randall Borges, *Pr*
Tracy Gable, *Prin*
Nicholas Vann, *Prin*
EMP: 8 **EST:** 2019
SALES (est): 868.92K **Privately Held**
Web: www.waterlinesystems.com
SIC: 3731 Shipbuilding and repairing

(G-8757)
WILLIAM STONE & TILE INC
1525 Freedom Way (28539-3641)
PHONE.................................910 353-0914
William S Cucksee, *CEO*
▲ **EMP:** 4 **EST:** 2005
SQ FT: 22,500
SALES (est): 475.41K **Privately Held**
Web: www.williamstoneandtile.com
SIC: 2541 5211 Counter and sink tops; Counter tops

(G-8758)
WINTER CUSTOM YACHTS INC
270 Hogans Rd (28539-4508)
P.O. Box 40 (28539-0040)
PHONE.................................910 325-7583
Katelyn Miller, *CEO*
EMP: 10 **EST:** 2018
SALES (est): 1.16MM **Privately Held**
Web: www.wintercustomyachts.com
SIC: 3732 Boat kits, not models

Hudson
Caldwell County

(G-8759)
ACTIONSIGNCOM
2640 Hickory Blvd (28638-9100)
PHONE.................................828 572-2308
EMP: 5 **EST:** 2013
SALES (est): 121.49K **Privately Held**
Web: www.actionsign.com
SIC: 3993 Signs and advertising specialties

(G-8760)
ADHEZION BIOMEDICAL LLC
506 Pine Mountain Rd (28638-8793)
PHONE.................................828 728-6116
Caridad Rahim, *Brnch Mgr*
EMP: 5
SALES (corp-wide): 3.51B **Publicly Held**
Web: www.adhezion.com
SIC: 3841 Surgical and medical instruments
HQ: Adhezion Biomedical, Llc
   1 Meridian Blvd Ste 1b02
   Wyomissing PA 19610

(G-8761)
ARCONA LEATHER COMPANY LLC (PA)
Also Called: JP Leather Arcona Division
2615 Mission Rd (28638-9043)
P.O. Box 399 (28638-0399)
PHONE.................................828 396-7728
Robert Hollar, *Pr*
▲ **EMP:** 9 **EST:** 1979
SALES (est): 2.53MM
SALES (corp-wide): 2.53MM **Privately Held**
Web: www.arconaleather.com
SIC: 5199 3111 Leather, leather goods, and furs; Leather tanning and finishing

(G-8762)
BEOCARE INC
1905 International Blvd (28638-2734)
PHONE.................................828 728-7300
▲ **EMP:** 105 **EST:** 2010
SQ FT: 85,000
SALES (est): 27.45MM
SALES (corp-wide): 12.8MM **Privately Held**
Web: www.beocare.net
SIC: 3842 Surgical appliances and supplies
PA: Fra Production Spa
   Via Delle Poste 16
   Dusino San Michele AT 14010
   014 197-9911

(G-8763)
BEOCARE GROUP INC (PA)
1905 International Blvd (28638-2734)
PHONE.................................828 728-7300
Peter Vanderbruggen, *CEO*
Matt Valego, *
Peter Vanderbruggen, *Pr*
Steve De Backer, *
James Verberg, *
◆ **EMP:** 104 **EST:** 2009
SQ FT: 85,000
SALES (est): 8.91MM
SALES (corp-wide): 8.91MM **Privately Held**
Web: www.beocare.net
SIC: 2399 Hand woven apparel

(G-8764)
CAJAH CORPORATION
Also Called: Cajah Mountain Hosiery Mills
1905 International Blvd (28638-2734)
P.O. Box 369 (28638-0369)

Hudson - Caldwell County (G-8765)

PHONE.................828 728-7300
Jim Verberg, *Mgr*
▲ **EMP:** 110 **EST:** 1993
SQ FT: 1,000
SALES (est): 9.42MM **Privately Held**
Web: www.mountzionhudson.org
SIC: 2251 Women's hosiery, except socks

(G-8765)
CALDWELL CABINETS NC LLC
Also Called: Caseworx
3441 Hickory Blvd (28638-9025)
P.O. Box 547 (28638-0547)
PHONE.................828 212-0000
Dianne Green, *
EMP: 28 **EST:** 2016
SQ FT: 20,000
SALES (est): 2.7MM **Privately Held**
Web: www.caseworxnc.com
SIC: 2434 Wood kitchen cabinets

(G-8766)
CAROLINA BASE - PAC CORP
3157 Freezer Locker Rd (28638-8759)
P.O. Box 783 (28638-0783)
PHONE.................828 728-7304
Weidner Abernathy, *Pr*
EMP: 50 **EST:** 1982
SQ FT: 25,000
SALES (est): 4.39MM **Privately Held**
Web: www.carolinabasepac.com
SIC: 2448 3089 Pallets, wood; Plastics processing

(G-8767)
CEDAR ROCK HOME FURNISHINGS
3483 Hickory Blvd (28638-9025)
P.O. Box 515 (28638-0515)
PHONE.................828 396-2361
Leonard G Widner, *Pr*
Jimmie Kaye Widner, *Sec*
EMP: 4 **EST:** 1986
SQ FT: 12,000
SALES (est): 821.39K **Privately Held**
Web: www.cedarrockfurniture.com
SIC: 5712 2512 Mattresses; Living room furniture: upholstered on wood frames

(G-8768)
CEDAR VALLEY HOSIERY MILL INC
3074 Deal Mill Rd (28638-9216)
PHONE.................828 396-1804
Monti Hall, *VP*
Carroll Hall, *Pr*
Dorothy Hall, *Sec*
Karen Roberts, *Treas*
EMP: 7 **EST:** 1979
SQ FT: 2,000
SALES (est): 428.09K **Privately Held**
SIC: 2252 Socks

(G-8769)
CONSUMER SPECIALTY INC
Also Called: American Classic Furniture
4003 Us Highway 321a (28638-9501)
P.O. Box 826 (28630-0826)
PHONE.................828 396-2195
Mark Kiser, *Pr*
Donald Heavner, *VP*
▲ **EMP:** 6 **EST:** 2015
SALES (est): 67.06K **Privately Held**
SIC: 2519 5021 Furniture, household: glass, fiberglass, and plastic; Office and public building furniture

(G-8770)
J & M WOODWORKING INC
432 Pine Mountain Rd (28638-2638)
P.O. Box 145 (28638-0145)
PHONE.................828 728-3253
Todd Bumgarner, *Pr*
Jerry A Bumgarner, *Sec*
▲ **EMP:** 10 **EST:** 1963
SQ FT: 11,250
SALES (est): 976.04K **Privately Held**
SIC: 2431 Millwork

(G-8771)
JP LEATHER COMPANY INC
2615 Mission Rd (28638-9043)
P.O. Box 11066 (28603-4566)
PHONE.................828 396-7728
Robert D Haller, *Pr*
▲ **EMP:** 6 **EST:** 1995
SQ FT: 20,000
SALES (est): 453.82K **Privately Held**
SIC: 2386 Leather and sheep-lined clothing

(G-8772)
KELLEYS SPORTS AND AWARDS INC
2636 Hickory Blvd (28638-9100)
P.O. Box 2579 (28645-2579)
PHONE.................828 728-4600
Robert Peircy, *Pr*
Robert Piercy, *Pr*
Todd Rayle, *VP*
▲ **EMP:** 9 **EST:** 1983
SQ FT: 10,000
SALES (est): 697.49K **Privately Held**
Web: www.kelleyssports.net
SIC: 2759 2395 5941 5999 Screen printing; Embroidery and art needlework; Sporting goods and bicycle shops; Trophies and plaques

(G-8773)
KINCAID FURNITURE COMPANY INC (HQ)
240 Pleasant Hill Rd (28638-2244)
P.O. Box 605 (28638-0605)
PHONE.................828 728-3261
Steven M Kincaid, *Pr*
Bob Lemons, *VP Sls*
Reggie Probst, *VP Opers*
Gary Lake, *Contrlr*
▲ **EMP:** 70 **EST:** 1946
SALES (est): 62.15MM
SALES (corp-wide): 2.35B **Publicly Held**
Web: www.kincaidfurniture.com
SIC: 2511 2512 Wood household furniture; Upholstered household furniture
PA: La-Z-Boy Incorporated
1 Lazboy Dr
Monroe MI 48162
734 242-1444

(G-8774)
LEA INDUSTRIES INC
240 Pleasant Hill Rd (28638-2244)
PHONE.................336 294-5233
Jack Richardson, *Pr*
▲ **EMP:** 250 **EST:** 1973
SALES (est): 47.63MM
SALES (corp-wide): 2.35B **Publicly Held**
SIC: 2511 Wood bedroom furniture
PA: La-Z-Boy Incorporated
1 Lazboy Dr
Monroe MI 48162
734 242-1444

(G-8775)
MARX INDUSTRIES INCORPORATED
Also Called: Marx Industries
4276 Helena St (28638-9023)
P.O. Box 826 (28630-0826)
PHONE.................828 396-6700
EMP: 50
SIC: 3069 3086 Foam rubber; Plastics foam products

(G-8776)
MODERN STRUCTURE SOLUTIONS LLC ✪
2601 Withers Dr (28638-9062)
PHONE.................984 286-2447
EMP: 5 **EST:** 2022
SALES (est): 79.3K **Privately Held**
SIC: 3441 7389 Fabricated structural metal; Business Activities at Non-Commercial Site

(G-8777)
RPM WOOD FINISHES GROUP INC
C C I Division
3190 Hickory Blvd (28638-2661)
PHONE.................828 728-8266
EMP: 100
SALES (corp-wide): 7.26B **Publicly Held**
Web: wfgpmt.rpmwfg.com
SIC: 2851 2893 3479 Lacquers, varnishes, enamels, and other coatings; Printing ink; Coating of metals and formed products
HQ: Rpm Wood Finishes Group, Inc.
2220 Us Highway 70 Se # 100
Hickory NC 28602
828 261-0325

(G-8778)
SATTLER CORP
Also Called: Outdura
447 Main St (28638-2329)
PHONE.................828 759-2100
◆ **EMP:** 80 **EST:** 2010
SQ FT: 175,000
SALES (est): 11.56MM
SALES (corp-wide): 176.69MM **Privately Held**
Web: usa.sattler.com
SIC: 2211 Broadwoven fabric mills, cotton
PA: Sattler Ag
SattlerstraBe 45
GOssendorf 8077
31641040

(G-8779)
SEALED AIR CORPORATION
Polyethylene Foam Div
2001 International Blvd (28638-2731)
PHONE.................828 728-6610
Ed Frost, *Mgr*
EMP: 100
SALES (corp-wide): 5.49B **Publicly Held**
Web: www.sealedair.com
SIC: 3087 3086 3089 2676 Custom compound purchased resins; Plastics foam products; Plastics containers, except foam; Sanitary paper products
PA: Sealed Air Corporation
2415 Cascade Pointe Blvd
Charlotte NC 28208
980 221-3535

(G-8780)
SIX WATERPOTS VINYRD & WINERY
4040 James Dr (28638-9413)
PHONE.................828 728-5099
EMP: 4 **EST:** 2018
SALES (est): 120.15K **Privately Held**
Web: www.sixwaterpots.com
SIC: 2084 Wines

(G-8781)
SUPERFAST PERFORMANCE PDTS INC
3379 Harvard Pl (28638-9227)
PHONE.................828 980-8072
Timothy Davison Obrien, *Admn*
EMP: 8 **EST:** 2017
SALES (est): 194.53K **Privately Held**
Web: www.superfastperformanceproducts.com

SIC: 3714 Motor vehicle parts and accessories

(G-8782)
SUPERIOR DRY KILNS INC
Also Called: Boldesigns
2601 Withers Dr (28638-9062)
P.O. Box 1586 (28645-1586)
PHONE.................828 754-7001
Brett Bollinger, *Pr*
EMP: 20 **EST:** 1984
SALES (est): 2.44MM **Privately Held**
Web: www.boldesigninc.com
SIC: 3559 3531 3541 3537 Kilns, lumber; Construction machinery; Machine tools, metal cutting type; Industrial trucks and tractors

(G-8783)
TIMBER WOLF FOREST PRODUCTS
3189 Freezer Locker Rd (28638-8759)
P.O. Box 608 (28638-0608)
PHONE.................828 728-7500
Randy Roper, *Pr*
Rita Roper, *VP*
EMP: 18 **EST:** 1998
SQ FT: 13,000
SALES (est): 4.67MM **Privately Held**
Web: www.timberwolfforest.com
SIC: 2431 Millwork

Huntersville
Mecklenburg County

(G-8784)
3D MATERNITEES LLC
9101 Torrence Creek Ct (28078-9132)
PHONE.................704 778-0633
Heather M Simica, *Admn*
EMP: 5 **EST:** 2016
SALES (est): 149.47K **Privately Held**
SIC: 2759 Screen printing

(G-8785)
760 CRAFT WORKS LLC
100 Gilead Rd (28078-7825)
PHONE.................704 274-5216
Knox Ramsey, *Managing Member*
EMP: 15 **EST:** 2019
SALES (est): 518.52K **Privately Held**
Web: www.760craftworks.com
SIC: 2082 5813 7389 Malt beverages; Drinking places; Business services, nec

(G-8786)
AKOUSTIS INC (HQ)
9805 Northcross Center Ct Ste A (28078-7327)
PHONE.................704 997-5735
Jeffrey Shealy, *Pr*
Lora Shealy, *
EMP: 44 **EST:** 2014
SQ FT: 2,000
SALES (est): 13.68MM
SALES (corp-wide): 27.12MM **Publicly Held**
Web: www.akoustis.com
SIC: 3674 4813 Integrated circuits, semiconductor networks, etc.; Data telephone communications
PA: Akoustis Technologies, Inc.
9805 Northcross Center Ct
Huntersville NC 28078
704 997-5735

(G-8787)
AKOUSTIS TECHNOLOGIES INC (PA)
9805 Northcross Center Ct Ste A (28078-7327)

PHONE.....................704 997-5735
Jeffrey B Shealy, Pr
Kenneth E Boller, CORP CTRL
David M Aichele, Development
EMP: 104 EST: 2013
SQ FT: 22,400
SALES (est): 27.12MM
SALES (corp-wide): 27.12MM Publicly Held
Web: www.akoustis.com
SIC: 3663 Amplifiers, RF power and IF

(G-8788)
ALPHA MEDSOURCE LLC
14009 Island Dr (28078-8954)
PHONE.....................704 408-8505
EMP: 4 EST: 2015
SALES (est): 160.85K Privately Held
Web: www.alphamedsource.com
SIC: 3841 Surgical and medical instruments

(G-8789)
AMERICAN CABINETRY
7918 Leisure Ln (28078-6399)
PHONE.....................704 502-4450
Harold Hickson, Mgr
EMP: 5 EST: 2011
SALES (est): 222.42K Privately Held
Web: www.americancabinetrync.com
SIC: 2434 Wood kitchen cabinets

(G-8790)
AMERICAN WOODMARK CORPORATION
Also Called: Timberlake Cabinet Company
9825 Northcross Center Ct Ste N (28078-7338)
P.O. Box 65524 (28216)
PHONE.....................704 947-3280
Tim Argall, Mgr
EMP: 21
SALES (corp-wide): 2.07B Publicly Held
Web: www.americanwoodmark.com
SIC: 2431 Millwork
PA: American Woodmark Corporation
    561 Shady Elm Rd
    Winchester VA 22602
    540 665-9100

(G-8791)
AMEROCK LLC (DH)
Also Called: Piedmont Hardware Brands
10115 Kincey Ave Ste 210 (28078-6483)
PHONE.....................800 435-6959
Ian T Graham, *
▲ EMP: 18 EST: 1928
SALES (est): 11.65MM
SALES (corp-wide): 2.67MM Privately Held
SIC: 3429 Cabinet hardware
HQ: Ferguson Enterprises, Llc
    751 Lakefront Cmns
    Newport News VA 23606
    757 969-4011

(G-8792)
APEX TOOL GROUP LLC
13620 Reese Blvrd Pkwy E Ste 410 (28078)
PHONE.....................410 773-7800
EMP: 65
SQ FT: 180,000
SALES (corp-wide): 1.8MM Privately Held
Web: www.apextoolgroup.com
SIC: 3423 Hand and edge tools, nec
HQ: Apex Tool Group, Llc
    910 Ridgebrook Rd Ste 200
    Sparks Glencoe MD 21152

(G-8793)
AREVA
11515 Vanstory Dr Ste 140 (28078-6388)
PHONE.....................704 805-2935
EMP: 11 EST: 2018
SALES (est): 126.37K Privately Held
SIC: 3823 Process control instruments

(G-8794)
ASHLAND PRODUCTS INC
Also Called: Ashland Hardware Systems
8936 N Exec Dr S 250 (28078)
PHONE.....................815 266-0250
▲ EMP: 200
SIC: 3089 Plastics hardware and building products

(G-8795)
ATOM POWER INC
Also Called: Atom Power
13245 Reese Blvd W Ste 130 (28078-6349)
PHONE.....................844 704-2866
Bharat Vats, CEO
Eric Dana, *
EMP: 98 EST: 2014
SALES (est): 16.47MM Privately Held
Web: www.atompower.com
SIC: 3699 Electrical equipment and supplies, nec

(G-8796)
AUTOMATED CONTROLS LLC
13416 S Old Statesville Rd (28078-7261)
P.O. Box 1952 (28070-1952)
PHONE.....................704 724-7625
Joshua J Penn, Prin
EMP: 17 EST: 2008
SQ FT: 1,500
SALES (est): 917.49K Privately Held
Web: www.automatedcontrolsnc.com
SIC: 1799 7382 1731 3446 Fence construction; Fire alarm maintenance and monitoring; Access control systems specialization; Gates, ornamental metal

(G-8797)
BELTSERVICE CORPORATION
9540 Julian Clark Ave (28078-3346)
PHONE.....................704 947-2264
Jim Mcnery, Mgr
EMP: 26
SALES (corp-wide): 135.54MM Privately Held
Web: www.beltservice.com
SIC: 3052 3535 Rubber belting; Conveyors and conveying equipment
PA: Beltservice Corporation
    4143 Rider Trl N
    Earth City MO 63045
    314 344-8500

(G-8798)
BURKERT USA CORPORATION
Also Called: Burkert Fluid Control Systems
11425 Mount Holly Hntrsvlle Rd (28078-7763)
PHONE.....................800 325-1405
Heribert Peter Rohrbeck, Ch Bd
Dietrich Glas, *
Marco Ivan Steinemann, *
EMP: 138 EST: 1984
SQ FT: 198,000
SALES (est): 50.31MM Privately Held
Web: www.burkert.com
SIC: 3491 Industrial valves
HQ: Burkert International Ag
    Bosch 71
    HUnenberg ZG 6331

(G-8799)
CABINET PLUS
13211 Willow Breeze Ln (28078-9620)
PHONE.....................917 698-7708
Mladen Licul, Prin
EMP: 5 EST: 2015
SALES (est): 165.44K Privately Held
Web: www.mycabinetsplus.com
SIC: 2434 Wood kitchen cabinets

(G-8800)
CAMERA TO CANDLE
16016 Loch Raven Rd (28078-0007)
PHONE.....................339 224-1073
EMP: 4 EST: 2016
SALES (est): 66.56K Privately Held
SIC: 3999 Candles

(G-8801)
CELESTIAL PRODUCTS INC
9632 Skybluff Cir (28078-2412)
PHONE.....................540 338-4040
Larry Bohlayer, Pr
Barbara C Bohlayer, VP
EMP: 4 EST: 1980
SALES (est): 315.39K Privately Held
SIC: 2752 Calendars, lithographed

(G-8802)
CENTRAL ARC WLDG SOLUTIONS LLC
12524 Vantage Point Ln (28078-7110)
PHONE.....................704 858-1614
Joanna L Von Staden, Prin
EMP: 5 EST: 2018
SALES (est): 61.53K Privately Held
SIC: 7692 Welding repair

(G-8803)
CITIZEN MEDIA INC
403 N Old Statesville Rd (28078-7203)
PHONE.....................704 363-6062
EMP: 4 EST: 2017
SALES (est): 62.99K Privately Held
SIC: 2711 Newspapers

(G-8804)
COBB CLARK RICHARD II
Also Called: Wrap Attack
12723 Cliffcreek Dr (28078-7893)
PHONE.....................704 274-5479
Clark R Cobb Ii, Prin
EMP: 4 EST: 2007
SALES (est): 110K Privately Held
Web: www.wrapattack.com
SIC: 3993 Signs and advertising specialties

(G-8805)
COMMON PART GROUPINGS LLC
Also Called: Cpg
11601 Hambright Rd (28078-7666)
P.O. Box 2368 (28070-2368)
PHONE.....................704 948-0097
▲ EMP: 10 EST: 2006
SQ FT: 48,000
SALES (est): 1.86MM Privately Held
Web: www.commonpartgroupings.com
SIC: 3441 Fabricated structural metal

(G-8806)
CORSAN LLC
13201 Reese Blvd W Ste 100 (28078-7945)
PHONE.....................704 765-9979
Rusty Broome, Managing Member
Brad Edwards, COO
EMP: 15 EST: 2013
SALES (est): 4.56MM Privately Held
Web: www.corsan.com

SIC: 5051 3999 Miscellaneous nonferrous products; Barber and beauty shop equipment

(G-8807)
COVIA HOLDINGS CORPORATION
Also Called: COVIA HOLDINGS CORPORATION
9930 Kincey Ave # 200 (28078-6541)
PHONE.....................980 495-2092
EMP: 5
SALES (corp-wide): 1.6B Privately Held
Web: www.coviacorp.com
SIC: 1446 Industrial sand
PA: Covia Holdings Llc
    3 Summit Park Dr Ste 700
    Independence OH 44131
    800 255-7263

(G-8808)
CRC PRINTING CO INC
15700 Old Statesville Rd (28078-7238)
PHONE.....................704 875-1804
Robin Holder, Pr
EMP: 4 EST: 1984
SQ FT: 2,660
SALES (est): 417.74K Privately Held
Web: www.crc123.net
SIC: 2752 Offset printing

(G-8809)
DOOR WORKS HUNTERSVILLE LLC
11701 Mccord Rd Bldg 11 (28078-7293)
P.O. Box 430 (28164-0430)
PHONE.....................704 947-1900
EMP: 24 EST: 2003
SALES (est): 2.07MM Privately Held
Web: www.doorworkscompany.com
SIC: 2431 Louver doors: wood

(G-8810)
DURAFIBER TECHNOLOGIES
13620 Reese Blvd E # 400 (28078-6417)
PHONE.....................704 912-3700
EMP: 1500
SALES (est): 103.96K
SALES (corp-wide): 17.78B Privately Held
SIC: 2824 Organic fibers, noncellulosic
HQ: Sun Performance Fibers, Llc
    5200 Town Center Cir # 470
    Boca Raton FL

(G-8811)
DURAFIBER TECHNOLOGIES (DFT) INC
13620 Reese Blvd E Ste 400 (28078-6415)
PHONE.....................704 912-3700
▲ EMP: 1200
SIC: 2824 Organic fibers, noncellulosic

(G-8812)
DURAFIBER TECHNOLOGIES (DFT) OPERATIONS LLC
13620 Reese Blvd E Ste 400 (28078-6417)
PHONE.....................704 912-3770
◆ EMP: 650
SIC: 2824 Organic fibers, noncellulosic

(G-8813)
EAGLE MACHINING USA INC
13728 Statesville Rd (28078-9038)
PHONE.....................717 235-9383
Anthony Lazarek, Pr
Dave Rietschy, *
Marc Childs, *
EMP: 18 EST: 1998
SALES (est): 700.01K Privately Held
SIC: 3599 Machine shop, jobbing and repair

Huntersville - Mecklenburg County (G-8814)

(G-8814)
EIGHTY ORCHARD PUBLISHING INC
15823 Kelly Park Cir (28078-2719)
PHONE..................................980 689-5406
Charles Devon Weaver, *Owner*
EMP: 4 **EST:** 2017
SALES (est): 64.1K **Privately Held**
SIC: 2741 Miscellaneous publishing

(G-8815)
ENSINGER POLYTECH INC (DH) ◆
13728 Statesville Rd (28078-9038)
PHONE..................................704 992-8100
John Tremblay, *VP*
EMP: 8 **EST:** 2022
SALES (est): 11.61MM
SALES (corp-wide): 632.07MM **Privately Held**
Web: www.ensingerplastics.com
SIC: 3577 Computer peripheral equipment, nec
HQ: Ensinger Precision Components, Inc.
11 Danco Rd
Putnam CT 06260

(G-8816)
ERYTHIS INC
8820 Singleton Ct (28078-3216)
PHONE..................................704 644-0963
Leonidas Kyriazis, *Prin*
EMP: 6 **EST:** 2008
SALES (est): 162.78K **Privately Held**
Web: www.bioselect-us.com
SIC: 2844 Perfumes, cosmetics and other toilet preparations

(G-8817)
ESHER LLC
9911 Rose Commons Dr (28078-0323)
PHONE..................................704 975-1463
Joslyn Fyffe, *Prin*
EMP: 5 **EST:** 2015
SALES (est): 241.1K **Privately Held**
SIC: 3446 Ornamental metalwork

(G-8818)
FANUC AMERICA CORPORATION
Also Called: Fanuc Robotics
13245 Reese Blvd W Ste 140 (28078-6307)
PHONE..................................704 596-5121
EMP: 6
Web: www.fanucrobotics.com
SIC: 3559 3548 3569 Metal finishing equipment for plating, etc.; Electric welding equipment; Robots, assembly line: industrial and commercial
HQ: Fanuc America Corporation
3900 W Hamlin Rd
Rochester Hills MI 48309
248 377-7000

(G-8819)
FIDELITY PHARMACEUTICALS LLC
11957 Ramah Church Rd (28078-7271)
PHONE..................................704 274-3192
Joseph Pfeiffer, *CEO*
Matthew Damato, *CEO*
EMP: 5 **EST:** 2021
SALES (est): 462.15K **Privately Held**
Web: www.fidelitypharmaceuticals.com
SIC: 2834 5122 5047 Pharmaceutical preparations; Drugs, proprietaries, and sundries; Medical and hospital equipment

(G-8820)
FINNORD NORTH AMERICA CORP
14514 Sunset Walk Ln (28078-0602)
PHONE..................................704 723-4913
Deln Murphy, *Genl Mgr*
▲ **EMP:** 15 **EST:** 2011
SALES (est): 2.25MM **Privately Held**
Web: www.finnord.it
SIC: 8711 3679 Engineering services; Electronic circuits
HQ: Meccanica Finnord Spa
Via Dante Alighieri 51
Jerago Con Orago VA 21040

(G-8821)
FIRELINE SHIELDS LLC
15336 Old Statesville Rd (28078-7234)
PHONE..................................704 948-3680
Gregory Braham, *Prin*
EMP: 6 **EST:** 2011
SALES (est): 193.3K **Privately Held**
Web: www.firelineshields.com
SIC: 3559 Special industry machinery, nec

(G-8822)
FORBO BELTING
12201 Vanstory Dr (28078-8395)
PHONE..................................704 948-0800
Natlie Deal, *Mgr*
EMP: 31 **EST:** 2007
SALES (est): 4.93MM **Privately Held**
Web: www.forbo.com
SIC: 3052 Rubber belting
HQ: Forbo Siegling, Llc
12201 Vanstory Dr
Huntersville NC 28078
704 948-0800

(G-8823)
FORBO SIEGLING LLC
13245 Reese Blvd W (28078-6307)
PHONE..................................704 948-0800
EMP: 7
Web: www.forbo.com
SIC: 3052 Rubber and plastics hose and beltings
HQ: Forbo Siegling, Llc
12201 Vanstory Dr
Huntersville NC 28078
704 948-0800

(G-8824)
FORBO SIEGLING LLC
12120 Herbert Wayne Ct (28078-6326)
PHONE..................................704 948-0800
EMP: 8
Web: www.forbo.com
SIC: 3052 Rubber belting
HQ: Forbo Siegling, Llc
12201 Vanstory Dr
Huntersville NC 28078
704 948-0800

(G-8825)
FORBO SIEGLING LLC (HQ)
12201 Vanstory Dr (28078-8395)
P.O. Box 60943 (28260-0943)
PHONE..................................704 948-0800
Wayne E Hoffman, *Pr*
Chris Flannigan, *
John Casali, *
Norm Nelson, *
This E Schneider, *
▲ **EMP:** 274 **EST:** 1956
SQ FT: 100,000
SALES (est): 117.39MM **Privately Held**
Web: www.forbo.com
SIC: 3052 3535 Rubber belting; Conveyors and conveying equipment
PA: Forbo Holding Ag
Lindenstrasse 8
Baar ZG 6340

(G-8826)
GF MACHINING SOLUTIONS
13245 Reese Blvd W Ste 100 (28078-6307)
PHONE..................................704 927-8929
EMP: 10 **EST:** 2016
SALES (est): 947.92K **Privately Held**
SIC: 3599 Machine shop, jobbing and repair

(G-8827)
GREAT STAR INDUSTRIAL USA LLC (DH)
9836 Northcross Center Ct Ste A (28078-7344)
PHONE..................................704 892-4965
▲ **EMP:** 4 **EST:** 2012
SQ FT: 5,000
SALES (est): 28.69MM **Privately Held**
SIC: 3423 Carpenters' hand tools, except saws: levels, chisels, etc.
HQ: Great Star Tools Usa, Inc.
271 Mayhill St
Saddle Brook NJ 07663
201 562-1232

(G-8828)
HAWE NORTH AMERICA INC (HQ)
Also Called: Hawe Hydraulics
13020 Jamesburg Dr Ste A (28078-5536)
PHONE..................................704 509-1599
Robert Pettit, *CEO*
Karl Haeusgen, *
Carl Haeusgen, *
Charles Houghton, *
▲ **EMP:** 27 **EST:** 1997
SQ FT: 5,100
SALES (est): 29.58MM
SALES (corp-wide): 514.14MM **Privately Held**
Web: www.hawe.com
SIC: 5085 3492 5084 Hydraulic and pneumatic pistons and valves; Control valves, fluid power: hydraulic and pneumatic; Hydraulic systems equipment and supplies
PA: Hawe Hydraulik Se
Einsteinring 17
Aschheim BY 85609
893791001000

(G-8829)
HEMP AND TEA COMPANY LLC
15906 Old Statesville Rd Ste 100 (28078-7207)
PHONE..................................704 248-8657
EMP: 4 **EST:** 2020
SALES (est): 107.4K **Privately Held**
Web: www.hempandteaco.com
SIC: 2099 Food preparations, nec

(G-8830)
HERALD HUNTERSVILLE
Also Called: Mechlanburg Newspaper Group
200 S Old Statesville Rd (28078-3924)
PHONE..................................704 766-2100
Tucker Mitchell, *Owner*
EMP: 9 **EST:** 2002
SALES (est): 204.16K **Privately Held**
Web: www.lakenormanpublications.com
SIC: 2711 Newspapers, publishing and printing

(G-8831)
HUO LI JUICE & CO LLC
11104 Bryton Pkwy # 5113 (28078-3791)
PHONE..................................804 299-0806
EMP: 12 **EST:** 2021
SALES (est): 536.46K **Privately Held**
SIC: 3556 Juice extractors, fruit and vegetable: commercial type

(G-8832)
HYCORR LLC
10115 Kincey Ave (28078-6469)
PHONE..................................216 570-7408
EMP: 9 **EST:** 2016
SALES (est): 283.56K **Privately Held**
SIC: 3565 Packaging machinery

(G-8833)
IDEA PEOPLE INC
14311 Reese Blvd W (28078-7954)
PHONE..................................704 398-4437
Jay Joyce, *Pr*
Bill Mccown, *VP*
EMP: 6 **EST:** 1994
SQ FT: 7,000
SALES (est): 883.47K **Privately Held**
Web: www.theideapeople.com
SIC: 7372 7311 5942 8748 Application computer software; Advertising agencies; Children's books; Publishing consultant

(G-8834)
INNOVASOURCE LLC
11515 Vanstory Dr Ste 110 (28078-6388)
PHONE..................................704 584-0072
▲ **EMP:** 10 **EST:** 2009
SQ FT: 12,000
SALES (est): 2.46MM
SALES (corp-wide): 2.96B **Publicly Held**
Web: www.innovasource.com
SIC: 2841 Soap and other detergents
PA: Energizer Holdings, Inc.
533 Maryville Univ Dr
Saint Louis MO 63141
314 985-2000

(G-8835)
INTERACTIVE SAFETY PDTS INC
9825 Northcross Center Ct Ste A (28078-7338)
P.O. Box 315 (18407-0315)
PHONE..................................704 664-7377
Jan Korny, *CFO*
▲ **EMP:** 43 **EST:** 1996
SQ FT: 15,000
SALES (est): 8.35MM
SALES (corp-wide): 95.04MM **Privately Held**
Web: www.gentexcorp.com
SIC: 3469 Helmets, steel
HQ: Helmet Integrated Systems Limited
Unit 3
Letchworth HERTS SG6 2
146 247-8000

(G-8836)
INTERNATIONAL MINUTE PRESS
9633 Sunset Grove Dr (28078-0640)
PHONE..................................704 827-7173
EMP: 4 **EST:** 2016
SALES (est): 67.02K **Privately Held**
SIC: 2752 Commercial printing, lithographic

(G-8837)
IRWIN
8936 N Pointe Executive P (28078-4810)
PHONE..................................704 987-4339
EMP: 6 **EST:** 2014
SALES (est): 93.46K **Privately Held**
Web: www.irwin.com
SIC: 3423 Hand and edge tools, nec

(G-8838)
IRWIN INDUSTRIAL TOOL COMPANY (HQ)
Also Called: Irwin Construction Accessories
8935 N Pointe Executive Park Dr (28078-4857)
PHONE..................................704 987-4555
Michael B Polk, *CEO*
Neil R Eibeler, *
◆ **EMP:** 200 **EST:** 1985
SALES (est): 334.56MM
SALES (corp-wide): 15.78B **Publicly Held**
Web: www.irwintools.com

GEOGRAPHIC SECTION
Huntersville - Mecklenburg County (G-8864)

SIC: **3423** 3545 3421 Screw drivers, pliers, chisels, etc. (hand tools); Drill bits, metalworking; Snips, tinners'
PA: Stanley Black & Decker, Inc.
1000 Stanley Dr
New Britain CT 06053
860 225-5111

(G-8839)
ISABELLAS FINE OLIVE OILS & VI
16835 Birkdale Commons Pkwy (28078)
PHONE..............................704 237-4949
EMP: 5 **EST:** 2017
SALES (est): 62.38K **Privately Held**
SIC: **2099** Vinegar

(G-8840)
JAG INDUSTRIES LLC
10408 Remembrance Trl (28078-5914)
PHONE..............................704 655-2507
Joseph Grouse, *Prin*
EMP: 4 **EST:** 2018
SALES (est): 77.07K **Privately Held**
Web: www.jagconstructioncorp.com
SIC: **3999** Manufacturing industries, nec

(G-8841)
JOHN GLEN ALEXANDER CORP
Also Called: Service Team Prfssnals Stop Ch
10015 Andres Duany Dr (28078-0087)
PHONE..............................704 309-7258
EMP: 5 **EST:** 2019
SALES (est): 240.82K **Privately Held**
SIC: **3732** Boatbuilding and repairing

(G-8842)
KEFFER AUTO HUNTERSVILLE LLC
13651 Statesville Rd (28078-9013)
PHONE..............................877 260-4062
James L Keffer, *Prin*
EMP: 8 **EST:** 2012
SALES (est): 234.01K **Privately Held**
SIC: **3559** Automotive related machinery

(G-8843)
KELLANOVA
Also Called: Kellog
13801 Reese Blvd W (28078-6308)
PHONE..............................704 370-1658
Michelle Piegaro, *Mgr*
EMP: 5
SALES (corp-wide): 15.31B **Publicly Held**
Web: www.kellanova.com
SIC: **2043** Cereal breakfast foods
PA: Kellanova
412 N Wells St
Chicago IL 60654
269 961-2000

(G-8844)
KELLER TECHNOLOGY CORPORATION
11905 Vanstory Dr (28078-8121)
PHONE..............................704 875-1605
Robert Paschka, *Brnch Mgr*
EMP: 40
SALES (corp-wide): 150MM **Privately Held**
Web: www.kellertechnology.com
SIC: **8711** 3569 Engineering services; Robots, assembly line: industrial and commercial
PA: Keller Technology Corporation
2320 Military Rd
Tonawanda NY 14150
716 693-3840

(G-8845)
KURZ TRANSFER PRODUCTS LP (HQ)
11836 Patterson Rd (28078-9732)
P.O. Box 63182 (28263-3182)
PHONE..............................704 927-3700
Walter Kurz, *Pt*
Kurz Charlotte, *Pt*
Peter Kurz, *Pt*
Konrad Kurz, *Pt*
▲ **EMP:** 100 **EST:** 1992
SALES (est): 67.2MM
SALES (corp-wide): 1B **Privately Held**
Web: www.kurzusa.com
SIC: **3497** Metal foil and leaf
PA: Leonhard Kurz Stiftung & Co. Kg
Schwabacher Str. 482
Furth BY 90763
91171410

(G-8846)
KWIK KOPY BUSINESS
16630 Northcross Dr Ste 102 (28078-5049)
PHONE..............................704 987-0111
Ron Gomilla, *Owner*
EMP: 5 **EST:** 2014
SALES (est): 204.53K **Privately Held**
Web: www.kwikkopy.com
SIC: **2752** Offset printing

(G-8847)
LAKESHORE CABINET
14034 Holly Springs Dr (28078-4240)
PHONE..............................847 508-3594
EMP: 5 **EST:** 2020
SALES (est): 246.32K **Privately Held**
Web: www.lakeshorecabinet.com
SIC: **2434** Wood kitchen cabinets

(G-8848)
LANART INTERNATIONAL INC
10325 Hambright Rd (28078-7655)
PHONE..............................704 875-1972
Angelo Ponce, *Pr*
EMP: 4 **EST:** 1979
SQ FT: 3,458
SALES (est): 363.26K **Privately Held**
Web: www.lanartalpaca.com
SIC: **2211** Alpacas, cotton

(G-8849)
LEHR LLC
12703 Commerce Station Dr (28078-6825)
PHONE..............................704 827-9368
Patrick Mccullagh, *CEO*
EMP: 18 **EST:** 2014
SALES (est): 1.35MM **Privately Held**
Web: www.golehr.com
SIC: **3519** Marine engines

(G-8850)
LENOX BIRKDALE LLC
16623 Birkdale Commons Pkwy (28078)
PHONE..............................704 997-8116
EMP: 8 **EST:** 2013
SALES (est): 451.6K **Privately Held**
SIC: **3585** Refrigeration and heating equipment

(G-8851)
LENOX LAND
15925 Bayshore Dr (28078-6862)
P.O. Box 673 (28070-0673)
PHONE..............................704 507-4877
Brian Hines, *Prin*
EMP: 4 **EST:** 2018
SALES (est): 79.98K **Privately Held**
SIC: **3585** Refrigeration and heating equipment

(G-8852)
LIECHTI AMERICA
13245 Reese Blvd W Ste 100 (28078-6307)
PHONE..............................704 948-1277
Philip Ward, *COO*
▲ **EMP:** 7 **EST:** 2012
SALES (est): 242.37K **Privately Held**
SIC: **3462** Pump, compressor, and turbine forgings

(G-8853)
MAX DAETWYLER CORP (DH)
Also Called: Daetwyler Cstm Fbrction McHnin
13420 Reese Blvd W (28078-7925)
PHONE..............................704 875-1200
Ralph Daetwyler, *Pr*
Walter Siegenthaler, *
Kurt Oegerli, *
▲ **EMP:** 21 **EST:** 1975
SQ FT: 72,000
SALES (est): 14.61MM **Privately Held**
Web: www.daetwyler-usa.com
SIC: **3599** Electrical discharge machining (EDM)
HQ: Mdc Max Daetwyler Ag
Flugplatz
Bleienbach BE 3368

(G-8854)
MICROBAN PRODUCTS COMPANY
Also Called: Microban
11400 Vanstory Dr (28078-8147)
PHONE..............................704 766-4267
David Mayers, *Pr*
Richard Chapman, *
Tom Bowlds, *
▲ **EMP:** 65 **EST:** 1987
SQ FT: 50,000
SALES (est): 23.65MM
SALES (corp-wide): 390.28MM **Privately Held**
Web: www.microban.com
SIC: **2842** 2819 2821 2899 Specialty cleaning; Industrial inorganic chemicals, nec ; Thermoplastic materials; Chemical preparations, nec
HQ: Microban International, Ltd.
11400 Vanstory Dr
Huntersville NC 28078

(G-8855)
MIRACLE RECREATION EQP CO
11515 Vanstory Dr Ste 100 (28078-6300)
PHONE..............................704 875-6550
Erin Hampton, *Prin*
EMP: 386
Web: www.miracle-recreation.com
SIC: **3949** Playground equipment
HQ: Miracle Recreation Equipment Company
878 E Us Highway 60
Monett MO 65708
888 458-2752

(G-8856)
MLB SCREEN PRINTING
12008 Regal Lily Ln (28078-2396)
PHONE..............................704 363-6124
Michelle L Backstrom, *Prin*
EMP: 5 **EST:** 2013
SALES (est): 143.5K **Privately Held**
SIC: **2752** Commercial printing, lithographic

(G-8857)
MOMENTIVE PERFORMANCE MTLS INC
Also Called: Momentive Performance Mtls USA
13620 Reese Blvd E Ste 310 (28078-6418)
PHONE..............................704 805-6200
EMP: 59
Web: www.momentive.com
SIC: **2869** Silicones
HQ: Momentive Performance Materials Inc.
2750 Balltown Rd
Niskayuna NY 12309

(G-8858)
NEWELL BRANDS INC
Also Called: Testing Facility
9815 Northcross Center Ct Ste 8 (28078-7340)
PHONE..............................704 987-4760
Gary Decarr, *Mgr*
EMP: 30
SALES (corp-wide): 8.13B **Publicly Held**
Web: www.newellbrands.com
SIC: **3089** Plastics kitchenware, tableware, and houseware
PA: Newell Brands Inc.
6655 Peachtree Dunwoody Rd
Atlanta GA 30328
770 418-7000

(G-8859)
NEWELL BRANDS INC
Rubbermaid
8935 N Pointe Executive Park Dr (28078-4857)
PHONE..............................704 895-8082
EMP: 38
SALES (corp-wide): 8.13B **Publicly Held**
Web: www.newellbrands.com
SIC: **3089** Plastics kitchenware, tableware, and houseware
PA: Newell Brands Inc.
6655 Peachtree Dunwoody Rd
Atlanta GA 30328
770 418-7000

(G-8860)
NINOS WLDG & CNSTR SVCS LLC
11901 Everett Keith Rd (28078-3661)
PHONE..............................980 214-5804
Joaquin Guevara Nino, *Prin*
EMP: 7 **EST:** 2016
SALES (est): 181.21K **Privately Held**
SIC: **7692** Welding repair

(G-8861)
NORMAN LAKE GRAPHICS INC
16630 Northcross Dr Ste 102 (28078-5048)
P.O. Box 2280 (28031-2280)
PHONE..............................704 896-8444
EMP: 5 **EST:** 1991
SQ FT: 4,500
SALES (est): 462.96K **Privately Held**
Web: www.lakenormanchamber.org
SIC: **2752** Commercial printing, lithographic

(G-8862)
NOVA WILDCAT DRAPERY HDWR LLC
Also Called: Drapery Hardware
10115 Kincey Ave Ste 210 (28078-6483)
PHONE..............................704 696-5110
EMP: 50 **EST:** 2013
SALES (est): 3.24MM **Privately Held**
SIC: **2591** Drapery hardware and window blinds and shades

(G-8863)
NSI HOLDINGS INC
9730 Northcross Center Ct (28078-7301)
PHONE..............................704 439-2420
G R Schrotenboer, *CEO*
EMP: 10 **EST:** 1989
SALES (est): 171.35K **Privately Held**
Web: www.nsiindustries.com
SIC: **3643** Current-carrying wiring services

(G-8864)
NSI HOLDINGS INC (PA)
13235 Reese Blvd W (28078-7935)

Huntersville - Mecklenburg County (G-8865)
GEOGRAPHIC SECTION

P.O. Box 2725 (28070-2725)
PHONE..................................914 664-3542
Glen Schrotenboer, *Pr*
Victoria White, *Ch Bd*
Leonard Caponigro, *VP Opers*
Nicholas Murlo, *VP Engg*
▲ **EMP:** 11 **EST:** 1934
SALES (est): 21.68MM
SALES (corp-wide): 21.68MM **Privately Held**
Web: www.nsiindustries.com
SIC: 3643 3585 Connectors and terminals for electrical devices; Refrigeration and heating equipment

(G-8865)
NSI INDUSTRIES
9730 Northcross Center Ct (28078-7301)
PHONE..................................800 321-5847
EMP: 100
SALES (corp-wide): 9.22MM **Privately Held**
SIC: 3625 Relays and industrial controls
PA: Nsi Industries
   9730 Northcross Center Ct
   Huntersville NC 28078
   914 664-3542

(G-8866)
NSI INDUSTRIES LLC (PA)
Also Called: Nsi Tork
13235 Reese Blvd W (28078-7935)
P.O. Box 2725 (28070-2725)
PHONE..................................800 321-5847
◆ **EMP:** 100 **EST:** 2004
SQ FT: 43,000
SALES (est): 173.63MM **Privately Held**
Web: www.nsiindustries.com
SIC: 3643 Connectors and terminals for electrical devices

(G-8867)
NUTEC INC
11830 Mount Holly Hntrsvlle Rd (28078-7628)
PHONE..................................877 318-2430
Gilberto Wells, *CEO*
EMP: 30 **EST:** 2015
SALES (est): 8.67MM **Privately Held**
Web: www.nutec.com
SIC: 3567 Heating units and devices, industrial: electric
PA: Grupo Nutec, S.A. De C.V.
   Jardin De San Jeronimo No. 225
   Monterrey NLE 64640

(G-8868)
OASIS MAGAZINE LLC
10225 Hickorywood Hill Ave (28078-3430)
PHONE..................................888 559-7549
EMP: 8 **EST:** 2008
SALES (est): 197.56K **Privately Held**
SIC: 2721 Magazines: publishing and printing

(G-8869)
OCUFII INC ⊖
11211 James Coy Rd (28078-5131)
PHONE..................................804 874-4036
William Sandoval, *Pr*
EMP: 4 **EST:** 2023
SALES (est): 168.32K **Privately Held**
SIC: 7372 7389 Prepackaged software; Business Activities at Non-Commercial Site

(G-8870)
OERLIKON AM US INC
12012 Vanstory Dr (28078-8324)
PHONE..................................980 260-2827
Roland Fischer, *CEO*
EMP: 50 **EST:** 2017
SALES (est): 16.97MM **Privately Held**
SIC: 5084 2851 Industrial machinery and equipment; Coating, air curing
PA: Oc Oerlikon Corporation Ag, Pfaffikon
   Churerstrasse 120
   PfAffikon SZ 8808

(G-8871)
OERLIKON METCO (US) INC
12012 Vanstory Dr (28078-8324)
PHONE..................................713 715-6300
EMP: 10
Web: www.oerlikon.com
SIC: 3399 5084 3479 Powder, metal; Industrial machinery and equipment; Coating of metals and formed products
HQ: Oerlikon Metco (Us) Inc.
   1101 Prospect Ave
   Westbury NY 11590
   516 334-1300

(G-8872)
ORANGE BAKERY INC
13400 Reese Blvd W (28078-7925)
PHONE..................................704 875-3003
Yoshiaki Okacaki, *Dir*
EMP: 30
SQ FT: 45,063
Web: www.orangebakery.com
SIC: 2038 2053 2051 Frozen specialties, nec ; Frozen bakery products, except bread; Bread, cake, and related products
HQ: Orange Bakery, Inc.
   17751 Cowan
   Irvine CA 92614
   949 863-1377

(G-8873)
PCS COLLECTIBLES LLC (PA)
Also Called: Culture Shock Toys
9825 Northcross Center Ct (28078-7339)
PHONE..................................805 306-1140
Anthony Adams, *Managing Member*
EMP: 9 **EST:** 2017
SALES (est): 8.28MM
SALES (corp-wide): 8.28MM **Privately Held**
Web: www.collectpcs.com
SIC: 3942 Dolls and stuffed toys

(G-8874)
PERFORMANCE FIBERS
12721 Longstock Ct (28078-5718)
PHONE..................................704 947-7193
Gareth Jones, *Prin*
EMP: 10 **EST:** 2010
SALES (est): 593.29K **Privately Held**
SIC: 2221 Polyester broadwoven fabrics

(G-8875)
PLASMA SURGICAL
9924 Bayart Way (28078-4900)
PHONE..................................704 608-6756
Brian Register, *Prin*
EMP: 5 **EST:** 2017
SALES (est): 105.43K **Privately Held**
SIC: 2836 Plasmas

(G-8876)
PLAYPOWER INC (DH)
11515 Vanstory Dr Ste 100 (28078-6300)
PHONE..................................704 949-1600
Bryan Yeazel, *CEO*
Michael Pruss, *
Lynn Vandever, *
Brenda Mcclelland, *Contrlr*
◆ **EMP:** 58 **EST:** 1993
SQ FT: 124,260
SALES (est): 167.16MM **Privately Held**
Web: www.playpower.com
SIC: 3949 Playground equipment
HQ: Playpower Holdings Inc.
   11515 Vanstory Dr Ste 100
   Huntersville NC 28078

(G-8877)
POLY-TECH INDUSTRIAL INC
11330 Vanstory Dr (28078-8143)
PHONE..................................704 992-8100
Daniel Cedrone, *Prin*
EMP: 6 **EST:** 2015
SALES (est): 2.26MM **Privately Held**
Web: www.ensinger-pc.com
SIC: 3089 Injection molding of plastics

(G-8878)
POLY-TECH INDUSTRIAL INC
13728 Statesville Rd (28078-9038)
PHONE..................................704 948-8055
EMP: 35 **EST:** 2015
SALES (est): 11.61MM
SALES (corp-wide): 632.07MM **Privately Held**
Web: www.ensinger-pc.com
SIC: 5162 3089 Plastics materials and basic shapes; Molding primary plastics
HQ: Ensinger Polytech, Inc.
   13728 Statesville Rd
   Huntersville NC 28078
   704 992-8100

(G-8879)
POPPIES LLC
16815 Cranlyn Rd Ste A (28078-1831)
PHONE..................................704 896-3433
Cydney White, *Prin*
EMP: 5 **EST:** 2001
SALES (est): 264.52K **Privately Held**
Web: www.poppiesgifts.com
SIC: 2759 5947 Invitation and stationery printing and engraving; Gift shop

(G-8880)
POWERBRAKE CORPORATION
14514 Sunset Walk Ln (28078-0602)
PHONE..................................704 804-2438
EMP: 7 **EST:** 2016
SALES (est): 67.19K **Privately Held**
Web: www.powerbrakeglobal.com
SIC: 3714 Motor vehicle parts and accessories

(G-8881)
PRATT MLLER ENGRG FBRCTION LLC
9801 Kincey Ave Ste 175 (28078-3104)
PHONE..................................704 977-0642
Christopher Gilligan, *Brnch Mgr*
EMP: 175
SALES (corp-wide): 9.66B **Publicly Held**
Web: www.prattmiller.com
SIC: 3711 8711 Automobile assembly, including specialty automobiles; Engineering services
HQ: Pratt & Miller Engineering & Fabrication, Llc
   29600 Wk Smith Dr
   New Hudson MI 48165

(G-8882)
PRINT ADVISORS LLC
15905 Brookway Dr Ste 4105 (28078-3240)
PHONE..................................704 385-4315
Greg Razewski, *Prin*
EMP: 7 **EST:** 2017
SALES (est): 250.66K **Privately Held**
Web: www.myprintadvisors.com
SIC: 2752 Commercial printing, lithographic

(G-8883)
PRINT SOCIAL
403 Gilead Rd Ste A (28078-6814)
PHONE..................................980 430-4483
EMP: 4 **EST:** 2016
SALES (est): 86.67K **Privately Held**
Web: www.primoprint.com
SIC: 2752 Commercial printing, lithographic

(G-8884)
PUZZLES FROM PAST LLC
17424 Invermere Ave (28078-4830)
PHONE..................................704 231-5878
Allison Hamme, *Prin*
EMP: 4 **EST:** 2019
SALES (est): 71.11K **Privately Held**
Web: www.puzzlesfromthepast.com
SIC: 3944 Puzzles

(G-8885)
REYNOLDS CONSUMER PRODUCTS INC
Also Called: Reynolds Consumer Products
14201 Meacham Farm Dr (28078-8000)
PHONE..................................704 371-5550
EMP: 856
Web: www.reynoldsbrands.com
SIC: 2673 3497 3089 2621 Food storage and trash bags (plastic); Metal foil and leaf; Plastics containers, except foam; Pressed and molded pulp and fiber products
HQ: Reynolds Consumer Products Inc.
   1900 W Field Ct
   Lake Forest IL 60045
   800 879-5067

(G-8886)
RICURA CORPORATION
11515 Vanstory Dr Ste 110 (28078-6388)
PHONE..................................704 875-0366
Glen Cueman, *Pr*
Barnwell Ramsey, *VP*
▲ **EMP:** 10 **EST:** 1996
SQ FT: 12,000
SALES (est): 2.01MM **Privately Held**
Web: www.ricura.com
SIC: 3564 5075 Filters, air: furnaces, air conditioning equipment, etc.; Air pollution control equipment and supplies

(G-8887)
ROYAL FAIRES INC (PA)
16445 Poplar Tent Rd (28078-4620)
PHONE..................................704 896-5555
Jeffrey Siegel, *Prin*
Robert Levine C F O, *Prin*
EMP: 12 **EST:** 1993
SALES (est): 4.1MM **Privately Held**
SIC: 7922 2731 Theatrical producers and services; Book publishing

(G-8888)
RUBBERMAID COMMERCIAL PDTS LLC (DH)
Also Called: Rubbermaid
8900 N Pointe Executive Park Dr (28078)
PHONE..................................540 667-8700
Mike Mcdermott, *CEO*
◆ **EMP:** 1000 **EST:** 1968
SQ FT: 750,000
SALES (est): 361.49MM
SALES (corp-wide): 8.13B **Publicly Held**
Web: www.rubbermaidcommercial.com
SIC: 3089 2673 Plastics containers, except foam; Bags: plastic, laminated, and coated
HQ: Rubbermaid Incorporated
   6655 Pachtree Dunwoody Rd
   Atlanta GA 30328
   888 895-2110

(G-8889)
RUBBERMAID INCORPORATED
Also Called: Rubbermaid

GEOGRAPHIC SECTION

Hurdle Mills - Person County (G-8914)

16905 Northcross Dr Ste 120 (28078)
PHONE..................................888 859-8294
David Walsh, *Brnch Mgr*
EMP: 1386
SALES (corp-wide): 8.13B **Publicly Held**
Web: www.rubbermaid.com
SIC: 3089 Buckets, plastics
HQ: Rubbermaid Incorporated
6655 Pachtree Dunwoody Rd
Atlanta GA 30328
888 895-2110

(G-8890)
RUBBERMAID INCORPORATED
Also Called: Rubbermaid
8936 N Pointe Executive Park Dr (28078)
PHONE..................................704 987-4339
Steve Taylor, *Brnch Mgr*
EMP: 1487
SALES (corp-wide): 8.13B **Publicly Held**
Web: www.rubbermaid.com
SIC: 3089 Buckets, plastics
HQ: Rubbermaid Incorporated
6655 Pachtree Dunwoody Rd
Atlanta GA 30328
888 895-2110

(G-8891)
SAERTEX MULTICOM LP (DH)
12200 Mount Holly Hntrsvlle Rd (28078-7632)
PHONE..................................704 946-9229
Frank Mersamann, *Pt*
▲ **EMP:** 10 **EST:** 2013
SQ FT: 100,000
SALES (est): 9.83MM
SALES (corp-wide): 404.25MM **Privately Held**
Web: www.saertex-multicom.de
SIC: 3312 Pipes and tubes
HQ: Saertex Holding Gmbh & Co.Kg
Brochterbecker Damm 52
Saerbeck NW 48369
25749020

(G-8892)
SAERTEX MULTICOM LP
12200 Mount Holly Hntrsvlle Rd Ste A (28078-7632)
PHONE..................................704 946-9229
Frank Mersamann, *Pt*
EMP: 20
SALES (corp-wide): 404.25MM **Privately Held**
Web: www.saertex-multicom.de
SIC: 3312 Pipes and tubes
HQ: Saertex Multicom Lp
12200 Mt Hly Hntrsvle Rd A
Huntersville NC 28078
704 946-9229

(G-8893)
SAERTEX USA LLC (DH)
12200 Mount Holly Hntrsvlle Rd (28078-7631)
PHONE..................................704 464-5998
Ulrich Tombuelt, *COO*
◆ **EMP:** 24 **EST:** 2000
SQ FT: 22,000
SALES (est): 45.65MM
SALES (corp-wide): 404.25MM **Privately Held**
Web: www.saertex.com
SIC: 2297 Nonwoven fabrics
HQ: Saertex Beteiligungsges. Mbh
Brochterbecker Damm 52
Saerbeck NW 48369
25749020

(G-8894)
SAINT-GOBAIN VETROTEX AMER INC
8936 N Pointe Executive Park Dr Ste 165 (28078-0806)
PHONE..................................704 895-5906
Miguel Furray, *Mgr*
EMP: 152
SALES (corp-wide): 397.78MM **Privately Held**
Web: www.saint-gobain-northamerica.com
SIC: 3089 Spouting, plastics and glass fiber reinforced
HQ: Saint-Gobain Vetrotex America, Inc.
20 Moores Rd
Valley Forge PA 19482

(G-8895)
SCALABLE SOFTWARE INC
9320 Old Barnette Pl (28078-8364)
PHONE..................................713 316-4900
EMP: 8 **EST:** 2017
SALES (est): 75.07K **Privately Held**
Web: www.scalable.com
SIC: 7372 Prepackaged software

(G-8896)
SEG SYSTEMS LLC
10701 Hambright Rd (28078-7659)
PHONE..................................704 579-5800
Reid Johnson, *Pr*
EMP: 13 **EST:** 2014
SALES (est): 5.05MM
SALES (corp-wide): 98.8MM **Privately Held**
Web: www.segsystems.com
SIC: 3354 Aluminum extruded products
PA: Orbus, Llc
9033 Murphy Rd
Woodridge IL 60517
630 226-1155

(G-8897)
SMC CORPORATION OF AMERICA
9801 Kincey Ave Ste 150 (28078-3106)
PHONE..................................704 947-7556
Lisa Shue, *Mgr*
EMP: 11
Web: www.smcusa.com
SIC: 3652 Prerecorded records and tapes
HQ: Smc Corporation Of America
10100 Smc Blvd
Noblesville IN 46060
317 899-4440

(G-8898)
SOUTHWIRE COMPANY LLC
Also Called: Southwire
12331 Commerce Station Dr (28078-6823)
PHONE..................................704 379-9600
EMP: 18
SALES (corp-wide): 1.7B **Privately Held**
Web: www.southwire.com
SIC: 3355 Aluminum rolling and drawing, nec
PA: Southwire Company, Llc
1 Southwire Dr
Carrollton GA 30119
770 832-4529

(G-8899)
STANLEY BLACK & DECKER
9829 Northcross Center Ct (28078-7302)
PHONE..................................704 987-2271
EMP: 32 **EST:** 2018
SALES (est): 243.81K **Privately Held**
Web: www.stanleyblackanddecker.com
SIC: 3546 Power-driven handtools

(G-8900)
STANLEY BLACK & DECKER INC
9930 Kincey Ave (28078-6541)
PHONE..................................704 293-9392
EMP: 5
SALES (corp-wide): 15.78B **Publicly Held**
Web: www.stanleyblackanddecker.com
SIC: 3545 Machine tool accessories
PA: Stanley Black & Decker, Inc.
1000 Stanley Dr
New Britain CT 06053
860 225-5111

(G-8901)
STITCH-N-SASSY
10303 Remembrance Trl (28078-5913)
PHONE..................................704 491-8274
Traci Wood, *Prin*
EMP: 4 **EST:** 2014
SALES (est): 44.26K **Privately Held**
SIC: 2395 Embroidery and art needlework

(G-8902)
SUNCAST CORPORATION
9801 Kincey Ave (28078-3110)
PHONE..................................704 274-5394
Jennifer Fensley, *Owner*
EMP: 24
SALES (corp-wide): 286.25MM **Privately Held**
Web: www.suncast.com
SIC: 2519 Lawn furniture, except wood, metal, stone, or concrete
PA: Suncast Corporation
701 N Kirk Rd
Batavia IL 60510
630 879-2050

(G-8903)
TRUNORTH WRRNTY PLANS N AMER L
16740 Birkdale Commons Pkwy (28078)
PHONE..................................800 903-7489
EMP: 34 **EST:** 2015
SALES (est): 4.15MM **Privately Held**
Web: www.trunorthwarranty.com
SIC: 3537 Trucks, tractors, loaders, carriers, and similar equipment

(G-8904)
TUDG MULTIMEDIA FIRM
Also Called: Grapgic Design
12523 Surreykirt Ln (28078-4306)
PHONE..................................704 916-9819
EMP: 7 **EST:** 2011
SALES (est): 191.31K **Privately Held**
SIC: 2741 Miscellaneous publishing

(G-8905)
VISION WOODWORKS LLC
9306 Stawell Dr (28078-9322)
PHONE..................................704 779-0734
EMP: 4 **EST:** 2015
SALES (est): 72.41K **Privately Held**
SIC: 2431 Millwork

(G-8906)
WIRENET INC
16740 Birkdale Commons Pkwy Ste 306 (28078)
PHONE..................................513 774-7759
Kenneth Cowan, *Pr*
EMP: 22 **EST:** 2000
SQ FT: 5,000
SALES (est): 1.01MM **Privately Held**
SIC: 1623 8742 3663 3441 Transmitting tower (telecommunication) construction; Management consulting services; Radio and t.v. communications equipment; Fabricated structural metal

(G-8907)
WRIGHT INDUSTRIES LLC
10841 Dry Stone Dr (28078-3632)
PHONE..................................919 824-2936
EMP: 5 **EST:** 2011
SALES (est): 54.89K **Privately Held**
SIC: 3999 Manufacturing industries, nec

(G-8908)
YAT USA INC
10506 Bryton Corporate Center Dr (28078-0142)
PHONE..................................480 584-4096
Todd Murphy, *Pr*
EMP: 8 **EST:** 2017
SALES (est): 529.42K **Privately Held**
SIC: 3545 5072 5251 Tools and accessories for machine tools; Power tools and accessories; Tools, power

Hurdle Mills
Person County

(G-8909)
KYSON LEATHER INCORPORATED
9333 Tapp Rd (27541-8018)
PHONE..................................919 245-0053
Sonya H Hschofield, *Pr*
EMP: 5 **EST:** 2016
SALES (est): 142.34K **Privately Held**
SIC: 3172 Personal leather goods, nec

(G-8910)
MAINES WOODWORKS CSTM MIL LLC
1224 Crowsnest Dr (27541-7425)
PHONE..................................336 263-0799
EMP: 4 **EST:** 2019
SALES (est): 54.13K **Privately Held**
SIC: 2431 Millwork

(G-8911)
MONTICELLO LABS INC
4604 Brodog Ter (27541-8918)
P.O. Box 610 (27278-0610)
PHONE..................................919 623-6390
Edward Eastman, *Pr*
EMP: 4 **EST:** 2002
SALES (est): 348.3K **Privately Held**
SIC: 2861 Gum and wood chemicals

(G-8912)
R&R CUSTOM EMBROIDERY LLC
26 Bridger Farm Rd (27541-7335)
PHONE..................................336 693-5029
Rachel Walker, *Ofcr*
EMP: 6 **EST:** 2018
SALES (est): 65.11K **Privately Held**
Web: www.rrcustomembroidery.com
SIC: 2759 Screen printing

(G-8913)
RED WOLFE INDUSTRIES LLC
1118 Crowsnest Dr (27541-7427)
PHONE..................................336 570-2282
Michael Seymour, *Admn*
EMP: 4 **EST:** 2019
SALES (est): 84.12K **Privately Held**
SIC: 3999 Manufacturing industries, nec

(G-8914)
ROCK AGES WINERY & VINYRD INC
1890 Charlie Long Rd (27541-7363)
PHONE..................................336 364-7625
EMP: 7 **EST:** 2020
SALES (est): 177.76K **Privately Held**
Web: www.rockofageswinery.com
SIC: 2084 Wines

(G-8915)
WILLOW OAK WOODWORKS
430 Charlie Monk Rd (27541-7836)
PHONE....................919 906-1232
Julia Alliger, *Prin*
EMP: 5 **EST:** 2015
SALES (est): 72.04K **Privately Held**
SIC: 2431 Millwork

Icard
Burke County

(G-8916)
ARTCRAFT PRESS INC
7814 Old Hwy 10 (28666)
P.O. Box 130 (28666-0130)
PHONE....................828 397-8612
Mike Wallace, *Pr*
EMP: 12 **EST:** 1947
SQ FT: 6,200
SALES (est): 419.81K **Privately Held**
Web: www.artcraftpress.org
SIC: 2752 2759 Offset printing; Letterpress printing

Indian Trail
Union County

(G-8917)
3 STAR ENTERPRISES LLC
Also Called: Bce South
115 Business Park Dr (28079-9432)
P.O. Box 829 (28079-0829)
PHONE....................704 821-7503
EMP: 20 **EST:** 1989
SQ FT: 5,600
SALES (est): 1.61MM **Privately Held**
Web: www.bcesouth.com
SIC: 2752 Visiting cards, lithographed

(G-8918)
ADD-ON TECHNOLOGIES INC
7000 Stinson Hartis Rd Ste D (28079-8807)
PHONE....................704 882-2227
Ray Van Vynckt, *Pr*
EMP: 10 **EST:** 1994
SALES (est): 1.52MM **Privately Held**
Web: www.addontechnologies.com
SIC: 7371 3578 Computer software development; Billing machines

(G-8919)
ANDARK GRAPHICS INC
7204 Stinson Hartis Rd Ste A (28079-8835)
PHONE....................704 882-1400
Rob Sellers, *Prin*
EMP: 6 **EST:** 2007
SALES (est): 470.65K **Privately Held**
Web: www.andarkgraphics.com
SIC: 3993 Signs and advertising specialties

(G-8920)
ANDRONICS CONSTRUCTION INC
Also Called: Andronx
110 Business Park Dr (28079-9432)
PHONE....................704 400-9562
Yelena Andronic, *Pr*
Ivan Andronic, *
EMP: 30 **EST:** 2005
SQ FT: 13,000
SALES (est): 3.29MM **Privately Held**
Web: www.andronx.com
SIC: 2431 1751 Staircases and stairs, wood; Cabinet building and installation

(G-8921)
AUDIO VDEO CONCEPTS DESIGN INC
Also Called: Co-Da
1409 Babbage Ln Ste B (28079-3458)
PHONE....................704 821-2823
Chris Wissa, *Pr*
Robert Burns, *VP*
EMP: 5 **EST:** 2011
SALES (est): 1.57MM **Privately Held**
Web: www.co-da.com
SIC: 3699 1731 Security control equipment and systems; Electronic controls installation

(G-8922)
AUSTIN BUSINESS FORMS INC
Also Called: Austin Print Solutions
241 Post Office Dr Ste A5 (28079-7676)
P.O. Box 1905 (28106-1905)
PHONE....................704 821-6165
Robert L Austin, *Pr*
Terry S Austin, *VP*
Bart Austin, *VP*
EMP: 10 **EST:** 1991
SALES (est): 1.74MM **Privately Held**
Web: austin.untapd.us
SIC: 5112 2759 Business forms; Commercial printing, nec

(G-8923)
B & B INDUSTRIES INC
4824 Unionville Indian Trail Rd W Ste A (28079-9567)
PHONE....................704 882-4688
Gary Beck, *Pr*
Sandra Beck, *Sec*
EMP: 6 **EST:** 1992
SQ FT: 7,000
SALES (est): 953.55K **Privately Held**
Web: www.coloradogolflinks.com
SIC: 3599 Machine shop, jobbing and repair

(G-8924)
BRANCH OFFICE SOLUTIONS INC
4391 Indian Trail Fairview Rd Ste A (28079-9656)
PHONE....................800 743-1047
Jeffrey Pitney, *Pr*
Jeffrey Pitney, *Pr*
Chris Heffner, *VP*
EMP: 6 **EST:** 2008
SQ FT: 4,000
SALES (est): 991.43K **Privately Held**
Web: www.branchcopy.com
SIC: 5044 3955 3577 7334 Office equipment ; Print cartridges for laser and other computer printers; Printers, computer; Photocopying and duplicating services

(G-8925)
CALL PRINTING & COPYING
311 Indian Trail Rd S (28079-9101)
P.O. Box 31 (28079-0031)
PHONE....................704 821-6554
Greg Rogers, *Owner*
EMP: 6 **EST:** 1981
SQ FT: 3,200
SALES (est): 286.44K **Privately Held**
Web: www.callprinting.com
SIC: 2752 Offset printing

(G-8926)
CAROLINA BLUE PUBLISHING LLC
5105 Candleglow Ct (28079-7697)
PHONE....................704 628-6290
Kimberley Miller, *Prin*
EMP: 4 **EST:** 2016
SALES (est): 77.73K **Privately Held**
SIC: 2711 Newspapers

(G-8927)
COATINGS TECHNOLOGIES INC
Also Called: C T I
214 Plyler Rd (28079-7589)
P.O. Box 2400 (28079-2400)
PHONE....................704 821-8231
David C Mccallister, *Pr*
David C Mc Callister Junior, *Pr*
Nancy Mc Callister, *Sec*
EMP: 18 **EST:** 1988
SQ FT: 3,200
SALES (est): 795.52K **Privately Held**
Web: www.coatingstechnologies.com
SIC: 3479 Coating of metals and formed products

(G-8928)
CRYSTAL IMPRESSIONS LTD
14200 E Independence Blvd (28079-7833)
P.O. Box 280 (28079-0280)
PHONE....................704 821-7678
Clive Berman, *Pr*
EMP: 10 **EST:** 1985
SALES (est): 387.89K **Privately Held**
Web: www.thecrystalshoppe.com
SIC: 2759 2396 Screen printing; Automotive and apparel trimmings

(G-8929)
DOODLE SASSER DISTILLING LLC
171 Associate Ln (28079-7840)
PHONE....................704 806-6594
Paul Collins, *Prin*
EMP: 7 **EST:** 2017
SALES (est): 127.45K **Privately Held**
Web: www.thegreenwagonfarm.com
SIC: 2085 Distilled and blended liquors

(G-8930)
DRYDOG BARRIERS LLC
2034 Van Buren Ave Ste C (28079-5596)
P.O. Box 743 (28106-0743)
PHONE....................704 334-8222
▲ **EMP:** 5
SIC: 1799 2385 Waterproofing; Aprons, waterproof: made from purchased materials

(G-8931)
ELIZABETH LOGISTIC LLC
1000 Loudoun Rd (28079-8478)
PHONE....................803 920-3931
Melody Williams, *Managing Member*
EMP: 65 **EST:** 2017
SALES (est): 2.5MM **Privately Held**
SIC: 4731 4214 7372 Freight forwarding; Local trucking with storage; Application computer software

(G-8932)
ETK INTERNATIONAL INC
1005 Andrea Pl (28079-5529)
P.O. Box 2394 (28079-2394)
PHONE....................704 819-1541
Douglas Todd, *Pr*
Dunja Todd, *Treas*
▲ **EMP:** 4 **EST:** 2003
SALES (est): 493.45K **Privately Held**
Web: www.etkinternational.com
SIC: 3553 Woodworking machinery

(G-8933)
EXHIBIT WORLD INC
13701 E Independence Blvd (28079-7600)
PHONE....................704 882-2272
Dennis J Rogers, *Pr*
Phyllis Rogers, *VP*
EMP: 6 **EST:** 1974
SQ FT: 35,000
SALES (est): 473.85K **Privately Held**
Web: www.exhibit-world.com
SIC: 7389 3993 Exhibit construction by industrial contractors; Signs and advertising specialties

(G-8934)
FERGUSON HIGHWAY PRODUCTS INC
212 Old Dutch Rd W (28079-8771)
PHONE....................704 320-3087
Helen Ferguson, *Pr*
Patrick Ferguson, *VP*
EMP: 5 **EST:** 2004
SALES (est): 499K **Privately Held**
Web: www.fergusonhp.com
SIC: 3531 Construction machinery

(G-8935)
FIRST DUE PRINTS INC
1202 Technology Dr Ste B (28079-7815)
PHONE....................704 320-1251
Lia Schwinghammer, *Prin*
EMP: 6 **EST:** 2013
SALES (est): 204.53K **Privately Held**
Web: www.firstdueprints.com
SIC: 2752 Offset printing

(G-8936)
GAME DAY CROCHET
1005 Dunard Ct (28079-5389)
PHONE....................704 635-7557
Becky Edwards, *Prin*
EMP: 4 **EST:** 2017
SALES (est): 55.11K **Privately Held**
Web: www.marlybird.com
SIC: 2399 Hand woven and crocheted products

(G-8937)
GENERAL ELECTRIC COMPANY
Also Called: GE
171 Associate Ln (28079-7840)
PHONE....................704 821-8260
Cheerie Shelton, *Brnch Mgr*
EMP: 10
SALES (corp-wide): 67.95B **Publicly Held**
Web: www.ge.com
SIC: 3829 Measuring and controlling devices, nec
PA: General Electric Company
    1 Financial Ctr Ste 3700
    Boston MA 02111
    617 443-3000

(G-8938)
HEAVY ARMOR DIVISION LLC
7916 Stinson Hartis Rd (28079-9699)
PHONE....................980 328-8883
Danny Hasty, *Prin*
EMP: 5 **EST:** 2016
SALES (est): 241.97K **Privately Held**
Web: www.heavyarmordivision.com
SIC: 3489 Ordnance and accessories, nec

(G-8939)
HITECH CIRCUITS INC
Also Called: Circuits
7711 Idlewild Rd (28079-7628)
P.O. Box 1796 (28079-1796)
PHONE....................336 838-3420
Jerambhai Patel, *Pr*
Ramesh M Sanghani, *VP*
Kiran Patel, *Prin*
Ramnik Sanghani, *Sec*
Mahesh Patel, *Treas*
EMP: 24 **EST:** 1987
SQ FT: 22,000
SALES (est): 487.63K **Privately Held**
SIC: 3672 Printed circuit boards

GEOGRAPHIC SECTION

Indian Trail - Union County (G-8967)

(G-8940)
KBK CABINETRY INC
9812 Running Cedar Ln (28079-7706)
PHONE.................................704 506-0088
Kenneth Kiser, *Prin*
EMP: 5 **EST:** 2010
SALES (est): 216.56K **Privately Held**
SIC: 2434 Wood kitchen cabinets

(G-8941)
KC STONE ENTERPRISE INC
3006 Sardis Dr (28079-3625)
PHONE.................................704 907-1361
Esselito Solano, *Pr*
EMP: 6 **EST:** 2015
SALES (est): 147.24K **Privately Held**
SIC: 2434 Wood kitchen cabinets

(G-8942)
KESSLER INC
7171 Stinson Hartis Rd (28079-9617)
PHONE.................................248 717-0027
Marius Frum, *Prin*
EMP: 9 **EST:** 2019
SALES (est): 601.3K **Privately Held**
Web: www.kessler-axles.com
SIC: 3714 Motor vehicle parts and accessories

(G-8943)
KNIGHT COMMUNICATIONS INC
Also Called: Carolina Fire Journal
6301 Creft Cir (28079-9544)
PHONE.................................704 568-7804
Randall Baxter Knight, *Pr*
EMP: 12 **EST:** 1974
SALES (est): 1.79MM **Privately Held**
Web: www.baxterknight.com
SIC: 2721 7389 Magazines: publishing and printing; Advertising, promotional, and trade show services

(G-8944)
LARU INDUSTRIES INC
Also Called: Bce South
115 Business Park Dr (28079-9432)
P.O. Box 829 (28079-0829)
PHONE.................................704 821-7503
Larry Kunar, *Pr*
Ruth Kunar, *Sec*
EMP: 10 **EST:** 1989
SQ FT: 5,500
SALES (est): 473.09K **Privately Held**
Web: www.bcesouth.com
SIC: 2759 Thermography

(G-8945)
LIQUID PROCESS SYSTEMS INC
1025 Technology Dr Ste A (28079-5514)
PHONE.................................704 821-1115
Judy Shums, *Pr*
▼ **EMP:** 5 **EST:** 1992
SQ FT: 5,600
SALES (est): 556.37K **Privately Held**
Web: www.lps-filtration.com
SIC: 3677 3569 Filtration devices, electronic; Filters

(G-8946)
LOGIC MANUFACTURING INC
4009 Fawnbrooke Dr (28079-3704)
PHONE.................................704 821-0535
Teresa Wilkie-hoefl, *Ch*
Robert Hoefl Ii, *Pr*
EMP: 27 **EST:** 1997
SQ FT: 10,000
SALES (est): 4.27MM **Privately Held**
Web: www.logicmfginc.com
SIC: 3599 Machine shop, jobbing and repair

(G-8947)
M & M TECHNOLOGY INC
7711 Idlewild Rd (28079-7628)
P.O. Box 1796 (28079-1796)
PHONE.................................704 882-9432
Majid Babaie, *CEO*
Jerambhai Patel, *
Ramnik Sanghani, *
▲ **EMP:** 26 **EST:** 1996
SQ FT: 24,000
SALES (est): 4.68MM **Privately Held**
Web: www.mandm-tech.com
SIC: 3672 Printed circuit boards

(G-8948)
MACHINE TOOL COMPONENTS LLC
1507 Turring Dr Ste D (28079-8473)
PHONE.................................866 466-0120
Dorian Popescu, *Managing Member*
▲ **EMP:** 6 **EST:** 2012
SQ FT: 3,000
SALES (est): 552.39K **Privately Held**
Web: www.machinetoolcomponents.com
SIC: 3541 5085 5084 Machine tool replacement & repair parts, metal cutting types; Industrial supplies; Industrial machine parts

(G-8949)
MICRO LENS TECHNOLOGY INC
2001 Van Buren Ave (28079-5573)
PHONE.................................704 893-2109
Mary Ellen Conley, *Mgr*
EMP: 7
SQ FT: 2,250
SALES (corp-wide): 787.9K **Privately Held**
Web: www.microlens.com
SIC: 3089 Injection molding of plastics
PA: Micro Lens Technology, Inc
 3308 Mikelynn Dr
 Matthews NC 28105
 704 847-9234

(G-8950)
MULCH SOLUTIONS LLC
1011 Thessallian Ln (28079-5793)
P.O. Box 2933 (28079-2933)
PHONE.................................704 893-5302
Mack Oneal Partee Junior, *Pr*
EMP: 7 **EST:** 2017
SALES (est): 498.52K **Privately Held**
Web: www.mulch-solutions.com
SIC: 2499 Mulch or sawdust products, wood

(G-8951)
NC CAROLINA VENOM
6100 Flagstone Ln Apt 204 (28079-8446)
PHONE.................................704 635-8696
EMP: 4 **EST:** 2018
SALES (est): 68.23K **Privately Held**
SIC: 2836 Venoms

(G-8952)
NORTHERN STAR TECHNOLOGIES INC
1712 Price Rd (28079-7512)
PHONE.................................516 353-3333
Chris Zbodula, *Pr*
EMP: 6 **EST:** 2002
SALES (est): 502.42K **Privately Held**
SIC: 3444 7389 Metal ventilating equipment; Business Activities at Non-Commercial Site

(G-8953)
OMEGA PRODUCTS
600 Radiator Rd (28079-5225)
PHONE.................................704 684-1920
EMP: 9 **EST:** 2010
SALES (est): 132.96K **Privately Held**
SIC: 3299 Stucco

(G-8954)
OPTO ALIGNMENT TECHNOLOGY INC
1034 Van Buren Ave Ste A (28079-5632)
PHONE.................................704 893-0399
Guy Pearlman, *Pr*
Sahsha Pearlman, *Pr*
Guy Pearlman, *Prin*
▲ **EMP:** 20 **EST:** 1992
SALES (est): 6.05MM **Privately Held**
Web: www.optoalignment.com
SIC: 3827 Optical instruments and lenses

(G-8955)
ORYX SYSTEMS INC
1064 Van Buren Ave Ste 6 (28079-5569)
PHONE.................................704 519-8803
David K Lacey, *Pr*
EMP: 5 **EST:** 1999
SALES (est): 1.01MM **Privately Held**
Web: www.oryxsystems.com
SIC: 3823 Process control instruments

(G-8956)
PETRA TECHNOLOGIES INC
3902 Alden St (28079-9522)
PHONE.................................704 577-0687
EMP: 4 **EST:** 2017
SALES (est): 79.6K **Privately Held**
Web: www.wmmartintransport.com
SIC: 1389 Oil field services, nec

(G-8957)
PIERCE FARRIER SUPPLY INC
9705 Pierce Rd (28079-7710)
PHONE.................................704 753-4358
Ben Pierce, *Owner*
EMP: 4 **EST:** 1988
SALES (est): 361.08K **Privately Held**
Web: www.piercefarriersupply.com
SIC: 3462 Horseshoes

(G-8958)
PREVENTIVE TECHNOLOGIES INC
Also Called: Preventech
4330 Matthews Indian Trail Rd (28079-3779)
PHONE.................................704 684-1211
Fred Alton King, *Pr*
EMP: 5 **EST:** 1995
SQ FT: 7,500
SALES (est): 988.29K **Privately Held**
Web: www.preventech.com
SIC: 3843 8021 Dental equipment; Offices and clinics of dentists

(G-8959)
RADIATOR SPECIALTY COMPANY (PA)
Also Called: Gunk
600 Radiator Rd (28079-5225)
P.O. Box 1890 (28079-1890)
PHONE.................................704 688-2302
Mike Guggenheimer, *CEO*
Alan Blumenthal, *Ch*
Ronald Weiner, *VP*
◆ **EMP:** 55 **EST:** 1923
SQ FT: 351,000
SALES (est): 45.45MM
SALES (corp-wide): 45.45MM **Privately Held**
Web: www.rscbrands.com
SIC: 2899 Chemical preparations, nec

(G-8960)
RAW DESIGN WOODWORKS LLC
3825 Monticello St (28079-3658)
PHONE.................................516 477-1963
Dimitri Vouvoudakis, *Prin*
EMP: 6 **EST:** 2019
SALES (est): 157.63K **Privately Held**
SIC: 2431 Millwork

(G-8961)
RSC CHEMICAL SOLUTIONS LLC
600 Radiator Rd (28079-5225)
P.O. Box 159 (28079-0159)
PHONE.................................704 821-7643
C Michale Guggenheimer, *Mgr*
EMP: 48 **EST:** 2010
SALES (est): 525.75K **Privately Held**
Web: www.rscbio.com
SIC: 2899 Chemical preparations, nec

(G-8962)
SHOWER GLASS LLC
1013 Tiger Eye Ave (28079-5543)
PHONE.................................980 785-4030
EMP: 4 **EST:** 2021
SALES (est): 70.82K **Privately Held**
Web: www.theshowerglass.com
SIC: 2431 Millwork

(G-8963)
SIGNS DESIGNED LLC
268 Unionville Indian Trail Rd W (28079-9500)
PHONE.................................704 332-4800
EMP: 6 **EST:** 2019
SALES (est): 235.6K **Privately Held**
Web: www.signsdesignedofcharlotte.com
SIC: 3993 Signs and advertising specialties

(G-8964)
SOUTHERN ELECTRICAL EQP CO INC
Also Called: Seeco
1015 Van Buren Ave (28079)
PHONE.................................704 392-1396
Kathleen Panto, *Mgr*
EMP: 7
SALES (corp-wide): 9.89MM **Privately Held**
Web: www.seecoswitch.com
SIC: 3625 3613 Relays and industrial controls; Switchgear and switchgear accessories, nec
PA: Southern Electrical Equipment Company, Inc.
 4045 Hargrove Ave
 Charlotte NC 28208
 704 392-1396

(G-8965)
STAFFORD CUTTING DIES INC
131 Business Park Dr (28079-9432)
P.O. Box 566 (28079-0566)
PHONE.................................704 821-6330
EMP: 97 **EST:** 1991
SALES (est): 9.62MM **Privately Held**
Web: www.gostafford.com
SIC: 3544 Special dies and tools

(G-8966)
SUNSEEKER US INC
311 Post Office Dr Ste 315 (28079-7835)
PHONE.................................443 253-1546
Terry Ma, *Pr*
Ned Cox, *General Vice President*
Justin Novosel, *Ex VP*
EMP: 6 **EST:** 2016
SQ FT: 1,800
SALES (est): 623.04K **Privately Held**
Web: www.shopsunseekertech.com
SIC: 3524 Blowers and vacuums, lawn

(G-8967)
TEES FOOTWEAR INC
2002 Filly Dr (28079-5723)

Indian Trail - Union County (G-8968)

PHONE..................704 628-0376
Tonya Mccarty, *Owner*
EMP: 4 **EST:** 2018
SALES (est): 59.77K **Privately Held**
SIC: 2389 Apparel and accessories, nec

(G-8968)
TEXTILE RUBBER AND CHEM CO INC
1020 Forsyth Ave Ste 100 (28079-0019)
PHONE..................704 376-3582
Chip Howalt, *Brnch Mgr*
EMP: 8
SALES (corp-wide): 225.27MM **Privately Held**
Web: www.trcc.com
SIC: 5169 2891 Chemicals and allied products, nec; Adhesives
PA: Textile Rubber And Chemical Company, Inc.
 1400 Tiarco Dr Sw
 Dalton GA 30721
 706 277-1300

(G-8969)
V/N WOODWORK
4106 Less Traveled Trl (28079-7802)
PHONE..................704 277-6336
Viktor Nikolayenko, *Prin*
EMP: 4 **EST:** 2019
SALES (est): 91.16K **Privately Held**
SIC: 2434 Wood kitchen cabinets

(G-8970)
VRG COMPONENTS INC
3056 Eaton Ave (28079-8830)
PHONE..................980 244-3862
Ruben Gutierrez, *CEO*
EMP: 19 **EST:** 2014
SALES (est): 12.58MM **Privately Held**
Web: www.vrgcomponents.com
SIC: 5065 3674 5084 Connectors, electronic ; Integrated circuits, semiconductor networks, etc.; Industrial machinery and equipment

(G-8971)
WINDCO LLC
1505 Turring Dr Ste B (28079-8475)
PHONE..................704 846-6029
EMP: 4 **EST:** 2017
SALES (est): 232.29K **Privately Held**
SIC: 3541 Machine tools, metal cutting type

(G-8972)
WMF AMERICAS INC
Also Called: Wmf USA
3521 Faith Church Rd (28079)
PHONE..................704 882-3898
♦ **EMP:** 50
Web: www.wmfamericas.com
SIC: 3589 Coffee brewing equipment

Iron Station
Lincoln County

(G-8973)
ACTEGA NORTH AMERICA INC
Also Called: Actega Wit
3840 E Highway 27 (28080-9797)
PHONE..................704 736-9389
EMP: 4
SALES (corp-wide): 4.22B **Privately Held**
Web: www.actega.com
SIC: 2851 2952 Paints and allied products; Coating compounds, tar
HQ: Actega North America, Inc.
 1450 Taylors Ln A
 Cinnaminson NJ 08077
 856 829-6300

(G-8974)
LINCOLNTON BEARING PLANT
1000 Timken Pl (28080-7788)
PHONE..................704 794-5964
EMP: 5 **EST:** 2015
SALES (est): 112.27K **Privately Held**
SIC: 3562 Ball and roller bearings

(G-8975)
PRINTING PRO
1310 L R Schronce Ln (28080-6731)
PHONE..................704 748-9396
Jonathan Lester, *Prin*
EMP: 4 **EST:** 2006
SQ FT: 1,809
SALES (est): 124.47K **Privately Held**
SIC: 2752 Commercial printing, lithographic

(G-8976)
R & R LOGGING INC
1040 N Ingleside Farm Rd (28080-9242)
PHONE..................704 483-5733
Mark A Reel, *Pr*
Ronald Reel, *Sec*
EMP: 7 **EST:** 1953
SALES (est): 748.44K **Privately Held**
SIC: 2411 Logging camps and contractors

(G-8977)
TIMKEN COMPANY
1000 Timken Pl (28080-8771)
PHONE..................704 736-2700
Todd Lautzenheiser, *Genl Mgr*
EMP: 248
SQ FT: 1,248
SALES (corp-wide): 4.77B **Publicly Held**
Web: www.timken.com
SIC: 3562 Ball and roller bearings
PA: The Timken Company
 4500 Mount Pleasant St Nw
 North Canton OH 44720
 234 262-3000

(G-8978)
WILLIS DEFENSE LLC
802 Amity Church Rd (28080-8716)
PHONE..................704 609-9953
Anne Shinall Willis, *Owner*
EMP: 5 **EST:** 2016
SALES (est): 207.25K **Privately Held**
Web: www.willisdefensenc.com
SIC: 3812 Defense systems and equipment

Ivanhoe
Sampson County

(G-8979)
AMERICAN MATERIALS COMPANY LLC
3596 Dr Kerr Rd (28447-9611)
PHONE..................910 532-6070
Tim Bizzal, *Mgr*
EMP: 50
SALES (corp-wide): 2.62B **Publicly Held**
Web: www.americanmaterialsco.com
SIC: 1442 Construction sand mining
HQ: American Materials Company, Llc
 1410 Commwl Dr Ste 201
 Wilmington NC 28403
 910 799-1411

(G-8980)
BLACK RIVER LOGGING INC
20289 North Carolina Hwy 210 E (28447-9552)
PHONE..................910 669-2850
Mike Squires, *Pr*
EMP: 7 **EST:** 1978
SALES (est): 516.35K **Privately Held**

SIC: 2411 Logging

(G-8981)
JOHNSON LUMBER PRODUCTS INC
911 Eddie L Jones Rd (28447-3601)
P.O. Box 37 (28447-0037)
PHONE..................910 532-4201
Earnest C Johnson, *Pr*
Mickey Johnson, *Admn*
EMP: 6 **EST:** 1975
SALES (est): 352K **Privately Held**
SIC: 2499 Surveyors' stakes, wood

Jackson
Northampton County

(G-8982)
HIGHWAY MAINTENANCE OFC
Hwy 305 (27845)
PHONE..................252 534-4031
Jack Liverman, *Prin*
EMP: 8 **EST:** 2002
SALES (est): 153.36K **Privately Held**
SIC: 2951 Asphalt paving mixtures and blocks

Jackson Springs
Moore County

(G-8983)
PHITECH LABORATORIES INC
12 Forest Lake Dr (27281-9745)
PHONE..................910 420-1020
Guy Peckitt, *Pr*
EMP: 9 **EST:** 2001
SALES (est): 156.6K **Privately Held**
Web: www.phitechlabs.com
SIC: 3861 3824 Cameras and related equipment; Fluid meters and counting devices

Jacksonville
Onslow County

(G-8984)
910 SIGN CO LLC
614 Richlands Hwy (28540-3655)
PHONE..................910 353-2298
Lisa Marshburn, *Managing Member*
Michael Marshburn, *Managing Member*
EMP: 4 **EST:** 2014
SALES (est): 300K **Privately Held**
SIC: 3993 Signs and advertising specialties

(G-8985)
AIRFIELD SOLUTIONS LLC (PA)
825 Gum Branch Rd Ste 102 (28540-6270)
P.O. Box 37211 (27627-7211)
PHONE..................919 348-4271
Erica Rogers, *Mgr*
EMP: 5 **EST:** 2013
SALES (est): 226.03K
SALES (corp-wide): 226.03K **Privately Held**
Web: www.airfield-solutions.com
SIC: 3812 8748 4959 7389 Search and navigation equipment; Business consulting, nec; Road, airport, and parking lot maintenance services; Business services, nec

(G-8986)
ALEXANDERS
165 Blue Creek School Rd (28540-3305)
PHONE..................910 938-0013
Kimberly Reust, *Genl Mgr*

EMP: 4 **EST:** 2006
SALES (est): 158.33K **Privately Held**
Web: www.alexandersofjacksonville.com
SIC: 2599 Bar, restaurant and cafeteria furniture

(G-8987)
ALLEN R GOODSON LOGGING CO
Also Called: Allen Goodson Logging Co
1417 Kellum Loop Rd (28546-3311)
PHONE..................910 455-4177
Allen R Goodson, *Pr*
Margaret Goodson, *Sec*
EMP: 9 **EST:** 1963
SALES (est): 394.96K **Privately Held**
SIC: 2411 Logging camps and contractors

(G-8988)
ATLANTIC COASTAL ENTERPRISES
300 New Bridge St (28540-4756)
PHONE..................910 478-0777
Brian Bryce, *Pr*
EMP: 9 **EST:** 2012
SALES (est): 213.25K **Privately Held**
Web: www.atlanticcoastalenterprises.com
SIC: 5211 1761 3448 Door and window products; Roofing contractor; Sunrooms, prefabricated metal

(G-8989)
BARNES DMND GLLERY JWLY MFRS I
120 College Plz (28546-6820)
PHONE..................910 347-4300
Carol T Barnes, *Pr*
Jimmy Barnes, *VP*
EMP: 6 **EST:** 1991
SQ FT: 2,100
SALES (est): 666.92K **Privately Held**
Web: www.barnesdiamondgallery.com
SIC: 5944 3911 Jewelry, precious stones and precious metals; Jewelry, precious metal

(G-8990)
BEAUTY ELEMENTS LLC
200 Doctors Dr Ste C (28546-6308)
PHONE..................910 333-9957
Joanna Israel, *Admn*
EMP: 6 **EST:** 2016
SALES (est): 170.02K **Privately Held**
Web: www.beautyelementsspa.com
SIC: 2819 Elements

(G-8991)
BPC PLASMA INC
113 Yopp Rd (28540-3509)
PHONE..................910 463-2603
EMP: 15
SQ FT: 15,000
Web: www.biotestplasma.com
SIC: 2834 Pharmaceutical preparations
HQ: Bpc Plasma, Inc.
 901 W Yamato Rd Ste 101
 Boca Raton FL 33431

(G-8992)
BUTLER TRIEU INC
1183 Kellum Loop Rd (28546-3305)
P.O. Box 343 (28541-0343)
PHONE..................910 346-4929
Tim Butler, *Pr*
Vy Trieu, *VP*
EMP: 8 **EST:** 2011
SQ FT: 5,000
SALES (est): 573.8K **Privately Held**
Web: www.butlertrieu.com

GEOGRAPHIC SECTION
Jacksonville - Onslow County (G-9022)

SIC: 4959 3589 0781 0782 Sweeping service: road, airport, parking lot, etc.; High pressure cleaning equipment; Landscape services; Landscape contractors

(G-8993)
CAMP LEJEUNE GLOBE
149 Rea St (28546-5773)
PHONE..............................910 939-0705
EMP: 7 **EST:** 2017
SALES (est): 114.18K **Privately Held**
Web: www.jdnews.com
SIC: 2711 Newspapers, publishing and printing

(G-8994)
CAROLINA COASTAL COATINGS
400 White St (28546-6732)
PHONE..............................910 346-9607
Jeffrey Bailey, *Sec*
EMP: 10 **EST:** 2018
SALES (est): 655.23K **Privately Held**
SIC: 3479 Painting, coating, and hot dipping

(G-8995)
CHRONICLES
121 Mendover Dr (28546-9207)
PHONE..............................252 617-1774
EMP: 4 **EST:** 2018
SALES (est): 102.72K **Privately Held**
Web: www.highlandsnews.com
SIC: 2711 Newspapers, publishing and printing

(G-8996)
D&M EMBROIDERY LLC
1324 Sofia Ct (28540-3353)
PHONE..............................910 467-3586
Sheila Covington, *Prin*
EMP: 4 **EST:** 2018
SALES (est): 31.29K **Privately Held**
SIC: 2395 Embroidery and art needlework

(G-8997)
DECOCRETE
1120 River St (28540-5705)
PHONE..............................910 358-4175
Doug Smith, *Mgr*
EMP: 4 **EST:** 2016
SALES (est): 65.93K **Privately Held**
Web: www.decocrete.net
SIC: 3272 Concrete products, nec

(G-8998)
DIABLO DISTILLERIES LLC
316 Royal Bluff Rd (28540-3822)
PHONE..............................910 467-5017
Phillip M O Hara, *Admn*
EMP: 6 **EST:** 2012
SALES (est): 217.8K **Privately Held**
Web: www.diablodistilleries.com
SIC: 2085 Distilled and blended liquors

(G-8999)
FLAMINGO GROUP LLC
1250 Western Blvd Ste L2 (28546-6755)
PHONE..............................910 478-9987
Ben Hodgins, *Managing Member*
EMP: 5 **EST:** 2018
SALES (est): 130.15K **Privately Held**
SIC: 2721 Magazines: publishing only, not printed on site

(G-9000)
FOUR POINTS RECYCLING LLC
309 King Rd (28540-8438)
P.O. Box 87 (28541-0287)
PHONE..............................910 333-5961
EMP: 12 **EST:** 2000
SALES (est): 1.05MM **Privately Held**
Web: www.fourpointsrecycling.com
SIC: 3531 1799 Graders, road (construction machinery); Construction site cleanup

(G-9001)
FURNITURE FAIR INC
418 White St (28546-6732)
PHONE..............................910 455-4044
EMP: 38
SALES (corp-wide): 20.72MM **Privately Held**
Web: www.furniture-fair.net
SIC: 5712 2273 Furniture stores; Carpets and rugs
PA: Furniture Fair, Inc.
    507 Bell Fork Rd
    Jacksonville NC 28540
    910 455-9595

(G-9002)
GEE SPOT MOBILE BAR LLC
12 East Dr (28546-8213)
PHONE..............................910 581-1786
EMP: 5 **EST:** 2020
SALES (est): 74.42K **Privately Held**
SIC: 2869 Alcohols, non beverage

(G-9003)
GOOD NEWS IPHC MINISTRIES INC
102 E Doris Ave (28540-5175)
PHONE..............................919 906-2104
Phillip Bland, *Religious Leader*
EMP: 6 **EST:** 2009
SALES (est): 130.31K **Privately Held**
Web: www.goodnewsjville.com
SIC: 2711 Newspapers, publishing and printing

(G-9004)
GOODSON S ALL TERRAIN LOG INC
173 Goodson Trl (28546-4127)
PHONE..............................910 347-7919
EMP: 14 **EST:** 1992
SALES (est): 896.44K **Privately Held**
SIC: 2411 Logging camps and contractors

(G-9005)
GOODSONS ALL TERRAIN LOG
137 Rustic Ln (28540-4108)
PHONE..............................910 934-8451
EMP: 4 **EST:** 2018
SALES (est): 173.84K **Privately Held**
SIC: 2411 Logging

(G-9006)
GRIDLOCK ENTERPRISES LLC
3165 Northwoods Dr (28540-3851)
PHONE..............................910 939-4867
EMP: 5 **EST:** 2014
SALES (est): 87.7K **Privately Held**
SIC: 3482 Small arms ammunition

(G-9007)
HOME TEAM ATHLETICS INC
242 Wilmington Hwy 17 (28540-3506)
PHONE..............................910 938-0862
EMP: 5 **EST:** 1993
SQ FT: 955
SALES (est): 476.91K **Privately Held**
Web: home-team-athletics.ueniweb.com
SIC: 5941 2395 2759 Team sports equipment; Embroidery products, except Schiffli machine; Screen printing

(G-9008)
ICEE COMPANY
13 E Doris Ave Ste H (28540-5149)
PHONE..............................910 346-3937
EMP: 4
SALES (corp-wide): 1.56B **Publicly Held**
Web: www.icee.com
SIC: 2038 Frozen specialties, nec
HQ: The Icee Company
    265 Mason Rd
    La Vergne TN 37086
    800 426-4233

(G-9009)
IRON FORGED WOODWORKS
400 Mccall Dr (28540-8076)
PHONE..............................910 581-6574
Matthew Dunlap, *Prin*
EMP: 4 **EST:** 2018
SALES (est): 60.94K **Privately Held**
SIC: 2431 Millwork

(G-9010)
JACKSONVILLE METAL MFG INC
181 Piney Green Rd (28546-8125)
PHONE..............................910 938-7635
William T Humphrey, *Pr*
EMP: 5 **EST:** 1989
SALES (est): 2.17MM
SALES (corp-wide): 64.45MM **Privately Held**
SIC: 3444 Ducts, sheet metal
PA: W. T. Humphrey, Inc.
    2423 N Marine Blvd
    Jacksonville NC 28546
    910 455-3555

(G-9011)
JTC AWARDS AND PRINTING
1423 N Marine Blvd (28540-6417)
PHONE..............................910 346-9522
Lloyd James, *Prin*
EMP: 5 **EST:** 2007
SALES (est): 202.67K **Privately Held**
SIC: 2759 5734 5999 Screen printing; Printers and plotters: computers; Trophies and plaques

(G-9012)
LACEYS TREE SERVICE
221 Jenkins Rd (28546-8434)
PHONE..............................910 330-2868
Jeremy Lacey, *Owner*
Jeremy Lacey, *Prin*
EMP: 4 **EST:** 2007
SALES (est): 240.14K **Privately Held**
SIC: 2411 Logging

(G-9013)
MICHAEL L GOODSON LOGGING INC
171 Goodson Trl (28546-4127)
PHONE..............................910 346-8399
Michael L Goodson, *Pr*
Cathy Goodson, *Sec*
EMP: 9 **EST:** 1991
SALES (est): 5.29MM **Privately Held**
SIC: 2411 Logging camps and contractors

(G-9014)
MINUTEMAN QUICK COPY SVC INC
207 W Bayshore Blvd (28540-5339)
PHONE..............................910 455-5353
Debbie Phillips, *Pr*
Dwain Phillips, *Sec*
EMP: 5 **EST:** 1977
SQ FT: 800
SALES (est): 349.6K **Privately Held**
SIC: 2752 Offset printing

(G-9015)
MSA SAFETY SALES LLC
352 White St (28546-6730)
PHONE..............................910 353-1540
J Ryan, *BD*
EMP: 80
SALES (corp-wide): 1.79B **Publicly Held**
Web: us.msasafety.com
SIC: 3842 Personal safety equipment
HQ: Msa Safety Sales, Llc
    1000 Cranberry Woods Dr
    Cranberry Township PA 16066
    800 672-2222

(G-9016)
NC LICENSE PLATE AGENCY
521 Yopp Rd (28540-3595)
PHONE..............................910 347-1000
Cecil Hargett, *Prin*
EMP: 9 **EST:** 1993
SALES (est): 909.5K **Privately Held**
SIC: 3469 Automobile license tags, stamped metal

(G-9017)
NEALS CARPENTRY & CNSTR
153 White Oak Blvd (28546-4538)
PHONE..............................910 346-6154
Robert Neal, *Pr*
EMP: 4 **EST:** 1992
SALES (est): 236.57K **Privately Held**
SIC: 1751 3448 1521 Cabinet and finish carpentry; Prefabricated metal buildings and components; Single-family home remodeling, additions, and repairs

(G-9018)
NEWTON SIGN CO INC
310 Preston Rd (28540-5655)
PHONE..............................910 347-1661
Richard S Newton, *Pr*
EMP: 5 **EST:** 1974
SALES (est): 413.99K **Privately Held**
SIC: 3993 Signs and advertising specialties

(G-9019)
PERSONAL DEFENSE TRAININ
213 Maplehurst Dr (28540-7815)
PHONE..............................910 455-4473
EMP: 4 **EST:** 2016
SALES (est): 205.5K **Privately Held**
SIC: 3812 Defense systems and equipment

(G-9020)
PETTEWAY BODY SHOP INC
Also Called: Petteway Rentals
1362 Old Maplehurst Rd (28540-3215)
PHONE..............................910 455-3272
EMP: 4 **EST:** 1972
SQ FT: 3,336
SALES (est): 340.96K **Privately Held**
SIC: 3599 Grinding castings for the trade

(G-9021)
PRINT EXPRESS INC
Also Called: Express Printing
117 N Marine Blvd (28540-6508)
PHONE..............................910 455-4554
Carol Cross, *VP*
EMP: 10 **EST:** 1984
SQ FT: 1,500
SALES (est): 611.11K **Privately Held**
SIC: 2752 7334 2759 Offset printing; Photocopying and duplicating services; Commercial printing, nec

(G-9022)
PROFESSNL ALTERATIONS EMB INC
Also Called: Shirleys Prof Alterations EMB
2113 Lejeune Blvd (28546-8251)
PHONE..............................910 577-8484
Shirley Stanley, *Pr*
EMP: 7 **EST:** 1991
SALES (est): 114.22K **Privately Held**

Jacksonville - Onslow County (G-9023)

SIC: **2395** 7219 7389 Embroidery products, except Schiffli machine; Garment alteration and repair shop; Personal service agents, brokers, and bureaus

(G-9023)
PROGRESSIVE SERVICE DIE CO
226 White St (28546-6318)
PHONE..............................910 353-4836
Brian France, *Pr*
George France, *VP*
EMP: 19 EST: 1913
SQ FT: 30,000
SALES (est): 2.35MM **Privately Held**
Web: www.psdcdies.com
SIC: **3544** Special dies and tools

(G-9024)
PULLOVER PAL
305 Thomas Dr (28546-7118)
PHONE..............................910 340-1801
Ronnie Fulcher, *Prin*
EMP: 5 EST: 2017
SALES (est): 63.78K **Privately Held**
Web: www.thepulloverpal.com
SIC: **3999** Manufacturing industries, nec

(G-9025)
RANDOLPH GOODSON LOGGING INC
170 Jenkins Rd (28540-8466)
PHONE..............................910 347-5117
Randolph D Goodson, *Pr*
Judy Carroll Goodson, *Sec*
EMP: 9 EST: 1987
SALES (est): 629.56K **Privately Held**
SIC: **2411** Logging camps and contractors

(G-9026)
RUSH MASONRY MANAGEMENT LLC
234 Clayton James Rd (28540-9549)
PHONE..............................910 787-9100
Kendra Blackmon, *Pr*
Travis Plymell, *VP*
EMP: 6 EST: 2011
SALES (est): 911.04K **Privately Held**
Web: www.rushconstruction.org
SIC: **3423** Masons' hand tools

(G-9027)
S A L T SOAK AWAY LFES TRUBLES
108 Skipping Stone Ln (28546-9516)
PHONE..............................910 238-2695
Donna Ferguson, *Prin*
EMP: 5 EST: 2013
SALES (est): 63.65K **Privately Held**
SIC: **2899** Salt

(G-9028)
SEMPER FI WATER LLC ◆
508 Cozy Crow Trl (28540-4818)
PHONE..............................910 381-3569
Norine Rosetti, *Managing Member*
EMP: 4 EST: 2022
SALES (est): 241.33K **Privately Held**
SIC: **3589** Water treatment equipment, industrial

(G-9029)
SERVICE AND EQUIPMENT COMPANY
521 Yopp Rd Ste 214 (28540-3597)
PHONE..............................910 545-5886
Terry Leach, *Pr*
EMP: 8 EST: 2013
SALES (est): 624.29K **Privately Held**
SIC: **5085** 7389 3536 Rope, except wire rope ; Crane and aerial lift service; Hand hoists

(G-9030)
SILKSCREEN SPECIALISTS
2239 Lejeune Blvd (28546-8253)
PHONE..............................910 353-8859
Jerry Copeland, *Owner*
EMP: 5 EST: 1991
SALES (est): 308.65K **Privately Held**
Web: www.silkscreenspecialists.com
SIC: **2759** Screen printing

(G-9031)
SL LIQUIDATION LLC
408 White St (28546-6732)
PHONE..............................910 353-3666
EMP: 77
SALES (corp-wide): 325.81MM **Privately Held**
Web: www.stanadyne.com
SIC: **3714** Motor vehicle parts and accessories
HQ: Sl Liquidation Llc
    405 White St
    Jacksonville NC 28546
    860 525-0821

(G-9032)
SL LIQUIDATION LLC (DH)
Also Called: Stanadyne LLC
405 White St (28546-6731)
PHONE..............................860 525-0821
John A Pinson, *CEO*
Costas Loukellis, *CFO*
◆ EMP: 272 EST: 1988
SALES (est): 209.85MM
SALES (corp-wide): 325.81MM **Privately Held**
Web: www.stanadyne.com
SIC: **3714** Fuel pumps, motor vehicle
HQ: Stanadyne Intermediate Holdings, Llc
    405 White St
    Jacksonville NC 28546

(G-9033)
SL LIQUIDATION LLC
Also Called: Stanadyne Diesel Systems
405 White St (28546-6731)
PHONE..............................910 353-3666
Rich Pasqualune, *Brnch Mgr*
EMP: 360
SALES (corp-wide): 325.81MM **Privately Held**
Web: www.stanadyne.com
SIC: **3714** 3561 3432 Fuel systems and parts, motor vehicle; Pumps and pumping equipment; Plumbing fixture fittings and trim
HQ: Sl Liquidation Llc
    405 White St
    Jacksonville NC 28546
    860 525-0821

(G-9034)
SONOCO PRODUCTS COMPANY
Also Called: Sonoco Recycling
417 Meadowview Rd (28540-7313)
PHONE..............................910 455-6903
Jim Foster, *Brnch Mgr*
EMP: 4
SALES (corp-wide): 6.78B **Publicly Held**
Web: www.sonoco.com
SIC: **2631** 3085 Cardboard; Plastics bottles
PA: Sonoco Products Company
    1 N 2nd St
    Hartsville SC 29550
    843 383-7000

(G-9035)
SOUNDSIDE ORTHTICS PRSTHTICS L
1715 Country Club Rd Ste B (28546-6009)
PHONE..............................910 238-2026
Stephen Truesdale, *Bd of Dir*
EMP: 4 EST: 2004
SALES (est): 244.19K **Privately Held**
SIC: **3842** Surgical appliances and supplies

(G-9036)
SOUTHEASTERN STEEL CNSTR INC
225 Ellis Blvd (28540-6332)
P.O. Box 190 (28541-0190)
PHONE..............................910 346-4462
Valerie Dail, *Pr*
EMP: 10 EST: 2003
SQ FT: 5,000
SALES (est): 1.27MM **Privately Held**
Web: www.southeasternsteel.com
SIC: **3441** Building components, structural steel

(G-9037)
SOUTHERN LEISURE BUILDERS INC
2444 Commerce Rd (28546-7560)
PHONE..............................910 381-0426
Shannon Kellum, *Mgr*
EMP: 4
SALES (corp-wide): 907.84K **Privately Held**
Web: www.southernleisurebuilders.com
SIC: **3448** Sunrooms, prefabricated metal
PA: Southern Leisure Builders Inc
    172 Willis Pkwy Ste A
    Jacksonville NC 28546
    910 219-0438

(G-9038)
STANADYNE INTRMDATE HLDNGS LLC (HQ)
405 White St (28546-6790)
PHONE..............................860 525-0821
David P Galuska, *CEO*
John A Pinson, *
Steve Rodgers, *
Stephen S Langin, *
▲ EMP: 250 EST: 1997
SALES (est): 325.81MM
SALES (corp-wide): 325.81MM **Privately Held**
Web: www.stanadyne.com
SIC: **3714** 3492 Fuel systems and parts, motor vehicle; Control valves, fluid power: hydraulic and pneumatic
PA: Stanadyne Parent Holdings, Inc.
    405 White St
    Jacksonville NC 28546
    860 525-0821

(G-9039)
STANADYNE JACKSONVILLE LLC ◆
405 White St (28546-6790)
PHONE..............................860 683-4553
Rob Mallory, *CEO*
EMP: 190 EST: 2023
SALES (est): 15.27MM
SALES (corp-wide): 90MM **Privately Held**
SIC: **3714** Motor vehicle engines and parts
PA: Stanadyne Operating Company Llc
    405 White St
    Jacksonville NC 28546
    910 353-3666

(G-9040)
STANADYNE OPERATING CO LLC (PA) ◆
405 White St (28546-6790)
PHONE..............................910 353-3666
Rob Mallory, *Managing Member*
EMP: 67 EST: 2023
SALES (est): 90MM
SALES (corp-wide): 90MM **Privately Held**
SIC: **3714** Motor vehicle parts and accessories

(G-9041)
STONE CLLINS MTR REWINDING INC
Also Called: Sams Motor Rewinding
111 Ramsey Rd (28546-9366)
PHONE..............................910 347-2775
Kevin Collins, *Pr*
Vernancia Collins, *VP*
EMP: 5 EST: 1970
SQ FT: 8,000
SALES (est): 432.78K **Privately Held**
SIC: **7694** 5063 Electric motor repair; Motors, electric

(G-9042)
TIMBER HARVESTER INC (PA)
3862 Richlands Hwy (28540-7123)
P.O. Box 164 (28541-0164)
PHONE..............................910 346-9754
Charles Rawls, *Pr*
Anthony Rawls, *VP*
Myrtie Rawls, *Sec*
EMP: 6 EST: 1984
SALES (est): 949.43K
SALES (corp-wide): 949.43K **Privately Held**
SIC: **2411** Logging camps and contractors

(G-9043)
VEXEA MX LLC
205 America Ct (28540-5060)
PHONE..............................910 787-9391
Adam Baldwin, *Prin*
EMP: 5 EST: 2015
SALES (est): 58.8K **Privately Held**
SIC: **3751** Gears, motorcycle and bicycle

(G-9044)
W T HUMPHREY INC (PA)
2423 N Marine Blvd (28546-6906)
P.O. Box 1268 (28541-1268)
PHONE..............................910 455-3555
Steven Wangerin, *CEO*
William Troy Humphrey, *
Wanda Flud, *
Frances Humphrey, *
EMP: 52 EST: 1967
SQ FT: 7,500
SALES (est): 64.45MM
SALES (corp-wide): 64.45MM **Privately Held**
Web: www.wthumphrey.com
SIC: **8741** 1711 1542 3444 Management services; Plumbing, heating, air-conditioning ; Commercial and office building, new construction; Ducts, sheet metal

(G-9045)
WALTONS DISTILLERY INC
261 Ben Williams Rd (28540-9213)
PHONE..............................910 347-7770
Donald Walton, *Pr*
EMP: 8 EST: 2015
SALES (est): 412.44K **Privately Held**
Web: www.waltonsdistillery.com
SIC: **2085** Distilled and blended liquors

(G-9046)
WETHERINGTON S MOBILE HOME
106 Marlo Cir (28540-4572)
PHONE..............................910 347-3664
A W Wetherington, *Prin*
EMP: 5 EST: 2005
SALES (est): 64.09K **Privately Held**
SIC: **2451** Mobile homes

(G-9047)
WORLD ART GALLERY INCORPORATED
Also Called: Carriage House Furniture Co
1116 Gum Branch Rd (28540-5743)

GEOGRAPHIC SECTION

Jamestown - Guilford County (G-9072)

PHONE.....................910 989-0203
Dora Smith, *Pr*
Richard Smith, *Sec*
EMP: 8 **EST:** 1971
SQ FT: 8,000
SALES (est): 1.2MM **Privately Held**
Web:
www.carriagehousefurnitureco.com
SIC: 5712 2499 5999 Furniture stores; Picture and mirror frames, wood; Art dealers

Jamestown
Guilford County

(G-9048)
CARSON DELLOSA PUBLISHING CO
3316 Morris Farm Dr (27282-8669)
PHONE.....................336 294-8176
Rob Shina, *Prin*
EMP: 6 **EST:** 2013
SALES (est): 155.99K **Privately Held**
Web: www.carsondellosa.com
SIC: 2741 Miscellaneous publishing

(G-9049)
FLOWERS BAKING CO NEWTON LLC (HQ)
Also Called: Flowers Bakery
801 W Main St (27282-9562)
P.O. Box 819 (27282-0819)
PHONE.....................336 841-8840
Roger Tooley, *Pr*
Paul Houser, *
EMP: 56 **EST:** 2000
SQ FT: 110,000
SALES (est): 28.96MM
SALES (corp-wide): 5.09B **Publicly Held**
SIC: 2051 Bread, all types (white, wheat, rye, etc); fresh or frozen
PA: Flowers Foods, Inc.
1919 Flowers Cir
Thomasville GA 31757
229 226-9110

(G-9050)
GEO-LIN INC
Also Called: Budget Printing
107 Hillstone Dr (27282-8924)
PHONE.....................336 884-0648
Jason Spangler, *Pr*
EMP: 4 **EST:** 1986
SQ FT: 1,700
SALES (est): 334.19K **Privately Held**
SIC: 2752 Offset printing

(G-9051)
GOCAISSONCOM
3210 Dillon Rd (27282-9129)
PHONE.....................336 454-4610
Jim Burns, *Prin*
EMP: 5 **EST:** 2016
SALES (est): 90.04K **Privately Held**
Web: www.gocaisson.com
SIC: 3679 Electronic components, nec

(G-9052)
HEMCO WIRE PRODUCTS INC
Also Called: Greensboro Metal Parts
301 Scientific St (27282-9537)
P.O. Box 1648 (27282-1648)
PHONE.....................336 454-7280
Mark Myers, *Pr*
EMP: 18 **EST:** 1943
SQ FT: 48,000
SALES (est): 479.82K **Privately Held**
SIC: 3496 3479 3694 2542 Miscellaneous fabricated wire products; Painting, coating, and hot dipping; Engine electrical equipment; Partitions and fixtures, except wood

(G-9053)
HIGHLAND CONTAINERS INC (DH)
100 Ragsdale Rd (27282-9874)
PHONE.....................336 887-5400
Doug Johnston, *Pr*
▲ **EMP:** 200 **EST:** 1992
SQ FT: 179,000
SALES (est): 48.76MM **Privately Held**
SIC: 2653 Boxes, corrugated: made from purchased materials
HQ: Stronghaven, Incorporated
2727 Paces Ferry Rd Se 1-1850
Atlanta GA 30339
678 235-2713

(G-9054)
HIGHLAND CONTAINERS INC
3520 Dillon Rd (27282-9802)
PHONE.....................336 887-5400
Travis Wright, *Brnch Mgr*
EMP: 250
Web: www.hoodcontainer.com
SIC: 2653 Boxes, corrugated: made from purchased materials
HQ: Highland Containers, Inc.
100 Ragsdale Rd
Jamestown NC 27282

(G-9055)
HOOD CONTAINER CORPORATION
3520 Dillon Rd (27282-9802)
PHONE.....................336 887-5400
EMP: 20
Web: www.hoodcontainer.com
SIC: 2653 Corrugated boxes, partitions, display items, sheets, and pad
HQ: Hood Container Corporation
2727 Paces Ferry Rd Se 1-1850
Atlanta GA 30339
855 605-6317

(G-9056)
IMAGE WORKS INC
120 Wade St Ste A (27282-9846)
PHONE.....................336 668-3338
Arnold Riewe, *Pr*
Linda Riewe, *Sec*
▲ **EMP:** 5 **EST:** 1994
SQ FT: 11,000
SALES (est): 367.73K **Privately Held**
SIC: 2752 Offset printing

(G-9057)
IMS INTRNATIONAL MFRS SHOWROOM
4250 Furniture Ave (27282-8743)
PHONE.....................336 454-0388
EMP: 4 **EST:** 2018
SALES (est): 101.6K **Privately Held**
Web: jamestown-nc.north-carolina-bd.com
SIC: 3999 Manufacturing industries, nec

(G-9058)
INSPIRATION LEATHER DESIGN INC
4713 Barrington Place Ct (27282-7976)
PHONE.....................336 420-2265
Vicki Ann Reed, *Pr*
Kenneth Reed, *Sec*
EMP: 6 **EST:** 2012
SALES (est): 487.51K **Privately Held**
SIC: 2386 3111 7389 Garments, leather; Upholstery leather; Business Activities at Non-Commercial Site

(G-9059)
JAMESTOWN NEWS
Also Called: Womack Newspapers
206 E Main St Ste 1a (27282-8005)
P.O. Box 307 (27282-0307)
PHONE.....................336 841-4933
Charles Womack, *Pr*
Carolyn Lewis, *Off Mgr*
EMP: 5 **EST:** 1990
SALES (est): 412.11K **Privately Held**
Web: www.yesweekly.com
SIC: 2711 Newspapers, publishing and printing

(G-9060)
MARIETTA MARTIN MATERIALS INC
Martin Marietta Aggregates
5725 Riverdale Dr (27282-9172)
P.O. Box 937 (27282-0937)
PHONE.....................336 886-5015
Steve Carter, *Genl Mgr*
EMP: 5
Web: www.martinmarietta.com
SIC: 1422 Crushed and broken limestone
PA: Martin Marietta Materials Inc
4123 Parklake Ave
Raleigh NC 27612

(G-9061)
MCKENZIE INDUSTRIES INC
216 Lady Slipper Ln (27282-8304)
P.O. Box 1177 (27282-1177)
PHONE.....................336 870-9229
John T Mckenzie Junior, *Pr*
EMP: 5 **EST:** 2010
SALES (est): 179.16K **Privately Held**
SIC: 3999 Manufacturing industries, nec

(G-9062)
NAVELITE LLC
3220 Peninsula Dr (27282-8700)
PHONE.....................336 509-9924
John Price, *Prin*
EMP: 5 **EST:** 2015
SALES (est): 195.23K **Privately Held**
Web: www.navelite.com
SIC: 3812 Search and navigation equipment

(G-9063)
NC SIGN AND LIGHTING SVC LLC
213 Hillstone Pl (27282-2000)
PHONE.....................586 764-0563
EMP: 11 **EST:** 2015
SALES (est): 864.73K **Privately Held**
Web: www.yesco.com
SIC: 3993 Signs and advertising specialties

(G-9064)
OAKDALE COTTON MILLS
409 E Main St (27282-9554)
P.O. Box 367 (27282-0367)
PHONE.....................336 454-1144
Billy Ragsdale, *Mgr*
EMP: 6 **EST:** 1900
SALES (est): 66.04K **Privately Held**
Web: www.oakdalecotton.com
SIC: 2211 Broadwoven fabric mills, cotton

(G-9065)
OAKDALE COTTON MILLS
710 Oakdale Rd (27282)
PHONE.....................336 454-1144
William Ragsdale, *Pr*
William G Ragsdale Iii, *Pr*
Norma Knight, *
EMP: 9 **EST:** 1865
SQ FT: 50,000
SALES (est): 272.62K **Privately Held**
SIC: 2281 2298 Yarn spinning mills; Twine, nec

(G-9066)
PERFORMANCE PLASTICS PDTS INC
126 Wade St Ste D (27282-9848)
PHONE.....................336 454-0350
James Mchon, *Brnch Mgr*
EMP: 91
SALES (corp-wide): 597.58K **Privately Held**
Web: www.3pcorporate.com
SIC: 3089 3498 3312 3084 Plastics hardware and building products; Fabricated pipe and fittings; Blast furnaces and steel mills; Plastics pipe
HQ: Performance Plastics Products, Inc.
11718 Mcgallion Rd
Houston TX

(G-9067)
QORVO US INC
4113 Devondale Ct (27282-7793)
PHONE.....................503 615-9000
Andrew Labaziewicz, *Brnch Mgr*
EMP: 9
SALES (corp-wide): 3.57B **Publicly Held**
Web: www.qorvo.com
SIC: 3674 Semiconductors and related devices
HQ: Qorvo Us, Inc.
2300 Ne Brookwood Pkwy
Hillsboro OR 97124
336 664-1233

(G-9068)
R & D LABEL LLC
117 Wade St (27282-9567)
P.O. Box 6 (27282-0006)
PHONE.....................336 889-2900
EMP: 7 **EST:** 2006
SALES (est): 503.26K **Privately Held**
Web: ns1.hxmi.com
SIC: 2752 Commercial printing, lithographic

(G-9069)
R D TILLSON & ASSOCIATES INC
Also Called: Tillson Engineering Laboratory
105 Cottonwood Dr (27282-9468)
PHONE.....................336 454-1410
David K Tillson, *Pr*
EMP: 4 **EST:** 1953
SALES (est): 277.82K **Privately Held**
SIC: 8711 3621 Consulting engineer; Motors and generators

(G-9070)
ROTHROCK INDUSTRIES
103 Newberry St (27282-9670)
PHONE.....................336 454-4549
Mark Joyner, *Prin*
EMP: 4 **EST:** 2013
SALES (est): 58.9K **Privately Held**
SIC: 3999 Manufacturing industries, nec

(G-9071)
SBS DIVERSIFIED TECH INC
Also Called: Diversified Technologies
125 Wade St (27282-9567)
P.O. Box 2039 (27282-2039)
PHONE.....................336 884-5564
William Sosnowski, *Pr*
Robert Sosnowski, *VP*
EMP: 15 **EST:** 1979
SQ FT: 21,000
SALES (est): 391.13K **Privately Held**
SIC: 3672 Printed circuit boards

(G-9072)
SERIGRAPH TECHNIQUES INC
101 Oakdale Rd # 1254 (27282-9299)
PHONE.....................336 454-5066

Jamestown - Guilford County (G-9073)

Roger Helmstetler, *Prin*
EMP: 6 **EST:** 2006
SALES (est): 117.92K **Privately Held**
SIC: 2759 Commercial printing, nec

(G-9073)
SWATCHCRAFT
203 Woodmont Rd (27282-8502)
PHONE..............................336 841-7113
EMP: 5 **EST:** 2017
SALES (est): 73.16K **Privately Held**
Web: www.swatchcraft.com
SIC: 2789 Binding and repair of books, magazines, and pamphlets

(G-9074)
TEKNOR APEX COMPANY
3518 Dillon Rd (27282-9802)
PHONE..............................401 642-3598
EMP: 50
SALES (corp-wide): 1.03B **Privately Held**
Web: www.teknorapex.com
SIC: 3087 3084 Custom compound purchased resins; Plastics pipe
PA: Teknor Apex Company
505 Central Ave
Pawtucket RI 02861
401 725-8000

(G-9075)
TLC ENTERPRISES
704 Ragsdale Rd (27282-9627)
PHONE..............................336 454-4981
EMP: 4 **EST:** 2013
SALES (est): 54.51K **Privately Held**
Web: www.nctlcenterprises.com
SIC: 2759 Screen printing

(G-9076)
UNIVERSAL PLASTIC PRODUCTS INC
3220 Peninsula Dr (27282-8700)
PHONE..............................336 856-0882
John K Price, *Prin*
EMP: 4 **EST:** 1996
SALES (est): 325.6K **Privately Held**
SIC: 3089 Injection molding of plastics

Jamesville
Martin County

(G-9077)
ARRANTS LOGGING INC
3600 Jerden Thicket Rd (27846-9151)
P.O. Box 30 (27846-0030)
PHONE..............................252 792-1889
Frankie Arrants, *Pr*
Danette Arrants, *Sec*
EMP: 17 **EST:** 1978
SQ FT: 3,600
SALES (est): 2.33MM **Privately Held**
SIC: 2411 Logging camps and contractors

(G-9078)
BARRY LANE PERRY
Also Called: Blp Logging Company
2465 Manning Rd (27846-9550)
PHONE..............................252 799-4334
Barry L Perry, *Owner*
EMP: 6 **EST:** 2009
SALES (est): 23.96K **Privately Held**
SIC: 2411 Logging

(G-9079)
CAROLINA STORE FIXTURES LLC
28333 Us Highway 64 (27846-9625)
PHONE..............................252 508-0110
EMP: 8 **EST:** 2011
SALES (est): 222.84K **Privately Held**
SIC: 2541 Wood partitions and fixtures

(G-9080)
EVANS LOGGING INC
1047 Fleming Cir (27846-9148)
P.O. Box 156 (27846-0156)
PHONE..............................252 792-3865
Gary Evans, *Pr*
Larry Evans, *VP*
EMP: 10 **EST:** 1925
SALES (est): 982.1K **Privately Held**
SIC: 2411 Logging camps and contractors

(G-9081)
PRICE LOGGING INC
1901 Mill Rd (27846-9237)
PHONE..............................252 792-5687
Alfred Price Senior, *Pr*
Alfred Price Junior, *VP*
EMP: 9 **EST:** 1983
SQ FT: 4,200
SALES (est): 495.31K **Privately Held**
SIC: 2411 2426 2421 Logging camps and contractors; Hardwood dimension and flooring mills; Sawmills and planing mills, general

(G-9082)
STEPHEN P WOLFE
Also Called: Wolfe Industries
28228 Us Highway 64 (27846-9624)
P.O. Box 220 (27846-0220)
PHONE..............................252 792-3001
Stephen P Wolfe, *Owner*
EMP: 5 **EST:** 1961
SALES (est): 109.83K **Privately Held**
Web: www.daswolf.com
SIC: 3089 2421 3429 Plastics processing; Sawmills and planing mills, general; Hardware, nec

Jarvisburg
Currituck County

(G-9083)
CAROLINA CSUAL OTDOOR FURN INC
Also Called: Salt Marsh Home
7359 Caratoke Hwy (27947-9705)
PHONE..............................252 491-5171
Michael Mcclanahan, *Pr*
Susan Mcclanahan, *VP*
EMP: 15 **EST:** 2016
SALES (est): 1.51MM **Privately Held**
Web: www.carolinacasual.com
SIC: 2511 5021 Porch furniture and swings: wood; Household furniture

(G-9084)
ERNIES BOAT CANVAS & AWNING C
101 Meadow Lake Cir 158 (27947-9720)
PHONE..............................252 491-8279
Ernie Dennison, *Owner*
EMP: 5 **EST:** 2008
SALES (est): 56.46K **Privately Held**
SIC: 2394 Canvas and related products

(G-9085)
SANCTUARY VINEYARDS
7005 Caratoke Hwy (27947-9727)
PHONE..............................252 491-2387
EMP: 7 **EST:** 2020
SALES (est): 62.38K **Privately Held**
Web: www.sanctuaryvineyards.com
SIC: 2084 Brandy

(G-9086)
SOUNDSIDE RECYCLING & MTLS INC
7565 Caratoke Hwy (27947-9709)
PHONE..............................252 491-8666
Kimberly Newbern, *CEO*
Kimberly Newbern, *Pr*
Horatio D Newbern Iv, *VP*
EMP: 8 **EST:** 1999
SQ FT: 1,000
SALES (est): 1.42MM **Privately Held**
Web: www.soundsiderecycling.com
SIC: 1442 1795 4953 1629 Construction sand and gravel; Concrete breaking for streets and highways; Recycling, waste materials; Waste disposal plant construction

Jefferson
Ashe County

(G-9087)
CARDINAL STONE COMPANY INC
1608 Us Highway 221 N (28640-9808)
P.O. Box 635 (28640-0635)
PHONE..............................336 846-7191
James M Vannoy, *Pr*
EMP: 38 **EST:** 1986
SALES (est): 737.32K **Privately Held**
Web: www.jrvannoy.com
SIC: 1429 3531 Igneous rock, crushed and broken-quarrying; Asphalt plant, including gravel-mix type

(G-9088)
FRANKLIN FOREST PRODUCTS LLC
1260 Old Highway 16 (28640-9755)
PHONE..............................336 982-5550
EMP: 4 **EST:** 2018
SALES (est): 121.97K **Privately Held**
SIC: 2431 Millwork

(G-9089)
HALCORE GROUP INC
American Emergency Vehicles
101 Gates Ln (28640-9704)
PHONE..............................336 982-9824
Mark Van Arnam, *Mgr*
EMP: 36
Web: www.hortonambulance.com
SIC: 3711 Ambulances (motor vehicles), assembly of
HQ: Halcore Group, Inc.
3800 Mcdowell Rd
Grove City OH 43123
614 539-8181

(G-9090)
HALCORE GROUP INC
Also Called: American Emergency Vehicles
101 Gates Ln (28640-9704)
PHONE..............................336 846-8010
Mark Van Arnam, *Pr*
Mark Van Arnam, *Prin*
Randy Hanson, *General Vice President*
Dino Cusumano, *
Chris Eppel, *
◆ **EMP:** 366 **EST:** 1997
SALES (est): 58.08MM **Publicly Held**
Web: www.aev.com
SIC: 3711 Ambulances (motor vehicles), assembly of
PA: Rev Group, Inc.
245 S Executive Dr # 100
Brookfield WI 53005

(G-9091)
MC FARLAND & COMPANY INC
960 Nc Highway 88 W (28640-8813)
P.O. Box 611 (28640-0611)
PHONE..............................336 246-4460
Robert Franklin, *Pr*
Rhonda Herman, *
Michael Strand, *
EMP: 48 **EST:** 1979
SQ FT: 6,500
SALES (est): 7.51MM **Privately Held**
Web: www.mcfarlandbooks.com
SIC: 2731 Books, publishing only

(G-9092)
NEXT SAFETY INC
676 S Main St (28640-9571)
P.O. Box 547 (28640-0547)
PHONE..............................336 246-7700
C Eric Hunter, *Ch*
Ron Criss, *Pr*
Lyndell Devall, *Sec*
EMP: 19 **EST:** 2002
SQ FT: 25,000
SALES (est): 1.6MM **Privately Held**
Web: www.nextsafety.net
SIC: 3841 Surgical and medical instruments

(G-9093)
VANNOY CONSTRUCTION ARCFT LLC
1608 Us Highway 221 N (28640-9808)
PHONE..............................336 846-7191
James B Maloney, *Prin*
EMP: 9 **EST:** 2008
SALES (est): 2.14MM **Privately Held**
Web: www.jrvannoy.com
SIC: 3728 Aircraft parts and equipment, nec

Jonesville
Yadkin County

(G-9094)
CHATEAU JOURDAIN LLC
2406 Swan Creek Rd (28642-9436)
PHONE..............................786 273-2869
Joseph Jourdain, *Prin*
Glennis Rodriguez, *Prin*
EMP: 4 **EST:** 2019
SALES (est): 245.03K **Privately Held**
Web: www.chateaujourdain.com
SIC: 2084 Wines

(G-9095)
CHRONICLE-OF-VICTORIACOM
110 S Arlington Ave (28642-2702)
PHONE..............................336 258-2022
EMP: 4 **EST:** 2017
SALES (est): 56.95K **Privately Held**
Web: www.chronicle-of-victoria.com
SIC: 2741 Miscellaneous publishing

(G-9096)
FOOTHILLS SUG CURED CNTRY HAMS
522 S Main St (28642-2726)
PHONE..............................336 835-2411
Greg Purdue, *Pt*
Stephen Edwards, *Pt*
EMP: 18 **EST:** 1997
SQ FT: 2,000
SALES (est): 918.13K **Privately Held**
SIC: 2011 Meat packing plants

(G-9097)
GENERATIONS L LLC
220 Winston Rd (28642-2209)
PHONE..............................336 835-3095
Doug Longworth, *Prin*
EMP: 4 **EST:** 2008
SALES (est): 429.73K **Privately Held**
SIC: 3421 Table and food cutlery, including butchers'

GEOGRAPHIC SECTION

Kannapolis - Cabarrus County (G-9124)

(G-9098)
GRANDEUR MANUFACTURING INC
Also Called: Salt Water Lite
2200 Nc Highway 67 (28642-9251)
P.O. Box 216 (28642-0216)
PHONE.............................336 526-2468
Mike Phillips, *Pr*
Tricia Phillips, *Sec*
Jennie Wilkins, *Adm/Asst*
EMP: 22 **EST:** 1989
SQ FT: 12,500
SALES (est): 4.09MM **Privately Held**
Web: www.grandeurcycle.com
SIC: 3599 Custom machinery

(G-9099)
K P WELDING INC
3133 Swan Creek Rd (28642-9441)
PHONE.............................540 250-7187
Amy Combs, *Prin*
EMP: 6 **EST:** 2017
SALES (est): 73.63K **Privately Held**
SIC: 7692 Welding repair

(G-9100)
MIDNIGHT MNDANCE VINEYARDS LLC
5040 Howell School Rd (28642-9560)
PHONE.............................336 835-6681
EMP: 4 **EST:** 2012
SALES (est): 68.62K **Privately Held**
SIC: 2084 Wines

(G-9101)
PARRISH TIRE COMPANY
547 Winston Rd (28642-2217)
PHONE.............................704 872-6565
Tim Chaffin, *Mgr*
EMP: 26
SALES (corp-wide): 378.88MM **Privately Held**
Web: www.parrishtire.com
SIC: 5531 5014 7534 Automotive tires; Tires and tubes; Tire recapping
PA: Parrish Tire Company
5130 Indiana Ave
Winston Salem NC 27106
800 849-8473

(G-9102)
TOWN OF JONESVILLE
Also Called: Jonesville Water Plant
399 Shaw St (28642-2155)
PHONE.............................336 835-2250
Scott Buffkin, *Mgr*
EMP: 5
Web: www.jonesvillenc.gov
SIC: 3589 Water treatment equipment, industrial
PA: Town Of Jonesville
1503 Nc Highway 67
Jonesville NC 28642
336 835-3426

(G-9103)
WOODTEKS LLC
5243 Captains Trl (28642-9398)
PHONE.............................336 244-1718
Jason Benge, *Prin*
EMP: 4 **EST:** 2015
SALES (est): 53.24K **Privately Held**
Web: www.woodteksllc.com
SIC: 2499 Wood products, nec

Julian
Guilford County

(G-9104)
BATTLGRUND STRTER GNERATOR INC
4497 Folger Rd (27283-8009)
PHONE.............................336 685-4511
Jerry Brown, *VP*
Sylvia C Brown, *Sec*
EMP: 4 **EST:** 1978
SQ FT: 2,400
SALES (est): 368.6K **Privately Held**
SIC: 3621 Starters, for motors

(G-9105)
HOMELAND CREAMERY LLC
6506 Bowman Dairy Rd (27283-9122)
PHONE.............................336 685-6455
Bowman Theresa, *Prin*
EMP: 4 **EST:** 2003
SQ FT: 2,069
SALES (est): 659.25K **Privately Held**
Web: www.homelandcreamery.com
SIC: 2024 Ice cream, bulk

(G-9106)
PLASTERING
5405 Woodlane Dr (27283-9196)
PHONE.............................336 402-0445
EMP: 5 **EST:** 2011
SALES (est): 73.92K **Privately Held**
SIC: 3299 Stucco

(G-9107)
PRINTS ON PARADE LLC
6148 Liberty Rd (27283-9166)
PHONE.............................713 387-9061
Ryan Davis, *Prin*
EMP: 5 **EST:** 2018
SALES (est): 76.07K **Privately Held**
SIC: 2752 Commercial printing, lithographic

(G-9108)
S ERNIE MACHINE CO INC
4722 Old Julian Rd (27283-9210)
P.O. Box 78182 (27427-8182)
PHONE.............................336 852-6355
Ernest R Ledford Junior, *Pr*
Eyvonne Ledford, *Sec*
Betty Aker, *VP*
EMP: 13 **EST:** 1977
SALES (est): 339.85K **Privately Held**
SIC: 3599 Machine shop, jobbing and repair

(G-9109)
YATES AMERICAN MACHINE COMPANY
5309 Burrow Rd (27283-8002)
PHONE.............................336 685-5118
EMP: 4 **EST:** 2016
SALES (est): 55.55K **Privately Held**
SIC: 3599 Machine shop, jobbing and repair

Kannapolis
Cabarrus County

(G-9110)
1ST PLACE EMBROIDERY INC
6749 Plyler Rd (28081-8795)
PHONE.............................704 239-8844
Zachary Conner, *Prin*
EMP: 4 **EST:** 2019
SALES (est): 50.74K **Privately Held**
SIC: 2395 Embroidery and art needlework

(G-9111)
BOMMERANG IMPRINTS
2305 Beaver Pond Rd (28083-6504)
PHONE.............................704 933-9075
EMP: 5 **EST:** 2007
SALES (est): 73.63K **Privately Held**
SIC: 3949 Boomerangs

(G-9112)
BRIGHT PATH LABORATORIES INC
150 N Research Campus Dr (28081-3384)
PHONE.............................858 281-8121
Tony Quinones, *Prin*
Phil Lichtenberger, *Prin*
John Lalonde, *Prin*
Matt Demarey, *Prin*
Todd Smith, *Prin*
EMP: 8 **EST:** 2017
SALES (est): 1.18MM **Privately Held**
Web: www.brightpathlabs.com
SIC: 2834 Pharmaceutical preparations

(G-9113)
BROWN CABINET CO
1510 N Ridge Ave (28083-1703)
P.O. Box 122 (28082-0122)
PHONE.............................704 933-2731
Doug Brown, *Owner*
EMP: 4 **EST:** 1935
SQ FT: 5,000
SALES (est): 226.57K **Privately Held**
Web: www.browncabinetcompany.com
SIC: 2511 2434 Wood household furniture; Wood kitchen cabinets

(G-9114)
CABARRUS CYCLING COMPANY
109 West Ave (28081-4332)
PHONE.............................704 938-8735
EMP: 6 **EST:** 2020
SALES (est): 246.35K **Privately Held**
Web: www.cabarruscyclingco.com
SIC: 3732 Boatbuilding and repairing

(G-9115)
CGI INC
712 N Cannon Blvd (28083-3704)
PHONE.............................704 932-1820
Christopher Gardner, *Pr*
EMP: 10 **EST:** 2008
SALES (est): 110.34K **Privately Held**
SIC: 3231 Products of purchased glass

(G-9116)
DALE RAY FABRICS LLC
1121 N Main St (28081-2256)
PHONE.............................704 932-6411
Dale Ray Cathcart, *Owner*
EMP: 7 **EST:** 1978
SQ FT: 10,000
SALES (est): 310K **Privately Held**
Web: www.dalerayfabrics.com
SIC: 2392 5719 5714 Cushions and pillows; Wicker, rattan, or reed home furnishings; Upholstery materials

(G-9117)
DIAGNOSTIC SHOP INC
Also Called: Diagnostic Shop and Repair
723 Fairview St (28083-5201)
PHONE.............................704 933-3435
Joshua Rachels, *Pr*
EMP: 5 **EST:** 2014
SQ FT: 4,500
SALES (est): 670.16K **Privately Held**
Web: www.diagnosticshop.guru
SIC: 3011 7549 7539 5531 Automobile tires, pneumatic; Emissions testing without repairs, automotive; Brake repair, automotive; Automotive tires

(G-9118)
ECS ENTERPRISES INC
7200 Devonshire Dr (28081-7722)
PHONE.............................704 786-1600
Cliff Sult, *CEO*
John Stilwell, *
EMP: 60 **EST:** 1990
SALES (est): 4.72MM **Privately Held**
SIC: 3993 3599 Displays and cutouts, window and lobby; Machine and other job shop work

(G-9119)
ENVIRNMNTAL CMFORT SLTIONS INC
1400 S Main St (28081-5918)
PHONE.............................980 272-7327
Michelle Setzekorn, *CEO*
Jonathan Setzekorn, *
EMP: 26 **EST:** 2005
SQ FT: 5,000
SALES (est): 3.06MM **Privately Held**
Web: www.environmentalcomfortsolutions.com
SIC: 5063 5075 3625 8748 Electrical apparatus and equipment; Warm air heating and air conditioning; Relays and industrial controls; Energy conservation consultant

(G-9120)
GENIXUS CORP (PA)
Also Called: Genixus
150 N Research Campus Dr (28081-3384)
PHONE.............................877 436-4987
Kendall Foster, *CEO*
EMP: 10 **EST:** 2020
SALES (est): 2.66MM
SALES (corp-wide): 2.66MM **Privately Held**
Web: www.genixus.com
SIC: 2834 Pharmaceutical preparations

(G-9121)
HANGING C FARMS
709 China Grove Rd (28083-8800)
PHONE.............................704 239-6691
EMP: 12 **EST:** 2011
SALES (est): 753.06K **Privately Held**
SIC: 3537 Industrial trucks and tractors

(G-9122)
HYGEIA CORPORATION
P.O. Box 210 (28082-0210)
PHONE.............................704 933-5190
EMP: 6 **EST:** 2012
SALES (est): 217.23K **Privately Held**
SIC: 3069 Fabricated rubber products, nec

(G-9123)
HYGEIA MARKETING CORPORATION
729 S Main St (28081-4915)
PHONE.............................704 933-5190
John A Bishop, *Pr*
Malcom Bishop, *VP*
EMP: 11 **EST:** 1986
SALES (est): 483.68K **Privately Held**
SIC: 3069 Birth control devices, rubber

(G-9124)
INNOVATIVE CUSTOM CABINETS INC
1018 Robinhood Ln (28081-5744)
PHONE.............................813 748-0655
Angel L Ortiz, *Prin*
EMP: 4 **EST:** 2011
SALES (est): 199.35K **Privately Held**
SIC: 2434 Wood kitchen cabinets

Kannapolis - Cabarrus County (G-9125) GEOGRAPHIC SECTION

(G-9125)
KANNAPOLIS AWARDS AND GRAPHICS
1103 Central Dr (28083-3736)
PHONE.................................704 224-3695
Derik Wieland, *Mgr*
EMP: 5 **EST:** 2017
SALES (est): 93.95K **Privately Held**
SIC: 2759 Screen printing

(G-9126)
LOLLIPOP CENRAL
3111 Mocking Bird Ln (28083-9225)
PHONE.................................704 934-0015
Crissie Cain, *Owner*
EMP: 5 **EST:** 2016
SALES (est): 64.26K **Privately Held**
SIC: 2064 Lollipops and other hard candy

(G-9127)
MRA SERVICES INC
2500 S Cannon Blvd (28083-6912)
PHONE.................................704 933-4300
James J Miller, *Pr*
EMP: 12 **EST:** 1986
SALES (est): 982.15K **Privately Held**
Web: www.mraservices.net
SIC: 2741 8711 Technical manual and paper publishing; Consulting engineer

(G-9128)
O GRAYSON COMPANY
6509 Grayson Ln (28081-9608)
PHONE.................................704 932-6195
Van D Stamey, *Pr*
G O'dell Stamey, *Sec*
▲ **EMP:** 50 **EST:** 1973
SQ FT: 52,000
SALES (est): 11.45MM **Privately Held**
SIC: 2844 Hair preparations, including shampoos

(G-9129)
PASB INC
303 N Cannon Blvd (28083-3822)
PHONE.................................704 490-2556
Lee N Forrest, *Pr*
EMP: 5 **EST:** 2003
SALES (est): 370.76K **Privately Held**
SIC: 2273 Art squares, textile fiber

(G-9130)
PHILLIPS MOBILE HOME VLG LLC
7740 Freeze Rd (28081-8963)
PHONE.................................704 298-4648
Richard Phillips, *Brnch Mgr*
EMP: 6
SALES (corp-wide): 65.02K **Privately Held**
SIC: 2451 Mobile homes
PA: Phillips Mobile Home Village, Llc
113 Crescent Place Ln
Mooresville NC

(G-9131)
SALUBRENT PHRMA SOLUTIONS CORP
150 N Research Campus Dr Ste 3700 (28081)
PHONE.................................301 980-7224
Terry Novak, *CEO*
EMP: 5 **EST:** 2020
SALES (est): 546.08K **Privately Held**
Web: www.salubrent.com
SIC: 2834 Pharmaceutical preparations

(G-9132)
SENTEK DYNAMICS INC
1548 Roger Dale Carter Dr Ste A (28081-7729)
PHONE.................................980 556-7081
EMP: 7 **EST:** 2011
SALES (est): 107.32K **Privately Held**
Web: www.sentekdynamics.com
SIC: 3829 Measuring and controlling devices, nec

(G-9133)
SMITHFIELD FOODS INC
2975 Dale Earnhardt Blvd (28083-1404)
PHONE.................................704 298-0936
EMP: 15
Web: www.smithfieldfoods.com
SIC: 2011 Meat packing plants
HQ: Smithfield Foods, Inc.
200 Commerce St
Smithfield VA 23430
757 365-3000

(G-9134)
SS MANUFACTURING INC
703 Mooresville Rd Ste B (28081-4309)
PHONE.................................770 317-8121
EMP: 6 **EST:** 2018
SALES (est): 89.9K **Privately Held**
Web: www.ss-manufacturing.com
SIC: 3999 Manufacturing industries, nec

(G-9135)
SUNDROP PRINTING
700 N Cannon Blvd (28083-3798)
PHONE.................................704 960-1592
EMP: 5 **EST:** 2016
SALES (est): 83.91K **Privately Held**
Web: www.sundropgraphics.com
SIC: 2752 Commercial printing, lithographic

(G-9136)
TOWEL CITY TIRE & WHEEL LLC
1601 N Ridge Ave (28083-2788)
PHONE.................................704 933-2143
Herbert O Cauble Iii, *Pr*
Herbert O Cauble Junior, *Treas*
Danny R Cauble, *VP*
EMP: 8 **EST:** 1935
SQ FT: 5,000
SALES (est): 807.15K **Privately Held**
Web: www.towelcityracingtires.com
SIC: 7534 5531 5014 Tire recapping; Automotive tires; Automobile tires and tubes

Kelly
Bladen County

(G-9137)
DANIEL A MALPASS LOGGING
21819 Nc Highway 53 E (28448-8441)
PHONE.................................910 669-2823
Daniel Malpass, *Prin*
EMP: 8 **EST:** 2007
SALES (est): 238.21K **Privately Held**
SIC: 2411 Logging

(G-9138)
HIGH VELOCITY ARCHERY LLC ◆
18879 Nc Highway 53 E (28448-8409)
P.O. Box 91 (28448-0091)
PHONE.................................910 620-5215
EMP: 4 **EST:** 2022
SALES (est): 79.3K **Privately Held**
SIC: 3949 7389 Archery equipment, general; Business services, nec

(G-9139)
TOPLINK PUBLISHING
2227 Natmore Rd (28448-8677)
PHONE.................................888 375-9818
EMP: 4 **EST:** 2017
SALES (est): 66.03K **Privately Held**
SIC: 2741 Miscellaneous publishing

Kenansville
Duplin County

(G-9140)
AG PROVISION LLC (PA)
277 Faison W Mcgowan Rd (28349-8948)
PHONE.................................910 296-0302
▲ **EMP:** 30 **EST:** 1990
SQ FT: 182,000
SALES (est): 39.76MM **Privately Held**
Web: www.agprovisionllc.com
SIC: 5191 2841 Chemicals, agricultural; Detergents, synthetic organic or inorganic alkaline

(G-9141)
COASTAL CAROLINA CLEAN PWR LLC
1838 N Nc 11 903 Hwy (28349-8729)
P.O. Box 809 (28349-0809)
PHONE.................................910 296-1909
Darren Stephens, *Pr*
Kyle Michael, *Managing Member*
Vince Cegielski, *CFO*
EMP: 10 **EST:** 2003
SALES (est): 478.79K **Privately Held**
Web: www.coastalccp.com
SIC: 3621 Power generators

(G-9142)
COX NRTH CRLINA PBLCATIONS INC
Also Called: Duplin Times
102 Front St (28349)
P.O. Box 69 (28349-0069)
PHONE.................................910 296-0239
EMP: 4
SALES (corp-wide): 2.85B **Privately Held**
Web: www.reflector.com
SIC: 2711 Newspapers: publishing only, not printed on site
HQ: Cox North Carolina Publications, Inc.
1150 Sugg Pkwy
Greenville NC 27834
252 329-9643

(G-9143)
GUILFORD PERFORMANCE TEXTILES ◆
1754 Nc-903 (28349)
PHONE.................................910 296-5362
EMP: 8 **EST:** 2022
SALES (est): 63.22K **Privately Held**
Web: www.lear.com
SIC: 3714 Motor vehicle parts and accessories

(G-9144)
LEAR CORPORATION
1754 N Nc 11 903 Hwy (28349)
P.O. Box 509 (28349-0509)
PHONE.................................910 296-8671
John Emmett, *Pr*
EMP: 50
SALES (corp-wide): 23.47B **Publicly Held**
Web: www.lear.com
SIC: 2258 2282 Cloth, warp knit; Acetate filament yarn: throwing, twisting, winding, spooling
PA: Lear Corporation
21557 Telegraph Rd
Southfield MI 48033
248 447-1500

(G-9145)
QUO VADEMUS LLC
277 Faison W Mcgowan Rd (28349-8948)
PHONE.................................910 296-1632
Gabriela Greilinger, *Managing Member*
EMP: 9 **EST:** 2008
SALES (est): 992.2K **Privately Held**
SIC: 2836 Veterinary biological products

Kenly
Johnston County

(G-9146)
CAROLINA EMBROIDERY KENLY INC
103 N Gardner Ave (27542-9608)
PHONE.................................919 279-2356
Mary Stuart Champion, *Admn*
EMP: 5 **EST:** 2014
SALES (est): 50.14K **Privately Held**
SIC: 2395 Embroidery and art needlework

(G-9147)
CCO HOLDINGS LLC
607 W 2nd St (27542-7723)
PHONE.................................919 502-4007
EMP: 107
SALES (corp-wide): 54.61B **Publicly Held**
SIC: 4841 3663 3651 Cable television services; Radio and t.v. communications equipment; Household audio and video equipment
HQ: Cco Holdings, Llc
400 Atlantic St
Stamford CT 06901
203 905-7801

(G-9148)
CONESTOGA WOOD SPC CORP
621 Johnston Pkwy (27542-7516)
PHONE.................................919 284-2258
Roger Anderson, *Brnch Mgr*
EMP: 100
SALES (corp-wide): 214.83MM **Privately Held**
Web: www.conestogawood.com
SIC: 2514 2434 Kitchen cabinets: metal; Wood kitchen cabinets
PA: Conestoga Wood Specialties Corporation
245 Reading Rd
East Earl PA 17519
717 445-6701

(G-9149)
CUMMINS ATLANTIC LLC
Also Called: Cummins
350 Cummins Dr (27542-7545)
PHONE.................................919 284-9111
Michael Stanford, *Mgr*
EMP: 48
SALES (corp-wide): 34.06B **Publicly Held**
SIC: 5084 3519 Engines and parts, diesel; Internal combustion engines, nec
HQ: Cummins Atlantic Llc
11101 Nations Ford Rd
Charlotte NC 28273

(G-9150)
CUMMINS INC
350 Cummins Dr (27542-7545)
PHONE.................................919 284-9111
Michael Stanford, *Brnch Mgr*
EMP: 5
SALES (corp-wide): 34.06B **Publicly Held**
Web: www.cummins.com
SIC: 3714 Motor vehicle parts and accessories
PA: Cummins Inc.
500 Jackson St
Columbus IN 47201
812 377-5000

GEOGRAPHIC SECTION
Kernersville - Forsyth County (G-9175)

(G-9151)
DAUGHTERS & RYAN INC
207 Johnston Pkwy (27542-7503)
PHONE.................................919 284-0153
EMP: 9
SALES (est): 142.68K **Privately Held**
SIC: 3069 Pipestems or bits, tobacco: hard rubber

(G-9152)
FUEL DOC 16
214 E 2nd St (27542)
PHONE.................................919 284-5400
Anne Sims, *Prin*
EMP: 6 **EST:** 2007
SALES (est): 104.41K **Privately Held**
SIC: 2869 Fuels

(G-9153)
HERSHEY COMPANY
Also Called: Hershey
104 Hershey Dr (27542-7536)
PHONE.................................919 284-0272
Ronald Wishall, *Mgr*
EMP: 10
SALES (corp-wide): 10.42B **Publicly Held**
Web: www.thehersheycompany.com
SIC: 2064 5143 Candy and other confectionery products; Dairy products, except dried or canned
PA: Hershey Company
19 E Chocolate Ave
Hershey PA 17033
717 534-4200

(G-9154)
PERDUE FARMS INC
Also Called: Perdue Farms
9266 Revell Rd (27542-9204)
PHONE.................................919 284-2033
Darryl Bryant, *Brnch Mgr*
EMP: 82
SALES (corp-wide): 1.24B **Privately Held**
Web: www.perdue.com
SIC: 2015 Poultry slaughtering and processing
PA: Perdue Farms Incorporated
31149 Old Ocean City Rd
Salisbury MD 21804
800 473-7383

(G-9155)
PETROLEUM TANK CORPORATION
Also Called: Petco
600 N Gardner Ave (27542)
P.O. Box 429 (27542-0429)
PHONE.................................919 284-2418
Greg Narron, *Pr*
Lois Narron, *Sec*
EMP: 16 **EST:** 1954
SQ FT: 1,000
SALES (est): 1.81MM **Privately Held**
Web: www.pettank.com
SIC: 3713 7699 5084 Tank truck bodies; Tank repair and cleaning services; Textile and leather machinery

(G-9156)
RICHARD D STEWART
Also Called: Kenly News
201 W 2nd St (27542-5001)
P.O. Box 39 (27542-0039)
PHONE.................................919 284-2295
Richard D Stewart, *Owner*
EMP: 7 **EST:** 1973
SQ FT: 6,000
SALES (est): 325.08K **Privately Held**
Web: www.kenlynews.com
SIC: 2711 2791 Newspapers, publishing and printing; Typesetting

(G-9157)
RPP ACQUISITION LLC
Also Called: Quantum Plastics Raleigh
131 Johnston Pkwy (27542-7504)
PHONE.................................919 248-9001
Ron Embree, *CEO*
Lisa Fiorenza, *
EMP: 25 **EST:** 2018
SQ FT: 45,000
SALES (est): 9.99MM **Privately Held**
SIC: 3089 Injection molded finished plastics products, nec
HQ: Qp Holdings, Llc
3730 Wheeler Ave
Fort Smith AR 72901
479 646-3473

Kernersville
Forsyth County

(G-9158)
A & S TOOL & DIE CO INC
1510 Brookford Industrial Dr (27284-9412)
P.O. Box 890 (27285-0890)
PHONE.................................336 993-3440
Jack Hale, *Pr*
Ken Hale, *VP*
EMP: 6 **EST:** 1958
SQ FT: 7,000
SALES (est): 497.39K **Privately Held**
SIC: 3599 Machine shop, jobbing and repair

(G-9159)
ADVANTAGE FITNESS PRODUCTS INC
115 Gralin St (27284-3998)
P.O. Box 710 (29566-0710)
PHONE.................................336 643-8810
Brent Johnson, *Pr*
EMP: 11 **EST:** 2005
SALES (est): 599.56K **Privately Held**
Web: www.afpnorthamerica.com
SIC: 3949 Exercise equipment

(G-9160)
ALLIED TOOL AND MACHINE CO (PA)
115 Corum St (27284-2927)
P.O. Box 706 (27285-0706)
PHONE.................................336 993-2131
Nan Kollar, *Pr*
Joe Kollar, *VP*
Mildred Ballard, *Sec*
EMP: 7 **EST:** 1945
SQ FT: 40,000
SALES (est): 2.45MM
SALES (corp-wide): 2.45MM **Privately Held**
SIC: 3469 3444 Appliance parts, porcelain enameled; Sheet metalwork

(G-9161)
ALTERNATIVE CARE GROUP LLC
931 S Main St Ste A (27284-7459)
PHONE.................................336 499-5644
EMP: 4 **EST:** 2009
SALES (est): 223.73K **Privately Held**
Web: www.alternativecaregroup.com
SIC: 3842 Prosthetic appliances

(G-9162)
AMANZI MARBLE & GRANITE LLC
703 Park Lawn Ct (27284-8967)
PHONE.................................336 993-9998
EMP: 6 **EST:** 2004
SALES (est): 1.63MM **Privately Held**
Web: www.amanzigranite.com
SIC: 3281 Granite, cut and shaped

(G-9163)
AMERICAN CYLINDER PRODUCTS INC
115 Furlong Industrial Dr (27284-3242)
P.O. Box 408 (27285-0408)
PHONE.................................336 993-7722
Phillip E Fuller Junior, *Pr*
Tony W Seaford, *VP*
Darlene S Fuller, *Treas*
EMP: 5 **EST:** 2010
SALES (est): 497.97K **Privately Held**
Web: www.americancylinderproducts.com
SIC: 3599 Machine shop, jobbing and repair

(G-9164)
AMERICAN WOOD REFACE OF TRIAD
5339 Valleydale Rd (27284-7874)
PHONE.................................336 345-2837
EMP: 5 **EST:** 2017
SALES (est): 64.21K **Privately Held**
Web: www.woodreface.com
SIC: 2434 Wood kitchen cabinets

(G-9165)
ARTWEAR EMBROIDERY INC (PA)
621 Indeneer Dr (27284-3581)
PHONE.................................336 992-2166
Cindy Cox-wilson, *Pr*
Jerry Davis, *VP*
EMP: 24 **EST:** 1993
SALES (est): 1.57MM **Privately Held**
Web: www.artwearinc.com
SIC: 2395 Embroidery products, except Schiffli machine

(G-9166)
ATLANTIC MANUFACTURING LLC
1322 S Park Dr (27284-3151)
PHONE.................................336 497-5500
EMP: 5 **EST:** 2017
SALES (est): 91.1K **Privately Held**
SIC: 3999 Manufacturing industries, nec

(G-9167)
BEESON SIGN CO INC
213 Berry Garden Rd (27284-9449)
PHONE.................................336 993-5617
Chris Beeson, *Pr*
Allan Lamper, *Mgr*
EMP: 6 **EST:** 1972
SALES (est): 495.29K **Privately Held**
Web: www.beesonsignco.com
SIC: 3993 Electric signs

(G-9168)
BELEWS CREEK VINEYARD
1952 Pondarosa Dr (27284-8065)
PHONE.................................904 345-1466
David Moore, *Prin*
EMP: 4 **EST:** 2018
SALES (est): 74.48K **Privately Held**
SIC: 2084 Wines

(G-9169)
BRIDGPORT RESTORATION SVCS INC
742 Park Lawn Ct (27284-8967)
P.O. Box 1051 (27285-1051)
PHONE.................................336 996-1212
EMP: 11 **EST:** 1987
SQ FT: 1,500
SALES (est): 432.19K **Privately Held**
Web: www.bridgeportrestoration.com
SIC: 7217 1799 2269 7342 Carpet and upholstery cleaning; Post disaster renovations; Finishing plants, nec; Disinfecting and deodorizing

(G-9170)
CARAUSTAR INDUS CNSMR PDTS GRO
Also Called: Kernersville Adhesives Plant
1485 Plaza South Dr (27284-3515)
PHONE.................................336 564-2163
EMP: 8
SALES (corp-wide): 5.22B **Publicly Held**
SIC: 2655 Fiber cans, drums, and similar products
HQ: Caraustar Industrial And Consumer Products Group Inc
5000 Austell Powder Ste
Austell GA 30106
803 548-5100

(G-9171)
CARAUSTAR INDUS CNSMR PDTS GRO
Also Called: Kernsville Tube Plant
1045 Industrial Park Dr (27284-9481)
PHONE.................................336 996-4165
David Partin, *Mgr*
EMP: 49
SALES (corp-wide): 5.22B **Publicly Held**
SIC: 2655 Fiber cans, drums, and similar products
HQ: Caraustar Industrial And Consumer Products Group Inc
5000 Austell Powder Ste
Austell GA 30106
803 548-5100

(G-9172)
CARAUSTAR INDUSTRIES INC
1496 Plaza South Dr (27284-3514)
PHONE.................................336 992-1053
Charlie Burton, *Manager*
EMP: 22
SALES (corp-wide): 5.22B **Publicly Held**
Web: www.greif.com
SIC: 2655 Tubes, fiber or paper: made from purchased material
HQ: Caraustar Industries, Inc.
5000 Astell Pwdr Sprng Rd
Austell GA 30106
770 948-3101

(G-9173)
CAROLINA NORTH MFG INC
1161 S Park Dr (27284-3114)
P.O. Box 339 (27358-0339)
PHONE.................................336 992-0082
Kent Southard, *Pr*
Linda Southard, *Sec*
▲ **EMP:** 6 **EST:** 1991
SQ FT: 9,000
SALES (est): 944.75K **Privately Held**
Web: www.roperatchet.com
SIC: 3429 Marine hardware

(G-9174)
CARTER PUBLISHING COMPANY INC
Also Called: Carter Office Supplies
300 E Mountain St (27284-2943)
P.O. Box 337 (27285-0337)
PHONE.................................336 993-2161
John Owensby, *Pr*
Connie Owensby, *
EMP: 18 **EST:** 1938
SQ FT: 20,000
SALES (est): 2.04MM **Privately Held**
Web: www.kernersvillenews.com
SIC: 2711 5943 2759 Commercial printing and newspaper publishing combined; Office forms and supplies; Letterpress printing

(G-9175)
CASTLE SHIRT COMPANY LLC
621 Indeneer Dr Ste 1 (27284-3570)

Kernersville - Forsyth County (G-9176)

P.O. Box 8666 (27419-0666)
PHONE..................................336 992-7727
Jenny Zmuda, *Managing Member*
Jinny Zmuda, *Managing Member*
▲ **EMP:** 10 **EST:** 1999
SALES (est): 448.49K **Privately Held**
SIC: 2759 Screen printing

(G-9176)
CGMI ACQUISITION COMPANY LLC
Also Called: Clearlight Glass and Mirror
1318 Shields Rd (27284-3532)
PHONE..................................919 533-6123
EMP: 15 **EST:** 2017
SALES (est): 2.48MM **Privately Held**
Web: www.clearlightglass.com
SIC: 3231 Mirrored glass

(G-9177)
CHICHIBONE INC (PA)
Also Called: McNamara & Company
P.O. Box 667 (27285-0667)
PHONE..................................919 785-0090
Pat Mcnamara, *Pr*
Phil Mcnamara, *Sr VP*
Dick Polenm, *CFO*
EMP: 15 **EST:** 1999
SALES (est): 26.15MM
SALES (corp-wide): 26.15MM **Privately Held**
Web: www.trs-sesco.com
SIC: 3585 7623 3561 Heating and air conditioning combination units; Refrigeration service and repair; Pumps and pumping equipment

(G-9178)
CHOPPERS AND HOTRODS
1527 Union Cross Rd (27284-6500)
PHONE..................................336 993-3939
Scottie Craven, *Owner*
EMP: 5 **EST:** 2008
SALES (est): 56.27K **Privately Held**
SIC: 3751 Motorcycles and related parts

(G-9179)
CINDY BLACKBURN
7650 Anthony Rd (27284-8720)
PHONE..................................336 643-3822
Cindy Blackburn, *Prin*
EMP: 5 **EST:** 2010
SALES (est): 135.32K **Privately Held**
SIC: 3911 Jewelry, precious metal

(G-9180)
CLARIOS LLC
Also Called: Johnson Controls
2701 Johnson Controls Dr (27284-5200)
P.O. Box 1667 (27285-1667)
PHONE..................................336 761-1550
Dick Tryor, *Mgr*
EMP: 270
SQ FT: 250,000
SALES (corp-wide): 4.48B **Privately Held**
Web: www.clarios.com
SIC: 2531 3692 3691 Seats, automobile; Primary batteries, dry and wet; Storage batteries
HQ: Clarios, Llc
   5757 N Green Bay Ave
   Milwaukee WI 53209

(G-9181)
COLUMBIANA HI TECH LLC (PA)
1621 Old Greensboro Rd (27284-6855)
PHONE..................................336 497-3600
EMP: 60 **EST:** 1985
SALES (est): 4.68MM
SALES (corp-wide): 4.68MM **Privately Held**

SIC: 3443 Nuclear shielding, metal plate

(G-9182)
CORILAM FABRICATING CO
5211 Macy Grove Rd (27284-0204)
P.O. Box 361 (27285-0361)
PHONE..................................336 993-2371
Bradley Robins, *Pr*
Brad Robins, *
Miles West, *
Andrew J Robins, *
Charles Gray, *
▲ **EMP:** 45 **EST:** 1975
SQ FT: 84,000
SALES (est): 7.65MM **Privately Held**
Web: www.corilam.com
SIC: 2541 2531 2521 2434 Wood partitions and fixtures; Public building and related furniture; Wood office furniture; Wood kitchen cabinets

(G-9183)
COVINGTON BARCODING INC
1800 Watmead Rd (27284-8761)
PHONE..................................336 996-5759
Mark Covington, *Prin*
EMP: 4 **EST:** 2015
SALES (est): 500.18K **Privately Held**
Web: www.covingtonbarcoding.com
SIC: 3577 7389 Bar code (magnetic ink) printers; Business services, nec

(G-9184)
CREATIVE FISH COMPANY INC
106 Short St (27284-2866)
PHONE..................................203 515-8631
James M Cheshire, *Admn*
EMP: 4 **EST:** 2013
SALES (est): 63.6K **Privately Held**
SIC: 3999 Manufacturing industries, nec

(G-9185)
CUSTOM MACHINING INC
121 Majestic Way Ct Ste D (27284-3259)
P.O. Box 1605 (27285-1605)
PHONE..................................336 996-0855
Alan Mellott, *Pr*
EMP: 6 **EST:** 1991
SQ FT: 2,000
SALES (est): 472.39K **Privately Held**
SIC: 3599 Machine shop, jobbing and repair

(G-9186)
CUSTOM PRINTING SOLUTIONS INC
1355 S Park Dr (27284-3150)
P.O. Box 450 (27285-0450)
PHONE..................................336 992-1161
Devin Lineberry, *Pr*
Jodi Lineberry, *VP*
EMP: 12 **EST:** 2004
SALES (est): 388.22K **Privately Held**
SIC: 2752 Offset printing

(G-9187)
DANBY BARCODING LLC
1800 Watmead Rd (27284-8761)
PHONE..................................770 416-9845
EMP: 5
SALES (est): 287.62K **Privately Held**
SIC: 3565 7389 Labeling machines, industrial ; Business Activities at Non-Commercial Site

(G-9188)
DANISSON USA TRADING LTD LLC
Also Called: Danisson Trading
210 Serenity Pointe Dr (27284-9822)
PHONE..................................704 965-8317
Efstratios Ferentinos, *Pr*
Nick Delis, *VP*

EMP: 8 **EST:** 2010
SALES (est): 209.11K **Privately Held**
SIC: 1389 5172 Cementing oil and gas well casings; Petroleum brokers

(G-9189)
DEERE & COMPANY
Also Called: Deere-Hitachi Cnstr McHy
1000 John Deere Rd (27284-2275)
PHONE..................................336 996-8100
EMP: 4
SALES (corp-wide): 61.25B **Publicly Held**
Web: www.deere.com
SIC: 3523 Farm machinery and equipment
PA: Deere & Company
   1 John Deere Pl
   Moline IL 61265
   309 765-8000

(G-9190)
DIXON CUSTOM CABINETRY LLC
129 Furlong Industrial Dr (27284-3242)
PHONE..................................336 992-3306
EMP: 10 **EST:** 2006
SALES (est): 964.5K **Privately Held**
Web: www.dixoncabinetry.com
SIC: 3553 5031 Cabinet makers' machinery; Kitchen cabinets

(G-9191)
DJ POWDERCOATING IRONWORK LLC
Also Called: Dj Powder Coating
232 Industrial Way Dr Ste A (27284-3260)
PHONE..................................336 310-4725
Marvin Young, *Managing Member*
Denny Young, *Managing Member*
EMP: 5 **EST:** 2008
SALES (est): 473.73K **Privately Held**
Web: www.djpowdercoating.com
SIC: 3479 Coating of metals and formed products

(G-9192)
DONE-GONE ADIOS INC
1318 Shields Rd (27284-3532)
PHONE..................................336 993-7300
EMP: 12 **EST:** 1994
SQ FT: 75,000
SALES (est): 2.11MM **Privately Held**
Web: www.clearlightglass.com
SIC: 5231 3231 Glass; Aquariums and reflectors, glass

(G-9193)
DREAM KREAMS LLC
549 Arbor Hill Rd Apt 5a (27284-3333)
PHONE..................................919 491-1984
Kendra Sharlese Vanhook, *CEO*
EMP: 4 **EST:** 2019
SALES (est): 238.98K **Privately Held**
SIC: 2024 Ice cream and frozen deserts

(G-9194)
EDC INC (PA)
950 Old Winston Rd (27284-8193)
PHONE..................................336 993-0468
EMP: 65 **EST:** 1981
SALES (est): 9.53MM
SALES (corp-wide): 9.53MM **Privately Held**
Web: www.edcinc.com
SIC: 3679 Electronic circuits

(G-9195)
EMERALD TOOL AND MOLD INC
106 Furlong Industrial Dr (27284-3241)
P.O. Box 2462 (27285-2462)
PHONE..................................336 996-6445
Joe Russell, *Pr*

Michael T Young, *VP*
▲ **EMP:** 13 **EST:** 1992
SQ FT: 4,800
SALES (est): 2.46MM **Privately Held**
Web: www.emeraldtoolandmold.com
SIC: 3544 Dies, plastics forming

(G-9196)
EMMCO SPORT LLC
1355 S Park Dr # A (27284-3150)
PHONE..................................336 354-7244
Daniel Emmi, *Managing Member*
EMP: 6 **EST:** 2011
SALES (est): 105.77K **Privately Held**
SIC: 3463 Aluminum forgings

(G-9197)
ENERJALI LLC
7567 Haw Meadows Dr (27284-6700)
PHONE..................................336 451-6479
EMP: 5 **EST:** 2017
SALES (est): 109.02K **Privately Held**
SIC: 3691 Batteries, rechargeable

(G-9198)
EUROGOLD ART
251 N Main St (27284-2879)
P.O. Box 2215 (27285-2215)
PHONE..................................336 989-6205
Mariam Martinca, *Prin*
EMP: 6 **EST:** 2005
SALES (est): 96.48K **Privately Held**
SIC: 3911 Jewelry, precious metal

(G-9199)
EXOTICS POWER COAT
745 Cinema Ct (27284-2494)
PHONE..................................336 831-3865
George Debidart Iii, *Prin*
EMP: 7 **EST:** 2014
SALES (est): 149.77K **Privately Held**
SIC: 3479 Coating of metals and formed products

(G-9200)
FELICE HOSIERY CO INC
118 Burke St (27284-2687)
P.O. Box 1116 (27285-1116)
PHONE..................................336 996-2371
Daniel Hayworth, *Mgr*
EMP: 42
SALES (corp-wide): 2.53MM **Privately Held**
Web: www.iwsocks.com
SIC: 2252 2251 Socks; Women's hosiery, except socks
PA: Felice Hosiery Co, Inc
   632 W Roosevelt Rd
   Chicago IL 60607
   312 922-3710

(G-9201)
FRANK G SHUMATE
145 Bluff School Rd (27284-8866)
PHONE..................................336 784-0828
Frank Shumate, *Owner*
EMP: 5 **EST:** 2018
SALES (est): 113.98K **Privately Held**
SIC: 3545 Machine tool accessories

(G-9202)
GET CUSTOM PRINT
504 Edgewood St (27284-3137)
PHONE..................................336 682-3891
Elmer Ramos, *Prin*
EMP: 4 **EST:** 2018
SALES (est): 178.92K **Privately Held**
SIC: 2752 Commercial printing, lithographic

GEOGRAPHIC SECTION
Kernersville - Forsyth County (G-9229)

(G-9203)
GRASS AMERICA INC
1202 Nc Highway 66 S (27284-3537)
PHONE.................................336 996-4041
Tom Kipp, *Pr*
Scott Bjork, *
Matthias Bulla, *
◆ **EMP:** 201 **EST:** 1977
SQ FT: 190,000
SALES (est): 89.74MM
SALES (corp-wide): 20.7B **Privately Held**
Web: www.grassusa.com
SIC: 5072 3429 Hardware; Furniture, builders' and other household hardware
HQ: Wurth Group Of North America Inc.
93 Grant St
Ramsey NJ 07446

(G-9204)
HEDRICK CONSTRUCTION
838 Crosscreek Rd (27284-8442)
PHONE.................................336 362-3443
Jeff Hedrick, *Owner*
EMP: 5 **EST:** 1995
SALES (est): 301.25K **Privately Held**
Web: www.hedrickconstructionco.com
SIC: 2431 Interior and ornamental woodwork and trim

(G-9205)
IDEAL PRINTING SERVICES INC
4240 Kernersville Rd Ste D (27284-8101)
P.O. Box 161 (27051-0161)
PHONE.................................336 784-0074
Bobby Wolfington, *Pr*
Mark Wolfington, *Sec*
EMP: 5 **EST:** 1964
SQ FT: 3,000
SALES (est): 325.4K **Privately Held**
SIC: 2752 Offset printing

(G-9206)
ILLINOIS TOOL WORKS INC
Texwipe
1210 S Park Dr (27284-3104)
PHONE.................................336 996-7046
Les Josey, *Genl Mgr*
EMP: 200
SALES (corp-wide): 15.93B **Publicly Held**
Web: www.itw.com
SIC: 2842 Specialty cleaning
PA: Illinois Tool Works Inc.
155 Harlem Ave
Glenview IL 60025
847 724-7500

(G-9207)
JOHN DEERE KERNERSVILLE LLC
1000 John Deere Rd (27284-2275)
P.O. Box 1187 (27285-1187)
PHONE.................................336 996-8100
John C May, *CEO*
▲ **EMP:** 691 **EST:** 1988
SALES (est): 125.19MM
SALES (corp-wide): 61.25B **Publicly Held**
Web: www.dhkernersville.com
SIC: 3531 Bituminous, cement and concrete related products and equip.
PA: Deere & Company
1 John Deere Pl
Moline IL 61265
309 765-8000

(G-9208)
LIBERTY PRESS
1356 Amylee Trl (27284-9470)
PHONE.................................336 996-3667
Darius Stewart, *Prin*
EMP: 6 **EST:** 2008
SALES (est): 65.12K **Privately Held**
SIC: 2741 Miscellaneous publishing

(G-9209)
LOFLIN CONCRETE CO INC
2105 Pisgah Church Rd (27284-8063)
PHONE.................................336 904-2788
Richard G Loflin, *Pr*
Denise Loflin, *Sec*
EMP: 35 **EST:** 1925
SQ FT: 23,000
SALES (est): 5.12MM **Privately Held**
Web: www.loflinconcrete.com
SIC: 3273 4214 Ready-mixed concrete; Local trucking with storage

(G-9210)
LOFLIN MATERIALS INC
4880 Old Hollow Rd (27284-9642)
PHONE.................................336 993-2432
EMP: 5 **EST:** 2004
SALES (est): 82.87K **Privately Held**
SIC: 3273 Ready-mixed concrete

(G-9211)
M & S SYSTEMS INC
Also Called: M & S Systems
951 Nc Highway 66 S Ste 6b (27284-3101)
P.O. Box 610 (27235-0610)
PHONE.................................336 996-7118
Marvin R Keel, *Pr*
EMP: 4 **EST:** 1987
SQ FT: 600
SALES (est): 485.96K **Privately Held**
Web: www.stenclabl.net
SIC: 2752 5999 Commercial printing, lithographic; Packaging materials: boxes, padding, etc.

(G-9212)
MARCHING ORDERS INCORPORATED
1014 Grays Land Ct Apt 125 (27284-0048)
PHONE.................................336 497-4251
Sequola Mcneill, *Prin*
EMP: 4 **EST:** 2015
SALES (est): 83.8K **Privately Held**
SIC: 2741 Miscellaneous publishing

(G-9213)
MARIETTA MARTIN MATERIALS INC
Also Called: Salem Stone Quarry
4572 High Point Rd (27284-9158)
PHONE.................................336 769-3803
David Thorne, *Bookkpr*
EMP: 5
Web: www.martinmarietta.com
SIC: 1422 5032 Crushed and broken limestone; Granite building stone
PA: Martin Marietta Materials Inc
4123 Parklake Ave
Raleigh NC 27612

(G-9214)
MARTINS FMOUS PSTRY SHOPPE INC
1031 E Mountain St Bldg 314 (27284-7998)
PHONE.................................800 548-1200
EMP: 5
SALES (corp-wide): 149.7MM **Privately Held**
Web: www.potatorolls.com
SIC: 2051 Rolls, bread type: fresh or frozen
PA: Martin's Famous Pastry Shoppe, Inc.
1000 Potato Roll Ln
Chambersburg PA 17202
800 548-1200

(G-9215)
MEPLA-ALFIT INCORPORATED
1202 Nc Highway 66 S (27284-3537)
PHONE.................................336 289-2300
▼ **EMP:** 45 **EST:** 1977
SQ FT: 100,000
SALES (est): 5.51MM
SALES (corp-wide): 12.52B **Privately Held**
SIC: 3429 Furniture hardware
HQ: Wurth Group Of North America Inc.
93 Grant St
Ramsey NJ 07446
201 818-8877

(G-9216)
METAL PROCESSORS INC
1010 W Mountain St (27284-2257)
P.O. Box 545 (27285-0545)
PHONE.................................336 993-2181
Donald Lee Ballard, *Pr*
Mildred Ballard, *Sec*
EMP: 11 **EST:** 1952
SQ FT: 46,000
SALES (est): 232.55K **Privately Held**
Web: www.metalprocessorsinc.com
SIC: 3452 Bolts, metal

(G-9217)
MJ PRINTING
1490 Plaza South Dr Ste 9 (27284-3530)
PHONE.................................336 992-3828
Mark Joyce, *Owner*
EMP: 4 **EST:** 2006
SALES (est): 299.1K **Privately Held**
Web: www.mjcustomprinting.com
SIC: 2752 Offset printing

(G-9218)
MOCHA MEMOIR PRESS
931 S Main St (27284-7493)
PHONE.................................336 404-7445
EMP: 5 **EST:** 2013
SALES (est): 118.33K **Privately Held**
Web: www.mochamemoirspress.com
SIC: 2741 Miscellaneous publishing

(G-9219)
MORE THAN BILLBOARDS INC
Also Called: Associated Posters
2737 W Mountain St (27284-9332)
PHONE.................................336 723-1018
Robert Arnold, *Pr*
Nina Hill, *VP*
EMP: 36 **EST:** 2017
SALES (est): 5.5MM **Privately Held**
Web: www.associatedposters.com
SIC: 2752 Commercial printing, lithographic

(G-9220)
MORGAN MANUFACTURING
211 Berry Garden Rd (27284-9449)
PHONE.................................336 497-5763
EMP: 4 **EST:** 2015
SALES (est): 100.17K **Privately Held**
SIC: 3999 Manufacturing industries, nec

(G-9221)
OLD CASTLE SERVICE INC
920 Old Winston Rd (27284-8119)
PHONE.................................336 992-1601
Bob Jackson, *Genl Mgr*
EMP: 6 **EST:** 2012
SALES (est): 80.11K **Privately Held**
SIC: 2541 Counter and sink tops

(G-9222)
OLIVE EURO OIL LLC
1369 S Park Dr (27284-3150)
PHONE.................................336 310-4624
Francesco Caccamo, *Managing Member*
EMP: 8 **EST:** 2018
SALES (est): 446.96K **Privately Held**
SIC: 2079 Olive oil

(G-9223)
PALADIN CUSTOM WORKS
230 Perry Rd (27284-2148)
PHONE.................................336 996-2796
Jason Oswalt, *Prin*
EMP: 11 **EST:** 2016
SALES (est): 807.66K **Privately Held**
Web: www.paladinattachments.com
SIC: 3531 Construction machinery

(G-9224)
PAM TRADING CORPORATION
1135 Snow Bridge Ln (27284-8429)
P.O. Box 819 (27235-0819)
PHONE.................................336 668-0901
▲ **EMP:** 38 **EST:** 1983
SALES (est): 8.71MM **Privately Held**
Web: www.paminjectionmolding.com
SIC: 5084 3089 Textile machinery and equipment; Injection molding of plastics

(G-9225)
PRINTING PARTNERS INC
365 W Bodenhamer St (27284-2528)
P.O. Box 837 (27235-0837)
PHONE.................................336 996-2268
Barbara A Hannon, *Pr*
EMP: 8 **EST:** 2002
SQ FT: 7,500
SALES (est): 907.27K **Privately Held**
SIC: 2752 2791 Offset printing; Typesetting

(G-9226)
PROCOATERS INC
216 Industrial Way Dr (27284-3200)
P.O. Box 426 (27285-0426)
PHONE.................................336 992-0012
EMP: 16 **EST:** 1995
SQ FT: 12,000
SALES (est): 1.11MM **Privately Held**
Web: www.procoatersinc.com
SIC: 3479 Painting of metal products

(G-9227)
QMF MTAL ELCTRNIC SLUTIONS INC
324 Berry Garden Rd (27284-9450)
PHONE.................................336 992-8002
Tina H Rierson, *Pr*
Clarence Rierson, *
▲ **EMP:** 85 **EST:** 2002
SQ FT: 75,000
SALES (est): 16.89MM **Privately Held**
SIC: 3444 3679 Sheet metal specialties, not stamped; Antennas, receiving

(G-9228)
QUALITY MACHINE & TOOL
1793 Union Cross Rd (27284-7582)
PHONE.................................336 769-9131
George Yountz, *Pr*
Zachary Yountz, *VP*
Juanita Yountz, *Sec*
EMP: 8 **EST:** 1978
SQ FT: 8,640
SALES (est): 597.85K **Privately Held**
SIC: 3599 Machine shop, jobbing and repair

(G-9229)
RUGBY ACQUISITION LLC
637 Graves St (27284-3205)
PHONE.................................336 993-8686
Doug Forstrom, *Genl Mgr*
EMP: 59
SALES (corp-wide): 2.58B **Privately Held**
Web: www.rugbyabp.com
SIC: 5031 2821 2541 2434 Lumber: rough, dressed, and finished; Plastics materials and resins; Wood partitions and fixtures; Wood kitchen cabinets
HQ: Rugby Acquisition Llc

Kernersville - Forsyth County (G-9230)

1 Pillsbury St Ste 302
Concord NH 03301
603 369-4710

(G-9230)
SAF-HOLLAND INC
952 Kensal Green Dr (27284-7668)
PHONE..................336 310-4595
EMP: 6 EST: 2017
SALES (est): 162.18K **Privately Held**
Web: www.safholland.com
SIC: 3714 Motor vehicle parts and accessories

(G-9231)
SALEM ONE INC
Also Called: Postmark
1155 Distribution Ct (27284-0039)
PHONE..................336 722-2886
John Bowman, Brnch Mgr
EMP: 15
SALES (corp-wide): 25.3MM **Privately Held**
Web: www.postmark.ws
SIC: 7331 8742 2752 Mailing service; Marketing consulting services; Commercial printing, lithographic
PA: Salem One, Inc.
  5670 Shattalon Dr
  Winston Salem NC 27105
  336 744-9990

(G-9232)
SANDALWOOD HEALING CENTER INC
935 E Mountain St Ste L (27284-3238)
PHONE..................828 228-4517
Ashly D Black, Pr
EMP: 6 EST: 2014
SALES (est): 109.04K **Privately Held**
SIC: 2499 Wood products, nec

(G-9233)
SIGN RESOURCES OF NC
673 Gralin St Ste B (27284-3457)
PHONE..................336 310-4611
James Braun, Prin
EMP: 4 EST: 2009
SALES (est): 482.52K **Privately Held**
Web: www.signresourcesnc.com
SIC: 3993 Signs and advertising specialties

(G-9234)
SIMREK CORPORATION
764 Eagle Point Dr (27284-7733)
PHONE..................336 497-5331
Nancy Simpson, Prin
EMP: 6 EST: 2015
SALES (est): 88.17K **Privately Held**
Web: www.driveshowers.com
SIC: 3714 Motor vehicle parts and accessories

(G-9235)
SOLO SOLUTIONS CORPORATION
102b Furlong Industrial Dr (27284-3241)
P.O. Box 2584 (27285-2584)
PHONE..................336 992-2585
Ron Styers, Prin
EMP: 8 EST: 2014
SALES (est): 320.32K **Privately Held**
SIC: 2842 Specialty cleaning

(G-9236)
SOUTH-EAST LUMBER COMPANY
1896 W Mountain St (27284-2140)
P.O. Box 745 (27285-0745)
PHONE..................336 996-5322
Steve Brackett, Pr
Thad Brackett, *
Teresa Brackett, *
EMP: 28 EST: 1960
SQ FT: 2,400
SALES (est): 16.75MM **Privately Held**
Web: www.south-eastlumber.com
SIC: 5031 2452 Lumber: rough, dressed, and finished; Log cabins, prefabricated, wood

(G-9237)
SPARTAN MANUFACTURING CORP (PA)
Also Called: Pressure Power Systems
1536 Brookford Industrial Dr (27284-9412)
P.O. Box 917 (27285-0917)
PHONE..................336 996-5585
Ronald W Robarge, Pr
Marilyn C Robarge, Stockholder*
EMP: 20 EST: 1974
SQ FT: 12,500
SALES (est): 2.47MM
SALES (corp-wide): 2.47MM **Privately Held**
Web: www.smcwashers.com
SIC: 3699 Cleaning equipment, ultrasonic, except medical and dental

(G-9238)
SPECIALTY NATIONAL INC
119 Furlong Industrial Dr Ste E (27284-3274)
P.O. Box 488 (27285-0488)
PHONE..................336 996-8783
Tom Corns, Pr
Ronald L Styers, *
EMP: 20 EST: 1989
SQ FT: 112,000
SALES (est): 1.03MM **Privately Held**
Web: www.specialtynational.com
SIC: 2841 Soap and other detergents

(G-9239)
STARR TRAINING
7715 Tall Meadows Dr (27284-6706)
PHONE..................336 644-0252
King Starr, Prin
EMP: 5 EST: 2002
SALES (est): 73.46K **Privately Held**
SIC: 7372 Prepackaged software

(G-9240)
SWEET WICK CANDLE COMPANY LLC
120 Serenity Pointe Dr (27284-9831)
PHONE..................770 687-1519
Jaime D Casstevens, Prin
EMP: 7 EST: 2017
SALES (est): 481.43K **Privately Held**
SIC: 3999 Candles

(G-9241)
TECGRACHEM INC
1957 Nc Highway 66 S (27284-3903)
P.O. Box 2120 (27285-2120)
PHONE..................336 993-6785
John R Peters, Pr
EMP: 5 EST: 1979
SQ FT: 542
SALES (est): 879.54K **Privately Held**
SIC: 2819 Industrial inorganic chemicals, nec

(G-9242)
TEX-TECH COATINGS LLC
215 Drummond St (27284-2849)
PHONE..................336 992-7500
EMP: 80
Web: www.textechindustries.com
SIC: 2296 Tire cord and fabrics
HQ: Tex-Tech Coatings, Llc
  1350 Bridgeport Dr Ste 1
  Kernersville NC 27284
  336 992-7500

(G-9243)
TEX-TECH COATINGS LLC (HQ)
1350 Bridgeport Dr Ste 1 (27284-3794)
PHONE..................336 992-7500
Ciaran Lynch, CEO
Peter Manos, Pr
John Stankiewicz, Treas
Stephen Judge, Ex VP
Erica Son, Asst VP
EMP: 15 EST: 2019
SALES (est): 41.27MM **Privately Held**
SIC: 2296 2261 Tire cord and fabrics; Finishing plants, cotton
PA: Tex-Tech Industries, Inc.
  1350 Bridgeport Dr Ste 1
  Kernersville NC 27284

(G-9244)
TEX-TECH ENGNRED CMPOSITES LLC
1350 Bridgeport Dr Ste 1 (27284-3794)
PHONE..................207 756-8606
EMP: 104
SALES (est): 327.09K **Privately Held**
SIC: 2655 Fiber cans, drums, and similar products
PA: Tex-Tech Industries, Inc.
  1350 Bridgeport Dr Ste 1
  Kernersville NC 27284

(G-9245)
TEX-TECH INDUSTRIES INC (PA)
Also Called: Tex Tech Industries
1350 Bridgeport Dr Ste 1 (27284-3794)
PHONE..................207 756-8606
Scott Burkhart, Pr
John Stankiewicz, *
Stephen Judge, *
▲ EMP: 185 EST: 1983
SQ FT: 3,000
SALES (est): 176.1MM **Privately Held**
Web: www.textechindustries.com
SIC: 2299 Batting, wadding, padding and fillings

(G-9246)
TORTILLERIA DUVY LLC ◆
1261 Nc Highway 66 S (27284-3550)
PHONE..................336 497-1510
EMP: 4 EST: 2022
SALES (est): 82.04K **Privately Held**
SIC: 2032 Tortillas: packaged in cans, jars, etc.

(G-9247)
TRIAD FABRICATION AND MCH INC
1080 Industrial Park Dr (27284-9410)
P.O. Box 1053 (27285-1053)
PHONE..................336 993-6042
John Ogle, Pr
Norman Bennett, VP
Avalon Potts, Treas
EMP: 19 EST: 1988
SQ FT: 20,000
SALES (est): 459.43K **Privately Held**
SIC: 3599 3444 Machine and other job shop work; Sheet metalwork

(G-9248)
TRS-SESCO LLC
721 Park Centre Dr Ste A (27284-3895)
PHONE..................336 996-2220
EMP: 95 EST: 2020
SALES (est): 28.71MM
SALES (corp-wide): 3.63B **Publicly Held**
Web: www.trs-sesco.com
SIC: 3585 7623 3561 Heating and air conditioning combination units; Refrigeration service and repair; Pumps and pumping equipment
HQ: Coolsys Commercial & Industrial Solutions, Inc.
  145 S State College Blvd
  Brea CA 92821

(G-9249)
US INDUSTRIAL PIPING INC
105 Woodland Trl (27284-2159)
P.O. Box 889 (27285-0889)
PHONE..................336 993-9505
John C Dixon, Pr
Cassius Dixon, *
EMP: 56 EST: 1992
SALES (est): 8.39MM **Privately Held**
Web: www.usindustrialpiping.com
SIC: 3498 Fabricated pipe and fittings

(G-9250)
VAULT OF FORSYTH INC
578 Arbor Hill Rd (27284-3346)
PHONE..................336 996-2044
Richard Kohl Senior, Pr
Richard Kohl Junior, VP
Nicholas Gervasi, *
EMP: 5 EST: 2007
SQ FT: 8,000
SALES (est): 228.61K **Privately Held**
Web: www.legendsofthepast.com
SIC: 3911 3499 Jewelry, precious metal; Novelties and specialties, metal

(G-9251)
VESTAL BUICK GMC INC
Also Called: Vestal Pontiac Buick GMC Truck
900 Hwy 66 South (27284)
PHONE..................336 310-0261
Timothy Vestal, Pr
EMP: 63 EST: 1966
SQ FT: 5,500
SALES (est): 20.36MM **Privately Held**
Web: www.parksbuickgmckernersville.com
SIC: 5511 7534 Automobiles, new and used; Tire repair shop

(G-9252)
VULCAN MATERIALS COMPANY
2874 Nc Highway 66 S (27284-9175)
PHONE..................336 869-2148
D Gray Kimel Junior, Prin
EMP: 5
Web: www.vulcanmaterials.com
SIC: 3273 Ready-mixed concrete
PA: Vulcan Materials Company
  1200 Urban Center Dr
  Vestavia AL 35242

(G-9253)
WILLIAMS UNITED LLC
843 Burke Hollow Rd (27284-2463)
PHONE..................336 251-7355
Arious L Williams, Prin
EMP: 7 EST: 2018
SALES (est): 109.73K **Privately Held**
Web: williams-united-llc.business.site
SIC: 3732 Boatbuilding and repairing

Kill Devil Hills
Dare County

(G-9254)
ATLANTIC COASTAL SHUTTERS LLC
2701 N Croatan Hwy (27948-9062)
P.O. Box 1243 (27948-1243)

GEOGRAPHIC SECTION

PHONE.....................252 441-4358
EMP: 6 **EST:** 2000
SALES (est): 495.97K **Privately Held**
Web:
www.atlanticcoastalshuttersobx.com
SIC: 3442 Shutters, door or window: metal

(G-9255)
COUNTY OF DARE
Dare County Water
600 S Mustian St (27948-8459)
P.O. Box 1000 (27954-1000)
PHONE.....................252 475-5990
Bob Oreskovich, *Mgr*
EMP: 106
Web: www.darenc.gov
SIC: 3589 Sewage and water treatment equipment
PA: County Of Dare
954 Marshall Collins Dr
Manteo NC 27954
252 475-5000

(G-9256)
EPIC KITES LLC
508 Schooner Ct (27948-9600)
PHONE.....................203 209-6831
Dimitri Maramedides, *Prin*
▲ **EMP:** 6 **EST:** 2009
SALES (est): 244.61K **Privately Held**
SIC: 3944 Kites

(G-9257)
FISHKILLERDAVES LLC
Also Called: USA Fuel Service
337 Sir Chandler Dr (27948-9056)
PHONE.....................252 441-7703
David Edouglas, *Prin*
EMP: 6 **EST:** 2010
SALES (est): 249.4K **Privately Held**
SIC: 2869 Fuels

(G-9258)
GMG GROUP LLC
Also Called: Good Measure Graphics
115 W Saint Clair St (27948-6955)
P.O. Box 7804 (27948-5804)
PHONE.....................252 441-8374
EMP: 5 **EST:** 2012
SALES (est): 270.16K **Privately Held**
Web: www.goodmeasuregraphics.com
SIC: 2759 3993 7336 5941 Commercial printing, nec; Signs and advertising specialties; Commercial art and graphic design; Sporting goods and bicycle shops

(G-9259)
OUTER BANKS INTERNET INC
3116 N Croatan Hwy Ste 104 (27948-6200)
P.O. Box 2560 (27948-2560)
PHONE.....................252 441-6698
Chris Hess, *Pr*
Tricia Honeycutt, *Corporate Secretary*
EMP: 4 **EST:** 1996
SALES (est): 301.3K **Privately Held**
Web: www.outerbanksinternet.com
SIC: 7374 2741 Computer graphics service; Internet publishing and broadcasting

(G-9260)
OUTER BANKS OLIVE OIL COMPANY
2200 N Croatan Hwy (27948-9542)
PHONE.....................252 449-8229
EMP: 4 **EST:** 2018
SALES (est): 215.03K **Privately Held**
Web: www.outerbanksolive.com
SIC: 2079 Olive oil

(G-9261)
PET LOVE PUBLISHING LLC
1229 S Virginia Dare Trl (27948-7748)
PHONE.....................252 489-3832
EMP: 5 **EST:** 2014
SALES (est): 62.37K **Privately Held**
SIC: 2741 Miscellaneous publishing

(G-9262)
PPG INDUSTRIES INC
Also Called: PPG 4655
2800 N Croatan Hwy (27948-9267)
PHONE.....................252 480-1970
Ryan Smithson, *Mgr*
EMP: 6
SALES (corp-wide): 17.65B **Publicly Held**
Web: www.ppg.com
SIC: 2851 Paints and allied products
PA: Ppg Industries, Inc.
1 Ppg Pl
Pittsburgh PA 15272
412 434-3131

(G-9263)
TIMES PRINTING COMPANY INC
1500 S Croatan Hwy (27948-8714)
PHONE.....................252 441-2223
EMP: 6
SALES (corp-wide): 1.5MM **Privately Held**
SIC: 2759 5943 2711 Commercial printing, nec; Office forms and supplies; Newspapers
PA: Times Printing Company Inc
501 Budleigh St
Manteo NC 27954
252 473-2105

King
Stokes County

(G-9264)
BLUE LIGHT IMAGES COMPANY INC
Also Called: Camel City Posters
428 Newsome Rd (27021-8508)
P.O. Box 2409 (27021-2409)
PHONE.....................336 983-4986
Danny Hoots, *Pr*
John Keats, *VP*
EMP: 25 **EST:** 1988
SALES (est): 2.64MM **Privately Held**
Web: www.camelcityposters.com
SIC: 3993 Signs and advertising specialties

(G-9265)
BUCK RACING ENGINES INC
205 Old Newsome Rd (27021-8532)
PHONE.....................336 983-6562
Charlie Buck, *Pr*
EMP: 6 **EST:** 1993
SALES (est): 497.23K **Privately Held**
Web: www.buckracingengines.com
SIC: 3537 Engine stands and racks, metal

(G-9266)
CAROLINA SIGNS & LIGHTING INC
928 Spainhour Rd (27021-9395)
P.O. Box 1037 (27045-1037)
PHONE.....................336 399-1400
Chris Smith, *Pr*
EMP: 4 **EST:** 2000
SALES (est): 480.33K **Privately Held**
Web: www.carolinasignsandlighting.com
SIC: 3993 Signs and advertising specialties

(G-9267)
CARROLL SIGNS & ADVERTISING
151 Jefferson Church Rd Ste B (27021-8605)
P.O. Box 809 (27021-0809)
PHONE.....................336 983-3415
Lewis N Carroll, *Owner*
EMP: 4 **EST:** 1966
SQ FT: 8,000
SALES (est): 476.38K **Privately Held**
Web: www.carrollsigns.com
SIC: 5199 2752 Advertising specialties; Commercial printing, lithographic

(G-9268)
CRES TOBACCO COMPANY LLC
Also Called: Alliance One International
3000 Big Oaks Rd (27021)
P.O. Box 2559 (27021-2559)
PHONE.....................336 983-7727
Pete Harrison, *Pr*
Ed Dilda, *
Mark W Kehaya, *
▲ **EMP:** 25 **EST:** 1994
SQ FT: 130,000
SALES (est): 6.04MM
SALES (corp-wide): 1.91B **Privately Held**
SIC: 2131 Chewing and smoking tobacco
PA: Pyxus International, Inc.
6001 Hospitality Ct # 100
Morrisville NC 27560
919 379-4300

(G-9269)
DM2
P.O. Box 429 (27021-0429)
PHONE.....................336 362-3425
EMP: 9 **EST:** 2013
SALES (est): 175.18K **Privately Held**
Web: www.dmxm.com
SIC: 3599 Machine shop, jobbing and repair

(G-9270)
DW BEAM PUBLISHING
222 Red Coat Ln (27021-9726)
PHONE.....................336 813-2451
Derrick Beam, *Prin*
EMP: 5 **EST:** 2017
SALES (est): 115.62K **Privately Held**
Web: www.dwbeampublishing.com
SIC: 2741 Miscellaneous publishing

(G-9271)
DYNAMIC MACHINING X MFG LLC
157 Industrial Dr (27021-8221)
P.O. Box 429 (27021-0429)
PHONE.....................336 362-3425
Joseph H Landry, *Managing Member*
Leonard Speaks, *VP*
EMP: 23 **EST:** 2004
SALES (est): 3.45MM **Privately Held**
Web: www.dmxm.com
SIC: 3599 Machine shop, jobbing and repair

(G-9272)
HIM INC
P.O. Box 851 (27021-0851)
PHONE.....................336 409-7795
Richard Hammon, *CEO*
Shannon Bowles, *Ofcr*
EMP: 12 **EST:** 2017
SALES (est): 877.99K **Privately Held**
SIC: 3442 Metal doors

(G-9273)
IMPERIAL VAULT COMPANY
1 Sun Dr (27021)
P.O. Box 950 (27021-0950)
PHONE.....................336 983-6343
Nancy Carter-griffin, *Pr*
Todd Carter, *
Terry Carter, *
Timothy Carter, *
EMP: 34 **EST:** 1935
SQ FT: 26,000
SALES (est): 2.67MM **Privately Held**
Web: www.imperialvaultcompany.com
SIC: 3272 5087 Burial vaults, concrete or precast terrazzo; Concrete burial vaults and boxes

(G-9274)
KING INTERNATIONAL CORPORATION
275 S Main St (27021-9012)
P.O. Box 1009 (27021-1009)
PHONE.....................336 983-5171
Shelby Smith, *Ch Bd*
George C Smith Senior, *Pr*
▲ **EMP:** 28 **EST:** 1964
SQ FT: 20,000
SALES (est): 3.59MM **Privately Held**
Web: www.ki-corp.com
SIC: 2752 2396 Decals, lithographed; Automotive and apparel trimmings

(G-9275)
MAGNET AMERICA INTL INC
Also Called: Magnet America
512 Newsome Rd (27021-8510)
PHONE.....................336 985-0320
Leigh Anne Parker, *CEO*
Paul Parker, *COO*
Chris Weeks, *VP Opers*
EMP: 20 **EST:** 2012
SQ FT: 10,000
SALES (est): 2MM **Privately Held**
Web: www.magnetamerica.com
SIC: 2759 Decals: printing, nsk

(G-9276)
MERFIN SYSTEMS LLC
105 Industrial Dr (27021-8221)
PHONE.....................800 874-6373
◆ **EMP:** 60
SQ FT: 92,000
SALES (est): 11.69MM
SALES (corp-wide): 40.63B **Privately Held**
Web: www.merfin.com
SIC: 2676 Towels, napkins, and tissue paper products
HQ: Buckeye Technologies Inc.
1001 Tillman St
Memphis TN 38112

(G-9277)
N C COIL INC
529b S Main St (27021-9015)
PHONE.....................336 983-4440
Danny Isaacs, *Prin*
EMP: 6 **EST:** 2008
SALES (est): 89.08K **Privately Held**
Web: www.nccoil.com
SIC: 3495 Wire springs

(G-9278)
NVIZION INC
129 Charles Rd (27021-8247)
P.O. Box 2424 (27021-2424)
PHONE.....................336 985-3862
Frank Lawson, *Pr*
EMP: 11 **EST:** 2008
SALES (est): 743.15K **Privately Held**
Web: www.nvizioninc.com
SIC: 2759 Screen printing

(G-9279)
PERFORMANCE MACHINE & FAB INC
1050 Denny Rd (27021-8312)
PHONE.....................336 983-0414
Joshua Pruitt, *Prin*
EMP: 10 **EST:** 2015
SALES (est): 259.68K **Privately Held**
Web: www.performancemfnc.com
SIC: 3599 Machine shop, jobbing and repair

(G-9280)
RONNIE A MABE
1122 Covington Rd (27021-7611)
PHONE..............................336 994-2257
Ronnie A Mabe, *Prin*
EMP: 5 **EST:** 2004
SALES (est): 137.65K **Privately Held**
SIC: 2411 Logging

(G-9281)
SCORPION PRODUCTS INC
741 Spainhour Rd (27021-9393)
P.O. Box 834 (27045-0834)
PHONE..............................336 813-3241
Joseph Sabo, *Prin*
▲ **EMP:** 7 **EST:** 2014
SALES (est): 478.59K **Privately Held**
SIC: 3714 Motor vehicle parts and accessories

(G-9282)
SIGNATURE CUSTOM WDWKG INC
1050 Denny Rd (27021-8312)
P.O. Box 345 (27021-0345)
PHONE..............................336 983-9905
Randy Bennett, *Pr*
EMP: 8 **EST:** 2004
SQ FT: 22,000
SALES (est): 984.81K **Privately Held**
Web: www.signaturecw.com
SIC: 2431 Millwork

(G-9283)
USA ATTACHMENTS INC
105 Industrial Dr (27021-8221)
PHONE..............................336 983-0763
Jeff Hamilton, *Pr*
▼ **EMP:** 25 **EST:** 2003
SQ FT: 10,000
SALES (est): 3.91MM **Privately Held**
Web: www.excavatorthumb.com
SIC: 3531 Construction machinery attachments

(G-9284)
WEST STKES WLDCAT GRDRON CLB I
321 Logan Ct (27021-9463)
PHONE..............................336 985-6152
Tonya Smith, *Prin*
EMP: 5 **EST:** 2016
SALES (est): 64.02K **Privately Held**
SIC: 2711 Newspapers, publishing and printing

(G-9285)
WHOLESALE DIRECT CARPORTS
731 E King St (27021-9166)
PHONE..............................336 399-3221
EMP: 5 **EST:** 2017
SALES (est): 228.91K **Privately Held**
Web: www.carportsandbuildingsdirect.com
SIC: 3448 Prefabricated metal buildings and components

(G-9286)
WINSTON TOOL COMPANY INC
1025 Gause Dr (27021-8096)
PHONE..............................336 983-3722
Herman Denny, *Pr*
Dennis Gause, *VP*
Ashley Bennett, *Sec*
EMP: 4 **EST:** 1975
SALES (est): 316.13K **Privately Held**
Web: www.winstontoolco.com
SIC: 3599 Machine shop, jobbing and repair

(G-9287)
WOODMASTERS WOODWORKING INC
Also Called: Woodmaster Woodworking
402 Newsome Rd (27021-8509)
PHONE..............................336 985-4000
Donnald L Dunnagan Junior, *Owner*
EMP: 4 **EST:** 1989
SALES (est): 258.78K **Privately Held**
SIC: 2434 Wood kitchen cabinets

Kings Mountain
Cleveland County

(G-9288)
ABB MOTORS AND MECHANICAL INC
101 Reliance Rd (28086-8512)
PHONE..............................704 734-2500
Brain Brehmer, *Brnch Mgr*
EMP: 300
Web: www.baldor.com
SIC: 3621 Electric motor and generator auxiliary parts
HQ: Abb Motors And Mechanical Inc.
5711 Rs Boreham Jr St
Fort Smith AR 72901
479 646-4711

(G-9289)
ADVANCE CONVEYING TECH LLC
171 Kings Rd (28086-2089)
P.O. Box 189 (28086-0189)
PHONE..............................704 710-4001
EMP: 20 **EST:** 2011
SQ FT: 26,500
SALES (est): 2.63MM **Privately Held**
Web: act.us.com
SIC: 3535 Conveyors and conveying equipment

(G-9290)
ALBEMARLE CORPORATION
348 Holiday Inn Dr (28086-3615)
PHONE..............................704 739-2501
EMP: 102
Web: www.albemarle.com
SIC: 2819 Industrial inorganic chemicals, nec
PA: Albemarle Corporation
4250 Congress St Ste 900
Charlotte NC 28209

(G-9291)
ALBEMARLE US INC (DH)
348 Holiday Inn Dr (28086-3615)
PHONE..............................704 739-2501
Steffen Haber, *Ch*
Thomas J Riordan, *
Robert J Zatta, *
Michael W Valente, *
Marcus Brune, *
◆ **EMP:** 112 **EST:** 1876
SQ FT: 6,500
SALES (est): 115.15MM **Publicly Held**
Web: www.albemarle.com
SIC: 2819 Lithium compounds, inorganic
HQ: Rockwood Specialties Group, Inc.
100 Overlook Ctr Ste 101
Princeton NJ 08540
609 514-0300

(G-9292)
ALCO METAL FABRICATORS INC
307 S Cansler St (28086-3501)
P.O. Box 1158 (28086-1158)
PHONE..............................704 739-1168
Charles D Cody, *Pr*
Jeffrey Cody, *VP*
Kevin Cody, *Sec*
EMP: 16 **EST:** 1999
SQ FT: 24,000
SALES (est): 2.43MM **Privately Held**
Web: www.alcometalfabricatorsinc.com
SIC: 3441 Fabricated structural metal

(G-9293)
B & D ENTERPRISES INC
Also Called: Tom's Coin Laundry
736 Stony Point Rd (28086-8567)
PHONE..............................704 739-2958
Thomas G Brooks, *Pr*
James Brooks, *VP*
Rose E Brooks, *Sec*
EMP: 12 **EST:** 1963
SQ FT: 2,000
SALES (est): 760.64K **Privately Held**
SIC: 5411 7692 7542 7033 Convenience stores, independent; Welding repair; Carwash, automatic; Trailer park

(G-9294)
BAY VALLEY FOODS LLC
120 Woodlake Pkwy (28086-9225)
PHONE..............................704 476-7141
EMP: 38
SALES (corp-wide): 3.43B **Publicly Held**
Web: www.bayvalleyfoods.com
SIC: 2099 Food preparations, nec
HQ: Bay Valley Foods, Llc
3200 Riverside Dr Ste A
Green Bay WI 54301
800 558-4700

(G-9295)
BLACHFORD RBR ACQUISITION CORP
Also Called: Blachford Rp Corporation
707 Broadview Dr (28086-3176)
PHONE..............................704 730-1005
John Blachford, *Pr*
Bill Hayes, *
▲ **EMP:** 26 **EST:** 2001
SALES (est): 10.2MM
SALES (corp-wide): 17.57MM **Privately Held**
Web: www.blachfordrp.com
SIC: 3069 Mats or matting, rubber, nec
HQ: Blachford Enterprises, Inc.
1400 Nuclear Dr
West Chicago IL 60185

(G-9296)
BUCKEYE FIRE EQUIPMENT COMPANY (PA)
110 Kings Rd (28086-2090)
P.O. Box 428 (28086-0428)
PHONE..............................704 739-7415
Kevin Bower, *Pr*
Thomas J Bower, *
William Cowley, *
◆ **EMP:** 45 **EST:** 1968
SQ FT: 265,000
SALES (est): 92MM
SALES (corp-wide): 92MM **Privately Held**
Web: www.buckeyef.com
SIC: 3569 Firefighting apparatus

(G-9297)
C & C PRECISION MACHINE INC
418 Canterbury Rd (28086-8627)
PHONE..............................704 739-0505
Joe Cunningham, *CEO*
Joseph S Cunningham, *Pr*
Jeff Cunningham, *VP*
EMP: 20 **EST:** 1990
SQ FT: 22,000
SALES (est): 4.5MM **Privately Held**
Web: www.e-ccpm.com
SIC: 3599 3545 Machine shop, jobbing and repair; Precision tools, machinists'

(G-9298)
CARDINAL PLASTICS INC
4910 Barrett Rd (28086-8547)
PHONE..............................704 739-9420
John F Hess, *VP*
Linda Hess, *Pr*
EMP: 5 **EST:** 1991
SQ FT: 6,000
SALES (est): 1MM **Privately Held**
Web: www.cardinal-plastics.com
SIC: 5162 3081 Plastics materials and basic shapes; Unsupported plastics film and sheet

(G-9299)
CAROLINA FINSHG & COATING INC
441 Countryside Rd (28086-8914)
PHONE..............................704 730-8233
Gorham J Samuel Iii, *Prin*
EMP: 12 **EST:** 2008
SALES (est): 2.3MM **Privately Held**
Web: www.cfcanodizing.com
SIC: 3471 Electroplating of metals or formed products

(G-9300)
CAROLINA PIPING SERVICES INC
307 S Cansler St (28086-3501)
P.O. Box 186 (28086-0186)
PHONE..............................704 405-0297
Harold K Green, *Pr*
Michele Green, *VP*
EMP: 9 **EST:** 2006
SALES (est): 1.77MM **Privately Held**
Web: www.carolinapiping.com
SIC: 3443 Fabricated plate work (boiler shop)

(G-9301)
CAROLINA TEX SLS GASTONIA INC
Also Called: Carolina Textile Sls Gastonia
521 N Sims St (28086-3261)
P.O. Box 637 (28086-0637)
PHONE..............................704 739-1646
Pam Grimsley, *CEO*
Greg Mccomas, *VP*
EMP: 13 **EST:** 1977
SQ FT: 8,000
SALES (est): 390.37K **Privately Held**
SIC: 3599 3552 3699 Machine and other job shop work; Textile machinery; Electrical equipment and supplies, nec

(G-9302)
CHAPMAN MACHINE
109 Joanne Dr (28086-7735)
PHONE..............................704 739-1834
Tim L Chapman, *Owner*
EMP: 4 **EST:** 1989
SALES (est): 234.91K **Privately Held**
SIC: 3599 Machine shop, jobbing and repair

(G-9303)
DIRECT WHOLESALE SIGNS LLC
711 York Rd (28086-3662)
PHONE..............................704 750-2842
Teresa Gardner Caldwell, *Admn*
EMP: 7 **EST:** 2016
SALES (est): 410.33K **Privately Held**
Web: www.directwholesalesigns.co
SIC: 3993 Signs and advertising specialties

(G-9304)
DIVERSIFIED TEXTILE MCHY CORP
Also Called: D T M
133 Kings Rd (28086-2089)
P.O. Box 809 (28086-0809)
PHONE..............................704 739-2121
Ronald Goble, *Pr*
Janice Goble, *VP*
Flay Washburn, *VP*
EMP: 8 **EST:** 1986

GEOGRAPHIC SECTION
Kings Mountain - Cleveland County (G-9326)

SQ FT: 30,000
SALES (est): 857.6K **Privately Held**
Web: www.diversifiedtextilemach.com
SIC: 3552 Creels, textile machinery

(G-9305)
EAS INCORPORATED
420 Canterbury Rd (28086-8627)
P.O. Box 2029 (28086-6029)
PHONE..............................704 734-4945
Jeff Fish, *Pr*
EMP: 8 **EST:** 1987
SALES (est): 1MM **Privately Held**
Web: www.eassheetmetal.com
SIC: 3564 Air cleaning systems

(G-9306)
EATON CORPORATION
Eaton Transmission Div
744 S Battleground Ave (28086-3610)
P.O. Box 1728 (28086-1728)
PHONE..............................704 937-7411
Jon Sczesny, *Brnch Mgr*
EMP: 121
Web: www.dix-eaton.com
SIC: 3714 Transmissions, motor vehicle
HQ: Eaton Corporation
1000 Eaton Blvd
Cleveland OH 44122
440 523-5000

(G-9307)
EDDIE HSR S PRCSION MCHNING IN
Also Called: Precision McHning Eddie Husers
613 Slater St (28086-3148)
P.O. Box 887 (28086-0887)
PHONE..............................704 750-4244
Eddie Houser, *Pr*
Joyce Houser, *Clerk*
EMP: 6 **EST:** 1989
SALES (est): 520.95K **Privately Held**
SIC: 3599 Machine shop, jobbing and repair

(G-9308)
FIRESTONE FIBERS TEXTILES LLC
100 Firestone Ln (28086-7706)
P.O. Box 1369 (28086-1369)
PHONE..............................704 734-2110
James Pridgen, *Pr*
◆ **EMP:** 520 **EST:** 2007
SQ FT: 400,000
SALES (est): 101.87MM **Privately Held**
Web: commercial.firestone.com
SIC: 2299 Textile mill waste and remnant processing
HQ: Bridgestone Americas, Inc.
200 4th Ave S Ste 100
Nashville TN 37201
615 937-1000

(G-9309)
IMERYS MICA KINGS MOUNTAIN INC
1469 S Battleground Ave (28086-3906)
PHONE..............................704 739-3616
Damien Caby, *VP*
◆ **EMP:** 44 **EST:** 2007
SALES (est): 2.58MM
SALES (corp-wide): 3.28MM **Privately Held**
SIC: 3295 Minerals, ground or treated
HQ: Imerys Usa, Inc.
100 Mansell Ct E Ste 300
Roswell GA 30076
770 645-3300

(G-9310)
J E HERNDON COMPANY (HQ)
1020 Je Herndon Access Rd (28086-2000)
P.O. Box 1608 (28086-1608)
PHONE..............................704 739-4711
Patrick Mullen, *Pr*

▼ **EMP:** 20 **EST:** 1928
SQ FT: 60,000
SALES (est): 1.95MM
SALES (corp-wide): 98.42MM **Privately Held**
Web: www.steinfibers.com
SIC: 2299 Fibers, textile: recovery from textile mill waste and rags
PA: Stein Fibers, Llc
4 Computer Dr W Ste 200
Albany NY 12205
518 489-5700

(G-9311)
KEYSTONE POWDERED METAL CO
779 Sunnyside Shady Rest Rd (28086-8404)
PHONE..............................704 730-8805
Monty Rhea, *Owner*
EMP: 44
Web: www.keystonepm.com
SIC: 2899 Fluxes: brazing, soldering, galvanizing, and welding
HQ: Keystone Powdered Metal Co
251 State St
Saint Marys PA 15857
814 781-1591

(G-9312)
KINGDOM WOODWORKS INC
405 Margrace Rd (28086-3873)
PHONE..............................704 678-8134
Bryan Morrow, *Prin*
EMP: 6 **EST:** 2009
SALES (est): 87.06K **Privately Held**
SIC: 2431 Millwork

(G-9313)
KINGS MOUNTAIN INTL INC
1755 S Battleground Ave (28086-9237)
PHONE..............................704 739-4227
Steve Wagenknight, *Pr*
John Spencer, *
◆ **EMP:** 65 **EST:** 2004
SQ FT: 140,000
SALES (est): 8.87MM **Privately Held**
Web: www.kmiinc.net
SIC: 3471 Electroplating of metals or formed products

(G-9314)
KINGS PLUSH INC
Also Called: STI
515 Marie St (28086-3147)
P.O. Box 398 (28086-0398)
PHONE..............................704 739-9931
John Kay, *Pr*
Sean D Gibbons, *
Mark Hovis, *
◆ **EMP:** 200 **EST:** 1964
SQ FT: 150,000
SALES (est): 43.77MM **Privately Held**
Web: www.stifabrics.com
SIC: 2221 Nylon broadwoven fabrics
PA: Specialty Textiles Inc
515 Marie St
Kings Mountain NC 28086

(G-9315)
KITCHEN VNTILATION SYSTEMS LLC
212 Commerce Blvd (28086-8905)
PHONE..............................704 476-3565
EMP: 9 **EST:** 2011
SALES (est): 217.99K **Privately Held**
Web: www.greenheck.com
SIC: 3564 Blowers and fans

(G-9316)
LNS TURBO INC (DH)
203 Turbo Dr (28086-7641)
PHONE..............................704 739-7111

▲ **EMP:** 100 **EST:** 1977
SALES (est): 27.72MM
SALES (corp-wide): 3.26B **Privately Held**
Web: www.lns-northamerica.com
SIC: 3535 Conveyors and conveying equipment
HQ: Lns Holding Sa
C/O Coworking Neuchatel Sarl
NeuchAtel NE 2000

(G-9317)
MARIETTA MARTIN MATERIALS INC
Also Called: Martin Marietta Aggregates
181 Quarry Rd (28086-3896)
P.O. Box 747 (28086-0747)
PHONE..............................704 739-4761
Donald Champion, *Brnch Mgr*
EMP: 7
Web: www.martinmarietta.com
SIC: 1422 Crushed and broken limestone
PA: Martin Marietta Materials Inc
4123 Parklake Ave
Raleigh NC 27612

(G-9318)
MAYFLOWER VEHICLE SYSTEMS LLC (HQ)
629 S Battleground Ave (28086)
P.O. Box 789 (28086-0789)
PHONE..............................704 937-4400
Darryl Rowlins, *Prin*
EMP: 69 **EST:** 2008
SALES (est): 24.33MM
SALES (corp-wide): 994.68MM **Publicly Held**
Web: www.cvgrp.com
SIC: 3714 Motor vehicle parts and accessories
PA: Commercial Vehicle Group, Inc.
7800 Walton Pkwy
New Albany OH 43054
614 289-5360

(G-9319)
MR TIRE INC
407 S Battleground Ave (28086-3603)
PHONE..............................704 739-6456
Stephen Honbaier, *Brnch Mgr*
EMP: 6
SALES (corp-wide): 1.33B **Publicly Held**
Web: mrtireinc.business.site
SIC: 5722 5014 7538 7534 Household appliance stores; Tires and tubes; General automotive repair shops; Tire recapping
HQ: Mr. Tire Inc.
2078 New York Ave Unit 2
Huntington Station NY 11746
631 499-3700

(G-9320)
NVR INC
Also Called: NVR Building Products
132 Riverside Ct (28086-8901)
PHONE..............................704 484-7170
Jim Kepple, *Mgr*
EMP: 100
Web: www.nvrinc.com
SIC: 1521 2439 New construction, single-family houses; Structural wood members, nec
PA: Nvr, Inc.
11700 Plaza America Dr # 500
Reston VA 20190

(G-9321)
PARKDALE AMERICA LLC
Plant 5
500 S Railroad Ave (28086-3351)
P.O. Box 709 (28086-0709)
PHONE..............................704 739-7411
Jonh Nims, *Pr*

EMP: 35
SALES (corp-wide): 1.44B **Privately Held**
Web: www.uscotton.com
SIC: 2281 Combed yarn, spun
HQ: Parkdale America, Llc
531 Cotton Blossom Cir
Gastonia NC 28054
704 874-5000

(G-9322)
PARKDALE MILLS INCORPORATED
Also Called: Parkdale Plant 5
500 S Railroad Ave (28086-3351)
PHONE..............................704 739-7411
Jeff Johnson, *Brnch Mgr*
EMP: 24
SALES (corp-wide): 1.44B **Privately Held**
Web: www.parkdalemills.com
SIC: 2281 Yarn spinning mills
HQ: Parkdale Mills, Incorporated
531 Cotton Blossom Cir
Gastonia NC 28054
704 874-5000

(G-9323)
PARKER-HANNIFIN CORPORATION
Also Called: Parker Hydraulics
101 Canterbury Rd (28086-9433)
P.O. Box 219 (28086-0219)
PHONE..............................704 739-9781
Bob Mcbride, *Brnch Mgr*
EMP: 350
SALES (corp-wide): 19.07B **Publicly Held**
Web: www.parker.com
SIC: 3594 Fluid power pumps and motors
PA: Parker-Hannifin Corporation
6035 Parkland Blvd
Cleveland OH 44124
216 896-3000

(G-9324)
PATRICK YARN MILL INC
Also Called: Patrick Yarns
501 York Rd (28086-3158)
P.O. Box 1847 (28086-1847)
PHONE..............................704 739-4119
Gilbert H Patrick, *Pr*
Janice Patrick, *VP*
Thomas Koval, *Treas*
▲ **EMP:** 190 **EST:** 1963
SQ FT: 200,000
SALES (est): 51.46MM
SALES (corp-wide): 1.58B **Privately Held**
Web: www.patrickyarns.com
SIC: 2281 Yarn spinning mills
PA: Coats Group Plc
4th Floor
London EC2V
208 210-5086

(G-9325)
PIONEER MOTOR BEARING COMPANY
129 Battleground Rd (28086-8260)
PHONE..............................704 937-7000
Gordon P Bardet, *CEO*
EMP: 32
Web: www.pioneer1.com
SIC: 3562 5085 Ball and roller bearings; Bearings, bushings, wheels, and gears
PA: Pioneer Motor Bearing Company
129 Battleground Rd
Kings Mountain NC 28086

(G-9326)
PLASTIC PRODUCTS INC
1051 York Rd (28086-9713)
PHONE..............................704 739-7463
Jay E Raxter, *Brnch Mgr*
EMP: 16
SALES (corp-wide): 8.58MM **Privately Held**

Kings Mountain - Cleveland County (G-9327)

Web: www.plastic-products.com
SIC: 3089 Injection molding of plastics
PA: Plastic Products, Inc.
1413 Bessemer City
Bessemer City NC 28016
704 739-7463

(G-9327)
QUALTECH INDUSTRIES INC
311 Industrial Dr (28086-3888)
PHONE....................704 734-0345
Jeffrey P Latchaw, *Prin*
EMP: 8 EST: 2009
SALES (est): 616.04K **Privately Held**
Web: www.qualtechindustries.com
SIC: 3999 Manufacturing industries, nec

(G-9328)
R AND L COLLISION CENTER INC
Also Called: R & L
1207 S Battleground Ave (28086-3901)
PHONE....................704 739-2500
EMP: 10 EST: 1995
SALES (est): 786.45K **Privately Held**
SIC: 7532 3993 Truck painting and lettering; Signs and advertising specialties

(G-9329)
RIDDLEY RETAIL FIXTURES INC
119 Bess Rd (28086-8106)
PHONE....................704 435-8829
Terry Riddley, *Prin*
Terry A Riddley, *
Alan Riddley, *
Lorie Riddley, *
EMP: 50 EST: 1990
SQ FT: 5,000
SALES (est): 9.19MM **Privately Held**
Web: www.riddleyinc.com
SIC: 1751 5046 2541 Cabinet and finish carpentry; Store fixtures and display equipment; Cabinets, lockers, and shelving

(G-9330)
ROCKWOOD LITHIUM
348 Holiday Inn Dr (28086-3615)
PHONE....................704 739-2501
EMP: 12 EST: 2019
SALES (est): 2.05MM **Privately Held**
Web: www.albemarle.com
SIC: 2819 Industrial inorganic chemicals, nec

(G-9331)
SCIVOLUTIONS INC
811 Floyd St (28086-3130)
P.O. Box 234 (28637-0234)
PHONE....................704 853-0100
Fritz Schulte, *CEO*
▲ EMP: 24 EST: 1986
SQ FT: 28,000
SALES (est): 462.06K **Privately Held**
SIC: 3842 Bandages and dressings

(G-9332)
SPECIALTY TEXTILES INC
Also Called: STI
822 Floyd St (28086-3131)
PHONE....................704 710-8657
EMP: 7
Web: www.stifabrics.com
SIC: 2299 Fibers, textile: recovery from textile mill waste and rags
PA: Specialty Textiles Inc
515 Marie St
Kings Mountain NC 28086

(G-9333)
SPECIALTY TEXTILES INC (PA)
Also Called: King Splash
515 Marie St (28086-3147)

P.O. Box 398 (27261-0398)
PHONE....................704 739-4503
John Kay, *Pr*
EMP: 150 EST: 2007
SQ FT: 250,000
SALES (est): 44.77MM **Privately Held**
Web: yuri-greene.squarespace.com
SIC: 2299 Fibers, textile: recovery from textile mill waste and rags

(G-9334)
STOUT BEVERAGES LLC (PA)
518 N Sims St (28086-3262)
PHONE....................704 293-7640
Cody Sommer, *Managing Member*
▲ EMP: 20 EST: 2011
SALES (est): 2.32MM
SALES (corp-wide): 2.32MM **Privately Held**
SIC: 2082 Beer (alcoholic beverage)

(G-9335)
STOUT BRANDS LLC
518 N Sims St (28086-3262)
PHONE....................704 293-7640
Cody Sommer, *Managing Member*
David Scott, *Bd of Dir*
▲ EMP: 29 EST: 2012
SQ FT: 21,000
SALES (est): 606.45K
SALES (corp-wide): 2.32MM **Privately Held**
SIC: 2082 Stout (alcoholic beverage)
PA: Stout Beverages, Llc
518 N Sims St
Kings Mountain NC 28086
704 293-7640

(G-9336)
STOUT BREWING COMPANY LLC
518 N Sims St (28086-3262)
PHONE....................704 288-4042
Cody Sommer, *Prin*
▲ EMP: 5 EST: 2013
SALES (est): 178.61K **Privately Held**
Web: www.stoutbrewingcompany.com
SIC: 2085 Cocktails, alcoholic

(G-9337)
SUDS ME UP BUTTERCUP
226 Marys Grove Church Rd (28086-9340)
PHONE....................704 419-2075
Kristy Mcswain, *Prin*
EMP: 4 EST: 2019
SALES (est): 112.78K **Privately Held**
SIC: 2844 Perfumes, cosmetics and other toilet preparations

(G-9338)
WEDE CORPORATION
133 Industrial Dr (28086-3889)
PHONE....................704 864-1313
Hans Wede, *Pr*
EMP: 16 EST: 1969
SQ FT: 20,000
SALES (est): 570.51K **Privately Held**
SIC: 3441 3444 Fabricated structural metal; Sheet metalwork

Kinston
Lenoir County

(G-9339)
ADAMSON GLOBAL TECHNOLOGY CORP (PA)
2018 W Vernon Ave (28504-0001)
P.O. Box 6246 (28501-0246)
PHONE....................252 523-5200
EMP: 5 EST: 1995

SQ FT: 10,000
SALES (est): 1.78MM **Privately Held**
Web: www.adamsontank.com
SIC: 3443 Tanks, standard or custom fabricated: metal plate

(G-9340)
ADDITIVE AMERICA INC
300 N Herritage St (28501-4824)
PHONE....................252 549-0247
Zachary Holcomb, *CEO*
Mitchel Sugg, *Prin*
William Wright, *Prin*
Gail Sugg, *Prin*
EMP: 4 EST: 2020
SALES (est): 502.76K **Privately Held**
Web: www.additiveamerica.com
SIC: 2823 Acetate fibers, triacetate fibers

(G-9341)
ADVANTAGE PRINTING & DESIGN
2425 N Herritage St (28501-1613)
PHONE....................252 523-8133
Gordon Vermillionee, *Pr*
EMP: 7 EST: 1988
SQ FT: 7,000
SALES (est): 739.38K **Privately Held**
SIC: 2752 Offset printing

(G-9342)
ALSIDE WINDOW CO
3800 Window Way (28504-8038)
PHONE....................407 293-9010
EMP: 9 EST: 2019
SALES (est): 376.76K **Privately Held**
Web: www.alside.com
SIC: 3442 Metal doors, sash, and trim

(G-9343)
ARGOS USA LLC
3350 Nc Highway 11 N (28501-7344)
PHONE....................252 527-8008
Ricky Gray, *Brnch Mgr*
EMP: 34
Web: www.argos-us.com
SIC: 3273 Ready-mixed concrete
HQ: Argos Usa Llc
3015 Windward Plz Ste 300
Alpharetta GA 30005
678 368-4300

(G-9344)
BARNHILL CONTRACTING COMPANY
604 E New Bern Rd (28504-6742)
PHONE....................252 527-8021
William F Davis, *Mgr*
EMP: 15
SALES (corp-wide): 389.14MM **Privately Held**
Web: www.barnhillcontracting.com
SIC: 1611 1771 3531 5032 Highway and street paving contractor; Parking lot construction; Asphalt plant, including gravel-mix type; Sand, construction
PA: Barnhill Contracting Company Inc
800 Tiffany Blvd Ste 200
Rocky Mount NC 27804
252 823-1021

(G-9345)
BLUE MOUNTAIN ENTERPRISES INC
Also Called: Blue Mountain Flavors
4000 Commerce Dr (28504-7906)
PHONE....................252 522-1544
▼ EMP: 37 EST: 1988
SALES (est): 6.07MM **Privately Held**
Web: www.bluemountainflavors.com
SIC: 2087 Extracts, flavoring

(G-9346)
BOBBY BENTON
396 Sandy Foundation Rd (28504-7022)
PHONE....................252 527-7023
Bobby Benton, *Prin*
EMP: 4 EST: 2008
SALES (est): 142.64K **Privately Held**
SIC: 1381 Service well drilling

(G-9347)
BRIDGESTONE RET OPERATIONS LLC
Also Called: Firestone
1901 W Vernon Ave (28504-3327)
PHONE....................252 522-5126
Ricky Morris, *Mgr*
EMP: 7
Web: www.bridgestoneamericas.com
SIC: 5531 7534 Automotive tires; Rebuilding and retreading tires
HQ: Bridgestone Retail Operations, Llc
333 E Lake St Ste 300
Bloomingdale IL 60108
630 259-9000

(G-9348)
BUFFALO INV GROUP NC LLC ◊
Also Called: Hoover Custom Tops
1592 Industrial Dr (28504-7589)
PHONE....................252 522-0050
EMP: 4 EST: 2022
SALES (est): 79.3K **Privately Held**
SIC: 2541 Table or counter tops, plastic laminated

(G-9349)
C & W MCH & FABRICATION INC
1206 Hugo Rd (28501-7149)
PHONE....................252 522-5476
EMP: 4 EST: 1992
SALES (est): 343.26K **Privately Held**
Web: md-rockville.doctors.at
SIC: 3599 Machine shop, jobbing and repair

(G-9350)
CAROLINA GREENHOUSE PLANTS INC
1504 Cunningham Rd (28501-1838)
P.O. Box 1140 (28503-1140)
PHONE....................252 523-9300
Dwight Howard, *Pr*
EMP: 15 EST: 1982
SQ FT: 6,000
SALES (est): 2.41MM **Privately Held**
Web: www.carolinagreenhouses.com
SIC: 3448 5191 Greenhouses, prefabricated metal; Greenhouse equipment and supplies

(G-9351)
CAROLINA ICE INC
2466 Old Poole Rd (28504-9234)
PHONE....................252 527-3178
TOLL FREE: 800
Thomas L Edwards, *Pr*
Merle Edwards, *
EMP: 30 EST: 1983
SALES (est): 4.14MM **Privately Held**
Web: www.carolinaice.com
SIC: 2097 Manufactured ice

(G-9352)
CAROLINA WELDING & CNSTR
1806 N Herritage St (28501-2216)
PHONE....................252 814-8740
Meldon Dail, *CEO*
EMP: 5 EST: 2012
SALES (est): 194.15K **Privately Held**
Web: www.carolinawelding.us
SIC: 7692 Welding repair

GEOGRAPHIC SECTION
Kinston - Lenoir County (G-9375)

(G-9353)
CAULEY CONSTRUCTION COMPANY
2385 Westdowns Ter (28504-7545)
PHONE..................252 522-1078
William B Cauley, *Pr*
C B Cauley, *VP*
Kattie L Cauley, *Sec*
EMP: 7 **EST:** 1962
SALES (est): 496.35K **Privately Held**
SIC: 2411 0191 0212 Logging camps and contractors; General farms, primarily crop; Beef cattle, except feedlots

(G-9354)
COCA-COLA CONSOLIDATED INC
Also Called: Coca-Cola
4194 W Vernon Ave (28504-9673)
P.O. Box 337 (28502-0337)
PHONE..................704 551-4500
Stene Walton, *Mgr*
EMP: 45
SALES (corp-wide): 6.65B **Publicly Held**
Web: www.cokeconsolidated.com
SIC: 2086 Bottled and canned soft drinks
PA: Coca-Cola Consolidated, Inc.
  4100 Coca Cola Plz # 100
  Charlotte NC 28211
  704 557-4400

(G-9355)
CROWN EQUIPMENT CORPORATION
Also Called: Crown Lift Trucks
2000 Dobbs Farm Rd (28504-8907)
PHONE..................252 522-3088
EMP: 325
SALES (corp-wide): 7.12B **Privately Held**
Web: www.crown.com
SIC: 3537 Forklift trucks
PA: Crown Equipment Corporation
  44 S Washington St
  New Bremen OH 45869
  419 629-2311

(G-9356)
DAILS PALLET & PRODUCE INC
2884 Neuse Rd (28501-9119)
PHONE..................252 717-1338
Gail Dail, *Prin*
EMP: 7 **EST:** 2009
SALES (est): 154.03K **Privately Held**
SIC: 2448 Pallets, wood

(G-9357)
DINGS ETC
572 Nc Hwy 58 S (28504-6808)
P.O. Box 1577 (28590-1577)
PHONE..................252 933-0208
Patrick Johnson, *Prin*
EMP: 5 **EST:** 2010
SALES (est): 71.51K **Privately Held**
SIC: 2842 Automobile polish

(G-9358)
DISCOVERY INSURANCE COMPANY
604 N Queen St (28501-4340)
P.O. Box 200 (28502-0200)
PHONE..................800 876-1492
EMP: 57 **EST:** 1993
SQ FT: 20,000
SALES (est): 39.01MM **Privately Held**
Web: www.discoveryinsurance.com
SIC: 6331 7372 Property damage insurance; Application computer software

(G-9359)
DOMESTIC FABRICS BLANKETS CORP
2002 W Vernon Ave (28504-3330)
PHONE..................252 523-7948
Donna Wilfong, *Ch*
David E Wilfong, *
Jonathan Wilfong, *
EMP: 46 **EST:** 2009
SQ FT: 70,000
SALES (est): 8.97MM **Privately Held**
Web: www.domesticfabrics.com
SIC: 5131 2396 Piece goods and notions; Apparel and other linings, except millinery

(G-9360)
EASTERN FUEL PROCUREMENT INC
3419 Buena Vista Ct (28504-8446)
PHONE..................252 523-2799
James R Creel, *Prin*
EMP: 7 **EST:** 2008
SALES (est): 247.38K **Privately Held**
SIC: 2869 Fuels

(G-9361)
EFFIKAL LLC
2630 Airport Rd (28504-7319)
PHONE..................252 522-3031
Patrick Holleran, *Pr*
▲ **EMP:** 9 **EST:** 1977
SQ FT: 30,000
SALES (est): 2.23MM
SALES (corp-wide): 1.21B **Privately Held**
Web: www.fieldcontrols.com
SIC: 3822 3444 Damper operators: pneumatic, thermostatic, electric; Sheet metalwork
HQ: Field Controls, L.L.C.
  2630 Airport Rd
  Kinston NC 28504
  252 208-7300

(G-9362)
EIDP INC
Also Called: Dupont
4693 Hwy 11 N (28502)
PHONE..................252 522-6286
Harold Thomas, *Manager*
EMP: 6
SALES (corp-wide): 17.23B **Publicly Held**
Web: www.dupont.com
SIC: 2821 Plastics materials and resins
HQ: Eidp, Inc.
  9330 Zionsville Rd
  Indianapolis IN 46268
  833 267-8382

(G-9363)
ELECTROLUX HOME PRODUCTS INC
ELECTROLUX HOME PRODUCTS, INC.
4850 W Vernon Ave (28504-7544)
PHONE..................252 527-5100
Bill Hilling, *Mgr*
EMP: 404
SALES (corp-wide): 12.86B **Privately Held**
Web: www.electroluxprofessional.com
SIC: 5722 3631 Household appliance stores; Household cooking equipment
HQ: Electrolux Home Products, Llc
  10200 David Taylor Dr
  Charlotte NC 28262

(G-9364)
FARVAL LUBRICATION SYSTEMS
2685 Airport Rd (28504-7335)
PHONE..................252 527-6001
John Short, *Manager*
EMP: 44
SALES (corp-wide): 545.92MM **Privately Held**
Web: www.bijurdelimon.com
SIC: 3569 Lubricating equipment
HQ: Farval Lubrication Systems, Inc
  808 Aviation Pkwy
  Kinston NC 28504

(G-9365)
FARVAL LUBRICATION SYSTEMS (DH)
808 Aviation Parkway (28504)
PHONE..................252 527-6001
Thomas W Arndt, *Pr*
Roger M Yamamoto, *VP Fin*
John V Curci, *Sec*
▲ **EMP:** 50 **EST:** 1993
SQ FT: 46,000
SALES (est): 14.05MM
SALES (corp-wide): 545.92MM **Privately Held**
Web: www.farval.com
SIC: 3569 Lubricating equipment
HQ: Industrial Manufacturing Company Llc
  8223 Brecksville Rd # 100
  Brecksville OH 44141
  440 838-4700

(G-9366)
FIELD CONTROLS LLC (DH)
2630 Airport Rd (28504-7319)
PHONE..................252 208-7300
Patrick T Holleran, *Pr*
Michael Afarian, *
Tony Schrank, *
Bobby Nelson, *
▲ **EMP:** 84 **EST:** 1927
SQ FT: 100,000
SALES (est): 31.3MM
SALES (corp-wide): 1.21B **Privately Held**
Web: www.fieldcontrols.com
SIC: 3829 3564 3444 Measuring and controlling devices, nec; Blowers and fans; Sheet metalwork
HQ: Pettibone L.L.C.
  27501 Bella Vista Pkwy
  Warrenville IL 60555
  630 353-5000

(G-9367)
FUSION FIBER OPTICS LLC
1935 Neuse Rd (28501-9188)
PHONE..................252 933-5244
Richard V Acevedo, *Owner*
EMP: 6 **EST:** 2017
SALES (est): 234.11K **Privately Held**
SIC: 3678 2298 Electronic connectors; Cable, fiber

(G-9368)
HARVEY FERTILIZER AND GAS CO
1291 Hwy 258 N (28504-7209)
PHONE..................252 523-9090
Frakie Hill, *CFO*
EMP: 12
SALES (corp-wide): 80.5MM **Privately Held**
Web: www.harveyfertilizerandgas.com
SIC: 5191 2873 2875 Fertilizer and fertilizer materials; Nitrogenous fertilizers; Fertilizers, mixing only
PA: Harvey Fertilizer And Gas Co.
  303 Bohannon Rd
  Kinston NC 28501
  252 526-4150

(G-9369)
HARVEY FERTILIZER AND GAS CO (PA)
Also Called: Harvey Gin & Cotton
303 Bohannon Rd (28501-7434)
P.O. Box 189 (28502-0189)
PHONE..................252 526-4150
Herbert Rouse, *Pr*
Llyod E Cooper, *
Frankie Hill, *
▲ **EMP:** 42 **EST:** 1871
SQ FT: 25,000
SALES (est): 80.5MM
SALES (corp-wide): 80.5MM **Privately Held**
Web: www.harveyfertilizerandgas.com
SIC: 2875 2873 5191 Fertilizers, mixing only; Nitrogenous fertilizers; Chemicals, agricultural

(G-9370)
JARED SASNETT LOGGING CO INC
1976 Neuse Rd (28501-9188)
PHONE..................252 939-6289
Jared Sasnett, *Owner*
EMP: 6 **EST:** 2008
SALES (est): 763.36K **Privately Held**
SIC: 2411 Logging camps and contractors

(G-9371)
KINSTON FREE PRESS COMPANY
Also Called: Free Press, The
2103 N Queen St (28501-1622)
P.O. Box 129 (28502-0129)
PHONE..................252 527-3191
Patrick Holmes, *Associate Publisher*
Lee Raynor, *Managing Editor**
EMP: 118 **EST:** 1882
SQ FT: 16,000
SALES (est): 2.3MM
SALES (corp-wide): 2.66B **Publicly Held**
Web: www.kinston.com
SIC: 2711 Newspapers, publishing and printing
HQ: Gatehouse Media, Llc
  175 Sullys Trl Ste 203
  Pittsford NY 14534
  585 598-0030

(G-9372)
KINSTON NEUSE CORPORATION
2000 Dobbs Farm Rd (28504-8907)
PHONE..................252 522-3088
◆ **EMP:** 250
Web: www.visitkinston.com
SIC: 3537 Pallet loaders and unloaders

(G-9373)
KINSTON OFFICE SUPPLY CO INC (PA)
Also Called: Corporate Resources
704 Plaza Blvd Ste B (28501-1554)
P.O. Box 696 (28502-0696)
PHONE..................252 523-7654
Scott H Bowen, *Pr*
Craig Bowen, *
Barbara Bowen, *
EMP: 26 **EST:** 1951
SQ FT: 30,000
SALES (est): 4.12MM
SALES (corp-wide): 4.12MM **Privately Held**
Web: ci.kinston.nc.us
SIC: 5712 5942 2752 Office furniture; Books, religious; Offset printing

(G-9374)
LYNN JONES RACE CARS
1168 Woodington Rd (28504-7057)
PHONE..................252 522-0705
Lynn Jones, *Owner*
EMP: 4 **EST:** 1999
SALES (est): 78.68K **Privately Held**
SIC: 3711 Cars, electric, assembly of

(G-9375)
MAGIC MILE MEDIA INC
Also Called: Davidson Daily
105 W Blount St (28501-4807)
PHONE..................252 572-1330
Bj Murphy, *CEO*
Aleatha Thrower, *VP*
EMP: 12 **EST:** 2016
SALES (est): 589.02K **Privately Held**

Kinston - Lenoir County (G-9376)   **GEOGRAPHIC SECTION**

Web: www.magicmilemedia.com
SIC: 2711 7379 Newspapers: publishing only, not printed on site; Online services technology consultants

(G-9376)
MASTERBRAND CABINETS INC
Also Called: MASTERBRAND CABINETS, INC.
651 Collier Loftin Rd (28504-6847)
P.O. Box 3567 (28502-3567)
PHONE..................252 523-4131
Steve Woolard, Mgr
EMP: 61
SALES (corp-wide): 2.73B Publicly Held
Web: www.masterbrand.com
SIC: 2434 Wood kitchen cabinets
HQ: Masterbrand Cabinets Llc
1 Masterbrand Cabinets Dr
Jasper IN 47546
812 482-2527

(G-9377)
MOTHER EARTH BREWING LLC
311 N Herritage St (28501-4823)
PHONE..................252 208-2437
Trent E Mooring, Managing Member
▲ EMP: 6 EST: 2008
SALES (est): 1.19MM Privately Held
Web: www.motherearthbrewing.com
SIC: 2082 Beer (alcoholic beverage)

(G-9378)
NARRON WOODWORKS
1209 Sutton Dr (28501-2605)
PHONE..................252 258-2151
Curtis Narron, Prin
EMP: 4 EST: 2019
SALES (est): 68.28K Privately Held
SIC: 2431 Millwork

(G-9379)
NORTH CRLINA DEPT CRIME CTRL P
Also Called: Highway Patrol
2214 W Vernon Ave (28504-3334)
PHONE..................252 522-1511
EMP: 6
Web: www.ncdps.gov
SIC: 3711 9229 Patrol wagons (motor vehicles), assembly of; Public order and safety, State government
HQ: North Carolina Department Of Crime Control And Public Safety
512 N Salisbury St
Raleigh NC 27604

(G-9380)
PACTIV LLC
1447 Enterprise Blvd (28504-7598)
PHONE..................252 527-6300
Mike Tutowski, Mgr
EMP: 56
Web: www.pactivevergreen.com
SIC: 2657 2671 2631 Food containers, folding; made from purchased material; Paper; coated and laminated packaging; Paperboard mills
HQ: Pactiv Llc
1900 W Field Ct
Lake Forest IL 60045
847 482-2000

(G-9381)
RS BOSTIC SERVICE INC
2280 Hwy 258 S (28504-6498)
PHONE..................252 527-4781
Richard S Bostic Junior, Pr
Sara Bostic, VP
EMP: 5 EST: 1986
SALES (est): 334.52K Privately Held

SIC: 3534 Escalators, passenger and freight

(G-9382)
S & W READY MIX CON CO LLC
604 E New Bern Rd (28504-6742)
PHONE..................252 527-1881
Johnny Jarman, Brnch Mgr
EMP: 15
SALES (corp-wide): 8.01MM Privately Held
SIC: 3273 Ready-mixed concrete
HQ: S & W Ready Mix Concrete Company Llc
217 Lisbon St
Clinton NC 28328
910 592-1733

(G-9383)
SANDERSON FARMS INC
Also Called: Production Division
1536 Smithfield Way (28504-9272)
PHONE..................252 208-0036
Wes Hall, Mgr
EMP: 27
SALES (corp-wide): 4.8B Privately Held
Web: www.sandersonfarms.com
SIC: 2015 Poultry slaughtering and processing
HQ: Sanderson Farms, Llc
127 Flynt Rd
Laurel MS 39443
601 649-4030

(G-9384)
SMITHFIELD FOODS INC
1780 Smithfield Way (28504-9244)
PHONE..................252 208-4700
Gerry Koster, Manager
EMP: 83
Web: www.smithfieldfoods.com
SIC: 2013 2011 Sausages and other prepared meats; Boxed beef, from meat slaughtered on site
HQ: Smithfield Foods, Inc.
200 Commerce St
Smithfield VA 23430
757 365-3000

(G-9385)
SOUTHERN VINYL MFG INC
2010 Smithfield Way (28504-6200)
PHONE..................252 523-2520
Wes Seegars, CEO
Dean Ervin, Pr
EMP: 12 EST: 1997
SALES (est): 1.9MM Privately Held
Web: www.svmnc.com
SIC: 3089 Fences, gates, and accessories: plastics

(G-9386)
SPIRIT AEROSYSTEMS INC
2600 Aerosystems Blvd (28504-7356)
PHONE..................252 208-4645
EMP: 3883
Web: www.spiritaero.com
SIC: 3728 3721 Aircraft parts and equipment, nec; Aircraft
HQ: Spirit Aerosystems, Inc.
3801 S Oliver St
Wichita KS 67201
316 526-9000

(G-9387)
TAR HEEL METAL STRUCTURES
2200 W Vernon Ave (28504-3368)
PHONE..................252 208-7171
Kim Thompson, Pr
EMP: 5 EST: 2011
SALES (est): 123.54K Privately Held
Web: www.tarheelmetal.com

SIC: 2865 Tar

(G-9388)
THREE STACKS DISTILLING CO LLC
Also Called: Three Stacks Distilling Co.
906 Atlantic Ave (28501-4109)
PHONE..................252 468-0779
EMP: 8 EST: 2017
SALES (est): 258.83K Privately Held
SIC: 2085 Distilled and blended liquors

(G-9389)
UNIFI KINSTON LLC
4693 Hwy 11 (28504)
PHONE..................252 522-6518
Bill Lowe, CEO
▲ EMP: 21 EST: 2004
SALES (est): 962.86K
SALES (corp-wide): 623.53MM Publicly Held
SIC: 2821 Polyesters
PA: Unifi, Inc.
7201 W Friendly Ave
Greensboro NC 27410
336 294-4410

(G-9390)
URBAN TACTICAL AND CSTM ARMORY
643 Tyree Rd (28504-6343)
PHONE..................252 686-0122
EMP: 5 EST: 2015
SALES (est): 170.86K Privately Held
SIC: 3484 Small arms

(G-9391)
VILLABONA IRON WORKS INC
1415 W New Bern Rd (28504-4717)
P.O. Box 6549 (28501-0549)
PHONE..................252 522-4005
EMP: 10 EST: 1994
SQ FT: 60,000
SALES (est): 501.05K Privately Held
SIC: 7692 Welding repair

(G-9392)
WEST PHARMACEUTICAL SVCS INC
1028 Innovation Way (28504-7616)
PHONE..................252 522-8956
Thomas Clagoen, Mgr
EMP: 4
SALES (corp-wide): 2.95B Publicly Held
Web: www.westpharma.com
SIC: 2834 Pharmaceutical preparations
PA: West Pharmaceutical Services, Inc.
530 Herman O West Dr
Exton PA 19341
610 594-2900

(G-9393)
WILLIAM BARNET & SON LLC
Kinston Division
1411 Hwy 258 S (28504-5379)
P.O. Box 3449 (28502-3449)
PHONE..................252 522-2418
Thomas Parker, Brnch Mgr
EMP: 200
SALES (corp-wide): 104.69MM Privately Held
Web: www.barnet.com
SIC: 2299 Textile mill waste and remnant processing
PA: William Barnet & Son, Llc
1300 Hayne St
Spartanburg SC 29301
864 576-7154

Kittrell
Vance County

(G-9394)
BUFFALOE MILLING COMPANY INC
196 Buffalo Mill Rd (27544-9048)
P.O. Box 145 (27544-0145)
PHONE..................252 438-8637
John D Spencer, Pr
James K Spencer Junior, VP
Marilove Spencer, Treas
Christina Spencer, Sec
EMP: 23 EST: 1855
SQ FT: 13,000
SALES (est): 1.01MM Privately Held
Web: www.buffaloemilling.com
SIC: 2041 Corn flour

(G-9395)
CAROLINA SUNROCK LLC
214 Sunrock Rd (27544-8012)
PHONE..................252 433-4617
EMP: 33
SALES (corp-wide): 68.06MM Privately Held
Web: www.thesunrockgroup.com
SIC: 3273 Ready-mixed concrete
HQ: Carolina Sunrock Llc
1001 W B St
Butner NC 27509
919 575-4502

(G-9396)
GES INDUSTRIES (PA)
78 Walter Grissom Rd (27544-9129)
PHONE..................252 430-8851
▲ EMP: 35
SALES (est): 3MM Privately Held
SIC: 2499 Laundry products, wood

(G-9397)
NC GRAPHIC PROS LLC
2232 Rocky Ford Rd (27544-9576)
PHONE..................252 492-7326
Jennifer Stanley, Prin
EMP: 4 EST: 2016
SALES (est): 207.54K Privately Held
Web: www.ncgraphicpros.com
SIC: 3993 7336 5131 5999 Letters for signs, metal; Commercial art and graphic design; Flags and banners; Trophies and plaques

(G-9398)
SHARP FIBERGLASS LLC
6032 Us 1 Byp S (27544-9365)
PHONE..................610 760-0638
Frank Meldau Iii, Admn
EMP: 6 EST: 2018
SALES (est): 62.63K Privately Held
Web: www.sharpfiberglass.com
SIC: 3296 Mineral wool

Kitty Hawk
Dare County

(G-9399)
ALPHA-ADVANTAGE INC
891 Emeline Ln (27949-4271)
PHONE..................252 441-3766
Robert Walde Junior, Pr
EMP: 5 EST: 1999
SALES (est): 879.58K Privately Held
Web: www.alpha-advantage.com
SIC: 3589 Water treatment equipment, industrial

GEOGRAPHIC SECTION

Knightdale - Wake County (G-9427)

(G-9400)
DISCOVERY MAP
176 S Dogwood Trl (27949-3103)
PHONE.....................435 901-1027
EMP: 5
SALES (est): 76.29K **Privately Held**
Web: www.discoverymap.com
SIC: 2741 Miscellaneous publishing

(G-9401)
DOOR SCREEN
1177 Duck Rd (27949-4553)
PHONE.....................406 531-4516
Craig Readman, *Prin*
EMP: 5 EST: 2012
SALES (est): 76.69K **Privately Held**
SIC: 3442 Screen and storm doors and windows

(G-9402)
DRUM BEAT FISHING LLC
Also Called: Kitty Hawk Chairs
105 Mariners Vw (27949-4718)
PHONE.....................252 455-5114
EMP: 5 EST: 2018
SALES (est): 68.6K **Privately Held**
SIC: 2426 Stock, chair, hardwood: turned, shaped, or carved

(G-9403)
DUSTY RHOADS HVAC INC
Also Called: Honeywell Authorized Dealer
3822 Elijah Baum Dr (27949-4253)
P.O. Box 444 (27949-0444)
PHONE.....................252 261-5892
Dusty Rhoads, *Pr*
Bonnie Rhoads, *Sec*
EMP: 7 EST: 1987
SALES (est): 460.3K **Privately Held**
Web: www.honeywell.com
SIC: 1711 3444 Warm air heating and air conditioning contractor; Sheet metalwork

(G-9404)
FAR NIENTE LLC
6021 Martins Point Rd (27949-3865)
P.O. Box 243 (27949-0243)
PHONE.....................252 715-0154
Elizabeth E Robbins, *Admn*
EMP: 4 EST: 2015
SALES (est): 69.41K **Privately Held**
Web: www.outerbankscarolinavacations.com
SIC: 2084 Wines

(G-9405)
FLYING SMILES INC
302 Sea Oats Trl (27949-3202)
PHONE.....................252 255-3054
Catherine Gephart Shook, *Prin*
EMP: 4 EST: 2008
SALES (est): 103.44K **Privately Held**
SIC: 3944 Kites

(G-9406)
GULFSTREAM PUBLICATIONS INC
Also Called: North Beach Sun
4425 N Croatan Hwy (27949-4123)
P.O. Box 28 (27948-0028)
PHONE.....................252 449-2222
Rex Peters, *Pr*
Victoria Peters, *VP*
EMP: 7 EST: 1987
SQ FT: 3,000
SALES (est): 731.7K **Privately Held**
Web: www.northbeachsun.com
SIC: 2711 2741 7336 Newspapers: publishing only, not printed on site; Directories, telephone: publishing only, not printed on site; Graphic arts and related design

(G-9407)
IDENTIFY YOURSELF LLC
6146 N Croatan Hwy Unit C (27949-3866)
P.O. Box 432 (27949-0432)
PHONE.....................252 202-1452
Alex Lefevre, *Prin*
Emily Ausband, *Prin*
EMP: 12 EST: 2004
SALES (est): 3.14MM **Privately Held**
Web: www.idyourself.com
SIC: 5199 2759 Advertising specialties; Promotional printing

(G-9408)
TNT SERVICES INC
3908 Poor Ridge Rd (27949-4332)
P.O. Box 296 (27966-0296)
PHONE.....................252 261-3073
Roy Lee Etheridge, *Pr*
Karen Etheridge, *VP*
EMP: 13 EST: 1981
SQ FT: 5,000
SALES (est): 414.29K **Privately Held**
SIC: 1771 1711 3272 1629 Driveway contractor; Septic system construction; Septic tanks, concrete; Land clearing contractor

Knightdale
Wake County

(G-9409)
ALLAN FITCH
212 Dwelling Pl (27545-9410)
PHONE.....................919 834-2593
Allen Fitch, *Owner*
EMP: 5 EST: 2015
SALES (est): 83.1K **Privately Held**
SIC: 3499 Fabricated metal products, nec

(G-9410)
ALLEGRA MARKETING PRINT MAIL
Also Called: Allegra Knightdale
1009 Steeple Square Ct (27545-8072)
PHONE.....................919 373-0531
EMP: 4 EST: 2015
SALES (est): 179.86K **Privately Held**
Web: www.allegramarketingprint.com
SIC: 2752 Offset printing

(G-9411)
AMETEK ELECTRONICS SYSTEMS
8001 Knightdale Blvd Ste 121 (27545-9023)
PHONE.....................800 645-9721
EMP: 24 EST: 2017
SALES (est): 2.5MM **Privately Held**
Web: www.ametekesp.com
SIC: 3629 Electronic generation equipment

(G-9412)
ANCHOR WELDING LLC
1310 Bristoe Dr Apt 201 (27545-6538)
PHONE.....................919 747-1926
Vanessa Flores, *Prin*
EMP: 4 EST: 2017
SALES (est): 59.37K **Privately Held**
SIC: 7692 Welding repair

(G-9413)
BHAKI BULLIES LLC
1301 Cherry Hollow Way (27545-5936)
PHONE.....................646 387-3974
EMP: 4 EST: 2021
SALES (est): 64.53K **Privately Held**
SIC: 2399 Pet collars, leashes, etc.: non-leather

(G-9414)
CAPITAL READY MIX CONCRETE LLC
512 Three Sisters Rd (27545-8202)
P.O. Box 1697 (27312-1697)
PHONE.....................919 217-0222
EMP: 35 EST: 2008
SALES (est): 10.11MM **Privately Held**
Web: www.capitalreadymixconcrete.com
SIC: 3273 Ready-mixed concrete

(G-9415)
CARTER PRINTING
1105 Great Falls Ct Ste A (27545-5800)
P.O. Box 385 (27545-0385)
PHONE.....................919 373-0531
Herb Steward, *Owner*
EMP: 5 EST: 2015
SALES (est): 77.41K **Privately Held**
SIC: 2752 Offset printing

(G-9416)
CARTER PRINTING & GRAPHICS INC
1001 Steeple Square Ct (27545-8072)
P.O. Box 385 (27545-0385)
PHONE.....................919 266-5280
Gene Carter, *Pr*
Joyce Carter, *
EMP: 22 EST: 1985
SQ FT: 33,000
SALES (est): 521.74K **Privately Held**
Web: www.carterprintingnc.com
SIC: 2752 Offset printing

(G-9417)
DUNKIN DONUTS
Also Called: Baskin-Robbins
7137 Knightdale Blvd Ste A (27545-6049)
PHONE.....................919 217-9603
Charlie Bed, *Owner*
EMP: 10 EST: 2000
SALES (est): 347.87K **Privately Held**
Web: www.dunkindonuts.com
SIC: 5461 2051 5812 Doughnuts; Doughnuts, except frozen; Ice cream stands or dairy bars

(G-9418)
HUMMINGBIRD NATURALS LLC
1304 Colton Creek Rd (27545-6383)
PHONE.....................774 276-0889
Katherine Franceschelli, *Prin*
EMP: 4 EST: 2018
SALES (est): 112.01K **Privately Held**
SIC: 2844 Perfumes, cosmetics and other toilet preparations

(G-9419)
LASSITER DISTILLING COMPANY
319 N 1st Ave (27545-8501)
P.O. Box 213 (27545-0213)
PHONE.....................919 295-0111
Rebecca Lassiter, *Prin*
EMP: 4 EST: 2017
SALES (est): 231.47K **Privately Held**
Web: www.lassiterdistilling.com
SIC: 2085 Distilled and blended liquors

(G-9420)
LEN CORPORATION
Also Called: Royce Company
525 Hinton Oaks Blvd (27545-5834)
PHONE.....................919 876-2964
Len Johnson, *Pr*
Scott Shulz, *VP*
EMP: 18 EST: 1982
SALES (est): 2.62MM
SALES (corp-wide): 170.37MM **Privately Held**
Web: www.roycecompany.com

SIC: 3444 Sheet metal specialties, not stamped
PA: N. B. Handy Operations, Llc
65 10th St
Lynchburg VA 24504
434 847-4495

(G-9421)
MOBILE MINI - STOR TANKS PUMPS
618 Nc-2655 (27545)
PHONE.....................919 365-0377
EMP: 5 EST: 2018
SALES (est): 80.58K **Privately Held**
SIC: 3448 Buildings, portable: prefabricated metal

(G-9422)
MOBILE MINI INC
618 Three Sisters Rd (27545-8204)
PHONE.....................480 894-6311
Chris Miner, *Brnch Mgr*
EMP: 6
SALES (corp-wide): 2.36B **Publicly Held**
Web: www.mobilemini.com
SIC: 3448 Buildings, portable: prefabricated metal
HQ: Mobile Mini, Inc.
4646 E Van Buren St # 400
Phoenix AZ 85008
480 894-6311

(G-9423)
MYRICKS CABINET SHOP INC
2329 Hodge Rd (27545-8601)
PHONE.....................919 266-3720
Steve Myrick, *Prin*
EMP: 6 EST: 2007
SALES (est): 390.65K **Privately Held**
Web: www.myrickscabinetshop.com
SIC: 2434 Wood kitchen cabinets

(G-9424)
OAK CITY WOODWORKS
904 Willow Ridge Dr (27545-8862)
PHONE.....................919 247-5984
EMP: 4 EST: 2016
SALES (est): 55.79K **Privately Held**
SIC: 2431 Millwork

(G-9425)
PCX HOLDING LLC
370 Spectrum Dr (27545-5144)
PHONE.....................919 550-2800
EMP: 74
SALES (corp-wide): 5.37B **Publicly Held**
Web: www.pcxcorp.com
SIC: 3699 Electrical equipment and supplies, nec
HQ: Pcx Holding Llc
33 Pony Farm Rd
Clayton NC 27520
919 550-2800

(G-9426)
PROGRESSIVE INTL ELEC INC
1106 Great Falls Ct (27545-5801)
PHONE.....................919 266-4442
Ted Warn, *Pr*
EMP: 8 EST: 1978
SQ FT: 5,000
SALES (est): 783.13K **Privately Held**
Web: www.pie-corp2.com
SIC: 3823 Process control instruments

(G-9427)
PROTRONICS INC
Also Called: Pro Tronics
861 Old Knight Rd Ste 102 (27545-6056)
PHONE.....................919 217-0007
Jan Alford, *Pr*

Knightdale - Wake County (G-9428)

Teresa Alford, *VP*
EMP: 15 **EST:** 1993
SQ FT: 5,300
SALES (est): 2.28MM **Privately Held**
Web: www.protronics-inc.com
SIC: 3672 7629 Circuit boards, television and radio printed; Circuit board repair

(G-9428)
SCHNEIDER ELECTRIC USA INC
Also Called: Schneider Electric
Hwy 64 East (27545)
PHONE.....................919 266-3671
Harry Hyatt, *Brnch Mgr*
EMP: 161
SALES (corp-wide): 82.05K **Privately Held**
Web: www.se.com
SIC: 3613 3625 Switchgear and switchboard apparatus; Relays and industrial controls
HQ: Schneider Electric Usa, Inc.
1 Boston Pl Ste 2700
Boston MA 02108
978 975-9600

(G-9429)
SUPERIOR ENVMTL SVCS LLC
4033 Village Park Dr Unit 220 (27545-7044)
PHONE.....................919 717-1199
EMP: 6
SALES (est): 79.3K **Privately Held**
SIC: 2842 Specialty cleaning

(G-9430)
THREE SISTERS READY MIX LLC
512 Three Sisters Rd (27545-8202)
PHONE.....................919 217-0222
EMP: 11 **EST:** 2009
SALES (est): 479.94K **Privately Held**
Web: www.capitalreadymixconcrete.com
SIC: 3273 Ready-mixed concrete

(G-9431)
TRADE VENTURE STONES LLC
Also Called: Tvs
365 Spectrum Dr Ste 100 (27545-5144)
PHONE.....................919 803-3923
David Kim, *Pr*
▲ **EMP:** 6 **EST:** 2015
SALES (est): 1.27MM **Privately Held**
Web: www.tvs-usa.com
SIC: 3281 5032 Table tops, marble; Granite building stone

(G-9432)
TRESMC LLC
2509 Ferdinand Dr (27545-7460)
PHONE.....................919 900-0868
Angela Clemmons, *Pr*
EMP: 5 **EST:** 2006
SALES (est): 461.22K **Privately Held**
SIC: 5699 5137 2311 Uniforms; Uniforms, women's and children's; Men's and boys' uniforms

(G-9433)
WAGCO OIL AND VINEGAR TAPROOM
861 Old Knight Rd Ste 113 (27545-7803)
PHONE.....................919 295-6134
Deanna Palo, *Prin*
EMP: 5 **EST:** 2017
SALES (est): 92.74K **Privately Held**
Web: wagcooilandvinegartaproom.wordpress.com
SIC: 2099 Vinegar

(G-9434)
WAKE STONE CORPORATION (PA)
6821 Knightdale Blvd (27545-9651)
P.O. Box 190 (27545-0190)
PHONE.....................919 266-1100
Samuel T Bratton, *Pr*
John R Bratton, *
Theodore D Bratton, *
Thomas B Oxholm, *
M Holt Browning, *
EMP: 48 **EST:** 1970
SQ FT: 8,500
SALES (est): 24.15MM
SALES (corp-wide): 24.15MM **Privately Held**
Web: www.wakestonecorp.com
SIC: 3281 Cut stone and stone products

Knotts Island
Currituck County

(G-9435)
OBX METALWORKS LLC
281 Woodleigh Rd (27950-9697)
PHONE.....................757 434-0211
EMP: 5 **EST:** 2019
SALES (est): 191.22K **Privately Held**
Web: www.obxmetalworks.com
SIC: 3444 Sheet metalwork

Kure Beach
New Hanover County

(G-9436)
ANDREWS VIOLINIST
546 Anchor Way (28449-4802)
PHONE.....................910 458-1226
EMP: 4 **EST:** 2012
SALES (est): 81.56K **Privately Held**
SIC: 3931 Violins and parts

(G-9437)
DNA SERVICES INC
Also Called: Fireplace Guy, The
770 Settlers Ln (28449-4907)
PHONE.....................910 279-2775
EMP: 6 **EST:** 2014
SALES (est): 73.45K **Privately Held**
Web: www.fireplaceguy.net
SIC: 3433 1799 Logs, gas fireplace; Prefabricated fireplace installation

La Grange
Lenoir County

(G-9438)
COOPER BUSSMANN LLC
Cooper Bussmann-Automotive
4758 Washington St (28551-8173)
PHONE.....................252 566-0278
Steve Tate, *Genl Mgr*
EMP: 189
SIC: 3613 3545 Fuses, electric; Machine tool accessories
HQ: Cooper Bussmann, Llc
114 Old State Rd
Ellisville MO 63021
636 394-2877

(G-9439)
COOPER CROUSE-HINDS LLC
4758 Washington St (28551-8173)
PHONE.....................252 566-3014
Alexander M Cutler, *CEO*
EMP: 42
Web: www.coopercrouse-hinds.com
SIC: 3069 3679 Hard rubber and molded rubber products; Electronic circuits
HQ: Cooper Crouse-Hinds, Llc
1201 Wolf St
Syracuse NY 13208
315 477-7000

(G-9440)
DUDLEYS FENCE COMPANY
4126 Fields Station Rd (28551-7933)
PHONE.....................252 566-5759
Sherman Dudley, *Pr*
EMP: 5 **EST:** 1997
SALES (est): 496.81K **Privately Held**
Web: dudleysfence.webs.com
SIC: 3446 5084 Fences, gates, posts, and flagpoles; Cleaning equipment, high pressure, sand or steam

(G-9441)
FOSS INDUSTRIAL RECYCLING LLC
7037 Us Highway 70 W (28551-8932)
PHONE.....................336 342-4812
Jimmie C Foss Junior, *Pr*
EMP: 18 **EST:** 2015
SALES (est): 2.82MM **Privately Held**
Web: www.fossrecycling.com
SIC: 3569 Baling machines, for scrap metal, paper, or similar material

(G-9442)
LITE LOGGING LLC
7091 Nc Highway 903 S (28551-8368)
PHONE.....................252 560-8131
EMP: 4 **EST:** 2020
SALES (est): 76.29K **Privately Held**
SIC: 2411 Logging

(G-9443)
M M M INC (PA)
501 W Railroad St (28551-1641)
P.O. Box 188 (28551-0188)
PHONE.....................252 527-0229
J Ward Mc Connell, *Ch Bd*
EMP: 6 **EST:** 1818
SQ FT: 48,000
SALES (est): 1.06MM
SALES (corp-wide): 1.06MM **Privately Held**
Web: www.mmmpots.com
SIC: 3443 Tanks, lined: metal plate

(G-9444)
P & D ARCHTECTURAL PRECAST INC
323 E Railroad St (28551-1844)
P.O. Box 477 (28551-0477)
PHONE.....................252 566-9811
Mark Fairman, *Pr*
EMP: 14 **EST:** 1980
SQ FT: 17,000
SALES (est): 5.76MM **Privately Held**
Web: www.pdarchprecast.com
SIC: 3272 Concrete products, precast, nec

(G-9445)
SALTY DOG SNACKS INC
507 W Washington St (28551-1625)
PHONE.....................252 532-2109
Gary B Marchant, *Pr*
EMP: 6 **EST:** 2016
SALES (est): 102.86K **Privately Held**
SIC: 2096 Potato chips and similar snacks

(G-9446)
SOUTHERN STONE CUTTING
108 N Caswell St (28551-1725)
PHONE.....................252 566-3116
Joseph M Price, *Prin*
EMP: 6 **EST:** 2010
SALES (est): 163.6K **Privately Held**
SIC: 3281 Marble, building: cut and shaped

Lake Lure
Rutherford County

(G-9447)
LAKE LURE MARINE
5911 Us 64 74a Hwy (28746-9234)
PHONE.....................828 200-5908
EMP: 4 **EST:** 2019
SALES (est): 85.49K **Privately Held**
Web: www.lakeluremarine.com
SIC: 3731 Shipbuilding and repairing

Lake Waccamaw
Columbus County

(G-9448)
COUNCIL TOOL COMPANY INC (PA)
345 Pecan Ln (28450-2325)
PHONE.....................910 646-3011
John M Council Iii, *Pr*
Virginia P Council, *VP*
▲ **EMP:** 50 **EST:** 1886
SQ FT: 2,500
SALES (est): 7.71MM
SALES (corp-wide): 7.71MM **Privately Held**
Web: www.counciltool.com
SIC: 3423 Carpenters' hand tools, except saws: levels, chisels, etc.

(G-9449)
TOP TOBACCO LP
204 Top Tobacco Rd (28450)
PHONE.....................910 646-3014
Claus Platt, *Pr*
EMP: 106
SALES (corp-wide): 40.41MM **Privately Held**
SIC: 2131 2141 0132 Smoking tobacco; Tobacco stemming and redrying; Tobacco
PA: Top Tobacco L.P.
2301 Ravine Way
Glenview IL 60025
847 832-9700

Landis
Rowan County

(G-9450)
CECO FRICTION PRODUCTS INC
2525 N Hwy 29 (28088)
P.O. Box 150 (28088-0150)
PHONE.....................704 857-1156
Phillip Coan, *Pr*
Thomas Young, *VP*
Paul B Coan, *Treas*
EMP: 14 **EST:** 1973
SQ FT: 18,000
SALES (est): 1.39MM **Privately Held**
Web: www.cecofriction.com
SIC: 3714 Motor vehicle brake systems and parts

(G-9451)
MARTIN MARIETTA MATERIALS INC
Also Called: Martin Marietta Aggregates
P.O. Box 8108 (28088-8108)
PHONE.....................704 932-4379
Ronnie Borum, *Brnch Mgr*
EMP: 10
Web: www.martinmarietta.com
SIC: 3273 Ready-mixed concrete
PA: Martin Marietta Materials Inc
4123 Parklake Ave
Raleigh NC 27612

GEOGRAPHIC SECTION

Laurinburg - Scotland County (G-9475)

(G-9452)
PARKDALE MILLS INCORPORATED
Also Called: Parkdale Plant 23
100 S Main St (28088-1310)
P.O. Box 1787 (28053-1787)
PHONE.................704 855-3164
Brett Lowder, *Brnch Mgr*
EMP: 46
SALES (corp-wide): 1.44B **Privately Held**
Web: www.parkdalemills.com
SIC: 2281 Yarn spinning mills
HQ: Parkdale Mills, Incorporated
531 Cotton Blossom Cir
Gastonia NC 28054
704 874-5000

(G-9453)
PARKDALE MILLS INC
Also Called: Parkdale Plant 24
414 N Meriah St (28088-1039)
PHONE.................704 857-3456
Brett Lowder, *Brnch Mgr*
EMP: 24
SALES (corp-wide): 1.44B **Privately Held**
Web: www.parkdalemills.com
SIC: 2281 Cotton yarn, spun
HQ: Parkdale Mills, Incorporated
531 Cotton Blossom Cir
Gastonia NC 28054
704 874-5000

Lansing
Ashe County

(G-9454)
DMA DESIGN PRINT
102 Grouse Rdg (28643-9258)
PHONE.................336 877-0068
EMP: 4 **EST:** 2016
SALES (est): 132.04K **Privately Held**
SIC: 2752 Commercial printing, lithographic

(G-9455)
JERRY BLEVINS
Also Called: High Country Chair Weaving
1162 Deep Ford Rd (28643-9240)
PHONE.................336 384-3726
Jerry Blevins, *Owner*
EMP: 6 **EST:** 1996
SQ FT: 2,400
SALES (est): 710.32K **Privately Held**
SIC: 5021 2426 Chairs; Chair seats, hardwood

(G-9456)
UNITED CHEMI-CON INC
185 Mcneil Rd (28643-8308)
PHONE.................336 384-6903
Noboru Tokushige, *Mgr*
EMP: 300
Web: www.chemi-con.com
SIC: 3675 5065 Electronic capacitors; Capacitors, electronic
HQ: United Chemi-Con, Inc.
1701 Golf Rd Ste 1-1200
Rolling Meadows IL 60008
847 696-2000

Lattimore
Cleveland County

(G-9457)
KLEAROPTICS INC
150 N Rsrch Cmpus Dr Ste (28089)
PHONE.................760 224-6770
Ali Dahi, *Pr*
Ramazan Benrashid, *VP*
EMP: 5 **EST:** 2017

SALES (est): 400K **Privately Held**
SIC: 7389 3827 Business Activities at Non-Commercial Site; Optical instruments and apparatus

(G-9458)
MARTINS WOODWORKING LLC
Also Called: Martins Woodworking
100 Martin St (28089)
P.O. Box 256 (28089-0256)
PHONE.................704 473-7617
Jackson Martin, *Managing Member*
EMP: 10 **EST:** 2011
SALES (est): 497.56K **Privately Held**
Web: www.martinswoodworking.com
SIC: 2431 Millwork

Laurel Hill
Scotland County

(G-9459)
EAST COAST UMBRELLA INC
6321 Andrew Jackson Hwy (28351-8561)
PHONE.................910 462-2500
Darrell L Day, *Pr*
Dewayne Day, *
Christine Oxendine, *
▲ **EMP:** 45 **EST:** 1987
SQ FT: 68,000
SALES (est): 4.42MM **Privately Held**
Web: www.eastcoastumbrella.com
SIC: 3999 2393 5712 Umbrellas, garden or wagon; Cushions, except spring and carpet: purchased materials; Outdoor and garden furniture

(G-9460)
HANESBRANDS INC
Also Called: Champion Products
18400 Fieldcrest Rd (28351-8351)
P.O. Box 70 (28351-0070)
PHONE.................910 462-2001
Stodd Mcewan, *Brnch Mgr*
EMP: 4
SQ FT: 165,000
Web: www.hanes.com
SIC: 5621 2253 Women's sportswear; Knit outerwear mills
PA: Hanesbrands Inc.
1000 E Hanes Mill Rd
Winston Salem NC 27105

(G-9461)
HYGIENE SYSTEMS INC
Also Called: Omni Systems
10442 Old Wire Rd (28351-9386)
PHONE.................910 462-2661
EMP: 30 **EST:** 1996
SALES (est): 3.31MM **Privately Held**
SIC: 2676 Sanitary paper products

(G-9462)
KORDSA INC
17780 Armstrong Rd (28351-9394)
PHONE.................910 462-2051
Daniel Pelton V Press, *Brnch Mgr*
EMP: 135
Web: careers.indokordsa.com
SIC: 2281 Nylon yarn, spinning of staple
HQ: Kordsa, Inc.
4501 N Access Rd
Chattanooga TN 37415
423 643-8300

(G-9463)
KRODSA USA INC
17780 Armstrong Rd (28351-9394)
PHONE.................910 462-2041
Thomas Harmen, *Ofcr*

EMP: 5 **EST:** 2014
SALES (est): 64.07K **Privately Held**
SIC: 2281 Yarn spinning mills

(G-9464)
LAWRENCE WILLIAMS
Also Called: Williams Machine & Tool
10200 Andrew Jackson Hwy (28351-9579)
PHONE.................910 462-2332
Lawrence Williams, *Owner*
EMP: 6 **EST:** 1995
SQ FT: 3,000
SALES (est): 425.23K **Privately Held**
Web: www.williamsmachineandtool.com
SIC: 3599 Machine shop, jobbing and repair

(G-9465)
TONY D HILDRETH
Also Called: Hildreth Mechanical & Maint
22945 Broadwell Rd (28351-9704)
PHONE.................910 276-1803
Tony D Hildreth, *Owner*
EMP: 10 **EST:** 1990
SQ FT: 6,000
SALES (est): 633.67K **Privately Held**
SIC: 1711 7389 3599 1799 Mechanical contractor; Crane and aerial lift service; Machine shop, jobbing and repair; Welding on site

Laurel Springs
Alleghany County

(G-9466)
L F DELP LUMBER CO INC
2601 Nc Highway 113 (28644-9149)
PHONE.................336 359-8202
Larry Delp, *Pr*
Linda Delp, *
EMP: 12 **EST:** 1979
SALES (est): 447.25K **Privately Held**
SIC: 2421 2426 Sawmills and planing mills, general; Hardwood dimension and flooring mills

(G-9467)
THISTLE MEADOW WINERY INC
102 Thistle Mdw (28644-8333)
PHONE.................800 233-1505
Thomas Burgess, *Pr*
EMP: 9 **EST:** 2003
SALES (est): 529.6K **Privately Held**
Web: www.thistlemeadowwinery.com
SIC: 2084 Wines

(G-9468)
TOM BURGISS
Also Called: Burgiss Farm Bed & Breakfast
294 Elk Knob Rd (28644-8374)
PHONE.................336 359-2995
Thomas Burgiss, *Owner*
EMP: 5 **EST:** 1987
SALES (est): 210K **Privately Held**
Web: www.thistlemeadowwinery.com
SIC: 2084 7011 Wines; Bed and breakfast inn

Laurinburg
Scotland County

(G-9469)
AVERITT ENTERPRISES INC
Also Called: Averitt Electric Motor Repair
14121 Highland Rd (28352-4045)
P.O. Box 1793 (28353-1793)
PHONE.................910 276-1294
Ronnie Averitt, *Pr*
Levinia Averitt, *Sec*

EMP: 10 **EST:** 1964
SQ FT: 10,500
SALES (est): 984.24K **Privately Held**
SIC: 7694 Electric motor repair

(G-9470)
BUIE MANUFACTURING COMPANY
Also Called: Buie and Company
105 Sterling Ln (28352-5526)
PHONE.................910 610-3504
Clifton Poole Buie, *Pr*
EMP: 25 **EST:** 2020
SALES (est): 1.49MM **Privately Held**
SIC: 3429 Furniture hardware

(G-9471)
CAROLINA CONTAINER LLC
Also Called: Carocon
16100 Joy St (28352)
P.O. Box 2166 (27261-2166)
PHONE.................910 277-0400
EMP: 18
SALES (corp-wide): 679.24MM **Privately Held**
Web: www.carolinacontainer.com
SIC: 2653 Boxes, corrugated: made from purchased materials
HQ: Carolina Container Company
909 Prospect St
High Point NC 27260
336 883-7146

(G-9472)
CAROLINA CRATING INC
430 Hillside Ave (28352-3046)
PHONE.................910 276-7170
Linda Pate, *Pr*
Catherine Boone, *
Archibald Mclean Junior, *VP*
EMP: 45 **EST:** 1971
SQ FT: 75,000
SALES (est): 3.54MM **Privately Held**
Web: www.carolinacratinginc.com
SIC: 2441 2448 Shipping cases, wood: nailed or lock corner; Pallets, wood

(G-9473)
CHAMPION MEDIA LLC
Also Called: Laurinburg Exchange
915 S Main St Ste H (28352-4700)
PHONE.................910 506-3021
EMP: 218
SALES (corp-wide): 9.61MM **Privately Held**
SIC: 2711 Newspapers, publishing and printing
PA: Champion Media Llc
116 Morlake Dr Ste 203
Mooresville NC 28117
704 746-3955

(G-9474)
CHARLES CRAFT INC (PA)
Also Called: Burch Industries
21381 Charles Craft Ln (28352)
P.O. Box 1049 (28353-1049)
PHONE.................910 844-3521
▲ **EMP:** 7 **EST:** 1966
SALES (est): 5.05MM
SALES (corp-wide): 5.05MM **Privately Held**
Web: www.charlescraftinc.com
SIC: 2281 2015 Manmade and synthetic fiber yarns, spun; Egg albumen

(G-9475)
EAST COAST SIGNS
9757 Mccoll Rd (28352-8901)
PHONE.................910 462-2632
James Williams, *Prin*
EMP: 5 **EST:** 2018

Laurinburg - Scotland County (G-9476) — GEOGRAPHIC SECTION

SALES (est): 50.69K **Privately Held**
Web: eastcoastsigns.business.site
SIC: 3993 Signs and advertising specialties

(G-9476)
ED S TIRE LAURINBURG INC
300 Biggs St (28352-3806)
PHONE.................910 277-0565
Alan Smith, *Pr*
Deneane Smith, *Sec*
EMP: 6 EST: 1982
SALES (est): 961.66K **Privately Held**
SIC: 5531 7534 5014 Automotive tires; Tire repair shop; Automobile tires and tubes

(G-9477)
EDWARDS WOOD PRODUCTS INC
19500 Old Lumberton Rd (28352-6632)
P.O. Box 1527 (28353-1527)
PHONE.................910 276-6870
EMP: 65 EST: 1989
SQ FT: 2,500
SALES (est): 5.36MM **Privately Held**
Web: www.ewpi.com
SIC: 2421 Sawmills and planing mills, general

(G-9478)
ELECTRICAL EQUIPMENT COMPANY
226 N Wilkinson Dr (28352-2927)
PHONE.................910 276-2141
Bill Litton, *Mgr*
EMP: 26
SALES (corp-wide): 225.44MM **Privately Held**
Web: www.eecoonline.com
SIC: 5063 7629 7694 Electrical supplies, nec; Electrical equipment repair services; Armature rewinding shops
PA: Electrical Equipment Company Inc
1440 Diggs Dr
Raleigh NC 27603
919 828-5411

(G-9479)
FCC (NORTH CAROLINA) LLC
Also Called: FCC
18000 Fieldcrest Rd (28352-6798)
PHONE.................910 462-4465
▲ EMP: 185 EST: 2001
SQ FT: 75,000
SALES (est): 38.77MM **Privately Held**
Web: www.fcc-na.com
SIC: 3714 Clutches, motor vehicle
PA: F.C.C.Co., Ltd.
7000-36, Hosoechonakagawa,
Hamana-Ku
Hamamatsu SZO 431-1

(G-9480)
FEEDER INNOVATIONS CORPORATION
9781 Mccoll Rd (28352-8901)
P.O. Box 816 (28031-0816)
PHONE.................910 276-3511
Douglas Bowen, *Pr*
Lawrence Bowen, *Sec*
EMP: 4 EST: 1985
SALES (est): 369.01K **Privately Held**
Web: www.feederinnovations.com
SIC: 3549 Metalworking machinery, nec

(G-9481)
HANEYS TIRE RECAPPING SVC LLC
Also Called: Haney's Tire
1663 S Main St (28352-5412)
PHONE.................910 276-2636
Mike Coughenour, *Managing Member*
EMP: 17 EST: 1961
SQ FT: 10,000
SALES (est): 951.67K **Privately Held**
Web: www.haneystire.com
SIC: 5531 7534 7538 5014 Automotive tires; Tire recapping; General automotive repair shops; Automobile tires and tubes

(G-9482)
JPH III LOGGING INC
11241 Barnes Bridge Rd (28352-1413)
P.O. Box 267 (28353-0267)
PHONE.................910 610-9338
EMP: 9 EST: 2017
SALES (est): 476.95K **Privately Held**
SIC: 2411 Logging

(G-9483)
KING BUSINESS SERVICE INC
Also Called: UPS Stores 2922, The
1680 S Main St (28352-5413)
PHONE.................910 610-1030
EMP: 8 EST: 1996
SQ FT: 1,750
SALES (est): 632.08K **Privately Held**
Web: www.theupsstore.com
SIC: 7389 7331 5943 5087 Mailbox rental and related service; Mailing service; Office forms and supplies; Moving equipment and supplies

(G-9484)
LAURINBURG MACHINE COMPANY
715 Park Cir (28352-4417)
PHONE.................910 276-0360
William D Lytch Junior, *Pr*
James A Lytch, *VP*
EMP: 6 EST: 1909
SQ FT: 35,000
SALES (est): 467.95K **Privately Held**
SIC: 3713 3599 5085 Truck and bus bodies; Machine shop, jobbing and repair; Mill supplies

(G-9485)
LUXURY TRESSES COLLECTION LLC
1301 Franklin Ave (28352-3426)
PHONE.................910 501-4451
EMP: 6 EST: 2020
SALES (est): 319.54K **Privately Held**
SIC: 3999 Hair and hair-based products

(G-9486)
M C C OF LAURINBURG INC
Also Called: Evans, Bill Co
200 Johns Rd (28352-4735)
P.O. Box 669 (28353-0669)
PHONE.................910 276-0519
M C Cathcart, *Pr*
EMP: 7 EST: 1937
SQ FT: 10,000
SALES (est): 430K **Privately Held**
Web: www.laurinburg.org
SIC: 2752 5712 5943 Offset printing; Office furniture; Office forms and supplies

(G-9487)
MARMON ENGINE CONTROLS LLC
Also Called: Marmonpowertrain
2519 Dana Dr (28352-4000)
PHONE.................843 701-5145
Jeff Mccurley, *Pr*
Patrick Fennell, *
EMP: 42 EST: 2017
SALES (est): 4.92MM **Privately Held**
SIC: 3714 Motor vehicle parts and accessories

(G-9488)
MARMON HOLDINGS INC
Also Called: Rostra Powertrain Controls
2519 Dana Dr (28352-4000)
PHONE.................910 291-2571
Justin Tatum, *Mgr*
EMP: 15
SALES (corp-wide): 364.48B **Publicly Held**
Web: www.rostrapowertrain.com
SIC: 3714 3679 Acceleration equipment, motor vehicle; Solenoids for electronic applications
HQ: Marmon Holdings, Inc.
181 W Madison St Ste 3900
Chicago IL 60602
312 372-9500

(G-9489)
MCKENZIE SUPPLY COMPANY
1600 Us Highway 401 Byp S (28352-5401)
P.O. Box 1068 (28353-1068)
PHONE.................910 276-1691
Fred Johnson, *Mgr*
EMP: 7
SALES (corp-wide): 11.53MM **Privately Held**
Web: www.mckenziesupplyco.com
SIC: 5074 5063 5064 3625 Plumbing fittings and supplies; Electrical supplies, nec; Water heaters, electric; Motor control accessories, including overload relays
PA: Mckenzie Supply Company
726 E 16th St
Lumberton NC 28358
910 738-4801

(G-9490)
MURPHY-BROWN LLC
Also Called: Laurinburg Feed Mill
19600 Andrew Jackson Hwy (28352-4067)
PHONE.................910 277-8999
Cesar Menendez Feedmill, *Mgr*
EMP: 66
Web: www.smithfieldfoods.com
SIC: 2048 Prepared feeds, nec
HQ: Murphy-Brown Llc
2822 Highway 24 W
Warsaw NC 28398
910 293-3434

(G-9491)
N2GOD PRINT CENTER LLC
202 S Caledonia Rd (28352-3810)
PHONE.................910 318-4259
EMP: 4 EST: 2020
SALES (est): 150.45K **Privately Held**
SIC: 2752 Commercial printing, lithographic

(G-9492)
PILKINGTON NORTH AMERICA INC
13121 S Rocky Ford Rd (28352-6216)
PHONE.................910 276-5630
David Robinson, *Brnch Mgr*
EMP: 27
Web: www.pilkington.com
SIC: 3211 Flat glass
HQ: Pilkington North America, Inc.
811 Madison Ave Fl 3
Toledo OH 43604
419 247-3731

(G-9493)
QUALPAK LLC
16000 Joy St (28352-0402)
P.O. Box 2277 (44309-2277)
PHONE.................910 610-1213
Dick Palin, *Managing Member*
Joseph S Kanfer, *Managing Member*
▲ EMP: 24 EST: 2003
SQ FT: 200,000
SALES (est): 988.9K
SALES (corp-wide): 425.22MM **Privately Held**
SIC: 2841 Soap: granulated, liquid, cake, flaked, or chip
PA: Gojo Industries, Inc.
1 Gojo Plz Ste 500
Akron OH 44311
330 255-6000

(G-9494)
SAM M BUTLER INC
Also Called: Service Thread Manufacturing
504 King St (28352-3735)
PHONE.................910 276-2360
Jim Myers, *Brnch Mgr*
EMP: 45
SQ FT: 115,000
SALES (corp-wide): 10.06MM **Privately Held**
Web: www.servicethread.com
SIC: 2282 Throwing and winding mills
PA: Sam M. Butler, Inc.
17900 Dana Dr
Laurinburg NC 28352
910 277-7456

(G-9495)
SAM M BUTLER INC (PA)
Also Called: Service Thread Manufacturing
17900 Dana Dr (28352-4031)
P.O. Box 673 (28353-0673)
PHONE.................910 277-7456
◆ EMP: 20 EST: 1949
SALES (est): 10.06MM
SALES (corp-wide): 10.06MM **Privately Held**
Web: www.servicethread.com
SIC: 2284 2295 3552 Thread mills; Yarns, plastic coated: made from purchased yarns; Textile machinery

(G-9496)
SHIRTAILS
115 E Bizzell St (28352-3107)
PHONE.................910 277-0960
Jim Willis, *Prin*
EMP: 5 EST: 2010
SALES (est): 62.2K **Privately Held**
Web: www.shirttalesnc.com
SIC: 2759 Screen printing

(G-9497)
SIGNS DONE RIGHT
12008 Purcell Rd (28352-2096)
PHONE.................910 384-2007
James Gibson, *Prin*
EMP: 4 EST: 2019
SALES (est): 46.08K **Privately Held**
SIC: 3993 Signs and advertising specialties

(G-9498)
SMC HOLDCO INC
22261 Skyway Church Rd (28353)
P.O. Box 1067 (28353-1067)
PHONE.................910 844-3956
Wayne Cain, *Prin*
EMP: 105 EST: 1991
SQ FT: 50,000
SALES (est): 20.69MM
SALES (corp-wide): 160.67MM **Privately Held**
Web: www.scotlandmanufacturing.com
SIC: 3469 Stamping metal for the trade
PA: Spartanburg Steel Products, Inc.
1290 New Cut Rd
Spartanburg SC 29303
864 585-5211

(G-9499)
THOMAS LCKLARS CBNETS LRNBURG
21720 Wagram Rd (28352-6770)
PHONE.................910 369-2094

GEOGRAPHIC SECTION

Thomas Locklear, *Pr*
Joann Locklear, *VP*
EMP: 8 **EST:** 1977
SALES (est): 680.03K **Privately Held**
SIC: 2434 1799 Wood kitchen cabinets; Kitchen cabinet installation

Lawndale
Cleveland County

(G-9500)
JA SMITH INC
Also Called: Smith Electric Co
305 Plainsview Church Rd (28090-7405)
P.O. Box 550 (28042-0550)
PHONE.................................704 860-4910
EMP: 4 **EST:** 1984
SALES (est): 331.68K **Privately Held**
Web: www.jasmithinc.com
SIC: 1731 8711 5063 3625 General electrical contractor; Engineering services; Electrical apparatus and equipment; Relays and industrial controls

(G-9501)
MCNEILLYS INC
Also Called: McNeilly Champion Furniture
229 Carpenters Grove Church Rd (28090-9256)
PHONE.................................704 300-1712
Leonard J Mcneilly, *Pr*
EMP: 35 **EST:** 2000
SALES (est): 2.03MM **Privately Held**
Web: www.mcneillychampionfurniture.com
SIC: 2512 5712 Chairs: upholstered on wood frames; Furniture stores

(G-9502)
NEW RIVER FABRICS INC
106 Oak St (28090-9457)
PHONE.................................704 462-1401
Jerry L Smith Junior, *Pr*
Jerry Smith Senior, *VP*
EMP: 8 **EST:** 1993
SQ FT: 26,000
SALES (est): 437.03K **Privately Held**
SIC: 2211 2257 5131 Broadwoven fabric mills, cotton; Weft knit fabric mills; Piece goods and other fabrics

Lawsonville
Stokes County

(G-9503)
HIGH-TECH FABRICATIONS INC
3045 Nc 704 Hwy E (27022-7851)
PHONE.................................336 871-2990
Jerry Lawrence, *Pr*
Jerry William Lawrence, *Pr*
Avalon Potts, *Sec*
Jerry W Lawrence, *Owner*
EMP: 10 **EST:** 1999
SQ FT: 14,500
SALES (est): 878.78K **Privately Held**
Web: www.high-techfab.com
SIC: 3441 Fabricated structural metal

(G-9504)
SPRINGMILL PRODUCTS INC
1147 Walter Mabe Rd (27022-8256)
P.O. Box 291 (27016-0291)
PHONE.................................336 406-9050
William F Fels, *Pr*
Thomas Sparacio, *VP*
Rhonda C Fels, *Sec*
▼ **EMP:** 5 **EST:** 2002
SQ FT: 75,000
SALES (est): 452.86K **Privately Held**
SIC: 2048 Dry pet food (except dog and cat)

Leasburg
Caswell County

(G-9505)
FUQUA LOGGING COMPANY INC
388 Fuqua Rd (27291-9778)
P.O. Box 216 (27291-0216)
PHONE.................................336 562-5178
Ralph Fuqua, *Owner*
EMP: 11 **EST:** 2002
SALES (est): 510.06K **Privately Held**
SIC: 2411 Logging camps and contractors

Leicester
Buncombe County

(G-9506)
ALTOM FUEL CELLS LLC
117 Jones Rd (28748-5128)
PHONE.................................828 231-6889
EMP: 4 **EST:** 2008
SALES (est): 240.34K **Privately Held**
SIC: 3621 Motors and generators

(G-9507)
BRANCHED OUT WOOD WORKS LLC
42 Gillespie Dr (28748-9649)
PHONE.................................828 515-0377
Douglas Coombs, *Prin*
EMP: 5 **EST:** 2012
SALES (est): 190.64K **Privately Held**
SIC: 2431 Millwork

(G-9508)
BRUCE STANLEY
Also Called: Smokey Mountain Logging
570 Clarks Branch Rd (28748-5612)
PHONE.................................828 683-1265
Bruce Stanley, *Owner*
EMP: 4 **EST:** 2014
SALES (est): 81.72K **Privately Held**
SIC: 2411 Logging

(G-9509)
CREATIVE WOODCRAFTERS INC
42 West Rd (28748-7739)
PHONE.................................828 252-9663
Michael Keleher, *Pr*
Jennifer P Keleher, *VP*
EMP: 4 **EST:** 1976
SQ FT: 12,000
SALES (est): 282.4K **Privately Held**
SIC: 2434 Wood kitchen cabinets

(G-9510)
DYNAMIC SYSTEMS INC
104 Morrow Branch Rd (28748-9635)
PHONE.................................828 683-3523
Robin Yost, *Pr*
▲ **EMP:** 24 **EST:** 1967
SQ FT: 16,000
SALES (est): 3.82MM **Privately Held**
Web: www.sunmatecushions.com
SIC: 3086 Insulation or cushioning material, foamed plastics

(G-9511)
FLAT IRON MILL WORKS LLC
22 Pear Tree Ln (28748-5500)
PHONE.................................828 768-7770
Rachel R Brown, *Owner*
EMP: 7 **EST:** 2017
SALES (est): 54.13K **Privately Held**
SIC: 2431 Millwork

(G-9512)
GREEN LINE DEFENSE LLC
36 Renaissance Pl (28748-8438)
PHONE.................................828 707-5236
Shawn Patrick Martin, *Owner*
EMP: 5 **EST:** 2017
SALES (est): 83.36K **Privately Held**
SIC: 3812 Defense systems and equipment

(G-9513)
INDUSTRIAL TLING SVCS ASHVLLE
1259 Alexander Rd (28748-6338)
P.O. Box 877 (28748-0877)
PHONE.................................828 683-4168
Cliff Johnson, *Pr*
EMP: 8 **EST:** 1973
SQ FT: 5,000
SALES (est): 607.11K **Privately Held**
SIC: 3599 Machine shop, jobbing and repair

(G-9514)
JHONS WOOD WORK LLC
255 Tipton Hill Rd (28748-6392)
PHONE.................................828 231-6240
Jhon Cartagena, *Prin*
EMP: 5 **EST:** 2019
SALES (est): 92.8K **Privately Held**
SIC: 2431 Millwork

(G-9515)
MELT YOUR HEART LLC
Also Called: Melt Your Heart
162 Brookshire Rd (28748-5140)
PHONE.................................828 989-6749
Steven Paulson, *Prin*
EMP: 5 **EST:** 2016
SALES (est): 108.22K **Privately Held**
SIC: 2599 Food wagons, restaurant

(G-9516)
NEWFOUND TIRE & QUICK LUBE INC
642 Newfound Rd (28748-9769)
PHONE.................................828 683-3232
Stacy Gossett, *Pr*
EMP: 4 **EST:** 2006
SQ FT: 4,000
SALES (est): 482.83K **Privately Held**
Web: www.newfoundtireandquicklube.com
SIC: 7549 7534 Lubrication service, automotive; Tire retreading and repair shops

(G-9517)
POPEMBROIDERYDESIGNS
37 Bakers Acres Ln (28748-8820)
PHONE.................................828 575-4252
Teresa Riley, *Prin*
EMP: 5 **EST:** 2015
SALES (est): 68.72K **Privately Held**
SIC: 2395 Embroidery and art needlework

(G-9518)
QUALITY INFORMATION PUBLS INC
84 Solomon Rd (28748-9342)
PHONE.................................919 593-4715
Lyndon Smith, *Pr*
EMP: 5 **EST:** 2013
SALES (est): 173.53K **Privately Held**
SIC: 2741 Miscellaneous publishing

(G-9519)
RON CLEARFIELD
21 Clear Water Creek Rd (28748-8856)
PHONE.................................828 683-4425
Rachel Clearfield, *Owner*
EMP: 4 **EST:** 2011
SALES (est): 51.29K **Privately Held**
Web: www.ronclearfield.com
SIC: 2741 Music book and sheet music publishing

(G-9520)
SEVEN THUNDERS PUBLISHING INC
6 Sunrise Vly (28748-6516)
PHONE.................................828 236-0221
Robert Lee Camp, *Pr*
EMP: 7 **EST:** 2013
SALES (est): 156K **Privately Held**
SIC: 2741 Miscellaneous publishing

(G-9521)
SOUTHERN SIGNWORKS
45 Single Tree Gap Rd (28748-4505)
PHONE.................................828 683-8726
Doc Welty, *Prin*
EMP: 5 **EST:** 2005
SALES (est): 128.27K **Privately Held**
SIC: 3993 Signs and advertising specialties

(G-9522)
YOUNG FABRICATION
265 Morgan Branch Rd (28748-7583)
PHONE.................................828 776-3203
James Young, *Prin*
EMP: 4 **EST:** 2017
SALES (est): 72.92K **Privately Held**
SIC: 7692 Welding repair

Leland
Brunswick County

(G-9523)
33RD STRIKE GROUP LLC
9101 Lackey Rd Ne Ste 4 (28451-3308)
PHONE.................................910 371-9688
Christopher Chen, *Pr*
▲ **EMP:** 7 **EST:** 2014
SQ FT: 106,000
SALES (est): 189.62K **Privately Held**
SIC: 3732 Boatbuilding and repairing

(G-9524)
ACCURATE FABRICATIONS INC
1987 Andrew Jackson Hwy Bldg B (28451)
P.O. Box 15836 (28408-5836)
PHONE.................................910 383-2140
Henry Clayton Williams Iii, *Pr*
H C Williams, *Prin*
Dottie Williams, *VP*
EMP: 9 **EST:** 1979
SALES (est): 316.29K **Privately Held**
Web: www.accuratefabrications.com
SIC: 2899 3569 3541 Fluxes: brazing, soldering, galvanizing, and welding; Assembly machines, non-metalworking; Machine tools, metal cutting type

(G-9525)
ADAMS BEVERAGES NC LLC
Also Called: Adams Beverages Leland
2265 Mercantile Dr (28451-4058)
PHONE.................................910 763-6216
Casey Cranor, *Mgr*
EMP: 75
SALES (corp-wide): 11.91MM **Privately Held**
Web: www.adamsbeverages.net
SIC: 2084 Wine coolers (beverages)
PA: Adams Beverages Of North Carolina, Llc
7505 Statesville Rd
Charlotte NC 28269
704 509-3000

(G-9526)
APRINNOVA LLC
2271 Andrew Jackson Hwy Ne (28451-9627)
PHONE.................................910 371-2234
EMP: 7 **EST:** 2016

Leland - Brunswick County (G-9527)

SALES (est): 73.71K **Privately Held**
SIC: **2844** Perfumes, cosmetics and other toilet preparations

(G-9527)
BOAT LIFT US INC
2216 Mercantile Dr (28451-4091)
PHONE..............................239 283-9040
Terry J Hamilton, *Prin*
▲ **EMP:** 7 **EST:** 2006
SALES (est): 404.56K **Privately Held**
Web: www.boatliftus.com
SIC: **3536** Boat lifts

(G-9528)
BOLIVIA LUMBER COMPANY LLC (PA)
405 Old Mill Rd Ne (28451-7594)
P.O. Box 1387 (28402-1387)
PHONE..............................910 371-2515
Thomas Garner, *Pr*
EMP: 15 **EST:** 1960
SQ FT: 75,000
SALES (est): 8.4MM
SALES (corp-wide): 8.4MM **Privately Held**
Web: www.bolivialumber.com
SIC: **2448** 5031 Pallets, wood; Lumber: rough, dressed, and finished

(G-9529)
BRADFORD PRODUCTS LLC (PA)
Also Called: Bradford Products
2101 Enterprise Dr Ne (28451-8807)
PHONE..............................910 791-2202
Dale Brodeur Junior, *Pr*
Dale Brodeur Senior, *Managing Member*
Mike Brodeur, *
Mark Miller, *
◆ **EMP:** 89 **EST:** 1997
SQ FT: 50,000
SALES (est): 18.78MM
SALES (corp-wide): 18.78MM **Privately Held**
Web: www.bradfordproducts.com
SIC: **3999** 1799 Hot tubs; Spa or hot tub installation or construction

(G-9530)
BRIDGEWATER BLINDS INTERI
1132 New Pointe Blvd Ste 5 (28451)
PHONE..............................910 408-1900
EMP: 5 **EST:** 2020
SALES (est): 238.85K **Privately Held**
SIC: **2591** Window blinds

(G-9531)
C&V POWDER COATING
1068 Ashland Way (28451-9112)
PHONE..............................910 228-1173
Nijel Richburg, *Prin*
EMP: 5 **EST:** 2018
SALES (est): 84.6K **Privately Held**
SIC: **3479** Coating of metals and formed products

(G-9532)
CAPE FEAR COFFEE LLC
511 Olde Waterford Way (28451-4118)
PHONE..............................910 383-2429
Crystal Garvey, *Prin*
EMP: 7 **EST:** 2013
SALES (est): 108.78K **Privately Held**
Web: www.capefearcoffee.com
SIC: **2499** Wood products, nec

(G-9533)
CAPEFEAR WOODWORKS
551 Town Creek Rd Ne (28451-7705)
PHONE..............................910 988-3306
Ron Colson, *Owner*

EMP: 5 **EST:** 2011
SALES (est): 68.29K **Privately Held**
SIC: **2434** Wood kitchen cabinets

(G-9534)
CDB CORPORATION
2304 Mercantile Dr Ne (28451-4066)
PHONE..............................910 383-6464
Markus Hirsch, *CEO*
H W Heipl, *
Eric Moschik, *
Hermann Hirsch, *
▲ **EMP:** 50 **EST:** 1989
SQ FT: 10,900
SALES (est): 8.23MM **Privately Held**
Web: www.cdbcorp.net
SIC: **3843** 8072 Orthodontic appliances; Dental laboratories

(G-9535)
CELEBRATION CANDLES INC
1333 Hydrangea Ct (28451-7796)
PHONE..............................610 360-1545
Faye Dorney-madgitz, *Prin*
EMP: 5 **EST:** 2015
SALES (est): 85.17K **Privately Held**
Web: www.celebrationcandleshop.com
SIC: **3999** Candles

(G-9536)
COASTAL TRIMWORKS INC
1114 Maplechase Dr Se (28451-9569)
PHONE..............................910 231-8532
Danielle D Permenter, *Pr*
EMP: 6 **EST:** 2006
SALES (est): 144.74K **Privately Held**
SIC: **3732** Boatbuilding and repairing

(G-9537)
COATINGS AND ADHESIVES CORP (PA)
1901 Popular St (28451-8181)
P.O. Box 1080 (28451-1080)
PHONE..............................910 371-3184
Richard Pasin, *Pr*
◆ **EMP:** 165 **EST:** 1986
SQ FT: 80,000
SALES (est): 44.94MM
SALES (corp-wide): 44.94MM **Privately Held**
Web: www.cacoatings.com
SIC: **5169** 2891 Chemicals and allied products, nec; Adhesives

(G-9538)
COCA-COLA CONSOLIDATED INC
Also Called: Coca-Cola
2210 Mercantile Dr (28451-4091)
PHONE..............................919 763-3172
Paul Summerlin, *Brnch Mgr*
EMP: 4
SALES (corp-wide): 6.65B **Publicly Held**
Web: www.coca-cola.com
SIC: **2086** Bottled and canned soft drinks
PA: Coca-Cola Consolidated, Inc.
4100 Coca Cola Plz # 100
Charlotte NC 28211
704 557-4400

(G-9539)
CUSTOM WOOD CREATIONS
9485 Night Harbor Dr Se (28451-9596)
PHONE..............................910 367-8747
James Curry, *Prin*
EMP: 4 **EST:** 2010
SALES (est): 66.37K **Privately Held**
SIC: **2431** Millwork

(G-9540)
EIDP INC
Also Called: Dupont
3500 Daniels Rd Ne (28451-4174)
PHONE..............................910 371-4000
Tom Harris, *Mgr*
EMP: 4
SALES (corp-wide): 17.23B **Publicly Held**
Web: www.dupont.com
SIC: **2819** Industrial inorganic chemicals, nec
HQ: Eidp, Inc.
9330 Zionsville Rd
Indianapolis IN 46268
833 267-8382

(G-9541)
FELLER LLC (DH)
9100 Industrial Blvd Ne (28451-9037)
PHONE..............................910 383-6920
Doug Fox, *
Rod Linville, *
▲ **EMP:** 25 **EST:** 1984
SQ FT: 30,000
SALES (est): 6.58MM
SALES (corp-wide): 242.12K **Privately Held**
Web: www.feller-us.com
SIC: **3699** Accelerating waveguide structures
HQ: Feller U.S. Corp.
9100 Industrial Blvd Ne
Leland NC 28451
910 383-6920

(G-9542)
FLOW SCIENCES INC
2025 Mercantile Dr (28451-4054)
PHONE..............................910 763-1717
Raymond F Ryan, *Pr*
Ruth Gensinger, *
▼ **EMP:** 38 **EST:** 1987
SQ FT: 37,000
SALES (est): 9.08MM **Privately Held**
Web: www.flowsciences.com
SIC: **3821** Laboratory equipment: fume hoods, distillation racks, etc.

(G-9543)
FLOWSERVE CORPORATION
Flowserve
2216 Mercantile Dr (28451-4091)
PHONE..............................910 371-9011
Sue Russell, *Mgr*
EMP: 7
SALES (corp-wide): 4.32B **Publicly Held**
Web: www.flowserve.com
SIC: **3561** Pumps and pumping equipment
PA: Flowserve Corporation
5215 N Ocnnor Blvd Ste 70 Connor
Irving TX 75039
972 443-6500

(G-9544)
FUNSTON COMPANY
1018 Grandiflora Dr (28451-7474)
PHONE..............................910 383-1425
Katie Funston, *Prin*
EMP: 6 **EST:** 2008
SALES (est): 529.88K **Privately Held**
Web: www.funstoncompany.com
SIC: **1382** Oil and gas exploration services

(G-9545)
GALE GLOBAL RESEARCH INC
Also Called: Ggr
7007 Robert Ruark Dr (28451)
PHONE..............................910 795-8595
William Gale, *Pr*
Joe Hatem, *VP*
EMP: 6 **EST:** 2013
SALES (est): 309.94K **Privately Held**
Web: www.galeglobalresearch.com

SIC: **2834** 8731 Druggists' preparations (pharmaceuticals); Medical research, commercial

(G-9546)
GENERAL WOOD PRESERVING CO INC
1901 Wood Treatment Rd Ne (28451-9655)
P.O. Box 370 (28451-0370)
PHONE..............................910 371-3131
Karl Boatright, *CEO*
EMP: 19 **EST:** 1979
SQ FT: 2,000
SALES (est): 303.95K **Privately Held**
SIC: **2491** 2411 Poles and pole crossarms, treated wood; Logging

(G-9547)
GLYCOTECH INC
2271 Andrew Jackson Hwy Ne (28451-9627)
P.O. Box 1956 (28451-1956)
PHONE..............................910 371-2234
Margaret Heitman Collins, *Pr*
Eddie Collins, *
EMP: 10 **EST:** 2008
SALES (est): 481.18K **Privately Held**
SIC: **2611** Pulp mills, chemical and semichemical processing

(G-9548)
HIGH RISE SERVICE COMPANY INC
1690 Royster Rd Ne (28451-7528)
P.O. Box 400 (28451-0400)
PHONE..............................910 371-2325
Andrew J Simmons Junior, *Pr*
Earl Simmons, *
EMP: 32 **EST:** 1970
SQ FT: 49,000
SALES (est): 2.09MM **Privately Held**
Web: www.highriseservices.org
SIC: **1721** 1799 7692 7699 Industrial painting ; Sandblasting of building exteriors; Welding repair; Tank repair and cleaning services

(G-9549)
INDUSTRIAL CTING SOLUTIONS INC
9049 Industrial Blvd Ne (28451-2067)
PHONE..............................910 398-7556
EMP: 6 **EST:** 2014
SALES (est): 216.94K **Privately Held**
SIC: **3479** Coating of metals and formed products

(G-9550)
KEVINS SHEET METAL
933 Forest Way Ne (28451-8775)
PHONE..............................910 253-6203
Kevin Mintz, *Prin*
EMP: 5 **EST:** 2009
SALES (est): 184.28K **Privately Held**
SIC: **3444** Sheet metalwork

(G-9551)
LELAND MACHINE SHOP INC
767 Village Rd Ne (28451-8469)
PHONE..............................910 371-0360
Glenn Johnson, *Pr*
EMP: 4 **EST:** 1990
SALES (est): 289.59K **Privately Held**
SIC: **3599** Machine shop, jobbing and repair

(G-9552)
LIBRA LIFE GROUP LLC
Also Called: Libra Logistics/Escort
9371 Cassadine Ct (28451-1860)
PHONE..............................910 550-8664
Lwanda Green, *CEO*
EMP: 8 **EST:** 2020

SALES (est): 335.71K **Privately Held**
SIC: 3799 Transportation equipment, nec

(G-9553)
LUMINA EMBROIDERY LLC
734 Remount Ct Se (28451-8549)
PHONE..................910 371-1384
Sarah Tillery, *Mgr*
EMP: 4 EST: 2016
SALES (est): 41.01K **Privately Held**
SIC: 2395 Embroidery and art needlework

(G-9554)
MANUFACTURING METHODS LLC
9244 Industrial Blvd Ne (28451-7517)
P.O. Box 2105 (28451-2105)
PHONE..................910 371-1700
Hanson Peterson, *Managing Member*
David Ott, *CFO*
EMP: 25 EST: 2007
SQ FT: 40,000
SALES (est): 4.67MM **Privately Held**
Web: www.manufacturingmethods.com
SIC: 3441 3549 Fabricated structural metal; Metalworking machinery, nec

(G-9555)
MARTIN MARIETTA MATERIALS INC
Also Called: Martin Marietta Aggregates
1635 Malmo Loop Rd Ne (28451-7866)
PHONE..................910 371-3848
Tommy Shepard, *Brnch Mgr*
EMP: 5
Web: www.martinmarietta.com
SIC: 1422 Crushed and broken limestone
PA: Martin Marietta Materials Inc
 4123 Parklake Ave
 Raleigh NC 27612

(G-9556)
MICROSOLV TECHNOLOGY CORP
9158 Industrial Blvd Ne (28451-9037)
PHONE..................720 949-1302
EMP: 11 EST: 2018
SALES (est): 2.63MM **Privately Held**
Web: www.mtc-usa.com
SIC: 3826 Analytical instruments

(G-9557)
QUAD CITY HIGH PRFMCE COATINGS
1427 Green Hill Rd Ne (28451-8619)
PHONE..................937 623-2282
Zachary Rgambrell, *Pr*
EMP: 11 EST: 2014
SALES (est): 588.72K **Privately Held**
SIC: 3479 Metal coating and allied services

(G-9558)
RAMCO MACHINE & PUMP SVC INC
1054 Thistle Downs St Se (28451-9550)
PHONE..................910 371-3388
Jimmy U Ramsey, *Pr*
J Scott Ramsey, *VP*
Phyllis Ramsey, *Sec*
Alecia Williams, *Treas*
EMP: 5 EST: 1993
SALES (est): 393.42K **Privately Held**
SIC: 3599 Machine shop, jobbing and repair

(G-9559)
RUDYS LOGGING LLC
4006 Long Bow Ct (28451-9705)
PHONE..................910 918-2993
Rutilo Andres, *Prin*
EMP: 6 EST: 2021
SALES (est): 343.3K **Privately Held**
SIC: 2411 Logging

(G-9560)
STEVE S SEAFOOD INC
6545 Angels Gift Trl Ne (28451-7747)
PHONE..................910 279-5711
Steven M Wein, *Pr*
EMP: 6 EST: 1985
SALES (est): 248.71K **Privately Held**
Web: www.stevesseafood.com
SIC: 2091 Canned and cured fish and seafoods

(G-9561)
THUNDER ALLEY ENTERPRISES
1224 Magnolia Village Way (28451-9464)
PHONE..................910 371-0119
Kevin Groves, *Mgr*
EMP: 6 EST: 2009
SALES (est): 341.81K **Privately Held**
Web: www.thunderalleybowling.com
SIC: 3949 Bowling balls

(G-9562)
TRI-TECH FORENSICS INC (PA)
Also Called: Tri Tech Forensics National La
3811 International Blvd Ne Ste 100 (28451)
PHONE..................910 457-6600
Jim Seidel, *CEO*
James Cesar, *
Jan Johnson, *
Eric Barton, *
EMP: 60 EST: 1983
SALES (est): 22.34MM
SALES (corp-wide): 22.34MM **Privately Held**
Web: www.tritechforensics.com
SIC: 3999 5049 Fingerprint equipment; Law enforcement equipment and supplies

(G-9563)
USW-MENARD INC
3600 Andrew Jackson Hwy Ne (28451-7988)
PHONE..................910 371-1899
Mark Palmatier, *Pr*
◆ EMP: 4 EST: 1994
SQ FT: 100,000
SALES (est): 2.59MM **Privately Held**
Web: www.menardusa.com
SIC: 3499 Drain plugs, magnetic

(G-9564)
VICTAULIC COMPANY
Also Called: Victaulic Leland Facility
2010 Enterprise Dr Ne (28451-8804)
PHONE..................910 371-5588
Ron Hower, *Mgr*
EMP: 33
SALES (corp-wide): 574.15MM **Privately Held**
Web: www.victaulic.com
SIC: 3494 3498 3432 3053 Couplings, except pressure and soil pipe; Fabricated pipe and fittings; Plumbing fixture fittings and trim; Gaskets; packing and sealing devices
PA: Victaulic Company
 4901 Kesslersville Rd
 Easton PA 18040
 610 559-3300

(G-9565)
WALEX PRODUCTS COMPANY INC (PA)
1949 Popular St (28451-8181)
P.O. Box 3785 (28406-0785)
PHONE..................910 371-2242
Bill Williams Walex, *Pr*
Bill Williams, *
William A Williams, *
Robert A Williams, *
◆ EMP: 16 EST: 1986
SQ FT: 60,000
SALES (est): 13.19MM
SALES (corp-wide): 13.19MM **Privately Held**
Web: www.walex.com
SIC: 2842 2844 Polishes and sanitation goods; Perfumes, cosmetics and other toilet preparations

Lenoir
Caldwell County

(G-9566)
A FORBES COMPANY
Also Called: Forbes Printing
1035 Harper Ave Sw (28645-5092)
EMP: 19 EST: 1984
SALES (est): 2.25MM **Privately Held**
Web: www.aforbescompany.com
SIC: 2752 Offset printing

(G-9567)
ACTION SIGN COMPANY LENOIR INC
Also Called: Actionsign Group
511 Creekway Dr Nw (28645-4958)
PHONE..................828 754-4116
Steve Harvey, *Pr*
Benny Hamby, *CEO*
EMP: 12 EST: 1978
SQ FT: 6,500
SALES (est): 469.25K **Privately Held**
Web: www.actionsign.com
SIC: 7312 3993 Billboard advertising; Electric signs

(G-9568)
AIKEN DEVELOPMENT LLC
Also Called: Aikencontrols
1028 West Ave Nw (28645-5127)
PHONE..................828 572-4040
Christopher E Aiken, *Pr*
EMP: 9 EST: 2006
SALES (est): 2.5MM **Privately Held**
Web: www.aikencontrols.com
SIC: 3625 7371 Control circuit relays, industrial; Computer software development and applications

(G-9569)
AIR SYSTEMS MFG OF LENOIR INC
2621 Hogan Dr (28645-9424)
P.O. Box 1736 (28645-1736)
PHONE..................828 757-3500
EMP: 30 EST: 1988
SALES (est): 4.79MM **Privately Held**
Web: www.airsystemsmfglenoir.com
SIC: 3564 Dust or fume collecting equipment, industrial

(G-9570)
ALAN WALSH LOGGING LLC
Also Called: Alan Walsh Logging
2687 Nc Highway 268 (28645-6544)
PHONE..................828 234-7500
EMP: 6 EST: 1980
SALES (est): 479.88K **Privately Held**
SIC: 2411 Logging camps and contractors

(G-9571)
ALBION MEDICAL HOLDINGS INC (DH)
Also Called: Stallergenes Greer
639 Nuway Cir (28645-3646)
P.O. Box 800 (28645-0800)
PHONE..................800 378-3906
EMP: 11 EST: 1999
SALES (est): 51.86MM **Privately Held**
Web: www.stallergenesgreer.com
SIC: 2836 8734 2834 Vaccines; Testing laboratories; Pharmaceutical preparations
HQ: Stallergenes Greer Ltd
 30 Old Bailey
 London EC4M
 203 910-7600

(G-9572)
AMERICAN & EFIRD LLC
619 Connelly Springs Rd Sw (28645-6331)
PHONE..................828 754-9066
Morris Dellinger, *Mgr*
EMP: 17
SALES (corp-wide): 1.98B **Privately Held**
Web: www.amefird.com
SIC: 2281 2284 Yarn spinning mills; Thread mills
HQ: American & Efird Llc
 22 American St
 Mount Holly NC 28120
 704 827-4311

(G-9573)
ANNAS MACHINE SHOP INC
1751 Main St Nw (28645-3955)
PHONE..................828 754-4184
Mark Annas, *Pr*
EMP: 5 EST: 1961
SQ FT: 500
SALES (est): 340K **Privately Held**
SIC: 3599 Machine shop, jobbing and repair

(G-9574)
ANYTHING OVERSTOCK
2135 Arrowhead Ln (28645-8868)
PHONE..................828 572-2157
EMP: 5 EST: 2010
SALES (est): 72.01K **Privately Held**
SIC: 3643 Outlets, electric: convenience

(G-9575)
ARIA DESIGNS LLC
800 Hickory Blvd Sw (28645-5858)
PHONE..................828 572-4303
Jeffrey Arditti, *CEO*
▲ EMP: 14 EST: 2011
SALES (est): 882K **Privately Held**
Web: www.ariadesigns.us
SIC: 7389 5712 2512 Design services; Furniture stores; Chairs; upholstered on wood frames

(G-9576)
AUTOMATED LUMBER HANDLING INC
723 Virginia St Sw (28645)
P.O. Box 796 (28645-0796)
PHONE..................828 754-4662
William Dugger, *Pr*
Teresa Dugger, *VP*
Tracy Richardson, *Engg Mgr*
Wayne Parton, *Mfg Mgr*
Rose Younce, *Sec*
EMP: 5 EST: 1988
SALES (est): 500.44K **Privately Held**
SIC: 3553 3535 Woodworking machinery; Conveyors and conveying equipment

(G-9577)
B & E WOODTURNING INC
2395 Howard Arnette Rd (28645-7012)
P.O. Box 469 (28645-0469)
PHONE..................828 758-2843
James Greer, *Pr*
Sandra Poarch, *VP*
Lewis F Bentley, *Sec*
EMP: 10 EST: 1969
SQ FT: 23,200
SALES (est): 291.25K **Privately Held**
Web: www.bandewoodturning.com

SIC: 2426 Turnings, furniture: wood

(G-9578)
BAREWOODWORKING INC
4400 Fox Rd (28645-7557)
PHONE.................................828 758-0694
Ron Bare, *Pr*
EMP: 13 EST: 2011
SALES (est): 498.31K **Privately Held**
Web: www.barewoodworking.com
SIC: 2431 Millwork

(G-9579)
BAT PUBLISHING
3125 Auld Farm Dr (28645-8916)
PHONE.................................828 754-2216
Jeff Norris Junior, *Prin*
EMP: 4 EST: 2010
SALES (est): 83.19K **Privately Held**
SIC: 2741 Miscellaneous publishing

(G-9580)
BEARD HOSIERY CO
652 Nuway Cir (28645-3646)
P.O. Box 2369 (28645-2369)
PHONE.................................828 758-1942
David W Beard, *Pr*
Joyce Beard, *
EMP: 52 EST: 1954
SQ FT: 10,000
SALES (est): 2.4MM **Privately Held**
SIC: 2252 Socks

(G-9581)
BEMIS MANUFACTURING COMPANY
Bemis Contract Group
201 Industrial Ct (28645-8174)
PHONE.................................828 754-1086
Jim Chapman, *Mgr*
EMP: 200
SALES (corp-wide): 636.83K **Privately Held**
Web: www.bemismfg.com
SIC: 0782 3083 Landscape contractors; Laminated plastics plate and sheet
PA: Bemis Manufacturing Company Inc
300 Mill St
Sheboygan Falls WI 53085
920 467-4621

(G-9582)
BERNHARDT FURNITURE COMPANY
Also Called: Bfc Plant 5a
1814 Morganton Blvd Sw (28645-5337)
PHONE.................................828 572-4664
Debbie Robbins, *Brnch Mgr*
EMP: 19
SALES (corp-wide): 252.62MM **Privately Held**
Web: www.bernhardt.com
SIC: 2512 Upholstered household furniture
HQ: Bernhardt Furniture Company
1839 Morganton Blvd Sw
Lenoir NC 28645
828 758-9811

(G-9583)
BERNHARDT FURNITURE COMPANY
Also Called: Bernhardt Design Plant 3
1502 Morganton Blvd Sw (28645-5561)
P.O. Box 740 (28645-0740)
PHONE.................................828 759-6245
Enno Roellgen, *Manager*
EMP: 19
SALES (corp-wide): 252.62MM **Privately Held**
Web: www.bernhardtdesign.com
SIC: 2521 2522 Wood office furniture; Office furniture, except wood
HQ: Bernhardt Furniture Company
1839 Morganton Blvd Sw
Lenoir NC 28645
828 758-9811

(G-9584)
BERNHARDT FURNITURE COMPANY
Also Called: Bfc Plant 2
1828 Morganton Blvd Sw (28645-5337)
P.O. Box 740 (28645-0740)
PHONE.................................828 759-6652
EMP: 19
SALES (corp-wide): 252.62MM **Privately Held**
Web: www.bernhardt.com
SIC: 2511 2512 Wood household furniture; Upholstered household furniture
HQ: Bernhardt Furniture Company
1839 Morganton Blvd Sw
Lenoir NC 28645
828 758-9811

(G-9585)
BERNHARDT FURNITURE COMPANY
Also Called: Plant 6
1840 Morganton Blvd Sw (28645-5337)
P.O. Box 740 (28645-0740)
PHONE.................................828 758-9811
Gary Shuffler, *Manager*
EMP: 19
SALES (corp-wide): 252.62MM **Privately Held**
Web: www.bernhardt.com
SIC: 2511 2521 2512 Wood household furniture; Wood office furniture; Upholstered household furniture
HQ: Bernhardt Furniture Company
1839 Morganton Blvd Sw
Lenoir NC 28645
828 758-9811

(G-9586)
BERNHARDT FURNITURE COMPANY (HQ)
1839 Morganton Blvd Sw (28645-5338)
P.O. Box 740 (28645-0740)
PHONE.................................828 758-9811
Alex Bernhardt Junior, *Pr*
Rountree Collett, *
◆ EMP: 200 EST: 1889
SQ FT: 55,000
SALES (est): 252.62MM
SALES (corp-wide): 252.62MM **Privately Held**
Web: www.bernhardt.com
SIC: 2511 2512 2521 2522 Dining room furniture: wood; Couches, sofas, and davenports: upholstered on wood frames; Desks, office: wood; Chairs, office: padded or plain: except wood
PA: Bernhardt Industries, Inc.
1839 Morganton Blvd Sw
Lenoir NC 28645
828 758-9811

(G-9587)
BERNHARDT FURNITURE COMPANY
Also Called: Bernhardt Design Plant 7
1402 Morganton Blvd Sw (28645-5508)
P.O. Box 740 (28645-0740)
PHONE.................................828 759-6205
EMP: 19
SALES (corp-wide): 252.62MM **Privately Held**
Web: www.bernhardt.com
SIC: 5712 2511 2521 2512 Furniture stores; Wood household furniture; Wood office furniture; Upholstered household furniture
HQ: Bernhardt Furniture Company
1839 Morganton Blvd Sw
Lenoir NC 28645
828 758-9811

(G-9588)
BERNHARDT INDUSTRIES INC (PA)
Also Called: Bernhardt Furniture Company
1839 Morganton Blvd Sw (28645-5338)
P.O. Box 740 (28645-0740)
PHONE.................................828 758-9811
Alex Bernhardt Junior, *Pr*
William B Collett, *
Harland Dick, *
J Rountree Collett Junior, *COO*
Peter W Craymer, *
◆ EMP: 146 EST: 1927
SALES (est): 252.62MM
SALES (corp-wide): 252.62MM **Privately Held**
Web: www.bernhardttextiles.com
SIC: 2511 2521 2512 2522 Wood household furniture; Wood office furniture; Upholstered household furniture; Office furniture, except wood

(G-9589)
BIOGENIV INC
640 Nuway Cir (28645-3646)
PHONE.................................828 850-1007
EMP: 8 EST: 2018
SALES (est): 323.16K **Privately Held**
SIC: 3841 Surgical and medical instruments

(G-9590)
BIONUTRA LIFE SCIENCES LLC ◯
2464 Norwood St Sw (28645-8924)
PHONE.................................828 572-2838
Meena Tummuru, *Pr*
Ranga Namburi, *Techl Dir*
EMP: 4 EST: 2022
SALES (est): 252.21K **Privately Held**
SIC: 2023 Dietary supplements, dairy and non-dairy based

(G-9591)
BLUE RDGE ELC MMBERS FNDTION I
Also Called: BLUE RIDGE ELECTRIC MEMBERS FOUNDATION, INC.
219 Nuway Cir (28645-3644)
PHONE.................................828 754-9071
Kenneth Greene, *Brnch Mgr*
EMP: 88
SALES (corp-wide): 150.28MM **Privately Held**
Web: www.blueridgeenergy.com
SIC: 3272 Fireplaces, concrete
PA: Blue Ridge Energy Members Foundation
1216 Blowing Rock Blvd
Lenoir NC 28645
828 758-2383

(G-9592)
BRUEX INC
312 Lutz St Sw (28645-5328)
P.O. Box 1623 (28645-1623)
PHONE.................................828 754-1186
Keith Johnston, *Pr*
Bruce Johnston Junior, *Pr*
EMP: 22 EST: 1993
SQ FT: 12,500
SALES (est): 2.39MM **Privately Held**
Web: www.bruexinc.net
SIC: 2426 Furniture stock and parts, hardwood

(G-9593)
CALDWELL WD CARVING TURNING CO
459 Abington Rd (28645-3964)
PHONE.................................828 758-0186
Ray Shew, *Owner*
EMP: 6 EST: 1976
SALES (est): 218.44K **Privately Held**
SIC: 2426 Turnings, furniture: wood

(G-9594)
CAROLINA LEG SUPPLY LLC
511 Golfview Ct (28645-5930)
PHONE.................................828 446-6838
Charles Roy Munday, *Managing Member*
William Hunter Munday, *Managing Member*
EMP: 6 EST: 2019
SALES (est): 245.71K **Privately Held**
SIC: 2426 Furniture stock and parts, hardwood

(G-9595)
CAROLINA PRIME PET INC
Also Called: Carolina Prime
2040 Morganton Blvd Sw (28645-4971)
P.O. Box 635 (28906-0635)
PHONE.................................888 370-2360
▲ EMP: 45 EST: 1997
SQ FT: 260,000
SALES (est): 9.49MM **Privately Held**
Web: www.carolinaprimepet.com
SIC: 2047 Dog food

(G-9596)
CAROLINA YOGURT INC
Also Called: TCBY
208 Morganton Blvd Sw (28645-5219)
PHONE.................................828 754-9685
Melanie Cromer, *Mgr*
EMP: 7
SALES (corp-wide): 1.66MM **Privately Held**
Web: www.tcby.com
SIC: 5812 2026 Frozen yogurt stand; Fluid milk
PA: Carolina Yogurt Inc
2170 E 116th St
Carmel IN
317 844-2885

(G-9597)
CCO HOLDINGS LLC
1048 Harper Ave Nw (28645-5085)
PHONE.................................828 394-0635
EMP: 107
SALES (corp-wide): 54.61B **Publicly Held**
SIC: 4841 3663 3651 Cable television services; Radio and t.v. communications equipment; Household audio and video equipment
HQ: Cco Holdings, Llc
400 Atlantic St
Stamford CT 06901
203 905-7801

(G-9598)
CHASE CORPORATION
2012 Hickory Blvd Sw (28645-6406)
PHONE.................................828 726-6023
EMP: 7
Web: www.chasecorp.com
SIC: 3644 Insulators and insulation materials, electrical
HQ: Chase Corporation
375 University Ave
Westwood MA 02090
781 332-0700

(G-9599)
CITY MACHINE COMPANY INC
723 Virginia St Sw (28645)
P.O. Box 723 (28645-0723)
PHONE.................................828 754-9661
Larry Setzer Senior, *Pr*
Mitchell Setzer Senior, *VP*
EMP: 25 EST: 1958
SQ FT: 40,000
SALES (est): 2.19MM **Privately Held**

GEOGRAPHIC SECTION

SIC: 3599 3441 Machine shop, jobbing and repair; Fabricated structural metal

(G-9600)
COMPAGNIE PARENTO INC
340 Industrial Ct (28645-8100)
PHONE.................828 758-2525
Roger T Kiley, *Pr*
Joyce Kiley, *VP*
EMP: 5 **EST:** 1920
SALES (est): 138K **Privately Held**
Web: www.compagnieparento.com
SIC: 2869 Perfume materials, synthetic

(G-9601)
CONSTRUCTION ATTACHMENTS INC
Also Called: Construction Attachments
1160 Cal Ct (28645-8124)
PHONE.................828 758-2674
Charles Corriher Junior, *Pr*
Michelle Clark, *
▲ **EMP:** 75 **EST:** 1976
SQ FT: 47,000
SALES (est): 11.04MM **Privately Held**
Web: www.constructionattachmentsinc.com
SIC: 3531 Construction machinery

(G-9602)
CUT ABOVE CONSTRUCTION
3815 Charles White Ln (28645-7535)
PHONE.................828 758-8557
Charles White, *Owner*
EMP: 4 **EST:** 1994
SALES (est): 170K **Privately Held**
SIC: 2434 Wood kitchen cabinets

(G-9603)
D R KINCAID CHAIR CO INC
3122 Sheely Rd (28645-9778)
P.O. Box 925 (28645-0925)
PHONE.................828 754-0255
▲ **EMP:** 45 **EST:** 1983
SALES (est): 2.82MM **Privately Held**
Web: www.drkincaidchair.com
SIC: 2512 Chairs: upholstered on wood frames

(G-9604)
DISTINCTIVE FURNITURE INC (PA)
1750 Taylorsville Rd Se (28645-8330)
PHONE.................828 754-3947
Edward Andrews, *Pr*
Phyllis Andrews, *Sec*
EMP: 5 **EST:** 1995
SALES (est): 493.01K **Privately Held**
SIC: 2512 5712 7389 5949 Upholstered household furniture; Furniture stores; Design, commercial and industrial; Fabric stores piece goods

(G-9605)
DREXEL HERITAGE FURNISHINGS
825 Visionary St (28645-8365)
PHONE.................828 391-6400
Robert Curby, *Maint Supr*
EMP: 5 **EST:** 2018
SALES (est): 96.09K **Privately Held**
SIC: 2511 Wood household furniture

(G-9606)
EONCOAT LLC
1333 Virginia St Sw (28645-8177)
PHONE.................941 928-9401
Tony Collins, *CEO*
EMP: 5
SALES (corp-wide): 2.56MM **Privately Held**
Web: www.eoncoat.com
SIC: 2899 Chemical preparations, nec
PA: Eoncoat, Llc
  3337 Air Park Rd Ste 6
  Fuquay Varina NC 27526
  941 928-9401

(G-9607)
EXELA DRUG SUBSTANCE LLC
1245 Blowing Rock Blvd (28645-3618)
PHONE.................828 758-5474
Phanesh Koneru, *Admn*
EMP: 21 **EST:** 2016
SALES (est): 592.79K **Privately Held**
Web: www.exelapharma.com
SIC: 2834 Pharmaceutical preparations

(G-9608)
EXELA PHARMA SCIENCES LLC (PA)
1245 Blowing Rock Blvd (28645-3618)
P.O. Box 818 (28645-0818)
PHONE.................828 758-5474
Phanesh Koneru, *CEO*
Jonathon Sterling, *Prin*
EMP: 21 **EST:** 2008
SALES (est): 18.25MM **Privately Held**
Web: www.exelapharma.com
SIC: 2834 Pharmaceutical preparations

(G-9609)
FAIRFIELD CHAIR COMPANY
606 Kincaid Cir (28645-9429)
PHONE.................828 785-5571
EMP: 27
SALES (corp-wide): 46.98MM **Privately Held**
Web: www.fairfieldchair.com
SIC: 2512 2511 Chairs: upholstered on wood frames; Wood household furniture
PA: Fairfield Chair Company
  1331 Harper Ave Sw
  Lenoir NC 28645
  828 758-5571

(G-9610)
FAIRFIELD CHAIR COMPANY (PA)
1331 Harper Ave Sw (28645-5098)
P.O. Box 1710 (28645-1710)
PHONE.................828 758-5571
J Harper Beall, *Ch*
J Harper Beall Iii, *CEO*
Dick Posey, *
Larry E Hollar, *
Alvin W Daughtridge, *TRAFFIC Customer Service*
◆ **EMP:** 129 **EST:** 1921
SQ FT: 500,000
SALES: 46.98MM
SALES (corp-wide): 46.98MM **Privately Held**
Web: www.fairfieldchair.com
SIC: 2512 2511 Chairs: upholstered on wood frames; Wood household furniture

(G-9611)
FAITH LOGGING
1722 White Rock Rd (28645-9731)
PHONE.................828 446-5671
Greg Rash, *Prin*
EMP: 7 **EST:** 2015
SALES (est): 150.57K **Privately Held**
SIC: 2411 Logging camps and contractors

(G-9612)
FLEETGENIUS OF NC INC
1808 Norwood St Sw (28645-6431)
PHONE.................828 726-3001
Andreas Y Gruson, *Pr*
▼ **EMP:** 131 **EST:** 1981
SQ FT: 55,000
SALES (est): 27.43MM
SALES (corp-wide): 27.43MM **Privately Held**
Web: www.fleetgenius.com
SIC: 3443 3411 Dumpsters, garbage; Metal cans
PA: Fleetgenius, Llc
  2525 Tarpon Rd
  Naples FL 34102
  714 912-8353

(G-9613)
GRAND MANOR FURNITURE INC
929 Harrisburg Dr Sw (28645-6126)
P.O. Box 1286 (28645-1286)
PHONE.................828 758-5521
William R Johnson, *CEO*
EMP: 100 **EST:** 1963
SQ FT: 70,000
SALES (est): 13.63MM **Privately Held**
Web: www.grandmanorfurniture.com
SIC: 2512 Chairs: upholstered on wood frames
HQ: Lacquer Craft Hospitality, Inc.
  2575 Penny Rd
  High Point NC 27265

(G-9614)
GREER LABORATORIES INC
Hwy 90 (28645)
P.O. Box 800 (28645-0800)
PHONE.................828 758-2388
EMP: 28
Web: www.stagrallergy.com
SIC: 2836 8734 Vaccines; Commercial physical research; Testing laboratories
HQ: Greer Laboratories, Inc.
  639 Nuway Cir
  Lenoir NC 28645
  828 754-5327

(G-9615)
GREER LABORATORIES INC (DH)
Also Called: Stallergenes Greer
639 Nuway Cir (28645-3646)
P.O. Box 800 (28645-0800)
PHONE.................828 754-5327
Rick Russell, *Pr*
Robert E Esch, *
Anthony Palombo, *
William White Junior, *Dir*
Terrance C Coyne, *Chief Medical Officer*
▲ **EMP:** 186 **EST:** 1946
SQ FT: 150,000
SALES (est): 51.86MM **Privately Held**
Web: www.stagrallergy.com
SIC: 2836 8734 2834 Vaccines; Testing laboratories; Pharmaceutical preparations
HQ: Albion Medical Holdings Inc
  639 Nuway Cir
  Lenoir NC 28645
  800 378-3906

(G-9616)
H PARSONS INCORPORATED
100 Parsons Park Dr (28645-8844)
PHONE.................828 757-9191
Harold V Parsons, *Pr*
EMP: 30 **EST:** 1986
SQ FT: 90,000
SALES (est): 2.87MM **Privately Held**
SIC: 2421 2448 Sawmills and planing mills, general; Pallets, wood

(G-9617)
H&H METAL FAB
3050 Mcmillan Pl (28645-7615)
PHONE.................828 757-3747
Shawn Haigler, *Owner*
EMP: 4 **EST:** 1997
SALES (est): 229.53K **Privately Held**
SIC: 3999 Parasols and frames: handles, parts, and trimmings

(G-9618)
HAMBY BROTHERS CONCRETE INC
2051 Morganton Blvd Sw (28645-4970)
P.O. Box 844 (28645-0844)
PHONE.................828 754-2176
Randall Hamby, *Pr*
EMP: 42 **EST:** 1979
SQ FT: 1,000
SALES (est): 2.12MM **Privately Held**
SIC: 3273 Ready-mixed concrete

(G-9619)
HICKORY SPRINGS MFG CO
Also Called: Hickory Springs Mfg Rubbr
2145 Norwood St Sw (28645-8921)
PHONE.................828 728-9274
John Paul Eisenhower, *Mgr*
EMP: 54
SALES (corp-wide): 430.3MM **Privately Held**
Web: www.hickorysprings.com
SIC: 3069 Foam rubber
PA: Hickory Springs Manufacturing Company
  235 2nd Ave Nw
  Hickory NC 28601
  828 328-2201

(G-9620)
HOLDERS RESTAURANT FURNITURE
2310 Morganton Blvd Sw (28645-4972)
P.O. Box 1198 (28638-1198)
PHONE.................828 754-8383
EMP: 6 **EST:** 1990
SQ FT: 10,000
SALES (est): 511.5K **Privately Held**
Web: www.holdersrestaurantfurniture.com
SIC: 2599 Carts, restaurant equipment

(G-9621)
I G P
1477 Connelly Springs Rd (28645-7824)
PHONE.................828 728-5338
Craig Osborne, *Owner*
EMP: 6 **EST:** 1982
SQ FT: 12,500
SALES (est): 634.56K **Privately Held**
Web: www.igptools.com
SIC: 3545 Diamond cutting tools for turning, boring, burnishing, etc.

(G-9622)
JBS USA LLC
Also Called: Jbs Case Ready
1450 Homegrown Ct (28645-8175)
PHONE.................828 725-7000
▲ **EMP:** 14 **EST:** 2020
SALES (est): 2.63MM **Privately Held**
Web: www.jbsfoodsgroup.com
SIC: 2011 Meat packing plants

(G-9623)
LAWS DISTILLERY INC
1889 Greasy Creek Rd (28645-8532)
PHONE.................828 726-3663
Holly Putnam, *Prin*
EMP: 4 **EST:** 2017
SALES (est): 74.62K **Privately Held**
SIC: 2085 Distilled and blended liquors

(G-9624)
LEGACY VULCAN LLC
2008 Wilkesboro Blvd (28645-4646)
P.O. Box 1796 (28645-1796)
PHONE.................828 754-5348

John Peck, *Brnch Mgr*
EMP: 4
Web: www.vulcanmaterials.com
SIC: 3273 Ready-mixed concrete
HQ: Legacy Vulcan, Llc
  1200 Urban Center Dr
  Vestavia AL 35242
  205 298-3000

(G-9625)
LENOIR CONCRETE CNSTR CO
562 Abington Rd (28645-3993)
PHONE.............................828 759-0449
Marie Sanders, *Owner*
EMP: 8 EST: 1961
SALES (est): 689.83K **Privately Held**
SIC: 3273 Ready-mixed concrete

(G-9626)
LENOIR MIRROR COMPANY
401 Kincaid St (28645-9476)
P.O. Box 1650 (28645-1650)
PHONE.............................828 728-3271
A G Jonas Junior, *Ch Bd*
Drew Mayberry, *
Myron L Moore Junior, *Treas*
Linda T Jonas, *
Joyce Bumgarner, *
▲ EMP: 155 EST: 1929
SQ FT: 260,000
SALES (est): 23.24MM **Privately Held**
Web: www.lenoirmirror.com
SIC: 3231 Mirrored glass

(G-9627)
LENOIR PRINTING INC
401 Harper Ave Sw (28645-5068)
P.O. Box 739 (28645-0739)
PHONE.............................828 758-7260
Robert P Booth Junior, *Pr*
Glenda Booth, *VP*
Jean Booth, *Prin*
EMP: 5 EST: 1987
SQ FT: 4,000
SALES (est): 410.65K **Privately Held**
Web: www.printdirtcheap.com
SIC: 2752 Offset printing

(G-9628)
M & S WAREHOUSE INC (PA)
Also Called: M & S Manufacturing
1712 Hickory Blvd (28645-6446)
P.O. Box 929 (28638-0929)
PHONE.............................828 728-3733
David Miller, *Pr*
Jane Miller, *VP*
Angie Coffey, *Sec*
◆ EMP: 20 EST: 1992
SQ FT: 5,000
SALES (est): 4.76MM **Privately Held**
SIC: 2426 7389 5712 Furniture stock and parts, hardwood; Furniture finishing; Furniture stores

(G-9629)
MANUFACTURING STRATEGIES LLC
1301 Mountain Circle Dr (28645-9141)
PHONE.............................828 758-9092
Michael Shows, *Prin*
EMP: 4 EST: 2017
SALES (est): 62.83K **Privately Held**
SIC: 3999 Manufacturing industries, nec

(G-9630)
MARK LINDSAY LOOPER
6290 Duck Creek Rd (28645-7206)
PHONE.............................828 234-5453
Mark Lindsay Looper, *Prin*
EMP: 6 EST: 2005
SALES (est): 134.03K **Privately Held**
SIC: 2411 Logging camps and contractors

(G-9631)
MARLIN COMPANY INC
1211 Underdown Ave Sw (28645-5552)
PHONE.............................828 758-9999
Marty Waters, *Brnch Mgr*
EMP: 5
Web: www.marlinchemical.net
SIC: 2891 2841 Glue; Soap and other detergents
HQ: Marlin Company, Inc.
  1333 Virginia St Sw
  Lenoir NC 28645

(G-9632)
MARLIN COMPANY INC (HQ)
1333 Virginia St Sw (28645-8177)
P.O. Box 639 (28645-0639)
PHONE.............................828 754-0980
Marty Waters, *Pr*
◆ EMP: 15 EST: 1992
SALES (est): 9.1MM **Privately Held**
Web: www.marlinchemical.net
SIC: 2891 2841 Glue; Soap and other detergents
PA: Brenntag Se
  Messeallee 11
  Essen NW 45131

(G-9633)
MARTIN MARIETTA MATERIALS INC
Also Called: Martin Marietta Aggregates
1325 Bradford Mountain Rd (28645-8117)
PHONE.............................828 754-3077
Linwood Hanrick, *Mgr*
EMP: 10
Web: www.martinmarietta.com
SIC: 1422 Crushed and broken limestone
PA: Martin Marietta Materials Inc
  4123 Parklake Ave
  Raleigh NC 27612

(G-9634)
MAYMEAD MATERIALS
2008 Wilkesboro Blvd (28645-4646)
PHONE.............................828 758-9299
Wiley Roarke, *Pr*
EMP: 6 EST: 2017
SALES (est): 102.41K **Privately Held**
Web: www.maymead.com
SIC: 2951 Asphalt paving mixtures and blocks

(G-9635)
MC GEES CRATING INC
1640 Wilkesboro Blvd (28645-8283)
P.O. Box 1588 (28645-1588)
PHONE.............................828 758-4660
Tommy L Mc Gee, *Pr*
Diane Davis, *
EMP: 30 EST: 1969
SQ FT: 32,000
SALES (est): 2.28MM **Privately Held**
SIC: 2441 2426 2448 Shipping cases, wood: nailed or lock corner; Furniture stock and parts, hardwood; Pallets, wood

(G-9636)
MCCOMBS STEEL
3620 Cameo Ln (28645-9365)
PHONE.............................828 572-7600
EMP: 4 EST: 2018
SALES (est): 86.93K **Privately Held**
Web: www.mccombs-steel.com
SIC: 3441 Fabricated structural metal

(G-9637)
MR TIRE INC
1306 Morganton Blvd Sw (28645-5506)
PHONE.............................828 758-0047
Clayton Brant, *Brnch Mgr*
EMP: 5
SQ FT: 4,028
SALES (corp-wide): 1.33B **Publicly Held**
Web: mrtireinc.business.site
SIC: 7549 7534 5014 7538 Automotive maintenance services; Tire recapping; Tires and tubes; General automotive repair shops
HQ: Mr. Tire Inc.
  2078 New York Ave Unit 2
  Huntington Station NY 11746
  631 499-3700

(G-9638)
MURPHY USA INC
Also Called: Murphy USA
915 Blowing Rock Blvd (28645-3711)
PHONE.............................828 758-7055
EMP: 29
Web: www.murphyusa.com
SIC: 5541 2911 Filling stations, gasoline; Petroleum refining
PA: Murphy Usa Inc.
  200 E Peach St
  El Dorado AR 71730

(G-9639)
NEPTCO INCORPORATED
Also Called: Neptco
2012 Hickory Blvd Sw (28645-6406)
P.O. Box 1766 (28645-1766)
PHONE.............................828 728-5951
Mark Kenroberts, *Mgr*
EMP: 243
Web: www.chasecorp.com
SIC: 2672 3357 Tape, pressure sensitive: made from purchased materials; Nonferrous wiredrawing and insulating
HQ: Neptco Incorporated
  295 University Ave
  Westwood MA 02090
  401 722-5500

(G-9640)
NERDY LLAMA LLC
904 Plantation Dr (28645-3854)
PHONE.............................571 431-8933
Hannah Romero, *Owner*
EMP: 5 EST: 2017
SALES (est): 92.36K **Privately Held**
SIC: 2752 Commercial printing, lithographic

(G-9641)
NORTH AMERCN BIO-ENERGIES LLC
815d Virginia St Sw (28645-6036)
P.O. Box 795 (28645-0795)
PHONE.............................828 759-7101
EMP: 7 EST: 2006
SALES (est): 984.1K **Privately Held**
SIC: 2869 Industrial organic chemicals, nec
PA: Incoming, Inc.
  244 5th Ave Ste V235
  New York NY 10001

(G-9642)
NPS HOLDINGS LLC
Blue Ridge Tissue
1427 Yadkin River Rd (28645-9041)
PHONE.............................828 757-7501
Jim Brown, *Pr*
EMP: 40
SALES (corp-wide): 11.86MM **Privately Held**
Web: www.npsholdings.com
SIC: 2679 Paper products, converted, nec
PA: Nps Holdings Llc
  3303 Spirit Way
  Green Bay WI 54304
  920 983-9223

(G-9643)
NUTEX CONCEPTS NC CORP
2424 Norwood St Sw (28645-8924)
P.O. Box 3359 (28645-3359)
PHONE.............................828 726-8801
Arnold D Moore Iii, *Pr*
◆ EMP: 25 EST: 2001
SQ FT: 35,000
SALES (est): 5.57MM **Privately Held**
Web: www.nutexconcepts.com
SIC: 2297 Nonwoven fabrics

(G-9644)
OBSCURA MFG LLC
3031 Sheely Rd (28645-9756)
PHONE.............................336 419-5648
EMP: 6 EST: 2019
SALES (est): 246.71K **Privately Held**
SIC: 3999 Manufacturing industries, nec

(G-9645)
PACTIV LLC
303 Advantage Ct (28645-8379)
PHONE.............................828 758-7580
Mike Crump, *Brnch Mgr*
EMP: 12
Web: www.pactivevergreen.com
SIC: 3086 5113 Packaging and shipping materials, foamed plastics; Industrial and personal service paper
HQ: Pactiv Llc
  1900 W Field Ct
  Lake Forest IL 60045
  847 482-2000

(G-9646)
PARSONS METAL FABRICATORS INC
265 Wildwood Rd (28645-8280)
P.O. Box 310 (28645-0310)
PHONE.............................828 758-7521
Kevin Parsons, *Pr*
Douglas Parsons, *VP*
Mark Parsons, *Asst VP*
Jill Parsons, *Sec*
EMP: 10 EST: 1981
SQ FT: 6,000
SALES (est): 887.69K **Privately Held**
SIC: 3441 Fabricated structural metal

(G-9647)
PMG ACQUISITION CORP
Also Called: PMG Acquisitions Group Div
123 Pennton Ave (28645-4313)
P.O. Box 1110 (28645-1110)
PHONE.............................828 758-7381
Deborah Murray, *Brnch Mgr*
EMP: 73
SALES (corp-wide): 243.17MM **Privately Held**
Web: www.newstopicnews.com
SIC: 2711 2752 Newspapers: publishing only, not printed on site; Commercial printing, lithographic
HQ: Pmg Acquisition Corp.
  201 S 4th St
  Paducah KY 42003

(G-9648)
POLYCHEM ALLOY INC
Also Called: PCA
240 Polychem Ct (28645-8688)
PHONE.............................828 754-7570
Chakra V Gupta, *CEO*
Heather Justice, *
▲ EMP: 35 EST: 1989
SQ FT: 5,000
SALES (est): 5.65MM **Privately Held**
Web: www.polychemalloy.com
SIC: 2821 Plastics materials and resins

GEOGRAPHIC SECTION
Lewisville - Forsyth County (G-9673)

(G-9649)
PRE FLIGHT INC
1035 Harper Ave Sw (28645-5092)
P.O. Box 2430 (28645-2430)
PHONE..............................828 758-1138
Esley S Forbes, *Pr*
EMP: 5 **EST:** 1994
SALES (est): 338.14K **Privately Held**
SIC: 2796 2759 Platemaking services; Ready prints

(G-9650)
ROBBINS SIGN SUPPLY INC
2435 Hunt Ln (28645-4737)
PHONE..............................828 758-1954
Gurney Robbins, *Pr*
Debbie Haigler, *VP*
EMP: 11 **EST:** 2000
SALES (est): 463.25K **Privately Held**
Web: www.robbinssignsupply.com
SIC: 3993 Signs and advertising specialties

(G-9651)
SANDERS ELECTRIC MOTOR SVC INC
Also Called: Sanders Electric Motor Svc
285 Wildwood Rd (28645-8280)
PHONE..............................828 754-0513
Roger Sanders, *Pr*
Mike Sanders, *
Fred M Sanders, *
EMP: 26 **EST:** 1985
SQ FT: 13,000
SALES (est): 10.24MM **Privately Held**
Web: www.sanderselectricmotors.com
SIC: 5063 5999 7694 Motors, electric; Motors, electric; Electric motor repair

(G-9652)
SEALED AIR CORPORATION
2075 Valway Rd (28645-3969)
P.O. Box 1018 (28645-1018)
PHONE..............................828 726-2100
Roger Jackson, *Mgr*
EMP: 103
SALES (corp-wide): 5.49B **Publicly Held**
Web: www.sealedair.com
SIC: 3086 Packaging and shipping materials, foamed plastics
PA: Sealed Air Corporation
2415 Cascade Pointe Blvd
Charlotte NC 28208
980 221-3235

(G-9653)
STRUCTURAL MATERIALS INC
802 Old North Rd Nw (28645-3916)
P.O. Box 598 (28645-0598)
PHONE..............................828 754-6413
E J Temple Junior, *Pr*
EMP: 6 **EST:** 1991
SQ FT: 8,000
SALES (est): 1.01MM **Privately Held**
Web: www.structuralmaterialsinc.com
SIC: 5085 3312 Industrial supplies; Structural shapes and pilings, steel

(G-9654)
TEIJIN AUTOMOTIVE TECH INC
2424 Norwood St Sw Unit 300 (28645-8924)
PHONE..............................828 757-8313
David Stearman, *Opers Mgr*
EMP: 5
SQ FT: 90,000
Web: www.teijinautomotive.com
SIC: 3089 Injection molding of plastics
HQ: Teijin Automotive Technologies, Inc.
255 Rex Blvd
Auburn Hills MI 48326
248 237-7800

(G-9655)
TEIJIN AUTOMOTIVE TECH INC
601 Hibriten Dr Sw (28645-6389)
P.O. Box 820 (28645-0820)
PHONE..............................828 754-8441
John Eller, *Mgr*
EMP: 107
Web: www.teijinautomotive.com
SIC: 3714 Motor vehicle parts and accessories
HQ: Teijin Automotive Technologies, Inc.
255 Rex Blvd
Auburn Hills MI 48326
248 237-7800

(G-9656)
THOMAS GARY HELTON
1523 Gilbert Ln (28645-7506)
PHONE..............................828 726-3694
Thomas Gary Helton, *Pr*
EMP: 6 **EST:** 2015
SALES (est): 142.18K **Privately Held**
SIC: 2411 Logging

(G-9657)
VERDANTE BIOENERGY SVCS LLC
Also Called: Verdante
628 Harper Ave Nw # D (28645-5056)
PHONE..............................828 394-1246
G David Waechter, *CEO*
EMP: 5 **EST:** 2014
SALES (est): 209.12K **Privately Held**
Web: www.verdantebioenergy.com
SIC: 7379 7372 8731 Computer related consulting services; Business oriented computer software; Natural resource research

(G-9658)
VULCAN CONSTRUCTION MTLS LLC
609 Wilkesboro Blvd Ne (28645-4638)
P.O. Box 1796 (28645-1796)
PHONE..............................828 754-3200
EMP: 18
Web: www.vulcanmaterials.com
SIC: 3273 Ready-mixed concrete
HQ: Vulcan Construction Materials, Llc
1200 Urban Center Dr
Vestavia AL 35242
205 298-3000

(G-9659)
W G CANNON PAINT CO INC (PA)
Also Called: Cannon Paint and Abbraisives
1015 Zacks Fork Rd (28645-8306)
P.O. Box 1976 (28645-1976)
PHONE..............................828 754-5376
Greg Pilkenton, *Pr*
Stephen Pilkenton, *Pr*
Charlie Pilkenton, *VP*
Jeff Pilkenton, *VP*
Pamela Pilkenton, *Sec*
EMP: 5 **EST:** 1946
SQ FT: 12,000
SALES (est): 1.05MM
SALES (corp-wide): 1.05MM **Privately Held**
Web: www.cannonpaint.com
SIC: 5231 3291 Paint and painting supplies; Abrasive buffs, bricks, cloth, paper, stones, etc.

(G-9660)
WATSON CONCRETE PIPE COMPANY
2532 Morganton Blvd Sw (28645-9692)
PHONE..............................828 754-6476
Thomas Ray Hoover, *Pr*
Elizabeth Davis, *Sec*
Monica T Hoover, *VP*
EMP: 6 **EST:** 1949
SQ FT: 4,700
SALES (est): 608.2K **Privately Held**
Web: www.watsonconcrete.com
SIC: 3272 Pipe, concrete or lined with concrete

(G-9661)
WOODSMITHS COMPANY
Also Called: Woodsmiths
418 Prospect St Nw (28645-5017)
P.O. Box 1318 (28645-1318)
PHONE..............................406 626-3102
Michael Munoz, *Pr*
EMP: 18 **EST:** 1977
SQ FT: 350,000
SALES (est): 385.26K **Privately Held**
Web: www.woodsmiths.com
SIC: 2599 2521 3281 2511 Cabinets, factory; Cabinets, office: wood; Table tops, marble; Wood household furniture

Lewiston Woodville
Bertie County

(G-9662)
PERDUE FARMS INC
Also Called: PERDUE FARMS INC.
3539 Governors Rd (27849-9241)
P.O. Box 460 (27849-0460)
PHONE..............................252 348-4200
Ron Flagg, *Prin*
EMP: 600
SALES (corp-wide): 1.24B **Privately Held**
Web: www.perdue.com
SIC: 2015 Chicken, processed, nsk
PA: Perdue Farms Incorporated
31149 Old Ocean City Rd
Salisbury MD 21804
800 473-7383

(G-9663)
VALLEY PROTEINS
3539 Governors Rd (27849-9241)
P.O. Box 10 (27849-0010)
PHONE..............................252 348-4200
EMP: 11 **EST:** 2012
SALES (est): 202.24K **Privately Held**
Web: www.darpro-solutions.com
SIC: 2077 Animal and marine fats and oils

Lewisville
Forsyth County

(G-9664)
AD RUNNER MBL OUTDOOR ADVG INC
2555 Williams Rd (27023-8298)
PHONE..............................336 945-1190
Zebulon Williams, *Owner*
EMP: 8 **EST:** 2005
SALES (est): 930.13K **Privately Held**
Web: www.adrunnertrucks.com
SIC: 3993 Signs and advertising specialties

(G-9665)
COMPONENT MANUFACTURING & MCH
P.O. Box 455 (27023-0455)
PHONE..............................336 699-4204
Kim Meyers, *Prin*
EMP: 5 **EST:** 2001
SALES (est): 90.53K **Privately Held**
SIC: 3999 Manufacturing industries, nec

(G-9666)
FIBER COMPANY
8863 Belhaven Ct (27023-7740)
PHONE..............................336 725-5277
EMP: 6 **EST:** 1985
SALES (est): 352.85K **Privately Held**
Web: fibercompany.blogspot.com
SIC: 2221 7336 Specialty broadwoven fabrics, including twisted weaves; Art design services

(G-9667)
GRYPHON HOUSE INC
Also Called: Robins Lane Press
1310 Lewisville Clemmons Rd (27023-9635)
P.O. Box 10 (27023-0010)
PHONE..............................800 638-0928
Matthew Marceron, *Pr*
▲ **EMP:** 24 **EST:** 1969
SQ FT: 43,000
SALES (est): 508.2K **Privately Held**
Web: www.gryphonhouse.com
SIC: 2731 5192 Textbooks: publishing only, not printed on site; Books

(G-9668)
JOHN JONES DBA GRASS CHOPPERS
393 Slater Rd (27023-8711)
PHONE..............................336 413-6613
EMP: 5 **EST:** 2009
SALES (est): 151.82K **Privately Held**
SIC: 3751 Motorcycles and related parts

(G-9669)
MEDALONI CELLARS LLC
470 Yadkin Valley Trl (27023-8733)
PHONE..............................305 509-2004
Joey Medaloni, *Owner*
EMP: 6 **EST:** 2019
SALES (est): 534.98K **Privately Held**
Web: www.medalonicellars.com
SIC: 2084 Wines

(G-9670)
PETERSON WELDING INC
107 Hillside Manor Dr (27023-9576)
PHONE..............................336 480-4152
EMP: 4 **EST:** 2007
SALES (est): 61.7K **Privately Held**
SIC: 7692 Welding repair

(G-9671)
POTTERWYX SCNTED CANDLES SOAPS
1351 Lwsville Clemmons Rd (27023-9635)
PHONE..............................336 245-8560
EMP: 4 **EST:** 2017
SALES (est): 43.66K **Privately Held**
SIC: 3999 Candles

(G-9672)
ROUSE CUSTOM STONE
6680 Shallowford Rd (27023-9504)
PHONE..............................336 655-1613
Aaron Rouse, *Prin*
EMP: 4 **EST:** 2016
SALES (est): 97.61K **Privately Held**
Web: www.langleyphoto.com
SIC: 1411 Dimension stone

(G-9673)
SIGN A RAMA INC
Also Called: Sign-A-Rama
5054 Styers Ferry Rd (27023-9634)
PHONE..............................336 893-8042
John Barnes, *Genl Mgr*
EMP: 4
Web: www.signarama.com
SIC: 3993 Signs and advertising specialties
HQ: Sign A Rama Inc.
2121 Vista Pkwy

West Palm Beach FL 33411
561 640-5570

(G-9674)
TARHEEL OLD ENGLISH SHEEPDOG
8088 Deverow Ct (27023-9708)
PHONE...................336 499-6788
Belinda Lamm, *Prin*
EMP: 5 **EST:** 2010
SALES (est): 65.76K **Privately Held**
Web: www.tarheeloesrescue.org
SIC: 3999 Pet supplies

(G-9675)
VERYLAK INC
116 Lowes Foods Dr (27023-8258)
PHONE...................812 442-7281
Rob Heckard, *Mgr*
EMP: 10 **EST:** 2017
SALES (est): 424.53K **Privately Held**
SIC: 2851 Epoxy coatings

Lexington
Davidson County

(G-9676)
2ND SHIFT CYCLES LLC
6670 Old Us Highway 52 (27295-5335)
PHONE...................336 462-3262
James Wayne Beasley, *Prin*
EMP: 5 **EST:** 2019
SALES (est): 128.69K **Privately Held**
Web: www.2ndshiftcycles.com
SIC: 3732 Boatbuilding and repairing

(G-9677)
A-1 FACE INC
480 Dixon St Ste C (27292-7594)
PHONE...................336 248-5555
Loyd Leonard, *Pr*
Leonard Loyd, *Pr*
EMP: 14 **EST:** 1988
SQ FT: 50,000
SALES (est): 925.71K **Privately Held**
SIC: 2435 2436 2499 Veneer stock, hardwood; Veneer stock, softwood; Veneer work, inlaid

(G-9678)
ALL PRO FABRICATION & WLDG LLC
241 Arnold Rd (27295-8736)
PHONE...................336 953-4082
Jason Altiers, *Prin*
EMP: 5 **EST:** 2015
SALES (est): 237.59K **Privately Held**
SIC: 7692 Welding repair

(G-9679)
AMERICAN ATTACHMENTS INC
702 N Silver St (27292-6192)
PHONE...................336 859-2002
EMP: 6 **EST:** 2018
SALES (est): 202.13K **Privately Held**
Web: www.americanattachments.com
SIC: 3531 Construction machinery

(G-9680)
ARNEG LLC
Also Called: Arneg USA
750 Old Hargrave Rd (27295-7514)
PHONE...................336 956-5300
Louis Moschetta, *Managing Member*
◆ **EMP:** 70 **EST:** 1988
SQ FT: 66,000
SALES (est): 20.72MM **Privately Held**
Web: www.arnegusa.com
SIC: 3585 Refrigeration equipment, complete
HQ: Arneg Spa
 Via Venezia 58
 Campo San Martino PD 35010
 049 969-9333

(G-9681)
ASCO POWER TECHNOLOGIES LP
325 Welcome Center Blvd (27295-9018)
PHONE...................336 731-5000
Bob Kinross, *Brnch Mgr*
EMP: 11
SALES (corp-wide): 82.05M **Privately Held**
Web: www.ascopower.com
SIC: 3699 Electrical equipment and supplies, nec
HQ: Asco Power Technologies, L.P.
 160 Park Ave
 Florham Park NJ 07932

(G-9682)
ASTROTURF
676 High Rock Shores Dr (27292-6460)
PHONE...................336 528-5496
EMP: 6 **EST:** 2018
SALES (est): 75.59K **Privately Held**
Web: www.astroturf.com
SIC: 3999 Manufacturing industries, nec

(G-9683)
ASTROTURF CORP
176 Windchime Ct (27295-9642)
PHONE...................336 238-9060
EMP: 6 **EST:** 2019
SALES (est): 72.98K **Privately Held**
Web: www.astroturf.com
SIC: 3999 Manufacturing industries, nec

(G-9684)
BB METALS INC
148 Primrose Dr (27292-4264)
PHONE...................336 345-3430
EMP: 6 **EST:** 2020
SALES (est): 243.13K **Privately Held**
SIC: 3441 Fabricated structural metal

(G-9685)
BLACK CONCRETE INC
705 Cotton Grove Rd (27292-3823)
P.O. Box 664 (27293-0664)
PHONE...................336 243-1388
TOLL FREE: 800
Jerry B Black, *Prin*
EMP: 18 **EST:** 1973
SQ FT: 2,500
SALES (est): 648.37K **Privately Held**
Web: www.blackconcreteinc.com
SIC: 3273 Ready-mixed concrete

(G-9686)
BORDER CONCEPTS INC
115 Lexington Pkwy (27295-8524)
PHONE...................336 248-2419
Neal Miller, *Pr*
EMP: 4
Web: www.borderconcepts.com
SIC: 3317 3469 3441 Steel pipe and tubes; Metal stampings, nec; Fabricated structural metal
PA: Border Concepts, Inc.
 15720 Brixham Hill Ave
 Charlotte NC 28277

(G-9687)
BURRIS WOODWORKS
1134 John Young Rd (27292-7030)
PHONE...................336 746-5286
Carroll Burris, *Prin*
EMP: 5 **EST:** 2008
SALES (est): 59.52K **Privately Held**
SIC: 2431 Millwork

(G-9688)
C & S CUSTOM
441 Pine Top Rd (27295-6266)
PHONE...................336 242-9730
EMP: 4 **EST:** 2013
SALES (est): 91K **Privately Held**
Web: www.garwoodcustomcycles.com
SIC: 3751 Motorcycles and related parts

(G-9689)
CARDINAL CONTAINER SVCS INC
138 Walser Rd (27295-1338)
P.O. Box 1866 (27293-1866)
PHONE...................336 249-6816
Ian Miller, *CFO*
▲ **EMP:** 52 **EST:** 1976
SQ FT: 60,000
SALES (est): 10.32MM
SALES (corp-wide): 2.83B **Privately Held**
SIC: 2653 5199 Corrugated and solid fiber boxes; Packaging materials
HQ: Schutz Container Systems, Inc.
 200 Aspen Hill Rd
 Branchburg NJ 08876

(G-9690)
CARTER MILLWORK INC
Also Called: Flex Tram
117 Cedar Lane Dr (27292-5709)
P.O. Box 189 (27299-0189)
PHONE...................800 861-0734
Greg Carter, *Pr*
Alan Carter, *
Lisa Carter, *
EMP: 60 **EST:** 1996
SQ FT: 28,000
SALES (est): 9.76MM **Privately Held**
Web: www.carterflex.com
SIC: 2431 Moldings, wood: unfinished and prefinished

(G-9691)
CEPRINT SOLUTIONS INC
Also Called: Carolina Envelope
564 Dixon St (27292-7516)
P.O. Box 1229 (27293-1229)
PHONE...................336 956-6327
Tony S Townsend, *CEO*
Tony S Townsend Junior, *CEO*
Carolyn Townsend, *
Michelle T O'bryant, *Ex VP*
Jill Koontz, *
EMP: 28 **EST:** 1979
SQ FT: 60,000
SALES (est): 4.55MM **Privately Held**
Web: www.ceprint.com
SIC: 2752 Offset printing

(G-9692)
CHILDRESS VINEYARDS LLC
1000 Childress Vinyard Rd (27295-2061)
P.O. Box 847 (27293-0847)
PHONE...................336 236-9463
▲ **EMP:** 20 **EST:** 2002
SALES (est): 3.36MM **Privately Held**
Web: www.childressvineyards.com
SIC: 2084 Wines

(G-9693)
CHILDRESS WINERY LLC
9160 Hampton Rd (27295-9785)
P.O. Box 847 (27293-0847)
PHONE...................336 775-0522
▲ **EMP:** 7 **EST:** 2002
SALES (est): 532.71K **Privately Held**
Web: www.childressvineyards.com
SIC: 2084 Wines

(G-9694)
CIDER BROS LLC
Also Called: Bull City Ciderworks
599 S Railroad St (27292-3318)
PHONE...................919 943-9692
John Clowney, *Mgr*
EMP: 13 **EST:** 2015
SQ FT: 2,000
SALES (est): 1.06MM **Privately Held**
Web: www.bullcityciderworks.com
SIC: 2084 Wines, brandy, and brandy spirits

(G-9695)
CITY OF LEXINGTON
Also Called: Lexington Gas Dept, City of
425 Carolina Ave (27292-4325)
PHONE...................336 248-3945
John Everhart, *Mgr*
EMP: 20
Web: www.lexingtonnc.gov
SIC: 1311 Natural gas production
PA: City Of Lexington
 28 W Center St
 Lexington NC 27292
 336 243-2489

(G-9696)
COL-EVE METAL PRODUCTS CO
702 Bryant Rd (27292-8117)
P.O. Box 2067 (27361-2067)
PHONE...................336 472-7039
Tammy Carrick, *Pr*
EMP: 5 **EST:** 1963
SQ FT: 8,000
SALES (est): 382.01K **Privately Held**
Web: www.coleve.com
SIC: 3469 Stamping metal for the trade

(G-9697)
COMER SANITARY SERVICE INC
Also Called: Comer Trucking
3039 Greensboro Street Ext (27295-4806)
P.O. Box 1083 (27293-1083)
PHONE...................336 629-8311
Charlie Comer, *Prin*
EMP: 10 **EST:** 1968
SQ FT: 1,092
SALES (est): 410.95K **Privately Held**
Web: www.comersanitary.com
SIC: 7359 4214 3431 4212 Portable toilet rental; Local trucking with storage; Metal sanitary ware; Dump truck haulage

(G-9698)
CPM ACQUISITION CORP
Also Called: TSA Griddle System
121 Proctor Ln (27292-7630)
PHONE...................972 243-8070
Ted Waitman, *Pr*
EMP: 10
SALES (corp-wide): 227.38MM **Privately Held**
Web: www.cpmroskamp.com
SIC: 3634 Griddles or grills, electric: household
HQ: Cpm Acquisition Corp.
 2975 Airline Cir
 Waterloo IA 50703
 319 232-8444

(G-9699)
CPM WOLVERINE PROCTOR LLC
121 Proctor Ln (27292-7630)
PHONE...................336 479-2983
David Scrauss, *Mgr*
EMP: 10
SALES (corp-wide): 227.38MM **Privately Held**
Web: www.wolverineproctor.com
SIC: 3542 Mechanical (pneumatic or hydraulic) metal forming machines

GEOGRAPHIC SECTION

Lexington - Davidson County (G-9724)

HQ: Cpm Wolverine Proctor, Llc
251 Gibraltar Rd
Horsham PA 19044

(G-9700)
CPM WOLVERINE PROCTOR LLC
Also Called: Wolverine Proctor
121 Proctor Ln (27292-7630)
PHONE...................336 248-5181
EMP: 100
SALES (corp-wide): 227.38MM **Privately Held**
Web: www.wolverineproctor.com
SIC: 3542 Mechanical (pneumatic or hydraulic) metal forming machines
HQ: Cpm Wolverine Proctor, Llc
251 Gibraltar Rd
Horsham PA 19044

(G-9701)
CSI ARMORING INC
425 Industrial Dr (27295-7542)
PHONE...................336 313-8561
Usman Bashir, *Pr*
▼ **EMP:** 8 **EST:** 2004
SQ FT: 20,000
SALES (est): 835.26K **Privately Held**
Web: www.csiarmoring.com
SIC: 3711 Automobile bodies, passenger car, not including engine, etc.

(G-9702)
CUNNINGHAM BRICK COMPANY
Also Called: Scenic Scape
701 N Main St (27292-2692)
P.O. Box 2063 (27293-2063)
PHONE...................336 248-8541
TOLL FREE: 800
EMP: 134
Web: cunninghambrik.openfos.com
SIC: 3251 Brick and structural clay tile

(G-9703)
CURVED PLYWOOD INC
111 E 7th Ave (27292-3861)
P.O. Box 1092 (27293-1092)
PHONE...................336 249-6901
Thomas S Payne, *Pr*
EMP: 4 **EST:** 1978
SALES (est): 294.88K **Privately Held**
SIC: 2426 Furniture stock and parts, hardwood

(G-9704)
DAVIDSON PRINTING INC
Also Called: Davidsonspeed Printing
223 S Main St Ste D (27292-3352)
P.O. Box 1534 (27293-1534)
PHONE...................336 357-0555
Ron Hutcheson, *Pr*
EMP: 5 **EST:** 1974
SALES (est): 442.53K **Privately Held**
Web: www.davidsonspeed.com
SIC: 2752 Offset printing

(G-9705)
DELIVERIGHT LOGISTICS INC
176 L F I Complex Ln (27295)
P.O. Box 20763 (10023-1488)
PHONE...................862 279-7332
Doug Ladden, *CEO*
Ori Anavim, *
EMP: 120 **EST:** 2015
SALES (est): 8.43MM **Privately Held**
Web: www.deliveright.com
SIC: 4731 7372 Truck transportation brokers ; Application computer software

(G-9706)
DERT SIGN CO
984 N Nc Highway 150 (27295-7680)
PHONE...................336 225-1800
EMP: 4 **EST:** 2019
SALES (est): 50.69K **Privately Held**
SIC: 3993 Signs and advertising specialties

(G-9707)
DIAMONDBACK INDUSTRIES LLC
4683 Old Salisbury Rd (27295-7826)
PHONE...................336 956-8871
EMP: 22 **EST:** 2018
SALES (est): 4.79MM **Privately Held**
Web: diamondback-industries-llc.business.site
SIC: 3441 Fabricated structural metal

(G-9708)
DIAMONDBACK PRODUCTS INC
40 W 12th Ave (27292-3126)
P.O. Box 2235 (27374-2235)
PHONE...................336 236-9800
Eric Surratt, *CEO*
▲ **EMP:** 7 **EST:** 1998
SALES (est): 623.89K **Privately Held**
Web: www.diamondbackproducts.com
SIC: 3714 Dump truck lifting mechanism

(G-9709)
DIRECT WOOD PRODUCTS
Also Called: DIRECT WOOD PRODUCTS
808 Grimes Blvd (27292-7640)
P.O. Box 856 (23181-0856)
PHONE...................336 238-2516
Chris Davis, *Mgr*
EMP: 5
SALES (corp-wide): 4.58MM **Privately Held**
Web: www.dwp-inc.com
SIC: 2448 Pallets, wood
PA: Direct Wood Products, Incorporated
18501 Eltham Rd
West Point VA 23181
804 843-4642

(G-9710)
DRAFT DOT INTERNATIONAL LLC
Also Called: DOT Master
5450 N Nc Highway 150 (27295-9754)
P.O. Box 2164 (27374-2164)
PHONE...................336 775-0525
Richard Everhart, *Pr*
Omaey Everhart, *VP*
EMP: 6 **EST:** 1972
SALES (est): 489.57K **Privately Held**
SIC: 2759 2672 Labels and seals: printing, nsk; Tape, pressure sensitive: made from purchased materials

(G-9711)
EBERT SIGN COMPANY INC
7815 N Nc Highway 150 (27295-9387)
P.O. Box 24274 (27114-4274)
PHONE...................336 768-2867
Roger Ebert, *Pr*
EMP: 7 **EST:** 1985
SALES (est): 451.38K **Privately Held**
Web: www.ebertsigns.com
SIC: 3993 1799 Electric signs; Sign installation and maintenance

(G-9712)
ELECTRIC GLASS FIBER AMER LLC
473 New Jersey Church Rd (27292-6726)
P.O. Box 949 (27293-0949)
PHONE...................336 357-8151
Todd Douthit, *Brnch Mgr*
EMP: 213
SIC: 2851 Paint removers

HQ: Electric Glass Fiber America, Llc
940 Washburn Switch Rd
Shelby NC 28150
704 434-2261

(G-9713)
ELEMENT WEST LLC
266 Haywood Rd (27295-9610)
PHONE...................336 853-6118
Erik A Ullring, *Prin*
EMP: 6 **EST:** 2015
SALES (est): 158.84K **Privately Held**
SIC: 2819 Industrial inorganic chemicals, nec

(G-9714)
ELIZABETH CARBIDE DIE CO INC
Elizabeth Carbide NC
5801 E Us Highway 64 (27292-6607)
PHONE...................336 472-5555
EMP: 58
SALES (corp-wide): 53.46MM **Privately Held**
Web: www.eliz.com
SIC: 3544 Special dies, tools, jigs, and fixtures
PA: Elizabeth Carbide Die Co., Inc.
601 Linden St
Mckeesport PA 15132
412 751-3000

(G-9715)
ELIZABETH CARBIDE NC INC
Also Called: Elizabeth Carbide Die Co
5801 E Us Highway 64 (27292-6607)
PHONE...................336 472-5555
EMP: 38 **EST:** 1979
SALES (est): 1.61MM
SALES (corp-wide): 53.46MM **Privately Held**
Web: www.eliz.com
SIC: 3544 Special dies and tools
PA: Elizabeth Carbide Die Co., Inc.
601 Linden St
Mckeesport PA 15132
412 751-3000

(G-9716)
ERLANGER AUTO CARE INC
905 W Center St (27292-2630)
PHONE...................336 249-9674
Raymond C Watkins, *Prin*
EMP: 8 **EST:** 2014
SALES (est): 291.18K **Privately Held**
Web: www.erlangerautocare.com
SIC: 3559 Automotive maintenance equipment

(G-9717)
ESC BRANDS LLC (PA)
664 Old Hargrave Rd (27295-7504)
PHONE...................888 331-8332
EMP: 6 **EST:** 2017
SQ FT: 25,000
SALES (est): 1.7MM
SALES (corp-wide): 1.7MM **Privately Held**
Web: www.escbrands.com
SIC: 2834 Antiseptics, medicinal

(G-9718)
FLETCHER MACHINE INDS INC
4305 E Us Highway 64 (27292-8041)
P.O. Box 2096 (27293-2096)
PHONE...................336 249-6101
Ray Fletcher, *Pr*
Bryan Eunlip, *General Vice President**
Carolyn Smith, *
EMP: 52 **EST:** 2014
SQ FT: 104,000
SALES (est): 7.57MM **Privately Held**
Web: www.fletcher-machine.com

SIC: 3553 Woodworking machinery

(G-9719)
FOSTER TIRE SALES INC
1609 S Main St (27292-2843)
P.O. Box 823 (27293-0823)
PHONE...................336 248-6726
Joe A Foster Junior, *Pr*
EMP: 4 **EST:** 1961
SQ FT: 6,000
SALES (est): 424.91K **Privately Held**
SIC: 7534 5531 Tire recapping; Automotive tires

(G-9720)
FRANKS MILLWRIGHT SERVICES
1207 Ashland Dr (27295-2631)
PHONE...................336 248-6692
Joe Frank, *Owner*
EMP: 4 **EST:** 1965
SALES (est): 134.9K **Privately Held**
SIC: 7692 7389 Welding repair; Business services, nec

(G-9721)
FRENZELIT INC
4165 Old Salisbury Rd (27295-6870)
P.O. Box 1853 (27293-1853)
PHONE...................336 814-4317
Phil Howell, *Pr*
Wolfgang Wagner Ph.d., *Ch Bd*
Thorsten Sowa, *OF TEXTILES**
Torsten Aeugle, *OF GASKETS**
Richard Hammer, *OF EXPANSION JOINTS**
EMP: 49 **EST:** 2017
SALES (est): 11.05MM
SALES (corp-wide): 107.26MM **Privately Held**
Web: www.frenzelit.com
SIC: 3069 3357 Expansion joints, rubber; Nonferrous wiredrawing and insulating
PA: Frenzelit Gmbh
Frankenhammer 7
Bad Berneck I. Fichtelgebirge BY 95460
9273720

(G-9722)
GAINSBOROUGH BATHS LLC
Also Called: Gainsbrough Specialist Bathing
41 Rogers Rd (27292-5802)
PHONE...................336 357-0797
Gordon T Farmiloe, *Managing Member*
Daniel Mills, *General Vice President**
Cynthia Byrd, *
▲ **EMP:** 18 **EST:** 2011
SQ FT: 45,000
SALES (est): 683.19K **Privately Held**
SIC: 3088 1799 Tubs (bath, shower, and laundry), plastics; Fiberglass work

(G-9723)
GB LABS LLC
794 American Way (27295-1156)
PHONE...................919 606-7253
Dave Obrien, *Managing Member*
Robert Lewis, *Managing Member*
EMP: 4 **EST:** 2019
SALES (est): 316.16K **Privately Held**
Web: www.gblabs.com
SIC: 3565 Bottling machinery: filling, capping, labeling

(G-9724)
GOOSE AND MONKEY BREWHOUSE LLC
Also Called: Goose and The Monkey Brewhouse
401 S Railroad St (27292-3337)
PHONE...................336 239-0206

Lexington - Davidson County (G-9725)

Ashlee Moore, *CEO*
Ashlee Moore, *Pr*
Brent Moore, *Pr*
EMP: 17 **EST:** 2019
SALES (est): 991K **Privately Held**
Web:
www.gooseandthemonkeybrewhouse.com
SIC: 2082 Ale (alcoholic beverage)

(G-9725)
GRIMES MILL LLC
4 E 1st Ave (27292-3302)
PHONE.................................336 470-6864
Dana Hamilton, *Prin*
EMP: 5 **EST:** 2018
SALES (est): 74.91K **Privately Held**
Web: www.grimesmillwinery.com
SIC: 2084 Wines

(G-9726)
H & V PROCESSING INC
251 Primrose Drive Ext (27292-0607)
P.O. Box 1172 (27293-1172)
PHONE.................................336 224-2985
James Harris, *Pr*
Bernice Volpe, *VP*
Hildur Harris, *Sec*
▲ **EMP:** 15 **EST:** 1997
SQ FT: 20,900
SALES (est): 496.25K **Privately Held**
Web: www.hvprocessing.com
SIC: 2621 Paper mills

(G-9727)
H HORSESHOE
194 Sandy Creek Ln (27295-0358)
PHONE.................................336 853-5913
Albert Bruce Hinson, *Admn*
EMP: 7 **EST:** 2010
SALES (est): 53.37K **Privately Held**
SIC: 3462 Horseshoes

(G-9728)
HARVEST HOMES AND HANDI HOUSES (PA)
2100 S Main St (27292-3624)
PHONE.................................336 243-2382
Elizabeth Bunce, *Pr*
Dearl L Bunce Ii, *VP*
EMP: 8 **EST:** 1986
SQ FT: 960
SALES (est): 2.27MM
SALES (corp-wide): 2.27MM **Privately Held**
Web: www.buncebuildings.com
SIC: 3448 Buildings, portable: prefabricated metal

(G-9729)
HEDRICK BROTHERS LUMBER CO INC
6736 Nc Highway 47 (27292-7764)
PHONE.................................336 746-5885
Terry Hedrick, *Pr*
Charles Ricky Hedrick, *Sec*
Danny Lee Hedrick, *VP*
William D Hedrick, *Stockholder*
EMP: 17 **EST:** 1920
SQ FT: 4,000
SALES (est): 1.36MM **Privately Held**
SIC: 2421 Sawmills and planing mills, general

(G-9730)
HIGH POINT PRECAST PDTS INC
4130 W Us Highway 64 (27292-7763)
PHONE.................................336 434-1815
James Shoaf, *Pr*
Carlton Shoaf, *VP*
EMP: 6 **EST:** 1997
SALES (est): 933.55K **Privately Held**
Web: www.hpprecast.com
SIC: 3272 5074 Precast terrazzo or concrete products; Plumbing fittings and supplies

(G-9731)
HITCH CRAFTERS LLC
853 Cid Rd (27292-6184)
PHONE.................................336 859-3257
Jason Hughes, *Managing Member*
EMP: 7 **EST:** 2005
SALES (est): 707.18K **Privately Held**
Web: www.hitchcrafter.com
SIC: 3714 Acceleration equipment, motor vehicle

(G-9732)
J E JONES LUMBER COMPANY
Also Called: Carolina Dry Kiln
7255 E Us Highway 64 (27292-7603)
PHONE.................................336 472-3478
Jim Leonard, *Brnch Mgr*
EMP: 25
SQ FT: 95,262
SALES (corp-wide): 4.15MM **Privately Held**
SIC: 5031 2421 Lumber, plywood, and millwork; Sawmills and planing mills, general
PA: J. E. Jones Lumber Company
1301 Kimberly Rd
New Bern NC 28562
252 638-5717

(G-9733)
JC WELDING AND MACHINE LLC
429 Hege Rd (27295-6440)
PHONE.................................336 306-2026
EMP: 4 **EST:** 2019
SALES (est): 27.6K **Privately Held**
SIC: 7692 Welding repair

(G-9734)
JEWEL MASTERS INC (PA)
Also Called: Ellis Jewelers
221 W Us Highway 64 (27295-2567)
PHONE.................................336 243-2711
Leonard M Defelice, *Pr*
▲ **EMP:** 17 **EST:** 1951
SQ FT: 4,500
SALES (est): 2.32MM
SALES (corp-wide): 2.32MM **Privately Held**
Web: www.ellisjewelers.com
SIC: 5944 3915 Jewelry, precious stones and precious metals; Jewelers' materials and lapidary work

(G-9735)
JKS MOTORSPORTS INC (PA)
301 Welcome Center Blvd (27295-9018)
P.O. Box 450 (27374-0450)
PHONE.................................336 722-4129
Will Spencer, *Pr*
EMP: 8 **EST:** 1984
SQ FT: 21,000
SALES (est): 8.25MM
SALES (corp-wide): 8.25MM **Privately Held**
Web: www.jksincorporated.com
SIC: 7389 3993 Sign painting and lettering shop; Signs and advertising specialties

(G-9736)
JOHNSON CONCRETE COMPANY
Also Called: Piedmont Block
514 Burgin Dr (27292-2740)
PHONE.................................336 248-2918
David Bates, *Mgr*
EMP: 33
SALES (corp-wide): 24.37MM **Privately Held**
Web: www.johnsonproductsusa.com
SIC: 3271 Blocks, concrete or cinder: standard
PA: Johnson Concrete Company
217 Klumac Rd
Salisbury NC 28144
704 636-5231

(G-9737)
K & K INDUSTRIES LLC
427 Hannersville Rd (27292-8926)
PHONE.................................336 689-4293
Kevin Karriker, *Prin*
EMP: 6 **EST:** 2010
SALES (est): 109.78K **Privately Held**
SIC: 3999 Manufacturing industries, nec

(G-9738)
K12 COMPUTERS ◆
1203 Winston Rd (27295-1754)
PHONE.................................336 754-6111
EMP: 6 **EST:** 2022
SALES (est): 342.96K **Privately Held**
Web: www.k12computers.us
SIC: 3571 Electronic computers

(G-9739)
KAUFMAN TRAILERS INC
702 N Silver St (27292-6192)
PHONE.................................336 790-6800
▼ **EMP:** 30 **EST:** 1986
SALES (est): 22.26MM **Privately Held**
Web: www.kaufmantrailers.com
SIC: 5599 5084 3799 3537 Utility trailers; Trailers, industrial; Trailers and trailer equipment; Industrial trucks and tractors

(G-9740)
KEPLEY-FRANK HARDWOOD CO INC
Also Called: Kfh
975 Conrad Hill Mine Rd (27292-7090)
PHONE.................................336 746-5419
Jim Kepley, *Pr*
J Herbert Frank Junior, *VP*
EMP: 50 **EST:** 1959
SQ FT: 10,000
SALES (est): 9.58MM **Privately Held**
Web: www.kepleyfrank.com
SIC: 2421 Sawmills and planing mills, general

(G-9741)
KOONTS MANUFACTURING INC
1447 Rowe Rd (27295-8265)
PHONE.................................336 300-8009
Eddy Koonts, *Owner*
EMP: 5 **EST:** 2011
SALES (est): 80.84K **Privately Held**
SIC: 3999 Manufacturing industries, nec

(G-9742)
KURZ TRANSFER PRODUCTS LP
4939 N Nc Highway 150 (27295-9749)
PHONE.................................336 764-4128
Richard Tilley, *Mgr*
EMP: 65
SQ FT: 37,118
SALES (corp-wide): 1B **Privately Held**
Web: www.kurzusa.com
SIC: 3497 Metal foil and leaf
HQ: Kurz Transfer Products, Lp
11836 Patterson Rd
Huntersville NC 28078
704 927-3700

(G-9743)
LACY J MILLER MACHINE
7987 Old Us Highway 52 (27295-7333)
PHONE.................................336 764-0518
Lacy Miller, *Prin*
EMP: 9 **EST:** 2005
SALES (est): 173.46K **Privately Held**
SIC: 3599 Machine shop, jobbing and repair

(G-9744)
LAKE CITY ELECTRIC MOTOR REPR
Also Called: Lexington Electric Motor Repr
915 S Talbert Blvd (27292-3937)
PHONE.................................336 248-2377
Joe Frye, *Pr*
EMP: 4 **EST:** 2010
SALES (est): 370.74K **Privately Held**
Web: www.lexingtonelectric.net
SIC: 7694 Electric motor repair

(G-9745)
LAYING DIMES WELDING & FAB LLC
1240 Regan Rd (27292-7116)
PHONE.................................704 677-5521
Jason Turner, *Prin*
EMP: 5 **EST:** 2020
SALES (est): 66.1K **Privately Held**
Web: www.layingdimes.com
SIC: 7692 Welding repair

(G-9746)
LEGGETT & PLATT
161 Proctor Ln (27292-7630)
PHONE.................................336 357-3641
EMP: 22 **EST:** 2019
SALES (est): 166.44K **Privately Held**
SIC: 2515 Mattresses and bedsprings

(G-9747)
LEXINGTON HOME BRANDS MFG
1893 Brown St (27292-8412)
PHONE.................................336 243-5740
EMP: 7 **EST:** 2019
SALES (est): 52.63K **Privately Held**
SIC: 3999 Manufacturing industries, nec

(G-9748)
LEXINGTON TIRE & AUTO LLC
1200 S Main St (27292-2836)
PHONE.................................336 249-2105
EMP: 7 **EST:** 2018
SALES (est): 257.17K **Privately Held**
Web: www.welcometire.net
SIC: 7534 Tire repair shop

(G-9749)
LIBERTY SIGN AND LIGHTING LLC
375 Ridge Rd (27295-9184)
P.O. Box 2152 (27293-2152)
PHONE.................................336 703-7465
Zach Wishon, *Prin*
EMP: 6 **EST:** 2018
SALES (est): 239.49K **Privately Held**
Web: www.libertysignllc.com
SIC: 3993 Signs and advertising specialties

(G-9750)
LINWOOD INC
3979 Old Linwood Rd (27292-7528)
P.O. Box 5129 (27113-5129)
PHONE.................................336 300-8307
Jimmy Kepley, *Pr*
▼ **EMP:** 11 **EST:** 2005
SQ FT: 47,611
SALES (est): 316.42K **Privately Held**
SIC: 2511 Wood household furniture

(G-9751)
LJM MACHINE CO INC
7987 Old Us Highway 52 (27295-7333)
PHONE.................................336 764-0518
James T Donley, *Owner*
Craig Donley, *
Nancy Donley, *
Jeff Lookabill, *

GEOGRAPHIC SECTION

Lexington - Davidson County (G-9778)

EMP: 16 **EST:** 1967
SQ FT: 51,000
SALES (est): 520.77K **Privately Held**
Web: www.ljmmachineco.com
SIC: 3599 Machine shop, jobbing and repair

(G-9752)
LRS TECHNOLOGY INC (PA)
1802 Cotton Grove Rd (27292-5720)
PHONE..................336 669-5982
Larry R Shackleford, *Pr*
EMP: 5 **EST:** 2016
SALES (est): 827.59K
SALES (corp-wide): 827.59K **Privately Held**
Web: www.lrstech.co
SIC: 3443 Metal parts

(G-9753)
M AND M DOCKS LLC
10235 Nc Highway 8 (27292-6495)
PHONE..................336 537-0092
EMP: 10 **EST:** 2021
SALES (est): 432.31K **Privately Held**
Web: www.mandmdocks.com
SIC: 1389 Construction, repair, and dismantling services

(G-9754)
MASTERBRAND CABINETS INC
632 Dixon St (27292-7558)
PHONE..................765 491-2385
EMP: 34 **EST:** 2015
SALES (est): 1.2MM **Privately Held**
Web: www.masterbrand.com
SIC: 2434 Wood kitchen cabinets

(G-9755)
MASTERWRAP INC
969 American Way (27295)
P.O. Box 1219 (27374-1219)
PHONE..................336 243-4515
Richard Goff, *Pr*
▲ **EMP:** 50 **EST:** 1994
SQ FT: 63,000
SALES (est): 6.93MM **Privately Held**
Web: www.masterwrap.com
SIC: 2431 Millwork

(G-9756)
MATCOR MTAL FBRCTION WLCOME IN
835 Salem Rd (27295-1086)
PHONE..................336 731-5700
Arthur Artuso, *Pr*
Frank Lucus, *
Rod Harrison, *
Manfred Kretschmer, *
Galliano Tiberini, *
▲ **EMP:** 140 **EST:** 2009
SALES (est): 24.37MM **Privately Held**
Web: www.matcormetalfab.com
SIC: 3541 Machine tools, metal cutting type

(G-9757)
MEDCOR INC
550 Scout Rd (27292-5215)
PHONE..................888 579-1050
EMP: 7 **EST:** 1996
SALES (est): 844.97K **Privately Held**
SIC: 5047 3841 Hospital equipment and supplies, nec; Surgical and medical instruments

(G-9758)
MYERS TOOL AND MACHINE CO INC
156 Dixon St (27292-7565)
P.O. Box 219 (27299-0219)
PHONE..................336 956-1324
H Donald Myers, *Pr*
Eric Myers, *
Judy Myers, *
EMP: 70 **EST:** 1982
SQ FT: 66,000
SALES (est): 9.51MM **Privately Held**
Web: www.myerstoolandmachine.com
SIC: 3599 Machine shop, jobbing and repair

(G-9759)
NC IMPRINTS INC
3199 E Holly Grove Rd (27292-9631)
PHONE..................336 790-4546
EMP: 5 **EST:** 2016
SALES (est): 116.28K **Privately Held**
SIC: 2752 Commercial printing, lithographic

(G-9760)
NC MOULDING ACQUISITION LLC
Also Called: North Carolina Moulding Co
808 Martin Luther King Jr Blvd (27292-3793)
PHONE..................336 249-7309
Kevin Mallory, *Managing Member*
EMP: 11 **EST:** 2018
SALES (est): 564.24K **Privately Held**
SIC: 2499 Picture frame molding, finished

(G-9761)
NIPPON ELECTRIC GLASS CO LTD
Also Called: Lexington Plant Nippon Elc GL
473 New Jersey Church Rd (27292-6726)
PHONE..................336 357-8151
Motoharu Matsumoto, *Pr*
EMP: 6
Web: www.neg.co.jp
SIC: 3229 Glassware, industrial
PA: Nippon Electric Glass Co., Ltd.
2-7-1, Seiran
Otsu SGA 520-0

(G-9762)
NORTH AMERICAN IMPLEMENTS
12608 E Old Us Highway 64 (27292-7324)
P.O. Box 2840 (27361-2840)
PHONE..................336 476-2904
Eric Garner, *Pr*
EMP: 45 **EST:** 2014
SALES (est): 2.26MM **Privately Held**
Web: www.northamericanimplements.com
SIC: 3537 Trucks, tractors, loaders, carriers, and similar equipment

(G-9763)
NORTH STATE MACHINE INC
1775 Tyro Rd (27295-7804)
PHONE..................336 956-1441
EMP: 12 **EST:** 1985
SALES (est): 1.87MM **Privately Held**
Web: www.northstatemachine.com
SIC: 3599 Machine shop, jobbing and repair

(G-9764)
NUTRA-PHARMA MFG CORP NC
130 Lexington Pkwy (27295-8524)
PHONE..................631 846-2500
Oscar Ramjeet, *Pr*
Joseph Kramer, *CFO*
EMP: 60 **EST:** 2014
SALES (est): 5.08MM **Privately Held**
SIC: 2834 Pharmaceutical preparations

(G-9765)
NUTRACEUTICAL LF SCIENCES INC
Also Called: Nls
130 Lexington Pkwy (27295-8524)
PHONE..................336 956-0800
EMP: 424 **EST:** 2007
SALES (est): 2.4MM
SALES (corp-wide): 148.26B **Publicly Held**
SIC: 2834 Tablets, pharmaceutical
HQ: Vitacost.Com Inc.
4700 Exchange Ct Ste 200
Boca Raton FL 33431

(G-9766)
PALLET RESOURCE OF NC INC
4572 N Nc Highway 150 (27295-9745)
PHONE..................336 731-8338
TOLL FREE: 800
Forrest M Grimes, *Pr*
Laura Grimes, *
EMP: 95 **EST:** 1970
SQ FT: 45,000
SALES (est): 9.84MM **Privately Held**
Web: www.prnc.com
SIC: 2448 Pallets, wood

(G-9767)
PAPS PERFORMANCE & MACHINE LLC
587 Lanier Rd (27295-8155)
PHONE..................336 225-1877
EMP: 4 **EST:** 2017
SALES (est): 85.78K **Privately Held**
SIC: 3999 Manufacturing industries, nec

(G-9768)
PARKDALE MILLS INCORPORATED
Also Called: Parkdale Plants 3 & 4
100 Mill St (27295-1624)
PHONE..................336 243-2141
Dan Thompson, *Brnch Mgr*
EMP: 46
SALES (corp-wide): 1.44B **Privately Held**
Web: www.parkdalemills.com
SIC: 2281 Polyester yarn, spun: made from purchased staple
HQ: Parkdale Mills, Incorporated
531 Cotton Blossom Cir
Gastonia NC 28054
704 874-5000

(G-9769)
PHASE II CREATIONS INC
109 E 7th Ave (27292-3861)
PHONE..................336 249-0673
John Adkins, *Prin*
EMP: 6 **EST:** 1987
SALES (est): 330.97K **Privately Held**
SIC: 2821 Acrylic resins

(G-9770)
PIEDMONT CANDY COMPANY (PA)
404 Market St (27292-1293)
P.O. Box 1722 (27293-1722)
PHONE..................336 248-2477
Mark Stephens, *CEO*
Chris Reid, *Pr*
J Douglas Reid, *Pr*
Heath Cagle, *VP*
Mary Cox, *VP*
▲ **EMP:** 76 **EST:** 1890
SQ FT: 38,000
SALES (est): 12.63MM
SALES (corp-wide): 12.63MM **Privately Held**
Web: www.redbirdcandies.com
SIC: 2064 Lollipops and other hard candy

(G-9771)
PMB INDUSTRIES INC
632 Dixon St (27292-7558)
PHONE..................336 453-3121
Diane Mcbride, *CFO*
EMP: 11 **EST:** 2013
SALES (est): 404.29K **Privately Held**
SIC: 3999 Barber and beauty shop equipment

(G-9772)
PRINTCRAFT COMPANY INC
259 City Lake Rd (27295-8437)
P.O. Box 1558 (28151-1558)
PHONE..................336 248-2544
Boyce J Hanna, *Pr*
EMP: 60 **EST:** 1953
SALES (est): 5.38MM **Privately Held**
Web: www.printcraftcompany.com
SIC: 2759 Tags: printing, nsk

(G-9773)
PRINTCRAFT COMPANY INC
259 City Lake Rd (27295-8437)
P.O. Box 477 (27293-0477)
PHONE..................336 248-2544
Boyce Hanna, *Pr*
Gene Dover, *VP*
Joan Hana, *Sec*
◆ **EMP:** 35
SALES (est): 2.36MM **Privately Held**
Web: www.printcraftcompany.com
SIC: 2759 2671 2297 Tags: printing, nsk; Paper; coated and laminated packaging; Nonwoven fabrics

(G-9774)
RIVERWOOD INC
Also Called: Riverwood Casual
632 Dixon St (27292-7558)
PHONE..................336 956-3034
EMP: 20
SIC: 2519 Garden furniture, except wood, metal, stone, or concrete

(G-9775)
RP FLETCHER MACHINE CO INC
4305 E Us Highway 64 (27292-8041)
PHONE..................336 249-6101
Richard Piselli, *Pr*
▲ **EMP:** 85 **EST:** 1962
SQ FT: 125,000
SALES (est): 8.48MM **Privately Held**
Web: www.ez-door.com
SIC: 3553 3545 3069 3544 Woodworking machinery; Diamond cutting tools for turning, boring, burnishing, etc.; Molded rubber products; Special dies, tools, jigs, and fixtures

(G-9776)
SAUERS & COMPANY INC
Also Called: Sauers & Co Processed Veneers
363 Dixon St (27292-7574)
PHONE..................336 956-1200
Laurence C Sauers, *Pr*
Laurence C Sauers Junior, *VP*
Jeffrey A Sauers, *VP*
▲ **EMP:** 10 **EST:** 1999
SQ FT: 15,000
SALES (est): 1.99MM **Privately Held**
Web: www.sveneers.com
SIC: 5031 2435 Veneer; Veneer stock, hardwood

(G-9777)
SCOOTATRAILERTM
1370 Payne Rd (27295-9027)
PHONE..................336 671-0444
Gregory W Tesh, *Prin*
EMP: 4 **EST:** 2008
SALES (est): 455.11K **Privately Held**
Web: www.scootatrailer.com
SIC: 3537 Forklift trucks

(G-9778)
SHOAF PRECAST SEPTIC TANK INC
Also Called: Shoaf Precasting
4130 W Us Highway 64 (27295-7763)
PHONE..................336 787-5826

Jimmy Shoaf, *Pr*
James Shoaf, *Pr*
Dennis Shoaf, *VP*
EMP: 9 **EST:** 1966
SQ FT: 20,000
SALES (est): 1.23MM **Privately Held**
Web: www.shoafprecast.com
SIC: 3272 Concrete products, precast, nec

(G-9779)
SIDES SPREADER AND EQP CO INC
1010 American Way (27295-0902)
P.O. Box 1969 (27374-1969)
PHONE 336 978-6732
Johnny Sides, *Prin*
Jon Babek, *Prin*
EMP: 13 **EST:** 2015
SALES (est): 1.38MM **Privately Held**
Web: www.sidesspreaders.com
SIC: 3523 3531 Spreaders, fertilizer; Aggregate spreaders

(G-9780)
SKYLINE WELDING LLC
2597 Michael Rd (27295-9669)
PHONE 336 479-0166
Minh D Pressley, *Admn*
EMP: 5 **EST:** 2017
SALES (est): 131.21K **Privately Held**
SIC: 7692 Welding repair

(G-9781)
SMITH COMPANIES LEXINGTON INC (PA)
720 W Center St (27292-2718)
P.O. Box 594 (27293-0594)
PHONE 336 249-4941
Jerry F Smith, *Pr*
M Steve Smith, *VP*
R B Smith, *Treas*
EMP: 5 **EST:** 1978
SALES (est): 18.27MM
SALES (corp-wide): 18.27MM **Privately Held**
Web: www.gwsmithlumber.com
SIC: 5211 2431 1531 Lumber and other building materials; Millwork; Speculative builder, single-family houses

(G-9782)
SMITH MILLWORK INC
920 Robbins Cir (27292-3138)
P.O. Box T (27293-9394)
PHONE 800 222-8498
Keith Smith, *Pr*
Jerry F Smith, *
M Steve Smith, *
R B Smith, *Stockholder*
▲ **EMP:** 30 **EST:** 1921
SQ FT: 99,000
SALES (est): 9.04MM
SALES (corp-wide): 18.27MM **Privately Held**
Web: www.smithmillwork.com
SIC: 5031 2431 Doors and windows; Windows and window parts and trim, wood
PA: Smith Companies Of Lexington, Inc.
  720 W Center St
  Lexington NC 27292
  336 249-4941

(G-9783)
SOUTHEASTERN INSTALLATION INC (PA)
Also Called: Sii Dry Kilns
207 Cedar Lane Dr (27292-5711)
P.O. Box I (27293-9383)
PHONE 704 352-7146
Dan R Mathews, *Pr*
Paula Turlington, *
EMP: 48 **EST:** 1969
SQ FT: 65,000
SALES (est): 19.07MM
SALES (corp-wide): 19.07MM **Privately Held**
Web: www.siidrykilns.com
SIC: 3559 3567 Kilns, lumber; Industrial furnaces and ovens

(G-9784)
SPECIAL FAB & MACHINE INC
Also Called: S F M
4133 Old Salisbury Rd (27295-6870)
P.O. Box 808 (27299-0808)
PHONE 336 956-2121
W Avalon Potts, *Pr*
Avalon Potts, *
EMP: 50 **EST:** 1993
SQ FT: 70,000
SALES (est): 7.16MM **Privately Held**
Web: www.specialfabinc.com
SIC: 3599 Machine shop, jobbing and repair

(G-9785)
STITCHERY INC
134 Elk St (27292-4028)
P.O. Box 1693 (27293-1693)
PHONE 336 248-5604
Todd A Klass, *Pr*
Amy S Klass, *Sec*
EMP: 5 **EST:** 1989
SQ FT: 8,500
SALES (est): 266.66K **Privately Held**
SIC: 2395 Emblems, embroidered

(G-9786)
STONE EQUIPMENT COMPANY INC
322 Old Hargrave Rd (27295-7513)
PHONE 980 202-4448
EMP: 115
SIC: 3523 Farm machinery and equipment
PA: Stone Equipment Company, Inc.
  210 West Blvd
  Montgomery AL 36108

(G-9787)
STURGEON CREEK HOME LLC
90 East 13th Ave (27292-2815)
PHONE 336 843-1403
EMP: 4 **EST:** 2020
SALES (est): 248.49K **Privately Held**
Web: www.sturgeoncreekhome.com
SIC: 2599 Factory furniture and fixtures

(G-9788)
SUPERIOR FINISHING SYSTEMS LLC
2132 Beckner Rd (27292-8884)
PHONE 336 956-2000
EMP: 9 **EST:** 1995
SALES (est): 805.22K **Privately Held**
Web: www.superiorfinishingsystems.com
SIC: 3569 3567 3444 3563 Gas producers, generators, and other gas related equipment; Paint baking and drying ovens; Booths, spray: prefabricated sheet metal; Spraying and dusting equipment

(G-9789)
TARHEEL CUSTOM WOODWORKING INC
2550 Jerusalem Rd (27292-7149)
PHONE 336 237-9344
Jonathan Rowe, *Prin*
EMP: 5 **EST:** 2015
SALES (est): 55.26K **Privately Held**
SIC: 2499 Wood products, nec

(G-9790)
TARHEEL PLASTICS LLC
2018 E Us Highway 64 (27292-8083)
EMP: 20
Web: www.tarheelplastics.com
SIC: 3089 Injection molded finished plastics products, nec

(G-9791)
THERMAL PANE INC
200 S Main St (27292-3324)
PHONE 336 722-9977
EMP: 5 **EST:** 2011
SALES (est): 106.64K **Privately Held**
SIC: 3724 Aircraft engines and engine parts

(G-9792)
THOMASVLLE MTAL FBRICATORS INC (PA)
200 Prospect Dr (27292-3751)
PHONE 336 248-4992
EMP: 25 **EST:** 1995
SQ FT: 40,000
SALES (est): 5.93MM **Privately Held**
Web: www.tier1isp.com
SIC: 3441 3444 2542 Fabricated structural metal; Sheet metalwork; Partitions and fixtures, except wood

(G-9793)
THOMSON PLASTICS INC
2018 E Us Highway 64 (27292-8083)
PHONE 336 843-4255
Genu Revattaro, *Genl Mgr*
EMP: 91
Web: www.thomsonplastics.com
SIC: 3949 3089 Sporting and athletic goods, nec; Plastics containers, except foam
PA: Thomson Plastics, Inc.
  130 Quality Dr
  Thomson GA 30824

(G-9794)
TIMELESS BEDDING INC
306 Beech Retreat Dr (27292-9195)
P.O. Box 336 (27350-0336)
PHONE 336 472-6603
Robert Allen, *Pr*
Betty Allen, *
Sharon Gainey, *
▼ **EMP:** 9 **EST:** 1983
SQ FT: 55,000
SALES (est): 126.93K **Privately Held**
SIC: 2515 Mattresses and bedsprings

(G-9795)
TODCO INC
1123 Roy Lopp Rd (27292)
PHONE 336 248-2001
EMP: 10 **EST:** 1992
SALES (est): 1.54MM **Privately Held**
Web: www.todcoinc.com
SIC: 4953 2611 Sanitary landfill operation; Pulp manufactured from waste or recycled paper

(G-9796)
TOM HEDRICK EXPRESS
8034 Nc Highway 8 (27292-6245)
PHONE 336 798-1293
Tomas Hedrick, *Prin*
EMP: 6 **EST:** 2006
SALES (est): 88.1K **Privately Held**
SIC: 2741 Miscellaneous publishing

(G-9797)
TUBULAR TEXTILE MACHINERY
85 Hargrave Rd (27293)
P.O. Box 2097 (27293-2097)
PHONE 336 956-6444
William Milligan, *Pr*
▲ **EMP:** 9 **EST:** 1965
SALES (est): 318.13K **Privately Held**
Web: www.hkwinc.com
SIC: 3552 Textile machinery

(G-9798)
TYSINGER HOSIERY MILL INC
1294 Old Nc Highway 109 (27292-9411)
PHONE 336 472-2148
Bradley Tysinger, *Pr*
E Vernon Tysinger, *VP*
Shirley Tysinger, *Sec*
EMP: 10 **EST:** 1974
SQ FT: 8,800
SALES (est): 656.08K **Privately Held**
SIC: 2252 Socks

(G-9799)
VALENDRAWERS INC
Also Called: Valendrawers
555 Dixon St Sapona Business Park (27293)
P.O. Box 1169 (27293-1169)
PHONE 336 956-2118
Amedeo D Valentina, *Ch Bd*
Piero Della Valentina, *
Carla Della Valentina, *
Diane Mcbride, *Sec*
Michele Cassin, *
▲ **EMP:** 50 **EST:** 1984
SQ FT: 75,000
SALES (est): 11.53MM **Privately Held**
Web: www.valenusa.com
SIC: 2426 Furniture stock and parts, hardwood

(G-9800)
WALKER AND ASSOCIATES INC (DH)
Also Called: Netceed
7129 Old Us Hwy 52 (27295-6160)
P.O. Box 639309 (45263-9309)
PHONE 336 731-6391
Virginia M Walker, *Ch Bd*
Mark Walker, *
Douglas Leckie, *
Chrystie Walker Brown, *
Marshall Rick Walker, *OF Development*
◆ **EMP:** 104 **EST:** 1970
SQ FT: 60,000
SALES (est): 192.18MM
SALES (corp-wide): 183.75MM **Privately Held**
Web: www.walkerfirst.com
SIC: 4813 5065 8731 8711 Telephone communication, except radio; Electronic parts and equipment, nec; Commercial physical research; Engineering services
HQ: Ustc-United States Technologies Communication Corp
  225 Raritan Center Pkwy
  Edison NJ 08837
  732 902-2358

(G-9801)
WEATHER MARINE CANVAS LLC
245 Creek Meadow Dr (27295-9201)
PHONE 336 764-4015
David M Canavan, *Prin*
EMP: 4 **EST:** 2008
SALES (est): 10.01K **Privately Held**
Web: www.weathermarinecanvas.com
SIC: 2211 Canvas

(G-9802)
WEATHERVANE WINERY INC
1452 Welcome Arcadia Rd (27295-5475)
PHONE 336 793-3366
EMP: 5 **EST:** 2010
SALES (est): 461.08K **Privately Held**
Web: www.weathervanewinery.com
SIC: 2084 Wines

(G-9803)
YOUNG GRAPHICS INC
10 Echoview Cir (27292-5529)
PHONE.................................336 249-3148
Bobby Young, *Pr*
Rodney Young, *VP*
Tanger Young, *Sec*
Theresa Young, *Stockholder*
EMP: 7 **EST:** 1976
SQ FT: 14,000
SALES (est): 326.69K **Privately Held**
SIC: 2752 Offset printing

Liberty
Randolph County

(G-9804)
ADVINTECH INC
2825 Nc Highway 62 E (27298-9118)
PHONE.................................336 327-2666
EMP: 5 **EST:** 2020
SALES (est): 88.38K **Privately Held**
SIC: 3663 Radio and t.v. communications equipment

(G-9805)
AERO PRECISION MACHINE INC
6024 Smithwood Rd (27298-9125)
P.O. Box 216 (27283-0216)
PHONE.................................336 685-0016
EMP: 10 **EST:** 1992
SALES (est): 957.07K **Privately Held**
Web: www.aeroprecisionmachine.com
SIC: 3599 Machine shop, jobbing and repair

(G-9806)
AMOR FURNITURE AND BEDDING LLC
Also Called: Amor Furniture
143 S Asheboro St (27298-7517)
P.O. Box 63 (27298-0063)
PHONE.................................336 795-0044
Spiro Laousis, *Banking Manager*
EMP: 10 **EST:** 2010
SQ FT: 10,000
SALES (est): 971.79K **Privately Held**
Web: www.amorfurniture.com
SIC: 2512 5021 Upholstered household furniture; Beds and bedding

(G-9807)
AMT/BCU INC
Also Called: American Modular Technologies
6306 Old 421 Rd (27298-8285)
P.O. Box 1069 (27298-1069)
PHONE.................................336 622-6200
EMP: 37
Web: www.americanmodulartechnologies.com
SIC: 3441 3448 Fabricated structural metal; Prefabricated metal buildings and components

(G-9808)
BRAFFORD WELDING
2262 Ramseur Julian Rd (27298-8578)
PHONE.................................336 318-5436
Andrew Brafford, *Prin*
EMP: 4 **EST:** 2018
SALES (est): 25.09K **Privately Held**
SIC: 7692 Welding repair

(G-9809)
CUMINS MACHINERY CORP
312 W Luther Ave (27298-8634)
PHONE.................................336 622-1000
Edward W Cumins, *Pr*
EMP: 6 **EST:** 1967
SQ FT: 12,000
SALES (est): 983.72K **Privately Held**
Web: www.cumins.com
SIC: 5084 2281 Textile machinery and equipment; Yarn spinning mills

(G-9810)
DANIELS LUMBER SALES INC
3224 Staley Store Rd (27298-9500)
PHONE.................................336 622-5486
Gene Aldridge, *Pr*
Nancy Aldridge, *VP*
EMP: 19 **EST:** 1980
SQ FT: 5,600
SALES (est): 500.3K **Privately Held**
Web: www.danielslumbersales.com
SIC: 2421 Planing mills, nec

(G-9811)
EDWARDS WOOD PRODUCTS INC
9979 Old Liberty Rd (27298-8628)
PHONE.................................704 624-5098
EMP: 62
SALES (corp-wide): 75.9MM **Privately Held**
Web: www.ewpi.com
SIC: 2421 Sawmills and planing mills, general
PA: Edwards Wood Products, Inc.
       2215 Old Lawyers Rd
       Marshville NC 28103
       704 624-3624

(G-9812)
EDWARDS WOOD PRODUCTS INC
3231 Staley Store Rd (27298-9500)
PHONE.................................336 622-7537
Don Blair, *Brnch Mgr*
EMP: 63
SQ FT: 34,116
SALES (corp-wide): 75.9MM **Privately Held**
Web: www.ewpi.com
SIC: 2421 Sawmills and planing mills, general
PA: Edwards Wood Products, Inc.
       2215 Old Lawyers Rd
       Marshville NC 28103
       704 624-3624

(G-9813)
EULISS OIL COMPANY INC
122 S Foster St (27298-9661)
P.O. Box 789 (27298-0789)
PHONE.................................336 622-3055
John K Stanley Junior, *Pr*
EMP: 8 **EST:** 1954
SQ FT: 3,500
SALES (est): 2.44MM **Privately Held**
Web: www.eulisspropane.com
SIC: 1321 5983 5172 5984 Propane (natural) production; Fuel oil dealers; Gasoline; Liquefied petroleum gas, delivered to customers' premises

(G-9814)
GENESIS WLDG & FABRICATION LLC
6029 Kirkman Street Ext (27298-8530)
PHONE.................................336 622-9533
Jonathan S Bautista Castro, *Prin*
EMP: 4 **EST:** 2019
SALES (est): 92.75K **Privately Held**
SIC: 7692 Welding repair

(G-9815)
GEORGE R HARDIE
Also Called: Hardie Wood Working
5529 Ferguson Rd (27298-9334)
PHONE.................................336 263-7920
George Hardie, *Prin*
EMP: 7 **EST:** 2005
SALES (est): 236.16K **Privately Held**
SIC: 2499 Decorative wood and woodwork

(G-9816)
HOLDER BACKHOE & HAULING INC
4660 Randolph Church Rd (27298-8108)
PHONE.................................336 622-7388
Christopher R Holder, *Pr*
EMP: 10 **EST:** 2014
SALES (est): 504.89K **Privately Held**
SIC: 3531 Backhoes

(G-9817)
INDIANA CHAIR FRAME COMPANY
Also Called: Indiana Chair Frame 3200
330 N Greensboro St (27298-2605)
PHONE.................................574 825-9355
Terry Gabhart, *Pr*
David Haffner, *
▲ **EMP:** 23 **EST:** 1985
SALES (est): 499.65K
SALES (corp-wide): 5.15B **Publicly Held**
Web: www.lpworkfurniture.com
SIC: 2512 Upholstered household furniture
PA: Leggett & Platt, Incorporated
       1 Leggett Rd
       Carthage MO 64836
       417 358-8131

(G-9818)
KENNY ROBINSON S WLDG SVC INC
8975 Moody Rd (27298-8923)
PHONE.................................760 213-6454
Kenny G Robinson, *Pr*
EMP: 5 **EST:** 1991
SALES (est): 102.64K **Privately Held**
SIC: 7692 Welding repair

(G-9819)
LEGGETT & PLATT INCORPORATED
Also Called: Cincro
330 N Greensboro St (27298-2605)
PHONE.................................336 622-0121
Terry Gabhart, *Brnch Mgr*
EMP: 16
SALES (corp-wide): 5.15B **Publicly Held**
Web: www.leggett.com
SIC: 2515 Mattresses and bedsprings
PA: Leggett & Platt, Incorporated
       1 Leggett Rd
       Carthage MO 64836
       417 358-8131

(G-9820)
LIBERTY DRY KILN CORP
3246 Staley Store Rd (27298-9500)
PHONE.................................336 622-5490
EMP: 4 **EST:** 1996
SALES (est): 213.35K **Privately Held**
SIC: 2421 Sawmills and planing mills, general

(G-9821)
LIBERTY LUMBER COMPANY
9979 Old Liberty Rd (27298-8628)
P.O. Box 271 (27248-0271)
PHONE.................................336 622-4901
Paul James Skiver Ii, *Pr*
EMP: 40 **EST:** 1974
SQ FT: 62,000
SALES (est): 3.89MM **Privately Held**
Web: www.ewpi.com
SIC: 5031 2421 Lumber: rough, dressed, and finished; Sawmills and planing mills, general

(G-9822)
LIBERTY TRAILERS LLC
5806 York Martin Rd (27298-8479)
PHONE.................................219 866-7141
EMP: 6 **EST:** 2014
SALES (est): 603.62K **Privately Held**
Web: www.libertytrailers.com
SIC: 3715 Bus trailers, tractor type

(G-9823)
LIBERTY WELDING
134 E Dameron Ave (27298-3329)
PHONE.................................336 964-0640
EMP: 5 **EST:** 2019
SALES (est): 84.33K **Privately Held**
SIC: 7692 Welding repair

(G-9824)
MAJIC TNT INC
419 E Starmount Ave (27298-3008)
PHONE.................................252 425-0489
Ellen Hayes, *Prin*
EMP: 4 **EST:** 2019
SALES (est): 87.26K **Privately Held**
SIC: 3715 Truck trailers

(G-9825)
NORCRAFT COMPANIES LP
Also Called: Ultra Craft Companies
6163 Old 421 Rd (27298-8283)
PHONE.................................336 622-4281
David Andrew, *Mgr*
EMP: 250
SQ FT: 217,457
SALES (corp-wide): 2.73B **Publicly Held**
Web: www.ultracraft.com
SIC: 2434 Wood kitchen cabinets
HQ: Norcraft Companies, L.P.
       1 Masterbrand Cabinets Dr
       Jasper IN 47546
       812 482-2527

(G-9826)
PALLET EXPRESS INC
6306 Old 421 Rd (27298-8285)
P.O. Box 1998 (27298-1998)
PHONE.................................336 621-2266
TOLL FREE: 800
EMP: 115 **EST:** 1993
SQ FT: 10,000
SALES (est): 19.8MM **Privately Held**
Web: www.palletexpress.com
SIC: 2448 Pallets, wood

(G-9827)
QUALITY VENEER COMPANY
237 Teague Ave (27298)
P.O. Box 10 (27298-0010)
PHONE.................................336 622-2211
James G Ritch Junior, *Pr*
David Ritch, *VP*
EMP: 16 **EST:** 1952
SQ FT: 15,000
SALES (est): 603.96K **Privately Held**
SIC: 2436 Veneer stock, softwood

(G-9828)
ROBINSONS WELDING SERVICE
3465 Staley Store Rd (27298-9527)
PHONE.................................336 622-3150
Kenny Robinson, *Pr*
Ronda W Robinson, *Sec*
EMP: 8 **EST:** 1989
SALES (est): 562.22K **Privately Held**
Web: www.robinsonsinc.net
SIC: 7692 1542 Welding repair; Commercial and office buildings, prefabricated erection

(G-9829)
ROD RAND INC
5524 Eulis Rd (27298-9306)
PHONE.................................336 565-4874
Barbara G Lowe, *Prin*
EMP: 5 **EST:** 2008

Liberty - Randolph County (G-9830)

SALES (est): 74.41K **Privately Held**
SIC: 3131 Rands

(G-9830)
RUBBER MILL INC
Also Called: Rubber Mill
9897 Old Liberty Rd (27298-8627)
P.O. Box 1329 (27298-1329)
PHONE.....................336 622-1680
▲ EMP: 20 EST: 1986
SALES (est): 2.64MM **Privately Held**
Web: www.rubbermill.com
SIC: 3069 5085 3569 3053 Molded rubber products; Rubber goods, mechanical; Filters; Gaskets; packing and sealing devices

(G-9831)
SFP RESEARCH INC
Also Called: Gen Trak
121 W Swannanoa Ave (27298-3215)
P.O. Box 1290 (27298-1290)
PHONE.....................336 622-5266
Steve Repp, Pr
EMP: 8 EST: 1991
SQ FT: 10,000
SALES (est): 651.63K **Privately Held**
Web: www.gentrakinc.com
SIC: 3841 Medical instruments and equipment, blood and bone work

(G-9832)
SUMMIT PEAK PENS AND WD WORKS
412 E Starmount Ave (27298-3008)
PHONE.....................336 404-8312
Joyce Simoes, Prin
EMP: 5 EST: 2010
SALES (est): 63.7K **Privately Held**
SIC: 2431 Millwork

(G-9833)
SUPERTEX INC
Also Called: Earthknit
312 W Luther Ave (27298-8634)
PHONE.....................336 622-1000
Edward Cumins, Pr
Howard Cumins, *
Cheryl Severson, *
▲ EMP: 35 EST: 1982
SQ FT: 350,000
SALES (est): 7.29MM **Privately Held**
Web: www.supertex-inc.com
SIC: 2258 Lace and warp knit fabric mills

(G-9834)
VISION METALS INC
Also Called: Ferree Trailer
5806 York Martin Rd (27298-8479)
P.O. Box 1169 (27298-1169)
PHONE.....................336 622-7300
EMP: 10 EST: 1992
SALES (est): 517.01K **Privately Held**
SIC: 3715 3596 Truck trailers; Weighing machines and apparatus

Lilesville
Anson County

(G-9835)
BONSAL AMERICAN INC
Building Products Division
351 Haileys Ferry Rd (28091-6055)
PHONE.....................704 848-4141
Dale Tomacin, Genl Mgr
EMP: 8
SALES (corp-wide): 32.72B **Privately Held**
SIC: 3272 3241 Concrete products, nec; Cement, hydraulic
HQ: Bonsal American, Inc.

625 Griffith Rd Ste 100
Charlotte NC 28217
704 525-1621

(G-9836)
COUNTY OF ANSON
Also Called: Anson County Water Treatment
567 Filtration Rd (28091-6086)
PHONE.....................704 848-4849
EMP: 9
Web: co.anson.nc.us
SIC: 3589 4941 Water treatment equipment, industrial; Water supply
PA: County Of Anson
101 S Green St
Wadesboro NC 28170
704 994-3200

(G-9837)
HEDRICK B V GRAVEL & SAND CO
403 Gravel Plant Rd (28091)
P.O. Box 418 (28091-0418)
PHONE.....................704 848-4165
Judith Johnson, Pt
EMP: 39 EST: 1925
SQ FT: 4,000
SALES (est): 4.68MM **Privately Held**
Web: www.hedrickind.com
SIC: 1442 Construction sand mining

(G-9838)
HORNWOOD INC (PA)
766 Haileys Ferry Rd (28091-6051)
PHONE.....................704 848-4121
Charles D Horne, Pr
Larry W Adams, *
Kenneth W Horne Junior, Ex VP
Paula Tice, *
◆ EMP: 320 EST: 1945
SQ FT: 230,000
SALES (est): 46.97MM
SALES (corp-wide): 46.97MM **Privately Held**
Web: www.hornwoodinc.com
SIC: 2258 Cloth, warp knit

(G-9839)
KING CHARLES INDUSTRIES LLC
766 Haileys Ferry Rd (28091-6051)
PHONE.....................704 848-4121
Charles Horne, Prin
EMP: 6 EST: 2016
SALES (est): 251.04K **Privately Held**
SIC: 3999 Manufacturing industries, nec

(G-9840)
MIKE GOODWIN LOGGING
338 Horseback Ln (28091-6083)
PHONE.....................704 848-8222
Joseph M Goodwin, Owner
EMP: 7 EST: 1978
SALES (est): 362.47K **Privately Held**
SIC: 2411 Logging

(G-9841)
TRIANGLE AUTO COMPONENTS LLC
766 Haileys Ferry Rd (28091-6051)
PHONE.....................704 848-4121
Chuck Horne, Managing Member
EMP: 10 EST: 2006
SALES (est): 186.8K **Privately Held**
SIC: 3714 Motor vehicle parts and accessories

Lillington
Harnett County

(G-9842)
ARMTEC ESTERLINE CORP
608 E Mcneill St (27546-9189)
PHONE.....................910 814-3029
Lena Olving, COO
EMP: 48 EST: 2006
SALES (est): 4.26MM
SALES (corp-wide): 6.58B **Publicly Held**
Web: www.armtecdefense.com
SIC: 3823 Process control instruments
HQ: Esterline Technologies Corp
1301 E 9th St Ste 3000
Cleveland OH 44114
216 706-2960

(G-9843)
BARLIN RANCH & PETS INC
390 D R Harvell Ln (27546-5512)
PHONE.....................910 814-1930
EMP: 4
SALES (est): 293.93K **Privately Held**
SIC: 3131 Quarters

(G-9844)
BOON EDAM INC (DH)
402 Mckinney Pkwy (27546-9336)
PHONE.....................910 814-3800
Mark G Borto, Ch Bd
Thomas Devine, *
Valerie Anderson, *
Daniel Camp, *
◆ EMP: 37 EST: 1981
SQ FT: 50,000
SALES (est): 46.21MM
SALES (corp-wide): 194.28MM **Privately Held**
Web: www.boonedam.com
SIC: 3829 Turnstiles, equipped with counting mechanisms
HQ: Boon Edam B.V.
Ambachtstraat 4
Edam NH 1135
299380808

(G-9845)
CAPITAL MARBLE CREATIONS INC
309 W Duncan St (27546-9462)
P.O. Box 1417 (27546-1417)
PHONE.....................910 893-2462
Thomas E Wood, Pr
Bruce W Morris, Sec
EMP: 19 EST: 1972
SQ FT: 29,540
SALES (est): 1.43MM **Privately Held**
Web: www.capitalmarblecreations.com
SIC: 3281 3431 Household articles, except furniture: cut stone; Metal sanitary ware

(G-9846)
CASE BY CASE LLC
162 Summerwood Ln (27546-5517)
PHONE.....................910 814-3288
Georjean Privette, Prin
EMP: 5 EST: 2016
SALES (est): 98.18K **Privately Held**
SIC: 3523 Farm machinery and equipment

(G-9847)
CFI READY MIX LLC
304 E Mcneill St (27546-8408)
P.O. Box 970 (27546-0970)
PHONE.....................910 814-4238
Wayne Underwood, Managing Member
EMP: 5 EST: 2007
SALES (est): 471.41K **Privately Held**

SIC: 3273 Ready-mixed concrete

(G-9848)
CHAMPION HOME BUILDERS INC
Also Called: Champion
4055 Us 401 S (27546-6829)
PHONE.....................910 893-5713
Gary Wilkinson, Mgr
EMP: 234
SALES (corp-wide): 2.61B **Publicly Held**
Web: www.championhomes.com
SIC: 1521 2451 New construction, single-family houses; Mobile homes, except recreational
HQ: Champion Home Builders, Inc.
755 W Big Beavr Rd # 1000
Troy MI 48084
248 614-8200

(G-9849)
CHEMTECH NORTH CAROLINA LLC
1030 S Main St (27546-5633)
P.O. Box 58 (27546-0058)
PHONE.....................910 514-9575
EMP: 26 EST: 2008
SALES (est): 2.75MM **Privately Held**
Web: www.chemtechglobal.com
SIC: 2899 Chemical preparations, nec

(G-9850)
DONALD R YOUNG LOGGING INC
165 Buie Farm Ln (27546-6180)
PHONE.....................910 934-6769
Donald R Young, Prin
EMP: 6 EST: 2010
SALES (est): 620.52K **Privately Held**
SIC: 2411 Logging camps and contractors

(G-9851)
ESTERLINE TECHNOLOGIES CORP
Also Called: Esterline Defense Technologies
608 E Mcneill St (27546-9189)
P.O. Box 1179 (27546-1179)
PHONE.....................910 814-1222
Robert W Cremin, CEO
R Brad Lawrence, CEO
Jerry D Leitman, Ch
EMP: 5 EST: 2009
SALES (est): 962.74K **Privately Held**
Web: www.armtecdefense.com
SIC: 3728 Aircraft parts and equipment, nec

(G-9852)
HEIDELBERG MTLS STHAST AGG LLC
Sr 2016 (27546)
PHONE.....................910 893-2111
EMP: 22
SALES (corp-wide): 21.19B **Privately Held**
Web: www.hansonbiz.com
SIC: 1423 Crushed and broken granite
HQ: Heidelberg Materials Southeast Agg Llc
3237 Satellite Blvd # 30
Duluth GA 30096
770 491-2756

(G-9853)
KELKEN ENTERPRISES LLC
12 Caco Dr (27546-7974)
PHONE.....................910 890-7211
Kelley Peregoy, Prin
EMP: 7 EST: 2017
SALES (est): 251.8K **Privately Held**
Web: www.kelkengolf.com
SIC: 3949 Sporting and athletic goods, nec

(G-9854)
KRIGEN PHARMACEUTICALS LLC
800 Edwards Dr (27546)
PHONE.....................919 523-7530

GEOGRAPHIC SECTION

Lincolnton - Lincoln County (G-9880)

Dhruvkumar Patel, *Prin*
EMP: 5 **EST:** 2018
SALES (est): 103.43K **Privately Held**
Web: www.krigenpharmaceuticals.com
SIC: 2834 Pharmaceutical preparations

(G-9855)
KRIGEN PHARMACEUTICALS LLC
800 Edwards Brothers Dr (27546-9401)
PHONE.................................919 961-3751
EMP: 5 **EST:** 2018
SALES (est): 239.96K **Privately Held**
Web: www.krigenpharmaceuticals.com
SIC: 2834 Pharmaceutical preparations

(G-9856)
MARLINWOODWORKS LLC
50 Otto Rd (27546-6276)
PHONE.................................919 343-2605
Doug Courtright, *Prin*
EMP: 7 **EST:** 2016
SALES (est): 470.89K **Privately Held**
SIC: 2499 Wood products, nec

(G-9857)
NERDPOPPRINTS
390 Kramer Rd (27546-8780)
PHONE.................................910 514-2279
Jason Dresser, *Prin*
EMP: 4 **EST:** 2016
SALES (est): 118.21K **Privately Held**
SIC: 2752 Commercial printing, lithographic

(G-9858)
POINT BLANK ENTERPRISES INC
Also Called: Gould & Goodrich
709 E Mcneill St (27546-9188)
PHONE.................................910 893-2071
Scott Nelson, *Brnch Mgr*
EMP: 67
Web: www.pointblankenterprises.com
SIC: 3199 2387 3172 2221 Holsters, leather; Apparel belts; Personal leather goods, nec; Broadwoven fabric mills, manmade
HQ: Point Blank Enterprises, Inc.
2102 Sw 2nd St
Pompano Beach FL 33069
954 630-0900

(G-9859)
SAAB BARRACUDA LLC
608 E Mcneill St (27546-9189)
PHONE.................................910 814-3088
▲ **EMP:** 27 **EST:** 2002
SQ FT: 156,000
SALES (est): 20.67MM
SALES (corp-wide): 2.29B **Privately Held**
SIC: 5511 1711 2399 Automobiles, new and used; Heating systems repair and maintenance; Parachutes
HQ: Saab, Inc.
20700 Loudoun County Pkwy # 100
Ashburn VA 20147
703 406-7200

(G-9860)
SORRELLS CABINET CO INC
490 Chesterfield Lake Rd (27546-8138)
PHONE.................................919 639-4320
Corbin Sorrell, *Pr*
Dann Sorrell, *VP*
Kathy Sorrell, *Sec*
EMP: 8 **EST:** 1977
SALES (est): 464.87K **Privately Held**
Web: www.sorrellscabinets.com
SIC: 2434 5211 Wood kitchen cabinets; Lumber and other building materials

(G-9861)
TIN CANS LLC
510 E Washington St (27546-8075)
P.O. Box 208 (27546-0208)
PHONE.................................910 322-2626
Mark L Centrella, *Prin*
EMP: 8 **EST:** 2014
SALES (est): 742.29K **Privately Held**
Web: www.calltincans.com
SIC: 3411 Tin cans

(G-9862)
ZOEYS BTQ STYLE SPCLTY TRATS
896 Shawtown Rd (27546-9080)
P.O. Box 721 (27546-0721)
PHONE.................................910 808-1778
EMP: 4 **EST:** 2021
SALES (est): 23K **Privately Held**
SIC: 2389 Apparel and accessories, nec

Lincolnton
Lincoln County

(G-9863)
A & D PRECAST INC
1032 N Flint St (28092-3026)
P.O. Box 1198 (28093-1198)
PHONE.................................704 735-3337
David C Gilbert, *Pr*
EMP: 5 **EST:** 2011
SALES (est): 590.5K **Privately Held**
Web: www.adprecast.com
SIC: 3272 Concrete products, precast, nec

(G-9864)
A R BYRD COMPANY INC
Also Called: A R Byrd Company
171 Joshua Ct (28092-7508)
PHONE.................................704 732-5675
Alan R Byrd, *Pr*
EMP: 5 **EST:** 1987
SALES (est): 461.33K **Privately Held**
Web: www.arbyrdcompany.com
SIC: 5712 1542 2522 1541 Cabinet work, custom; Nonresidential construction, nec; Cabinets, office: except wood; Renovation, remodeling and repairs: industrial buildings

(G-9865)
ACTEGA WIT INC
125 Technolgy Dr (28092-4290)
P.O. Box 10 (28093-0010)
PHONE.................................704 735-8282
▲ **EMP:** 150
Web: www.inkmiser2.com
SIC: 2893 Printing ink

(G-9866)
ACTIVE CONCEPTS
109 Technolgy Dr (28092-4290)
PHONE.................................704 276-7386
EMP: 4 **EST:** 2017
SALES (est): 80.87K **Privately Held**
Web: www.activeconceptsllc.com
SIC: 2844 Cosmetic preparations

(G-9867)
ACTIVE CONCEPTS LLC ✪
110 Technolgy Dr (28092-4288)
PHONE.................................704 276-7372
EMP: 4 **EST:** 2022
SALES (est): 63.22K **Privately Held**
Web: www.activeconceptsllc.com
SIC: 2844 Cosmetic preparations

(G-9868)
ACTIVE CONCEPTS LLC
107 Technolgy Dr (28092-4290)
PHONE.................................704 276-7100
Durant Scholz, *Managing Member*
▲ **EMP:** 33 **EST:** 2012
SQ FT: 7,000
SALES (est): 7.62MM **Privately Held**
Web: www.activeconceptsllc.com
SIC: 2844 Cosmetic preparations

(G-9869)
AIRBORN INDUSTRIES INC
115 Industrial Park Rd (28092-8359)
PHONE.................................704 483-5000
Donald J Barry, *Pr*
EMP: 25 **EST:** 2002
SALES (est): 4.66MM **Privately Held**
Web: www.airbornusa.com
SIC: 3523 3639 Balers, farm: hay, straw, cotton, etc.; Trash compactors, household

(G-9870)
ALLIED MANUFACTURING TECH INC
1477 Roseland Dr (28092-7007)
P.O. Box 248 (28093-0248)
PHONE.................................704 276-8192
Joseph Navarro, *Pr*
▲ **EMP:** 16 **EST:** 1999
SALES (est): 448.71K **Privately Held**
SIC: 3829 Geophysical and meteorological testing equipment

(G-9871)
AMERICAN CONVERTING CO LTD LLC
Also Called: Amerikrate
1161 Burris Blvd (28092-6014)
PHONE.................................704 479-5025
Tom Eubanks, *Managing Member*
EMP: 25 **EST:** 2003
SQ FT: 210,000
SALES (est): 7.67MM **Privately Held**
Web: www.americanconverting.com
SIC: 2679 Paper products, converted, nec

(G-9872)
ANNIHILARE MEDICAL SYSTEMS INC
311 Motz Ave # E (28092-2532)
PHONE.................................855 545-5677
Parker Sipes, *Pr*
Steve Cobb, *CFO*
Marty Paris, *CEO*
Bill Bath, *Dir*
Diana Seifert, *Dir*
EMP: 10 **EST:** 2015
SALES (est): 947.47K **Privately Held**
Web: www.annihilare.com
SIC: 8099 2842 Medical services organization; Polishes and sanitation goods

(G-9873)
APTARGROUP INC
3300 Finger Mill Rd (28092-6129)
PHONE.................................828 970-6300
Tim Decrow, *Brnch Mgr*
EMP: 150
Web: www.aptar.com
SIC: 3586 Measuring and dispensing pumps
PA: Aptargroup, Inc.
265 Exchange Dr Ste 100
Crystal Lake IL 60014

(G-9874)
ARBOR ORGANIC TECHNOLOGIES LLC
107 Technolgy Dr (28092-4290)
PHONE.................................704 276-7100
Durant Scholz, *Managing Member*
EMP: 25 **EST:** 2011
SALES (est): 1.86MM **Privately Held**

SIC: 2834 Extracts of botanicals: powdered, pilular, solid, or fluid

(G-9875)
BETH WISEMAN
224 Hollow Rd (28092-8434)
PHONE.................................704 735-4469
Beth Wiseman, *Prin*
EMP: 4 **EST:** 2010
SALES (est): 92.79K **Privately Held**
SIC: 2269 8999 Embossing: linen broadwoven fabrics; Art related services

(G-9876)
BR LEE INDUSTRIES INC
500 Lincoln County Parkway Ext (28092-6132)
PHONE.................................704 966-3317
Calvin Majeskie, *Prin*
EMP: 6 **EST:** 2010
SALES (est): 198.38K **Privately Held**
SIC: 3999 Manufacturing industries, nec

(G-9877)
BURGESS DUKE HWARD KTRINA KNER
Also Called: Burgess Logging
4659 Asbury Church Rd (28092-8102)
PHONE.................................704 732-0547
EMP: 8 **EST:** 1997
SQ FT: 1,188
SALES (est): 240.3K **Privately Held**
SIC: 2411 Logging

(G-9878)
CAMPBELL & SONS MACHINING CO
230 W Congress St (28092-2507)
PHONE.................................704 394-0291
Leroy Campbell, *Pr*
Ronnie Campbell, *VP*
Steven Campbell, *Sec*
EMP: 5 **EST:** 1979
SQ FT: 128
SALES (est): 471.17K **Privately Held**
Web: www.lincolneda.org
SIC: 3599 7699 Machine shop, jobbing and repair; Industrial machinery and equipment repair

(G-9879)
CATALER NORTH AMERICA CORP (DH)
2002 Cataler Dr (28092-6138)
PHONE.................................828 970-0026
Hiroaki Sunakawa, *Pr*
Rikizo Yoshikawa, *
Albert Alvarez, *
Hironao Kawai, *
▲ **EMP:** 197 **EST:** 2001
SQ FT: 200,000
SALES (est): 51.59MM **Privately Held**
Web: www.cataler.co.jp
SIC: 3714 Exhaust systems and parts, motor vehicle
HQ: Cataler Corporation
7800, Chihama
Kakegawa SZO 437-1

(G-9880)
CCO HOLDINGS LLC
644 Center Dr (28092-3712)
PHONE.................................704 308-3361
EMP: 107
SALES (corp-wide): 54.61B **Publicly Held**
SIC: 4841 3663 3651 Cable television services; Radio and t.v. communications equipment; Household audio and video equipment
HQ: Cco Holdings, Llc
400 Atlantic St

Lincolnton - Lincoln County (G-9881)   GEOGRAPHIC SECTION

Stamford CT 06901
203 905-7801

(G-9881)
CHARLOTTE METAL FINISHING INC
Also Called: CMF
2708 E Main St (28092-4281)
PHONE.....................704 732-7570
Michael Wise, *Mgr*
Thomas L Finger, *Pr*
Kay C Finger, *Sec*
EMP: 10 **EST:** 1983
SQ FT: 10,000
SALES (est): 1.05MM
SALES (corp-wide): 15.33MM **Privately Held**
Web: www.t-fab.com
SIC: 3471 Electroplating of metals or formed products
PA: T L F Inc
    280 Cane Creek Rd
    Fletcher NC 28732
    828 681-5343

(G-9882)
CHRISCO MACHINE SHOP LLC
4280 Maiden Hwy (28092-4904)
PHONE.....................828 428-9966
Jeffrey Dean Chrisco, *Prin*
EMP: 6 **EST:** 2010
SALES (est): 172.75K **Privately Held**
SIC: 3599 Machine shop, jobbing and repair

(G-9883)
COMMERCIAL PRTG LINCOLNTON NC
Also Called: Commercial Printing
523 N Aspen St (28092-2105)
P.O. Box 675 (28093-0675)
PHONE.....................704 735-6831
Russell Cornwell Ii, *Pr*
Dorothy Cornwell, *Sec*
Debra Cornwell, *VP*
♦ **EMP:** 4 **EST:** 1958
SQ FT: 4,600
SALES (est): 292.55K **Privately Held**
SIC: 2752 Offset printing

(G-9884)
CORIANDER DESIGNS
2141 Heavner Rd (28092-8552)
PHONE.....................425 402-8001
Dean Root, *Mgr*
EMP: 4 **EST:** 2019
SALES (est): 121.38K **Privately Held**
Web: www.corianderdesigns.com
SIC: 2522 Office furniture, except wood

(G-9885)
COSETTE PHARMACEUTICALS INC
1877 Kawai Rd (28092-5905)
PHONE.....................704 735-5700
Greg Sherwood, *Mgr*
EMP: 180
SALES (corp-wide): 91.68MM **Privately Held**
Web: www.cosettepharma.com
SIC: 2834 Pharmaceutical preparations
PA: Cosette Pharmaceuticals, Inc.
    101 Coolidge St
    South Plainfield NJ 07080
    800 922-1038

(G-9886)
COSETTE PHRMCTCALS NC LABS LLC
1877 Kawai Rd (28092-5905)
PHONE.....................908 753-2000
▲ **EMP:** 150 **EST:** 2014
SALES (est): 43.95MM

SALES (corp-wide): 91.68MM **Privately Held**
SIC: 2834 Pharmaceutical preparations
PA: Cosette Pharmaceuticals, Inc.
    101 Coolidge St
    South Plainfield NJ 07080
    800 922-1038

(G-9887)
CREATIVE PRINTING STANLEY INC
4147 Stoney Creek Dr (28092-6107)
PHONE.....................704 732-6398
Gary Wooten, *Prin*
EMP: 5 **EST:** 2010
SALES (est): 98.3K **Privately Held**
SIC: 2752 Offset printing

(G-9888)
CUSTOM GEARS INC
3565 Hwy 155 S (28092)
P.O. Box 1736 (28093-1736)
PHONE.....................704 735-6883
George Bundy, *Pr*
Brenda Bundy, *Sec*
EMP: 4 **EST:** 1990
SQ FT: 3,500
SALES (est): 168.13K **Privately Held**
SIC: 2299 Fibers, textile: recovery from textile mill waste and rags

(G-9889)
D BLOCK METALS LLC
1808 Indian Creek Rd (28092-6916)
PHONE.....................980 238-2600
EMP: 4
SALES (corp-wide): 2.13MM **Privately Held**
Web: www.dblockmetals.com
SIC: 3399 Powder, metal
PA: D Block Metals, Llc
    1111 Jenkins Rd
    Gastonia NC 28052
    704 705-5895

(G-9890)
DIRTY DOG THREADS LLC
1841 Wisteria Ln (28092-7199)
PHONE.....................704 240-3668
Jesse Freeman, *Prin*
EMP: 5 **EST:** 2019
SALES (est): 90.96K **Privately Held**
SIC: 2759 Screen printing

(G-9891)
DUSTIN ELLIS LOGGING
1186 Confederate Rd (28092-9091)
PHONE.....................704 732-6027
Dustin Ellis, *Owner*
Wendy Ellis, *Owner*
EMP: 5 **EST:** 1985
SALES (est): 455.12K **Privately Held**
Web: rambo.sites.c21.homes
SIC: 2411 Logging

(G-9892)
EXCEL INC
509 Lee Ave (28092-2522)
P.O. Box 459 (28093-0459)
PHONE.....................704 735-6535
Charles Eurey, *Pr*
Paul Eurey, *Sec*
▼ **EMP:** 15 **EST:** 1945
SQ FT: 40,000
SALES (est): 922.08K **Privately Held**
Web: www.excelhandling.com
SIC: 3552 Textile machinery

(G-9893)
FMS ENTERPRISES USA INC
2001 Kawai Rd (28092-6976)

PHONE.....................704 735-4249
Daniel Blum, *Pr*
Avi Blum, *VP*
♦ **EMP:** 55 **EST:** 2005
SQ FT: 65,000
SALES (est): 4.56MM **Privately Held**
SIC: 2396 Linings, apparel: made from purchased materials

(G-9894)
GAME PROCESSING LEONARDS WILD
167 Car Farm Rd (28092-7102)
PHONE.....................980 429-7042
EMP: 4 **EST:** 2015
SALES (est): 63.44K **Privately Held**
SIC: 2015 Chicken slaughtering and processing

(G-9895)
HUGGER INC
1443 E Gaston St (28092-4401)
P.O. Box 489 (28093-0489)
PHONE.....................704 735-7422
Carol Grove, *Pr*
Thomas D Grove, *
Harris Jones, *VP Fin*
Sonnie G Herbert, *
EMP: 150 **EST:** 1977
SQ FT: 100,000
SALES (est): 9.08MM **Privately Held**
SIC: 2253 2335 T-shirts and tops, knit; Women's, junior's, and misses' dresses

(G-9896)
J WISE INC
Also Called: Vapor Honing Technologies
313a Motz Ave (28092-2532)
PHONE.....................828 202-5563
Johnathan Wise, *Pr*
EMP: 25 **EST:** 2013
SQ FT: 4,000
SALES (est): 3.09MM **Privately Held**
Web: www.vaporhoningtechnologies.com
SIC: 5993 3549 Tobacco stores and stands; Assembly machines, including robotic

(G-9897)
JAX BROTHERS INC
Also Called: Gametime Imagewear
536 N Generals Blvd (28092-3561)
PHONE.....................704 732-3351
Michael Hopkins, *Pr*
EMP: 5 **EST:** 2008
SALES (est): 243.1K **Privately Held**
Web: www.gametimeimagewear.com
SIC: 2759 Screen printing

(G-9898)
LAWING MARBLE CO INC
2523 E Highway 150 (28092-4188)
PHONE.....................704 732-0360
Candace Heavner, *Pr*
Candance Heavner, *Pr*
EMP: 5 **EST:** 1989
SQ FT: 3,000
SALES (est): 337.8K **Privately Held**
Web: www.brothertonmarble.com
SIC: 3281 5719 Marble, building: cut and shaped; Bath accessories

(G-9899)
LEDFORD UPHOLSTERY
Also Called: Ledford Upholstery & Fabrics
202 W Pine St (28092-2159)
PHONE.....................704 732-0233
Bill Ledford, *Owner*
EMP: 5 **EST:** 1978
SALES (est): 317.13K **Privately Held**
Web: ledfordupholstery.theinfocity.com

SIC: 2221 7641 5949 Upholstery fabrics, manmade fiber and silk; Upholstery work; Fabric stores piece goods

(G-9900)
LINCOLN COUNTY FABRICATORS INC
513 Jason Rd (28092-6451)
PHONE.....................704 735-1398
Kenneth Carpenter, *Pr*
David Carpenter, *
▼ **EMP:** 29 **EST:** 1972
SALES (est): 4.99MM **Privately Held**
Web: www.lincolncountyfabricators.com
SIC: 3552 Knitting machines

(G-9901)
LINCOLN HERALD LLC
611 N Laurel St (28092-2917)
PHONE.....................704 735-3620
Jacob Dellinger, *Prin*
EMP: 9 **EST:** 2012
SALES (est): 76.33K **Privately Held**
Web: www.lincolnherald.com
SIC: 2711 Newspapers, publishing and printing

(G-9902)
LITTLE BEEKEEPER LLC
3978 Stoney Creek Dr (28092-6105)
PHONE.....................704 215-9690
Johnnie Hunt, *CEO*
EMP: 5 **EST:** 2018
SALES (est): 125K **Privately Held**
Web: www.thelittlebeekeeper.com
SIC: 2087 Syrups, drink

(G-9903)
LUCKY COUNTRY USA LLC
3333 Finger Mill Rd (28092-6129)
PHONE.....................828 428-8313
▲ **EMP:** 30 **EST:** 2000
SALES (est): 9.79MM **Privately Held**
SIC: 2064 Licorice candy
HQ: Darrell Lea Confectionery Co Pty Ltd
    3 Brooks Rd
    Ingleburn NSW 2565

(G-9904)
MAIN FILTER LLC
1443 E Gaston St (28092-4401)
PHONE.....................704 735-0009
Andrew Perkel, *Pr*
Todd Crawford, *CFO*
EMP: 27 **EST:** 2021
SALES (est): 2.67MM **Privately Held**
Web: www.mainfilter.com
SIC: 3569 Filter elements, fluid, hydraulic line

(G-9905)
MARILYN COOK
Also Called: Gerald's Yarns
2628 Buffalo Forest Rd (28092-7271)
PHONE.....................704 735-4414
Marilyn Cook, *Owner*
EMP: 4 **EST:** 1980
SQ FT: 5,000
SALES (est): 240.22K **Privately Held**
SIC: 2282 2281 Rewinding of yarn; Yarn spinning mills

(G-9906)
MCMURRAY FABRICS INC
1140 N Flint St (28092-5238)
P.O. Box 893 (28093-0893)
PHONE.....................704 732-9613
Johnathan Yoder, *Mgr*
EMP: 54
SALES (corp-wide): 77.47MM **Privately Held**

GEOGRAPHIC SECTION

Lincolnton - Lincoln County (G-9929)

Web: www.mcmurrayfabrics.com
SIC: 2262 2261 5949 Finishing plants, manmade; Finishing plants, cotton; Fabric stores piece goods
PA: Mcmurray Fabrics, Inc.
105 Vann Pl
Aberdeen NC 28315
910 944-2128

(G-9907)
METAL INC TRIAD
108 Industrial Park Rd (28092-8358)
PHONE..................980 429-2278
EMP: 6 **EST:** 2014
SALES (est): 186.14K **Privately Held**
SIC: 3444 Metal roofing and roof drainage equipment

(G-9908)
MOHICAN MILLS INC
1419 E Gaston St (28092-4425)
P.O. Box 190 (28093-0190)
PHONE..................704 735-3343
▼ **EMP:** 307
Web: www.mohicanmills.com
SIC: 2258 Cloth, warp knit

(G-9909)
MOORES UPHOLSTERING INTERIORS
Also Called: AMF Custom Upholstery
308 S Poplar St (28092-3324)
PHONE..................704 240-8393
Alex F Moore, *Pr*
Karen Moore, *VP*
EMP: 5 **EST:** 1985
SQ FT: 1,100
SALES (est): 246.93K **Privately Held**
SIC: 7641 2512 Reupholstery; Upholstered household furniture

(G-9910)
MR TIRE INC
609 E Main St (28092-3411)
PHONE..................704 735-8024
Thomas Hand, *Brnch Mgr*
EMP: 9
SALES (corp-wide): 1.33B **Publicly Held**
Web: mrtireinc.business.site
SIC: 5941 5014 7538 5531 Bicycle and bicycle parts; Tires and tubes; General automotive repair shops; Automotive tires
HQ: Mr. Tire Inc.
2078 New York Ave Unit 2
Huntington Station NY 11746
631 499-3700

(G-9911)
NORTH CRLINA SPNNING MILLS INC
104 Industrial Park Rd (28092-8358)
P.O. Box 818 (28093-0818)
PHONE..................704 732-1171
William Kaplan, *Pr*
Robert Lehrer, *
Sharon Hovis, *
▲ **EMP:** 32 **EST:** 1964
SQ FT: 150,000
SALES (est): 1.96MM **Privately Held**
SIC: 2281 Yarn spinning mills

(G-9912)
PACKAGING UNLIMITED NC INC (DH)
1880 Riverview Rd (28092-6909)
PHONE..................704 732-7100
Pete Hanekamp, *Pr*
Jim Story, *Prin*
▲ **EMP:** 100 **EST:** 1986
SALES (est): 3.65MM **Privately Held**
Web: www.hoodcontainer.com
SIC: 2653 7389 5199 5113 Boxes, corrugated: made from purchased materials; Packaging and labeling services; Packaging materials; Corrugated and solid fiber boxes
HQ: Packaging Unlimited, Llc
1729 Mccloskey Ave
Louisville KY 40210
502 515-3900

(G-9913)
PUNKER LLC
1112 Lincoln County Pkwy (28092-6135)
PHONE..................828 322-1951
Ryan Kilkelly, *Managing Member*
▲ **EMP:** 18 **EST:** 2011
SALES (est): 4.84MM
SALES (corp-wide): 66.07MM **Privately Held**
Web: www.punker-usa.com
SIC: 3564 Blowers and fans
HQ: Punker Gmbh
Niewark 1
Eckernforde SH 24340
43514720

(G-9914)
R W GARCIA CO INC
3181 Progress Dr (28092-5203)
PHONE..................828 428-0115
Greg Taylor, *Managing Member*
EMP: 20
SALES (corp-wide): 1.44B **Publicly Held**
Web: www.rwgarcia.com
SIC: 2096 Tortilla chips
HQ: R. W. Garcia Co., Inc.
900 High St
Hanover PA 17331
408 287-4616

(G-9915)
ROBERT BOSCH TOOL CORPORATION
Vermont American Tool Company
1980 Indian Creek Rd (28092-6939)
PHONE..................704 735-7464
Shane Jones, *Genl Mgr*
EMP: 33
SALES (corp-wide): 230.19MM **Privately Held**
Web: www.boschtools.com
SIC: 3425 5085 Saw blades and handsaws; Tools, nec
HQ: Robert Bosch Tool Corporation
1800 W Central Rd
Mount Prospect IL 60056

(G-9916)
RR POWDER COATINGS
569 S Grove Street Ext (28092-7012)
PHONE..................704 240-3266
EMP: 7 **EST:** 2014
SALES (est): 136.14K **Privately Held**
Web: www.rrpowdercoating.com
SIC: 3479 Coating of metals and formed products

(G-9917)
RSI HOME PRODUCTS INC
General Marble
838 Lincoln County Pkwy (28092-6126)
PHONE..................828 428-6300
Karen Eakins, *Prin*
EMP: 132
SALES (corp-wide): 2.07B **Publicly Held**
Web: www.americanwoodmark.com
SIC: 3281 5031 Cut stone and stone products; Lumber, plywood, and millwork
HQ: Rsi Home Products Llc
400 E Orangethorpe Ave
Anaheim CA 92801
714 449-2200

(G-9918)
SIA ABRASIVES INC USA
Also Called: Abrasives Industries AG
1980 Indian Creek Rd (28092-6939)
PHONE..................704 587-7355
▲ **EMP:** 100 **EST:** 1995
SQ FT: 70,000
SALES (est): 27.43MM
SALES (corp-wide): 230.19MM **Privately Held**
Web: www.siaabrasives.com
SIC: 3291 Abrasive products
HQ: Sia Abrasives Industries Ag
Muhlewiesenstrasse 20
Frauenfeld TG 8501

(G-9919)
SOUTHERN FIBER INC (PA)
1041 S Grove Extension (28093)
PHONE..................704 736-0011
Robert Ruberti, *Pr*
▼ **EMP:** 20 **EST:** 1996
SQ FT: 65,000
SALES (est): 8.5MM
SALES (corp-wide): 8.5MM **Privately Held**
Web: www.southernfiberinc.com
SIC: 2824 Polyester fibers

(G-9920)
SPANTEK EXPANDED METAL INC
352 N Generals Blvd (28092-3557)
PHONE..................704 479-6210
Mike Gilboy, *Pr*
EMP: 26 **EST:** 1970
SQ FT: 60,000
SALES (est): 13.58MM
SALES (corp-wide): 54.97MM **Privately Held**
Web: www.spantek.com
SIC: 3312 Blast furnaces and steel mills
PA: Umi Company, Inc.
1520 5th St S
Hopkins MN 55343
952 935-8431

(G-9921)
ST ENGINEERING LEEBOY INC
Also Called: Leeboy
500 Lincoln County Parkway Ext (28092-6132)
PHONE..................704 966-3300
Christopher Barnard, *CEO*
EMP: 8 **EST:** 2019
SALES (est): 2.21MM **Privately Held**
Web: www.leeboy.com
SIC: 3531 Railway track equipment

(G-9922)
STEPHANIE BAXTER
1089 Peach Tree St (28092-8699)
PHONE..................803 203-8467
Stephanie Baxter, *Owner*
EMP: 7
SALES (est): 226.85K **Privately Held**
SIC: 2519 7389 Household furniture, nec; Business services, nec

(G-9923)
SUPERIOR CABLING SOLUTIONS LLC
824 Madison St (28092-2450)
PHONE..................704 736-9017
Maria Ruth Madrigal, *Owner*
EMP: 5 **EST:** 2017
SALES (est): 177.38K **Privately Held**
SIC: 2834 Digitalis pharmaceutical preparations

(G-9924)
SVCM
Also Called: Svcm International
536 N Generals Blvd (28092-3561)
PHONE..................305 767-3595
Stanley Clark-munoz, *Owner*
EMP: 5 **EST:** 2017
SALES (est): 181.37K **Privately Held**
SIC: 2299 4226 5131 2221 Textile goods, nec; Textile warehousing; Textiles, woven, nec; Textile mills, broadwoven: silk and manmade, also glass

(G-9925)
TENOWO INC (DH)
1968 Kawai Rd (28092-5916)
PHONE..................704 732-3525
◆ **EMP:** 14 **EST:** 1991
SALES (est): 122.28MM
SALES (corp-wide): 690.5MM **Privately Held**
Web: www.tenowo.com
SIC: 2297 Nonwoven fabrics
HQ: Tenowo Gmbh
Fabrikzeile 21
Hof BY 95028
9281490

(G-9926)
TENOWO INC
1582 Startown Rd (28092-8040)
PHONE..................704 732-3525
EMP: 1486
SALES (corp-wide): 690.5MM **Privately Held**
Web: www.tenowo.com
SIC: 3714 Motor vehicle parts and accessories
HQ: Tenowo Inc.
1968 Kawai Rd
Lincolnton NC 28092

(G-9927)
TEXTILE PIECE DYEING CO INC
319 N Generals Blvd (28092-3558)
P.O. Box 370 (28093-0370)
PHONE..................704 732-4200
Dan Doherr, *Pr*
Thomas A Rosse, *
EMP: 114 **EST:** 1986
SQ FT: 200,000
SALES (est): 766.51K **Privately Held**
SIC: 2253 Dyeing and finishing knit outerwear, excl. hosiery and glove
PA: Dartmouth Textile International Inc
185 Devonshire St Fl 9
Boston MA

(G-9928)
TEXTURE PLUS INC
1477 Roseland Dr (28092-7007)
PHONE..................631 218-9200
EMP: 40 **EST:** 1980
SQ FT: 16,000
SALES (est): 3.19MM **Privately Held**
Web: www.textureplus.com
SIC: 2952 Siding materials

(G-9929)
THORNBURG MACHINE & SUP CO INC
1699 Smith Farm Rd (28092-0902)
P.O. Box 981 (28093-0981)
PHONE..................704 735-5421
B C Lineberger, *Pr*
Mike Nale, *
EMP: 28 **EST:** 1926
SQ FT: 31,000
SALES (est): 2.92MM **Privately Held**
Web: www.thornburgmachine.com

Lincolnton - Lincoln County (G-9930)

SIC: 7692 3599 Welding repair; Machine shop, jobbing and repair

(G-9930)
TWO PERCENT LLC
204 N Laurel St (28092-3408)
P.O. Box 15 (28093-0015)
PHONE..................301 401-2750
Allison Levitt, *Prin*
EMP: 4 **EST:** 2015
SALES (est): 252.42K **Privately Held**
Web: www.barebites.com
SIC: 2048 Canned pet food (except dog and cat)

(G-9931)
UCS INC
Also Called: U C S
511 Hoffman Rd (28092-8230)
P.O. Box 657 (28093-0657)
PHONE..................704 732-9922
◆ **EMP:** 70 **EST:** 2005
SALES (est): 11.01MM **Privately Held**
Web: www.ucsspirit.com
SIC: 3949 Track and field athletic equipment

(G-9932)
UMI COMPANY INC
Also Called: Cemco
352 N Generals Blvd (28092-3557)
PHONE..................704 479-6210
Vince Hendrickson, *Mgr*
EMP: 9
SALES (corp-wide): 54.97MM **Privately Held**
Web: www.spantek.com
SIC: 3469 3449 Cash and stamp boxes, stamped metal; Miscellaneous metalwork
PA: Umi Company, Inc.
1520 5th St S
Hopkins MN 55343
952 935-8431

(G-9933)
UNITED CANVAS & SLING INC
Also Called: U C S
511 Hoffman Rd (28092-8230)
P.O. Box 657 (28093-0657)
PHONE..................704 732-9922
Jeffrey Schwartz, *Pr*
Lawrence Schwartz, *
Jason Schwartz, *
◆ **EMP:** 50 **EST:** 1967
SQ FT: 130,000
SALES (est): 9.67MM **Privately Held**
Web: www.ucsspirit.com
SIC: 3949 Track and field athletic equipment

(G-9934)
VT LEEBOY INC
Also Called: Leeboy
500 Lincoln County Parkway Ext (28092-6132)
P.O. Box 370 (28093-0370)
PHONE..................704 966-3300
Christopher A Barnard, *CEO*
William Robert Grail Junior, *Pr*
Kevin B Murphy, *CFO*
Scott S Thomas, *Sec*
◆ **EMP:** 120 **EST:** 1978
SQ FT: 150,000
SALES (est): 72.21MM **Privately Held**
Web: www.leeboy.com
SIC: 3531 Drags, road (construction and road maintenance equipment)
HQ: St Engineering North America, Inc.
99 Canal Center Plz # 220
Alexandria VA 22314
703 739-2610

(G-9935)
WALTER REYNOLDS (PA)
Also Called: T&J Sales
216 Old Lincolnton Crouse Rd (28092-7040)
P.O. Box 1858 (28093-1858)
PHONE..................704 735-6050
Walter Reynolds, *Owner*
EMP: 6 **EST:** 1994
SALES (est): 429.17K **Privately Held**
SIC: 2329 2339 5137 5136 Men's and boys' sportswear and athletic clothing; Women's and misses' athletic clothing and sportswear; Women's and children's clothing; Men's and boy's clothing

(G-9936)
WEST DYNAMICS US INC
1443 E Gaston St (28092-4401)
PHONE..................704 735-0009
Steve Turmaine, *Pr*
EMP: 30 **EST:** 2011
SALES (est): 8.21MM **Privately Held**
Web: www.mainfilter.com
SIC: 5084 3569 Industrial machinery and equipment; Assembly machines, non-metalworking

(G-9937)
ZWZ BEARING USA INC
Also Called: Zwz Bearing USA
1574 Startown Rd (28092-8040)
PHONE..................734 456-6206
Robert Waters, *Sls Mgr*
EMP: 22
SALES (corp-wide): 4.63MM **Privately Held**
Web: www.zwzamerica.com
SIC: 3366 Bushings and bearings
PA: Zwz Bearing Usa Inc.
535 Brea Canyon Rd
City Of Industry CA 91789
909 598-6238

Linden
Cumberland County

(G-9938)
A HOUSE OF HEMP LLC
235 Shepard Dr (28356-9589)
PHONE..................910 984-1441
Sheila Hill, *CEO*
EMP: 5 **EST:** 2019
SALES (est): 468.19K **Privately Held**
Web: www.ahouseofhemp.com
SIC: 2833 5999 5169 Botanical products, medicinal: ground, graded, or milled; Essential oils

(G-9939)
DAVID RAYNOR LOGGING INC
4718 Long St (28356-8008)
P.O. Box 70 (28356-0070)
PHONE..................910 980-0129
David Raynor, *Pr*
Sue Raynor, *Sec*
EMP: 22 **EST:** 1973
SALES (est): 2.46MM **Privately Held**
SIC: 2411 2426 2421 Logging camps and contractors; Hardwood dimension and flooring mills; Sawmills and planing mills, general

(G-9940)
DELTA CONTRACTORS INC
6309 Castlebrooke Ln (28356-8046)
P.O. Box 68 (28356-0068)
PHONE..................817 410-9481
Maria Madriz, *CEO*

EMP: 10 **EST:** 2009
SALES (est): 965.03K **Privately Held**
SIC: 2851 7363 Removers and cleaners; Temporary help service

(G-9941)
PAGES HYDRO DIPPING COATINGS
7455 Lane Rd (28356-9125)
PHONE..................910 322-2077
Stephen Page, *Prin*
EMP: 5 **EST:** 2017
SALES (est): 87.31K **Privately Held**
SIC: 3479 Metal coating and allied services

(G-9942)
SOLARA OF CAROLINAS
10255 Ramsey St (28356-8943)
PHONE..................910 723-1270
EMP: 4 **EST:** 2015
SALES (est): 95.58K **Privately Held**
Web: www.solaranc.com
SIC: 3999 Manufacturing industries, nec

Linwood
Davidson County

(G-9943)
EGGER WOOD PRODUCTS LLC
Also Called: Egger
300 Egger Pkwy (27299-9030)
PHONE..................336 843-7000
Gerald Jobst, *Managing Member*
Michael Egger, *
Fritz Egger, *
EMP: 284 **EST:** 2016
SALES (est): 80.78MM
SALES (corp-wide): 355.83K **Privately Held**
Web: www.egger.com
SIC: 2493 Particleboard, plastic laminated
PA: Egger Gmbh
Dollach 23
Liezen
361 282-6300

(G-9944)
EVERETTES COMPANY INC
4805 Old Linwood Rd (27299-9614)
P.O. Box 640 (27299-0640)
PHONE..................336 956-2097
Ronald M Everette, *Pr*
Geraldine Everette, *Pr*
EMP: 11 **EST:** 1978
SALES (est): 248.73K **Privately Held**
SIC: 3599 Machine shop, jobbing and repair

(G-9945)
FERGUSON COMPANIES
Also Called: Ferguson Fibers
1638 Clyde Fitzgerald Rd (27299-9264)
▲ **EMP:** 8 **EST:** 1972
SQ FT: 78,000
SALES (est): 905.92K **Privately Held**
SIC: 3552 3589 Textile machinery; Car washing machinery

(G-9946)
LIVENGOOD INNOVATIONS LLC
12068 S Nc Highway 150 (27299-9677)
PHONE..................336 925-7604
EMP: 4
SALES (est): 100.05K **Privately Held**
SIC: 1389 7389 Construction, repair, and dismantling services; Business Activities at Non-Commercial Site

(G-9947)
OLDE LEXINGTON PRODUCTS INC
480 Cedarwood Dr (27299)
P.O. Box 673 (27293-0673)
PHONE..................336 956-2355
Barry Sink, *Pr*
Renee Sink, *Sec*
EMP: 5 **EST:** 1990
SALES (est): 443.25K **Privately Held**
Web: www.oldelexington.com
SIC: 2431 5712 Moldings, wood: unfinished and prefinished; Furniture stores

Little Switzerland
Mcdowell County

(G-9948)
EMERALD VILLAGE INC
387 Mckinney Mine Rd (28749)
P.O. Box 98 (28749-0098)
PHONE..................828 765-6463
Robert Schabilion, *Pr*
Allan Schabilion, *Pr*
EMP: 12 **EST:** 1980
SQ FT: 40,000
SALES (est): 399.37K **Privately Held**
Web: www.emeraldvillage.com
SIC: 8412 1499 Museum; Gem stones (natural) mining, nec

Littleton
Halifax County

(G-9949)
89 INDUSTRIES
14711 Nc Highway 48 (27850-8979)
PHONE..................303 681-3188
Dean Gary, *Admn*
EMP: 6 **EST:** 2016
SALES (est): 39.69K **Privately Held**
SIC: 3999 Manufacturing industries, nec

(G-9950)
AIRBOSS HEATING AND COOLG INC
Also Called: Honeywell Authorized Dealer
127 W South Main St (27850-0046)
P.O. Box 25 (27850-0025)
PHONE..................252 586-0500
Joanne Lynch, *Prin*
EMP: 5 **EST:** 2004
SALES (est): 845.38K **Privately Held**
Web: www.airbossheatingandcooling.com
SIC: 3585 1711 Air conditioning units, complete: domestic or industrial; Plumbing, heating, air-conditioning

(G-9951)
ENTERPRISE LOGGERS COMPANY INC
681 Enterprise Rd (27850-8179)
PHONE..................252 586-4805
Burnice Hilliard, *Pr*
Teresa W Hilliard, *Sec*
Ronnie West, *VP*
Lynne West, *Treas*
EMP: 10 **EST:** 1987
SALES (est): 860.96K **Privately Held**
SIC: 2411 Logging camps and contractors

(G-9952)
GLOVERS WELDING LLC
638 Oak Grove Church Rd (27850)
P.O. Box 1109 (27850-1109)
PHONE..................252 586-7692
EMP: 10 **EST:** 2006
SQ FT: 8,000
SALES (est): 975.75K **Privately Held**

Web: www.gloverswelding.com
SIC: 7692 3441 Welding repair; Fabricated structural metal for ships

(G-9953)
STONE HOUSE CREEK LOGGING
615 Fleming Dairy Rd (27850-7722)
PHONE..................252 586-4477
EMP: 7 EST: 1997
SQ FT: 800
SALES (est): 522.88K Privately Held
SIC: 2411 Logging camps and contractors

(G-9954)
WOMACK PUBLISHING CO INC
Also Called: Lake Gaston Gazette
378 Lizard Creek Rd (27850-8390)
P.O. Box 1166 (27850-1166)
PHONE..................252 586-2700
EMP: 5
SALES (corp-wide): 21.7MM Privately Held
Web: www.womackpublishing.com
SIC: 2711 Newspapers: publishing only, not printed on site
PA: Womack Publishing Company, Inc.
    28 N Main St
    Chatham VA 24531
    434 432-2791

Locust
Stanly County

(G-9955)
CARNES-MILLER GEAR COMPANY INC
362 Browns Hill Rd (28097-6614)
P.O. Box 268 (28097-0268)
PHONE..................704 888-4448
Daniel M Tweed Junior, Pr
EMP: 17 EST: 1974
SQ FT: 20,000
SALES (est): 1.9MM Privately Held
Web: www.cmgear.us
SIC: 3599 Machine shop, jobbing and repair

(G-9956)
CHICAGO TUBE AND IRON COMPANY
Also Called: Chicago Tube and Iron
421 Browns Hill Rd (28097-6615)
P.O. Box 548 (28129-0548)
PHONE..................704 781-2060
Jerry Osborne, Brnch Mgr
EMP: 65
SALES (corp-wide): 2.16B Publicly Held
Web: www.chicagotube.com
SIC: 5051 7699 3498 3443 Steel; Boiler repair shop; Fabricated pipe and fittings; Fabricated plate work (boiler shop)
HQ: Chicago Tube And Iron Company
    1 Chicago Tube Dr
    Romeoville IL 60446
    815 834-2500

(G-9957)
DIARKIS LLC
142 Cara Ct (28097-9740)
PHONE..................704 888-5244
EMP: 4 EST: 2007
SQ FT: 500
SALES (est): 237.46K Privately Held
Web: www.diarkis.com
SIC: 2843 Surface active agents

(G-9958)
EAST COAST BAT COMPANY INC
8427 Dawson Ln (28097-9418)
PHONE..................704 305-3649
Derek Shoe, Prin
EMP: 4 EST: 2011
SALES (est): 92.73K Privately Held
Web: www.eastcoastbats.com
SIC: 3949 Bases, baseball

(G-9959)
ENZYME CUSTOMS
515 Redah Ave (28097-8708)
PHONE..................704 888-8278
Mason Mcnaught, Prin
EMP: 5 EST: 2013
SALES (est): 98.04K Privately Held
SIC: 2869 Enzymes

(G-9960)
FLEXTROL CORPORATION
192 Browns Hill Rd (28097-6609)
PHONE..................704 888-1120
Richard B Patterson, Pr
William R Patterson, Stockholder
EMP: 15 EST: 1982
SQ FT: 8,000
SALES (est): 2.35MM Privately Held
Web: www.flextrol.com
SIC: 3052 3568 Rubber hose; Joints and couplings

(G-9961)
KENZIE LAYNE COMPANY
506 Running Creek Ch Rd (28097-6213)
PHONE..................704 485-2282
Darryl Page, Pr
James Page, VP
EMP: 6 EST: 1993
SQ FT: 4,050
SALES (est): 767.61K Privately Held
SIC: 2511 Wood household furniture

(G-9962)
LOCUST MONUMENT LLC
713 Main St W (28097-9715)
P.O. Box 221 (28097-0221)
PHONE..................704 888-5600
Stan Dry, Owner
EMP: 5 EST: 1960
SALES (est): 354.86K Privately Held
Web: www.locustnc.com
SIC: 3281 Monuments, cut stone (not finishing or lettering only)

(G-9963)
LOUISE L NONA L C
25425 Rowland Rd (28097-7266)
PHONE..................704 242-0929
Taylor Gibson, Managing Member
EMP: 7 EST: 2019
SALES (est): 228.35K Privately Held
Web: www.nonalouisenc.com
SIC: 2395 Embroidery and art needlework

(G-9964)
NORMAC KITCHENS INC
607 N Central Ave (28097-7131)
PHONE..................704 485-1911
Robin Zaretsky, Brnch Mgr
EMP: 49
SALES (corp-wide): 29.62MM Privately Held
Web: www.normackitchens.com
SIC: 3553 Cabinet makers' machinery
HQ: Normac Kitchens, Inc.
    226 S Main St
    Oakboro NC 28129

(G-9965)
OHILDA BOMBARDIER
221 Woodwinds St (28097-8510)
PHONE..................704 658-7134
EMP: 4 EST: 2017

SALES (est): 69.9K Privately Held
SIC: 3743 Railroad equipment

(G-9966)
PSI LIQUIDATING INC
605 N Central Ave Ste A (28097-7312)
PHONE..................704 888-9930
Christopher Meurett, Pr
EMP: 7 EST: 2006
SALES (est): 939.33K Privately Held
Web: www.powerstreamindustries.com
SIC: 3599 Machine shop, jobbing and repair

(G-9967)
READY MIX OF CAROLINAS INC
364 Browns Hill Rd (28097-6614)
P.O. Box 325 (28097-0325)
PHONE..................704 888-3027
EMP: 26 EST: 2015
SALES (est): 9.47MM Privately Held
Web: ready-mix-of-the-carolinas-inc.business.site
SIC: 3273 Ready-mixed concrete

(G-9968)
RED AAMEROSA LEATHERWORKS LLC
26381 Red Barn Trl (28097-7260)
PHONE..................717 991-0308
Hanna Turner, Prin
EMP: 5 EST: 2019
SALES (est): 61.31K Privately Held
SIC: 3199 Leather goods, nec

(G-9969)
REDY MIX OF CAROLINAS INC
364 Browns Hill Rd (28097-6614)
P.O. Box 325 (28097-0325)
PHONE..................704 888-2224
Rick Alexander, Pr
EMP: 7 EST: 2015
SALES (est): 808.97K Privately Held
Web: ready-mix-of-the-carolinas-inc.business.site
SIC: 3273 Ready-mixed concrete

(G-9970)
SERVICE ELECTRIC AND CONTROL
703 Redah Ave (28097-8712)
P.O. Box 969 (28097-0969)
PHONE..................704 888-5100
Ronald Wolfarth, Pr
EMP: 7 EST: 2012
SALES (est): 991.61K Privately Held
Web: www.seac-inc.com
SIC: 3699 1731 Electrical equipment and supplies, nec; Electrical work

(G-9971)
SOUTHERN ESTATES METAL ROOFING
614 Maple St (28097-9447)
PHONE..................704 245-2023
Zack Criscoe, Pr
EMP: 4 EST: 1996
SALES (est): 187.29K Privately Held
SIC: 1389 1761 Construction, repair, and dismantling services; Roofing contractor

(G-9972)
STEEL CONSTRUCT SYSTEMS LLC
118 Pine Forest Rd (28097-9404)
PHONE..................704 781-5575
EMP: 20 EST: 2011
SALES (est): 2.42MM Privately Held
Web: www.lgscs.com
SIC: 3441 Fabricated structural metal

(G-9973)
STREETS AUTO SALES & FOUR WD
814 Main St W (28097-9716)
PHONE..................704 888-8686
EMP: 4 EST: 2011
SALES (est): 94.06K Privately Held
SIC: 5511 5012 3711 New and used car dealers; Busses; Buses, all types, assembly of

(G-9974)
T W HATHCOCK LOGGING INC
25341 Millingport Rd (28097-8327)
PHONE..................704 485-9457
Todd Hathcock, Prin
EMP: 7 EST: 2010
SALES (est): 244.84K Privately Held
SIC: 2411 Logging

(G-9975)
TARHEEL MARBLE COMPANY INC
123 Jefferson Dr (28097-9527)
PHONE..................704 888-6003
EMP: 14 EST: 1996
SALES (est): 663.84K Privately Held
Web: www.tarheelmarble.com
SIC: 3281 5032 Marble, building: cut and shaped; Marble building stone

(G-9976)
UFP SITE BUILT LLC
Also Called: Ufp Mid-Atlantic
147 Locust Level Dr (28097-8715)
PHONE..................704 781-2520
Corie Misenheimer, Brnch Mgr
EMP: 52
SALES (corp-wide): 7.22B Publicly Held
Web: www.ufpi.com
SIC: 2439 Trusses, except roof: laminated lumber
HQ: Ufp Site Built, Llc
    2801 E Beltline Ave Ne
    Grand Rapids MI 49525
    616 634-6161

(G-9977)
UNITED PROTECTIVE TECH LLC
142 Cara Ct (28097-9740)
P.O. Box 1149 (28097-1149)
PHONE..................704 888-2470
EMP: 20 EST: 2002
SQ FT: 20,000
SALES (est): 3MM Privately Held
Web: www.upt-usa.com
SIC: 3842 Clothing, fire resistant and protective

Louisburg
Franklin County

(G-9978)
ADVANTAGE MARKETING
129 Bartholomew Rd (27549-8267)
PHONE..................919 872-8610
John A Parrish, Owner
EMP: 4 EST: 1984
SALES (est): 171.72K Privately Held
SIC: 2759 Screen printing

(G-9979)
ALBERT E MANN
106 Clifton Ridge Ct (27549-9030)
PHONE..................919 497-0815
Albert Mann, Ch
EMP: 4 EST: 2016
SALES (est): 67K Privately Held
SIC: 3571 Electronic computers

Louisburg - Franklin County (G-9980)

(G-9980)
BLACK BUSINESS UNIVERSE LLC
113 Fox Park Rd (27549-8704)
PHONE.....................215 279-1509
Kianna Foster, *CEO*
EMP: 5 **EST:** 2020
SALES (est): 375.48K **Privately Held**
SIC: 2741 Internet publishing and broadcasting

(G-9981)
BRODIE-JONES PRINTING CO INC
Also Called: Finch's Print Shop
253 Ronald Tharrington Rd (27549-7418)
PHONE.....................252 438-7992
Thomas Finch, *Pr*
EMP: 5 **EST:** 1972
SALES (est): 481.39K **Privately Held**
SIC: 2752 Offset printing

(G-9982)
CAROLINA DESIGN & MFG INC
Also Called: CDM Wireless
239 Wiggins Rd (27549-9161)
P.O. Box 865 (27596-0865)
PHONE.....................919 554-1823
Thomas G Albright, *CEO*
EMP: 5 **EST:** 2006
SALES (est): 681.72K **Privately Held**
Web: www.cdmwireless.com
SIC: 3663 Radio and t.v. communications equipment

(G-9983)
CHEMTECH INDUSTRIAL INC
61 T Kemp Rd (27549-6707)
PHONE.....................919 400-5743
EMP: 9 **EST:** 2010
SQ FT: 37,000
SALES (est): 1.02MM **Privately Held**
SIC: 2869 Industrial organic chemicals, nec

(G-9984)
DANA INDUSTRIES
Timberlake Rd (27549)
PHONE.....................919 496-3262
EMP: 6 **EST:** 1996
SALES (est): 185.7K **Privately Held**
Web: www.danaindustries.com
SIC: 3823 Industrial flow and liquid measuring instruments

(G-9985)
DEFENSE OF IMPLICIT
144 S Creek Dr (27549-9736)
PHONE.....................919 554-2735
Russell Reed, *Owner*
EMP: 5 **EST:** 2017
SALES (est): 185.51K **Privately Held**
SIC: 3812 Defense systems and equipment

(G-9986)
EASTERN CORNERSTONE CNSTR LLC
105 S Creek Dr (27549-9736)
PHONE.....................919 702-3583
Robert Stitt, *Prin*
EMP: 6 **EST:** 2019
SALES (est): 361.7K **Privately Held**
SIC: 2431 Millwork

(G-9987)
EN FLEUR CORPORATION
Also Called: Paramason
124 Fairview Rd (27549-9792)
PHONE.....................919 556-1623
Brenda D Lewis, *Pr*
EMP: 5 **EST:** 1984
SALES (est): 339.61K **Privately Held**

SIC: 7372 Prepackaged software

(G-9988)
FRANKLIN COUNTY NEWSPAPERS INC
Also Called: Franklin Times
109 S Bickett Blvd (27549-2468)
P.O. Box 119 (27549-0119)
PHONE.....................919 496-6503
Gary R Cunard, *Pr*
EMP: 13 **EST:** 1952
SALES (est): 300.38K **Privately Held**
Web: www.thefranklintimes.com
SIC: 2711 Newspapers, publishing and printing

(G-9989)
FRED R HARRRIS LOGGING INC
527 Schloss Rd (27549-8037)
PHONE.....................919 853-2266
Fred R Harris, *Pr*
Rachel Harris, *Sec*
EMP: 6 **EST:** 1975
SALES (est): 522.06K **Privately Held**
SIC: 2411 Logging camps and contractors

(G-9990)
H&M WOODWORKS INC
504 S Bickett Blvd (27549-2804)
PHONE.....................919 496-5993
John Daniel, *Pr*
EMP: 10 **EST:** 2020
SALES (est): 1.08MM **Privately Held**
Web: www.hmwoodworksnc.com
SIC: 2431 Millwork

(G-9991)
HUNT LOGGING CO
2233 Person Rd (27549-8030)
PHONE.....................919 853-2850
James T Hunt, *Pt*
Lonnie Hunt, *Pt*
EMP: 4 **EST:** 1984
SALES (est): 277.34K **Privately Held**
SIC: 2411 Logging

(G-9992)
INTEGRITY WELDING LLC
75 Eastwind Rd (27549-6445)
PHONE.....................919 556-5144
Daniel Jeremiah Erb, *Owner*
EMP: 5 **EST:** 2017
SALES (est): 130.52K **Privately Held**
SIC: 7692 Welding repair

(G-9993)
JIMMY D NELMS LOGGING INC
Also Called: Jimmie Nelms Trucking
4021 Nc 561 Hwy (27549-9677)
PHONE.....................919 853-2597
Jimmie D Nelms, *Pr*
EMP: 10 **EST:** 1968
SALES (est): 411.9K **Privately Held**
SIC: 2411 Logging camps and contractors

(G-9994)
NORTH STATE STEEL INC
Also Called: North State Steel At Louisburg
1801 Nc 98 Hwy W (27549-7612)
PHONE.....................919 496-2506
EMP: 16
SALES (corp-wide): 10.24MM **Privately Held**
Web: www.northstatesteel.com
SIC: 3441 Building components, structural steel
PA: North State Steel, Inc.
1010 W Gum Rd
Greenville NC 27834
252 830-8884

(G-9995)
PACKO BOTTLING INC
Also Called: Bobbees Bottling
42 Golden Leaf Dr (27549-2853)
PHONE.....................919 496-4286
Jack Pyritz, *Pr*
Patty Pyritz, *VP*
◆ **EMP:** 20 **EST:** 1982
SQ FT: 89,000
SALES (est): 6.79MM **Privately Held**
Web: www.bobbeesbottling.com
SIC: 2086 Bottled and canned soft drinks

(G-9996)
PALZIV NORTH AMERICA INC
Also Called: Palziv North America
7966 Nc 56 Hwy (27549-8633)
PHONE.....................919 497-0010
Paul Robertson, *COO*
Rick Merkley, *
▲ **EMP:** 190 **EST:** 2008
SQ FT: 200,000
SALES (est): 49.28MM **Privately Held**
Web: www.palzivna.com
SIC: 3086 Packaging and shipping materials, foamed plastics
PA: Palziv Ein Hanaziv Agricultural Coop Society Ltd.
Kibbutz
Ein Hanatziv 10805

(G-9997)
PUETT TRUCKING & LOGGING
1796 Person Rd (27549-7936)
PHONE.....................919 853-2071
Gene Puett, *Owner*
EMP: 5 **EST:** 1988
SALES (est): 315.35K **Privately Held**
SIC: 2411 Logging camps and contractors

(G-9998)
QUALITY PRECAST INC
100 Gayline Dr (27549-8612)
PHONE.....................919 497-0660
Roland Lindsay, *Pr*
Timothy Gessaman, *VP*
Linda Lindsay, *Treas*
EMP: 5 **EST:** 2003
SALES (est): 1.02MM
SALES (corp-wide): 98.36MM **Privately Held**
SIC: 3272 Precast terrazzo or concrete products
PA: Lindsay Precast, Llc
6845 Erie Ave Nw
Canal Fulton OH 44614
800 837-7788

(G-9999)
REGIMENTAL FLAG & T SHIRTS
29 Secession Ln (27549-7065)
PHONE.....................919 496-2888
Jane Langley, *Owner*
EMP: 5 **EST:** 2002
SALES (est): 248.97K **Privately Held**
Web: www.kudzutshirts.com
SIC: 2396 Screen printing on fabric articles

(G-10000)
RICHARD C JONES
Also Called: B J Logging
7823 Nc 561 Hwy (27549-8862)
PHONE.....................919 853-2096
Richard Jones, *Owner*
EMP: 8 **EST:** 1997
SQ FT: 1,620
SALES (est): 403.89K **Privately Held**
SIC: 2411 Logging camps and contractors

(G-10001)
SANDY CREEK WOODWORKS
115 Leonard Rd (27549-8414)
PHONE.....................919 853-3415
Dennis Hess, *Prin*
EMP: 4 **EST:** 2010
SALES (est): 137.83K **Privately Held**
Web: www.sandycreekwwks.com
SIC: 2431 Millwork

(G-10002)
SMITHS MOWER MARINE & WLDG LLC
1149 Ronald Tharrington Rd (27549-7411)
PHONE.....................919 729-0070
George Smith, *Prin*
EMP: 5 **EST:** 2016
SALES (est): 67.44K **Privately Held**
SIC: 7692 Welding repair

(G-10003)
SWEET TEES SCREEN PRINTING LLC
651 Woodland Trl (27549-9339)
P.O. Box 338 (27549-0338)
PHONE.....................919 497-0500
Alice Riggan, *Prin*
EMP: 4 **EST:** 2010
SALES (est): 150.72K **Privately Held**
Web: www.sweetteesnc.com
SIC: 2759 Screen printing

(G-10004)
TAR RIVER THINNING INC
176 Paul Sledge Rd (27549-7040)
PHONE.....................919 497-1647
David Jones, *Pr*
Rebecca Jones, *
EMP: 12 **EST:** 2001
SALES (est): 456.54K **Privately Held**
SIC: 2411 Logging camps and contractors

(G-10005)
TONEY LUMBER COMPANY INC
309 Bunn Rd (27549-2707)
P.O. Box 447 (27549-0447)
PHONE.....................919 496-5711
Roger Melvin, *Pr*
Elizabeth Toney Melvin, *
Susan Toney, *
Conrad Sturges, *
EMP: 68 **EST:** 1948
SQ FT: 2,600
SALES (est): 23.16MM **Privately Held**
Web: www.toneyhardware.com
SIC: 5031 2421 Lumber: rough, dressed, and finished; Sawmills and planing mills, general

(G-10006)
WOOD BARN INC (PA)
206 Clifton Ridge Ct (27549-9031)
P.O. Box 819 (27549-0819)
PHONE.....................919 496-6714
Jerry Faulkner, *Pr*
EMP: 20 **EST:** 1992
SQ FT: 150,000
SALES (est): 1.8MM **Privately Held**
Web: www.woodbarn.com
SIC: 2431 Staircases and stairs, wood

Lowell
Gaston County

(G-10007)
CHOICE USA BEVERAGE INC (PA)
Also Called: Sun-Drop Bottling Co
603 Groves St (28098-1702)
PHONE.....................704 823-1651

GEOGRAPHIC SECTION

Lumberton - Robeson County (G-10030)

James P Falls Senior, *Ch Bd*
Linda Medley, *
Sam L Robinson, *
J Falls Junior, *Owner*
EMP: 75 **EST:** 1933
SQ FT: 18,000
SALES (est): 30.99MM
SALES (corp-wide): 30.99MM **Privately Held**
Web: www.choiceusabeverage.com
SIC: 2086 2087 Carbonated beverages, nonalcoholic; pkged. in cans, bottles; Syrups, drink

(G-10008)
FRYEDAY COFFEE ROASTERS LLC
106 E 1st St Unit B (28098-1573)
PHONE.................................704 879-9083
Alisa Frye, *Managing Member*
EMP: 6 **EST:** 2017
SALES (est): 178.13K **Privately Held**
Web: www.fryedaycoffeeroasters.com
SIC: 2095 Coffee roasting (except by wholesale grocers)

(G-10009)
IMPERIAL PRINTING PDTS CO INC
141 Robins St (28098-1940)
P.O. Box 240905 (28224-0905)
PHONE.................................704 554-1188
Stuart Cojac, *Pr*
EMP: 20 **EST:** 1936
SQ FT: 25,000
SALES (est): 375.46K **Privately Held**
SIC: 2752 Offset printing

(G-10010)
INDIAN MOTORCYCLE COMPANY
Also Called: Indian Motorcycle Charlotte
110 Indian Walk (28098-2030)
PHONE.................................704 879-4560
EMP: 7
SALES (corp-wide): 8.93B **Publicly Held**
Web: www.indianmotorcyclecharlotte.com
SIC: 3751 7699 Motorcycles and related parts; Motorcycle repair service
HQ: Indian Motorcycle Company
2100 Highway 55
Hamel MN 55340
763 542-0500

(G-10011)
S & L CREATIONS INC
120 E 1st St (28098-1573)
P.O. Box 334 (28098-0334)
PHONE.................................704 824-1930
James F Smith, *Pr*
Pamela Smith, *Sec*
EMP: 5 **EST:** 1984
SQ FT: 2,700
SALES (est): 369.63K **Privately Held**
SIC: 2261 5999 Screen printing of cotton broadwoven fabrics; Trophies and plaques

(G-10012)
U S ALLOY CO
Also Called: Washington Alloy
825 Groves St (28098-1706)
PHONE.................................888 522-8296
Joe Dearborn, *Mgr*
EMP: 16
SALES (corp-wide): 13.17MM **Privately Held**
Web: www.washingtonalloy.com
SIC: 3548 Welding wire, bare and coated
PA: U. S. Alloy Co.
8885 White Oak Ave Ste 10
Rancho Cucamonga CA 91730
800 830-9033

Lowgap
Surry County

(G-10013)
G & G LOGGING
401 Ramey Orchard Rd (27024-9255)
PHONE.................................336 352-5586
EMP: 5 **EST:** 2017
SALES (est): 83.69K **Privately Held**
SIC: 2411 Logging camps and contractors

Lowland
Pamlico County

(G-10014)
LOWLAND SEAFOOD INC
569 Kelly Watson Rd (28552-9653)
PHONE.................................252 745-3751
Carol Potter, *Pr*
EMP: 7 **EST:** 1975
SALES (est): 553.08K **Privately Held**
SIC: 5146 2092 Seafoods; Fresh or frozen packaged fish

(G-10015)
TRAWLER INCORPORATED
569 Kelly Watson Rd (28552-9653)
PHONE.................................252 745-3751
Carol Potter, *Prin*
EMP: 7 **EST:** 2002
SALES (est): 174.49K **Privately Held**
SIC: 3732 Fishing boats: lobster, crab, oyster, etc.: small

Lucama
Wilson County

(G-10016)
CRAFTEX REWORK INC
500 Woodcrest St (27851-9153)
P.O. Box 146 (27851-0146)
PHONE.................................252 239-0123
Bobby O'neal, *Prin*
EMP: 6 **EST:** 2005
SALES (est): 103.29K **Privately Held**
SIC: 2389 Academic vestments (caps and gowns)

(G-10017)
JOHNSON INDUSTRIAL MCHY SVCS
7160 Us Highway 117 (27851-8805)
P.O. Box 3877 (27895-3877)
PHONE.................................252 239-1944
Jimmy R Johnson, *Pr*
Lynda Johnson, *
Angela Fulghum, *
EMP: 25 **EST:** 1972
SQ FT: 7,500
SALES (est): 1.88MM **Privately Held**
Web: www.jimsinc.net
SIC: 1796 3523 3599 Machinery installation; Farm machinery and equipment; Machine shop, jobbing and repair

(G-10018)
R & J ROAD SERVICE INC
5014 Saint Marys Church Rd (27851-9699)
PHONE.................................252 239-1404
Rufus Gallyn, *Pr*
EMP: 4 **EST:** 2005
SALES (est): 727.18K **Privately Held**
Web: www.rjroadservice.com
SIC: 3669 Emergency alarms

(G-10019)
WORLD OF RC PARTS
5320 Us Highway 301 (27851-9533)
PHONE.................................252 291-4088
Chad Bunn, *Owner*
EMP: 8 **EST:** 2005
SALES (est): 405.3K **Privately Held**
Web: www.worldofrcparts.com
SIC: 3944 5092 Board games, puzzles, and models, except electronic; Model kits

Lumber Bridge
Robeson County

(G-10020)
MOUNTAIRE FARMS LLC
Also Called: Mountaire Farms, L.L.C.
17269 N Carolina Hwy 71 (28357-8089)
PHONE.................................910 843-5942
EMP: 124
SALES (corp-wide): 2.07B **Privately Held**
Web: www.mountaire.com
SIC: 2015 Poultry slaughtering and processing
HQ: Mountaire Farms Inc.
1901 Napa Valley Dr
Little Rock AR 72212
501 372-6524

(G-10021)
MOUNTAIRE FARMS LLC
Also Called: Piedmont Poultry
17269 Nc 71 Hwy N (28357)
P.O. Box 129 (28357-0129)
PHONE.................................910 843-3332
EMP: 139
SALES (corp-wide): 2.07B **Privately Held**
Web: www.mountaire.com
SIC: 2015 Poultry slaughtering and processing
HQ: Mountaire Farms Inc.
1901 Napa Valley Dr
Little Rock AR 72212
501 372-6524

(G-10022)
MOUNTAIRE FARMS INC
17269 Hwy 71 (28357)
P.O. Box 339 (28357-0339)
PHONE.................................910 843-5942
EMP: 825
SALES (corp-wide): 2.07B **Privately Held**
Web: www.mountaire.com
SIC: 2015 Poultry slaughtering and processing
HQ: Mountaire Farms Inc.
1901 Napa Valley Dr
Little Rock AR 72212
501 372-6524

Lumberton
Robeson County

(G-10023)
ADAMS BEVERAGES NC LLC
Also Called: Adams Beverages Lumberton
797 Caton Rd (28360-0457)
PHONE.................................910 738-8165
Casey Cranor, *Mgr*
EMP: 75
SALES (corp-wide): 11.91MM **Privately Held**
Web: www.adamsbeverages.net
SIC: 2084 Wine coolers (beverages)
PA: Adams Beverages Of North Carolina, Llc
7505 Statesville Rd
Charlotte NC 28269
704 509-3000

(G-10024)
ALAMAC AMERICAN KNITS LLC
1885 Alamac Rd (28358-8859)
P.O. Box 1347 (28359-1347)
PHONE.................................910 618-2248
◆ **EMP:** 240
Web: www.alamacknits.com
SIC: 2211 Broadwoven fabric mills, cotton

(G-10025)
ALLENS GUTTER SERVICE
209 T P Rd (28358-7897)
PHONE.................................910 738-9509
Jerry C Allen, *Owner*
EMP: 5 **EST:** 1978
SQ FT: 5,000
SALES (est): 230.34K **Privately Held**
SIC: 1761 5051 3444 Gutter and downspout contractor; Metals service centers and offices; Sheet metalwork

(G-10026)
ASBURY GRAPHITE MILLS
191 Magna Blvd (28360-4807)
PHONE.................................910 671-4141
EMP: 8 **EST:** 2019
SALES (est): 748.57K **Privately Held**
Web: www.asbury.com
SIC: 3624 Carbon and graphite products

(G-10027)
BFT LUMBERTON OPS CORP
Also Called: Bft Lumberton
1000 Noir St (28358-6660)
PHONE.................................910 737-3200
James Posa, *CEO*
▲ **EMP:** 30 **EST:** 1968
SQ FT: 150,000
SALES (est): 5.32MM **Privately Held**
SIC: 2611 Pulp produced from non-wood fiber base, nec
HQ: Bast Fibre Technologies Usa Inc.
148 River St Ste 202
Greenville SC 29601
778 433-2278

(G-10028)
BUNZL PROCESSOR DIST LLC
124 Hornets Rd (28358-5879)
PHONE.................................910 738-8111
James Jacobs, *Mgr*
EMP: 9
SALES (corp-wide): 14.5B **Privately Held**
Web: www.bunzlpd.com
SIC: 5046 5084 3565 Restaurant equipment and supplies, nec; Industrial machinery and equipment; Packaging machinery
HQ: Bunzl Processor Distribution, Llc
5710 Nw 41st St
Riverside MO 64150
816 448-4300

(G-10029)
CAROLINA MNUFACTURED HOMES LLC
Also Called: Carolina Homes
386 Brookgreen Dr (28358-2618)
PHONE.................................910 374-6889
EMP: 4 **EST:** 2020
SALES (est): 39.69K **Privately Held**
SIC: 3999 Manufacturing industries, nec

(G-10030)
CONTEMPORA FABRICS INC
351 Contempora Dr (28358-0445)
PHONE.................................910 345-0150
Ronald Roach, *Pr*
Carey M Read, *
Gerald Cauthen, *PROD**
EMP: 145 **EST:** 1972

Lumberton - Robeson County (G-10031) — GEOGRAPHIC SECTION

SQ FT: 150,000
SALES (est): 23.02MM **Privately Held**
Web: www.contemporafabrics.com
SIC: **2253** 5949 2257 Dresses and skirts; Sewing, needlework, and piece goods; Weft knit fabric mills

(G-10031)
DANGELICO GUITARS
4111 W 5th St (28358-0411)
PHONE..................908 451-9606
John M Ferolito, *CEO*
EMP: 6 EST: 2014
SALES (est): 170.07K **Privately Held**
Web: www.dangelicoguitars.com
SIC: **3931** Guitars and parts, electric and nonelectric

(G-10032)
DUE PROCESS STABLE TRDG CO LLC
4111 W 5th St (28358-0411)
PHONE..................910 608-0284
David Grasse, *Managing Member*
▲ EMP: 25 EST: 2004
SALES (est): 2.28MM **Privately Held**
SIC: **2273** 1771 Carpets and rugs; Flooring contractor

(G-10033)
EARNHARDT MANUFACTURING
606 E 1st St (28358-5838)
PHONE..................910 738-9426
Monroe William, *Prin*
Monroe William, *Mgr*
EMP: 6 EST: 2009
SALES (est): 244.95K **Privately Held**
SIC: **3999** Manufacturing industries, nec

(G-10034)
ELKAY OHIO PLUMBING PDTS CO
880 Caton Rd (28360-0458)
PHONE..................910 739-8181
EMP: 3525
Web: www.elkay.com
SIC: **3431** Sinks: enameled iron, cast iron, or pressed metal
HQ: Elkay Ohio Plumbing Products Company
    7634 New West Rd
    Toledo OH 43617
    419 841-1820

(G-10035)
EXPRESSIVE SCREEN PRINTING
504 Peterson Dr (28358-2600)
PHONE..................910 739-3221
EMP: 4 EST: 1983
SQ FT: 3,000
SALES (est): 205.97K **Privately Held**
SIC: **2759** 2396 Screen printing; Automotive and apparel trimmings

(G-10036)
FAITH COMPUTER REPAIRS
3404 Nc Highway 211 W (28360-3571)
PHONE..................910 730-1731
EMP: 6 EST: 2011
SQ FT: 2,000
SALES (est): 240K **Privately Held**
SIC: **3577** Computer peripheral equipment, nec

(G-10037)
FEX STRAW MANUFACTURING INC
191 Magna Blvd (28360-4807)
PHONE..................910 671-4141
Jim Mcalpine, *Pr*
▲ EMP: 7 EST: 2003
SALES (est): 217.19K **Privately Held**
SIC: **2399** Horse and pet accessories, textile

(G-10038)
FLO-TITE INC VALVES & CONTRLS
4815 W 5th St (28358-0425)
P.O. Box 1293 (28359-1293)
PHONE..................910 738-8904
Martin Gibbons, *CEO*
▲ EMP: 47 EST: 2004
SALES (est): 18MM **Privately Held**
Web: www.flotite.com
SIC: **3492** 5085 Control valves, aircraft: hydraulic and pneumatic; Valves and fittings

(G-10039)
GUNMAR MACHINE CORPORATION
310 Hines St (28358-6624)
PHONE..................910 738-6295
Dennis Martin, *Pr*
Joanne Martin, *Sec*
EMP: 10 EST: 1972
SQ FT: 7,900
SALES (est): 916.94K **Privately Held**
SIC: **3599** 7692 Machine shop, jobbing and repair; Welding repair

(G-10040)
INTERNATIONAL PAPER COMPANY
Also Called: International Paper
2060 W 5th St (28358-5453)
PHONE..................910 738-8930
EMP: 5
SALES (corp-wide): 18.92B **Publicly Held**
Web: www.internationalpaper.com
SIC: **2621** Paper mills
PA: International Paper Company
    6400 Poplar Ave
    Memphis TN 38197
    901 419-7000

(G-10041)
INTERNATIONAL PAPER COMPANY
International Paper
820 Caton Rd (28360-0458)
PHONE..................910 738-6214
Mark Witt, *Genl Mgr*
EMP: 89
SALES (corp-wide): 18.92B **Publicly Held**
Web: www.internationalpaper.com
SIC: **2653** Boxes, corrugated: made from purchased materials
PA: International Paper Company
    6400 Poplar Ave
    Memphis TN 38197
    901 419-7000

(G-10042)
J&B WELDING LLC
2188 Moores Ln (28358-8695)
PHONE..................910 316-5838
Mauro Vazquez Nava, *Prin*
EMP: 5 EST: 2019
SALES (est): 25.09K **Privately Held**
SIC: **7692** Welding repair

(G-10043)
KR PUBLICATIONS
4100 Nelson Way (28360-9102)
PHONE..................910 852-1525
Kadan Thompson, *Owner*
EMP: 4 EST: 2018
SALES (est): 99.81K **Privately Held**
SIC: **2731** Books, publishing only

(G-10044)
MELODIA GOODS AND EMBROIDERY
1306 Redwood Ct (28358-2335)
PHONE..................910 674-3934
Adina Morando, *Prin*
EMP: 4 EST: 2017
SALES (est): 49.58K **Privately Held**
Web: melodia.espwebsite.com
SIC: **2395** Embroidery and art needlework

(G-10045)
MILITARY WRAPS INC
Also Called: Mw Defense Systems
3400a David St (28358-6900)
PHONE..................910 671-0008
Trevor Kracker, *Pr*
EMP: 10 EST: 2007
SALES (est): 480.63K **Privately Held**
Web: www.militarywraps.com
SIC: **2824** Vinyl fibers

(G-10046)
NUCOR HARRIS REBAR NC INC
Also Called: NUCOR HARRIS REBAR NORTH CAROLINA INC.
2790 Kenny Biggs Rd (28358-3771)
PHONE..................910 739-9747
EMP: 117
SALES (corp-wide): 50.22MM **Privately Held**
Web: www.harrisrebar.com
SIC: **3441** Fabricated structural metal
HQ: Nucor Rebar Fabrication North Carolina Inc.
    803 S Market St
    Benson NC 27504
    919 894-3900

(G-10047)
NYP CORP FRMRLY NEW YRKR-PTERS
Ampack
299 Osterneck Robetex Dr (28358-0804)
PHONE..................910 739-4403
Chris Labelle, *Brnch Mgr*
EMP: 10
SALES (corp-wide): 32.82MM **Privately Held**
Web: www.nyp-corp.com
SIC: **2393** Textile bags
PA: Nyp Corp. (Formerly New Yorker-Peters Corporation)
    1640 Vauxhall Rd
    Union NJ 07083
    908 351-6550

(G-10048)
PERDUE FARMS INC
Also Called: PERDUE FARMS INC.
1801 Godwin Ave (28358-3193)
PHONE..................910 738-8581
W Parker, *Pr*
EMP: 24
SALES (corp-wide): 1.24B **Privately Held**
Web: www.perdue.com
SIC: **2015** Poultry slaughtering and processing
PA: Perdue Farms Incorporated
    31149 Old Ocean City Rd
    Salisbury MD 21804
    800 473-7383

(G-10049)
QUICKIE MANUFACTURING CORP
2880 Kenny Biggs Rd (28358-6332)
PHONE..................910 737-6500
Bob Carson, *VP*
EMP: 147
SALES (corp-wide): 8.13B **Publicly Held**
Web: www.quickie.com
SIC: **3991** 2392 Brooms and brushes; Mops, floor and dust
HQ: Quickie Manufacturing Corp
    3124 Valley Ave
    Winchester VA 22601
    856 829-7900

(G-10050)
QUIK PRINT INC
232 E 4th St (28358-5525)
P.O. Box 805 (28359-0805)
PHONE..................910 738-6775
Betty M Evans, *Pr*
EMP: 6 EST: 1985
SQ FT: 4,500
SALES (est): 536.53K **Privately Held**
SIC: **2752** 2759 Offset printing; Commercial printing, nec

(G-10051)
REMPAC LLC
2005 Starlite Dr (28358-6951)
PHONE..................910 737-6557
Mike Vanepen, *Dir Opers*
EMP: 33
SALES (corp-wide): 16.29MM **Privately Held**
Web: www.rempac.com
SIC: **3069** 3053 Sponge rubber and sponge rubber products; Gaskets; packing and sealing devices
PA: Rempac Llc
    370 W Passaic St Ste A
    Rochelle Park NJ 07662
    201 843-4585

(G-10052)
RIVERBANK SCREEN PRINTING CO
470 Sherwood Rd (28358-9189)
PHONE..................910 248-4647
EMP: 4 EST: 2015
SALES (est): 55.47K **Privately Held**
Web: www.riverbankscreenprinting.com
SIC: **2752** Commercial printing, lithographic

(G-10053)
ROBETEX INC (PA)
2504 Fayetteville Rd (28358-3114)
P.O. Box 1489 (30740-1489)
PHONE..................910 671-8787
David G Talbot, *Ch Bd*
Cary Talbot, *Pr*
John Moravec, *Sec*
Kerry Talbot, *Prin*
▲ EMP: 19 EST: 1994
SALES (est): 4.75MM **Privately Held**
Web: www.robetexinc.com
SIC: **3089** 3083 3082 Reinforcing mesh, plastics; Laminated plastics plate and sheet ; Unsupported plastics profile shapes

(G-10054)
ROGERS SCREENPRINTING EMB INC
1988 N Roberts Ave (28358-3120)
PHONE..................910 738-6208
Keith Rogers, *Brnch Mgr*
EMP: 5
SALES (corp-wide): 2.37MM **Privately Held**
Web: www.rogersseinc.com
SIC: **2759** Screen printing
PA: Rogers Screenprinting & Embroidery, Inc.
    10306 Nc Highway 41 S
    Fairmont NC 28340
    910 628-1983

(G-10055)
SOUTHEASTERN OUTDOOR PDTS INC
1825 N Roberts Ave (28358-3117)
P.O. Box 779 (28329-0779)
PHONE..................910 608-0015
Henry Lawson, *Pr*
Owen D White, *Sec*
EMP: 30 EST: 1997

▲ = Import ▼ = Export
◆ = Import/Export

SALES (est): 2.12MM **Privately Held**
Web: www.qualityoutdoor.net
SIC: 3448 Garages, portable: prefabricated metal

(G-10056)
SUMMIT LOGGING LLC
1485 Beulah Church Rd (28358-8115)
PHONE................................910 734-8787
Thomas L Odum, *Prin*
EMP: 7 **EST:** 2014
SALES (est): 218.71K **Privately Held**
SIC: 2411 Logging

(G-10057)
TAYLCO INC
Also Called: Green State Landscape & Nrsry
2643 W Carthage Rd (28360-8859)
PHONE................................910 739-0405
Myra Norton, *Pr*
G Keith Taylor, *
Myra T Norton, *
EMP: 30 **EST:** 1985
SQ FT: 4,000
SALES (est): 4.33MM **Privately Held**
SIC: 3271 0181 0782 1711 Blocks, concrete; landscape or retaining wall; Flowers: grown under cover (e.g., greenhouse production); Landscape contractors; Irrigation sprinkler system installation

(G-10058)
TITAN FLOW CONTROL INC (PA)
290 Corporate Dr (28358-1110)
P.O. Box 7408 (28359-3096)
PHONE................................910 735-0000
Martin Gibbons, *Pr*
◆ **EMP:** 20 **EST:** 2000
SQ FT: 10,000
SALES (est): 14.46MM
SALES (corp-wide): 14.46MM **Privately Held**
Web: www.titanfci.com
SIC: 3494 Valves and pipe fittings, nec

(G-10059)
TOKYOS EXPRESS
2716 N Roberts Ave (28358-2856)
PHONE................................910 735-0412
Douglas J Barbera, *Owner*
EMP: 6 **EST:** 2005
SALES (est): 120K **Privately Held**
SIC: 2741 Miscellaneous publishing

(G-10060)
WILBERT BURIAL VAULT COMPANY
1015 Roberts Ave (28358)
P.O. Box 934 (28359-0934)
PHONE................................910 739-7276
Wanda Ouzts, *Pr*
EMP: 20 **EST:** 1959
SQ FT: 8,000
SALES (est): 408.63K **Privately Held**
Web: www.wilbert.com
SIC: 3272 Burial vaults, concrete or precast terrazzo

(G-10061)
XAVIER POWER SYSTEMS
885 Shawn Rd (28358-8953)
P.O. Box 234 (28384-0234)
PHONE................................910 734-7813
EMP: 10
SALES (est): 142.73K **Privately Held**
Web: www.xavier.edu
SIC: 3621 Motors, electric

(G-10062)
ZURN ELKAY WTR SOLUTIONS CORP
102 Elkay Way (28358-2476)
PHONE................................910 501-1853
Todd A Adams, *Ch Bd*
EMP: 10
SIC: 3491 Industrial valves
PA: Zurn Elkay Water Solutions Corporation
511 W Freshwater Way
Milwaukee WI 53204

Lynn
Polk County

(G-10063)
PURE COUNTRY INC
Also Called: Fine Art Tapestries
81 Skylar Dr (28750)
P.O. Box 407 (28750-0407)
PHONE................................828 859-9916
George Clark, *Pr*
Ann Wetherill, *
Mark Majewski, *
▲ **EMP:** 90 **EST:** 1988
SQ FT: 35,000
SALES (est): 10.5MM **Privately Held**
Web: www.purecountry.com
SIC: 2392 2211 Household furnishings, nec; Broadwoven fabric mills, cotton

Macclesfield
Edgecombe County

(G-10064)
CALHOUN WELDING INC
7367 Tory Pl (27852-9512)
PHONE................................252 281-1455
Joe Calhoun, *Prin*
EMP: 8 **EST:** 2012
SALES (est): 247.04K **Privately Held**
SIC: 7692 Welding repair

(G-10065)
HALES WELDING AND FABRICATION
900 Carr Farm Rd (27852-9040)
PHONE................................252 907-5508
Charles Hales, *Owner*
Stephanie Spencer C.p.a., *Prin*
EMP: 5 **EST:** 2012
SALES (est): 117.08K **Privately Held**
SIC: 7692 Welding repair

(G-10066)
RAMONS CUSTOM FRAMING LLC
3720 Buck Moore Rd (27852-9749)
PHONE................................252 208-8093
Ramon A Nunez Arellano, *Prin*
EMP: 4 **EST:** 2018
SALES (est): 72.94K **Privately Held**
SIC: 2499 Picture frame molding, finished

(G-10067)
WIZARDS WOOD WERKS
7114 Shallingtons Mill Rd (27852-9803)
PHONE................................252 813-3929
Walt Williams, *Prin*
EMP: 5 **EST:** 2016
SALES (est): 54.13K **Privately Held**
SIC: 2431 Millwork

Macon
Warren County

(G-10068)
ARCOLA LOGGING CO INC
134 Chip Capps Rd (27551-8929)
PHONE................................252 257-3205
Weldon C Capps Junior, *Pr*
Sarah P Capps, *Sec*
EMP: 15 **EST:** 1986
SQ FT: 3,000
SALES (est): 946.36K **Privately Held**
SIC: 2411 Logging camps and contractors

Madison
Rockingham County

(G-10069)
ACE INDUSTRIES INC
213 Carlton Rd (27025)
P.O. Box 891 (27025-0891)
PHONE................................336 427-5316
Jim L Allred Senior, *Pr*
EMP: 4 **EST:** 1977
SQ FT: 5,000
SALES (est): 547.61K **Privately Held**
Web: www.aceindustries.com
SIC: 5087 2842 Service establishment equipment; Cleaning or polishing preparations, nec

(G-10070)
COMPTON TAPE & LABEL INC
Also Called: Compton Tape and Converting
3520 Us Highway 220 (27025-8310)
P.O. Box 370 (27025-0370)
PHONE................................336 548-4400
EMP: 12 **EST:** 1996
SQ FT: 8,800
SALES (est): 1.76MM **Privately Held**
SIC: 2259 Convertors, knit goods

(G-10071)
CUSTOM SCREENS INC
Also Called: Cs Ink
2216 Us Highway 311 (27025-8456)
P.O. Box 368 (27025-0368)
PHONE................................336 427-0265
John Pleas Mcmichael, *CEO*
Chris Mcmichael, *VP*
EMP: 25 **EST:** 1961
SQ FT: 41,000
SALES (est): 441.98K **Privately Held**
Web: www.csink.net
SIC: 2262 2396 Screen printing: manmade fiber and silk broadwoven fabrics; Automotive and apparel trimmings

(G-10072)
DEEP SOUTH HOLDING COMPANY INC
Also Called: Csi
2216 Us Highway 311 (27025-8456)
P.O. Box 250 (27025-0250)
PHONE................................336 427-0265
William Hemrck, *Pr*
▲ **EMP:** 100 **EST:** 2009
SQ FT: 40,000
SALES (est): 4.78MM **Privately Held**
SIC: 2759 Screen printing

(G-10073)
DICKS STORE
547 Mccollum Rd (27025-7808)
PHONE................................336 548-9358
Richard R Cartwright, *Owner*
EMP: 5 **EST:** 1962
SALES (est): 254.88K **Privately Held**
SIC: 2396 5199 Screen printing on fabric articles; Advertising specialties

(G-10074)
JOB SHOP FABRICATORS INC
3522 Us Highway 220 (27025-8310)
P.O. Box 1003 (27025-1003)
PHONE................................336 427-7300
Jerry Hilliard, *Ch Bd*
Gerald Hudson, *Pr*
Elaine Hudson, *Treas*
Judy Hilliard, *Sec*
EMP: 8 **EST:** 1989
SQ FT: 10,000
SALES (est): 943.6K **Privately Held**
SIC: 3443 Fabricated plate work (boiler shop)

(G-10075)
JOEYS WOODWORKING GIFTS
1601 Gold Hill Rd (27025-7739)
PHONE................................336 427-5263
Joey Brewer, *Prin*
EMP: 5 **EST:** 2017
SALES (est): 59.85K **Privately Held**
SIC: 2431 Millwork

(G-10076)
KREBS CORPORATION
Also Called: Seal Master
703 W Decatur St (27025-1817)
P.O. Box 826 (27025-0826)
PHONE................................336 548-3250
Robert Krebs, *Pr*
EMP: 9 **EST:** 2004
SALES (est): 1.99MM **Privately Held**
Web: www.sealmaster.net
SIC: 2951 Asphalt paving mixtures and blocks

(G-10077)
LIBERTY EMBROIDERY INC
301 K Fork Rd (27025-7532)
P.O. Box 707 (27025-0707)
PHONE................................336 548-1802
EMP: 600 **EST:** 1980
SQ FT: 87,000
SALES (est): 18.34MM **Privately Held**
SIC: 2395 Embroidery products, except Schiffli machine

(G-10078)
LICHTENBERG INC
Also Called: Hell On Horsecreek Brewing
107 E Murphy St (27025-1919)
PHONE................................336 949-9438
David Peters, *Pr*
EMP: 4 **EST:** 2018
SALES (est): 76.29K **Privately Held**
SIC: 2391 Curtains and draperies

(G-10079)
MADISON COMPANY INC (PA)
Also Called: Gem-Dandy
200 W Academy St (27025-2002)
P.O. Box 657 (27025-0657)
PHONE................................336 548-9624
Fred Burke, *Pr*
George R Penn, *VP*
Donald Wilson, *VP*
▲ **EMP:** 20 **EST:** 1921
SQ FT: 107,000
SALES (est): 5.63MM
SALES (corp-wide): 5.63MM **Privately Held**
Web: www.gem-dandy.com
SIC: 2387 2389 5136 2386 Apparel belts; Suspenders; Men's and boy's clothing; Leather and sheep-lined clothing

(G-10080)
MARTIN WOOD PRODUCTS INC
Also Called: McW Custom Doors
680 Bald Hill Loop (27025-7613)
PHONE................................336 548-3470
Eddie Martin, *Owner*
EMP: 5 **EST:** 1994
SQ FT: 4,050
SALES (est): 493.42K **Privately Held**
Web: www.mcwcustomdoors.com

Madison - Rockingham County (G-10081)

SIC: 2431 Woodwork, interior and ornamental, nec

(G-10081)
NATURESRULES INC
2094 Ellisboro Rd (27025-8063)
PHONE..................336 427-2526
EMP: 6 EST: 2019
SALES (est): 225.78K Privately Held
Web: www.naturesrules.com
SIC: 2034 Dried and dehydrated fruits, vegetables and soup mixes

(G-10082)
PIEDMONT DISTILLERS INC
3960 Us Highway 220 (27025-8314)
P.O. Box 472 (27025-0472)
PHONE..................336 445-0055
Joseph Michalek, Pr
Katherine Michalek, *
Candy W Bowlin, *
EMP: 82 EST: 1997
SALES (est): 10.34MM Privately Held
Web: www.piedmontdistillers.com
SIC: 2085 Distiller's dried grains and solubles, and alcohol

(G-10083)
PINE HALL BRICK CO INC
634 Lindsey Bridge Rd (27025-9477)
P.O. Box 836 (27025-0836)
PHONE..................336 721-7500
W Steele, Brnch Mgr
EMP: 14
SALES (corp-wide): 79.78MM Privately Held
Web: www.pinehallbrick.com
SIC: 3259 5211 Adobe brick; Brick
PA: Pine Hall Brick Co., Inc.
2701 Shorefair Dr
Winston Salem NC 27105
336 721-7500

(G-10084)
PMG SM HOLDINGS LLC
Also Called: Seal Master
703 W Decatur St (27025-1817)
PHONE..................336 548-3250
EMP: 11 EST: 2020
SALES (est): 1.02MM Privately Held
Web: www.sealmaster.net
SIC: 2851 Wood fillers or sealers

(G-10085)
REMINGTON ARMS COMPANY LLC
H&R 1871
870 Remington Dr (27025-8331)
P.O. Box 1849 (45071-1849)
PHONE..................800 544-8892
Rebecca Wood, Brnch Mgr
EMP: 343
SALES (corp-wide): 491.13MM Privately Held
Web: www.remington.com
SIC: 3484 Guns (firearms) or gun parts, 30 mm. and below
PA: Remington Arms Company, Llc
2592 Arkansas Hwy 15n
Lonoke AR 72086
336 548-8700

(G-10086)
REMINGTON ARMS COMPANY LLC
Marlin Firearms Company
870 Remington Dr (27025-8331)
P.O. Box 1849 (45071-1849)
PHONE..................800 544-8892
Robert Behn, Brnch Mgr
EMP: 120
SALES (corp-wide): 491.13MM Privately Held
Web: www.remington.com
SIC: 3484 Rifles or rifle parts, 30 mm. and below
PA: Remington Arms Company, Llc
2592 Arkansas Hwy 15n
Lonoke AR 72086
336 548-8700

(G-10087)
SOUTHERN STEEL AND WIRE INC
100 Minich Rd (27025-8474)
PHONE..................336 548-9611
EMP: 95
SQ FT: 37,520
SIC: 3544 3315 Wire drawing and straightening dies; Steel wire and related products
HQ: Southern Steel And Wire, Incorporated
1111 6th St
Highland IL 62249
618 654-2161

(G-10088)
THE MADISON COMPANY INC
Also Called: Gem-Dandy
200 W Academy St (27025-2002)
PHONE..................336 548-9624
EMP: 25
SALES (corp-wide): 5.63MM Privately Held
Web: www.gem-dandy.com
SIC: 2387 2341 2389 Apparel belts; Women's and children's undergarments; Suspenders
PA: The Madison Company Inc
200 W Academy St.
Madison NC 27025
336 548-9624

(G-10089)
TOP HAT BBCAT BACKHOE SVCS INC
530 Gold Hill Rd (27025-8072)
PHONE..................336 382-0068
Phillip S Nugent, Pr
EMP: 7 EST: 2013
SALES (est): 219.17K Privately Held
SIC: 3531 Backhoes

(G-10090)
UNIFI INC
Also Called: Unifi Plant 3
805 Island Dr (27025-8419)
P.O. Box 737 (27025-0737)
PHONE..................336 427-1890
Carol Sparks, Mgr
EMP: 201
SALES (corp-wide): 623.53MM Publicly Held
Web: www.unifi.com
SIC: 2281 Manmade and synthetic fiber yarns, spun
PA: Unifi, Inc.
7201 W Friendly Ave
Greensboro NC 27410
336 294-4410

(G-10091)
WENTWORTH CORPORATION
301 K Fork Rd (27025-7532)
PHONE..................336 548-1802
Phillip Ray Junior, Pr
Betty S Harter, Sec
John B Sealy Junior, Prin
Steve Hassenfelt, Prin
Donald Orr, Prin
▲ EMP: 10 EST: 1971
SQ FT: 24,000
SALES (est): 232.17K Privately Held
Web: www.wentworthcorp.com
SIC: 2387 Apparel belts

(G-10092)
WRIGHT PRINTING SERVICE INC
1510 W Academy St (27025-9320)
P.O. Box 483 (27025-0483)
PHONE..................336 427-4768
Daniel F Wright, Pr
EMP: 6 EST: 1986
SQ FT: 4,800
SALES (est): 485.19K Privately Held
Web: www.wrightprinting.net
SIC: 2752 5943 Offset printing; Office forms and supplies

Maggie Valley
Haywood County

(G-10093)
B C WINERY
2499 Soco Rd (28751-7858)
PHONE..................828 550-3610
Chris Choinski, Owner
EMP: 4 EST: 2008
SALES (est): 84.69K Privately Held
Web: www.bcwinerync.com
SIC: 2084 Wines

(G-10094)
HINSON METAL FABRICATION
30 Tess Ln (28751-7676)
PHONE..................828 944-0908
EMP: 4 EST: 2017
SALES (est): 59.8K Privately Held
SIC: 3499 Fabricated metal products, nec

(G-10095)
HMS PROTEC INC
5667 Soco Rd (28751-9524)
PHONE..................954 803-2319
Douglas K Stafford, Prin
EMP: 6 EST: 2009
SALES (est): 323.65K Privately Held
Web: www.hmsprotec.com
SIC: 3479 Coating of metals and formed products

(G-10096)
TOWN OF MAGGIE VALLEY INC
Also Called: Maggie Valley Sanitary Dst
45 Water Plant Rd (28751)
P.O. Box 1029 (28751-1029)
PHONE..................828 926-0145
Niel Carpenter, Mgr
EMP: 10
Web: maggiewater.myruralwater.com
SIC: 3589 6531 Water treatment equipment, industrial; Real estate agents and managers
PA: Town Of Maggie Valley Inc
3987 Soco Rd
Maggie Valley NC 28751
828 926-0866

(G-10097)
WOODLEY ENTERPRISES LLC
22 Turtle Dr (28751-9590)
PHONE..................828 944-0653
EMP: 5 EST: 2016
SALES (est): 64.95K Privately Held
SIC: 2499 Wood products, nec

Magnolia
Duplin County

(G-10098)
OLD DELL DESIGNS
199 E Magnolia Lisbon Rd (28453-7853)
PHONE..................910 532-6066
Daisy Chestnutt, Owner
EMP: 5 EST: 1993
SQ FT: 5,500
SALES (est): 73.8K Privately Held
SIC: 2339 Women's and misses' athletic clothing and sportswear

Maiden
Catawba County

(G-10099)
BEN PUSHPA INC
2896 E Maiden Rd (28650-9605)
PHONE..................828 428-8590
Nayana Patel, Prin
EMP: 11 EST: 2005
SALES (est): 661.67K Privately Held
SIC: 3873 Watches, clocks, watchcases, and parts

(G-10100)
C O JELLIFF CORPORATION
Also Called: L G M
4292 Providence Mill Rd (28650-8593)
P.O. Box 456 (28650-0456)
PHONE..................828 428-3672
EMP: 8
SALES (corp-wide): 9.42MM Privately Held
Web: www.jelliff.com
SIC: 3357 3825 Automotive wire and cable, except ignition sets: nonferrous; Ignition testing instruments
PA: C. O. Jelliff Corporation
354 Pequot Ave Ste 300
Southport CT 06890
203 259-1615

(G-10101)
CALDWELLS MT PROCESS ABATTOIRS
3726 Goodson Rd (28650-8216)
PHONE..................828 428-8833
Kevin Caldwell, Owner
EMP: 4 EST: 1971
SALES (est): 163.29K Privately Held
SIC: 2011 Meat packing plants

(G-10102)
CAROLINA MILLS INCORPORATED (PA)
618 N Carolina Ave (28650-1170)
P.O. Box 157 (28650-0157)
PHONE..................828 428-9911
Bryan E Beal, Pr
George A Moretz, *
◆ EMP: 460 EST: 1928
SQ FT: 100,000
SALES (est): 40.93MM
SALES (corp-wide): 40.93MM Privately Held
Web: www.carolinamills.com
SIC: 2281 2211 2221 2257 Knitting yarn, spun; Upholstery fabrics, cotton; Upholstery fabrics, manmade fiber and silk; Dyeing and finishing circular knit fabrics

(G-10103)
CAROLINA MILLS WAREHOUSE
624 N Carolina Ave (28650-1100)
PHONE..................828 428-9911
EMP: 7 EST: 2019
SALES (est): 27.98K Privately Held
Web: www.carolinamills.com
SIC: 2281 Yarn spinning mills

(G-10104)
CAROLINA NONWOVENS LLC
Also Called: Cnc
1106 Jw Abernathy Plant Rd (28650-9697)

PHONE...............................704 735-5600
Frederick Fink, *Pr*
S Paul Whitaker, *Ex VP*
▲ **EMP:** 15 **EST:** 2006
SQ FT: 75,000
SALES (est): 2.48MM
SALES (corp-wide): 102.19MM **Privately Held**
Web: www.carolinanonwovens.com
SIC: 2297 Nonwoven fabrics
PA: National Spinning Co., Inc.
1481 W 2nd St Ste 103
Washington NC 27889
252 975-7111

(G-10105)
CLOVER GARDEN SOAPS
506 E Main St (28650-1418)
PHONE...............................828 970-7289
Claire Teegardin, *Prin*
EMP: 4 **EST:** 2015
SALES (est): 98.6K **Privately Held**
Web: www.clovergardensoaps.com
SIC: 2844 Perfumes, cosmetics and other toilet preparations

(G-10106)
DRIVER DISTRIBUTION INC (PA)
Also Called: Eastern Bikes
624 N Carolina Ave Bldg 4 (28650-1100)
P.O. Box 1287 (27512-1287)
PHONE...............................984 204-2929
Jon Byers, *CEO*
Mike Corley, *VP*
EMP: 5 **EST:** 2015
SALES (est): 448.57K
SALES (corp-wide): 448.57K **Privately Held**
Web: www.easternbikes.com
SIC: 3751 Motorcycles and related parts

(G-10107)
ETHAN ALLEN RETAIL INC
Also Called: Ethan Allen Maiden Division
700 S Main Ave (28650-8211)
PHONE...............................828 428-9361
Wade Spears, *Mgr*
EMP: 38
Web: www.ethanallen.com
SIC: 5712 2511 2426 Furniture stores; Wood household furniture; Hardwood dimension and flooring mills
HQ: Ethan Allen Retail, Inc.
25 Lake Avenue Ext
Danbury CT 06811
203 743-8000

(G-10108)
FAIRVIEW WOODCARVING INC
2092 Anaconda Ln (28650-9361)
PHONE...............................828 428-9491
Samuel Dellinger, *Pr*
Sherry Dellinger, *Sec*
EMP: 6 **EST:** 1989
SALES (est): 402.93K **Privately Held**
SIC: 2499 Carved and turned wood

(G-10109)
GREGORY HILL FRAME
108 W Cemetery St (28650-1172)
PHONE...............................828 428-0007
EMP: 10 **EST:** 1994
SALES (est): 781.08K **Privately Held**
SIC: 2426 Frames for upholstered furniture, wood

(G-10110)
JTS VENOM PERFORMANCE
108 Bost Nursery Rd (28650-9524)
PHONE...............................704 214-7849
EMP: 4 **EST:** 2011
SALES (est): 214.94K **Privately Held**
SIC: 2836 Venoms

(G-10111)
KEENER WOOD PRODUCTS INC
4274 Providence Mill Rd (28650-8593)
P.O. Box 566 (28650-0566)
PHONE...............................828 428-1562
Ronnie Keener, *VP*
Chad Dale Keener, *Pr*
EMP: 4 **EST:** 1997
SALES (est): 483.72K **Privately Held**
Web: www.keenerwoodproducts.com
SIC: 2421 2499 Wood chips, produced at mill ; Carved and turned wood

(G-10112)
MAIDEN CASTING COMPANY
3540 Anderson Mountain Rd (28650-9595)
PHONE...............................704 735-6812
William Saunders, *Pr*
EMP: 5 **EST:** 1989
SQ FT: 4,500
SALES (est): 476.4K **Privately Held**
SIC: 3366 3365 Castings (except die), nec, brass; Machinery castings, aluminum

(G-10113)
MCFARLIN CABINETS
108 W Cemetery St (28650-1172)
PHONE...............................828 310-9906
Sam Mcfarlin, *Prin*
EMP: 5 **EST:** 2010
SALES (est): 154.53K **Privately Held**
SIC: 2434 Wood kitchen cabinets

(G-10114)
NOVAK INDUSTRIES LLC
3898 Joe Crouse Rd (28650-9159)
PHONE...............................704 662-2982
EMP: 4 **EST:** 2017
SALES (est): 47.38K **Privately Held**
SIC: 3999 Manufacturing industries, nec

(G-10115)
PARKER SOUTHERN INC
15 W Holly St (28650-8596)
P.O. Box 568 (28650-0568)
PHONE...............................828 428-3506
Tony Parker, *Pr*
Gary Parker, *VP*
EMP: 10 **EST:** 1991
SQ FT: 60,000
SALES (est): 757.73K
SALES (corp-wide): 11.03MM **Privately Held**
Web: www.parkersouthern.com
SIC: 2512 2521 Upholstered household furniture; Wood office furniture
PA: Temple, Inc.
102 S 7th Avenue Ext
Maiden NC 28650
828 428-8031

(G-10116)
SIMPLE GRAPHX LLC
3554 Walker Rd (28650-9567)
PHONE...............................828 428-1567
Cindy Lancaster, *Admn*
EMP: 5 **EST:** 2012
SALES (est): 57.13K **Privately Held**
SIC: 2752 Commercial printing, lithographic

(G-10117)
SOUTH FORK INDUSTRIES INC
100 W Pine St (28650-1261)
P.O. Box 742 (28650-0742)
PHONE...............................828 428-9921
EMP: 75 **EST:** 1988
SALES (est): 5.29MM **Privately Held**
Web: www.southforkind.com
SIC: 2257 2269 2261 Dyeing and finishing circular knit fabrics; Finishing plants, nec; Finishing plants, cotton

(G-10118)
TCC MANUFACTURING
4418 Providence Mill Rd (28650-8520)
PHONE...............................828 970-7270
EMP: 4 **EST:** 2017
SALES (est): 68.4K **Privately Held**
SIC: 3999 Manufacturing industries, nec

(G-10119)
TEMPLE INC (PA)
Also Called: Temple Furniture
102 S 7th Avenue Ext (28650-1451)
P.O. Box 185 (28650-0185)
PHONE...............................828 428-8031
Tony A Parker, *Pr*
Gary Parker, *
Adrian Parker, *
EMP: 85 **EST:** 1977
SQ FT: 67,500
SALES (est): 11.03MM
SALES (corp-wide): 11.03MM **Privately Held**
Web: www.templefurniture.com
SIC: 2512 Couches, sofas, and davenports: upholstered on wood frames

(G-10120)
TOUCH UP SOLUTIONS INC
4372 Providence Mill Rd (28650-8594)
P.O. Box 368 (28650-0368)
PHONE...............................828 428-9094
Troy W Pait, *Pr*
William T Brown, *VP*
EMP: 22 **EST:** 2006
SQ FT: 44,760
SALES (est): 3.88MM **Privately Held**
Web: www.touchupsolutions.com
SIC: 2599 7641 Factory furniture and fixtures ; Furniture repair and maintenance

(G-10121)
UNRIVALED METAL BUILDINGS LLC
814 E Boyd St (28650-1715)
P.O. Box 241 (28650-0241)
PHONE...............................844 848-8676
EMP: 5 **EST:** 2019
SALES (est): 153.4K **Privately Held**
Web: www.unrivaledmetalbuildings.com
SIC: 3448 Prefabricated metal buildings and components

Manns Harbor
Dare County

(G-10122)
MANN CUSTOM BOATS INC
6300 Us Highway 64 # 264 (27953-9574)
P.O. Box 239 (27953-0239)
PHONE...............................252 473-1716
EMP: 20 **EST:** 1987
SQ FT: 8,000
SALES (est): 2.06MM **Privately Held**
Web: www.paulmanncustomboats.com
SIC: 3732 5551 Boats, fiberglass: building and repairing; Boat dealers

(G-10123)
SPENCER YACHTS INC
5698 Us Highway 64 # 264 (27953-9517)
P.O. Box 210 (27953-0210)
PHONE...............................252 473-2660
Paul Spencer, *Pr*
Shelly Spencer, *
EMP: 19 **EST:** 1997
SQ FT: 8,000
SALES (est): 803.29K **Privately Held**
Web: www.spenceryachtsinc.com
SIC: 3732 Fishing boats: lobster, crab, oyster, etc.: small

Manson
Vance County

(G-10124)
INTERNATIONAL PAPER COMPANY
Also Called: International Paper
967 Us Highway 1 S (27553-9085)
P.O. Box 338 (27553-0338)
PHONE...............................252 456-3111
EMP: 5
SALES (corp-wide): 18.92B **Publicly Held**
Web: www.internationalpaper.com
SIC: 2653 Boxes, corrugated: made from purchased materials
PA: International Paper Company
6400 Poplar Ave
Memphis TN 38197
901 419-7000

(G-10125)
SCM PUBLISHING LLC
489 Liberation Rd (27553-9088)
PHONE...............................252 456-2132
S C Mckissick-melton, *Prin*
EMP: 4 **EST:** 2018
SALES (est): 72.83K **Privately Held**
SIC: 2741 Miscellaneous publishing

Manteo
Dare County

(G-10126)
ARTHUR DEMAREST
Also Called: Art Press
419 Skyco Rd (27954-9394)
P.O. Box 580 (27981-0580)
PHONE...............................252 473-1449
Arthur Demarest, *Owner*
EMP: 5 **EST:** 1923
SQ FT: 20,000
SALES (est): 198.07K **Privately Held**
Web: www.artpressprinters.com
SIC: 2752 Offset printing

(G-10127)
CHAIR MAN
118 Fort Hugar Way (27954-9479)
PHONE...............................610 809-0871
Theodore Moore, *Prin*
EMP: 4 **EST:** 2015
SALES (est): 79.61K **Privately Held**
Web: www.thechairmanweb.com
SIC: 2512 Upholstered household furniture

(G-10128)
OUTER BANKS CRAFT DISTLG LLC
Also Called: Outer Banks Distilling
510 Budleigh St (27954)
P.O. Box 531 (27949-0531)
PHONE...............................252 423-3011
EMP: 6 **EST:** 2013
SALES (est): 354.33K **Privately Held**
SIC: 5182 2085 Bottling wines and liquors; Distilled and blended liquors

(G-10129)
RAPID CONNECTOR
136 Carolina Ct W (27954-9545)
PHONE...............................843 315-4700
EMP: 4 **EST:** 2019
SALES (est): 88.38K **Privately Held**

SIC: 3646 Commercial lighting fixtures

(G-10130)
TIMES PRINTING COMPANY (PA)
Also Called: Coastland Times
501 Budleigh St (27954)
P.O. Box 400 (27954-0400)
PHONE..................................252 473-2105
Francis W Meekins, *Pr*
Susan M Simpson, *
EMP: 40 EST: 1935
SQ FT: 10,000
SALES (est): 2.01MM
SALES (corp-wide): 2.01MM **Privately Held**
Web: www.thecoastlandtimes.com
SIC: **2711** 5943 Commercial printing and newspaper publishing combined; Office forms and supplies

Maple Hill
Pender County

(G-10131)
CAROLINA COASTAL COATINGS INC
375 Padgett Rd (28454-8576)
PHONE..................................910 346-9607
Jenaca Wasicki, *Prin*
Jeffrey D Bailey, *Prin*
EMP: 10 EST: 2018
SALES (est): 445.15K **Privately Held**
SIC: **3479** 7389 Painting, coating, and hot dipping; Business Activities at Non-Commercial Site

(G-10132)
SEASHORE BUILDERS INC
266 Nelson Park Rd (28454-8569)
PHONE..................................910 259-3404
Elizabeth Raynor, *Pr*
Elizabeth G Raynor, *
Stephen L Raynor, *
EMP: 26 EST: 2001
SALES (est): 2.44MM **Privately Held**
Web: www.seashorebuilders.net
SIC: **1522** 1541 1542 1751 Residential construction, nec; Industrial buildings and warehouses; Commercial and office buildings, renovation and repair; Framing contractor

Marble
Cherokee County

(G-10133)
PAMELA STOEPPELWERTH
Also Called: Mountain Manner Exotic Jellies
929 Coalville Rd (28905-8519)
PHONE..................................828 837-7293
Pamela Stoeppelwerth, *Owner*
EMP: 4 EST: 1997
SALES (est): 165.59K **Privately Held**
Web: www.mountainmanna.net
SIC: **2033** Jams, jellies, and preserves, packaged in cans, jars, etc.

(G-10134)
STROUD LOGGING
480 Coalville Rd (28905-8887)
PHONE..................................828 541-2721
Johnny Paul Stroud, *Prin*
EMP: 5 EST: 2017
SALES (est): 86.6K **Privately Held**
SIC: **2411** Logging

(G-10135)
VALWOOD CORPORATION
35 Coalville Rd (28905-8888)
PHONE..................................828 321-4717
Chris Logan, *Pr*
Tom Buchanon, *VP*
EMP: 10 EST: 1972
SALES (est): 605.5K **Privately Held**
SIC: **2421** Wood chips, produced at mill

Margarettsville
Northampton County

(G-10136)
COUNTRY ROADS LOGGING LLC
332 Providence Ln (27853-8904)
PHONE..................................252 578-8191
EMP: 5 EST: 2018
SALES (est): 162.92K **Privately Held**
SIC: **2411** Logging

Marion
Mcdowell County

(G-10137)
ABB MOTORS AND MECHANICAL INC
Also Called: Marian Manufacturing Plant
510 Rockwell Dr (28752-8821)
PHONE..................................479 646-4711
Ronald E Tucker, *CEO*
EMP: 8
Web: www.baldor.com
SIC: **3621** Electric motor and generator parts
HQ: Abb Motors And Mechanical Inc.
5711 Rs Boreham Jr St
Fort Smith AR 72901
479 646-4711

(G-10138)
AJS DEZIGNS INC
Also Called: Allied Industrial
Ashworth Rd (28752)
P.O. Box 1360 (28762-1360)
PHONE..................................828 652-6304
Len Warren, *Pr*
Anita F Warren, *Treas*
EMP: 8 EST: 1987
SQ FT: 8,400
SALES (est): 915.11K **Privately Held**
Web: www.alliedindustrial.net
SIC: **2541** 2431 Cabinets, except refrigerated: show, display, etc.: wood; Millwork

(G-10139)
AMERICAN PLASTIC INC
136 W Marion Business Park (28752-5574)
P.O. Box 1269 (28752-1269)
PHONE..................................828 652-3511
Jim Hall, *Pr*
EMP: 9 EST: 1997
SQ FT: 5,000
SALES (est): 960K **Privately Held**
Web: www.americanplastics.com
SIC: **3089** Injection molding of plastics

(G-10140)
B V HEDRICK GRAVEL & SAND CO
Also Called: Cumberland Gravel
1182 Old Glenwood Rd (28752-7785)
PHONE..................................828 738-0332
John Brown, *Mgr*
EMP: 9
SALES (corp-wide): 238.17MM **Privately Held**
Web: www.hedrickind.com

SIC: **1442** Construction sand and gravel
PA: B. V. Hedrick Gravel & Sand Company
120 1/2 N Church St
Salisbury NC 28144
704 633-5982

(G-10141)
BALDOR DODGE RELIANCE
510 Rockwell Dr (28752-8821)
PHONE..................................828 652-0074
▲ EMP: 13 EST: 2008
SALES (est): 2.23MM **Privately Held**
SIC: **3562** Ball bearings and parts

(G-10142)
BAXTER HEALTHCARE CORPORATION
Also Called: Baxter US
65 Pitts Station Rd (28752-7925)
P.O. Box 1390 (28752-1390)
PHONE..................................828 756-6600
Tony Johnson, *Mgr*
EMP: 329
SALES (corp-wide): 14.81B **Publicly Held**
Web: www.baxter.com
SIC: **2834** Pharmaceutical preparations
HQ: Baxter Healthcare Corporation
1 Baxter Pkwy
Deerfield IL 60015
224 948-2000

(G-10143)
BAXTER HEALTHCARE CORPORATION
65 Pitts Station Rd (28752)
PHONE..................................828 756-6623
Keely Elkins, *Mgr*
EMP: 10
SALES (corp-wide): 15.11B **Publicly Held**
Web: www.baxter.com
SIC: **2834** Pharmaceutical preparations
HQ: Baxter Healthcare Corporation
1 Baxter Pkwy
Deerfield IL 60015
224 948-2000

(G-10144)
BOYD STONE & QUARRIES
2207 Cannon Rd (28752-2944)
P.O. Box 579 (28752-0579)
PHONE..................................828 659-6862
Mark Boyd, *Pt*
EMP: 5 EST: 1987
SALES (est): 509.44K **Privately Held**
SIC: **1422** Crushed and broken limestone

(G-10145)
BUECHEL STONE CORP
7274 Us 221 N (28752-6103)
PHONE..................................800 236-4474
EMP: 70
SALES (corp-wide): 15.32MM **Privately Held**
Web: www.buechelstone.com
SIC: **3281** Cut stone and stone products
PA: Buechel Stone Corp.
W3639 County Road H
Chilton WI 53014
920 922-4790

(G-10146)
CAROLINA CHOCOLATIERS INC
20 N Main St (28752-3936)
PHONE..................................828 652-4496
Kelly Lewis, *Pr*
EMP: 5 EST: 1981
SALES (est): 433.33K **Privately Held**
SIC: **2064** Chocolate candy, except solid chocolate

(G-10147)
CAROLINA PALLET RECYCLING INC
2855 Nc 226 I 40 (28752-7775)
P.O. Box 1233 (28752-1233)
PHONE..................................828 652-6818
EMP: 11 EST: 1992
SQ FT: 30,000
SALES (est): 430.65K **Privately Held**
SIC: **2448** Pallets, wood

(G-10148)
CHATTER FREE TLING SLTIONS INC
1877 Rutherford Rd (28752-4764)
PHONE..................................828 659-7379
Joel Hardin, *Prin*
EMP: 7 EST: 2011
SALES (est): 98.38K **Privately Held**
SIC: **3999** Manufacturing industries, nec

(G-10149)
EDWARDS WOOD PDTS INC/ WOODLAWN
8482 Us 221 N (28752-7564)
P.O. Box 219 (28103-0219)
PHONE..................................828 756-4758
EMP: 6 EST: 2010
SALES (est): 138.94K **Privately Held**
Web: www.ewpi.com
SIC: **2421** Sawmills and planing mills, general

(G-10150)
HALDEX INC
5334 Us Hwy 221 N (28752-6100)
P.O. Box 1129 (28752-1129)
PHONE..................................828 652-9308
EMP: 115
SALES (corp-wide): 472.17MM **Privately Held**
SIC: **3714** 3568 3561 Motor vehicle brake systems and parts; Power transmission equipment, nec; Pumps and pumping equipment
HQ: Haldex, Inc.
10930 N Pomona Ave
Kansas City MO 64153
816 891-2470

(G-10151)
HUNTER LIVER MUSH INC
98 Poteat Rd (28752-9014)
PHONE..................................828 652-7902
Jerry Hunter, *Pr*
Carolyn Hunter, *VP*
Phyllis Harmon, *Sec*
Louise Rumfelt, *Treas*
EMP: 9 EST: 1959
SQ FT: 5,000
SALES (est): 982.23K **Privately Held**
SIC: **2013** Sausages and other prepared meats

(G-10152)
ITL CORP
203 College Dr (28752-7723)
PHONE..................................828 659-9663
EMP: 16
Web: www.itlcorp.com
SIC: **2421** Sawmills and planing mills, general
HQ: Itl Corp.
23925 Commerce Park
Cleveland OH 44122
216 831-3140

(G-10153)
JELD-WEN INC
Also Called: Fiber N C Div
100 Henry Mccall Rd (28752-7412)
PHONE..................................828 724-9511

Jim English, *Mgr*
EMP: 60
Web: www.jeld-wen.com
SIC: 2431 Doors, wood
HQ: Jeld-Wen, Inc.
2645 Silver Crescent Dr
Charlotte NC 28273
800 535-3936

(G-10154)
JOHNSON PAVING COMPANY INC
3101 Us 221 North (28752)
P.O. Box 1066 (28752-1066)
PHONE..............................828 652-4911
Gregory Johnson, *Pr*
Virginia Johnson, *Sec*
EMP: 12 **EST:** 1968
SQ FT: 150
SALES (est): 938.78K **Privately Held**
Web: www.johnsonpavingcompany.com
SIC: 1499 1611 2951 Asphalt mining and bituminous stone quarrying; Highway and street paving contractor; Asphalt paving mixtures and blocks

(G-10155)
JOSEPH SOTANSKI
Also Called: Forever Outdoors
632 College Dr (28752-8729)
PHONE..............................407 324-6187
Joseph Sotanski, *Owner*
EMP: 30
SALES (corp-wide): 1.89MM **Privately Held**
SIC: 2519 3999 Garden furniture, except wood, metal, stone, or concrete; Lawn ornaments
PA: Joseph Sotanski
2260 Old Lake Mary Rd
Sanford FL 32771
407 324-6187

(G-10156)
KEY GAS COMPONENTS INC (PA)
160 Clay St (28752-3570)
PHONE..............................828 655-1700
Roy Kuhn, *CEO*
Jim Kuhn, *
Mary Ann Kuhn, *Stockholder**
Henderson Cathcart, *
Michelle Cline, *
▲ **EMP:** 34 **EST:** 1986
SQ FT: 50,000
SALES (est): 12.19MM
SALES (corp-wide): 12.19MM **Privately Held**
Web: www.keygas.com
SIC: 3498 3491 3494 3432 Manifolds, pipe: fabricated from purchased pipe; Gas valves and parts, industrial; Valves and pipe fittings, nec; Plumbing fixture fittings and trim

(G-10157)
MARION CULTURED MARBLE INC
Also Called: Wilson Marble
4805 Highway 70 W (28752)
P.O. Box 2562 (28752-2562)
PHONE..............................828 724-4782
Randy Wilson, *Pr*
Kenny Wilson, *VP*
Bernice Wilson, *Treas*
EMP: 15 **EST:** 1972
SQ FT: 26,250
SALES (est): 481.21K **Privately Held**
SIC: 3281 3088 Marble, building: cut and shaped; Plastics plumbing fixtures

(G-10158)
MARION MACHINE LLC
169 Machine Shop Rd (28752-2812)
PHONE..............................800 627-1639
Howard Mcneil, *Brnch Mgr*
EMP: 200
SALES (corp-wide): 140.26MM **Privately Held**
Web: www.marionmachinellc.com
SIC: 3599 Machine shop, jobbing and repair
HQ: Marion Machine Llc
14937 Warfordsburg Rd
Hancock MD 21750
301 678-2000

(G-10159)
MASTERS HAND PRINT WORKS INC
5 Old Greenlee Rd W (28752-6226)
P.O. Box 190 (28752-0190)
PHONE..............................828 652-5833
Brian K Johnston, *Pr*
Linda Johnston, *Stockholder*
EMP: 4 **EST:** 2006
SALES (est): 262.61K **Privately Held**
Web: www.mastershandprint.com
SIC: 2752 2759 Offset printing; Commercial printing, nec

(G-10160)
MCC HOLDINGS INC
Also Called: Crane Resistoflex
1 Quality Way (28752-9410)
PHONE..............................828 724-4000
EMP: 170
SALES (corp-wide): 1.39B **Publicly Held**
Web: www.cranecpe.com
SIC: 3492 Control valves, fluid power: hydraulic and pneumatic
HQ: Mcc Holdings, Inc.
4526 Res Frest Dr Ste 400
The Woodlands TX 77381
936 271-6500

(G-10161)
MCDOWELL CEMENT PRODUCTS CO (HQ)
S Garden St (28752)
PHONE..............................828 652-5721
Robert H Boone, *Pr*
John Boone, *VP*
Susan B Gardin, *Sec*
EMP: 11 **EST:** 1947
SALES (est): 2.29MM
SALES (corp-wide): 4.16MM **Privately Held**
SIC: 3273 Ready-mixed concrete
PA: Explosives Supply Company
167 Roan Rd
Spruce Pine NC 28777
828 765-2762

(G-10162)
MCDOWELL COUNTY MILLWORK LLC
4 Old West Henderson St (28752-7889)
P.O. Box 726 (28714-0726)
PHONE..............................828 682-6215
Deanna French, *Mgr*
EMP: 10 **EST:** 2006
SALES (est): 934.53K **Privately Held**
SIC: 2434 Wood kitchen cabinets

(G-10163)
MCDOWELL PRESSURE WASHING
129 Hill Rd (28752-3579)
PHONE..............................828 620-2141
Robby Preswood, *Prin*
EMP: 5 **EST:** 2019
SALES (est): 89.17K **Privately Held**
SIC: 2711 Newspapers, publishing and printing

(G-10164)
MCNEELY ACCOUNTING & TAX SVC
3562 Us 221 S (28752-7016)
PHONE..............................828 652-7405
Misty Mcneely, *Prin*
EMP: 6 **EST:** 2015
SALES (est): 98.88K **Privately Held**
Web: www.mcneelyaccounting.com
SIC: 2411 Logging

(G-10165)
MELISSAE MEADERY & WINERY LLC
272 Plantation Dr (28752-7101)
PHONE..............................336 207-7097
EMP: 4 **EST:** 2015
SALES (est): 99.15K **Privately Held**
SIC: 2084 Wines

(G-10166)
MOUNTAIN SNOW LLC
172 Mountain View Rd (28752-6466)
PHONE..............................828 403-7535
Jaysun Lyles, *Prin*
EMP: 8 **EST:** 2017
SQ FT: 3,200
SALES (est): 239.29K **Privately Held**
SIC: 2024 Ices, flavored (frozen dessert)

(G-10167)
MPV MORGANTON PRESSU
1 Alfredo Baglioni Dr (28752-5104)
PHONE..............................828 652-3704
EMP: 11
SALES (est): 3.71MM **Privately Held**
Web: www.morgantonpv.com
SIC: 1382 Oil and gas exploration services

(G-10168)
MPV MRGNTON PRSSURE VSSELS NC
Also Called: Morganton Pressure Vessels LLC
1 Alfredo Baglioni Dr (28752-5104)
PHONE..............................828 652-3704
Franco Tartaglino, *Managing Member*
▲ **EMP:** 118 **EST:** 2006
SQ FT: 110,000
SALES (est): 23.25MM **Privately Held**
Web: www.morgantonpv.com
SIC: 3491 Pressure valves and regulators, industrial
HQ: Baglioni Spa
Strada Biandrate 24
Novara NO 28100

(G-10169)
NEW WORLD TECHNOLOGIES INC
Also Called: Midnight Machining
78 W Marion Business Park (28752-5041)
PHONE..............................828 652-8662
Alex Lee Hawkins, *Treas*
Misty Callahan, *Sec*
Greg Ward, *Pr*
EMP: 10 **EST:** 1997
SQ FT: 8,200
SALES (est): 178.14K **Privately Held**
SIC: 3599 Machine shop, jobbing and repair

(G-10170)
ORA INC
315 Baldwin Ave (28752-6656)
PHONE..............................540 903-7177
Steven Parks, *Pr*
EMP: 7 **EST:** 2016
SQ FT: 20,000
SALES (est): 577.16K **Privately Held**
SIC: 3542 3569 3599 3442 High energy rate metal forming machines; Testing chambers for altitude, temperature, ordnance, power; Custom machinery; Metal doors

(G-10171)
PEPSICO INC
Also Called: Pepsico
8337 Us 221 N (28752-9647)
P.O. Box 486 (28777-0486)
PHONE..............................828 756-4662
Dan Revis, *Brnch Mgr*
EMP: 4
SALES (corp-wide): 86.39B **Publicly Held**
Web: www.pepsico.com
SIC: 2086 Carbonated soft drinks, bottled and canned
PA: Pepsico, Inc.
700 Anderson Hill Rd
Purchase NY 10577
914 253-2000

(G-10172)
PLEASANT GARDENS MACHINE INC
2708 Us 70 W (28752-8815)
PHONE..............................828 724-4173
Michael L Queen, *Pr*
Lawrence Queen, *Treas*
EMP: 18 **EST:** 1965
SQ FT: 43,000
SALES (est): 564.03K **Privately Held**
Web: www.pgmachine.com
SIC: 3599 Machine shop, jobbing and repair

(G-10173)
RATOON AGROPROCESSING LLC
5290 Nc 226 S (28752-8733)
PHONE..............................828 273-9114
EMP: 6 **EST:** 2019
SALES (est): 249.21K **Privately Held**
Web: www.ratoonagroprocessing.com
SIC: 3999 Manufacturing industries, nec

(G-10174)
ROCKWELL AUTOMATION INC
510 Rockwell Dr (28752-8821)
PHONE..............................828 652-0074
Mark Early, *Mgr*
EMP: 12
Web: www.rockwellautomation.com
SIC: 3625 Electric controls and control accessories, industrial
PA: Rockwell Automation, Inc.
1201 S 2nd St
Milwaukee WI 53204

(G-10175)
ROSS SKID PRODUCTS INC
7 Landis Rd (28752-7711)
P.O. Box 1455 (28752-1455)
PHONE..............................828 652-7450
Perry Jack Ross, *Pr*
EMP: 20 **EST:** 1972
SQ FT: 6,000
SALES (est): 1.28MM **Privately Held**
SIC: 2448 Pallets, wood

(G-10176)
SILVER MILLER HOLDINGS LLC
70 Anderson Dr (28752-5449)
PHONE..............................828 652-6677
Matthew Todd Miller, *Prin*
EMP: 5 **EST:** 2019
SALES (est): 113.19K **Privately Held**
SIC: 2711 Newspapers, publishing and printing

(G-10177)
SMITHS CUSTOM KITCHEN INC
58 Butterfly Dr (28752-7848)
PHONE..............................828 652-9033
EMP: 5 **EST:** 1982
SALES (est): 316.39K **Privately Held**
SIC: 2434 Wood kitchen cabinets

Marion - Mcdowell County (G-10178)

(G-10178)
SOLAR CONNECTION LLC
632 College Dr (28752-8729)
PHONE..................................828 484-9163
EMP: 5 EST: 2014
SALES (est): 125.13K Privately Held
SIC: 3433 Solar heaters and collectors

(G-10179)
SPEER OPERATIONAL TECH LLC
315 Baldwin Ave (28752-6656)
PHONE..................................864 631-2512
EMP: 4 EST: 2007
SALES (est): 491.26K Privately Held
SIC: 5099 3999 5999 5047 Safety equipment and supplies; Fire extinguishers, portable; Alarm and safety equipment stores ; Instruments, surgical and medical

(G-10180)
SSS LOGGING INC
29 Liberty Drive Marion (28752)
P.O. Box 281 (28752-0281)
PHONE..................................828 467-1155
Doyle Shuford, Pr
EMP: 7 EST: 2002
SALES (est): 1.2MM Privately Held
SIC: 2411 Logging

(G-10181)
SUPERIOR MACHINE CO SC INC
Also Called: Marion Machine Div
169 Machine Shop Rd (28752-2812)
PHONE..................................828 652-6141
E L Cunningham, Brnch Mgr
EMP: 35
SALES (corp-wide): 20.69MM Privately Held
Web: www.smco.net
SIC: 3599 7629 3444 Machine shop, jobbing and repair; Electrical repair shops; Sheet metalwork
PA: Superior Machine Co. Of South Carolina, Inc.
692 N Cashua Dr
Florence SC 29501
843 468-9200

(G-10182)
TILSON MACHINE INC (PA)
632 College Dr (28752-8729)
PHONE..................................828 668-4416
EMP: 81 EST: 1988
SALES (est): 9.51MM
SALES (corp-wide): 9.51MM Privately Held
Web: www.tilsonmachine.com
SIC: 3599 Machine and other job shop work

(G-10183)
TOOLCRAFT INC NORTH CAROLINA (PA)
1877 Rutherford Rd (28752-4764)
PHONE..................................828 659-7379
Darvy Hensley, Pr
EMP: 15 EST: 1978
SQ FT: 40,000
SALES (est): 4.58MM
SALES (corp-wide): 4.58MM Privately Held
Web: www.toolcraftinc.com
SIC: 3545 3469 Tools and accessories for machine tools; Machine parts, stamped or pressed metal

(G-10184)
UNIVERSAL MACHINE AND TOOL INC
1114 W Marion Business Park (28752)
P.O. Box 756 (28762-0756)
PHONE..................................828 659-2002
David Lytle, Pr
EMP: 7 EST: 1995
SQ FT: 5,000
SALES (est): 794.51K Privately Held
SIC: 3599 Machine shop, jobbing and repair

(G-10185)
WAYCASTER NICK STONE CO
Also Called: Waycaster Stone Co
5455 Us 221 N (28752-7236)
PHONE..................................828 756-4011
Nick Waycaster, Owner
EMP: 6 EST: 1968
SQ FT: 1,000
SALES (est): 330.89K Privately Held
SIC: 1411 3281 Dimension stone; Cut stone and stone products

(G-10186)
WESTROCK RKT LLC
468 Carolina Ave (28752-2846)
PHONE..................................828 655-1303
Pat Warner, Brnch Mgr
EMP: 5
SALES (corp-wide): 20.31B Publicly Held
Web: www.westrock.com
SIC: 2653 Boxes, corrugated: made from purchased materials
HQ: Westrock Rkt, Llc
1000 Abernathy Rd Ste 125
Atlanta GA 30328
770 448-2193

(G-10187)
WESTROCK RKT LLC
1659 E Court St (28752-4565)
PHONE..................................770 448-2193
Steve Arrell, Mgr
EMP: 258
SALES (corp-wide): 20.31B Publicly Held
Web: www.westrock.com
SIC: 2657 2752 Folding paperboard boxes; Commercial printing, lithographic
HQ: Westrock Rkt, Llc
1000 Abernathy Rd Ste 125
Atlanta GA 30328
770 448-2193

(G-10188)
WNC DRY KILN INC (PA)
65 Jacktown Rd (28752-9206)
P.O. Box 777 (28752-0777)
PHONE..................................828 652-0050
Joe Lyle, Pr
Tom Thrash, VP
Tommy Orr, Sec
EMP: 10 EST: 2003
SQ FT: 10,000
SALES (est): 2.19MM
SALES (corp-wide): 2.19MM Privately Held
Web: www.wncpallet.com
SIC: 5093 2421 Lumber scrap; Lumber: rough, sawed, or planed

(G-10189)
WOODLAWN QUALITY PLUS
3086 Us 221 N (28752-9824)
PHONE..................................828 659-7721
EMP: 4 EST: 2015
SALES (est): 39K Privately Held
Web: www.qualityplusnc.com
SIC: 2499 Wood products, nec

(G-10190)
WOODLAWN TIRE AND ALGNMT INC
Also Called: Woodlawn Tire & Alignment
8021 Us 221 N (28752-7565)
PHONE..................................828 756-4212
Andrew Winters, CEO
EMP: 6 EST: 2006
SALES (est): 462.97K Privately Held
SIC: 7534 Tire repair shop

Mars Hill
Madison County

(G-10191)
ADVANCED SUPERABRASIVES INC
1270 N Main St (28754-7500)
P.O. Box 1390 (28754-1390)
PHONE..................................828 689-3200
Jonathan Szucs, Pr
Attila Szucs, *
EMP: 28 EST: 1993
SQ FT: 34,000
SALES (est): 6.05MM Privately Held
Web: www.asiwheels.com
SIC: 3545 3291 Diamond cutting tools for turning, boring, burnishing, etc.; Abrasive products

(G-10192)
B-LED INC
400 Hickory Dr (28754-0470)
PHONE..................................828 680-1444
William Boyle, Prin
EMP: 6 EST: 2018
SALES (est): 138.56K Privately Held
SIC: 3993 Signs and advertising specialties

(G-10193)
BILLY RICE
365 Horace Rice Rd (28754-6510)
PHONE..................................828 691-4831
Billy Rice, Prin
EMP: 6 EST: 2011
SALES (est): 119.41K Privately Held
Web: www.legendoutdoorfurnace.com
SIC: 3567 Industrial furnaces and ovens

(G-10194)
DANCING MOON PRINT SLTIONS INC
16 N Main St (28754-9503)
PHONE..................................828 689-9353
Kim Barnes, Prin
EMP: 6 EST: 2007
SALES (est): 51.39K Privately Held
Web: www.dancingmoonprintsolutions.com
SIC: 2752 Offset printing

(G-10195)
GOOD BROS GINGER BREW LLC
516 Roy Forrester Rd (28754-6511)
PHONE..................................828 279-2512
EMP: 4 EST: 2015
SALES (est): 114.65K Privately Held
SIC: 2082 Malt beverages

(G-10196)
JIM HAMMONDS ENTERPRISES LLC
349 Miller Branch Rd (28754-9260)
PHONE..................................828 775-8805
EMP: 5 EST: 2020
SALES (est): 261.92K Privately Held
SIC: 1389 Construction, repair, and dismantling services

(G-10197)
TREE CRAFT LOG HOMES INC
43 Back Hollow Rd (28754-6702)
PHONE..................................828 689-2240
Don Fosson, Pr
Edward A Fosson, VP
Nancy A Fosson, Sec
EMP: 5 EST: 1978
SQ FT: 6,400
SALES (est): 302.91K Privately Held
Web: www.treecraft.net
SIC: 2452 Log cabins, prefabricated, wood

(G-10198)
WAGON WHEEL
89 Carl Eller Road (28754)
P.O. Box 411 (28754-0411)
PHONE..................................828 689-4755
Camille Taylor, Prin
EMP: 7 EST: 2010
SALES (est): 153.84K Privately Held
SIC: 3312 Wheels

Marshall
Madison County

(G-10199)
ASHEVILLE KOMBUCHA MAMAS LLC (PA)
Also Called: Buchi Kombucha
242 Derringer Dr (28753-8909)
PHONE..................................828 394-2360
Jeannine Buscher, Managing Member
Sarah I Schomber, *
EMP: 10 EST: 2009
SALES (est): 11.02MM
SALES (corp-wide): 11.02MM Privately Held
Web: www.drinkbuchi.com
SIC: 2086 Carbonated beverages, nonalcoholic: pkged. in cans, bottles

(G-10200)
BIG PINE LOG AND LUMBER INC
14245 Us 25/70 Hwy (28753-8333)
PHONE..................................828 656-2754
EMP: 6 EST: 2017
SALES (est): 171.99K Privately Held
SIC: 2421 5211 Sawmills and planing mills, general; Planing mill products and lumber

(G-10201)
DERINGER-NEY INC
155 Deringer Dr (28753)
P.O. Box 159 (28753-0159)
PHONE..................................828 649-3232
Richard Rzeszotarski, Brnch Mgr
EMP: 43
SALES (corp-wide): 98.41MM Privately Held
Web: www.deringerney.com
SIC: 3643 Contacts, electrical
PA: Deringer-Ney Inc.
353 Woodland Ave
Bloomfield CT 06002
860 242-2281

(G-10202)
GANNETT MEDIA CORP
News Record & Sentinal
58 Back St (28753)
P.O. Box 369 (28753-0369)
PHONE..................................828 649-1075
Christina Rice, Brnch Mgr
EMP: 6
SALES (corp-wide): 2.66B Publicly Held
Web: www.gannett.com
SIC: 2711 Newspapers, publishing and printing
HQ: Gannett Media Corp.
7950 Jones Branch Dr Fl 8
Mc Lean VA 22102
703 854-6000

(G-10203)
KD CABINETS INC
474 Wolf Branch Rd (28753-6016)
PHONE..................................828 689-3848
James Cady, Owner

EMP: 5 **EST:** 2006
SALES (est): 77.97K **Privately Held**
SIC: 2434 Wood kitchen cabinets

(G-10204)
LONGLEAF VINEYARD
36 Hallaran Dr (28753-6195)
PHONE..................828 435-3555
EMP: 4 **EST:** 2018
SALES (est): 90.89K **Privately Held**
Web: www.longleafvineyard.com
SIC: 2084 Wines

(G-10205)
MEDICAL MISSIONARY PRESS
491 Blue Hill Rd (28753-5366)
PHONE..................828 649-3976
Bob Jorgensen, *Dir*
EMP: 4 **EST:** 1985
SQ FT: 4,500
SALES (est): 284.05K **Privately Held**
Web: www.mmpress.info
SIC: 2741 Miscellaneous publishing

(G-10206)
PRINTPACK INC
Also Called: Printpack Medical Store
100 Kenpak Ln (28753-0770)
PHONE..................828 649-3800
EMP: 188
SALES (corp-wide): 1.3B **Privately Held**
Web: www.printpack.com
SIC: 3081 Film base, cellulose acetate or nitrocellulose plastics
HQ: Printpack, Inc.
2800 Overlook Pkwy Ne
Atlanta GA 30339
404 460-7000

(G-10207)
RED SHED WOODWORKS INC
200 Carl Bowman Rd (28753-4409)
P.O. Box 53 (28753-0053)
PHONE..................828 768-3854
Matt Yeakley, *Pr*
Morgan Yeakley, *VP*
EMP: 8 **EST:** 2004
SALES (est): 992.31K **Privately Held**
Web: www.redshedwoodworks.com
SIC: 2431 Millwork

(G-10208)
WEN BIZ JOURNAL
5150 Us 25/70 Hwy (28753-6448)
PHONE..................509 663-6730
Carol Forhan, *Prin*
EMP: 5 **EST:** 2012
SALES (est): 68.67K **Privately Held**
SIC: 2711 Commercial printing and newspaper publishing combined

Marshallberg
Carteret County

(G-10209)
BUDSIN WOOD CRAFT
142 Moore Ln (28553-9713)
PHONE..................252 729-1540
Tom Hesselink, *Owner*
EMP: 4 **EST:** 1987
SALES (est): 248.63K **Privately Held**
Web: www.budsin.com
SIC: 3732 Boats, fiberglass: building and repairing

Marshville
Union County

(G-10210)
ALLYN INTERNATIONAL TRDG CORP (PA)
412 College St (28103-1343)
P.O. Box 1682 (28111-1682)
PHONE..................877 858-2482
Ernest Allen, *Pr*
EMP: 8 **EST:** 2016
SQ FT: 28,000
SALES (est): 952.77K
SALES (corp-wide): 952.77K **Privately Held**
Web: www.aitc-steel.com
SIC: 8741 5085 2297 3842 Management services; Industrial supplies; Nonwoven fabrics; Surgical appliances and supplies

(G-10211)
CAROLINA WD PDTS MRSHVILLE INC
1112 Doctor Blair Rd (28103-9704)
P.O. Box 523 (28103-0523)
PHONE..................704 624-2119
Robert Horne Junior, *CEO*
Ronald Horne, *
Randy Horne, *
Frances Horne, *
EMP: 65 **EST:** 1969
SQ FT: 70,220
SALES (est): 4.86MM **Privately Held**
Web: www.carolinawood.net
SIC: 2448 2449 2441 Pallets, wood; Wood containers, nec; Nailed wood boxes and shook

(G-10212)
CORNERSTONE MFG CO LLC
4104 Philadelphia Church Rd (28103-8708)
PHONE..................704 624-6145
Ernest Scott Haigler, *Owner*
EMP: 4 **EST:** 2017
SALES (est): 72.17K **Privately Held**
SIC: 3999 Manufacturing industries, nec

(G-10213)
D C CUSTOM FREIGHT LLC
Also Called: Fiber Fuels
1901 Landsford Rd (28103-9718)
P.O. Box 430 (29718-0430)
PHONE..................843 658-6484
Don Underhill, *Owner*
EMP: 22 **EST:** 2004
SALES (est): 2.01MM **Privately Held**
SIC: 4731 2499 2421 Transportation agents and brokers; Mulch or sawdust products, wood; Sawdust, shavings, and wood chips

(G-10214)
DP CUSTOM WORKS LLC
5210 Horne Rd (28103-8005)
PHONE..................704 221-7291
EMP: 5 **EST:** 2017
SALES (est): 79.43K **Privately Held**
Web: www.dpcustomworksllc.com
SIC: 3599 Machine shop, jobbing and repair

(G-10215)
EDWARDS TIMBER COMPANY INC (PA)
2215 Old Lawyers Rd (28103-8002)
P.O. Box 219 (28103-0219)
PHONE..................704 624-5098
Carroll Edwards, *CEO*
EMP: 6 **EST:** 1969
SALES (est): 2.29MM
SALES (corp-wide): 2.29MM **Privately Held**
Web: www.ewpi.com
SIC: 2421 Sawmills and planing mills, general

(G-10216)
EDWARDS WOOD PRODUCTS INC (PA)
Also Called: Edwards Transportation
2215 Old Lawyers Rd (28103-8002)
P.O. Box 219 (28103-0219)
PHONE..................704 624-3624
Jeffrey G Edwards, *Pr*
Tina Edwards, *
Elona Edwards, *
Michelle Medlin, *
Lisa E Ammons, *
◆ **EMP:** 250 **EST:** 1969
SQ FT: 48,000
SALES (est): 75.9MM
SALES (corp-wide): 75.9MM **Privately Held**
Web: www.ewpi.com
SIC: 2448 2421 2631 2426 Pallets, wood; Sawmills and planing mills, general; Chip board; Hardwood dimension and flooring mills

(G-10217)
GRIFFIN INDUSTRIES LLC
Also Called: Bakery Feeds
5805 Highway 74 E (28103-7035)
PHONE..................704 624-9140
EMP: 44
SALES (corp-wide): 6.53B **Publicly Held**
Web: www.griffinind.com
SIC: 5083 2048 Agricultural machinery and equipment; Prepared feeds, nec
HQ: Griffin Industries Llc
4221 Alexandria Pike
Cold Spring KY 41076
859 781-2010

(G-10218)
HIGHS WELDING SHOP
1027 Unarco Rd (28103-9328)
P.O. Box 312 (28103-0312)
PHONE..................704 624-5707
Thomas High, *Owner*
Douglas High Junior, *Prin*
EMP: 6 **EST:** 1973
SQ FT: 11,500
SALES (est): 294.37K **Privately Held**
SIC: 7692 Welding repair

(G-10219)
HOP A CHOPPER INC
6703 Old Pglnd Marshvl Rd (28103-6702)
PHONE..................704 624-6794
Glenda T Lee, *Owner*
EMP: 5 **EST:** 2010
SALES (est): 183.23K **Privately Held**
SIC: 3751 Motorcycles and related parts

(G-10220)
MR FABRICATIONS LLC
Also Called: Elders MBL Grinding & Recycl
9403 Highway 742 (28103-7605)
PHONE..................980 785-3943
Mathew Rodriguez, *Prin*
EMP: 9 **EST:** 2017
SALES (est): 77.4K **Privately Held**
SIC: 7692 Welding repair

(G-10221)
PAUL HOGE CREATIONS INC
Also Called: Candlevision
7105 E Marshville Blvd (28103-1237)
P.O. Box 540 (28103-0540)
PHONE..................704 624-6860
Paul Hoge, *Pr*
◆ **EMP:** 15 **EST:** 1976
SQ FT: 15,000
SALES (est): 3MM **Privately Held**
Web: www.paulhogecreations.com
SIC: 3999 Candles

(G-10222)
PILGRIMS PRIDE CORPORATION
5901 Hwy 74 E (28103)
PHONE..................704 624-2171
EMP: 293
Web: www.pilgrims.com
SIC: 2015 0254 0252 2048 Chicken, slaughtered and dressed; Chicken hatchery; Chicken eggs; Poultry feeds
HQ: Pilgrim's Pride Corporation
1770 Promontory Cir
Greeley CO 80634
970 506-8000

(G-10223)
POLY PLASTIC PRODUCTS NC INC
1206 Traywick Rd (28103-9502)
PHONE..................704 624-2555
Steve Redlich, *Pr*
▼ **EMP:** 78 **EST:** 2003
SALES (est): 17.75MM **Privately Held**
Web: www.sigmaplasticsgroup.com
SIC: 2673 Plastic bags: made from purchased materials
PA: Alpha Industries Management, Inc.
2919 Center Port Cir
Pompano Beach FL 33064

(G-10224)
SEAFARER LLC (PA)
Also Called: Seagoing Uniform
220 E Main St (28103-1149)
PHONE..................704 624-3200
Hugh M Efird, *Pr*
Aaron H Efird, *VP*
Debbie Gibson, *Off Mgr*
EMP: 4 **EST:** 1938
SQ FT: 14,000
SALES (est): 15.75MM
SALES (corp-wide): 15.75MM **Privately Held**
SIC: 2326 2339 5136 5137 Work shirts: men's, youths', and boys'; Women's and misses' outerwear, nec; Men's and boy's clothing; Women's and children's clothing

(G-10225)
STONY KNOLL FORGE
1309 Hamiltons Cross Rd (28103-9513)
P.O. Box 3352 (28111-3352)
PHONE..................704 507-0179
William Kiker, *Prin*
EMP: 4 **EST:** 2018
SALES (est): 122.56K **Privately Held**
Web: www.stonyknollforge.com
SIC: 3446 Architectural metalwork

(G-10226)
UNION PLASTICS COMPANY
132 E Union St (28103-1141)
P.O. Box 512 (28103-0512)
PHONE..................704 624-2112
Carroll H Osborn, *Pr*
Sandra Osborn, *Sec*
EMP: 8 **EST:** 1967
SQ FT: 7,500
SALES (est): 962.52K **Privately Held**
SIC: 3432 Plastic plumbing fixture fittings, assembly

(G-10227)
VICTORY INFRSTRCTURE CNSTR LLC
1511 Doctor Blair Rd (28103-8302)
P.O. Box 720 (28103-0720)
PHONE..................704 572-8247

Marshville - Union County (G-10228)

EMP: 5 EST: 2016
SALES (est): 367.64K **Privately Held**
SIC: **1389** Construction, repair, and dismantling services

(G-10228)
WALCO INTERNATIONAL
531 E Main St Ste B (28103-1503)
PHONE..................................704 624-2473
Dale Zaimey, *Prin*
EMP: 6 EST: 2009
SALES (est): 151.91K **Privately Held**
SIC: **3999** Pet supplies

Marston
Richmond County

(G-10229)
AROMATHERAPY BY IRENE LLC
27041 Hoffman Rd (28363-8119)
PHONE..................................404 457-1871
EMP: 4 EST: 2018
SALES (est): 69.14K **Privately Held**
SIC: **3841** Inhalation therapy equipment

Matthews
Mecklenburg County

(G-10230)
AARONS QUALITY SIGNS
524 E Charles St (28105-4788)
PHONE..................................704 841-7733
EMP: 5 EST: 1986
SALES (est): 249.3K **Privately Held**
Web: www.aqsigns.com
SIC: **3993** Signs, not made in custom sign painting shops

(G-10231)
AGVE INC
13029 Bleinheim Ln Ste B (28105-4236)
PHONE..................................704 243-8300
EMP: 7 EST: 2014
SALES (est): 169.51K **Privately Held**
Web: www.agvegroup.com
SIC: **3714** Motor vehicle parts and accessories

(G-10232)
AL-TEX DYES CO LLC
1531 Wickerby Ct (28105-0323)
PHONE..................................704 849-9727
Mike Austell, *Prin*
EMP: 4 EST: 2019
SALES (est): 80.17K **Privately Held**
SIC: **2819** Industrial inorganic chemicals, nec

(G-10233)
ALTITUDE SIGN COMPANY LLC
900 Winter Wood Dr (28105-3810)
PHONE..................................980 339-8160
Steven Kenneth Kreis, *Owner*
EMP: 4 EST: 2015
SALES (est): 86.37K **Privately Held**
Web: www.altitudesigncompany.com
SIC: **3993** Signs and advertising specialties

(G-10234)
BODY ENGINEERING INC
701 Matthews Mint Hill Rd (28105-1706)
PHONE..................................704 650-3434
Kathy Feldman, *CEO*
Ross Leveque, *Pr*
EMP: 6 EST: 2003
SALES (est): 550K **Privately Held**
SIC: **2023** Dietary supplements, dairy and non-dairy based

(G-10235)
BORNEMANN PUMPS INC
901a Matthews Mint Hill Rd (28105-1704)
P.O. Box 1769 (28106-1769)
PHONE..................................704 849-8636
Tim Mabes, *Prin*
EMP: 6 EST: 2013
SALES (est): 220.33K **Privately Held**
SIC: **3561** Pumps and pumping equipment

(G-10236)
CAROLINA BG
624 Matthews Mint Hill Rd Ste B (28105-1761)
PHONE..................................704 847-8840
Thomas Scott, *Mgr*
EMP: 5 EST: 2008
SALES (est): 961.28K **Privately Held**
Web: www.carolinabg.com
SIC: **5169** 2911 Oil additives; Fuel additives

(G-10237)
CAROLINA CONCRETE INC (PA)
1316 Waxhaw Rd (28105)
PHONE..................................704 821-7645
James R Mc Clain, *Pr*
C Louise Mc Clain, *
EMP: 30 EST: 1972
SQ FT: 3,000
SALES (est): 2.9MM
SALES (corp-wide): 2.9MM **Privately Held**
SIC: **3273** Ready-mixed concrete

(G-10238)
CAROTEK INC (HQ)
Also Called: Carotek
700 Sam Newell Rd (28105-4515)
P.O. Box 1395 (28106-1395)
PHONE..................................704 844-1100
▲ EMP: 80 EST: 1965
SALES (est): 43.67MM
SALES (corp-wide): 664.84MM **Privately Held**
Web: www.carotek.com
SIC: **7692** 5084 Welding repair; Industrial machinery and equipment
PA: Sts Operating, Inc.
    2301 W Windsor Ct
    Addison IL 60101
    630 317-2700

(G-10239)
CCS INTERNATIONAL CIRCUITS LLC
1408 Wyndmere Hills Ln (28105-6810)
PHONE..................................704 907-1208
Joseph Fortmuller, *Brnch Mgr*
EMP: 7
Web: www.ccsintlcircuits.com
SIC: **3679** Electronic circuits
PA: Ccs International Circuits Llc
    523 S Paula Dr
    Dunedin FL 34698

(G-10240)
CHANNELTIVITY LLC
301 E John St (28106-4201)
P.O. Box 3449 (28106-3449)
PHONE..................................704 408-3560
EMP: 10 EST: 2007
SALES (est): 1.01MM **Privately Held**
Web: www.channeltivity.com
SIC: **7372** Business oriented computer software

(G-10241)
CHARLOTTE OBSERVER PUBG CO
Also Called: Charlotte Observer
10810 Independence Pointe Pkwy Ste H (28105-1754)
PHONE..................................704 358-6020
Glenn Hargett, *Brnch Mgr*
EMP: 38
SALES (corp-wide): 709.52MM **Privately Held**
SIC: **2711** 2741 Newspapers, publishing and printing; Miscellaneous publishing
HQ: The Charlotte Observer Publishing Company
    550 S Caldwell St Fl 10
    Charlotte NC 28202
    704 358-5000

(G-10242)
CITY PRINTS LLC
5008 Helena Park Ln (28105-7718)
PHONE..................................404 273-5741
Anthony N Rodono, *Prin*
EMP: 6 EST: 2013
SALES (est): 284.27K
SALES (corp-wide): 97.7MM **Privately Held**
Web: www.cityprintsmapart.com
SIC: **2752** Commercial printing, lithographic
PA: Vertitex Spa
    Via Pietro Ferloni 42
    Bulgarograsso CO 22070
    031 687-6400

(G-10243)
COC USA INC ◆
624 Matthews Mint Hill Rd Ste C (28105-1761)
PHONE..................................888 706-0059
Eiichi Kobayashi, *CEO*
Devin Ware, *Pr*
EMP: 5 EST: 2022
SALES (est): 482.37K **Privately Held**
SIC: **3562** Ball and roller bearings

(G-10244)
COG GLBAL MEDIA/CONSULTING LLC
738 Ablow Dr (28105-8905)
PHONE..................................980 239-8042
EMP: 20 EST: 2014
SALES (est): 301.86K **Privately Held**
SIC: **7812** 4841 2741 Audio-visual program production; Subscription television services; Miscellaneous publishing

(G-10245)
CUSTOM EXPRESS
1400 Industrial Dr (28105-5308)
P.O. Box 1377 (28105-1377)
PHONE..................................704 845-0900
EMP: 5 EST: 2019
SALES (est): 212.7K **Privately Held**
Web: www.yourcustomexpress.com
SIC: **2759** Screen printing

(G-10246)
DELCOR POLYMERS INC
2536 Winterbrooke Dr (28105-8859)
PHONE..................................704 847-0640
John Buhlinger, *Pr*
Jenevieve Buhlinger, *VP*
EMP: 5 EST: 1999
SQ FT: 1,500
SALES (est): 494.95K **Privately Held**
Web: www.delcorpolymers.com
SIC: **2821** Plastics materials and resins

(G-10247)
EVERGLOW NA INC
1122 Industrial Dr Ste 112 (28105-5419)
P.O. Box 830 (28106-0830)
PHONE..................................704 841-2580
Markus Thrun, *Pr*
Charles Barlow, *VP*
EMP: 20 EST: 2004
SALES (est): 2.55MM

SALES (corp-wide): 438.26K **Privately Held**
Web: www.everglow.us
SIC: **3993** 1799 Signs, not made in custom sign painting shops; Sign installation and maintenance
HQ: Everglow Gmbh
    Draisstr. 19a-B
    Muggensturm BW 76461

(G-10248)
EVERGREEN SILKS NC INC
Also Called: Evergreen Silks
901 Sam Newell Rd Ste I (28105-9400)
P.O. Box 1138 (28106-1138)
PHONE..................................704 845-5577
Mary Fehl, *Pr*
Jim Fehl, *VP*
EMP: 11 EST: 1992
SQ FT: 12,000
SALES (est): 922.26K **Privately Held**
Web: www.anysizeart.com
SIC: **3999** Artificial trees and flowers

(G-10249)
GALAXY GRAPHICS INC
1028 Brenham Ln (28105-8815)
P.O. Box 2191 (28106-2191)
PHONE..................................704 724-9057
Roger Walton, *Owner*
EMP: 5 EST: 1991
SALES (est): 93.46K **Privately Held**
Web: www.galaxygraphicsprinting.com
SIC: **2752** Offset printing

(G-10250)
H2H BLINDS
13137 Bleinheim Ln (28105-5092)
PHONE..................................704 628-5084
EMP: 10 EST: 2019
SALES (est): 450.81K **Privately Held**
Web: www.h2hinstall.com
SIC: **2591** Window blinds

(G-10251)
HAINES CORPORATION
3622 Glen Lyon Dr (28105-1000)
PHONE..................................704 545-4361
EMP: 4 EST: 2019
SALES (est): 56.97K **Privately Held**
SIC: **2741** Miscellaneous publishing

(G-10252)
HARRIS TEETER LLC
Also Called: Harris Teeter 157
1811 Matthews Township Pkwy (28105-4659)
PHONE..................................704 846-7117
EMP: 90
SALES (corp-wide): 148.26B **Publicly Held**
Web: www.harristeeter.com
SIC: **5411** 5992 5912 2051 Supermarkets, chain; Florists; Drug stores and proprietary stores; Bread, cake, and related products
HQ: Harris Teeter, Llc
    701 Crestdale Rd
    Matthews NC 28105
    704 844-3100

(G-10253)
HIGH MOBILITY SOLUTIONS INC
Also Called: Hsm
648 Matthews Mint Hill Rd Ste D (28105-1767)
P.O. Box 1299 (28106-1299)
PHONE..................................704 849-8242
EMP: 8 EST: 1976
SALES (est): 413.09K **Privately Held**

GEOGRAPHIC SECTION

Matthews - Mecklenburg County (G-10279)

SIC: 3695 Computer software tape and disks: blank, rigid, and floppy

(G-10254)
HOLLINGSWORTH & VOSE COMPANY
143 Sardis Pointe Rd (28105-5326)
PHONE.............................704 708-5913
John Fry, *Genl Mgr*
EMP: 5
SALES (corp-wide): 584.59MM **Privately Held**
Web: www.hollingsworth-vose.com
SIC: 2621 Paper mills
PA: Hollingsworth & Vose Company
112 Washington St
East Walpole MA 02032
508 850-2000

(G-10255)
INTERNATIONAL MINUTE PRESS
11100 Monroe Rd Ste H (28105-1322)
PHONE.............................704 246-3758
Randy Pellisero, *Owner*
EMP: 5 **EST:** 2017
SALES (est): 139.56K **Privately Held**
SIC: 2752 Offset printing

(G-10256)
JODY STOWE
Also Called: Charlottes Crown
2848 Lakeview Cir (28105-7562)
PHONE.............................704 519-6560
EMP: 5 **EST:** 1997
SALES (est): 224.57K **Privately Held**
SIC: 2431 Interior and ornamental woodwork and trim

(G-10257)
KALEIDA SYSTEMS INC
2530 Plantation Center Dr Ste A (28105-5298)
PHONE.............................704 814-4429
David Glenn, *Pr*
Russell Roux, *Prin*
EMP: 8 **EST:** 2001
SALES (est): 1.24MM **Privately Held**
Web: www.kaleidasystems.com
SIC: 7372 Business oriented computer software

(G-10258)
KARL OGDEN ENTERPRISES INC
Also Called: Ogden Enterprises
1320 Industrial Dr (28105-5307)
PHONE.............................704 845-2785
Karl Ogden, *Pr*
Brenley Ogden, *Sec*
◆ **EMP:** 9 **EST:** 1983
SQ FT: 20,000
SALES (est): 1.02MM **Privately Held**
Web: www.ogden-group.com
SIC: 3553 Woodworking machinery

(G-10259)
KERN-LIEBERS USA TEXTILE INC
921 Matthews Mint Hill Rd (28105-1776)
P.O. Box 519 (28106-0519)
PHONE.............................704 329-7153
Tasslo Baeuerle, *Pr*
Larry Ausley, *Contrlr*
▲ **EMP:** 21 **EST:** 2004
SQ FT: 9,600
SALES (est): 1.42MM **Privately Held**
SIC: 3552 Textile machinery

(G-10260)
KME CONSOLIDATED INC
Also Called: Ballabox
529 Crestdale Rd (28105)
P.O. Box 851 (28106-0851)
PHONE.............................704 847-9888
Kate B Young, *Pr*
Jim Kutcher, *
EMP: 30 **EST:** 1957
SQ FT: 51,300
SALES (est): 3.93MM **Privately Held**
Web: www.ballabox.com
SIC: 2657 2631 Folding paperboard boxes; Folding boxboard

(G-10261)
KRAL USA INC
901a Matthews Mint Hill Rd (28105-1704)
P.O. Box 2990 (28106-2990)
PHONE.............................704 814-6164
Otmar E Krautler, *Pr*
Richard Meighan, *Sec*
▲ **EMP:** 9 **EST:** 2001
SALES (est): 976.1K **Privately Held**
Web: www.kral-usa.com
SIC: 3561 Industrial pumps and parts

(G-10262)
LAUNDRY SVC TECH LTD LBLTY CO
Also Called: Pro Laundry Equipment
2217 Matthews Township Pkwy Ste D (28105-4815)
PHONE.............................908 327-1997
EMP: 6 **EST:** 2008
SALES (est): 416.2K **Privately Held**
Web: www.mylaundrycare.com
SIC: 3582 5087 Commercial laundry equipment; Laundry equipment and supplies

(G-10263)
LIZZYS LOGOS INC
3118 Savannah Hills Dr (28105-6732)
PHONE.............................704 321-2588
Elizabeth Thomas, *Prin*
EMP: 4 **EST:** 2010
SALES (est): 120.72K **Privately Held**
Web: www.lizzyslogosembroidery.com
SIC: 2323 Men's and boy's neckwear

(G-10264)
LUXEBRIGHT SKIN CARE LLC
Also Called: Luxebright Skin Care
2704 Cross Point Cir Apt 21 (28105-8406)
PHONE.............................877 614-9128
Simone L Mowatt, *CEO*
EMP: 4 **EST:** 2020
SALES (est): 20K **Privately Held**
SIC: 2844 5999 Face creams or lotions; Hair care products

(G-10265)
MACHINE CONTROL COMPANY INC LLC
1030 Industrial Dr (28105-5371)
P.O. Box 703 (28106-0703)
PHONE.............................704 708-5782
Chris Trapp, *Pr*
EMP: 4 **EST:** 1995
SALES (est): 718.77K **Privately Held**
Web: www.machinecontrolco.com
SIC: 3699 Electrical equipment and supplies, nec

(G-10266)
MANA NUTRITIVE AID PDTS INC (PA)
Also Called: Mana Nutrition
130 Library Ln Ste A (28105-5345)
P.O. Box 763 (28106-0763)
PHONE.............................855 438-6262
▼ **EMP:** 6 **EST:** 2009
SQ FT: 3,000
SALES (est): 29.22MM **Privately Held**
Web: www.mananutrition.org
SIC: 2099 Food preparations, nec

(G-10267)
MARTIN MARIETTA MATERIALS INC
Also Called: Martin Marietta Aggregates
1601 Sam Newell Rd (28105-7572)
P.O. Box 2198 (28106-2198)
PHONE.............................704 847-3087
EMP: 8
Web: www.martinmarietta.com
SIC: 1422 Crushed and broken limestone
PA: Martin Marietta Materials Inc
4123 Parklake Ave
Raleigh NC 27612

(G-10268)
MATTHEWS BUILDING SUPPLY CO
325 W Matthews St (28105-5320)
P.O. Box 607 (28106-0607)
PHONE.............................704 847-2106
Eric Hulsey, *Pr*
EMP: 50 **EST:** 1946
SQ FT: 30,000
SALES (est): 3.31MM **Privately Held**
Web: www.matthewsbuildingsupply.com
SIC: 5211 5251 2431 Lumber products; Hardware stores; Millwork

(G-10269)
MCGEE CORPORATION
12100 Stallings Commerce Dr (28105-5098)
PHONE.............................980 721-1911
EMP: 41 **EST:** 2019
SALES (est): 1.59MM **Privately Held**
Web: www.mcgeecorp.com
SIC: 3448 Prefabricated metal buildings and components

(G-10270)
MCGEE CORPORATION
Also Called: North Carolina McGee
12701 E Independence Blvd (28105-4103)
P.O. Box 1375 (28106-1375)
PHONE.............................704 882-1500
Richard M Mc Gee, *Pr*
John C Oakes, *
Arthur K Cates, *
Tommy L Broome, *
▼ **EMP:** 80 **EST:** 1948
SQ FT: 175,000
SALES (est): 20.24MM **Privately Held**
Web: www.mcgeecorp.com
SIC: 3448 3441 3444 Prefabricated metal buildings and components; Fabricated structural metal; Sheet metalwork

(G-10271)
METALFAB OF NORTH CAROLINA LLC
Also Called: Select Stainless
11145 Monroe Rd (28105-6564)
PHONE.............................704 841-1090
EMP: 160
SIC: 3431 3469 5078 2431 Metal sanitary ware; Kitchen fixtures and equipment: metal, except cast aluminum; Refrigerators, commercial (reach-in and walk-in); Millwork

(G-10272)
MICRO LENS TECHNOLOGY INC (PA)
3308 Mikelynn Dr (28105-3885)
P.O. Box 656 (28691-0656)
PHONE.............................704 847-9234
Kenneth Conley, *Pr*
Mary Ellen Conley, *VP Fin*
▲ **EMP:** 8 **EST:** 1997
SQ FT: 2,000
SALES (est): 787.9K
SALES (corp-wide): 787.9K **Privately Held**
Web: www.microlens.com

SIC: 3089 Engraving of plastics

(G-10273)
MID CAROLINA CABINETS INC
Also Called: Kitchen Distributors of South
1418 Industrial Dr (28105-5414)
PHONE.............................704 358-9950
Andrew H Estes, *Pr*
EMP: 6 **EST:** 2004
SALES (est): 313.9K **Privately Held**
Web: www.jwcabinets.com
SIC: 2434 Wood kitchen cabinets

(G-10274)
NATIONWIDE ANALGESICS LLC
3116 Weddington Rd # 900 (28105-9406)
PHONE.............................704 651-5551
Marcy Huey, *Prin*
EMP: 6 **EST:** 2010
SALES (est): 165.76K **Privately Held**
SIC: 2834 Analgesics

(G-10275)
NATSOL LLC
11100 Muses Ct (28105-1249)
PHONE.............................704 302-1246
Rfichard Clay, *Owner*
Richard Clay, *Owner*
EMP: 16 **EST:** 2016
SALES (est): 869.87K **Privately Held**
Web: natsolbodyshape.blogspot.com
SIC: 2833 Vitamins, natural or synthetic: bulk, uncompounded

(G-10276)
NONTOXIC PTHGEN ERDCTION CONS
1258 Mann Dr Ste 200 (28105-5548)
PHONE.............................800 308-1094
Charles Cole, *Managing Member*
Neal Speight, *Managing Member*
EMP: 8 **EST:** 2020
SALES (est): 512.36K **Privately Held**
SIC: 2834 Pharmaceutical preparations

(G-10277)
OFFERISOR LLC
1014 Brightmoor Dr (28105-2428)
PHONE.............................704 970-9700
Balasanyan Davit, *Prin*
EMP: 4 **EST:** 2012
SALES (est): 155.62K **Privately Held**
Web: www.offerisor.com
SIC: 7372 Prepackaged software

(G-10278)
OMNIA INDUSTRIES LLC
1430 Industrial Dr Ste A (28105-5300)
PHONE.............................704 707-6062
Denise Skinner, *Managing Member*
David Klinko, *Managing Member*
EMP: 4 **EST:** 2019
SALES (est): 260.36K **Privately Held**
SIC: 3429 Keys, locks, and related hardware

(G-10279)
ORACLE SYSTEMS CORPORATION
Also Called: Oracle
1608 Nightshade Pl (28105-0308)
PHONE.............................704 423-1426
Emily Kao, *Brnch Mgr*
EMP: 5
SALES (corp-wide): 49.95B **Publicly Held**
SIC: 7372 Prepackaged software
HQ: Oracle Systems Corporation
500 Oracle Pkwy
Redwood City CA 94065

Matthews - Mecklenburg County (G-10280)

(G-10280)
PACELINE INC (PA)
Also Called: Rx Textiles
10737 Independence Pointe Pkwy Ste 103 (28105-2885)
PHONE..................704 290-5007
Joseph Davant, *Pr*
Anne S Davant, *
Herman Pfisterer, *
▲ **EMP:** 42 **EST:** 1985
SQ FT: 15,000
SALES (est): 9.57MM
SALES (corp-wide): 9.57MM Privately Held
Web: www.paceline.com
SIC: 3842 2259 Prosthetic appliances; Stockinettes, knit

(G-10281)
POWER BUSINESS PRODUCTS LLC
1001 Somersby Ln (28105-1508)
PHONE..................704 604-2844
EMP: 4 **EST:** 2013
SALES (est): 246.45K Privately Held
Web: www.powerbusinessproducts.com
SIC: 2752 Commercial printing, lithographic

(G-10282)
PPG ARCHITECTURAL FINISHES INC
Also Called: Glidden Professional Paint Ctr
1600 Matthews Mint Hill Rd Ste B (28105-1848)
PHONE..................704 847-7251
Doug Ernhart, *Brnch Mgr*
EMP: 4
SALES (corp-wide): 17.65B Publicly Held
Web: www.glidden.com
SIC: 2851 Paints and allied products
HQ: Ppg Architectural Finishes, Inc.
1 Ppg Pl
Pittsburgh PA 15272
412 434-3131

(G-10283)
PUBLISHING GROUP INC
Also Called: Publishing Group, The
211 W Matthews St Ste 105 (28105-1310)
PHONE..................704 847-7150
Eddis Fulghum, *Pr*
EMP: 6 **EST:** 1988
SQ FT: 1,323
SALES (est): 471.9K Privately Held
Web: www.thevolunteerfiremanonline.com
SIC: 2741 Miscellaneous publishing

(G-10284)
R82 INC
13137 Bleinheim Ln (28105-5092)
P.O. Box 1739 (28106-1739)
PHONE..................704 882-0668
Ryan Williams, *Pr*
Ro Octave, *
▲ **EMP:** 25 **EST:** 1987
SQ FT: 25,000
SALES (est): 8.31MM
SALES (corp-wide): 1.76B Privately Held
Web: www.etac.com
SIC: 3842 Orthopedic appliances
HQ: Etac Ab
Farogatan 33
Kista 164 4
86334700

(G-10285)
REHAB SOLUTIONS INC
3029 Senna Dr (28105-6727)
PHONE..................800 273-3418
EMP: 6 **EST:** 2019
SALES (est): 198.37K Privately Held
SIC: 2741 Miscellaneous publishing

(G-10286)
RFSPROTECH LLC
1320 Industrial Dr (28105-5307)
PHONE..................704 845-2785
Russell Hass, *
▼ **EMP:** 25 **EST:** 2006
SQ FT: 20,000
SALES (est): 2.55MM Privately Held
Web: www.ogden-group.com
SIC: 3553 Woodworking machinery

(G-10287)
RSA SECURITY LLC
250 N Trade St (28105-9449)
PHONE..................704 847-4725
Jim Fisher, *Brnch Mgr*
EMP: 19
SALES (corp-wide): 1.44B Privately Held
Web: www.rsa.com
SIC: 3577 Computer peripheral equipment, nec
PA: Rsa Security Llc
2 Burlington Woods Dr # 2
Burlington MA 01803
800 995-5095

(G-10288)
SECOND MAIN PHASE SLUTIONS LLC
407 Clairview Ln (28105-0208)
PHONE..................704 303-0090
Jason Lu, *Prin*
EMP: 5 **EST:** 2019
SALES (est): 210.38K Privately Held
SIC: 7372 Prepackaged software

(G-10289)
SIGN O RAMA
3601 Matthews Mint Hill Rd (28105-4130)
PHONE..................704 443-0092
EMP: 4 **EST:** 2017
SALES (est): 46.08K Privately Held
SIC: 3993 Signs and advertising specialties

(G-10290)
SIGNAL PATH INTERNATIONAL LLC
Also Called: Peachtree Audio
13087 Bleinheim Ln Ste C (28105-4240)
PHONE..................704 391-9337
Andrew Clark, *Pr*
Jim Spainhour, *VP*
EMP: 5 **EST:** 2017
SALES (est): 204K Privately Held
Web: www.peachtreeaudio.com
SIC: 3651 Amplifiers: radio, public address, or musical instrument

(G-10291)
SOUTHERN CABINET CO INC
1418 Industrial Dr (28105-5414)
PHONE..................704 373-2299
James F Freeze Junior, *Pr*
Brian Freeze, *
Steve Foster, *
EMP: 18 **EST:** 1989
SQ FT: 40,000
SALES (est): 763.45K Privately Held
Web: www.lathamremodel.com
SIC: 2434 Wood kitchen cabinets

(G-10292)
SPEEDWAY LINK INC
3727 Weddington Ridge Ln (28105-7700)
PHONE..................704 338-2028
Mykoala Nagornyy, *Pr*
EMP: 10 **EST:** 2005
SQ FT: 8,000
SALES (est): 164.28K Privately Held
Web: www.speedway.com
SIC: 3715 4789 Truck trailers; Pipeline terminal facilities, independently operated

(G-10293)
STEVEN MESEROLL
202 Demaree Ln (28105-5637)
PHONE..................850 264-6079
EMP: 7 **EST:** 2016
SALES (est): 243.95K Privately Held
Web: www.procast-metals.com
SIC: 3444 Sheet metalwork

(G-10294)
STRONGHAVEN INCORPORATED
11135 Monroe Rd (28105-6564)
P.O. Box 1300 (28106-1300)
PHONE..................770 739-6080
Rodney Benson, *Genl Mgr*
EMP: 100
Web: www.hoodcontainer.com
SIC: 2653 Boxes, corrugated: made from purchased materials
HQ: Stronghaven, Incorporated
2727 Paces Ferry Rd Se 1-1850
Atlanta GA 30339
678 235-2713

(G-10295)
TOTAL CONTROLS INC
4420 Friendship Dr Ste A (28105-5902)
P.O. Box 629 (28106-0629)
PHONE..................704 821-6341
EMP: 8 **EST:** 1995
SQ FT: 4,000
SALES (est): 987.7K Privately Held
Web: www.totalcontrols.com
SIC: 3625 1731 Relays and industrial controls; Electronic controls installation

(G-10296)
TRANSCONTINENTAL AC US LLC (HQ)
700 Crestdale Rd (28105-4700)
PHONE..................704 847-9171
Francois Olivier, *Managing Member*
▲ **EMP:** 19 **EST:** 2007
SALES (est): 24.17MM
SALES (corp-wide): 2.15B Privately Held
Web: www.transcontinentaladvancedcoatings.com
SIC: 2631 2621 Container, packaging, and boxboard; Wrapping and packaging papers
PA: Transcontinental Inc
1 Place Ville-Marie Bureau 3240
Montreal QC H3B 0
514 954-4000

(G-10297)
TVL INTERNATIONAL LLC
165 S Trade St (28105-5771)
P.O. Box 2278 (28106-2278)
PHONE..................704 814-0930
▲ **EMP:** 4 **EST:** 2004
SALES (est): 423.26K Privately Held
Web: www.gaswatch.com
SIC: 3491 Process control regulator valves

(G-10298)
VIGOR LLC
9905 Devereaux Dr (28105-6705)
PHONE..................704 661-0891
EMP: 4 **EST:** 2016
SALES (est): 70.55K Privately Held
SIC: 3731 Shipbuilding and repairing

(G-10299)
WATKINS CABINETS LLC
1418 Industrial Dr (28105-5414)
PHONE..................704 634-1724
John Watkins Estes, *Prin*
EMP: 7 **EST:** 2013
SALES (est): 221.22K Privately Held
SIC: 2434 Wood kitchen cabinets

Matthews
Union County

(G-10300)
ACM PANELS
708 Kelly Dr (28104-5142)
PHONE..................704 839-0104
Julio Gonzalez, *Prin*
EMP: 7 **EST:** 2019
SALES (est): 64.34K Privately Held
Web: www.metalimpressionsinc.com
SIC: 3444 Sheet metalwork

(G-10301)
ASSOCIATED BATTERY COMPANY
3469 Gribble Rd (28104-8114)
P.O. Box 1590 (28079-1590)
PHONE..................704 821-8311
Dwight Hobbs, *Pr*
EMP: 10 **EST:** 1980
SALES (est): 196.79K Privately Held
Web: www.associatedbattery.com
SIC: 3691 Storage batteries

(G-10302)
ATLANTIC PINSTRIPING ATL WRAPS
4108 Matthews Indian Trail Rd (28104-5008)
PHONE..................704 201-4406
EMP: 5 **EST:** 2019
SALES (est): 209.72K Privately Held
Web: www.atlanticcustomwraps.com
SIC: 3993 Signs and advertising specialties

(G-10303)
B P PRINTING AND COPYING INC
3756 Pleasant Plains Rd (28104-5960)
PHONE..................704 821-8219
Boyce Paysoyce, *Pr*
EMP: 4 **EST:** 1998
SALES (est): 295.31K Privately Held
SIC: 2752 Offset printing

(G-10304)
BERRY GLOBAL FILMS LLC
303 Seaboard Dr (28104-8155)
PHONE..................704 821-2316
Donald L Brafford, *Mgr*
EMP: 247
Web: www.berryglobal.com
SIC: 3081 2673 Polyethylene film; Bags: plastic, laminated, and coated
HQ: Berry Global Films, Llc
95 Chestnut Ridge Rd
Montvale NJ 07645
201 641-6600

(G-10305)
BRICKS & QUARTERS LLC
3014 Shalford Ln (28104-6879)
PHONE..................704 321-0124
Tracey Rogers, *Prin*
EMP: 4 **EST:** 2020
SALES (est): 76.29K Privately Held
SIC: 3131 Quarters

(G-10306)
BULLDOG MACHINE INC
3330 Smith Farm Rd (28104-5040)
PHONE..................704 200-7838
James Rublee, *Pr*
EMP: 5 **EST:** 2017
SALES (est): 123.87K Privately Held

GEOGRAPHIC SECTION

Matthews - Union County (G-10334)

SIC: **3599** Machine shop, jobbing and repair

(G-10307)
CEM CORPORATION (HQ)
Also Called: Innovtors In McRwave Technolgy
3100 Smith Farm Rd (28104-5044)
P.O. Box 200 (28106-0200)
PHONE.................................704 821-7015
Michael J Collins, *Pr*
Richard N Decker, *
◆ EMP: 180 EST: 1971
SQ FT: 70,000
SALES (est): 81.54MM **Privately Held**
Web: www.cem.com
SIC: **3826** 3679 Moisture analyzers; Microwave components
PA: Cem Holdings Corporation
3100 Smith Farm Rd
Matthews NC 28104

(G-10308)
CEM HOLDINGS CORPORATION (PA)
3100 Smith Farm Rd (28104-5044)
P.O. Box 200 (28106-0200)
PHONE.................................704 821-7015
EMP: 27 EST: 1971
SALES (est): 81.94MM **Privately Held**
Web: www.cem.com
SIC: **3826** Moisture analyzers

(G-10309)
CHOICE AWARDS & SIGNS
4036 Matthews Indian Trail Rd (28104-3920)
PHONE.................................704 844-0860
Deforest Kenemer, *Owner*
EMP: 6 EST: 1994
SQ FT: 5,000
SALES (est): 419.42K **Privately Held**
Web: choice-awards-signs.hub.biz
SIC: **3993** Signs, not made in custom sign painting shops

(G-10310)
CONSOLIDATED EMC INC
2240 Stevens Mill Rd (28104-4204)
PHONE.................................980 245-2859
EMP: 5 EST: 2014
SALES (est): 117.57K **Privately Held**
SIC: **3572** Computer storage devices

(G-10311)
DAVIS STEEL AND IRON CO INC
1035 Commercial Dr (28104-5001)
P.O. Box 3450 (28106-3450)
PHONE.................................704 821-7676
EMP: 37 EST: 1967
SALES (est): 4.92MM **Privately Held**
Web: www.davissteel.com
SIC: **3441** 3449 3446 Fabricated structural metal; Miscellaneous metalwork; Ornamental metalwork

(G-10312)
DN YAGER WOODWORKS
709 Catawba Cir N (28104-5111)
PHONE.................................704 236-3481
Dennis Yager, *Prin*
EMP: 5 EST: 2011
SALES (est): 112.16K **Privately Held**
Web: www.dnywoodworks.com
SIC: **2431** Millwork

(G-10313)
ELEKTRIKREDD LLC
2123 Stevens Mill Rd (28104-4248)
PHONE.................................704 805-0110
EMP: 5 EST: 2020
SALES (est): 100K **Privately Held**

SIC: **3537** Trucks: freight, baggage, etc.: industrial, except mining

(G-10314)
EZ CUSTOM SCREEN PRINTING
600 Union West Blvd Ste B (28104-8841)
PHONE.................................704 821-8488
Ed Jones, *Owner*
EMP: 23 EST: 2014
SALES (est): 980.09K **Privately Held**
Web: www.ezcustomscreenprinting.com
SIC: **2759** Screen printing

(G-10315)
EZ CUSTOM SCRNPRINTING EMB INC
200 Foxton Rd (28104-7307)
PHONE.................................704 821-9641
Ez Jones, *Owner*
EMP: 7 EST: 2006
SALES (est): 366.03K **Privately Held**
Web: www.ezcustomscreenprinting.com
SIC: **2759** Screen printing

(G-10316)
FIRE RETARDANT CHEM TECH LLC
Also Called: Frct
3465 Gribble Rd (28104-8114)
PHONE.................................980 253-8880
Futong Cui, *Pr*
EMP: 5 EST: 2014
SQ FT: 2,000
SALES (est): 1.2MM
SALES (corp-wide): 7.22B **Publicly Held**
SIC: **2899** 8733 Fire retardant chemicals; Research institute
HQ: Prowood, Llc
2801 E Beltline Ave Ne
Grand Rapids MI

(G-10317)
FRESH AIR TECHNOLOGIES LLC
2246 Stevens Mill Rd Ste B (28104-4210)
PHONE.................................704 622-7877
EMP: 17 EST: 2010
SALES (est): 2.49MM **Privately Held**
Web: www.thefreshaircompanies.com
SIC: **3563** Air and gas compressors

(G-10318)
GLOBAL SYNERGY GROUP INC
13663 Providence Rd Ste 370 (28104-9373)
PHONE.................................704 254-9886
Larayne Whitehead, *CEO*
EMP: 5 EST: 2009
SALES (est): 106.76K **Privately Held**
SIC: **3482** Small arms ammunition

(G-10319)
GRUND AMERICA LLC
220 Reefton Rd (28104-6002)
PHONE.................................704 287-1805
America Grund, *CEO*
▲ EMP: 25 EST: 2014
SALES (est): 2.22MM **Privately Held**
Web: www.livegrund.com
SIC: **2273** Carpets and rugs

(G-10320)
HMF INC
3479 Gribble Rd (28104-8114)
PHONE.................................704 821-6765
Robert T Hucks, *Pr*
Kathy T Hucks, *Sec*
EMP: 8 EST: 1985
SQ FT: 9,500
SALES (est): 1.12MM **Privately Held**
Web: www.hmf.com

SIC: **3599** Machine shop, jobbing and repair

(G-10321)
HUNTER MILLWORK INC
422 Seaboard Dr (28104-5073)
P.O. Box 2483 (28106-2483)
PHONE.................................704 821-0144
Glenn Ronald Hunter, *Pr*
EMP: 14 EST: 1997
SALES (est): 2.04MM **Privately Held**
Web: www.huntermillwork.com
SIC: **5211** 2431 Door and window products; Awnings, blinds and shutters: wood

(G-10322)
INTERNATIONAL CNSTR EQP INC (PA)
Also Called: Ice
301 Warehouse Dr (28104-8100)
PHONE.................................704 821-8200
T Richard Morris, *Pr*
Thomas P Cunningham, *
Kurt W Seufort, *
Brock Hemmingsen, *
Dick Morris, *
◆ EMP: 25 EST: 1974
SQ FT: 50,000
SALES (est): 14.99MM
SALES (corp-wide): 14.99MM **Privately Held**
Web: www.iceusa.com
SIC: **7353** 3531 Heavy construction equipment rental; Vibrators for concrete construction

(G-10323)
ITC MILLWORK LLC (PA)
Also Called: Interior Trim Creations
3619 Gribble Rd (28104-8112)
P.O. Box 1618 (28079-1618)
PHONE.................................704 821-1470
EMP: 85 EST: 1999
SQ FT: 49,000
SALES (est): 9.85MM
SALES (corp-wide): 9.85MM **Privately Held**
Web: www.itcmillwork.com
SIC: **2431** Moldings and baseboards, ornamental and trim

(G-10324)
J J JENKINS INCORPORATED
3380 Smith Farm Rd (28104-5040)
P.O. Box 1949 (28106-1949)
PHONE.................................704 821-6648
EMP: 27 EST: 1984
SALES (est): 4.63MM **Privately Held**
Web: www.jjjenkinsinc.com
SIC: **8711** 5084 3552 Designing: ship, boat, machine, and product; Textile machinery and equipment; Textile machinery

(G-10325)
J&J WOODWORKING LLC
1004 Raywood Ct (28104-8547)
PHONE.................................704 941-9537
EMP: 5 EST: 2019
SALES (est): 54.13K **Privately Held**
SIC: **2431** Millwork

(G-10326)
JOHN W FOSTER SALES INC
3491 Gribble Rd (28104-8114)
P.O. Box 2883 (28106-2883)
PHONE.................................704 821-3822
Debi Long, *Pr*
John W Foster, *Pr*
Debbie Long, *VP*
EMP: 9 EST: 1973
SALES (est): 423.46K **Privately Held**

SIC: **3569** Filters, general line: industrial

(G-10327)
KC STONE INC
3821 Wesley Chapel Rd (28104-6371)
PHONE.................................704 907-1361
EMP: 7 EST: 2018
SALES (est): 260.05K **Privately Held**
Web: www.kcstoneinc.com
SIC: **2434** Wood kitchen cabinets

(G-10328)
LIQUID ICE CORPORATION
500 Union West Blvd Ste C (28104-8802)
PHONE.................................704 882-3505
Henry Rabinovich, *Pr*
EMP: 10 EST: 2002
SALES (est): 954.45K **Privately Held**
Web: www.liquidicecoolant.com
SIC: **2899** Chemical preparations, nec

(G-10329)
M3 PRODUCTS COM
Also Called: Scienscope Products
1537 Golden Rain Dr (28104-6215)
P.O. Box 1657 (28106-1657)
PHONE.................................631 938-1245
Susan Vincenti, *Pt*
EMP: 5 EST: 2008
SALES (est): 263.12K **Privately Held**
Web: www.scienscopeproducts.com
SIC: **3827** Optical instruments and lenses

(G-10330)
MANG SYSTEMS INC
500 Union West Blvd Ste B (28104-8802)
PHONE.................................704 292-1041
EMP: 5 EST: 1988
SQ FT: 16,000
SALES (est): 757.36K **Privately Held**
Web: www.pdm-at.com
SIC: **5084** 3599 Industrial machinery and equipment; Machine shop, jobbing and repair

(G-10331)
MASTER FORM INC
500 Union West Blvd Ste B (28104-8802)
PHONE.................................704 292-1041
Heinz Roth, *Pr*
▲ EMP: 26 EST: 1993
SQ FT: 16,000
SALES (est): 1.05MM **Privately Held**
SIC: **3471** 3444 3441 Finishing, metals or formed products; Sheet metalwork; Fabricated structural metal

(G-10332)
MASTER KRAFT INC
3350 Smith Farm Rd (28104-5040)
PHONE.................................704 234-2673
Michael Kovalev, *Prin*
EMP: 30 EST: 2006
SALES (est): 2.78MM **Privately Held**
Web: www.masterkraftinc.com
SIC: **2431** Millwork

(G-10333)
MASTERPIECE STAIRCASE LLC ✪
3368 Smith Farm Rd (28104-5040)
PHONE.................................704 806-2894
Jonathan Wisher, *Managing Member*
EMP: 5 EST: 2022
SALES (est): 63.22K **Privately Held**
SIC: **2431** Staircases and stairs, wood

(G-10334)
MCNEELY MOTORSPORTS INC
340 Seaboard Dr (28104-8119)
PHONE.................................704 426-7430

(PA)=Parent Co (HQ)=Headquarters
✪ = New Business established in last 2 years

Matthews - Union County (G-10335)

Myra Holt Mcneely, *Prin*
EMP: 4 **EST:** 2011
SALES (est): 162.78K **Privately Held**
SIC: 3949 Sporting and athletic goods, nec

(G-10335)
MELLTRONICS INDUSTRIAL INC
(PA)
3479 Gribble Rd (28104-8114)
P.O. Box 2368 (28079-2368)
PHONE..............................704 821-6651
Frederick Mellon, *Pr*
Gregory Barker, *Sec*
Scott W Mellon, *VP*
EMP: 5 **EST:** 1993
SQ FT: 2,000
SALES (est): 3.21MM **Privately Held**
Web: www.melltronics.com
SIC: 3625 Motor controls and accessories

(G-10336)
MMDI INC
Also Called: Steelpoint
200 Beltway Blvd (28104-8807)
PHONE..............................704 882-4550
Michael J Edwards, *Pr*
Deborah L Edwards, *
EMP: 55 **EST:** 2010
SQ FT: 60,000
SALES (est): 9.01MM **Privately Held**
Web: www.mmdicorp.com
SIC: 3441 Fabricated structural metal

(G-10337)
NORTHEAST TOOL AND MFG COMPANY
15200 Idlewild Rd (28104-1418)
P.O. Box 55 (28079-0055)
PHONE..............................704 882-1187
EMP: 45 **EST:** 1964
SALES (est): 9.94MM **Privately Held**
Web: www.northeasttool.us
SIC: 3444 3495 3544 3541 Sheet metalwork; Mechanical springs, precision; Special dies and tools; Grinding machines, metalworking

(G-10338)
OPTOMILL SOLUTIONS LLC
1223 Clover Ln (28104-6119)
PHONE..............................704 560-4037
Colleen A Davies, *Managing Member*
EMP: 4 **EST:** 2017
SALES (est): 153.54K **Privately Held**
SIC: 3999 Manufacturing industries, nec

(G-10339)
ORNAMENTAL SPECIALTIES INC
3488 Gribble Rd (28104-8105)
P.O. Box 1980 (28079-1980)
PHONE..............................704 821-9154
EMP: 12 **EST:** 1994
SALES (est): 2.01MM **Privately Held**
Web: www.ornamentalspecialties.com
SIC: 3446 Ornamental metalwork

(G-10340)
PRECISION MACHINE TOOLS CORP
500 Union West Blvd Ste A (28104-8802)
PHONE..............................704 882-3700
Henry S Rabinovich, *Pr*
Susan Rabinovich, *Sec*
EMP: 6 **EST:** 1988
SQ FT: 8,000
SALES (est): 510.06K **Privately Held**
Web: www.pmtcorporation.com
SIC: 3599 Machine shop, jobbing and repair

(G-10341)
PROSTAR PRINTING PROM PRO
6010 Bluebird Hill Ln (28104-7258)
PHONE..............................704 839-0253
EMP: 4 **EST:** 2019
SALES (est): 114.89K **Privately Held**
Web: www.prostarprinting.com
SIC: 2752 Commercial printing, lithographic

(G-10342)
SCR CONTROLS INC
Also Called: SCR/ Melltronics
3479 Gribble Rd (28104-8114)
P.O. Box 2368 (28079-2368)
PHONE..............................704 821-6651
Fred Mellon, *Pr*
Scott Mellon, *VP*
Pamela Holly, *Sec*
EMP: 12 **EST:** 1981
SQ FT: 6,000
SALES (est): 3.21MM **Privately Held**
Web: www.scrcontrols.com
SIC: 3621 7629 8711 Electric motor and generator parts; Electronic equipment repair; Electrical or electronic engineering
PA: Melltronics Industrial, Inc.
     3479 Gribble Rd
     Matthews NC 28104

(G-10343)
SIGNARC OF MATTHEWS LLC
14101 E Independence Blvd (28104-5104)
PHONE..............................704 209-4444
Thomas A Greene, *Admn*
EMP: 5 **EST:** 2016
SALES (est): 226.9K **Privately Held**
SIC: 3993 Signs and advertising specialties

(G-10344)
SORBE LTD
111 Cupped Oak Dr Ste A (28104-8823)
P.O. Box 457 (28106-0457)
PHONE..............................704 562-2991
▲ **EMP:** 5 **EST:** 1995
SQ FT: 17,000
SALES (est): 437.05K **Privately Held**
SIC: 2339 5137 Sportswear, women's; Women's and children's clothing

(G-10345)
SOUTHERN MLLWK BY DESIGN INC
2105 Blue Iris Dr (28104-4107)
PHONE..............................704 309-8854
EMP: 5 **EST:** 2006
SALES (est): 57.06K **Privately Held**
SIC: 2431 Millwork

(G-10346)
STEELCO INC
1020 Commercial Dr (28104-5004)
PHONE..............................704 896-1207
Brooks Davis, *Pr*
Jean Davis, *Sec*
EMP: 10 **EST:** 1993
SQ FT: 14,000
SALES (est): 1.23MM **Privately Held**
Web: www.steelco.co
SIC: 3441 Fabricated structural metal

(G-10347)
STS SCREEN PRINTING INC
107 Industrial Dr (28104-5147)
PHONE..............................704 821-8488
Devonne Smith, *Pr*
EMP: 6 **EST:** 1994
SQ FT: 5,000
SALES (est): 598.39K **Privately Held**
SIC: 2759 2395 Screen printing; Embroidery and art needlework

(G-10348)
SURFACE RENEWAL SYSTEMS LLC
Also Called: SRS Partners
5024 Saddle Horn Trl (28104-7751)
PHONE..............................704 207-3596
Mark Gavrilov, *Ex Dir*
EMP: 4 **EST:** 2020
SALES (est): 116.89K **Privately Held**
SIC: 1389 1799 1721 Construction, repair, and dismantling services; Coating, caulking, and weather, water, and fireproofing; Bridge painting

(G-10349)
TECHSOUTH INC
601 Union West Blvd (28104-8820)
P.O. Box 1799 (28106-1799)
PHONE..............................704 334-1100
Joe Kloiber, *Pr*
▲ **EMP:** 9 **EST:** 1983
SQ FT: 15,000
SALES (est): 1.67MM **Privately Held**
Web: www.techsouthinc.com
SIC: 3545 7699 Cutting tools for machine tools; Welding equipment repair

(G-10350)
WATSON STEEL & IRON WORKS LLC
3624 Gribble Rd (28104-8107)
PHONE..............................704 821-7140
Douglas B Watson, *Managing Member*
EMP: 23 **EST:** 1975
SQ FT: 2,400
SALES (est): 2.34MM **Privately Held**
Web: www.watsonsteelandiron.com
SIC: 1791 3446 7389 Iron work, structural; Architectural metalwork; Crane and aerial lift service

(G-10351)
WILDCAT PETROLEUM SERVICE INC
326 Hawksnest Ct (28104-4261)
P.O. Box 690816 (28227-7014)
PHONE..............................704 379-0132
EMP: 10 **EST:** 1999
SALES (est): 560.14K **Privately Held**
Web: www.wildcatpetroleuminc.com
SIC: 3728 Refueling equipment for use in flight, airplane

(G-10352)
WOODWORKING BY ROBT WADDE
218 K Line Dr Ste A (28104-5996)
PHONE..............................704 236-0883
Robert Waddell, *Prin*
EMP: 6 **EST:** 2011
SALES (est): 152.23K **Privately Held**
SIC: 2431 Millwork

Maxton
Robeson County

(G-10353)
3 D FOOTPRINTS LOGGING INC
145 Cabinet Shop Rd (28364-8964)
PHONE..............................910 521-2640
EMP: 4 **EST:** 2018
SALES (est): 192.45K **Privately Held**
SIC: 2411 Logging

(G-10354)
ADVANCED CUTTING TECH INC
Also Called: Adcut
12760 Airport Rd (28364-9429)
PHONE..............................910 944-3028
EMP: 8 **EST:** 1995
SQ FT: 6,750
SALES (est): 992.99K **Privately Held**

Web: www.adcut.net
SIC: 3599 Machine shop, jobbing and repair

(G-10355)
EMBREX POULTRY HEALTH LLC
22300 Skyway Church Rd (28364-6412)
P.O. Box 190 (28364-0190)
PHONE..............................910 844-5566
EMP: 14 **EST:** 2003
SALES (est): 878.03K
SALES (corp-wide): 8.08B **Publicly Held**
SIC: 2834 Pharmaceutical preparations
PA: Zoetis Inc.
     10 Sylvan Way Ste 100
     Parsippany NJ 07054
     973 822-7000

(G-10356)
HUVEPHARMA INC
22300 Skyway Church Rd (28364-6412)
PHONE..............................910 506-4649
Glen Wilkinson, *Pr*
EMP: 13 **EST:** 2016
SALES (est): 1.43MM **Privately Held**
Web: www.huvepharma.com
SIC: 2834 Veterinary pharmaceutical preparations

(G-10357)
JASON CULBERTSON
Also Called: Rocks Remodeling Dirt & Gravel
357 Lighthouse Rd (28364-7583)
PHONE..............................910 733-6794
Jason Culbertson, *Owner*
EMP: 4 **EST:** 2021
SALES (est): 66.08K **Privately Held**
SIC: 1442 Construction sand and gravel

(G-10358)
K & W WELDING LLC
12721 Airport Rd (28364-9430)
PHONE..............................910 844-2288
EMP: 4 **EST:** 2015
SALES (est): 49.35K **Privately Held**
Web: www.kwwllc.com
SIC: 7692 Welding repair

(G-10359)
MERITOR INC
Also Called: Arvinmeritor Automotive
22021 Skyway Church Rd Ste B (28364-6946)
PHONE..............................910 844-9401
Rick Martello, *Mgr*
EMP: 17
SALES (corp-wide): 34.06B **Publicly Held**
Web: www.meritor.com
SIC: 3714 Motor vehicle parts and accessories
HQ: Meritor, Inc.
     2135 W Maple Rd
     Troy MI 48084

(G-10360)
MERITOR INC
Also Called: Transmission Div
22021 Skyway Church Rd Ste A (28364-6946)
PHONE..............................910 844-9401
David Coleman, *Manager*
EMP: 100
SALES (corp-wide): 34.06B **Publicly Held**
Web: www.meritor.com
SIC: 3714 3568 Motor vehicle parts and accessories; Power transmission equipment, nec
HQ: Meritor, Inc.
     2135 W Maple Rd
     Troy MI 48084

GEOGRAPHIC SECTION

Mc Leansville - Guilford County (G-10384)

(G-10361)
MOUNTAIRE FARMS INC
10800 Pell Dr (28364-5641)
PHONE..................910 844-3126
Gary Scott, *Brnch Mgr*
EMP: 58
SALES (corp-wide): 2.07B **Privately Held**
Web: www.mountaire.com
SIC: **2048** 5191 Prepared feeds, nec; Animal feeds
HQ: Mountaire Farms Inc.
1901 Napa Valley Dr
Little Rock AR 72212
501 372-6524

(G-10362)
RAILROAD FRICTION PDTS CORP
13601 Airport Rd (28364-6819)
P.O. Box 1349 (28353-1349)
PHONE..................910 844-9709
Rafael Santana, *CEO*
Matthew Jurinski, *
◆ EMP: 150 EST: 1954
SQ FT: 800
SALES (est): 43.48MM **Publicly Held**
Web: www.wabteccorp.com
SIC: **3743** Railroad equipment, except locomotives
PA: Westinghouse Air Brake Technologies Corporation
30 Isabella St
Pittsburgh PA 15212

Mayodan
Rockingham County

(G-10363)
BMS INVESTMENT HOLDINGS LLC
225 Commerce Ln (27027-8597)
P.O. Box 37 (27027-0037)
PHONE..................336 949-4107
Scott Mcneil, *Genl Mgr*
Sara Brust, *
▼ EMP: 45 EST: 2009
SQ FT: 2,500
SALES (est): 8.81MM **Privately Held**
Web: www.blowmoldedsolutions.com
SIC: **3089** Injection molding of plastics

(G-10364)
JOHN K CHENAUSKY
Also Called: John K Chenausky, Owner
3494 Ayersville Rd (27027-8241)
PHONE..................336 427-2495
John K Chenausky, *Prin*
EMP: 6 EST: 2004
SALES (est): 83.27K **Privately Held**
SIC: **2421** Sawmills and planing mills, general

(G-10365)
MCMICHAEL MILLS INC (PA)
130 Shakey Rd (27027-8587)
P.O. Box 507 (27025-0507)
PHONE..................336 548-4242
Dalton L Mcmichael Junior, *Pr*
Martha Ford, *
Brac Brigman, *
◆ EMP: 200 EST: 1993
SQ FT: 87,000
SALES (est): 34.55MM **Privately Held**
Web: www.mcmichaelmills.com
SIC: **2241** Rubber and elastic yarns and fabrics

(G-10366)
MILLIKEN & COMPANY
Also Called: Two Rivers Plant
109 Turner Rd (27027-8251)
PHONE..................336 548-5680
Mark Rice, *Brnch Mgr*
EMP: 19
SALES (corp-wide): 1.69B **Privately Held**
Web: www.milliken.com
SIC: **2281** Yarn spinning mills
PA: Milliken & Company
920 Milliken Rd
Spartanburg SC 29303
864 503-2020

(G-10367)
SHILOH PRODUCTS INC
203 N 1st Ave (27027-2401)
PHONE..................336 548-6035
EMP: 5 EST: 2019
SALES (est): 47.23K **Privately Held**
Web: www.durashiloh.com
SIC: **3465** Automotive stampings

(G-10368)
STURM RUGER & COMPANY INC
271 Cardwell Rd (27027-8043)
PHONE..................336 427-0286
EMP: 388
SALES (corp-wide): 595.84MM **Publicly Held**
Web: www.ruger.com
SIC: **5941** 3489 Firearms; Artillery or artillery parts, over 30 mm.
PA: Sturm, Ruger & Company, Inc.
1 Lacey Pl
Southport CT 06890
203 259-7843

Maysville
Jones County

(G-10369)
BRADLEY TODD BAUGUS
6444 White Oak River Rd (28555-7081)
PHONE..................252 665-4901
Bradley Todd Baugus, *Prin*
EMP: 7 EST: 2016
SALES (est): 149.59K **Privately Held**
SIC: **2411** Logging

(G-10370)
C MURRELLS EVENT PLANNING LLC
1004 Main St (28555-5000)
PHONE..................910 382-2742
Nichole Murrell, *Prin*
EMP: 4 EST: 2019
SALES (est): 46.58K **Privately Held**
SIC: **2211** Canvas

(G-10371)
CUTTING UP LOGGING LLC
1507 White Oak River Rd (28555-9327)
PHONE..................910 389-3539
EMP: 5 EST: 2017
SALES (est): 89.89K **Privately Held**
SIC: **2411** Logging camps and contractors

(G-10372)
FAERIE STAR FORGE
206 Halibut Ct (28555-9612)
PHONE..................910 743-2862
Anna Meredith, *Owner*
EMP: 4 EST: 2015
SALES (est): 102.94K **Privately Held**
Web: www.faeriestarforge.com
SIC: **3911** Jewelry, precious metal

(G-10373)
JAMIE M DOLLAHAN
112 Hardin Dr (28555-9378)
PHONE..................571 435-2060
Jamie Dollahan, *Owner*
EMP: 4 EST: 2015
SALES (est): 42.32K **Privately Held**
SIC: **3269** Cookware: stoneware, coarse earthenware, and pottery

(G-10374)
MARIETTA MARTIN MATERIALS INC
Also Called: Martin Marietta Aggregates
2998 Belgrade Swansboro Rd (28555-9427)
P.O. Box 99 (28555-0099)
PHONE..................910 743-6471
Jerry Fraizer, *Mgr*
EMP: 5
Web: www.martinmarietta.com
SIC: **1422** Cement rock, crushed and broken-quarrying
PA: Martin Marietta Materials Inc
4123 Parklake Ave
Raleigh NC 27612

(G-10375)
STELLA CABINET WORKS
218 Starlight Ln (28555-9486)
PHONE..................910 358-4248
David Cain, *Mgr*
EMP: 5 EST: 2009
SALES (est): 73.71K **Privately Held**
SIC: **2434** Wood kitchen cabinets

(G-10376)
STEVE & RAY BANKS LOGGING INC
Also Called: Banks, Steve and Ray Logging
7625 New Bern Hwy (28555-9322)
P.O. Box 448 (28555-0448)
PHONE..................910 743-3051
Steven Banks, *Pr*
Ray Bank, *VP*
Ruth Banks, *Sec*
EMP: 4 EST: 1953
SALES (est): 496K **Privately Held**
SIC: **2411** Pulpwood contractors engaged in cutting

Mc Adenville
Gaston County

(G-10377)
COATS HP INC
Also Called: Pharr Ph/Crescent Plant
300 Dickson Rd (28101)
PHONE..................704 824-9904
▲ EMP: 323
SQ FT: 2,268
SALES (corp-wide): 1.58B **Privately Held**
SIC: **2281** 2282 2824 Manmade and synthetic fiber yarns, spun; Manmade and synthetic fiber yarns, twisting, winding, etc.; Acrylic fibers
HQ: Coats Hp Inc.
14120 Balntyn Corp Pl # 300
Charlotte NC 28277
704 329-5800

(G-10378)
EXTRA-DIMENSIONAL PUBG LLC
516 Academy St (28101-9004)
PHONE..................704 574-4652
David Wilson Brown, *Admn*
EMP: 5 EST: 2013
SALES (est): 112.13K **Privately Held**
SIC: **2741** Miscellaneous publishing

(G-10379)
MANNINGTON MILLS INC
Also Called: Pharr Fibers and Yarns
200 Saxony Dr (28101)
PHONE..................704 824-3551
EMP: 45
SALES (corp-wide): 686.34MM **Privately Held**
Web: www.mannington.com
SIC: **2281** 2824 Manmade and synthetic fiber yarns, spun; Acrylic fibers
PA: Mannington Mills Inc.
75 Mannington Mills Rd
Salem NJ 08079
800 356-6787

(G-10380)
PHARR MCADENVILLE CORPORATION (PA)
100 Main St (28101)
P.O. Box 1939 (28101-1939)
PHONE..................704 824-3551
William J P Carstarphen, *Pr*
EMP: 72 EST: 2003
SALES (est): 102.45MM
SALES (corp-wide): 102.45MM **Privately Held**
Web: www.pharrcorp.com
SIC: **6719** 2281 2282 2824 Investment holding companies, except banks; Manmade and synthetic fiber yarns, spun; Manmade and synthetic fiber yarns, twisting, winding, etc.; Acrylic fibers

Mc Farlan
Anson County

(G-10381)
HOW GREAT THOU ART PUBLICATION
Hwy 52 Sr 1003 Ste 357 (28102)
P.O. Box 48 (28102-0048)
PHONE..................704 851-3117
Barry Stebbing, *Owner*
EMP: 4 EST: 1991
SQ FT: 700
SALES (est): 226.23K **Privately Held**
Web: www.howgreatthouart.com
SIC: **2731** Book publishing

Mc Grady
Wilkes County

(G-10382)
WILKES WELDING AND MCH CO INC
1018 Mulberry Rd (28649-9618)
P.O. Box 1067 (28659-1067)
PHONE..................336 670-2742
Jeral Sebastian, *Pr*
Doris Sebastian, *Treas*
EMP: 5 EST: 1955
SQ FT: 6,500
SALES (est): 483.65K **Privately Held**
SIC: **3599** 7692 Machine shop, jobbing and repair; Welding repair

Mc Leansville
Guilford County

(G-10383)
BIG TIRE OUTFITTERS
5210 Cragganmore Dr (27301-9524)
PHONE..................919 568-9605
Brian Roberts, *Owner*
EMP: 8 EST: 2015
SALES (est): 216.78K **Privately Held**
SIC: **7534** Rebuilding and retreading tires

(G-10384)
BLUE RIDGE PROPELLER REPR LLC
5307 Verna Rd (27301-9616)

Mc Leansville - Guilford County (G-10385)

PHONE..................................276 340-1597
Jason E Spence, *Admn*
EMP: 4 **EST:** 2014
SALES (est): 215.43K **Privately Held**
Web: proprepairs.wordpress.com
SIC: 3366 Propellers

(G-10385)
BLUEWATER PALLET SOLUTIONS
5517 Burlington Rd (27301-9622)
PHONE..................................336 697-9109
Marc Scudder, *Owner*
EMP: 4 **EST:** 2009
SALES (est): 332.46K **Privately Held**
SIC: 2448 Pallets, wood

(G-10386)
CONTINENTAL MANUFACTURING CO
814c Knox Rd Ste E (27301-9227)
PHONE..................................336 697-2591
Briz Walia, *Owner*
EMP: 4 **EST:** 2004
SALES (est): 241.01K **Privately Held**
SIC: 2899 3999 Concrete curing and hardening compounds; Manufacturing industries, nec

(G-10387)
COOPER THOMAS & BENTON PRTG CO
829 Knox Rd (27301-9227)
PHONE..................................336 698-0951
Glenn Benton, *Owner*
EMP: 4 **EST:** 2018
SALES (est): 69.95K **Privately Held**
SIC: 2752 Offset printing

(G-10388)
DECAL SOURCE INC
804 Knox Rd (27301-9227)
PHONE..................................336 574-3141
Anthony Johnson, *Pr*
Jeffrey L Fischer, *Stockholder**
Brian T Fleming, *Stockholder**
Vass A Barbour, *Stockholder**
Charlie L Christopher, *Stockholder**
▲ **EMP:** 24 **EST:** 1998
SQ FT: 1,500
SALES (est): 4.22MM **Privately Held**
Web: www.thedecalsource.com
SIC: 2752 Decals, lithographed

(G-10389)
DONS STITCHES
4705 Benttree Dr (27301-8107)
PHONE..................................336 554-6697
Donald Williams, *Prin*
EMP: 4 **EST:** 2015
SALES (est): 46.79K **Privately Held**
SIC: 2395 Embroidery and art needlework

(G-10390)
GENERAL DYNAMICS CORPORATION
5440 Millstream Rd Ste W300 (27301)
PHONE..................................336 698-8571
Earl Mc Bride, *Brnch Mgr*
EMP: 28
SALES (corp-wide): 42.27B **Publicly Held**
Web: www.gd.com
SIC: 7372 Prepackaged software
PA: General Dynamics Corporation
11011 Sunset Hills Rd
Reston VA 20190
703 876-3000

(G-10391)
GENERAL DYNMICS MSSION SYSTEMS
5440 Millstream Rd Ste W300 (27301-9274)
PHONE..................................336 698-8000
Harry Grant, *Prin*
EMP: 234
SALES (corp-wide): 42.27B **Publicly Held**
Web: www.gdmissionsystems.com
SIC: 3669 3812 7373 8711 Emergency alarms; Search and navigation equipment; Computer integrated systems design; Engineering services
HQ: General Dynamics Mission Systems, Inc.
12450 Fair Lakes Cir
Fairfax VA 22033
877 449-0600

(G-10392)
H & H WOODWORKING LLC
4159 Keeley Rd (27301-9746)
PHONE..................................336 676-6524
Rhonda Holbrook, *Prin*
EMP: 4 **EST:** 2018
SALES (est): 54.13K **Privately Held**
SIC: 2431 Millwork

(G-10393)
IRSI AUTOMATION INC
3703 Hines Chapel Rd (27301-9113)
PHONE..................................336 303-5320
Kenneth Moore, *Pr*
Gary Floyd, *Treas*
EMP: 5 **EST:** 2015
SALES (est): 334.51K **Privately Held**
SIC: 3569 7699 8711 8742 Liquid automation machinery and equipment; Industrial machinery and equipment repair; Machine tool design; Automation and robotics consultant

(G-10394)
MMS LOGISTICS INCORPORATED
1509 Guinness Dr (27301-9512)
PHONE..................................336 214-3552
Ranaldo Harden, *CEO*
EMP: 5 **EST:** 2016
SALES (est): 274.41K **Privately Held**
SIC: 4789 3537 Transportation services, nec; Trucks: freight, baggage, etc.: industrial, except mining

(G-10395)
QUICK COLOR SOLUTIONS
829 Knox Rd (27301-9227)
PHONE..................................336 698-0951
Mary Benton, *Prin*
EMP: 6 **EST:** 2009
SALES (est): 517.13K **Privately Held**
Web: www.quickcolorsolutions.com
SIC: 2752 Offset printing

Mebane
Alamance County

(G-10396)
AKG NORTH AMERICA INC
7315 Oakwood Street Ext (27302-9211)
P.O. Box 365 (27302-0365)
PHONE..................................919 563-4286
Ralf Hutter, *VP*
Richard White, ***
Peter Feuerle, ***
Ron Prichard, *VP*
Alexander Gress, *VP*
◆ **EMP:** 28 **EST:** 1981
SALES (est): 9.58MM **Privately Held**
Web: www.akg-america.com
SIC: 3443 Fabricated plate work (boiler shop)

(G-10397)
AKG NRTH AMERCN OPERATIONS INC (DH)
7315 Oakwood Street Ext (27302-9211)
PHONE..................................919 563-4286
◆ **EMP:** 11 **EST:** 2010
SALES (est): 97.94MM
SALES (corp-wide): 1.2MM **Privately Held**
Web: www.akg-america.com
SIC: 3443 Cooling towers, metal plate
HQ: Autokuhler Gmbh & Co. Kg
Am Hohlen Weg 31
Hofgeismar HE 34369
56718831172

(G-10398)
AKG OF AMERICA INC (DH)
7315 Oakwood Street Ext (27302-9211)
P.O. Box 370 (27302-0370)
PHONE..................................919 563-4286
G Richard White, *Pr*
◆ **EMP:** 36 **EST:** 1981
SQ FT: 100,000
SALES (est): 76.53MM
SALES (corp-wide): 1.2MM **Privately Held**
Web: www.akg-america.com
SIC: 3443 Heat exchangers, condensers, and components
HQ: Autokuhler Gmbh & Co. Kg
Am Hohlen Weg 31
Hofgeismar HE 34369
56718831172

(G-10399)
ARMACELL US HOLDINGS LLC
7600 Oakwood Street Ext (27302-9577)
PHONE..................................919 304-3846
Ulrich Weimer, *Pr*
James F Mars Junior, *VP*
EMP: 200 **EST:** 2000
SALES (est): 30.58MM **Privately Held**
Web: www.armacell.com
SIC: 3086 Plastics foam products
PA: Insulation United States Holdings, Llc
7600 Oakwood Street Ext
Mebane NC 27302

(G-10400)
BIOMERICS LLC ✪
1413 S Third St (27302-8186)
PHONE..................................336 810-7178
EMP: 6 **EST:** 2023
SALES (est): 79.3K **Privately Held**
SIC: 3089 Plastics products, nec

(G-10401)
BROADSIGHT SYSTEMS INC
1023 Corporate Park Dr (27302-8368)
PHONE..................................336 837-1272
Takeshi Fujita, *Pr*
▲ **EMP:** 5 **EST:** 2011
SALES (est): 991.5K **Privately Held**
Web: www.broadsightsystems.com
SIC: 7539 3599 Machine shop, automotive; Machine and other job shop work
HQ: Cbc America Holding Corp
1023 Corporate Park Dr
Mebane NC 27302
919 230-8700

(G-10402)
CAMBBRO MANUFACTURING COMPANY
1268 W Holt St (27302-8174)
PHONE..................................919 568-8506
EMP: 15 **EST:** 2016
SALES (est): 660.02K **Privately Held**
SIC: 3999 Atomizers, toiletry

(G-10403)
CAMBRO
1268 Holt St (27302-9148)
PHONE..................................919 563-0761
Jon Skiffington, *Pr*
EMP: 6 **EST:** 2015
SALES (est): 193.54K **Privately Held**
Web: blog.cambro.com
SIC: 3999 Manufacturing industries, nec

(G-10404)
CARRIER FIRE SEC AMERICAS CORP
Also Called: CARRIER FIRE & SECURITY AMERICAS CORPORATION
1027 Corporate Park Dr (27302-8368)
PHONE..................................919 563-5911
Scott Little, *Brnch Mgr*
EMP: 46
SALES (corp-wide): 22.1B **Publicly Held**
Web: corporate.carrier.com
SIC: 3669 Burglar alarm apparatus, electric
HQ: Carrier Fire & Security Americas, Llc
13995 Pasteur Blvd
Palm Beach Gardens FL 33418

(G-10405)
COMFORTLAND INTERNATIONAL LLC
709 A O Smith Rd (27302-2752)
PHONE..................................866 277-3135
Lois Tsui, *Pr*
◆ **EMP:** 12 **EST:** 2010
SQ FT: 10,000
SALES (est): 1MM **Privately Held**
Web: www.comfortlandmed.com
SIC: 3842 Orthopedic appliances

(G-10406)
D & S INTERNATIONAL INC
700 Trollingwood Hawflds Rd (27302-8169)
P.O. Box 40 (27302-0040)
PHONE..................................336 578-3800
Frank Strohlein, *Pr*
Emy Strohlein, *VP*
Bonnie Philips, *VP*
◆ **EMP:** 14 **EST:** 1982
SQ FT: 102,000
SALES (est): 2.21MM **Privately Held**
Web: www.dandsinternational.com
SIC: 3552 Textile machinery

(G-10407)
DORMER PRAMET LLC
1483 Dogwood Way (27302-9115)
PHONE..................................800 877-3745
◆ **EMP:** 282 **EST:** 2010
SALES (est): 2.5MM
SALES (corp-wide): 11.77B **Privately Held**
Web: www.dormerpramet.com
SIC: 3545 Drills (machine tool accessories)
HQ: Sandvik, Inc.
1483 Dogwood Way
Mebane NC 27302
919 563-5008

(G-10408)
EAST COAST DIGITAL INC
100 E Ruffin St (27302-2441)
P.O. Box 483 (27302-0483)
PHONE..................................919 304-1142
John Cornett, *Pr*
Glenn Cornett, *VP*
Christie Aaron, *Sec*
EMP: 10 **EST:** 2004
SALES (est): 558.71K **Privately Held**
SIC: 3651 Household audio equipment

GEOGRAPHIC SECTION

Mebane - Alamance County (G-10432)

(G-10409)
FORMA-FAB METALS INC
5816 Us 70 W (27302-8807)
P.O. Box 710 (27302-0710)
PHONE..................919 563-5630
EMP: 35 **EST:** 1995
SQ FT: 50,000
SALES (est): 4.47MM **Privately Held**
Web: www.formafab.com
SIC: 3441 Fabricated structural metal

(G-10410)
GENERAL ELECTRIC COMPANY
Also Called: GE
I-85 Buckhorn Rd (27302)
PHONE..................919 563-7445
Rodger Gasaway, *Brnch Mgr*
EMP: 15
SALES (corp-wide): 67.95B **Publicly Held**
Web: www.ge.com
SIC: 3625 3537 Control circuit relays, industrial; Industrial trucks and tractors
PA: General Electric Company
1 Financial Ctr Ste 3700
Boston MA 02111
617 443-3000

(G-10411)
GENERAL ELECTRIC COMPANY
GE
6801 Industrial Dr (27302-8603)
PHONE..................919 563-5561
Eric Tate, *Mgr*
EMP: 460
SQ FT: 9,514
SALES (corp-wide): 67.95B **Publicly Held**
Web: www.ge.com
SIC: 3625 3537 3613 Control circuit relays, industrial; Industrial trucks and tractors; Switchgear and switchboard apparatus
PA: General Electric Company
1 Financial Ctr Ste 3700
Boston MA 02111
617 443-3000

(G-10412)
GKN DNA INC
Also Called: Alamance Facility
1067 Trollingwood Hawflds Rd (27302-9740)
PHONE..................919 304-7378
EMP: 8 **EST:** 2010
SALES (est): 707.89K **Privately Held**
SIC: 3714 Universal joints, motor vehicle

(G-10413)
GKN DRIVELINE NORTH AMER INC
1067 Trollingwood Hawflds Rd (27302-9740)
P.O. Box 220 (27302-0220)
PHONE..................919 304-7252
Jeff Brooks, *Prin*
EMP: 23
SALES (corp-wide): 4.25MM **Privately Held**
SIC: 3714 Universal joints, motor vehicle
HQ: Gkn Driveline North America, Inc.
2200 N Opdyke Rd
Auburn Hills MI 48326
248 296-7000

(G-10414)
HARMONY FARM CANDLES
404 S First St (27302-3102)
PHONE..................919 698-5200
Erin Hils, *Prin*
EMP: 5 **EST:** 2016
SALES (est): 95.68K **Privately Held**
SIC: 3999 Candles

(G-10415)
KINGSDOWN INCORPORATED (HQ)
110 S Fourth St (27302-2640)
P.O. Box 388 (27302-0388)
PHONE..................919 563-3531
Frank Hood, *Pr*
Timothy Price, *
◆ **EMP:** 25 **EST:** 1904
SALES (est): 84.16MM
SALES (corp-wide): 84.16MM **Privately Held**
Web: www.kingsdown.com
SIC: 2515 5712 5023 Mattresses, innerspring or box spring; Mattresses; Homefurnishings
PA: Kingsdown Holdings Inc.
110 S Fourth St
Mebane NC 27302
919 563-3531

(G-10416)
LIGGETT GROUP LLC (DH)
100 Maple Ln (27302-8160)
PHONE..................919 304-7700
James A Taylor, *
Steven H Erikson, *
Jerry R Loftin, *
John R Long, *
▲ **EMP:** 372 **EST:** 1911
SQ FT: 300,000
SALES (est): 112.29MM **Publicly Held**
Web: www.liggettvectorbrands.com
SIC: 2111 Cigarettes
HQ: Vgr Holding Llc
4400 S Biscayne Blvd # 10
Miami FL 33131

(G-10417)
LOTUS BAKERIES US LLC
2010 Park Center Dr (27302-9817)
PHONE..................415 956-8956
Jan Boone, *CEO*
Ignace Heyman, *COO*
EMP: 5 **EST:** 2017
SALES (est): 1.03MM
SALES (corp-wide): 183.75K **Privately Held**
SIC: 5963 5145 5149 2052 Food services, direct sales; Snack foods; Health foods; Bakery products, dry
HQ: Lotus Bakeries North America, Inc.
1000 Sansome St Ste 350
San Francisco CA 94111

(G-10418)
MAJORPOWER CORPORATION
7011 Industrial Dr (27302-8605)
PHONE..................919 563-6610
Oren Nutik, *Pr*
Samuel Norman, *
▲ **EMP:** 25 **EST:** 1990
SQ FT: 20,000
SALES (est): 3.48MM **Privately Held**
Web: www.majorpower.com
SIC: 5065 3629 Communication equipment; Inverters, nonrotating: electrical

(G-10419)
MEBANE MACHINE & TOOL LLC
317 Canterwood Dr (27302-9709)
PHONE..................919 597-1169
EMP: 4 **EST:** 2015
SALES (est): 119.59K **Privately Held**
SIC: 3599 Machine shop, jobbing and repair

(G-10420)
MORINAGA AMERICA FOODS INC
Also Called: Morinaga America
4391 Wilson Rd (27302-9823)
PHONE..................919 643-2439
Toshiaki Fukunaga, *CEO*
Masao Hoshino, *Pr*
Teruhiro Kawabe, *COO*
Tomohiko Nakatogawa, *CFO*
▲ **EMP:** 31 **EST:** 2013
SALES (est): 5.05MM **Privately Held**
Web: www.morinaga-america-foods.com
SIC: 2064 Chewing candy, not chewing gum

(G-10421)
NYPRO INC
Also Called: Nypro Mebane
1018 Corporate Park Dr (27302-8368)
PHONE..................919 304-1400
Gordon Lankton, *Brnch Mgr*
EMP: 4011
SALES (corp-wide): 34.7B **Publicly Held**
Web: www.jabil.com
SIC: 3089 Injection molding of plastics
HQ: Nypro Inc.
101 Union St
Clinton MA 01510
978 365-9721

(G-10422)
PAK-LITE INC
6508 E Washington Street Ext (27302-7222)
PHONE..................919 563-1097
Jimmy Reily, *Brnch Mgr*
EMP: 37
SALES (corp-wide): 58.39MM **Privately Held**
Web: www.pliusa.com
SIC: 3086 Packaging and shipping materials, foamed plastics
PA: Pak-Lite, Inc.
550 Old Peachtree Rd Nw
Suwanee GA 30024
770 447-5123

(G-10423)
PARK COURT PROPERTIES RE INC
1404 Dogwood Way Unit C (27302-9586)
PHONE..................919 304-3110
Doug Mahar, *Mgr*
EMP: 10
SALES (corp-wide): 4.28MM **Privately Held**
SIC: 3823 Water quality monitoring and control systems
PA: Park Court Properties Real Estate, Inc.
207a Park Ct
Ridgeland MS 39157
601 605-3000

(G-10424)
PIEDMONT METALWORKS LLC
5902 Us 70 W (27302-8808)
PHONE..................919 598-6500
Ron Hamilton, *Pr*
Ron Hamilton, *Pr*
EMP: 5 **EST:** 2007
SALES (est): 913.94K **Privately Held**
Web: www.piedmontmetalworks.com
SIC: 3441 Fabricated structural metal

(G-10425)
PRECISION CONCEPTS MEBANE LLC (DH)
1405 Dogwood Way (27302-9115)
PHONE..................919 563-9292
James M Piermarini, *Pr*
▲ **EMP:** 76 **EST:** 1984
SQ FT: 50,000
SALES (est): 24.69MM **Privately Held**
Web: www.pcinternational.com
SIC: 3089 Injection molding of plastics
HQ: Biomerics, Llc
6030 W Harold Gatty Dr
Salt Lake City UT 84116

(G-10426)
PRECISION PRTCLE MSREMENTS INC
1514 Saddle Club Rd (27302-8509)
PHONE..................919 667-6960
Gary Linz, *Pr*
Bary Linz, *Pr*
EMP: 5 **EST:** 2015
SALES (est): 65.48K **Privately Held**
SIC: 3826 Analytical instruments

(G-10427)
SANDVIK INC (HQ)
Also Called: Sandvik Coromant
1483 Dogwood Way (27302-9115)
P.O. Box 428 (07410-0428)
PHONE..................919 563-5008
Rick Askin, *Pr*
◆ **EMP:** 250 **EST:** 1919
SALES (est): 911.74MM
SALES (corp-wide): 11.77B **Privately Held**
Web: www.home.sandvik
SIC: 3316 3317 3356 3315 Strip, steel, cold-rolled, nec: from purchased hot-rolled,; Tubes, seamless steel; Zirconium and zirconium alloy: rolling, drawing,or extruding ; Wire products, ferrous/iron: made in wiredrawing plants
PA: Sandvik Ab
Hogbovagen 45
Sandviken 811 3
26260000

(G-10428)
SANDVIK MCHNING SLTONS USA LLC
295 Maple Ln (27302-0748)
PHONE..................919 563-5008
EMP: 14
SALES (corp-wide): 11.77B **Privately Held**
SIC: 3545 Machine tool accessories
HQ: Sandvik Machining Solutions Usa Llc
2424 Sandifer Blvd
Westminster SC 29693
800 726-3845

(G-10429)
SANDVIK TOOLING
1483 Dogwood Way (27302-9115)
PHONE..................919 563-5008
Jogendra Saxena, *Mgr*
EMP: 4 **EST:** 2010
SALES (est): 423.71K **Privately Held**
SIC: 3541 Drilling machine tools (metal cutting)

(G-10430)
TATUMS TRUCKING & WELDING LLC
1804 Mill Creek Rd (27302-8830)
PHONE..................919 697-6913
Addison Tatum, *Admn*
EMP: 6 **EST:** 2020
SALES (est): 88.73K **Privately Held**
SIC: 7692 Welding repair

(G-10431)
TEA DOGU
102 Village Dr Apt 426 (27302-9856)
PHONE..................818 404-6523
Eric Lane, *Prin*
EMP: 5 **EST:** 2011
SALES (est): 73.33K **Privately Held**
Web: www.teadogu.com
SIC: 2499 Wood products, nec

(G-10432)
TECH MEDICAL PLASTICS INC
1403 Dogwood Way (27302-9115)
PHONE..................919 563-9272

Mebane - Alamance County (G-10433)

James Piermarini, *Pr*
Alberto Rossato, *VP Opers*
Pamela Ward, *CFO*
EMP: 15 **EST:** 1989
SQ FT: 15,000
SALES (est): 243.09K **Privately Held**
SIC: 3089 3083 Injection molded finished plastics products, nec; Laminated plastics plate and sheet

(G-10433)
THOMPSON MILLWORK LLC
200 Redman Xing (27302-8625)
P.O. Box 11349 (27703-0349)
PHONE.................................919 596-8236
Matt Thompson, *CEO*
Becky Crapo, *
Wayne Wickham, *
EMP: 74 **EST:** 2018
SQ FT: 123,000
SALES (est): 5.32MM **Privately Held**
Web: www.thompsonmillwork.com
SIC: 2541 1522 2431 Wood partitions and fixtures; Residential construction, nec; Millwork

(G-10434)
UNIVERSAL PRESERVACHEM INC
Also Called: Upi Chem Distribution Center
2390 Park Center Dr (27302-9848)
PHONE.................................732 568-1266
Daniel Ravitz, *Pr*
Herbert Ravitz, *
Michael Ravitz, *
Jim Sardi, *
◆ **EMP:** 81 **EST:** 1969
SALES (est): 28.96MM **Privately Held**
Web: www.upichem.com
SIC: 5169 2844 2834 Chemicals and allied products, nec; Perfumes, cosmetics and other toilet preparations; Pharmaceutical preparations

(G-10435)
WALTER KIDDE PORTABLE EQP INC (HQ)
Also Called: Kidde Safety
1016 Corporate Park Dr (27302-8368)
PHONE.................................919 563-5911
Isis Wu, *Pr*
Kenneth Cammarato, *
Jack Parow, *
Chris Rovenstine, *
◆ **EMP:** 269 **EST:** 1987
SQ FT: 100,000
SALES (est): 105.5MM
SALES (corp-wide): 22.1B **Publicly Held**
Web: www.kidde.com
SIC: 3669 5099 Smoke detectors; Fire extinguishers
PA: Carrier Global Corporation
13995 Pasteur Blvd
Palm Beach Gardens FL 33418
561 365-2000

(G-10436)
WALTON LUMBER CO
302 Circle Dr (27302-2726)
P.O. Box 218 (27302-0218)
PHONE.................................919 563-6565
Sam L White, *Pt*
Ellen White Turner, *Pt*
EMP: 7 **EST:** 1950
SALES (est): 775.31K **Privately Held**
SIC: 2426 5211 Lumber, hardwood dimension; Planing mill products and lumber

(G-10437)
WOMACK PUBLISHING CO INC
Also Called: Mebane Enterprise
106 N Fourth St (27302-2428)
PHONE.................................919 563-3555
Jackie Brown, *Mgr*
EMP: 5
SQ FT: 1,850
SALES (corp-wide): 21.7MM **Privately Held**
Web: www.womackpublishing.com
SIC: 2711 Newspapers: publishing only, not printed on site
PA: Womack Publishing Company, Inc.
28 N Main St
Chatham VA 24531
434 432-2791

(G-10438)
WRKCO INC
7411 Oakwood Street Ext (27302-9212)
PHONE.................................919 304-0300
Joe Royal, *Owner*
EMP: 4
SALES (corp-wide): 20.31B **Publicly Held**
SIC: 2631 Paperboard mills
HQ: Wrkco Inc.
1000 Abernathy Rd Ste 12
Atlanta GA 30328
770 448-2193

Merritt
Pamlico County

(G-10439)
CUSTOM STEEL BOATS INC
102 Yacht Dr (28556-9433)
P.O. Box 148 (28556-0148)
PHONE.................................252 745-7447
Rodney Flowers, *Pr*
Teresa Flowers, *VP*
EMP: 15 **EST:** 1981
SQ FT: 16,000
SALES (est): 1.65MM **Privately Held**
Web: www.customsteelboats.com
SIC: 3732 1799 1721 Boats, fiberglass: building and repairing; Sandblasting of building exteriors; Commercial painting

Merry Hill
Bertie County

(G-10440)
AVOCA LLC (DH)
841 Avoca Rd (27957)
P.O. Box 129 (27957-0129)
PHONE.................................252 482-2133
Augustinus Gerritsen, *Pr*
Robin E Lampkin, *
Donald E Meyer, *
Matthew K Spence, *
William C Whitaker, *
▲ **EMP:** 100 **EST:** 1962
SQ FT: 172,000
SALES (est): 33.13MM
SALES (corp-wide): 2.19B **Publicly Held**
Web: www.avocainc.com
SIC: 2099 Food preparations, nec
HQ: Ashland Chemco Inc.
1979 Atlas St
Columbus OH 43228
859 815-3333

(G-10441)
TATE & LYLE SOLUTIONS USA LLC
841 Avoca Farm Rd Ste 2 (27957)
PHONE.................................252 482-0402
Michele Mcguire, *Quality*
EMP: 50
SALES (corp-wide): 1.16B **Privately Held**
Web: www.tateandlyle.com
SIC: 2099 Food preparations, nec
HQ: Tate & Lyle Solutions Usa Llc
5450 Prairie Stone Pkwy # 170
Hoffman Estates IL 60192
217 423-4411

Micaville
Yancey County

(G-10442)
BOONE-WOODY MINING COMPANY INC
Also Called: B & W Stone Company
4456 E Us Hwy 19 E (28755)
P.O. Box 209 (28755-0209)
PHONE.................................828 675-5188
Tim Boone, *Pr*
Paul Boone, *Sec*
Chris Boone, *VP*
EMP: 6 **EST:** 1961
SQ FT: 560
SALES (est): 483.48K **Privately Held**
SIC: 3281 Stone, quarrying and processing of own stone products

Middleburg
Vance County

(G-10443)
GEORGIA-PACIFIC LLC
Also Called: Georgia-Pacific
Hwy 158 And Interstate 85 (27556)
P.O. Box 99 (27556-0099)
PHONE.................................252 438-2238
Mark Tucker, *Mgr*
EMP: 5
SALES (corp-wide): 36.93B **Privately Held**
Web: www.gp.com
SIC: 2621 Paper mills
HQ: Georgia-Pacific Llc
133 Peachtree St Nw
Atlanta GA 30303
404 652-4000

Middlesex
Nash County

(G-10444)
ALLSTEEL WELDING LLC
11936 W Nc 97 (27557-8146)
PHONE.................................919 429-0468
EMP: 4 **EST:** 2019
SALES (est): 107.22K **Privately Held**
SIC: 7692 Welding repair

(G-10445)
CONCEPT FUSION LLC
Also Called: Concept Fusion
8200 Planer Mill Rd (27557-7439)
PHONE.................................252 406-7052
Nathan Brindle, *Pr*
EMP: 6 **EST:** 2015
SALES (est): 320.73K **Privately Held**
Web: www.conceptfusionmanufacturing.com
SIC: 3446 Architectural metalwork

(G-10446)
EAGLE SPORTSWEAR LLC
10447 S Nash St (27557-7825)
P.O. Box 430 (27557-0430)
PHONE.................................252 235-4082
William Lucas, *Prin*
EMP: 7 **EST:** 2014
SALES (est): 245.35K **Privately Held**
SIC: 2339 Women's and misses' outerwear, nec

(G-10447)
EASTCOAST PACKAGING INC
Also Called: E C P
10235 E Finch Ave (27557-7400)
P.O. Box 279 (27557-0279)
PHONE.................................919 562-6060
Kevin Carden, *Pr*
Jimmy Royall, *
Crystal Nines, *
▲ **EMP:** 35 **EST:** 1995
SQ FT: 70,000
SALES (est): 4.06MM **Privately Held**
Web: www.ecpkg.com
SIC: 2675 2671 2652 5113 Paperboard die-cutting; Paper; coated and laminated packaging; Setup paperboard boxes; Folding paperboard boxes

(G-10448)
FREDERICK AND FREDERICK ENTP
Also Called: Shutter Works, The
8520 Hilliard Rd (27557-9350)
PHONE.................................252 235-4849
Judith Frederick, *Pr*
Walter Frederick, *VP*
EMP: 10 **EST:** 1993
SQ FT: 15,000
SALES (est): 757.25K **Privately Held**
Web: www.shutterworksandblinds.com
SIC: 2431 Millwork

(G-10449)
G&N LOGGING LLC
11727 Nc 222 Hwy W (27557-8399)
PHONE.................................919 524-1555
EMP: 5 **EST:** 2018
SALES (est): 171.98K **Privately Held**
SIC: 2411 Logging

(G-10450)
GERSON & GERSON INC
10601 E Finch Ave (27557-9223)
P.O. Box 97 (27557-0097)
PHONE.................................252 235-2441
Barbara Bowen, *Mgr*
EMP: 50
SALES (corp-wide): 22.9MM **Privately Held**
Web: www.gersonandgerson.com
SIC: 5137 2335 Women's and children's clothing; Women's, junior's, and misses' dresses
PA: Gerson & Gerson, Inc.
100 W 33rd St Ste 911
New York NY 10001
212 244-6775

(G-10451)
MIDDLESEX PLANT
8171 Planer Mill Rd (27557-7407)
PHONE.................................252 235-2121
EMP: 6 **EST:** 2010
SALES (est): 285.74K **Privately Held**
SIC: 3625 Relays and industrial controls

(G-10452)
NORTH CAROLINA MULCH INC
3277 Prong Creek Rd (27557-7969)
PHONE.................................252 478-4609
Kurk Stickland, *Pr*
EMP: 4 **EST:** 1997
SALES (est): 495.88K **Privately Held**
Web: www.northcarolinamulch.com
SIC: 2499 Mulch, wood and bark

GEOGRAPHIC SECTION

Midland - Cabarrus County (G-10479)

(G-10453)
PENCCO INC
10143 Us 264a (27557)
PHONE.................................252 235-5300
Jerry Murphy, *Brnch Mgr*
EMP: 10
SALES (corp-wide): 23.22MM **Privately Held**
Web: www.pencco.com
SIC: 2899 5169 2819 Water treating compounds; Chemicals and allied products, nec; Industrial inorganic chemicals, nec
PA: Pencco, Inc.
831 Bartlett Rd
Sealy TX 77474
979 885-0005

(G-10454)
PHYNIX PC INC ✪
51 Abba Cir (27557-7301)
PHONE.................................503 890-1444
Angel Klett, *Pr*
EMP: 14 **EST:** 2022
SALES (est): 575.36K **Privately Held**
SIC: 3575 7389 Computer terminals, monitors and components; Business services, nec

(G-10455)
QUINN POWDER COATING
8246 Planer Mill Rd (27557-7439)
PHONE.................................252 235-0200
Ricky Quinn, *Prin*
EMP: 5 **EST:** 2008
SALES (est): 228.94K **Privately Held**
Web: www.quinnpowdercoating.com
SIC: 3399 Powder, metal

Midland
Cabarrus County

(G-10456)
BARRACUDA DISPLAYS
3305 Muddy Creek Rd (28107-7807)
PHONE.................................704 322-0971
George Evanoff, *Owner*
EMP: 5 **EST:** 2015
SALES (est): 98.36K **Privately Held**
SIC: 3993 Signs and advertising specialties

(G-10457)
BENCHMARK SCREEN PTG DESIGN
12416 Pine Bluff Rd (28107-6777)
PHONE.................................704 785-7826
Philip Depasquale, *Prin*
EMP: 4 **EST:** 2016
SALES (est): 57.65K **Privately Held**
Web: www.benchmarkscreenprinting.net
SIC: 2759 Screen printing

(G-10458)
BRUN MILLWORKS LLC
16300 Blackberry Hills Dr (28107-9045)
PHONE.................................704 989-3145
EMP: 5 **EST:** 2019
SALES (est): 242.47K **Privately Held**
Web: www.brunmillworks.com
SIC: 2431 Millwork

(G-10459)
CARRIFF CORPORATION INC (PA)
Also Called: Carriff Engineered Fabrics
3500 Fieldstone Trce (28107-9534)
PHONE.................................704 888-3330
◆ **EMP:** 7 **EST:** 1993
SALES (est): 2.26MM **Privately Held**
Web: www.carriff.com
SIC: 2221 Polyester broadwoven fabrics

(G-10460)
CF STEEL LLC
12322 Old Camden Rd (28107-7463)
P.O. Box 148 (28129-0148)
PHONE.................................704 516-1750
Tim Liescheidt, *Managing Member*
EMP: 6 **EST:** 2011
SALES (est): 957.18K **Privately Held**
Web: www.flattruss.com
SIC: 3448 Prefabricated metal buildings and components

(G-10461)
CHROME MAN
10090 Bethel Church Rd (28107-8703)
PHONE.................................704 550-6423
Kevin Parks, *Prin*
EMP: 5 **EST:** 2017
SALES (est): 161.29K **Privately Held**
SIC: 3471 Electroplating of metals or formed products

(G-10462)
CLARK CO CSTM TRIM & WDWKG INC
3031 Valley Acres Dr (28107-4704)
PHONE.................................704 905-7131
EMP: 5 **EST:** 2018
SALES (est): 54.13K **Privately Held**
Web: www.clarkcompanytrim.com
SIC: 2431 Millwork

(G-10463)
CM WELDING
9851 Reed Mine Rd (28107-9675)
PHONE.................................704 791-0572
EMP: 5 **EST:** 2017
SALES (est): 34.53K **Privately Held**
Web: midland-nc.auto-usa.org
SIC: 7692 Welding repair

(G-10464)
CORNING INCORPORATED
Also Called: Corning
14556 S Us Hwy 601 (28107-9245)
P.O. Box 1700 (28026-1700)
PHONE.................................704 569-6000
Tom Nettleman, *Brnch Mgr*
EMP: 99
SALES (corp-wide): 12.59B **Publicly Held**
Web: www.corning.com
SIC: 3211 3357 Flat glass; Nonferrous wiredrawing and insulating
PA: Corning Incorporated
1 Riverfront Plz
Corning NY 14831
607 974-9000

(G-10465)
CROSSROADS TIRE STORE INC
4430 Albemarle Rd (28107-9722)
P.O. Box 13 (28107-0013)
PHONE.................................704 888-2064
Dennis Hathcock, *Pr*
Claudia Hathcock, *Treas*
EMP: 5 **EST:** 1962
SQ FT: 6,000
SALES (est): 772.21K **Privately Held**
SIC: 5531 7534 Automotive tires; Tire recapping

(G-10466)
DARRELL SCOTT CARRIKER
P.O. Box 377 (28107-0377)
PHONE.................................704 201-7465
Darrell Carriker, *Prin*
EMP: 5 **EST:** 2012
SALES (est): 70.5K **Privately Held**
SIC: 2434 Wood kitchen cabinets

(G-10467)
E T SALES INC
Also Called: Carolina Counters
13570 Broadway Ave (28107-9733)
P.O. Box 39 (28107-0039)
PHONE.................................704 888-4010
Nell M Eudy, *Pr*
Henry Eudy, *
Mark Eudy, *
EMP: 35 **EST:** 1982
SQ FT: 30,000
SALES (est): 1.99MM **Privately Held**
Web: www.carolinacounters.com
SIC: 3281 2541 Cut stone and stone products; Wood partitions and fixtures

(G-10468)
H & R MULLIS MACHINE INC
151 Highway 24 27 E (28107-6420)
P.O. Box 229 (28107-0229)
PHONE.................................704 791-4149
Ronald L Mullis, *Pr*
Harold C Mullis, *Stockholder*
EMP: 14 **EST:** 1978
SQ FT: 10,000
SALES (est): 420.55K **Privately Held**
Web: www.hrmullis.com
SIC: 3599 Machine shop, jobbing and repair

(G-10469)
INTERTAPE POLYMER CORP
Also Called: Intertape Polymer Group
13722 Bill Mcgee Rd (28107-9539)
PHONE.................................980 907-4871
Jason Brauch, *Opers Mgr*
EMP: 55
SALES (corp-wide): 571.43MM **Privately Held**
Web: www.itape.com
SIC: 2672 Paper; coated and laminated, nec
HQ: Intertape Polymer Corp.
100 Paramount Dr Ste 300
Sarasota FL 34232
888 898-7834

(G-10470)
KNAPHEIDE TRCK EQP CO MIDSOUTH
Also Called: Knapheide Truck Equipment Ctrs
3572 Fieldstone Trce (28107-9534)
P.O. Box 318 (28107-0318)
PHONE.................................910 484-0558
Harold W Knapheide, *Pr*
Hardy Harris, *
EMP: 35 **EST:** 2004
SALES (est): 3.93MM
SALES (corp-wide): 93.38MM **Privately Held**
Web: www.knapheide.com
SIC: 3713 Truck bodies (motor vehicles)
PA: The Knapheide Manufacturing Company
1848 Westphalia Strasse
Quincy IL 62305
217 222-7131

(G-10471)
METAL BUILDINGS CHARLOTTE
420 Highway 24 27 W (28107-7421)
PHONE.................................980 365-6583
EMP: 5 **EST:** 2017
SALES (est): 123.62K **Privately Held**
Web: www.metalbuildingsclt.com
SIC: 3448 Prefabricated metal buildings and components

(G-10472)
OLIN BLACK ENTERPRISE LLC
11695 Troutman Rd (28107-6768)
PHONE.................................704 363-5675
Black Olin, *Prin*
EMP: 8 **EST:** 2016
SALES (est): 262.26K **Privately Held**
Web: www.olin.com
SIC: 2819 Industrial inorganic chemicals, nec

(G-10473)
PEPSI BOTTLING GROUP INC
Also Called: Pepsico
5047 Highway 24 27 E (28107-5762)
PHONE.................................704 507-4031
EMP: 7
SIC: 2086 Carbonated soft drinks, bottled and canned

(G-10474)
PLANTATION SHUTTER PROS INC
5811 Kristi Ln (28107-6802)
PHONE.................................843 591-6834
Fred Erwin Trull Junior, *Owner*
EMP: 5 **EST:** 2018
SALES (est): 187.3K **Privately Held**
Web: www.plantationshutterpros.com
SIC: 3442 Shutters, door or window: metal

(G-10475)
POEHLER ENTERPRISES INC
10515 Jim Sossoman Rd (28107-7707)
PHONE.................................704 239-1166
Sylvia Poehler, *Pr*
David F Poehler Junior, *VP*
EMP: 5 **EST:** 1997
SALES (est): 476.81K **Privately Held**
Web: www.poentinc.com
SIC: 3446 1796 3534 Architectural metalwork; Installing building equipment; Elevators and moving stairways

(G-10476)
PREMIER MFG CO
3520 Fieldstone Trce (28107-9534)
PHONE.................................704 781-4001
EMP: 50 **EST:** 2019
SQ FT: 36,000
SALES (est): 9.43MM **Privately Held**
Web: www.premier-mfg.com
SIC: 3599 Machine shop, jobbing and repair
HQ: Drt Precision Mfg., Llc
1985 Campbell Rd
Sidney OH 45365
937 507-4308

(G-10477)
QUARRY & KILN LLC
1334 Nc-24 W (28107)
P.O. Box 23027 (28227-0272)
PHONE.................................704 888-0775
EMP: 10 **EST:** 2016
SALES (est): 837.75K **Privately Held**
Web: www.quarryandkiln.com
SIC: 3559 Kilns

(G-10478)
ROCKY RIVER VINEYARDS LLC
11685 Reed Mine Rd (28107-8617)
PHONE.................................704 781-5035
David Elliott, *Managing Member*
EMP: 7 **EST:** 2005
SALES (est): 481.41K **Privately Held**
Web: www.rockyrivervineyards.com
SIC: 2084 Wines

(G-10479)
SOTA VISION INC
1325 Aj Tucker Loop (28107-0030)
PHONE.................................800 807-7187
Daniel Ilnitskiy, *CEO*
EMP: 38 **EST:** 2018
SALES (est): 2.38MM **Privately Held**
Web: www.sotavision.com

(PA)=Parent Co (HQ)=Headquarters
✪ = New Business established in last 2 years

2024 Harris North Carolina Manufacturers Directory

Midland - Cabarrus County (G-10480)   **GEOGRAPHIC SECTION**

SIC: 3823 Process control instruments

(G-10480)
SQUEEGEE TEES & MORE INC
12410 Grey Commercial Rd (28107-9400)
P.O. Box 159 (28107-0159)
PHONE.................................704 888-0336
Laurie Levinsky, Pr
Diane Levinsky, Sec
EMP: 6 EST: 1990
SQ FT: 6,000
SALES (est): 487K **Privately Held**
SIC: 2759 Screen printing

(G-10481)
WHITLEY HOLDING COMPANY (PA)
Also Called: Whitley Manufacturing
3827 Whitley Rd (28107-7242)
P.O. Box 112 (28107-0112)
PHONE.................................704 888-2625
Arlene Whitley, Pr
▲ EMP: 30 EST: 1960
SALES (est): 6.98MM **Privately Held**
Web: www.whitleyhandle.com
SIC: 2499 Handles, wood

(G-10482)
WHITLEY/MONAHAN HANDLE LLC
3827 Whitley Rd (28107-7242)
P.O. Box 112 (28107-0112)
PHONE.................................704 888-2625
Patrick Peeples, *
◆ EMP: 40 EST: 2007
SALES (est): 3.4MM **Privately Held**
Web: www.whitleyhandle.com
SIC: 2499 Handles, wood

Mill Spring
Polk County

(G-10483)
AMERI-CON MATERIALS INC
2554 Deep Gap Farm Rd (28756-9721)
PHONE.................................828 863-0444
Jason C Deck, Pr
EMP: 16 EST: 2000
SALES (est): 1.06MM **Privately Held**
SIC: 3273 Ready-mixed concrete

(G-10484)
C & M INDUSTRIAL SUPPLY CO
748 N Hwy 16 (28756)
P.O. Box 911 (28037-0911)
PHONE.................................704 483-4001
Susan Donaldson, Pr
EMP: 4 EST: 2008
SALES (est): 229.93K **Privately Held**
SIC: 5251 5211 3069 Hardware stores; Home centers; Tubing, rubber

(G-10485)
GREENVILLE WOOD RENEWAL INC
836 Hawk Ridge Dr (28756-5509)
PHONE.................................828 894-5376
Sebastian Terrana, Prin
EMP: 5 EST: 2016
SALES (est): 41.52K **Privately Held**
SIC: 2499 Wood products, nec

(G-10486)
HELPING HANDS CONCRETE LLC
Also Called: Landscaping/Construction
112 Carson Cove Rd (28756-4713)
PHONE.................................828 817-1288
Nicholas Logan, CEO
EMP: 6 EST: 2018
SALES (est): 140K **Privately Held**
SIC: 3271 Blocks, concrete: landscape or retaining wall

(G-10487)
HTC LOGGING INC
1055 Cooper Gap Rd (28756-9670)
PHONE.................................828 625-1601
Hoyle Jackson, Pr
EMP: 5 EST: 1988
SALES (est): 342K **Privately Held**
SIC: 2411 Logging camps and contractors

(G-10488)
M&M BIOPLASTIC LLC ✪
4021 Highway 108 E (28756-5824)
PHONE.................................877 366-5227
Jeffrey Phillip Hendricks, Prin
EMP: 5 EST: 2022
SALES (est): 63.22K **Privately Held**
SIC: 7389 2834 Design services; Adrenal pharmaceutical preparations

(G-10489)
PACK BROTHERS LOGGING
Also Called: Pack Brothers Log & Grading
1559 Highway 9 S (28756-4716)
PHONE.................................828 894-2191
Kevin Pack, Pt
Kyle Pack, Pt
Bryan Pack, Pt
EMP: 5 EST: 1999
SALES (est): 516.75K **Privately Held**
SIC: 2411 Logging

(G-10490)
PARKER-BINNS VINEYARD LLC
7382 Highway 108 E (28756-4707)
PHONE.................................828 894-0154
Karen Parker-binns, Prin
EMP: 8 EST: 2010
SALES (est): 417.31K **Privately Held**
Web: www.parkerbinnsvineyard.com
SIC: 2084 Wines

(G-10491)
SUNNY VIEW PALLET COMPANY
3057 Big Level Rd (28756-6714)
PHONE.................................828 625-9907
James V Searcy, Owner
EMP: 4 EST: 1978
SALES (est): 231.25K **Privately Held**
SIC: 2448 Pallets, wood

Millers Creek
Wilkes County

(G-10492)
CHURCH & CHURCH LUMBER LLC
Also Called: Select Hardwoods Div
185 Hensley Eller Rd (28651-9132)
P.O. Box 619 (28651-0619)
PHONE.................................336 838-1256
EMP: 12
SALES (corp-wide): 15.41MM **Privately Held**
Web: www.churchandchurchlumber.com
SIC: 2426 2421 Hardwood dimension and flooring mills; Sawmills and planing mills, general
PA: Church & Church Lumber, Llc
    863 New Browns Ford Rd
    Wilkesboro NC 28697
    336 973-5700

(G-10493)
KEITH CALL LOGGING LLC
P.O. Box 1407 (28651-1407)
PHONE.................................336 262-3681
Keith Call, Prin
EMP: 7 EST: 2001
SALES (est): 487.27K **Privately Held**

SIC: 2411 Logging camps and contractors

(G-10494)
OPENFIRE SYSTEMS
5450 Boone Trl (28651-9197)
PHONE.................................336 251-3991
Daniel Pereira, Pr
EMP: 8 EST: 2013
SALES (est): 390.8K **Privately Held**
Web: www.openfiresystems.com
SIC: 3949 7371 Target shooting equipment; Computer software systems analysis and design, custom

(G-10495)
RETAIL INSTALLATION SVCS LLC
142 Lexi Dr (28651-9241)
PHONE.................................336 818-1333
Jonathan Gorich, Owner
Steven Kilbey, Dir Opers
EMP: 9 EST: 2010
SALES (est): 408.78K **Privately Held**
SIC: 3993 1799 1542 Signs and advertising specialties; Office furniture installation; Commercial and office building, new construction

(G-10496)
WILLIAM SHAWN STALEY
Also Called: Staley Logging & Grading
838 Green Acres Mill Rd (28651-8756)
P.O. Box 800 (28651-0800)
PHONE.................................336 838-9193
William S Staley, Owner
EMP: 4 EST: 2000
SALES (est): 246.97K **Privately Held**
SIC: 2411 Logging

Mills River
Henderson County

(G-10497)
A & M TOOL INC
125 School House Rd (28759-9742)
P.O. Box 309 (28742-0309)
PHONE.................................828 891-9990
James Awald, Pr
Anna Awald, VP
EMP: 19 EST: 1980
SQ FT: 9,000
SALES (est): 2.31MM **Privately Held**
Web: www.amtoolusa.com
SIC: 3544 Forms (molds), for foundry and plastics working machinery

(G-10498)
ALAN KIMZEY
Also Called: National Wood Products
42 Sawmill Rd (28759-9730)
PHONE.................................828 891-8720
Billy Kimzey, Owner
EMP: 6 EST: 1979
SALES (est): 368.64K **Privately Held**
SIC: 2421 2448 Sawmills and planing mills, general; Wood pallets and skids

(G-10499)
BALDWIN WOOD WORKS LLC
143 Knoll Ridge Rd (28759-8531)
PHONE.................................828 974-2716
EMP: 5 EST: 2014
SALES (est): 126.3K **Privately Held**
SIC: 2431 Millwork

(G-10500)
BLUE RIDGE CAB CONNECTION LLC
7 Brandy Branch Rd (28759-8715)
PHONE.................................828 891-2281
EMP: 4 EST: 2018

SALES (est): 234.08K **Privately Held**
Web: www.blueridgecabinetconnection.com
SIC: 2434 Wood kitchen cabinets

(G-10501)
BOLD ROCK PARTNERS LP
Also Called: Bold Rock Hard Cider
72 School House Rd (28759-9712)
PHONE.................................828 595-9940
Brian Shanks, Pt
▲ EMP: 15 EST: 2011
SALES (est): 2.48MM
SALES (corp-wide): 5.3MM **Privately Held**
Web: www.boldrock.com
SIC: 5813 2085 Bars and lounges; Applejack (alcoholic beverage)
PA: Craft Revolution, Llc
    4001 Yancey Rd Ste A
    Charlotte NC 28217
    347 924-7540

(G-10502)
DOVER FOODS INC
Also Called: American Quality Foods
353 Banner Farm Rd (28759-8707)
P.O. Box 519 (28704-0519)
PHONE.................................800 348-7416
Kathy S Milner, Pr
Joseph Mckay, VP
EMP: 32 EST: 1994
SQ FT: 17,000
SALES (est): 7.02MM **Privately Held**
Web: www.americanqualityfoods.com
SIC: 2099 Food preparations, nec

(G-10503)
HIGHLAND TOOL AND GAUGE INC
Also Called: Highland Tool
5500 Old Haywood Rd (28759-2008)
PHONE.................................828 891-8557
Bill Lafever, Pr
Lillie Lafever, Sec
EMP: 15 EST: 1985
SQ FT: 9,500
SALES (est): 429.23K **Privately Held**
SIC: 3599 Machine shop, jobbing and repair

(G-10504)
HILLS MACHINERY COMPANY LLC
5481 Old Haywood Rd (28759-2007)
PHONE.................................828 820-5265
EMP: 7
SALES (corp-wide): 27.87MM **Privately Held**
Web: www.hillsmachinery.com
SIC: 3531 Construction machinery
PA: Hills Machinery Company, Llc
    1014 Atlas Way
    Columbia SC 29209
    803 658-0200

(G-10505)
JABIL INC
724 Broadpointe Dr (28759-0018)
PHONE.................................828 209-4202
Drew Friedman, Mgr
EMP: 5
SALES (corp-wide): 34.7B **Publicly Held**
SIC: 3672 Printed circuit boards
PA: Jabil Inc.
    10800 Roosevelt Blvd N
    Saint Petersburg FL 33716
    727 577-9749

(G-10506)
LINAMAR LIGHT METAL S-MR LLC
490 Ferncliff Park Dr (28732-8633)
PHONE.................................828 348-4010
Eric Showalter, Managing Member
EMP: 505 EST: 2016

GEOGRAPHIC SECTION

SALES (est): 85.51MM
SALES (corp-wide): 5.89B Privately Held
SIC: 3363 Aluminum die-castings
PA: Linamar Corporation
287 Speedvale Ave W
Guelph ON N1H 1
587 206-6590

(G-10507)
MEDICAL CABLE SPECIALISTS INC
Also Called: M T I
2133 Old Fanning Bridge Rd (28759-3418)
PHONE.................................828 890-2888
EMP: 20
SIC: 3089 Injection molded finished plastics products, nec

(G-10508)
MICROTECH KNIVES INC (PA)
Also Called: Microtech
321 Fanning Fields Rd (28759-4610)
PHONE.................................828 684-4355
Anthony L Marfione, Pr
Susan A Marfione, VP
EMP: 58 EST: 2005
SALES (est): 10.05MM
SALES (corp-wide): 10.05MM Privately Held
Web: www.microtechknives.com
SIC: 3423 Hand and edge tools, nec

(G-10509)
PRINCE GROUP LLC
Also Called: Prince Mfg - Greenville
209 Broadpointe Dr (28759-4995)
PHONE.................................828 681-8860
Bill White, Prin
EMP: 50
SALES (corp-wide): 133.52MM Privately Held
Web: www.princemanufacturing.com
SIC: 3479 3471 Coating of metals and formed products; Plating and polishing
HQ: Prince Group, Llc
3227 Sunset Blvd Ste E101
West Columbia SC 29169
803 708-4789

(G-10510)
PRINCE MANUFACTURING CORP
Also Called: Prince Mfg - Asheville
209 Broadpointe Dr (28759-4995)
PHONE.................................828 681-8860
Steven Floyd, Mgr
EMP: 150
SALES (corp-wide): 133.52MM Privately Held
Web: www.princemanufacturing.com
SIC: 2759 3479 Commercial printing, nec; Coating of metals and formed products
HQ: Prince Manufacturing Corporation
203 W Main St Ste A3
Lexington SC 29072
803 708-4789

(G-10511)
SKYLINE PLASTIC SYSTEMS INC
2220 Jeffress Rd (28759-4192)
PHONE.................................828 891-2515
Dean Smithson, Pr
Deborah P Smithson, Sec
Wayne Parrish, Dir
Doctor S A Burnette, Dir
EMP: 14 EST: 1990
SQ FT: 3,000
SALES (est): 3.63MM Privately Held
Web: www.skylineplastics.com
SIC: 3089 Injection molding of plastics

(G-10512)
UPM RAFLATAC INC (HQ)
400 Broadpointe Dr (28759-4652)
P.O. Box 13457 (19101-3457)
PHONE.................................828 651-4800
Jussi Vanhanen, Pr
Mark Pollard, *
Greg Owen, Business*
◆ EMP: 315 EST: 1985
SQ FT: 235,000
SALES (est): 223.96MM Privately Held
Web: www.upmraflatac.com
SIC: 2672 3083 Labels (unprinted), gummed: made from purchased materials; Laminated plastics plate and sheet
PA: Upm-Kymmene Oyj
Alvar Aallon Katu 1
Helsinki 00100

(G-10513)
VAN WINGERDEN GRNHSE CO INC
Also Called: Vwgc
4078 Haywood Rd (28759-9762)
PHONE.................................828 891-7389
Richard Van Wingerden, Pr
James Gapinski, *
◆ EMP: 25 EST: 1972
SQ FT: 83,000
SALES (est): 7.39MM Privately Held
Web: www.van-wingerden.com
SIC: 3448 3231 Greenhouses, prefabricated metal; Products of purchased glass

(G-10514)
WESTERN CRLINA TL MOLD CORP IN
Also Called: Repair Services
3 Brandy Branch Rd (28759-8708)
PHONE.................................828 890-4448
Woody Scott, Pr
Alan W Scott Junior, Pr
Danny Grant, VP
David Holland, VP
Aubrey Laubter, VP
EMP: 21 EST: 1997
SQ FT: 7,000
SALES (est): 524.21K Privately Held
Web: www.wescartool.com
SIC: 7699 3544 Miscellaneous building item repair services; Special dies, tools, jigs, and fixtures

Milton
Caswell County

(G-10515)
HIGH STREET BAPTIST CHURCH
11759 Academy St (27305-9746)
PHONE.................................336 234-0400
Angel Lee, Religious Leader
EMP: 6 EST: 2001
SALES (est): 90.18K Privately Held
SIC: 3714 Motor vehicle parts and accessories

(G-10516)
RFH TACTICAL MOBILITY INC
748 Dotmond Rd (27305-9660)
PHONE.................................910 916-0284
EMP: 15 EST: 2008
SALES (est): 2.21MM Privately Held
Web: www.rfhtacticalmobility.com
SIC: 3711 8299 Ambulances (motor vehicles), assembly of; Vehicle driving school

Mineral Springs
Union County

(G-10517)
JAB-C LLC
5912 Waxhaw Hwy (28108-9800)
PHONE.................................704 507-6196
EMP: 5 EST: 2018
SALES (est): 91.37K Privately Held
SIC: 3273 Ready-mixed concrete

(G-10518)
MINERAL SPRINGS FERTILIZER INC
5901 Eubanks (28108)
P.O. Box 8 (28108-0008)
PHONE.................................704 843-2683
Burt Fincher, Pr
Crystal F Hinson, VP
EMP: 6 EST: 1957
SQ FT: 15,000
SALES (est): 773.85K Privately Held
Web: www.mineralspringsfertilizer.com
SIC: 2873 0723 5261 Nitrogenous fertilizers; Grain milling; custom services; Nursery stock, seeds and bulbs

(G-10519)
PARKDALE MILLS INCORPORATED
Also Called: Plant 21
Hwy 75 (28108)
PHONE.................................704 292-1255
EMP: 28
SALES (corp-wide): 1.44B Privately Held
Web: www.parkdalemills.com
SIC: 2281 Yarn spinning mills
HQ: Parkdale Mills, Incorporated
531 Cotton Blossom Cir
Gastonia NC 28054
704 874-5000

Mint Hill
Mecklenburg County

(G-10520)
ATLANTIC TUBE & FITTING LLC
4475 Morris Park Dr Ste L (28227-8260)
P.O. Box 690366 (28227-7007)
PHONE.................................704 545-6166
EMP: 5 EST: 2011
SALES (est): 632.17K Privately Held
Web: www.atlantictubeandfitting.com
SIC: 3494 Pipe fittings

(G-10521)
ATRIUM HLTH BSPCMEN REPOSITORY ✪
10545 Blair Rd Ste 1001 (28227-2806)
PHONE.................................704 863-4001
EMP: 5 EST: 2022
SALES (est): 79.3K Privately Held
SIC: 3826 Analytical instruments

(G-10522)
BIG FISH DPI
9740 Lawyers Rd (28227-5134)
PHONE.................................704 545-8112
Jeff Love, Pt
EMP: 6 EST: 2012
SALES (est): 462.66K Privately Held
Web: www.bigfishdpi.com
SIC: 2754 7336 7374 Commercial printing, gravure; Commercial art and graphic design; Computer graphics service

(G-10523)
BLUE DOT READI-MIX LLC (PA)
11330 Bain School Rd (28227-7550)
P.O. Box 23027 (28227-0272)
PHONE.................................704 971-7676
Jj Dixon, Managing Member
EMP: 15 EST: 2004
SALES (est): 45.71MM
SALES (corp-wide): 45.71MM Privately Held
Web: www.bluedotreadimix.com
SIC: 3273 Ready-mixed concrete

(G-10524)
C & M ENTERPRISE INC
Also Called: C & M Tag
6808 Wilgrove Mint Hill Rd (28227-3428)
P.O. Box 23226 (28227-0275)
PHONE.................................704 545-1180
Charles S Jones, Pr
Marlene Jones, VP
EMP: 8 EST: 1982
SQ FT: 2,000
SALES (est): 2.19MM Privately Held
Web: www.cmenterprise.net
SIC: 5199 7519 2759 Advertising specialties; Trailer rental; Tags: printing, nsk

(G-10525)
CABINET KING REFINISHING
8500 Pine Hill Rd (28227-8540)
PHONE.................................704 241-6405
EMP: 4 EST: 2013
SALES (est): 58.87K Privately Held
Web: www.cabinetkingrefinishing.com
SIC: 2434 Wood kitchen cabinets

(G-10526)
CARDINAL GRAPHICS INC
4475 Morris Park Dr Ste H (28227-8260)
P.O. Box 23367 (28227-0276)
PHONE.................................704 545-4144
Kelly Moore, Ch Bd
Ray Dulin, Pr
EMP: 5 EST: 1983
SQ FT: 4,000
SALES (est): 475.45K Privately Held
SIC: 2752 Offset printing

(G-10527)
CAROLINA STAKE AND WD PDTS INC
11223 Blair Rd Ste 4 (28227-6870)
PHONE.................................704 545-7774
EMP: 5 EST: 1993
SALES (est): 490.14K Privately Held
Web: www.carolinawoodstakes.com
SIC: 2499 Surveyors' stakes, wood

(G-10528)
DATASCOPE NORTH AMERICA INC
4427 Wilgrove Mint Hill Rd (28227-3468)
PHONE.................................980 819-5244
Anton Jurgens, Pr
EMP: 27 EST: 2016
SALES (est): 1.15MM Privately Held
Web: www.datascopewms.com
SIC: 7372 Prepackaged software

(G-10529)
DIA-BE-TEES LLC
Also Called: Personalized Learning
6501 Hollow Oak Dr (28227-9578)
PHONE.................................330 687-7792
Rachael Price, Prin
EMP: 5 EST: 2018
SALES (est): 73.28K Privately Held
SIC: 2759 Screen printing

(G-10530)
DOWNS&MOSS A1 TRUCKING LLC
7319 Mtthews Mint HI Rd S (28227-7594)
PHONE.................................704 981-0880

Mint Hill - Mecklenburg County (G-10531)

Ketjuan Moss, *Mgr*
EMP: 6 **EST:** 2021
SALES (est): 200K **Privately Held**
SIC: 3537 Trucks, tractors, loaders, carriers, and similar equipment

(G-10531)
FAT MAN FABRICATIONS INC
8621c Fairview Rd (28227-7619)
PHONE..................704 545-0369
Brent K Vandervort, *Pr*
Deborah Vandervort, *
EMP: 29 **EST:** 1985
SQ FT: 13,000
SALES (est): 4.81MM **Privately Held**
Web: www.fatmanfab.com
SIC: 3714 Frames, motor vehicle

(G-10532)
FIND YOUR VOICE LLC
5101 Stoney Pond Ln Apt W (28227-6076)
PHONE..................301 922-0978
Elaine M Isaacson, *Prin*
EMP: 4 **EST:** 2018
SALES (est): 74.93K **Privately Held**
SIC: 2741 Miscellaneous publishing

(G-10533)
GAYLORD INC
Also Called: Medical Spec Mfg
4600 Lebanon Rd Ste K (28227-8252)
P.O. Box 977 (28170-0977)
PHONE..................704 694-2434
John F Gaylord Junior, *Pr*
Lewis H Parham Junior, *Sec*
Rick Gaylord, *
Scott Gaylord, *
EMP: 89 **EST:** 1967
SQ FT: 40,000
SALES (est): 8.01MM **Privately Held**
Web: www.medspec.com
SIC: 3086 3081 Plastics foam products; Unsupported plastics film and sheet

(G-10534)
GERRARD FAMILY LLC
7218 Ashbourne Ln (28227-8511)
PHONE..................704 545-5117
Jerry Gerrard, *Brnch Mgr*
EMP: 8
SALES (corp-wide): 65.74K **Privately Held**
SIC: 3011 Tire and inner tube materials and related products
PA: Gerrard Family Llc
15026 Davis Trace Dr
Mint Hill NC

(G-10535)
GRID RESEARCH LLC
13310 Fairington Oaks Dr (28227-4624)
PHONE..................704 345-9774
Adam Walsh, *Ofcr*
EMP: 4 **EST:** 2014
SALES (est): 56.54K **Privately Held**
SIC: 7372 Prepackaged software

(G-10536)
HARRIS INDUSTRIES LLC
7136 Friar Tuck Ln (28227-6126)
PHONE..................410 924-3894
Michael Harris, *Prin*
EMP: 4 **EST:** 2018
SALES (est): 64.11K **Privately Held**
SIC: 3999 Manufacturing industries, nec

(G-10537)
JOHNSTON KNIFE AND TOOL INC
6400 Lake Rd (28227-5533)
PHONE..................704 208-9191
Thomas Johnston, *Prin*
EMP: 5 **EST:** 2016
SALES (est): 44.02K **Privately Held**
SIC: 3599 Machine shop, jobbing and repair

(G-10538)
MAIN STREET RAG PUBLISHING CO
4614 Wilgrove Mint Hill Rd Ste G3 (28227-0130)
P.O. Box 690100 (28227-7001)
PHONE..................704 573-2516
M Scott Douglass, *Pt*
EMP: 6 **EST:** 1996
SALES (est): 499.97K **Privately Held**
Web: www.mainstreetrag.com
SIC: 2741 Miscellaneous publishing

(G-10539)
MEUSBURGER US INC
4600 Lebanon Rd Ste A-1 (28227-8252)
PHONE..................704 526-0330
Reinhard Von Hennigs, *Prin*
Michael Winship, *Prin*
▲ **EMP:** 19 **EST:** 2011
SALES (est): 905.71K **Privately Held**
Web: www.meusburger.com
SIC: 3544 Diamond dies, metalworking

(G-10540)
MINT HILL INDUSTRIES
7313 Old Oak Ln (28227-5122)
PHONE..................704 545-8852
Raymond Filz, *Prin*
EMP: 7 **EST:** 2008
SALES (est): 75.01K **Privately Held**
Web: www.minthill.com
SIC: 3999 Manufacturing industries, nec

(G-10541)
MOSACK GROUP LLC
Also Called: Apollo By Mosack Group
11210 Allen Station Dr (28227-7105)
P.O. Box 247 (28106-0247)
PHONE..................888 229-2874
Glenn Mosack, *CEO*
Taylor Nelson, *
EMP: 75 **EST:** 2018
SALES (est): 6.64MM **Privately Held**
Web: www.apolloflow.com
SIC: 3494 Valves and pipe fittings, nec

(G-10542)
MT PRESS SERVICES INC
7928 Goodall Ct (28227-0033)
PHONE..................647 979-8675
Kevin Fernandes, *Pr*
EMP: 5 **EST:** 2019
SALES (est): 210.92K **Privately Held**
SIC: 3589 Service industry machinery, nec

(G-10543)
QUAILWOOD SCREEN PRTG & EMB
4804 Quail Ridge Dr (28227-8240)
PHONE..................704 910-2385
Christopher Maultsby, *Prin*
EMP: 5 **EST:** 2016
SALES (est): 67.06K **Privately Held**
SIC: 2752 Commercial printing, lithographic

(G-10544)
S Y SHOP INC
4475 Morris Park Dr Ste G (28227-8285)
PHONE..................704 545-7710
Sam Yue, *Pr*
EMP: 6 **EST:** 1991
SQ FT: 2,500
SALES (est): 309.26K **Privately Held**
Web: www.syshopinc.com
SIC: 3999 Models, general, except toy

(G-10545)
TARLTON CABINET SHOP
5532 Gristmill Ln (28227-9259)
PHONE..................704 573-7064
EMP: 4 **EST:** 2019
SALES (est): 108.08K **Privately Held**
Web: www.tarltoncabinetshop.com
SIC: 2434 Wood kitchen cabinets

(G-10546)
UTD TECHNOLOGY CORP
4455 Morris Park Dr Ste J (28227-8264)
PHONE..................704 612-0121
Johan Marte, *Prin*
EMP: 6 **EST:** 2010
SALES (est): 527.23K **Privately Held**
Web: www.utdtechnology.com
SIC: 3571 5999 7372 7373 Electronic computers; Audio-visual equipment and supplies; Home entertainment computer software; Computer integrated systems design

(G-10547)
VINTNERS HILL
3453 Mayhew Forrest Ln (28227-9436)
PHONE..................704 737-8023
Christine Liescheidt, *Owner*
EMP: 5 **EST:** 2015
SALES (est): 75.34K **Privately Held**
Web: www.vintnershill.com
SIC: 2084 Wines

(G-10548)
WHELAN INDUSTRIES LLC
8621 Fairview Rd Ste I (28227-2900)
PHONE..................704 506-9515
Jay Whelan, *Prin*
EMP: 5 **EST:** 2004
SALES (est): 142.01K **Privately Held**
SIC: 3999 Manufacturing industries, nec

(G-10549)
WOOD COUNTRY CREATIONS LLC
7901 Allen Black Rd (28227-9622)
PHONE..................704 545-5966
EMP: 7 **EST:** 2021
SALES (est): 405.69K **Privately Held**
Web: www.woodcountrycreations.com
SIC: 2511 5031 2521 Wood household furniture; Pallets, wood; Wood office furniture

Mocksville
Davie County

(G-10550)
48 CUSTOMS INC
896 Pine Ridge Rd (27028-6756)
PHONE..................336 403-0731
Jessica Phelps, *Pr*
EMP: 19 **EST:** 2017
SALES (est): 1.1MM **Privately Held**
Web: www.48customs.com
SIC: 3441 Fabricated structural metal

(G-10551)
ABLE GRAPHICS COMPANY LLC
126 Horn St (27028-2449)
PHONE..................336 753-1812
William R Freeman, *Prin*
EMP: 6 **EST:** 2010
SALES (est): 455.39K **Privately Held**
Web: www.ablegraphicsprinting.com
SIC: 2752 Offset printing

(G-10552)
ALTERNATIVE BRANDS INC
321 Farmington Rd (27028-7638)
P.O. Box 2338 (27402-2338)
PHONE..................336 751-4818
Calvin Phelps, *Pr*
Lisa Yamaoka, *
◆ **EMP:** 355 **EST:** 1998
SALES (est): 4.47MM **Privately Held**
Web: www.renegadetobaccousa.com
SIC: 2111 Cigarettes
PA: Renegade Holdings Inc
321 Farmington Rd
Mocksville NC 27028

(G-10553)
AMARR COMPANY
275 Enterprise Way (27028-4417)
PHONE..................336 936-0010
EMP: 6
SALES (corp-wide): 11.51B **Privately Held**
Web: www.amarr.com
SIC: 1751 3442 2431 5031 Garage door, installation or erection; Baseboards, metal; Doors and door parts and trim, wood; Lumber, plywood, and millwork
HQ: Amarr Company
165 Carriage Ct
Winston Salem NC 27105
336 744-5100

(G-10554)
ATEC COATINGS LLC
111 Bailey St (27028-2408)
PHONE..................336 753-8888
EMP: 9 **EST:** 2009
SALES (est): 453.06K **Privately Held**
Web: www.ateccoatings.com
SIC: 2851 Coating, air curing

(G-10555)
ATEC WIND ENERGY PRODUCTS LLC
Also Called: Atec
111 Bailey St (27028-2408)
PHONE..................336 753-8888
EMP: 9 **EST:** 2009
SALES (est): 468.16K **Privately Held**
Web: www.ateccoatings.com
SIC: 2851 Undercoatings, paint

(G-10556)
AVGOL AMERICA INC
Also Called: Avgol Nonwovens
178 Avgol Dr (27028-2558)
PHONE..................336 936-2500
Shlomo Liran, *CEO*
Nir Peleg, *
Kazann Joyner, *
Shachar Rachim, *
◆ **EMP:** 140 **EST:** 2001
SALES (est): 55.5MM **Privately Held**
Web: www.avgol.com
SIC: 2297 Nonwoven fabrics
PA: Avgol Industries 1953 Ltd
9 Shimshon
Petah Tikva 49527

(G-10557)
BEAR CREEK LOG TMBER HOMES LLC
371 Valley Rd (27028-2080)
PHONE..................336 751-6180
Kevin Nunn, *Owner*
EMP: 5 **EST:** 2005
SALES (est): 473.07K **Privately Held**
Web: www.loghomesofnc.com
SIC: 2452 Log cabins, prefabricated, wood

GEOGRAPHIC SECTION

Mocksville - Davie County (G-10582)

(G-10558)
BUS SAFETY INC
Also Called: Bus Safety Solutions
133 Avgol Dr (27028-2559)
  PHONE..............................336 671-0838
Scott Geyer, *Pr*
Robert Geyer, *Pr*
Scott Geyer, *VP*
EMP: 6 **EST:** 2017
SALES (est): 975.13K **Privately Held**
Web: www.bussafetysolutions.com
SIC: 8741 3711 Business management; Buses, all types, assembly of

(G-10559)
CAROLINA PRCSION MACHINING INC
1500 N Main St (27028-2719)
  PHONE..............................336 751-7788
Steven B Vick, *Pr*
Jansen Vick, *Mgr*
EMP: 44 **EST:** 1994
SQ FT: 15,000
SALES (est): 5.6MM **Privately Held**
Web: www.cpmmachining.com
SIC: 3599 Machine shop, jobbing and repair

(G-10560)
CAROLINA PRECISION MACHINING
130 Funder Dr (27028-2884)
  PHONE..............................336 751-7788
Steve Vick, *Pr*
EMP: 13 **EST:** 2016
SALES (est): 444.5K **Privately Held**
Web: www.cpmmachining.com
SIC: 3599 Machine shop, jobbing and repair

(G-10561)
CAROLINA PRECISION PLAS LLC
Also Called: Cpp Global
111 Cpp Global Dr (27028-5979)
  PHONE..............................336 283-4700
Tim Stafford, *Mgr*
EMP: 100
SALES (corp-wide): 480.33MM **Privately Held**
Web: www.cppglobal.com
SIC: 3089 Injection molding of plastics
HQ: Carolina Precision Plastics, L.L.C.
  405 Commerce Pl
  Asheboro NC 27203
  336 498-2654

(G-10562)
CAROLINA SQUARE INC
Also Called: Diamond Apparel
1164 Cherry Hill Rd (27028-6629)
  PHONE..............................336 793-3222
Dan Cagle, *Pr*
Janet J Cagle, *VP*
EMP: 5 **EST:** 1993
SALES (est): 617.51K **Privately Held**
Web: www.diamondgolfshirts.com
SIC: 2491 Structural lumber and timber, treated wood

(G-10563)
CHESTNUT TRAIL VINEYARD LLC
640 Cedar Grove Church Rd (27028-7117)
  PHONE..............................336 655-4755
Sherry Ellis, *Owner*
EMP: 6 **EST:** 2013
SALES (est): 167.26K **Privately Held**
Web: www.chestnuttrail.com
SIC: 2084 Wines

(G-10564)
COIL MASTERS LLC
139 White Dove Way (27028-5962)
  PHONE..............................704 500-8341
EMP: 5 **EST:** 2020
SALES (est): 85.67K **Privately Held**
SIC: 3498 Coils, pipe: fabricated from purchased pipe

(G-10565)
DAVIE COUNTY PUBLISHING CO (HQ)
Also Called: Clemmons Courier
171 S Main St (27028-2424)
P.O. Box 99 (27028-0099)
  PHONE..............................336 751-2120
Dwight Sparks, *Pr*
EMP: 13 **EST:** 1920
SALES (est): 1.67MM
SALES (corp-wide): 233.03MM **Privately Held**
Web: www.ourdavie.com
SIC: 2711 5735 Newspapers: publishing only, not printed on site; Records
PA: Epi Group, Llc.
  4020 Stirrup Creek Dr
  Durham NC 27703
  843 577-7111

(G-10566)
DOVE VINE LLC
261 Scenic Dr (27028-8357)
  PHONE..............................336 751-3794
Nathan Dove, *Admn*
EMP: 4 **EST:** 2019
SALES (est): 62.38K **Privately Held**
Web: www.dovevinebev.com
SIC: 2084 Wines

(G-10567)
DUNLOP AIRCRAFT TYRES INC
205 Enterprise Way (27028-4417)
  PHONE..............................336 283-0979
John Seawell, *Mgr*
◆ **EMP:** 30 **EST:** 2015
SQ FT: 110,000
SALES (est): 4.64MM
SALES (corp-wide): 76.77MM **Privately Held**
Web: www.dunlopaircrafttyres.co.uk
SIC: 7534 5014 Rebuilding and retreading tires; Tires and tubes
HQ: Dunlop Aircraft Tyres Limited
  40 Fort Parkway
  Birmingham W MIDLANDS B24 9

(G-10568)
DWIGGINS METAL MASTERS INC
122 Wilkesboro St (27028-2322)
  PHONE..............................336 751-2379
Mike Dwiggins, *Pr*
David Dwiggins, *VP*
Peggy Dwiggins, *Sec*
EMP: 7 **EST:** 1922
SQ FT: 3,200
SALES (est): 510K **Privately Held**
SIC: 3446 3449 3444 3441 Stairs, staircases, stair treads: prefabricated metal; Miscellaneous metalwork; Sheet metalwork; Fabricated structural metal

(G-10569)
EEKKOHART FLOORS & LBR CO INC
1133 N Main St (27028-2215)
  PHONE..............................336 409-2672
EMP: 8 **EST:** 2010
SALES (est): 243.41K **Privately Held**
SIC: 2426 Hardwood dimension and flooring mills

(G-10570)
FAST LANE SIGNS
115 Spry Ln (27028-7409)
  PHONE..............................336 745-5257
Clarence Hill, *Prin*
EMP: 5 **EST:** 2016
SALES (est): 63.57K **Privately Held**
SIC: 3993 Signs and advertising specialties

(G-10571)
FILET OF CHICKEN
251 Eaton Rd (27028-8653)
  PHONE..............................336 751-4752
Marty Gautreau, *Owner*
EMP: 23 **EST:** 2015
SALES (est): 209.54K **Privately Held**
Web: www.houseofraeford.com
SIC: 2015 Chicken, processed: cooked

(G-10572)
FOX BRIAR FURNITURE & WDWKG
3580 Us Highway 158 (27028-7842)
  PHONE..............................980 254-8433
Stacey L Gretka, *Owner*
EMP: 4 **EST:** 2018
SALES (est): 54.13K **Privately Held**
SIC: 2431 Millwork

(G-10573)
FULLER WLDG & FABRICATORS INC
980 Salisbury Rd (27028-9301)
  PHONE..............................336 751-3712
Phillip E Fuller Junior, *Pr*
Darlene Fuller, *Sec*
EMP: 21 **EST:** 1972
SQ FT: 30,000
SALES (est): 4.07MM **Privately Held**
Web: www.fullerwelding.com
SIC: 3441 Fabricated structural metal

(G-10574)
FUNDER AMERICA INC (HQ)
200 Funder Dr (27028-2886)
P.O. Box 729 (27028-0729)
  PHONE..............................336 751-3501
Peter Funder, *Pr*
Lisl Funder, *
Erhard Grossnigg, *
◆ **EMP:** 110 **EST:** 1972
SQ FT: 120,000
SALES (est): 26.59MM
SALES (corp-wide): 114.8MM **Privately Held**
Web: www.funderamerica.com
SIC: 2431 Millwork
PA: Genesis Products, Llc
  2608 Almac Ct
  Elkhart IN 46514
  877 266-8292

(G-10575)
FUNDER AMERICA INC
Ilbau America
200 Funder Dr (27028-2886)
  PHONE..............................336 751-3501
Peter Funder, *Brnch Mgr*
EMP: 18
SALES (corp-wide): 114.8MM **Privately Held**
Web: www.funderamerica.com
SIC: 5021 2431 Furniture; Panel work, wood
HQ: Funder America, Inc.
  200 Funder Dr
  Mocksville NC 27028
  336 751-3501

(G-10576)
GENTLE MACHINE AND TOOL INC
2716 Us Highway 601 N (27028-5952)
  PHONE..............................336 492-5055
Jimmy Gentle, *Pr*
Melinda Gentle, *VP*
EMP: 4 **EST:** 1970
SQ FT: 4,000
SALES (est): 349K **Privately Held**
SIC: 3599 Machine shop, jobbing and repair

(G-10577)
GESIPA FASTENERS USA INC
Also Called: Tooling Division
126 Quality Dr (27028-4415)
  PHONE..............................336 751-1555
Milo Edwards, *Brnch Mgr*
EMP: 21
SALES (corp-wide): 22.96MM **Privately Held**
Web: www.gesipausa.com
SIC: 3599 3542 3965 3452 Machine shop, jobbing and repair; Riveting machines; Fasteners; Rivets, metal
PA: Gesipa Fasteners Usa, Inc.
  126 Quality Dr
  Mocksville NC 27028
  609 208-1740

(G-10578)
GESIPA FASTENERS USA INC (PA)
126 Quality Dr (27028-4415)
  PHONE..............................609 208-1740
Guy C Krone, *Pr*
Erik Olshall, *General Vice President*
Bill Schuler, *VP*
◆ **EMP:** 12 **EST:** 1975
SALES (est): 9.57MM
SALES (corp-wide): 9.57MM **Privately Held**
Web: www.gesipausa.com
SIC: 5251 3542 3965 3599 Builders' hardware; Riveting machines; Fasteners; Machine shop, jobbing and repair

(G-10579)
HEALTH WYZE MEDIA
Also Called: Health Wyze Report, The
142 Redwood Dr (27028-5434)
  PHONE..............................336 528-4120
Sarah C Corriher, *Prin*
EMP: 5 **EST:** 2011
SALES (est): 100.86K **Privately Held**
Web: www.healthwyze.org
SIC: 2741 Shopping news: publishing and printing

(G-10580)
HOUSE OF RAEFORD FARMS LA LLC
251 Eaton Rd (27028-8653)
  PHONE..............................336 751-4752
EMP: 160
SALES (corp-wide): 1.79B **Privately Held**
Web: www.houseofraeford.com
SIC: 2015 Poultry slaughtering and processing
HQ: House Of Raeford Farms Of Louisiana, L.L.C.
  3867 2nd St
  Arcadia LA 71001
  318 263-9004

(G-10581)
HUNCKLER FABRICATION LLC
123 S Park Pl (27028-9305)
  PHONE..............................336 753-0905
EMP: 14 **EST:** 2009
SALES (est): 1.44MM **Privately Held**
Web: www.magneshade.com
SIC: 3716 5719 Motor homes; Window shades, nec

(G-10582)
JONES DOORS & WINDOWS INC
533 Joe Rd (27028-7253)
  PHONE..............................336 998-8624
David Tkach, *Pr*
Albert Tkach, *VP*
EMP: 12 **EST:** 1996

Mocksville - Davie County (G-10583)   GEOGRAPHIC SECTION

SQ FT: 15,000
SALES (est): 5.91MM **Privately Held**
Web: www.jonesdoors.net
SIC: 2431   Millwork

(G-10583)
LANDMARK COATINGS LLC
Also Called: Landmark Coatings
933 Danner Rd (27028-5731)
P.O. Box 1602 (27028-1602)
PHONE.................................336 492-2492
EMP: 5 EST: 1997
SQ FT: 10,000
SALES (est): 485.11K **Privately Held**
Web: www.landmarkcoatings.com
SIC: 3479   Coating of metals and formed products

(G-10584)
LATHAMSCU
376 Ben Anderson Rd (27028-5638)
PHONE.................................336 477-5008
Justin Latham, *Owner*
EMP: 6 EST: 2009
SALES (est): 115.9K **Privately Held**
SIC: 3089   Fences, gates, and accessories: plastics

(G-10585)
LEWTAK PIPE ORGAN BUILDERS INC
211 Parsley Ln (27028-6771)
PHONE.................................336 554-2251
Tomasz Lewtak, *Pr*
▲ EMP: 4 EST: 2008
SALES (est): 372.6K **Privately Held**
Web: www.lewtak.com
SIC: 1521 3931   New construction, single-family houses; Musical instruments

(G-10586)
MCDANIEL DELMAR (PA)
Also Called: Uniform Express
144 Whetstone Dr (27028-6932)
PHONE.................................336 284-6377
Delmar Mc Daniel, *Owner*
EMP: 24 EST: 1984
SQ FT: 35,000
SALES (est): 1.72MM
SALES (corp-wide): 1.72MM **Privately Held**
Web: www.duckscrubs.com
SIC: 2311 2339 2326 5699   Men's and boys' uniforms; Women's and misses' outerwear, nec; Men's and boy's work clothing; Uniforms and work clothing

(G-10587)
MEGA MACHINE SHOP INC
130 Macy Langston Ln (27028-6227)
P.O. Box 1252 (27028-1252)
PHONE.................................336 492-2728
Kimberly Howard, *Pr*
Todd Howard, *VP*
EMP: 8 EST: 1993
SQ FT: 5,500
SALES (est): 698.52K **Privately Held**
Web: www.megamachineinc.com
SIC: 3599   Machine shop, jobbing and repair

(G-10588)
MENDEZ WELDING LLC
133 Hillcrest St (27028-4804)
PHONE.................................336 618-9337
Jose A Gama-mendez, *Owner*
EMP: 5 EST: 2018
SALES (est): 208.29K **Privately Held**
SIC: 7692   Welding repair

(G-10589)
METAL SALES MANUFACTURING CORP
188 Quality Dr (27028-4415)
PHONE.................................704 859-0550
Jerry Ace, *Mgr*
EMP: 24
SALES (corp-wide): 347.39MM **Privately Held**
Web: metalsales.us.com
SIC: 3444   Roof deck, sheet metal
HQ: Metal Sales Manufacturing Corporation
    545 S 3rd St Ste 200
    Louisville KY 40202
    502 855-4300

(G-10590)
MILLER SHEET METAL CO INC
2038 Us Highway 601 S (27028-6904)
P.O. Box 158 (27028-0158)
PHONE.................................336 751-2304
Cletus R Miller, *Pr*
Mildred M Miller, *Sec*
Ed Miller, *VP*
EMP: 4 EST: 1969
SQ FT: 1,025
SALES (est): 415.62K **Privately Held**
SIC: 1711 7692   Warm air heating and air conditioning contractor; Welding repair

(G-10591)
MOCK TIRE & AUTOMOTIVE INC
Also Called: Beroth Tire of Mocksville
132 Interstate Dr (27028-4195)
PHONE.................................336 753-8473
EMP: 36
SALES (corp-wide): 18.02MM **Privately Held**
Web: www.mockberothtire.com
SIC: 5531 7539 7534   Automotive tires; Auto front end repair; Tire repair shop
PA: Mock Tire & Automotive Inc
    4752 Country Club Rd
    Winston Salem NC 27104
    336 768-1010

(G-10592)
MONOGRAM THIS
784 Sheffield Rd (27028-8408)
PHONE.................................336 528-9980
Jennifer Dehring, *Prin*
EMP: 4 EST: 2017
SALES (est): 39.91K **Privately Held**
SIC: 2395   Pleating and stitching

(G-10593)
MOUNTAINTOP CHEESECAKES LLC
209 Sunburst Ln (27028-5378)
PHONE.................................336 391-9127
Dustin Horner, *Owner*
EMP: 6 EST: 2017
SALES (est): 120.67K **Privately Held**
SIC: 2591   Window blinds

(G-10594)
NEWRIVERWELDING
271 Merrells Lake Rd (27028-7321)
PHONE.................................336 413-3040
EMP: 6 EST: 2014
SALES (est): 225.24K **Privately Held**
SIC: 7692   Welding repair

(G-10595)
NPC CORPORATION
140 Theodore Dr (27028)
P.O. Box 2011 (27006-2011)
PHONE.................................336 998-2386
Jerry Smith, *CEO*
Brock Agee, *Pr*
Eddie Scott, *Contrlr*
Kathy Woodrum, *Dir*
Ashley Seamon, *Dir*
EMP: 11 EST: 2006
SALES (est): 1.58MM **Privately Held**
Web: www.naturespearlproducts.com
SIC: 2023   Dietary supplements, dairy and non-dairy based

(G-10596)
OLON INDUSTRIES INC (US)
Also Called: Eurodrawer
279 Bethel Church Rd (27028-2871)
P.O. Box 669 (47501-0669)
PHONE.................................630 232-4705
Dagmar Deich, *Mgr*
EMP: 13
SALES (corp-wide): 38.47MM **Privately Held**
Web: www.olon.ca
SIC: 2493 3081   Particleboard products; Unsupported plastics film and sheet
HQ: Olon Industries Inc. (Us)
    411 Union St
    Geneva IL 60134
    630 232-4705

(G-10597)
PALLETONE NORTH CAROLINA INC
Pallet One
165 Turkey Foot Rd (27028-5930)
PHONE.................................336 492-5565
Brian Dyson, *Brnch Mgr*
EMP: 98
SALES (corp-wide): 7.22B **Publicly Held**
Web: www.palletone.com
SIC: 2448   Pallets, wood
HQ: Palletone Of North Carolina, Inc.
    2340 Ike Brooks Rd
    Siler City NC 27344
    704 462-1882

(G-10598)
PREVETTE & SONS HAULING LLC
566 Duke Whittaker Rd (27028-5744)
PHONE.................................336 909-2717
Ryan Marvin Prevette, *Owner*
EMP: 4 EST: 2021
SALES (est): 95.58K **Privately Held**
SIC: 3537   Trucks, tractors, loaders, carriers, and similar equipment

(G-10599)
PRO REFRIGERATION INC
319 Farmington Rd (27028-7638)
PHONE.................................336 283-7281
James L Vander Giessen Senior, *Pr*
EMP: 25
Web: www.prochiller.com
SIC: 3585   Refrigeration equipment, complete
PA: Pro Refrigeration Inc.
    326 8th St Sw
    Auburn WA 98001

(G-10600)
QST INDUSTRIES INC
Quick Service Textiles
140 Lionheart Dr (27028-9440)
PHONE.................................336 751-1000
Nathan Varner, *Mgr*
EMP: 15
SALES (corp-wide): 65.4MM **Privately Held**
Web: www.qst.com
SIC: 2396   Waistbands, trouser
PA: Qst Industries, Inc.
    1755 Park St Ste 200
    Naperville IL 60563
    312 930-9400

(G-10601)
REEB MILLWORK CORPORATION
346 Bethel Church Rd (27028-2872)
PHONE.................................336 751-4650
EMP: 8
SALES (corp-wide): 790.63MM **Privately Held**
Web: www.reeb.com
SIC: 2431   Millwork
HQ: Reeb Millwork Corporation
    1000 Maloney Cir
    Bethlehem PA 18015
    610 867-6160

(G-10602)
SCOTT BADER INC
212 Quality Dr (27028-4430)
PHONE.................................330 920-4410
Kevin Matthews, *Pr*
EMP: 11 EST: 2008
SALES (est): 1.33MM **Privately Held**
SIC: 2891   Adhesives and sealants

(G-10603)
SIGNLITE SERVICES INC
151 Industrial Blvd (27028-2773)
P.O. Box 1207 (27028-1207)
PHONE.................................336 751-9543
Daniel Des Noyers, *Pr*
EMP: 4 EST: 1987
SQ FT: 3,000
SALES (est): 418.58K **Privately Held**
Web: www.signliteonline.com
SIC: 7312 3993   Outdoor advertising services; Signs, not made in custom sign painting shops

(G-10604)
SOISA INC
111 Dalton Business Ct Ste 101 (27028-5195)
PHONE.................................336 940-4006
Van Fulp, *Prin*
Roberto Romero, *CEO*
Jacobo Mesta, *VP*
Jesus Mesta, *Prin*
Javier Mesta, *Prin*
EMP: 5 EST: 2019
SALES (est): 297.34K **Privately Held**
SIC: 2396 3728   Automotive trimmings, fabric; Aircraft parts and equipment, nec

(G-10605)
SPECTACLE ENVY
143 Summit Dr (27028-7262)
PHONE.................................336 231-3135
Kelley J Taylor, *Owner*
EMP: 4 EST: 2016
SALES (est): 64.28K **Privately Held**
Web: spectacle-envy.business.site
SIC: 3851   Spectacles

(G-10606)
SPORTSFIELD SPECIALTIES INC
Also Called: Sportsfield Specialties
155 Boyce Dr (27028-4187)
P.O. Box 2489 (28145-2489)
PHONE.................................704 637-2140
EMP: 11
Web: www.sportsfield.com
SIC: 3949   Sporting and athletic goods, nec
PA: Sportsfield Specialties, Inc.
    41155 State Highway 10
    Delhi NY 13753

(G-10607)
TAR HEEL LANDWORKS LLC
6858 Nc Highway 801 S (27028-6733)
PHONE.................................336 941-3009
Brian R Williams, *Owner*

GEOGRAPHIC SECTION   Monroe - Union County (G-10634)

EMP: 11 EST: 2018
SALES (est): 1.49MM Privately Held
SIC: 2865 Cyclic crudes and intermediates

(G-10608)
TRANE TECHNOLOGIES COMPANY LLC
Ingersoll-Rand
501 Sanford Ave (27028-2919)
P.O. Box 868 (27028-0868)
PHONE..................................336 751-3561
Carl Nascar, Brnch Mgr
EMP: 450
Web: www.tranetechnologies.com
SIC: 3621 3563 3441 Motors and generators; Air and gas compressors; Fabricated structural metal
HQ: Trane Technologies Company Llc
    800 Beaty St Ste E
    Davidson NC 28036
    704 655-4000

(G-10609)
TRIM INC
351 Bethel Church Rd (27028-2873)
P.O. Box 905 (27028-0905)
PHONE..................................336 751-3591
Paul Hauser, Pr
Neil Hauser, Sec
EMP: 18 EST: 1970
SQ FT: 45,000
SALES (est): 305.75K Privately Held
SIC: 2431 3442 Moldings and baseboards, ornamental and trim; Metal doors, sash, and trim

(G-10610)
WNYH LLC
155 Boyce Dr (27028-4187)
PHONE..................................716 853-1800
▲ EMP: 250
SIC: 3841 Medical instruments and equipment, blood and bone work

Moncure
Chatham County

(G-10611)
3M COMPANY
3M
4191 Hwy 87 S (27559)
PHONE..................................919 642-0006
John Lowery, Mgr
EMP: 100
SALES (corp-wide): 34.23B Publicly Held
Web: www.3m.com
SIC: 3295 Roofing granules
PA: 3m Company
    3m Center
    Saint Paul MN 55144
    651 733-1110

(G-10612)
ACONCAGUA TIMBER CORP
Also Called: Franklin Partleboard
985 Corinth Rd (27559-9740)
PHONE..................................919 542-2128
◆ EMP: 500
SIC: 2493 Particleboard products

(G-10613)
ARAUCO NORTH AMERICA INC
985 Corinth Rd (27559-9740)
PHONE..................................919 542-2128
EMP: 88
Web: www.arauco.com
SIC: 2493 Reconstituted wood products
HQ: Arauco North America, Inc.
    400 Prmter Ctr Ter Ste 7
    Atlanta GA 30346

(G-10614)
ARCLIN USA LLC
Also Called: Dynea
790 Corinth Rd (27559-9345)
PHONE..................................919 542-2526
Larry Sanders, Brnch Mgr
EMP: 9
SALES (corp-wide): 151.11MM Privately Held
Web: www.arclin.com
SIC: 2821 2891 Plastics materials and resins; Adhesives and sealants
HQ: Arclin Usa Llc
    1150 Sanctuary Pkwy # 100
    Alpharetta GA 30009
    678 999-2100

(G-10615)
ATC PANELS
985 Corinth Rd (27559-9740)
PHONE..................................888 200-7955
Juan Obach, Ch
EMP: 7 EST: 2019
SALES (est): 433.25K Privately Held
SIC: 2493 Reconstituted wood products

(G-10616)
CABINET CREATIONS INC
585 Carl Foushee Rd (27559-9220)
PHONE..................................919 542-3722
Wayne Foushee, Pr
Kathie Foushee, VP
EMP: 8 EST: 1980
SALES (est): 556.55K Privately Held
Web: www.cabinetcreations.info
SIC: 2434 Wood kitchen cabinets

(G-10617)
CAPITAL RDYMX PITTSBORO LLC
270 Moncure Pittsboro Rd (27559-9721)
PHONE..................................919 217-0222
EMP: 10 EST: 2017
SALES (est): 1.96MM Privately Held
Web: www.capitalreadymixconcrete.com
SIC: 3273 Ready-mixed concrete

(G-10618)
CENTRAL CAROLINA FORKLIFT LLC
156 Carl Foushee Rd (27559-9108)
PHONE..................................919 545-9749
Alfred James Ryan, Owner
EMP: 5 EST: 2016
SALES (est): 246.44K Privately Held
SIC: 3537 Forklift trucks

(G-10619)
EAST COAST FIREWOOD LLC
840 Moncure Pittsboro Rd (27559-9222)
PHONE..................................919 542-0792
J Perry Hunt, Managing Member
EMP: 10 EST: 2016
SALES (est): 651.19K Privately Held
Web: www.ecfirewood.com
SIC: 2421 Lumber: rough, sawed, or planed

(G-10620)
EDDIE TA MENDENHALL LOGGING
314 Mendenhall Farm Ln (27559-9098)
PHONE..................................919 718-9293
EMP: 4 EST: 2019
SALES (est): 157.07K Privately Held
SIC: 2411 Logging

(G-10621)
ELKINS SAWMILL INC
670 King Rd (27559-9653)
PHONE..................................919 362-1235
Billy H Elkins, Prin
EMP: 28
SALES (corp-wide): 4.99MM Privately Held
Web: www.elkinssawmill.com
SIC: 2421 Sawmills and planing mills, general
PA: Elkins Sawmill, Inc.
    6855 Pittsboro Rd
    Goldston NC 27252
    919 898-4689

(G-10622)
GENERAL SHALE BRICK INC
300 Brick Plant Rd (27559-9519)
PHONE..................................919 775-2121
Jerry Whitfield, Mgr
EMP: 30
SALES (corp-wide): 5.17B Privately Held
Web: www.generalshale.com
SIC: 3251 3271 Brick clay: common face, glazed, vitrified, or hollow; Concrete block and brick
HQ: General Shale Brick, Inc.
    3015 Bristol Hwy
    Johnson City TN 37601
    423 282-4661

(G-10623)
GREY STAR WOODWORKS
421 Bruce Burns Rd (27559-9399)
PHONE..................................919 903-8471
Colin M Starnes, Prin
EMP: 6 EST: 2019
SALES (est): 125.3K Privately Held
Web: greystarwoodworks.blogspot.com
SIC: 2431 Millwork

(G-10624)
HEARTWOOD PINE FLOORS INC
2722 Nc 87 S (27559-9780)
PHONE..................................919 542-4394
▼ EMP: 8 EST: 2004
SALES (est): 729.51K Privately Held
Web: www.heartwoodpine.com
SIC: 5713 2499 Floor covering stores; Applicators, wood

(G-10625)
LUCK STONE CORPORATION
Also Called: Luck Stone - Pittsboro
4189 Nc Highway 87 S (27559)
P.O. Box 59 (27312-0059)
PHONE..................................919 545-0027
Steve Demeyer, Prin
EMP: 20
SALES (corp-wide): 366.46MM Privately Held
Web: www.luckstone.com
SIC: 1429 Grits mining (crushed stone)
PA: Luck Stone Corporation
    515 Stone Mill Dr
    Manakin Sabot VA 23103
    804 784-6300

(G-10626)
SOUTHERN VNEER SPCLTY PDTS LLC
306 Corinth Rd (27559-9295)
PHONE..................................919 642-7004
EMP: 13 EST: 2019
SALES (est): 1.82MM Privately Held
SIC: 2435 5031 Hardwood plywood, prefinished; Veneer

(G-10627)
TRIANGLE BRICK COMPANY
Also Called: Triangle Brick Merryoaks Plant
294 King Rd (27559-9580)
PHONE..................................919 387-9257
EMP: 77
SALES (corp-wide): 48.2MM Privately Held
Web: www.trianglebrick.com
SIC: 3251 Brick and structural clay tile
PA: Triangle Brick Company
    6523 Nc Highway 55
    Durham NC 27713
    919 544-1796

(G-10628)
UNIBOARD USA LLC
985 Corinth Rd (27559-9740)
PHONE..................................919 542-2128
◆ EMP: 250
SIC: 2493 Reconstituted wood products

(G-10629)
WAKE STONE CORPORATION
9725 Stone Quarry Rd (27559)
P.O. Box 158 (27559-0158)
PHONE..................................919 775-7349
Floyd Drake, Brnch Mgr
EMP: 25
SALES (corp-wide): 24.15MM Privately Held
Web: www.wakestonecorp.com
SIC: 1423 5032 Crushed and broken granite; Stone, crushed or broken
PA: Wake Stone Corporation
    6821 Knightdale Blvd
    Knightdale NC 27545
    919 266-1100

(G-10630)
WILLIAMS LOGGING INC
2371 Charlie Brooks Rd (27559-9325)
PHONE..................................919 542-2740
Richard Williams, Pr
EMP: 5 EST: 1989
SALES (est): 601.85K Privately Held
SIC: 2411 Logging camps and contractors

Monroe
Union County

(G-10631)
A C S ENTERPRISES NC INC
Also Called: Whitecaps
307 N Secrest Ave (28110-3801)
PHONE..................................704 226-9898
Jeffrey W White, Pr
EMP: 17 EST: 1989
SALES (est): 697.8K Privately Held
SIC: 3444 Sheet metalwork

(G-10632)
AAA MACHINE SHOP
904 Clarence Secrest Rd (28110-8050)
PHONE..................................704 989-1385
Dean Preston, Prin
EMP: 5 EST: 2014
SALES (est): 67.59K Privately Held
SIC: 3599 Machine shop, jobbing and repair

(G-10633)
ABC CABINETRY LLC
5600 Lander Benton Rd (28110-6970)
PHONE..................................704 307-8310
EMP: 4 EST: 2018
SALES (est): 138.31K Privately Held
SIC: 2434 Wood kitchen cabinets

(G-10634)
ACHEM INDUSTRY AMERICA INC
2910 Stitt St (28110-3914)
PHONE..................................704 283-6144
Kenny Liu, Brnch Mgr
EMP: 8
SALES (corp-wide): 24.61MM Privately Held

Monroe - Union County (G-10635)

Web: www.achem.com.tw
SIC: 2672 Tape, pressure sensitive: made from purchased materials
PA: Achem Industry America, Inc.
4250 N Harbor Blvd
Fullerton CA 92835
562 802-0998

(G-10635)
ACME NAMEPLATE & MFG INC
300 Acme Dr (Off Hwy 74 E) (28112-4199)
PHONE...................704 283-8175
Bromley B Schuett, *Ch Bd*
Peter C Collias, *
Stephen L Ebbers, *
Jack L Sharrett, *
EMP: 21 EST: 1937
SQ FT: 60,000
SALES (est): 389.7K Privately Held
Web: www.boydcorp.com
SIC: 3479 3089 Name plates: engraved, etched, etc.; Engraving of plastics

(G-10636)
ADVANCED DIGITAL TEXTILES LLC
600 Broome St (28110-3947)
PHONE...................704 226-9600
Nicola Del Verme, *Pt*
▲ EMP: 20 EST: 2006
SQ FT: 34,000
SALES (est): 2.62MM Privately Held
Web: www.advdigitaltextiles.com
SIC: 2269 2261 2262 Linen fabrics: dyeing, finishing, and printing; Printing of cotton broadwoven fabrics; Printing, manmade fiber and silk broadwoven fabrics

(G-10637)
ADVANCED PLATING TECHNOLOGIES
2600 Stitt St (28110-3836)
PHONE...................704 291-9325
EMP: 8 EST: 1996
SQ FT: 10,000
SALES (est): 1.01MM Privately Held
Web: www.advplating.com
SIC: 3356 3471 Nickel and nickel alloy pipe, plates, sheets, etc.; Plating and polishing

(G-10638)
ADVPLATING LLC
2600 Stitt St (28110-3836)
PHONE...................704 291-9325
Kyle Caniglia, *Managing Member*
EMP: 9 EST: 2015
SQ FT: 17,000
SALES (est): 989.39K Privately Held
Web: www.advplating.com
SIC: 3471 Electroplating of metals or formed products

(G-10639)
AFL NETWORK SERVICES INC
2807 Gray Fox Rd (28110-6405)
P.O. Box 2580 (28111-2580)
PHONE...................704 289-5522
Dick Phillips, *Brnch Mgr*
EMP: 30
Web: www.aflglobal.com
SIC: 3357 Nonferrous wiredrawing and insulating
HQ: Afl Network Services, Inc.
170 Ridgeview Center Dr
Duncan SC 29334
864 433-0333

(G-10640)
AIR-WE-GO LLC
Also Called: Aie We Go
4507 W Highway 74 (28110-0430)
PHONE...................704 289-6565

Andrew A Adams, *Managing Member*
Margret England, *Mgr*
EMP: 39
SALES (est): 2.22MM Privately Held
SIC: 3728 Aircraft parts and equipment, nec

(G-10641)
ALLIED PRESSROOM PRODUCTS INC (PA)
4814 Persimmon Ct (28110-9313)
PHONE...................954 920-0909
Richard H Sures, *Pr*
Jeffrey H Rose, *
▼ EMP: 20 EST: 1952
SQ FT: 1,530
SALES (est): 4.14MM
SALES (corp-wide): 4.14MM Privately Held
Web: www.alliedpressroomproducts.com
SIC: 2893 2851 Printing ink; Paints: oil or alkyd vehicle or water thinned

(G-10642)
AMERICAN REWINDING NC INC
Also Called: American Rewinding Co
1825 N Rocky River Rd (28110-7961)
P.O. Box 890377 (28289-0377)
PHONE...................704 289-4177
Paula Huber, *CEO*
Michael Huber, *
Lewis Stegall, *
Danny Plyler, *
EMP: 40 EST: 1972
SQ FT: 15,000
SALES (est): 9.62MM Privately Held
Web: www.americanmts.com
SIC: 7694 3599 Rewinding services; Machine shop, jobbing and repair

(G-10643)
AMERICAN REWINDING OF NC INC
1825 N Rocky River Rd (28110-7961)
PHONE...................704 589-1020
EMP: 20 EST: 2002
SALES (est): 1.03MM Privately Held
Web: www.americanmts.com
SIC: 7694 Electric motor repair

(G-10644)
AMERICAN WICK DRAIN CORP
1209 Airport Rd (28110-7389)
PHONE...................704 296-5801
T Richard Morris, *Pr*
Thomas P Cunningham, *
▼ EMP: 35 EST: 1974
SQ FT: 105,000
SALES (est): 5.6MM Privately Held
Web: www.awd-usa.com
SIC: 3444 3089 Sheet metalwork; Thermoformed finished plastics products, nec

(G-10645)
AMERICAN WOOD REFACE INC
509 Jim Parker Rd (28110-7318)
PHONE...................704 577-2948
Paul Brese, *Brnch Mgr*
EMP: 5
SALES (corp-wide): 457.15K Privately Held
Web: www.woodreface.com
SIC: 2434 Wood kitchen cabinets
PA: American Wood Reface Inc.
854 Medina Rd
Medina OH 44256
440 944-3750

(G-10646)
AMSTED INDUSTRIES INCORPORATED

4515 Corporate Dr (28110)
PHONE...................704 226-5243
EMP: 4
SALES (corp-wide): 3.96B Privately Held
Web: www.conmet.com
SIC: 3714 Motor vehicle parts and accessories
PA: Amsted Industries Incorporated
111 S Wacker Dr Ste 4400
Chicago IL 60606
312 645-1700

(G-10647)
ANCIENT MARINER INC
1402 Walkup Ave (28110-3524)
P.O. Box 1277 (28111-1277)
PHONE...................704 635-7911
Jessica Cann, *Pr*
EMP: 15 EST: 2016
SALES (est): 1.08MM Privately Held
Web: www.ancientmarinersigns.com
SIC: 3993 Signs and advertising specialties

(G-10648)
AP&T NORTH AMERICA INC
4817 Persimmon Ct (28110-9314)
PHONE...................704 292-2900
Adam Allansson, *Pr*
◆ EMP: 15 EST: 1990
SQ FT: 5,800
SALES (est): 5.25MM
SALES (corp-wide): 801.74K Privately Held
Web: www.aptgroup.com
SIC: 3499 5084 Aerosol valves, metal; Hydraulic systems equipment and supplies
HQ: Automation, Press And Tooling, A.P.& T. Ab
Ronnasgatan 3a
Ulricehamn 523 3

(G-10649)
AQUA LOGIC INC
2806 Gray Fox Rd (28110-8422)
PHONE...................858 292-4773
Douglas Russell, *Pr*
▼ EMP: 20 EST: 1989
SQ FT: 20,000
SALES (est): 4.82MM Privately Held
Web: www.aqualogicinc.com
SIC: 3585 Refrigeration and heating equipment

(G-10650)
ARC3 GASES INC
2411 Nelda Dr (28110-8583)
PHONE...................704 220-1029
Matthew Wright, *Mgr*
EMP: 13
SALES (corp-wide): 204.15MM Privately Held
SIC: 2813 5084 5169 7359 Industrial gases; Industrial machinery and equipment; Chemicals and allied products, nec; Equipment rental and leasing, nec
PA: Arc3 Gases, Inc.
1600 Us 301 S
Dunn NC 28334
910 892-4016

(G-10651)
AS INC
Also Called: St.clair Coatings
1920 Tower Industrial Dr (28110-8513)
PHONE...................704 225-1700
EMP: 5 EST: 2010
SALES (est): 464.93K Privately Held
Web: www.stclaircoatings.com
SIC: 3479 Coating of metals and formed products

(G-10652)
ASSA ABLOY AB
1902 Airport Rd (28110-7396)
PHONE...................704 283-2101
▲ EMP: 79 EST: 2010
SALES (est): 9.06MM Privately Held
SIC: 3695 Magnetic and optical recording media

(G-10653)
ASSA ABLOY ACC DOOR CNTRLS GRO (DH)
Also Called: Assa Abloy
1902 Airport Rd (28110-7396)
PHONE...................877 974-2255
Lucas Boselli, *Pr*
Page Heslin, *
Joseph Hurley, *
◆ EMP: 200 EST: 1864
SQ FT: 130,000
SALES (est): 208.04MM
SALES (corp-wide): 11.51B Privately Held
SIC: 3429 3466 Locks or lock sets; Crowns and closures
HQ: Assa Abloy Inc.
110 Sargent Dr
New Haven CT 06511

(G-10654)
ASSA ABLOY ACCESSORIES AND
Also Called: Norton Door Controls Yale SEC
3000 E Highway 74 (28112-9152)
PHONE...................704 233-4011
Doug Millikan, *Mgr*
EMP: 276
SALES (corp-wide): 11.51B Privately Held
SIC: 3429 3812 3699 Door locks, bolts, and checks; Search and navigation equipment; Electrical equipment and supplies, nec
HQ: Assa Abloy Accessories And Door Controls Group, Inc.
1902 Airport Rd
Monroe NC 28110
877 974-2255

(G-10655)
ASSA ABLOY ENTRNCE SYSTEMS US (DH)
Also Called: Besam Entrance Solution
1900 Airport Rd Ste B (28110-7396)
PHONE...................704 357-9924
Michael Mccaslin, *Pr*
Michael Fisher, *
Michael W Griffin, *
Michael Drury, *
◆ EMP: 120 EST: 1975
SALES (est): 450.22MM
SALES (corp-wide): 11.51B Privately Held
Web: www.assaabloyentrance.com
SIC: 3699 1796 3442 Door opening and closing devices, electrical; Installing building equipment; Metal doors
HQ: Assa Abloy Entrance Systems Ab
Lodjursgatan 10
Landskrona 261 4
104747000

(G-10656)
ASSA ABLOY INC
Rixson Speciality Door Contrls
3000 E Highway 74 (28112-9152)
PHONE...................704 776-8773
EMP: 14
SALES (corp-wide): 11.51B Privately Held
Web: www.assaabloydss.com
SIC: 3568 Pivots, power transmission
HQ: Assa Abloy Inc.
110 Sargent Dr
New Haven CT 06511

GEOGRAPHIC SECTION

Monroe - Union County (G-10680)

(G-10657)
ATI ALLVAC
6400 Alloy Way (28110-8329)
PHONE..................541 967-9000
EMP: 5 **EST:** 2020
SALES (est): 223.07K **Privately Held**
Web: www.atimaterials.com
SIC: 3356 Battery metal

(G-10658)
AUSTIN PRINTING COMPANY INC
1823 Morgan Mill Rd (28110-3644)
PHONE..................704 289-1445
Jeff Austin, *Pr*
Debbie Austin, *VP*
Donna Austin Whitley, *Pt*
EMP: 4 **EST:** 1976
SQ FT: 2,400
SALES (est): 359.17K **Privately Held**
Web: www.austinprinting.com
SIC: 2752 2791 Offset printing; Typesetting

(G-10659)
B+E MANUFACTURING CO INC
Also Called: Stainless Valve Co
4811 Persimmon Ct (28110-9314)
PHONE..................704 236-8439
EMP: 22 **EST:** 1993
SALES (est): 4.54MM
SALES (corp-wide): 6.23MM **Privately Held**
Web: www.bemfg.com
SIC: 3599 Machine and other job shop work
PA: Dal Investment Inc.
4811 Persimmon Ct
Monroe NC 28110
704 847-1423

(G-10660)
BARNYARD UTLITY BLDNGS-STRG/TL
3906 W Highway 74 (28110-8445)
PHONE..................704 226-9454
EMP: 4
SALES (corp-wide): 2.21MM **Privately Held**
Web: www.4barnyard.com
SIC: 3448 Prefabricated metal buildings and components
PA: Barnyard Utility Buildings-Storage/Utility, S.C. Corp.
707 N Main St
Clover SC 29710
803 831-9408

(G-10661)
BERRY GLOBAL INC
3414 Wesley Chapel Stouts Rd (28110-7945)
PHONE..................704 289-1526
Jeff Godsey, *Brnch Mgr*
EMP: 101
Web: www.berryglobal.com
SIC: 3089 3081 Bottle caps, molded plastics; Unsupported plastics film and sheet
HQ: Berry Global, Inc.
101 Oakley St
Evansville IN 47710

(G-10662)
BGM INC
2524 Old Charlotte Hwy (28110-2100)
P.O. Box 2072 (28111-2072)
PHONE..................704 776-4086
▲ **EMP:** 6 **EST:** 2010
SALES (est): 210.93K **Privately Held**
SIC: 3552 Knitting machines

(G-10663)
BMC SOFTWARE INC
Also Called: BMC Software
2980 Mason St (28110-3942)
PHONE..................704 283-8179
Randy Rogers, *Brnch Mgr*
EMP: 5
SALES (corp-wide): 1.5B **Privately Held**
Web: www.bmc.com
SIC: 7372 Prepackaged software
PA: Bmc Software, Inc.
2103 Citywest Blvd
Houston TX 77042
713 918-8800

(G-10664)
BOGGS MATERIALS INC (PA)
Also Called: Boggs Materials Plant 1
1613 W Roosevelt Blvd (28110-2754)
P.O. Box 689 (28111-0689)
PHONE..................704 289-8482
Drew Boggs, *Pr*
Chris Boggs, *
EMP: 6 **EST:** 1997
SALES (est): 7.81MM
SALES (corp-wide): 7.81MM **Privately Held**
Web: www.truerockholdings.com
SIC: 2951 Asphalt and asphaltic paving mixtures (not from refineries)

(G-10665)
BOGGS TRANSPORT INC
Also Called: Boggs Group
2318 Concord Hwy (28110-8768)
PHONE..................704 289-8482
Carl A Boggs Junior, *Pr*
David Boggs, *VP*
EMP: 25 **EST:** 1997
SALES (est): 960.82K **Privately Held**
Web: www.truerockholdings.com
SIC: 2951 Asphalt and asphaltic paving mixtures (not from refineries)

(G-10666)
BONA USA
4275 Corporate Center Dr (28110-1314)
PHONE..................704 220-6943
EMP: 11 **EST:** 2018
SALES (est): 3.3MM **Privately Held**
Web: www.bona.com
SIC: 2426 Flooring, hardwood

(G-10667)
BONAKEMI USA INCORPORATED
Also Called: Bona US
4275 Corporate Center Dr (28110-1314)
PHONE..................704 218-3917
Paul England, *VP Opers*
EMP: 101
SALES (corp-wide): 343.3MM **Privately Held**
SIC: 5198 2431 Stain; Awnings, blinds and shutters: wood
HQ: Bonakemi Usa, Incorporated
24 Inverness Pl E Ste 100
Englewood CO 80112
303 371-1411

(G-10668)
BOYD GMN INC
Also Called: GM Nameplate NC Division
300 Acme Dr (28112-4199)
PHONE..................206 284-2200
Jack Sharrett, *Mgr*
EMP: 165
SQ FT: 58,408
Web: www.boydcorp.com
SIC: 3479 3089 3993 Name plates: engraved, etched, etc.; Engraving of plastics; Signs and advertising specialties
HQ: Boyd Gmn, Inc.
2040 15th Ave W
Seattle WA 98119
206 284-2200

(G-10669)
BROOKS TOOL INC
524 Marshall St (28112-4676)
P.O. Box 1695 (28111-1695)
PHONE..................704 283-0112
Randy Brooks, *Pr*
Mandy Brooks, *Sec*
EMP: 5 **EST:** 1985
SQ FT: 5,000
SALES (est): 552.72K **Privately Held**
Web: www.kutcheyfamilyfarm.com
SIC: 3544 Industrial molds

(G-10670)
BROWN EQUIPMENT AND CAPITL INC
650 Broome St (28110-3947)
P.O. Box 32214 (28232-2214)
PHONE..................704 921-4644
Neil N Brown, *Pr*
Patrick N Brown, *VP*
EMP: 17 **EST:** 1946
SQ FT: 33,000
SALES (est): 2.41MM **Privately Held**
Web: www.bemlaser.com
SIC: 3541 Machine tools, metal cutting type

(G-10671)
BUMGARNERS WELDING
8701 Landsford Rd (28112-8233)
PHONE..................704 764-7041
EMP: 5 **EST:** 1998
SALES (est): 37.81K **Privately Held**
SIC: 7692 Welding repair

(G-10672)
CARDINAL BAG & ENVELOPE CO INC
2861 Gray Fox Rd (28110-6405)
PHONE..................704 225-9636
David T Van Blarcom, *Pr*
▲ **EMP:** 25 **EST:** 1957
SQ FT: 34,000
SALES (est): 4.14MM **Privately Held**
Web: www.cardinalbag.com
SIC: 2674 Paper bags: made from purchased materials

(G-10673)
CARLSON ENVIRONMENTAL CONS PC (PA)
Also Called: Carlson Envmtl Cons Prof Corp
1127 Curtis St Ste 110 (28112-5090)
PHONE..................704 283-9765
Kristofer L Carlson, *Pr*
Seth Nunes, *
Jeff Mcnabb, *VP*
EMP: 73 **EST:** 2004
SQ FT: 5,000
SALES (est): 45.28MM
SALES (corp-wide): 45.28MM **Privately Held**
Web: www.cecenv.com
SIC: 8711 4959 1381 1623 Consulting engineer; Sanitary services, nec; Drilling oil and gas wells; Oil and gas pipeline construction

(G-10674)
CAROLINA BOTTLE MFR LLC
2630 Nelda Dr Ste B (28110-8485)
PHONE..................704 635-8759
EMP: 5 **EST:** 2017
SALES (est): 253.04K **Privately Held**
Web: www.carolinabottle.com

SIC: 2899 Distilled water

(G-10675)
CAROLINA CLASSIFIEDSCOM LLC (PA)
Also Called: Carolina Money Saver
1609 Airport Rd (28110-7393)
PHONE..................704 246-0900
Scott Patterson, *Managing Member*
EMP: 68 **EST:** 2006
SALES (est): 4.73MM **Privately Held**
Web: www.carolinamoneysaver.com
SIC: 2759 Advertising literature: printing, nsk

(G-10676)
CAROLINA ELECTRIC MTR REPR LLC
1812 Skyway Dr (28110-2715)
PHONE..................704 289-3732
EMP: 7 **EST:** 2016
SALES (est): 243.95K **Privately Held**
SIC: 7699 3699 Repair services, nec; Electrical equipment and supplies, nec

(G-10677)
CAROLINA READY-MIX LLC
1901 Valley Pkwy Ste 100 (28110-6515)
PHONE..................704 225-1112
Eric W Mccomb, *Prin*
EMP: 5 **EST:** 2008
SALES (est): 1.41MM **Privately Held**
Web: www.carolinareadymix.com
SIC: 3273 Ready-mixed concrete

(G-10678)
CCBCC OPERATIONS LLC
Also Called: Coca-Cola
4268 Capital Dr (28110-7681)
PHONE..................704 225-1973
Devin Dunway, *Brnch Mgr*
EMP: 67
SALES (corp-wide): 6.65B **Publicly Held**
Web: www.coca-cola.com
SIC: 2086 Bottled and canned soft drinks
HQ: Ccbcc Operations, Llc
4100 Coca Cola Plz
Charlotte NC 28211
704 364-8728

(G-10679)
CEDAR VALLEY FINISHING CO INC
603 Broome St (28110-3946)
PHONE..................704 289-9546
Richard Quick, *Pr*
EMP: 10 **EST:** 1982
SQ FT: 20,000
SALES (est): 650K **Privately Held**
Web: www.wcfcourier.com
SIC: 2262 Finishing plants, manmade

(G-10680)
CHARLOTTE PIPE AND FOUNDRY CO
Also Called: Charlotte Plastics
4210 Old Charlotte Hwy (28110-7333)
P.O. Box 1339 (28111-1339)
PHONE..................704 372-3650
Charles E Cobb, *VP*
EMP: 550
SALES (corp-wide): 841.88MM **Privately Held**
Web: www.charlottepipe.com
SIC: 3084 Plastics pipe
PA: Charlotte Pipe And Foundry Company
2109 Randolph Rd
Charlotte NC 28207
704 372-5030

Monroe - Union County (G-10681) GEOGRAPHIC SECTION

(G-10681)
CHARLOTTE PIPE INC
P.O. Box 1338 (28111-1338)
PHONE................................704.291-3269
EMP: 7 **EST:** 2009
SALES (est): 209.01K **Privately Held**
Web: www.charlottepipe.com
SIC: 3084 Plastics pipe

(G-10682)
CIRCOR PRECISION METERING LLC (DH)
1710 Airport Rd (28110-7394)
P.O. Box 5020 (28111-5020)
PHONE................................704 289-6511
Darryl Mayhorn, *CEO*
▲ **EMP:** 63 **EST:** 2000
SALES (est): 260.74MM **Publicly Held**
Web: www.zenithpumps.com
SIC: 3561 Pumps and pumping equipment
HQ: Circor International, Inc.
  30 Corporate Dr Ste 200
  Burlington MA 01803
  781 270-1200

(G-10683)
CIRCOR PUMPS NORTH AMERICA LLC (DH)
1710 Airport Rd (28110-7394)
PHONE................................704 289-6511
EMP: 58 **EST:** 2017
SALES (est): 107.76MM **Publicly Held**
Web: www.circor.com
SIC: 3561 3829 Pumps and pumping equipment; Aircraft and motor vehicle measurement equipment
HQ: Circor International, Inc.
  30 Corporate Dr Ste 200
  Burlington MA 01803
  781 270-1200

(G-10684)
CIRCOR PUMPS NORTH AMERICA LLC
Also Called: Circor Pumping Technologies
1710 Airport Rd (28110-7394)
PHONE................................877 853-7867
EMP: 211
Web: www.circor.com
SIC: 3491 Industrial valves
HQ: Circor Pumps North America, Llc
  1710 Airport Rd
  Monroe NC 28110
  704 289-6511

(G-10685)
CLASSIC SIGN SERVICES LLC
Also Called: Fastsigns
2242 W Roosevelt Blvd Ste F (28110-3070)
PHONE................................704 401-1466
Judith Stuebs, *Prin*
EMP: 4 **EST:** 2018
SALES (est): 46.08K **Privately Held**
Web: www.fastsigns.com
SIC: 3993 Signs and advertising specialties

(G-10686)
COCHRANE STEEL INDUSTRIES INC
Also Called: Cochrane Steel
5529 Cannon Dr (28110-7982)
PHONE................................704 291-9330
John Turnblom, *Pr*
EMP: 17 **EST:** 1974
SQ FT: 13,500
SALES (est): 2.51MM **Privately Held**
Web: www.cochranesteelusa.com
SIC: 3441 Fabricated structural metal

(G-10687)
COLFAX AMRCAS ENGNERED SYSTEMS
1710 Airport Rd (28110-7394)
P.O. Box 5020 (28111-5020)
PHONE................................704 289-6511
▲ **EMP:** 9 **EST:** 2015
SALES (est): 207.89K **Privately Held**
Web: www.zenithpumps.com
SIC: 3561 Pumps and pumping equipment

(G-10688)
COLFAX PUMP GROUP
Also Called: IMO Pump
1710 Airport Rd (28110-7394)
PHONE................................704 289-6511
▲ **EMP:** 200
SIC: 3561 Industrial pumps and parts

(G-10689)
COLONY GUMS LLC
2626 Executive Point Dr (28110-8523)
PHONE................................704 226-9666
Robert Muhlsteff, *Pr*
Christopher Muhlsteff, *VP*
♦ **EMP:** 29 **EST:** 1938
SQ FT: 20,000
SALES (est): 6.62MM **Privately Held**
Web: www.colonygums.com
SIC: 2041 Sorghum grain flour
PA: Brenntag Se
  Messeallee 11
  Essen NW 45131

(G-10690)
CONN-SELMER INC
Also Called: Ludwig Industries
2806 Mason St (28110-3826)
PHONE................................704 289-6459
Jim Kinsey, *Mgr*
EMP: 74
SALES (corp-wide): 528.25MM **Privately Held**
Web: www.conn-selmer.com
SIC: 3161 3931 Musical instrument cases; Musical instruments
HQ: Conn-Selmer, Inc.
  600 Industrial Pkwy
  Elkhart IN 46516
  574 522-1675

(G-10691)
CONSOLIDATED METCO INC
780 Patton Ave (28110-2438)
P.O. Box 907 (28111-0907)
PHONE................................704 289-6492
Wayne Duncan, *Genl Mgr*
EMP: 11
SQ FT: 6,000
SALES (corp-wide): 3.96B **Privately Held**
Web: www.conmet.com
SIC: 3365 Aluminum and aluminum-based alloy castings
HQ: Consolidated Metco, Inc.
  5701 Se Columbia Way
  Vancouver WA 98661
  360 828-2599

(G-10692)
CONSOLIDATED METCO INC
1700 N Charlotte Ave (28110-8481)
PHONE................................704 289-6491
EMP: 88
SALES (corp-wide): 3.96B **Privately Held**
Web: www.conmet.com
SIC: 3365 Aluminum and aluminum-based alloy castings
HQ: Consolidated Metco, Inc.
  5701 Se Columbia Way
  Vancouver WA 98661
  360 828-2599

(G-10693)
CONSOLIDATED METCO INC
Also Called: Conmet
4220 Propel Way (28110-8399)
PHONE................................704 226-5246
Thomas White, *Mgr*
EMP: 64
SALES (corp-wide): 3.96B **Privately Held**
Web: www.conmet.com
SIC: 3714 Motor vehicle parts and accessories
HQ: Consolidated Metco, Inc.
  5701 Se Columbia Way
  Vancouver WA 98661
  360 828-2599

(G-10694)
CONSOLIDATED PRESS
2106 W Roosevelt Blvd (28110-3793)
PHONE................................704 283-0776
EMP: 5 **EST:** 2018
SALES (est): 108.91K **Privately Held**
Web: www.consolidatedpress.net
SIC: 2741 Miscellaneous publishing

(G-10695)
COOLANT & CLEANING TECH INC
7421 Morgan Mill Rd (28110-7546)
PHONE................................704 753-1333
C A Williams, *Pr*
Eric D Williams, *VP*
Betty Williams, *Sec*
EMP: 4 **EST:** 1998
SQ FT: 22,500
SALES (est): 309.49K **Privately Held**
SIC: 3714 Cleaners, air, motor vehicle

(G-10696)
COX MACHINE CO INC
2336 Concord Hwy (28110-8768)
P.O. Box 1979 (28079-1979)
PHONE................................704 296-0118
Douglas L Cox, *Pr*
Sue Cox, *Sec*
EMP: 17 **EST:** 1987
SQ FT: 1,500
SALES (est): 989.04K **Privately Held**
SIC: 3559 3714 3444 Degreasing machines, automotive and industrial; Motor vehicle parts and accessories; Sheet metalwork

(G-10697)
CPS RESOURCES INC
5712 Stockbridge Dr (28110-9188)
PHONE................................704 628-7678
Craig Smith, *Pr*
Paul Smith, *
▲ **EMP:** 26 **EST:** 1987
SQ FT: 9,000
SALES (est): 2.51MM **Privately Held**
Web: www.cpsresources.com
SIC: 3089 5084 2791 2752 Injection molding of plastics; Plastic products machinery; Typesetting; Commercial printing, lithographic

(G-10698)
CREATIVEMINDS DESIGN LLC
Also Called: Creativeminds Design
5051 Waldorf Ave (28110-0059)
PHONE................................678 457-6148
Mark Fritz, *Brnch Mgr*
EMP: 8
SALES (corp-wide): 130.54K **Privately Held**
SIC: 3993 3231 Electric signs; Reflector glass beads, for highway signs or reflectors
PA: Creativeminds Design Llc
  5051 Waldorf Ave
  Monroe NC 28110
  336 763-4446

(G-10699)
CRH AMERICAS INC
1139 N Charlotte Ave (28110-2512)
PHONE................................704 282-8443
Randy Lake, *CEO*
EMP: 118
SALES (corp-wide): 32.72B **Privately Held**
Web: www.crhamericas.com
SIC: 3273 Ready-mixed concrete
HQ: Crh Americas, Inc.
  900 Ashwood Pkwy Ste 600
  Atlanta GA 30338
  770 804-3363

(G-10700)
CUSTOM AUTOMATED MACHINES INC
509 E Windsor St (28112-4831)
PHONE................................704 289-7038
Tom Land, *Pr*
EMP: 4 **EST:** 1993
SQ FT: 6,000
SALES (est): 909.02K **Privately Held**
Web: www.customautomatedmachines.com
SIC: 3599 Machine shop, jobbing and repair

(G-10701)
CYRIL BATH COMPANY (PA)
1610 Airport Rd (28110-7393)
PHONE................................704 289-8531
Patrick Braun, *Prin*
♦ **EMP:** 18 **EST:** 1999
SQ FT: 65,000
SALES (est): 8.49MM
SALES (corp-wide): 8.49MM **Privately Held**
Web: www.cyrilbath.com
SIC: 3542 Machine tools, metal forming type

(G-10702)
D WINCHESTER DESIGNS
3121 Duck Point Dr (28110-8880)
PHONE................................704 607-0678
Debbie Winchester, *Prin*
EMP: 4 **EST:** 2016
SALES (est): 78.24K **Privately Held**
Web: www.dwinchesterdesigns.com
SIC: 3914 Silverware and plated ware

(G-10703)
DARNEL INC
1809 Airport Rd (28110-7395)
PHONE................................704 625-9869
Charles Odle, *Dir Opers*
Albert Tverus, *Pr*
♦ **EMP:** 5 **EST:** 2006
SALES (est): 4.92MM **Privately Held**
Web: www.darnelgroup.com
SIC: 2821 Plastics materials and resins

(G-10704)
DECORE-ATIVE SPC NC LLC
701 Industrial Dr (28110-8155)
PHONE................................704 291-9669
EMP: 111
SALES (corp-wide): 202.63MM **Privately Held**
Web: www.decore.com
SIC: 2431 Doors, wood
PA: Decore-Ative Specialties Nc Llc
  2772 Peck Rd
  Monrovia CA 91016
  626 254-9191

(G-10705)
DENTONICS INC
Also Called: Microbrush International
2833 Top Hill Rd (28110-9310)
PHONE................................704 238-0245

GEOGRAPHIC SECTION

Monroe - Union County (G-10728)

Randall Leander, *Pr*
Elaine Leander, *Sec*
▲ **EMP**: 16 **EST**: 1988
SALES: 2.26MM **Privately Held**
Web: www.dentonics.com
SIC: 5047 3843 Dentists' professional supplies; Dental equipment and supplies

(G-10706)
DOT BLUE READI-MIX LLC
1703 Morgan Mill Rd (28110-3642)
PHONE.................704 247-2777
Monny Taylor, *Manager*
EMP: 27
SALES (corp-wide): 45.71MM **Privately Held**
Web: www.bluedotreadimix.com
SIC: 3273 Ready-mixed concrete
PA: Blue Dot Readi-Mix, Llc
 11330 Bain School Rd
 Mint Hill NC 28227
 704 971-7676

(G-10707)
DP WOODWORKS INC
5631 Cannon Dr Ste A (28110-9139)
PHONE.................704 821-7799
Richard Turner, *Pr*
Charles R Turner Junior, *Sec*
EMP: 4 **EST**: 1999
SALES (est): 594.75K
SALES (corp-wide): 2.48MM **Privately Held**
Web: www.dpwoodworksllc.com
SIC: 2521 Cabinets, office: wood
PA: Design Plus Store Fixtures, Inc.
 5631 Cannon Dr
 Monroe NC 28110
 704 821-7799

(G-10708)
DUCO-SCI INC
6004 Stitt St (28110-8186)
PHONE.................704 289-9502
Joanne South, *Prin*
EMP: 21 **EST**: 2007
SALES (est): 504.82K
SALES (corp-wide): 24.67MM **Privately Held**
SIC: 3264 Insulators, electrical: porcelain
PA: Du-Co Ceramics Company
 155 S Rebecca St
 Saxonburg PA 16056
 724 352-1511

(G-10709)
DUNN MANUFACTURING CORP (PA)
Also Called: Mutual Dropcloth
1400 Goldmine Rd (28110-2664)
P.O. Box 810 (28111-0810)
PHONE.................704 283-2147
◆ **EMP**: 210 **EST**: 1905
SALES (est): 22.22MM
SALES (corp-wide): 22.22MM **Privately Held**
Web: www.mutualdropcloth.com
SIC: 2241 2394 2399 Cotton narrow fabrics; Canvas and related products; Flags, fabric

(G-10710)
DYNA-TECH MANUFACTURING INC
5639 Cannon Dr (28110-9139)
PHONE.................704 839-0203
Ronald Elliott Eodom, *Pr*
EMP: 19 **EST**: 2013
SALES (est): 471.27K **Privately Held**
SIC: 3599 Machine shop, jobbing and repair

(G-10711)
EDUCATRX INC
504 Kintyre Dr (28112-4111)
PHONE.................980 328-0013
Tony Burrus, *VP*
EMP: 4 **EST**: 2015
SALES (est): 155.97K **Privately Held**
SIC: 8742 7389 7372 Management consulting services; Business services, nec; Educational computer software

(G-10712)
ELEMENT COUNTERTOPS INC
1724 Clontz Long Rd (28110-8265)
PHONE.................704 641-7145
EMP: 5 **EST**: 2018
SALES (est): 242.35K **Privately Held**
SIC: 2819 Elements

(G-10713)
EMINESS TECHNOLOGIES INC
1412 Airport Rd (28110-7391)
PHONE.................704 283-2600
Boyd Brown, *Mgr*
EMP: 24
SALES (corp-wide): 5.06MM **Privately Held**
Web: www.pureon.com
SIC: 2842 5169 Cleaning or polishing preparations, nec; Polishes, nec
PA: Eminess Technologies, Inc.
 7272 E Indian School Rd # 350
 Scottsdale AZ 85251
 480 505-3409

(G-10714)
ENGINEERING MFG SVCS CO
5634 Cannon Dr (28110-9139)
P.O. Box 1771 (28079-1771)
PHONE.................704 821-7325
Gale Orem, *Pr*
EMP: 18 **EST**: 1985
SQ FT: 12,400
SALES (est): 2.35MM **Privately Held**
Web: www.emsco-nc.com
SIC: 3491 Industrial valves

(G-10715)
ENOVIS CORPORATION
Colfax Fluid Handling
1710 Airport Rd (28110-7394)
PHONE.................704 289-6511
Barry Butler, *Prin*
EMP: 16
SALES (corp-wide): 1.71B **Publicly Held**
Web: www.enovis.com
SIC: 3561 Pump jacks and other pumping equipment
PA: Enovis Corporation
 2711 Centerville Rd # 400
 Wilmington DE 19808
 301 252-9160

(G-10716)
EQUIPMENT & SUPPLY INC
4507 W Highway 74 (28110-0430)
PHONE.................704 289-6565
Andrew A Adams, *Pr*
Geroge Griffith, *
L Jester, *
EMP: 41 **EST**: 1972
SQ FT: 140,000
SALES (est): 9.13MM **Privately Held**
Web: www.equipsy.com
SIC: 3728 3423 Aircraft parts and equipment, nec; Hand and edge tools, nec

(G-10717)
EUCLID CHEMICAL COMPANY
914 N Johnson St (28110-4676)
PHONE.................704 283-2544
EMP: 5
SALES (corp-wide): 7.26B **Publicly Held**
Web: www.euclidchemical.com
SIC: 2899 Chemical preparations, nec
HQ: The Euclid Chemical Company
 19215 Redwood Rd
 Cleveland OH 44110
 800 321-7628

(G-10718)
FAIZON GLOBAL INC
Also Called: Kraze Custom Prints
2115 W Roosevelt Blvd # 70 (28110-2712)
PHONE.................704 774-1141
EMP: 5
SIC: 2211 Print cloths, cotton

(G-10719)
FERNCREST FASHIONS INC
4813 Starcrest Dr (28110-8496)
PHONE.................704 283-6422
Steve Seaborn, *Pr*
Daniel Seaborn, *
John Seaborn, *Stockholder**
▲ **EMP**: 60 **EST**: 1978
SQ FT: 30,000
SALES (est): 4.35MM **Privately Held**
SIC: 2211 2391 Draperies and drapery fabrics, cotton; Curtains and draperies

(G-10720)
FLOWERS BKG CO JAMESTOWN LLC
Also Called: FLOWERS BAKING CO. OF JAMESTOWN, LLC
5524 W Highway 74 (28110-8461)
PHONE.................704 296-1000
EMP: 7
SALES (corp-wide): 5.09B **Publicly Held**
SIC: 2051 Bread, cake, and related products
HQ: Flowers Baking Co. Of Newton, Llc
 801 W Main St
 Jamestown NC 27282
 336 841-8840

(G-10721)
FORWARD DESIGN & PRINT CO INC
1903 Tom Williams Rd (28112-9610)
PHONE.................704 776-9304
David W Nowlan, *Pr*
Angela R Ammons, *VP*
EMP: 6 **EST**: 2010
SALES (est): 196.18K **Privately Held**
SIC: 2752 Offset printing

(G-10722)
GARY FORTE WOODWORKING INC
1424 Forest Ln (28112-7716)
PHONE.................704 780-0095
Gary Forte, *Prin*
EMP: 4 **EST**: 2009
SALES (est): 452.95K **Privately Held**
Web: www.garyfortewoodworking.com
SIC: 2431 Millwork

(G-10723)
GLENMARK PHRMCEUTICALS INC USA
Glenmark Generics
4147 Goldmine Rd (28110-7759)
PHONE.................704 218-2600
EMP: 60
Web: www.glenmarkpharma-us.com
SIC: 5122 2834 Pharmaceuticals; Adrenal pharmaceutical preparations
HQ: Glenmark Pharmaceuticals Inc., Usa
 750 Corporate Dr
 Mahwah NJ 07430
 201 684-8000

(G-10724)
GLOBAL SOFTWARE LABS LLC
304 W Franklin St (28112-4704)
PHONE.................404 550-4390
Michael Thomas Duke, *Admn*
EMP: 4 **EST**: 2010
SALES (est): 84.59K **Privately Held**
SIC: 7372 Prepackaged software

(G-10725)
GOODRICH CORPORATION
Also Called: Customer Service Spare
4115 Corporate Center Dr (28110-1313)
PHONE.................704 282-2500
Christa Mcmanus, *Admn*
EMP: 5
SALES (corp-wide): 68.92B **Publicly Held**
Web: www.collinsaerospace.com
SIC: 3728 Aircraft parts and equipment, nec
HQ: Goodrich Corporation
 2730 W Tyvola Rd
 Charlotte NC 28217
 704 423-7000

(G-10726)
GOODRICH CORPORATION
Also Called: Customer Service Center Repair
4115 Corporate Center Dr (28110-1313)
PHONE.................704 282-2500
Robert Butz, *Genl Mgr*
EMP: 160
SALES (corp-wide): 68.92B **Publicly Held**
Web: www.collinsaerospace.com
SIC: 3728 Aircraft parts and equipment, nec
HQ: Goodrich Corporation
 2730 W Tyvola Rd
 Charlotte NC 28217
 704 423-7000

(G-10727)
GOULSTON TECHNOLOGIES INC (HQ)
700 N Johnson St (28110-2650)
PHONE.................704 289-6464
Frederick Edwards, *Pr*
Hisao Yamamoto, *
Andrew Starzecki, *
Alan Gold, *
◆ **EMP**: 43 **EST**: 1956
SQ FT: 300,000
SALES (est): 50.96MM **Privately Held**
Web: www.goulston.com
SIC: 2899 Chemical preparations, nec
PA: Takemoto Oil & Fat Co., Ltd.
 2-5, Minatomachi
 Gamagori AIC 443-0

(G-10728)
GREINER BIO-ONE NORTH AMER INC (DH)
Also Called: Greiner-Bio-One
4238 Capital Dr (28110-7681)
PHONE.................704 261-7800
A C Marchionne, *Ch Bd*
Eric J Mcinnis, *VP Fin*
Roland Keller, *Operations**
▲ **EMP**: 260 **EST**: 1997
SQ FT: 180,000
SALES (est): 98.33MM
SALES (corp-wide): 2.3B **Privately Held**
Web: www.gbo.com
SIC: 5047 3841 Medical laboratory equipment; Surgical and medical instruments
HQ: Greiner Bio-One Gmbh
 Bad HallerstraBe 32
 KremsmUnster 4550
 758367910

Monroe - Union County (G-10729)   GEOGRAPHIC SECTION

(G-10729)
H & H FARM MACHINE CO INC
7916 Unionville Brief Rd (28110-9025)
PHONE.............................704 753-1555
Brian Nance, Pr
EMP: 24 EST: 1981
SQ FT: 4,500
SALES (est): 1.98MM Privately Held
Web: www.hhspray.com
SIC: 3523 3524 Sprayers and spraying machines, agricultural; Lawn and garden equipment

(G-10730)
HELMS MACHINE COMPANY
216 N Bivens Rd (28110-8110)
P.O. Box 1355 (28111-1355)
PHONE.............................704 289-5571
Walter C Helms, Pr
Jane Helms, Sec
EMP: 9 EST: 1972
SQ FT: 10,500
SALES (est): 780.8K Privately Held
SIC: 3599 Machine shop, jobbing and repair

(G-10731)
HILTON VINEYARDS LLC
3310 Crow Rd (28112-7558)
PHONE.............................704 776-9656
EMP: 4 EST: 2015
SALES (est): 99.95K Privately Held
Web: www.hiltonvineyardatthevine.com
SIC: 2084 Wines

(G-10732)
HOPEWRITERS LLC
4405 Gwen Hartis Ct (28110-6718)
PHONE.............................317 414-3342
Gary Morland, Prin
EMP: 49 EST: 2020
SALES (est): 349.66K Privately Held
Web: www.hopewriters.com
SIC: 2741 Miscellaneous publishing

(G-10733)
HOS WOODWORKING INC
2704 Old Course Rd (28112-7629)
PHONE.............................712 298-1985
Brian Hospelhorn, Owner
EMP: 5 EST: 2018
SALES (est): 180.77K Privately Held
SIC: 2431 Millwork

(G-10734)
HOSER INC
1132 Curtis St (28112-5058)
PHONE.............................704 989-7151
Joseph Paul Dugick, Pr
EMP: 10 EST: 2020
SALES (est): 995.21K Privately Held
Web: www.hoserinc.com
SIC: 3599 Hose, flexible metallic

(G-10735)
HUNEYWOOD INC
Also Called: Huneywood Frames
7123 Sugar And Wine Rd (28110-1072)
PHONE.............................704 385-9785
Wayne Huneycutt, Pr
EMP: 6 EST: 1984
SALES (est): 358.87K Privately Held
Web: huneywood-inc.hub.biz
SIC: 2499 Picture frame molding, finished

(G-10736)
IDENTIGRAPH SIGNS & AWNINGS
1132 Curtis St (28112-5058)
PHONE.............................704 635-7911
Bill Petroff, CEO
EMP: 6 EST: 2011
SQ FT: 1,000
SALES (est): 608.97K Privately Held
Web: www.identigraphsigns.com
SIC: 3089 Awnings, fiberglass and plastics combination

(G-10737)
IMO INDUSTRIES INC (HQ)
Also Called: Zenith Pumps
420 National Business Pkwy Fl 5 (28110)
P.O. Box 5020 (28111-5020)
PHONE.............................301 323-9000
Darryl Mayhorn, CEO
▲ EMP: 61 EST: 1931
SALES (est): 83.87MM
SALES (corp-wide): 1.71B Publicly Held
Web: www.imo-pump.com
SIC: 3561 3829 Pumps and pumping equipment; Aircraft and motor vehicle measurement equipment
PA: Enovis Corporation
    2711 Centerville Rd # 400
    Wilmington DE 19808
    301 252-9160

(G-10738)
IMO INDUSTRIES INC
IMO Pump Division
1710 Airport Rd (28110-7394)
P.O. Box 5020 (28111-5020)
PHONE.............................704 289-6511
Christian Sahlman, Prin
EMP: 188
SQ FT: 268,488
SALES (corp-wide): 1.71B Publicly Held
Web: www.imo-pump.com
SIC: 5084 3561 Pumps and pumping equipment, nec; Cylinders, pump
HQ: Imo Industries Inc.
    420 Ntional Bus Pkwy Fl 5 Flr 5
    Monroe NC 28110
    301 323-9000

(G-10739)
INSTRUMENT TRANS EQP CORP
2402 Walkup Ave (28110-3842)
P.O. Box 129 (28111-0129)
PHONE.............................704 282-4331
John P Cochran, CEO
Paul E Millward, *
Kevin Ball, *
▲ EMP: 60 EST: 1993
SALES (est): 15.86MM Privately Held
Web: www.itec-ctvt.com
SIC: 3612 Specialty transformers
PA: Falfurrias Capital Partners, L.P.
    100 N Tryon St Ste 4100
    Charlotte NC 28202

(G-10740)
INTERORDNANCE AMER LTD PARTNR
Also Called: Moses, David
3305 Westwood Indus Dr (28110-5204)
PHONE.............................321 212-7801
EMP: 4 EST: 2019
SALES (est): 123.98K Privately Held
SIC: 3482 Cartridge cases for ammunition, 30 mm. and below

(G-10741)
ITEC
2402 Walkup Ave (28110-3842)
PHONE.............................704 282-4331
EMP: 11 EST: 2019
SALES (est): 2.32MM Privately Held
Web: www.itec-ctvt.com
SIC: 3612 Transformers, except electric

(G-10742)
IVEY FIXTURE & DESIGN INC
2814 N Rocky River Rd (28110-9266)
PHONE.............................704 283-4398
Tim Ivey, Pr
J B Ivey, Pr
Barbara Ivey, Sec
Tim Ivey, VP
Marty Barbee, VP
EMP: 4 EST: 1977
SQ FT: 7,000
SALES (est): 469.36K Privately Held
SIC: 2541 Store fixtures, wood

(G-10743)
J & M PAVERS LLC
1504 Citrus Dr (28110-2876)
PHONE.............................704 776-6613
Misael Castillo, Prin
EMP: 5 EST: 2017
SALES (est): 132.93K Privately Held
SIC: 3531 Pavers

(G-10744)
J L ANDERSON CO INC
Also Called: Palmetto Brick-Florence
4812 W Highway 74 (28110-8454)
PHONE.............................704 289-9599
Ricky Taylor, Brnch Mgr
EMP: 7
SALES (corp-wide): 32.63MM Privately Held
Web: www.palmettobrick.com
SIC: 3251 Brick clay: common face, glazed, vitrified, or hollow
PA: J. L. Anderson Co., Inc.
    3501 Brickyard Rd
    Wallace SC 29596
    843 537-7861

(G-10745)
J&P METAL ARTS INC
5923 Stockbridge Dr Ste B (28110-8127)
PHONE.............................704 684-5140
Jorge E Galindo, Pr
EMP: 4 EST: 2014
SALES (est): 121.63K Privately Held
Web: www.jpmetalartsinc.com
SIC: 1799 3353 Ornamental metal work; Aluminum sheet, plate, and foil

(G-10746)
JAMES IRON & STEEL INC
2819 Top Hill Rd (28110-9310)
PHONE.............................704 283-2299
Eric James, Pr
Robert James, Contrlr
Robert Darren, VP
EMP: 26 EST: 1952
SQ FT: 8,500
SALES (est): 703.02K Privately Held
Web: www.jamesironandsteel.com
SIC: 1799 3446 Ornamental metal work; Stairs, staircases, stair treads: prefabricated metal

(G-10747)
JAMES RIVER EQUIPMENT
Also Called: John Deere Authorized Dealer
2112 Morgan Mill Rd (28110-8845)
PHONE.............................704 821-7399
James D Black, Pr
EMP: 27 EST: 1988
SALES (est): 1.18MM Privately Held
Web: www.jamesriverequipment.com
SIC: 3523 5082 Tractors, farm; Construction and mining machinery

(G-10748)
JD APPAREL INC
Also Called: Pine Island Sportswear
1680 Williams Rd (28110-8563)
PHONE.............................704 289-5600
Jaime Winter, Pr
◆ EMP: 20 EST: 2006
SQ FT: 15,000
SALES (est): 1.36MM Privately Held
SIC: 2321 Polo shirts, men's and boys': made from purchased materials

(G-10749)
JESKRI ASSOCIATES INC
1821 N Rocky River Rd (28110-7961)
PHONE.............................704 291-9991
Josef Pennigar, Pr
EMP: 9 EST: 2004
SALES (est): 709.61K Privately Held
SIC: 2899 Drug testing kits, blood and urine

(G-10750)
JLS MASONRY INC
4509 Parkwood School Rd (28112-7553)
PHONE.............................704 307-1219
EMP: 6 EST: 2018
SALES (est): 249.97K Privately Held
SIC: 2024 Yogurt desserts, frozen

(G-10751)
KEFI WINERY INC
3109 Plyler Mill Rd (28112-8817)
PHONE.............................704 591-5791
Vasiliki Collins, Pr
EMP: 5 EST: 2018
SALES (est): 140.68K Privately Held
Web: www.kefiwinery.com
SIC: 2084 Wines

(G-10752)
KELLANOVA
Also Called: Kellogg
1007 Omaha Dr (28110-7693)
PHONE.............................704 241-6977
EMP: 4
SALES (corp-wide): 15.31B Publicly Held
Web: www.kellanova.com
SIC: 2043 Cereal breakfast foods
PA: Kellanova
    412 N Wells St
    Chicago IL 60654
    269 961-2000

(G-10753)
KELLER COSMETICS INC
Also Called: Hazel Keller Cosmetics
2620 Stitt St (28110)
P.O. Box 77064 (28271-7000)
PHONE.............................704 399-2226
Amy Kramer Kennedy, Pr
EMP: 4 EST: 1956
SALES (est): 834.4K Privately Held
Web: www.kellercosmetics.com
SIC: 5122 2844 Cosmetics; Cosmetic preparations

(G-10754)
LADYBUGS MEDIBLES LLC
2003 Shady Ln (28110-7970)
PHONE.............................704 635-7596
Kendra Jeffress, Prin
EMP: 4 EST: 2016
SALES (est): 71.53K Privately Held
SIC: 2099 Food preparations, nec

(G-10755)
LANDSDOWN MINING CORPORATION
7406 Concord Hwy (28110-6927)
PHONE.............................704 753-5400

GEOGRAPHIC SECTION
Monroe - Union County (G-10780)

EMP: 10 EST: 2018
SALES (est): 2.28MM **Privately Held**
SIC: **1442** Sand mining

(G-10756)
LD DAVIS INDUSTRIES INC
Also Called: L D Davis
2031 E Roosevelt Blvd (28112-4133)
PHONE..................................704 289-4551
Barry Barto, *Mgr*
EMP: 43
SALES (corp-wide): 15.72MM **Privately Held**
Web: www.lddavis.com
SIC: **2891** Adhesives
PA: L.D. Davis Industries, Inc.
   1725 The Fairway
   Jenkintown PA 19046
   800 883-6199

(G-10757)
LEGACY MECHANICAL
2715 Gray Fox Rd (28110-8421)
PHONE..................................704 225-8558
Melvin Thomas, *Prin*
Melvin Thomas Senior, *VP*
▲ EMP: 10 EST: 1987
SQ FT: 7,000
SALES (est): 1.72MM **Privately Held**
SIC: **3542** Robots for metal forming: pressing, extruding, etc.

(G-10758)
LIMESTONE PRODUCTS INC (PA)
3302 W Highway 74 B (28110-8439)
P.O. Box 1309 (28111-1309)
PHONE..................................704 283-9492
Larry Rogers, *Pr*
Thomas L Broome, *VP*
Arthur K Cates, *VP*
Jerry Sutton, *Sec*
EMP: 6 EST: 1985
SALES (est): 2.71MM
SALES (corp-wide): 2.71MM **Privately Held**
Web: www.limestoneproductsinc.com
SIC: **1422** Lime rock, ground

(G-10759)
LLEWELLYN MTAL FABRICATORS INC
4816 Persimmon Ct (28110-9313)
PHONE..................................704 283-4816
Joe Llewellyn, *Pr*
Brenda Llewellyn, *VP*
EMP: 11 EST: 1986
SALES (est): 465.46K **Privately Held**
Web: www.lmetalfabrication.com
SIC: **3441** Fabricated structural metal

(G-10760)
LOGO DOGZ
4808 Persimmon Ct (28110-9313)
PHONE..................................888 827-8866
Traci Mcdonald, *Owner*
EMP: 4 EST: 2018
SALES (est): 132.16K **Privately Held**
Web: www.logodogz.com
SIC: **2759** Screen printing

(G-10761)
M & J STUCCO LLC
P.O. Box 513 (29714-0513)
PHONE..................................704 634-2249
Jennifer Lloyd, *Managing Member*
Mark Lloyd, *Managing Member*
EMP: 4 EST: 2011
SALES (est): 148.45K **Privately Held**
Web: www.mandjstucco.com
SIC: **3299** Stucco

(G-10762)
M AND H MASONRY
503 N Bragg St (28112-4627)
PHONE..................................704 858-7230
Melinda Nelson, *Prin*
EMP: 5 EST: 2018
SALES (est): 90.62K **Privately Held**
SIC: **2024** Yogurt desserts, frozen

(G-10763)
MACHINING TECHNOLOGY SERVICES
1817 N Rocky River Rd (28110-7961)
PHONE..................................704 282-1071
Sherrill Connell, *Pr*
Lindy Williams, *VP*
Terry Thompson, *Sec*
EMP: 6 EST: 1988
SQ FT: 4,000
SALES (est): 942.33K **Privately Held**
Web: www.machiningtechnologyservices.com
SIC: **3433** Stokers, mechanical: domestic or industrial

(G-10764)
MANUFACTURING SYSTEMS EQP INC
2812 Chamber Dr (28110-8473)
PHONE..................................704 283-2086
Charles Earhart, *CEO*
Keith Earhart, *Pr*
Ruth Earhart, *Sec*
Kerry Earhart, *VP Fin*
Kim Earhart, *VP Mktg*
▲ EMP: 18 EST: 1987
SQ FT: 33,300
SALES (est): 2.31MM **Privately Held**
SIC: **5063** 3612 3694 Transformers and transmission equipment; Power transformers, electric; Engine electrical equipment

(G-10765)
MARIETTA MARTIN MATERIALS INC
Also Called: Martin Marietta Aggregates
2111 N Rocky River Rd (28110-7964)
P.O. Box 458 (28110-0458)
PHONE..................................704 283-4915
Larry Thomas, *Mgr*
EMP: 7
Web: www.martinmarietta.com
SIC: **1422** Crushed and broken limestone
PA: Martin Marietta Materials Inc
   4123 Parklake Ave
   Raleigh NC 27612

(G-10766)
MASTER SCREENS SOUTH LLC
600 Broome St (28110-3947)
PHONE..................................704 226-9600
▲ EMP: 7 EST: 1997
SQ FT: 30,000
SALES (est): 459.64K **Privately Held**
SIC: **2754** Rotogravure printing

(G-10767)
MATTHEWS MILLWORK INC
1105 Jim Cir (28110-5101)
PHONE..................................704 821-4499
Roger I Leslie, *Pr*
EMP: 7 EST: 1987
SQ FT: 7,000
SALES (est): 802.99K **Privately Held**
Web: www.matthewsmillwork.com
SIC: **2431** Millwork

(G-10768)
MBP ACQUISITION LLC
Also Called: Hamilton Drywall Products
6090 Willis Way (28110-8365)
PHONE..................................704 349-5055
Mark Hamilton, *Managing Member*
EMP: 14 EST: 2017
SALES (est): 536.96K **Privately Held**
Web: www.hamiltondrywallproducts.com
SIC: **3275** Acoustical plaster, gypsum

(G-10769)
MCDONALD SERVICES INC (PA)
7427 Price Tucker Rd (28110-8297)
P.O. Box 1192 (28070-1192)
PHONE..................................704 753-9669
Jim Mcdonald, *Pr*
Margaret Mcdonald, *VP*
EMP: 4 EST: 1983
SQ FT: 30,000
SALES (est): 4.54MM
SALES (corp-wide): 4.54MM **Privately Held**
Web: www.msibalers.com
SIC: **5084** 3559 Industrial machinery and equipment; Recycling machinery

(G-10770)
MINT HILL CABINET SHOP INC
Also Called: Mint Hill Cabinet Shop
5519 Cannon Dr (28110-7982)
P.O. Box 2069 (28079-2069)
PHONE..................................704 821-9373
John Carriker, *Pr*
Richard Carriker, *
EMP: 30 EST: 1961
SQ FT: 25,000
SALES (est): 3.6MM **Privately Held**
Web: www.minthillcabinets.com
SIC: **2434** 5031 5211 Wood kitchen cabinets ; Kitchen cabinets; Cabinets, kitchen

(G-10771)
MITCHELL MEDLIN MACHINE SHOP
1394 Walkup Ave Ste C (28110-3565)
PHONE..................................704 289-2840
Louceil Medlin, *Pr*
EMP: 6 EST: 1979
SQ FT: 3,500
SALES (est): 461.58K **Privately Held**
SIC: **3599** Machine shop, jobbing and repair

(G-10772)
MONARCH KNITTING MCHY CORP
Also Called: Vanguard Supreme Div
601 Mcarthur Cir (28110-3622)
PHONE..................................704 283-8171
William Moody, *Brnch Mgr*
EMP: 22
SALES (corp-wide): 9.53MM **Privately Held**
Web: www.monarchknitting.org
SIC: **3552** Knitting machines
PA: Monarch Knitting Machinery Corp.
   115 N Secrest Ave
   Monroe NC 28110
   704 291-3300

(G-10773)
MONARCH KNITTING MCHY CORP (PA)
Also Called: Monarch Manufacturing
115 N Secrest Ave (28110-6807)
P.O. Box 5009 (28111-5009)
PHONE..................................704 291-3300
David Pernick, *Ch Bd*
Bruce Pernick, *Pr*
Jose Rodriguez, *CFO*
Stewart Bader, *Sec*
◆ EMP: 15 EST: 1964
SQ FT: 6,000
SALES (est): 9.53MM
SALES (corp-wide): 9.53MM **Privately Held**
Web: www.monarchknitting.org
SIC: **3552** 5084 Knitting machines; Textile machinery and equipment

(G-10774)
MONARCH MANUFACTURING CORP
Also Called: Vanguard Supreme
115 N Secrest Ave (28110-6807)
P.O. Box 9 (28111-0009)
PHONE..................................704 283-8171
David Pernick, *Pr*
◆ EMP: 10 EST: 1986
SALES (est): 2.04MM
SALES (corp-wide): 9.53MM **Privately Held**
SIC: **3552** Knitting machines
PA: Monarch Knitting Machinery Corp.
   115 N Secrest Ave
   Monroe NC 28110
   704 291-3300

(G-10775)
MONROE METAL MANUFACTURING INC
Also Called: Monroe Metal Manufacturing
6025 Stitt St (28110-8187)
PHONE..................................800 366-1391
Bobby F Pope, *Pr*
Janice Pope, *
▼ EMP: 55 EST: 1968
SQ FT: 180,000
SALES (est): 5.24MM **Privately Held**
SIC: **3444** Ducts, sheet metal

(G-10776)
MULLIS MECHANICAL INC
609 Belmont Church Rd (28112-7436)
PHONE..................................704 254-5229
EMP: 5 EST: 2019
SALES (est): 102.23K **Privately Held**
SIC: **7692** Welding repair

(G-10777)
MYCOATINGSOLUTIONS
1410 Crown Forest Ln (28112-9021)
PHONE..................................704 619-0308
Anthony Belk, *Prin*
EMP: 5 EST: 2011
SALES (est): 190.37K **Privately Held**
SIC: **3829** Measuring and controlling devices, nec

(G-10778)
NC AGRICULTURE TEACHERS ASSOC
722 Brewer Dr (28112-6193)
PHONE..................................704 290-1513
EMP: 6 EST: 2019
SALES (est): 98.52K **Privately Held**
SIC: **3399** Primary metal products

(G-10779)
NEWGARD INDUSTRIES INC
3132 Drake Ln (28110-8895)
PHONE..................................704 283-6011
Curt Peterson, *Pr*
EMP: 10 EST: 1954
SQ FT: 15,000
SALES (est): 162.45K **Privately Held**
SIC: **2221** 2241 Nylon broadwoven fabrics; Braids, tubular nylon or plastic

(G-10780)
NORTHSTAR COMPUTER TECH INC
5014 Hampton Meadows Rd (28110-9351)
PHONE..................................980 272-1969
Daniel Beltz, *CEO*
EMP: 4 EST: 2008
SALES (est): 260.21K **Privately Held**
Web: www.northstarcomp.com

SIC: **5734** 3812 3674 Computer and software stores; Defense systems and equipment; Microcircuits, integrated (semiconductor)

(G-10781)
NORTON DOOR CONTROLS
3000 E Highway 74 (28112-9152)
PHONE..................................704 233-4011
◆ **EMP:** 45 **EST:** 1957
SALES (est): 9.98MM **Privately Held**
Web: www.nortonrixson.com
SIC: **3429** 5099 Locks or lock sets; Locks and lock sets

(G-10782)
ODELL CUSTOM CABINETS
5424 Concord Hwy (28110-9281)
PHONE..................................704 201-6975
EMP: 4 **EST:** 2017
SALES (est): 77.11K **Privately Held**
Web: www.odellcustomcabinets.com
SIC: **2434** Wood kitchen cabinets

(G-10783)
ORO MANUFACTURING COMPANY
5000 Stitt St (28110-4000)
PHONE..................................704 283-2186
Robert Engel, *Pr*
Patricia Engel, *
Robert Engel, *VP*
Nancy Engel, *
Susan Hagarty, *
EMP: 41 **EST:** 1945
SQ FT: 80,000
SALES (est): 8.08MM **Privately Held**
Web: www.oromfg.com
SIC: **2542** 3499 3728 3444 Fixtures, office: except wood; Wheels: wheelbarrow, stroller, etc.: disc, stamped metal; Aircraft assemblies, subassemblies, and parts, nec; Sheet metalwork

(G-10784)
PAXTON MEDIA GROUP
Also Called: Inquire Journal, The
1508 Skyway Dr (28110-3008)
PHONE..................................704 289-1541
Marvin Enderle, *Publisher*
EMP: 15 **EST:** 1997
SALES (est): 421.23K **Privately Held**
Web: www.paducahsun.com
SIC: **2711** Newspapers, publishing and printing

(G-10785)
PEARL RIVER GROUP LLC
Also Called: Altior Industries
6027 Stitt St (28110-8370)
PHONE..................................704 283-4667
◆ **EMP:** 6 **EST:** 1996
SQ FT: 16,000
SALES (est): 950.96K **Privately Held**
SIC: **2389** Disposable garments and accessories

(G-10786)
PEELLE COMPANY
115 N Secrest Ave (28110-6807)
PHONE..................................631 231-6000
C J Wagenhauser, *Prin*
EMP: 8
SALES (corp-wide): 5.12MM **Privately Held**
Web: www.peelledoor.com
SIC: **3442** Metal doors
PA: The Peelle Company
   373 Smithtown Byp 311
   Hauppauge NY 11788
   631 231-6000

(G-10787)
PIEDMONT SIGNS
2330 Concord Hwy (28110-8768)
PHONE..................................704 291-2345
Clay Helms, *Owner*
EMP: 6 **EST:** 2006
SALES (est): 179.39K **Privately Held**
Web: www.piedmontsignsnc.com
SIC: **3993** Signs and advertising specialties

(G-10788)
POPLIN & SONS MACHINE CO INC
2118 Stafford Street Ext (28110-9650)
PHONE..................................704 289-2079
Ronny Poplin, *Pr*
Gary Poplin, *Treas*
Kathy Presson, *Sec*
EMP: 11 **EST:** 1975
SQ FT: 12,300
SALES (est): 980.38K **Privately Held**
SIC: **3599** Machine shop, jobbing and repair

(G-10789)
PRIVETTE ENTERPRISES INC
2751 Old Charlotte Hwy (28110-9107)
P.O. Box 1189 (28111-1189)
PHONE..................................704 634-3291
David Privette, *Pr*
EMP: 22 **EST:** 2001
SALES (est): 4.16MM **Privately Held**
Web: www.peigrading.com
SIC: **5211** 2499 2879 4212 Sand and gravel; Mulch, wood and bark; Soil conditioners; Dump truck haulage

(G-10790)
PUREON INC
1412 Airport Rd (28110-7391)
PHONE..................................480 505-3409
Daniel Spring, *CEO*
Martin Spring, *
Karen Miles, *
Jeanie Coudright Ctrl, *Prin*
EMP: 52 **EST:** 2007
SALES (est): 4.35MM **Privately Held**
Web: www.pureon.com
SIC: **2842** Polishes and sanitation goods

(G-10791)
QSPAC INDUSTRIES INC
506 Miller St (28110-3180)
PHONE..................................704 635-7815
EMP: 28
Web: www.qspac.com
SIC: **3999** Atomizers, toiletry
PA: Qspac Industries, Inc.
   15020 Marquardt Ave
   Santa Fe Springs CA 90670

(G-10792)
RANDALL SUPPLY INC (PA)
2409 Walkup Ave (28110-3841)
PHONE..................................704 289-6479
Kenneth R Randall Junior, *Pr*
Eleanor Randall, *
EMP: 24 **EST:** 1954
SQ FT: 19,000
SALES (est): 2.41MM
SALES (corp-wide): 2.41MM **Privately Held**
Web: www.randallsupply.com
SIC: **7694** 5063 Electric motor repair; Motors, electric

(G-10793)
RECORD USA INC (PA)
4324 Phil Hargett Ct (28110-7671)
P.O. Box 3099 (28110-3099)
PHONE..................................704 289-9212
Marty Licciardello, *Pr*
▲ **EMP:** 50 **EST:** 1995
SQ FT: 35,000
SALES (est): 60.55MM **Privately Held**
Web: www.recorddoors.com
SIC: **3699** Electrical equipment and supplies, nec

(G-10794)
REFINED OUTDOORS LLC
2004 Ridge Rd (28110-9222)
PHONE..................................704 634-4027
Jordan A Edwards, *Prin*
EMP: 5 **EST:** 2015
SALES (est): 205.18K **Privately Held**
Web: www.refinedoutdoors.com
SIC: **2323** Men's and boy's neckwear

(G-10795)
RELIABLE CONSTRUCTION CO INC
100 N Sutherland Ave Ste A (28110-3992)
P.O. Box 688 (28111-0688)
PHONE..................................704 289-1501
Douglas S Moore, *Pr*
Galard C Moore Junior, *VP*
Phyllis Garrison, *Sec*
EMP: 21 **EST:** 1965
SQ FT: 3,000
SALES (est): 951.69K **Privately Held**
SIC: **1542** 2541 2431 Bank building construction; Wood partitions and fixtures; Millwork

(G-10796)
RELIANCE MANAGEMENT GROUP INC
Also Called: Logodogz
4910 Starcrest Dr (28110-8497)
PHONE..................................704 282-2255
Rodney Mcdonald, *Pr*
Anthony Mizzi, *VP*
George Bohle, *VP*
EMP: 12 **EST:** 2000
SALES (est): 2.47MM **Privately Held**
SIC: **2759** Screen printing

(G-10797)
ROBERT HAMMS LLC
Also Called: Custom Wood Products
3028 Proverbs Ct (28110-7896)
PHONE..................................704 605-8057
Robert Hamm, *Managing Member*
EMP: 7 **EST:** 2016
SALES (est): 400K **Privately Held**
SIC: **2499** 7699 Applicators, wood; Customizing services

(G-10798)
ROVERTYM
3308 Westwood Industrial Dr Ste E (28110)
PHONE..................................704 635-7305
Larry Harrell, *Pr*
EMP: 4 **EST:** 2011
SALES (est): 203.01K **Privately Held**
SIC: **3441** Fabricated structural metal

(G-10799)
ROZ INC
206 N Hayne St Ste C (28112-4866)
PHONE..................................704 737-7940
Rosalind Blakeney, *Prin*
EMP: 5 **EST:** 2009
SALES (est): 134.69K **Privately Held**
SIC: **2752** Commercial printing, lithographic

(G-10800)
RS INDUSTRIES INC
Also Called: Classic Molders
524 Marshall St (28112-4676)
P.O. Box 1051 (28111-1051)
PHONE..................................704 289-2734
Robert Snyder, *Pr*
Mary Snyder, *VP*
EMP: 8 **EST:** 1990
SQ FT: 15,000
SALES (est): 997.85K **Privately Held**
Web: www.classicmolders.com
SIC: **3089** Injection molding of plastics

(G-10801)
SAFE FIRE DETECTION INC
Also Called: Westek
5915 Stockbridge Dr (28110-8106)
PHONE..................................704 821-7920
Ronald Robertson, *Pr*
▲ **EMP:** 18 **EST:** 1995
SALES (est): 4.33MM **Privately Held**
Web: www.safefiredetection.com
SIC: **3669** Fire alarm apparatus, electric

(G-10802)
SCOTT TECHNOLOGIES INC (HQ)
Also Called: Scott Safety
4320 Goldmine Rd (28110-7355)
P.O. Box 569 (28111-0569)
PHONE..................................704 291-8300
Andrew Chrostowski, *Pr*
◆ **EMP:** 44 **EST:** 1983
SQ FT: 10,000
SALES (est): 386.75MM
SALES (corp-wide): 34.23B **Publicly Held**
Web: scottu.3m.com
SIC: **3569** Firefighting and related equipment
PA: 3m Company
   3m Center
   Saint Paul MN 55144
   651 733-1110

(G-10803)
SCOTT TECHNOLOGIES INC
Scott Safety
4320 Goldmine Rd (28110-7355)
P.O. Box 569 (28111-0569)
PHONE..................................704 291-8300
Mike Ryan, *Brnch Mgr*
EMP: 500
SQ FT: 201,214
SALES (corp-wide): 34.23B **Publicly Held**
Web: scottu.3m.com
SIC: **3569** 3842 Firefighting apparatus; Respiratory protection equipment, personal
HQ: Scott Technologies, Inc.
   4320 Goldmine Rd
   Monroe NC 28110
   704 291-8300

(G-10804)
SDFC LLC
Also Called: Mocaro Dyeing & Finishing
3511 Essex Pointe Dr (28110-7733)
PHONE..................................704 878-6645
Abid Ali, *Managing Member*
EMP: 14 **EST:** 2016
SALES (est): 2.48MM **Privately Held**
Web: www.mocaro.com
SIC: **2257** Dyeing and finishing circular knit fabrics

(G-10805)
SELECT AIR SYSTEMS USA INC
Also Called: Select Air Systems
2716 Chamber Dr (28110-8472)
PHONE..................................704 289-1122
Gary D Smith, *Pr*
Trecia Thomas, *Pr*
Jody Reynolds, *VP*
EMP: 20 **EST:** 2001
SQ FT: 150,000
SALES (est): 4.17MM **Privately Held**
Web: www.selectairsystemsinc.com
SIC: **3564** Ventilating fans: industrial or commercial

GEOGRAPHIC SECTION
Monroe - Union County (G-10831)

(G-10806)
SEW BLESSED EMBROIDERY
1775 E Brief Rd (28110-9032)
PHONE...................704 840-7571
Jeanette Baucom, *Owner*
EMP: 4 **EST:** 2015
SALES (est): 45.44K **Privately Held**
SIC: 2395 Embroidery and art needlework

(G-10807)
SIGNATURE CUSTOM CABINETS LLC
2106 E Highway 218 (28110-7031)
PHONE...................704 753-4874
Charles Medlin Junior, *Prin*
EMP: 4 **EST:** 2011
SALES (est): 228.44K **Privately Held**
SIC: 2434 Wood kitchen cabinets

(G-10808)
SMALL BROTHERS TIRE CO INC
Also Called: Small Tire Company
1725 Concord Ave (28110-2917)
P.O. Box 852 (28111-0852)
PHONE...................704 289-3531
Alan L Small, *Pr*
Sadie H Small, *Sec*
EMP: 6 **EST:** 1945
SQ FT: 8,000
SALES (est): 921.08K **Privately Held**
Web: www.monroetiresnc.com
SIC: 5531 7534 Automotive tires; Tire recapping

(G-10809)
SMOOTHIE FABRICATION LLC
1809 Timber Lane Dr (28110-7836)
PHONE...................704 291-7728
Marty Roberson, *Prin*
EMP: 4 **EST:** 2014
SALES (est): 111.31K **Privately Held**
Web: www.smoothiefab.com
SIC: 2037 Frozen fruits and vegetables

(G-10810)
SOUTHERN RANGE BREWING LLC
151 S Stewart St (28112-5548)
PHONE...................704 289-4049
Dustin Gatliff, *Managing Member*
EMP: 8 **EST:** 2016
SALES (est): 745.39K **Privately Held**
Web: www.southernrangebrewing.com
SIC: 2082 2084 Beer (alcoholic beverage); Wines

(G-10811)
SPT TECHNOLOGY INC
3107 Chamber Dr (28110-0439)
PHONE...................612 332-1880
Daryl Sandberg, *Pr*
Mary Van Horne, *Ex VP*
▲ **EMP:** 14 **EST:** 1996
SQ FT: 6,280
SALES (est): 2.31MM
SALES (corp-wide): 9.57MM **Privately Held**
Web: www.paceline.com
SIC: 2821 3229 2241 2299 Polyesters; Yarn, fiberglass; Tie tapes, woven or braided; Scouring and carbonizing of textile fibers
PA: Paceline, Inc.
10737 Indpndnce Pnte Pkwy
Matthews NC 28105
704 290-5007

(G-10812)
SPT TECHNOLOGY INC
Also Called: Paceline
4808 Persimmon Ct (28110-9313)
PHONE...................704 290-5007
Anthony Mizzi, *Prin*
EMP: 8 **EST:** 2012
SALES (est): 248.24K **Privately Held**
Web: www.paceline.com
SIC: 2821 Plastics materials and resins

(G-10813)
STAFFORD WELDING
1806 Starnes Cemetary Rd (28112-9605)
PHONE...................704 774-1837
Sarah Stafford, *Prin*
EMP: 4 **EST:** 2019
SALES (est): 61.74K **Privately Held**
SIC: 7692 Welding repair

(G-10814)
STAINLESS SUPPLY INC
Also Called: JW Metal Products
307 N Secrest Ave (28110-3801)
PHONE...................704 635-2064
Jeffrey White, *Prin*
EMP: 19 **EST:** 2012
SALES (est): 4.84MM **Privately Held**
Web: www.stainlesssupply.com
SIC: 3444 Sheet metalwork

(G-10815)
STEGALL PETROLEUM INC
Also Called: SPI Express
1907 Old Charlotte Hwy (28110-9146)
P.O. Box 766 (28111-0766)
PHONE...................704 283-5058
Danny Seagall, *Owner*
EMP: 5 **EST:** 2005
SALES (est): 250.71K **Privately Held**
Web: www.marathonoil.com
SIC: 2741 Miscellaneous publishing

(G-10816)
STUDLEYS INDEPENDENT RODS
3229 Waxhaw Hwy (28112-6729)
PHONE...................704 296-9036
Kim S Studley Phillips, *Pr*
EMP: 8 **EST:** 2016
SALES (est): 498.94K **Privately Held**
Web: www.hotrodit.com
SIC: 3714 Motor vehicle parts and accessories

(G-10817)
SUN VALLEY STL FABRICATION INC
1810 Tower Industrial Dr (28110-8575)
PHONE...................704 289-5830
Timothy Curtis Meggs, *Pr*
Debbie Meggs, *Sec*
EMP: 10 **EST:** 1989
SALES (est): 2.11MM **Privately Held**
SIC: 5051 3599 Steel; Machine shop, jobbing and repair

(G-10818)
SWANSON SHEETMETAL INC
320 Broome St (28110-3908)
PHONE...................704 283-3955
Karen Swanson, *Pr*
EMP: 17 **EST:** 1991
SQ FT: 30,000
SALES (est): 2.33MM **Privately Held**
Web: www.swansonsheetmetal.com
SIC: 3444 Sheet metal specialties, not stamped

(G-10819)
SYNTHOMER INC
Also Called: Printworld
2011 N Rocky River Rd (28110-7963)
PHONE...................704 225-1872
Rick Creedmore, *Dir*
EMP: 52
SQ FT: 78,502
SALES (corp-wide): 2.87B **Privately Held**
Web: www.omnova.com
SIC: 2621 2754 Paper mills; Commercial printing, gravure
HQ: Synthomer Inc.
25435 Harvard Rd
Beachwood OH 44122
216 682-7000

(G-10820)
TAYLOR COMMUNICATIONS INC
1803 N Rocky River Rd (28110-7961)
P.O. Box 989 (28111-0989)
PHONE...................704 282-0989
EMP: 32
SALES (corp-wide): 3.81B **Privately Held**
Web: www.taylor.com
SIC: 2761 Manifold business forms
HQ: Taylor Communications, Inc.
1725 Roe Crest Dr
North Mankato MN 56003
866 541-0937

(G-10821)
TEXTROL LABORATORIES INC
111 W Sandy Ridge Rd (28112-9541)
PHONE...................704 764-3400
E F White, *Pr*
Francis H White, *
B E Wallace, *
▲ **EMP:** 30 **EST:** 1971
SQ FT: 22,000
SALES (est): 2.4MM **Privately Held**
Web: www.textrol.com
SIC: 3625 8711 3552 Electric controls and control accessories, industrial; Consulting engineer; Textile machinery

(G-10822)
TORTILLERIA LOS PAISANOS
1404 Skyway Dr (28110-3085)
PHONE...................704 283-8508
Alfonso Garcia, *Prin*
EMP: 5 **EST:** 2014
SALES (est): 161.96K **Privately Held**
SIC: 2099 Tortillas, fresh or refrigerated

(G-10823)
TRIMWORKS INC
Also Called: Haigler Electric & Cnstr
4705 Carriker Rd (28110-7491)
PHONE...................704 753-4149
Michelle Haiger, *Pr*
Ronnie Haiger, *VP*
Michelle Haigler, *Pr*
EMP: 4 **EST:** 1993
SQ FT: 2,000
SALES (est): 464.47K **Privately Held**
SIC: 2431 Moldings and baseboards, ornamental and trim

(G-10824)
TS WOODWORKS & RAD DESIGN INC
3213 Westwood Industrial Dr (28110-5228)
PHONE...................704 238-1015
Toral Jagani, *Pr*
Kamlesh Jagani, *VP*
EMP: 12 **EST:** 2015
SQ FT: 18,000
SALES (est): 1.27MM **Privately Held**
Web: www.tswoodworks.com
SIC: 2431 2541 2434 Millwork; Table or counter tops, plastic laminated; Vanities, bathroom: wood

(G-10825)
TSERINGS LLC
1414 Ellen St (28112-5173)
PHONE....!..................704 283-8811
EMP: 5 **EST:** 2019
SALES (est): 112.45K **Privately Held**
SIC: 3281 Cut stone and stone products

(G-10826)
TYSON FOODS INC
Also Called: Tyson
2023 Hasty St (28112-5997)
PHONE...................704 283-7571
EMP: 6
SALES (corp-wide): 52.88B **Publicly Held**
Web: www.tysonfoods.com
SIC: 2015 Poultry slaughtering and processing
PA: Tyson Foods, Inc.
2200 W Don Tyson Pkwy
Springdale AR 72762
479 290-4000

(G-10827)
UNCLE BROWNS SCENTED CANDLES
2311 Honeycutt Simpson Rd (28110-1410)
PHONE...................704 993-0409
Stacy Brown, *Prin*
EMP: 4 **EST:** 2018
SALES (est): 62.54K **Privately Held**
SIC: 3999 Candles

(G-10828)
VANGUARD PAI LUNG LLC
Also Called: Vanguard Pailung
601 Mcarthur Cir (28110-3622)
P.O. Box 9 (28111-0009)
PHONE...................704 283-8171
Christopher Skinner, *Pr*
Chien Chang James Wang, *Ch*
◆ **EMP:** 9 **EST:** 2009
SALES (est): 4.83MM **Privately Held**
Web: www.vanguardpailung.com
SIC: 5084 3552 Textile machinery and equipment; Knitting machines

(G-10829)
VANN S WLDG & ORNA WORKS INC
709 Sikes Mill Rd (28110-9759)
PHONE...................704 289-6056
Vann Mcmanus, *Pr*
Judy Mc Manus, *Sec*
EMP: 17 **EST:** 1983
SQ FT: 10,000
SALES (est): 2.19MM **Privately Held**
Web: www.vannsweldingnc.com
SIC: 3446 3441 Ornamental metalwork; Fabricated structural metal

(G-10830)
W F HARRIS LIGHTING INC
4015 Airport Extension Rd (28110-7398)
P.O. Box 5023 (28111-5023)
PHONE...................704 283-7477
▲ **EMP:** 18 **EST:** 1971
SALES (est): 3.43MM **Privately Held**
Web: www.wfharris.com
SIC: 3646 3645 3648 Fluorescent lighting fixtures, commercial; Fluorescent lighting fixtures, residential; Lighting equipment, nec

(G-10831)
WDM INC
Also Called: Wood Designs
608 Broome St (28110-3947)
P.O. Box 1308 (28111-1308)
PHONE...................704 283-7508
Dennis Gosney, *Pr*
Deborah Gosney, *
◆ **EMP:** 50 **EST:** 1981
SQ FT: 70,000
SALES (est): 8.35MM **Privately Held**
Web: www.wooddesigns.com

Monroe - Union County (G-10832)

SIC: 2511 Children's wood furniture

(G-10832)
WEISS USA LLC
2213 Stafford Street Ext (28110-9651)
P.O. Box 509 (28111-0509)
PHONE.................704 282-4496
T W Kirkpatrick, Pr
▲ **EMP:** 4 **EST:** 2009
SALES (est): 482.05K **Privately Held**
Web: www.weiss-usa.com
SIC: 2891 Adhesives

(G-10833)
WILLIAM GOODYEAR CO (PA)
2802 Gray Fox Rd (28110-8422)
PHONE.................704 283-7824
Edward W Goodyear Junior, Pr
Sylvia Goodyear, Sec
▲ **EMP:** 19 **EST:** 1986
SQ FT: 16,400
SALES (est): 4.74MM
SALES (corp-wide): 4.74MM **Privately Held**
Web: www.wmgoodyear.com
SIC: 3069 Hard rubber and molded rubber products

(G-10834)
WILLIAMS READY MIX PDTS INC
2465 Old Charlotte Hwy (28110-7366)
PHONE.................704 283-1137
Mitchell C Crook, Pr
Paula W Crook, Sec
EMP: 19 **EST:** 1987
SQ FT: 500
SALES (est): 1.8MM **Privately Held**
Web: ivj.sgz.mybluehost.me
SIC: 3273 Ready-mixed concrete

(G-10835)
WINDSOR WINDOW COMPANY
2210 Stafford Street Ext (28110-9651)
PHONE.................704 283-7459
EMP: 7
Web: www.woodgrain.com
SIC: 2431 Millwork
HQ: Windsor Window Company
  300 Nw 16th St
  Fruitland ID 83619
  800 452-3801

(G-10836)
WINDSOR WINDOW COMPANY
2210 Stafford Street Ext (28110-9651)
PHONE.................704 283-7459
Richard Stephens, Prin
EMP: 150
Web: www.woodgrain.com
SIC: 2431 3231 Windows and window parts and trim, wood; Products of purchased glass
HQ: Windsor Window Company
  300 Nw 16th St
  Fruitland ID 83619
  800 452-3801

(G-10837)
WPT LLC
1416 E Highway 218 (28110-7024)
PHONE.................704 770-1311
EMP: 4 **EST:** 2015
SALES (est): 186.81K **Privately Held**
SIC: 2869 Ethylene

Mooresboro
Cleveland County

(G-10838)
FULTON TECHNOLOGY CORPORATION
337 S Pea Ridge Rd (28114-7681)
P.O. Box 159 (28019-0159)
PHONE.................828 657-1611
Jane Fulton, Pr
Nathan Fulton, VP
EMP: 5 **EST:** 1999
SQ FT: 10,000
SALES (est): 1.27MM **Privately Held**
Web: www.fultontechnology.com
SIC: 3599 Machine shop, jobbing and repair

(G-10839)
MICKEY BLANTON LOGGING
277 Henry Jenkins Rd (28114-8257)
PHONE.................828 289-9344
EMP: 4 **EST:** 2018
SALES (est): 81.72K **Privately Held**
SIC: 2411 Logging

(G-10840)
ROGERS GROUP INC
1385 Ferry Rd (28114-8649)
PHONE.................828 657-9331
EMP: 9
SALES (corp-wide): 1.05B **Privately Held**
Web: www.rogersgroupincint.com
SIC: 1442 Construction sand and gravel
PA: Rogers Group, Inc.
  421 Great Circle Rd
  Nashville TN 37228
  615 242-0585

(G-10841)
SUNRISE DEVELOPMENT LLC
Also Called: Sunrise Development USA
650 Nc 120 Hwy (28114-6713)
P.O. Box 35 (28040-0035)
PHONE.................828 453-0590
Quinxin Zhu, Pr
▲ **EMP:** 12 **EST:** 2009
SQ FT: 50,000
SALES (est): 979.52K **Privately Held**
Web: www.sunrise-usa.com
SIC: 2299 2221 2392 5137 Batting, wadding, padding and fillings; Bedding, manmade or silk fabric; Pillows, bed: made from purchased materials; Baby goods

(G-10842)
THOMPSON PRINTING & PACKG INC ✪
2457 Mccraw Rd (28114-7721)
PHONE.................704 313-7323
Robert Thompson, CEO
EMP: 5 **EST:** 2022
SALES (est): 289.37K **Privately Held**
Web: www.tpphome.com
SIC: 7389 3086 5199 2752 Packaging and labeling services; Packaging and shipping materials, foamed plastics; Packaging materials; Commercial printing, lithographic

(G-10843)
U-HEAR OF HICKORY
1227 Mount Pleasant Church Rd (28114-8719)
PHONE.................704 434-2062
Angelia Goode, Owner
EMP: 5 **EST:** 2013
SALES (est): 241.36K **Privately Held**
SIC: 3842 Surgical appliances and supplies

Mooresville
Iredell County

(G-10844)
27 SOFTWARE US INC
Also Called: Dxterity Solutions
153 Farm Knoll Way (28117-0010)
PHONE.................704 968-2879
Darrel Woodruff, CEO
EMP: 10 **EST:** 2018
SALES (est): 403.01K **Privately Held**
Web: www.dxteritysolutions.com
SIC: 7371 7372 Computer software systems analysis and design, custom; Prepackaged software

(G-10845)
ACCELRTED SVCS MOORESVILLE INC
107 Rinehardt Rd (28115-7979)
PHONE.................704 658-6666
EMP: 7 **EST:** 2012
SALES (est): 61.91K **Privately Held**
Web: www.towingmooresvillenc.com
SIC: 7549 4789 3715 Towing services; Transportation services, nec; Truck trailers

(G-10846)
ACCESS MANUFACTURING TECH LLC
163 Cooley Rd (28117-9253)
PHONE.................224 610-0171
Tom Rissmanno, Prin
▲ **EMP:** 6 **EST:** 2009
SALES (est): 289.7K **Privately Held**
SIC: 3999 Manufacturing industries, nec

(G-10847)
ACCESS TECHNOLOGIES LLC
163 Cooley Rd (28117-9253)
PHONE.................574 286-1255
Stefan Savastano, Managing Member
EMP: 5 **EST:** 2005
SALES (est): 786.58K **Privately Held**
SIC: 2819 5169 Industrial inorganic chemicals, nec; Industrial chemicals

(G-10848)
ADDENDUM LLC
119 Sunhaven Ln (28117-5947)
PHONE.................704 664-9898
EMP: 4 **EST:** 2017
SALES (est): 39.69K **Privately Held**
SIC: 3999 Manufacturing industries, nec

(G-10849)
ADITI 108 INC
132 Joe Knox Ave Ste 111 (28117-9203)
PHONE.................704 763-3741
Divyesh Bhingradia, Pr
EMP: 5 **EST:** 2017
SALES (est): 300K **Privately Held**
SIC: 3993 Signs and advertising specialties

(G-10850)
ADVANCED DETECTION TECH LLC
215 Overhill Dr 1 (28117-7036)
PHONE.................704 663-1949
Jan Zickerman, Managing Member
EMP: 20 **EST:** 2006
SQ FT: 4,000
SALES (est): 4.83MM **Privately Held**
Web: www.advanced-detection-technology.com
SIC: 7382 3812 Security systems services; Search and detection systems and instruments

(G-10851)
AIDLEYCO LLC
532 Patterson Ave # 220 (28115-2139)
PHONE.................704 782-0648
Abraham L Kraus, Managing Member
EMP: 7 **EST:** 2007
SALES (est): 222.94K **Privately Held**
Web: www.ivyleaguetots.com
SIC: 5641 5999 2511 Children's and infants' wear stores; Baby carriages and strollers; Children's wood furniture

(G-10852)
ALCON COMPONENTS USA INC
Also Called: Alcon Components
121 Oakpark Dr (28115-7811)
PHONE.................704 799-2723
EMP: 6 **EST:** 2018
SALES (est): 239.46K **Privately Held**
Web: www.alcon.co.uk
SIC: 3625 Electromagnetic clutches or brakes

(G-10853)
ALEXANDERS HAM COMPANY INC
5920 Highway 152 W (28115-7330)
P.O. Box 57 (28088-0057)
PHONE.................704 857-9222
Carl W Alexander Junior, Pr
Kathy Teague, Sec
Ricky Lipe, VP
Harry K Smith, VP
EMP: 10 **EST:** 1952
SQ FT: 6,300
SALES (est): 973.24K **Privately Held**
Web: www.alexanderham.com
SIC: 5147 2013 2011 Meats, cured or smoked; Sausages and other prepared meats; Meat packing plants

(G-10854)
ALTERNATIVE HEALTH DIST LLC
106 N Commercial Dr Ste A (28115-7801)
PHONE.................336 465-6618
Lee Vantine Iii, CEO
Yasser Abdelhalim, CFO
Nicholas Groat, COO
EMP: 9 **EST:** 2016
SALES (est): 226.63K **Privately Held**
SIC: 2833 Drugs and herbs: grading, grinding, and milling

(G-10855)
AMERICAN ACRYLIC ADHESIVES
111 Montrose Dr (28115-3459)
PHONE.................520 954-1700
EMP: 5 **EST:** 2018
SALES (est): 123.28K **Privately Held**
Web: www.aaaglue.com
SIC: 2891 Adhesives

(G-10856)
AMERICAN DURAFILM CO INC
117 Infield Ct (28117-8026)
PHONE.................704 895-7701
Jeff Allegrti, Pr
EMP: 5 **EST:** 2017
SALES (est): 237.88K **Privately Held**
Web: www.americandurafilm.com
SIC: 2821 Plastics materials and resins

(G-10857)
AMERITECH DIE & MOLD INC
107 Knob Hill Rd (28117-6847)
PHONE.................704 664-0801
Steven Rotman, Prin
Mark Rotman, Prin
EMP: 20 **EST:** 1985
SALES (est): 3.07MM **Privately Held**
Web: www.amdiemold.com

GEOGRAPHIC SECTION

Mooresville - Iredell County (G-10882)

SIC: 3544 Industrial molds

(G-10858)
AMERITECH DIE & MOLD SOUTH INC (PA)
107 Knob Hill Rd (28117-6847)
PHONE.................................704 664-0801
Steven J Rotman, *Pr*
Wayne E Rotman, *VP*
EMP: 10 **EST:** 1985
SQ FT: 26,000
SALES (est): 4.09MM
SALES (corp-wide): 4.09MM **Privately Held**
Web: www.amdiemold.com
SIC: 3544 Industrial molds

(G-10859)
AMIAD FILTRATION SYSTEMS LTD (PA)
Also Called: Amiad Water Systems
120 Talbert Rd Ste J (28117-7119)
PHONE.................................805 377-0288
Michael Poth, *Pr*
Matthew Miles, *
◆ **EMP:** 24 **EST:** 2012
SALES (est): 4.85MM
SALES (corp-wide): 4.85MM **Privately Held**
Web: www.amiad.com
SIC: 3677 3589 Filtration devices, electronic; Water treatment equipment, industrial

(G-10860)
AMIAD USA INC (DH)
120 Talbert Rd Ste J (28117-7119)
PHONE.................................704 662-3133
Tom Akehurst, *Pr*
▲ **EMP:** 17 **EST:** 2011
SALES (est): 9.18MM **Privately Held**
Web: us.amiad.com
SIC: 3589 Water treatment equipment, industrial
HQ: Amiad Filtration Solutions (2004) Ltd
    Kibbutz
    Amiad 12335

(G-10861)
ANTHONY FABRICATION
254 Rolling Hill Rd (28117-6937)
PHONE.................................704 658-1519
EMP: 7 **EST:** 2012
SALES (est): 223.58K **Privately Held**
SIC: 3441 Fabricated structural metal

(G-10862)
ARGOS USA LLC
Also Called: Redi-Mix Concrete
Hwy 150 E (28115)
PHONE.................................704 872-9566
John Wood, *Brnch Mgr*
EMP: 5
Web: www.argos-us.com
SIC: 3273 Ready-mixed concrete
HQ: Argos Usa Llc
    3015 Windward Plz Ste 300
    Alpharetta GA 30005
    678 368-4300

(G-10863)
ATLANTIC WOODWORKING
154 Kiskadee Dr (28117-5214)
PHONE.................................704 680-8802
EMP: 4 **EST:** 2019
SALES (est): 54.13K **Privately Held**
Web: www.atlanticwoodworkschool.com
SIC: 2431 Millwork

(G-10864)
ATTIC TENT INC
Also Called: Insulsure
164 Mill Pond Ln (28115-7777)
PHONE.................................704 892-5399
▲ **EMP:** 5 **EST:** 1996
SQ FT: 1,200
SALES (est): 504.79K **Privately Held**
Web: www.attictent.com
SIC: 2493 1711 1742 Insulation and roofing material, reconstituted wood; Plumbing, heating, air-conditioning; Insulation, buildings

(G-10865)
AUTOMAIL LLC
2987 Charlotte Hwy (28117-8052)
PHONE.................................704 677-0152
Kent Hovey, *Prin*
EMP: 10 **EST:** 2012
SALES (est): 413.24K **Privately Held**
Web: www.automail1.com
SIC: 2711 Commercial printing and newspaper publishing combined

(G-10866)
AVANT PUBLICATIONS LLC
116 Morlake Dr Ste 203 (28117-9211)
PHONE.................................704 897-6048
Scott Champion, *CEO*
Corey Champion, *CFO*
EMP: 7 **EST:** 2019
SALES (est): 238.11K **Privately Held**
SIC: 2759 Publication printing

(G-10867)
AVINTIV SPECIALTY MTLS INC
111 Excellance Ln (28115-9305)
PHONE.................................704 660-6242
Fernando Apolinario, *Bd of Dir*
EMP: 93
Web: www.berryglobal.com
SIC: 2297 Nonwoven fabrics
HQ: Avintiv Specialty Materials Inc.
    9335 Hrris Crners Pkwy St
    Charlotte NC 28269

(G-10868)
AVP VACCINES LLC
112 Lightship Dr (28117-7109)
PHONE.................................704 799-0161
Paul J Wilson, *Owner*
EMP: 5 **EST:** 2018
SALES (est): 74.42K **Privately Held**
SIC: 2836 Vaccines

(G-10869)
B & B FABRICATION INC
Also Called: Billy Boat Performance Exhaust
125 Infield Ct (28117-8026)
PHONE.................................623 581-7600
William Boat, *Pr*
Andrea Boat, *VP*
▲ **EMP:** 10 **EST:** 1986
SALES (est): 2.42MM **Privately Held**
Web: www.bbexhaust.com
SIC: 3714 Exhaust systems and parts, motor vehicle

(G-10870)
BAY STATE MILLING COMPANY
448 N Main St (28115-2456)
P.O. Box 358 (28115-0358)
PHONE.................................704 664-4873
Leslie A Lovett, *Mgr*
EMP: 30
SALES (corp-wide): 131.82MM **Privately Held**
Web: www.baystatemilling.com

SIC: 2041 2048 Flour: blended, prepared, or self-rising; Prepared feeds, nec
PA: Bay State Milling Company
    100 Congress St Ste 2
    Quincy MA 02169
    617 328-4400

(G-10871)
BELK CONSTRUCTION INC
358 Montibello Dr (28117-8222)
PHONE.................................704 507-6327
Nick Belk, *Prin*
EMP: 5 **EST:** 2010
SALES (est): 107.73K **Privately Held**
Web: www.belkhomes.com
SIC: 3993 Signs and advertising specialties

(G-10872)
BEN HUFFMAN ENTERPRISES LLC
516 River Hwy Ste D (28117-6830)
PHONE.................................704 724-4705
EMP: 6 **EST:** 2018
SALES (est): 609.78K **Privately Held**
SIC: 3714 Motor vehicle parts and accessories

(G-10873)
BERRY GLOBAL INC
Also Called: Berry Plastics
111 Excellance Ln (28115-9305)
PHONE.................................704 664-3733
Steve Ford, *Prin*
EMP: 101
Web: www.berryglobal.com
SIC: 3089 Plastics containers, except foam
HQ: Berry Global, Inc.
    101 Oakley St
    Evansville IN 47710

(G-10874)
BESTCO HOLDINGS INC
288 Mazeppa Rd (28117-7928)
P.O. Box 329 (28115-0329)
PHONE.................................704 664-4300
Richard Zulman, *CEO*
Tim Condron, *Pr*
Mark Knight, *Ex VP*
Steve Berkowitz, *Ex VP*
Scott Wattenberg, *CFO*
◆ **EMP:** 424 **EST:** 1990
SQ FT: 140,000
SALES (est): 88.68MM **Privately Held**
Web: www.bestco.com
SIC: 2064 Candy and other confectionery products

(G-10875)
BESTCO LLC
Also Called: Accounting Office
137 Bestco Ln (28115)
PHONE.................................704 664-4300
Richard Zulman, *Brnch Mgr*
EMP: 40
SALES (corp-wide): 299.17MM **Privately Held**
Web: www.bestco.com
SIC: 2023 Dietary supplements, dairy and non-dairy based
PA: Bestco Llc
    288 Mazeppa Rd
    Mooresville NC 28115
    704 664-4300

(G-10876)
BESTCO LLC
119 E Super Sport Dr (28117-6311)
PHONE.................................704 664-4300
EMP: 34
SALES (corp-wide): 299.17MM **Privately Held**
Web: www.bestco.com

SIC: 2834 Pharmaceutical preparations
PA: Bestco Llc
    288 Mazeppa Rd
    Mooresville NC 28115
    704 664-4300

(G-10877)
BESTCO LLC
139 Cam Ct (28115)
P.O. Box 329 (28115-0329)
PHONE.................................704 664-4300
Tim Condron, *Brnch Mgr*
EMP: 150
SALES (corp-wide): 299.17MM **Privately Held**
Web: www.bestco.com
SIC: 2834 Pharmaceutical preparations
PA: Bestco Llc
    288 Mazeppa Rd
    Mooresville NC 28115
    704 664-4300

(G-10878)
BESTCO LLC
208 Manufacturers Blvd (28115-6001)
PHONE.................................704 664-4300
Tim Condron, *CEO*
EMP: 250
SALES (corp-wide): 299.17MM **Privately Held**
Web: www.bestco.com
SIC: 2834 Pharmaceutical preparations
PA: Bestco Llc
    288 Mazeppa Rd
    Mooresville NC 28115
    704 664-4300

(G-10879)
BESTCO LLC (PA)
288 Mazeppa Rd (28115-7928)
P.O. Box 329 (28115-0329)
PHONE.................................704 664-4300
Tim Condron, *Pr*
John Dahldorf, *
Mark Knight, *
Andrew B Hochman, *
Amy Rockwell, *
◆ **EMP:** 133 **EST:** 2013
SQ FT: 334,000
SALES (est): 299.17MM
SALES (corp-wide): 299.17MM **Privately Held**
Web: www.bestco.com
SIC: 2834 Lozenges, pharmaceutical

(G-10880)
BIFFLE STEEL SERVICES LLC
140 Pintail Run Ln (28117-8120)
PHONE.................................704 626-0909
EMP: 5 **EST:** 2017
SALES (est): 122.3K **Privately Held**
SIC: 3441 Fabricated structural metal

(G-10881)
BIZ TECHNOLOGY SOLUTIONS LLC
353 Oates Rd (28117-6824)
PHONE.................................704 658-1707
Mahmoud Chouffani, *Pr*
Reda Chouffani, *OK Vice President*
EMP: 40 **EST:** 2001
SQ FT: 8,000
SALES (est): 5.41MM **Privately Held**
Web: www.biztechnologysolutions.com
SIC: 7378 7372 Computer maintenance and repair; Prepackaged software

(G-10882)
BLACK & DECKER CORPORATION
Also Called: Black & Decker
134 Talbert Pointe Dr (28117-4377)
PHONE.................................704 799-3929

Mooresville - Iredell County (G-10883)

EMP: 5
SALES (corp-wide): 15.78B **Publicly Held**
Web: www.blackanddecker.com
SIC: 3546 Power-driven handtools
HQ: The Black & Decker Corporation
    701 E Joppa Rd
    Towson MD 21286
    410 716-3900

(G-10883)
BOARDS AND BOWLS LLC
141 Brookleaf Ln (28115-6788)
PHONE..................................704 293-2004
David Paventi, *Prin*
EMP: 5 EST: 2019
SALES (est): 95.41K **Privately Held**
Web: www.spencerpeterman.com
SIC: 2499 Wood products, nec

(G-10884)
BODYCOTE THERMAL PROC INC
Also Called: Bodycote Thermal Processing
128 Speedway Ln (28117-6879)
PHONE..................................704 664-1808
EMP: 11
SALES (corp-wide): 895.27MM **Privately Held**
Web: www.bodycote.com
SIC: 3398 Metal heat treating
HQ: Bodycote Thermal Processing, Inc.
    12750 Merit Dr Ste 1400
    Dallas TX 75251
    214 904-2420

(G-10885)
BRANDSPEED
915 River Hwy (28117-9245)
PHONE..................................410 204-1032
EMP: 6 EST: 2018
SALES (est): 131.66K **Privately Held**
Web: www.brandspeed.us
SIC: 2299 Textile goods, nec

(G-10886)
BRANFORD FILTRATION LLC (PA)
Also Called: Fibrix Filtration
119 Poplar Pointe Dr Ste C (28117-9427)
PHONE..................................704 394-2111
Keith White, *CEO*
Michael Rush, *CFO*
Jr Baccus, *Pr*
EMP: 51 EST: 2020
SALES (est): 71.9MM
SALES (corp-wide): 71.9MM **Privately Held**
SIC: 3677 Filtration devices, electronic

(G-10887)
BRAVO TEAM LLC
603 N Church St (28115-2303)
PHONE..................................704 309-1918
EMP: 24 EST: 2018
SALES (est): 5.93MM **Privately Held**
Web: www.bravoteam.tech
SIC: 3451 7371 Screw machine products; Computer software development and applications

(G-10888)
BRIGHT FABRICATION LLC
133 Waderich Ln (28117-5409)
PHONE..................................704 660-3151
EMP: 5 EST: 2018
SALES (est): 43.73K **Privately Held**
SIC: 7692 Welding repair

(G-10889)
BRUMLEY/SOUTH INC
Also Called: Brumley-South
422 N Broad St (28115-3040)
P.O. Box 1237 (28115-1237)
PHONE..................................704 664-9251
Thomas Norment, *Pr*
Cindy Norment, *Treas*
▲ EMP: 7 EST: 1992
SQ FT: 25,000
SALES (est): 1.05MM **Privately Held**
Web: www.brumleysouth.com
SIC: 3674 Wafers (semiconductor devices)

(G-10890)
BSCI INC (PA)
170 Barley Park Ln (28115-7912)
P.O. Box 1203 (28115-1203)
PHONE..................................704 664-3005
Karen B Ray, *Pr*
Luke Ray, *VP*
▲ EMP: 7 EST: 1990
SQ FT: 6,000
SALES (est): 856.35K
SALES (corp-wide): 856.35K **Privately Held**
Web: www.rollbarpadding.com
SIC: 3069 Foam rubber

(G-10891)
BUCHER MUNICIPAL N AMER INC
Also Called: Jna
105 Motorsports Rd (28115-8258)
P.O. Box 388 (28115-0388)
PHONE..................................704 658-1333
Todd Parsons, *Pr*
Todd W Parsons, *
Bob Ohara, *
Colin Madden, *
◆ EMP: 33 EST: 2011
SQ FT: 12,000
SALES (est): 10.21MM **Privately Held**
Web: www.buchermunicipal.com
SIC: 3711 Motor vehicles and car bodies
HQ: Bucher Municipal Limited
    Gate 3
    Dorking RH4 1
    130 688-4722

(G-10892)
BUDDY BOOK PUBLISHING
104 Nathaniel Ct (28115-6712)
PHONE..................................704 657-6909
David Harrison, *Prin*
EMP: 4 EST: 2016
SALES (est): 67.27K **Privately Held**
SIC: 2741 Miscellaneous publishing

(G-10893)
C&K PLASTICS NC LLC
Also Called: C&K Plastics North Carolina
164 Mckenzie Rd (28115-9302)
PHONE..................................833 232-4848
EMP: 11 EST: 2021
SALES (est): 774.02K **Privately Held**
SIC: 3089 Plastics containers, except foam

(G-10894)
CAIRN STUDIO LTD
200 Mckenzie Rd (28115-7975)
P.O. Box 400 (28036-0400)
PHONE..................................704 664-7128
Clarence Atwell, *Mgr*
EMP: 28
SALES (corp-wide): 1.75MM **Privately Held**
Web: www.cairnstudio.com
SIC: 3269 3544 4226 Figures: pottery, china, earthenware, and stoneware; Special dies, tools, jigs, and fixtures; Special warehousing and storage, nec
PA: Cairn Studio, Ltd.
    121 N Main St
    Davidson NC 28036
    704 892-3581

(G-10895)
CARDINAL GLASS INDUSTRIES INC
Also Called: Cardinal Fg
342 Mooresville Blvd (28115-7909)
PHONE..................................704 660-0900
Jim Stevens, *Manager*
EMP: 250
SALES (corp-wide): 1B **Privately Held**
Web: www.cardinalcorp.com
SIC: 3211 Float glass
PA: Cardinal Glass Industries Inc
    775 Pririe Ctr Dr Ste 200
    Eden Prairie MN 55344
    952 229-2600

(G-10896)
CAROLINA BEVERAGE GROUP LLC (HQ)
Also Called: Carolina Beer Company
110 Barley Park Ln (28115-7912)
P.O. Box 1183 (28115-1183)
PHONE..................................704 799-2337
Brian Demos, *CEO*
Brian Demos, *Pr*
J Michael Smith, *Managing Member**
John Stritch, *
Eric Pearce, *
▲ EMP: 40 EST: 1997
SQ FT: 30,000
SALES (est): 105.25MM
SALES (corp-wide): 167.48MM **Privately Held**
Web: www.carolinabeveragegroup.com
SIC: 2082 Beer (alcoholic beverage)
PA: Cold Spring Brewing Company
    219 Red River Ave N
    Cold Spring MN 56320
    320 685-8686

(G-10897)
CAROLINA BUILDING SERVICES INC (PA)
Also Called: CBS Windows & Doors
207 Timber Rd (28115-7868)
P.O. Box 414 (28123-0414)
PHONE..................................704 664-7110
John S Alden, *Pr*
Garry Dunne, *VP*
EMP: 15 EST: 1992
SQ FT: 5,000
SALES (est): 6.09MM **Privately Held**
Web: www.carolinabuildingservices.com
SIC: 2431 Windows and window parts and trim, wood

(G-10898)
CAROLINA PRECISION TECH LLC
1055 Gateway Dr Ste A (28115-8342)
PHONE..................................215 675-4590
Kevin Burke, *Managing Member*
EMP: 47 EST: 1998
SALES (est): 5.65MM **Privately Held**
Web: www.carolinaprecision.com
SIC: 3841 3724 Surgical and medical instruments; Aircraft engines and engine parts

(G-10899)
CASETEC PRECISION MACHINE LLC
Also Called: Casetec
178 Attleboro Pl (28117-7106)
PHONE..................................704 663-6043
Jon R Carlson, *Managing Member*
▲ EMP: 8 EST: 2006
SQ FT: 2,500
SALES (est): 474.6K **Privately Held**
SIC: 3599 3541 Machine shop, jobbing and repair; Numerically controlled metal cutting machine tools

(G-10900)
CAVOTEC USA INC (DH)
500 S Main St # 1 (28115-3228)
PHONE..................................704 873-3009
◆ EMP: 24 EST: 1990
SALES (est): 20.66MM **Privately Held**
Web: www.cavotec.com
SIC: 5082 3568 Cranes, construction; Pulleys, power transmission
HQ: Cavotec Group Holdings N.V.
    Meent 106 Minervahuis
    Rotterdam ZH 3011
    348460160

(G-10901)
CB INDUSTRIES
125 Infield Ct (28117-8026)
PHONE..................................704 660-1955
EMP: 5 EST: 2017
SALES (est): 222.75K **Privately Held**
SIC: 3999 Manufacturing industries, nec

(G-10902)
CHARMED WRIGHT LLC
108 Saye Pl (28115-5813)
PHONE..................................704 850-8186
EMP: 4 EST: 2020
SALES (est): 139.88K **Privately Held**
SIC: 3911 Jewelry, precious metal

(G-10903)
CJM INDUSTRIES LLC
276 Whippoorwill Rd (28115-5803)
PHONE..................................704 506-5926
EMP: 7 EST: 2020
SALES (est): 234.07K **Privately Held**
SIC: 3999 Manufacturing industries, nec

(G-10904)
CKS PACKAGING
289 Rolling Hill Rd (28117-6845)
PHONE..................................704 663-6510
Marshall Henderson, *Pr*
EMP: 23 EST: 1983
SQ FT: 40,000
SALES (est): 1.35MM **Privately Held**
Web: www.ckspackaging.com
SIC: 3089 Plastics containers, except foam

(G-10905)
CKS PACKAGING INC
289 Rolling Hill Rd (28117-6845)
PHONE..................................704 663-6510
Marshall Henderson, *Prin*
EMP: 50
SALES (corp-wide): 483.16MM **Privately Held**
Web: www.ckspackaging.com
SIC: 3089 2656 Plastics containers, except foam; Sanitary food containers
PA: C.K.S. Packaging, Inc.
    350 Great Sw Pkwy
    Atlanta GA 30336
    404 691-8900

(G-10906)
CLARIANT CORPORATION
337 Timber Rd (28115-7855)
PHONE..................................704 235-5700
Raymond Sloan, *Brnch Mgr*
EMP: 23
Web: www.clariant.com
SIC: 2869 Industrial organic chemicals, nec
HQ: Clariant Corporation
    500 E Morehead St Ste 400
    Charlotte NC 28202
    704 331-7000

GEOGRAPHIC SECTION
Mooresville - Iredell County (G-10934)

(G-10907)
CLEOS ALPACAS LLC
585 Isle Of Pines Rd (28117-7479)
PHONE.................704 663-9785
Cleoi Ellen Kuhl, *Prin*
EMP: 5 **EST:** 2016
SALES (est): 111.5K **Privately Held**
SIC: 2231 Alpacas, mohair: woven

(G-10908)
COCONUT PARADISE INC
803 Performance Rd (28115-9597)
PHONE.................704 662-3443
George Brunnhoelzl, *Pr*
Robin Hansen, *Sec*
EMP: 8 **EST:** 1993
SQ FT: 18,000
SALES (est): 834.87K **Privately Held**
Web: www.brunnhoelzl.com
SIC: 3423 3714 Jacks: lifting, screw, or ratchet (hand tools); Motor vehicle parts and accessories

(G-10909)
COMMONWEALTH GRAPHICS INC
191 Knoxview Ln (28117-7554)
PHONE.................704 997-8501
Kim Shaffer, *Prin*
EMP: 9 **EST:** 2015
SALES (est): 472.05K **Privately Held**
SIC: 2759 Screen printing

(G-10910)
COMPOSITE FACTORY LLC
255 Raceway Dr (28117-6510)
PHONE.................484 264-3306
EMP: 10 **EST:** 2019
SALES (est): 620.51K **Privately Held**
Web: www.fibreworkscomposites.com
SIC: 3449 Bars, concrete reinforcing: fabricated steel

(G-10911)
COOK GROUP INC
Also Called: Logo Shop, The
147 Forest Glen Rd (28115-9702)
PHONE.................336 605-5557
Celia B Cook, *Pr*
David Cook, *Sec*
EMP: 4 **EST:** 1990
SALES (est): 328.19K **Privately Held**
Web: www.yourlogoshop.com
SIC: 2395 3993 Embroidery and art needlework; Signs and advertising specialties

(G-10912)
COPPER LINE CUSTOM
213 English Hills Dr (28115-5783)
PHONE.................704 956-0734
Fred Nydegger, *Prin*
EMP: 4 **EST:** 2019
SALES (est): 94.54K **Privately Held**
SIC: 3444 Sheet metalwork

(G-10913)
CORAMDEO LIGHTING INDUSTRIES
116 Gasoline Aly Ste 119 (28117-6507)
PHONE.................704 906-8864
EMP: 4 **EST:** 2019
SALES (est): 80.76K **Privately Held**
SIC: 3999 Manufacturing industries, nec

(G-10914)
COREGRP LLC
Also Called: Coregroup Displays
631 Brawley School Rd (28117-6204)
P.O. Box 210 (12534-0210)
PHONE.................845 876-5109
Daniel Riso, *Pr*
◆ **EMP:** 15 **EST:** 2003
SALES (est): 2.35MM **Privately Held**
Web: www.coregroupdisplays.com
SIC: 2542 Partitions and fixtures, except wood

(G-10915)
COUNTER ART
132 Joe Knox Ave Ste 106 (28117-9203)
PHONE.................704 658-0312
Steve Farmer, *Pr*
EMP: 6 **EST:** 2004
SALES (est): 185.92K **Privately Held**
SIC: 3211 Plate and sheet glass

(G-10916)
CP COMPONENTS LLC
151 Gray Cliff Dr (28117-8517)
PHONE.................330 715-1837
Christopher Petit, *Prin*
EMP: 5 **EST:** 2015
SALES (est): 63.79K **Privately Held**
SIC: 3441 Fabricated structural metal

(G-10917)
CRC
Also Called: CRC Powder Coating
2425 Statesville Hwy (28115-7968)
PHONE.................704 664-1242
Paul Daigrepont, *Prin*
EMP: 7 **EST:** 2015
SALES (est): 414.67K **Privately Held**
Web: www.crcpowdercoating.com
SIC: 3479 Coating of metals and formed products

(G-10918)
CRP USA LLC
127 Goodwin Cir (28115-7971)
P.O. Box 728 (28115-0728)
PHONE.................704 660-0258
Stewart Davis, *Dir Opers*
EMP: 8 **EST:** 2009
SALES (est): 951.77K **Privately Held**
Web: www.crp-usa.net
SIC: 3087 Custom compound purchased resins

(G-10919)
CURTIS L MACLEAN L C
227 Manufacturers Blvd (28115-6001)
PHONE.................704 940-5531
Paul R Hojnacki, *Pr*
EMP: 110
SQ FT: 55,000
SALES (corp-wide): 1.15B **Privately Held**
SIC: 3451 3714 Screw machine products; Motor vehicle parts and accessories
HQ: Curtis L Maclean L C
50 Thielman Dr
Buffalo NY 14206
716 898-7800

(G-10920)
CUSTOM PRODUCTS INC
1618 Landis Hwy (28115-6906)
P.O. Box 1141 (28115-1141)
PHONE.................704 663-4159
▲ **EMP:** 99
SIC: 2531 Seats, aircraft

(G-10921)
CUTTING EDGE STONEWORKS INC
Also Called: Cutting Edge Stoneworks
161 Mckenzie Rd (28115-7976)
P.O. Box 4931 (28117-4931)
PHONE.................704 799-1227
Michael Giordano, *Pr*
EMP: 5 **EST:** 2008
SALES (est): 899.08K **Privately Held**
Web: www.cuttingedgestoneworks.com
SIC: 2541 Counter and sink tops

(G-10922)
CYCLE PRO LLC
261 Rolling Hill Rd Ste 1a (28117-6505)
PHONE.................704 662-6682
▲ **EMP:** 10 **EST:** 2000
SALES (est): 455.09K **Privately Held**
Web: www.cycleprollc.com
SIC: 8748 3714 Business consulting, nec; Motor vehicle parts and accessories

(G-10923)
DANBARTEX LLC
120 Commercial Dr Ste A (28115-8039)
P.O. Box 681748 (28216-0033)
PHONE.................704 323-8728
Danny L Barrett, *Managing Member*
▲ **EMP:** 6 **EST:** 2007
SALES (est): 542.29K **Privately Held**
Web: www.danbartex.com
SIC: 5999 2426 Business machines and equipment; Hardwood dimension and flooring mills

(G-10924)
DAP PRODUCTS INC
125 Infield Ct (28117-8026)
PHONE.................704 799-9640
Michael Morris, *Prin*
EMP: 16
SALES (corp-wide): 7.26B **Publicly Held**
Web: www.dap.com
SIC: 2891 Caulking compounds
HQ: Dap Products Inc.
2400 Boston St Ste 200
Baltimore MD 21224
800 543-3840

(G-10925)
DARYL DUFF LOCKYER
Also Called: Dkd Apparel
170 Gabriel Dr (28115-9400)
PHONE.................704 658-0695
Daryl D Lockyer, *Owner*
EMP: 5 **EST:** 2010
SALES (est): 12.79K **Privately Held**
SIC: 2759 Screen printing

(G-10926)
DCE INC
138 Cayuga Dr Ste C (28117-8260)
PHONE.................704 230-4649
David Cunliffe, *Pr*
Sandra Cunliffe, *VP*
◆ **EMP:** 8 **EST:** 2012
SQ FT: 2,500
SALES (est): 2.3MM
SALES (corp-wide): 1.2MM **Privately Held**
Web: us.dcemotorsport.com
SIC: 3714 Automotive wiring harness sets
PA: D.C. Electronics Motorsport Specialist Limited
Unit 1
Maldon CM9 5

(G-10927)
DEBOTECH INC
130 Infield Ct (28117-8026)
PHONE.................704 664-1361
Hans Debot, *CEO*
Hans Debot, *Pr*
Jamye Debot, *
▼ **EMP:** 150 **EST:** 1998
SQ FT: 25,000
SALES (est): 24.84MM **Privately Held**
Web: www.debotech.com
SIC: 3089 3624 Automotive parts, plastic; Carbon and graphite products

(G-10928)
DEJ HOLDINGS LLC (PA)
349 Cayuga Dr (28117-8216)
P.O. Box 330 (28115-0330)
PHONE.................704 799-4800
Dale Earnhardt Junior, *Managing Member*
EMP: 25 **EST:** 1999
SALES (est): 4.43MM **Privately Held**
Web: www.thedalejrfoundation.org
SIC: 3711 Motor vehicles and car bodies

(G-10929)
DETMER METALS LLC
168 Beracah Rd (28115-9737)
P.O. Box 113 (28036-0113)
PHONE.................704 997-6114
Damon Detmer, *Prin*
EMP: 5 **EST:** 2019
SALES (est): 89.18K **Privately Held**
SIC: 3441 Fabricated structural metal

(G-10930)
DEUCES CUSTOM
240 Commodore Loop (28117-7416)
PHONE.................704 658-1777
Yoshikazu Imagawa, *Prin*
EMP: 6 **EST:** 2004
SALES (est): 111.63K **Privately Held**
SIC: 3714 Propane conversion equipment, motor vehicle

(G-10931)
DYNAMIC MOUNTING
120b Pitt Rd (28115-6782)
PHONE.................704 978-8723
EMP: 4 **EST:** 2019
SALES (est): 39.69K **Privately Held**
Web: www.mantelmount.com
SIC: 3999 Manufacturing industries, nec

(G-10932)
E G A PRODUCTS INC
Also Called: Ega Southeast
208 Mckenzie Rd (28115-7975)
PHONE.................704 664-1221
Gary Green, *Prin*
EMP: 10
SALES (corp-wide): 6.57MM **Privately Held**
Web: www.egaproducts.com
SIC: 3542 2542 Machine tools, metal forming type; Partitions and fixtures, except wood
PA: E G A Products, Inc.
4275 N 127th St
Brookfield WI 53005
262 781-7899

(G-10933)
E-LIQUID BRANDS LLC
120 Commercial Dr (28115-8036)
PHONE.................828 385-5090
EMP: 30 **EST:** 2014
SALES (est): 1.14MM **Privately Held**
Web: www.eliquidbrands.com
SIC: 3999 Cigarette and cigar products and accessories

(G-10934)
EARTH-KIND INC
Also Called: Crane Creek Garden
346 E Plaza Dr Ste D (28115-8050)
PHONE.................701 751-4456
EMP: 5 **EST:** 1993
SALES (est): 2.11MM **Privately Held**
Web: www.earthkind.com
SIC: 3999 Artificial trees and flowers

Mooresville - Iredell County (G-10935)

(G-10935)
EAST BAY WOODWORKS
249 Woodstream Cir (28117-7469)
PHONE..................................503 313-4079
Michael Puncochar, *Prin*
EMP: 4 **EST:** 2019
SALES (est): 54.13K **Privately Held**
SIC: 2431 Millwork

(G-10936)
EAST WEST MANUFACTURING LLC
Also Called: East West Design Mfg Dist
1133 N Main St (28115-2359)
PHONE..................................704 663-5975
EMP: 9
SALES (corp-wide): 490.36MM **Privately Held**
Web: www.ewmfg.com
SIC: 3549 3841 3594 5065 Assembly machines, including robotic; Surgical and medical instruments; Motors: hydraulic, fluid power, or air; Electronic parts
PA: East West Manufacturing, Llc
  4170 Ashford Dnwody Rd St
  Brookhaven GA 30319
  404 252-9441

(G-10937)
ECLIPSE COMPOSITE ENGINEERING
Also Called: Eclipse Composites Engineering
138 Cedar Pointe Dr (28117-6880)
PHONE..................................801 601-8559
Obie Johnson, *CEO*
EMP: 20 **EST:** 2018
SALES (est): 1.91MM **Privately Held**
Web: www.eclipsecomposites.com
SIC: 3679 Antennas, receiving

(G-10938)
EL VALLE OF LAKE NORMAN INC
835 Williamson Rd (28117-8505)
PHONE..................................704 658-0212
Jose Ayala, *Owner*
EMP: 6 **EST:** 2010
SALES (est): 195.34K **Privately Held**
SIC: 2711 Newspapers

(G-10939)
ENGAGE2EXCEL INC (PA)
115 Corporate Center Dr Ste E (28117-0080)
P.O. Box 1719 (28687-1719)
PHONE..................................704 872-5231
EMP: 75 **EST:** 2010
SALES (est): 58.32MM **Privately Held**
Web: www.engage2excel.com
SIC: 3911 Pins (jewelry), precious metal

(G-10940)
EXECUTIVE PROMOTIONS INC
Also Called: Mailing Solutions Plus
2987 Charlotte Hwy 21 (28117-8052)
PHONE..................................704 663-4000
Kent Hovey, *Pr*
Kirsten Hovey, *VP*
EMP: 12 **EST:** 1990
SQ FT: 4,000
SALES (est): 458.33K **Privately Held**
SIC: 2754 7311 Commercial printing, gravure; Advertising agencies

(G-10941)
FABRINEERING LLC
1035 Mecklenburg Hwy (28115-7853)
PHONE..................................704 999-9906
EMP: 7 **EST:** 2015
SALES (est): 483.36K **Privately Held**
Web: www.fabrineering.co
SIC: 3441 Fabricated structural metal

(G-10942)
FABRINEERING LLC
8955 W Nc 152 Hwy (28115-4240)
PHONE..................................704 661-4877
Becky Stutts, *Prin*
EMP: 7 **EST:** 2015
SALES (est): 374.42K **Privately Held**
SIC: 3441 Fabricated structural metal

(G-10943)
FASTSIGNS
Also Called: Fastsigns
119 Midnight Ln (28117-8803)
PHONE..................................704 360-3805
EMP: 7 **EST:** 2017
SALES (est): 46.08K **Privately Held**
Web: www.fastsigns.com
SIC: 3993 Signs and advertising specialties

(G-10944)
FIBREWORKS COMPOSITES LLC
143 Thunder Rd (28115-6000)
PHONE..................................704 696-1084
Gunther Steiner, *CEO*
Joseph G Hofmann, *
EMP: 36 **EST:** 2008
SALES (est): 5.29MM **Privately Held**
Web: www.fibreworkscomposites.com
SIC: 3089 7948 Composition stone, plastics; Stock car racing

(G-10945)
FIRERESQ INCORPORATED
Also Called: Fire Hose Direct
115 Corporate Center Dr Ste J (28117-0080)
P.O. Box 3455 (28117-3455)
PHONE..................................888 975-0858
▼ **EMP:** 10 **EST:** 2011
SQ FT: 12,000
SALES (est): 1.22MM **Privately Held**
Web: www.fireresq.com
SIC: 3429 3569 5999 5087 Nozzles, fire fighting; Firefighting and related equipment; Alarm and safety equipment stores; Firefighting equipment

(G-10946)
FITT USA INC
136 Corporate Park Dr Ste I (28117-6960)
PHONE..................................866 348-8872
Federico Cuman, *Pr*
Andrea Budano, *Sec*
EMP: 15 **EST:** 2018
SALES (est): 5.98MM
SALES (corp-wide): 317.29MM **Privately Held**
Web: usa.fitt.com
SIC: 3084 Plastics pipe
HQ: Fitt Group Spa
  Viale Del Mercato Nuovo 44/G
  Vicenza VI 36100
  044 457-0505

(G-10947)
FLYNN BURNER CORPORATION
225 Mooresville Blvd (28115-7965)
PHONE..................................704 660-1500
Dom Medina, *Pr*
Edward Flynn, *
Julian Modzeleski, *
◆ **EMP:** 50 **EST:** 1946
SQ FT: 25,000
SALES (est): 9.12MM **Privately Held**
Web: www.flynnburner.com
SIC: 3433 Gas burners, industrial

(G-10948)
FORGED TIMBER COMPANY
802e Performance Rd (28115-9597)
PHONE..................................704 351-7712
EMP: 4 **EST:** 2019
SALES (est): 249.83K **Privately Held**
Web: www.forgedtimbercompany.com
SIC: 2431 Millwork

(G-10949)
FOUR CORNERS FRMNG GALLERY INC
148 N Main St (28115-2526)
PHONE..................................704 662-7154
Kim Saragoni, *Owner*
EMP: 5 **EST:** 2006
SALES (est): 414.98K **Privately Held**
Web: www.fcfgframing.com
SIC: 5999 5023 3499 2499 Picture frames, ready made; Frames and framing, picture and mirror; Picture frames, metal; Picture and mirror frames, wood

(G-10950)
FOX FACTORY INC
169 Gasoline Aly (28117-6515)
PHONE..................................831 421-1791
EMP: 5 **EST:** 2019
SALES (est): 156.91K **Privately Held**
Web: www.ridefox.com
SIC: 3714 Motor vehicle parts and accessories

(G-10951)
FUNNY BONE EMB & SCREENING
829 Plaza Ln (28115-9555)
PHONE..................................704 663-4711
Daniel Dougherty, *Owner*
EMP: 6 **EST:** 2003
SALES (est): 470.6K **Privately Held**
Web: www.funnybonenc.com
SIC: 2395 5699 2759 Embroidery products, except Schiffli machine; Miscellaneous apparel and accessory stores; Screen printing

(G-10952)
G-LOC BRAKES LLC
Also Called: Gee-Lock
503 Performance Rd (28115-9594)
PHONE..................................704 765-0213
James Rogerson, *Managing Member*
EMP: 7 **EST:** 2016
SALES (est): 243.49K **Privately Held**
Web: www.g-locbrakes.com
SIC: 3714 Air brakes, motor vehicle

(G-10953)
GA COMMUNICATIONS INC
136 Fairview Rd Ste 220 (28117-8547)
PHONE..................................704 360-1860
Mike Hynson, *Mgr*
EMP: 31
Web: www.purered.net
SIC: 2796 Color separations, for printing
PA: Ga Communications, Inc.
  2196 W Park Ct
  Stone Mountain GA 30087

(G-10954)
GARRETTCOM INC (HQ)
Also Called: Califrnia Grrett Cmmnctons Inc
1113 N Main St (28115-2359)
PHONE..................................510 438-9071
EMP: 62 **EST:** 1989
SALES (est): 28.47MM
SALES (corp-wide): 2.51B **Publicly Held**
Web: www.belden.com
SIC: 3577 Input/output equipment, computer
PA: Belden Inc.
  1 N Brentwood Blvd Fl 15
  Saint Louis MO 63105
  314 854-8000

(G-10955)
GEAR FX DRIVELINE LLC
185 Mckenzie Rd (28115-7976)
PHONE..................................704 799-9117
Kyle G Tucker, *Prin*
EMP: 8 **EST:** 2018
SALES (est): 369.96K **Privately Held**
Web: www.gearfxdriveline.com
SIC: 3714 Motor vehicle parts and accessories

(G-10956)
GENERAL MCROCIRCUITS - E W LLC
1133 N Main St (28115-2359)
P.O. Box 748 (28115-0748)
PHONE..................................704 663-5975
EMP: 112
SALES (corp-wide): 490.36MM **Privately Held**
Web: www.ewmfg.com
SIC: 3672 Circuit boards, television and radio printed
HQ: General Microcircuits - East West, Llc
  4170 Ashford Dnwody Rd St
  Brookhaven GA 30319
  404 252-9441

(G-10957)
GENERAL MICROCIRCUITS INC
1133 N Main St (28115-2359)
P.O. Box 748 (28115-0748)
PHONE..................................704 663-5975
EMP: 38 **EST:** 1980
SALES (est): 4.75MM **Privately Held**
SIC: 3672 Circuit boards, television and radio printed

(G-10958)
GEOSURFACES SOUTHEAST INC
Also Called: Medallion Athletic Products
150 River Park Rd (28117-8929)
PHONE..................................704 660-3000
Charles Dawson, *CEO*
EMP: 20 **EST:** 2018
SALES (est): 4.83MM
SALES (corp-wide): 9.39MM **Privately Held**
Web: www.geosurfaces.com
SIC: 3949 Sporting and athletic goods, nec
PA: Geosurfaces, Inc.
  7080 Saint Gabriel Ave A
  Saint Gabriel LA 70776
  877 663-5968

(G-10959)
GLACIER FORESTRY INC
135 Jocelyn Ln Apt 108 (28117-5270)
PHONE..................................704 902-2594
Jaime L Hutton, *Pr*
EMP: 7 **EST:** 2015
SALES (est): 374.64K **Privately Held**
SIC: 2411 Logging camps and contractors

(G-10960)
GO GREEN RACING
409 Performance Rd (28115-9593)
PHONE..................................916 295-2621
Tim Barile, *CEO*
EMP: 8 **EST:** 2015
SALES (est): 711.72K **Privately Held**
Web: www.gofasracing.com
SIC: 3711 Automobile assembly, including specialty automobiles

(G-10961)
GOLD STAR
129 Oak Park Dr. (28115-8124)
PHONE..................................704 651-8186
EMP: 5 **EST:** 2016
SALES (est): 77.06K **Privately Held**

SIC: 2023 Dietary supplements, dairy and non-dairy based

(G-10962)
GRACIE & LUCAS LLC
Also Called: Transmission Unlimited
224 Wiredell Ave (28115)
PHONE.................704 707-3207
EMP: 5 EST: 2017
SALES (est): 234.72K Privately Held
SIC: 3714 Wheels, motor vehicle

(G-10963)
GRAY OX INC
155 Quiet Cove Rd (28117-8892)
PHONE.................704 662-8247
Roger M Oxidine, Pr
Troy C Graham, Sec
EMP: 10 EST: 2001
SALES (est): 496.36K Privately Held
Web: www.grayox.com
SIC: 3253 Ceramic wall and floor tile

(G-10964)
GREENBROOK TMS NEUROHEALTH CTR
Also Called: Tms Neurohealth Centers
149 Plantation Ridge Dr Ste 150 (28117-9174)
PHONE.................855 910-4867
EMP: 4
SALES (corp-wide): 29.8MM Privately Held
Web: www.greenbrooktms.com
SIC: 3312 Blast furnaces and steel mills
PA: Tms Neurohealth Centers Tysons Corner, Llc
8405 Greensboro Dr # 120
Mc Lean VA 22102
703 356-1568

(G-10965)
GREENWORKS NORTH AMERICA LLC (PA)
Also Called: Greenworks Tools
500 S Main St Ste 450 (28115-3550)
PHONE.................704 658-0539
Dave Pelichet, Pr
◆ EMP: 100 EST: 2006
SQ FT: 2,000
SALES (est): 58.49MM Privately Held
SIC: 5072 3423 Power tools and accessories ; Garden and farm tools, including shovels

(G-10966)
GS FAB INC
235 Rolling Hill Rd Ste 10 (28117-6528)
P.O. Box 4931 (28117-4931)
PHONE.................704 799-1227
Michael Giordano, Prin
EMP: 5 EST: 2019
SALES (est): 83.9K Privately Held
SIC: 7692 Welding repair

(G-10967)
H M ELLIOTT INC
387 Pitt Rd (28115-6777)
PHONE.................704 663-8226
Brenda Elliott, Pr
▲ EMP: 13 EST: 1990
SQ FT: 12,000
SALES (est): 421.05K Privately Held
Web: www.hmelliottcoatings.com
SIC: 3479 Coating of metals and formed products

(G-10968)
H&S AUTOSHOT LLC
302 Rolling Hill Rd (28117-6846)
PHONE.................847 662-8500
EMP: 20 EST: 2016
SALES (est): 1.66MM Privately Held
Web: www.hsautoshot.com
SIC: 3444 Studs and joists, sheet metal

(G-10969)
HAGER CABINET WORKS JOHN E HAG
111 Barksdale Ln (28117-6613)
PHONE.................704 799-8113
EMP: 4 EST: 2010
SALES (est): 90.35K Privately Held
SIC: 2434 Wood kitchen cabinets

(G-10970)
HASTY PRINT WORKS
821 Heatherly Rd (28115-2778)
PHONE.................704 964-6401
EMP: 4 EST: 2018
SALES (est): 83.91K Privately Held
SIC: 2752 Commercial printing, lithographic

(G-10971)
HEALTH SUPPLY US LLC
205 Raceway Dr Ste 3 (28117-6524)
PHONE.................888 408-1694
Christopher Garcia, CEO
EMP: 12 EST: 2020
SALES (est): 1.83MM Privately Held
Web: www.healthsupplyus.com
SIC: 5047 3841 3842 2389 Medical equipment and supplies; Surgical and medical instruments; Personal safety equipment; Hospital gowns

(G-10972)
HENKEL US OPERATIONS CORP
150 Fairview Rd Ste 225 (28117-9515)
PHONE.................704 799-0385
Kevin Kruger, Mgr
EMP: 5
SALES (corp-wide): 23.39B Privately Held
Web: www.henkel.com
SIC: 2891 Adhesives
HQ: Henkel Us Operations Corporation
1 Henkel Way
Rocky Hill CT 06067
860 571-5100

(G-10973)
HI & DRI BOAT LIFT SYSTEMS INC
1277 River Hwy (28117-9088)
P.O. Box 3744 (28117-3744)
PHONE.................704 663-5438
EMP: 4 EST: 1988
SALES (est): 317.67K Privately Held
Web: hi-dri-boat-lift-systems.business.site
SIC: 3536 Boat lifts

(G-10974)
HIGHLINE PERFORMANCE GROUP
Also Called: Fitzbradshaw Racing
114 Meadow Hill Cir (28117-8089)
PHONE.................704 799-3500
Armando Fitz, Pr
EMP: 50 EST: 2000
SQ FT: 20,000
SALES (est): 3.23MM Privately Held
Web: www.fitzbradshawracing.com
SIC: 3711 Automobile assembly, including specialty automobiles

(G-10975)
HOLZ-HER US INC (DH)
124 Crosslake Park Dr (28117-8016)
P.O. Box 3158 (28117-3158)
PHONE.................704 587-3400
Wulf W Reich, Ch
Stephen Carey, *
Richard Hannigan, *
◆ EMP: 70 EST: 1984
SQ FT: 83,000
SALES (est): 15.07MM Privately Held
Web: www.weinig.com
SIC: 3553 Furniture makers machinery, woodworking
HQ: Weinig Holz-Her Usa, Inc.
124 Crosslake Park Dr
Mooresville NC 28117
704 799-0100

(G-10976)
HOOTENANNY BREWING COMPANY LLC
Also Called: Hoptown
187 Shinnville Rd (28115-9372)
PHONE.................704 254-6190
EMP: 5 EST: 2018
SALES (est): 245.05K Privately Held
SIC: 2082 Malt beverages

(G-10977)
HOTCHKIS BRYDE INCORPORATED
118 Infield Ct Ste A (28117-8212)
PHONE.................704 660-3060
Kevin Bryde, Prin
EMP: 6 EST: 2013
SALES (est): 241.38K Privately Held
Web: www.hotchkis.net
SIC: 3714 Motor vehicle parts and accessories

(G-10978)
HOTCHKIS PERFORMANCE MFG INC
118 Infield Ct Ste A (28117-8212)
PHONE.................704 660-3060
John Hotchkis, Pr
EMP: 8 EST: 2013
SALES (est): 968.27K Privately Held
Web: www.hotchkis.net
SIC: 3446 Acoustical suspension systems, metal

(G-10979)
HYDROHOIST OF NORTH CAROLINA
Also Called: Hydrohoist of The Carolinas
1258 River Hwy (28117-9088)
PHONE.................704 799-1910
Mike Lineberger, Owner
EMP: 5 EST: 2004
SQ FT: 600
SALES (est): 376.58K Privately Held
Web: www.hydrohoistofthecarolinas.com
SIC: 3536 Boat lifts

(G-10980)
ICKLER MANUFACTURING LLC
229 Pitt Rd (28115-6783)
PHONE.................704 658-1195
Brian Ickler, Managing Member
EMP: 5 EST: 2014
SQ FT: 13,000
SALES (est): 270.45K Privately Held
Web: www.icklermfg.com
SIC: 3841 3812 Diagnostic apparatus, medical; Search and navigation equipment

(G-10981)
ILMOR MARINE LLC
186 Penske Way (28115-8094)
PHONE.................704 360-1901
Paul Ray, Pr
Ronald Brown, *
Julie Bernard, *
John Fraas, *
Edwin Baumgartner, *
▲ EMP: 25 EST: 2008
SQ FT: 50,000
SALES (est): 9.89MM Privately Held
Web: www.ilmor.com
SIC: 3519 Marine engines
PA: Ilmor Engineering Inc.
43939 Plymouth Oaks Blvd
Plymouth MI 48170

(G-10982)
INNOVATIVE TECHNOLOGY MFG LLC
136 Lugnut Ln Ste C (28117-9398)
PHONE.................980 248-3731
Matthew Blankenship, Prin
EMP: 7 EST: 2019
SALES (est): 474.63K Privately Held
SIC: 3999 Manufacturing industries, nec

(G-10983)
INTERNTNAL AGRCLTURE GROUP LLC
106 Langtree Village Dr Ste 301 (28117-7593)
PHONE.................908 323-3246
Maurice Moragne, Managing Member
David Skea, Managing Member
Humberto Wedderburn, Managing Member
Julio Vasquez, Managing Member
EMP: 10 EST: 2017
SALES (est): 2MM Privately Held
Web: www.iagnubana.com
SIC: 2833 5149 5122 2034 Vitamins, natural or synthetic: bulk, uncompounded; Flour; Vitamins and minerals; Fruit flour, meal, and powder

(G-10984)
IQMETRIX USA INC
184 Longboat Rd (28117-8202)
PHONE.................704 987-9903
Erick Stachowski, Pr
EMP: 65 EST: 2010
SALES (est): 19.85MM
SALES (corp-wide): 17.2MM Privately Held
Web: www.iqmetrix.com
SIC: 7372 Business oriented computer software
PA: Iqmetrix Software Development Corp
250 Howe St Suite 1210
Vancouver BC V6C 3
866 476-3874

(G-10985)
ISLAND MACHINING LLC
Also Called: Machine Shop
265 Pitt Rd (28115-6783)
PHONE.................704 278-3553
Melissa Fleming, Owner
Melissa Fleming, Prin
EMP: 4 EST: 2007
SALES (est): 284.97K Privately Held
Web: www.islandmachiningllc.com
SIC: 3599 Machine shop, jobbing and repair

(G-10986)
JAMES EMBROIDERY COMPANY
3270 Jackson Rd (28115-7571)
PHONE.................704 467-1224
James Policastro, Prin
EMP: 6 EST: 2018
SALES (est): 37.85K Privately Held
SIC: 2395 Embroidery and art needlework

(G-10987)
JASPER ENGINE EXCHANGE INC
Also Called: Jasper Motor Sports
200 Penske Way (28115-8022)
PHONE.................704 664-2300
EMP: 40
SALES (corp-wide): 650.44MM Privately Held
Web: www.jasperengines.com

Mooresville - Iredell County (G-10988)

SIC: 3714 3711 Rebuilding engines and transmissions, factory basis; Motor vehicles and car bodies
PA: Jasper Engine Exchange, Inc.
815 Wernsing Rd
Jasper IN 47546
812 482-1041

(G-10988)
JOSEPH AND JERRY CURTIS
342 Kistler Farm Rd (28115-5734)
PHONE..................704 663-4811
Joseph C Curtis, Prin
EMP: 7 EST: 2010
SALES (est): 186.81K Privately Held
SIC: 2411 Logging

(G-10989)
JRI DEVELOPMENT GROUP LLC
136 Knob Hill Rd (28117-6847)
PHONE..................704 660-8346
Dan Kungl, Managing Member
▲ EMP: 12 EST: 2007
SQ FT: 2,500
SALES (est): 2.52MM Privately Held
Web: www.jrishocks.com
SIC: 3714 Motor vehicle parts and accessories

(G-10990)
JRI SHOCKS LLC
116 Infield Ct (28117-8026)
PHONE..................704 660-8346
Det Cullum, Prin
EMP: 17 EST: 2018
SALES (est): 3.86MM Privately Held
Web: www.jrishocks.com
SIC: 3714 Motor vehicle parts and accessories

(G-10991)
JTEC RADIOWAVE
129 Loc Doc Pl # B (28115-8015)
PHONE..................704 799-1658
EMP: 5 EST: 2010
SALES (est): 242.67K Privately Held
Web: www.jtecrc.com
SIC: 3429 Aircraft hardware

(G-10992)
JUNES CRAFTMANSHIP INC
185 Oliphant Rd (28115-7953)
PHONE..................704 230-0901
Robert June, Prin
EMP: 5 EST: 2016
SALES (est): 117.69K Privately Held
Web: www.junescraftmanship.com
SIC: 2434 Wood kitchen cabinets

(G-10993)
JUSTICE BEARING LLC
Also Called: Justice Bearings
243 Overhill Dr Ste D (28117-7019)
PHONE..................800 355-2500
Shawn Barnett Sabatino, CEO
John E Miller Iii, Pr
EMP: 4 EST: 2015
SALES (est): 570.26K Privately Held
Web: www.justicebearing.com
SIC: 3562 5085 7389 Ball and roller bearings ; Industrial supplies; Business services, nec

(G-10994)
KAHNE SCREEN PRINT LLC
265 Cayuga Dr (28117-8179)
PHONE..................704 663-8549
EMP: 5 EST: 2019
SALES (est): 212.4K Privately Held
Web: www.kahnescreenprint.com
SIC: 2759 Screen printing

(G-10995)
KEMMLER PRODUCTS INC
250 Canvasback Rd (28117-8109)
PHONE..................704 663-5678
Bruce Kemmler, Pr
Tom Pearce, Ex VP
EMP: 5 EST: 2001
SALES (est): 260.37K Privately Held
Web: www.shocktec.com
SIC: 2299 Padding and wadding, textile

(G-10996)
KENNYS FIBERGLASS RESTORATION
210 Sparta Dr (28117-9503)
PHONE..................704 252-0979
EMP: 4 EST: 2019
SALES (est): 70.38K Privately Held
Web: www.lknfiberglass.com
SIC: 3732 Boatbuilding and repairing

(G-10997)
KGT ENTERPRISES INC
Also Called: Dse
185 Mckenzie Rd (28115-7976)
PHONE..................704 662-3272
Kyle G Tucker, Pr
Stacy Tucker, *
EMP: 49 EST: 2006
SQ FT: 30,000
SALES (est): 9.3MM Privately Held
Web: www.detroitspeed.com
SIC: 3714 5531 Motor vehicle parts and accessories; Automotive parts

(G-10998)
KIDSVIDZ PRODUCTIONS
694 Big Indian Loop (28117-9047)
PHONE..................704 663-4487
EMP: 4 EST: 2016
SALES (est): 107.32K Privately Held
Web: www.jcrproductions.com
SIC: 3674 Semiconductors and related devices

(G-10999)
KINGS QUEENS PLUS SIZE FASHION
107 Assembly Dr Unit 110 (28117-5439)
PHONE..................704 223-4277
EMP: 4 EST: 2016
SALES (est): 48.23K Privately Held
Web: kings-and-queens-plus-size-fashions.ueniweb.com
SIC: 2299 Jute and flax textile products

(G-11000)
L B PLASTICS INCORPORATED
482 E Plaza Dr (28115-8021)
P.O. Box 907 (28115-0907)
PHONE..................704 663-1543
Matt Cobb, Pr
▲ EMP: 60 EST: 1977
SQ FT: 279,000
SALES (est): 16.53MM Privately Held
Web: www.lbplastics.com
SIC: 3089 2522 3069 Plastics hardware and building products; Office cabinets and filing drawers, except wood; Mats or matting, rubber, nec

(G-11001)
L G SOURCING INC (HQ)
Also Called: Lowes Global Sourcing
1000 Lowes Blvd (28117-8520)
P.O. Box 1111 (28659-1111)
PHONE..................704 758-1000
Robert F Posthauer, Pr
David R Green, VP
Amber Lason, Sec
Benjamin S Adams Junior, Treas
◆ EMP: 26 EST: 1997
SALES (est): 81.15MM
SALES (corp-wide): 97.06B Publicly Held
Web: www.loweslink.com
SIC: 5031 2499 5023 Building materials, exterior; Picture and mirror frames, wood; Decorative home furnishings and supplies
PA: Lowe's Companies, Inc.
1000 Lowes Blvd
Mooresville NC 28117
704 758-1000

(G-11002)
L MICHELLE LLC
137 Autry Ave (28117-9135)
PHONE..................980 946-0204
Latoya Russell, CEO
EMP: 5 EST: 2021
SALES (est): 94.56K Privately Held
SIC: 8748 3421 Business consulting, nec; Clippers, fingernail and toenail

(G-11003)
LAKE NRMAN SCREEN PRTG FCTRY L
915 River Hwy (28117-9245)
PHONE..................704 664-8337
Norman Lake, Prin
EMP: 7 EST: 2009
SALES (est): 573.16K Privately Held
Web: www.lknprints.com
SIC: 2759 Screen printing

(G-11004)
LASER DYNAMICS INC
104 Performance Rd (28115-9590)
PHONE..................704 658-9769
Patrick Folmar, Owner
EMP: 7 EST: 2004
SALES (est): 834.59K Privately Held
Web: www.laserdynamicsinc.com
SIC: 3599 Machine shop, jobbing and repair

(G-11005)
LELANTOS GROUP INC
132 Joe Knox Ave Ste 100 (28117-9203)
PHONE..................704 780-4127
Michael Strohl, CEO
Derek Strohl, Sr VP
John Barb, COO
Monique Nicolai, Admn
EMP: 95 EST: 2013
SALES (est): 2.32MM Privately Held
Web: www.lelantosgroup.com
SIC: 7382 3312 2311 3711 Protective devices, security; Armor plate; Military uniforms, men's and youths': purchased materials; Universal carriers, military, assembly of

(G-11006)
LI-ION MOTORS CORP
158 Rolling Hill Rd (28117-8804)
PHONE..................704 662-0827
Stacey Fling, Pr
Benjamin Roseberry, *
EMP: 8 EST: 2006
SQ FT: 40,000
SALES (est): 164.62K Privately Held
SIC: 3621 Motors and generators

(G-11007)
LIBURDI DIMETRICS CORPORATION
Also Called: Liburdi
2599 Charlotte Hwy (28117-9463)
PHONE..................704 230-2510
Joe Liburdi, Pr
▲ EMP: 35 EST: 1997
SQ FT: 15,000
SALES (est): 14.23MM
SALES (corp-wide): 25.02MM Privately Held
Web: www.liburdi.com
SIC: 3612 3548 Transformers, except electric ; Welding and cutting apparatus and accessories, nec
PA: Liburdi Engineering Limited
400 Hwy 6 N
Dundas ON L9H 7
905 689-0734

(G-11008)
LIBURDI TURBINE SERVICES LLC
2599 Charlotte Hwy (28117-9463)
PHONE..................704 230-2510
Joe Liburdi, Prin
▲ EMP: 24 EST: 2008
SALES (est): 1.07MM Privately Held
Web: www.liburditurbineservices.com
SIC: 3823 Turbine flow meters, industrial process type

(G-11009)
LIFT EQUIPMENT INC
660 Millswood Dr (28115-7718)
PHONE..................704 799-3355
Robert E Ward, Pr
EMP: 5 EST: 2002
SALES (est): 69.68K Privately Held
SIC: 2721 Periodicals

(G-11010)
LITEX INDUSTRIES INC
120 N Commercial Dr (28115-7801)
PHONE..................704 799-3758
Greg Tronti, VP
EMP: 5 EST: 2001
SALES (est): 340K Privately Held
SIC: 2844 Cosmetic preparations

(G-11011)
LOGONATION INC
128 Overhill Dr Ste 102 (28117-8025)
P.O. Box 3847 (28117-3847)
PHONE..................704 799-0612
Denny Watson, Pr
Jennifer Watson, *
EMP: 48 EST: 1998
SQ FT: 4,000
SALES (est): 1.95MM Privately Held
Web: www.logonation.com
SIC: 2759 Screen printing

(G-11012)
M 5 SCENTIFIC GLASSBLOWING INC
Also Called: Edge Welding Supply
706c Performance Rd (28115-9596)
PHONE..................704 663-0101
Eric Mueller, Pr
Stacia Mueller, VP
EMP: 5 EST: 2012
SQ FT: 2,500
SALES (est): 426.06K Privately Held
Web: www.m5glassblowing.com
SIC: 3231 3229 Scientific and technical glassware: from purchased glass; Scientific glassware

(G-11013)
M I CONNECTION
435 S Broad St (28115-3208)
P.O. Box 90 (28115-0090)
PHONE..................704 662-3255
EMP: 17 EST: 2009
SALES (est): 490.01K Privately Held
Web: www.ourtds.com
SIC: 7389 7372 4841 4813 Telephone services; Prepackaged software; Cable and other pay television services; Online service providers

GEOGRAPHIC SECTION

Mooresville - Iredell County (G-11041)

(G-11014)
MAMMOTH MACHINE AND DESIGN LLC
197 Pitt Rd (28115-6782)
PHONE..................704 727-3330
Ali Bahar, *CEO*
Eric Winkler, *Genl Mgr*
EMP: 7 **EST:** 2016
SALES (est): 596.45K **Privately Held**
Web: www.mammothmachine.com
SIC: 3599 3999 Machine shop, jobbing and repair; Barber and beauty shop equipment

(G-11015)
MASCO CORPORATION
Also Called: Masco
344 E Plaza Dr (28115-8041)
PHONE..................704 658-9646
EMP: 5
SALES (corp-wide): 8.68B **Publicly Held**
Web: www.masco.com
SIC: 3432 Faucets and spigots, metal and plastic
PA: Masco Corporation
17450 College Pkwy
Livonia MI 48152
313 274-7400

(G-11016)
MASTERS IMAGING SCREEN PR
220 W Wilson Ave (28115-3237)
PHONE..................704 500-1039
EMP: 4 **EST:** 2018
SALES (est): 135.52K **Privately Held**
SIC: 2759 Screen printing

(G-11017)
MATT BIENEMAN ENTERPRISES LLC
1375 Deal Rd (28115-6721)
PHONE..................704 856-0200
EMP: 4 **EST:** 2002
SQ FT: 3,000
SALES (est): 492.91K **Privately Held**
Web: www.mbellc.com
SIC: 3469 Machine parts, stamped or pressed metal

(G-11018)
MAXAM NORTH AMERICA INC (PA)
133 River Park Rd Ste 106 (28117-8929)
P.O. Box 140906 (75014-0906)
PHONE..................214 736-8100
German Morales, *CEO*
James Bryan, *CAO*
Rocio Summers, *CFO*
Stanton Johnso, *Pr*
John Watson, *VP*
◆ **EMP:** 17 **EST:** 2000
SQ FT: 3,000
SALES (est): 27.56MM
SALES (corp-wide): 27.56MM **Privately Held**
SIC: 2892 5169 Explosives; Explosives

(G-11019)
MCLAUGHLIN FARMHOUSE
15725 Mooresville Rd (28115-6925)
PHONE..................704 660-0971
William Mclaughlin, *Prin*
EMP: 8 **EST:** 2007
SALES (est): 473.54K **Privately Held**
SIC: 2013 Corned meats, from purchased meat

(G-11020)
MEMORIES OF ORANGEBURG INC
Also Called: Memories
126 Foxfield Park Dr (28115-7885)
PHONE..................803 533-0035
Jay C Pearson, *Pr*
James Avinger, *Sec*
Robert F Fulmur, *VP*
EMP: 8 **EST:** 1972
SQ FT: 3,800
SALES (est): 483.82K **Privately Held**
SIC: 2759 5199 5099 Screen printing; Advertising specialties; Novelties, durable

(G-11021)
METAL STRUCTURES PLUS LLC
561 Oak Tree Rd (28117-5919)
PHONE..................704 896-7155
EMP: 7 **EST:** 2013
SALES (est): 205.77K **Privately Held**
SIC: 3399 3444 Primary metal products; Sheet metalwork

(G-11022)
MI SCREEN PRINTING INC
114 Vincent Pl Apt 106 (28115-0109)
PHONE..................704 500-1039
EMP: 5 **EST:** 2019
SALES (est): 242.14K **Privately Held**
SIC: 2759 Screen printing

(G-11023)
MITSUBISHI MATERIALS USA CORP
105 Corporate Center Dr Ste A (28117-0078)
PHONE..................980 312-3100
EMP: 43 **EST:** 2019
SALES (est): 3.85MM **Privately Held**
Web: www.mmus.com
SIC: 3545 Angle rings

(G-11024)
MOORESVILLE ICE CREAM COMPANY LLC
Also Called: Front Porch Ice Cream
172 N Brd St (28115)
P.O. Box 118 (28115-0118)
PHONE..................704 664-5456
▲ **EMP:** 20 **EST:** 2009
SALES (est): 2.19MM **Privately Held**
Web: www.visitmooresville.com
SIC: 2024 5451 Ice cream and ice milk; Ice cream (packaged)

(G-11025)
MOORESVILLE NC
174 Mandarin Dr (28117-8156)
PHONE..................704 909-6459
EMP: 6 **EST:** 2018
SALES (est): 182.2K **Privately Held**
Web: www.mooresvilletribune.com
SIC: 2711 Newspapers, publishing and printing

(G-11026)
MOORESVILLE PARLOR LLC
168 N Broad St (28115-3234)
PHONE..................704 450-1836
Glenn Patcha, *COO*
EMP: 5 **EST:** 2017
SALES (est): 82.32K **Privately Held**
SIC: 2711 Newspapers, publishing and printing

(G-11027)
MOORESVILLE TAX SERVICE INC
907 Brawley School Rd (28117-8993)
PHONE..................704 360-1040
Craig Lancaster, *Prin*
EMP: 4 **EST:** 2018
SALES (est): 135.72K **Privately Held**
Web: www.mooresvilletax.com
SIC: 2711 Newspapers, publishing and printing

(G-11028)
MOORESVLLE BLUE DVIL BAND BSTE
659 E Center Ave (28115-2592)
PHONE..................704 787-2994
EMP: 9 **EST:** 2010
SALES (est): 212.41K **Privately Held**
Web: www.mooresvillebands.com
SIC: 2711 Newspapers, publishing and printing

(G-11029)
MOORESVLLE PUB WRKS SNTTION DE
2523 Charlotte Hwy (28117-9463)
P.O. Box 878 (28115-0878)
PHONE..................704 664-4278
Ryan Rafe, *Dir*
John Yvars Sanitation, *Superintnt*
EMP: 9 **EST:** 2002
SQ FT: 1,210
SALES (est): 242.81K **Privately Held**
Web: www.mooresvillenc.gov
SIC: 2842 Sanitation preparations

(G-11030)
MOTORING INC
139 Golden Pond Ln (28117-8875)
PHONE..................704 809-1265
Jayme H Freitas, *Pr*
EMP: 7 **EST:** 2016
SALES (est): 173.62K **Privately Held**
SIC: 3714 Motor vehicle parts and accessories

(G-11031)
MOULDING SOURCE INCORPORATED
184 Azalea Rd (28115-7252)
PHONE..................704 658-1111
Rick Dinardo, *Pr*
EMP: 4 **EST:** 1996
SALES (est): 399.17K **Privately Held**
Web: www.themouldingsource.com
SIC: 2431 5031 Moldings, wood: unfinished and prefinished; Lumber, plywood, and millwork

(G-11032)
MSI DEFENSE SOLUTIONS LLC
Also Called: MSI
136 Knob Hill Rd (28115-6847)
P.O. Box 5506 (28117-0506)
PHONE..................704 660-8348
David Holden, *Pr*
David J Holden, *
Eric Dana, *
EMP: 64 **EST:** 2007
SQ FT: 69,000
SALES (est): 11.39MM **Privately Held**
Web: www.msidefense.com
SIC: 8711 3714 Engineering services; Motor vehicle parts and accessories

(G-11033)
NATIONAL PRINT SERVICES INC
678 Big Indian Loop (28117-9047)
P.O. Box 2055 (28031-2055)
PHONE..................704 892-9209
Daniel Preiss, *Prin*
▲ **EMP:** 6 **EST:** 2009
SALES (est): 530.33K **Privately Held**
SIC: 2752 Color lithography

(G-11034)
NC SOFTBALL SALES
117 E Statesville Ave (28115-2321)
PHONE..................704 663-2134
EMP: 4 **EST:** 2007
SALES (est): 160.23K **Privately Held**
Web: www.ncsoftballsales.com
SIC: 3949 Sporting and athletic goods, nec

(G-11035)
NGK CERAMICS USA INC (HQ)
119 Mazeppa Rd (28115-7927)
PHONE..................704 664-7000
◆ **EMP:** 11 **EST:** 1988
SALES (est): 93.53MM **Privately Held**
Web: www.ngkceramics.com
SIC: 3559 Automotive related machinery
PA: Ngk Insulators, Ltd.
2-56, Sudacho, Mizuho-Ku
Nagoya AIC 467-0

(G-11036)
NIAGARA BOTTLING LLC
178 Mooresville Blvd (28115-7433)
PHONE..................909 815-6310
EMP: 6
SALES (corp-wide): 120MM **Privately Held**
Web: www.niagarawater.com
SIC: 2086 Water, natural: packaged in cans, bottles, etc.
PA: Niagara Bottling, Llc
1440 Bridgegate Dr
Diamond Bar CA 91765
909 230-5000

(G-11037)
NISSENS COOLING SOLUTIONS INC
110 Oakpark Dr Ste 105 (28115-0137)
PHONE..................704 696-8575
Alan Steighner, *Pr*
EMP: 10 **EST:** 2014
SALES (est): 343.7K **Privately Held**
SIC: 3585 Parts for heating, cooling, and refrigerating equipment

(G-11038)
NITRO MANUFACTURING INC
510 Performance Rd (28115-9594)
PHONE..................704 663-3155
Danny Timmons, *Pr*
Valerie Timmons, *Sec*
EMP: 10 **EST:** 1998
SQ FT: 12,000
SALES (est): 1.22MM **Privately Held**
Web: www.nitromfg.com
SIC: 3444 Sheet metalwork

(G-11039)
NORMAN LAKE HIGH
135 Northbridge Dr (28115-7191)
PHONE..................336 971-7348
EMP: 4 **EST:** 2018
SALES (est): 94.89K **Privately Held**
Web: www.mooresvilletribune.com
SIC: 2711 Newspapers, publishing and printing

(G-11040)
NORTHEAST TEXTILES
105 Oakpark Dr Ste A (28115-8029)
P.O. Box 2147 (29342-2147)
PHONE..................704 799-2235
Denise Evans, *Owner*
EMP: 5 **EST:** 2015
SALES (est): 103.75K **Privately Held**
SIC: 2299 Textile goods, nec

(G-11041)
OILKLEEN INC
123 Poplar Pointe Dr Ste G (28117)
PHONE..................480 650-8711
EMP: 9 **EST:** 2010
SALES (est): 896.5K **Privately Held**
Web: www.oilkleen.com

Mooresville - Iredell County (G-11042) — GEOGRAPHIC SECTION

SIC: 1381 3731 Drilling oil and gas wells; Shipbuilding and repairing

(G-11042)
OILKLEEN LLC (PA)
123 Poplar Pointe Dr Unit G (28117-9596)
PHONE.............................480 650-8711
EMP: 12 EST: 2005
SQ FT: 8,000
SALES (est): 2.46MM Privately Held
Web: www.oilkleen.com
SIC: 3714 3731 Filters: oil, fuel, and air, motor vehicle; Shipbuilding and repairing

(G-11043)
OLEKSYNPRANNYK LLC
Also Called: Olpr.leather Goods Co.
149 Cayuga Dr Ste A3 (28117-8343)
PHONE.............................704 450-0182
Pavlo Prannyk, CEO
EMP: 12 EST: 2015
SALES (est): 459.81K Privately Held
SIC: 3199 2399 5947 3999 Leather goods, nec; Fabricated textile products, nec; Gift shop; Manufacturing industries, nec

(G-11044)
ONE SOURCE SEC & SOUND INC
122 Summerville Dr Ste 101 (28115-8037)
PHONE.............................281 850-9487
Jason Smith, Pr
EMP: 7
SALES (corp-wide): 8.78MM Privately Held
Web: www.os2s.com
SIC: 7382 3578 7539 Security systems services; Calculating and accounting equipment; Automotive repair shops, nec
PA: One Source Security & Sound, Inc.
    2925 Fm 1960 Rd E
    Humble TX 77338
    888 848-6727

(G-11045)
OVER RAINBOW PUBLISHING
262 Stonemarker Rd (28117-6669)
PHONE.............................704 360-4075
Kara M Payton, Owner
EMP: 4 EST: 2016
SALES (est): 65.27K Privately Held
SIC: 2741 Miscellaneous publishing

(G-11046)
PACKAGING CORPORATION AMERICA
Also Called: Pca/Regional Design Center
307 Oates Rd Ste B (28117-6985)
PHONE.............................704 664-5010
Carmine Buclo, Brnch Mgr
EMP: 14
SALES (corp-wide): 8.48B Publicly Held
Web: www.packagingcorp.com
SIC: 2653 5113 Boxes, corrugated: made from purchased materials; Corrugated and solid fiber boxes
PA: Packaging Corporation Of America
    1 N Field Ct
    Lake Forest IL 60045
    847 482-3000

(G-11047)
PARKER-HANNIFIN CORPORATION
Also Called: Parker Service Center
2559 Charlotte Hwy (28117-9463)
PHONE.............................704 664-1922
Tom Boyer, Brnch Mgr
EMP: 9
SQ FT: 48,602
SALES (corp-wide): 19.07B Publicly Held
Web: www.parker.com
SIC: 3429 5012 Clamps and couplings, hose ; Automobiles and other motor vehicles
PA: Parker-Hannifin Corporation
    6035 Parkland Blvd
    Cleveland OH 44124
    216 896-3000

(G-11048)
PEGGS RECREATION INC
408 N Main St (28115-2456)
P.O. Box 917 (28115-0917)
PHONE.............................704 660-0007
Eric Lowder, Prin
EMP: 4 EST: 2011
SALES (est): 493.96K Privately Held
Web: www.peggsrecreation.com
SIC: 3949 Playground equipment

(G-11049)
PENROCK LLC
Also Called: Leviosa Motor Shades
251 Knoxview Ln (28117-9689)
PHONE.............................704 800-6722
David Biedermann, Dir
Caroline Biedermann, Dir
EMP: 27 EST: 2016
SQ FT: 3,000
SALES (est): 1.84MM Privately Held
Web: www.leviosashades.com
SIC: 2591 Window shades

(G-11050)
PENSKE RACING SOUTH INC (DH)
Also Called: Team Penske
200 Penske Way (28115-8022)
P.O. Box 500 (28115-0500)
PHONE.............................704 664-2300
Roger S Penske, Ch Bd
Timothy J Cindric, *
David N Hoffert, *
Michael Nelson Junior, VP
Lawrence N Bluth, *
▲ EMP: 200 EST: 1990
SQ FT: 427,000
SALES (est): 63.05MM
SALES (corp-wide): 5.16B Privately Held
Web: www.teampenske.com
SIC: 3711 8711 8731 7948 Motor vehicles and car bodies; Engineering services; Commercial physical research; Motor vehicle racing and drivers
HQ: Penske Company Llc
    2555 S Telegraph Rd
    Bloomfield Hills MI 48302
    248 648-2000

(G-11051)
PEP FILTERS INC
Also Called: Pep Filters
120 Talbert Rd Ste J (28117-7119)
PHONE.............................704 662-3133
Michael Poth, Pr
▲ EMP: 42 EST: 1975
SQ FT: 20,000
SALES (est): 7.82MM Privately Held
Web: www.pepfilters.com
SIC: 3589 Water treatment equipment, industrial

(G-11052)
PERFORMANCE PARTS INTL LLC
Also Called: Ppi
104 Blue Ridge Trl (28117-8477)
PHONE.............................704 660-1084
John Vitale, Pr
EMP: 11 EST: 2020
SALES (est): 1.3MM Privately Held
Web: www.thepropad.com
SIC: 3751 7389 Motorcycles and related parts; Business Activities at Non-Commercial Site

(G-11053)
PERFORMANCE RACING WHSE INC
Also Called: Performance Center
145 Blossom Ridge Dr (28117-5834)
PHONE.............................704 838-1400
Roger Johnson Iii, Pr
Kim Kurzejewski, VP
EMP: 6 EST: 2010
SALES (est): 377.09K Privately Held
Web: www.performancenter.com
SIC: 3711 Cars, electric, assembly of

(G-11054)
POLISHED PEN
128 Shagbark Ln (28115-9703)
PHONE.............................704 451-4077
Nancy Wiseheart, Prin
EMP: 5 EST: 2010
SALES (est): 102.22K Privately Held
SIC: 2741 Miscellaneous publishing

(G-11055)
POLYTEC INC (PA)
191 Barley Park Ln (28115-7912)
P.O. Box 659 (28115-0659)
PHONE.............................704 277-3960
Jack Harmon, Pr
▲ EMP: 23 EST: 1994
SQ FT: 33,000
SALES (est): 25.74MM Privately Held
Web: www.polytecinc.net
SIC: 5169 2899 Industrial chemicals; Chemical preparations, nec

(G-11056)
PPG ARCHITECTURAL FINISHES INC
Also Called: Glidden Professional Paint Ctr
142 S Cardigan Way (28117-8536)
PHONE.............................704 658-9250
Charles Bunch, Brnch Mgr
EMP: 6
SALES (corp-wide): 17.65B Publicly Held
Web: www.ppg.com
SIC: 2851 Paints and allied products
HQ: Ppg Architectural Finishes, Inc.
    1 Ppg Pl
    Pittsburgh PA 15272
    412 434-3131

(G-11057)
PPG INDUSTRIES INC
128 Overhill Dr Ste 104 (28115-8025)
PHONE.............................704 658-9250
Kevin Braun, Mgr
EMP: 7
SALES (corp-wide): 17.65B Publicly Held
Web: www.ppg.com
SIC: 2851 Paints and allied products
PA: Ppg Industries, Inc.
    1 Ppg Pl
    Pittsburgh PA 15272
    412 434-3131

(G-11058)
PRECISION CONCEPTS INTL LLC (PA)
136 Fairview Rd Ste 320 (28117-9519)
PHONE.............................704 360-8923
Ray Grupinski, CEO
Dave Bell, CFO
EMP: 7 EST: 2011
SALES (est): 106.91MM
SALES (corp-wide): 106.91MM Privately Held
Web: www.pcinternational.com
SIC: 3085 3221 7336 Plastics bottles; Glass containers; Package design

(G-11059)
PRECISION METAL FINISHING INC
962 N Main St (28115-2356)
PHONE.............................704 799-0250
Eric Wilkinson, Owner
EMP: 5 EST: 2007
SALES (est): 239.98K Privately Held
SIC: 3471 Finishing, metals or formed products

(G-11060)
PRIME CREDIT LLC
118 Morlake Dr Ste 204 (28117-9259)
PHONE.............................704 729-7000
EMP: 4 EST: 2019
SALES (est): 116.87K Privately Held
SIC: 2741 Miscellaneous publishing

(G-11061)
PRIME WIRE AND CABLE
179 Gasoline Aly Ste 103 (28117-6533)
PHONE.............................704 799-6000
Bill Ferlauto, Pr
EMP: 5 EST: 2013
SALES (est): 445.76K Privately Held
Web: www.primewirecable.com
SIC: 3661 Telephone cords, jacks, adapters, etc.

(G-11062)
PRO-FIT BOAT CANVAS LLC
134 Palmer Marsh Pl (28117-6413)
PHONE.............................704 340-7733
Brett A White, Pr
EMP: 5 EST: 2016
SALES (est): 56.36K Privately Held
SIC: 2211 Canvas

(G-11063)
PRO-MOTOR ENGINES INC
Also Called: PME
102 S Iredell Industrial Park Rd (28115-7128)
PHONE.............................704 664-6800
Peter F Guild, Pr
Ann Guild, Sec
EMP: 7 EST: 1992
SQ FT: 15,000
SALES (est): 1.83MM Privately Held
Web: www.pmeengines.com
SIC: 5013 8732 7699 7549 Automotive supplies and parts; Research services, except laboratory; Marine engine repair; High performance auto repair and service

(G-11064)
PRO-SYSTEM INC
121 Oakpark Dr (28115-7811)
P.O. Box 685 (28115-0685)
PHONE.............................704 799-8100
EMP: 10 EST: 1994
SQ FT: 8,400
SALES (est): 935.82K Privately Held
Web: www.prosystembrakes.com
SIC: 2396 5012 Automotive and apparel trimmings; Automobiles and other motor vehicles

(G-11065)
PSALM 32 PUBLISHING LLC
200 Collingswood Rd (28117-9472)
PHONE.............................704 799-7637
John R Lamb, Prin
EMP: 5 EST: 2016
SALES (est): 59.23K Privately Held
SIC: 2741 Miscellaneous publishing

(G-11066)
QUEEN CITY PASTRY LLC
137 Speedway Ln (28117-6879)

GEOGRAPHIC SECTION

Mooresville - Iredell County (G-11095)

PHONE..................704 660-5706
EMP: 45 **EST:** 1996
SQ FT: 6,500
SALES (est): 4.8MM **Privately Held**
Web: www.queencitypastry.com
SIC: 2051 5143 Bakery: wholesale or wholesale/retail combined; Frozen dairy desserts

(G-11067)
R JONES FABRICATION LLC
270 Deerfield Dr (28115-9573)
PHONE..................937 779-0826
Joseph Ryan Jones, *Prin*
EMP: 8 **EST:** 2015
SALES (est): 248.07K **Privately Held**
Web: www.rjonesfab.com
SIC: 7692 Welding repair

(G-11068)
REVOULTION OIL INC
291 Cayuga Dr (28117-8179)
PHONE..................704 577-2546
EMP: 4 **EST:** 2011
SALES (est): 144.97K **Privately Held**
SIC: 2992 Lubricating oils and greases

(G-11069)
RILEY TECHNOLOGIES LLC
170 Overhill Dr (28117-8006)
P.O. Box 4447 (28117-4447)
PHONE..................704 663-6319
Bob Riley, *Pr*
Bill Riley, *
▲ **EMP:** 35 **EST:** 1990
SQ FT: 57,000
SALES (est): 5MM **Privately Held**
Web: www.rileytech.com
SIC: 3711 7389 Automobile assembly, including specialty automobiles; Design services

(G-11070)
RITCHIE FOAM COMPANY INC
214 E Waterlynn Rd (28117-8075)
PHONE..................704 663-2533
Ted W Ritchie, *Pr*
Wayne Ritchie, *VP*
EMP: 4 **EST:** 1980
SALES (est): 481.07K **Privately Held**
Web: www.ritchiefoam.com
SIC: 3086 Plastics foam products

(G-11071)
RMI PLASTIC
184 Ringneck Trl (28117-8124)
PHONE..................704 995-9489
EMP: 8 **EST:** 2016
SALES (est): 190.3K **Privately Held**
SIC: 3089 Injection molding of plastics

(G-11072)
ROOSTERFISH MEDIA LLC
Also Called: Real Producers
129 Ashford Hollow Ln (28117-9695)
PHONE..................980 722-7454
Tom Bramhall, *Owner*
EMP: 7 **EST:** 2018
SALES (est): 122.18K **Privately Held**
Web: www.roosterfish.media
SIC: 2741 Miscellaneous publishing

(G-11073)
ROUSH & YATES RACING ENGS LLC
Also Called: Roush Yates Mfg Solutions
112 Byers Creek Rd (28117-4376)
PHONE..................704 799-6216
EMP: 55
SALES (corp-wide): 43.73MM **Privately Held**
Web: www.roushyates.com
SIC: 3462 Automotive forgings, ferrous: crankshaft, engine, axle, etc.
PA: Roush & Yates Racing Engines Llc
297 Rolling Hill Rd
Mooresville NC 28117
704 799-6216

(G-11074)
ROUSH & YATES RACING ENGS LLC (PA)
297 Rolling Hill Rd (28117-6845)
P.O. Box 3788 (28117-3788)
PHONE..................704 799-6216
Jack Roush, *
Robert Yates, *
▲ **EMP:** 110 **EST:** 2003
SQ FT: 12,000
SALES (est): 43.73MM
SALES (corp-wide): 43.73MM **Privately Held**
Web: www.roushyates.com
SIC: 3462 Automotive forgings, ferrous: crankshaft, engine, axle, etc.

(G-11075)
ROWDY MANUFACTURING LLC
Also Called: Rowdy Manufacturing
161 Byers Creek Rd (28117-4440)
PHONE..................704 662-0000
Kyle Busch, *Managing Member*
EMP: 4 **EST:** 2010
SALES (est): 1.11MM **Privately Held**
Web: www.rowdymfg.com
SIC: 3711 3599 Automobile assembly, including specialty automobiles; Machine and other job shop work

(G-11076)
RTST LLC
243 Collingswood Rd (28117-9472)
P.O. Box 5362 (28117-0362)
PHONE..................704 999-9906
Richard L Touchette, *Admn*
EMP: 5 **EST:** 2010
SALES (est): 75.81K **Privately Held**
SIC: 3823 Process control instruments

(G-11077)
RUST-OLEUM CORPORATION
Also Called: Rust-Oleum
157 Cedar Pointe Dr Ste A (28117-6975)
PHONE..................704 662-7730
Norm Bowman, *Brnch Mgr*
EMP: 4
SALES (corp-wide): 7.26B **Publicly Held**
Web: www.rustoleum.com
SIC: 2851 Paints and allied products
HQ: Rust-Oleum Corporation
11 E Hawthorn Pkwy
Vernon Hills IL 60061
847 367-7700

(G-11078)
SATO INC
136 Acorn Ln (28117-6919)
PHONE..................980 613-2022
EMP: 4 **EST:** 2020
SALES (est): 92.36K **Privately Held**
SIC: 2759 Labels and seals: printing, nsk

(G-11079)
SAUDER WOODWORKING CO
119 Magnolia Park Dr (28117-8928)
PHONE..................704 799-6782
EMP: 5 **EST:** 2019
SALES (est): 54.13K **Privately Held**
SIC: 2431 Millwork

(G-11080)
SCOTTS COMPANY LLC
319 Oates Rd Ste A (28117-7041)
PHONE..................704 663-6088
Pete Carpentier, *Mgr*
EMP: 10
SALES (corp-wide): 3.55B **Publicly Held**
Web: www.scotts.com
SIC: 2873 2874 2879 Fertilizers: natural (organic), except compost; Phosphates; Fungicides, herbicides
HQ: The Scotts Company Llc
14111 Scottslawn Rd
Marysville OH 43040
937 644-0011

(G-11081)
SCREENS STITCHES & STONES LLC
208 Waterlynn Ridge Rd Unit E (28117-5481)
PHONE..................704 622-1660
EMP: 4 **EST:** 2019
SALES (est): 183.49K **Privately Held**
SIC: 2759 Screen printing

(G-11082)
SEALCO MANUFACTURING LLC
105 Keel Ct (28117-6619)
P.O. Box 4313 (28117-2313)
PHONE..................704 662-2850
Jeffrey D Saal, *Prin*
EMP: 5 **EST:** 2016
SALES (est): 127.23K **Privately Held**
SIC: 3999 Manufacturing industries, nec

(G-11083)
SHEETS LAUNDRY CLUB INC
211 Mckenzie Rd (28115-7975)
PHONE..................704 662-8696
Chris Videau, *Prin*
EMP: 10 **EST:** 2019
SALES (est): 756.5K **Privately Held**
Web: www.sheetslaundryclub.com
SIC: 2841 Soap and other detergents

(G-11084)
SHOCKTEC INC
250 Canvasback Rd (28117-8109)
PHONE..................704 663-5678
EMP: 4 **EST:** 2020
SALES (est): 117.22K **Privately Held**
Web: www.shocktec.com
SIC: 3999 Manufacturing industries, nec

(G-11085)
SHUR LINE INC
116 Exmore Rd (28117-9422)
PHONE..................317 442-8850
EMP: 39 **EST:** 2017
SALES (est): 2.19MM **Privately Held**
Web: www.shurline.com
SIC: 3991 Brooms and brushes

(G-11086)
SHURTECH BRANDS LLC
150 Fairview Rd (28117-9504)
PHONE..................704 799-0779
EMP: 5
SALES (corp-wide): 787.56MM **Privately Held**
Web: www.shurtapetech.com
SIC: 2671 Plastic film, coated or laminated for packaging
HQ: Shurtech Brands, Llc
32150 Just Imagine Dr
Avon OH 44011

(G-11087)
SIGN ON TIME
124 Avalon Reserve Dr (28115-7012)
PHONE..................704 507-2486
Crystal Michelle Pedrero, *Prin*
EMP: 5 **EST:** 2019
SALES (est): 234.56K **Privately Held**
SIC: 3993 Signs and advertising specialties

(G-11088)
SIR SPEEDY PRINTING
Also Called: Sir Speedy
124 E Plaza Dr Ste C (28115-8103)
PHONE..................704 664-1911
EMP: 8 **EST:** 2017
SALES (est): 181.87K **Privately Held**
Web: www.sirspeedy.com
SIC: 2752 Commercial printing, lithographic

(G-11089)
SKIN WELLNESS BY PATRICIA INC
158 Saye Pl (28115-5813)
PHONE..................704 634-6635
Patricia Coolidge, *Prin*
EMP: 5 **EST:** 2019
SALES (est): 59.54K **Privately Held**
SIC: 2431 Millwork

(G-11090)
SMITH FABRICATION INC
2136 Coddle Creek Hwy (28115-8250)
PHONE..................704 660-5170
Jeffery Brian Smith, *Pr*
EMP: 5 **EST:** 1996
SALES (est): 319.32K **Privately Held**
SIC: 3599 3711 3444 Machine and other job shop work; Motor vehicles and car bodies; Sheet metalwork

(G-11091)
SNIFF N RESCUE CANDLES LLC
159 Pampas Ln (28117-9438)
PHONE..................704 909-9853
Laura Weber, *Prin*
EMP: 4 **EST:** 2018
SALES (est): 86.78K **Privately Held**
Web: www.sniffnrescuecandles.org
SIC: 3999 Candles

(G-11092)
SNYDER CUSTOM CREATIONS LLC
163 Sundown Rd (28117-9168)
PHONE..................704 743-3386
EMP: 5 **EST:** 2018
SALES (est): 117.18K **Privately Held**
SIC: 2431 Millwork

(G-11093)
SOWERS WELDING SERVICE
111 Red Arrow Pl (28117-6918)
PHONE..................704 929-5617
EMP: 4 **EST:** 2017
SALES (est): 47.63K **Privately Held**
SIC: 7692 Welding repair

(G-11094)
SPECTRE CUSTOM SOLUTIONS LLC
142 Hampshire Dr (28115-8501)
PHONE..................704 450-4428
EMP: 4 **EST:** 2019
SALES (est): 64.64K **Privately Held**
SIC: 3999 Manufacturing industries, nec

(G-11095)
SPECTRUM BRANDS INC
307 Oates Rd Ste F (28117-6985)
PHONE..................704 658-2060
Jeff Johnson, *Brnch Mgr*
EMP: 5
SALES (corp-wide): 2.92B **Publicly Held**
Web: www.spectrumbrands.com
SIC: 3691 Alkaline cell storage batteries
HQ: Spectrum Brands, Inc.

Mooresville - Iredell County (G-11096)

3001 Deming Way
Middleton WI 53562
608 275-3340

(G-11096)
SPEEDPRO IMAGING
103 Masthead Ct (28117-6043)
PHONE.....................704 495-6749
EMP: 4 **EST:** 2018
SALES (est): 25.81K **Privately Held**
Web: www.speedpro.com
SIC: 3993 Signs and advertising specialties

(G-11097)
SRI PERFORMANCE LLC
122 Knob Hill Rd (28117-6847)
P.O. Box 5478 (28117-0478)
PHONE.....................704 662-6982
EMP: 43 **EST:** 2016
SALES (est): 4.66MM **Privately Held**
Web: www.sriperformance.com
SIC: 3714 Motor vehicle parts and accessories

(G-11098)
SS HANDCRAFTED ART LLC
107 Glade Valley Ave (28117-8705)
PHONE.....................704 664-2544
◆ **EMP:** 6
SALES (corp-wide): 476.27K **Privately Held**
Web: www.sshandart.com
SIC: 2395 Embroidery and art needlework
PA: Ss Handcrafted Art Llc
    195 E Waterlynn Rd
    Mooresville NC 28117
    866 352-9377

(G-11099)
STARHGEN AROSPC COMPONENTS LLC
333 Oates Rd (28117-6824)
PHONE.....................704 660-1001
◆ **EMP:** 13 **EST:** 2012
SALES (est): 3.65MM **Privately Held**
SIC: 3728 Aircraft parts and equipment, nec

(G-11100)
STEEL FAB
161 Gray Cliff Dr (28117-8517)
PHONE.....................980 721-8969
Luke Miller, *Prin*
EMP: 4 **EST:** 2016
SALES (est): 43.21K **Privately Held**
Web: www.steelfabinc.com
SIC: 3441 Fabricated structural metal

(G-11101)
STEIN-PALMER PRINTING CO
124 Tulip Dr (28117-6060)
PHONE.....................740 633-3894
Thomas Palmer, *Owner*
EMP: 4 **EST:** 2015
SALES (est): 51.49K **Privately Held**
SIC: 2752 Offset printing

(G-11102)
STITCH 2 FIT
295 Alcove Rd (28117-7519)
PHONE.....................704 677-4842
James W Finnerty Junior, *Prin*
EMP: 5 **EST:** 2009
SALES (est): 43.09K **Privately Held**
SIC: 2395 Embroidery and art needlework

(G-11103)
STITCH 98 INC
154 Talbert Pointe Dr Ste 101 (28117-4314)
PHONE.....................704 235-5783
Marci Athey, *Pr*
EMP: 18 **EST:** 2007
SALES (est): 883.32K **Privately Held**
Web: www.stitch98.com
SIC: 2395 Embroidery products, except Schiffli machine

(G-11104)
STONERY LLC
1077 Mecklenburg Hwy (28115-7853)
PHONE.....................704 662-8702
EMP: 7 **EST:** 2006
SALES (est): 164.08K **Privately Held**
Web: www.thestonery.com
SIC: 2541 Counter and sink tops

(G-11105)
STORAGEMOTION INC
216 Overhill Dr Ste 104 (28117-7000)
PHONE.....................704 746-3700
Kurtis Krohn, *Pr*
Tina Krohn, *Sec*
▲ **EMP:** 6 **EST:** 2005
SALES (est): 674.91K **Privately Held**
Web: www.storagemotion.com
SIC: 2511 China closets

(G-11106)
STRUCTURE MEDICAL LLC
123 Cayuga Dr (28117-8239)
PHONE.....................704 799-3450
Robert Boody, *Mgr*
EMP: 90
Web: www.structuremedical.com
SIC: 3842 Orthopedic appliances
HQ: Structure Medical, Llc
    9935 Business Cir
    Naples FL 34112
    239 262-5551

(G-11107)
SUGAR POPS
248 N Main St (28115-2528)
PHONE.....................704 799-0959
EMP: 5 **EST:** 2012
SALES (est): 246.09K **Privately Held**
SIC: 3421 7299 5441 Table and food cutlery, including butchers'; Party planning service; Candy

(G-11108)
SYSMETRIC USA
107 Infield Ct (28117-8026)
PHONE.....................704 522-8778
Itzhak Livni, *Pr*
EMP: 9 **EST:** 2016
SALES (est): 220.37K **Privately Held**
Web: sysmetric-usa.business.site
SIC: 3089 Plastics containers, except foam

(G-11109)
TALTIC PROPERTIES LLC
206 Joe Knox Ave Ste C (28117-7912)
PHONE.....................731 656-2735
EMP: 4 **EST:** 2016
SALES (est): 137.73K **Privately Held**
SIC: 2844 Perfumes, cosmetics and other toilet preparations

(G-11110)
TEXTILE DESIGNED MACHINE CO
1320 Shearers Rd (28115-7778)
PHONE.....................704 664-1374
Dan Newton, *Pr*
Richard Newton, *Pr*
EMP: 10 **EST:** 1961
SQ FT: 12,000
SALES (est): 980.26K **Privately Held**
Web: www.tdmc-rolls.com
SIC: 3599 Machine shop, jobbing and repair

(G-11111)
THOMAS MENDOLIA MD
Also Called: Tri County Gastroenterology
116 Quincy Ct (28117-7340)
PHONE.....................336 835-5688
Thomas Mendolia Md, *Owner*
EMP: 6 **EST:** 1991
SALES (est): 280K **Privately Held**
SIC: 8011 3845 Gastronomist; Colonoscopes, electromedical

(G-11112)
THYSSENKRUPP BILSTEIN AMER INC
Also Called: Shock Absorber Division
293 Timber Rd (28115-7868)
PHONE.....................704 663-7563
Scott Mcdonald, *Brnch Mgr*
EMP: 10
SALES (corp-wide): 40.78B **Privately Held**
Web: www.bilstein.com
SIC: 3714 Motor vehicle parts and accessories
HQ: Thyssenkrupp Bilstein Of America, Inc.
    8685 Bilstein Blvd
    Hamilton OH 45015
    513 881-7600

(G-11113)
TIGER PRECISION PRODUCTS LLC
138 Cedar Pointe Dr (28117-6880)
PHONE.....................714 360-4134
EMP: 8 **EST:** 2020
SALES (est): 1.1MM **Privately Held**
Web: www.tigerpp.com
SIC: 3599 Machine shop, jobbing and repair

(G-11114)
TREADZ LLC
2118 Charlotte Hwy (28117-9468)
PHONE.....................704 664-0995
James Hubschmitt, *Pr*
James Hubschmitt, *Managing Member*
EMP: 4 **EST:** 2017
SALES (est): 487.33K **Privately Held**
Web: www.treadznc.com
SIC: 7699 5531 7539 7534 Motorcycle repair service; Automotive accessories; Automotive repair shops, nec; Tire repair shop

(G-11115)
TRIBODYN TECHNOLOGIES INC
109 Summerville Dr (28115-8043)
PHONE.....................859 750-6299
Mark Wheatley, *Pr*
EMP: 10 **EST:** 2012
SALES (est): 1.95MM **Privately Held**
Web: www.tribodyn.com
SIC: 2899 Chemical preparations, nec

(G-11116)
UNITED WELDING AND IRON WORK
115 Denver Business Park Dr Ste D (28115-5901)
PHONE.....................704 281-3706
EMP: 4 **EST:** 2019
SALES (est): 84.54K **Privately Held**
SIC: 7692 Welding repair

(G-11117)
UTSEY DUSKIE & ASSOCIATES
243 Overhill Dr Ste B (28117-7016)
PHONE.....................704 663-0036
Libby Duskie, *Prin*
EMP: 8
SALES (corp-wide): 602.69K **Privately Held**
SIC: 3556 Food products machinery
PA: Utsey Duskie & Associates
    386 Williamson Rd
    Mooresville NC 28117
    704 663-0036

(G-11118)
VICTORY 1 PERFORMANCE INC
159 Lugnut Ln (28117-9300)
PHONE.....................704 799-1955
EMP: 15 **EST:** 1980
SQ FT: 18,000
SALES (est): 5.03MM
SALES (corp-wide): 195.05MM **Privately Held**
Web: www.titaniumvalve.com
SIC: 3462 Automotive and internal combustion engine forgings
PA: Race Winning Brands, Inc.
    7201 Industrial Park Blvd
    Mentor OH 44060
    440 951-6600

(G-11119)
VICTORY PRESS LLC
114 Eastbend Ct Ste 4 (28117-4310)
PHONE.....................704 660-0348
EMP: 9 **EST:** 2006
SALES (est): 796.47K **Privately Held**
Web: www.victorypress.biz
SIC: 2752 Offset printing

(G-11120)
VINE & BRANCH WOODWORKS LLC
388 E Plaza Dr (28115-8047)
PHONE.....................704 663-0077
Shawn A Copeland, *Admn*
EMP: 6 **EST:** 2016
SALES (est): 610.42K **Privately Held**
Web: www.vineandbranchwoodworks.com
SIC: 2434 Wood kitchen cabinets

(G-11121)
VM PUBLISHING
106 Colonial Ridge Cir # 22 (28117-8103)
PHONE.....................704 547-4322
Viola Mclelland, *Prin*
EMP: 4 **EST:** 2018
SALES (est): 78.04K **Privately Held**
SIC: 2741 Miscellaneous publishing

(G-11122)
WALK IN FAITH LLC
Also Called: Nufced Custom T-Shirts & More
2785 Charlotte Hwy (28117-8050)
P.O. Box 3862 (28117-3862)
PHONE.....................704 660-8337
EMP: 5 **EST:** 2014
SALES (est): 397.72K **Privately Held**
Web: www.nufced.co
SIC: 2759 Screen printing

(G-11123)
WATER TECH SOLUTIONS INC
178 Cayuga Dr (28117-8239)
PHONE.....................704 408-8391
Greg Sanders, *Pr*
EMP: 5 **EST:** 2004
SALES (est): 842.71K **Privately Held**
Web: www.ozonesalesandservice.com
SIC: 3823 Process control instruments

(G-11124)
WEBER SCREWDRIVING SYSTEMS INC
149 Knob Hill Rd (28117-6847)
PHONE.....................704 360-5820
EMP: 35 **EST:** 1979
SALES (est): 9.62MM
SALES (corp-wide): 88.99MM **Privately Held**

Web: www.weberusa.com
SIC: 3546 Power-driven handtools
PA: Weber Schraubautomaten
Gesellschaft Mit Beschrankter Haftung
Hans-Urmiller-Ring 56
Wolfratshausen BY 82515
817 140-6580

(G-11125)
WEBER STEPHEN PRODUCTS LLC
200 Overhill Dr (28117-7033)
PHONE.........................704 662-0335
EMP: 12 EST: 2015
SALES (est): 747.33K **Privately Held**
SIC: 3631 Household cooking equipment

(G-11126)
WERNER CO
307 Oask Rd Ste D (28115-3055)
PHONE.........................704 235-5660
EMP: 8
Web: www.wernerco.com
SIC: 3499 Aerosol valves, metal
HQ: Werner Co.
555 W Pierce Rd Ste 300
Itasca IL 60143

(G-11127)
WESLACOVA CORP
719 Pinewood Cir (28115-3422)
PHONE.........................704 607-1449
Scott Mauney, *Pr*
EMP: 7 EST: 2020
SALES (est): 128.82K **Privately Held**
Web: www.weslacova.com
SIC: 3841 Surgical and medical instruments

(G-11128)
WESTROCK - SOUTHERN CONT LLC
279 Mooresville Blvd (28115-7965)
P.O. Box 1009 (28115-1009)
PHONE.........................704 662-8496
EMP: 63
SALES (corp-wide): 20.31B **Publicly Held**
Web: www.westrock.com
SIC: 2653 Boxes, corrugated: made from purchased materials
HQ: Westrock - Southern Container, Llc
1000 Abernathy Rd
Atlanta GA 30328
770 448-2193

(G-11129)
WESTROCK RKT LLC
279 Mooresville Blvd (28115-7965)
P.O. Box 1009 (28115-1009)
PHONE.........................704 662-8494
Don Kasun, *Brnch Mgr*
EMP: 33
SALES (corp-wide): 20.31B **Publicly Held**
Web: www.westrock.com
SIC: 2653 2652 2631 Boxes, corrugated: made from purchased materials; Setup paperboard boxes; Paperboard mills
HQ: Westrock Rkt, Llc
1000 Abernathy Rd Ste 125
Atlanta GA 30328
770 448-2193

(G-11130)
WHITE STONE LABS INC
178 Cayuga Dr (28117-8239)
PHONE.........................704 775-5274
Gregory Sanders, *Pr*
EMP: 4
SALES (est): 243.09K **Privately Held**
SIC: 2833 Medicinals and botanicals

(G-11131)
WOMACK PUBLISHING CO INC
Also Called: Lake Norman Times
548 Williamson Rd Ste 3 (28117-9111)
PHONE.........................704 660-5520
Chris Montgomery, *Dir*
EMP: 10
SALES (corp-wide): 21.7MM **Privately Held**
Web: www.womackpublishing.com
SIC: 2711 Newspapers: publishing only, not printed on site
PA: Womack Publishing Company, Inc.
28 N Main St
Chatham VA 24531
434 432-2791

(G-11132)
WYOMING WHISKEY INC
170 Mooresville Commons Way Unit 218 (28117)
PHONE.........................561 573-5605
Sammy Di Nardo, *Prin*
EMP: 4 EST: 2016
SALES (est): 51.92K **Privately Held**
Web: www.wyomingwhiskey.com
SIC: 2085 Distilled and blended liquors

(G-11133)
XRE PERFORMANCE ENGINES LLC
138 Quiet View Dr (28115-6985)
PHONE.........................704 663-3505
Rebecca Ghent, *Prin*
EMP: 7 EST: 2008
SALES (est): 184.5K **Privately Held**
SIC: 3519 Internal combustion engines, nec

(G-11134)
XTREME GRAPHIX
10060 Unity Church Rd (28115-7364)
PHONE.........................704 746-5744
EMP: 4 EST: 2009
SALES (est): 82.57K **Privately Held**
Web: www.branded.ink
SIC: 3993 Signs and advertising specialties

(G-11135)
XXXTREME MOTORSPORT
292 Rolling Hill Rd (28115-6845)
PHONE.........................704 663-1500
John Cohen, *Owner*
EMP: 7 EST: 2012
SALES (est): 422.1K **Privately Held**
SIC: 3799 Recreational vehicles

(G-11136)
YATES PRECISION MACHINING LLC
133 Byers Creek Rd Unit D (28117-4376)
P.O. Box 5450 (28117-0450)
PHONE.........................704 662-7165
EMP: 10 EST: 2008
SALES (est): 747.33K **Privately Held**
SIC: 3462 Iron and steel forgings

(G-11137)
YOUNG & SON MFG LLC
129 Loc Doc Pl Unit B (28115-8015)
PHONE.........................704 799-1658
EMP: 4 EST: 2012
SALES (est): 39.69K **Privately Held**
SIC: 3999 Manufacturing industries, nec

(G-11138)
YUMMY TUMMY GA LLC
Also Called: Planet Smoothie
2105 Brawley School Rd (28117-7081)
PHONE.........................704 658-0445
Bill Renton, *Pr*
Mo Rafiq, *VP*
EMP: 35 EST: 2007
SALES (est): 357.96K **Privately Held**
Web: www.planetsmoothie.com
SIC: 5812 2024 Soft drink stand; Ice cream and frozen deserts

(G-11139)
ZEKELMAN INDUSTRIES INC
Wheatland Tube A Div Zklman In
111 Pin Oak Ln (28117-7501)
PHONE.........................704 560-6768
EMP: 10
Web: www.zekelman.com
SIC: 3317 Pipes, seamless steel
PA: Zekelman Industries, Inc.
227 W Monroe St Ste 2600
Chicago IL 60606

(G-11140)
ZIBRA LLC (PA)
172 Broad Sound Pl (28117-6050)
PHONE.........................704 271-4503
▲ EMP: 4 EST: 2004
SALES (est): 1.02MM **Privately Held**
Web: www.enjoyzibra.com
SIC: 3991 3699 Brushes, household or industrial; Household electrical equipment

Moravian Falls
Wilkes County

(G-11141)
AMERICAN ALCOHOLLERY LLC
385 Hose Rd (28654-9671)
PHONE.........................704 960-7243
Amanda Holman, *Prin*
EMP: 5 EST: 2015
SALES (est): 80.68K **Privately Held**
SIC: 2084 Wines

(G-11142)
BROCK AND TRIPLETT MACHINE SP
Also Called: Brock & Triplett Machine
285 E Meadows Rd (28654-9600)
PHONE.........................336 667-6951
Donnie A Brock, *Pr*
Warren E Triplett, *VP*
EMP: 4 EST: 1961
SALES (est): 377.23K **Privately Held**
Web: www.discoverymobilehomes.com
SIC: 3599 Custom machinery

(G-11143)
BRUSHY MTN CSTM WOODWORKS INC
10350 Brushy Mountain Rd (28654-9654)
PHONE.........................336 921-3510
Janet Owens Estep, *Prin*
EMP: 5 EST: 2014
SALES (est): 223.74K **Privately Held**
Web: www.bmcwinc.com
SIC: 2431 Millwork

(G-11144)
CHARLES FERGUSON LOGGING
245 Jack Russell Rd (28654-9641)
P.O. Box 235 (28606-0235)
PHONE.........................336 921-3126
Charles F Ferguson, *Owner*
EMP: 4 EST: 1984
SALES (est): 303.37K **Privately Held**
SIC: 2411 Logging camps and contractors

(G-11145)
JOINES CUSTOM WOODWORK
485 Pennell Rd (28654-9786)
PHONE.........................336 984-7237
EMP: 4 EST: 2018
SALES (est): 81.72K **Privately Held**
SIC: 2431 Millwork

(G-11146)
NI4L ANTENNAS AND ELEC LLC
Also Called: Unadilla Antenna Mfg Co
3861 Mount Olive Church Rd (28654-9576)
PHONE.........................828 738-6445
EMP: 5 EST: 2013
SALES (est): 461K **Privately Held**
Web: www.ni4l.com
SIC: 3663 5063 5731 7389 Antennas, transmitting and communications; Antennas, receiving, satellite dishes; Antennas; Business Activities at Non-Commercial Site

(G-11147)
STAFFORD LOGGING LLC
905 Cove Gap Rd (28654-9464)
PHONE.........................828 635-8584
Brooks B Stafford, *Owner*
EMP: 6 EST: 2015
SALES (est): 199.05K **Privately Held**
SIC: 2411 Logging

Morehead City
Carteret County

(G-11148)
ACE MARINE RIGGING & SUPPLY INC (PA)
600 Arendell St (28557-4233)
PHONE.........................252 726-6620
◆ EMP: 12 EST: 1990
SALES (est): 2.47MM **Privately Held**
Web: www.acemarinerigging.com
SIC: 5031 5251 5551 2298 Building materials, exterior; Hardware stores; Marine supplies, nec; Slings, rope

(G-11149)
AQUA 10 CORPORATION
Also Called: Bio D
5112 Midyette Ave (28557-2694)
PHONE.........................252 726-5421
William E Campell Iii, *Pr*
EMP: 8 EST: 1972
SQ FT: 12,000
SALES (est): 573.3K **Privately Held**
SIC: 2879 Agricultural chemicals, nec

(G-11150)
ASPHALT EMULSION INDS LLC
107 Arendell St (28557-4248)
PHONE.........................252 726-0653
Carter Dabney, *Managing Member*
EMP: 4 EST: 2011
SALES (est): 349.31K **Privately Held**
Web: www.asphalt-emulsion.com
SIC: 5032 3531 Paving materials; Aggregate spreaders

(G-11151)
BALLY REFRIGERATED BOXES INC (PA)
135 Little Nine Rd (28557-8483)
PHONE.........................252 240-2829
◆ EMP: 175 EST: 1995
SQ FT: 200,000
SALES (est): 62.45MM **Privately Held**
Web: www.ballyrefboxes.com
SIC: 5078 3585 Refrigeration equipment and supplies; Air conditioning condensers and condensing units

(G-11152)
BIG ROCK INDUSTRIES INC
Also Called: Big Rock Propellers
111 Turners Dairy Rd Ste A (28557-4530)
PHONE.........................252 222-3618
Adam Pierce, *Pr*

Morehead City - Carteret County (G-11153)

GEOGRAPHIC SECTION

Thomas Healey, *Sec*
EMP: 4 **EST:** 2014
SALES (est): 327.13K **Privately Held**
Web: www.bigrockpropellers.com
SIC: 8711 3731 Marine engineering; Fishing vessels, large: building and repairing

(G-11153)
BIRCHER INCORPORATED
Also Called: Beaufort Naval Armorers
119 Industrial Dr (28557-8481)
PHONE..........................252 726-5470
James T Bircher, *Pr*
EMP: 5 **EST:** 1984
SQ FT: 7,200
SALES (est): 431.7K **Privately Held**
Web: www.bircherinc.com
SIC: 3599 Machine shop, jobbing and repair

(G-11154)
BLACKBEARDS BOATWORKS
4531 Arendell St (28557-2707)
PHONE..........................252 726-6161
Joy Edmundson, *Prin*
EMP: 7 **EST:** 2016
SALES (est): 82.41K **Privately Held**
Web: www.shearlineboatworks.com
SIC: 3732 Boatbuilding and repairing

(G-11155)
BOARDWALK INC
4911 Bridges St Ext # A (28557-8978)
PHONE..........................252 240-1095
Garry Mckeel, *Pr*
EMP: 5 **EST:** 1994
SALES (est): 265.76K **Privately Held**
Web: www.boardwalkscreenprinting.com
SIC: 2396 5999 Screen printing on fabric articles; Trophies and plaques

(G-11156)
CABINET SHOP INC
4915 Arendell St Ste 309 (28557-2659)
PHONE..........................252 726-6965
Paul Pagliughi, *Pr*
EMP: 6 **EST:** 1983
SQ FT: 24,090
SALES (est): 479.57K **Privately Held**
Web: www.cabinet-shop.com
SIC: 2434 Wood kitchen cabinets

(G-11157)
CAPE LOOKOUT CANVAS & CUSTOMS
4444 Arendell St Ste D (28557-2701)
PHONE..........................252 726-3751
William Hoke Page Junior, *Owner*
EMP: 4 **EST:** 2003
SALES (est): 181.31K **Privately Held**
SIC: 2394 Canvas and related products

(G-11158)
CAROLINA CUSTOM TOWERS LLC
311 Facility Dr (28557-6322)
PHONE..........................252 671-3779
EMP: 7 **EST:** 2008
SALES (est): 290.93K **Privately Held**
SIC: 3441 Fabricated structural metal

(G-11159)
CARTERET PUBLISHING COMPANY (PA)
Also Called: This Week Magazine
5039 Executive Dr Ste 300 (28557-2579)
P.O. Box 1679 (28557-1679)
PHONE..........................252 726-7081
Bonnie Pollock, *Managing Editor*
Walter D Phillips, *
Lockwood B Phillips, *
EMP: 100 **EST:** 1944
SALES (est): 7.75MM
SALES (corp-wide): 7.75MM **Privately Held**
Web: www.carolinacoastonline.com
SIC: 2711 Newspapers, publishing and printing

(G-11160)
CASE-CLOSED INVESTIGATIONS
5032 Hwy 70 W (28557-4502)
P.O. Box 218 (28557-0218)
PHONE..........................336 794-2274
EMP: 6 **EST:** 2013
SALES (est): 156.56K **Privately Held**
Web: www.case-closed.com
SIC: 3523 Farm machinery and equipment

(G-11161)
CHRISTIAN FOCUS MAGAZINE
Also Called: Creative Clout Agency
706 Wagon Cir (28557-3172)
P.O. Box 102 (28557-0102)
PHONE..........................252 240-1656
Janet Landenburger, *Owner*
EMP: 5 **EST:** 2004
SALES (est): 116.1K **Privately Held**
SIC: 2721 Magazines: publishing only, not printed on site

(G-11162)
COASTAL AWNINGS INC
Also Called: Coastal Awngs Hrrcane Shutters
5300 High St Unit 0 (28557-4520)
PHONE..........................252 222-0707
Bobby Berckman, *Pr*
Judy Berckman, *Sec*
EMP: 13 **EST:** 1999
SALES (est): 820.13K **Privately Held**
Web: www.crystalcoastawnings.com
SIC: 2394 3442 Awnings, fabric: made from purchased materials; Louvers, shutters, jalousies, and similar items

(G-11163)
COASTAL PRESS INC
Also Called: Down East Printing
502 Arendell St (28557-4232)
PHONE..........................252 726-1549
Steve Brock, *Pr*
Chris Brock, *VP*
EMP: 7 **EST:** 1949
SQ FT: 2,600
SALES (est): 768.33K **Privately Held**
Web: www.coastalpressinc.com
SIC: 2759 5943 2791 2789 Letterpress printing; Office forms and supplies; Typesetting; Bookbinding and related work

(G-11164)
CONSUMER CONCEPTS
Also Called: ASAP Embroideries
1506 Bridges St (28557-3649)
PHONE..........................252 247-7000
Sara West, *Pr*
Nancy Carrier, *Prin*
EMP: 10 **EST:** 1976
SQ FT: 2,000
SALES (est): 2.4MM **Privately Held**
Web: www.ncpromotionalproducts.com
SIC: 5199 2759 3993 2396 Advertising specialties; Commercial printing, nec; Signs and advertising specialties; Automotive and apparel trimmings

(G-11165)
CRYSTAL COAST COMPOSITES INC (PA)
1707 River Dr (28557-6120)
PHONE..........................252 838-0025
William Brown Coulter, *Prin*
EMP: 5 **EST:** 2010
SALES (est): 240.14K
SALES (corp-wide): 240.14K **Privately Held**
Web: www.crystalcoastnc.org
SIC: 3732 Boatbuilding and repairing

(G-11166)
CULLIGAN WATER CONDITIONING
4911 Bridges St Ext (28557-8978)
PHONE..........................252 646-3800
EMP: 5 **EST:** 2019
SALES (est): 79.98K **Privately Held**
SIC: 3585 Refrigeration and heating equipment

(G-11167)
DEEP RIVER PRESS INC
412 Virginia Ave (28557-2662)
PHONE..........................910 249-9552
EMP: 4 **EST:** 2019
SALES (est): 101.1K **Privately Held**
SIC: 2741 Miscellaneous publishing

(G-11168)
DIVINE CREATIONS
216 Glenn Abby Dr (28557-2578)
PHONE..........................704 364-5844
Donna Snipes, *Owner*
EMP: 8 **EST:** 1988
SALES (est): 387.14K **Privately Held**
Web: www.divinecreationsusa.com
SIC: 2339 Women's and misses' outerwear, nec

(G-11169)
DUOCRAFT CABINETS & DIST CO (PA)
1306 Bridges St (28557-3757)
PHONE..........................252 240-1476
Alan Tate, *Prin*
EMP: 5 **EST:** 2006
SALES (est): 390.01K **Privately Held**
Web: www.duocraft.com
SIC: 2434 Wood kitchen cabinets

(G-11170)
EAST CAROLINA BRACE LIMB INC
209 N 35th St Ste 1 (28557-3179)
PHONE..........................252 726-8068
Cynthia T Monroe, *Brnch Mgr*
EMP: 9
SALES (corp-wide): 2.12MM **Privately Held**
Web: www.ecblnc.com
SIC: 3842 Limbs, artificial
PA: East Carolina Brace & Limb Co., Inc.
4110 M L King Jr Blvd C
New Bern NC 28562
252 638-1312

(G-11171)
ESKIMO 7 LIMITED
Also Called: Windows & More
5317 Hwy 70 W (28557-4509)
PHONE..........................252 726-8181
Sharon Yeomans, *Owner*
EMP: 7 **EST:** 2006
SALES (est): 732.44K **Privately Held**
Web: www.windows-and-more.com
SIC: 2426 Flooring, hardwood

(G-11172)
GOVERNMENT SALES LLC
4644 Arendell St Ste A (28557-2759)
PHONE..........................252 726-6315
Charles Robinson, *Managing Member*
EMP: 6 **EST:** 1993
SQ FT: 800
SALES (est): 2.4MM **Privately Held**
Web: www.governmentsalesllc.com
SIC: 5046 5193 5023 2599 Restaurant equipment and supplies, nec; Artificial flowers; Homefurnishings; Factory furniture and fixtures

(G-11173)
GWG BOATWORKS LLC
902 Oxford Dr (28557-3050)
PHONE..........................252 422-0757
Gary Gargone, *Owner*
EMP: 5 **EST:** 2017
SALES (est): 94.65K **Privately Held**
SIC: 3732 Boatbuilding and repairing

(G-11174)
HEIDELBERG MTLS STHAST AGG LLC
5101 Business Dr (28557-6313)
PHONE..........................252 222-0812
Joseph Martin, *Brnch Mgr*
EMP: 6
SALES (corp-wide): 21.19B **Privately Held**
Web: www.hansonbiz.com
SIC: 1423 Crushed and broken granite
HQ: Heidelberg Materials Southeast Agg Llc
3237 Satellite Blvd # 30
Duluth GA 30096
770 491-2756

(G-11175)
HERALD PRINTING INC
201 N 17th St (28557-3627)
PHONE..........................252 726-3534
Pete Wenk, *Pr*
EMP: 9 **EST:** 1983
SQ FT: 1,000
SALES (est): 176.3K **Privately Held**
SIC: 2752 2759 Offset printing; Commercial printing, nec

(G-11176)
HERITAGE CABINET COMPANY INC
5030 Business Dr (28557-6327)
P.O. Box 127 (28557-0127)
PHONE..........................252 648-8151
EMP: 10 **EST:** 2008
SALES (est): 458.12K **Privately Held**
Web: www.hercabcon.com
SIC: 2434 Wood kitchen cabinets

(G-11177)
IVP FOREST PRODUCTS LLC
125 Horton Dr (28557-4528)
PHONE..........................252 241-8126
Ingrid Pfaff-niebauer, *CEO*
Carl Heinz Pfaff, *CSO*
◆ **EMP:** 15 **EST:** 2012
SALES (est): 1.85MM **Privately Held**
Web: www.ivplogs.com
SIC: 2411 0831 Wooden logs; Gathering of forest products

(G-11178)
JONES BROTHERS MARINE MFG INC
Also Called: Jbm Manufacturing
100 Bateau Blvd (28557-6314)
PHONE..........................252 240-1995
Mary Raines Jones, *VP*
Donnie H Jones Iii, *Pr*
EMP: 10 **EST:** 1993
SQ FT: 46,520
SALES (est): 809.45K **Privately Held**
Web: www.jonesbrothersmarine.com
SIC: 3732 Motorized boat, building and repairing

(G-11179)
KNOOOSC INC
208 Lord Granville Dr (28557-8952)

PHONE..............................415 640-0080
George Iv, *CEO*
EMP: 4
SALES (est): 182.43K **Privately Held**
SIC: 3732 7389 Yachts, building and repairing; Business services, nec

(G-11180)
KNUCKLEHEADZ KUSTOMZ INC
5306 High St (28557-4520)
PHONE..............................252 646-3354
Scott Grady, *Owner*
EMP: 8 **EST:** 2010
SALES (est): 108.28K **Privately Held**
Web: www.knuckleheadzkustomz.com
SIC: 3444 Sheet metalwork

(G-11181)
LAMCO MACHINE TOOL INC
135 Industrial Dr (28557-8481)
P.O. Box 2357 (28557-2357)
PHONE..............................252 247-4360
Lois Fowler, *Pr*
EMP: 15 **EST:** 1990
SQ FT: 40,000
SALES (est): 1.46MM **Privately Held**
Web: www.lamcomachine.com
SIC: 3089 Injection molding of plastics

(G-11182)
LOOKOUT BOAT WINDOW FRAMES LLC
2500 Bridges St Ste W19 (28557-3386)
PHONE..............................252 723-2222
EMP: 4 **EST:** 2019
SALES (est): 188.58K **Privately Held**
Web: www.boatwindowframes.com
SIC: 5031 2431 Windows; Door frames, wood

(G-11183)
NCOAST COMMUNICATIONS (PA)
Also Called: Coaster Magazine Carteret Cnty
201 N 17th St (28557-3627)
PHONE..............................252 247-7442
Jennifer Star, *Pr*
EMP: 19 **EST:** 1984
SALES (est): 1.94MM **Privately Held**
SIC: 2721 Magazines: publishing only, not printed on site

(G-11184)
QUILLEN WELDING SERVICES LLC
110 Bonner Ave (28557-3212)
PHONE..............................252 269-4908
Jared Quillen, *Pr*
EMP: 6 **EST:** 2017
SALES (est): 175K **Privately Held**
Web: www.quillenwelding.com
SIC: 7692 Welding repair

(G-11185)
QWS LLC
110 Bonner Ave (28557-3212)
PHONE..............................252 723-2106
Jared Quillen, *Managing Member*
EMP: 25 **EST:** 2017
SALES (est): 1.22MM **Privately Held**
Web: www.quillenwelding.com
SIC: 3548 Electric welding equipment

(G-11186)
S & W READY MIX CON CO LLC
5161 Business Dr (28557-6313)
PHONE..............................252 726-2566
EMP: 15
SALES (corp-wide): 8.01MM **Privately Held**
SIC: 3273 Ready-mixed concrete

HQ: S & W Ready Mix Concrete Company Llc
217 Lisbon St
Clinton NC 28328
910 592-1733

(G-11187)
SEA STRIKER INC
158 Little Nine Rd (28557-8482)
P.O. Box 459 (28557-0459)
PHONE..............................252 247-4113
Phyllis Henry, *Pr*
Troy D Henry Junior, *VP*
Troy D Henry Iii, *Stockholder*
Phillip Henry, *Stockholder*
◆ **EMP:** 20 **EST:** 1992
SQ FT: 8,000
SALES (est): 357.43K **Privately Held**
Web: www.calcuttaoutdoors.com
SIC: 3949 Fishing tackle, general

(G-11188)
SEW TRENDY
3906b Arendell St (28557-2924)
PHONE..............................252 240-9796
Phil Panzarella, *Mgr*
EMP: 5 **EST:** 2016
SALES (est): 45.04K **Privately Held**
SIC: 2399 Fabricated textile products, nec

(G-11189)
SHEARLINE BOATWORKS LLC
127 Hestron Dr (28557-6303)
P.O. Box 579 (28557-0579)
PHONE..............................252 726-6916
EMP: 8 **EST:** 2000
SALES (est): 642.78K **Privately Held**
Web: www.shearlineboatworks.com
SIC: 3732 Boats, fiberglass: building and repairing

(G-11190)
SIMMONS CSTM CBNETRY MLLWK INC
5312 High St (28557-4520)
PHONE..............................252 240-1020
Daniel Simmons, *Pr*
EMP: 6 **EST:** 2017
SALES (est): 205.84K **Privately Held**
Web: www.simmonscustomcabinetryandmillwork.com
SIC: 2434 Wood kitchen cabinets

(G-11191)
SOUTHEAST BLASTG & COATING LLC
1705 Olde Farm Rd (28557-0029)
PHONE..............................252 725-0010
Trey Perry, *Prin*
EMP: 5 **EST:** 2017
SALES (est): 81.52K **Privately Held**
SIC: 3479 Coating of metals and formed products

(G-11192)
SOUTHEASTERN ELEVATOR LLC
143 Industrial Dr (28557-8481)
P.O. Box 2148 (28557-2148)
PHONE..............................252 726-9983
EMP: 6 **EST:** 2013
SALES (est): 445.49K **Privately Held**
Web: www.southeasternelevatorllc.com
SIC: 1796 3534 Elevator installation and conversion; Elevators and equipment

(G-11193)
SURGICAL CENTER OF MOREHEA
3714 Guardian Ave Ste W (28557-2975)
PHONE..............................252 247-0314

Thomas Bates, *Pr*
EMP: 14 **EST:** 2011
SALES (est): 1.53MM **Privately Held**
Web: www.surgicalcenterofmhc.com
SIC: 3842 8011 Trusses, orthopedic and surgical; Plastic surgeon

(G-11194)
TAYLOR BOAT WORKS
200 Pensacola Ave (28557-2730)
P.O. Box 1346 (28557-1346)
PHONE..............................252 726-6374
John Mc Callum, *Owner*
EMP: 6 **EST:** 1965
SALES (est): 344.67K **Privately Held**
SIC: 3732 Boatbuilding and repairing

(G-11195)
V M TRUCKING INC
4915 Arendell St (28557-2659)
PHONE..............................984 239-4853
Franco Hill, *Pr*
EMP: 4 **EST:** 2017
SALES (est): 256.32K **Privately Held**
SIC: 4212 3537 7513 Dump truck haulage; Trucks: freight, baggage, etc.: industrial, except mining; Truck leasing, without drivers

Morganton
Burke County

(G-11196)
ALL 4 U HOME MEDICAL LLC
617 S Green St Ste 100 (28655-3517)
P.O. Box 1393 (28680-1393)
PHONE..............................828 437-0684
Jerrol Smith, *Managing Member*
Wesley Smith, *Opers Mgr*
Laura Clark, *Treas*
EMP: 8 **EST:** 2010
SQ FT: 2,800
SALES (est): 978.7K **Privately Held**
Web: www.all4uhomemedical.com
SIC: 5999 3842 Medical apparatus and supplies; Wheelchairs

(G-11197)
AMERICAN ROLLER BEARING INC (HQ) ✪
307 Burke Dr (28655-5334)
PHONE..............................828 624-1460
Michael J Connors, *Pr*
Hansal N Patel, *Sec*
Teresa L Wilson, *Treas*
EMP: 13 **EST:** 2022
SALES (est): 45.94MM
SALES (corp-wide): 4.77B **Publicly Held**
SIC: 3562 Roller bearings and parts
PA: The Timken Company
4500 Mount Pleasant St Nw
North Canton OH 44720
234 262-3000

(G-11198)
ARPRO M-TEC LLC
Also Called: Whole Sale Printing Inks
212 E Fleming Dr (28655-3676)
PHONE..............................828 433-0699
EMP: 15 **EST:** 2011
SALES (est): 1.36MM **Privately Held**
Web: www.arproinks.com
SIC: 2893 Printing ink

(G-11199)
BAREFOOT CNC INC
Also Called: H D Technologies
333 Sanford Dr (28655-2555)
PHONE..............................828 438-5038
James Wakeford, *Pr*

EMP: 7 **EST:** 1997
SALES (est): 1.09MM **Privately Held**
Web: www.barefootcnc.com
SIC: 5734 3451 Software, business and non-game; Screw machine products

(G-11200)
BEDARD CUSTOM WOODWORKS
1513 Southpointe Dr (28655-6141)
P.O. Box 1655 (28680-1655)
PHONE..............................828 432-6556
EMP: 4 **EST:** 2008
SALES (est): 126.97K **Privately Held**
SIC: 2431 Millwork

(G-11201)
BEELITE INC
3292 Norman Dr (28655-8865)
PHONE..............................828 584-1488
Timothy Trescott, *Pr*
EMP: 7 **EST:** 2017
SALES (est): 233.45K **Privately Held**
Web: www.beelitecandles.com
SIC: 3999 Candles

(G-11202)
BORDEN CHEMICAL
Also Called: Borden
114 Industrial Blvd (28655-8285)
PHONE..............................828 584-3800
Rooney Borden, *Prin*
EMP: 7 **EST:** 2014
SALES (est): 146.57K **Privately Held**
SIC: 2819 Industrial inorganic chemicals, nec

(G-11203)
BURKE VENEERS INC
2170 Fr Coffey Rd (28655-9399)
PHONE..............................828 437-8510
Wendell Powell, *Pr*
Carolyn Powell, *
EMP: 20 **EST:** 1980
SQ FT: 10,500
SALES (est): 885.71K **Privately Held**
SIC: 2435 Hardwood veneer and plywood

(G-11204)
CHESTERFIELD WOOD PRODUCTS INC
1810 Us 64 (28655-8868)
P.O. Box 1792 (28680-1792)
PHONE..............................828 433-0042
Wendell Powell, *Pr*
Robin Powell, *Sec*
EMP: 13 **EST:** 1991
SQ FT: 20,000
SALES (est): 1.08MM **Privately Held**
SIC: 2499 2435 Furniture inlays (veneers); Hardwood veneer and plywood

(G-11205)
CITY OF MORGANTON
100 Coulter St (28655-4114)
PHONE..............................828 584-1460
EMP: 10
Web: ci.morganton.nc.us
SIC: 3569 Filters
PA: City Of Morganton
305 E Union St Ste A100
Morganton NC 28655
828 438-5376

(G-11206)
COMMERCIAL PRTG SOLUTUTIONS
3640 Nc 18 S (28655-7445)
PHONE..............................828 764-4137
EMP: 4 **EST:** 2017
SALES (est): 83.91K **Privately Held**
SIC: 2752 Commercial printing, lithographic

Morganton - Burke County (G-11207)

(G-11207)
CONSOLIDATED ELEC DISTRS INC
Also Called: Ced
208 W Fleming Dr Ste D (28655-3969)
PHONE..................................828 433-4689
EMP: 6
SALES (corp-wide): 1.5B Privately Held
Web: www.cedcareers.com
SIC: 5099 3699 Firearms and ammunition, except sporting; High-energy particle physics equipment
PA: Consolidated Electrical Distributors, Inc.
    1920 Westridge Dr
    Irving TX 75038
    972 582-5300

(G-11208)
CONTINENTAL AUTO SYSTEMS INC
Also Called: Continental Teves
1103 Jamestown Rd (28655-9285)
PHONE..................................828 584-4500
David Jones, *Brnch Mgr*
EMP: 252
SALES (corp-wide): 40.93B Privately Held
Web: www.continental-automotive.com
SIC: 3714 Motor vehicle brake systems and parts
HQ: Continental Automotive Systems, Inc.
    1 Continental Dr
    Auburn Hills MI 48326
    248 393-5300

(G-11209)
DYNAMIC FABRICATION & WLDG INC
4620 Amber Ln (28655-7908)
PHONE..................................828 390-8377
EMP: 4 EST: 2019
SALES (est): 27.6K Privately Held
SIC: 7692 Welding repair

(G-11210)
E J VICTOR INC (PA)
Also Called: E J Victor Furniture
110 Wamsutta Mill Rd (28655-5551)
P.O. Box 309 (28680-0309)
PHONE..................................828 437-1991
John Victor Jokinen, *Pr*
Edward W Phifer Iii, *Sr VP*
Daniel C Breeden, *
William G Morrison Junior, *VP*
◆ EMP: 160 EST: 1989
SQ FT: 232,000
SALES (est): 24.34MM Privately Held
Web: www.ejvictor.com
SIC: 2512 2511 Couches, sofas, and davenports: upholstered on wood frames; Dining room furniture: wood

(G-11211)
EMERY CORPORATION
1523 N Green St (28655-6744)
P.O. Box 1104 (28680-1104)
PHONE..................................828 433-1536
Beverly Emery, *CEO*
Mark Emery, *
Meryl Taulbee, *
Ronald Emery, *
Sheryl Emery Burdick, *
◆ EMP: 75 EST: 1955
SQ FT: 80,000
SALES (est): 9.85MM Privately Held
Web: www.emerycorp.com
SIC: 3542 3545 3544 Machine tools, metal forming type; Gauges (machine tool accessories); Jigs: inspection, gauging, and checking

(G-11212)
ENVIRONMENTAL INKS AND COATINGS CANADA LTD
1 Quality Products Rd (28655-4759)
PHONE..................................828 433-1922
▲ EMP: 200
Web: www.siegwerk.com
SIC: 2893 Printing ink

(G-11213)
FERGUSON CABINET WORKS
4188 Nc 181 (28655-7597)
P.O. Box 925 (28680-0925)
PHONE..................................828 433-8710
James Ferguson, *Owner*
EMP: 4 EST: 1987
SQ FT: 7,000
SALES (est): 193.63K Privately Held
Web: www.fergusoncabinetworks.com
SIC: 2434 Wood kitchen cabinets

(G-11214)
G & G MOULDING INC
Also Called: G and G Art and Frame
801 N Green St (28655-5611)
P.O. Box 830 (28680-0830)
PHONE..................................828 438-1112
▲ EMP: 37
Web: www.internationalmoulding.com
SIC: 5023 2499 5719 Decorative home furnishings and supplies; Picture and mirror frames, wood; Lighting, lamps, and accessories

(G-11215)
GERRESHEIMER GLASS INC
114 Wamsutta Mill Rd (28655-5551)
PHONE..................................828 433-5000
Jim Baldwin, *Mgr*
EMP: 17
SALES (corp-wide): 2.1B Privately Held
Web: www.gerresheimer.com
SIC: 3221 3231 Glass containers; Products of purchased glass
HQ: Gerresheimer Glass Inc.
    537 Crystal Ave
    Vineland NJ 08360

(G-11216)
GRAPHX PRINTING INC
1243 Burkemont Ave Ste A (28655-4560)
PHONE..................................828 475-4970
EMP: 5 EST: 2019
SALES (est): 81.43K Privately Held
Web: www.graphxinc.com
SIC: 2752 Commercial printing, lithographic

(G-11217)
GUY CHADDOCK AND COMPANY LLC
Also Called: Chaddock Home
100 Reep Dr (28655-8441)
PHONE..................................828 584-0664
Andrew Crone, *Pr*
EMP: 200 EST: 2004
SALES (est): 8.86MM Privately Held
SIC: 2511 Wood household furniture

(G-11218)
HAIRFIELD WILBERT BURIAL VLT
3098 Morganton Furniture Rd (28655)
P.O. Box 146 (28680-0146)
PHONE..................................828 437-4319
Joseph B Hairfield, *Pr*
Steven Hairfield, *VP*
EMP: 21 EST: 1952
SQ FT: 7,500
SALES (est): 847.62K Privately Held
SIC: 3272 Burial vaults, concrete or precast terrazzo

(G-11219)
HEXION INC
114 Industrial Blvd (28655-8285)
PHONE..................................828 584-3800
EMP: 20
SQ FT: 1,872
SALES (corp-wide): 1.26B Privately Held
Web: www.hexion.com
SIC: 2821 Plastics materials and resins
PA: Hexion Inc.
    180 E Broad St
    Columbus OH 43215
    888 443-9466

(G-11220)
HFI WIND DOWN INC
109 E Fleming Dr 7 (28655-3675)
PHONE..................................828 438-5767
EMP: 180
SQ FT: 1,707
SALES (corp-wide): 511.79MM Privately Held
SIC: 5712 2512 2426 Furniture stores; Upholstered household furniture; Hardwood dimension and flooring mills
PA: Hfi Wind Down, Inc.
    1925 Eastchester Dr
    High Point NC 27265
    336 888-4800

(G-11221)
HFI WIND DOWN INC
410 Hogan St (28655-3616)
PHONE..................................828 430-3355
EMP: 133
SALES (corp-wide): 511.79MM Privately Held
SIC: 2511 Wood household furniture
PA: Hfi Wind Down, Inc.
    1925 Eastchester Dr
    High Point NC 27265
    336 888-4800

(G-11222)
ICE RIVER SPRINGS USA INC (HQ)
Also Called: Ice River Springs Water
601 E Union St (28655-3457)
PHONE..................................519 925-2929
EMP: 11 EST: 2005
SALES (est): 44.22MM
SALES (corp-wide): 143.34MM Privately Held
SIC: 2086 Water, natural: packaged in cans, bottles, etc.
PA: Ice River Springs Water Co. Inc
    485387 Sideroad 30 Dufferin County Rd 11
    Shelburne ON
    844 764-7336

(G-11223)
JACKSON CORRUGATED LLC
1000 Chain Dr (28655-7239)
PHONE..................................828 608-0931
EMP: 51 EST: 2019
SALES (est): 15.84MM Privately Held
Web: www.sustainablecorrugated.com
SIC: 2653 Boxes, corrugated: made from purchased materials
PA: Jackson Paper Manufacturing Company
    152 W Main St
    Sylva NC 28779

(G-11224)
JAMES TOOL MACHINE & ENGRG INC (PA)
Also Called: James Tool Company
130 Reep Dr (28655-8441)
P.O. Box 1665 (28680-1665)
PHONE..................................828 584-8722
Jeff Toner, *Pr*
Elizabeth Burleson, *
Kevin Moses, *
Tim King, *
▲ EMP: 115 EST: 1987
SALES (est): 23.23MM
SALES (corp-wide): 23.23MM Privately Held
Web: www.jamestool.com
SIC: 3599 3724 3728 3764 Machine and other job shop work; Aircraft engines and engine parts; Aircraft parts and equipment, nec; Space propulsion units and parts

(G-11225)
JARRETT BROTHERS
200 Carbondale Ln (28655-4381)
PHONE..................................828 433-8036
Kirby Jarrett, *Pt*
Michael Jarrett, *Pt*
▼ EMP: 9 EST: 1979
SQ FT: 8,000
SALES (est): 399.02K Privately Held
SIC: 2512 Upholstered household furniture

(G-11226)
JE EKORNES USA INC
115 Wamsutta Mill Rd (28655-5524)
PHONE..................................828 764-4001
Rolf Aarseth, *Pr*
Randall Tallent, *
Christopher R Casey, *
◆ EMP: 74 EST: 2011
SQ FT: 100,000
SALES (est): 10.18MM
SALES (corp-wide): 2.67MM Privately Held
Web: www.ekornes.com
SIC: 2426 Carvings, furniture: wood
HQ: Ekornes As
    Industrivegen 1
    Ikornnes 6222

(G-11227)
LEGACY VULCAN LLC
Mideast Division
Causby Quarry Rd (28655)
P.O. Box 69 (28680-0069)
PHONE..................................828 437-2616
EMP: 5
Web: www.vulcanmaterials.com
SIC: 3273 Ready-mixed concrete
HQ: Legacy Vulcan, Llc
    1200 Urban Center Dr
    Vestavia AL 35242
    205 298-3000

(G-11228)
LEVITON MANUFACTURING CO INC
113 Industrial Blvd (28655-8285)
PHONE..................................828 584-1611
Leonard Causby, *Brnch Mgr*
EMP: 24
SALES (corp-wide): 1.46B Privately Held
Web: www.leviton.com
SIC: 3643 3357 Current-carrying wiring services; Nonferrous wiredrawing and insulating
PA: Leviton Manufacturing Co., Inc.
    201 N Service Rd
    Melville NY 11747
    800 323-8920

(G-11229)
LLC FERGUSON COPELAND (HQ)
Also Called: Chaddock
100 Reep Dr (28655-8441)
P.O. Box 10 (28680-0010)
PHONE..................................828 584-0664
◆ EMP: 120 EST: 1996
SQ FT: 110,000

GEOGRAPHIC SECTION
Morganton - Burke County (G-11254)

SALES (est): 24.96MM
SALES (corp-wide): 25.47MM **Privately Held**
Web: www.fergusoncopeland.com
SIC: 2512 Chairs: upholstered on wood frames
PA: Eighteen Seventy Corporation
  1700 E Putnam Ave Ste 202
  Old Greenwich CT 06870
  203 769-1873

(G-11230)
MAIA LLC
Also Called: Maia Stave
3327 Henderson Mill Rd (28655-8710)
PHONE 828 612-6109
EMP: 5 **EST:** 2019
SALES (est): 88.01K **Privately Held**
Web: www.maiawine.com
SIC: 2084 Wines

(G-11231)
MATERIAL RETURN LLC
Also Called: Chrysalis
647 Hopewell Rd (28655-8267)
P.O. Box 71 (28680-0071)
PHONE 828 234-5368
EMP: 7 **EST:** 2018
SALES (est): 406.34K **Privately Held**
Web: www.thematerialreturn.com
SIC: 2282 Acetate filament yarn: throwing, twisting, winding, spooling

(G-11232)
MERITOR INC
105 Wamsutta Mill Rd (28655-5552)
PHONE 828 433-4600
Brad Kendall, *Manager*
EMP: 250
SQ FT: 5,970
SALES (corp-wide): 34.06B **Publicly Held**
Web: www.meritor.com
SIC: 3312 3714 3713 Axles, rolled or forged: made in steel mills; Motor vehicle parts and accessories; Truck and bus bodies
HQ: Meritor, Inc.
  2135 W Maple Rd
  Troy MI 48084

(G-11233)
MGE PRODUCTS LLC
4830 Crawley Dale St (28655-9624)
PHONE 828 443-3214
EMP: 4 **EST:** 2017
SALES (est): 39.69K **Privately Held**
SIC: 3999 Manufacturing industries, nec

(G-11234)
MOLDED FIBR GL CMPNY/NRTH CRLI
Also Called: Molded Fiber Glass
213 Reep Dr (28655-8253)
PHONE 828 584-4974
Richard S Morrison, *Pr*
Joseph A Cotman, *
Stuart W Cordell, *
EMP: 215 **EST:** 1994
SQ FT: 110,000
SALES (est): 49.89MM
SALES (corp-wide): 360.86MM **Privately Held**
Web: www.moldedfiberglass.com
SIC: 3089 Air mattresses, plastics
PA: Molded Fiber Glass Companies
  2925 Mfg Pl
  Ashtabula OH 44004
  440 997-5851

(G-11235)
MORGANTON SERVICE LEAGUE INC
Also Called: Morganton Service League
112 Terrace Pl (28655-3774)
P.O. Box 792 (28680-0792)
PHONE 828 439-9525
Vivian Radford, *Pr*
Katherine M Lindquist, *Dir*
EMP: 8 **EST:** 1989
SALES (est): 114.13K **Privately Held**
Web: www.morganton.com
SIC: 2711 Newspapers, publishing and printing

(G-11236)
MULLS CON & SEPTIC TANKS INC
Also Called: Mull's Concrete & Septic Tanks
2416 Mount Home Church Rd (28655-6405)
PHONE 828 437-0959
Richard Mulls, *Pr*
Susan Mulls, *VP*
EMP: 8 **EST:** 1969
SALES (est): 482.49K **Privately Held**
SIC: 7699 3273 Septic tank cleaning service; Ready-mixed concrete

(G-11237)
MYERS BROTHERS LOGGING LLC
1222 Myers Ridge Ln S (28655-0136)
PHONE 828 432-9738
EMP: 4 **EST:** 2018
SALES (est): 234.86K **Privately Held**
SIC: 2411 Logging camps and contractors

(G-11238)
NELSON RODRIGUEZ
341 E Parker Rd (28655-5112)
PHONE 828 433-1223
Nelson Rodriguez, *Prin*
EMP: 7 **EST:** 2010
SALES (est): 121.85K **Privately Held**
SIC: 3843 Enamels, dentists'

(G-11239)
NORELL INC
1377 Old Dry Creek Rd (28655-0002)
P.O. Box 1707 (28680-1707)
PHONE 828 584-2600
Gregory Norell, *Ch*
Theresa Norell, *VP*
EMP: 8 **EST:** 1967
SALES (est): 726.9K **Privately Held**
Web: shop.nmrtubes.com
SIC: 3231 2821 Laboratory glassware; Polytetrafluoroethylene resins, teflon

(G-11240)
OPTICONCEPTS INC
911 W Union St (28655-4253)
PHONE 828 874-0667
Chris Tons, *Mgr*
EMP: 7 **EST:** 2015
SALES (est): 90.27K **Privately Held**
Web: www.opticoncepts.com
SIC: 3229 Pressed and blown glass, nec

(G-11241)
PACKAGING CORPORATION AMERICA
Also Called: Pca/Morganton 354
114 Dixie Blvd (28655-8244)
PHONE 828 584-1511
Rich De Augustinis, *Brnch Mgr*
EMP: 74
SALES (corp-wide): 8.48B **Publicly Held**
Web: www.packagingcorp.com
SIC: 2653 Boxes, corrugated: made from purchased materials
PA: Packaging Corporation Of America
  1 N Field Ct
  Lake Forest IL 60045
  847 482-3000

(G-11242)
PPG ARCHITECTURAL FINISHES INC
Also Called: Glidden Professional Paint Ctr
511 Burkemont Ave (28655-4409)
PHONE 828 438-9210
Richard Sharp, *Mgr*
EMP: 5
SALES (corp-wide): 17.65B **Publicly Held**
Web: www.glidden.com
SIC: 2851 Paints and allied products
HQ: Ppg Architectural Finishes, Inc.
  1 Ppg Pl
  Pittsburgh PA 15272
  412 434-3131

(G-11243)
R & R IRONWORKS INC
Also Called: R&R Iron Works
501 Salem Rd (28655-4718)
PHONE 828 448-0524
Roy Moseley, *Pr*
EMP: 10 **EST:** 2014
SALES (est): 988.99K **Privately Held**
Web: www.rrironworks.com
SIC: 3441 Expansion joints (structural shapes), iron or steel

(G-11244)
R S SKILLEN
2080 Us 70 E (28655-8952)
PHONE 828 433-5353
Kwang Chung, *Prin*
EMP: 6 **EST:** 2007
SALES (est): 100.65K **Privately Held**
SIC: 3728 Aircraft parts and equipment, nec

(G-11245)
R S WELDING LLC
5697 Morris Loop (28655-8606)
PHONE 828 437-0768
Ricky E Smith, *Owner*
EMP: 5 **EST:** 2017
SALES (est): 44.95K **Privately Held**
SIC: 7692 Welding repair

(G-11246)
ROBERT BERGELIN COMPANY (PA)
120 S Sterling St (28655-3441)
PHONE 828 437-6409
EMP: 25 **EST:** 1995
SQ FT: 48,000
SALES (est): 1.44MM **Privately Held**
Web: www.rbcfurn.com
SIC: 2511 Wood household furniture

(G-11247)
RONALD
205 N Sterling St (28655-3344)
PHONE 828 433-1377
EMP: 4 **EST:** 2017
SALES (est): 86.6K **Privately Held**
SIC: 2752 Offset printing

(G-11248)
S&S WELDING
105 Old Hickory Dr (28655-2771)
PHONE 828 408-2794
EMP: 4 **EST:** 2014
SALES (est): 33.06K **Privately Held**
SIC: 7692 Welding repair

(G-11249)
SACK-UPS CORPORATION
Also Called: Sandviper
1611 Jamestown Rd (28655-9289)
P.O. Box 3051 (28680-3051)
PHONE 828 584-4579
Warren Norman, *VP*
EMP: 10 **EST:** 2014
SQ FT: 20,000
SALES (est): 817.93K **Privately Held**
Web: www.sackups.com
SIC: 2282 Knitting yarn: twisting, winding, or spooling

(G-11250)
SEIREN NORTH AMERICA LLC (HQ)
1500 E Union St (28655-5325)
P.O. Box 130 (28680-0130)
PHONE 828 430-3456
Jeff Kale, *
▲ **EMP:** 19 **EST:** 2001
SQ FT: 437,000
SALES (est): 48.19MM **Privately Held**
Web: www.seiren-na.com
SIC: 2221 Automotive fabrics, manmade fiber
PA: Seiren Co.,Ltd.
  1-10-1, Keya
  Fukui FKI 918-8

(G-11251)
SGL CARBON LLC
Also Called: S G L Carbon
307 Jamestown Rd (28655-9948)
PHONE 828 437-3221
Andy Stinson, *Genl Mgr*
EMP: 4
SALES (corp-wide): 1.18B **Privately Held**
Web: www.sglcarbon.com
SIC: 3624 3823 Carbon and graphite products; Process control instruments
HQ: Sgl Carbon, Llc
  10715 David Taylor Dr # 4
  Charlotte NC 28262
  704 593-5100

(G-11252)
SHERRILL FURNITURE COMPANY
Also Called: Motioncraft By Sherrill Div
516 Drexel Rd (28655-8949)
P.O. Box 9145 (28603-9145)
PHONE 828 437-2256
Johnny Suddreth, *Brnch Mgr*
EMP: 12
SQ FT: 52,000
SALES (corp-wide): 104.33MM **Privately Held**
Web: www.sherrillfurniture.com
SIC: 2512 Upholstered household furniture
PA: Sherrill Furniture Company Inc
  2405 Highland Ave Ne
  Hickory NC 28601
  828 322-2640

(G-11253)
SIEGWERK EIC LLC (DH)
Also Called: Environmental Inks
1 Quality Products Rd (28655-4759)
PHONE 800 368-4657
Herbert Forkner, *CEO*
▲ **EMP:** 11 **EST:** 2010
SALES (est): 13.79MM
SALES (corp-wide): 2.67MM **Privately Held**
Web: www.siegwerk.com
SIC: 2893 Printing ink
HQ: Siegwerk Usa Inc.
  3535 Sw 56th St
  Des Moines IA 50321
  515 471-2100

(G-11254)
SKELLY INC
628 E Meeting St (28655-3435)
P.O. Box 3853 (28680-3853)
PHONE 828 433-7070

Morganton - Burke County (G-11255)

Robert Skelly, *Pr*
EMP: 11 EST: 2003
SALES (est): 1.01MM **Privately Held**
Web: www.skellyinc.net
SIC: **3069** Foam rubber

(G-11255)
SOUTH MOUNTAIN CRAFTS
Also Called: Craft Village
300 Enola Rd (28655-4608)
PHONE..................828 433-2607
June Hollingsworth, *Mgr*
EMP: 8 EST: 2001
SALES (est): 248.96K **Privately Held**
SIC: **2511** 3944 5999 Wood household furniture; Craft and hobby kits and sets; Miscellaneous retail stores, nec

(G-11256)
SOUTHERN DEVICES INC
113 Industrial Blvd (28655-8285)
PHONE..................828 584-1611
Grady Redis, *Prin*
EMP: 6 EST: 2014
SALES (est): 97.91K **Privately Held**
SIC: **3643** Current-carrying wiring services

(G-11257)
STEVE NOGGLE TURNED WOOD
638 Enola Rd (28655-7635)
PHONE..................828 437-8017
EMP: 5 EST: 2014
SALES (est): 57.47K **Privately Held**
Web: www.stevenoggle.com
SIC: **2431** Millwork

(G-11258)
SUPERIOR VENEERS INC
1405 Mountain Shadows Dr (28655-9617)
PHONE..................828 433-6986
Virgil Crawley, *Pr*
Hazel Crawley, *VP*
Tanya Crawley-yearick, *Sec*
EMP: 18 EST: 1972
SALES (est): 953.81K **Privately Held**
SIC: **2435** Hardwood veneer and plywood

(G-11259)
T DISTRIBUTION NC INC
Also Called: International Moulding NC
801 N Green St (28655-5611)
PHONE..................828 438-1112
Jason Whisnant, *Pr*
EMP: 28 EST: 2014
SQ FT: 82,000
SALES (est): 5MM
SALES (corp-wide): 5MM **Privately Held**
SIC: **5023** 2499 Frames and framing, picture and mirror; Picture frame molding, finished
PA: International Mouldings, Inc.
33 Omega St S
Birmingham AL 35205
205 324-5783

(G-11260)
TABLE ROCK PRINTERS LLC
205 N Sterling St (28655-3344)
PHONE..................828 433-1377
Ronald Perry, *Owner*
EMP: 5 EST: 1986
SALES (est): 361.77K **Privately Held**
Web: www.tablerockprinters.com
SIC: **2752** Offset printing

(G-11261)
TONER MACHINING TECH INC
1523 N Green St (28655-6744)
P.O. Box 2876 (28680-2876)
PHONE..................828 432-8007
James C Toner Junior, *Pr*

EMP: 80 EST: 2001
SQ FT: 25,000
SALES (est): 15MM **Privately Held**
Web: www.tonermachining.com
SIC: **3469** 3544 3545 Machine parts, stamped or pressed metal; Special dies, tools, jigs, and fixtures; Machine tool accessories

(G-11262)
TONER MACHINING TECHNOLOGIES
212 E Fleming Dr (28655-3676)
P.O. Box 2876 (28680-2876)
PHONE..................828 432-8007
EMP: 10
SALES (est): 254.85K **Privately Held**
Web: www.tonermachining.com
SIC: **3599** Machine shop, jobbing and repair

(G-11263)
UNIX PACKAGING LLC
100 Ceramic Tile Dr (28655-6772)
PHONE..................310 877-7979
Kouresh Melamed, *Pr*
EMP: 21 EST: 2020
SALES (est): 1.26MM **Privately Held**
Web: www.unixpackaging.com
SIC: **2086** Mineral water, carbonated: packaged in cans, bottles, etc.

(G-11264)
VEKA EAST INC
90 Ceramic Tile Dr (28655-6734)
PHONE..................800 654-5589
EMP: 496 EST: 2017
SALES (est): 5.7MM
SALES (corp-wide): 1.92B **Privately Held**
Web: www.vekainc.com
SIC: **3089** Injection molding of plastics
HQ: Veka Inc.
100 Veka Dr
Fombell PA 16123
800 654-5589

(G-11265)
VLR LLC
Also Called: Stone & Leigh Furniture
1020 N Green St (28655-9029)
PHONE..................252 355-4610
Brad Garner, *Managing Member*
EMP: 31 EST: 2018
SQ FT: 25,000
SALES (est): 4.54MM **Privately Held**
SIC: **2211** Upholstery fabrics, cotton

(G-11266)
VX AEROSPACE CORPORATION
2080 Us 70 E (28655-8952)
PHONE..................828 433-5353
Raymond Jones, *Pr*
Robert Skillen, *CEO*
EMP: 14 EST: 2006
SALES (est): 2.03MM **Privately Held**
Web: www.vxaerospace.com
SIC: **3721** 3728 Research and development on aircraft by the manufacturer; Aircraft parts and equipment, nec

(G-11267)
VX AEROSPACE HOLDINGS INC
2080 Us 70 E (28655)
PHONE..................828 433-5353
Robert Skillen, *CEO*
EMP: 10 EST: 2016
SALES (est): 514.94K **Privately Held**
Web: www.vxaerospace.com
SIC: **3721** Helicopters

(G-11268)
WB EMBROIDERY INC
Also Called: Wendy Bs Cstm EMB Screen Prtg
3076 Nc 18 S (28655-7476)
PHONE..................828 432-0076
Wendy Bradshaw, *Pr*
Linda Norville, *Sec*
EMP: 5 EST: 2004
SQ FT: 4,300
SALES (est): 420.12K **Privately Held**
Web: www.wbembinc.com
SIC: **2395** Embroidery products, except Schiffli machine

(G-11269)
WOLFPIT TACTICAL
1528 N Green St (28655-6744)
PHONE..................828 234-1279
John Hamer, *Prin*
EMP: 5 EST: 2016
SALES (est): 64.6K **Privately Held**
SIC: **3489** Ordnance and accessories, nec

(G-11270)
WOODYS WELDING LLC
4576 Saint Pauls Church Rd (28655-7850)
PHONE..................828 391-1484
Christopher Steven Woody, *Prin*
EMP: 5 EST: 2018
SALES (est): 95.81K **Privately Held**
SIC: **7692** Welding repair

Morrisville
Wake County

(G-11271)
3SHAPE INC
2800 Perimeter Park Dr Ste E (27560-8429)
PHONE..................919 813-8694
EMP: 7 EST: 2008
SALES (est): 82.58K **Privately Held**
SIC: **3841** Surgical and medical instruments

(G-11272)
623 MEDICAL LLC
Also Called: 623 Medical
635 Davis Dr Ste 100 (27560-7183)
PHONE..................877 455-0112
Ty Schandler, *CEO*
EMP: 10 EST: 2020
SALES (est): 456.73K **Privately Held**
Web: www.623medical.com
SIC: **3841** Anesthesia apparatus

(G-11273)
6TH SENSE ANALYTICS
1 Copley Pkwy Ste 560 (27560-7424)
PHONE..................919 439-4740
Gregory Burnell, *CEO*
EMP: 4 EST: 2019
SALES (est): 91.13K **Privately Held**
SIC: **7372** Prepackaged software

(G-11274)
AAA MOBILE SIGNS LLC
Also Called: Signs Now
10404 Chapel Hill Rd Ste 110 (27560-0218)
PHONE..................919 463-9768
Lisa Dyrd, *Mgr*
EMP: 5
SALES (corp-wide): 2.4MM **Privately Held**
Web: www.signsnow.com
SIC: **3993** Signs and advertising specialties
PA: Aaa Mobile Signs, L.C.
1570 Lakeview Dr Ste 108
Sebring FL 33870
863 471-1800

(G-11275)
AAR KEY ENTERPRISES INC
1209 Justice Walk Ave (27560-5301)
PHONE..................919 337-9706
Rakesh Sharma, *Prin*
EMP: 4 EST: 2017
SALES (est): 75.44K **Privately Held**
SIC: **3728** Aircraft parts and equipment, nec

(G-11276)
ACCULABS TECHNOLOGIES INC
1018 Morrisville Pkwy Ste E (27560-0308)
P.O. Box 1579 (27312-1579)
PHONE..................919 468-8780
Tom Wilkie, *Pr*
Cameron Stephens, *Treas*
EMP: 5 EST: 1997
SALES (est): 471.58K **Privately Held**
Web: www.acculabstech.com
SIC: **3564** Air cleaning systems

(G-11277)
ACTERNA LLC
1100 Perimeter Park Dr Ste 101 (27560-9119)
PHONE..................919 388-5100
John Govert, *Brnch Mgr*
EMP: 19
SALES (corp-wide): 1.11B **Publicly Held**
SIC: **3669** 7379 3825 5065 Intercommunication systems, electric; Computer related consulting services; Instruments to measure electricity; Electronic parts and equipment, nec
HQ: Acterna Llc
20250 Century Blvd # 100
Germantown MD 20874
301 353-1550

(G-11278)
ADAMS PRODUCTS COMPANY
5701 Mccrimmon Pkwy Ste 201 (27560-8340)
P.O. Box 189 (27560-0189)
PHONE..................919 467-2218
Joseph Mc Cullough, *V Ch Bd*
Michael Lynch, *Sec*
▲ EMP: 180 EST: 1946
SQ FT: 11,000
SALES (est): 25.51MM
SALES (corp-wide): 32.72B **Privately Held**
Web: www.adamsproducts.com
SIC: **3271** 5032 3272 Blocks, concrete or cinder: standard; Concrete building products; Concrete products, nec
HQ: Crh Americas, Inc.
900 Ashwood Pkwy Ste 600
Atlanta GA 30338
770 804-3363

(G-11279)
ADR HYDRO-CUT INC
125 International Dr Ste E (27560-7390)
PHONE..................919 388-2251
David Brooks, *Pr*
Al Ely, *VP*
Ron Harris, *VP*
EMP: 5 EST: 1998
SQ FT: 10,000
SALES (est): 725.11K **Privately Held**
Web: www.adrhydrocut.com
SIC: **3589** Water treatment equipment, industrial

(G-11280)
ADVANCED MICRO DEVICES INC
3000 Rdu Center Dr Ste 230 (27560-7671)
PHONE..................919 840-8080
Ted Donnelly, *Mgr*
EMP: 9
SALES (corp-wide): 22.68B **Publicly Held**

GEOGRAPHIC SECTION

Morrisville - Wake County (G-11304)

Web: www.amd.com
SIC: **3674** Integrated circuits, semiconductor networks, etc.
PA: Advanced Micro Devices, Inc.
   2485 Augustine Dr
   Santa Clara CA 95054
   408 749-4000

(G-11281)
ALCAMI CAROLINAS CORPORATION
627 Davis Dr Ste 100 (27560-7101)
PHONE..................910 254-7000
EMP: 7
SALES (corp-wide): 418.48MM **Privately Held**
Web: www.alcami.com
SIC: **2834** Pharmaceutical preparations
HQ: Alcami Carolinas Corporation
   2320 Scientific Park Dr
   Wilmington NC 28405

(G-11282)
ALCAMI CAROLINAS CORPORATION
419 Davis Dr Ste 300 (27560-7552)
PHONE..................910 254-7000
EMP: 8
SALES (corp-wide): 418.48MM **Privately Held**
Web: www.alcami.com
SIC: **2834** Drugs affecting neoplasms and endrocrine systems
HQ: Alcami Carolinas Corporation
   2320 Scientific Park Dr
   Wilmington NC 28405

(G-11283)
ALCAMI CAROLINAS CORPORATION
200 Innovation Ave Ste 150 (27560-8562)
PHONE..................910 254-7000
EMP: 8
SALES (corp-wide): 418.48MM **Privately Held**
Web: www.alcami.com
SIC: **2834** 8731 Drugs affecting neoplasms and endrocrine systems; Biological research
HQ: Alcami Carolinas Corporation
   2320 Scientific Park Dr
   Wilmington NC 28405

(G-11284)
ALTERNATIVE PWR SLS & RENT LLP
1000 Northgate Ct (27560-6295)
PHONE..................919 467-8001
Don Bitting Mg, *Pt*
Don Bitting, *Mng Pt*
EMP: 6 EST: 2004
SALES (est): 678.81K **Privately Held**
Web: www.alternativepower.com
SIC: **3621** Motors and generators

(G-11285)
ALTERRA LABS LLC
1316 Sorrel Park Dr (27560-5450)
PHONE..................704 770-7695
EMP: 6 EST: 2020
SALES (est): 363.81K **Privately Held**
SIC: **3577** Printers, computer

(G-11286)
AMG CASEWORK LLC
10315 Chapel Hill Rd (27560-8707)
P.O. Box 1338 (27560-1338)
PHONE..................919 462-9203
Anita Mcleod, *Managing Member*
EMP: 10 EST: 2019
SALES (est): 928.34K **Privately Held**
Web: www.amgcasework.com
SIC: **2599** Cabinets, factory

(G-11287)
ANUTRA MEDICAL INC
1000 Perimeter Park Dr Ste E (27560-9658)
PHONE..................919 648-1215
Derek Lorati, *Admn*
EMP: 17 EST: 2013
SALES (est): 4.8MM **Privately Held**
Web: www.anutramedical.com
SIC: **3843** Dental equipment

(G-11288)
ANUVA SERVICES INC
Also Called: Anuva
140 Southcenter Ct Ste 600 (27560)
PHONE..................919 468-6441
▲ EMP: 14
Web: www.anuvaservices.com
SIC: **3679** 7629 Electronic circuits; Electronic equipment repair

(G-11289)
APEX MARBLE AND GRANITE INC
10315b Chapel Hill Rd (27560-8707)
P.O. Box 1338 (27560-1338)
PHONE..................919 462-9202
Nathan Mcleod, *Pr*
Anital Mcleod, *Sec*
EMP: 24 EST: 1999
SQ FT: 100
SALES (est): 2.34MM **Privately Held**
Web: www.apexmarbleandgranite.com
SIC: **3281** 1743 Granite, cut and shaped; Marble installation, interior

(G-11290)
APJET INC (PA)
523 Davis Dr Ste 100 (27560-6554)
PHONE..................919 595-5538
John A Emrich, *CEO*
EMP: 6 EST: 2014
SALES (est): 853.22K
SALES (corp-wide): 853.22K **Privately Held**
Web: www.apjet.com
SIC: **3599** Industrial machinery, nec

(G-11291)
ARRAY BIOPHARMA INC
3005 Carrington Mill Blvd (27560-8885)
PHONE..................303 381-6600
Tricia Haugeto, *Off Mgr*
EMP: 85
SALES (corp-wide): 100.33B **Publicly Held**
Web: www.pfizer.com
SIC: **2834** Pharmaceutical preparations
HQ: Array Biopharma Inc.
   3200 Walnut St
   Boulder CO 80301
   303 381-6600

(G-11292)
ARRIVO MANAGEMENT LLC
3000 Rdu Center Dr (27560-7643)
PHONE..................919 460-9500
Michael Ackermann, *Mgr*
EMP: 8 EST: 2015
SALES (est): 949.52K **Privately Held**
Web: www.arrivobio.com
SIC: **2834** Proprietary drug products

(G-11293)
ASCOM (US) INC
300 Perimeter Park Dr Ste D (27560-9703)
PHONE..................877 712-7266
Tim Whelehan, *Pr*
Tom Mckearney, *VP*
Robert Goldman,   *
Nancy Duffy,   *
EMP: 150 EST: 2000
SQ FT: 10,000
SALES (est): 37.8MM **Privately Held**
Web: www.ascom.com
SIC: **3663** Radio broadcasting and communications equipment
HQ: Ascom (Sweden) Ab
   Grimbodalen 2
   GOteborg 417 0
   31559300

(G-11294)
ASKLEPIOS BOPHARMACEUTICAL INC (HQ)
Also Called: Askbio
507 Airport Blvd Ste 111 (27560-8200)
PHONE..................919 561-6210
Gustavo Pesquin, *CEO*
Philippe Moullier, *CSO*
Martin K Childers, *CMO*
Don Haut, *Chief Business Officer*
EMP: 114 EST: 2001
SALES (est): 59.7MM
SALES (corp-wide): 51.78B **Privately Held**
Web: www.askbio.com
SIC: **2834** Pharmaceutical preparations
PA: Bayer Ag
   Kaiser-Wilhelm-Allee 1
   Leverkusen NW 51373
   214301

(G-11295)
ATC PANELS INC
2000 Aerial Center Pkwy Ste 113 (27560-9294)
PHONE..................919 653-6053
Rony Obach, *Pr*
Jim Skinner, *VP*
◆ EMP: 11 EST: 2005
SALES (est): 181.57K **Privately Held**
SIC: **2493** Reconstituted wood products

(G-11296)
ATLAS SIGNS
951 Aviation Pkwy Ste 1000 (27560-8462)
PHONE..................919 238-5078
Jim Adinolfe, *Owner*
EMP: 5 EST: 2017
SALES (est): 91.01K **Privately Held**
Web: www.atlasbtw.com
SIC: **3993** Signs and advertising specialties

(G-11297)
AUTOMATED MACHINE TECHNOLOGIES
10404 Chapel Hill Rd Ste 100 (27560-6900)
P.O. Box 1186 (27560-1186)
PHONE..................919 361-0121
Ted Kemnitz, *Pr*
EMP: 8 EST: 1994
SQ FT: 2,000
SALES (est): 518.08K **Privately Held**
Web: www.amtliquidfilling.com
SIC: **3565** 5084 3599 Packaging machinery; Packaging machinery and equipment; Custom machinery

(G-11298)
B-LIGHT PUBLISHING LLC
309 Durants Neck Ln (27560-5849)
PHONE..................919 957-8997
Tolu Adeniji, *Prin*
EMP: 4 EST: 2019
SALES (est): 73.2K **Privately Held**
SIC: **2741** Miscellaneous publishing

(G-11299)
BASF CORPORATION
3500 Paramount Pkwy (27560-7218)
PHONE..................919 461-6500
EMP: 34
SALES (corp-wide): 74.89B **Privately Held**
Web: www.basf.com
SIC: **2869** Industrial organic chemicals, nec
HQ: Basf Corporation
   100 Park Ave
   Florham Park NJ 07932
   800 962-7831

(G-11300)
BAYER HEALTHCARE LLC
Also Called: Bayer Technology and Services
3500 Paramount Pkwy (27560-7218)
PHONE..................919 461-6525
Neil Cleveland, *Brnch Mgr*
EMP: 42
SALES (corp-wide): 51.78B **Privately Held**
Web: www.bayercare.com
SIC: **2834** Pharmaceutical preparations
HQ: Bayer Healthcare Llc
   100 Bayer Blvd
   Whippany NJ 07981
   862 404-3000

(G-11301)
BEAZER EAST INC
3131 Rdu Center Dr Ste 220 (27560-7687)
PHONE..................919 380-2610
Jim Sprinkle, *Mgr*
EMP: 8
SQ FT: 1,836
SALES (corp-wide): 21.19B **Privately Held**
SIC: **3272** Concrete products, nec
HQ: Beazer East, Inc.
   600 River Ave Ste 200
   Pittsburgh PA 15212
   412 428-9407

(G-11302)
BIJUR DELIMON INTL INC (DH)
1 Copley Pkwy Ste 104 (27560-9693)
PHONE..................919 465-4448
Roger M Yamamoto, *Pr*
Roger M Yamamoto, *CFO*
John V Curci,   *
Karen Johnson,   *
Nancy S Lenhart,   *
▲ EMP: 40 EST: 1965
SALES (est): 21.52MM
SALES (corp-wide): 545.92MM **Privately Held**
Web: www.bijurdelimon.com
SIC: **3569** Lubricating equipment
HQ: Industrial Manufacturing Company Llc
   8223 Brecksville Rd # 100
   Brecksville OH 44141
   440 838-4700

(G-11303)
BIOGEN PHARMA ✿
3798 Hopson Rd (27560-9016)
PHONE..................919 993-1100
EMP: 4 EST: 2022
SALES (est): 63.22K **Privately Held**
Web: www.biogen.com
SIC: **2834** Pharmaceutical preparations

(G-11304)
BIOSUPPLYNET INC
Also Called: Sciquest
3020 Carrington Mill Blvd Ste 100 (27560-5432)
PHONE..................919 659-2121
EMP: 10 EST: 1996
SALES (est): 12.18MM
SALES (corp-wide): 174.61MM **Privately Held**
Web: www.blaze.ae

Morrisville - Wake County (G-11305) — GEOGRAPHIC SECTION

SIC: 5049 2721 Scientific and engineering equipment and supplies; Periodicals, publishing only
HQ: Jaggaer, Llc
3020 Carrington Mill Blvd # 100
Morrisville NC 27560
919 659-2100

(G-11305)
BLUE FORCE TECHNOLOGIES LLC
627 Distribution Dr Ste D (27560-7100)
PHONE..................919 443-1660
EMP: 90 EST: 2011
SALES (est): 19.52MM
SALES (corp-wide): 558.6MM Privately Held
Web: www.blueforcetech.com
SIC: 3728 Fuselage assembly, aircraft
PA: Anduril Industries, Inc.
1400 Anduril
Costa Mesa CA 92626
949 891-1607

(G-11306)
BRACELETS AND MORE
306 Millet Dr (27560-6893)
PHONE..................419 236-4933
Patricia Buchanan, Prin
EMP: 4 EST: 2015
SALES (est): 101.08K Privately Held
SIC: 3961 Bracelets, except precious metal

(G-11307)
BRAVOSOLUTION US INC (DH)
3020 Carrington Mill Blvd Ste 100 (27560-5432)
PHONE..................312 373-3100
▲ EMP: 25 EST: 1995
SALES (est): 21.31MM
SALES (corp-wide): 174.61MM Privately Held
SIC: 7372 Prepackaged software
HQ: Jaggaer, Llc
3020 Carrington Mill Blvd # 100
Morrisville NC 27560
919 659-2100

(G-11308)
BROWN BUILDING CORPORATION
1111 Copeland Oaks Dr (27560-6611)
P.O. Box 91206 (27675-1206)
PHONE..................919 782-1800
Peter D Brown, Pr
Jan Brown, Sec
EMP: 10 EST: 1993
SALES (est): 1.1MM Privately Held
SIC: 1521 1389 1611 Single-family housing construction; Construction, repair, and dismantling services; General contractor, highway and street construction

(G-11309)
BUEHLER MOTOR INC (HQ)
1100 Perimeter Park Dr Ste 118 (27560-9119)
PHONE..................919 380-3333
Peter Muhr, CEO
Ray Welterlin, *
Stephanie Denkowicz, *
Karl Wagner, *
◆ EMP: 25 EST: 2004
SALES (est): 46.3MM
SALES (corp-wide): 272.59MM Privately Held
Web: www.buehlermotor.com
SIC: 3621 Motors, electric
PA: Buhler Motor Gmbh
Anne-Frank-Str. 33-35
Nurnberg BY 90459
91145040

(G-11310)
BURTS BEES INC
900 Aviation Pkwy Ste 400 (27560-9218)
PHONE..................919 238-6450
Brian Buchanan, Dir
EMP: 257
SALES (corp-wide): 7.39B Publicly Held
Web: www.burtsbees.com
SIC: 2844 5122 Perfumes, cosmetics and other toilet preparations; Drugs, proprietaries, and sundries
HQ: Burt's Bees, Inc.
210 W Pettigrew St
Durham NC 27701

(G-11311)
BUSIAPP CORPORATION
Also Called: Lightjunction
400 Innovation Ave Ste 150 (27560-8557)
PHONE..................877 558-2518
Yi Zhou, Pr
▲ EMP: 10 EST: 2013
SALES (est): 2.49MM Privately Held
Web: www.lightjunction.com
SIC: 3648 Lighting equipment, nec

(G-11312)
CARRIER CORPORATION
200 Perimeter Park Dr Ste A (27560-9714)
PHONE..................704 494-2600
Ronald Reitler, Brnch Mgr
EMP: 4
SALES (corp-wide): 22.1B Publicly Held
Web: www.carrier.com
SIC: 3585 Refrigeration and heating equipment
HQ: Carrier Corporation
13995 Pasteur Blvd
Palm Beach Gardens FL 33418
561 365-2000

(G-11313)
CATALENT PHARMA SOLUTIONS LLC
140 Southcenter Ct (27560-8538)
PHONE..................919 481-4855
EMP: 13
SALES (est): 572.01K Privately Held
Web: catalent.dejobs.org
SIC: 2834 Pharmaceutical preparations

(G-11314)
CATALENT PHARMA SOLUTIONS LLC
160 N Pharma Dr (27560-9570)
PHONE..................919 481-4855
Chris Gregory, Brnch Mgr
EMP: 193
Web: www.catalent.com
SIC: 2834 8734 Pharmaceutical preparations; Product testing laboratories
HQ: Catalent Pharma Solutions, Llc
14 Schoolhouse Rd
Somerset NJ 08873

(G-11315)
CATALENT PHARMA SOLUTIONS INC
120 Southcenter Ct Ste 100 (27560)
PHONE..................919 481-2614
Russ Winstead, Brnch Mgr
EMP: 10
Web: www.catalent.com
SIC: 2834 Pharmaceutical preparations
HQ: Catalent Pharma Solutions, Inc.
14 Schoolhouse Rd
Somerset NJ 08873

(G-11316)
CDV LLC (PA)
Also Called: Trimaco
2300 Gateway Centre Blvd Ste 200 (27560-9669)
PHONE..................919 674-3460
◆ EMP: 18 EST: 2002
SQ FT: 22,000
SALES (est): 102.72MM
SALES (corp-wide): 102.72MM Privately Held
SIC: 2851 2621 2672 2679 Paints and allied products; Poster and art papers; Masking tape: made from purchased materials; Building paper, laminated: made from purchased material

(G-11317)
CHANNELADVISOR CORPORATION (DH)
Also Called: Channeladvisor
1010 Sync St (27560-9044)
PHONE..................919 228-4700
Bryan Dove, CEO
EMP: 85 EST: 2001
SALES (est): 167.73MM
SALES (corp-wide): 226.42MM Privately Held
Web: www.rithum.com
SIC: 7372 Application computer software
HQ: Rithum Holdings Inc.
800 Troy Schenectady Rd
Latham NY 12110
518 810-0700

(G-11318)
CHARLES & COLVARD LTD (PA)
Also Called: Charles & Colvard
170 Southport Dr (27560-7327)
PHONE..................919 468-0399
Don O'connell, Pr
Neal I Goldman, Ch Bd
▲ EMP: 19 EST: 1995
SQ FT: 36,350
SALES (est): 29.95MM
SALES (corp-wide): 29.95MM Publicly Held
Web: www.charlesandcolvard.com
SIC: 3911 Jewelry, precious metal

(G-11319)
CHARLES & COLVARD DIRECT LLC
300 Perimeter Park Dr Ste A (27560-9703)
PHONE..................919 468-0399
Randall N Mccullough, CEO
EMP: 13 EST: 2011
SALES (est): 8.56K
SALES (corp-wide): 29.95MM Publicly Held
SIC: 3915 Jewelers' materials and lapidary work
PA: Charles & Colvard, Ltd.
170 Southport Dr
Morrisville NC 27560
919 468-0399

(G-11320)
CHARLESANDCOLVARDCOM LLC
Also Called: Moissanite.com, LLC
170 Southport Dr (27560-7327)
PHONE..................877 202-5467
EMP: 21 EST: 2011
SALES (est): 2.57MM
SALES (corp-wide): 29.95MM Publicly Held
Web: www.charlesandcolvard.com
SIC: 3915 Jewelers' materials and lapidary work
PA: Charles & Colvard, Ltd.
170 Southport Dr
Morrisville NC 27560
919 468-0399

(G-11321)
CHICHIBONE INC
600 Airport Blvd Ste 1400 (27560-9138)
PHONE..................919 785-0090
Pat Mcnamara, Pr
EMP: 7
SALES (corp-wide): 26.15MM Privately Held
Web: www.trs-sesco.com
SIC: 3561 1711 Pumps and pumping equipment; Heating and air conditioning contractors
PA: Chichibone, Inc.
Kernersville NC 27284
919 785-0090

(G-11322)
CHRONICLE RESEARCH INC
409 Walnut Woods Dr (27560-6772)
PHONE..................919 259-0970
Drew C Rivers, Prin
EMP: 5 EST: 2008
SALES (est): 81.97K Privately Held
SIC: 2711 Newspapers

(G-11323)
CISCO SYSTEMS INC
Also Called: Cisco Systems
7100 Kit Creek Rd (27560-8663)
PHONE..................919 392-2000
John Chambers, CEO
EMP: 17
SALES (corp-wide): 57B Publicly Held
Web: www.cisco.com
SIC: 3577 3578 Data conversion equipment, media-to-media: computer; Automatic teller machines (ATM)
PA: Cisco Systems, Inc.
170 W Tasman Dr
San Jose CA 95134
408 526-4000

(G-11324)
CISCO SYSTEMS INC
Also Called: Cisco Systems
7025 Kit Creek Rd (27560-9741)
P.O. Box 14987 (27709-4987)
PHONE..................919 392-2000
EMP: 2500
SALES (corp-wide): 57B Publicly Held
Web: www.cisco.com
SIC: 3577 8731 Data conversion equipment, media-to-media: computer; Commercial physical research
PA: Cisco Systems, Inc.
170 W Tasman Dr
San Jose CA 95134
408 526-4000

(G-11325)
CORTINA SYSTEMS
523 Davis Dr Ste 300 (27560-7165)
PHONE..................919 226-1800
George Kaldani, Prin
EMP: 4 EST: 2007
SALES (est): 474.33K Privately Held
SIC: 3674 Semiconductors and related devices

(G-11326)
CURRENT ENTERPRISES INC
125 International Dr Ste J (27560-7390)
PHONE..................919 469-1227
Eugene Creech, Pr
George Welch, Sec
EMP: 6 EST: 1977
SQ FT: 10,130
SALES (est): 461.55K Privately Held
SIC: 3599 Machine shop, jobbing and repair

GEOGRAPHIC SECTION

(G-11327)
DAILY GRIND
10970 Chapel Hill Rd Ste 122 (27560-6237)
PHONE..................919 864-8775
Jay Ahmad, *Mgr*
EMP: 5 **EST:** 2015
SALES (est): 206.86K **Privately Held**
SIC: 3599 Grinding castings for the trade

(G-11328)
DAUNTLESS DISCOVERY LLC
808 Aviation Pkwy Ste 1200 (27560-6663)
PHONE..................610 909-7383
EMP: 123 **EST:** 2017
SALES (est): 2.05MM **Privately Held**
Web: www.dauntlessdiscovery.com
SIC: 7372 Prepackaged software

(G-11329)
DCS USA CORPORATION
3000 Bear Cat Way Ste 118 (27560-7353)
PHONE..................919 535-8000
Annesophie Dorey, *Pr*
EMP: 5 **EST:** 2014
SALES (est): 720.77K **Privately Held**
Web: www.converting-systems.com
SIC: 3549 3423 3621 Cutting and slitting machinery; Cutting dies, except metal cutting; Rotary converters (electrical equipment)

(G-11330)
DELARRIVO INC
3000 Rdu Center Dr (27560-7643)
PHONE..................919 460-9500
Stephen E Butts, *Pr*
EMP: 7 **EST:** 2018
SALES (est): 195.96K **Privately Held**
SIC: 2834 Pharmaceutical preparations

(G-11331)
DIGITAL RECORDERS INC
598 Airport Blvd Ste 300 (27560-7214)
PHONE..................919 361-2155
Francis X Coleman Iii, *Prin*
Francis X Coleman Iii, *Pr*
Francis J Ingrassia, *VP*
Andrew Stanton, *COO*
EMP: 241 **EST:** 2012
SALES (est): 220.27K
SALES (corp-wide): 127.61MM **Privately Held**
SIC: 3652 Prerecorded records and tapes
PA: Clever Devices Ltd.
300 Crossways Park Dr
Woodbury NY 11797
516 433-6100

(G-11332)
DISCO HI-TEC AMERICA INC
3000 Aerial Center Pkwy Ste 140 (27560-9132)
PHONE..................919 468-6003
Joel Sigmund, *Mgr*
EMP: 7
Web: www.dicing-grinding.com
SIC: 5065 3674 Semiconductor devices; Semiconductors and related devices
HQ: Disco Hi-Tec America, Inc.
5921 Optical Ct
San Jose CA 95138
408 987-3776

(G-11333)
DOBLE ENGINEERING COMPANY
2200 Gateway Centre Blvd Ste 207 (27560)
PHONE..................919 380-7461
Lawrence H Nordt, *Brnch Mgr*
EMP: 6
Web: www.doble.com
SIC: 8711 1389 Electrical or electronic engineering; Pipe testing, oil field service
HQ: Doble Engineering Company
123 Felton St
Marlborough MA 01752
617 926-4900

(G-11334)
DOCU SOURCE OF NC
951 Aviation Pkwy Ste 600 (27560-6636)
PHONE..................919 459-5900
Derek Dorroh, *Prin*
EMP: 17 **EST:** 2013
SALES (est): 2.32MM **Privately Held**
Web: www.docusourceofnc.com
SIC: 2752 Offset printing

(G-11335)
DOCUSOURCE NORTH CAROLINA LLC
2800 Slater Rd (27560-8436)
PHONE..................919 459-5900
EMP: 35 **EST:** 2001
SQ FT: 26,500
SALES (est): 4.88MM **Privately Held**
Web: www.docusourceofnc.com
SIC: 2759 2789 2796 Publication printing; Bookbinding and related work; Platemaking services

(G-11336)
DSK BIOPHARMA INC (PA)
112 Nova Dr (27560-8244)
P.O. Box 253 (27560-0253)
PHONE..................919 465-9104
Krishnudu Kasireddy, *Pr*
Rama Pidadarthi, *Prin*
EMP: 5 **EST:** 2014
SALES (est): 265.27K
SALES (corp-wide): 265.27K **Privately Held**
Web: www.dskbiopharma.com
SIC: 2834 Pharmaceutical preparations

(G-11337)
EMITBIO INC
615 Davis Dr (27560-6845)
PHONE..................919 321-1726
Neal Hunter, *Ofcr*
David Emerson, *CEO*
John C Oakley, *CFO*
EMP: 6 **EST:** 2020
SALES (est): 819.72K
SALES (corp-wide): 3.04MM **Privately Held**
Web: www.emitbio.com
SIC: 3841 Surgical and medical instruments
PA: Know Bio, Llc
615 Davis Dr Ste 800
Morrisville NC 27560
919 321-1726

(G-11338)
ENDAXI COMPANY INC
Also Called: Business Card Express Raleigh
137 Trans Air Dr (27560-7211)
P.O. Box 565 (27560-0565)
PHONE..................919 467-8895
Marshall Bates, *Pr*
Lyle Blue, *
Marilyn S Bates, *
EMP: 32 **EST:** 1989
SQ FT: 10,000
SALES (est): 2.24MM **Privately Held**
Web: www.bcesouth.com
SIC: 2759 Thermography

(G-11339)
EXTREME NETWORKS INC (PA)
Also Called: Extreme
2121 Rdu Center Dr Ste 300 (27560-6250)
PHONE..................408 579-2800
◆ **EMP:** 400 **EST:** 1996
SQ FT: 54,530
SALES (est): 1.31B **Publicly Held**
Web: www.extremenetworks.com
SIC: 3661 7373 7372 Telephone and telegraph apparatus; Computer integrated systems design; Prepackaged software

(G-11340)
FINELINE PROTOTYPING INC
3700 Pleasant Grove Church Rd (27560-8942)
PHONE..................919 781-7702
Robert I Connelly, *Pr*
EMP: 53 **EST:** 2000
SQ FT: 11,000
SALES (est): 9.97MM
SALES (corp-wide): 503.88MM **Publicly Held**
Web: www.protolabs.com
SIC: 3089 Injection molding of plastics
PA: Proto Labs, Inc.
5540 Pioneer Creek Dr
Maple Plain MN 55359
763 479-3680

(G-11341)
FLEXTRONICS INTL USA INC
1000 Innovation Ave (27560-8532)
PHONE..................919 998-4000
Debrie Johnson, *Brnch Mgr*
EMP: 214
Web: www.flex.com
SIC: 3672 8711 Printed circuit boards; Engineering services
HQ: Flextronics International Usa, Inc.
6201 America Center Dr
San Jose CA 95002

(G-11342)
FLOLOGIC INC
1015 Aviation Pkwy Ste 900 (27560)
PHONE..................919 878-1808
Charles Desmet, *Pr*
▼ **EMP:** 5 **EST:** 1997
SQ FT: 4,200
SALES (est): 717.56K **Privately Held**
Web: www.flologic.com
SIC: 5999 3432 5074 Plumbing and heating supplies; Plumbing fixture fittings and trim; Plumbing fittings and supplies

(G-11343)
FUJIFILM DSYNTH BTCHNLGIES USA (DH)
101 J Morris Commons Ln Ste 300 (27560-0287)
PHONE..................919 337-4400
EMP: 217 **EST:** 2011
SQ FT: 137,000
SALES (est): 152.61MM **Privately Held**
Web: www.fujifilmdiosynth.com
SIC: 2834 Pharmaceutical preparations
HQ: Fujifilm Holdings America Corporation
200 Summit Lake Dr Fl 2
Valhalla NY 10595

(G-11344)
FURIEX PHARMACEUTICALS LLC
3900 Paramount Pkwy Ste 150 (27560)
PHONE..................919 456-7800
EMP: 20 **EST:** 2009
SQ FT: 4,650
SALES (est): 3.04MM
SALES (corp-wide): 54.32B **Publicly Held**
Web: news.abbvie.com
SIC: 2834 Pharmaceutical preparations
HQ: Allergan Sales, Llc
2525 Dupont Dr
Irvine CA 92612

(G-11345)
GAINSPAN CORPORATION
3131 Rdu Center Dr Ste 135 (27560-7687)
PHONE..................408 627-6500
EMP: 58 **EST:** 2006
SALES (est): 4.74MM **Privately Held**
Web: www.telit.com
SIC: 3674 Semiconductors and related devices

(G-11346)
GANNETT MEDIA CORP
U S A Today
107b Quail Fields Ct (27560-8798)
PHONE..................919 467-1402
Paul Cimino Circulation, *Mgr*
EMP: 10
SALES (corp-wide): 2.66B **Publicly Held**
Web: www.gannett.com
SIC: 2711 Newspapers, publishing and printing
HQ: Gannett Media Corp.
7950 Jones Branch Dr Fl 8
Mc Lean VA 22102
703 854-6000

(G-11347)
GILMORE GLOBL LGSTICS SVCS INC
101 Southcenter Ct Ste 100-E (27560)
PHONE..................919 277-2700
Bob Gilmore, *CEO*
Brian Wright, *
Dennis Quon, *
Robert E Gilmore, *Prin*
EMP: 100 **EST:** 1999
SQ FT: 50,000
SALES (est): 24.69MM
SALES (corp-wide): 96.89MM **Privately Held**
SIC: 7389 2752 2759 Printing broker; Commercial printing, lithographic; Commercial printing, nec
PA: Gilmore, R. E. Investments Corp
120 Herzberg Rd
Kanata ON K2K 3
613 592-2944

(G-11348)
GLAXOSMITHKLINE LLC
7030 Kit Creek Rd (27560-9761)
PHONE..................919 628-3630
EMP: 4
SALES (corp-wide): 35.31B **Privately Held**
Web: us.gsk.com
SIC: 2834 Pharmaceutical preparations
HQ: Glaxosmithkline Llc
2929 Walnut St Ste 1700
Philadelphia PA 19104
888 825-5249

(G-11349)
GLOBAL RESOURCE CORPORATION
Also Called: (A Development Stage Company)
9400 Globe Center Dr # 101 (27560-6213)
PHONE..................919 972-7803
Peter A Worthington, *CEO*
Peter A Worthington, *Interim Chairman of the Board*
Jeffrey J Andrews, *CFO*
Ken Kinsella, *Pr*
▲ **EMP:** 10 **EST:** 2000
SQ FT: 5,124
SALES (est): 234.76K **Privately Held**
SIC: 3559 Automotive related machinery

Morrisville - Wake County (G-11350)

(G-11350)
HAIR SOCIETY INC
117 Station Dr (27560-9237)
PHONE....................919 588-1453
Tina Silver, *CEO*
EMP: 5 **EST:** 2019
SALES (est): 50.1K **Privately Held**
SIC: 3999 Barber and beauty shop equipment

(G-11351)
HAP INNOVATIONS LLC
2501 Aerial Center Pkwy Ste 100 (27560-7655)
PHONE....................919 650-6497
Thomas Rhoads, *CEO*
Nancy Thomason, *
EMP: 42 **EST:** 2015
SALES (est): 3.56MM **Privately Held**
SIC: 3829 8082 Measuring and controlling devices, nec; Home health care services

(G-11352)
HATTERAS NETWORKS INC
637 Davis Dr (27560-6835)
PHONE....................919 991-5440
Mike Aquino, *Pr*
Kevin Sheehan, *CEO*
Jeff White, *Pr*
Vincent Zumbo, *CFO*
▲ **EMP:** 24 **EST:** 1999
SQ FT: 16,275
SALES (est): 1.15MM **Privately Held**
Web: www.hatterasnetworks.com
SIC: 3661 Telephone and telegraph apparatus

(G-11353)
HB FULLER CO
523 Davis Dr (27560-7165)
PHONE....................415 878-7202
EMP: 8 **EST:** 2015
SALES (est): 276.73K **Privately Held**
Web: www.hbfuller.com
SIC: 2891 Adhesives

(G-11354)
HEXATECH INC
991 Aviation Pkwy Ste 800 (27560-8458)
PHONE....................919 481-4412
John Goehrke, *CEO*
Zlatko Sitar, *Pr*
Raoul Schleffer, *VP*
Kathy Morris, *CFO*
▲ **EMP:** 13 **EST:** 2001
SALES (est): 3.55MM **Privately Held**
Web: www.hexatechinc.com
SIC: 3674 Semiconductors and related devices

(G-11355)
HZO INC (PA)
Also Called: Hzo
5151 Mccrimmon Pkwy Ste 208 (27560-0177)
PHONE....................919 439-0505
Richard Holder, *CEO*
Glen Marder, *
EMP: 52 **EST:** 2009
SALES (est): 23.48MM
SALES (corp-wide): 23.48MM **Privately Held**
Web: www.hzo.com
SIC: 2899 Waterproofing compounds

(G-11356)
ICONTACT LLC
Also Called: Broadwick
2450 Perimeter Park Dr Ste 105 (27560-8443)
PHONE....................919 957-6150
Nate Simmons, *Pr*
EMP: 67 **EST:** 2003
SALES (est): 13.66MM
SALES (corp-wide): 934.8MM **Privately Held**
Web: www.icontact.com
SIC: 7372 Business oriented computer software
HQ: Cision Us Inc.
    300 S Riverside Plz
    Chicago IL 60606
    312 922-2400

(G-11357)
IFS INDUSTRIES INC
Also Called: Ifs Industries
100 Southcenter Ct Ste 300 (27560-9125)
PHONE....................919 234-1397
EMP: 24
SALES (corp-wide): 76.91MM **Privately Held**
Web: www.ifscos.com
SIC: 2899 Chemical preparations, nec
PA: Ifs Industries, Inc.
    400 Orton Ave
    Reading PA 19603
    610 378-1381

(G-11358)
IMBRIUM THERAPEUTICS LP
400 Park Offices Dr Ste Ll 102 (27560)
PHONE....................984 439-1075
David Igo, *Brnch Mgr*
EMP: 11
SALES (corp-wide): 790.3MM **Privately Held**
Web: www.purduepharma.com
SIC: 2834 Pharmaceutical preparations
HQ: Imbrium Therapeutics L.P.
    201 Tresser Blvd
    Stamford CT 06901
    888 827-0622

(G-11359)
INI POWER SYSTEMS INC
Also Called: I N I
137 Trans Air Dr (27560-7211)
PHONE....................919 677-7112
EMP: 12
Web: www.inipowersystems.com
SIC: 3621 Motors and generators

(G-11360)
INSTANT IMPRINTS
10970 Chapel Hill Rd Ste 118 (27560-6237)
P.O. Box 99082 (27624-9082)
PHONE....................919 468-9808
EMP: 5 **EST:** 2016
SALES (est): 106.08K **Privately Held**
Web: www.instantimprints.com
SIC: 2752 Commercial printing, lithographic

(G-11361)
INTERPACE PHARMA SOLUTIONS INC
133 Southcenter Ct Ste 400 (27560)
PHONE....................919 678-7024
EMP: 6 **EST:** 2019
SALES (est): 362.1K **Privately Held**
Web: www.interpace.com
SIC: 2834 Pharmaceutical preparations

(G-11362)
JAGGAER LLC (HQ)
Also Called: Jaggaer
3020 Carrington Mill Blvd Ste 100 (27560-5433)
PHONE....................919 659-2100
Jim Bureau, *CEO*
Jeff Laborde, *
Eva Skidmore, *CMO**
EMP: 89 **EST:** 1996
SQ FT: 78,500
SALES (est): 174.61MM
SALES (corp-wide): 174.61MM **Privately Held**
Web: www.jaggaer.com
SIC: 7372 Business oriented computer software
PA: Sciquest Parent, Llc
    3020 Carrington Mill Blvd
    Morrisville NC 27560
    919 659-2100

(G-11363)
JOHNSON CONTROLS INC
2700 Perimeter Park Dr (27560-8448)
PHONE....................866 285-8345
George Oliver, *CEO*
Joanne Birtwistle, *VP*
Tomas Brannemo, *VP*
EMP: 7 **EST:** 1926
SALES (est): 121.27K **Privately Held**
SIC: 1389 7372 4911 Grading oil and gas well foundations; Prepackaged software; Transmission, electric power

(G-11364)
KDY AUTOMATION SOLUTIONS INC
150 Dominion Dr Ste E (27560-9205)
PHONE....................888 219-0049
Allan Salant, *Pr*
Douglas Mecvey, *VP*
EMP: 6 **EST:** 2006
SALES (est): 1.16MM **Privately Held**
Web: www.kdyautomation.com
SIC: 7371 8711 3429 3823 Computer software development; Engineering services; Hardware, nec; Industrial process control instruments

(G-11365)
KEEL LABS INC
1015 Aviation Pkwy Ste 400 (27560)
PHONE....................917 848-9066
Aaron Nesser, *CEO*
Aleksandra Gosiewski, *Dir*
Wayne Cheng, *Prin*
EMP: 5 **EST:** 2019
SALES (est): 513.09K **Privately Held**
Web: www.keellabs.com
SIC: 7389 2282 Design services; Acetate filament yarn: throwing, twisting, winding, spooling

(G-11366)
KODAK
Also Called: Kodak
1100 Perimeter Park Dr Ste 108 (27560-9119)
PHONE....................919 559-7232
Chuck Bowen, *Mgr*
EMP: 8 **EST:** 2011
SALES (est): 251.75K **Privately Held**
Web: www.kodakalaris.com
SIC: 3861 Photographic equipment and supplies

(G-11367)
KORBER MEDIPAK SYSTEMS NA INC
Also Called: Korber Medipak Systems N Amer
1001 Aviation Pkwy Ste 200 (27560)
PHONE....................727 538-4644
Kerry Fillmore, *Pr*
EMP: 37
SALES (corp-wide): 2.09MM **Privately Held**
Web: www.koerber-pharma.com
SIC: 3565 Packaging machinery
HQ: Korber Pharma, Inc.
    969 34th St N
    Fargo ND 58102
    701 232-1780

(G-11368)
KOWA RESEARCH INSTITUTE INC
430 Davis Dr Ste 200 (27560-6802)
PHONE....................919 433-1600
Gary Gordon, *Pr*
EMP: 21 **EST:** 2003
SALES (est): 5.47MM **Privately Held**
Web: www.kowaus.com
SIC: 2834 Pharmaceutical preparations
HQ: Kowa Holdings America, Inc.
    55 E 59th St Fl 19a
    New York NY 10022

(G-11369)
KSEP SYSTEMS LLC
598 Airport Blvd Ste 600 (27560-7205)
PHONE....................919 339-1850
Sunil Mehta, *Pr*
Tod Herman, *Dir*
EMP: 10 **EST:** 2011
SALES (est): 245.25K **Privately Held**
SIC: 2834 Pharmaceutical preparations

(G-11370)
LAIRD THERMAL SYSTEMS INC
629 Davis Dr Ste 200 (27560-7890)
PHONE....................919 597-7300
Karine Brand, *CEO*
Robert Baxter, *Sec*
◆ **EMP:** 23 **EST:** 2019
SQ FT: 14,150
SALES (est): 10.98MM
SALES (corp-wide): 12.07B **Publicly Held**
Web: www.lairdthermal.com
SIC: 3629 Electronic generation equipment
HQ: Laird Technologies, Inc.
    16401 Swingley Ridge Rd
    Chesterfield MO 63017
    636 898-6000

(G-11371)
LAMBDA TECHNOLOGIES INC
2200 Gateway Centre Blvd (27560-6217)
PHONE....................919 462-1919
Richard Garard, *Pr*
▲ **EMP:** 20 **EST:** 1994
SQ FT: 15,000
SALES (est): 4.61MM **Privately Held**
Web: www.microcure.com
SIC: 3567 Heating units and devices, industrial: electric

(G-11372)
LANDSHIRE INC
150 Dominion Dr Ste G (27560-9205)
PHONE....................919 650-3544
Terry Lange, *Pr*
EMP: 5 **EST:** 2014
SALES (est): 125.85K **Privately Held**
SIC: 2099 Food preparations, nec

(G-11373)
LED LIGHTING FIXTURES INC
Also Called: Llf
617 Davis Dr Ste 200 (27560-7171)
PHONE....................919 991-0700
Neal Hunter, *CEO*
▲ **EMP:** 8 **EST:** 2005
SALES (est): 118.07K **Privately Held**
Web: www.llfinc.com
SIC: 3646 Commercial lighting fixtures

(G-11374)
LENOVO (UNITED STATES) INC
5241 Paramount Pkwy (27560-8496)
PHONE....................919 486-9627
Julia Deigh, *Brnch Mgr*

GEOGRAPHIC SECTION
Morrisville - Wake County (G-11398)

EMP: 5
Web: www.lenovo.com
SIC: 3571 Electronic computers
HQ: Lenovo (United States) Inc.
8001 Development Dr
Morrisville NC 27560
855 253-6686

(G-11375)
LENOVO (UNITED STATES) INC
7001 Development Dr Bldg 7 (27560)
PHONE..................919 237-8389
EMP: 85
Web: www.lenovo.com
SIC: 3571 Electronic computers
HQ: Lenovo (United States) Inc.
8001 Development Dr
Morrisville NC 27560
855 253-6686

(G-11376)
LENOVO (UNITED STATES) INC (HQ)
Also Called: Lenovo International
8001 Development Dr (27560-7416)
PHONE..................855 253-6686
Yang Yuanqing, *CEO*
Gianfranco Lanci, *
Liu Chuanzhi, *
Wong W Ming, *
David Roman, *
▲ **EMP:** 1518 **EST:** 2005
SALES (est): 653.89MM **Privately Held**
Web: www.lenovo.com
SIC: 3571 7371 Electronic computers; Computer software development and applications
PA: Lenovo Group Limited
23/F Taikoo Place Lincoln Hse
Quarry Bay HK

(G-11377)
LENOVO HOLDING COMPANY INC (HQ)
8001 Development Dr (27560-7416)
PHONE..................855 253-6686
Kurt Cranor, *Pr*
EMP: 14 **EST:** 2007
SALES (est): 45.65MM **Privately Held**
Web: www.lenovocareers.com
SIC: 3571 Personal computers (microcomputers)
PA: Lenovo Group Limited
23/F Taikoo Place Lincoln Hse
Quarry Bay HK

(G-11378)
LENOVO US FULFILLMENT CTR LLC
1009 Think Pl (27560-9002)
P.O. Box 1009 (27560-1009)
PHONE..................855 253-6686
Yang Yuanqing, *CEO*
John Pershke, *Managing Member**
▲ **EMP:** 136 **EST:** 2007
SALES (est): 45.65MM **Privately Held**
Web: www.lenovo.com
SIC: 3571 Electronic computers
HQ: Lenovo Holding Company, Inc.
8001 Development Dr
Morrisville NC 27560
855 253-6686

(G-11379)
LIBERTY INVESTMENT & MGT CORP
Also Called: Metaltek
455 Kitty Hawk Dr (27560-8515)
P.O. Box 30399 (27622-0399)
PHONE..................919 544-0344
Alfred F Yarur, *Pr*
Nickolas J Yarur, *VP*
▲ **EMP:** 15 **EST:** 1973
SQ FT: 10,000

SALES (est): 2.32MM **Privately Held**
Web: www.playmatetennis.com
SIC: 3949 Tennis equipment and supplies

(G-11380)
LIGHTJUNCTION
400 Innovation Ave # 150 (27560-8557)
PHONE..................919 607-9717
EMP: 5 **EST:** 2014
SALES (est): 205.1K **Privately Held**
Web: www.lightjunction.com
SIC: 3648 Lighting equipment, nec

(G-11381)
LIPOSCIENCE INC
Also Called: Liposcience
100 Perimeter Park Dr Ste C (27560-9203)
PHONE..................919 212-1999
Howard B Doran, *Pr*
William C Cromwell, *Chief Medical Officer**
Lucy G Martindale, *
James D Otvos, *
EMP: 239 **EST:** 2000
SQ FT: 83,000
SALES (est): 45.42MM **Publicly Held**
Web: www.liposcience.com
SIC: 8071 2835 Testing laboratories; Diagnostic substances
HQ: Laboratory Corporation Of America
531 S Spring St
Burlington NC 27215
336 229-1127

(G-11382)
LONZA RTP
523 Davis Dr Ste 400 (27560-7165)
PHONE..................800 748-8979
EMP: 6
SALES (est): 260.38K **Privately Held**
Web: www.lonza.com
SIC: 2834 Pharmaceutical preparations

(G-11383)
LQ3 PHARMACEUTICALS INC
Also Called: Lq3 Pharmaceuticals
419 Davis Dr Ste 100 (27560-7551)
PHONE..................919 794-7391
Kyle Chenet, *CEO*
Kevin Herlihy, *Dir*
Drew Folk, *Dir*
Enrique Alvarez, *Prin*
EMP: 9 **EST:** 2013
SALES (est): 361.44K **Privately Held**
Web: www.lq3pharma.com
SIC: 2834 Pharmaceutical preparations

(G-11384)
LULAZA AEROSPACE LLC
627 Distribution Dr Ste D (27560-7100)
PHONE..................919 371-4240
EMP: 5 **EST:** 2017
SALES (est): 116.66K **Privately Held**
SIC: 3721 Aircraft

(G-11385)
LULU TECHNOLOGY CIRCUS INC
Also Called: Lulu.com
860 Aviation Pkwy Ste 300 (27560-7396)
PHONE..................919 459-5858
Robert Young, *CEO*
Gart Davis, *
Tim Albury, *
Bryce Boothby Junior, *COO*
EMP: 50 **EST:** 2002
SQ FT: 13,800
SALES (est): 3.79MM **Privately Held**
SIC: 8299 2731 Educational services; Books, publishing and printing

(G-11386)
MACOM TECHNOLOGY SOLUTIONS INC
523 Davis Dr Ste 500 (27560-7165)
PHONE..................919 807-9100
EMP: 37
Web: www.macom.com
SIC: 3674 Semiconductors and related devices
HQ: Macom Technology Solutions Inc.
100 Chelmsford St
Lowell MA 01851

(G-11387)
MARVELL SEMICONDUCTOR INC
3015 Carrington Mill Blvd (27560-5437)
PHONE..................408 222-2500
EMP: 204
SALES (corp-wide): 5.92B **Publicly Held**
Web: www.marvell.com
SIC: 3674 Semiconductors and related devices
HQ: Marvell Semiconductor, Inc.
5488 Marvell Ln
Santa Clara CA 95054

(G-11388)
MATERIAL HANDLING TECHNOLOGIES INC (PA)
Also Called: Material Handling Tech - NC
113 International Dr (27560-8792)
PHONE..................919 388-0050
EMP: 60 **EST:** 1992
SALES (est): 20.51MM **Privately Held**
Web: www.materialhandlingtech.com
SIC: 5084 3535 Materials handling machinery; Conveyors and conveying equipment

(G-11389)
MAXIMUM ASP
9221 Globe Center Dr # 120 (27560-6205)
PHONE..................919 544-7900
D Foster C, *Technology Officer*
EMP: 9 **EST:** 2015
SALES (est): 103.77K **Privately Held**
SIC: 3841 Surgical and medical instruments

(G-11390)
MICROPORE TECHNOLOGIES INC
2121 Tw Alexander Dr Ste 124-8 (27560-6815)
PHONE..................984 344-7499
Dai Hayward, *CEO*
EMP: 16 **EST:** 2019
SALES (est): 1.36MM **Privately Held**
Web: www.microporetech.com
SIC: 3559 Pharmaceutical machinery

(G-11391)
MOTOROLA MOBILITY LLC
7001 Development Dr (27560-8105)
PHONE..................919 294-1289
EMP: 36
Web: www.motorola.com
SIC: 3663 Mobile communication equipment
HQ: Motorola Mobility Llc
222 Mdse Mart Plz # 1800
Chicago IL 60654

(G-11392)
NCONTACT SURGICAL LLC
Also Called: Atricure
1001 Aviation Pkwy Ste 400 (27560)
EMP: 20 **EST:** 2004
SQ FT: 3,500
SALES (est): 836.61K **Privately Held**
Web: www.ncontactinc.com
SIC: 3841 Surgical and medical instruments

(G-11393)
NEOMONDE BAKING COMPANY (PA)
Also Called: Neomonde Bakery
220 Dominion Dr Ste A (27560-7307)
PHONE..................919 469-8009
Sam Saleh, *Pr*
Joseph Saleh, *
Mounir Saleh, *
EMP: 50 **EST:** 1977
SALES (est): 10.69MM
SALES (corp-wide): 10.69MM **Privately Held**
Web: www.neomonde.com
SIC: 2051 5812 Bakery: wholesale or wholesale/retail combined; Delicatessen (eating places)

(G-11394)
NEURONEX INC
9001 Aerial Center Pkwy Ste 110 (27560-9731)
PHONE..................919 460-9500
EMP: 5 **EST:** 2010
SALES (est): 984.72K **Publicly Held**
SIC: 2834 Pharmaceutical preparations
PA: Acorda Therapeutics, Inc.
2 Blue Hill Plz Ste 1703
Pearl River NY 10965

(G-11395)
NEXT GENERATION SNACKS INC
615 Davis Dr Ste 900 (27560-6346)
P.O. Box 110263 (27709-5263)
PHONE..................919 797-9623
Edison Hudson, *CEO*
Raymond Szafranski Junior, *Treas*
EMP: 5 **EST:** 2012
SQ FT: 8,000
SALES (est): 94.12K **Privately Held**
SIC: 2099 Food preparations, nec

(G-11396)
NHANCED SEMICONDUCTORS INC
800 Perimeter Park Dr Ste B (27560-7271)
PHONE..................630 561-6813
Robert Patti, *Pr*
EMP: 20
SALES (corp-wide): 5.96MM **Privately Held**
Web: www.nhanced-semi.com
SIC: 3674 Semiconductors and related devices
PA: Nhanced Semiconductors, Inc.
1201 N Raddant Rd
Batavia IL 60510
331 701-7070

(G-11397)
NITRONEX LLC
523 Davis Dr Ste 500 (27560-7165)
PHONE..................919 807-9100
Greg Baker, *Pr*
EMP: 30 **EST:** 1999
SQ FT: 12,000
SALES (est): 8.73MM **Publicly Held**
Web: www.macom.com
SIC: 3674 Semiconductors and related devices
HQ: Macom Technology Solutions Inc.
100 Chelmsford St
Lowell MA 01851

(G-11398)
NORTHROP GRUMMAN SYSTEMS CORP
Also Called: Northrop Grumman Info Systems
3005 Carrington Mill Blvd (27560-8885)
PHONE..................919 465-5020
EMP: 57
Web: www.northropgrumman.com

Morrisville - Wake County (G-11399)   GEOGRAPHIC SECTION

SIC: 3812 Search and navigation equipment
HQ: Northrop Grumman Systems
    Corporation
    2980 Fairview Park Dr
    Falls Church VA 22042
    703 280-2900

(G-11399)
NOVOZYMES NORTH AMERICA INC
9000 Development Dr (27560-7427)
PHONE.................................919 494-3220
EMP: 42
SALES (corp-wide): 2.45B Privately Held
Web: www.novozymes.com
SIC: 2869 Industrial organic chemicals, nec
HQ: Novozymes North America, Inc.
    77 Perry Chapel Church Rd
    Franklinton NC 27525
    919 494-2014

(G-11400)
NOXON AUTOMATION USA LLC
150 Dominion Dr Ste B (27560-9205)
PHONE.................................919 390-1560
Marcel Zachmann, *Managing Member*
EMP: 5 EST: 2015
SALES (est): 476.85K Privately Held
Web: www.noxon-automation.com
SIC: 3599 Custom machinery

(G-11401)
ONION PEEL SOFTWARE INC
1 Copley Pkwy Ste 480 (27560-7423)
PHONE.................................919 460-1789
EMP: 10 EST: 1994
SQ FT: 15,000
SALES (est): 175.92K Privately Held
SIC: 7372 7379 7371 Business oriented
    computer software; Computer related
    consulting services; Custom computer
    programming services

(G-11402)
ORACLE CORPORATION
Also Called: Oracle
5200 Paramount Pkwy Ste 100
(27560-5470)
PHONE.................................919 595-2500
EMP: 6
SALES (corp-wide): 49.95B Publicly Held
Web: www.oracle.com
SIC: 7372 Prepackaged software
PA: Oracle Corporation
    2300 Oracle Way
    Austin TX 78741
    737 867-1000

(G-11403)
ORACLE CORPORATION
Also Called: Oracle
5200 Paramount Pkwy Ste 100
(27560-5470)
PHONE.................................919 205-6000
Patricia Stephens, *Ex VP*
EMP: 76
SALES (corp-wide): 49.95B Publicly Held
Web: www.oracle.com
SIC: 7372 3577 Prepackaged software;
    Computer peripheral equipment, nec
PA: Oracle Corporation
    2300 Oracle Way
    Austin TX 78741
    737 867-1000

(G-11404)
ORGANIZED CABINET LLC
100 Dominion Dr Ste 102 (27560-9257)
PHONE.................................517 402-8639
Carter Chill, *Prin*
▲ EMP: 4 EST: 2013
SALES (est): 79.6K Privately Held

SIC: 2434 Wood kitchen cabinets

(G-11405)
PARK COMMUNICATIONS LLC (HQ)
Also Called: Millenium Print Group
9301 Globe Center Dr Ste 120
(27560-6203)
PHONE.................................919 852-1117
Terry Pegram, *Managing Member*
EMP: 9 EST: 2014
SALES (est): 44.76MM Privately Held
Web: www.mprintgroup.com
SIC: 2759 Commercial printing, nec
PA: Pokemon Company, The
    6-10-1, Roppongi
    Minato-Ku TKY 106-0

(G-11406)
PATHEON CALCULUS MERGER LLC
3900 Paramount Pkwy (27560-7200)
PHONE.................................919 226-3200
EMP: 7 EST: 2018
SALES (est): 912.02K
SALES (corp-wide): 44.91B Publicly Held
SIC: 2834 Pharmaceutical preparations
PA: Thermo Fisher Scientific Inc.
    168 3rd Ave
    Waltham MA 02451
    781 622-1000

(G-11407)
PATHEON PHARMACEUTICALS INC (DH)
Also Called: Patheon
3900 Paramount Pkwy (27560-7200)
PHONE.................................919 226-3200
James C Mullen, *CEO*
Frank Mccune, *Sec*
Bradley Mitchell, *Treas*
Michael Lehmann, *Pr*
Stuart Grant, *Ex VP*
◆ EMP: 58 EST: 2002
SALES (est): 89.15MM
SALES (corp-wide): 44.91B Publicly Held
SIC: 2834 Pharmaceutical preparations
HQ: Patheon U.S. Holdings Inc.
    4815 Emperor Blvd Ste 110
    Durham NC 27703

(G-11408)
PATHEON PHRMCEUTICALS SVCS INC (DH)
Also Called: Patheon
3900 Paramount Pkwy (27560-7200)
PHONE.................................919 226-3200
James Mullen, *CEO*
EMP: 48 EST: 2009
SALES (est): 60.91MM
SALES (corp-wide): 44.91B Publicly Held
Web: www.patheon.com
SIC: 2834 Pharmaceutical preparations
HQ: Patheon U.S. Holdings Inc.
    4815 Emperor Blvd Ste 110
    Durham NC 27703

(G-11409)
PATHOLDCO INC (HQ)
108 Nova Dr (27560-8244)
P.O. Box 46449 (27620-6449)
PHONE.................................919 212-1300
EMP: 9 EST: 1994
SALES (est): 2.51MM
SALES (corp-wide): 15.19MM Privately Held
Web: www.precisionairtechnology.com
SIC: 3564 Filters, air: furnaces, air
    conditioning equipment, etc.
PA: Technical Safety Services, Llc
    4225 Executive Sq Ste 370
    La Jolla CA 92037
    510 845-5591

(G-11410)
POBLOCKI SIGN COMPANY LLC
210 Kitty Hawk Dr Ste 100 (27560-8547)
PHONE.................................919 354-3800
Renee Underwood, *Brnch Mgr*
EMP: 52
SALES (corp-wide): 48.69MM Privately Held
Web: www.poblocki.com
SIC: 3993 Signs and advertising specialties
PA: Poblocki Sign Company Llc
    922 S 70th St
    Milwaukee WI 53214
    414 453-4010

(G-11411)
PRACTICHEM LLC
Also Called: Practichem
10404 Chapel Hill Rd Ste 112 (27560-6900)
PHONE.................................919 714-8430
Nicholas Demarco, *Prin*
EMP: 7 EST: 2010
SALES (est): 538.63K Privately Held
Web: www.practichem.com
SIC: 3826 Chromatographic equipment,
    laboratory type

(G-11412)
PROGRESS SOFTWARE CORP
3005 Carrington Mill Blvd (27560-8885)
PHONE.................................919 461-4200
EMP: 21 EST: 2014
SALES (est): 904.79K Privately Held
Web: www.progress.com
SIC: 7372 Business oriented computer
    software

(G-11413)
PROTO LABS INC
3700 Pleasant Grove Church Rd
(27560-8942)
PHONE.................................833 245-8827
Craig Goss, *of Strat*
EMP: 103
SALES (corp-wide): 503.88MM Publicly Held
Web: www.protolabs.com
SIC: 3089 Plastics containers, except foam
PA: Proto Labs, Inc.
    5540 Pioneer Creek Dr
    Maple Plain MN 55359
    763 479-3680

(G-11414)
QUATROBIO LLC
3000 Rdu Center Dr (27560-7643)
PHONE.................................919 460-9500
EMP: 5 EST: 2016
SALES (est): 246.1K Privately Held
Web: www.arrivobio.com
SIC: 2834 Pharmaceutical preparations

(G-11415)
QUEST SOFTWARE INC
Also Called: QUEST SOFTWARE, INC.
133 Southcenter Ct (27560-8537)
PHONE.................................919 337-4719
Mike Sharrett, *Brnch Mgr*
EMP: 4
SALES (corp-wide): 647.68MM Privately Held
Web: www.quest.com
SIC: 7372 Prepackaged software
PA: Quest Software Inc.
    20 Enterprise Ste 100
    Aliso Viejo CA 92656
    949 754-8000

(G-11416)
RECIPHARM LABORATORIES INC
511 Davis Dr Ste 100 (27560-6804)
P.O. Box 14748 (27709-4748)
PHONE.................................919 884-2064
Roger Francis, *
Anne Flodin, *
EMP: 50 EST: 1997
SQ FT: 29,811
SALES (est): 19.62MM Privately Held
SIC: 2834 Pharmaceutical preparations
PA: Kemwell Biopharma Private Limited
    Kemell House No.11,
    Bengaluru KA 56002

(G-11417)
RFHIC US CORPORATION
920 Morrisville Pkwy (27560-8799)
PHONE.................................919 677-8780
Stella Bae, *Pr*
EMP: 8 EST: 2012
SALES (est): 3.11MM Privately Held
Web: www.rfhic.com
SIC: 3674 Integrated circuits, semiconductor
    networks, etc.
PA: Rfhic Corporation
    41-14 Burim-Ro 170beon-Gil, Dongan-
    Gu
    Anyang 14055

(G-11418)
SCHELLING AMERICA INC
301 Kitty Hawk Dr (27560-8581)
P.O. Box 80367 (27623-0367)
PHONE.................................919 544-0430
▲ EMP: 30 EST: 1986
SALES (est): 19.67MM Privately Held
Web: www.imaschelling.us
SIC: 5084 3541 Woodworking machinery;
    Machine tools, metal cutting type
HQ: Ima Schelling Austria Gmbh
    Gebhard Schwarzler-StraBe 34
    Schwarzach 6858
    55723960

(G-11419)
SCHNEIDER ELECTRIC USA INC
Also Called: Schneider Electric
1101 Shiloh Glenn Dr # 100 (27560-5419)
PHONE.................................888 778-2733
Charlie Denny, *Brnch Mgr*
EMP: 152
SALES (corp-wide): 82.05K Privately Held
Web: www.se.com
SIC: 3613 Switchgear and switchboard
    apparatus
HQ: Schneider Electric Usa, Inc.
    1 Boston Pl Ste 2700
    Boston MA 02108
    978 975-9600

(G-11420)
SCHUNK INTEC INC
Also Called: Schunk
211 Kitty Hawk Dr (27560-8548)
P.O. Box 91023 (27675-1023)
PHONE.................................919 572-2705
Milton Guerry, *Pr*
Heinz D Schunk, *
Henrik Schunk, *
◆ EMP: 80 EST: 1992
SQ FT: 37,000
SALES (est): 24.11MM
SALES (corp-wide): 47.12MM Privately Held
Web: www.schunk.com
SIC: 3542 5084 3594 3544 Machine tools,
    metal forming type; Machine tools and
    metalworking machinery; Fluid power
    pumps and motors; Special dies, tools, jigs,
    and fixtures

PA: Schunk Se & Co. Kg Spanntechnik
Greiftechnik Automatisierungstechnik
Bahnhofstr. 106-134
Lauffen Am Neckar BW 74348
71331030

(G-11421)
SCIQUEST HOLDINGS INC
5151 Mccrimmon Pkwy Ste 216 (27560-0177)
PHONE..........................919 659-2100
Stephen J Wiehe, *CEO*
EMP: 89 **EST:** 2004
SALES (est): 2.27MM **Privately Held**
SIC: 7372 Educational computer software

(G-11422)
SCIQUEST PARENT LLC (PA)
3020 Carrington Mill Blvd Ste 100 (27560-5432)
PHONE..........................919 659-2100
EMP: 11 **EST:** 2016
SALES (est): 174.61MM
SALES (corp-wide): 174.61MM **Privately Held**
Web: www.jaggaer.com
SIC: 7372 Business oriented computer software

(G-11423)
SCORPIUS HOLDINGS INC (PA)
627 Davis Dr Ste 400 (27560-6847)
PHONE..........................919 240-7133
Jeffrey Wolf, *Ch Bd*
William L Ostrander, *CTRL*
EMP: 24 **EST:** 2008
SQ FT: 15,996
SALES (est): 6.38MM **Publicly Held**
Web: www.nighthawkbio.com
SIC: 2834 Pharmaceutical preparations

(G-11424)
SENSUS USA INC
639 Davis Dr (27560-6835)
PHONE..........................919 879-3200
Darrin Sutherland, *Brnch Mgr*
EMP: 444
Web: www.sensus.com
SIC: 3824 Gasmeters, domestic and large capacity: industrial
HQ: Sensus Usa Inc.
637 Davis Dr
Morrisville NC 27560

(G-11425)
SENSUS USA INC (HQ)
Also Called: Sensus
637 Davis Dr (27560-6835)
P.O. Box 30160 (77842-3160)
PHONE..........................919 845-4000
◆ **EMP:** 24 **EST:** 1989
SALES (est): 453.29MM **Publicly Held**
Web:
SIC: 3824 3363 2891 3491 Gasmeters, domestic and large capacity: industrial; Aluminum die-castings; Sealants; Industrial valves
PA: Xylem Inc.
301 Water St Se Ste 201
Washington DC 20003

(G-11426)
SENSUS USA INC
Also Called: Sensus Metering Systems
400 Perimeter Park Dr Ste K (27560-9744)
Rural Route 639 Davis Dr (27560)
PHONE..........................919 576-6185
EMP: 200
Web: www.sensus.com

SIC: 3824 3363 3491 2891 Gasmeters, domestic and large capacity: industrial; Aluminum die-castings; Industrial valves; Sealants
HQ: Sensus Usa Inc.
637 Davis Dr
Morrisville NC 27560

(G-11427)
SHIFTWIZARD INC
909 Aviation Pkwy Ste 700 (27560-6632)
PHONE..........................866 828-3318
Christain Pardue, *Pr*
David Moes, *VP*
Shane Pearker, *VP*
EMP: 10 **EST:** 2005
SQ FT: 1,000
SALES (est): 4.47MM **Publicly Held**
Web: www.shiftwizard.com
SIC: 3571 Electronic computers
PA: Healthstream, Inc.
500 11th Ave N Ste 1000
Nashville TN 37203

(G-11428)
SICEL TECHNOLOGIES INC
3800 Gateway Centre Blvd (27560)
PHONE..........................919 465-2236
Charles Scarantino, *Ch Bd*
Michael D Riddle, *
Jennifer Pierce, *
EMP: 48 **EST:** 1994
SQ FT: 17,625
SALES (est): 5.12MM **Privately Held**
SIC: 3841 Diagnostic apparatus, medical

(G-11429)
SIGNATURE FLIGHT AIR INC
Also Called: TAC Air
1725 E International Dr (27560-7690)
P.O. Box 90995 (27675-0995)
PHONE..........................919 840-4400
Greg Arnold, *CEO*
EMP: 30
SALES (corp-wide): 703.02MM **Privately Held**
Web: www.tacenergy.com
SIC: 3721 Aircraft
PA: Signature Flight Air Inc.
100 Crescent Ct Ste 1600
Dallas TX 75201
903 794-3835

(G-11430)
SMG HEARTH AND HOME LLC
Also Called: Comfort Bilt
9241 Globe Center Dr Ste 120 (27560-6204)
PHONE..........................919 973-4079
▲ **EMP:** 10 **EST:** 2014
SALES (est): 2.5MM **Privately Held**
Web: www.comfortbilt.net
SIC: 3433 Gas infrared heating units

(G-11431)
SOLARA SOLUTIONS LLC
Also Called: Solara Automation
155 Kitty Hawk Dr (27560-8511)
PHONE..........................919 534-1500
Harry Steven Crouch, *Pt*
EMP: 14 **EST:** 2004
SQ FT: 10,000
SALES (est): 4.97MM **Privately Held**
Web: www.solaraautomation.com
SIC: 3569 Assembly machines, non-metalworking

(G-11432)
SOUTHERN COMFORT A SYSTEMS LLC (PA)
141 Kitty Hawk Dr (27560-8511)

PHONE..........................919 324-6336
Steve Kearney, *Pr*
Mark Cassidy, *VP*
EMP: 6 **EST:** 2013
SALES (est): 441.75K
SALES (corp-wide): 441.75K **Privately Held**
SIC: 3444 1711 Ducts, sheet metal; Plumbing, heating, air-conditioning

(G-11433)
SOUTHPORT GRAPHICS LLC
9400 Globe Center Dr Ste 101 (27560-6213)
P.O. Box 91709 (27675-1709)
PHONE..........................919 650-3822
EMP: 6 **EST:** 2010
SQ FT: 5,600
SALES (est): 1.32MM **Privately Held**
Web: www.southportgraphics.com
SIC: 2752 Offset printing

(G-11434)
STOP N GO LLC
2916 Homebrook Ln (27560-7174)
PHONE..........................919 523-7355
EMP: 13
SALES (corp-wide): 1.84MM **Privately Held**
Web: www.kwiktrip.com
SIC: 2911 Petroleum refining
PA: Stop N Go Llc
2028 Mill Gate Ln
Cary NC

(G-11435)
SUNTECH MEDICAL INC
5827 S Miami Blvd Ste 100 (27560-8394)
PHONE..........................919 654-2300
▼ **EMP:** 80 **EST:** 1983
SALES (est): 28.74MM
SALES (corp-wide): 2.23B **Privately Held**
Web: www.suntechmed.com
SIC: 5047 3841 Medical equipment and supplies; Anesthesia apparatus
HQ: Halma Holdings Inc.
535 Sprngfeld Ave Ste 110
Summit NJ 07901
513 772-5501

(G-11436)
SYNEOS HEALTH CONSULTING INC
1030 Sync St (27560-5468)
PHONE..........................866 462-7373
Michael Brooks, *COO*
EMP: 93 **EST:** 1997
SALES (est): 12.41MM
SALES (corp-wide): 5.39B **Privately Held**
Web: www.syneoshealth.com
SIC: 2834 Pharmaceutical preparations
PA: Syneos Health, Inc.
1030 Sync St
Morrisville NC 27560
919 876-9300

(G-11437)
SYNOPSYS INC
710 Slater Rd (27560-6438)
PHONE..........................919 941-6600
Jonathan White, *Brnch Mgr*
EMP: 11
SALES (corp-wide): 5.84B **Publicly Held**
Web: www.synopsys.com
SIC: 7372 7371 5065 Application computer software; Custom computer programming services; Semiconductor devices
PA: Synopsys, Inc.
675 Almanor Ave
Sunnyvale CA 94085
650 584-5000

(G-11438)
TARHEEL WOOD TREATING COMPANY
10309 Chapel Hill Rd (27560-5413)
P.O. Box 480 (27560-0480)
PHONE..........................919 467-9176
James S Gallup, *Pr*
Vickie Gallup, *Sec*
EMP: 10 **EST:** 1956
SQ FT: 3,000
SALES (est): 1.76MM **Privately Held**
Web: www.tarheelwoodtreating.com
SIC: 2491 Structural lumber and timber, treated wood

(G-11439)
TEARSCIENCE INC
5151 Mccrimmon Pkwy Ste 250 (27560-0177)
PHONE..........................919 459-4880
Steve Grenon, *VP*
Brian Regan, *
Doug Pinotti, *
Donald Korb, *
Joe Boorady, *
▲ **EMP:** 90 **EST:** 2005
SALES (est): 11.74MM
SALES (corp-wide): 85.16B **Publicly Held**
Web: www.jnjvisionpro.com
SIC: 3845 Electromedical equipment
PA: Johnson & Johnson
1 Johnson And Johnson Plz
New Brunswick NJ 08933
732 524-0400

(G-11440)
TECHNOLIO INC
114 Bristolwood Cir (27560-6733)
PHONE..........................919 481-4454
Alexander Wechsler, *Prin*
EMP: 5 **EST:** 2009
SALES (est): 80.88K **Privately Held**
Web: www.iwechsler.com
SIC: 3652 Prerecorded records and tapes

(G-11441)
TECHNOSOFT INNOVATIONS INC
900 Perimeter Park Dr Ste C (27560-8725)
PHONE..........................919 388-3360
EMP: 7 **EST:** 2016
SALES (est): 238.81K **Privately Held**
Web: www.technosoftinv.com
SIC: 3841 Surgical and medical instruments

(G-11442)
TEKELEC INC
5200 Paramount Pkwy (27560-5469)
▲ **EMP:** 233 **EST:** 2012
SALES (est): 8.25MM
SALES (corp-wide): 49.95B **Publicly Held**
SIC: 3661 3825 7371 Telephone and telegraph apparatus; Test equipment for electronic and electrical circuits; Computer software development and applications
PA: Oracle Corporation
2300 Oracle Way
Austin TX 78741
737 867-1000

(G-11443)
TEKELEC GLOBAL INC
Also Called: Tekelec
5200 Paramount Pkwy (27560-5469)
PHONE..........................919 460-5500
EMP: 1291
SIC: 3661 3825 7371 Telephone and telegraph apparatus; Test equipment for electronic and electrical circuits; Computer software development and applications

Morrisville - Wake County (G-11444)   GEOGRAPHIC SECTION

(G-11444)
TELEFLEX INCORPORATED
Also Called: Teleflex
3015 Carrington Mill Blvd (27560-5437)
PHONE..................919 544-8000
EMP: 19
SALES (corp-wide): 2.97B Publicly Held
Web: www.teleflex.com
SIC: 3841 Catheters
PA: Teleflex Incorporated
    550 E Swedesford Rd # 400
    Wayne PA 19087
    610 225-6800

(G-11445)
TELEFLEX MEDICAL INCORPORATED (HQ)
3015 Carrington Mill Blvd (27560-5438)
P.O. Box 12600 (27709-2600)
PHONE..................919 544-8000
Liam Kelly, CEO
George Babich Junior, CEO
Gregg W Winter, VP
Cynthia Sharo, Sec
C Jeffrey Jacobs, Treas
◆ EMP: 79 EST: 1955
SALES (est): 412.29MM
SALES (corp-wide): 2.97B Publicly Held
Web: www.teleflex.com
SIC: 3841 Surgical and medical instruments
PA: Teleflex Incorporated
    550 E Swedesford Rd # 400
    Wayne PA 19087
    610 225-6800

(G-11446)
TG THERAPEUTICS INC (PA)
Also Called: TG THERAPEUTICS
3020 Carrington Mill Blvd Ste 475 (27560-5435)
PHONE..................212 554-4484
Michael S Weiss, Ch Bd
Sean A Power, Corporate Secretary
EMP: 57 EST: 1993
SALES (est): 233.66MM Publicly Held
Web: www.tgtherapeutics.com
SIC: 2834 Pharmaceutical preparations

(G-11447)
THOMAS CONCRETE CAROLINA INC
220 International Dr (27560-8708)
PHONE..................919 460-5317
Justin Hartley, Mgr
EMP: 11
SQ FT: 9,595
SALES (corp-wide): 1.01B Privately Held
Web: www.thomasconcrete.com
SIC: 3273 Ready-mixed concrete
HQ: Thomas Concrete Of Carolina, Inc.
    1131 N West St
    Raleigh NC 27603
    919 832-0451

(G-11448)
TICKETS PLUS INC (PA)
Also Called: Star Tickets Plus
909 Aviation Pkwy Ste 900 (27560-9000)
PHONE..................616 222-4000
Jack Krasula, Pr
Henry Mast, *
Robert Struyk, *
Larry D Fredericks, *
Kevin Einfeld, *
EMP: 35 EST: 1994
SALES (est): 3.97MM Privately Held
SIC: 2759 7999 Tickets: printing, nsk; Ticket sales office for sporting events, contract

(G-11449)
TRANE US INC
Also Called: Trane
401 Kitty Hawk Dr (27560-8271)
PHONE..................919 781-0458
Randy Zatz, Mgr
EMP: 6
Web: www.trane.com
SIC: 3585 Refrigeration and heating equipment
HQ: Trane U.S. Inc.
    800 Beaty St Ste E
    Davidson NC 28036
    704 655-4000

(G-11450)
TRANSENTERIX SURGICAL INC
635 Davis Dr Ste 300 (27560-7199)
PHONE..................919 765-8400
Todd M Pope, Pr
David N Gill, *
Richard M Mueller, *
▲ EMP: 65 EST: 2006
SALES (est): 3.34MM Publicly Held
Web: www.asensus.com
SIC: 3841 Surgical and medical instruments
PA: Asensus Surgical, Inc.
    1 Tw Alexander Dr Ste 160
    Durham NC 27703

(G-11451)
TRIANGLE COATINGS INC
6721 Mount Herman Rd (27560-9223)
PHONE..................919 781-6108
Terry Overton, Pr
Deborah Overton, Sec
EMP: 9 EST: 1978
SQ FT: 10,000
SALES (est): 757.44K Privately Held
Web: www.trianglepowdercoating.com
SIC: 3479 Coating of metals and formed products

(G-11452)
TRIANGLE INNER VISION COMPANY
Also Called: Speedpro of Northwest Raleigh
100 Dominion Dr Ste 110 (27560-9257)
PHONE..................919 460-6013
Jerry Parise, Pr
Kim Parise, VP
EMP: 4 EST: 2009
SQ FT: 3,000
SALES (est): 446.25K Privately Held
SIC: 3993 Signs and advertising specialties

(G-11453)
TRIANGLE PIPE FTTING SLTONS IN
Also Called: Triangle Service Solutions
102 Stardale Rd (27560-7064)
PHONE..................919 696-8635
Heidy Giron Espinoza, Prin
EMP: 7 EST: 2019
SALES (est): 534.37K Privately Held
SIC: 3494 Pipe fittings

(G-11454)
TRIANGLE READY MIX LLC
241 International Dr (27560-8411)
PHONE..................919 859-4190
Nelson Loureiro, Managing Member
EMP: 20
SALES (est): 2.77MM Privately Held
SIC: 3273 Ready-mixed concrete

(G-11455)
TRIMACO INC (PA)
2300 Gateway Centre Blvd Ste 200 (27560)
PHONE..................919 674-3460
Drew Cook, Sec
EMP: 5 EST: 2018

SALES (est): 10.55MM
SALES (corp-wide): 10.55MM Privately Held
Web: www.trimaco.com
SIC: 2394 Canvas covers and drop cloths

(G-11456)
TRIO LABS INC
133 Southcenter Ct Ste 900 (27560)
P.O. Box 13169 (27709-3169)
PHONE..................919 818-9646
Adam Steege, CEO
Ken Purchase, COO
Scott Schiller, CCO
EMP: 15 EST: 2015
SALES (est): 1.01MM Privately Held
Web: www.triolabs.com
SIC: 3555 Printing trades machinery

(G-11457)
TRIPHARM SERVICES INC
627 Davis Dr Ste 100 (27560-7101)
PHONE..................984 243-0800
Patrick Walsh, CEO
EMP: 10 EST: 2019
SALES (est): 2.08MM
SALES (corp-wide): 418.48MM Privately Held
Web: www.alcami.com
SIC: 2834 Solutions, pharmaceutical
PA: Alcami Corporation
    2320 Scientific Park Dr
    Wilmington NC 28405
    910 254-7000

(G-11458)
TUFF SHED INC
409 Airport Blvd (27560-8426)
PHONE..................919 413-2494
EMP: 6
SALES (corp-wide): 347.42MM Privately Held
Web: www.tuffshed.com
SIC: 2452 Prefabricated wood buildings
PA: Tuff Shed, Inc.
    1777 S Harrison St # 600
    Denver CO 80210
    303 753-8833

(G-11459)
TYRATECH INC
5151 Mccrimmon Pkwy Ste 275 (27560-5425)
PHONE..................919 415-4275
Bruno Jactel, CEO
Alan Reid, *
Peter K Jerome, *
Vincent T Morgus, *
EMP: 35 EST: 2007
SALES (est): 9.2MM
SALES (corp-wide): 609.62MM Publicly Held
Web: www.tyratech.com
SIC: 2879 Insecticides, agricultural or household
PA: American Vanguard Corporation
    4695 Macarthur Ct
    Newport Beach CA 92660
    949 260-1200

(G-11460)
UNLIMITED POTENTIAL SANFORD INC
Also Called: Millennium Print Group
9301 Globe Center Dr Ste 120 (27560-6203)
PHONE..................919 852-1117
Darren Spivey, Pr
David Lane, VP
EMP: 21 EST: 1989
SALES (est): 1.96MM Privately Held

SIC: 7334 2752 Photocopying and duplicating services; Offset printing

(G-11461)
VASONOVA INC
3015 Carrington Mill Blvd (27560-5437)
PHONE..................650 327-1412
▲ EMP: 17
SIC: 3841 Surgical and medical instruments

(G-11462)
VAST THERAPEUTICS INC
Also Called: Novoclem
615 Davis Dr Ste 800 (27560-6845)
PHONE..................919 321-1403
Neal Hunter, CEO
John Oakley, CFO
EMP: 6 EST: 2017
SALES (est): 2.61MM Privately Held
Web: www.vasttherapeutics.com
SIC: 2834 Drugs acting on the respiratory system

(G-11463)
VECTOR TOBACCO INC
3800 Paramount Pkwy Ste 250 (27560)
P.O. Box 2010 (27560-2010)
PHONE..................919 990-3500
Howard M Lorber, Prin
EMP: 26 EST: 2011
SALES (est): 990.08K Privately Held
Web: www.liggettvectorbrands.com
SIC: 2111 Cigarettes

(G-11464)
VIAVI SOLUTIONS INC
1100 Perimeter Park Dr Ste 101 (27560-9119)
PHONE..................919 388-5100
EMP: 4
SALES (corp-wide): 1.11B Publicly Held
Web: www.viavisolutions.com
SIC: 3674 Semiconductors and related devices
PA: Viavi Solutions Inc.
    1445 S Spectrum Blvd # 102
    Chandler AZ 85286
    408 404-3600

(G-11465)
WEBSTER FINE ART LIMITED (PA)
2800 Perimeter Park Dr Ste A (27560-0176)
PHONE..................919 349-8455
Brandin Myers, Pr
Tim Myers, VP
◆ EMP: 4 EST: 1987
SALES (est): 432.42K Privately Held
Web: www.websterspages.com
SIC: 2741 Art copy: publishing only, not printed on site

(G-11466)
WESTROCK PAPER AND PACKG LLC
Also Called: Kapstone Paper Packaging
5150 Mccrimmon Pkwy (27560-0179)
PHONE..................919 463-3100
EMP: 198
SALES (corp-wide): 20.31B Publicly Held
Web: www.westrock.com
SIC: 2653 Boxes, corrugated: made from purchased materials
HQ: Westrock Paper And Packaging, Llc
    1000 Abernathy Rd
    Atlanta GA 30328

(G-11467)
XSCHEM INC (PA)
Also Called: Nterline
1500 Perimeter Park Dr Ste 300 (27560-0195)

GEOGRAPHIC SECTION

Mount Airy - Surry County (G-11491)

PHONE.............................919 379-3500
Fulton Breen, CEO
Bill Barton, COO
EMP: 20 EST: 1998
SALES (est): 4.6MM
SALES (corp-wide): 4.6MM Privately Held
SIC: 7372 Business oriented computer software

(G-11468)
YOUR CABINET CONNECTION INC
10315 Chapel Hill Rd (27560-8707)
P.O. Box 1507 (27502-3507)
PHONE.............................919 641-2877
Marvin Eugene Allen Iii, Pr
EMP: 8 EST: 2017
SALES (est): 231.46K Privately Held
Web: www.yourcabinetconnectionnc.com
SIC: 2434 Wood kitchen cabinets

(G-11469)
ZEBRA COMMUNICATIONS INC (PA)
Also Called: Zebra Print Solutions
9401 Globe Center Dr Ste 130 (27560-6211)
PHONE.............................919 314-3700
Charlotte Dileonardo, CEO
Patrick Dileonardo, Pr
EMP: 21 EST: 1991
SQ FT: 10,000
SALES (est): 2.41MM
SALES (corp-wide): 2.41MM Privately Held
Web: www.zebraprintsolutions.com
SIC: 7334 2752 7336 Photocopying and duplicating services; Offset printing; Graphic arts and related design

(G-11470)
ZIPTRONIX INC
800 Perimeter Park Dr Ste B (27560-7271)
PHONE.............................919 459-2400
Dan Donabedian, CEO
EMP: 16 EST: 2003
SQ FT: 1,200
SALES (est): 3.87MM
SALES (corp-wide): 388.79MM Publicly Held
Web: www.ziptronix.com
SIC: 3674 Semiconductors and related devices
HQ: Tessera Technologies, Inc.
    3025 Orchard Pkwy
    San Jose CA 95134
    408 321-6000

Morven
Anson County

(G-11471)
I I G LOGGING INC
10342 Highway 145 (28119-7735)
P.O. Box 608 (28119-0608)
PHONE.............................704 984-3175
EMP: 4 EST: 2015
SALES (est): 68.65K Privately Held
SIC: 2411 Logging

Mount Airy
Surry County

(G-11472)
ACME STONE COMPANY INC
1700 Fancy Gap Rd (27030-1800)
P.O. Box 925 (27030-0925)
PHONE.............................336 786-6978
▲ EMP: 22 EST: 1957
SQ FT: 2,250
SALES (est): 925.17K Privately Held
Web: www.acmestonenc.com
SIC: 3281 5999 1799 Monument or burial stone, cut and shaped; Monuments and tombstones; Counter top installation

(G-11473)
ADVANCED ELECTRONIC SVCS INC (PA)
Also Called: Ces
101 Technology Ln (27030-6683)
PHONE.............................336 789-0792
▲ EMP: 90 EST: 1992
SQ FT: 2,800
SALES (est): 21.27MM Privately Held
Web: www.aesintl.com
SIC: 7629 3699 Electronic equipment repair; Accelerating waveguide structures

(G-11474)
ADVENTURE SIGN AND LTG LLC
473 Oak Ridge Dr (27030-8766)
PHONE.............................336 401-3410
John Brandon Mchone, Pr
EMP: 4 EST: 2017
SALES (est): 168.96K Privately Held
SIC: 3993 Signs and advertising specialties

(G-11475)
ALTEC INDUSTRIES INC
Also Called: Altec Inds Mt Airy Operations
200 Altec Way (27030-9934)
PHONE.............................336 786-3623
EMP: 19
SALES (corp-wide): 1.21B Privately Held
Web: www.altec.com
SIC: 3531 Derricks, except oil and gas field
HQ: Altec Industries, Inc.
    210 Inverness Center Dr
    Birmingham AL 35242
    205 991-7733

(G-11476)
AMERICAN CARPORTS STRUCTURES
152 Eastwind Ct (27030-7818)
PHONE.............................336 710-1091
EMP: 4 EST: 2018
SALES (est): 99.72K Privately Held
Web: www.carportcentral.com
SIC: 3448 Prefabricated metal buildings and components

(G-11477)
AMERICAN CARPORTS STUCTURES
155 Mount View Dr (27030-2454)
PHONE.............................844 628-4973
EMP: 4 EST: 2018
SALES (est): 95.5K Privately Held
Web: www.carportcentral.com
SIC: 3448 Prefabricated metal buildings and components

(G-11478)
AWESOME PRODUCTS INC
1625 Sheep Farm Rd (27030-6379)
PHONE.............................336 374-5900
Loksarang D Hardas, Admn
EMP: 6 EST: 2013
SALES (est): 570.96K Privately Held
Web: www.lastotallyawesome.com
SIC: 2842 Cleaning or polishing preparations, nec

(G-11479)
B & M WHOLESALE INC
Also Called: B & M Wholesale
1800 Sparger Rd (27030-7565)
PHONE.............................336 789-3916
Michael B Waddell, Pr
Blanche Waddell, Sec
Buernie Waddell, VP
EMP: 6 EST: 1949
SALES (est): 733.44K Privately Held
Web: b-m-wholesale.edan.io
SIC: 5099 5085 2252 Novelties, durable; Industrial tools; Socks

(G-11480)
BARES BACKHOE & SEPTIC SYSTEM
2020 Haystack Rd (27030-9087)
PHONE.............................336 352-3951
Mathew Brain Bare, Prin
EMP: 5 EST: 2017
SALES (est): 79.14K Privately Held
Web: www.baresbackhoe.com
SIC: 3531 Backhoes

(G-11481)
BARNHARDT MANUFACTURING CO
Also Called: Ncfi Polyurethanes
1515 Carter St (27030-5721)
P.O. Box 1528 (27030-1528)
PHONE.............................336 789-9161
EMP: 170
SALES (corp-wide): 268.75MM Privately Held
Web: www.barnhardt.net
SIC: 3086 Plastics foam products
PA: Barnhardt Manufacturing Company
    1100 Hawthorne Ln
    Charlotte NC 28205
    800 277-0377

(G-11482)
BED IN A BOX
199 Woltz St (27030)
PHONE.............................800 588-5720
EMP: 5 EST: 2020
SALES (est): 40.95K Privately Held
Web: www.bedinabox.com
SIC: 2392 Mattress pads

(G-11483)
BGI RECOVERY LLC
127 Belvue Dr (27030-5190)
PHONE.............................336 429-6976
Tonya Ferguson, Prin
EMP: 5 EST: 2010
SALES (est): 133.89K Privately Held
SIC: 3531 Automobile wrecker hoists

(G-11484)
BOBCAT OF MOUNT AIRY
825 W Lebanon St Ste 101 (27030-2219)
PHONE.............................336 459-3844
EMP: 5 EST: 2018
SALES (est): 60.08K Privately Held
Web: www.curtis-lane.com
SIC: 3531 Construction machinery

(G-11485)
BOTTOMLEY ENTERPRISES INC
452 Oak Grove Church Rd (27030-8769)
P.O. Box 70 (28623-0070)
PHONE.............................336 657-6400
Mitchell Bottomley, CEO
Deanna Bottomley, *
Michelle Voss, *
EMP: 84 EST: 2004
SALES (est): 24.68MM Privately Held
Web: www.bottomleyenterprises.com
SIC: 3537 Trucks: freight, baggage, etc.: industrial, except mining

(G-11486)
BRAY S RECAPPING SERVICE INC (PA)
1120 W Lebanon St (27030-2226)
P.O. Box 804 (27030-0804)
PHONE.............................336 786-6182
E Dean Bray Iii, Pr
E Dean Bray Junior, VP
Rebecca Bray, VP
Shannon Bray, VP
EMP: 22 EST: 1930
SALES (est): 1.42MM
SALES (corp-wide): 1.42MM Privately Held
SIC: 7534 5531 Tire recapping; Automotive tires

(G-11487)
CARDINAL CT COMPANY
630 Derby St (27030-4400)
PHONE.............................336 719-6857
EMP: 246
SALES (corp-wide): 1B Privately Held
Web: www.cardinalcorp.com
SIC: 3211 Tempered glass
HQ: Cardinal Ct Company
    775 Pririe Ctr Dr Ste 200
    Eden Prairie MN 55344

(G-11488)
CAROLINA CONNECTIONS INC
Also Called: Unique Background Solutions
805 Merita St (27030-2763)
P.O. Box 1604 (27030-1604)
PHONE.............................336 786-7030
Norwood A Barnes Junior, Pr
Michael Barnes, VP
EMP: 9 EST: 2002
SALES (est): 950.88K Privately Held
Web: www.uniquebackground.com
SIC: 7389 2899 7375 Personal service agents, brokers, and bureaus; Drug testing kits, blood and urine; Information retrieval services

(G-11489)
CAROLINA EXPEDITERS LLC
1415 Fancy Gap Rd (27030-1821)
P.O. Box 207 (27030-0207)
PHONE.............................888 537-5330
Jason Lee Ring, Mgr
EMP: 4 EST: 2008
SALES (est): 478.6K Privately Held
Web: www.freightemergency.com
SIC: 3537 4789 Containers (metal), air cargo ; Cargo loading and unloading services

(G-11490)
CAROLINA NORTH GRANITE CORP
151 Granite Quarry Trl (27030-3970)
PHONE.............................336 719-2600
C Richard Vaughn, Ch Bd
Donald R Shelton, *
Joan H Gammons, *
D Sam Brintle, *
◆ EMP: 90 EST: 1889
SQ FT: 25,000
SALES (est): 13.96MM
SALES (corp-wide): 2.1MM Privately Held
Web: www.polycor.com
SIC: 3281 Building stone products
HQ: Polycor Inc
    100-76 Rue Saint-Paul
    Quebec QC G1K 3
    418 692-4695

(G-11491)
CARPORT CENTRAL INC
1372 Boggs Dr (27030-2144)
P.O. Box 1308 (27030-1308)
PHONE.............................980 321-9898
Alvaro Lara, Pr
EMP: 75 EST: 2014
SALES (est): 10.8MM Privately Held

Mount Airy - Surry County (G-11492)

(G-11492)
CARPORT COMMANDER LLC
238 Willow St Ste 102 (27030-3683)
PHONE................................800 688-6151
EMP: 4 **EST:** 2019
SALES (est): 67.71K **Privately Held**
Web: www.carportcommander.com
SIC: 3448 Prefabricated metal buildings and components

(G-11493)
CARPORT DIRECT INC
737 S Main St (27030-4723)
PHONE................................336 715-8217
EMP: 5 **EST:** 2017
SALES (est): 70.28K **Privately Held**
Web: www.carportdirect.com
SIC: 3448 Prefabricated metal buildings and components

(G-11494)
CCBCC OPERATIONS LLC
Also Called: Coca-Cola
2516 W Pine St (27030-8544)
PHONE................................336 789-7111
Sid Harris, *Brnch Mgr*
EMP: 45
SALES (corp-wide): 6.65B **Publicly Held**
Web: www.coca-cola.com
SIC: 2086 Bottled and canned soft drinks
HQ: Ccbcc Operations, Llc
4100 Coca Cola Plz
Charlotte NC 28211
704 364-8728

(G-11495)
CENTRAL STATES MFG INC
751 Piedmont Triad West Dr (27030-9851)
PHONE................................336 719-3280
Charlie Cox, *Brnch Mgr*
EMP: 157
SALES (corp-wide): 148.14MM **Privately Held**
Web: www.centralstatesco.com
SIC: 3353 3448 Aluminum sheet, plate, and foil; Prefabricated metal buildings and components
PA: Central States Manufacturing, Inc.
171 Naples St
Tontitown AR 72762
800 356-2733

(G-11496)
CENTRAL STEEL BUILDINGS INC
Also Called: Carport Central
181 Woltz St (27030-7832)
PHONE................................336 789-7896
Albert Lara, *Pr*
Zack Mcmillian, *Genl Mgr*
Jody Casstevens, *Genl Mgr*
Eric Aparicio, *Genl Mgr*
Rick York, *Prin*
▲ **EMP:** 10 **EST:** 2015
SALES (est): 1.36MM **Privately Held**
Web: www.carportcentral.com
SIC: 3448 1541 Carports, prefabricated metal ; Steel building construction

(G-11497)
COAST TO COAST CARPORTS INC
Also Called: COAST TO COAST CARPORTS INC.
170 Holly Springs Rd (27030-6688)
P.O. Box 100 (72845-0100)
PHONE................................336 783-3015
Primo Castillo, *Prin*
EMP: 28
SALES (corp-wide): 23.06MM **Privately Held**
Web: www.coast-to-coastcarports.com
SIC: 3448 Carports, prefabricated metal
PA: Coast To Coast Carports, Inc.
22525 I 40 Knoxville
Knoxville AR 72845
479 885-1258

(G-11498)
CREATIVE LIQUID COATINGS INC
710 Piedmont Triad West Dr (27030-9851)
PHONE................................336 415-6214
Josh Ault, *Brnch Mgr*
EMP: 73
Web: www.creativeliquidcoatings.com
SIC: 3089 Injection molding of plastics
PA: Creative Liquid Coatings, Inc.
2620 Marion Dr
Kendallville IN 46755

(G-11499)
D & D WELDING & REPAIR LLC
350 Slate Mountain Rd (27030-4902)
PHONE................................336 648-1393
EMP: 4 **EST:** 2016
SALES (est): 47.65K **Privately Held**
Web: mountairyncwelder-d-d-welding-repair.business.site
SIC: 7692 Welding repair

(G-11500)
DESENA COMMERCIAL SERVICES LLC
525 Holly Springs Rd (27030-8081)
PHONE................................336 786-1111
Tom Desena, *Prin*
EMP: 8 **EST:** 2008
SALES (est): 260.44K **Privately Held**
Web: www.desenacommercialservices.com
SIC: 3993 Signs and advertising specialties

(G-11501)
DESENA COMMERCIAL SVC
268 Old Highway 601 (27030-5974)
PHONE................................336 786-1111
Tom Desena, *Owner*
EMP: 4 **EST:** 2015
SALES (est): 45.07K **Privately Held**
Web: www.desenacommercialservices.com
SIC: 3993 Signs and advertising specialties

(G-11502)
DIRECT DISCOUNT CARPORTS
743 Slate Mountain Rd (27030-4883)
PHONE................................888 642-1910
Penny Mccoy, *Prin*
EMP: 5 **EST:** 2016
SALES (est): 113.04K **Privately Held**
Web: www.tntcarports.com
SIC: 3448 Prefabricated metal buildings and components

(G-11503)
EAGLE CARPORTS INC (PA)
210 Airport Rd (27030-7950)
PHONE................................800 579-8589
Gabriel Torrez, *Pr*
EMP: 25 **EST:** 1997
SQ FT: 1,800
SALES (est): 25.61MM
SALES (corp-wide): 25.61MM **Privately Held**
Web: www.eaglecarports.com
SIC: 1541 3448 Steel building construction; Buildings, portable: prefabricated metal

(G-11504)
EASTCOAST CARPORTS
510 Riverside Dr (27030-3688)
PHONE................................336 755-3409
EMP: 6 **EST:** 2019
SALES (est): 501.43K **Privately Held**
Web: www.carportcentral.com
SIC: 3448 Prefabricated metal buildings and components

(G-11505)
EASYGLASS INC
Also Called: Andrew Pearson Design
1 Andrew Pearson Dr (27030-2124)
PHONE................................336 786-1800
Harold Brownfield, *Pr*
Susanne Brownfield Ph.d., *Ex VP*
▲ **EMP:** 22 **EST:** 1990
SQ FT: 70,000
SALES (est): 494.99K **Privately Held**
SIC: 3229 2511 3231 Pressed and blown glass, nec; Wood household furniture; Furniture tops, glass: cut, beveled, or polished

(G-11506)
EDWARDS LOGGING INC
119 Crabapple Ln (27030-8892)
PHONE................................336 783-0833
EMP: 4 **EST:** 2019
SALES (est): 98.88K **Privately Held**
SIC: 2411 Logging

(G-11507)
ESTES MACHINE CO
256 Snowhill Dr (27030-4392)
PHONE................................336 786-7680
EMP: 14 **EST:** 1990
SQ FT: 10,000
SALES (est): 218.76K **Privately Held**
SIC: 3599 7692 Machine shop, jobbing and repair; Welding repair

(G-11508)
EVERVIEW
201 Technology Ln (27030-6684)
PHONE................................800 549-4722
Eric W Ek, *CEO*
EMP: 6 **EST:** 2018
SALES (est): 68.72K **Privately Held**
SIC: 7372 Prepackaged software

(G-11509)
FIBRECRETE PPRSRVTION TECH INC
Also Called: Fpt Infrastructure
131 Saint James Way (27030-6068)
PHONE................................336 789-7259
Jonathan Simmons, *Pr*
Mark O'neal, *VP*
Rick Marion, *Contrlr*
Mark E Mcgonigle, *Treas*
Edward W Moore, *Sec*
EMP: 9 **EST:** 2016
SALES (est): 5.77MM
SALES (corp-wide): 7.26B **Publicly Held**
Web: www.fptinfrastructure.com
SIC: 2951 Road materials, bituminous (not from refineries)
HQ: Rpm Performance Coatings Group, Inc.
280 West Ave
Long Branch NJ 07740
888 788-4323

(G-11510)
GENESYS TECHNOLOGY INC
506 Bennett St (27030-5873)
PHONE................................336 789-0763
Mark E Coleman, *Owner*
EMP: 12 **EST:** 2003
SALES (est): 98.99K **Privately Held**
Web: www.genesys.com
SIC: 7372 Business oriented computer software

(G-11511)
GEORGIA-CAROLINA QUARRIES INC (PA)
1700 Fancy Gap Rd (27030-1800)
P.O. Box 925 (27030-0925)
PHONE................................336 786-6978
Bob Stevens, *Pr*
Mary Laura Stevens, *Sec*
Mark Steven, *VP*
EMP: 20 **EST:** 1979
SQ FT: 50
SALES (est): 5.18MM
SALES (corp-wide): 5.18MM **Privately Held**
SIC: 1423 3281 Crushed and broken granite; Curbing, granite or stone

(G-11512)
GRANITE MEMORIALS INC
636 S Main St (27030-4722)
P.O. Box 790 (27041-0790)
PHONE................................336 786-6596
EMP: 8
SALES (est): 400K **Privately Held**
SIC: 3281 5999 Cut stone and stone products; Monuments and tombstones

(G-11513)
GRANITE TACTICAL VEHICLES INC
915 Newsome St (27030-5421)
PHONE................................336 789-5555
Christopher Berman, *Pr*
Tammy Geldenhuys, *VP*
EMP: 12 **EST:** 2006
SALES (est): 2.49MM **Privately Held**
Web: www.granitetacticalvehicles.com
SIC: 3711 Cars, armored, assembly of

(G-11514)
GUNS WELDING LLC
496 Belton Rd (27030-8232)
PHONE................................336 786-1020
Timothy T Minter, *Admn*
EMP: 5 **EST:** 2013
SALES (est): 119.03K **Privately Held**
SIC: 7692 Welding repair

(G-11515)
HANESBRANDS INC
Also Called: L'Eggs - Hanes - Bali
645 W Pine St (27030-4439)
PHONE................................336 789-6118
Doug St Louis, *Mgr*
EMP: 5
Web: www.hanes.com
SIC: 2251 2252 Women's hosiery, except socks; Hosiery, nec
PA: Hanesbrands Inc.
1000 E Hanes Mill Rd
Winston Salem NC 27105

(G-11516)
HAO WEI LAI INC
2021 Rockford St (27030-5203)
PHONE................................336 789-9969
Wu Lin, *Prin*
EMP: 7 **EST:** 2012
SALES (est): 85.58K **Privately Held**
SIC: 3421 Table and food cutlery, including butchers'

(G-11517)
HARVEST TIME BREAD COMPANY
501 Piedmont Triad W Dr (27030-9850)
EMP: 100

SIC: 2051 Breads, rolls, and buns

(G-11518)
HICKS WTERSTOVES SOLAR SYSTEMS
Also Called: Hicks Mechanical
2649 S Main St (27030-7219)
PHONE..............................336 789-4977
Mark Hicks, *Pr*
Mark Hicks, *Pr*
Carol Hicks, *VP*
EMP: 11 **EST:** 1981
SQ FT: 13,000
SALES (est): 1.97MM **Privately Held**
Web: www.hickswaterstoves.com
SIC: 1711 3433 3441 Process piping contractor; Heating equipment, except electric; Fabricated structural metal

(G-11519)
HULL BROTHERS LUMBER CO INC
579 Maple Hollow Rd (27030-9731)
PHONE..............................336 789-5252
Howard W Hull, *Pr*
Chad H Hull, *Sec*
Brent Hull, *VP*
Howard Hull Junior, *Asst VP*
EMP: 22 **EST:** 1943
SQ FT: 900
SALES (est): 941.21K **Privately Held**
SIC: 2421 2426 Sawmills and planing mills, general; Hardwood dimension and flooring mills

(G-11520)
INSTEEL INDUSTRIES INC (PA)
Also Called: Insteel
1373 Boggs Dr (27030-2145)
PHONE..............................336 786-2141
H O Woltz Iii, *Pr*
Richard T Wagner, *Sr VP*
James R York, *Sr VP*
Scot R Jafroodi, *VP*
Elizabeth C Southern, *CLO*
◆ **EMP:** 124 **EST:** 1953
SALES (est): 649.19MM
SALES (corp-wide): 649.19MM **Publicly Held**
Web: www.insteel.com
SIC: 3441 Fabricated structural metal

(G-11521)
INSTEEL WIRE PRODUCTS COMPANY (HQ)
1373 Boggs Dr (27030-2145)
PHONE..............................336 719-9000
H O Woltz Iii, *Pr*
James F Petelle, *Admn Execs*
Richard Wagner, *General Vice President*
Michael C Gazmarian, *VP*
Lyle Bullington, *Vice-President Information Systems*
◆ **EMP:** 101 **EST:** 1981
SQ FT: 43,000
SALES (est): 480.78MM
SALES (corp-wide): 649.19MM **Publicly Held**
Web: www.insteel.com
SIC: 3315 Welded steel wire fabric
PA: Insteel Industries Inc.
1373 Boggs Dr
Mount Airy NC 27030
336 786-2141

(G-11522)
INTERCONTINENTAL METALS CORP
1373 Boggs Dr (27030-2145)
PHONE..............................336 786-2141
Howard Woltz Iii, *Pr*
Gary Kniskern, *
EMP: 75 **EST:** 1955

SALES (est): 9.19MM
SALES (corp-wide): 649.19MM **Publicly Held**
SIC: 3496 Concrete reinforcing mesh and wire
PA: Insteel Industries Inc.
1373 Boggs Dr
Mount Airy NC 27030
336 786-2141

(G-11523)
INTERLAM CORPORATION
391 Hickory St (27030-2264)
PHONE..............................336 786-6254
Alvin Eckenrod, *Pr*
◆ **EMP:** 20 **EST:** 1987
SQ FT: 70,000
SALES (est): 4.72MM **Privately Held**
Web: www.interlam-design.com
SIC: 2541 5162 Bar fixtures, wood; Plastics materials and basic shapes

(G-11524)
INTERSTATE SIGN COMPANY INC
1990 Rockford St (27030-5202)
PHONE..............................336 789-3069
Ricky Shelton, *Pr*
Steve Barnard, *Sec*
EMP: 23 **EST:** 1991
SQ FT: 6,000
SALES (est): 2.43MM **Privately Held**
Web: www.interstatesign.com
SIC: 1799 3993 Sign installation and maintenance; Electric signs

(G-11525)
JANTEC SIGN GROUP LLC
196 Sexton Rd (27030-8784)
PHONE..............................336 429-5010
Jan Day Legere, *Mgr*
EMP: 34 **EST:** 2017
SALES (est): 2.6MM **Privately Held**
Web: www.jantecneon.com
SIC: 3993 Signs and advertising specialties

(G-11526)
JIM JOHN
1223 Laurel Springs Church Rd (27030-9720)
PHONE..............................336 352-4650
Walter Johnson, *Prin*
EMP: 5 **EST:** 2016
SALES (est): 52.1K **Privately Held**
Web: www.mtairynews.com
SIC: 2711 Newspapers, publishing and printing

(G-11527)
K & D SIGNS LLC
1078 S Main St (27030-4730)
P.O. Box 1546 (27030-1546)
PHONE..............................336 786-1111
Tony Kirby, *Admn*
EMP: 10 **EST:** 2014
SALES (est): 959.46K **Privately Held**
Web: www.kdsignllc.com
SIC: 3993 Signs and advertising specialties

(G-11528)
KAT DESIGNS INC
Also Called: T W Signs & Graphics
280 Hickory St (27030-2212)
PHONE..............................336 789-7288
EMP: 6 **EST:** 1996
SALES (est): 461.24K **Privately Held**
Web: www.twsigns.net
SIC: 3993 Signs, not made in custom sign painting shops

(G-11529)
KB SOCKS INC
661 Linville Rd (27030-3101)
P.O. Box 908 (27030-0908)
PHONE..............................336 719-8000
Karen Bell, *CEO*
EMP: 21 **EST:** 2011
SALES (est): 4.8MM
SALES (corp-wide): 3.26B **Privately Held**
Web: www.kbellsocks.com
SIC: 2252 Socks
HQ: Renfro Llc
661 Linville Rd
Mount Airy NC 27030
336 719-8000

(G-11530)
KEN HORTON LOGGING LLC
120 W Elm St (27030-3502)
PHONE..............................336 789-2849
Ken Horton, *Owner*
EMP: 4 **EST:** 1985
SALES (est): 463.39K **Privately Held**
Web: www.getfitwithida.com
SIC: 2411 Logging camps and contractors

(G-11531)
KIEFFER STARLITE COMPANY
609 Junction St (27030-3719)
PHONE..............................800 659-2493
EMP: 4 **EST:** 2019
SALES (est): 171.21K **Privately Held**
SIC: 2752 Commercial printing, lithographic

(G-11532)
KINGS PRTBLE WLDG FBRCTION LLC
832 W Lebanon St (27030-2220)
PHONE..............................336 789-2372
Jack King, *Owner*
EMP: 4 **EST:** 1971
SQ FT: 4,500
SALES (est): 420.1K **Privately Held**
Web: kings-portable-welding-fabrication-llc.business.site
SIC: 7692 3443 Welding repair; Fabricated plate work (boiler shop)

(G-11533)
KUSTOM KRAFT WDWRKS MT AIRY IN
Also Called: Surry Collection
3096 Westfield Rd (27030-9553)
PHONE..............................336 786-2831
Claybern Taylor, *Pr*
Peggy Taylor, *VP*
EMP: 4 **EST:** 1976
SQ FT: 8,500
SALES (est): 332.4K **Privately Held**
SIC: 2511 Wood household furniture

(G-11534)
LAB DESIGNS LLC (PA)
Also Called: Lab Dsgns Archtctural Laminate
391 Hickory St (27030-2264)
PHONE..............................336 429-4114
Joseph Ervin, *Managing Member*
▲ **EMP:** 7 **EST:** 2010
SQ FT: 10,000
SALES (est): 1.56MM
SALES (corp-wide): 1.56MM **Privately Held**
Web: www.labdesignlaminate.com
SIC: 3299 Mica, laminated

(G-11535)
LAZEREDGE LLC
244 Brunswick Ln (27030-3765)
PHONE..............................336 480-7934

William Pfitzner, *Brnch Mgr*
EMP: 5
SALES (corp-wide): 2.14MM **Privately Held**
Web: www.lazeredge.com
SIC: 3555 Blocks, wood: engravers'
PA: Lazeredge, Llc
244 Brunswick Ln
Mount Airy NC 27030
336 480-7934

(G-11536)
LAZEREDGE LLC (PA)
244 Brunswick Ln (27030-3765)
P.O. Box 15 (27030-0015)
PHONE..............................336 480-7934
William Pfitzner, *Prin*
EMP: 5 **EST:** 2015
SALES (est): 2.14MM
SALES (corp-wide): 2.14MM **Privately Held**
Web: www.lazeredge.com
SIC: 3555 Blocks, wood: engravers'

(G-11537)
LEAR METAL CARPORTS LLC
149 Tanglewood Dr (27030-7777)
PHONE..............................877 219-4677
EMP: 5 **EST:** 2017
SALES (est): 68.6K **Privately Held**
Web: www.learmetalcarports.com
SIC: 3448 Prefabricated metal buildings and components

(G-11538)
LEONARD ALUM UTLITY BLDNGS INC (PA)
Also Called: Leonard Building & Trck Covers
630 W Independence Blvd Ste 3 (27030-3568)
P.O. Box 1728 (27030-1728)
PHONE..............................336 789-5018
Sandra P Leonard, *Pr*
David Oneal, *
Michael J Leonard, *
Bruce Strohl, *
EMP: 75 **EST:** 1967
SQ FT: 100,000
SALES (est): 98.91MM
SALES (corp-wide): 98.91MM **Privately Held**
Web: www.leonardusa.com
SIC: 5531 3448 Truck equipment and parts; Prefabricated metal buildings

(G-11539)
LL CULTURED MARBLE INC
1184 Maple Grove Church Rd (27030-7552)
PHONE..............................336 789-3908
Doris Holder, *Pr*
EMP: 12 **EST:** 1976
SALES (est): 912.63K **Privately Held**
Web: www.llmarble.com
SIC: 2493 3088 Marbleboard (stone face hard board); Plastics plumbing fixtures

(G-11540)
LS STARRETT COMPANY
1372 Boggs Dr (27030-2144)
PHONE..............................336 789-5141
EMP: 25
SALES (corp-wide): 256.18MM **Publicly Held**
Web: www.starrett.com
SIC: 3545 Machine tool accessories
PA: The L S Starrett Company
121 Crescent St
Athol MA 01331
978 249-3551

Mount Airy - Surry County (G-11541)

(G-11541)
LUCK STONE CORPORATION
525 Quarry Rd (27030-9959)
PHONE....................................336 786-4693
Charles S Luck Iii, *Ch Bd*
EMP: 28
SALES (corp-wide): 366.46MM **Privately Held**
Web: www.luckstone.com
SIC: 1423 Crushed and broken granite
PA: Luck Stone Corporation
515 Stone Mill Dr
Manakin Sabot VA 23103
804 784-6300

(G-11542)
LYONS HOSIERY INC
719 S South St (27030-4425)
P.O. Box 1833 (27030-6833)
PHONE....................................336 789-2651
Clancy Lyons, *Pr*
Trent Lyons, *Stockholder*
Sandy Lyons, *Sec*
Susan Simmons, *Stockholder*
▲ **EMP:** 11 **EST:** 1980
SQ FT: 40,000
SALES (est): 287.94K **Privately Held**
Web: www.bargain-bulk-sock-sales.com
SIC: 2252 Socks

(G-11543)
M & M SIGNS AND AWNINGS INC
1465 Ladonia Church Rd (27030-9080)
PHONE....................................336 352-4300
TOLL FREE: 800
Dale Golding, *Pr*
Melissa Golding, *Sec*
EMP: 10 **EST:** 1970
SQ FT: 2,500
SALES (est): 990.29K **Privately Held**
Web: www.mmsignsinc.com
SIC: 3993 2394 Signs, not made in custom sign painting shops; Canvas and related products

(G-11544)
MAYBERRY DISTILLERY
461 N South St (27030-3533)
PHONE....................................336 719-6860
James Mayberry, *Prin*
Vann Mccoy, *Managing Member*
EMP: 6 **EST:** 2013
SALES (est): 243.25K **Privately Held**
Web: www.mayberryspirits.com
SIC: 2085 Distilled and blended liquors

(G-11545)
METALLUM STRUCTURES INC
1618 S Main St (27030-5528)
PHONE....................................877 517-4422
W David White, *Prin*
EMP: 7 **EST:** 2018
SALES (est): 169.27K **Privately Held**
Web: www.metalcarports.com
SIC: 3448 Prefabricated metal buildings and components

(G-11546)
MICHAEL TATE
Also Called: Mike's Hosiery
1455 Simpson Mill Rd (27030-8573)
PHONE....................................336 374-4695
Michael Tate, *Owner*
EMP: 4 **EST:** 1981
SALES (est): 163.18K **Privately Held**
SIC: 2252 Hosiery, nec

(G-11547)
MOUNT AIRY SIGNS & LETTERS INC
1543 Fancy Gap Rd (27030-1823)
PHONE....................................336 786-5777
Bobby Bodenhamer, *Pr*
EMP: 16 **EST:** 1990
SQ FT: 8,000
SALES (est): 1.95MM **Privately Held**
SIC: 3993 Neon signs

(G-11548)
MT AIRY MEAT CENTER INC
133 Old Buck Shoals Rd (27030-7597)
PHONE....................................336 786-2023
Gray Gwyn, *Pr*
Wade Johnson, *Sec*
EMP: 13 **EST:** 1977
SQ FT: 6,000
SALES (est): 789.7K **Privately Held**
Web: www.mtairyncchamber.org
SIC: 2011 5421 Meat packing plants; Meat markets, including freezer provisioners

(G-11549)
MVP GROUP INTERNATIONAL INC
830 Fowler Rd (27030-2750)
PHONE....................................336 527-2238
EMP: 35
Web: www.mvpgroupint.com
SIC: 3999 Candles
HQ: Mvp Group International, Inc.
430 Gentry Rd
Elkin NC 28621
843 216-8380

(G-11550)
NC QUALITY SALES LLC
136 Greyhound Rd (27030-4885)
PHONE....................................336 786-7211
EMP: 10 **EST:** 2010
SQ FT: 20,000
SALES (est): 779.14K **Privately Held**
Web: www.ncqualitysales.net
SIC: 2252 Socks

(G-11551)
NCFI POLYURETHANES
Also Called: Ncfi
1515 Carter St (27030-5721)
P.O. Box 1528 (27030-1528)
PHONE....................................336 789-9161
◆ **EMP:** 200 **EST:** 1964
SQ FT: 3,000
SALES (est): 47.2MM
SALES (corp-wide): 268.75MM **Privately Held**
Web: www.ncfi.com
SIC: 3086 Insulation or cushioning material, foamed plastics
PA: Barnhardt Manufacturing Company
1100 Hawthorne Ln
Charlotte NC 28205
800 277-0537

(G-11552)
NESTER HOSIERY INC
Also Called: NESTER HOSIERY, INC.
1400 Carter St (27030-5711)
PHONE....................................336 789-0026
EMP: 70
Web: www.nesterhosiery.com
SIC: 2252 Socks
PA: Nester Hosiery, Llc
1546 Carter St
Mount Airy NC 27030

(G-11553)
NESTER HOSIERY LLC (PA)
Also Called: Nester Hosiery
1546 Carter St (27030-5720)
P.O. Box 1343 (27030-1343)
PHONE....................................336 789-0026
Kelly Nester, *CEO*
Dusty Wade Nester, *Sec*
Keith Nester, *CFO*
Donna Anderson, *VP*
▲ **EMP:** 30 **EST:** 1993
SQ FT: 50,000
SALES (est): 25.45MM **Privately Held**
Web: www.nesterhosiery.com
SIC: 2252 Socks

(G-11554)
OLD NORTH STATE WINERY INC
Also Called: Fish Hippie
308 N Main St (27030-3812)
PHONE....................................336 789-9463
EMP: 11 **EST:** 2006
SALES (est): 1.79MM **Privately Held**
Web: www.oldnorthstatewinery.com
SIC: 2084 Wines

(G-11555)
OTTENWELLER CO INC
401 Technology Ln (27030-5039)
PHONE....................................336 783-6959
Carl Brodhun, *Brnch Mgr*
EMP: 13
SALES (corp-wide): 28.75MM **Privately Held**
Web: www.ottenweller.com
SIC: 3441 Fabricated structural metal
PA: Ottenweller Co., Inc.
3011 Congressional Pkwy
Fort Wayne IN 46808
260 484-3166

(G-11556)
PILOT RACK COMPANY
2220 Riverside Dr (27030-2506)
PHONE....................................336 351-5851
Brandon Sawyers, *Prin*
EMP: 6 **EST:** 2019
SALES (est): 493.23K **Privately Held**
Web: www.pilotrackco.com
SIC: 3441 Fabricated structural metal

(G-11557)
PINE STATE CORPORATE AP LLC
Also Called: Pine State Corporative Apparel
219 Frederick St (27030-5603)
PHONE....................................336 789-9437
EMP: 10 **EST:** 2003
SALES (est): 573.73K **Privately Held**
SIC: 2395 5621 Embroidery and art needlework; Women's clothing stores

(G-11558)
PIONEER PRINTING COMPANY INC
203 N South St (27030-3560)
P.O. Box 407 (27030-0407)
PHONE....................................336 789-4011
Robin Owens, *Pr*
Anita Nichols, *Treas*
Vicky Fields, *Sec*
Douglas Nichols, *VP*
EMP: 6 **EST:** 1971
SQ FT: 5,000
SALES (est): 487.86K **Privately Held**
Web: www.pioneerprintingco.com
SIC: 2752 Offset printing

(G-11559)
POP DESIGNS MKTG SOLUTIONS LLC
1153 Holly Springs Rd (27030-9539)
PHONE....................................336 444-4033
Rick G Hunter, *CEO*
Teresa Martin, *COO*
EMP: 7 **EST:** 2014
SALES (est): 331.06K **Privately Held**
SIC: 2759 Screen printing

(G-11560)
PROFESSIONAL SHEET METAL LLC
2957 Park Dr (27030-5768)
PHONE....................................336 755-3794
EMP: 4 **EST:** 2019
SALES (est): 218.43K **Privately Held**
SIC: 3444 Sheet metalwork

(G-11561)
PSM ENTERPRISES INC
219 Frederick St (27030-5603)
PHONE....................................336 789-8888
Alfred S Holcomb Junior, *Pr*
EMP: 10 **EST:** 2006
SALES (est): 952.03K **Privately Held**
Web: www.pinestatemarketing.com
SIC: 2396 5199 Fabric printing and stamping ; Advertising specialties

(G-11562)
RENFRO LLC
801 W Lebanon St (27030-2219)
PHONE....................................336 719-8290
EMP: 75
SALES (corp-wide): 3.26B **Privately Held**
Web: www.renfro.com
SIC: 2252 Socks
HQ: Renfro Llc
661 Linville Rd
Mount Airy NC 27030
336 719-8000

(G-11563)
RENFRO LLC (HQ)
Also Called: Renfro Brands
661 Linville Rd (27030-3101)
P.O. Box 908 (27030-0908)
PHONE....................................336 719-8000
Stanley Jewell, *CEO*
David Dinkins, *
Susan Bevard, *
Kieth Venable, *
◆ **EMP:** 350 **EST:** 1921
SQ FT: 180,000
SALES (est): 662.45MM
SALES (corp-wide): 3.26B **Privately Held**
Web: www.renfro.com
SIC: 2252 Socks
PA: The Renco Group Inc
1 Rockefeller Plz Fl 29
New York NY 10020
212 541-6000

(G-11564)
RENFRO LLC
Also Called: Willow Street Plant
304 Willow St (27030-3550)
PHONE....................................336 786-3000
Norman Smith, *Mgr*
EMP: 25
SALES (corp-wide): 3.26B **Privately Held**
Web: www.renfro.com
SIC: 2252 Hosiery, nec
HQ: Renfro Llc
661 Linville Rd
Mount Airy NC 27030
336 719-8000

(G-11565)
RENFRO MEXICO HOLDINGS LLC
661 Linville Rd (27030-3101)
PHONE....................................336 786-3501
EMP: 16 **EST:** 2002
SALES (est): 275.74K **Privately Held**
Web: www.renfro.com
SIC: 2252 Socks

(G-11566)
RIVERSIDE KNITTING DEPT
661 Linville Rd (27030-3101)

PHONE..........................336 719-8252
Andy Anderson, *Mgr*
EMP: 7 **EST:** 2010
SALES (est): 173.75K **Privately Held**
Web: www.renfro.com
SIC: 2252 Socks

(G-11567)
ROGERS KNITTING INC
181 Beasley Rd (27030-9212)
PHONE..........................336 789-4155
Roger Delnorman, *Pr*
Tina Marshall, *Sec*
EMP: 5 **EST:** 1988
SQ FT: 2,400
SALES (est): 319.63K **Privately Held**
SIC: 2251 7389 Women's hosiery, except socks; Textile and apparel services

(G-11568)
ROUND PEAK VINEYARDS LLC
765 Round Peak Church Rd (27030-8421)
PHONE..........................336 352-5595
George Little, *Managing Member*
Susan Little, *Managing Member*
Ken Gulaian, *Managing Member*
Kari Heerdt, *Managing Member*
EMP: 7 **EST:** 2004
SALES (est): 237.03K **Privately Held**
Web: www.roundpeak.com
SIC: 2084 Wines

(G-11569)
S&S METAL STRUCTURES LLC
102 Solo Ln (27030-4488)
PHONE..........................336 466-7929
Tameka Sanchez, *Prin*
EMP: 5 **EST:** 2019
SALES (est): 60.64K **Privately Held**
SIC: 3441 Fabricated structural metal

(G-11570)
SARA LEE SOCKS
100 Woltz St (27030-7832)
PHONE..........................336 789-6118
EMP: 4
SALES (est): 285.72K **Privately Held**
SIC: 2252 Socks

(G-11571)
SAWYERS SIGN SERVICE INC
608 Allred Mill Rd (27030-2204)
EMP: 19 **EST:** 1996
SQ FT: 30,000
SALES (est): 933.79K **Privately Held**
SIC: 1799 2394 3993 Sign installation and maintenance; Canvas and related products; Signs and advertising specialties

(G-11572)
SIGN MEDIC INC
1410 Boggs Dr (27030-2146)
PHONE..........................336 789-5972
Scott Simmons, *Pr*
▼ **EMP:** 8 **EST:** 2000
SQ FT: 30,000
SALES (est): 921.5K **Privately Held**
Web: www.signmedicinc.com
SIC: 3993 Electric signs

(G-11573)
SOLID WOODWORKER
305 Tanglewood Dr (27030-7782)
PHONE..........................336 786-7385
EMP: 4 **EST:** 2010
SALES (est): 139.75K **Privately Held**
SIC: 2431 Millwork

(G-11574)
SOUTHEASTERN SIGN WORKS INC
609 Junction St (27030-3719)
P.O. Box 1206 (27030-1206)
PHONE..........................336 789-5516
Teresa Martin, *Pr*
Bob Gravley, *VP*
Rick Vaughn, *Treas*
EMP: 15 **EST:** 1999
SALES (est): 489.71K **Privately Held**
SIC: 3993 5046 Electric signs; Signs, electrical

(G-11575)
SOUTHERN STATES COOP INC
Also Called: S S C 7793-7
202 Snowhill Dr (27030-4392)
PHONE..........................336 786-7545
Mike Midkiff, *Mgr*
EMP: 31
SALES (corp-wide): 1.71B **Privately Held**
Web: www.southernstates.com
SIC: 2048 2873 0181 2874 Prepared feeds, nec; Nitrogenous fertilizers; Bulbs and seeds; Phosphatic fertilizers
PA: Southern States Cooperative, Incorporated
6606 W Broad St Ste B
Richmond VA 23230
804 281-1000

(G-11576)
SPECIFIED METALS INC
391 Hickory St (27030-2264)
PHONE..........................336 786-6254
Alvin Eckenrod, *Pr*
Catherine Eckenrod, *VP*
EMP: 8 **EST:** 2015
SALES (est): 114.4K **Privately Held**
Web: www.specifiedmetals.com
SIC: 3444 Sheet metalwork

(G-11577)
SPENCERS INC MOUNT AIRY N C (PA)
290 Quarry Rd (27030-5728)
P.O. Box 988 (27030-0988)
PHONE..........................336 789-9111
James H Crossingham Junior, *CEO*
Helen C Rowe, *
Henry Rowe, *
◆ **EMP:** 179 **EST:** 1926
SQ FT: 275,000
SALES (est): 21.82MM
SALES (corp-wide): 21.82MM **Privately Held**
Web: www.mountairy.org
SIC: 2341 Women's and children's undergarments

(G-11578)
STORAGE SYSTEM SOLUTIONS INC
590 Crossingham Rd (27030-9170)
PHONE..........................336 710-5600
Debra B Dowell, *Prin*
EMP: 6 **EST:** 2015
SALES (est): 245.65K **Privately Held**
Web: www.cardinalcarports.com
SIC: 3448 Prefabricated metal buildings and components

(G-11579)
SUITS USA INC
Also Called: Suits US
1219a W Lebanon St (27030-2227)
PHONE..........................336 786-8808
EMP: 9 **EST:** 1995
SALES (est): 493.3K **Privately Held**
Web: www.suitsusainc.com
SIC: 3842 Suits, firefighting (asbestos)

(G-11580)
SURRY CHEMICALS INCORPORATED
241 Hickory St (27030-2211)
P.O. Box 1447 (27030-1447)
PHONE..........................336 786-4607
Sherman H Shepherd, *Pr*
Vicki Shepherd, *
William Shepherd, *
◆ **EMP:** 28 **EST:** 1977
SQ FT: 50,000
SALES (est): 4.84MM **Privately Held**
Web: www.surrychemicals.co
SIC: 2843 2841 2899 Textile finishing agents ; Soap and other detergents; Chemical preparations, nec

(G-11581)
SURRY ELC MTR & CONTRLS INC
Also Called: Core Electric Rebuilders
425 Hadley St (27030-4517)
P.O. Box 446 (27030-0446)
PHONE..........................336 786-1717
Fred O'neal, *Pr*
Faye O'neal, *VP*
Amy O'neal, *Treas*
EMP: 12 **EST:** 1985
SQ FT: 5,100
SALES (est): 251.25K **Privately Held**
SIC: 7694 5063 5999 Electric motor repair; Motors, electric; Motors, electric

(G-11582)
SURRY LOGISTIX LLC
535 E Pine St (27030-3951)
PHONE..........................336 710-3446
EMP: 6 **EST:** 2012
SALES (est): 161.14K **Privately Held**
Web: www.surrylogistix.com
SIC: 4789 3541 3542 Transportation services, nec; Deburring machines; Bending machines

(G-11583)
SURRY SCENE
319 N Renfro St (27030-3838)
PHONE..........................336 786-4141
John Peters, *Editor*
EMP: 6 **EST:** 2018
SALES (est): 62.71K **Privately Held**
Web: www.mtairynews.com
SIC: 2711 Newspapers, publishing and printing

(G-11584)
SYNERGEM TECHNOLOGIES INC
371 Windrush Ln (27030-7930)
PHONE..........................866 859-0911
EMP: 25 **EST:** 2019
SALES (est): 4.79MM **Privately Held**
Web: www.synergemtech.com
SIC: 7379 7372 Computer related consulting services; Business oriented computer software

(G-11585)
T P SUPPLY CO INC
Also Called: Material Handling
483 Belvue Dr (27030-5196)
P.O. Box 1543 (27030-1543)
PHONE..........................336 789-2337
Troy Payne Junior, *Pr*
EMP: 22 **EST:** 1979
SQ FT: 4,500
SALES (est): 4.81MM **Privately Held**
Web: www.tpsupplyco.com
SIC: 2448 5084 5085 Pallets, wood and metal combination; Materials handling machinery; Mill supplies

(G-11586)
T-N-T CARPORTS INC
1050 Worth St (27030-4453)
PHONE..........................336 789-3818
EMP: 8
SALES (corp-wide): 8.47MM **Privately Held**
Web: www.tntcarports.com
SIC: 3448 Prefabricated metal buildings and components
PA: T-N-T Carports, Inc.
170 Holly Springs Rd
Mount Airy NC 27030
336 789-3818

(G-11587)
T-N-T CARPORTS INC (PA)
170 Holly Springs Rd (27030-6688)
PHONE..........................336 789-3818
Venancio Torres, *CEO*
▼ **EMP:** 26 **EST:** 1995
SQ FT: 12,000
SALES (est): 8.47MM
SALES (corp-wide): 8.47MM **Privately Held**
Web: www.tntcarports.com
SIC: 3448 Carports, prefabricated metal

(G-11588)
TIGER STEEL INC (PA)
1425 Mckinney Rd (27030-5773)
PHONE..........................336 624-4481
Arturo Lopez, *Pr*
EMP: 4 **EST:** 2020
SALES (est): 978.1K
SALES (corp-wide): 978.1K **Privately Held**
SIC: 3291 Abrasive metal and steel products

(G-11589)
TRAVIS L BUNKER
Also Called: L C B of Mount Airy
6198 W Pine St (27030-6185)
PHONE..........................336 352-3289
Travis L Bunker, *Owner*
EMP: 4 **EST:** 1983
SALES (est): 147.31K **Privately Held**
SIC: 2261 Finishing plants, cotton

(G-11590)
TRI-STATE CARPORTS INC (PA)
304 Franklin St (27030-4588)
PHONE..........................276 755-2081
Torres Gabriel, *Pr*
Florencio Torres, *VP*
Hilario Torres, *Sec*
EMP: 7 **EST:** 2000
SALES (est): 2.49MM
SALES (corp-wide): 2.49MM **Privately Held**
Web: www.tristatecarports.com
SIC: 3448 Carports, prefabricated metal

(G-11591)
TRITON INDUSTRIES LLC ✪
830 Fowler Rd (27030-2750)
PHONE..........................336 816-3794
EMP: 10 **EST:** 2022
SALES (est): 1.02MM **Privately Held**
SIC: 3448 Prefabricated metal buildings and components

(G-11592)
UNITED PLASTICS CORPORATION
511 Hay St (27030-5629)
P.O. Box 807 (27030-0807)
PHONE..........................336 786-2127

Monty K Venable, *Ch Bd*
Nick Antonnechia, *
Johnny Collins, *
▲ **EMP:** 105 **EST:** 1947
SQ FT: 143,000
SALES (est): 21.22MM **Privately Held**
Web: www.unitedplastics.com
SIC: 3082 5162 Unsupported plastics profile shapes; Plastics sheets and rods

(G-11593)
WEDDLES SIGNS
144 Ridgeview Dr (27030-9297)
PHONE..................276 779-9218
Greg Weddle, *Prin*
EMP: 4 **EST:** 2017
SALES (est): 46.08K **Privately Held**
Web: www.weddlesignsandgraphics.com
SIC: 3993 Signs and advertising specialties

(G-11594)
WHATZ COOKIN LLC ✪
123 Old Brintle St (27030-5970)
PHONE..................336 353-0227
Bernetta Simmons, *Managing Member*
EMP: 4 **EST:** 2022
SALES (est): 182.43K **Privately Held**
SIC: 2599 7389 Food wagons, restaurant; Business services, nec

(G-11595)
WILLOW TEX LLC
Also Called: Izitleather
501 Piedmont Triad West Dr (27030-9850)
PHONE..................336 789-1009
Dew Claybough, *
▲ **EMP:** 24 **EST:** 1964
SQ FT: 18,000
SALES (est): 4.56MM **Privately Held**
Web: www.izitleather.com
SIC: 3111 Upholstery leather

(G-11596)
WISE STORAGE SOLUTIONS LLC
1372 Boggs Dr (27030-2144)
P.O. Box 804 (27030-0804)
PHONE..................336 789-5141
Neil Willard, *Brnch Mgr*
EMP: 45
SALES (corp-wide): 1.67MM **Privately Held**
SIC: 3545 Machine tool accessories
PA: Wise Storage Solutions, Llc
1219 N South St
Mount Airy NC 27030
336 786-6182

(G-11597)
WP SIMMONS INC
Also Called: Simmon, W P
205 N South St (27030-3560)
P.O. Box 1045 (27030-1045)
PHONE..................336 789-3114
Hm Loy, *Pr*
EMP: 10 **EST:** 1975
SQ FT: 3,500
SALES (est): 394.16K **Privately Held**
SIC: 3272 3281 Burial vaults, concrete or precast terrazzo; Monuments, cut stone (not finishing or lettering only)

(G-11598)
YADKIN VALLEY CABINET CO INC
135 Red Laurel Ln (27030-7920)
P.O. Box 6048 (27030-6048)
PHONE..................336 786-9860
Thelma Hill, *Pr*
EMP: 8 **EST:** 2006
SALES (est): 669.44K **Privately Held**
Web: www.yvccinc.com

SIC: 2434 Wood kitchen cabinets

Mount Gilead
Montgomery County

(G-11599)
CAPITOL FUNDS INC
Also Called: Piedmont Components
409 N Main St (27306-9038)
P.O. Box 1253 (27306-1253)
PHONE..................910 439-5275
EMP: 16
SALES (corp-wide): 18.32MM **Privately Held**
Web: www.capitolfundsinc.com
SIC: 6552 5231 5251 2439 Land subdividers and developers, commercial; Paint; Hardware stores; Structural wood members, nec
PA: Capitol Funds, Inc.
720 S Lafayette St
Shelby NC 28150
704 487-8547

(G-11600)
GIBRALTAR PACKAGING INC
5465 Nc Highway 73 W (27306-9316)
P.O. Box 700 (27306-0700)
PHONE..................910 439-6137
Jim Downey, *Brnch Mgr*
EMP: 120
Web: www.onepaperworks.com
SIC: 2752 2759 Offset printing; Commercial printing, nec
HQ: Gibraltar Packaging Inc.
2000 Summit Ave
Hastings NE 68901
402 463-1366

(G-11601)
J R B AND J KNITTING INC
4543 Nc Highway 109 S (27306-9496)
P.O. Box 833 (27306-0833)
PHONE..................910 439-4242
Jessie R Bowles Junior, *Pr*
Joyce T Sedberry, *VP*
Marty B Richardson, *Sec*
Jessie Bowles Junior, *Pr*
EMP: 4 **EST:** 1981
SQ FT: 2,400
SALES (est): 298.13K **Privately Held**
SIC: 2252 Socks

(G-11602)
JORDAN LUMBER & SUPPLY INC
Also Called: Cotton Creek Chip Co
1939 Nc Highway 109 S (27306-8455)
P.O. Box 98 (27306-0098)
PHONE..................910 439-6121
Bob Jordan, *Brnch Mgr*
EMP: 106
SALES (corp-wide): 48.73MM **Privately Held**
Web: www.jordanlumber.com
SIC: 2421 Lumber: rough, sawed, or planed
PA: Jordan Lumber & Supply, Inc.
1939 Nc Highway 109 S
Mount Gilead NC 27306
910 439-6121

(G-11603)
JORDAN LUMBER & SUPPLY INC (PA)
1939 Nc Highway 109 S (27306-8455)
P.O. Box 98 (27306-0098)
PHONE..................910 439-6121
Bob Jordan, *Pr*
Jack P Jordan, *
Robert B Jordan Iv, *VP*

EMP: 250 **EST:** 1939
SQ FT: 6,000
SALES (est): 48.73MM
SALES (corp-wide): 48.73MM **Privately Held**
Web: www.jordanlumber.com
SIC: 2421 Lumber: rough, sawed, or planed

(G-11604)
MCLENDON LOGGING INCORPORATED
671 Nc Highway 731 W (27306-8608)
PHONE..................910 439-6223
Tommy Mclendon, *Pr*
EMP: 4 **EST:** 1980
SALES (est): 340K **Privately Held**
SIC: 2411 Logging camps and contractors

(G-11605)
MCRAE INDUSTRIES INC
Mc Rae Footwear
125 Wadeville Fire Station Rd (27306-6004)
P.O. Box 1239 (27306-1239)
PHONE..................910 439-6149
Kelly Hamilton, *CFO*
EMP: 180
SALES (corp-wide): 40.36MM **Publicly Held**
Web: www.mcraeindustries.com
SIC: 5139 6153 3021 Boots; Short-term business credit institutions, except agricultural; Arctics, rubber or rubber soled fabric
PA: Mcrae Industries, Inc.
400 N Main St
Mount Gilead NC 27306
910 439-6147

(G-11606)
MCRAE INDUSTRIES INC (PA)
400 N Main St (27306-9038)
P.O. Box 1239 (27306-1239)
PHONE..................910 439-6147
D Gary Mc Rae, *Ch Bd*
Victor A Karam, *FOOTWEAR**
Harold W Smith, *
James W Mc Rae, *
▲ **EMP:** 40 **EST:** 1959
SQ FT: 71,000
SALES (est): 40.36MM
SALES (corp-wide): 40.36MM **Publicly Held**
Web: www.mcraeindustries.com
SIC: 3143 3144 Boots, dress or casual: men's; Women's footwear, except athletic

(G-11607)
MEGAWOOD INC
670 Allenton St (27306-9238)
P.O. Box 464 (27371-0464)
PHONE..................910 572-3796
Billy Hamilton, *Pr*
Sue Hamilton, *VP*
EMP: 17 **EST:** 1985
SQ FT: 7,200
SALES (est): 511.98K **Privately Held**
SIC: 2421 Cants, resawed (lumber)

(G-11608)
MEGAWOOD HOLDINGS INC
610 W Allenton St (27306-9238)
P.O. Box 1227 (27306-1227)
PHONE..................910 439-2124
EMP: 6 **EST:** 2015
SALES (est): 237.33K **Privately Held**
SIC: 2499 Wood products, nec

(G-11609)
MOHAWK INDUSTRIES INC
Unilin US Mdf
149 Homanit Usa Rd (27306-8649)
P.O. Box 69 (27306-0069)
PHONE..................910 439-6959
Gunter Heyen, *Pr*
EMP: 197
Web: www.mohawkind.com
SIC: 2493 Insulation board, cellular fiber
PA: Mohawk Industries, Inc.
160 S Industrial Blvd
Calhoun GA 30701

(G-11610)
MT GILEAD CUT & SEW INC
112 N Main St (27306-9276)
PHONE..................910 439-9909
Geraldine Craven, *Pr*
EMP: 10 **EST:** 2019
SALES (est): 703.41K **Privately Held**
SIC: 3639 Sewing equipment

(G-11611)
PAPERWORKS INDUSTRIES INC
5465 Nc Highway 73 W (27306-9316)
PHONE..................910 439-6137
EMP: 227
Web: www.onepaperworks.com
SIC: 2653 Boxes, corrugated: made from purchased materials
PA: Paperworks Industries, Inc.
1300 Virginia Dr Ste 220
Fort Washington PA 19034

(G-11612)
RANDY CHAPPELL LOGGING LLC
142 Hamilton Dr (27306-9344)
PHONE..................910 439-6690
EMP: 4 **EST:** 2010
SALES (est): 95K **Privately Held**
SIC: 2411 Logging

(G-11613)
TIMBER STAND IMPROVEMENTS INC
1939 Nc Highway 109 S (27306-8455)
P.O. Box 98 (27306-0098)
PHONE..................910 439-6121
Bruce Evans, *Pr*
Jack P Jordan, *Sec*
EMP: 8 **EST:** 1988
SQ FT: 6,000
SALES (est): 1.01MM **Privately Held**
Web: www.jordanlumber.com
SIC: 2411 Logging camps and contractors

(G-11614)
TOBE MANUFACTURING INC
603 W Allenton St (27306-9238)
P.O. Box 447 (27306-0447)
PHONE..................910 439-6203
Gary Haywood, *Pr*
Brenda Haywood, *CFO*
EMP: 15 **EST:** 1983
SQ FT: 30,000
SALES (est): 1.88MM **Privately Held**
Web: www.tobemfg.com
SIC: 3599 Machine shop, jobbing and repair

(G-11615)
WAYNE DUNN LOGGING LLC
656 Bowles Rd (27306-8502)
PHONE..................910 439-5478
Wayne Dunn, *Prin*
EMP: 6 **EST:** 2016
SALES (est): 207.39K **Privately Held**
SIC: 2411 Logging

GEOGRAPHIC SECTION

Mount Holly - Gaston County (G-11640)

(G-11616)
WOODLAND HOSIERY INC
118 Hudson Ln (27306-8972)
PHONE.................................910 439-4843
Jimmy Bowles, *Pr*
EMP: 10 EST: 1997
SALES (est): 433.64K **Privately Held**
Web: www.woodlandhosiery.com
SIC: 2252 Socks

Mount Holly
Gaston County

(G-11617)
AMERICAN & EFIRD GLOBAL LLC (DH)
22 American St (28120-2150)
P.O. Box 507 (28120-0507)
PHONE.................................704 827-4311
Mary Ann Sigler, *
EMP: 29 EST: 1968
SALES (est): 11.46MM
SALES (corp-wide): 1.98B **Privately Held**
Web: www.amefird.com
SIC: 2284 Thread mills
HQ: Elevate Textiles, Inc.
    121 W Trade St Ste 1700
    Charlotte NC 28202

(G-11618)
AMERICAN & EFIRD LLC
Regal Thread & Notions
22 American St (28120-2150)
PHONE.................................704 827-4311
Jerome Golden, *Mgr*
EMP: 12
SALES (corp-wide): 1.98B **Privately Held**
Web: www.amefird.com
SIC: 2284 Thread from natural fibers
HQ: American & Efird Llc
    24 American St
    Mount Holly NC 28120
    704 827-4311

(G-11619)
AMERICAN & EFIRD LLC (DH)
24 American St (28120-2150)
P.O. Box 507 (28120-0507)
PHONE.................................704 827-4311
Les Miller, *CEO*
Lindell Stoker, *
L Richard Heavener, *Credit Vice President**
Ronnie Ensley, *
Al Irvine, *
◆ **EMP: 200 EST:** 1891
SQ FT: 20,000
SALES (est): 514.67MM
SALES (corp-wide): 1.98B **Privately Held**
Web: www.amefird.com
SIC: 2284 Thread from natural fibers
HQ: Elevate Textiles, Inc.
    121 W Trade St Ste 1700
    Charlotte NC 28202

(G-11620)
AMERICAN & EFIRD LLC
101 Mill St (28120-1534)
PHONE.................................704 823-2501
Eddie Eaker, *Mgr*
EMP: 16
SALES (corp-wide): 1.98B **Privately Held**
Web: www.amefird.com
SIC: 2284 Sewing thread
HQ: American & Efird Llc
    24 American St
    Mount Holly NC 28120
    704 827-4311

(G-11621)
ARROCHEM INC
201 Westland Farm Rd (28120-9533)
P.O. Box 5 (28120-0005)
PHONE.................................704 827-0216
David A Hostetler, *Pr*
Patty M Hostetler, *VP*
EMP: 15 EST: 1979
SQ FT: 18,000
SALES (est): 2.29MM **Privately Held**
Web: www.arrochem.com
SIC: 2843 Emulsifiers, except food and pharmaceutical

(G-11622)
BELMONT TEXTILE MACHINERY CO
1212 W Catawba Ave (28120-1111)
P.O. Box 568 (28120-0568)
PHONE.................................704 827-5836
Walter P Rhyne, *CEO*
Jeff T Rhyne, *
▲ **EMP: 48 EST:** 1955
SQ FT: 59,000
SALES (est): 4.47MM **Privately Held**
Web: www.btmc.com
SIC: 3552 Winders, textile machinery

(G-11623)
BUCKEYE TECHNOLOGIES INC
Also Called: BUCKEYE TECHNOLOGIES INC.
100 Buckeye Dr (28120-1278)
PHONE.................................704 822-6400
John Crows, *Prin*
EMP: 219
SALES (corp-wide): 36.93B **Privately Held**
Web: www.bkitech.com
SIC: 2611 2621 Pulp mills; Paper mills
HQ: Georgia-Pacific Nonwovens Llc
    1001 Tillman St
    Memphis TN 38112

(G-11624)
CAROLINA FAB INC
2129 Charles Raper Jonas Hwy (28120-1276)
P.O. Box 672 (28120-0672)
PHONE.................................704 820-8694
Deborah Evans, *Pr*
William Evans, *VP*
Christian Evans, *VP*
EMP: 17 EST: 1998
SALES (est): 3.52MM **Privately Held**
Web: www.carolinafabinc.com
SIC: 3441 Fabricated structural metal

(G-11625)
CEKAL SPECIALTIES INC
101 Brickyard Rd (28120-8800)
P.O. Box 788 (28120-0788)
PHONE.................................704 822-6206
Dallas Crotts, *Pr*
Jimmy Lawing, *Stockholder*
Jeff Lawing, *VP*
◆ **EMP: 20 EST:** 1992
SQ FT: 10,000
SALES (est): 4.57MM **Privately Held**
Web: www.cekalspecialties.com
SIC: 2393 Textile bags

(G-11626)
CHARAH LLC
175 Steam Plant Rd (28120-9740)
PHONE.................................502 873-6993
EMP: 138
SALES (corp-wide): 293.17MM **Publicly Held**
Web: www.charah.com
SIC: 1081 Metal mining exploration and development services
HQ: Charah, Llc
    12601 Plantside Dr
    Louisville KY 40299

(G-11627)
CLARIANT CORPORATION
Also Called: Mount Holly West Plant
625 E Catawba Ave (28120-2270)
PHONE.................................704 822-2100
EMP: 40
Web: www.clariant.com
SIC: 2869 Industrial organic chemicals, nec
HQ: Clariant Corporation
    500 E Morehead St Ste 400
    Charlotte NC 28202
    704 331-7000

(G-11628)
CLIFT INDUSTRIES INC
201 Westland Farm Rd (28120-9533)
PHONE.................................704 752-0031
Layne Finchur, *Pr*
EMP: 5
SALES (corp-wide): 2.42MM **Privately Held**
Web: www.cliftindustries.com
SIC: 2819 Industrial inorganic chemicals, nec
PA: Clift Industries, Inc.
    3033 Eaton Ave
    Indian Trail NC 28079
    704 752-0031

(G-11629)
CRAZIE TEES
177 Brookstone Dr (28120-2811)
PHONE.................................704 898-2272
Theresa Wilson, *Prin*
EMP: 4 EST: 2018
SALES (est): 90.31K **Privately Held**
SIC: 2759 Screen printing

(G-11630)
DAVID VIZARD MOTORTEC FEATURES
109 Mistywood Dr (28120-9267)
PHONE.................................865 850-0666
EMP: 4 EST: 2017
SALES (est): 148.96K **Privately Held**
SIC: 3714 Motor vehicle parts and accessories

(G-11631)
DIVERSFIED HOLDINGS DALLAS INC
124 W Catawba Ave (28120-1602)
P.O. Box 515 (28034-0515)
PHONE.................................704 922-5293
David W Hoyle Junior, *Pr*
EMP: 10 EST: 2009
SALES (est): 907.87K **Privately Held**
SIC: 3499 Fabricated metal products, nec

(G-11632)
ENVIRNMNTAL PRCESS SYSTEMS INC
227 Lamplighter Ln (28120-9243)
PHONE.................................704 827-0740
EMP: 6 EST: 1996
SQ FT: 4,000
SALES (est): 480.02K **Privately Held**
Web: www.epsiusa.com
SIC: 3589 Water treatment equipment, industrial

(G-11633)
EPSIUSA
1124 W Charlotte Ave (28120-1212)
PHONE.................................704 827-0740
Ben Taylor, *Prin*
EMP: 7 EST: 2010
SALES (est): 115.92K **Privately Held**
SIC: 3589 Service industry machinery, nec

(G-11634)
GASTON COUNTY DYEING MACHINE COMPANY
Also Called: Gaston Fabrication
1310 Charles Raper Jonas Hwy (28120-1234)
PHONE.................................704 822-5000
▼ **EMP: 100 EST:** 1921
SALES (est): 15.07MM **Privately Held**
Web: www.gaston-county.com
SIC: 3443 3552 Tanks, standard or custom fabricated: metal plate; Dyeing machinery, textile

(G-11635)
GASTONIA ORNAMENTAL WLDG INC
Also Called: Gastonia Iron Works
624 Legion Rd (28120-1424)
P.O. Box 748 (28120-0748)
PHONE.................................704 827-1146
Katherine C Pace, *Pr*
Jerry N Pace Senior, *VP*
EMP: 15 EST: 1940
SQ FT: 2,400
SALES (est): 2.22MM **Privately Held**
SIC: 3449 1799 Bars, concrete reinforcing: fabricated steel; Ornamental metal work

(G-11636)
GIVING TREE WOODWORKS LLC
204 Brookstone Dr (28120-2812)
PHONE.................................704 930-5847
EMP: 4 EST: 2021
SALES (est): 54.13K **Privately Held**
SIC: 2431 Millwork

(G-11637)
GLATFELTER MT HOLLY LLC
100 Buckeye Dr (28120-1278)
PHONE.................................704 812-2299
◆ **EMP: 98 EST:** 1999
SQ FT: 15,563
SALES (est): 26.06MM
SALES (corp-wide): 1.49B **Publicly Held**
Web: www.mtholly.us
SIC: 2611 Pulp produced from non-wood fiber base, nec
PA: Glatfelter Corporation
    4350 Congress St Ste 600
    Charlotte NC 28209
    704 885-2555

(G-11638)
GLOBAL SENSORS
123 N Main St (28120-1793)
PHONE.................................704 827-4331
David Caskey, *Prin*
▲ **EMP: 5 EST:** 2004
SALES (est): 106.08K **Privately Held**
Web: www.global-sensors.com
SIC: 3823 Process control instruments

(G-11639)
J & B TOOL MAKING INC
14522 Lucia Riverbend Hwy (28120-9703)
PHONE.................................704 827-4805
Jim Barker, *Pr*
Vicki Barker, *VP*
EMP: 6 EST: 1985
SQ FT: 7,000
SALES (est): 597.22K **Privately Held**
SIC: 3541 Drilling machine tools (metal cutting)

(G-11640)
LEONINE PROTECTION SYSTEMS LLC
309 Dutchmans Meadow Dr (28120-3015)

Mount Holly - Gaston County (G-11641)

PHONE.................................704 296-2675
EMP: 6 EST: 2003
SALES (est): 310.05K **Privately Held**
SIC: 3699 Security control equipment and systems

(G-11641)
MAC/FAB COMPANY INC
913 W Catawba Ave (28120-1411)
P.O. Box 452 (28120-0452)
PHONE.................................704 822-1103
R G Pfaff, *Pr*
Jeffery Pfaff, *VP*
EMP: 20 EST: 1982
SQ FT: 10,000
SALES (est): 4.66MM **Privately Held**
Web: www.macfab.net
SIC: 3444 3469 3599 Sheet metalwork; Metal stampings, nec; Machine and other job shop work

(G-11642)
METRO PRINT INC
800 W Central Ave (28120-1675)
P.O. Box 374 (28120-0374)
PHONE.................................704 827-3796
Frank Kemp, *Pr*
Angela Kemp, *Sec*
EMP: 10 EST: 2011
SQ FT: 10,000
SALES (est): 927.47K **Privately Held**
Web: www.signsbymetroprint.com
SIC: 3993 Signs and advertising specialties

(G-11643)
MODERN MOLD & TOOL COMPANY
Also Called: Machine Shop of Charlotte, The
1050 Ironwood Dr (28120-8108)
P.O. Box 5313 (28299-5313)
PHONE.................................704 377-2300
Robin Hood, *Pr*
Dora A Hood, *VP*
Elizabeth Patton, *Sec*
EMP: 6 EST: 1968
SALES (est): 779.27K **Privately Held**
Web: www.tonerplastics.com
SIC: 3544 Special dies and tools

(G-11644)
N2 PUBLISHING
516 Ernst Pt (28120-9355)
PHONE.................................410 370-5530
EMP: 4
SALES (est): 74.89K **Privately Held**
Web: www.strollmag.com
SIC: 2741 Miscellaneous publishing

(G-11645)
NATIONAL COLOR GRAPHICS INC
98 Rutledge Rd (28120-9407)
PHONE.................................704 263-3187
Hugh Taylor, *Pr*
EMP: 4 EST: 1980
SALES (est): 298.24K **Privately Held**
SIC: 3555 Plates, offset

(G-11646)
PARKDALE MILLS INCORPORATED
Also Called: Parkdale Plant 68
101 Mill St (28120-1534)
PHONE.................................704 822-0778
EMP: 24
SALES (corp-wide): 1.44B **Privately Held**
Web: www.parkdalemills.com
SIC: 2281 Cotton yarn, spun
HQ: Parkdale Mills, Incorporated
531 Cotton Blossom Cir
Gastonia NC 28054
704 874-5000

(G-11647)
PROCESS ELECTRONICS CORP
100 Brickyard Rd (28120-8800)
P.O. Box 505 (28120-0505)
PHONE.................................704 827-9019
Carolyn Berry, *Ch Bd*
EMP: 19 EST: 1984
SQ FT: 16,000
SALES (est): 1.86MM **Privately Held**
Web: www.pecrectifier.com
SIC: 3699 Accelerating waveguide structures

(G-11648)
PROFORM FINISHING PRODUCTS LLC
1725 Wester Rd (28120-9483)
PHONE.................................704 398-3900
Thomas Nelson, *Prin*
EMP: 25
SALES (corp-wide): 795.88MM **Privately Held**
Web: www.nationalgypsum.com
SIC: 3275 Gypsum products
HQ: Proform Finishing Products, Llc
2001 Rexford Rd
Charlotte NC 28211

(G-11649)
PURE SOY SCENTS
1245 Blake Dr (28120-9605)
PHONE.................................980 722-1483
EMP: 4 EST: 2010
SALES (est): 56.38K **Privately Held**
Web: www.puresoyscents.com
SIC: 2844 Perfumes, cosmetics and other toilet preparations

(G-11650)
RINKER MATERIALS
1725 Drywall Dr (28120-8453)
PHONE.................................704 827-8175
Earl Wood, *Prin*
EMP: 7 EST: 2010
SALES (est): 98.49K **Privately Held**
SIC: 3273 Ready-mixed concrete

(G-11651)
S & S DEER PROCESSING
216 Helms Dr (28120-9406)
PHONE.................................704 827-6884
EMP: 5 EST: 2008
SALES (est): 50K **Privately Held**
SIC: 2011 Meat packing plants

(G-11652)
WARREN PLASTICS INC
511 Rankin Ave (28120-1565)
PHONE.................................704 827-9887
Mark V Warren, *Pr*
Betty Warren, *VP*
EMP: 5 EST: 1981
SQ FT: 5,500
SALES (est): 470.12K **Privately Held**
Web: www.warrenplasticsinc.com
SIC: 3089 Injection molding of plastics

Mount Olive
Wayne County

(G-11653)
AFL NETWORK SERVICES INC
Also Called: Impulse NC
100 Impulse Way (28365-8691)
P.O. Box 889 (28365-0889)
PHONE.................................919 658-2311
EMP: 25
Web: www.aflglobal.com
SIC: 3357 Nonferrous wiredrawing and insulating
HQ: Afl Network Services, Inc.
170 Ridgeview Center Dr
Duncan SC 29334
864 433-0333

(G-11654)
B E R TRUCKING AND GRAVEL
594 Pineview Cemetery Rd (28365-8212)
PHONE.................................919 738-5928
EMP: 4 EST: 2016
SALES (est): 126.37K **Privately Held**
SIC: 1442 Construction sand and gravel

(G-11655)
BENMOT PUBLISHING COMPANY INC
Also Called: Mount Olive Tribune
214 N Center St (28365-1702)
PHONE.................................919 658-9456
Larry Mcphail, *Genl Mgr*
EMP: 4 EST: 2012
SALES (est): 210.1K **Privately Held**
SIC: 2711 Newspapers, publishing and printing

(G-11656)
BOBBY A HERRING LOGGING
324 Alum Springs Rd (28365-9270)
PHONE.................................919 658-9768
Bobby Herring, *Owner*
EMP: 7 EST: 1982
SALES (est): 419.73K **Privately Held**
SIC: 2411 Logging camps and contractors

(G-11657)
BUTTERBALL LLC
Also Called: Carolina Turkeys
1628 Garner Chapel Rd (28365-6167)
P.O. Box 599 (28365-0599)
PHONE.................................919 658-6743
EMP: 99
SALES (corp-wide): 11.24B **Publicly Held**
Web: www.butterballfoodservice.com
SIC: 2015 Turkey, processed, nsk
HQ: Butterball, Llc
1 Butterball Ln
Garner NC 27529
919 255-7900

(G-11658)
CAROLINA NUT INC
Also Called: Golden Grove USA
1180 Stanley Chapel Church Rd (28365-8614)
PHONE.................................910 293-4209
Nicholas Swinson, *Pr*
EMP: 10 EST: 2017
SALES (est): 936.73K **Privately Held**
Web: www.carolinanutcracker.com
SIC: 2068 Nuts: dried, dehydrated, salted or roasted

(G-11659)
CASE FARMS LLC
Also Called: Calypso Feed Mill
188 Broadhurst Rd (28365-9541)
PHONE.................................919 635-2390
Johnny Milkovits, *Mgr*
EMP: 91
Web: www.casefarms.com
SIC: 2015 Poultry slaughtering and processing
PA: Case Farms, L.L.C.
385 Pilch Rd
Troutman NC 28166

(G-11660)
CONSOLIDATED INSPECTIONS INC
526 Norwood Ezzell Rd (28365-5361)
P.O. Box 450 (28365-0450)
PHONE.................................919 658-5800
EMP: 5 EST: 1991
SALES (est): 341.18K **Privately Held**
Web: www.conspect.com
SIC: 3599 Machine shop, jobbing and repair

(G-11661)
GOSHEN ENGINEERING INC
439 Nc Highway 55 E (28365-8001)
P.O. Box 1170 (28365-3170)
PHONE.................................919 429-9798
Jason Stevens, *Dir*
EMP: 4 EST: 2006
SALES (est): 577.27K **Privately Held**
Web: www.goshenengineering.com
SIC: 8711 8742 3599 Electrical or electronic engineering; Automation and robotics consultant; Custom machinery

(G-11662)
IMPULSE NC LLC
100 Impulse Way (28365-8691)
PHONE.................................919 658-2311
▲ EMP: 25
SIC: 3612 Transformers, except electric

(G-11663)
JACKSON LOGGING
2936 Summerlins Crossroad Rd (28365-6416)
PHONE.................................919 658-2757
Ricki Jackson, *Owner*
EMP: 4 EST: 1980
SALES (est): 246.02K **Privately Held**
SIC: 2411 Logging camps and contractors

(G-11664)
KELLYS EMBROIDERY
843 Norwood Ezzell Rd (28365-5368)
PHONE.................................919 738-5072
Phyllis Tucker, *Prin*
EMP: 5 EST: 2017
SALES (est): 63.73K **Privately Held**
SIC: 2395 Embroidery and art needlework

(G-11665)
KORNEGAY LOGGING & TIMBER CO
1404 Red Hill Rd (28365-5412)
P.O. Box 764 (28365-0764)
PHONE.................................919 658-5716
Gerald Kornegay, *Owner*
EMP: 7 EST: 1992
SALES (est): 441.61K **Privately Held**
SIC: 4212 2411 Timber trucking, local; Logging

(G-11666)
MOUNT OLIVE PICKLE COMPANY INC (PA)
Also Called: That's Picklicious
1 Cucumber Blvd (28365-1210)
P.O. Box 609 (28365-0609)
PHONE.................................919 658-2535
William H Bryan, *Ch*
Robert D Frye Junior, *Pr*
A Douglas Brock, *
Richard D Bowen, *
◆ EMP: 431 EST: 1926
SQ FT: 400,000
SALES (est): 835.67K
SALES (corp-wide): 835.67K **Privately Held**
Web: www.mtolivepickles.com
SIC: 2035 Pickles, vinegar

(G-11667)
SASSY STITCHES-N-SUCH INC
608 N Breazeale Ave (28365-1204)
PHONE.................................919 658-6105
Sherry Alee, *Pr*

EMP: 6 EST: 2016
SALES (est): 48.5K **Privately Held**
SIC: 2395 Embroidery and art needlework

(G-11668)
SOUTHERN MACHINE SERVICES INC
300 Waller Rd (28365-7570)
PHONE..................919 658-9300
EMP: 4 EST: 1996
SQ FT: 2,500
SALES (est): 242.04K **Privately Held**
SIC: 3599 3569 Machine shop, jobbing and repair; Robots, assembly line: industrial and commercial

(G-11669)
SOUTHERN STATES COOP INC
Also Called: S S C 7795-7
301 N Chestnut St (28365-1615)
P.O. Box 419 (28365-0419)
PHONE..................919 658-5061
Sammy Fields, Mgr
EMP: 21
SALES (corp-wide): 1.71B **Privately Held**
Web: www.southernstates.com
SIC: 2048 2873 0181 2874 Prepared feeds, nec; Nitrogenous fertilizers; Bulbs and seeds; Phosphatic fertilizers
PA: Southern States Cooperative, Incorporated
6606 W Broad St Ste B
Richmond VA 23230
804 281-1000

(G-11670)
SWELL HOME SOLUTIONS INC
109 Barfield St (28365-2624)
PHONE..................919 440-4692
EMP: 4 EST: 2017
SALES (est): 200.39K **Privately Held**
SIC: 3524 Lawn and garden equipment

(G-11671)
TORTILLERIA LOS REMNEDIOS II
902 N Breazeale Ave (28365-1104)
PHONE..................919 658-1714
Juliana Pacheco, Owner
EMP: 6 EST: 2007
SALES (est): 145.97K **Privately Held**
SIC: 2099 Tortillas, fresh or refrigerated

Mount Pleasant
Cabarrus County

(G-11672)
CABARRUS HOSIERY DIST INC
8215 W Franklin St (28124-8510)
PHONE..................704 436-3575
Jerry E Bennick, Pr
EMP: 9 EST: 1988
SALES (est): 476.66K **Privately Held**
SIC: 2252 Socks

(G-11673)
CREATIONS BY TAYLOR
2892 Long Run Farm Rd (28124-8830)
PHONE..................410 269-6430
Barry Taylor, Owner
EMP: 8 EST: 1986
SALES (est): 500.69K **Privately Held**
Web: www.creationsbytaylor.com
SIC: 2512 Upholstered household furniture

(G-11674)
IVEY ICENHOUR DBA
5690 Barrier Georgeville Rd (28124-9158)
PHONE..................704 786-0676
Ivey Icenhour, Prin
EMP: 6 EST: 2010

SALES (est): 250.08K **Privately Held**
SIC: 2411 Logging

(G-11675)
PASTURE MANAGEMENT SYSTEMS INC
10325 Nc Highway 49 N (28124-9666)
P.O. Box 1120 (28124-1120)
PHONE..................704 436-6401
David A Hill, Pr
W C Cannon Junior, Sec
▲ EMP: 17 EST: 1991
SQ FT: 23,500
SALES (est): 2.16MM **Privately Held**
Web: www.pasturemgmt.com
SIC: 3523 Farm machinery and equipment

(G-11676)
PIEDMONT HARDWOOD LBR CO INC
9000 Nc Highway 49 N (28124-9656)
P.O. Box 535 (28124-0535)
PHONE..................704 436-9311
L Joe Stirewalt, Pr
Curtis L Stirewalt, VP
Randy Bingham, Off Mgr
EMP: 23 EST: 1960
SQ FT: 1,200
SALES (est): 2.16MM **Privately Held**
SIC: 2421 2426 Lumber: rough, sawed, or planed; Hardwood dimension and flooring mills

(G-11677)
RAM WELDING & FABRICATION INC
1903 Lorelei Ct (28124-8554)
PHONE..................704 985-8486
Randy Mullins, Prin
EMP: 4 EST: 2019
SALES (est): 63.04K **Privately Held**
SIC: 7692 Welding repair

(G-11678)
TOMMY W SMITH INC
Also Called: Cabinet Creations
9825 Bowman Barrier Rd (28124-8713)
P.O. Box 267 (28124-0267)
PHONE..................704 436-6616
Tommy W Smith, Owner
Tommy W Smith, Pr
Debbie Smith, VP
EMP: 5 EST: 1988
SQ FT: 5,000
SALES (est): 385.47K **Privately Held**
SIC: 2434 Wood kitchen cabinets

(G-11679)
TRINWELD WELDING SERVICES LLC
6895 Mission Rd (28124-8900)
PHONE..................704 721-5944
EMP: 4 EST: 2019
SALES (est): 139.44K **Privately Held**
Web: www.trinweld.com
SIC: 7692 Welding repair

(G-11680)
TUSCARORA YARNS INC
8760 Franklin St E (28124-8788)
P.O. Box 218 (28124-0218)
PHONE..................704 436-6527
◆ EMP: 305
Web: www.tuscarorayarns.com
SIC: 2281 Knitting yarn, spun

Mount Ulla
Rowan County

(G-11681)
CAROLINA STAIRS INC
255 Belk Rd (28125-9769)

P.O. Box 572 (28125-0572)
PHONE..................704 664-5032
Charles Johnson, Pr
EMP: 17 EST: 1981
SQ FT: 16,000
SALES (est): 2.31MM **Privately Held**
Web: www.bigframer.com
SIC: 2431 Staircases and stairs, wood

(G-11682)
CWC FABRICATING
2530 Graham Rd (28125-9652)
PHONE..................704 360-8264
EMP: 4 EST: 2017
SALES (est): 225.7K **Privately Held**
SIC: 3441 Fabricated structural metal

(G-11683)
HODGE FARMS LLC
11235 Nc Highway 801 (28125-8640)
PHONE..................704 278-2684
EMP: 4 EST: 1962
SALES (est): 291.46K **Privately Held**
SIC: 2048 Rolled oats, prepared as animal feed

(G-11684)
KENNEDY WOODWORKING LLC
955 Umberger Rd (28125-7714)
PHONE..................704 278-9444
Onathan B Kennedy, Prin
EMP: 5 EST: 2018
SALES (est): 54.13K **Privately Held**
SIC: 2431 Millwork

(G-11685)
PIEDMONT WELL COVERS INC
1135 Mazeppa Rd (28125-9703)
PHONE..................704 664-8488
William Wainscott, Pr
Pam Wainscott, VP
EMP: 10 EST: 1994
SALES (est): 894.17K **Privately Held**
Web: www.piedmontwellcovers.com
SIC: 3432 1799 3443 3229 Plumbing fixture fittings and trim; Fiberglass work; Heat exchangers, condensers, and components; Glass fiber products

(G-11686)
PROTECH FABRICATION INC
575 Edmiston Rd (28125-8746)
PHONE..................704 663-1721
Harold G Moore, Pr
Christy Moore, Sec
EMP: 24 EST: 1992
SQ FT: 7,500
SALES (est): 931.8K **Privately Held**
Web: www.protechnc.net
SIC: 3498 3441 Fabricated pipe and fittings; Fabricated structural metal

(G-11687)
WAGGONER MANUFACTURING CO
1065 Hall Rd (28125-9668)
PHONE..................704 278-2000
Luther W Waggoner, Owner
Luther W Waggoner, Pr
Peggy Waggoner, Sec
EMP: 20 EST: 1964
SQ FT: 1,350
SALES (est): 4.08MM **Privately Held**
Web: www.waggonermanufacturing.com
SIC: 3498 7699 Fabricated pipe and fittings; Industrial machinery and equipment repair

(G-11688)
WILLIAMS PERFORMANCE INC
3140 Corriher Grange Rd (28125-7820)
PHONE..................704 603-4431

Nicholas Williams, Pr
▲ EMP: 6 EST: 2005
SQ FT: 9,000
SALES (est): 772.6K **Privately Held**
Web: www.williamsperformance.net
SIC: 3559 Automotive related machinery

Mountain Home
Henderson County

(G-11689)
HAYNES INTERNATIONAL INC
Also Called: Haynes Wire Company
158 N Edgerton Rd (28758)
PHONE..................765 456-6000
EMP: 30
SALES (corp-wide): 589.96MM **Publicly Held**
Web: www.haynesintl.com
SIC: 3356 Nickel
PA: Haynes International, Inc.
1020 W Park Ave
Kokomo IN 46901
765 456-6000

(G-11690)
HAYNES WIRE COMPANY
Also Called: Haynes International
158 N Edgerton Rd (28758)
P.O. Box 677 (28758-0677)
PHONE..................828 692-5791
TOLL FREE: 800
▲ EMP: 52
SIC: 3315 Wire and fabricated wire products

Moyock
Currituck County

(G-11691)
ANDREA L GRIZZLE
Also Called: Unified Logistics NC
101 Trinity Ln Box 751 (27958-5900)
PHONE..................252 202-3278
Andrea Grizzle, Owner
Lorie Grizzle, Prin
Mary Dorsey, Prin
Andre Grizzle, Prin
EMP: 4 EST: 2010
SALES (est): 208.65K **Privately Held**
Web: www.unifiedlogisticsnc.com
SIC: 3661 2621 Telephone central office equipment, dial or manual; Cleansing paper

(G-11692)
BAY PAINTING CONTRACTORS
128 Bayside Dr (27958-9056)
PHONE..................252 435-5374
Brad Forehand, Owner
EMP: 4 EST: 2008
SALES (est): 172.53K **Privately Held**
SIC: 2851 Paints and allied products

(G-11693)
BUILT TO LAST NC LLC
417h Caratoke Hwy (27958-8608)
PHONE..................252 232-0055
Daniel W Aston, Managing Member
EMP: 17 EST: 2019
SALES (est): 1.05MM **Privately Held**
SIC: 2519 Fiberglass and plastic furniture

(G-11694)
CARE A LOT PET SUPPLY
102 Lark Dr (27958-8719)
PHONE..................757 457-9425
EMP: 5 EST: 2019
SALES (est): 39.69K **Privately Held**
Web: www.carealotpets.com

Moyock - Currituck County (G-11695)

SIC: 3999 Pet supplies

(G-11695)
COMMERCIAL READY MIX PDTS INC
115 Windchaser Way (27958-8794)
PHONE..................252 232-1250
EMP: 13
SALES (corp-wide): 52.99MM **Privately Held**
Web: www.crmpinc.com
SIC: 3273 Ready-mixed concrete
PA: Commercial Ready Mix Products, Inc.
115 Hwy 158 W
Winton NC 27986
252 358-5461

(G-11696)
EASTCAROLINACUSTOMCABINETS
122 Quail Run Dr (27958-9489)
PHONE..................757 450-7385
Tony Thomas, *Prin*
EMP: 5 EST: 2015
SALES (est): 57.63K **Privately Held**
SIC: 2434 Wood kitchen cabinets

(G-11697)
QUALITY MCH & FABRICATION INC
444 Guinea Mill Rd (27958-9293)
P.O. Box 460 (27958-0460)
PHONE..................252 435-6041
Deborah Brackett, *Pr*
EMP: 5 EST: 1990
SALES (est): 352.99K **Privately Held**
Web: www.qualitymachineandfabrication.com
SIC: 3599 Machine shop, jobbing and repair

Murfreesboro
Hertford County

(G-11698)
BORNEO INC
10 Commerce St (27855)
PHONE..................252 398-3100
Jacques Y Gamard, *Pr*
Peter Martone, *
EMP: 18 EST: 1987
SQ FT: 85,000
SALES (est): 629.26K **Privately Held**
SIC: 3089 Plastics kitchenware, tableware, and houseware

(G-11699)
JIF LOGGING INC
411 E Woodrow School Rd (27855-9417)
PHONE..................252 398-2249
John Futrell, *Pr*
Debra H Futrell, *Sec*
EMP: 7 EST: 1993
SALES (est): 508.17K **Privately Held**
SIC: 2411 Logging camps and contractors

(G-11700)
METAL TECH MURFREESBORO INC (PA)
Also Called: Metal Tech of Murfreesboro
314 W Broad St (27855-1442)
PHONE..................252 398-4041
Ray Felton, *Pr*
Edward Drock, *
Judy H Felton, *
Brock Felton, *
▲ EMP: 45 EST: 1971
SQ FT: 21,500
SALES (est): 15.33MM
SALES (corp-wide): 15.33MM **Privately Held**
Web: www.metaltechnc.com

SIC: 3441 Fabricated structural metal

(G-11701)
PERDUE FARMS INC
Also Called: Perdue Farms
Hwy 158 W (27855)
P.O. Box 532 (27855-0532)
PHONE..................252 398-5112
Dale Evans, *Mgr*
EMP: 106
SALES (corp-wide): 1.24B **Privately Held**
Web: www.perdue.com
SIC: 2015 Poultry slaughtering and processing
PA: Perdue Farms Incorporated
31149 Old Ocean City Rd
Salisbury MD 21804
800 473-7383

(G-11702)
PRODUCERS GIN MURFREESBORO LLC
336 Benthall Bridge Rd (27855-9672)
PHONE..................252 398-3762
EMP: 6 EST: 2010
SALES (est): 256.28K **Privately Held**
SIC: 3999 Manufacturing industries, nec

(G-11703)
TUFF TEMP CORP
310 W Broad St (27855-1442)
PHONE..................252 398-3400
EMP: 10 EST: 2009
SALES (est): 246.86K **Privately Held**
SIC: 3398 Metal heat treating

Murphy
Cherokee County

(G-11704)
ACORN WOODWORKS NC LLC
1221 Warren Dr (28906-3102)
PHONE..................828 361-9953
John Lachance, *Prin*
EMP: 5 EST: 2019
SALES (est): 65.49K **Privately Held**
SIC: 2431 Millwork

(G-11705)
AEGIS POWER SYSTEMS INC
805 Greenlawn Cemetery Rd (28906-9137)
P.O. Box 429 (28906-0429)
PHONE..................828 837-4029
EMP: 25 EST: 1995
SQ FT: 10,000
SALES (est): 4.06MM **Privately Held**
Web: www.aegispower.com
SIC: 3699 Electrical equipment and supplies, nec

(G-11706)
BEAR PAGES
99 Smoke Rise Cir (28906-9005)
PHONE..................828 837-0785
Weldon Beach, *Owner*
EMP: 6 EST: 2007
SALES (est): 159.65K **Privately Held**
Web: www.bearpagespaperarts.com
SIC: 3069 3953 5084 5945 Rubber tape; Embossing seals and hand stamps; Industrial machinery and equipment; Hobbies, nec

(G-11707)
CHI RESOURCES
Also Called: Indian Health Spring Water
1115 Horton Rd (28906-3580)
P.O. Box 860 (28906-0860)
PHONE..................828 835-7878

David Lawrence, *Pr*
EMP: 4 EST: 1997
SALES (est): 271.9K **Privately Held**
SIC: 3221 Water bottles, glass

(G-11708)
DOCKERY LOGGING
2020 Bell Hill Rd (28906-7336)
PHONE..................828 557-9149
EMP: 4 EST: 2018
SALES (est): 89.89K **Privately Held**
SIC: 2411 Logging camps and contractors

(G-11709)
FERTILITY TECH RESOURCES INC
211 Paradise Rd (28906-7002)
PHONE..................404 626-9786
EMP: 5 EST: 2019
SALES (est): 133.02K **Privately Held**
SIC: 3841 Surgical and medical instruments

(G-11710)
INDIAN HEAD INDUSTRIES INC
Also Called: MGM Brakes
229 Park Ave (28906-2745)
P.O. Box 70 (28906-0070)
PHONE..................704 547-7411
Robin Jenkins, *Mgr*
EMP: 88
SALES (corp-wide): 52.66MM **Privately Held**
Web: www.mgmbrakes.com
SIC: 3714 Motor vehicle brake systems and parts
PA: Indian Head Industries, Inc.
6200 Hars Tech Blvd
Charlotte NC 28269
704 547-7411

(G-11711)
LEDFORD LOGGING CO INC
1737 Sunny Point Rd (28906-7393)
PHONE..................828 644-5410
Robert Ledford, *Pr*
Robert Buddy Ledford, *Pr*
Linda Ledford, *Mgr*
Linda Ledford, *Sec*
EMP: 4 EST: 1967
SALES (est): 385.03K **Privately Held**
SIC: 2411 Logging camps and contractors

(G-11712)
MCLOUD MEDIA
Also Called: Late Model Digest
1192 Andrews Rd Ste H (28906-2809)
P.O. Box 340 (28906-0340)
PHONE..................828 837-9539
Carolyn Mcloud, *Owner*
EMP: 5 EST: 1989
SALES (est): 258.39K **Privately Held**
SIC: 2711 Newspapers: publishing only, not printed on site

(G-11713)
MOOG INC
Also Called: Moog Components Group
1995 Nc Highway 141 (28906-6864)
P.O. Box 160 (28906-0160)
PHONE..................828 837-5115
Terry Martin, *Brnch Mgr*
EMP: 400
SQ FT: 130,000
SALES (corp-wide): 3.32B **Publicly Held**
Web: www.moog.com
SIC: 3625 Relays and industrial controls
PA: Moog Inc.
400 Jamison Rd
Elma NY 14059
716 652-2000

(G-11714)
MURPHY PRINTING & VINYL LLC
180 Beulah Ln (28906-5185)
PHONE..................828 835-4848
Michael A Catuto, *Prin*
EMP: 4 EST: 2007
SALES (est): 174.55K **Privately Held**
SIC: 2752 Offset printing

(G-11715)
SCRAPPYS METAL LLC
701 Regal St (28906-5150)
P.O. Box 962 (28906-0962)
PHONE..................828 557-5861
EMP: 5 EST: 2018
SALES (est): 149.42K **Privately Held**
SIC: 3471 Plating and polishing

(G-11716)
SIGNAL SIGNS OF GA INC
15 Running Bear Rd (28906-1925)
PHONE..................828 494-4913
Carl Dills, *Pr*
EMP: 8
SALES (corp-wide): 2.16MM **Privately Held**
Web: www.signalsignscorp.com
SIC: 3993 1799 Advertising artwork; Antenna installation
PA: Signal Signs Of Ga, Inc.
440 Six Flags Pkwy
Mableton GA 30126
770 941-9900

(G-11717)
SNAP-ON POWER TOOLS INC
Also Called: Snap-On Tools
250 Snap On Dr (28906-9033)
P.O. Box 1596 (28906-1596)
PHONE..................828 835-4400
Thomas Kassouf, *Ch Bd*
Thomas Kassouf, *Ch Bd*
Daniel Garramone, *
Richard Kobor, *
◆ EMP: 250 EST: 1914
SQ FT: 150,000
SALES (est): 31.92MM
SALES (corp-wide): 4.73B **Publicly Held**
Web: www.siouxtools.com
SIC: 5251 3546 Tools; Power-driven handtools
PA: Snap-On Incorporated
2801 80th St
Kenosha WI 53143
262 656-5200

(G-11718)
WESTERN CRLINA MUTL BRIAL ASSN
138 Peachtree St (28906-2910)
P.O. Box 10 (28906-0010)
PHONE..................828 837-2577
Frank R Grose Junior, *Owner*
EMP: 5 EST: 2001
SALES (est): 87.28K **Privately Held**
SIC: 3272 6311 Burial vaults, concrete or precast terrazzo; Burial insurance societies

Nags Head
Dare County

(G-11719)
COASTAL IMPRESSIONS INC
3022 S Croatan Hwy (27959-9029)
P.O. Box 1055 (27959-1055)
PHONE..................252 480-1717
Patrick Cahill, *Pr*
Douglas Stoddart, *VP*
EMP: 6 EST: 1994

SQ FT: 1,000
SALES (est): 911.22K **Privately Held**
Web: www.coastalimpressions.com
SIC: 2752 Offset printing

(G-11720)
ISLAND XPRTEES OF OTER BNKS IN
2224 S Lark Ave (27959-9433)
PHONE.................................252 480-3990
James Kenny, *Pr*
Gary High, *
EMP: 25 EST: 1991
SQ FT: 9,000
SALES (est): 3.77MM **Privately Held**
Web: www.islandxpertees.com
SIC: 2396 3993 Screen printing on fabric articles; Signs and advertising specialties

(G-11721)
JEWELRY BY GAIL INC
207 E Driftwood St (27959-9172)
PHONE.................................252 441-5387
Gail Kowalski, *Pr*
David Stewart, *Sec*
EMP: 6 EST: 1981
SQ FT: 2,500
SALES (est): 789.17K **Privately Held**
Web: www.jewelrybygail.com
SIC: 3911 5944 Jewelry, precious metal; Jewelry stores

(G-11722)
KITTY HAWK KITES INC
3933 S Croatan Hwy (27959-9796)
PHONE.................................252 441-4124
Kristi Geske, *Brnch Mgr*
EMP: 11
SALES (corp-wide): 24.3MM **Privately Held**
Web: www.kittyhawk.com
SIC: 3944 Kites
PA: Kitty Hawk Kites, Inc.
    306 W Lake Dr Unit K
    Kill Devil Hills NC 27948
    252 441-4124

(G-11723)
MOTOR RACEWAYS INC
4025 W Soundside Rd (27959-9148)
PHONE.................................252 715-3990
Michelle M Chimento, *Pr*
EMP: 5 EST: 2017
SALES (est): 88.38K **Privately Held**
SIC: 3644 Raceways

(G-11724)
NAGS HEAD HAMMOCKS LLC (PA)
Also Called: Nags Head Hammock Co
1801 Croatan Hwy (27959)
P.O. Box 250 (27959-0250)
PHONE.................................252 441-6115
Ja Branch, *Managing Member*
EMP: 8 EST: 1974
SQ FT: 3,024
SALES (est): 4.52MM
SALES (corp-wide): 4.52MM **Privately Held**
Web: www.nagsheadhammocks.com
SIC: 5712 2399 Outdoor and garden furniture ; Hammocks, fabric: made from purchased materials

(G-11725)
SECRET SPOT INC
Also Called: Secret Spot Surf Shop
2815 S Croatan Hwy (27959-9025)
PHONE.................................252 441-4030
Steve Hess, *Pr*
Christine Hill, *Sec*
Stuart Taylor, *VP*

▲ EMP: 4 EST: 1977
SQ FT: 1,800
SALES (est): 531.43K **Privately Held**
Web: www.secretspotsurfshop.com
SIC: 5651 3949 Family clothing stores; Surfboards

(G-11726)
SLAM PUBLICATIONS LLC
Also Called: Outer Banks Centinel
2910 S Croatan Hwy Unit 19 (27959-9026)
P.O. Box 546 (27959-0546)
PHONE.................................252 480-2234
EMP: 10 EST: 2014
SALES (est): 442.74K **Privately Held**
Web: www.obsentinel.com
SIC: 2711 Newspapers: publishing only, not printed on site

(G-11727)
SURFLINE INC
3335 S Virginia Dare Trl (27959-9267)
PHONE.................................252 715-1630
EMP: 6 EST: 2012
SALES (est): 87.71K **Privately Held**
Web: www.surfline.com
SIC: 3949 Surfboards

(G-11728)
VIRGINN-PLOT MDIA CMPANIES LLC
2224 S Croatan Hwy (27959-8813)
P.O. Box 10 (27959-0010)
PHONE.................................252 441-3628
EMP: 7
Web: www.pilotonline.com
SIC: 2711 Newspapers, publishing and printing
HQ: Virginian-Pilot Media Companies, Llc
    5457 Greenwich Rd
    Virginia Beach VA 23462
    757 446-9000

(G-11729)
WICKED OCEANS
3431 S Buccaneer Dr (27959-9777)
PHONE.................................252 269-0488
EMP: 4 EST: 2014
SALES (est): 88.21K **Privately Held**
Web: www.wickedoceans.com
SIC: 2323 Men's and boy's neckwear

(G-11730)
WOMACK PUBLISHING CO INC
Outer Banks Sentinel Pubg
2910 S Croatan Hwy Ste 19 (27959-9026)
P.O. Box 546 (27959-0546)
PHONE.................................252 480-2234
EMP: 54
SALES (corp-wide): 21.7MM **Privately Held**
Web: www.womackpublishing.com
SIC: 2711 Newspapers: publishing only, not printed on site
PA: Womack Publishing Company, Inc.
    28 N Main St
    Chatham VA 24531
    434 432-2791

Nakina
Columbus County

(G-11731)
SKJ MOORE LOGGING LLC
351 Sp Long Rd (28455-9488)
PHONE.................................910 642-5724
EMP: 7 EST: 2014
SALES (est): 227.16K **Privately Held**
SIC: 2411 Logging

(G-11732)
TRU LUCK WOODWORKS
2122 Pine Level Church Rd (28455-9114)
PHONE.................................910 642-2753
Tommie Ward, *Owner*
EMP: 5 EST: 2015
SALES (est): 203.09K **Privately Held**
SIC: 2429 Special product sawmills, nec

Nashville
Nash County

(G-11733)
ASTERRA LABS LLC
800 Cooke Rd (27856-7004)
PHONE.................................800 430-9074
Joe Cascone, *Managing Member*
EMP: 7 EST: 2019
SALES (est): 784.2K **Privately Held**
Web: www.asterralabs.com
SIC: 3999

(G-11734)
ATLANTIC NATURAL FOODS LLC
110 Industry Ct (27856-8895)
P.O. Box 985 (27856-0985)
PHONE.................................888 491-0524
Kelly Krause, *CEO*
J Hines, *Prin*
Desiree Wilson, *Corporate Secretary**
Kathy Werner, *
▲ EMP: 75 EST: 2008
SQ FT: 53,000
SALES (est): 23.58MM
SALES (corp-wide): 23.58MM **Privately Held**
Web: www.atlanticnaturalfoods.com
SIC: 5499 2032 Health foods; Baby foods, including meats: packaged in cans, jars, etc.
PA: Aft Holdings, Inc.
    10380 Perkins Rd 84427
    Baton Rouge LA 70810
    504 737-1000

(G-11735)
BOUNCERS AND SLIDES INC
2218 N Nc Highway 58 (27856-9006)
PHONE.................................252 908-2292
EMP: 5 EST: 2011
SALES (est): 48.51K **Privately Held**
Web: www.bounceandslides.com
SIC: 3999 Preparation of slides and exhibits

(G-11736)
BRASWELL MILLING COMPANY (PA)
Also Called: Braswell Foods
105 E Cross St (27856-1360)
P.O. Box 669 (27856-0669)
PHONE.................................252 459-2143
Ronald S Braswell Junior, *Pr*
Dixie Manning, *
Russell V Powell Junior, *Asst VP*
Robert Pike, *
Trey Braswell, *
EMP: 38 EST: 1950
SQ FT: 5,900
SALES (est): 13.02MM
SALES (corp-wide): 13.02MM **Privately Held**
Web: www.braswellfamilyfarms.com
SIC: 2048 2047 Chicken feeds, prepared; Dog and cat food

(G-11737)
BRIG HOMES NC
1001 Eastern Ave (27856-1717)
PHONE.................................252 459-7026
A Schindehette, *Pur Agt*
EMP: 7 EST: 2018

SALES (est): 239.98K **Privately Held**
SIC: 2451 Mobile homes

(G-11738)
BUTTERFIELDS CANDY LLC
Also Called: Butterfields Candies
2155 S Old Franklin Rd (27856-8952)
PHONE.................................252 459-2577
EMP: 8 EST: 2013
SALES (est): 762.04K **Privately Held**
Web: www.butterfieldscandies.com
SIC: 5441 2064 Candy; Breakfast bars

(G-11739)
CAROLINA EGG COMPANIES INC
10927 Cooper Rd (27856-9192)
P.O. Box 669 (27856-0669)
PHONE.................................252 459-2143
Ronald Braswell Junior, *Prin*
EMP: 60 EST: 1970
SQ FT: 50,000
SALES (est): 17.9MM **Privately Held**
SIC: 5144 2015 Eggs; Poultry slaughtering and processing

(G-11740)
CAROLINA INNVTIVE FD INGRDNTS
4626 Coleman Dr (27856)
P.O. Box 519 (27856-0519)
PHONE.................................804 359-9311
James Nagy, *Pr*
Ronald J Taylor, *VP Fin*
Catherine H Claiborne, *Sec*
John Kimber, *COO*
Candace C Formacek, *Treas*
EMP: 5 EST: 2014
SALES (est): 2.43MM
SALES (corp-wide): 2.57B **Publicly Held**
SIC: 2099 2034 Food preparations, nec; Dried and dehydrated fruits
PA: Universal Corporation
    9201 Forest Hill Ave
    Richmond VA 23235
    804 359-9311

(G-11741)
CAVALIER HOME BUILDERS LLC
1001 Eastern Ave (27856-1717)
P.O. Box 1007 (27856-1007)
PHONE.................................252 459-7026
Eric Bibb, *Mgr*
EMP: 183
SALES (corp-wide): 364.48B **Publicly Held**
Web: www.cavalieralabama.com
SIC: 2451 Mobile homes
HQ: Cavalier Home Builders, Llc
    32 Wilson Blvd 100
    Addison AL 35540
    256 747-1575

(G-11742)
CRUMP GROUP USA INC
4626 Coleman Dr (27856-7768)
PHONE.................................936 465-5870
Todd Fraysier, *Prin*
EMP: 19 EST: 2021
SALES (est): 3.11MM
SALES (corp-wide): 121.85MM **Privately Held**
SIC: 2047 7389 Dog and cat food; Business services, nec
PA: The Crump Group Inc
    2050 Drew Rd
    Mississauga ON L5S 1
    905 584-6781

(G-11743)
CSC FAMILY HOLDINGS INC
341 Corbett Rd (27856-8207)
PHONE.................................252 459-7116

Nashville - Nash County (G-11744)

Roger Breeden, *Mgr*
EMP: 7
SALES (corp-wide): 17.66MM **Privately Held**
Web: www.wwafcosteel.com
SIC: **3441** Fabricated structural metal
PA: Csc Family Holdings, Inc.
101 Centreport Dr Ste 400
Greensboro NC 27409
336 275-9711

(G-11744)
FAWN INDUSTRIES INC
100 Industry Ct (27856-8895)
PHONE..................................252 462-4700
Arthur Rutledge, *Brnch Mgr*
EMP: 71
SALES (corp-wide): 36.42MM **Privately Held**
Web: www.fawnplastics.com
SIC: **3089** Injection molding of plastics
PA: Fawn Industries, Inc.
225 Intrntl Cir Ste 200
Cockeysville MD 21030
410 308-9200

(G-11745)
GEORGES SAUCES LLC
Also Called: George's Bbq Sauce
1173 Womble Rd (27856-9131)
P.O. Box 99 (27856-0099)
PHONE..................................252 459-3084
Ashley Hassell, *Pr*
Elizabeth Chappell, *Managing Member*
EMP: 8 EST: 1992
SALES (est): 727.68K **Privately Held**
Web: www.georgesbbqsauce.com
SIC: **2035** **7389** Seasonings and sauces, except tomato and dry; Business Activities at Non-Commercial Site

(G-11746)
KEY PRINTING INC
1036 E Washington St (27856-1673)
PHONE..................................252 459-4783
Craig Glasgow, *Pr*
Richard Winstead, *VP*
EMP: 10 EST: 1989
SQ FT: 10,000
SALES (est): 958.67K **Privately Held**
Web: www.keyprinting.com
SIC: **2752** Offset printing

(G-11747)
NASH COUNTY NEWSPAPERS INC
Also Called: Nashville Graphic
203 W Washington St (27856-1263)
PHONE..................................252 459-7101
Gary Cunard, *Pr*
Joan Cooper, *Mgr*
EMP: 10 EST: 1996
SALES (est): 999.03K **Privately Held**
SIC: **2711** Commercial printing and newspaper publishing combined

(G-11748)
PERDUE FARMS INC
Also Called: Perdue Farms
1835 Us Highway 64a (27856-8202)
PHONE..................................252 459-9763
Ellen Skinner, *Mgr*
EMP: 165
SALES (corp-wide): 1.24B **Privately Held**
Web: www.perdue.com
SIC: **2015** Poultry slaughtering and processing
PA: Perdue Farms Incorporated
31149 Old Ocean City Rd
Salisbury MD 21804
800 473-7381

(G-11749)
RTS SCREEN PRINTING
2259 Sandy Cross Rd (27856-8628)
P.O. Box 8003 (27804-1003)
PHONE..................................252 972-3599
Ronnie West, *Owner*
EMP: 5 EST: 2017
SALES (est): 146.27K **Privately Held**
Web: www.rtsscreenprinting.com
SIC: **2759** Screen printing

(G-11750)
SIGNS NOW OF GREENVILLE
Also Called: Signs Now
6703 N Nc Highway 58 (27856-8401)
PHONE..................................252 382-0020
EMP: 5 EST: 2015
SALES (est): 50.69K **Privately Held**
SIC: **3993** Signs and advertising specialties

(G-11751)
TNT WEB & GRAFIX LLC
619 Western Ave (27856-1136)
PHONE..................................252 289-8846
EMP: 4 EST: 2016
SALES (est): 120.42K **Privately Held**
Web: www.tntwebandgrafix.com
SIC: **2759** Screen printing

(G-11752)
TORTILLAS SAN ANTONIO INC
4981 Old Bailey Hwy (27856-8537)
P.O. Box 1134 (27856-2134)
PHONE..................................252 459-5459
Richard Joyner, *Pr*
Antonio Armandariz, *VP*
EMP: 7 EST: 1998
SQ FT: 5,000
SALES (est): 125K **Privately Held**
SIC: **2099** Tortillas, fresh or refrigerated

(G-11753)
W&W-AFCO STEEL LLC
341 Corbett Rd (27856-8207)
PHONE..................................252 459-7116
Roger Breeden, *Brnch Mgr*
EMP: 46
SALES (corp-wide): 364.48B **Publicly Held**
Web: www.wwafcosteel.com
SIC: **3441** Fabricated structural metal
HQ: W&W-Afco Steel Llc
1730 W Reno Ave
Oklahoma City OK 73106
405 235-3621

(G-11754)
WAR SPORT MANUFACTURING LLC
111 W Church St (27856-1327)
PHONE..................................252 220-6505
EMP: 5 EST: 2017
SALES (est): 145.97K **Privately Held**
SIC: **3999** Manufacturing industries, nec

(G-11755)
WELDINGART4U LLC
624 Wollett Mill Rd (27856-7831)
PHONE..................................252 220-0294
Jason Ashley Knapp, *Managing Member*
EMP: 4 EST: 2013
SALES (est): 52.57K **Privately Held**
SIC: **7692** Welding repair

(G-11756)
WINGFIELD HOUSE OF PEACE
2024 Trinity Dr (27856-7860)
PHONE..................................719 251-0618
EMP: 5 EST: 2018
SALES (est): 169.75K **Privately Held**
Web: www.houseofpeacepubs.com

SIC: **2741** Miscellaneous publishing

Navassa
Brunswick County

(G-11757)
CAPE FEAR BOAT WORKS INC
1690 Royster Rd Ne (28451-7528)
P.O. Box 2195 (28451-2195)
PHONE..................................910 371-3460
Andrew J Simmons Junior, *Pr*
EMP: 10 EST: 2008
SQ FT: 22,000
SALES (est): 454.14K **Privately Held**
Web: www.capefearboatworks.com
SIC: **4493** **3732** Boat yards, storage and incidental repair; Boatbuilding and repairing

(G-11758)
PACON MANUFACTURING CORP LLC
Also Called: Baumgartner Associates
100 Quality Dr Ne (28451-7666)
PHONE..................................732 764-9070
Dorothy H Shannon, *Ch Bd*
A Vernon Shannon Iii, *Pr*
Lawrence H Shannon, *
Micheal Shannon, *
▲ EMP: 125 EST: 1946
SQ FT: 168,000
SALES (est): 22.69MM **Privately Held**
Web: www.paconmfg.com
SIC: **2676** **3821** **3842** Sanitary paper products; Incubators, laboratory; Surgical appliances and supplies

Nebo
Mcdowell County

(G-11759)
BLANKENSHIP LOGGING
397 Biggerstaff Loop (28761-5746)
PHONE..................................828 652-2250
Ray Blankenship, *Pt*
EMP: 5 EST: 1955
SALES (est): 492.62K **Privately Held**
SIC: **2411** Logging camps and contractors

(G-11760)
FOREST CITY PALLETT CO INC
5159 Harmony Grove Rd (28761-7734)
PHONE..................................828 652-8432
Clyde Robinson, *Pr*
Michael Robinson, *VP*
Billy Warren, *VP*
Sandy Mckinney, *Treas*
Debbie Warren, *Sec*
EMP: 9 EST: 1970
SQ FT: 10,000
SALES (est): 358K **Privately Held**
SIC: **2448** Pallets, wood

(G-11761)
MICHAEL D PRESSLEY
198 Emerson Ln (28761-5509)
PHONE..................................828 652-8292
Michael D Pressley, *Prin*
EMP: 7 EST: 2013
SALES (est): 196.01K **Privately Held**
SIC: **2759** Screen printing

(G-11762)
MUDDY CREEK MILL WORKS INC
2854 Muddy Creek Rd (28761-0106)
PHONE..................................828 659-5558
Teele H Dockery Junior, *Admn*
EMP: 6 EST: 2015

SALES (est): 87.17K **Privately Held**
SIC: **2431** Millwork

(G-11763)
RDM INDUSTRIAL ELECTRONICS INC (PA)
Also Called: Wellness Robotronic Industries
850 Harmony Grove Rd (28761-9504)
P.O. Box 969 (28761-0961)
PHONE..................................828 652-8346
Doug Long, *Pr*
Rick Long, *
Teresa Long, *
EMP: 65 EST: 1988
SQ FT: 21,000
SALES (est): 9.88MM **Privately Held**
Web: www.rdm.net
SIC: **3699** Electrical equipment and supplies, nec

(G-11764)
TAYLOR STAVE LLC
2854 Muddy Creek Rd (28761-0106)
PHONE..................................828 659-8880
Natalie B Taylor, *Pr*
EMP: 8 EST: 2015
SALES (est): 534.34K **Privately Held**
Web: www.taylorstave.com
SIC: **2499** Wood products, nec

New Bern
Craven County

(G-11765)
ACCUKING INC
Also Called: King Aerospace and Tech
3458 Martin Dr (28562-5145)
PHONE..................................252 649-2323
EMP: 4 EST: 2014
SQ FT: 10,000
SALES (est): 270.09K **Privately Held**
Web: www.accukinginc.com
SIC: **3451** Screw machine products

(G-11766)
ALAMO PUBLISHING SERVICES
316 Shoreline Dr (28562-9522)
PHONE..................................252 269-1513
Oliver Moore, *Prin*
EMP: 5 EST: 2013
SALES (est): 108.79K **Privately Held**
SIC: **2741** Miscellaneous publishing

(G-11767)
AMERICAN EAGLE MFG LLC
3280 Us Highway 70 E (28560-6928)
PHONE..................................252 633-0603
Robert L Liland, *Managing Member*
EMP: 8 EST: 2009
SALES (est): 1.7MM **Privately Held**
Web: www.americaneaglemanufacturing.com
SIC: **3999** Barber and beauty shop equipment

(G-11768)
AMERICAN FABRICATORS
4395 Us Highway 17 S (28562-8308)
PHONE..................................252 637-2600
Jean Wachter, *Pr*
EMP: 6 EST: 2005
SALES (est): 457.12K **Privately Held**
Web: www.americanfabricatorsnc.com
SIC: **3496** Miscellaneous fabricated wire products

GEOGRAPHIC SECTION

New Bern - Craven County (G-11795)

(G-11769)
AMERICAN LGACY TIMELINE PRINTS
905 Coral Ct (28560-9731)
PHONE.....................252 514-0225
Sandra Casado, *Owner*
EMP: 5 **EST:** 2017
SALES (est): 63.01K **Privately Held**
SIC: 2752 Commercial printing, lithographic

(G-11770)
AMEROCHEM CORPORATION
1885 Old Airport Rd (28562-9453)
P.O. Box 3009 (28564-3009)
PHONE.....................252 634-9344
Harvey W Wright, *Pr*
Paula E Norman, *VP*
Ida M Wright, *Sec*
EMP: 21 **EST:** 1990
SALES (est): 2.87MM **Privately Held**
Web: www.amerochem.com
SIC: 3589 4489 Sewage and water treatment equipment; Water taxis

(G-11771)
ANDREWS GRAPHICS LLC
Also Called: Alphagraphcis of New Bern
3731 Trent Rd (28562-2221)
PHONE.....................252 633-3199
EMP: 6 **EST:** 2011
SALES (est): 450K **Privately Held**
Web: www.alphagraphicsnewbern.com
SIC: 2752 Offset printing

(G-11772)
ATLANTIC LOGGING INC
232 Stony Branch Rd (28562-9329)
PHONE.....................252 229-9997
Robert F Dail Junior, *Pr*
EMP: 10 **EST:** 2017
SALES (est): 247.97K **Privately Held**
SIC: 2411 Logging camps and contractors

(G-11773)
AWCNC LLC
401 Industrial Dr (28562-5437)
PHONE.....................252 633-5757
EMP: 47 **EST:** 1978
SQ FT: 50,000
SALES (est): 2.47MM **Privately Held**
Web: www.aylward-usa.com
SIC: 3565 Packaging machinery

(G-11774)
AYLWARD ENTERPRISES LLC (PA)
401 Industrial Dr (28562-5437)
PHONE.....................252 639-9242
EMP: 30 **EST:** 2007
SQ FT: 50,000
SALES (est): 6.91MM **Privately Held**
Web: www.aylward-usa.com
SIC: 3559 3565 Pharmaceutical machinery; Packaging machinery

(G-11775)
B & J SEAFOOD CO INC
1101 Us Highway 70 E (28560-6617)
P.O. Box 3321 (28564-3321)
PHONE.....................252 637-0483
Catherine Fulcher, *Prin*
EMP: 23 **EST:** 1998
SALES (est): 8.55MM **Privately Held**
SIC: 5146 2092 Seafoods; Fresh or frozen packaged fish

(G-11776)
BANNISTER INC
Also Called: Ultra Precision Machining
303 Crescent St (28560-3227)
P.O. Box 12848 (28561-2848)
PHONE.....................252 638-6611
Al Bannister Junior, *Pr*
EMP: 19 **EST:** 1983
SALES (est): 485.43K **Privately Held**
SIC: 3599 Machine shop, jobbing and repair

(G-11777)
BENDER APPAREL & SIGNS INC
1841 Old Airport Rd (28562-9453)
PHONE.....................252 636-8337
John Berry Bender, *Pr*
Wade Bender, *VP*
EMP: 8 **EST:** 1996
SQ FT: 2,400
SALES (est): 968.69K **Privately Held**
Web: www.bendershirts.com
SIC: 2759 Screen printing

(G-11778)
BROADWAY LOGGING CO INC
Also Called: Broadway Chipping Co.
1525 Saints Delight Church Rd (28560-7305)
PHONE.....................252 633-2693
B F Broadway, *Pr*
Gail Broadway, *
EMP: 50 **EST:** 1978
SALES (est): 3.54MM **Privately Held**
SIC: 2411 Logging camps and contractors

(G-11779)
BSH HOME APPLIANCES CORP
120 Bosch Blvd (28562-6924)
PHONE.....................252 636-4454
Clemence Schaller, *Brnch Mgr*
EMP: 34
SALES (corp-wide): 230.19MM **Privately Held**
Web: www.bsh-group.com
SIC: 3631 Convection ovens, including portable: household
HQ: Bsh Home Appliances Corporation
1901 Main St Ste 600
Irvine CA 92614

(G-11780)
BSH HOME APPLIANCES CORP
Also Called: Bsh International Trade
100 Bosch Blvd (28562-6924)
PHONE.....................252 672-9155
Clemens Schaller, *Brnch Mgr*
EMP: 400
SALES (corp-wide): 230.19MM **Privately Held**
Web: www.bsh-group.com
SIC: 7629 3632 Electrical household appliance repair; Household refrigerators and freezers
HQ: Bsh Home Appliances Corporation
1901 Main St Ste 600
Irvine CA 92614

(G-11781)
BSH HOME APPLS A LTD PARTNR
100 Bosch Blvd (28562-6924)
PHONE.....................252 636-4200
EMP: 270 **EST:** 1996
SQ FT: 160,000
SALES (est): 53.33MM
SALES (corp-wide): 230.19MM **Privately Held**
SIC: 3639 Dishwashing machines, household
HQ: Bsh Hausgerate Gmbh
Carl-Wery-Str. 34
Munchen BY 81739
89459001

(G-11782)
BURKETT WELDING SERVICES INC
1401 B St (28560-9300)
P.O. Box 314 (28586-0314)
PHONE.....................252 635-2814
Kevin L Burkett, *Pr*
EMP: 10 **EST:** 2008
SALES (est): 1.15MM **Privately Held**
SIC: 1799 3441 Welding on site; Fabricated structural metal

(G-11783)
CARAWAY LOGGING INC
1939 Olympia Rd (28560-5110)
PHONE.....................252 633-1230
John Dee Caraway, *Pr*
John Dee Caraway Iii, *VP*
EMP: 8 **EST:** 1990
SALES (est): 476.72K **Privately Held**
SIC: 2411 Logging camps and contractors

(G-11784)
CAROLINA EAST TIMBER INC
2145 Saints Delight Church Rd (28560-7317)
PHONE.....................252 638-1914
EMP: 5 **EST:** 1992
SALES (est): 300.63K **Privately Held**
SIC: 2411 Logging camps and contractors

(G-11785)
CAROLINA GROUND SVC EQP INC (PA)
Also Called: Carolina GSE
430 Executive Pkwy (28562-9794)
PHONE.....................252 565-0288
John Werner, *Pr*
EMP: 14 **EST:** 2002
SALES (est): 2.4MM
SALES (corp-wide): 2.4MM **Privately Held**
Web: www.carolinagse.com
SIC: 3728 5088 Aircraft parts and equipment, nec; Aircraft and parts, nec

(G-11786)
CAROLINA HOME EXTERIORS LLC
252 Kale Rd (28562-7055)
PHONE.....................252 637-6599
David Thereault, *Managing Member*
EMP: 17 **EST:** 1980
SQ FT: 23,000
SALES (est): 2.33MM **Privately Held**
Web: www.carolinahomeexteriorsenc.com
SIC: 1521 3089 5033 Patio and deck construction and repair; Window screening, plastics; Siding, except wood

(G-11787)
CAT LOGISTICS INC
Also Called: Caterpillar
7970 Hwy 70 E (28560-8487)
PHONE.....................252 447-2490
Daniel Shannon, *Mgr*
EMP: 10
SALES (corp-wide): 67.06B **Publicly Held**
SIC: 3365 Aerospace castings, aluminum
HQ: C.A.T. Logistics Inc.
500 N Morton Ave
Morton IL 61560
309 675-1000

(G-11788)
CHATSWORTH PRODUCTS INC
Also Called: CPI
701 Industrial Dr (28562-5447)
PHONE.....................252 514-2779
David Parker, *Genl Mgr*
EMP: 110
Web: www.chatsworth.com
SIC: 3499 3496 3444 3441 Machine bases, metal; Miscellaneous fabricated wire products; Sheet metalwork; Fabricated structural metal
PA: Chatsworth Products, Inc.
4175 Guardian St
Simi Valley CA 93063

(G-11789)
COASTAL CABINETS OF NEW BERN
121 Premier Dr (28562-9591)
PHONE.....................252 514-5030
EMP: 5 **EST:** 2013
SALES (est): 62.53K **Privately Held**
SIC: 2434 Wood kitchen cabinets

(G-11790)
COASTAL CUSTOM WOOD WORKS LLC
111 Premier Dr (28562-9591)
PHONE.....................252 675-8732
Eric Williams Massey, *VP*
EMP: 6 **EST:** 2013
SALES (est): 128.51K **Privately Held**
SIC: 2431 Millwork

(G-11791)
COUNTER EFFECT
115 Justin Dr (28562-9143)
PHONE.....................252 636-0080
Chuck Arcomdak, *Dir*
EMP: 5 **EST:** 2011
SALES (est): 263.2K **Privately Held**
Web: www.countereffect.net
SIC: 3131 Counters

(G-11792)
CRAVEN TIRE INC
318 1st St (28560-5506)
PHONE.....................252 633-0200
Robert R Northington, *Pr*
Tim Tart, *VP*
EMP: 6 **EST:** 1975
SQ FT: 4,820
SALES (est): 875.98K **Privately Held**
Web: www.craventiresales.com
SIC: 5999 3272 Concrete products, pre-cast; Concrete products, nec

(G-11793)
CREEKRAFT CULTURED MARBLE INC
3205 Old Cherry Point Rd (28560-6967)
P.O. Box 3413 (28564-3413)
PHONE.....................252 636-5488
Guy Hopewell, *Pr*
EMP: 12 **EST:** 1990
SQ FT: 10,000
SALES (est): 447.31K **Privately Held**
Web: www.creekraftmarble.com
SIC: 3088 Hot tubs, plastics or fiberglass

(G-11794)
CUSTOM CANVAS INC 2
225b S Front St (28560-2135)
PHONE.....................252 633-0754
David T Crawford, *Pr*
EMP: 7 **EST:** 2017
SALES (est): 229.94K **Privately Held**
SIC: 2211 Canvas

(G-11795)
CUSTOM MARINE FABRICATION INC
2401 Us Highway 70 E (28560-6795)
PHONE.....................252 638-5422
Donald A Willis Senior, *Pr*
Donald Willis Junior, *VP*
EMP: 8 **EST:** 1986
SQ FT: 12,500
SALES (est): 807.45K **Privately Held**
Web: www.nccustommarine.com
SIC: 5091 3732 5941 Boat accessories and parts; Boatbuilding and repairing; Fishing equipment

New Bern - Craven County (G-11796)

(G-11796)
CUSTOM SURFACES CORPORATION
115 Justin Dr (28562-9143)
P.O. Box 12849 (28561-2849)
PHONE.................................252 638-3800
Denny Murdock, *Pr*
Charles Murdock, *VP*
Amy Upton, *Off Mgr*
EMP: 8 **EST:** 2015
SQ FT: 3,600
SALES (est): 515.68K **Privately Held**
SIC: 2434 2541 Wood kitchen cabinets; Table or counter tops, plastic laminated

(G-11797)
D2 GOVERNMENT SOLUTIONS LLC (PA)
820 Aviation Dr Ste 1 (28562-8117)
PHONE.................................662 655-4554
EMP: 35 **EST:** 2015
SALES (est): 24.28MM **Privately Held**
Web: www.d2-gs.com
SIC: 3728 4512 4522 4581 Aircraft parts and equipment, nec; Air transportation, scheduled; Air transportation, nonscheduled ; Aircraft maintenance and repair services

(G-11798)
DAMCO INC
1103 Us Highway 17 N (28560-5061)
P.O. Box 1656 (28563-1656)
PHONE.................................252 633-1404
Asa Dail, *Pr*
Beverly Dail, *Sec*
EMP: 15 **EST:** 1975
SQ FT: 20,000
SALES (est): 2.6MM **Privately Held**
Web: www.damcoinc.net
SIC: 3599 Machine shop, jobbing and repair

(G-11799)
DECORATIVE PLASTICS LLC
203 River Bluffs Dr (28560-8494)
PHONE.................................252 638-6684
Michelle Faulkner, *Pr*
EMP: 6 **EST:** 2015
SALES (est): 204.57K **Privately Held**
SIC: 3089 Injection molding of plastics

(G-11800)
DERROW ENTERPRISES INC
Also Called: Trailer Plus
7001 Us Highway 70 E (28562-8716)
PHONE.................................252 635-3375
Scott Derrow, *Pr*
EMP: 7 **EST:** 2013
SALES (est): 415.72K **Privately Held**
SIC: 3011 3792 5014 5561 Tires and inner tubes; Travel trailers and campers; Tires and tubes; Recreational vehicle parts and accessories

(G-11801)
DIVISION SIX INCORPORATED
115 Justin Dr (28562-9143)
PHONE.................................910 420-3305
Chuck Murdock, *Pr*
EMP: 5 **EST:** 2019
SALES (est): 476.97K **Privately Held**
SIC: 2431 Millwork

(G-11802)
DRADURA USA CORP
197 Bosch Blvd (28562-6924)
PHONE.................................252 637-9660
Wolfgang Stein, *Pr*
▲ **EMP:** 90 **EST:** 2007
SALES (est): 25.83MM
SALES (corp-wide): 2.67MM **Privately Held**

Web: www.dradura.com
SIC: 3496 Miscellaneous fabricated wire products
HQ: Dradura Holding Gmbh & Co. Kg
    Talstr. 2
    Altleiningen RP 67317
    63569660

(G-11803)
ELLIS PUBLISHING COMPANY INC
Also Called: The Havelock News
3200 Wellons Blvd (28562-5234)
P.O. Box 777 (28532-0777)
PHONE.................................252 444-1999
Gene Mace, *Pr*
Lea Stifflemire, *Sec*
EMP: 12 **EST:** 1985
SALES (est): 171.28K **Privately Held**
Web: www.havenews.com
SIC: 2711 Newspapers, publishing and printing

(G-11804)
FRANKIE YORK LOGGING CO
2250 Us Highway 17 N (28560-9660)
PHONE.................................252 633-4825
Frankie York, *Owner*
EMP: 4 **EST:** 1971
SALES (est): 243.34K **Privately Held**
SIC: 2411 Logging camps and contractors

(G-11805)
G & H BROADWAY LOGGING INC
145 Territorial Rd (28560-8894)
PHONE.................................252 229-4594
Gregory A Broadway, *Pr*
EMP: 9 **EST:** 2016
SALES (est): 464.82K **Privately Held**
SIC: 2411 Logging camps and contractors

(G-11806)
GENERAL WHOLESALE BLDG SUP CO (PA)
Also Called: Eastern Building Components
3321 Neuse Blvd (28560-4109)
P.O. Box 12305 (28561-2305)
PHONE.................................252 638-5861
J V Williams Junior, *Pr*
Gary Hardison, *
EMP: 75 **EST:** 1954
SQ FT: 45,000
SALES (est): 9.15MM
SALES (corp-wide): 9.15MM **Privately Held**
SIC: 5211 2439 Lumber and other building materials; Trusses, wooden roof

(G-11807)
GERALD FISHERIES LLC
104 Coree Way (28562-9095)
PHONE.................................907 518-0004
Darian Gerald, *Prin*
EMP: 4 **EST:** 2021
SALES (est): 64.64K **Privately Held**
SIC: 2389 5092 5149 Apparel and accessories, nec; Toys and hobby goods and supplies; Groceries and related products, nec

(G-11808)
HATTERAS YACHTS INC
110 N Glenburnie Rd (28560-2703)
PHONE.................................252 633-3101
◆ **EMP:** 1320
SIC: 3732 Yachts, building and repairing

(G-11809)
HOLLANDS FLOOR COVERING LLC
203 Nydegg Rd (28562-7042)
PHONE.................................602 703-1951

Mark Holland, *Owner*
EMP: 5 **EST:** 2008
SALES (est): 146.16K **Privately Held**
Web: www.az-flooring.com
SIC: 2752 Commercial printing, lithographic

(G-11810)
INNOVATIVE LAMINATIONS COMPANY
51a Halls Creek Rd (28560-5766)
PHONE.................................252 745-8133
Andreas Penz, *Pr*
Peter Hofmann, *Sec*
EMP: 18 **EST:** 2000
SQ FT: 21,000
SALES (est): 8.15MM
SALES (corp-wide): 323.59MM **Privately Held**
Web: www.innovative-laminations.com
SIC: 3083 Laminated plastics sheets
HQ: Trodat Gmbh
    Linzer StraBe 156
    Wels 4600
    72422390

(G-11811)
INTERNATIONAL PAPER COMPANY
Also Called: International Paper
1785 Weyerhaeuser Rd (28563)
PHONE.................................252 633-7407
EMP: 5
SALES (corp-wide): 18.92B **Publicly Held**
Web: www.internationalpaper.com
SIC: 2653 Boxes, corrugated: made from purchased materials
PA: International Paper Company
    6400 Poplar Ave
    Memphis TN 38197
    901 419-7000

(G-11812)
J & S TOOLS INC
100 Liestal Ln (28562-8969)
PHONE.................................252 514-7805
Danielle Goforth, *Prin*
EMP: 6 **EST:** 2019
SALES (est): 86.57K **Privately Held**
SIC: 3599 Machine shop, jobbing and repair

(G-11813)
JOESIGNS INC
2617 Trent Rd (28562-2025)
PHONE.................................252 638-1622
Joey Pontiff, *Pr*
Paige Pontiff, *Sec*
EMP: 4 **EST:** 1992
SALES (est): 254.21K **Privately Held**
Web: www.joesigns.com
SIC: 3993 Signs, not made in custom sign painting shops

(G-11814)
JOHNSON MACHINE CO INC
8 Batts Hill Rd (28562-7364)
PHONE.................................252 638-2620
Junius P Johnson Junior, *Pr*
Paul Johnson, *Pr*
EMP: 6 **EST:** 1944
SQ FT: 2,500
SALES (est): 331.87K **Privately Held**
SIC: 7538 5013 3599 Engine rebuilding: automotive; Automotive supplies and parts; Machine shop, jobbing and repair

(G-11815)
KENS CUSTOM CABINETS INC
4685 E Us 70 Hwy (28562-7036)
PHONE.................................252 637-3378
William K Stembridge Junior, *CEO*
EMP: 7 **EST:** 2000
SALES (est): 241.3K **Privately Held**

SIC: 2434 Wood kitchen cabinets

(G-11816)
M & K LOGGING LLC
310 Parker Rd (28562-9215)
PHONE.................................252 349-8975
Miguel Bryant, *Prin*
EMP: 8 **EST:** 2016
SALES (est): 361.75K **Privately Held**
SIC: 2411 Logging camps and contractors

(G-11817)
MAOLA MILK AND ICE CREAM CO
307 N First Ave (28560-2850)
PHONE.................................844 287-1970
Dwayne Myers, *Prin*
EMP: 20 **EST:** 1945
SALES (est): 468.69K **Privately Held**
Web: www.maolamilk.com
SIC: 2026 Acidophilus milk

(G-11818)
MARCO PRODUCTS INC
Also Called: Marco Pproducts
214 Kale Rd (28562-7055)
P.O. Box 826 (28571-0826)
PHONE.................................215 956-0313
Arden Martenz, *Pr*
Cameon Funk, *VP*
EMP: 10 **EST:** 1983
SALES (est): 877.66K **Privately Held**
Web: www.youthlight.com
SIC: 2731 Books, publishing only

(G-11819)
MARSHALL GROUP OF NC INC
2400 Trent Rd (28562-2020)
PHONE.................................252 638-8585
Jason Voyce, *Prin*
EMP: 5 **EST:** 1991
SQ FT: 2,000
SALES (est): 328.35K **Privately Held**
Web: www.themarshallgroup.net
SIC: 2531 Public building and related furniture

(G-11820)
MARTIN MARIETTA MATERIALS INC
Also Called: Martin Marietta Aggregates
1315 Old Us 70 W (28560)
P.O. Box 12326 (28561-2326)
PHONE.................................252 633-5308
EMP: 7
Web: www.martinmarietta.com
SIC: 1422 Crushed and broken limestone
PA: Martin Marietta Materials Inc
    4123 Parklake Ave
    Raleigh NC 27612

(G-11821)
MASS ENTERPRISES LLC
Also Called: Pocket Yacht Company
4310 Us Highway 70 E (28560-7913)
PHONE.................................443 585-0732
Mark Schulstad, *Managing Member*
EMP: 19 **EST:** 2011
SALES (est): 1.11MM **Privately Held**
SIC: 3732 Yachts, building and repairing

(G-11822)
MILLER SAWS & SUPPLIES INC
115 Ridgewood Trl (28560-9462)
PHONE.................................252 636-3347
EMP: 5
SALES (est): 631.62K **Privately Held**
SIC: 3524 Lawn and garden equipment

(G-11823)
MINGES BOTTLING GROUP
256 Middle St (28560-2142)

GEOGRAPHIC SECTION

New Bern - Craven County

PHONE..................252 636-5898
Larry Cook, *Prin*
EMP: 17 **EST:** 2011
SALES (est): 242.05K **Privately Held**
Web: www.mbgpepsi.com
SIC: 2086 Soft drinks: packaged in cans, bottles, etc.

(G-11824)
MOEN INCORPORATED
Also Called: Moen
101 Industrial Dr (28562-9607)
PHONE..................252 638-3300
Brian Donato, *Brnch Mgr*
EMP: 50
SQ FT: 60,000
SALES (corp-wide): 4.63B **Publicly Held**
Web: www.moen.com
SIC: 3088 Shower stalls, fiberglass and plastics
HQ: Moen Incorporated
25300 Al Moen Dr
North Olmsted OH 44070
800 289-6636

(G-11825)
MONTE ENTERPRISES INC
Also Called: Monte Printing Co
3204 Neuse Blvd (28560-4113)
P.O. Box 12391 (28561-2391)
PHONE..................252 637-5803
Peter T Monte, *Pr*
EMP: 5 **EST:** 1952
SALES (est): 403.21K **Privately Held**
Web: www.monteprinting.com
SIC: 2752 Offset printing

(G-11826)
MORRIS GROUP
1707 Pennyroyal Rd (28562-4918)
PHONE..................973 713-2211
Ed Morris, *Prin*
EMP: 6 **EST:** 2019
SALES (est): 66.55K **Privately Held**
Web: www.morrisgroupinc.com
SIC: 3599 Machine shop, jobbing and repair

(G-11827)
MULBERRY STREET INC
101 Timberwolf Ct (28560-8940)
PHONE..................252 638-3195
Robert S Fugate, *Pr*
EMP: 6 **EST:** 1991
SALES (est): 218.22K **Privately Held**
Web: www.mulberrystreetinc.com
SIC: 2361 2329 2369 Girl's and children's dresses, blouses; Shirt and slack suits: men's, youths', and boys'; Girl's and children's outerwear, nec

(G-11828)
MULLIS MILLWORK INC
904 Jewell Ct (28560-9016)
PHONE..................919 496-5993
Steve Sherwood, *Owner*
Steve Sherwood, *Pr*
Virginia Sherwood, *Sec*
EMP: 10 **EST:** 1991
SALES (est): 825.5K **Privately Held**
Web: www.mullismillwork.com
SIC: 2431 Millwork

(G-11829)
NEW BERN CRAVEN CO BD OF EDUC
2922 Trent Rd (28562-2030)
PHONE..................252 635-1822
EMP: 4 **EST:** 2019
SALES (est): 67.45K **Privately Held**

SIC: 2711 Commercial printing and newspaper publishing combined

(G-11830)
NEW BERN MAGAZINE
219 Pecan Grove Ct (28562-9836)
PHONE..................252 626-5812
Matt Farver, *Prin*
EMP: 6 **EST:** 2019
SALES (est): 93.11K **Privately Held**
Web: www.newbernmagazine.com
SIC: 2721 Magazines: publishing and printing

(G-11831)
NOMAD HOUSEBOATS INC
208 Outrigger Rd (28562-8844)
PHONE..................252 288-5670
Warren Lloyd, *Pr*
Judy Lloyd, *Sec*
EMP: 5 **EST:** 2000
SQ FT: 5,000
SALES (est): 584.08K **Privately Held**
Web: www.nomadhouseboats.com
SIC: 5551 3732 Motor boat dealers; Boatbuilding and repairing

(G-11832)
OWEN G DUNN CO INC (PA)
3731 Trent Rd (28562-2221)
P.O. Box 13216 (28561-3216)
PHONE..................252 633-3197
Owen D Andrews, *Pr*
Donald R Andrews Junior, *VP*
Debra C Andrews, *Sec*
EMP: 8 **EST:** 1902
SQ FT: 18,000
SALES (est): 4.63MM
SALES (corp-wide): 4.63MM **Privately Held**
Web: www.printelect.com
SIC: 2752 5943 2791 2789 Commercial printing, lithographic; Office forms and supplies; Typesetting; Bookbinding and related work

(G-11833)
PCS PHOSPHATE
535 Prescott Rd (28560-5912)
PHONE..................252 402-5779
Timothy Jestness, *Engr*
EMP: 5 **EST:** 2018
SALES (est): 197.04K **Privately Held**
SIC: 1475 Phosphate rock

(G-11834)
PEPSI-COLA BTLG NEW BERN INC (PA)
Also Called: Pepsi-Cola
3610 Dr M L King Jr Blvd (28562)
P.O. Box 520 (28513-0520)
PHONE..................252 522-0232
Jeffrey Minges, *Pr*
Ty Minges, *
Tom Minges, *
EMP: 45 **EST:** 1946
SQ FT: 15,000
SALES (est): 3.75MM
SALES (corp-wide): 3.75MM **Privately Held**
Web: www.pepsico.com
SIC: 2086 Carbonated soft drinks, bottled and canned

(G-11835)
PHILLIP DUNN LOGGING CO INC
508 Madam Moores Ln (28562-6440)
PHONE..................252 633-4577
Phillip Dunn, *Pr*
EMP: 10 **EST:** 1970
SALES (est): 528.91K **Privately Held**

SIC: 2411 Logging camps and contractors

(G-11836)
PIEDMONT COCA-COLA BTLG PARTNR
Also Called: Coca-Cola
3710 Dr M L King Jr Blvd (28562)
PHONE..................252 637-3157
George Walker, *Mgr*
EMP: 123
SALES (corp-wide): 6.65B **Publicly Held**
Web: www.cokeconsolidated.com
SIC: 2086 Bottled and canned soft drinks
HQ: Piedmont Coca-Cola Bottling Partnership
4115 Coca Cola Plz
Charlotte NC 28211
704 551-4400

(G-11837)
PINECONE PUBLISHING LLC
Also Called: Discovery Map
4910 Spring Green Pass (28562-5754)
PHONE..................252 649-0973
EMP: 4 **EST:** 2019
SALES (est): 80.05K **Privately Held**
Web: www.discoverymap.com
SIC: 2741 Miscellaneous publishing

(G-11838)
PUCUDA INC
Also Called: Leading Edge Safety Systems
3100 Oaks Rd (28560-2841)
P.O. Box 471 (06443-0471)
PHONE..................860 526-8004
John Rexroad, *Pr*
◆ **EMP:** 15 **EST:** 1992
SQ FT: 12,500
SALES (est): 4.04MM **Privately Held**
Web: www.netting.com
SIC: 3089 Netting, plastics

(G-11839)
R E BENGEL SHEET METAL CO
1311 N Craven St (28560-3249)
PHONE..................252 637-3404
Steve Bengel, *Pr*
Ella Bengel, *Sec*
Sabrina Bengel, *Treas*
EMP: 20 **EST:** 1912
SQ FT: 3,000
SALES (est): 461.83K **Privately Held**
Web: www.rebengel.com
SIC: 1761 3444 Sheet metal work, nec; Sheet metalwork

(G-11840)
ROBERT LASKOWSKI
232 Stony Branch Rd (28562-9329)
PHONE..................203 732-0846
Robert Laskowski, *Prin*
EMP: 6 **EST:** 2012
SALES (est): 104.71K **Privately Held**
SIC: 2711 Newspapers, publishing and printing

(G-11841)
S & W READY MIX CON CO LLC
1300 Us Highway 17 N (28560-5013)
PHONE..................252 633-2115
Daniel Bordeaux, *Mgr*
EMP: 19
SALES (corp-wide): 8.01MM **Privately Held**
SIC: 3273 Ready-mixed concrete
HQ: S & W Ready Mix Concrete Company Llc
217 Lisbon St
Clinton NC 28328
910 592-1733

(G-11842)
S T WOOTEN CORPORATION
Also Called: New Bern Asphalt Plant
245 Parker Rd (28562-9214)
PHONE..................252 636-2568
Scott Wooten, *Pr*
EMP: 22
SALES (corp-wide): 319.83MM **Privately Held**
Web: www.stwcorp.com
SIC: 3531 Asphalt plant, including gravel-mix type
PA: S. T. Wooten Corporation
3801 Black Creek Rd Se
Wilson NC 27893
252 291-5165

(G-11843)
S ZAYTOUN CUSTOM CABINETS INC
1206 Pollock St (28560-5538)
PHONE..................252 638-8390
John E Zaytoun Junior, *Pr*
Michael F Zaytoun, *VP*
Michael Zaytoun Junior, *Treas*
EMP: 19 **EST:** 1972
SQ FT: 25,000
SALES (est): 877.4K **Privately Held**
Web: www.zaytouncustomcabinets.com
SIC: 2541 2434 Cabinets, lockers, and shelving; Wood kitchen cabinets

(G-11844)
SCHLAADT PLASTICS LIMITED
198 Bosch Blvd (28562-6924)
P.O. Box 15409 (28561-5409)
PHONE..................252 634-9494
Stefan Schlaadt, *Pr*
▲ **EMP:** 15 **EST:** 2005
SALES (est): 4.38MM
SALES (corp-wide): 355.83K **Privately Held**
Web: www.schlaadt.de
SIC: 2821 Plastics materials and resins
HQ: Schlaadt-Plastics Gesellschaft Mit Beschrankter Haftung
Schwalbacher Str. 123
Lorch HE 65391
67268030

(G-11845)
SHOPPER
Also Called: Shopper The
3200 Wellons Blvd (28562-5234)
P.O. Box 12367 (28561-2367)
PHONE..................252 633-1153
Judy Avery, *Pr*
EMP: 9 **EST:** 1968
SQ FT: 3,600
SALES (est): 237.03K **Privately Held**
Web: www.theshopper.com
SIC: 2711 Newspapers: publishing only, not printed on site

(G-11846)
SIKORSKY AIRCRAFT CORPORATION
Us Highway 70 East (28560)
PHONE..................252 447-5050
EMP: 5 **EST:** 2018
SALES (est): 78.31K **Privately Held**
SIC: 3429 Aircraft hardware

(G-11847)
SMYRNA READY MIX CONCRETE LLC
Also Called: Ready Mixed Concrete
1715 Race Track Rd (28562-4117)
P.O. Box 877 (27835-0877)
PHONE..................252 637-4155
Carl Norris, *Manager*

New Bern - Craven County (G-11848)

EMP: 12
SALES (corp-wide): 1.05B **Privately Held**
Web: www.argos-us.com
SIC: 3273 Ready-mixed concrete
PA: Smyrna Ready Mix Concrete, Llc
1000 Hollingshead Cir
Murfreesboro TN 37129
615 355-1028

(G-11848)
SUN-JOURNAL INCORPORATED
4901 Us Highway 17 S (28562-8880)
PHONE..................252 638-8101
Mike Distelhorst, *Prin*
David Threshie, *Ch*
Richard A Wallace, *
Albert W Bassett, *
EMP: 30 EST: 1929
SALES (est): 5.58MM
SALES (corp-wide): 2.66B **Publicly Held**
Web: www.newbernsj.com
SIC: 2711 Commercial printing and newspaper publishing combined
HQ: Gatehouse Media, Llc
175 Sullys Trl Ste 203
Pittsford NY 14534
585 598-0030

(G-11849)
TEST ME OUT INC
Also Called: Second Nature
3262 Wellons Blvd (28562-5234)
PHONE..................252 635-6770
Janis T Gaskill, *Pr*
Anna Hardison, *VP*
EMP: 5 EST: 2009
SALES (est): 406.8K **Privately Held**
Web: www.secondnatureme.com
SIC: 3842 5047 Surgical appliances and supplies; Medical equipment and supplies

(G-11850)
THERMIK CORPORATION
3498a Martin Dr (28562-5145)
P.O. Box 12786 (28561-2786)
PHONE..................252 636-5720
Fred Goeckerman, *Pr*
Terry Dixon, *Sec*
EMP: 20 EST: 1987
SQ FT: 5,000
SALES (est): 4.99MM
SALES (corp-wide): 48.38MM **Privately Held**
Web: www.thermik.de
SIC: 3822 Air conditioning and refrigeration controls
HQ: Thermik Geratebau Gmbh
Salzstr. 11
Sondershausen TH 99706
363254120

(G-11851)
TRIAD MARINE CENTER INC
Also Called: Boats Unlimited
4316 Us Highway 70 E (28560-7913)
PHONE..................252 634-1880
Jerry Bryant, *Prin*
EMP: 6
SALES (corp-wide): 6.69MM **Privately Held**
SIC: 5551 3732 Motor boat dealers; Boatbuilding and repairing
PA: Triad Marine Center, Inc.
2102 N Elm St Ste E
Greensboro NC 27408
336 379-7000

(G-11852)
TRYHARD INFINITY LLC ◆
3019 Brunswick Ave (28562-4126)
PHONE..................252 269-0985
EMP: 4 EST: 2022
SALES (est): 173.48K **Privately Held**
SIC: 7372 7389 Prepackaged software; Business Activities at Non-Commercial Site

(G-11853)
URETHANE INNOVATORS INC
403 Industrial Dr (28562-5437)
PHONE..................252 637-7110
▲ EMP: 40 EST: 1983
SALES (est): 6.72MM **Privately Held**
Web: www.urethaneusa.com
SIC: 3562 Roller bearings and parts

(G-11854)
US ARMS & AMMUNITION LLC
119 Mellen Rd (28562-8766)
PHONE..................252 652-7400
EMP: 8 EST: 2019
SALES (est): 498.66K **Privately Held**
Web: www.usarmsandammo.com
SIC: 3484 Small arms

(G-11855)
WHEATSTONE CORPORATION (PA)
600 Indl Dr (28562)
PHONE..................252 638-7000
Gary C Snow, *Pr*
Kathleen Snow, *
Denny Murdock, *
▲ EMP: 97 EST: 1974
SQ FT: 51,000
SALES (est): 11.22MM
SALES (corp-wide): 11.22MM **Privately Held**
Web: www.wheatstone.com
SIC: 3663 3651 2522 Radio and t.v. communications equipment; Household audio and video equipment; Office furniture, except wood

(G-11856)
WHITE RIVER MARINE GROUP LLC
Also Called: Hatteras Yachts
110 N Glenburnie Rd (28560-2703)
PHONE..................252 633-3101
Don Farlow, *Mgr*
EMP: 139
Web: www.trackerboats.com
SIC: 3519 3732 Outboard motors; Yachts, building and repairing
HQ: White River Marine Group, Llc
2500 E Kearney St
Springfield MO 65898
417 873-5900

(G-11857)
WHITES TIRE SVC NEW BERN INC
2813 Neuse Blvd (28562-2838)
PHONE..................252 633-1170
Samuel E White, *Pr*
Victoria White, *Sec*
EMP: 4 EST: 1961
SQ FT: 10,000
SALES (est): 582.23K **Privately Held**
Web: www.whitestireserviceinc.com
SIC: 5531 7534 5014 Automotive tires; Tire recapping; Automobile tires and tubes

(G-11858)
WILSONEPES PRINTING
1714 Neuse Blvd (28560-2304)
PHONE..................252 224-0248
EMP: 4 EST: 2017
SALES (est): 81.92K **Privately Held**
SIC: 2752 Commercial printing, lithographic

(G-11859)
WIRTHWEIN NEW BERN CORP
901 Industrial Dr (28562-5403)
PHONE..................252 634-2871
Udo Wirthwein, *Pr*
Marh Hansen Om, *Prin*
◆ EMP: 150 EST: 2002
SQ FT: 101,000
SALES (est): 27.15MM
SALES (corp-wide): 377.18MM **Privately Held**
Web: www.wirthwein.de
SIC: 3089 Injection molding of plastics
PA: Wirthwein Se
Walter-Wirthwein-Str. 2-10
Creglingen BW 97993
79337020

New Hill
Wake County

(G-11860)
DAS OIL WERKS LLC
198 Hidden Field Ln (27562-8847)
PHONE..................919 267-5781
William M White, *Prin*
▲ EMP: 9 EST: 2012
SALES (est): 1.43MM **Privately Held**
SIC: 1382 Oil and gas exploration services

(G-11861)
JC POWDER COATING LLC
9016 Barker Rd (27562-9788)
PHONE..................919 362-9311
Justin Trepper, *Prin*
EMP: 6 EST: 2017
SALES (est): 153.77K **Privately Held**
Web: www.jcpowdercoating.com
SIC: 3479 Coating of metals and formed products

(G-11862)
LOGGER HEAD LOGGING
538 Pea Ridge Rd (27562-8950)
PHONE..................919 842-0249
EMP: 6 EST: 2016
SALES (est): 89.89K **Privately Held**
SIC: 2411 Logging

(G-11863)
PLAN B ENTERPRISES LLC
3217 Hinsley Rd (27562-8978)
PHONE..................919 387-4856
Michael P Klatt, *Ch*
EMP: 5 EST: 2000
SALES (est): 370.39K **Privately Held**
Web: www.planbenterprises.com
SIC: 3699 8711 Security control equipment and systems; Consulting engineer

(G-11864)
SIGNATURE MAILINGS
3194 Retama Run (27562-9345)
PHONE..................919 981-5736
EMP: 4 EST: 2019
SALES (est): 172.56K **Privately Held**
Web: www.signaturemailings.com
SIC: 2752 Offset printing

(G-11865)
STRANDH WOODWORKS LLC
3501 Johnson Grant Dr (27562-9313)
PHONE..................919 703-8056
Daniel Patrick Strandh, *Prin*
EMP: 5 EST: 2019
SALES (est): 244.95K **Privately Held**
SIC: 2431 Millwork

New London
Stanly County

(G-11866)
ARTECH GRAPHICS INC
176 Yadkin Falls Rd (28127-9135)
PHONE..................704 545-9804
David Carpenter, *Pr*
EMP: 9 EST: 1969
SQ FT: 4,200
SALES (est): 699.34K **Privately Held**
Web: www.artechgraphicsinc.com
SIC: 2752 Offset printing

(G-11867)
CAPITAL WOOD PRODUCTS INC
38081 Saw Mill Rd (28127-9569)
PHONE..................704 982-2417
Ronnie Carter, *Pr*
Allen Herlocker, *VP*
EMP: 6 EST: 1980
SQ FT: 30,000
SALES (est): 941.03K **Privately Held**
SIC: 2421 Sawmills and planing mills, general

(G-11868)
DEBERRY PRECISION MACHINE INC
40018 Palmerville Rd (28127-9683)
PHONE..................704 422-3274
Charles K Deberry, *Prin*
EMP: 7 EST: 2004
SQ FT: 3,383
SALES (est): 200.77K **Privately Held**
SIC: 3599 Machine shop, jobbing and repair

(G-11869)
FIBER COMPOSITES LLC
Also Called: Fiberon Recycling
44017 Us 52 Hwy N (28127-9726)
PHONE..................704 463-7118
Susan Saunders, *Mgr*
EMP: 62
SALES (corp-wide): 4.63B **Publicly Held**
Web: www.fiberondecking.com
SIC: 3089 4953 Air mattresses, plastics; Recycling, waste materials
HQ: Fiber Composites, Llc
181 Random Dr
New London NC 28127
704 463-7120

(G-11870)
FIBER COMPOSITES LLC (HQ)
Also Called: Fiberon
181 Random Dr (28127-8735)
PHONE..................704 463-7120
◆ EMP: 290 EST: 1997
SQ FT: 300,000
SALES (est): 227.4MM
SALES (corp-wide): 4.63B **Publicly Held**
Web: www.fiberondecking.com
SIC: 2899 Plastic wood
PA: Fortune Brands Innovations, Inc.
520 Lake Cook Rd
Deerfield IL 60015
847 484-4400

(G-11871)
H W CULP LUMBER COMPANY
491 Us Hwy 52 N (28127)
PHONE..................704 463-7311
H W Culp Junior, *Pr*
H W Culp Iii, *VP*
Amy Shelton, *
Jewel Culp, *
EMP: 92 EST: 1924
SQ FT: 5,000
SALES (est): 17.45MM **Privately Held**

GEOGRAPHIC SECTION

Newport - Carteret County (G-11897)

Web: www.culplumber.com
SIC: 2421 Sawmills and planing mills, general

(G-11872)
HARRIS WOOD PRODUCTS INC
40425 Tower Rd (28127-8527)
PHONE.....................704 550-5494
James Harris, *Pr*
Susan Harris, *VP*
EMP: 9 EST: 1985
SALES (est): 999.77K **Privately Held**
SIC: 5031 2541 Millwork; Cabinets, except refrigerated: show, display, etc.: wood

(G-11873)
HERD WOODWORKING LLC
36589 Millingport Rd (28127-7786)
PHONE.....................704 778-0556
Michael C Cowles, *Prin*
EMP: 5 EST: 2018
SALES (est): 216.9K **Privately Held**
SIC: 2431 Millwork

(G-11874)
MOOSE-TEK INDUSTRIES INC
595 Lake Forest Dr (28127-7607)
PHONE.....................336 416-7034
James Hastings, *Pr*
EMP: 4 EST: 2019
SALES (est): 63.91K **Privately Held**
SIC: 3999 Manufacturing industries, nec

(G-11875)
POTTS LOGGING INC
39342 Holly Ridge Rd (28127-8517)
PHONE.....................704 463-7549
James L Potts, *Pr*
Linda Potts, *VP*
Randy Potts, *Mgr*
EMP: 9 EST: 1975
SALES (est): 683.49K **Privately Held**
SIC: 2411 Logging camps and contractors

(G-11876)
PREFORMED LINE PRODUCTS CO
Also Called: Preformed Line Products Co
446 Glenbrook Spg (28127-9140)
PHONE.....................336 461-3513
EMP: 6
SALES (corp-wide): 669.68MM **Publicly Held**
Web: www.plp.com
SIC: 3644 Noncurrent-carrying wiring devices
PA: Preformed Line Products Company
  660 Beta Dr
  Mayfield Village OH 44143
  440 461-5200

(G-11877)
RUSSELL CUSTOM STONE LLC
2741 Highway 49 (28127-7649)
PHONE.....................336 859-5755
EMP: 6 EST: 2021
SALES (est): 214.35K **Privately Held**
Web: www.russellcustomstone.com
SIC: 3281 Table tops, marble

(G-11878)
SOUTHERN PIPE INC (PA)
135 Random Dr (28127-8735)
P.O. Box 606 (28127-0606)
PHONE.....................704 463-5202
Bryan Mitchell, *Pr*
Kevin Mitchell, *
Patricia Mitchell, *
▼ EMP: 39 EST: 2005
SQ FT: 55,475
SALES (est): 14.87MM
SALES (corp-wide): 14.87MM **Privately Held**

Web: www.southern-pipe.com
SIC: 3084 Plastics pipe

(G-11879)
STANLY TRACTOR COMPANY
37931 Us 52 Hwy N (28127-9733)
PHONE.....................704 983-1106
EMP: 6 EST: 2020
SALES (est): 70.49K **Privately Held**
Web: www.stanlytractor.com
SIC: 7353 5261 3545 3523 Heavy construction equipment rental; Retail nurseries and garden stores; Machine tool accessories; Farm machinery and equipment

(G-11880)
UFP NEW LONDON LLC
Also Called: U F P
174 Random Dr (28127-8735)
PHONE.....................704 463-1400
John Devitto, *Mgr*
EMP: 38 EST: 2011
SALES (est): 1.08MM
SALES (corp-wide): 7.22B **Publicly Held**
SIC: 2452 2436 2435 2439 Prefabricated wood buildings; Softwood veneer and plywood; Hardwood veneer and plywood; Trusses, except roof: laminated lumber
HQ: Ufp Factory Built, Llc
  2801 E Beltline Ave Ne
  Grand Rapids MI 49525
  616 364-6161

Newland
Avery County

(G-11881)
AVERY COUNTY RECAPPING CO INC
Also Called: Avery County Tire
405 Linville St (28657-8029)
P.O. Box 505 (28657-0505)
PHONE.....................828 733-0161
John Phillips, *Pr*
James Phillips, *
EMP: 25 EST: 1964
SQ FT: 12,000
SALES (est): 2.44MM **Privately Held**
Web: www.averytirepros.com
SIC: 5531 7539 7534 Automotive tires; Automotive repair shops, nec; Tire recapping

(G-11882)
BRASWELL REALTY
320 Linville St (28657-8037)
P.O. Box 1208 (28657-1208)
PHONE.....................828 733-5800
EMP: 7 EST: 1992
SALES (est): 521.18K **Privately Held**
Web: www.braswellrealty.com
SIC: 6531 2452 Real estate agent, commercial; Log cabins, prefabricated, wood

(G-11883)
CCO HOLDINGS LLC
520 Pineola St (28657-7604)
PHONE.....................828 528-4004
EMP: 107
SALES (corp-wide): 54.61B **Publicly Held**
SIC: 4841 3663 3651 Cable television services; Radio and t.v. communications equipment; Household audio and video equipment
HQ: Cco Holdings, Llc
  400 Atlantic St
  Stamford CT 06901
  203 905-7801

(G-11884)
DAUGHTRYS CREATIONS LLC
2134 Land Hbr (28657-7928)
PHONE.....................704 929-8717
Jerry G Daughtry, *Prin*
EMP: 4 EST: 2018
SALES (est): 79.66K **Privately Held**
SIC: 2431 Millwork

(G-11885)
DICKIE JONES
Also Called: Bowman Distribution
883 Whitaker Branch Rd (28657-9170)
PHONE.....................828 733-5084
EMP: 5 EST: 1996
SALES (est): 80.32K **Privately Held**
SIC: 3492 Hose and tube fittings and assemblies, hydraulic/pneumatic

(G-11886)
FORAGE SOAPS LLC
20 Randall Ln (28657-9607)
P.O. Box 1324 (28657-1324)
PHONE.....................828 737-9088
Chad Smith, *Prin*
EMP: 4 EST: 2016
SALES (est): 139.49K **Privately Held**
Web: www.smellslikebooks.com
SIC: 3999 Candles

(G-11887)
GARDEN METALWORK
3640 Rd (28657)
P.O. Box 41 (28662-0041)
PHONE.....................828 733-1077
Bruce Yak, *Owner*
EMP: 5 EST: 2008
SALES (est): 230.18K **Privately Held**
Web: www.gardenmetalwork.com
SIC: 1791 3442 Iron work, structural; Sash, door or window: metal

(G-11888)
HIGH COUNTRY MEDIA LLC
Also Called: Avery Journal Times
428 Pineola St (28657-7603)
PHONE.....................828 733-2448
Sam Calhoun, *Editor*
EMP: 4 EST: 1959
SALES (est): 280.46K **Privately Held**
Web: www.averyjournal.com
SIC: 2711 Newspapers, publishing and printing

(G-11889)
LINVILLE FALLS WINERY
9557 Linville Falls Hwy (28657-8920)
P.O. Box 517 (28657-0517)
PHONE.....................828 733-9021
EMP: 6 EST: 2014
SALES (est): 106.97K **Privately Held**
Web: www.linvillefallswinery.com
SIC: 2084 Wines

(G-11890)
MOUNTAIN RCRTION LOG CBINS LLC
8007 Linville Falls Hwy (28657-8293)
PHONE.....................828 387-6688
Shane Ollis, *Prin*
EMP: 5 EST: 2011
SALES (est): 120K **Privately Held**
Web: www.mountainrecreationlogcabins.com
SIC: 2452 Log cabins, prefabricated, wood

(G-11891)
NORTH CAROLINA DEPT TRNSP
Also Called: Equipment Shop
North Carolina Hwy 181 (28657-7818)

P.O. Box 631 (28657-0631)
PHONE.....................828 733-9002
Nathan Clark, *Mgr*
EMP: 4
Web: www.ncdot.gov
SIC: 3799 9621 Trailers and trailer equipment; Regulation, administration of transportation
HQ: North Carolina Department Of Transportation
  1 S Wilmington St
  Raleigh NC 27601

(G-11892)
PARKWAY VINEYARD & WINERY LLC
9557 Linville Falls Hwy (28657-8920)
P.O. Box 517 (28657-0517)
PHONE.....................828 765-1400
EMP: 5 EST: 2014
SALES (est): 133.31K **Privately Held**
SIC: 2084 Wines

(G-11893)
S BANNER CABINETS INCORPORATED
299 Watauga St (28657-7100)
P.O. Box 1390 (28657-1390)
PHONE.....................828 733-2031
Joseph E Banner Senior, *Pr*
Joseph E Banner Junior, *VP*
Debbie Banner, *
EMP: 38 EST: 1942
SQ FT: 55,000
SALES (est): 2.88MM **Privately Held**
Web: www.bannerscabinets.com
SIC: 2434 5712 2431 Wood kitchen cabinets ; Cabinet work, custom; Millwork

(G-11894)
SUGAR MOUNTAIN WOODWORKS INC
3030 Sugar Mountain 2 Rd (28657-8397)
PHONE.....................423 292-6245
EMP: 8 EST: 2020
SALES (est): 236.16K **Privately Held**
SIC: 2431 Millwork

(G-11895)
T&L NURSERY AND LOGGING LLC
325 Clarktown Rd (28657-8941)
PHONE.....................828 387-0448
Tyler Buchanan, *Prin*
EMP: 5 EST: 2020
SALES (est): 136.05K **Privately Held**
SIC: 2411 Logging

Newport
Carteret County

(G-11896)
ABC SIGNS
214 Roberts Rd (28570-7932)
PHONE.....................252 223-5900
Joyce Tferrell, *Prin*
EMP: 4 EST: 2011
SALES (est): 56.78K **Privately Held**
Web: www.abcsigns.biz
SIC: 3993 Signs and advertising specialties

(G-11897)
ARGOS USA LLC
Also Called: Readymixed
247 Carl Garner Rd (28570-7956)
PHONE.....................252 223-4348
Duncan Kimbro, *Genl Mgr*
EMP: 8
Web: www.argos-us.com

Newport - Carteret County (G-11898)

SIC: 3273 Ready-mixed concrete
HQ: Argos Usa Llc
3015 Windward Plz Ste 300
Alpharetta GA 30005
678 368-4300

(G-11898)
BOGUE SOUND DISTILLERY INC
108 Bogue Commercial Dr (28570-8224)
PHONE..................................252 241-1606
EMP: 8 EST: 2019
SALES (est): 470.01K Privately Held
Web: www.boguesounddistillery.com
SIC: 2085 Distilled and blended liquors

(G-11899)
CAROLINA TAILORS INC (PA)
Also Called: Promotional Products Plus
2896 Highway 24 Ste D (28570-5088)
PHONE..................................252 247-6469
George Gardner, Pr
EMP: 10 EST: 1979
SALES (est): 1.68MM Privately Held
Web: www.ctailors.com
SIC: 5136 2759 Uniforms, men's and boys';
Screen printing

(G-11900)
CLOUD NINE FOODS INC
160 Live Oak Rd (28570-5140)
PHONE..................................817 909-8988
George Nicolle, Pr
EMP: 4 EST: 2014
SALES (est): 74.19K Privately Held
SIC: 3949 Sporting and athletic goods, nec

(G-11901)
DL HOPPER & ASSOCIATES INC
402 Sea Gate Dr (28570-6270)
PHONE..................................252 838-1062
David Hopper, Ch
Elizabeth Hopper, CFO
B D Hall, VP
EMP: 4 EST: 1994
SQ FT: 3,500
SALES (est): 336.6K Privately Held
SIC: 7372 Prepackaged software

(G-11902)
OFFSHORE MARINE ELEC LLC
1381 Old Winberry Rd (28570-6163)
PHONE..................................252 504-2624
EMP: 7 EST: 2007
SALES (est): 917.63K Privately Held
SIC: 3699 Electrical equipment and supplies, nec

(G-11903)
OLE PELICANS CUSTOM WDWKG
337 E Southwinds Dr (28570-9150)
PHONE..................................252 808-7633
Christopher Kent, Prin
EMP: 5 EST: 2018
SALES (est): 68.35K Privately Held
SIC: 2431 Millwork

(G-11904)
PRISCLLAS CRYSTAL CAST WNES IN
187 Hibbs Road Ext (28570-9172)
PHONE..................................252 422-8336
Priscilla Livingston, Pr
EMP: 4 EST: 2007
SALES (est): 190.2K Privately Held
SIC: 2084 Wines, brandy, and brandy spirits

(G-11905)
RIGEM RIGHT
173 Hankison Dr (28570-9170)
PHONE..................................252 726-9508

Matthew Cagle, Managing Member
▲ EMP: 11 EST: 2011
SALES (est): 417.82K Privately Held
Web: www.rigemright.com
SIC: 3949 Hunting equipment

(G-11906)
SALT BOATWORKS INC
117 Adams Ct (28570-9009)
PHONE..................................919 394-3795
Robert Adam Parchman, Prin
EMP: 5 EST: 2016
SALES (est): 59.45K Privately Held
Web: www.saltboatworks.com
SIC: 3732 Boatbuilding and repairing

(G-11907)
SHORTWAY BREWING COMPANY LLC (PA)
228 Chatham St (28570-8515)
PHONE..................................252 777-3065
Matt Shortway, Prin
EMP: 6 EST: 2017
SALES (est): 494.6K
SALES (corp-wide): 494.6K Privately Held
Web: www.shortwaybrewing.com
SIC: 5813 2082 Bars and lounges; Malt beverages

(G-11908)
THAT WELDER GUY
468 Bogue Loop Rd (28570-5186)
PHONE..................................252 342-0391
EMP: 5 EST: 2016
SALES (est): 45.87K Privately Held
Web: www.thatwelderguy.net
SIC: 7692 Welding repair

(G-11909)
TRF MANUFACTURING NC INC
Also Called: Frank Door Company
413 Howard Blvd (28570-9530)
P.O. Box 1720 (28570-1720)
PHONE..................................252 223-1112
▲ EMP: 38 EST: 1996
SQ FT: 50,000
SALES (est): 8.6MM Privately Held
Web: www.frankdoor.com
SIC: 3822 5078 5211 Refrigeration/air-conditioning defrost controls; Commercial refrigeration equipment; Door and window products

(G-11910)
VENEER TECHNOLOGIES INC (PA)
Also Called: Cloverdale Co Inc Roanoke Co
611 Verdun St (28570-8088)
P.O. Box 1145 (28570-1145)
PHONE..................................252 223-5600
Christian Weygoldt, Pr
Michael Kraszeksi, *
Ilse Moehring, *
▲ EMP: 135 EST: 1992
SQ FT: 100,000
SALES (est): 22.77MM Privately Held
Web: www.veneertech.com
SIC: 2435 2426 2421 Veneer stock, hardwood; Hardwood dimension and flooring mills; Sawmills and planing mills, general

---

Newton
Catawba County

(G-11911)
ABZORBIT INC
2628 Northwest Blvd (28658-3729)
P.O. Box 1538 (28613-1538)
PHONE..................................828 464-9944

EMP: 10 EST: 1994
SQ FT: 15,000
SALES (est): 996.25K Privately Held
Web: www.abzorbit.com
SIC: 2621 2842 Absorbent paper; Polishes and sanitation goods

(G-11912)
ADVANCED GRADING & EXCVTG LLC
4360 Caldwell Rd (28658-8104)
PHONE..................................828 320-7465
Jonathan Setzer, Prin
EMP: 7 EST: 2013
SALES (est): 466.72K Privately Held
SIC: 3531 Plows: construction, excavating, and grading

(G-11913)
ASHFAR ENTERPRISES INC
Also Called: Catawba Valley Mills
3772 Plateau Rd (28658-8812)
P.O. Box 10233 (28603)
PHONE..................................704 462-4672
Anis Satar, Mgr
EMP: 10
SALES (corp-wide): 4.74MM Privately Held
Web: www.ashfar.com
SIC: 2221 Broadwoven fabric mills, manmade
PA: Ashfar Enterprises Inc.
200 Metroplex Dr Ste 275
Edison NJ 08817
848 202-1581

(G-11914)
BA ROBBINS COMPANY LLC
110 E 15th St (28658-2957)
P.O. Box 645 (28658-0645)
PHONE..................................828 466-3900
Adam Robbins, Owner
EMP: 7 EST: 2002
SALES (est): 366.46K Privately Held
Web: www.windingnc.com
SIC: 2282 Winding yarn

(G-11915)
BASSETT FURNITURE INDS INC
Also Called: Bassett Upholstery Division
111 E 20th St (28658)
P.O. Box 47 (28658-0047)
PHONE..................................828 465-7700
Mark Jordan, Brnch Mgr
EMP: 64
SALES (corp-wide): 390.14MM Publicly Held
Web: www.bassettfurniture.com
SIC: 2512 5712 Upholstered household furniture; Furniture stores
PA: Bassett Furniture Industries Incorporated
3525 Fairystone Park Hwy
Bassett VA 24055
276 629-6000

(G-11916)
BOX SCIENTIFIC LLC
Also Called: Box Scientific
2805 Rosewood Ln (28658-8424)
PHONE..................................408 361-8631
EMP: 4 EST: 2017
SALES (est): 183.11K Privately Held
Web: www.boxscientific.com
SIC: 3826 Analytical instruments

(G-11917)
CATAWBA FARMS ENTERPRISES LLC
1670 Southwest Blvd (28658-7439)

PHONE..................................828 464-5780
Michael Waltuch, Pt
Twyla Mcdermott, Pt
James D Baucom, Pt
EMP: 10 EST: 2015
SQ FT: 1,481,040
SALES (est): 1.03MM Privately Held
Web: www.catawbafarms.com
SIC: 5153 7011 2084 0191 Field beans; Vacation lodges; Wines, brandy, and brandy spirits; General farms, primarily crop
PA: Second Nature Technology Inc.
19 N College Ave
Newton NC 28658

(G-11918)
CATAWBA VALLEY FINISHING LLC (PA)
1609 Northwest Blvd (28658-3759)
P.O. Box 410 (28658-0410)
PHONE..................................828 464-2252
Renee Woody, CEO
EMP: 45 EST: 1941
SQ FT: 68,000
SALES (est): 4.77MM
SALES (corp-wide): 4.77MM Privately Held
SIC: 2252 2251 Men's, boys', and girls' hosiery; Women's hosiery, except socks

(G-11919)
CLEVELAND-CLIFFS PLATE LLC
Also Called: Cleveland-Cliffs Piedmont
2027 S Mclin Creek Rd (28658-1957)
PHONE..................................828 464-9214
Debbie Mccurry, Brnch Mgr
EMP: 979
SALES (corp-wide): 22B Publicly Held
SIC: 3312 Plate, steel
HQ: Cleveland-Cliffs Plate Llc
139 Modena Rd
Coatesville PA 19320
610 383-2000

(G-11920)
COCA-COLA CONSOLIDATED INC
Also Called: Coca-Cola
820 E 1st St (28658-1803)
PHONE..................................828 322-5096
Frank Wood, Brnch Mgr
EMP: 44
SALES (corp-wide): 6.65B Publicly Held
Web: www.cokeconsolidated.com
SIC: 2086 Bottled and canned soft drinks
PA: Coca-Cola Consolidated, Inc.
4100 Coca Cola Plz # 100
Charlotte NC 28211
704 557-4400

(G-11921)
COMMERCIAL FABRICATORS INC
2045 Industrial Dr (28658-7703)
P.O. Box 165 (28658-0165)
PHONE..................................828 465-1010
Richard J Tucker, Pr
Richard J Tucker, VP
Diann B Icenhour, *
EMP: 30 EST: 1962
SQ FT: 34,600
SALES (est): 8.58MM Privately Held
Web: www.commfab.com
SIC: 3441 3446 Fabricated structural metal; Architectural metalwork

(G-11922)
COMMSCOPE INC NORTH CAROLINA
Also Called: Comm Scope Network Cable Div
1545 Saint James Church Rd (28658-8938)
PHONE..................................828 466-8600
Randy Crenshaw, Brnch Mgr

EMP: 12
Web: www.commscope.com
SIC: 3663 Radio and t.v. communications equipment
HQ: Commscope, Inc. Of North Carolina
3642 E Us Highway 70
Claremont NC 28610
828 324-2200

(G-11923)
COMMUNITY BREWING VENTURES LLC (PA)
Also Called: Bevana
116 W A St (28658-3342)
PHONE.............................800 579-6539
Andrew Durstewitz, CEO
EMP: 8 EST: 2019
SALES (est): 1MM
SALES (corp-wide): 1MM Privately Held
Web: www.communitybrewingventures.com
SIC: 5084 3556 Brewery products manufacturing machinery, commercial; Beverage machinery

(G-11924)
CONCEPT FRAMES INC
2015 Industrial Dr (28658-7703)
P.O. Box 248 (28658-0248)
PHONE.............................828 465-2015
C John Wiley, Pr
Diann B Icenhour, *
Daniel L Gibbs, *
Cindy L Payne, *
EMP: 60 EST: 1984
SQ FT: 35,000
SALES (est): 8.7MM Privately Held
Web: www.conceptframes.com
SIC: 3441 Fabricated structural metal

(G-11925)
CORNING INCORPORATED
Also Called: Corning
1500 Prodelin Dr (28658-7819)
PHONE.............................828 465-0016
EMP: 11
SALES (corp-wide): 12.59B Publicly Held
Web: www.corning.com
SIC: 3229 Glass fiber products
PA: Corning Incorporated
1 Riverfront Plz
Corning NY 14831
607 974-9000

(G-11926)
COUNTRY AT HOME FURNITURE INC
2010 Log Barn Rd (28658-8889)
P.O. Box 39 (28637-0039)
PHONE.............................828 464-7498
William Coulter, Pr
Robert Davis, VP
EMP: 10 EST: 2003
SALES (est): 797.27K Privately Held
SIC: 2512 Upholstered household furniture

(G-11927)
CRAFT DOORS USA LLC
1516 Mount Olive Church Rd (28658-1706)
PHONE.............................828 469-7029
EMP: 10 EST: 2020
SALES (est): 696.21K Privately Held
Web: www.craftdoorsusa.com
SIC: 2431 Garage doors, overhead, wood

(G-11928)
CREATIVE LABEL SOLUTIONS
1132 Bugle Ln (28658-8013)
PHONE.............................828 315-9500
Allen Watson, Owner
EMP: 4 EST: 2016
SALES (est): 174.84K Privately Held
Web: www.creativelabelsolutions.com
SIC: 2759 Commercial printing, nec

(G-11929)
CUSTOM SOCKS INK INC
Also Called: Csi
2011 N Main Ave (28658-2825)
P.O. Box 14 (28658-0014)
PHONE.............................828 695-9869
Alton Rockett, Pr
Ranae Woody, *
EMP: 29 EST: 2014
SALES (est): 1.85MM
SALES (corp-wide): 4.77MM Privately Held
Web: www.customsocksink.com
SIC: 2252 Socks
PA: Catawba Valley Finishing, Llc
1609 Northwest Blvd
Newton NC 28658
828 464-2252

(G-11930)
ELITE WOOD PRODUCTS
1600 N College Ave (28658-2126)
PHONE.............................828 994-4446
Charles Bandy, VP
EMP: 5 EST: 2017
SALES (est): 77.85K Privately Held
SIC: 5712 2426 Furniture stores; Chair seats, hardwood

(G-11931)
ERIC ARNOLD KLEIN
Also Called: Pioneer Diversities
504a W 25th St (28658-3701)
PHONE.............................828 464-0001
Eric A Klein, Owner
EMP: 10 EST: 1990
SQ FT: 10,000
SALES (est): 779.4K Privately Held
SIC: 3479 Painting, coating, and hot dipping

(G-11932)
FORMING BELT SERVICE LLC
3280 20th Ave Se (28658-8572)
P.O. Box 37 (28603-0037)
PHONE.............................828 465-0001
Drago Gorupic, Managing Member
EMP: 4 EST: 2018
SALES (est): 77.45K Privately Held
Web: www.formingbeltservice.com
SIC: 3052 Rubber and plastics hose and beltings

(G-11933)
GKN DRIVELINE NEWTON LLC (HQ)
Also Called: GKN Automotive
1848 Gkn Way (28658-9072)
PHONE.............................828 428-3711
Markus Bannert, CEO
Sean Bannon, *
Thierry Minel, CPO*
Mark Gabriel, CCO*
◆ EMP: 551 EST: 1980
SQ FT: 250,000
SALES (est): 166.16MM
SALES (corp-wide): 4.25MM Privately Held
SIC: 3462 3714 Iron and steel forgings; Gears, motor vehicle
PA: Dowlais Group Plc
2nd Floor
London SW1E

(G-11934)
GKN DRIVELINE NEWTON LLC
Also Called: GKN Automotive
2900 S Us 321 Hwy (28658-8154)
PHONE.............................828 428-5292
EMP: 27

SALES (corp-wide): 4.25MM Privately Held
SIC: 3714 Motor vehicle parts and accessories
HQ: Gkn Driveline Newton, Llc
1848 Gkn Way
Newton NC 28658
828 428-3711

(G-11935)
GLENN MAUSER COMPANY INC
3240 20th Ave Se (28658-8572)
PHONE.............................828 464-8996
H Glenn Mauser, Pr
EMP: 10 EST: 1983
SQ FT: 25,000
SALES (est): 914.61K Privately Held
Web: www.glennmauserplastics.com
SIC: 3089 Injection molding of plastics

(G-11936)
GOLD TOE STORES INC (DH)
514 W 21st St (28658-3763)
PHONE.............................828 464-0751
John M Moretz, CEO
◆ EMP: 8 EST: 1982
SQ FT: 42,600
SALES (est): 24MM
SALES (corp-wide): 3.24B Privately Held
SIC: 2252 5136 Hosiery, nec; Men's and boy's clothing
HQ: Gold Toe Moretz Holdings Corp.
2121 Heilig Rd
Salisbury NC 28146
828 464-0751

(G-11937)
GOLDTOEMORETZ LLC
514 W 21st St (28658-3763)
P.O. Box 580 (28658-0580)
PHONE.............................828 464-0751
◆ EMP: 500
SIC: 2251 2252 Women's hosiery, except socks; Socks

(G-11938)
GREEN QUEST INC
1555 N Rankin Ave (28658-2028)
PHONE.............................828 464-7336
EMP: 6 EST: 2018
SALES (est): 209.67K Privately Held
Web: www.greenquestnc.com
SIC: 3433 Heating equipment, except electric

(G-11939)
HANES INDUSTRIES-NEWTON
2042 Fairgrove Church Rd (28658-8598)
P.O. Box 457 (28613-0457)
PHONE.............................828 469-2000
Tyler Newton, Prin
▲ EMP: 13 EST: 2004
SALES (est): 428.46K Privately Held
Web: www.hanescompanies.com
SIC: 3999 Barber and beauty shop equipment

(G-11940)
HM FRAME COMPANY INC
1903 Gkn Way (28658-9073)
PHONE.............................828 428-3354
Kevin Hefner, Pr
Daren Hefner, *
Jan S Hefner, *
EMP: 30 EST: 1984
SQ FT: 55,000
SALES (est): 1.61MM Privately Held
Web: www.hmwoodworkinginc.com
SIC: 2512 2511 2435 2426 Upholstered household furniture; Wood household furniture; Hardwood veneer and plywood; Hardwood dimension and flooring mills

(G-11941)
HORIZON PUBLICATIONS INC
Also Called: Observer News Enterprise
309 N College Ave (28658-3255)
P.O. Box 48 (28658-0048)
PHONE.............................828 464-0221
Seth Mabry, Mgr
EMP: 12
SALES (corp-wide): 47.1MM Privately Held
Web: www.horizonpublicationsinc.com
SIC: 2711 Newspapers, publishing and printing
PA: Horizon Publications, Inc.
1120 N Carbon St Ste 100
Marion IL 62959
618 993-1711

(G-11942)
IMAGE INDUSTRIES NC INC
1848 Saint Pauls Church Rd (28658-9521)
PHONE.............................828 464-8882
Jerry Mallonee Junior, CEO
Tony Trado, Pr
▲ EMP: 19 EST: 1997
SQ FT: 15,000
SALES (est): 2.18MM Privately Held
Web: www.iionc.com
SIC: 3955 Ribbons, inked: typewriter, adding machine, register, etc.

(G-11943)
INDUSTRIAL RECYCLING SERVICES
Also Called: A Palletone Company
2815 Woodtech Dr (28658-8967)
PHONE.............................704 462-1882
EMP: 8 EST: 2015
SALES (est): 116.13K Privately Held
SIC: 2448 Pallets, wood

(G-11944)
INK TEC INC
1838 Saint Pauls Church Rd (28658-9521)
P.O. Box 909 (28671-0909)
PHONE.............................828 465-6411
Ivan Livas, CEO
Renato Livas, Pr
Myrna Livas, VP
▲ EMP: 15 EST: 1995
SQ FT: 14,000
SALES (est): 1.66MM Privately Held
Web: www.inktecinc.com
SIC: 2893 Printing ink

(G-11945)
INTER-CONTINENTAL CORPORATION
2575 N Ashe Ave (28658-2766)
P.O. Box 1119 (28613-1119)
PHONE.............................828 464-8250
David B Radke, Ch Bd
Mark Radke, *
Steve Radke, *
▲ EMP: 70 EST: 1969
SQ FT: 70,000
SALES (est): 12.35MM Privately Held
Web: www.iccboxes.com
SIC: 2653 3412 Boxes, corrugated: made from purchased materials; Metal barrels, drums, and pails

(G-11946)
INTERNATIONAL PAPER COMPANY
International Paper
1525 Mount Olive Church Rd (28658-1740)
PHONE.............................828 464-3841
Larry Wise, Mgr
EMP: 51
SALES (corp-wide): 18.92B Publicly Held
Web: www.internationalpaper.com
SIC: 2621 Paper mills

Newton - Catawba County (G-11947)

PA: International Paper Company
6400 Poplar Ave
Memphis TN 38197
901 419-7000

(G-11947)
LEE INDUSTRIES LLC
402 W 25th St (28658-3755)
PHONE..................828 464-8318
EMP: 219
SALES (corp-wide): 87.21MM **Privately Held**
Web: www.leeindustries.com
SIC: 2512 Chairs: upholstered on wood frames
PA: Lee Industries, Llc
210 4th St Sw
Conover NC 28613
828 464-8318

(G-11948)
LEE INDUSTRIES LLC
1620 Fisher Ct (28658-7821)
PHONE..................828 464-8318
EMP: 219
SALES (corp-wide): 87.21MM **Privately Held**
Web: www.leeindustries.com
SIC: 2512 Couches, sofas, and davenports: upholstered on wood frames
PA: Lee Industries, Llc
210 4th St Sw
Conover NC 28613
828 464-8318

(G-11949)
LLC STANTON GRAY
202 N Main Ave (28658-3216)
PHONE..................704 975-9392
EMP: 5 **EST:** 2017
SALES (est): 39.69K **Privately Held**
Web: www.stantongray.com
SIC: 3999 Manufacturing industries, nec

(G-11950)
LOOC STUDIO INC
2066 Industrial Dr (28658-7703)
P.O. Box 697 (28613-0697)
PHONE..................336 472-6877
▲ **EMP:** 6 **EST:** 2012
SALES (est): 103.21K **Privately Held**
SIC: 2519 2521 Bean bag Chairs; Wood office furniture

(G-11951)
MCCREARY MODERN INC (PA)
2564 S Us 321 Hwy (28658-9349)
P.O. Box 130 (28658-0130)
PHONE..................828 464-6465
Robert Mccreary, *CEO*
Bob Mccreary, *Ch Bd*
Rick Coffey, *
Michele Mccreary, *Sec*
Doug Yoder, *
◆ **EMP:** 425 **EST:** 1985
SQ FT: 160,000
SALES (est): 98.54MM
SALES (corp-wide): 98.54MM **Privately Held**
Web: www.mccrearymodern.com
SIC: 2512 2421 Living room furniture: upholstered on wood frames; Kiln drying of lumber

(G-11952)
MENNEL MIL & BKY MIX NC LLC
11 N Brady Ave (28658-3245)
PHONE..................828 468-6015
EMP: 9 **EST:** 2016
SALES (est): 600.44K **Privately Held**
Web: www.mennel.com
SIC: 2051 Bread, cake, and related products

(G-11953)
MIDSTATE MILLS INC
Also Called: Tenda Bake
11 N Brady Ave (28658-3245)
P.O. Box 350 (28658-0350)
PHONE..................828 464-1611
Steven Arndt, *Pr*
Cindy Gabriel, *
Dianne Fulbright, *
Cynthia Drum, *
EMP: 120 **EST:** 1935
SQ FT: 10,000
SALES (est): 14.9MM **Privately Held**
Web: www.midstatemills.com
SIC: 2041 2048 Wheat flour; Prepared feeds, nec

(G-11954)
OBSERVER NEWS ENTERPRISE INC
Also Called: County Nws-Ntrprs-Maiden Times
309 N College Ave (28658-3255)
P.O. Box 48 (28658-0048)
PHONE..................828 464-0221
Steve Garland, *Publisher*
EMP: 23 **EST:** 1879
SQ FT: 10,000
SALES (est): 490.92K
SALES (corp-wide): 47.1MM **Privately Held**
Web: www.observernewsonline.com
SIC: 2711 2752 Newspapers, publishing and printing; Commercial printing, lithographic
PA: Horizon Publications, Inc.
1120 N Carbon St Ste 100
Marion IL 62959
618 993-1711

(G-11955)
OLD HICKORY TANNERY INC (PA)
970 Locust St (28658-9235)
PHONE..................828 465-6599
Willard G Black, *Pr*
Clint Black, *
Sharee Huffman, *
▲ **EMP:** 38 **EST:** 1962
SQ FT: 80,000
SALES (est): 7.59MM
SALES (corp-wide): 7.59MM **Privately Held**
Web: www.ohtfurniture.com
SIC: 2522 2512 Office furniture, except wood ; Upholstered household furniture

(G-11956)
OWENS QUILTING INC
101 E 11th St Ste 13 (28658-2274)
PHONE..................828 695-1495
William Douglas Owens, *Pr*
Diane Owens, *VP*
EMP: 4 **EST:** 2001
SQ FT: 4,000
SALES (est): 229.33K **Privately Held**
Web: www.losego.net
SIC: 2392 7299 Slip covers and pads; Quilting for individuals

(G-11957)
P1 CATAWBA DEVELOPMENT CO LLC
2815 Woodtech Dr (28658-8967)
PHONE..................704 462-1882
Howe Wallace, *Pr*
EMP: 9 **EST:** 2010
SALES (est): 1.62MM
SALES (corp-wide): 7.22B **Publicly Held**
SIC: 2448 Pallets, wood
HQ: Palletone, Inc.
6001 Foxtrot Ave
Bartow FL 33830
866 336-6032

(G-11958)
PAUL P POOVEY JR
Also Called: Poovey Frame
2538 (28658)
PHONE..................828 465-2975
Paul P Poovey Junior, *Owner*
EMP: 5 **EST:** 1990
SQ FT: 20,000
SALES (est): 104.99K **Privately Held**
SIC: 2426 Furniture stock and parts, hardwood

(G-11959)
PERRYS FRAME INC
3785 Thompson St (28658-9528)
PHONE..................828 327-4681
Ricky Travis, *Pr*
Christine Travis, *VP*
EMP: 13 **EST:** 1965
SALES (est): 1.43MM **Privately Held**
SIC: 2426 Frames for upholstered furniture, wood

(G-11960)
PIEDMONT BUSINESS FORMS INC
Also Called: Piedmont Office Products
703 W C St (28658-4304)
P.O. Box 281 (28658-0281)
PHONE..................828 464-0010
Ken Ferguson, *Pr*
Gary Wagner, *VP*
EMP: 12 **EST:** 1955
SQ FT: 13,000
SALES (est): 391.46K **Privately Held**
SIC: 2752 2789 2759 Offset printing; Bookbinding and related work; Commercial printing, nec

(G-11961)
POWDER RIVER TECHNOLOGIES INC
1987 Industrial Dr (28658-7702)
PHONE..................828 465-2894
Mark Sigmon, *Pr*
Myron Yount, *VP*
EMP: 8 **EST:** 1980
SALES (est): 968.2K **Privately Held**
Web: www.powderriverinc.com
SIC: 2514 Chairs, household: metal

(G-11962)
PRECISION CABINETRY INC (PA)
200 W 4th St (28658-3227)
PHONE..................828 465-3341
Keith Mayberry, *Owner*
EMP: 4 **EST:** 2008
SALES (est): 312.41K **Privately Held**
Web: www.precisioncabinetry.com
SIC: 2434 Wood kitchen cabinets

(G-11963)
RENWOOD MILLS LLC
Also Called: Renwood Mills
11 N Brady Ave (28658-3245)
P.O. Box 350 (28658-0350)
PHONE..................828 465-0302
Tommy Lynn, *CEO*
Robin Sigmon, *
EMP: 94 **EST:** 2013
SALES (est): 31.72MM
SALES (corp-wide): 211.12MM **Privately Held**
Web: www.homegrownfamilyfood.com
SIC: 0723 2041 Flour milling, custom services; Cake flour
PA: The Mennel Milling Company
319 S Vine St
Fostoria OH 44830
419 435-8151

(G-11964)
RMC ADVANCED TECHNOLOGIES INC
1400 Burris Rd (28658-1753)
PHONE..................704 325-7100
Soroush Nazarpour, *Pr*
Aly Karnib, *VP Opers*
EMP: 52 **EST:** 2019
SALES (est): 8.76MM
SALES (corp-wide): 90.32MM **Privately Held**
SIC: 3448 Prefabricated metal components
PA: Nanoxplore Inc
4500 Boul Thimens
Montreal QC H4R 2
514 935-1377

(G-11965)
RUDISILL FRAME SHOP INC
780 Buchanan Pl (28658-8595)
PHONE..................828 464-7020
EMP: 23 **EST:** 1982
SALES (est): 1.66MM **Privately Held**
Web: www.yardstickinteriors.com
SIC: 2426 Furniture stock and parts, hardwood

(G-11966)
SARSTEDT INC (PA)
1025 Saint James Church Rd (28658-8937)
P.O. Box 468 (28658-0468)
PHONE..................828 465-4000
Walter Sarstedt, *Pr*
▲ **EMP:** 198 **EST:** 1973
SALES (est): 53.23MM
SALES (corp-wide): 53.23MM **Privately Held**
Web: www.sarstedt.com
SIC: 5047 3821 Medical laboratory equipment; Laboratory apparatus and furniture

(G-11967)
SHERRILL FURNITURE COMPANY
Also Called: Precedent Furniture
1425 Smyre Farm Rd (28658-9361)
P.O. Box 730 (28658-0730)
PHONE..................828 465-0844
Woody Williams, *Brnch Mgr*
EMP: 94
SQ FT: 103,000
SALES (corp-wide): 104.33MM **Privately Held**
Web: www.sherrillfurniture.com
SIC: 2512 Upholstered household furniture
PA: Sherrill Furniture Company Inc
2405 Highland Ave Ne
Hickory NC 28601
828 322-2640

(G-11968)
SMITH WOODTURNING INC
2427 Claremont Rd (28658-9615)
PHONE..................828 464-2230
Linda Smith, *Prin*
EMP: 4 **EST:** 2005
SALES (est): 488.35K **Privately Held**
SIC: 3553 Woodworking machinery

(G-11969)
SNYDER PAPER CORPORATION
Also Called: Snyder Paper
1813 Mount Olive Church Rd (28658-1642)
PHONE..................828 464-1189
Bill Schultz, *Brnch Mgr*
EMP: 7
SALES (corp-wide): 75.1MM **Privately Held**
Web: www.snydersolutions.com

GEOGRAPHIC SECTION

Newton Grove - Sampson County (G-11992)

SIC: 5199 2392 Foams and rubber; Household furnishings, nec
PA: Snyder Paper Corporation
250 26th Street Dr Se
Hickory NC 28602
828 328-2501

(G-11970)
SOUTHERN GLOVE INC
749 Ac Little Dr (28658-3769)
PHONE.................................828 464-4884
Brent A Fidler, *Pr*
Jeff Carter, *VP*
Doug Dickson, *CFO*
◆ **EMP:** 300 **EST:** 1945
SQ FT: 34,440
SALES (est): 29.94MM
SALES (corp-wide): 80.12MM **Privately Held**
Web: www.twusa.com
SIC: 2381 Gloves, work: woven or knit, made from purchased materials
PA: Techniweld Usa, Inc.
6205 Boat Rock Blvd Sw
Atlanta GA 30336
404 699-9900

(G-11971)
SPECIALTY TRNSP SYSTEMS INC
Also Called: Specialty Transportation
2720 N Main Ave (28658-2732)
P.O. Box 334 (28658-0334)
PHONE.................................828 464-9738
Dexter Warren, *Pr*
Carry Warren, *VP*
EMP: 4 **EST:** 1992
SALES (est): 290.95K **Privately Held**
SIC: 7549 5047 3999 Automotive customizing services, nonfactory basis; Medical equipment and supplies; Wheelchair lifts

(G-11972)
SPECIALTY WELDING & MCH INC
505 E 16th St (28658-2102)
PHONE.................................828 464-1104
Dennis Hefner, *Pr*
Gail Hefner, *Sec*
EMP: 8 **EST:** 1993
SQ FT: 16,000
SALES (est): 747.95K **Privately Held**
Web: www.specweld.biz
SIC: 3441 1799 Fabricated structural metal; Welding on site

(G-11973)
STANLEYS WOODWORKING
3006 Jack Whitener Rd (28658-9375)
PHONE.................................828 612-4286
Jerry Stanley, *Prin*
EMP: 5 **EST:** 2019
SALES (est): 92.5K **Privately Held**
SIC: 2431 Millwork

(G-11974)
SUN CLEANERS & LAUNDRY INC
Also Called: Frsteam By Sun Cleaners
2306 N Main Ave (28658-2724)
PHONE.................................704 325-3722
Nick Babamov, *Pr*
Ashley Babamov, *Sec*
EMP: 4 **EST:** 2001
SALES (est): 359.5K **Privately Held**
SIC: 2842 Polishes and sanitation goods

(G-11975)
SUNQEST INC (PA)
1555 N Rankin Ave (28658-2028)
PHONE.................................828 325-4910
Greg Baer, *Pr*
Delores Baer, *VP*
EMP: 8 **EST:** 1988
SQ FT: 12,000
SALES (est): 1.51MM
SALES (corp-wide): 1.51MM **Privately Held**
Web: www.sunqest.com
SIC: 3433 5074 8711 1799 Solar heaters and collectors; Heating equipment (hydronic); Engineering services; Home/office interiors finishing, furnishing and remodeling

(G-11976)
TECHNIBILT LTD (DH)
Also Called: Wanzl North America
700 Technibilt Dr (28658-8991)
P.O. Box 310 (28658-0310)
PHONE.................................828 464-7388
Ben Hinnen, *Pr*
Lynda Farrell, *
◆ **EMP:** 47 **EST:** 1946
SQ FT: 300,000
SALES (est): 114.62MM
SALES (corp-wide): 983.85MM **Privately Held**
Web: www.technibilt.com
SIC: 3799 2542 5046 3496 Pushcarts; Partitions and fixtures, except wood; Shelving, commercial and industrial; Grocery carts, made from purchased wire
HQ: Wanzl Gmbh & Co. Kgaa
Rudolf-Wanzl-Str. 4
Leipheim BY 89340
82217290

(G-11977)
TEIJIN AUTOMOTIVE TECH INC
1400 Burris Rd (28658-1753)
PHONE.................................828 466-7000
Rick Spaulding, *Mgr*
EMP: 97
Web: www.teijinautomotive.com
SIC: 3714 Motor vehicle parts and accessories
HQ: Teijin Automotive Technologies, Inc.
255 Rex Blvd
Auburn Hills MI 48326
248 237-7800

(G-11978)
TEMPRANO TECHVESTORS INC
2105 Northwest Blvd (28658-3723)
PHONE.................................877 545-1509
Luke Walling, *Pr*
EMP: 18 **EST:** 2005
SQ FT: 8,000
SALES (est): 3.16MM **Privately Held**
Web: www.temprano.com
SIC: 7372 Business oriented computer software

(G-11979)
TREE MASTERS INC
101 E 11th St Ste 1 (28658-2275)
P.O. Box 1095 (28658-1095)
PHONE.................................828 464-9443
Robert Baker Junior, *Pr*
Edsel Shusort, *
Cecelia Baker, *
◆ **EMP:** 45 **EST:** 1997
SQ FT: 75,000
SALES (est): 3.44MM **Privately Held**
Web: www.treemastersinc.com
SIC: 3999 Artificial trees and flowers

(G-11980)
UNIFOUR TECH INC
2845 Robinson Rd (28658-8547)
P.O. Box 1235 (28613-1235)
PHONE.................................828 256-4962
Spencer Fredell, *Pr*
EMP: 6 **EST:** 1996
SQ FT: 5,000
SALES (est): 804.89K **Privately Held**
SIC: 3625 Relays and industrial controls

(G-11981)
UNITED GLOVE INC
2017 N Stewart Ave (28658-2800)
P.O. Box 7 (28658-0007)
PHONE.................................828 464-2510
Dan Long, *Pr*
Michael C Long, *
◆ **EMP:** 50 **EST:** 1984
SQ FT: 33,000
SALES (est): 5.74MM **Privately Held**
Web: www.unitedglove.com
SIC: 2259 2381 Gloves and mittens, knit; Gloves, work: woven or knit, made from purchased materials

(G-11982)
WALLACE PRINTING INC
2032 Fairgrove Church Rd (28658-8598)
P.O. Box 1238 (28658-1238)
PHONE.................................828 466-3300
Kim Wallace, *Pr*
Danny Wallace, *VP*
EMP: 11 **EST:** 1989
SQ FT: 5,000
SALES (est): 984.13K **Privately Held**
Web: www.wallaceprinting.com
SIC: 2752 Offset printing

(G-11983)
WAREHOUSE DISTILLERY LLC
2628 Northwest Blvd (28658-3729)
PHONE.................................828 464-5183
EMP: 4 **EST:** 2015
SALES (est): 240.69K **Privately Held**
Web: www.warehousedistillery.com
SIC: 4225 2085 Miniwarehouse, warehousing ; Applejack (alcoholic beverage)

(G-11984)
WAYNE FARMS LLC
332 E A St (28658-2304)
P.O. Box 383 (27017-0383)
PHONE.................................770 538-2120
Andrea Stewart, *Acctnt*
EMP: 13 **EST:** 2000
SALES (est): 2.44MM **Privately Held**
Web: www.waynesandersonfarms.com
SIC: 2015 Poultry slaughtering and processing

(G-11985)
WEYERHAEUSER CO
1525 Mount Olive Church Rd (28658-1740)
P.O. Box 408 (28658-0408)
PHONE.................................828 464-3841
Jerry Thomas, *Genl Mgr*
EMP: 13 **EST:** 2009
SALES (est): 149.18K **Privately Held**
Web: www.weyerhaeuser.com
SIC: 2653 Corrugated and solid fiber boxes

(G-11986)
ZF CHASSIS COMPONENTS LLC
Also Called: ZF Lemforder
1570 E P Street Ext (28658-7803)
PHONE.................................828 468-3711
Mike Curtis, *Manager*
EMP: 128
SQ FT: 188,250
SALES (corp-wide): 144.19K **Privately Held**
Web: www.zf.com
SIC: 3714 Steering mechanisms, motor vehicle
HQ: Zf Chassis Components, Llc
3300 John Conley Dr
Lapeer MI 48446
810 245-2000

Newton Grove
Sampson County

(G-11987)
ALPHA SIGNS & LIGHTING INC
515 Old Crow Rd (28366-7151)
PHONE.................................910 567-5813
Donald Bain, *Pr*
EMP: 11 **EST:** 2016
SALES (est): 510.07K **Privately Held**
Web: www.alphasignsnc.com
SIC: 3993 Signs and advertising specialties

(G-11988)
HOG SLAT INCORPORATED (PA)
Also Called: Georgia Poultry Equipment Co
206 Fayetteville St (28366-9071)
P.O. Box 300 (28366-0300)
PHONE.................................800 949-4647
William Herring Senior, *Ch Bd*
William Herring Ii, *Pr*
Mark Herring, *
David Herring, *
◆ **EMP:** 360 **EST:** 1970
SQ FT: 16,000
SALES (est): 538.94MM
SALES (corp-wide): 538.94MM **Privately Held**
Web: www.hogslat.com
SIC: 1542 3272 3523 0213 Farm building construction; Floor slabs and tiles, precast concrete; Hog feeding, handling, and watering equipment; Hogs

(G-11989)
HOG SLAT INCORPORATED
117 W Weeksdale St (28366-7762)
PHONE.................................800 949-4647
EMP: 21
SALES (corp-wide): 538.94MM **Privately Held**
Web: www.hogslat.com
SIC: 3523 Balers, farm: hay, straw, cotton, etc.
PA: Hog Slat, Incorporated
206 Fayetteville St
Newton Grove NC 28366
800 949-4647

(G-11990)
MACS FARMS SAUSAGE CO INC
209 Raleigh Rd (28366-7613)
P.O. Box 190 (28366-0190)
PHONE.................................910 594-0095
EMP: 6 **EST:** 1994
SALES (est): 477.77K **Privately Held**
SIC: 2013 Sausages and other prepared meats

(G-11991)
NEW VISION LOGGING LLC
180 Kenan Weeks Rd (28366-6421)
PHONE.................................910 594-0571
Marcos Navarro, *Prin*
EMP: 6 **EST:** 2018
SALES (est): 80.48K **Privately Held**
SIC: 2411 Logging

(G-11992)
SAMPSON GIN COMPANY INC
Also Called: Cotton Gin and Warehouse
5625 Newton Grove Hwy (28366-6255)
P.O. Box 526 (28366-0526)
PHONE.................................910 567-5111
Henry F Chancy, *Prin*
Henry F Chancy, *Pr*

Newton Grove - Sampson County (G-11993)

Arthur T Lee, *
R Gerald Warren, *
EMP: 10 **EST:** 1990
SQ FT: 71,800
SALES (est): 393.18K **Privately Held**
SIC: 0724 2211 Cotton ginning; Broadwoven fabric mills, cotton

(G-11993)
STICKY LIFE
321 Goldsboro St (28366-7705)
P.O. Box 10 (28366-0010)
PHONE.............................910 817-4531
EMP: 4 **EST:** 2013
SALES (est): 112.19K **Privately Held**
Web: www.stickylife.com
SIC: 3993 Signs and advertising specialties

(G-11994)
TRANSFORMER SALES & SERVICE
1392 Massey Rd (28366-8542)
P.O. Box 808 (27577-0808)
PHONE.............................910 594-1495
Roger C Mayo, Pr
Daryl Mayo, Treas
William F Outlaw, VP Opers
EMP: 8 **EST:** 1979
SALES (est): 155.97K **Privately Held**
SIC: 7629 3612 Electrical equipment repair, high voltage; Power transformers, electric

Norlina
Warren County

(G-11995)
CLAYPRO LLC
Also Called: Orca Tactical
343 Warren Plains Norlina Rd (27563)
P.O. Box 1024 (27563-1024)
PHONE.............................828 301-6309
EMP: 6
SALES (est): 246.6K **Privately Held**
SIC: 3949 Sporting and athletic goods, nec

North Wilkesboro
Wilkes County

(G-11996)
4 HOME PRODUCTS INC
201 Elkin Hwy Ste I (28659-3464)
PHONE.............................888 609-8222
Randy Whittington, Pr
EMP: 8 **EST:** 2015
SALES (est): 374.52K **Privately Held**
Web: www.fourseasonsoutdoorproduct.com
SIC: 2499 Fencing, docks, and other outdoor wood structural products

(G-11997)
ANCHOR COFFEE CO INC
Also Called: Anchor Coffee Co.
313b 9th St Ste 1 (28659-4168)
PHONE.............................336 265-7458
Nathaniel Griffin, Pr
Greg Brady, VP
Barry Mitchell, Sec
EMP: 5 **EST:** 2014
SQ FT: 6,000
SALES (est): 245.04K **Privately Held**
Web: shop.anchorcoffeeco.com
SIC: 5812 2095 Coffee shop; Roasted coffee

(G-11998)
B & C CONCRETE PRODUCTS INC
228 New Brickyard Rd (28659-8961)
P.O. Box 1014 (28659-1014)
PHONE.............................336 838-4201
EMP: 5 **EST:** 1977
SQ FT: 6,000
SALES (est): 946.6K **Privately Held**
Web: www.bc-concrete.com
SIC: 3272 Concrete products, precast, nec

(G-11999)
BLISSFULL MEMORIES
101 6th St (28659-4238)
PHONE.............................336 903-1835
EMP: 4 **EST:** 2007
SALES (est): 177.99K **Privately Held**
Web: www.blissfulmemories.com
SIC: 2782 Scrapbooks

(G-12000)
CARTER-HUBBARD PUBLISHING CO
711 Main St (28659-4279)
P.O. Box 70 (28659-0070)
PHONE.............................336 838-4117
Julius C Hubbard Junior, Pr
John W Hubbard, Treas
EMP: 12 **EST:** 1933
SQ FT: 15,000
SALES (est): 360.05K **Privately Held**
Web: www.journalpatriot.com
SIC: 2752 2711 2796 2791 Offset printing; Newspapers: publishing only, not printed on site; Platemaking services; Typesetting

(G-12001)
CERTAINTEED LLC
1149 Abtco Rd (28659-9633)
PHONE.............................336 696-2007
Don Veronie, Mgr
EMP: 11
SALES (corp-wide): 397.78MM **Privately Held**
Web: www.certainteed.com
SIC: 3292 Asbestos building materials, except asbestos paper
HQ: Certainteed Llc
   20 Moores Rd
   Malvern PA 19355
   610 893-5000

(G-12002)
COMMERCIAL PROPERTY LLC
Also Called: Carolina Heritage Cabinetry
209 Elkin Hwy (28659-3478)
PHONE.............................336 818-1078
Scott Nase, Pt
Jeff Sigmon, Genl Mgr
EMP: 23 **EST:** 2002
SALES (est): 2.15MM **Privately Held**
Web: www.chcabinetry.com
SIC: 2434 Wood kitchen cabinets

(G-12003)
COPPER BARREL DISTILLERY LLC
508 Main St (28659-4406)
PHONE.............................336 262-6500
George L Smith, CEO
EMP: 7 **EST:** 2015
SALES (est): 497.46K **Privately Held**
Web: www.copperbarrel.com
SIC: 2085 Distilled and blended liquors

(G-12004)
CUB CREEK KITCHENS & BATHS INC
309 Wilkesboro Ave (28659-4227)
PHONE.............................336 651-8983
William M Walker, Pr
Debbie Walker, Sec
EMP: 14 **EST:** 1999
SALES (est): 1.95MM **Privately Held**
Web: www.cubcreekkitchensandbaths.com
SIC: 2542 2541 Partitions and fixtures, except wood; Wood partitions and fixtures

(G-12005)
D & D DISPLAYS INC
126 Shaver St (28659-3403)
P.O. Box 1809 (28659-1809)
PHONE.............................336 667-8765
Glenn Harrs, Pr
J D Brown, *
◆ **EMP:** 30 **EST:** 2000
SQ FT: 100,000
SALES (est): 3.3MM **Privately Held**
SIC: 2541 Display fixtures, wood

(G-12006)
ECMD INC (PA)
Also Called: East Coast Mouldings
2 Grandview St (28659-3109)
P.O. Box 278 (28659-0278)
PHONE.............................336 667-5976
▲ **EMP:** 100 **EST:** 1981
SALES (est): 186.49MM
SALES (corp-wide): 186.49MM **Privately Held**
Web: www.ecmd.com
SIC: 2431 5031 Moldings, wood: unfinished and prefinished; Millwork

(G-12007)
FISH STICKS LLC
622 Moore Rd (28659-8521)
PHONE.............................336 984-1791
Christopher Kirk Privette, Owner
EMP: 5 **EST:** 2018
SALES (est): 134.67K **Privately Held**
Web: www.fish-sticks.net
SIC: 2092 Fish sticks

(G-12008)
FORD DIVISION
1422 2nd St (28659-3853)
PHONE.............................336 838-4155
Andrew Kilby, Mgr
EMP: 5 **EST:** 2019
SALES (est): 87.26K **Privately Held**
Web: www.ford.com
SIC: 3711 Motor vehicles and car bodies

(G-12009)
GARDNER GLASS PRODUCTS INC
Carolina Mirror Division
201 Elkin Hwy (28659-3463)
PHONE.............................336 838-2151
Mike Jordan, Mgr
EMP: 12
SALES (corp-wide): 49.88MM **Privately Held**
Web: www.dreamwalls.com
SIC: 3231 Mirrored glass
PA: Gardner Glass Products, Inc.
   301 Elkin Hwy
   North Wilkesboro NC 28659
   336 651-9300

(G-12010)
GARDNER GLASS PRODUCTS INC (PA)
Also Called: Gardner Glass Products
301 Elkin Hwy (28659-3444)
P.O. Box 1570 (28659-1570)
PHONE.............................336 651-9300
Randy Brooks, CEO
Melissa Lackey, *
Tommy Huskey, *
Edd Gardner, *
◆ **EMP:** 175 **EST:** 1961
SQ FT: 70,000
SALES (est): 49.88MM
SALES (corp-wide): 49.88MM **Privately Held**
Web: www.dreamwalls.com
SIC: 3231 Mirrored glass

(G-12011)
GREENE MOUNTAIN OUTDOORS LLC
2321 Yellow Banks Rd (28659-8700)
PHONE.............................336 670-2186
EMP: 14 **EST:** 2008
SALES (est): 1.29MM **Privately Held**
Web: www.greenemountain.net
SIC: 2311 3111 3199 3792 Coats, overcoats and vests; Die-cutting of leather; Holsters, leather; Pickup covers, canopies or caps

(G-12012)
GREENE PRODUCTS INC
2321 Yellow Banks Rd (28659-8700)
PHONE.............................336 670-2186
James H Greene, Prin
EMP: 6 **EST:** 2012
SALES (est): 105.01K **Privately Held**
Web: www.greenemountain.net
SIC: 3949 Sporting and athletic goods, nec

(G-12013)
HAMBY BROTHER S INCORPORATED
Us Hwy 421 (28659)
P.O. Box 973 (28659-0973)
PHONE.............................336 667-1154
Joe D Hamby, Pr
Gail Hamby, Sec
EMP: 10 **EST:** 1963
SQ FT: 500
SALES (est): 1.13MM **Privately Held**
SIC: 3273 Ready-mixed concrete

(G-12014)
HIGH COUNTRY ELECTRIC MTRS LLC
1268 Suncrest Orchard Rd (28659-9461)
P.O. Box 1262 (28659-1262)
PHONE.............................336 838-4808
EMP: 6 **EST:** 2005
SALES (est): 481.01K **Privately Held**
SIC: 7694 5999 Electric motor repair; Motors, electric

(G-12015)
HOBES COUNTRY HAMS INC (PA)
389 Elledge Mill Rd (28659-9241)
P.O. Box 350 (28697-0350)
PHONE.............................336 670-3401
Hobert D Gambill, Pr
David Gambill, *
Carolyn Wagoner, *
EMP: 35 **EST:** 1977
SALES (est): 5.53MM
SALES (corp-wide): 5.53MM **Privately Held**
Web: www.hobescountryham.com
SIC: 2013 2011 Prepared pork products, from purchased pork; Meat packing plants

(G-12016)
JELD-WEN INC
Also Called: Jeld-Wen Composite
205 Lanes Dr (28659-8376)
P.O. Box 1329 (97601-0268)
PHONE.............................336 838-0292
Arnie Hoyle, Brnch Mgr
EMP: 125
Web: www.jeld-wen.com
SIC: 2421 3442 3089 2448 Sawmills and planing mills, general; Metal doors, sash, and trim; Windows, plastics; Pallets, wood
HQ: Jeld-Wen, Inc.
   2645 Silver Crescent Dr
   Charlotte NC 28273
   800 535-3936

GEOGRAPHIC SECTION

Norwood - Stanly County (G-12041)

(G-12017)
JENKINS PROPERTIES INC
Also Called: Jenkins Interiors
102 Chestnut St Ste 101 (28659-4450)
P.O. Box 1509 (28659-1509)
PHONE.................................336 667-4282
Lewis Jenkins Senior, *Pr*
Ira D Morris, *
Lewis H Jenkins Junior, *VP*
EMP: 25 **EST:** 1950
SQ FT: 50,000
SALES (est): 1.98MM **Privately Held**
SIC: 6512 5199 7532 3714 Commercial and industrial building operation; Leather, leather goods, and furs; Antique and classic automobile restoration; Motor vehicle body components and frame

(G-12018)
JOHNSTON CASUALS FURNITURE INC
121 Shaver St (28659-3445)
P.O. Box 668 (28659-0668)
PHONE.................................336 838-5178
Joe Johnston, *Pr*
Gary Cogdill, *
▼ **EMP:** 100 **EST:** 1955
SQ FT: 100,000
SALES (est): 11.01MM **Privately Held**
Web: www.johnstoncasuals.com
SIC: 2511 Wood household furniture

(G-12019)
JORDAN PIPING INC
300 8th St (28659-0100)
PHONE.................................336 818-9252
James Jordan, *Prin*
EMP: 8 **EST:** 2018
SALES (est): 850.14K **Privately Held**
Web: www.jpiping.com
SIC: 1389 Oil field services, nec

(G-12020)
JUSTRITE MANUFACTURING
2745 Statesville Rd (28659-9122)
PHONE.................................336 990-0918
EMP: 4 **EST:** 2019
SALES (est): 39.69K **Privately Held**
Web: www.justrite.com
SIC: 3999 Manufacturing industries, nec

(G-12021)
LEGACY VULCAN LLC
Mideast Division
776 Quarry Rd # 115 (28659-7806)
PHONE.................................336 838-8072
Bob Church, *Mgr*
EMP: 4
Web: www.vulcanmaterials.com
SIC: 3273 Ready-mixed concrete
HQ: Legacy Vulcan, Llc
    1200 Urban Center Dr
    Vestavia AL 35242
    205 298-3000

(G-12022)
LIFESPAN INCORPORATED
Ls Solutions
2070 River Rd Liberty Grove Rd (28659)
PHONE.................................336 838-2614
Scott Mauney, *Genl Mgr*
EMP: 84
SALES (corp-wide): 19.26MM **Privately Held**
Web: www.lifespanservices.org
SIC: 8211 3842 School for retarded, nec; Surgical appliances and supplies
PA: Lifespan Incorporated
    1511 Shopton Rd Ste A
    Charlotte NC 28217
    704 944-5100

(G-12023)
LIFT BODIES INC
1675 Elkin Hwy 268 (28659-8827)
P.O. Box 1321 (28659-1321)
PHONE.................................336 667-2588
Danny Wagoner, *Pr*
Phyllis Wagoner, *Sec*
EMP: 7 **EST:** 1982
SQ FT: 21,000
SALES (est): 638.91K **Privately Held**
Web: www.liftbodies.com
SIC: 3713 Dump truck bodies

(G-12024)
LOUISIANA-PACIFIC CORPORATION
Also Called: L P
1068 Abtco Rd (28659-9632)
P.O. Box 98 (28669-0098)
PHONE.................................336 696-2751
Mike Blosser, *Mgr*
EMP: 194
SALES (corp-wide): 4.55B **Publicly Held**
Web: www.lpcorp.com
SIC: 2493 Hardboard
PA: Louisiana-Pacific Corporation
    1610 West End Ave Ste 200
    Nashville TN 37203
    615 986-5600

(G-12025)
LURAY TEXTILES INC
Also Called: Luray Textiles & Knitting
300 Luray Rd (28659-9709)
PHONE.................................336 670-3725
Raymond Church, *Pr*
Diane Royall, *
EMP: 24 **EST:** 1986
SQ FT: 18,000
SALES (est): 937.88K **Privately Held**
Web: www.luraytextiles.com
SIC: 2257 2211 Jersey cloth; Terry woven fabrics, cotton

(G-12026)
MATHIS QUARRIES INC
873 Cove Creek Dr (28659-7829)
PHONE.................................336 984-4010
EMP: 4 **EST:** 2010
SALES (est): 428.7K **Privately Held**
SIC: 3295 Minerals, ground or treated

(G-12027)
MEADOWS MILLS INC
1352 W D St (28659-3506)
P.O. Box 1288 (28659-1288)
PHONE.................................336 838-2282
Robert Hege Iii, *Pr*
Bob Hege, *
June Hege, *
Brian Hege, *
Corey Sheets, *
▼ **EMP:** 37 **EST:** 1902
SQ FT: 52,000
SALES (est): 5.39MM **Privately Held**
Web: www.meadowsmills.com
SIC: 3531 3553 3556 3599 Hammer mills (rock and ore crushing machines), portable; Sawmill machines; Food products machinery; Machine shop, jobbing and repair

(G-12028)
MICHAEL S NORTH WILKESBORO INC
Also Called: Michaels Jewelry
900 Main St (28659-4216)
PHONE.................................336 838-5964
Michael Parsons, *Pr*
Vickie Parsons, *Sec*
EMP: 5 **EST:** 1985
SQ FT: 1,250
SALES (est): 540.46K **Privately Held**
Web: www.michaelsjewelry.com
SIC: 5944 3911 5947 Jewelry, precious stones and precious metals; Jewelry, precious metal; Gift shop

(G-12029)
MILLER BEE SUPPLY INC
496 Yellow Banks Rd (28659-8773)
PHONE.................................336 670-2249
Presley Miller, *Pr*
EMP: 12 **EST:** 2003
SALES (est): 852.67K **Privately Held**
Web: www.millerbeesupply.com
SIC: 2499 3999 Beekeeping supplies, wood; Beekeepers' supplies

(G-12030)
PLYCEM USA LLC
Allura Fiber Cement
1149 Abtco Rd (28659-9633)
PHONE.................................336 696-2007
Jerry Shermer, *Mgr*
EMP: 90
Web: www.allurausa.com
SIC: 2952 3292 5032 Roof cement: asphalt, fibrous, or plastic; Siding, asbestos cement; Cement
HQ: Plycem Usa Llc
    396 W Greens Rd Ste 300
    Houston TX 77067
    844 525-5872

(G-12031)
RAGG CO INC
627 Elkin Hwy (28659-3405)
PHONE.................................336 838-4895
Tim R Clonch, *Pr*
EMP: 4 **EST:** 1987
SALES (est): 276.25K **Privately Held**
Web: www.theraggcompany.com
SIC: 2759 Screen printing

(G-12032)
RICKY WYATT LOGGING
5209 Speedway Rd (28659-7523)
PHONE.................................336 984-3145
Janice Turbeville, *Prin*
EMP: 5 **EST:** 2010
SALES (est): 213.94K **Privately Held**
SIC: 2411 Logging

(G-12033)
ROTENS LOGGING LLC
466 Dowell Ridge Ln (28659-7648)
PHONE.................................336 981-7019
Kenneth Roten, *Prin*
EMP: 6 **EST:** 2016
SALES (est): 249.18K **Privately Held**
SIC: 2411 Logging

(G-12034)
TAYLOR BUSINESS FORMS INC
Also Called: Taylor Business Products
177 Business Center Dr (28659-7411)
PHONE.................................336 667-0300
Philip G Taylor, *Pr*
Patricia Taylor, *Sec*
EMP: 8 **EST:** 1986
SQ FT: 10,000
SALES (est): 472.9K **Privately Held**
SIC: 5112 2752 Business forms; Commercial printing, lithographic

(G-12035)
THOMAS BROTHERS SLAUGHTER HSE
Also Called: Thomas Brothers Meat Proc
347 Thomas St (28659-3168)
PHONE.................................336 667-1346
Buddy Joe Thomas, *Pt*
Charlie P Thomas, *Pt*
EMP: 5 **EST:** 1971
SQ FT: 4,000
SALES (est): 293.56K **Privately Held**
SIC: 0751 2011 Slaughtering: custom livestock services; Meat packing plants

Norwood
Stanly County

(G-12036)
AQUADALE QUERY
12423 Old Aquadale Rd (28128-7548)
P.O. Box 987 (28002-0987)
PHONE.................................704 474-3165
Jeffrey Goodman, *Owner*
EMP: 9 **EST:** 2008
SALES (est): 282.63K **Privately Held**
Web: www.hedrickind.com
SIC: 1442 Construction sand and gravel

(G-12037)
CAROLINA STALITE CO LTD PARTNR
12423 Old Aquadale Rd (28128-7548)
PHONE.................................704 474-3165
Mike Farrington, *Brnch Mgr*
EMP: 16
SALES (corp-wide): 22.99MM **Privately Held**
Web: www.stalite.com
SIC: 3281 Slate products
PA: Carolina Stalite Company Limited Partnership
    205 Klumac Rd
    Salisbury NC 28144
    704 637-1515

(G-12038)
CUMBERLAND SAND AND GRAVEL
12423 Old Aquadale Rd (28128-7548)
PHONE.................................704 474-3165
EMP: 9 **EST:** 2010
SALES (est): 454.27K **Privately Held**
Web: www.hedrickind.com
SIC: 1442 Construction sand and gravel

(G-12039)
KENNEL-AIRE LLC (PA)
17382 Randalls Ferry Rd (28128-7458)
PHONE.................................704 459-0044
E Michael Powers, *Managing Member*
Trygve Pederson, *CFO*
◆ **EMP:** 45 **EST:** 1956
SQ FT: 44,000
SALES (est): 3.02MM
SALES (corp-wide): 3.02MM **Privately Held**
SIC: 3999 5999 Pet supplies; Pet supplies

(G-12040)
M & R RETREADING & OIL CO INC
337 W Whitley St (28128-8712)
PHONE.................................704 474-4101
Reggie Barfield, *Pr*
Mitchell Barfield, *Pr*
Reggie Barfield, *Dir*
Wesley Smith, *Dir*
EMP: 11 **EST:** 1971
SQ FT: 15,000
SALES (est): 2.21MM **Privately Held**
Web: mr-retreading.business.site
SIC: 5014 5531 7534 5983 Automobile tires and tubes; Automotive tires; Tire recapping; Fuel oil dealers

(G-12041)
NEW FINISH INC
8353 Us 52 Hwy S (28128-6592)

PHONE..................................704 474-4116
Steve Bradley, *Pr*
Brenda Bradley, *
EMP: 47 **EST:** 2001
SALES (est): 7.05MM **Privately Held**
Web: www.newfinishinc.com
SIC: 2851 4212 Epoxy coatings; Local trucking, without storage

(G-12042)
NORWOOD MANUFACTURING INC
680 Lanier Rd (28128-8448)
PHONE..................................704 474-0505
Allen Kuehl, *Pr*
EMP: 47 **EST:** 2004
SQ FT: 77,920
SALES (est): 8.95MM
SALES (corp-wide): 240.55MM **Publicly Held**
SIC: 3448 Prefabricated metal components
PA: Burnham Holdings, Inc.
1241 Harrisburg Ave
Lancaster PA 17603
717 390-7800

(G-12043)
RUSCO FIXTURE COMPANY INC
Also Called: Rusco Fixture
11635 Nc 138 Hwy (28128-7509)
P.O. Box 598 (28129-0598)
PHONE..................................704 474-3184
EMP: 37 **EST:** 1976
SALES (est): 3.96MM **Privately Held**
SIC: 2541 Store fixtures, wood

(G-12044)
STANLY FIXS ACQUISITION LLC
Also Called: Stanly Fixtures
11635 Nc 138 Hwy (28128-7509)
P.O. Box 616 (28128-0616)
PHONE..................................704 474-3184
Kinny Bowers, *
Boyce Thompson, *
EMP: 30 **EST:** 1959
SQ FT: 128,000
SALES (est): 2.43MM **Privately Held**
Web: www.stanlyfixtures.com
SIC: 2541 Store fixtures, wood

(G-12045)
STANLY FIXTURES COMPANY INC
11635 Nc 138 Hwy (28128-7509)
P.O. Box 616 (28128-0616)
PHONE..................................704 474-3184
Todd Curlee, *Pr*
EMP: 12 **EST:** 2006
SALES (est): 871.3K **Privately Held**
SIC: 2542 Partitions and fixtures, except wood

(G-12046)
TILLERY ACCESSORIES INC
7041 Riverview Rd (28128-9623)
PHONE..................................704 474-3013
Yvonne Pinion, *Pr*
Roger Pinion, *VP*
EMP: 7 **EST:** 1993
SQ FT: 3,000
SALES (est): 119.35K **Privately Held**
SIC: 2326 Work uniforms

(G-12047)
UWHARRIE KNITS INC
957 N Main St (28128-6526)
P.O. Box 890 (28128-0890)
PHONE..................................704 474-4123
Doug Forman, *Pr*
▲ **EMP:** 12 **EST:** 1999
SALES (est): 2.48MM **Privately Held**
SIC: 5949 2258 Knitting goods and supplies; Lace and warp knit fabric mills

Oak Island
Brunswick County

(G-12048)
BURLINGTON OUTLET (PA)
5817 E Oak Island Dr (28465-5040)
PHONE..................................910 278-3442
James R Taylor, *Owner*
EMP: 7 **EST:** 1983
SQ FT: 8,000
SALES (est): 526.21K
SALES (corp-wide): 526.21K **Privately Held**
Web: www.burlingtonoutlet.com
SIC: 2339 5945 5947 Beachwear: women's, misses', and juniors'; Toys and games; Gift shop

(G-12049)
ELITE WOOD CLASSICS INC
4392 Long Beach Rd Se (28461-8617)
PHONE..................................910 454-8745
Merrideth Herr, *Prin*
EMP: 9 **EST:** 2005
SALES (est): 291.44K **Privately Held**
SIC: 2431 Millwork

(G-12050)
HAVE A SHIRT MADE
106 Se 58th St (28465-5021)
PHONE..................................910 201-9911
EMP: 4 **EST:** 2012
SALES (est): 363.35K **Privately Held**
Web: www.haveashirtmade.com
SIC: 2759 Screen printing

(G-12051)
JAMES IRON & STEEL INC
3010 W Beach Dr (28465-7735)
PHONE..................................704 309-8507
EMP: 5 **EST:** 2018
SALES (est): 109.84K **Privately Held**
Web: www.jamesironandsteel.com
SIC: 2591 Drapery hardware and window blinds and shades

(G-12052)
LAKEBROOK CORPORATION
Also Called: Leonard Products
3506 E Yacht Dr (28465-5721)
PHONE..................................207 947-4051
Elizabeth A R Long, *Pr*
EMP: 4 **EST:** 1997
SALES (est): 351.15K **Privately Held**
SIC: 2672 2675 Tape, pressure sensitive: made from purchased materials; Die-cut paper and board

(G-12053)
PARKWOOD CORPORATION
3506 E Yacht Dr (28465-5721)
PHONE..................................910 815-4300
Robert L Long, *Pr*
EMP: 5 **EST:** 2003
SALES (est): 350K **Privately Held**
SIC: 2631 Paperboard mills

(G-12054)
RC BOLDT PUBLISHING LLC (PA)
804 Ocean Dr (28465-8217)
PHONE..................................904 624-0033
EMP: 6 **EST:** 2016
SALES (est): 72.02K
SALES (corp-wide): 72.02K **Privately Held**
SIC: 2741 Miscellaneous publishing

(G-12055)
SELDON CELE
126 Ne 25th St (28465-6225)
PHONE..................................910 274-8070
Cele Seldon, *Prin*
EMP: 5 **EST:** 2016
SALES (est): 61.4K **Privately Held**
SIC: 2741 Miscellaneous publishing

(G-12056)
VALLEE INDUSTRIES INC
5400 E Yacht Dr Apt C1 (28465-4900)
PHONE..................................910 477-0092
Scott Rowe, *Prin*
EMP: 5 **EST:** 2010
SALES (est): 64.11K **Privately Held**
SIC: 3999 Manufacturing industries, nec

Oak Ridge
Guilford County

(G-12057)
B & B WELDING INC
Also Called: Spencer Bowman Customs
2900 Oak Ridge Rd (27310-8705)
PHONE..................................336 643-5702
Spencer G Bowman, *Pr*
Spencer E Bowman, *VP*
Wanda Bowman, *Sec*
EMP: 7 **EST:** 1971
SQ FT: 5,000
SALES (est): 566.56K **Privately Held**
SIC: 3751 7538 Motorcycles and related parts; General automotive repair shops

(G-12058)
BLUM INC
594 Carson Ridge Dr (27310-9693)
PHONE..................................919 345-6214
EMP: 6 **EST:** 2010
SALES (est): 116.77K **Privately Held**
Web: www.blum.com
SIC: 3429 Hardware, nec

(G-12059)
EDUCATION CENTER LLC
Also Called: Mailbox, The
8886 Rymack Dr (27310-8804)
PHONE..................................336 854-0309
EMP: 49 **EST:** 2012
SALES (est): 5.39MM **Privately Held**
Web: www.themailbox.com
SIC: 2721 Periodicals

(G-12060)
MEADOWS FROZEN CUSTAR
2205 Oak Ridge Rd Ste F (27310-8729)
P.O. Box 407 (27310-0407)
PHONE..................................336 298-7246
EMP: 7 **EST:** 2010
SALES (est): 171.56K **Privately Held**
Web: www.meadowsfrozencustard.com
SIC: 2024 Ice cream, bulk

(G-12061)
NUCLAMP SYSTEM LLC
Also Called: Nuclamp
8585 Benbow Merrill Rd (27310-9509)
PHONE..................................336 643-1766
EMP: 5 **EST:** 2011
SALES (est): 236.18K **Privately Held**
Web: www.nuclamp.com
SIC: 3429 Clamps, metal

(G-12062)
OAKBROOK SOLUTIONS INC
Also Called: Cornerstone Software
5930 Tarleton Dr (27310-9632)
PHONE..................................336 714-0321
Craig Cook, *Brnch Mgr*
EMP: 38
SALES (corp-wide): 8.23MM **Privately Held**
Web: www.f2strategy.com
SIC: 7372 Prepackaged software
HQ: Oakbrook Solutions, Inc.
301 N Main St Ste 2424
Winston Salem NC 27101
336 714-0321

(G-12063)
OTTER PUBLICATIONS
8011 Pate Dr (27310-8706)
PHONE..................................336 643-5387
Jennifer Otter, *Prin*
EMP: 4 **EST:** 2010
SALES (est): 119.33K **Privately Held**
SIC: 2741 Music book and sheet music publishing

(G-12064)
PARRISH WELDING
6711 Sandylea Rd (27310-9702)
PHONE..................................336 707-3878
Christopher Parrish, *Prin*
EMP: 4 **EST:** 2009
SALES (est): 51.42K **Privately Held**
SIC: 7692 Welding repair

(G-12065)
PHYLLIS PULLING
5935 Tarleton Dr (27310-9106)
PHONE..................................336 643-8201
Phyllis Pulling, *Prin*
EMP: 5 **EST:** 2010
SALES (est): 86.67K **Privately Held**
SIC: 1389 Construction, repair, and dismantling services

(G-12066)
PIEDMONT MARBLE INC
5014 Robdot Dr (27310-9208)
P.O. Box 1047 (27402-1047)
PHONE..................................336 274-1800
Tony Parrish, *Pr*
Rene Parrish, *VP*
Louise Hobbs, *Off Mgr*
EMP: 8 **EST:** 1985
SALES (est): 500K **Privately Held**
SIC: 3281 Household articles, except furniture: cut stone

(G-12067)
SOUTHLAND COATINGS TECH LLC
1683 Deer Run Ct (27310-9687)
PHONE..................................336 644-8919
Dave Maxson, *Owner*
EMP: 6 **EST:** 2015
SALES (est): 69.26K **Privately Held**
Web: www.southlandcoatings.com
SIC: 3479 Metal coating and allied services

Oakboro
Stanly County

(G-12068)
BUHLMANN NORTH AMERICA LP
Also Called: Buhlmann Group
527 S Main St (28129-8888)
PHONE..................................704 485-4144
Oliver Buhlmann, *Prin*
EMP: 7 **EST:** 2014
SALES (est): 74.3K **Privately Held**
SIC: 3317 Steel pipe and tubes

GEOGRAPHIC SECTION

Ocean Isle Beach - Brunswick County (G-12095)

(G-12069)
CHARLOTTE PIPE AND FOUNDRY CO
10145 Lighthouse Rd (28129-8988)
P.O. Box 36487 (28236-6487)
PHONE.................704 887-8015
Mike Hall, *Manager*
EMP: 510
SALES (corp-wide): 841.88MM **Privately Held**
Web: www.charlottepipe.com
SIC: 3084 Plastics pipe
PA: Charlotte Pipe And Foundry Company
2109 Randolph Rd
Charlotte NC 28207
704 372-5030

(G-12070)
CONCRETE PIPE & PRECAST LLC
20047 Silver Rd (28129-8986)
PHONE.................704 485-4614
James B Kennedy, *Pr*
EMP: 32
SALES (corp-wide): 61.95MM **Privately Held**
Web: www.concretepandp.com
SIC: 3272 Precast terrazzo or concrete products
PA: Concrete Pipe & Precast, Llc
11352 Virginia Precast Rd
Ashland VA 23005
804 798-6068

(G-12071)
CT COMMERCIAL PAPER LLC
349 S Main St (28129-7719)
PHONE.................704 485-3212
EMP: 52 **EST:** 2014
SALES (est): 10.06MM
SALES (corp-wide): 1.71B **Privately Held**
Web: www.ctcpaper.com
SIC: 3089 2621 Tissue dispensers, plastics; Towels, tissues and napkins; paper and stock
PA: Pmc Global, Inc.
12243 Branford St
Sun Valley CA 91352
818 896-1101

(G-12072)
DOVER POWER LLC
Also Called: Diy Performance
16400 Buster Rd (28129-8921)
PHONE.................704 485-2020
EMP: 5 **EST:** 2014
SALES (est): 100.67K **Privately Held**
Web: www.doverpoweronlinestore.com
SIC: 3714 Motor vehicle parts and accessories

(G-12073)
ENTERPRISE RENDERING COMPANY
28821 Bethlehem Church Rd (28129-8758)
PHONE.................704 485-3018
Carroll Braun Senior, *Pr*
EMP: 9 **EST:** 1964
SQ FT: 8,000
SALES (est): 1.23MM **Privately Held**
Web: www.enterpriserendering.com
SIC: 2077 Bone meal, except as animal feed

(G-12074)
FAB-CON MACHINERY DEV CORP (PA)
Also Called: Fab-Con
201 E 10th St (28129-9621)
P.O. Box 591 (11050-0250)
PHONE.................704 486-7120
Frank Catallo, *Pr*
James Catallo, *

◆ **EMP:** 70 **EST:** 1966
SQ FT: 20,000
SALES (est): 15.67MM
SALES (corp-wide): 15.67MM **Privately Held**
Web: www.fab-con.com
SIC: 5084 3552 Textile machinery and equipment; Knitting machines

(G-12075)
LIN-INK PUBLISHING LLC
825 Old Farm Rd (28129-7743)
PHONE.................704 485-5823
Reese Linnell, *Prin*
EMP: 5 **EST:** 2017
SALES (est): 77.62K **Privately Held**
SIC: 2741 Miscellaneous publishing

(G-12076)
LITTLE LOGGING INC
1513 N Main St (28129-9012)
PHONE.................704 201-8185
Michael D Little Ii, *Pr*
Ashlee N Little, *VP*
EMP: 10 **EST:** 2007
SALES (est): 1MM **Privately Held**
SIC: 2411 Logging camps and contractors

(G-12077)
MARCOTT HOSIERY LLC
349 Rocky River Rd (28129)
P.O. Box 28 (28129-0028)
PHONE.................704 485-8702
EMP: 33
Web: www.marcotthosiery.com
SIC: 2252 Socks
PA: Marcott Hosiery, Llc
3028 S Kilbourn Ave
Chicago IL 60623

(G-12078)
MORGANS CABINETS INC
8056 Rocky River Rd (28129-8879)
P.O. Box 269 (28129-0269)
PHONE.................704 485-8693
Claude Morgan, *Prin*
EMP: 10 **EST:** 1995
SALES (est): 836.59K **Privately Held**
SIC: 2434 Wood kitchen cabinets

(G-12079)
NORMAC KITCHENS INC (HQ)
226 S Main St (28129-7718)
P.O. Box 479 (28129-0479)
PHONE.................704 485-1911
Hans Marcus, *Pr*
EMP: 10 **EST:** 1993
SQ FT: 5,000
SALES (est): 16.48MM
SALES (corp-wide): 29.62MM **Privately Held**
Web: www.normackitchens.com
SIC: 2434 2541 2431 Wood kitchen cabinets; Wood partitions and fixtures; Millwork
PA: Normac Kitchens Limited
59 Glen Cameron Rd
Thornhill ON L3T 5
905 889-1342

(G-12080)
RMB CUSTOM LEATHER LLC
966 Bay Dr (28129-9030)
PHONE.................704 762-1614
Sonya Palmer Bennett, *Prin*
EMP: 4 **EST:** 2013
SALES (est): 126.78K **Privately Held**
Web: www.rmbcl.com
SIC: 3199 Leather goods, nec

(G-12081)
SIMPSON SAWMILL LLC
12733 Hazard Rd (28129-8724)
PHONE.................704 485-8814
Jeffrey Simpson, *Prin*
EMP: 5 **EST:** 2017
SALES (est): 83.8K **Privately Held**
SIC: 2431 Millwork

(G-12082)
SWB LOGGING LLC
213 Glenwood Dr (28129-9406)
PHONE.................704 485-3411
Scott Broadaway, *Pr*
EMP: 5 **EST:** 2001
SALES (est): 564.92K **Privately Held**
SIC: 2411 Logging camps and contractors

(G-12083)
TA LOGGING LLC
16537 Big Lick Rd (28129-8965)
PHONE.................704 485-8337
Tyler Almond, *Pr*
EMP: 8 **EST:** 2013
SALES (est): 493.23K **Privately Held**
SIC: 2411 Logging camps and contractors

(G-12084)
VALLEY PROTEINS (DE) INC
Also Called: Valley Proteins (de), Inc.
28844 Bethlehem Church Rd (28129-8758)
PHONE.................540 877-2533
EMP: 145
SALES (corp-wide): 6.53B **Publicly Held**
Web: www.darpro-solutions.com
SIC: 2077 Animal and marine fats and oils
HQ: Valley Proteins (De), Llc
151 Randall Stuewe Dr
Winchester VA 22603
540 877-2533

(G-12085)
WEST STANLY FABRICATION INC
16431 Sr 24 27 (28129)
PHONE.................704 254-2967
Christopher West, *Pr*
EMP: 5 **EST:** 2007
SALES (est): 129.68K **Privately Held**
SIC: 7692 Welding repair

Ocean Isle Beach
Brunswick County

(G-12086)
ALTERNATIVE CUTTING TOOLS LLC
1628 Waterway Cove Dr Sw (28469-4805)
PHONE.................484 684-9924
EMP: 4 **EST:** 2015
SALES (est): 109.44K **Privately Held**
SIC: 3545 Cutting tools for machine tools

(G-12087)
BRUNSWICK SCREEN PRTG & EMB
570 Meadow Summit Dr (28469-6185)
PHONE.................910 579-1234
Paul Saah, *Prin*
EMP: 11 **EST:** 2016
SALES (est): 601.97K **Privately Held**
SIC: 2759 Commercial printing, nec

(G-12088)
CENTRAL SITE GROUP LLC
15 Scotland St (28469-7629)
PHONE.................336 380-4121
Travis E Sharpe, *Managing Member*
EMP: 6 **EST:** 2016
SALES (est): 500K **Privately Held**

SIC: 1389 Construction, repair, and dismantling services

(G-12089)
CREATIVE CLOSETS AND CABINETRY
6576 Annesbrook Pl Sw (28469-5695)
PHONE.................570 952-1702
Ronnie Olesnovich, *Prin*
EMP: 4 **EST:** 2018
SALES (est): 64.93K **Privately Held**
SIC: 2434 Wood kitchen cabinets

(G-12090)
EAST END MLLWK DBA AVVENTO INC
1772 Rosebay Ct Sw (28469-5772)
PHONE.................516 313-7739
David Foley, *Pr*
EMP: 5 **EST:** 2020
SALES (est): 54.13K **Privately Held**
SIC: 2431 Millwork

(G-12091)
EDD LOFTIS BACKHOE SERVIC
6484 Carrick Bend Trl Sw (28469-4810)
PHONE.................919 971-5740
EMP: 4 **EST:** 2018
SALES (est): 192.26K **Privately Held**
SIC: 3531 Backhoes

(G-12092)
ICE BOX COMPANY INC
570 Meadow Summit Dr Ste 19 (28469)
PHONE.................910 579-3273
Stephen C Rhodes Senior, *Pr*
▼ **EMP:** 10 **EST:** 1984
SALES (est): 476.24K **Privately Held**
Web: www.1800icebags.com
SIC: 2673 Plastic bags: made from purchased materials

(G-12093)
MOORE DUMPSTER SERVICE LLC
1617 Salmon Ln Sw (28469-6021)
PHONE.................704 560-4410
Adam Moore, *Prin*
EMP: 5 **EST:** 2017
SALES (est): 161.67K **Privately Held**
SIC: 3443 Dumpsters, garbage

(G-12094)
OCEAN WOODWORKING INC
6863 Beach Dr Sw (28469-5747)
PHONE.................910 579-2233
Laurence Moore, *Pr*
Rita Moore, *VP*
EMP: 4 **EST:** 1999
SQ FT: 8,000
SALES (est): 433.73K **Privately Held**
Web: www.oceanwoodworking.com
SIC: 2521 2517 Cabinets, office: wood; Home entertainment unit cabinets, wood

(G-12095)
UNIQUE-SKILL PRECISION INC
90 Fairmont St (28469-7637)
PHONE.................910 393-0090
Richard Smith, *Prin*
▲ **EMP:** 6 **EST:** 2015
SALES (est): 158.52K **Privately Held**
SIC: 3599 Machine shop, jobbing and repair

Ocracoke
Hyde County

(G-12096)
OCRACOKE SAUCE COMPANY LLC ✪
58 Water Plant Rd (27960-9617)
PHONE..............................443 904-7972
Mike Dalgleish, *Managing Member*
EMP: 6 **EST:** 2022
SALES (est): 63.22K **Privately Held**
SIC: 2099 Sauce, gravy, dressing, and dip mixes

(G-12097)
ODENS FISH & OIL CO INC
P.O. Box 1269 (27960-1269)
PHONE..............................252 588-0036
EMP: 5 **EST:** 2004
SALES (est): 201.1K **Privately Held**
SIC: 2077 Fish oil

Old Fort
Mcdowell County

(G-12098)
AURIA OLD FORT LLC (DH)
1506 E Main St (28762-0168)
PHONE..............................828 668-7601
Brian Pour, *Pr*
▲ **EMP:** 206 **EST:** 2007
SALES (est): 128.92MM **Privately Held**
Web: www.auriasolutions.com
SIC: 3714 Motor vehicle parts and accessories
HQ: Auria Solutions Usa Inc.
26999 Centrl Pk Blvd # 30
Southfield MI 48076
248 728-8000

(G-12099)
AURIA OLD FORT II LLC
1542 E Main St (28762-0168)
PHONE..............................828 668-3277
Brian Pour, *Pr*
▲ **EMP:** 71 **EST:** 2007
SALES (est): 22.2MM **Privately Held**
SIC: 3714 Motor vehicle parts and accessories
HQ: Auria Solutions Usa Inc.
26999 Centrl Pk Blvd # 30
Southfield MI 48076
248 728-8000

(G-12100)
COLUMBIA PLYWOOD CORPORATION
Also Called: Columbia Carolina Division
369 Columbia Carolina Rd (28762-8629)
P.O. Box 1148 (28762-1148)
PHONE..............................828 724-4191
Jeff Tuckey, *Mgr*
EMP: 447
SALES (corp-wide): 494.11K **Privately Held**
Web: www.columbiaforestproducts.com
SIC: 2435 2426 Plywood, hardwood or hardwood faced; Hardwood dimension and flooring mills
HQ: Columbia Plywood Corporation
222 Sw Columbia St # 1575
Portland OR 97201
503 224-5300

(G-12101)
HI-TEC MACHINE CORP
2082 Silvers Welch Rd (28762-8728)
PHONE..............................828 652-1060
Russell D Wysong Iii, *Pr*
Todd Mustin, *
Richard T Mustin, *
EMP: 25 **EST:** 1998
SQ FT: 5,000
SALES (est): 4.65MM **Privately Held**
Web: www.hitechmachines.com
SIC: 3599 Machine shop, jobbing and repair

(G-12102)
JANESVILLE LLC
157 Lackey Town Rd (28762-7758)
P.O. Box 1209 (28762-1209)
PHONE..............................828 668-9251
John Berghammer, *Brnch Mgr*
EMP: 180
SIC: 3086 Insulation or cushioning material, foamed plastics
HQ: Janesville, Llc
23028 Commerce Dr
Farmington Hills MI 48335
248 948-1811

(G-12103)
LEWIS MACHINE COMPANY INC
712 Catawba River Rd (28762-7642)
PHONE..............................828 668-7752
Gary Lewis, *Pr*
EMP: 8 **EST:** 1985
SQ FT: 2,500
SALES (est): 548.57K **Privately Held**
SIC: 3599 Machine shop, jobbing and repair

(G-12104)
PARKER HOSIERY COMPANY INC
Also Called: Parker Legwear
78 Catawba Ave (28762-8920)
P.O. Box 1799 (28762-1799)
PHONE..............................828 668-7628
Jeffrey W Parker, *Pr*
Amy L Parker, *
◆ **EMP:** 30 **EST:** 1946
SQ FT: 100,000
SALES (est): 2.52MM **Privately Held**
Web: www.parkerhosiery.com
SIC: 5137 2252 Gloves, women's and children's; Hosiery, nec

(G-12105)
POPPY HANDCRAFTED POPCORN LLC
Also Called: Poppy Handcrafted Popcorn LLC
78 Catawba Ave Ste A (28762-8920)
PHONE..............................828 552-3149
Carmen Cabrera, *Mgr*
EMP: 10
SALES (corp-wide): 2.68MM **Privately Held**
Web: www.poppyhandcraftedpopcorn.com
SIC: 2099 Food preparations, nec
PA: Poppy Handcrafted Popcorn Inc.
127 Old Us Hwy 70 E
Black Mountain NC 28711
828 552-3149

(G-12106)
ULTIMATE CLEANING SERVCES DEAN
225 Chinqunpin Trl (28762-8731)
PHONE..............................865 382-2433
EMP: 4 **EST:** 2016
SALES (est): 65.5K **Privately Held**
SIC: 1389 Cleaning wells

Olin
Iredell County

(G-12107)
CONTROLLED ROCK DRILLILNG & BL
1047 Olin Loop (28660-8415)
PHONE..............................704 876-9004
EMP: 5 **EST:** 2014
SALES (est): 193.55K **Privately Held**
SIC: 3546 Power-driven handtools

(G-12108)
WOODWORKING UNLIMITED INC
675 Bussell Rd (28660-9450)
PHONE..............................704 903-8080
David Haynes, *Prin*
EMP: 6 **EST:** 2007
SALES (est): 141.56K **Privately Held**
SIC: 2431 Millwork

Oriental
Pamlico County

(G-12109)
COLLIN MFG INC
99 Pelican Cir (28571-9808)
PHONE..............................919 917-6264
Steve Price, *Prin*
EMP: 5 **EST:** 2005
SALES (est): 109.59K **Privately Held**
SIC: 3999 Manufacturing industries, nec

(G-12110)
J C LAWRENCE CO
Also Called: Medlin Office Supply
9526 Connie Cove Rd (28571-9493)
PHONE..............................919 553-3044
Jennifer Lawrence, *Pr*
Charels Chuck Lawrence, *VP*
EMP: 5 **EST:** 1985
SALES (est): 281.82K **Privately Held**
SIC: 5932 2759 Used merchandise stores; Commercial printing, nec

(G-12111)
M & J MARINE LLC
Also Called: Sailcraft Service
1218 Lupton Dr (28571-9629)
PHONE..............................252 249-0522
Jennifer Pawlikowski, *Managing Member*
EMP: 10 **EST:** 2018
SALES (est): 942.08K **Privately Held**
SIC: 5551 3731 7699 3732 Boat dealers; Shipbuilding and repairing; Recreational sporting equipment repair services; Motorized boat, building and repairing

(G-12112)
ONC TEES
204 Freemason St (28571-9202)
P.O. Box 192 (28571-0192)
PHONE..............................252 671-7576
EMP: 4 **EST:** 2018
SALES (est): 124.25K **Privately Held**
SIC: 2759 Screen printing

(G-12113)
VILLAGE GRAPHICS
204 Freemason St (28571-9202)
P.O. Box 61 (28509-0061)
PHONE..............................252 745-4600
Greg Winfrey, *Owner*
EMP: 4 **EST:** 1986
SALES (est): 470.82K **Privately Held**
SIC: 7336 2752 Graphic arts and related design; Commercial printing, lithographic

(G-12114)
WATERDOG WOOD WORKS LLC
195 Port Dr (28571-8907)
PHONE..............................252 808-7978
Aldo H Cristiani, *Owner*
EMP: 5 **EST:** 2017
SALES (est): 242.12K **Privately Held**
SIC: 2431 Millwork

Orrum
Robeson County

(G-12115)
CHAMELEON WRAPS & DESIGNS
3273 Fire Tower Rd (28369-8705)
PHONE..............................910 544-9801
Michael Middleton, *Prin*
EMP: 4 **EST:** 2016
SALES (est): 52.02K **Privately Held**
SIC: 3993 Signs and advertising specialties

(G-12116)
PRO-KAY SUPPLY INC
5032 Atkinson Rd (28369-9057)
P.O. Box 93 (28369-0093)
PHONE..............................910 628-0882
Wilton P Caulder, *Pr*
Sabrina Caulder, *Sec*
EMP: 16 **EST:** 1984
SALES (est): 1.03MM **Privately Held**
Web: www.prokaysupply.com
SIC: 2431 Millwork

(G-12117)
RICHARD LEWIS VON
1928 Indian Swamp Rd (28369-9650)
PHONE..............................910 628-9292
Richard Lewis, *Owner*
EMP: 7 **EST:** 2017
SALES (est): 208.88K **Privately Held**
SIC: 2411 Logging

Otto
Macon County

(G-12118)
J CULPEPPER & CO
Also Called: Infinity Stingray Products
8285 Georgia Rd (28763-8339)
P.O. Box 690 (28763-0690)
PHONE..............................828 524-6842
Joe Culpepper, *Pr*
Kristi Culpepper, *VP*
▲ **EMP:** 5 **EST:** 1995
SALES (est): 340.79K **Privately Held**
Web: www.knifehandles.com
SIC: 3421 Cutlery

Oxford
Granville County

(G-12119)
CENTAUR LABORATORIES INC
7715 Peck Watts Rd (27565-8224)
PHONE..............................919 249-5072
Michael Abruzzo, *Brnch Mgr*
EMP: 13
SALES (corp-wide): 246.31K **Privately Held**
SIC: 8731 3599 3589 Energy research; Oil filters, internal combustion engine, except auto; Water filters and softeners, household type

GEOGRAPHIC SECTION
Oxford - Granville County (G-12145)

PA: Centaur Laboratories, Inc.
115 Virgilina Rd
Roxboro NC

(G-12120)
CERTAINTEED LLC
200 Certainteed Dr (27565-3597)
PHONE..................919 603-1971
Mark Hielman, *Mgr*
EMP: 250
SALES (corp-wide): 397.78MM **Privately Held**
Web: www.certainteed.com
SIC: 2952 Roofing felts, cements, or coatings, nec
HQ: Certainteed Llc
20 Moores Rd
Malvern PA 19355
610 893-5000

(G-12121)
CHAMPION BURLEY
Also Called: Champion & Company
1168 Us Highway 158 Ste A (27565-6248)
PHONE..................919 693-6285
Burley Champion, *Owner*
EMP: 5 **EST:** 1971
SALES (est): 235.24K **Privately Held**
SIC: 2429 Shingle and shingle mills

(G-12122)
COBLE PRINTING CO INC
120 Hillsboro St (27565-3212)
P.O. Box 667 (27565-0667)
PHONE..................919 693-4622
Kevin King, *Pr*
Laurie Stephens, *Sec*
Claudia King, *VP*
EMP: 4 **EST:** 1928
SQ FT: 3,000
SALES (est): 335.21K **Privately Held**
Web: www.cobleprinting.com
SIC: 2752 Offset printing

(G-12123)
CREATIVE TEXTILES INC
615 Hillsboro St (27565-3102)
P.O. Box 587 (27565-0587)
PHONE..................919 693-4427
Michael Newton, *Pr*
Thomas D Newton Junior, *VP*
EMP: 7 **EST:** 1984
SQ FT: 16,000
SALES (est): 812.79K **Privately Held**
Web: www.notiremarks.com
SIC: 2299 2392 Quilt fillings: curled hair, cotton waste, moss, hemp tow; Pillows, bed: made from purchased materials

(G-12124)
CROSCILL HOME LLC
200 Ne Outer Loop (27565-5014)
PHONE..................919 735-7111
EMP: 169
SALES (corp-wide): 1.17K **Privately Held**
Web: www.croscill.com
SIC: 3431 Bathroom fixtures, including sinks
HQ: Croscill Home Llc
1333 Broadway Fl 8
New York NY 10018

(G-12125)
CURVEMAKERS INC
115 Corporation Dr (27565-4000)
PHONE..................919 690-1121
EMP: 9
SALES (corp-wide): 2.15MM **Privately Held**
Web: www.curvemakers.com
SIC: 2431 Millwork
PA: Curvemakers, Inc.

703 W Johnson St
Raleigh NC 27603
919 821-5792

(G-12126)
DAN MORTON LOGGING
1671 Sunset Rd (27565-8213)
PHONE..................919 693-1898
Martha Morton, *Prin*
EMP: 5 **EST:** 2017
SALES (est): 66.84K **Privately Held**
SIC: 2411 Logging

(G-12127)
DILL AIR CONTROLS PRODUCTS LLC
1500 Williamsboro St (27565-3461)
P.O. Box 159 (27565-0159)
PHONE..................919 692-2300
Brian Rigney, *Genl Mgr*
Larry Schlesinger, *
Tony Monfrado, *
▲ **EMP:** 160 **EST:** 2005
SALES (est): 27.91MM **Privately Held**
Web: www.dillvalves.com
SIC: 3714 Tire valve cores

(G-12128)
DON KOONS INC
4662 Antioch Rd (27565-9424)
PHONE..................919 603-0948
Don Koons, *Prin*
EMP: 24 **EST:** 2008
SALES (est): 302.69K **Privately Held**
SIC: 2844 Perfumes, cosmetics and other toilet preparations

(G-12129)
GATE PRECAST COMPANY
3800 Oxford Loop (27565)
P.O. Box 1604 (27565-1604)
PHONE..................919 603-1633
EMP: 120
SALES (corp-wide): 708.16K **Privately Held**
Web: www.gateprecast.com
SIC: 3272 Concrete products, nec
HQ: Gate Precast Company
9540 San Jose Blvd
Jacksonville FL 32257
904 732-7668

(G-12130)
GRANVILLE EQUIPMENT LLC
4602a Watkins Rd (27565-7995)
PHONE..................919 693-1425
Don Watkins, *Prin*
▲ **EMP:** 12 **EST:** 2005
SALES (est): 1.56MM **Privately Held**
Web: www.granvilleequipment.com
SIC: 3523 Farm machinery and equipment

(G-12131)
GRANVILLE PALLET CO INC
3566 Us Highway 15 (27565-8519)
PHONE..................919 528-2347
J Glen Watkins, *Pr*
Angela Watkins, *
EMP: 68 **EST:** 1979
SQ FT: 25,000
SALES (est): 9.15MM **Privately Held**
Web: www.granvillepallet.com
SIC: 2448 Pallets, wood

(G-12132)
IDAHO WOOD INC
114 Southgate Dr (27565-3280)
PHONE..................208 263-9521
J T Vaughn, *Pr*
EMP: 10 **EST:** 2021

SALES (est): 998.65K **Privately Held**
SIC: 2431 3646 Woodwork, interior and ornamental, nec; Commercial lighting fixtures

(G-12133)
IDEAL FASTENER CORPORATION (PA)
Also Called: Ideal Accessories
603 W Industry Dr (27565-3593)
P.O. Box 548 (27565-0548)
PHONE..................919 693-3115
TOLL FREE: 800
Ralph Gut, *Pr*
Carol Critcher, *
◆ **EMP:** 150 **EST:** 1936
SQ FT: 105,000
SALES (est): 24.77MM
SALES (corp-wide): 24.77MM **Privately Held**
Web: www.idealfastener.com
SIC: 3965 5085 Buckles and buckle parts; Fasteners, industrial: nuts, screws, etc.

(G-12134)
JOEY MANIC INC
122 Wall St (27565-3255)
PHONE..................919 772-7756
EMP: 6 **EST:** 2007
SALES (est): 134.13K **Privately Held**
SIC: 2499 Wood products, nec

(G-12135)
LEDGER PUBLISHING COMPANY
Also Called: Oxford Public Ledger
200 W Spring St (27565-3247)
P.O. Box 643 (27565-0643)
PHONE..................919 693-2646
Ronnie Critcher, *Pr*
Charles Critcher, *VP*
EMP: 13 **EST:** 1932
SQ FT: 6,400
SALES (est): 458.76K **Privately Held**
Web: www.oxfordledger.com
SIC: 2711 Newspapers, publishing and printing

(G-12136)
NELSON LOGGING COMPANY INC
9557 Nc Highway 96 (27565-7647)
PHONE..................919 849-2547
James Ray Nelson, *Pr*
Connie Nelson, *Treas*
EMP: 22 **EST:** 2004
SALES (est): 2.32MM **Privately Held**
SIC: 2421 Sawmills and planing mills, general

(G-12137)
OLD MADE QUILTS
1156 Grassy Crk Virgilina (27565-8851)
PHONE..................919 692-1060
Beverly Vollaire Ferro, *Owner*
EMP: 5 **EST:** 2012
SALES (est): 228.29K **Privately Held**
Web: www.oldmadequilts.com
SIC: 3552 Fabric forming machinery and equipment

(G-12138)
OMNIA LLC
Also Called: Omnia Products
115 Certainteed Dr (27565-3587)
PHONE..................919 696-2193
EMP: 5 **EST:** 1994
SQ FT: 6,000
SALES (est): 811.44K **Privately Held**
Web: www.omnia-products.com

SIC: 5131 2295 Piece goods and other fabrics; Coated fabrics, not rubberized

(G-12139)
OMNIA PRODUCTS LLC
115 Certainteed Dr (27565-3587)
PHONE..................919 514-3977
John Dispennette, *Pr*
EMP: 4 **EST:** 2011
SQ FT: 6,000
SALES (est): 497.24K **Privately Held**
Web: www.omnia-products.com
SIC: 2824 Organic fibers, noncellulosic

(G-12140)
PERRY BROTHERS TIRE SVC INC
Also Called: Goodyear
606 Lewis St (27565-3524)
P.O. Box 869 (27565-0869)
PHONE..................919 693-2128
Harry Wilkins, *Mgr*
EMP: 10
SALES (corp-wide): 8.2MM **Privately Held**
Web: www.blackstire.com
SIC: 5531 7534 5731 5014 Automotive tires; Tire recapping; Television sets; Automobile tires and tubes
PA: Perry Brothers Tire Service, Inc.
610 Wicker St
Sanford NC 27330
919 775-7225

(G-12141)
PHILLIP RICE WOODWORKING LLC
113 Rayland St (27565-2544)
PHONE..................919 339-4543
Phillip Rice, *Prin*
EMP: 8 **EST:** 2004
SALES (est): 419K **Privately Held**
SIC: 2431 Millwork

(G-12142)
PLANTD INC
3220 Knotts Grove Rd (27565-7421)
PHONE..................434 906-3445
Nathan Silvernail, *CEO*
Huade Tan, *
EMP: 57 **EST:** 2021
SALES (est): 3.21MM **Privately Held**
SIC: 3999 Grasses, artificial and preserved

(G-12143)
PLASTIC INGENUITY INC
113 Certainteed Dr (27565-3587)
PHONE..................919 693-2009
Charles Polichnowski, *Mgr*
EMP: 83
SALES (corp-wide): 136.45MM **Privately Held**
Web: www.plasticingenuity.com
SIC: 3089 3081 Plastics containers, except foam; Packing materials, plastics sheet
PA: Plastic Ingenuity, Inc.
1017 Park St
Cross Plains WI 53528
608 798-3071

(G-12144)
PLUTO LABS LLC
1217 Lewis St (27565)
PHONE..................919 691-3550
EMP: 6 **EST:** 2020
SALES (est): 378.45K **Privately Held**
Web: www.plutolabs.us
SIC: 5159 3999

(G-12145)
PRECISION WELDING MNTNC
5612 Hebron Rd (27565-8256)
P.O. Box 965 (27565-0965)

Oxford - Granville County (G-12146)   GEOGRAPHIC SECTION

PHONE..................................336 504-5894
James Fields, *Prin*
EMP: 5 **EST:** 2016
SALES (est): 27.6K **Privately Held**
SIC: 7692 Welding repair

(G-12146)
PREMIER QUILTING CORPORATION
720 W Industry Dr (27565-3599)
PHONE..................................919 693-1151
Louis Lobraico, *Pr*
Louis J Lobraico, *
EMP: 18 **EST:** 1965
SQ FT: 52,000
SALES (est): 460.23K **Privately Held**
Web: www.premierquiltingcorp.com
SIC: 2221 Comforters and quilts, manmade fiber and silk

(G-12147)
PROMETALS INC
510 1/2 Hillsboro St (27565-3218)
P.O. Box 532 (27565-0532)
PHONE..................................919 693-8884
Tim Sobolak, *Pr*
Jean Sobolak, *Treas*
EMP: 7 **EST:** 1962
SALES (est): 456.06K **Privately Held**
Web: www.prometals.com
SIC: 3599 Machine shop, jobbing and repair

(G-12148)
REVLON INC
Also Called: Revlon Accounts Payable
1501 Williamsboro St (27565-3461)
P.O. Box 6114 (27565-2114)
PHONE..................................919 603-2782
EMP: 153
Web: www.revloncorp.com
SIC: 2844 Cosmetic preparations
HQ: Revlon, Inc.
55 Water St Fl 43
New York NY 10041

(G-12149)
REVLON INC
1501 Williamsboro St (27565-3461)
P.O. Box 6111 (27565-6111)
PHONE..................................919 603-2000
William Conover, *Brnch Mgr*
EMP: 50
Web: www.revloncorp.com
SIC: 2844 5122 Cosmetic preparations; Drugs, proprietaries, and sundries
HQ: Revlon, Inc.
55 Water St Fl 43
New York NY 10041

(G-12150)
REVLON CONSUMER PRODUCTS CORP
Also Called: Cnd
1501 Williamsboro St (27565-3461)
P.O. Box 6112 (27565-2112)
PHONE..................................919 603-2000
Art Curtis, *Brnch Mgr*
EMP: 100
Web: www.revlon.com
SIC: 2844 Cosmetic preparations
HQ: Revlon Consumer Products Llc
1 New York Plz
New York NY 10004

(G-12151)
RFR METAL FABRICATION INC
Also Called: Rfr
3204 Knotts Grove Rd (27565-7421)
P.O. Box 1627 (27565-1627)
PHONE..................................919 693-1354
Randall Williams, *Pr*
EMP: 58 **EST:** 1999

SQ FT: 20,000
SALES (est): 18.86MM **Privately Held**
Web: www.rfr-metalfab.com
SIC: 3444 3331 3469 Sheet metal specialties, not stamped; Bars (primary), copper; Electronic enclosures, stamped or pressed metal

(G-12152)
ROOSTEM HUNTING PRODUCTS LLC
3000 Roostem Way (27565-5230)
PHONE..................................919 693-3359
Jeffrey Lee Wade, *Prin*
EMP: 5 **EST:** 2014
SALES (est): 173.19K **Privately Held**
Web: www.roostemhuntingproducts.com
SIC: 3949 Sporting and athletic goods, nec

(G-12153)
SANTA FE NATURAL TOB CO INC
104 Enterprise Ct (27565-6179)
P.O. Box 3000 (27102-3000)
PHONE..................................919 690-1905
Michael R Ball, *Pr*
Alden H Smith, *Sec*
John R Whitener, *Treas*
EMP: 11 **EST:** 2016
SALES (est): 9.73MM **Privately Held**
Web: www.americanspirit.com
SIC: 2121 Cigars
HQ: Santa Fe Natural Tobacco Company Foundation
401 N Main St
Winston Salem NC 27101
800 332-5595

(G-12154)
SANTA FE NTURAL TOB FOUNDATION
3220 Knotts Grove Rd (27565-7421)
P.O. Box 129 (27565-0129)
PHONE..................................919 690-0880
EMP: 140
SIC: 2111 Cigarettes
HQ: Santa Fe Natural Tobacco Company Foundation
401 N Main St
Winston Salem NC 27101
800 332-5595

(G-12155)
SHALAG US INC
Also Called: Shalag Nonwovents
917 Se Industry Dr (27565)
P.O. Box 225 (27565-0225)
PHONE..................................919 690-0250
▲ **EMP:** 95 **EST:** 2009
SQ FT: 12,000
SALES (est): 45.09MM **Privately Held**
Web: www.shalag.com
SIC: 2297 Nonwoven fabrics
HQ: Shalag Industries Ltd
Kibbutz
Shamir 12135

(G-12156)
SOUTHERN DATA SYSTEMS INC
7758 Nc Highway 96 (27565-8841)
P.O. Box 65 (23962-0065)
PHONE..................................919 781-7603
Robert Drew, *Pr*
Michelle Sparrow, *VP*
EMP: 10 **EST:** 1979
SQ FT: 5,500
SALES (est): 668.26K **Privately Held**
SIC: 7379 3577 Computer related consulting services; Computer peripheral equipment, nec

(G-12157)
SOUTHERN STATES COOP INC
Also Called: S S C Oxford Svc
607 Hillsboro St (27565-3102)
PHONE..................................919 693-6136
Steve Timberlake, *Mgr*
EMP: 31
SALES (corp-wide): 1.71B **Privately Held**
Web: www.southernstates.com
SIC: 2048 5999 Prepared feeds, nec; Farm equipment and supplies
PA: Southern States Cooperative, Incorporated
6606 W Broad St Ste B
Richmond VA 23230
804 281-1000

(G-12158)
SOUTHERN WOODCRAFT DESIGN LLC
114 Southgate Dr (27565-3280)
PHONE..................................919 693-8995
EMP: 7 **EST:** 2005
SALES (est): 745.32K **Privately Held**
Web: www.southernwoodcraft.net
SIC: 2431 Millwork

(G-12159)
TED WHEELER
Also Called: Ted's Service Company
2651 Hwy 158 (27565-8478)
P.O. Box 1457 (27302-1457)
PHONE..................................252 438-0820
Ted Wheeler, *Owner*
EMP: 4 **EST:** 2005
SALES (est): 201.41K **Privately Held**
SIC: 2099 Food preparations, nec

(G-12160)
TRUE MACHINE LLC
6575 Huntsboro Rd (27565-7548)
P.O. Box 1607 (27565-1607)
PHONE..................................919 270-2552
Sylvester Moltisanti, *Admn*
EMP: 6 **EST:** 2015
SALES (est): 223.03K **Privately Held**
Web: www.truemachineautomation.com
SIC: 3599 Machine shop, jobbing and repair

(G-12161)
WINSTONS WOODWORKS
600 Sunset Ave (27565-2842)
PHONE..................................919 693-4120
EMP: 5 **EST:** 1985
SALES (est): 247.43K **Privately Held**
Web: www.winstonswoodworks.com
SIC: 2434 Wood kitchen cabinets

Pantego
Beaufort County

(G-12162)
COASTAL CAROLINA GIN LLC
Also Called: Coastal Carolina Gin
4851 Terra Ceia Rd (27860-9315)
PHONE..................................252 943-6990
EMP: 11 **EST:** 1996
SQ FT: 4,000
SALES (est): 912.73K **Privately Held**
Web: www.coastalcarolinagin.com
SIC: 0724 3559 Cotton ginning; Cotton ginning machinery

(G-12163)
EAST CRLINA OLSEED PRCSSORS LL
Also Called: Perdue Ecop Crushing
2015 Nc Highway 45 N (27860-9110)
PHONE..................................252 935-5553

EMP: 80 **EST:** 2011
SALES (est): 887.03K
SALES (corp-wide): 1.24B **Privately Held**
SIC: 5159 3556 Oil nuts, kernels, seeds; Oilseed crushing and extracting machinery
HQ: Perdue Agribusiness Llc
31149 Old Ocean City Rd
Salisbury MD 21804

(G-12164)
IBX LUMBER LLC
405 Mainstem Rd (27860-9214)
PHONE..................................252 935-4050
Leland Hershey, *Managing Member*
EMP: 15 **EST:** 2016
SALES (est): 1.1MM **Privately Held**
SIC: 2421 Sawmills and planing mills, general

(G-12165)
J&R COHOON LOGGING & TIDEWATER
25912 Us Highway 264 E (27860-9404)
P.O. Box 429 (27860-0429)
PHONE..................................252 943-6300
Barbara Cahoon, *Owner*
EMP: 10 **EST:** 2005
SALES (est): 562.04K **Privately Held**
SIC: 2411 Logging camps and contractors

(G-12166)
LIGHTWAVE FABRICATION MCH LLC
333 Windley Canal Rd (27860-9485)
PHONE..................................252 927-1591
EMP: 5 **EST:** 2019
SALES (est): 103.91K **Privately Held**
SIC: 3599 Machine shop, jobbing and repair

(G-12167)
MARTIN LUMBER & MULCH LLC
301 Mainstem Rd (27860-9212)
PHONE..................................252 935-5294
Malvrin Martin, *Managing Member*
EMP: 14 **EST:** 1996
SALES (est): 1.36MM **Privately Held**
Web: www.martinlumberllc.com
SIC: 5031 2499 Lumber: rough, dressed, and finished; Mulch or sawdust products, wood

(G-12168)
MENDOZA LOGGING INC
115 Loop Road Number 1 (27860-9646)
PHONE..................................252 935-5560
EMP: 6 **EST:** 2017
SALES (est): 81.72K **Privately Held**
SIC: 2411 Logging

(G-12169)
NATHAN BEILER
Also Called: Pungo River Timber Company
2685 Nc Highway 45 N (27860-9108)
PHONE..................................252 935-5141
Nathan Beiler, *Pt*
Tom Beiler, *Pt*
Brenda Beiler, *Sec*
EMP: 6 **EST:** 1992
SALES (est): 349.16K **Privately Held**
SIC: 2411 Logging

(G-12170)
PRECISION PALLET LLC
405 Mainstem Rd (27860-9214)
PHONE..................................252 935-5355
EMP: 11 **EST:** 2005
SALES (est): 2.25MM **Privately Held**
Web: www.precisionpallet.net
SIC: 2448 Pallets, wood

Parkton
Robeson County

(G-12171)
READERS PUBLISHING LLC
307 N Green St (28371-9174)
P.O. Box 433 (28371-0433)
PHONE..............................910 728-2911
Douglas Smith, *Owner*
EMP: 4 **EST:** 2020
SALES (est): 83.46K **Privately Held**
SIC: 2741 Miscellaneous publishing

Paw Creek
Mecklenburg County

(G-12172)
LETS TALK SOME SHIT
7400 Old Mount Holly Rd (28130-2001)
PHONE..............................704 264-6212
Orlando Parker, *CEO*
EMP: 4 **EST:** 2020
SALES (est): 261.67K **Privately Held**
SIC: 3663 Television broadcasting and communications equipment

Peachland
Anson County

(G-12173)
DAVIS MECHANICAL INC
4368 Nc 218 (28133-9179)
P.O. Box 488 (28103-0488)
PHONE..............................704 272-9366
Robert Delane Davis, *Pr*
Robert Delane Davis Ii, *VP*
EMP: 17 **EST:** 2002
SALES (est): 4.48MM **Privately Held**
SIC: 1623 2431 Water, sewer, and utility lines ; Millwork

(G-12174)
PEACHLAND DSIGN FBRICATION LLC
3129 Deep Springs Church Rd (28133-9056)
PHONE..............................704 272-9296
Dona F Black, *CEO*
Tom Black, *VP*
EMP: 13 **EST:** 2016
SALES (est): 1.73MM **Privately Held**
Web: www.peachlanddesignandfabrication.com
SIC: 3441 Fabricated structural metal

(G-12175)
QUIKRETE COMPANIES LLC
Also Called: Quikrete Peachland
13471 Us Highway 74 W (28133-9524)
P.O. Box 99 (28133-0099)
PHONE..............................704 272-7677
EMP: 37
Web: www.quikrete.com
SIC: 3272 3273 Concrete products, nec; Ready-mixed concrete
HQ: The Quikrete Companies Llc
   5 Concourse Pkwy Ste 1900
   Atlanta GA 30328
   404 634-9100

(G-12176)
SOUTHERN PDMONT PPING FBRCTION
2798 Lower White Store Rd (28133-8227)
P.O. Box 100 (28133-0100)
PHONE..............................704 272-7936
Katrenia M Davis, *Pr*
Kristina Forbes, *VP*
EMP: 13 **EST:** 1983
SQ FT: 3,500
SALES (est): 2.23MM **Privately Held**
Web: www.southernpiedmontpiping.com
SIC: 1711 3444 Process piping contractor; Sheet metalwork

Pelham
Caswell County

(G-12177)
NORAG TECHNOLOGY LLC (PA)
1214 Nc Highway 700 (27311-8913)
PHONE..............................336 316-0417
Floyd Guidry, *CEO*
Eresterine Guidiy, *CFO*
▼ **EMP:** 5 **EST:** 2007
SALES (est): 1.07MM **Privately Held**
Web: www.noragtech.com
SIC: 2869 Industrial organic chemicals, nec

(G-12178)
SOUTHSIDE MATERIALS LLC
1524 Rock Quarry Rd (27311-8719)
PHONE..............................336 388-5613
EMP: 6 **EST:** 2019
SALES (est): 918.23K **Privately Held**
SIC: 1442 Construction sand and gravel

(G-12179)
VERNONS MOBILE WELDING LLC
5566 Park Springs Rd (27311-8836)
PHONE..............................336 388-0415
EMP: 4 **EST:** 2017
SALES (est): 29.69K **Privately Held**
SIC: 7692 Welding repair

Pembroke
Robeson County

(G-12180)
ARROW EDUCATIONAL PRODUCTS INC
208 Union Chapel Rd 101 (28372-7419)
P.O. Box 1287 (28372-1287)
PHONE..............................910 521-0840
Riginald Oxendine, *Pr*
Reginald Oxendine Junior, *CEO*
EMP: 5 **EST:** 1988
SQ FT: 1,000
SALES (est): 426.33K **Privately Held**
SIC: 7372 Prepackaged software

(G-12181)
COLLEGE SUN DO
701 W 3rd St (28372-7979)
P.O. Box 1575 (28372-1575)
PHONE..............................910 521-9189
Edsel Lowry, *Owner*
Kelby Lowry, *Owner*
EMP: 4 **EST:** 1981
SQ FT: 2,000
SALES (est): 475.79K **Privately Held**
SIC: 5541 7534 Filling stations, gasoline; Tire retreading and repair shops

(G-12182)
DESIGNER WOODWORK
1616 Hiawatha Rd (28372)
P.O. Box 2663 (28372-2663)
PHONE..............................910 521-1252
Elwood Deese, *Owner*
EMP: 6 **EST:** 1982
SQ FT: 5,000
SALES (est): 393.67K **Privately Held**
SIC: 2434 Vanities, bathroom: wood

(G-12183)
SIMMIE BULLARD
Also Called: Simmie Bullard Construction
787 Goins Rd (28372-8341)
PHONE..............................910 600-3191
Simmie Bullard, *Owner*
EMP: 7 **EST:** 2020
SALES (est): 167.53K **Privately Held**
SIC: 1389 Construction, repair, and dismantling services

(G-12184)
STEVEN-ROBERT ORIGINALS LLC
Also Called: Steven-Robert Original Dessert
701 S Jones St (28372-9696)
PHONE..............................910 521-0199
EMP: 150
Web: www.originaldesserts.com
SIC: 2052 Cookies and crackers
PA: Steven-Robert Originals, Llc
   2780 Tower Rd
   Aurora CO 80011

Pendleton
Northampton County

(G-12185)
COMMERCIAL READY MIX PDTS INC
1231 Vougemills Rd (27862)
P.O. Box 189 (27986-0189)
PHONE..............................252 585-1777
Laverne Howell, *Brnch Mgr*
EMP: 13
SALES (corp-wide): 52.99MM **Privately Held**
Web: www.crmpinc.com
SIC: 3273 Ready-mixed concrete
PA: Commercial Ready Mix Products, Inc.
   115 Hwy 158 W
   Winton NC 27986
   252 358-5461

Penrose
Transylvania County

(G-12186)
MERRILL RESOURCES INC
99 Cascade Lake Rd (28766-8716)
PHONE..............................828 877-4450
Dustin Merrill, *Pr*
EMP: 14 **EST:** 1946
SQ FT: 2,000
SALES (est): 894.36K **Privately Held**
Web: www.merrillresources.com
SIC: 5251 1781 3561 1623 Pumps and pumping equipment; Water well drilling; Pumps and pumping equipment; Pumping station construction

Pfafftown
Forsyth County

(G-12187)
CLASSIC PACKAGING COMPANY
5570 Bethania Rd (27040-9596)
P.O. Box 310 (27010-0310)
PHONE..............................336 922-4224
Geraldine Pilla, *CEO*
Joseph Pilla, *
▲ **EMP:** 80 **EST:** 1990
SQ FT: 41,000
SALES (est): 22.28MM **Privately Held**
Web: www.classicpackaging.com
SIC: 2673 3086 Bags: plastic, laminated, and coated; Packaging and shipping materials, foamed plastics

(G-12188)
NORTHWEST COATINGS SYSTEMS INC
5640 Clinedale Ct (27040-9308)
PHONE..............................336 924-1459
William Miller, *Pr*
EMP: 5 **EST:** 1980
SALES (est): 284.31K **Privately Held**
SIC: 2851 Paints and allied products

(G-12189)
OBERLE GROUP
4721 Sherborne Dr (27040-8731)
PHONE..............................336 399-6833
Valerie Oberle, *Owner*
EMP: 5 **EST:** 1997
SALES (est): 127.7K **Privately Held**
Web: www.oberlegroup.com
SIC: 3651 8742 8299 Speaker monitors; Management consulting services; Schools and educational services, nec

(G-12190)
SPEVCO INC
8118 Reynolda Rd (27040-9661)
P.O. Box 11845 (27116-1845)
PHONE..............................336 924-8100
Frank M Tharpe Junior, *CEO*
Fran Weller, *
Frank M Tharpe Iii, *Pr*
EMP: 65 **EST:** 1979
SQ FT: 40,000
SALES (est): 14.99MM **Privately Held**
Web: www.spevco.com
SIC: 3711 Trucks, pickup, assembly of

Pikeville
Wayne County

(G-12191)
BASF
703 Nor Am Rd (27863-8420)
PHONE..............................919 731-1700
EMP: 8 **EST:** 2019
SALES (est): 372.03K **Privately Held**
SIC: 2869 Industrial organic chemicals, nec

(G-12192)
BENTON & SONS FABRICATION INC
1921 N Nc 581 Hwy (27863-8756)
PHONE..............................919 734-1700
Binford Benton, *Pr*
Binford Benton Junior, *VP*
Cheryl Benton, *
Bruce Benton, *
Donna Myers, *
EMP: 38 **EST:** 1981
SQ FT: 70,000
SALES (est): 7.46MM **Privately Held**
Web: www.bentonsfabrication.com
SIC: 3599 3444 Machine shop, jobbing and repair; Sheet metalwork

(G-12193)
PAULAS PRETTY THINGS INC
770 Vail Rd (27863-9446)
PHONE..............................919 656-1163
Paula Fleming, *Pr*
EMP: 7 **EST:** 2019
SALES (est): 64.19K **Privately Held**
SIC: 3161 Clothing and apparel carrying cases

Pikeville - Wayne County (G-12194)

(G-12194)
STEEL SMART INCORPORATED
1042 Airport Rd Ne (27863-9130)
PHONE.....................919 736-0681
Brandon Hall, *Pr*
April Hall, *Sec*
Gerald Hall, *VP*
Linda Hall, *Treas*
EMP: 20 **EST:** 1962
SQ FT: 5,000
SALES (est): 3MM **Privately Held**
Web: www.steelsmartinc.com
SIC: 3446 3449 Architectural metalwork; Miscellaneous metalwork

(G-12195)
WHEELER INDUSTRIES INC
Also Called: Wheeler Industries
4573 Us Highway 117 N (27863-9016)
P.O. Box 1521 (27533-1521)
PHONE.....................919 736-4256
Horace Gillett, *Pr*
EMP: 10 **EST:** 1992
SQ FT: 17,000
SALES (est): 469.44K **Privately Held**
Web: www.wheeler-industries.com
SIC: 2448 4214 Pallets, wood; Local trucking with storage

Pilot Mountain
Surry County

(G-12196)
BROWN & CHURCH NECK WEAR CO
118 Mary Moore Ln (27041-8692)
PHONE.....................336 368-5502
Larry Marshall, *COO*
▲ **EMP:** 45 **EST:** 1980
SQ FT: 7,500
SALES (est): 4.53MM
SALES (corp-wide): 421.83MM **Privately Held**
Web: www.brownandchurch.com
SIC: 2323 Men's and boy's neckwear
PA: Tom James Company
263 Seaboard Ln
Franklin TN 37067
615 771-1122

(G-12197)
IMAGE SOLUTIONS
332b Shellybrook Dr (27041-7572)
PHONE.....................336 769-8403
EMP: 4 **EST:** 2019
SALES (est): 85.05K **Privately Held**
Web: www.gotdesigned.com
SIC: 2752 Offset printing

(G-12198)
JAMN TEES
244 Ararat Longhill Rd (27041-8165)
PHONE.....................336 444-4327
Jimmy Stewart, *Mgr*
EMP: 4 **EST:** 2013
SALES (est): 246.87K **Privately Held**
Web: www.jamntees.com
SIC: 2759 Screen printing

(G-12199)
JOLO WINERY & VINEYARDS LLC
219 Jolo Winery Ln (27041-8717)
PHONE.....................954 816-5649
Kristen Ray, *Prin*
EMP: 14 **EST:** 2012
SALES (est): 864.15K **Privately Held**
Web: www.jolovineyards.com
SIC: 2084 Wines

(G-12200)
PROTECHNOLOGIES INC
Also Called: Pti
331 Shellybrook Dr (27041-7572)
P.O. Box 950 (27041-0950)
PHONE.....................336 368-1375
Ian Edmonds, *CEO*
Raymond H Roc, *Pr*
Iris Stonestreet, *
Julie Sanson Rees, *
▲ **EMP:** 31 **EST:** 1985
SQ FT: 20,000
SALES (est): 7.71MM
SALES (corp-wide): 86.13MM **Privately Held**
Web: www.protechnologies.com
SIC: 3679 Harness assemblies, for electronic use: wire or cable
PA: Universal Power Group, Inc.
488 S Royal Ln
Coppell TX 75019
469 892-1122

(G-12201)
RACK WORKS INC
207 Premier Ln (27041-9108)
PHONE.....................336 368-1302
Michael Francis, *Pr*
Sandra Francis, *
EMP: 35 **EST:** 1990
SQ FT: 3,500
SALES (est): 4.36MM **Privately Held**
Web: www.rackworksinc.com
SIC: 3496 3315 5021 3443 Miscellaneous fabricated wire products; Baskets, steel wire; Racks; Fabricated plate work (boiler shop)

(G-12202)
SPORTS SOLUTIONS INC
Also Called: No Sweat Specialties
614 E Main St (27041-8517)
P.O. Box 596 (27041-0596)
PHONE.....................336 368-1100
Charles Badgett, *Pr*
EMP: 18 **EST:** 2001
SALES (est): 2.33MM **Privately Held**
Web: www.nosweatspecialties.com
SIC: 2252 Socks

(G-12203)
TWIN CARPORTS LLC (PA)
202 Hamlin Dr (27041-8707)
PHONE.....................866 486-3924
Nain Rodriguez-armenta, *Pr*
EMP: 6 **EST:** 2017
SALES (est): 1.12MM
SALES (corp-wide): 1.12MM **Privately Held**
Web: www.twincarports.com
SIC: 3448 Prefabricated metal buildings and components

(G-12204)
VEGA CONSTRUCTION COMPANY INC
137 W Main St Unit 8 (27041-9304)
P.O. Box 1901 (27030-6901)
PHONE.....................336 756-3477
Carlos Vega, *CEO*
Socorro Vega, *
EMP: 28 **EST:** 2018
SALES (est): 4.82MM **Privately Held**
SIC: 3241 1741 Masonry cement; Masonry and other stonework

(G-12205)
WELLINGTON LEISURE PRODUCTS
309 Nelson St (27041-8618)
PHONE.....................336 342-4701
Jay Cecil, *Maint Mgr*
EMP: 6 **EST:** 2018
SALES (est): 98.66K **Privately Held**
SIC: 2299 Textile goods, nec

Pine Hall
Stokes County

(G-12206)
WIELAND COPPER PRODUCTS LLC
3990 Us 311 Hwy N (27042-8166)
P.O. Box 160 (27042-0160)
PHONE.....................336 445-4500
▲ **EMP:** 470 **EST:** 1988
SQ FT: 560,000
SALES (est): 110.38MM **Privately Held**
Web: www.wieland.com
SIC: 3351 Bands, copper and copper alloy
HQ: Wieland-Werke Ag
Graf-Arco-Str. 36
Ulm BW 89079
7319440

Pine Level
Johnston County

(G-12207)
CUSTOM ASSEMBLIES INC
330 E Main St (27568-9210)
P.O. Box 177 (27568-0177)
PHONE.....................919 202-4533
EMP: 43 **EST:** 1996
SQ FT: 18,500
SALES (est): 5.51MM **Privately Held**
Web: www.customassemblies.com
SIC: 3069 3841 Medical and laboratory rubber sundries and related products; Surgical and medical instruments

(G-12208)
CUSTOM MEDICAL SPECIALTIES INC
330 E Main St (27568-9210)
P.O. Box 177 (27568-0177)
PHONE.....................919 202-8462
Jack Peacock, *CEO*
Jim Perkins, *Pr*
▼ **EMP:** 10 **EST:** 1999
SALES (est): 252.88K **Privately Held**
Web: www.custommedicalspecialties.com
SIC: 3842 Surgical appliances and supplies

(G-12209)
GENERAL METALS INC
Also Called: G M I
328 E Main St (27568-9210)
P.O. Box 99 (27568-0099)
PHONE.....................919 202-0100
EMP: 25 **EST:** 1994
SQ FT: 25,000
SALES (est): 8.82MM **Privately Held**
Web: www.generalmetalsllc.com
SIC: 3444 Sheet metalwork

(G-12210)
HINNANT FARMS VINEYARD LLC
826 Pine Level Micro Road (27568)
P.O. Box 189 (27568-0189)
PHONE.....................919 965-3350
EMP: 18 **EST:** 1990
SALES (est): 883.17K **Privately Held**
Web: www.hinnantvineyards.com
SIC: 0172 2084 Grapes; Brandy

(G-12211)
JABB OF CAROLINAS INC
302 E Brown St (27568-9062)
P.O. Box 310 (27568-0310)
PHONE.....................919 965-9007
EMP: 6 **EST:** 1994
SQ FT: 6,000
SALES (est): 712.62K **Privately Held**
Web: www.jabbofthecarolinas.com
SIC: 2879 Insecticides, agricultural or household

(G-12212)
NEW INNOVATIVE PRODUCTS INC
Also Called: Starlight Cases
2180 Hyw 70 E (27568)
PHONE.....................919 631-6759
Steve L Ramos Senior, *Pr*
Betty Ramos, *Pr*
Steve L Ramos, *VP*
▲ **EMP:** 8 **EST:** 1994
SQ FT: 10,000
SALES (est): 932.9K **Privately Held**
Web: www.starlightcases.com
SIC: 3669 3089 Emergency alarms; Plastics containers, except foam

Pinebluff
Moore County

(G-12213)
BALLISTIC RECOVERY SYSTEMS INC (PA)
Also Called: Brs Aerospace
41383 Us 1 Hwy (28373-8330)
PHONE.....................651 457-7491
Fernando De Caralt, *CEO*
Robert L Nelson, *Sec*
▲ **EMP:** 30 **EST:** 1980
SALES (est): 26.83MM
SALES (corp-wide): 26.83MM **Publicly Held**
Web: www.brsaerospace.com
SIC: 3728 2399 Aircraft parts and equipment, nec; Parachutes

(G-12214)
BLUE MAIDEN DEFENSE
165 Laurel Oak Ln (28373-8020)
PHONE.....................678 292-8342
Christy Wentzell, *Prin*
EMP: 4 **EST:** 2018
SALES (est): 220.96K **Privately Held**
SIC: 3812 Defense systems and equipment

(G-12215)
MANNING FABRICS INC
42028 Us 1 Hwy (28373)
PHONE.....................910 295-1970
Ned Manning, *Mgr*
EMP: 33
SALES (corp-wide): 6.69MM **Privately Held**
Web: www.manningcorporation.com
SIC: 2211 Broadwoven fabric mills, cotton
PA: Manning Fabrics, Inc.
650a Page St
Pinehurst NC 28374
910 295-1970

(G-12216)
PINS AND NEEDLES
110 N Ridgecrest St (28373-8190)
PHONE.....................910 639-9662
Casidy S Taylor, *Owner*
EMP: 5 **EST:** 2016
SALES (est): 64.13K **Privately Held**
SIC: 3452 Pins

Pinehurst
Moore County

(G-12217)
CAROLINA PERFUMER INC (PA)
102 Berwick Ct (28374-8142)
PHONE..................910 295-5600
Janet Coffman, *Pr*
Ronald L Coffman, *Sec*
EMP: 9 **EST:** 1981
SQ FT: 6,000
SALES (est): 1.87MM
SALES (corp-wide): 1.87MM **Privately Held**
SIC: 3999 2844 5947 Potpourri; Perfumes and colognes; Gift shop

(G-12218)
CAROLINA VINYL PRINTING
14 Troon Dr (28374-6710)
PHONE..................910 603-3036
Yolanda Mccarty, *Prin*
EMP: 4 **EST:** 2018
SALES (est): 128.24K **Privately Held**
SIC: 2752 Commercial printing, lithographic

(G-12219)
CUSTOM MARBLE CORPORATION (PA)
150 Safford Dr (28374-8221)
PHONE..................910 215-0679
Anthony J Leo Junior, *Pr*
Christine Leo, *Sec*
EMP: 9 **EST:** 1974
SQ FT: 25,000
SALES (est): 783.88K
SALES (corp-wide): 783.88K **Privately Held**
SIC: 3261 5031 3431 3281 Bathroom accessories/fittings, vitreous china or earthenware; Lumber, plywood, and millwork; Metal sanitary ware; Cut stone and stone products

(G-12220)
DISCOVERY MAP
P.O. Box 1834 (28370-1834)
PHONE..................910 315-3145
EMP: 4
SALES (est): 76.29K **Privately Held**
Web: www.discoverymap.com
SIC: 2741 Miscellaneous publishing

(G-12221)
EATON CORPORATION
Also Called: Golf Pride
15 Centennial Blvd (28374-0400)
P.O. Box 58 (28388-0058)
PHONE..................910 695-2900
James Ledford, *Mgr*
EMP: 107
Web: www.golfpride.com
SIC: 3069 3568 Grips or handles, rubber; Power transmission equipment, nec
HQ: Eaton Corporation
   1000 Eaton Blvd
   Cleveland OH 44122
   440 523-5000

(G-12222)
GHOST HAWK INTEL LLC
1 Troy Ct (28374-8413)
PHONE..................910 235-0323
Thomas Beers, *Owner*
EMP: 5 **EST:** 2017
SALES (est): 99.04K **Privately Held**
SIC: 3674 Microprocessors

(G-12223)
GILLEY PRINTERS INC
Also Called: Village Printers
22 Rattlesnake Trl (28374-7612)
P.O. Box 2139 (28370-2139)
PHONE..................910 295-6317
Kim Gilley, *Pr*
Tony Gilley, *VP*
EMP: 5 **EST:** 1951
SALES (est): 491.42K **Privately Held**
Web: www.villageprinters.com
SIC: 2752 Offset printing

(G-12224)
GOLFSTAR TECHNOLOGY LLC
75 Lakewood Dr (28374-8292)
PHONE..................910 420-3122
Graham Ballingall, *CEO*
EMP: 6 **EST:** 2010
SALES (est): 321.16K **Privately Held**
SIC: 5091 3663 Golf equipment; Global positioning systems (GPS) equipment

(G-12225)
GREEN GATE OLIVE OILS INC
105 Cherokee Rd Ste 1b (28374-0082)
PHONE..................910 986-0880
Keith Mcdaniel, *Pr*
EMP: 7 **EST:** 2011
SALES (est): 243.2K **Privately Held**
Web: www.thepinehurstoliveoilco.com
SIC: 2079 Olive oil

(G-12226)
KS PRECIOUS METALS LLC
P.O. Box 3686 (28374-3686)
PHONE..................910 687-0244
EMP: 5 **EST:** 2008
SALES (est): 167.83K **Privately Held**
Web: www.pinehurstcoins.com
SIC: 3339 Precious metals

(G-12227)
M & P POLYMERS INC
135 Applecross Rd (28374-8521)
P.O. Box 2229 (28388-2229)
PHONE..................910 246-6585
Maurice V Smith, *Pr*
◆ **EMP:** 8 **EST:** 2008
SALES (est): 253.11K **Privately Held**
SIC: 2822 Ethylene-propylene rubbers, EPDM polymers

(G-12228)
MANNING FABRICS INC (PA)
Also Called: Manning and Co.
650a Page St (28374)
P.O. Box 6300 (28374-6300)
PHONE..................910 295-1970
Edward N Manning Senior, *Ch Bd*
Edward N Manning Junior, *Pr*
EMP: 7 **EST:** 1967
SQ FT: 3,000
SALES (est): 6.69MM
SALES (corp-wide): 6.69MM **Privately Held**
Web: www.manningcorporation.com
SIC: 2211 3083 3089 2891 Broadwoven fabric mills, cotton; Laminated plastics plate and sheet; Extruded finished plastics products, nec; Adhesives and sealants

(G-12229)
MCDONALDS
Also Called: McDonald's
260 Ivey Ln (28374-9818)
PHONE..................910 295-1112
EMP: 14 **EST:** 2020
SALES (est): 57.19K **Privately Held**
Web: www.mcdonalds.com

SIC: 5813 5812 5499 2038 Drinking places; Eating places; Miscellaneous food stores; Frozen specialties, nec

(G-12230)
PAPER PERFECTOR LLC
125 Brookfield Dr (28374-8783)
PHONE..................910 695-1092
EMP: 5 **EST:** 2018
SALES (est): 82.48K **Privately Held**
SIC: 2621 Paper mills

(G-12231)
PRINT PROFESSIONALS
280 Oakmont Cir (28374-8343)
PHONE..................607 279-3335
Edward Emnett, *Pr*
EMP: 5 **EST:** 2010
SALES (est): 175.15K **Privately Held**
SIC: 2752 Offset printing

(G-12232)
PROTECH METALS LLC
3619 Murdocksville Rd (28374)
P.O. Box 1925 (28370-1925)
PHONE..................910 295-6905
Wiliiam Hall, *Mng Pt*
EMP: 20 **EST:** 2011
SALES (est): 1.43MM **Privately Held**
Web: www.protechmetals.net
SIC: 3599 3479 3449 3446 Machine and other job shop work; Metal coating and allied services; Miscellaneous metalwork; Architectural metalwork

(G-12233)
REFINERY 56 LLC
8 Apawamis Rd (28374-9049)
PHONE..................910 215-0596
David Ennis, *Prin*
EMP: 4 **EST:** 2015
SALES (est): 155.82K **Privately Held**
SIC: 1311 Crude petroleum and natural gas

(G-12234)
RILEY POWER GROUP LLC
Also Called: Riley Power Group
100 Magnolia Rd Ste 2207 (28374-9820)
PHONE..................910 420-6999
David Riley, *CEO*
Bill Felt, *
EMP: 130 **EST:** 2013
SALES (est): 12.11MM **Privately Held**
Web: www.rileypowergroup.com
SIC: 1711 3731 3599 3317 Boiler maintenance contractor; Shipbuilding and repairing; Machine shop, jobbing and repair ; Welded pipe and tubes

(G-12235)
ROOT SPRING SCRAPER CO
1 York Pl (28374-8512)
PHONE..................269 382-2025
Frederick Root Junior, *Pr*
Rodney Root, *
William Root, *
▼ **EMP:** 18 **EST:** 1891
SALES (est): 432.67K **Privately Held**
Web: www.rootsnowplows.com
SIC: 3531 3524 Snow plow attachments; Lawn and garden equipment

(G-12236)
SHADES AND SHELVES LLC
105 Spring Lake Dr (28374-7002)
PHONE..................910 603-4906
Amy P Killam, *Prin*
EMP: 7 **EST:** 2007
SALES (est): 126.84K **Privately Held**

SIC: 2673 Wardrobe bags (closet accessories): from purchased materials

(G-12237)
SHUTTERBUG GRAFIX & SIGNS
300 Kelly Rd Ste B3 (28374-8276)
PHONE..................910 315-1556
EMP: 4 **EST:** 2014
SALES (est): 83.04K **Privately Held**
Web: www.shutterbuggrafixnc.com
SIC: 3993 Signs and advertising specialties

(G-12238)
TERIDA LLC
40 Augusta National Dr (28374-7140)
P.O. Box 5897 (28374-5897)
PHONE..................910 693-1633
Teri Prince, *Pr*
EMP: 10 **EST:** 2003
SALES (est): 754.09K **Privately Held**
Web: www.terida.com
SIC: 7379 7371 7372 Online services technology consultants; Computer software systems analysis and design, custom; Application computer software

Pinetops
Edgecombe County

(G-12239)
ABB INC
Also Called: A B B Power Technolgies
3022 Nc 43 N (27864-9575)
P.O. Box 22114 (27420)
PHONE..................252 827-2121
Tobias Lynch, *Mgr*
EMP: 1007
Web: new.abb.com
SIC: 5063 3613 Motor controls, starters and relays: electric; Switchgear and switchboard apparatus
HQ: Abb Inc.
   305 Gregson Dr
   Cary NC 27511

(G-12240)
ABB INC
Us Hwy 43 (27864)
P.O. Box 687 (27864-0687)
PHONE..................252 827-2121
Julius Wooten, *Brnch Mgr*
EMP: 38
Web: new.abb.com
SIC: 3612 Transformers, except electric
HQ: Abb Inc.
   305 Gregson Dr
   Cary NC 27511

(G-12241)
C B BUNTING & SONS INC
266 Bunting Ln (27864-9398)
PHONE..................252 813-4237
EMP: 5 **EST:** 2018
SALES (est): 99.09K **Privately Held**
SIC: 2011 Meat packing plants

(G-12242)
HARRIS-ROBINETTE INC
412 Harris Acre Ln (27864-7026)
P.O. Box 158 (27864-0158)
PHONE..................252 813-5794
Harris Robinette, *Pr*
EMP: 7 **EST:** 2012
SALES (est): 368.12K **Privately Held**
Web: www.harrisrobinette.com
SIC: 2013 Prepared beef products, from purchased beef

Pinetown
Beaufort County

(G-12243)
ACRE STATION MEAT FARM INC
Also Called: Meat Farm
17076 Nc Highway 32 N (27865-9502)
PHONE..................................252 927-3700
- Ronald Huettmann, *Pr*
- Richard Huettmann, *VP*
- Nancy Huettmann, *Treas*
EMP: 17 **EST:** 1977
SQ FT: 2,000
SALES (est): 875.5K **Privately Held**
Web: www.acrestationmeatfarm.com
SIC: 5421 2011 Meat markets, including freezer provisioniers; Meat packing plants

(G-12244)
C J MANUFACTURING INC
2331 Pocosin Rd (27865-9429)
PHONE..................................252 927-4913
Charlie Oden Alligood, *Admn*
EMP: 4 **EST:** 2016
SALES (est): 96.19K **Privately Held**
SIC: 3999 Manufacturing industries, nec

(G-12245)
CAHOON BROTHERS LOGGING LLC
6073 Free Union Church Rd (27865-9533)
PHONE..................................252 943-9901
Ronnie Cahoon, *Managing Member*
Ronnie W Cahoon, *Managing Member*
EMP: 11 **EST:** 2003
SALES (est): 801.23K **Privately Held**
SIC: 2411 Logging camps and contractors

(G-12246)
CAHOON LOGGING COMPANY INC
Also Called: Cahoon Logging
6848 Free Union Church Rd (27865-9539)
P.O. Box 579 (27860-0579)
PHONE..................................252 943-6805
Christine Cahoon, *Pr*
EMP: 9 **EST:** 1994
SALES (est): 1.03MM **Privately Held**
SIC: 2411 Logging camps and contractors

(G-12247)
COASTAL WOOD PRODUCTS INC
6650 Free Union Church Rd (27865-9537)
PHONE..................................252 943-6650
EMP: 5 **EST:** 1992
SALES (est): 441.61K **Privately Held**
Web: www.coastalwoodproductsinc.com
SIC: 2511 Porch furniture and swings: wood

(G-12248)
E JS LOGGING INC
420 Long Ridge Rd (27865-9605)
PHONE..................................252 927-3539
Edwin Tetterton, *Pr*
EMP: 8 **EST:** 2003
SALES (est): 240.93K **Privately Held**
SIC: 2411 Logging camps and contractors

(G-12249)
R W BRITT LOGGING INC
7281 Long Ridge Rd (27865-9668)
PHONE..................................252 799-7682
EMP: 9 **EST:** 2019
SALES (est): 238.49K **Privately Held**
SIC: 2411 Logging camps and contractors

(G-12250)
TERRY LEGGETT LOGGING CO INC
4403 Long Ridge Rd (27865-9618)
PHONE..................................252 927-4671
Terry W Leggett, *Pr*
Gretta Leggett, *VP*
EMP: 21 **EST:** 1984
SQ FT: 6,400
SALES (est): 2.73MM **Privately Held**
SIC: 2411 Logging camps and contractors

(G-12251)
WADE BIGGS LOGGING INC
2173 Biggs Rd (27865-9471)
PHONE..................................252 927-4470
Wade T Biggs, *Pr*
Caroline Biggs, *Sec*
EMP: 17 **EST:** 1985
SALES (est): 799.61K **Privately Held**
SIC: 2411 Logging camps and contractors

Pineville
Mecklenburg County

(G-12252)
AMERICAN MOISTENING CO INC
Also Called: Amoco
10402 Rodney St (28134-8832)
P.O. Box 1066 (28134-1066)
PHONE..................................704 889-7281
James O Alexander, *CEO*
Mario Giammattei, *Pr*
EMP: 15 **EST:** 1983
SQ FT: 50,000
SALES (est): 2.37MM **Privately Held**
Web: www.amco.com
SIC: 3585 3613 Humidifiers and dehumidifiers; Control panels, electric

(G-12253)
AMERICAN SPRINKLE CO INC
11240 Rivers Edge Rd (28134-7385)
PHONE..................................800 408-6708
William Brockmann, *Pr*
Kenneth Brockmann, *Prin*
Robert Brockmann, *Prin*
Douglas Brockmann, *Prin*
EMP: 35 **EST:** 2001
SQ FT: 60,000
SALES (est): 5.82MM **Privately Held**
Web: www.americansprinkle.com
SIC: 2064 Candy and other confectionery products

(G-12254)
B G V INC
12245 Nations Ford Rd Ste 503 (28134-8444)
P.O. Box 7725 (28241-7725)
PHONE..................................704 588-3047
John H Hopkins, *Pr*
Ida Mae Hopkins, *Sec*
EMP: 5 **EST:** 1969
SQ FT: 3,000
SALES (est): 975.14K **Privately Held**
Web: sell.sawbrokers.com
SIC: 3823 Process control instruments

(G-12255)
BLACK BOX CORPORATION
10817 Southern Loop Blvd (28134-7384)
PHONE..................................704 248-6430
EMP: 6
Web: www.blackbox.com
SIC: 3577 Computer peripheral equipment, nec
HQ: Black Box Corporation
  1000 Park Dr
  Lawrence PA 15055
  724 746-5500

(G-12256)
BLP PRODUCTS AND SERVICES INC
Also Called: Embroidery 2
605 N Polk St Ste D (28134-7435)
PHONE..................................704 899-5505
Nick Vona, *CEO*
EMP: 4 **EST:** 2010
SALES (est): 386.42K **Privately Held**
Web: www.embroidery2.com
SIC: 2759 Screen printing

(G-12257)
BUILDING CENTER INC (PA)
10201 Industrial Dr (28134-6520)
P.O. Box 357 (28134-0357)
PHONE..................................704 889-8182
Edgar L Norris Senior, *Ch Bd*
Edgar L Norris Junior, *Pr*
Judith Norris, *
Grant Phillip, *
Amanda N Arnett, *
EMP: 96 **EST:** 1977
SQ FT: 52,000
SALES (est): 106.3MM
SALES (corp-wide): 106.3MM **Privately Held**
Web: www.thebuildingcenterinc.com
SIC: 5031 2431 Lumber, plywood, and millwork; Millwork

(G-12258)
CABLE DEVICES INCORPORATED
10540 Southern Loop Blvd (28134-7383)
PHONE..................................704 588-0859
EMP: 10
SIC: 3663 Radio and t.v. communications equipment
HQ: Cable Devices Incorporated
  1100 Commscope Pl Se
  Hickory NC 28602
  714 554-4370

(G-12259)
CAROLINA CARTON
8800 Crump Rd (28134-8607)
PHONE..................................704 554-5796
Bob Cichanski, *Mgr*
EMP: 7 **EST:** 2008
SALES (est): 210.22K **Privately Held**
SIC: 2655 Fiber cans, drums, and similar products

(G-12260)
CAROLINA URBAN LUMBER
10412 Rodney St (28134-8832)
PHONE..................................704 755-5110
EMP: 6 **EST:** 2017
SALES (est): 264.85K **Privately Held**
Web: www.carolinaurbanlumber.com
SIC: 2431 Millwork

(G-12261)
CONTAINER GRAPHICS CORP
Also Called: Cgc
10430 Southern Loop Blvd (28134-8468)
PHONE..................................704 588-7230
Bill Farber, *Mgr*
EMP: 44
SQ FT: 3,168
SALES (corp-wide): 4MM **Privately Held**
Web: www.containergraphics.com
SIC: 5084 3544 2796 Machine tools and accessories; Special dies, tools, jigs, and fixtures; Platemaking services
PA: Container Graphics Corp.
  114 Ednbrgh S Dr Ste 104
  Cary NC 27511
  919 481-4200

(G-12262)
CONTROLS SOUTHEAST INC
Also Called: Csi
12201 Nations Ford Rd (28134-9457)
P.O. Box 7500 (28241-7500)
PHONE..................................704 644-5000
Fred H Stubblefield Iii, *Pr*
Fred Stubblefield Junior, *Sec*
Michael D Cockram, *Design Vice President*
Jackson Roper, *VP*
Brian Walsh, *VP*
◆ **EMP:** 220 **EST:** 1962
SQ FT: 150,000
SALES: 42.07MM
SALES (corp-wide): 6.6B **Publicly Held**
Web: www.csiheat.com
SIC: 3498 3494 3312 Piping systems for pulp, paper, and chemical industries; Valves and pipe fittings, nec; Blast furnaces and steel mills
PA: Ametek, Inc.
  1100 Cassatt Rd
  Berwyn PA 19312
  610 647-2121

(G-12263)
CREATIVE TOOLING SOLUTIONS INC
10809 Southern Loop Blvd (28134-7425)
PHONE..................................704 504-5415
▲ **EMP:** 7 **EST:** 2010
SALES (est): 300.06K **Privately Held**
Web: www.creativetoolingsolutions.net
SIC: 3545 Tools and accessories for machine tools

(G-12264)
CUMMINS INC
11101 Nations Ford Rd (28134-9437)
PHONE..................................704 588-1240
Russell Dallas, *Brnch Mgr*
EMP: 4
SALES (corp-wide): 28.07B **Publicly Held**
Web: www.cummins.com
SIC: 3519 3714 3694 3621 Internal combustion engines, nec; Motor vehicle parts and accessories; Engine electrical equipment; Generator sets: gasoline, diesel, or dual-fuel
PA: Cummins Inc.
  500 Jackson St
  Columbus IN 47201
  812 377-3842

(G-12265)
DIENES APPARATUS INC
9220 Rodney St (28134-9200)
P.O. Box 549 (28134-0549)
PHONE..................................704 525-3770
Dan Miller, *Pr*
▲ **EMP:** 6 **EST:** 1981
SQ FT: 12,000
SALES (est): 1.31MM
SALES (corp-wide): 1.64MM **Privately Held**
Web: www.dienes.net
SIC: 3585 Refrigeration and heating equipment
PA: Dienes Apparatebau Gesellschaft Mit Beschrankter Haftung
  Philipp-Reis-Str. 16
  Muhlheim Am Main HE 63165
  61087070

(G-12266)
DIVERSIFIED WELDING AND STEEL
10801 Nations Ford Rd (28134-9440)
PHONE..................................704 504-1111
EMP: 6 **EST:** 2016
SALES (est): 151.79K **Privately Held**
Web: www.diversifiedweldingllc.com
SIC: 7692 Welding repair

GEOGRAPHIC SECTION

Pineville - Mecklenburg County (G-12291)

(G-12267)
ELNIK SYSTEMS LLC
12004 Carolina Logistics Dr Ste A
(28134-1400)
PHONE..........................973 239-6066
EMP: 8 EST: 2002
SALES (est): 109.11K Privately Held
SIC: 3621 Motors and generators

(G-12268)
FERGUSON WATERWORKS
10039 Industrial Dr (28134-8384)
P.O. Box 1147 (28134-1147)
PHONE..........................704 540-7225
Trae Farthing, *Mgr*
EMP: 6 EST: 2018
SALES (est): 148.68K Privately Held
SIC: 3589 Service industry machinery, nec

(G-12269)
FORKLIFT PRO INC
Also Called: Bellatony
9801 Industrial Dr (28134-6515)
P.O. Box 99 (28134-0099)
PHONE..........................704 716-3636
Bill Zemak, *Pr*
Jaclyn Smith Ctrl, *Prin*
◆ EMP: 18 EST: 1999
SQ FT: 21,200
SALES (est): 5.02MM Privately Held
Web: www.theforkliftpro.com
SIC: 3537 Forklift trucks

(G-12270)
GALAXY PRESSURE WASHING INC
10810 Southern Loop Blvd Ste 12
(28134-8365)
P.O. Box 832 (28106-0832)
PHONE..........................888 299-3129
Saqer Hejji, *Pr*
EMP: 5 EST: 2011
SALES (est): 383.03K Privately Held
Web: www.galaxypressurewashing.com
SIC: 7389 7699 7349 3589 Business Activities at Non-Commercial Site; Cleaning services; Building cleaning service; Commercial cleaning equipment

(G-12271)
GRIFFITHS CORPORATION
Wrico Stamping Co NC
10134 Industrial Dr (28134-6516)
PHONE..........................704 552-6793
Ed Schleicher, *Mgr*
EMP: 100
SALES (corp-wide): 147.92MM Privately Held
Web: www.griffithscorp.com
SIC: 3469 Stamping metal for the trade
HQ: Griffiths Corporation
    2717 Niagara Ln N
    Minneapolis MN 55447
    763 557-8935

(G-12272)
GRIFFITHS CORPORATION
Also Called: K-Tek Crlina Prcsion Spclty Mf
10240 Industrial Dr (28134-6517)
PHONE..........................704 554-5657
John Kirkpatrick, *Mgr*
EMP: 65
SALES (corp-wide): 147.92MM Privately Held
Web: www.griffithscorp.com
SIC: 3469 3544 3444 3451 Stamping metal for the trade; Special dies, tools, jigs, and fixtures; Sheet metal specialties, not stamped; Screw machine products
HQ: Griffiths Corporation
    2717 Niagara Ln N
    Minneapolis MN 55447
    763 557-8935

(G-12273)
HLMF LOGISTICS INC
11516 Downs Rd (28134-8416)
PHONE..........................704 782-0356
Amy Bush, *Pr*
EMP: 4 EST: 2003
SALES (est): 490.62K Privately Held
SIC: 3621 7699 Electric motor and generator parts; Filter cleaning

(G-12274)
HYPER NETWORKS LLC ✪
12249 Nations Ford Rd (28134-9457)
PHONE..........................704 837-8411
Ryan Draayer, *Managing Member*
EMP: 15 EST: 2022
SALES (est): 614.6K Privately Held
Web: www.hypernetworksinc.com
SIC: 1623 3531 Pipeline wrapping; Cranes, nec

(G-12275)
IPEX USA LLC (DH)
10100 Rodney St (28134-7538)
P.O. Box 240696 (28224-0696)
PHONE..........................704 889-2431
Thomas E Torokvei, *CEO*
Katherine Serafino, *
◆ EMP: 130 EST: 2000
SALES (est): 294.62MM
SALES (corp-wide): 87.53MM Privately Held
Web: www.ipexna.com
SIC: 3084 Plastics pipe
HQ: Ipex Inc
    3-1425 North Service Rd E
    Oakville ON L6H 1
    289 881-0120

(G-12276)
IPEX USA LLC
Eslon Thermo Plastics
10100 Rodney St (28134-7538)
P.O. Box 240696 (28224-0696)
PHONE..........................704 889-2431
Wayne Peterson, *Mgr*
EMP: 12
SALES (corp-wide): 87.53MM Privately Held
Web: www.ipexna.com
SIC: 3084 3498 Plastics pipe; Fabricated pipe and fittings
HQ: Ipex Usa Llc
    10100 Rodney St
    Pineville NC 28134

(G-12277)
JD STEEL LLC
12324 Buxton Dr (28134-6354)
PHONE..........................843 367-7456
EMP: 5 EST: 2016
SALES (est): 103.91K Privately Held
SIC: 3441 Fabricated structural metal

(G-12278)
JGI INC (PA)
Also Called: Signs Etc
10108 Industrial Dr (28134-6516)
PHONE..........................704 522-8860
Spencer Brower, *Pr*
Sherry Brower, *Sec*
EMP: 20 EST: 1980
SALES (est): 2.42MM
SALES (corp-wide): 2.42MM Privately Held
SIC: 3993 Signs, not made in custom sign painting shops

(G-12279)
KRANKEN SIGNS VEHICLE WRAPS
310 N Polk St (28134-8133)
P.O. Box 1025 (28134-1025)
PHONE..........................704 339-0059
Clifford Smith, *Owner*
EMP: 4 EST: 2013
SALES (est): 252.02K Privately Held
Web: www.krankensigns.com
SIC: 3993 Signs and advertising specialties

(G-12280)
LEKE LLC
Also Called: A S I
10800 Nations Ford Rd (28134-9431)
PHONE..........................704 523-1452
Lawrence Eichorn, *Pr*
Kevin Eichorn, *
EMP: 24 EST: 1929
SQ FT: 20,000
SALES (est): 1.58MM Privately Held
SIC: 2819 2869 5169 Industrial inorganic chemicals, nec; Industrial organic chemicals, nec; Industrial chemicals
HQ: Colonial Chemical Solutions, Inc.
    916 W Lathrop Ave
    Savannah GA 31415
    912 236-7891

(G-12281)
LOCK DRIVES INC
11198 Downs Rd (28134-8445)
P.O. Box 501 (28134-0501)
PHONE..........................704 588-1844
John Walters, *Pr*
▲ EMP: 4 EST: 2008
SALES (est): 404.55K Privately Held
Web: www.lockdrives.com
SIC: 3523 1542 3448 5084 Barn, silo, poultry, dairy, and livestock machinery; Commercial and office buildings, renovation and repair; Greenhouses, prefabricated metal; Industrial machinery and equipment

(G-12282)
LSC COMMUNICATIONS INC
10519 Industrial Dr (28134-6527)
PHONE..........................704 889-5800
EMP: 11
SALES (corp-wide): 8.23B Privately Held
Web: www.lsccom.com
SIC: 2732 Book printing
HQ: Lsc Communications, Inc.
    4101 Winfield Rd
    Warrenville IL 60555
    773 272-9200

(G-12283)
MEXICHEM SPCALTY COMPOUNDS INC
9635 Industrial Dr (28134-8835)
P.O. Box 490 (28134-0490)
PHONE..........................704 889-7821
Robert N Gingue, *Brnch Mgr*
EMP: 80
SQ FT: 60,000
Web: www.alphagary.com
SIC: 2821 Plastics materials and resins
HQ: Mexichem Specialty Compounds, Inc.
    170 Pioneer Dr
    Leominster MA 01453
    978 537-8071

(G-12284)
MPE USA INC
10424 Rodney St (28134-8832)
P.O. Box 713 (28134-0713)
PHONE..........................704 340-4910
Barbara Duncan, *Off Mgr*
▲ EMP: 21 EST: 2003
SQ FT: 70,000
SALES (est): 10.59MM
SALES (corp-wide): 63.27MM Privately Held
Web: www.mpeplastics.com
SIC: 5162 3089 Plastics materials and basic shapes; Injection molding of plastics
PA: M.P.E. Srl
    Via Dell'industria 15
    Villanova Canavese TO 10070
    011 926-1811

(G-12285)
NCSMJ INC
Also Called: Skatells Mfg Jewelers
9433 Pineville Matthews Rd (28134-6588)
PHONE..........................704 544-1118
EMP: 10 EST: 1994
SQ FT: 14,638
SALES (est): 643.69K Privately Held
Web: www.skatellsnc.com
SIC: 3911 5094 5944 5045 Jewelry, precious metal; Jewelry and precious stones; Jewelry stores; Computers, peripherals, and software

(G-12286)
O P S HOLDING COMPANY LLC
12243 Nations Ford Rd (28134-9457)
PHONE..........................361 446-8376
EMP: 5 EST: 2018
SALES (est): 98.84K Privately Held
SIC: 2252 Socks

(G-12287)
OMEGA STUDIOS INC
10519 Industrial Dr (28134-6527)
PHONE..........................704 889-5800
Tom Palmer, *Pr*
EMP: 7 EST: 2017
SALES (est): 83.91K Privately Held
SIC: 2752 Commercial printing, lithographic

(G-12288)
ORAMENTAL POST
10108 Industrial Dr (28134-6516)
PHONE..........................704 376-8111
John Iyoob, *Pr*
▲ EMP: 13 EST: 1984
SQ FT: 10,000
SALES (est): 468.83K Privately Held
Web: www.ornamentalpost.com
SIC: 3993 Signs and advertising specialties

(G-12289)
PATE INDUSTRIES
9920 Pineville Matthews Rd (28134-7551)
PHONE..........................704 889-2376
EMP: 4 EST: 2015
SALES (est): 80.86K Privately Held
SIC: 3999 Manufacturing industries, nec

(G-12290)
PINNACLE CONVERTING EQP & SVCS
11325 Nations Ford Rd Ste A (28134-8319)
PHONE..........................704 376-3855
Thomas Kepper, *Prin*
EMP: 20 EST: 2014
SALES (est): 1.18MM Privately Held
Web: www.pinnacleconverting.com
SIC: 3599 Machine and other job shop work

(G-12291)
PINNACLE CONVERTING EQP INC (PA)
11325 Nations Ford Rd Ste A (28134-8319)
PHONE..........................704 376-3855
EMP: 23 EST: 1983
SALES (est): 6.91MM Privately Held
Web: www.pinnacleconverting.com

Pineville - Mecklenburg County (G-12292)

SIC: 3599 3621 Machine and other job shop work; Motors and generators

(G-12292)
PYRAMID CEMENT PRODUCTS INC
9724 Industrial Dr (28134-8385)
PHONE.....................704 373-2529
Michael Yon, *Pr*
EMP: 16 EST: 2002
SQ FT: 18,500
SALES (est): 684.12K **Privately Held**
Web: www.byvip03.com
SIC: 2891 Sealants

(G-12293)
QMAX INDUSTRIES LLC
Also Called: QMAX Industries
520 Eagleton Downs Dr Ste A (28134-7453)
P.O. Box 470924 (28247-0924)
PHONE.....................704 643-7299
EMP: 8 EST: 2010
SALES (est): 2.1MM **Privately Held**
Web: www.qmaxindustries.com
SIC: 3823 Industrial process measurement equipment

(G-12294)
R S INTEGRATORS INC
11172 Downs Rd (28134-8445)
PHONE.....................704 588-8288
EMP: 6 EST: 1995
SQ FT: 4,000
SALES (est): 540.46K **Privately Held**
Web: www.rsintegrators.com
SIC: 3613 7539 Control panels, electric; Electrical services

(G-12295)
ROARK PRINTING INC
Also Called: International Minute Press
209 Main St (28134-7528)
PHONE.....................704 889-5544
Jacky Roark, *Pr*
EMP: 8 EST: 2003
SALES (est): 95.93K **Privately Held**
Web: pineville.intlminutepress.com
SIC: 2752 Offset printing

(G-12296)
ROCCO MARIE VENTURES LLC
Also Called: Minuteman Press
209 Main St (28134-7528)
PHONE.....................704 341-8800
EMP: 9 EST: 2021
SALES (est): 862.14K **Privately Held**
Web: www.minuteman.com
SIC: 2752 Commercial printing, lithographic

(G-12297)
ROYAL WELDING INC
413 N Polk St (28134-7457)
PHONE.....................704 750-9353
EMP: 11 EST: 2018
SALES (est): 1.09MM **Privately Held**
Web: www.royalweldingandsteelfabricationofcharlotte.com
SIC: 3441 Fabricated structural metal

(G-12298)
ROYAL WELDING LLC
413 N Polk St Unit H (28134-7457)
PHONE.....................704 750-9353
EMP: 8 EST: 2009
SQ FT: 2,400
SALES (est): 754.82K **Privately Held**
Web: www.royalweldingandsteelfabricationofcharlotte.com
SIC: 7692 Welding repair

(G-12299)
RUSSELL FINEX INC
625 Eagleton Downs Dr (28134-7424)
P.O. Box 69 (28134-0069)
PHONE.....................704 588-9808
Rob Ward, *Pr*
John Edwards, *Pr*
Ernest W Reigel, *Sec*
◆ EMP: 16 EST: 1970
SQ FT: 25,000
SALES (est): 10.84MM
SALES (corp-wide): 60.21MM **Privately Held**
Web: www.russellfinex.com
SIC: 5084 3569 Industrial machinery and equipment; Assembly machines, non-metalworking
PA: Russell Finex Limited
Russell House
Feltham MIDDX TW13
208 818-2000

(G-12300)
RUTLAND GROUP INC (HQ)
10021 Rodney St (28134-8574)
PHONE.....................704 553-0046
Jeff Leone, *CEO*
Hortensia Ladr, *
◆ EMP: 110 EST: 1986
SQ FT: 75,000
SALES (est): 34.65MM **Publicly Held**
SIC: 3087 2821 Custom compound purchased resins; Plastics materials and resins
PA: Avient Corporation
33587 Walker Rd
Avon Lake OH 44012

(G-12301)
RUTLAND HOLDINGS LLC (PA)
Also Called: Rutland Plastic Technologies
10021 Rodney St (28134-8574)
P.O. Box 339 (28134-0339)
PHONE.....................704 553-0046
◆ EMP: 33 EST: 2004
SALES (est): 10.55MM **Privately Held**
Web: www.avientspecialtyinks.com
SIC: 3087 2821 Custom compound purchased resins; Plastics materials and resins

(G-12302)
SAPPHIRE TCHNCAL SOLUTIONS LLC
10230 Rodney St (28134-7539)
PHONE.....................704 561-3100
Michael Piscitelli, *Managing Member*
EMP: 9 EST: 2005
SQ FT: 21,000
SALES (est): 2.51MM **Privately Held**
Web: www.sapphirests.com
SIC: 8734 3829 3823 3826 Testing laboratories; Measuring and controlling devices, nec; Industrial process measurement equipment; Analytical instruments

(G-12303)
SAS INDUSTRIES COMPANY LLC
12208 Winghurst Dr (28134-9127)
PHONE.....................704 323-9098
Arthur Sanoyan, *Admn*
EMP: 4 EST: 2014
SALES (est): 79.04K **Privately Held**
SIC: 3999 Manufacturing industries, nec

(G-12304)
SCI SHARP CONTROLS INC
11331 Downs Rd (28134-8441)
PHONE.....................704 394-1395
Chrinstine Lopez-blossfled, *CEO*
EMP: 6 EST: 2007
SALES (est): 827.07K **Privately Held**
Web: www.sharpcontrols.com
SIC: 3494 3492 3594 Valves and pipe fittings, nec; Fluid power valves and hose fittings; Fluid power pumps and motors

(G-12305)
SCRIBBLES SOFTWARE LLC
10617 Southern Loop Blvd (28134-7381)
PHONE.....................704 390-5690
EMP: 18 EST: 2016
SALES (est): 2.63MM **Privately Held**
Web: www.scribsoft.com
SIC: 7372 Prepackaged software

(G-12306)
SIGNS NOW CHARLOTTE
Also Called: Signs Now
600 Towne Centre Blvd Ste 404 (28134)
PHONE.....................704 844-0552
EMP: 4 EST: 1996
SALES (est): 486.9K **Privately Held**
Web: www.signsnow.com
SIC: 3993 Signs and advertising specialties

(G-12307)
SIQNARAMA PINEVILLW
10615 Industrial Dr Ste 200 (28134-6526)
PHONE.....................704 835-1123
EMP: 4 EST: 2018
SALES (est): 46.08K **Privately Held**
SIC: 3993 Signs and advertising specialties

(G-12308)
STRONG MEDICAL PARTNERS LLC (PA)
Also Called: Strong Manufacturers
11519 Nations Ford Rd Ste 200 (28134-9447)
PHONE.....................716 626-9400
Alan Bagliore, *CEO*
EMP: 27 EST: 2016
SALES (est): 9.54MM
SALES (corp-wide): 9.54MM **Privately Held**
Web: www.strongmanufacturers.com
SIC: 3841 Surgical and medical instruments

(G-12309)
STRONG MEDICAL PARTNERS LLC
Also Called: Strong Manufacturers
11515 Nations Ford Rd (28134-9540)
PHONE.....................716 507-4476
EMP: 93
SALES (corp-wide): 9.54MM **Privately Held**
Web: www.strongmanufacturers.com
SIC: 3841 Surgical and medical instruments
PA: Strong Medical Partners Llc
11519 Nations Ford Rd # 2
Pineville NC 28134
716 626-9400

(G-12310)
STUDIO DISPLAYS INC
11150 Rivers Edge Rd (28134-8478)
PHONE.....................704 588-6590
EMP: 13
SALES (corp-wide): 4.94MM **Privately Held**
Web: www.studiodisplays.com
SIC: 3993 7336 Signs and advertising specialties; Graphic arts and related design
PA: Studio Displays, Inc.
9081 Northfield Dr
Indian Land SC 29707
704 588-6590

(G-12311)
SUCCESSION SOLUTIONS INC
11108 Downs Rd (28134-8412)
PHONE.....................704 631-9004
William T Walker, *Pr*
Scott Rossi, *VP*
Bill Walker, *Prin*
EMP: 14 EST: 2009
SQ FT: 6,000
SALES (est): 1.65MM **Privately Held**
Web: www.ss-nc.com
SIC: 7379 2752 Diskette duplicating service; Commercial printing, lithographic

(G-12312)
SUPERIOR FIRE HOSE CORP
10000 Industrial Dr Ste B (28134-8624)
P.O. Box 3527 (91744-0527)
PHONE.....................704 643-5888
▲ EMP: 27 EST: 1996
SQ FT: 56,000
SALES (est): 2.44MM **Privately Held**
Web: www.superiorfirehose.com
SIC: 3052 Fire hose, rubber

(G-12313)
URBAN INDUSTRIES CORP
12245 Nations Ford Rd Ste 505 (28134-7456)
PHONE.....................980 209-9471
Mark Urban, *Prin*
EMP: 10 EST: 2017
SALES (est): 814.19K **Privately Held**
Web: www.urbanind.com
SIC: 3999 Manufacturing industries, nec

Pink Hill
Lenoir County

(G-12314)
BACKWOODS LOGGING LLC
1066 Sumner Rd (28572-7918)
PHONE.....................910 298-3786
EMP: 6 EST: 2012
SALES (est): 769.71K **Privately Held**
SIC: 2411 Logging camps and contractors

(G-12315)
BACKWOODS LOGGING PINK HL INC
1066 Sumner Rd (28572-7918)
PHONE.....................910 298-1284
EMP: 8 EST: 2014
SALES (est): 258.88K **Privately Held**
SIC: 2411 Logging

(G-12316)
CORDSET DESIGNS INC
100 W New St (28572-8569)
P.O. Box 528 (31007-0528)
PHONE.....................252 568-4001
Steven Peltz, *Pr*
Gary Payne, *VP*
Ben Byrnside, *Sec*
▲ EMP: 21 EST: 1991
SQ FT: 43,000
SALES (est): 4.42MM **Privately Held**
Web: www.cordsetdesigns.com
SIC: 3357 3699 Appliance fixture wire, nonferrous; Electrical equipment and supplies, nec

(G-12317)
TRAINING GRUND PBLICATIONS LLC
4028 Duplin County Rd (28572-9687)
PHONE.....................252 568-3922
Mac E Whitfield Junior, *Prin*
EMP: 4 EST: 2019
SALES (est): 68.11K **Privately Held**

SIC: 2741 Miscellaneous publishing

(G-12318)
WAYNE WOODWORKS
880 Sumner Rd (28572-7914)
PHONE..............................910 298-5669
EMP: 4 EST: 2010
SALES (est): 59.49K **Privately Held**
SIC: 2431 Millwork

Pinnacle
Stokes County

(G-12319)
B & B HOSIERY MILL
3608 Volunteer Rd (27043-8525)
PHONE..............................336 368-4849
Bernie Young, *Owner*
EMP: 5 EST: 1981
SALES (est): 260.32K **Privately Held**
SIC: 2252 Socks

(G-12320)
EMERALD PRINTING INC
2616 Shoals Rd (27043-9278)
PHONE..............................336 325-3522
EMP: 5 EST: 2017
SALES (est): 96.1K **Privately Held**
SIC: 2752 Offset printing

(G-12321)
FELTS LUMBER CO INC
1377 Perch Rd (27043-8314)
P.O. Box 8 (27043-0008)
PHONE..............................336 368-5667
Brent Felts, *Pr*
Debra Felts, *Sec*
EMP: 7 EST: 1972
SALES (est): 564.34K **Privately Held**
SIC: 2421 Lumber: rough, sawed, or planed

(G-12322)
PILOT MOUNTAIN VINEYARDS LLC
1162 Bradley Rd (27043-8411)
PHONE..............................828 400-9533
EMP: 4 EST: 2018
SALES (est): 248.32K **Privately Held**
Web: www.pilotmtnvineyards.com
SIC: 2084 Wines

Pisgah Forest
Transylvania County

(G-12323)
GLATFELTER CORPORATION
Also Called: Glatfelter Composite Fibers NA
2795 King Rd (28768-7880)
PHONE..............................828 877-2110
Jim Turra, *Genl Mgr*
EMP: 6
SALES (corp-wide): 1.49B **Publicly Held**
Web: www.glatfelter.com
SIC: 2621 Specialty papers
PA: Glatfelter Corporation
    4350 Congress St Ste 600
    Charlotte NC 28209
    704 885-2555

(G-12324)
JONATHAN STAMEY
Also Called: Brevard Laser
1 Old Hendersonville Hwy (28768-0080)
PHONE..............................828 577-0450
Jonathan Stamey, *Owner*
EMP: 4 EST: 2020
SALES (est): 69.98K **Privately Held**
Web: www.stameyconstruction.com

SIC: 3479 Aluminum coating of metal products

(G-12325)
KEOWEE PUBLISHING CO INC
96 Merle Farm Ln (28768-9960)
PHONE..............................828 877-4742
Gerald Harris, *Prin*
EMP: 9 EST: 2002
SALES (est): 513.78K **Privately Held**
SIC: 2741 Miscellaneous publishing

(G-12326)
MCJAST INC
Also Called: American Carolina Lighting
6497 Old Hendersonville Hwy (28768-8851)
P.O. Box 1079 (28729-1079)
PHONE..............................828 884-4809
Janet Mcnabb, *Pr*
Steve Mcnabb, *CEO*
EMP: 10 EST: 1987
SQ FT: 8,000
SALES (est): 810.59K **Privately Held**
Web: www.americancarolinalight.net
SIC: 3496 3599 3469 3452 Miscellaneous fabricated wire products; Grinding castings for the trade; Metal stampings, nec; Bolts, nuts, rivets, and washers

(G-12327)
PISGAH LABORATORIES INC
3222 Old Hendersonville Hwy (28768-9213)
PHONE..............................828 884-2789
David W Bristol, *Pr*
Cliff King, *VP*
Belinda Novick, *Sec*
▲ EMP: 20 EST: 1979
SQ FT: 30,000
SALES (est): 5.01MM **Privately Held**
SIC: 2833 2869 Medicinals and botanicals; Industrial organic chemicals, nec
PA: Ipca Laboratories Limited
    125, Kandivli Industrial Estate, Kandivli (West),
    Mumbai MH 40006

(G-12328)
TNW VENTURES INC
60 Bishop Ln (28768-7602)
P.O. Box 152 (28768-0152)
PHONE..............................828 216-4089
Tammy Woods, *Pr*
EMP: 6 EST: 2004
SALES (est): 69.94K **Privately Held**
SIC: 2064 Breakfast bars

(G-12329)
TREND PERFORMANCE PRODUCTS
114 Lime Kiln Ln (28768-8914)
PHONE..............................828 862-8290
Robert Fox, *Brnch Mgr*
EMP: 5
SALES (corp-wide): 2.2MM **Privately Held**
Web: www.trendperform.com
SIC: 3714 Motor vehicle parts and accessories
PA: Trend Performance Products Inc
    23444 Schoenherr Rd
    Warren MI 48089
    586 447-0400

(G-12330)
WINS SMOKEHOUSE SERVICES LTD
45 S Ridge Rd (28768-8506)
PHONE..............................828 884-7476
EMP: 6 EST: 1996
SALES (est): 936.68K **Privately Held**
Web: www.winssmokehouse.com

SIC: 3556 Smokers, food processing equipment

Pittsboro
Chatham County

(G-12331)
BIOLEX THERAPEUTICS INC
158 Credle St (27312-4130)
PHONE..............................919 542-9901
Jan Turek, *Pr*
Dale A Sander, *
David Spencer Ph.d., *COO*
Glen Williams, *
Bipin Dalmia Ph.d., *Sr VP*
EMP: 46 EST: 1998
SALES (est): 5.19MM **Privately Held**
Web: www.biolex.com
SIC: 2834 Digitalis pharmaceutical preparations

(G-12332)
BITE MY COOKIES BREWING CO INC
Also Called: BMC Brewing
213 Lorax Ln (27312-8850)
PHONE..............................919 602-7636
John Rice, *Prin*
EMP: 7 EST: 2019
SALES (est): 277.83K **Privately Held**
SIC: 2082 Malt beverages

(G-12333)
BUDDY CUT INC
760 Redgate Rd (27312-7936)
P.O. Box 160 (27312-0160)
PHONE..............................888 608-4701
Joshua Esnard, *CEO*
EMP: 5 EST: 2017
SALES (est): 477.07K **Privately Held**
Web: www.thecutbuddy.com
SIC: 5961 3999 Electronic shopping; Barber and beauty shop equipment

(G-12334)
CARR AMPLIFERS
23 Rectory St Ste E (27312-4160)
PHONE..............................919 545-0747
EMP: 5 EST: 2016
SALES (est): 143.1K **Privately Held**
Web: www.carramps.com
SIC: 3651 Amplifiers: radio, public address, or musical instrument

(G-12335)
CARR AMPLIFIERS INC
433 W Salisbury St (27312-9451)
PHONE..............................919 545-0747
Steve Carr, *Pr*
EMP: 10 EST: 1998
SQ FT: 2,800
SALES (est): 597.8K **Privately Held**
Web: www.carramps.com
SIC: 3651 Amplifiers: radio, public address, or musical instrument

(G-12336)
CHANDLER CONCRETE INC
Also Called: Chandler Concrete Company
246 Chatham Forest Dr (27312-5729)
PHONE..............................919 542-4242
EMP: 7
Web: www.chandlerconcrete.com
SIC: 3273 Ready-mixed concrete
PA: Chandler Concrete Co., Inc.
    1006 S Church St
    Burlington NC 27215

(G-12337)
COUNTRY CORNER
2193 Us 64 Business E (27312-7672)
PHONE..............................919 444-9663
Alicia Womble, *Owner*
EMP: 6 EST: 2004
SALES (est): 207.85K **Privately Held**
SIC: 3581 Automatic vending machines

(G-12338)
DEVMIR LEGWEAR INC
136 Fayetteville St (27312-0750)
PHONE..............................919 545-5500
Altug Sipal, *Pr*
▲ EMP: 4 EST: 2010
SALES (est): 417.74K **Privately Held**
Web: www.devmir.com
SIC: 2252 Anklets (hosiery)

(G-12339)
DLSS MANUFACTURING LLC
697 Hillsboro St (27312-5979)
P.O. Box 1549 (27312-1549)
PHONE..............................919 619-7594
Erik Berg, *Managing Member*
EMP: 4 EST: 2010
SALES (est): 451.17K **Privately Held**
Web: www.dlssmfg.com
SIC: 3446 Architectural metalwork

(G-12340)
DLSS MFG
2458 Hamlets Chapel Rd (27312-8787)
PHONE..............................919 619-6184
EMP: 4 EST: 2019
SALES (est): 73.81K **Privately Held**
SIC: 3999 Manufacturing industries, nec

(G-12341)
DONS DISPOSAL
3692 Nc Highway 87 N (27312-7264)
PHONE..............................919 542-2208
EMP: 6 EST: 2008
SALES (est): 246.24K **Privately Held**
SIC: 3089 Garbage containers, plastics

(G-12342)
HOMESERVE NC LLC ✪
2225 Castle Rock Farm Rd (27312-9648)
PHONE..............................740 552-8497
EMP: 4 EST: 2022
SALES (est): 102.19K **Privately Held**
SIC: 1389 Construction, repair, and dismantling services

(G-12343)
NVN LIQUIDATION INC (PA)
P.O. Box 64 (27312-0064)
PHONE..............................919 485-8080
Paula B Stafford, *Ch Bd*
Paula Brown Stafford, *Ch Bd*
John M Gay, *Corporate Secretary*
EMP: 8 EST: 2006
SALES (est): 23.68MM **Publicly Held**
Web: www.pelthos.com
SIC: 2834 Dermatologicals

(G-12344)
PENNY CONNECTED CAFE LLC
66 Easy St (27312-5846)
PHONE..............................984 214-2131
Jimmy Penny, *Mgr*
EMP: 4
SALES (est): 62.38K **Privately Held**
SIC: 2099 Food preparations, nec

(G-12345)
PROPELLA THERAPEUTICS INC
120 Mosaic Blvd Ste 120-3 (27312-4966)
PHONE..............................703 631-7523

Pittsboro - Chatham County (G-12346)

William Moore, *Pr*
EMP: 6 **EST:** 2020
SALES (est): 868.42K **Privately Held**
Web: www.propellatx.com
SIC: 2834 Pharmaceutical preparations
PA: Astellas Pharma Inc.
2-5-1, Nihombashihoncho
Chuo-Ku TKY 103-0

(G-12346)
RANCHO PARK PUBLISHING INC
8 Matchwood (27312-8601)
PHONE.................................919 942-9493
Stan Cheren, *Pr*
EMP: 5 **EST:** 1992
SALES (est): 414.38K **Privately Held**
Web: www.ranchopark.com
SIC: 2741 Miscellaneous publishing

(G-12347)
REVOLUTION PD LLC
379 White Smith Rd (27312-6028)
PHONE.................................919 949-0241
EMP: 8 **EST:** 2011
SALES (est): 412.49K **Privately Held**
SIC: 3089 3465 Molding primary plastics; Moldings or trim, automobile: stamped metal

(G-12348)
ROLLS ENTERPRISES INC
2277 Otis Johnson Rd (27312-6275)
PHONE.................................919 545-9401
Rollo T Varkey, *Pr*
▲ **EMP:** 4 **EST:** 2000
SALES (est): 385.86K **Privately Held**
Web: www.keralacurry.com
SIC: 2099 Ready-to-eat meals, salads, and sandwiches

(G-12349)
SIGN AND PRINT SHOP
295 Hillsboro St (27312-5906)
PHONE.................................919 542-0727
EMP: 5 **EST:** 2015
SALES (est): 97.53K **Privately Held**
SIC: 2752 Offset printing

(G-12350)
SNIPES GROUP LLC
Also Called: Coloring Pen The
90 Lucy Mae Page Rd (27312-9852)
PHONE.................................757 266-0488
Claude Snipes, *Pr*
EMP: 4 **EST:** 2021
SALES (est): 71.21K **Privately Held**
SIC: 5999 2389 Miscellaneous retail stores, nec; Apparel and accessories, nec

(G-12351)
STARRLIGHT MEAD
130 Lorax Ln (27312-5763)
PHONE.................................919 533-6314
EMP: 4 **EST:** 2020
SALES (est): 227.49K **Privately Held**
Web: www.starrlightmead.com
SIC: 2084 Wines, brandy, and brandy spirits

(G-12352)
TYNDALL MACHINE TOOL INC
Also Called: Tyndall Machine Technologies
154 Dogwood Ln (27312-4119)
PHONE.................................919 542-4014
Dwight Tyndall, *Pr*
EMP: 6 **EST:** 1983
SALES (est): 252.69K **Privately Held**
SIC: 3599 Machine shop, jobbing and repair

(G-12353)
US MICROWAVE INC
164 Fearrington Post (27312-8553)

PHONE.................................520 891-2444
Ana C Brownstein, *Pr*
Dennis Brownstein, *VP*
EMP: 6 **EST:** 1984
SALES (est): 408.31K **Privately Held**
SIC: 3679 5065 Microwave components; Communication equipment

(G-12354)
WARMING SUN MUSIC PUBLISHING
107 Deep Crk (27312-9596)
PHONE.................................714 390-8010
Douglas Boughter, *Owner*
EMP: 5 **EST:** 2011
SALES (est): 54K **Privately Held**
Web: www.warmingsunmusic.com
SIC: 2741 Miscellaneous publishing

(G-12355)
WHOLESEAL INTERNATIONAL
192c Lorax Ln (27312)
PHONE.................................919 346-0788
Patrick Wilson, *Pr*
EMP: 5 **EST:** 2016
SALES (est): 135.61K **Privately Held**
SIC: 2891 Sealing compounds, synthetic rubber or plastic

Pleasant Garden
Guilford County

(G-12356)
ASK ELEVATOR SERVICE INC
6000 Spring Forest Ct (27313-9707)
PHONE.................................336 674-2715
Randall G Clark, *Prin*
EMP: 6 **EST:** 2001
SALES (est): 102.1K **Privately Held**
SIC: 3999 5084 Wheelchair lifts; Elevators

(G-12357)
LEGACY NATIONAL INSTALLERS LLC
425 E Steeple Chase Rd (27313-9239)
PHONE.................................336 804-1990
EMP: 5 **EST:** 2016
SALES (est): 136.68K **Privately Held**
SIC: 3993 Signs and advertising specialties

(G-12358)
MEDLEY S GARAGE WELDING
5879 Cherokee Trl (27313-9600)
PHONE.................................336 674-0422
Garland Medley, *Prin*
EMP: 7 **EST:** 2008
SALES (est): 277.68K **Privately Held**
SIC: 7692 Welding repair

(G-12359)
PLEASANT GARDEN DRY KILN
1221 Briarcrest Dr (27313-9234)
P.O. Box 457 (27313-0457)
PHONE.................................336 674-2863
Derrick Milliken, *Pt*
EMP: 9 **EST:** 1969
SQ FT: 200
SALES (est): 647.25K **Privately Held**
SIC: 2421 Kiln drying of lumber

(G-12360)
SIZEMORE CUSTOM JEWELRY REPAIR
6212 Russwood Dr (27313-9536)
PHONE.................................336 633-8979
Joseph Sizemore, *Prin*
EMP: 5 **EST:** 2014
SALES (est): 26.07K **Privately Held**

SIC: 7699 2752 Repair services, nec; Commercial printing, lithographic

(G-12361)
SMITH FAMILY SCREEN PRINTING
5311 Appomattox Rd (27313-8255)
PHONE.................................336 317-4849
Anthony Smith, *Prin*
EMP: 4 **EST:** 2017
SALES (est): 83.91K **Privately Held**
SIC: 2752 Commercial printing, lithographic

(G-12362)
TARHEEL SOLUTIONS LLC
6463 Walter Wright Rd (27313-9715)
PHONE.................................336 420-9265
Marcus B Talcott, *Pr*
EMP: 6 **EST:** 2014
SALES (est): 92.36K **Privately Held**
SIC: 2834 Pharmaceutical preparations

(G-12363)
WYRICK MACHINE AND TOOL CO
1215 Kearns Hackett Rd (27313-8217)
P.O. Box 573 (27313-0573)
PHONE.................................336 841-8261
Chet Wyrick, *Pr*
Ann Wyrick, *Treas*
EMP: 6 **EST:** 1987
SQ FT: 2,000
SALES (est): 529.96K **Privately Held**
SIC: 3599 Machine shop, jobbing and repair

Pleasant Hill
Northampton County

(G-12364)
GLOVER MATERIALS INC (PA)
4493 Us Highway 301 (27866-9687)
P.O. Box 40 (27866-0040)
PHONE.................................252 536-2660
EMP: 5 **EST:** 1987
SALES (est): 2.43MM **Privately Held**
Web: www.gloverconstruction.com
SIC: 5211 1442 Masonry materials and supplies; Construction sand mining

Plymouth
Washington County

(G-12365)
BARNES LOGGING CO INC
308 Golf Rd (27962-1114)
P.O. Box 665 (27962-0665)
PHONE.................................252 799-6016
Jack O Barnes Junior, *Pr*
Jack O Barnes Senior, *VP*
Connie Barnes, *Treas*
Christine Barnes, *Sec*
EMP: 14 **EST:** 1984
SQ FT: 1,100
SALES (est): 1.53MM **Privately Held**
SIC: 2411 Logging camps and contractors

(G-12366)
BASTROP SKID COMPANY (PA)
111 W Water St (27962-1305)
PHONE.................................252 793-6600
Thomas Harrison, *Pr*
Rexanne Harrison, *VP*
Trudy C Respess, *Sec*
EMP: 9 **EST:** 1982
SQ FT: 1,000
SALES (est): 2.17MM
SALES (corp-wide): 2.17MM **Privately Held**

SIC: 2448 5031 Pallets, wood; Lumber: rough, dressed, and finished

(G-12367)
CAROLINA MAT INCORPORATED
193 Hwy 149 N (27962-9309)
P.O. Box 339 (27962-0339)
PHONE.................................252 793-1111
Susan Harrison, *Pr*
Margaret Harrison, *Pr*
Susan Harrison, *VP*
EMP: 15 **EST:** 1985
SQ FT: 6,000
SALES (est): 2.19MM **Privately Held**
Web: www.carolinamat.com
SIC: 2448 Pallets, wood

(G-12368)
CBR LOGGING LLC
105 Ange Dr (27962-9113)
PHONE.................................252 791-0494
EMP: 9 **EST:** 2019
SALES (est): 432.28K **Privately Held**
SIC: 2411 Logging

(G-12369)
CROSSTIES PLUS LLC
383 Industrial Park Rd (27962-9695)
PHONE.................................252 943-7437
Ernest Derstine, *Managing Member*
EMP: 10 **EST:** 2011
SALES (est): 640.03K **Privately Held**
SIC: 2421 Sawmills and planing mills, general

(G-12370)
DIVERSIFIED WOOD PRODUCTS INC
Also Called: Dwp
111 W Water St Ste 1 (27962-1347)
P.O. Box 706 (27962-0706)
PHONE.................................252 793-6600
EMP: 15 **EST:** 1995
SQ FT: 10,000
SALES (est): 2.16MM **Privately Held**
Web: www.dwpworks.com
SIC: 2448 Pallets, wood

(G-12371)
DOMTAR PAPER COMPANY LLC
Also Called: Plymouth Mill
1375 Nc Hwy 149 N (27962)
P.O. Box 747 (27962-0747)
PHONE.................................252 793-8111
Jack Bray, *Brnch Mgr*
EMP: 375
Web: www.domtar.com
SIC: 2621 2631 2421 Paper mills; Paperboard mills; Sawmills and planing mills, general
HQ: Domtar Paper Company, Llc
234 Kingsley Park Dr
Fort Mill SC 29715

(G-12372)
EDSEL G BARNES JR INC
1458 Morrattock Rd (27962-8401)
PHONE.................................252 793-4170
Edsel G Barnes Jr, *Pr*
EMP: 9 **EST:** 2013
SALES (est): 279.4K **Privately Held**
SIC: 2411 Logging

(G-12373)
GEO SPECIALTY CHEMICALS INC
Main St Extension (27962)
P.O. Box 68 (27962-0068)
PHONE.................................252 793-2121
Herb Myers, *Mgr*
EMP: 4
SALES (corp-wide): 41.27MM **Privately Held**

Web: www.geosc.com
SIC: 2819 Industrial inorganic chemicals, nec
HQ: Geo Specialty Chemicals, Inc.
105 N Axtel Ave
Milford IL 60953

(G-12374)
H & L LOGGING INC
1166 Long Ridge Rd (27962-8707)
PHONE..................................252 793-2778
Louis E White, *Pr*
Vanessa White, *VP*
EMP: 15 EST: 1999
SALES (est): 968.47K **Privately Held**
Web: www.renttoownlewistonme.com
SIC: 2411 Logging camps and contractors

(G-12375)
KITTEN KABOODLE ALPACAS
327 Fairlane Rd (27962-9650)
PHONE..................................252 289-5654
Rachel Jeans, *Prin*
EMP: 4 EST: 2018
SALES (est): 87.64K **Privately Held**
SIC: 2231 Alpacas, mohair: woven

(G-12376)
M M & D HARVESTING INC
385 Roxie Reese Rd (27962-9084)
PHONE..................................252 793-4074
EMP: 5 EST: 1994
SALES (est): 600.88K **Privately Held**
SIC: 2411 Logging

(G-12377)
RICHARD WEST CO INC
1174 Us Highway 64 W (27962-8846)
P.O. Box 868 (27962-0868)
PHONE..................................252 793-4440
Harvey West, *Pr*
Richard G West, *VP*
Ethel West, *Sec*
EMP: 8 EST: 1937
SQ FT: 22,000
SALES (est): 676.33K **Privately Held**
Web: www.richardwestcompany.com
SIC: 2448 Pallets, wood

(G-12378)
WASHINGTON CNTY NEWSPAPERS INC
Also Called: Roanke Beacon, The
212 W Water St (27962-1212)
P.O. Box 726 (27962-0726)
PHONE..................................252 793-2123
Gary R Cunard, *Pr*
EMP: 4 EST: 1998
SALES (est): 272.8K **Privately Held**
Web: www.roanokebeacon.com
SIC: 2711 Newspapers: publishing only, not printed on site

(G-12379)
WEYERHAEUSER COMPANY
1000 Nc Hwy 149 N (27962-9544)
P.O. Box 787 (27962-0787)
PHONE..................................252 791-3200
Kenneth Mcride, *Mgr*
EMP: 10
SALES (corp-wide): 7.67B **Publicly Held**
Web: www.weyerhaeuser.com
SIC: 5031 2421 Lumber: rough, dressed, and finished; Lumber: rough, sawed, or planed
PA: Weyerhaeuser Company
220 Occidental Ave S
Seattle WA 98104
206 539-3000

Point Harbor
Currituck County

(G-12380)
BUFFALO CITY DISTILLERY LLC
8821 Caratoke Hwy (27964-9602)
PHONE..................................252 256-1477
Clifford C Byrum Junior, *Managing Member*
EMP: 5 EST: 2018
SALES (est): 49.63K **Privately Held**
SIC: 2085 Distilled and blended liquors

(G-12381)
POINT HARBOR ART
103 Sumac Ln (27964-1404)
P.O. Box 66 (27964-0066)
PHONE..................................804 852-3633
Ray Edmonds, *Prin*
EMP: 5 EST: 2016
SALES (est): 51.08K **Privately Held**
Web: www.pointharborart.com
SIC: 3993 Signs and advertising specialties

Polkton
Anson County

(G-12382)
A B METALS OF POLKTON LLC
6245 Us Highway 74 W (28135-8432)
PHONE..................................704 694-6635
EMP: 6 EST: 2020
SALES (est): 364.61K **Privately Held**
Web: www.abmetalsllc.com
SIC: 3444 Metal roofing and roof drainage equipment

(G-12383)
AMERICAN BUILDERS ANSON INC (PA)
8564 Hwy 74 W (28135-8446)
P.O. Box 8 (28135-0008)
PHONE..................................704 272-7655
W Bruce Thomas, *Pr*
Walter G Thomas Junior, *VP*
Ralph E Thomas, *VP*
Patricia M Thomas, *Sec*
EMP: 20 EST: 1972
SQ FT: 2,400
SALES (est): 2.26MM
SALES (corp-wide): 2.26MM **Privately Held**
SIC: 1542 3325 Farm building construction; Rolling mill rolls, cast steel

(G-12384)
ANSON MACHINE WORKS INC
505 Hwy 74 (28135)
PHONE..................................704 272-7657
EMP: 8 EST: 2016
SALES (est): 204.04K **Privately Held**
Web: www.ansonmachine.com
SIC: 3599 Machine shop, jobbing and repair

(G-12385)
ANSON MACHINE WORKS INC
100 Efird Cir (28135-2100)
P.O. Box 269 (28133-0269)
PHONE..................................704 272-7657
Steve Garris, *Pr*
Lynn Godwin, *VP*
Randy Smith, *Sec*
Joel L Godwin, *Treas*
EMP: 22 EST: 1988
SQ FT: 17,500
SALES (est): 2.46MM **Privately Held**
Web: www.ansonmachine.com
SIC: 3599 Machine shop, jobbing and repair

(G-12386)
D & T SOY CANDLES
152 Hawk Rd (28135-7223)
PHONE..................................704 320-2804
Teresa Mercer, *Prin*
EMP: 4 EST: 2015
SALES (est): 70.95K **Privately Held**
SIC: 3999 Candles

(G-12387)
H & H LOGIN
2355 Tarpin Town Rd (28135-8773)
PHONE..................................704 272-8763
Donald K Hildreth, *Owner*
EMP: 6 EST: 2001
SALES (est): 206.2K **Privately Held**
SIC: 2411 Logging

(G-12388)
JRT LOGGING INC
117 Pine Log Rd (28135-6221)
PHONE..................................704 322-0458
EMP: 5 EST: 2017
SALES (est): 81.72K **Privately Held**
SIC: 2411 Logging

(G-12389)
PRECISION SAW WORKS INC
10424 Highway 742 N # 742n (28135-7712)
PHONE..................................704 272-8326
Frank Curran, *Owner*
EMP: 40 EST: 1986
SQ FT: 1,900
SALES (est): 1.93MM **Privately Held**
Web: www.precisionsawworks.com
SIC: 7699 3425 Knife, saw and tool sharpening and repair; Saw blades and handsaws

(G-12390)
SOUTHERN FABRICATORS INC
8188 Us Highway 74 W (28135-8442)
P.O. Box 97 (28135-0097)
PHONE..................................704 272-7615
Ken Carpenter Senior, *Pr*
Hugh Efird, *Stockholder**
Ken Carpenter Junior, *Prin*
▲ EMP: 80 EST: 1968
SQ FT: 100,000
SALES (est): 22.22MM **Privately Held**
Web: www.southernfabricators.net
SIC: 3444 Sheet metalwork

Pollocksville
Jones County

(G-12391)
ADVANCED PLASTIC EXTRUSION LLC
Also Called: Apex
213 Sermon Rd (28573-9218)
PHONE..................................252 224-1444
Ronald Buck, *Managing Member*
EMP: 7 EST: 2014
SALES (est): 1.02MM **Privately Held**
Web: www.apex-extrusion.com
SIC: 3089 Injection molding of plastics

(G-12392)
BENDER SIGNS
8400 Us Highway 17 (28573-8787)
PHONE..................................252 631-5144
EMP: 4 EST: 2018
SALES (est): 202.83K **Privately Held**
Web: www.bendersigns.com
SIC: 3993 Signs and advertising specialties

(G-12393)
MARINE & INDUSTRIAL PLASTICS
Hwy 17 Sermon Lane (28573)
PHONE..................................252 224-1000
C Hunter Williams, *Pr*
Susan T Williams, *Sec*
EMP: 8 EST: 1991
SALES (est): 117.37K **Privately Held**
SIC: 3089 3081 Plastics boats and other marine equipment; Unsupported plastics film and sheet

(G-12394)
MIKE S CUSTOM CABINETS INC
587 Island Creek Rd (28573-9451)
PHONE..................................252 224-5351
Michael Meadows, *Pr*
Kimberly A Meadows, *Sec*
EMP: 8 EST: 1991
SALES (est): 688.76K **Privately Held**
Web: www.mikescustomcabinetsinc.com
SIC: 2434 Wood kitchen cabinets

Potecasi
Northampton County

(G-12395)
BRANT & LASSITER SEPTIC TANK
Hwy 35 (27867)
P.O. Box 157 (27867-0157)
PHONE..................................252 587-4321
David Cooper, *Pr*
Felisia Cooper, *VP*
EMP: 6 EST: 1968
SQ FT: 3,000
SALES (est): 525.4K **Privately Held**
Web: www.bryantandlassiter.com
SIC: 3272 7699 Septic tanks, concrete; Aircraft and heavy equipment repair services

Powells Point
Currituck County

(G-12396)
CAROLINA CUSTOM CABINETS INC
Also Called: Carolina Cstm Cabinets & Furn
102 Park Dr (27966-9616)
P.O. Box 252 (27949-0252)
PHONE..................................252 491-5475
Rex Filion, *Pr*
Arlene Filion, *Sec*
EMP: 8 EST: 1989
SQ FT: 5,000
SALES (est): 892.44K **Privately Held**
Web: www.carolinacustomcabinet.com
SIC: 2434 Wood kitchen cabinets

(G-12397)
HARCO AIR LLC
116 Ballast Rock Rd Unit L (27966-9614)
PHONE..................................252 491-5220
Phillip Rose, *Managing Member*
Robert Harwood Junior, *Managing Member*
EMP: 8 EST: 2017
SALES (est): 600K **Privately Held**
SIC: 1711 3444 Heating and air conditioning contractors; Ducts, sheet metal

(G-12398)
JAMES LAMMERS
Also Called: Lammers Glass & Design
7715 Caratoke Hwy (27966-9738)
P.O. Box 428 (27966-0428)
PHONE..................................252 491-2303
James Lammers, *Owner*

Princeton - Johnston County (G-12399)

Theresa G Lammers, *Genl Mgr*
EMP: 4 **EST:** 1972
SALES (est): 245.52K **Privately Held**
Web: www.lammersglass.com
SIC: 5947 3231 Gift shop; Stained glass; made from purchased glass

Princeton
Johnston County

(G-12399)
CAROLINA PRINTING CO
640 Quarterhorse Rd (27569-8645)
PHONE..................................919 834-0433
Steve Yancey, *Owner*
EMP: 4 **EST:** 1982
SALES (est): 241.5K **Privately Held**
Web: www.carolinaprintingcompany.com
SIC: 2752 2759 Offset printing; Letterpress printing

(G-12400)
HEIDELBERG MTLS STHAST AGG LLC
476 Edwards Rd (27569-7041)
P.O. Box 180 (27569-0180)
PHONE..................................919 936-4221
Jesse Bizzell, *Mgr*
EMP: 22
SALES (corp-wide): 21.19B **Privately Held**
Web: www.hansonbiz.com
SIC: 1422 1521 Crushed and broken limestone; Single-family housing construction
HQ: Heidelberg Materials Southeast Agg Llc
3237 Satellite Blvd # 30
Duluth GA 30096
770 491-2756

(G-12401)
HYDRANT MECHANICS
7303 Hickory Crossroads Rd (27569-8119)
PHONE..................................919 922-3829
EMP: 6 **EST:** 2014
SALES (est): 466.75K **Privately Held**
Web: www.hydrantmechanic.com
SIC: 3491 Industrial valves

(G-12402)
POWERSECURE INC
Also Called: Southern Flow Companies
6137 Princeton Kenly Rd (27569-7955)
PHONE..................................919 818-8700
Christ Edge, *Brnch Mgr*
EMP: 9
SALES (corp-wide): 25.25B **Publicly Held**
Web: www.powersecure.com
SIC: 3621 Power generators
HQ: Powersecure, Inc.
4068 Stirrup Creek Dr
Durham NC 27703
919 556-3056

(G-12403)
S T WOOTEN CORPORATION
Also Called: Princeton Asphalt Plant
6401 Us Highway 70 E (27569-7828)
PHONE..................................919 965-7176
David Fountain, *Mgr*
EMP: 22
SALES (corp-wide): 319.83MM **Privately Held**
Web: www.stwcorp.com
SIC: 3531 Asphalt plant, including gravel-mix type
PA: S. T. Wooten Corporation
3801 Black Creek Rd Se
Wilson NC 27893
252 291-5165

(G-12404)
S T WOOTEN CORPORATION
Princeton Commercial Cnstr Off
6401 Us Highway 70 E (27569-7828)
PHONE..................................919 965-9880
Reade Dawson, *Mgr*
EMP: 22
SALES (corp-wide): 319.83MM **Privately Held**
Web: www.stwcorp.com
SIC: 2951 1611 1794 Asphalt paving mixtures and blocks; Highway and street construction; Excavation work
PA: S. T. Wooten Corporation
3801 Black Creek Rd Se
Wilson NC 27893
252 291-5165

(G-12405)
STEVES CABINETS PLUS INC
121 Christopher Ave (27569-9065)
PHONE..................................919 351-0454
John S Williamson, *Prin*
EMP: 5 **EST:** 2008
SALES (est): 83.35K **Privately Held**
SIC: 2434 Wood kitchen cabinets

Princeville
Edgecombe County

(G-12406)
SOUTHERN STATES COOP INC
Also Called: Tarboro Serv
142 Commercial Rd (27886-9728)
P.O. Box 1214 (27886-1214)
PHONE..................................252 823-2520
Joe Dupree, *Mgr*
EMP: 7
SALES (corp-wide): 1.71B **Privately Held**
Web: www.southernstates.com
SIC: 2048 5999 Prepared feeds, nec; Farm equipment and supplies
PA: Southern States Cooperative, Incorporated
6606 W Broad St Ste B
Richmond VA 23230
804 281-1000

Prospect Hill
Caswell County

(G-12407)
L & W GL MIRROR & WD WORKS LLC
14480 Nc Highway 86 S (27314-9491)
PHONE..................................336 562-2155
Illiam F Hill, *Prin*
EMP: 5 **EST:** 2018
SALES (est): 102.77K **Privately Held**
SIC: 2431 Millwork

(G-12408)
ROYAL PARK UNIFORMS INC
14139 Nc Highway 86 S (27314-9488)
P.O. Box 24 (27314-0024)
PHONE..................................336 562-3345
William K Royal, *Pr*
Geraldine Royal, *
Steven R Royal, *
Gregory W Royal, *
◆ **EMP:** 49 **EST:** 1973
SQ FT: 175,000
SALES (est): 1.5MM **Privately Held**
Web: www.royal-park.com
SIC: 2389 Uniforms and vestments

(G-12409)
W T MANDER & SON INC
1587 Egypt Rd (27314-9525)
PHONE..................................336 562-5755
Tom Mander, *Pr*
Joy Mander, *VP*
Jacob Mander, *Treas*
EMP: 5 **EST:** 1998
SALES (est): 363.35K **Privately Held**
SIC: 3545 Machine tool accessories

Purlear
Wilkes County

(G-12410)
DANNY HUFFMAN LOGGING LLC
154 Fletcher Creek Ln (28665-9062)
PHONE..................................336 973-0555
EMP: 6 **EST:** 2012
SALES (est): 81.72K **Privately Held**
SIC: 2411 Logging camps and contractors

(G-12411)
GLYPHUS LLC
4159 Summit Rd (28665-9217)
PHONE..................................336 973-4793
Joni Meredth, *Pr*
EMP: 4 **EST:** 2018
SALES (est): 54.51K **Privately Held**
SIC: 2741 Miscellaneous publishing

(G-12412)
GREENE LOGGING
9145 Boone Trl (28665-9191)
PHONE..................................336 667-6960
Scott Greene, *Owner*
EMP: 5 **EST:** 2000
SALES (est): 275.29K **Privately Held**
Web: www.greenelogging.com
SIC: 2411 Logging camps and contractors

(G-12413)
SPRING ROCK FARMS INC
4701 Parsonsville Rd (28665-8833)
PHONE..................................336 973-1447
Jonathan Watson, *Pr*
EMP: 4 **EST:** 2014
SALES (est): 114.39K **Privately Held**
SIC: 3999 Candles

Raeford
Hoke County

(G-12414)
BENNETT ELEC MAINT & CNSTR LLC
Also Called: Electrical
586 Allegiance St (28376-8656)
PHONE..................................910 231-0300
Jimmy Bennett, *CEO*
EMP: 5 **EST:** 2001
SALES (est): 253.17K **Privately Held**
Web: www.fayetteville-nc-electrician.com
SIC: 1521 1389 1731 Single-family housing construction; Construction, repair, and dismantling services; Electrical work

(G-12415)
BUTTERBALL LLC
1140 E Central Ave (28376-3000)
PHONE..................................910 875-8711
EMP: 275
SALES (corp-wide): 11.24B **Publicly Held**
Web: www.butterballfoodservice.com
SIC: 2015 Turkey, processed, nsk
HQ: Butterball, Llc
1 Butterball Ln
Garner NC 27529
919 255-7900

(G-12416)
CONOPCO INC
Also Called: Unilever
100 Faberge Blvd (28376-3406)
PHONE..................................910 875-4121
Kevin Beck, *Genl Mgr*
EMP: 290
SALES (corp-wide): 62.39B **Privately Held**
Web: www.autoclor.com
SIC: 2844 Perfumes, cosmetics and other toilet preparations
HQ: Conopco, Inc.
700 Sylvan Ave
Englewood Cliffs NJ 07632
201 894-7760

(G-12417)
COPIA LABS INC
2501 Us Hwy 401 Bus (28376-5776)
P.O. Box 447 (28376-0447)
PHONE..................................910 904-1000
J Todd Sumner, *Pr*
Frances Sumner, *Sec*
EMP: 5 **EST:** 1994
SQ FT: 6,700
SALES (est): 497.37K **Privately Held**
Web: www.copialabs.net
SIC: 2899 Chemical preparations, nec

(G-12418)
CURRIE MOTORSPORTS INC
Also Called: CMS Printing Services
611 College Dr (28376-2403)
P.O. Box 972 (28376-0972)
PHONE..................................910 580-1765
Robie W Currie, *CEO*
Linda Cadlett, *Sec*
EMP: 4 **EST:** 2007
SALES (est): 356.38K **Privately Held**
SIC: 2752 Commercial printing, lithographic

(G-12419)
CW MEDIA INC
Also Called: Mommy's Numbers
220 Crestwood Ln (28376-7828)
PHONE..................................910 302-3066
Crystal Waddell, *CEO*
EMP: 5 **EST:** 2017
SALES (est): 120.95K **Privately Held**
Web: www.collageandwood.com
SIC: 2399 2499 Military insignia, textile; Signboards, wood

(G-12420)
FARM CHEMICALS INC (PA)
Also Called: Fci-An Agricultural Service Co
2274 Saint Pauls Dr (28376-5616)
P.O. Box 667 (28376-0667)
PHONE..................................910 875-4277
Alfred K Leach Junior, *Pr*
Earl Hendrix, *Sec*
▲ **EMP:** 12 **EST:** 1964
SQ FT: 2,500
SALES (est): 23.11MM
SALES (corp-wide): 23.11MM **Privately Held**
Web: www.fciag.com
SIC: 5153 2873 Grains; Nitrogen solutions (fertilizer)

(G-12421)
GARNERS SEPTIC TANK INC
8574 Turnpike Rd (28376-6327)
PHONE..................................919 718-5181
Eddie Garner, *Pr*
EMP: 9 **EST:** 2017
SALES (est): 1.19MM **Privately Held**
Web: www.garnerssseptictanks.com

GEOGRAPHIC SECTION   Raleigh - Wake County (G-12451)

SIC: 3272 Septic tanks, concrete

(G-12422)
GINAS PROCESSING & PRTG CTR
114 Harris Ln (28376-9647)
PHONE..................................910 476-0037
EMP: 4 EST: 2014
SALES (est): 83.91K **Privately Held**
SIC: 2752 Commercial printing, lithographic

(G-12423)
HOUSE OF RAEFORD FARMS INC
1000 E Central Ave (28376-3039)
P.O. Box 3628 (29070-1628)
PHONE..................................910 289-3191
Donald Taber, Ch
EMP: 840
SALES (corp-wide): 1.79B **Privately Held**
Web: www.houseofraeford.com
SIC: 2015 Poultry slaughtering and processing
HQ: House Of Raeford Farms, Inc.
    3333 S Us Highway 117
    Rose Hill NC 28458
    912 222-4090

(G-12424)
I T G RAEFORD
1001 Turnpike Rd (28376-8566)
PHONE..................................910 875-3736
Barry Tapp, Prin
EMP: 8 EST: 2010
SALES (est): 267.74K **Privately Held**
SIC: 2231 Broadwoven fabric mills, wool

(G-12425)
KINETIC PERFORMANCE LLC
393 Gable Dr (28376-6919)
PHONE..................................910 248-2121
Keith Pilgrim, Prin
EMP: 5 EST: 2016
SALES (est): 57.23K **Privately Held**
Web: www.kineticperformancellc.com
SIC: 3999 Manufacturing industries, nec

(G-12426)
MOES HNDY SVCS FNCE INSTL MNO ✪
185 Desert Orchid Cir (28376-1546)
PHONE..................................910 712-1402
Jamie Mclaurin, CEO
EMP: 5 EST: 2022
SALES (est): 75.42K **Privately Held**
SIC: 7699 3312 Repair services, nec; Fence posts, iron and steel

(G-12427)
NATURES CUP LLC
1930 Club Pond Rd (28376-8691)
PHONE..................................910 795-2700
Aundrea Dinkins, Managing Member
EMP: 6 EST: 2021
SALES (est): 150K **Privately Held**
SIC: 2099 Tea blending

(G-12428)
PARACLETE XP SKY VENTURE LLC
190 Paraclete Dr (28376-6844)
PHONE..................................910 848-2600
EMP: 13 EST: 2009
SALES (est): 252.27K **Privately Held**
Web: www.paracletexp.com
SIC: 7999 2759 Instruction schools, camps, and services; Screen printing

(G-12429)
PARACLETE XP SKYVENTURE LLC
925 Doc Brown Rd (28376-8081)
PHONE..................................910 904-0027
Timothy D'annunzio, Managing Member

EMP: 35 EST: 2007
SALES (est): 1.29MM **Privately Held**
Web: www.paracletexp.com
SIC: 7999 2759 Instruction schools, camps, and services; Screen printing

(G-12430)
PARISH SIGN & SERVICE INC
627 Laurinburg Rd (28376-2526)
P.O. Box 766 (28376-0766)
PHONE..................................910 875-6121
William R Parish, Pr
Linda Parish, Sec
EMP: 20 EST: 1982
SQ FT: 7,000
SALES (est): 2.43MM **Privately Held**
Web: www.parishsigns.com
SIC: 3993 1799 Electric signs; Sign installation and maintenance

(G-12431)
PENNSYLVANIA TRANS TECH INC
Also Called: Pennsylvania Transformer Co
201 Carolina Dr (28376-9272)
PHONE..................................910 875-7600
EMP: 65
Web: www.patransformer.com
SIC: 3612 Distribution transformers, electric
HQ: Pennsylvania Transformer Technology, Llc
    30 Curry Ave Ste 2
    Canonsburg PA 15317
    724 873-2100

(G-12432)
PRECISE SHEET METAL MECH LLC
124 Winterfield Dr (28376-5408)
PHONE..................................336 693-3246
Adela Garcia, Prin
EMP: 6 EST: 2019
SALES (est): 120.32K **Privately Held**
SIC: 3444 Sheet metalwork

(G-12433)
QUINNESSENTIAL TOOLS COMPANY
117 Kirkland Pl (28376-5919)
PHONE..................................540 623-7965
Anthony Quinn, Prin
EMP: 7 EST: 2016
SALES (est): 247.06K **Privately Held**
SIC: 3599 Industrial machinery, nec

(G-12434)
RAINEY AND WILSON LOGISTICS
1308 Checker Dr (28376-5041)
PHONE..................................910 736-8540
Lawerence Rainey, Prin
EMP: 4 EST: 2020
SALES (est): 170K **Privately Held**
SIC: 3537 Trucks, tractors, loaders, carriers, and similar equipment

(G-12435)
REBECCA TRICKEY
Also Called: Rebecca Kaye International
389 Gibson Dr (28376-5569)
PHONE..................................910 584-5549
EMP: 6 EST: 2012
SALES (est): 361.67K **Privately Held**
SIC: 2844 7389 Hair preparations, including shampoos; Business Activities at Non-Commercial Site

(G-12436)
ROCKFISH CREEK WINERY LLC
1709 Arabia Rd (28376-7062)
PHONE..................................910 729-0648
Imberly Rulli, Prin
EMP: 9 EST: 2018
SALES (est): 371.15K **Privately Held**

Web: www.rockfishcreekwinery.com
SIC: 2084 Wines

(G-12437)
SAL AND SONS WOODWORKING LLC
1402 Saint Johns Loop (28376-7249)
PHONE..................................910 489-5373
Alvatore E Candela, Prin
EMP: 4 EST: 2018
SALES (est): 54.13K **Privately Held**
SIC: 2431 Millwork

(G-12438)
SAPPS VENTURES
994 Wayside Rd (28376-6404)
PHONE..................................910 824-0762
EMP: 4 EST: 2011
SALES (est): 77.4K **Privately Held**
SIC: 3645 Table lamps

(G-12439)
SOUTHERN ELEGANCE CANDLE LLC
174 Stream Fall Ct (28376-8542)
PHONE..................................706 825-7658
D'shawn Russell, Owner
EMP: 8 EST: 2015
SALES (est): 477.16K **Privately Held**
Web: www.secandleco.com
SIC: 3999 Candles

(G-12440)
SPC-USA INC
Also Called: Sun Path Contracting
404 W Edinborough Ave (28376-2832)
PHONE..................................910 875-9002
Patricia Thomas, Pr
EMP: 11 EST: 2005
SALES (est): 225.14K **Privately Held**
Web: www.sunpath.com
SIC: 2399 Fabricated textile products, nec

(G-12441)
ST LUCIE WOODWORKS INC
366 Bostic Rd (28376-6104)
PHONE..................................772 626-4778
Robert M Mcnaughton, Prin
EMP: 5 EST: 2017
SALES (est): 98.91K **Privately Held**
SIC: 2431 Millwork

(G-12442)
SUN PATH PRODUCTS INC
404 W Edinborough Ave (28376-2832)
PHONE..................................910 875-9002
Patricia Thomas, Pr
EMP: 90 EST: 1986
SQ FT: 28,000
SALES (est): 9.87MM **Privately Held**
Web: www.sunpath.com
SIC: 3429 Parachute hardware

(G-12443)
TYTON NC BIOFUELS LLC
800 Pate Rd (28376-9189)
PHONE..................................910 878-7820
Benjamin Steves, *
EMP: 45 EST: 2014
SQ FT: 4,000
SALES (est): 7.05MM **Privately Held**
Web: www.tytonbiofuels.com
SIC: 2869 Ethyl alcohol, ethanol

(G-12444)
UNILEVER
4152 Turnpike Rd (28376-7343)
PHONE..................................910 988-1054
Lauren Garner, Prin
EMP: 9 EST: 2019

SALES (est): 299.41K **Privately Held**
Web: www.unilever.com
SIC: 2844 Perfumes, cosmetics and other toilet preparations

(G-12445)
WILLIAM BRANTLEY
Also Called: Professnal Prprty Prservations
637 Dunrobin Dr (28376-9149)
PHONE..................................910 627-7286
William Brantley, Owner
EMP: 4 EST: 2020
SALES (est): 83K **Privately Held**
SIC: 1389 Construction, repair, and dismantling services

Raleigh
Wake County

(G-12446)
2391 EATONS FERRY RD ASSOC LLC
7610 Six Forks Rd Ste 200 (27615-5049)
PHONE..................................919 844-0565
Rabon Robert Gary, Prin
EMP: 5 EST: 2014
SALES (est): 114.25K **Privately Held**
SIC: 3625 Motor controls and accessories

(G-12447)
4 OVER LLC
Also Called: ASAP Printing
5609 Departure Dr (27616-1842)
PHONE..................................919 875-3187
Ed Dignam, Brnch Mgr
EMP: 15
SALES (corp-wide): 172.36MM **Privately Held**
Web: www.4over.com
SIC: 2752 Offset printing
HQ: 4 Over, Llc
    1225 Los Angeles St
    Glendale CA 91204
    818 246-1170

(G-12448)
522 FLIPPER LLC
4301 Worley Dr (27613-1593)
PHONE..................................919 785-3417
James Morton, Prin
EMP: 4 EST: 2019
SALES (est): 88.38K **Privately Held**
SIC: 3651 Video triggers (remote control TV devices)

(G-12449)
78C SPIRITS
2660 Discovery Dr (27616-1906)
PHONE..................................919 615-0839
EMP: 5 EST: 2015
SALES (est): 188.09K **Privately Held**
SIC: 2085 Distilled and blended liquors

(G-12450)
919 MOTORING LLC
5540 Atlantic Springs Rd Ste 109 (27616-1860)
PHONE..................................919 872-4996
Shaun R Reilly, Prin
EMP: 6 EST: 2008
SALES (est): 463.42K **Privately Held**
Web: www.919motoring.com
SIC: 3465 Hub caps, automobile: stamped metal

(G-12451)
A & B CHEM-DRY
4208 Bertram Dr (27604-2658)
PHONE..................................919 878-0288
EMP: 16 EST: 1999

Raleigh - Wake County (G-12452)

SALES (est): 272.74K **Privately Held**
Web: www.abchemdry.com
SIC: 7349 2842 Building maintenance services, nec; Polishes and sanitation goods

(G-12452)
A PLUS KITCHEN BATH CABINETS
120 Saint Albans Dr Apt 291 (27609-6399)
PHONE..................................919 622-0515
Margaret Tobin, *Prin*
EMP: 4 EST: 2016
SALES (est): 58.22K **Privately Held**
Web: www.apluskitchenbathremodeling.com
SIC: 2434 Wood kitchen cabinets

(G-12453)
A1GUMBALLS
Also Called: A1 Vending
316 W Millbrook Rd Ste 113 (27609)
PHONE..................................919 494-1322
Scott Tidball, *Owner*
EMP: 5 EST: 2000
SALES (est): 486K **Privately Held**
Web: www.frugalburger.com
SIC: 3556 Chewing gum machinery

(G-12454)
AARDVARK SCREEN PRINTING
1600 Automotive Way (27604-2050)
PHONE..................................919 829-9058
Greg A Clayton, *Pt*
EMP: 5 EST: 1999
SALES (est): 331.55K **Privately Held**
Web: www.aardvarkscreenprinting.net
SIC: 2759 Screen printing

(G-12455)
ABB ENTERPRISE SOFTWARE INC
Also Called: Power Technologies
1021 Main Campus Dr (27606-5238)
P.O. Box 90999 (27675-0999)
PHONE..................................919 582-3283
Jamie Travino, *Dir*
EMP: 150
Web: new.abb.com
SIC: 3612 8711 3613 3625 Transformers, except electric; Engineering services; Switchgear and switchboard apparatus; Relays and industrial controls
HQ: Abb Inc.
  305 Gregson Dr
  Cary NC 27511

(G-12456)
ABB INC
901 Main Campus Dr Ste 300 (27606-5293)
PHONE..................................919 856-3920
EMP: 95
Web: new.abb.com
SIC: 3612 Transformers, except electric
HQ: Abb Inc.
  305 Gregson Dr
  Cary NC 27511

(G-12457)
ABB INC
Also Called: ABB Power Systems
1021 Main Campus Dr (27606-5239)
P.O. Box 91209 (27675-1209)
PHONE..................................919 856-2360
Greg Scheu, *Brnch Mgr*
EMP: 76
Web: new.abb.com
SIC: 3613 3675 3612 Switchgear and switchboard apparatus; Electronic capacitors; Power and distribution transformers
HQ: Abb Inc.
  305 Gregson Dr
  Cary NC 27511

(G-12458)
ABB POWER SYSTEMS INC
901 Main Campus Dr Ste 300 (27606-5293)
PHONE..................................919 856-2389
EMP: 10 EST: 2016
SALES (est): 238K **Privately Held**
SIC: 3612 Transformers, except electric
PA: Abb Ltd
  Affolternstrasse 44
  ZUrich ZH 8050

(G-12459)
ABB POWER T & D COMPANY INC
1021 Main Campus Dr (27606-5238)
P.O. Box 91471 (27675-1471)
PHONE..................................919 856-3806
Enrique Santacana, *Pr*
▼ **EMP: 1300 EST:** 1988
SALES (est): 210.32MM **Privately Held**
SIC: 3612 Distribution transformers, electric
HQ: Abb Inc.
  305 Gregson Dr
  Cary NC 27511

(G-12460)
ABBOTT SALES LLC
1309 Hedgelawn Way (27615-6908)
PHONE..................................919 523-5478
Robert Abbott, *Prin*
EMP: 5 EST: 2012
SALES (est): 88.14K **Privately Held**
SIC: 2834 Pharmaceutical preparations

(G-12461)
ABC FITNESS PRODUCTS LLC (PA)
8541 Glenwood Ave (27612-7358)
PHONE..................................704 649-0000
▲ **EMP: 6 EST:** 2011
SALES (est): 482.29K
SALES (corp-wide): 482.29K **Privately Held**
Web: www.abcfitnessproducts.com
SIC: 3949 Exercise equipment

(G-12462)
ABC PUBLICATION
924 Blenheim Dr (27612-4907)
PHONE..................................919 614-3451
Charles O'bryant, *Prin*
EMP: 8 EST: 2017
SALES (est): 117.27K **Privately Held**
Web: abc.nc.gov
SIC: 2741 Miscellaneous publishing

(G-12463)
ABLE SOFTSYSTEMS CORP
1017 Main Campus Dr Ste 1501 (27606-5204)
PHONE..................................919 241-7907
John Kahsai, *Pr*
Ruth Kahsai, *Prin*
EMP: 5 EST: 2002
SALES (est): 342.81K **Privately Held**
SIC: 7372 7371 Prepackaged software; Software programming applications

(G-12464)
ABS SOUTHEAST LLC (PA)
5902 Fayetteville Rd (27603-4530)
PHONE..................................919 329-0014
Wayne Sullivan, *Managing Member*
EMP: 10 EST: 2012
SALES (est): 23.49MM
SALES (corp-wide): 23.49MM **Privately Held**
Web: www.truteam.com

SIC: 3089 1742 Gutters (glass fiber reinforced), fiberglass or plastics; Insulation, buildings

(G-12465)
ABSOLENT INC
6541 Meridien Dr Ste 125 (27616-3211)
P.O. Box 1279 (27596-1279)
PHONE..................................919 570-2862
Joshua Hannah, *Pr*
Edwin Sithes, *Pr*
Charles Sithes, *VP*
Brittany Long, *Mgr*
▲ **EMP: 17 EST:** 2006
SALES (est): 4.95MM **Privately Held**
Web: www.avanienvironmental.com
SIC: 3564 Air purification equipment

(G-12466)
ACC SPORTS JOURNAL
3012 Highwoods Blvd Ste 200 (27604-1037)
PHONE..................................919 846-7502
David Glenn, *Editor*
EMP: 10 EST: 2010
SALES (est): 333.45K **Privately Held**
Web: www.accsports.com
SIC: 2711 Newspapers, publishing and printing

(G-12467)
ACCORD HEALTHCARE INC (HQ)
8041 Arco Corporate Dr Ste 200 (27617)
PHONE..................................919 941-7878
Gerald Price, *Pr*
Burt Sullivan, *
▼ **EMP: 35 EST:** 2005
SQ FT: 6,160
SALES (est): 14.75MM **Privately Held**
Web: www.accordhealthcare.us
SIC: 2834 8011 Pharmaceutical preparations; Oncologist
PA: Intas Pharmaceuticals Limited
  Corporate House, Plot No. 255,
  Magnet Corporate Park,
  Ahmedabad GJ 380 0

(G-12468)
ACCUMED CORP (HQ)
160 Mine Lake Ct Ste 200 (27615-6417)
PHONE..................................800 278-6796
Jason Cardew, *CEO*
EMP: 100 EST: 2014
SALES (est): 117.13MM
SALES (corp-wide): 20.89B **Publicly Held**
Web: www.accumedtech.com
SIC: 3841 Medical instruments and equipment, blood and bone work
PA: Lear Corporation
  21557 Telegraph Rd
  Southfield MI 48033
  248 447-1500

(G-12469)
ACCURATE MACHINE & TOOL LLC
5124 Trademark Dr (27610-3024)
PHONE..................................919 212-0266
EMP: 14 EST: 2003
SQ FT: 20,300
SALES (est): 1.39MM **Privately Held**
Web: www.accuratemachining.com
SIC: 3599 Machine shop, jobbing and repair

(G-12470)
ACHILLI USA INC
4030 Wake Forest Rd Ste 349 (27609)
PHONE..................................704 940-0115
EMP: 4 EST: 2018
SALES (est): 179.35K **Privately Held**
Web: www.achilliusa.com

SIC: 3541 Grinding machines, metalworking

(G-12471)
ACORN CLIMBING LLC
8309 Davishire Dr (27615-1848)
PHONE..................................919 518-5022
EMP: 5 EST: 2018
SALES (est): 107.4K **Privately Held**
SIC: 3949 Sporting and athletic goods, nec

(G-12472)
ACOUSTIC IMAGE LLC
Also Called: Acoustic Image
839 The Village Cir (27615-6863)
PHONE..................................919 785-1280
▲ **EMP: 4 EST:** 1997
SALES (est): 396.88K **Privately Held**
Web: www.acousticimg.com
SIC: 3651 Amplifiers: radio, public address, or musical instrument

(G-12473)
ACROPLIS CNTRLS ENGINEERS PLLC
313 S Blount St Ste 200d (27601-1861)
PHONE..................................919 275-3884
Terence Morrison, *Pr*
EMP: 15 EST: 2014
SALES (est): 997.56K **Privately Held**
Web: www.acropoliscontrols.com
SIC: 8711 7373 3613 Electrical or electronic engineering; Turnkey vendors, computer systems; Control panels, electric

(G-12474)
ACW TECHNOLOGY INC
3725 Althorp Dr (27616-8457)
▲ **EMP:** 530
SIC: 3699 3841 Electrical equipment and supplies, nec; Medical instruments and equipment, blood and bone work

(G-12475)
ADAPTIVE TECHNOLOGIES LLC
Also Called: Beacon Prosthetics & Orthotics
3224 Lake Woodard Dr Ste 100 (27604-3659)
PHONE..................................919 231-6890
Eddie White, *Brnch Mgr*
EMP: 6
SALES (corp-wide): 24.99MM **Privately Held**
Web: www.beaconpo.com
SIC: 3842 Prosthetic appliances
HQ: Adaptive Technologies, Llc
  3224 Lake Woodard Dr # 100
  Raleigh NC 27604
  919 231-6890

(G-12476)
ADEMCO INC
Also Called: ADI Global Distribution
2741 Noblin Rd Ste 101 (27604-3381)
PHONE..................................919 872-5556
Johnny Hudson, *Brnch Mgr*
EMP: 8
SALES (corp-wide): 6.24B **Publicly Held**
Web: www.adiglobaldistribution.com
SIC: 5063 3669 3822 Electrical apparatus and equipment; Emergency alarms; Environmental controls
HQ: Ademco Inc.
  275 Broadhollow Rd # 400
  Melville NY 11747
  631 692-1000

(G-12477)
ADS PRINTING CO INC
733 W Hargett St (27603-1601)
P.O. Box 25667 (27611-5667)

GEOGRAPHIC SECTION
Raleigh - Wake County (G-12504)

PHONE.................................919 834-0579
W Bruce Cash, *Pr*
Sylvia M Cash, *VP*
EMP: 9 **EST:** 1958
SQ FT: 7,500
SALES (est): 940.25K **Privately Held**
SIC: 2752 Lithographing on metal

(G-12478)
ADVANCED BRACE & LIMB INC
3617 Nightfall Ct (27607-6370)
PHONE.................................919 818-0359
Carl Bruce Casciere, *Pr*
EMP: 7 **EST:** 2015
SALES (est): 288.25K **Privately Held**
Web: www.advancedbraceandlimb.com
SIC: 3842 Limbs, artificial

(G-12479)
ADVANCED NON-LETHAL TECH INC
8311 Brier Creek Pkwy (27617-7328)
PHONE.................................847 812-6450
David Chlystek, *Managing Member*
Felix Batts, *CEO*
Deloris E Jordan, *COO*
Dave Chlystek, *VP*
EMP: 6 **EST:** 2019
SALES (est): 404.66K **Privately Held**
SIC: 8731 7389 3489 Engineering laboratory, except testing; Design services; Smoke generators (ordnance)

(G-12480)
AEROFABB LLC
3312 Marcony Way (27610-4076)
PHONE.................................919 793-8487
EMP: 4 **EST:** 2018
SALES (est): 231.8K **Privately Held**
SIC: 3714 Motor vehicle parts and accessories

(G-12481)
AFI CAPITAL INC
801 Beacon Lake Dr (27610-1377)
PHONE.................................919 212-6400
Gregory W Page, *Pr*
Craven B Page, *
Greg Newey, *
▼ **EMP:** 120 **EST:** 1972
SQ FT: 82,000
SALES (est): 46.05MM **Privately Held**
Web: www.accufabnc.com
SIC: 3444 Sheet metal specialties, not stamped

(G-12482)
AIR PURIFICATION INC (PA)
8121 Ebenezer Church Rd (27612-7307)
PHONE.................................919 783-6161
TOLL FREE: 800
Ron Stumpo, *Pr*
Duane Dorsay, *VP*
EMP: 16 **EST:** 1986
SQ FT: 10,000
SALES (est): 2.16MM
SALES (corp-wide): 2.16MM **Privately Held**
Web: www.airpurificationinc.com
SIC: 3564 Blowers and fans

(G-12483)
AJC CRAFTWORKS INC
8900 Miranda Dr (27617-7682)
PHONE.................................919 279-1621
Adam Christopherson, *Pr*
EMP: 4 **EST:** 2017
SALES (est): 92.36K **Privately Held**
SIC: 3999 Manufacturing industries, nec

(G-12484)
AJINOMOTO HLTH NTRTN N AMER IN
Also Called: Ajinomoto
4020 Ajinomoto Dr (27610-2911)
PHONE.................................919 231-0100
Brad Bigger, *Brnch Mgr*
EMP: 140
Web: www.ajihealthandnutrition.com
SIC: 2099 Food preparations, nec
HQ: Ajinomoto Health & Nutrition North America, Inc.
250 E Devon Ave
Itasca IL 60143
630 931-6800

(G-12485)
ALAMO NORTH TEXAS RAILROAD CO
2710 Wycliff Rd (27607-3033)
PHONE.................................919 787-9504
EMP: 8 **EST:** 2009
SALES (est): 2.45MM **Publicly Held**
SIC: 1423 Crushed and broken granite
PA: Martin Marietta Materials Inc
4123 Parklake Ave
Raleigh NC 27612

(G-12486)
ALCON
6425 Belle Crest Dr (27612-2871)
PHONE.................................919 624-5868
Julie Johnson, *Prin*
EMP: 6 **EST:** 2010
SALES (est): 47.45K **Privately Held**
Web: www.alcon.com
SIC: 3841 Surgical and medical instruments

(G-12487)
ALERT PROTECTION SYSTEMS INC
1401 Monkwood Pl (27603-3952)
PHONE.................................919 467-4357
Larry Beaton, *Pr*
Brian Beaton, *Cnslt*
EMP: 9 **EST:** 1985
SALES (est): 877.48K **Privately Held**
SIC: 3699 5065 Security devices; Security control equipment and systems

(G-12488)
ALK INVESTMENTS LLC
Also Called: Batteries Plus
6812 Glenwood Ave Ste 100 (27612-7133)
PHONE.................................984 233-5353
Mark Doggett, *Pr*
EMP: 9 **EST:** 2011
SALES (est): 914.24K **Privately Held**
Web: www.batteriesplus.com
SIC: 3621 3612 5063 3641 Storage battery chargers, motor and engine generator type; Ballasts for lighting fixtures; Flashlights; Electric light bulbs, complete

(G-12489)
ALL IN ONE PRINTING
4607 Grinding Stone Dr Apt A (27604-3028)
PHONE.................................919 360-8092
EMP: 4 **EST:** 2019
SALES (est): 83.91K **Privately Held**
SIC: 2752 Offset printing

(G-12490)
ALLEN KELLY & CO INC
Also Called: Honeywell Authorized Dealer
220 Tryon Rd Ste A (27603-3587)
PHONE.................................919 779-4197
Allen Kelly, *Pr*
Joan Kelly, *
Jc Moeller, *CFO*
EMP: 77 **EST:** 1986
SQ FT: 5,000
SALES (est): 24.41MM **Privately Held**
Web: www.allenkelly.com
SIC: 1711 3444 1731 Warm air heating and air conditioning contractor; Sheet metalwork; Electrical work

(G-12491)
ALLERGAN INC
Also Called: Allergan
7701 Umstead Forest Dr (27612-7362)
PHONE.................................704 301-7790
Terry Coleman, *Brnch Mgr*
EMP: 4
SALES (corp-wide): 54.32B **Publicly Held**
Web: www.abbvie.com
SIC: 2834 Drugs acting on the central nervous system & sense organs
HQ: Allergan, Inc.
1 N Waukegan Rd
North Chicago IL 60064
862 261-7000

(G-12492)
ALOSSI RENEWAL SPA LLC
300 Okamato St (27603-1996)
PHONE.................................406 338-7700
EMP: 4 **EST:** 2019
SALES (est): 138.9K **Privately Held**
Web: www.alossispa.com
SIC: 3792 Travel trailers and campers

(G-12493)
ALPHAGRAPHICS NORTH RALEIGH
Also Called: AlphaGraphics
8321 Bandford Way Ste 1 (27615-2762)
PHONE.................................919 322-2257
EMP: 7 **EST:** 2019
SALES (est): 90.24K **Privately Held**
Web: www.alphagraphics.com
SIC: 2752 Commercial printing, lithographic

(G-12494)
ALTERA CORPORATION
5540 Centerview Dr Ste 318 (27606-3363)
PHONE.................................919 852-1004
EMP: 6
SALES (corp-wide): 54.23B **Publicly Held**
Web: www.intel.com
SIC: 3674 7372 3577 Metal oxide silicon (MOS) devices; Application computer software; Data conversion equipment, media-to-media: computer
HQ: Altera Corporation
101 Innovation Dr
San Jose CA 95134
408 544-7000

(G-12495)
ALYWILLOW
5301 Hillsborough St Ste 100 (27606-6343)
PHONE.................................919 454-4826
Angela Suggs, *Owner*
EMP: 5 **EST:** 2017
SALES (est): 177.69K **Privately Held**
Web: www.alywillow.com
SIC: 2844 Perfumes, cosmetics and other toilet preparations

(G-12496)
AMBER ALERT INTERNATIONAL TM (PA)
6537 English Oaks Dr (27615-6306)
PHONE.................................919 641-8773
James M Thrasher, *Pr*
EMP: 4 **EST:** 2006
SALES (est): 401.6K **Privately Held**
SIC: 2754 Business form and card printing, gravure

(G-12497)
AMBER BROOKS PUBLISHING LLC
7233 Mine Shaft Rd (27615-6019)
PHONE.................................704 582-1035
Amber Brooks, *Prin*
EMP: 4 **EST:** 2017
SALES (est): 64.05K **Privately Held**
SIC: 2741 Miscellaneous publishing

(G-12498)
AMBIANCE DOORS LLC
3208 Wellington Ct Ste 109 (27615-4121)
PHONE.................................919 855-9220
Andrew Nippert, *Managing Member*
EMP: 5 **EST:** 2015
SALES (est): 242.03K **Privately Held**
Web: www.ambiancedoors.com
SIC: 2431 Doors and door parts and trim, wood

(G-12499)
AMERICAN SOIL AND MULCH INC
1109 Athens Dr (27606-2420)
PHONE.................................919 460-1349
Russell W Tarlton, *Pr*
EMP: 10 **EST:** 1966
SALES (est): 464.78K **Privately Held**
Web: www.americansoilandmulch.com
SIC: 2499 5261 Mulch, wood and bark; Top soil

(G-12500)
AMERICAN SOLUTIONS FOR BU
9201 Leesville Rd Ste 120 (27613-7540)
PHONE.................................919 848-2442
Michael P Arata, *Prin*
EMP: 5 **EST:** 2006
SALES (est): 100K **Privately Held**
SIC: 2759 Commercial printing, nec

(G-12501)
AMERICAN WELDING & GAS INC (PA)
Also Called: Compressed Gas Solutions
4900 Falls Of Neuse Rd Ste 150 (27609-5490)
PHONE.................................984 222-2600
EMP: 6 **EST:** 1983
SALES (est): 166.62MM
SALES (corp-wide): 166.62MM **Privately Held**
Web: www.awggases.com
SIC: 3548 Gas welding equipment

(G-12502)
AMS USA INC
Also Called: AMS
353 E Six Forks Rd Ste 250 (27609-7881)
P.O. Box 97414 (27624-7414)
PHONE.................................919 755-2889
Ravi Jhota, *Prin*
EMP: 26 **EST:** 2007
SALES (est): 655.59K **Privately Held**
SIC: 3674 Infrared sensors, solid state

(G-12503)
AMTAI MEDICAL EQUIPMENT INC
5605 Primavera Ct (27616-1840)
PHONE.................................919 872-1803
Alan Sou Cheng Lee, *VP*
▲ **EMP:** 14 **EST:** 2008
SALES (est): 2.4MM **Privately Held**
Web: www.amtai.com
SIC: 5047 3842 Medical equipment and supplies; Surgical appliances and supplies

(G-12504)
ANALOG DEVICES INC
223 S West St Ste 1400 (27603-4094)
PHONE.................................919 831-2790

Raleigh - Wake County (G-12505) — GEOGRAPHIC SECTION

Tony Montalvo, *Mgr*
EMP: 6
SALES (corp-wide): 12.31B **Publicly Held**
Web: www.analog.com
SIC: 3674 Integrated circuits, semiconductor networks, etc.
PA: Analog Devices, Inc.
  1 Analog Way
  Wilmington MA 01887
  781 935-5565

(G-12505)
ANDREWS INDUSTRIES LLC
1700 Rocky Falls Ct (27610-8610)
PHONE..............................919 266-9656
Mackenzie Andrews, *Prin*
EMP: 4 **EST:** 2018
SALES (est): 46.23K **Privately Held**
SIC: 3999 Manufacturing industries, nec

(G-12506)
ANDRITZ FABRICS AND ROLLS INC (HQ)
Also Called: Xerium
8521 Six Forks Rd (27615-5278)
PHONE..............................919 526-1400
Mark Staton, *Pr*
Clifford E Pietrafitta, *
William S Butterfield, *
Phillip B Kennedy, *
EMP: 73 **EST:** 2002
SALES (est): 955.05MM
SALES (corp-wide): 7.83B **Privately Held**
Web: www.andritz.com
SIC: 2221 3069 Broadwoven fabric mills, manmade; Printers' rolls and blankets: rubber or rubberized fabric
PA: Andritz Ag
  Stattegger StraBe 18
  Graz 8045
  31669020

(G-12507)
ANGEL INDUSTRIES INC
905 Capital Blvd (27603-1109)
PHONE..............................919 264-0765
Michael Ward, *Prin*
EMP: 6 **EST:** 2008
SALES (est): 75K **Privately Held**
Web: www.angelindustriesnc.org
SIC: 3999 Manufacturing industries, nec

(G-12508)
ANOTHER CREATION BY LADY J
7636 Silver View Ln (27613-1439)
PHONE..............................919 334-9797
Judy Mcclendon-redmond, *Prin*
EMP: 4 **EST:** 2010
SALES (est): 82.46K **Privately Held**
Web: www.anothercreationbyladyj.com
SIC: 3552 Embroidery machines

(G-12509)
ANTKAR LLC
Also Called: Flavors Ice Cream
2831 Jones Franklin Rd (27606-4007)
PHONE..............................919 322-4100
EMP: 6 **EST:** 2020
SALES (est): 327.7K **Privately Held**
Web: www.flavorsicecream.net
SIC: 2024 Dairy based frozen desserts

(G-12510)
ANTLER AND OAK JOINERY LLC
6436 Cape Charles Dr (27617-7641)
PHONE..............................845 505-6185
Matthew Berrian, *Prin*
EMP: 4 **EST:** 2019
SALES (est): 54.13K **Privately Held**
SIC: 2431 Millwork

(G-12511)
ANUMA AEROSPACE LLC
720 Pebblebrook Dr (27609-5345)
PHONE..............................919 600-0142
Diana Little, *CEO*
EMP: 4 **EST:** 2021
SALES (est): 266.08K **Privately Held**
Web: www.anumaaerospace.com
SIC: 3721 Aircraft

(G-12512)
APAC-ATLANTIC INC (DH)
Also Called: APAC
2626 Glenwood Ave Ste 550 (27608-1370)
P.O. Box 399 (28502-0399)
PHONE..............................336 412-6800
David L Schwartz, *Pr*
David H Kilpatrick, *VP*
Thomas G Kindred, *VP*
E S Arthur Junior, *VP*
Barry L Johnson, *VP*
EMP: 100 **EST:** 1945
SQ FT: 5,000
SALES (est): 146.96MM
SALES (corp-wide): 32.72B **Privately Held**
Web: www.harrisoncc.com
SIC: 1611 1771 3531 5032 Highway and street paving contractor; Parking lot construction; Asphalt plant, including gravel-mix type; Sand, construction
HQ: Crh Americas Materials, Inc.
  900 Ashwood Pkwy Ste 700
  Atlanta GA 30338

(G-12513)
APEX PUBLISHING LLC
3434 Edwards Mill Rd Ste 112 (27612-4275)
PHONE..............................919 886-7153
C Barnette, *Prin*
EMP: 6 **EST:** 2010
SALES (est): 10.37K **Privately Held**
SIC: 2741 Miscellaneous publishing

(G-12514)
APEX STEEL CORP
301 Petfinder Ln (27603-2874)
PHONE..............................919 362-6611
Bridgette Burks, *Pr*
Ronald E Clemmons, *
Teresa L Clemmons, *
EMP: 45 **EST:** 1985
SQ FT: 20,000
SALES (est): 8.89MM **Privately Held**
Web: www.apexsteelcorp.com
SIC: 1791 3446 1799 Iron work, structural; Ornamental metalwork; Welding on site

(G-12515)
AQUARIUS DESIGNS & LOGO WEAR
4429 Beryl Rd (27606-1457)
PHONE..............................919 821-4646
Michel Kelkalezic, *Owner*
EMP: 5 **EST:** 1983
SALES (est): 352.93K **Privately Held**
SIC: 2759 Screen printing

(G-12516)
AQUATIC PRESSURE WASHING
6534 English Oaks Dr (27615-6325)
PHONE..............................910 232-3723
Scott Kelly, *Prin*
EMP: 4 **EST:** 2001
SALES (est): 123.55K **Privately Held**
Web: www.raleighpowerwashing.com
SIC: 3589 High pressure cleaning equipment

(G-12517)
ARBOR PHARMACEUTICALS INC
5511 Capital Center Dr Ste 224 (27606-3380)
PHONE..............................919 792-1700
Ed Schutter, *CEO*
EMP: 9 **EST:** 2018
SALES (est): 1.3MM **Privately Held**
SIC: 2834 Pharmaceutical preparations

(G-12518)
ARCHANGEL ARMS LLC
3405 Banks Rd (27603-8998)
PHONE..............................984 235-2536
Jeremy Jones, *Managing Member*
EMP: 7 **EST:** 2011
SALES (est): 225K **Privately Held**
Web: www.archangelarms.com
SIC: 3949 Sporting and athletic goods, nec

(G-12519)
ARGOS READY MIX (CAROLINAS) CORP
Also Called: Ready Mixed Concrete Company
3610 Bush St (27609-7511)
P.O. Box 27326 (27611-7326)
PHONE..............................919 790-1520
EMP: 475
SIC: 3273 Ready-mixed concrete

(G-12520)
ARGOS USA LLC
Also Called: Ready Mixed Concrete Co
3200 Spring Forest Rd Ste 210 (27616)
PHONE..............................919 828-3695
George Turner, *Pr*
EMP: 10
Web: www.argos-us.com
SIC: 3273 Ready-mixed concrete
HQ: Argos Usa Llc
  3015 Windward Plz Ste 300
  Alpharetta GA 30005
  678 368-4300

(G-12521)
ARGOS USA LLC
Also Called: Ready Mix Concrete of Sanford
3200 Spring Forest Rd Ste 210 (27616-2811)
PHONE..............................919 775-5441
Mike Sakzer, *Mgr*
EMP: 10
Web: www.argos-us.com
SIC: 3273 Ready-mixed concrete
HQ: Argos Usa Llc
  3015 Windward Plz Ste 300
  Alpharetta GA 30005
  678 368-4300

(G-12522)
ARGOS USA LLC
Also Called: Argos Ready Mix
3200 Spring Forest Rd Ste 210 (27616-2811)
PHONE..............................919 790-1520
EMP: 42
Web: www.argos-us.com
SIC: 3273 Ready-mixed concrete
HQ: Argos Usa Llc
  3015 Windward Plz Ste 300
  Alpharetta GA 30005
  678 368-4300

(G-12523)
ARK INC
Also Called: Ark Shores
555 Fayetteville St # 201 (27601-3030)
PHONE..............................919 841-3637
Dante Smith, *Managing Member*
EMP: 4 **EST:** 2019
SALES (est): 293.27K **Privately Held**
SIC: 3441 Railroad car racks, for transporting vehicles: steel

(G-12524)
ARMAC INC
4027 Atlantic Ave (27604-1732)
P.O. Box 1985 (27526-2985)
PHONE..............................919 878-9836
Rusty Young, *CEO*
Sue Parker, *
Dorothy Young, *Stockholder*
EMP: 48 **EST:** 1983
SQ FT: 21,000
SALES (est): 2.14MM **Privately Held**
Web: www.tecgraphics.com
SIC: 2759 Screen printing

(G-12525)
ARTIST STUDIO PROJECT PUBG LLC
5620 Millrace Trl (27606-9227)
PHONE..............................919 233-3873
Rafael A Osuba, *Owner*
EMP: 5 **EST:** 2017
SALES (est): 81.79K **Privately Held**
Web: www.artiststudioprojectpublishing.com
SIC: 2741 Miscellaneous publishing

(G-12526)
ASAP COMPONENTS
410 Lord Berkley Rd (27610-2467)
PHONE..............................919 258-2230
EMP: 6 **EST:** 2019
SALES (est): 204.45K **Privately Held**
Web: www.asap-components.com
SIC: 3728 Aircraft parts and equipment, nec

(G-12527)
ASCEPI MEDICAL GROUP LLC
3344 Hillsborough St Ste 100 (27607-5469)
PHONE..............................919 336-4246
EMP: 7 **EST:** 2020
SALES (est): 100K **Privately Held**
Web: www.ascepimed.com
SIC: 3841 Medical instruments and equipment, blood and bone work

(G-12528)
ASEPTIA INC
723 W Johnson St Ste 100 (27603-1244)
PHONE..............................678 373-6751
David Clark, *Pr*
Michael Drozd, *
Mac Mcaulay, *CFO*
John Winnie, *
Lindsey Lacy, *
EMP: 125 **EST:** 2006
SALES (est): 22.77MM **Privately Held**
Web: www.wrightfoods.com
SIC: 3356 5199 5148 Battery metal; Packaging materials; Fresh fruits and vegetables

(G-12529)
ASSYST BULLMER INC
3221 Durham Dr Ste 101 (27603-3507)
PHONE..............................919 467-2211
EMP: 4 **EST:** 2020
SALES (est): 125.56K **Privately Held**
SIC: 7372 Prepackaged software

(G-12530)
ATLANTIC GROUP USA INC (PA)
3401 Gresham Lake Rd Ste 118 (27615-4243)
PHONE..............................919 623-7824
Brett Block, *CEO*
EMP: 10 **EST:** 1990
SQ FT: 1,000
SALES (est): 13.7MM **Privately Held**
Web: www.agunc.com

GEOGRAPHIC SECTION

Raleigh - Wake County (G-12556)

SIC: **6411** 8748 1522 3999 Insurance adjusters; Business consulting, nec; Residential construction, nec; Atomizers, toiletry

(G-12531)
ATRC INC
Also Called: Acroprint Time Recorders
1200 Melton Ct (27615-1125)
PHONE.................................919 872-5800
Glenn Robbins, *Pr*
Tula C Robbins, *
Katherine R Niquette, *
◆ **EMP:** 100 **EST:** 1968
SALES (est): 23.39MM **Privately Held**
Web: www.acroprint.com
SIC: **5112** 3579 File cards; Time clocks and time recording devices

(G-12532)
ATTENDS HEALTHCARE PRODUCTS INC (PA)
8020 Arco Corporate Dr Ste 200 (27617)
PHONE.................................800 428-8363
◆ **EMP:** 280 **EST:** 2002
SALES (est): 103.92MM
SALES (corp-wide): 103.92MM **Privately Held**
Web: www.attends.com
SIC: **2676** Sanitary paper products

(G-12533)
ATTINDAS HYGIENE PARTNERS INC (PA)
8020 Arco Corporate Dr Ste 200 (27617)
PHONE.................................919 237-4000
Harold H Mackay, *Ch Bd*
EMP: 9 **EST:** 2013
SALES (est): 18.86MM
SALES (corp-wide): 18.86MM **Privately Held**
Web: www.attindas.com
SIC: **2621** Paper mills

(G-12534)
AUDIO ADVICE INC
8621 Glenwood Ave Ste 117 (27617-7427)
PHONE.................................919 881-2005
EMP: 92 **EST:** 1978
SALES (est): 10.98MM **Privately Held**
Web: www.audioadvice.com
SIC: **3663** Studio equipment, radio and television broadcasting

(G-12535)
AUTO CARE & TRUCK WASH LLC
1316 S Blount St (27601-2625)
PHONE.................................704 363-6341
EMP: 5 **EST:** 2013
SALES (est): 108.32K **Privately Held**
SIC: **7534** 7542 Tire retreading and repair shops; Truck wash

(G-12536)
AXIAL EXCHANGE INC
1111 Haynes St Ste 113 (27604-1454)
P.O. Box 6486 (27628-6486)
PHONE.................................919 576-9988
Joanne Rohde, *Pr*
John Casey, *VP*
EMP: 5 **EST:** 2012
SALES (est): 397.76K **Privately Held**
Web: www.axialexchange.com
SIC: **7372** Business oriented computer software

(G-12537)
AXITARE CORPORATION
1717 Brassfield Rd (27614-9448)
PHONE.................................919 256-8196
Jim Passe, *Pr*
EMP: 4 **EST:** 2005
SALES (est): 350K **Privately Held**
SIC: **2834** Pharmaceutical preparations

(G-12538)
AXON LLC
Also Called: Axon Styrotech
3080 Business Park Dr Ste 103 (27610)
PHONE.................................919 772-8383
▲ **EMP:** 44 **EST:** 1991
SALES (est): 11.96MM **Privately Held**
Web: www.axoncorp.com
SIC: **3565** Packaging machinery
HQ: Pro Mach, Inc.
  50 E Rvrcnter Blvd Ste 18
  Covington KY 41011
  513 831-8778

(G-12539)
B&B CAP LINERS LLC
3208 Spottswood St Ste 115 (27615-8130)
PHONE.................................585 598-1828
EMP: 6 **EST:** 2011
SALES (est): 243.08K **Privately Held**
Web: www.bbcapliners.com
SIC: **3443** Liners, industrial: metal plate

(G-12540)
B&C XTERIOR CLEANING SVC INC
Also Called: Xterior Sales & Service
142 Annaron Ct (27603-3640)
PHONE.................................919 779-7905
C Mike Baker, *Pr*
Mary Baker, *VP*
EMP: 8 **EST:** 1977
SQ FT: 3,000
SALES (est): 655.84K **Privately Held**
Web: www.landanc.com
SIC: **3589** 5251 7699 7542 High pressure cleaning equipment; Hardware stores; Cleaning services; Carwashes

(G-12541)
B6USA INC
Also Called: Bay Six
414 Dupont Cir (27603-2076)
PHONE.................................919 833-3851
Katherine Hite, *Pr*
EMP: 11 **EST:** 2005
SALES (est): 256.29K **Privately Held**
SIC: **2395** Embroidery products, except Schiffli machine

(G-12542)
BAD CAT PRESS LLC
13200 Strickland Rd Ste 114-215 (27613-5212)
PHONE.................................919 870-4908
Michael Santos, *Prin*
EMP: 5 **EST:** 2018
SALES (est): 82.63K **Privately Held**
Web: www.michaelsantosauthor.com
SIC: **2741** Miscellaneous publishing

(G-12543)
BAR SQUARED INC
Also Called: Caromed
5605 Spring Ct (27616-2920)
P.O. Box 4360 (18043-4360)
PHONE.................................919 878-0578
Thomas Barnett, *Pr*
Barbara Beck, *VP*
EMP: 18 **EST:** 1992
SALES (est): 162.04K **Privately Held**
Web: www.caromed.us
SIC: **3842** Bandages and dressings

(G-12544)
BAR-S FOODS CO
2101 Westinghouse Blvd Ste 109 (27604)
PHONE.................................847 652-3238
EMP: 37
Web: www.bar-s.com
SIC: **2013** Sausages and other prepared meats
HQ: Bar-S Foods Co.
  18700 N Hayden Rd Ste 545
  Scottsdale AZ 85255
  602 264-7272

(G-12545)
BAREFOOT PRESS INC
731 Pershing Rd (27608-2711)
PHONE.................................919 283-6396
Richard Kilby, *Pr*
EMP: 5 **EST:** 1987
SQ FT: 6,500
SALES (est): 968.1K **Privately Held**
Web: www.barefootpress.com
SIC: **2752** Offset printing

(G-12546)
BAYER HLTHCARE PHARMACEUTICALS
1820 Liatris Ln (27613-6583)
PHONE.................................602 469-6846
Vilushis Byrd, *Sls Mgr*
EMP: 5 **EST:** 2017
SALES (est): 155.22M **Privately Held**
SIC: **2834** Pharmaceutical preparations

(G-12547)
BAYSIX USA
414 Dupont Cir (27603-2076)
PHONE.................................919 833-3851
Katherine Hite, *Prin*
▲ **EMP:** 18 **EST:** 2010
SALES (est): 1.16MM **Privately Held**
Web: www.wearebaysix.com
SIC: **2395** Embroidery products, except Schiffli machine

(G-12548)
BEACON PROSTHETICS & ORTHOTICS
3224 Lake Woodard Dr (27604-3659)
PHONE.................................919 231-6890
EMP: 4 **EST:** 2019
SALES (est): 105.57K **Privately Held**
Web: www.beaconpo.com
SIC: **3842** 3841 Surgical appliances and supplies; Surgical and medical instruments

(G-12549)
BEAKER INC
700 Spring Forest Rd Ste 121 (27609)
PHONE.................................919 803-7422
Jeffrey Clark, *CEO*
EMP: 14 **EST:** 2013
SALES (est): 957.54K **Privately Held**
Web: www.beaker.com
SIC: **2834** Pharmaceutical preparations

(G-12550)
BEAUTIMAR MANUFACTURED MBL INC
1221 Home Ct (27603-4541)
PHONE.................................919 779-1181
Howard B Mills, *Pr*
Gail Mills, *Sec*
EMP: 12 **EST:** 1969
SQ FT: 9,000
SALES (est): 378.81K **Privately Held**
Web: www.beautimar.com
SIC: **3281** Marble, building: cut and shaped

(G-12551)
BELKOZ INC
4900 Thornton Rd (27616-5878)
PHONE.................................919 703-0694
Zoltan Laszlovszky, *Prin*
EMP: 4 **EST:** 2012
SALES (est): 459.74K **Privately Held**
Web: www.belkoz.com
SIC: **3541** 3423 8711 Milling machines; Soldering tools; Engineering services

(G-12552)
BEST BAR EVER INC
P.O. Box 37146 (27627-7146)
PHONE.................................910 508-3628
EMP: 5 **EST:** 2015
SALES (est): 62.38K **Privately Held**
SIC: **2064** Candy bars, including chocolate covered bars

(G-12553)
BEYOND ELECTRONICS CORP
Also Called: BEC
12405 Cilcain Ct (27614-8959)
PHONE.................................919 231-8000
Richard Goodell, *Pr*
EMP: 5 **EST:** 2005
SALES (est): 454.74K **Privately Held**
Web: www.beyondelectronics.us
SIC: **3812** Acceleration indicators and systems components, aerospace

(G-12554)
BFS ASSET HOLDINGS LLC (HQ)
4800 Falls Of Neuse Rd Ste 400 (27609-8141)
PHONE.................................303 784-4288
David Flitman, *Managing Member*
Peter Jackson, *
Timothy Johnson, *
▲ **EMP:** 240 **EST:** 1987
SALES (est): 479.55MM
SALES (corp-wide): 17.1B **Publicly Held**
SIC: **5211** 2431 2439 5031 Lumber and other building materials; Millwork; Trusses, wooden roof; Lumber, plywood, and millwork
PA: Builders Firstsource, Inc.
  6031 Connection Dr # 400
  Irving TX 75039
  214 880-3500

(G-12555)
BFS OPERATIONS LLC (HQ)
4800 Falls Of Neuse Rd (27609-8141)
PHONE.................................919 431-1000
David Keltner, *Pr*
James F Major Junior, *Ex VP*
Lisa Hamblet, *
Mike Mtgaugh, *
Donna Thagard, *
▲ **EMP:** 1500 **EST:** 1922
SALES (est): 1B
SALES (corp-wide): 17.1B **Publicly Held**
SIC: **5211** 2431 5031 5713 Millwork and lumber; Millwork; Lumber: rough, dressed, and finished; Floor covering stores
PA: Builders Firstsource, Inc.
  6031 Connection Dr # 400
  Irving TX 75039
  214 880-3500

(G-12556)
BIG OAK COATINGS LLC
1148 Vannstone Dr (27603-8479)
PHONE.................................919 771-8470
Ronald Oakley, *Prin*
EMP: 5 **EST:** 2016
SALES (est): 206.19K **Privately Held**
SIC: **3479** Metal coating and allied services

Raleigh - Wake County (G-12557)   GEOGRAPHIC SECTION

(G-12557)
BIOFLUIDICA INC
176 Mine Lake Ct (27615-6417)
PHONE......................858 535-6493
Rolf Muller, *CEO*
Samuel Tetlow, *Ch Bd*
David Claypool, *COO*
Mateusz Hupert, *Research & Development*
EMP: 7 **EST:** 2007
SQ FT: 523
SALES (est): 440.28K **Privately Held**
Web: www.biofluidica.com
SIC: 3826 Analytical instruments

(G-12558)
BIOLOGICS INC
625 Oberlin Rd (27605-1126)
PHONE......................919 546-9810
EMP: 8 **EST:** 2019
SALES (est): 301.46K **Privately Held**
SIC: 2514 Metal household furniture

(G-12559)
BIOMERIEUX INC
3300 Tarheel Dr (27609-7538)
PHONE......................800 682-2666
EMP: 5
SALES (corp-wide): 7.5MM **Privately Held**
Web: www.biomerieux-usa.com
SIC: 3829 Ion chambers
HQ: Biomerieux, Inc.
100 Rodolphe St
Durham NC 27712
919 620-2000

(G-12560)
BIZNET SOFTWARE INC
8529 Six Forks Rd Ste 400 (27615-4972)
PHONE......................919 872-7800
George Mcmann, *Pr*
Paula Anthony Mcmann, *Sec*
Lori Shwenn, *CFO*
EMP: 12 **EST:** 1996
SALES (est): 3.51MM
SALES (corp-wide): 113.32MM **Privately Held**
Web: www.insightsoftware.com
SIC: 7372 Business oriented computer software
PA: Insightsoftware, Llc
8529 Six Forks Rd
Raleigh NC 27615
919 872-7800

(G-12561)
BLACK & DECKER CORPORATION
Also Called: Black & Decker
2930 Capital Blvd (27604-3235)
PHONE......................919 878-0357
Benjamin G Beeker, *Mgr*
EMP: 5
SALES (corp-wide): 15.78B **Publicly Held**
Web: www.blackanddecker.com
SIC: 3546 Power-driven handtools
HQ: The Black & Decker Corporation
701 E Joppa Rd
Towson MD 21286
410 716-3900

(G-12562)
BLACKHAWK DIVERSIFIED SVCS INC
5618 Deblyn Ave (27612-2606)
PHONE......................919 279-5679
EMP: 6 **EST:** 2016
SALES (est): 108.51K **Privately Held**
Web: www.cleanoil.info
SIC: 1382 Oil and gas exploration services

(G-12563)
BLU DISTILLING COMPANY LLC (PA)
Also Called: Liberty & Plenty Distilling
3420 Landor Rd (27609-7015)
PHONE......................919 999-6736
EMP: 6 **EST:** 2019
SALES (est): 70.88K
SALES (corp-wide): 70.88K **Privately Held**
SIC: 2085 Distilled and blended liquors

(G-12564)
BLUE WOLF TECHNOLOGIES LLP
9650 Strickland Rd Ste 103 (27615-1902)
PHONE......................919 810-1508
Ernest Johnson, *Pt*
Joseph E Freed, *Pt*
EMP: 6 **EST:** 2012
SALES (est): 354.44K **Privately Held**
SIC: 7372 7373 7379 Business oriented computer software; Local area network (LAN) systems integrator; Online services technology consultants

(G-12565)
BLUEBIRD CUPCAKES
2524 Beech Gap Ct (27603-5876)
PHONE......................919 616-7347
Cynthia Mcgee, *Prin*
EMP: 5 **EST:** 2011
SALES (est): 190.21K **Privately Held**
SIC: 2051 Bread, cake, and related products

(G-12566)
BMI WOOD PRODUCTS INC
2506 Yonkers Rd (27604-2241)
PHONE......................919 829-9505
Sandy Mullin, *Pr*
Courtney Mullin, *CEO*
EMP: 7 **EST:** 1975
SALES (est): 162.54K **Privately Held**
Web: www.barrmullin.com
SIC: 3553 Sawmill machines

(G-12567)
BO TAYLOR CUSTOM WDWKG LLC
417 Eby Dr (27610-4605)
PHONE......................919 839-7175
Albert Zachary Iii, *Mgr*
EMP: 7 **EST:** 2005
SALES (est): 241.57K **Privately Held**
SIC: 2431 Millwork

(G-12568)
BONAVENTURE GROUP INC
Also Called: Afex
6031 Oak Forest Dr (27616-1903)
PHONE......................919 781-6610
EMP: 14 **EST:** 1986
SALES (est): 3.35MM **Privately Held**
Web: www.afexsystems.com
SIC: 3999 Fire extinguishers, portable

(G-12569)
BOND TECHNOLOGIES
909 Walkertown Dr (27614-7177)
PHONE......................919 866-0075
Brian Scarboro, *Prin*
EMP: 6 **EST:** 2010
SALES (est): 68.16K **Privately Held**
Web: www.bondtechnologies.net
SIC: 3599 Machine shop, jobbing and repair

(G-12570)
BORDENTOWN HIGHWAY SIGN LLC
9921 Waterview Rd (27615-1555)
PHONE......................919 870-8116
Robert C White, *Mgr*
EMP: 4 **EST:** 2018
SALES (est): 46.08K **Privately Held**
SIC: 3993 Signs and advertising specialties

(G-12571)
BOSS KEY PRODUCTIONS INC
230 Fayetteville St Ste 300 (27601-1587)
P.O. Box 90126 (27675-0126)
PHONE......................919 659-5704
Cliff Bleszinski, *CEO*
Arjan Brussee, * *
EMP: 57 **EST:** 2014
SQ FT: 5,000
SALES (est): 4.83MM **Privately Held**
Web: www.bosskey.com
SIC: 7372 Home entertainment computer software

(G-12572)
BRANDILLY OF NC INC
Also Called: Brandilly Marketing Creative
1053 E Whitaker Mill Rd Ste 115 (27604-5311)
PHONE......................919 278-7896
Kemah Washington, *Pr*
EMP: 10 **EST:** 2015
SALES (est): 315.5K **Privately Held**
Web: www.bcgnc.com
SIC: 7336 2752 Graphic arts and related design; Commercial printing, lithographic

(G-12573)
BRIDGESTONE RET OPERATIONS LLC
Also Called: Firestone
5058 N New Hope Rd (27604-4400)
PHONE......................919 872-6402
Nathan Barbour, *Mgr*
EMP: 6
Web: www.bridgestoneamericas.com
SIC: 5531 7534 Automotive tires; Rebuilding and retreading tires
HQ: Bridgestone Retail Operations, Llc
333 E Lake St Ste 300
Bloomingdale IL 60108
630 259-9000

(G-12574)
BRIDGESTONE RET OPERATIONS LLC
Also Called: Firestone
4305 Wake Forest Rd (27609-6276)
PHONE......................919 872-6566
Paul Morton, *Brnch Mgr*
EMP: 8
SQ FT: 7,744
Web: www.bridgestoneamericas.com
SIC: 5531 7534 Automotive tires; Rebuilding and retreading tires
HQ: Bridgestone Retail Operations, Llc
333 E Lake St Ste 300
Bloomingdale IL 60108
630 259-9000

(G-12575)
BRIGHTWILL TECHNOLOGIES LLC
3613 Cathedral Bell Rd (27614-8374)
PHONE......................919 757-3176
EMP: 4 **EST:** 2008
SALES (est): 43.62K **Privately Held**
Web: www.preeminent-outsource.com
SIC: 7372 Prepackaged software

(G-12576)
BROOKHURST ASSOCIATES
Also Called: Fundamental Playgrounds
2400 Saint Pauls Sq (27614-7424)
PHONE......................919 792-0987
G Mark Hockenyos, *Owner*
EMP: 4 **EST:** 1995
SALES (est): 159.19K **Privately Held**
SIC: 3949 6531 Playground equipment; Real estate agents and managers

(G-12577)
BUMPKIN SKATEBOARDS LLC
4924 Kundinger Ct (27606-9341)
PHONE......................919 821-2037
Justin Hill, *Brnch Mgr*
EMP: 5
SALES (corp-wide): 65.3K **Privately Held**
SIC: 3949 Skateboards
PA: Bumpkin Skateboards Llc
68 Golfers Ridge Ct
Chapel Hill NC

(G-12578)
BUSINESS MOGUL LLC
2120 Breezeway Dr Unit 112 (27614-7461)
PHONE......................919 605-2165
Sheria Rowe, *Pr*
EMP: 6 **EST:** 2018
SALES (est): 281.89K **Privately Held**
Web: www.thebusinessmogul.com
SIC: 2759 2836 Publication printing; Culture media

(G-12579)
BUSINESS TO BUSINESS INC (PA)
Also Called: Business Leader
3801 Wake Forest Rd Ste 102 (27609)
PHONE......................919 872-7077
Chris Verk, *Prin*
Daniel Davies, *Prin*
Martin Feligson, *VP*
EMP: 7 **EST:** 1989
SQ FT: 18,000
SALES (est): 850K **Privately Held**
Web: www.businessleader.com
SIC: 2721 Magazines: publishing only, not printed on site

(G-12580)
BUSY BS MONOGRAMMING LLC
1500 Bedford Hills Ct (27613-7492)
PHONE......................919 870-6106
Dara Bonner, *Owner*
EMP: 5 **EST:** 2014
SALES (est): 49.7K **Privately Held**
SIC: 2395 Embroidery and art needlework

(G-12581)
BYRNES ENTERPRISES
3216 Wellington Ct # 107 (27615-4122)
PHONE......................919 876-3223
Derick Byrne, *Owner*
EMP: 6 **EST:** 1963
SQ FT: 2,400
SALES (est): 421K **Privately Held**
SIC: 3425 Saw blades and handsaws

(G-12582)
C&M WOODWORKS
2800 Mattlyn Ct (27613-6510)
PHONE......................919 280-9896
EMP: 5 **EST:** 2013
SALES (est): 165.52K **Privately Held**
SIC: 2431 Millwork

(G-12583)
CABINET SALES LLC
8705 Cliff Top Ct (27613-1103)
PHONE......................919 604-9536
Matthew May, *Prin*
EMP: 5 **EST:** 2016
SALES (est): 103.91K **Privately Held**
SIC: 2434 Wood kitchen cabinets

(G-12584)
CABINETWORKS GROUP MICH LLC
6221 Westgate Rd Ste 100 (27617-4722)

GEOGRAPHIC SECTION

Raleigh - Wake County (G-12611)

PHONE.....................919 868-8174
EMP: 29
SALES (corp-wide): 1.6B **Privately Held**
Web: www.cabinetworksgroup.com
SIC: 2434 Wood kitchen cabinets
PA: Cabinetworks Group Michigan, Llc
20000 Victor Pkwy Ste 100
Livonia MI 48152
734 205-4600

(G-12585)
CAKERATOR INC
5924 Swales Way (27603-8710)
PHONE.....................919 270-5899
Luis Campos, *Prin*
EMP: 5 EST: 2011
SALES (est): 63.15K **Privately Held**
Web: www.cakerator.com
SIC: 3421 Table and food cutlery, including butchers'

(G-12586)
CANALTA ENTERPRISES LLC
Also Called: Phillips Iron Works
4809 Auburn Knightdale Rd (27610-8230)
PHONE.....................919 615-1570
Maryanne Mah-throndson, *CEO*
Ronald Throndson, *Pr*
EMP: 25 EST: 2013
SALES (est): 2.72MM **Privately Held**
Web: www.phillipsiw.com
SIC: 3449 1791 Miscellaneous metalwork; Structural steel erection

(G-12587)
CANDYPEARLS HAIR LLC
2417 Blackwolf Run Ln (27604-5453)
PHONE.....................252 558-7202
EMP: 4 EST: 2020
SALES (est): 39.69K **Privately Held**
SIC: 3999 Hair and hair-based products

(G-12588)
CAPITAL CITY CUISINE LLC
4808 Wallingford Dr (27616-7032)
PHONE.....................919 432-2126
EMP: 4 EST: 2021
SALES (est): 155.83K **Privately Held**
SIC: 2599 7389 Food wagons, restaurant; Business services, nec

(G-12589)
CAPITAL CITY SEALANTS LLC
3101 Stony Brook Dr Ste 166 (27604-3786)
P.O. Box 41014 (27629-1014)
PHONE.....................919 427-4077
EMP: 8 EST: 2010
SALES (est): 978.99K **Privately Held**
SIC: 2891 Sealants

(G-12590)
CAPITAL LGHTNING PRTECTION INC
Also Called: Quality Lightning Protection
743 Pershing Rd (27608-2711)
P.O. Box 162 (27602-0162)
PHONE.....................919 832-5574
Thomas J Cottle Junior, *Pr*
Charles Stephenson, *VP*
EMP: 6 EST: 1944
SQ FT: 5,000
SALES (est): 858.74K
SALES (corp-wide): 2.46MM **Privately Held**
SIC: 3643 Lightning protection equipment
PA: Quality Lightning Protection, Inc.
743 Pershing Rd
Raleigh NC 27608
919 832-9399

(G-12591)
CAPITAL SIGN SOLUTIONS LLC
5800 Mchines Pl Ste 110 (27616-1952)
PHONE.....................919 789-1452
EMP: 28 EST: 2011
SALES (est): 3.15MM **Privately Held**
Web: www.capitalsignsolutions.com
SIC: 3993 Signs and advertising specialties

(G-12592)
CAPPER MCCALL CO
9650 Strickland Rd Ste 103420 (27615-1902)
PHONE.....................919 270-8813
EMP: 9 EST: 2019
SALES (est): 464.6K **Privately Held**
Web: www.cappermccall.com
SIC: 3599 Industrial machinery, nec

(G-12593)
CAPTIVE-AIRE SYSTEMS INC (PA)
Also Called: Aqua-Matic
4641 Paragon Park Rd Ste 104 (27616-3407)
PHONE.....................919 882-2410
Robert L Luddy, *Pr*
William H Francis Junior, *VP Fin*
◆ EMP: 130 EST: 1978
SQ FT: 90,000
SALES (est): 485.13MM
SALES (corp-wide): 485.13MM **Privately Held**
Web: www.captiveaire.com
SIC: 3444 Restaurant sheet metalwork

(G-12594)
CARDINAL CABINETWORKS INC
4900 Craftsman Dr Ste A (27609-5665)
PHONE.....................919 829-3634
L Hardin Sigmon, *Pr*
EMP: 9 EST: 1994
SALES (est): 989.7K **Privately Held**
Web: www.cardinalcabinetworks.com
SIC: 2434 Wood kitchen cabinets

(G-12595)
CAROLINA COUNTERTOPS OF GARNER
3800 Tryon Rd Ste F (27606-4247)
PHONE.....................919 832-3335
Robert Lilly, *Pr*
Hal Lilly, *VP*
A Lilly, *Sec*
EMP: 15 EST: 1985
SQ FT: 9,000
SALES (est): 997.26K **Privately Held**
SIC: 2541 Counters or counter display cases, wood

(G-12596)
CAROLINA EAR HRING AID ASSOC L
5900 Six Forks Rd Ste 200 (27609-8226)
PHONE.....................919 876-4327
EMP: 5 EST: 2014
SALES (est): 211.8K **Privately Held**
Web: www.carolinaear.com
SIC: 3842 Hearing aids

(G-12597)
CAROLINA FABRICATORS LLC
Also Called: Carolina Fabricators
6016 Triangle Dr (27617-4743)
PHONE.....................919 510-8410
Scott Kisner, *Managing Member*
EMP: 18 EST: 1998
SQ FT: 16,000
SALES (est): 8.06MM
SALES (corp-wide): 8.06MM **Privately Held**
Web: www.carolinametalfabricators.com
SIC: 3441 Fabricated structural metal
PA: Directus Holdings, Llc
6016 Triangle Dr
Raleigh NC 27617
919 510-8410

(G-12598)
CAROLINA FUR DRESSING COMPANY
900 Freedom Dr (27610-1424)
PHONE.....................919 231-0086
Rick Morgan, *Pr*
▲ EMP: 28 EST: 1980
SQ FT: 30,000
SALES (est): 2.33MM **Privately Held**
Web: www.carolinafurdressing.com
SIC: 3111 Leather tanning and finishing

(G-12599)
CAROLINA LASERS
Also Called: Clausen Carolina Lasers
5508 Old Wake Forest Rd (27609-5279)
PHONE.....................919 872-8001
Wayne Clausen, *Prin*
EMP: 5 EST: 2009
SALES (est): 376.31K **Privately Held**
Web: www.carolinalasers.com
SIC: 3829 Measuring and controlling devices, nec

(G-12600)
CAROLINA PACKAGING & SUP INC (PA)
5609 Departure Dr (27616-1842)
PHONE.....................919 201-5592
EMP: 61 EST: 1994
SALES (est): 7.04MM **Privately Held**
Web: www.carolinapackaging.com
SIC: 2653 Boxes, corrugated: made from purchased materials

(G-12601)
CAROLINA SUNROCK LLC
8620 Barefoot Industrial Rd (27617-4703)
PHONE.....................919 861-1860
Bryan Postol, *Owner*
EMP: 33
SALES (corp-wide): 68.06MM **Privately Held**
Web: www.thesunrockgroup.com
SIC: 3273 Ready-mixed concrete
HQ: Carolina Sunrock Llc
1001 W B St
Butner NC 27509
919 575-4502

(G-12602)
CAROLINIAN PUBG GROUP LLC
1504 New Bern Ave (27610-2536)
P.O. Box 25308 (27611-5308)
PHONE.....................919 834-5558
Adria Jervay, *Pr*
EMP: 7 EST: 1940
SALES (est): 395.75K **Privately Held**
Web: www.thecarolinian.com
SIC: 2711 Newspapers, publishing and printing

(G-12603)
CAROMED INTERNATIONAL INC
Also Called: Polli Garment
5605 Spring Ct (27616-2920)
P.O. Box 4360 (18043-4360)
PHONE.....................919 878-0578
Barbara Beck, *Pr*
Thomas A Barnett, *
Brian Madigan, *
EMP: 16 EST: 1983
SQ FT: 15,000
SALES (est): 330.73K **Privately Held**
Web: www.caromed.us
SIC: 3842 Bandages and dressings

(G-12604)
CARROLL RUSSELL MFG INC
2009 Carr Pur Dr (27603-8885)
PHONE.....................919 779-2273
John Kissock, *Ch*
Russell K Carroll Junior, *Pr*
Donna Watkins, *
Connie Carroll, *
EMP: 45 EST: 1976
SQ FT: 52,000
SALES (est): 9.77MM **Privately Held**
Web: www.russwood.com
SIC: 2511 Wood household furniture

(G-12605)
CARY AUDIO DESIGN LLC
6301 Chapel Hill Rd (27607-5115)
PHONE.....................919 355-0010
William W Wright Junior, *Managing Member*
▲ EMP: 24 EST: 1989
SQ FT: 10,000
SALES (est): 4.42MM **Privately Held**
Web: www.caryaudio.com
SIC: 3651 Household audio equipment

(G-12606)
CARY PRINTING
1528 Crickett Rd (27610-9300)
PHONE.....................919 266-9005
EMP: 5 EST: 2010
SALES (est): 159.76K **Privately Held**
SIC: 2752 Commercial printing, lithographic

(G-12607)
CARYPRESS PUBLISHING
8801 Fast Park Dr Ste 301 (27617-4853)
PHONE.....................919 346-4907
EMP: 4 EST: 2019
SALES (est): 97.23K **Privately Held**
Web: www.carypress.com
SIC: 2741 Miscellaneous publishing

(G-12608)
CAS MACHINE DESIGN LLC
210 Cox Ave Apt A (27605-1845)
PHONE.....................919 515-2834
Christopher A Sanford, *Prin*
EMP: 7 EST: 2018
SALES (est): 172.67K **Privately Held**
Web: www.casmachinedesign.com
SIC: 3599 Machine shop, jobbing and repair

(G-12609)
CASA DI CUPCAKES
2120 Woodwyck Way (27604-6127)
PHONE.....................919 255-9994
Jennifer Humeniuk, *Prin*
EMP: 5 EST: 2010
SALES (est): 66.5K **Privately Held**
SIC: 2051 Bread, cake, and related products

(G-12610)
CASCADAS NYE CORPORATION
Also Called: Sir Speedy
2109 Avent Ferry Rd Ste 103 (27606-2198)
PHONE.....................919 834-8128
Phillip Nye, *Pr*
Margaret Nye, *Stockholder*
Edith Nye, *Stockholder*
EMP: 10 EST: 1989
SALES (est): 952.03K **Privately Held**
Web: www.sirspeedy.com
SIC: 2752 Commercial printing, lithographic

(G-12611)
CASE SPECIALISTS
2033 Longwood Dr (27612-2814)

Raleigh - Wake County (G-12612)

PHONE..................919 818-4476
Wayne Evans, *Owner*
EMP: 5 **EST:** 2003
SALES (est): 285.68K **Privately Held**
Web: www.casespecialists.com
SIC: 2449 Shipping cases and drums, wood: wirebound and plywood

(G-12612)
CAST IRON ELEGANCE INC
Also Called: Elite Custom Coatings
831 Purser Dr Ste 103 (27603-4181)
PHONE..................919 662-8777
Matt Vaughn, *CEO*
EMP: 15 **EST:** 2005
SALES (est): 1.25MM **Privately Held**
Web: www.castironelegance.com
SIC: 3446 2851 Architectural metalwork; Coating, air curing

(G-12613)
CCL LABEL
308 S Rogers Ln (27610-2925)
PHONE..................919 713-0388
▲ **EMP:** 10 **EST:** 2011
SALES (est): 1.2MM **Privately Held**
Web: www.ccllabel.com
SIC: 2759 Labels and seals: printing, nsk

(G-12614)
CCL LABEL INC
308 S Rogers Ln Ste 120 (27610-2925)
PHONE..................919 713-0388
Geoff Martin, *CEO*
EMP: 48
SALES (corp-wide): 4.75B **Privately Held**
Web: www.cclind.com
SIC: 2759 Labels and seals: printing, nsk
HQ: Ccl Label, Inc.
    161 Worcester Rd Ste 403
    Framingham MA 01701
    508 872-4511

(G-12615)
CELTIC CERAMICS
4140 Mardella Dr (27613-1529)
PHONE..................919 510-6817
Edward Gallagher, *Prin*
EMP: 5 **EST:** 2010
SALES (est): 245.5K **Privately Held**
SIC: 3269 Pottery products, nec

(G-12616)
CENGAGE LEARNING INC
Also Called: Webassign
1791 Varsity Dr Ste 200 (27606-5242)
P.O. Box 37665 (27627-7665)
PHONE..................919 829-8181
Michael Hansen, *Brnch Mgr*
EMP: 25
Web: www.webassign.com
SIC: 4813 7372 Internet connectivity services; Educational computer software
HQ: Cengage Learning, Inc.
    5191 Natorp Blvd
    Mason OH 45040

(G-12617)
CENTICE CORPORATION
7283 Nc Highway 42 Ste 102 (27603-7529)
PHONE..................919 653-0424
John Goehrke, *CEO*
Rob Mclaughlin, *Sec*
Prasant Potuluri, *
EMP: 45 **EST:** 2003
SQ FT: 14,000
SALES (est): 4.38MM **Privately Held**
Web: www.centice.com

SIC: 3823 3826 5049 Process control instruments; Spectroscopic and other optical properties measuring equip.; Precision tools

(G-12618)
CHEF MARTINI LLC
1908 Falls Of Neuse Rd Ste 215 (27615)
P.O. Box 99806 (27624-9806)
PHONE..................919 327-3183
EMP: 1129 **EST:** 1989
SQ FT: 2,500
SALES (est): 26.09MM **Privately Held**
SIC: 5149 5046 2035 2023 Natural and organic foods; Commercial cooking and food service equipment; Seasonings, meat sauces (except tomato and dry); Canned milk, whole

(G-12619)
CHESNICK CORPORATION
3236 Lake Woodard Dr (27604-3659)
PHONE..................919 231-2899
Mark A Chesnick, *Pr*
Charlie Lingenfelser, *VP*
Susan Latta, *Sec*
EMP: 15 **EST:** 1996
SQ FT: 20,000
SALES (est): 2.45MM **Privately Held**
Web: www.chesnick.com
SIC: 2431 2434 Moldings and baseboards, ornamental and trim; Wood kitchen cabinets

(G-12620)
CHOICE PRINTING LLC
4100 Wingate Dr (27609-6053)
PHONE..................919 790-0680
EMP: 5 **EST:** 2001
SALES (est): 115.3K **Privately Held**
SIC: 2752 Offset printing

(G-12621)
CHRISTOPHER RIDLEY
8426 Old Ponderosa Cir (27603-8598)
PHONE..................919 291-9999
EMP: 4 **EST:** 2016
SALES (est): 109.23K **Privately Held**
Web: www.cplatoon.org
SIC: 3572 Computer storage devices

(G-12622)
CINTERS INC
4501 New Bern Ave # 130-308 (27610-1549)
PHONE..................336 267-3051
Jacob Adelowo, *Pr*
Emmanuel Adelowo, *Sec*
Christy Adelowo, *Treas*
Howard Williams, *VP*
EMP: 7 **EST:** 2002
SQ FT: 6,000
SALES (est): 184.29K **Privately Held**
SIC: 3061 Mechanical rubber goods

(G-12623)
CIRCLE GRAPHICS INC
10700 World Trade Blvd (27617-4220)
PHONE..................919 864-4518
Hank Ridless, *Pr*
EMP: 250
SALES (corp-wide): 509.22MM **Privately Held**
Web: www.circlegraphicsonline.com
SIC: 2759 Commercial printing, nec
PA: Circle Graphics, Inc.
    120 9th Ave
    Longmont CO 80501
    303 532-2370

(G-12624)
CIVES CORP
1621 Morning Mountain Rd (27614-9388)
PHONE..................919 518-2140
Howard Lachlar, *Owner*
EMP: 4 **EST:** 2002
SALES (est): 215.43K **Privately Held**
SIC: 3441 Fabricated structural metal

(G-12625)
CLARK ART SHOP INC
12705 Scenic Dr (27614-9183)
PHONE..................919 832-8319
Owen Walker Iii, *Pr*
Doris C Walker, *Sec*
EMP: 8 **EST:** 1923
SQ FT: 4,000
SALES (est): 241.67K **Privately Held**
Web: www.clarknow.org
SIC: 7999 2394 1799 Art gallery, commercial; Awnings, fabric: made from purchased materials; Window treatment installation

(G-12626)
CLASSIC CLEANING LLC
Also Called: Commercial Cnstr Jantr Svcs
8601 Six Forks Rd Ste 400 (27615-2965)
PHONE..................800 220-7101
Patricia Mathis, *Pr*
Marcus Brinson, *
EMP: 30 **EST:** 2016
SALES (est): 1.07MM **Privately Held**
SIC: 7699 0782 3315 7349 Cleaning services; Lawn care services; Chain link fencing; Janitorial service, contract basis

(G-12627)
CLEAN-SWEEP SOLUTIONS INC ✪
1017 Main Campus Dr (27606-5204)
PHONE..................469 450-8317
EMP: 6 **EST:** 2023
SALES (est): 332.38K **Privately Held**
SIC: 3571 Electronic computers

(G-12628)
CLICK ELECTRONICS LLC
4030 Wake Forest Rd Ste 349 (27609-0010)
PHONE..................704 840-6855
Jovan Ortiz, *Mgr*
EMP: 12
SALES (est): 777.96K **Privately Held**
Web: www.clickic.net
SIC: 3679 Electronic components, nec

(G-12629)
CLINETIC INC
520 Guilford Cir (27608-1698)
PHONE..................513 295-1332
Thomas Kaminski, *CEO*
EMP: 10 **EST:** 2017
SALES (est): 500K **Privately Held**
Web: www.clinetic.com
SIC: 7372 Business oriented computer software

(G-12630)
CLOSURE MEDICAL CORPORATION
5250 Greens Dairy Rd (27616-4612)
PHONE..................919 876-7800
Daniel A Pelak, *Pr*
EMP: 123 **EST:** 1987
SQ FT: 69,000
SALES (est): 29.15MM
SALES (corp-wide): 85.16B **Publicly Held**
SIC: 2834 Pharmaceutical preparations
HQ: Ethicon Inc.
    1000 Route 202
    Raritan NJ 08869
    800 384-4266

(G-12631)
CLOUD SFTWR GROUP HOLDINGS INC
Also Called: Citrix Sharefile
120 S West St (27603-1834)
PHONE..................919 839-6139
EMP: 600
SALES (corp-wide): 4.38B **Privately Held**
Web: www.sharefile.com
SIC: 7372 Business oriented computer software
HQ: Cloud Software Group Holdings, Inc.
    851 W Cypress Creek Rd
    Fort Lauderdale FL 33309
    954 267-3000

(G-12632)
COHERA MEDICAL INC (PA)
227 Fayetteville St Ste 900 (27601-1574)
PHONE..................800 641-7458
Patrick Daly, *CEO*
Eric Beckman, *Pr*
Richard Wonsettler, *Sec*
William M Cotter, *VP*
Dottie Clower, *VP*
EMP: 7 **EST:** 2004
SQ FT: 8,000
SALES (est): 1.29MM
SALES (corp-wide): 1.29MM **Privately Held**
Web: www.coheramedical.com
SIC: 2891 Adhesives

(G-12633)
COLD OFF PRESS LLC
416 W South St Ste 100 (27601-2242)
PHONE..................984 444-9006
EMP: 5 **EST:** 2018
SALES (est): 218.39K **Privately Held**
Web: www.coldoffthepress.com
SIC: 2741 Miscellaneous publishing

(G-12634)
COMPETITIVE SOLUTIONS INC (PA)
8340 Bandford Way Ste 103 (27615-2755)
PHONE..................919 851-0058
John Pyecha, *CEO*
Anna Versteeg, *
John Pyecha, *Treas*
Shane Yount, *
EMP: 25 **EST:** 1991
SALES (est): 3.81MM **Privately Held**
Web: www.csipbl.com
SIC: 8742 7372 8741 8748 Business management consultant; Business oriented computer software; Business management; Business consulting, nec

(G-12635)
COMPLETE COMP ST OF RALGH INC
Also Called: Digitz
3016 Hillsborough St Ste 100 (27607-0149)
P.O. Box 847 (27522-0847)
PHONE..................919 828-5227
Joseph K Alukal, *Pr*
Maria J Alukal, *VP*
EMP: 20 **EST:** 1984
SQ FT: 7,700
SALES (est): 2.06MM **Privately Held**
SIC: 5734 7378 3955 Personal computers; Computer and data processing equipment repair/maintenance; Print cartridges for laser and other computer printers

(G-12636)
COMPUTER TASK GROUP INC
8801 Fast Park Dr Ste 101 (27617-4853)
PHONE..................919 677-1313
Tom Stephenson, *Owner*

GEOGRAPHIC SECTION

Raleigh - Wake County (G-12663)

EMP: 6
SALES (corp-wide): 325.08MM **Privately Held**
Web: www.ctg.com
SIC: 7371 7379 7374 7372 Custom computer programming services; Computer related consulting services; Data processing and preparation; Prepackaged software
PA: Computer Task Group, Incorporated
300 Corp Pkwy Ste 214n
Amherst NY 14226
716 882-8000

(G-12637)
CONNECTMEDIA VENTURES LLC
425 N Boylan Ave (27603-1200)
PHONE.................................773 551-7446
EMP: 6 **EST:** 2009
SQ FT: 1,500
SALES (est): 455.66K **Privately Held**
Web: www.cmvmobile.com
SIC: 7372 Prepackaged software

(G-12638)
CONSOLIDATED MFG INTL LLC (PA)
Also Called: C M I
5816 Triangle Dr (27617-4705)
PHONE.................................919 781-3411
◆ **EMP:** 6 **EST:** 2002
SQ FT: 12,600
SALES (est): 3.44MM
SALES (corp-wide): 3.44MM **Privately Held**
Web: www.cmiwebsite.com
SIC: 3699 Electrical equipment and supplies, nec

(G-12639)
CONSOLIDATED SCIENCES INC
Also Called: Micro Technology Unlimited
8390 Six Forks Rd Ste 101 (27615-3060)
P.O. Box 80124 (27623-0124)
PHONE.................................919 870-0344
David B Cox, *Pr*
Bryan Cox, *VP*
Benjamin Bryan Cox, *VP*
EMP: 5 **EST:** 1977
SQ FT: 1,500
SALES (est): 419.1K **Privately Held**
SIC: 3695 Computer software tape and disks: blank, rigid, and floppy

(G-12640)
CONTECH ENGNERED SOLUTIONS LLC
4917 Waters Edge Dr Ste 271 (27606-5416)
PHONE.................................919 858-7820
Brent Brewbaker, *Mgr*
EMP: 6
Web: www.conteches.com
SIC: 3443 Fabricated plate work (boiler shop)
HQ: Contech Engineered Solutions Llc
9025 Centre Pointe Dr # 400
West Chester OH 45069
513 645-7000

(G-12641)
CONTECH ENGNERED SOLUTIONS LLC
6115 Chapel Hill Rd (27607-5111)
PHONE.................................919 851-2880
Greg Demerjian, *Mgr*
EMP: 9
Web: www.conteches.com
SIC: 3443 Fabricated plate work (boiler shop)
HQ: Contech Engineered Solutions Llc
9025 Centre Pointe Dr # 400
West Chester OH 45069
513 645-7000

(G-12642)
CONTEGO MEDICAL INC
3801 Lake Boone Trl Ste 100 (27607-2994)
PHONE.................................919 606-3917
Ravish Sachar, *CEO*
Jay Yadav, *CEO*
Nathalie Greene, *VP*
EMP: 26 **EST:** 2010
SALES (est): 3.4MM **Privately Held**
Web: www.contegomedical.com
SIC: 3841 Surgical and medical instruments

(G-12643)
CONTEMPORARY PUBLISHING CO
1460 Diggs Dr Ste C (27603-2771)
P.O. Box 767 (27502-0767)
PHONE.................................919 834-4432
Ronald B Rose, *Pr*
Ellen Rose, *VP*
EMP: 5 **EST:** 1975
SALES (est): 300K **Privately Held**
SIC: 2731 Textbooks: publishing only, not printed on site

(G-12644)
CONTRACT PRINTING & GRAPHICS
2417 Bertie Dr (27610-1730)
PHONE.................................919 832-7178
Charles L Ethridge, *Owner*
EMP: 5 **EST:** 1975
SALES (est): 174.07K **Privately Held**
SIC: 7336 2759 Commercial art and graphic design; Commercial printing, nec

(G-12645)
COOL RUNNINGS JAMAICAN LLC (PA)
Also Called: Millys Jamaican Jerk Seasoning
2700 Hidden Glen Ln (27606-8307)
PHONE.................................919 818-9220
Stephen Millington, *Managing Member*
EMP: 8 **EST:** 2019
SALES (est): 54.38K
SALES (corp-wide): 54.38K **Privately Held**
SIC: 2099 Seasonings and spices

(G-12646)
COOPERCRAFT PENS
2816 Fowler Ave (27607-7064)
PHONE.................................910 603-1191
Don Cooper, *Prin*
EMP: 4 **EST:** 2008
SALES (est): 72.59K **Privately Held**
SIC: 3951 Pens and mechanical pencils

(G-12647)
CORE SOUND IMAGING INC
5510 Six Forks Rd Ste 200 (27609-8620)
PHONE.................................919 277-0636
Mark Smith, *Pr*
Laurie Smith, *VP*
EMP: 30 **EST:** 2007
SALES (est): 2.39MM **Privately Held**
Web: app.corestudycast.com
SIC: 3841 Surgical and medical instruments

(G-12648)
CORNERSTONE KITCHENS INC
6300 Westgate Rd Ste C (27617-4754)
PHONE.................................919 510-4200
Scott Baltz, *Pr*
EMP: 4 **EST:** 1983
SALES (est): 416.7K **Privately Held**
Web: www.cornerstonekitchensnc.com
SIC: 2434 Wood kitchen cabinets

(G-12649)
COTTAGE
1430 Canterbury Rd (27608-1948)
P.O. Box 14 (27894-0014)
PHONE.................................919 872-1441
EMP: 4 **EST:** 2010
SALES (est): 74.55K **Privately Held**
SIC: 2754 Stationery and invitation printing, gravure

(G-12650)
COVIDIEN HOLDING INC
8800 Durant Rd (27616-3104)
PHONE.................................919 878-2930
Bob Hassebrock, *Brnch Mgr*
EMP: 151
SQ FT: 121,800
Web: www.covidien.com
SIC: 3841 Surgical and medical instruments
HQ: Covidien Holding Inc.
710 Medtronic Pkwy
Minneapolis MN 55432

(G-12651)
CRANKY CREATIVE GROUP
5812 Triangle Dr (27617-4705)
PHONE.................................877 775-9727
EMP: 4 **EST:** 2016
SALES (est): 103.05K **Privately Held**
Web: www.crankycreative.com
SIC: 3993 Signs and advertising specialties

(G-12652)
CRAWLSPACE PRESS LLC
2821 Knowles St (27603-2555)
PHONE.................................919 645-7075
Eric Gilmore, *Prin*
EMP: 5 **EST:** 2018
SALES (est): 117.57K **Privately Held**
Web: www.thecrawlspacepress.com
SIC: 2741 Miscellaneous publishing

(G-12653)
CREATIONS CABINETRY DESIGN LLC
3825 Junction Blvd (27603-5264)
PHONE.................................919 865-5979
EMP: 7 **EST:** 2013
SALES (est): 137.5K **Privately Held**
Web: www.creationscabinetry.com
SIC: 2434 Wood kitchen cabinets

(G-12654)
CREATIVE T-SHIRTS IMAGING LLC
2526 Hillsborough St Ste 101 (27607-7275)
PHONE.................................919 828-0204
Geraldine Jones, *Owner*
EMP: 5 **EST:** 2016
SALES (est): 149.91K **Privately Held**
Web: www.creativeteesraleigh.com
SIC: 2759 Screen printing

(G-12655)
CREATIVE TEES
2526 Hillsborough St (27607-7298)
PHONE.................................919 828-0204
Roland Jones, *Mgr*
EMP: 6 **EST:** 2008
SALES (est): 277.41K **Privately Held**
Web: www.creativeteesraleigh.com
SIC: 2759 Screen printing

(G-12656)
CRMNEXT INC
702 Oberlin Rd Ofc Ofc (27605-1357)
PHONE.................................415 424-4644
Joseph Salesky, *Prin*
EMP: 30 **EST:** 2016
SALES (est): 1.06MM **Privately Held**
Web: www.businessnext.com
SIC: 7372 Business oriented computer software
PA: Acidaes Solutions Private Limited
Unitech Infospace, Block B, Plot No.2, Tower 1
Noida UP 20130

(G-12657)
CRUDE LLC
501 E Davie St (27601-1917)
PHONE.................................919 391-8185
Craig Rudewicz, *Managing Member*
EMP: 6 **EST:** 2015
SALES (est): 70.77K **Privately Held**
Web: www.crudebitters.com
SIC: 2087 Flavoring extracts and syrups, nec

(G-12658)
CRYOGEN LLC
Also Called: Glia Beauty
2626 Glenwood Ave Ste 140 (27608-1367)
PHONE.................................919 649-7027
Criollo Vinueza, *Managing Member*
Valeria Margarita, *Managing Member*
EMP: 15 **EST:** 2021
SQ FT: 1,174
SALES (est): 573.25K **Privately Held**
SIC: 2844 Perfumes, cosmetics and other toilet preparations

(G-12659)
CTI PROPERTY SERVICES INC
Also Called: C T I Pressure Washing
5450 Old Wake Forest Rd (27609-5012)
P.O. Box 58635 (27658-8635)
PHONE.................................919 787-3789
Tim Felton, *Pr*
EMP: 37 **EST:** 1995
SALES (est): 4.77MM **Privately Held**
Web: www.ctipropertyservices.com
SIC: 0783 3271 1721 Removal services, bush and tree; Blocks, concrete: insulating; Painting and paper hanging

(G-12660)
CUPCAKE A LA MO LLC
8110 Farmlea Cir (27616-7706)
PHONE.................................919 322-8824
Monique Butler, *Prin*
EMP: 4 **EST:** 2015
SALES (est): 180.8K **Privately Held**
SIC: 2051 Bread, cake, and related products

(G-12661)
CUPCAKE STOP SHOP LLC ✪
6902 Cameron Crest Cir Apt 118 (27613-7348)
PHONE.................................919 457-7900
Stephanie Jones, *CEO*
EMP: 4 **EST:** 2022
SALES (est): 182.43K **Privately Held**
SIC: 2051 7389 Cakes, bakery: except frozen ; Business Activities at Non-Commercial Site

(G-12662)
CURVEMAKERS INC (PA)
703 W Johnson St (27603-1295)
P.O. Box 33706 (27636-3706)
PHONE.................................919 821-5792
John Thomas, *Pr*
EMP: 9 **EST:** 1996
SQ FT: 20,000
SALES (est): 2.15MM
SALES (corp-wide): 2.15MM **Privately Held**
Web: www.curvemakers.com
SIC: 2431 Doors, wood

(G-12663)
CUSTOM BRICK COMPANY INC
Also Called: Custom Brick and Supplied Co.
1833 Capital Blvd (27604-2144)

Raleigh - Wake County (G-12664) — GEOGRAPHIC SECTION

P.O. Box 6245 (27628-6245)
PHONE.................................919 832-2804
TOLL FREE: 800
Tom G Fisher, *Pr*
Steve Frazier, *VP*
Grant Fisher, *Treas*
EMP: 22 EST: 1961
SQ FT: 6,000
SALES (est): 8.81MM **Privately Held**
Web: www.custombrick.com
SIC: **5032** 3271 2951 3272 Brick, stone, and related material; Concrete block and brick; Paving blocks; Cast stone, concrete

(G-12664)
CUSTOM CONTROLS UNLIMITED LLC
2600 Garner Station Blvd (27603-4187)
PHONE.................................919 812-6553
Melissa Carroll, *Pr*
Devin Carrol, *VP*
EMP: 18 EST: 2000
SQ FT: 16,000
SALES (est): 4.51MM **Privately Held**
Web: www.ccuinc.com
SIC: **7373** 1731 3625 8711 Systems engineering, computer related; Electronic controls installation; Electric controls and control accessories, industrial; Engineering services

(G-12665)
CUSTOM NANO INC
1509 Lorimer Rd (27606-2623)
PHONE.................................919 608-3540
Roger Russell, *CEO*
Sam Rogers, *COO*
EMP: 6 EST: 2015
SALES (est): 119.22K **Privately Held**
SIC: **5169** 2869 7389 Industrial chemicals; Laboratory chemicals, organic; Business services, nec

(G-12666)
CUSTOM PATCH HATS LLC
1505 Capital Blvd Ste 14b (27603-1199)
PHONE.................................919 424-7723
Scott Alexander, *Managing Member*
EMP: 6 EST: 2018
SALES (est): 602.17K **Privately Held**
Web: www.custompatchhats.com
SIC: **2353** 2389 Hats, caps, and millinery; Apparel and accessories, nec

(G-12667)
CYBER IMAGING SYSTEMS INC
8300 Falls Of Neuse Rd (27615-3449)
PHONE.................................919 872-5179
Hal E Wilson, *Pr*
James Welch, *Sec*
EMP: 10 EST: 1996
SQ FT: 2,000
SALES (est): 1.09MM **Privately Held**
Web: www.cyber-imaging.com
SIC: **7372** Prepackaged software

(G-12668)
D & B PRINTING CO
3000 Trawick Rd (27604-3753)
PHONE.................................919 876-3530
Shirley Blake, *Owner*
EMP: 6 EST: 1975
SQ FT: 3,000
SALES (est): 369.23K **Privately Held**
SIC: **2752** Offset printing

(G-12669)
D J LOGGING INC
5199 Hillsborough St (27606-1335)
PHONE.................................919 219-6853
EMP: 6 EST: 2020
SALES (est): 483.17K **Privately Held**
SIC: **2411** Logging

(G-12670)
DAIRY SERVICES
100 Cordova Ct (27606)
PHONE.................................919 303-2442
Tyrone Tazewell, *Owner*
EMP: 4 EST: 1989
SALES (est): 197.33K **Privately Held**
SIC: **3523** Dairy equipment (farm), nec

(G-12671)
DALES WELDING SERVICE
7352 Berkshire Downs Dr (27616-5636)
PHONE.................................919 872-6969
Dale Kraynak, *Owner*
EMP: 5 EST: 1986
SALES (est): 425.83K **Privately Held**
Web: www.daleswelding.com
SIC: **7692** Welding repair

(G-12672)
DAN FORREST WOODWORKS WRAP UP
4209 Waterbury Rd (27604-3448)
PHONE.................................919 532-9190
Danny Forrest, *Prin*
EMP: 5 EST: 2018
SALES (est): 54.13K **Privately Held**
SIC: **2431** Millwork

(G-12673)
DATASPECTRUM
4700 Falls Of Neuse Rd (27609-6200)
PHONE.................................919 341-3300
David E Williams, *Prin*
EMP: 7 EST: 2004
SALES (est): 166.79K **Privately Held**
SIC: **2834** Pharmaceutical preparations

(G-12674)
DAVCOM ENTERPRISES INC
Also Called: Fastsigns
2621 Spring Forest Rd Ste 105 (27616-1830)
PHONE.................................919 872-9522
Tonya Davis, *Pr*
EMP: 8 EST: 1989
SQ FT: 2,800
SALES (est): 898.19K **Privately Held**
Web: www.fastsigns.com
SIC: **3993** Signs and advertising specialties

(G-12675)
DAVID ALLEN COMPANY INC (PA)
150 Rush St (27603-3594)
P.O. Box 27705 (27611-7705)
PHONE.................................919 821-7100
Robert C Roberson, *Ch*
Donald R Scott, *
David Roberson, *
Philip Halcomb, *
Martin Howard, *
▲ EMP: 150 EST: 1920
SQ FT: 25,000
SALES (est): 63.51MM
SALES (corp-wide): 63.51MM **Privately Held**
Web: www.davidallen.com
SIC: **1743** 3272 Tile installation, ceramic; Areaways, basement window: concrete

(G-12676)
DDI PRINT
Also Called: Ddi
5210 Western Blvd (27604-1642)
PHONE.................................919 829-8810
EMP: 8 EST: 2010
SALES (est): 98.5K **Privately Held**
Web: www.documentsdirectinc.com
SIC: **2752** Commercial printing, lithographic

(G-12677)
DESCHER LLC
Also Called: Descher Automation
1613 Old Louisburg Rd (27604-1300)
PHONE.................................919 828-7708
EMP: 5 EST: 2008
SQ FT: 4,500
SALES (est): 498.33K **Privately Held**
Web: www.descher-automation.com
SIC: **3569** 8711 7373 Assembly machines, non-metalworking; Machine tool design; Computer-aided design (CAD) systems service

(G-12678)
DESIGN SPECIALTIES INC
Also Called: Presicion Wall
3640 Banks Rd (27603-8918)
PHONE.................................919 772-6955
Loy C Allen, *Pr*
Loy C Allen Junior, *VP*
Gary Roth, *Sec*
Jim Womble, *Sec*
EMP: 22 EST: 1985
SQ FT: 2,000
SALES (est): 648.32K **Privately Held**
SIC: **5032** 5039 3355 Brick, stone, and related material; Architectural metalwork; Aluminum rolling and drawing, nec

(G-12679)
DESIGN SURFACES INC
Also Called: Design Surfaces of Raleigh
1212 Front St (27609-7527)
PHONE.................................919 781-0310
▲ EMP: 11 EST: 1989
SALES (est): 1.68MM **Privately Held**
SIC: **5031** 2499 5211 Structural assemblies, prefabricated: wood; Decorative wood and woodwork; Counter tops

(G-12680)
DESIGNELEMENT
972 Trinity Rd (27607-4940)
PHONE.................................919 383-5561
EMP: 13 EST: 2019
SALES (est): 542.2K **Privately Held**
Web: www.designelement-us.com
SIC: **3993** Signs and advertising specialties

(G-12681)
DEXTER INC (PA)
Also Called: Dexter Furniture
8411 Glenwood Ave Ste 101 (27612-7312)
PHONE.................................919 510-5050
Thomas Collins, *Pr*
EMP: 4 EST: 1985
SALES (est): 1.1MM
SALES (corp-wide): 1.1MM **Privately Held**
Web: www.dexterfurniture.com
SIC: **5712** 2512 Mattresses; Upholstered household furniture

(G-12682)
DG PRINTING SOLUTIONS
5412 Overdale Ln (27603-7861)
PHONE.................................919 779-0225
EMP: 5 EST: 2018
SALES (est): 126.43K **Privately Held**
SIC: **2752** Commercial printing, lithographic

(G-12683)
DIGI RONIN GAMES LLC
12308 Glenlivet Way (27613-6852)
PHONE.................................919 845-9960
EMP: 4 EST: 2019
SALES (est): 60.53K **Privately Held**
SIC: **3652** Prerecorded records and tapes

(G-12684)
DIMILL ENTERPRISES LLC
Also Called: Prism Specialties NC
531 Pylon Dr (27606-1414)
PHONE.................................919 629-2011
EMP: 9 EST: 2012
SALES (est): 246.75K **Privately Held**
Web: www.prismspecialties.com
SIC: **7699** 3571 8999 5045 Antique repair and restoration, except furniture, autos; Electronic computers; Art restoration; Computers and accessories, personal and home entertainment

(G-12685)
DIRECT LEGAL MAIL LLC
8800 Westgate Park Dr Ste 110 (27617-4833)
PHONE.................................919 353-9158
Steve Darren Immelman, *Managing Member*
EMP: 4 EST: 2019
SALES (est): 226.2K **Privately Held**
Web: www.directlegalmail.com
SIC: **2741** Miscellaneous publishing

(G-12686)
DIRECTUS HOLDINGS LLC (PA)
Also Called: Carolina Metal Fabricators
6016 Triangle Dr (27617-4743)
PHONE.................................919 510-8410
Jeffrey Matuszak, *Managing Member*
EMP: 5 EST: 1998
SALES (est): 8.06MM
SALES (corp-wide): 8.06MM **Privately Held**
SIC: **3441** Fabricated structural metal

(G-12687)
DISCOVER NIGHT LLC
Also Called: Night
4030 Wake Forest Rd Ste 349 (27609)
PHONE.................................888 825-6282
Kalle Simpson, *Managing Member*
EMP: 12 EST: 2021
SALES (est): 1.31MM **Privately Held**
Web: www.discovernight.com
SIC: **2392** Pillows, bed: made from purchased materials

(G-12688)
DIVERSE SECURITY SYSTEMS INC
8831 Westgate Park Dr Ste 100 (27617-4815)
PHONE.................................919 848-9599
Alan Brain, *Pr*
EMP: 8 EST: 1999
SALES (est): 485.06K **Privately Held**
Web: www.diversesecuritysystemsinc.com
SIC: **3699** Security control equipment and systems

(G-12689)
DIVISION 10
10111 Division Dr (27603-5664)
PHONE.................................919 661-1101
EMP: 6 EST: 2020
SALES (est): 245.31K **Privately Held**
Web: www.div10csi.com
SIC: **5211** 3429 Lumber and other building materials; Hardware, nec

(G-12690)
DNA GROUP INC (PA)
2841 Plaza Pl Ste 200 (27612-6746)
PHONE.................................919 881-0889
Eric Vaughn, *CEO*

GEOGRAPHIC SECTION

Raleigh - Wake County (G-12717)

W Michael Owens, *
Bill Romick, Prin
▲ EMP: 46 EST: 1987
SQ FT: 25,000
SALES (est): 21.92MM Privately Held
Web: www.dnagroup.com
SIC: 5063 3822 3643 3621 Electrical apparatus and equipment; Environmental controls; Current-carrying wiring services; Motors and generators

(G-12691)
DOCMAGNET INC
6220 Angus Dr Ste 100 (27617-4752)
PHONE..................................919 788-7999
▲ EMP: 4
Web: www.docmagnet.com
SIC: 3499 Magnets, permanent: metallic

(G-12692)
DOCUMENT DIRECTS INC
5210 Western Blvd (27606-1642)
PHONE..................................919 829-8810
Quinn Wesson, Pr
EMP: 6 EST: 2005
SALES (est): 464.96K Privately Held
Web: www.documentsdirectinc.com
SIC: 2759 Commercial printing, nec

(G-12693)
DOCUMENT IMAGING SYSTEMS INC
Also Called: Engineering Reprographics
8709 Stage Ford Rd (27615-1826)
PHONE..................................919 460-9440
Laura Evans-sharp, Pr
Laura Evans, Pr
EMP: 4 EST: 1993
SALES (est): 346.6K Privately Held
Web: www.documentimagingsystems.com
SIC: 7334 2741 Blueprinting service; Art copy: publishing and printing

(G-12694)
DOLAN LLC
Also Called: North Carolina Lawyers Weekly
107 Fayetteville St 3rd Fl (27601-1398)
PHONE..................................919 829-9333
Liz Irwin, Brnch Mgr
EMP: 8
SALES (corp-wide): 316.47MM Privately Held
Web: www.bridgetowermedia.com
SIC: 2711 Newspapers, publishing and printing
HQ: Dolan Llc
222 S 9th St Ste 2300
Minneapolis MN 55402

(G-12695)
DOMIMEX
421 Chapanoke Rd (27603-3689)
PHONE..................................919 602-3921
EMP: 4 EST: 2014
SALES (est): 91.72K Privately Held
Web: www.theflowerbakery.com
SIC: 2844 Perfumes, cosmetics and other toilet preparations

(G-12696)
DOOR STORE OF AMERICA INC
Also Called: DSA Master Crafted Doors
10681 World Trade Blvd (27617-4304)
PHONE..................................919 781-3200
Eric Burkam, Pr
Eddie Wang, VP
▲ EMP: 19 EST: 2001
SQ FT: 25,000
SALES (est): 6.25MM Privately Held
Web: www.dsadoors.com
SIC: 2431 Doors, wood

(G-12697)
DORIS E INC
1027 Lake Moraine Pl (27607-3619)
PHONE..................................919 858-5419
EMP: 4 EST: 2019
SALES (est): 78.44K Privately Held
SIC: 2893 Printing ink

(G-12698)
DOWNTOWN RALEIGH
402 Glenwood Ave (27603-1220)
PHONE..................................919 821-7897
EMP: 5 EST: 2014
SALES (est): 160.51K Privately Held
Web: www.gladwellorthodontics.com
SIC: 2752 Commercial printing, lithographic

(G-12699)
DRAMEN OF RALEIGH LLC
547 Pylon Dr (27606-1414)
PHONE..................................919 828-5464
Don Brod, Mgr
EMP: 6 EST: 2020
SALES (est): 486.56K Privately Held
Web: www.dramen.com
SIC: 3571 Electronic computers

(G-12700)
DREAMCATCHERS PUBLISHING
4008 Mitchell Mill Rd (27616-8894)
PHONE..................................336 441-2255
EMP: 4 EST: 2015
SALES (est): 45.48K Privately Held
SIC: 2741 Miscellaneous publishing

(G-12701)
DREAMSHIP INC
Also Called: Dreamshipper
12212 Kyle Abbey Ln (27613-6271)
PHONE..................................908 601-8152
William G Bricker Iii, CEO
EMP: 4 EST: 2018
SALES (est): 421.42K Privately Held
Web: www.dreamship.com
SIC: 7372 7389 Prepackaged software; Business services, nec

(G-12702)
DRIVER DISTRIBUTION INC
Also Called: Eastern Bikes
9413 Owls Nest Dr (27613-7526)
PHONE..................................984 204-2929
Jon Byers, CEO
EMP: 6
SALES (corp-wide): 448.57K Privately Held
Web: www.easternbikes.com
SIC: 3751 Motorcycles and related parts
PA: Driver Distribution, Inc.
624 N Carolina Ave Bldg 4
Maiden NC 28650
984 204-2929

(G-12703)
DROPPING GEMZ NAIL STUDIO LLC (PA)
7400 Six Forks Rd Ste 4 (27615-6190)
PHONE..................................919 440-4744
EMP: 8 EST: 2020
SALES (est): 40K
SALES (corp-wide): 40K Privately Held
SIC: 3999 Fingernails, artificial

(G-12704)
DRS TRANSPORTATION INC
Also Called: Drs Consulting
10820 Oliver Rd Apt 101 (27614-7341)
PHONE..................................919 215-2770
Lenny Gibson, Prin
EMP: 4 EST: 2013

SALES (est): 344.12K Privately Held
SIC: 3537 7389 Trucks: freight, baggage, etc.: industrial, except mining; Business Activities at Non-Commercial Site

(G-12705)
DSKOW PUBLISHING LLC
301 Fayetteville St Unit 3309 (27601)
PHONE..................................321 506-0004
EMP: 4 EST: 2014
SALES (est): 55.74K Privately Held
Web: www.dskow.com
SIC: 2741 Miscellaneous publishing

(G-12706)
DSM INC
266 W Millbrook Rd (27609-4684)
PHONE..................................919 876-2802
Ralph Mullins, Prin
EMP: 10 EST: 2009
SALES (est): 137.89K Privately Held
Web: www.dsm.com
SIC: 2834 Pharmaceutical preparations

(G-12707)
DUCDUC LLC
Also Called: Ducduc Nyc
3200 Wake Forest Rd Ste 204 (27609)
PHONE..................................212 226-1868
Philip Eidles, Managing Member
EMP: 8
Web: www.ducducnyc.com
SIC: 2511 Children's wood furniture
PA: Ducduc Llc
200 Lexington Ave Rm 715
New York NY 10016

(G-12708)
DUKE ENERGY CENTER
2 E South St (27601-2337)
PHONE..................................919 464-0960
EMP: 22 EST: 2019
SALES (est): 474.4K Privately Held
Web: www.martinmariettacenter.com
SIC: 1389 Oil field services, nec

(G-12709)
DUNCAN DESIGN LTD
2308 Wake Forest Rd Ste E (27608-1756)
PHONE..................................919 834-7713
Todd Duncan, Pr
Susan Duncan, VP
EMP: 4 EST: 1986
SQ FT: 1,600
SALES (est): 295.48K Privately Held
SIC: 3911 5094 5944 Jewelry, precious metal; Jewelry; Jewelry stores

(G-12710)
DUPONT
5816 Raddington St (27613-5719)
PHONE..................................919 414-0089
EMP: 6 EST: 2017
SALES (est): 230.15K Privately Held
Web: www.dupont.com
SIC: 2879 Agricultural chemicals, nec

(G-12711)
DURHAM COCA-COLA BOTTLING CO
Also Called: Coca-Cola
1 Floretta Pl (27613)
PHONE..................................919 510-0574
Tommy Dorsett, Mgr
EMP: 4
SALES (corp-wide): 45.47MM Privately Held
Web: www.durhamcocacola.com
SIC: 2086 Bottled and canned soft drinks
PA: Durham Coca-Cola Bottling Company
3214 Hillsborough Rd
Durham NC 27705
919 383-1531

(G-12712)
E I DU PONT DE NEMOURS
509 Grosvenor Dr (27615-2053)
PHONE..................................919 518-1332
EMP: 5 EST: 2017
SALES (est): 92.37K Privately Held
SIC: 2879 Agricultural chemicals, nec

(G-12713)
EAGLE ROCK CONCRETE LLC (PA)
8310 Bandford Way (27615-2752)
PHONE..................................919 781-3744
Jay Loftin, Pr
Henry Willeym, *
Adam Loftin, *
Lyman Austin, *
Dexter Tart, *
EMP: 25 EST: 2011
SALES (est): 22.33MM
SALES (corp-wide): 22.33MM Privately Held
Web: www.eaglerockconcrete.com
SIC: 3273 Ready-mixed concrete

(G-12714)
EAGLE ROCK CONCRETE LLC
Also Called: Raleigh Plant
8311 Bandford Way Ste 7 (27615-2761)
PHONE..................................919 281-0120
Jay Loftin, Pr
EMP: 44
SALES (corp-wide): 22.33MM Privately Held
Web: www.eaglerockconcrete.com
SIC: 3273 Ready-mixed concrete
PA: Eagle Rock Concrete Llc
8310 Bandford Way
Raleigh NC 27615
919 781-3744

(G-12715)
EARTH DOG ENTERPRISES LLC
2231 E Millbrook Rd Ste 111 (27604)
PHONE..................................919 876-7768
EMP: 6 EST: 2016
SALES (est): 243.8K Privately Held
Web: www.minuteman.com
SIC: 2752 Commercial printing, lithographic

(G-12716)
EAST CRLINA METAL TREATING INC (PA)
Also Called: Virginia Mtal Trting Lynchburg
1117 Capital Blvd (27603-1113)
PHONE..................................919 834-2100
Roscoe L Strickland Iii, Pr
Don Bryant, *
James D Ramm, *
EMP: 33 EST: 1976
SQ FT: 45,000
SALES (est): 6.13MM
SALES (corp-wide): 6.13MM Privately Held
Web: www.ecmtinc.com
SIC: 3398 Metal heat treating

(G-12717)
EASTER SEALS UCP NC & VA INC
Also Called: Copymatic Document Solutions
2533 Atlantic Ave (27604-1567)
PHONE..................................919 856-0250
Greg Card, Mgr
EMP: 55
SALES (corp-wide): 91.81MM Privately Held
Web: www.eastersealsucp.com

Raleigh - Wake County (G-12718)   GEOGRAPHIC SECTION

SIC: 8748 2759 Business consulting, nec; Commercial printing, nec
PA: Easter Seals Ucp North Carolina & Virginia, Inc.
5171 Glenwood Ave Ste 211
Raleigh NC 27612
919 832-3787

(G-12718)
EASTERN ELEVATOR INC
176 Mine Lake Ct (27615-6417)
PHONE...............................877 840-2638
Rob Rauch, *VP*
EMP: 6 **EST:** 2015
SALES (est): 216.81K **Privately Held**
SIC: 3534 Stair elevators, motor powered

(G-12719)
EASYNOTES LLC
Also Called: Easynotes Pro
412 Kaywoody Ct (27615-1532)
PHONE...............................919 870-5228
EMP: 5 **EST:** 2002
SALES (est): 450.31K **Privately Held**
Web: www.easynotespro.com
SIC: 7372 Educational computer software

(G-12720)
EATON CORPORATION
8609 Six Forks Rd (27615-2966)
PHONE...............................919 870-3000
EMP: 227
Web: www.dix-eaton.com
SIC: 3625 Motor controls and accessories
HQ: Eaton Corporation
1000 Eaton Blvd
Cleveland OH 44122
440 523-5000

(G-12721)
EATON CORPORATION
Also Called: Eaton US Raleigh
8380 Capital Blvd (27616-3146)
PHONE...............................864 433-1603
Steve Laughinghouse, *Mgr*
EMP: 74
Web: www.dix-eaton.com
SIC: 3629 7629 Power conversion units, a.c. to d.c.: static-electric; Electrical equipment repair services
HQ: Eaton Corporation
1000 Eaton Blvd
Cleveland OH 44122
440 523-5000

(G-12722)
EATON CORPORATION
3301 Spring Forest Rd (27616-2922)
PHONE...............................919 872-3020
Mark Ascolese, *Pr*
EMP: 110
Web: www.dix-eaton.com
SIC: 3629 7629 3699 Power conversion units, a.c. to d.c.: static-electric; Electrical equipment repair services; Electrical equipment and supplies, nec
HQ: Eaton Corporation
1000 Eaton Blvd
Cleveland OH 44122
440 523-5000

(G-12723)
EATON POWER QUALITY CORP
8609 Six Forks Rd (27615-2966)
P.O. Box 58189 (27658-8189)
PHONE...............................919 872-3020
A M Cutler, *Pr*
Thomas Gutierrez, *Power Systems Division President*
Richard Nicholas, *Controller Power Systems Division*

R W Carson, *VP*
R H Fearon, *VP*
EMP: 102 **EST:** 1962
SQ FT: 93,000
SALES (est): 5.35MM **Privately Held**
SIC: 3629 7629 Power conversion units, a.c. to d.c.: static-electric; Electrical equipment repair services
HQ: Eaton Corporation
1000 Eaton Blvd
Cleveland OH 44122
440 523-5000

(G-12724)
EATON POWER QUALITY GROUP INC (DH)
8609 Six Forks Rd (27615-2966)
PHONE...............................919 872-3020
A M Cutler, *Pr*
David P Johnson, *VP*
Earl R Franklin, *VP*
Herve Tardy, *VP*
Loraine Leavell, *Prin*
▲ **EMP:** 13 **EST:** 2004
SALES (est): 3.1MM **Privately Held**
SIC: 3629 7629 Power conversion units, a.c. to d.c.: static-electric; Electrical equipment repair services
HQ: Eaton Corporation
1000 Eaton Blvd
Cleveland OH 44122
440 523-5000

(G-12725)
EATON SCIENTIFIC INC
2105 Osprey Cir (27615-5573)
PHONE...............................919 855-9886
Susan Eaton, *Pr*
EMP: 6 **EST:** 2015
SALES (est): 227.36K **Privately Held**
SIC: 3625 Relays and industrial controls

(G-12726)
ECO-KIDS LLC
6316 J Richard Dr Ste C (27617-4614)
PHONE...............................207 899-2752
Cammie Weeks, *CEO*
Edward Weeks, *Pr*
EMP: 9 **EST:** 2008
SALES (est): 561.33K **Privately Held**
Web: www.ecokidsusa.com
SIC: 3952 Crayons: chalk, gypsum, charcoal, fusains, pastel, wax, etc.

(G-12727)
EDTECH SYSTEMS LLC
6115 Corporate Ridge Rd (27607-5473)
PHONE...............................919 341-0613
EMP: 5 **EST:** 2007
SALES (est): 460.1K **Privately Held**
SIC: 2676 Sanitary paper products

(G-12728)
EISAI INC
4130 Parklake Ave Ste 500 (27612-4462)
PHONE...............................919 941-6920
EMP: 13
Web: www.eisai.com
SIC: 2834 Pharmaceutical preparations
HQ: Eisai Inc.
200 Metro Blvd
Nutley NJ 07110
201 692-1100

(G-12729)
EIZI GROUP LLC
9008 Riverview Park Dr (27613-5392)
PHONE...............................919 397-3638
Gaurav Sharma, *Mng Pt*
EMP: 5 **EST:** 2016
SALES (est): 206.84K **Privately Held**

SIC: 3589 5063 3491 3312 Water treatment equipment, industrial; Electrical fittings and construction materials; Pressure valves and regulators, industrial; Galvanized pipes, plates, sheets, etc.: iron and steel

(G-12730)
ELECTRO SWITCH CORP
Also Called: Electroswitch
2010 Yonkers Rd (27604-2258)
P.O. Box 41129 (27629-1129)
PHONE...............................919 833-0707
Kyle Martin, *Brnch Mgr*
EMP: 105
SALES (corp-wide): 103.82MM **Privately Held**
Web: www.electroswitch.com
SIC: 3613 Switches, electric power except snap, push button, etc.
HQ: Electro Switch Corp.
775 Pleasant St Ste 1
Weymouth MA 02189
781 335-1195

(G-12731)
ELLEDGE FAMILY INC
Also Called: A Place To Copy
2900 Spring Forest Rd Ste 101 (27616-1895)
PHONE...............................919 876-2300
Keith Ford, *Admn Mgr*
Susan Ford, *Sec*
Christoper Ford, *Dir*
EMP: 10 **EST:** 1990
SQ FT: 8,000
SALES (est): 817.5K **Privately Held**
Web: www.aplacetocopy.com
SIC: 2752 Offset printing

(G-12732)
ELSTER SOLUTIONS LLC (DH)
Also Called: Electric Meter Division
208 S Rogers Ln (27610-2144)
PHONE...............................919 212-4800
Mark Munday, *Pr*
Mark Fronmuller, *
Patrick Corrigan, *
◆ **EMP:** 415 **EST:** 2002
SQ FT: 115,500
SALES (est): 137.33MM
SALES (corp-wide): 36.66B **Publicly Held**
Web: ess.honeywell.com
SIC: 3825 Meters: electric, pocket, portable, panelboard, etc.
HQ: Elster Gmbh
Steinern Str. 19-21
Mainz-Kastel HE 55252
61346050

(G-12733)
ELSTER SOLUTIONS LLC
Also Called: Elster Electricity
201 S Rogers Ln (27610-4336)
PHONE...............................919 212-4819
Ray Schmitt, *Brnch Mgr*
EMP: 300
SALES (corp-wide): 36.66B **Publicly Held**
Web: portal.elstersolutions.com
SIC: 3613 Panel and distribution boards and other related apparatus
HQ: Elster Solutions, Llc
208 S Rogers Ln
Raleigh NC 27610
919 212-4800

(G-12734)
EMBROIDERY NURSE LLC
1812 Falls River Ave (27614-7737)
PHONE...............................919 630-5261
Kelly Payne, *Prin*
EMP: 5 **EST:** 2016

SALES (est): 31.29K **Privately Held**
SIC: 2395 Embroidery and art needlework

(G-12735)
EMC CORPORATION
701 Corporate Center Dr Ste 425 (27607-5245)
PHONE...............................919 851-3241
Randall Gresset, *Mgr*
EMP: 16
Web: www.emc.com
SIC: 3572 Computer storage devices
HQ: Emc Corporation
176 South St
Hopkinton MA 01748
508 435-1000

(G-12736)
EMPOWERED DEFENSE LLC
3602 Mill Run (27612-5218)
PHONE...............................919 624-1304
Melissa Palmer, *Prin*
EMP: 5 **EST:** 2018
SALES (est): 81.4K **Privately Held**
SIC: 3812 Defense systems and equipment

(G-12737)
ENA ADVANCED RUBBER TECH
3032 Barrow Dr (27616-3015)
PHONE...............................919 235-0245
EMP: 9 **EST:** 2016
SALES (est): 168.88K **Privately Held**
Web: www.enarubber.com
SIC: 3069 Fabricated rubber products, nec

(G-12738)
ENEPAY CORPORATION
7226 Summit Waters Ln (27613-7479)
PHONE...............................919 788-1454
Gary Stewart, *Prin*
EMP: 5 **EST:** 2008
SALES (est): 290.11K **Privately Held**
Web: www.enepay.com
SIC: 3999 Manufacturing industries, nec

(G-12739)
ENGAGING SIGNS & GRAPHICS
11705 Dellcain Ct (27617-4253)
PHONE...............................919 371-0885
Melissa Kitts, *Prin*
EMP: 4 **EST:** 2017
SALES (est): 78.66K **Privately Held**
Web: www.signscientist.com
SIC: 3993 Signs and advertising specialties

(G-12740)
ENTERPRINT CORP
606 Wade Ave Ste 100 (27605-1391)
PHONE...............................919 821-7897
EMP: 5 **EST:** 2019
SALES (est): 63.37K **Privately Held**
SIC: 2752 Offset printing

(G-12741)
ENVIRO-COMPANIES LLC
Also Called: Adams 919 Plumbing
3305 Durham Dr Ste 119 (27603-3579)
PHONE...............................919 758-6246
John Carbone, *Managing Member*
EMP: 7 **EST:** 2008
SALES (est): 208.7K **Privately Held**
SIC: 1711 3432 Plumbing, heating, air-conditioning; Plumbing fixture fittings and trim

(G-12742)
ENVIRONMENTAL SPECIALTIES LLC (DH)
4412 Tryon Rd (27606-4246)
PHONE...............................919 829-9300

Tim Whitener, *CEO*
Steve Draper, *
Chris Berrier, *
John Walters, *
EMP: 100 **EST:** 1973
SQ FT: 20,000
SALES (est): 45.25MM
SALES (corp-wide): 12.58B **Publicly Held**
Web: www.eschambers.com
SIC: 3826 7623 3564 Environmental testing equipment; Refrigeration service and repair; Blowers and fans
HQ: Bahnson, Inc.
    4731 Commercial Park Ct
    Clemmons NC 27012

(G-12743)
ENVISION INC
625 Hutton St Ste 102 (27606-6321)
PHONE...............................919 832-8962
James Friedrich, *Pr*
EMP: 6
Web: www.envisionllc.com
SIC: 3669 Intercommunication systems, electric
PA: Envision Inc
    1025 Old Monrovia Rd Nw
    Huntsville AL 35806

(G-12744)
EQUAGEN ENGINEERS PLLC
Also Called: Equagen Engineers
8045 Arco Corporate Dr Ste 220 (27617)
PHONE...............................919 444-5442
Moti Kc, *CEO*
Moti Kc, *Prin*
EMP: 44 **EST:** 2018
SALES (est): 2.61MM **Privately Held**
Web: www.equagen.com
SIC: 8711 3999 3629 8741 Engineering services; Barber and beauty shop equipment; Electronic generation equipment; Construction management

(G-12745)
ESCAZU ARTISAN CHOCOLATE LLC
936 N Blount St (27604-1128)
PHONE...............................919 832-3433
EMP: 10 **EST:** 2007
SQ FT: 1,650
SALES (est): 912.14K **Privately Held**
Web: www.escazuchocolates.com
SIC: 5149 2066 Chocolate; Chocolate

(G-12746)
ESCO GROUP LLC
3221 Durham Dr Ste 118 (27603-3507)
PHONE...............................919 900-8226
Dean Heaney, *Mgr*
EMP: 8
SALES (corp-wide): 2.98B **Privately Held**
Web: www.global.weir
SIC: 3535 Conveyors and conveying equipment
HQ: Esco Group Llc
    2141 Nw 25th Ave
    Portland OR 97210
    503 228-2141

(G-12747)
ESEQUENCE INC
412 W Jones St (27603-1341)
PHONE...............................919 831-1995
Eric Hawkins, *Pr*
Raymond Orospesa, *Prin*
Rosemarie Bae, *Prin*
EMP: 6 **EST:** 1999
SALES (est): 146.08K **Privately Held**
Web: www.esequence.com

SIC: 7372 7373 7389 8721 Business oriented computer software; Systems integration services; Printing broker; Accounting services, except auditing

(G-12748)
ESYMPHONY SOFTWARE SOLUTIONS I
9220 Clubvalley Way (27617-7577)
PHONE...............................919 293-0233
Tony Wang, *Prin*
EMP: 5 **EST:** 2005
SALES (est): 114.08K **Privately Held**
SIC: 7372 Prepackaged software

(G-12749)
ETHEREON SOFTWARE CORP
8013 Tylerton Dr (27613-1557)
PHONE...............................919 510-5112
Grant King, *Supervisor*
EMP: 5 **EST:** 2007
SALES (est): 84.68K **Privately Held**
SIC: 7372 Prepackaged software

(G-12750)
EVANS AND MCCLAIN LLC
555 Fayetteville St # 201 (27601-3030)
PHONE...............................919 374-5578
EMP: 4 **EST:** 2021
SALES (est): 200K **Privately Held**
SIC: 2326 Men's and boy's work clothing

(G-12751)
EVERGREEN PACKAGING LLC
Also Called: Raleigh Facility
2215 S Wilmington St (27603-2541)
PHONE...............................919 828-9134
Tom David, *Brnch Mgr*
EMP: 100
Web: www.pactivevergreen.com
SIC: 2621 Paper mills
HQ: Evergreen Packaging Llc
    5350 Poplar Ave Ste 400
    Memphis TN 38119

(G-12752)
EVOLUTION TECHNOLOGIES INC
1121 Situs Ct Ste 130 (27606-4164)
PHONE...............................919 544-3777
Bradley Deifer, *Pr*
Donald Deifer, *VP*
▼ **EMP:** 6 **EST:** 2000
SQ FT: 3,100
SALES (est): 359.86K **Privately Held**
SIC: 3651 Household audio and video equipment

(G-12753)
EXECUTIVE GROOMING LLC
5910 Duraleigh Rd Ste 133 (27612-2581)
PHONE...............................919 706-5382
EMP: 5 **EST:** 2017
SALES (est): 76.05K **Privately Held**
Web: executive-grooming-services.business.site
SIC: 7241 7372 Hair stylist, men; Application computer software

(G-12754)
EXPOSURE SOFTWARE LLC
1111 Haynes St Ste 107 (27604-1454)
PHONE...............................919 832-4124
EMP: 16 **EST:** 1993
SALES (est): 1.59MM **Privately Held**
Web: www.exposure.software
SIC: 7372 Application computer software

(G-12755)
EXPRESS YOURSELF
10351 Crestgate Ter Apt 206 (27617-1809)

PHONE...............................919 526-0611
EMP: 4 **EST:** 2012
SALES (est): 81.16K **Privately Held**
Web: www.expressyourselfpaint.com
SIC: 3578 Automatic teller machines (ATM)

(G-12756)
EXPROLINK CORP
5025 Departure Dr Ste A (27616-1972)
PHONE...............................919 215-4675
Mike Woinicki, *Sls Mgr*
EMP: 6
SALES (est): 79.3K **Privately Held**
SIC: 3711 Brooms, powered (motor vehicles), assembly of

(G-12757)
EXQUISITE AIR AND WATER
1011 Beach Pointe Ave (27604-8747)
PHONE...............................919 524-4625
Stuart French, *Prin*
EMP: 4 **EST:** 2010
SALES (est): 121.62K **Privately Held**
Web: www.exquisiteair-water.com
SIC: 3564 5074 Air purification equipment; Water purification equipment

(G-12758)
EXTRON ELECTRONICS
2500 N Raleigh Blvd (27604-2478)
PHONE...............................919 850-1000
Robert Barra, *Prin*
EMP: 6 **EST:** 2019
SALES (est): 3.06MM **Privately Held**
SIC: 5065 3578 Sound equipment, electronic; Automatic teller machines (ATM)

(G-12759)
FAIRWAY OUTDOOR ADVG LLC
FAIRWAY OUTDOOR ADVERTISING LLC
508 Capital Blvd (27603-1318)
PHONE...............................919 755-1900
Paul Hitman, *Mgr*
EMP: 11
SQ FT: 2,200
SALES (corp-wide): 24.76MM **Privately Held**
SIC: 7312 3993 Billboard advertising; Signs and advertising specialties
PA: Fairway Outdoor Advertising Llc
    420 The Pkwy Bldg H
    Greer SC 29650

(G-12760)
FAIRWAY PRINTING INC
821 Purser Dr Ste A (27603-4185)
P.O. Box 37429 (27627-7429)
PHONE...............................919 779-4797
Don Beasley, *Pr*
James Nichols, *Sec*
Neal Champion, *VP*
Jeanette Burlock, *VP*
EMP: 9 **EST:** 1988
SQ FT: 6,500
SALES (est): 693.6K **Privately Held**
Web: www.fairwayprintingofnc.com
SIC: 2752 Offset printing

(G-12761)
FALLS OF NEUSE MANAGEMENT LLC
Also Called: National Coatings & Supplies
4900 Falls Of Neuse Rd Ste 150 (27609-5490)
PHONE...............................919 573-2900
Temple O Sloan Junior, *Managing Member*
EMP: 3599 **EST:** 2012
SALES (est): 126.54MM **Privately Held**
Web: www.fnmllc.com

SIC: 3559 Automotive maintenance equipment

(G-12762)
FAMILY INDUSTRIES INC
Also Called: Woodplay
631 Macon Pl (27609-5649)
P.O. Box 97995 (27624-7995)
PHONE...............................919 875-4499
James Sally, *Pr*
John Sally Junior, *Stockholder*
James W Sally, *
Thomas Marenyi, *Stockholder*
EMP: 14 **EST:** 1976
SQ FT: 70,000
SALES (est): 565.97K **Privately Held**
SIC: 3949 7336 Playground equipment; Commercial art and graphic design

(G-12763)
FEEDTRAIL INCORPORATED
811 Handsworth Ln Apt 108 (27607-5260)
PHONE...............................757 618-7760
Paul Jaglowski, *Pr*
EMP: 14 **EST:** 2017
SALES (est): 1.22MM **Privately Held**
Web: www.feedtrail.com
SIC: 7372 Operating systems computer software

(G-12764)
FIELDX INC
7504 Deer Track Dr (27613-3508)
PHONE...............................919 926-7001
EMP: 9 **EST:** 2015
SALES (est): 162.21K **Privately Held**
Web: www.fieldx.com
SIC: 7372 Prepackaged software

(G-12765)
FIESTIC INC
555 Fayetteville St Ste 201 (27601-3030)
PHONE...............................888 935-3999
Jacob Ongwiseth, *CEO*
Nipith Ongwiseth, *CEO*
Jacob Ongwiseth, *Pr*
EMP: 15 **EST:** 2014
SQ FT: 1,200
SALES (est): 1.01MM **Privately Held**
Web: www.fiestic.com
SIC: 7372 7336 7371 Business oriented computer software; Commercial art and graphic design; Software programming applications

(G-12766)
FIL-CHEM INC
3808 Evander Way (27613-5370)
P.O. Box 90833 (27675-0833)
PHONE...............................919 878-1270
Jerome Bogus, *Pr*
Felice Bogus, *VP*
EMP: 6 **EST:** 1966
SQ FT: 7,500
SALES (est): 571.3K **Privately Held**
Web: www.fil-chem.com
SIC: 2819 5169 3559 3812 Industrial inorganic chemicals, nec; Chemical additives; Metal finishing equipment for plating, etc.; Search and navigation equipment

(G-12767)
FINTRONX LLC
5995 Chapel Hill Rd Ste 119 (27607-0118)
PHONE...............................919 324-3960
Brenda Yatef, *CFO*
Pat Forbis, *Ch Bd*
▲ **EMP:** 10 **EST:** 2002
SQ FT: 7,000
SALES (est): 9MM **Privately Held**

Raleigh - Wake County (G-12768)

Web: www.fxlsolutions.com
SIC: **3641** 5719 5063 Electric light bulbs, complete; Lighting, lamps, and accessories; Light bulbs and related supplies

(G-12768)
FIREHOUSE PUBLICATIONS
5924 Lunenburg Dr (27603-8043)
PHONE..................609 298-3742
EMP: 4 **EST:** 2019
SALES (est): 70.7K **Privately Held**
Web: www.firehousepublications.com
SIC: **2741** Miscellaneous publishing

(G-12769)
FISHSTICKS
7145 North Ridge Dr (27615-7038)
PHONE..................919 900-8998
Scott Parsons, *Prin*
EMP: 6 **EST:** 2010
SALES (est): 196.94K **Privately Held**
SIC: **2092** Fish sticks

(G-12770)
FIT1MEDIA LLC
8601 Six Forks Rd Ste 400 (27615-2965)
PHONE..................919 925-2200
EMP: 4 **EST:** 2018
SALES (est): 511.26K **Privately Held**
Web: www.fit1media.com
SIC: **2741** 7311 Internet publishing and broadcasting; Advertising agencies

(G-12771)
FIVE POINTS BAKING COMPANY LLC
2009 Carroll Dr (27608-1630)
PHONE..................919 349-2033
Todd A Jones, *Prin*
EMP: 5 **EST:** 2012
SALES (est): 109.53K **Privately Held**
Web: www.fivepointsbakingco.com
SIC: **2051** Bread, cake, and related products

(G-12772)
FLAMEOFF COATINGS INC (PA)
3915 Beryl Rd Ste 130 (27607-5609)
PHONE..................888 816-7468
Jim Turner, *Pr*
EMP: 8 **EST:** 2014
SALES (est): 1.39MM
SALES (corp-wide): 1.39MM **Privately Held**
Web: www.flameoffcoatings.com
SIC: **3569** 7371 Firefighting and related equipment; Computer software development and applications

(G-12773)
FLORALEADS GROUP
5308 Dutchman Dr (27606-9792)
P.O. Box 5546 (27512-5546)
PHONE..................919 303-1420
Alex Korneyed, *Pt*
EMP: 4 **EST:** 1995
SALES (est): 243.69K **Privately Held**
Web: www.floraleads.com
SIC: **2844** Lotions, shaving

(G-12774)
FLORES WELDING INC
961 Palace Garden Way (27603-2892)
PHONE..................919 838-1060
EMP: 10 **EST:** 1996
SQ FT: 4,000
SALES (est): 598.6K **Privately Held**
Web: www.floresweldinginc.com
SIC: **7692** Welding repair

(G-12775)
FLORIDA PROGRESS CORPORATION (DH)
Also Called: Progress Energy Florida
410 S Wilmington St (27601-1849)
PHONE..................704 382-3853
Richard D Keller, *CEO*
William D Johnson, *
Peter M Scott Iii, *Ex VP*
Robert B Mcgehee, *Ex VP*
EMP: 241 **EST:** 1982
SQ FT: 35,000
SALES (est): 7.04B
SALES (corp-wide): 29.06B **Publicly Held**
Web: www.duke-energy.com
SIC: **1221** 4911 4011 4449 Bituminous coal and lignite-surface mining; Generation, electric power; Railroads, line-haul operating; River transportation, except on the St. Lawrence Seaway
HQ: Progress Energy, Inc.
    410 S Wilmington St
    Raleigh NC 27601
    704 382-3853

(G-12776)
FLOWSERVE US INC
1900 S Saunders St (27603-2318)
P.O. Box 1961 (27602-1961)
PHONE..................972 443-6500
EMP: 11
SALES (corp-wide): 4.32B **Publicly Held**
Web: www.flowserve.com
SIC: **3561** Pump jacks and other pumping equipment
HQ: Flowserve Us Inc.
    5215 N Ocnnor Blvd Ste 70 Connor
    Irving TX 75039
    972 443-6500

(G-12777)
FOCUSALES INC
6113 Chowning Ct (27612-6704)
PHONE..................919 614-3076
Terry J Carlton, *Pr*
EMP: 10 **EST:** 2004
SALES (est): 432.36K **Privately Held**
Web: www.focusalesinc.com
SIC: **2782** Account books

(G-12778)
FOOTHOLD PUBLICATIONS INC
2656 Garden Knoll Ln (27614-8970)
PHONE..................770 891-3423
Phillip A Lombardi, *CEO*
EMP: 5 **EST:** 2015
SALES (est): 48.89K **Privately Held**
SIC: **2741** Miscellaneous publishing

(G-12779)
FORTOVIA THERAPEUTICS INC (PA)
8540 Colonnade Center Dr Ste 101 (27615-3052)
PHONE..................919 872-5578
Peter Melnyk, *CEO*
Craig Cook, *CMO*
Tim Sparey, *Chief Business Officer*
Dan Palmer, *CSO*
Ernest De Paolantonio, *CFO*
EMP: 8 **EST:** 1993
SQ FT: 7,520
SALES (est): 2.45MM **Privately Held**
Web: www.fortovia.com
SIC: **2834** Pharmaceutical preparations

(G-12780)
FRANKLIN BAKING COMPANY LLC
1404 S Bloodworth St (27610-3902)
PHONE..................919 832-7942
Robert Reegs, *Mgr*
EMP: 6
SQ FT: 12,768
SALES (corp-wide): 5.09B **Publicly Held**
Web: franklin-co4goldsboro.edan.io
SIC: **2051** Bread, cake, and related products
HQ: Franklin Baking Company, Llc
    500 W Grantham St
    Goldsboro NC 27530
    919 735-0344

(G-12781)
FREEMAN CUSTOM WELDING INC
2108 Langdon Rd (27604-3616)
PHONE..................919 210-6267
Sie Freeman, *Pt*
EMP: 4 **EST:** 2006
SALES (est): 210.8K **Privately Held**
SIC: **7692** Welding repair

(G-12782)
FRESH LLC
4700 Archean Way Apt 107 (27616-5828)
P.O. Box 97324 (27624-7324)
PHONE..................919 592-7255
EMP: 7
SALES (est): 79.3K **Privately Held**
SIC: **2389** Apparel and accessories, nec

(G-12783)
FROEHLING & ROBERTSON INC
310 Hubert St (27603-2302)
PHONE..................804 264-2701
Daniel Schaefer, *Mgr*
EMP: 41
SQ FT: 13,570
SALES (corp-wide): 85.98MM **Privately Held**
Web: www.fandr.com
SIC: **7389** 8711 3829 8734 Inspection and testing services; Engineering services; Measuring and controlling devices, nec; Testing laboratories
PA: Froehling & Robertson Inc
    3015 Dumbarton Rd
    Richmond VA 23228
    804 264-2701

(G-12784)
FSC HOLDINGS INC
Also Called: Asphalt Plant 1
6001 Westgate Rd (27617-5222)
PHONE..................919 782-1247
Donald Schell, *Mgr*
EMP: 5
SALES (corp-wide): 42.22MM **Privately Held**
Web: www.fredsmithcompany.net
SIC: **2951** Asphalt paving mixtures and blocks
PA: Fsc Holdings, Inc.
    6105 Chapel Hill Rd
    Raleigh NC 27607
    919 783-5700

(G-12785)
FSC II LLC (HQ)
Also Called: Fred Smith Company
701 Corporate Center Dr Ste 101 (27607-5084)
PHONE..................919 783-5700
Fred Smith Iii, *Pr*
Jule Smith, *Pr*
EMP: 15 **EST:** 1998
SALES (est): 56.92MM
SALES (corp-wide): 1.56B **Publicly Held**
Web: www.fredsmithcompany.net
SIC: **5032** 1499 Asphalt mixture; Asphalt (native) mining
PA: Construction Partners, Inc.
    290 Healthwest Dr Ste 2
    Dothan AL 36303
    334 673-9763

(G-12786)
FUN PUBLICATIONS INC
12513 Birchfalls Dr (27614-9675)
PHONE..................919 847-5263
EMP: 5 **EST:** 1992
SALES (est): 298.49K **Privately Held**
SIC: **2711** Newspapers: publishing only, not printed on site

(G-12787)
FUNNY GIRL PRESS
6511 Creedmoor Rd Ste 204 (27613-1687)
PHONE..................919 247-8861
EMP: 4 **EST:** 2019
SALES (est): 79.17K **Privately Held**
SIC: **2741** Miscellaneous publishing

(G-12788)
G B TECHNOLOGIES
3222 Wellington Ct Ste 104 (27615-4124)
PHONE..................919 954-0721
Gene Braswell, *Owner*
EMP: 5 **EST:** 2010
SALES (est): 73.66K **Privately Held**
SIC: **3825** Electrical power measuring equipment

(G-12789)
G H GROUP LLC
Also Called: Wag Pet Boutique
2001 Yorkgate Dr (27612-3451)
PHONE..................919 264-0939
Dan Hendrick, *Managing Member*
Pamela Guthrie, *Managing Member*
EMP: 5 **EST:** 2004
SALES (est): 186.04K **Privately Held**
SIC: **3999** Pet supplies

(G-12790)
GATEWAY CAMPUS
1306 Hillsborough St (27605-1827)
PHONE..................919 833-0096
Wendy Banister, *Prin*
EMP: 8 **EST:** 2007
SALES (est): 467.83K **Privately Held**
Web: www.gatewaywomens.care
SIC: **2835** Pregnancy test kits

(G-12791)
GEAMI LTD
3401 Gresham Lake Rd Ste 110 (27615-4243)
P.O. Box 8004 (44077-8004)
PHONE..................919 654-7700
EMP: 25
Web: www.ranpak.com
SIC: **2621** 5199 Packaging paper; Packaging materials

(G-12792)
GELDER & ASSOCIATES INC
3901 Gelder Dr (27603-5699)
PHONE..................919 772-6895
EMP: 109 **EST:** 1953
SALES (est): 15.81MM
SALES (corp-wide): 1.56B **Publicly Held**
Web: www.gelderandassociates.com
SIC: **2951** 1611 Asphalt paving mixtures and blocks; Surfacing and paving
PA: Construction Partners, Inc.
    290 Healthwest Dr Ste 2
    Dothan AL 36303
    334 673-9763

(G-12793)
GENERAL SHALE BRICK INC
8820 Westgate Park Dr (27617-4775)
PHONE..................919 828-0541
Alex Allen, *Mgr*
EMP: 6

GEOGRAPHIC SECTION

Raleigh - Wake County (G-12818)

SALES (corp-wide): 5.17B **Privately Held**
Web: www.generalshale.com
SIC: 5032 3251 Brick, except refractory; Brick and structural clay tile
HQ: General Shale Brick, Inc.
3015 Bristol Hwy
Johnson City TN 37601
423 282-4661

(G-12794)
GENERATOR SUPERCENTER RALEIGH
8601 Glenwood Ave (27617-7000)
PHONE.................................919 925-3434
EMP: 7 **EST:** 2019
SALES (est): 998.36K **Privately Held**
Web: www.generatorshopraleigh.com
SIC: 3621 Motors and generators

(G-12795)
GEORGE CLINICAL INC
120 Penmarc Dr (27603-2574)
PHONE.................................919 789-2022
EMP: 5 **EST:** 2017
SALES (est): 193.75K **Privately Held**
Web: www.georgeclinical.com
SIC: 2834 Pharmaceutical preparations

(G-12796)
GEORGIA PRATT BOX INC
5620 Departure Dr (27616-1841)
PHONE.................................919 872-3007
EMP: 103
Web: www.prattindustries.com
SIC: 2653 Boxes, corrugated: made from purchased materials
HQ: Georgia Pratt Box Inc
1800 Sarasot Bus Pkwy Ne
Conyers GA 30013
864 963-0992

(G-12797)
GEOSONICS INC
5874 Faringdon Pl Ste 100 (27609-3932)
PHONE.................................919 790-9500
William Powell, *Genl Mgr*
EMP: 5
SALES (corp-wide): 9.71MM **Privately Held**
Web: www.geosonicsvibratech.com
SIC: 8999 3829 Geological consultant; Seismographs
PA: Geosonics, Inc.
359 Northgate Dr Ste 200
Warrendale PA 15086
724 934-2900

(G-12798)
GERDAU AMERISTEEL US INC
Ameristeel Rligh Fab Rnfrcing
2126 Garner Rd (27610-4608)
PHONE.................................919 833-9737
Ron Long, *Brnch Mgr*
EMP: 23
SQ FT: 36,484
Web: gerdau.com
SIC: 3449 3441 Miscellaneous metalwork; Fabricated structural metal
HQ: Gerdau Ameristeel Us Inc.
4221 W Boy Scout Blvd # 600
Tampa FL 33607
813 286-8383

(G-12799)
GETBRIDGE LLC
Also Called: Bridge
434 Fayetteville St Fl 9 (27601-1891)
PHONE.................................919 645-2800
Peter Brussard, *Pr*
Jocelyn Karney, *CFO*
Eric Fairbanks, *CMO*
EMP: 155 **EST:** 2020
SALES (est): 25MM
SALES (corp-wide): 718.65MM **Privately Held**
Web: www.getbridge.com
SIC: 7372 Educational computer software
HQ: Learning Technologies Group Inc.
300 5th Ave
Waltham MA 02451
781 530-2000

(G-12800)
GIK INC
Also Called: Sir Speedy
1801 Saint Albans Dr Ste B (27609-6286)
PHONE.................................919 872-9498
Lloyd Newton, *Pr*
Colleen Newton, *Sec*
Frank Shepphard Stkldr, *Prin*
EMP: 12 **EST:** 1981
SQ FT: 6,000
SALES (est): 2.34MM **Privately Held**
Web: www.sirspeedy.com
SIC: 2752 7334 2791 2789 Commercial printing, lithographic; Photocopying and duplicating services; Typesetting; Bookbinding and related work

(G-12801)
GILEAD SCIENCES INC
305 Church At North Hills St (27609-2666)
PHONE.................................650 574-3000
EMP: 4
SALES (corp-wide): 27.12B **Publicly Held**
Web: www.gilead.com
SIC: 2834 Pharmaceutical preparations
PA: Gilead Sciences, Inc.
333 Lakeside Dr
Foster City CA 94404
650 574-3000

(G-12802)
GK SOFTWARE USA INC
Also Called: GK Software USA
9121 Anson Way Ste 150 (27615-5858)
PHONE.................................984 255-7995
Michael Jaszczyk, *Pr*
EMP: 45 **EST:** 2013
SALES (est): 10.06MM
SALES (corp-wide): 157.92MM **Privately Held**
Web: www.gk-software.com
SIC: 7372 Business oriented computer software
PA: Gk Software Se
Waldstr. 7
Schoneck/Vogtl. SN 08261
37464840

(G-12803)
GLASER DESIGNS INC
2825 Seclusion Ct Apt A (27612-6632)
PHONE.................................415 552-3188
Myron Glaser, *Pr*
Kari Glaser, *VP*
EMP: 10 **EST:** 1975
SALES (est): 876.32K **Privately Held**
Web: www.shapingsoundco.com
SIC: 3171 3172 3161 Handbags, women's; Personal leather goods, nec; Clothing and apparel carrying cases

(G-12804)
GLOBAL FILTER SOURCE LLC
6212 Westgate Rd Ste A (27617-4847)
P.O. Box 99215 (27624-9215)
PHONE.................................919 571-4945
Paul Bryant, *Owner*
EMP: 4 **EST:** 2005
SALES (est): 346.05K **Privately Held**
Web: www.globalfiltersource.com
SIC: 3569 Filters

(G-12805)
GLOBAL SOFTWARE LLC
Also Called: GLOBAL SOFTWARE, LLC
3200 Atlantic Ave Ste 200 (27604-1668)
PHONE.................................919 872-7800
Zack Michael Schuch, *Owner*
EMP: 8
SALES (corp-wide): 113.32MM **Privately Held**
Web: www.insightsoftware.com
SIC: 7372 Prepackaged software
PA: Insightsoftware, Llc
8529 Six Forks Rd
Raleigh NC 27615
919 872-7800

(G-12806)
GLOBALECTRONICS INC
8608 Harps Mill Rd (27615-3884)
PHONE.................................919 599-6680
EMP: 7 **EST:** 2009
SALES (est): 73.61K **Privately Held**
SIC: 3679 Electronic components, nec

(G-12807)
GLOVER CORPORATION INC
Also Called: Glover Printing Company
2401 Atlantic Ave (27604-1409)
PHONE.................................919 821-5535
Louis M Goldberg, *Pr*
Brian Goldberg, *Sec*
EMP: 38 **EST:** 1963
SALES (est): 10.98MM **Privately Held**
Web: www.discoverglover.com
SIC: 5045 5084 2752 Printers, computer; Packaging machinery and equipment; Offset and photolithographic printing

(G-12808)
GLYCYX PHARMACEUTICALS LTD
8510 Colonnade Center Dr (27615-5860)
PHONE.................................919 862-1097
EMP: 5 **EST:** 2015
SALES (est): 187.81K **Privately Held**
Web: www.salix.com
SIC: 2834 Pharmaceutical preparations

(G-12809)
GOGOPANELS
1600 Carson St (27608-2606)
PHONE.................................702 800-1941
Christian Etheridge, *Prin*
EMP: 4 **EST:** 2015
SALES (est): 179.79K **Privately Held**
SIC: 3993 Signs and advertising specialties

(G-12810)
GOUNMANNED LLC
533 Pylon Dr (27606-1414)
PHONE.................................919 835-2140
Maria Kolar, *Prin*
EMP: 7 **EST:** 2017
SALES (est): 179.48K **Privately Held**
Web: www.gounmanned.com
SIC: 3728 Aircraft parts and equipment, nec

(G-12811)
GP TECHNOLOGY LLC
Also Called: Sitech Precision
4807 Beryl Rd (27606-1406)
PHONE.................................919 876-3666
EMP: 7 **EST:** 2020
SALES (est): 209.19K **Privately Held**
SIC: 1389 Construction, repair, and dismantling services

(G-12812)
GRACEFULLY GIFTED HANDS LLC
8480 Honeycutt Rd Ste 200 (27615-2261)
PHONE.................................845 248-8743
Crystal Hines, *Managing Member*
EMP: 5 **EST:** 2019
SALES (est): 205.73K **Privately Held**
SIC: 3944 Craft and hobby kits and sets

(G-12813)
GRANVILLE MILLER LLC
5305 Burning Oak Ct (27606-9595)
PHONE.................................919 865-0602
Granville Miller, *CEO*
EMP: 4 **EST:** 2018
SALES (est): 105.1K **Privately Held**
Web: www.extremedevelopmenttools.com
SIC: 7372 Prepackaged software

(G-12814)
GREENE IMAGING & DESIGN INC
Also Called: Image 360, Raleigh-Rtp
6320 Angus Dr Ste E (27617-4756)
PHONE.................................919 787-3737
Robert N Greene, *Pr*
EMP: 5 **EST:** 2007
SQ FT: 1,800
SALES (est): 393.83K **Privately Held**
SIC: 3993 Signs and advertising specialties

(G-12815)
GREENOLOGY PRODUCTS LLC
7020 Cynrow Blvd (27615-5739)
PHONE.................................877 473-3650
Adam Mccarthy, *CEO*
Adam Mccarthy, *Pr*
Shanna Redkey, *Marketing**
Frank Lemanski, *
▼ **EMP:** 25 **EST:** 2008
SQ FT: 3,000
SALES (est): 25.04MM **Privately Held**
Web: www.greenshieldorganic.com
SIC: 5169 2841 Detergents; Soap and other detergents

(G-12816)
GREENWICH BAY TRADING CO INC
5809 Triangle Dr Ste C (27617-4809)
P.O. Box 90787 (27675-0787)
PHONE.................................919 781-5008
Richard Huntwork, *Mgr*
EMP: 23
SALES (corp-wide): 4.2MM **Privately Held**
Web: www.gbsoaps.com
SIC: 2844 2841 Perfumes, cosmetics and other toilet preparations; Soap and other detergents
PA: Greenwich Bay Trading Co Inc
216 Spencer Ave
East Greenwich RI 02818
401 885-0144

(G-12817)
GREER AND ASSOCIATES INC
Also Called: Sign-A-Rama
972 Trinity Rd (27607-4940)
PHONE.................................919 383-3500
Robert D Greer, *CEO*
Philip Greer, *Pr*
EMP: 6 **EST:** 1991
SALES (est): 837.74K **Privately Held**
Web: www.thegreergroup.com
SIC: 3993 Signs and advertising specialties

(G-12818)
GREGORY POOLE EQUIPMENT CO
2620 Discovery Dr (27616-1817)
PHONE.................................919 872-2691
EMP: 14

Raleigh - Wake County (G-12819)

SALES (corp-wide): 585.63MM **Privately Held**
Web: www.gregorypoolelift.com
SIC: 7359 5084 5082 3569 Garage facility and tool rental; Industrial machinery and equipment; Construction and mining machinery; Assembly machines, non-metalworking
HQ: Gregory Poole Equipment Company
4807 Beryl Rd
Raleigh NC 27606
919 828-0641

(G-12819)
GREYBERRY PRINTING
8301 Hempshire Pl Apt 106 (27613-5442)
PHONE.................................919 649-3187
EMP: 4 EST: 2011
SALES (est): 77.91K **Privately Held**
SIC: 2752 Offset printing

(G-12820)
GRIFFIN PRINTING INC
500 Uwharrie Ct Ste A (27606-1469)
P.O. Box 10812 (27605-0812)
PHONE.................................919 832-6931
Jack Griffin, *Pr*
▲ EMP: 4 EST: 1976
SALES (est): 407.61K **Privately Held**
Web: www.griffinprint.com
SIC: 2752 Offset printing

(G-12821)
GRIFOLS THERAPEUTICS LLC
1017 Main Campus Dr Ste 2580 (27606-5204)
PHONE.................................919 316-6612
Greg Rich, *Brnch Mgr*
EMP: 4120
SIC: 2836 Blood derivatives
HQ: Grifols Therapeutics Llc
79 Tw Alexander Dr
Durham NC 27709

(G-12822)
GRIP POD SYSTEMS INTL LLC
6321 Swallow Cove Ln (27614-7161)
PHONE.................................239 233-3694
Joseph Gaddini, *Managing Member*
EMP: 5 EST: 2012
SALES (est): 357.03K **Privately Held**
Web: www.grippod.com
SIC: 3484 Guns (firearms) or gun parts, 30 mm. and below

(G-12823)
GRT ELECTRONICS LLC
Also Called: G R T Electronics
3805 Beryl Rd (27607-5244)
PHONE.................................919 821-1996
▲ EMP: 19 EST: 2001
SQ FT: 6,000
SALES (est): 3.94MM **Privately Held**
Web: www.grtelectronics.com
SIC: 3672 Circuit boards, television and radio printed

(G-12824)
GT RHYNO CONSTRUCTION LLC
7061 Fox Meadow Ln Apt 911 (27616-7649)
PHONE.................................919 737-3620
EMP: 6
SALES (est): 145.03K **Privately Held**
SIC: 1389 7389 Construction, repair, and dismantling services; Business Activities at Non-Commercial Site

(G-12825)
GW INDUSTRIES LLC
Also Called: Cabinet Cures of The Carolinas
2013 New Hope Church Rd (27604-2272)
PHONE.................................919 608-1911
Gregory R Wood, *Prin*
EMP: 5 EST: 2019
SALES (est): 163.93K **Privately Held**
SIC: 3999 Manufacturing industries, nec

(G-12826)
HAIRCUTTERS OF RALEIGH INC
4024 Barrett Dr Ste 102 (27609-6625)
PHONE.................................919 781-3465
Renee Tilley, *Owner*
EMP: 4 EST: 1985
SQ FT: 1,000
SALES (est): 175.74K **Privately Held**
SIC: 7231 2844 Hairdressers; Manicure preparations

(G-12827)
HALEY PROMOTIONS INC
200 Park At North Hills St Apt 1606 (27609-2656)
PHONE.................................336 402-7450
EMP: 5 EST: 2019
SALES (est): 203.16K **Privately Held**
Web: haleypromotions.espwebsite.com
SIC: 2752 Offset printing

(G-12828)
HAMILTON MACHINE WORKS LLC
908 Withers Rd (27603-6095)
P.O. Box 37516 (27627-7516)
PHONE.................................919 779-6892
Robert Hamilton Junior, *Pt*
Linwood Hamilton, *Pt*
EMP: 8 EST: 1967
SQ FT: 4,400
SALES (est): 906.83K **Privately Held**
Web: www.hamiltonmachineworks.com
SIC: 3599 Machine shop, jobbing and repair

(G-12829)
HANTA RODS AND LURES LLC
6612 Viceroy Dr (27613-7366)
PHONE.................................919 480-5138
Anthony Dillon, *Admn*
EMP: 4 EST: 2016
SALES (est): 95.61K **Privately Held**
Web: www.hantarodsandlures.com
SIC: 3949 Lures, fishing: artificial

(G-12830)
HARGROVE COUNTERTOPS & ACC INC
Also Called: Atlantic Counter Top & ACC
5250 Old Wake Forest Rd Ste 100 (27609-5275)
PHONE.................................919 981-0163
Michael Orlikoff, *Pr*
EMP: 20 EST: 1994
SQ FT: 12,000
SALES (est): 2.13MM **Privately Held**
Web: www.atlanticcountertops.com
SIC: 2541 5211 5084 Counter and sink tops; Counter tops; Countersinks

(G-12831)
HARRIS TEETER LLC
Also Called: Harris Teeter 038
5563 Western Blvd Ste 38 (27606-1595)
PHONE.................................919 859-0110
EMP: 51
SALES (corp-wide): 148.26B **Publicly Held**
Web: www.harristeeter.com
SIC: 5411 2051 Supermarkets, chain; Bread, cake, and related products
HQ: Harris Teeter, Llc
701 Crestdale Rd
Matthews NC 28105
704 844-3100

(G-12832)
HEALTHLINK EUROPE
611 Creekside Dr (27609-7807)
PHONE.................................919 368-2187
EMP: 10 EST: 2015
SALES (est): 218.05K **Privately Held**
Web: www.healthlinkeurope.com
SIC: 3841 Surgical and medical instruments

(G-12833)
HEALTHLINK EUROPE
3737 Glenwood Ave Ste 100 (27612-5515)
PHONE.................................919 783-4142
Richard Hughes, *Pr*
Rick Hughes, *Pr*
EMP: 18 EST: 2010
SALES (est): 813.05K **Privately Held**
Web: www.healthlinkeurope.com
SIC: 3841 Medical instruments and equipment, blood and bone work

(G-12834)
HEALTHLINK INTERNATIONAL INC
Also Called: Healthlink Europe & Intl
211 E Six Forks Rd Ste 209a (27609-7745)
PHONE.................................877 324-2837
EMP: 12 EST: 2013
SALES (est): 803.47K **Privately Held**
SIC: 3841 Muscle exercise apparatus, ophthalmic
HQ: Healthlink Europe B.V.
Pettelaarpark 114
's-Hertogenbosch NB 5216
135479300

(G-12835)
HEAVY METAL SUPPLY
1010 S Saunders St (27603-2202)
PHONE.................................919 625-3508
EMP: 6 EST: 2017
SALES (est): 223.82K **Privately Held**
Web: www.heavymetalsupply.com
SIC: 3441 Fabricated structural metal

(G-12836)
HEIDELBERG MTLS STHAST AGG LLC
5001 Duraleigh Rd (27612-7627)
P.O. Box 52039 (27612-0039)
PHONE.................................919 787-0613
Kenneth W Kennedy, *Mgr*
EMP: 30
SALES (corp-wide): 21.19B **Privately Held**
Web: www.hansonbiz.com
SIC: 1429 Igneus rock, crushed and broken-quarrying
HQ: Heidelberg Materials Southeast Agg Llc
3237 Satellite Blvd # 30
Duluth GA 30096
770 491-2756

(G-12837)
HELIUM AGENCY LLC
2207 Alexander Rd (27608-1644)
PHONE.................................919 833-1358
Wilbur Garner Lingo Iii, *Owner*
EMP: 5 EST: 2018
SALES (est): 131.44K **Privately Held**
Web: www.helium-agency.com
SIC: 2813 Helium

(G-12838)
HELP/SYSTEMS LLC
2435 Lynn Rd Ste 100 (27612-6756)
PHONE.................................844 425-2966
Ray Wright, *Pr*
EMP: 4 EST: 2018
SALES (est): 56.54K **Privately Held**
SIC: 7372 Business oriented computer software

(G-12839)
HEXATECH INC
8311 Brier Creek Pkwy (27617-7328)
PHONE.................................919 633-0583
Raoul Schlesser, *Prin*
EMP: 7 EST: 2010
SALES (est): 220.5K **Privately Held**
Web: www.hexatechinc.com
SIC: 3674 Semiconductors and related devices

(G-12840)
HEYEL CUSTOM METAL
1224 Home Ct (27603-4541)
PHONE.................................919 957-8442
EMP: 7
SALES (est): 123.72K **Privately Held**
Web: www.heyelcustommetal.com
SIC: 3441 Fabricated structural metal

(G-12841)
HEYEL CUSTOM METAL INC
1224 Home Ct (27603-4541)
P.O. Box 13527 (27709-3527)
PHONE.................................919 957-8442
EMP: 10 EST: 1995
SQ FT: 7,000
SALES (est): 971.07K **Privately Held**
Web: www.heyelcustommetal.com
SIC: 3441 Fabricated structural metal

(G-12842)
HI-TECH FABRICATION INC
222 Glenwood Ave Apt 503 (27603-1496)
P.O. Box 80668 (27623-0668)
PHONE.................................919 781-6150
▲ EMP: 145
Web: www.htfi.com
SIC: 3469 3444 3479 3471 Stamping metal for the trade; Sheet metalwork; Painting of metal products; Chromium plating of metals or formed products

(G-12843)
HIGH PERFORMANCE MARKETING INC
158 Wind Chime Ct (27615-6433)
PHONE.................................919 870-9915
Jay Langley, *CEO*
EMP: 7 EST: 1991
SQ FT: 2,000
SALES (est): 812.8K **Privately Held**
Web: www.hpmmail.com
SIC: 7336 2759 Commercial art and graphic design; Commercial printing, nec

(G-12844)
HIGH TECH SIGNS INC
8601 Battom Ct (27613-1201)
PHONE.................................919 859-3206
James Watts, *Owner*
EMP: 4 EST: 2018
SALES (est): 74.64K **Privately Held**
SIC: 3993 Signs and advertising specialties

(G-12845)
HILL PRINTING COMPANY
606 Glenwood Ave (27603-1224)
PHONE.................................919 833-5934
EMP: 7 EST: 1997
SALES (est): 90.04K **Privately Held**
SIC: 2752 Offset printing

GEOGRAPHIC SECTION
Raleigh - Wake County (G-12873)

(G-12846)
HIPRA SCIENTIFIC USA
1001 William Moore Dr (27607-6379)
PHONE..................919 605-8256
EMP: 10 EST: 2019
SALES (est): 299.1K **Privately Held**
Web: www.hipra.com
SIC: 2834 Pharmaceutical preparations

(G-12847)
HISTORIC INTERPRETATIONS INC
P.O. Box 61277 (27661-1277)
PHONE..................919 339-1558
EMP: 6 EST: 2011
SALES (est): 62.33K **Privately Held**
Web: www.historicinterpretations.org
SIC: 3999 Framed artwork

(G-12848)
HITACHI ENERGY USA INC
Also Called: Hitachi ABB Power Grids
901 Main Campus Dr (27606-5293)
PHONE..................919 649-7022
Yoann Barbosa, *CFO*
EMP: 19
SIC: 7372 Prepackaged software
HQ: Hitachi Energy Usa Inc
 901 Main Campus Dr
 Raleigh NC 27606
 919 856-2360

(G-12849)
HITACHI ENERGY USA INC
1345 Express Dr (27603-4156)
PHONE..................919 324-5403
EMP: 14
SIC: 3675 Electronic capacitors
HQ: Hitachi Energy Usa Inc
 901 Main Campus Dr
 Raleigh NC 27606
 919 856-2360

(G-12850)
HITACHI ENERGY USA INC (HQ)
901 Main Campus Dr (27606-5293)
P.O. Box 90774 (27675-0774)
PHONE..................919 856-2360
Yoann Barbosa, *CEO*
Anthony Allard, *
EMP: 200 EST: 1997
SQ FT: 10,000
SALES (est): 503.54MM **Privately Held**
SIC: 3675 3699 3621 Electronic capacitors;
 Electrical equipment and supplies, nec;
 Motors and generators
PA: Hitachi, Ltd.
 1-6-6, Marunouchi
 Chiyoda-Ku TKY 100-0

(G-12851)
HOLLEY SELINDA
Also Called: Helpmehelpu
700 Peterson St (27610-0053)
PHONE..................919 351-9466
Selinda Holley, *Owner*
Selinda Holley, *Mgr*
EMP: 5 EST: 2015
SALES (est): 134.31K **Privately Held**
SIC: 2761 Manifold business forms

(G-12852)
HOLLISTER INCORPORATED
5959 Triangle Town Blvd Ste 1085
(27616-3270)
PHONE..................919 792-2095
Caroline Knorr, *Brnch Mgr*
EMP: 6
SALES (corp-wide): 709.48MM **Privately Held**
Web: www.hollister.com
SIC: 3842 Surgical appliances and supplies
PA: Hollister Incorporated
 2000 Hollister Dr
 Libertyville IL 60048
 847 680-1000

(G-12853)
HOLMES WELDING LLC
9408 Middleberry Ln (27603-9211)
PHONE..................919 779-8844
Leroy Holmes, *Prin*
EMP: 6 EST: 2014
SALES (est): 70.37K **Privately Held**
Web: www.raleighwelder.com
SIC: 7692 Welding repair

(G-12854)
HOLTEN INDUSTRIES LLC
2009 Lake Trout Ln (27610-5565)
PHONE..................919 810-8467
EMP: 4 EST: 2013
SALES (est): 93.43K **Privately Held**
SIC: 3999 Manufacturing industries, nec

(G-12855)
HOLY MOUNTAIN PRINTING
301 Catalpa Ct (27609-3853)
PHONE..................801 634-3462
EMP: 4 EST: 2017
SALES (est): 83.91K **Privately Held**
Web: www.holymountainprinting.com
SIC: 2752 Commercial printing, lithographic

(G-12856)
HOME IMPRV SOLUTIONS NC LLC
Also Called: Shelf Genie
2013 New Hope Church Rd Ste K
(27604-1660)
PHONE..................919 876-3230
Andy Pittman, *Managing Member*
EMP: 8 EST: 2014
SQ FT: 1,500
SALES (est): 192.82K **Privately Held**
Web: www.cabinetcurestriangle.com
SIC: 2434 Wood kitchen cabinets

(G-12857)
HONEYWELL INTERNATIONAL INC
Also Called: Honeywell
201 S Rogers Ln (27610-4336)
PHONE..................919 662-7539
Vince Iamunno, *Brnch Mgr*
EMP: 657
SALES (corp-wide): 36.66B **Publicly Held**
Web: www.honeywell.com
SIC: 3724 Aircraft engines and engine parts
PA: Honeywell International Inc.
 855 S Mint St
 Charlotte NC 28202
 704 627-6200

(G-12858)
HOOKS VINEYARD
8145 Caliber Woods Dr (27616-8665)
PHONE..................919 917-5658
EMP: 4 EST: 2017
SALES (est): 74.48K **Privately Held**
SIC: 2084 Wines

(G-12859)
HORBALLS INC
1009 Lila Ln (27614-9118)
PHONE..................919 925-0483
EMP: 5 EST: 2017
SALES (est): 230.21K **Privately Held**
Web: www.horballs.com
SIC: 2099 Food preparations, nec

(G-12860)
HORIZON FREST PDTS WLMNGTON LP
Also Called: Horizon Forest Products
4115 Commodity Pkwy (27610-2973)
P.O. Box 46809 (27620-6809)
PHONE..................919 424-8265
Jeff Myer, *Pr*
David Wiilliams, *VP*
EMP: 100 EST: 1992
SQ FT: 10,000
SALES (est): 10.86MM **Privately Held**
Web: www.horizonforest.com
SIC: 2426 Flooring, hardwood

(G-12861)
HORIZON LAB SYSTEMS LLC
8601 Six Forks Rd Ste 160 (27615-2965)
PHONE..................919 896-7737
Michael Simpson, *CEO*
EMP: 33 EST: 1987
SQ FT: 7,452
SALES (est): 9.59MM
SALES (corp-wide): 5.37B **Publicly Held**
Web: www.clinisys.com
SIC: 7372 7371 Prepackaged software;
 Custom computer programming services
HQ: Qsc 1209 Limited
 Rutland House
 Birmingham W MIDLANDS

(G-12862)
HORSEWARE TRIPLE CROWN BLANKET
1030 N Rogers Ln (27610-6083)
P.O. Box 6328 (28501-0328)
PHONE..................252 208-0080
▲ EMP: 18 EST: 1996
SALES (est): 1.04MM **Privately Held**
SIC: 2399 Horse blankets

(G-12863)
HOUSE OF HOPS
6909 Glenwood Ave (27612-7100)
PHONE..................919 819-0704
EMP: 7 EST: 2015
SALES (est): 236.32K **Privately Held**
Web: www.houseofhopsnc.com
SIC: 2082 Malt beverages

(G-12864)
HRTMS INCORPORATED
801 Corporate Center Dr Ste 130
(27607-5243)
PHONE..................919 741-5099
Andrew Ellerhorst, *Pr*
EMP: 9 EST: 2005
SALES (est): 1.61MM **Privately Held**
Web: www.jdxpert.com
SIC: 7372 7389 Prepackaged software;
 Business services, nec

(G-12865)
HUBER USA INC
1101 Nowell Rd # 110 (27607-5242)
PHONE..................919 674-4266
Georg Kiefer, *CEO*
EMP: 19 EST: 2014
SALES (est): 4.86MM
SALES (corp-wide): 166.62K **Privately Held**
Web: www.huber-usa.com
SIC: 3822 Environmental controls
PA: Huber Kg
 Werner-Von-Siemens-Str. 1
 Offenburg BW
 78196030

(G-12866)
HUMBLY MADE BRAND
2411 Still Forest Pl Apt 303 (27607)
PHONE..................740 506-1554
Mitch Shepherd, *Prin*
EMP: 4 EST: 2019
SALES (est): 121.98K **Privately Held**
Web: www.humblymade.com
SIC: 2759 Screen printing

(G-12867)
HUMBOLDT MFG CO INC
2525 Atlantic Ave (27604-1411)
PHONE..................919 832-6509
Mahir Alnadaf, *VP*
EMP: 6 EST: 2015
SALES (est): 143.4K **Privately Held**
Web: www.humboldtmfg.com
SIC: 3999 Manufacturing industries, nec

(G-12868)
HUNT KENDALL PUBLISHING
11717 Stannary Pl (27613-7814)
PHONE..................919 510-0160
Brianne Racer, *Mgr*
EMP: 7 EST: 2011
SALES (est): 71.7K **Privately Held**
SIC: 2741 Miscellaneous publishing

(G-12869)
HUNTER INNOVATIONS LTD
1201 Corporation Pkwy (27610-1349)
P.O. Box 17105 (27619-7105)
PHONE..................919 848-8814
Al Hunter, *Pr*
Nancy Hunter, *VP*
EMP: 7 EST: 1986
SQ FT: 17,000
SALES (est): 743.16K **Privately Held**
Web: www.oakcitycolumns.com
SIC: 2431 5031 Millwork; Millwork

(G-12870)
HYDROTEX USA INC
1065 Bullard Ct (27615-6801)
PHONE..................919 876-4170
Mike Mcintyre, *Pr*
EMP: 7 EST: 2001
SALES (est): 504.55K **Privately Held**
Web: www.hydrotexusa.com
SIC: 2899 Chemical cotton (processed cotton linters)

(G-12871)
HYSUCAT USA LLC
12608 Leatherwood Ct (27613-5303)
PHONE..................919 345-0240
EMP: 7 EST: 2016
SALES (est): 114.3K **Privately Held**
SIC: 3732 Boatbuilding and repairing

(G-12872)
I MUST GARDEN LLC
1500 Garner Rd Ste D (27610-6669)
PHONE..................919 929-2299
▲ EMP: 5 EST: 2004
SALES (est): 706.29K **Privately Held**
Web: www.imustgarden.com
SIC: 5261 5941 2879 Lawn and garden equipment; Golf goods and equipment; Agricultural disinfectants

(G-12873)
I2M LLC
801 Corporate Center Dr Ste 128
(27607-5243)
PHONE..................984 202-0582
Stuart Miller, *Pr*
Christian Aue, *VP*
W Patrick Dreisig, *Sec*

Raleigh - Wake County (G-12874)   GEOGRAPHIC SECTION

Charles Vaillant, *Prin*
EMP: 4 EST: 2015
SALES (est): 1.74MM
SALES (corp-wide): 5.01B **Privately Held**
Web: www.i-2-m.com
SIC: 3589 Water filters and softeners, household type
PA: Mann + Hummel International Gmbh & Co. Kg
Schwieberdinger Str. 126
Ludwigsburg BW 71636
7141980

(G-12874)
ICARE USA INC
Also Called: Icare Tonomoter
809 Faulkner Pl (27609-5943)
PHONE...............................919 877-9607
EMP: 4
SALES (corp-wide): 100.72MM **Privately Held**
Web: www.icare-world.com
SIC: 3822 Hydronic pressure or temperature controls
HQ: Icare Finland Oy
Ayritie 22
Vantaa 01510

(G-12875)
IDAEL MFG CO
6300 Creedmoor Rd (27612-6730)
PHONE...............................919 480-1329
Dkr Y'srael, *Prin*
EMP: 4 EST: 2015
SALES (est): 87.09K **Privately Held**
SIC: 3999 Manufacturing industries, nec

(G-12876)
IDEA SOFTWARE INC
10814 Greater Hills St (27614-8653)
PHONE...............................407 453-3883
EMP: 5 EST: 2009
SALES (est): 123.95K **Privately Held**
SIC: 7372 Prepackaged software

(G-12877)
IDEAL PRECISION METER INC
5816 Creedmoor Rd Ste 103 (27612-2310)
PHONE...............................919 571-2000
Mohamed El-refai, *Pr*
EMP: 21 EST: 1972
SQ FT: 25,000
SALES (est): 532.29K **Privately Held**
Web: www.idealmeter.com
SIC: 3825 Indicating instruments, electric

(G-12878)
ILUKA RESOURCES INC
4208 Six Forks Rd Ste 1000 (27609-5733)
PHONE...............................904 284-9832
Matthew Blackwell, *Pr*
◆ EMP: 120 EST: 1984
SALES (est): 14.09MM **Privately Held**
Web: www.iluka.com
SIC: 1499 Peat mining and processing
HQ: Iluka Resources Inc
12472 St John Church Rd
Stony Creek VA 23882

(G-12879)
IMAGE360 NORTH RALEIGH NC
8471 Garvey Dr Ste 101 (27616-3370)
PHONE...............................919 307-4119
EMP: 4 EST: 2016
SALES (est): 29.17K **Privately Held**
Web: www.image360.com
SIC: 3993 Signs and advertising specialties

(G-12880)
IN ACORDA THERAPEUTICS
5300 Balmy Dawn Ct (27613-1039)
PHONE...............................914 347-4300
EMP: 5 EST: 2017
SALES (est): 190.48K **Privately Held**
SIC: 2834 Pharmaceutical preparations

(G-12881)
INDIE PUBLISHING
2623 Hamlet Green Dr (27614-8076)
PHONE...............................919 435-6215
Dana Grizzel, *Prin*
EMP: 4 EST: 2015
SALES (est): 60.21K **Privately Held**
SIC: 2741 Miscellaneous publishing

(G-12882)
INDIVIOR MANUFACTURING LLC ✪
8900 Capital Blvd (27616-3117)
PHONE...............................804 594-0974
Mark Erossley, *Managing Member*
EMP: 65 EST: 2023
SALES (est): 9.62MM
SALES (corp-wide): 901MM **Privately Held**
SIC: 2834 Pharmaceutical preparations
HQ: Indivior Inc.
10710 Midlothian Tpke # 430
North Chesterfield VA 23235

(G-12883)
INDUCTION FOOD SYSTEMS INC
2609 Discovery Dr Ste 115 (27616-1905)
PHONE...............................919 907-0179
Francesco Aimone, *CEO*
George Sadler, *Pr*
EMP: 5 EST: 2017
SALES (est): 484.89K **Privately Held**
Web: www.inductionfoodsystems.com
SIC: 3556 5499 Food products machinery; Gourmet food stores

(G-12884)
INDUSTRIAL AUTOMATION COMPANY
544 Pylon Dr (27606-1415)
PHONE...............................877 727-8757
Will Jacobson, *Owner*
EMP: 12 EST: 2019
SALES (est): 2.83MM **Privately Held**
Web: www.industrialautomationco.com
SIC: 3569 Liquid automation machinery and equipment

(G-12885)
INDUSTRIAL HEAT LLC
1017 Main Campus Dr (27606-5505)
PHONE...............................919 743-5727
Thomas Francis Darden, *Pr*
J T Vaughn, *VP*
EMP: 10 EST: 2012
SALES (est): 486.19K **Privately Held**
SIC: 3822 Environmental controls

(G-12886)
INDY WEEK
709 W Jones St (27603-1426)
PHONE...............................919 832-8774
Pete Weber, *Pr*
EMP: 7 EST: 2015
SALES (est): 112.14K **Privately Held**
Web: www.indyweek.com
SIC: 2711 Newspapers, publishing and printing

(G-12887)
INEOS AUTOMOTIVE AMERICAS LLC
2020 Progress Ct Ste 100-112 (27608-2767)
PHONE...............................404 513-8577
EMP: 8
SALES (est): 535.81K **Privately Held**
SIC: 3694 Distributors, motor vehicle engine

(G-12888)
INFORMATION TECH WORKS LLC (HQ)
4809 Little Falls Dr (27609-5983)
PHONE...............................919 232-5332
Jim Wrenn, *Pr*
EMP: 10 EST: 2001
SALES (est): 445.07K
SALES (corp-wide): 8.19MM **Privately Held**
SIC: 7372 7371 5734 Prepackaged software; Software programming applications; Computer software and accessories
PA: Cayuse, Llc
121 Sw Salmon St Ste 900
Portland OR 97204
503 297-2108

(G-12889)
INNOWERA LTD LIABILITY COMPANY
8529 Six Forks Rd Ste 400 (27615-4972)
PHONE...............................214 295-9508
Mickey Shah, *SAP SOLUTIONS ARC*
EMP: 6 EST: 2007
SALES (est): 2.32MM
SALES (corp-wide): 113.32MM **Privately Held**
Web: www.insightsoftware.com
SIC: 7372 Application computer software
HQ: Magnitude Software, Inc.
8904 Westminster Glen Ave
Austin TX 78730
866 466-3849

(G-12890)
INOVAETION INC
8601 Six Forks Rd Ste 400 (27615-2965)
PHONE...............................919 651-1628
Kimthanh Do Le, *Pr*
EMP: 11 EST: 2015
SIC: 7372 Application computer software

(G-12891)
INPRIMO SOLUTIONS INC
7925 Vandemere Ct (27615-4601)
PHONE...............................919 390-7776
Vann R James, *Prin*
EMP: 6 EST: 2013
SALES (est): 91.31K **Privately Held**
Web: www.inprimosolutions.com
SIC: 2752 Offset printing

(G-12892)
INSIGHTSOFTWARE LLC (PA)
Also Called: Insightsoftware
8529 Six Forks Rd (27615-4971)
PHONE...............................919 872-7800
Michael Sullivan, *CEO*
Matthew Kupferman, *
Spencer Kupferman, *
EMP: 50 EST: 1981
SALES (est): 113.32MM
SALES (corp-wide): 113.32MM **Privately Held**
Web: www.insightsoftware.com
SIC: 7371 7372 Computer software development; Application computer software

(G-12893)
INSPECTIONXPERT CORPORATION
1 Glenwood Ave Ste 500 (27603-2580)
P.O. Box 991 (24063-0991)
PHONE...............................919 249-6442
Jeff Cope, *CEO*
EMP: 14 EST: 2004
SALES (est): 3.17MM
SALES (corp-wide): 355.83K **Privately Held**
Web: www.inspectionxpert.com
SIC: 7372 7371 Prepackaged software; Computer software development
HQ: Ideagen Limited
Mere Way Ruddington Fields Business Park
Nottingham NOTTS NG11
162 969-9100

(G-12894)
INSURANCE SYSTEMS GROUP INC
Also Called: I S G
827 N Bloodworth St (27604-1231)
PHONE...............................919 834-4907
Charles Kerr, *CEO*
Duncan Kerr, *VP*
EMP: 10 EST: 1984
SALES (est): 630.66K **Privately Held**
Web: www.isg-online.com
SIC: 7372 Business oriented computer software

(G-12895)
INTAS PHARMACEUTICALS LIMITED
8041 Arco Corporate Dr Ste 200 (27617)
PHONE...............................919 941-7878
EMP: 66 EST: 2006
SALES (est): 6.47MM **Privately Held**
Web: www.intaspharma.com
SIC: 2834 Pharmaceutical preparations
PA: Intas Pharmaceuticals Limited
Corporate House, Plot No. 255,
Magnet Corporate Park,
Ahmedabad GJ 380 0

(G-12896)
INTEGRATED ROE SECURITY LLC
2308 Basil Dr (27612-2872)
PHONE...............................919 297-8036
Roe Brandon Stephens, *Asst Sec*
EMP: 7 EST: 2018
SALES (est): 120.44K **Privately Held**
Web: www.roeintegrated.com
SIC: 3699 1731 6211 7382 Security control equipment and systems; Access control systems specialization; Dealers, security; Fire alarm maintenance and monitoring

(G-12897)
INTELLIGENT APPS LLC
12113 Oakwood View Dr Apt 202 (27614-6878)
PHONE...............................919 628-6256
Ruba Abughazaleh, *VP*
EMP: 4 EST: 2014
SALES (est): 226.04K **Privately Held**
Web: www.intelligentappsinc.com
SIC: 7371 7372 8742 7389 Computer software systems analysis and design, custom; Application computer software; Management consulting services; Business services, nec

(G-12898)
INTERECO USA BELT FILTER PRESS
7474 Creedmoor Rd (27613-1663)
PHONE...............................919 349-6041
Stephanie Richardson, *Prin*
▲ EMP: 6 EST: 2008
SALES (est): 94.15K **Privately Held**
SIC: 2741 Miscellaneous publishing

(G-12899)
INTERNATIONAL PAPER COMPANY
Also Called: International Paper
5 W Hargett St Rm 914 (27601-2936)
PHONE...............................919 831-4764

Deano Orr, *Brnch Mgr*
EMP: 5
SALES (corp-wide): 18.92B **Publicly Held**
Web: www.internationalpaper.com
SIC: 2621 Paper mills
PA: International Paper Company
6400 Poplar Ave
Memphis TN 38197
901 419-7000

(G-12900)
INTERNATIONAL PET ACC LLC
11842 Canemount St (27614-8385)
PHONE..................................919 964-0738
Rufus Coley Junior, *Managing Member*
EMP: 4 **EST:** 2014
SALES (est): 58.61K **Privately Held**
SIC: 2399 5199 Pet collars, leashes, etc.: non-leather; Pet supplies

(G-12901)
IRON BOX LLC
Also Called: Iron Box
1349 Express Dr (27603-4156)
P.O. Box 19422 (27619-9422)
PHONE..................................919 890-0025
Elizabeth Knout, *Pt*
Christopher Knout, *VP*
Brittany Dedafoe, *Genl Mgr*
Elizabeth Knout, *Pr*
▲ **EMP:** 21 **EST:** 2021
SALES (est): 10.23MM **Privately Held**
Web: www.customavrack.com
SIC: 5051 5063 3679 Metals service centers and offices; Wire and cable; Harness assemblies, for electronic use: wire or cable

(G-12902)
IRONLUNGS BOXING & PERSONAL
5608 Spring Ct (27616-2873)
PHONE..................................919 332-8966
EMP: 5 **EST:** 2017
SALES (est): 86.67K **Privately Held**
SIC: 3842 Iron lungs

(G-12903)
ISSUER DIRECT CORPORATION (PA)
Also Called: Issuer Direct
1 Glenwood Ave Ste 1001 (27603-2582)
PHONE..................................919 481-4000
Brian R Balbirnie, *Pr*
Timothy Pitoniak, *CFO*
EMP: 83 **EST:** 1988
SQ FT: 9,766
SALES (est): 33.38MM **Publicly Held**
Web: www.issuerdirect.com
SIC: 7372 Application computer software

(G-12904)
ITG BRANDS
900 E Six Forks Rd Unit 210 (27604-1822)
PHONE..................................919 366-0220
Steven Brooks, *Brnch Mgr*
EMP: 57
Web: www.itgbrands.com
SIC: 2111 Cigarettes
HQ: Itg Brands
714 Green Valley Rd
Greensboro NC 27408
336 335-7000

(G-12905)
ITRON INC
8529 Six Forks Rd Ste 100 (27615-4972)
PHONE..................................919 876-2600
Dave Godwin, *Dir*
EMP: 85
SALES (corp-wide): 2.17B **Publicly Held**
Web: na.itron.com
SIC: 3663 3571 Radio and t.v. communications equipment; Electronic computers
PA: Itron, Inc.
2111 N Molter Rd
Liberty Lake WA 99019
509 924-9900

(G-12906)
J & E DIGITAL PRINTING INC
3524 Pinnacle Peak Dr (27604-9700)
PHONE..................................919 803-8913
William L Moody, *Prin*
EMP: 5 **EST:** 2008
SALES (est): 226.16K **Privately Held**
Web: www.jeprinting.com
SIC: 2752 Offset printing

(G-12907)
J A KING
7239 Acc Blvd Ste 101 (27617-4882)
PHONE..................................800 327-7727
EMP: 12 **EST:** 2018
SALES (est): 155.53K **Privately Held**
Web: www.crossco.com
SIC: 7692 Welding repair

(G-12908)
J E INGRAM LLC
5401 Amsterdam Pl (27606-9709)
PHONE..................................770 354-5599
John Edward Ingram, *CEO*
EMP: 5 **EST:** 2014
SALES (est): 76.87K **Privately Held**
SIC: 2599 Furniture and fixtures, nec

(G-12909)
J M I BARCODES
9400 Ransdell Rd Ste 9 (27603-8980)
PHONE..................................919 289-4125
James Jourdan, *Prin*
EMP: 5 **EST:** 2010
SALES (est): 203.95K **Privately Held**
Web: www.jmibarcodes.com
SIC: 7372 Prepackaged software

(G-12910)
JACK PAGAN & ASSOC INC
1001 Thoreau Dr (27609-6040)
PHONE..................................919 872-0159
Jack Pagan, *Owner*
EMP: 5 **EST:** 2000
SALES (est): 169.54K **Privately Held**
SIC: 3569 General industrial machinery, nec

(G-12911)
JADAS HATS
5812 Magellan Way Apt 102 (27612-2281)
PHONE..................................919 561-4373
EMP: 4 **EST:** 2017
SALES (est): 153.14K **Privately Held**
SIC: 2353 Hats, caps, and millinery

(G-12912)
JANCO LLC
128 Yorkchester Way (27615-2979)
PHONE..................................919 847-8816
EMP: 10 **EST:** 2012
SALES (est): 150.59K **Privately Held**
SIC: 3089 Injection molding of plastics

(G-12913)
JARRETT BAY OFFSHORE
4209 Lassiter Mill Rd Ste 126 (27609-5794)
PHONE..................................919 803-1990
EMP: 6 **EST:** 2017
SALES (est): 49.42K **Privately Held**
Web: shop.jarrettbay.com
SIC: 3732 Boatbuilding and repairing

(G-12914)
JARRETT PRESS PUBLICATIONS
2805 Spring Forest Rd Ste 201 (27616)
PHONE..................................919 862-0551
EMP: 4 **EST:** 2020
SALES (est): 101.64K **Privately Held**
SIC: 2741 Miscellaneous publishing

(G-12915)
JEFFREY SHEFFER
Also Called: Atc Conversions
3901 Commerce Park Dr (27610-2776)
PHONE..................................919 861-9126
Jeffrey Sheffer, *Owner*
EMP: 7 **EST:** 2014
SQ FT: 1,600
SALES (est): 424.61K **Privately Held**
SIC: 3499 Automobile seat frames, metal

(G-12916)
JEREMY WEITZEL
Also Called: Allkindsa Signs
1228 United Dr (27603-2241)
P.O. Box 883 (27526-0883)
PHONE..................................919 878-4474
Jeremy Weitzel, *Pr*
EMP: 5 **EST:** 1985
SALES (est): 245.88K **Privately Held**
Web: www.allkindsa.com
SIC: 3993 Signs and advertising specialties

(G-12917)
JESTER-CROWN INC
Also Called: Sign-A-Rama
4721 Atlantic Ave Ste 119 (27604-8106)
PHONE..................................919 872-1070
Randy Warren, *Owner*
EMP: 4 **EST:** 1990
SQ FT: 1,050
SALES (est): 311.03K **Privately Held**
Web: www.signarama.com
SIC: 3993 Signs and advertising specialties

(G-12918)
JOHN LINDENBERGER
6429 Grassy Knoll Ln (27616-8875)
PHONE..................................919 337-6741
John Lindenberger, *Prin*
EMP: 5 **EST:** 2017
SALES (est): 76.15K **Privately Held**
SIC: 2431 Millwork

(G-12919)
JOHN WEST AUTO SERVICE INC
3216 Lake Woodard Dr (27604-3659)
PHONE..................................919 250-0825
John West, *Pr*
EMP: 7 **EST:** 1976
SQ FT: 10,000
SALES (est): 495.68K **Privately Held**
Web: www.johnwestautorepairservice.com
SIC: 3599 7538 Machine shop, jobbing and repair; General automotive repair shops

(G-12920)
JOHNSON CONTROLS INC
Also Called: Johnson Controls
633 Hutton St Ste 104 (27606-6319)
PHONE..................................919 743-3500
EMP: 74
Web: www.johnsoncontrols.com
SIC: 2531 7623 Seats, automobile; Air conditioning repair
HQ: Johnson Controls, Inc.
5757 N Green Bay Ave
Milwaukee WI 53209
920 245-6409

(G-12921)
JOHNSON HARN VNGAR GEE GL PLLC
434 Fayetteville St Ste 2200 (27601-1701)
PHONE..................................919 213-6163
Samuel H Johnson, *Prin*
EMP: 7 **EST:** 2017
SALES (est): 399.52K **Privately Held**
Web: www.jhvgglaw.com
SIC: 2099 Vinegar

(G-12922)
JOSEPH C WOODARD PRTG CO INC
2815 S Saunders St (27603-3519)
PHONE..................................919 829-0634
Joyce W Woodard, *Pr*
Kimberly W Hall, *VP*
Joseph C Woodard Junior, *VP*
Ryan S Woodard, *VP*
Jason H Woodard, *VP*
EMP: 19 **EST:** 1967
SQ FT: 11,000
SALES (est): 2.51MM **Privately Held**
Web: www.josephcwoodard.com
SIC: 2752 2791 2789 Offset printing; Typesetting; Bookbinding and related work

(G-12923)
JPS COMMUNICATIONS INC
5800 Departure Dr (27616-1857)
PHONE..................................919 534-1168
Carl S Kist, *Pr*
Rochelle Graham,
EMP: 60 **EST:** 1988
SQ FT: 16,000
SALES (est): 25.01K
SALES (corp-wide): 68.92B **Publicly Held**
Web: www.jps.com
SIC: 8748 3577 3663 3661 Communications consulting; Computer peripheral equipment, nec; Radio and t.v. communications equipment; Telephone and telegraph apparatus
HQ: Raytheon Company
870 Winter St
Waltham MA 02451
781 522-3000

(G-12924)
JPS INTRPRBILITY SOLUTIONS INC
5800 Departure Dr (27616-1857)
PHONE..................................919 332-5009
Donald Scott, *CEO*
Arthur Powers, *VP*
EMP: 18 **EST:** 2016
SALES (est): 2.63MM **Privately Held**
Web: www.jps.com
SIC: 3663 Receivers, radio communications

(G-12925)
JS PRINTING LLC
Also Called: International Minute Press
1824 Garner Station Blvd (27603-3643)
PHONE..................................919 773-1103
EMP: 6 **EST:** 1999
SQ FT: 2,000
SALES (est): 465.99K **Privately Held**
Web: www.minuteman.com
SIC: 2752 Offset printing

(G-12926)
JSBD SOFTWARE LLC
5409 Wynneford Way (27614-8341)
PHONE..................................919 841-1218
James Macon, *Prin*
EMP: 5 **EST:** 2011
SALES (est): 123.58K **Privately Held**
SIC: 7372 Prepackaged software

Raleigh - Wake County (G-12927)   GEOGRAPHIC SECTION

(G-12927)
JULIAS SOUTHERN FOODS LLC
Also Called: Julia's Pantry
5608 Primavera Ct Ste G (27616-1848)
PHONE.............................919 609-6745
Reta Washington, *Managing Member*
EMP: 6 **EST:** 2011
SALES (est): 485.27K **Privately Held**
Web: www.juliaspantry.com
SIC: 2096 2099 2045 Pork rinds; Seasonings: dry mixes; Pancake mixes, prepared: from purchased flour

(G-12928)
JUNIPER NETWORKS INC
1730 Varsity Dr Ste 10 (27606-2188)
PHONE.............................888 586-4737
EMP: 12
Web: www.juniper.net
SIC: 7373 7372 Computer integrated systems design; Prepackaged software
PA: Juniper Networks, Inc.
1133 Innovation Way
Sunnyvale CA 94089

(G-12929)
KALEIDO INC
16 W Martin St Fl 7 (27601-1341)
PHONE.............................984 205-9436
Steve Cerveny, *CEO*
Sophia Lopez, *Prin*
Joseph Lubin, *Prin*
EMP: 19 **EST:** 2020
SALES (est): 1.28MM **Privately Held**
Web: www.kaleido.io
SIC: 7372 Prepackaged software

(G-12930)
KARAMEDICA INC
509 W North St (27603-1414)
PHONE.............................919 302-1325
Andrew Crofton, *CEO*
Wolff Kirsch, *CEO*
Taub Swartz, *CFO*
Andrew Crofton, *COO*
Sam Hudson, *Ofcr*
EMP: 7 **EST:** 2016
SALES (est): 802.58K **Privately Held**
Web: www.karamedica.com
SIC: 3841 5122 Surgical and medical instruments; Biotherapeutics

(G-12931)
KARL RL MANUFACTURING
11937 Appaloosa Run E (27613-7111)
PHONE.............................919 846-3801
Randy Karl, *Prin*
EMP: 5 **EST:** 2010
SALES (est): 63.74K **Privately Held**
SIC: 3999 Manufacturing industries, nec

(G-12932)
KBERG PRODUCTIONS LLC
Also Called: Kberg Consultants
4234 Massey Preserve Trl (27616-3381)
PHONE.............................910 232-0342
Lisa Kohnberg, *Prin*
Jim Roessner, *Prin*
EMP: 7 **EST:** 2010
SALES (est): 459.04K **Privately Held**
Web: www.kbergconsultants.com
SIC: 8748 3826 2899 1799 Business consulting, nec; Water testing apparatus; Food contamination testing or screening kits; Decontamination services

(G-12933)
KCP INC
6807 Breezewood Rd (27607-4704)
PHONE.............................919 854-7824
Douglas Walters Ph.d. Csp, *Pr*
EMP: 7 **EST:** 2010
SALES (est): 220K **Privately Held**
SIC: 3444 Sheet metalwork

(G-12934)
KEGLERS WOODWORKS LLC
330 Dupont Cir (27603-1928)
PHONE.............................919 608-7220
Allen Keglers, *Prin*
EMP: 7 **EST:** 2007
SALES (est): 163.5K **Privately Held**
SIC: 2431 Millwork

(G-12935)
KENN M LLC
6046 Inona Pl (27606-1198)
PHONE.............................678 755-6607
Kenneth C Mathara, *CEO*
EMP: 5 **EST:** 2019
SALES (est): 228.14K **Privately Held**
SIC: 7389 4731 3799 Business Activities at Non-Commercial Site; Freight transportation arrangement; Transportation equipment, nec

(G-12936)
KERYFLEX PODADVANCE INC
9132 Fawn Hill Ct (27617-7768)
PHONE.............................888 763-2382
EMP: 5 **EST:** 2010
SALES (est): 61.05K **Privately Held**
SIC: 3999 Fingernails, artificial

(G-12937)
KI AGENCY LLC
Also Called: Capital Wraps
5812 Triangle Dr (27617-4705)
P.O. Box 80371 (27623-0371)
PHONE.............................919 977-7075
EMP: 8 **EST:** 2010
SALES (est): 1.21MM **Privately Held**
Web: www.capitalwraps.com
SIC: 3993 Signs and advertising specialties

(G-12938)
KING TUTT GRAPHICS
1100 Corporation Pkwy Ste 122 (27610)
PHONE.............................919 977-6901
EMP: 4 **EST:** 2019
SALES (est): 145.16K **Privately Held**
Web: www.kingtuttgraphics.com
SIC: 3993 Signs and advertising specialties

(G-12939)
KING TUTT GRAPHICS LLC
1113 Transport Dr (27603-4146)
PHONE.............................877 546-4888
EMP: 7 **EST:** 2019
SALES (est): 488.46K **Privately Held**
Web: www.kingtuttgraphics.com
SIC: 3993 Signs and advertising specialties

(G-12940)
KINGTUTTGRAPHICS
8809 Amerjack Ct (27603-9173)
PHONE.............................919 748-0843
Steven Michaels, *Prin*
EMP: 5 **EST:** 2018
SALES (est): 218.91K **Privately Held**
Web: www.kingtuttgraphics.com
SIC: 3993 Signs and advertising specialties

(G-12941)
KISNER CORPORATION
Also Called: Carolina Fabricators
6016 Triangle Dr (27617-4743)
PHONE.............................919 510-8410
Scott Kisner, *Pr*
EMP: 10 **EST:** 2007
SALES (est): 208.88K **Privately Held**
Web: www.carolinametalfabricators.com
SIC: 3441 Fabricated structural metal

(G-12942)
KITCHEN BATH GLLRIES N HLLS LL
Also Called: K&B Galleries
4209 Lassiter Mill Rd Ste 130 (27609-5794)
PHONE.............................919 600-6200
Rachel Roberts, *Owner*
EMP: 7 **EST:** 2008
SALES (est): 944.82K **Privately Held**
Web: www.kandbgalleries.com
SIC: 3429 Cabinet hardware

(G-12943)
KITCHEN CABINET DESIGNERS LLC
Also Called: Kitchen Cabinet Distributors
2114 Atlantic Ave Ste 106 (27604-1555)
PHONE.............................919 833-6532
Randy Goldstein, *CEO*
Richard Gambill, *
Patrcik Dickinson, *Managing Member**
Michael Weiner, *
Pauline Gambill, *
▲ **EMP:** 119 **EST:** 2008
SQ FT: 68,500
SALES (est): 17MM **Privately Held**
Web: www.kcdus.com
SIC: 2434 Wood kitchen cabinets

(G-12944)
KNOWLEDGE MANAGEMENT ASSOC LLC
Also Called: Metal Graphic
8529 Six Forks Rd Ste 400 (27615-4972)
PHONE.............................781 250-2001
David Goldstein, *Managing Member*
Jorge Rodriguez, *Sec*
▼ **EMP:** 9 **EST:** 1995
SALES (est): 960.22K **Privately Held**
Web: www.mekkographics.com
SIC: 7372 Prepackaged software

(G-12945)
KOL INCORPORATED
Also Called: Ward's Grocery
5700 Buffaloe Rd (27616-6036)
PHONE.............................919 872-2340
Byung Kim, *Pr*
EMP: 6 **EST:** 1953
SALES (est): 301.15K **Privately Held**
SIC: 3949 5411 Hunting equipment; Grocery stores

(G-12946)
KRAFT CABIN LLC
3928 Tyler Bluff Ln (27616-8330)
PHONE.............................224 409-4374
EMP: 4 **EST:** 2020
SALES (est): 64.95K **Privately Held**
SIC: 2022 Processed cheese

(G-12947)
KSW LOGISTICS & TRANSPORT LLC
6048 Beale Loop (27616-3473)
PHONE.............................919 578-5788
EMP: 4 **EST:** 2017
SALES (est): 65K **Privately Held**
SIC: 3537 Trucks: freight, baggage, etc.: industrial, except mining

(G-12948)
KUENZ AMERICA INC
9321 Focal Pt Ste 8 (27617-8770)
PHONE.............................984 255-1018
▲ **EMP:** 19 **EST:** 1997
SQ FT: 6,000
SALES (est): 2.89MM **Privately Held**
Web: www.kuenz.com
SIC: 3536 3589 Cranes, industrial plant; Commercial cooking and foodwarming equipment

(G-12949)
KYMA TECHNOLOGIES INC
Also Called: Carolina Sputter Solutions
8829 Midway West Rd (27617-4606)
PHONE.............................919 789-8880
Keith R Evans, *Pr*
Mark Williams, *COO*
Karen Nield, *Dir Fin*
Edward Preble, *VP*
▼ **EMP:** 13 **EST:** 1998
SQ FT: 7,000
SALES (est): 5.35MM **Privately Held**
Web: www.kymatech.com
SIC: 3674 Integrated circuits, semiconductor networks, etc.

(G-12950)
LABEL & PRINTING SOLUTIONS INC
201 Buncombe St (27609)
P.O. Box 18647 (27619-8647)
PHONE.............................919 782-1242
Michael Tollison, *CEO*
EMP: 5 **EST:** 1996
SALES (est): 460.21K **Privately Held**
Web: www.labelandprinting.com
SIC: 2679 2759 7389 2752 Tags and labels, paper; Decals: printing, nsk; Packaging and labeling services; Commercial printing, lithographic

(G-12951)
LACERATION LURES LLC
5333 Durham Rd (27613-7435)
PHONE.............................919 612-3368
Joseph Raymond Massey, *Admn*
EMP: 5 **EST:** 2016
SALES (est): 150.74K **Privately Held**
SIC: 3949 Lures, fishing: artificial

(G-12952)
LAKE HOUSE ENTERPRISES INC
Also Called: Mr Handyman Western Wake Cnty
4104 Ridgebluffs Ct (27603-8822)
PHONE.............................919 424-3780
Bruce Foster, *Prin*
EMP: 7 **EST:** 2010
SALES (est): 88.95K **Privately Held**
SIC: 3732 Boatbuilding and repairing

(G-12953)
LAND AND LOFT LLC
Also Called: Lie Loft
701 Georgetown Rd (27608-2703)
PHONE.............................315 560-7060
Luke Davis, *CEO*
EMP: 5 **EST:** 2015
SALES (est): 239.04K **Privately Held**
SIC: 2741 5941 Art copy: publishing and printing; Golf goods and equipment

(G-12954)
LANDMARK PRINTING INC
901 W Hodges St (27608-1704)
PHONE.............................919 833-5151
Teresa Davis, *Prin*
Jerry Davis, *Prin*
EMP: 6 **EST:** 1989
SALES (est): 461.82K **Privately Held**
Web: www.landmarkprintingink.com
SIC: 2752 Offset printing

(G-12955)
LANDMARK PRINTING CO INC
901 W Hodges St (27608-1704)
PHONE.............................919 833-5151

GEOGRAPHIC SECTION
Raleigh - Wake County (G-12979)

Teresa Davis, *Pr*
Tim Davis, *Pr*
Jerry Davis, *VP*
EMP: 6 **EST:** 1982
SQ FT: 3,500
SALES (est): 477.31K **Privately Held**
SIC: 2752 Offset printing

(G-12956)
LANE CONSTRUCTION CORPORATION
3010 Gresham Lake Rd (27615-4221)
PHONE.................919 876-4550
Eddie Spencer, *Mgr*
EMP: 298
SALES (corp-wide): 7.95B **Privately Held**
Web: www.laneconstruct.com
SIC: 1611 2951 Highway and street paving contractor; Asphalt paving mixtures and blocks
HQ: The Lane Construction Corporation
90 Fieldstone Ct
Cheshire CT 06410
203 235-3351

(G-12957)
LANGLEY & HUTHER RF TECH
3304 E Annaley Dr (27604-3957)
PHONE.................919 880-4968
Evan Pallesen, *Owner*
EMP: 4 **EST:** 2012
SALES (est): 140K **Privately Held**
SIC: 3825 Radio frequency measuring equipment

(G-12958)
LARRYS BEANS INC
1507 Gavin St (27608-2613)
PHONE.................919 828-1234
Larry Larson, *Pr*
Kevin Bobal, *VP*
▲ **EMP:** 25 **EST:** 1993
SQ FT: 8,700
SALES (est): 4.87MM **Privately Held**
Web: www.larryscoffee.com
SIC: 5149 2095 2087 Coffee, green or roasted; Roasted coffee; Flavoring extracts and syrups, nec

(G-12959)
LATINO COMMUNICATIONS INC
150 Fayetteville St Ste 110 (27601-1395)
PHONE.................919 645-1680
Federico Van Gelderen, *Brnch Mgr*
EMP: 18
SALES (corp-wide): 4.65MM **Privately Held**
Web: www.quepasamedia.com
SIC: 2711 7313 4832 Newspapers: publishing only, not printed on site; Newspaper advertising representative; Radio broadcasting stations
PA: Latino Communications, Inc.
3067 Waughtown St
Winston Salem NC 27107
336 714-2823

(G-12960)
LAWS SIGN GROUP LLC
3119 Belvin Dr (27609-7801)
PHONE.................919 755-3632
Tanya Haley, *Admn*
EMP: 5 **EST:** 2015
SALES (est): 82.74K **Privately Held**
SIC: 3993 Signs and advertising specialties

(G-12961)
LC FOODS LLC
3809 Frazier Dr Ste 101 (27610-1358)
PHONE.................919 510-6688
Glen A Frederich, *Prin*
EMP: 6 **EST:** 2010
SALES (est): 676.89K **Privately Held**
Web: www.lowcarbfoods.com
SIC: 5499 2051 2099 2046 Health foods; Bread, cake, and related products; Pasta, uncooked: packaged with other ingredients; Wheat gluten

(G-12962)
LE SOIGNEUR CANVAS LLC
10611 Lanier Club Dr Apt 305 (27617-8536)
PHONE.................910 670-3620
Aysa Lane, *Owner*
EMP: 4 **EST:** 2020
SALES (est): 73.4K **Privately Held**
SIC: 2211 Canvas

(G-12963)
LEA AID ACQUISITION COMPANY
Also Called: Lea Aid
1717 S Saunders St (27603-2313)
P.O. Box 26688 (27611-6688)
PHONE.................919 872-6210
Paige Briggs, *Pr*
EMP: 16 **EST:** 2012
SALES (est): 5.57MM **Privately Held**
Web: www.leacorp.com
SIC: 5049 5099 3663 3577 Law enforcement equipment and supplies; Video and audio equipment; Radio broadcasting and communications equipment; Encoders, computer peripheral equipment

(G-12964)
LEARNPLATFORM INC
Also Called: Lea R N
509 W North St (27603-1414)
PHONE.................919 247-5998
Karl Rectanus, *CEO*
EMP: 4 **EST:** 2014
SALES (est): 1.05MM **Privately Held**
Web: www.learnplatform.com
SIC: 7372 7379 8748 Educational computer software; Online services technology consultants; Test development and evaluation service

(G-12965)
LEGALIS DMS LLC
1315 Oakwood Ave (27610-2247)
PHONE.................919 741-8260
Craig Mcgannon, *CEO*
Robert Almoney, *Pr*
Brandie Beebe, *COO*
EMP: 11 **EST:** 2014
SQ FT: 27,000
SALES (est): 883.46K **Privately Held**
Web: www.legalis.com
SIC: 7334 4226 7389 7374 Photocopying and duplicating services; Document and office records storage; Document storage service; Optical scanning data service

(G-12966)
LEIVA STRINGS INC
3653 Campbell Rd (27606-4433)
PHONE.................919 538-6269
Ahmad Abdel-ghani, *Prin*
EMP: 5 **EST:** 2010
SALES (est): 165.47K **Privately Held**
Web: www.mauriciovelez.com
SIC: 3931 Violins and parts

(G-12967)
LEOFORCE LLC
500 W Peace St (27603-1102)
PHONE.................919 539-5434
Madhusudan Modugu, *Managing Member*
Amit Singh, *
EMP: 28 **EST:** 2013
SALES (est): 4.33MM **Privately Held**
Web: www.leoforce.com
SIC: 7372 Application computer software

(G-12968)
LEONARD ALUM UTLITY BLDNGS INC
Also Called: Leonard Building & Truck ACC
4239 Capital Blvd (27604-4310)
PHONE.................919 872-4442
Thomas Brown, *Mgr*
EMP: 7
SALES (corp-wide): 98.91MM **Privately Held**
Web: www.leonardusa.com
SIC: 3448 3713 3089 3714 Prefabricated metal buildings; Truck tops; Molding primary plastics; Motor vehicle parts and accessories
PA: Leonard Aluminum Utility Buildings, Inc.
630 W Indpndnce Blvd
Mount Airy NC 27030
336 789-5018

(G-12969)
LIEBEL-FLARSHEIM COMPANY LLC
8800 Durant Rd (27616-3104)
PHONE.................919 878-2930
Chris Guerdan, *Mgr*
EMP: 137
SALES (corp-wide): 477.14MM **Privately Held**
SIC: 3841 2835 Diagnostic apparatus, medical; Diagnostic substances
HQ: Liebel-Flarsheim Company Llc
1034 S Brentwood Blvd
Saint Louis MO 63117
314 376-4768

(G-12970)
LIGHTING
1608 N Market Dr (27609-2501)
PHONE.................919 828-0351
EMP: 4 **EST:** 2020
SALES (est): 26.29K **Privately Held**
SIC: 7629 5719 3646 1731 Electrical repair shops; Miscellaneous homefurnishings; Commercial lighting fixtures; Electrical work

(G-12971)
LIGHTNING PRTCTION SYSTEMS LLC
Also Called: VFC Lightning Protection
5901 Triangle Dr (27617-4742)
PHONE.................252 213-9900
Kirk John Partridge, *Brnch Mgr*
EMP: 76
Web: www.vfclp.com
SIC: 3643 Lightning protection equipment
PA: Lightning Protection Systems, Llc
90 Cutler Dr
North Salt Lake UT 84054

(G-12972)
LILLIANONLINE LLC
3641 Top Of The Pines Ct (27604-5053)
P.O. Box 40066 (27629-0066)
PHONE.................919 850-4594
Lillian L Thompson, *Owner*
EMP: 5 **EST:** 2018
SALES (est): 49.59K **Privately Held**
Web: www.lillianonline.us
SIC: 2741 Miscellaneous publishing

(G-12973)
LINES AND LINEAGE LLC
809 Munt Vrnon Rd Ste 103 (27607)
PHONE.................919 783-7517
Richard Guirlinger, *Prin*
EMP: 5 **EST:** 2015
SALES (est): 81.71K **Privately Held**
SIC: 2741 Miscellaneous publishing

(G-12974)
LIPSTICK MINISTRIES INC
4809 Elmhurst Ridge Ct (27616-5063)
PHONE.................910 228-0097
Rochelle Merrell, *Prin*
EMP: 4 **EST:** 2015
SALES (est): 59.76K **Privately Held**
SIC: 2844 Lipsticks

(G-12975)
LITHO PRITING INC
Also Called: Lithography Design
1501 S Blount St (27603-2507)
P.O. Box 26344 (27611-6344)
PHONE.................919 755-9542
Carl Dereth, *Pr*
Elizabeth Dereth, *VP*
EMP: 5 **EST:** 1990
SQ FT: 19,000
SALES (est): 491.75K **Privately Held**
SIC: 2752 Offset printing

(G-12976)
LLS INVESTMENTS INC (PA)
Also Called: Craters and Freighters Raleigh
3400 Lake Woodard Dr (27604-3854)
P.O. Box 98895 (27624-8895)
PHONE.................919 662-7283
Evan Lennon, *Pr*
John Lennon, *Treas*
EMP: 10 **EST:** 2011
SALES (est): 2.12MM
SALES (corp-wide): 2.12MM **Privately Held**
Web: www.cratersandfreightersraleigh.com
SIC: 4783 2653 5113 4731 Packing and crating; Corrugated and solid fiber boxes; Shipping supplies; Freight transportation arrangement

(G-12977)
LM SHEA LLC
8201 Candelaria Dr (27616-5860)
PHONE.................919 608-1901
EMP: 4 **EST:** 2020
SALES (est): 54K **Privately Held**
SIC: 2339 6799 Women's and misses' accessories; Real estate investors, except property operators

(G-12978)
LOBBYGUARD SOLUTIONS LLC
4700 Six Forks Rd Ste 300 (27609-5244)
P.O. Box 4458 (77210-4458)
PHONE.................919 785-3301
Kevin Allen, *Pr*
EMP: 15 **EST:** 2005
SALES (est): 2.52MM
SALES (corp-wide): 11.35MM **Privately Held**
Web: www.lobbyguard.com
SIC: 7372 Business oriented computer software
PA: Raptor Technologies, Llc
2900 North Loop W Ste 900
Houston TX 77092
713 880-8902

(G-12979)
LONG LIFE LIGHTING INC
8810 Westgate Park Dr Ste 100 (27617-4821)
P.O. Box 91057 (27675-1057)
PHONE.................919 833-1292
William P Flythe, *Pr*
EMP: 4 **EST:** 1967

Raleigh - Wake County (G-12980)

SQ FT: 5,000
SALES (est): 954.92K **Privately Held**
Web: www.lightbulbspecialist.com
SIC: **5063** 3531 Light bulbs and related supplies; Ballast distributors

(G-12980)
LS OF RALEIGH
10208 Cerny St Ste 210 (27617-7885)
PHONE..................................919 457-0340
EMP: 5 EST: 2018
SALES (est): 69.4K **Privately Held**
SIC: **3993** Signs and advertising specialties

(G-12981)
LUMEOVA INC
3801 Lake Boone Trl Ste 260 (27607-0044)
PHONE..................................908 229-4651
Mohammad Khatibzadeh, *CEO*
EMP: 5 EST: 2014
SALES (est): 500.7K **Privately Held**
Web: www.lumeova.com
SIC: **3674** Monolithic integrated circuits (solid state)

(G-12982)
LUXEMARK COMPANY
6909 Glenwood Ave Ste 106 (27612-7101)
PHONE..................................919 863-0101
Michael Armstrong, *Pr*
EMP: 4 EST: 2008
SALES (est): 465.9K **Privately Held**
Web: www.luxemarkcompany.com
SIC: **2434** Wood kitchen cabinets

(G-12983)
LUXURY ESCAPES LLC
8480 Honeycutt Rd Ste 200 (27615-2261)
PHONE..................................706 373-8500
Jasmyne Snow, *Managing Member*
EMP: 12
SALES (corp-wide): 198.48K **Privately Held**
SIC: **2411** Logging
PA: Luxury Escapes Llc
 7319 Mtthews Mint Hl Rd S
 Mint Hill NC 28227
 706 373-8500

(G-12984)
LXD RESEARCH & DISPLAY LLC
7516 Precision Dr Ste 100 (27617-8748)
PHONE..................................919 600-6440
▲ EMP: 15 EST: 2010
SALES (est): 2.19MM **Privately Held**
Web: www.lxdinc.com
SIC: **3679** Liquid crystal displays (LCD)

(G-12985)
M2 OPTICS INC
5621 Departure Dr Ste 117 (27616-1911)
PHONE..................................919 342-5619
Kevin Miller, *CEO*
EMP: 4
SALES (corp-wide): 714.47K **Privately Held**
Web: www.m2optics.com
SIC: **1731** 3699 3675 3082 Electrical work; Electrical equipment and supplies, nec; Electronic capacitors; Unsupported plastics profile shapes
PA: M2 Optics, Inc.
 100 Parksouth Ln
 Holly Springs NC 27540
 919 342-5619

(G-12986)
MADIX
2326 Hales Rd (27608-1446)
PHONE..................................804 456-3007
Clayton Allen, *Prin*
EMP: 7 EST: 2010
SALES (est): 75.77K **Privately Held**
Web: www.madixinc.com
SIC: **2542** Partitions and fixtures, except wood

(G-12987)
MAGAZINE NAKIA LASHAWN
Also Called: Hair Collection, The
2833 Roundleaf Ct (27604-5474)
PHONE..................................919 875-1156
Nakia L Magazine, *Owner*
EMP: 7 EST: 2007
SALES (est): 200.87K **Privately Held**
SIC: **2721** Magazines: publishing and printing

(G-12988)
MAGNA READY LLC
7721 Harps Mill Rd (27615-5426)
PHONE..................................617 909-4166
EMP: 4 EST: 2019
SALES (est): 115.38K **Privately Held**
Web: www.magnaready.com
SIC: **2381** Fabric dress and work gloves

(G-12989)
MAJORPHARMA US INC
4801 Glenwood Ave (27612-3856)
PHONE..................................919 799-2010
EMP: 5 EST: 2017
SALES (est): 403.43K **Privately Held**
Web: www.major-pharma.com
SIC: **2834** Pharmaceutical preparations

(G-12990)
MAKHTESHIM AGAN NORTH AMER INC (DH)
Also Called: Adama US
8601 Six Forks Rd Ste 300 (27615-2965)
PHONE..................................919 256-9300
Jake Brodsgaard, *CEO*
Joseph Mark Hough,
Craig Lupton-smith, *CFO*
◆ EMP: 50 EST: 1991
SQ FT: 12,000
SALES (est): 107.43MM **Privately Held**
Web: www.manainc.com
SIC: **2879** Agricultural chemicals, nec
HQ: Adama Ltd.
 No.93, Beijing East Road, Shashi Dist.
 Jingzhou HB 43400

(G-12991)
MALLINCKRODT LLC
8801 Capital Blvd (27616-3116)
PHONE..................................919 878-2800
Keitha Buckingham, *Brnch Mgr*
EMP: 18
Web: www.mallinckrodt.com
SIC: **2834** Pharmaceutical preparations
HQ: Mallinckrodt Llc
 675 Jmes S Mcdonnell Blvd
 Hazelwood MO 63042
 314 654-2000

(G-12992)
MALLINCKRODT LLC
8800 Durant Rd (27616-3104)
PHONE..................................919 878-2900
Michael Collins, *Brnch Mgr*
EMP: 6
Web: www.mallinckrodt.com
SIC: **2834** 3829 3841 2833 Pharmaceutical preparations; Medical diagnostic systems, nuclear; Catheters; Codeine and derivatives
HQ: Mallinckrodt Llc
 675 Jmes S Mcdonnell Blvd
 Hazelwood MO 63042
 314 654-2000

(G-12993)
MAMMOTH INDUSTRIES LLC
8013 Wesley Farm Dr (27616-3255)
PHONE..................................919 749-8183
Kevin Murray, *Prin*
EMP: 4 EST: 2018
SALES (est): 64.56K **Privately Held**
SIC: **3999** Manufacturing industries, nec

(G-12994)
MARIETTA MARTIN MATERIALS INC
Also Called: Martin Marietta Aggregates
6028 Triangle Dr (27617-4743)
PHONE..................................919 788-4392
Todd Tucker, *Mgr*
EMP: 15
Web: www.martinmarietta.com
SIC: **1422** Crushed and broken limestone
PA: Martin Marietta Materials Inc
 4123 Parklake Ave
 Raleigh NC 27612

(G-12995)
MARISCOS NAYARIT CORP INC
1428 Garner Station Blvd (27603-3600)
PHONE..................................919 615-4347
Ruth Guerra, *CEO*
EMP: 28
SALES (est): 1.2MM **Privately Held**
SIC: **2599** Bar, restaurant and cafeteria furniture

(G-12996)
MARK JOHNSON
204 Plainview Ave (27604-2330)
PHONE..................................919 834-1157
Mark Johnson, *Prin*
EMP: 4 EST: 2017
SALES (est): 68.79K **Privately Held**
SIC: **3861** Photographic equipment and supplies

(G-12997)
MARK L WOOD
1140 Stone Kirk Dr (27614-7289)
PHONE..................................919 977-6507
Mark L Wood, *Prin*
EMP: 4 EST: 2015
SALES (est): 122.26K **Privately Held**
SIC: **2431** Millwork

(G-12998)
MARKET OF RALEIGH LLC
4111 New Bern Ave (27610-1372)
PHONE..................................919 212-2100
EMP: 4 EST: 2019
SALES (est): 300K **Privately Held**
Web: www.theraleighmarket.com
SIC: **2519** Furniture, household: glass, fiberglass, and plastic

(G-12999)
MARTIN MARIETTA MATERIALS INC
Also Called: Aggregates Div
4123 Parklake Ave (27612-2309)
P.O. Box 30013 (27622-0013)
PHONE..................................360 424-3441
Rosa Naprstek, *CFO*
EMP: 11
Web: www.martinmarietta.com
SIC: **1422** 1442 Cement rock, crushed and broken-quarrying; Construction sand and gravel
PA: Martin Marietta Materials Inc
 4123 Parklake Ave
 Raleigh NC 27612

(G-13000)
MARTIN MARIETTA MATERIALS INC
Also Called: Martin Marietta Aggregates
2501 Blue Ridge Rd (27607-0159)
PHONE..................................919 863-4305
EMP: 7
Web: www.martinmarietta.com
SIC: **1423** Crushed and broken granite
PA: Martin Marietta Materials Inc
 4123 Parklake Ave
 Raleigh NC 27612

(G-13001)
MARTIN MARIETTA MATERIALS INC (PA)
Also Called: Martin Marietta
4123 Parklake Ave (27612-2309)
P.O. Box 30013 (27622-0013)
PHONE..................................919 781-4550
C Howard Nye, *Ch Bd*
Roselyn R Bar, *Corporate Secretary*
James A J Nickolas, *Sr VP*
Craig M Latorre, *Chief Human Resources Officer*
Robert J Cardin, *CAO*
◆ EMP: 150 EST: 1993
SALES (est): 6.16B **Publicly Held**
Web: www.martinmarietta.com
SIC: **1423** 1422 1442 3295 Crushed and broken granite; Crushed and broken limestone; Construction sand and gravel; Magnesite, crude: ground, calcined, or dead-burned

(G-13002)
MARTIN MARIETTA MATERIALS INC
2235 Gateway Access Pt Ste 400 (27607-3076)
PHONE..................................919 664-1700
Ron Kopplin, *Div Pres*
EMP: 9
Web: www.martinmarietta.com
SIC: **3273** Ready-mixed concrete
PA: Martin Marietta Materials Inc
 4123 Parklake Ave
 Raleigh NC 27612

(G-13003)
MARTINEZ WLDG FABRICATION CORP
2901 Carpenter Pond Rd (27613-8165)
PHONE..................................919 957-8904
EMP: 18 EST: 2020
SALES (est): 972.72K **Privately Held**
SIC: **3441** Fabricated structural metal

(G-13004)
MASTER MARKETING GROUP LLC (PA)
4801 Glenwood Ave Ste 310 (27612-3857)
PHONE..................................870 932-4491
Eran Salu, *Managing Member*
EMP: 4 EST: 2014
SALES (est): 4.11MM
SALES (corp-wide): 4.11MM **Privately Held**
SIC: **2752** Offset printing

(G-13005)
MASTERS CRAFTSMAN
832 Purser Dr Ste 202 (27603-4167)
PHONE..................................919 800-0096
EMP: 5 EST: 2012
SALES (est): 70.3K **Privately Held**
Web: www.raleighmurphybeds.com
SIC: **2431** Millwork

(G-13006)
MASTERS MOVING SERVICES INC
4220 Gallatree Ln (27616-0728)
PHONE..................................919 523-9836
William Porter, *Pr*
EMP: 6 EST: 2008

GEOGRAPHIC SECTION
Raleigh - Wake County (G-13028)

SALES (est): 274.84K **Privately Held**
SIC: **2519** Household furniture, nec

(G-13007)
MATRIX TECHNOLOGIES INC
3109 Poplarwood Ct Ste 217 (27604)
PHONE..............................414 291-1000
Novena Droneblli, *Prin*
EMP: 8 EST: 2017
SALES (est): 66.08K **Privately Held**
Web: www.matrixti.com
SIC: **7372** Prepackaged software

(G-13008)
MAVERICK METALWORKS LLC
1108 Vannstone Dr (27603-8479)
PHONE..............................919 609-1274
Ryan Holmes, *Prin*
EMP: 5 EST: 2019
SALES (est): 193.16K **Privately Held**
SIC: **7692** Welding repair

(G-13009)
MAYNE PHARMA COMMERCIAL LLC
3301 Benson Dr Ste 401 (27609-7380)
PHONE..............................984 242-1400
Shawn Patrick O'brien, *CEO*
Wes Edwards, *
EMP: 350 EST: 1994
SQ FT: 44,000
SALES (est): 198.86MM **Publicly Held**
Web: www.maynepharma.com
SIC: **2834** Pharmaceutical preparations
PA: Mayne Pharma Group Limited
    1538 Main North Road
    Salisbury South SA 5106

(G-13010)
MAYNE PHARMA VENTURES LLC
3301 Benson Dr Ste 401 (27609-7380)
PHONE..............................252 752-3800
Shawn O'brien, *CEO*
Stefan Cross, *Pr*
John Ross, *VP*
Nick Freeman, *CFO*
EMP: 5 EST: 2014
SALES (est): 974.92K **Publicly Held**
Web: www.maynepharma.com
SIC: **2834** Pharmaceutical preparations
PA: Mayne Pharma Group Limited
    1538 Main North Road
    Salisbury South SA 5106

(G-13011)
MC CLATCHY INTERACTIVE USA
1101 Haynes St (27604-1455)
PHONE..............................919 861-1200
Christian A Hendrick, *Prin*
EMP: 12 EST: 2013
SALES (est): 879.67K **Privately Held**
Web: www.mcclatchy.com
SIC: **2711** Newspapers, publishing and printing

(G-13012)
MECHA INC
6204 Daimler Way Ste 107 (27607-5479)
PHONE..............................919 858-0372
Bobby Boyd, *Pr*
EMP: 13 EST: 2008
SQ FT: 6,000
SALES (est): 1.3MM **Privately Held**
Web: www.mechainc.com
SIC: **3599** 3499 Custom machinery; Metal household articles

(G-13013)
MEDAPTUS INC
4917 Waters Edge Dr Ste 135 (27606-2380)
PHONE..............................617 896-4000
Dennis Mitchelle, *Brnch Mgr*
EMP: 8
SALES (corp-wide): 4.64MM **Privately Held**
Web: www.medaptus.com
SIC: **7372** Business oriented computer software
PA: Medaptus, Inc.
    176 Federal St Fl 3
    Boston MA 02110
    617 896-4000

(G-13014)
MEDVERTICAL LLC
Also Called: Beewell
3725 National Dr Ste 160 (27612-4832)
PHONE..............................919 867-4268
Alden Parsons, *Managing Member*
EMP: 6 EST: 2015
SALES (est): 455.29K **Privately Held**
SIC: **7372** Application computer software

(G-13015)
MERCHANTS METALS LLC
Also Called: Merchants Metals
6512 Mount Herman Rd (27617-9401)
PHONE..............................919 598-8471
EMP: 7
SALES (corp-wide): 1.06B **Privately Held**
Web: www.merchantsmetals.com
SIC: **3496** Miscellaneous fabricated wire products
HQ: Merchants Metals Llc
    3 Ravinia Dr Ste 1750
    Atlanta GA 30346
    770 741-0300

(G-13016)
MERGE LLC
1410 Hillsborough St (27605-1829)
PHONE..............................919 832-3924
EMP: 9 EST: 2003
SQ FT: 2,000
SALES (est): 978.24K **Privately Held**
Web: www.mergellc.com
SIC: **7336** 3993 Commercial art and graphic design; Advertising artwork

(G-13017)
MERHI GLASS INC
6925 Old Wake Forest Rd (27616-3414)
PHONE..............................919 961-5930
EMP: 4 EST: 2019
SALES (est): 207.86K **Privately Held**
Web: www.merhiglass.com
SIC: **3442** 1799 1522 1521 Metal doors, sash, and trim; Special trade contractors, nec; Residential construction, nec; Single-family housing construction

(G-13018)
MERIDIAN GRANITE COMPANY
2710 Wycliff Rd (27607-3033)
PHONE..............................919 781-4550
EMP: 24 EST: 1997
SALES (est): 2.02MM **Publicly Held**
SIC: **1423** Crushed and broken granite
PA: Martin Marietta Materials Inc
    4123 Parklake Ave
    Raleigh NC 27612

(G-13019)
MERZ INCORPORATED
Also Called: Merz
6501 Six Forks Rd (27615-6515)
P.O. Box 18806 (27419-8806)
PHONE..............................919 582-8196
▲ EMP: 135 EST: 1986
SQ FT: 60,000
SALES (est): 79.98MM
SALES (corp-wide): 2.67MM **Privately Held**
Web: www.merzusa.com
SIC: **2834** Pharmaceutical preparations
HQ: Merz Pharma Gmbh & Co. Kgaa
    Eckenheimer Landstr. 100
    Frankfurt Am Main HE 60318
    6915030

(G-13020)
MERZ NORTH AMERICA INC (DH)
Also Called: Neocutis
6501 Six Forks Rd (27615-6515)
PHONE..............................919 582-8000
Bob Rhatigan, *CEO*
Patrick Urban, *Pr*
Alana Sine, *VP*
Matt Anderson, *Technology Operations Vice President*
Joseph Barry, *CCO*
EMP: 16 EST: 1999
SQ FT: 20,000
SALES (est): 149.66MM
SALES (corp-wide): 2.67MM **Privately Held**
Web: www.merzusa.com
SIC: **2834** Pharmaceutical preparations
HQ: Merz Pharma Gmbh & Co. Kgaa
    Eckenheimer Landstr. 100
    Frankfurt Am Main HE 60318
    6915030

(G-13021)
MERZ PHARMACEUTICALS LLC
6601 Six Forks Rd Ste 430 (27615-6590)
PHONE..............................919 582-8000
Kevin O Brien, *Pr*
Terry Crandall, *
Chad Duncan, *
Alana Sine, *
Bill Edwards, *
▲ EMP: 90 EST: 1951
SALES (est): 49.91MM
SALES (corp-wide): 2.67MM **Privately Held**
Web: www.merz.com
SIC: **2834** Pharmaceutical preparations
HQ: Merz Pharmaceuticals Gmbh
    Eckenheimer Landstr. 100
    Frankfurt Am Main HE 60318
    6915031

(G-13022)
METRO PRODUCTIONS INC
6005 Chapel Hill Rd (27607-5109)
PHONE..............................919 851-6420
Charles Underwood Senior, *Pr*
Charles Underwood Junior, *VP*
Clara Underwood, *Sec*
EMP: 12 EST: 1988
SQ FT: 6,500
SALES (est): 949.48K **Privately Held**
Web: www.metroproductions.com
SIC: **2752** 7336 7812 7331 Offset printing; Commercial art and graphic design; Video production; Mailing service

(G-13023)
METTECH INC (PA)
105 S Wilmington St (27601-1431)
P.O. Box 25609 (27611-5609)
PHONE..............................919 833-9460
Michael Mettrey, *Pr*
Iris Mettrey, *VP*
▲ EMP: 9 EST: 1970
SQ FT: 9,000
SALES (est): 1.19MM
SALES (corp-wide): 1.19MM **Privately Held**
Web: www.met-techbilliards.com
SIC: **5941** 5091 3949 Pool and billiard tables; Billiard equipment and supplies; Billiard and pool equipment and supplies, general

(G-13024)
MICHAEL PARKER CABINETRY
Also Called: Eidolon Designs
414 Dupont Cir Ste 4 (27603-2083)
PHONE..............................919 833-5117
Micheal Parker, *Pr*
Anne Cowperthwaite, *VP*
EMP: 5 EST: 1984
SALES (est): 486.92K **Privately Held**
Web: www.eidolondesigns.com
SIC: **2511** 2521 2541 Wood household furniture; Wood office furniture; Wood partitions and fixtures

(G-13025)
MICRO EPSILON AMER LTD PARTNR (PA)
Also Called: Micro Epsilon America
8120 Brownleigh Dr (27617-7410)
PHONE..............................919 787-9707
Richard Auxer, *Genl Pt*
Karl Wisspeintner, *Pt*
▲ EMP: 5 EST: 1998
SQ FT: 1,000
SALES (est): 1.62MM
SALES (corp-wide): 1.62MM **Privately Held**
Web: www.micro-epsilon.com
SIC: **3829** Measuring and controlling devices, nec

(G-13026)
MICRO-OHM CORPORATION
14460 Falls Of Neuse Rd Ste 149-273 (27614-8227)
P.O. Box 99748 (27624-9748)
PHONE..............................800 845-5167
EMP: 4 EST: 2010
SALES (est): 1.63MM
SALES (corp-wide): 8.25B **Publicly Held**
Web: www.microohm.com
SIC: **3674** Solar cells
PA: On Semiconductor Corporation
    5701 N Pima Rd
    Scottsdale AZ 85250
    602 244-6600

(G-13027)
MICROCHIP TECHNOLOGY INC
7901 Strickland Rd Ste 101 (27615-3189)
PHONE..............................919 844-7510
EMP: 10
SALES (corp-wide): 8.44B **Publicly Held**
Web: www.microchip.com
SIC: **3674** Microcircuits, integrated (semiconductor)
PA: Microchip Technology Inc
    2355 W Chandler Blvd
    Chandler AZ 85224
    480 792-7200

(G-13028)
MICROTHERMICS INC
3216 Wellington Ct Ste 102 (27615-4122)
PHONE..............................919 878-8045
John J Miles, *Pr*
David M Miles, *VP*
▲ EMP: 12 EST: 1989
SQ FT: 7,200
SALES (est): 2.49MM **Privately Held**
Web: www.microthermics.com
SIC: **3556** 8742 Beverage machinery; Food and beverage consultant

Raleigh - Wake County (G-13029)

(G-13029)
MID-ATLANTIC CRANE AND EQP CO
3224 Northside Dr (27615-4125)
PHONE................919 790-3535
Mitchell E Filip, *Pr*
▲ **EMP:** 25 **EST:** 1980
SQ FT: 10,000
SALES (est): 12.82MM **Privately Held**
Web: www.midatlanticcrane.com
SIC: 5084 3531 Materials handling machinery; Aerial work platforms: hydraulic/elec. truck/carrier mounted

(G-13030)
MID-ATLANTIC SPECIALTIES INC
5200 Trademark Dr Ste 102 (27610-3087)
P.O. Box 98749 (27624-8749)
PHONE................919 212-1939
Thomas Harward, *Prin*
EMP: 4 **EST:** 2007
SALES (est): 951.27K **Privately Held**
Web: www.midatlanticspecialties.com
SIC: 5033 3296 Insulation materials; Acoustical board and tile, mineral wool

(G-13031)
MIDLAND BOTTLING LLC
4141 Parklake Ave Ste 600 (27612-2380)
PHONE................919 865-2300
David Obryant, *Admn*
EMP: 6 **EST:** 2013
SALES (est): 162.08K **Privately Held**
SIC: 2086 Carbonated soft drinks, bottled and canned

(G-13032)
MILL ART WOOD
1500 Capital Blvd (27603-1122)
PHONE................919 828-7376
Rob Christian, *Pr*
EMP: 7 **EST:** 2011
SALES (est): 362.29K **Privately Held**
Web: www.millwoodart.com
SIC: 3553 Woodworking machinery

(G-13033)
MINCAR GROUP INC
215 Tryon Rd (27603-3527)
PHONE................919 772-7170
Josephine D Jones, *Pr*
Ronnie Jones, *VP*
Dwight Jones, *Sec*
EMP: 9 **EST:** 1995
SQ FT: 7,500
SALES (est): 1.01MM **Privately Held**
Web: www.morethanamailbox.com
SIC: 3444 Mail (post office) collection or storage boxes, sheet metal

(G-13034)
MIRCHANDANI INC
3904 Peppertree Pl (27604-3443)
PHONE................919 872-8871
Mike Mirchandani, *Prin*
EMP: 4 **EST:** 2002
SALES (est): 386.53K **Privately Held**
SIC: 2893 Printing ink

(G-13035)
MISSION SRGCAL INNOVATIONS LLC
9004 Shellwood Ct (27617-7354)
PHONE................810 965-7455
EMP: 5 **EST:** 2019
SALES (est): 284.9K **Privately Held**
Web: www.safeviewsurgery.com
SIC: 3841 Surgical and medical instruments

(G-13036)
MJPC TRANSPORT LLC (PA)
3201 Edwards Mill Rd Ste 141 (27612-5385)
PHONE................877 590-9512
EMP: 7 **EST:** 2021
SALES (est): 100K
SALES (corp-wide): 100K **Privately Held**
Web: www.24hourpassportandvisas.com
SIC: 3537 Trucks, tractors, loaders, carriers, and similar equipment

(G-13037)
MLF COMPANY LLC
3248 Lake Woodard Dr (27604-3659)
PHONE................919 231-9401
Michael Ficalora, *Pr*
EMP: 14 **EST:** 2000
SQ FT: 8,000
SALES (est): 2MM **Privately Held**
Web: www.ficaloramfg.com
SIC: 2514 3446 Household furniture: upholstered on metal frames; Architectural metalwork

(G-13038)
MON MACARON LLC
111 Seaboard Ave Ste 118 (27604-1152)
PHONE................984 200-1387
Autumn C Butler, *Managing Member*
EMP: 8 **EST:** 2019
SALES (est): 453.55K **Privately Held**
Web: www.monmacaron.us
SIC: 2051 Bakery: wholesale or wholesale/retail combined

(G-13039)
MONTH9 BOOKS LLC (PA)
4208 Six Forks Rd Ste 1000 (27609-5733)
PHONE................919 645-5786
EMP: 5 **EST:** 2014
SALES (est): 555.87K
SALES (corp-wide): 555.87K **Privately Held**
Web: www.month9books.com
SIC: 2741 Miscellaneous publishing

(G-13040)
MOON AND LOLA INC (PA)
2024 Saint Marys St (27608-2249)
PHONE................919 306-2257
Kelly Shatat, *Pr*
EMP: 6 **EST:** 2012
SALES (est): 2.33MM
SALES (corp-wide): 2.33MM **Privately Held**
Web: www.moonandlola.com
SIC: 5137 3915 Women's and children's accessories; Jewel cutting, drilling, polishing, recutting, or setting

(G-13041)
MOORE PRINTING & GRAPHICS INC
Also Called: Lewis Moore Prtg & Graphics
5320 Departure Dr (27616-1836)
PHONE................919 821-3293
Sharry Layton, *Pr*
Barbara Moore, *Sec*
EMP: 24 **EST:** 1977
SQ FT: 4,500
SALES (est): 715.14K **Privately Held**
Web: www.mooreprintingandgraphics.com
SIC: 7334 2752 Photocopying and duplicating services; Offset printing

(G-13042)
MORDECAI BEVERAGE CO
2425 Crabtree Blvd (27604-2232)
PHONE................919 831-9125
EMP: 4 **EST:** 2020
SALES (est): 127.8K **Privately Held**
Web: www.mordecaibev.co
SIC: 2082 Beer (alcoholic beverage)

(G-13043)
MOTOR RITE INC
1001 Corporation Pkwy Ste 100 (27610)
PHONE................919 625-3653
David Brooks, *Prin*
EMP: 10 **EST:** 2002
SALES (est): 966.09K **Privately Held**
Web: www.motorrite.com
SIC: 3621 Electric motor and generator parts

(G-13044)
MOVEX USA INC
1311 Rio Falls Dr (27614-7551)
PHONE................434 616-2590
Garland Jones, *Pr*
Bill Grady, *VP*
EMP: 6 **EST:** 2015
SALES (est): 256.04K **Privately Held**
Web: www.movexii.com
SIC: 3535 Conveyors and conveying equipment

(G-13045)
MPRESSIVE SHIRT WORKS LLC
3402 Tuckland Dr (27610-3685)
PHONE................919 395-8295
Marlan A Blount, *Prin*
EMP: 5 **EST:** 2018
SALES (est): 65.02K **Privately Held**
SIC: 2752 Commercial printing, lithographic

(G-13046)
MR HARDWOOD FLOORS INC
9650 Neils Branch Rd (27603-8449)
PHONE................919 369-8027
Ronald D Howell, *Prin*
EMP: 6 **EST:** 2000
SALES (est): 182.93K **Privately Held**
SIC: 2426 Flooring, hardwood

(G-13047)
MR TOBACCO
4011 Capital Blvd Ste 125 (27604-3486)
PHONE................919 747-9052
EMP: 4 **EST:** 2012
SALES (est): 190.63K **Privately Held**
SIC: 5194 2111 Smoking tobacco; Cigarettes

(G-13048)
MRF TECHNOLOGIES LLC
622 Devereux St (27605-1504)
PHONE................919 714-2852
EMP: 5 **EST:** 2013
SALES (est): 64.49K **Privately Held**
SIC: 7372 Prepackaged software

(G-13049)
MRR SOUTHERN LLC
5842 Faringdon Pl Ste 1 (27609-3930)
PHONE................919 436-3571
Francis Hector, *Prin*
EMP: 10 **EST:** 2015
SALES (est): 640.8K **Privately Held**
SIC: 3443 Dumpsters, garbage

(G-13050)
MULCH MASTERS OF NC INC
Also Called: Mulch Masters
10200 Durant Rd (27614-9783)
PHONE................919 676-0031
Randolph Keith Caruthers, *Pr*
Catherine Caruthers, *VP*
EMP: 15 **EST:** 1993
SALES (est): 623.05K **Privately Held**
Web: www.themulchmasters.com
SIC: 2499 Mulch, wood and bark

(G-13051)
MY ALABASTER BOX LLC
5412 Cahaba Way (27616-3192)
PHONE................919 873-1442
Barbara Lennon, *Owner*
EMP: 5 **EST:** 2017
SALES (est): 76.33K **Privately Held**
Web: www.myalabasterboxllc.com
SIC: 2741 Miscellaneous publishing

(G-13052)
MYFUTURENC INC
311 New Bern Ave Unit 26246 (27611-0801)
PHONE................919 649-7834
Cecilia Holden, *Pr*
EMP: 18 **EST:** 2019
SALES (est): 1.25MM **Privately Held**
Web: www.myfuturenc.org
SIC: 3999 Education aids, devices and supplies

(G-13053)
NATIONAL AIR FILTERS INC
1109 N New Hope Rd (27610-1415)
PHONE................919 231-8596
EMP: 10 **EST:** 2010
SALES (est): 2.13MM **Privately Held**
Web: www.filtersonline.com
SIC: 3564 Filters, air: furnaces, air conditioning equipment, etc.

(G-13054)
NATIONAL CTR FOR SOCIAL IMPACT
1053 E Whitaker Mill Rd Ste 115 (27604-5311)
PHONE................984 212-2285
Daniel Demaionewton, *Ex Dir*
EMP: 6 **EST:** 2016
SALES (est): 349.67K **Privately Held**
SIC: 8742 4832 8299 3999 Human resource consulting services; Educational; Educational services; Education aids, devices and supplies

(G-13055)
NATIONAL MASTERCRAFT INDS INC
Also Called: Mastercraft
14 Glenwood Ave Ste 22 (27603-1700)
P.O. Box 27643 (27611-7643)
PHONE................919 896-8858
Barry W Carter, *Pr*
Sherry O Stegall, *Sec*
EMP: 10 **EST:** 1936
SQ FT: 12,000
SALES (est): 488.4K **Privately Held**
SIC: 2391 Curtains, window: made from purchased materials

(G-13056)
NATURAL GRANITE & MARBLE INC
3100 Stony Brook Dr Ste N1 (27604-3768)
PHONE................919 872-1508
Issam Hachicho, *Pr*
Sam Coelho, *Genl Mgr*
▲ **EMP:** 7 **EST:** 2008
SQ FT: 3,000
SALES (est): 700K **Privately Held**
Web: www.naturalgranitemarble.com
SIC: 3281 Marble, building: cut and shaped

(G-13057)
NAVIA INC
4313 Quail Hollow Dr (27609-6015)
PHONE................626 372-9791
Leonard Nelson, *Owner*
EMP: 5 **EST:** 2018
SALES (est): 47.88K **Privately Held**

Web: www.navia.ai
SIC: 7372 Prepackaged software

(G-13058)
NC SOLAR NOW INC
Also Called: NC Solar
2517 Atlantic Ave (27604-1411)
PHONE.................................919 833-9096
Stephen Nicolas, Pr
EMP: 15 EST: 2010
SALES (est): 4.89MM Privately Held
Web: www.ncsolarnow.com
SIC: 1711 3699 Solar energy contractor; Electrical equipment and supplies, nec

(G-13059)
NCI GROUP INC
Also Called: Metal Depots
5115 New Bern Ave (27610-1429)
PHONE.................................919 926-4800
Ed Collier, Mgr
EMP: 9
SALES (corp-wide): 5.58B Privately Held
Web: www.bluescopecoatedproducts.com
SIC: 3448 3446 Prefabricated metal buildings; Architectural metalwork
HQ: Nci Group, Inc.
10943 N Sam Huston Pkwy W
Houston TX 77064
281 897-7788

(G-13060)
NCLOGOWEARCOM
414 Dupont Cir (27603-2076)
PHONE.................................919 821-4646
Dave Bovue, Mgr
EMP: 5 EST: 2015
SALES (est): 293.2K Privately Held
Web: www.nclogowear.com
SIC: 2759 Screen printing

(G-13061)
NEIGHBORHOOD SMOOTHIE LLC
10115 Second Star Ct (27613-4157)
PHONE.................................919 845-5513
John Agori, Prin
EMP: 8 EST: 2014
SALES (est): 359.99K Privately Held
SIC: 2037 Frozen fruits and vegetables

(G-13062)
NEW PHOENIX AEROSPACE INC
6008 Triangle Dr Ste 101 (27617-4784)
PHONE.................................919 380-8500
Cynthia Ezami, Pr
EMP: 15 EST: 2004
SALES (est): 1.62MM Privately Held
Web: www.npaero.com
SIC: 3812 Acceleration indicators and systems components, aerospace

(G-13063)
NEWS AND OBSERVER PUBG CO (DH)
Also Called: Gold Leaf Publishers
421 Fayetteville St Ste 104 (27601-3010)
PHONE.................................919 829-4500
Orage Quarles Iii, Pr
George Mccanless, VP
▲ EMP: 700 EST: 1894
SQ FT: 20,000
SALES (est): 96.05MM
SALES (corp-wide): 709.52MM Privately Held
SIC: 2711 2741 2721 2752 Newspapers, publishing and printing; Shopping news: publishing and printing; Magazines: publishing and printing; Commercial printing, lithographic
HQ: Mcclatchy Newspapers, Inc.

1601 Alhambra Blvd # 100
Sacramento CA 95816
916 321-1855

(G-13064)
NINE THIRTEEN LLC
Also Called: Instant Imprints
5300 Atlantic Ave Ste 105 (27609-1123)
PHONE.................................919 876-8070
Sharon Sawyer, Owner
Tyron Freeman, Store Mgr
EMP: 4 EST: 2006
SALES (est): 278.13K Privately Held
Web: www.instantimprints.com
SIC: 2752 Commercial printing, lithographic

(G-13065)
NOBLE PRINTERS
5812 Triangle Dr (27617-4705)
PHONE.................................877 786-6253
EMP: 6 EST: 2017
SALES (est): 96.71K Privately Held
Web: www.nobleprinters.com
SIC: 2752 Commercial printing, lithographic

(G-13066)
NOKIA OF AMERICA CORPORATION
Also Called: Alcatel-Lucent USA
2301 Sugar Bush Rd Ste 300 (27601)
PHONE.................................919 850-6000
EMP: 7
SALES (corp-wide): 25.87B Privately Held
Web: www.nokia.com
SIC: 3674 Integrated circuits, semiconductor networks, etc.
HQ: Nokia Of America Corporation
600 Mountain Ave Ste 700
New Providence NJ 07974

(G-13067)
NORCA ENGINEERED PRODUCTS LLC
7201 Creedmoor Rd Ste 150 (27613-1688)
PHONE.................................919 846-2010
Jim Pollan, Pr
EMP: 28 EST: 1988
SALES (est): 2.5MM Privately Held
Web: www.norcaeng.com
SIC: 3325 Alloy steel castings, except investment

(G-13068)
NORTH CAROLINA DEPT LABOR
Also Called: Elevator & Amusement DVC Bur
1101 Mail Service Ctr (27699-0001)
PHONE.................................919 807-2770
Jonathan Brooks, Pr
EMP: 16
Web: labor.nc.gov
SIC: 9311 3599 Finance, taxation, and monetary policy, State government; Amusement park equipment
HQ: North Carolina Department Of Labor
4 W Edenton St
Raleigh NC 27601

(G-13069)
NORTH CAROLINA DEPT PUB SAFETY
Also Called: Enterprise Metal Tag Plant
1150 Martin Luther King Jr Blvd (27601)
PHONE.................................919 733-0867
Yonny Mclamb, Mgr
EMP: 7
SQ FT: 706,810
Web: www.correctionenterprises.com
SIC: 3555 9223 Plates, metal: engravers'; Correctional institutions

HQ: North Carolina Department Of Adult Corrections
214 W Jones St
Raleigh NC 27603

(G-13070)
NORTH CAROLINA STATE UNIV
Also Called: North Carolina State Dar Plant
Food Science Bldg Rm 12 (27695-0001)
P.O. Box 7624 (27695-0001)
PHONE.................................919 515-2760
Gary Cartwright, Mgr
EMP: 9
SALES (corp-wide): 4.81B Privately Held
Web: www.ncsu.edu
SIC: 2024 8221 Ice cream and frozen deserts; University
HQ: North Carolina State University
2601 Wolf Village Way
Raleigh NC 27607
919 515-2011

(G-13071)
NORTH CRLINA RNWABLE PRPTS LLC
176 Mine Lake Ct Ste 100 (27615-6417)
PHONE.................................407 536-5346
EMP: 5 EST: 2011
SALES (est): 1.52MM
SALES (corp-wide): 29.06B Publicly Held
SIC: 3674 Semiconductors and related devices
PA: Duke Energy Corporation
526 S Church St
Charlotte NC 28202
704 382-3853

(G-13072)
NORTH STATE SIGNS INC
553 Pylon Dr Ste D (27606-1466)
PHONE.................................919 977-7053
Cyrus Gill, Owner
EMP: 7 EST: 2016
SALES (est): 233.25K Privately Held
Web: www.northstatesigns.com
SIC: 3993 Signs and advertising specialties

(G-13073)
NORTRIA INC
8801 Fast Park Dr Ste 301 (27617-4853)
PHONE.................................919 440-3253
Bobby Butler, CEO
EMP: 12 EST: 2019
SALES (est): 1.2MM Privately Held
SIC: 2834 Pharmaceutical preparations

(G-13074)
NOVISYSTEMS INC
1315 Ileagnes Rd (27603-3432)
PHONE.................................919 205-5005
John Bass, Ex Dir
John Bass, Prin
Michael Kowolenko, CEO
EMP: 4 EST: 2018
SALES (est): 303.84K Privately Held
Web: www.novisurvey.net
SIC: 7371 7372 Computer software development; Business oriented computer software

(G-13075)
NSI LAB SOLUTIONS INC
7212 Acc Blvd (27617-8736)
PHONE.................................919 789-3000
Mark Hammersla, Pr
Deborah Hammersla, Sec
EMP: 15 EST: 1991
SQ FT: 10,000
SALES (est): 3.3MM Privately Held
Web: www.nsilabsolutions.com

SIC: 2899 Chemical preparations, nec

(G-13076)
OAK & BULL DISTILLING LLC
916 Palace Garden Way (27603-2891)
PHONE.................................978 732-4531
EMP: 5 EST: 2017
SALES (est): 64.16K Privately Held
SIC: 2085 Distilled and blended liquors

(G-13077)
OAK CITY ARTISANS LLC
2325 Woodrow Dr (27609-7626)
PHONE.................................347 738-1228
EMP: 4 EST: 2019
SALES (est): 110.68K Privately Held
Web: www.oakcityartisans.com
SIC: 2431 Millwork

(G-13078)
OAK CITY COLUMNS LLC ✪
1201 Corporation Pkwy (27610-1349)
PHONE.................................919 848-8814
James Brandon Willis, Managing Member
Leslie Willis, Managing Member
EMP: 6 EST: 2022
SALES (est): 63.22K Privately Held
SIC: 3272 Columns, concrete

(G-13079)
OAK CITY DISTILLING INC
514 Daniels St (27605-1317)
PHONE.................................919 520-4102
Philip Morris Junior, Owner
EMP: 6 EST: 2018
SALES (est): 136.25K Privately Held
SIC: 2085 Distilled and blended liquors

(G-13080)
OAK CITY SIGN SOLUTIONS INC
4904 Alpinis Dr Ste 108 (27616-1888)
PHONE.................................919 792-8077
EMP: 4 EST: 2019
SALES (est): 88.22K Privately Held
Web: www.oakcitysigns.com
SIC: 3993 Signs and advertising specialties

(G-13081)
OBJECTIVE SECURITY CORPORATION
555 Fayetteville St Ste 201 (27601-3034)
PHONE.................................415 997-9967
Grace Nordin, CEO
Thomas Nordin, Pr
EMP: 15 EST: 2003
SALES (est): 701.29K Privately Held
Web: www.objectivefs.com
SIC: 7372 Application computer software

(G-13082)
OLDCASTLE INFRASTRUCTURE INC
Also Called: NC Products
920 Withers Rd (27603-6095)
P.O. Box 27077 (27611-7077)
PHONE.................................919 772-6269
EMP: 26
SALES (corp-wide): 32.72B Privately Held
Web: www.oldcastleinfrastructure.com
SIC: 1791 3272 5013 Precast concrete structural framing or panels, placing of; Concrete products, nec; Automobile glass
HQ: Oldcastle Infrastructure, Inc.
7000 Central Pkwy Ste 800
Atlanta GA 30328
770 270-5000

(G-13083)
OLIVE WAGON LLC
8490 Honeycutt Rd Ste 106 (27615-2263)
PHONE.................................919 559-0845

Raleigh - Wake County (G-13084)

Whitney L Brown, *Prin*
EMP: 5 EST: 2012
SALES (est): 216.66K **Privately Held**
Web: www.theolivewagon.com
SIC: 2079 Olive oil

(G-13084)
OLIVENTURES INC (PA)
6325 Falls Of Neuse Rd Ste 35-122 (27615-6877)
PHONE................................800 231-2619
EMP: 4 EST: 2009
SALES (est): 228.35K
SALES (corp-wide): 228.35K **Privately Held**
SIC: 2079 Olive oil

(G-13085)
ONLY BITTERS
517 W Cabarrus St Ste A (27603-2087)
PHONE................................617 413-6571
EMP: 5 EST: 2016
SALES (est): 55.55K **Privately Held**
Web: www.crudebitters.com
SIC: 2087 Flavoring extracts and syrups, nec

(G-13086)
ONTARGET LABS INC (PA)
8605 Bell Grove Way (27615-3168)
PHONE................................919 846-3877
EMP: 5 EST: 2010
SALES (est): 260.55K **Privately Held**
SIC: 2834 Pharmaceutical preparations

(G-13087)
OPTOPOL USA INC
3915 Beryl Rd Ste 130 (27607-5609)
PHONE................................833 678-6765
Robert Padula, *Pr*
EMP: 4 EST: 2020
SALES (est): 335.5K **Privately Held**
Web: www.optopolusa.com
SIC: 3841 Ophthalmic instruments and apparatus

(G-13088)
OPULENCE OF SOUTHERN PINE
400 Daniels St (27605-1315)
PHONE................................919 467-1781
EMP: 7 EST: 2013
SALES (est): 301.67K **Privately Held**
Web: www.opulenceofsouthernpines.com
SIC: 2299 Linen fabrics

(G-13089)
ORACLE OF GOD MINISTRIES NC
Also Called: Oracle
5731 New Bern Ave (27610-9305)
PHONE................................919 522-2113
EMP: 6 EST: 2015
SALES (est): 126.29K **Privately Held**
SIC: 7372 Prepackaged software

(G-13090)
ORACLE SYSTEMS CORPORATION
Also Called: Oracle
8081 Arco Corporate Dr Ste 270 (27617)
PHONE................................919 257-2300
Frank Myers, *Brnch Mgr*
EMP: 9
SALES (corp-wide): 49.95B **Publicly Held**
SIC: 7372 Prepackaged software
HQ: Oracle Systems Corporation
500 Oracle Pkwy
Redwood City CA 94065

(G-13091)
ORIGINAL IMAGE
229 Rosehaven Dr (27609-3881)
PHONE................................919 781-0064
Gerry Belsha, *Prin*
EMP: 5 EST: 2016
SALES (est): 85.99K **Privately Held**
SIC: 3571 Electronic computers

(G-13092)
OSLO PRESS INC
2316 Foxtrot Rd (27610-5048)
PHONE................................919 606-2028
Morris Glenwood, *Prin*
EMP: 4 EST: 2008
SALES (est): 127.4K **Privately Held**
SIC: 2741 Miscellaneous publishing

(G-13093)
PACKAGING SERVICES
4112 Willow Oak Rd (27604-4729)
PHONE................................919 630-4145
EMP: 5 EST: 2010
SALES (est): 102.41K **Privately Held**
SIC: 2631 Container, packaging, and boxboard

(G-13094)
PALACE GREEN LLC
Also Called: Palace Green
4701 Violet Fields Way (27612-5661)
P.O. Box 308 (27512-0308)
PHONE................................919 827-7950
EMP: 4 EST: 2013
SALES (est): 215.78K **Privately Held**
SIC: 2033 Jams, jellies, and preserves, packaged in cans, jars, etc.

(G-13095)
PALETRIA LA MNRCA MCHACANA LLC
3901 Capital Blvd Ste 155 (27604-6072)
PHONE................................919 803-0636
Azucena Morales, *Managing Member*
EMP: 4 EST: 2015
SALES (est): 135.31K **Privately Held**
SIC: 5451 2024 Ice cream (packaged); Ice cream and frozen deserts

(G-13096)
PAMELA A ADAMS
Also Called: Insty-Prints
3812 Tarheel Dr Ste D (27609-7535)
PHONE................................919 876-5949
Pamela J Atkins Adams, *Owner*
EMP: 4 EST: 1983
SQ FT: 1,575
SALES (est): 199.66K **Privately Held**
Web: www.instyprints.com
SIC: 2752 2791 2789 Commercial printing, lithographic; Typesetting; Bookbinding and related work

(G-13097)
PAMOR FINE PRINT
5924 Crepe Myrtle Ct (27609-4245)
PHONE................................919 559-2846
Bill Griggs, *Owner*
EMP: 6 EST: 2010
SALES (est): 106.73K **Privately Held**
Web: www.pamorfineprint.com
SIC: 2752 Offset printing

(G-13098)
PAMPERING MOMS NTRAL SKIN CARE
6401 Ashire Xing Apt G (27616)
PHONE................................706 490-3083
Joselyn Sullivan, *Managing Member*
EMP: 4 EST: 2020
SALES (est): 82.4K **Privately Held**
SIC: 2844 7389 Perfumes, cosmetics and other toilet preparations; Business Activities at Non-Commercial Site

(G-13099)
PAPER SPECIALTIES INC
2708 Discovery Dr Ste J (27616-1961)
PHONE................................919 431-0028
Henry K Tingley, *Pr*
Charles Tingley, *VP*
EMP: 5 EST: 1981
SQ FT: 6,000
SALES (est): 504.81K **Privately Held**
SIC: 2675 Paper die-cutting

(G-13100)
PASCHAL ASSOCIATES LTD
324 S Wilmington St (27601-1847)
PHONE................................336 625-2535
EMP: 10 EST: 2016
SALES (est): 926.89K **Privately Held**
Web: www.paschalassociates.com
SIC: 3532 Mining machinery

(G-13101)
PATHWAY TECHNOLOGIES INC (PA)
8400 Six Forks Rd Ste 202 (27615-3068)
PHONE................................919 847-2680
Donald Frazier, *Pr*
EMP: 5 EST: 2008
SQ FT: 1,000
SALES (est): 2.57MM
SALES (corp-wide): 2.57MM **Privately Held**
Web: www.pathwaytech.com
SIC: 3699 Security control equipment and systems

(G-13102)
PATTY KNIO
Also Called: Tube-Tech Solar
3008 Campbell Rd (27606-4422)
PHONE................................919 995-2670
Patty Knio, *Owner*
EMP: 8 EST: 2010
SALES (est): 312.93K **Privately Held**
SIC: 5013 3533 Pumps, oil and gas; Oil and gas field machinery

(G-13103)
PB & J INDUSTRIES INC
8805 Running Oak Dr (27617-4621)
PHONE................................919 661-2738
Jonathan Pulverhouse, *CEO*
EMP: 18 EST: 2006
SALES (est): 2.46MM **Privately Held**
Web: www.pbandjindustries.com
SIC: 2434 Wood kitchen cabinets

(G-13104)
PDM LIGHTING LLC
3737 Glenwood Ave Ste 100 (27612-5515)
P.O. Box 61151 (27661-1151)
PHONE................................919 771-3230
Ponce D Moody, *Owner*
Ponce D Moody, *Prin*
EMP: 9 EST: 2015
SALES (est): 495.3K **Privately Held**
Web: www.poncemoody.com
SIC: 3648 Lighting equipment, nec

(G-13105)
PELICAN VENTURES LLC
5924 Wild Orchid Trl (27613-8550)
PHONE................................919 518-8203
Jim Tarleton, *Mgr*
EMP: 7 EST: 2010
SALES (est): 58.35K **Privately Held**
SIC: 3648 Lighting equipment, nec

(G-13106)
PENDULUM ELECTROMAGNETICS INC
Also Called: Pendel
6304 Westgate Rd Ste D (27617-4750)
PHONE................................919 571-9970
Carl A Everleigh, *Pr*
Mike Everleigh, *Admn Execs*
John Gatsis, *VP Engg*
EMP: 13 EST: 1994
SQ FT: 15,000
SALES (est): 897.85K **Privately Held**
Web: www.pendel.com
SIC: 3663 Microwave communication equipment

(G-13107)
PEPSI BOTTLING VENTURES LLC (DH)
Also Called: Pepsi-Cola
4141 Parklake Ave Ste 600 (27612-2380)
PHONE................................919 865-2300
Derek Hill, *Pr*
Derek Hill, *CFO*
Matthew Bucherati, *
Mark Johnson, *
Claire Niver, *
▲ EMP: 60 EST: 1980
SQ FT: 3,000
SALES (est): 521.69MM **Privately Held**
Web: www.pepsibottlingventures.com
SIC: 2086 Carbonated soft drinks, bottled and canned
HQ: Suntory International
4141 Parklake Ave Ste 600
Raleigh NC 27612
917 756-2747

(G-13108)
PERFECT CUBE LLC
2405 Paula St (27608-1755)
PHONE................................970 481-5785
EMP: 8 EST: 2019
SALES (est): 499.68K **Privately Held**
SIC: 2752 Commercial printing, lithographic

(G-13109)
PHILANTROPHY JOURNAL
220 Fayetteville St (27601-1358)
PHONE................................919 890-6240
Todd Cohen, *Owner*
EMP: 7 EST: 2004
SALES (est): 209.96K **Privately Held**
SIC: 2711 Newspapers, publishing and printing

(G-13110)
PINE TOP DISTILLERY LLC
3036 Farrior Rd (27607-3725)
PHONE................................888 261-5287
Gabriel Guillois, *Prin*
EMP: 4 EST: 2014
SALES (est): 232.03K **Privately Held**
Web: www.pinetopdistillery.com
SIC: 2085 Distilled and blended liquors

(G-13111)
PIPE BRIDGE PRODUCTS INC
5208 Rembert Dr (27612-6244)
P.O. Box 10544 (27605-0544)
PHONE................................919 786-4499
David Clemmer, *Pr*
EMP: 5 EST: 1999
SALES (est): 397.99K **Privately Held**
Web: www.daveclemmer.com
SIC: 3272 Sewer pipe, concrete

(G-13112)
PITNEY BOWES INC
Also Called: Pitney Bowes

Raleigh - Wake County (G-13136)

3150 Spring Forest Rd Ste 122 (27616)
P.O. Box 27407 (27611-7407)
PHONE..............................919 785-3480
Elisabeth Crut, *Brnch Mgr*
EMP: 4
SALES (corp-wide): 3.27B **Publicly Held**
Web: www.pitneybowes.com
SIC: 3579 Postage meters
PA: Pitney Bowes Inc.
3001 Summer St
Stamford CT 06905
203 356-5000

(G-13113)
PLASMA GAMES
208 Bracken Ct (27615-6101)
PHONE..............................252 721-3294
Hunter Moore, *Prin*
EMP: 4 **EST:** 2018
SALES (est): 74.42K **Privately Held**
SIC: 2836 Plasmas

(G-13114)
PLASMA GAMES INC
112 Wind Chime Ct (27615-6433)
PHONE..............................919 627-1252
Hunter Moore, *Prin*
EMP: 27 **EST:** 2019
SALES (est): 651.81K **Privately Held**
Web: www.plasma.games
SIC: 2836 Plasmas

(G-13115)
PLASTIC ART DESIGN INC
5811 Mchines Pl (27616-1914)
PHONE..............................919 878-1672
Ricky Chua, *Pr*
EMP: 4 **EST:** 1986
SQ FT: 4,000
SALES (est): 354.11K **Privately Held**
Web: www.plasticartdesign.com
SIC: 3993 5712 Displays and cutouts, window and lobby; Customized furniture and cabinets

(G-13116)
PLEXUS CORP
5511 Capital Center Dr Ste 600 (27606-3365)
PHONE..............................919 807-8000
Randy Hrnick, *Mgr*
EMP: 55
SALES (corp-wide): 4.21B **Publicly Held**
Web: www.plexus.com
SIC: 3841 3672 Surgical and medical instruments; Printed circuit boards
PA: Plexus Corp.
1 Plexus Way
Neenah WI 54956
920 969-6000

(G-13117)
PLUSHH LLC
3633 Top Of The Pines Ct (27604-5053)
PHONE..............................919 647-7911
Bianca Williams, *Managing Member*
EMP: 7 **EST:** 2015
SALES (est): 100K **Privately Held**
SIC: 5699 3999 Costumes and wigs; Wigs, including doll wigs, toupees, or wiglets

(G-13118)
POGO SOFTWARE INC
Also Called: Pogo
8212 Oak Leaf Ct (27615-5116)
PHONE..............................407 267-4864
Joseph Farrell, *Pr*
EMP: 18 **EST:** 2010
SALES (est): 195.06K **Privately Held**
Web: www.pogocorporation.com

SIC: 7372 7371 Prepackaged software; Computer software development

(G-13119)
POGOMAXY INC
3737 Benson Dr (27609-7324)
P.O. Box 2477 (27602-2477)
PHONE..............................919 623-0118
Murali Bashyam, *CEO*
EMP: 4 **EST:** 2015
SQ FT: 2,800
SALES (est): 108.21K **Privately Held**
SIC: 7372 Application computer software

(G-13120)
POOLE PRINTING COMPANY INC
1400 Mapleside Ct (27609-4075)
P.O. Box 58487 (27658-8487)
PHONE..............................919 876-5260
A Richard Poole, *Pr*
Henry W Poole Junior, *Sec*
EMP: 7 **EST:** 1947
SQ FT: 8,500
SALES (est): 934.1K **Privately Held**
Web: www.pooleprinting.com
SIC: 2752 2759 Offset printing; Letterpress printing

(G-13121)
POWDER COAT USA
4200 Atlantic Ave Ste 130 (27604-1752)
PHONE..............................919 954-7170
Debbie Ainolhayat, *Prin*
EMP: 7 **EST:** 2008
SALES (est): 590.31K **Privately Held**
Web: www.powdercoatusa.com
SIC: 3479 Coating of metals and formed products

(G-13122)
POWERAMERICA INSTITUTE
930 Main Campus Dr Ste 20 (27606-5560)
PHONE..............................919 515-6013
Victor Veliadis, *Ex Dir*
EMP: 11 **EST:** 2017
SALES (est): 162.07K **Privately Held**
Web: www.poweramericainstitute.org
SIC: 3674 Semiconductors and related devices

(G-13123)
POWERHOUSE RESOURCES INTL LLC
2710 Wycliff Rd Ste 105 (27607-3033)
PHONE..............................919 291-1783
EMP: 59 **EST:** 2010
SQ FT: 16,000
SALES (est): 4.91MM
SALES (corp-wide): 7.24MM **Privately Held**
Web: www.powerhrllc.com
SIC: 4581 3559 Aircraft maintenance and repair services; Automotive maintenance equipment
PA: Vetpride Services, Inc
2710 Wycliff Rd Ste 105
Raleigh NC 27607
910 920-2220

(G-13124)
POWERLYTE PAINTBALL GAME PDTS
5811 Mchines Pl Ste 105 (27616-1914)
PHONE..............................919 713-4317
Paul Fernandez, *Pr*
Carson Fernandez, *VP*
▲ **EMP:** 11 **EST:** 1999
SALES (est): 197.21K **Privately Held**
SIC: 3398 7389 Tempering of metal; Design services

(G-13125)
POZEN INC
8310 Bandford Way (27615-2752)
PHONE..............................919 913-1030
EMP: 12
SIC: 2834 Pharmaceutical preparations

(G-13126)
PPG ARCHITECTURAL FINISHES INC
Also Called: Porter Paints
5500 Atlantic Springs Rd Ste 110-112 (27616-1856)
PHONE..............................919 981-0600
Jeff Cornet, *Mgr*
EMP: 4
SALES (corp-wide): 17.65B **Publicly Held**
Web: www.ppg.com
SIC: 2851 Paints and allied products
HQ: Ppg Architectural Finishes, Inc.
1 Ppg Pl
Pittsburgh PA 15272
412 434-3131

(G-13127)
PPG ARCHITECTURAL FINISHES INC
Also Called: Glidden Professional Paint Ctr
2205 Westinghouse Blvd 11 (27604-2495)
PHONE..............................919 872-6500
Pom Joens, *Mgr*
EMP: 5
SALES (corp-wide): 17.65B **Publicly Held**
Web: www.ppg.com
SIC: 2851 Paints and allied products
HQ: Ppg Architectural Finishes, Inc.
1 Ppg Pl
Pittsburgh PA 15272
412 434-3131

(G-13128)
PPG ARCHITECTURAL FINISHES INC
Also Called: Glidden Professional Paint Ctr
1458 Garner Station Blvd (27603-3600)
PHONE..............................919 779-5400
EMP: 6
SALES (corp-wide): 17.65B **Publicly Held**
Web: www.glidden.com
SIC: 2851 Paints and allied products
HQ: Ppg Architectural Finishes, Inc.
1 Ppg Pl
Pittsburgh PA 15272
412 434-3131

(G-13129)
PPG INDUSTRIES INC
Also Called: PPG 4669
5500 Atlantic Springs Rd (27616-1856)
PHONE..............................919 981-0600
David Brady, *Brnch Mgr*
EMP: 4
SALES (corp-wide): 17.65B **Publicly Held**
Web: www.ppgpaints.com
SIC: 2851 Paints and allied products
PA: Ppg Industries, Inc.
1 Ppg Pl
Pittsburgh PA 15272
412 434-3131

(G-13130)
PRACTICE FUSION INC (DH)
Also Called: Ringadoc
305 Church At North Hills St Ste 100 (27609-2667)
PHONE..............................415 346-7700
Tom Langan, *CEO*
Jonathan Malek, *
▲ **EMP:** 103 **EST:** 2005
SALES (est): 23.02MM
SALES (corp-wide): 1.5B **Publicly Held**
Web: www.practicefusion.com
SIC: 7372 Prepackaged software
HQ: Veradigm Llc

305 Church At North Hills
Raleigh NC 27609
919 847-8102

(G-13131)
PRATT INDUSTRIES INC
Also Called: Converting Division
5620 Departure Dr (27616-1841)
PHONE..............................919 334-7400
Mike Keepers, *Brnch Mgr*
EMP: 52
Web: www.prattindustries.com
SIC: 2653 5113 Boxes, corrugated: made from purchased materials; Corrugated and solid fiber boxes
PA: Pratt Industries, Inc.
1800 Sarasota Pkwy Ne C
Conyers GA 30013

(G-13132)
PRECAST TERRAZZO ENTPS INC
1107 N New Hope Rd (27610-1415)
PHONE..............................919 231-6200
EMP: 25 **EST:** 1996
SQ FT: 15,000
SALES (est): 4.94MM **Privately Held**
Web: www.precastterrazzo.com
SIC: 3272 3253 2511 Concrete products, nec ; Ceramic wall and floor tile; Wood household furniture

(G-13133)
PRECISION ALLOYS INC
1040 Corp Pkwy Ste T (27610)
P.O. Box 41143 (27629-1143)
PHONE..............................919 231-6329
William L Russell Junior, *Pr*
Richard W Zendzian, *VP*
EMP: 15 **EST:** 1988
SQ FT: 4,500
SALES (est): 361.47K **Privately Held**
SIC: 3471 Finishing, metals or formed products

(G-13134)
PRECISION MCH FABRICATION INC
1100 N New Hope Rd (27610-1416)
PHONE..............................919 231-8648
Gene Richardson, *Pr*
Don Turner, *
Richard Wheeler, *
▲ **EMP:** 65 **EST:** 1978
SQ FT: 100,000
SALES (est): 9.88MM **Privately Held**
Web: www.pmfweb.com
SIC: 3599 3613 3444 Machine shop, jobbing and repair; Switchgear and switchboard apparatus; Sheet metalwork

(G-13135)
PREDATAR INC
4208 Six Forks Rd Ste 1000 (27609-5733)
PHONE..............................919 827-4516
Brandon S Neuman, *Prin*
EMP: 8 **EST:** 2021
SALES (est): 518.03K **Privately Held**
Web: www.predatar.com
SIC: 7371 7372 Custom computer programming services; Application computer software

(G-13136)
PREISS PAPER & PRINTING
1618 Weatherford Cir (27604-2382)
PHONE..............................919 325-3790
Walter Nelson, *Prin*
EMP: 5 **EST:** 2010
SALES (est): 72.69K **Privately Held**
SIC: 2752 Commercial printing, lithographic

Raleigh - Wake County (G-13137) GEOGRAPHIC SECTION

(G-13137)
PREMIER CAKES LLC
Also Called: Premier Cakes
6617 Falls Of Neuse Rd Ste 105 (27615-6879)
PHONE.....................919 274-8511
EMP: 5 EST: 2008
SQ FT: 1,700
SALES (est): 478.3K Privately Held
Web: www.premier-cakes.com
SIC: 2051 Cakes, bakery: except frozen

(G-13138)
PREMIER STUCCO LLC
10009 Friedel Pl (27613-7561)
PHONE.....................919 676-2306
Wojciech Radziwanowski, Prin
EMP: 6 EST: 2011
SALES (est): 150.28K Privately Held
SIC: 3299 Stucco

(G-13139)
PRESTIGE FARMS INC
2414 Crabtree Blvd (27604-2233)
PHONE.....................919 861-8867
Chandler Thompson, Mgr
EMP: 34
SALES (corp-wide): 38.89MM Privately Held
Web: www.prestigefarms.com
SIC: 2015 Poultry slaughtering and processing
PA: Prestige Farms, Inc.
7120 Orr Rd
Charlotte NC 28213
704 596-2824

(G-13140)
PRIME WATER SERVICES INC
9400 Ransdell Rd Ste 9 (27603-8980)
PHONE.....................919 504-1020
Phillip Minor, Pr
EMP: 8 EST: 2015
SQ FT: 2,000
SALES (est): 344.75K Privately Held
Web: www.primewaterservices.com
SIC: 1711 3639 4941 Plumbing contractors; Hot water heaters, household; Water supply

(G-13141)
PRIMEVIGILANCE INC
5430 Wade Park Blvd Ste 208 (27607-4191)
PHONE.....................781 703-5540
Aleksandra Seisert, Off Mgr
EMP: 6 EST: 2016
SALES (est): 746.76K Privately Held
Web: www.primevigilance.com
SIC: 3821 Clinical laboratory instruments, except medical and dental

(G-13142)
PRINTER SOLUTIONS INC
5100 Pointe Water Ct (27603-8138)
PHONE.....................919 592-1077
Jeffrey Rubin, Pr
EMP: 5 EST: 2015
SALES (est): 109.44K Privately Held
SIC: 2752 Offset printing

(G-13143)
PRINTSURGE INCORPORATED
2308 Beaver Oaks Ct (27606-9287)
PHONE.....................919 854-4376
Greg Card, Prin
EMP: 6 EST: 2007
SALES (est): 251.47K Privately Held
SIC: 2752 Offset printing

(G-13144)
PRINTWORKS INC
7649 Summerglen Dr (27615-6167)
PHONE.....................919 649-1547
EMP: 4 EST: 2009
SALES (est): 69.58K Privately Held
SIC: 2741 Miscellaneous publishing

(G-13145)
PRISM RESEARCH GLASS INC
6004 Triangle Dr Ste B (27617-4743)
P.O. Box 14187 (27709-4187)
PHONE.....................919 571-0078
John Foscato, Pr
Steve Foscato, VP
▲ EMP: 15 EST: 1990
SQ FT: 17,000
SALES (est): 2.38MM Privately Held
Web: www.prismresearchglass.com
SIC: 3231 Laboratory glassware

(G-13146)
PRO CHOICE CONTRACTORS CORP
2405 Churchill Rd (27608-1927)
PHONE.....................919 696-7383
Frank Marina, Pr
EMP: 10 EST: 2007
SALES (est): 432.93K Privately Held
SIC: 1521 1542 1799 2449 General remodeling, single-family houses; Commercial and office building contractors; Post disaster renovations; Shipping cases and drums, wood: wirebound and plywood

(G-13147)
PRO FARM GROUP INC (PA)
Also Called: Marrone Bio Innovations
7780 Brier Creek Pkwy Ste 420 (27617-7849)
PHONE.....................530 750-2800
Kevin Helash, CEO
Robert A Woods, *
Ladon Johnson, Interim Chief Financial Officer
Linda V Moore, CCO
Amit Vasavada, Sr VP
▲ EMP: 59 EST: 2006
SQ FT: 2,291
SALES (est): 44.31MM Privately Held
Web: www.marronebio.com
SIC: 2879 Agricultural chemicals, nec

(G-13148)
PROBLEM SOLVER INC
3200 Glen Royal Rd Ste 112 (27617-7419)
PHONE.....................919 596-5555
Robert A Wiener, Pr
▼ EMP: 10 EST: 2009
SALES (est): 931.94K Privately Held
Web: www.businessfurnitureshop.com
SIC: 3562 3499 Casters; Furniture parts, metal

(G-13149)
PRODUCTION MEDIA INC
Also Called: Church Production Magazine
2501 Blue Ridge Rd Ste 250 (27607-6346)
PHONE.....................919 325-0120
Brian Blackmore, Pr
Terri L South, VP
EMP: 10 EST: 1998
SQ FT: 1,500
SALES (est): 808.68K Privately Held
Web: www.churchproduction.com
SIC: 2741 7389 Miscellaneous publishing; Decoration service for special events

(G-13150)
PROGRESS SOLAR SOLUTIONS LLC
Also Called: Manufacturing
1108 N New Hope Rd (27610-1416)
P.O. Box 19540 (27619-9540)
PHONE.....................919 363-3738
Dan Mckenzie, Pr
◆ EMP: 16 EST: 2008
SQ FT: 25,000
SALES (est): 2.41MM Privately Held
Web: www.progresssolarsolutions.com
SIC: 3645 3621 3648 1711 Residential lighting fixtures; Generator sets: gasoline, diesel, or dual-fuel; Lighting equipment, nec; Solar energy contractor

(G-13151)
PROMETHERA BIOSCIENCES LLC (PA)
4700 Falls Of Neuse Rd Ste 400 (27609-6200)
PHONE.....................919 354-1933
Mark B Johnston, Pr
EMP: 7 EST: 2016
SALES (est): 2MM
SALES (corp-wide): 2MM Privately Held
Web: www.cellaion.com
SIC: 2834 Pharmaceutical preparations

(G-13152)
PROMETHEUS GROUP HOLDINGS LLC
4601 Six Forks Rd Ste 220 (27609-5210)
PHONE.....................919 835-0810
Eric Huang, CEO
EMP: 85 EST: 2015
SALES (est): 4.48MM Privately Held
SIC: 7372 Business oriented computer software

(G-13153)
PROPHARMA GROUP LLC (HQ)
Also Called: Acadeus
107 W Hargett St (27601-1700)
P.O. Box 12090 (66282-2090)
PHONE.....................888 242-0559
Dawn Sherman, CEO
Jeff Hargroves, *
Robert Chestnut, *
Joe Biehl, *
Steve Swantek, *
EMP: 60 EST: 2001
SALES (est): 102.88MM
SALES (corp-wide): 188.16MM Privately Held
Web: www.propharmagroup.com
SIC: 8742 8731 7372 Quality assurance consultant; Commercial physical research; Prepackaged software
PA: Linden, Llc
111 S Wacker Dr Ste 3350
Chicago IL 60606
312 506-5657

(G-13154)
PROSAPIENT INC
Also Called: Prosapient
555 Fayetteville St Ste 700 (27601-3030)
PHONE.....................984 282-2823
Jordan Shlosberg, Pr
EMP: 16 EST: 2019
SALES (est): 276.45K
SALES (corp-wide): 35.38MM Privately Held
SIC: 7372 Prepackaged software
PA: Prosapient Limited
5 Floor
London EC1N
208 505-0500

(G-13155)
PROVEER
331 Sherwee Dr (27603-3521)
PHONE.....................800 542-9941
EMP: 5 EST: 2017
SALES (est): 53.23K Privately Held
Web: www.grimco.ca
SIC: 3993 Signs and advertising specialties

(G-13156)
PROXIMAL DESIGN LABS LLC
1421 Carolina Pines Ave (27603-2739)
PHONE.....................919 599-5742
EMP: 4 EST: 2020
SALES (est): 98.37K Privately Held
SIC: 7372 Educational computer software

(G-13157)
PT MARKETING INCORPORATED
Also Called: Tech Marketing
8360 Six Forks Rd Ste 204 (27615-5087)
PHONE.....................412 471-8995
Patrick Teen, Pr
Aileen Bryant, Admn
EMP: 9 EST: 1994
SALES (est): 956.44K Privately Held
Web: www.techmarketing.biz
SIC: 3679 Electronic circuits

(G-13158)
PUNY HUMAN LLC
6278 Glenwood Ave (27612-2723)
PHONE.....................919 420-4538
Michael Sanders, Prin
EMP: 16 EST: 2011
SALES (est): 623.5K Privately Held
Web: www.punyhuman.com
SIC: 3652 Prerecorded records and tapes

(G-13159)
PYRAMID SOFTWARE INC
7410 Denlee Rd (27603-5108)
PHONE.....................336 209-2684
Kevin E Fenters, Pr
EMP: 4 EST: 2017
SALES (est): 94.33K Privately Held
Web: www.cimpyramid.com
SIC: 7372 Prepackaged software

(G-13160)
QPLOT CORPORATION
3245 Lewis Farm Rd (27607-6761)
PHONE.....................949 302-7928
Zhengzheng Hu, CEO
EMP: 5 EST: 2011
SALES (est): 246.65K Privately Held
Web: www.qplot.com
SIC: 7373 7371 8748 7372 Systems engineering, computer related; Custom computer programming services; Systems engineering consultant, ex. computer or professional; Application computer software

(G-13161)
QUALCOMM DATACENTER TECH INC
8045 Arco Corporate Dr (27617-2025)
PHONE.....................858 567-1121
EMP: 61
SALES (corp-wide): 35.82B Publicly Held
SIC: 3674 Integrated circuits, semiconductor networks, etc.
HQ: Qualcomm Datacenter Technologies, Inc.
5775 Morehouse Dr
San Diego CA 92121
858 567-1121

GEOGRAPHIC SECTION
Raleigh - Wake County (G-13188)

(G-13162)
QUALIA NETWORKS INC
Also Called: Qni
3732 Westbury Lake Dr (27603-5187)
PHONE..............................805 637-2083
George Wayne, *Pr*
Edward Carney, *Bd of Dir*
Byron Shaw, *Bd of Dir*
Michael Wayne, *VP*
EMP: 6 **EST:** 2013
SALES (est): 335.76K **Privately Held**
SIC: 3674 3663 3812 3822 Integrated circuits, semiconductor networks, etc.; Antennas, transmitting and communications; Aircraft control systems, electronic; Environmental controls

(G-13163)
QUALITY CONTEMPORARY FURNITURE
2517 Floyd Dr B (27610-5529)
PHONE..............................919 758-7277
Milton Simpkins, *Pr*
EMP: 5 **EST:** 2009
SALES (est): 155.9K **Privately Held**
SIC: 2511 Wood household furniture

(G-13164)
QUALITY LGHTNING PRTECTION INC (PA)
Also Called: Capital Lightng Protection
743 Pershing Rd (27608-2711)
P.O. Box 162 (27602-0162)
PHONE..............................919 832-9399
TOLL FREE: 800
Thomas J Cottle Junior, *Pr*
Charles Stephenson, *VP*
Marsha S Caviness, *Treas*
EMP: 12 **EST:** 1976
SQ FT: 8,000
SALES (est): 2.46MM
SALES (corp-wide): 2.46MM **Privately Held**
Web: www.qualitylightning.com
SIC: 3643 Current-carrying wiring services

(G-13165)
QUALITY PRINTING SOLUTIONS INC
4800 Frenchill Cir (27610-8602)
PHONE..............................919 261-9527
Christopher D Oconnor, *Pr*
EMP: 5 **EST:** 2004
SALES (est): 127.7K **Privately Held**
SIC: 2752 Offset printing

(G-13166)
QUANTUM NEWSWIRE
150 Fayetteville St 2800d108 (27601-1395)
PHONE..............................919 439-8800
EMP: 4 **EST:** 2019
SALES (est): 118.96K **Privately Held**
Web: www.quantumnewswire.app
SIC: 3572 Computer storage devices

(G-13167)
R JACOBS FINE PLBG & HDWR INC
8613 Glenwood Ave Ste 103 (27617-7553)
PHONE..............................919 720-4202
Nikole B Mariencheck, *Prin*
EMP: 11 **EST:** 2012
SALES (est): 403.45K **Privately Held**
Web: www.rjacobsfph.com
SIC: 3261 5074 Vitreous plumbing fixtures; Plumbing fittings and supplies

(G-13168)
RABBIT PRESS LLC
2029 Rabbit Run (27603-2783)
PHONE..............................919 703-8206
EMP: 4 **EST:** 2020
SALES (est): 76.29K **Privately Held**
Web: www.rabbitpressprint.com
SIC: 2741 Miscellaneous publishing

(G-13169)
RACHEL DUBOIS
Also Called: Moondance Soaps & More
6013 Old Horseman Trl (27613-8104)
PHONE..............................919 870-8063
Rachel Dubois, *Owner*
EMP: 6 **EST:** 1999
SALES (est): 393.56K **Privately Held**
Web: www.moondancesoaps.com
SIC: 2841 7215 Soap: granulated, liquid, cake, flaked, or chip; Coin-operated laundries and cleaning

(G-13170)
RACKWISE INC
Also Called: Rackwise
4020 Westchase Blvd Ste 470 (27607-3938)
PHONE..............................919 533-5533
EMP: 10
Web: www.rackwise.com
SIC: 7372 Business oriented computer software
PA: Rackwise, Inc.
1610 Wynkoop St Ste 400
Denver CO 80202

(G-13171)
RAINFOREST NUTRITIONALS INC
9201 Leesville Rd Ste 120c (27613-7540)
PHONE..............................919 847-2221
Paul J Bobrowski, *Pr*
Donna Theriot, *Sec*
EMP: 7 **EST:** 2002
SALES (est): 564.16K **Privately Held**
Web: www.rainforest-inc.com
SIC: 2023 2834 Dietary supplements, dairy and non-dairy based; Pharmaceutical preparations

(G-13172)
RALEIGH
1216 Nikole Ct (27612-2475)
PHONE..............................919 306-3208
EMP: 7 **EST:** 2015
SALES (est): 105.97K **Privately Held**
Web: www.visitraleigh.com
SIC: 2752 Offset printing

(G-13173)
RALEIGH AREA MASTERS
13200 Falls Of Neuse Rd (27614-8239)
PHONE..............................919 233-6713
EMP: 6 **EST:** 2010
SALES (est): 128.59K **Privately Held**
SIC: 2273 Carpets and rugs

(G-13174)
RALEIGH CABINET WORKS
4713 Grand Cypress Ct (27604-5877)
PHONE..............................919 412-7750
EMP: 4 **EST:** 2013
SALES (est): 65.97K **Privately Held**
SIC: 2434 Wood kitchen cabinets

(G-13175)
RALEIGH CUSTOM WOODWORK INC
4712 Radcliff Rd (27609-5316)
P.O. Box 17434 (27619-7434)
PHONE..............................919 522-6621
Matthew Kesterson, *Pr*
EMP: 5 **EST:** 2014
SALES (est): 72.04K **Privately Held**
Web: www.raleighcustom.com
SIC: 2431 Millwork

(G-13176)
RALEIGH DOWNTOWNER
Also Called: Downtown Raleigh Publishing
12 E Hargett St (27601-1426)
P.O. Box 27603 (27611-7603)
PHONE..............................919 821-9000
Crash Gregg, *Prin*
EMP: 8 **EST:** 2007
SALES (est): 250.37K **Privately Held**
Web: www.welovedowntown.com
SIC: 2711 5994 Newspapers, publishing and printing; Newsstand

(G-13177)
RALEIGH ENGRAVING CO
Also Called: Raleigh Engraving Press
806 N West St (27603-1138)
P.O. Box 2854 (27602-2854)
PHONE..............................919 832-5557
Edwin G Brandle, *Pr*
Jacqueline Brandle, *Prin*
Greg Brandle, *VP*
EMP: 5 **EST:** 1955
SQ FT: 6,000
SALES (est): 272.85K **Privately Held**
Web: www.customengravingandtrophy.com
SIC: 2791 2759 Typesetting; Engraving, nec

(G-13178)
RALEIGH MAGAZINE
6511 Creedmoor Rd Ste 207 (27613-1687)
PHONE..............................919 307-3047
EMP: 8 **EST:** 2019
SALES (est): 178.02K **Privately Held**
Web: www.raleighmag.com
SIC: 2721 Magazines: publishing only, not printed on site

(G-13179)
RALEIGH MECHANICAL & MTLS INC
7405 Acc Blvd (27617-8406)
PHONE..............................919 598-4601
Peter Manuel, *Pr*
EMP: 12 **EST:** 1984
SQ FT: 15,000
SALES (est): 2.04MM **Privately Held**
Web: www.raleighmech.com
SIC: 1711 1761 3444 Mechanical contractor; Sheet metal work, nec; Awnings and canopies

(G-13180)
RALEIGH POWDER COATING CO
2100 Garner Rd (27610-6890)
PHONE..............................919 301-8065
EMP: 4 **EST:** 2019
SALES (est): 93.93K **Privately Held**
Web: www.raleighpowdercoating.com
SIC: 3479 Coating of metals and formed products

(G-13181)
RALEIGH PRINTING & TYPING INC
Also Called: Raleigh Printing
5415 Fayetteville Rd (27603-4182)
PHONE..............................919 662-8001
Patricia Simmons, *Pr*
Clyde E Simmons, *VP*
EMP: 9 **EST:** 1972
SQ FT: 3,000
SALES (est): 836.41K **Privately Held**
Web: www.raleighprintinginc.com
SIC: 2752 7338 Offset printing; Secretarial and typing service

(G-13182)
RALEIGH RINGERS INC
2200 E Millbrook Rd Ste 113 (27604)
PHONE..............................919 847-7574
David Harris, *Admn*
David Harris, *Dir*
EMP: 9 **EST:** 1990
SALES (est): 267.69K **Privately Held**
Web: www.rr.org
SIC: 3931 Bells (musical instruments)

(G-13183)
RALEIGH ROLLS
411 W Morgan St (27603-1825)
PHONE..............................919 559-0451
EMP: 6 **EST:** 2018
SALES (est): 115.32K **Privately Held**
Web: www.raleighrolls.com
SIC: 2024 Ice cream and frozen deserts

(G-13184)
RALEIGH SAW CO INC
5805 Departure Dr Ste C (27616-1859)
PHONE..............................919 832-2248
William J Shields, *Pr*
▲ **EMP:** 8 **EST:** 1950
SQ FT: 9,600
SALES (est): 498.48K **Privately Held**
Web: www.raleighsaw.com
SIC: 7699 3425 Knife, saw and tool sharpening and repair; Saw blades, for hand or power saws

(G-13185)
RALEIGH SHIRT PRINTER
3125 Gresham Lake Rd Ste 104 (27615-4233)
PHONE..............................919 261-6628
Bob Liddle, *Pr*
EMP: 5 **EST:** 2016
SALES (est): 81.59K **Privately Held**
Web: www.raleighshirtprinter.com
SIC: 2759 Screen printing

(G-13186)
RALEIGH SIGN SOLUTIONS LLC
6548 English Oaks Dr (27615-6326)
PHONE..............................919 578-7255
Carlo Morbidini, *Owner*
EMP: 4 **EST:** 2016
SALES (est): 111.02K **Privately Held**
Web: www.raleighsignsolutions.com
SIC: 3993 Signs and advertising specialties

(G-13187)
RALEIGH TEES
4909 Alpinis Dr Ste 113 (27616-1957)
PHONE..............................919 850-3378
Roland Jones, *Pr*
Willie Sinclair, *Pt*
Geraldine Jones, *Pr*
EMP: 5 **EST:** 1988
SQ FT: 6,000
SALES (est): 415.83K **Privately Held**
Web: www.123raleightees.com
SIC: 7389 2261 Embroidery advertising; Screen printing of cotton broadwoven fabrics

(G-13188)
RALEIGH WORKSHOP INC
Also Called: Raleigh Denim
319 W Martin St (27601-1352)
PHONE..............................919 917-8969
Victor Lytvinenko, *Pr*
Sarah Lytvinenko, *
◆ **EMP:** 24 **EST:** 2012
SQ FT: 7,000
SALES (est): 2.42MM **Privately Held**
Web: www.raleighdenimworkshop.com
SIC: 2211 5651 5137 5136 Denims; Family clothing stores; Women's and children's clothing; Men's and boy's clothing

Raleigh - Wake County (G-13189)

(G-13189)
RAMA SADRI
4420 Jacqueline Ln (27616-5693)
PHONE.....................919 875-8088
Sadri Rama, *Prin*
EMP: 6 **EST:** 2007
SALES (est): 150.09K **Privately Held**
SIC: 3993 Signs and advertising specialties

(G-13190)
RANPAK CORP
3401 Gresham Lake Rd (27615-4243)
PHONE.....................919 790-8225
EMP: 5
SALES (corp-wide): 492.28MM **Publicly Held**
Web: www.ranpak.com
SIC: 2621 Packaging paper
HQ: Ranpak Corp.
    7990 Auburn Rd
    Concord Township OH 44077
    440 354-4445

(G-13191)
RDD PHARMA INC
8480 Honeycutt Rd Ste 120 (27615-2261)
PHONE.....................302 319-9970
John Temperato, *CEO*
Mark Sirgo, *Ch Bd*
Arie Giniger, *Bd of Dir*
Nir Barak, *Prin*
EMP: 5 **EST:** 2013
SQ FT: 150
SALES (est): 300.71K **Privately Held**
Web: www.9meters.com
SIC: 3841 Surgical and medical instruments

(G-13192)
RE-CRTION SSTAINABLE WDWKG LLC
315 Yadkin Dr (27609-6362)
PHONE.....................919 612-4791
EMP: 4 **EST:** 2017
SALES (est): 68.56K **Privately Held**
SIC: 3999 Manufacturing industries, nec

(G-13193)
READABLE COMMUNICATIONS INC
Also Called: Poole Printing Company
2609 Spring Forest Rd (27616-1825)
PHONE.....................919 876-5260
Mory Read, *Pr*
EMP: 8 **EST:** 2015
SQ FT: 8,400
SALES (est): 825.77K **Privately Held**
SIC: 2731 2752 Pamphlets: publishing and printing; Offset and photolithographic printing

(G-13194)
READILITE & BARRICADE INC (PA)
708 Freedom Dr (27610-1402)
P.O. Box 58280 (27658-8280)
PHONE.....................919 231-8309
Larry J Cashwell, *Pr*
Deborah Cashwell, *VP*
EMP: 18 **EST:** 1965
SQ FT: 5,000
SALES (est): 2.15MM
SALES (corp-wide): 2.15MM **Privately Held**
Web: www.unitedsiteservices.com
SIC: 7519 3993 3431 2451 Trailer rental; Signs and advertising specialties; Metal sanitary ware; Mobile homes

(G-13195)
RED DOG PUBLICATIONS INC
3804 City Of Oaks Wynd (27612-5305)
PHONE.....................919 782-4422
Richard Williams, *Prin*
EMP: 5 **EST:** 2003
SALES (est): 10.68K **Privately Held**
SIC: 2741 Miscellaneous publishing

(G-13196)
RED HAT INC (HQ)
Also Called: Centos Project
100 E Davie St (27601-1806)
PHONE.....................919 754-3700
EMP: 610 **EST:** 1998
SQ FT: 380,000
SALES (est): 2.72B
SALES (corp-wide): 60.53B **Publicly Held**
Web: www.redhat.com
SIC: 7371 7372 Computer software development; Prepackaged software
PA: International Business Machines Corporation
    1 New Orchard Rd Ste 1 # 1
    Armonk NY 10504
    914 499-1900

(G-13197)
RED HAT SA I LLC (DH)
100 E Davie St (27601-1806)
PHONE.....................919 754-3700
EMP: 26 **EST:** 2006
SALES (est): 1.83MM
SALES (corp-wide): 60.53B **Publicly Held**
Web: www.redhat.com
SIC: 7371 7372 Computer software development; Prepackaged software
HQ: Red Hat, Inc.
    100 E Davie St
    Raleigh NC 27601

(G-13198)
RED HOUSE CABINETS LLC
9660 Falls Of Neuse Rd (27615-2473)
PHONE.....................919 201-2101
EMP: 5 **EST:** 2016
SALES (est): 53.79K **Privately Held**
Web: www.redhousecabinets.com
SIC: 2434 Wood kitchen cabinets

(G-13199)
REDBIRD SCREEN PRINTING LLC
8711 Owl Roost Pl (27617-8731)
PHONE.....................919 946-0005
EMP: 5 **EST:** 2014
SALES (est): 81.6K **Privately Held**
Web: www.redbirdscreenprinting.com
SIC: 2752 Offset printing

(G-13200)
REDDICK & REDDICK LLC
5500 Somerford Ln (27614-9840)
PHONE.....................919 845-7333
Douglas Freeman, *Prin*
EMP: 5 **EST:** 2019
SALES (est): 76.16K **Privately Held**
SIC: 3523 Farm machinery and equipment

(G-13201)
REDHAWK PUBLISHING
2312 Quartz Ct (27610-5856)
PHONE.....................919 274-6477
EMP: 4 **EST:** 2015
SALES (est): 59.98K **Privately Held**
SIC: 2741 Miscellaneous publishing

(G-13202)
REDHILL BIOPHARMA INC
8045 Arco Corporate Dr (27617-2025)
PHONE.....................984 444-7010
Rick Scruggs, *Pr*
Guy Goldberg, *Chief Business Officer**
June Almenoff, *CSO**
EMP: 74 **EST:** 2017
SALES (est): 15.43MM **Privately Held**
Web: www.redhillbio.com
SIC: 2834 Pharmaceutical preparations

(G-13203)
REFAB WOOD LLC
1501 S Blount St (27603-2507)
PHONE.....................919 272-2589
EMP: 5 **EST:** 2017
SALES (est): 240.27K **Privately Held**
Web: www.refabwood.com
SIC: 2431 Millwork

(G-13204)
RESOURCE MANAGEMENT ASSOCIATES
5720 Six Forks Rd Ste 201 (27609-8618)
PHONE.....................919 841-9642
Eugene Langley, *Pr*
EMP: 6 **EST:** 2011
SALES (est): 62.35K **Privately Held**
SIC: 3589 Service industry machinery, nec

(G-13205)
REVWARE INC
1645 Old Louisburg Rd (27604-1376)
P.O. Box 90786 (27675-0786)
PHONE.....................919 790-0000
Thomas Welsh, *Pr*
EMP: 7 **EST:** 1992
SQ FT: 6,000
SALES (est): 1.45MM **Privately Held**
Web: www.revware.net
SIC: 3577 7372 3829 Computer peripheral equipment, nec; Prepackaged software; Measuring and controlling devices, nec

(G-13206)
RFMD INFRSTRCTURE PDT GROUP IN
327 Hillsborough St (27603-1725)
PHONE.....................704 996-2997
Robert A Bruggeworth, *Pr*
William A Priddy Junior, *CFO*
Alan Hallberg, ***
J Forrest Moore, ***
EMP: 22 **EST:** 2004
SALES (est): 3.55MM
SALES (corp-wide): 3.57B **Publicly Held**
SIC: 3674 Semiconductors and related devices
HQ: Qorvo Us, Inc.
    2300 Ne Brookwood Pkwy
    Hillsboro OR 97124
    336 664-1233

(G-13207)
RICHARDS SOUTHERN SOUL FD LLC
6500 Paces Arbor Cir Apt 113 (27609-5381)
PHONE.....................919 210-8275
EMP: 5
SALES (est): 79.3K **Privately Held**
SIC: 2656 7389 Frozen food containers: made from purchased material; Business Activities at Non-Commercial Site

(G-13208)
RIDDLE INC
9117 Colony Village Ln (27617-5963)
P.O. Box 30395 (27622-0395)
PHONE.....................919 724-3272
Anna Lipscomb, *Prin*
EMP: 5 **EST:** 2017
SALES (est): 65.53K **Privately Held**
Web: www.agriddle.com
SIC: 2741 Miscellaneous publishing

(G-13209)
RIVERSIDE CEMENT CO
2710 Wycliff Rd (27607-3033)
PHONE.....................760 245-5321
EMP: 5 **EST:** 2015
SALES (est): 149.05K **Privately Held**
SIC: 3273 Ready-mixed concrete

(G-13210)
ROBERT GREGORY
Also Called: Industrial Services
309 Burkwood Ln (27609-3851)
PHONE.....................919 821-9188
Robert Gregory, *Owner*
EMP: 6 **EST:** 2018
SALES (est): 238.46K **Privately Held**
SIC: 7692 Welding repair

(G-13211)
ROBERT ST CLAIR CO INC
7701 Leesville Rd (27613-4028)
PHONE.....................919 847-8611
Robert Stclaire, *Pr*
Toni Stclaire, *VP*
▲ **EMP:** 10 **EST:** 1986
SALES (est): 592.01K **Privately Held**
SIC: 2426 Flooring, hardwood

(G-13212)
ROBERTS FAMILY ENTERPRISES LLP
7101 Ebenezer Church Rd (27612-1856)
PHONE.....................919 785-3111
Roy Roberts, *Mng Pt*
EMP: 7 **EST:** 2005
SALES (est): 444.61K **Privately Held**
SIC: 3312 Blast furnaces and steel mills

(G-13213)
ROCKY MOUNT MILL LLC
2619 Western Blvd (27606-2125)
PHONE.....................919 890-6000
James F Goodmon, *CEO*
EMP: 10 **EST:** 2012
SALES (est): 280.7K **Privately Held**
Web: www.capitolbroadcasting.com
SIC: 2281 Cotton yarn, spun

(G-13214)
ROYAL BLUNTS CONNECTIONS INC
4900 Thornton Rd Ste 109 (27616-5879)
PHONE.....................919 961-4910
Louis Wilson, *Pr*
EMP: 4 **EST:** 2002
SQ FT: 8,800
SALES (est): 721.67K **Privately Held**
Web: www.royalbc.com
SIC: 5194 3634 Smokeless tobacco; Vaporizers, electric: household

(G-13215)
ROYAL CHEESECAKE VARIETIES LLC
8458 Reedy Ridge Ln (27613-6884)
PHONE.....................919 670-8766
Kenneth Jwilliams, *Admn*
EMP: 4 **EST:** 2017
SALES (est): 247.1K **Privately Held**
Web: www.rcvcakes.com
SIC: 2591 Window blinds

(G-13216)
ROYAL OAK STAIRS INC
3201 Wellington Ct Ste 104 (27615-5494)
PHONE.....................919 855-8988
Christopher Morley, *Pr*
Cathy Morley, *VP*
EMP: 11 **EST:** 2000
SQ FT: 4,900
SALES (est): 454.23K **Privately Held**

GEOGRAPHIC SECTION
Raleigh - Wake County (G-13242)

Web: www.royaloakstairs.net
SIC: 2431 Staircases and stairs, wood

(G-13217)
RSR FITNESS INC
Also Called: Batca Fitness Systems
1207 N New Hope Rd (27610-1413)
P.O. Box 28328 (27611-8328)
PHONE.................................919 255-1233
▲ EMP: 11 EST: 1994
SQ FT: 30,000
SALES (est): 1.42MM Privately Held
Web: www.batcafitness.com
SIC: 3949 Exercise equipment

(G-13218)
RT CARDIAC SYSTEMS INC
5420 Deer Forest Trl (27614-8221)
PHONE.................................954 908-1074
Jeffrey Larose, CEO
Al Basilico, Prin
Ernie Baker, Sec
Daiga Koenig, Mgr
EMP: 9 EST: 1998
SQ FT: 8,100
SALES (est): 975.37K Privately Held
Web: www.rtcardiacsystems.us
SIC: 3674 Microcircuits, integrated (semiconductor)

(G-13219)
RUSTIC INNOVATIONS LLC
3138 Groveshire Dr (27616-8396)
PHONE.................................804 822-2492
Sean Kudlacz, Prin
EMP: 4 EST: 2019
SALES (est): 75.4K Privately Held
SIC: 2431 Millwork

(G-13220)
RUSTIC OAK SIGN CO
4717 Longhill Ln (27612-6839)
PHONE.................................919 619-4452
Jessica Lombardo, Prin
EMP: 4 EST: 2018
SALES (est): 46.08K Privately Held
SIC: 3993 Signs and advertising specialties

(G-13221)
S CHAMBLEE INCORPORATED
Also Called: Chamblee Graphics
1300 Hodges St (27604-1414)
P.O. Box 40727 (27629-0727)
PHONE.................................919 833-7561
EMP: 22 EST: 1966
SALES (est): 2.38MM Privately Held
Web: www.chambleeinc.com
SIC: 2752 2791 2789 Offset printing; Typesetting; Bookbinding and related work

(G-13222)
S P CO INC
Also Called: Spco.
200 W Millbrook Rd (27609-4304)
PHONE.................................919 848-3599
▼ EMP: 4 EST: 1983
SALES (est): 246.27K Privately Held
SIC: 7389 2048 Brokers' services; Feed supplements

(G-13223)
S T WOOTEN CORPORATION
Rdu Airport Concrete Plant
9001 Fortune Way (27613)
PHONE.................................919 783-5507
Eric Henderson, Mgr
EMP: 10
SALES (corp-wide): 319.83MM Privately Held
Web: www.stwcorp.com

SIC: 3272 Concrete products, nec
PA: S. T. Wooten Corporation
3801 Black Creek Rd Se
Wilson NC 27893
252 291-5165

(G-13224)
S T WOOTEN CORPORATION
Also Called: Gresham Lake Concrete Plant
6937 Capital Blvd (27616-3029)
PHONE.................................252 291-5165
Eric Henderson, Mgr
EMP: 23
SALES (corp-wide): 319.83MM Privately Held
Web: www.stwcorp.com
SIC: 3531 Concrete plants
PA: S. T. Wooten Corporation
3801 Black Creek Rd Se
Wilson NC 27893
252 291-5165

(G-13225)
SAFARILAND GROUP
3319 Anvil Pl (27603-3514)
PHONE.................................919 779-6141
EMP: 4 EST: 2018
SALES (est): 77.33K Privately Held
Web: inside.safariland.com
SIC: 3949 Sporting and athletic goods, nec

(G-13226)
SAFETY WHEELCHAIR COMPANY
108 Seastone St (27603-3100)
PHONE.................................919 819-3775
Donald Bagwell, Prin
EMP: 5 EST: 2010
SALES (est): 68.88K Privately Held
SIC: 3842 Wheelchairs

(G-13227)
SAGENT PHARMACEUTICALS INC
8900 Capital Blvd (27616-3117)
PHONE.................................919 327-5500
David Vogt, Dir
EMP: 249
Web: www.sagentpharma.com
SIC: 2834 Pharmaceutical preparations
HQ: Sagent Pharmaceuticals, Inc.
1901 N Roselle Rd Ste 450
Schaumburg IL 60195

(G-13228)
SANTARUS INC
8510 Colonnade Center Dr (27615-5860)
PHONE.................................919 862-1000
Gerald T Proehl, Pr
Debra P Crawford, Sr VP
Carey J Fox, Sr VP
Michael D Step, Senior Vice President Corporate Development
Teri L Chuppe, Corporate Controller
EMP: 290 EST: 1998
SQ FT: 40,000
SALES (est): 98.15MM
SALES (corp-wide): 8.05B Privately Held
Web: www.salix.com
SIC: 2834 Pharmaceutical preparations
HQ: Salix Pharmaceuticals, Ltd.
400 Smrst Corp Blvd # 500
Bridgewater NJ 08807

(G-13229)
SAPIENS AMERICAS CORPORATION (DH)
801 Corporate Center Dr Ste 310 # 320 (27607-5486)
PHONE.................................919 405-1500
Ronnie Al-dor, CEO
Andrew Treitel, *
Gina Rubendall, *

EMP: 18 EST: 1991
SQ FT: 9,000
SALES (est): 120.91MM Privately Held
Web: www.sapiens.com
SIC: 7372 Application computer software
HQ: Sapiens International Corporation B.V.
Onbekend Nederlands Adres
Onbekend
97237902000

(G-13230)
SASH AND SABER CASTINGS
119 Dublin Rd (27609-3822)
PHONE.................................919 870-5513
EMP: 6 EST: 2011
SALES (est): 88.73K Privately Held
Web: www.sashandsaber.com
SIC: 3812 Defense systems and equipment

(G-13231)
SAVAGE PROS LLC
1213 Brown Straw Dr (27610-3102)
PHONE.................................919 971-3153
Terry Hawkins, Prin
EMP: 5 EST: 2015
SALES (est): 105.66K Privately Held
SIC: 2741 Miscellaneous publishing

(G-13232)
SAVOYE SOLUTIONS INC
5408 Von Hoyt Dr (27613-6820)
PHONE.................................919 466-9784
EMP: 6 EST: 2009
SALES (est): 117.88K Privately Held
SIC: 3577 Computer peripheral equipment, nec

(G-13233)
SAVVY MILLWORK LLC
4504 Fox Rd (27616-5265)
PHONE.................................919 625-5387
EMP: 6 EST: 2015
SALES (est): 105.16K Privately Held
SIC: 2499 Wood products, nec

(G-13234)
SAVVY PARROT PARTNERS
3914 Center Creek Cir (27612-6261)
PHONE.................................919 417-8865
Wesley Mcclure, Mng Pt
Susan Mcclure, Ch Bd
EMP: 6 EST: 2014
SALES (est): 48.56K Privately Held
SIC: 2741 Miscellaneous publishing

(G-13235)
SBM INDUSTRIES LLC
3948 Browning Pl Ste 208 (27609-6512)
PHONE.................................919 625-3672
Gustavo Velazquez, Admn
EMP: 8 EST: 2016
SALES (est): 437.06K Privately Held
SIC: 3999 Manufacturing industries, nec

(G-13236)
SCATTERED WRENCHES INC
Also Called: Matt's Auto Shop
130 Annaron Ct (27603-3640)
PHONE.................................919 480-1605
Matt Simmons, Pr
EMP: 7
SALES (corp-wide): 197.46K Privately Held
Web: www.raleighev.com
SIC: 7539 7699 3694 Automotive repair shops, nec; Miscellaneous automotive repair services; Automotive electrical equipment, nec
PA: Scattered Wrenches Inc.
267 Timber Dr Unit 1248

Garner NC
919 454-4782

(G-13237)
SCHMALZ INC
5850 Oak Forest Dr (27616-2968)
PHONE.................................919 713-0880
Volker Schmitz, Pr
Gary Vickerson, *
▲ EMP: 110 EST: 1999
SQ FT: 5,000
SALES (est): 45.66MM
SALES (corp-wide): 146.36MM Privately Held
Web: www.schmalz.com
SIC: 5084 3563 Materials handling machinery; Vacuum (air extraction) systems, industrial
PA: Schmalz-International Gmbh
Johannes-Schmalz-Str. 1
Glatten BW 72293
744324030

(G-13238)
SCHNEIDER AUTOMATION INC
2641 Sumner Blvd (27616-3234)
PHONE.................................919 855-1262
Gregr Odiheim, Brnch Mgr
EMP: 133
SALES (corp-wide): 82.05M Privately Held
Web: www.telemecanique.com
SIC: 3699 Electrical equipment and supplies, nec
HQ: Schneider Automation Inc.
800 Federal St
Andover MA 01810
978 794-0800

(G-13239)
SCINOVIA CORP
8801 Fast Park Dr Ste 301 (27617-4853)
PHONE.................................703 957-0396
Scinovia Address, CEO
James Sund, CEO
EMP: 12 EST: 2014
SQ FT: 2,300
SALES (est): 1.1MM Privately Held
Web: www.scinovia.com
SIC: 3841 Diagnostic apparatus, medical

(G-13240)
SEAL INNOVATION INC
2520 Kenmore Dr (27608-1420)
PHONE.................................919 302-7870
Graham Snyder, CEO
Cassandra Taylor, Contrlr
EMP: 10 EST: 2013
SALES (est): 102.31K Privately Held
Web: www.swimsealsafe.com
SIC: 3669 Emergency alarms

(G-13241)
SEAMARE PRESS LLC
2004 Falls Farm Xing (27614-7894)
PHONE.................................919 846-3540
Shonette Charles, Owner
EMP: 5 EST: 2015
SALES (est): 50.03K Privately Held
Web: www.seamarepress.com
SIC: 2741 Miscellaneous publishing

(G-13242)
SEAS PUBLICATIONS
3608 Ladywood Ct (27616-9769)
PHONE.................................919 266-0035
Susan W Crumpler, Owner
EMP: 5 EST: 2014
SALES (est): 65.22K Privately Held
SIC: 2741 Miscellaneous publishing

Raleigh - Wake County (G-13243)

(G-13243)
SECURED SHRED
Also Called: Shred Instead
3901 Barrett Dr Ste 306 (27609-6653)
PHONE.................443 288-6375
James Knight, *Owner*
EMP: 7 **EST:** 2006
SALES (est): 486.41K **Privately Held**
SIC: 3589 7389 Shredders, industrial and commercial; Business Activities at Non-Commercial Site

(G-13244)
SELECTBUILD CONSTRUCTION INC
Also Called: BMC Construction
4800 Falls Of Neuse Rd Ste 400 (27609-8141)
PHONE.................208 331-4300
Stanley M Wilson, *Pr*
EMP: 34 **EST:** 1999
SALES (est): 2.06MM
SALES (corp-wide): 22.15B **Publicly Held**
SIC: 1521 1771 1751 2431 Single-family housing construction; Concrete work; Framing contractor; Windows and window parts and trim, wood
PA: Builders Firstsource, Inc.
6031 Connection Dr # 400
Irving TX 75039
214 880-3500

(G-13245)
SEVENTY EIGHT C INC
2660 Discovery Dr Ste 136 (27616-1907)
PHONE.................919 602-0677
EMP: 4 **EST:** 2015
SALES (est): 48.86K **Privately Held**
SIC: 2085 Distilled and blended liquors

(G-13246)
SHARE ADVENTURES PUBG INC
10110 Knotty Pine Ln (27617-8218)
PHONE.................919 973-1299
Kyra Burton, *Prin*
EMP: 4 **EST:** 2017
SALES (est): 69.43K **Privately Held**
SIC: 2741 Miscellaneous publishing

(G-13247)
SHEET METAL PRODUCTS INC
3728 Overlook Rd (27616-3039)
PHONE.................919 954-9950
Ryan Wilson, *Mgr*
EMP: 6 **EST:** 2004
SALES (est): 646.35K **Privately Held**
Web: www.smpnc.com
SIC: 3444 Sheet metalwork

(G-13248)
SHERWIN-WILLIAMS COMPANY
Also Called: Sherwin-Williams
5301 Capital Blvd (27616-2956)
PHONE.................919 436-2460
Jeff Allen, *Prin*
EMP: 6
SALES (corp-wide): 22.15B **Publicly Held**
Web: www.sherwin-williams.com
SIC: 2851 5198 Paints and allied products; Paint brushes, rollers, sprayers
PA: The Sherwin-Williams Company
101 W Prospect Ave # 1020
Cleveland OH 44115
216 566-2000

(G-13249)
SHOE VENOM
5433 Neuse View Dr (27610-1528)
PHONE.................919 763-4512
Candace Marie Brangan, *Pr*
EMP: 6 **EST:** 2015
SALES (est): 121.58K **Privately Held**
SIC: 2836 Venoms

(G-13250)
SHOWLINE INC (PA)
Also Called: US Soaps Manufacturing Co
2114 Atlantic Ave Ste 160 (27604-1555)
PHONE.................919 255-9160
Patrick Diehl, *Pr*
▲ **EMP:** 17 **EST:** 2009
SQ FT: 65,000
SALES (est): 2.59MM
SALES (corp-wide): 2.59MM **Privately Held**
SIC: 2841 Soap and other detergents

(G-13251)
SHOWLINE AUTOMOTIVE PDTS INC (PA)
1108 N New Hope Rd (27610-1416)
PHONE.................919 255-9160
Patrick Diehl, *CEO*
Robert Patrick Diehl Junior, *Pr*
EMP: 9 **EST:** 1999
SQ FT: 16,000
SALES (est): 1.82MM
SALES (corp-wide): 1.82MM **Privately Held**
SIC: 2841 Detergents, synthetic organic or inorganic alkaline

(G-13252)
SHRED-TECH USA LLC
4701 Trademark Dr (27610-3051)
PHONE.................919 387-8220
Tim Fields, *Managing Member*
EMP: 4 **EST:** 2007
SQ FT: 5,000
SALES (est): 1.07MM **Privately Held**
Web: www.shred-tech.com
SIC: 3559 Recycling machinery
HQ: Shred-Tech Corporation
295 Pinebush Rd
Cambridge ON N1T 1
519 621-3560

(G-13253)
SIDE HUSTLE VENTURES LLC
Also Called: Altered State Brewing Company
8471 Garvey Dr Ste 115 (27616-3370)
PHONE.................919 816-2324
Andrew Adams, *Mgr*
EMP: 5 **EST:** 2020
SALES (est): 105.21K **Privately Held**
SIC: 2082 Malt beverages

(G-13254)
SIGN SCIENTIST LLC
335 Sherwee Dr Ste 103 (27603-3510)
PHONE.................919 685-7641
David Bogart, *Pr*
EMP: 5 **EST:** 2014
SALES (est): 215.33K **Privately Held**
Web: www.signscientist.com
SIC: 3993 Signs and advertising specialties

(G-13255)
SIGN-A-RAMA
Also Called: Sign A Rama
972 Trinity Rd (27607-4940)
P.O. Box 51004 (27717-1004)
PHONE.................919 383-5561
Thomas Zelaney, *Pr*
Brian Cox, *Sec*
EMP: 8 **EST:** 1990
SALES (est): 922.36K **Privately Held**
Web: www.signarama.com
SIC: 3993 Signs and advertising specialties

(G-13256)
SIGNERGY LLC
12208 Warwickshire Way (27613-6024)
PHONE.................919 876-1370
Douglas Whiteley, *Prin*
EMP: 4 **EST:** 2014
SALES (est): 224.04K **Privately Held**
Web: www.signergy.us
SIC: 3993 Signs and advertising specialties

(G-13257)
SIGNIFICANT OTHERS
2201 Digby Ct (27613-4320)
PHONE.................919 539-7551
Ellen Condelli, *Prin*
EMP: 5 **EST:** 2010
SALES (est): 85.75K **Privately Held**
SIC: 3993 Signs and advertising specialties

(G-13258)
SIGNS BY DESIGN
10350 Sugarberry Ct # 204 (27614-6479)
PHONE.................919 217-8000
Maggie Clark, *Prin*
EMP: 4 **EST:** 2016
SALES (est): 60.14K **Privately Held**
SIC: 3993 Signs and advertising specialties

(G-13259)
SIGNS BY DESIGN
4112 Pleasant Valley Rd Ste 120 (27612-6256)
PHONE.................919 217-8000
Susan Clark, *Sls Mgr*
EMP: 5 **EST:** 2006
SALES (est): 69.2K **Privately Held**
Web: www.signsbydesignnc.com
SIC: 3993 Signs and advertising specialties

(G-13260)
SIGNS NOW
2424 Atlantic Ave (27604-1410)
PHONE.................919 546-0006
EMP: 6 **EST:** 1995
SALES (est): 367.95K **Privately Held**
Web: www.signsnow.com
SIC: 3993 Signs and advertising specialties

(G-13261)
SILANNA SEMICDTR N AMER INC
1130 Situs Ct Ste 100 (27606-3372)
PHONE.................984 444-6500
EMP: 84
Web: www.silanna.com
SIC: 3674 3625 3679 Semiconductor circuit networks; Switches, electronic applications; Electronic switches
HQ: Silanna Semiconductor North America, Inc.
4795 Estgate Mall Ste 100
San Diego CA 92121
858 373-0440

(G-13262)
SIMON INDUSTRIES INC
Also Called: Wakefield Solutions
2910 Industrial Dr (27609-7529)
PHONE.................919 469-2004
David Stone, *Pr*
Wayne Frerichs, *
James J Polakiewicz, *
EMP: 42 **EST:** 1997
SQ FT: 50,000
SALES (est): 7.4MM **Privately Held**
Web: www.wakefieldthermal.com
SIC: 3444 8711 Forming machine work, sheet metal; Engineering services
HQ: Wakefield Thermal Solutions, Inc.
120 Northwest Blvd
Nashua NH 03063
603 635-2800

(G-13263)
SIMPLIFYBER INC ◊
625 Hutton St Ste 106 (27606-6321)
PHONE.................919 396-8355
Philip Cohen, *Pr*
EMP: 6 **EST:** 2022
SALES (est): 79.3K **Privately Held**
SIC: 2221 Bedspreads, silk and manmade fiber

(G-13264)
SINNOVATEK INC
2609 Discovery Dr Ste 115 (27616-1905)
PHONE.................919 694-0974
Michael Druga, *Pr*
Amanda Vargochik, *VP*
Josip Simunovic, *CSO*
EMP: 7 **EST:** 2016
SALES (est): 2.5MM **Privately Held**
Web: www.sinnovatek.com
SIC: 5084 3499 3589 3556 Food product manufacturing machinery; Fire- or burglary-resistive products; Commercial cooking and foodwarming equipment; Food products machinery

(G-13265)
SINNOVITA INC
2609 Discovery Dr Ste 115 (27616-1905)
PHONE.................919 694-0974
Michael Druga, *Pr*
EMP: 8 **EST:** 2016
SALES (est): 555.5K **Privately Held**
Web: www.sinnovatek.com
SIC: 2099 Food preparations, nec

(G-13266)
SINOWEST MFG LLC
5915 Oak Frest Dr Ste 103 (27616)
PHONE.................919 289-9337
Abdulhameed Manadath, *Prin*
EMP: 4 **EST:** 2017
SALES (est): 332.37K **Privately Held**
SIC: 2911 Diesel fuels

(G-13267)
SIR PLASMA
9005 Brook Garden Ct (27615-3756)
PHONE.................919 232-1961
EMP: 6 **EST:** 2017
SALES (est): 95.42K **Privately Held**
SIC: 2836 Plasmas

(G-13268)
SIRE TEES
6104 Westgate Rd Ste 115 (27617-4618)
PHONE.................919 787-6843
Brian Unger, *Prin*
EMP: 4 **EST:** 2011
SALES (est): 199.91K **Privately Held**
Web: www.sirescreenprinting.com
SIC: 2752 Offset printing

(G-13269)
SITELINK SOFTWARE LLC
3301 Atlantic Ave (27604-1658)
P.O. Box 19744 (27619-9744)
PHONE.................919 865-0789
Chuck Gordon, *CEO*
Ross Lampe, *
Luke Lenzen, *
EMP: 96 **EST:** 2006
SALES (est): 10.93MM
SALES (corp-wide): 25.78MM **Privately Held**
Web: www.sitelink.com
SIC: 7372 Prepackaged software
PA: Sparefoot, Llc
11000 N Mopac Expy # 300
Austin TX 78759
844 264-4136

GEOGRAPHIC SECTION

Raleigh - Wake County (G-13297)

(G-13270)
SKAN US INC
7409 Acc Blvd Ste 200 (27617-1920)
PHONE............919 354-6380
Sonia White, *Prin*
◆ **EMP:** 12 **EST:** 2011
SALES (est): 10.86MM **Privately Held**
Web: www.skan.com
SIC: 3674 Semiconductors and related devices
HQ: Skan Ag
Kreuzstrasse 5
Allschwil BL 4123

(G-13271)
SMALL BUSINESS SOFTWARE LLC
5117 Wickham Rd (27606-2547)
PHONE............919 400-8298
Brett J Stephenson, *Admn*
EMP: 5 **EST:** 2010
SALES (est): 106.54K **Privately Held**
SIC: 7372 Prepackaged software

(G-13272)
SMART CAST GROUP
Also Called: Fortis Track
5540 Centerview Dr Ste 204 (27606-3363)
PHONE............855 971-2287
Puia Purkyan, *Brnch Mgr*
EMP: 10 **EST:** 2017
SALES (est): 533.6K **Privately Held**
SIC: 3011 3531 Industrial tires, pneumatic; Tractors, tracklaying

(G-13273)
SMT INC
7300 Acc Blvd (27617-8407)
PHONE............919 782-4804
EMP: 64 **EST:** 1969
SALES (est): 14.18MM **Privately Held**
Web: www.smtcoinc.com
SIC: 3444 Sheet metalwork

(G-13274)
SO & SO SOCKS
6325 Falls Of Neuse Rd (27615-6877)
PHONE............919 437-6458
Martrenia Carr, *Prin*
EMP: 5 **EST:** 2016
SALES (est): 80.38K **Privately Held**
SIC: 2252 Socks

(G-13275)
SOFTWARE PROFESSIONALS INC
8529 Six Forks Rd Ste 400 (27615-4972)
PHONE............503 860-4507
EMP: 8 **EST:** 2018
SALES (est): 648.29K **Privately Held**
SIC: 7372 Prepackaged software

(G-13276)
SOLAR HOT LIMITED
Also Called: Solar Hot USA
1105 Transport Dr (27604-4146)
PHONE............919 439-2387
Dan Gretsch, *VP*
EMP: 7 **EST:** 2007
SALES (est): 700.25K **Privately Held**
Web: www.solarhotusa.com
SIC: 3433 5074 Solar heaters and collectors; Heating equipment and panels, solar

(G-13277)
SOLAR PACK
Also Called: Solarpack
1791 Varsity Dr (27606-5241)
PHONE............919 515-2194
Bryon Spells, *VP*
Hannah Schauer, *
EMP: 42 **EST:** 2016
SQ FT: 78,022
SALES (est): 1.46MM **Privately Held**
SIC: 3711 Cars, electric, assembly of

(G-13278)
SOLARBROOK WATER AND PWR CORP (PA)
1220 Corporation Pkwy Ste 103 (27610)
PHONE............919 231-3205
George A Moore, *CEO*
Shane Traveller, *Dir*
Ross W Smith, *Dir*
Michael Griffith, *COO*
EMP: 4 **EST:** 1999
SQ FT: 4,550
SALES (est): 704.93K
SALES (corp-wide): 704.93K **Privately Held**
Web: www.solarbrookwaterandpower.com
SIC: 3589 6799 3823 5999 Water treatment equipment, industrial; Investors, nec; Process control instruments; Water purification equipment

(G-13279)
SOLARH2OT LTD
Also Called: Solarhot
1105 Transport Dr (27604-4146)
PHONE............919 439-2387
Jeanette Gretsch, *Pr*
Daniel Gretsch, *VP*
Dan Gretsch, *VP*
▲ **EMP:** 6 **EST:** 2006
SQ FT: 8,750
SALES (est): 719.44K **Privately Held**
Web: www.solarhotusa.com
SIC: 3433 6531 Solar heaters and collectors; Real estate managers

(G-13280)
SOLVAY USA INC
Also Called: SOLVAY USA INC.
9650 Strickland Rd Ste 103 (27615-1902)
PHONE............919 786-4555
Glewn Simon, *Brnch Mgr*
EMP: 201
SALES (corp-wide): 146.05MM **Privately Held**
Web: www.solvay.com
SIC: 2819 Industrial inorganic chemicals, nec
HQ: Solvay Usa Llc
504 Carnegie Ctr
Princeton NJ 08540
609 860-4000

(G-13281)
SOUTHEASTERN MBL WLDG REPR LLC
1321 Greenbranch Ln (27603-2051)
PHONE............919 521-7039
Terry Fish, *Managing Member*
EMP: 5 **EST:** 2016
SALES (est): 169.23K **Privately Held**
SIC: 7692 Welding repair

(G-13282)
SOUTHERN CUSTOM DOORS JAMES NA
2025 Travianna Ct (27609-4168)
PHONE............919 986-6943
EMP: 4 **EST:** 2015
SALES (est): 69.35K **Privately Held**
Web: www.southerncustomdoor.com
SIC: 2431 Millwork

(G-13283)
SOUTHERN CUSTOM DOORS LLC
8308 Grey Abbey Pl (27615-2823)
PHONE............919 889-5404
EMP: 5 **EST:** 2018
SALES (est): 56.29K **Privately Held**
Web: www.southerncustomdoor.com
SIC: 2431 Millwork

(G-13284)
SOUTHERN WICKED DISTILLERY INC
3211 Imperial Oaks Dr (27614-7881)
PHONE............919 539-1620
Tolan Lucas, *Prin*
EMP: 5 **EST:** 2015
SALES (est): 169.8K **Privately Held**
SIC: 2082 Malt beverages

(G-13285)
SOUTHSTERN EDCTL TOY BK DSTRS
3071 Business Park Dr # 116 (27610-3057)
PHONE............919 954-0140
Gary Odom, *CEO*
EMP: 22 **EST:** 2008
SALES (est): 335.83K **Privately Held**
SIC: 2759 Advertising literature: printing, nsk

(G-13286)
SPECGX LLC
8801 Capital Blvd (27616-3116)
PHONE............919 878-4706
Keitha Buckingham, *Brnch Mgr*
EMP: 250
Web: www.mallinckrodt.com
SIC: 2834 2899 Analgesics; Chemical preparations, nec
HQ: Specgx Llc
385 Marshall Ave
Webster Groves MO

(G-13287)
SPECTRA INTEGRATED SYSTEMS INC
4805 Green Rd Ste 110 (27616-2848)
PHONE............919 876-3666
EMP: 5
SALES (corp-wide): 4.54MM **Privately Held**
SIC: 3699 Laser systems and equipment
PA: Spectra Integrated Systems, Inc.
8100 Arrowridge Blvd G
Charlotte NC 28273
704 525-7099

(G-13288)
SPECTRUM NEWS
2505 Atlantic Ave Ste 102 (27604-1593)
PHONE............919 882-4009
EMP: 10 **EST:** 2019
SALES (est): 232.97K **Privately Held**
SIC: 2721 Periodicals

(G-13289)
SPEEDPRO IMAGING
2400 Sumner Blvd Ste 110 (27616-6676)
PHONE............919 578-4338
EMP: 5 **EST:** 2017
SALES (est): 204.16K **Privately Held**
Web: www.speedpro.com
SIC: 3993 Signs and advertising specialties

(G-13290)
SPIRAL GRAPHICS INC
8821 Gulf Ct Ste A (27617-4612)
PHONE............919 571-3371
Donnie Williams, *Owner*
EMP: 9 **EST:** 1993
SQ FT: 3,500
SALES (est): 651.23K **Privately Held**
Web: www.spiralgraphics.com
SIC: 2759 Screen printing

(G-13291)
SPIRE INDUSTRIES INC
2524 S Wilmington St (27603-2548)
PHONE............435 994-4756
Jimmy Lynn, *Prin*
EMP: 4 **EST:** 2018
SALES (est): 39.69K **Privately Held**
SIC: 3999 Manufacturing industries, nec

(G-13292)
SPIRIT AEROSYSTEMS NC INC
2626 Glenwood Ave Ste 550 (27608-1370)
PHONE............252 208-4645
Jeff Turner, *CEO*
◆ **EMP:** 10 **EST:** 2006
SALES (est): 2.61MM **Publicly Held**
Web: www.spiritaero.com
SIC: 3728 Aircraft parts and equipment, nec
PA: Spirit Aerosystems Holdings, Inc.
3801 S Oliver St
Wichita KS 67210

(G-13293)
SPOONS BOWLS N BAKING PANS LLC
101 Saint Mellion St (27603-4174)
PHONE............919 662-0494
Devonne Daniels, *Prin*
EMP: 5 **EST:** 2014
SALES (est): 82.72K **Privately Held**
SIC: 2051 Bread, cake, and related products

(G-13294)
SPROUT PHARMACEUTICALS INC
4350 Lassiter At North Hills Ave Ste 260 (27609-5743)
PHONE............919 882-0850
Cynthia Whitehead, *CEO*
Robert Whitehead, *COO*
Eric Atkins, *CFO*
EMP: 10 **EST:** 2011
SALES (est): 5.41MM
SALES (corp-wide): 5.41MM **Privately Held**
Web: www.sproutpharmaceuticals.com
SIC: 2834 Pharmaceutical preparations
PA: Sprout2 Inc.
4208 Six Forks Rd # 1010
Raleigh NC 27609
844 746-5745

(G-13295)
SSI SERVICES INC
7231 Acc Blvd Ste 107 (27617-4886)
PHONE............919 867-1450
Bryan Johnson, *Pr*
Cindy Anderson, *CFO*
EMP: 5 **EST:** 2012
SQ FT: 2,000
SALES (est): 1.36MM **Privately Held**
Web: www.ssiservicesusa.com
SIC: 4783 8711 3613 Crating goods for shipping; Engineering services; Control panels, electric

(G-13296)
STACLEAR INC
7250 Acc Blvd (27617-8736)
PHONE............919 838-2844
Vinay Sakhrani, *Pr*
EMP: 4
SALES (est): 182.43K **Privately Held**
SIC: 3841 Surgical and medical instruments

(G-13297)
STAINLESS STEEL SPC INC
2025 Carr Pur Dr (27603-8885)
PHONE............919 779-4290
Ricky Ennis, *Pr*
Brenda Ennis, *Sec*

Amanda Daley, *Brnch Mgr*
EMP: 12 **EST:** 1989
SQ FT: 9,500
SALES (est): 2.27MM **Privately Held**
Web: www.ssspec.com
SIC: 3441 Fabricated structural metal

(G-13298)
STAINLESS STL FABRICATORS INC
5325 Departure Dr (27616-1835)
P.O. Box 58459 (27658-8459)
PHONE..................919 833-3520
William E Bolton Iii, *Pr*
EMP: 19 **EST:** 2000
SQ FT: 30,000
SALES (est): 2.44MM **Privately Held**
Web: www.sstlf.com
SIC: 3441 Fabricated structural metal

(G-13299)
STARTA DEVELOPMENT INC
Also Called: Cstruct
2610 Wycliff Rd Ste 19 (27607-3073)
PHONE..................919 865-7700
Gordon Blackwell, *Prin*
Dave Demski, *Prin*
EMP: 7 **EST:** 2000
SQ FT: 5,000
SALES (est): 346.5K **Privately Held**
Web: www.startadev.com
SIC: 7372 Business oriented computer software

(G-13300)
STAY ALERT SAFETY SERVICES INC
Also Called: STAY ALERT SAFETY SERVICES, INC.
1240 Kirkland Rd (27603-2850)
P.O. Box 467 (27285-0467)
PHONE..................919 828-5399
Melissa Babcock, *Brnch Mgr*
EMP: 40
SALES (corp-wide): 539.72MM **Privately Held**
Web: www.stayalertsafety.com
SIC: 3993 Signs and advertising specialties
HQ: Stay Alert Safety Services, Llc
272 Clayton Forest Rd
Kernersville NC 27284
336 993-2828

(G-13301)
STEELFAB OF VIRGINIA INC (HQ)
5105 Bur Oak Cir Ste 100 (27612-3160)
PHONE..................919 828-9545
EMP: 21 **EST:** 1990
SALES (est): 102.65MM
SALES (corp-wide): 327.38MM **Privately Held**
SIC: 3449 3441 Miscellaneous metalwork; Fabricated structural metal
PA: Steelfab, Inc.
3025 Westport Rd
Charlotte NC 28208
704 394-5376

(G-13302)
STERLING PUBLICATIONS LLC
3809 Sparrow Pond Ln (27606-8505)
PHONE..................919 656-5042
EMP: 5 **EST:** 2019
SALES (est): 195.64K **Privately Held**
SIC: 2741 Miscellaneous publishing

(G-13303)
STEVE BROOKS
4725 Regalwood Dr (27613-7040)
PHONE..................919 248-1458
Steve Brooks, *Prin*
EMP: 5 **EST:** 2017
SALES (est): 85.99K **Privately Held**

SIC: 3571 Electronic computers

(G-13304)
STEVENS FOODSERVICE
8392 Six Forks Rd Ste 202 (27615-3061)
PHONE..................919 322-5470
EMP: 6 **EST:** 2010
SALES (est): 355.93K **Privately Held**
SIC: 2032 Canned specialties

(G-13305)
STOCK BUILDING SUPPLY HOLDINGS LLC
8020 Arco Corp Dr Ste 400 (27617)
P.O. Box 90068 (27675-0068)
PHONE..................919 431-1000
▲ **EMP:** 2557
SIC: 5211 2431 5031 5713 Millwork and lumber; Millwork; Lumber: rough, dressed, and finished; Floor covering stores

(G-13306)
STOWE WOODWARD LICENSCO LLC
8537 Six Forks Rd Ste 300 (27615-6545)
PHONE..................919 526-1400
EMP: 8 **EST:** 1988
SALES (est): 151.47K **Privately Held**
SIC: 2221 Broadwoven fabric mills, manmade

(G-13307)
STRATEGIC 3D SOLUTIONS INC
Also Called: Strategic3dsolutions
4805 Green Rd Ste 114 (27616-2848)
PHONE..................919 451-5963
EMP: 10 **EST:** 2011
SALES (est): 207.07K **Privately Held**
Web: www.strategic3dsolutions.com
SIC: 3577 Printers and plotters

(G-13308)
STRONGER BY SCIENCE TECH LLC
514 Daniels St 101 (27605-1317)
PHONE..................336 391-9377
EMP: 5 **EST:** 2021
SALES (est): 117.25K **Privately Held**
Web: www.strongerbyscience.com
SIC: 7372 Application computer software

(G-13309)
STRUCTURAL PLANNERS INC
312 Dalton Dr (27615-1654)
PHONE..................919 848-8964
Thomas J Vassallo, *Pr*
Pauline Vassallo, *Sec*
EMP: 10 **EST:** 1977
SALES (est): 831.54K **Privately Held**
Web: www.structuralplannersinc.com
SIC: 3441 Fabricated structural metal

(G-13310)
STRYKER CORP
525 Pylon Dr (27606-1414)
PHONE..................919 455-6755
EMP: 9 **EST:** 2019
SALES (est): 465.4K **Privately Held**
Web: www.stryker.com
SIC: 3841 Surgical and medical instruments

(G-13311)
SUCCESS IN MARKETPLACE LLC
5300 Six Forks Rd Ste 213 (27609-4465)
PHONE..................919 608-1259
Tonja Austin, *Prin*
EMP: 5 **EST:** 2018
SALES (est): 91.31K **Privately Held**
SIC: 3429 Hardware, nec

(G-13312)
SUCCESS PUBLISHING INC
Also Called: Success Magazine
150 Fayetteville St M (27601-1395)
PHONE..................919 807-1100
Victoria Conte, *Pr*
Chris Reid, *Sec*
EMP: 109 **EST:** 1999
SALES (est): 409.69K **Privately Held**
SIC: 2721 Magazines: publishing only, not printed on site
PA: The Successful Company Llc
150 Fayetteville St
Raleigh NC 27601

(G-13313)
SUMITOMO ELC LIGHTWAVE CORP
201 S Rogers Ln Ste 100 (27610-4336)
PHONE..................919 541-8100
Koji Niikura, *Pr*
Junichiro Hanai, *
Barrett Mills, *
Kevin Mistele, *Marketing**
Patria Smith, *Corporate Secretary**
▼ **EMP:** 200 **EST:** 1994
SALES (est): 92.46MM **Privately Held**
Web: www.sumitomoelectriclightwave.com
SIC: 3357 Communication wire
PA: Sumitomo Electric Industries, Ltd.
4-5-33, Kitahama, Chuo-Ku
Osaka OSK 541-0

(G-13314)
SUNDAY DRIVE HOLDINGS INC
421 Fayetteville St # 1100 (27601-1792)
P.O. Box 98084 (27624-8084)
PHONE..................919 825-5613
Francesco Gozzo, *Pr*
Robert Woodruff, *Prin*
EMP: 9 **EST:** 2002
SALES (est): 235K **Privately Held**
SIC: 7372 Business oriented computer software

(G-13315)
SUNROCK GROUP HOLDINGS CORP (PA)
200 Horizon Dr Ste 100 (27615-4947)
PHONE..................919 747-6400
Bryan M Pfohl, *Ch*
Gregg W Bowler, *
Katherine Pfohl Tejano, *
Elisabeth A Pfohl Sasser, *
John A Tankard Iii, *General Vice President*
EMP: 80 **EST:** 2004
SALES (est): 68.06MM
SALES (corp-wide): 68.06MM **Privately Held**
Web: www.thesunrockgroup.com
SIC: 1429 3273 2951 1411 Trap rock, crushed and broken-quarrying; Ready-mixed concrete; Asphalt paving mixtures and blocks; Dimension stone

(G-13316)
SUNTORY INTERNATIONAL (DH)
4141 Parklake Ave Ste 600 (27612-2380)
PHONE..................917 756-2747
Tsuyoshi Nishizaki, *Pr*
Yoshihiko Kunimoto, *Ex VP*
Tsutomu Santoki, *CFO*
Yoshito Shihara, *Treas*
Masaru Ijima, *Sec*
◆ **EMP:** 13 **EST:** 1967
SQ FT: 5,100
SALES (est): 1.26B **Privately Held**
Web: www.beamsuntory.com

SIC: 5149 2084 2086 5499 Mineral or spring water bottling; Wines, brandy, and brandy spirits; Bottled and canned soft drinks; Health and dietetic food stores
HQ: Suntory Spirits Limited
2-3-3, Daiba
Minato-Ku TKY 135-0

(G-13317)
SUPREME T-SHIRTS & APPAREL
2813 Banks Rd (27603-8943)
PHONE..................919 772-9040
Paulette Disbrow, *Pr*
EMP: 17 **EST:** 2017
SALES (est): 157.5K **Privately Held**
Web: www.shopsupremets.com
SIC: 2759 Screen printing

(G-13318)
SURTRONICS INC
4001 Beryl Rd (27606-1451)
P.O. Box 33459 (27636-3459)
PHONE..................919 834-8027
Angela D Stanley, *CEO*
EMP: 47 **EST:** 1965
SQ FT: 41,000
SALES (est): 6.48MM **Privately Held**
Web: www.surtronics.com
SIC: 3471 Electroplating of metals or formed products

(G-13319)
SYMBRIUM INC (PA)
Also Called: Factory Systems
6021 Triangle Dr (27617-4744)
P.O. Box 90514 (27675-0514)
PHONE..................919 879-2470
Alicia A Blankenship, *Prin*
G Wesley Blankenship, *COO*
EMP: 15 **EST:** 2013
SQ FT: 25,000
SALES (est): 2.38MM
SALES (corp-wide): 2.38MM **Privately Held**
Web: www.symbrium.com
SIC: 7372 3823 Application computer software; Computer interface equipment, for industrial process control

(G-13320)
SYNCHRONO GROUP INC
8601 Six Forks Rd Ste 400 (27615-2965)
PHONE..................888 389-0439
EMP: 47 **EST:** 2019
SALES (est): 3.14MM **Privately Held**
Web: www.synchronosure.com
SIC: 3695 Computer software tape and disks: blank, rigid, and floppy

(G-13321)
SYNTEGON TECHNOLOGY SVCS LLC (PA)
2440 Sumner Blvd (27616-3275)
PHONE..................919 877-0886
Gary Anderton, *Pr*
Brian Dieter, *
Shane Larsen, *
▲ **EMP:** 44 **EST:** 2000
SALES (est): 25.49MM
SALES (corp-wide): 25.49MM **Privately Held**
Web: www.syntegon.com
SIC: 3599 3565 Machine shop, jobbing and repair; Packaging machinery

(G-13322)
T HOFF MANUFACTURING CORP (PA)
4500 Preslyn Dr D (27603)
PHONE..................919 833-8671

GEOGRAPHIC SECTION

Raleigh - Wake County (G-13349)

Theodore C Hoffman, *Pr*
Bill White, *CFO*
EMP: 4 **EST:** 1968
SQ FT: 19,000
SALES (est): 546.56K
SALES (corp-wide): 546.56K **Privately Held**
Web: www.t-hoff.com
SIC: 3599 Machine shop, jobbing and repair

(G-13323)
TACTILE WORKSHOP LLC
1001 S Saunders St (27603-2201)
PHONE...............................919 738-9924
EMP: 7 **EST:** 2014
SALES (est): 421.59K **Privately Held**
Web: www.tactilewksp.com
SIC: 3541 Home workshop machine tools, metalworking

(G-13324)
TAG-M PRINTS
8318 Tierra Del Sol Way (27616-3512)
PHONE...............................919 615-4222
Tyronza Lewis, *Prin*
EMP: 4 **EST:** 2016
SALES (est): 101.02K **Privately Held**
SIC: 2752 Commercial printing, lithographic

(G-13325)
TAGTRAUM INDUSTRIES INC
724 Nash Dr (27608-2420)
PHONE...............................919 809-7797
Hendrik Schreiber, *Pr*
EMP: 4 **EST:** 2004
SALES (est): 105.57K **Privately Held**
Web: www.tagtraum.com
SIC: 3999 Manufacturing industries, nec

(G-13326)
TALLAHASSEE DEMOCRAT
4600 Trinity Rd (27607-3924)
PHONE...............................919 832-9430
Steve Clark, *Prin*
EMP: 9 **EST:** 2007
SALES (est): 98.33K **Privately Held**
Web: www.tallahassee.com
SIC: 2711 Newspapers, publishing and printing

(G-13327)
TANNIS ROOT PRODUCTIONS INC
Also Called: Cognito Promo
1720 Capital Blvd (27604-1362)
PHONE...............................919 832-8552
Barbara Herring, *Pr*
William Mooney, *VP*
▲ **EMP:** 9 **EST:** 1992
SQ FT: 4,600
SALES (est): 825.56K **Privately Held**
Web: www.tannisroot.com
SIC: 2759 5199 7336 Screen printing; Advertising specialties; Graphic arts and related design

(G-13328)
TAR HEEL ENDDNTIC EDCTL FNDTIO
2920 Ballybunion Way (27613-5402)
PHONE...............................207 843-6703
EMP: 4 **EST:** 2019
SALES (est): 66.08K **Privately Held**
SIC: 1442 Construction sand and gravel

(G-13329)
TC2 LABS LLC
3948 Browning Pl Ste 334 (27609-6534)
PHONE...............................919 380-2171
EMP: 5 **EST:** 2015
SALES (est): 480.29K **Privately Held**
Web: www.tc2.com

SIC: 3823 7371 Infrared instruments, industrial process type; Software programming applications

(G-13330)
TD CLOUD SERVICES
Also Called: Td Cloud
3129 Oaklyn Springs Dr (27606-8311)
PHONE...............................518 258-6788
Christopher Groff, *Mng Pt*
EMP: 5 **EST:** 2013
SALES (est): 205.83K **Privately Held**
SIC: 7372 7389 Business oriented computer software; Business services, nec

(G-13331)
TEA AND HONEY BLENDS LLC
444 S Blount St Ste 115b (27601-2087)
PHONE...............................919 673-4273
EMP: 5 **EST:** 2008
SALES (est): 236.34K **Privately Held**
SIC: 2844 Perfumes, cosmetics and other toilet preparations

(G-13332)
TEAM TRIANGLE CABINETS
3209 Gresham Lake Rd Ste 105 (27615-4131)
PHONE...............................919 609-1332
EMP: 4 **EST:** 2018
SALES (est): 156.46K **Privately Held**
SIC: 2434 Wood kitchen cabinets

(G-13333)
TEBO DISPLAYS LLC
2609 Discovery Dr Ste 105 (27616-1905)
PHONE...............................919 832-8525
Joseph White, *Managing Member*
EMP: 6 **EST:** 2012
SALES (est): 482.2K **Privately Held**
Web: www.jwimageco.com
SIC: 3993 Signs and advertising specialties

(G-13334)
TECHJOURNAL SOUTH
211 N Boylan Ave (27603-1424)
PHONE...............................919 832-1858
Richard Giersh, *Dir*
EMP: 6 **EST:** 2010
SALES (est): 101.41K **Privately Held**
Web: www.techjournalsouth.com
SIC: 2721 Magazines: publishing only, not printed on site

(G-13335)
TEKTRONIX INC
Also Called: Tektronix
5608 Pine Dr (27606-8944)
PHONE...............................919 233-9490
Richard Willis, *CEO*
EMP: 5
SALES (corp-wide): 6.07MM **Publicly Held**
Web: www.tek.com
SIC: 3825 Test equipment for electronic and electric measurement
HQ: Tektronix, Inc.
    14150 Sw Karl Braun Dr
    Beaverton OR 97005
    800 833-9200

(G-13336)
TELECMMNCTONS RESOURCE MGT INC
Also Called: TRM
156 Annaron Ct (27603-3640)
PHONE...............................919 779-0776
Thomas Mcdowell, *Pr*
Thomas Mcdowell, *Pr*
Tammy Mcdowell, *Sec*

Kevin Sullivan, *VP*
EMP: 12 **EST:** 1997
SQ FT: 45,000
SALES (est): 2.43MM **Privately Held**
Web: www.trminc.net
SIC: 5999 1731 3429 5065 Telephone equipment and systems; Fiber optic cable installation; Security cable locking systems; Security control equipment and systems

(G-13337)
TELEPATHIC GRAPHICS INC (PA)
6001 Chapel Hill Rd Ste 106 (27607-0119)
PHONE...............................919 342-4603
Bob Boyle, *Pr*
Mark Gauley, *
EMP: 35 **EST:** 2004
SQ FT: 9,700
SALES (est): 10.56MM **Privately Held**
Web: www.telepathicgraphics.com
SIC: 2759 7374 Publication printing; Computer graphics service

(G-13338)
TELETEC CORPORATION
5617 Departure Dr Ste 107 (27616-1913)
PHONE...............................919 954-7300
Nader Al Farouqi, *Pr*
Harry F Taji, *Pr*
EMP: 18 **EST:** 1983
SQ FT: 3,000
SALES (est): 1.45MM **Privately Held**
Web: www.teleteccorporation.com
SIC: 8748 7382 3663 Telecommunications consultant; Security systems services; Encryption devices

(G-13339)
TERADATA CORPORATION
5565 Centerview Dr Ste 300 (27606-3563)
PHONE...............................919 816-1900
Charles Douthart, *Brnch Mgr*
EMP: 19
Web: www.teradata.com
SIC: 3571 Electronic computers
PA: Teradata Corporation
    17095 Via Del Campo
    San Diego CA 92127

(G-13340)
TETHIS INC
3401 Spring Forest Rd (27616-2948)
PHONE...............................919 808-2866
Robin Weitkamp, *CEO*
EMP: 40 **EST:** 2012
SQ FT: 1,200
SALES (est): 4.29MM **Privately Held**
Web: www.tethis.com
SIC: 2822 Ethylene-propylene rubbers, EPDM polymers

(G-13341)
TETHIS MANUFACTURING LLC
3401 Spring Forest Rd (27616-2948)
PHONE...............................919 808-2866
EMP: 5 **EST:** 2017
SALES (est): 121.34K **Privately Held**
Web: www.tethis.com
SIC: 3999 Manufacturing industries, nec

(G-13342)
THE TARHEEL ELECTRIC MEMBERSHIP ASSOCIATION INCORPORATED
Also Called: T E M A
8730 Wadford Dr (27616-9027)
P.O. Box 61050 (27661-1050)
PHONE...............................919 876-4603
EMP: 17 **EST:** 1950
SALES (est): 4.91MM **Privately Held**

Web: www.tema.coop
SIC: 3264 5722 Porcelain electrical supplies; Electric ranges

(G-13343)
THERAPEUTICS
Also Called: Self Helpers
309 Seawell Ave (27601-1255)
PHONE...............................919 695-7291
Hailey M Okamoto, *Admn*
EMP: 5 **EST:** 2015
SALES (est): 98.19K **Privately Held**
Web: www.plan-it-therapy.com
SIC: 2834 Pharmaceutical preparations

(G-13344)
THERMO FISHER SCIENTIFIC INC
3315 Atlantic Ave (27604-1680)
PHONE...............................919 876-2352
EMP: 27
SALES (corp-wide): 44.91B **Publicly Held**
Web: www.thermofisher.com
SIC: 3826 Analytical instruments
PA: Thermo Fisher Scientific Inc.
    168 3rd Ave
    Waltham MA 02451
    781 622-1000

(G-13345)
THIRDPARTY LABS
220 Fayetteville St Ste 200 (27601-1358)
PHONE...............................919 741-5118
EMP: 4 **EST:** 2016
SALES (est): 79.47K **Privately Held**
Web: www.thirdpartylabs.com
SIC: 7372 Prepackaged software

(G-13346)
THOMAS CONCRETE CAROLINA
609 Tucker St (27603-1231)
PHONE...............................919 828-6923
EMP: 6 **EST:** 2019
SALES (est): 124.72K **Privately Held**
SIC: 3273 Ready-mixed concrete

(G-13347)
THOMAS CONCRETE CAROLINA INC (DH)
1131 Nw Street (27603-1143)
P.O. Box 12544 (27605-2544)
PHONE...............................919 832-0451
John N Holding Junior, *Pr*
EMP: 10 **EST:** 1959
SQ FT: 3,000
SALES (est): 23.47MM
SALES (corp-wide): 1.01B **Privately Held**
Web: www.thomasconcrete.com
SIC: 3273 Ready-mixed concrete
HQ: Thomas Concrete, Inc.
    2500 Cumberland Pkwy Se # 200
    Atlanta GA 30339
    770 431-3300

(G-13348)
THORWORKS INDUSTRIES INC
Also Called: Sealmaster
550 Corporate Center Dr (27607-0153)
PHONE...............................919 852-3714
EMP: 5
Web: www.sealmaster.net
SIC: 2951 Asphalt paving mixtures and blocks
PA: Thorworks Industries, Inc.
    2520 Campbell St
    Sandusky OH 44870

(G-13349)
THUNDERBIRD TECHNOLOGIES INC
5540 Centerview Dr Ste 200 (27606-3363)
PHONE...............................919 481-3239

Raleigh - Wake County (G-13350) — GEOGRAPHIC SECTION

Andrew C Vinal, *Pr*
Michael W Dennen, *Ex VP*
Laura Perry, *CFO*
EMP: 5 **EST:** 1989
SQ FT: 3,200
SALES (est): 556.36K **Privately Held**
SIC: 3674 Semiconductors and related devices

(G-13350)
TICE KITCHENS & INTERIORS LLC
1504 Capital Blvd (27603-1122)
PHONE...................919 366-4117
EMP: 10 **EST:** 2014
SQ FT: 700
SALES (est): 776.49K **Privately Held**
Web: www.ticekitchensandinteriors.com
SIC: 1799 2599 5211 2434 Kitchen and bathroom remodeling; Cabinets, factory; Cabinets, kitchen; Wood kitchen cabinets

(G-13351)
TOBACCO MRCHNTS ASSN OF US INC
Also Called: Tobacco Merchants Association of The United States Inc.
901 Jones Franklin Rd Ste 102 (27606-5441)
PHONE...................919 872-5040
EMP: 13
SALES (corp-wide): 4.72MM **Privately Held**
Web: www.tma.org
SIC: 2721 Magazines: publishing only, not printed on site
PA: Tobacco Merchants Association Of The United States Inc.
231 Clarksville Rd Ste 6
Princeton Junction NJ 08550
609 275-4900

(G-13352)
TOPQUADRANT INC
930 Main Campus Dr Ste 300 (27606-5560)
PHONE...................919 300-7945
Nimit Mehta, *CEO*
Irene Polikoff, *Pr*
Robert Coyne, *VP*
Ralph Hodgson, *Ex VP*
EMP: 20 **EST:** 2001
SQ FT: 4,400
SALES (est): 2.63MM **Privately Held**
Web: www.topquadrant.com
SIC: 7372 Prepackaged software

(G-13353)
TOTAL SOLUTION INDUSTRIES INC
7613 Pats Branch Dr (27612-7323)
PHONE...................919 900-8801
EMP: 10 **EST:** 2011
SALES (est): 81.78K **Privately Held**
Web: www.ts-industries.com
SIC: 3089 Injection molding of plastics

(G-13354)
TOUCH TONE TEES LLC ◊
3316c Capital Blvd Ste 8 (27604-3340)
PHONE...................919 358-5536
Antonio Blanding, *CEO*
EMP: 5 **EST:** 2022
SALES (est): 73.28K **Privately Held**
SIC: 2759 Screen printing

(G-13355)
TOWER ENGRG PROFESSIONALS INC (PA)
Also Called: Southern Environmental Cons
326 Tryon Rd (27603-3530)
PHONE...................919 661-6351

Pete Jernigan, *Pr*
Andrew Haldane, *
Michael L Gardner, *
EMP: 224 **EST:** 1997
SQ FT: 29,000
SALES (est): 99.02MM
SALES (corp-wide): 99.02MM **Privately Held**
Web: www.tepgroup.net
SIC: 8711 3441 Consulting engineer; Fabricated structural metal

(G-13356)
TRAINING INDUSTRY INC
Also Called: TRAININGINDUSTRY.COM
110 Horizon Dr Ste 110 (27615-4927)
PHONE...................919 653-4990
William Douglas Harward, *CEO*
Doug Harward, *CEO*
Ken Taylor, *Pr*
EMP: 70 **EST:** 2005
SQ FT: 6,000
SALES (est): 363.43K **Privately Held**
Web: www.trainingindustry.com
SIC: 8742 8249 2741 Marketing consulting services; Business training services; Internet publishing and broadcasting

(G-13357)
TRAJAN INC
2942 Imperial Oaks Dr (27614-6919)
PHONE...................919 435-1105
EMP: 4 **EST:** 2017
SALES (est): 47.92K **Privately Held**
Web: www.trajanscimed.com
SIC: 3826 Analytical instruments

(G-13358)
TREKLITE INC
904 Dorothea Dr (27603-2140)
PHONE...................919 610-1788
Joseph Huberman, *Pr*
Ruth Bromer, *Sec*
EMP: 6 **EST:** 1977
SQ FT: 2,000
SALES (est): 367.09K **Privately Held**
Web: www.treklite.com
SIC: 3299 3949 2399 Architectural sculptures: gypsum, clay, papier mache, etc.; Sporting and athletic goods, nec; Sleeping bags

(G-13359)
TRIANGLE MICROSYSTEMS INC
Also Called: T M S
1807 Garner Station Blvd (27603-3644)
PHONE...................919 878-1880
Tommy Goodson, *Pr*
George King, *Pr*
Earl Parks, *VP*
Jeffrey Luther, *VP*
EMP: 10 **EST:** 1979
SQ FT: 11,500
SALES (est): 1.04MM **Privately Held**
Web: www.trianglemicrosystems.net
SIC: 3824 3823 3625 Gasoline dispensing meters; Process control instruments; Relays and industrial controls

(G-13360)
TRIANGLE MICROWORKS INC
2840 Plaza Pl Ste 205 (27612-6343)
PHONE...................919 870-5101
EMP: 10 **EST:** 1994
SALES (est): 1.52MM **Privately Held**
Web: www.trianglemicroworks.com
SIC: 7372 Application computer software

(G-13361)
TRIANGLE PLASTICS INC
6435 Mount Herman Rd (27617-8962)
P.O. Box 32222 (27622-2222)
PHONE...................919 598-8839
Jeanene Rose Martin, *CEO*
Eric Martin, *Pr*
◆ **EMP:** 5 **EST:** 1991
SQ FT: 20,000
SALES (est): 997.04K **Privately Held**
Web: www.triangleplas.com
SIC: 3089 Injection molding of plastics

(G-13362)
TRIANGLE REGULATORY PUBG LLC
7780 Brier Creek Pkwy (27617-7849)
P.O. Box 91594 (27675-1594)
PHONE...................919 886-4587
Irisha Johnson, *Prin*
EMP: 5 **EST:** 2010
SALES (est): 254.9K **Privately Held**
Web: www.triangleregulatorypublishing.com
SIC: 2741 8748 Miscellaneous publishing; Publishing consultant

(G-13363)
TRIANGLE TRGGR-PINT THRAPY INC
184 Wind Chime Ct Ste 202 (27615-6485)
PHONE...................919 845-1818
Terrie Mendenhall, *Pr*
EMP: 4 **EST:** 1989
SALES (est): 241.72K **Privately Held**
Web: www.triangletrigger.com
SIC: 7299 3999 Massage parlor; Massage machines, electric: barber and beauty shops

(G-13364)
TRIBOFILM RESEARCH INC
7250 Acc Blvd (27617-8736)
PHONE...................919 838-2844
Vinay Sakhrani, *CEO*
Robert A Mineo Esq, *VP Legal*
EMP: 7 **EST:** 1997
SALES (est): 999.25K **Privately Held**
Web: www.tribofilmresearch.com
SIC: 3999 8731 Barber and beauty shop equipment; Commercial physical research

(G-13365)
TRIMED LLC
7429 Acc Blvd Ste 105 (27617-8401)
PHONE...................919 615-2784
Michael Jones, *Managing Member*
EMP: 9 **EST:** 2011
SALES (est): 468.7K **Privately Held**
SIC: 3842 3841 7699 Ligatures, medical; Surgical and medical instruments; Medical equipment repair, non-electric

(G-13366)
TRITECH VENTURES INC
9801 Saint Stephan Ct (27615-1622)
PHONE...................919 846-3415
EMP: 6 **EST:** 2010
SALES (est): 56.45K **Privately Held**
Web: www.tritechventures.com
SIC: 7372 Prepackaged software

(G-13367)
TROPHY ON MAYWOOD LLC
656 Maywood Ave (27603-2340)
PHONE...................919 803-1333
EMP: 15 **EST:** 2014
SQ FT: 11,000
SALES (est): 1.71MM **Privately Held**
Web: www.trophybrewing.com
SIC: 2082 Beer (alcoholic beverage)

(G-13368)
TRTL INC
120 Penmarc Dr Ste 118 (27603-2400)
PHONE...................844 811-5816
Micheal Corrigan, *CEO*
Cara Hunt, *Brand Relations*
◆ **EMP:** 7 **EST:** 2016
SALES (est): 485.36K **Privately Held**
Web: www.trtltravel.com
SIC: 2392 Cushions and pillows

(G-13369)
TRUSWOOD INC (PA)
8816 Running Oak Dr (27617-4617)
P.O. Box 90035 (27675-0035)
PHONE...................800 473-8787
Richard Watts, *Pr*
Jeff Landon, *
▲ **EMP:** 50 **EST:** 1980
SQ FT: 30,000
SALES (est): 20.39MM
SALES (corp-wide): 20.39MM **Privately Held**
Web: www.truswood.com
SIC: 2439 Trusses, wooden roof

(G-13370)
TRYTON MEDICAL INC
1 Floretta Pl Rm 208 (27676-9803)
PHONE...................919 226-1490
Carl J St Bernard, *Pr*
Brett Farabaugh, *CFO*
H Richard Davis, *COO*
EMP: 8 **EST:** 2008
SALES (est): 1.01MM **Privately Held**
Web: www.trytonmedical.com
SIC: 3841 Surgical and medical instruments

(G-13371)
TURNER BOYS CARRIER SVC LLC
1012 Southern Living Dr (27610-9301)
PHONE...................919 946-7553
EMP: 4 **EST:** 2021
SALES (est): 65K **Privately Held**
SIC: 3799 Transportation equipment, nec

(G-13372)
TWISTED INFUSIONZ LLC
14460 Falls Of Neuse Rd Ste 149339 (27614-8227)
PHONE...................252 432-4215
Garrette Martin, *Managing Member*
EMP: 6 **EST:** 2021
SALES (est): 279.47K **Privately Held**
SIC: 2024 Ice cream and frozen deserts

(G-13373)
TWO ENGRAVERS LLC
5100 Western Blvd (27606-1640)
PHONE...................919 526-0102
Sofya Gekht, *Managing Member*
EMP: 5 **EST:** 2017
SALES (est): 73.28K **Privately Held**
SIC: 2759 Engraving, nec

(G-13374)
UDM SYSTEMS LLC
6621 Fleetwood Dr (27612-1838)
PHONE...................919 789-0777
Andre Cates, *Mgr*
EMP: 4
Web: www.udmsystems.com
SIC: 2891 Adhesives
PA: Udm Systems Llc
8311 Brier Creek Pkwy
Raleigh NC 27617

(G-13375)
UDM SYSTEMS LLC (PA)
Also Called: Fleetwood

GEOGRAPHIC SECTION
Raleigh - Wake County (G-13401)

8311 Brier Creek Pkwy Ste 105-159 (27617-7328)
PHONE..............................919 789-0777
▲ EMP: 6 EST: 2005
SALES (est): 2.75MM Privately Held
Web: www.udmsystems.com
SIC: 2891 Adhesives

(G-13376)
UGLY ESSENTIALS LLC
8601 Six Forks Rd Ste 400 (27615-2965)
PHONE..............................910 319-9945
EMP: 15 EST: 2020
SALES (est): 522.12K Privately Held
SIC: 8743 5087 2844 5122 Sales promotion; Beauty salon and barber shop equipment and supplies; Face creams or lotions; Cosmetics, perfumes, and hair products

(G-13377)
ULTIMATE PRODUCTS INC (PA)
3201 Wellington Ct Ste 115 (27615-5494)
PHONE..............................919 836-1627
Carey Dean Debnam, *Pr*
Stephanie Fanjul, *Sec*
▲ EMP: 15 EST: 1989
SQ FT: 28,000
SALES (est): 4.27MM
SALES (corp-wide): 4.27MM Privately Held
SIC: 5075 5031 3442 Warm air heating equipment and supplies; Doors, garage; Metal doors, sash, and trim

(G-13378)
UMETHOD HEALTH INC
9660 Falls Of Neuse Rd Ste 138-146 (27615-2473)
PHONE..............................984 232-6699
Vikas Chandra, *CEO*
EMP: 16 EST: 2014
SALES (est): 4.56MM Privately Held
Web: www.umethod.com
SIC: 2834 Pharmaceutical preparations

(G-13379)
UMICORE USA INC (HQ)
3600 Glenwood Ave Ste 250 (27612-4945)
PHONE..............................919 874-7171
◆ EMP: 23 EST: 1993
SQ FT: 9,000
SALES (est): 199.37MM
SALES (corp-wide): 6.78B Privately Held
Web: www.umicore.com
SIC: 5052 3339 5051 5169 Metallic ores; Cobalt refining (primary); Nonferrous metal sheets, bars, rods, etc., nec; Industrial chemicals
PA: Umicore
    Rue Du Marais 31
    Bruxelles 1000
    22277111

(G-13380)
UNDER ONE CROWN PUBLISHING LLC
4826 Rembert Dr (27612-6236)
PHONE..............................919 812-4930
EMP: 5 EST: 2019
SALES (est): 100.52K Privately Held
SIC: 2741 Miscellaneous publishing

(G-13381)
UNDERGROUND RENOVATIONS LLC
2834 Friar Tuck Rd (27610-3654)
PHONE..............................202 316-9286
Scott Fairman, *Prin*
EMP: 4 EST: 2019
SALES (est): 39.69K Privately Held
SIC: 3999 Candles

(G-13382)
UNION MASONRY INC
4708 Forestville Rd (27616-9678)
PHONE..............................919 217-7806
Mardelo Adueoar, *Pr*
EMP: 4 EST: 2001
SALES (est): 193.37K Privately Held
SIC: 3271 Blocks, concrete or cinder: standard

(G-13383)
UNIVERSAL TIRE SERVICE INC
4608 Fayetteville Rd (27603-3616)
PHONE..............................919 779-8798
Ray Sears, *Pr*
EMP: 9 EST: 1989
SALES (est): 1.08MM Privately Held
Web: www.universaltireservice.com
SIC: 5531 7538 7534 Automotive tires; General automotive repair shops; Tire retreading and repair shops

(G-13384)
UPFRONT WELL OF THE CAROLINAS
8800 Westgate Park Dr Ste 108 (27617-4832)
PHONE..............................919 415-6000
EMP: 6 EST: 2020
SALES (est): 338.94K Privately Held
Web: www.upfrontwells.com
SIC: 1381 Drilling oil and gas wells

(G-13385)
US MIRRORS
5995 Chapel Hill Rd # 119 (27607-0118)
PHONE..............................919 561-6800
EMP: 4 EST: 2018
SALES (est): 39.74K Privately Held
SIC: 3231 Products of purchased glass

(G-13386)
US TOBACCO COOPERATIVE INC (PA)
1304 Annapolis Dr (27608-2130)
PHONE..............................919 821-4560
Keith H Merrick, *CFO*
Stuart Thompson, *
Tommy Bunn, *
Kenneth M Bopp, *
Wayne Crawford, *
◆ EMP: 75 EST: 1946
SQ FT: 35,000
SALES (est): 36.68MM
SALES (corp-wide): 36.68MM Privately Held
Web: www.usleaf.com
SIC: 8611 2111 Growers' associations; Cigarettes

(G-13387)
USEABLE PRODUCTS
P.O. Box 97482 (27624-7482)
PHONE..............................919 870-6693
Lisa Carson, *Owner*
EMP: 5 EST: 2007
SALES (est): 102.25K Privately Held
SIC: 3999 Manufacturing industries, nec

(G-13388)
V1 PHARMA LLC (PA)
Also Called: V1 Pharma
353 E Six Forks Rd # 220 (27609-7881)
PHONE..............................919 338-5744
Luis Banks, *Managing Member*
EMP: 5 EST: 2015
SALES (est): 479.07K
SALES (corp-wide): 479.07K Privately Held
SIC: 2834 5122 Druggists' preparations (pharmaceuticals); Drugs and drug proprietaries

(G-13389)
VAIBAS INDUSTRIES LLC
6108 Big Sandy Dr (27616-5790)
PHONE..............................919 749-4422
Cameron Hill, *Prin*
EMP: 5 EST: 2017
SALES (est): 87.13K Privately Held
SIC: 3999 Manufacturing industries, nec

(G-13390)
VALENCELL INC
4601 Six Forks Rd Ste 103 (27609-5272)
PHONE..............................919 747-3668
Kent Novak, *CEO*
Steven Leboeuf, *Pr*
Jesse Tucker, *VP*
Michael Aumer, *VP*
Todd Ackman, *VP*
EMP: 9 EST: 2006
SALES (est): 2.65MM Privately Held
Web: www.valencell.com
SIC: 3841 Diagnostic apparatus, medical

(G-13391)
VAN DUYN WOODWORK
9533 Bells Valley Dr (27617-7604)
PHONE..............................919 760-0327
EMP: 4 EST: 2014
SALES (est): 59.54K Privately Held
Web: www.vanduynwoodwork.com
SIC: 2431 Millwork

(G-13392)
VAN PRODUCTS INC (PA)
2521 Noblin Rd (27604-2415)
PHONE..............................919 878-7110
David H Wendt, *Ch Bd*
Libby Wendt, *
W H Wendt Iii, *VP*
EMP: 26 EST: 1975
SQ FT: 21,000
SALES (est): 4.95MM
SALES (corp-wide): 4.95MM Privately Held
Web: www.vanproducts.com
SIC: 7514 5531 3716 Passenger car rental; Automotive accessories; Motor homes

(G-13393)
VANS INC
5959 Triangle Town Blvd Ste 1152 (27616-3268)
PHONE..............................919 792-2555
Crystal Pool, *Brnch Mgr*
EMP: 5
SALES (corp-wide): 11.61B Publicly Held
Web: www.vans.com
SIC: 3021 Rubber and plastics footwear
HQ: Vans, Inc.
    1588 S Coast Dr
    Costa Mesa CA 92626
    714 755-4000

(G-13394)
VAUGHAN ENTERPRISES INC
Also Called: Toddler Tables
834 Purser Dr Ste 102 (27603-4177)
PHONE..............................919 772-4765
Tom Vaughan, *Pr*
▼ EMP: 4 EST: 1982
SQ FT: 2,500
SALES (est): 385.21K Privately Held
SIC: 2531 Chairs, table and arm

(G-13395)
VENTILATION DIRECT
14460 Falls Of Neuse Rd # 14 (27614-8227)
PHONE..............................919 573-1522
Bob Luddy, *Owner*
▼ EMP: 5 EST: 2004
SALES (est): 506.92K Privately Held
Web: www.ventilationdirect.com
SIC: 3444 Sheet metalwork

(G-13396)
VENTURE SHADES LLC
900 E Six Forks Rd Unit 211 (27604-1818)
PHONE..............................804 240-2854
Joseph Williams, *Pr*
EMP: 4 EST: 2017
SALES (est): 128.2K Privately Held
Web: www.ventureshades.com
SIC: 2323 Men's and boy's neckwear

(G-13397)
VERADIGM LLC (HQ)
Also Called: Veradigm
305 Church At North Hills St Ste 100 (27609-2667)
PHONE..............................919 847-8102
Melinda Whittington, *CFO*
Dennis Olis Senior, *VP*
John P Mcconnell, *Pt*
Eric Jacobson, *Sec*
EMP: 1150 EST: 1982
SALES (est): 727.22MM
SALES (corp-wide): 1.5B Publicly Held
Web: www.allscripts.com
SIC: 7372 Prepackaged software
PA: Veradigm Inc.
    222 Merchandise Mart Plz
    Chicago IL 60654
    800 334-8534

(G-13398)
VERITABLE AEROSPACE
410 Lord Berkley Rd (27610-2467)
PHONE..............................919 258-2230
EMP: 6 EST: 2019
SALES (est): 190.56K Privately Held
Web: www.veritableaerospace.com
SIC: 3728 Aircraft parts and equipment, nec

(G-13399)
VIDEO FUEL
6417 Lakeland Dr (27612-6524)
PHONE..............................919 676-9940
Alain Tartevet, *Prin*
EMP: 5 EST: 2011
SALES (est): 248.24K Privately Held
Web: www.mainehealthalliance.com
SIC: 2869 Fuels

(G-13400)
VILLAGE TIRE CENTER INC
Also Called: Duty Tire and Service Center
5220 Atlantic Ave (27616-1870)
PHONE..............................919 862-8500
David Duty, *Pr*
Steve Duty, *VP*
EMP: 9 EST: 1975
SQ FT: 5,000
SALES (est): 1.6MM Privately Held
Web: www.dutytire.com
SIC: 5531 7534 Automotive tires; Tire repair shop

(G-13401)
VIM PRODUCTS INC
5060 Trademark Dr (27610-3054)
PHONE..............................919 277-0267
Gary Phillips, *Pr*
EMP: 8 EST: 2012

Raleigh - Wake County (G-13402)   GEOGRAPHIC SECTION

SALES (est): 399.13K **Privately Held**
Web: www.vimproducts.com
SIC: 3272 Shower receptors, concrete

(G-13402)
VIOLET STUDIO GAMES LLC
5417 Parkwood Dr (27612-6228)
PHONE....................919 785-1989
Abrina Marie Boone, Prin
EMP: 4 EST: 2018
SALES (est): 55.69K **Privately Held**
SIC: 2741 Miscellaneous publishing

(G-13403)
VIOVIO INC
310 W Whitaker Mill Rd (27608-2442)
PHONE....................919 827-1932
Christian A Fowler, Prin
EMP: 5 EST: 2006
SALES (est): 234.26K **Privately Held**
Web: www.prestophoto.com
SIC: 2752 Commercial printing, lithographic

(G-13404)
VIRTUE LABS LLC (PA)
426 S Dawson St (27601-1723)
PHONE....................844 782-4247
Melisse Shavan, Pr
Julieanne Danniels, VP
EMP: 5 EST: 2013
SALES (est): 11.23MM
SALES (corp-wide): 11.23MM **Privately Held**
Web: www.virtuelabs.com
SIC: 2844 Hair preparations, including shampoos

(G-13405)
VISHAY PRECISION GROUP INC
Micro-Measurements (27611)
P.O. Box 2777 (27602-2777)
PHONE....................919 374-5555
EMP: 10
SALES (corp-wide): 355.05MM **Publicly Held**
Web: www.vpgsensors.com
SIC: 3823 Pressure measurement instruments, industrial
PA: Vishay Precision Group, Inc.
    3 Great Valley Pkwy # 150
    Malvern PA 19355
    484 321-5300

(G-13406)
VISIONS STAIRWAYS AND MILLWORK
Also Called: VISIONS STAIRWAYS AND MILLWORK
2200 Westinghouse Blvd Ste 108 (27604-2491)
PHONE....................919 878-5622
Andrew F Lund, Admn
EMP: 44
SALES (corp-wide): 11.97MM **Privately Held**
Web: www.visionstairwaysandmillwork.com
SIC: 2431 Millwork
PA: Vision Stairways & Millwork, Llc
    105 Smoke Hill Ln Ste 180
    Woodstock GA 30188
    678 701-5520

(G-13407)
VISTA PRINT
5007 N New Hope Rd Apt A2 (27604-7303)
PHONE....................919 400-2736
Yesenia Lopez, Prin
EMP: 5 EST: 2017
SALES (est): 59.83K **Privately Held**
SIC: 2752 Offset printing

(G-13408)
VOLTA GROUP CORPORATION LLC
Also Called: Consulting & Management Svcs
300 Fayetteville St Unit 1344 (27602)
PHONE....................919 637-0273
Nana Ansah, CEO
Anan Ansah, Pr
Joan Atkins, VP
EMP: 21 EST: 2008
SALES (est): 958.76K **Privately Held**
SIC: 8711 5172 2911 1799 Engineering services; Crude oil; Petroleum refining; Petroleum storage tanks, pumping and draining

(G-13409)
VONTIER CORPORATION (PA)
5438 Wade Park Blvd Ste 601 (27607-3651)
PHONE....................984 275-6000
Mark D Morelli, Pr
David H Naemura, Sr VP
Kathryn K Rowen, Sr VP
EMP: 100 EST: 2019
SALES (est): 3.1B
SALES (corp-wide): 3.1B **Publicly Held**
Web: www.vontier.com
SIC: 3824 Fluid meters and counting devices

(G-13410)
VORTEX-CYCLONE TECHNOLOGIES
Also Called: Vortex
4400 Blossom Hill Ct (27613-6323)
PHONE....................919 225-1724
Jason Janet, Prin
EMP: 10 EST: 2006
SALES (est): 677.72K **Privately Held**
SIC: 3699 Electrical equipment and supplies, nec

(G-13411)
WAKE CROSS ROADS EXPRESS LLC
3501 Forestville Rd (27616-9531)
PHONE....................919 266-7966
Charlotte Thaxton, Pr
EMP: 4 EST: 2006
SQ FT: 6,356
SALES (est): 330.78K **Privately Held**
Web: www.wakecrossroads.com
SIC: 2741 Miscellaneous publishing

(G-13412)
WASTE INDUSTRIES USA LLC (DH)
Also Called: Gfl Environmental Company
3301 Benson Dr Ste 601 (27609-7331)
PHONE....................919 325-3000
Patrick Dovigi, CEO
Ven Poole, Prin
Lonnie C Poole Junior, Ch Bd
Stephen Grissom, VP
Harrell J Auten Iii, S&M/VP
EMP: 95 EST: 1970
SQ FT: 33,730
SALES (est): 547.53MM
SALES (corp-wide): 5.03B **Privately Held**
Web: www.gflenv.com
SIC: 4953 3443 Rubbish collection and disposal; Dumpsters, garbage
HQ: Wrangler Super Holdco Corp.
    3301 Benson Dr Ste 601
    Raleigh NC 27609
    919 325-3000

(G-13413)
WASTEZERO INC (PA)
4208 Six Forks Rd Ste 1000 (27609-5738)
PHONE....................919 322-1208
Mark A Dancy, Pr
James Calvin Cunningham, VP
William J Easton, VP

▲ EMP: 20 EST: 1991
SALES (est): 17.36MM **Privately Held**
Web: www.wastezero.com
SIC: 4953 2673 Refuse systems; Bags: plastic, laminated, and coated

(G-13414)
WAVE FRONT COMPUTERS LLC
Also Called: Wave Front Studios
8015 Creedmoor Rd Ste 201 (27613-4397)
PHONE....................919 896-6121
EMP: 4 EST: 2011
SQ FT: 1,800
SALES (est): 297.56K **Privately Held**
SIC: 7372 Home entertainment computer software

(G-13415)
WAVETHERM CORPORATION
5995 Chapel Hill Rd Ste 119 (27607-5148)
PHONE....................919 307-8071
EMP: 26 EST: 2008
SQ FT: 1,500
SALES (est): 5.64MM **Privately Held**
Web: shop.wavetherm.com
SIC: 3429 Hardware, nec

(G-13416)
WE PARTNERS LLC
324 Buncombe St (27609-6312)
PHONE....................360 750-3500
EMP: 8 EST: 2008
SALES (est): 227.5K **Privately Held**
SIC: 3443 Fabricated plate work (boiler shop)

(G-13417)
WEDPICS
6413 Rushingbrook Dr (27612-6547)
PHONE....................919 699-5676
EMP: 5 EST: 2018
SALES (est): 58.27K **Privately Held**
SIC: 2741 Miscellaneous publishing

(G-13418)
WELLOYT ENTERPRISES INC
Also Called: International Minute Press
221 W Martin St (27601-1323)
PHONE....................919 821-7897
George Wells, Pr
Linda D Wells, VP
EMP: 4 EST: 1985
SQ FT: 1,900
SALES (est): 300K **Privately Held**
SIC: 2752 Offset printing

(G-13419)
WESTROCK MWV LLC
Also Called: Meadwestvaco Research Center
1021 Main Campus Dr (27606-5238)
PHONE....................919 334-3200
James Wright, Brnch Mgr
EMP: 6
SALES (corp-wide): 20.31B **Publicly Held**
Web: www.westrock.com
SIC: 2631 2671 2678 2677 Linerboard; Paper; coated and laminated packaging; Stationery products; Envelopes
HQ: Westrock Mwv, Llc
    3500 45th St Sw
    Lanett AL 36863
    804 444-1000

(G-13420)
WHATS YOUR SIGN LLC
720 Sawmill Rd (27615-4847)
PHONE....................919 274-5703
EMP: 5 EST: 2017
SALES (est): 93.64K **Privately Held**
Web: www.signsofnc.com

SIC: 3993 Signs and advertising specialties

(G-13421)
WHITAKER MILL WORKS LLC
3801 Beryl Rd (27607-5244)
PHONE....................919 772-3030
Richard Stephenson, Pt
Tom Rickman, Pt
EMP: 8 EST: 2013
SALES (est): 991.86K **Privately Held**
Web: www.whitakermillworks.com
SIC: 2431 Millwork

(G-13422)
WHITE PACKING CO INC -VA
5404 Hillsborough St Ste A (27606-1339)
P.O. Box 7067 (22404-7067)
PHONE....................540 373-9883
Karl White, Pr
Kris White, Sec
Collin White, CFO
EMP: 7 EST: 1971
SQ FT: 60,000
SALES (est): 964.91K **Privately Held**
SIC: 2013 2011 Bacon, side and sliced: from purchased meat; Meat packing plants

(G-13423)
WILLIAMS INDUSTRIES INC (PA)
1128 Tyler Farms Dr (27603-7949)
P.O. Box 1770 (20108-1770)
PHONE....................919 604-1746
Frank E Williams Iii, Ch Bd
Danny C Dunlap, *
Marianne Pastor, *
▲ EMP: 200 EST: 1970
SALES (est): 77.4MM
SALES (corp-wide): 77.4MM **Privately Held**
Web: www.wmsi.com
SIC: 3441 1531 1541 3315 Fabricated structural metal for bridges; Operative builders; Steel building construction; Steel wire and related products

(G-13424)
WIND CHIME PLAZA
185 Wind Chime Ct Ste 104 (27615-6481)
PHONE....................919 848-9715
EMP: 4 EST: 2017
SALES (est): 94.3K **Privately Held**
SIC: 3999 Wind chimes

(G-13425)
WITHERSPOON WOODWORKS LLC
812 Bryan St (27605-1104)
PHONE....................919 669-9103
Laura Witherspoon, Prin
EMP: 6 EST: 2010
SALES (est): 247.01K **Privately Held**
Web: www.witherspoonwoodworks.com
SIC: 2431 Millwork

(G-13426)
WMB OF WAKE COUNTY INC
Also Called: Glenwood Village Exxon
2601 Glenwood Ave (27608-1003)
PHONE....................919 782-0419
William Barker, Pr
Bryan Barker, VP
EMP: 14 EST: 2006
SALES (est): 708.51K **Privately Held**
Web: www.glenwoodvillageexxon.com
SIC: 3011 5014 Tires and inner tubes; Tires and tubes

(G-13427)
WORKDAY INC
4801 Glenwood Ave Ste 300 (27612-3857)
PHONE....................919 703-2559

GEOGRAPHIC SECTION

Randleman - Randolph County (G-13453)

EMP: 5
Web: www.workday.com
SIC: 7372 Prepackaged software
PA: Workday, Inc.
 6110 Stoneridge Mall Rd
 Pleasanton CA 94588

(G-13428)
WORLDGRANITE & STONEART INC
4600 Twisted Oaks Dr Apt 1505 (27612-2505)
PHONE...............................919 871-0078
Mel Neale, *Pr*
Emily Rosevage, *VP*
EMP: 9 EST: 2001
SQ FT: 7,000
SALES (est): 801.51K **Privately Held**
Web: www.worldgranite.biz
SIC: 1411 Granite, dimension-quarrying

(G-13429)
X-JET TECHNOLOGIES INC
142 Annaron Ct (27603-3640)
PHONE...............................800 983-7467
Kenneth L Sapic Ii, *Pr*
Dana Sapic, *VP*
EMP: 9 EST: 2015
SALES (est): 514.28K **Privately Held**
Web: www.xjetnozzle.com
SIC: 3429 Hardware, nec

(G-13430)
XELAQUA INC
404b Glenwood Ave (27603-1220)
PHONE...............................919 964-4181
Graham A Crispin, *CEO*
EMP: 4 EST: 2013
SALES (est): 372.73K **Privately Held**
Web: www.xelaqua.com
SIC: 3589 Sewage and water treatment equipment

(G-13431)
XILINX INC
220 Horizon Dr Ste 114 (27615-4928)
PHONE...............................919 846-3922
Tony Scarangella, *Brnch Mgr*
EMP: 10
SALES (corp-wide): 22.68B **Publicly Held**
Web: www.amd.com
SIC: 3674 Microcircuits, integrated (semiconductor)
HQ: Xilinx, Inc.
 2100 Logic Dr
 San Jose CA 95124
 408 559-7778

(G-13432)
XPC CORPORATION
3070 Business Park Dr Ste 108 (27610-3592)
PHONE...............................919 210-1756
EMP: 17
Web: www.xpcc.com
SIC: 3629 Power conversion units, a.c. to d.c.: static-electric
PA: Xpc Corporation
 230 Yuma St
 Denver CO 80223

(G-13433)
XPC CORPORATION
Also Called: Xtreme Power Conversion
7239 Acc Blvd (27617-4881)
PHONE...............................800 582-4524
EMP: 17
SIC: 3629 Power conversion units, a.c. to d.c.: static-electric
PA: Xpc Corporation
 230 Yuma St
 Denver CO 80223

(G-13434)
YENTIYAHS NATURALS LLC
3601 Deering Dr (27616-8655)
PHONE...............................919 295-4279
Tara White, *Owner*
EMP: 5 EST: 2017
SALES (est): 109.34K **Privately Held**
SIC: 2844 Perfumes, cosmetics and other toilet preparations

(G-13435)
Z-BAKE CUSTOM PICTURE FRAMING
8412 Aptos Ct (27613-1264)
PHONE...............................919 848-4931
Gary Baker, *Prin*
EMP: 5 EST: 2011
SALES (est): 96.95K **Privately Held**
SIC: 2499 Picture frame molding, finished

(G-13436)
ZENECAR LLC
Also Called: Enwood Structures
10224 Durant Rd Ste 201 (27614-6468)
PHONE...............................919 518-0464
EMP: 8 EST: 2011
SALES (est): 905.1K **Privately Held**
Web: www.enwood.com
SIC: 2426 Frames for upholstered furniture, wood

(G-13437)
ZOETIC DIGITAL DEVELOPMENT
401 Scripps Lane Unit 104 (27610-6636)
PHONE...............................919 720-5945
Shontae Hogan, *Prin*
EMP: 5 EST: 2017
SALES (est): 65.15K **Privately Held**
SIC: 1521 1522 1389 1623 Single-family housing construction; Multi-family dwelling construction, nec; Construction, repair, and dismantling services; Underground utilities contractor

(G-13438)
ZONKD LLC
2419 Atlantic Ave (27604-1598)
P.O. Box 6492 (27628-6492)
PHONE...............................919 977-6463
Ryan Graven, *Pr*
Ashley Holder, *
EMP: 49 EST: 2013
SALES (est): 4.35MM **Privately Held**
Web: www.zonkd.com
SIC: 2299 Upholstery filling, textile

Ramseur
Randolph County

(G-13439)
ANA MUF CORPORATION
2530 Nc Highway 49 N (27316-8532)
PHONE...............................336 653-3509
Miguel Uribe, *Pr*
Javier Uribe, *Contrlr*
EMP: 8 EST: 2021
SALES (est): 529.92K **Privately Held**
SIC: 2426 Frames for upholstered furniture, wood

(G-13440)
AUTO-SYSTEMS AND SERVICE INC
839 Crestwick Rd (27316-8726)
P.O. Box 1180 (27316-1180)
PHONE...............................336 824-3580
Jimmy Wayne Harris, *Pr*
EMP: 14 EST: 1976
SQ FT: 24,000
SALES (est): 1.47MM **Privately Held**

SIC: 3559 Brick making machinery

(G-13441)
BOBBY BARNS WOODWORKING
1337 Nc Hwy 22 S (27316-8790)
PHONE...............................336 824-2821
EMP: 4 EST: 2011
SALES (est): 171.57K **Privately Held**
SIC: 2431 Millwork

(G-13442)
CRAWFORD KNITTING COMPANY INC
7718 Us Highway 64 E (27316-8861)
P.O. Box 1360 (27316-1360)
PHONE...............................336 824-1065
John C Mccuiston, *Pr*
Peggy Mccuiston, *Sec*
▲ EMP: 95 EST: 1975
SQ FT: 10,000
SALES (est): 8.75MM **Privately Held**
Web: www.crawfordknitting.com
SIC: 2252 2251 Men's, boys', and girls' hosiery; Women's hosiery, except socks

(G-13443)
JERRY COX LOGGING
7598 Old Siler City Rd (27316-8575)
P.O. Box 663 (27316-0663)
PHONE...............................919 742-6089
Jerry Y Cox, *Prin*
EMP: 9 EST: 2002
SALES (est): 237.41K **Privately Held**
SIC: 2411 Logging camps and contractors

(G-13444)
KN FURNITURE INC
244 Nc Highway 22 N (27316-8774)
PHONE...............................336 953-3259
Kevin Arevalo, *Pr*
EMP: 24 EST: 2018
SALES (est): 1.14MM **Privately Held**
SIC: 2511 2522 2512 Bed frames, except water bed frames: wood; Office furniture, except wood; Upholstered household furniture

(G-13445)
KRAFTSMAN INC
10051 Us Highway 64 E (27316-8699)
PHONE...............................336 824-1114
Paul Kaufman, *Pr*
Jenatte Kaufman, *
EMP: 52 EST: 2000
SQ FT: 9,000
SALES (est): 14.49MM **Privately Held**
Web: www.kraftsmantrailers.com
SIC: 5599 3715 Utility trailers; Bus trailers, tractor type

(G-13446)
LINE DRIVE SPORTS CENTER INC
Also Called: Beet River Traders
161 Crestwick Rd (27316-8720)
P.O. Box 346 (27316-0346)
PHONE...............................336 824-1692
Doug Langley, *Pr*
Doug Langley, *Pr*
Pat Pate, *Genl Mgr*
EMP: 7 EST: 1992
SQ FT: 40,000
SALES (est): 800K **Privately Held**
Web: www.linedrivegraphics.com
SIC: 5941 7374 2396 Sporting goods and bicycle shops; Computer graphics service; Screen printing on fabric articles

(G-13447)
MARCH FURNITURE MANUFACTURING INC

447 Reed Creek Rd (27316-8890)
P.O. Box 875 (27316-0875)
PHONE...............................336 824-4413
◆ EMP: 240
SIC: 2512 Living room furniture: upholstered on wood frames

(G-13448)
NC STAIRS AND RAILS INC
5504 Foushee Rd (27316-8332)
P.O. Box 664 (27316-0664)
PHONE...............................336 460-5687
Terri Swaney, *Pr*
EMP: 7 EST: 2010
SALES (est): 430.92K **Privately Held**
SIC: 3446 Stairs, staircases, stair treads: prefabricated metal

(G-13449)
QUICK N EASY 12 NC739
8112 Us Highway 64 E (27316-8649)
PHONE...............................336 824-3832
Donna Woodard, *Pr*
Burnan Major, *Owner*
EMP: 4 EST: 2003
SALES (est): 112.98K **Privately Held**
SIC: 1389 Gas field services, nec

(G-13450)
TOWER COMPONENTS INC
Also Called: TCI
5960 Us Highway 64 E (27316-8858)
PHONE...............................336 824-2102
William G Bartley, *Pr*
Tom Byrne, *General Vice President**
▼ EMP: 90 EST: 1990
SQ FT: 250,000
SALES (est): 9.61MM **Privately Held**
Web: www.towercomponentsinc.com
SIC: 3443 Fabricated plate work (boiler shop)

(G-13451)
UNIFIED SCRNING CRSHING - NC I (PA)
136 Crestwick Rd (27316-8720)
P.O. Box 486 (27316-0486)
PHONE...............................336 824-2151
Troy Hartman, *Pr*
Pete Smith, *Dir*
◆ EMP: 6 EST: 1997
SALES (est): 1.14MM
SALES (corp-wide): 1.14MM **Privately Held**
Web: www.unifiedscreening.com
SIC: 3496 Miscellaneous fabricated wire products

Randleman
Randolph County

(G-13452)
AMERICA PRINTER
5349 Racine Rd (27317-7888)
PHONE...............................336 465-0269
Amber Adams, *Prin*
EMP: 5 EST: 2010
SALES (est): 66.39K **Privately Held**
SIC: 2752 Offset printing

(G-13453)
BUTLER TRAILER MFG CO INC
259 Hockett Dairy Rd (27317-8037)
PHONE...............................336 674-8850
Cornelius Butler Junior, *Pr*
EMP: 10 EST: 1965
SQ FT: 900
SALES (est): 2.03MM **Privately Held**

Randleman - Randolph County (G-13454)

SIC: **3537** 5031 Truck trailers, used in plants, docks, terminals, etc.; Lumber: rough, dressed, and finished

(G-13454)
BWH FOAM AND FIBER INC
605 Sunset Dr (27317-1917)
P.O. Box 370 (27317-0370)
PHONE..................................336 498-6949
Bruce W Hughes, *Pr*
EMP: 14 **EST:** 2005
SALES (est): 99.86K **Privately Held**
SIC: **3086** Plastics foam products

(G-13455)
CARAUSTAR CSTM PACKG GROUP INC
Also Called: Randleman Carton Plant
4139 Us Hwy 311 (27317-7314)
P.O. Box 609 (27317-0609)
PHONE..................................336 498-2631
Doris Rigud, *Brnch Mgr*
EMP: 123
SALES (corp-wide): 5.22B **Publicly Held**
SIC: **2652** 2657 Setup paperboard boxes; Folding paperboard boxes
HQ: Caraustar Custom Packaging Group, Inc.
5000 Austell Powder Sprin
Austell GA 30106

(G-13456)
CARAUSTAR INDUSTRIES INC
4139 Us Highway 311 (27317-7314)
PHONE..................................336 498-2631
Doug Wagner, *Genl Mgr*
EMP: 10
SALES (corp-wide): 5.22B **Publicly Held**
Web: www.greif.com
SIC: **2655** 2631 2679 2656 Tubes, fiber or paper: made from purchased material; Paperboard mills; Paperboard products, converted, nec; Food containers (liquid tight), including milk cartons
HQ: Caraustar Industries, Inc.
5000 Astell Pwdr Sprng Rd
Austell GA 30106
770 948-3101

(G-13457)
CARER WELDING
10553 Randleman Rd Bldg 6 (27317-8217)
PHONE..................................336 558-3906
Angel Carter, *Prin*
EMP: 5 **EST:** 2017
SALES (est): 44.19K **Privately Held**
Web: carter-welding.business.site
SIC: **7692** Welding repair

(G-13458)
CAUDLE BEDDING SUPPLIES
216 Russell Walker Ave (27317-9480)
PHONE..................................336 498-2600
Grover Hancock, *Owner*
EMP: 7 **EST:** 2017
SALES (est): 78.71K **Privately Held**
Web: www.caudlesew.com
SIC: **2515** Mattresses and bedsprings

(G-13459)
COMMONWEALTH HOSIERY MILLS INC
Also Called: Commonwealth Hosiery
4964 Island Ford Rd (27317-7209)
P.O. Box 939 (27317-0939)
PHONE..................................336 498-2621
▲ **EMP:** 65 **EST:** 1916
SALES (est): 4.89MM **Privately Held**
Web: www.commonwealth-hosiery.com

SIC: **2251** 2252 Panty hose; Socks

(G-13460)
COTNER CABINET
7653 Adams Farm Rd (27317-7392)
PHONE..................................336 498-6199
EMP: 4 **EST:** 2015
SALES (est): 107.05K **Privately Held**
SIC: **2434** Wood kitchen cabinets

(G-13461)
CUSTOM STEEL FABRICATORS INC
362 Providence Church Rd (27317-7876)
P.O. Box 128 (27317-0128)
PHONE..................................336 498-5099
Marvin Tickle, *Pr*
J R Criscoe, *VP*
EMP: 24 **EST:** 1992
SQ FT: 4,000
SALES (est): 1.68MM **Privately Held**
SIC: **3441** Fabricated structural metal

(G-13462)
D & D ENTPS GREENSBORO INC
10458 Us Highway 220 Bus N (27317-8121)
PHONE..................................336 495-3407
Ralph Davis, *Pr*
Harold Davis, *
EMP: 40 **EST:** 1976
SQ FT: 38,000
SALES (est): 5.33MM **Privately Held**
Web: www.ddent-usa.com
SIC: **3599** Machine shop, jobbing and repair

(G-13463)
DART CONTAINER CORP GEORGIA
3219 Wesleyan Rd (27317-7667)
PHONE..................................336 495-1101
Steve Ridgill, *Mgr*
EMP: 233
SQ FT: 507,092
SALES (corp-wide): 139.75MM **Privately Held**
SIC: **3086** Plastics foam products
PA: Dart Container Corporation Of Georgia
500 Hogsback Rd
Mason MI 48854
517 676-3800

(G-13464)
DIGGER SPECIALTIES INC
Also Called: Polyvnyl Fnce By Digger Spc In
4256 Heath Dairy Rd (27317-7489)
PHONE..................................336 495-1517
EMP: 9
SALES (corp-wide): 22.78MM **Privately Held**
Web: www.diggerspecialties.com
SIC: **3089** 1799 Plastics hardware and building products; Fence construction
PA: Digger Specialties, Inc.
3446 Us Highway 6
Bremen IN 46506
574 546-5999

(G-13465)
DST MANUFACTURING LLC
166 Regal Dr (27317-8148)
P.O. Box 295 (27317-0295)
PHONE..................................336 676-6096
EMP: 5 **EST:** 2010
SALES (est): 493.14K **Privately Held**
Web: www.nviroclean.net
SIC: **2899** Chemical preparations, nec

(G-13466)
DWD INDUSTRIES LLC
151 Southern Dr (27317)
PHONE..................................336 498-6327

Mike Schoolcraft, *Mgr*
EMP: 47
Web: www.estevesgroup.com
SIC: **5084** 3544 Industrial machinery and equipment; Special dies, tools, jigs, and fixtures
HQ: Dwd Industries, Llc
1921 Patterson St
Decatur IN 46733
260 728-9272

(G-13467)
E F P INC
8013 Adams Farm Rd (27317-7384)
PHONE..................................336 498-4134
Frank Moore, *Pr*
Glenda Moore, *VP*
EMP: 11 **EST:** 1983
SQ FT: 40,000
SALES (est): 862.69K **Privately Held**
Web: www.efpfactorydirect.com
SIC: **3599** Machine shop, jobbing and repair

(G-13468)
EAST COAST FAB LLC
195 Labrador Dr (27317-8050)
PHONE..................................336 285-7444
EMP: 15 **EST:** 2016
SALES (est): 727.43K **Privately Held**
SIC: **3441** Fabricated structural metal

(G-13469)
ESCO INDUSTRIES INC
4717 Island Ford Rd (27317-7208)
PHONE..................................336 495-3772
James Cossee, *Genl Mgr*
EMP: 13
SALES (corp-wide): 22.41MM **Privately Held**
Web: www.escoindustries.com
SIC: **3275** 7389 2451 2435 Wallboard, gypsum; Laminating service; Mobile homes ; Hardwood veneer and plywood
PA: Esco Industries, Inc.
185 Sink Hole Rd
Douglas GA 31533
912 384-1417

(G-13470)
FROZEN DESSERT SPECIALISTS LLC
10922 Randleman Rd (27317-8083)
PHONE..................................336 362-8707
Joseph Preston Byrd, *Prin*
EMP: 5 **EST:** 2013
SALES (est): 168.06K **Privately Held**
Web: www.frozendessertspecialists.org
SIC: **2024** Ice cream and frozen deserts

(G-13471)
GERALD HARTSOE
Also Called: Precision Enterprises
3109 Tom Brown Rd (27317)
PHONE..................................336 498-3233
Gerald Hartsoe, *Owner*
EMP: 4 **EST:** 1984
SALES (est): 207.96K **Privately Held**
SIC: **3544** 3823 3469 Special dies and tools; Process control instruments; Metal stampings, nec

(G-13472)
HITECH CONTROLS INC
1348 Plantation Ct (27317-8186)
PHONE..................................336 498-1534
Jack Phan, *Owner*
EMP: 4 **EST:** 2003
SALES (est): 255.6K **Privately Held**
Web: www.hitechcontrols.com

SIC: **3625** Industrial controls: push button, selector switches, pilot

(G-13473)
HUGHES FURNITURE INDS INC (PA)
Also Called: H F I
952 S Stout Rd (27317-7638)
P.O. Box 486 (27317-0486)
PHONE..................................336 498-8700
Bruce W Hughes, *Pr*
Steve Hunsucker, *
◆ **EMP:** 250 **EST:** 1963
SQ FT: 140,000
SALES (est): 45.05MM **Privately Held**
Web: www.hughesfurniture.com
SIC: **2512** 7641 2426 Living room furniture: upholstered on wood frames; Upholstery work; Furniture stock and parts, hardwood

(G-13474)
IRON MEN FABRICATION
1296 Little Point Rd (27317-7549)
PHONE..................................336 929-6263
Clarence Brady, *Prin*
EMP: 5 **EST:** 2018
SALES (est): 72.1K **Privately Held**
Web: iron-men-fabrication.business.site
SIC: **7692** Welding repair

(G-13475)
J C STAIR ERECTORS
7981 Us Highway 220 Bus N (27317-7304)
PHONE..................................336 240-0560
EMP: 4 **EST:** 2015
SALES (est): 103.34K **Privately Held**
SIC: **3446** Stairs, staircases, stair treads: prefabricated metal

(G-13476)
LUCK FABRICATION INCORPORATED
616 New Salem Rd (27317-7819)
PHONE..................................336 498-0905
William Luck, *Prin*
EMP: 5 **EST:** 2020
SALES (est): 64.64K **Privately Held**
SIC: **7692** Welding repair

(G-13477)
MARTIN MARIETTA MATERIALS INC
Also Called: Martin Marietta Aggregates
2757 Hopewood Rd (27317-7518)
PHONE..................................336 672-1501
Doyle Carlise, *Brnch Mgr*
EMP: 5
Web: www.martinmarietta.com
SIC: **1422** Crushed and broken limestone
PA: Martin Marietta Materials Inc
4123 Parklake Ave
Raleigh NC 27612

(G-13478)
MARTIN MARIETTA MATERIALS INC
Also Called: Martin Marietta
2757 Hopewood Rd (27317-7518)
P.O. Box 1084 (27317-1084)
PHONE..................................336 672-1501
EMP: 5
Web: www.martinmarietta.com
SIC: **1422** Crushed and broken limestone
PA: Martin Marietta Materials Inc
4123 Parklake Ave
Raleigh NC 27612

(G-13479)
MMJ MACHINING AND FABG INC
1332 Gene Allred Dr (27317-7769)
PHONE..................................336 495-1029
EMP: 10 **EST:** 1993
SALES (est): 1.21MM **Privately Held**

GEOGRAPHIC SECTION
Red Springs - Robeson County (G-13503)

Web: www.mmjmachine.com
SIC: 5084 3599 Textile machinery and equipment; Machine shop, jobbing and repair

(G-13480)
MYERS QUALITY MACHINE CO INC
1120 N Main St (27317-7225)
PHONE...............................336 498-4187
Bobby Myers Senior, *Pr*
Bobby Myers Junior, *VP*
Jane Myers, *Sec*
EMP: 16 **EST:** 1982
SQ FT: 2,700
SALES (est): 356.96K **Privately Held**
SIC: 3552 3441 Knitting machines; Fabricated structural metal

(G-13481)
NORTH CAROLINA LUMBER COMPANY
Also Called: Motion-Eaze
1 Parrish Dr (27317-9598)
P.O. Box 486 (27317-0486)
PHONE...............................336 498-6600
Bruce W Hughes, *Pr*
R Wilbur Hughes, *
A Stephen Hunsucker, *
◆ **EMP:** 19 **EST:** 1985
SQ FT: 156,000
SALES (est): 371.92K **Privately Held**
SIC: 2426 2392 2512 Lumber, hardwood dimension; Cushions and pillows; Upholstered household furniture

(G-13482)
OUTKAST TIMBER HARVESTING LLC
7209 Cedar Square Rd (27317-7125)
PHONE...............................336 906-0962
Cory Steed, *Prin*
EMP: 6 **EST:** 2019
SALES (est): 103.91K **Privately Held**
SIC: 2411 Logging

(G-13483)
PILGRIM TRACT SOCIETY INC
105 Depot St (27317-1705)
P.O. Box 126 (27317-0126)
PHONE...............................336 495-1241
Chris Hancock, *Pr*
Sandra Hancock, *Sec*
John Henderson, *Mgr*
EMP: 8 **EST:** 1938
SQ FT: 7,400
SALES (est): 331.97K **Privately Held**
Web: www.pilgrimtract.org
SIC: 2752 Offset printing

(G-13484)
POLYMER CONCEPTS INC
124 Regal Dr (27317-8148)
PHONE...............................336 495-7713
Larry A Draughn, *Pr*
Rickey Barker, *VP*
◆ **EMP:** 10 **EST:** 1999
SQ FT: 9,000
SALES (est): 411.22K **Privately Held**
Web: www.polymerconcepts.com
SIC: 3089 Injection molding of plastics

(G-13485)
POWERFAB
1410 Coltrane Mill Rd (27317-8021)
PHONE...............................336 674-0624
EMP: 4 **EST:** 2019
SALES (est): 99.74K **Privately Held**
SIC: 3444 Sheet metalwork

(G-13486)
R M GEAR HARNESS
420 High Point St (27317-1531)
PHONE...............................336 498-1169
Richard Mellentine, *Prin*
EMP: 7 **EST:** 2010
SALES (est): 170.56K **Privately Held**
SIC: 3714 Automotive wiring harness sets

(G-13487)
RANDOLPH MACHINE INC
498 Pointe South Dr (27317-9502)
PHONE...............................336 799-1039
EMP: 4
Web: www.randolphmachine.com
SIC: 3479 Coating of metals and formed products
PA: Randolph Machine, Inc.
1206 Uwharrie St
Asheboro NC 27203

(G-13488)
RHEEM MANUFACTURING COMPANY
Also Called: Rheem Sales Company
4744 Island Ford Rd (27317-7208)
PHONE...............................336 495-6800
Don Harter, *Dir*
EMP: 237
Web: www.rheem.com
SIC: 5075 3585 Electrical heating equipment; Air conditioning condensers and condensing units
HQ: Rheem Manufacturing Company Inc
1100 Abernathy Rd # 1700
Atlanta GA 30328
770 351-3000

(G-13489)
SAFE AIR SYSTEMS INC
210 Labrador Dr (27317-8165)
PHONE...............................336 674-0749
Joseph C Smith, *Pr*
EMP: 20 **EST:** 1992
SALES (est): 2.42MM **Privately Held**
Web: www.safeairsystems.com
SIC: 7699 3563 Industrial equipment services; Air and gas compressors including vacuum pumps

(G-13490)
SALEM NECKWEAR CORPORATION
116 W Academy St (27317-1558)
P.O. Box 38 (27317-0038)
PHONE...............................336 498-2022
James L Trogdon Junior, *Pr*
Rene Trogdon, *
▲ **EMP:** 5 **EST:** 1964
SQ FT: 8,200
SALES (est): 148.93K **Privately Held**
Web: www.salemneckwear.com
SIC: 2323 Men's and boys' neckties and bow ties

(G-13491)
SKIDRIL INDUSTRIES LLC
235 Labrador Dr (27317-8165)
P.O. Box 8041 (27419-0041)
PHONE...............................800 843-3745
Mark T Salman, *Admn*
▲ **EMP:** 10 **EST:** 2008
SALES (est): 249.02K **Privately Held**
Web: www.skidril.com
SIC: 3999 Barber and beauty shop equipment

(G-13492)
SUB-AQUATICS INC
Also Called: Breathingair Systems
210 Labrador Dr (27317-8165)

PHONE...............................336 674-0749
EMP: 20
SALES (corp-wide): 22.14MM **Privately Held**
Web: www.breathingair.com
SIC: 7699 3563 Industrial equipment services; Air and gas compressors including vacuum pumps
PA: Sub-Aquatics, Inc.
8855 E Broad St
Reynoldsburg OH
614 864-1235

(G-13493)
TECHNIMARK
208 Nc Highway 62 W (27317-9774)
PHONE...............................336 736-9366
EMP: 6 **EST:** 2018
SALES (est): 83.71K **Privately Held**
Web: www.technimark.com
SIC: 3089 Injection molding of plastics

(G-13494)
UNITED BRASS WORKS INC (HQ)
Also Called: United Brass Works
714 S Main St (27317-2100)
PHONE...............................336 498-2661
Michael Berkelhammer, *CEO*
Anthony Forman, *
▲ **EMP:** 153 **EST:** 1910
SQ FT: 70,000
SALES (est): 48.05MM
SALES (corp-wide): 94.97MM **Privately Held**
Web: www.ubw.com
SIC: 3491 3494 3369 Industrial valves; Valves and pipe fittings, nec; Nonferrous foundries, nec
PA: Bradford Equities Management Llc
360 Hamilton Ave Ste 425
White Plains NY 10601
914 922-7171

Red Springs
Robeson County

(G-13495)
AMERICAN PLUSH TEX MILLS LLC
213 S Edinborough St (28377-1233)
PHONE...............................765 609-0456
Virgil E Stanley, *Prin*
EMP: 15 **EST:** 2011
SALES (est): 1.02MM **Privately Held**
Web: www.americanplush.com
SIC: 5199 2326 Fabrics, yarns, and knit goods; Aprons, work, except rubberized and plastic: men's

(G-13496)
CAROLINA TEXTILE SERVICES INC (PA)
Off Hwy 211 (28377)
P.O. Box 205 (28377-0205)
PHONE...............................910 843-3033
Morris Pounds, *Pr*
EMP: 7 **EST:** 1992
SALES (est): 518.36K **Privately Held**
SIC: 7699 8748 3552 Industrial machinery and equipment repair; Business consulting, nec; Textile machinery

(G-13497)
DAYCO PRODUCTS LLC
Also Called: Red Springs Distribution Ctr
16824 Nc Highway 211 W (28377-8887)
PHONE...............................910 843-1024
Anna Contoleon, *Brnch Mgr*
EMP: 89
SALES (corp-wide): 211.24MM **Privately Held**

Web: www.daycoproducts.com
SIC: 3052 Rubber and plastics hose and beltings
HQ: Dayco Products, Llc
16000 Common Rd
Roseville MI 48066

(G-13498)
DESIGNTEK FABRICATION INC
16824 A Hwy 211 (28377)
PHONE...............................910 359-0130
Kevin Mauldin, *Pr*
EMP: 17 **EST:** 2012
SALES (est): 1.94MM **Privately Held**
SIC: 3556 3559 Food products machinery; Pharmaceutical machinery

(G-13499)
ECO BUILDING CORPORATION
Also Called: Emerging Technology Institute
16824 A Nc-211 (28377)
PHONE...............................910 736-1540
James Freeman, *Pr*
Jeff Collins, *Ex VP*
EMP: 4 **EST:** 2017
SALES (est): 485.43K **Privately Held**
SIC: 3812 8742 Acceleration indicators and systems components, aerospace; Management consulting services

(G-13500)
ELEVATED CNSTR RENOVATIONS LLC
1279 Lewis Mcneill Rd (28377-9647)
PHONE...............................910 301-4243
Larry Mcmillan, *CEO*
EMP: 4 **EST:** 2021
SALES (est): 100.05K **Privately Held**
SIC: 1389 7389 Construction, repair, and dismantling services; Business Activities at Non-Commercial Site

(G-13501)
INDUSTRIAL AND AGRICULTURAL CHEMICALS INCORPORATED
Also Called: I A C
2042 Buie Philadelphus Rd (28377-6052)
PHONE...............................910 843-2121
◆ **EMP:** 20 **EST:** 1972
SALES (est): 2MM **Privately Held**
Web: www.industrial-agricultural-chemicals-inc.com
SIC: 2819 5191 Industrial inorganic chemicals, nec; Chemicals, agricultural

(G-13502)
MCCABES INDUS MLLWRGHT MFG INC
9502 Nc Highway 71 N (28377-7608)
P.O. Box 32 (28377-0032)
PHONE...............................910 843-8699
Robert Mccabe, *Pr*
EMP: 26 **EST:** 2001
SALES (est): 1.28MM **Privately Held**
SIC: 3441 Fabricated structural metal

(G-13503)
S & S TRUCKING COMPANY
604 E 4th Ave (28377-1667)
PHONE...............................910 843-6264
EMP: 6 **EST:** 2010
SALES (est): 86.7K **Privately Held**
SIC: 3537 Trucks, tractors, loaders, carriers, and similar equipment

Reidsville
Rockingham County

(G-13504)
ALBAAD USA INC
Also Called: Albaad Fem US
1900 Barnes St (27320-6410)
P.O. Box 1825 (27323-1825)
PHONE....................336 634-0091
Boaz Roseman, *CEO*
Adi Maor, *CFO*
◆ **EMP:** 350 **EST:** 2003
SQ FT: 146,622
SALES (est): 87.14MM **Privately Held**
Web: www.albaad.com
SIC: 2844 Towelettes, premoistened
HQ: Albaad Massuot Yitzhak Ltd
 Moshav
 Massuot Itzhak 79858

(G-13505)
ALCORNS CUSTOM WOODWORKING INC
941 Flat Rock Rd (27320-7645)
PHONE....................336 342-0908
Richie Alcorn, *Owner*
EMP: 4 **EST:** 1990
SALES (est): 491.85K **Privately Held**
Web: www.alcornswoodworking.com
SIC: 1751 2499 Cabinet building and installation; Applicators, wood

(G-13506)
ALTIUM PACKAGING LP
Envision Ecoplast Group
606 Walters St Unit B (27320-2609)
PHONE....................336 342-4749
EMP: 62
SALES (corp-wide): 15.9B **Publicly Held**
Web: www.altiumpkg.com
SIC: 3089 Plastics containers, except foam
HQ: Altium Packaging Lp
 3101 Towercreek Pkwy Se
 Atlanta GA 30339
 678 742-4600

(G-13507)
BALL METAL BEVERAGE CONT CORP
Also Called: Ball Metal Beverage Cont Div
1900 Barnes St (27320-6410)
P.O. Box 1170 (27323-1170)
PHONE....................336 342-4711
Joseph Corbett, *Mgr*
EMP: 232
SALES (corp-wide): 14.03B **Publicly Held**
Web: www.ball.com
SIC: 3411 Beer cans, metal
HQ: Ball Metal Beverage Container Corp.
 9300 W 108th Cir
 Westminster CO 80021

(G-13508)
BEJEWELED CREATIONS
386 River Run Dr (27320-9037)
PHONE....................336 552-0841
Barbara Conroy, *Prin*
EMP: 5 **EST:** 2010
SALES (est): 90K **Privately Held**
SIC: 3911 Jewelry apparel

(G-13509)
BETA FUELING SYSTEMS LLC
Also Called: Beta Fluid Systems
1209 Freeway Dr (27320-7103)
P.O. Box 1737 (27323-1737)
PHONE....................336 342-0306
John Ingold, *CEO*
Jonathan Deline, *Managing Member**
Marcel Haar, **
▲ **EMP:** 51 **EST:** 1972
SQ FT: 76,000
SALES (est): 18.47MM
SALES (corp-wide): 355.83K **Privately Held**
Web: www.betafueling.com
SIC: 3728 Aircraft parts and equipment, nec
PA: Dome Gmbh & Co. Kg
 Bauernallee 7
 Ludwigslust MV
 387466300

(G-13510)
BOEHME-FILATEX INC
209 Watlington Industrial Dr (27320-8147)
PHONE....................336 342-4507
Rene A Eckert, *CEO*
Phil Goodman, **
George Sembert, **
Judy Pope, **
◆ **EMP:** 140 **EST:** 1981
SQ FT: 40,000
SALES (est): 32.69MM
SALES (corp-wide): 3.16MM **Privately Held**
Web: www.boehme-chemie.com
SIC: 2869 Industrial organic chemicals, nec
PA: Boehme Systems Ohg
 An Der Triebe 12-14
 Moritzburg SN 01468
 351 838-2603

(G-13511)
CAMCO MANUFACTURING INC
Also Called: CAMCO MANUFACTURING, INC.
2900 Vance Street Ext (27320-9499)
PHONE....................336 348-6609
EMP: 5
SALES (corp-wide): 100.88MM **Privately Held**
Web: www.camco.net
SIC: 2899 3714 3822 5013 Antifreeze compounds; Motor vehicle parts and accessories; Water heater controls; Motor vehicle supplies and new parts
PA: Camco Manufacturing, Llc
 121 Landmark Dr
 Greensboro NC 27409
 800 334-2004

(G-13512)
CAROLINA CORE MACHINE LLC
638 Tamco Rd (27320-8690)
PHONE....................336 342-1141
Brent Allen, *Managing Member*
EMP: 25 **EST:** 2021
SALES (est): 3.21MM **Privately Held**
SIC: 3599 Machine and other job shop work

(G-13513)
CARTER THOMAS WAYNE SR
Also Called: T C Logging
2141 Moir Mill Rd (27320-8074)
PHONE....................336 623-2177
Thomas B Carter Senior, *Prin*
EMP: 4
SALES (est): 20.16K **Privately Held**
SIC: 2411 Logging

(G-13514)
CONTINENTAL STONE COMPANY
159 Harvest Rd (27320-8820)
PHONE....................336 951-2945
Lloyd C Prontaut Junior, *Owner*
EMP: 4 **EST:** 1982
SALES (est): 214.4K **Privately Held**
Web: www.continentalstone.com
SIC: 3272 Concrete products, precast, nec

(G-13515)
CREIGHTON AB INC
205 Watlington Industrial Dr (27320-8147)
P.O. Box 1797 (27323-1797)
PHONE....................336 349-8275
EMP: 5 **EST:** 2010
SALES (est): 558.62K **Privately Held**
Web: www.abelectricalserv.com
SIC: 2326 Men's and boy's work clothing

(G-13516)
DAVID ROTHSCHILD CO INC
618 Grooms Rd (27320-8673)
PHONE....................336 342-0035
Walter Rothschild, *Pr*
EMP: 65
SALES (corp-wide): 9.11MM **Privately Held**
Web: www.davidrothschildco.com
SIC: 2221 Acetate broadwoven fabrics
PA: David Rothschild Co., Inc.
 512 12th St
 Columbus GA 31901
 706 324-2411

(G-13517)
DIVINE LEMONADES LLC
1605 Withersea Ln (27320-8621)
PHONE....................336 255-0739
EMP: 5 **EST:** 2020
SALES (est): 196.99K **Privately Held**
Web: www.divinelemonades.com
SIC: 2086 Lemonade: packaged in cans, bottles, etc.

(G-13518)
DYSTAR LP
209 Watlington Industrial Dr (27320-8147)
PHONE....................336 342-6631
EMP: 75
Web: www.dystar.com
SIC: 2865 Dyes and pigments
HQ: Dystar L.P.
 9844 Southern Pine Blvd A
 Charlotte NC 28273

(G-13519)
GENERAL MACHINING INC
37 W Plymouth (27320)
PHONE....................336 342-2759
James Putnam, *Pr*
EMP: 4 **EST:** 1980
SQ FT: 4,000
SALES (est): 392.98K **Privately Held**
SIC: 3599 Custom machinery

(G-13520)
GLOBAL TEXTILE ALLIANCE INC (PA)
Also Called: G.T.a
2361 Holiday Loop (27320-8684)
PHONE....................336 217-1300
Timothy M Dolan, *CEO*
Steven M Graven, **
◆ **EMP:** 8 **EST:** 2001
SALES (est): 12.89MM
SALES (corp-wide): 12.89MM **Privately Held**
Web: www.globaltextileallianceinc.com
SIC: 2299 5131 Broadwoven fabrics: linen, jute, hemp, and ramie; Piece goods and notions

(G-13521)
GP FABRICATION INC
9968 Us 158 (27320-9543)
PHONE....................336 361-0410
Gerald Pruitt, *Pr*
EMP: 24 **EST:** 2001
SQ FT: 800
SALES (est): 2.27MM **Privately Held**
Web: www.gpfabrication.com
SIC: 3441 Fabricated structural metal

(G-13522)
GRAILGAME INC ✪
301 N Scales St (27320-2906)
P.O. Box 3003 (23228-9701)
PHONE....................804 517-3102
Evans Richards, *Pr*
Christopher Farrar, *CFO*
EMP: 5 **EST:** 2023
SALES (est): 222K **Privately Held**
SIC: 5961 3944 Electronic shopping; Electronic games and toys

(G-13523)
GREGORY PALLET CO
11177 Cherry Grove Rd (27320-0249)
PHONE....................336 349-2212
Maynard Gregory, *Owner*
EMP: 6 **EST:** 1970
SALES (est): 351.05K **Privately Held**
Web: www.gregorypalletcompany.com
SIC: 2448 Pallets, wood

(G-13524)
HANKS GAME CALLS
140 Hanks Trl (27320-8523)
PHONE....................336 317-3530
Kimmy Hanks, *Prin*
EMP: 4 **EST:** 2017
SALES (est): 47.08K **Privately Held**
SIC: 3949 Game calls

(G-13525)
HAT CREEK ALPACAS
2141 Moir Mill Rd (27320-8074)
PHONE....................336 552-2284
Lisa Moore, *Prin*
EMP: 5 **EST:** 2016
SALES (est): 62.19K **Privately Held**
SIC: 2231 Alpacas, mohair: woven

(G-13526)
HENNIGES AUTOMOTIVE N AMER INC (DH)
226 Watlington Industrial Dr (27320-8147)
PHONE....................336 342-9300
Mark Drumheller, *Pr*
Larry Williams, *VP*
▲ **EMP:** 98 **EST:** 1994
SQ FT: 250,000
SALES (est): 56MM **Privately Held**
Web: www.hennigesautomotive.com
SIC: 3053 Gaskets and sealing devices
HQ: Schlegel Corporation
 2750 High Meadow Cir
 Auburn Hills MI 48326
 248 340-4100

(G-13527)
ISOMETRICS INC
7537 Nc Highway 87 (27320-8803)
PHONE....................336 342-4150
Gary Mcgrath, *Mgr*
EMP: 10
SALES (corp-wide): 10.08MM **Privately Held**
Web: www.isometrics-inc.com
SIC: 3728 3714 Fuel tanks, aircraft; Gas tanks, motor vehicle
PA: Isometrics, Inc.
 1266 N Scales St
 Reidsville NC 27320
 336 349-2329

(G-13528)
ISOMETRICS INC (PA)
1266 N Scales St (27320-8306)

GEOGRAPHIC SECTION

Richfield - Stanly County (G-13554)

P.O. Box 660 (27323-0660)
PHONE.................................336 349-2329
Dennis Bracy, *Ch Bd*
David Mccollum, *VP*
Gail Martin, *
◆ **EMP:** 40 **EST:** 1973
SQ FT: 80,000
SALES (est): 10.08MM
SALES (corp-wide): 10.08MM **Privately Held**
Web: www.isometrics-inc.com
SIC: 3714 3728 Gas tanks, motor vehicle; Fuel tanks, aircraft

(G-13529)
KEYSTONE FOODS LLC
Equity Group
227 Equity Dr (27320-7000)
P.O. Box 1436 (27323-1436)
PHONE.................................336 342-6601
Tom Harris, *Manager*
EMP: 150
SALES (corp-wide): 52.88B **Publicly Held**
Web: www.tysonfoods.com
SIC: 2015 Chicken, processed, nsk
HQ: Keystone Foods Llc
   905 Airport Rd Ste 400
   West Chester PA 19380
   610 667-6700

(G-13530)
MARIETTA MARTIN MATERIALS INC
Also Called: Martin Marietta Aggregates
7639 Nc Highway 87 (27320-8818)
PHONE.................................336 349-3333
Kenneth Roberts, *Brnch Mgr*
EMP: 6
Web: www.martinmarietta.com
SIC: 1422 Crushed and broken limestone
PA: Martin Marietta Materials Inc
   4123 Parklake Ave
   Raleigh NC 27612

(G-13531)
MINUTEMAN PROVISION CO LLC
8740 Us 158 (27320-7611)
PHONE.................................252 996-0856
Lane Miller, *Owner*
EMP: 5 **EST:** 2016
SALES (est): 82.35K **Privately Held**
Web: www.minutemanstove.com
SIC: 2711 Newspapers

(G-13532)
MIRROR TECH INC
1011 Freeway Dr (27320-7101)
P.O. Box 468 (27357-0468)
PHONE.................................336 342-6041
Paul Potter, *Pr*
▲ **EMP:** 6 **EST:** 1991
SQ FT: 1,200
SALES (est): 951.31K **Privately Held**
SIC: 2869 Industrial organic chemicals, nec

(G-13533)
MORRISETTE PAPER COMPANY INC
Also Called: Paper Development
105 E Harrison St (27320-3901)
P.O. Box 786 (27323-0786)
PHONE.................................336 342-5570
Rodney Martin, *Brnch Mgr*
EMP: 8
SALES (corp-wide): 100.46MM **Privately Held**
Web: www.morrisette.com
SIC: 2621 2675 2631 Paper mills; Die-cut paper and board; Paperboard mills
PA: Morrisette Packaging, Inc.
   5925 Summit Ave
   Browns Summit NC 27214
   336 375-1515

(G-13534)
MQH LLC
1625 Grooms Rd (27320-9280)
PHONE.................................570 417-3165
EMP: 5 **EST:** 2015
SALES (est): 93.97K **Privately Held**
SIC: 3131 Quarters

(G-13535)
MY THREESONS GOURMET
2138 Wentworth St (27320-7304)
PHONE.................................336 324-5638
Cheryl Bennett, *Owner*
EMP: 5 **EST:** 2011
SALES (est): 230.45K **Privately Held**
SIC: 2099 Food preparations, nec

(G-13536)
NEWS & RECORD
1921 Vance St (27320-3254)
PHONE.................................336 627-1781
Karl Miller, *Prin*
EMP: 15 **EST:** 2011
SALES (est): 158.19K **Privately Held**
Web: www.greensboro.com
SIC: 2711 Newspapers, publishing and printing

(G-13537)
OSCEOLA CUSTOM WOODWORKS
1551 Brooks Rd (27320-7585)
PHONE.................................336 514-3720
EMP: 4 **EST:** 2014
SALES (est): 54.13K **Privately Held**
SIC: 2431 Millwork

(G-13538)
ROCKINGHAM NOW
1921 Vance St (27320-3254)
PHONE.................................336 349-4331
EMP: 6 **EST:** 2019
SALES (est): 78.68K **Privately Held**
Web: www.greensboro.com
SIC: 2711 Newspapers, publishing and printing

(G-13539)
S BOYD WELDING
10044 Nc Highway 87 (27320-7374)
PHONE.................................336 349-8349
EMP: 4 **EST:** 2017
SALES (est): 41.46K **Privately Held**
SIC: 7692 Welding repair

(G-13540)
SMITH-CAROLINA CORPORATION
Also Called: S C C
654 Freeway Dr (27320-7207)
PHONE.................................336 349-2905
Wes Taylor, *Sec*
EMP: 27 **EST:** 1977
SALES (est): 3.31MM **Publicly Held**
Web: www.smithmidland.com
SIC: 3272 Concrete products, precast, nec
PA: Smith-Midland Corporation
   5119 Catlett Rd
   Midland VA 22728

(G-13541)
TIM NICHOLSON RACE CARS LLC
205 Se Market St B (27320-3802)
PHONE.................................336 253-6767
EMP: 4 **EST:** 2015
SALES (est): 218.57K **Privately Held**
SIC: 3711 Automobile assembly, including specialty automobiles

(G-13542)
TIRE KOUNTRY LLC ✪
2300 Freeway Dr (27320-7208)
PHONE.................................336 637-8320
EMP: 5 **EST:** 2022
SALES (est): 419.68K **Privately Held**
Web: tirekountry.business.site
SIC: 7549 5015 3714 Automotive services, nec; Motor vehicle parts, used; Motor vehicle parts and accessories

(G-13543)
TOYMAKERZ LLC
2358 Holiday Loop (27320-8684)
PHONE.................................843 267-3477
David Ankin, *CEO*
David Young, *Prin*
EMP: 10 **EST:** 2017
SALES (est): 918.64K **Privately Held**
Web: www.toymakerz.com
SIC: 3711 7922 Motor vehicles and car bodies; Television program, including commercial producers

(G-13544)
UNIFI INC
Also Called: Unifi Plant 2
2920 Vance Street Ext (27320-9499)
P.O. Box 1437 (27323-1437)
PHONE.................................336 348-6539
Ron Mangrun, *Mgr*
EMP: 58
SALES (corp-wide): 623.53MM **Publicly Held**
Web: www.unifi.com
SIC: 2269 2281 Finishing: raw stock, yarn, and narrow fabrics; Yarn spinning mills
PA: Unifi, Inc.
   7201 W Friendly Ave
   Greensboro NC 27410
   336 294-4410

(G-13545)
WESTERN TECHNOLOGY INC
711 County Line Rd (27320-1697)
P.O. Box 3580 (27515-3580)
PHONE.................................336 361-0402
EMP: 10 **EST:** 1992
SALES (est): 491.05K **Privately Held**
Web: www.westerntechnology.net
SIC: 2046 Industrial starch

(G-13546)
WLC FORKLIFT SERVICES LLC
640 Tamco Rd (27320-8690)
PHONE.................................336 345-2571
William Conklin, *Managing Member*
EMP: 9 **EST:** 2014
SALES (est): 776.77K **Privately Held**
Web: www.wlcforkliftservicesllc.com
SIC: 3537 Forklift trucks

(G-13547)
WP REIDSVILLE LLC
109 Sands Rd (27320-6521)
P.O. Box 368 (46507-0368)
PHONE.................................336 342-1200
▼ **EMP:** 125
SIC: 2821 Molding compounds, plastics

Research Triangle Pa
Durham County

(G-13548)
AVAYA LLC
4001 E Chapel Hl (27709)
PHONE.................................919 425-8268
EMP: 255
Web: www.avaya.com

SIC: 3661 Telephone and telegraph apparatus
HQ: Avaya Llc
   350 Mount Kemble Ave # 1
   Morristown NJ 07960
   908 953-6000

(G-13549)
CYBERLUX CORPORATION (PA)
800 Park Offices Dr Ste 3209 (27709)
PHONE.................................984 363-6894
Mark Schmidt, *CEO*
Mark D Schmidt, *CEO*
David D Downing, *Treas*
EMP: 16 **EST:** 2000
SQ FT: 7,472
SALES (est): 15.58MM
SALES (corp-wide): 15.58MM **Publicly Held**
Web: www.cyberlux.com
SIC: 3728 3721 3648 7371 Target drones; Aircraft; Arc lighting fixtures; Computer software development and applications

(G-13550)
DZONE INC
Also Called: Devada
600 Park Offices Dr Ste 150 (27709)
P.O. Box 12077 (27709-2077)
PHONE.................................919 678-0300
Terry Walters, *Pr*
EMP: 15 **EST:** 2005
SQ FT: 6,000
SALES (est): 2.67MM **Privately Held**
Web: www.dzone.com
SIC: 7319 7372 Media buying service; Publisher's computer software

(G-13551)
GLAXOSMITHKLINE LLC
52069 Five Moore Dr (27709)
P.O. Box 13358 (27709-3358)
PHONE.................................919 483-5006
EMP: 21
SALES (corp-wide): 35.31B **Privately Held**
Web: us.gsk.com
SIC: 2834 Pharmaceutical preparations
HQ: Glaxosmithkline Llc
   2929 Walnut St Ste 1700
   Philadelphia PA 19104
   888 825-5249

Richfield
Stanly County

(G-13552)
MAGNA MACHINING INC
111 3rd Park Dr (28137-7500)
PHONE.................................704 463-9904
George Williams Junior, *Pr*
Nancy Williams, *VP*
EMP: 21 **EST:** 1998
SQ FT: 5,000
SALES (est): 2.2MM **Privately Held**
Web: www.magnamachining.com
SIC: 3599 Machine shop, jobbing and repair

(G-13553)
ORION MANUFACTURING LLC
20016 Bear Creek Ch Rd (28137-7640)
PHONE.................................714 633-5850
EMP: 8 **EST:** 2003
SALES (est): 76.37K **Privately Held**
SIC: 2431 Millwork

(G-13554)
RICHFELD PRTABLE BUILDINGS INC
Also Called: Pro Storage Plus
321 W Church St (28137-5717)

PHONE.....................704 463-1802
Marvin Robinson, Prin
EMP: 5 **EST:** 2018
SALES (est): 239.74K **Privately Held**
Web: www.richfieldportablebuildings.com
SIC: 3448 Prefabricated metal buildings and components

Richlands
Onslow County

(G-13555)
HOUSE OF GUNS INC
377 Bannermans Mill Rd (28574-8105)
PHONE.....................910 381-0732
Joshua M Barney, Pr
EMP: 4 **EST:** 2012
SALES (est): 74.25K **Privately Held**
SIC: 3489 Ordnance and accessories, nec

(G-13556)
MARTIN MARIETTA MATERIALS INC
Also Called: Martin Marietta Aggregates
131 Duffy Field Rd (28574-2300)
P.O. Box 67 (28574-0067)
PHONE.....................910 324-7430
Greg Meadows, Mgr
EMP: 4
Web: www.martinmarietta.com
SIC: 3273 Ready-mixed concrete
PA: Martin Marietta Materials Inc
4123 Parklake Ave
Raleigh NC 27612

Riegelwood
Columbus County

(G-13557)
BEST WORKERS COMPANY
5494 Port Royal Rd Ne (28456-9314)
PHONE.....................336 665-0076
EMP: 5 **EST:** 1987
SALES (est): 173.81K **Privately Held**
SIC: 3272 Burial vaults, concrete or precast terrazzo

(G-13558)
FRASER WEST INC
361 Federal Rd (28456-7117)
PHONE.....................910 655-4106
Kelly Hoffman, Dir Opers
EMP: 46 **EST:** 2000
SALES (est): 6.26MM **Privately Held**
SIC: 2421 Sawmills and planing mills, general

(G-13559)
INTERNATIONAL PAPER COMPANY
Also Called: International Paper
1865 John Riegel Rd (28456)
PHONE.....................910 655-2211
EMP: 5
SALES (corp-wide): 18.92B **Publicly Held**
Web: www.internationalpaper.com
SIC: 2621 Paper mills
PA: International Paper Company
6400 Poplar Ave
Memphis TN 38197
901 419-7000

(G-13560)
INTERNATIONAL PAPER COMPANY
Also Called: International Paper
865 John L Regel Rd (28456-9581)
P.O. Box 825 (28456-0825)
PHONE.....................910 362-4900
Scott Grimes, Mgr

EMP: 248
SALES (corp-wide): 18.92B **Publicly Held**
Web: www.internationalpaper.com
SIC: 2621 2631 Paper mills; Paperboard mills
PA: International Paper Company
6400 Poplar Ave
Memphis TN 38197
901 419-7000

(G-13561)
OAK-BARK CORPORATION
Also Called: Wright
1507 Cronly Dr (28456-9504)
PHONE.....................910 655-2263
William Oakley, Brnch Mgr
EMP: 20
SALES (corp-wide): 8.63MM **Privately Held**
Web: www.oakbark12.com
SIC: 2869 Industrial organic chemicals, nec
PA: Oak-Bark Corporation
514 Wayne Dr
Wilmington NC 28403

(G-13562)
REEVES INDUS WLDG FABRICATION
5479 Goose Neck Rd Ne (28456-9337)
PHONE.....................910 399-7127
Rebecca Potter, Prin
EMP: 5 **EST:** 2017
SALES (est): 96.27K **Privately Held**
SIC: 7692 Welding repair

(G-13563)
SILAR LLC (DH)
Also Called: Silar Laboratories
333 Neils Eddy Rd (28456-9570)
PHONE.....................910 655-4212
Martha Neely, Prin
◆ **EMP:** 35 **EST:** 2008
SALES (est): 12.27MM
SALES (corp-wide): 3.52B **Publicly Held**
Web: www.silar.com
SIC: 2869 Industrial organic chemicals, nec
HQ: Mpd Holdings, Llc
340 Mathers Rd
Ambler PA 19002

Roanoke Rapids
Halifax County

(G-13564)
3D PRINT LODGE LLC
620 E Littleton Rd (27870-4830)
PHONE.....................804 309-6028
EMP: 4 **EST:** 2021
SALES (est): 83.91K **Privately Held**
SIC: 2752 Commercial printing, lithographic

(G-13565)
ALLIE M POWELL III
Also Called: Powell's Ready-Mix
3692 Nc Highway 48 (27870-8474)
P.O. Box 395 (27870-0395)
PHONE.....................252 535-9717
Allie M Powell Iii, Owner
EMP: 4 **EST:** 1994
SQ FT: 1,200
SALES (est): 236.95K **Privately Held**
SIC: 3273 Ready-mixed concrete

(G-13566)
ARGOS USA LLC
Also Called: Ready Mixed Concrete Co
75 W 13th St (27870-3725)
P.O. Box 2065 (27533-2065)
PHONE.....................252 443-5046
EMP: 4

Web: www.argos-us.com
SIC: 3273 Ready-mixed concrete
HQ: Argos Usa Llc
3015 Windward Plz Ste 300
Alpharetta GA 30005
678 368-4300

(G-13567)
AUTOVERTERS INC
2212 W 10th St (27870-9295)
P.O. Box 850 (27870-0850)
PHONE.....................252 537-0426
Barbara A Dickens, Pr
Shawn Burke, Sec
▲ **EMP:** 16 **EST:** 1976
SQ FT: 87,700
SALES (est): 1.5MM **Privately Held**
Web: www.autovertersinc.com
SIC: 7389 3999 Textile folding and packing services; Advertising curtains

(G-13568)
BUCK LUCAS LOGGING COMPANIES
812 W Hawkins Rd (27870-9519)
PHONE.....................252 410-0160
Jonathan Vance Lucas, Prin
EMP: 9 **EST:** 2007
SALES (est): 488.47K **Privately Held**
SIC: 2411 Logging camps and contractors

(G-13569)
BUTCHERS BEST INC
944 Raleigh St (27870-2923)
PHONE.....................252 533-0961
Chris Rice, Owner
EMP: 4 **EST:** 2002
SALES (est): 313.78K **Privately Held**
SIC: 3421 Cutlery

(G-13570)
C&A HOCKADAY TRANSPORT LLC
1660 Hill St (27870-4210)
PHONE.....................252 676-5956
EMP: 4
SALES (est): 182.43K **Privately Held**
SIC: 3537 7389 Trucks: freight, baggage, etc.: industrial, except mining; Business Activities at Non-Commercial Site

(G-13571)
COASTAL TREATED PRODUCTS LLC
1433 Georgia Ave (27870-4653)
PHONE.....................252 410-0180
EMP: 22 **EST:** 2012
SALES (est): 646.51K
SALES (corp-wide): 8.39B **Publicly Held**
SIC: 2491 Wood preserving
PA: Boise Cascade Company
1111 W Jefferson St # 100
Boise ID 83702
208 384-6161

(G-13572)
CULPEPER ROANOKE RAPIDS LLC
2262 W 10th St (27870-9295)
PHONE.....................252 678-3804
EMP: 8 **EST:** 2017
SALES (est): 301.51K **Privately Held**
Web: www.culpeperwood.com
SIC: 2491 Wood preserving

(G-13573)
CURLEYS PLUMBING
190 Fairlane Dr (27870-9005)
PHONE.....................252 578-8666
Joe Curley, Owner
EMP: 6 **EST:** 2014
SALES (est): 154.81K **Privately Held**
SIC: 3469 Enameled ware, except plumbers' supplies: porcelain

(G-13574)
FRANKLIN BAKING COMPANY LLC
610 Julian R Allsbrook Hwy (27870-4613)
PHONE.....................252 410-0255
Tim Hales, Mgr
EMP: 10
SALES (corp-wide): 5.09B **Publicly Held**
Web: franklin-co4goldsboro.edan.io
SIC: 2051 Bread, all types (white, wheat, rye, etc); fresh or frozen
HQ: Franklin Baking Company, Llc
500 W Grantham St
Goldsboro NC 27530
919 735-0344

(G-13575)
HERALD PRINTING CO INC
916 Roanoke Ave (27870-2720)
PHONE.....................252 537-2505
Stephen Woody, VP
Walter M Wick, *
Robert J Wick, Treas
EMP: 20 **EST:** 1947
SQ FT: 9,000
SALES (est): 220.52K **Privately Held**
Web: www.rrdailyherald.com
SIC: 2711 Newspapers, publishing and printing

(G-13576)
J E KERR TIMBER CO CORP
1005 Old Halifax Rd (27870-8572)
PHONE.....................252 537-0544
James Kerr, Pr
Charlotte Kerr, *
Joan Kerr, *
EMP: 18 **EST:** 1975
SQ FT: 1,500
SALES (est): 1.09MM **Privately Held**
SIC: 5031 2411 Lumber: rough, dressed, and finished; Logging

(G-13577)
LOTS OF LABELS
210 E 10th St (27870-3821)
PHONE.....................252 410-1611
EMP: 5 **EST:** 2014
SALES (est): 89.33K **Privately Held**
Web: www.elliottscomputers.com
SIC: 2759 Labels and seals: printing, nsk

(G-13578)
LYNCHS OFFICE SUPPLY CO INC (PA)
921 Roanoke Ave (27870-2719)
PHONE.....................252 537-6041
TOLL FREE: 800
Cecil T Lynch Junior, Pr
Lynne S Lynch, VP
Christian T Lynch, VP
Kevin S Lynch, VP
EMP: 10 **EST:** 1961
SALES (est): 2.41MM
SALES (corp-wide): 2.41MM **Privately Held**
Web: www.lynchsofficesupply.com
SIC: 5943 5999 2752 Office forms and supplies; Business machines and equipment; Offset printing

(G-13579)
MCPHERSON BEVERAGES INC
Also Called: Pepsico
1330 Stancell St (27870-4824)
PHONE.....................252 537-3571
Russell M Hull, Pr
EMP: 47 **EST:** 1932
SQ FT: 15,000
SALES (est): 5.35MM **Privately Held**
Web: www.pepsico.com

SIC: 2086 Bottled and canned soft drinks

(G-13580)
PRINT EXPRESS PLUS
310 Roanoke Ave (27870-1918)
PHONE..................................252 541-4444
Rachelle Harris, *Prin*
EMP: 4 **EST:** 2016
SALES (est): 179.86K **Privately Held**
SIC: 2752 Offset printing

(G-13581)
ROANOKE TRUSS INC
711 E 15th St (27870-4441)
PHONE..................................252 537-0012
James D Cagle, *Pr*
Linda Mozingo, *VP*
EMP: 8 **EST:** 1984
SQ FT: 3,500
SALES (est): 800K **Privately Held**
SIC: 2439 Trusses, wooden roof

(G-13582)
THOMPSON WELDING & MECHCL SVC
115 W 13th St (27870-3727)
PHONE..................................252 536-9431
Tony Thompson, *Owner*
EMP: 7 **EST:** 2015
SALES (est): 40.23K **Privately Held**
Web: www.thompsonwam.com
SIC: 7692 Welding repair

(G-13583)
THOMPSON WLDG & MECH SVC LLC
P.O. Box 1482 (27870-7482)
PHONE..................................252 535-4269
Tony Thompson, *Prin*
EMP: 5 **EST:** 2010
SALES (est): 86.95K **Privately Held**
SIC: 7692 Welding repair

(G-13584)
VULTARE LOGGING LLC
Also Called: Big E'S Hauling
81 Johnson St (27870-9442)
PHONE..................................252 578-0377
Kevin Michael Edmondson, *Admn*
EMP: 7 **EST:** 2016
SALES (est): 217.77K **Privately Held**
SIC: 2411 Logging camps and contractors

(G-13585)
WELLS MECHANICAL SERVICES LLC
628 Raleigh Dr (27870-3915)
PHONE..................................252 532-2632
Michael Wells, *Prin*
EMP: 8 **EST:** 2013
SALES (est): 242.21K **Privately Held**
SIC: 7692 Welding repair

(G-13586)
WESTROCK KRAFT PAPER LLC
100 Gaston Rd (27870-1900)
PHONE..................................252 533-6000
EMP: 5
SALES (corp-wide): 20.31B **Publicly Held**
Web: www.westrock.com
SIC: 2621 Specialty papers
HQ: Westrock Kraft Paper, Llc
1000 Abernathy Rd
Atlanta GA 30328
770 448-2193

(G-13587)
WESTROCK PAPER AND PACKG LLC
Also Called: Kapstone Kraft Paper
100 Gaston Rd (27870-1900)
PHONE..................................252 533-6000

Anitra Collins, *Brnch Mgr*
EMP: 500
SALES (corp-wide): 20.31B **Publicly Held**
Web: www.westrock.com
SIC: 2631 2611 2621 Paperboard mills; Pulp mills; Paper mills
HQ: Westrock Paper And Packaging, Llc
1000 Abernathy Rd
Atlanta GA 30328

(G-13588)
WHIPPOORWILL HILLS INC
1509 E 10th St (27870-4101)
P.O. Box 56 (27832-0056)
PHONE..................................252 537-2765
Philipp Moncure, *Pr*
EMP: 6 **EST:** 2010
SALES (est): 192.11K **Privately Held**
SIC: 2519 Household furniture, nec

(G-13589)
WICK COMMUNICATIONS CO
Also Called: Daily Herald
1025 Roanoke Ave (27870-3701)
P.O. Box 520 (27870-0520)
PHONE..................................252 537-2505
Stephen Woody, *Publisher*
EMP: 23
SALES (corp-wide): 87.63MM **Privately Held**
Web: www.wickcommunications.com
SIC: 2711 2752 Newspapers, publishing and printing; Commercial printing, lithographic
HQ: Wick Communications Co.
333 W Wilcox Dr Ste 302
Sierra Vista AZ 85635
520 458-0200

(G-13590)
WILLIAMS & SON LOGGING LLC
112 Steeplechase Run (27870-3239)
PHONE..................................252 533-9201
Jeffrey W Williams, *Prin*
EMP: 7 **EST:** 2017
SALES (est): 490.26K **Privately Held**
SIC: 2411 Logging camps and contractors

(G-13591)
WRIGHT & HOBBS INC
105 W Becker Dr (27870-4800)
P.O. Box 696 (27832-0696)
PHONE..................................252 537-5817
Leslie Wright Junior, *Pr*
EMP: 26 **EST:** 1967
SQ FT: 4,000
SALES (est): 2.33MM **Privately Held**
SIC: 2411 2426 2421 Timber, cut at logging camp; Hardwood dimension and flooring mills; Sawmills and planing mills, general

Roaring River
Wilkes County

(G-13592)
COMBS WELDING LLC
976 Dellaplane Rd (28669-9244)
PHONE..................................336 984-3832
Matthew J Combs, *Prin*
EMP: 5 **EST:** 2016
SALES (est): 30.36K **Privately Held**
SIC: 7692 Welding repair

(G-13593)
GENTRYS CABNT DOORS
2872 Austin Little Mtn Rd (28669-9190)
PHONE..................................336 957-8787
Scott Gentry, *Prin*
EMP: 7 **EST:** 2010
SALES (est): 191K **Privately Held**

SIC: 2434 7389 Wood kitchen cabinets; Business Activities at Non-Commercial Site

(G-13594)
LOUISIANA-PACIFIC CORPORATION
1151 Abtco Rd (28669)
PHONE..................................336 696-2751
EMP: 8
SALES (corp-wide): 4.55B **Publicly Held**
Web: www.lpcorp.com
SIC: 2493 Strandboard, oriented
PA: Louisiana-Pacific Corporation
1610 West End Ave Ste 200
Nashville TN 37203
615 986-5600

(G-13595)
SMITH MILLING COMPANY
1265 Wagon Ridge Rd (28669-9169)
PHONE..................................336 957-8108
Sheila S Smith, *Prin*
EMP: 6 **EST:** 2008
SALES (est): 50.1K **Privately Held**
SIC: 2041 Flour and other grain mill products

Robbins
Moore County

(G-13596)
AMERICAN GROWLER INC (PA)
121 N Green St (27325-9480)
P.O. Box 430 (27325-0430)
PHONE..................................352 671-5393
Terry Crews, *Pr*
EMP: 30 **EST:** 1992
SALES (est): 4.62MM
SALES (corp-wide): 4.62MM **Privately Held**
Web: www.growlerme.com
SIC: 3799 Off-road automobiles, except recreational vehicles

(G-13597)
CAROLINA GROWLER INC
Also Called: Growler Manufacturing & Engrg
121 N Green St (27325-9480)
PHONE..................................910 948-2114
Curtis Crews, *CEO*
Terry Crews, *
John Crews, *
EMP: 30 **EST:** 2007
SALES (est): 4.69MM **Privately Held**
Web: www.growlerme.com
SIC: 3699 Security devices

(G-13598)
GRASSY RIDGE LOGGING CO
315 Hallison Highfalls Rd (27325-9318)
PHONE..................................919 935-5355
EMP: 5 **EST:** 2016
SALES (est): 89.89K **Privately Held**
SIC: 2411 Logging

(G-13599)
KEY PACKING COMPANY INC
596 Maness Rd (27325-8243)
PHONE..................................910 464-5054
Gilbert M Key, *Pr*
Elizabeth Key, *Sec*
Mitchell Key, *VP*
EMP: 8 **EST:** 1975
SALES (est): 911.82K **Privately Held**
Web: www.keypackingcompany.com
SIC: 2011 Beef products, from beef slaughtered on site

(G-13600)
MCI PACKING COMPANY LLC
596 Maness Rd (27325-8243)
PHONE..................................910 464-3507
Mitchell G Key, *Managing Member*
EMP: 5 **EST:** 2015
SALES (est): 768K **Privately Held**
SIC: 2011 Meat packing plants

(G-13601)
MINHAS FURNITURE HOUSE INC
Also Called: Flair Designs
6844 Nc 705 Hwy (27325-7828)
PHONE..................................910 898-0808
Bill Minhas, *Pr*
Kamanjeet Minhas, *
◆ **EMP:** 30 **EST:** 2012
SQ FT: 125,000
SALES (est): 4.95MM
SALES (corp-wide): 17.39MM **Privately Held**
SIC: 2512 5021 Upholstered household furniture; Furniture
PA: Minhas Furniture House Ltd
3916 72 Ave Se
Calgary AB T2C 2
403 219-1006

(G-13602)
PORTERS TAVERN WOOD WORKS
731 Jesse Phillips Rd (27325-8220)
PHONE..................................910 639-4519
EMP: 4 **EST:** 2015
SALES (est): 101.97K **Privately Held**
Web: www.porterstavernwoodworks.com
SIC: 2431 Millwork

(G-13603)
VANDERBILT MINERALS LLC
Also Called: Standard Mineral Division
400 Spies Rd (27325-7395)
P.O. Box 279 (27325-0279)
PHONE..................................910 948-2266
James Faile, *Genl Mgr*
EMP: 26
SALES (corp-wide): 266.87MM **Privately Held**
Web: www.vanderbiltminerals.com
SIC: 1499 3295 Pyrophyllite mining; Minerals, ground or treated
HQ: Vanderbilt Minerals, Llc
33 Winfield St
Norwalk CT 06855
203 295-2140

Robbinsville
Graham County

(G-13604)
BEASLEY CONTRACTING
756 Gladdens Creek Rd (28771-6909)
PHONE..................................828 479-3775
Gary Beasley, *Owner*
EMP: 4 **EST:** 2009
SALES (est): 178.92K **Privately Held**
SIC: 3531 Construction machinery

(G-13605)
BLUE ROCK MATERIALS LLC
750 Tallulah Rd (28771-9461)
PHONE..................................828 479-3581
EMP: 10 **EST:** 2010
SALES (est): 991.26K **Privately Held**
Web: www.bluerocknc.com
SIC: 1423 1442 Crushed and broken granite; Construction sand and gravel

Robbinsville - Graham County (G-13606)

(G-13606)
COMMUNITY NEWSPAPERS INC
Also Called: The Graham Star
720 Tallulah Rd (28771-9461)
P.O. Box 69 (28771-0069)
PHONE.................................828 479-3383
Gary Corsair, Mgr
EMP: 4
SALES (corp-wide): 49.22MM Privately Held
Web: www.cninewspapers.com
SIC: 2711 Newspapers, publishing and printing
PA: Community Newspapers, Inc.
2365 Prince Ave A
Athens GA 30606
706 548-0010

(G-13607)
DENTON WREATH COMPANY
692 Slaybacon Rd (28771-8619)
PHONE.................................828 479-4992
Peggy Denton, Prin
EMP: 4 EST: 2017
SALES (est): 49.9K Privately Held
SIC: 3999 Wreaths, artificial

(G-13608)
HOLDER MACHINE & MFG CO
1483 Fontana Rd (28771-5661)
PHONE.................................828 479-8627
Tony Holder, Pr
EMP: 5 EST: 1985
SQ FT: 7,000
SALES (est): 267.67K Privately Held
SIC: 7699 3599 Industrial machinery and equipment repair; Custom machinery

(G-13609)
MEDACCESS INC
1236 Gladdens Creek Rd (28771-6913)
PHONE.................................828 264-4085
Daniel K Stover, Pr
EMP: 4 EST: 2001
SALES (est): 243.32K Privately Held
Web: www.medaccessinc.com
SIC: 5999 7352 7359 8099 Wheelchair lifts; Medical equipment rental; Equipment rental and leasing, nec; Medical services organization

(G-13610)
ROBBINSVILLE CSTM MOLDING INC
Also Called: CM Supply
1450 Old Hwy 129 (28771-6807)
P.O. Box 817 (28771-0817)
PHONE.................................828 479-2317
John Garland, Pr
EMP: 13 EST: 1987
SQ FT: 5,000
SALES (est): 2.48MM Privately Held
Web: www.custommoulding.com
SIC: 1521 2434 2435 2431 New construction, single-family houses; Wood kitchen cabinets; Panels, hardwood plywood ; Moldings, wood: unfinished and prefinished

(G-13611)
SMOKEY MOUNTAIN AMUSEMENTS
5660 Tallulah Rd (28771-7535)
PHONE.................................828 479-2814
Billy J Clark, Prin
▲ EMP: 8 EST: 2002
SALES (est): 177.13K Privately Held
SIC: 3599 Industrial machinery, nec

(G-13612)
SMOKY MTN NATIV PLANT ASSN
546 Upper Tuskeegee Rd (28771-9012)
P.O. Box 761 (28771-0761)
PHONE.................................828 479-8788
Beverley Whitehead, Dir
EMP: 4 EST: 2008
SALES (est): 243.23K Privately Held
Web: www.smnpa.org
SIC: 8731 3523 Environmental research; Incubators and brooders, farm

(G-13613)
SNOWBIRD LOGGING LLC
270 Dick Branch Rd (28771-7951)
PHONE.................................828 479-6635
Walter Hooper, Pt
Tommy Cable, Pt
Jason Hooper, Pt
Lucas Hooper, Pt
EMP: 7 EST: 1994
SALES (est): 655.99K Privately Held
SIC: 2411 Logging camps and contractors

Robersonville
Martin County

(G-13614)
ANNS HOUSE OF NUTS
1159 Robersonville Products Rd (27871)
PHONE.................................252 795-6500
EMP: 4 EST: 2020
SALES (est): 226.93K Privately Held
SIC: 2034 Soup mixes

(G-13615)
CAROLINA EASTERN INC
Also Called: Eastern Crlina Agrculture Svcs
6940 Us Highway 64 (27871-9654)
P.O. Box 989 (27871-0989)
PHONE.................................252 795-3128
EMP: 5
SALES (corp-wide): 122.88MM Privately Held
Web: www.carolina-eastern.com
SIC: 2873 Nitrogenous fertilizers
PA: Carolina Eastern, Inc.
1820 Savannah Hwy Ste G1
Charleston SC 29407
843 571-0411

(G-13616)
FLAGSTONE FOODS LLC
201 E 3rd St (27871-9756)
PHONE.................................252 795-6500
Steve Gandy, Mgr
EMP: 421
SALES (corp-wide): 1.09B Privately Held
Web: www.flagstonefoods.com
SIC: 3556 Food products machinery
HQ: Flagstone Foods Llc
323 Washington Ave N # 400
Minneapolis MN 55401
612 222-3800

Rockingham
Richmond County

(G-13617)
ADVANCED MACHINE SERVICES
835 N Us Highway 220 (28379-6809)
PHONE.................................910 410-0099
Jermey Festheran, Owner
EMP: 4 EST: 2007
SALES (est): 354.18K Privately Held
SIC: 3365 Machinery castings, aluminum

(G-13618)
ADVANCED MACHINE SERVICES LLC
128 Industrial Park Dr (28379-3536)
P.O. Box 2512 (28380-2512)
PHONE.................................910 410-0099
EMP: 6 EST: 2020
SALES (est): 412.51K Privately Held
SIC: 7692 Welding repair

(G-13619)
ALLEN BROTHERS TIMBER COMPANY
Also Called: Crestview Trading Post
723 N Us Highway 220 (28379-6807)
PHONE.................................910 997-6412
Bruce G Allen, Pr
Craig Allen, Sec
Clay Allen, VP
EMP: 21 EST: 1968
SALES (est): 955.51K Privately Held
SIC: 2411 Logging camps and contractors

(G-13620)
B&D SPINDLES LLC
216 Lakeshore Dr (28379-9709)
PHONE.................................910 895-9769
Sherry Byrd, Owner
EMP: 5 EST: 2017
SALES (est): 103.91K Privately Held
Web: www.bdspindles.com
SIC: 3599 Machine shop, jobbing and repair

(G-13621)
CASCADES MOULDED PULP INC
112 Cascades Way (28379-3689)
P.O. Box 609 (28380-0609)
PHONE.................................910 997-2775
Gary A Hayden, Pr
Alain Lemaire, *
Guy Prenevost, *
Debbie Lear, *
Shannon Willart, *
EMP: 30 EST: 1986
SQ FT: 250,000
SALES (est): 10.4MM
SALES (corp-wide): 3.32B Privately Held
Web: www.cascades.com
SIC: 2621 Paper mills
PA: Cascades Inc
404 Boul Marie-Victorin
Kingsey Falls QC J0A 1
819 363-5100

(G-13622)
CASCADES TISSUE GROUP - NC INC
Also Called: Cascades Tissue Group
805 Midway Rd (28379-4101)
P.O. Box 578 (28380-0578)
PHONE.................................910 895-4033
Alain Lemaire, Pr
Suzanne Blanchet, *
◆ EMP: 130 EST: 1983
SQ FT: 155,000
SALES (est): 47.23MM
SALES (corp-wide): 46.25MM Privately Held
Web: www.cascades.com
SIC: 2676 2621 Toilet paper: made from purchased paper; Tissue paper
HQ: Cascades Fine Papers Group Inc.
7280 West Credit Ave
Mississauga ON L5N 5
905 813-9400

(G-13623)
DIRECT PACK EAST LLC
612 Airport Rd (28379-7494)
PHONE.................................910 331-0071
EMP: 25 EST: 2017
SALES (est): 8.59MM
SALES (corp-wide): 1.71B Privately Held
Web: www.directpackinc.com

SIC: 3565 Aerating machines, for beverages
PA: Pmc Global, Inc.
12243 Branford St
Sun Valley CA 91352
818 896-1101

(G-13624)
DORSETT PRINTING COMPANY
1203 Rockingham St (28379-4958)
P.O. Box 428 (28380-0428)
PHONE.................................910 895-3520
Karen Dunn, Pt
Susan Martin, Pt
EMP: 5 EST: 1966
SQ FT: 6,000
SALES (est): 487.58K Privately Held
SIC: 2752 Offset printing

(G-13625)
ELEKTRAN INC
220 River Rd (28379-4219)
P.O. Box 1027 (28380-1027)
PHONE.................................910 997-6640
Richard Adams, Pr
Brian Fournier, VP
EMP: 12 EST: 1977
SQ FT: 9,900
SALES (est): 1.85MM Privately Held
Web: www.elektran.com
SIC: 5063 7694 Power transmission equipment, electric; Electric motor repair

(G-13626)
EMBROIDERY CORNER
136 Glendale Dr (28379-9405)
PHONE.................................910 817-7586
Colleen Rene Parsons, Owner
EMP: 5 EST: 2015
SALES (est): 41.5K Privately Held
SIC: 2395 Embroidery and art needlework

(G-13627)
GGI GLASS DISTRIBUTORS CORP
Also Called: General Glass International
208 Silver Grove Church Rd (28379-5401)
PHONE.................................910 895-2022
EMP: 30
Web: www.generalglass.com
SIC: 3231 Products of purchased glass
PA: Ggi Glass Distributors Corp.
101 Venture Way
Secaucus NJ 07094

(G-13628)
HENSON FAMILY INVESTMENTS LLC
Also Called: Unique Stone
395 Ledbetter Rd (28379-7819)
PHONE.................................910 817-9450
Douglas Henson, Managing Member
EMP: 20 EST: 2015
SALES (est): 2.31MM Privately Held
Web: www.uniquestone.com
SIC: 3272 Art marble, concrete

(G-13629)
HILDRETH READY MIX LLC
518 W Us Highway 74 (28379-7006)
P.O. Box 1098 (28170-1098)
PHONE.................................704 694-2034
Melissa Renea Hildreth, Managing Member
EMP: 9 EST: 2008
SALES (est): 548.86K Privately Held
SIC: 3273 Ready-mixed concrete

(G-13630)
HUDSON PAVING INC
120 Yates Hill Rd (28379-3374)
P.O. Box 1232 (28380-1232)
PHONE.................................910 895-5910
Eugene Tom Hudson Junior, Pr

Ronnie Hudson, *
Brenda W Herring, *
EMP: 53 **EST:** 1961
SALES (est): 14.46MM **Privately Held**
Web:
www.hudsonpavingrockinghamnc.com
SIC: 1611 2951 1771 Surfacing and paving; Asphalt paving mixtures and blocks; Concrete work

(G-13631)
HUGHES WELDING & CRANE SVC LLC
121 Mill Rd (28379-4247)
PHONE.................910 895-9767
Robert Hughes, *Pr*
EMP: 6 **EST:** 2016
SALES (est): 240.57K **Privately Held**
Web:
hughes-welding-crane-services.business.site
SIC: 7692 Welding repair

(G-13632)
K & W WELDING LLC
180 Old 74 Hwy (28379)
P.O. Box 430 (28380-0430)
PHONE.................910 895-9220
EMP: 6 **EST:** 2006
SALES (est): 771.31K **Privately Held**
Web: www.kandwwelding.com
SIC: 7692 Welding repair

(G-13633)
LEGACY VULCAN LLC
Mideast Division
353 Galestown Rd (28379-7486)
P.O. Box 547 (28380-0547)
PHONE.................910 895-2415
TOLL FREE: 800
Charles Heatherly, *Mgr*
EMP: 6
Web: www.vulcanmaterials.com
SIC: 3273 Ready-mixed concrete
HQ: Legacy Vulcan, Llc
1200 Urban Center Dr
Vestavia AL 35242
205 298-3000

(G-13634)
MCKAY LOGGING INC
151 Glendale Dr (28379-9406)
PHONE.................910 334-3448
Daniel J Mckay, *Owner*
EMP: 7 **EST:** 2016
SALES (est): 237.42K **Privately Held**
SIC: 2411 Logging camps and contractors

(G-13635)
MOSS BROTHERS TIRES & SVC INC
190 W Us Highway 74 (28379-3488)
PHONE.................910 895-4572
William Moss, *Pr*
Elaine N Moss, *Sec*
EMP: 5 **EST:** 1988
SALES (est): 699.96K **Privately Held**
Web: www.mossbrotherstires.com
SIC: 5531 5014 7534 Automotive tires; Automobile tires and tubes; Tire retreading and repair shops

(G-13636)
NORTH CAROLINA INDUSTRIAL SAND
943 Airport Rd (28379-4709)
PHONE.................910 205-8535
EMP: 4 **EST:** 2016
SALES (est): 50.1K **Privately Held**
SIC: 1446 Industrial sand

(G-13637)
NPX ONE LLC
112 Sonoco Paper Mill Rd (28379-9535)
P.O. Box 1747 (28380-1747)
PHONE.................910 997-2217
Michael Hardy, *Brnch Mgr*
EMP: 213
SALES (corp-wide): 8.23B **Privately Held**
Web: www.novipax.com
SIC: 3086 2671 Packaging and shipping materials, foamed plastics; Paper; coated and laminated packaging
HQ: Npx One Llc
4275 Reading Crest Ave
Reading PA 19605
866 764-8338

(G-13638)
PERDUE FARMS INCORPORATED
Also Called: Rockingham Plant
416 S Long Dr (28379-3965)
P.O. Box 1357 (28380-1357)
PHONE.................910 997-8600
Jim Booth, *Brnch Mgr*
EMP: 824
SALES (corp-wide): 1.24B **Privately Held**
Web: www.perdue.com
SIC: 2015 Poultry, slaughtered and dressed
PA: Perdue Farms Incorporated
31149 Old Ocean City Rd
Salisbury MD 21804
800 473-7383

(G-13639)
PLASTEK GROUP
206 Enterprise Dr (28379-6997)
PHONE.................910 895-2089
EMP: 7 **EST:** 2019
SALES (est): 234.64K **Privately Held**
Web: www.plastekgroup.com
SIC: 3089 Injection molding of plastics

(G-13640)
RICHMOND INVESTMENT (PA)
611 Airport Rd (28379-7495)
PHONE.................910 410-8200
William D Maness, *Pr*
Terence B Lewis, *
Patsy Maness, *
Mandy Luther, *
EMP: 30 **EST:** 1956
SALES (est): 1.88MM **Privately Held**
SIC: 7534 5531 Tire recapping; Automotive tires

(G-13641)
RICHMOND MILLWORK LLC
707 Haywood St (28379-4216)
PHONE.................910 331-1009
EMP: 5 **EST:** 2000
SALES (est): 313.36K **Privately Held**
Web: www.richmondmillwork.com
SIC: 2431 Millwork

(G-13642)
RICHMOND OBSERVER LLP
505 Rockingham Rd (28379-3615)
P.O. Box 2662 (28380-2662)
PHONE.................910 817-3169
Charles Melvin, *Prin*
EMP: 7 **EST:** 2017
SALES (est): 119.15K **Privately Held**
Web: www.richmondobserver.com
SIC: 2711 Newspapers, publishing and printing

(G-13643)
RICHMOND STEEL WELDING
895 Airport Rd (28379-4707)
PHONE.................910 582-4026

EMP: 4 **EST:** 2020
SALES (est): 27.6K **Privately Held**
SIC: 3441 Fabricated structural metal

(G-13644)
THOMPSON SUNNY ACRES INC
150 Thompson Farm Rd (28379-8976)
PHONE.................910 206-1801
William Thompson, *Pr*
Dewey Thompson, *VP*
Dianne Thompson, *Sec*
Kris Thompson, *Treas*
EMP: 4 **EST:** 1975
SALES (est): 401.68K **Privately Held**
Web: www.thompsonsunnyacres.com
SIC: 3663 5191 0139 Satellites, communications; Farm supplies; Hay farm

(G-13645)
UNIQUE STONE INCORPORATED
222 Lakeshore Dr (28379-9709)
P.O. Box 460 (28380-0460)
PHONE.................910 817-9450
Alex Perakis, *Pr*
Jason Perakis, *VP*
EMP: 7 **EST:** 1992
SALES (est): 977.59K **Privately Held**
Web: www.uniquestone.com
SIC: 3281 5199 Monument or burial stone, cut and shaped; Statuary

(G-13646)
WADE MANUFACTURING COMPANY
235 River Rd (28379-4252)
PHONE.................910 895-0276
Bernard Hodges, *Mgr*
EMP: 42
SALES (corp-wide): 22.87MM **Privately Held**
Web: www.waremfg.com
SIC: 2211 2221 Cotton broad woven goods; Polyester broadwoven fabrics
PA: Wade Manufacturing Company Inc
76 Mill St
Wadesboro NC 28170
704 694-2131

Rockwell
Rowan County

(G-13647)
CAROLINA CUSTOM COATING
380 Neazer St (28138-7002)
PHONE.................704 224-1503
Craig Carr, *Owner*
EMP: 6 **EST:** 2014
SALES (est): 85.92K **Privately Held**
SIC: 3479 Coating of metals and formed products

(G-13648)
CASES FOR A CAUSE
1034 Quail Haven Ln (28138-8518)
PHONE.................704 239-3269
Alexander Hiatt, *Prin*
EMP: 6 **EST:** 2019
SALES (est): 238.5K **Privately Held**
Web: www.casesforacausenc.org
SIC: 3523 Farm machinery and equipment

(G-13649)
CMH MANUFACTURING INC
Also Called: CMH
508 Palmer Rd (28138-9318)
P.O. Box 700 (28138-0700)
PHONE.................704 279-4659
Joe Earnhadt, *Genl Mgr*
EMP: 800
SALES (corp-wide): 364.48B **Publicly Held**

Web: www.claytonhomes.com
SIC: 2451 Mobile homes, except recreational
HQ: Cmh Manufacturing, Inc.
5000 Clayton Rd
Maryville TN 37804
865 380-3000

(G-13650)
CONSOLIDATED TRUCK PARTS INC
7665 Hwy 52 North (28138)
P.O. Box 697 (28138-0697)
PHONE.................704 279-5543
EMP: 7 **EST:** 1985
SALES (est): 1.31MM **Privately Held**
Web: www.consolidatedtruckparts.com
SIC: 5531 5013 7694 Truck equipment and parts; Truck parts and accessories; Electric motor repair

(G-13651)
DAILY MANUFACTURING INC
4820 Pless Rd (28138-8921)
P.O. Box 7 (28138-0007)
PHONE.................704 782-0700
James Daily Iii, *Pr*
EMP: 15 **EST:** 1979
SQ FT: 7,000
SALES (est): 3.87MM **Privately Held**
Web: www.dailymfg.com
SIC: 5499 2834 Vitamin food stores; Adrenal pharmaceutical preparations

(G-13652)
FILLTECH INC
228 W Main St (28138-8582)
P.O. Box 1209 (28138-1209)
PHONE.................704 279-4300
EMP: 18 **EST:** 2019
SALES (est): 1.39MM **Privately Held**
Web: www.filltechus.com
SIC: 2844 Perfumes, cosmetics and other toilet preparations

(G-13653)
FILLTECH USA LLC
380 Palmer Cir (28138-8585)
P.O. Box 1209 (28138-1209)
PHONE.................704 279-4300
EMP: 47 **EST:** 1995
SQ FT: 9,300
SALES (est): 9.49MM **Privately Held**
Web: www.filltechusa.com
SIC: 2844 Perfumes, cosmetics and other toilet preparations

(G-13654)
FRANCHISE SIGNS INTERNATIONAL
9905 Old Beatty Ford Rd (28138-9498)
PHONE.................704 209-1087
Regina Halpin, *Prin*
EMP: 5 **EST:** 2010
SALES (est): 61.85K **Privately Held**
Web:
staging.franchisesignsinternational.com
SIC: 3993 Signs and advertising specialties

(G-13655)
LIME-CHEM INC
8135 Red Rd (28138-8557)
PHONE.................910 843-2121
EMP: 5
SIC: 2899 Chemical preparations, nec
PA: Lime-Chem Inc
2042 Buie Philadelphus Rd
Red Springs NC 28377

(G-13656)
N2 EVERYTHING LLC
1070 Cannon St (28138-9489)
PHONE.................704 232-1407

Rockwell - Rowan County (G-13657)

Kevin Trexler, *Owner*
EMP: 5 **EST:** 2018
SALES (est): 51.46K **Privately Held**
SIC: 2741 Miscellaneous publishing

(G-13657)
RED MAPLE LOGGING COMPANY INC
10007 Meismer Ln (28138-9753)
PHONE..........................704 279-6379
Danny Scott, *Prin*
EMP: 6 **EST:** 2000
SALES (est): 664.41K **Privately Held**
SIC: 2411 Logging camps and contractors

(G-13658)
SNIDERS MACHINE SHOP INC
8025 Highway 52 (28138-8543)
PHONE..........................704 279-6129
EMP: 4 **EST:** 1996
SALES (est): 300.45K **Privately Held**
SIC: 3599 Machine shop, jobbing and repair

(G-13659)
SUNSHINE MNFCTRED STRCTRES INC
850 Gold Hill Ave (28138-7763)
P.O. Box 1000 (28138-1000)
PHONE..........................704 279-6600
Dean Bodine, *Pr*
John D Bodine, *
Nancy Bodine, *
EMP: 35 **EST:** 1984
SQ FT: 55,000
SALES (est): 480.79K **Privately Held**
Web: www.sunshinemodulars.com
SIC: 2452 3448 2451 Prefabricated buildings, wood; Buildings, portable: prefabricated metal; Mobile homes

(G-13660)
SUPPLYONE ROCKWELL INC
729 Palmer Rd (28138-8578)
P.O. Box 1469 (28138-1469)
PHONE..........................704 279-5650
William T Leith, *CEO*
Kevin M O'brien, *Pr*
George Ruth, *
Ryan S Northington, *
EMP: 150 **EST:** 1985
SQ FT: 85,000
SALES (est): 45.49MM
SALES (corp-wide): 838.82MM **Privately Held**
Web: www.supplyone.com
SIC: 2631 2653 Container, packaging, and boxboard; Display items, corrugated: made from purchased materials
PA: Supplyone Holdings Company, Inc.
11 Campus Blvd Ste 150
Newtown Square PA 19073
484 582-5005

(G-13661)
THORNEBURG HOSIERY MILLS INC
Also Called: Thor.lo
319 Link St (28138-7500)
PHONE..........................704 279-7247
Kevin Goodden, *Mgr*
EMP: 26
SALES (corp-wide): 45.57MM **Privately Held**
Web: www.thmills.com
SIC: 2252 2251 Socks; Women's hosiery, except socks
PA: Thorneburg Hosiery Mills, Inc.
2210 Newton Dr
Statesville NC 28677
704 872-6522

(G-13662)
UFP ROCKWELL LLC
Also Called: Ufp Rockwell
175 Old Mail Rd (28138-6823)
PHONE..........................704 279-0744
Jeff Richards, *Mgr*
EMP: 9 **EST:** 2016
SALES (est): 1.62MM
SALES (corp-wide): 7.22B **Publicly Held**
SIC: 2491 Millwork, treated wood
HQ: Prowood, Llc
2801 E Beltline Ave Ne
Grand Rapids MI

Rocky Mount
Edgecombe County

(G-13663)
ACME UNITED CORPORATION
2280 Tanner Rd (27801-2731)
P.O. Box 458 (27830-0458)
PHONE..........................252 822-5051
Larry Buchkmann, *Brnch Mgr*
EMP: 29
SALES (corp-wide): 191.5MM **Publicly Held**
Web: www.acmeunited.com
SIC: 3841 5112 Surgical and medical instruments; Office supplies, nec
PA: Acme United Corporation
1 Waterview Dr Ste 200
Shelton CT 06484
203 254-6060

(G-13664)
BERRY GLOBAL INC
6941 Corporation Pkwy (27801)
PHONE..........................252 984-4104
Mark Powell, *Genl Mgr*
EMP: 65
Web: www.berryglobal.com
SIC: 3089 Plastics containers, except foam
HQ: Berry Global, Inc.
101 Oakley St
Evansville IN 47710

(G-13665)
DAUGHTRIDGE ENTERPRISES INC
Also Called: Tharrington Parts
1200 East St (27801-5484)
P.O. Box 1680 (27802-1680)
PHONE..........................252 977-7775
Tony Gay, *Brnch Mgr*
EMP: 5
SALES (corp-wide): 8.85MM **Privately Held**
Web: www.citgo.com
SIC: 3523 Tobacco curers
PA: Daughtridge Enterprises Inc
1200 East St
Rocky Mount NC 27801
252 446-6137

(G-13666)
DOZIER INDUSTRIAL ELECTRIC INC
1151 Atlantic Ave (27801-2707)
PHONE..........................252 451-0020
Blake Dozier, *Pr*
Janie Houfe, *
EMP: 10 **EST:** 2005
SQ FT: 5,000
SALES (est): 381.47K **Privately Held**
SIC: 3625 Industrial electrical relays and switches

(G-13667)
ENC CONVEYANCE LLC
Also Called: Enc Conveyance
4314 Bulluck School Rd (27801-9190)
PHONE..........................252 378-9990
EMP: 6 **EST:** 2019
SALES (est): 200K **Privately Held**
SIC: 3711 Truck and tractor truck assembly

(G-13668)
GUY N LANGLEY
2026 Leggett Rd (27801-2810)
PHONE..........................252 972-9875
Guy N Langley, *Prin*
EMP: 7 **EST:** 2001
SALES (est): 218.62K **Privately Held**
SIC: 3713 Dump truck bodies

(G-13669)
HOSPIRA INC
Highway 301 North (27801)
P.O. Box 2226 (27802-2226)
PHONE..........................252 977-5500
Marty Nealey, *Prin*
EMP: 234
SALES (corp-wide): 100.33B **Publicly Held**
Web: www.pfizer.com
SIC: 2834 Pharmaceutical preparations
HQ: Hospira, Inc.
275 N Field Dr
Lake Forest IL 60045
224 212-2000

(G-13670)
NUTRIEN AG SOLUTIONS INC
CPS
1160 Brake Rd (27801-8347)
PHONE..........................252 977-2025
Jeff Griffin, *Mgr*
EMP: 10
SALES (corp-wide): 27.71B **Privately Held**
Web: www.nutrienagsolutions.com
SIC: 2875 5191 2048 2874 Fertilizers, mixing only; Pesticides; Prepared feeds, nec ; Phosphatic fertilizers
HQ: Nutrien Ag Solutions, Inc.
3005 Rocky Mountain Ave
Loveland CO 80538
970 685-3300

(G-13671)
PRECISION STEEL WORKS LLC
1100 Atlantic Ave (27801-2708)
PHONE..........................252 467-0338
Clyde Dishner, *Mgr*
EMP: 8 **EST:** 2013
SALES (est): 225.97K **Privately Held**
Web: www.precisionsteelworks.com
SIC: 3441 Fabricated structural metal

(G-13672)
TELEPATHIC GRAPHICS INC
1131 Atlantic Ave (27801-2707)
PHONE..........................919 342-4603
Bob Boyle, *CEO*
EMP: 12
Web: www.telepathicgraphics.com
SIC: 2752 Offset printing
PA: Telepathic Graphics, Inc.
6001 Chapel Hill Rd # 106
Raleigh NC 27607

(G-13673)
TO THE TOP TIRES AND SVC LLC
327 E Raleigh Blvd Ste 943 (27801)
P.O. Box 943 (27802-0943)
PHONE..........................252 886-3286
Shabere Dorsett, *Managing Member*
EMP: 6 **EST:** 2018
SALES (est): 489.73K **Privately Held**
Web: tothetoptires.business.site
SIC: 7534 Tire retreading and repair shops

(G-13674)
TRANS-TECH ENERGY INC (PA)
Also Called: T 2 E
14527 Us Highway 64 Alt W (27801)
P.O. Box 8197 (27804-1197)
PHONE..........................252 446-4357
Greg Ezzell, *Pr*
◆ **EMP:** 7 **EST:** 1998
SQ FT: 2,500
SALES (est): 100.26MM
SALES (corp-wide): 100.26MM **Privately Held**
Web: www.transtechenergy.com
SIC: 1389 Gas field services, nec

(G-13675)
TRANS-TECH ENERGY LLC
14527 Us Highway 64 Alt W (27801-9806)
PHONE..........................254 840-3355
EMP: 9 **EST:** 2012
SALES (est): 2.92MM **Privately Held**
SIC: 1311 Natural gas production

(G-13676)
TRI-COUNTY INDUSTRIES INC
1250 Atlantic Ave (27801-2710)
PHONE..........................252 977-3800
Brenda Cogdell, *Pr*
EMP: 140 **EST:** 1966
SQ FT: 43,500
SALES (est): 2.76MM **Privately Held**
Web: www.tricountyind.com
SIC: 8331 2448 Vocational rehabilitation agency; Wood pallets and skids

(G-13677)
WILSON IRON WORKS INCORPORATED (PA)
Also Called: Eastern Hydraulic & Pwr Transm
600 S Washington St (27801-5669)
P.O. Box 552 (27802-0552)
PHONE..........................252 291-4465
EMP: 69 **EST:** 1933
SQ FT: 40,500
SALES (est): 24.35MM **Privately Held**
Web: www.wilsonironworks.com
SIC: 3599 Machine shop, jobbing and repair

Rocky Mount
Nash County

(G-13678)
AAA MOBILE SIGNS LLC
Also Called: Signs Now
106 Zebulon Ct (27804-2420)
PHONE..........................252 446-9777
John Mooring, *Mgr*
EMP: 7
SALES (corp-wide): 2.4MM **Privately Held**
Web: www.signsnow.com
SIC: 3993 Signs and advertising specialties
PA: Aaa Mobile Signs, L.C.
1570 Lakeview Dr Ste 108
Sebring FL 33870
863 471-1800

(G-13679)
ACS ADVNCED CLOR SOLUTIONS INC
120 S Business Ct (27804-6543)
PHONE..........................252 442-0098
Franco Furlin, *Owner*
▲ **EMP:** 9 **EST:** 2005
SALES (est): 714.72K **Privately Held**
SIC: 3429 Keys, locks, and related hardware

GEOGRAPHIC SECTION
Rocky Mount - Nash County (G-13702)

(G-13680)
ALLSTAR WASTE SYSTEMS INC
4270 S Browntown Rd (27804-9296)
P.O. Box 9012 (27804-7012)
PHONE.................................252 343-5156
James I Tanner Junior, *Prin*
EMP: 6 **EST:** 2008
SALES (est): 219.77K **Privately Held**
Web: www.allstarwasteinc.com
SIC: 3089 Garbage containers, plastics

(G-13681)
AMERICAN PRINTERS INC
120 Sorsbys Aly (27804-5723)
PHONE.................................252 977-7468
John S Taylor, *Pr*
Everett K Nightingale, *Sec*
EMP: 6 **EST:** 2000
SQ FT: 10,000
SALES (est): 535.6K **Privately Held**
SIC: 2752 Offset printing

(G-13682)
BABINGTON TECHNOLOGY LLC
Also Called: Manufacturing
159 Fabrication Way (27804-9356)
PHONE.................................252 984-0349
Andrew Babington, *Prin*
Robert Babington, *Managing Member*
▲ **EMP:** 29 **EST:** 2006
SQ FT: 12,500
SALES (est): 5.7MM **Privately Held**
Web: www.babingtontechnology.com
SIC: 3441 Fabricated structural metal

(G-13683)
BABINGTON TECHNOLOGY INC (PA)
159 Fabrication Way (27804-9356)
PHONE.................................252 984-0349
Andrew Babington, *CEO*
Robert Babington, *Prin*
Andrew Babington, *Prin*
EMP: 6 **EST:** 1965
SALES (est): 13.71MM
SALES (corp-wide): 13.71MM **Privately Held**
Web: www.babingtontechnology.com
SIC: 5084 3556 Food product manufacturing machinery; Food products machinery

(G-13684)
BEFCO INC
1781 S Wesleyan Blvd (27803-5629)
P.O. Box 6036 (27802-6036)
PHONE.................................252 977-9920
Pio Figna, *Pr*
Francesco Figna, *
Rina Figna, *
Merle Hendricks, *
Bobby Davis, *
◆ **EMP:** 45 **EST:** 1980
SQ FT: 80,000
SALES (est): 10.85MM
SALES (corp-wide): 9.46MM **Privately Held**
Web: www.befco.com
SIC: 3523 3531 3524 Grounds mowing equipment; Posthole diggers, powered; Lawn and garden equipment
PA: Rotomec Spa
Via Molino Di Sopra 56
Nogara VR 37054
044 251-0400

(G-13685)
BOWDEN ELECTRIC MOTOR SVC INC
1681 S Wesleyan Blvd (27803-5627)
P.O. Box 1874 (27802-1874)
PHONE.................................252 446-4203
David E Bowden, *Pr*
Richard E Bowden, *VP*
Charlotte Briley, *Sec*
EMP: 6 **EST:** 1965
SQ FT: 12,500
SALES (est): 475.73K **Privately Held**
SIC: 7694 5063 Electric motor repair; Motors, electric

(G-13686)
C D J & P INC
Also Called: PIP Printing
1911 N Wesleyan Blvd (27804-6634)
PHONE.................................252 446-3611
Laura Friedrich, *Pr*
Peter Friedrich, *Sec*
EMP: 4 **EST:** 1990
SQ FT: 1,600
SALES (est): 384.94K **Privately Held**
Web: www.pip.com
SIC: 2752 Offset printing

(G-13687)
CAROL WILLIAMS
745 Foxridge Ct (27804-8215)
PHONE.................................252 883-7968
EMP: 4 **EST:** 2017
SALES (est): 40.95K **Privately Held**
Web: www.carolwilliamsphotography.com
SIC: 2394 Canvas and related products

(G-13688)
COLONY TIRE CORPORATION
1463 N Wesleyan Blvd (27804-1843)
PHONE.................................252 973-0004
Lee Hadison, *Brnch Mgr*
EMP: 8
SALES (corp-wide): 138.19MM **Privately Held**
Web: locations.mrtire.com
SIC: 5531 7534 Automotive tires; Tire retreading and repair shops
PA: Colony Tire Corporation
1429 N Broad St
Edenton NC 27932
252 482-5521

(G-13689)
DAVIS DAVIS MCH & WLDG CO INC
4956 Community Dr (27804-3065)
P.O. Box 8558 (27804-1558)
PHONE.................................252 443-2652
Michael Davis, *Pr*
Phil Davis, *VP*
Robert K Davis, *Treas*
Tim Davis, *Sec*
John S Davis Junior, *Stockholder*
EMP: 14 **EST:** 1972
SQ FT: 6,000
SALES (est): 2.16MM **Privately Held**
SIC: 3599 7692 Machine shop, jobbing and repair; Welding repair

(G-13690)
DRAKA ELEVATOR PRODUCTS INC (DH)
2151 N Church St (27804-2026)
PHONE.................................252 984-5100
Kent Sterrett Lloyd Iii, *Pr*
◆ **EMP:** 160 **EST:** 1999
SQ FT: 158,000
SALES (est): 99.36MM **Privately Held**
Web: www.prysmian.com
SIC: 3315 3357 Cable, steel: insulated or armored; Nonferrous wiredrawing and insulating
HQ: Prysmian Cables And Systems Usa, Llc
4 Tesseneer Dr
Highland Heights KY 41076
859 572-8000

(G-13691)
DRILL & FILL MFG LLC
5484 S Old Carriage Rd (27803-8372)
PHONE.................................252 937-4555
EMP: 4 **EST:** 2006
SQ FT: 5,000
SALES (est): 486.99K **Privately Held**
Web: www.drillandfillmfg.com
SIC: 3541 Drilling and boring machines

(G-13692)
DUNCAN-PARNELL INC
2741 N Wesleyan Blvd (27804-8664)
P.O. Box 7517 (27804-0517)
PHONE.................................252 977-7832
James May, *Mgr*
EMP: 7
SALES (corp-wide): 22.61MM **Privately Held**
Web: www.duncan-parnell.com
SIC: 5049 5999 2752 Scientific and engineering equipment and supplies; Drafting equipment and supplies; Offset printing
PA: Duncan-Parnell, Inc.
900 S Mcdowell St
Charlotte NC 28204
704 372-7764

(G-13693)
EAST INDUSTRIES INC
1114 Instrument Dr (27804-9002)
P.O. Box 7724 (27804-0724)
PHONE.................................252 442-9662
David W Wilson, *Pr*
EMP: 55 **EST:** 1975
SQ FT: 63,000
SALES (est): 10.34MM **Privately Held**
Web: www.eastindustries.com
SIC: 5031 2448 Pallets, wood; Pallets, wood

(G-13694)
ELECTRIC MTR SP WAKE FREST INC
Also Called: Electric Motor Shop
2421 W Raleigh Blvd (27804-2757)
PHONE.................................252 446-4173
Kevin Lee, *Brnch Mgr*
EMP: 33
SALES (corp-wide): 15.64MM **Privately Held**
Web: www.electricmotorshopnc.com
SIC: 7694 Electric motor repair
PA: Electric Motor Shop Of Wake Forest, Inc.
1225 N White St
Wake Forest NC 27587
919 556-3229

(G-13695)
ENGINE SYSTEMS INC (HQ)
175 Freight Rd (27804-8002)
PHONE.................................252 977-2720
Dorman L Strahan, *Pr*
J H Pyne, *Ex VP*
Norman Nolen, *VP*
◆ **EMP:** 80 **EST:** 1984
SALES (est): 18.27MM
SALES (corp-wide): 3.09B **Publicly Held**
Web: www.enginesystems.com
SIC: 5084 3519 Engines and parts, diesel; Diesel engine rebuilding
PA: Kirby Corporation
55 Waugh Dr Ste 1000
Houston TX 77007
713 435-1000

(G-13696)
ESSAY OPERATIONS INC (PA)
Also Called: Essay Polyfab
3701 Winchester Rd (27804-3340)
PHONE.................................252 443-6010
FAX: 252 443-6529
EMP: 4
SALES (est): 511.73K
SALES (corp-wide): 511.73K **Privately Held**
SIC: 3061 2821 3949 Appliance rubber goods (mechanical); Plastics materials and resins; Sporting and athletic goods, nec

(G-13697)
EVELYN T BURNEY
Also Called: Plott Bakery Products
2551 N Church St (27804-2040)
PHONE.................................336 473-9794
EMP: 5 **EST:** 1983
SALES (est): 784.56K **Privately Held**
SIC: 5142 2052 2051 2521 Bakery products, frozen; Bakery products, dry; Bread, cake, and related products; Tables, office: wood

(G-13698)
FREEDOM INDUSTRIES INC
4000 E Old Spring Hope Rd (27804-7727)
P.O. Box 7099 (27804-0099)
PHONE.................................252 984-0007
Derrick Vick, *CEO*
Douglas Ezzell, *
EMP: 150 **EST:** 2003
SQ FT: 40,000
SALES (est): 27.12MM **Privately Held**
Web: www.freedomind.us
SIC: 3449 1731 1711 Bars, concrete reinforcing: fabricated steel; Electrical work; Mechanical contractor

(G-13699)
GARLAND LANGLEY GRAVEL
2933 Old Mill Rd (27803-3024)
PHONE.................................252 450-9022
EMP: 4 **EST:** 2019
SALES (est): 66.08K **Privately Held**
SIC: 1442 Construction sand and gravel

(G-13700)
HINSON INDUSTRIES INC
Also Called: Allegra Print & Imaging
109 Zebulon Ct (27804-2420)
P.O. Box 8003 (27804-1003)
PHONE.................................252 937-7171
Henry Hinson, *Pr*
Mark Hinson, *VP*
Todd Hinson, *VP*
Lucy Hinson, *Sec*
EMP: 9 **EST:** 1956
SQ FT: 4,800
SALES (est): 919.86K **Privately Held**
Web: www.allegramarketingprint.com
SIC: 2752 6411 Offset printing; Insurance agents, brokers, and service

(G-13701)
HONEYWELL INTERNATIONAL INC
Honeywell
3475 N Wesleyan Blvd (27804-8677)
PHONE.................................252 977-2100
Juergen Heller, *Mgr*
EMP: 104
SALES (corp-wide): 36.66B **Publicly Held**
Web: www.honeywell.com
SIC: 3812 3728 Search and navigation equipment; Aircraft parts and equipment, nec
PA: Honeywell International Inc.
855 S Mint St
Charlotte NC 28202
704 627-6200

(G-13702)
HOSPIRA INC
4285 N Wesleyan Blvd (27804-8612)
PHONE.................................252 977-5111

Rocky Mount - Nash County (G-13703)

Rick Isaza, *Pr*
EMP: 762
SALES (corp-wide): 100.33B **Publicly Held**
Web: www.pfizer.com
SIC: **2834** Pharmaceutical preparations
HQ: Hospira, Inc.
275 N Field Dr
Lake Forest IL 60045
224 212-2000

(G-13703)
ILCO UNICAN HOLDING CORP
400 Jeffreys Rd (27804-6624)
P.O. Box 2627 (27802-2627)
PHONE.............................252 446-3321
Aaron M Fish, *Ch Bd*
▲ EMP: 98 EST: 1988
SALES (est): 4.84MM **Privately Held**
Web: www.ilco.us
SIC: **3429** Keys, locks, and related hardware
HQ: Dormakaba Schweiz Ag
Kempten
Wetzikon ZH 8623

(G-13704)
KABA ILCO CORP (HQ)
400 Jeffreys Rd (27804-6624)
P.O. Box 2627 (27802-2627)
PHONE.............................252 446-3321
Frank Belflower, *Pr*
Tom Boswell, *
◆ EMP: 700 EST: 1981
SQ FT: 323,000
SALES (est): 240.08MM **Privately Held**
Web: www.ilco.us
SIC: **3429** Keys, locks, and related hardware
PA: Dormakaba Holding Ag
Hofwisenstrasse 24
RUmlang ZH 8153

(G-13705)
KAMLAR CORPORATION (PA)
444 Kamlar Rd (27804-8175)
PHONE.............................252 443-2576
Richard C Seale, *Pr*
Albert Oettinger Junior, *VP*
EMP: 20 EST: 1966
SQ FT: 6,500
SALES (est): 4.55MM
SALES (corp-wide): 4.55MM **Privately Held**
Web: www.kamlar.com
SIC: **2499** 2873 2421 Mulch, wood and bark; Nitrogenous fertilizers; Sawmills and planing mills, general

(G-13706)
KOI POND BREWING COMPANY LLC
1107 Falls Rd (27804)
P.O. Box 4307 (27803-0307)
PHONE.............................252 231-1660
EMP: 7 EST: 2014
SQ FT: 1,823
SALES (est): 233.42K **Privately Held**
Web: www.koipondbrewingcompany.com
SIC: **5813** 2082 5181 5921 Bars and lounges ; Beer (alcoholic beverage); Beer and ale; Beer (packaged)

(G-13707)
LARRY S CABINET SHOP INC
4217 S Church St (27803-5710)
PHONE.............................252 442-4330
Larry Gupton, *Pr*
EMP: 5 EST: 1976
SQ FT: 2,000
SALES (est): 300K **Privately Held**
SIC: **2434** Wood kitchen cabinets

(G-13708)
LOG CABIN HOMES LTD (PA)
Also Called: Cabin Craft American Homes
513 Keen St # 515 (27804-4824)
P.O. Box 1457 (27802-1457)
PHONE.............................252 454-1500
Thomas Vesce, *Pr*
◆ EMP: 60 EST: 1987
SALES (est): 9.77MM
SALES (corp-wide): 9.77MM **Privately Held**
Web: www.logcabinhomes.com
SIC: **2452** 5031 Log cabins, prefabricated, wood; Lumber: rough, dressed, and finished

(G-13709)
MALINDA RACKLEY
Also Called: KBK Cstom Dsgns Essential Oils
1384 Northridge Dr (27804-8324)
PHONE.............................252 886-3315
Malinda Rackley, *Owner*
EMP: 4 EST: 2021
SALES (est): 100K **Privately Held**
SIC: **1389** Construction, repair, and dismantling services

(G-13710)
MARTIN MANUFACTURING CO LLC
Also Called: Martin Innovations
2585 Eastern Ave (27804-8179)
PHONE.............................919 741-5439
EMP: 9 EST: 2004
SALES (est): 738.85K **Privately Held**
Web: www.martininnovations.com
SIC: **3841** Surgical and medical instruments

(G-13711)
MATTRESS FIRM
794 Sutters Creek Blvd (27804-8429)
PHONE.............................252 443-1259
EMP: 5 EST: 2016
SALES (est): 84.07K **Privately Held**
Web: www.mattressfirm.com
SIC: **5712** 5021 2515 Mattresses; Mattresses ; Mattresses and bedsprings

(G-13712)
MIJO ENTERPRISES INC
Also Called: Natures Own Gallery
2220 N Wesleyan Blvd (27804-8636)
PHONE.............................252 442-6806
Tom Minges, *Pr*
Morrie Minges, *Sec*
EMP: 8 EST: 1982
SQ FT: 12,000
SALES (est): 713.43K **Privately Held**
Web: www.mbuddies.com
SIC: **7389** 2542 Interior designer; Counters or counter display cases, except wood

(G-13713)
MILWAUKEE INSTRUMENTS INC
2950 Business Park Dr (27804-2818)
PHONE.............................252 443-3630
Bryan Moore, *Genl Mgr*
EMP: 5 EST: 1998
SALES (est): 464.13K **Privately Held**
Web: www.milwaukeeinstruments.com
SIC: **3829** Measuring and controlling devices, nec

(G-13714)
NEW STANDARD CORPORATION
3883 S Church St (27803-5702)
PHONE.............................252 446-5481
C Meckley, *Pr*
EMP: 173
SALES (corp-wide): 117.56MM **Privately Held**
Web: www.newstandard.com
SIC: **3469** Stamping metal for the trade
PA: New Standard Corporation
74 Commerce Way
York PA 17406
717 757-9450

(G-13715)
NORTH STATE MILLWORK
2950 Raleigh Rd (27803-4626)
PHONE.............................252 442-9090
EMP: 5 EST: 2020
SALES (est): 215.79K **Privately Held**
SIC: **2431** Millwork

(G-13716)
O D EYECARECENTER P A
Also Called: Opticare
3044 Sunset Ave (27804-3647)
PHONE.............................252 443-7011
Rick Adams, *Mgr*
EMP: 7
SALES (corp-wide): 45.77MM **Privately Held**
Web: www.eyecarecenter.com
SIC: **8042** 5995 3851 Offices and clinics of optometrists; Optical goods stores; Ophthalmic goods
PA: O D Eyecarecenter P A
2325 Sunset Ave
Rocky Mount NC

(G-13717)
O R PRDGEN SONS SPTIC TANK I
4824 S Halifax Rd (27803-5897)
PHONE.............................252 442-3338
Dale M Pridgen, *Pr*
Cindy Pridgen, *VP*
EMP: 5 EST: 1973
SALES (est): 471.81K **Privately Held**
SIC: **3272** 1711 Septic tanks, concrete; Septic system construction

(G-13718)
PEN-CELL PLASTICS INC
546 English Rd (27804-9517)
PHONE.............................252 467-2210
Robert R Schlegel, *Pr*
◆ EMP: 50 EST: 2010
SQ FT: 90,000
SALES (est): 24.28MM
SALES (corp-wide): 5.37B **Publicly Held**
SIC: **3089** Injection molding of plastics
PA: Hubbell Incorporated
40 Waterview Dr
Shelton CT 06484
800 626-0005

(G-13719)
PEPSI BOTTLING VENTURES LLC
Also Called: Pepsi-Cola
620 Health Dr (27804-9445)
PHONE.............................252 451-1811
Evelyn Cowan, *Off Mgr*
EMP: 45
Web: www.pepsibottlingventures.com
SIC: **2086** 5149 Carbonated soft drinks, bottled and canned; Groceries and related products, nec
HQ: Pepsi Bottling Ventures Llc
4141 Parklake Ave Ste 600
Raleigh NC 27612
919 865-2300

(G-13720)
PEPSI-COLA METRO BTLG CO INC
Also Called: Pepsi-Cola
620 Health Dr (27804-9445)
PHONE.............................252 446-7181
Alan Sleischer, *Mgr*
EMP: 6
SALES (corp-wide): 86.39B **Publicly Held**
Web: www.pepsico.com
SIC: **2086** Soft drinks: packaged in cans, bottles, etc.
HQ: Pepsi-Cola Metropolitan Bottling Company, Inc.
700 Anderson Hill Rd
Purchase NY 10577
914 767-6000

(G-13721)
PFIZER INC
4285 N Wesleyan Blvd (27804-8612)
PHONE.............................252 977-5111
EMP: 22
SALES (corp-wide): 100.33B **Publicly Held**
Web: www.pfizer.com
SIC: **2834** Pharmaceutical preparations
PA: Pfizer Inc.
66 Hudson Blvd E
New York NY 10001
800 879-3477

(G-13722)
POWER WASHER PROS
8740 Bend Of The River Rd (27803-8888)
PHONE.............................252 446-4643
Steve Saal, *Owner*
EMP: 4 EST: 2004
SALES (est): 97.42K **Privately Held**
Web: www.powerwasherpros.com
SIC: **3452** Washers

(G-13723)
PRESSED DESIGN & PRINTING LLC
8884 Taylor Woods Cir (27803-8711)
PHONE.............................252 314-6036
EMP: 4 EST: 2021
SALES (est): 83.91K **Privately Held**
SIC: **2752** Commercial printing, lithographic

(G-13724)
PRINT SHOPPE OF ROCKY MT INC
140 S Business Ct (27804-6543)
PHONE.............................252 442-9912
Andy Dickerson, *Pr*
Randall Pridgen, *Sec*
EMP: 10 EST: 1999
SQ FT: 4,000
SALES (est): 435.6K **Privately Held**
Web: www.printshoppeofrockymount.com
SIC: **2752** Offset printing

(G-13725)
QCS ACQUISITION CORPORATION
Also Called: Quality Conveyor Solutions
130 N Business Ct (27804-6546)
PHONE.............................252 446-5000
EMP: 6
Web: www.qualityconveyorsolutions.com
SIC: **3535** Belt conveyor systems, general industrial use
HQ: Qcs Acquisition Corporation
971b Russell Dr
Salem VA 24153
540 427-7705

(G-13726)
R/W CONNECTION INC
Also Called: Virginia Carolina Belting
136 S Business Ct (27804-6543)
PHONE.............................252 446-0114
Al Blonberg, *Brnch Mgr*
EMP: 4
SALES (corp-wide): 4.71B **Privately Held**
Web: www.rwconnection.com
SIC: **2399** Belting and belt products
HQ: R/W Connection, Inc.
936 Links Ave
Landisville PA 17538

GEOGRAPHIC SECTION

Rocky Point - Pender County (G-13753)

(G-13727)
RBI MANUFACTURING INC
Also Called: Rbi Precision
4642 S Us Highway 301 (27803-8641)
P.O. Box 250 (27878-0250)
PHONE...................................252 977-6764
Edward Bunch Junior, *Pr*
EMP: 12 EST: 1994
SQ FT: 12,000
SALES (est): 11.34MM **Privately Held**
Web: www.rbimfg.com
SIC: 3599 Machine shop, jobbing and repair

(G-13728)
RIPE REVIVAL PRODUCE LLC
161 English Rd (27804-8206)
PHONE...................................252 567-8305
EMP: 7 EST: 2019
SALES (est): 614.7K **Privately Held**
Web: www.riperevivalmarket.com
SIC: 2096 Cheese curls and puffs

(G-13729)
RIVERS EDGE WOODWORKERS LLC
2728 Buff Rd (27803-1606)
PHONE...................................252 443-5099
Jason Roebuck, *Prin*
EMP: 7 EST: 2019
SALES (est): 318.98K **Privately Held**
Web:
rivers-edge-woodworkers-llc.business.site
SIC: 2431 Millwork

(G-13730)
ROCKY MOUNT AWNING & TENT CO
Also Called: Carolina Awning and Tent
602 N Church St (27804-4910)
PHONE...................................252 442-0184
TOLL FREE: 800
Joseph R Daniel Iii, *Pr*
Bobby Pridgen, *Sec*
EMP: 17 EST: 1925
SQ FT: 10,000
SALES (est): 507.17K **Privately Held**
Web: www.rockymountawning.com
SIC: 2394 3444 Awnings, fabric: made from purchased materials; Sheet metalwork

(G-13731)
ROCKY MOUNT CORD COMPANY
Also Called: Romoco
381 N Grace St (27804-5317)
P.O. Box 4304 (27803-0304)
PHONE...................................252 977-9130
Joseph E Bunn, *Pr*
Thomas B Battle, *
Andrew K Barker, *
Dawn Fowler, *
▲ **EMP: 75 EST:** 1946
SQ FT: 110,000
SALES (est): 9.18MM **Privately Held**
Web: www.rmcord.com
SIC: 2298 Cord, braided

(G-13732)
ROCKY MOUNT ELECTRIC MOTOR LLC
3870 S Church St (27803-5701)
P.O. Box 1063 (27802-1063)
PHONE...................................252 446-1510
Timmy Thorne, *VP*
Deborah Vick, *Off Mgr*
EMP: 8 EST: 1972
SQ FT: 3,300
SALES (est): 2.06MM **Privately Held**
Web: www.rmemnc.com
SIC: 5063 7694 Motors, electric; Electric motor repair

(G-13733)
STEEL TECHNOLOGY INC (PA)
2620 Business Park Dr (27804)
P.O. Box 7217 (27804-0217)
PHONE...................................252 937-7122
William H Pruden Iii, *Pr*
Lillian M Pruden, *Sec*
EMP: 8 EST: 1999
SALES (est): 4.87MM
SALES (corp-wide): 4.87MM **Privately Held**
Web: www.steeltechnc.com
SIC: 3441 Fabricated structural metal

(G-13734)
STONEWORX INC
7015 Stanley Park Dr (27804-3046)
P.O. Box 109 (15376-0109)
PHONE...................................252 937-8080
Elizabeth S Hunt, *Pr*
Frank Hunt, *VP*
EMP: 7 EST: 2003
SQ FT: 6,000
SALES (est): 626.77K **Privately Held**
SIC: 3281 Marble, building: cut and shaped

(G-13735)
SUN-DROP BTLG ROCKY MT NC INC
Also Called: Sun Drop Bottling
2406 W Raleigh Blvd (27803-2751)
PHONE...................................252 977-4586
Michael K Berry, *Sec*
John D Berry, *Pr*
Stephen L Berry, *VP*
EMP: 16 EST: 1955
SQ FT: 20,000
SALES (est): 945.81K **Privately Held**
SIC: 2086 Soft drinks: packaged in cans, bottles, etc.

(G-13736)
SWEET TATERS LLC
1121 Falls Rd (27804-4407)
PHONE...................................252 969-0229
EMP: 4 EST: 2017
SALES (est): 70.8K **Privately Held**
SIC: 2082 Malt beverages

(G-13737)
TORPEDO SPECIALTY WIRE INC
1115 Instrument Dr (27804-9003)
P.O. Box 21 (27868-0021)
PHONE...................................252 977-3900
▲ **EMP:** 100
Web: www.summitplating.com
SIC: 3315 3351 3356 Wire and fabricated wire products; Copper rolling and drawing; Nickel and nickel alloy: rolling, drawing, or extruding

(G-13738)
TRIPLE R MBL CIGR LOUNGE LLC
163 S Winstead Ave Ste A (27804-1000)
PHONE...................................252 281-7738
EMP: 6
SALES (est): 490.11K **Privately Held**
SIC: 3711 Mobile lounges (motor vehicle), assembly of

(G-13739)
WARD SPECIALTY PHARMACY LLC
3646 Sunset Ave Ste 110 (27804-3499)
P.O. Box 8573 (27804-1573)
PHONE...................................252 459-5544
Gary R Glisson, *Admn*
EMP: 8 EST: 2013
SALES (est): 1.33MM **Privately Held**
Web: www.warddrug.com
SIC: 2834 Syrups, pharmaceutical

(G-13740)
WATERS BROTHERS CONTRS INC
511 Instrument Dr (27804-8614)
PHONE...................................252 446-7141
Trudy Waters, *Pr*
Lou Carson, *Treasurer Finance*
EMP: 11 EST: 1921
SQ FT: 22,500
SALES (est): 1MM **Privately Held**
Web: www.watersbros.com
SIC: 3441 Fabricated structural metal

(G-13741)
WILDWOOD LAMPS & ACCENTS INC (PA)
516 Paul St (27803-3545)
P.O. Box 672 (27802-0672)
PHONE...................................252 446-3266
William H Kincheloe, *Pr*
Russ Barnes, *
John B Kincheloe, *
◆ **EMP:** 40 **EST:** 1968
SQ FT: 150,000
SALES (est): 9.06MM **Privately Held**
Web: www.wildwoodhome.com
SIC: 3645 Table lamps

(G-13742)
WOOD MACHINE SERVICE INC
2 Great State Ln (27803-8747)
PHONE...................................252 446-2142
William T Wood, *Pr*
EMP: 10 EST: 1983
SALES (est): 993.44K **Privately Held**
Web: www.woodsmachine.com
SIC: 3599 Machine shop, jobbing and repair

Rocky Point
Pender County

(G-13743)
CARLTON ENTERPRIZES LLC
Also Called: General Contracting
195 Rocky Point Trng Sch Rd (28457-7321)
P.O. Box 986 (28457-0986)
PHONE...................................919 534-5424
Terrell Carlton, *Admn*
EMP: 8 EST: 2012
SALES (est): 289.71K **Privately Held**
SIC: 1611 0782 1389 7389 General contractor, highway and street construction; Landscape contractors; Construction, repair, and dismantling services; Business services, nec

(G-13744)
CINCINNATI THERMAL SPRAY INC
Also Called: CTS
11766 Nc Hwy 210 (28457-8560)
PHONE...................................910 675-2909
Will Reed, *Brnch Mgr*
EMP: 50
Web: www.cts-inc.net
SIC: 3479 Coating of metals and formed products
PA: Cincinnati Thermal Spray, Inc.
10904 Deerfield Rd
Blue Ash OH 45242

(G-13745)
FUSION WELDING
37 Brandon Ln (28457-7673)
PHONE...................................508 320-3525
Francine Darling, *Prin*
EMP: 5 EST: 2016
SALES (est): 55.68K **Privately Held**
SIC: 7692 Welding repair

(G-13746)
H & P WOOD TURNINGS INC
9375 Us Hwy 117 S (28457-8028)
P.O. Box 505 (28457-0505)
PHONE...................................910 675-2784
Neal Cavanaugh, *Pr*
Richard Cavanaugh, *VP*
EMP: 14 EST: 1965
SQ FT: 13,000
SALES (est): 852.06K **Privately Held**
Web: www.hpwoodturnings.com
SIC: 2499 Decorative wood and woodwork

(G-13747)
HEATH AND SONS MGT SVCS LLC
Also Called: Heath and Sons Management
514 Complex Rd (28457-7724)
P.O. Box 11280 (28404-1280)
PHONE...................................910 679-6142
Micheal Heath, *Managing Member*
EMP: 12 EST: 2018
SALES (est): 400K **Privately Held**
Web: www.handsmgmt.com
SIC: 1771 1629 1711 1389 Concrete work; Drainage system construction; Plumbing contractors; Construction, repair, and dismantling services

(G-13748)
JOHN H PETERSON JR
51 Feather Ln (28457-1322)
PHONE...................................910 762-9957
John H Peterson Junior, *Prin*
EMP: 5 EST: 2011
SALES (est): 68.73K **Privately Held**
SIC: 2431 Millwork

(G-13749)
SEA MARK BOATS INC
Also Called: Entropy
13991 Nc Hwy 210 (28457-8523)
PHONE...................................910 675-1877
EMP: 6 EST: 1969
SALES (est): 399.02K **Privately Held**
Web: www.seamarkboats.com
SIC: 3732 Boatbuilding and repairing

(G-13750)
SOUTHERN STYLE LOGGING LLC
3595 Little Kelly Rd (28457-8659)
PHONE...................................910 259-9897
EMP: 8 EST: 2014
SALES (est): 474.59K **Privately Held**
SIC: 2411 Logging

(G-13751)
STROUDCRAFT MARINE LLC
13991 Nc Hwy 210 (28457-8523)
PHONE...................................910 623-4055
EMP: 10
SALES (est): 555.24K **Privately Held**
SIC: 3732 Boatbuilding and repairing

(G-13752)
SUPERIOR MACHINE SHOP INC
354 Sawdust Rd (28457-9379)
P.O. Box 308 (28457-0308)
PHONE...................................910 675-1336
Ronald D Graves, *Pr*
John O Keel Iii, *VP*
EMP: 15 EST: 1969
SQ FT: 9,000
SALES (est): 250.59K **Privately Held**
SIC: 3599 Machine shop, jobbing and repair

(G-13753)
TANK FAB INC
8787 Us Hwy 117 S (28457-6001)
P.O. Box 680 (28457-0680)
PHONE...................................910 675-8999

EMP: 10 EST: 1995
SQ FT: 30,000
SALES (est): 2.26MM **Privately Held**
Web: www.tankfab.com
SIC: 3441 3443 Fabricated structural metal; Tanks, standard or custom fabricated: metal plate

(G-13754)
TRIN-I-TEE DESIGNZ LLC
300 Preswick Dr (28457-9620)
PHONE..................................910 520-2032
Brenda Thorpe, *Bd of Dir*
EMP: 4 EST: 2019
SALES (est): 76.29K **Privately Held**
SIC: 2759 Screen printing

(G-13755)
WOODTREATERS INC
224 Sawdust Rd (28457)
P.O. Box 557 (28457-0557)
PHONE..................................910 675-0038
Ronnie Graves, *Pr*
John Keel, *Sec*
EMP: 7 EST: 1976
SQ FT: 4,000
SALES (est): 792.61K **Privately Held**
SIC: 2491 Wood preserving

Rodanthe
Dare County

(G-13756)
RIDE BEST LLC
Also Called: Best Kiteboarding
24267 Hwy 12 (27968)
P.O. Box 571 (11561-0571)
PHONE..................................252 489-2959
◆ EMP: 6 EST: 2003
SQ FT: 5,000
SALES (est): 2.1MM **Privately Held**
SIC: 3721 Hang gliders
PA: Pure Action Sports Worldwide, Inc.
2016 Autumn Dr Nw
Alexandria MN 56308

Rolesville
Wake County

(G-13757)
GORILLA OFFROAD COMPANY
414 Virginia Water Dr (27571-9585)
P.O. Box 526 (27571-0526)
PHONE..................................815 715-6003
Derek T Versteegen, *Mgr*
EMP: 5 EST: 2017
SALES (est): 47.8K **Privately Held**
SIC: 3449 Bars, concrete reinforcing: fabricated steel

(G-13758)
MURDOCK BUILDING COMPANY
Also Called: Murdock Bldg Portable Sawmill
109 Watkins Farm Rd (27571-9510)
PHONE..................................919 669-1859
Jack C Murdock, *Prin*
EMP: 8 EST: 2002
SALES (est): 260.46K **Privately Held**
Web: www.ncsawmill.com
SIC: 1799 2426 Antenna installation; Hardwood dimension and flooring mills

(G-13759)
POLYONE DISTRIBUTION
118 Brandi Dr (27571-9432)
PHONE..................................919 413-4547
Abel Salgado, *Prin*
EMP: 4 EST: 2018

SALES (est): 74.42K **Privately Held**
SIC: 2821 Thermoplastic materials

(G-13760)
TEAM X-TREME LLC
600 S Main St Ste C (27571-9309)
PHONE..................................919 562-8100
EMP: 8 EST: 1983
SQ FT: 4,800
SALES (est): 682.08K **Privately Held**
SIC: 7538 5531 7534 General automotive repair shops; Automotive tires; Tire retreading and repair shops

(G-13761)
WAKE MONUMENT COMPANY INC (PA)
213 N Main St (27571-9646)
P.O. Box 130 (27571-0130)
PHONE..................................919 556-3422
Carolyn Bartholomew, *Pr*
Ron Bartholomew, *VP*
Cathy Batts, *Sec*
EMP: 9 EST: 1934
SALES (est): 1.1MM
SALES (corp-wide): 1.1MM **Privately Held**
Web: www.wakemonument.com
SIC: 3281 5999 Monuments, cut stone (not finishing or lettering only); Monuments, finished to custom order

(G-13762)
WIGGINS NORTH STATE CO INC (PA)
204 S Main St (27571-8702)
P.O. Box 70 (27571-0070)
PHONE..................................919 556-3231
Bertie Wiggins, *Pr*
Alvin T Wiggins Junior, *VP*
James W Wiggins, *Treas*
EMP: 5 EST: 1962
SALES (est): 982.39K
SALES (corp-wide): 982.39K **Privately Held**
SIC: 3281 7261 Tombstones, cut stone (not finishing or lettering only); Funeral service and crematories

Ronda
Wilkes County

(G-13763)
CAROLINA PRCSION FBERS SPV LLC
145 Factory St (28670-9236)
PHONE..................................336 527-4140
Alfred Vincelli, *Pr*
EMP: 21 EST: 2017
SALES (est): 6.93MM **Privately Held**
Web: www.carolinafibers.com
SIC: 2823 5039 Cellulosic manmade fibers; Soil erosion control fabrics

(G-13764)
CAROLINA PRECISION FIBERS INC
145 Factory St (28670-9236)
P.O. Box 624 (28621-0624)
PHONE..................................336 527-4140
EMP: 30
SIC: 2679 Paper products, converted, nec

(G-13765)
COMBS WELDING LLC
290 Froglevel Rd (28670-8941)
PHONE..................................336 452-1386
EMP: 4 EST: 2016
SALES (est): 25.09K **Privately Held**
SIC: 7692 Welding repair

(G-13766)
NC RIVER RIDERS LLC
201 Big Bend Rd (28670-9100)
PHONE..................................336 244-6220
EMP: 5 EST: 2016
SALES (est): 50.92K **Privately Held**
Web: www.northcarolinariverriders.com
SIC: 3317 Steel pipe and tubes

(G-13767)
PICCIONE VINYARDS
2364 Cedar Forest Rd (28670-9107)
PHONE..................................312 342-0181
William Piccione, *Prin*
EMP: 5 EST: 2017
SALES (est): 94.11K **Privately Held**
Web: www.piccionevineyards.com
SIC: 2084 Wines

(G-13768)
PRECISION FABRICATORS INC (PA)
Hwy 268 (28670)
P.O. Box 69 (28670-0069)
PHONE..................................336 835-4763
James K Willis, *Pr*
Brenda P Willis, *Sec*
EMP: 6 EST: 1980
SQ FT: 1,700
SALES (est): 500K
SALES (corp-wide): 500K **Privately Held**
Web: www.precision-fab.com
SIC: 3599 1796 7692 3444 Custom machinery; Millwright; Welding repair; Sheet metalwork

(G-13769)
RAFFALDINI VNEYARDS WINERY LLC
450 Groce Rd (28670-9134)
PHONE..................................336 835-9463
Jerome Raffaldini, *Managing Member*
▲ EMP: 15 EST: 2001
SALES (est): 2.19MM **Privately Held**
Web: www.raffaldini.com
SIC: 2084 Wines

Roper
Washington County

(G-13770)
PC SATELLITE SOLUTIONS
325 Jones White Rd (27970-9598)
PHONE..................................252 217-7237
Keith Patrick, *Pt*
EMP: 8 EST: 2009
SALES (est): 416.37K **Privately Held**
SIC: 3651 Household audio and video equipment

(G-13771)
T AND T TIMBER
910 Breezy Banks Rd (27970-9491)
PHONE..................................252 799-6077
EMP: 8 EST: 2014
SALES (est): 231.34K **Privately Held**
SIC: 2411 Logging

(G-13772)
TIM CON WOOD PRODUCTS INC
1438 Cross Rd (27970-9406)
P.O. Box 600 (27846-0600)
PHONE..................................252 793-4819
Billy Corey, *Pr*
Sharon Corey, *Sec*
EMP: 22 EST: 1985
SALES (est): 2.14MM **Privately Held**
SIC: 2411 Logging camps and contractors

Rose Hill
Duplin County

(G-13773)
AMERICAN MATERIALS COMPANY LLC
9763 Taylors Bridge Hwy (28458-8661)
PHONE..................................910 532-6659
EMP: 50
SALES (corp-wide): 2.62B **Publicly Held**
Web: www.americanmaterialsco.com
SIC: 3599 Machine shop, jobbing and repair
HQ: American Materials Company, Llc
1410 Commwl Dr Ste 201
Wilmington NC 28403
910 799-1411

(G-13774)
COOPER TECHNICAL SERVICES INC
4527 S Us Highway 117 (28458-8910)
P.O. Box 398 (28458-0398)
PHONE..................................910 285-2925
John C Cooper Iii, *Pr*
Deborah Cooper, *Sec*
EMP: 8 EST: 1989
SQ FT: 4,500
SALES (est): 894.89K **Privately Held**
Web: www.coopertechnicalservices.com
SIC: 3821 Laboratory equipment: fume hoods, distillation racks, etc.

(G-13775)
DARLING INGREDIENTS INC
469 Yellowcut Rd (28458)
P.O. Box 1026 (28458-1026)
PHONE..................................910 289-2083
Stan Rutherford, *Brnch Mgr*
EMP: 5
SQ FT: 10,000
SALES (corp-wide): 6.53B **Publicly Held**
Web: www.darpro-solutions.com
SIC: 2077 Animal and marine fats and oils
PA: Darling Ingredients Inc.
5601 N Macarthur Blvd
Irving TX 75038
972 717-0300

(G-13776)
DUPLIN WINE CELLARS INC (PA)
Also Called: Cape Fear Vineyards
505 N Sycamore St (28458-8423)
P.O. Box 756 (28458-0756)
PHONE..................................910 289-3888
David G Fussell Junior, *Pr*
Jonathan Fussell, *
Jeff Craft, *
EMP: 30 EST: 1972
SQ FT: 20,000
SALES (est): 10.2MM
SALES (corp-wide): 10.2MM **Privately Held**
Web: www.duplinwinery.com
SIC: 2084 Wines

(G-13777)
HOUSE OF RAEFORD FARMS INC (HQ)
3333 S Us Highway 117 (28458-8493)
P.O. Box 3628 (29070-1628)
PHONE..................................912 222-4090
Robert Johnson, *CEO*
Donald Taber, *
Ken Qualls, *
Marvin Johnson, *
◆ EMP: 1500 EST: 1925
SQ FT: 400,000
SALES (est): 476.58MM
SALES (corp-wide): 1.79B **Privately Held**
Web: www.houseofraeford.com

SIC: 2015 Turkey, slaughtered and dressed
PA: Nash Johnson & Sons Farms, Inc.
3385 S Us Highway 117
Rose Hill NC 28458
910 289-3113

(G-13778)
JOHNSON NASH & SONS FARMS INC (PA)
3385 Us Hwy 117 S (28458-8493)
P.O. Box 699 (28458-0699)
PHONE..............................910 289-3113
Robert C Johnson, *CEO*
E Marvin Johnson, *
Don Taber, *
Dennis E Abraczinskas, *
Glenn Fox, *
◆ **EMP:** 400 **EST:** 1934
SQ FT: 2,000
SALES (est): 1.79B
SALES (corp-wide): 1.79B Privately Held
Web: www.houseofraeford.com
SIC: 2015 0254 0253 0251 Poultry, slaughtered and dressed; Poultry hatcheries; Turkey farm; Broiler, fryer, and roaster chickens

(G-13779)
MURPHY-BROWN LLC
Also Called: Chief Feed Mill
210 Chief Ln (28458)
PHONE..............................910 293-3434
Greg Ewing, *Mgr*
EMP: 94
Web: www.smithfieldfoods.com
SIC: 2048 Prepared feeds, nec
HQ: Murphy-Brown Llc
2822 Highway 24 W
Warsaw NC 28398
910 293-3434

(G-13780)
MURPHY-BROWN LLC
Smithfeld Hog Prodn S Cntl Div
152 Farrow To Finish Ln (28458-1500)
P.O. Box 759 (28458-0759)
PHONE..............................910 282-4264
Jaz Kydes, *Mgr*
EMP: 132
Web: www.smithfieldfoods.com
SIC: 0213 2048 Hogs; Prepared feeds, nec
HQ: Murphy-Brown Llc
2822 Highway 24 W
Warsaw NC 28398
910 293-3434

(G-13781)
SHUTTER PRODUCTION INC
227 1st St (28458-0106)
P.O. Box 446 (28458-0446)
PHONE..............................910 289-2620
Patrick Byrd, *Pr*
EMP: 8 **EST:** 1997
SALES (est): 948.62K Privately Held
Web: www.shutterproduction.com
SIC: 5211 2431 Door and window products; Awnings, blinds and shutters: wood

Roseboro
Sampson County

(G-13782)
A+ CUSTOM CUT PRINT PRESS LLC
708 N Broad St (28382-8750)
PHONE..............................910 337-1033
EMP: 4 **EST:** 2020
SALES (est): 76.29K Privately Held
Web: www.acustomcutprintpresses.com

SIC: 2741 Miscellaneous publishing

(G-13783)
CAROLINA CUSTOM CABINETS
104 Andrews Chapel Rd (28382-8611)
PHONE..............................910 525-3096
EMP: 5 **EST:** 1995
SQ FT: 2,400
SALES (est): 282.15K Privately Held
Web: www.carolinacustomcabinet.com
SIC: 2434 Wood kitchen cabinets

(G-13784)
CRUMPLER PLASTIC PIPE INC
852 Autry Hwy 24 (28382-8307)
P.O. Box 2068 (28382-2068)
PHONE..............................910 525-4046
Houston Crumpler Junior, *Pr*
Houston Temple Iii, *VP*
Richard Brian Temple, *
▼ **EMP:** 65 **EST:** 1975
SALES (est): 10MM Privately Held
Web: www.cpp-pipe.com
SIC: 3084 Plastics pipe

(G-13785)
GREENES LOGGING
760 Mill Creek Church Rd (28382-8603)
PHONE..............................910 533-2021
EMP: 4 **EST:** 2019
SALES (est): 76.25K Privately Held
SIC: 2411 Logging

Rosman
Transylvania County

(G-13786)
M-B INDUSTRIES INC
Also Called: Sunbelt Spring & Stamping
9205 Rosman Hwy (28772-0378)
PHONE..............................828 862-4201
Edwin E Morrow, *Pr*
Carla Morrow, *
▲ **EMP:** 130 **EST:** 1894
SQ FT: 110,000
SALES (est): 20.14MM Privately Held
Web: www.mb-industries.com
SIC: 3495 3469 3552 3496 Wire springs; Stamping metal for the trade; Textile machinery; Miscellaneous fabricated wire products

Rougemont
Durham County

(G-13787)
MOVING SCREENS INCORPORATED
7807 Helena Moriah Rd (27572-7522)
PHONE..............................336 364-9259
Wesley Winstead, *Pr*
Greg Fogleman, *Treas*
EMP: 4 **EST:** 1989
SQ FT: 6,000
SALES (est): 364.5K Privately Held
Web: www.blsales.net
SIC: 7336 2395 2759 Silk screen design; Embroidery products, except Schiffli machine; Screen printing

(G-13788)
RUGERS WELDING
3617 Red Mountain Rd (27572-9436)
PHONE..............................919 471-8795
EMP: 4 **EST:** 2011
SALES (est): 57.22K Privately Held
SIC: 7692 Welding repair

Rowland
Robeson County

(G-13789)
HELENA AGRI-ENTERPRISES LLC
13866 Hwy 301 S (28383)
P.O. Box 1027 (28383-1027)
PHONE..............................910 422-8901
William Bates, *Brnch Mgr*
EMP: 10
Web: www.helenaagri.com
SIC: 2873 5191 Fertilizers: natural (organic), except compost; Fertilizers and agricultural chemicals
HQ: Helena Agri-Enterprises, Llc
225 Schilling Blvd
Collierville TN 38017
901 761-0050

(G-13790)
LOCKLEAR CABINETS WDWRK SP INC
Also Called: Locklear Cabinet and Woodworks
4659 Cabinet Shop Rd (28383-9257)
PHONE..............................910 521-4463
Harold B Locklear, *Pr*
Janie Locklear Davis, *VP*
EMP: 5 **EST:** 1949
SQ FT: 4,500
SALES (est): 431.75K Privately Held
Web: www.locklearcabinets.com
SIC: 5712 2591 Cabinet work, custom; Curtain and drapery rods, poles, and fixtures

(G-13791)
MJ SOFFE LLC
Also Called: M.J. SOFFE, LLC
13750 Us Highway 301 S (28383-6648)
PHONE..............................910 422-9002
James Taylor, *Mgr*
EMP: 47
SALES (corp-wide): 415.35MM Publicly Held
Web: www.soffe.com
SIC: 2389 2329 2321 2339 Men's miscellaneous accessories; Athletic clothing, except uniforms: men's, youths' and boys'; Men's and boy's furnishings; Athletic clothing: women's, misses', and juniors'
HQ: M. J. Soffe Co.
1 Soffe Dr
Fayetteville NC 28312
910 435-3138

Roxboro
Person County

(G-13792)
ABSOLUTE SECURITY & LOCK INC
216 S Main St (27573-5546)
P.O. Box 3250 (27573-3250)
PHONE..............................336 322-4598
Scott Spencer, *Pr*
EMP: 5 **EST:** 2003
SALES (est): 364.53K Privately Held
Web: www.absolutesecurityandlock.com
SIC: 7699 3429 7382 1731 Locksmith shop; Door opening and closing devices, except electrical; Burglar alarm maintenance and monitoring; Access control systems specialization

(G-13793)
ACCELERATED MEDIA TECHNOLOGIES
4400 Semora Rd (27574-6624)

PHONE..............................336 599-2070
Wilbur Brann, *Mgr*
EMP: 8 **EST:** 2018
SALES (est): 86.63K Privately Held
Web: www.acceleratedmt.com
SIC: 3441 Fabricated structural metal

(G-13794)
B & B DISTRIBUTING INC
Also Called: Brady's Baked Goods
2888 Durham Rd Ste 102 (27573-6178)
PHONE..............................336 592-5665
Tr Brady, *Pr*
EMP: 6 **EST:** 1978
SALES (est): 366.83K Privately Held
SIC: 2011 Pork products, from pork slaughtered on site

(G-13795)
BOISE CASCADE WOOD PDTS LLC
Also Called: Roxboro Ewp Mill
1000 N Park Dr (27573-2474)
PHONE..............................336 598-3001
EMP: 5
SALES (corp-wide): 8.39B Publicly Held
Web: www.bc.com
SIC: 2491 Structural lumber and timber, treated wood
HQ: Boise Cascade Wood Products, L.L.C.
1111 W Jefferson St # 300
Boise ID 83728
208 384-6161

(G-13796)
BOLEEF INDUSTRIES
368 Nelson Loop Rd (27574-6421)
PHONE..............................336 330-0404
Bobby Farrish, *Pr*
EMP: 4 **EST:** 2014
SALES (est): 59.49K Privately Held
Web: www.boleefindustries.com
SIC: 3999 Manufacturing industries, nec

(G-13797)
CAMP CHEMICAL CORPORATION (PA)
200 Hester St (27573-5957)
P.O. Box 521 (27573-0521)
PHONE..............................336 597-2214
EMP: 19 **EST:** 1929
SALES (est): 9.74MM
SALES (corp-wide): 9.74MM Privately Held
Web: www.campchemical.com
SIC: 2875 5999 5191 Fertilizers, mixing only; Feed and farm supply; Seeds: field, garden, and flower

(G-13798)
CENTEREDGE SOFTWARE
5050 Durham Rd (27574-9811)
P.O. Box 1359 (27573-1359)
PHONE..............................336 598-5934
EMP: 8 **EST:** 2013
SALES (est): 1.73MM Privately Held
Web: www.centeredgesoftware.com
SIC: 7372 Business oriented computer software

(G-13799)
CHANDLER CONCRETE INC
Also Called: CHANDLER CONCRETE INC
121 Burch Ave (27573-4738)
P.O. Box 1732 (27573-1732)
PHONE..............................336 599-8343
Michael Owen, *Genl Mgr*
EMP: 14
Web: www.chandlerconcrete.com
SIC: 3273 Ready-mixed concrete
PA: Chandler Concrete Co., Inc.
1006 S Church St

Roxboro - Person County (G-13800) GEOGRAPHIC SECTION

Burlington NC 27215

(G-13800)
DEEP CREEK MOTORS INC
625 N Madison Blvd (27573-4660)
PHONE..................................336 599-0000
EMP: 6 **EST:** 2014
SALES (est): 316.86K **Privately Held**
SIC: 3599 Machine shop, jobbing and repair

(G-13801)
EATON CORPORATION
Also Called: Air Controls Division
2564 Durham Rd (27573-6172)
P.O. Box 241 (27573-0241)
PHONE..................................336 322-0696
David Sintson, *Brnch Mgr*
EMP: 440
Web: www.dix-eaton.com
SIC: 3714 Motor vehicle parts and accessories
HQ: Eaton Corporation
1000 Eaton Blvd
Cleveland OH 44122
440 523-5000

(G-13802)
EPIC RESTORATIONS LLC
118 Commerce Dr (27573-3812)
P.O. Box 3010 (27573-3010)
PHONE..................................866 597-2733
EMP: 4 **EST:** 2003
SALES (est): 1.46MM **Privately Held**
Web: www.strutmasters.com
SIC: 3714 Motor vehicle parts and accessories

(G-13803)
FORCE PROTECTION INC
3300 Jim Thorpe Hwy (27574-5445)
PHONE..................................336 597-2381
Ernie Nagy, *Dir*
EMP: 10
SALES (corp-wide): 42.27B **Publicly Held**
SIC: 3711 Motor vehicles and car bodies
HQ: Force Protection, Inc.
9801 Highway 78 Bldg 1
Ladson SC 29456

(G-13804)
GO ASK ERIN LLC
328 Virgilina Rd (27573-4422)
PHONE..................................336 747-3777
Erin Miller, *Pr*
EMP: 5 **EST:** 2018
SALES (est): 48.16K **Privately Held**
Web: www.goaskerinllc.com
SIC: 3448 Prefabricated metal buildings and components

(G-13805)
JH LOGGING
1300 Virgilina Rd (27573-4461)
PHONE..................................336 599-0278
James H Heath, *Owner*
James Heath, *Owner*
EMP: 5 **EST:** 1993
SALES (est): 309.21K **Privately Held**
SIC: 2411 Logging camps and contractors

(G-13806)
LOUISIANA-PACIFIC CORPORATION
Also Called: Louisiana-Pacific Southern Div
10475 Boston Rd (27574-6774)
PHONE..................................336 599-8080
EMP: 112
SALES (corp-wide): 4.55B **Publicly Held**
Web: www.lpcorp.com
SIC: 2431 2493 Millwork; Reconstituted wood products

PA: Louisiana-Pacific Corporation
1610 West End Ave Ste 200
Nashville TN 37203
615 986-5600

(G-13807)
NEWELL & SONS INC
Also Called: Newell
211 Clayton Ave (27573-4641)
P.O. Box 1098 (27573-1098)
PHONE..................................336 597-2248
David Newell, *Pr*
Linda Newell Garza, *Sec*
EMP: 10 **EST:** 1967
SQ FT: 15,000
SALES (est): 412.5K **Privately Held**
Web: www.newellandsons.com
SIC: 2392 Mops, floor and dust

(G-13808)
NEWELL NOVELTY CO INC
Also Called: Roxboro Broom Works
25 Weeks Dr (27573-5954)
P.O. Box 949 (27573-0949)
PHONE..................................336 597-2246
Henry Newell Junior, *Pr*
David Newell, *VP*
Jean Newell, *Prin*
▲ **EMP:** 4 **EST:** 1920
SQ FT: 20,000
SALES (est): 244.7K **Privately Held**
Web: www.roxborobroom.com
SIC: 3991 5169 Brooms; Chemicals and allied products, nec

(G-13809)
NORTH AMERCN AERODYNAMICS INC (PA)
1803 N Main St (27573-4047)
PHONE..................................336 599-9266
John P Higgins, *Pr*
Jim Barker, *
EMP: 82 **EST:** 1964
SQ FT: 56,000
SALES (est): 4.73MM
SALES (corp-wide): 4.73MM **Privately Held**
Web: www.naaero.com
SIC: 2399 Parachutes

(G-13810)
NORTH CRLINA DEPT CRIME CTRL P
Also Called: State Hwy Patrol-Troop D
3434 Burlington Rd (27574-7742)
PHONE..................................336 599-9233
Robert Pearson, *Prin*
EMP: 6
Web: www.ncdps.gov
SIC: 3711 9229 Patrol wagons (motor vehicles), assembly of; Public order and safety, State government
HQ: North Carolina Department Of Crime Control And Public Safety
512 N Salisbury St
Raleigh NC 27604

(G-13811)
OLD BELT EXTRACTS LLC
Also Called: Open Book Extracts
317 Lucy Garrett Rd (27574-9789)
P.O. Box 1328 (27573-1328)
PHONE..................................336 530-5784
Oscar Hackett, *Pr*
David Neundorfer, *
EMP: 50 **EST:** 2019
SALES (est): 5.18MM **Privately Held**
Web: www.oldbeltextracts.com
SIC: 2899 Oils and essential oils

(G-13812)
OLIVE HL WLDG FABRICATION INC
Also Called: Olive Hill Wldg & Fabrication
1940 Semora Rd (27574-6654)
PHONE..................................336 597-0737
Charles Dickerson, *Pr*
Charles E Dickerson, *
EMP: 32 **EST:** 1982
SQ FT: 4,500
SALES (est): 3.6MM **Privately Held**
Web: www.olivehillwelding.com
SIC: 7692 Welding repair

(G-13813)
OUR PRIDE FOODS ROXBORO INC
Also Called: Our Pride Foods
1128 N Main St (27573-4402)
PHONE..................................336 597-4978
Malcolm Wooten, *Pr*
Ray Dunlap, *VP*
Danny Hodge, *Sec*
EMP: 8 **EST:** 1990
SQ FT: 18,000
SALES (est): 667.1K **Privately Held**
Web: www.ourpridepimentocheese.com
SIC: 2022 Cheese spreads, dips, pastes, and other cheese products

(G-13814)
OWENS CORNING SALES LLC
Owens Corning
3321 Durham Rd (27573-2713)
P.O. Box 61 (27573-0061)
PHONE..................................419 248-8000
Tom Mc Elveen, *Mgr*
EMP: 26
SIC: 3442 3444 3354 Screen doors, metal; Sheet metalwork; Aluminum extruded products
HQ: Owens Corning Sales, Llc
1 Owens Corning Pkwy
Toledo OH 43659
419 248-8000

(G-13815)
P&A INDSTRIAL FABRICATIONS LLC (PA)
Also Called: Epoch Solutions
1841 N Main St (27573-4047)
P.O. Box 28 (27573-0028)
PHONE..................................336 322-1766
Don Millwater, *Contrlr*
▲ **EMP:** 34 **EST:** 2006
SALES (est): 77.94MM **Privately Held**
Web: www.paifllc.com
SIC: 3991 2221 Paint rollers; Automotive fabrics, manmade fiber

(G-13816)
PANELS BY PAITH INC
2728 Allensville Rd (27574-7278)
PHONE..................................336 599-3437
Don C Paith, *Pr*
Greta S Paith, *Sec*
EMP: 5 **EST:** 1975
SALES (est): 380.44K **Privately Held**
SIC: 2541 5712 3442 Partitions for floor attachment, prefabricated: wood; Cabinet work, custom; Moldings and trim, except automobile: metal

(G-13817)
PERSON COUNTY RECYCLE CENTER
Madison Blvd (27573)
PHONE..................................336 597-4437
Paul Bailey, *Mgr*
EMP: 7 **EST:** 2001
SALES (est): 89.3K **Privately Held**
Web: www.personcountync.gov

SIC: 2611 Pulp manufactured from waste or recycled paper

(G-13818)
PERSON PRINTING COMPANY INC
Also Called: Taylor Printing & Office Sup
115 Clayton Ave (27573-4611)
P.O. Box 681 (27573-0681)
PHONE..................................336 599-2146
Donald Ray Wilkins, *Pr*
EMP: 20 **EST:** 1945
SQ FT: 7,950
SALES (est): 4.56MM **Privately Held**
Web: www.taylorbusinessproducts.com
SIC: 2752 2791 2789 5112 Offset printing; Typesetting; Bookbinding and related work; Stationery and office supplies

(G-13819)
PIEDMONT PARACHUTE INC
2712 Durham Rd (27573-6176)
PHONE..................................336 597-2225
Carolyn Oakley, *Pr*
EMP: 6 **EST:** 2008
SALES (est): 434.12K **Privately Held**
Web: www.triangleparachute.com
SIC: 2399 Parachutes

(G-13820)
R & S SPORTING GOODS CTR INC
Also Called: Sign and Graphics
515 S Morgan St (27573-5451)
PHONE..................................336 599-0248
Wayne T Roberts, *Pr*
Doris Winstead, *VP*
EMP: 4 **EST:** 1977
SQ FT: 3,200
SALES (est): 363K **Privately Held**
SIC: 2396 5941 Screen printing on fabric articles; Sporting goods and bicycle shops

(G-13821)
ROXBORO WELDING
3735 Cates Mill Rd (27574-7992)
PHONE..................................336 364-2307
Daniel Hutchinson, *Prin*
EMP: 5 **EST:** 2017
SALES (est): 62.77K **Privately Held**
Web: www.olivehillwelding.com
SIC: 7692 Welding repair

(G-13822)
S OAKLEY MACHINE SHOP INC
126 W Gordon St (27573-5211)
PHONE..................................336 599-6105
Charles R Oakley, *Pr*
Arthur R Oakley, *VP*
Marie Oakley, *Sec*
EMP: 6 **EST:** 1942
SQ FT: 10,000
SALES (est): 468.21K **Privately Held**
SIC: 7692 3599 Welding repair; Machine shop, jobbing and repair

(G-13823)
SIGNARAMA OF ROXBORO
Also Called: Sign-A-Rama
1680 Gentry Dunkley Rd (27574-8285)
PHONE..................................336 322-1663
Sita Makowske, *Prin*
EMP: 6 **EST:** 2019
SALES (est): 127.86K **Privately Held**
Web: www.signarama.com
SIC: 3993 Signs and advertising specialties

(G-13824)
SOUTHERN STATES COOP INC
Also Called: S S C 7883-7
1112 N Main St (27573-4402)
PHONE..................................336 599-2185

Donald Bowes, *Mgr*
EMP: 10
SALES (corp-wide): 1.71B **Privately Held**
Web: www.southernstates.com
SIC: 2048 5261 Prepared feeds, nec; Retail nurseries and garden stores
PA: Southern States Cooperative, Incorporated
6606 W Broad St Ste B
Richmond VA 23230
804 281-1000

(G-13825)
SPUNTECH INDUSTRIES INC
555 N Park Dr (27573-2477)
PHONE.................................336 330-9000
Hezi Yeheskel Nissan, *Ch*
Tomer Duash, *Sec*
Moshe Zorea, *Treas*
Ilan Pickman, *Sec*
Yiftah Sharrown, *Treas*
◆ **EMP:** 210 **EST:** 2003
SQ FT: 250,000
SALES (est): 61.8MM **Privately Held**
Web: www.spuntech.com
SIC: 2299 2841 2241 Upholstery filling, textile; Textile soap; Lacings, textile
HQ: N.R. Spuntech Industries Ltd.
Tiberias

(G-13826)
STOKES MFG LLC
140 Somerset Church Rd (27573-6069)
PHONE.................................336 270-8746
EMP: 6 **EST:** 2018
SALES (est): 296.16K **Privately Held**
Web: www.stokesmfg.com
SIC: 3999 Manufacturing industries, nec

(G-13827)
SUSPENSION EXPERTS LLC
Also Called: Strutmasters
118 Commerce Dr (27573-3812)
PHONE.................................855 419-3072
Chip Lofton, *Managing Member*
EMP: 24 **EST:** 1999
SALES (est): 3.26MM **Privately Held**
Web: www.strutmasters.com
SIC: 3751 Motorcycles and related parts

(G-13828)
TUNNEL CREEK VENUES LLC
1576 Berryhill Rd (27574-6707)
PHONE.................................336 322-3600
Sharon Holler, *Prin*
Larry Holler, *Prin*
EMP: 5 **EST:** 2018
SALES (est): 111.3K **Privately Held**
Web: www.tunnelcreekvineyards.com
SIC: 2084 Wines

Roxobel
Bertie County

(G-13829)
BAKERS SOUTHERN TRADITIONS INC
Also Called: Bakers Sthern Trdtions Peanuts
704 E Church St (27872-9612)
P.O. Box 62 (27872-0062)
PHONE.................................252 344-2120
Danielle Baker, *Pr*
EMP: 4 **EST:** 2007
SALES (est): 496.62K **Privately Held**
Web: www.bakerspeanuts.com
SIC: 2096 5963 5499 5149 Cheese curls and puffs; Snacks, direct sales; Gourmet food stores; Groceries and related products, nec

Rtp
Durham County

(G-13830)
CERTIRX CORPORATION
2 Davis Dr (27709-0003)
PHONE.................................919 354-1029
EMP: 4 **EST:** 2011
SALES (est): 274.01K **Privately Held**
Web: www.certirx.com
SIC: 2834 Pharmaceutical preparations

(G-13831)
GRACILI THERAPEUTICS INC
15 Tw Alexander Dr (27709-0152)
PHONE.................................617 331-4110
EMP: 6 **EST:** 2019
SALES (est): 170.91K **Privately Held**
Web: www.g1therapeutics.com
SIC: 2834 Pharmaceutical preparations

Rural Hall
Forsyth County

(G-13832)
A & J PALLETS INC
121 Anderson St (27045-9147)
PHONE.................................336 969-0265
Richard Scott, *Brnch Mgr*
EMP: 7
SALES (corp-wide): 654.03K **Privately Held**
Web: www.ajpalletsandmulch.com
SIC: 2448 2499 Pallets, wood; Mulch, wood and bark
PA: A & J Pallets, Inc.
195 Apache Dr
Winston Salem NC 27107
336 407-4368

(G-13833)
BBF PRINTING SOLUTIONS
1190 Old Beltway (27045-9537)
PHONE.................................336 969-2323
EMP: 6 **EST:** 2017
SALES (est): 147.67K **Privately Held**
Web: www.bbfprinting.com
SIC: 2752 Offset printing

(G-13834)
BUSICK BROTHERS MACHINE INC
262 Northstar Dr (27045-9949)
P.O. Box 1009 (27045-1009)
PHONE.................................336 969-2717
EMP: 17 **EST:** 1990
SQ FT: 7,000
SALES (est): 874.03K **Privately Held**
Web: www.busickbrothers.com
SIC: 3599 Machine shop, jobbing and repair

(G-13835)
CAROLON COMPANY
601 Forum Pkwy (27045-8934)
P.O. Box 1329 (27045-1329)
PHONE.................................336 969-6001
▲ **EMP:** 100 **EST:** 1973
SALES (est): 9.13MM **Privately Held**
Web: www.carolon.com
SIC: 3842 Surgical appliances and supplies

(G-13836)
CASE SMITH INC
625 Montroyal Rd (27045-9550)
PHONE.................................336 969-9786
EMP: 16 **EST:** 2011
SQ FT: 30,000
SALES (est): 1.07MM **Privately Held**
Web: www.smithcase.com
SIC: 3161 Cases, carrying, nec

(G-13837)
CAVERT WIRE COMPANY INC (HQ)
Also Called: Cavert Red Line Wire Division
620 Forum Pkwy (27045-8934)
P.O. Box 725 (27045-0725)
PHONE.................................800 969-2601
▲ **EMP:** 45 **EST:** 1910
SALES (est): 22.5MM
SALES (corp-wide): 105.79MM **Privately Held**
Web: www.accentwiretie.com
SIC: 3315 3496 Wire products, ferrous/iron: made in wiredrawing plants; Miscellaneous fabricated wire products
PA: Accent Packaging, Inc.
10131 Fm 2920 Rd
Tomball TX 77375
281 255-4881

(G-13838)
CHERRY CONTRACTING INC
Also Called: Cherry Precast
8640 Broad St (27045-9458)
P.O. Box 368 (27023-0368)
PHONE.................................336 969-1825
Cherry K Fulcher, *Pr*
Nelson T Fulcher, *
EMP: 95 **EST:** 2001
SQ FT: 50,000
SALES (est): 17.04MM **Privately Held**
Web: www.cherrycontracting.com
SIC: 3272 Concrete products, precast, nec

(G-13839)
DAC PRODUCTS INC
Also Called: D A C
625 Montroyal Rd (27045-9550)
PHONE.................................336 969-9786
Durward Smith Iii, *Pr*
Chris Smith, *
Chris Hodges, *
Squire Irwin, *
◆ **EMP:** 35 **EST:** 1987
SALES (est): 5.51MM **Privately Held**
Web: www.dacproducts.com
SIC: 2541 2431 2449 3442 Display fixtures, wood; Door frames, wood; Wood containers, nec; Metal doors, sash, and trim

(G-13840)
FORSYTH PRINTING COMPANY INC
627 Forum Pkwy (27045-8934)
PHONE.................................336 969-0383
Ricky Jones, *Pr*
Wiley R Jones Senior, *Sec*
EMP: 4 **EST:** 1977
SQ FT: 5,000
SALES (est): 367.33K **Privately Held**
Web: www.burkleeprinting.com
SIC: 2752 Offset printing

(G-13841)
FORSYTH REDI-MIX INC
100 Anderson St (27045-9147)
P.O. Box 95 (27045-0095)
PHONE.................................336 969-0446
Jason Scott Speer, *Prin*
EMP: 15 **EST:** 2012
SALES (est): 2.36MM **Privately Held**
SIC: 3273 Ready-mixed concrete

(G-13842)
GRAPHIC REWARDS INC
130 Northstar Dr Ste B (27045-9450)
P.O. Box 1166 (27021-1166)
PHONE.................................336 969-2733
EMP: 8 **EST:** 1996
SQ FT: 10,000
SALES (est): 254.58K **Privately Held**
SIC: 2752 Business form and card printing, lithographic

(G-13843)
HANESBRANDS INC
710 Almondridge Dr (27045-9576)
PHONE.................................336 519-8080
EMP: 113 **EST:** 2006
SALES (est): 1.56MM **Privately Held**
SIC: 2252 Socks

(G-13844)
KEN GARNER MFG - RHO INC
Also Called: Ken Garner Mfg
8610 Chipboard Rd (27045-9503)
PHONE.................................336 969-0416
Jerry Prince, *Pr*
EMP: 47 **EST:** 2006
SALES (est): 7.75MM
SALES (corp-wide): 21.16MM **Privately Held**
Web: www.kgarnermfg.com
SIC: 3531 Aerial work platforms: hydraulic/elec. truck/carrier mounted
PA: Ken Garner Manufacturing, Inc.
1201 E 28th St
Chattanooga TN 37404
423 698-6200

(G-13845)
KIMMYS CUSTOMS LLC
2339 Whisperwood St (27045-9816)
PHONE.................................904 699-2933
Kimberly Smith, *Prin*
EMP: 5 **EST:** 2020
SALES (est): 241.93K **Privately Held**
Web: www.kimmyscustomllc.com
SIC: 2211 2299 5699 5023 Apparel and outerwear fabrics, cotton; Yarns, specialty and novelty; Uniforms; Decorative home furnishings and supplies

(G-13846)
LANGENTHAL CORPORATION
1300 Langenthal Dr (27045-9800)
P.O. Box 965 (27045-0965)
PHONE.................................336 969-9551
Urs Baumann, *Ch Bd*
EMP: 10 **EST:** 1972
SALES (est): 232.92K **Privately Held**
Web: www.lantal.com
SIC: 2221 5131 Broadwoven fabric mills, manmade; Textiles, woven, nec

(G-13847)
LANTAL TEXTILES INC (HQ)
1300 Langenthal Dr (27045-9800)
P.O. Box 965 (27045-0965)
PHONE.................................336 969-9551
Urs Baumann, *Ch Bd*
Scott C Walker, *Pr*
Kim Lawson, *Prin*
Jamey Hughes, *Treas*
▲ **EMP:** 147 **EST:** 1979
SQ FT: 50,000
SALES (est): 24.73MM **Privately Held**
Web: www.lantal.com
SIC: 2231 2211 5131 Upholstery fabrics, wool; Upholstery fabrics, cotton; Upholstery fabrics, woven
PA: Lantal Textiles Ag
Dorfgasse 5
Langenthal BE 4900

(G-13848)
LEISTRIZ ADVANCED TURBINE COMPONENTS INC
3050 Wstnghuse Rd Ste 190 (27045)
P.O. Box 790 (16117-0790)
PHONE.................................336 969-1352

Rural Hall - Forsyth County (G-13849)

▲ **EMP:** 165
SIC: 3511 Turbines and turbine generator set units, complete

(G-13849)
LOGOWEAR
8003 Mathison Creek Dr (27045-9882)
PHONE.................336 969-0444
Kent Hunter, *Owner*
EMP: 5 **EST:** 2017
SALES (est): 82.68K **Privately Held**
SIC: 2395 Pleating and stitching

(G-13850)
NORTHLINE NC LLC
262 Northstar Dr Ste 122 (27045-9180)
PHONE.................336 283-4811
Tonya Morris, *Prin*
EMP: 13 **EST:** 2013
SALES (est): 3.19MM **Privately Held**
Web: www.northlinenc.com
SIC: 5084 3825 Industrial machinery and equipment; Test equipment for electronic and electrical circuits

(G-13851)
ROBERT H WAGER COMPANY INC
Also Called: Wager
570 Montroyal Rd (27045-9233)
PHONE.................336 969-6909
Robert Wager Senior, *CEO*
Lynn Wager Powers, *Ex VP*
Mike Wager, *Pr*
▲ **EMP:** 18 **EST:** 1933
SQ FT: 20,000
SALES (est): 5.51MM **Privately Held**
Web: www.wagerusa.com
SIC: 3491 3823 Valves, automatic control; Process control instruments

(G-13852)
SBRC HOBBIES & RACEWAY LLC
341 W Wall St (27045-9307)
PHONE.................336 782-8420
Carol H Smith, *Owner*
EMP: 4 **EST:** 2018
SALES (est): 88.38K **Privately Held**
SIC: 3644 Raceways

(G-13853)
SIEMENS ENERGY INC
Also Called: Power Generation Mfg Oper Div
3050 Westinghouse Rd (27045-9570)
PHONE.................336 969-1351
Amogh Bhonde, *Mgr*
EMP: 192
SALES (corp-wide): 33.81B **Privately Held**
Web: new.siemens.com
SIC: 3621 3511 Motors and generators; Turbines and turbine generator sets
HQ: Siemens Energy, Inc.
4400 N Alafaya Trl
Orlando FL 32826
407 736-2000

(G-13854)
WE CBD LLC
8701 Jefferson Church Rd (27045-9420)
PHONE.................336 969-0400
Daniel Martin, *Prin*
EMP: 6 **EST:** 2016
SALES (est): 75.53K **Privately Held**
SIC: 3999

(G-13855)
WESTROCK SHARED SERVICES LLC
Also Called: Westrock Merchandising Display
520 Northridge Park Dr (27045-9575)
PHONE.................336 642-4165
Stephanie W Bignon, *Mgr*
EMP: 846
SALES (corp-wide): 20.31B **Publicly Held**
Web: www.westrock.com
SIC: 2621 2631 Packaging paper; Container, packaging, and boxboard
HQ: Westrock Shared Services, Llc
1000 Abernathy Rd
Atlanta GA 30328

(G-13856)
WILLIAMS PRINTING INC
286 Northstar Dr Ste 118 (27045-9445)
P.O. Box 1166 (27021-1166)
PHONE.................336 969-2733
Kevin Williams, *Pr*
EMP: 7 **EST:** 2005
SALES (est): 468.49K **Privately Held**
Web: www.wpicolor.com
SIC: 2752 Offset printing

(G-13857)
WILLIAMS PRINTING INC
268 Northstar Dr Ste 118 (27045-9182)
PHONE.................336 969-2733
Kevin Williams, *Prin*
EMP: 8 **EST:** 2017
SALES (est): 922.34K **Privately Held**
Web: www.wpicolor.com
SIC: 2752 Offset printing

Rutherford College
Burke County

(G-13858)
AQUAFIL OMARA INC
Also Called: Omtex
160 Fashion Ave (28671)
P.O. Box 970 (28671-0970)
PHONE.................828 874-2100
Gary Bradley, *Pr*
Joseph Leirer, *
Andrea Pugnali, *
Angela Elliott, *
◆ **EMP:** 150 **EST:** 1970
SALES (est): 22.74MM
SALES (corp-wide): 712.35MM **Privately Held**
Web: www.aquafil.com
SIC: 2282 2281 5199 Textured yarn; Yarn spinning mills; Fabrics, yarns, and knit goods
HQ: Aquafil U.S.A., Inc.
1 Aquafil Dr
Cartersville GA 30120
678 605-8100

(G-13859)
FILTEX INC
160 Fashion Ave (28671)
P.O. Box 970 (28671-0970)
PHONE.................828 874-2100
Joseph J O'mara Junior, *Pr*
Joe Leirer Junior, *Sec*
▲ **EMP:** 75 **EST:** 1987
SQ FT: 27,000
SALES (est): 6.49MM **Privately Held**
Web: www.aquafil.com
SIC: 2221 Shirting fabrics, manmade fiber and silk

Rutherfordton
Rutherford County

(G-13860)
3TEX INC
208 Laurel Hill Dr (28139-2599)
P.O. Box 97544 (27624-7544)
PHONE.................919 481-2500
◆ **EMP:** 42
Web: www.3tex.com
SIC: 3297 Heat resistant mixtures

(G-13861)
ALLRAIL INC
289 Calton Hill Ln (28139-9181)
PHONE.................828 287-3747
Thomas Calton, *Pr*
▲ **EMP:** 8 **EST:** 2008
SALES (est): 992.88K **Privately Held**
Web: www.allrail.us
SIC: 3317 Steel pipe and tubes

(G-13862)
AMBRO-SOL USA LLC
286 Industrial Park Rd (28139-2526)
PHONE.................844 824-6959
EMP: 4 **EST:** 2018
SALES (est): 190.84K **Privately Held**
Web: www.ambro-solusa.com
SIC: 2813 Aerosols

(G-13863)
AMERICAN MISO COMPANY INC
4225 Maple Creek Rd (28139-7521)
PHONE.................828 287-2940
Barry Evans, *Pr*
Jan Paige, *VP*
EMP: 11 **EST:** 1982
SALES (est): 612.97K **Privately Held**
Web: www.greateasternsun.com
SIC: 2099 Sauces: dry mixes

(G-13864)
ASSOCIATED PRINTING & SVCS INC
905 N Main St (28139-2523)
P.O. Box 905 (28139-0905)
PHONE.................828 286-9064
Ginny Wells, *Pr*
Eric Wells, *VP*
Joe Wells, *Sec*
EMP: 10 **EST:** 1967
SQ FT: 20,000
SALES (est): 1.21MM **Privately Held**
Web: www.associatedprinting.biz
SIC: 2752 2789 Offset printing; Swatches and samples

(G-13865)
BADGER WELDING INCORPORATED
387 Creek Rd (28139-6720)
PHONE.................828 863-2078
Stanley Badger, *Pr*
Lori Badger, *VP*
EMP: 4 **EST:** 1985
SALES (est): 423.2K **Privately Held**
Web: www.badgerweld.net
SIC: 7692 Welding repair

(G-13866)
BLUE RIDGE ARMOR LLC
340 Industrial Park Rd (28139-2541)
PHONE.................844 556-6855
James D Taylor, *Pr*
Dale Taylor, *Managing Member*
EMP: 7 **EST:** 2014
SALES (est): 602.43K **Privately Held**
Web: www.blueridgearmor.com
SIC: 3812 Defense systems and equipment

(G-13867)
BOONES SAWMILL INC
182 Goldfinch Ln (28139-8386)
PHONE.................828 287-8774
Jesse Boone, *Pr*
EMP: 5 **EST:** 2013
SALES (est): 449.55K **Privately Held**
Web: www.boonessawmill.com

SIC: 2421 Lumber: rough, sawed, or planed

(G-13868)
BROAD RIVER FOREST PRODUCTS
2250 Us 221 Hwy N (28139-8686)
PHONE.................828 287-8003
Tim Parton, *Pr*
William Parton, *VP*
Mike Parton, *Treas*
EMP: 7 **EST:** 1998
SALES (est): 970.44K **Privately Held**
SIC: 2611 Pulp mills

(G-13869)
CARPENTER DESIGN INC
Also Called: Carpenter Design
330 Broyhill Rd (28139-9612)
PHONE.................828 248-9070
Thomas Carpenter, *Pr*
EMP: 15 **EST:** 1989
SQ FT: 30,000
SALES (est): 3.99MM **Privately Held**
Web: www.carpenterpallet.com
SIC: 2448 Pallets, wood

(G-13870)
COUNTRY HEART BRAIDING
955 Hopper Rd (28139-8749)
PHONE.................828 245-0562
Joyce Shires, *Owner*
EMP: 8 **EST:** 1988
SALES (est): 282.8K **Privately Held**
SIC: 2273 Rugs, braided and hooked

(G-13871)
DAILY COURIER
162 N Main St (28139-2502)
PHONE.................828 245-6431
Jim Brown, *Mgr*
EMP: 24 **EST:** 1969
SALES (est): 948.25K **Privately Held**
Web: www.thedigitalcourier.com
SIC: 2711 Newspapers, publishing and printing

(G-13872)
GILKEY LUMBER CO INC
2250 Us 221 Hwy N (28139-8686)
PHONE.................828 286-9069
William Parton, *CEO*
EMP: 6 **EST:** 2011
SALES (est): 998.19K **Privately Held**
Web: www.gilkeylumber.com
SIC: 2421 Sawmills and planing mills, general

(G-13873)
GOOD EARTH MINISTRIES
156 River Ridge Pkwy (28139-8478)
PHONE.................828 287-9826
EMP: 6 **EST:** 1998
SALES (est): 452.07K **Privately Held**
SIC: 3271 Blocks, concrete: landscape or retaining wall

(G-13874)
GRAYSTONE MANOR LAKE LURE LLC
730 N Washington St (28139-2418)
PHONE.................828 395-2099
Michelle Gref, *Prin*
EMP: 5 **EST:** 2019
SALES (est): 79.08K **Privately Held**
SIC: 3949 Sporting and athletic goods, nec

(G-13875)
GUERRERO ENTERPRISES INC
1621 Poors Ford Rd (28139-8728)
P.O. Box 103 (28139-0103)
PHONE.................828 286-4900

EMP: 4 **EST:** 2005
SALES (est): 252.72K **Privately Held**
Web: www.dssignsandgraphics.com
SIC: 3993 1799 Signs and advertising specialties; Sign installation and maintenance

(G-13876)
HARRIS CUSTOM CABINETRY LLC
471 Ivy Dr (28139-3234)
PHONE.................................828 289-5620
EMP: 5 **EST:** 2010
SALES (est): 156.28K **Privately Held**
SIC: 2434 Wood kitchen cabinets

(G-13877)
HARRIS LUMBER COMPANY INC
1266 Big Island Rd (28139-8761)
PHONE.................................828 245-2664
Dwayne Harris, *Pr*
EMP: 4 **EST:** 2000
SALES (est): 421.95K **Privately Held**
Web: www.broadriverhomes.com
SIC: 2421 Lumber: rough, sawed, or planed

(G-13878)
HEAL
Also Called: H.E.A.L. Marketplace
360 Carpenter Rd (28139-8552)
PHONE.................................828 287-8787
Michael Dietz, *Prin*
EMP: 7 **EST:** 2010
SALES (est): 67.15K **Privately Held**
SIC: 3421 Table and food cutlery, including butchers'

(G-13879)
HENDRENS RACG ENGS CHASSIS INC
1310 Us 221 Hwy N (28139-9507)
PHONE.................................828 286-0780
Bill Hendren, *Pr*
Steve Hendren, *VP*
Bettie Hendren, *Sec*
▼ **EMP:** 6 **EST:** 1977
SQ FT: 7,500
SALES (est): 554.16K **Privately Held**
Web: www.hendrensracingengines.com
SIC: 3714 Motor vehicle parts and accessories

(G-13880)
MN LOGGING LLC
449 Mountain Creek Rd (28139-8634)
PHONE.................................828 286-9262
EMP: 6 **EST:** 2020
SALES (est): 246.89K **Privately Held**
SIC: 2411 Logging

(G-13881)
PACKAGING CORPORATION AMERICA
Pca/Rutherfordton 373
321 Industrial Park Rd (28139-2542)
PHONE.................................828 286-9356
Peter Anzenberger, *Mgr*
EMP: 50
SALES (corp-wide): 8.48B **Publicly Held**
Web: www.packagingcorp.com
SIC: 2653 Boxes, corrugated: made from purchased materials
PA: Packaging Corporation Of America
 1 N Field Ct
 Lake Forest IL 60045
 847 482-3000

(G-13882)
PARTON FOREST PRODUCTS INC
251 Parton Rd (28139-8116)
PHONE.................................828 287-4257
Furman Parton, *Pr*
Patrick Parton, *Sec*
▼ **EMP:** 4 **EST:** 1996
SALES (est): 844.23K
SALES (corp-wide): 16.52MM **Privately Held**
Web: www.partonlumber.com
SIC: 2421 Sawmills and planing mills, general
PA: Parton Lumber Company, Inc.
 251 Parton Rd
 Rutherfordton NC 28139
 828 287-4257

(G-13883)
PARTON LUMBER COMPANY INC (PA)
Also Called: Parton Export
251 Parton Rd (28139-8116)
PHONE.................................828 287-4257
Carl F Parton, *Pr*
Scott Hughes, *
▼ **EMP:** 83 **EST:** 1937
SQ FT: 1,500
SALES (est): 16.52MM
SALES (corp-wide): 16.52MM **Privately Held**
Web: www.partonlumber.com
SIC: 2421 2426 Planing mills, nec; Lumber, hardwood dimension

(G-13884)
PEPSI BOTTLING GROUP
Also Called: Pepsico
1621 Poors Ford Rd (28139-8728)
PHONE.................................828 286-4406
EMP: 6 **EST:** 2018
SALES (est): 135.03K **Privately Held**
Web: www.pepsibottlingventures.com
SIC: 2086 Carbonated soft drinks, bottled and canned

(G-13885)
PRITCHARD LOGGING LLC
1651 Piney Knob Rd (28139-8528)
PHONE.................................828 447-4354
Ethan Pritchard, *Managing Member*
EMP: 6 **EST:** 2017
SALES (est): 258.77K **Privately Held**
SIC: 2411 Logging

(G-13886)
RCM INDUSTRIES INC
Also Called: Aallied Die Casting of N C
401 Aallied Dr (28139-2990)
PHONE.................................828 286-4003
Mike Nowak, *Mgr*
EMP: 150
Web: www.rcmindustries.com
SIC: 3363 3365 Aluminum die-castings; Aluminum foundries
PA: R.C.M. Industries, Inc.
 3021 Cullerton St
 Franklin Park IL 60131

(G-13887)
RUFFTON BREWHOUSE
177 N Main St (28139-2501)
P.O. Box 1095 (28139-1095)
PHONE.................................828 289-8060
Mary Mooney, *Prin*
EMP: 5 **EST:** 2016
SALES (est): 150.2K **Privately Held**
Web: www.rufftonbrewhouse.com
SIC: 3949 Hunting equipment

(G-13888)
S & B SCENTS INC
555 Mcentire Rd (28139-7652)
PHONE.................................828 287-9410
David C Smith, *Prin*
EMP: 6 **EST:** 2010
SALES (est): 66.33K **Privately Held**
SIC: 2844 Perfumes, cosmetics and other toilet preparations

(G-13889)
S RUPPE INC
Also Called: Liberty Press
137 Taylor St (28139-2558)
P.O. Box 837 (28139-0837)
PHONE.................................828 287-4936
Edward R Ruppe, *Pr*
Ethel Ruppe, *
Diane Ruppe, *
EMP: 24 **EST:** 1940
SALES (est): 2MM **Privately Held**
Web: www.libertypressonline.com
SIC: 5112 2752 2791 2789 Business forms; Offset printing; Typesetting; Bookbinding and related work

(G-13890)
SAVATECH CORP
715 Railroad Ave (28139-2207)
PHONE.................................386 760-0706
Izidor Debenc, *Pr*
David Lander, *Ex VP*
▲ **EMP:** 6 **EST:** 1999
SQ FT: 8,000
SALES (est): 1.95MM **Privately Held**
Web: www.savatrade.com
SIC: 3069 Hard rubber and molded rubber products
HQ: Sava, D.D.
 Dunajska Cesta 152
 Ljubljana 1000

(G-13891)
STEVE WHITESIDE LOGGING LLC
136 Matthew Church Rd (28139-8359)
PHONE.................................828 287-5862
Charles Steven Whiteside, *Admn*
EMP: 5 **EST:** 2017
SALES (est): 98.88K **Privately Held**
SIC: 2411 Logging

(G-13892)
SUNRAY INC
4761 Us 64 74a Hwy (28139-6322)
PHONE.................................828 287-7030
EMP: 30 **EST:** 1976
SALES (est): 5.38MM **Privately Held**
Web: www.sunray-inc.com
SIC: 3089 2822 3429 Molding primary plastics; Synthetic rubber; Hardware, nec

(G-13893)
TOOL-WELD LLC
180 Cross Ridge Dr (28139-6437)
PHONE.................................843 986-4931
Juhn Anthony Zucker Senior, *Pr*
Rose Mary Zucker, *VP*
▼ **EMP:** 4 **EST:** 1960
SALES (est): 900K **Privately Held**
Web: www.toolweld.com
SIC: 7692 Welding repair

(G-13894)
TRELLEBORG CTD SYSTEMS US INC
Also Called: Atg Division
715 Railroad Ave (28139-2207)
P.O. Box 929 (28139-0929)
PHONE.................................864 576-1210
EMP: 211
SALES (corp-wide): 276.11MM **Privately Held**
SIC: 2261 2231 Finishing plants, cotton; Fabric finishing: wool, mohair, or similar fibers
PA: Trelleborg Coated Systems Us, Inc.
 715 Railroad Ave
 Rutherfordton NC 28139
 828 286-9126

(G-13895)
TRELLEBORG CTD SYSTEMS US INC
Also Called: Engineered Coated Fabrics
631 Rock Rd (28139-8123)
PHONE.................................828 286-9126
EMP: 48
SALES (corp-wide): 276.11MM **Privately Held**
SIC: 2295 Coated fabrics, not rubberized
PA: Trelleborg Coated Systems Us, Inc.
 715 Railroad Ave
 Rutherfordton NC 28139
 828 286-9126

(G-13896)
TRELLEBORG CTD SYSTEMS US INC (PA)
715 Railroad Ave (28139-2207)
PHONE.................................828 286-9126
Patric Vestlund, *Pr*
Jessie Marlowe, *
Jennifer Walker, *
Thomas Yaczik, *
▲ **EMP:** 170 **EST:** 1937
SQ FT: 43,000
SALES (est): 276.11MM
SALES (corp-wide): 276.11MM **Privately Held**
SIC: 2295 2221 2394 2396 Coated fabrics, not rubberized; Manmade and synthetic broadwoven fabrics; Tarpaulins, fabric: made from purchased materials; Automotive and apparel trimmings

(G-13897)
TRELLEBORG CTD SYSTEMS US INC
Also Called: Industrial Ctd Fabrics Group
715 Railroad Ave (28139-2207)
PHONE.................................828 286-9126
Mark Patterson, *Brnch Mgr*
EMP: 121
SALES (corp-wide): 276.11MM **Privately Held**
Web: www.trelleborg.com
SIC: 3069 2824 Rubber coated fabrics and clothing; Vinyl fibers
PA: Trelleborg Coated Systems Us, Inc.
 715 Railroad Ave
 Rutherfordton NC 28139
 828 286-9126

(G-13898)
ULTIMATE TEXTILE INC
1437 Us 221 Hwy S (28139)
P.O. Box 1465 (28139-1465)
PHONE.................................828 286-8880
▲ **EMP:** 35 **EST:** 1994
SQ FT: 100,000
SALES (est): 7.17MM **Privately Held**
Web: www.ultimatetextileinc.com
SIC: 2269 2261 Finishing plants, nec; Finishing plants, cotton

(G-13899)
URETEK LLC
715 Railroad Ave (28139-2207)
PHONE.................................203 468-0342
Milton Berlinski, *Managing Member*
Stuart Press, *
◆ **EMP:** 48 **EST:** 2006
SALES (est): 1.91MM **Privately Held**
Web: www.trelleborg.com
SIC: 2295 Resin or plastic coated fabrics

(G-13900)
US PRECISION CABINETRY LLC
Also Called: Touchstone Fine Cabinetry
160 Executive Dr (28139-2929)

Rutherfordton - Rutherford County (G-13901)   GEOGRAPHIC SECTION

P.O. Box 2141 (28139-4341)
PHONE..................................828 351-2020
Chris Britton, *Managing Member*
EMP: 100 EST: 2018
SALES (est): 8MM **Privately Held**
SIC: 2434 Wood kitchen cabinets

(G-13901)
WATKINS WLDG FABRICATIONS LLC
1583 Big Island Rd (28139-8764)
PHONE..................................828 429-2369
Deborah Watkins, *Prin*
EMP: 5 EST: 2019
SALES (est): 74.65K **Privately Held**
SIC: 7692 Welding repair

(G-13902)
WHITE WOLF PRESS LLC
961 Painters Gap Rd (28139-9519)
PHONE..................................828 288-2077
Brian K Rathbone, *Prin*
EMP: 5 EST: 2008
SALES (est): 180K **Privately Held**
SIC: 2741 Miscellaneous publishing

(G-13903)
WRKCO INC
300 Broyhill Rd (28139-9612)
PHONE..................................828 287-9430
EMP: 4
SALES (corp-wide): 20.31B **Publicly Held**
SIC: 2653 Boxes, corrugated: made from purchased materials
HQ: Wrkco Inc.
    1000 Abernathy Rd Ste 12
    Atlanta GA 30328
    770 448-2193

Saint Pauls
Robeson County

(G-13904)
CORNEY TRANSPORTATION INC
19214 Us Highway 301 N (28384-7443)
P.O. Box 385 (28384-0385)
PHONE..................................800 354-9111
Bobby R Corney, *Pr*
EMP: 23 EST: 1996
SALES (est): 12.24MM **Privately Held**
Web: www.corneytransportation.com
SIC: 2653 Boxes, corrugated: made from purchased materials

(G-13905)
ELIZONDO LLC
Also Called: Tortillas Carolina
106 W Clark St Ste B (28384-1712)
PHONE..................................910 590-6550
EMP: 5 EST: 2015
SALES (est): 165.02K **Privately Held**
SIC: 2099 Tortillas, fresh or refrigerated

(G-13906)
MUELLER STEAM SPECIALTY (DH)
Also Called: Mueller Steam Specialty
1491 Nc Highway 20 W (28384-9209)
PHONE..................................910 865-8241
David Palmer, *CEO*
Cameron Sheets, *
◆ EMP: 89 EST: 1956
SALES (est): 25.31MM
SALES (corp-wide): 2.06B **Publicly Held**
Web: www.watts.com
SIC: 3491 Industrial valves
HQ: Watts Regulator Co.
    815 Chestnut St
    North Andover MA 01845
    978 689-6000

(G-13907)
PEPSI BOTTLING VENTURES LLC
Also Called: Pepsico
137 Pepsi Way (28384-5400)
PHONE..................................910 865-1600
David Graham, *Mgr*
EMP: 96
Web: www.pepsibottlingventures.com
SIC: 2086 Carbonated soft drinks, bottled and canned
HQ: Pepsi Bottling Ventures Llc
    4141 Parklake Ave Ste 600
    Raleigh NC 27612
    919 865-2300

(G-13908)
PRESTAGE FOODS INC
4470 Nc Hwy 20 E (28384)
PHONE..................................910 865-6611
John Prestage, *Pr*
John Hott, *
Scott Prestage, *
Ron Prestage, *
▼ EMP: 350 EST: 2000
SQ FT: 210,000
SALES (est): 72.84MM
SALES (corp-wide): 174.84MM **Privately Held**
Web: www.prestagefarms.com
SIC: 2015 Turkey, processed, nsk
PA: Prestage Farms, Inc.
    4651 Taylors Bridge Hwy
    Clinton NC 28328
    910 596-5700

(G-13909)
SANDERSON FARMS LLC PROC DIV
Also Called: St Pauls, NC Processing Plant
2076 Nc Highway 20 W (28384-5501)
PHONE..................................910 274-0220
EMP: 896
SALES (corp-wide): 4.8B **Privately Held**
Web: www.sandersonfarms.com
SIC: 2015 Chicken, slaughtered and dressed
HQ: Sanderson Farms, Llc (Processing Division)
    127 Flynt Rd
    Laurel MS 39443
    601 649-4030

(G-13910)
WATTS REGULATOR
1491 Nc Highway 20 W (28384-9209)
PHONE..................................978 689-6066
EMP: 9 EST: 2020
SALES (est): 1.1MM **Privately Held**
Web: www.watts.com
SIC: 3491 Industrial valves

Salisbury
Rowan County

(G-13911)
A-1 COATINGS
525 Linda St (28146-1158)
PHONE..................................704 790-9528
EMP: 5
SALES (est): 237.93K **Privately Held**
SIC: 3479 Metal coating and allied services

(G-13912)
ABILITY ORTHOPEDICS
209 Statesville Blvd (28144-2313)
P.O. Box 9526 (28603-9526)
PHONE..................................704 630-6789
James P Rubel, *Owner*
EMP: 4 EST: 2000
SQ FT: 1,260
SALES (est): 420.77K **Privately Held**
Web: www.ncability.com
SIC: 3842 Orthopedic appliances

(G-13913)
ACCEL DISCOUNT TIRE (PA)
201 E Liberty St (28144)
PHONE..................................704 636-0323
Darryl White, *Owner*
EMP: 6 EST: 1935
SQ FT: 7,000
SALES (est): 921.18K
SALES (corp-wide): 921.18K **Privately Held**
Web: www.micasakb.com
SIC: 5531 7389 7534 5722 Automotive tires; Drive-a-way automobile service; Tire recapping; Electric household appliances

(G-13914)
ADVANCED MACHINING TOOLING LLC
Also Called: Advanced Machining
215 Forbes Ave (28147-6930)
PHONE..................................704 633-8157
Keith A Felts, *Pr*
Bobby L Miller, *VP*
EMP: 8 EST: 1985
SQ FT: 4,800
SALES (est): 1.06MM **Privately Held**
Web: www.advancedmachiningcnc.com
SIC: 3599 Machine shop, jobbing and repair

(G-13915)
AGILITY FUEL SYSTEMS LLC
1010 Corporate Center Dr (28146-8626)
PHONE..................................704 870-3520
Shawn Adelsberger, *Mgr*
EMP: 6
Web: www.hexagonagility.com
SIC: 1389 1623 3443 Gas compressing (natural gas) at the fields; Natural gas compressor station construction; Tank towers, metal plate
HQ: Agility Fuel Systems, Llc
    1815 Carnegie Ave
    Santa Ana CA 92705

(G-13916)
AIRGAS USA LLC
Also Called: Airgas
1924 S Main St (28146-6714)
P.O. Box 2125 (28145-2125)
PHONE..................................704 636-5049
Steve Simpson, *Mgr*
EMP: 8
SALES (corp-wide): 101.26MM **Privately Held**
Web: www.airgas.com
SIC: 5084 7692 Welding machinery and equipment; Welding repair
HQ: Airgas Usa, Llc
    259 N Radnor Chester Rd
    Radnor PA 19087
    216 642-6600

(G-13917)
ALAN LANE WESLEY
580 Daves Dr (28146-9440)
PHONE..................................704 433-8338
EMP: 4 EST: 2018
SALES (est): 57.99K **Privately Held**
SIC: 2451 Mobile homes

(G-13918)
ALDO PRODUCTS COMPANY INC
1320 Litton Dr (28147-9379)
PHONE..................................704 932-3054
Robert Brenk, *Pr*
Willi Kramer, *Ch*
Christine Brenk, *Stockholder*
▲ EMP: 9 EST: 1980
SQ FT: 10,000
SALES (est): 2.69MM **Privately Held**
Web: www.aldocoatings.com
SIC: 2851 2891 Coating, air curing; Adhesives

(G-13919)
ALLISON BROTHERS RACE CARS INC
7920 Statesville Blvd (28147-7498)
PHONE..................................704 278-0174
Kenneth J Allison, *Pr*
Ronald J Allison, *Sec*
EMP: 15 EST: 1988
SALES (est): 394.73K **Privately Held**
Web: www.allisonlegacy.com
SIC: 3711 Automobile assembly, including specialty automobiles

(G-13920)
ALLOYWORKS LLC
814 W Innes St (28144-4152)
PHONE..................................704 645-0511
William Russell Chinnis, *Pt*
▲ EMP: 15 EST: 2001
SALES (est): 2.55MM **Privately Held**
SIC: 3339 Precious metals

(G-13921)
AMREP INC
1405 Julian Rd (28146-2322)
PHONE..................................704 949-2595
EMP: 51
Web: www.amrepproducts.com
SIC: 3713 Truck bodies (motor vehicles)
HQ: Amrep, Inc.
    6525 Carnegie Blvd # 300
    Charlotte NC 28211
    909 923-0430

(G-13922)
APPLE BAKING COMPANY INC
4470 Hampton Rd (28144-1202)
PHONE..................................704 637-6800
Robert Watts, *Pr*
Jeff Haas, *Contrlr*
EMP: 20 EST: 1984
SALES (est): 1.7MM **Privately Held**
Web: www.applebaking.com
SIC: 2051 Bread, cake, and related products

(G-13923)
ARTCRAFT TUMBLERS
3220 Old Union Church Rd (28146-7930)
PHONE..................................704 798-6115
Paulette Nicholas, *Prin*
EMP: 4 EST: 2019
SALES (est): 117.55K **Privately Held**
SIC: 2813 Neon

(G-13924)
ATHENA MARBLE INCORPORATED
7400 Bringle Ferry Rd (28146-7154)
PHONE..................................704 636-7810
Alan R Jones, *Pr*
Jean Jones, *Treas*
EMP: 12 EST: 1973
SQ FT: 6,000
SALES (est): 448.41K **Privately Held**
SIC: 3261 3281 Vitreous plumbing fixtures; Bathroom fixtures, cut stone

(G-13925)
ATLANTIC MFG & FABRICATION INC
705 S Railroad St Unit 1 (28144-5665)
PHONE..................................704 647-6200
EMP: 5 EST: 2009
SALES (est): 156.03K **Privately Held**
SIC: 3999 Manufacturing industries, nec

GEOGRAPHIC SECTION

Salisbury - Rowan County (G-13949)

(G-13926)
AZ FAUX
1910 Saint Luke Church Rd (28146-7956)
PHONE..............................704 279-0114
EMP: 5 EST: 2019
SALES (est): 448.65K Privately Held
Web: www.azfauxbeams.com
SIC: 2431 Millwork

(G-13927)
B & B MACHINE CO INC
1890 Barringer Rd (28147-9518)
PHONE..............................704 637-2356
Danny Bogle, Pr
Rick Bogle, VP
EMP: 8 EST: 1986
SQ FT: 7,000
SALES (est): 828.15K Privately Held
SIC: 3599 Machine shop, jobbing and repair

(G-13928)
B V HEDRICK GRAVEL & SAND CO (PA)
Also Called: Grove Stone & Sand Division
120 1/2 N Church St (28144-4311)
P.O. Box 1040 (28145-1040)
PHONE..............................704 633-5982
Jeffrey V Goodman, Pr
Frances H Johnson, *
Jane B Arnold, *
Joanne Johnson, *
Artie Hattaway, *
EMP: 50 EST: 1924
SQ FT: 2,000
SALES (est): 238.17MM
SALES (corp-wide): 238.17MM Privately Held
Web: www.hedrickind.com
SIC: 1442 7359 6512 3273 Construction sand mining; Equipment rental and leasing, nec; Commercial and industrial building operation; Ready-mixed concrete

(G-13929)
BAILEYS QUICK COPY SHOP INC (PA)
Also Called: Quick Copy Print Shop
324 E Fisher St (28144-5002)
P.O. Box 1527 (28145-1527)
PHONE..............................704 637-2020
Robert R Bailey, Pr
Mary Ellen Bailey, Ex VP
EMP: 14 EST: 1973
SQ FT: 4,320
SALES (est): 1.3MM
SALES (corp-wide): 1.3MM Privately Held
SIC: 2752 Offset printing

(G-13930)
BOSMERE INC
Also Called: The Wynsum Gardener
2701 S Main St (28147-7901)
P.O. Box 2267 (28145-2267)
PHONE..............................704 784-1608
Patrick Rykens, Pr
Susan Rykens, VP
▲ EMP: 12 EST: 1988
SQ FT: 20,000
SALES (est): 1.73MM Privately Held
Web: www.bosmereusa.com
SIC: 3524 Lawn and garden equipment

(G-13931)
CANVAS OF FLESH
6295 S Main St (28147-8301)
PHONE..............................980 234-5957
EMP: 4 EST: 2009
SALES (est): 67.98K Privately Held
SIC: 2211 Canvas

(G-13932)
CAROLINA BEVERAGE CORPORATION (PA)
Also Called: Cheerwine
1413 Jake Alexander Blvd S (28146-8359)
P.O. Box 697 (28145-0697)
PHONE..............................704 636-2191
Cliff Ritchie, CEO
Mark Ritchie, *
Raymond Ritchie, *
Tommy Page, *
EMP: 25 EST: 1917
SQ FT: 35,000
SALES (est): 16.65MM
SALES (corp-wide): 16.65MM Privately Held
Web: www.cheerwine.com
SIC: 2086 Bottled and canned soft drinks

(G-13933)
CAROLINA BOTTLING COMPANY
1413 Jake Alexander Blvd S (28146-8359)
P.O. Box 697 (28145-0697)
PHONE..............................704 637-5869
EMP: 72 EST: 1994
SQ FT: 35,000
SALES (est): 4.65MM
SALES (corp-wide): 16.65MM Privately Held
Web: www.cheerwine.com
SIC: 2086 Bottled and canned soft drinks
PA: Carolina Beverage Corporation
    1413 Jake Alxander Blvd S
    Salisbury NC 28146
    704 636-2191

(G-13934)
CAROLINA CUSTOM RUBBER INC
5415 Statesville Blvd (28147-7473)
P.O. Box 459 (27013-0459)
PHONE..............................704 636-6989
Bob Clester, Pr
Karen Clester, Sec
EMP: 8 EST: 1983
SQ FT: 2,000
SALES (est): 676.84K Privately Held
Web: www.carolinacustomrubber.com
SIC: 3069 3061 Foam rubber; Mechanical rubber goods

(G-13935)
CAROLINA PRINT WORKS INC
Also Called: Lewis Frank Specialty Products
600 N Long St Ste B (28144-4421)
P.O. Box 2581 (28145-2581)
PHONE..............................704 637-6902
▲ EMP: 10 EST: 1992
SQ FT: 20,000
SALES (est): 869.39K Privately Held
Web: www.carolinaprintworks.com
SIC: 3089 Novelties, plastics

(G-13936)
CAROLINA QUARRIES INC (PA)
Also Called: Rock of Ages
805 Harris Granite Rd (28146-7810)
PHONE..............................704 633-0201
EMP: 60 EST: 1991
SALES (est): 8.26MM Privately Held
SIC: 1411 3281 Dimension stone; Granite, cut and shaped

(G-13937)
CAROLINA STALITE CO LTD PARTNR (PA)
205 Klumac Rd (28144-6723)
P.O. Box 1037 (28145-1037)
PHONE..............................704 637-1515
Frances H Johnson, Mng Pt
EMP: 10 EST: 1972
SALES (est): 22.99MM
SALES (corp-wide): 22.99MM Privately Held
Web: www.stalite.com
SIC: 3281 0711 Slate products; Soil chemical treatment services

(G-13938)
CAROLINA STAMPING COMPANY
701 Corporate Cir (28147-7220)
PHONE..............................704 637-0260
Daniel Cronin, Pr
EMP: 55 EST: 1977
SQ FT: 27,000
SALES (est): 9.43MM
SALES (corp-wide): 18.64MM Privately Held
Web: www.carolinastamping.com
SIC: 3469 Stamping metal for the trade
PA: W.L.S. Stamping Co.
    3292 E 80th St
    Cleveland OH 44104
    216 271-5100

(G-13939)
CHANDLER CONCRETE INC
Also Called: Chandler Concrete & Bldg Sup
400 N Long St (28144-4455)
P.O. Box 139 (28145-0139)
PHONE..............................704 636-4711
Ed Williams, Genl Mgr
EMP: 77
Web: www.chandlerconcrete.com
SIC: 3273 1771 Ready-mixed concrete; Concrete work
PA: Chandler Concrete Co., Inc.
    1006 S Church St
    Burlington NC 27215

(G-13940)
CHARTER DURA-BAR INC
Also Called: Durabar Metals Services Div
770 Cedar Springs Rd (28147-9252)
PHONE..............................704 637-1906
Jim Lewis, Opers Mgr
EMP: 19
SALES (corp-wide): 570.48MM Privately Held
Web: www.dura-barms.com
SIC: 5051 3599 Steel; Machine shop, jobbing and repair
HQ: Charter Dura-Bar, Inc.
    2100 W Lake Shore Dr
    Woodstock IL 60098
    815 338-3900

(G-13941)
CHROMA COLOR CORPORATION
100 E 17th St (28144-2980)
PHONE..............................704 637-7000
Matt Barr, Prin
EMP: 141
SALES (corp-wide): 117.78MM Privately Held
Web: www.chromacolors.com
SIC: 2821 Plastics materials and resins
PA: Chroma Color Corporation
    3900 W Dayton St
    Mchenry IL 60050
    877 385-8777

(G-13942)
CLAY TAYLOR PRODUCTS INC
1225 Chuck Taylor Ln (28147-9813)
P.O. Box 2128 (28145-2128)
PHONE..............................704 636-2411
Charles D Taylor Junior, Pr
Barbara Johnson, *
Burton Benfield, *
▲ EMP: 100 EST: 1949
SQ FT: 212,000
SALES (est): 15.2MM Privately Held
Web: www.taylorclaybrick.com
SIC: 3251 Brick and structural clay tile

(G-13943)
CMW MANUFACTURING LLC
1217 Speedway Blvd (28146-7448)
PHONE..............................704 216-0171
Scott Lowrie, Pr
EMP: 35 EST: 2014
SQ FT: 40,000
SALES (est): 4.32MM Privately Held
Web: www.cmwmfg.com
SIC: 3441 Fabricated structural metal

(G-13944)
COMPASS WOODWORKS CO
440 Waters Rd (28146-7984)
PHONE..............................704 232-0272
Bradford Taylor, Prin
EMP: 5 EST: 2018
SALES (est): 74.37K Privately Held
Web: www.compasswoodworksco.com
SIC: 2431 Millwork

(G-13945)
CONCISE MANUFACTURING INC
630 Corporate Cir (28147-9004)
PHONE..............................704 796-8419
EMP: 8 EST: 2019
SALES (est): 506.91K Privately Held
Web: www.concisecnc.com
SIC: 3999 Manufacturing industries, nec

(G-13946)
CONTEMPORARY FURNISHINGS CORP (PA)
Also Called: Carter Furniture
1000 N Long St (28144-3834)
P.O. Box 117 (28388-0117)
PHONE..............................704 633-8000
Robert Logan, Ch Bd
Lloyd Davis, *
Bill Ward, *
Luke Fisher, *
Michael Murray, *
◆ EMP: 85 EST: 1968
SQ FT: 121,000
SALES (est): 4.35MM
SALES (corp-wide): 4.35MM Privately Held
SIC: 2512 2599 Couches, sofas, and davenports; upholstered on wood frames; Hotel furniture

(G-13947)
CONVEYING SOLUTIONS LLC
Also Called: Conveying Solutions LLC NC
804 Julian Rd (28147-9080)
PHONE..............................704 636-4241
EMP: 10 EST: 2009
SALES (est): 942.9K Privately Held
Web: www.csllc.us
SIC: 3535 Conveyors and conveying equipment

(G-13948)
CROCHET BY SUE
533 Fairbluff Ave (28146-4711)
PHONE..............................201 723-4906
Assunta Peluso, Prin
EMP: 4 EST: 2017
SALES (est): 44.65K Privately Held
SIC: 2399 Hand woven and crocheted products

(G-13949)
CUMBERLAND GRAVEL & SAND CO
P.O. Box 1040 (28145-1040)
PHONE..............................704 633-4241

Salisbury - Rowan County (G-13950)

Donald B Hensley, *Pr*
Robert Settle Iii, *VP*
Anthony M Arnold, *VP*
F Joanne Johnson, *Sec*
Jeffrey V Goodman, *Treas*
EMP: 12 **EST:** 1949
SALES (est): 289.04K **Privately Held**
SIC: 1442 Construction sand and gravel

(G-13950)
CUSTOM CABINETS BY LIVENGOOD
490 Parks Rd (28146-1189)
PHONE.................................704 279-3031
Billy Livengood, *Owner*
EMP: 6 **EST:** 1961
SQ FT: 15,000
SALES (est): 470.16K **Privately Held**
SIC: 2434 2521 Wood kitchen cabinets; Cabinets, office: wood

(G-13951)
CUSTOM DESIGN INC
2001 S Main St (28144-6833)
P.O. Box 835 (28145-0835)
PHONE.................................704 637-7110
Lynn Butler, *Pr*
EMP: 9 **EST:** 2006
SALES (est): 958.19K **Privately Held**
Web: www.hydraulicdepotnc.com
SIC: 3449 Miscellaneous metalwork

(G-13952)
CUSTOM GOLF CAR SUPPLY INC
Also Called: Custom Plastic Forming
1735 Heilig Rd (28146-2314)
PHONE.................................704 855-1130
Jeffrey S Martin, *Pr*
◆ **EMP:** 174 **EST:** 1991
SQ FT: 86,000
SALES (est): 26.17MM **Privately Held**
Web: www.doubletakegolfcar.com
SIC: 2394 3949 Canopies, fabric: made from purchased materials; Golf equipment

(G-13953)
DIMENSIONAL METALS INC
819 S Salisbury Ave (28146)
PHONE.................................704 279-9691
Steve Wissman, *Pr*
EMP: 7
Web: www.dmimetals.com
SIC: 3531 1761 Roofing equipment; Roofing, siding, and sheetmetal work
PA: Dimensional Metals, Inc.
58 Klema Dr N
Reynoldsburg OH 43068

(G-13954)
DOWNTOWN GRAPHICS NETWORK INC
1409 S Fulton St (28144-6411)
P.O. Box 4216 (28145-4216)
PHONE.................................704 637-0855
Diane M Young, *Pr*
Michael Young, *VP*
◆ **EMP:** 7 **EST:** 1988
SQ FT: 3,500
SALES (est): 596.46K **Privately Held**
Web: www.materialpromotions.com
SIC: 2399 2674 1521 Banners, made from fabric; Shopping bags: made from purchased materials; Single-family housing construction

(G-13955)
DUDLEY INC
Old Carolina Brick Company
475 Majolica Rd (28147-8010)
PHONE.................................704 636-8850
Art Burkhart, *VP*
EMP: 9

SALES (corp-wide): 4.83MM **Privately Held**
Web: www.handmadebrick.com
SIC: 3251 Brick clay: common face, glazed, vitrified, or hollow
PA: Dudley Inc
705 Quintard Ave
Anniston AL 36201
256 237-2890

(G-13956)
DURAFIBER TECHNOLOGIES DFT INC
7401 Statesville Blvd (28147-7493)
PHONE.................................704 639-2722
EMP: 7
SALES (corp-wide): 17.78B **Privately Held**
SIC: 2824 Organic fibers, noncellulosic
HQ: Durafiber Technologies (Dft), Inc.
13620 Reese Blvd E # 400
Huntersville NC 28078
704 912-3700

(G-13957)
EASTERN WHOLESALE FENCE LLC
7401 Statesville Blvd (28147-1000)
PHONE.................................631 698-0975
EMP: 94
SALES (corp-wide): 96.51MM **Privately Held**
Web: www.easternfence.com
SIC: 5039 3496 Wire fence, gates, and accessories; Barbed wire, made from purchased wire
PA: Eastern Wholesale Fence Llc
266 Middle Island Rd A
Medford NY 11763
631 698-0900

(G-13958)
EPK LLC
Also Called: Epk Industrial Solutions
425 Klumac Rd (28144-6727)
PHONE.................................980 643-4787
Paul Kennedy, *VP Engg*
EMP: 10 **EST:** 2018
SALES (est): 910K **Privately Held**
SIC: 3711 Motor vehicles and car bodies

(G-13959)
EVER GLO SIGN CO INC
4975 S Main St (28147-9388)
P.O. Box 1349 (28145-1349)
PHONE.................................704 633-3324
Robert Gainer, *Pr*
Joseph J Gainer, *Sec*
EMP: 7 **EST:** 1920
SQ FT: 15,000
SALES (est): 247.16K **Privately Held**
SIC: 3993 3441 Electric signs; Fabricated structural metal

(G-13960)
EXTENSIVE BUILDERS LLC
2604 Old Wilkesboro Rd (28144-3073)
PHONE.................................980 621-3793
EMP: 5
SALES (est): 126.55K **Privately Held**
SIC: 1389 7389 Construction, repair, and dismantling services; Business services, nec

(G-13961)
FAB DESIGNS INCORPORATED
2231 Old Wilkesboro Rd (28144-3042)
PHONE.................................704 636-2349
Lee Gillespie, *Pr*
EMP: 5 **EST:** 2002
SALES (est): 892.24K **Privately Held**
Web: www.fabdesignsinc.com

SIC: 3441 Fabricated structural metal

(G-13962)
FADING D FARM LLC
295 Fading D Farm Rd (28144-9562)
PHONE.................................704 633-3888
David Diloreto, *Prin*
EMP: 4 **EST:** 2014
SALES (est): 96.38K **Privately Held**
Web: www.fadingdfarm.com
SIC: 0191 2022 0241 General farms, primarily crop; Natural cheese; Dairy farms

(G-13963)
FAITH FARM INC
585 W Ritchie Rd Ste A (28147-8176)
PHONE.................................704 431-4566
Tim Ervin, *Pr*
Pam Ervin, *VP*
EMP: 4 **EST:** 1995
SALES (est): 584.26K **Privately Held**
Web: www.faithfarm.com
SIC: 3799 5999 Trailers and trailer equipment; Alarm and safety equipment stores

(G-13964)
FEE KEES WREATHS LLC
1047 Landsdown Dr (28147-9048)
PHONE.................................704 636-1008
EMP: 5 **EST:** 2020
SALES (est): 150.7K **Privately Held**
SIC: 3999 Wreaths, artificial

(G-13965)
FISHER ATHLETIC EQUIPMENT INC
2060 Cauble Rd (28144-1506)
P.O. Box 1985 (28145-1985)
PHONE.................................704 636-5713
Robert Pritchard, *Pr*
Brian Pritchard, *
EMP: 45 **EST:** 1959
SQ FT: 50,000
SALES (est): 13.47MM
SALES (corp-wide): 13.47MM **Privately Held**
SIC: 3949 2393 Sporting and athletic goods, nec; Textile bags
PA: Pritchard Enterprises, Inc.
2060 Cauble Rd
Salisbury NC 28144
704 636-5713

(G-13966)
FREIRICH FOODS INC
815 W Kerr St (28144-3241)
P.O. Box 1529 (28145-1529)
PHONE.................................704 636-2621
Paul Bardinas, *Pr*
Digna Freirich, *Sec*
Jerry Freirich, *Ch*
Doug Sokolwski, *CFO*
EMP: 105 **EST:** 1921
SQ FT: 50,000
SALES (est): 24.72MM **Privately Held**
Web: www.freirich.com
SIC: 2011 2013 Meat packing plants; Sausages and other prepared meats

(G-13967)
GGS WOODWORKING
1725 Lower Palmer Rd (28146-8195)
PHONE.................................704 279-5482
Joe Freeze, *Prin*
EMP: 5 **EST:** 2010
SALES (est): 158.34K **Privately Held**
SIC: 2431 Millwork

(G-13968)
GILDAN YARNS LLC
2121 Heilig Rd (28146-2316)
PHONE.................................704 633-5133
Shannon Preston, *VP*
Andrew Colvin, *Sec*
◆ **EMP:** 5 **EST:** 2003
SALES (est): 2.54MM
SALES (corp-wide): 3.24B **Privately Held**
Web: www.gildanyarns.com
SIC: 2281 Yarn spinning mills
PA: Les Vetements De Sport Gildan Inc
600 Boul De Maisonneuve O 33eme Etage
Montreal QC H3A 3
514 735-2023

(G-13969)
GILLESPIES FBRCTION DESIGN INC
Also Called: Gillespies Fabrication Design
2231 Old Wilkesboro Rd (28144-3042)
PHONE.................................704 636-2349
Ligon Lee Gillespie, *Pr*
EMP: 5 **EST:** 1927
SQ FT: 40,000
SALES (est): 452.44K **Privately Held**
Web: www.fabdesignsinc.com
SIC: 1799 3599 3949 Welding on site; Machine shop, jobbing and repair; Sporting and athletic goods, nec

(G-13970)
GLOBAL ENVMTL CTRL III INC
585 Bonanza Dr (28144-9424)
PHONE.................................704 603-6155
Osiris L Coello, *Prin*
EMP: 4 **EST:** 2019
SALES (est): 88.96K **Privately Held**
SIC: 3822 Environmental controls

(G-13971)
GOLF SHOP
747 Club Dr (28144)
PHONE.................................704 636-7070
Randy Padavic, *Owner*
EMP: 5 **EST:** 1983
SALES (est): 247.12K **Privately Held**
Web: www.ccofsalisbury.com
SIC: 3949 Golf equipment

(G-13972)
GOODMAN MILLWORK INC
201 Lumber St (28144-6553)
P.O. Box 859 (28145-0859)
PHONE.................................704 633-2421
Francis E Goodman, *Pr*
Brenda M Goodman, *
EMP: 25 **EST:** 1907
SQ FT: 67,000
SALES (est): 1.87MM **Privately Held**
Web: www.goodmanmillwork.com
SIC: 2431 5211 Millwork; Lumber and other building materials

(G-13973)
GRANGES AMERICAS INC
1709 Jake Alexander Blvd S (28146-8365)
PHONE.................................704 633-6020
Bean Stout, *Mgr*
EMP: 105
SQ FT: 11,310
SALES (corp-wide): 2.31B **Privately Held**
Web: www.granges.com
SIC: 3353 3497 Foil, aluminum; Metal foil and leaf
HQ: Granges Americas Inc.
501 Corporate Centre Dr # 280
Franklin TN 37067
615 778-2004

GEOGRAPHIC SECTION

Salisbury - Rowan County (G-13997)

(G-13974)
GRINDTEC ENTERPRISES CORP
3402 Mooresville Rd (28147-8828)
PHONE..................704 636-1825
Julius Waggoner, *Pr*
Dan Waggoner, *Ex VP*
▲ **EMP:** 9 **EST:** 1982
SQ FT: 4,500
SALES (est): 952.6K **Privately Held**
SIC: 3541 7699 Drilling and boring machines; Industrial tool grinding

(G-13975)
HARVEST HOMES AND HANDI HOUSES
Also Called: Bunce Buildings
3711 Statesville Blvd (28147-7456)
PHONE..................704 637-3878
EMP: 5
SALES (corp-wide): 2.27MM **Privately Held**
Web: www.buncebuildings.com
SIC: 3448 5999 Buildings, portable: prefabricated metal; Awnings
PA: Harvest Homes And Handi Houses Inc
2100 S Main St
Lexington NC 27292
336 243-2382

(G-13976)
HENKEL CORPORATION
Also Called: Henkel Corporation
485 Cedar Springs Rd (28147-9249)
PHONE..................704 633-1731
EMP: 52
SALES (corp-wide): 23.39B **Privately Held**
Web: www.henkel.com
SIC: 2843 Surface active agents
HQ: Henkel Us Operations Corporation
1 Henkel Way
Rocky Hill CT 06067
860 571-5100

(G-13977)
HENKEL US OPERATIONS CORP
Also Called: Henkel Electronic Materials
825 Cedar Springs Rd (28147-9253)
PHONE..................704 647-3500
Katrina Brown, *Brnch Mgr*
EMP: 50
SQ FT: 111,824
SALES (corp-wide): 23.39B **Privately Held**
Web: www.henkel.com
SIC: 2891 Adhesives
HQ: Henkel Us Operations Corporation
1 Henkel Way
Rocky Hill CT 06067
860 571-5100

(G-13978)
HERITAGE STEEL LLC
3870 Statesville Blvd (28147-7457)
P.O. Box 217 (27013-0217)
PHONE..................704 431-4097
Jadon Lavern Martin, *Managing Member*
EMP: 11 **EST:** 2018
SALES (est): 1.19MM **Privately Held**
SIC: 3448 Prefabricated metal buildings and components

(G-13979)
HESS MANUFACTURING INC
Also Called: Blast-It-All
185 Piper Ln (28147-7949)
P.O. Box 1615 (28145-1615)
PHONE..................704 637-3300
TOLL FREE: 800
EMP: 29 **EST:** 1978
SALES (est): 4.07MM **Privately Held**
Web: www.blast-it-all.com

SIC: 3589 Sandblasting equipment

(G-13980)
HIGH VELOCITY DEFENSE
195 Lone Star St (28146-9632)
PHONE..................704 738-3574
Eric Dougherty, *Prin*
EMP: 5 **EST:** 2017
SALES (est): 177.42K **Privately Held**
SIC: 3812 Defense systems and equipment

(G-13981)
HIS SPECIALTY FAB LLC
3250 Poole Rd (28146-5559)
PHONE..................704 279-1638
Mark White, *Prin*
EMP: 7 **EST:** 2018
SALES (est): 134.2K **Privately Held**
SIC: 7692 Welding repair

(G-13982)
IMS FABRICATION INC
150 Summit Park Dr (28146-6325)
PHONE..................704 216-0255
Andrew Clayton, *Brnch Mgr*
EMP: 35
Web: www.imsfabrication.com
SIC: 3549 Metalworking machinery, nec
PA: Ims Fabrication, Inc.
1278 Highway 461
Somerset KY 42503

(G-13983)
INDUSTRIAL SUP SOLUTIONS INC (PA)
Also Called: Issi
804 Julian Rd (28147-9080)
PHONE..................704 636-4241
R Frank Carmazzi, *Pr*
Joe Carmazzi, *
Perry Bernhardt, *
Mike Lear, *
◆ **EMP:** 43 **EST:** 1988
SQ FT: 70,000
SALES (est): 91.21MM **Privately Held**
Web: www.issimro.com
SIC: 5084 5085 3535 3511 Hydraulic systems equipment and supplies; Industrial supplies; Belt conveyor systems, general industrial use; Turbines and turbine generator sets and parts

(G-13984)
INNOSPEC ACTIVE CHEMICALS LLC
Also Called: Innospec Performance Chemicals
500 Hinkle Ln (28144-8574)
PHONE..................704 633-8028
EMP: 22
SALES (corp-wide): 1.95B **Publicly Held**
Web: www.innospec.com
SIC: 2869 Industrial organic chemicals, nec
HQ: Innospec Active Chemicals Llc
510 W Grimes Ave
High Point NC 27260
336 882-3308

(G-13985)
INNOSPEC INC
Also Called: Innospec Performance Chemicals
500 Hinkle Ln (28144-8574)
PHONE..................704 633-8028
◆ **EMP:** 35
SIC: 2819 Catalysts, chemical

(G-13986)
INNOSPEC INC
Also Called: Innospec Performance Chemicals

500 Hinkle Ln (28144-8574)
PHONE..................704 633-8028
EMP: 35
SALES (corp-wide): 1.95B **Publicly Held**
Web: www.innospec.com
SIC: 2819 Catalysts, chemical
PA: Innospec Inc.
8310 S Valley Hwy Ste 350
Englewood CO 80112
303 792-5554

(G-13987)
INTERSTATE FABRICATIONS LLC
121 N Salisbury Gq Ave (28146)
P.O. Box 777 (28072-0777)
PHONE..................704 209-0263
EMP: 5 **EST:** 2015
SALES (est): 79.41K **Privately Held**
Web: www.interstate-fab.com
SIC: 3446 Fences, gates, posts, and flagpoles

(G-13988)
INTERTAPE POLYMER CORP
Also Called: Maiweave
3725 Faith Rd (28146-8336)
PHONE..................704 279-3011
EMP: 25
SQ FT: 41,000
SALES (corp-wide): 571.43MM **Privately Held**
Web: www.itape.com
SIC: 2231 Overcoatings: wool, mohair, or similar fibers
HQ: Intertape Polymer Corp.
100 Paramount Dr Ste 300
Sarasota FL 34232
888 898-7834

(G-13989)
INVISTA CAPITAL MANAGEMENT LLC
Hwy 70 W (28145)
PHONE..................704 636-6000
EMP: 89
SALES (corp-wide): 36.93B **Privately Held**
Web: www.invista.com
SIC: 2821 2823 2281 2284 Polyethylene resins; Cellulosic manmade fibers; Yarn spinning mills; Sewing thread
HQ: Invista Capital Management, Llc
2801 Centerville Rd
Wilmington DE 19808
302 683-3000

(G-13990)
JEAN DUPREE
476 Pepperstone Dr (28146-0008)
PHONE..................919 821-4020
Jean Dupree, *Prin*
EMP: 5 **EST:** 2017
SALES (est): 74.5K **Privately Held**
SIC: 3572 Computer storage devices

(G-13991)
JESTINES JEWELS INC
512 Klumac Rd Ste 4 (28144-6752)
PHONE..................704 904-0191
Tracey Bost, *Pr*
Keith Bost, *VP*
EMP: 5 **EST:** 2016
SQ FT: 1,000
SALES (est): 312.96K **Privately Held**
Web: www.jestinesjewels.com
SIC: 5621 2335 2389 8742 Boutiques; Women's, junior's, and misses' dresses; Men's miscellaneous accessories; Management consulting services

(G-13992)
JKA IDUSTRIES
353 Grayson Dr (28147-8111)
PHONE..................980 225-5350
Stacey Blashfield, *Owner*
EMP: 6 **EST:** 2013
SALES (est): 210K **Privately Held**
SIC: 3993 2542 2531 Signs and advertising specialties; Postal lock boxes, mail racks, and related products; Public building and related furniture

(G-13993)
JOHNSON CONCRETE COMPANY (PA)
Also Called: Johnson Concrete Products
217 Klumac Rd (28144-6723)
P.O. Box 1037 (28145-1037)
PHONE..................704 636-5231
Judith Johnson, *Pr*
Joanne Johnson, *Sec*
Kathryn Johnson, *Treas*
◆ **EMP:** 30 **EST:** 1947
SQ FT: 4,000
SALES (est): 24.37MM
SALES (corp-wide): 24.37MM **Privately Held**
Web: www.johnsonproductsusa.com
SIC: 3271 3272 Blocks, concrete or cinder: standard; Pipe, concrete or lined with concrete

(G-13994)
JONES MARINE INC
10285 Bringle Ferry Rd (28146-9566)
PHONE..................704 639-0173
Brian Jones, *Pr*
Larry Jones, *Sec*
EMP: 4 **EST:** 2002
SALES (est): 943.32K **Privately Held**
Web: www.jonesmarine.net
SIC: 5551 3519 5088 3732 Marine supplies, nec; Marine engines; Marine crafts and supplies; Motorboats, inboard or outboard: building and repairing

(G-13995)
JPI COASTAL
1114 Old Concord Rd (28146-1353)
PHONE..................704 310-5867
Henry Van Hoy Ii, *Admn*
EMP: 11 **EST:** 2015
SALES (est): 647.95K **Privately Held**
Web: www.jpindustrial.com
SIC: 2821 Plastics materials and resins

(G-13996)
JULIAN FREIRICH COMPANY INC
815 W Kerr St (28144-3241)
P.O. Box 1529 (28145-1529)
PHONE..................704 636-2621
Jeff Freirich, *Pr*
EMP: 50
SALES (corp-wide): 5.01MM **Privately Held**
SIC: 2013 Prepared beef products, from purchased beef
PA: Julian Freirich Company, Inc.
4601 5th St
Long Island City NY 11101
718 361-9111

(G-13997)
JULIAN FREIRICH FOOD PRODUCTS
Also Called: Julian Freirich Co
815 W Kerr St (28144-3241)
P.O. Box 1529 (28145-1529)
PHONE..................704 636-2621
Jerry Freirich, *Ch*
Jeff Freirich, *Pr*
Digna Freirich, *Sec*

EMP: 20 EST: 1957
SQ FT: 32,000
SALES (est): 2.58MM **Privately Held**
Web: www.freirich.com
SIC: **5147** 2013 2011   Meats and meat products; Sausages and other prepared meats; Meat packing plants

(G-13998)
KETCHIE MARBLE CO INC
1920 Saint Luke Church Rd (28146-7956)
PHONE.................................704 279-8377
Bobby Ketchie, *Pr*
Jancy Ketchie, *VP*
EMP: 8 EST: 1986
SQ FT: 20,000
SALES (est): 462.95K **Privately Held**
SIC: **3281**   Marble, building: cut and shaped

(G-13999)
KIMBALLS SCREEN PRINT INC
1315 Union Church Rd (28146-7979)
PHONE.................................704 636-0488
Tommy Kimball, *Pr*
Todd Kimball, *VP*
Carlen Kimball, *Sec*
EMP: 5 EST: 1988
SALES (est): 323.42K **Privately Held**
SIC: **2759**   Screen printing

(G-14000)
KITCHEN MASTERS CHARLOTTE LLC
504 Sarazen Way (28144-8426)
PHONE.................................704 375-3320
David Garst, *Owner*
EMP: 12 EST: 2004
SALES (est): 1.36MM **Privately Held**
Web: www.kitchenmastersclt.com
SIC: **2434**   Wood kitchen cabinets

(G-14001)
KNORR BRAKE TRUCK SYSTEMS CO
115 Summit Park Dr (28146-6325)
PHONE.................................888 836-6922
EMP: 674
SALES (corp-wide): 2.67MM **Privately Held**
Web: www.knorr-bremse.us
SIC: **3743**   Railroad equipment
HQ: Knorr Brake Truck Systems Company
    748 Starbuck Ave
    Watertown NY 13601

(G-14002)
KRIEGER CABINETS DEWAYNE
415 Sailboat Dr (28146-2539)
PHONE.................................704 630-0609
EMP: 4 EST: 2011
SALES (est): 63.58K **Privately Held**
SIC: **2434**   Wood kitchen cabinets

(G-14003)
LGC CONSULTING INC
Also Called: Cmw Holding
1217 Speedway Blvd (28146-7448)
PHONE.................................704 216-0171
▼ EMP: 20
SIC: **3069**   Rubber automotive products

(G-14004)
LINGLE ELECTRIC REPAIR INC
600 N Main St (28144-3644)
PHONE.................................704 636-5591
Mary Ann S Lingle, *Pr*
Hilton Lingle, *Mgr*
EMP: 12 EST: 1936
SQ FT: 9,000
SALES (est): 1.09MM **Privately Held**

Web: www.lingleelectric.com
SIC: **7694** 5063   Electric motor repair; Motors, electric

(G-14005)
LOCKREY COMPANY LLC (PA)
Also Called: Liquid Moly
614 Emerald Bay Dr (28146-1595)
PHONE.................................856 665-4794
EMP: 8 EST: 1940
SALES (est): 753.97K **Privately Held**
SALES (corp-wide): 753.97K **Privately Held**
SIC: **2992**   Re-refining lubricating oils and greases, nec

(G-14006)
LOCUST PLASTICS INC
630 Industrial Ave (28144-3013)
PHONE.................................704 636-2742
Russell Hayes, *Pr*
Russell B Hayes, *
▲ EMP: 72 EST: 2008
SQ FT: 80,000
SALES (est): 15.38MM **Privately Held**
Web: www.locustplastics.com
SIC: **3089**   Injection molding of plastics

(G-14007)
LOG HOME BUILDERS INC
Also Called: Locktite Log Systems
470 B Leazer Rd (28147-8261)
PHONE.................................704 638-0677
Jim Kilgore, *Pr*
Debra Kilgore, *VP*
EMP: 7 EST: 1991
SALES (est): 535.72K **Privately Held**
Web: www.locktitelogs.com
SIC: **2411** 2439   Timber, cut at logging camp; Timbers, structural: laminated lumber

(G-14008)
MAGNA COMPOSITES LLC
6701 Statesville Blvd (28147-7486)
PHONE.................................704 797-8744
▲ EMP: 323
SIC: **3714**   Motor vehicle parts and accessories

(G-14009)
MARIETTA MARTIN MATERIALS INC
Also Called: Martin Marietta Aggregates
3825 Trexler St (28147-8378)
PHONE.................................704 636-6372
Damon Allen, *Brnch Mgr*
EMP: 11
Web: www.martinmarietta.com
SIC: **1422**   Crushed and broken limestone
PA: Martin Marietta Materials Inc
    4123 Parklake Ave
    Raleigh NC 27612

(G-14010)
MCDANIEL AWNING CO
Also Called: McDaniel Awning Manufacturing
225 White Farm Rd (28147-7730)
PHONE.................................704 636-8503
Joseph M Mcdaniel, *Pr*
Dale G Mcdaniel, *Admn*
EMP: 5 EST: 1966
SQ FT: 5,200
SALES (est): 725K **Privately Held**
Web: www.mcdanielawning.com
SIC: **1521** 3446 3444 3442   Single-family home remodeling, additions, and repairs; Architectural metalwork; Sheet metalwork; Metal doors, sash, and trim

(G-14011)
MCKENZIE SPORTS PRODUCTS LLC (PA)
Also Called: Mc Kenzie Taxidermy Supply
1910 Saint Luke Church Rd (28146-7956)
P.O. Box 480 (28072-0480)
PHONE.................................704 279-7985
▲ EMP: 125 EST: 1974
SQ FT: 120,000
SALES (est): 48.61MM
SALES (corp-wide): 48.61MM **Privately Held**
Web: www.mckenziesp.com
SIC: **3949** 3423   Targets, archery and rifle shooting; Taxidermist tools and equipment

(G-14012)
MDI SOLUTIONS LLC
760 Choate Rd (28146-3211)
PHONE.................................845 721-6758
Matthew Tomosivitch, *Pr*
EMP: 12 EST: 2014
SALES (est): 431.65K **Privately Held**
SIC: **3999**   Manufacturing industries, nec

(G-14013)
MERIDIAN BRICK LLC
700 S Long St (28144)
P.O. Box 1249 (28145-1249)
PHONE.................................704 636-0131
EMP: 63
SALES (corp-wide): 5.17B **Privately Held**
Web: www.meridianbrick.com
SIC: **3251**   Brick clay: common face, glazed, vitrified, or hollow
HQ: Meridian Brick Llc
    3015 Bristol Hwy
    Johnson City TN 37601
    770 645-4500

(G-14014)
MPX MANUFACTURING INC
1531 S Main St (28144-6705)
PHONE.................................704 762-9207
Jeffrey Goodman, *Pr*
EMP: 4 EST: 2019
SALES (est): 100K **Privately Held**
SIC: **3999**   Manufacturing industries, nec

(G-14015)
NATIONAL CARTON AND COATING CO
215 Newport Dr (28144-1262)
PHONE.................................704 647-0705
EMP: 6 EST: 2017
SALES (est): 79.91K **Privately Held**
SIC: **3479**   Metal coating and allied services

(G-14016)
NC DIESEL PERFORMANCE LLC
5213 Mooresville Rd (28147-7658)
PHONE.................................704 431-3257
Brandon Lottes, *Pr*
Brandon Lottes, *Managing Member*
EMP: 4 EST: 2018
SALES (est): 359.93K **Privately Held**
SIC: **7389** 7538 3443 3519   Business Activities at Non-Commercial Site; General automotive repair shops; Tanks, standard or custom fabricated: metal plate; Diesel engine rebuilding

(G-14017)
NEET SCRUBS
618 E Franklin St (28144-4524)
PHONE.................................704 431-5019
Otis West Junior, *Prin*
EMP: 5 EST: 2010
SALES (est): 80.3K **Privately Held**

SIC: **2844**   Perfumes, cosmetics and other toilet preparations

(G-14018)
NEW SARUM BREWING CO LLC
109 N Lee St (28144-5033)
PHONE.................................704 310-5048
Tony Hornick, *Pdt Mgr*
Gian-mauro Moscardini, *Sls Dir*
Gianni Moscardini, *CEO*
Edward Moscardini, *COO*
EMP: 6 EST: 2012
SALES (est): 520.13K **Privately Held**
Web: www.newsarumbrewing.com
SIC: **2082**   Beer (alcoholic beverage)

(G-14019)
NEW YORK AIR BRAKE LLC
Premtec Division
985 Whitney Dr (28147-8394)
P.O. Box 6760 (13601-6760)
PHONE.................................315 786-5200
EMP: 60
SALES (corp-wide): 2.67MM **Privately Held**
Web: www.nyab.com
SIC: **3743**   Brakes, air and vacuum: railway
HQ: New York Air Brake Llc
    748 Starbuck Ave
    Watertown NY 13601

(G-14020)
NORTH CAROLINA DEPT TRNSP
Also Called: Driver License
5780 S Main St (28147-9396)
PHONE.................................704 633-5873
R Crowe, *Brnch Mgr*
EMP: 44
Web: www.nc.gov
SIC: **3469**   Automobile license tags, stamped metal
HQ: North Carolina Department Of Transportation
    1 S Wilmington St
    Raleigh NC 27601

(G-14021)
OPTIMAL INDUSTRIES LLC
285 Cauble Stout Cir (28146-5001)
PHONE.................................601 530-5222
Shawn Christian, *Prin*
EMP: 4 EST: 2019
SALES (est): 155.42K **Privately Held**
Web: www.optimalindustriesllc.com
SIC: **3999**   Manufacturing industries, nec

(G-14022)
P P KILN ERECTORS
5351 Faith Rd (28146-0365)
PHONE.................................980 825-2263
EMP: 5 EST: 2018
SALES (est): 122.52K **Privately Held**
SIC: **3559**   Kilns

(G-14023)
PACKAGING CORPORATION AMERICA
Also Called: Pca/Salisbury 375
1302 N Salisbury Ave (28144-8543)
PHONE.................................704 633-3611
Pete Esenburger, *Mgr*
EMP: 97
SALES (corp-wide): 8.48B **Publicly Held**
Web: www.packagingcorp.com
SIC: **2653**   Boxes, corrugated: made from purchased materials
PA: Packaging Corporation Of America
    1 N Field Ct
    Lake Forest IL 60045
    847 482-3000

GEOGRAPHIC SECTION

Salisbury - Rowan County (G-14047)

(G-14024)
PERMA FLEX ROLLER TECHNOLOGY (PA)
1415 Jake Alexander Blvd S (28146-8359)
PHONE..............................704 633-1201
Michael Berwick, *Pr*
Linda Elkins, *
▲ **EMP:** 30 **EST:** 2001
SALES (est): 11.75MM
SALES (corp-wide): 11.75MM **Privately Held**
SIC: 3069 Rubber rolls and roll coverings

(G-14025)
PERMA-FLEX ROLLERS INC
Also Called: Perma Flex Rller Tchnlgy-Rgnge
1415 Jake Alexander Blvd S (28146-8359)
P.O. Box 2389 (28145-2389)
PHONE..............................704 633-1201
Michael Berwick, *Pr*
Doug Angel, *
▲ **EMP:** 75 **EST:** 1977
SQ FT: 22,000
SALES (est): 1.71MM
SALES (corp-wide): 11.75MM **Privately Held**
SIC: 3069 Printers' rolls and blankets: rubber or rubberized fabric
PA: Perma Flex Roller Technology- Organge, Llc
1415 Jake Alxander Blvd S
Salisbury NC 28146
704 633-1201

(G-14026)
POST PUBLISHING COMPANY
Also Called: Salisbury Post
131 W Innes St (28144-4338)
P.O. Box 4639 (28145-4639)
PHONE..............................704 633-8950
EMP: 88 **EST:** 1905
SALES (est): 10.69MM
SALES (corp-wide): 233.03MM **Privately Held**
Web: www.salisburypost.com
SIC: 2711 Newspapers, publishing and printing
PA: Epi Group, Llc.
4020 Stirrup Creek Dr
Durham NC 27703
843 577-7111

(G-14027)
POWER CURBERS INC (PA)
727 Bendix Dr (28146-5876)
P.O. Box 1639 (28145-1639)
PHONE..............................704 636-5871
Dwight F Messinger, *Pr*
Stephen B Bullock, *
Deborah W Messinger, *
◆ **EMP:** 82 **EST:** 1953
SQ FT: 90,500
SALES (est): 24.98MM
SALES (corp-wide): 24.98MM **Privately Held**
Web: www.powercurbers.com
SIC: 3531 Road construction and maintenance machinery

(G-14028)
PPG ARCHITECTURAL FINISHES INC
Also Called: Glidden Professional Paint Ctr
1333 Klumac Rd (28147-9086)
PHONE..............................704 633-0673
Regina O'brien, *Mgr*
EMP: 4
SALES (corp-wide): 17.65B **Publicly Held**
Web: www.glidden.com
SIC: 2851 Paints and allied products
HQ: Ppg Architectural Finishes, Inc.
1 Ppg Pl
Pittsburgh PA 15272
412 434-3131

(G-14029)
PRATTGEARS
113 Churchill Dr (28144-8306)
PHONE..............................414 704-3912
Nancy Pratt, *Owner*
EMP: 4 **EST:** 2016
SALES (est): 90.84K **Privately Held**
Web: www.prattgears.com
SIC: 3542 Gear rolling machines

(G-14030)
PRETTY BABY HERBAL SOAPS
1050 Winding Brook Ln (28146-9428)
P.O. Box 555 (28023-0555)
PHONE..............................704 209-0669
Terrianne Taylor, *Owner*
EMP: 5 **EST:** 1992
SALES (est): 226.32K **Privately Held**
Web: www.nakedbarnaturals.com
SIC: 2841 Soap: granulated, liquid, cake, flaked, or chip

(G-14031)
PRO CUSTOM CABINETS LLC
1440 Upper Palmer Rd (28146-8178)
PHONE..............................704 239-6054
EMP: 4 **EST:** 2013
SALES (est): 44.19K **Privately Held**
Web: www.procustomcabinets.com
SIC: 2499 Decorative wood and woodwork

(G-14032)
PROTEX SPORT PRODUCTS INC
1029 S Main St (28144-6421)
P.O. Box 106 (28159-0106)
PHONE..............................336 956-2419
Tim Clancy, *Pr*
Dawn Clancy, *VP*
EMP: 14 **EST:** 1993
SQ FT: 4,000
SALES (est): 1.21MM **Privately Held**
Web: www.protexsportproducts.com
SIC: 3949 Sporting and athletic goods, nec

(G-14033)
PYROTEK INCORPORATED
Also Called: Neco Division
970 Grace Church Rd (28147-9694)
PHONE..............................704 642-1993
Denny Weis, *Mgr*
EMP: 47
SQ FT: 9,000
SALES (corp-wide): 462.43MM **Privately Held**
Web: www.pyrotek.com
SIC: 3255 3544 3264 Clay refractories; Special dies, tools, jigs, and fixtures; Porcelain electrical supplies
PA: Pyrotek Incorporated
705 W 1st Ave
Spokane WA 99201
509 926-6212

(G-14034)
QUALITY BEVERAGE LLC (PA)
Also Called: Quality Beverage Brands
1413 Jake Alexander Blvd S (28146-8359)
P.O. Box 778 (28145-0778)
PHONE..............................704 637-5881
EMP: 4 **EST:** 1998
SALES (est): 10.39MM
SALES (corp-wide): 10.39MM **Privately Held**
Web: www.cheerwine.com
SIC: 2086 Bottled and canned soft drinks

(G-14035)
QUICK PRINT OF CONCORD
Also Called: Quick Print
700 N Long St Ste C (28144-4463)
PHONE..............................704 782-6634
Orbe A Garcia, *Pr*
Nina H Garcia, *VP*
EMP: 5 **EST:** 1985
SALES (est): 298.53K **Privately Held**
SIC: 2752 Offset printing

(G-14036)
RETROFIX SCREWS LLC
821 Mitchell Ave (28144-6252)
PHONE..............................980 432-8412
Teresa Miller, *Managing Member*
EMP: 5 **EST:** 2017
SALES (est): 198.15K **Privately Held**
Web: www.retrofixscrews.com
SIC: 3841 Surgical and medical instruments

(G-14037)
ROWAN MONUMENTS LLC
116 Statesville Blvd Ste B (28144-2363)
PHONE..............................704 905-6651
Nancy Poe, *Prin*
EMP: 4 **EST:** 2012
SALES (est): 79.9K **Privately Held**
Web: www.rowanmonuments.com
SIC: 3272 Monuments and grave markers, except terrazzo

(G-14038)
ROYCE APPAREL INC
408 Long Meadow Dr (28147-8201)
PHONE..............................704 933-6000
James Whitney, *Brnch Mgr*
EMP: 25
SALES (corp-wide): 16.79MM **Privately Held**
Web: www.royceapparel.com
SIC: 2331 T-shirts and tops, women's: made from purchased materials
PA: Royce Apparel, Inc.
5800 Royce St
Kannapolis NC 28083
704 933-6000

(G-14039)
S LOFLIN ENTERPRISES INC
Also Called: Thread Shed Clothing Company
133 S Main St (28144-4941)
PHONE..............................704 633-1159
Alan D Loflin, *Pr*
Cynthia Loflin, *VP*
Adam D Loflin Field, *Ofcr*
Annalacy Loflin Field, *Ofcr*
EMP: 10 **EST:** 1963
SQ FT: 5,000
SALES (est): 852.21K **Privately Held**
SIC: 2326 2399 2499 Work uniforms; Military insignia, textile; Shoe and boot products, wood

(G-14040)
SALISBURY MILLWORK INC
1910 S Martin Luther King Jr. Ave (28144)
PHONE..............................704 603-4501
EMP: 9 **EST:** 2009
SALES (est): 304.65K **Privately Held**
Web: www.salisburymillwork.com
SIC: 2431 Millwork

(G-14041)
SALISBURY MTAL FABRICATION LLC
565 Trexler Loop (28144-9060)
P.O. Box 2591 (28145-2591)
PHONE..............................704 278-0785
Debi Malone, *Managing Member*
EMP: 12 **EST:** 2014
SALES (est): 519.94K **Privately Held**
SIC: 3441 Fabricated structural metal

(G-14042)
SHAT-R-SHIELD LIGHTING INC
116 Ryan Patrick Dr (28147-5624)
PHONE..............................800 223-0853
Robert Nolan, *CEO*
Karen Clause, *
Margaret Nolan, *
▲ **EMP:** 64 **EST:** 1968
SQ FT: 46,000
SALES (est): 13.59MM **Privately Held**
Web: www.shatrshield.com
SIC: 3646 Commercial lighting fixtures

(G-14043)
SHIELD & STEEL ENTERPRISES LLC
Also Called: Impeccable Improvements NC
417b Peach Orchard Rd (28147-8325)
PHONE..............................704 607-0869
Simon Wentzel, *Prin*
EMP: 6 **EST:** 2015
SALES (est): 51.89K **Privately Held**
Web: www.shatrshield.com
SIC: 3646 Commercial lighting fixtures

(G-14044)
SNOW ON GO TRUCKING LLC
201 S Institute St (28144-4019)
PHONE..............................980 892-1791
Timothy Scott, *Prin*
EMP: 4 **EST:** 2020
SALES (est): 39.69K **Privately Held**
SIC: 3999 Manufacturing industries, nec

(G-14045)
SOUTHERN CONCRETE MTLS INC
1155 Chuck Taylor Ln (28147-9812)
PHONE..............................877 788-3001
EMP: 16
SALES (corp-wide): 238.17MM **Privately Held**
Web: www.scmusa.com
SIC: 3273 1771 Ready-mixed concrete; Concrete work
HQ: Southern Concrete Materials, Inc.
35 Meadow Rd
Asheville NC 28803
828 253-6421

(G-14046)
SPEED BRITE INC
Also Called: Windsor Gallery
1810 W Innes St (28144-2554)
P.O. Box 1766 (28145-1766)
PHONE..............................704 639-9771
Jim Rabon, *Pr*
Carol Rabon, *Sec*
EMP: 6 **EST:** 1991
SQ FT: 3,800
SALES (est): 486.28K **Privately Held**
Web: www.speedbrite.com
SIC: 2842 5944 Specialty cleaning; Jewelry stores

(G-14047)
STACLEAN DIFFUSER COMPANY LLC (PA)
Also Called: Staclean Diffuser
2205 Executive Dr (28147-9008)
P.O. Box 1147 (28145-1147)
PHONE..............................704 636-8697
EMP: 12 **EST:** 1980
SQ FT: 57,000
SALES (est): 5.27MM
SALES (corp-wide): 5.27MM **Privately Held**
Web: www.staclean.com

Salisbury - Rowan County (G-14048)

SIC: 3564 3826 Air purification equipment; Environmental testing equipment

(G-14048)
TARHEEL TOOL & GAUGE LLC
4665 Miller Rd (28147-7636)
PHONE...................704 213-6924
Dale W Brown, *Owner*
EMP: 6 EST: 2016
SALES (est): 137.8K **Privately Held**
Web: www.tarheeltoolgauge.com
SIC: 3599 Machine shop, jobbing and repair

(G-14049)
TEIJIN AUTOMOTIVE TECH INC
Also Called: Salisbury Operations
6701 Statesville Blvd (28147-7486)
PHONE...................704 797-8744
Nick Jockheck, *Brnch Mgr*
EMP: 350
Web: www.teijinautomotive.com
SIC: 3089 Injection molding of plastics
HQ: Teijin Automotive Technologies, Inc.
255 Rex Blvd
Auburn Hills MI 48326
248 237-7800

(G-14050)
TEXAS REFINERY
175 Frances St (28147-9009)
PHONE...................704 213-4990
Bill Wallin, *Prin*
EMP: 7 EST: 2010
SALES (est): 116.25K **Privately Held**
Web: www.texasrefinery.com
SIC: 3559 Refinery, chemical processing, and similar machinery

(G-14051)
TEXTILE PRODUCTS INC
119 121 N Main St (28144)
PHONE...................704 636-6221
EMP: 25 EST: 1994
SQ FT: 10,000
SALES (est): 627.68K **Privately Held**
Web: www.textileproducts.com
SIC: 5714 7389 2392 2391 Drapery and upholstery stores; Interior design services; Household furnishings, nec; Curtains and draperies

(G-14052)
THREESIXTY GRAPHIX INC
465 Airport Rd (28147-8903)
PHONE...................704 960-4467
EMP: 6 EST: 2015
SALES (est): 99.83K **Privately Held**
Web: www.threesixtygraphix.com
SIC: 2759 Screen printing

(G-14053)
TIVOLI WOODWORKS LLC
4850 Bringle Ferry Rd (28146-7108)
PHONE...................336 602-3512
Tivoli Woodworks, *Prin*
EMP: 5 EST: 2011
SALES (est): 173.08K **Privately Held**
SIC: 2431 Millwork

(G-14054)
TOOL RENTAL DEPOT LLC
2001 S Main St (28144-6833)
PHONE...................704 636-6400
Philip Butler, *Owner*
EMP: 4 EST: 2012
SQ FT: 72,000
SALES (est): 597.15K **Privately Held**
Web: www.toolrentaldepot.com

SIC: 3599 7699 Machine shop, jobbing and repair; Industrial machinery and equipment repair
PA: Hydraulics Depot, L.L.C.
2001 S Main St
Salisbury NC 28144

(G-14055)
TRELLEBORG SALISBURY INC
510 Long Meadow Dr (28147-8202)
PHONE...................704 797-8030
D C Howard, *Pr*
Denise Reid, *
◆ EMP: 45 EST: 1997
SQ FT: 5,600
SALES (est): 27.97MM
SALES (corp-wide): 4.26B **Privately Held**
SIC: 3089 Automotive parts, plastic
HQ: Trelleborg Corporation
200 Veterans Blvd Ste 3
South Haven MI 49090
269 639-9891

(G-14056)
TURNKEY TECHNOLOGIES INC
402 Bringle Ferry Rd (28144-4417)
PHONE...................704 245-6437
Tony Ward, *Pr*
Michael Brusich, *VP*
Paul Galvin, *VP*
EMP: 9 EST: 1999
SQ FT: 6,100
SALES (est): 2.9MM **Privately Held**
Web: www.turnkeytechnologies.net
SIC: 3599 Custom machinery

(G-14057)
UFP SALISBURY LLC
Also Called: UFP SALISBURY, LLC
520 Grace Church Rd (28147-9690)
PHONE...................704 855-1600
EMP: 300
SALES (corp-wide): 7.22B **Publicly Held**
SIC: 2491 Wood preserving
HQ: Ufp Salisbury Llc
358 Woodmill Rd
Salisbury NC 28147
704 855-1600

(G-14058)
UFP SALISBURY LLC (DH)
Also Called: U F P
358 Woodmill Rd (28147)
P.O. Box 1635 (28145-1635)
PHONE...................704 855-1600
EMP: 11 EST: 2012
SALES (est): 12.26MM
SALES (corp-wide): 7.22B **Publicly Held**
SIC: 2491 Wood preserving
HQ: Ufp Structural Packaging, Llc
5840 Wi 60
Hartford WI 53027
262 673-6090

(G-14059)
UNDERBRINKS LLC
705 Hedrick St (28144-3154)
P.O. Box 5194 (28117-5194)
PHONE...................866 495-4465
Billie Underbrink, *Managing Member*
EMP: 5 EST: 2018
SALES (est): 447.81K **Privately Held**
SIC: 3449 Bars, concrete reinforcing: fabricated steel

(G-14060)
USA MADE BLADE
134 N Lee St (28144-5068)
P.O. Box 3385 (28145-3385)
PHONE...................704 798-6478
Andy Roy, *Owner*

EMP: 4 EST: 2015
SALES (est): 58.32K **Privately Held**
Web: www.usamadeblade.com
SIC: 3423 Knives, agricultural or industrial

(G-14061)
VALUE CLOTHING INC (PA)
Also Called: Value Clothing
1310 Richard St (28144-3732)
PHONE...................704 638-6111
Doctor Richard Williams, *Pr*
Richard Williams Junior, *VP*
Elaine Williams, *
Wendy Workman, *
Candy Trivette, *
▼ EMP: 50 EST: 1968
SQ FT: 90,000
SALES (est): 5.4MM
SALES (corp-wide): 5.4MM **Privately Held**
Web: www.valueclothing.us
SIC: 2211 1521 5141 Broadwoven fabric mills, cotton; General remodeling, single-family houses; Food brokers

(G-14062)
VIRGINIA CAROLINA REFR INC (PA)
Also Called: Refractory Construction
1123 Speedway Blvd (28146-8389)
P.O. Box 761 (28037-0761)
PHONE...................704 216-0223
TOLL FREE: 800
Tony R Basinger, *Pr*
EMP: 7 EST: 1989
SQ FT: 6,000
SALES (est): 3.67MM **Privately Held**
Web: www.vcref.com
SIC: 3297 Nonclay refractories

(G-14063)
W A BROWN & SON INCORPORATED (PA)
209 Long Meadow Dr (28147-9299)
PHONE...................704 636-5131
Jacob Werner, *Pr*
Robert L Rouse, *
EMP: 40 EST: 1910
SQ FT: 111,000
SALES (est): 5.06MM
SALES (corp-wide): 5.06MM **Privately Held**
Web: www.imperialbrown.com
SIC: 3585 3822 5078 Refrigeration equipment, complete; Environmental controls; Refrigerators, commercial (reach-in and walk-in)

(G-14064)
WALDOS WLDG MET FBRICATION LLC
3185 Bringle Ferry Rd (28146-9243)
PHONE...................704 638-0462
Austin Waller, *Prin*
EMP: 4 EST: 2018
SALES (est): 54.36K **Privately Held**
SIC: 3499 Fabricated metal products, nec

(G-14065)
WELDING ON WHEELS
3215 Old Union Church Rd (28146-7930)
PHONE...................704 239-7831
Dan Mcgrew, *Prin*
EMP: 4 EST: 2018
SALES (est): 142.75K **Privately Held**
SIC: 3499 Fabricated metal products, nec

(G-14066)
WHITE TIRE AND SERVICE LLC ✪
200 E Liberty St (28144-5041)
PHONE...................704 636-0323
Jeremy White, *Managing Member*

EMP: 6 EST: 2023
SALES (est): 567.11K **Privately Held**
SIC: 7534 Tire repair shop

(G-14067)
WOODSHED SOFTWARE
925 Mainsail Rd (28146-1459)
PHONE...................941 240-1780
Stephen Wood, *Prin*
EMP: 5 EST: 2008
SALES (est): 182.94K **Privately Held**
SIC: 7372 Prepackaged software

(G-14068)
YALE ROPE TECHNOLOGIES INC
634 Industrial Ave (28144-3013)
PHONE...................704 630-0331
Tom Yale, *Pr*
▲ EMP: 8 EST: 2006
SALES (est): 536.23K **Privately Held**
SIC: 2298 Cordage and twine

(G-14069)
ZEON TECHNOLOGIES INC
425 Lash Dr (28147-9153)
PHONE...................704 680-9160
Richard F Zopf Junior, *Pr*
Michael A Burnett, *VP*
▲ EMP: 4 EST: 1990
SQ FT: 32,000
SALES (est): 750.19K **Privately Held**
Web: www.zeontech.net
SIC: 3087 Custom compound purchased resins

Saluda
Polk County

(G-14070)
FOSTER JACKSON & SONS LLC
10363 Holbert Cove Rd (28773-9536)
P.O. Box 68 (28756-0068)
PHONE...................828 674-7941
Foster Jackson, *Prin*
EMP: 8 EST: 2002
SALES (est): 256.29K **Privately Held**
SIC: 2411 Logging camps and contractors

(G-14071)
JERKY MAN INC
4035 Fork Creek Rd (28773-9678)
PHONE...................828 749-3685
Gale O Kelly, *Prin*
EMP: 7 EST: 2008
SALES (est): 113.13K **Privately Held**
SIC: 2013 Snack sticks, including jerky: from purchased meat

(G-14072)
MILL CREEK POST & BEAM CO
1970 Holbert Cove Rd (28773-8520)
P.O. Box 580 (28773-0580)
PHONE...................828 749-8000
Mark Wray, *Pr*
EMP: 9 EST: 1985
SQ FT: 1,500
SALES (est): 426.73K **Privately Held**
Web: www.millcreekinfo.com
SIC: 2452 1521 Log cabins, prefabricated, wood; Single-family housing construction

(G-14073)
SALUDA YARN CO INC
Greenville & Walnut Streets (28773)
PHONE...................828 749-2861
Ray P Reid, *Pr*
Ellen B Reid, *Sec*
EMP: 12 EST: 1962
SQ FT: 11,200

GEOGRAPHIC SECTION

SALES (est): 494.49K **Privately Held**
SIC: **2299** Yarns, specialty and novelty

(G-14074)
SAWGRASS INDUSTRIES
1298 Ozone Dr (28773-9607)
PHONE.....................................912 884-4008
Wayne Phillips, *Prin*
EMP: **7** EST: 2012
SALES (est): 146.56K **Privately Held**
Web: www.sawgrassindustries.com
SIC: **3999** Manufacturing industries, nec

(G-14075)
WILDFLOUR BAKERY INC
Also Called: Wildflour Bakery & Cafe
173 Main St (28773-9796)
PHONE.....................................828 749-9224
Debi K Thomas, *Pt*
Joy Hersberger, *Pt*
EMP: **8** EST: 1981
SALES (est): 229.64K **Privately Held**
Web: www.wildflourbakerync.com
SIC: **2051** 5461 5812 Bread, cake, and related products; Retail bakeries; Cafeteria

Sandy Ridge
Stokes County

(G-14076)
BHAKTIVEDANTA ARCHIVES
Also Called: BBT ARCHIVES
1453 Tom Shelton Rd (27046-7026)
P.O. Box 255 (27046-0255)
PHONE.....................................336 871-3636
Eddy Gaasbeek, *Pr*
▲ EMP: **9** EST: 1989
SQ FT: 5,500
SALES (est): 94K **Privately Held**
Web: www.prabhupada.com
SIC: **2731** 2741 3999 Books, publishing only; Miscellaneous publishing; Education aids, devices and supplies

(G-14077)
CRISTAL DRAGON CANDLE COMPANY
3271 Moir Farm Rd (27046-7504)
PHONE.....................................336 997-4210
EMP: **5** EST: 2014
SALES (est): 53.54K **Privately Held**
SIC: **3999** Candles

(G-14078)
DUNCAN JUNIOR D
Also Called: Duncan, JD Logging
1165 Troy Brown Rd (27046-7426)
PHONE.....................................336 871-3599
Junior David Duncan, *Owner*
EMP: **4** EST: 1982
SALES (est): 238.03K **Privately Held**
SIC: **2411** Logging camps and contractors

(G-14079)
FERGUSON LUMBER INC
2634 Amostown Rd (27046-7409)
P.O. Box 250 (27046-0250)
PHONE.....................................336 871-2591
Daula Ferguson, *Pr*
David Ferguson, *VP*
EMP: **8** EST: 1980
SQ FT: 7,100
SALES (est): 778.75K **Privately Held**
Web: www.fergusonlumber.com
SIC: **2421** Sawmills and planing mills, general

Sanford
Lee County

(G-14080)
3M COMPANY
Also Called: 3M
3010 Lee Ave (27332-6210)
PHONE.....................................919 774-3808
Michael Swartz, *Brnch Mgr*
EMP: **5**
SALES (corp-wide): 34.23B **Publicly Held**
Web: www.3m.com
SIC: **3629** Static elimination equipment, industrial
PA: 3m Company
    3m Center
    Saint Paul MN 55144
    651 733-1110

(G-14081)
ACE LASER RECYCLING INC
1808 Rice Rd (27330-9045)
P.O. Box 151 (27331-0151)
PHONE.....................................919 775-5521
Phillip C Kelly, *Pr*
EMP: **4** EST: 1998
SALES (est): 248.04K **Privately Held**
SIC: **3955** Print cartridges for laser and other computer printers

(G-14082)
ACU TROL INC
1620 Hawkins Ave (27330-9501)
PHONE.....................................919 566-8332
Jeff Sanchez, *Mgr*
EMP: **9** EST: 2010
SALES (est): 160.99K **Privately Held**
SIC: **3999** Manufacturing industries, nec

(G-14083)
AIR SYSTEM COMPONENTS INC
Also Called: ASC
275 Pressly Foushee Rd (27330-7595)
PHONE.....................................919 279-8868
EMP: **86**
Web: www.airsysco.com
SIC: **3585** Air conditioning equipment, complete
HQ: Air System Components, Inc.
    605 Shiloh Rd
    Plano TX 75074
    972 212-4888

(G-14084)
AIR SYSTEM COMPONENTS INC
Also Called: Trion Iaq
101 Mcneill Rd (27330-9451)
PHONE.....................................919 775-2201
William Crawford, *Contrlr*
EMP: **100**
Web: www.airsysco.com
SIC: **3585** Air conditioning equipment, complete
HQ: Air System Components, Inc.
    605 Shiloh Rd
    Plano TX 75074
    972 212-4888

(G-14085)
ALPACA
813 S Horner Blvd (27330-5309)
PHONE.....................................919 628-9686
EMP: **9** EST: 2015
SALES (est): 238.89K **Privately Held**
Web: www.alpacachicken.com
SIC: **2231** Alpacas, mohair: woven

(G-14086)
APEX INDUSTRIAL GROUP LLC
2903 Lee Ave (27332-6207)
PHONE.....................................919 578-9039
Jon Link, *Pr*
Perry Corker, *Prin*
EMP: **8** EST: 2014
SQ FT: 12,000
SALES (est): 1.51MM **Privately Held**
Web: www.apexmro.com
SIC: **3429** 5084 Clamps, couplings, nozzles, and other metal hose fittings; Hydraulic systems equipment and supplies

(G-14087)
ARDEN COMPANIES LLC
Also Called: Arden
1611 Broadway Rd (27332-9795)
PHONE.....................................919 258-3081
Alice Edmisten, *Brnch Mgr*
EMP: **26**
SALES (corp-wide): 3.31B **Publicly Held**
Web: www.ardencompanies.com
SIC: **2392** 3999 Cushions and pillows; Umbrellas, canes, and parts
HQ: Arden Companies, Llc
    30400 Telg Rd Ste 200
    Bingham Farms MI 48025
    248 415-8500

(G-14088)
ARDEN COMPANIES LLC
Also Called: Arden Companies
1611 Broadway Rd (27332-9795)
PHONE.....................................919 258-3081
Al Smith, *Prin*
EMP: **53**
SALES (corp-wide): 3.31B **Publicly Held**
Web: www.ardencompanies.com
SIC: **2519** 2515 2392 Lawn and garden furniture, except wood and metal; Mattresses and bedsprings; Household furnishings, nec
HQ: Arden Companies, Llc
    30400 Telg Rd Ste 200
    Bingham Farms MI 48025
    248 415-8500

(G-14089)
ASTELLAS GENE THERAPIES INC
6074 Enterprise Park Dr (27330-9709)
PHONE.....................................415 638-6561
EMP: **89**
Web: www.astellasgenetherapies.com
SIC: **2836** Biological products, except diagnostic
HQ: Astellas Gene Therapies, Inc.
    480 Forbes Blvd
    South San Francisco CA 94080
    415 818-1001

(G-14090)
ATKINS UNLIMITED LLC
127 Atkins Ln (27330-7926)
PHONE.....................................704 984-8595
Vickie Atkins, *Prin*
EMP: **5** EST: 2019
SALES (est): 59.69K **Privately Held**
SIC: **2099** Food preparations, nec

(G-14091)
ATLANTIC HYDRAULICS SVCS LLC
5225 Womack Rd (27330-9517)
P.O. Box 5225 (27331-5225)
PHONE.....................................919 542-2985
Tiffany Roberts, *Pr*
▲ EMP: **30** EST: 1981
SQ FT: 8,000
SALES (est): 7.11MM **Privately Held**
Web: www.atlantic-hydraulics.com

SIC: **1799** 3594 3541 3593 Hydraulic equipment, installation and service; Motors: hydraulic, fluid power, or air; Lathes, metal cutting and polishing; Fluid power cylinders and actuators

(G-14092)
BATTLE TRUCKING INC
Also Called: Battle Trucking Company
911 San Lee Dr (27330-9067)
PHONE.....................................919 708-2288
Howard Battle, *Owner*
EMP: **4** EST: 1976
SALES (est): 283.73K **Privately Held**
Web: www.atticmoldremediation.com
SIC: **3715** Truck trailers

(G-14093)
BHARAT FORGE ALUMINUM USA INC (DH)
777 Kalyani Way (27330-9713)
PHONE.....................................585 576-7483
EMP: **192** EST: 2019
SALES (est): 42.33MM **Privately Held**
SIC: **3353** Aluminum sheet and strip
HQ: Bharat Forge America Inc.
    2105 Schmiede St
    Surgoinsville TN 37873

(G-14094)
BNP INC
Also Called: J M C Tool and Machine
5910 Elwin Buchanan Dr (27330-9525)
PHONE.....................................919 775-7070
Glen Berry, *Pr*
Howard Nystrom, *VP*
Frank Patkunas, *VP*
EMP: **10** EST: 1993
SQ FT: 5,000
SALES (est): 3.15MM **Privately Held**
Web: www.jmctool.com
SIC: **3469** 3544 Machine parts, stamped or pressed metal; Special dies, tools, jigs, and fixtures

(G-14095)
BOST DISTRIBUTING COMPANY INC
2209 Boone Trail Rd (27330-8641)
P.O. Box 447 (27331-0447)
PHONE.....................................919 775-5931
James H Bost Junior, *Pr*
Jim Bost, *
EMP: **21** EST: 1987
SALES (est): 681.36K **Privately Held**
Web: www.bostdistributingcompany.com
SIC: **2032** 2099 Chili, with or without meat: packaged in cans, jars, etc.; Gravy mixes, dry

(G-14096)
BROADWIND INDUS SOLUTIONS LLC
1824 Boone Trail Rd (27330-8662)
PHONE.....................................919 777-2907
Gil Mayo, *Pr*
▲ EMP: **40** EST: 2007
SQ FT: 125,000
SALES (est): 13.81MM **Publicly Held**
Web: www.bwen.com
SIC: **4783** 3599 8742 8734 Packing and crating; Machine and other job shop work; Materials mgmt. (purchasing, handling, inventory) consultant; Calibration and certification
PA: Broadwind, Inc.
    3240 S Central Ave
    Cicero IL 60804

Sanford - Lee County (G-14097)   GEOGRAPHIC SECTION

(G-14097)
CAROLINA CREATIVE CABINETS INC
517 N Franklin Dr (27330-7647)
PHONE..............................919 842-2060
William H Stamey Iii, *Prin*
EMP: 5 **EST:** 2007
SALES (est): 183.59K **Privately Held**
SIC: 2434 Wood kitchen cabinets

(G-14098)
CATERPILLAR INC
Also Called: Caterpillar
5000 Womack Rd (27330-9594)
P.O. Box 3667 (27331-3667)
PHONE..............................919 777-2000
Bill Allenbough, *Brnch Mgr*
EMP: 51
SALES (corp-wide): 67.06B **Publicly Held**
Web: www.caterpillar.com
SIC: 3531 3519 3511 3537 Construction machinery; Internal combustion engines, nec; Turbines and turbine generator sets; Industrial trucks and tractors
PA: Caterpillar Inc.
   5205 N Ocnnor Blvd Ste 10
   Irving TX 75039
   972 891-7700

(G-14099)
CENTURY STONE LLC
624 Fairway Dr (27330-9267)
PHONE..............................919 774-3334
Kevin Noel, *Managing Member*
EMP: 5 **EST:** 2005
SALES (est): 379.83K **Privately Held**
SIC: 3281 Curbing, granite or stone

(G-14100)
CERTIFIED MACHINING INC
2710 Wilkins Dr (27330-9400)
PHONE..............................919 777-9608
Tim Coggins, *Pr*
Lisa Coggins, *Sec*
EMP: 17 **EST:** 1996
SQ FT: 9,600
SALES (est): 998.79K **Privately Held**
Web: www.dnzproducts.com
SIC: 3599 Machine shop, jobbing and repair

(G-14101)
CHALLNGE PRTG OF CRLNAS INC TH
5905 Clyde Rhyne Dr (27330-9508)
PHONE..............................919 777-2820
Thomas Forrest, *Prin*
EMP: 8 **EST:** 2013
SALES (est): 199.27K **Privately Held**
Web: www.challengeprintingco.com
SIC: 2671 Paper; coated and laminated packaging

(G-14102)
CIRCOR PRECISION METERING LLC
Zenith Pumps Division
5910 Elwin Buchanan Dr (27330-9525)
PHONE..............................919 774-7667
Bill Roller, *Brnch Mgr*
EMP: 548
Web: www.zenithpumps.com
SIC: 3728 3724 3561 3541 Pumps, propeller feathering; Lubricating systems, aircraft; Pump jacks and other pumping equipment; Drilling machine tools (metal cutting)
HQ: Circor Precision Metering, Llc
   1710 Airport Rd
   Monroe NC 28110
   704 289-6511

(G-14103)
CONVEYOR TECHNOLOGIES OF SANFORD NC INC
Also Called: CTI Systems
5313 Womack Rd (27330-9517)
PHONE..............................919 776-7227
◆ **EMP:** 80
Web: www.conveyor-technologies.com
SIC: 3535 Conveyors and conveying equipment

(G-14104)
COOMERS WELDING LLC
473 Peele Ln (27332-2347)
PHONE..............................919 708-8087
John Coomer, *Prin*
EMP: 5 **EST:** 2017
SALES (est): 28.27K **Privately Held**
SIC: 7692 Welding repair

(G-14105)
COTY INC
Also Called: Coty Sanford Factory
1400 Broadway Rd (27332-7739)
PHONE..............................919 895-5000
EMP: 86
Web: www.coty.com
SIC: 2844 Perfumes, cosmetics and other toilet preparations
PA: Coty Inc.
   350 5th Ave Ste 2700
   New York NY 10118

(G-14106)
COTY US LLC
Also Called: Coty
1400 Broadway Rd (27332-7713)
PHONE..............................919 895-5374
EMP: 850
SQ FT: 435,000
Web: www.coty.com
SIC: 2844 Perfumes, natural or synthetic
HQ: Coty Us Llc
   350 5th Ave
   New York NY 10118

(G-14107)
DESCO INDUSTRIES INC
Also Called: Jj Electronic Solutions Div
920 J R Industrial Dr (27332-9733)
PHONE..............................919 718-0000
Tommie Lee, *Mgr*
EMP: 13
SALES (corp-wide): 49.98MM **Privately Held**
Web: www.descoindustries.com
SIC: 3081 Plastics film and sheet
PA: Desco Industries, Inc.
   3651 Walnut Ave
   Chino CA 91710
   909 627-8178

(G-14108)
DESCO INDUSTRIES INC
917 J R Industrial Dr (27332-9733)
PHONE..............................919 718-0000
Tommie Lee, *Mgr*
EMP: 21
SALES (corp-wide): 49.98MM **Privately Held**
Web: www.descoindustries.com
SIC: 3629 Static elimination equipment, industrial
PA: Desco Industries, Inc.
   3651 Walnut Ave
   Chino CA 91710
   909 627-8178

(G-14109)
DESCO INDUSTRIES INC
914 J R Industrial Dr (27332-9733)
PHONE..............................919 718-0000
Tommie Lee, *Mgr*
EMP: 12
SALES (corp-wide): 49.98MM **Privately Held**
Web: www.descoindustries.com
SIC: 3841 Surgical instruments and apparatus
PA: Desco Industries, Inc.
   3651 Walnut Ave
   Chino CA 91710
   909 627-8178

(G-14110)
DESCO INDUSTRIES INC
Electronic Solutions Division
926 J R Industrial Dr (27332-9733)
PHONE..............................919 718-0000
Vladimir Kraz, *Brnch Mgr*
EMP: 37
SALES (corp-wide): 49.98MM **Privately Held**
Web: www.descoindustries.com
SIC: 3829 Measuring and controlling devices, nec
PA: Desco Industries, Inc.
   3651 Walnut Ave
   Chino CA 91710
   909 627-8178

(G-14111)
DURAFIBER TECHNOLOGIES DFT INC
672 Douglas Farm Rd (27332-1831)
PHONE..............................919 356-3824
EMP: 4
SALES (corp-wide): 17.78B **Privately Held**
SIC: 2824 Organic fibers, noncellulosic
HQ: Durafiber Technologies (Dft), Inc.
   13620 Reese Blvd E # 400
   Huntersville NC 28078
   704 912-3700

(G-14112)
EARLS PRECISION MACHINING
365 Taylors Chapel Rd (27330-0988)
PHONE..............................919 542-1869
EMP: 4 **EST:** 1989
SALES (est): 378.71K **Privately Held**
Web: www.earlspm.com
SIC: 3599 Machine shop, jobbing and repair

(G-14113)
EDELBROCK LLC
5715 Clyde Rhyne Dr (27330-9563)
PHONE..............................919 718-9737
Terry Pattigno, *Manager*
EMP: 76
Web: www.edelbrock.com
SIC: 3751 3714 Motorcycle accessories; Gas tanks, motor vehicle
HQ: Edelbrock, Llc
   8649 Hacks Cross Rd
   Olive Branch MS 38654
   310 781-2222

(G-14114)
ELIO INC
2555 Hawkins Ave (27330-9236)
PHONE..............................919 708-5554
Elio Castiglia, *Owner*
EMP: 8 **EST:** 2011
SALES (est): 140.95K **Privately Held**
SIC: 3711 Motor vehicles and car bodies

(G-14115)
ELIZABETH S JAVA EXPRESS
120 S Moore St (27330-4224)
PHONE..............................919 777-5282
Jeff Sadlick, *Owner*
EMP: 4 **EST:** 2006
SALES (est): 142.36K **Privately Held**
SIC: 2741 Miscellaneous publishing

(G-14116)
ENTERGY GROUP LLC
500 Westover Dr Ste 10447 (27330-8941)
PHONE..............................866 988-8884
EMP: 7 **EST:** 2011
SALES (est): 90.04K **Privately Held**
Web: www.entergy.com
SIC: 3679 Electronic loads and power supplies

(G-14117)
ENVIRCO CORPORATION (PA)
101 Mcneill Rd (27330-9451)
PHONE..............................919.775-2201
Paul Christiansen, *Sls Dir*
▲ **EMP:** 27 **EST:** 1965
SQ FT: 45,000
SALES (est): 2.49MM
SALES (corp-wide): 2.49MM **Privately Held**
Web: www.envirco-hvac.com
SIC: 3564 Purification and dust collection equipment

(G-14118)
FLOWERS BKG CO JAMESTOWN LLC
Also Called: Flowers Bakery
708 E Main St (27332-6126)
PHONE..............................919 776-8932
Mike Waites, *Mgr*
EMP: 44
SALES (corp-wide): 5.09B **Publicly Held**
SIC: 2051 Bread, all types (white, wheat, rye, etc); fresh or frozen
HQ: Flowers Baking Co. Of Newton, Llc
   801 W Main St
   Jamestown NC 27282
   336 841-8840

(G-14119)
FOELL PACKING COMPANY OF NC
2209 Boone Trail Rd (27330-8641)
P.O. Box 2340 (27331-2340)
PHONE..............................919 776-0592
Jim Bost, *Pr*
EMP: 11 **EST:** 1919
SQ FT: 32,000
SALES (est): 226.05K **Privately Held**
SIC: 2013 2099 Canned meats (except baby food), from purchased meat; Ready-to-eat meals, salads, and sandwiches

(G-14120)
FOILED AGIN CHOCLAT COINS LLC
1488 Mcneill Rd # A (27330-9526)
PHONE..............................919 342-4601
Scott Wayne, *Pr*
EMP: 4 **EST:** 2011
SALES (est): 304.53K **Privately Held**
Web: www.foiledagainchocolate.com
SIC: 2064 Chocolate candy, except solid chocolate

(G-14121)
FRONTIER YARNS INC (HQ)
1823 Boone Trail Rd (27330-8662)
PHONE..............................919 776-9940
Robin Perkins, *CEO*
EMP: 36 **EST:** 2019
SALES (est): 25.49MM

GEOGRAPHIC SECTION
Sanford - Lee County (G-14146)

SALES (corp-wide): 3.24B **Privately Held**
Web: www.gildanyarns.com
SIC: 2281 Yarn spinning mills
PA: Les Vetements De Sport Gildan Inc
600 Boul De Maisonneuve O 33eme Etage
Montreal QC H3A 3
514 735-2023

(G-14122)
FRONTIER YARNS INC
1823 Boone Trail Rd (27330-8662)
PHONE.................................919 776-9940
EMP: 68
SALES (corp-wide): 33.59MM **Privately Held**
SIC: 2281 Spinning yarn
PA: Frontier Yarns, Inc.
1823 Boone Trail Rd
Sanford NC 27330
919 776-9940

(G-14123)
FSM LIQUIDATION CORP
1823 Boone Trail Rd (27330-8662)
PHONE.................................919 776-9940
◆ EMP: 1200
SIC: 2281 Spinning yarn

(G-14124)
GENERAL SHALE BRICK INC
2507 Jefferson Davis Hwy (27332-7106)
PHONE.................................919 775-2121
Bill Brown, *Principal B*
EMP: 9
SALES (corp-wide): 5.17B **Privately Held**
Web: www.generalshale.com
SIC: 3251 5032 Brick and structural clay tile; Brick, stone, and related material
HQ: General Shale Brick, Inc.
3015 Bristol Hwy
Johnson City TN 37601
423 282-4661

(G-14125)
GLENDON PYROPHYLLITE INC
Also Called: Glendon Pyrophllite Rock Quar
1789 Clarence Mckeithen Rd (27330-8780)
PHONE.................................919 464-5243
Benny Lee, *Mgr*
EMP: 6
SALES (corp-wide): 976.41K **Privately Held**
SIC: 3295 Pyrophyllite, ground or otherwise treated
PA: Glendon Pyrophyllite Inc
1789 Mckeithan Rd
Sanford NC
919 774-6602

(G-14126)
GODFREY INDUSTRIAL WELDING
439 Ragan Rd (27330-3171)
PHONE.................................919 604-0498
Matthew Godfrey, *Prin*
EMP: 4 EST: 2017
SALES (est): 37.45K **Privately Held**
SIC: 7692 Welding repair

(G-14127)
GORDON ENTERPRISES
3125 Hawkins Ave (27330-6916)
PHONE.................................919 776-8784
William A Gordon, *Owner*
EMP: 6 EST: 1978
SALES (est): 462.64K **Privately Held**
SIC: 3599 Custom machinery

(G-14128)
GRP INC
1823 Boone Trail Rd (27330-8662)
PHONE.................................919 776-9940
EMP: 8 EST: 2010
SALES (est): 215K **Privately Held**
SIC: 2281 Cotton yarn, spun

(G-14129)
HAWK DISTRIBUTORS INC
2980 Lee Ave (27332-6208)
PHONE.................................888 334-1307
Terry Earle, *Pr*
EMP: 8 EST: 2012
SALES (est): 708.22K **Privately Held**
Web: www.hawkdistributors.com
SIC: 2337 2311 2387 3949 Women's and misses' suits and coats; Coats, overcoats and vests; Apparel belts; Hunting equipment

(G-14130)
HERALD SANFORD INC
208 Saint Clair Ct (27330-3916)
PHONE.................................919 708-9000
J Fred Paxton, *Pr*
W E Horner Iii, *Publisher*
Doug Rowe, *Advt Dir*
EMP: 53 EST: 1930
SQ FT: 16,000
SALES (est): 2.37MM
SALES (corp-wide): 243.17MM **Privately Held**
Web: www.sanfordherald.com
SIC: 2711 Newspapers, publishing and printing
PA: Paxton Media Group, Llc
100 Television Ln
Paducah KY 42003
270 575-8630

(G-14131)
HERITAGE CONCRETE SERVICE CORP (PA)
Also Called: Heritage Concrete
140 Deep River Rd (27330-6528)
P.O. Box 964 (27331-0964)
PHONE.................................919 775-5014
Cliff Stephens, *Pr*
Ovide De St Aubin Junior, *Sec*
Dennis D Aubin, *Prin*
EMP: 19 EST: 1986
SQ FT: 5,000
SALES (est): 3.24MM
SALES (corp-wide): 3.24MM **Privately Held**
Web: www.heritageconcreteservice.com
SIC: 3273 Ready-mixed concrete

(G-14132)
HERITAGE WOODWORKS LLC
205 Mciver St (27330-4342)
PHONE.................................919 774-1554
EMP: 7 EST: 2021
SALES (est): 393.97K **Privately Held**
SIC: 2431 Millwork

(G-14133)
HFC PRESTIGE PRODUCTS INC
1400 Broadway Rd (27332-7713)
PHONE.................................919 895-5300
Mark Duncan, *Brnch Mgr*
EMP: 7
SIC: 2844 Perfumes, cosmetics and other toilet preparations
HQ: Hfc Prestige Products, Inc.
350 5th Ave Fl 19
New York NY 10118

(G-14134)
HUGGER MUGGER LLC
Also Called: Brick City Phenomicon
229 Wicker St (27330-4253)
PHONE.................................910 585-2749
Tim Emmert, *Managing Member*
EMP: 11 EST: 2015
SALES (est): 600K **Privately Held**
Web: www.huggermuggerbrewing.com
SIC: 2082 Beer (alcoholic beverage)

(G-14135)
HUMBER STREET FACILITY INC
105 E Humber St (27330-5844)
P.O. Box 2705 (27331-2705)
PHONE.................................919 775-3628
Allen Heckle, *Genl Mgr*
Kirby Weisner, *
Martin Marks, *
EMP: 26 EST: 1946
SQ FT: 50,000
SALES (est): 665.61K **Privately Held**
Web: www.hallmanfoundryusa.com
SIC: 3321 Gray iron castings, nec

(G-14136)
HYDRO TUBE ENTERPRISES INC
2645 Mount Pisgah Church Rd (27332-8508)
PHONE.................................919 258-3070
EMP: 35
SALES (corp-wide): 22.56MM **Privately Held**
Web: www.hydrotube.com
SIC: 3292 Tubing and piping, asbestos and asbestos cement
PA: Hydro Tube Enterprises, Inc.
137 Artino St
Oberlin OH 44074
440 774-1022

(G-14137)
HYDRO TUBE SOUTH LLC
2645 Mount Pisgah Church Rd (27332-8508)
PHONE.................................919 258-3070
Lawrence L Reining, *Managing Member*
EMP: 13 EST: 1997
SQ FT: 40,000
SALES (est): 984.53K **Privately Held**
Web: www.hydrotube.com
SIC: 3498 Tube fabricating (contract bending and shaping)

(G-14138)
INGRAM WOODYARDS INC
1925 Jefferson Davis Hwy (27330-9123)
P.O. Box 828 (27209-0828)
PHONE.................................910 556-1250
Wayne Ingram, *Pr*
Scott Ingram, *VP*
EMP: 10 EST: 1998
SALES (est): 901.73K **Privately Held**
SIC: 2611 Pulp mills

(G-14139)
JEFFERS LOGGING INC
279 Garner Rd (27330-9684)
PHONE.................................919 708-2193
Johnny D Jeffers, *Pr*
EMP: 5 EST: 1992
SALES (est): 583.34K **Privately Held**
SIC: 2411 Logging camps and contractors

(G-14140)
JMC TOOL & MACHINE CO
5910 Elwin Buchanan Dr (27330-9525)
PHONE.................................919 775-7070
Anthony Butler, *Managing Member*
Glenn Berry, *
EMP: 44 EST: 1997
SALES (est): 5.44MM **Privately Held**
Web: www.jmctool.com
SIC: 3599 Machine shop, jobbing and repair

(G-14141)
JONES PRINTING COMPANY INC
104 Hawkins Ave (27330-4322)
P.O. Box 1089 (27331-1089)
PHONE.................................919 774-9442
Dale Harrison, *Pr*
John Lemon, *VP*
Michael Thomas, *Sec*
David G Spivey, *Treas*
P J Patterson, *Off Mgr*
EMP: 17 EST: 1924
SQ FT: 6,000
SALES (est): 905.67K **Privately Held**
Web: www.jonesprintingco.com
SIC: 2752 Offset printing

(G-14142)
JORDAN ELECTRIC MOTORS INC
3307 Lee Ave (27332-8495)
PHONE.................................919 708-7010
Don Jordan, *Pr*
EMP: 13 EST: 2004
SQ FT: 25,000
SALES (est): 670.41K **Privately Held**
Web: www.djeminc.com
SIC: 7694 Electric motor repair

(G-14143)
KEEBLER COMPANY
Also Called: Keebler
5801 Mockingbird Ln (27332-7811)
PHONE.................................919 774-6431
EMP: 75
SALES (corp-wide): 15.31B **Publicly Held**
Web: www.keebler.com
SIC: 2052 Cookies
HQ: Keebler Company
1 Kellogg Sq
Battle Creek MI 49017
269 961-2000

(G-14144)
KELLER COMPANIES INC
1600 Colon Rd (27330-9577)
PHONE.................................919 776-4641
EMP: 6 EST: 2012
SALES (est): 111.37K **Privately Held**
SIC: 2421 Building and structural materials, wood

(G-14145)
L F I SERVICES INC
1136 Broadway Rd (27332-9793)
PHONE.................................215 343-0411
Lucille Jones, *Pr*
Salvatore J Stea, *
Larry Jones, *
Virginia Stea, *Stockholder*
EMP: 7 EST: 1978
SQ FT: 7,000
SALES (est): 208.74K **Privately Held**
SIC: 3567 Heating units and devices, industrial: electric

(G-14146)
LEE BRICK & TILE COMPANY
3704 Hawkins Ave (27330-9519)
P.O. Box 1027 (27331-1027)
PHONE.................................919 774-4800
Don Perry, *Pr*
Paul Perry, *
Gil Perry, *
Frank G Perry Junior, *VP*
Michael Lilly, *
EMP: 54 EST: 1946
SQ FT: 2,000

Sanford - Lee County (G-14147)

SALES (est): 7.42MM **Privately Held**
Web: www.leebrickonline.com
SIC: 3259 Adobe brick

(G-14147)
LEE BUILDER MART INC
1000 N Homer Blvd (27330-9401)
EMP: 23 **EST:** 1956
SALES (est): 4.27MM **Privately Held**
Web: www.leebuildermart.com
SIC: 5211 2431 Home centers; Millwork

(G-14148)
LEE COUNTY INDUSTRIES INC
Also Called: LCI
2711 Tramway Rd (27332-7140)
P.O. Box 973 (27331-0973)
PHONE...........................919 775-3439
Meg Moss, *Ex Dir*
Sue Marshburn, *Dir*
EMP: 21 **EST:** 1967
SQ FT: 30,000
SALES (est): 945.86K **Privately Held**
Web: www.lciinc.org
SIC: 8331 3412 2796 2789 Vocational rehabilitation agency; Metal barrels, drums, and pails; Platemaking services; Bookbinding and related work

(G-14149)
MARTIN MARIETTA MATERIALS INC
Also Called: Martin Marietta Aggregates
1227 Willett Rd (27332-0805)
P.O. Box 247 (28355-0247)
PHONE...........................919 788-4391
Ray Thatcher, *Mgr*
EMP: 6
Web: www.martinmarietta.com
SIC: 1422 Crushed and broken limestone
PA: Martin Marietta Materials Inc
   4123 Parklake Ave
   Raleigh NC 27612

(G-14150)
MATTHEW JOHNSON LOGGING
536 Farrell Rd (27330-7961)
PHONE...........................919 291-0197
Matthew Johnson, *Owner*
EMP: 6 **EST:** 1999
SALES (est): 556.76K **Privately Held**
SIC: 2411 Logging

(G-14151)
MAX PATTERSON
1910 Autumn Ct (27330-8144)
PHONE...........................910 947-2524
Max Patterson, *Prin*
EMP: 4
SALES (est): 34.42K **Privately Held**
SIC: 7692 Welding repair

(G-14152)
MERTEK SOLUTIONS INC
3913 Hawkins Ave (27330-9419)
PHONE...........................919 774-7827
EMP: 37 **EST:** 2010
SQ FT: 25,000
SALES (est): 7.98MM **Privately Held**
Web: www.merteknc.com
SIC: 3599 Machine shop, jobbing and repair

(G-14153)
MIDPINES HOSIERY INC
Also Called: Mid Pines Hosiery Company
840 White Hill Rd (27332-7582)
P.O. Box 1093 (27331-1093)
PHONE...........................919 774-3888
Beverly T Gautier Senior, *Pr*
Beverly T Gautier Iii, *VP*
Greg Gautier, *VP*
Patricia J Gautier, *Sec*
EMP: 7 **EST:** 1991
SQ FT: 22,500
SALES (est): 386.72K **Privately Held**
Web: www.mid-pineshosiery.com
SIC: 2252 Anklets and socks

(G-14154)
MODERN MACHINING INC
115 Brady Rd (27330-9503)
PHONE...........................919 775-7332
John Clark, *Pr*
EMP: 5 **EST:** 1986
SQ FT: 8,000
SALES (est): 416.33K **Privately Held**
Web: modern-machining.business.site
SIC: 3599 Machine shop, jobbing and repair

(G-14155)
MTZ WELDING INC
1108 Lemmond Dr (27330-7639)
PHONE...........................919 708-8288
EMP: 4 **EST:** 2018
SALES (est): 150.44K **Privately Held**
SIC: 7692 Welding repair

(G-14156)
N & N INDUSTRIES INC
5319 Womack Rd (27330-9517)
PHONE...........................919 770-1311
Novella Richardson, *Pr*
EMP: 4 **EST:** 2020
SALES (est): 114.06K **Privately Held**
SIC: 3999 Manufacturing industries, nec

(G-14157)
NC LOGGING & CLEARING LLC
207 Wilson Rd (27332-9648)
PHONE...........................919 524-4878
Johnny Fernando Fonseca, *Owner*
EMP: 7 **EST:** 2018
SALES (est): 284.77K **Privately Held**
SIC: 2411 Logging

(G-14158)
NEW BOSTON FRUIT SLICE & CONFE
Also Called: Boston Fruit Slice & Conf
2627 Watson Ave (27332-6146)
PHONE...........................919 775-2471
Michael Hiera, *Pr*
EMP: 24 **EST:** 2001
SQ FT: 1,800
SALES (est): 2.59MM **Privately Held**
Web: www.bostonfruitslice.com
SIC: 2064 Candy and other confectionery products

(G-14159)
NOBLE OIL SERVICES INC
5617 Clyde Rhyne Dr (27330-9562)
PHONE...........................919 774-8180
James Noble, *Pr*
Richard Kalin, *
EMP: 120 **EST:** 1983
SQ FT: 1,800
SALES (est): 31.56MM **Privately Held**
Web: www.nobleoil.com
SIC: 1799 4953 7699 1795 Decontamination services; Recycling, waste materials; Tank repair and cleaning services; Dismantling steel oil tanks

(G-14160)
OLIVIA MACHINE & TOOL INC
815 Seawell Rosser Rd (27332-2411)
P.O. Box 351 (28368-0351)
PHONE...........................919 499-6021
Terry W Thomas, *Pr*
Sam Thomas, *VP*
Waylon W Thomas, *Sec*
Sammy D Thomas, *Sec*
Wayne W Thomas, *Treas*
EMP: 18 **EST:** 1981
SQ FT: 30,000
SALES (est): 2.51MM **Privately Held**
Web: www.oliviamachine.com
SIC: 3599 Machine shop, jobbing and repair

(G-14161)
PACKET PUSHERS INTERACTIVE LLC
500 Westover Dr Ste 16993 (27330-8941)
PHONE...........................928 793-2450
Ethan Banks, *Managing Member*
EMP: 7 **EST:** 2012
SALES (est): 173.8K **Privately Held**
Web: www.packetpushers.net
SIC: 3545 Pushers

(G-14162)
PAPER ROUTE TRANSPORTATION LLC
347 Longstreet Rd (27330-0655)
PHONE...........................919 478-6615
Bradley Brown Senior, *CEO*
Bradley Brown Senior, *Managing Member*
EMP: 5 **EST:** 2021
SALES (est): 245.46K **Privately Held**
SIC: 7389 3537 Business Activities at Non-Commercial Site; Trucks: freight, baggage, etc.: industrial, except mining

(G-14163)
PARKDALE MILLS INCORPORATED
Also Called: Parkdale Plant 29
1921 Boone Trail Rd (27330-9414)
PHONE...........................919 774-7401
Robert Ward, *Prin*
EMP: 57
SALES (corp-wide): 1.44B **Privately Held**
Web: www.parkdalemills.com
SIC: 2281 Yarn spinning mills
HQ: Parkdale Mills, Incorporated
   531 Cotton Blossom Cir
   Gastonia NC 28054
   704 874-5000

(G-14164)
PCC AIRFOILS LLC
Also Called: Sherwood Refractores
5105 Rex Mcleod Dr (27330-9539)
PHONE...........................919 774-4300
Steve Chance, *Mgr*
EMP: 395
SALES (corp-wide): 364.48B **Publicly Held**
Web: www.pccairfoils.com
SIC: 3369 3728 3714 3297 Castings, except die-castings, precision; Aircraft parts and equipment, nec; Motor vehicle parts and accessories; Castable refractories, nonclay
HQ: Pcc Airfoils, Llc
   3401 Entp Pkwy Ste 200
   Cleveland OH 44122
   216 831-3590

(G-14165)
PEARSON TEXTILES INC
7975 Villanow Dr (27332-7595)
P.O. Box 1289 (27331-1289)
PHONE...........................919 776-8730
Mike W Gonella, *Pr*
Cynthia Gonella, *
EMP: 6 **EST:** 1974
SQ FT: 40,000
SALES (est): 383.25K **Privately Held**
SIC: 5131 2281 Textiles, woven, nec; Knitting yarn, spun

(G-14166)
PENTAIR WATER POOL AND SPA INC (DH)
Also Called: Pentair Pool Products
1620 Hawkins Ave (27330-9501)
PHONE...........................919 566-8000
Mario R D'ovidio, *Pr*
Karl Frykman, *Pr*
Robert D Miller, *VP*
Dave Murray, *VP Sls*
◆ **EMP:** 600 **EST:** 1971
SALES (est): 557.81MM **Privately Held**
Web: www.pentairpool.com
SIC: 3589 3561 3569 3648 Swimming pool filter and water conditioning systems; Pumps, domestic: water or sump; Heaters, swimming pool: electric; Underwater lighting fixtures
HQ: Pentair, Inc.
   5500 Wayzata Blvd Ste 900
   Minneapolis MN 55416
   763 545-1730

(G-14167)
PERRY BROTHERS TIRE SVC INC (PA)
610 Wicker St (27330-4141)
P.O. Box 968 (27331-0968)
PHONE...........................919 775-7225
Hugh P Perry, *CEO*
Paul Steven Perry, *Pr*
Charles Ross Perry, *VP*
Hal Chaplan Perry, *VP*
Paul Horton, *VP*
EMP: 21 **EST:** 1932
SQ FT: 8,000
SALES (est): 8.2MM
SALES (corp-wide): 8.2MM **Privately Held**
Web: www.blackstire.com
SIC: 5531 5722 5014 7534 Automotive tires; Household appliance stores; Automobile tires and tubes; Tire recapping

(G-14168)
PFIZER INC
Wyeth
4300 Oak Park Rd (27330-9550)
PHONE...........................919 775-7100
Bruce Kaylos, *Brnch Mgr*
EMP: 125
SALES (corp-wide): 100.33B **Publicly Held**
Web: www.pfizer.com
SIC: 2836 5122 2834 Biological products, except diagnostic; Biologicals and allied products; Pharmaceutical preparations
PA: Pfizer Inc.
   66 Hudson Blvd E
   New York NY 10001
   800 879-3477

(G-14169)
PHILOSOPHY INC (HQ)
Also Called: Biotech Research Laboratories
1400 Broadway Rd (27332-7713)
PHONE...........................602 794-8701
▲ **EMP:** 40 **EST:** 1996
SQ FT: 55,000
SALES (est): 27.46MM **Publicly Held**
Web: www.philosophy.com
SIC: 5122 2844 Cosmetics; Perfumes, cosmetics and other toilet preparations
PA: Coty Inc.
   350 5th Ave Ste 2700
   New York NY 10118

(G-14170)
PIEDMONT SALES & RENTALS LLC
Also Called: Piedmont Sales
5074 Nc 87 N (27332-2858)
P.O. Box 516 (28368-0516)

GEOGRAPHIC SECTION
Sanford - Lee County (G-14194)

PHONE..............................919 499-9888
EMP: 6 **EST:** 1995
SQ FT: 5,750
SALES (est): 616.8K **Privately Held**
Web: www.piedmontutilitybuildings.com
SIC: 2452 Prefabricated buildings, wood

(G-14171)
PILGRIMS PRIDE CORPORATION
484 Zimmerman Rd (27330-0519)
PHONE..............................919 774-7333
Phil Brooks, *Mgr*
EMP: 39
Web: www.pilgrims.com
SIC: 2015 Poultry slaughtering and processing
HQ: Pilgrim's Pride Corporation
  1770 Promontory Cir
  Greeley CO 80634
  970 506-8000

(G-14172)
PRS GROUP LLC
500 Westover Dr (27330-8941)
PHONE..............................910 550-0088
EMP: 4 **EST:** 2019
SALES (est): 155.63K **Privately Held**
SIC: 2741 Miscellaneous publishing

(G-14173)
RALPH B HALL
Also Called: M & G Screen Service
804 Cox Maddox Rd (27332-8505)
PHONE..............................919 258-3634
Ralph B Hall, *Owner*
EMP: 8 **EST:** 1965
SALES (est): 487.38K **Privately Held**
SIC: 3569 Filters

(G-14174)
ROCTOOL INC
5900 Westover Dr #15609 (27330)
PHONE..............................888 364-6321
Mathieu Boulanger, *Pr*
EMP: 7 **EST:** 2013
SALES (est): 1.89MM
SALES (corp-wide): 8.1MM **Privately Held**
Web: www.roctool.com
SIC: 3585 Parts for heating, cooling, and refrigerating equipment
PA: Roctool
  Modul R Savoie Technolac
  Le Bourget Du Lac 73270
  479262707

(G-14175)
RODECO COMPANY
5811 Elwin Buchanan Dr (27330-9541)
PHONE..............................919 775-7149
Ryan Murphy, *Pr*
EMP: 19 **EST:** 1961
SQ FT: 28,000
SALES (est): 4.84MM **Privately Held**
Web: www.rodeco.com
SIC: 5084 3471 Metalworking machinery; Anodizing (plating) of metals or formed products

(G-14176)
ROGER D THOMAS
8313 Hillcrest Farm Rd (27330-9006)
PHONE..............................919 258-3148
Roger D Thomas, *Prin*
EMP: 7 **EST:** 2005
SALES (est): 132.59K **Privately Held**
SIC: 3827 Optical instruments and lenses

(G-14177)
ROGUE CUSTOM KOTE LLC
347 Altons Ln (27332-6922)
PHONE..............................919 498-5000
Matt Rosser, *Prin*
EMP: 4 **EST:** 2018
SALES (est): 169.58K **Privately Held**
Web: www.roguecustomkote.com
SIC: 3479 Coating of metals and formed products

(G-14178)
S T WOOTEN CORPORATION
Also Called: Sanford Asphalt Plant
966 Rocky Fork Church Rd (27332-0838)
PHONE..............................919 776-2736
Scott Wooten, *Pr*
EMP: 40
SALES (corp-wide): 319.83MM **Privately Held**
Web: www.stwcorp.com
SIC: 3531 Asphalt plant, including gravel-mix type
PA: S. T. Wooten Corporation
  3801 Black Creek Rd Se
  Wilson NC 27893
  252 291-5165

(G-14179)
SANDHILLS CNSLD SVCS INC
Also Called: Scs Wood Products
200 E Williams St (27332-6149)
P.O. Box 2592 (27331-2592)
PHONE..............................919 718-7909
Jerry Davis, *CEO*
Michelle Davis, *
EMP: 38 **EST:** 2009
SALES (est): 4.41MM **Privately Held**
Web: www.scswoodproducts.com
SIC: 2448 Pallets, wood

(G-14180)
SANFORD COCA-COLA BOTTLING CO
Also Called: Coca-Cola
1605 Hawkins Ave (27330-9501)
P.O. Box 1207 (27331-1207)
PHONE..............................919 774-4111
Charles A Ingram, *Pr*
Margaret Harrington, *
EMP: 20 **EST:** 1907
SQ FT: 30,000
SALES (est): 1.23MM **Privately Held**
Web: www.coca-cola.com
SIC: 2086 Bottled and canned soft drinks

(G-14181)
SANFORD KITCHEN & BATH INC
1062 Hickory House Rd (27332-9132)
PHONE..............................919 708-9080
EMP: 6 **EST:** 2010
SALES (est): 150.91K **Privately Held**
Web: www.sanfordkitchenandbath.com
SIC: 2434 Wood kitchen cabinets

(G-14182)
SANFORD TRANSITION COMPANY INC
5108 Rex Mcleod Dr (27330-9539)
P.O. Box 421 (28350-0421)
PHONE..............................919 775-4989
▲ **EMP:** 50 **EST:** 1995
SQ FT: 50,000
SALES (est): 33.57MM
SALES (corp-wide): 3.85B **Privately Held**
Web: www.fuchs.com
SIC: 2992 7389 Lubricating oils and greases ; Packaging and labeling services
HQ: Fuchs Lubricants Co.
  17050 Lathrop Ave
  Harvey IL 60426
  708 333-8900

(G-14183)
SEAL IT SERVICES INC
3301 Industrial Dr (27326-6072)
PHONE..............................919 777-0374
David Moore, *Pr*
EMP: 12 **EST:** 2016
SQ FT: 30,000
SALES (est): 6.11MM
SALES (corp-wide): 542.1K **Privately Held**
Web: www.sealitgroup.com
SIC: 2822 Silicone rubbers
PA: Bond It Limited
  231-233 Elliott Street
  Manchester M29 8
  161 737-6270

(G-14184)
SILLAMAN & SONS INC
Also Called: PIP Printing
356 Wilson Rd (27332-9616)
PHONE..............................919 774-6324
Samuel W Sillaman, *Pr*
EMP: 4 **EST:** 1986
SQ FT: 3,500
SALES (est): 250K **Privately Held**
Web: www.pip.com
SIC: 2752 7334 2741 Offset printing; Photocopying and duplicating services; Miscellaneous publishing

(G-14185)
SK ENTERPRISES MFG LLC
129 Flowers Ln (27332-7584)
PHONE..............................919 721-1458
Sheryl Krieger, *Prin*
EMP: 6 **EST:** 2008
SALES (est): 141.48K **Privately Held**
Web: www.brandpa.com
SIC: 3999 Manufacturing industries, nec

(G-14186)
SLOANS MACHINE SHOP
1186 Walker Rd (27332-9650)
P.O. Box 2261 (27331-2261)
PHONE..............................919 499-5655
Jerry Sloan, *Owner*
EMP: 6 **EST:** 1991
SALES (est): 335.15K **Privately Held**
SIC: 3599 Machine shop, jobbing and repair

(G-14187)
SOUTHERN ELC & AUTOMTN CORP
Also Called: Direct South Logistics
800 Hawkins Ave (27330-3312)
P.O. Box 733 (27331-0733)
PHONE..............................919 718-0122
David Griffith, *Pr*
◆ **EMP:** 13 **EST:** 2002
SQ FT: 1,500
SALES (est): 1.03MM **Privately Held**
Web: www.seacorpservices.com
SIC: 1731 3825 3661 General electrical contractor; Integrating electricity meters; Data sets, telephone or telegraph

(G-14188)
SOUTHERN ELEMENTS HARDSCAPES
301 Bruce Coggins Rd (27332-9113)
PHONE..............................240 626-1586
Leslie Driver, *Prin*
EMP: 4 **EST:** 2016
SALES (est): 144.79K **Privately Held**
SIC: 3271 0781 0782 Blocks, concrete: landscape or retaining wall; Landscape planning services; Landscape contractors

(G-14189)
SPANSET INC (HQ)
3125 Industrial Dr (27332-6068)

P.O. Box 2828 (27331-2828)
PHONE..............................919 774-6316
Kenneth Milligan, *CEO*
William Lyn Roberts, *
◆ **EMP:** 36 **EST:** 1980
SQ FT: 42,000
SALES (est): 14.8MM **Privately Held**
Web: www.spanset.com
SIC: 2241 Fabric tapes
PA: Spanset Inter Ag
  Samstagernstrasse 45
  Wollerau SZ 8832

(G-14190)
SRI VENTURES INC
3415 Hawkins Ave (27330-6944)
PHONE..............................919 427-1681
Ashley Bethea, *Brnch Mgr*
EMP: 9
SALES (corp-wide): 4.74MM **Privately Held**
Web: www.sri.com
SIC: 2741 Telephone and other directory publishing
PA: Sri Ventures, Inc.
  1071 Classic Rd
  Apex NC 27539
  919 465-2300

(G-14191)
STATIC CONTROL COMPONENTS INC (DH)
Also Called: Static Control
3010 Lee Ave (27332-6210)
P.O. Box 152 (27331-0152)
PHONE..............................919 774-3808
Juan Carlos Bonell, *Ch*
Michael L Swartz, *
◆ **EMP:** 1190 **EST:** 1987
SALES (est): 297.93MM **Privately Held**
Web: www.scc-inc.com
SIC: 3629 3955 Static elimination equipment, industrial; Print cartridges for laser and other computer printers
HQ: Jihai Microelectronics Co., Ltd.
  F1, F2 Area A, F3, F5, F6, F7, F8, F9, Block 01, No.83 Guangwan
  Zhuhai GD

(G-14192)
STATIC CONTROL IC-DISC INC
3010 Lee Ave (27332-6210)
P.O. Box 152 (27331-0152)
PHONE..............................919 774-3808
William London, *VP*
EMP: 37 **EST:** 1987
SALES (est): 529.75K **Privately Held**
Web: www.scc-inc.com
SIC: 3629 Blasting machines, electrical

(G-14193)
STEEL AND PIPE CORPORATION
3709 Hawkins Ave (27330-9519)
P.O. Box 700 (27331-0700)
PHONE..............................919 776-0751
EMP: 37 **EST:** 1961
SALES (est): 22.23MM **Privately Held**
Web: www.steelandpipecorp.com
SIC: 5051 3441 Steel; Fabricated structural metal

(G-14194)
STI POLYMER INC
5618 Clyde Rhyne Dr (27330-9562)
PHONE..............................800 874-5878
Jeffrey A Lamb, *Pr*
▲ **EMP:** 20 **EST:** 1978
SQ FT: 30,000
SALES (est): 8.31MM **Privately Held**
Web: www.stipolymer.com
SIC: 2891 Adhesives

Sanford - Lee County (G-14195)

(G-14195)
TED M HART LOGGING INC
3760 S Plank Rd (27330-7557)
PHONE...............................919 776-7237
EMP: 5 EST: 2019
SALES (est): 234.78K Privately Held
SIC: 2411 Logging

(G-14196)
THOMAS & GENDICS INC
2428 Hickory House Rd (27332-9195)
PHONE...............................919 842-7860
Joe Gendics, Prin
EMP: 5 EST: 2013
SALES (est): 144.46K Privately Held
SIC: 3499 Fabricated metal products, nec

(G-14197)
TOWER HOUSE PUBLISHING LLC
500 Westover Dr Ste 11228 (27330-8941)
PHONE...............................917 284-0619
EMP: 7
SALES (est): 79.3K Privately Held
SIC: 2731 Books, publishing and printing

(G-14198)
TRAMWAY VENEERS INC
2603 Tramway Rd (27332-9175)
P.O. Box 322 (27331-0322)
PHONE...............................919 776-7606
Lowell W Rickard, Ch Bd
Tim Mcfarland, VP
Linda Bryant, Sec
Carroll Rickard, Sls Dir
EMP: 25 EST: 1965
SQ FT: 26,000
SALES (est): 1.66MM Privately Held
Web: www.yorkflowershop.com
SIC: 2435 Hardwood veneer and plywood

(G-14199)
TRANSDATA SOLUTIONS INC
221 N Horner Blvd (27330-3965)
P.O. Box 110021 (27709-5021)
PHONE...............................919 770-9329
Matthew Sakurad, CEO
EMP: 7 EST: 2017
SALES (est): 231.97K Privately Held
Web: www.transdatasolutions.com
SIC: 7372 Business oriented computer software

(G-14200)
TRIAD CORRUGATED METAL INC
Also Called: Triad Corrugated Metal
109 Mcneill Rd (27330-9451)
PHONE...............................919 775-1663
EMP: 15
SALES (corp-wide): 19.39MM Privately Held
Web: www.triadcorrugatedmetal.com
SIC: 3444 Sheet metalwork
PA: Triad Corrugated Metal, Inc.
208 Luck Rd
Asheboro NC 27205
336 625-9727

(G-14201)
TYSON MEXICAN ORIGINAL INC
800 E Main St (27332-9708)
PHONE...............................919 777-9428
Richard Price, Mgr
EMP: 98
SALES (corp-wide): 52.88B Publicly Held
Web: www.tysonfoods.com
SIC: 2032 2099 2096 Mexican foods, nec; packaged in cans, jars, etc.; Food preparations, nec; Potato chips and similar snacks
HQ: Tyson Mexican Original, Inc.
2200 W Don Tyson Pkwy
Springdale AR 72762
479 290-6111

(G-14202)
UNIFI INC
1921 Boone Trail Rd (27330-9414)
PHONE...............................919 774-7401
EMP: 4
SALES (corp-wide): 623.53MM Publicly Held
Web: www.unifi.com
SIC: 2281 Cotton yarn, spun
PA: Unifi, Inc.
7201 W Friendly Ave
Greensboro NC 27410
336 294-4410

(G-14203)
VIOLET SANFORD HOLDINGS LLC
Also Called: Boone Brands
2209 Boone Trail Rd (27330-8641)
PHONE...............................919 775-5931
EMP: 50 EST: 2014
SALES (est): 5.03MM Privately Held
Web: www.boonebrands.com
SIC: 2099 Sauce, gravy, dressing, and dip mixes

(G-14204)
VIVID PRO SIGNS
1671 S Plank Rd (27330-3067)
PHONE...............................919 352-8485
Katti Sheffield, Prin
EMP: 4 EST: 2016
SALES (est): 69.11K Privately Held
SIC: 3993 Signs and advertising specialties

(G-14205)
WHITE TIGER BTQ & CANDLE CO ◆
3206 Smokey Path (27330-0907)
PHONE...............................919 610-7244
Keiomi Woodson, CEO
EMP: 5 EST: 2023
SALES (est): 229.6K Privately Held
SIC: 3999 7389 Candles; Business Activities at Non-Commercial Site

(G-14206)
WILLIAMS ELECTRIC MTR REPR INC
2515 Cox Mill Rd Ste A (27332-7701)
PHONE...............................919 859-9790
George Williams, Pr
EMP: 4 EST: 2008
SALES (est): 422.26K Privately Held
SIC: 7694 5531 Electric motor repair; Auto and home supply stores

(G-14207)
WILSON MACHINE & TOOL INC
4956 Womack Rd (27330-9592)
P.O. Box 773 (27331-0773)
PHONE...............................919 776-0043
EMP: 8 EST: 1992
SQ FT: 10,000
SALES (est): 981.64K Privately Held
Web: www.wmtusa.com
SIC: 3599 Machine shop, jobbing and repair

(G-14208)
WOLVERINE MTAL STMPING SLTONS
Also Called: Metal Stamping Solutions
5720 Clyde Rhyne Dr (27330-9563)
PHONE...............................919 774-4729
Rick Dresser, Managing Member
EMP: 20 EST: 2002
SQ FT: 38,000
SALES (est): 1.66MM Privately Held
Web: www.stampingsolutionsnc.com
SIC: 3469 Stamping metal for the trade

(G-14209)
WORLD STONE OF SANFORD LLC
3201 Industrial Dr (27332-6070)
PHONE...............................919 468-8450
EMP: 12 EST: 2013
SALES (est): 545.11K Privately Held
SIC: 3281 Cut stone and stone products

(G-14210)
WYETH HOLDINGS LLC
Also Called: Wyeth Pharmaceutical Division
4300 Oak Park Rd (27330-9550)
PHONE...............................919 775-7100
EMP: 1401
SALES (corp-wide): 100.33B Publicly Held
SIC: 2834 Pharmaceutical preparations
HQ: Wyeth Holdings Llc
5 Giralda Farms
Madison NJ 07940

(G-14211)
ZURN ELKAY WTR SOLUTIONS CORP
5900 Elwin Buchanan Dr (27330-9525)
PHONE...............................855 663-9876
EMP: 7
SIC: 3491 Water works valves
PA: Zurn Elkay Water Solutions Corporation
511 W Freshwater Way
Milwaukee WI 53204

(G-14212)
ZURN INDUSTRIES LLC
Zurn Commercial Brass
5900 Elwin Buchanan Dr (27330-9525)
PHONE...............................919 775-2255
EMP: 22
Web: www.zurn.com
SIC: 5074 3499 Plumbing and hydronic heating supplies; Aerosol valves, metal
HQ: Zurn Industries, Llc
511 W Freshwater Way
Milwaukee WI 53204
855 663-9876

Sapphire
Transylvania County

(G-14213)
LBM INDUSTRIES INC
Also Called: Toxaway Concrete
17668 Rosman Hwy (28774)
P.O. Box 40 (28774-0040)
PHONE...............................828 966-4270
EMP: 10
SALES (corp-wide): 9.72MM Privately Held
Web: www.mcneelycompanies.com
SIC: 3281 5032 1475 Stone, quarrying and processing of own stone products; Stone, crushed or broken; Phosphate rock
PA: Lbm Industries, Inc.
2000 Whitewater Rd
Sapphire NC 28774
828 966-4270

(G-14214)
LBM INDUSTRIES INC (PA)
Also Called: McNeelys Store Rental & Eqp
2000 Whitewater Rd (28774)
P.O. Box 40 (28774-0040)
PHONE...............................828 966-4270
William L Mc Neely Junior, Pr
William L Mc Neely Iii, VP
Grace Mc Neely, Treas
Kathy Fisher, Sec
EMP: 11 EST: 1976
SQ FT: 8,000
SALES (est): 9.72MM
SALES (corp-wide): 9.72MM Privately Held
Web: www.lbmindustries.com
SIC: 1411 5231 Dimension stone; Paint, glass, and wallpaper stores

(G-14215)
MCNEELY TRUCKING CO
17692 Rosman Hwy (28774)
P.O. Box 40 (28774-0040)
PHONE...............................828 966-4270
William L Mcneely Junior, Pr
Grace Mc Neely, Treas
EMP: 42 EST: 1971
SQ FT: 3,000
SALES (est): 1.73MM Privately Held
Web: www.mcneelycompanies.com
SIC: 1411 Dimension stone

Saratoga
Wilson County

(G-14216)
OLD SARATOGA INC
6351 Nc Hwy 222 (27873)
P.O. Box 270 (27873-0270)
PHONE...............................252 238-2175
Fitzgerald D Hudson, Ch
M Grady Golson, *
Christopher A Hudson, *
Keith Johnston, *
EMP: 25 EST: 1993
SQ FT: 45,000
SALES (est): 2.24MM Privately Held
Web: www.oldsaratogainc.com
SIC: 2086 5963 Bottled and canned soft drinks; Bottled water delivery

Saxapahaw
Alamance County

(G-14217)
HAW RIVER FARMHOUSE ALES LLC
1713 Sax-Beth Church Rd (27340)
P.O. Box 390 (27340-0390)
PHONE...............................336 525-9270
EMP: 9 EST: 2011
SALES (est): 516.22K Privately Held
Web: www.hawriverstore.com
SIC: 2082 Beer (alcoholic beverage)

Scotland Neck
Halifax County

(G-14218)
AIRBOSS RBR COMPOUNDING NC LLC
Also Called: Airboss Rubber Solutions
500 Airboss Pkwy (27874-1567)
PHONE...............................252 826-4919
Robert Hagerman, Pr
Wendy Ford, *
Earl Laurie, *
Yvan Ambeault, *
Lisa Swartzman, *
▲ EMP: 40 EST: 2004
SALES (est): 14.37MM
SALES (corp-wide): 477.15MM Privately Held
Web: www.airboss.com
SIC: 3011 Automobile tires, pneumatic
PA: Airboss Of America Corp
16441 Yonge St
Newmarket ON L3X 2
905 751-1188

GEOGRAPHIC SECTION

Seagrove - Randolph County (G-14246)

(G-14219)
JOSEY LUMBER COMPANY INC
476 Lees Meadow Rd (27874-8778)
P.O. Box 447 (27874-0447)
PHONE.....................252 826-5614
Joey Josey, *Pr*
Deborah G Josey, *
EMP: 40 **EST:** 1983
SQ FT: 1,200
SALES (est): 5.5MM **Privately Held**
SIC: 2421 2426 Lumber: rough, sawed, or planed; Hardwood dimension and flooring mills

(G-14220)
SCOTLAND NECK HEART PINE INC
25574 Hwy 125 (27874)
P.O. Box 536 (27874-0536)
PHONE.....................252 826-2755
Hodge Kitchin, *Owner*
Hodge Kitchin, *Pr*
EMP: 9 **EST:** 2003
SALES (est): 722.87K **Privately Held**
Web: www.snheartpine.com
SIC: 2439 Arches, laminated lumber

(G-14221)
SHENANDOAH WOOD PRESERVERS INC
301 E 16th St (27874-1707)
P.O. Box 310 (27874-0310)
PHONE.....................252 826-4151
Courtney Hutcherson, *Pr*
J Eldrige Wimmer, *Prin*
Steve Michael, *VP*
Brenda Jones, *Treas*
Anthony Bailey, *Dir*
EMP: 23 **EST:** 1987
SQ FT: 2,000
SALES (est): 1.83MM **Privately Held**
SIC: 2491 Wood preserving

(G-14222)
SOUTH EASTERN ELECTRIC WHL
34747 Nc 903 (27874)
PHONE.....................252 826-0123
EMP: 4 **EST:** 2016
SALES (est): 169.4K **Privately Held**
SIC: 5099 3699 Durable goods, nec; Electrical equipment and supplies, nec

(G-14223)
W H BUNTING THINNING
2305 Bynums Bridge Rd (27874-8970)
PHONE.....................252 826-4025
William Bunting, *Owner*
EMP: 4 **EST:** 1995
SALES (est): 277.85K **Privately Held**
SIC: 2411 Logging

(G-14224)
WIGGINS DESIGN FABRICATION INC
140 Edwards Fork Rd (27874-8692)
P.O. Box 252 (27874-0252)
PHONE.....................252 826-5239
James C Wiggins, *Pr*
Kelvin L Wiggins, *VP*
Lendo M Wiggins, *Treas*
Linda Wiggins, *Pr*
EMP: 9 **EST:** 1972
SQ FT: 21,000
SALES (est): 987.74K **Privately Held**
Web: www.wigginsdesign.com
SIC: 3443 Fabricated plate work (boiler shop)

(G-14225)
WOOD BARN INC
476 Lees Meadow Rd (27874-8778)
PHONE.....................252 826-5538
Ken Baisey, *Brnch Mgr*
EMP: 12
Web: www.woodbarn.com
SIC: 2431 Staircases and stairs, wood
PA: The Wood Barn Inc
206 Clifton Ridge Ct
Louisburg NC 27549

Seaboard
Northampton County

(G-14226)
BLAST OFF INTL CHEM & MFG CO
199 Crocker St (27876-9713)
PHONE.....................509 885-4525
Ellen Mclaughlin, *Pr*
Liana Mclaughlin, *Pr*
Shelley Van Dyk, *VP*
EMP: 4 **EST:** 1979
SALES (est): 1.3MM **Privately Held**
SIC: 2899 Chemical preparations, nec

(G-14227)
CAROLINA BARK PRODUCTS LLC
Hwy 186 E (27876)
P.O. Box 395 (27876-0395)
PHONE.....................252 589-1324
EMP: 8 **EST:** 2002
SALES (est): 535.77K **Privately Held**
Web: www.carolinabarkproducts.com
SIC: 2499 Mulch, wood and bark

(G-14228)
ELSCO INC (PA)
199 Crocker St (27876-9713)
P.O. Box 99 (27876-0099)
PHONE.....................509 885-4525
Earl Smith, *Pr*
Liana Mclaughlin, *Mgr*
EMP: 4 **EST:** 1952
SQ FT: 1,488
SALES (est): 784.79K
SALES (corp-wide): 784.79K **Privately Held**
SIC: 2842 Cleaning or polishing preparations, nec

(G-14229)
MILLER MEAT PROCESSING LLC
2365 Big Johns Store Rd (27876-9531)
PHONE.....................252 589-0004
Titus Miller, *Owner*
EMP: 5 **EST:** 2014
SALES (est): 232.24K **Privately Held**
Web: www.customestatespainting.com
SIC: 2011 Meat packing plants

(G-14230)
WEST FRASER INC
4400 Nc Hwy 186 (27876)
P.O. Box 459 (27876-0459)
PHONE.....................252 589-2011
Carl Buck, *Mgr*
EMP: 189
SALES (corp-wide): 7.22B **Privately Held**
SIC: 2421 Sawmills and planing mills, general
HQ: Fraser West Inc
1900 Exeter Rd Ste 105
Germantown TN 38138
901 620-4200

Seagrove
Randolph County

(G-14231)
4 SEASONS FURNITURE INDUST LLC
236 N Broad St (27341-9202)
P.O. Box 10 (27341-0010)
PHONE.....................336 873-7245
Kenneth H Hill, *Managing Member*
▼ **EMP:** 14 **EST:** 1999
SALES (est): 926.23K **Privately Held**
Web: www.shopfourseasonsfurniture.com
SIC: 2512 Couches, sofas, and davenports: upholstered on wood frames

(G-14232)
A & S LOGGING LLC
4170 Maness Rd (27341-8611)
PHONE.....................336 879-4364
EMP: 5 **EST:** 2016
SALES (est): 213.3K **Privately Held**
SIC: 2411 Logging camps and contractors

(G-14233)
CAGLE FRAMES LLC
978 Brewer Rd (27341-7282)
PHONE.....................910 464-1170
Frankie J Cagle, *Managing Member*
EMP: 8 **EST:** 2010
SALES (est): 424.75K **Privately Held**
SIC: 2426 Hardwood dimension and flooring mills

(G-14234)
CALDWELL HOHL ARTWORKS
155 Cabin Trl (27341-8606)
PHONE.....................336 879-9090
Debbie Struz, *Prin*
EMP: 5 **EST:** 2010
SALES (est): 65.25K **Privately Held**
SIC: 3999 Framed artwork

(G-14235)
CAROLINA BRONZE SCULPTURE INC
Also Called: Carolina Bronze
6108 Maple Springs Rd (27341-9047)
PHONE.....................336 873-8291
EMP: 9 **EST:** 1990
SQ FT: 8,200
SALES (est): 1.07MM **Privately Held**
Web: www.carolinabronze.com
SIC: 3366 Copper foundries

(G-14236)
CAROLINA FURNITURE MFRS INC
1776 Pleasant Ridge Rd (27341)
PHONE.....................336 873-7355
Richard Williamson, *Prin*
EMP: 5 **EST:** 2008
SALES (est): 150.8K **Privately Held**
SIC: 2531 2521 2511 Public building and related furniture; Wood office furniture; Wood household furniture

(G-14237)
E Z FRAMES
978 Brewer Rd (27341-7282)
PHONE.....................910 464-1813
Frankie Cagle, *Owner*
EMP: 4 **EST:** 2000
SALES (est): 266.69K **Privately Held**
SIC: 2426 Frames for upholstered furniture, wood

(G-14238)
EVIL SWINGARMS 1 LLC
4342 Woodfern Rd (27341-8534)
PHONE.....................336 847-2476
EMP: 5 **EST:** 2016
SALES (est): 266.75K **Privately Held**
SIC: 3751 Motorcycles, bicycles and parts

(G-14239)
H & H FURNITURE MFRS INC
Also Called: Casual Crates
236 N Broad St (27341-9202)
P.O. Box 10 (27341-0010)
PHONE.....................336 873-7245
Ken H Hill, *Pr*
Jerry Hill, *
EMP: 120 **EST:** 1979
SQ FT: 290,000
SALES (est): 4.53MM **Privately Held**
Web: www.americanloftandlounge.com
SIC: 2511 3949 Wood household furniture; Sporting and athletic goods, nec

(G-14240)
JOSH ALLRED
335 N Broad St (27341-8540)
PHONE.....................336 873-1006
Josh Allred, *Prin*
EMP: 7 **EST:** 2011
SALES (est): 177.24K **Privately Held**
SIC: 3621 Generators and sets, electric

(G-14241)
JUGTOWN POTTERY
330 Jugtown Rd (27341-7402)
PHONE.....................910 464-3266
Vernon Owens, *Owner*
EMP: 6 **EST:** 1920
SALES (est): 222.81K **Privately Held**
Web: www.jugtownware.com
SIC: 3269 5719 Pottery products, nec; Pottery

(G-14242)
K & J ASHWORTH LOGGING LLC
8797 Erect Rd (27341-9098)
PHONE.....................336 879-2388
EMP: 5 **EST:** 2018
SALES (est): 215.26K **Privately Held**
SIC: 2411 Logging

(G-14243)
KNOWLTON WOODWORKING LLC
523 Gap Rd (27341-9505)
PHONE.....................336 588-3502
Robert Knowlton, *Prin*
EMP: 4 **EST:** 2019
SALES (est): 54.13K **Privately Held**
SIC: 2431 Millwork

(G-14244)
MCNEILL FRAME INC
3631 Alternate Rd (27341)
PHONE.....................336 873-7934
Gene Mcneill, *Pr*
EMP: 24 **EST:** 2001
SQ FT: 40,000
SALES (est): 964.46K **Privately Held**
SIC: 2426 Frames for upholstered furniture, wood

(G-14245)
REEDER PALLET COMPANY INC
435 Reeder Rd (27341-7470)
P.O. Box 540 (27341-0540)
PHONE.....................336 879-3095
Cecil Reeder, *Pr*
EMP: 16 **EST:** 1989
SQ FT: 3,000
SALES (est): 792.43K **Privately Held**
Web: www.reederpallet.com
SIC: 2448 Pallets, wood

(G-14246)
RITTER FAB LLC
5829 Riverside Rd (27341-8415)
PHONE.....................336 879-2428
Joseph Ritter, *Prin*

EMP: 6 **EST:** 2015
SALES (est): 247.34K **Privately Held**
SIC: 3999 Manufacturing industries, nec

(G-14247)
SAPONA PLASTIC LLC
798 Nc Highway 705 (27341-8665)
PHONE..................................336 873-7201
EMP: 8 **EST:** 2013
SALES (est): 355.8K **Privately Held**
Web: www.saponaplastics.com
SIC: 3089 Injection molding of plastics

(G-14248)
SEAGROVE LUMBER LLC
558 Little River Golf Dr (27341-9308)
PHONE..................................910 428-9663
Philip Sechrest, *Mgr*
EMP: 10 **EST:** 2010
SALES (est): 916.53K **Privately Held**
Web: www.discoverseagrove.com
SIC: 2511 Bed frames, except water bed frames: wood

(G-14249)
STUDIO TOUYA
4911 Busbee Rd (27341-7281)
PHONE..................................910 464-3116
Hitomi Shibata, *Prin*
EMP: 5 **EST:** 2016
SALES (est): 62.56K **Privately Held**
Web: www.studiotouya.com
SIC: 3269 Pottery products, nec

Selma
Johnston County

(G-14250)
3DDUCTCLEANING LLC ◎
207 Merriman Dr (27576-3656)
PHONE..................................919 723-4512
EMP: 4 **EST:** 2022
SALES (est): 175.11K **Privately Held**
SIC: 3582 7389 Dryers, laundry: commercial, including coin-operated; Business services, nec

(G-14251)
AIRFLOW PRODUCTS COMPANY INC
100 Oak Tree Dr (27576-3540)
PHONE..................................919 975-0240
Roy Boswell, *Pr*
Jeff Holt, *
▲ **EMP:** 165 **EST:** 2002
SQ FT: 100,000
SALES (est): 23.65MM **Privately Held**
Web: viewer.zmags.com
SIC: 3564 Filters, air: furnaces, air conditioning equipment, etc.

(G-14252)
APC LLC
Also Called: Atlantic Coast Protein Co
1451 W Noble St (27576-3639)
PHONE..................................919 965-2051
Matt Ruppert, *Mgr*
EMP: 32
SALES (corp-wide): 192.23MM **Privately Held**
Web: www.apcproteins.com
SIC: 2048 Feed supplements
HQ: Apc, Llc
2425 Se Oak Tree Ct
Ankeny IA 50021
515 289-7600

(G-14253)
ATKINSON MILLING COMPANY
Also Called: Atkinson's Mill
95 Atkinson Mill Rd Intersection Hwy 42 & 39 (27576-9067)
PHONE..................................919 965-3547
Glen R Wheeler Junior, *Pr*
Tim Wheeler, *
▲ **EMP:** 60 **EST:** 1951
SQ FT: 2,500
SALES (est): 9.24MM **Privately Held**
Web: www.atkinsonmilling.com
SIC: 2041 Corn meal

(G-14254)
DREWS CABINETS AND CASES
8100 Nc Highway 42 E (27576-7940)
PHONE..................................919 796-3985
Drew Roy, *Owner*
EMP: 4 **EST:** 1997
SALES (est): 152.37K **Privately Held**
Web: www.drewscabinets.com
SIC: 2599 Cabinets, factory

(G-14255)
EATON CORPORATION
Cuttler Hmmer Cmrcl Cntrls Div
1100 E Preston St (27576-3162)
P.O. Box 57 (27576-0057)
PHONE..................................919 965-2341
Michael K Carper, *Brnch Mgr*
EMP: 200
Web: www.dix-eaton.com
SIC: 3643 Electric switches
HQ: Eaton Corporation
1000 Eaton Blvd
Cleveland OH 44122
440 523-5000

(G-14256)
GUYCLEE MILLWORK
1251 S Pollock St (27576-3401)
PHONE..................................919 202-5738
Rodney Chambers, *Genl Mgr*
EMP: 10 **EST:** 2006
SALES (est): 840.93K **Privately Held**
Web: www.guyclee.com
SIC: 2431 Doors, wood

(G-14257)
JOHNSTON COUNTY INDUSTRIES INC
Also Called: J C I
1100 E Preston St (27576-3162)
PHONE..................................919 743-8700
C W Sharek Junior, *CEO*
Lina Sanders-johnson, *Sec*
Durwood Woodall V, *Ch Bd*
EMP: 195 **EST:** 1975
SQ FT: 90,000
SALES (est): 8.3MM **Privately Held**
Web: www.jcindustries.com
SIC: 2448 3694 2452 Wood pallets and skids; Engine electrical equipment; Prefabricated wood buildings

(G-14258)
MIKE ATKINS & SON LOGGING INC
Also Called: Atkins, Mike & Son Logging
4336 Browns Pond Rd (27576-8119)
PHONE..................................919 965-8002
Mike Atkins, *Pr*
Jeff Atkins, *VP*
Betty Atkins, *Sec*
EMP: 4 **EST:** 1998
SALES (est): 525.24K **Privately Held**
SIC: 2411 Logging camps and contractors

(G-14259)
POWER LOGISTIXS LLC
108 Shady Grove Ct (27576-3674)
PHONE..................................919 799-0303
EMP: 4 **EST:** 2021
SALES (est): 149.8K **Privately Held**
SIC: 3743 Freight cars and equipment

(G-14260)
SONA AUTOCOMP USA LLC
500 Oak Tree Dr (27576-3544)
PHONE..................................919 965-5555
EMP: 165 **EST:** 2008
SALES (est): 32.26MM
SALES (corp-wide): 240.01MM **Privately Held**
SIC: 3542 3462 Machine tools, metal forming type; Automotive forgings, ferrous: crankshaft, engine, axle, etc.
HQ: Sona Blw Prazisionsschmiede Gmbh
Papenberger Str. 37
Remscheid NW 42859
2191150

(G-14261)
SONA BLW PRECISION FORGE INC
500 Oak Tree Dr (27576-3544)
PHONE..................................919 828-3375
◆ **EMP:** 145
SIC: 3542 3462 Machine tools, metal forming type; Automotive forgings, ferrous: crankshaft, engine, axle, etc.

(G-14262)
TRANSMONTAIGNE TERMINALING INC
Also Called: TransMontaigne
2600 W Oak St (27576-9199)
PHONE..................................303 626-8200
EMP: 18 **EST:** 2020
SALES (est): 167.99K **Privately Held**
Web: www.transmontaignepartners.com
SIC: 1389 Gas field services, nec

(G-14263)
WILLIAMSBURG WOODCRAFT INC
4901 Nc Highway 96 N (27576-6016)
PHONE..................................919 965-3363
Tim Stevens, *Pr*
Linda Stevens, *VP*
EMP: 12 **EST:** 1980
SQ FT: 22,400
SALES (est): 398.85K **Privately Held**
Web: www.williamsburgwoodcraft.com
SIC: 2431 Doors, wood

Semora
Person County

(G-14264)
PROASH LLC (HQ)
1514 Dunnaway Rd (27343-9057)
PHONE..................................336 597-8734
Jim Simon, *Mgr*
EMP: 8 **EST:** 1997
SALES (est): 3.54MM **Privately Held**
SIC: 1481 Nonmetallic mineral services
PA: Separation Technologies, Llc
101 Hampton Ave
Needham MA

(G-14265)
SEPARATION TECHNOLOGIES LLC
1514 Dunnaway Rd (27343-9057)
PHONE..................................336 597-9814
Randy Dunlap, *Brnch Mgr*
EMP: 151
SALES (corp-wide): 8.01MM **Privately Held**
Web: www.proash.com
SIC: 3612 Transformers, except electric
HQ: Separation Technologies Llc
188 Summerfield Ct # 101
Roanoke VA 24019

Seven Springs
Wayne County

(G-14266)
CONVENIENT PALLETS LLC
379 Savannah Rd (28578-9071)
PHONE..................................919 648-3396
EMP: 8 **EST:** 2019
SALES (est): 225.46K **Privately Held**
SIC: 2448 Pallets, wood

(G-14267)
GOALS IN SERVICE LLC
103 Richard Dupree Ln (28578-7604)
PHONE..................................919 440-2656
EMP: 8 **EST:** 2018
SALES (est): 435.86K **Privately Held**
SIC: 3535 Conveyors and conveying equipment

Severn
Northampton County

(G-14268)
NORTHAMPTON PEANUT COMPANY
413 Main St (27877-9901)
P.O. Box 149 (27877-0149)
PHONE..................................252 585-0916
Dallas Barnes, *Pr*
William E Mckeown, *VP*
Jane Taylor, *
▼ **EMP:** 85 **EST:** 1989
SQ FT: 50,000
SALES (est): 48.94MM
SALES (corp-wide): 1.13B **Privately Held**
SIC: 5159 5441 2068 Peanuts (bulk), unroasted; Nuts; Nuts: dried, dehydrated, salted or roasted
HQ: Severn Peanut Company, Inc.
413 Main St
Severn NC 27877
252 585-0838

(G-14269)
RESINALL CORP
Also Called: RESINALL CORP.
302 Water St (27877)
P.O. Box 195 (27877-0195)
PHONE..................................252 585-1445
Paul Pierce, *Mgr*
EMP: 118
SALES (corp-wide): 1.44B **Privately Held**
Web: www.resinall.com
SIC: 2821 Plastics materials and resins
HQ: Resinall Corp Of North Carolina
3065 High Ridge Rd
Stamford CT 06903
203 329-7100

Shallotte
Brunswick County

(G-14270)
BRUNSWICK BEACON INC
208 Smith Ave (28470-4458)
P.O. Box 2558 (28459-2558)
PHONE..................................910 754-6890
Edward M Sweatt, *Pr*
Carolyn Sweatt, *Sec*
EMP: 14 **EST:** 1962

GEOGRAPHIC SECTION

Shelby - Cleveland County (G-14294)

SALES (est): 366.17K **Privately Held**
Web: www.newsargus.com
SIC: **2711** 6531 Newspapers: publishing only, not printed on site; Real estate agents and managers

(G-14271)
COASTAL CABINETRY INC
5017 Songline St (28470-6700)
PHONE..................................910 367-8864
Laura Scinto, *Prin*
EMP: **4 EST:** 2010
SALES (est): 251.17K **Privately Held**
SIC: **2434** Wood kitchen cabinets

(G-14272)
COASTAL MACHINE & WELDING INC
146 Wall St (28470-4510)
P.O. Box 617 (28462-0617)
PHONE..................................910 754-6476
Gene A Smith, *Pr*
Beverly A Smith, *Sec*
EMP: **6 EST:** 1955
SQ FT: 15,000
SALES (est): 774.35K **Privately Held**
Web: www.carolinacraneservice.com
SIC: **3448** 3842 7692 Prefabricated metal buildings; Surgical appliances and supplies; Welding repair

(G-14273)
FREEDOM ENTERPRISE LLC
Also Called: Weathersby Guild Louisville
5028 Pender Rd (28470-4430)
PHONE..................................502 510-7296
Jeffrey Walton, *Pt*
Doug Roye, *Pt*
EMP: **6 EST:** 2014
SALES (est): 321.95K **Privately Held**
Web: www.weathersbyguild.com
SIC: **2431** 2441 7641 Moldings, wood: unfinished and prefinished; Chests and trunks, wood; Office furniture repair and maintenance

(G-14274)
KART PRECISION BARREL CORP
3975 Garner St Sw (28470-5645)
PHONE..................................910 754-5212
Frederick Kart, *Pr*
Conrad Bulak, *Sec*
EMP: **4 EST:** 1989
SQ FT: 5,000
SALES (est): 350K **Privately Held**
Web: www.kartbarrel.com
SIC: **3484** Small arms

(G-14275)
KOOLABREW LLC
44 Red Bug Rd Sw (28470-5943)
PHONE..................................910 579-6711
EMP: **4 EST:** 2019
SALES (est): 62.38K **Privately Held**
Web: www.yardtimegym.com
SIC: **2082** Malt beverages

(G-14276)
LLOYDS OYSTER HOUSE INC
Also Called: Milliken Calabash Seafood
1642 Village Point Rd Sw (28470-5581)
PHONE..................................910 754-6958
Lloyd R Milliken, *Pr*
Jeffrey Milliken, *
EMP: **30 EST:** 1960
SQ FT: 6,000
SALES (est): 1.33MM **Privately Held**
SIC: **0913** 5146 2091 Oysters, dredging or tonging of; Seafoods; Canned and cured fish and seafoods

(G-14277)
QUALITY WELDING
4916 Arnold St (28470-4500)
PHONE..................................910 754-3232
Preston Conley, *Pr*
EMP: **6 EST:** 2017
SALES (est): 39.47K **Privately Held**
Web: www.qualityweldingnc.com
SIC: **7692** Welding repair

(G-14278)
SKIPPER GRAPHICS
209 Village Rd Sw (28470-4441)
P.O. Box 989 (28459-0989)
PHONE..................................910 754-8729
Barbara S Stanley, *Owner*
EMP: **4 EST:** 1987
SQ FT: 2,400
SALES (est): 249.7K **Privately Held**
Web: www.skippergraphics.com
SIC: **7336** 2759 3993 Commercial art and illustration; Letterpress printing; Signs, not made in custom sign painting shops

(G-14279)
SUN & SURF CONTAINERS INC
2589 Sun And Surf Ln Nw (28470-5978)
PHONE..................................910 754-9600
Henry B Tonking Junior, *Pr*
Mary Lou Tonking, *Sec*
EMP: **8 EST:** 1984
SQ FT: 20,000
SALES (est): 813.29K **Privately Held**
Web: www.sunandsurfcontainers.com
SIC: **2653** Boxes, corrugated: made from purchased materials

Sharpsburg
Nash County

(G-14280)
SCOGGINS INDUSTRIAL INC
Also Called: Langley Indus McHning Fbrction
4842 Us-301 (27878)
P.O. Box 1939 (27878-1939)
PHONE..................................252 977-9222
Gregory Scoggins, *Pr*
EMP: **17 EST:** 2021
SALES (est): 1.5MM **Privately Held**
SIC: **3599** 7389 Machine and other job shop work; Business Activities at Non-Commercial Site

Shelby
Cleveland County

(G-14281)
ABERCROMBIE TEXTILES INC (PA)
3051 River Rd (28152-8644)
PHONE..................................704 487-0935
Johnathan H Abercrombie, *Pr*
EMP: **6 EST:** 1984
SALES (est): 398.95K
SALES (corp-wide): 398.95K **Privately Held**
SIC: **7349** 3552 7389 Janitorial service, contract basis; Textile machinery; Business Activities at Non-Commercial Site

(G-14282)
ABERCROMBIE TEXTILES I LLC (PA)
1322 Mount Sinai Church Rd (28152-0755)
P.O. Box 427 (28024-0427)
PHONE..................................704 487-1245
John Regan, *CEO*
Kim Thompson, *
▲ EMP: **18 EST:** 2006
SQ FT: 43,000
SALES (est): 5.15MM
SALES (corp-wide): 5.15MM **Privately Held**
Web: www.cryptonmills.com
SIC: **2221** 2522 Automotive fabrics, manmade fiber; Office furniture, except wood

(G-14283)
ALPHA MAILING SERVICE INC
501 N Washington St (28150-4409)
P.O. Box 231 (28151-0231)
PHONE..................................704 484-1711
Oliver Emmert, *Pr*
EMP: **42 EST:** 1978
SQ FT: 23,000
SALES (est): 1.51MM **Privately Held**
Web: www.alphamail.com
SIC: **7331** 2782 Mailing service; Account books

(G-14284)
ALPHA PRINTING & MAILING
501 N Washington St (28150-4409)
PHONE..................................704 751-4930
EMP: **4 EST:** 2020
SALES (est): 83.91K **Privately Held**
SIC: **2752** Commercial printing, lithographic

(G-14285)
AMERICAN SAFETY UTILITY CORP
529 Caleb Rd (28152-7956)
P.O. Box 1740 (28151-1740)
PHONE..................................704 482-0601
Charles R Buddy Price, *Pr*
▼ EMP: **44 EST:** 1982
SQ FT: 30,000
SALES (est): 17.2MM **Privately Held**
Web: www.americansafety.com
SIC: **5099** 8734 2326 2311 Safety equipment and supplies; Testing laboratories; Men's and boy's work clothing; Men's and boy's suits and coats

(G-14286)
AMES COPPER GROUP LLC
125 Old Boiling Springs Rd (28152-0648)
PHONE..................................860 622-7626
Sean Meyer, *Managing Member*
EMP: **15 EST:** 2020
SALES (est): 3.8MM **Privately Held**
Web: www.amescoppergroup.com
SIC: **1021** Copper ore mining and preparation

(G-14287)
BARRS COMPETITION
124 Drum Rd (28152-0907)
PHONE..................................704 482-5169
Robert L Barr, *Owner*
EMP: **10 EST:** 1971
SQ FT: 6,000
SALES (est): 946.77K **Privately Held**
Web: www.barrscompetition.net
SIC: **3714** 3751 5571 7538 Motor vehicle engines and parts; Motorcycles and related parts; Motorcycle dealers; General automotive repair shops

(G-14288)
BARTLETT MILLING COMPANY LP
1101 Airport Rd (28150-3640)
PHONE..................................704 487-5061
Tom Wortman, *Mgr*
EMP: **35**
SALES (corp-wide): 1.73B **Privately Held**
Web: www.bartlettco.com
SIC: **2048** 5122 Prepared feeds, nec; Vitamins and minerals
HQ: Bartlett Milling Company, L.P.
  4900 Main St Ste 1200
  Kansas City MO 64112
  816 753-6300

(G-14289)
BRADLEYS INC
Also Called: Bradley Screen Printing
2522 W Dixon Blvd (28152-9007)
PHONE..................................704 484-2077
Marty Bradley, *Pr*
EMP: **22 EST:** 1990
SQ FT: 2,400
SALES (est): 2.2MM **Privately Held**
Web: www.bradleysinc.com
SIC: **2759** 2395 Screen printing; Embroidery products, except Schiffli machine

(G-14290)
BUILDINGS R US
1703 E Dixon Blvd (28152-6947)
PHONE..................................704 482-3166
Joe Ruppe, *Owner*
EMP: **5 EST:** 2014
SALES (est): 126.3K **Privately Held**
Web: www.buildingsrusllc.com
SIC: **3448** 4225 Carports, prefabricated metal ; General warehousing

(G-14291)
CAPITOL FUNDS INC (PA)
Also Called: Piedmont Components Division
720 S Lafayette St (28150-5860)
P.O. Box 146 (28150-0146)
PHONE..................................704 487-8547
David W Royster Iii, *Pr*
James B Taylor, *
Ann R Taylor, *
EMP: **40 EST:** 1949
SQ FT: 6,400
SALES (est): 18.32MM
SALES (corp-wide): 18.32MM **Privately Held**
Web: www.capitolfundsinc.com
SIC: **6552** 5231 5251 2439 Land subdividers and developers, commercial; Paint; Hardware stores; Structural wood members, nec

(G-14292)
CAPITOL FUNDS INC
Also Called: Piedmont Components Division
649 Washburn Switch Rd (28150-7712)
P.O. Box 878 (28151-0878)
PHONE..................................704 482-0645
Joel Hoard, *Mgr*
EMP: **74**
SALES (corp-wide): 18.32MM **Privately Held**
Web: www.capitolfundsinc.com
SIC: **2439** 3441 2435 Trusses, wooden roof; Fabricated structural metal; Hardwood veneer and plywood
PA: Capitol Funds, Inc.
  720 S Lafayette St
  Shelby NC 28150
  704 487-8547

(G-14293)
CAROLINA PRINTING ASSOCIATES
1707 N Post Rd (28150-9296)
PHONE..................................704 477-0626
EMP: **6 EST:** 2019
SALES (est): 83.91K **Privately Held**
SIC: **2752** Commercial printing, lithographic

(G-14294)
CHOICE USA BEVERAGE INC
Also Called: Sun Drop Bottling Co
2440 S Lafayette St (28152-7579)
P.O. Box 40 (28098-0040)
PHONE..................................704 487-6951
Reggie Bean, *Mgr*

Shelby - Cleveland County (G-14295)

EMP: 5
SALES (corp-wide): 30.99MM **Privately Held**
Web: www.choiceusabeverage.com
SIC: **2086** 5149 Bottled and canned soft drinks; Soft drinks
PA: Choice U.S.A. Beverage, Inc.
603 Groves St
Lowell NC 28098
704 823-1651

(G-14295)
CITY OF SHELBY
Also Called: Gas Dept
824 W Grover St (28150-2920)
P.O. Box 207 (28151-0207)
PHONE..............................704 484-6840
EMP: 32
SALES (corp-wide): 29.67MM **Privately Held**
Web: www.cityofshelby.com
SIC: **1311** Natural gas production
PA: City Of Shelby
300 S Washington St
Shelby NC 28150
704 484-6801

(G-14296)
CLEARWATER PAPER SHELBY LLC
671 Washburn Switch Rd (28150-7712)
PHONE..............................704 476-3802
Michael Urlick, *Managing Member*
EMP: 300 EST: 2020
SALES (est): 88.32MM **Publicly Held**
Web: www.clearwaterpaper.com
SIC: **2621** Paper mills
PA: Clearwater Paper Corporation
601 W Riverside Ave # 1100
Spokane WA 99201

(G-14297)
CLEVELAND COMPOUNDING INC
701 E Grover St # 2 (28150-4035)
PHONE..............................704 487-1971
Gary Harden, *Pr*
EMP: 4 EST: 2008
SALES (est): 238.46K **Privately Held**
SIC: **8748** 2834 Business consulting, nec; Pharmaceutical preparations

(G-14298)
CLEVELAND LUMBER COMPANY (PA)
Also Called: Benjamin Moore Authorized Ret
217 Arrowood Dr (28150-4300)
P.O. Box 1559 (28151-1559)
PHONE..............................704 487-5263
M Garland Johnson Junior, *Pr*
Jane Hunter, *
EMP: 39 EST: 1937
SQ FT: 13,200
SALES (est): 4.89MM
SALES (corp-wide): 4.89MM **Privately Held**
Web: www.clevelandlumbercompany.com
SIC: **5211** 2431 2426 5231 Lumber products; Millwork; Hardwood dimension and flooring mills; Paint, glass, and wallpaper stores

(G-14299)
CLEVELAND YUTAKA CORPORATION
2081 W Dixon Blvd (28152-9017)
PHONE..............................704 480-9290
Mototsugu Watanabe, *Pr*
▲ EMP: 94 EST: 1995
SQ FT: 56,788
SALES (est): 11.04MM **Privately Held**
Web: www.clevelandyutaka.com
SIC: **3714** Acceleration equipment, motor vehicle
PA: Yutaka Industry Co.,Ltd.
1-17, Hiyoshi, Satocho
Anjo AIC 446-0

(G-14300)
COLONIAL BRAIDED RUG CO NC
3414 W Stage Coach Trl (28150-9580)
PHONE..............................704 538-1824
Donna Noblitt, *Pr*
EMP: 7 EST: 1958
SALES (est): 381.19K **Privately Held**
Web: www.colonialrug.com
SIC: **2273** 5713 Rugs, braided and hooked; Rugs

(G-14301)
COLORED METAL PRODUCTS INC
Also Called: Awning Shop
103 Cameron St (28152-6601)
P.O. Box 2572 (28151-2572)
PHONE..............................704 482-1407
Jim Robinson, *Pr*
▼ EMP: 12 EST: 1983
SQ FT: 3,900
SALES (est): 839.39K **Privately Held**
Web: www.theawningshop.com
SIC: **2394** 3444 3949 Awnings, fabric: made from purchased materials; Awnings, sheet metal; Soccer equipment and supplies

(G-14302)
COMMUNITY FIRST MEDIA INC
503 N Lafayette St (28150-4426)
PHONE..............................704 482-4142
Greg Ledford, *Prin*
EMP: 8 EST: 2008
SALES (est): 169.39K **Privately Held**
Web: www.cfmedia.info
SIC: **2711** Newspapers, publishing and printing

(G-14303)
CONTROLLED RELEASE TECH INC
1016 Industry Dr (28152-8550)
PHONE..............................704 487-0878
Rachelle Cunningham, *Pr*
EMP: 9 EST: 1985
SQ FT: 20,000
SALES (est): 1.65MM **Privately Held**
Web: www.cleanac.com
SIC: **2842** 2841 5198 Polishes and sanitation goods; Soap and other detergents; Paints

(G-14304)
CREATIVE CONQUEST LLC
728 Mcswain Rd (28150-7786)
PHONE..............................720 481-4372
Peter Anderson, *CEO*
EMP: 5 EST: 2021
SALES (est): 88K **Privately Held**
Web: www.creativeconquests.com
SIC: **7336** 2211 7311 5043 Commercial art and graphic design; Print cloths, cotton; Advertising agencies; Printing apparatus, photographic

(G-14305)
CURTISS-WRIGHT CONTROLS INC
Flight Systms- PDT Support Div
201 Old Boiling Springs Rd (28152-0649)
PHONE..............................704 869-2300
EMP: 50
SALES (corp-wide): 2.85B **Publicly Held**
Web: www.cwcontrols.com
SIC: **3724** 3812 3728 3625 Aircraft engines and engine parts; Search and navigation equipment; Aircraft parts and equipment, nec; Relays and industrial controls
HQ: Curtiss-Wright Controls, Inc.
15801 Brixham Hill Ave # 200
Charlotte NC 28277
704 869-4600

(G-14306)
CURTISS-WRIGHT CONTROLS INC
Actuation Division - Aerospace
201 Old Boiling Springs Rd (28152-0649)
PHONE..............................704 481-1150
EMP: 25
SALES (corp-wide): 2.85B **Publicly Held**
Web: www.cwcontrols.com
SIC: **3593** Fluid power cylinders and actuators
HQ: Curtiss-Wright Controls, Inc.
15801 Brixham Hill Ave # 200
Charlotte NC 28277
704 869-4600

(G-14307)
CURTISS-WRIGHT CORPORATION
Actuation Division
201 Old Boiling Springs Rd (28152-0649)
PHONE..............................704 481-1150
EMP: 8
SALES (corp-wide): 2.85B **Publicly Held**
SIC: **3491** Industrial valves
PA: Curtiss-Wright Corporation
130 Harbour Place Dr # 300
Davidson NC 28036
704 869-4600

(G-14308)
CUTTING EDGE PIPING SVCS LLC
115 Ralph Green Rd (28152-8008)
PHONE..............................704 419-3995
EMP: 5 EST: 2019
SALES (est): 215.98K **Privately Held**
SIC: **7692** Welding repair

(G-14309)
D M & E CORPORATION
833 S Post Rd (28152-6932)
P.O. Box 580 (28151-0580)
PHONE..............................704 482-8876
Van D Durrett, *VP*
▲ EMP: 30 EST: 1976
SQ FT: 6,000
SALES (est): 9.41MM **Privately Held**
Web: www.dmecutter.com
SIC: **5085** 3559 3552 Industrial supplies; Electronic component making machinery; Textile machinery

(G-14310)
DALE ADVERTISING INC
2523 Taylor Rd (28152-7942)
PHONE..............................704 484-0971
Lanny R Newton, *Pr*
Cathy Newton, *Sec*
EMP: 4 EST: 1973
SQ FT: 3,000
SALES (est): 259.82K **Privately Held**
SIC: **2759** 2395 5199 7311 Screen printing; Embroidery products, except Schiffli machine; Advertising specialties; Advertising agencies

(G-14311)
DAVIS RUG COMPANY
Also Called: Davis Rug
3938 Barclay Rd (28152-9562)
P.O. Box 217 (28017-0217)
PHONE..............................704 434-7231
Harvey Davis, *Pr*
Brenda Davis, *Sec*
▲ EMP: 9 EST: 1976
SQ FT: 7,800
SALES (est): 994.68K **Privately Held**
SIC: **2273** Scatter rugs, except rubber or plastic

(G-14312)
DICEY MILLS INC
Also Called: Dicey Fabrics
430 Neisler St (28152-5000)
P.O. Box 1090 (28151-1090)
PHONE..............................704 487-6324
◆ EMP: 19 EST: 1957
SALES (est): 651.78K **Privately Held**
SIC: **2221** Upholstery fabrics, manmade fiber and silk

(G-14313)
ELECTRIC GLASS FIBER AMER LLC (DH)
Also Called: Nippon Electric Glass
940 Washburn Switch Rd (28150-9089)
PHONE..............................704 434-2261
Shigeru Goto, *CEO*
▲ EMP: 500 EST: 1998
SQ FT: 1,001,880
SALES (est): 439.09MM **Privately Held**
Web: www.neg.co.jp
SIC: **2851** Paints and allied products
HQ: Nippon Electric Glass America, Inc.
1515 E Wdfield Rd Ste 720
Schaumburg IL 60173
630 285-8500

(G-14314)
ELECTRIC MOTOR SERVICE OF SHELBY INC
1143 Airport Rd (28150-3723)
PHONE..............................704 482-9979
EMP: 16
SIC: **7694** 5999 7629 5063 Motor repair services; Motors, electric; Tool repair, electric; Motors, electric

(G-14315)
ELLIS LUMBER COMPANY INC
Also Called: Ellis Lumber Co and Logs
1681 S Lafayette St (28152-7152)
PHONE..............................704 482-1414
Yancey Ellis, *Pr*
W Yancey Ellis, *Pr*
Scott Ellis, *VP*
Tim Ellis, *VP*
Brenda Arton, *Mgr*
EMP: 18 EST: 1946
SALES (est): 993.89K **Privately Held**
Web: www.ellislumbercompany.com
SIC: **2421** Lumber: rough, sawed, or planed

(G-14316)
EMERSON ELECTRIC CO
Also Called: Emerson
Plant 4I-32 4401 East Dix (28150)
PHONE..............................704 480-8519
Eric Emerson, *Mgr*
EMP: 5
SALES (corp-wide): 15.16B **Publicly Held**
Web: www.emerson.com
SIC: **3823** Process control instruments
PA: Emerson Electric Co.
8000 West Florissant Ave
Saint Louis MO 63136
314 553-2000

(G-14317)
FITCH SIGN COMPANY INC
341 N Post Rd (28152-4948)
P.O. Box 1316 (28151-1316)
PHONE..............................704 482-2916
Thomas Fitch, *Pr*
Charlene Fitch, *VP*
EMP: 4 EST: 1977
SQ FT: 1,500

GEOGRAPHIC SECTION

Shelby - Cleveland County (G-14340)

SALES (est): 308.02K **Privately Held**
Web: www.fitchsigncoinc.com
SIC: **3993** 7389 1799 Signs, not made in custom sign painting shops; Sign painting and lettering shop; Sign installation and maintenance

(G-14318)
FLINT HILL TEXTILES INC
2240 Flint Hill Church Rd (28152-8137)
PHONE.................................704 434-9331
Billy E Pearson, *Owner*
Edith E Pearson, *Owner*
EMP: 5 **EST:** 1970
SALES (est): 254.79K **Privately Held**
SIC: **2273** 2399 Carpets and rugs; Seat covers, automobile

(G-14319)
GEOCOMP INC
Also Called: Geo Comp
1901 W Dixon Blvd (28152-9018)
P.O. Box 2642 (28151-2642)
PHONE.................................704 480-7688
▲ **EMP:** 14 **EST:** 1995
SALES (est): 407.03K **Privately Held**
Web: www.geocomp.com
SIC: **3081** Unsupported plastics film and sheet

(G-14320)
GLENN LUMBER COMPANY INC
145 Rockford Rd (28152-0667)
P.O. Box 756 (28017-0756)
PHONE.................................704 434-7873
John C Glenn, *Pr*
EMP: 25 **EST:** 1948
SALES (est): 1.87MM **Privately Held**
Web: www.glennlumber.com
SIC: **5211** 2448 2426 2421 Planing mill products and lumber; Wood pallets and skids; Hardwood dimension and flooring mills; Sawmills and planing mills, general

(G-14321)
GREENHECK FAN CORPORATION
2000 Partnership Dr (28150-9424)
PHONE.................................704 476-3700
EMP: 4
SALES (corp-wide): 1.29B **Privately Held**
Web: www.greenheck.com
SIC: **3564** Blowers and fans
PA: Greenheck Fan Corporation
  1100 Greenheck Dr
  Schofield WI 54476
  715 359-6171

(G-14322)
GROUND CONTROL LANDSCAPE MGT
506 W Dixon Blvd (28152-6555)
P.O. Box 357 (28151-0357)
PHONE.................................704 472-3448
EMP: 5 **EST:** 2015
SALES (est): 205.35K **Privately Held**
Web: www.groundcontrolinc.com
SIC: **5083** 3524 Cultivating machinery and equipment; Lawn and garden mowers and accessories

(G-14323)
HACKNER HOME LLC
806 W Warren St (28150-5024)
PHONE.................................980 552-9573
Jona Hackner, *CEO*
Cristoph Hackner, *Managing Member*
EMP: 7 **EST:** 2013
SALES (est): 350.78K **Privately Held**
Web: www.hacknerhome.com
SIC: **2211** Pillowcases

(G-14324)
HAMRICK PRECAST LLC
415 W College Ave (28152-8190)
P.O. Box 755 (28017-0755)
PHONE.................................704 434-6551
Ryan Hamrick, *Managing Member*
EMP: 8
SALES (est): 565.88K **Privately Held**
SIC: **3273** Ready-mixed concrete

(G-14325)
HANWHA ADVANCED MTLS AMER LLC
Also Called: Hanwha Shelby
925 Washburn Switch Rd (28150-7008)
PHONE.................................704 434-2271
Philip Welton, *Mgr*
EMP: 35
Web: www.hanwhaus.com
SIC: **3714** 2821 Motor vehicle parts and accessories; Plastics materials and resins
HQ: Hanwha Advanced Materials America Llc
  4400 N Park Dr
  Opelika AL 36801
  334 741-7725

(G-14326)
HEADRICK OTDOOR MDIA OF CRLNAS
Also Called: Creative Outdoor Advertising
600 S Morgan St (28150-5832)
P.O. Box 248 (28151-0248)
PHONE.................................704 487-5971
Max Padgett Butler, *Pr*
Earnest Johnson, *VP*
Phyllis B Wortman, *Sec*
EMP: 10 **EST:** 1945
SQ FT: 20,000
SALES (est): 396.81K **Privately Held**
Web: www.creativesignservice.com
SIC: **3993** Signs and advertising specialties

(G-14327)
HUDSON INDUSTRIES LLC
439 Neisler St (28152-5001)
PHONE.................................704 480-0014
EMP: 6 **EST:** 2006
SALES (est): 333.9K **Privately Held**
SIC: **3999** Manufacturing industries, nec

(G-14328)
HURST JAWS OF LIFE INC (HQ)
711 N Post Rd (28150-4246)
PHONE.................................704 487-6961
Bruce Lear, *VP*
◆ **EMP:** 150 **EST:** 1917
SQ FT: 185,000
SALES (est): 94.63MM
SALES (corp-wide): 3.27B **Publicly Held**
Web: www.jawsoflife.com
SIC: **3569** 3561 3594 Firefighting apparatus; Industrial pumps and parts; Fluid power pumps and motors
PA: Idex Corporation
  3100 Sanders Rd Ste 301
  Northbrook IL 60062
  847 498-7070

(G-14329)
IF ARMOR INTERNATIONAL LLC
Also Called: Man Lift
2501 W Dixon Blvd (28152-9012)
PHONE.................................704 482-1399
Roger Bingham, *Managing Member*
EMP: 150 **EST:** 2019
SALES (est): 27.96MM
SALES (corp-wide): 31MM **Privately Held**
Web: www.if-armor.com

(G-14330)
IMC-METALSAMERICA LLC (HQ)
Also Called: IMC
135 Old Boiling Springs Rd (28152-0648)
PHONE.................................704 482-8200
Bernard C Shilberg, *Managing Member*
Nathan B Shilberg, *
◆ **EMP:** 5 **EST:** 2009
SQ FT: 165,000
SALES (est): 17.56MM
SALES (corp-wide): 145.97MM **Privately Held**
Web: www.imc-ma.com
SIC: **3331** Primary copper smelter products
PA: Prime Materials Recovery Inc.
  99 E River Dr
  East Hartford CT 06108
  860 622-7626

(G-14331)
IVARS DISPLAY
2001 Partnership Dr (28150-9424)
PHONE.................................909 923-2761
EMP: 27
SALES (corp-wide): 18.21MM **Privately Held**
Web: www.ivarsdisplay.com
SIC: **2541** Partitions for floor attachment, prefabricated: wood
PA: Ivar's Display
  2314 E Locust Ct
  Ontario CA 91761
  909 923-2761

(G-14332)
JENKINS FOODS INC
2119 New House Rd (28150-7923)
PHONE.................................704 434-2347
Harry Mauney, *Pr*
Mark Mauney, *
Diane Mauney, *Stockholder**
Rachel Mauney, *Stockholder**
EMP: 20 **EST:** 1933
SQ FT: 24,000
SALES (est): 711.67K **Privately Held**
SIC: **2013** 2035 2099 Sausages, from purchased meat; Spreads, sandwich: salad dressing base; Food preparations, nec

(G-14333)
JOE ROBIN DARNELL
Also Called: First Choice Properties
2115 Chatfield Rd (28150-9491)
PHONE.................................704 482-1186
Joe R Darnell, *Prin*
EMP: 6 **EST:** 2011
SALES (est): 49K **Privately Held**
SIC: **7692** 6531 Welding repair; Real estate brokers and agents

(G-14334)
KEMET ELECTRONICS CORPORATION
2501 W Dixon Blvd (28152-9012)
PHONE.................................864 963-6300
Bruce White, *Mgr*
EMP: 26
Web: www.kemet.com
SIC: **3675** Electronic capacitors
HQ: Kemet Electronics Corporation
  1 E Broward Blvd Fl 2
  Fort Lauderdale FL 33301
  864 963-6700

(G-14335)
KSM CASTINGS USA INC (DH)
Also Called: Ksm
120 Blue Brook Dr (28150-1500)
PHONE.................................704 751-0559
Mark Bradley, *Pr*
John Rollins, *
▲ **EMP:** 40 **EST:** 2012
SALES (est): 47.07MM **Privately Held**
Web: www.ksmcastings.com
SIC: **3363** Aluminum die-castings
HQ: Dicastal North America, Inc.
  1 Dicastal Dr
  Greenville MI 48838
  616 619-7500

(G-14336)
LAVENDER INC
769 Ware Rd (28152-7952)
PHONE.................................704 481-8327
Johnny M Lavender, *Pr*
Martha Lavender, *VP*
EMP: 20 **EST:** 1972
SQ FT: 50,000
SALES (est): 121.86K **Privately Held**
SIC: **3441** Fabricated structural metal

(G-14337)
LEONARD MCSWAIN SPTIC TANK SVC
3020 Ramseur Church Rd (28150-9308)
PHONE.................................704 482-1380
Leonard L Mcswain, *Pr*
EMP: 5 **EST:** 1963
SALES (est): 468.72K **Privately Held**
Web: www.leonardmcswainseptic.com
SIC: **3272** 1711 Septic tanks, concrete; Septic system construction

(G-14338)
LINNIG CORPORATION
Also Called: Kendrion
1100 Airport Rd (28150-3639)
PHONE.................................704 482-9582
▲ **EMP:** 100 **EST:** 1994
SQ FT: 5,000
SALES (est): 6.93MM
SALES (corp-wide): 459.03MM **Privately Held**
Web: www.kendrion.com
SIC: **3714** Clutches, motor vehicle
HQ: Kendrion (Markdorf) Gmbh
  Riedheimer Str. 5
  Markdorf BW 88677
  75449640

(G-14339)
LIZMERE CAVALIERS
403 S Washington St (28150-5902)
PHONE.................................704 418-2543
EMP: 6 **EST:** 2010
SALES (est): 49.9K **Privately Held**
Web: www.lizmere.com
SIC: **3999** Pet supplies

(G-14340)
MACHINE BUILDERS & DESIGN INC
806 N Post Rd (28150-4247)
PHONE.................................704 482-3456
Daryl Mims, *Pr*
Teresa Miller, *
Gonzalo Penya, *
Brad Hogan, *
◆ **EMP:** 40 **EST:** 1974
SQ FT: 15,000
SALES (est): 8.02MM **Privately Held**
Web: www.mbd-inc.com
SIC: **3599** Custom machinery

Shelby - Cleveland County (G-14341)

(G-14341)
MACK S LIVER MUSH INC
Also Called: Mack's Livermush & Meats
6126 Mckee Rd (28150-7102)
P.O. Box 227 (28136-0227)
PHONE..................704 434-6188
B Ron Mckee, *Pr*
EMP: 19 **EST:** 1944
SQ FT: 8,000
SALES (est): 521.19K **Privately Held**
SIC: 2013 Puddings, meat, from purchased meat

(G-14342)
MACO INC
521 Plato Lee Rd (28150-9418)
PHONE..................704 434-6800
EMP: 48 **EST:** 1979
SALES (est): 9.22MM **Privately Held**
Web: www.macoincorporated.com
SIC: 3441 Building components, structural steel

(G-14343)
MAFIC USA LLC
119 Metrolina Plz (28150-7708)
PHONE..................704 967-8006
Mike Levine, *CEO*
Dwight Lacelle, *CFO*
EMP: 13 **EST:** 2015
SALES (est): 2.08MM **Privately Held**
Web: www.mafic.com
SIC: 1429 Basalt, crushed and broken-quarrying

(G-14344)
MAN LIFT MFG CO
2501 W Dixon Blvd (28152-9012)
P.O. Box 1466 (28151-1466)
PHONE..................414 486-1760
Phil Sprio, *Pr*
EMP: 44 **EST:** 2000
SQ FT: 33,000
SALES (est): 16.29MM
SALES (corp-wide): 37.52MM **Privately Held**
SIC: 3531 8711 Aerial work platforms: hydraulic/elec. truck/carrier mounted; Professional engineer
PA: Universal Mfg. Co.
1128 Lincoln Mall Ste 301
Lincoln NE 68508
402 261-3851

(G-14345)
MAXXDRIVE LLC
1847 E Dixon Blvd (28152-6901)
PHONE..................704 600-8684
EMP: 8 **EST:** 2016
SALES (est): 977.3K **Privately Held**
Web: www.maxxdrive.us
SIC: 3711 Motor vehicles and car bodies

(G-14346)
MEDICAL ENGINEERING LABS
Also Called: Mel
3039 Longwood Dr (28152-8638)
P.O. Box 2423 (28151-2423)
PHONE..................704 487-0166
William J Young Junior, *Pr*
EMP: 5 **EST:** 1973
SQ FT: 8,000
SALES (est): 290.73K **Privately Held**
SIC: 3841 Surgical instruments and apparatus

(G-14347)
METAL WORKS MFG CO
2501 W Dixon Blvd (28152-9012)
PHONE..................704 482-1399
Phil Sprio, *Pr*
EMP: 80 **EST:** 2015
SQ FT: 219,000
SALES (est): 21.23MM
SALES (corp-wide): 37.52MM **Privately Held**
Web: www.metalworksmfg.com
SIC: 3441 Fabricated structural metal
PA: Universal Mfg. Co.
1128 Lincoln Mall Ste 301
Lincoln NE 68508
402 261-3851

(G-14348)
MODERN DENSIFYING INC
Also Called: M D I
662 Plato Lee Rd (28150-7769)
P.O. Box 2312 (28151-2312)
PHONE..................704 434-8335
Andy Ball, *VP*
Joe Morgan, *Pr*
EMP: 18 **EST:** 1992
SALES (est): 2.05MM **Privately Held**
SIC: 2821 Plastics materials and resins

(G-14349)
MOIRE CREATIONS AMERICA LLC (PA)
1808 Country Garden Dr (28150-6165)
PHONE..................704 482-9860
John O Salazar, *Pr*
EMP: 40 **EST:** 1933
SALES (est): 3.83MM
SALES (corp-wide): 3.83MM **Privately Held**
SIC: 2221 2269 2262 2261 Broadwoven fabric mills, manmade; Finishing plants, nec ; Finishing plants, manmade; Finishing plants, cotton

(G-14350)
MR TIRE INC
315 S Dekalb St (28150-5403)
PHONE..................704 484-0816
Darren Davis, *Brnch Mgr*
EMP: 7
SALES (corp-wide): 1.33B **Publicly Held**
Web: mrtireinc.business.site
SIC: 5941 5531 5014 7534 Bicycle and bicycle parts; Automotive tires; Tires and tubes; Tire recapping
HQ: Mr. Tire Inc.
2078 New York Ave Unit 2
Huntington Station NY 11746
631 499-3700

(G-14351)
NANE PUBLISHING LLC
106 Southern Pines Dr (28152-8166)
PHONE..................704 477-3462
Lisa Byrum, *Pr*
EMP: 5 **EST:** 2015
SALES (est): 89.6K **Privately Held**
SIC: 2741 Miscellaneous publishing

(G-14352)
NEWGRASS BREWING COMPANY LLC
101 Columns Cir (28150-4865)
PHONE..................704 477-2795
EMP: 5 **EST:** 2015
SALES (est): 447.55K **Privately Held**
Web: www.newgrassbrewing.com
SIC: 2082 Beer (alcoholic beverage)

(G-14353)
OAKIE S TIRE & RECAPPING INC
800 W Warren St (28150-5024)
PHONE..................704 482-5629
Oakie Canipe, *Pr*
Chris Canipe, *VP*
Ken Canipe, *VP*
Rachel Canipe, *Sec*
EMP: 11 **EST:** 1958
SQ FT: 7,000
SALES (est): 905.01K **Privately Held**
SIC: 5531 7534 5014 Automotive tires; Tire recapping; Automobile tires and tubes

(G-14354)
OPERATING SHELBY LLC TAG ✪
2501 W Dixon Blvd (28152-9012)
PHONE..................704 482-1399
Robert Pazderka, *Managing Member*
EMP: 50 **EST:** 2022
SALES (est): 6.21MM **Privately Held**
SIC: 3711 Military motor vehicle assembly
PA: The Armored Group Llc
5050 E Red Rock Dr
Phoenix AZ 85018

(G-14355)
PLASTIC ODDITIES INC
1701 Burke Rd (28152-8116)
PHONE..................704 484-1830
Lewis B Izzi Senior, *Ch Bd*
Loretta B Izzi, *
Hilda Blanton, *
Bobby G Guffey, *
Thomas Clint Shuford Contl, *Prin*
EMP: 21 **EST:** 1975
SQ FT: 6,000
SALES (est): 448.31K **Privately Held**
SIC: 3088 5074 Plastics plumbing fixtures; Plumbing and hydronic heating supplies

(G-14356)
PPG-DEVOLD LLC
940 Washburn Switch Rd (28150-9400)
PHONE..................704 434-2261
▲ **EMP:** 21 **EST:** 2007
SALES (est): 1.18MM **Privately Held**
SIC: 3229 Pressed and blown glass, nec

(G-14357)
PRINTING & PACKAGING INC
1015 Buffalo St (28150-4047)
P.O. Box 1558 (28151-1558)
PHONE..................704 482-3866
Boyce J Hanna, *Pr*
Joan Hanna, *
EMP: 27 **EST:** 1947
SQ FT: 26,000
SALES (est): 3.94MM **Privately Held**
Web: www.pandpinc.com
SIC: 2631 2752 2791 Folding boxboard; Offset printing; Typesetting

(G-14358)
PROPAK LOGISTICS
200 Wal Mart Dr (28150-3717)
PHONE..................704 471-1070
James Henson, *Mgr*
EMP: 7 **EST:** 2005
SALES (est): 79.23K **Privately Held**
SIC: 2448 Pallets, wood and metal combination

(G-14359)
RAFTERS AND WALLS LLC
2312 W Randolph Rd (28150-7785)
PHONE..................980 404-0209
Richard Peddy, *Managing Member*
EMP: 20 **EST:** 2015
SALES (est): 1.56MM **Privately Held**
Web: www.rafterswalls.com
SIC: 2439 5031 Structural wood members, nec; Lumber, plywood, and millwork

(G-14360)
RIDDLEY METALS INC
639 Washburn Switch Rd (28150-7712)
P.O. Box 2406 (28151-2406)
PHONE..................704 435-8829
EMP: 17 **EST:** 2020
SALES (est): 2.22MM **Privately Held**
Web: www.riddleyinc.com
SIC: 3441 Fabricated structural metal

(G-14361)
RUFUS N IVIE III
Also Called: Southern Machining
4007 Hillview Dr (28152-8978)
PHONE..................704 482-2559
Rufus N Ivie Iii, *Owner*
EMP: 7 **EST:** 1990
SALES (est): 597.51K **Privately Held**
SIC: 3599 Machine shop, jobbing and repair

(G-14362)
SAIN GRADING & BACKHOE
121 Melton Dr (28152-8790)
PHONE..................704 481-9179
Gregory Dean Sain, *Pr*
EMP: 5 **EST:** 2015
SALES (est): 79.96K **Privately Held**
SIC: 3531 Backhoes

(G-14363)
SHELBY BUSINESS CARDS
2020 E Dixon Blvd (28152-6958)
P.O. Box 2344 (28151-2344)
PHONE..................704 481-8341
Boyd H Hendrick, *Owner*
EMP: 4 **EST:** 1965
SQ FT: 1,800
SALES (est): 234.79K **Privately Held**
Web: www.westmorelandprinters.com
SIC: 2752 Offset printing

(G-14364)
SHELBY ELASTICS OF NORTH CAROLINA LLC
Also Called: Shelby Elastics
639 N Post Rd (28150-4965)
P.O. Box 2405 (28151-2405)
PHONE..................704 487-4301
EMP: 60
SIC: 2259 Convertors, knit goods

(G-14365)
SHELBY FREEDOM STAR INC
Also Called: Shelby Star The
315 E Graham St (28150-5452)
P.O. Box 48 (28151-0048)
PHONE..................704 484-7000
Johnathan Segal, *Pr*
Richard Wallace, *
EMP: 104 **EST:** 1800
SALES (est): 2.21MM
SALES (corp-wide): 2.66B **Publicly Held**
Web: www.shelbystar.com
SIC: 2711 Newspapers, publishing and printing
HQ: Gatehouse Media, Llc
175 Sullys Trl Ste 203
Pittsford NY 14534
585 598-0030

(G-14366)
SHELBY KENDRION INC
1100 Airport Rd (28150-3639)
PHONE..................704 482-9582
Piet Veenema, *CEO*
William Brown, *
Tom Paisley, *
Jimmy Yarboro, *
Delon Hoffa, *
▲ **EMP:** 118 **EST:** 2007

GEOGRAPHIC SECTION

SQ FT: 180,000
SALES (est): 24.07MM
SALES (corp-wide): 539.34MM **Privately Held**
Web: www.kendrion.com
SIC: 3822 3643 3625 3613 Built-in thermostats, filled system and bimetal types ; Current-carrying wiring services; Relays and industrial controls; Switchgear and switchboard apparatus
PA: Kendrion N.V.
Herikerbergweg 213
Amsterdam NH 1101
850731500

(G-14367)
SILVER INK PUBLISHING INC
Also Called: Publishing/Education
917 Beau Rd (28152-9686)
PHONE................................704 473-0192
Jill P Nolen, *Managing Member*
▲ **EMP:** 4 **EST:** 2003
SALES (est): 221.86K **Privately Held**
Web: www.silverinkpublishing.com
SIC: 2741 Miscellaneous publishing

(G-14368)
SMITH HOLDINGS
411 Beaumonde Ave (28150-6001)
PHONE................................704 472-4937
EMP: 4
SALES (est): 76.29K **Privately Held**
SIC: 3949 Golf equipment

(G-14369)
SOUTHCO INDUSTRIES INC
1840 E Dixon Blvd (28152-6902)
PHONE................................704 482-1477
J Steve Goforth, *Pr*
Dennis G Goforth, *
Richard Goforth, *
EMP: 130 **EST:** 1985
SQ FT: 15,000
SALES (est): 22.19MM **Privately Held**
Web: www.southcoindustries.com
SIC: 3713 3535 3711 3441 Truck bodies (motor vehicles); Conveyors and conveying equipment; Motor vehicles and car bodies; Fabricated structural metal

(G-14370)
SQUARE ONE MACHINE LLC
658 Washburn Switch Rd (28150-9480)
PHONE................................704 600-6296
Terry Beck, *Owner*
EMP: 7 **EST:** 2018
SALES (est): 225.9K **Privately Held**
SIC: 3599 Machine shop, jobbing and repair

(G-14371)
TACTICAL COATINGS INC
1028 Railroad Ave (28152-6681)
P.O. Box 1042 (28151-1042)
PHONE................................704 692-4511
David Bryant, *Pr*
Kelly Bryant, *VP*
EMP: 4 **EST:** 2009
SALES (est): 252.13K **Privately Held**
Web: www.tacticalcoatings.net
SIC: 3479 Metal coating and allied services

(G-14372)
TAK MANUFACTURING LLC
2322 Kings Rd (28152-6232)
PHONE................................704 473-6391
Kimberly Denise Hunt, *Prin*
EMP: 5 **EST:** 2019
SALES (est): 128.7K **Privately Held**
SIC: 3999 Manufacturing industries, nec

(G-14373)
TIME WARNER CABLE INC
2020 E Dixon Blvd (28152-6958)
PHONE................................704 751-5207
EMP: 5 **EST:** 2019
SALES (est): 83.91K **Privately Held**
SIC: 2752 Commercial printing, lithographic

(G-14374)
TNT SIGNS & GRAPHICS
3131 Suffolk Dr (28152-7537)
PHONE................................704 460-5050
EMP: 4 **EST:** 2007
SALES (est): 9.54K **Privately Held**
SIC: 3993 Signs and advertising specialties

(G-14375)
TRIPLE D PUBLISHING INC
Also Called: Onsat Magazine
1300 S Dekalb St (28152-7210)
PHONE................................704 482-9673
Douglas G Brown, *Pr*
▲ **EMP:** 17 **EST:** 1977
SQ FT: 100,000
SALES (est): 380.04K **Privately Held**
SIC: 2721 Magazines: publishing only, not printed on site

(G-14376)
TUBE ENTERPRISES INCORPORATED
Also Called: Integrity Medical Solutions
1028 Railroad Ave (28152-6681)
P.O. Box 2206 (28086-6206)
PHONE................................941 629-9267
Robert A Wright, *Pr*
Alfred A Taylor, *VP*
EMP: 12 **EST:** 2004
SALES (est): 2.07MM **Privately Held**
Web: www.integritymedicalsolutions.com
SIC: 2514 Lawn furniture: metal

(G-14377)
TWIN OAKS GALLERY & FRMNG LLC
2017 Fairview Rd (28150-9235)
PHONE................................704 466-3889
Stacey Straight, *Prin*
EMP: 5 **EST:** 2016
SALES (est): 88.2K **Privately Held**
SIC: 2499 Picture frame molding, finished

(G-14378)
TWIN OAKS SERVICE SOUTH INC
1320 Stony Point Rd (28150-8198)
PHONE................................704 914-7142
William Straight, *Pr*
Stacey Straight, *CFO*
EMP: 7 **EST:** 1996
SQ FT: 15,000
SALES (est): 1.98MM **Privately Held**
Web: www.twinoaksservicessouthinc.com
SIC: 3743 Railroad equipment

(G-14379)
ULTRA MACHINE & FABRICATION INC
Also Called: Ultra
2501 W Dixon Blvd (28152-9012)
P.O. Box 335 (28086-0335)
PHONE................................704 482-1399
EMP: 103
SIC: 3542 3599 Machine tools, metal forming type; Machine shop, jobbing and repair

(G-14380)
VARIETY CONSULT LLC
3735 Robert Riding Rd (28150-7038)
PHONE................................704 275-2284
EMP: 6 **EST:** 2003
SALES (est): 2.5K **Privately Held**
SIC: 3641 Health lamps, infrared or ultraviolet

(G-14381)
WALKER WOODWORKING INC (PA)
Also Called: Greenbrook Design Center
112 N Lafayette St (28150-4446)
PHONE................................704 434-0823
Travis Walker, *CEO*
EMP: 27 **EST:** 1997
SALES (est): 2.63MM
SALES (corp-wide): 2.63MM **Privately Held**
Web: www.walkerwoodworking.com
SIC: 2434 Wood kitchen cabinets

(G-14382)
WESTMORELAND PRINTERS INC
Also Called: Copyrite
2020 E Dixon Blvd (28152-6958)
PHONE................................704 482-9100
Wes Westmoreland, *Pr*
EMP: 10 **EST:** 1999
SQ FT: 13,000
SALES (est): 939.85K **Privately Held**
Web: www.westmorelandprinters.com
SIC: 2759 5943 Screen printing; Office forms and supplies

Sherrills Ford
Catawba County

(G-14383)
AT THE LAKE CANVAS AND COVERS
4059 Shasta Ln (28673-9761)
PHONE................................704 966-1586
EMP: 4 **EST:** 2015
SALES (est): 58.16K **Privately Held**
Web: www.atthelakecanvasandcovers.com
SIC: 2211 Canvas

(G-14384)
BR549 ENTERPRISES LLC
1558 Sherwood Ct (28673-7271)
PHONE................................704 799-0955
Kyle Tucker, *Owner*
EMP: 5 **EST:** 2018
SALES (est): 87.26K **Privately Held**
SIC: 3714 Motor vehicle parts and accessories

(G-14385)
I-LEADR INC
2220 Lazy Ln (28673-9734)
P.O. Box 625 (28673-0625)
PHONE................................910 431-5252
Brie Beane, *Prin*
EMP: 14 **EST:** 2014
SALES (est): 235.62K **Privately Held**
Web: www.ileadr.com
SIC: 8748 7372 Educational consultant; Educational computer software

(G-14386)
JONES SIGN
9325 Azalea Rd (28673-7268)
P.O. Box 127 (28673-0127)
PHONE................................828 478-4780
EMP: 8 **EST:** 2008
SALES (est): 224.47K **Privately Held**
SIC: 3993 Signs and advertising specialties

(G-14387)
LA WEST INC
8815 Colebridge Ct (28673-7298)
PHONE................................704 685-2833
Vern Kauffman, *Pr*
EMP: 5 **EST:** 2017
SALES (est): 39.69K **Privately Held**
SIC: 3999 Manufacturing industries, nec

(G-14388)
NATIONAL SIGN & DECAL INC
2199 Lynmore Dr (28673-9740)
P.O. Box 189 (28673-0189)
PHONE................................828 478-2123
Carin A Hooper, *Pr*
Meagan Suggs, *Opers Mgr*
EMP: 6 **EST:** 1971
SQ FT: 7,000
SALES (est): 480.18K **Privately Held**
Web: www.nationalsignanddecalinc.com
SIC: 2759 3953 Screen printing; Screens, textile printing

(G-14389)
NORTHSOUTH BIOMAGNETICS INC
3682 Burton St (28673-9800)
P.O. Box 6 (28673-0006)
PHONE................................828 478-2277
Donna Mendenhall, *Pr*
EMP: 6 **EST:** 2007
SALES (est): 190.79K **Privately Held**
Web: www.promagnet.com
SIC: 3499 7389 Magnetic shields, metal; Business services, nec

(G-14390)
UNRULY MUTT PUBLISHING LLC
2612 Penngate Dr (28673-9128)
PHONE................................828 478-9097
Chad Starnes, *Prin*
EMP: 5 **EST:** 2016
SALES (est): 41.35K **Privately Held**
SIC: 2741 Miscellaneous publishing

Shiloh
Camden County

(G-14391)
ED MAJKA LLC
459 Wickham Rd (27974-7227)
PHONE................................570 985-9677
Ed Majka, *Admn*
EMP: 4 **EST:** 2017
SALES (est): 50.12K **Privately Held**
SIC: 7692 Welding repair

(G-14392)
RICKYS WELDING INC
899 S Sandy Hook Rd (27974-7213)
P.O. Box 336 (27974-0336)
PHONE................................252 336-4437
Ricky Lee Edwards, *Pr*
Shelia Edwards, *Sec*
EMP: 9 **EST:** 1983
SQ FT: 5,000
SALES (est): 931.59K **Privately Held**
Web: www.rickyswelding.com
SIC: 7692 Welding repair

(G-14393)
STAIR TAMER LLC
Also Called: Stair Tamer Cargo Lifts
899 S Sandy Hook Rd (27974-7213)
PHONE................................252 336-4437
Ricky Edwards, *Pr*
EMP: 4 **EST:** 2015
SALES (est): 265.55K **Privately Held**
Web: www.stairtamercargolifts.com
SIC: 3499 Stabilizing bars (cargo), metal

Siler City
Chatham County

(G-14394)
A AND J TA LOGGING
186 Epps Clark Rd (27344-9106)
PHONE..............................919 663-1110
EMP: 4 EST: 2019
SALES (est): 84.04K Privately Held
SIC: 2411 Logging

(G-14395)
ACME - MCCRARY CORPORATION
Also Called: ACME - MCCRARY CORPORATION
1311 E 11th St (27344-2772)
PHONE..............................336 625-2161
Neal Anderson, Brnch Mgr
EMP: 10
Web: www.acme-mccrary.com
SIC: 2251 Women's hosiery, except socks
HQ: Acme-Mccrary Corporation
  162 N Cherry St
  Asheboro NC 27203
  336 625-2161

(G-14396)
ACME-MCCRARY CORPORATION
1200 E 3rd St (27344-2732)
P.O. Box 686 (27344-0686)
PHONE..............................919 663-2200
Dave Foster, Mgr
EMP: 129
Web: www.acme-mccrary.com
SIC: 2251 Panty hose
HQ: Acme-Mccrary Corporation
  162 N Cherry St
  Asheboro NC 27203
  336 625-2161

(G-14397)
AD TUBI USA INC
3031 Hamp Stone Rd (27344-1426)
PHONE..............................919 930-3023
Craig Sullivan, Pr
EMP: 20 EST: 2018
SALES (est): 9.08MM Privately Held
Web: www.adtubi.com
SIC: 3312 Tubes, steel and iron
PA: A.D. Tubi Inossidabili Spa
  Via Adige 2
  Casnate Con Bernate CO 22070

(G-14398)
AXCHEM SOLUTIONS INC
1325 N 2nd Ave (27344-1841)
PHONE..............................919 742-9810
Richard Joy, Mgr
EMP: 6 EST: 2006
SALES (est): 648.67K Privately Held
Web: www.axchemgroup.com
SIC: 2822 Ethylene-propylene rubbers, EPDM polymers

(G-14399)
BASIC MACHINERY COMPANY INC
Also Called: Basic Group, The
1220 Harold Andrews Rd (27344-9170)
P.O. Box 688 (27344-0688)
PHONE..............................919 663-2244
William F Milholen, CEO
William S Robinson, *
Harold J Milholon Junior, VP
William J Milholon, *
▲ EMP: 58 EST: 1975
SALES (est): 19.35MM Privately Held
Web: www.basicmachinery.com

SIC: 5084 3535 3537 Materials handling machinery; Conveyors and conveying equipment; Industrial trucks and tractors

(G-14400)
BOYD MANUFACTURING INC
222 W Raleigh St (27344-3420)
PHONE..............................336 301-6433
Paul D Thompson, Prin
EMP: 11 EST: 2012
SALES (est): 997.11K Privately Held
SIC: 3999 Barber and beauty shop equipment

(G-14401)
BROOKWOOD FARMS INC
1015 Alston Bridge Rd (27344-9573)
P.O. Box 277 (27344-0277)
PHONE..............................919 663-3612
EMP: 68 EST: 1959
SALES (est): 12.26MM Privately Held
Web: www.brookwoodfarms.com
SIC: 2033 Barbecue sauce: packaged in cans, jars, etc.

(G-14402)
CCO HOLDINGS LLC
466 Vineyard Rdg (27344-4366)
PHONE..............................919 200-6260
EMP: 107
SALES (corp-wide): 54.61B Publicly Held
SIC: 4841 3663 3651 Cable television services; Radio and t.v. communications equipment; Household audio and video equipment
HQ: Cco Holdings, Llc
  400 Atlantic St
  Stamford CT 06901
  203 905-7801

(G-14403)
CECIL BUDD TIRE COMPANY LLC
394 Pine Forest Dr (27344-7995)
PHONE..............................919 742-2322
Michael Budd, Managing Member
John Grimes, Pt
Ruth Budd, Pt
EMP: 10 EST: 1936
SALES (est): 862.93K Privately Held
SIC: 5531 7534 5014 Automotive tires; Tire recapping; Automobile tires and tubes

(G-14404)
CELEBRITY DAIRY LLC
198 Celebrity Dairy Way (27344-6761)
PHONE..............................919 742-4931
EMP: 5 EST: 1987
SALES (est): 222.64K Privately Held
Web: www.celebritydairy.com
SIC: 7011 2022 5143 Bed and breakfast inn; Cheese; natural and processed; Frozen dairy desserts

(G-14405)
CHANDLER CONCRETE CO
804 S Chatham Ave (27344-3914)
PHONE..............................919 742-2627
Norman Suits, Mgr
EMP: 6 EST: 2020
SALES (est): 96.58K Privately Held
Web: www.chandlerconcrete.com
SIC: 3273 Ready-mixed concrete

(G-14406)
CHATHAM NEWS PUBLISHING CO (PA)
Also Called: Chatham News
303 W Raleigh St (27344-3725)
P.O. Box 290 (27344-0290)
PHONE..............................919 663-4042

Alan D Resch, Pr
Mary L Resch, Sec
EMP: 4
SQ FT: 5,600
SALES (est): 1.12MM
SALES (corp-wide): 1.12MM Privately Held
Web: www.thechathamnews.com
SIC: 2711 5812 Newspapers, publishing and printing; Eating places

(G-14407)
DAKOTA FAB & WELDING INC
1420 W 3rd St (27344-3626)
PHONE..............................919 881-0027
Chris Lonski, Pr
EMP: 4 EST: 1996
SALES (est): 485.68K Privately Held
Web: www.dakotafabwelding.com
SIC: 3446 Architectural metalwork

(G-14408)
DF FRAMING LLC
510 N Garden Ave (27344-2902)
PHONE..............................919 368-7903
EMP: 12 EST: 2021
SALES (est): 607.29K Privately Held
SIC: 2426 Frames for upholstered furniture, wood

(G-14409)
EAGLE ROCK INDUSTRIES LLC
2271 S Chatham Avenue Ext (27344-4356)
PHONE..............................919 799-1021
Mark A Middeke, Prin
EMP: 5 EST: 2010
SALES (est): 78.72K Privately Held
SIC: 3999 Manufacturing industries, nec

(G-14410)
ENGINRED PLSTIC COMPONENTS INC
Also Called: Silver City
920 E Raleigh St (27344-2708)
PHONE..............................919 663-3141
Irving Glasgow, Mgr
EMP: 120
Web: www.epcmfg.com
SIC: 3089 3086 Injection molding of plastics; Carpet and rug cushions, foamed plastics
PA: Engineered Plastic Components, Inc.
  4500 Westown Pkwy Ste 277
  West Des Moines IA 50266

(G-14411)
FLOORAZZO
Also Called: Floor Azzo
215 W 3rd St (27344-3443)
P.O. Box 380 (27344-0380)
PHONE..............................919 663-1684
Donna Sich, Managing Member
EMP: 5 EST: 2002
SALES (est): 304.14K Privately Held
Web: www.floorazzo.com
SIC: 3253 Ceramic wall and floor tile

(G-14412)
FLOORAZZO TILE LLC
1217 Harold Andrews Rd (27344-9171)
P.O. Box 380 (27344-0380)
PHONE..............................919 663-1684
Donna Sich, Managing Member
EMP: 17 EST: 2002
SALES (est): 1.56MM Privately Held
Web: www.floorazzo.com
SIC: 3272 Floor tile, precast terrazzo

(G-14413)
GATHERING PLACE PUBG CO LLC
274 Lambert Chapel Rd (27344-6307)

PHONE..............................919 742-5850
Timothy J Moore, Prin
EMP: 4 EST: 2011
SALES (est): 69.27K Privately Held
SIC: 2741 Miscellaneous publishing

(G-14414)
HOG SLAT INCORPORATED
17720 Us Highway 64 W (27344-1629)
PHONE..............................919 663-3321
Dwight Jenkins, Brnch Mgr
EMP: 21
SALES (corp-wide): 538.94MM Privately Held
Web: www.hogslat.com
SIC: 3523 Farm machinery and equipment
PA: Hog Slat, Incorporated
  206 Fayetteville St
  Newton Grove NC 28366
  800 949-4647

(G-14415)
IMMIXT LLC
9743 Silk Hope Liberty Rd (27344-4482)
PHONE..............................336 207-8679
EMP: 5 EST: 2009
SALES (est): 212.96K Privately Held
SIC: 3713 Truck and bus bodies

(G-14416)
INTERNATIONAL PRECAST INC
2469 Old Us 421 N (27344-1548)
PHONE..............................919 742-4241
Gregory M Lask, Pr
Stephen G Lask, *
▲ EMP: 25 EST: 2002
SALES (est): 4.98MM Privately Held
Web: www.international-precast.com
SIC: 3272 Concrete products, precast, nec

(G-14417)
INTERNATIONAL VAULT INC (PA)
Also Called: International Vault
2469 Old Us 421 N (27344)
PHONE..............................919 742-3132
EMP: 25 EST: 1982
SALES (est): 4.74MM Privately Held
Web: www.internationalvault.com
SIC: 3499 3272 Fire- or burglary-resistive products; Burial vaults, concrete or precast terrazzo

(G-14418)
JJ HERNANDEZ LOGGING LLC
4272 Piney Grove Church Rd (27344-5458)
PHONE..............................919 742-3381
EMP: 5 EST: 2019
SALES (est): 242.39K Privately Held
SIC: 2411 Logging

(G-14419)
JUAN J HERNANDEZ
4272 Piney Grove Church Rd (27344-5458)
PHONE..............................919 742-3381
Juan J Hernandez, Owner
EMP: 6 EST: 2015
SALES (est): 174.83K Privately Held
SIC: 2411 Logging

(G-14420)
LAZAR INDUSTRIES LLC (PA)
3025 Hamp Stone Rd (27344-1426)
PHONE..............................919 742-9303
Robert Luce, Managing Member
David Sowinski, *
James Baker, *
Wayne Gilman, *
Gary Piper, *
◆ EMP: 150 EST: 1983
SQ FT: 78,000

SALES (est): 26.21MM
SALES (corp-wide): 26.21MM **Privately Held**
Web: www.lazarind.com
SIC: **2512** Upholstered household furniture

(G-14421)
LAZAR INDUSTRIES EAST INC
Also Called: Textile Trends
3025 Hamp Stone Rd (27344-1426)
PHONE..................................919 742-9303
Barry Lazar, *Pr*
EMP: **11** EST: 1990
SALES (est): 500.21K **Privately Held**
Web: www.lazarind.com
SIC: **2512** Upholstered household furniture

(G-14422)
LINRENE FURNITURE INC
2535 Us Hwy 421 N (27344)
P.O. Box 408 (27344-0408)
PHONE..................................919 742-9391
EMP: **8** EST: 1994
SQ FT: 30,000
SALES (est): 238.8K **Privately Held**
Web: www.linreneinc.com
SIC: **2512** Upholstered household furniture

(G-14423)
LODGING BY LIBERTY INC
Also Called: Charter Furniture
50 Industrial Park Dr (27344-1318)
PHONE..................................336 622-2201
Gene J Moriarty, *Pr*
Jeff Leonard, *
Frederick King, *
EMP: **200** EST: 2000
SALES (est): 7.82MM **Privately Held**
SIC: **2512** 5021 Upholstered household furniture; Furniture

(G-14424)
MOUNTAIRE FARMS LLC
Also Called: Master Hatchery
4555 Old Us Hwy 421 N (27344-7381)
P.O. Box 175 (27344-0175)
PHONE..................................919 663-1768
David Pogge, *Brnch Mgr*
EMP: **232**
SALES (corp-wide): 2.07B **Privately Held**
Web: www.mountaire.com
SIC: **2015** Poultry slaughtering and processing
HQ: Mountaire Farms Inc.
1901 Napa Valley Dr
Little Rock AR 72212
501 372-6524

(G-14425)
MOUNTAIRE FARMS INC
1101 E 3rd St (27344-2729)
PHONE..................................919 663-0848
EMP: **353**
SALES (corp-wide): 2.07B **Privately Held**
Web: www.mountaire.com
SIC: **2015** Poultry slaughtering and processing
HQ: Mountaire Farms Inc.
1901 Napa Valley Dr
Little Rock AR 72212
501 372-6524

(G-14426)
MOYA CUSTOM DESIGNS LLC
789 Ss Edwards Rd (27344-7907)
PHONE..................................984 208-3118
EMP: **4** EST: 2021
SALES (est): 91.34K **Privately Held**
SIC: **3999** 7389 Candles; Business services, nec

(G-14427)
NATIONAL WDEN PLLET CONT ASSOC
2340 Ike Brooks Rd (27344-8769)
PHONE..................................919 837-2105
Kenny Reavis, *Prin*
EMP: **11** EST: 2014
SALES (est): 1.13MM **Privately Held**
Web: www.palletone.com
SIC: **2448** Pallets, wood

(G-14428)
ONEIDA MOLDED PLASTICS LLC
920 E Raleigh St (27344-2708)
PHONE..................................919 663-3141
Irvin Glasgow, *Brnch Mgr*
EMP: **10**
SALES (corp-wide): 23.25MM **Privately Held**
Web: www.oneidamoldedplastics.com
SIC: **3089** Injection molding of plastics
PA: Oneida Molded Plastics, Llc
104 S Warner St
Oneida NY 13421
315 363-7980

(G-14429)
ORARE INC
Also Called: Glass & Window Warehouse
812 E 3rd St (27344-2724)
PHONE..................................919 742-1003
Judy Harrelson, *Pr*
Michael Harrelson, *VP*
EMP: **5** EST: 2007
SALES (est): 490K **Privately Held**
Web: www.mikeharrelson.net
SIC: **1793** 3231 5231 7536 Glass and glazing work; Products of purchased glass; Glass; Automotive glass replacement shops

(G-14430)
PALLETONE NORTH CAROLINA INC (HQ)
Also Called: Palletone
2340 Ike Brooks Rd (27344-8769)
PHONE..................................704 462-1882
Howe Wallace, *Pr*
Casey Fletcher, *
EMP: **93** EST: 1993
SALES (est): 46.25MM
SALES (corp-wide): 7.22B **Publicly Held**
Web: www.palletone.com
SIC: **2448** 2426 2421 Pallets, wood; Hardwood dimension and flooring mills; Sawmills and planing mills, general
PA: Ufp Industries, Inc.
2801 E Beltline Ave Ne
Grand Rapids MI 49525
616 364-6161

(G-14431)
SOUTHERN TRADITIONS TWO INC
55 Industrial Park Dr (27344-1300)
P.O. Box 523 (27344-0523)
PHONE..................................919 742-4692
James Lloyd, *Prin*
EMP: **6** EST: 2010
SALES (est): 177.52K **Privately Held**
SIC: **2599** Furniture and fixtures, nec

(G-14432)
SOUTHERN TRUCKING & BACKHOE
165 Riverside Rd (27344-9416)
PHONE..................................919 548-9723
Gerald Palmer, *Prin*
EMP: **5** EST: 2013
SALES (est): 67.56K **Privately Held**
SIC: **3531** Backhoes

(G-14433)
WATER TREATMENT FACILITY
955 Water Plant Rd (27344)
PHONE..................................919 742-2939
Philip Parkins, *Superintnt*
EMP: **5** EST: 2008
SALES (est): 128.47K **Privately Held**
SIC: **3069** Water bottles, rubber

(G-14434)
WHOLESALE KENNEL SUPPLY CO
163 Stockyard Rd (27344)
P.O. Box 745 (27344-0745)
PHONE..................................919 742-2515
Thomas E Dewitt, *Owner*
EMP: **9** EST: 1959
SQ FT: 13,200
SALES (est): 702.7K **Privately Held**
Web: www.wholesalekennel.com
SIC: **5199** 5999 2834 Pet supplies; Pet food; Veterinary pharmaceutical preparations

(G-14435)
WRENN BROTHERS INC
902 S Chatham Ave (27344-4302)
PHONE..................................919 742-3329
EMP: **7**
SALES (corp-wide): 62.34K **Privately Held**
Web: www.wrennwood.com
SIC: **2421** Sawmills and planing mills, general
PA: Wrenn Brothers, Inc.
36 Pine Court Dr
Siler City NC

(G-14436)
WRENN BROTHERS INC
1311 N 2nd Ave (27344-1841)
PHONE..................................919 742-3717
EMP: **5** EST: 2019
SALES (est): 86.73K **Privately Held**
Web: www.wrennwood.com
SIC: **2421** Sawmills and planing mills, general

Simpson
Pitt County

(G-14437)
COASTAL CABINETS & GRANITE LLC
2845b Edwards Drive (27879-9703)
P.O. Box 125 (27879-0125)
PHONE..................................252 717-0611
EMP: **6** EST: 2017
SALES (est): 176.81K **Privately Held**
Web: www.coastalcabinetsandgranite.com
SIC: **2434** Wood kitchen cabinets

(G-14438)
JOHNSON CABINET CO
P.O. Box 355 (27879-0355)
PHONE..................................252 714-2051
EMP: **4** EST: 2009
SALES (est): 121.85K **Privately Held**
SIC: **2434** Wood kitchen cabinets

Sims
Wilson County

(G-14439)
ARGOS USA LLC
Also Called: Ready Mix Concrete Co
6823 Bruce Rd (27880-9208)
P.O. Box 280 (27880-0280)
PHONE..................................252 291-8888
Tim Jacobs, *Mgr*
EMP: **8**
Web: www.argos-us.com
SIC: **3273** Ready-mixed concrete
HQ: Argos Usa Llc
3015 Windward Plz Ste 300
Alpharetta GA 30005
678 368-4300

(G-14440)
CAROLINA FLARE SPORTFISHNG LLC
5166 Mamie Rd (27880-9375)
PHONE..................................252 205-5563
Joseph Russell Tyler, *Owner*
EMP: **5** EST: 2017
SALES (est): 107.04K **Privately Held**
SIC: **2899** Flares

(G-14441)
DAVIS CABINET CO WILSON INC
6116 Green Pond Rd (27880-9672)
P.O. Box 295 (27880-0295)
PHONE..................................252 291-9052
Stanley G Davis, *Pr*
Keith Davis, *VP*
Susan Davis, *Sec*
EMP: **13** EST: 1981
SQ FT: 26,000
SALES (est): 447.41K **Privately Held**
Web: www.daviscabinet.com
SIC: **2434** 2541 2431 Wood kitchen cabinets; Cabinets, except refrigerated: show, display, etc.: wood; Millwork

(G-14442)
FLOWERS SLAUGHTERHOUSE LLC
5154a Saint Rose Church Rd (27880-9419)
PHONE..................................252 235-4106
Alan Sharp, *Prin*
Pender Sharp, *Prin*
EMP: **12** EST: 2019
SALES (est): 697.04K **Privately Held**
SIC: **2011** Meat packing plants

(G-14443)
HEIDELBERG MATERIALS US INC
Also Called: Neverson Quarry
7225 Neverson Rd (27880-9476)
PHONE..................................252 235-4162
Rodney Godwin, *Brnch Mgr*
EMP: **22**
SALES (corp-wide): 21.19B **Privately Held**
Web: www.heidelbergmaterials.us
SIC: **3273** Ready-mixed concrete
HQ: Heidelberg Materials Us, Inc.
300 E John Carpenter Fwy
Irving TX 75062

(G-14444)
ROUNDWOOD LOGGING INC
8421 Amber Rd (27880-9382)
PHONE..................................252 230-9980
EMP: **6** EST: 2015
SALES (est): 98.88K **Privately Held**
SIC: **2411** Logging

(G-14445)
TRI-STEEL FABRICATORS INC
6864 Wagon Wheel Rd (27880-9694)
P.O. Box 250 (27880-0250)
PHONE..................................252 291-7900
Tom Robertson, *Pr*
Ronald Cook, *
Steve Gibbon, *
EMP: **35** EST: 1996
SQ FT: 40,000
SALES (est): 7.78MM **Privately Held**
Web: www.tri-steel.net

SIC: 3441 Fabricated structural metal

Sjafb
Wayne County

(G-14446)
BOEING COMPANY
Also Called: Kc-46a Pegasus
1155 Blakeslee Ave (27531-2263)
PHONE..................................919 722-1983
EMP: 5 EST: 2020
SALES (est): 190.72K **Privately Held**
Web: jobs.boeing.com
SIC: 3721 Airplanes, fixed or rotary wing

Smithfield
Johnston County

(G-14447)
A WINDOW TREATMENT CO INC
525 S Brightleaf Blvd (27577-4076)
P.O. Box 2388 (27577-2388)
PHONE..................................919 934-7100
Bill Kimball, *Pr*
Thomas Berkau, *Prin*
Daniel Matthews, *Sec*
▲ EMP: 10 EST: 1988
SQ FT: 13,000
SALES (est): 739.74K **Privately Held**
SIC: 2591 2391 Window blinds; Curtains and draperies

(G-14448)
ACE FABRICATION INC
Also Called: M & W Fab
2880 Us Highway 70 Bus W (27577-9360)
P.O. Box 2769 (27577-2769)
PHONE..................................919 934-3251
Michael Prince, *Pr*
Mike Munden, *Pr*
Mike Watkins, *VP*
EMP: 16 EST: 1966
SQ FT: 13,200
SALES (est): 2.02MM **Privately Held**
Web: www.acefab.com
SIC: 3441 Fabricated structural metal

(G-14449)
APERGY ARTFL LIFT INTL LLC
3250 Us Highway 70 Bus E (27577-7777)
PHONE..................................919 934-1533
Jim Weber, *Mgr*
EMP: 11
SALES (corp-wide): 3.76B **Publicly Held**
Web: www.championx.com
SIC: 1389 5172 1799 Oil field services, nec; Service station supplies, petroleum; Service station equipment installation, maint., and repair
HQ: Apergy Artificial Lift International, Llc
2445 Tech Frest Blvd Bldg
The Woodlands TX 77381
281 403-5742

(G-14450)
BAKERS STNLESS FABRICATION INC
1520 Freedom Rd (27577-8131)
PHONE..................................919 934-2707
Billy Baker, *Pr*
Sandy Baker, *VP*
Margie Crumley, *Sec*
EMP: 9 EST: 1996
SQ FT: 5,000
SALES (est): 925.02K **Privately Held**
SIC: 3441 Fabricated structural metal

(G-14451)
BRIGHTLEAF WLDG & MCH REPR LLC
2850 S Brightleaf Blvd (27577-8357)
PHONE..................................919 934-3300
Jeffery Carawan, *Admn*
EMP: 5 EST: 2015
SALES (est): 25.09K **Privately Held**
SIC: 7692 Welding repair

(G-14452)
CAROLINA ELCTRNIC ASSMBLERS IN
132 Citation Ln (27577-6969)
PHONE..................................919 938-1086
Steven S Yauch, *Pr*
Kimberly N Godfrey, *
◆ EMP: 50 EST: 2000
SQ FT: 50,000
SALES (est): 6.64MM **Privately Held**
Web: www.ceamanufacturing.com
SIC: 3679 3613 Electronic circuits; Switchgear and switchboard apparatus

(G-14453)
CAROLINA PACKERS INC (PA)
2999 S Brightleaf Blvd (27577-5251)
P.O. Box 1109 (27577-1109)
PHONE..................................919 934-2181
EMP: 80 EST: 1940
SQ FT: 100,000
SALES (est): 11.57MM
SALES (corp-wide): 11.57MM **Privately Held**
Web: www.carolinapackers.com
SIC: 2011 2013 Meat packing plants; Sausages, from purchased meat

(G-14454)
CLARITY VISION OF SMITHFIELD
1680 E Booker Dairy Rd (27577-9405)
PHONE..................................919 938-6101
EMP: 4 EST: 2015
SALES (est): 111.77K **Privately Held**
Web: www.findclarityvision.com
SIC: 3851 5995 Ophthalmic goods; Eyeglasses, prescription

(G-14455)
CLASSIC INDUSTRIAL SERVICES
Also Called: Classic Industrial Services
1305 S Brightleaf Blvd Ste 103 (27577-4260)
PHONE..................................919 209-0909
Michael Landes, *Pr*
Mark Beuerle, *
EMP: 49 EST: 1987
SQ FT: 89,000
SALES (est): 15.19MM
SALES (corp-wide): 6.93B **Publicly Held**
Web: www.classicindustrial.com
SIC: 1499 7359 Corundum mining; Equipment rental and leasing, nec
HQ: Api Group, Inc.
1100 Old Highway 8 Nw
New Brighton MN 55112
651 636-4320

(G-14456)
CMC SENCON INC (PA)
132 Citation Ln (27577-6969)
PHONE..................................919 938-3216
▲ EMP: 33 EST: 1992
SQ FT: 4,000
SALES (est): 2.83MM **Privately Held**
SIC: 3625 Relays and industrial controls

(G-14457)
COMMSCOPE TECHNOLOGIES LLC
1315 Industrial Park Dr (27577)
PHONE..................................919 934-9711
Danny Ricker, *Brnch Mgr*
EMP: 11
SIC: 3663 3357 3679 3812 Microwave communication equipment; Coaxial cable, nonferrous; Waveguides and fittings; Search and navigation equipment
HQ: Commscope Technologies Llc
4 Westbrook Corp Ctr
Westchester IL 60154
800 366-3891

(G-14458)
CREATIVE BREWING COMPANY LLC
809 S 2nd St (27577-4347)
PHONE..................................919 297-8182
EMP: 4 EST: 2013
SALES (est): 173.61K **Privately Held**
SIC: 7389 2082 Business Activities at Non-Commercial Site; Ale (alcoholic beverage)

(G-14459)
EAST CAST TRCKG BCKHOE SVCS LL
708 Nc Highway 210 (27577-9155)
PHONE..................................919 209-0198
Pamela Lucious Christmas, *Owner*
EMP: 5 EST: 2018
SALES (est): 210.04K **Privately Held**
SIC: 3531 Backhoes

(G-14460)
FLANDERS CORPORATION
Also Called: Flanders Precisionaire
2121 Wal Pat Rd (27577-8375)
PHONE..................................919 934-3020
EMP: 151
Web: www.flanderscorp.com
SIC: 3569 Filters
HQ: Flanders Corporation
531 Flanders Filter Rd
Washington NC 27889

(G-14461)
FLANDERS FILTERS INC
1418 Wal Pat Rd (27577-8394)
PHONE..................................252 217-3978
EMP: 5
Web: www.aafintl.com
SIC: 3569 Filters
HQ: Flanders Filters, Inc.
531 Flanders Filter Rd
Washington NC 27889
252 946-8081

(G-14462)
HINSONS TYPING & PRINTING
Also Called: Henson's Printing
1294 W Market St (27577-3337)
P.O. Box 87 (27577-0087)
PHONE..................................919 934-9036
Amy Stanley, *Pr*
Nolan Hinson, *Owner*
Joanne Hinson, *VP*
James L Stanley Junior, *Treas*
Jamie Stanley, *VP*
EMP: 7 EST: 1983
SALES (est): 423.49K **Privately Held**
Web: www.hinsprint.com
SIC: 2752 2389 8742 Offset printing; Apparel for handicapped; Marketing consulting services

(G-14463)
J & B LOGGING AND TIMBER CO
524 Brogden Rd (27577-4306)
P.O. Box 2430 (27577-2430)
PHONE..................................919 934-4115
John Mark Williams, *Pr*
Andy Lee, *Contrlr*
▼ EMP: 22 EST: 1987

SQ FT: 3,000
SALES (est): 492.1K **Privately Held**
Web: www.jerrygwilliamslumber.com
SIC: 2421 Sawmills and planing mills, general

(G-14464)
JERRY G WILLIAMS & SONS INC
524 Brogden Rd (27577-4306)
P.O. Box 59 (27577-0059)
PHONE..................................919 934-4115
J Mark Williams, *Pr*
Virginia M Williams, *Sec*
Kevin D Williams, *VP*
EMP: 23 EST: 1986
SALES (est): 2.26MM **Privately Held**
Web: www.jerrygwilliamslumber.com
SIC: 2421 Sawmills and planing mills, general

(G-14465)
JERRY WILLIAMS & SON INC
524 Brogden Rd (27577-4306)
P.O. Box 2430 (27577-2430)
PHONE..................................919 934-4115
John Mark Williams, *Pr*
Lynette Williams, *
EMP: 100 EST: 1938
SQ FT: 3,500
SALES (est): 9.73MM **Privately Held**
Web: www.jerrygwilliamslumber.com
SIC: 2421 Lumber: rough, sawed, or planed

(G-14466)
JMW LOGGING LLC
524 Brogden Rd (27577-4306)
P.O. Box 2430 (27577-2430)
PHONE..................................919 934-4115
EMP: 5 EST: 2015
SALES (est): 98.88K **Privately Held**
Web: www.jmwlogging.com
SIC: 2411 Logging

(G-14467)
KEENER LUMBER COMPANY INC (PA)
1209 W Market St (27577-3338)
P.O. Box 2323 (27577-2323)
PHONE..................................919 934-1087
Wade M Stewart, *Pr*
Reid Stewart, *
Steve Clark, *CIO*
Wayne Stewart, *
Ralph Stewart, *
EMP: 95 EST: 1935
SQ FT: 1,800
SALES (est): 7.88MM
SALES (corp-wide): 7.88MM **Privately Held**
Web: www.keenerlumber.com
SIC: 2421 Sawmills and planing mills, general

(G-14468)
KRATOS ANTENNA SOLUTIONS CORP
1315 Industrial Park Dr (27577)
PHONE..................................919 934-9711
Danny Ricker, *Mgr*
EMP: 5
Web: www.kratosdefense.com
SIC: 3679 Antennas, satellite: household use
HQ: Kratos Antenna Solutions Corporation
3801 E Plano Pkwy Ste 200
Plano TX 75074

(G-14469)
LAMPE & MALPHRUS LUMBER CO
37 E Peedin Rd (27577-4709)
P.O. Box 150 (27577-0150)

PHONE..............................919 934-6152
EMP: 15
SALES (corp-wide): 10.05MM Privately Held
Web: www.lampemalphrus.com
SIC: 2421 Sawmills and planing mills, general
PA: Lampe & Malphrus Lumber Company
37 E Peedin Rd
Smithfield NC 27577
919 934-6152

(G-14470)
LAMPE & MALPHRUS LUMBER CO (PA)
Also Called: Geecee
37 E Peedin Rd (27577-4709)
P.O. Box 150 (27577-0150)
PHONE..............................919 934-6152
James Malphrus, Pr
▼ EMP: 84 EST: 1986
SQ FT: 3,600
SALES (est): 10.05MM
SALES (corp-wide): 10.05MM Privately Held
Web: www.lampemalphrus.com
SIC: 2421 Sawmills and planing mills, general

(G-14471)
LAMPE & MALPHRUS LUMBER CO
210 N 10th St (27577-4658)
P.O. Box 150 (27577-0150)
PHONE..............................919 934-1124
EMP: 15
SALES (corp-wide): 10.05MM Privately Held
Web: www.lampemalphrus.com
SIC: 2421 3543 Sawmills and planing mills, general; Industrial patterns
PA: Lampe & Malphrus Lumber Company
37 E Peedin Rd
Smithfield NC 27577
919 934-6152

(G-14472)
MITCHELL CONCRETE PRODUCTS INC
490 W Market St (27577-3321)
P.O. Box 585 (27577-0585)
PHONE..............................919 934-4333
Nelson Mitchell, Pr
EMP: 9 EST: 1958
SQ FT: 85,000
SALES (est): 1.01MM Privately Held
SIC: 3272 Concrete products, nec

(G-14473)
OLT LOGGING INC
451 Marshall Ln (27577-7492)
PHONE..............................919 894-4506
Donald Czysz, Pr
EMP: 7 EST: 1994
SALES (est): 960.66K Privately Held
SIC: 2411 Logging camps and contractors

(G-14474)
OPW FLING CNTNMENT SYSTEMS INC (DH)
3250 Us Highway 70 Bus W (27577-6954)
PHONE..............................919 209-2280
David Crouse, Pr
Susan Hathaway, CFO
◆ EMP: 29 EST: 2006
SQ FT: 190,000
SALES (est): 93.79MM
SALES (corp-wide): 8.44B Publicly Held
Web: www.opwglobal.com

SIC: 3089 3084 3561 Plastics processing; Plastics pipe; Pumps and pumping equipment
HQ: Opw Fluid Transfer Group
4304 Nw Mattox Rd
Kansas City MO 64150

(G-14475)
OPW FUELING COMPONENTS INC
Also Called: Opw Feling Containment Systems
3250 Us Highway 70 Bus W (27577)
PHONE..............................919 464-4569
EMP: 45
SALES (corp-wide): 8.51B Publicly Held
Web: www.opwglobal.com
SIC: 2899 Fuel treating compounds
HQ: Opw Fueling Components Inc.
9393 Prnceton Glendale Rd
West Chester OH 45011

(G-14476)
PENN COMPRESSION MOULDING INC (PA)
Also Called: Penn
309 Components Dr (27577-6030)
PHONE..............................919 934-5144
Richard S Robinson, Pr
EMP: 5 EST: 1995
SQ FT: 2,000
SALES (est): 21.24MM
SALES (corp-wide): 21.24MM Privately Held
Web: www.penncompression.com
SIC: 3089 3644 Molding primary plastics; Insulators and insulation materials, electrical

(G-14477)
POST EC HOLDINGS INC
207a Computer Dr (27577-3156)
PHONE..............................919 989-0175
G Steve Arnold, CEO
Stephen Butts, *
Francis Koh, *
▲ EMP: 35 EST: 2006
SQ FT: 40,000
SALES (est): 6.2MM Privately Held
Web: www.envicor.com
SIC: 3089 Injection molding of plastics

(G-14478)
RAVEN ANTENNA SYSTEMS INC
Also Called: Global Skyware
1315 Outlet Center Dr (27577-6024)
PHONE..............................919 934-9711
David C Mccourt, Pr
Michael Kevin Jackson, *
Hamid Moheb, *
◆ EMP: 200 EST: 2004
SQ FT: 75,200
SALES (est): 56.23MM Privately Held
Web: www.globalinvacom.com
SIC: 3663 Television antennas (transmitting) and ground equipment
PA: Global Invacom Group Limited
7 Temasek Boulevard
Singapore 03898

(G-14479)
RDC DEBRIS REMOVAL CNSTR LLC
149 Rainbow Ln (27577-6801)
PHONE..............................323 614-2353
EMP: 50 EST: 2019
SALES (est): 1.88MM Privately Held
SIC: 1521 1771 0782 1081 Single-family housing construction; Stucco, gunite, and grouting contractors; Lawn and garden services; Metal mining exploration and development services

(G-14480)
RETAIL MARKET PLACE
950 W Market St (27577-3331)
PHONE..............................984 201-1948
Brian Parker, Owner
EMP: 4 EST: 2016
SQ FT: 10,000
SALES (est): 140.54K Privately Held
SIC: 2051 Bakery: wholesale or wholesale/retail combined

(G-14481)
SANDY RIDGE PORK
2080 Wilsons Mills Rd (27577-7657)
PHONE..............................919 989-8878
Whitley Stevenson, Owner
EMP: 8 EST: 2004
SALES (est): 227.29K Privately Held
SIC: 2011 Pork products, from pork slaughtered on site

(G-14482)
SHALLCO INC
308 Components Dr (27577-6029)
P.O. Box 1089 (27577-1089)
PHONE..............................919 934-3135
Jason Shallcross, Pr
▲ EMP: 40 EST: 1967
SQ FT: 15,000
SALES (est): 6.9MM Privately Held
Web: www.shallco.com
SIC: 3613 3679 Switches, electric power except snap, push button, etc.; Attenuators

(G-14483)
SMITHFIELD CED
412 S 7th St (27577-4414)
P.O. Box 861 (27577-0861)
PHONE..............................919 934-5041
EMP: 5 EST: 2015
SALES (est): 251.03K Privately Held
Web: cedsmithfieldnc.portalced.com
SIC: 3699 Electrical equipment and supplies, nec

(G-14484)
SNAPZ SOFTWARE INC
52 Quince Ct (27577-8930)
PHONE..............................302 234-0402
Jared Menzie, Pr
EMP: 4 EST: 2018
SALES (est): 62.19K Privately Held
Web: www.snapz.com
SIC: 7372 Prepackaged software

(G-14485)
SOUTHMARK FOREST PRODUCTS
1209 W Market St (27577-3338)
PHONE..............................919 300-1596
EMP: 5 EST: 2015
SALES (est): 103.19K Privately Held
Web: www.southmarkforest.com
SIC: 5031 2421 Lumber: rough, dressed, and finished; Lumber: rough, sawed, or planed

(G-14486)
TAR HEEL TLING PRCSION MCHNING
3290 Us Highway 70 E (27577-7771)
P.O. Box 1063 (27577-1063)
PHONE..............................919 965-6160
Bobby G Pilkington, Pr
Durwood D Woodall, VP
Charles L Pilkington, Treas
Cecil C Woodall, Sec
EMP: 23 EST: 1978
SQ FT: 15,000
SALES (est): 2.5MM Privately Held
Web: www.tarheeltooling.com

SIC: 3599 3545 Custom machinery; Tools and accessories for machine tools

(G-14487)
VIDA WOOD US INC
219 Peedin Rd Ste 102 (27577-4738)
PHONE..............................919 934-9904
Kenny W Woodard, Pr
EMP: 4 EST: 2008
SALES (est): 575.88K Privately Held
Web: www.vidawoodus.com
SIC: 2421 Outdoor wood structural products

(G-14488)
WALLACE WELDING INC
403 W Market St (27577-3322)
PHONE..............................919 934-2488
Garrett Wallace, Pr
EMP: 10 EST: 1945
SQ FT: 3,500
SALES (est): 850.85K Privately Held
SIC: 3441 3599 7692 Fabricated structural metal; Machine shop, jobbing and repair; Welding repair

(G-14489)
WILSON BILLBOARD ADVG INC
Also Called: Wilson Signs
212 Bridge St (27577-3963)
P.O. Box 910 (27577-0910)
PHONE..............................919 934-2421
EMP: 8 EST: 1986
SALES (est): 515.25K Privately Held
SIC: 7312 3993 Billboard advertising; Signs and advertising specialties

Smyrna
Carteret County

(G-14490)
SAVVY - DISCOUNTSCOM NEWS LTR
195 Old Nassau Road Williston (28579-9519)
P.O. Box 117 (28579-0117)
PHONE..............................252 729-8691
Rick Doble, Owner
EMP: 10 EST: 1994
SALES (est): 339.21K Privately Held
Web: www.savvy-discounts.com
SIC: 2741 Business service newsletters: publishing and printing

Sneads Ferry
Onslow County

(G-14491)
HOPE COUNSELING CTR
971 Chadwick Shores Dr (28460-9213)
PHONE..............................910 741-0538
Kathy Bornarth, CEO
EMP: 5 EST: 2015
SALES (est): 62.99K Privately Held
SIC: 2711 Newspapers

(G-14492)
MCLEAN PRECISION CABINETRY INC
2507 Nc Highway 172 (28460-6637)
PHONE..............................910 327-9217
John Mclean, Prin
EMP: 4 EST: 2007
SALES (est): 430.64K Privately Held
Web: www.mcleanprecisioncabinetry.com
SIC: 2434 Wood kitchen cabinets

Sneads Ferry - Onslow County (G-14493)

(G-14493)
WALRATH WELDING
1360 Chadwick Shores Dr (28460-9274)
P.O. Box 54 (28173-1038)
PHONE..................704 771-6640
Jeremiah Walrath, *Prin*
EMP: 5 **EST:** 2015
SALES (est): 28.6K **Privately Held**
Web: www.walrathwelding.com
SIC: 7692 Welding repair

(G-14494)
ZERI CONSULTING INC
Also Called: Minuteman Press
114 Salt Marsh Cv (28460-9592)
PHONE..................412 512-2027
Aurelio Gomes, *Prin*
EMP: 6 **EST:** 2021
SALES (est): 25.81K **Privately Held**
Web: www.minuteman.com
SIC: 2752 Commercial printing, lithographic

Snow Camp
Alamance County

(G-14495)
CHARLIES HEATING & COOLING LLC
8277 Bethel South Fork Rd (27349-9879)
PHONE..................336 260-1973
EMP: 4
SALES (est): 168.32K **Privately Held**
SIC: 7389 3585 Business Activities at Non-Commercial Site; Heating and air conditioning combination units

(G-14496)
COLE MACHINE INC
6144 Patterson Rd (27349-9911)
PHONE..................336 222-8381
Harry Cole, *Pr*
Jason Cole, *VP*
EMP: 8 **EST:** 1990
SQ FT: 4,000
SALES (est): 583.26K **Privately Held**
SIC: 3599 Machine and other job shop work

(G-14497)
RGF PRINTING
6965 Snow Camp Rd (27349-9154)
PHONE..................201 832-5233
Francis Arrigo, *Prin*
EMP: 6 **EST:** 2019
SALES (est): 85.69K **Privately Held**
SIC: 2752 Commercial printing, lithographic

Snow Hill
Greene County

(G-14498)
BOAT LIFT WAREHOUSE LLC
900 Hwy 258 S (28580-8964)
P.O. Box 798 (28580-0798)
PHONE..................877 468-5438
▼ **EMP:** 6 **EST:** 2009
SQ FT: 7,000
SALES (est): 881.11K **Privately Held**
Web: www.boatliftwarehouse.com
SIC: 3536 Boat lifts

(G-14499)
BUILDING ENVLOPE ERCTION SVCS (PA)
1441 Nahunta Rd (28580-7557)
PHONE..................252 747-2015
John Taylor Iii, *Pr*
William R Brown, *VP*
Richard Logan, *Sec*
EMP: 12 **EST:** 2013
SQ FT: 30,000
SALES (est): 2.5MM
SALES (corp-wide): 2.5MM **Privately Held**
Web: www.beesinc.net
SIC: 1793 3442 Glass and glazing work; Baseboards, metal

(G-14500)
CAROLINA FARMSTEAD LLC
1012 Hardy Rd (28580-7389)
PHONE..................800 822-6219
Wayne Noble, *Owner*
EMP: 6 **EST:** 2015
SALES (est): 112.56K **Privately Held**
Web: www.carolinafarmstead.com
SIC: 2511 Bed frames, except water bed frames: wood

(G-14501)
CD SNOW HILL LLC
Also Called: Nwl Capacitors
204 Carolina Dr (28580-1646)
PHONE..................252 747-5943
James Kaplan, *CEO*
EMP: 85 **EST:** 2020
SALES (est): 16.25MM
SALES (corp-wide): 707.6MM **Publicly Held**
Web: www.nwl.com
SIC: 3679 Power supplies, all types: static
HQ: Cornell-Dubilier Electronics, Inc.
140 Technology Pl
Liberty SC 29657
864 843-2277

(G-14502)
DEHYDRATION LLC
963 Hwy 258 S (28580-8964)
PHONE..................252 747-8200
EMP: 7 **EST:** 2015
SALES (est): 168.52K **Privately Held**
Web: www.hamfarms.com
SIC: 2034 Dried and dehydrated fruits, vegetables and soup mixes

(G-14503)
HAPPY JACK INCORPORATED
Also Called: E- Stitch.com
2122 Hwy 258 S (28580-9016)
P.O. Box 475 (28580-0475)
PHONE..................252 747-2911
EMP: 8 **EST:** 1946
SALES (est): 1.03MM **Privately Held**
Web: www.happyjackinc.com
SIC: 2834 5699 Veterinary pharmaceutical preparations; Sports apparel

(G-14504)
METAL SOLUTIONS LLC
4865 Hwy 258 S (28580-8920)
PHONE..................252 702-7523
Benito P Rodriguez, *Owner*
EMP: 5 **EST:** 2014
SALES (est): 86.05K **Privately Held**
SIC: 7692 Welding repair

(G-14505)
NWL INC
Also Called: N W L Capacitors
204 Carolina Dr (28580-1646)
P.O. Box 97 (28580-0097)
PHONE..................252 747-5943
Stewart Irvin, *Opers Mgr*
EMP: 42
SQ FT: 35,000
SALES (corp-wide): 102.3MM **Privately Held**
Web: www.nwl.com
SIC: 3612 3675 3629 Power transformers, electric; Electronic capacitors; Capacitors and condensers
HQ: Nwl, Inc.
312 Rising Sun Rd
Bordentown NJ 08505
609 298-7300

(G-14506)
PARKERS EQUIPMENT COMPANY
3204 Hwy 258 S (28580-8914)
PHONE..................252 560-0088
Richard Parker, *Owner*
Richard Dick Parker, *Prin*
EMP: 4 **EST:** 2001
SALES (est): 195.27K **Privately Held**
SIC: 3537 Forklift trucks

(G-14507)
PRECISION GRAPHICS INC
429 Kingold Blvd (28580-1307)
PHONE..................252 917-3174
EMP: 6 **EST:** 2021
SALES (est): 79.3K **Privately Held**
SIC: 3679 Electronic components, nec

(G-14508)
SMART PLAY USA
417 Kingold Blvd (28580-1307)
PHONE..................252 747-2587
John Colombu, *Owner*
▲ **EMP:** 6 **EST:** 2007
SALES (est): 235.11K **Privately Held**
SIC: 2759 7699 Commercial printing, nec; Customizing services

(G-14509)
VERTICAL ACCESS LLC
900 Hwy 258 S (28580-8964)
P.O. Box 737 (28580-0737)
PHONE..................800 325-1116
Francis Shackelford, *Pr*
EMP: 7 **EST:** 2015
SALES (est): 797.65K **Privately Held**
Web: www.vertical-access.com
SIC: 3534 Elevators and equipment

(G-14510)
WORTH PRODUCTS LLC
856 Hwy 258 S (28580-8963)
P.O. Box 491 (28580-0491)
PHONE..................252 747-9994
Kenneth Letchworth, *Owner*
EMP: 18 **EST:** 2004
SQ FT: 28,000
SALES (est): 2.3MM **Privately Held**
Web: www.worthproducts.com
SIC: 3544 3599 Jigs and fixtures; Custom machinery

(G-14511)
YAMCO LLC
310 Kingold Blvd (28580-1306)
P.O. Box 42 (28580-0042)
PHONE..................252 747-9267
EMP: 4 **EST:** 2004
SALES (est): 1.02MM **Privately Held**
Web: www.yamco.net
SIC: 2033 Vegetable purees: packaged in cans, jars, etc.

(G-14512)
YANEK LLC
303 Elm St (28580-1750)
PHONE..................252 558-3757
Daneka Sheppard, *Mgr*
EMP: 5 **EST:** 2021
SALES (est): 90.74K **Privately Held**
Web: yanek.business.site
SIC: 2911 Aromatic chemical products

Sophia
Randolph County

(G-14513)
BUNTING EQUIPMENT COMPANY INC
Also Called: Exact Fit
3846 Caraway Mountain Rd (27350-8557)
P.O. Box 4414 (27204-4414)
PHONE..................336 626-7300
Larry L Bunting, *Pr*
Gregg Bunting, *VP*
Betty Bunting, *Sec*
EMP: 15 **EST:** 1992
SQ FT: 72,000
SALES (est): 896.52K **Privately Held**
SIC: 3086 3599 3296 Insulation or cushioning material, foamed plastics; Custom machinery; Mineral wool

(G-14514)
COTNER CABINET
3004 Old County Farm Rd (27350-8862)
PHONE..................336 672-1560
Raymond Dalton Cotner, *Owner*
EMP: 6 **EST:** 1978
SALES (est): 380.89K **Privately Held**
Web: www.cotnercabinet.com
SIC: 2434 Wood kitchen cabinets

(G-14515)
ENGINEERED STEEL PRODUCTS LLC
4977 Plainfield Rd (27350-8895)
PHONE..................336 495-5266
Rick Ramsey, *Pr*
EMP: 30 **EST:** 1989
SALES (est): 7.15MM
SALES (corp-wide): 7.15MM **Privately Held**
Web: www.engineeredsteel.com
SIC: 3441 Fabricated structural metal
PA: New Page Capital, Llc
100 N Greene St Ste 600
Greensboro NC 27401
770 853-6748

(G-14516)
ENGINEERED STEEL PRODUCTS INC
4977 Plainfield Rd (27350-8895)
P.O. Box 967 (27317-0967)
PHONE..................336 495-5266
EMP: 30
SIC: 3441 Fabricated structural metal

(G-14517)
G T RACING HEADS INC
2735 Banner Whitehead Rd (27350-9119)
PHONE..................336 905-7988
Gregory B Burkhart, *Pr*
EMP: 4 **EST:** 2003
SQ FT: 7,200
SALES (est): 449.01K **Privately Held**
SIC: 3549 7539 3599 Metalworking machinery, nec; Machine shop, automotive; Machine shop, jobbing and repair

(G-14518)
HAYES WELDING
5033 Walker Mill Rd (27350-9249)
PHONE..................336 989-6171
Gene Hayes, *Prin*
EMP: 4 **EST:** 2019
SALES (est): 25.09K **Privately Held**
SIC: 7692 Welding repair

GEOGRAPHIC SECTION

Southern Pines - Moore County (G-14545)

(G-14519)
K&S CUSTOM LLC
2316 Windsong Rd (27350-8942)
PHONE................................336 861-1607
Steven W Harris, *Owner*
EMP: 5 EST: 2017
SALES (est): 231.86K **Privately Held**
Web: www.kscustommillwork.com
SIC: **2431** Millwork

(G-14520)
PLAN B CHIPPING AND LOGGING
2539 Beckerdite Rd (27350-8510)
PHONE................................336 942-2692
Toby Montgomery, *Prin*
EMP: 5 EST: 2019
SALES (est): 81.72K **Privately Held**
SIC: **2411** Logging

(G-14521)
RBC INC (PA)
Also Called: Braxton Culler
7310 Us Highway 311 (27350-8981)
P.O. Box 248 (27261-0248)
PHONE................................336 889-7333
Braxton Culler, *Pr*
Steve Greene, *
Ashley Culler, *
◆ EMP: 160 EST: 1975
SQ FT: 465,000
SALES (est): 23.83MM
SALES (corp-wide): 23.83MM **Privately Held**
Web: www.braxtonculler.com
SIC: **5021** 2512 2519 Household furniture; Upholstered household furniture; Wicker and rattan furniture

(G-14522)
SOUTHERN CLASSIC SEATING LLC
7064 Us Highway 311 (27350-8978)
PHONE................................336 498-3130
EMP: 19 EST: 1972
SQ FT: 20,000
SALES (est): 2.42MM **Privately Held**
SIC: **7532** 2531 Customizing services, nonfactory basis; Seats, miscellaneous public conveyances

(G-14523)
TAR HEEL FENCE & VINYL
5279 Branson Davis Rd (27350-9015)
PHONE................................336 465-1297
Benny Cruthis, *Owner*
EMP: 6 EST: 2005
SALES (est): 90.81K **Privately Held**
SIC: **2865** Tar

South Mills
Camden County

(G-14524)
JAB LURES
105 Taylor Leigh Dr (27976-9427)
PHONE................................860 885-9314
Jeffrey Baur, *Prin*
EMP: 4 EST: 2018
SALES (est): 47.08K **Privately Held**
SIC: **3949** Sporting and athletic goods, nec

(G-14525)
SWAIN & TEMPLE INC
149 Lilly Rd (27976-9533)
PHONE................................252 771-8147
Tracy Swain, *Pr*
Douglas Temple, *
EMP: 26 EST: 1993
SALES (est): 1.05MM **Privately Held**

SIC: **2411** Logging camps and contractors

Southern Pines
Moore County

(G-14526)
AMP PROS LLC
105 Stornoway Dr (28387-7544)
PHONE................................910 315-1620
Martin Williamson, *Prin*
EMP: 7 EST: 2008
SALES (est): 242.97K **Privately Held**
SIC: **2752** Commercial printing, lithographic

(G-14527)
ARTISTIC KITCHENS & BATHS LLC
683 Sw Broad St (28387-5925)
PHONE................................910 692-4000
John Wilson, *Pr*
EMP: 9 EST: 2009
SQ FT: 3,700
SALES (est): 715.9K **Privately Held**
Web: www.artistic-kitchens.com
SIC: **2434** Wood kitchen cabinets

(G-14528)
AZALEA ART PRESS
210a S Valley Rd (28387-5731)
PHONE................................510 919-6117
Karen Smith, *Prin*
EMP: 4 EST: 2015
SALES (est): 65.06K **Privately Held**
Web: azaleaartpress.blogspot.com
SIC: **2741** Miscellaneous publishing

(G-14529)
BIOMEDICAL INNOVATIONS INC
410 N Bennett St (28387-4815)
PHONE................................910 603-0267
Melissa Justice, *Pr*
EMP: 4 EST: 2002
SALES (est): 223.43K **Privately Held**
SIC: **3842** Surgical appliances and supplies

(G-14530)
CAROLINA CANNERS INC
750 S Bennett St (28387-5922)
PHONE................................843 537-5281
Brantley Burnett, *Prin*
EMP: 80
SALES (corp-wide): 81.18MM **Privately Held**
Web: www.carolinacanners.com
SIC: **2033** Canned fruits and specialties
PA: Carolina Canners, Inc.
300 Highway 1 S
Cheraw SC 29520
843 537-5281

(G-14531)
COTE TIMEWORKS LLC
106 E Connecticut Ave (28387-5528)
PHONE................................910 246-1767
Jonathan Cote, *Owner*
EMP: 5 EST: 2013
SALES (est): 247.1K **Privately Held**
Web: www.cotetimeworks.com
SIC: **3732** Boatbuilding and repairing

(G-14532)
CRYOTHERAPY OF PINES LLC
122 Brucewood Rd (28387-5143)
PHONE................................910 988-0357
EMP: 5 EST: 2019
SALES (est): 170.45K **Privately Held**
Web: www.thryvewellness.com
SIC: **2711** Newspapers, publishing and printing

(G-14533)
DIRECT ACTION K-9 LLC
160 E Massachusetts Ave (28387-6132)
PHONE................................910 246-0806
Catrina Kelley, *Prin*
EMP: 4 EST: 2012
SALES (est): 103.49K **Privately Held**
Web: www.directactionk9.com
SIC: **3131** Footwear cut stock

(G-14534)
E-Z DUMPER PRODUCTS LLC
150 Vardon Ct (28387-2987)
PHONE................................717 762-8432
EMP: 10 EST: 1972
SQ FT: 40,000
SALES (est): 661.64K **Privately Held**
SIC: **3537** 3594 Trucks, tractors, loaders, carriers, and similar equipment; Fluid power pumps and motors

(G-14535)
EPIC ENTERPRISES INC (PA)
845 Valley View Rd (28387-2575)
P.O. Box 979 (28388-0979)
PHONE................................910 692-5750
Edward P Crenshaw, *Pr*
John Shaw, *
▲ EMP: 47 EST: 1977
SQ FT: 37,000
SALES (est): 18.83MM
SALES (corp-wide): 18.83MM **Privately Held**
Web: www.epicenterprises.com
SIC: **5084** 3499 Textile machinery and equipment; Aerosol valves, metal

(G-14536)
FLETCHER INDUSTRIES INC
1485 Central Dr 22 (28387-2105)
PHONE................................910 692-7133
John H Taws, *Pr*
Carol F Prevatte, *
◆ EMP: 25 EST: 1960
SQ FT: 60,000
SALES (est): 3.07MM **Privately Held**
Web: www.fletcherindustries.com
SIC: **3552** Textile machinery

(G-14537)
INTERNATIONAL MINUTE PRESS
280 Pinehurst Ave Ste 6 (28387-7089)
PHONE................................910 725-1148
EMP: 4 EST: 2016
SALES (est): 67.85K **Privately Held**
SIC: **2741** Miscellaneous publishing

(G-14538)
K2 SOLUTIONS INC
5735 Us Hwy 1 N (28387)
P.O. Box 690 (28388-0690)
PHONE................................910 692-6898
Lane Kjellsen, *Pr*
James A Lynch, *
Susan Kjellsen, *
Robert Spivey, *
EMP: 275 EST: 2003
SALES (est): 26.15MM **Privately Held**
Web: www.k2si.com
SIC: **8742** 2892 8731 General management consultant; Explosives; Commercial physical research

(G-14539)
LONGWORTH INDUSTRIES INC (DH)
Also Called: Polarmax/Xgo
565 Air Tool Dr Ste K (28387-3469)
P.O. Box 2716 (28388-2716)
PHONE................................910 673-5290
▼ EMP: 19 EST: 1985

SALES (est): 23.17MM
SALES (corp-wide): 99.5MM **Privately Held**
Web: www.proxgo.com
SIC: **2341** 2322 Women's and children's undergarments; Underwear, men's and boys': made from purchased materials
HQ: Stanfield's Limited
1 Logan St
Truro NS B2N 5
902 895-5406

(G-14540)
M VISION SOFTWARE INC
58 Highland View Dr (28387-2151)
PHONE................................703 530-9900
Michael Fitzgerald, *Pr*
EMP: 4 EST: 1992
SALES (est): 318.7K **Privately Held**
Web: www.mvisionsoftware.com
SIC: **7372** Prepackaged software

(G-14541)
MEMORIES IN STITCHES
1150 Old Us 1 Hwy Ste 10 (28387-6341)
PHONE................................910 725-0512
EMP: 4 EST: 2017
SALES (est): 103.13K **Privately Held**
Web: www.memoriesinstitches.com
SIC: **2395** Embroidery and art needlework

(G-14542)
MISS KLLYS JLLIES JAMS SUCH LL
Also Called: Miss Kelly's Cookin'
540 Highland Rd (28387-6632)
P.O. Box 1843 (28388-1843)
PHONE................................910 988-8042
Kelly Patterson, *Prin*
EMP: 5 EST: 2016
SALES (est): 154.67K **Privately Held**
SIC: **2033** Jams, jellies, and preserves, packaged in cans, jars, etc.

(G-14543)
PERFORMANCE ADDITIVES LLC
160 W New York Ave Unit 2b (28387-5417)
PHONE................................215 321-4388
Arthur Van Nostrand, *Pr*
▲ EMP: 15 EST: 2005
SALES (est): 2.28MM **Privately Held**
Web: www.performanceadditives.us
SIC: **2821** 7389 Plastics materials and resins ; Business Activities at Non-Commercial Site

(G-14544)
PERFORMANCE APPAREL LLC
Also Called: Hot Chillys
565 Air Tool Dr Ste K (28387-3469)
P.O. Box 2716 (28388-2716)
PHONE................................805 541-0989
▲ EMP: 10 EST: 1997
SALES (est): 2.17MM
SALES (corp-wide): 99.5MM **Privately Held**
Web: www.hotchillys.com
SIC: **2339** Athletic clothing: women's, misses', and juniors'
HQ: Stanfield's Limited
1 Logan St
Truro NS B2N 5
902 895-5406

(G-14545)
PILOT LLC
375 E Connecticut Ave (28387-5601)
P.O. Box 58 (28388-0058)
PHONE................................864 430-6337
EMP: 4
SALES (corp-wide): 4.45MM **Privately Held**

Southern Pines - Moore County (G-14546)

Web: www.thepilot.com
SIC: 2711 Newspapers, publishing and printing
PA: The Pilot Llc
145 W Pennsylvania Ave
Southern Pines NC 28387
910 692-7271

(G-14546)
PILOT LLC (PA)
145 W Pennsylvania Ave (28387-5428)
PHONE.............................910 692-7271
David Woronoff, *Managing Member*
Jack Andrews, *
Lee Dirks, *
EMP: 70 EST: 1996
SQ FT: 5,000
SALES (est): 4.45MM
SALES (corp-wide): 4.45MM **Privately Held**
Web: www.thepilot.com
SIC: 2711 2752 2791 Newspapers, publishing and printing; Offset printing; Typesetting

(G-14547)
PILOT PRESS LLC
175 Davis St (28387-7068)
PHONE.............................910 692-8366
Timothy E King, *Prin*
EMP: 8 EST: 1920
SALES (est): 315.53K **Privately Held**
SIC: 2741 Miscellaneous publishing

(G-14548)
PINELAND CUTLERY INC
625 Se Service Rd (28387-6062)
PHONE.............................910 757-0035
EMP: 6 EST: 2019
SALES (est): 62.98K **Privately Held**
SIC: 3421 Carving sets

(G-14549)
POWER COOLANT & CHEMICAL LLC
109 Tanglewood Ct (28387-4353)
PHONE.............................704 759-3435
Chuck Austin, *Mgr*
EMP: 9 EST: 2000
SALES (est): 484.48K **Privately Held**
Web: www.chuckaustinrealty.com
SIC: 2992 Lubricating oils and greases

(G-14550)
R RIVETER LLC
154 Nw Broad St (28387-4801)
PHONE.............................406 321-2315
EMP: 7 EST: 2015
SALES (est): 604.62K **Privately Held**
Web: www.rriveter.com
SIC: 5621 3171 Boutiques; Handbags, women's

(G-14551)
RYJAK ENTERPRISES LLC
1050 N May St (28387-4206)
PHONE.............................910 638-0716
Rhonda Sweet, *Prin*
EMP: 10 EST: 2015
SALES (est): 437.75K **Privately Held**
SIC: 2711 Newspapers, publishing and printing

(G-14552)
SALON COUTURE
180 Council Way (28387-1000)
PHONE.............................910 693-1611
Lisa O Goneau, *Owner*
Lisa O Goneau Junior, *Owner*
EMP: 4 EST: 1997

SALES (est): 58.78K **Privately Held**
SIC: 7299 2361 Tanning salon; T-shirts and tops: girls', children's, and infants'

(G-14553)
SIERRA NEVADA CORPORATION
795 Sw Broad St (28387-5926)
PHONE.............................775 331-0222
Fatih Ozmen, *CEO*
EMP: 15
SALES (corp-wide): 2.38B **Privately Held**
Web: www.sncorp.com
SIC: 3812 Search and navigation equipment
PA: Sierra Nevada Corporation
444 Salomon Cir
Sparks NV 89434
775 331-0222

(G-14554)
SOUTHERN PINE WOODWORKING LLC
230 S Bennett St (28387-5402)
PHONE.............................910 690-9800
EMP: 4 EST: 2019
SALES (est): 103.89K **Privately Held**
Web: www.theheritageflag.com
SIC: 2431 Millwork

(G-14555)
SOUTHERN SOFTWARE INC
150 Perry Dr (28387-7020)
PHONE.............................336 879-3350
Jennifer Maggs, *CEO*
John Roscoe, *
EMP: 70 EST: 1988
SQ FT: 10,000
SALES (est): 9.63MM **Privately Held**
Web: www.southernsoftware.com
SIC: 7372 Business oriented computer software

(G-14556)
SPARTAN BLADES LLC
625 Se Service Rd (28387-6062)
PHONE.............................910 757-0035
EMP: 4 EST: 2008
SALES (est): 497.1K **Privately Held**
Web: www.spartanbladesusa.com
SIC: 3421 Cutlery

(G-14557)
SPENCER LOGGING
P.O. Box 512 (28388-0512)
PHONE.............................910 638-4899
EMP: 5 EST: 2009
SALES (est): 71.77K **Privately Held**
SIC: 2411 Logging

(G-14558)
TRANE TECHNOLOGIES COMPANY LLC
Also Called: Ingersoll-Rand
1725 Us 1 Hwy N (28387-2362)
P.O. Box 8000 (28388)
PHONE.............................910 692-8700
Mark Amlot, *Brnch Mgr*
EMP: 250
Web: www.tranetechnologies.com
SIC: 3519 3714 3546 3423 Parts and accessories, internal combustion engines; Motor vehicle parts and accessories; Power-driven handtools; Hand and edge tools, nec
HQ: Trane Technologies Company Llc
800 Beaty St Ste E
Davidson NC 28036
704 655-4000

(G-14559)
TURNBERRY PRESS
150 Crest Rd (28387-3149)

PHONE.............................860 670-4892
EMP: 4 EST: 2016
SALES (est): 46.57K **Privately Held**
SIC: 2741 Miscellaneous publishing

(G-14560)
WHISTLE STOP PRESS INC
175 Davis St (28387-7068)
PHONE.............................910 695-1403
Thomas L West, *Pr*
Sandra S West, *Sec*
▲ EMP: 15 EST: 1985
SQ FT: 13,000
SALES (est): 985.41K **Privately Held**
Web: www.gowhistlestop.com
SIC: 2752 Offset printing

Southern Shores
Dare County

(G-14561)
BOWED UP LURES
25 12th Ave (27949-9015)
PHONE.............................757 376-7944
William Gorham, *Prin*
EMP: 4 EST: 2019
SALES (est): 47.08K **Privately Held**
Web: www.boweduplures.com
SIC: 3949 Bobsleds

Southmont
Davidson County

(G-14562)
VETERAN SAFETY SOLUTIONS LLC
10584 Nc Highway 8 S Unit 286 (27351-0938)
PHONE.............................980 339-2721
Jessica Colbert, *Prin*
EMP: 4 EST: 2019
SALES (est): 93.51K **Privately Held**
Web: www.safetyvets.com
SIC: 3993 Signs and advertising specialties

Southport
Brunswick County

(G-14563)
ABOARD TRADE LLC
Also Called: Kalinka Arms
4705 Southport Supply Rd Se Ste 208 (28461)
PHONE.............................919 341-7045
EMP: 5
SALES (corp-wide): 495.2K **Privately Held**
Web: www.aboardtrade.com
SIC: 3484 Small arms
PA: Aboard Trade, Llc
16192 Coastal Hwy
Lewes DE 19958
919 341-7045

(G-14564)
AMYS CUSTOM CANVAS
4677 Southgate Blvd Se (28461-8750)
PHONE.............................910 713-8481
Amy Parrish, *Prin*
EMP: 5 EST: 2017
SALES (est): 46.58K **Privately Held**
SIC: 2211 Canvas

(G-14565)
ARCHER-DANIELS-MIDLAND COMPANY
Also Called: ADM
1730 E Moore St (28461-9418)

P.O. Box 10640 (28461-0640)
PHONE.............................910 457-5011
Eric Warner, *Brnch Mgr*
EMP: 150
SQ FT: 16,463
SALES (corp-wide): 101.56B **Publicly Held**
Web: www.adm.com
SIC: 2041 2869 Flour and other grain mill products; Industrial organic chemicals, nec
PA: Archer-Daniels-Midland Company
77 W Wacker Dr Ste 4600
Chicago IL 60601
312 634-8100

(G-14566)
ASSOCIATED ARTISTS SOUTHPORT
130 E West St (28461-3950)
PHONE.............................910 457-5450
Donna Mandell, *Owner*
EMP: 7 EST: 1997
SALES (est): 123.67K **Privately Held**
Web: www.saucysoutherner.com
SIC: 2411 Logging

(G-14567)
BETHANY SMALL
4353 Marsh Elder Ct Se (28461-8461)
PHONE.............................910 409-2167
Bethany Small, *Prin*
EMP: 5 EST: 2017
SALES (est): 43.66K **Privately Held**
SIC: 3999 Candles

(G-14568)
CWI SERVICES LLC
3382 Willow Cir Se (28461-8545)
PHONE.............................704 560-9755
Barbara Clark, *Prin*
William Clark, *Prin*
EMP: 4
SALES (est): 101.56K **Privately Held**
SIC: 7692 Welding repair

(G-14569)
DAH INC
3940 Old Bridge Rd Se (28461-8448)
PHONE.............................910 887-3675
Dustin Hewett, *Prin*
EMP: 9 EST: 2016
SALES (est): 247.63K **Privately Held**
SIC: 7692 Welding repair

(G-14570)
DAMSEL DEDICATED TO DEFENSE
4392 Eagle Bluff Ln (28461-1040)
PHONE.............................910 546-5603
Krystal Tarlton, *Prin*
EMP: 5 EST: 2017
SALES (est): 176.58K **Privately Held**
SIC: 3812 Defense systems and equipment

(G-14571)
GTG ENGINEERING INC
4956 Long Beach Rd Se Ste 14 (28461-8498)
PHONE.............................910 457-0068
Michael Leblanc, *Pr*
EMP: 5
SALES (corp-wide): 1.41MM **Privately Held**
Web: www.gtgengineering.com
SIC: 2899 Chemical preparations, nec
PA: Gtg Engineering, Inc.
766 Furnie Hammond Rd
Clarendon NC 28432
877 569-8572

GEOGRAPHIC SECTION

(G-14572)
LEE CONTROLS LLC
8250 River Rd (28461-8911)
PHONE..................732 752-5200
Glen Michalske, Pr
Jim Ashworth, *
▲ EMP: 16 EST: 1972
SQ FT: 42,000
SALES (est): 336.23K Privately Held
SIC: 3312 Primary finished or semifinished shapes

(G-14573)
LEE LINEAR
8250 River Rd (28461-8911)
P.O. Box 10100 (28461-0100)
PHONE..................800 221-0811
EMP: 9 EST: 2015
SALES (est): 248.78K Privately Held
Web: www.leelinear.com
SIC: 3999 Manufacturing industries, nec

(G-14574)
LUTHERAN SVCS FOR THE AGING
4843 Southport Supply Rd Se (28461)
PHONE..................910 457-5604
William Sraver, Ch
EMP: 7 EST: 2008
SALES (est): 464.52K Privately Held
Web: www.brunswickcountync.gov
SIC: 3825 Instruments to measure electricity

(G-14575)
PARTY TIME INC
1658 N Howe St Ste 1 (28461-7940)
PHONE..................910 454-4577
EMP: 6 EST: 1995
SQ FT: 6,100
SALES (est): 498.08K Privately Held
Web: www.partytime28461.com
SIC: 5947 2759 Party favors; Invitation and stationery printing and engraving

(G-14576)
PRINT DOC PACK AND
114 E Nash St (28461-3984)
PHONE..................910 454-9104
Susan Davis, Owner
EMP: 6 EST: 2005
SALES (est): 122.06K Privately Held
SIC: 2752 Commercial printing, lithographic

(G-14577)
RAPPORT MAGAZINE INC
4262 Cherry Laurel Dr Se (28461-9238)
PHONE..................919 435-7690
Howard Christine, Prin
EMP: 5 EST: 2010
SALES (est): 148.89K Privately Held
Web: www.rapportmagazine.com
SIC: 2721 Periodicals

(G-14578)
RC BOLDT PUBLISHING LLC
701 N Howe St Ste 6 (28461-3475)
PHONE..................904 624-0033
Rc Boldt, Brnch Mgr
EMP: 8
SALES (corp-wide): 72.02K Privately Held
SIC: 2741 Miscellaneous publishing
PA: Rc Boldt Publishing Llc
    804 Ocean Dr
    Oak Island NC 28465
    904 624-0033

(G-14579)
SEAWAY PRINTING COMPANY
Also Called: Seaway Printing & Mailing
4130 Long Beach Rd Se (28461-8653)
PHONE..................910 457-6158
Gary Mattingry, Owner
EMP: 8 EST: 1967
SQ FT: 4,000
SALES (est): 805.1K Privately Held
Web: www.seawayprintingnc.com
SIC: 2752 Offset printing

(G-14580)
SINCERE SCENTS CO LLC ✪
7300 River Rd Se Trlr 84 (28461-9608)
PHONE..................910 616-4697
EMP: 5 EST: 2022
SALES (est): 63.22K Privately Held
Web: www.sincerescentsco.com
SIC: 3999 Candles

(G-14581)
SOUTHPORT NC
5105 Bent Oak Ln (28461-3133)
PHONE..................910 524-7425
EMP: 5 EST: 2016
SALES (est): 99.09K Privately Held
Web: www.southportmag.com
SIC: 3519 Internal combustion engines, nec

(G-14582)
SOUTHPORT SMOOTHIES LLC
3703 Cinnamon Fern Dr (28461-8222)
PHONE..................910 363-4526
Lori B Gezelman, Owner
EMP: 5 EST: 2013
SALES (est): 232.89K Privately Held
SIC: 2037 Frozen fruits and vegetables

(G-14583)
SPEED KING MANUFACTURING INC
8128 River Rd (28461-8972)
PHONE..................910 457-1995
Tammy C Johnston, Prin
EMP: 6 EST: 2012
SALES (est): 168.95K Privately Held
SIC: 3999 Manufacturing industries, nec

(G-14584)
SPOD INC
316 Cedar Rd (28461-7701)
PHONE..................910 477-6297
Christie Walker, Prin
EMP: 6 EST: 2016
SALES (est): 116.06K Privately Held
Web: www.4x4spod.com
SIC: 3714 Motor vehicle parts and accessories

(G-14585)
SWANSON CUSTOM WOODWORKING INC
98 N Fayetteville Rd (28461-9744)
PHONE..................910 465-3199
Jeffrey Swanson, Pr
EMP: 4 EST: 2018
SALES (est): 54.13K Privately Held
SIC: 2431 Millwork

(G-14586)
WAHAH ELECTRIC SUPPLY ✪
3698 Wingfoot Dr (28461-8101)
PHONE..................717 208-2260
EMP: 5 EST: 2023
SALES (est): 79.3K Privately Held
SIC: 3699 Electrical equipment and supplies, nec

Sparta
Alleghany County

(G-14587)
ALLEGHANY GARBAGE SERVICE INC
Also Called: Alleghany Garbage Service
453 N Main St (28675-8608)
P.O. Box 1538 (28675-1538)
PHONE..................336 372-4413
Kenneth Nichols, Pr
Don Nichols, VP
EMP: 4 EST: 1972
SALES (est): 479.56K Privately Held
SIC: 4953 3469 Refuse collection and disposal services; Garbage cans, stamped and pressed metal

(G-14588)
AMANO PIONEER ECLIPSE CORP (DH)
Also Called: Pioneer
1 Eclipse Rd (28675-9233)
P.O. Box 909 (28675-0909)
PHONE..................336 372-8080
Thomas Benton, Pr
Byron Snyder, *
Thomas Ording, *
Robert Allen, Plant Operations*
Nurzat Jumukova, *
◆ EMP: 73 EST: 1978
SQ FT: 105,000
SALES (est): 39.79MM Privately Held
Web: www.pioneereclipse.com
SIC: 3589 2842 Floor washing and polishing machines, commercial; Cleaning or polishing preparations, nec
HQ: Amano Usa Holdings, Inc.
    29j Commerce Way
    Totowa NJ 07512

(G-14589)
BICKERSTAFF TREES INC
866 Nc Highway 18 S (28675-8477)
PHONE..................336 372-8866
Frank B Bickerstaff, Pr
Ruth Bickerstaff, *
EMP: 7 EST: 1978
SALES (est): 245.16K Privately Held
SIC: 0783 3999 5199 Planting, pruning, and trimming services; Wreaths, artificial; Christmas trees, including artificial

(G-14590)
BLUE RIDGE SUN INC
32 W Whitehead St (28675-8927)
P.O. Box 757 (28675-0757)
PHONE..................336 372-5490
Milly Richardson, Pr
EMP: 5 EST: 1979
SALES (est): 167.57K Privately Held
Web: www.blueridgesun.com
SIC: 2711 Newspapers

(G-14591)
CHANDLER CONCRETE INC
Also Called: CHANDLER CONCRETE INC
23 Birch Ln (28675-8741)
PHONE..................336 372-4348
Jess Millan, Mgr
EMP: 13
Web: www.chandlerconcrete.com
SIC: 3273 Ready-mixed concrete
PA: Chandler Concrete Co., Inc.
    1006 S Church St
    Burlington NC 27215

(G-14592)
DAVID PRESNELL
Also Called: Presnells Prtg & Photography
1397 Us Highway 21 S (28675-8640)
P.O. Box 26 (28675-0026)
PHONE..................336 372-5989
David Presnell, Owner
EMP: 6 EST: 1999
SQ FT: 1,500
SALES (est): 406.56K Privately Held
Web: www.presnellsonline.com
SIC: 7335 7221 2789 2759 Commercial photography; Photographer, still or video; Bookbinding and related work; Commercial printing, nec

(G-14593)
DESIGNS IN WOOD
Also Called: Carolina Farm Table
122 E Doughton St (28675-9127)
P.O. Box 788 (28675-0788)
PHONE..................336 372-8995
John Ulery, Owner
Penny Ulery, Owner
EMP: 5 EST: 1973
SQ FT: 6,000
SALES (est): 311.41K Privately Held
Web: www.carolinafarmtable.com
SIC: 2426 Carvings, furniture: wood

(G-14594)
HARTMAN WELDING
23 Rivers Edge Rd (28675-9766)
PHONE..................336 372-2220
EMP: 4 EST: 2015
SALES (est): 49.02K Privately Held
SIC: 7692 Welding repair

(G-14595)
INTERNTNAL INSTLLTION GROUP LL
312 Riverside Dr (28675-9064)
P.O. Box 1057 (28675-1057)
PHONE..................704 231-1868
EMP: 10 EST: 2003
SALES (est): 976.73K Privately Held
Web: www.internationalinstallationgroup.us
SIC: 1389 Construction, repair, and dismantling services

(G-14596)
MARTIN MARIETTA MATERIA
140 S Sparta Pkwy (28675-8223)
PHONE..................336 372-6311
EMP: 4 EST: 2019
SALES (est): 262.68K Privately Held
Web: www.martinmarietta.com
SIC: 1422 Crushed and broken limestone

(G-14597)
NAPCO INC (DH)
Also Called: Napco
120 Trojan Ave (28675-9073)
P.O. Box 1029 (28675-1029)
PHONE..................336 372-5214
James R Proffit, Pr
Henry Hayes, *
▲ EMP: 113 EST: 1977
SQ FT: 62,000
SALES (est): 39.76MM
SALES (corp-wide): 5.58B Privately Held
Web: www.napcousa.com
SIC: 2631 2782 Setup boxboard; Looseleaf binders and devices
HQ: Ply Gem Holdings, Inc.
    5020 Weston Pkwy Ste 400
    Cary NC 27513
    919 677-3900

Sparta - Alleghany County (G-14598)

(G-14598)
PERRYCRAFT INC
1549 Us Highway 21 S (28675-8924)
PHONE..................336 372-2545
Dan Epting, *Pr*
▲ **EMP:** 10 **EST:** 1982
SQ FT: 15,000
SALES (est): 947.57K **Privately Held**
Web: www.perrycraft.com
SIC: 3429 3069 Luggage racks, car top; Grips or handles, rubber

(G-14599)
SHAW FINE WOODWORKING
241 Rifle Range Rd (28675-8301)
PHONE..................336 529-4080
John Shaw, *Prin*
EMP: 5 **EST:** 2016
SALES (est): 216.02K **Privately Held**
SIC: 2431 Millwork

(G-14600)
TRUSS SHOP INC
Also Called: Tri State Componenets
84 Buffalo Rd (28675-9491)
P.O. Box 1795 (28675-1795)
PHONE..................336 372-6260
John Miller, *Pr*
EMP: 35 **EST:** 2000
SQ FT: 4,000
SALES (est): 9.78MM **Privately Held**
Web: www.tristatecomponents.com
SIC: 2439 Trusses, wooden roof

Spencer
Rowan County

(G-14601)
MATTHEWS INDUSTRIAL
216 N Yadkin Ave (28159-2434)
PHONE..................704 239-5925
Jesse Matthews, *Prin*
EMP: 4 **EST:** 2015
SALES (est): 47.62K **Privately Held**
Web: www.matw.com
SIC: 3366 Copper foundries

(G-14602)
RABID GAMES LLC
404 S Carolina Ave (28159-2212)
PHONE..................704 754-6382
George Young, *CEO*
EMP: 13 **EST:** 2021
SALES (est): 340.32K **Privately Held**
SIC: 7372 Prepackaged software

Spindale
Rutherford County

(G-14603)
BACKYARD ENTPS & SVCS LLC
281 Spindale St (28160-2415)
P.O. Box 888 (28139-0888)
PHONE..................828 755-4960
Michael M Galloway, *Managing Member*
David Russel, *Managing Member*
EMP: 8 **EST:** 2011
SALES (est): 559.51K **Privately Held**
SIC: 3563 Air and gas compressors including vacuum pumps

(G-14604)
BURNETT DARRILL STEPHEN
Also Called: Tri-City Tire Service
137 Williamsburg Dr (28160-1155)
PHONE..................828 287-8778
EMP: 4 **EST:** 2012
SALES (est): 78.67K **Privately Held**
SIC: 7534 Tire repair shop

(G-14605)
CARDINAL TISSUE LLC
207 Oakland Rd (28160-2117)
PHONE..................815 503-2096
Steven Reese, *Managing Member*
EMP: 51 **EST:** 2017
SALES (est): 13.17MM **Privately Held**
Web: www.cardinal-tissue.com
SIC: 2676 Cleansing tissues: made from purchased paper

(G-14606)
DIAMONDBACK ARMOR
207 Oakland Rd (28160-2117)
PHONE..................828 288-6680
EMP: 4 **EST:** 2010
SALES (est): 60.99K **Privately Held**
SIC: 2389 Apparel and accessories, nec

(G-14607)
LAKESIDE MILLS INC (PA)
Also Called: Yelton Milling Co
398 W Main St (28160-1594)
P.O. Box 230 (28139-0230)
PHONE..................828 286-4866
Bryan A King, *Pr*
Aaron King, *VP*
Kim Allen King, *Sec*
EMP: 11 **EST:** 1936
SALES (est): 3.2MM
SALES (corp-wide): 3.2MM **Privately Held**
Web: lakeside-mills.mybigcommerce.com
SIC: 2041 Corn meal

(G-14608)
MANROY USA LLC
Also Called: Manroy Defense Systems
159 Yelton St (28160-1179)
PHONE..................828 286-9274
John P Buckner, *Managing Member*
EMP: 5 **EST:** 2009
SALES (est): 758.35K **Privately Held**
Web: www.manroy-usa.com
SIC: 3484 Small arms

(G-14609)
WATTS DRAINAGE PRODUCTS INC
Also Called: Enpoco
100 Watts Rd (28160-2211)
PHONE..................828 288-2179
William C Mccartney, *Pr*
Timothy M Macphee, *CFO*
Kristine Uttley, *Treas*
Lester J Taufen, *Sec*
◆ **EMP:** 10 **EST:** 1987
SALES (est): 4.55MM
SALES (corp-wide): 2.06B **Publicly Held**
SIC: 3432 Plumbing fixture fittings and trim
PA: Watts Water Technologies, Inc.
  815 Chestnut St
  North Andover MA 01845
  978 688-1811

(G-14610)
WATTS REGULATOR CO
Regtrol Division
100 Watts Rd (28160-2211)
PHONE..................828 286-4151
Tommy Horton, *Brnch Mgr*
EMP: 700
SALES (corp-wide): 2.06B **Publicly Held**
Web: www.watts.com
SIC: 3491 Pressure valves and regulators, industrial
HQ: Watts Regulator Co.
  815 Chestnut St
  North Andover MA 01845
  978 689-6000

(G-14611)
WHITE OAK CARPET MILLS INC
Also Called: White Oak
1553 Old Ballpark Rd (28160-2177)
PHONE..................828 287-8892
▲ **EMP:** 7 **EST:** 1996
SQ FT: 25,000
SALES (est): 491.24K **Privately Held**
SIC: 2273 Carpets and rugs

Spring Hope
Nash County

(G-14612)
ARTCRAFT SIGN CO
205 N Louisburg Rd (27882-8572)
PHONE..................919 841-7686
EMP: 4 **EST:** 2019
SALES (est): 91.48K **Privately Held**
SIC: 3993 Signs and advertising specialties

(G-14613)
BASS FARMS INC
Also Called: Bass Farm Sausage
6685 Highway 64 Alt East (27882)
P.O. Box 126 (27882-0126)
PHONE..................252 478-4147
Kenneth Edwards, *Pr*
John Bass, *
Kenneth Edwards, *VP*
Brent Edwards, *
EMP: 21 **EST:** 1979
SALES (est): 2.17MM **Privately Held**
Web: www.bassfarmsausage.com
SIC: 2011 5147 2013 Meat packing plants; Meats, fresh; Sausages and other prepared meats

(G-14614)
BELT CONCEPTS AMERICA INC
605 N Pine St (27882-7875)
P.O. Box 340 (27882-0340)
PHONE..................888 598-2358
Cris Balint, *Pr*
▲ **EMP:** 15 **EST:** 1993
SQ FT: 150,000
SALES (est): 5.58MM
SALES (corp-wide): 44.45MM **Privately Held**
Web: www.belt-concepts.com
SIC: 3496 3535 Conveyor belts; Conveyors and conveying equipment
PA: Right Lane Industries Llc
  111 W Jackson Blvd # 1700
  Chicago IL 60604
  857 869-4132

(G-14615)
BK SEAMLESS GUTTERS LLC
Also Called: Bk Seamless Gutters
1705 Old Us 64 (27882-7518)
PHONE..................252 955-5414
Brandon King, *Owner*
EMP: 4 **EST:** 2011
SALES (est): 241.01K **Privately Held**
Web: www.bkroofingandgutters.com
SIC: 3589 High pressure cleaning equipment

(G-14616)
CAROLINA DUCT FABRICATION INC
360 Barbee St (27882-7957)
P.O. Box 820 (27882-0820)
PHONE..................252 478-9955
J Derrill Edwards, *Pr*
Nathan Edward, *VP*
EMP: 4 **EST:** 2006
SALES (est): 455.59K **Privately Held**
Web: www.carolinaduct.com
SIC: 3441 Fabricated structural metal

(G-14617)
ERADER MILLS SEPTIC TANK INC
8374 Savage Rd (27882-9224)
PHONE..................252 478-5960
A T Mills Junior, *Pr*
Stanley Mills, *VP*
Erader Mills, *VP*
Judith Mills, *Sec*
EMP: 11 **EST:** 1968
SALES (est): 448.95K **Privately Held**
Web: www.eradermills.com
SIC: 3272 Septic tanks, concrete

(G-14618)
JHRG LLC
303 S Pine St (27882-9551)
P.O. Box D (27882-0930)
PHONE..................252 478-4997
EMP: 8 **EST:** 2000
SALES (est): 427.98K **Privately Held**
Web: www.hsarmor.com
SIC: 3842 Clothing, fire resistant and protective

(G-14619)
JHRG MANUFACTURING LLC
303 S Pine St (27882-9551)
P.O. Box D (27882-0930)
PHONE..................252 478-4977
John Holland, *Managing Member*
EMP: 9 **EST:** 2012
SQ FT: 25,000
SALES (est): 330.72K **Privately Held**
SIC: 2298 3842 3537 Ropes and fiber cables ; Life preservers, except cork and inflatable; Containers (metal), air cargo

(G-14620)
PURE WATER INNOVATIONS INC
272 Williams Rd (27882-7521)
P.O. Box 567 (27597-0567)
PHONE..................919 301-8189
Vicky Hortman, *Pr*
Vicky Hortman, *Pr*
Bill Land, *VP*
Natalie Land, *Off Mgr*
EMP: 4 **EST:** 2009
SQ FT: 4,500
SALES (est): 175.04K **Privately Held**
SIC: 2086 Pasteurized and mineral waters, bottled and canned

(G-14621)
RSF SOLID STATE LIGHTING INC
3469 Peachtree Hills Rd (27882-8286)
P.O. Box 383 (27882-0383)
PHONE..................252 478-9915
EMP: 8 **EST:** 1995
SQ FT: 5,000
SALES (est): 237.99K **Privately Held**
SIC: 3646 Commercial lighting fixtures

(G-14622)
SPRING HOPE ENTERPRISE INC
113 N Ash St (27882-7711)
P.O. Box 2447 (27894-2447)
PHONE..................252 478-3651
Ken Ripley, *Pr*
Vickie Ripley, *VP*
EMP: 5 **EST:** 1947
SQ FT: 1,800
SALES (est): 436.53K **Privately Held**
Web: www.restorationnewsmedia.com
SIC: 2711 Job printing and newspaper publishing combined

GEOGRAPHIC SECTION

Spruce Pine - Mitchell County (G-14646)

(G-14623)
STRICKLAND BROS ENTPS INC
3622 Wiggins Rd (27882-8846)
P.O. Box 536 (27882-0536)
PHONE..................................252 478-3058
Terry Strickland, *Pr*
EMP: 19 **EST:** 1987
SQ FT: 10,000
SALES (est): 2.47MM **Privately Held**
Web: www.stricklandbros.com
SIC: 3523 7692 Farm machinery and equipment; Welding repair

Spring Lake
Cumberland County

(G-14624)
A-I VNYL GRPHICS PRTG SLUTIONS
154 Rosebud St (28390-7710)
PHONE..................................910 436-4880
Rodney Federspiel, *Prin*
EMP: 5 **EST:** 2013
SALES (est): 63.97K **Privately Held**
SIC: 2752 Commercial printing, lithographic

(G-14625)
EXTERIORS INC LTD
650 W Manchester Rd (28390-2314)
PHONE..................................919 325-2251
Michelle Kettering, *CEO*
EMP: 8 **EST:** 2016
SALES (est): 996.88K **Privately Held**
SIC: 1542 3259 7389 5033 Commercial and office buildings, renovation and repair; Roofing tile, clay; Business Activities at Non-Commercial Site; Roofing, asphalt and sheet metal

(G-14626)
RUHL INC
Also Called: Ruhl Tech Engineering
26 Mockingbird Ln (28390-8715)
PHONE..................................910 497-3172
EMP: 6 **EST:** 1999
SQ FT: 2,800
SALES (est): 1.07MM **Privately Held**
Web: www.ruhltech.us
SIC: 3441 Fabricated structural metal

(G-14627)
S & W READY MIX CON CO LLC
545 W Manchester Rd (28390-2311)
PHONE..................................910 496-3232
Tony Lee, *Mgr*
EMP: 19
SALES (corp-wide): 8.01MM **Privately Held**
SIC: 3273 Ready-mixed concrete
HQ: S & W Ready Mix Concrete Company Llc
217 Lisbon St
Clinton NC 28328
910 592-1733

(G-14628)
STITCH IN TIME INC
412 S Main St (28390-3907)
PHONE..................................910 497-4171
EMP: 6 **EST:** 1994
SQ FT: 6,000
SALES (est): 399.47K **Privately Held**
Web: www.customplaquesusa.com
SIC: 2395 7216 Embroidery products, except Schiffli machine; Drycleaning plants, except rugs

---

Spruce Pine
Mitchell County

(G-14629)
BARK HOUSE SUPPLY COMPANY
534 Oak Ave (28777-2728)
PHONE..................................828 765-9010
Christie Mccurry, *Pr*
EMP: 5 **EST:** 2008
SALES (est): 304.08K **Privately Held**
Web: www.barkhouse.com
SIC: 3999 Manufacturing industries, nec

(G-14630)
BRP US INC
Also Called: Brp Spruce Pine Distribution
12934 S Highway 226 (28777-6345)
PHONE..................................828 766-1164
EMP: 7 **EST:** 2019
SALES (est): 270.6K **Privately Held**
Web: www.brp.com
SIC: 3732 Boatbuilding and repairing

(G-14631)
BRP US INC
Also Called: Brp Spruce Pine
1211 Greenwood Rd (28777-8808)
PHONE..................................828 766-1100
Bill Johnson, *Mgr*
EMP: 92
SALES (corp-wide): 7.38B **Privately Held**
Web: www.brp.com
SIC: 3732 Motorboats, inboard or outboard: building and repairing
HQ: Brp Us Inc.
10101 Science Dr
Sturtevant WI 53177
262 884-5000

(G-14632)
BUCHANAN GEM STONE MINES INC
Also Called: Gem Mountain
13780 S 226 Hwy (28777-6343)
P.O. Box 488 (28777-0488)
PHONE..................................828 765-6130
Madonna K Buchanan, *Pr*
Danyeale Forbes, *VP*
▲ **EMP:** 10 **EST:** 1985
SQ FT: 3,500
SALES (est): 833.41K **Privately Held**
Web: www.gemmountain.com
SIC: 1499 3915 5999 5944 Gemstone and industrial diamond mining; Gems, real and imitation: preparation for settings; Gems and precious stones; Jewelry stores

(G-14633)
COMMUNITY NEWSPAPERS INC
261 Locust St (28777-2713)
P.O. Box 339 (28777-0339)
PHONE..................................828 765-7169
Andy Ashuhet, *Mgr*
EMP: 7
SALES (corp-wide): 49.22MM **Privately Held**
Web: www.cninewspapers.com
SIC: 2711 Newspapers, publishing and printing
PA: Community Newspapers, Inc.
2365 Prince Ave A
Athens GA 30606
706 548-0010

(G-14634)
COVIA HOLDINGS CORPORATION
Also Called: COVIA HOLDINGS CORPORATION
Rag Branch Rd (28777)
P.O. Box 588 (28777-0588)
PHONE..................................828 765-4823
EMP: 8
SALES (corp-wide): 1.6B **Privately Held**
Web: www.coviacorp.com
SIC: 1446 Industrial sand
PA: Covia Holdings Llc
3 Summit Park Dr Ste 700
Independence OH 44131
800 255-7263

(G-14635)
COVIA HOLDINGS LLC
7638 S 226 Hwy (28777-0538)
PHONE..................................828 765-1215
EMP: 5
SALES (corp-wide): 1.6B **Privately Held**
Web: www.coviacorp.com
SIC: 1446 Industrial sand
PA: Covia Holdings Llc
3 Summit Park Dr Ste 700
Independence OH 44131
800 255-7263

(G-14636)
COVIA HOLDINGS LLC
Us Hwy 19 E (28777)
P.O. Box 588 (28777-0588)
PHONE..................................828 765-4251
Carl Horbat, *Mgr*
EMP: 9
SALES (corp-wide): 1.6B **Privately Held**
Web: www.coviacorp.com
SIC: 1446 Industrial sand
PA: Covia Holdings Llc
3 Summit Park Dr Ste 700
Independence OH 44131
800 255-7263

(G-14637)
COVIA HOLDINGS LLC
Bakersville Rd (28777)
P.O. Box 588 (28777-0588)
PHONE..................................828 765-4283
Karl Kuchta, *Mgr*
EMP: 42
SALES (corp-wide): 1.6B **Privately Held**
Web: www.coviacorp.com
SIC: 1459 3295 Feldspar mining; Minerals, ground or treated
PA: Covia Holdings Llc
3 Summit Park Dr Ste 700
Independence OH 44131
800 255-7263

(G-14638)
COVIA HOLDINGS LLC
Also Called: Crystal Plant
136 Crystal Dr (28777-8726)
P.O. Box 588 (28777-0588)
PHONE..................................828 765-1114
Mike Bensill, *Mgr*
EMP: 4
SALES (corp-wide): 1.6B **Privately Held**
Web: www.coviacorp.com
SIC: 1446 Industrial sand
PA: Covia Holdings Llc
3 Summit Park Dr Ste 700
Independence OH 44131
800 255-7263

(G-14639)
DESIGNS BY RACHEL
Also Called: Graphic Design
220 Reservoir Rd (28777-2532)
PHONE..................................828 783-0698
Rachel Wheeler, *Owner*
EMP: 5 **EST:** 2016
SALES (est): 179.29K **Privately Held**
SIC: 7336 3952 Commercial art and graphic design; Pastels, artists'

(G-14640)
EXPLOSIVES SUPPLY COMPANY (PA)
167 Roan Rd (28777-2638)
P.O. Box 217 (28777-0217)
PHONE..................................828 765-2762
Robert H Boone, *Pr*
John H Boone, *VP*
Susan S Gardin, *Sec*
EMP: 15 **EST:** 1940
SQ FT: 800
SALES (est): 4.16MM
SALES (corp-wide): 4.16MM **Privately Held**
Web: www.explosivessupply-mcdowellcement.com
SIC: 5032 3273 5039 5169 Stone, crushed or broken; Ready-mixed concrete; Septic tanks; Explosives

(G-14641)
FEC INC
284 Roan Rd (28777-2624)
PHONE..................................828 765-4599
Scott Pearson, *Pr*
EMP: 6 **EST:** 2010
SALES (est): 867.53K **Privately Held**
SIC: 3715 Truck trailers

(G-14642)
HIGHLAND CRAFTSMEN INC
534 Oak Ave (28777-2728)
PHONE..................................828 765-9010
Marty Mccurry, *CEO*
Chris Mccurry, *VP*
EMP: 18 **EST:** 2002
SALES (est): 889.65K **Privately Held**
Web: www.barkhouse.com
SIC: 2499 Mulch, wood and bark

(G-14643)
HOLLIFIELD ENTERPRISES
10 Ellis Road Ext (28777-8761)
PHONE..................................828 766-7552
Robert Hollifield, *Prin*
EMP: 5 **EST:** 2010
SALES (est): 100.4K **Privately Held**
SIC: 3711 Automobile assembly, including specialty automobiles

(G-14644)
INNIAH PRODUCTION INCORPORATED
Also Called: Blue Ridge Christian News
152 Summit Ave (28777-2980)
PHONE..................................828 765-6800
Doug Harrell, *Pr*
Clint Pollard, *Editor*
Barbara Harrell, *Sec*
EMP: 4 **EST:** 2014
SALES (est): 206.59K **Privately Held**
Web: www.blueridgechristiannews.com
SIC: 2759 Publication printing

(G-14645)
MARKETS GLOBAL PUBLISHING
15 Deer Park Loop Apt A1 (28777-2866)
P.O. Box 523 (28777-0523)
PHONE..................................828 783-0599
Raymond Casper, *Prin*
EMP: 4 **EST:** 2015
SALES (est): 60.15K **Privately Held**
SIC: 2741 Miscellaneous publishing

(G-14646)
MCDOWELL CEMENT PRODUCTS CO
167 Roan Rd (28777-2638)
P.O. Box 217 (28777-0217)
PHONE..................................828 765-2762

Spruce Pine - Mitchell County (G-14647)

Robert H Boone, *Pr*
EMP: 4
SALES (corp-wide): 4.16MM **Privately Held**
SIC: 3273 Ready-mixed concrete
HQ: Mcdowell Cement Products Company
S Garden St
Marion NC 28752
828 652-5721

(G-14647)
MCGEE BROTHERS MACHINE & WLDG
Also Called: McGee Brothers Mch & Wldg Co
2585 Halltown Rd (28777-5461)
PHONE.................................828 766-9122
Donny Mcgee, *Pt*
Ted Mcgee, *Pt*
Jerry Mcgee, *Pt*
EMP: 6 **EST:** 1997
SALES (est): 961.01K **Privately Held**
SIC: 3599 Machine shop, jobbing and repair

(G-14648)
MCKINNEY ELECTRIC & MCH CO INC
12923 S 226 Hwy (28777-6345)
PHONE.................................828 765-7910
Richard Mckinney, *Pr*
Angela Mckinney, *Sec*
Scott Mckinney, *Treas*
Bruce Mckinney, *VP*
EMP: 5 **EST:** 1978
SQ FT: 1,600
SALES (est): 417.57K **Privately Held**
SIC: 7694 5063 5999 7699 Electric motor repair; Motors, electric; Motors, electric; Pumps and pumping equipment repair

(G-14649)
MCKINNEY LWNCARE GRBAGE SVC LL
Also Called: McKinney Garbage Service
1113 Dale Rd (28777-6301)
PHONE.................................828 766-9490
Tracey Mckinney, *Managing Member*
EMP: 6 **EST:** 2015
SALES (est): 152.45K **Privately Held**
SIC: 0782 3639 Lawn care services; Garbage disposal units, household

(G-14650)
MICHAEL RAY MCKINNEY
1202 Mckinney Mine Rd (28777-6458)
PHONE.................................828 765-7001
Brenda Mckinney, *Prin*
EMP: 5 **EST:** 2015
SALES (est): 68.7K **Privately Held**
SIC: 3482 Small arms ammunition

(G-14651)
MITCHELL WELDING INC
7080 Us 19e (28777-5806)
PHONE.................................828 765-2620
John C Stout, *Pr*
Clarann S Dixon, *
Boyd W Dixon, *
EMP: 25 **EST:** 1983
SQ FT: 6,000
SALES (est): 1.09MM **Privately Held**
Web: www.mitchellweldinginc.com
SIC: 7692 3444 Welding repair; Sheet metalwork

(G-14652)
MY COUNTY METAL OPERATIONS LLC
163 Tempie Mountain Rd (28777-5416)
PHONE.................................828 765-5265
EMP: 5 **EST:** 2019
SALES (est): 185.64K **Privately Held**

SIC: 3444 Sheet metalwork

(G-14653)
QUARTZ CORP USA
797 Altapass Hwy (28777-8927)
P.O. Box 99 (28777-0099)
PHONE.................................828 765-8950
Jerry Prosser, *Mgr*
EMP: 108
SALES (corp-wide): 3.28MM **Privately Held**
Web: www.thequartzcorp.com
SIC: 1459 3295 Feldspar mining; Minerals, ground or treated
HQ: The Quartz Corp Usa
8342 S 226 Byp Bypass
Spruce Pine NC 28777
828 766-2104

(G-14654)
QUARTZ CORP USA (DH)
Also Called: Quartz
8342 S 226 Bypass (28777)
P.O. Box 309 (28777-0309)
PHONE.................................828 766-2104
Jeffrey Curtis, *Ex Dir*
Thomas Guillaume, *CEO*
Benny Hallam, *VP*
Robert Kolakowski, *CFO*
◆ **EMP:** 52 **EST:** 1957
SQ FT: 2,000
SALES (est): 50.98MM
SALES (corp-wide): 3.28MM **Privately Held**
Web: www.thequartzcorp.com
SIC: 3295 Feldspar, ground or otherwise treated
HQ: Imerys Usa, Inc.
100 Mansell Ct E Ste 300
Roswell GA 30076
770 645-3300

(G-14655)
SIBELCO
107 Harris Mining Company Rd (28777-4506)
PHONE.................................828 765-1114
EMP: 29 **EST:** 2019
SALES (est): 3.53MM **Privately Held**
Web: www.sibelco.com
SIC: 2819 Industrial inorganic chemicals, nec

(G-14656)
SIBELCO NORTH AMERICA INC
74 Harris Mining Company Rd (28777-4521)
PHONE.................................828 766-6050
EMP: 100
SALES (corp-wide): 130.49MM **Privately Held**
Web: www.sibelco.com
SIC: 2851 Paints and allied products
HQ: Sibelco North America, Inc.
3426 Toringdon Way # 400
Charlotte NC 28277
704 420-7905

(G-14657)
SIBELCO NORTH AMERICA INC
136 Crystal Dr (28777-8726)
PHONE.................................828 766-6050
EMP: 100
SALES (corp-wide): 130.49MM **Privately Held**
Web: www.sibelco.com
SIC: 1499 Quartz crystal (pure) mining
HQ: Sibelco North America, Inc.
3426 Toringdon Way # 400
Charlotte NC 28277
704 420-7905

(G-14658)
SPRUCE PINE BATCH INC
2490 Us 19e (28777)
P.O. Box 159 (28777-0159)
PHONE.................................828 765-9876
◆ **EMP:** 6 **EST:** 1986
SQ FT: 11,000
SALES (est): 483.72K **Privately Held**
Web: www.sprucepinebatch.com
SIC: 3229 Pressed and blown glass, nec

(G-14659)
SPRUCE PINE MICA COMPANY
132 Mountain Laurel Dr (28777-9231)
P.O. Box 219 (28777-0219)
PHONE.................................828 765-4241
Richard Montague, *Pr*
Linda Lonen, *Treas*
EMP: 15 **EST:** 1924
SQ FT: 16,000
SALES (est): 1.54MM **Privately Held**
Web: www.spruce-pine-mica.com
SIC: 3679 3469 Electronic circuits; Machine parts, stamped or pressed metal

(G-14660)
UNITED STATES GYPSUM COMPANY
510 Altapass Hwy (28777-3013)
PHONE.................................828 765-9481
Randy Ruddell, *Brnch Mgr*
EMP: 10
SALES (corp-wide): 14.2B **Privately Held**
Web: www.usg.com
SIC: 3275 Wallboard, gypsum
HQ: United States Gypsum Company
550 W Adams St Ste 1300
Chicago IL 60661
312 606-4000

(G-14661)
WOODYS CHAIR SHOP
784 Dale Rd (28777-6314)
PHONE.................................828 765-9277
James Woody, *Owner*
EMP: 4 **EST:** 1944
SALES (est): 252.37K **Privately Held**
Web: www.woodyschairshop.com
SIC: 2511 Chairs, household, except upholstered: wood

(G-14662)
ZEMEX INDUSTRIAL MINERALS INC
797 Altapass Hwy (28777-8927)
P.O. Box 99 (28777-0099)
PHONE.................................828 765-5500
Richard L Lister, *Dir*
EMP: 9 **EST:** 2000
SALES (est): 126.64K **Privately Held**
SIC: 1499 Talc mining

Staley
Randolph County

(G-14663)
CHAUDHRY MEAT COMPANY
380 Stockyard Rd (27355-8376)
P.O. Box 1019 (27344-1019)
PHONE.................................919 742-9292
Abdul Chaudhry, *Pr*
Shamin Chaudhry, *Sec*
EMP: 10 **EST:** 1996
SQ FT: 8,600
SALES (est): 984.3K **Privately Held**
SIC: 2011 Meat packing plants

(G-14664)
CLIFFORD W ESTES CO INC
2637 Old 421 Rd (27355-8244)
P.O. Box 127 (27355-0127)
PHONE.................................336 622-6410
Peter Osborne, *VP*
EMP: 50
SQ FT: 22,000
SALES (corp-wide): 10.84MM **Privately Held**
Web: www.estesco.com
SIC: 3299 3281 1442 Gravel painting; Cut stone and stone products; Construction sand and gravel
PA: Clifford W. Estes Co., Inc.
182 Fairfield Rd
Fairfield NJ 07004
800 962-5128

(G-14665)
DISCOUNT BOX & PALLET INC (PA)
3174 Weeden St (27355-8305)
P.O. Box 459 (27298-0459)
PHONE.................................336 272-2220
Jeffrey W Coble, *Pr*
EMP: 31 **EST:** 1997
SQ FT: 20,000
SALES (est): 4.23MM **Privately Held**
Web: www.dboxpinc.com
SIC: 2448 5031 Pallets, wood; Lumber, plywood, and millwork

(G-14666)
JP MECHANIC & WELDING INC
1924 Stockyard Rd (27355-9113)
PHONE.................................919 650-7438
Prieto Jeronimo, *Pr*
EMP: 5 **EST:** 2014
SALES (est): 75.39K **Privately Held**
SIC: 7692 Welding repair

(G-14667)
MANHATTAN AMRCN TERRAZZO STRIP
2433 Us Hwy 421 (27355)
P.O. Box 7 (27355-0007)
PHONE.................................336 622-4247
Jim Behuniak, *Pr*
Tom Tassis, *
▲ **EMP:** 121
SQ FT: 25,000
SALES (est): 22.14MM
SALES (corp-wide): 27.58MM **Privately Held**
Web: www.manhattanamerican.com
SIC: 3272 3351 3316 Terrazzo products, precast, nec; Copper rolling and drawing; Cold finishing of steel shapes
PA: The Platt Brothers & Company
2670 S Main St
Waterbury CT 06706
203 753-4194

(G-14668)
MIDCOASTAL DEVELOPMENT CORP
Also Called: Southern Aggregates
2435 Old 421 Rd (27355-8242)
P.O. Box 70 (27355-0070)
PHONE.................................336 622-3091
Johnny Justice Iii, *Pr*
▲ **EMP:** 8 **EST:** 1981
SQ FT: 800
SALES (est): 2.28MM
SALES (corp-wide): 2.54MM **Privately Held**
SIC: 3281 Stone, quarrying and processing of own stone products
PA: Justice Products, Llc
301 Habersham St
Savannah GA 31401
855 720-2388

GEOGRAPHIC SECTION Stanley - Gaston County (G-14693)

(G-14669)
PILGRIMS PRIDE CORPORATION
Also Called: Staley Feed Mill
2607 Old 421 Rd (27355-8244)
PHONE..............................336 622-4251
Dale Kidd, *Mgr*
EMP: 25
Web: www.pilgrims.com
SIC: 2015 Poultry slaughtering and processing
HQ: Pilgrim's Price Corporation
1770 Promontory Cir
Greeley CO 80634
970 506-8000

(G-14670)
QUALITY FABRICATORS
1151 Langley Rd (27355-8068)
PHONE..............................336 622-3402
Curtis Coble, *Pt*
James Rex Johnson, *Pt*
EMP: 5 **EST:** 1984
SQ FT: 4,000
SALES (est): 498.97K **Privately Held**
SIC: 2426 Furniture stock and parts, hardwood

Stallings
Union County

(G-14671)
IPC CORPORATION
3330 Smith Farm Rd (28104-5040)
PHONE..............................704 821-7084
James A Massey, *Pr*
EMP: 10 **EST:** 1972
SALES (est): 2.22MM **Privately Held**
Web: www.ipc.org
SIC: 3354 5051 Aluminum extruded products; Aluminum bars, rods, ingots, sheets, pipes, plates, etc.

(G-14672)
METROLINA WOODWORKS INC
3475 Gribble Rd (28104-8114)
PHONE..............................704 821-9095
Fred W Crawford Ii, *Pr*
EMP: 10 **EST:** 2010
SALES (est): 794.63K **Privately Held**
Web: www.metrolinaww.com
SIC: 2431 Millwork

Stanfield
Stanly County

(G-14673)
ACTA PRINT & MARKETING LLC
224 Deerwood Ln (28163-5599)
PHONE..............................704 773-1493
Scott E Yarbrough, *Prin*
EMP: 4 **EST:** 2019
SALES (est): 106.48K **Privately Held**
SIC: 2752 Commercial printing, lithographic

(G-14674)
AMERICAN RACG HDERS EXHUST INC
Also Called: Arh
120 Riverstone Dr (28163-0078)
PHONE..............................631 608-1986
Nicholas Filippides, *CEO*
Jose Cruz, *
Yaquelin Cruz, *
Paul J Thau, *
EMP: 40 **EST:** 2005
SALES (est): 6.97MM **Privately Held**
SIC: 3542 3714 Headers; Motor vehicle parts and accessories

(G-14675)
AVDEL USA LLC (HQ)
Also Called: Stanley Engineered Fastening
614 Nc Hwy 200 S (28163-6715)
PHONE..............................704 888-7100
John Wyatt, *Pr*
▲ **EMP:** 36 **EST:** 2005
SALES (est): 30.27MM
SALES (corp-wide): 15.78B **Publicly Held**
Web: www.stanleyengineeredfastening.com
SIC: 3965 3452 Fasteners, buttons, needles, and pins; Bolts, nuts, rivets, and washers
PA: Stanley Black & Decker, Inc.
1000 Stanley Dr
New Britain CT 06053
860 225-5111

(G-14676)
BONDO INNOVATIONS LLC
14904 Barbee Rd (28163-8539)
PHONE..............................704 888-9910
EMP: 4 **EST:** 2008
SALES (est): 496.82K **Privately Held**
Web: www.bondoinnovations.com
SIC: 3441 Fabricated structural metal

(G-14677)
DE LITTLE CABINET INC
8267 Nc Hwy 200 (28163-9554)
PHONE..............................704 888-5994
EMP: 5 **EST:** 2008
SALES (est): 67.16K **Privately Held**
SIC: 2434 Wood kitchen cabinets

(G-14678)
EUDYS CABINET MANUFACTURING
Also Called: Kbs Sales Co
12303 Renee Ford Rd (28163-7692)
P.O. Box 639 (28163-0639)
PHONE..............................704 888-4454
Jeral Eudy, *Pr*
Rommie Gene Aldridge, *
Gary Eudy, *
Betty Eudy, *
EMP: 25 **EST:** 1964
SQ FT: 55,000
SALES (est): 1.89MM **Privately Held**
Web: www.eudyscabinets.com
SIC: 2434 Wood kitchen cabinets

(G-14679)
GLH SYSTEMS & CONTROLS INC
4667 Love Mill Rd (28163-7625)
PHONE..............................980 581-1304
Lee Hallock, *Pr*
EMP: 5 **EST:** 2004
SQ FT: 1,500
SALES (est): 506.73K **Privately Held**
Web: www.kspanglerrealtor.com
SIC: 3613 1731 Control panels, electric; Electrical work

(G-14680)
GRAPHICAL CREATIONS INC
106 Conveyor Beltway Dr (28163-9528)
P.O. Box 850 (28097-0850)
PHONE..............................704 888-8870
David Schopler, *Pr*
Marla Schopler, *VP*
EMP: 17 **EST:** 1995
SQ FT: 12,000
SALES (est): 2.47MM **Privately Held**
Web: www.graphi-cal.com
SIC: 3993 2531 Signs, not made in custom sign painting shops; Public building and related furniture

(G-14681)
OLD SCHOOL MILL INC (PA)
139 Concord St Unit 4 (28169-9619)
PHONE..............................704 781-5451
Robin Hinson, *Pr*
Parker D Hinson, *VP*
Virginia H Sedhom, *Sec*
EMP: 5 **EST:** 1995
SALES (est): 540.76K
SALES (corp-wide): 540.76K **Privately Held**
Web: www.oldschool.com
SIC: 2041 Corn grits and flakes, for brewers' use

(G-14682)
S EUDY CABINET SHOP INC
Also Called: Eudy's Cabinet Manufacturing
12303 Renee Ford Rd (28163-7692)
P.O. Box 639 (28163-0639)
PHONE..............................704 888-4454
Ernest L Eudy, *Ch Bd*
Jerel Eudy, *
Rommie G Aldridge, *
Betty Eudy, *
Gary Eudy, *
EMP: 23 **EST:** 1963
SQ FT: 185,000
SALES (est): 893.09K **Privately Held**
Web: www.eudyscabinets.com
SIC: 2434 Wood kitchen cabinets

Stanley
Gaston County

(G-14683)
ACCEL WLDG & FABRICATION LLC
389 Glencrest Dr (28164-9737)
PHONE..............................980 722-7198
Terry Small, *Pr*
EMP: 6 **EST:** 2014
SALES (est): 43.4K **Privately Held**
SIC: 7699 3441 1799 Welding equipment repair; Fabricated structural metal; Fiberglass work

(G-14684)
AVIENT PROTECTIVE MTLS LLC
1101 S Highway 27 (28164-2206)
PHONE..............................704 862-5100
EMP: 68
SIC: 2834 Pharmaceutical preparations
HQ: Avient Protective Materials Llc
5750 Mrtin Lther King Jr
Greenville NC 27834
252 707-2547

(G-14685)
B & B STUCCO AND STONE LLC
816 Joseph Antoon Cir (28164-4112)
P.O. Box 119 (28164-0119)
PHONE..............................704 524-1230
Amy Brunner, *Prin*
EMP: 14 **EST:** 2010
SALES (est): 408.76K **Privately Held**
SIC: 3299 Stucco

(G-14686)
B V HEDRICK GRAVEL & SAND CO
Also Called: Hedrick Industries
6941 Quarry Ln (28164-6778)
PHONE..............................704 827-8114
Jeffrey Goodman, *Mgr*
EMP: 102
SALES (corp-wide): 238.17MM **Privately Held**
Web: www.hedrickind.com
SIC: 1442 Construction sand and gravel
PA: B. V. Hedrick Gravel & Sand Company
120 1/2 N Church St
Salisbury NC 28144
704 633-5982

(G-14687)
BLUM INC
7733 Old Plank Rd (28164-7774)
PHONE..............................704 827-1345
Shannon Lafferty, *Pr*
Stephen Regele, *
Donna Springs, *
◆ **EMP:** 400 **EST:** 1977
SQ FT: 300,000
SALES (est): 116.23MM
SALES (corp-wide): 2.83B **Privately Held**
Web: www.blum.com
SIC: 3429 Furniture hardware
HQ: Julius Blum Gmbh
IndustriestraBe 1
HOchst 6973
55787050

(G-14688)
CHESAPEAKE GRAPHICS INC
8261 Nc 73 Hwy Ste A (28164-7815)
PHONE..............................704 827-7172
Byron O Long, *Pr*
Carol Long, *VP*
EMP: 9 **EST:** 1983
SQ FT: 12,000
SALES (est): 217.14K **Privately Held**
Web: www.chesapeakegraphics.com
SIC: 2759 Screen printing

(G-14689)
COLLIER INDUSTRIES NC
716 Murphy St (28164-1424)
PHONE..............................980 263-0510
Alexander Collier, *Prin*
EMP: 4 **EST:** 2018
SALES (est): 71.79K **Privately Held**
SIC: 3999 Manufacturing industries, nec

(G-14690)
DEB SBS INC
1100 S Highway 27 (28164-2205)
PHONE..............................704 263-4240
Allen Soden, *Pr*
EMP: 13 **EST:** 2015
SALES (est): 941.3K **Privately Held**
SIC: 2844 Perfumes, cosmetics and other toilet preparations

(G-14691)
DSM DESOTECH INC
Also Called: Perkem Technology
1101 N Carolina 27 (28164)
PHONE..............................704 862-5000
John Aviles, *Brnch Mgr*
EMP: 5
SQ FT: 14,922
Web: www.dsm.com
SIC: 2893 Printing ink
HQ: Dsm Desotech Inc.
1122 Saint Charles St
Elgin IL 60120

(G-14692)
ENTERPRISE TWD
7482 Nc 73 Hwy (28164)
PHONE..............................704 822-6166
Tim Dellinger, *Owner*
EMP: 4 **EST:** 2007
SALES (est): 227.05K **Privately Held**
SIC: 3713 Dump truck bodies

(G-14693)
ERA POLYMERS CORPORATION
1101 S Highway 27 (28164-2206)
P.O. Box 548 (28164-0548)

Stanley - Gaston County (G-14694) GEOGRAPHIC SECTION

PHONE..............................704 931-3675
George Papamanuel, *Pr*
Alex Papamanuel, *VP*
John Eve, *Sec*
Tina Papamanuel, *Treas*
Reynaldo Lopez, *Prin*
EMP: 12 **EST:** 2018
SALES (est): 2.81MM **Privately Held**
Web: www.erapol.com.au
SIC: 2822 Ethylene-propylene rubbers, EPDM polymers

(G-14694)
GASTON SYSTEMS INC
200 S Main St (28164-2011)
PHONE..............................704 263-6000
Gary Harris, *Pr*
▲ **EMP:** 17 **EST:** 1997
SALES (est): 2.48MM **Privately Held**
Web: www.gastonsystems.com
SIC: 2672 Chemically treated papers, made from purchased materials

(G-14695)
H AND H WOODWORKS
121 Griffin Rd (28164-9633)
PHONE..............................704 827-4506
EMP: 4 **EST:** 2019
SALES (est): 54.13K **Privately Held**
SIC: 2431 Millwork

(G-14696)
HEED GROUP INC
107 Redding Rd (28164-1118)
P.O. Box 7804 (28241-7804)
PHONE..............................877 938-8853
Patrick Barber, *CEO*
Tonya Barber, *VP*
Haywood Phifer, *Treas*
Sherry Adams, *Sec*
EMP: 5 **EST:** 1986
SQ FT: 1,000
SALES (est): 241.59K **Privately Held**
Web: www.theheedgroupinc.com
SIC: 2842 3993 8742 3999 Polishes and sanitation goods; Signs and advertising specialties; Training and development consultant; Artificial flower arrangements

(G-14697)
I C E S GASTON COUNTY INC
102 Mariposa Rd (28164-0049)
P.O. Box 89 (28164-0089)
PHONE..............................704 263-1418
Ronnie Lay, *Pr*
Jesse W Huffstickler, *Pr*
Jerry Haines, *Treas*
Darrell Kiser, *Sec*
EMP: 7 **EST:** 1985
SQ FT: 17,000
SALES (est): 2.13MM **Privately Held**
Web: www.ices-inc.com
SIC: 5084 3625 Textile machinery and equipment; Electric controls and control accessories, industrial

(G-14698)
J&L MACHINE & FABRICATION INC
201 S Buckoak St (28164-1744)
P.O. Box 579 (28164-0579)
PHONE..............................704 755-5552
EMP: 23 **EST:** 2015
SALES (est): 1.7MM **Privately Held**
Web: www.jlmaf.com
SIC: 3599 Machine shop, jobbing and repair

(G-14699)
KETER US INC
2369 Charles Raper Jonas Hwy (28164-2246)
PHONE..............................704 263-1967

EMP: 65
Web: www.keter.com
SIC: 2519 Fiberglass and plastic furniture
HQ: Keter Us, Inc.
6435 S Scatterfield Rd
Anderson IN 46013
317 575-4700

(G-14700)
LEES POLISHING & POWDERCOATIN
922 S Nc 16 Business Hwy (28164-8819)
PHONE..............................704 827-4309
Marsha R Washam, *Prin*
EMP: 6 **EST:** 2008
SALES (est): 101.42K **Privately Held**
SIC: 3471 Polishing, metals or formed products

(G-14701)
MACHINERY SALES
Also Called: Machinery Sales and Service
7659 Old Plank Rd (28164-7773)
PHONE..............................704 822-0110
EMP: 7 **EST:** 1992
SALES (est): 570.3K **Privately Held**
SIC: 3089 Injection molding of plastics

(G-14702)
METAL ROOFING SYSTEMS LLC
Also Called: Central Carolina Steel
7687 Mikron Dr (28164-4500)
P.O. Box 1534 (28037-1534)
PHONE..............................704 820-3110
Gavin Seale, *
EMP: 30 **EST:** 2001
SQ FT: 40,000
SALES (est): 13.77MM
SALES (corp-wide): 76.48MM **Privately Held**
Web: www.metalroofingsystems.com
SIC: 1761 2952 3444 3531 Roofing contractor; Roofing materials; Metal roofing and roof drainage equipment; Roofing equipment
PA: Atlantic Squared Supply Llc
155 Professional Park Dr
Cumming GA 30040
470 598-1010

(G-14703)
MICHELLES SCRUBS AND MORE
829 Joseph Antoon Cir (28164-4113)
PHONE..............................980 215-9461
EMP: 4 **EST:** 2016
SALES (est): 76.82K **Privately Held**
Web: www.michellesscrubsandmore.com
SIC: 2844 Perfumes, cosmetics and other toilet preparations

(G-14704)
OH SO NICE
112 Rollins St (28164-1426)
PHONE..............................704 263-2668
EMP: 4 **EST:** 2007
SALES (est): 5.39K **Privately Held**
SIC: 2395 Embroidery and art needlework

(G-14705)
ONYX ENVIRONMENTAL SOLUTIONS INC
Also Called: Onyx
7781 S Little Egypt Rd (28164-8732)
PHONE..............................800 858-3533
▲ **EMP:** 20
Web: www.onyxsolutions.com
SIC: 3589 Floor washing and polishing machines, commercial

(G-14706)
SAMOS POLYMERS CORPORATION
1101 S Highway 27 (28164-2206)
P.O. Box 548 (28164-0548)
PHONE..............................704 241-2065
EMP: 11 **EST:** 2019
SALES (est): 1.07MM **Privately Held**
Web: www.erapolymersusa.com
SIC: 2821 Plastics materials and resins

(G-14707)
SC JOHNSON PROF USA INC
1100 S Highway 27 (28164-2205)
PHONE..............................704 263-4240
John Campbell, *Prin*
EMP: 54
Web: www.scjp.com
SIC: 2844 Face creams or lotions
HQ: Sc Johnson Professional Usa, Inc.
2815 Clseum Cntre Dr Ste
Charlotte NC 28217

(G-14708)
SC JOHNSON PROFESSIONAL
1100 S Hwy (28164)
PHONE..............................704 263-4240
Michael Bogdanski, *Pr*
◆ **EMP:** 62 **EST:** 2014
SQ FT: 60,000
SALES (est): 10.2MM **Privately Held**
Web: www.scjp.com
SIC: 2841 Textile soap
HQ: Sc Johnson Professional Usa, Inc.
2815 Clseum Cntre Dr Ste
Charlotte NC 28217

(G-14709)
TWS SPECIALTY WOODWORKING
609 Killian Rd (28164-6761)
PHONE..............................315 492-1697
Thomas Skrocki, *Owner*
EMP: 5 **EST:** 2015
SALES (est): 135K **Privately Held**
SIC: 2429 Special product sawmills, nec

(G-14710)
ULTIMATE QM INC
7149 Brandywine Ln (28164-7843)
PHONE..............................704 500-9035
EMP: 7 **EST:** 2021
SALES (est): 63.22K **Privately Held**
Web: www.ultimateqm.com
SIC: 3714 Motor vehicle parts and accessories

Stantonsburg
Wilson County

(G-14711)
DAVIDSON PRINTING & MACHINERY
6173 Nc Highway 58 S (27883-9680)
PHONE..............................202 558-2055
Sean Behan, *Owner*
EMP: 4 **EST:** 2006
SALES (est): 59.13K **Privately Held**
SIC: 2752 Commercial printing, lithographic

(G-14712)
NORTH CAROLINA TOBACCO MFG LLC
7427 N. Carolina Way (27883)
PHONE..............................252 238-6514
George Aguerriberry, *Managing Member*
EMP: 14 **EST:** 2014
SALES (est): 8.89MM **Privately Held**
Web: www.nctob.com
SIC: 2121 Cigars

(G-14713)
WREATHSPLUSBYLYN
7050 Gardners School Rd (27883-9787)
PHONE..............................252 281-3674
Lynne Bachelder, *Owner*
EMP: 4 **EST:** 2014
SALES (est): 51.08K **Privately Held**
SIC: 3999 Wreaths, artificial

Star
Montgomery County

(G-14714)
C & J CROSSPIECES LLC
126 S Lancer Rd (27356-7329)
P.O. Box 732 (27209-0732)
PHONE..............................910 652-4955
EMP: 5 **EST:** 2007
SALES (est): 393.19K **Privately Held**
SIC: 2421 Building and structural materials, wood

(G-14715)
FREEMAN TRANSPORT AND LOGGING
1163 Tarry Church Rd (27356-7818)
PHONE..............................910 220-5358
Jeremy Wayne Freeman, *Pr*
EMP: 6 **EST:** 2017
SALES (est): 308.06K **Privately Held**
SIC: 2411 Logging camps and contractors

(G-14716)
JOHNSON CNC LLC
133 S Main St (27356-7961)
PHONE..............................910 428-1245
Ryan Johnson, *Managing Member*
EMP: 22 **EST:** 2011
SALES (est): 2.52MM **Privately Held**
Web: www.johnsoncnc.com
SIC: 3599 Machine shop, jobbing and repair

(G-14717)
JORDAN LUMBER & SUPPLY INC
Also Called: Cotton Creek Chip Company
4483 Spies Rd (27356-7938)
P.O. Box 822 (27356-0822)
PHONE..............................910 428-9048
Doug Richardson, *Brnch Mgr*
EMP: 6
SALES (corp-wide): 48.73MM **Privately Held**
Web: www.jordanlumber.com
SIC: 2421 Wood chips, produced at mill
PA: Jordan Lumber & Supply, Inc.
1939 Nc Highway 109 S
Mount Gilead NC 27306
910 439-6121

(G-14718)
LAGAEL MANUFACTURING LLC
Also Called: D&P Pallet
205 Frame Shop Rd (27356-7643)
P.O. Box 112 (27247-0112)
PHONE..............................910 428-9383
Vance Richardson, *Owner*
EMP: 6 **EST:** 1999
SALES (est): 66.61K **Privately Held**
SIC: 2448 Pallets, wood

(G-14719)
LANCER INCORPORATED
135 S Lancer Rd (27356-7329)
P.O. Box 848 (27356-0848)
PHONE..............................910 428-2181
Randy Deese, *Ch*
Peggy Thompson, *
Fred Ingle, *
EMP: 120 **EST:** 1969

GEOGRAPHIC SECTION

SQ FT: 96,000
SALES (est): 9.18MM **Privately Held**
Web: www.lancerfurniture.com
SIC: 2512 Upholstered household furniture

(G-14720)
MAYNARD FRAME SHOP INC
306 Mcbride Lumber Rd (27356-7513)
P.O. Box 182 (27247-0182)
PHONE..............................910 428-2033
Johnny Maynard, *Pr*
Teresa Maynard, *
EMP: 14 **EST:** 1984
SQ FT: 50,000
SALES (est): 371.2K **Privately Held**
SIC: 2511 2426 Unassembled or unfinished furniture, household: wood; Hardwood dimension and flooring mills

(G-14721)
MCBRIDE LUMBER CO PARTNR LLC
668 Mcbride Lumber Rd (27356-7516)
P.O. Box 91 (27356-0091)
PHONE..............................910 428-2747
EMP: 16 **EST:** 1964
SALES (est): 912.36K **Privately Held**
SIC: 2449 2448 Rectangular boxes and crates, wood; Wood pallets and skids

(G-14722)
PRESTIGE MILLWORK INC
671 Spies Rd (27356-7867)
P.O. Box 250 (27356-0250)
PHONE..............................910 428-2360
Stephen Bracey, *Pr*
David Allen, *VP*
EMP: 14 **EST:** 1992
SQ FT: 28,000
SALES (est): 941.11K **Privately Held**
Web: www.prestigemillworknc.com
SIC: 2431 2521 2434 Millwork; Wood office furniture; Wood kitchen cabinets

(G-14723)
SUTTON SCIENTIFICS INC
246 W College St (27356-7987)
P.O. Box 310 (27356-0310)
PHONE..............................910 428-1600
Steven Sutton, *Pr*
Elizabeth Sutton, *VP*
EMP: 5 **EST:** 2005
SQ FT: 36,000
SALES (est): 475.76K **Privately Held**
Web: www.suttonscientifics.com
SIC: 8748 3999 Business consulting, nec; Barber and beauty shop equipment

(G-14724)
TYSINGER LOGGING INC
499 Brewer St (27356-7535)
PHONE..............................910 220-5053
Roger D Tysinger, *Pr*
EMP: 8 **EST:** 2010
SALES (est): 209.23K **Privately Held**
SIC: 2411 Logging

(G-14725)
WET DOG GLASS LLC
100 Russell Dr (27356-7001)
P.O. Box 96 (27356-0096)
PHONE..............................910 428-4111
Edward B Bernard, *Managing Member*
▼ **EMP:** 8 **EST:** 2000
SQ FT: 7,000
SALES (est): 1MM **Privately Held**
Web: www.wdg-us.com
SIC: 3559 Glass making machinery: blowing, molding, forming, etc.

State Road
Surry County

(G-14726)
GRASSY CREEK VINEYARD & WINERY
235 Chatham Cottage Ln (28676-8836)
PHONE..............................336 835-2458
Cynthia Douthit, *Prin*
EMP: 6 **EST:** 2012
SALES (est): 244.23K **Privately Held**
Web: www.grassycreekvineyard.com
SIC: 2084 Wines

(G-14727)
HOT SHOT SERVICES LLC
2202 Us 21 (28676-9017)
PHONE..............................336 244-0331
Billy Hudspeth, *Prin*
EMP: 5 **EST:** 2016
SALES (est): 79.25K **Privately Held**
Web: hotshotservicesllc.business.site
SIC: 1389 Hot shot service

(G-14728)
PHARMDAWG VINEYARDS LLC
501 Mining School Rd (28676-9173)
PHONE..............................770 596-0960
EMP: 4 **EST:** 2018
SALES (est): 89.47K **Privately Held**
SIC: 2084 Wines

(G-14729)
PINE LOG CO INC
Also Called: Pine Log 118 Trdtnal Living Rd
118 Traditonal Living Rd (28676-8708)
P.O. Box 858 (28621-0858)
PHONE..............................336 366-2770
Charles W Woodie, *Pt*
Randy Miller, *Pt*
EMP: 30 **EST:** 1992
SALES (est): 2.48MM **Privately Held**
SIC: 2421 Sawmills and planing mills, general

(G-14730)
RALPH HARRIS LEATHER INC
219 Pat Nixon Rd (28676-9193)
PHONE..............................336 874-2100
Mabeline Harris, *Pr*
Phil Harris, *VP*
Edwin R Harris, *VP*
EMP: 5 **EST:** 1976
SQ FT: 2,400
SALES (est): 458.6K **Privately Held**
Web: www.harrisleather.com
SIC: 3199 Equestrian related leather articles

(G-14731)
WATSON METALS CO
2693 Poplar Springs Rd (28676-8842)
PHONE..............................336 366-4500
Hassell Watson, *Pr*
Nancy Watson, *VP*
EMP: 6 **EST:** 1988
SQ FT: 3,575
SALES (est): 476.76K **Privately Held**
SIC: 3441 Fabricated structural metal

Statesville
Iredell County

(G-14732)
3A COMPOSITES USA INC (HQ)
3480 Taylorsville Hwy (28625-2587)
P.O. Box 507 (42025-0507)
PHONE..............................704 872-8974
Brendan Cooper, *Pr*
◆ **EMP:** 125 **EST:** 1978
SQ FT: 6,000
SALES (est): 437.02MM **Privately Held**
Web: www.3acompositesusa.com
SIC: 3334 2679 3081 3449 Primary aluminum; Paper products, converted, nec; Unsupported plastics film and sheet; Curtain wall, metal
PA: Schweiter Technologies Ag
  Hinterbergstrasse 20
  Steinhausen ZG 6312

(G-14733)
A & A DRONE SERVICE LLC
166 Ralph Rd (28625-2135)
PHONE..............................704 928-5054
EMP: 5 **EST:** 2019
SALES (est): 86.08K **Privately Held**
SIC: 3728 Aircraft parts and equipment, nec

(G-14734)
ABT FOAM INC
Also Called: Multidrain Systems, Inc.
1405 Industrial Dr (28625-6263)
P.O. Box 88 (28010-0088)
PHONE..............................800 433-1119
Ralph Brafford, *Pr*
▲ **EMP:** 10 **EST:** 2002
SALES (est): 2.46MM **Privately Held**
Web: www.multidrainsystems.com
SIC: 3321 Cast iron pipe and fittings
PA: Abt, Inc.
  259 Murdock Rd
  Troutman NC 28166

(G-14735)
ABT FOAM LLC
Also Called: A B T
1405 Industrial Dr (28625-6263)
P.O. Box 7107 (28687-7107)
PHONE..............................704 508-1010
EMP: 12 **EST:** 2008
SALES (est): 930.21K **Privately Held**
Web: www.abtfoam.com
SIC: 3086 Plastics foam products

(G-14736)
ABT MANUFACTURING LLC
Also Called: ABT
1903 Weinig St (28677-3190)
P.O. Box 188 (28106-0188)
PHONE..............................704 847-9188
Robert G Estridge, *Managing Member*
W Kress Query, *Managing Member*
EMP: 34 **EST:** 1954
SQ FT: 55,000
SALES (est): 10.81MM **Privately Held**
Web: www.abtmetals.com
SIC: 3469 3544 Stamping metal for the trade ; Special dies and tools

(G-14737)
ABUNDANT MANUFACTURING INC
820 Cochran St (28677-5657)
PHONE..............................704 871-9911
Richard Piselli, *CEO*
Kevin A Smith, *
Eddie Oelenberger, *
Greg Watson, *
▲ **EMP:** 40 **EST:** 2003
SQ FT: 55,000
SALES (est): 3.01MM **Privately Held**
Web: www.abundantmfg.com
SIC: 3714 3566 Gears, motor vehicle; Speed changers, drives, and gears

(G-14738)
ACCUMA CORPORATION (DH)
133 Fanjoy Rd (28625-8567)
PHONE..............................704 873-1488
Francesca Inzernizzi, *Ch*
Steve Lepow, *
Paolo Invernizzi, *
Matthew Gillespie, *
◆ **EMP:** 112 **EST:** 1985
SQ FT: 160,000
SALES (est): 58.66MM
SALES (corp-wide): 166.09MM **Privately Held**
Web: www.accuma.com
SIC: 3089 Injection molding of plastics
HQ: Accuma Plastics Limited
  26 Princewood Road Earlstree
  Industrial Estate
  Corby NORTHANTS NN17
  153 626-3461

(G-14739)
ACME LIQUIDATING COMPANY LLC
Also Called: Acme Metal Products
1784 Salisbury Rd (28677-6264)
P.O. Box 1263 (28687-1263)
PHONE..............................704 873-3731
David Barnes, *Managing Member*
▲ **EMP:** 20 **EST:** 2007
SALES (est): 2.23MM **Privately Held**
Web: www.acmemetalproducts.com
SIC: 3497 Metal foil and leaf

(G-14740)
ACME RENTAL COMPANY
1784 Salisbury Rd (28677-6264)
P.O. Box 1263 (28687-1263)
PHONE..............................704 873-3731
William B Raymer Senior, *Pr*
J T Alexander Junior, *VP*
▲ **EMP:** 17 **EST:** 1946
SQ FT: 32,000
SALES (est): 697.89K **Privately Held**
SIC: 3429 Furniture hardware

(G-14741)
AGROFUEL LLC
964 Snow Creek Rd (28625-2147)
PHONE..............................704 876-6667
Harry Mclain, *Mgr*
EMP: 5 **EST:** 2006
SALES (est): 445.77K **Privately Held**
SIC: 2911 Oils, fuel

(G-14742)
AIR CRAFTSMEN INC
2503 Northside Dr (28625-3182)
P.O. Box 5547 (28687-5547)
PHONE..............................336 248-5777
Ken Hodges, *Pr*
EMP: 15 **EST:** 1981
SQ FT: 6,500
SALES (est): 1.44MM **Privately Held**
Web: www.aircraftsmen.com
SIC: 3564 Dust or fume collecting equipment, industrial

(G-14743)
AIRBOX LLC
2668 Peachtree Rd (28625-8252)
PHONE..............................855 927-1386
Timothy Self, *Managing Member*
EMP: 9 **EST:** 2017
SALES (est): 992.05K **Privately Held**
Web: www.airboxamerica.com
SIC: 3564 3634 Air purification equipment; Air purifiers, portable

(G-14744)
ALLESON OF ROCHESTER INC (DH)
Also Called: Alleson Athletic
111 Badger Ln (28625-2758)
PHONE..............................585 272-0606
Todd Levine, *CEO*
Pete Palermo Iii, *COO*

Statesville - Iredell County (G-14745)

Bob Baker, *CFO*
◆ **EMP:** 100 **EST:** 1966
SQ FT: 128,000
SALES (est): 32.25MM **Privately Held**
Web: www.foundersport.com
SIC: 2339 2329 Women's and misses' athletic clothing and sportswear; Athletic clothing, except uniforms: men's, youths' and boys'
HQ: Badger Sportswear, Llc
  111 Badger Ln
  Statesville NC 28625
  704 871-0990

(G-14745)
ALPHA SIGNS & EMBROIDERY INC
321 S Tradd St (28677-5842)
PHONE............................704 878-8870
EMP: 4 **EST:** 2016
SALES (est): 73.43K **Privately Held**
Web: www.asegraphics.com
SIC: 3993 Signs and advertising specialties

(G-14746)
ALTIUM PACKAGING LLC
124 Commerce Blvd (28625-8526)
PHONE............................704 873-6729
Les Smith, *Mgr*
EMP: 14
SALES (corp-wide): 15.9B **Publicly Held**
Web: www.altiumpkg.com
SIC: 3089 Plastics containers, except foam
HQ: Altium Packaging Llc
  2500 Windy Ridge Pkwy Se # 1400
  Atlanta GA 30339
  678 742-4600

(G-14747)
AMESBURY ACQSTION HLDNGS 2 INC (HQ)
Also Called: Balance Systems
2061 Sherrill Dr (28625-9025)
PHONE............................704 924-8586
Johnnthan Petromelis, *Pr*
Jeffrey Murphy, *Corporate Controller**
◆ **EMP:** 250 **EST:** 1980
SQ FT: 100,000
SALES (est): 264.28MM
SALES (corp-wide): 861.44MM **Privately Held**
SIC: 3429 Hardware, nec
PA: Tyman Plc
  29 Queen Annes Gate
  London SW1H
  207 976-8000

(G-14748)
AMESBURY GROUP INC
Amesbury Textile Division
125 Amesbury Truth Dr (28625-8578)
PHONE............................704 978-2883
EMP: 92
SQ FT: 37,920
SALES (corp-wide): 861.44MM **Privately Held**
SIC: 3442 3089 2221 3086 Sash, door or window: metal; Boxes, plastics; Pile fabrics, manmade fiber and silk; Plastics foam products
HQ: Amesbury Group, Inc.
  5001 W Delbridge St
  Sioux Falls SD 57107
  978 388-0581

(G-14749)
AMESBURY GROUP INC
Amesbury Balance Systems Div
1920 Flintstone Dr (28677-2996)
PHONE............................704 924-7694
Eddie Kistler, *Mgr*
EMP: 26

SALES (corp-wide): 861.44MM **Privately Held**
Web: www.amesburytruth.com
SIC: 3053 3442 3086 2221 Gaskets; packing and sealing devices; Sash, door or window: metal; Plastics foam products; Pile fabrics, manmade fiber and silk
HQ: Amesbury Group, Inc.
  5001 W Delbridge St
  Sioux Falls SD 57107
  978 388-0581

(G-14750)
AMESBURY INDUSTRIES INC
125 Amesbury Truth Dr (28625-8578)
PHONE............................704 978-3250
Jeffrey Graby, *Pr*
Jeffrey Murphy, *Sec*
EMP: 50 **EST:** 1980
SALES (est): 975.71K
SALES (corp-wide): 861.44MM **Privately Held**
Web: www.amesburytruth.com
SIC: 3272 Concrete window and door components, sills and frames
PA: Tyman Plc
  29 Queen Annes Gate
  London SW1H
  207 976-8000

(G-14751)
ANA GIZZI
124 Hatfield Rd (28625-8999)
PHONE............................908 334-8733
Ana Gizzi, *Prin*
EMP: 9 **EST:** 2016
SALES (est): 81.32K **Privately Held**
Web: www.westsideindustries.us
SIC: 3599 Machine shop, jobbing and repair

(G-14752)
ARGOS USA LLC
Also Called: Unicon Concrete
2289 Salisbury Hwy (28677)
P.O. Box 6388 (28677-6388)
PHONE............................704 872-9566
Chet Miller, *Brnch Mgr*
EMP: 135
Web: www.argos-us.com
SIC: 3273 3271 3272 Ready-mixed concrete; Blocks, concrete or cinder: standard; Septic tanks, concrete
HQ: Argos Usa Llc
  3015 Windward Plz Ste 300
  Alpharetta GA 30005
  678 368-4300

(G-14753)
ARMS RACE NUTRITION LLC
1415 Wilkesboro Hwy (28625-3262)
PHONE............................888 978-2332
EMP: 8 **EST:** 2019
SALES (est): 1.13MM **Privately Held**
Web: www.armsracenutrition.com
SIC: 2023 Dietary supplements, dairy and non-dairy based

(G-14754)
ASMO NORTH AMERICA LLC
470 Crawford Rd (28625-8545)
PHONE............................704 872-2319
▲ **EMP:** 2000
SIC: 3089 3621 Plastics and fiberglass tanks; Motors, electric

(G-14755)
AUTEC INC
2500 W Front St (28677-2998)
PHONE............................704 871-9141
Thomas J Hobby, *Pr*
Lynn Hobby, *

◆ **EMP:** 50 **EST:** 1981
SQ FT: 104,000
SALES (est): 12.7MM **Privately Held**
Web: www.autec-carwash.com
SIC: 3559 2842 Automotive related machinery; Specialty cleaning

(G-14756)
B & J KNITS INC
3492 Wilkesboro Hwy (28625-1250)
PHONE............................704 876-1498
Roger Mclelland, *Pr*
EMP: 9 **EST:** 1973
SQ FT: 16,000
SALES (est): 124.83K **Privately Held**
Web: www.bandjknits.com
SIC: 2253 Warm weather knit outerwear, including beachwear

(G-14757)
BADGER SPORTSWEAR LLC
Also Called: Taurus Textiles
111 Badger Ln (28625-2758)
PHONE............................704 871-0990
Jeff Jones, *Mgr*
EMP: 62
Web: www.foundersport.com
SIC: 5199 5137 5136 2339 Knit goods; Women's and children's clothing; Men's and boy's clothing; Women's and misses' outerwear, nec
HQ: Badger Sportswear, Llc
  111 Badger Ln
  Statesville NC 28625
  704 871-0990

(G-14758)
BADGER SPORTSWEAR LLC (HQ)
Also Called: Garb Athletics
111 Badger Ln (28625-2758)
P.O. Box 447 (28687-0447)
PHONE............................704 871-0990
▲ **EMP:** 129 **EST:** 1971
SALES (est): 101.02MM **Privately Held**
Web: www.foundersport.com
SIC: 2329 2339 Men's and boys' sportswear and athletic clothing; Sportswear, women's
PA: Platinum Equity, Llc
  360 N Crescent Dr Bldg S
  Beverly Hills CA 90210

(G-14759)
BARTLETT MILLING COMPANY LP
701 S Center St (28677-6732)
P.O. Box 831 (28687-0831)
PHONE............................704 872-9581
Joe Mitchell, *Prin*
EMP: 67
SALES (corp-wide): 1.73B **Privately Held**
Web: www.bartlettco.com
SIC: 2041 2048 Wheat flour; Prepared feeds, nec
HQ: Bartlett Milling Company, L.P.
  4900 Main St Ste 1200
  Kansas City MO 64112
  816 753-6300

(G-14760)
BEBIDA BEVERAGE COMPANY
1304 N Barkley Rd (28677-9728)
P.O. Box 125 (28115-0125)
PHONE............................704 660-0226
Brian Weber, *CEO*
▼ **EMP:** 21 **EST:** 2009
SALES (est): 1.63MM **Privately Held**
Web: www.bebevco.com
SIC: 2086 Bottled and canned soft drinks

(G-14761)
BEC-CAR PRINTING CO INC (PA)
Also Called: Ber-Car Printing
970 Davie Ave (28677-5302)
P.O. Box 569 (28687-0569)
PHONE............................704 873-1911
Delan White, *Pr*
Rebecca White Poplin, *VP*
Michelle White Baggarley, *Treas*
EMP: 12 **EST:** 1924
SQ FT: 4,000
SALES (est): 961.99K
SALES (corp-wide): 961.99K **Privately Held**
SIC: 2752 Offset printing

(G-14762)
BETCO INC (DH)
Also Called: Mini Storage of North Carolina
228 Commerce Blvd (28625-8549)
PHONE............................704 872-2999
Samir Sabri, *CEO*
Fred Barnard, *
Chris Gilbert, *
◆ **EMP:** 95 **EST:** 1984
SQ FT: 40,000
SALES (est): 68.57MM
SALES (corp-wide): 1.02B **Publicly Held**
Web: www.betcoinc.com
SIC: 3448 Buildings, portable: prefabricated metal
HQ: Janus International Group, Llc
  135 Janus Intl Blvd
  Temple GA 30179
  770 562-2850

(G-14763)
BH LOGGING
130 Hugo Ln (28677-1702)
PHONE............................980 330-0229
Beau Heald, *Prin*
EMP: 4 **EST:** 2018
SALES (est): 88.83K **Privately Held**
SIC: 2411 Logging

(G-14764)
BILL MARTIN INC
106 Martin Ln (28625-2250)
PHONE............................704 873-0241
Bill R Martin Senior, *Pr*
Bill Martin Junior, *VP*
John Martin, *Sec*
EMP: 12 **EST:** 1968
SQ FT: 4,141
SALES (est): 469.26K **Privately Held**
Web: www.billmartintires.com
SIC: 5531 7534 Automotive tires; Tire recapping

(G-14765)
BLIMP WORKS INC
156 Barnes Airship Dr (28625-9244)
PHONE............................704 876-2378
Tracy Barnes, *Pr*
Kay Truitt, *Sec*
EMP: 12 **EST:** 1982
SQ FT: 15,000
SALES (est): 218.26K **Privately Held**
Web: www.theblimpworks.com
SIC: 3721 Blimps

(G-14766)
BRUNING AND FEDERLE MFG CO (PA)
2503 Northside Dr (28625-3182)
P.O. Box 5547 (28687-5547)
PHONE............................704 873-7237
Thomas H Bass, *Pr*
Michael D Hepler, *General Vice President**
▲ **EMP:** 50 **EST:** 1963
SQ FT: 30,000

SALES (est): 9.75MM
SALES (corp-wide): 9.75MM **Privately Held**
Web: www.bruning-federle.com
SIC: **3564** Dust or fume collecting equipment, industrial

(G-14767)
BUCKS WRECKER SERVICE
2493 Hickory Hwy (28677-2513)
PHONE.................................704 776-0899
EMP: 6 EST: 2020
SALES (est): 87.33K **Privately Held**
Web: www.buckstowingandrecovery.com
SIC: **7549** 4789 3715 3713 Towing service, automotive; Transportation services, nec; Truck trailers; Truck and bus bodies

(G-14768)
BUSCH ENTERPRISES INC
908 Cochran St (28677-5655)
PHONE.................................704 878-2067
Ted Busch, *Pr*
Carolyn Busch, *Sec*
EMP: 6 EST: 1980
SQ FT: 12,000
SALES (est): 785.13K **Privately Held**
Web: www.buschpolishes.com
SIC: **2842** 5999 Cleaning or polishing preparations, nec; Cleaning equipment and supplies

(G-14769)
CABINET MAKERS INC
534 Jane Sowers Rd (28625-8929)
PHONE.................................704 876-2808
Kenny Harris, *Pr*
Jonathan Baumgarner, *
Jodie Harris, *
Crystal Baumgarner, *
Jesse Barnett, *Stockholder**
EMP: 23 EST: 1965
SQ FT: 54,000
SALES (est): 434.54K **Privately Held**
SIC: **2511** 2434 Wood household furniture; Wood kitchen cabinets

(G-14770)
CAPSTAR CORPORATION
600 Park Dr (28677-4937)
P.O. Box 5369 (28687-5369)
PHONE.................................704 878-2007
Aimee Toth, *CEO*
Aimee A Toth, *
Gregg Show, *
▼ EMP: 180 EST: 1988
SQ FT: 45,000
SALES (est): 15.57MM **Privately Held**
Web: www.capstarcorp.com
SIC: **2329** 2339 Men's and boys' sportswear and athletic clothing; Women's and misses' athletic clothing and sportswear

(G-14771)
CARDINAL AMERICA INC
165 Commerce Blvd (28625-8526)
PHONE.................................704 810-1620
EMP: 9 EST: 2018
SALES (est): 238.91K **Privately Held**
SIC: **3452** Bolts, metal

(G-14772)
CAROLINA PATCH & LEATHER LLC
203 Old Airport Rd (28677-8717)
PHONE.................................704 880-7724
Zachary Joseph Ponton, *Owner*
EMP: 4 EST: 2017
SALES (est): 51.92K **Privately Held**
Web: carolina-patch-and-leather.business.site

SIC: **2395** Embroidery products, except Schiffli machine

(G-14773)
CARPET RENTALS INC
Also Called: Piedmont First Aid
1002 Winston Ave (28677-6500)
P.O. Box 5386 (28687-5386)
PHONE.................................704 872-4461
TOLL FREE: 800
James A Gardner Junior, *Pr*
A James Gardner Junior, *Pr*
Brenda Gardner, *
EMP: 38 EST: 1966
SQ FT: 24,000
SALES (est): 8.66MM **Privately Held**
Web: www.carpetrentals.com
SIC: **2679** Pressed fiber and molded pulp products, except food products

(G-14774)
CCBCC OPERATIONS LLC
Also Called: Coca-Cola
2111 W Front St (28677-3650)
PHONE.................................704 872-3634
Richard Brogdon, *Brnch Mgr*
EMP: 43
SALES (corp-wide): 6.65B **Publicly Held**
Web: www.coca-cola.com
SIC: **2086** Bottled and canned soft drinks
HQ: Ccbcc Operations, Llc
    4100 Coca Cola Plz
    Charlotte NC 28211
    704 364-8728

(G-14775)
CELESTIAL COCOA CO (PA)
165 Bowman Rd (28625-8747)
PHONE.................................704 871-2495
Dawn Witherspoon, *Owner*
EMP: 6 EST: 1999
SALES (est): 58.22K
SALES (corp-wide): 58.22K **Privately Held**
Web: www.celestialcocoa.com
SIC: **2066** Powdered cocoa

(G-14776)
CEMEX CNSTR MTLS ATL LLC
2067 Salisbury Hwy (28677-2779)
PHONE.................................704 873-3263
Scott Matthews, *Brnch Mgr*
EMP: 5
SQ FT: 4,108
SIC: **3273** Ready-mixed concrete
HQ: Cemex Construction Materials Atlantic, Llc
    1501 Belvedere Rd
    West Palm Beach FL 33406
    561 833-5555

(G-14777)
COMPETITIVE EDGE INC
535 Davie Ave (28677-5322)
PHONE.................................704 881-4157
John Berkley, *Pr*
EMP: 8 EST: 2010
SALES (est): 202.49K **Privately Held**
Web: www.cedgeinc.com
SIC: **1531** 2621 Operative builders; Shipping sack paper

(G-14778)
CONSTRUCTION METAL PDTS INC
2204 W Front St (28677-2917)
PHONE.................................704 871-8704
Michael J Morton, *Ch Bd*
Robert M Noble, *
Staci M Ivester, *
EMP: 30 EST: 1993
SQ FT: 43,000
SALES (est): 9.52MM **Privately Held**

Web: www.cmpmetalsystems.com
SIC: **3444** Metal roofing and roof drainage equipment

(G-14779)
CROSSROADS COATINGS INC
Also Called: Crossroads Coatings
208 Bucks Industrial Rd (28625-2813)
P.O. Box 1508 (28687-1508)
PHONE.................................704 873-2244
William Lodgek, *Pr*
▲ EMP: 10 EST: 1958
SQ FT: 35,000
SALES (est): 1.46MM **Privately Held**
Web: www.crossroadscoatings.com
SIC: **2851** Paints and paint additives

(G-14780)
D & D MACHINE WORKS INC
Also Called: Machining
111 Dealwood Dr (28625-9143)
PHONE.................................704 878-0117
Aaron Jones, *Pr*
EMP: 8 EST: 1976
SQ FT: 5,500
SALES (est): 941.06K **Privately Held**
Web: www.ddmachineworks.net
SIC: **3599** Machine shop, jobbing and repair

(G-14781)
D & F CONSOLIDATED INC
Also Called: Car-Mel Products
2205 Mocaro Dr (28677-3668)
P.O. Box 5877 (28687-5877)
PHONE.................................704 664-6660
William Greg Glasby, *Pr*
Melvin J Skerpon, *Sr VP*
Carl E Tompkins Junior, *Sr VP*
Terry L Skerpon, *Sec*
EMP: 5 EST: 2009
SQ FT: 15,000
SALES (est): 1.13MM **Privately Held**
SIC: **5131** 2269 Labels; Labels, cotton: printed

(G-14782)
DANDY LIGHT TRAPS INC
1256 N Barkley Rd (28677-9726)
PHONE.................................980 223-2744
Kenneth W Teeters, *Pr*
Beverly R Frye, *Sec*
EMP: 5 EST: 2015
SALES (est): 690.88K **Privately Held**
Web: www.dandylighttraps.com
SIC: **3648** 5046 Lighting equipment, nec; Commercial equipment, nec

(G-14783)
DAYTON BAG & BURLAP CO
233 Commerce Blvd (28625-8549)
PHONE.................................704 873-7271
Mitch Perkins, *Brnch Mgr*
EMP: 4
SALES (corp-wide): 46.25MM **Privately Held**
Web: www.daybag.com
SIC: **2396** 2299 2393 2674 Automotive trimmings, fabric; Burlap, jute; Textile bags; Bags: uncoated paper and multiwall
PA: The Dayton Bag & Burlap Co
    322 Davis Ave
    Dayton OH 45403
    937 258-8000

(G-14784)
DEAL MACHINE SHOP INC
400 Beulah Rd (28625-2537)
PHONE.................................704 872-7618
Wayne G Deal Senior, *Pr*
Wayne G Deal Junior, *VP*
Gary Deal, *Sec*

EMP: 14 EST: 1968
SQ FT: 6,000
SALES (est): 257.82K **Privately Held**
Web: www.dealmachineshop.com
SIC: **3599** Machine shop, jobbing and repair

(G-14785)
DEAL-RITE FEEDS INC
109 Anna Dr (28625-8743)
P.O. Box 29 (28687-0029)
PHONE.................................704 873-8646
Ronald Deal, *Pr*
Diane Williams, *
EMP: 30 EST: 1962
SQ FT: 6,400
SALES (est): 6.43MM **Privately Held**
Web: www.deal-ritefeeds.com
SIC: **2048** Cereal-, grain-, and seed-based feeds

(G-14786)
DENSO MANUFACTURING NC INC (DH)
470 Crawford Rd (28625-8545)
PHONE.................................704 878-6663
Masanori Iyama, *Pr*
Daisuke Ishikawa, *Treas*
◆ EMP: 251 EST: 1988
SQ FT: 1,229,683
SALES (est): 264.89MM **Privately Held**
SIC: **3621** Motors and generators
HQ: Denso International America, Inc.
    24777 Denso Dr
    Southfield MI 48033
    248 350-7500

(G-14787)
DESCO EQUIPMENT COMPANY INC
1031 S Meeting St (28677-6655)
P.O. Box 6298 (28687-6298)
PHONE.................................704 873-2844
Nute H Shelton, *Pr*
Connie Shelton, *Sec*
EMP: 7 EST: 1983
SALES (est): 657.63K **Privately Held**
Web: www.descoequip.com
SIC: **3589** 5169 High pressure cleaning equipment; Specialty cleaning and sanitation preparations

(G-14788)
DONALD AUTON
Also Called: Bill's Welding & Son
841 Reynolds Rd (28677-3062)
PHONE.................................704 872-7528
Donald Auton, *Owner*
EMP: 4 EST: 2016
SALES (est): 123.96K **Privately Held**
SIC: **7692** Automotive welding

(G-14789)
DOOSAN BOBCAT NORTH AMER INC
Doosan Infracore Portable Pwr
1293 Glenway Dr (28625-9218)
PHONE.................................704 883-3500
EMP: 152
Web: www.bobcat.com
SIC: **3714** Motor vehicle parts and accessories
HQ: Doosan Bobcat North America, Inc.
    250 E Beaton Dr
    West Fargo ND 58078
    701 241-8700

(G-14790)
DOT BLUE READI-MIX LLC
158 Intercraft Dr (28625-2737)
PHONE.................................704 978-2331
John Wood, *Manager*
EMP: 27
SALES (corp-wide): 45.71MM **Privately Held**

Statesville - Iredell County (G-14791)

Web: www.bluedotreadimix.com
SIC: 3273 Ready-mixed concrete
PA: Blue Dot Readi-Mix, Llc
11330 Bain School Rd
Mint Hill NC 28227
704 971-7676

(G-14791)
DYNAMIC NUTRACEUTICALS LLC
(PA)
1441 Wilkesboro Hwy (28625-3262)
PHONE..................704 380-2324
Jason Dean Wolff, Pr
EMP: 25 EST: 2018
SQ FT: 15,000
SALES (est): 8.94MM
SALES (corp-wide): 8.94MM **Privately Held**
Web: www.dynamicnutraceuticals.com
SIC: 2834 Vitamin, nutrient, and hematinic preparations for human use

(G-14792)
EK AIR LLC
143 Southview Dr (28677-2608)
PHONE..................704 881-1959
Eric Kofke, Prin
EMP: 6 EST: 2011
SALES (est): 237.54K **Privately Held**
SIC: 3724 Aircraft engines and engine parts

(G-14793)
ELITE METAL PERFORMANCE LLC
Also Called: Emp Services
132 Conifer Dr (28625-9020)
PHONE..................704 660-0006
EMP: 10 EST: 2012
SALES (est): 893.74K **Privately Held**
Web: www.elitemetalperformance.com
SIC: 3792 3841 3714 3599 Travel trailer chassis; Surgical and medical instruments; Motor vehicle parts and accessories; Machine and other job shop work

(G-14794)
ELLENBURG SHEET METAL
353 Stamey Farm Rd (28625-2531)
P.O. Box 5638 (28687-5638)
PHONE..................704 872-2089
Tony Ellenburg, Owner
EMP: 4 EST: 1969
SALES (est): 269.38K **Privately Held**
Web: www.ellenburgs.com
SIC: 3444 1711 Sheet metalwork; Plumbing, heating, air-conditioning

(G-14795)
ETMO TEC LLC
111 Crofton Ct (28677-2089)
PHONE..................704 878-9979
Andreas Melville, Owner
EMP: 5 EST: 2017
SALES (est): 78.03K **Privately Held**
SIC: 2895 Carbon black

(G-14796)
FIBRIX LLC
Also Called: Cumulus - Statesville West
166 Orbit Rd (28677-8634)
PHONE..................704 872-5223
Gene Bardakjy, Brnch Mgr
EMP: 22
SALES (corp-wide): 47.37MM **Privately Held**
Web: www.fibrix.com
SIC: 2297 Nonwoven fabrics
HQ: Fibrix, Llc
1820 Evans St Ne
Conover NC 28613

(G-14797)
FIBRIX LLC
Also Called: Cumulus Fibres - Statesville
1004 Bucks Industrial Rd (28625-2813)
PHONE..................704 878-0027
Bucky Bradford, Mgr
EMP: 22
SALES (corp-wide): 47.37MM **Privately Held**
Web: www.fibrix.com
SIC: 2297 2824 2221 2299 Nonwoven fabrics; Organic fibers, noncellulosic; Broadwoven fabric mills, manmade; Batting, wadding, padding and fillings
HQ: Fibrix, Llc
1820 Evans St Ne
Conover NC 28613

(G-14798)
FIRE FLY BALLONS 2006 LLC
850 Meacham Rd (28677-2982)
PHONE..................704 878-9501
EMP: 11 EST: 1972
SQ FT: 28,000
SALES (est): 751.03K **Privately Held**
SIC: 3721 Balloons, hot air (aircraft)

(G-14799)
FIREFLY BALLOONS 2010 INC
850 Meacham Rd (28677-2982)
PHONE..................704 878-9501
Brian K Gantt, Admn
EMP: 6 EST: 2010
SALES (est): 340K **Privately Held**
Web: www.fireflyballoons.net
SIC: 3721 Balloons, hot air (aircraft)

(G-14800)
FIREFLY BALLOONS INC
810 Salisbury Rd (28677-6224)
PHONE..................704 878-9501
EMP: 9 EST: 2005
SALES (est): 99.49K **Privately Held**
Web: www.fireflyballoons.net
SIC: 3564 Blowers and fans

(G-14801)
FULLY INVOLVED LEATHERWORKS
147 Stonefield Dr (28677-9079)
PHONE..................704 799-9938
EMP: 4 EST: 2018
SALES (est): 239.47K **Privately Held**
Web: www.fullyinvolvedleatherworks.com
SIC: 3199 Leather goods, nec

(G-14802)
G & M MILLING CO INC
4000 Taylorsville Hwy (28625-1842)
PHONE..................704 873-5758
Jeffrey C Mcneely, Pr
Nancy S Mcneely, Sec
EMP: 28 EST: 1960
SQ FT: 6,400
SALES (est): 3.79MM **Privately Held**
SIC: 2048 5191 5451 Poultry feeds; Animal feeds; Dairy products stores

(G-14803)
GABDEN LLC
Also Called: Gabden Entertainment
232 N Center St (28677-5236)
PHONE..................704 451-8646
EMP: 6 EST: 2017
SALES (est): 120K **Privately Held**
SIC: 2024 Ices, flavored (frozen dessert)

(G-14804)
GODFREY LUMBER COMPANY INC
(PA)
1715 Amity Hill Rd (28677-7201)
P.O. Box 615 (28687-0615)
PHONE..................704 872-6366
Chester Godfrey, Pr
John Godfrey, Treas
William Godfrey, VP
Barry Godfrey, VP
▲ EMP: 16 EST: 1954
SQ FT: 75,000
SALES (est): 2.43MM
SALES (corp-wide): 2.43MM **Privately Held**
Web: www.godfreylumber.com
SIC: 2421 Wood chips, produced at mill

(G-14805)
GOODWILL EMPLOYMENT & TRAINING
124 Fourth Crescent Pl (28625-3004)
PHONE..................704 873-5005
EMP: 4 EST: 2019
SALES (est): 83.44K **Privately Held**
Web: www.goodwillnwnc.org
SIC: 2653 Corrugated and solid fiber boxes

(G-14806)
GOODYEAR TIRE & RUBBER COMPANY
Also Called: Goodyear
108 Business Park Dr (28677-9133)
PHONE..................704 928-4500
EMP: 63
SALES (corp-wide): 20.07MM **Publicly Held**
Web: www.goodyear.com
SIC: 3544 Forms (molds), for foundry and plastics working machinery
PA: The Goodyear Tire & Rubber Company
200 E Innovation Way
Akron OH 44316
330 796-2121

(G-14807)
GREEN KARMA LABS LLC ✪
3226 Taylorsville Hwy (28625-2965)
PHONE..................704 746-2363
Kevin Rose, Managing Member
EMP: 4 EST: 2022
SALES (est): 72.81K **Privately Held**
SIC: 2064 Candy and other confectionery products

(G-14808)
HARLEY OWNERS GROUP STTSVLLE I
1226 Morland Dr (28677-6949)
PHONE..................704 872-3883
William Tilley, Prin
EMP: 6 EST: 2017
SALES (est): 102.3K **Privately Held**
Web: www.statesville.com
SIC: 2711 Newspapers, publishing and printing

(G-14809)
HEINTZ BROS AUTOMOTIVES INC
1475 Old Mountain Rd (28677-2085)
PHONE..................704 872-8081
Steve B Heintz, Pr
Shirley C Heintz, Sec
Scott Heintz, VP
EMP: 8 EST: 1965
SQ FT: 6,000
SALES (est): 1.02MM **Privately Held**
Web: www.heintzbrothersautomotive.com
SIC: 5013 5531 3599 Automotive supplies and parts; Automotive parts; Machine shop, jobbing and repair

(G-14810)
HERFF JONES LLC
307 E Front St (28677-5906)
PHONE..................704 873-5563
EMP: 6
SALES (corp-wide): 2.02B **Privately Held**
Web: www.yearbookdiscoveries.com
SIC: 3911 Rings, finger: precious metal
HQ: Herff Jones, Llc
4501 W 62nd St
Indianapolis IN 46268
317 297-3741

(G-14811)
HERITAGE BUILDING COMPANY LLC
114 N Center St Ste 300 (28677-5273)
PHONE..................704 431-4494
James N Paquette, Prin
EMP: 15 EST: 2019
SALES (est): 2.45MM **Privately Held**
Web: www.heritagebuildings.com
SIC: 3448 Buildings, portable: prefabricated metal

(G-14812)
HERITAGE KNITTING CO LLC
240 Wilson Park Rd (28625-8525)
P.O. Box 1408 (28687-1408)
PHONE..................704 872-7653
Charles S Dockery Junior, Managing Member
EMP: 20 EST: 1994
SQ FT: 22,000
SALES (est): 1.27MM **Privately Held**
Web: www.heritageknitting.com
SIC: 2257 2211 Pile fabrics, circular knit; Broadwoven fabric mills, cotton

(G-14813)
HEXPOL COMPOUNDING NC INC
Also Called: Hexpol
280 Crawford Rd (28625-8541)
PHONE..................704 872-1585
Tracy Garrison, Pr
◆ EMP: 3100 EST: 1997
SQ FT: 44,000
SALES (est): 309.01MM
SALES (corp-wide): 2.12B **Privately Held**
Web: www.hexpol.com
SIC: 3069 3087 2891 Rubber automotive products; Custom compound purchased resins; Adhesives and sealants
HQ: Hexpol Holding Inc.
14330 Kinsman Rd
Burton OH 44021
440 834-4644

(G-14814)
HI-TEC PLATING INC
North Carolina Division
1603 Salisbury Rd (28677-6270)
PHONE..................704 872-8969
Buddy G Bray, Mgr
EMP: 10
SQ FT: 7,123
SALES (corp-wide): 4.91MM **Privately Held**
Web: www.hitecplating.com
SIC: 3471 Electroplating of metals or formed products
PA: Hi-Tec Plating, Inc.
219 Hitec Rd
Seneca SC 29678
864 882-3311

(G-14815)
HIDDEN PATH PUBLICATION INC
304 Brierwood Rd (28677-5410)
PHONE..................704 878-6986
EMP: 5 EST: 2010
SALES (est): 43.95K **Privately Held**

Statesville - Iredell County

SIC: 2741 Miscellaneous publishing

(G-14816)
HIGH COTTON SCREENPRINTING
809 Sharon School Rd (28625-1634)
PHONE.................704 872-7630
Frank Shook, *Owner*
EMP: 6 **EST:** 2005
SALES (est): 80K **Privately Held**
SIC: 2759 Screen printing

(G-14817)
HPC NC
280 Crawford Rd (28625-8541)
PHONE.................704 978-0103
EMP: 7 **EST:** 2010
SALES (est): 353.81K **Privately Held**
SIC: 3562 Ball and roller bearings

(G-14818)
HUGHS SHEET MTAL STTSVLLE LLC
Also Called: Hugh's Sheet Metal
1312 N Barkley Rd (28677-9728)
PHONE.................704 872-4621
Darrell Moose, *Pr*
Bonnie Moose, *Sec*
EMP: 12 **EST:** 1969
SQ FT: 8,000
SALES (est): 1.6MM **Privately Held**
Web: www.hughssheetmetal.com
SIC: 3441 1761 3564 3444 Fabricated structural metal; Sheet metal work, nec; Blowers and fans; Sheet metalwork

(G-14819)
I-40 MACHINE AND TOOL INC
223 Commerce Blvd (28625-8549)
PHONE.................704 881-0242
Alvin Anderson, *Pr*
Dan Anderson, *Sec*
EMP: 5 **EST:** 1987
SQ FT: 6,000
SALES (est): 424.15K **Privately Held**
Web: www.i40machine.com
SIC: 3599 Machine shop, jobbing and repair

(G-14820)
INTERNATIONAL PAPER COMPANY
International Paper
930 Meacham Rd (28677-2990)
PHONE.................704 872-6541
Tom Hamic, *Brnch Mgr*
EMP: 62
SQ FT: 158,047
SALES (corp-wide): 18.92B **Publicly Held**
Web: www.internationalpaper.com
SIC: 2621 Paper mills
PA: International Paper Company
6400 Poplar Ave
Memphis TN 38197
901 419-7000

(G-14821)
IPS PERFORATING INC
1821 Weinig St (28677-3187)
PHONE.................704 881-0050
Trish Idler, *Prin*
▲ **EMP:** 15 **EST:** 2005
SALES (est): 2.2MM **Privately Held**
Web: www.ipsperforating.com
SIC: 3443 Perforating on heavy metal

(G-14822)
IREDELL FIBER INC
Also Called: Division of Leggett Platt
124 Fanjoy Rd (28625-8567)
P.O. Box 5728 (28687-5728)
PHONE.................704 878-0884
Jerry Wahrmund, *Mgr*
▲ **EMP:** 53 **EST:** 1987

SALES (est): 3.43MM
SALES (corp-wide): 5.15B **Publicly Held**
SIC: 2515 Mattresses and bedsprings
PA: Leggett & Platt, Incorporated
1 Leggett Rd
Carthage MO 64836
417 358-8131

(G-14823)
JAX SPECIALTY WELDING LLC
621 Bristol Dr (28677-3011)
PHONE.................704 380-3548
Michael T Jackson, *Prin*
EMP: 5 **EST:** 2019
SALES (est): 113.51K **Privately Held**
SIC: 7692 Welding repair

(G-14824)
JENNIFER E SMITH ND
110 Stockton St Ste J (28677-5253)
PHONE.................704 871-1229
Jennifer Smith, *Prin*
EMP: 4 **EST:** 2008
SALES (est): 59.22K **Privately Held**
Web: www.jennifer-smith-nd.com
SIC: 3221 Medicine bottles, glass

(G-14825)
JMS SOUTHEAST INC
105 Temperature Ln (28677-9639)
PHONE.................704 873-1835
Frank L Johnson, *CEO*
Mitchell Johnson, *Pr*
Linda Johnson, *VP*
Frank Phillips, *Sec*
▲ **EMP:** 50 **EST:** 1980
SQ FT: 40,000
SALES (est): 11.95MM **Privately Held**
Web: www.jms-se.com
SIC: 3822 3829 3823 3812 Temperature controls, automatic; Measuring and controlling devices, nec; Process control instruments; Search and navigation equipment

(G-14826)
JPS COMPOSITE MATERIALS CORP
535 Connor St (28677-5757)
P.O. Box 871 (28687-0871)
PHONE.................704 872-9831
Mike Marshall, *Brnch Mgr*
EMP: 107
SALES (corp-wide): 1.91B **Publicly Held**
Web: www.jpscm.com
SIC: 2821 Plastics materials and resins
HQ: Jps Composite Materials Corp.
2200 S Murray Ave
Anderson SC 29624
800 431-1110

(G-14827)
JR MOORESVILLE INC
1515 E Broad St (28625-4301)
PHONE.................973 434-6453
Robert Maneson, *Pr*
Wanda Rosella, *Sec*
EMP: 9 **EST:** 1993
SALES (est): 119.47K **Privately Held**
SIC: 2711 Newspapers, publishing and printing

(G-14828)
JS FIBER CO INC (PA)
290 Marble Rd (28625-2351)
PHONE.................704 871-1582
◆ **EMP:** 86 **EST:** 1989
SQ FT: 70,000
SALES (est): 10.11MM **Privately Held**
Web: www.jsfiber.com
SIC: 3949 2392 Sporting and athletic goods, nec; Cushions and pillows

(G-14829)
JS LINENS AND CURTAIN OUTLET (PA)
290 Marble Rd (28625-2351)
PHONE.................704 871-1582
Morris Long, *Pr*
EMP: 18 **EST:** 2010
SALES (est): 4.44MM
SALES (corp-wide): 4.44MM **Privately Held**
SIC: 5999 2392 Alcoholic beverage making equipment and supplies; Mattress pads

(G-14830)
KESELOWSKI ADVANCED MFG LLC
258 Aviation Dr (28677-2516)
PHONE.................704 799-0206
EMP: 42 **EST:** 2018
SALES (est): 5.29MM **Privately Held**
Web: www.kamsolutions.com
SIC: 3291 Abrasive metal and steel products

(G-14831)
KEWAUNEE SCIENTIFIC CORP (PA)
2700 W Front St (28677-2894)
P.O. Box 1842 (28687-1842)
PHONE.................704 873-7202
Thomas D Hull Iii, *Pr*
Keith M Gehl, *
Donald T Gardner Iii, *VP Fin*
Elizabeth D Phillips, *Pers/VP*
Ryan S Noble, *AMERICAS*
EMP: 916 **EST:** 1906
SQ FT: 413,000
SALES (est): 219.49MM
SALES (corp-wide): 219.49MM **Publicly Held**
Web: www.kewaunee.com
SIC: 3821 2599 Laboratory furniture; Factory furniture and fixtures

(G-14832)
KONPTEC PUBLISHING LLC
142 Sweet Gum Ln (28625-9179)
PHONE.................704 873-4262
Henry Shephard, *Prin*
EMP: 4 **EST:** 2018
SALES (est): 73.81K **Privately Held**
SIC: 2741 Miscellaneous publishing

(G-14833)
KOOKS CUSTOM HEADERS
2333 Salisbury Hwy (28677-1129)
PHONE.................704 838-1110
Auke De Pater, *Pr*
EMP: 7 **EST:** 2016
SALES (est): 212.07K **Privately Held**
Web: www.kooksheaders.com
SIC: 3714 Motor vehicle parts and accessories

(G-14834)
KOOKS CUSTOM HEADERS INC
141 Advantage Pl (28677-9793)
PHONE.................704 768-2288
▲ **EMP:** 30 **EST:** 1995
SQ FT: 45,000
SALES (est): 9.84MM **Privately Held**
Web: www.kooksheaders.com
SIC: 3498 Fabricated pipe and fittings

(G-14835)
LEGGETT & PLATT INCORPORATED
Also Called: Super Sagless
178 Orbit Rd (28677-8634)
PHONE.................704 380-6208
EMP: 4
SALES (corp-wide): 5.15B **Publicly Held**
Web: www.leggett.com

SIC: 2515 2514 3495 2392 Furniture springs ; Frames for box springs or bedsprings: metal; Wire springs; Mattress pads
PA: Leggett & Platt, Incorporated
1 Leggett Rd
Carthage MO 64836
417 358-8131

(G-14836)
MACHINE NUNN CNC SHOP LLC
1235 Old Mountain Rd (28677-2084)
PHONE.................704 873-4931
EMP: 4 **EST:** 2019
SALES (est): 89.64K **Privately Held**
Web: www.machinenunn.com
SIC: 3599 Machine shop, jobbing and repair

(G-14837)
MACK MOLDING COMPANY INC
149 Water Tank Rd (28677-8637)
PHONE.................704 878-9641
Joe Carinci, *Mgr*
EMP: 150
SALES (corp-wide): 856.43MM **Privately Held**
Web: www.mack.com
SIC: 3089 Injection molding of plastics
HQ: Mack Molding Company, Inc.
608 Warm Brook Rd
Arlington VT 05250
802 375-2511

(G-14838)
MANHATTAN WOODWORKING INC
302 Compton Park Rd (28677-8407)
PHONE.................704 528-5733
EMP: 5 **EST:** 2011
SALES (est): 70.23K **Privately Held**
SIC: 2431 Millwork

(G-14839)
MARIETTA MARTIN MATERIALS INC
Also Called: Martin Marietta Aggregates
220 Quarry Rd (28677)
PHONE.................704 873-8191
Paul Wear, *Mgr*
EMP: 5
Web: www.martinmarietta.com
SIC: 1422 Crushed and broken limestone
PA: Martin Marietta Materials Inc
4123 Parklake Ave
Raleigh NC 27612

(G-14840)
MCCOMBS STEEL COMPANY INC (PA)
117 Slingshot Rd (28677-8604)
PHONE.................704 873-7563
Marvin W Mccombs Iii, *Pr*
John L Payne, *
Peggy Mccombs, *Sec*
EMP: 49 **EST:** 1915
SQ FT: 34,000
SALES (est): 12.01MM
SALES (corp-wide): 12.01MM **Privately Held**
Web: www.mccombs-steel.com
SIC: 3441 5051 Building components, structural steel; Steel

(G-14841)
MERCHANTS METALS LLC
Also Called: Merchants Metals
165 Fanjoy Rd (28625-8567)
PHONE.................704 878-8706
Harshad Londhe, *Mgr*
EMP: 90
SQ FT: 68,612
SALES (corp-wide): 1.06B **Privately Held**
Web: www.merchantsmetals.com

Statesville - Iredell County (G-14842) — GEOGRAPHIC SECTION

SIC: **3315** 3496 Chain link fencing; Miscellaneous fabricated wire products
HQ: Merchants Metals Llc
3 Ravinia Dr Ste 1750
Atlanta GA 30346
770 741-0300

(G-14842)
MERICA LABZ LLC (PA)
1415 Wilkesboro Hwy (28625-3262)
PHONE.................................844 445-5335
EMP: 6 EST: 2016
SALES (est): 519.17K
SALES (corp-wide): 519.17K **Privately Held**
Web: www.mericalabz.com
SIC: **2023** Dietary supplements, dairy and non-dairy based

(G-14843)
MIL-COMM PRODUCTS INC
1010 Salisbury Rd (28677-6227)
PHONE.................................704 450-6415
EMP: 6 EST: 2018
SALES (est): 212.69K **Privately Held**
Web: www.mil-comm.com
SIC: **2992** Lubricating oils

(G-14844)
MOCARO DYEING & FINISHING INC
2201 Mocaro Dr (28677-3668)
P.O. Box 6689 (28687-6689)
PHONE.................................704 878-6645
EMP: 100
SQ FT: 250,000
SALES (est): 13.86MM **Privately Held**
SIC: **2257** Dyeing and finishing circular knit fabrics

(G-14845)
MOCARO INDUSTRIES INC
2201 Mocaro Dr (28677-3668)
P.O. Box 6689 (28687-6689)
PHONE.................................704 878-6645
T C Spell, *Pr*
George S Simon, *
Harry C Spell, *
EMP: 21 EST: 1987
SQ FT: 90,000
SALES (est): 782.32K **Privately Held**
Web: www.mocaro.com
SIC: **2257** 2269 Jersey cloth; Finishing plants, nec

(G-14846)
MODERN INFORMATION SVCS INC
Also Called: Sir Speedy
436 S Center St (28677-5841)
PHONE.................................704 872-1020
EMP: 8 EST: 1995
SQ FT: 1,300
SALES (est): 1.21MM **Privately Held**
Web: www.sirspeedy.com
SIC: **2752** Commercial printing, lithographic

(G-14847)
MOUNTAIRE FARMS LLC
Also Called: Statesville Breeder Feedmill
2206 W Front St (28677-2917)
PHONE.................................704 978-3055
EMP: 107
SALES (corp-wide): 2.07B **Privately Held**
Web: www.mountaire.com
SIC: **2048** Livestock feeds
HQ: Mountaire Farms Inc.
1901 Napa Valley Rd
Little Rock AR 72212
501 372-6524

(G-14848)
MOUNTAIRE FARMS INC
2206 W Front St (28677-2917)
PHONE.................................704 978-3055
Dabbs Cavin, *CFO*
EMP: 13 EST: 2014
SALES (est): 493.16K **Privately Held**
Web: www.mountaire.com
SIC: **2015** Poultry slaughtering and processing

(G-14849)
MR TIRE INC
149 E Front St (28677-5851)
PHONE.................................704 872-4127
Derek Jackson, *Brnch Mgr*
EMP: 8
SALES (corp-wide): 1.33B **Publicly Held**
Web: mrtireinc.business.site
SIC: **5531** 5941 5014 7534 Automotive tires; Bicycle and bicycle parts; Tires and tubes; Tire recapping
HQ: Mr. Tire Inc.
2078 New York Ave Unit 2
Huntington Station NY 11746
631 499-3700

(G-14850)
NATIONAL PEENING INC (DH)
Also Called: Wilmington National Peening
1902 Weinig St (28677-3189)
PHONE.................................704 872-0113
Richard Stewart, *Pr*
Tom Wolf, *Prin*
Chuck Amaspas, *Prin*
EMP: 18 EST: 1986
SQ FT: 24,000
SALES (est): 12.85MM **Privately Held**
Web: www.sintoamerica.com
SIC: **3398** Shot peening (treating steel to reduce fatigue)
HQ: Sinto America, Inc.
150 Orchard St
Grand Ledge MI 48837

(G-14851)
NORTH CAROLINA CONVERTING LLC
1001 Bucks Industrial Rd (28625-2575)
P.O. Box 18493 (28218-0493)
PHONE.................................704 871-2912
Michael J Dortch, *Managing Member*
EMP: 11 EST: 2008
SALES (est): 954.96K **Privately Held**
SIC: **2611** Pulp mills

(G-14852)
NORTH IREDELL GRINDING INC
542 Fairmount Rd (28625-9552)
PHONE.................................704 902-4771
EMP: 12 EST: 2011
SALES (est): 456.39K **Privately Held**
SIC: **3599** Grinding castings for the trade

(G-14853)
OAK STREET MFG
1903 Clayton St (28677-3144)
PHONE.................................877 465-4344
EMP: 5 EST: 2018
SALES (est): 235.43K **Privately Held**
Web: www.oakstreetmfg.com
SIC: **3999** Manufacturing industries, nec

(G-14854)
OHIO FOAM CORPORATION
Also Called: Ofc Fabricators
2185 Salisbury Hwy (28677-2780)
PHONE.................................704 883-8402
Sam Ross, *Brnch Mgr*
EMP: 10

SALES (corp-wide): 7.68MM **Privately Held**
Web: www.ohiofoam.com
SIC: **3069** Foam rubber
PA: Ohio Foam Corporation
820 Plymouth St
Bucyrus OH 44820
419 563-0399

(G-14855)
ORIGIN FOOD GROUP LLC
306 Stamey Farm Rd (28677-8326)
P.O. Box 7621 (28687-7621)
PHONE.................................704 768-9000
Barbara Alarcon, *
David Stamey, *
▲ EMP: 24 EST: 2010
SQ FT: 34,000
SALES (est): 8.32MM **Privately Held**
Web: www.originfoodgroup.com
SIC: **2026** Yogurt

(G-14856)
PARKER-HANNIFIN CORPORATION
Precision Fluidics
149 Crawford Rd (28625-8546)
PHONE.................................704 662-3500
EMP: 8
SALES (corp-wide): 19.07B **Publicly Held**
Web: www.parker.com
SIC: **3339** Primary nonferrous metals, nec
PA: Parker-Hannifin Corporation
6035 Parkland Blvd
Cleveland OH 44124
216 896-3000

(G-14857)
PASHES LLC
328 E Broad St (28677-5327)
PHONE.................................704 682-6535
Ernestina Peter, *Managing Member*
EMP: 6 EST: 2020
SALES (est): 379.93K **Privately Held**
SIC: **5641** 3999 8742 Children's and infants' wear stores; Hair and hair-based products; Retail trade consultant

(G-14858)
PEPSI BOTTLING VENTURES LLC
Also Called: Pepsi-Cola
1703 Gregory Rd (28677-3162)
PHONE.................................704 873-0249
Tom Byerly, *Mgr*
EMP: 49
Web: www.pepsico.com
SIC: **2086** Carbonated soft drinks, bottled and canned
HQ: Pepsi Bottling Ventures Llc
4141 Parklake Ave Ste 600
Raleigh NC 27612
919 865-2300

(G-14859)
PIEDMONT FIBERGLASS INC
1166 Bunch Dr (28677-3261)
PHONE.................................828 632-8883
EMP: 30
Web: www.piedmontcomposites.com
SIC: **5999** 3544 7389 3949 Fiberglass materials, except insulation; Forms (molds), for foundry and plastics working machinery; Crane and aerial lift service; Sporting and athletic goods, nec

(G-14860)
PINE VIEW BUILDINGS LLC
933 Tomlin Mill Rd (28625-1597)
P.O. Box 120 (28688-0120)
PHONE.................................704 876-1501
EMP: 85 EST: 2013
SALES (est): 8.66MM **Privately Held**

Web: www.pineviewbuildings.com
SIC: **3448** Prefabricated metal buildings and components

(G-14861)
PLASGAD USA LLC
933 Meacham Rd Ste C (28677-2985)
PHONE.................................704 775-6461
Ido Shifroni, *CEO*
EMP: 29 EST: 2019
SALES (est): 5.21MM **Privately Held**
Web: www.plasgad.com
SIC: **3089** Plastics containers, except foam

(G-14862)
PLASTIFLEX NORTH CAROLINA LLC
2101 Sherrill Dr (28625-9052)
PHONE.................................704 871-8448
Peter Dirkx, *COO*
Hennie Kunneke, *
EMP: 53 EST: 2000
SALES (est): 19.12MM
SALES (corp-wide): 857.59K **Privately Held**
Web: www.plastiflex.com
SIC: **3052** Rubber and plastics hose and beltings
HQ: Plastiflex Company Inc.
601 E Palomar St Ste 424
Chula Vista CA 91911

(G-14863)
POLY ONE DISTRIBUTION
114 Morehead Rd (28677-2744)
PHONE.................................704 872-8168
Greg Mason, *Mgr*
EMP: 5 EST: 2014
SALES (est): 123.68K **Privately Held**
SIC: **2821** Thermoplastic materials

(G-14864)
POLYONE CORPORATION
POLYONE CORPORATION
114 Morehead Rd (28677-2744)
PHONE.................................704 838-0457
Greg Mason, *Mgr*
EMP: 4
Web: www.avient.com
SIC: **2821** Plastics materials and resins
PA: Avient Corporation
33587 Walker Rd
Avon Lake OH 44012

(G-14865)
PRATT (JET CORR) INC
Also Called: Pratt Industries USA
185 Deer Ridge Dr (28625-2502)
PHONE.................................704 878-6615
Bill Lefler, *Genl Mgr*
EMP: 629
Web: www.prattindustries.com
SIC: **2653** 2631 Boxes, corrugated: made from purchased materials; Paperboard mills
HQ: Pratt (Jet Corr), Inc.
1800 Sarasot Bus Pkwy Ne B
Conyers GA 30013
770 929-1300

(G-14866)
PRATT INDUSTRIES INC
185 Deer Ridge Dr (28625-2502)
PHONE.................................704 878-6615
Anthony Pratt, *Brnch Mgr*
EMP: 260
Web: www.prattindustries.com
SIC: **2653** Boxes, corrugated: made from purchased materials
PA: Pratt Industries, Inc.
1800 Sarasota Pkwy Ne C
Conyers GA 30013

GEOGRAPHIC SECTION
Statesville - Iredell County (G-14893)

(G-14867)
PRECISION MINDSET PLLC
130 April Showers Ln (28677-8003)
PHONE.................704 508-1314
Ronnie Fesperman, *Prin*
EMP: 5 **EST:** 2015
SALES (est): 76.72K **Privately Held**
SIC: 3599 Industrial machinery, nec

(G-14868)
PRETINNED CARBIDE CO INC
251 Commerce Blvd Unit G (28625-8565)
PHONE.................704 871-9644
Shelba Bissel, *Owner*
EMP: 10 **EST:** 2007
SALES (est): 494.71K **Privately Held**
Web: www.pretinnedcarbide.com
SIC: 2819 Industrial inorganic chemicals, nec

(G-14869)
PRINTCRAFTERS INCORPORATED
115 W Water St (28677-5250)
P.O. Box 343 (28687-0343)
PHONE.................704 873-7387
Joseph Tomlin Junior, *Pr*
Sarah Tomlin, *Sec*
EMP: 6 **EST:** 1949
SQ FT: 8,000
SALES (est): 526.61K **Privately Held**
Web: www.printcraftersnc.com
SIC: 2752 Offset printing

(G-14870)
PRO-TECH INC
1256 N Barkley Rd (28677-9726)
PHONE.................704 872-6227
Jim Sutton, *Pr*
Keith Norris, *VP*
J Christopher Sutton, *VP*
▲ **EMP:** 7 **EST:** 1975
SALES (est): 898.05K **Privately Held**
Web: www.pro-techinc.com
SIC: 3625 Control equipment, electric

(G-14871)
PROEDGE PRECISION LLC
113 Hatfield Rd (28625-8999)
PHONE.................704 872-3393
Joseph Chambers, *Pr*
EMP: 20 **EST:** 2012
SALES (est): 1.81MM **Privately Held**
Web: www.proedgeprecision.com
SIC: 3599 3728 Machine shop, jobbing and repair; Aircraft parts and equipment, nec

(G-14872)
PROVIDENCIA USA INC
200 Deer Ridge Dr (28625-2526)
PHONE.................704 881-2837
Herminio Freitas, *Pr*
Gene Konczal, *
Jian Wend, *
▲ **EMP:** 98 **EST:** 2008
SQ FT: 176,000
SALES (est): 10.18MM **Privately Held**
SIC: 2297 Spunbonded fabrics

(G-14873)
PURINA MILLS LLC
Also Called: Purina Mills
173 Mcness Rd (28677-2742)
PHONE.................704 872-0456
EMP: 53
SALES (corp-wide): 2.89B **Privately Held**
Web: www.purina-mills.com
SIC: 2048 Prepared feeds, nec
HQ: Purina Mills, Llc
    555 Mryvlle Univ Dr Ste 2
    Saint Louis MO 63141

(G-14874)
R GREGORY JEWELERS INC (PA)
122 W Broad St (28677-5256)
PHONE.................704 872-6669
Rick Gregory, *Pr*
Pamela Gregory, *Sec*
EMP: 10 **EST:** 1981
SQ FT: 4,000
SALES (est): 1.42MM
SALES (corp-wide): 1.42MM **Privately Held**
Web: www.rgregoryjewelers.com
SIC: 5944 3911 7631 Jewelry, precious stones and precious metals; Jewelry, precious metal; Jewelry repair services

(G-14875)
REAGAN ENTERPRISES LLC
183 Natures Trl (28625-2005)
PHONE.................704 564-7588
EMP: 4 **EST:** 2019
SALES (est): 218.19K **Privately Held**
Web: www.reaganenterprises.com
SIC: 3444 Sheet metalwork

(G-14876)
REISSMANN ENTERTAINMENT INC
126 Upper Lake Dr (28677-9304)
PHONE.................734 641-4434
EMP: 4 **EST:** 2018
SALES (est): 63.64K **Privately Held**
SIC: 3952 Lead pencils and art goods

(G-14877)
ROADMASTERS TRAFFIC CTRL LLC
120 Tweety Bird Ln (28625-1883)
P.O. Box 7351 (28687-7351)
PHONE.................704 585-9635
EMP: 5 **EST:** 2012
SALES (est): 224.45K **Privately Held**
Web: www.roadmasterstrafficcontrol.com
SIC: 7389 3669 Flagging service (traffic control); Pedestrian traffic control equipment

(G-14878)
ROTARY CLUB STATESVILLE
318 N Center St (28677-4064)
PHONE.................704 872-6851
EMP: 10 **EST:** 2010
SALES (est): 89.95K **Privately Held**
Web: www.statesville.com
SIC: 2711 Newspapers, publishing and printing

(G-14879)
RPAC RACING LLC
Also Called: Richard Petty Motorsports
310 Aviation Dr (28677-2509)
PHONE.................704 696-8650
EMP: 93 **EST:** 2010
SALES (est): 9.98MM **Privately Held**
Web: www.legacymotorclub.com
SIC: 7948 3444 Race car drivers; Sheet metalwork

(G-14880)
RPM PLASTICS INC
Also Called: RPM Plastics
2301 Speedball Rd (28677-2989)
PHONE.................704 871-0518
John R Hobson, *Pr*
EMP: 17 **EST:** 2008
SALES (est): 827.69K **Privately Held**
SIC: 3089 Injection molding of plastics

(G-14881)
RPM PLASTICS LLC
933 Meacham Rd (28677-2985)
PHONE.................704 871-0518
John Hobson, *Managing Member*
Kim Lookadoo, *
EMP: 50 **EST:** 2009
SALES (est): 9.84MM **Privately Held**
SIC: 3089 1796 5084 Injection molding of plastics; Machine moving and rigging; Industrial machinery and equipment

(G-14882)
RPM PRODUCTS INC
2301 Speedball Rd (28677-2989)
PHONE.................704 871-0518
John R Hobson, *Pr*
EMP: 13 **EST:** 2005
SQ FT: 4,000
SALES (est): 806.39K **Privately Held**
SIC: 5047 3089 Medical and hospital equipment; Injection molding of plastics

(G-14883)
SACKNER PRODUCTS INC
178 Orbit Rd (28677-8634)
PHONE.................704 873-1086
EMP: 6 **EST:** 1966
SALES (est): 264.53K **Privately Held**
SIC: 2298 Cordage and twine

(G-14884)
SHADOW CREEK CONSULTING INC
124 Commerce Blvd (28625-8526)
PHONE.................716 860-7397
Karen Erickson, *Pr*
Pauly Erickson, *VP*
EMP: 20 **EST:** 2012
SALES (est): 1.15MM **Privately Held**
SIC: 2899 Essential oils

(G-14885)
SHERWIN-WILLIAMS COMPANY
Also Called: Sherwin-Williams
188 Side Track Dr (28625-2543)
PHONE.................704 881-0245
EMP: 28
SALES (corp-wide): 22.15B **Publicly Held**
Web: www.sherwin-williams.com
SIC: 2851 Paints and paint additives
PA: The Sherwin-Williams Company
    101 W Prospect Ave # 1020
    Cleveland OH 44115
    216 566-2000

(G-14886)
SKLAR BOV SOLUTIONS INC
Also Called: Bov Solutions
1105 E Garner Bagnal Blvd (28677-6967)
PHONE.................704 872-7277
John Scheld, *Mgr*
EMP: 12
SALES (corp-wide): 12MM **Privately Held**
Web: www.bovsolutions.com
SIC: 2844 Concentrates, perfume
PA: Sklar Bov Solutions, Inc.
    3137 E 26th St
    Vernon CA 90058
    352 746-6731

(G-14887)
SLADE OPERATING COMPANY LLC
Also Called: Slade
181 Crawford Rd (28625-8546)
PHONE.................704 873-1366
Greg Raty, *Pr*
EMP: 25 **EST:** 2021
SQ FT: 62,000
SALES (est): 2.41MM
SALES (corp-wide): 5.69MM **Privately Held**
Web: www.egcgraphite.com
SIC: 3053 3624 2891 Gaskets; packing and sealing devices; Carbon and graphite products; Adhesives and sealants
PA: Egc Operating Company, Llc
    140 Parker Ct
    Chardon OH 44024
    440 285-5835

(G-14888)
SLANE O W GLASS CO INC
606 Meacham Rd (28677-2978)
P.O. Box 449 (28166-0449)
PHONE.................704 872-4291
Tom Slane, *Pr*
T Clayton Slane, *VP*
Pam Childers, *Sec*
◆ **EMP:** 10 **EST:** 1906
SQ FT: 70,000
SALES (est): 374.41K **Privately Held**
SIC: 3231 3229 Mirrored glass; Pressed and blown glass, nec

(G-14889)
SOUTHEAST TUBULAR PRODUCTS INC
Also Called: Stpi
1308 Industrial Dr (28625-6249)
PHONE.................704 883-8883
Thomas O Loftin, *
Thomas O Loftin, *
Fred H Stubblefield Junior, *VP*
Neil Loftin, *
Brenda S Loftin, *
EMP: 45 **EST:** 2000
SQ FT: 55,000
SALES (est): 9.17MM **Privately Held**
Web: www.setube.com
SIC: 3312 Tubes, steel and iron

(G-14890)
SOUTHEASTERN CONCRETE PDTS CO
2325 Salisbury Hwy (28677-1129)
P.O. Box 5188 (28687-5188)
PHONE.................704 873-2226
Herman Hammer, *Mgr*
EMP: 58 **EST:** 2002
SALES (est): 1.67MM
SALES (corp-wide): 24.3MM **Privately Held**
SIC: 3271 3272 Concrete block and brick; Pipe, concrete or lined with concrete
PA: Southeastern Concrete Products Company
    917 Frink St
    Cayce SC 29033
    803 794-7363

(G-14891)
SOUTHERN DISTILLING CO LLC
Also Called: Southern Distilling Company
211 Jennings Rd (28625-9447)
PHONE.................704 677-4069
Stacey Barger, *Managing Member*
EMP: 4 **EST:** 2021
SALES (est): 1.02MM **Privately Held**
Web: www.southerndistillingcompany.com
SIC: 2429 2085 Barrels and barrel parts; Distilled and blended liquors

(G-14892)
SOUTHERN HARDSCAPE PDTS INC
126 Orbit Rd (28677-5097)
PHONE.................704 528-6726
EMP: 7 **EST:** 2013
SALES (est): 380.73K **Privately Held**
SIC: 3271 Concrete block and brick

(G-14893)
SOUTHERN PRESTIGE INDUSTRIES INC
Also Called: Precision Processing System

Statesville - Iredell County (G-14894)

113 Hatfield Rd (28625-8999)
PHONE...................704 872-9524
EMP: 50
SIC: 3599 Machine and other job shop work

(G-14894)
SOUTHERN PRESTIGE INTL LLC
113 Hatfield Rd (28625-8999)
PHONE...................704 872-9524
Jeffrey Eidson, *
James Wilson, *
EMP: 13 EST: 2015
SALES (est): 2.47MM Privately Held
Web: www.southernprestige.com
SIC: 3081 3599 3728 Polyvinyl film and sheet ; Electrical discharge machining (EDM); Aircraft parts and equipment, nec

(G-14895)
SOUTHERN STAR CSTM FBRCTION LL
1033 Buffalo Shoals Rd (28677-8673)
PHONE...................704 880-8948
EMP: 5 EST: 2019
SALES (est): 68.6K Privately Held
SIC: 7692 Welding repair

(G-14896)
SOUTHERN STATES COOP INC
Also Called: S S C 7912-7
2504 Davie Ave (28625-9249)
PHONE...................704 872-6364
Roger Clement, Mgr
EMP: 31
SQ FT: 9,270
SALES (corp-wide): 1.71B Privately Held
Web: www.southernstates.com
SIC: 2048 2873 0181 2874 Prepared feeds, nec; Nitrogenous fertilizers; Bulbs and seeds; Phosphatic fertilizers
PA: Southern States Cooperative, Incorporated
    6606 W Broad St Ste B
    Richmond VA 23230
    804 281-1000

(G-14897)
SPECIALTY PERF LLC
228 Crawford Rd (28625-8541)
PHONE...................704 872-9980
EMP: 6 EST: 2015
SALES (est): 423.84K Privately Held
Web: www.specialtyperforating.com
SIC: 3081 3599 3728 Polyvinyl film and sheet ; Electrical discharge machining (EDM); Aircraft parts and equipment, nec

(G-14898)
SPEEDBALL ART PRODUCTS CO LLC
Also Called: Speedball Art Products
2301 Speedball Rd (28677-2989)
PHONE...................800 898-7424
◆ EMP: 55 EST: 1997
SQ FT: 224,000
SALES (est): 13.73MM Privately Held
Web: www.speedballart.com
SIC: 3952 Artists' materials, except pencils and leads

(G-14899)
SPINTECH LLC
159 Walker Rd (28625-2535)
PHONE...................704 885-4758
Jian Weng, Managing Member
EMP: 40 EST: 2020
SALES (est): 5MM Privately Held
Web: www.spintech-usa.com
SIC: 3842 Personal safety equipment

(G-14900)
STAR MILLING COMPANY
247 Commerce Blvd Unit F (28625-8564)
P.O. Box 5067 (28687-5067)
PHONE...................704 873-9561
James T Cashion Junior, Pr
James T Cashion Iii, Sec
Julia Cashion Johnson, Stockholder
EMP: 5 EST: 1910
SQ FT: 2,000
SALES (est): 859.3K Privately Held
Web: www.starmilling.com
SIC: 2048 Prepared feeds, nec

(G-14901)
STATESVILLE BRICK COMPANY
391 Brick Yard Rd (28677-9383)
P.O. Box 471 (28687-0471)
PHONE...................704 872-4123
EMP: 75 EST: 1903
SALES (est): 9.03MM Privately Held
Web: www.statesvillebrick.com
SIC: 3251 Brick clay: common face, glazed, vitrified, or hollow

(G-14902)
STATESVILLE HIGH
474 N Center St (28677-4022)
PHONE...................704 873-3491
Ted Millsaps, Prin
EMP: 10 EST: 2008
SALES (est): 240.08K Privately Held
Web: www.statesville.com
SIC: 2711 Newspapers, publishing and printing

(G-14903)
STATESVILLE LLC
151 Walker Rd (28625-2535)
PHONE...................704 872-3303
EMP: 6 EST: 2018
SALES (est): 197.72K Privately Held
Web: www.statesville.com
SIC: 2711 Newspapers, publishing and printing

(G-14904)
STATESVILLE MED MGT SVCS LLC
1503 E Broad St (28625-4301)
PHONE...................704 996-6748
EMP: 14 EST: 2011
SALES (est): 1.29MM Privately Held
Web: www.statesvillechamber.org
SIC: 8062 3841 8011 General medical and surgical hospitals; Surgical and medical instruments; Medical centers

(G-14905)
STATESVILLE SANDLOT BASBAL INC
165 Eastwood Dr (28625-4556)
PHONE...................704 880-1334
Mike Grant, Prin
EMP: 6 EST: 2019
SALES (est): 111.88K Privately Held
SIC: 2711 Newspapers, publishing and printing

(G-14906)
STEELCRAFT STRUCTURES LLC
1841 Amity Hill Rd (28677-7203)
P.O. Box 6177 (28687-6177)
PHONE...................980 434-5400
James Paquette, Managing Member
EMP: 7 EST: 2020
SALES (est): 943.66K Privately Held
Web: www.steelcraftmetal.com
SIC: 3441 Fabricated structural metal

(G-14907)
STOVERS PRECISION TOOLING INC
239 Treebark Rd (28625-1262)
PHONE...................704 876-3673
EMP: 6 EST: 1994
SALES (est): 490.07K Privately Held
SIC: 3599 Machine shop, jobbing and repair

(G-14908)
SUMTER PACKAGING CORPORATION
844 Meacham Rd (28677-2982)
PHONE...................704 873-0583
EMP: 5
SALES (corp-wide): 13.87MM Privately Held
Web: www.sumterpackaging.com
SIC: 2653 Boxes, corrugated: made from purchased materials
PA: Sumter Packaging Corporation
    2341 Corporate Way
    Sumter SC 29154
    803 481-2003

(G-14909)
T & J PANEL SYSTEMS INC
269 Marble Rd (28625-2351)
PHONE...................704 924-8600
Timothy Johnson, Pr
EMP: 9 EST: 1997
SALES (est): 718.28K Privately Held
Web: www.tjpanel.com
SIC: 2522 Panel systems and partitions, office: except wood

(G-14910)
TALLENT WOOD WORKS
113 Kammerer Dr (28625-1651)
PHONE...................704 592-2013
EMP: 4 EST: 2017
SALES (est): 54.13K Privately Held
SIC: 2431 Millwork

(G-14911)
THORNEBURG HOSIERY MILLS INC
1515 W Front St (28677-3638)
P.O. Box 5399 (28687-5399)
PHONE...................704 872-6522
James L Thorneburg, Mgr
EMP: 27
SALES (corp-wide): 45.57MM Privately Held
Web: www.thmills.com
SIC: 2252 Socks
PA: Thorneburg Hosiery Mills, Inc.
    2210 Newton Dr
    Statesville NC 28677
    704 872-6522

(G-14912)
THORNEBURG HOSIERY MILLS INC (PA)
Also Called: Th Mills
2210 Newton Dr (28677-4850)
P.O. Box 5399 (28687-5399)
PHONE...................704 872-6522
James L Thorneburg, CEO
Richard Oliver Junior, Pr
Robert B Tucker Junior, Sec
◆ EMP: 131 EST: 1952
SQ FT: 85,000
SALES (est): 45.57MM
SALES (corp-wide): 45.57MM Privately Held
Web: www.thmills.com
SIC: 2252 Socks

(G-14913)
THORNEBURG HOSIERY MILLS INC
1519 W Front St (28677-3638)
PHONE...................704 838-6329
Richard Oliver, Mgr
EMP: 26
SALES (corp-wide): 45.57MM Privately Held
Web: www.thmills.com
SIC: 2252 2251 Socks; Women's hosiery, except socks
PA: Thorneburg Hosiery Mills, Inc.
    2210 Newton Dr
    Statesville NC 28677
    704 872-6522

(G-14914)
TIMBER SPECIALISTS INC
2123 Shelton Ave (28677-2761)
PHONE...................704 902-5146
James E Johnson, Pr
EMP: 8 EST: 2005
SALES (est): 944.25K Privately Held
SIC: 2411 Timber, cut at logging camp

(G-14915)
TIMBER SPECIALISTS LLC
2511 Heritage Cir (28625-4411)
PHONE...................704 873-5756
James Johnson, Prin
EMP: 10 EST: 1999
SALES (est): 955.54K Privately Held
SIC: 2411 Logging camps and contractors

(G-14916)
TOTER LLC (DH)
841 Meacham Rd (28677-2983)
P.O. Box 5338 (28687-5338)
PHONE...................800 424-0422
John Scott, Pr
Steve Svetik, *
◆ EMP: 69 EST: 1983
SQ FT: 200,000
SALES (est): 46.17MM Privately Held
Web: www.toter.com
SIC: 3089 3536 3469 3412 Garbage containers, plastics; Hoists; Metal stampings, nec; Metal barrels, drums, and pails
HQ: Wastequip, Llc
    6525 Carnegie Blvd # 300
    Charlotte NC 28211

(G-14917)
TRICK KARTS INC
Also Called: Tubular Resources
935 Shelton Ave (28677-6726)
PHONE...................704 883-0089
Mark Mode, Pr
EMP: 4 EST: 1975
SALES (est): 279.68K Privately Held
Web: www.trickolimpic.com
SIC: 3799 5531 Go-carts, except children's; Auto and home supply stores

(G-14918)
TRIVANTAGE
1803 Salisbury Rd (28677-6219)
PHONE...................800 438-1061
EMP: 7 EST: 2019
SALES (est): 221.3K Privately Held
Web: www.trivantage.com
SIC: 2394 Canvas and related products

(G-14919)
TSAI WINDDOWN INC
607 Meacham Rd (28677-2979)
PHONE...................704 873-3106
▲ EMP: 21
SIC: 2511 Wood household furniture

GEOGRAPHIC SECTION

(G-14920)
TUBE SPECIALTIES CO INC
Also Called: PS Cisco
1401 Industrial Dr (28625-6263)
PHONE.................................704 818-8933
Gerald Mckley, *Brnch Mgr*
EMP: 150
Web: www.nelsongp.com
SIC: 3498 Tube fabricating (contract bending and shaping)
HQ: Tube Specialties Co., Inc.
   1459 Nw Sundial Rd
   Troutdale OR 97060
   503 674-8705

(G-14921)
UNIQUE IMPRESSIONS
1906 E Broad St (28625-4310)
PHONE.................................704 873-3241
Donna Kendall, *Prin*
EMP: 5 **EST:** 2010
SALES (est): 115.16K **Privately Held**
SIC: 2759 Screen printing

(G-14922)
US PLASTIC MOLDINGS
1711 Gregory Rd (28677-3162)
PHONE.................................800 262-2111
EMP: 4 **EST:** 2019
SALES (est): 64.65K **Privately Held**
Web: www.usplasticmoldings.com
SIC: 3089 Injection molding of plastics

(G-14923)
WASTEQUIP
841 Meacham Rd (28677-2983)
PHONE.................................800 255-4126
EMP: 13 **EST:** 2018
SALES (est): 2.14MM **Privately Held**
Web: www.wastequip.com
SIC: 3559 Special industry machinery, nec

(G-14924)
WEST SIDE INDUSTRIES LLC
124 Hatfield Rd (28625-8999)
PHONE.................................980 223-8665
David Gizzi, *Pt*
David Gizzi, *Admn*
EMP: 6 **EST:** 2013
SALES (est): 711.04K **Privately Held**
Web: www.westsideindustries.us
SIC: 3999 3499 3451 Barber and beauty shop equipment; Fire- or burglary-resistive products; Screw machine products

(G-14925)
WEST SIDE PRCSION MCH PDTS INC
124 Hatfield Rd (28625-8999)
PHONE.................................908 647-4903
David Gizzi, *Pr*
Joseph Petitti, *VP*
▼ **EMP:** 10 **EST:** 1944
SQ FT: 5,000
SALES (est): 949.57K **Privately Held**
Web: www.westsideindustries.us
SIC: 3599 Machine shop, jobbing and repair

(G-14926)
WIND DEFENDER LLC
2690 Salisbury Hwy (28677-1154)
PHONE.................................410 913-4660
EMP: 5 **EST:** 2019
SALES (est): 472.25K **Privately Held**
SIC: 2299 Upholstery filling, textile

(G-14927)
WINECOFF MMRALS STTESVILLE INC
Also Called: Winecoff Memorials
2120 Newton Dr (28677-4848)
PHONE.................................704 873-9661
Steve Bridle, *Pr*
Elizabeth Bridle, *VP*
EMP: 9 **EST:** 2000
SQ FT: 6,000
SALES (est): 940.06K **Privately Held**
Web: www.winecoff.com
SIC: 5999 3281 Gravestones, finished; Tombstones, cut stone (not finishing or lettering only)

(G-14928)
WOOD TONE MUSIC PUBLISHING
287 Massey Deal Rd (28625-8822)
PHONE.................................704 659-1064
Jason Wood, *Prin*
EMP: 4 **EST:** 2015
SALES (est): 60.44K **Privately Held**
SIC: 2741 Miscellaneous publishing

(G-14929)
WWJ LLC (PA)
Also Called: Acoustek Nonwovens
1002 Bucks Industrial Rd (28625-2581)
P.O. Box 4846 (28117-4846)
PHONE.................................704 871-8500
▼ **EMP:** 45 **EST:** 1990
SQ FT: 80,000
SALES (est): 9.99MM **Privately Held**
SIC: 3296 Fiberglass insulation

(G-14930)
XCELERATOR BOATWORKS INC (PA)
154 Commerce Blvd (28625-8526)
PHONE.................................704 622-8978
Joel Kauffman, *Prin*
EMP: 5 **EST:** 2010
SALES (est): 382.49K
SALES (corp-wide): 382.49K **Privately Held**
SIC: 3732 Boatbuilding and repairing

(G-14931)
YANJAN USA LLC
159 Walker Rd (28625-2535)
PHONE.................................704 380-6230
Jian Weng, *Pr*
Gene Konzzal, *CFO*
▲ **EMP:** 115 **EST:** 2017
SQ FT: 50,000
SALES (est): 10.18MM **Privately Held**
SIC: 2297 Nonwoven fabrics
PA: Xiamen Yanjan New Material Co.Ltd.
   No.666, Houdi Road, Industrial Cluster Zone, Xiang'an District
   Xiamen FJ 36119

(G-14932)
ZNDUS INC (DH)
214 James Farm Rd (28625-2714)
PHONE.................................704 981-8660
James Murphy, *Pr*
EMP: 4 **EST:** 2019
SALES (est): 4.49MM **Privately Held**
Web: www.znd.com
SIC: 3315 Fence gates, posts, and fittings: steel
HQ: Znd Group B.V.
   John F. Kennedylaan 22
   Valkenswaard NB

Stedman
Cumberland County

(G-14933)
AUTRY LOGGING INC
824 Magnolia Church Rd (28391-8677)
PHONE.................................910 303-4943
Jamey Autry, *Pr*
EMP: 4 **EST:** 2012
SALES (est): 318.55K **Privately Held**
SIC: 2411 Logging

(G-14934)
CYNTHIA SAAR
Also Called: Cardinal Cabinets Distinction
5139 Front St (28391-9603)
PHONE.................................910 480-2523
Cynthia Saar, *Owner*
EMP: 4 **EST:** 2010
SALES (est): 219.19K **Privately Held**
SIC: 2434 5712 2521 Wood kitchen cabinets ; Customized furniture and cabinets; Wood office filing cabinets and bookcases

(G-14935)
FARMHOUSE STITCHING
1029 Horne Farm Rd (28391-8454)
PHONE.................................910 308-7308
EMP: 5 **EST:** 2013
SALES (est): 49.02K **Privately Held**
SIC: 2395 Embroidery and art needlework

(G-14936)
POSH PAD
700 Mill Bay Dr (28391-8453)
PHONE.................................910 988-4800
Jacqueline Alphin, *Prin*
EMP: 5 **EST:** 2011
SALES (est): 170K **Privately Held**
SIC: 3699 Christmas tree lighting sets, electric

(G-14937)
TARHEEL ENVIROMENTAL LLC
633 Fred Hall Rd (28391-8408)
PHONE.................................910 425-4939
EMP: 4 **EST:** 2008
SALES (est): 390K **Privately Held**
SIC: 2875 Compost

Stella
Carteret County

(G-14938)
WETHERINGTON LOGGING INC
245 Walters Ln (28582-9744)
PHONE.................................252 393-8435
Walter Jon, *Pr*
Dora Wetherington, *Sec*
EMP: 9 **EST:** 1975
SALES (est): 395.19K **Privately Held**
SIC: 2411 Logging camps and contractors

Stem
Granville County

(G-14939)
TRIANGLE HRSE BLANKET SVCS LLC
3528 Fletchers Way (27581-9348)
PHONE.................................919 945-9560
Sapphhira Lamarche, *Prin*
EMP: 4 **EST:** 2018
SALES (est): 62.29K **Privately Held**
SIC: 2399 Horse blankets

Stokesdale
Guilford County

(G-14940)
CULP INC
Culps Knits
7209 Us Highway 158 (27357-9344)
P.O. Box 488 (27357-0488)
PHONE.................................336 885-2800
Denise Miles, *Mgr*
EMP: 49
SALES (corp-wide): 234.93MM **Publicly Held**
Web: www.culp.com
SIC: 2515 Mattresses and bedsprings
PA: Culp, Inc.
   1823 Eastchester Dr
   High Point NC 27265
   336 889-5161

(G-14941)
CULP INC
Also Called: Culp Ticking
7209 Us Highway 158 (27357-9344)
P.O. Box 488 (27357-0488)
PHONE.................................336 643-7751
Elena Arnold Knit, *Dir*
EMP: 172
SALES (corp-wide): 234.93MM **Publicly Held**
Web: www.culp.com
SIC: 2211 2396 Tickings; Automotive and apparel trimmings
PA: Culp, Inc.
   1823 Eastchester Dr
   High Point NC 27265
   336 889-5161

(G-14942)
FRIDDLES CUSTOM SAWING
117 Thrush Rd (27357-8530)
PHONE.................................336 210-0144
Harvey Friddle, *Prin*
EMP: 5 **EST:** 2011
SALES (est): 246.43K **Privately Held**
Web: www.friddlewood.com
SIC: 2421 Sawmills and planing mills, general

(G-14943)
JR S CUSTOM WOODWORKS
7951 Lester Rd (27357-8301)
PHONE.................................336 643-1524
EMP: 4 **EST:** 2017
SALES (est): 88.66K **Privately Held**
SIC: 2431 Millwork

(G-14944)
KALO FOODS LLC
Also Called: Kalo Foods
119 Carlton Park Dr (27357-8578)
PHONE.................................336 949-4802
Michael Cusato, *Pt*
EMP: 8 **EST:** 2012
SQ FT: 7,800
SALES (est): 965.67K **Privately Held**
Web: www.kalofoods.com
SIC: 2038 2053 2052 Frozen specialties, nec ; Frozen bakery products, except bread; Cookies

(G-14945)
LAMINATION SERVICES INC
6919 Us Highway 158 (27357-9341)
P.O. Box 188 (27358-0188)
PHONE.................................336 643-7369
Mark Stroud, *Pr*
EMP: 22 **EST:** 1989
SQ FT: 25,000
SALES (est): 4.93MM **Privately Held**
Web: www.laminationservicesinc.com
SIC: 3089 Plastics processing

(G-14946)
MIRROR IMAGE PUBLISHING LLC
9091 Us Highway 158 (27357-9275)
PHONE.................................336 643-7638
Cornella Jackson, *Prin*
EMP: 4 **EST:** 2016

Stokesdale - Guilford County (G-14947)

SALES (est): 59.23K **Privately Held**
SIC: 2741 Miscellaneous publishing

(G-14947)
ONTEX OPERATIONS USA LLC (HQ)
Also Called: Ontex North America
9300 Nc Highway 65 (27357-8436)
PHONE 770 346-9250
James Alan Skinner, *Pr*
EMP: 53 **EST:** 2020
SALES (est): 26.69MM
SALES (corp-wide): 2.67MM **Privately Held**
SIC: 2676 Feminine hygiene paper products
PA: Ontex Group
  Korte Keppestraat 21
  Aalst 9320
  53333600

(G-14948)
S SHELTON INC
9037 Ellisboro Rd (27357-9213)
PHONE 336 643-5916
EMP: 4 **EST:** 2019
SALES (est): 91.5K **Privately Held**
SIC: 2434 Wood kitchen cabinets

(G-14949)
SOUTHERN SPRING & STAMPING
2089 Us Highway 220 (27357-8540)
PHONE 336 548-3520
Jeff Artz, *Mgr*
EMP: 17
SALES (corp-wide): 12MM **Privately Held**
Web: www.southernspring.com
SIC: 3469 5085 Stamping metal for the trade; Springs
PA: Southern Spring & Stamping Inc
  401 Substation Rd
  Venice FL 34285
  941 488-2276

(G-14950)
STACKZ WELDING
8301 Zebedee Ln (27357-9200)
PHONE 336 564-5481
Xaiver Delan Campbell, *Prin*
EMP: 4 **EST:** 2019
SALES (est): 64.24K **Privately Held**
SIC: 7692 Welding repair

(G-14951)
STONEFIELD CELLARS LLC
8220 Nc Highway 68 N (27357-9330)
PHONE 336 632-2391
EMP: 6 **EST:** 2009
SALES (est): 329.89K **Privately Held**
Web: www.stonefieldcellars.com
SIC: 2084 Wines

(G-14952)
WOODWIZARDS INC
4214 Ellisboro Rd (27357-8053)
PHONE 336 427-7698
Randy Neal, *Pr*
Pamela Neal, *Sec*
EMP: 5 **EST:** 2003
SALES (est): 357.38K **Privately Held**
SIC: 2431 Woodwork, interior and ornamental, nec

Stoneville
Rockingham County

(G-14953)
AMERICAN WOODMARK CORPORATION
300 S Henry St (27048-8070)
PHONE 540 665-9100
EMP: 6
SALES (corp-wide): 2.07B **Publicly Held**
Web: www.americanwoodmark.com
SIC: 2434 Vanities, bathroom: wood
PA: American Woodmark Corporation
  561 Shady Elm Rd
  Winchester VA 22602
  540 665-9100

(G-14954)
CAROLINA-VIRGINIA MFG CO INC
2873 Nc Highway 135 (27048-7571)
PHONE 336 623-1307
EMP: 5 **EST:** 2018
SALES (est): 94.54K **Privately Held**
SIC: 3444 Sheet metalwork

(G-14955)
CLAYBROOK TIRE INC
101 N Glenn St (27048-8641)
P.O. Box 92 (27048-0092)
PHONE 336 573-3135
L Mike Claybrook, *Pr*
Jessica Reeder, *Sec*
EMP: 10 **EST:** 1946
SQ FT: 1,800
SALES (est): 1.18MM **Privately Held**
Web: www.claybrooktires.com
SIC: 5531 7534 7539 Automotive tires; Tire recapping; Wheel alignment, automotive

(G-14956)
CREATIVE LIGHTS
2541 River Rd (27048-8532)
PHONE 336 209-8209
Kenny Harris, *Prin*
EMP: 4 **EST:** 2017
SALES (est): 48.34K **Privately Held**
SIC: 3999 Manufacturing industries, nec

(G-14957)
FULP LUMBER COMPANY INC
280 Fulp Sawmill Rd (27048-8144)
PHONE 336 573-3113
Steven Martin, *Pr*
Patricia Shields, *Sec*
EMP: 11 **EST:** 1958
SALES (est): 496.34K **Privately Held**
SIC: 2421 Sawmills and planing mills, general

(G-14958)
GITSUM PRECISION LLC
390 Duggins Rd (27048-8134)
PHONE 336 453-3998
Sara Cutlip, *CEO*
Joshua Cutlip, *VP*
EMP: 5 **EST:** 2016
SALES (est): 305.04K **Privately Held**
SIC: 3484 3483 Small arms; Ammunition, except for small arms, nec

(G-14959)
GOINS SIGNS INC
1811 Victory Hill Church Rd (27048-8058)
PHONE 336 427-5783
Paula Goins, *Pr*
EMP: 5 **EST:** 2001
SALES (est): 205.83K **Privately Held**
SIC: 3993 Signs and advertising specialties

(G-14960)
KURRENT WLDG & FABRICATION INC
187 Deertract Loop (27048-8419)
PHONE 800 738-6114
EMP: 4 **EST:** 2018
SALES (est): 78.09K **Privately Held**
SIC: 7692 Welding repair

(G-14961)
LONDON GARMENT MFG LLC
1731 Price Grange Rd (27048-8238)
PHONE 336 573-9300
Joseph T London, *Pr*
Cynthia A Smith, *VP*
EMP: 5 **EST:** 2019
SALES (est): 125.23K **Privately Held**
Web: www.londongarmentmanufacturing.com
SIC: 2311 Vests: made from purchased materials

(G-14962)
NEAT FEET HOSIERY INC
304 Main St (27048-7663)
P.O. Box 23 (27048-0023)
PHONE 336 573-2177
Branch Bobbitt, *Pr*
Josh Bobbitt, *VP*
Patricia Bobbitt, *Sec*
EMP: 6 **EST:** 1992
SQ FT: 18,000
SALES (est): 237.7K **Privately Held**
SIC: 2252 2251 Socks; Women's hosiery, except socks

(G-14963)
NORMAN E CLARK
251 Duck Rd (27048-8130)
PHONE 336 573-9629
Norman Clark, *Prin*
EMP: 5 **EST:** 2005
SALES (est): 130.35K **Privately Held**
SIC: 2711 Newspapers, publishing and printing

(G-14964)
PAPA LONNIES INC
154 Dogwood Rd (27048-8424)
PHONE 336 573-9313
James M Bragdon, *Pr*
Carl S Bragdon, *VP*
EMP: 6 **EST:** 2002
SALES (est): 424.9K **Privately Held**
SIC: 2033 Barbecue sauce: packaged in cans, jars, etc.

(G-14965)
PRESS GLASS INC (HQ)
8901 Us Highway 220 (27048-8301)
P.O. Box 938 (27048-0938)
PHONE 336 573-2393
Michael Lankford, *Pr*
▲ **EMP:** 52 **EST:** 1985
SQ FT: 100,000
SALES (est): 47.66MM
SALES (corp-wide): 48.63MM **Privately Held**
Web: www.pressglass.us
SIC: 3231 Insulating glass: made from purchased glass
PA: Press Glass Na, Inc.
  1345 Ave Of The Amrcas Fl
  New York NY 10105
  212 631-3044

(G-14966)
SHELTON LOGGING & CHIPPING INC
2861 Anglin Mill Rd (27048-7824)
PHONE 336 548-3860
David M Shelton, *Pr*
EMP: 7 **EST:** 1996
SALES (est): 659.2K **Privately Held**
SIC: 2411 Logging camps and contractors

(G-14967)
SOUTHERN FINISHING COMPANY INC (PA)
100 W Main St (27048)
P.O. Box 888 (27048-0888)
PHONE 336 573-3741
Ed Brown, *Pr*
Kathy Brown, *Sec*
◆ **EMP:** 16 **EST:** 1978
SQ FT: 10,000
SALES (est): 47.85MM
SALES (corp-wide): 47.85MM **Privately Held**
Web: www.southernfinishing.com
SIC: 2499 2511 Furniture inlays (veneers); Wood household furniture

(G-14968)
STITCH-A-DOOZY
140 Salems Ln (27048-8605)
PHONE 336 573-2339
Marla Joyce-nelson, *Prin*
EMP: 5 **EST:** 2010
SALES (est): 56.02K **Privately Held**
SIC: 2395 Embroidery and art needlework

(G-14969)
STONEVILLE LUMBER COMPANY INC
3442 Nc Highway 135 (27048-7578)
PHONE 336 623-4311
James Tuttle, *Pr*
EMP: 10 **EST:** 1998
SALES (est): 450.08K **Privately Held**
SIC: 2421 Lumber: rough, sawed, or planed

(G-14970)
TIGERTEK INDUSTRIAL SVCS LLC
Also Called: Tigertek Industrial Services
2741 Nc Highway 135 (27048-7570)
P.O. Box 5097 (27289-5097)
PHONE 336 623-1717
Hadi Sayess, *CEO*
EMP: 40 **EST:** 1983
SQ FT: 12,000
SALES (est): 7.23MM
SALES (corp-wide): 7.23MM **Privately Held**
Web: www.tigertek.com
SIC: 7694 3599 Electric motor repair; Machine shop, jobbing and repair
PA: Omninvest, Llc
  4213 Abernathy Pl
  Harrisburg NC 28075
  336 623-1717

Stony Point
Alexander County

(G-14971)
DADDY PETES PLANT PLEASER
1210 Smith Farm Rd (28678-9158)
PHONE 704 585-2355
EMP: 6 **EST:** 2019
SALES (est): 228.74K **Privately Held**
Web: www.daddypetes.com
SIC: 2875 Fertilizers, mixing only

(G-14972)
EDDIES WELDING INC
213 Halyburton Rd (28678-9243)
PHONE 704 585-2024
Eddie Dillinger, *Prin*
EMP: 7 **EST:** 1994
SQ FT: 7,750
SALES (est): 944.82K **Privately Held**
Web: www.ewifab.com
SIC: 7692 Welding repair

(G-14973)
SENSE AND DEFENSEABILITY LLC
149 Walk On Rd (28678-8812)
PHONE 704 880-0165

Gary Wayne, *Prin*
EMP: 5 **EST:** 2012
SALES (est): 167.74K **Privately Held**
SIC: 3812 Defense systems and equipment

Summerfield
Guilford County

(G-14974)
A STITCH TO REMEMBER
7621 Whitaker Dr (27358-9369)
PHONE..................................336 202-0026
Yigael Gavish, *Prin*
EMP: 5 **EST:** 2010
SALES (est): 47.39K **Privately Held**
SIC: 2395 Embroidery and art needlework

(G-14975)
ADPRESS PRINTING INCORPORATED
Also Called: Ad Press Printing
7000 Morganshire Ct (27358-7804)
PHONE..................................336 294-2244
Larry Swaney, *Pr*
Carl Swaney, *Sec*
EMP: 9 **EST:** 1986
SQ FT: 3,000
SALES (est): 835.21K **Privately Held**
Web: www.adpressprinting.com
SIC: 2752 2789 Offset printing; Bookbinding and related work

(G-14976)
BIG CHAIR PUBLISHING LLC
7902 Thoroughbred Dr (27358-9742)
PHONE..................................336 207-4139
Adrian Harris, *Prin*
EMP: 4 **EST:** 2016
SALES (est): 64.5K **Privately Held**
SIC: 2741 Miscellaneous publishing

(G-14977)
CANDACE RAND
8306 Spotswood Rd (27358-9722)
PHONE..................................336 643-7082
Matthew Rand, *Prin*
EMP: 5 **EST:** 2009
SALES (est): 234.42K **Privately Held**
SIC: 3131 Rands

(G-14978)
CEMCO PARTITIONS INC
5340 Us Highway 220 N (27358-9727)
P.O. Box 839 (27358-0839)
PHONE..................................336 643-6316
Larry D Guinn, *Pr*
Marilyn Guinn, *Sec*
Brian Guinn, *VP*
EMP: 5 **EST:** 1971
SQ FT: 12,000
SALES (est): 684.63K **Privately Held**
Web: www.cemcopartitions.com
SIC: 2542 Partitions for floor attachment, prefabricated: except wood

(G-14979)
CURIOUS DISCOVERIES INC
7911 Windspray Dr (27358-9715)
PHONE..................................336 643-0432
EMP: 4 **EST:** 1995
SALES (est): 225K **Privately Held**
SIC: 3944 Board games, puzzles, and models, except electronic

(G-14980)
DOVE MEDICAL SUPPLY LLC
8164 Mabe Marshall Rd Bldg 2 (27358-9225)
PHONE..................................336 643-9367
Tammy Bridges, *CEO*
EMP: 32 **EST:** 2013
SALES (est): 3.87MM **Privately Held**
Web: www.mydovestore.com
SIC: 3069 5047 3821 Laboratory sundries: cases, covers, funnels, cups, etc.; Medical and hospital equipment; Laboratory apparatus and furniture

(G-14981)
EM2 MACHINE CORP
7939 Highfill Rd (27358-9707)
PHONE..................................336 297-4110
Vince Simmons, *Pr*
Tana Simmons, *Sec*
EMP: 5 **EST:** 2005
SALES (est): 899K **Privately Held**
SIC: 3545 Machine tool accessories

(G-14982)
FRANK FICCA WOODWORKING
6300 Wescott Dr (27358-8002)
PHONE..................................336 937-2985
EMP: 4 **EST:** 2019
SALES (est): 67.76K **Privately Held**
SIC: 2431 Millwork

(G-14983)
FRED L BROWN
2913 Pleasant Ridge Rd (27358-9094)
PHONE..................................336 643-7523
Fred L Brown, *Owner*
EMP: 5 **EST:** 2010
SALES (est): 240.65K **Privately Held**
SIC: 3571 7379 Electronic computers; Computer related consulting services

(G-14984)
FUTURE ENERGY SVC PUBLISHING
5302 Chestnut Ridge Dr (27358-7807)
PHONE..................................336 298-8036
Bo Zhang, *Prin*
EMP: 5 **EST:** 2014
SALES (est): 49.77K **Privately Held**
Web: www.form-a-tread.com
SIC: 2741 Miscellaneous publishing

(G-14985)
LOGO WEAR GRAPHICS LLC
300 Norman Farm Rd (27358-9525)
PHONE..................................336 382-0455
Angela Scott, *Managing Member*
EMP: 10 **EST:** 2010
SALES (est): 488.14K **Privately Held**
Web: www.logoweargraphics.com
SIC: 7336 2759 Graphic arts and related design; Letterpress and screen printing

(G-14986)
LONG ASP PAV TRCKG OF GRNSBURG
4349 Us Highway 220 N (27358-9401)
PHONE..................................336 643-4121
James Long, *Pr*
EMP: 12 **EST:** 1983
SALES (est): 263.13K **Privately Held**
Web: www.asphaltpavingofgso.com
SIC: 4212 2951 1771 1611 Dump truck haulage; Asphalt paving mixtures and blocks; Concrete work; Highway and street construction

(G-14987)
LURES GALORE LLC
5243 Larue Ct (27358-8282)
PHONE..................................336 643-0948
Bob Mendez, *Brnch Mgr*
EMP: 8
SALES (corp-wide): 108.81K **Privately Held**
SIC: 3949 Lures, fishing: artificial
PA: Lures Galore Llc
  201 Kemp Rd E
  Greensboro NC

(G-14988)
M & M TIRE AND AUTO INC
5570 Spotswood Cir (27358-9805)
P.O. Box 625 (27358-0625)
PHONE..................................336 643-7877
Mark Middleton, *Pr*
EMP: 6 **EST:** 1989
SALES (est): 709.3K **Privately Held**
Web: www.mmtiresummerfield.com
SIC: 5531 7534 Automotive tires; Tire retreading and repair shops

(G-14989)
MERCHANT 1 MANUFACTURING LLC
200 Starview Ln (27358-9606)
PHONE..................................336 617-3008
Clarence Lawrence, *Brnch Mgr*
EMP: 4
SALES (corp-wide): 977.68K **Privately Held**
Web: www.merchant1manufacturing.com
SIC: 3499 7389 Nozzles, spray: aerosol, paint, or insecticide; Business Activities at Non-Commercial Site
PA: Merchant 1 Manufacturing Llc
  1203 Freeway Dr
  Reidsville NC 27320
  336 580-1873

(G-14990)
PACKAGING PLUS NORTH CAROLINA
8301 Sangor Dr (27358-9732)
PHONE..................................336 643-4097
Robert Wray, *Owner*
EMP: 10 **EST:** 1999
SALES (est): 446.06K **Privately Held**
SIC: 3053 Packing materials

(G-14991)
RITENIS WOODWORKS
3205 Oak Ridge Rd (27358-9161)
PHONE..................................336 643-6426
Steven Ritenis, *Prin*
EMP: 5 **EST:** 2009
SALES (est): 104.84K **Privately Held**
SIC: 2431 Millwork

(G-14992)
TRIAD HOSTING INC
4602 Joseph Hoskins Rd (27358-9513)
P.O. Box 1018 (27358-1018)
PHONE..................................336 497-1932
EMP: 5 **EST:** 1999
SALES (est): 133.18K **Privately Held**
Web: www.triadhosting.com
SIC: 2741 Miscellaneous publishing

(G-14993)
WHAM AVIATION LLC
2611 Oxmoor Rd (27358-9786)
PHONE..................................336 605-4663
Hampton Haucke, *Prin*
EMP: 5 **EST:** 2007
SALES (est): 110K **Privately Held**
SIC: 3721 Aircraft

(G-14994)
WILSON LOGGING NC LLC
6308 Autumn Crest Ct (27358-9357)
PHONE..................................336 280-8648
EMP: 5 **EST:** 2019
SALES (est): 236.43K **Privately Held**
SIC: 2411 Logging camps and contractors

Sunbury
Gates County

(G-14995)
CLASSIC STEEL BUILDINGS INC
530 Folly Rd (27979-9412)
PHONE..................................252 465-4184
Calvin R Eason, *Pr*
EMP: 6 **EST:** 2006
SALES (est): 820.51K **Privately Held**
SIC: 3448 Buildings, portable: prefabricated metal

(G-14996)
GEORGE P GATLING LOGGING
223 Nc Highway 32 S (27979-9545)
PHONE..................................252 465-8983
George P Gatling, *Owner*
EMP: 9 **EST:** 1977
SALES (est): 535.46K **Privately Held**
SIC: 2411 Logging

(G-14997)
HOFLER H S & SONS LUMBER CO
577 Nc Highway 32 N (27979-9418)
P.O. Box 130 (27979-0130)
PHONE..................................252 465-8603
James M Hofler, *Pr*
Bernard S Hofler Junior, *Sec*
James M Hofler, *Treas*
EMP: 18 **EST:** 1960
SQ FT: 570
SALES (est): 213.7K **Privately Held**
SIC: 2421 2426 Lumber: rough, sawed, or planed; Hardwood dimension and flooring mills

(G-14998)
HOFLER LOGGING INC
491 Nc Highway 32 S (27979-9550)
PHONE..................................252 465-8921
Charles T Hofler, *Pr*
Thomas Hofler, *VP*
Barbara Hofler, *Sec*
EMP: 9 **EST:** 1935
SALES (est): 787.06K **Privately Held**
SIC: 2411 Logging camps and contractors

Sunset Beach
Brunswick County

(G-14999)
HOME ELEVATORS & LIFT PDTS LLC
Also Called: Home Elevators & Lift
8311 Ocean Hwy W (28468-6118)
PHONE..................................910 427-0006
EMP: 20 **EST:** 2016
SQ FT: 8,000
SALES (est): 4.34MM **Privately Held**
Web: www.homeelevatorsandlift.com
SIC: 3534 1796 Elevators and equipment; Elevator installation and conversion

(G-15000)
LEES SCREEN ENCLOSURES & MORE
403 Bayberry Ln (28468-4207)
PHONE..................................843 283-7227
EMP: 5 **EST:** 2015
SALES (est): 105.27K **Privately Held**
Web: www.leesscreenenclosuresandmore.com
SIC: 3448 Screen enclosures

(G-15001)
MEDICAL SPCLTIES OF CRLNAS INC
565 Meadow Ridge (28468)

P.O. Box 7087 (28469-1087)
PHONE..................910 575-4542
James W Hardie, Pr
EMP: 5 EST: 1998
SQ FT: 2,333
SALES (est): 248.52K Privately Held
SIC: 3842 Surgical appliances and supplies

(G-15002)
OLIVE PRESS LLC
7645 High Market St Unit 4 (28468-4571)
PHONE..................910 622-6718
Barbara Martin, Pr
EMP: 5 EST: 2015
SALES (est): 246.05K Privately Held
Web: www.theolivepressnc.com
SIC: 2741 Miscellaneous publishing

(G-15003)
ROD JAHNER
157 Crooked Gulley Cir (28468-4438)
PHONE..................919 435-7580
Rod Jahner, Prin
EMP: 4 EST: 2016
SALES (est): 50.37K Privately Held
Web: www.justrodbooks.com
SIC: 2741 Miscellaneous publishing

(G-15004)
WOOD WORKS
9040 Forest Dr Sw (28468-5020)
PHONE..................910 579-1487
Kevin Scott, Prin
EMP: 5 EST: 2015
SALES (est): 105.11K Privately Held
SIC: 2431 Millwork

Supply
Brunswick County

(G-15005)
A-1 HITCH & TRAILORS SALES INC
360 Ocean Hwy E (28462-3348)
PHONE..................910 755-6025
Don Carson, Pr
Cheryl Winans, Sec
EMP: 11 EST: 1996
SQ FT: 300
SALES (est): 477.29K Privately Held
Web: www.a1hitchandtrailers.com
SIC: 3799 5599 5013 Trailers and trailer equipment; Utility trailers; Trailer parts and accessories

(G-15006)
BCAC HOLDINGS LLC
Also Called: Brunswick Cabinets Countertops
674 Ocean Hwy W (28462-4048)
PHONE..................910 754-5689
Chris Gibson, Mgr
Todd Stancombe, Mgr
EMP: 7 EST: 2019
SALES (est): 256.94K Privately Held
Web: www.brunswickcabinetsandcountertops.com
SIC: 2434 Wood kitchen cabinets

(G-15007)
CAROLINA PRTG WILMINGTON INC
2790 Sea Vista Dr Sw (28462-5612)
PHONE..................910 762-2453
Kenneth Kalaher, Owner
EMP: 4 EST: 1995
SALES (est): 272.77K Privately Held
Web: www.printingwilmingtonnc.com
SIC: 2752 Offset printing

(G-15008)
PRECISION TIME SYSTEMS INC
959 Little Macedonia Rd Nw (28462-3749)
P.O. Box 171 (28422-0171)
PHONE..................910 253-9850
▲ EMP: 10 EST: 1993
SALES (est): 345.16K Privately Held
Web: www.precisiontime.com
SIC: 3613 Time switches, electrical switchgear apparatus

(G-15009)
RHYTHMS WELDING LLC
596 Makatoka Rd Nw (28462-3438)
PHONE..................910 477-7150
Cary Levon Lee Junior, Prin
EMP: 5 EST: 2019
SALES (est): 85.59K Privately Held
SIC: 7692 Welding repair

(G-15010)
S & S TRAWL SHOP INC
896 Stanbury Rd Sw (28462-6024)
P.O. Box 789 (28462-0789)
PHONE..................910 842-9197
Steve Parrish, Pr
Sabrina Parrish, Sec
Henry Steven Parrish Junior, VP
EMP: 4 EST: 1980
SQ FT: 1,800
SALES (est): 242.22K Privately Held
SIC: 2399 5091 Fishing nets; Fishing equipment and supplies

(G-15011)
SIGN SHOPPE INC
782 Ocean Hwy W (28462-4056)
P.O. Box 1037 (28462-1037)
PHONE..................910 754-5144
Jerome Munna, Prin
EMP: 4 EST: 1987
SQ FT: 5,000
SALES (est): 301.3K Privately Held
Web: www.signshoppe.org
SIC: 3993 Signs and advertising specialties

(G-15012)
STUMP LOGGING
61 Supply St Se (28462-3367)
PHONE..................910 620-7000
Tonia Twigg, Prin
EMP: 6 EST: 2016
SALES (est): 143.34K Privately Held
SIC: 2411 Logging

(G-15013)
TRADEMARK LANDSCAPE GROUP INC
Also Called: Trademark Ldscp Cntg Trdmark O
360 Ocean Hwy E (28462-3348)
PHONE..................910 253-0560
Tracy Dale Wheeler, CEO
EMP: 11 EST: 1999
SALES (est): 669.64K Privately Held
Web: www.trademarklandscaping.biz
SIC: 8741 3271 1629 Construction management; Blocks, concrete: landscape or retaining wall; Irrigation system construction

(G-15014)
VERMONT DESIGNS UNLIMITED LLC
2900 E Lakeview Dr Sw (28462-2117)
PHONE..................910 846-4477
Patricia Roelants, Prin
EMP: 5 EST: 2015
SALES (est): 147.06K Privately Held

SIC: 3999 Manufacturing industries, nec

Surf City
Onslow County

(G-15015)
DAILY GRIND LLC
114 N Topsail Dr (28445-6718)
P.O. Box 2519 (28445-0028)
PHONE..................910 541-0471
Margaret Hutchison Allan, Mgr
EMP: 6 EST: 2011
SALES (est): 260.73K Privately Held
Web: the-daily-grind-surf-city.business.site
SIC: 3599 Grinding castings for the trade

(G-15016)
SALTY TURTLE BEER COMPANY
103 Triton Ln (28445-6923)
PHONE..................910 803-2019
Dan Callander, Pr
EMP: 20 EST: 2017
SALES (est): 578.23K Privately Held
Web: www.saltyturtlebeer.com
SIC: 5813 2082 5181 Bars and lounges; Beer (alcoholic beverage); Beer and ale

Swannanoa
Buncombe County

(G-15017)
APPALACHIAN TOOL & MACHINE INC
121 Lytle Cove Rd (28778-3702)
PHONE..................828 669-0142
Grace Frizsell, Pr
Ed Frizsell, VP
EMP: 20 EST: 1990
SQ FT: 10,000
SALES (est): 4.59MM Privately Held
Web: www.appalachiantool.com
SIC: 3599 Custom machinery

(G-15018)
ASSURANCE PUBLICATIONS INC
101 College Cir (28778-2032)
PHONE..................423 473-3000
Jeff Thomas Shepherd, Prin
EMP: 6 EST: 2019
SALES (est): 65.16K Privately Held
SIC: 2741 Miscellaneous publishing

(G-15019)
AVADIM HOLDINGS INC (PA)
Also Called: Avadim Health
4 Old Patton Cove Rd (28778-2853)
PHONE..................877 677-2723
Keith Daniels, CEO
EMP: 35 EST: 2021
SALES (est): 12.03MM
SALES (corp-wide): 12.03MM Privately Held
Web: www.avadimhealth.com
SIC: 2834 Medicines, capsuled or ampuled

(G-15020)
B V HEDRICK GRAVEL & SAND CO
Also Called: Grove Stone & Sand
Old Us 70 (28778)
P.O. Box 425 (28778-0425)
PHONE..................828 686-3844
Robert Graham, Mgr
EMP: 155
SALES (corp-wide): 238.17MM Privately Held
Web: www.hedrickind.com

SIC: 1429 1442 Igneous rock, crushed and broken-quarrying; Construction sand and gravel
PA: B. V. Hedrick Gravel & Sand Company
120 1/2 N Church St
Salisbury NC 28144
704 633-5982

(G-15021)
BRUSHY MOUNTAIN PUBLISHING
221 Long Branch Rd (28778-3524)
PHONE..................828 298-6687
Leland K Davis, Pr
EMP: 5 EST: 2005
SALES (est): 90.45K Privately Held
Web: www.brushymountainpublishing.com
SIC: 2741 Miscellaneous publishing

(G-15022)
CAROLINA CONCRETE MATERIALS
650 Old Us 70 Hwy (28778-2645)
PHONE..................828 686-3040
Beth Wilson, Pr
Emmett Wilson, Sec
EMP: 8 EST: 1979
SQ FT: 250
SALES (est): 580.98K Privately Held
SIC: 3273 Ready-mixed concrete

(G-15023)
CAROLINA READY MIX & BUILD (PA)
606 Old Us 70 Hwy (28778-2645)
PHONE..................828 686-3041
Mark Mcmeans, Prin
EMP: 5 EST: 2008
SALES (est): 4.91MM
SALES (corp-wide): 4.91MM Privately Held
Web: www.carolinareadymixinc.com
SIC: 3273 Ready-mixed concrete

(G-15024)
CUMBERLAND GRAV & SAND MIN CO (PA)
Also Called: Piedmont Sand
Old Us Highway 70 (28778)
PHONE..................828 686-3844
Jeffrey V Goodman, Pr
Charles E Brady, Ch Bd
Don Hensley, VP
EMP: 10 EST: 1949
SQ FT: 3,000
SALES (est): 3.24MM
SALES (corp-wide): 3.24MM Privately Held
Web: www.hedrickind.com
SIC: 1442 Common sand mining

(G-15025)
DUNCAN JOSEPH E & DUNCAN BILLY
423 Christian Creek Rd (28778-2734)
PHONE..................828 299-8464
Joseph Duncan, Prin
EMP: 5 EST: 2009
SALES (est): 63.39K Privately Held
SIC: 7692 Welding repair

(G-15026)
GARNER WOODWORKS LLC
304 Patton Hill Rd (28778-2470)
P.O. Box 868 (28778-0868)
PHONE..................828 775-1790
Micdalia Cairns, Managing Member
EMP: 4 EST: 2002
SALES (est): 492.3K Privately Held
Web: www.garnerwoodworks.com
SIC: 2431 Millwork

(G-15027)
JBS2 INC
Also Called: National Wiper Alliance
875 Warren Wilson Rd (28778-2039)
P.O. Box 367 (28778-0367)
PHONE.................................828 236-1300
◆ **EMP:** 75 **EST:** 1996
SQ FT: 110,000
SALES (est): 69.23MM
SALES (corp-wide): 15.32B **Publicly Held**
Web: www.nationalwiper.com
SIC: 2392 Towels, dishcloths and dust cloths
PA: Ecolab Inc.
1 Ecolab Pl
Saint Paul MN 55102
800 232-6522

(G-15028)
LINKOUS CARPENTRY & WDWKG LLC
415 Melody Cir (28778-2213)
PHONE.................................828 460-5610
Mark Linkous, *Prin*
EMP: 5 **EST:** 2015
SALES (est): 75.77K **Privately Held**
SIC: 2431 Millwork

(G-15029)
MIXX-POINT 5 PROJECT LLC
Also Called: Mixx Pt 5
107 W Buckeye Rd (28778-2747)
PHONE.................................858 298-4625
Tom Dawson, *Prin*
Michele Dawson, *Prin*
EMP: 6 **EST:** 2021
SALES (est): 297.93K **Privately Held**
SIC: 2834 Pharmaceutical preparations

(G-15030)
NEW LIFE CBD
339 Lytle Cove Rd (28778-3706)
PHONE.................................828 545-7203
Marisa Hinchcliff, *Prin*
EMP: 5 **EST:** 2018
SALES (est): 137.25K **Privately Held**
Web: www.thenewlifecbd.com
SIC: 3999

(G-15031)
NONWOVENS OF AMERICA INC
Also Called: Noa
875 Warren Wilson Rd (28778-2039)
P.O. Box 367 (28778-0367)
PHONE.................................828 236-1300
Jeffrey Slosman, *Pr*
EMP: 11 **EST:** 2012
SQ FT: 200,000
SALES (est): 406.63K **Privately Held**
Web: www.nationalwiper.com
SIC: 2679 Insulating paper: batts, fills, and blankets

(G-15032)
ONIXX MANUFACTURING LLC
107 W Buckeye Rd (28778-2747)
PHONE.................................828 298-4625
EMP: 5
SALES (est): 229.77K **Privately Held**
SIC: 2844 Cosmetic preparations

(G-15033)
REDTAIL GROUP LLC ✪
2131 Us 70 Hwy Unit C (28778-9201)
P.O. Box 1188 (28778-1188)
PHONE.................................828 539-4700
EMP: 4 **EST:** 2022
SALES (est): 373.62K **Privately Held**
Web: www.redtailwire.com
SIC: 3496 Barbed wire, made from purchased wire

(G-15034)
RISE OVER RUN INC (PA)
2131 Us 70 Hwy Unit C (28778-9201)
PHONE.................................303 819-1566
Ryan Brazell, *Pr*
EMP: 6 **EST:** 2017
SALES (est): 227.48K
SALES (corp-wide): 227.48K **Privately Held**
SIC: 2084 Wines

(G-15035)
SARAZ MUSICAL INSTRUMENTS
90 Sean Dr (28778-2754)
PHONE.................................828 782-8896
Steven Mark Popie Garner, *Owner*
EMP: 4 **EST:** 2015
SALES (est): 45.13K **Privately Held**
SIC: 3931 Musical instruments

(G-15036)
SMITH CREATIONS LLC
56 Harrison Hill Rd (28778-2202)
PHONE.................................704 771-6749
EMP: 5 **EST:** 2018
SALES (est): 212.46K **Privately Held**
SIC: 2431 Millwork

(G-15037)
SOUTHEASTERN HARDWOODS INC
Also Called: Bee Tree Hardwoods
734 Bee Tree Rd (28778-3403)
PHONE.................................828 581-0197
Phillip Long, *Pr*
EMP: 5 **EST:** 2003
SQ FT: 400
SALES (est): 452.18K **Privately Held**
Web: www.beetreehardwoods.com
SIC: 2421 5211 Kiln drying of lumber; Lumber products

(G-15038)
WRIGHT MACHINE & TOOL CO INC
101 Jims Branch Rd (28778-3604)
PHONE.................................828 298-8440
Doris Wright, *Sec*
Frank A Wright, *
David Thomas, *
◆ **EMP:** 50 **EST:** 1970
SQ FT: 100,000
SALES (est): 6.81MM **Privately Held**
Web: www.wrightmachtool.com
SIC: 3599 3544 Machine shop, jobbing and repair; Special dies and tools

Swanquarter
Hyde County

(G-15039)
MATTAMUSKEET SEAFOOD INC
24694 Us Highway 264 (27885-9536)
PHONE.................................252 926-2431
Robert Eugene Carawan, *Pr*
Gary Mayo, *
Patty Jarvis, *
Charles Carawan, *
EMP: 100 **EST:** 1984
SQ FT: 5,000
SALES (est): 8.21MM **Privately Held**
Web: www.mattamuskeetseafoodnc.com
SIC: 2091 Bouillon, clam: packaged in cans, jars, etc.

(G-15040)
PAMLICO SHORES INC
14166 Us Highway 264 (27885-9661)
P.O. Box 218 (27824-0218)
PHONE.................................252 926-0011
Hunter Gibbs, *Pr*
EMP: 40 **EST:** 2012
SALES (est): 3.68MM **Privately Held**
Web: www.pamlicoshores.com
SIC: 2499 Food handling and processing products, wood

Swansboro
Onslow County

(G-15041)
3D OIL INC
316 Silver Creek Landing Rd (28584-7788)
PHONE.................................609 408-9159
Steven S Boljen, *Prin*
EMP: 4 **EST:** 2019
SALES (est): 54.23K **Privately Held**
SIC: 1382 Oil and gas exploration services

(G-15042)
CAROLINA CABINETS OF CEDAR PT
136 Vfw Rd (28584-8085)
PHONE.................................252 393-6236
Paul Westmeier, *Owner*
EMP: 4 **EST:** 2003
SALES (est): 249.58K **Privately Held**
Web: www.carolina-cabinets.com
SIC: 2434 Wood kitchen cabinets

(G-15043)
CARTERET PUBLISHING COMPANY
Also Called: Tideland News
774 W Corbett Ave (28584-8452)
P.O. Box 1000 (28584-1000)
PHONE.................................910 326-5066
Jimmy Williams, *Mgr*
EMP: 6
SALES (corp-wide): 7.75MM **Privately Held**
Web: www.carolinacoastonline.com
SIC: 2711 Commercial printing and newspaper publishing combined
PA: Carteret Publishing Company
5039 Executive Dr Ste 300
Morehead City NC 28557
252 726-7081

(G-15044)
DEVILS KINDRED MC
310 S Chestnut St (28584-9538)
PHONE.................................336 712-7689
James F Killian, *VP*
James F Killian, *VP*
EMP: 20 **EST:** 2016
SALES (est): 591.07K **Privately Held**
SIC: 3751 Motorcycles, bicycles and parts

(G-15045)
HIGH SPEED GEAR INC
Also Called: H S G
87 Old Hammock Rd (28584-8661)
P.O. Box 940 (28584-0940)
PHONE.................................910 325-1000
Gene Higdon, *Ch*
Becky Higdon, *Pr*
EMP: 11 **EST:** 1999
SQ FT: 6,000
SALES (est): 2.58MM **Privately Held**
Web: www.highspeedgear.com
SIC: 2824 Nylon fibers

(G-15046)
NC STEEL SERVICES INC
141 Seth Thomas Ln (28584-8538)
PHONE.................................252 393-7888
Maria Parrish, *Pr*
Mark Parrish, *VP*
EMP: 10 **EST:** 2004
SQ FT: 40,000
SALES (est): 995.77K **Privately Held**
Web: www.ncsteelservicesinc.com
SIC: 3441 Fabricated structural metal

(G-15047)
OLIVE BEAUFORT OIL COMPANY
105 W Church St (28584-9018)
PHONE.................................910 325-1556
Natalie Parker, *Genl Mgr*
EMP: 6 **EST:** 2014
SALES (est): 132.87K **Privately Held**
Web: www.beaufortoliveoil.com
SIC: 2079 Olive oil

(G-15048)
OPTOMETRIC EYECARE CENTER INC
775 W Corbett Ave (28584-8562)
PHONE.................................910 326-3050
Tina Siegel, *Pr*
EMP: 8 **EST:** 1996
SALES (est): 510.79K **Privately Held**
Web: www.eyecarecenter.com
SIC: 3211 Optical glass, flat

(G-15049)
WARREN OIL CO INC LOUISBURG
307 Duck Hvn (28584-9402)
PHONE.................................252 764-2171
Mark L Warren, *Prin*
EMP: 6 **EST:** 2004
SALES (est): 166.23K **Privately Held**
SIC: 1311 Crude petroleum and natural gas

Swepsonville
Alamance County

(G-15050)
AMERICAN HONDA MOTOR CO INC
3721 Nc Hwy 119 (27359)
PHONE.................................336 578-6300
Hiroki Chubachi, *Mgr*
EMP: 335
Web: www.honda.com
SIC: 3524 Lawn and garden mowers and accessories
HQ: American Honda Motor Co., Inc.
1919 Torrance Blvd
Torrance CA 90501
310 783-2000

Sylva
Jackson County

(G-15051)
828 CUSTOM PRINTING LLC
321 Jackson Plz Ste B (28779-2552)
PHONE.................................828 586-1828
EMP: 4 **EST:** 2020
SALES (est): 83.91K **Privately Held**
Web: www.828customprinting.com
SIC: 2752 Commercial printing, lithographic

(G-15052)
APPALACHIAN TIMBER COMPANY
151 Posey Blanton Rd (28779-8963)
PHONE.................................828 507-6505
Stacy Lane Henson, *Owner*
EMP: 5 **EST:** 2017
SALES (est): 55.82K **Privately Held**
SIC: 2411 Logging

(G-15053)
BANKS WELDING
465 Old Settlement Rd (28779-6781)
PHONE.................................828 586-2258
R A Banks, *Prin*
EMP: 5 **EST:** 2009

Sylva - Jackson County (G-15054)

SALES (est): 160.02K **Privately Held**
Web: www.aboutdelta.com
SIC: 7692 Welding repair

(G-15054)
BILLET SPEED INC
488 Fairview Rd (28779-9099)
PHONE..................828 226-8127
Matt Welsh, *Pr*
EMP: 6 EST: 2016
SALES (est): 152.64K **Privately Held**
Web: www.billet-speed.com
SIC: 3714 Motor vehicle parts and accessories

(G-15055)
BLUE DIAMOND DEFENSE LLC
245 Old Indian Flatts Ln (28779-9659)
PHONE..................334 905-0246
Otis F Farris Junior, *Prin*
EMP: 5 EST: 2012
SALES (est): 178.46K **Privately Held**
SIC: 3812 Defense systems and equipment

(G-15056)
ECOMARC LLC
1207 Posey Blanton Rd (28779-8967)
PHONE..................828 226-4780
EMP: 5 EST: 2019
SALES (est): 215.44K **Privately Held**
SIC: 7692 Welding repair

(G-15057)
GRAY WOLF LOG HOMES INC
538 Big Oak Springs Rd (28779-1223)
P.O. Box 636 (28725-0636)
PHONE..................828 586-4662
Larry Phillips, *Pr*
Pat Phillips, *Park Ranger*
EMP: 5 EST: 1992
SALES (est): 395.41K **Privately Held**
SIC: 2452 Log cabins, prefabricated, wood

(G-15058)
INNOVATION BREWING LLC
414 W Main St (28779-5548)
PHONE..................828 586-9678
Charles Owen, *Prin*
EMP: 7 EST: 2013
SALES (est): 445.26K **Privately Held**
Web: www.innovation-brewing.com
SIC: 5813 2082 Bars and lounges; Ale (alcoholic beverage)

(G-15059)
JACKSON ARTS MARKET LLC
533 W Main St (28779-5551)
PHONE..................415 659-0710
Joshua Murch, *CEO*
EMP: 5 EST: 2021
SALES (est): 34.67K **Privately Held**
Web: www.jacksonartsmarket.com
SIC: 3231 Aquariums and reflectors, glass

(G-15060)
JACKSON PAPER MANUFACTURING CO (PA)
152 W Main St (28779-2928)
P.O. Box 667 (28779-0667)
PHONE..................828 586-5534
Tim Campbell, *CEO*
Nicki Slusser, *Pr*
Tim Campbell, *VP*
Jeff Murphy, *VP*
Tammy Francis, *VP*
▲ EMP: 73 EST: 1994
SALES (est): 98.11MM **Privately Held**
Web: www.jacksonpaper.net
SIC: 2621 Paper mills

(G-15061)
JONES WELDING
512 Country Knoll Dr (28779-7030)
PHONE..................828 508-0080
Toby Jones, *Prin*
EMP: 4 EST: 2018
SALES (est): 28.12K **Privately Held**
Web: jones-welding-inc.business.site
SIC: 7692 Welding repair

(G-15062)
LBM INDUSTRIES INC
Also Called: Mc Neely's Store Rental & Eqpt
21 E Hall Hts (28779-2800)
PHONE..................828 631-1227
Luke Fisher, *Brnch Mgr*
EMP: 5
SALES (corp-wide): 9.72MM **Privately Held**
Web: www.mcneelycompanies.com
SIC: 1411 Dimension stone
PA: Lbm Industries, Inc.
2000 Whitewater Rd
Sapphire NC 28774
828 966-4270

(G-15063)
LUCY IN RYE LLC
612 W Main St (28779-5449)
PHONE..................828 586-4601
Constantinos Mitsides, *Mgr*
EMP: 7 EST: 2020
SALES (est): 568.74K **Privately Held**
SIC: 2099 Food preparations, nec

(G-15064)
NEAR URBAN LLC
714 W Main St (28779-5554)
PHONE..................828 631-6213
EMP: 5 EST: 2017
SALES (est): 166.44K **Privately Held**
SIC: 2711 Newspapers: publishing only, not printed on site

(G-15065)
Q C APPAREL INC
330 Scotts Creek Rd (28779-5237)
PHONE..................828 586-5663
Clemmey Queen, *Pr*
Carley Queen, *Sec*
▲ EMP: 10 EST: 1993
SQ FT: 70,000
SALES (est): 399.45K **Privately Held**
SIC: 2392 Household furnishings, nec

(G-15066)
QUARTZ MATRIX LLC
283 Winding Ridge Dr (28779-7616)
PHONE..................828 631-3207
Ofelia C Balta, *Prin*
EMP: 6 EST: 2012
SALES (est): 184.87K **Privately Held**
Web: www.quartzmatrixllc.com
SIC: 3599 Machine shop, jobbing and repair

(G-15067)
SHIRA FORGE
502 Utica Trl (28779-6697)
PHONE..................828 226-5687
EMP: 5 EST: 2017
SALES (est): 129.98K **Privately Held**
Web: www.shiraforge.com
SIC: 3423 Hand and edge tools, nec

(G-15068)
SIMPLY TS INC
50 W Sylva Shopping Area (28779-5264)
PHONE..................828 586-1113
EMP: 4 EST: 2015
SALES (est): 143.56K **Privately Held**

SIC: 2759 Screen printing

(G-15069)
SOUTHERN CONCRETE MTLS INC
1362 W Main St (28779-5213)
PHONE..................828 586-5280
EMP: 10
SALES (corp-wide): 238.17MM **Privately Held**
Web: www.scmusa.com
SIC: 3273 Ready-mixed concrete
HQ: Southern Concrete Materials, Inc.
35 Meadow Rd
Asheville NC 28803
828 253-6421

(G-15070)
SYLVA HERALD AND RURALITE
Also Called: Sylva Herald, The
539 W Main St (28779-5551)
P.O. Box 307 (28779-0307)
PHONE..................828 586-2611
Steve Gray, *Pr*
James A Gray, *VP*
EMP: 21 EST: 1926
SQ FT: 5,000
SALES (est): 475.4K **Privately Held**
Web: www.thesylvaherald.com
SIC: 2711 2752 Newspapers, publishing and printing; Commercial printing, lithographic

(G-15071)
SYLVA HERALD PUBG CO INC THE
539 W Main St (28779-5551)
P.O. Box 307 (28779-0307)
PHONE..................828 586-2611
James A Gray Junior, *VP*
EMP: 10 EST: 2012
SALES (est): 248.62K **Privately Held**
Web: www.thesylvaherald.com
SIC: 2711 Newspapers, publishing and printing

(G-15072)
T & S HARDWOODS INC
3635 Skyland Dr (28779-8359)
P.O. Box 1004 (28779-1004)
PHONE..................828 586-4044
Jack Swanner, *Mgr*
EMP: 90
SALES (corp-wide): 9.4MM **Privately Held**
Web: www.tshardwoods.com
SIC: 2421 2426 Lumber: rough, sawed, or planed; Hardwood dimension and flooring mills
PA: T & S Hardwoods, Inc.
293 Harrisburg Rd Sw
Milledgeville GA 31061
478 454-3400

(G-15073)
VISTA TRANQUILA PUBLISHERS LLC
53 Lands End Dr (28779-7037)
PHONE..................828 586-8401
Kimberly Mathis Pitts, *Prin*
EMP: 4 EST: 2019
SALES (est): 77.96K **Privately Held**
Web: www.vistatranquila.com
SIC: 2741 Miscellaneous publishing

(G-15074)
WEBSTER ENTPS JACKSON CNTY INC
140 Little Savannah Rd (28779-6852)
P.O. Box 220 (28788-0220)
PHONE..................828 586-8981
Bob Cochran, *Treas*
EMP: 24 EST: 1976
SQ FT: 18,000
SALES (est): 1.68MM **Privately Held**
Web: www.websterenterprises.org

SIC: 3841 8331 Surgical and medical instruments; Skill training center

(G-15075)
WILDCRAFT EXTRACTS LLC
64 Landmark Dr (28779-5465)
PHONE..................828 273-8173
EMP: 4 EST: 2018
SALES (est): 86.52K **Privately Held**
SIC: 2836 Extracts

(G-15076)
WNC WHITE CORPORATION
Also Called: Industrial Construction
3563 Skyland Dr (28779-6146)
P.O. Box 630 (28779-0630)
PHONE..................828 477-4895
Greg White, *CEO*
Greg White, *Pr*
Andy White, *VP*
EMP: 20 EST: 2007
SQ FT: 3,000
SALES (est): 4.28MM **Privately Held**
Web: www.wncwhitecorporation.com
SIC: 1629 1623 3443 Industrial plant construction; Water and sewer line construction; Fabricated plate work (boiler shop)

Tabor City
Columbus County

(G-15077)
ATLANTIC AUTOMOTIVE ENTPS LLC
Also Called: Atlantic Enterprises
1007 Pireway Rd Ste B (28463-9457)
PHONE..................910 377-4108
Maria Treece, *Managing Member*
▲ EMP: 17 EST: 2002
SQ FT: 45,000
SALES (est): 1.07MM **Privately Held**
SIC: 3089 Automotive parts, plastic

(G-15078)
BYRON DALE SPIVEY
2009 Reynolds Rd (28463-7385)
PHONE..................910 653-3128
Byron Dale Spivey, *Prin*
EMP: 4 EST: 2011
SALES (est): 76.79K **Privately Held**
Web: www.shamrockboxers.com
SIC: 3861 Tanks, photographic developing, fixing, and washing

(G-15079)
CAROLINA PACKING HOUSE SUPS
305 Green Sea Rd (28463-2499)
PHONE..................910 653-3438
Paul Hathaway, *Pr*
EMP: 5 EST: 1954
SQ FT: 6,000
SALES (est): 339.33K **Privately Held**
SIC: 3556 Packing house machinery

(G-15080)
DOWN SOUTH LOGGING LLC
121 Lake Tabor Dr (28463-2268)
PHONE..................843 333-1649
Steven Wayne Stanley, *Prin*
EMP: 8 EST: 2014
SALES (est): 177.97K **Privately Held**
SIC: 2411 Logging camps and contractors

(G-15081)
E A DUNCAN CNSTR CO INC
1475 Savannah Rd (28463-9156)
PHONE..................910 653-3535
Edgar A Duncan, *Pr*
EMP: 4 EST: 2000

SALES (est): 721.75K **Privately Held**
Web: www.eaduncanconstruction.com
SIC: **1521** 3448 New construction, single-family houses; Prefabricated metal buildings and components

(G-15082)
FILTEC PRECISE INC
218 N Us Highway 701 Byp (28463-2238)
P.O. Box 755 (28463-0755)
PHONE..................................910 653-5200
James Bailey, *Pr*
Dieter Vande Kamp, *
▲ **EMP:** 40 **EST:** 1989
SQ FT: 48,000
SALES (est): 6.04MM
SALES (corp-wide): 19MM **Privately Held**
Web: www.filtec-precise.com
SIC: **2281** Yarn spinning mills
PA: Filament-Technik Gesellschaft Fur Technische Garne Mbh & Cie. Kg
Hermann-Hollerith-Str. 13
Baesweiler NW 52499
240 193-3000

(G-15083)
KRS PLASTICS INC
26 Tabor Industrial Park Rd (28463)
P.O. Box 693 (28463-0693)
PHONE..................................910 653-3602
Billy Douglas, *Pr*
Charles Balkcum, *VP*
Lindsey Smith, *VP*
EMP: 15 **EST:** 1982
SQ FT: 9,000
SALES (est): 3.11MM **Privately Held**
Web: www.krsplastics.com
SIC: **3081** Vinyl film and sheet

(G-15084)
MILLIGAN HOUSE MOVERS INC (PA)
2115 Swamp Fox Hwy E (28463-7451)
PHONE..................................910 653-2272
EMP: 4 **EST:** 1968
SALES (est): 386.86K **Privately Held**
Web: www.milliganhousemovers.com
SIC: **1799** 3448 4212 Building mover, including houses; Prefabricated metal buildings and components; Moving services

(G-15085)
PATRICKS SMALL ENGINES
16624 Seven Creeks Hwy (28463-9009)
PHONE..................................910 653-2061
EMP: 5 **EST:** 2013
SALES (est): 149.43K **Privately Held**
SIC: **3519** Internal combustion engines, nec

(G-15086)
SMITHS LOGGING
13169 Swamp Fox Hwy E (28463-9166)
PHONE..................................910 653-4422
Leo Smith, *Owner*
EMP: 4 **EST:** 1984
SALES (est): 218.71K **Privately Held**
SIC: **2411** Logging camps and contractors

(G-15087)
TABOR CITY LUMBER COMPANY (PA)
510 N Main St (28463-8500)
P.O. Box 37 (28463-0037)
PHONE..................................910 653-3162
Roderick D Sanders, *Pr*
Daniel M Sanders, *
Anne M Sanders, *
EMP: 25 **EST:** 1946
SALES (est): 7.51MM
SALES (corp-wide): 7.51MM **Privately Held**
Web: www.taborcitylumber.com

SIC: **5031** 2421 Lumber: rough, dressed, and finished; Lumber: rough, sawed, or planed

(G-15088)
TWIGS SCREEN PRINTING
5474 Sidney Cherry Grove Rd (28463-8714)
PHONE..................................910 770-1605
Justin Worley, *Prin*
EMP: 4 **EST:** 2017
SALES (est): 83.91K **Privately Held**
SIC: **2752** Commercial printing, lithographic

Tar Heel
Bladen County

(G-15089)
MARK III LOGGING INC
16324 Nc Highway 87 W (28392-9302)
PHONE..................................910 862-4820
Shannon Woodell, *Managing Member*
EMP: 6 **EST:** 2006
SALES (est): 452.89K **Privately Held**
SIC: **2411** Logging camps and contractors

(G-15090)
SMITHFELD FRESH MEATS SLS CORP
15855 Hwy 87 W (28392)
PHONE..................................910 862-7675
EMP: 364
Web: smithfield.sfdbrands.com
SIC: **2011** Pork products, from pork slaughtered on site
HQ: Smithfield Fresh Meats Sales Corp.
200 Commerce St
Smithfield VA 23430
757 357-3131

(G-15091)
SMITHFIELD FOODS INC
16261 Nc Highway 87 W (28392-9322)
PHONE..................................910 241-2022
EMP: 20
Web: www.smithfieldfoods.com
SIC: **2011** Meat packing plants
HQ: Smithfield Foods, Inc.
200 Commerce St
Smithfield VA 23430
757 365-3000

(G-15092)
SMITHFIELD FOODS INC
15855 Nc Highway 87 W (28392-9307)
PHONE..................................910 862-7675
EMP: 228 **EST:** 1994
SALES (est): 13.04MM **Privately Held**
Web: smithfield.sfdbrands.com
SIC: **2011** Meat packing plants

Tarboro
Edgecombe County

(G-15093)
AIR SYSTEM COMPONENTS INC
Also Called: ASC
3301 N Main St (27886-1926)
PHONE..................................252 641-5900
EMP: 80
Web: www.airsysco.com
SIC: **3585** Air conditioning equipment, complete
HQ: Air System Components, Inc.
605 Shiloh Rd
Plano TX 75074
972 212-4888

(G-15094)
AIR SYSTEM COMPONENTS INC
Also Called: Titus
3301 N Main St (27886-1926)
PHONE..................................252 641-0875
Barry Beyer, *Pr*
EMP: 188
Web: www.airsysco.com
SIC: **3585** Air conditioning equipment, complete
HQ: Air System Components, Inc.
605 Shiloh Rd
Plano TX 75074
972 212-4888

(G-15095)
AMERICAN COMPOSITES ENGRG (HQ)
Also Called: Ace
1090 W Saint James St (27886-4822)
PHONE..................................252 641-9866
Ronnie Walker, *Pr*
EMP: 11 **EST:** 1994
SALES (est): 2.31MM
SALES (corp-wide): 2.48MM **Privately Held**
Web: www.qualityfrp.com
SIC: **3089** Synthetic resin finished products, nec
PA: Hornet Capital, Llc
1090 W Saint James St
Tarboro NC 27886
252 641-8000

(G-15096)
BIMBO BAKERIES USA INC
Also Called: Sara Lee Bakery Outlet
110 Sara Lee Rd (27886-5269)
PHONE..................................252 641-2200
Jim Dibble, *Mgr*
EMP: 1100
Web: www.arnoldbread.com
SIC: **2053** 2051 Frozen bakery products, except bread; Bread, cake, and related products
HQ: Bimbo Bakeries Usa, Inc.
355 Business Center Dr
Horsham PA 19044
215 347-5500

(G-15097)
BONES GRILL LLC
2404 Summerfield Dr (27886-5647)
PHONE..................................252 827-0454
Leatrice Pitt, *Mgr*
EMP: 5 **EST:** 2016
SALES (est): 143.46K **Privately Held**
SIC: **2599** Bar, restaurant and cafeteria furniture

(G-15098)
BRYANTS FIRE EXTINGUISHER CO
108 W Granville St (27886-5004)
PHONE..................................252 563-4111
EMP: 4 **EST:** 2017
SALES (est): 73.39K **Privately Held**
SIC: **3999** Fire extinguishers, portable

(G-15099)
CAMP PUBLICATIONS LLC
1505 Captains Rd (27886-2623)
PHONE..................................252 908-3684
Gene Hudson, *Prin*
EMP: 5 **EST:** 2014
SALES (est): 120.62K **Privately Held**
SIC: **2741** Miscellaneous publishing

(G-15100)
CORNING INCORPORATED
Also Called: Corning

7708 Us Highway 64 Alternate W (27886)
PHONE..................................252 316-4500
EMP: 19
SALES (corp-wide): 12.59B **Publicly Held**
Web: www.corning.com
SIC: **3229** 3357 3661 3674 Glass fiber products; Fiber optic cable (insulated); Telephone and telegraph apparatus; Semiconductors and related devices
PA: Corning Incorporated
1 Riverfront Plz
Corning NY 14831
607 974-9000

(G-15101)
DFA DAIRY BRANDS FLUID LLC
1079 W Saint James St (27886-4860)
PHONE..................................336 714-9032
Michael Hardcastle, *Brnch Mgr*
EMP: 6
SALES (corp-wide): 24.52B **Privately Held**
Web: www.dfamilk.com
SIC: **2026** Fluid milk
HQ: Dfa Dairy Brands Fluid, Llc
1405 N 98th St
Kansas City KS 66111
816 801-6455

(G-15102)
EASTERN CAROLINA MFG CO LLC
179 Nc Highway 97 E (27886-9090)
PHONE..................................252 824-3794
EMP: 4 **EST:** 2018
SALES (est): 116.54K **Privately Held**
SIC: **3999** Manufacturing industries, nec

(G-15103)
FIFTY COMBS LLC
611 Martin Luther King Jr Dr (27886-3103)
PHONE..................................252 406-6242
EMP: 4 **EST:** 2021
SALES (est): 39.69K **Privately Held**
SIC: **3999** Hair and hair-based products

(G-15104)
FOCAL POINT PRODUCTS INC
Also Called: Focal Point Architectural Pdts
3006 Anaconda Rd (27886-8836)
PHONE..................................252 824-0015
▲ **EMP:** 100
SIC: **3271** Architectural concrete: block, split, fluted, screen, etc.

(G-15105)
GEM BUOY INCORPORATED
3004 Lansdowne Dr (27886-1700)
PHONE..................................252 469-3680
James Buie, *Prin*
EMP: 6 **EST:** 2008
SALES (est): 135.09K **Privately Held**
SIC: **3732** Boatbuilding and repairing

(G-15106)
GENERAL FOAM PLASTICS CORP
501 Daniel St (27886-2249)
P.O. Box 2196 (23450-2196)
PHONE..................................757 857-0153
EMP: 7 **EST:** 2019
SALES (est): 483.54K **Privately Held**
SIC: **3999** Manufacturing industries, nec

(G-15107)
HC COMPOSITES LLC
Also Called: Powercat Group
1090 W Saint James St (27886-4822)
PHONE..................................252 641-8000
EMP: 166 **EST:** 2002
SQ FT: 145,000
SALES (est): 40.45MM **Privately Held**
Web: www.worldcat.com

Tarboro - Edgecombe County (G-15108)

SIC: 3732 Boatbuilding and repairing

(G-15108)
HOLLINGSWORTH HEATING AIR COND
1893 Mcnair Rd (27886-9054)
PHONE..................................252 824-0355
Johnnie Hollingsworth, *Prin*
EMP: 4 EST: 2004
SALES (est): 280.96K **Privately Held**
Web: www.tarboroheatingandair.com
SIC: 3699 1711 Electrical equipment and supplies, nec; Heating systems repair and maintenance

(G-15109)
HORNET CAPITAL LLC (PA)
1090 W Saint James St (27886-4822)
PHONE..................................252 641-8000
EMP: 7 EST: 1999
SALES (est): 2.48MM
SALES (corp-wide): 2.48MM **Privately Held**
Web: www.hornetcapital.com
SIC: 3089 Synthetic resin finished products, nec

(G-15110)
JEM ACRES INC
506 Trade St (27886-4322)
PHONE..................................252 823-3483
Jessie Smoot, *Prin*
EMP: 9 EST: 2004
SALES (est): 69.65K **Privately Held**
SIC: 3711 Buses, all types, assembly of

(G-15111)
LONG TRAILER CO INC
313 Bass Ln (27886-7921)
PHONE..................................252 823-8828
Lisa Gay, *Pr*
Linda Johnson, *
E L Elrod, *Stockholder**
EMP: 7 EST: 1958
SQ FT: 3,000
SALES (est): 649.59K **Privately Held**
Web: www.longtrailer.com
SIC: 3799 Boat trailers

(G-15112)
LS CABLE & SYSTEM USA INC
2801 Anaconda Rd (27886-8833)
PHONE..................................252 824-3553
David Han, *Manager*
EMP: 150
Web: www.lscsusa.com
SIC: 3357 2298 5063 Aircraft wire and cable, nonferrous; Ropes and fiber cables; Electrical apparatus and equipment
HQ: Ls Cable & System U.S.A., Inc.
  6625 The Crners Pkwy Ste
  Peachtree Corners GA 30092
  770 657-6000

(G-15113)
MADEM-MOORECRAFT REELS USA INC
3006 Anaconda Rd (27886-8836)
P.O. Box 1528 (27886-1528)
PHONE..................................252 823-2510
Stephen Redhage, *Prin*
Fatima Bellini, *
EMP: 107 EST: 2017
SALES (est): 19.65MM **Privately Held**
Web: www.madem-moorecraft.com
SIC: 2499 Reels, plywood

(G-15114)
MAYO KNITTING MILL INC (PA)
Also Called: Mayo

2204 W Austin St (27886-2467)
P.O. Box 160 (27886-0160)
PHONE..................................252 823-3101
Ben C Mayo Ii, *Pr*
C W Mayo Iv, *VP*
Bryan T Mayo, *
▲ EMP: 101 EST: 1931
SQ FT: 100,000
SALES (est): 21.63MM
SALES (corp-wide): 21.63MM **Privately Held**
Web: www.mayoknitting.com
SIC: 2252 5949 2251 Socks; Sewing, needlework, and piece goods; Women's hosiery, except socks

(G-15115)
MOORECRAFT REELS INC
101 Royster St (27886-8845)
P.O. Box 1528 (27886-1528)
PHONE..................................252 823-2510
Stephen J Redhage, *Pr*
Steve Redhage, *
Marvin Horton, *
Sharon Horton, *
Sharon H Redhage, *
EMP: 58 EST: 1992
SQ FT: 12,000
SALES (est): 5.32MM **Privately Held**
SIC: 2499 Spools, reels, and pulleys: wood

(G-15116)
MOORECRAFT WOOD PROUCTS INC
101 Royster St (27886-8845)
P.O. Box 1528 (27886-1528)
PHONE..................................252 823-2510
Marvin V Horton, *Pr*
Sharon L Horton, *Ch Bd*
Sharon H Redhage, *Sec*
EMP: 8 EST: 1966
SQ FT: 80,000
SALES (est): 923.81K **Privately Held**
SIC: 6512 2449 Commercial and industrial building operation; Rectangular boxes and crates, wood

(G-15117)
MURDOCK WEBBING COMPANY INC
Also Called: Phoenix Trimming
1052 W Saint James St (27886-4822)
P.O. Box 609 (27886-0609)
PHONE..................................252 823-1131
Vann Cummings, *Off Mgr*
EMP: 42
SALES (corp-wide): 23.07MM **Privately Held**
Web: www.murdockwebbing.com
SIC: 2241 Webbing, woven
PA: Murdock Webbing Company, Inc.
  27 Foundry St
  Central Falls RI 02863
  401 724-3000

(G-15118)
NASH BUILDING SYSTEMS INC
1803 Anaconda Rd (27886-8811)
P.O. Box 1320 (27886-1320)
PHONE..................................252 823-1905
EMP: 16 EST: 2014
SALES (est): 5.19MM **Privately Held**
Web: www.nashbuildingsystems.com
SIC: 3448 Prefabricated metal buildings and components

(G-15119)
NGX
3002 Anaconda Rd (27886-8836)
PHONE..................................866 782-7749
Steve Thompson, *Managing Member*
▼ EMP: 29 EST: 2007
SALES (est): 4.68MM

SALES (corp-wide): 95.55MM **Privately Held**
SIC: 3086 Packaging and shipping materials, foamed plastics
PA: Noel Group, Llc
  501 Innovative Way
  Zebulon NC 27597
  919 269-6500

(G-15120)
S & W METAL WORKS INC
1813 Anaconda Rd (27886-8811)
PHONE..................................252 641-0912
Ray Whitehurst, *Pr*
Kevin Comb, *VP*
EMP: 9 EST: 1987
SQ FT: 10,000
SALES (est): 832.01K **Privately Held**
SIC: 3599 Machine shop, jobbing and repair

(G-15121)
SUPERIOR ESSEX INC
2801 Anaconda Rd (27886-8833)
PHONE..................................252 823-5111
Jim Berry, *Brnch Mgr*
EMP: 87
Web: www.superioressex.com
SIC: 3357 Nonferrous wiredrawing and insulating
HQ: Superior Essex Inc.
  5770 Powers Ferry Rd
  Atlanta GA 30327
  770 657-6000

(G-15122)
SUPERIOR ESSEX INTL LP
Also Called: SUPERIOR ESSEX INTERNATIONAL LP
2801 Anaconda Rd (27886-8833)
PHONE..................................252 823-5111
EMP: 107
Web: www.superioressex.com
SIC: 3357 Communication wire
HQ: Superior Essex International Inc.
  5770 Powers Ferry Rd # 40
  Atlanta GA 30327
  770 657-6000

(G-15123)
SWIMWAYS
3002 Anaconda Rd (27886-8836)
PHONE..................................252 563-1101
EMP: 17 EST: 2018
SALES (est): 1.96MM **Privately Held**
SIC: 3086 Plastics foam products

(G-15124)
TOWN OF TARBORO
Also Called: Waterplant
600 Albemarle Ave (27886-4300)
P.O. Box 220 (27886-0220)
PHONE..................................252 641-4284
Harry Penwell, *Brnch Mgr*
EMP: 21
Web: www.tarboro-nc.com
SIC: 3589 Water treatment equipment, industrial
PA: Town Of Tarboro
  500 N Main St
  Tarboro NC 27886
  252 641-4250

(G-15125)
W R LONG INC
1607 Cedar St (27886-2464)
P.O. Box 460 (27886-0460)
PHONE..................................252 823-4570
Z Vance Long, *Pr*
▲ EMP: 20 EST: 1987
SQ FT: 27,000
SALES (est): 5.68MM **Privately Held**

Web: www.wrlonginc.com
SIC: 3531 Buckets, excavating: clamshell, concrete, dragline, etc.

Taylorsville
Alexander County

(G-15126)
ACCURATE WELD LLC
2374 Friendship Church Rd (28681-8873)
PHONE..................................828 310-1517
Terry Meadows, *Owner*
EMP: 6 EST: 2008
SALES (est): 78.33K **Privately Held**
SIC: 3699 Electrical welding equipment

(G-15127)
ADVANTAGE NN-WVENS CNVRTING LL
173 Wittenburg Industrial Dr (28681-8259)
P.O. Box 996 (28613-0996)
PHONE..................................828 635-1880
EMP: 6 EST: 2016
SALES (est): 245.23K **Privately Held**
Web: www.advantagenonwovens.com
SIC: 2297 Nonwoven fabrics

(G-15128)
ALEXANDER CRUSH INC
452 Paynes Dairy Rd (28681-6221)
PHONE..................................828 635-7136
Darryl Pritchard, *Prin*
EMP: 4 EST: 2016
SALES (est): 75.48K **Privately Held**
SIC: 2084 Wines

(G-15129)
ANCHOR-RICHEY EMERGENCY VEHICL
Also Called: Anchor Richey E V S
241 Advent Church Rd (28681-4622)
P.O. Box 6342 (28603-6342)
PHONE..................................828 495-8145
Matthew Richey, *Pr*
Bill Mccormick, *VP*
EMP: 23 EST: 1979
SQ FT: 6,000
SALES (est): 3.24MM **Privately Held**
Web: www.anchor-richeyevs.com
SIC: 3713 Specialty motor vehicle bodies

(G-15130)
BOREALIS COMPOUNDS INC
401 We Baab Industrial Dr (28681-6027)
PHONE..................................908 798-7497
Roland Janssen, *Brnch Mgr*
EMP: 30
SALES (corp-wide): 9.69B **Privately Held**
Web: www.borealisgroup.com
SIC: 3087 Custom compound purchased resins
HQ: Borealis Compounds Inc.
  176 Thomas Rd
  Port Murray NJ 07865

(G-15131)
BORN IN A BARN INC
1542 Rocky Face Church Rd (28681-3937)
PHONE..................................828 635-5808
EMP: 5 EST: 2006
SALES (est): 94.79K **Privately Held**
Web: www.borninabarncabinetry.com
SIC: 2431 Millwork

(G-15132)
BROWN BROTHERS LUMBER
1388 Little River Church Rd (28681-3644)
PHONE..................................828 632-6486
Rickey Brown, *Prin*

GEOGRAPHIC SECTION — Taylorsville - Alexander County (G-15155)

EMP: 6 EST: 2012
SALES (est): 350.61K Privately Held
SIC: 2411 Logging camps and contractors

(G-15133)
CARPENTER CO
Hwy 90 E (28681)
P.O. Box 455 (28681-0455)
PHONE...............................828 632-7061
Tom Dunston, *Brnch Mgr*
EMP: 32
SALES (corp-wide): 1.85B Privately Held
Web: www.carpenter.com
SIC: 3086 2821 2392 Insulation or cushioning material, foamed plastics; Plastics materials and resins; Household furnishings, nec
PA: Carpenter Co.
5016 Monument Ave
Richmond VA 23230
804 359-0800

(G-15134)
CHASE LAMINATING INC
138 Wittenburg Rd (28681-6515)
PHONE...............................828 632-6666
Al Stozer, *Mgr*
EMP: 11 EST: 2004
SALES (est): 537.83K Publicly Held
SIC: 2295 Coated fabrics, not rubberized
HQ: Chase Corporation
375 University Ave
Westwood MA 02090
781 332-0700

(G-15135)
COMPOSITE FABRICS AMERICA LLC
105 Pierpoint Ln (28681-3827)
P.O. Box 609 (28681-0609)
PHONE...............................828 632-5220
Matthew M Mcpherson, *Managing Member*
▲ EMP: 4 EST: 2009
SALES (est): 563.8K
SALES (corp-wide): 48.15MM Privately Held
Web: www.cfamills.com
SIC: 5949 2221 Fabric stores piece goods; Acetate broadwoven fabrics
PA: Schneider Mills, Inc.
1170 Nc Highway 16 N
Taylorsville NC 28681
828 632-8181

(G-15136)
COUNTY OF ALEXANDER
Also Called: Department of Solid Waste
255 Liledoun Rd (28681-2576)
P.O. Box 12 (28681-0012)
PHONE...............................828 632-1101
Rick French, *Mgr*
EMP: 28
Web: www.alexandercountync.gov
SIC: 3089 Garbage containers, plastics
PA: County Of Alexander
151 W Main Ave Ste 1
Taylorsville NC 28681
828 632-9332

(G-15137)
CUSTOM EDUCATIONAL FURN LLC
Also Called: CEF
2696 Nc Highway 16 S (28681-8952)
PHONE...............................800 255-9189
Scott Mchugh, *Managing Member*
EMP: 15 EST: 2014
SALES (est): 2.11MM
SALES (corp-wide): 5.59MM Privately Held
Web: www.cefinc.com
SIC: 2531 2541 School furniture; Office fixtures, wood
PA: Precision Materials, Llc
6246 Nc Highway 16 S
Taylorsville NC 28681
828 632-8851

(G-15138)
CUSTOM POWDER WORX
4911 Church Rd (28681-8713)
PHONE...............................828 310-1373
EMP: 5 EST: 2017
SALES (est): 89.13K Privately Held
Web: www.custompowderworx.com
SIC: 3479 Coating of metals and formed products

(G-15139)
D J ENVIRO SOLUTIONS
334 Riverview Rd (28681-7651)
PHONE...............................828 495-7448
Dennis Gillen, *Prin*
EMP: 6 EST: 2010
SALES (est): 85.48K Privately Held
SIC: 3564 Air cleaning systems

(G-15140)
DANIELS WOODCARVING CO INC
2325 Nc Highway 90 E (28681-3750)
PHONE...............................828 632-7336
David L Daniels, *Pr*
Paula Daniels, *
EMP: 10 EST: 1972
SQ FT: 45,000
SALES (est): 317.14K Privately Held
SIC: 2426 2512 Carvings, furniture: wood; Upholstered household furniture

(G-15141)
DURA-CRAFT DIE INC
1442 Liledoun Rd (28681-3090)
PHONE...............................828 632-1944
J Mark Warren, *Pr*
J M Warren, *Pr*
Ricky Bowman, *VP*
John C Warren, *Sec*
EMP: 4 EST: 1993
SQ FT: 400
SALES (est): 426.08K Privately Held
Web: www.duracraftdie.com
SIC: 3544 Special dies and tools

(G-15142)
FLAVOR SCIENCES INC
715 Houck Mountain Rd (28681-7714)
PHONE...............................828 758-2525
Roger E Kiley, *Pr*
Joyce Kiley, *VP*
EMP: 20 EST: 1969
SALES (est): 1.64MM Privately Held
Web: www.flavorsciences.com
SIC: 2087 Extracts, flavoring

(G-15143)
FRIENDSHIP UPHOLSTERY CO INC
6035 Church Rd (28681-8207)
PHONE...............................828 632-9836
Greg Hefner, *Pr*
EMP: 25 EST: 1972
SQ FT: 40,000
SALES (est): 1.18MM Privately Held
Web: www.friendshipupholstery.com
SIC: 2512 Upholstered household furniture

(G-15144)
HANCOCK & MOORE LLC (HQ)
Also Called: Cabot Wrenn
166 Hancock And Moore Ln (28681-7679)
P.O. Box 3444 (28603-3444)
PHONE...............................828 495-8235
John Glasheen, *CEO*
Timothy Rogers, *
Jimmy Moore, *
Brandon Hucks, *
EMP: 86 EST: 2015
SQ FT: 150,000
SALES (est): 53.64MM
SALES (corp-wide): 212.17MM Privately Held
Web: www.hancockandmoore.com
SIC: 2512 Upholstered household furniture
PA: Rhf Investments, Inc.
401 11th St Nw
Hickory NC 28601
828 326-8350

(G-15145)
HANCOCK & MOORE LLC
Also Called: Cabot Wrenn
405 Rink Dam Rd (28681-6726)
PHONE...............................828 495-8235
Bryan Craft, *Brnch Mgr*
EMP: 206
SALES (corp-wide): 212.17MM Privately Held
Web: www.hancockandmoore.com
SIC: 2512 2511 2521 Upholstered household furniture; Wood household furniture; Wood office furniture
HQ: Hancock & Moore, Llc
166 Hancock And Moore Ln
Taylorsville NC 28681
828 495-8235

(G-15146)
HEFNER REELS LLC
34 Wittenburg Industrial Dr (28681-8255)
PHONE...............................828 632-5717
Vicki Heffner, *
Hal Ray Hefner, *
Kim Ferguson, *
EMP: 45 EST: 2007
SALES (est): 7.15MM Privately Held
SIC: 2499 Spools, reels, and pulleys: wood

(G-15147)
HUNTINGTON HOUSE INC
210 Bethlehem Park Ln (28681-7682)
PHONE...............................828 495-4400
Monty Meadlock, *Mgr*
EMP: 50
SALES (corp-wide): 19.15MM Privately Held
Web: www.huntingtonhouse.com
SIC: 2512 Upholstered household furniture
PA: Huntington House, Inc.
661 Rink Dam Rd
Hickory NC 28601
828 495-4400

(G-15148)
IDEAL LIQUIDATION INC
171 5th Ave Sw (28681-3022)
P.O. Box 935 (28681-0935)
PHONE...............................828 632-3771
William Lackey, *Pr*
EMP: 16 EST: 1958
SQ FT: 58,000
SALES (est): 422.65K Privately Held
Web: www.idealframeco.com
SIC: 2426 Hardwood dimension and flooring mills

(G-15149)
ISENHOUR FURNITURE COMPANY (PA)
486 S Center St (28681-3027)
P.O. Box 1089 (28603-1089)
PHONE...............................828 632-8849
Dwight Isenhour, *Pr*
▲ EMP: 87 EST: 1989
SQ FT: 100,000
SALES (est): 4.72MM
SALES (corp-wide): 4.72MM Privately Held
Web: www.isenhourfurn.com
SIC: 2512 Upholstered household furniture

(G-15150)
LITTLE STITCHES EMB & PRTG LLC
196 Westgate Dr (28681-2300)
PHONE...............................828 352-7550
Traci Fox, *Prin*
EMP: 5 EST: 2016
SALES (est): 130.92K Privately Held
SIC: 2752 Commercial printing, lithographic

(G-15151)
MASTERFIELD FURNITURE CO INC
6463 Church Rd (28681-6413)
PHONE...............................828 632-8535
Jeffrey Hefner, *Pr*
Johnny Hefner, *
EMP: 50 EST: 1976
SQ FT: 95,000
SALES (est): 4.95MM Privately Held
Web: www.masterfieldfurniturecompany.com
SIC: 2512 Living room furniture: upholstered on wood frames

(G-15152)
MITCHELL GOLD CO LLC
804 Old Landfill Rd (28681-9087)
PHONE...............................828 632-7916
EMP: 64
SALES (corp-wide): 197.18MM Privately Held
Web: www.mgbwhome.com
SIC: 2512 Upholstered household furniture
PA: The Mitchell Gold Co Llc
135 One Comfortable Pl
Taylorsville NC 28681

(G-15153)
MITCHELL GOLD CO LLC (PA)
Also Called: Mitchell Gold Bob Williams
135 One Comfortable Pl (28681-3783)
◆ EMP: 228 EST: 1989
SQ FT: 575,000
SALES (est): 197.18MM
SALES (corp-wide): 197.18MM Privately Held
Web: www.mgbwhome.com
SIC: 5712 2512 Furniture stores; Chairs: upholstered on wood frames

(G-15154)
PARAGON FILMS INC
255 We Baab Industrial Dr (28681-6013)
PHONE...............................828 632-5552
Michael J Baab, *Brnch Mgr*
EMP: 15
SALES (corp-wide): 111.43MM Privately Held
Web: www.paragon-films.com
SIC: 3081 2671 Polyethylene film; Plastic film, coated or laminated for packaging
PA: Paragon Films, Inc.
3500 W Tacoma St
Broken Arrow OK 74012
918 250-3456

(G-15155)
PAUL ROBERT CHAIR INC (PA)
Also Called: Paul Robert
266 Martin Luther King Dr (28681-3065)
P.O. Box 969 (28681-0969)
PHONE...............................828 632-7021
Paul Robert Dickinson, *Pr*
Daniel Y Dickinson, *
Patricia M Dickinson, *

Taylorsville - Alexander County (G-15156)

◆ **EMP:** 69 **EST:** 1983
SQ FT: 125,000
SALES (est): 9.53MM
SALES (corp-wide): 9.53MM **Privately Held**
Web: www.paulrobert.com
SIC: 2512 Chairs: upholstered on wood frames

(G-15156)
PIEDMONT CMPOSITES TOOLING LLC
33 Lewittes Rd (28681-2873)
PHONE.................................828 632-8883
EMP: 55 **EST:** 2018
SALES (est): 6.01MM **Privately Held**
Web: www.piedmontcomposites.com
SIC: 2221 Fiberglass fabrics

(G-15157)
PIEDMONT WOOD PRODUCTS INC
1924 Black Oak Ridge Rd (28681-3309)
P.O. Box 307 (28681-0307)
PHONE.................................828 632-4077
Gary Coffey, *Pr*
Malcolm Reese, *VP*
EMP: 13 **EST:** 1972
SQ FT: 16,500
SALES (est): 1.05MM **Privately Held**
Web: www.piedmontwood.com
SIC: 2431 Millwork

(G-15158)
PRECISION LOG & CHIPPING LLC
330 Dee Loudermelk Ln (28681-8560)
PHONE.................................828 446-1592
Russell Lynn Loudermelk, *Admn*
EMP: 7 **EST:** 2014
SALES (est): 391.07K **Privately Held**
SIC: 2411 Logging camps and contractors

(G-15159)
PRECISION MATERIALS LLC (PA)
6246 Nc Highway 16 S (28681-6354)
P.O. Box 848 (28681-0848)
PHONE.................................828 632-8851
EMP: 17 **EST:** 2009
SALES (est): 5.59MM
SALES (corp-wide): 5.59MM **Privately Held**
Web: www.pmatnc.com
SIC: 2521 2531 2511 Wood office furniture; School furniture; Wood household furniture

(G-15160)
RELIC WOOD LLC
1050 Sipe Rd (28681-8689)
PHONE.................................828 855-8924
EMP: 4
SALES (est): 178.98K **Privately Held**
SIC: 2541 Wood partitions and fixtures

(G-15161)
RHF INVESTMENTS INC
165 Matheson Park Ave (28681-2435)
PHONE.................................828 632-7070
Dennis Lockhart, *Mgr*
EMP: 6
SALES (corp-wide): 212.17MM **Privately Held**
Web: www.centuryfurniture.com
SIC: 2426 Frames for upholstered furniture, wood
PA: Rhf Investments, Inc.
 401 11th St Nw
 Hickory NC 28601
 828 326-8350

(G-15162)
ROYALE COMFORT SEATING INC
140 Alspaugh Dam Rd (28681-4632)
P.O. Box 235 (28681-0235)
PHONE.................................828 352-9021
Clyde Goble, *Pr*
Harrison Reid Junior, *VP*
David Lawson, *
Fred Crump, *
EMP: 100 **EST:** 1987
SQ FT: 37,500
SALES (est): 5.08MM **Privately Held**
Web: www.royalecomfort.com
SIC: 2392 3089 Cushions and pillows; Fiber, vulcanized

(G-15163)
ROYALE KOMFORT BEDDING INC
2320 All Healing Springs Rd (28681-7273)
P.O. Box 549 (28681-0549)
PHONE.................................828 632-5631
EMP: 14 **EST:** 1997
SALES (est): 421.89K **Privately Held**
Web: www.royalekomfortbedding.com
SIC: 2515 Mattresses, innerspring or box spring

(G-15164)
RUSSELL LOUDERMILK LOGGING
330 Dee Loudermilk Ln (28681-8560)
PHONE.................................828 632-4968
Russell Loudermilk, *Owner*
EMP: 4 **EST:** 1985
SALES (est): 251.62K **Privately Held**
Web: www.grandmarquis.com
SIC: 2411 Logging camps and contractors

(G-15165)
SCHNEIDER MILLS INC (PA)
1170 Nc Highway 16 N (28681-2468)
PHONE.................................828 632-8181
Peter M Campanelli, *Pr*
Mark A Labbe, *VP*
EMP: 12 **EST:** 1921
SQ FT: 4,500
SALES (est): 48.15MM
SALES (corp-wide): 48.15MM **Privately Held**
Web: www.schneidermills.com
SIC: 2221 Manmade and synthetic broadwoven fabrics

(G-15166)
SHINERS STASH JERKY
272 Moore Ln (28681-7416)
PHONE.................................828 302-6359
Swen Altis, *Prin*
EMP: 5 **EST:** 2016
SALES (est): 134.34K **Privately Held**
Web: www.shinersstashjerky.com
SIC: 2013 Sausages and other prepared meats

(G-15167)
SIPE LUMBER COMPANY INC
2750 Us Highway 64 90 W (28681-7579)
PHONE.................................828 632-4679
EMP: 28 **EST:** 1941
SALES (est): 4.62MM **Privately Held**
Web: www.sipelumber.com
SIC: 5031 5211 2421 Building materials, exterior; Lumber and other building materials; Lumber: rough, sawed, or planed

(G-15168)
STIKELEATHER INC
146 Windsor Dr (28681-6910)
PHONE.................................828 352-9095
Timothy D Stikeleather, *Prin*
EMP: 6 **EST:** 2012

SALES (est): 225.16K **Privately Held**
SIC: 3199 Leather goods, nec

(G-15169)
TAILOR CUT WOOD PRODUCTS INC
35 Wittenburg Industrial Dr (28681-8250)
P.O. Box 99 (28681-0099)
PHONE.................................828 632-2808
Ricky Price, *Pr*
Hal Hefner, *VP*
EMP: 19 **EST:** 1989
SQ FT: 31,500
SALES (est): 438.55K **Privately Held**
SIC: 2435 Panels, hardwood plywood

(G-15170)
TAYLOR KING FURNITURE INC
286 County Home Rd (28681-9375)
PHONE.................................828 632-7731
John G Mullins, *CEO*
Del Starnes, *
Ron Downs, *
Dana Beach, *
Tanya Comer, *
▲ **EMP:** 120 **EST:** 1974
SQ FT: 160,000
SALES (est): 17.3MM **Privately Held**
Web: www.taylorking.com
SIC: 2512 Upholstered household furniture

(G-15171)
TAYLORSVILLE PRECAST MOLDS INC
128 Taylorsville Mfg Rd (28681-4005)
PHONE.................................828 632-4608
David R Mecimore, *Pr*
Sharon Mecimore, *Sec*
EMP: 6 **EST:** 1989
SQ FT: 6,000
SALES (est): 727.48K **Privately Held**
SIC: 1761 3444 Sheet metal work, nec; Sheet metalwork

(G-15172)
TAYLORSVILLE TIMES
24 E Main Ave (28681-2541)
P.O. Box 279 (28681-0279)
PHONE.................................828 632-2532
Walter Lee Sharpe, *Owner*
EMP: 16 **EST:** 1930
SQ FT: 8,000
SALES (est): 499.05K **Privately Held**
Web: www.taylorsvilletimes.com
SIC: 2711 Commercial printing and newspaper publishing combined

(G-15173)
TEXTILE MANUFACTURING TECH LLC
3215 Rink Dam Rd (28681-4250)
PHONE.................................828 632-3012
Stewart Bowman, *Prin*
EMP: 4 **EST:** 2015
SALES (est): 146.43K **Privately Held**
SIC: 8731 5199 3999 Commercial physical research; Fabrics, yarns, and knit goods; Manufacturing industries, nec

(G-15174)
THOMAS LEE FORTNER SAWMILL
70 Mount Olive Church Rd (28681-4335)
PHONE.................................828 632-9525
Thomas Lee Fortner, *Owner*
EMP: 8 **EST:** 1983
SALES (est): 583.43K **Privately Held**
SIC: 2421 Sawmills and planing mills, general

(G-15175)
VINTAGE EDITIONS INC
88 Buff Ln (28681-3352)
PHONE.................................828 632-4185
Perry L Austin, *Pr*
▲ **EMP:** 10 **EST:** 2002
SQ FT: 25,000
SALES (est): 941.79K **Privately Held**
Web: www.vintageeditions.com
SIC: 2499 3993 Decorative wood and woodwork; Signs and advertising specialties

(G-15176)
WATTS BUMGARNER & BROWN INC
9541 Us Highway 64 90 W (28681-7543)
PHONE.................................828 632-4797
Greg Bumgarner, *Pr*
Danny Bumgarner, *VP*
Patsy Wilson, *Sec*
EMP: 13 **EST:** 1964
SALES (est): 475.47K **Privately Held**
SIC: 2421 Lumber: rough, sawed, or planed

Teachey
Duplin County

(G-15177)
INDUSTRIAL METAL MAINT INC
164 John Deere Rd (28464-9446)
PHONE.................................910 285-3240
Jennifer Crist, *Pr*
EMP: 5 **EST:** 2001
SALES (est): 461.11K **Privately Held**
Web: imm.embarqspace.com
SIC: 7692 Welding repair

(G-15178)
RICKY DON THORNTON
Also Called: Thornton Trucking & Logging
131 Whitted Ln (28464-9471)
PHONE.................................910 271-2989
Ricky D Thornton, *Owner*
EMP: 6 **EST:** 2018
SALES (est): 247.08K **Privately Held**
SIC: 2411 Logging

Terrell
Catawba County

(G-15179)
GREENSTORY GLOBL GVRNMENT MLTA
3811 Gordon St (28682-9731)
PHONE.................................828 446-9278
Meghan Stout, *Ch Bd*
EMP: 16 **EST:** 2019
SALES (est): 649.09K **Privately Held**
SIC: 3589 Water filters and softeners, household type

(G-15180)
TRIPLE B STONE LLC
319 Doolie Road (28682)
PHONE.................................704 663-5860
EMP: 5 **EST:** 2011
SALES (est): 259.44K **Privately Held**
Web: www.triplebstone.com
SIC: 1481 Mine and quarry services, nonmetallic minerals

Thomasville
Davidson County

(G-15181)
ADVANCED MOTOR SPORTS COATINGS

GEOGRAPHIC SECTION

Thomasville - Davidson County (G-15206)

17 High Tech Blvd (27360-5560)
PHONE...................................336 472-5518
Brett Watkins, *Genl Mgr*
EMP: 8 **EST:** 2004
SALES (est): 488.41K **Privately Held**
Web: www.advancedmotorsportscoatings.com
SIC: 3471 Plating and polishing

(G-15182)
ALBRIGHT QULTY WD TURNING INC
193 Black Farm Rd (27360-6804)
PHONE...................................336 475-1434
Fred Albright, *Owner*
EMP: 8 **EST:** 2001
SALES (est): 416.36K **Privately Held**
Web: www.lakesbci.com
SIC: 2499 Carved and turned wood

(G-15183)
ALTIUM PACKAGING LLC
1408 Unity St (27360-4957)
PHONE...................................336 472-1500
Jeff Fay, *Brnch Mgr*
EMP: 54
SALES (corp-wide): 15.9B **Publicly Held**
Web: www.altiumpkg.com
SIC: 3089 Plastics containers, except foam
HQ: Altium Packaging Llc
2500 Windy Ridge Pkwy Se # 1400
Atlanta GA 30339
678 742-4600

(G-15184)
AM HAIRE MFG & SVC CORP
516 Pineywood Rd (27360-2763)
PHONE...................................336 472-4444
EMP: 150 **EST:** 2010
SQ FT: 68,300
SALES (est): 25.17MM **Privately Held**
Web: www.amhairecorp.com
SIC: 3713 Truck bodies (motor vehicles)

(G-15185)
AMERICAN RNOVATION SYSTEMS LLC
208 Bell Dr (27360-7960)
PHONE...................................336 313-6210
EMP: 6 **EST:** 2013
SALES (est): 163.42K **Privately Held**
Web: www.arsfixit.com
SIC: 1389 7389 Construction, repair, and dismantling services; Business services, nec

(G-15186)
AMT
113 Sunrise Center Dr (27360-4928)
PHONE...................................617 549-4395
EMP: 5 **EST:** 2019
SALES (est): 87.26K **Privately Held**
SIC: 3714 Motor vehicle parts and accessories

(G-15187)
ATTL PRODUCTS INC
216 E Holly Hill Rd (27360-5820)
PHONE...................................336 475-8101
Randy Ramsom, *Owner*
EMP: 4 **EST:** 2008
SALES (est): 428.5K **Privately Held**
Web: www.tracktac.com
SIC: 2899 Chemical preparations, nec

(G-15188)
BARTIMAEUS BY DESIGN INC
1010 Randolph St (27360-5877)
PHONE...................................336 475-4346
Eddie Brinkley, *Pr*
Chadwick Brinkley, *

Gloria Brinkley, *
EMP: 110 **EST:** 2001
SALES (est): 19.18MM **Privately Held**
Web: www.bartbydesign.com
SIC: 2426 3441 Frames for upholstered furniture, wood; Fabricated structural metal

(G-15189)
BRASSCRAFT
1024 Randolph St (27360-5877)
PHONE...................................336 475-2131
Don Woddy, *Pr*
▲ **EMP:** 131 **EST:** 1962
SQ FT: 200,000
SALES (est): 32.21MM
SALES (corp-wide): 7.97B **Publicly Held**
Web: www.brasscraft.com
SIC: 5074 3491 Plumbers' brass goods and fittings; Automatic regulating and control valves
HQ: Brasscraft Manufacturing Company
39600 Orchard Hill Pl
Novi MI 48375
248 305-6000

(G-15190)
BRASSCRAFT MANUFACTURING CO
Also Called: Brasscraft Brownstown
1024 Randolph St (27360-5877)
PHONE...................................336 475-2131
EMP: 12
SALES (corp-wide): 7.97B **Publicly Held**
Web: www.brasscraft.com
SIC: 3432 Plumbing fixture fittings and trim
HQ: Brasscraft Manufacturing Company
39600 Orchard Hill Pl
Novi MI 48375
248 305-6000

(G-15191)
BRYSON INDUSTRIES INC
416 Albertson Rd (27360-8985)
PHONE...................................336 931-0026
David Lancaster, *Pr*
Tommy Lancaster, *Sr VP*
EMP: 14 **EST:** 2001
SQ FT: 10,000
SALES (est): 7.74MM **Privately Held**
Web: www.brysonusa.com
SIC: 2819 Industrial inorganic chemicals, nec

(G-15192)
C & B FRAME CO INC
1506 Lexington Ave (27360-3329)
PHONE...................................336 475-0194
Jack W Medlin, *Pr*
Judith Medlin, *VP*
Don Lee Cooper, *Sec*
EMP: 12 **EST:** 1977
SQ FT: 7,500
SALES (est): 355.31K **Privately Held**
SIC: 2426 Frames for upholstered furniture, wood

(G-15193)
C & D WOODWORKING INC
7139 Wright Rd (27360-8342)
P.O. Box 1913 (27361-1913)
PHONE...................................336 476-8722
David Trimnal, *Pr*
EMP: 5 **EST:** 1990
SQ FT: 15,000
SALES (est): 369.4K **Privately Held**
SIC: 2499 Laundry products, wood

(G-15194)
CAROLINA ATTACHMENTS LLC
704 Pineywood Rd (27360-2753)
PHONE...................................336 474-7309
Wesley C Blackburn, *Pr*
EMP: 10 **EST:** 2013

SALES (est): 951.54K **Privately Held**
Web: www.carolinaattachments.com
SIC: 3714 Steering mechanisms, motor vehicle

(G-15195)
CAROLINA CONTAINER LLC
1205 Trinity St (27360-8821)
P.O. Box 2166 (27261-2166)
PHONE...................................336 883-7146
EMP: 18
SALES (corp-wide): 679.24MM **Privately Held**
Web: www.carolinacontainer.com
SIC: 5999 2672 Packaging materials: boxes, padding, etc.; Adhesive backed films, foams and foils
HQ: Carolina Container Company
909 Prospect St
High Point NC 27260
336 883-7146

(G-15196)
CAROLINA FAIRWAY CUSHIONS LLC
15 N Robbins St (27360-8970)
PHONE...................................336 434-4292
Nicole L Gardner, *Prin*
EMP: 8 **EST:** 2011
SALES (est): 859.74K **Privately Held**
Web: www.carolinafairwaycushions.com
SIC: 2392 Cushions and pillows

(G-15197)
CAROLINA INTERNATIONAL INC (HQ)
Also Called: Carolina Underwear
110 W Guilford St (27360-3919)
PHONE...................................336 472-7788
N C English Iii, *Pr*
Jim W English, *Sec*
▲ **EMP:** 22 **EST:** 1972
SQ FT: 95,000
SALES (est): 797.42K
SALES (corp-wide): 3.64MM **Privately Held**
SIC: 2341 2322 Women's and children's underwear; Nightwear, men's and boys': from purchased materials
PA: Carolina Underwear Company
110 W Guilford St
Thomasville NC 27360
336 472-7788

(G-15198)
CAROLINA MATTRESS GUILD INC
385 North Dr (27360-8944)
PHONE...................................336 841-8529
▲ **EMP:** 85
Web: www.carolinamattressguild.com
SIC: 2515 Mattresses and bedsprings

(G-15199)
CAROLINA MOVILE BUS SYSTEMS
771 Old Emanuel Church Rd (27360-7508)
PHONE...................................336 475-0983
Larry Shockley, *Owner*
▼ **EMP:** 5 **EST:** 2005
SQ FT: 10,000
SALES (est): 192.29K **Privately Held**
SIC: 3711 Motor vehicles and car bodies

(G-15200)
CAROLINA UNDERWEAR COMPANY (PA)
110 W Guilford St (27360-3919)
PHONE...................................336 472-7788
N C English Iii, *Pr*
Walter Jones, *VP*

James W English, *Sec*
◆ **EMP:** 20 **EST:** 1928
SQ FT: 140,000
SALES (est): 3.64MM
SALES (corp-wide): 3.64MM **Privately Held**
SIC: 2341 2322 Women's and children's undergarments; Nightwear, men's and boys': from purchased materials

(G-15201)
CELAND YARN DYERS INC
606 Davidson St (27360-3628)
P.O. Box 2127 (27361-2127)
PHONE...................................336 472-4400
Margaret Hill Norton, *Pr*
Rebecca Hill Leonard, *
Steve Yokeley, *
EMP: 9 **EST:** 1955
SQ FT: 49,500
SALES (est): 119.81K **Privately Held**
SIC: 2269 Dyeing: raw stock, yarn, and narrow fabrics

(G-15202)
CEMEX MATERIALS LLC
208 Randolph St (27360-4642)
PHONE...................................800 627-2986
Mike Shook, *Mgr*
EMP: 51
SIC: 3273 Ready-mixed concrete
HQ: Cemex Materials Llc
1720 Centrepark Dr E # 100
West Palm Beach FL 33401
561 833-5555

(G-15203)
CLA PROPERTIES LLC
200 Echo Trl (27360-8096)
PHONE...................................336 476-7828
Linda Douglas, *Prin*
EMP: 5 **EST:** 2008
SALES (est): 107.13K **Privately Held**
SIC: 6512 3678 Nonresidential building operators; Electronic connectors

(G-15204)
COMBINTONS SCREEN PRTG EMB INC
Also Called: Combinations Embroidery
4 N Robbins St (27360-8970)
P.O. Box 1857 (27361-1857)
PHONE...................................336 472-4420
Mark Berrier, *Pr*
Douglas Berrier, *VP*
June Berrier, *Sec*
EMP: 6 **EST:** 1985
SQ FT: 10,000
SALES (est): 350.39K **Privately Held**
SIC: 2396 2395 Screen printing on fabric articles; Embroidery products, except Schiffli machine

(G-15205)
COMFORT SLEEP LLC
1100 National Hwy Ste L (27360-2342)
P.O. Box 1351 (27361-1351)
PHONE...................................336 267-5853
EMP: 11 **EST:** 2019
SALES (est): 150K **Privately Held**
Web: www.comfortsleep.com
SIC: 2515 Mattresses and foundations

(G-15206)
CON-TAB INC
4001 Ball Park Rd (27360-8976)
P.O. Box 1369 (27361-1369)
PHONE...................................336 476-0104
EMP: 16

Thomasville - Davidson County (G-15207)

SIC: 2522 5072 5021 Tables, office: except wood; Hardware; Office furniture, nec

(G-15207)
CRAFTSMAN FOAM FABRICATORS INC
196 Mason Way (27360-4921)
PHONE................................336 476-5655
Olin Hill, *Pr*
Michael Hill, *
EMP: 14 **EST:** 1985
SQ FT: 22,000
SALES (est): 434.18K **Privately Held**
SIC: 3069 Foam rubber

(G-15208)
CUSTOM DESIGNS AND UPHOLSTERY
1372 Unity St # B (27360-3223)
PHONE................................336 882-1516
Mitzi Marlowe, *Pr*
Missy Marlowe, *Pr*
David Marlowe, *VP*
Will Swain, *Treas*
EMP: 10 **EST:** 2005
SALES (est): 416.9K **Privately Held**
SIC: 2512 Upholstered household furniture

(G-15209)
CUSTOM FABRIC SAMPLES INC
261 Sunset Dr (27360-9190)
P.O. Box 6632 (27262-6632)
PHONE................................336 472-1854
Brad Moser, *Pr*
▲ **EMP:** 8 **EST:** 2000
SALES (est): 568.11K **Privately Held**
SIC: 2241 Fabric tapes

(G-15210)
DAN MOORE INC
405 Albertson Rd (27360-8986)
PHONE................................336 475-8350
A Daniel Moore Junior, *Pr*
Martha Moore, *Sec*
EMP: 6 **EST:** 1975
SQ FT: 9,000
SALES (est): 563.29K **Privately Held**
SIC: 1611 3531 Highway and street construction; Construction machinery

(G-15211)
DANTHERM FILTRATION INC
Also Called: Nordfab
150 Transit Ave (27360-8927)
P.O. Box 429 (27361-0429)
PHONE................................336 889-5599
EMP: 13
SQ FT: 45,000
SIC: 3564 3444 Dust or fume collecting equipment, industrial; Ducts, sheet metal
HQ: Dantherm Filtration, Inc.
    150 Transit Ave
    Thomasville NC 27360
    336 821-0800

(G-15212)
DESIGN PRINTING INC
1107 Trinity St (27360-8819)
PHONE................................336 472-3333
Larry Utz, *Pr*
EMP: 8 **EST:** 1979
SQ FT: 20,000
SALES (est): 647.4K **Privately Held**
Web: www.dprintla.com
SIC: 2752 Commercial printing, lithographic

(G-15213)
DIE-TECH INC
4 Stanley Ave (27360-8969)
PHONE................................336 475-9186
Russell Hall, *Pr*
Norma Hall, *
Russell Hall, *VP*
EMP: 19 **EST:** 1966
SALES (est): 579.41K **Privately Held**
Web: www.dietechonline.com
SIC: 3544 Special dies and tools

(G-15214)
DIRECTIONAL BUYING GROUP INC
Also Called: Directional
201 E Holly Hill Rd (27360-5819)
PHONE................................336 472-6187
Tom Powell, *Pr*
EMP: 23 **EST:** 1965
SQ FT: 100,000
SALES (est): 238.25K **Privately Held**
Web: www.directionalinc.com
SIC: 2512 Chairs: upholstered on wood frames

(G-15215)
DOUGLAS WOLCOTT
48 High Tech Blvd Unit C (27360-5639)
PHONE................................336 475-0052
Doug Wolcott, *Prin*
EMP: 5 **EST:** 2017
SALES (est): 84.54K **Privately Held**
Web: www.cantina-loca.com
SIC: 3544 Special dies, tools, jigs, and fixtures

(G-15216)
DSI INNOVATIONS LLC
42 High Tech Blvd (27360-5560)
P.O. Box 1127 (27023-1127)
PHONE................................336 893-8385
Jason Dupre, *CEO*
Jason Dupre, *Managing Member*
Bobby Cole, *
Damien Johns, *
EMP: 45 **EST:** 2008
SALES (est): 8.62MM **Privately Held**
Web: www.dsiinnovations.com
SIC: 3625 3599 Relays and industrial controls; Custom machinery

(G-15217)
DURHAM RACING ENGINES INC
205 Old Embler Rd (27360-7291)
PHONE................................336 471-1830
Andy Durham, *Owner*
EMP: 7 **EST:** 2014
SALES (est): 160.02K **Privately Held**
Web: www.durhamracingengines.com
SIC: 3714 Motor vehicle engines and parts

(G-15218)
ELITE DISPLAYS & DESIGN INC
6771 Pikeview Dr (27360-8924)
P.O. Box 1949 (27361-1949)
PHONE................................336 472-8200
Thomas Waterhouse, *Pr*
Rusty Slate, *
▲ **EMP:** 75 **EST:** 2002
SQ FT: 60,000
SALES (est): 18.39MM **Privately Held**
Web: www.elitedisplays.net
SIC: 2542 Bar fixtures, except wood

(G-15219)
ENNIS-FLINT
505 County Line Rd (27360-5979)
PHONE................................336 477-8439
EMP: 6 **EST:** 2019
SALES (est): 197.38K **Privately Held**
Web: www.ennisflint.com
SIC: 2851 Paints and allied products

(G-15220)
ENNIS-FLINT INC
115 Todd Ct (27360-3233)
PHONE................................800 331-8118
EMP: 4
SALES (corp-wide): 17.65B **Publicly Held**
Web: www.ennisflintamericas.com
SIC: 2851 3953 Paints and allied products; Marking devices
HQ: Ennis-Flint, Inc.
    4161 Piedmont Pkwy # 370
    Greensboro NC 27410
    800 331-8118

(G-15221)
FINCH INDUSTRIES INCORPORATED
104 Williams St (27360-3600)
P.O. Box 1847 (27361-1847)
PHONE................................336 472-4499
◆ **EMP:** 90 **EST:** 1978
SALES (est): 8.21MM **Privately Held**
Web: www.finchindustries.com
SIC: 3231 2759 2396 Products of purchased glass; Screen printing; Automotive and apparel trimmings

(G-15222)
FLINT ACQUISITION CORP
115 Todd Ct (27360-3233)
P.O. Box 160 (27361-0160)
PHONE................................336 475-6600
Steven Vetter, *CEO*
Michael Murren, *
EMP: 76 **EST:** 2004
SALES (est): 23.97MM
SALES (corp-wide): 17.65B **Publicly Held**
SIC: 2851 Paints and allied products
HQ: Road Infrastructure Investment Holdings, Inc.
    115 Todd Ct
    Thomasville NC 27360
    336 475-6600

(G-15223)
FLINT TRADING INC
505 County Line Rd (27360-5979)
PHONE................................336 308-3770
EMP: 10 **EST:** 2017
SALES (est): 454.95K **Privately Held**
Web: www.ennisflint.com
SIC: 2851 Paints and allied products

(G-15224)
FLINT TRADING INC
Also Called: Ennis-Flint
115 Todd Ct (27360-3233)
P.O. Box 160 (27361-0160)
PHONE................................336 475-6600
▲ **EMP:** 73
Web: www.ennisflint.com
SIC: 3953 Marking devices

(G-15225)
FRANKLIN AEROSPACE INC
147 Commercial Park Dr (27360-9478)
PHONE................................336 474-1960
George Gillespie, *Prin*
EMP: 7 **EST:** 2013
SALES (est): 147.88K **Privately Held**
Web: www.franklinaerospace.us
SIC: 3721 Aircraft

(G-15226)
FURNITURE MFRS CLARING HSE INC
107 Sunrise Center Dr (27360-4928)
PHONE................................866 477-8468
EMP: 5 **EST:** 2004
SALES (est): 62.54K **Privately Held**
SIC: 3999 Manufacturing industries, nec

(G-15227)
GARY J YOUNTS MACHINE COMPANY
4786 Turnpike Ct (27360-8842)
PHONE................................336 476-7930
Gary J Younts, *Pr*
Pat Younts, *Sec*
EMP: 10 **EST:** 1987
SQ FT: 8,400
SALES (est): 936.12K **Privately Held**
Web: www.christmaswithelvis.com
SIC: 3451 Screw machine products

(G-15228)
GRESCO MANUFACTURING INC
216 E Holly Hill Rd (27360-5820)
PHONE................................336 475-8101
R E Ransom, *Pr*
R E Ransom, *Pr*
EMP: 7 **EST:** 1984
SQ FT: 30,000
SALES (est): 1.05MM **Privately Held**
Web: www.tracktac.com
SIC: 2819 Industrial inorganic chemicals, nec

(G-15229)
HIGH POINT ENTERPRISE INC
Thomasville Times, The
512 Turner St (27360-2646)
PHONE................................336 472-9500
Sara Smith, *Mgr*
EMP: 16
SQ FT: 17,810
SALES (corp-wide): 7.91MM **Privately Held**
Web: www.hpenews.com
SIC: 2711 Commercial printing and newspaper publishing combined
PA: The High Point Enterprise Inc
    213 Woodbine St
    High Point NC 27260
    336 888-3500

(G-15230)
HILL HOSIERY MILL INC
Also Called: Hill Spinning Division
602 Davidson St (27360-3628)
P.O. Box 2127 (27361-2127)
PHONE................................336 472-7908
Chris Yokeley, *Pr*
Mark Leonard, *
Steve Yokeley, *
▼ **EMP:** 14 **EST:** 1941
SQ FT: 90,000
SALES (est): 383.7K **Privately Held**
SIC: 2252 Socks

(G-15231)
HILLIARD FABRICATORS LLC
501 Carolina Ave (27360-4807)
P.O. Box 239 (27370-0239)
PHONE................................336 861-8833
EMP: 10 **EST:** 1986
SALES (est): 871.31K **Privately Held**
SIC: 3069 Foam rubber

(G-15232)
HUGHES SUP OF THOMASVILLE INC
175 Kanoy Rd (27360-8703)
P.O. Box 1003 (27361-1003)
PHONE................................336 475-8146
Jeffrey T Hughes, *Pr*
Terri Saintsing, *
Crystal Brock, *
Melissa Lawrence, *Stockholder**
Jimmy Saintsing, *
▲ **EMP:** 91 **EST:** 1973
SQ FT: 70,000
SALES (est): 15.09MM **Privately Held**

GEOGRAPHIC SECTION

Thomasville - Davidson County (G-15258)

Web: www.hughessupplyco.com
SIC: 3089 Injection molding of plastics

(G-15233)
HUNT COUNTRY COMPONENT LLC
1120 Trinity St (27360-8818)
PHONE..................................336 475-7000
▲ EMP: 5 EST: 2003
SALES (est): 644.98K Privately Held
Web: www.huntcc.com
SIC: 3469 Furniture components, porcelain enameled

(G-15234)
I MIX 4 U LLC
219 Santa Fe Cir (27360-3373)
PHONE..................................336 307-6297
Tiffaney Singleton, Prin
EMP: 4 EST: 2019
SALES (est): 75.7K Privately Held
SIC: 3273 Ready-mixed concrete

(G-15235)
IMAFLEX USA INC
7137 Prospect Church Rd (27360-8839)
P.O. Box 1719 (27361-1719)
PHONE..................................336 885-8131
Daniel A Jones, Opers Mgr
EMP: 35
SALES (corp-wide): 83.03MM Privately Held
Web: www.imaflex.com
SIC: 2673 Plastic bags: made from purchased materials
HQ: Imaflex Usa, Inc.
1200 Unity St
Thomasville NC 27360

(G-15236)
IMAFLEX USA INC (HQ)
1201 Unity St (27360-3220)
P.O. Box 1550 (27261-1550)
PHONE..................................336 474-1190
Joseph Abbandonato, Pr
EMP: 32 EST: 2005
SQ FT: 93,000
SALES (est): 22.76MM
SALES (corp-wide): 83.03MM Privately Held
Web: www.imaflex.com
SIC: 2821 Plastics materials and resins
PA: Imaflex Inc
5710 Rue Notre-Dame O
Montreal QC H4C 1
514 935-5710

(G-15237)
IMAGES OF AMERICA INC
Also Called: Ioa Healthcare Furniture
829 Blair St (27360-4302)
PHONE..................................336 475-7106
▲ EMP: 60 EST: 1969
SALES (est): 9.64MM Privately Held
Web: www.ioa-hcf.com
SIC: 2522 2512 Office furniture, except wood; Wood upholstered chairs and couches

(G-15238)
INTERNATIONAL FURNISHINGS INC
1506 Lexington Ave (27360-3329)
P.O. Box 722 (27361-0722)
PHONE..................................336 472-8422
Jack W Medlin, Pt
Judy Medlin, Pt
EMP: 9 EST: 1984
SALES (est): 776.44K Privately Held
Web: www.internationalfurnishingsinc.com
SIC: 2512 Chairs: upholstered on wood frames

(G-15239)
JOHN CONRAD INC
Also Called: Conrad Tire & Automotive
1028 Johnsontown Rd (27360-4416)
PHONE..................................336 475-8144
Robert Bergsma, Pr
Robert Conrad, Pr
Carol Conrad, Sec
EMP: 7 EST: 1969
SQ FT: 1,500
SALES (est): 924.55K Privately Held
Web: www.conradtireandauto.com
SIC: 5531 7534 7539 Automotive tires; Tire recapping; Auto front end repair

(G-15240)
LATHAM-HALL CORPORATION
5003 Ball Park Rd (27360-7911)
PHONE..................................336 475-9723
Gary Dellinger, Pr
Jeanna Latham Dellinger, Sec
EMP: 20 EST: 1972
SQ FT: 23,000
SALES (est): 1.6MM Privately Held
SIC: 3599 Machine shop, jobbing and repair

(G-15241)
LEXINGTON FURNITURE INDS INC (PA)
Also Called: Lexington Home Brands
1300 National Hwy (27360-2318)
PHONE..................................336 474-5300
Phil Haney, Pr
◆ EMP: 250 EST: 1936
SQ FT: 25,000
SALES (est): 195.76MM
SALES (corp-wide): 195.76MM Privately Held
Web: www.lexington.com
SIC: 2512 5021 5712 Upholstered household furniture; Furniture; Furniture stores

(G-15242)
LILLYS INTERIORS CSTM QUILTING
Also Called: Lillies Intriors Cstm Quilting
1165 Hillside Dr (27360-0526)
PHONE..................................336 475-1421
Marty Gallimore, Pr
Betty Gallimore, Sec
EMP: 6 EST: 1967
SQ FT: 6,000
SALES (est): 495.64K Privately Held
SIC: 2211 Bedspreads, cotton

(G-15243)
LKF INC
111 Todd Ct (27360-3233)
PHONE..................................336 475-7400
EMP: 10 EST: 1994
SQ FT: 37,000
SALES (est): 318.42K Privately Held
SIC: 2821 Plastics materials and resins

(G-15244)
LLOYDS FABRICATING SOLUTIONS
5896 Denton Rd (27360-8270)
PHONE..................................336 250-0154
Robert Lloyd, Admn
EMP: 8 EST: 2017
SALES (est): 245.56K Privately Held
SIC: 7692 Welding repair

(G-15245)
MARIETTA MARTIN MATERIALS INC
Also Called: Martin Marietta Aggregates
691 Upper Lake Rd (27360-0216)
P.O. Box 1666 (27361-1666)
PHONE..................................336 475-9134
Wonda Moretz, Mgr
EMP: 5
Web: www.martinmarietta.com
SIC: 1422 Crushed and broken limestone
PA: Martin Marietta Materials Inc
4123 Parklake Ave
Raleigh NC 27612

(G-15246)
MCINTYRE MANUFACTURING GROUP INC
310 Kendall Mill Rd (27360-5524)
PHONE..................................336 476-3646
▲ EMP: 60 EST: 1985
SALES (est): 12.22MM Privately Held
Web: www.mcintyremetals.com
SIC: 2542 3537 3496 Racks, merchandise display or storage: except wood; Industrial trucks and tractors; Miscellaneous fabricated wire products

(G-15247)
MESA INTERNATIONAL
1408 Unity St (27360-4957)
PHONE..................................207 774-5946
EMP: 6 EST: 2019
SALES (est): 85.19K Privately Held
Web: www.mesa.org
SIC: 3085 Plastics bottles

(G-15248)
MICKEY TRUCK BODIES INC
Also Called: Reconditioning Dept
Hwy 29-70 (27360)
P.O. Box 2044 (27261-2044)
PHONE..................................336 882-6806
Greg Mclaughlin, Mgr
EMP: 8
SALES (corp-wide): 213.06K Privately Held
Web: www.mickeybody.com
SIC: 3713 Truck and bus bodies
PA: Mickey Truck Bodies Inc.
1305 Trinity Ave
High Point NC 27260
336 882-6806

(G-15249)
MIKES WELDING & FABRICATING
2871 Old Highway 29 (27360-0040)
PHONE..................................336 472-5804
Michael Hillard, Pr
EMP: 4 EST: 1975
SQ FT: 4,200
SALES (est): 370.31K Privately Held
SIC: 7692 Welding repair

(G-15250)
MIKES WELDING & FABRICATION
2871 Old Highway 29 (27360-0040)
P.O. Box 128 (27360-0128)
PHONE..................................336 472-5804
EMP: 7 EST: 2012
SALES (est): 247.03K Privately Held
SIC: 3441 Fabricated structural metal

(G-15251)
MILL-CHEM MANUFACTURING INC
650 Bassett Dr (27360-8991)
P.O. Box 1455 (27261-1455)
PHONE..................................336 889-8038
Ernest Miller, Pr
EMP: 25 EST: 1989
SQ FT: 21,000
SALES (est): 2.78MM Privately Held
Web: www.millchem.com
SIC: 2842 Specialty cleaning

(G-15252)
MINNEWAWA INC
130 Sunrise Center Dr (27360-4900)
PHONE..................................865 522-8103
Lloyd Horner, CEO
Robert Puvey, Pr
EMP: 17 EST: 1939
SALES (est): 377.37K Privately Held
Web: www.minnewawa.com
SIC: 2241 2269 Labels, woven; Labels, cotton: printed
PA: Ctc Holdings, Llc
165 Bluedevil Dr
Gastonia NC 28056

(G-15253)
MOHAWK INDUSTRIES INC
Also Called: Mohawk Laminate & Hardwood
550 Cloniger Dr (27360-4960)
PHONE..................................336 313-4156
EMP: 8
Web: www.mohawkind.com
SIC: 3253 Ceramic wall and floor tile
PA: Mohawk Industries, Inc.
160 S Industrial Blvd
Calhoun GA 30701

(G-15254)
MOTORSPORTS MACHINING TECH LLC
37 High Tech Blvd (27360-5560)
P.O. Box 915 (27361-0915)
PHONE..................................336 475-3742
EMP: 10 EST: 1999
SALES (est): 128.93K Privately Held
SIC: 3599 3714 Machine shop, jobbing and repair; Motor vehicle parts and accessories

(G-15255)
NEDERMAN INC
150 Transit Ave (27360-8927)
PHONE..................................336 821-0827
◆ EMP: 92 EST: 1980
SQ FT: 28,000
SALES (est): 12.34MM Privately Held
Web: www.nederman.com
SIC: 5084 3564 Pollution control equipment, air (environmental); Blowers and fans
PA: Nederman Holding Ab
Sydhamnsgatan 2
Helsingborg 252 2

(G-15256)
NEXT WORLD DESIGN INC
Also Called: Cycra Racing Systems
42 High Tech Blvd (27360-5560)
PHONE..................................800 448-1223
Glen Laivins, Pr
Kenneth T Laivins, VP
▲ EMP: 17 EST: 1992
SALES (est): 573.63K Privately Held
SIC: 3751 7389 Motorcycles and related parts; Design services

(G-15257)
NIVEDTECH
1101 Mendenhall St (27360-8974)
PHONE..................................336 823-9501
EMP: 4 EST: 2015
SALES (est): 91.09K Privately Held
SIC: 7372 Application computer software

(G-15258)
NORDFAB LLC
150 Transit Ave (27360-8927)
P.O. Box 190 (27361-0190)
PHONE..................................336 821-0829
Tomas Hagstrom, CEO
Henrik Bjerregaard, *
EMP: 137 EST: 1979
SALES (est): 43.9MM Privately Held
Web: www.nordfab.com

Thomasville - Davidson County (G-15259)

SIC: 3443 Ducting, metal plate
HQ: Nederman Holding Usa, Inc.
4404a Chesapeake Dr
Charlotte NC 28216
704 859-2723

(G-15259)
NORTH AMERICAN IMPLEMENTS INC
215 Washboard Rd (27360-7900)
P.O. Box 2840 (27361-2840)
PHONE.....................336 476-2904
Eric Garner, *Prin*
EMP: 7 **EST:** 2012
SALES (est): 2.41MM **Privately Held**
Web: www.northamericanimplements.com
SIC: 5083 3531 3523 Agricultural machinery and equipment; Construction machinery; Farm machinery and equipment

(G-15260)
OTB MACHINERY INC
51 Proctor Rd (27360-9266)
PHONE.....................336 323-1035
Kevin J Arvin, *Pr*
Sallie Ann Church, *VP*
▲ **EMP:** 5 **EST:** 2003
SALES (est): 688.86K **Privately Held**
Web: www.otbmachinery.com
SIC: 3553 Woodworking machinery

(G-15261)
PARKDALE MILLS INCORPORATED
Also Called: Plant 6 & 7
400 Carmalt St (27360-4611)
PHONE.....................336 476-3181
Charles Russell, *Brnch Mgr*
EMP: 59
SALES (corp-wide): 1.44B **Privately Held**
Web: www.parkdalemills.com
SIC: 2281 Yarn spinning mills
HQ: Parkdale Mills, Incorporated
531 Cotton Blossom Cir
Gastonia NC 28054
704 874-5000

(G-15262)
PAYLOAD TRAILERS INC
4001 Ball Park Rd (27360-8976)
PHONE.....................833 239-6565
EMP: 5 **EST:** 2020
SALES (est): 166.86K **Privately Held**
Web: paysera.dream.press
SIC: 3715 Bus trailers, tractor type

(G-15263)
PETROLIANCE LLC
Also Called: Rex Oil Company
814 Lexington Ave (27360-3518)
PHONE.....................336 472-3000
EMP: 190
SALES (corp-wide): 676.37MM **Privately Held**
Web: www.petroliance.com
SIC: 3569 Lubricating equipment
HQ: Petroliance Llc
640 Freedom Bus Ctr Dr # 400
King Of Prussia PA 19406

(G-15264)
PIEDMONT TURNING & WDWKG CO
328 Jarrett Rd (27360-6018)
PHONE.....................336 475-7161
Jimmy Jones, *Pr*
EMP: 5 **EST:** 2002
SQ FT: 12,002
SALES (est): 499.47K **Privately Held**
Web: turningandcarving.tripod.com
SIC: 2431 Millwork

(G-15265)
POWDER WORKS INC
6698 Pikeview Dr (27360-9223)
P.O. Box 65 (27361-0065)
PHONE.....................336 475-7715
Jonathan C Hall, *Pr*
EMP: 19 **EST:** 2000
SALES (est): 1.46MM **Privately Held**
Web: www.powderworksinc.com
SIC: 3479 Painting of metal products

(G-15266)
PRIME SYNTEX LLC
6980 Pikeview Dr (27360-8803)
PHONE.....................828 324-5496
EMP: 23 **EST:** 2015
SALES (est): 847.81K **Privately Held**
Web: www.primesyntex.com
SIC: 2299 Upholstery filling, textile

(G-15267)
PROMINENCE FURNITURE INC
415 Commercial Park Dr (27360-9591)
PHONE.....................336 475-6505
Paul M Buch, *Prin*
EMP: 20 **EST:** 2007
SALES (est): 1.08MM **Privately Held**
Web: www.prominence-furniture.com
SIC: 2512 Chairs: upholstered on wood frames

(G-15268)
QUALITY MARBLE
416 Julian Ave (27360-4835)
PHONE.....................336 472-1000
Victor Chamorro, *Prin*
EMP: 5 **EST:** 2007
SALES (est): 78.33K **Privately Held**
SIC: 3281 Cut stone and stone products

(G-15269)
QUALITY SALVAGE INDUSTRIES
1433 National Hwy (27360-2319)
PHONE.....................336 884-4433
EMP: 4 **EST:** 2015
SALES (est): 64.44K **Privately Held**
SIC: 3999 Manufacturing industries, nec

(G-15270)
RAND ANGE ENTERPRISES INC
800 Bryan Rd (27360-5430)
PHONE.....................336 472-7313
EMP: 5 **EST:** 2008
SALES (est): 227.09K **Privately Held**
SIC: 3131 Rands

(G-15271)
ROAD INFRSTRCTURE INV HLDNGS I (HQ)
Also Called: Ennis-Flint
115 Todd Ct (27360-3233)
PHONE.....................336 475-6600
Steve Vetter, *CEO*
Michael Murren, *CFO*
EMP: 23 **EST:** 2012
SQ FT: 70,000
SALES (est): 200.17MM
SALES (corp-wide): 17.65B **Publicly Held**
SIC: 2851 Paints and allied products
PA: Ppg Industries, Inc.
1 Ppg Pl
Pittsburgh PA 15272
412 434-3131

(G-15272)
ROYAL COLONY FURNITURE INC
20 Carolina Ave (27360-4760)
P.O. Box 2402 (27361-2402)
PHONE.....................336 472-8833
James Beck, *Pr*
EMP: 6 **EST:** 1979
SQ FT: 8,256
SALES (est): 350.5K **Privately Held**
SIC: 2511 5712 Wood household furniture; Furniture stores

(G-15273)
S & S SAMPLES INC
880 Whitehart School Rd (27360-8465)
PHONE.....................336 472-0402
Sharon H Stone, *Pr*
Don Stone, *Sec*
EMP: 6 **EST:** 1997
SALES (est): 315K **Privately Held**
SIC: 2299 Textile mill waste and remnant processing

(G-15274)
S AND R SHEET METAL INC
521 Broad St (27360-5359)
PHONE.....................336 476-1069
Sammy Strickland, *Pr*
EMP: 6 **EST:** 1997
SALES (est): 961.99K **Privately Held**
Web: www.sandrsheetmetal.com
SIC: 3444 Sheet metal specialties, not stamped

(G-15275)
S DORSETT UPHOLSTERY INC
406 Aycock St (27360-4804)
PHONE.....................336 472-7076
Ronald Dorsett, *Pr*
Teresa Dorsett Holt, *Sec*
EMP: 4 **EST:** 1978
SQ FT: 7,000
SALES (est): 297.88K **Privately Held**
Web: www.dorsettupholsteryinc.com
SIC: 2512 7641 Upholstered household furniture; Reupholstery and furniture repair

(G-15276)
SHANES CAROLINA JERKY LLC
220 Cedar Lodge Rd (27360-6231)
PHONE.....................336 653-3673
EMP: 5 **EST:** 2019
SALES (est): 170.13K **Privately Held**
SIC: 2013 Snack sticks, including jerky: from purchased meat

(G-15277)
SHELBY CANDLES
900 Alice Dr (27360-5804)
PHONE.....................336 804-4182
Karen Mobley, *Prin*
EMP: 4 **EST:** 2017
SALES (est): 62.54K **Privately Held**
SIC: 3999 Candles

(G-15278)
SOUTHERN AERO LLC
142 Commercial Park Dr (27360-9478)
PHONE.....................336 476-9094
Robert Still, *Prin*
EMP: 6 **EST:** 2010
SALES (est): 408.06K **Privately Held**
Web: www.southernaero.com
SIC: 3721 Research and development on aircraft by the manufacturer

(G-15279)
SOUTHERN RESIN INC
3440 Denton Rd (27360-6168)
P.O. Box 4186 (28603-4186)
PHONE.....................336 475-1348
E J Temple Junior, *Pr*
E J Temple Iii, *VP*
EMP: 38 **EST:** 1987
SALES (est): 8.58MM **Privately Held**
Web: www.tailoredchemical.com

SIC: 2891 Adhesives and sealants

(G-15280)
SOUTHILL INDUSTRIAL CARVING
1861 N Nc Highway 109 (27360-7489)
P.O. Box 2126 (27361-2126)
PHONE.....................336 472-5311
Bob Hill, *Owner*
EMP: 4 **EST:** 1980
SALES (est): 390.8K **Privately Held**
SIC: 2426 7389 Carvings, furniture: wood; Furniture finishing

(G-15281)
SPRINKLE OF SUGAR LLC
11 E Main St (27360-4043)
PHONE.....................336 474-8620
Bobby Hall, *Pr*
Joy Hall Thompson, *Prin*
EMP: 9 **EST:** 2011
SALES (est): 297.96K **Privately Held**
SIC: 5461 2051 Retail bakeries; Bakery: wholesale or wholesale/retail combined

(G-15282)
STAMPER SHEET METAL INC
357 Bud Kanoy Rd (27360-0811)
PHONE.....................336 476-5145
EMP: 6 **EST:** 1994
SQ FT: 6,300
SALES (est): 855.12K **Privately Held**
Web: www.cameroncanine.com
SIC: 3444 1799 Sheet metalwork; Welding on site

(G-15283)
STEEDS SERVICE CO
109 Pineywood St (27360-3434)
PHONE.....................336 748-1587
Robbie Greer, *Owner*
EMP: 7 **EST:** 2015
SALES (est): 98.25K **Privately Held**
Web: www.steedsrepro.com
SIC: 7334 2759 Photocopying and duplicating services; Commercial printing, nec

(G-15284)
STN CUSHION COMPANY
3 Regency Industrial Blvd (27360-4940)
P.O. Box 2510 (27361-2510)
PHONE.....................336 476-9100
Steve Cothran, *Pr*
EMP: 100 **EST:** 1994
SQ FT: 55,000
SALES (est): 6.56MM **Privately Held**
Web: www.stncushion.com
SIC: 2392 2515 Cushions and pillows; Mattresses and bedsprings

(G-15285)
STONE MARBLE CO INC
Also Called: Stone International USA
7004 Pikeview Dr (27360-8875)
PHONE.....................773 227-1161
Katherine J Mark, *Pr*
Anselmo Mannelli, *VP*
Nate Grossman, *Sec*
▲ **EMP:** 6 **EST:** 1992
SQ FT: 700
SALES (est): 1.19MM
SALES (corp-wide): 237.69K **Privately Held**
Web: www.stoneinternational.it
SIC: 5021 7641 2512 2511 Furniture; Reupholstery and furniture repair; Upholstered household furniture; Wood household furniture
HQ: Stone Italia Srl
Via Caravaggio 41/43
Barberino Tavarnelle FI 50028
055755657

GEOGRAPHIC SECTION
Thurmond - Wilkes County (G-15310)

(G-15286)
SUPERIOR WOOD PRODUCTS INC
10190 E Us Highway 64 (27360-7749)
PHONE.................336 472-2237
Billy C Noah, *Pr*
EMP: 10 **EST:** 1961
SQ FT: 47,902
SALES (est): 484.04K **Privately Held**
Web: www.superiorwoodproducts.com
SIC: 2531 2511 2512 Public building and related furniture; Wood household furniture; Upholstered household furniture

(G-15287)
SV PLASTICS LLC
Also Called: Cycra Racing
42 High Tech Blvd (27360-5560)
P.O. Box 915 (27361-0915)
PHONE.................336 472-2242
Jim Zoretich, *Managing Member*
▲ **EMP:** 4 **EST:** 2013
SALES (est): 1.5MM
SALES (corp-wide): 16.53MM **Privately Held**
SIC: 3751 7389 Motorcycles and related parts; Design services
PA: Xceldyne Group, Llc
  37 High Tech Blvd
  Thomasville NC 27360
  336 472-2242

(G-15288)
THEODORE ALEXANDER UPHL LLC
Also Called: Trs
1 Regency Industrial Blvd (27360-4940)
PHONE.................336 472-7540
EMP: 9 **EST:** 2012
SALES (est): 353.98K **Privately Held**
SIC: 2211 Upholstery fabrics, cotton

(G-15289)
THOMAS MFG CO INC THOMASVILLE
1024 Randolph St (27360-5877)
PHONE.................336 474-6030
Donald Green, *Prin*
EMP: 6 **EST:** 2018
SALES (est): 85.67K **Privately Held**
SIC: 3494 Valves and pipe fittings, nec

(G-15290)
TIMOTHY LEE BLACJMON ✪
Also Called: 62 Woodworking
2658 Johnsontown Rd (27360-7597)
PHONE.................336 481-9038
Timothy Lee Blacjmon, *Owner*
EMP: 5 **EST:** 2022
SALES (est): 257.89K **Privately Held**
SIC: 2426 Frames for upholstered furniture, wood

(G-15291)
TOMARJO CORP
105 Julian Ave Ste A (27360-4828)
PHONE.................336 762-0065
EMP: 6 **EST:** 2020
SALES (est): 220.83K **Privately Held**
Web: www.tomarjo.com
SIC: 3451 Screw machine products

(G-15292)
TOMLINSON OF ORLANDO INC
Also Called: Carter
201 E Holly Hill Rd (27360-5819)
PHONE.................336 475-8000
William Lambeth, *Pr*
Howard Williams, *
EMP: 15 **EST:** 2015
SALES (est): 255.28K **Privately Held**
Web: www.tomlinsoncompanies.com

SIC: 2599 Boards: planning, display, notice

(G-15293)
TOMLINSON/ERWIN-LAMBETH INC
201 E Holly Hill Rd (27360-5819)
PHONE.................336 472-5005
William Roderick Lambeth, *Pr*
Howard L Williams, *
▲ **EMP:** 85 **EST:** 1900
SQ FT: 90,000
SALES (est): 9.2MM **Privately Held**
Web: www.tomlinsonerwinlambeth.com
SIC: 2512 Upholstered household furniture

(G-15294)
TRANSCONTINENTAL TVL LLC
1308 Blair St (27360-3249)
PHONE.................336 476-3131
EMP: 53 **EST:** 2003
SALES (est): 2.44MM
SALES (corp-wide): 2.15B **Privately Held**
SIC: 2673 Bags: plastic, laminated, and coated
PA: Transcontinental Inc
  1 Place Ville-Marie Bureau 3240
  Montreal QC H3B 0
  514 954-4000

(G-15295)
TRIAD PRECISION PRODUCTS INC
128 Sunrise Center Dr (27360-4900)
PHONE.................336 474-0980
Ken Maines, *Pr*
Donald Maines, *VP*
Marcia Maines, *Sec*
EMP: 12 **EST:** 1991
SQ FT: 10,000
SALES (est): 2.23MM **Privately Held**
Web: www.triadpp.com
SIC: 3599 Machine shop, jobbing and repair

(G-15296)
TRIMFIT INC
605 Pineywood Rd (27360-2750)
P.O. Box 699 (27361-0699)
PHONE.................336 476-6154
EMP: 102
SALES (corp-wide): 11.58MM **Privately Held**
Web: www.trimfit.com
SIC: 2252 4226 Socks; Special warehousing and storage, nec
PA: Trimfit, Inc.
  463 Fashion Ave Rm 1501
  New York NY 10018
  215 245-1122

(G-15297)
UNILIN FLOORING NC LLC (HQ)
550 Cloniger Dr (27360-4960)
PHONE.................336 313-4000
Jeffrey Lorberbaum, *Prin*
Barbara M Goetz, *VP*
◆ **EMP:** 206 **EST:** 2004
SQ FT: 75,000
SALES (est): 221.77MM **Publicly Held**
SIC: 2421 2426 Flooring (dressed lumber), softwood; Hardwood dimension and flooring mills
PA: Mohawk Industries, Inc.
  160 S Industrial Blvd
  Calhoun GA 30701

(G-15298)
UNIVERSAL STEEL NC LLC
630 Bassett Dr (27360-8991)
PHONE.................336 476-3105
Bill Noethling, *Managing Member*
EMP: 50 **EST:** 1972
SQ FT: 40,000
SALES (est): 9.79MM **Privately Held**

Web: www.universalsteelinc.com
SIC: 3441 3449 3444 Joists, open web steel: long-span series; Bars, concrete reinforcing: fabricated steel; Roof deck, sheet metal

(G-15299)
VICTORIA SWEET LLC
1122 Randolph St Unit 1 (27360-5175)
PHONE.................336 474-8008
Tamara L Joyce, *Admn*
EMP: 7 **EST:** 2013
SALES (est): 249.55K **Privately Held**
SIC: 2026 Yogurt

(G-15300)
WHITEWOOD INDUSTRIES INC (PA)
Also Called: Whitewood
100 Liberty Dr (27360-4837)
P.O. Box 1087 (27361-1087)
PHONE.................336 472-0303
◆ **EMP:** 75 **EST:** 1982
SALES (est): 20.02MM
SALES (corp-wide): 20.02MM **Privately Held**
Web: www.whitewood.net
SIC: 5021 2511 Dining room furniture; Bed frames, except water bed frames: wood

(G-15301)
WILDCAT TERRITORY INC
110 W Guilford St (27360-3919)
P.O. Box 2005 (27361-2005)
PHONE.................718 361-6726
Nancy F Reib, *Pr*
Ibrahim Coban, *VP*
▲ **EMP:** 14 **EST:** 1992
SQ FT: 10,000
SALES (est): 431.08K **Privately Held**
Web: www.wildcatterritory.com
SIC: 2392 2391 Household furnishings, nec; Curtains and draperies

(G-15302)
WINSTON CONCEPT FURNITURE
1110 Lexington Ave (27360-3415)
PHONE.................336 472-7839
Jerry Kearns, *Owner*
EMP: 5 **EST:** 1979
SQ FT: 5,000
SALES (est): 314.01K **Privately Held**
SIC: 2511 Wood household furniture

(G-15303)
WOEMPNER MACHINE COMPANY INC
Also Called: Wmc
385 Lloyd Murphy Rd (27360-7447)
PHONE.................336 475-2268
Scott Woempner, *Pr*
Peggy Woempner, *CEO*
Ken Woempner, *VP*
EMP: 8 **EST:** 1978
SQ FT: 13,000
SALES (est): 826.89K **Privately Held**
Web: www.woempner.com
SIC: 3599 Machine shop, jobbing and repair

(G-15304)
WOODLINE INC
4695 Turnpike Ct (27360-8841)
PHONE.................336 476-7100
Gail Lewis, *Pr*
Nancy Lewis, *Sec*
EMP: 9 **EST:** 1978
SQ FT: 6,000
SALES (est): 464.2K **Privately Held**
Web: www.woodline.com
SIC: 2426 2491 Furniture stock and parts, hardwood; Wood preserving

(G-15305)
WRIGHT OF THOMASVILLE INC (PA)
Also Called: Global Graphics Solution
5115 Prospect St (27360-8849)
P.O. Box 1069 (27361-1069)
PHONE.................336 472-4200
▲ **EMP:** 10 **EST:** 1961
SALES (est): 7.99MM
SALES (corp-wide): 7.99MM **Privately Held**
Web: www.wrightlabels.com
SIC: 2679 2759 2241 Tags, paper (unprinted): made from purchased paper; Commercial printing, nec; Narrow fabric mills

(G-15306)
XCELDYNE LLC
37 High Tech Blvd (27360-5560)
PHONE.................336 472-2242
Corey Smith, *Managing Member*
EMP: 84 **EST:** 2011
SALES (est): 11.5MM **Privately Held**
Web: www.xceldyneusa.com
SIC: 3714 Motor vehicle parts and accessories

(G-15307)
XCELDYNE GROUP LLC (PA)
Also Called: C.V.products
37 High Tech Blvd (27360-5560)
P.O. Box 915 (27361-0915)
PHONE.................336 472-2242
James Zoretich, *Pr*
Larry Nichols, *
Clyde Vickers, *
▲ **EMP:** 68 **EST:** 1988
SQ FT: 42,000
SALES (est): 16.53MM
SALES (corp-wide): 16.53MM **Privately Held**
Web: www.cvproducts.com
SIC: 3089 3599 3471 Plastics containers, except foam; Crankshafts and camshafts, machining; Electroplating and plating

(G-15308)
XCELDYNE TECHNOLOGIES LLC
37 High Tech Blvd (27360-5560)
P.O. Box 915 (27361-0915)
PHONE.................336 475-0201
Larry W Nichols, *Managing Member*
EMP: 75 **EST:** 2004
SQ FT: 30,000
SALES (est): 9.33MM **Privately Held**
Web: www.cvproducts.com
SIC: 3714 Motor vehicle engines and parts

(G-15309)
XTREME FABRICATION LTD
25b High Tech Blvd (27360-5560)
PHONE.................336 472-4562
Dan Kingen, *Pr*
Larry Nichols, *VP*
Clyde Vickers, *Sec*
EMP: 14 **EST:** 2001
SALES (est): 1.48MM **Privately Held**
Web: www.xtremefabrication.com
SIC: 3714 5013 Fuel pumps, motor vehicle; Pumps, oil and gas

Thurmond
Wilkes County

(G-15310)
JONES VONDREHLE VINEYARDS LLC
Also Called: Jones Vndrhle Vineyards Winery
964 Old Railroad Grade Rd (28683-9709)

P.O. Box 25 (28683-0025)
PHONE.................................336 874-2800
EMP: 10 EST: 2008
SALES (est): 712.6K Privately Held
Web: www.jonesvondrehle.com
SIC: 2084 Wines

(G-15311)
LYON LOGGING
3256 S Center Church Rd (28683-9770)
PHONE.................................336 957-3131
Steven A Lyon, *Prin*
EMP: 5 EST: 2005
SALES (est): 182.76K Privately Held
SIC: 2411 Logging

(G-15312)
MCRITCHIE WINE COMPANY LLC
315 Thurmond Rd (28683-9699)
PHONE.................................336 874-3003
Patricia Mcritchie, *Owner*
EMP: 5 EST: 2006
SALES (est): 118.04K Privately Held
Web: www.mcritchiewine.com
SIC: 2084 Wines

Timberlake
Person County

(G-15313)
CARDEN PRINTING COMPANY
52 Hunters Ln (27583-8781)
PHONE.................................336 364-2923
Skip Carden, *Prin*
EMP: 6 EST: 2010
SALES (est): 244.25K Privately Held
SIC: 2752 Commercial printing, lithographic

(G-15314)
GKN DRIVELINE NORTH AMER INC
Also Called: GKN Driveline Roxboro
6400 Durham Rd (27583-9587)
PHONE.................................336 364-6200
Sherry Folkestad, *Brnch Mgr*
EMP: 189
SALES (corp-wide): 4.25MM Privately Held
SIC: 3694 3714 3568 Engine electrical equipment; Motor vehicle parts and accessories; Power transmission equipment, nec
HQ: Gkn Driveline North America, Inc.
   2200 N Opdyke Rd
   Auburn Hills MI 48326
   248 296-7000

(G-15315)
MEDALLION COMPANY INC (HQ)
250 Crown Blvd (27583-8507)
PHONE.................................919 990-3500
EMP: 105 EST: 1996
SQ FT: 100,000
SALES (est): 24.05MM Publicly Held
SIC: 3999 2111 Cigarette and cigar products and accessories; Cigarettes
PA: Vector Group Ltd.
   4400 Biscayne Blvd
   Miami FL 33137

Tobaccoville
Forsyth County

(G-15316)
ANGEL KARDEES PUBLISHING
7509 Meadowgreen Ct (27050-9701)
PHONE.................................336 983-0600
Deanna Stalnaker, *Prin*
EMP: 5 EST: 2015

SALES (est): 45.48K Privately Held
SIC: 2741 Miscellaneous publishing

(G-15317)
DREAM DOERS PUBLISHING LLC
110 Norwood Forest Ln (27050-9498)
PHONE.................................336 413-7101
Bonnie Schaefer, *Prin*
EMP: 5 EST: 2008
SALES (est): 119.58K Privately Held
Web: www.dreamdoerspublishing.com
SIC: 2741 Miscellaneous publishing

(G-15318)
ON DEMAND HEMP COMPANY LLC
6880 Rolling View Dr (27050-9681)
PHONE.................................336 757-0320
EMP: 7 EST: 2020
SALES (est): 424.56K Privately Held
SIC: 2111 Cigarettes

(G-15319)
R J REYNOLDS TOBACCO COMPANY
100 Moore-Rjr Dr (27050-9816)
PHONE.................................336 741-0400
EMP: 69
Web: www.rjrt.com
SIC: 2131 Smoking tobacco
HQ: R. J. Reynolds Tobacco Company
   401 N Main St
   Winston Salem NC 27101
   336 741-5000

(G-15320)
REAPER CUSTOM FABRICATION LLC
7245 Donnaha Rd (27050-9452)
PHONE.................................336 972-4065
Matthew Greene, *Prin*
EMP: 5 EST: 2008
SALES (est): 382.79K Privately Held
Web: www.reapercustomfabrication.com
SIC: 3441 Fabricated structural metal

(G-15321)
STEWARTS GARAGE AND WELDING CO
6544 Doral Dr (27050-9562)
P.O. Box 88 (27050-0088)
PHONE.................................336 983-5563
Daniel L Stewart, *Pr*
Jackie Stewart, *Sec*
Daniel L Stewart Junior, *VP*
EMP: 6 EST: 1962
SQ FT: 2,000
SALES (est): 717.18K Privately Held
SIC: 1799 7692 Welding on site; Welding repair

(G-15322)
TOBACCOVILLE WELDING LLC
4040 Elizabeth Park Dr (27050-9000)
PHONE.................................336 287-7323
Russell Tuttle, *Prin*
EMP: 4 EST: 2018
SALES (est): 52.11K Privately Held
SIC: 7692 Welding repair

Todd
Ashe County

(G-15323)
M & M STONE SCULPTING & ENGRV
498 Carter Miller Rd (28684-9416)
PHONE.................................336 877-3842
David Mason, *Owner*
EMP: 5 EST: 2005

SALES (est): 116.64K Privately Held
SIC: 0781 1741 1799 3281 Landscape services; Stone masonry; Sandblasting of building exteriors; Cut stone and stone products

(G-15324)
ORIANNA NATURALS LLC
241 Great Sky Vly (28684-9620)
PHONE.................................336 877-1560
Richard Roberts, *Managing Member*
EMP: 6 EST: 2015
SALES (est): 134.56K Privately Held
Web: www.oriannabath.com
SIC: 2841 5999 Soap and other detergents; Toiletries, cosmetics, and perfumes

Topton
Cherokee County

(G-15325)
BAKCHOE SERVICES
545 Long Branch Rd (28781-7321)
PHONE.................................828 321-3360
EMP: 4 EST: 2008
SALES (est): 197.88K Privately Held
SIC: 3531 Backhoes

(G-15326)
NANTAHALA TALC & LIMESTONE CO
Also Called: NANTAHALA TALC & LIMESTONE CO
720 Hewitts Rd (28781-7510)
P.O. Box 174 (28781-0174)
PHONE.................................828 321-4239
EMP: 17
SALES (corp-wide): 2.43MM Privately Held
Web: www.mcneelycompanies.com
SIC: 1411 Limestone, dimension-quarrying
PA: Nantahala Talc & Limestone Co Inc
   840 Main St
   Andrews NC
   828 321-3284

Traphill
Wilkes County

(G-15327)
SMITH UTILITY BUILDINGS
Also Called: B & W Enterprises
13721 Longbottom Rd (28685-8724)
PHONE.................................336 957-8211
David Smith, *Owner*
Bert Smith, *Owner*
EMP: 6 EST: 1982
SALES (est): 388.22K Privately Held
Web: www.design1usa.com
SIC: 3691 4222 Storage batteries; Refrigerated warehousing and storage

Trent Woods
Craven County

(G-15328)
J E CARPENTER LOGGING CO INC
4911 Hermitage Rd (28562-7558)
PHONE.................................252 633-0037
Jerry E Carpenter, *Pr*
EMP: 15 EST: 1979
SALES (est): 574.82K Privately Held
SIC: 2411 Logging camps and contractors

(G-15329)
LITHOLYTE CORPORATION LLC
3505 Barons Way (28562-4549)

PHONE.................................252 671-2032
Ryan Holland, *Prin*
EMP: 6 EST: 2016
SALES (est): 110.89K Privately Held
SIC: 2869 Industrial organic chemicals, nec

(G-15330)
MCBRYDE PUBLISHING LLC
905 Hampton Way (28562-4530)
PHONE.................................252 638-8094
Paul W Crayton Junior, *Admn*
EMP: 5 EST: 2010
SALES (est): 98.03K Privately Held
Web: www.mcbrydepublishing.com
SIC: 2741 Miscellaneous publishing

(G-15331)
UNITED DECORATIVE PLAS NC INC
Also Called: Udp
812 Llewellyn Dr (28562-8339)
PHONE.................................252 637-1803
Robert H Barnhill, *Pr*
Susy Barnhill, *VP*
EMP: 4 EST: 1989
SQ FT: 6,000
SALES (est): 370.34K Privately Held
SIC: 3089 Injection molding of plastics

Trenton
Jones County

(G-15332)
ANTHONY B ANDREWS LOGGING INC
1000 Phillps Rd (28585-9356)
PHONE.................................252 448-8901
Anthony B Andrews, *Pr*
Betty Andrews, *Sec*
EMP: 9 EST: 1987
SALES (est): 970.17K Privately Held
SIC: 2411 Logging camps and contractors

(G-15333)
NEIGHBORHOOD UNION BURIAL SOC
387 1st Ave (28585-9519)
P.O. Box 637 (28585-0637)
PHONE.................................252 448-0581
Emmit Flemmings, *Prin*
EMP: 6 EST: 2013
SALES (est): 67.45K Privately Held
SIC: 3272 Burial vaults, concrete or precast terrazzo

(G-15334)
ROWMARK LLC
Color Path Technologies
182 Industrial Park Dr (28585-9593)
PHONE.................................252 448-9900
EMP: 6
SALES (corp-wide): 91.84MM Privately Held
Web: www.rowmark.com
SIC: 3089 Extruded finished plastics products, nec
PA: Rowmark Llc
   5409 Hamlet Dr
   Findlay OH 45840
   419 425-8974

(G-15335)
TRENTON EMERGENCY MED SVCS INC
Also Called: Trenton Ems
105 Cherry St (28585-7714)
P.O. Box 309 (28585-0309)
PHONE.................................252 448-2646
Edward V Eubanks, *Prin*
Michael Jarman, *Prin*

GEOGRAPHIC SECTION

EMP: 10 **EST:** 1959
SALES (est): 183.65K **Privately Held**
SIC: 3711 Fire department vehicles (motor vehicles), assembly of

(G-15336)
TRIPLE E EQUIPMENT LLC
Also Called: A.E. Logging
3899 Nc Highway 58 N (28585-9415)
PHONE..................................252 448-1002
EMP: 7 **EST:** 2020
SALES (est): 466.79K **Privately Held**
SIC: 2411 Logging

(G-15337)
WOLPHS WOOD WORKS LTD
374 Andrews Rd (28585-7624)
PHONE..................................719 629-6350
Paul E Buck, *Prin*
EMP: 4 **EST:** 2018
SALES (est): 59.54K **Privately Held**
SIC: 2431 Millwork

Trinity
Randolph County

(G-15338)
APPLIED NANO SOLUTIONS INC
106 Lake Dr (27370-9403)
PHONE..................................336 687-6517
Ronnie L Bolick, *Pr*
EMP: 5 **EST:** 2014
SALES (est): 210.32K **Privately Held**
SIC: 2819 Silica compounds

(G-15339)
BATT FABRICATORS INC
12957 Trinity Rd (27370-8306)
PHONE..................................336 431-9334
Robert T Hoover, *Pr*
Tara Hoover, *Sec*
EMP: 10 **EST:** 2006
SQ FT: 48,000
SALES (est): 1.09MM **Privately Held**
SIC: 3357 Nonferrous wiredrawing and insulating

(G-15340)
DUSTIN LYNN SINK
5869 Lacey Ct (27370-8978)
PHONE..................................336 442-5602
Dustin Sink, *Prin*
EMP: 5 **EST:** 2016
SALES (est): 98.88K **Privately Held**
SIC: 2411 Logging

(G-15341)
FURNITURE AT WORK
6089 Kennedy Rd (27370-7365)
PHONE..................................336 472-6619
Abby Williams, *Pr*
EMP: 10 **EST:** 1998
SALES (est): 173.4K **Privately Held**
Web: www.trinityfurniture.com
SIC: 5021 3469 Furniture; Metal stampings, nec

(G-15342)
GILBERT HARDWOODS INC (PA)
Also Called: Gilbert Hardwood Centers
12990 Trinity Rd (27370-8306)
P.O. Box 129 (27370-0129)
PHONE..................................336 431-2127
EMP: 11 **EST:** 1996
SALES (est): 13.94MM **Privately Held**
Web: www.gilberthardwood.com
SIC: 5031 2499 Lumber: rough, dressed, and finished; Applicators, wood

(G-15343)
GRUBB & SON SAWMILL INC
1498 Summey Town Rd (27370-7155)
PHONE..................................336 241-2252
Ronald Grubb, *Pr*
EMP: 4 **EST:** 1995
SALES (est): 445.74K **Privately Held**
SIC: 2421 Sawmills and planing mills, general

(G-15344)
HAULCO LLC
9057 Hillsville Rd (27370-7341)
PHONE..................................336 781-0468
EMP: 5 **EST:** 2018
SALES (est): 367.78K **Privately Held**
SIC: 4212 2951 1611 4789 Dump truck haulage; Asphalt paving mixtures and blocks; Grading; Transportation services, nec

(G-15345)
HILLSVILLE WELDING
9055 Hillsville Rd (27370-7341)
PHONE..................................336 861-0732
Steven Hodge, *Owner*
EMP: 5 **EST:** 2014
SALES (est): 45.54K **Privately Held**
SIC: 7692 Welding repair

(G-15346)
INDUSTRIAL ANODIZING
112 School Rd (27370-9425)
PHONE..................................336 434-2110
Bill Smith, *Pr*
EMP: 12 **EST:** 2017
SALES (est): 84.68K **Privately Held**
Web: www.industrialanodizinginc.com
SIC: 3471 Anodizing (plating) of metals or formed products

(G-15347)
JALCO INC
Also Called: C R Currin Company
3621 Steeplegate Dr (27370-7768)
PHONE..................................336 434-5909
Crawford Currin, *Pr*
Rebecca Currin, *Sec*
EMP: 6 **EST:** 1986
SQ FT: 85,000
SALES (est): 285.94K **Privately Held**
Web: www.reewesing.com
SIC: 7389 2511 Styling of fashions, apparel, furniture, textiles, etc.; Wood household furniture

(G-15348)
LABONTE RACING INC
5740 Hopewell Church Rd (27370-7646)
P.O. Box 370 (27370-0370)
PHONE..................................336 431-1004
Terry Labonte, *Pr*
Kim Labonte, *Sec*
EMP: 12 **EST:** 1986
SQ FT: 16,000
SALES (est): 254.86K **Privately Held**
Web: www.justinlabonte.com
SIC: 7948 5651 3711 Motor vehicle racing and drivers; Unisex clothing stores; Motor vehicles and car bodies

(G-15349)
OHIO MAT LCNSING CMPNNTS GROUP (DH)
1 Office Parkway Rd (27370-9449)
PHONE..................................336 861-3500
Lawrence Rogers, *Pr*
Kenneth L Walker, *VP*
◆ **EMP:** 5 **EST:** 1933
SQ FT: 179,000
SALES (est): 412.25MM
SALES (corp-wide): 4.93B **Publicly Held**
SIC: 2515 6794 Box springs, assembled; Franchises, selling or licensing
HQ: Sealy Mattress Company
1 Office Parkway Rd
Trinity NC 27370
336 861-3500

(G-15350)
OHIO-SEALY MATTRESS MFG CO
1 Office Parkway Rd (27370-9449)
PHONE..................................336 861-3500
EMP: 150 **EST:** 1936
SQ FT: 35,000
SALES (est): 27.73MM
SALES (corp-wide): 4.93B **Publicly Held**
SIC: 2515 Mattresses, innerspring or box spring
HQ: Sealy Mattress Company
1 Office Parkway Rd
Trinity NC 27370
336 861-3500

(G-15351)
P P M CYCLE AND CUSTOM
112 School Rd (27370-9425)
PHONE..................................336 434-5243
Tom Zales, *Pt*
Bill Smith, *Pt*
EMP: 5 **EST:** 2005
SALES (est): 212.44K **Privately Held**
SIC: 3751 Motorcycle accessories

(G-15352)
PACKAGING CORPORATION AMERICA
Also Called: PCA/High Point 334
212 Roelee St (27370-8263)
PHONE..................................336 434-0600
Dean Carter, *Brnch Mgr*
EMP: 60
SQ FT: 102,458
SALES (corp-wide): 8.48B **Publicly Held**
Web: www.packagingcorp.com
SIC: 2653 Boxes, corrugated: made from purchased materials
PA: Packaging Corporation Of America
1 N Field Ct
Lake Forest IL 60045
847 482-3000

(G-15353)
PALLET PLUS INC
12990 Trinity Rd (27370-8306)
PHONE..................................336 887-1810
William E Mcbride Junior, *Pr*
Keith Fraley, *VP*
EMP: 4 **EST:** 1998
SQ FT: 6,500
SALES (est): 345.4K **Privately Held**
SIC: 2448 Pallets, wood

(G-15354)
RABBIT TOWN MOLDING & TRIM LLC
3429 Miller Farm Dr (27370-7418)
PHONE..................................336 688-2162
EMP: 4 **EST:** 2020
SALES (est): 64.64K **Privately Held**
SIC: 2431 Millwork

(G-15355)
SEALY CORPORATION (HQ)
Also Called: Sealy & Company
1 Office Parkway Rd (27370-9449)
PHONE..................................336 861-3500
Lawrence J Rogers, *Pr*
Jeffrey C Ackerman, *
Louis R Bachicha, *
Jodi Allen, *
Michael Q Murray, *
◆ **EMP:** 130 **EST:** 1907
SALES: 362.21MM
SALES (corp-wide): 4.93B **Publicly Held**
Web: www.sealy.com
SIC: 2515 Mattresses, innerspring or box spring
PA: Tempur Sealy International, Inc.
1000 Tempur Way
Lexington KY 40511
800 878-8889

(G-15356)
SEALY MATTRESS CO SW VIRGINIA
1 Office Parkway Rd (27370-9449)
PHONE..................................336 861-3500
EMP: 6 **EST:** 2013
SALES (est): 99K **Privately Held**
SIC: 2515 Mattresses, innerspring or box spring

(G-15357)
SEALY MATTRESS COMPANY (DH)
1 Office Parkway Rd (27370-9449)
PHONE..................................336 861-3500
Larry Rogers, *Pr*
Kenneth L Walker, *
Jim Hirshorn, *
Lawrence J Rogers, *
Jeffrey C Ackerman, *
◆ **EMP:** 150 **EST:** 1881
SALES (est): 555.79MM
SALES (corp-wide): 4.93B **Publicly Held**
Web: www.sealy.com
SIC: 2515 Mattresses, innerspring or box spring
HQ: Sealy Mattress Corporation
1 Office Way
Trinity NC 27370
336 861-3500

(G-15358)
SEALY MATTRESS MFG CO LLC
Also Called: Sealy Mattress
239 Sealy Dr (27370-9405)
PHONE..................................336 861-2900
Tom Boggs, *Mgr*
EMP: 101
SQ FT: 97,400
SALES (corp-wide): 4.93B **Publicly Held**
Web: www.sealy.com
SIC: 2515 Mattresses, containing felt, foam rubber, urethane, etc.
HQ: Sealy Mattress Manufacturing Company, Llc
1000 Tempur Way
Lexington KY 40511
859 455-1000

(G-15359)
SPECTRUM INTEGRITY INC
2973 Autumn Acres Ln (27370-9304)
PHONE..................................805 426-4267
Robert Blomquist, *Prin*
EMP: 13 **EST:** 2007
SALES (est): 231.63K **Privately Held**
SIC: 3672 Printed circuit boards

(G-15360)
STEWART SREEN PRINTING
3757 Lynn Oaks Dr (27370-9445)
PHONE..................................336 434-4444
John Stewart, *Pr*
EMP: 6 **EST:** 2005
SALES (est): 122.18K **Privately Held**
SIC: 2759 Screen printing

Trinity - Randolph County (G-15361)

(G-15361)
TEMPUR SEALY INTERNATIONAL INC
1 Office Parkway Rd (27370-9449)
PHONE..................................336 861-2900
EMP: 42
SALES (corp-wide): 4.93B **Publicly Held**
Web: www.tempursealy.com
SIC: 2515 2392 Mattresses and foundations; Pillows, bed: made from purchased materials
PA: Tempur Sealy International, Inc.
  1000 Tempur Way
  Lexington KY 40511
  800 878-8889

(G-15362)
UNIQUE CARVING INC
2285 Todd Dr (27370-7801)
PHONE..................................336 472-6215
EMP: 7 **EST:** 1994
SQ FT: 40,000
SALES (est): 109.24K **Privately Held**
SIC: 2426 Carvings, furniture: wood

Troutman
Iredell County

(G-15363)
ABT INC
Sportsedge
259 Murdock Rd (28166-9695)
PHONE..................................314 610-8798
Cory Formyduval, *Mgr*
EMP: 5
Web: www.abtdrains.com
SIC: 3272 Concrete products used to facilitate drainage
PA: Abt, Inc.
  259 Murdock Rd
  Troutman NC 28166

(G-15364)
ABT INC (PA)
259 Murdock Rd (28166-9695)
P.O. Box 837 (28166-0837)
PHONE..................................704 528-9806
Ralph Brafford, *Pr*
◆ **EMP:** 40 **EST:** 1988
SQ FT: 32,000
SALES (est): 21.36MM **Privately Held**
Web: www.abtdrains.com
SIC: 2821 3272 Plastics materials and resins; Concrete products used to facilitate drainage

(G-15365)
AE TECHNOLOGY INC
Also Called: Atlantic Engineering
150 Ostwalt Amity Rd (28166-8834)
PHONE..................................704 528-2000
Dennis Lauffenburger, *Pr*
Virginia Lauffenburger, *VP*
EMP: 10 **EST:** 1995
SQ FT: 5,000
SALES (est): 1.79MM **Privately Held**
SIC: 2899 Chemical preparations, nec

(G-15366)
AMERICAN STAINLESS TUBING LLC
129 Honeycutt Rd (28166-7610)
PHONE..................................704 878-8823
EMP: 180
SALES (corp-wide): 414.15MM **Publicly Held**
Web: www.asti-nc.com
SIC: 3312 1799 Stainless steel; Fiberglass work
HQ: American Stainless Tubing, Llc
  160 Mine Lake Ct Ste 200
  Raleigh NC 27615
  804 822-3260

(G-15367)
ATMO-TEC
130 Ostwalt Amity Rd (28166-7743)
PHONE..................................704 528-3935
EMP: 7 **EST:** 2011
SALES (est): 156.7K **Privately Held**
SIC: 3398 Metal heat treating

(G-15368)
C R ONSRUD INC (PA)
120 Technology Dr (28166-8537)
P.O. Box 419 (28166-0419)
PHONE..................................704 508-7000
Thomas Onsrud, *CEO*
Charles R Onsrud, *
Thomas C Onsrud, *
John Onsrud, *
Bill Onsrud, *
▲ **EMP:** 46 **EST:** 1976
SQ FT: 60,000
SALES (est): 37.61MM
SALES (corp-wide): 37.61MM **Privately Held**
Web: www.cronsrud.com
SIC: 5084 3545 Industrial machinery and equipment; Machine tool accessories

(G-15369)
CAROLINA CEMETERY PARK CORP
Also Called: Ostwalt-Vault Co
344 Field Dr (28166-9737)
PHONE..................................704 528-5543
Avory Tucker, *Mgr*
EMP: 8
SALES (corp-wide): 2.45MM **Privately Held**
Web: www.carolinacemetery.com
SIC: 3272 Burial vaults, concrete or precast terrazzo
PA: Carolina Cemetery Park Corp
  601 Mount Olivet Rd
  Kannapolis NC
  704 786-2161

(G-15370)
CASE FARMS LLC (PA)
Also Called: Case Foods
385 Pilch Rd (28166-8782)
P.O. Box 729 (28166-0729)
PHONE..................................704 528-4501
EMP: 15 **EST:** 1995
SQ FT: 4,500
SALES (est): 304.63MM **Privately Held**
Web: www.casefarms.com
SIC: 2015 8731 Poultry slaughtering and processing; Commercial physical research

(G-15371)
CASE FARMS PROCESSING INC
Also Called: Case Farms
385 Pilch Rd (28166-8782)
P.O. Box 308 (28680-0308)
PHONE..................................704 528-4501
Thomas R Shelton, *Pr*
Michael Popowycz, *
Kevin Phillips, *
◆ **EMP:** 35 **EST:** 1943
SQ FT: 11,200
SALES (est): 10.28MM
SALES (corp-wide): 490.71MM **Privately Held**
Web: www.casefarms.com
SIC: 2015 Poultry slaughtering and processing
PA: Case Foods, Inc.
  385 Pilch Rd
  Troutman NC 28166
  704 528-4501

(G-15372)
CASE FOODS INC (PA)
385 Pilch Rd (28166-8782)
P.O. Box 729 (28166-0729)
PHONE..................................704 528-4501
Thomas Shelton, *Pr*
David Van Hoose, *Pr*
Michael Popowycz, *Sec*
▼ **EMP:** 15 **EST:** 1986
SALES (est): 490.71MM
SALES (corp-wide): 490.71MM **Privately Held**
Web: www.casefarms.com
SIC: 2015 Poultry, processed, nsk

(G-15373)
CAST FIRST STONE MINISTRY
106 Justin Dr (28166-8797)
PHONE..................................704 437-1053
EMP: 5 **EST:** 2013
SALES (est): 74.27K **Privately Held**
SIC: 3272 Concrete products, nec

(G-15374)
CNC CREATIONS
120 Corporate Dr (28166-8508)
PHONE..................................704 508-2668
EMP: 4 **EST:** 2017
SALES (est): 75.29K **Privately Held**
Web: www.cnccreationsshop.com
SIC: 3999 Manufacturing industries, nec

(G-15375)
ESSENCE CANDLES
576 Perry Rd (28166-9581)
PHONE..................................980 785-4309
EMP: 4 **EST:** 2017
SALES (est): 39.69K **Privately Held**
SIC: 3999 Candles

(G-15376)
FIBERLINK
151 Flower House Loop (28166-9569)
PHONE..................................901 826-8126
EMP: 12 **EST:** 2016
SALES (est): 827.84K **Privately Held**
SIC: 3661 Data sets, telephone or telegraph

(G-15377)
FIVE STAR BODIES
177 Houston Rd (28166-8740)
PHONE..................................262 325-9126
EMP: 6 **EST:** 2015
SALES (est): 271.69K **Privately Held**
Web: www.fivestarbodies.com
SIC: 3714 Motor vehicle parts and accessories

(G-15378)
FULLY INVLVED LEATHERWORKS LLC
147 Houston Rd Ste E (28166-8841)
PHONE..................................704 799-9938
EMP: 5 **EST:** 2020
SALES (est): 210.86K **Privately Held**
Web: www.fullyinvolvedleatherworks.com
SIC: 3199 Leather goods, nec

(G-15379)
GET WICKD CANDLES
366 Weathers Creek Rd (28166-8763)
PHONE..................................704 437-9062
Tiffany Marton, *Prin*
EMP: 4 **EST:** 2017
SALES (est): 51.62K **Privately Held**
SIC: 3999 Candles

(G-15380)
GLOBAL EMSSONS SYSTEMS INC-USA
158 Houston Rd (28166-8740)
PHONE..................................704 585-8490
Eric Latino, *Pr*
EMP: 8 **EST:** 2021
SALES (est): 956.58K **Privately Held**
SIC: 3621 Frequency converters (electric generators)

(G-15381)
HLM LEGACY GROUP INC
129 Honeycutt Rd (28166-7610)
P.O. Box 909 (28166-0909)
PHONE..................................704 878-8823
Tommy Mccoy, *Pr*
Fred Lampe, *VP*
Maria Haughton, *Prin*
▼ **EMP:** 200 **EST:** 1994
SQ FT: 82,000
SALES (est): 32.2MM **Privately Held**
Web: www.asti-nc.com
SIC: 3317 6719 Tubing, mechanical or hypodermic sizes: cold drawn stainless; Personal holding companies, except banks

(G-15382)
J & J METAL FABRICATION LLC
170 Rooster Tail Ln (28166-9628)
PHONE..................................704 746-5279
EMP: 4 **EST:** 2019
SALES (est): 138.4K **Privately Held**
SIC: 3499 Fabricated metal products, nec

(G-15383)
J & S FAB INC
354 S Eastway Dr (28166-8614)
P.O. Box 240 (28166-0240)
PHONE..................................704 528-4251
Joe N Fox, *Pr*
EMP: 5 **EST:** 2000
SQ FT: 18,560
SALES (est): 650.76K **Privately Held**
Web: www.jandsfab.com
SIC: 3441 Fabricated structural metal

(G-15384)
JASPER SEATING COMPANY INC
Also Called: Jasper Library Furniture
694 N Main St (28166-8529)
PHONE..................................704 528-4506
Anthony Moore, *Brnch Mgr*
EMP: 169
SALES (corp-wide): 128.3MM **Privately Held**
Web: jaspergroup.us.com
SIC: 2521 Wood office furniture
PA: Jasper Seating Company Inc
  225 Clay St
  Jasper IN 47546
  812 482-3204

(G-15385)
LEGACY PRE-FINISHING INC
450 S Eastway Dr (28166-8613)
P.O. Box 768 (28166-0768)
PHONE..................................704 528-7136
Jonathan Myers, *Pr*
EMP: 11 **EST:** 2009
SALES (est): 1.86MM **Privately Held**
Web: www.legacyprefinishing.com
SIC: 2421 Cants, resawed (lumber)

(G-15386)
LIAT LLC
Also Called: Jasper Library Furniture
694 N Main St (28166-8529)
P.O. Box 70 (28010-0070)
PHONE..................................704 528-4506

EMP: 53 EST: 2010
SALES (est): 4.44MM Privately Held
Web: www.liatfurniture.com
SIC: 2531 Library furniture

(G-15387)
MACHINING SOLUTIONS INC
102 Corporate Dr (28166-8508)
P.O. Box 300 (28166-0300)
PHONE..............................704 528-5436
Curtis Goodman, Pr
Harold Knight, VP
EMP: 13 EST: 1988
SQ FT: 7,000
SALES (est): 459.81K Privately Held
Web: www.msiracingproducts.com
SIC: 3599 Machine shop, jobbing and repair

(G-15388)
OSTWALT LEASING CO INC
867 S Main (28166-8739)
P.O. Box 419 (28166-0419)
PHONE..............................704 528-4528
Charlie Onsrud, Pr
Tom Onsrud, CEO
John Onsrud, Ex VP
Bill Onsrud, VP Engg
EMP: 4 EST: 1990
SALES (est): 1.22MM
SALES (corp-wide): 37.61MM Privately Held
SIC: 3553 Woodworking machinery
PA: C. R. Onsrud, Inc.
120 Technology Dr
Troutman NC 28166
704 508-7000

(G-15389)
OSTWALT MACHINE COMPANY INC
140 Apple Hill Rd (28166-9570)
PHONE..............................704 528-5730
Reginald K Ostwalt, Pr
Derek Ostwalt, VP
Melissa O Willis, Sec
Joanne Ostwalt, Treas
EMP: 5 EST: 1964
SQ FT: 5,500
SALES (est): 465.19K Privately Held
SIC: 3599 Machine shop, jobbing and repair

(G-15390)
PETRO EQUIPMENT SLS & SVC LLC
151 Flower House Loop (28166-9569)
PHONE..............................828 492-0700
EMP: 4 EST: 2009
SALES (est): 270.46K Privately Held
SIC: 3559 Petroleum refinery equipment

(G-15391)
ROCKET INSTALLATION LLC
329 Talley St (28166-7622)
PHONE..............................704 657-9492
EMP: 12 EST: 2020
SALES (est): 400K Privately Held
SIC: 3446 Stairs, fire escapes, balconies, railings, and ladders

(G-15392)
SCHAFER MANUFACTURING CO LLC
551 N Main St (28166-8526)
P.O. Box 388 (28166-0388)
PHONE..............................704 528-5321
Carlene C Schafer, Managing Member
EMP: 5 EST: 1955
SQ FT: 30,000
SALES (est): 394.95K Privately Held
Web: www.church-steeples.com
SIC: 3315 Staples, steel: wire or cut

(G-15393)
SERENITY HOME SERVICES LLC
767 Morrison Farm Rd (28166-7625)
PHONE..............................910 233-8733
James Shields, Managing Member
EMP: 5 EST: 2019
SALES (est): 117.4K Privately Held
SIC: 1389 7389 Construction, repair, and dismantling services; Business Activities at Non-Commercial Site

(G-15394)
TROUTMAN CARECONNECT CORP
191 Timber Lake Dr (28166-7687)
PHONE..............................704 838-9389
EMP: 10 EST: 2019
SALES (est): 102.03K Privately Held
Web: www.troutman.com
SIC: 2511 Wood household furniture

(G-15395)
TROUTMAN CHAIR COMPANY LLC
134 Rocker Ln (28166)
P.O. Box 208 (28166-0208)
PHONE..............................704 872-7625
Edward Land, *
▲ EMP: 43 EST: 1924
SQ FT: 50,000
SALES (est): 4.93MM Privately Held
Web: www.troutmanchairs.com
SIC: 2511 Rockers, except upholstered: wood

(G-15396)
U S PROPELLER SERVICE INC
844 S Main St (28166-8514)
PHONE..............................704 528-9515
Steve Rogers, Pr
Dee Dee Rogers, Sec
EMP: 5 EST: 1980
SALES (est): 390.23K Privately Held
Web: www.uspropellerservice.com
SIC: 7699 3732 Marine propeller repair; Boatbuilding and repairing

(G-15397)
UP ON HILL
Also Called: Precious Oils Up On The Hill
129 Fesperman Cir (28166)
P.O. Box 2036 (28031-2036)
PHONE..............................704 664-7971
Cynthia Hillson, Owner
EMP: 4 EST: 1989
SALES (est): 198.35K Privately Held
Web: preciousoils.wordpress.com
SIC: 2844 Perfumes, natural or synthetic

(G-15398)
VIBRATION SOLUTIONS
130 Ostwalt Amity Rd (28166-7743)
PHONE..............................704 754-3118
EMP: 5 EST: 2019
SALES (est): 135.08K Privately Held
Web: www.vibration-solutions.com
SIC: 3999 Manufacturing industries, nec

(G-15399)
WURTZ WOODWORKS LLC
117 Misty Spring Rd (28166-8804)
PHONE..............................704 657-6584
Katherine M Wurtz, Prin
EMP: 4 EST: 2019
SALES (est): 54.13K Privately Held
SIC: 2431 Millwork

Troy
Montgomery County

(G-15400)
ALANDALE INDUSTRIES INC
208 Burnette St (27371-3067)
P.O. Box 804 (27371-0804)
PHONE..............................910 576-1291
Laurie Gutschmit, Pr
▼ EMP: 8 EST: 1986
SALES (est): 964.64K Privately Held
Web: www.alandale.net
SIC: 3552 Knitting machines

(G-15401)
AURIA TROY LLC
163 Glen Rd (27371-8320)
P.O. Box B (27371-0455)
PHONE..............................910 572-3721
Brian Pour, Pr
EMP: 91 EST: 2007
SQ FT: 120,000
SALES (est): 25.34MM Privately Held
Web: www.auriasolutions.com
SIC: 3714 Motor vehicle parts and accessories
HQ: Auria Solutions Usa Inc.
26999 Centrl Pk Blvd # 30
Southfield MI 48076
248 728-8000

(G-15402)
CAPEL INCORPORATED (PA)
Also Called: Capel Rugs
831 N Main St (27371-2507)
P.O. Box 826 (27371-0826)
PHONE..............................910 572-7000
John A Magee, Pr
Bud Young, *
Mary Clara Capel, *
N C Capel, *
Arron W E Capel Iii, Dir
◆ EMP: 60 EST: 1957
SQ FT: 80,000
SALES (est): 23.65MM
SALES (corp-wide): 23.65MM Privately Held
Web: www.capelrugs.com
SIC: 5023 2273 Rugs; Rugs, braided and hooked

(G-15403)
DEBERRY LAND & TIMBER INC
112 Leslie St (27371-2506)
P.O. Box 622 (27371-0622)
PHONE..............................910 572-2698
Danny V Deberry, Owner
EMP: 6 EST: 1984
SALES (est): 884.26K Privately Held
SIC: 5099 2411 Pulpwood; Pulpwood contractors engaged in cutting

(G-15404)
DEX N DOX
225 Basswood Rd (27371-9765)
P.O. Box 618 (28009-0618)
PHONE..............................910 576-4644
Georgia Inskeep, Owner
Rick Inskeep, Mgr
EMP: 4 EST: 1986
SQ FT: 3,200
SALES (est): 260.72K Privately Held
SIC: 5031 2452 Lumber: rough, dressed, and finished; Log cabins, prefabricated, wood

(G-15405)
EMC CONTRACTOR LLC
3154 Love Joy Rd (27371-7214)
PHONE..............................910 576-7101
Edna Callicutt, Prin
EMP: 5 EST: 2013
SALES (est): 191.74K Privately Held
SIC: 3572 Computer storage devices

(G-15406)
HICKMAN OIL & ICE CO INC
Also Called: Hickman Oil & Ice
165 Lemonds Drywall Rd (27371-8587)
P.O. Box 563 (27371-0563)
PHONE..............................910 576-2501
Ricky L Harris, Pr
Ivey H Harris, Sec
EMP: 9 EST: 1986
SQ FT: 2,184
SALES (est): 460.43K Privately Held
Web: www.patpoor.us
SIC: 2097 5983 Manufactured ice; Fuel oil dealers

(G-15407)
HURLEYS ORNAMENTAL IRON
2179 Love Joy Rd (27371-7205)
P.O. Box 502 (27371-0502)
PHONE..............................910 576-4731
David Hurley, Owner
EMP: 4 EST: 1997
SALES (est): 179.03K Privately Held
Web: hurleysiron.wordpress.com
SIC: 3446 Architectural metalwork

(G-15408)
MONTGOMERY HERALD
341 N Main St # B (27371-3017)
P.O. Box 466 (27371-0466)
PHONE..............................910 576-6051
Charles Womack, CEO
EMP: 5 EST: 1880
SALES (est): 108.85K Privately Held
Web: www.montgomeryherald.com
SIC: 2711 Newspapers, publishing and printing

(G-15409)
MONTGOMERY LOGGING INC
207 Atkins Dairy Rd (27371-8502)
PHONE..............................910 572-2806
Bill Lynthacum, Pr
EMP: 8 EST: 1993
SALES (est): 864.45K Privately Held
Web: www.postroadliquors.com
SIC: 2411 7389 Logging; Brokers, contract services

(G-15410)
NC PALLET MANUFACTURER LLC
105 Poole Rd (27371-9300)
PHONE..............................910 576-4902
EMP: 4 EST: 2019
SALES (est): 99.39K Privately Held
SIC: 3999 Manufacturing industries, nec

(G-15411)
PRO PALLET SOUTH INC
105 Poole Rd (27371-9300)
PHONE..............................910 576-4902
EMP: 110 EST: 2007
SQ FT: 42,000
SALES (est): 9.38MM Privately Held
Web: www.propalletsouth.com
SIC: 2448 Pallets, wood

(G-15412)
ROBINWOOD ENTERPRISES
725 Railroad Ave (27371-2718)
P.O. Box 707 (27371-0707)
PHONE..............................910 571-0145
Terry Britt, Owner
▲ EMP: 6 EST: 1988

Troy - Montgomery County (G-15413)

SQ FT: 10,000
SALES (est): 240.23K **Privately Held**
Web: www.robinwoodenterprises.com
SIC: 2252 Socks

(G-15413)
RUSSELL-FSHION FOOT HSY MLLS I
875 N Main St (27371-2517)
P.O. Box 732 (27371-0732)
PHONE..................................336 299-0741
William J Sullivan, *Pr*
EMP: 5 EST: 1988
SALES (est): 307.52K **Privately Held**
Web: www.russellsocks.com
SIC: 2252 Socks

(G-15414)
SAPUTO CHEESE USA INC
131 Wright Way (27371-8715)
PHONE..................................847 267-1100
Lino A Saputo Junior, *CEO*
EMP: 131
SALES (corp-wide): 3.79B **Privately Held**
Web: www.saputousafoodservice.com
SIC: 2022 Natural cheese
HQ: Saputo Cheese Usa Inc.
    10700 W Res Dr Ste 400
    Milwaukee WI 53226

(G-15415)
SHEPHERD FAMILY LOGGING LLC
138 Ivey St (27371-8437)
PHONE..................................910 572-4098
EMP: 8 EST: 2016
SALES (est): 371.79K **Privately Held**
SIC: 2411 Logging

(G-15416)
SHORELINE INDUSTRIES INC
798 Nc Highway 109 N (27371-2963)
PHONE..................................910 571-0111
Nancy Starr, *Prin*
EMP: 5 EST: 2010
SALES (est): 195.09K **Privately Held**
SIC: 3999 Manufacturing industries, nec

(G-15417)
SUGARSHACK BAKERY AND EMB
275 Sugar Loaf Rd (27371-1978)
PHONE..................................803 920-3311
Vickie Barfield, *Prin*
EMP: 4 EST: 2015
SALES (est): 69.51K **Privately Held**
SIC: 2395 Embroidery and art needlework

(G-15418)
TROY READY - MIX INC
1739 Nc Highway 24 27 109 W (27371-8337)
P.O. Box 137 (27371-0137)
PHONE..................................910 572-1011
James Macon, *Pr*
Robert Foushee, *VP*
Jeff Macon, *Sec*
EMP: 9 EST: 1969
SQ FT: 7,000
SALES (est): 1.64MM **Privately Held**
SIC: 3272 5032 Concrete products, nec; Concrete mixtures

(G-15419)
UWHARRIE LUMBER CO
335 Page St (27371-2837)
P.O. Box 533 (27371-0533)
PHONE..................................910 572-3731
Ray Allen, *Pr*
John Fred Allen, *
Kerry Anderson, *
Becky Saunders, *
EMP: 20 EST: 1983
SQ FT: 522,720
SALES (est): 2.33MM **Privately Held**
Web: www.uwharrielumber.com
SIC: 2426 2421 Hardwood dimension and flooring mills; Sawmills and planing mills, general

(G-15420)
WOOD RIGHT LUMBER COMPANY
225 Basswood Rd (27371-9765)
P.O. Box 618 (28009-0618)
PHONE..................................910 576-4642
Gergio Inskeep, *Owner*
Gergia Inskeep, *Owner*
Rick Inskeep, *Owner*
▲ EMP: 4 EST: 1985
SALES (est): 304.41K **Privately Held**
SIC: 5031 2452 Lumber, plywood, and millwork; Prefabricated wood buildings

Tryon
Polk County

(G-15421)
ARC WOODWORKING
84 Brewery Ln (28782-8782)
PHONE..................................828 863-4994
EMP: 5 EST: 2013
SALES (est): 60.05K **Privately Held**
SIC: 2431 Millwork

(G-15422)
CAROLINA YARN PROCESSORS INC
Also Called: Cyp
250 Screvens Rd (28782-2720)
PHONE..................................828 859-5891
Steve Silvia, *Pr*
EMP: 155 EST: 1957
SALES (est): 528.59K **Privately Held**
SIC: 2269 2389 Finishing: raw stock, yarn, and narrow fabrics; Handkerchiefs, except paper
HQ: Fendrich Industries, Inc.
    7025 Augusta Rd
    Greenville SC 29605
    864 299-0600

(G-15423)
COMMUNITYS KITCHEN L3C
835 N Trade St Ste A (28782-5630)
PHONE..................................828 817-2308
Carol Lynn Jackson, *CEO*
EMP: 5 EST: 2013
SALES (est): 84.12K **Privately Held**
SIC: 0723 2099 5411 7299 Crop preparation services for market; Food preparations, nec; Cooperative food stores; Banquet hall facilities

(G-15424)
D&S ASPHALT MATERIALS INC
265 Hugh Champion Rd (28782-8888)
PHONE..................................828 894-2778
James Deck, *Pr*
Christopher Stott, *VP*
James Shehan, *Treas*
EMP: 6 EST: 1998
SALES (est): 983.7K **Privately Held**
SIC: 5032 2951 Asphalt mixture; Asphalt and asphaltic paving mixtures (not from refineries)

(G-15425)
MG12 LP
874 S Trade St (28782-3720)
P.O. Box 429 (27357-0429)
PHONE..................................828 440-1144
Thomas Strader, *Managing Member*
Rhett Greene, *Sls Dir*
EMP: 8 EST: 2014
SALES (est): 1.15MM **Privately Held**
Web: www.mg12.com
SIC: 3356 Magnesium

(G-15426)
OWNER TRYON BACKDOOR DIST
11 Depot St (28782-3359)
PHONE..................................864 237-1667
Jocelyn Davis, *Pr*
EMP: 6 EST: 2017
SALES (est): 107.02K **Privately Held**
SIC: 2711 Newspapers, publishing and printing

(G-15427)
POLK SAWMILL LLC
206 Will Green Rd (28782-8879)
PHONE..................................828 863-0436
Patrick Parton, *Admn*
EMP: 5 EST: 2016
SALES (est): 110.21K **Privately Held**
SIC: 2421 Sawmills and planing mills, general

(G-15428)
SEALED EDGE CUTTING
2400 Us 176 Hwy (28782-8632)
PHONE..................................828 859-2840
Christopher Dannels, *Prin*
EMP: 5 EST: 2006
SALES (est): 156.25K **Privately Held**
SIC: 3873 Clocks, assembly of

(G-15429)
TRYON FINISHING CORPORATION
250 Screvens Rd (28782-2720)
PHONE..................................828 859-5891
Naiden Kremenliev, *Pr*
EMP: 10 EST: 2020
SALES (est): 244.56K **Privately Held**
Web: www.tryonfinishing.com
SIC: 2261 Screen printing of cotton broadwoven fabrics

(G-15430)
TRYON NEWSMEDIA LLC
Also Called: Appointments
16 N Trade St (28782-6656)
PHONE..................................828 859-9151
Teddy Ramsey, *Pr*
EMP: 14 EST: 1928
SQ FT: 6,000
SALES (est): 427.74K **Privately Held**
Web: www.tryondailybulletin.com
SIC: 2711 2752 Newspapers, publishing and printing; Commercial printing, lithographic

(G-15431)
WILLIAM L DAY COMPANIES INC
Also Called: Framingsupplies.com
3325 Nc 9 Hwy (28782-6848)
PHONE..................................828 693-1333
Gail Day, *Pr*
William L Day, *Pr*
Richard Day, *VP*
Gail Day, *Sec*
▲ EMP: 16 EST: 1972
SALES (est): 319.87K **Privately Held**
Web: www.framingsupplies-shop.com
SIC: 2499 5961 Picture and mirror frames, wood; Arts and crafts equipment and supplies, mail order

(G-15432)
WOVENART INC
Also Called: Wovern Art
687 N Trade St (28782-5596)
P.O. Box 271 (28722-0271)
PHONE..................................828 859-6349
Caryn Cunningham, *Pr*
EMP: 10 EST: 1998
SALES (est): 766.94K **Privately Held**
Web: www.wovenart.net
SIC: 2399 5131 Hand woven and crocheted products; Linen piece goods, woven

Tyner
Chowan County

(G-15433)
BILLY HARRELL LOGGING INC
152 County Line Rd (27980-9690)
PHONE..................................252 221-4995
William H Harrell Senior, *Pr*
Doris Harrell, *Sec*
William H Harrell Junior, *VP*
EMP: 15 EST: 1990
SALES (est): 981.19K **Privately Held**
SIC: 2411 Logging camps and contractors

(G-15434)
J R NIXON WELDING
212 Center Hill Rd (27980-9774)
PHONE..................................252 221-4574
James R Nixon, *Owner*
EMP: 4 EST: 1980
SALES (est): 227.66K **Privately Held**
SIC: 7692 Welding repair

Union Grove
Iredell County

(G-15435)
CRAFTED HART HAND
176 Butch Branch Rd (28689-9132)
PHONE..................................704 539-4808
EMP: 5 EST: 2010
SALES (est): 53.16K **Privately Held**
SIC: 2431 Millwork

(G-15436)
CUTTING SYSTEMS INC
774 Zeb Rd (28689-9148)
PHONE..................................704 592-2451
▲ EMP: 60 EST: 1995
SQ FT: 80,000
SALES (est): 12.2MM **Privately Held**
Web: www.cuttingsys.com
SIC: 5271 5082 3537 3531 Mobile home equipment; Logging equipment and supplies; Industrial trucks and tractors; Construction machinery

(G-15437)
G & G FOREST PRODUCTS
147 Lumber Dr (28689)
P.O. Box 99 (28689-0099)
PHONE..................................704 539-5110
EMP: 9 EST: 2014
SALES (est): 186.5K **Privately Held**
Web: www.gandgforestproducts.com
SIC: 0831 2421 Forest products; Building and structural materials, wood

(G-15438)
UNION GROVE SAW & KNIFE INC
157 Sawtooth Lane (28689)
PHONE..................................704 539-4442
Edward A Bissell, *Pr*
Shelba Bissell, *
▲ EMP: 67 EST: 1981
SQ FT: 20,400
SALES (est): 4.98MM **Privately Held**
Web: www.sawandknife.com

SIC: 3425 3541 7699 Saws, hand: metalworking or woodworking; Machine tools, metal cutting type; Knife, saw and tool sharpening and repair

Union Mills
Rutherford County

(G-15439)
CABINETS AND THINGS
141 Bill Deck Rd (28167-7608)
PHONE..............................828 652-1734
Kenneth Smalley, *Prin*
EMP: 5 EST: 2010
SALES (est): 189.35K **Privately Held**
SIC: 2434 Wood kitchen cabinets

(G-15440)
CVMR (USA) INC
2702 Centennial Rd (28167-9617)
PHONE..............................828 288-3768
Michael C Hargett, *Pr*
Kamran M Khozan, *Ch*
John R Finley, *Sec*
Nanthakumar Victor Emmanuel, *VP*
John D Wagoner, *Dir*
EMP: 165 EST: 2007
SALES (est): 7.3B
SALES (corp-wide): 44.56MM **Privately Held**
Web: www.cvmr.ca
SIC: 3339 7389 Primary nonferrous metals, nec; Business services, nec
PA: Cvmr Corporation
    35 Kenhar Dr
    North York ON M9L 1
    416 743-2746

(G-15441)
JOSH LANE LOGGING LLC
2575 Camp Creek Rd (28167-9654)
PHONE..............................828 289-4052
EMP: 6 EST: 2016
SALES (est): 89.89K **Privately Held**
SIC: 2411 Logging

Valdese
Burke County

(G-15442)
BURKE MILLS INC
191 Sterling St Nw (28690-2649)
P.O. Box 190 (28690-0190)
PHONE..............................828 874-6341
Humayun N Shaikh, *Ch Bd*
Thomas I Nail, *
Richard F Byers, *
Pender R Mcelroy, *Sec*
William E Singleton, *VP Mfg*
◆ EMP: 43 EST: 1948
SALES (est): 749.41K **Privately Held**
SIC: 2299 Yarns and thread, made from non-fabric materials
PA: Naseus Inc.
    C/O: Franco Y Franco
    Panama City

(G-15443)
BY-DESIGN BLACK OXIDE & TL LLC
1260 Margaret St Nw (28690-2148)
PHONE..............................828 874-0610
EMP: 10 EST: 2012
SALES (est): 452.26K **Privately Held**
Web: www.bydesignblackoxideandtool.com
SIC: 7389 3398 Design services; Annealing of metal

(G-15444)
C & S WOODWORKING
833 Summers Rd (28690-9547)
PHONE..............................828 437-5024
Howard Crump, *Owner*
EMP: 5 EST: 1976
SQ FT: 11,250
SALES (est): 250K **Privately Held**
SIC: 2426 Frames for upholstered furniture, wood

(G-15445)
CCO HOLDINGS LLC
240 Main St W (28690-2835)
PHONE..............................828 368-4161
EMP: 107
SALES (corp-wide): 54.61B **Publicly Held**
SIC: 4841 3663 3651 Cable television services; Radio and t.v. communications equipment; Household audio and video equipment
HQ: Cco Holdings, Llc
    400 Atlantic St
    Stamford CT 06901
    203 905-7801

(G-15446)
CONTINENTAL AUTO SYSTEMS INC
1103 Johnstown Rd (28690)
PHONE..............................828 584-4500
EMP: 80
SALES (corp-wide): 40.93B **Privately Held**
Web: www.continental.com
SIC: 3714 Motor vehicle parts and accessories
HQ: Continental Automotive Systems, Inc.
    1 Continental Dr
    Auburn Hills MI 48326
    248 393-5300

(G-15447)
CUSTOM SEATINGS
3011 High Peak Rd (28690-9464)
P.O. Box 602 (28619-0602)
PHONE..............................828 879-1964
EMP: 8 EST: 1983
SQ FT: 12,000
SALES (est): 471.32K **Privately Held**
SIC: 3429 Furniture, builders' and other household hardware

(G-15448)
HUDDLE FURNITURE INC (PA)
1801 Main St E (28690-8733)
PHONE..............................828 874-8888
Gideon C Huddle, *CEO*
Candace H Payne, *
Damaris Huddle, *
John P Payne, *
▲ EMP: 50 EST: 1981
SQ FT: 50,000
SALES (est): 24.39MM
SALES (corp-wide): 24.39MM **Privately Held**
Web: www.shenandoahfurniture.com
SIC: 2512 Upholstered household furniture

(G-15449)
KELLEX CORP
Kellex Seating
501 Hoyle St Sw (28690-2605)
PHONE..............................828 874-0389
Larry Parsons, *VP*
EMP: 148
SQ FT: 298,000
Web: www.kellex.com
SIC: 2512 Chairs: upholstered on wood frames
PA: Kellex Corp.
    33390 Liberty Pkwy
    North Ridgeville OH 44039

(G-15450)
MERIDIAN SPCALTY YRN GROUP INC (HQ)
312 Colombo St Sw (28690-2750)
P.O. Box 10 (28690-0010)
PHONE..............................828 874-2151
Tim Manson, *Pr*
Bruce Eben Pindyck, *
Mary Ellen Pindyck, *
Douglas C Miller, *
Joseph B Tyson, *
◆ EMP: 300 EST: 2006
SALES (est): 44.68MM
SALES (corp-wide): 331.16MM **Privately Held**
Web: www.msyg.com
SIC: 5949 2282 Knitting goods and supplies; Acetate filament yarn: throwing, twisting, winding, spooling
PA: Meridian Industries, Inc.
    735 N Water St Ste 630
    Milwaukee WI 53202
    414 224-0610

(G-15451)
NOTEWORTHY SOFTWARE INC
5291 Mineral Springs Mountain Ave (28690-8792)
PHONE..............................828 604-1123
Heile Beth Zimmerman, *Prin*
EMP: 5 EST: 2013
SALES (est): 128.9K **Privately Held**
Web: www.noteworthycomposer.com
SIC: 7372 Prepackaged software

(G-15452)
PIEDMONT CORRUGATED SPECIALTY
Also Called: Piedmont Corrugated
340 Morgan St Se (28690-2930)
P.O. Box 68 (28690-0068)
PHONE..............................828 874-1153
Boyd Baird, *Pr*
Charles Baird, *
Dorothy Bauguess, *
Frank Welch, *General Vice President*
EMP: 60 EST: 1974
SQ FT: 32,000
SALES (est): 5.42MM **Privately Held**
Web: www.piedmontcorrugated.com
SIC: 2653 Boxes, corrugated: made from purchased materials

(G-15453)
ROBINSON HOSIERY MILL INC
113 Robinson St Se (28690-8813)
PHONE..............................828 874-2228
Kenneth Robinson, *Pr*
Alton Robinson, *
EMP: 18 EST: 1956
SQ FT: 1,500
SALES (est): 488.77K **Privately Held**
SIC: 2252 Socks

(G-15454)
SAFT AMERICA INC
Lithium Battery Div
313 Crescent St Ne (28690-9643)
PHONE..............................828 874-4111
John Lundeen, *Brnch Mgr*
EMP: 275
SQ FT: 20,346
SALES (corp-wide): 7.96B **Publicly Held**
Web: www.saft.com
SIC: 3692 3691 Primary batteries, dry and wet; Batteries, rechargeable
HQ: Saft America Inc
    13575 Waterworks St
    Jacksonville FL 32221
    904 861-1501

(G-15455)
TIN MAN CUSTOMS NORTH CAROLINA
1424 Drexel Rd (28690-9008)
PHONE..............................828 391-8080
EMP: 6 EST: 2019
SALES (est): 77.61K **Privately Held**
SIC: 3444 Sheet metalwork

(G-15456)
VALDESE PACKAGING & LABEL INC (PA)
302 Saint Germain Ave Se (28690)
P.O. Box 1215 (28690-1215)
PHONE..............................828 879-9772
Darren Little, *Pr*
Doyle Little, *
David Little, *
▼ EMP: 25 EST: 1993
SQ FT: 40,000
SALES (est): 3.61MM **Privately Held**
Web: www.visitvaldese.com
SIC: 2671 2752 2759 Paper; coated and laminated packaging; Offset and photolithographic printing; Flexographic printing

(G-15457)
VALDESE PACKAGING & LABEL INC
302 Saint Germain Ave Sw (28690-2734)
PHONE..............................828 879-9772
Darren Little, *Brnch Mgr*
EMP: 15
Web: www.visitvaldese.com
SIC: 2752 2759 Offset and photolithographic printing; Flexographic printing
PA: Valdese Packaging & Label, Inc.
    302 Saint Germain Ave Se
    Valdese NC 28690

(G-15458)
VALDESE TEXTILES INC
1901 Main St E (28690-8734)
P.O. Box 490 (28690-0490)
PHONE..............................828 874-4216
Yasmine Safadi, *Pr*
EMP: 10 EST: 1987
SQ FT: 20,000
SALES (est): 231.2K **Privately Held**
Web: www.valdeseweavers.com
SIC: 2221 2211 Broadwoven fabric mills, manmade; Broadwoven fabric mills, cotton

(G-15459)
VALDESE WEAVERS LLC
705 Lovelady Rd Ne (28690-8856)
P.O. Box 23000 (28603-0230)
PHONE..............................828 874-2181
Scott Malcolm, *Brnch Mgr*
▲ EMP: 4
SALES (corp-wide): 104.96MM **Privately Held**
Web: www.valdeseweavers.com
SIC: 2211 Broadwoven fabric mills, cotton
PA: Valdese Weavers, Llc
    1000 Perkins Rd Se
    Valdese NC 28690
    828 874-2181

(G-15460)
VALDESE WEAVERS LLC
Also Called: C V Industries
280 Crescent St Ne (28690-8914)
P.O. Box 70 (28690-0070)
PHONE..............................828 874-2181
EMP: 949
SALES (corp-wide): 104.96MM **Privately Held**
Web: www.valdeseweavers.com

Valdese - Burke County (G-15461)

SIC: 2211 2221 Broadwoven fabric mills, cotton; Broadwoven fabric mills, manmade
PA: Valdese Weavers, Llc
1000 Perkins Rd Se
Valdese NC 28690
828 874-2181

(G-15461)
VALDESE WEAVERS LLC (PA)
Also Called: Valdese Weavers
1000 Perkins Rd Se (28690-9749)
P.O. Box 70 (28690-0070)
PHONE..................................828 874-2181
Blake Millinor, *CEO*
Richard Reese, *
Snyder Garrison, *
◆ **EMP:** 450 **EST:** 1915
SALES (est): 104.96MM
SALES (corp-wide): 104.96MM Privately Held
Web: www.valdeseweavers.com
SIC: 2675 2221 Jacquard (textile weaving) cards: from purchased materials; Upholstery fabrics, manmade fiber and silk

Vale
Lincoln County

(G-15462)
ABERNETHY WELDING & REPAIR INC
2267 Welding Shop Rd (28168-9553)
PHONE..................................828 324-7361
Billy J Abernethy, *Pr*
Frances J Abernethy, *VP*
EMP: 6 **EST:** 1962
SQ FT: 8,000
SALES (est): 691.42K Privately Held
Web: www.abernethywelding.com
SIC: 3713 3589 3443 Stake, platform truck bodies; Sewage and water treatment equipment; Fabricated plate work (boiler shop)

(G-15463)
AMERICAN SAMPLE HOUSE INC
2105 Cat Square Rd (28168-8766)
P.O. Box 6 (28168-0006)
PHONE..................................704 276-1970
Thomas R Lackey, *Pr*
Judy Lackey, *Sec*
EMP: 6 **EST:** 1985
SQ FT: 8,268
SALES (est): 226.55K Privately Held
Web: americansamplehouse.godaddysites.com
SIC: 2789 5087 2782 Swatches and samples ; Upholsterers' equipment and supplies; Blankbooks and looseleaf binders

(G-15464)
CUSTOM METAL CREATION LLC
4395 Macedonia Church Rd (28168-8707)
PHONE..................................828 302-0623
EMP: 5 **EST:** 2016
SALES (est): 72.79K Privately Held
SIC: 3444 3993 Sheet metalwork; Letters for signs, metal

(G-15465)
ETHICS ARCHERY LLC
Also Called: Ethics Bullets
2664 Sam Houser Rd (28168-9365)
PHONE..................................980 429-2070
Scott Gizowski, *CEO*
Deborah Kelley, *VP Opers*
EMP: 7 **EST:** 2010
SALES (est): 444.29K Privately Held
Web: www.ethicsarchery.com

SIC: 3949 Sporting and athletic goods, nec

(G-15466)
EXTREME STUD WELDING LLC
2949 Cat Square Rd (28168-9438)
PHONE..................................828 217-2587
Brian N Rinehardt, *Managing Member*
EMP: 4 **EST:** 2015
SALES (est): 69.35K Privately Held
SIC: 7692 Welding repair

(G-15467)
FUSION FABRICATION & WLDG LLC
4720 Reepsville Rd (28168-9770)
PHONE..................................704 240-9416
Tanner C Springs, *Owner*
EMP: 5 **EST:** 2016
SALES (est): 117.34K Privately Held
SIC: 7692 Welding repair

(G-15468)
HASHTAG SCREEN PRINTING
5392 W Highway 27 (28168-8432)
PHONE..................................980 429-5447
Adam Roper, *Prin*
EMP: 4 **EST:** 2017
SALES (est): 58.12K Privately Held
SIC: 2752 Commercial printing, lithographic

(G-15469)
MEGHAN BLAKE INDUSTRIES INC
Also Called: Hickory Leather Company
7514 W Nc 10 Hwy (28168-9511)
PHONE..................................704 462-2988
Brian Litten, *Pr*
Melinda M Litten, *
▲ **EMP:** 50 **EST:** 2007
SALES (est): 9.34MM Privately Held
Web: www.hickorycontract.com
SIC: 5047 3999 Hospital furniture; Wheelchair lifts

(G-15470)
PITMAN KNITS INC
7625 Palm Tree Church Rd (28168-7463)
PHONE..................................704 276-3262
Fred Pitman, *VP*
Fred L Pitman, *VP*
Tracy Pitman, *Sec*
EMP: 7 **EST:** 1997
SALES (est): 490K Privately Held
SIC: 2253 Knit outerwear mills

(G-15471)
RONALD LEE FULBRIGHT LBR INC
6092 Smith Rd (28168-9564)
PHONE..................................704 462-1421
Ronald L Fulbright, *Pr*
Martha Fulbright, *Sec*
EMP: 10 **EST:** 1963
SQ FT: 2,000
SALES (est): 406.35K Privately Held
Web: www.ronaldleefulbrightlumberinc.com
SIC: 2421 5211 Sawmills and planing mills, general; Planing mill products and lumber

(G-15472)
WEST EXPRESS
4472 W Highway 27 (28168-9656)
PHONE..................................704 276-9001
Ronald Burton, *Pr*
EMP: 4 **EST:** 2006
SALES (est): 188.06K Privately Held
Web: www.westexpress.lt
SIC: 2741 Miscellaneous publishing

(G-15473)
WOODMILL WINERY INC
1350 Woodmill Winery Ln (28168-6796)
PHONE..................................704 276-9911
Larry Gene Cagle Junior, *Pr*
EMP: 7 **EST:** 2005
SALES (est): 491.63K Privately Held
Web: www.woodmillwinery.com
SIC: 2084 Wines

Vanceboro
Craven County

(G-15474)
A & J CANVAS INC
2450 Streets Ferry Rd (28586-8349)
PHONE..................................252 244-1509
Jerry L Shoe, *Pr*
Ada Shoe, *VP*
Georgia Kirkman, *Sec*
EMP: 22 **EST:** 1982
SQ FT: 960
SALES (est): 856.92K Privately Held
SIC: 2394 3732 Canvas and related products ; Boatbuilding and repairing

(G-15475)
ALL IN 1 HOME IMPROVEMENT
261 Streets Ferry Rd (28586)
PHONE..................................252 725-4560
Marvin Alston, *Owner*
EMP: 5 **EST:** 2018
SALES (est): 131.61K Privately Held
SIC: 1389 Construction, repair, and dismantling services

(G-15476)
DPS MOLDING INC
276 Bailey Ln (28586-8226)
PHONE..................................732 763-4811
Roger Clark, *Pr*
◆ **EMP:** 11 **EST:** 2010
SALES (est): 597.35K Privately Held
Web: www.dpsmolding.com
SIC: 3089 Injection molding of plastics

(G-15477)
FUSION INCORPORATED (PA)
276 Bailey Ln (28586-8226)
PHONE..................................252 244-4300
◆ **EMP:** 20 **EST:** 1994
SQ FT: 50,000
SALES (est): 2.62MM Privately Held
Web: www.fusion-inc.com
SIC: 3069 Brushes, rubber

(G-15478)
IDUSTRIAL BURKETT SERVICES
2050 Nc Highway 43 (28586-8916)
PHONE..................................252 244-0143
EMP: 10 **EST:** 2013
SALES (est): 73.15K Privately Held
SIC: 7692 Welding repair

(G-15479)
INTERNATIONAL PAPER COMPANY
Also Called: International Paper
1785 Weyerhaeuser Rd (28586-7606)
PHONE..................................252 633-7509
Donna Cannon, *Owner*
EMP: 52
SALES (corp-wide): 18.92B Publicly Held
Web: www.internationalpaper.com
SIC: 2621 Paper mills
PA: International Paper Company
6400 Poplar Ave
Memphis TN 38197
901 419-7000

(G-15480)
MCKEEL & SONS LOGGING INC
170 Spruill Town Rd (28586-8086)
PHONE..................................252 244-3903
Edward W Mckeel, *Pr*
EMP: 4 **EST:** 1986
SALES (est): 398.11K Privately Held
SIC: 2411 Logging camps and contractors

(G-15481)
MILLER LOGGING CO INC
7901 Main St (28586-9151)
PHONE..................................252 229-9860
Gregory S Miller, *Pr*
Carol Harper, *Sec*
EMP: 5 **EST:** 1988
SQ FT: 1,200
SALES (est): 535.55K Privately Held
SIC: 2411 Logging camps and contractors

(G-15482)
NORALEX INC (PA)
Also Called: Noralex Timber
215 Wilmar Rd (28586-8961)
PHONE..................................252 974-1253
John Hines, *Pr*
EMP: 8 **EST:** 1985
SQ FT: 5,000
SALES (est): 999.47K Privately Held
SIC: 2411 Timber, cut at logging camp

(G-15483)
STEVEN C HADDOCK DBA HADDOCK
4122 Leary Mills Rd (28586-9551)
PHONE..................................252 714-2431
Steven C Haddock, *Prin*
EMP: 6 **EST:** 2005
SQ FT: 1,782
SALES (est): 407.82K Privately Held
SIC: 2411 Logging

(G-15484)
VANCEBORO APPAREL INC
7906 Main St (28586-9150)
P.O. Box 716 (28586-0716)
PHONE..................................252 244-2780
Shirley Williams, *Pr*
EMP: 7 **EST:** 2001
SALES (est): 182.78K Privately Held
SIC: 2369 2389 2339 2341 Girl's and children's outerwear, nec; Men's miscellaneous accessories; Women's and misses' accessories; Women's and children's underwear

(G-15485)
WEYERHAEUSER COMPANY
Also Called: Pulp Mill
1785 Weyerhaeuser Rd (28586-7606)
PHONE..................................252 633-7100
John Ashley, *Manager*
EMP: 25
SALES (corp-wide): 7.67B Publicly Held
Web: www.weyerhaeuser.com
SIC: 2621 2421 2611 Paper mills; Sawmills and planing mills, general; Pulp mills
PA: Weyerhaeuser Company
220 Occidental Ave S
Seattle WA 98104
206 539-3000

(G-15486)
WEYERHAEUSER NEW BERN
Also Called: Weyerhaeuser
1785 Weyerhaeuser Rd (28586-7606)
PHONE..................................252 633-7100
EMP: 41 **EST:** 2015
SALES (est): 12.17MM
SALES (corp-wide): 7.67B Publicly Held

SIC: 2631 Container, packaging, and boxboard
PA: Weyerhaeuser Company
220 Occidental Ave S
Seattle WA 98104
206 539-3000

(G-15487)
WEYERHAEUSER NR COMPANY
1482 Weyerhaeuser Rd (28586-9244)
PHONE.................................252 633-7100
EMP: 100
SALES (corp-wide): 7.67B Publicly Held
Web: www.weyerhaeuser.com
SIC: 2421 Lumber: rough, sawed, or planed
HQ: Weyerhaeuser Nr Company
220 Occidental Ave S
Seattle WA 98104

(G-15488)
WEYERHAEUSER NR CO
1785 Weyerhaeuser Rd (28586-7606)
PHONE.................................252 633-7252
EMP: 8 EST: 2018
SALES (est): 164.46K Privately Held
SIC: 2611 Pulp mills

Vandemere
Pamlico County

(G-15489)
PAMLICO PACKING CO INC
28 N First St (28587)
P.O. Box 336 (28529-0336)
PHONE.................................252 745-3688
Ed Cross, Prin
EMP: 10
SALES (corp-wide): 5.49MM Privately Held
SIC: 2092 2091 5146 Seafoods, fresh: prepared; Bouillon, clam: packaged in cans, jars, etc.; Fish and seafoods
PA: Pamlico Packing Co., Inc.
66 Cross Rd S
Grantsboro NC 28529
252 745-3688

Vass
Moore County

(G-15490)
BOB MARTIN
1248 Greenbriar Dr (28394-9200)
PHONE.................................910 245-3593
Bob Martin, Prin
EMP: 8 EST: 2009
SALES (est): 125.79K Privately Held
SIC: 3599 Machine shop, jobbing and repair

(G-15491)
CAROLINA CRATE & PALLET INC
3281 Us 1 Hwy (28394-9314)
P.O. Box 279 (28394-0279)
PHONE.................................910 245-4001
Wallace Wilson, Pr
EMP: 35 EST: 1979
SQ FT: 40,000
SALES (est): 3.59MM Privately Held
Web: www.carolinacrate.com
SIC: 2441 2448 2499 2449 Boxes, wood; Pallets, wood; Reels, plywood; Wood containers, nec

(G-15492)
KENDALL E KRAUSE
Also Called: Ken Krause Co
148 Rice Rd (28394-9661)
PHONE.................................910 690-4119
Kendall E Krause, Owner
EMP: 5 EST: 2002
SALES (est): 187.68K Privately Held
SIC: 2499 3399 4731 4212 Carved and turned wood; Nails: aluminum, brass, or other nonferrous metal or wire; Freight forwarding; Moving services

(G-15493)
PACE INCORPORATED (PA)
Also Called: Pace Worldwide
346 Grant Rd (28394-9338)
PHONE.................................910 695-7223
Erick Siegel, Ch Bd
Eric Siegel, *
◆ EMP: 40 EST: 1958
SQ FT: 37,000
SALES (est): 9.09MM
SALES (corp-wide): 9.09MM Privately Held
Web: www.paceworldwide.com
SIC: 3699 Electrical equipment and supplies, nec

(G-15494)
TIER 1 HEATING AND AIR LLC
3459 Us Hwy 1 (28394)
PHONE.................................910 556-1444
EMP: 12 EST: 2020
SALES (est): 1.01MM Privately Held
SIC: 3585 Heating and air conditioning combination units

Vilas
Watauga County

(G-15495)
FLEMING WOOD & ROD LLC
5001 Us Highway 421 N (28692-9490)
PHONE.................................828 278-9194
EMP: 5 EST: 2018
SALES (est): 64.64K Privately Held
SIC: 2431 Millwork

(G-15496)
INTERSPORT GROUP INC
336 Willowdale Church Rd (28692-8961)
PHONE.................................814 968-3085
EMP: 4
SALES (est): 300.03K Privately Held
SIC: 2326 7389 Work uniforms; Business Activities at Non-Commercial Site

(G-15497)
MIXON MILLS INC
4965 Us Highway 421 N (28692-9489)
PHONE.................................828 297-5431
Ernest Mixon, Pr
Nancy Mixon, Sec
EMP: 5 EST: 1995
SALES (est): 330K Privately Held
SIC: 2421 5084 Sawmills and planing mills, general; Industrial machinery and equipment

(G-15498)
MW ENTERPRISES INC
Also Called: Muncy Winds
5014 Nc Highway 105 S (28692-9015)
P.O. Box 422 (28679-0422)
PHONE.................................828 963-7083
Philip Muncy, Pr
Pam Muncy, VP
◆ EMP: 6 EST: 1987
SQ FT: 4,000
SALES (est): 467.38K Privately Held
Web: www.muncywinds.com
SIC: 5736 3931 Pianos; Clarinets and parts

(G-15499)
WILSON WLDG & LINE BORING LLC
1263 Charlie Thompson Rd (28692-9640)
PHONE.................................828 406-2078
Tanner Wilson, Prin
EMP: 5 EST: 2018
SALES (est): 38.07K Privately Held
SIC: 7692 Welding repair

Wadesboro
Anson County

(G-15500)
ANSON EXPRESS
Also Called: Express, The
205 W Morgan St (28170-2147)
PHONE.................................704 694-2480
Alan Lyon Junior, Owner
EMP: 6 EST: 1993
SALES (est): 354.51K Privately Held
SIC: 2711 Newspapers, publishing and printing

(G-15501)
ANSON WOOD PRODUCTS
Parsons St (28170)
P.O. Box 247 (28170-0247)
PHONE.................................704 694-5390
EMP: 6 EST: 1969
SALES (est): 379.86K Privately Held
SIC: 2411 Wood chips, produced in the field

(G-15502)
BILL RATLIFF JR LOGGING I
4437 Beck Rd (28170-6380)
PHONE.................................704 694-5403
William H Ratliff Junior, Prin
EMP: 8 EST: 2005
SQ FT: 2,304
SALES (est): 134.74K Privately Held
SIC: 2411 Logging camps and contractors

(G-15503)
BRASINGTONS INC
1515 Us Highway 74 W (28170-7550)
P.O. Box 411 (28170-0411)
PHONE.................................704 694-5191
B C Brasington Junior, Pr
B C Brasington Iii, VP
Patsy Brasington, Sec
EMP: 5 EST: 1953
SQ FT: 7,200
SALES (est): 497.2K Privately Held
SIC: 5331 7692 Variety stores; Welding repair

(G-15504)
BROWN CREEK TIMBER COMPANY INC
2691 Nc 742 N (28170-8712)
PHONE.................................704 694-3529
Edward Flake, Pr
EMP: 5 EST: 1989
SALES (est): 343.31K Privately Held
SIC: 2411 Logging camps and contractors

(G-15505)
BUDS LOGGING AND TRUCKING
1561 Stanbackfry Ice Plnt Rd (28170-9236)
PHONE.................................704 465-8016
Buddy H Jarrell, Pr
Emily Jarrell, Sec
EMP: 6 EST: 2002
SALES (est): 564.73K Privately Held
SIC: 2411 Logging

(G-15506)
CAROLINA APPAREL GROUP INC
425 Us Highway 52 S (28170-6466)
P.O. Box 827 (28170-0827)
PHONE.................................704 694-6544
Don W Trexler, Pr
Laurie G Trexler, *
Michael A Gutschmit, *
▼ EMP: 60 EST: 1999
SALES (est): 7.1MM
SALES (corp-wide): 21.43MM Privately Held
SIC: 2322 Men's and boy's underwear and nightwear
PA: Coville, Inc.
8065 N Point Blvd Ste O
Winston Salem NC 27106
336 759-0115

(G-15507)
COLUMBUS MCKINNON CORPORATION
Also Called: Columbus McKinnon
2020 Country Club Rd (28170-3204)
P.O. Box 779 (28170-0779)
PHONE.................................704 694-2156
John Farnandez, Brnch Mgr
EMP: 78
SALES (corp-wide): 936.24MM Publicly Held
Web: www.cmco.com
SIC: 3536 Hoists
PA: Columbus Mckinnon Corporation
205 Crosspoint Pkwy
Getzville NY 14068
716 689-5400

(G-15508)
CORE BEGINNINGS
420 E Wade St (28170-2334)
PHONE.................................614 551-1963
Leshia Adams, Pr
EMP: 4 EST: 2019
SALES (est): 39.69K Privately Held
SIC: 3999 Education aids, devices and supplies

(G-15509)
DARLING INGREDIENTS INC
656 Little Duncan Rd (28170)
P.O. Box 718 (28170-0718)
PHONE.................................704 694-3701
Dean Deivert, Genl Mgr
EMP: 12
SALES (corp-wide): 6.53B Publicly Held
Web: www.darlingii.com
SIC: 2048 2077 Feed supplements; Rendering
PA: Darling Ingredients Inc.
5601 N Macarthur Blvd
Irving TX 75038
972 717-0300

(G-15510)
GLENN TREXLER & SONS LOG INC
1095 Bethel Rd (28170-7309)
PHONE.................................704 694-5644
Franklin G Trexler, Pr
EMP: 13 EST: 1970
SALES (est): 512.87K Privately Held
SIC: 2411 Logging camps and contractors

(G-15511)
HILDRETH WOOD PRODUCTS INC
825 Mount Vernon Rd (28170-7108)
PHONE.................................704 826-8326
Blake Hildreth Junior, Pr
EMP: 8 EST: 1968
SQ FT: 10,000
SALES (est): 386.87K Privately Held
Web: www.hildrethwoodproducts.com

SIC: **2448** 2449 Pallets, wood; Shipping cases and drums, wood: wirebound and plywood

(G-15512)
HORNWOOD INC
204 E Wade St (28170-2265)
PHONE..................................704 694-3009
Kenneth W Horne Senior, *Brnch Mgr*
EMP: 50
SALES (corp-wide): 46.97MM **Privately Held**
Web: www.hornwoodinc.com
SIC: **2258** Cloth, warp knit
PA: Hornwood, Inc.
766 Haileys Ferry Rd
Lilesville NC 28091
704 848-4121

(G-15513)
J4 CONSTRUCTION LLC ○
2634 E Hwy 74 W (28170-6108)
P.O. Box 756 (28097-0756)
PHONE..................................704 550-7970
Adrian Kennedy, *Managing Member*
EMP: 5 **EST:** 2022
SALES (est): 335.89K **Privately Held**
SIC: **3446** Lintels, light gauge steel

(G-15514)
JAMES L JOHNSON
Also Called: Deep Creek Timber
2151 Beaver Rd (28170-7360)
PHONE..................................704 694-0103
James L Johnson, *Prin*
EMP: 7 **EST:** 2012
SALES (est): 232.52K **Privately Held**
SIC: **2411** Logging

(G-15515)
LOBA-WAKOL LLC
2732 Us Highway 74 W (28170-7558)
P.O. Box 829 (28170-0829)
PHONE..................................704 527-5919
Ashley Carter, *Managing Member*
▲ **EMP:** 22 **EST:** 2009
SALES (est): 4.91MM
SALES (corp-wide): 154.09MM **Privately Held**
Web: www.loba-wakol.com
SIC: **2891** Adhesives and sealants
PA: Wakol Gmbh
Bottenbacher Str. 30
Pirmasens RP 66954
633180010

(G-15516)
MEDICAL SPECIALTIES INC
308 Parson St (28170-9623)
P.O. Box 977 (28170-0977)
PHONE..................................704 694-2434
Scott Gaylord, *Mgr*
EMP: 6
SALES (corp-wide): 4.21MM **Privately Held**
Web: www.medspec.com
SIC: **3842** Orthopedic appliances
PA: Medical Specialties Incorporated
4600 Lebanon Rd Ste K
Mint Hill NC 28227
704 573-4040

(G-15517)
TREXLER LOGGING INC
2292 Bethel Rd (28170-7321)
PHONE..................................704 694-5272
Robert Trexler, *Pr*
EMP: 5 **EST:** 2006
SALES (est): 385.3K **Privately Held**
SIC: **2411** Logging camps and contractors

(G-15518)
TRIANGLE BRICK COMPANY
2960 Us Highway 52 N (28170-9122)
PHONE..................................704 695-1420
Howard Brown, *Mgr*
EMP: 49
SALES (corp-wide): 48.2MM **Privately Held**
Web: www.trianglebrick.com
SIC: **3251** 5211 Brick and structural clay tile; Brick
PA: Triangle Brick Company
6523 Nc Highway 55
Durham NC 27713
919 544-1796

(G-15519)
WADE MANUFACTURING COMPANY (PA)
76 Mill St (28170-2410)
P.O. Box 32 (28170-0032)
PHONE..................................704 694-2131
Bernard M Hodges, *Pr*
Carl A Holt, *
Shelton Faulkner, *
▲ **EMP:** 200 **EST:** 1923
SQ FT: 300,000
SALES (est): 22.87MM
SALES (corp-wide): 22.87MM **Privately Held**
Web: www.waremfg.com
SIC: **2211** 2221 Cotton broad woven goods; Polyester broadwoven fabrics

(G-15520)
XCEL HRMETIC MTR REWINDING INC
2356 Bethel Rd (28170-7322)
P.O. Box 799 (28170-0799)
PHONE..................................704 694-6001
EMP: 8 **EST:** 1996
SQ FT: 30,000
SALES (est): 939.35K **Privately Held**
Web: www.xcelhermeticmotors.com
SIC: **7694** Electric motor repair

Wagram
Scotland County

(G-15521)
CASCADES TSSUE GROUP - ORE INC
Also Called: Cascades Tissue Group-Oregon
19320 Airbase Rd (28396-6102)
PHONE..................................503 397-2900
Suzanne Blanchet, *Pr*
Craig Nelson, *
Guy Prenevost, *
EMP: 70 **EST:** 2002
SALES (est): 28.02MM
SALES (corp-wide): 3.32B **Privately Held**
SIC: **2621** Paper mills
HQ: Cascades Canada Ulc
404 Boul Marie-Victorin
Kingsey Falls QC J0A 1
819 363-5100

(G-15522)
CYPRESS BEND VINEYARDS INC
21904 Riverton Rd (28396-8700)
PHONE..................................910 369-0411
Daniel Smith, *Pr*
Tina Smith, *VP*
EMP: 5 **EST:** 2003
SQ FT: 5,000
SALES (est): 441.23K **Privately Held**
Web: www.cypressbendvineyards.com
SIC: **2084** Wines

(G-15523)
DIRECT DISTRIBUTION INDS INC
24581 Main St (28396-9465)
P.O. Box 947 (28396-0947)
PHONE..................................910 217-0000
Neill Shaw, *Prin*
EMP: 6 **EST:** 2004
SALES (est): 241.28K **Privately Held**
SIC: **3999** Manufacturing industries, nec

(G-15524)
WESTPOINT HOME INC
Also Called: Biddeford Mill
19320 Airbase Rd (28396-6102)
PHONE..................................910 369-2231
Roger F Carr Junior, *Brnch Mgr*
EMP: 371
Web: www.westpointhome.com
SIC: **2211** 2269 2392 2297 Blankets and blanketings, cotton; Bleaching: raw stock, yarn, and narrow fabrics; Household furnishings, nec; Nonwoven fabrics
HQ: Westpoint Home Llc
777 3rd Ave Fl 7
New York NY 10017
212 930-2000

Wake Forest
Wake County

(G-15525)
ADS N ART SCREENPRINTING & EMB
929 Heritage Lake Rd Ste 400 (27587-4387)
PHONE..................................919 453-0400
Steve Fleming, *Pr*
EMP: 5 **EST:** 2014
SALES (est): 151.3K **Privately Held**
Web: www.adsnartscreenprinting.com
SIC: **2759** Screen printing

(G-15526)
ADVANCED SYSTEMS INTGRTION LLC (PA)
8512 Mangum Hollow Dr (27587-6127)
PHONE..................................260 447-5555
Christopher J Albertson, *Managing Member*
EMP: 4 **EST:** 2004
SALES (est): 2.24MM **Privately Held**
Web: www.asifabrication.com
SIC: **3498** Fabricated pipe and fittings

(G-15527)
AMS SOFTWARE INC
2012 S Main St (27587-5008)
PHONE..................................919 570-6001
EMP: 10 **EST:** 2019
SALES (est): 374.09K **Privately Held**
Web: www.ams-software.com
SIC: **7372** Prepackaged software

(G-15528)
ARGOS USA LLC
Also Called: Unicon Concrete
5025 Unicon Dr (27587-7794)
PHONE..................................919 554-2087
EMP: 34
Web: www.argos-us.com
SIC: **3273** Ready-mixed concrete
HQ: Argos Usa Llc
3015 Windward Plz Ste 300
Alpharetta GA 30005
678 368-4300

(G-15529)
B F I INDUSTRIES INC
3650 Rogers Rd # 334 (27587-9306)
PHONE..................................919 229-4509
Scott Skoll, *Pr*
Sharon Skoll, *VP*
EMP: 4 **EST:** 1986
SALES (est): 384.7K **Privately Held**
Web: www.bfiindustries.com
SIC: **5199** 2752 Advertising specialties; Promotional printing, lithographic

(G-15530)
BALLPOINTE PUBG & DESIGN LLC
1200 Crozier Ct (27587-4235)
PHONE..................................919 453-0449
Kent Lower, *Prin*
EMP: 5 **EST:** 2015
SALES (est): 134.18K **Privately Held**
SIC: **2711** Newspapers

(G-15531)
BIG SHOW FOODS INC
3959 Hwy 39 S (27588)
P.O. Box 3182 (27830-3182)
PHONE..................................919 242-7769
Tom Price, *Pr*
EMP: 10 **EST:** 1999
SQ FT: 75,000
SALES (est): 483.23K **Privately Held**
Web: www.bigshowfoods.com
SIC: **2099** Food preparations, nec

(G-15532)
BIKER SOFTWARE
1165 Litchborough Way (27587-3616)
PHONE..................................919 761-1681
Christopher Meuser, *Prin*
EMP: 5 **EST:** 2010
SALES (est): 71.51K **Privately Held**
SIC: **7372** Prepackaged software

(G-15533)
BIOLOGCAL INNVTION OPTMZTIONS
Also Called: Bios Lighting
224 E Holding Ave # 2116 (27587-2903)
PHONE..................................321 260-2467
EMP: 11
SALES (corp-wide): 2.5MM **Privately Held**
Web: www.bioslighting.com
SIC: **3646** Commercial lighting fixtures
PA: Biological Innovation And Optimization Systems, Llc
2355 Camino Vida Roble
Carlsbad CA 92011
321 260-2467

(G-15534)
BODY SHOP INC (DH)
Also Called: Body Shop
5036 One World Way (27587-7732)
PHONE..................................919 554-4900
Peter Saunders, *CEO*
Peter Ridler, *
David Bellamy, *
Anthea Borum, *
◆ **EMP:** 250 **EST:** 1987
SQ FT: 100,000
SALES (est): 451.42MM
SALES (corp-wide): 500.31K **Privately Held**
Web: www.thebodyshop.com
SIC: **5999** 6794 2844 Perfumes and colognes; Franchises, selling or licensing; Perfumes, cosmetics and other toilet preparations
HQ: The Body Shop International Limited
C/O Frp Advisory Trading Limited
London EC4N
167 051-3328

GEOGRAPHIC SECTION

Wake Forest - Wake County (G-15562)

(G-15535)
BRANDYWINE COMMUNICATIONS
1204 Golden Star Way (27587-3934)
PHONE..............................770 853-1799
Gene Long, *Dir*
EMP: 5 **EST:** 2016
SALES (est): 90.39K **Privately Held**
Web: www.brandywinecomm.com
SIC: 3663 Radio and t.v. communications equipment

(G-15536)
BTC ELECTRONIC COMPONENTS LLC (DH)
Also Called: Btc Electronic Components Inc
2709 Connector Dr (27587-4363)
PHONE..............................919 229-2162
Paul Mosely, *Pr*
EMP: 39 **EST:** 1980
SQ FT: 17,600
SALES (est): 10.95MM
SALES (corp-wide): 533.52MM **Privately Held**
Web: www.btcelectronics.com
SIC: 3812 5065 Search and navigation equipment; Electronic parts
HQ: Fastener Distribution Holdings, Llc
5200 Sheila St
Commerce CA 90040
213 620-9950

(G-15537)
C3 SEALCOATING LLC
101 Jordan Ln (27587-7140)
PHONE..............................919 880-5515
Calvin Anderson Ray Iii, *Prin*
EMP: 8 **EST:** 2019
SALES (est): 939.25K **Privately Held**
Web: www.c3sealcoating.com
SIC: 2952 Asphalt felts and coatings

(G-15538)
CAROLINA SUNROCK LLC
5043 Unicon Dr (27587-7794)
PHONE..............................919 554-0500
Carl Williams, *Mgr*
EMP: 33
SALES (corp-wide): 68.06MM **Privately Held**
Web: www.thesunrockgroup.com
SIC: 3273 Ready-mixed concrete
HQ: Carolina Sunrock Llc
1001 W B St
Butner NC 27509
919 575-4502

(G-15539)
CHANMALA GALLERY FINE ART PRTG
306 S White St (27587-2917)
PHONE..............................704 975-7695
Adriana Chanmala, *Prin*
EMP: 5 **EST:** 2016
SALES (est): 116.64K **Privately Held**
SIC: 2752 Commercial printing, lithographic

(G-15540)
CHURCH INITIATIVE INC
Also Called: DIVORCECARE
250 S Allen Rd (27587-2608)
P.O. Box 1739 (27588-1739)
PHONE..............................919 562-2112
EMP: 31 **EST:** 1993
SQ FT: 12,000
SALES (est): 5.67MM **Privately Held**
Web: www.churchinitiative.org
SIC: 2731 8661 2741 Book publishing; Religious organizations; Miscellaneous publishing

(G-15541)
CJC ENTERPRISES
Also Called: Vaughan Logging
7608 Ligon Mill Rd (27587-8888)
PHONE..............................919 266-3158
Charles L Vaughan, *Owner*
EMP: 20 **EST:** 1976
SQ FT: 2,400
SALES (est): 1.93MM **Privately Held**
SIC: 1623 1611 2411 Water, sewer, and utility lines; Grading; Timber, cut at logging camp

(G-15542)
CLEAR STONE COATING INC
608 Wahlbrink Dr (27587-5301)
PHONE..............................424 543-0811
EMP: 5 **EST:** 2016
SALES (est): 246.82K **Privately Held**
SIC: 3479 Metal coating and allied services

(G-15543)
CMD LAND SERVICES LLC
532 S Wingate St (27587-2820)
PHONE..............................919 554-2281
Rebecca Tiffany, *Managing Member*
EMP: 4 **EST:** 2005
SALES (est): 223.63K **Privately Held**
SIC: 2875 8999 Compost; Services, nec

(G-15544)
COLLIN MANUFACTURING INC
12271 Capital Blvd (27587-6200)
PHONE..............................919 917-5969
EMP: 5 **EST:** 2017
SALES (est): 180.51K **Privately Held**
SIC: 3999 Manufacturing industries, nec

(G-15545)
DEALER TRACK INC
1890 S Main St Ste 106 (27587-9726)
PHONE..............................919 554-0972
EMP: 5 **EST:** 2019
SALES (est): 166.32K **Privately Held**
SIC: 7372 Prepackaged software

(G-15546)
DIAZIT COMPANY INC
8120 Diazit Dr (27587-6683)
PHONE..............................919 556-5188
Bruce Barsalona, *Brnch Mgr*
EMP: 5
SALES (corp-wide): 4.04MM **Privately Held**
Web: www.diazit.com
SIC: 3555 Printing trades machinery
PA: Diazit Company, Inc.
941 Us Hwy 1
Youngsville NC
919 556-5188

(G-15547)
DISTINCTIVE MILLWORKS LLC
3650 Rogers Rd Ste 201 (27587-9306)
PHONE..............................919 263-4337
Timothy Kaiser, *Managing Member*
EMP: 5 **EST:** 2015
SALES (est): 243.87K **Privately Held**
Web: www.distinctivemillworks.com
SIC: 2431 Millwork

(G-15548)
DOCUREP LLC
8617 Territory Trl (27587-4412)
PHONE..............................919 280-4723
EMP: 5 **EST:** 2013
SALES (est): 158.12K **Privately Held**
SIC: 7372 Prepackaged software

(G-15549)
EAST WEST DIVERSIFIED LLC
1609 Gracie Girl Way (27587-5942)
PHONE..............................919 671-0301
EMP: 4 **EST:** 2017
SALES (est): 39.69K **Privately Held**
SIC: 3999 Manufacturing industries, nec

(G-15550)
ECS GROUP-NC LLC
Also Called: Elevator Controls and Security
6424 Zebulon Rd (27587-8359)
P.O. Box 41327 (27629-1327)
PHONE..............................919 830-1171
EMP: 4 **EST:** 2013
SALES (est): 386.54K **Privately Held**
Web: www.ecsgroupnc.com
SIC: 3534 Elevators and equipment

(G-15551)
EDWARDS LAWNMOWER & WLDG REPR
1616 Wake Dr (27587-8803)
PHONE..............................919 235-7173
EMP: 5 **EST:** 2015
SALES (est): 58.07K **Privately Held**
SIC: 7692 Welding repair

(G-15552)
ELECTRIC MTR SP WAKE FREST INC (PA)
1225 N White St (27587-7120)
P.O. Box 1885 (27588-1885)
PHONE..............................919 556-3229
Thomas Richard Wright Junior, *Pr*
Jennifer Wright, *
Hollie Wright, *
EMP: 36 **EST:** 1952
SQ FT: 30,000
SALES (est): 15.64MM
SALES (corp-wide): 15.64MM **Privately Held**
Web: www.electricmotorshopnc.com
SIC: 7694 5063 Electric motor repair; Motors, electric

(G-15553)
ENERTIA BUILDING SYSTEMS INC
13312 Garffe Sherron Rd (27587-8942)
PHONE..............................919 556-2391
Marvin Sykes, *Mgr*
EMP: 4
SALES (corp-wide): 482.57K **Privately Held**
Web: www.enertiahomes.com
SIC: 2452 Prefabricated buildings, wood
PA: Enertia Building Systems, Inc.
1472 Us Hwy 1 N
Youngsville NC 27596
919 556-2391

(G-15554)
EPL & SOLAR CORP
Also Called: Epl
5517 Sedge Wren Dr (27587-4992)
PHONE..............................201 577-8966
Man Park, *Pr*
EMP: 5 **EST:** 2018
SALES (est): 990.18K **Privately Held**
SIC: 5063 3648 Lighting fixtures, commercial and industrial; Lighting fixtures, except electric; residential

(G-15555)
EZ SIGN SERVICE
2513 Burlington Mills Rd (27587-8854)
PHONE..............................919 604-3508
EMP: 5 **EST:** 2017
SALES (est): 116.68K **Privately Held**
Web: www.ezsignservice.com
SIC: 3993 Signs and advertising specialties

(G-15556)
FIRE FLUTES
906 Bear Branch Way # 301 (27587-3880)
PHONE..............................321 230-3878
Craig Noss, *Prin*
EMP: 4 **EST:** 2010
SALES (est): 56.68K **Privately Held**
SIC: 3931 Musical instruments

(G-15557)
GAINS FITNESS GEAR LLC
224 E Holding Ave Unit 1616 (27588)
PHONE..............................800 403-2904
Chris Frazer, *Prin*
Chandra Frazer, *Prin*
Julian David, *Prin*
EMP: 8 **EST:** 2019
SALES (est): 231.53K **Privately Held**
SIC: 3949 Sporting and athletic goods, nec

(G-15558)
GARNETT COMPONENT SALES INC
2824 Penfold Ln (27587-5498)
PHONE..............................919 562-5158
Tommy Garnett, *Pr*
EMP: 4 **EST:** 2008
SALES (est): 840.84K **Privately Held**
Web: www.garnettcomponentsales.com
SIC: 3444 Bins, prefabricated sheet metal

(G-15559)
GIANT WAKE FOREST LLC
11216 Capital Blvd Ste 108 (27587-4530)
PHONE..............................919 556-7433
EMP: 4 **EST:** 2018
SALES (est): 131.49K **Privately Held**
Web: www.giantwakeforest.com
SIC: 3732 Boatbuilding and repairing

(G-15560)
GLOBAL ECOSCIENCES INC
7723 Benthill Ct (27587-5828)
PHONE..............................252 631-6266
Jan Levine, *Pr*
Gilmore Ching, *COO*
EMP: 5
SALES (est): 499.41K **Privately Held**
Web: global.wfu.edu
SIC: 2812 2842 4953 4959 Alkalies and chlorine; Polishes and sanitation goods; Refuse systems; Oil spill cleanup

(G-15561)
GMA CREATIVE INC
504 S White St (27587-2921)
P.O. Box 2072 (27588-2072)
PHONE..............................919 435-6984
Ginger Allen, *Owner*
EMP: 5 **EST:** 2014
SALES (est): 240.91K **Privately Held**
Web: www.gingermeekallen.com
SIC: 3911 5094 5944 Jewelry, precious metal ; Jewelry and precious stones; Jewelry stores

(G-15562)
GOODBERRY CREAMERY INC (PA)
Also Called: Goodberrys Creamery Rest
305 Capcom Ave (27587-6598)
P.O. Box 58307 (27658-8307)
PHONE..............................919 878-8870
Harry Brathwaite, *Pr*
EMP: 10 **EST:** 1987
SALES (est): 8.61MM **Privately Held**
Web: www.goodberrys.com
SIC: 5451 2024 Ice cream (packaged); Ice cream and ice milk

Wake Forest - Wake County (G-15563)

(G-15563)
GREEN STREAM TECHNOLOGIES INC
3331 Heritage Trade Dr Ste 101 (27587-4346)
PHONE..................844 499-8880
James Gray, *Pr*
Karen Lindquist Lee, *COO*
EMP: 4 **EST:** 2017
SALES (est): 331.3K **Privately Held**
Web: www.greenstream.com
SIC: 3822 3826 Hardware for environmental regulators; Environmental testing equipment

(G-15564)
HEIDELBERG MTLS STHAST AGG LLC
10501 Capital Blvd (27587-7795)
PHONE..................919 556-4011
EMP: 35
SALES (corp-wide): 21.19B **Privately Held**
Web: www.hansonbiz.com
SIC: 3273 Ready-mixed concrete
HQ: Heidelberg Materials Southeast Agg Llc
3237 Satellite Blvd # 30
Duluth GA 30096
770 491-2756

(G-15565)
JACKSON PRODUCTS INC
1109 Monterey Bay Dr (27587-9573)
PHONE..................704 598-4949
Robert Elkin, *Pr*
Chris Anderson, *Prin*
EMP: 10 **EST:** 1997
SALES (est): 596.23K **Privately Held**
SIC: 3842 Personal safety equipment

(G-15566)
KAY & SONS WOODWORKS INC
2040 Forestville Rd (27587-8130)
PHONE..................919 556-1060
Venica Hill, *Pr*
M Kay Hill, *VP*
S Kay Hill, *VP*
EMP: 10 **EST:** 1973
SQ FT: 5,700
SALES (est): 532.53K **Privately Held**
Web: www.kayandsonswoodworks.com
SIC: 2434 Wood kitchen cabinets

(G-15567)
KENSON PARENTING SOLUTIONS
1404 Wall Rd Ste 200 (27587-7470)
PHONE..................919 637-1499
Jennifer Kent, *Pr*
Jennifer Edmundson, *VP*
EMP: 6 **EST:** 2010
SALES (est): 170.52K **Privately Held**
Web: www.kensonparenting.com
SIC: 8322 3944 Individual and family services; Craft and hobby kits and sets

(G-15568)
KETTU WOODWORKS
7409 Lakefall Dr (27587-5797)
PHONE..................919 699-4173
Dave Skibo, *Prin*
EMP: 5 **EST:** 2017
SALES (est): 76.85K **Privately Held**
SIC: 2431 Millwork

(G-15569)
KITCHEN CABINETS OF RALEIGH
2816 Kimmon Way (27587-5442)
PHONE..................919 291-4397
EMP: 4 **EST:** 2014
SALES (est): 68.47K **Privately Held**
Web: www.raleigh-cabinets.com
SIC: 2434 Wood kitchen cabinets

(G-15570)
MAGNA SIGN INTL
2200 Prairie Dog Dr (27587-5062)
PHONE..................813 727-0205
EMP: 4 **EST:** 2016
SALES (est): 46.08K **Privately Held**
SIC: 3993 Signs, not made in custom sign painting shops

(G-15571)
MATHESON TRI-GAS INC
326 Forestville Rd (27587-9418)
PHONE..................919 556-6461
Brad Phillips, *Brnch Mgr*
EMP: 11
Web: www.mathesongas.com
SIC: 5084 2813 Welding machinery and equipment; Nitrogen
HQ: Matheson Tri-Gas, Inc.
3 Mountainview Rd Ste 3 # 3
Warren NJ 07059
908 991-9200

(G-15572)
MONOLITH CORPORATION (HQ)
12339 Wake Union Church Rd Ste 107 (27587-4512)
PHONE..................919 878-1900
Shawn Raynor, *CEO*
EMP: 47 **EST:** 1984
SQ FT: 23,000
SALES (est): 4.14MM
SALES (corp-wide): 6.62B **Privately Held**
Web: www.monolith.com
SIC: 3577 3571 Computer peripheral equipment, nec; Personal computers (microcomputers)
PA: Constellation Software Inc
20 Adelaide St E Suite 1200
Toronto ON M5C 2
416 861-9677

(G-15573)
N-ZYME SPECIALIST LLC
8121 Hawkshead Rd (27587-6680)
PHONE..................919 349-2429
James S Crawford, *Pr*
EMP: 5 **EST:** 2015
SALES (est): 134.3K **Privately Held**
SIC: 2869 Enzymes

(G-15574)
NORTH CRLINA ORTHTICS PRSTHTIC
2717 Leighton Ridge Dr (27587-5987)
PHONE..................919 210-0906
Damon Johncour, *Owner*
EMP: 22 **EST:** 2013
SALES (est): 1.95MM **Privately Held**
Web: www.ncopi.com
SIC: 3842 Orthopedic appliances

(G-15575)
OPERABLE INC
1209 Winkworth Way (27587-1308)
PHONE..................757 617-0935
Glen E Caplan, *Prin*
EMP: 6 **EST:** 2015
SALES (est): 75.78K **Privately Held**
Web: www.operable.io
SIC: 3652 Prerecorded records and tapes

(G-15576)
POWERSECURE INTERNATIONAL INC
Also Called: Powersecure
1609 Heritage Commerce Ct (27587-4245)
PHONE..................919 556-3056
▲ **EMP:** 1235
SIC: 3629 4931 Electronic generation equipment; Cogeneration of electric power

(G-15577)
PRP VENTURES INC
2811 Superior Dr Ste 101 (27587-7799)
P.O. Box 18207 (27619-8207)
PHONE..................919 554-8734
EMP: 15 **EST:** 1994
SQ FT: 20,000
SALES (est): 1.01MM **Privately Held**
SIC: 2541 1799 Counters or counter display cases, wood; Counter top installation

(G-15578)
PUFFING MONKEY
2115 S Main St (27587-5011)
PHONE..................919 556-7779
EMP: 4 **EST:** 2014
SALES (est): 141.62K **Privately Held**
SIC: 3634 Cigarette lighters, electric

(G-15579)
RAXTER CUSTOM BAGS
1129 Brason Ln (27587-5266)
PHONE..................864 421-5181
EMP: 4 **EST:** 2010
SALES (est): 104.04K **Privately Held**
Web: www.raxtercustombags.com
SIC: 3111 Bag leather

(G-15580)
RB3 ENTERPRISES INC
Also Called: Rb3 Digital Graphics
4701 Rogers Rd (27587-7653)
PHONE..................919 795-5822
Rose Beck, *Pr*
Robert D Beck Iii, *VP*
Rose M Beck, *Pr*
EMP: 6 **EST:** 2003
SQ FT: 6,000
SALES (est): 494.17K **Privately Held**
Web: www.rb3enterprises.com
SIC: 3861 Printing equipment, photographic

(G-15581)
RCNC INC
8817 Timberland Dr (27587-5353)
PHONE..................919 728-6691
EMP: 6 **EST:** 2019
SALES (est): 159.59K **Privately Held**
SIC: 3089 Plastics products, nec

(G-15582)
RECLAIM FILTERS AND SYSTEMS (PA)
Also Called: Reclaim
1129 Hidden Hills Dr (27587-5788)
PHONE..................919 528-1787
Russell J Keller, *Pr*
EMP: 4 **EST:** 2002
SALES (est): 771.85K
SALES (corp-wide): 771.85K **Privately Held**
Web: www.waterreclaim.com
SIC: 3569 5085 Filters, general line: industrial; Filters, industrial

(G-15583)
RENEWCO-MEADOW BRANCH LLC
1609 Heritage Commerce Ct (27587-4245)
PHONE..................404 584-3552
Eric Dupont, *CMO*
EMP: 6 **EST:** 2010
SALES (est): 1.89MM
SALES (corp-wide): 25.25B **Publicly Held**
SIC: 1311 Natural gas production
HQ: Powersecure, Inc.
4068 Stirrup Creek Dr
Durham NC 27703
919 556-3056

(G-15584)
RSK INDUSTRIES LLC
841 Traditions Ridge Dr (27587-9524)
PHONE..................216 905-4014
Rudolph Kandrach, *Prin*
EMP: 4 **EST:** 2017
SALES (est): 124.81K **Privately Held**
SIC: 3999 Manufacturing industries, nec

(G-15585)
RUFCO INC (PA)
Also Called: Rainbow Upholstery & Furniture
5101 Unicon Dr (27587-5066)
PHONE..................919 829-1332
Charles Bullock, *Pr*
Karla Bullock, *Prin*
EMP: 6 **EST:** 1986
SQ FT: 3,800
SALES (est): 917.91K
SALES (corp-wide): 917.91K **Privately Held**
Web: www.rainbowonwest.com
SIC: 7641 2512 Reupholstery; Upholstered household furniture

(G-15586)
S CHOICE BAKER INC
343 S White St Ste B (27587-1902)
PHONE..................919 556-1188
EMP: 4
SALES (est): 258.41K **Privately Held**
SIC: 2851 Shellac (protective coating)

(G-15587)
SALON & SPA DESIGN SERVICES
7208 Ledford Grove Ln (27587-1727)
PHONE..................919 556-6380
Denisa Ramirez, *Prin*
EMP: 4 **EST:** 2016
SALES (est): 55.16K **Privately Held**
SIC: 7389 3999 Design services; Barber and beauty shop equipment

(G-15588)
SCION INTERNATIONAL US
2520 Laurelford Ln (27587-4963)
PHONE..................919 570-9303
EMP: 7 **EST:** 1992
SALES (est): 97.06K **Privately Held**
SIC: 3679 Electronic components, nec

(G-15589)
SCOTTS CABINET STORE LLC
605 Rookwood Ct (27587-2295)
PHONE..................919 725-2530
EMP: 5 **EST:** 2018
SALES (est): 59.16K **Privately Held**
Web: www.scottscabinetstore.com
SIC: 2434 Wood kitchen cabinets

(G-15590)
SEA SUPREME INC
343 S White St Ste B (27587-1902)
PHONE..................919 556-1188
EMP: 8 **EST:** 1993
SQ FT: 4,500
SALES (est): 964.75K **Privately Held**
SIC: 2092 Crabmeat, frozen

(G-15591)
SEEMA INTL CUSTOM CABINETRY
1012 Lightfoot Ct (27587-9342)
PHONE..................917 703-0820
Jozsef Ignacz, *Prin*
EMP: 5 **EST:** 2018
SALES (est): 241.9K **Privately Held**
Web: www.seemawork.com

SIC: 2434 Wood kitchen cabinets

(G-15592)
SHOP DAWG SIGNS LLC
Also Called: Signcraft Solutions
4154 Shearon Farms Ave Ste 109 (27587)
PHONE..................................919 556-2672
Matthew Key, *Managing Member*
EMP: 7 **EST:** 2009
SALES (est): 119.89K **Privately Held**
SIC: 3993 Advertising artwork

(G-15593)
SONOCO PRODUCTS COMPANY
243 Tillamook Dr (27587-4957)
PHONE..................................919 556-1504
EMP: 5
SALES (corp-wide): 6.78B **Publicly Held**
Web: www.sonoco.com
SIC: 2631 Paperboard mills
PA: Sonoco Products Company
1 N 2nd St
Hartsville SC 29550
843 383-7000

(G-15594)
SOUTHERN DESIGN CABINETRY LLC
740 Merritt Capital Dr Ste 120 (27587-3742)
PHONE..................................919 340-1858
Heather T Dean, *Prin*
EMP: 10 **EST:** 2019
SALES (est): 473.61K **Privately Held**
Web: www.southerndesignandcabinetry.com
SIC: 2434 Wood kitchen cabinets

(G-15595)
SPORTS PRODUCTS LLC
1608 Heritage Commerce Ct Ste 100 (27587-6685)
PHONE..................................919 562-4074
Randy Mcintyre, *Managing Member*
▲ **EMP:** 5 **EST:** 1996
SALES (est): 446.95K **Privately Held**
Web: www.thesportsproductsgroup.com
SIC: 3949 Hunting equipment

(G-15596)
SPOTA LLC
Also Called: Stop-Painting.com
1505 Basley St (27587-6192)
PHONE..................................919 569-6765
Clifford A Lowe, *Managing Member*
▲ **EMP:** 15 **EST:** 2001
SQ FT: 2,500
SALES (est): 4.49MM **Privately Held**
Web: www.stop-painting.com
SIC: 3069 Rubber tape

(G-15597)
SPUNKY SPORTS LLC
7305 Mithrasdowne Ct (27587-5396)
PHONE..................................919 435-0198
Hurtford Smith Junior, *Prin*
EMP: 4 **EST:** 2016
SALES (est): 62.79K **Privately Held**
SIC: 2741 Miscellaneous publishing

(G-15598)
STEVES TS & UNIFORMS INC
3129 Heritage Trade Dr Ste 108 (27587-4296)
P.O. Box 1396 (27588-1396)
PHONE..................................919 554-4221
Steven Davis, *Owner*
EMP: 6 **EST:** 2000
SALES (est): 623.13K **Privately Held**
Web: www.stevestees.net

SIC: 2759 Screen printing

(G-15599)
STITCHES ON CRITTER POND
7333 Critter Pond Rd (27587-5503)
PHONE..................................919 624-5886
EMP: 4 **EST:** 2017
SALES (est): 40.31K **Privately Held**
SIC: 2395 Embroidery and art needlework

(G-15600)
SUPERIOR TOOLING INC
2800 Superior Dr (27587-7799)
PHONE..................................919 570-9762
EMP: 19 **EST:** 1985
SALES (est): 3.74MM **Privately Held**
Web: www.sti-nc.com
SIC: 3544 Dies, plastics forming

(G-15601)
SYNTHONIX INC
2713 Connector Dr (27587-4363)
PHONE..................................919 875-9277
Gary Allred, *Pr*
Jonathan Scoggins, *VP*
EMP: 12 **EST:** 2007
SQ FT: 10,000
SALES (est): 2.5MM **Privately Held**
Web: www.synthonix.com
SIC: 2834 Druggists' preparations (pharmaceuticals)

(G-15602)
TFS INC
P.O. Box 1408 (27588-1408)
PHONE..................................919 556-9161
Tom Oswald, *Prin*
EMP: 6 **EST:** 2011
SALES (est): 255.94K **Privately Held**
SIC: 3674 Semiconductors and related devices

(G-15603)
TIM P KRAHULEC
Also Called: Reliant Rubber Co
5107 Unicon Dr Ste H (27587-5020)
PHONE..................................919 554-1331
Tim P Krahulec, *Owner*
Tim Krahulec, *Owner*
▲ **EMP:** 6 **EST:** 1984
SQ FT: 2,000
SALES (est): 487.05K **Privately Held**
Web: www.greatlakesrubber.com
SIC: 3053 Gaskets, all materials

(G-15604)
TRIANGLE SIGN SOLUTIONS
5101 Unicon Dr Ste B (27587-5021)
PHONE..................................919 302-2482
EMP: 4 **EST:** 2019
SALES (est): 123.17K **Privately Held**
SIC: 3993 Signs and advertising specialties

(G-15605)
TRIANGLE WOODWORKS INC
7608 Fullard Dr (27587-6697)
PHONE..................................919 570-0337
Brian Sandy, *Prin*
EMP: 4 **EST:** 2001
SALES (est): 394.3K **Privately Held**
SIC: 2431 Millwork

(G-15606)
TRICKFIT & SUEPACK TRAINING
Also Called: Gym 30
918 Gateway Commons Cir (27587-5992)
PHONE..................................919 737-2231
EMP: 4 **EST:** 2017
SALES (est): 100K **Privately Held**
Web: www.gymthirty.com

SIC: 7991 7372 Physical fitness facilities; Application computer software

(G-15607)
TWIN ATTIC PUBLISHING HSE INC
1415 Cedar Branch Ct (27587-9208)
P.O. Box 51531 (27717-1531)
PHONE..................................919 426-0322
Crishna Murray, *Prin*
EMP: 6 **EST:** 2012
SALES (est): 9.74K **Privately Held**
Web: www.twinatticpublishinghouse.com
SIC: 2741 Miscellaneous publishing

(G-15608)
ULTRA ELEC OCEAN SYSTEMS INC
204 Capcom Ave (27587-6509)
PHONE..................................781 848-3400
EMP: 8
SALES (corp-wide): 2.67MM **Privately Held**
Web: www.ultra.group
SIC: 3812 Search and navigation equipment
HQ: Ultra Electronics Ocean Systems Inc.
115 Bay State Dr
Braintree MA 02184
781 848-3400

(G-15609)
VASILIY YAVDOSHNYAK
3517 Trawden Dr (27587-5073)
PHONE..................................919 995-9469
Vasiliy Yavdoshnyak, *Prin*
EMP: 4 **EST:** 2010
SALES (est): 135.08K **Privately Held**
Web: www.vintagewings-millersfield.com
SIC: 2741 Miscellaneous publishing

(G-15610)
VIRGILIOS PREMIUM VINEGARS
113 S White St (27587-2739)
PHONE..................................919 717-3373
EMP: 5 **EST:** 2017
SALES (est): 97.45K **Privately Held**
Web: www.virgiliosvinegarnoil.com
SIC: 2099 Vinegar

(G-15611)
WAKE FOREST GAZETTE
1255 S Main St (27587-9282)
PHONE..................................919 556-3409
EMP: 5 **EST:** 2017
SALES (est): 120.32K **Privately Held**
Web: www.wakeforestgazette.com
SIC: 2711 Newspapers, publishing and printing

(G-15612)
WELL-BEAN COFFEE & CRUMBS LLC
Also Called: Well-Bean Coffee Company
4154 Shearon Farms Ave Ste 106 (27587)
PHONE..................................833 777-2326
Melissa Brown, *Pt*
Melissa Brown, *Genl Pt*
EMP: 5 **EST:** 2013
SALES (est): 941.04K **Privately Held**
Web: www.wellbean.com
SIC: 5499 2095 Coffee; Coffee roasting (except by wholesale grocers)

Walkertown
Forsyth County

(G-15613)
AMERICAN TCHNCAL SOLUTIONS INC
Also Called: Atsi
4790 Walkertown Plaza Blvd (27051-9772)

P.O. Box 10 (27051-0010)
PHONE..................................336 595-2763
Robert Sandee, *Pr*
Gettys H Knox, *
EMP: 93 **EST:** 1994
SQ FT: 20,000
SALES (est): 7MM **Privately Held**
Web: www.atsi-online.com
SIC: 2221 Slip cover fabrics, manmade fiber and silk

(G-15614)
IDEAL PRINTING
4926 Harley Dr (27051-9131)
PHONE..................................336 754-4050
Bobby Wolfington, *Mgr*
EMP: 4 **EST:** 2018
SALES (est): 99.01K **Privately Held**
SIC: 2752 Offset printing

(G-15615)
ITS YOUR TIME BUSINESS CENTER
2735 Old Hollow Rd (27051-9529)
PHONE..................................336 754-4456
EMP: 5 **EST:** 2011
SALES (est): 77.45K **Privately Held**
SIC: 2752 Business form and card printing, lithographic

(G-15616)
STOLTZ AUTOMOTIVE INC
4861 New Walkertown Rd (27051-9556)
P.O. Box 998 (27051-0998)
PHONE..................................336 595-4218
Aubrey Stoltz, *Owner*
Jean S Stoltz, *Pt*
James Eugene Stoltz, *Pt*
Michael R Stoltz, *Pt*
EMP: 5 **EST:** 1938
SQ FT: 2,400
SALES (est): 495.78K **Privately Held**
SIC: 7538 7534 7539 General automotive repair shops; Tire repair shop; Frame and front end repair services

(G-15617)
TIM HLLEY EXCVTG DRCTNAL DRLG
5350 Main St (27051-9697)
P.O. Box 133 (27051-0133)
PHONE..................................336 595-3320
Timothy Holley, *Pr*
EMP: 8 **EST:** 2011
SALES (est): 233.56K **Privately Held**
SIC: 3531 1381 Buckets, excavating: clamshell, concrete, dragline, etc.; Directional drilling oil and gas wells

Wallace
Duplin County

(G-15618)
360 FOREST PRODUCTS INC
113 N Rockfish St (28466-2917)
P.O. Box 157 (28466-0157)
PHONE..................................910 285-5838
Larry Batchelor, *Pr*
Ricky Pope, *VP*
EMP: 6 **EST:** 1997
SALES (est): 638.6K **Privately Held**
Web: www.360forestproducts.com
SIC: 2411 Logging camps and contractors

(G-15619)
C AND D WELDERS LLC
3620 S Nc 41 Hwy (28466-7310)
PHONE..................................910 552-3294
Mabelyn Z Duarte Melgar, *Prin*
EMP: 8 **EST:** 2018
SALES (est): 221.52K **Privately Held**

Wallace - Duplin County (G-15620)

SIC: 7692 Welding repair

(G-15620)
CAPE FEAR NEWSPAPERS INC
107 N College St (28466-2707)
P.O. Box 69 (28349-0069)
PHONE..................................910 285-2178
Myrna Fountain Fusco, *Prin*
EMP: 7 EST: 2010
SALES (est): 134.79K **Privately Held**
SIC: 2711 Newspapers, publishing and printing

(G-15621)
DUPLIN FOREST PRODUCTS INC
312 Jack Dale Rd (28466-6019)
PHONE..................................910 285-5381
Terry Hill Rivenbark, *Pr*
Ramona Rivenbark, *Sec*
EMP: 16 EST: 1970
SQ FT: 4,000
SALES (est): 571.74K **Privately Held**
SIC: 2411 2421 Logging camps and contractors; Sawmills and planing mills, general

(G-15622)
EMERGENCY ENERGY SYSTEMS INC
116 W Southerland St (28466-2130)
PHONE..................................910 285-6400
EMP: 6 EST: 2008
SALES (est): 301.1K **Privately Held**
SIC: 3621 Generators and sets, electric

(G-15623)
HOLMES LOGGING - WALLACE LLC
2788 Lightwood Bridge Rd (28466-7358)
PHONE..................................910 271-1216
EMP: 10 EST: 2010
SALES (est): 392.29K **Privately Held**
SIC: 2411 Logging camps and contractors

(G-15624)
LSG LLC
Also Called: Large & Small Graphics
268 Hc Powers Rd (28466-8263)
PHONE..................................919 878-5500
EMP: 31 EST: 2001
SQ FT: 3,300
SALES (est): 610.56K **Privately Held**
SIC: 2759 Screen printing

(G-15625)
S & W READY MIX CON CO LLC
768 Sw Railroad St (28466-8210)
PHONE..................................910 285-2191
Robert Long, *Mgr*
EMP: 15
SALES (corp-wide): 8.01MM **Privately Held**
SIC: 3273 Ready-mixed concrete
HQ: S & W Ready Mix Concrete Company Llc
217 Lisbon St
Clinton NC 28328
910 592-1733

(G-15626)
SAWYER CREEK SOAPS LLC
181 Sawyer Ln (28466-9079)
PHONE..................................910 231-5013
EMP: 5 EST: 2020
SALES (est): 101.84K **Privately Held**
Web: www.sawyercreeksoaps.com
SIC: 2844 Perfumes, cosmetics and other toilet preparations

(G-15627)
SOUTHEAST WOOD PRODUCTS INC
444 Jack Dale Rd (28466-6021)
PHONE..................................910 285-4359
David Rivenbark Junior, *Pr*
Judy Rivenbark, *Sec*
▲ EMP: 10 EST: 1982
SALES (est): 1.12MM **Privately Held**
SIC: 2411 4213 Logging camps and contractors; Contract haulers

(G-15628)
SOUTHERN STATES COOP INC
939 Nw Railroad St (28466-5700)
PHONE..................................910 285-8213
EMP: 10
SALES (corp-wide): 1.71B **Privately Held**
Web: www.southernstates.com
SIC: 2048 0181 2873 2874 Prepared feeds, nec; Bulbs and seeds; Nitrogenous fertilizers; Phosphatic fertilizers
PA: Southern States Cooperative, Incorporated
6606 W Broad St Ste B
Richmond VA 23230
804 281-1000

(G-15629)
VILLAGE AT DUPLIN WINERY LLC
109 Candlewood Dr (28466-6098)
PHONE..................................910 285-6814
EMP: 4 EST: 2018
SALES (est): 105.81K **Privately Held**
Web: www.duplinwinery.com
SIC: 2084 Wines

Walnut Cove
Stokes County

(G-15630)
AGRICLTRAL-INDUSTRIAL FABR INC
Also Called: Thrift-Tents
223 S Main St (27052)
PHONE..................................336 591-3690
Donald C Brinkley, *Pr*
Charles Couch, *VP*
EMP: 5 EST: 1974
SALES (est): 195.61K **Privately Held**
SIC: 2394 Tents: made from purchased materials

(G-15631)
BILL SLATE GRATING
1045 Slate Farm Rd (27052-5610)
PHONE..................................336 591-8607
Bill Slate, *Prin*
EMP: 6 EST: 2004
SALES (est): 237.04K **Privately Held**
SIC: 3446 Gratings, tread: fabricated metal

(G-15632)
LINES UNLIMITED INC
1114 Oakwood Dr (27052-7274)
PHONE..................................336 996-6603
Deborah Dunbar, *Pr*
EMP: 7 EST: 1981
SALES (est): 60.54K **Privately Held**
SIC: 2426 Hardwood dimension and flooring mills

(G-15633)
MITCHELLS MEAT PROCESSING
Also Called: Mitchell Meat Processing
401 Mitchell St (27052-7321)
P.O. Box 421 (27052-0421)
PHONE..................................336 591-7420
EMP: 10 EST: 2018
SALES (est): 500K **Privately Held**
Web: www.mitchellsmeatnc.com

SIC: 5421 2011 0751 Meat and fish markets; Meat packing plants; Slaughtering: custom livestock services

(G-15634)
MONITOR ROLLER MILL INC
109 E 4th St (27052)
P.O. Box 393 (27052-0393)
PHONE..................................336 591-4126
William F Southern, *Pr*
Ron Southern, *Sec*
Patricia Southern, *VP*
EMP: 6 EST: 1909
SQ FT: 8,500
SALES (est): 450K **Privately Held**
SIC: 5999 2048 Feed and farm supply; Prepared feeds, nec

(G-15635)
PARKDALE MILLS INCORPORATED
Also Called: Parkdale Plant 26
1660 Us 311 Hwy N (27052-6930)
PHONE..................................336 591-4644
Robert Lawrence, *Brnch Mgr*
EMP: 58
SALES (corp-wide): 1.44B **Privately Held**
Web: www.parkdalemills.com
SIC: 2281 Yarn spinning mills
HQ: Parkdale Mills, Incorporated
531 Cotton Blossom Cir
Gastonia NC 28054
704 874-5000

(G-15636)
WALNUT COVE FURNITURE INC
4730 Nc 89 Hwy E (27052-6904)
PHONE..................................336 591-8008
Douglas Stephens, *CEO*
Wendell Dodson, *Sec*
Douglas Stephens, *Pr*
EMP: 6 EST: 2003
SALES (est): 877.57K **Privately Held**
Web: www.walnutcovefurniture.com
SIC: 2599 5722 Factory furniture and fixtures ; Household appliance stores

Walstonburg
Greene County

(G-15637)
GAYCO
893 Gay Rd (27888-9370)
PHONE..................................252 753-4777
EMP: 4 EST: 2019
SALES (est): 102.79K **Privately Held**
SIC: 7372 Prepackaged software

(G-15638)
JAK MOULDING & SUPPLY INC
1565 Strickland Rd (27888-9478)
PHONE..................................252 753-5546
Tony Holloman, *Pr*
John Holloman, *VP*
Rose Holloman, *Sec*
EMP: 12 EST: 2002
SQ FT: 20,000
SALES (est): 2.14MM **Privately Held**
Web: www.jakmoulding.com
SIC: 2491 5211 Millwork, treated wood; Lumber and other building materials

(G-15639)
KS CUSTOM WOODWORKS INC
3205 Fire Tower Rd (27888-9111)
P.O. Box 224 (27888-0224)
PHONE..................................252 714-3957
Kevin Holloman, *Prin*
EMP: 6 EST: 2015
SALES (est): 54.13K **Privately Held**

SIC: 2431 Millwork

(G-15640)
MOORES FIBERGLASS INC
926 Howell Swamp Church Rd (27888-9517)
P.O. Box 219 (27888-0219)
PHONE..................................252 753-2583
Hardy Moore, *Pr*
Chris Moore, *VP*
EMP: 10 EST: 1986
SQ FT: 2,600
SALES (est): 906.92K **Privately Held**
Web: www.mooresfiberglass.com
SIC: 1799 3088 Fiberglass work; Plastics plumbing fixtures

Wanchese
Dare County

(G-15641)
BAYLISS BOATWORKS INC
600 Harbor Rd (27981-9588)
P.O. Box 300 (27981-0300)
PHONE..................................252 473-9797
John Bayliss, *Pr*
▲ EMP: 45 EST: 2002
SQ FT: 10,000
SALES (est): 7.09MM **Privately Held**
Web: www.baylissboatworks.com
SIC: 3732 Boats, fiberglass: building and repairing

(G-15642)
BAYLISS BOATYARD INC
600 Harbor Rd (27981-9588)
P.O. Box 300 (27981-0300)
PHONE..................................252 473-9797
John Bayliss, *CEO*
Christopher Parker Ctrl, *Prin*
EMP: 15 EST: 2007
SQ FT: 1,500
SALES (est): 985.68K **Privately Held**
Web: www.baylissboatworks.com
SIC: 3732 Fishing boats: lobster, crab, oyster, etc.: small

(G-15643)
BRIGGS BOAT WORKS INCORPORATED
370 Harbor Rd (27981-9648)
P.O. Box 277 (27981-0277)
PHONE..................................252 473-2393
Thomas H Briggs Iii, *Pr*
Deanna Briggs, *Sec*
◆ EMP: 10 EST: 1980
SQ FT: 4,800
SALES (est): 264.39K **Privately Held**
SIC: 3732 Boats, fiberglass: building and repairing

(G-15644)
CRAIG & SANDRA BLACKWELL INC
Also Called: Blackwell Boatwork
932 Harbor Rd (27981-9617)
P.O. Box 580 (27981-0580)
PHONE..................................252 473-1803
EMP: 8 EST: 1989
SALES (est): 795.33K **Privately Held**
Web: www.blackwellboatworks.com
SIC: 3732 Motorized boat, building and repairing

(G-15645)
CROSWAIT CUSTOM COMPOSITES INC
90 Dusty Ln (27981-9535)
P.O. Box 478 (27981-0478)
PHONE..................................252 423-1245

GEOGRAPHIC SECTION

EMP: 7 **EST:** 2014
SALES (est): 713.48K **Privately Held**
Web: www.croswait.com
SIC: 3732 Boatbuilding and repairing

(G-15646)
GUNBOAT INTERNATIONAL LTD
829 Harbor Rd (27981-9646)
PHONE.................................252 305-8700
Peter L Johnstone, *CEO*
◆ **EMP:** 17 **EST:** 2011
SQ FT: 30,000
SALES (est): 632.7K **Privately Held**
Web: www.gunboat.com
SIC: 3732 Boatbuilding and repairing

(G-15647)
HARBOR WELDING INC
935 Harbor Rd (27981-9617)
P.O. Box 720 (27981-0720)
PHONE.................................252 473-3777
Wayne Umphlett, *Pr*
EMP: 6 **EST:** 1986
SALES (est): 493.19K **Privately Held**
Web: www.harborwelding.com
SIC: 7692 Welding repair

(G-15648)
ISLAND WOOD CRAFTS LTD
776 Old Wharf Rd (27981-9600)
P.O. Box 448 (27981-0448)
PHONE.................................252 473-5363
EMP: 9 **EST:** 1972
SALES (est): 474.94K **Privately Held**
Web: www.islandwoodcrafts.com
SIC: 2434 Wood kitchen cabinets

(G-15649)
MARINE FABRICATIONS LLC
31 Beverly Dr (27981-9652)
P.O. Box 240 (27981-0240)
PHONE.................................252 473-4767
Paul Spencer, *Mgr*
EMP: 6 **EST:** 2007
SALES (est): 467.62K **Privately Held**
SIC: 7692 3599 Welding repair; Machine shop, jobbing and repair

(G-15650)
RICHARD SCARBOROUGH BOAT WORKS
Ficket Lump Rd (27981)
P.O. Box 191 (27981-0191)
PHONE.................................252 473-3646
Ricky Scarborough, *Pr*
Annette Scarborough, *Sec*
EMP: 9 **EST:** 1974
SALES (est): 365.55K **Privately Held**
Web: www.scarboroughboatworks.com
SIC: 3732 Boats, fiberglass: building and repairing

(G-15651)
WANCHESE DOCK AND HAUL LLC
593 Baumtown Rd (27981-9502)
P.O. Box 415 (27981-0415)
PHONE.................................252 473-6424
Winston Silver, *Prin*
EMP: 7 **EST:** 2008
SALES (est): 140.93K **Privately Held**
Web: www.wanchesefirearms.com
SIC: 3732 Boatbuilding and repairing

(G-15652)
WATKINS CUSTOM SEWING INC
911 Harbor Rd (27981-9617)
P.O. Box 784 (27959-0784)
PHONE.................................252 996-0642
Lorna Watkins, *Pr*
EMP: 5 **EST:** 2007

SALES (est): 102.8K **Privately Held**
SIC: 2394 Canvas and related products

Warrensville
Ashe County

(G-15653)
ROLAND BROTHERS LLC
649 Carl Eastridge Rd (28693-9120)
PHONE.................................336 385-9013
EMP: 4 **EST:** 2019
SALES (est): 114.43K **Privately Held**
SIC: 2411 Logging

Warrenton
Warren County

(G-15654)
ARCOLA HARDWOOD COMPANY INC
2316 Nc Highway 43 (27589-9294)
PHONE.................................252 257-4484
Gary C Harris, *Pr*
EMP: 10 **EST:** 1966
SALES (est): 404.21K **Privately Held**
SIC: 2449 Wood containers, nec

(G-15655)
ARCOLA LUMBER COMPANY INC
2316 Nc Highway 43 (27589-9294)
PHONE.................................252 257-4923
Elmer W Harris Senior, *Pr*
Garry C Harris, *
EMP: 32 **EST:** 1952
SQ FT: 1,200
SALES (est): 2.25MM **Privately Held**
SIC: 2421 2449 2441 Tobacco hogshead stock; Wood containers, nec; Nailed wood boxes and shook

(G-15656)
ARCOLA SAWMILL
2316 Nc Highway 43 (27589-9294)
PHONE.................................252 257-1139
Gary Harris, *Prin*
EMP: 5 **EST:** 1952
SALES (est): 223.07K **Privately Held**
Web: www.danaweb.com
SIC: 2421 2426 2449 2441 Sawmills and planing mills, general; Hardwood dimension and flooring mills; Wood containers, nec; Nailed wood boxes and shook

(G-15657)
CAST STONE SYSTEMS INC
532 N Main St (27589-1633)
PHONE.................................252 257-1599
Ted Echols, *Pr*
Thomas Edward Echols Junior, *Pr*
Margaret Echols, *
EMP: 25 **EST:** 1998
SQ FT: 600,000
SALES (est): 4.68MM **Privately Held**
Web: www.caststonesystems.com
SIC: 3272 Concrete products, nec

(G-15658)
ELBERTA CRATE & BOX CO
619 N Main St (27589-1634)
P.O. Box 760 (39818-0760)
PHONE.................................252 257-4659
EMP: 105
SALES (corp-wide): 49.09MM **Privately Held**
Web: www.elbertacrate.com
SIC: 2449 Wood containers, nec
PA: Elberta Crate & Box Co.

606 Dothan Rd
Bainbridge GA 39817
229 243-1268

(G-15659)
ELITE WLDG & FABRICATIONS LLC
150 Ridgeway Warrenton Rd (27589-1641)
PHONE.................................919 224-6007
Daniel Rivera, *Managing Member*
EMP: 6 **EST:** 2016
SALES (est): 88.73K **Privately Held**
SIC: 7692 Welding repair

(G-15660)
RABBIT BOTTOM LOGGING CO INC
Also Called: Rabbit Bottom Logging Co
Hc 151 (27589)
PHONE.................................252 257-3585
Johnny M Coleman, *Prin*
EMP: 13 **EST:** 1980
SALES (est): 681.75K **Privately Held**
SIC: 2411 Logging camps and contractors

(G-15661)
SIDNEY PERRY COOPER III
445 Nc Highway 58 (27589-9161)
PHONE.................................252 257-3886
Sidney Perry Cooper Iii, *Prin*
EMP: 4 **EST:** 2010
SALES (est): 120.47K **Privately Held**
SIC: 3993 Signs and advertising specialties

(G-15662)
SMOKE HOUSE LUMBER COMPANY
2711 Nc Highway 58 (27589-9284)
PHONE.................................252 257-3303
Warren Griffin, *Pr*
EMP: 32 **EST:** 1980
SALES (est): 2.94MM **Privately Held**
Web: www.smokehouselumber.com
SIC: 2421 Lumber: rough, sawed, or planed

(G-15663)
WOMACK PUBLISHING CO INC
Also Called: Warren Record, The
112 N Main St (27589-1922)
P.O. Box 70 (27589-0070)
PHONE.................................252 257-3341
Jennifer Harris, *Prin*
EMP: 6
SALES (corp-wide): 21.7MM **Privately Held**
Web: www.warrenrecord.com
SIC: 2711 Newspapers: publishing only, not printed on site
PA: Womack Publishing Company, Inc.
28 N Main St
Chatham VA 24531
434 432-2791

Warsaw
Duplin County

(G-15664)
ACCU-FORM POLYMERS INC
170 Water Tank Rd (28398-7821)
P.O. Box 445 (28398-0445)
PHONE.................................910 293-6961
Pat Renfro, *Pr*
Don Greg, *
▲ **EMP:** 45 **EST:** 1990
SQ FT: 60,000
SALES (est): 4.83MM **Privately Held**
Web: www.accuform-polymers.com
SIC: 3089 Molding primary plastics

(G-15665)
BUNGE OILS INC
376 W Park Dr (28398-6400)
PHONE.................................910 293-7917
EMP: 27
SALES (corp-wide): 3.23B **Privately Held**
SIC: 2079 2013 2087 Edible fats and oils; Lard, from purchased meat products; Flavoring extracts and syrups, nec
HQ: Bunge Oils, Inc.
1391 Tmbarlake Manor Pkwy
Chesterfield MO 63017
314 292-2000

(G-15666)
DESIGN WORKSHOP INCORPORATED
1696 Nc 24 And 50 Hwy (28398-8675)
P.O. Box 451 (28398-0451)
PHONE.................................910 293-7329
David Carlton, *Pr*
Julie Carlton, *VP*
Jean Carlton, *Sec*
◆ **EMP:** 18 **EST:** 1992
SQ FT: 20,000
SALES (est): 2.39MM **Privately Held**
Web: www.designworkshop.us
SIC: 2511 Wood household furniture

(G-15667)
ELIAS GONZALEZ
Also Called: El Mexicano Tires
516 S Pine St (28398-2341)
PHONE.................................910 271-9514
Elias Gonzalez, *Owner*
EMP: 4 **EST:** 2017
SALES (est): 40.34K **Privately Held**
Web: www.elmexicanotires.com
SIC: 7534 Tire repair shop

(G-15668)
GINNY O S INC
946 Penny Branch Rd (28398-7762)
P.O. Box 6475 (27628-6475)
PHONE.................................919 816-7276
Ginny Johnson, *Pr*
Beverly Johnson, *VP*
EMP: 12 **EST:** 2001
SALES (est): 716.17K **Privately Held**
Web: www.ginnyo.com
SIC: 2096 Cheese curls and puffs

(G-15669)
HURRICANE AQUA SPORTS INC
Also Called: Hurricane Kayaks
170 Water Tank Rd (28398-7821)
P.O. Box 445 (28398-0445)
PHONE.................................910 293-2941
Patrick L Renfro, *Pr*
EMP: 9 **EST:** 1978
SALES (est): 306.48K **Privately Held**
Web: www.hurricaneaquasports.com
SIC: 3732 Kayaks, building and repairing

(G-15670)
J&D LOGGING INC
1644 Veachs Mill Rd (28398-8585)
PHONE.................................910 271-0750
EMP: 5 **EST:** 2016
SALES (est): 217.09K **Privately Held**
SIC: 2411 Logging

(G-15671)
MURPHY-BROWN LLC (DH)
Also Called: Smithfield Hog Production
2822 Highway 24 W (28398)
P.O. Box 856 (28398-0856)
PHONE.................................910 293-3434
Gregg Schmidt, *Pr*
Joan Lee, *CTRL*

Warsaw - Duplin County (G-15672)

Joe Szaloky, *Dir*
▲ **EMP:** 100 **EST:** 2001
SALES (est): 465.04MM **Privately Held**
Web: www.smithfieldfoods.com
SIC: 0213 2011 Hogs; Bacon, slab and sliced, from meat slaughtered on site
HQ: Smithfield Foods, Inc.
200 Commerce St
Smithfield VA 23430
757 365-3000

(G-15672)
PARKS FAMILY MEATS LLC
1618 Nc 24 And 50 Hwy (28398-8675)
PHONE 217 446-4600
▼ **EMP:** 13 **EST:** 1995
SALES (est): 362.76K **Privately Held**
Web: www.parkslivestock.com
SIC: 0751 2011 Slaughtering: custom livestock services; Meat packing plants

(G-15673)
PORK COMPANY
139 Carter Best Rd (28398-8682)
PHONE 910 293-2157
Joseph P Villari, *Pr*
Chris Villari, *
▲ **EMP:** 120 **EST:** 1996
SALES (est): 23.7MM
SALES (corp-wide): 48.3MM **Privately Held**
Web: www.villarifood.com
SIC: 2011 Meat packing plants
PA: Villari Food Group, Llc
1015 Ashes Dr Ste 102
Wilmington NC 28405
910 293-2157

(G-15674)
SOUTHERN BLOCK COMPANY
510 W Hill St (28398-1700)
PHONE 910 293-7844
David Houston, *Pr*
Ronnie Miller, *VP*
Larry Benson, *Treas*
EMP: 11 **EST:** 1952
SQ FT: 1,800
SALES (est): 870K **Privately Held**
SIC: 3272 3271 Septic tanks, concrete; Concrete block and brick

(G-15675)
VILLARI BROS FOODS LLC
135 Carter Best Rd (28398-8682)
P.O. Box 485 (28398-0485)
PHONE 910 293-2157
EMP: 36 **EST:** 2010
SALES (est): 2.69MM **Privately Held**
Web: www.villarifood.com
SIC: 2011 Pork products, from pork slaughtered on site

(G-15676)
WARSAW WELDING SERVICE INC
824 N Pine St (28398-1444)
P.O. Box 161 (28398-0161)
PHONE 910 293-4261
Bill Grady, *Pr*
EMP: 11 **EST:** 1986
SQ FT: 12,000
SALES (est): 472.09K **Privately Held**
SIC: 1799 7692 Welding on site; Welding repair

(G-15677)
WHOLE HARVEST FOODS LLC
Also Called: Whole Harvest
376 W Park Dr (28398-6400)
P.O. Box 527 (28398-0527)
PHONE 910 293-7917
EMP: 35

SIC: 5411 2079 Cooperative food stores; Cooking oils, except corn: vegetable refined

Washington
Beaufort County

(G-15678)
AAA GLASS COMPANY
2513 W 5th St (27889-9078)
PHONE 252 946-2396
EMP: 4 **EST:** 2019
SALES (est): 73.59K **Privately Held**
SIC: 2519 Household furniture, nec

(G-15679)
ABHW CONCRETE CO
347 S Wharton Station Rd (27889-6817)
PHONE 252 940-1002
Manfred Alligood Junior, *Owner*
EMP: 5 **EST:** 2008
SALES (est): 986.53K **Privately Held**
Web: www.abhwconcrete.com
SIC: 3273 Ready-mixed concrete

(G-15680)
ALLIGOOD BROTHERS LOGGING
436 Mill Hole Rd (27889-7011)
PHONE 252 927-2358
EMP: 9 **EST:** 1979
SALES (est): 600K **Privately Held**
Web: www.worldwar-2.net
SIC: 2411 Logging camps and contractors

(G-15681)
ALLIGOOD CABINET SHOP
Also Called: Alligood Cabinets
121 Alligood Dr (27889-8689)
PHONE 252 927-3201
Julie Alligood, *Owner*
EMP: 6 **EST:** 1979
SALES (est): 396.12K **Privately Held**
SIC: 2599 5712 5211 Cabinets, factory; Cabinet work, custom; Counter tops

(G-15682)
ARGOS USA LLC
Also Called: Ready Mix Concrete
1020 E 5th St (27889-4631)
PHONE 252 946-4704
Quin Baughn, *Brnch Mgr*
EMP: 7
SQ FT: 2,400
Web: www.argos-us.com
SIC: 3273 Ready-mixed concrete
HQ: Argos Usa Llc
3015 Windward Plz Ste 300
Alpharetta GA 30005
678 368-4300

(G-15683)
BAJA MARINE INC
1653 Whichards Beach Road (27889)
PHONE 252 975-2000
Reginald M Fountain Junior, *CEO*
John E Walker, *
John S Delong, *
Nick Miller, *
EMP: 20 **EST:** 2008
SALES (est): 437.14K **Privately Held**
Web: www.bajamarine.com
SIC: 3732 Boatbuilding and repairing

(G-15684)
CAM ENTERPRISES INC
5601 Us Highway 264 W (27889-7690)
PHONE 252 946-4877
Keith Manming, *
EMP: 10 **EST:** 1994
SALES (est): 747.62K **Privately Held**

Web: www.camenterprisesonline.com
SIC: 3524 5999 Cultivators (garden tractor equipment); Farm equipment and supplies

(G-15685)
CAMFIL USA INC
Also Called: Metalcraft Air Filtration
200 Creekside Dr (27889-9093)
PHONE 252 975-1141
Howard Campbell, *Prin*
EMP: 90
SALES (corp-wide): 1.18B **Privately Held**
Web: www.camfil.com
SIC: 3564 Blowers and fans
HQ: Camfil Usa, Inc.
1 N Corporate Dr
Riverdale NJ 07457
973 616-7300

(G-15686)
CAROLINA CATCH INC
Also Called: Washington Crab
321 N Pierce St (27889-4841)
PHONE 252 946-5796
Jason Hall, *Pr*
EMP: 65 **EST:** 2020
SALES (est): 5.83MM **Privately Held**
Web: www.washingtoncrab.com
SIC: 2092 Crab meat, fresh: packaged in nonsealed containers

(G-15687)
CHIRAZYME LABS INC
1520 Whootentown Rd (27889-6858)
PHONE 252 717-1112
Lowell Hager, *Pr*
EMP: 5 **EST:** 2009
SALES (est): 203.82K **Privately Held**
Web: www.chirazyme.com
SIC: 2869 Laboratory chemicals, organic

(G-15688)
CLARCOR ENG MBL SOLUTIONS LLC
Also Called: Clarcor
230 Clarks Neck Rd (27889-8976)
PHONE 860 992-3496
◆ **EMP:** 112 **EST:** 2014
SALES (est): 14.72MM **Privately Held**
SIC: 3714 Motor vehicle engines and parts

(G-15689)
CLAYTON WELDING
451 Barwick Dr (27889-8306)
PHONE 252 717-5909
EMP: 4 **EST:** 2013
SALES (est): 52.98K **Privately Held**
SIC: 7692 Welding repair

(G-15690)
CLEANAIRE INC
Also Called: Pamlico Air
112 S Respess St (27889-4956)
PHONE 252 623-4010
Shawn Windley, *Pr*
Harry Smith, *
R Leonard Rowe Junior, *Sec*
Matthew Cloninger, *
Kishore Abburu, *
▲ **EMP:** 500 **EST:** 2018
SALES (est): 24.67MM **Privately Held**
Web: airfiltration.mann-hummel.com
SIC: 3564 Filters, air: furnaces, air conditioning equipment, etc.

(G-15691)
COASTAL SALES INC
164 Periwinkle Ln (27889-9536)
PHONE 252 717-3542
Jeff Hendricks, *Pr*

EMP: 5 **EST:** 2017
SALES (est): 33.59K **Privately Held**
SIC: 7692 Welding repair

(G-15692)
COEUR INC
209 Creekside Dr (27889-9094)
P.O. Box 2125 (27889-2125)
PHONE 252 946-1963
Jay Cude, *Brnch Mgr*
EMP: 6
SALES (corp-wide): 15.93B **Publicly Held**
Web: www.itwmedical.com
SIC: 3089 Injection molding of plastics
HQ: Coeur, Inc.
100 Physicians Way # 200
Lebanon TN 37090
615 547-7923

(G-15693)
COMPMILLENNIA LLC
706 Hackney Ave (27889-4250)
PHONE 252 628-8065
◆ **EMP:** 10 **EST:** 2009
SALES (est): 464.12K **Privately Held**
Web: www.compmillennia.com
SIC: 2295 Coated fabrics, not rubberized

(G-15694)
DAVID J SPAIN
Also Called: J & K Logging
8851 Cherry Run Rd (27889-5575)
PHONE 252 902-6900
EMP: 4 **EST:** 2019
SALES (est): 81.72K **Privately Held**
SIC: 2411 Logging

(G-15695)
DIVINE CONNECTION
408 N Market St (27889-4936)
PHONE 252 975-1320
EMP: 5 **EST:** 2012
SALES (est): 50.93K **Privately Held**
SIC: 2741 Miscellaneous publishing

(G-15696)
DONZI MARINE LLC
1653 Whichards Beach Rd (27889)
PHONE 252 975-2000
EMP: 14 **EST:** 2001
SALES (est): 78K **Privately Held**
Web: www.donzimarine.com
SIC: 3732 Boatbuilding and repairing

(G-15697)
DOWNEAST MARINE CANVAS LLC
387 S Asbury Church Rd (27889-9372)
PHONE 252 495-2631
Irvin Francis Krick Iii, *Owner*
EMP: 5 **EST:** 2017
SALES (est): 46.58K **Privately Held**
Web: www.downeastmarinecanvas.com
SIC: 2211 Canvas

(G-15698)
EGRET BOATS LLC
715 Page Rd (27889-9540)
PHONE 252 948-0004
▼ **EMP:** 7 **EST:** 2005
SALES (est): 484.21K **Privately Held**
Web: www.egretboats.com
SIC: 3732 Boatbuilding and repairing

(G-15699)
FLANDERS CORPORATION (DH)
Also Called: AAF Flanders
531 Flanders Filter Rd (27889-7805)
PHONE 252 946-8081
◆ **EMP:** 14 **EST:** 1986
SQ FT: 285,000

GEOGRAPHIC SECTION

Washington - Beaufort County (G-15720)

SALES (est): 193.74MM **Privately Held**
Web: www.flanderscorp.com
SIC: 3564 Filters, air; furnaces, air conditioning equipment, etc.
HQ: Flanders Holdings Llc
531 Flanders Filter Rd
Washington NC 27889
252 946-8081

(G-15700)
FLANDERS CORPORATION
Flanders Precisionaire
531 Flanders Filter Rd (27889-7805)
PHONE.................................252 946-0744
Deb Murphy, *Mgr*
EMP: 66
SQ FT: 92,000
Web: www.flanderscorp.com
SIC: 3564 Filters, air; furnaces, air conditioning equipment, etc.
HQ: Flanders Corporation
531 Flanders Filter Rd
Washington NC 27889

(G-15701)
FLANDERS FILTERS INC (DH)
531 Flanders Filter Rd (27889-7805)
PHONE.................................252 946-8081
Peter Jones, *CEO*
Robert R Amerson, *Pr*
Debra Hill, *Sec*
Scott Brown, *CFO*
◆ **EMP:** 230 **EST:** 1971
SQ FT: 114,000
SALES (est): 50.99MM **Privately Held**
Web: residential.aafintl.com
SIC: 3564 Air purification equipment
HQ: Flanders Corporation
531 Flanders Filter Rd
Washington NC 27889

(G-15702)
FLANDERS/CSC LLC
531 Flanders Filter Rd (27889-7805)
P.O. Box 3 (27889-0003)
PHONE.................................252 946-8081
Harry Smith, *CEO*
James Keith, *VP Fin*
▲ **EMP:** 55 **EST:** 2006
SQ FT: 25,000
SALES (est): 24.76MM **Privately Held**
Web: www.flanders-csc.com
SIC: 3564 5084 Air cleaning systems; Industrial machinery and equipment
HQ: Flanders Corporation
531 Flanders Filter Rd
Washington NC 27889

(G-15703)
FOUNTAIN POWERBOAT INDS INC (HQ)
1653 Whichards Beach Rd (27889)
P.O. Box 457 (27889-0457)
PHONE.................................252 975-2000
Ronald Glass, *Prin*
Reginald M Fountain Junior, *Ch Bd*
Irving L Smith, *CFO*
EMP: 175 **EST:** 1979
SQ FT: 14,020
SALES (est): 45.57MM
SALES (corp-wide): 62.66MM **Privately Held**
Web: www.fountainpowerboats.com
SIC: 3732 Motorboats, inboard or outboard: building and repairing
PA: Iconic Marine Group, Llc
1653 Whichards Beach Rd
Chocowinity NC 27817
252 975-2000

(G-15704)
FOUNTAIN POWERBOATS INC
Also Called: Fountain Powerboats
1653 Whichards Beach Rd (27889)
PHONE.................................252 975-2000
John Walker, *Pr*
William R Gates, *Prin*
Joseph Wortley, *Prin*
EMP: 95 **EST:** 1979
SQ FT: 235,000
SALES (est): 21.96MM
SALES (corp-wide): 62.66MM **Privately Held**
Web: www.fountainpowerboats.com
SIC: 3732 Motorboats, inboard or outboard: building and repairing
HQ: Fountain Powerboat Industries, Inc.
1653 Whichards Beach Rd
Washington NC 27889
252 975-2000

(G-15705)
FRANKLIN BAKING COMPANY LLC
5398 Us Highway 264 E (27889-7889)
PHONE.................................252 946-3340
Jerry Hicks, *Mgr*
EMP: 7
SALES (corp-wide): 5.09B **Publicly Held**
Web: franklin-co4goldsboro.edan.io
SIC: 2051 Bread, cake, and related products
HQ: Franklin Baking Company, Llc
500 W Grantham St
Goldsboro NC 27530
919 735-0344

(G-15706)
GRIFFIN AUTOMOTIVE MARINE INC
450 Herring Club Rd (27889-9276)
PHONE.................................252 940-0714
Joseph L Griffin, *Pr*
EMP: 4 **EST:** 1980
SALES (est): 383.07K **Privately Held**
SIC: 3519 7538 Outboard motors; Engine rebuilding: automotive

(G-15707)
HACKNEY & SONS MIDWEST INC
911 W 5th St (27889-4205)
P.O. Box 880 (27889-0880)
PHONE.................................252 946-6521
James A Hackney Junior, *Ch Bd*
James A Hackney Iii, *V Ch Bd*
R Hodges Hackney, *Pr*
Keith D Hackney, *Sec*
Raymond R Bergevin, *Treas*
EMP: 5 **EST:** 1972
SQ FT: 130,000
SALES (est): 2.43MM **Privately Held**
Web: www.hackneyusa.com
SIC: 3713 Truck bodies (motor vehicles)

(G-15708)
HAMILTON BEACH BRANDS INC
234 Springs Rd (27889-9368)
PHONE.................................252 975-0444
Louis Whitford, *Mgr*
EMP: 5
SALES (corp-wide): 640.95MM **Publicly Held**
Web: www.hamiltonbeach.com
SIC: 3634 Toasters, electric: household
HQ: Hamilton Beach Brands, Inc.
4421 Waterfront Dr
Glen Allen VA 23060
804 273-9777

(G-15709)
HAMPTON ART INC
1481 W 2nd St Ste 109 (27889-4294)
P.O. Box 236 (27889-0236)
PHONE.................................252 975-7207
▲ **EMP:** 145 **EST:** 1980
SQ FT: 200,000
SALES (est): 9.69MM
SALES (corp-wide): 102.19MM **Privately Held**
Web: www.vista-art.com
SIC: 2281 5949 Yarn spinning mills; Sewing, needlework, and piece goods
PA: National Spinning Co., Inc.
1481 W 2nd St Ste 103
Washington NC 27889
252 975-7111

(G-15710)
IDX CORPORATION
Also Called: Idx North Carolina
234 Springs Rd (27889-9368)
PHONE.................................252 948-2048
EMP: 144
SALES (corp-wide): 7.22B **Publicly Held**
Web: www.idxcorporation.com
SIC: 2542 Partitions and fixtures, except wood
HQ: Idx Corporation
2801 E Beltline Ave Ne
Grand Rapids MI 49525
844 249-4633

(G-15711)
IDX IMPRESSIONS LLC (DH)
234 Springs Rd (27889-9368)
PHONE.................................703 550-6902
Eric T Gerber, *Pr*
John J Hendley, *
Kevin R Goodale, *
▲ **EMP:** 180 **EST:** 1982
SALES (est): 23.62MM
SALES (corp-wide): 7.22B **Publicly Held**
SIC: 2541 2431 2521 2434 Store fixtures, wood; Millwork; Wood office furniture; Wood kitchen cabinets
HQ: Idx Corporation
2801 E Beltline Ave Ne
Grand Rapids MI 49525
844 249-4633

(G-15712)
INGALLS ALTON
Also Called: Ingalls and Associates
115 N Respess St (27889-4953)
P.O. Box 1386 (27889-1386)
PHONE.................................252 975-2056
Alton Ingalls, *Owner*
EMP: 4 **EST:** 1979
SQ FT: 4,000
SALES (est): 246.94K **Privately Held**
Web: www.printerested.com
SIC: 2752 2759 Offset printing; Letterpress printing

(G-15713)
INTERMARKET TECHNOLOGY INC
932 Page Rd (27889-9788)
PHONE.................................252 623-2199
◆ **EMP:** 50 **EST:** 1995
SALES (est): 4.94MM **Privately Held**
Web: www.intmarktech.com
SIC: 2541 2653 Showcases, except refrigerated: wood; Display items, corrugated: made from purchased materials

(G-15714)
KIDKUSION INC
623 River Rd (27889-3922)
P.O. Box 1686 (27889-1686)
PHONE.................................252 946-7162
Cindy Bowen, *Pr*
Lee Bowen, *VP*
▲ **EMP:** 18 **EST:** 1991
SALES (est): 2.29MM **Privately Held**
Web: www.kidkusion.com
SIC: 3086 Plastics foam products

(G-15715)
MID-ATLANTIC TOOL AND DIE INC
Also Called: Mid Atlantic Hydraulics & Mch
5324 Us Highway 264 W (27889-7697)
P.O. Box 2594 (27889-2594)
PHONE.................................252 946-2598
Mitchell Woolard, *Pr*
Preston Alligood, *Sec*
EMP: 10 **EST:** 1985
SQ FT: 15,000
SALES (est): 958.96K **Privately Held**
SIC: 3599 Machine shop, jobbing and repair

(G-15716)
MIZELLE INDUSTRIES LLC
2032 Nc Highway 171 N (27889-8182)
PHONE.................................252 940-5506
Elizabeth W Mizelle, *Owner*
EMP: 6 **EST:** 2017
SALES (est): 249.36K **Privately Held**
SIC: 3999 Manufacturing industries, nec

(G-15717)
NATIONAL SPINNING CO INC (PA)
1481 W 2nd St Ste 103 (27889-4294)
PHONE.................................252 975-7111
James Chesnutt, *Ch*
James Booterbaugh, *
Morgan Miller, *
Bob Millere, *
Linda Fanton, *
◆ **EMP:** 200 **EST:** 1900
SQ FT: 2,500
SALES (est): 102.19MM
SALES (corp-wide): 102.19MM **Privately Held**
Web: www.natspin.com
SIC: 2281 Wool yarn, spun

(G-15718)
NATIONAL SPNNING OPRATIONS LLC
1481 W 2nd St Ste 103 (27889-4293)
PHONE.................................252 975-7111
James Booterbaugh, *CEO*
Dan K Martin, *CFO*
Hr Miller, *Ch Bd*
▲ **EMP:** 11 **EST:** 2000
SALES (est): 495.62K **Privately Held**
Web: www.natspin.com
SIC: 2281 Wool yarn, spun

(G-15719)
NEU SPICE AND SEASONINGS LLC
4571 Us Highway 264 W (27889-6622)
PHONE.................................252 378-7912
Michele Neuhoff, *Managing Member*
Jay Neuhoff, *Sec*
EMP: 6 **EST:** 2019
SQ FT: 4,000
SALES (est): 265.37K **Privately Held**
SIC: 2099 Chicory root, dried

(G-15720)
OAK RIDGE INDUSTRIES LLC
1228 Page Rd (27889-6520)
P.O. Box 1748 (27889-1748)
PHONE.................................252 833-4061
Kevin Boyd, *Prin*
Harry Smith, *
EMP: 50 **EST:** 2006
SALES (est): 10.96MM **Privately Held**
Web: www.oakridgemw.com
SIC: 3444 1761 Sheet metal specialties, not stamped; Sheet metal work, nec

Washington - Beaufort County (G-15721)

(G-15721)
P & G MANUFACTURING WASH INC
339 Old Bath Hwy (27889-7760)
P.O. Box 369 (27889-0369)
PHONE..................252 946-9110
Charlie Rasmussen, *CEO*
EMP: 8 **EST:** 1976
SQ FT: 16,000
SALES (est): 2.86MM **Privately Held**
Web: www.pgmfg.com
SIC: 3564 Air cleaning systems

(G-15722)
PACIFIC SEACRAFT LLC
1481 W 2nd St (27889-4293)
P.O. Box 189 (27889-0189)
PHONE..................252 948-1421
Steve Brodie, *Owner*
EMP: 9 **EST:** 2008
SALES (est): 513.7K **Privately Held**
Web: www.pacificseacraft.com
SIC: 3732 Boatbuilding and repairing

(G-15723)
PAIR MARINE INC
Also Called: Pair Cutoms Boats
106 Tarheel Dr (27889-4733)
PHONE..................252 717-7009
EMP: 15 **EST:** 2014
SALES (est): 970.88K **Privately Held**
Web: www.pairmarine.com
SIC: 3732 Boats, fiberglass: building and repairing

(G-15724)
PAMLICO AIR INC (DH)
112 S Respess St (27889-4956)
P.O. Box 579 (27920-0579)
PHONE..................252 995-6267
EMP: 12 **EST:** 1990
SALES (est): 23.9MM
SALES (corp-wide): 1.42MM **Privately Held**
Web: www.pamlicoair.com
SIC: 1711 3564 Warm air heating and air conditioning contractor; Blowers and fans
HQ: Tri-Dim Filter Corporation
93 Industrial Dr
Louisa VA 23093
540 967-2600

(G-15725)
PAMLICO SCREEN PRINTING INC
7669 Broad Creek Rd (27889-7796)
PHONE..................252 944-6001
EMP: 4 **EST:** 2014
SALES (est): 81.95K **Privately Held**
SIC: 2752 Commercial printing, lithographic

(G-15726)
PAS USA INC
2010 W 15th St (27889-3590)
PHONE..................252 974-5500
Glenn Sparrow, *CEO*
Stefan Kaiser, *
David Greco, *
April Woolard, *
▲ **EMP:** 141 **EST:** 2003
SQ FT: 50,000
SALES (est): 49.28MM
SALES (corp-wide): 437.55MM **Privately Held**
SIC: 3822 Appliance controls,except air-conditioning and refrigeration
HQ: Pas Management Holding Gmbh
Wilhelm-Bartelt-Str. 10-14
Neuruppin BB 16816

(G-15727)
PRECISIONAIRE INC (DH)
Also Called: Precisionaire of Smithfield
531 Flanders Filter Rd (27889-7805)
PHONE..................252 946-8081
Ted Beneski, *Ch*
Harry Smith, *
Mark Sokolowski, *
Warren Bonham, *
Eliot Kerlin, *
◆ **EMP:** 92 **EST:** 1970
SQ FT: 25,000
SALES (est): 100.6MM **Privately Held**
SIC: 3564 Filters, air: furnaces, air conditioning equipment, etc.
HQ: Flanders Corporation
531 Flanders Filter Rd
Washington NC 27889

(G-15728)
PROTOTECH MANUFACTURING INC ✿
514 Telfair St (27889-4520)
PHONE..................508 646-8849
Brett Palaschak, *Pr*
Jesus Chavez Lopez, *VP*
EMP: 11 **EST:** 2024
SALES (est): 452.49K **Privately Held**
SIC: 2821 3086 3069 7389 Plastics materials and resins; Plastics foam products; Floor coverings, rubber; Business Activities at Non-Commercial Site

(G-15729)
RONDOL CORDON LOGGING INC
101 Raccoon Run (27889-7680)
P.O. Box 1746 (27889-1746)
PHONE..................252 944-9220
EMP: 8 **EST:** 2010
SALES (est): 173.99K **Privately Held**
SIC: 2411 Logging camps and contractors

(G-15730)
SESAME TECHNOLOGIES INC
3718 River Rd (27889-7526)
P.O. Box 803 (27889-0803)
PHONE..................252 964-2205
Sue Faircloth, *Pr*
Ernest T Jefferson, *VP*
EMP: 10 **EST:** 1989
SQ FT: 3,200
SALES (est): 1.64MM **Privately Held**
Web: www.sesametech.com
SIC: 3052 Rubber and plastics hose and beltings

(G-15731)
SHUTTER FACTORY INC
6139w Us Highway 264 W (27889-8028)
PHONE..................252 974-2795
Reed Boseman, *Pr*
EMP: 5 **EST:** 1997
SALES (est): 480.86K **Privately Held**
Web: www.theshutterfactoryinc.com
SIC: 3442 5023 Shutters, door or window: metal; Vertical blinds

(G-15732)
SPINRITE YARNS LP
190 Plymouth St (27889-4291)
PHONE..................252 833-4970
EMP: 6 **EST:** 2018
SALES (est): 159.18K **Privately Held**
Web: www.spinriteyarns.com
SIC: 2281 Yarn spinning mills

(G-15733)
STARCRAFT DIAMONDS INC
444 Stewart Pkwy (27889-4974)
PHONE..................252 717-2548
James M Fortescue Senior, *Pr*
Elvira W Fortescue, *VP*
James M Fortescue Junior, *Treas*
Haywood P Fortescue, *Sec*
▲ **EMP:** 10 **EST:** 1962
SQ FT: 7,500
SALES (est): 488.57K **Privately Held**
Web: www.guyharveyjewelry.com
SIC: 5944 3911 Jewelry, precious stones and precious metals; Jewelry, precious metal

(G-15734)
TRANSPORTATION TECH INC (DH)
Also Called: Hackney
911 W 5th St (27889-4205)
P.O. Box 880 (27889-0880)
PHONE..................252 946-6521
Michael A Tucker, *Pr*
Jeffery T Joyner, *VP*
Sandra W Tankard, *Sec*
▲ **EMP:** 165 **EST:** 1989
SALES (est): 186.39MM **Privately Held**
Web: www.vthackney.com
SIC: 3713 Truck bodies (motor vehicles)
HQ: St Engineering North America, Inc.
99 Canal Center Plz # 220
Alexandria VA 22314
703 739-2610

(G-15735)
UNIFORMS GALORE
Also Called: Stitchworks Embroidery
628 River Rd (27889-3923)
PHONE..................252 975-5878
EMP: 5 **EST:** 1992
SQ FT: 12,500
SALES (est): 496.67K **Privately Held**
Web: www.buyworkwearforless.com
SIC: 2395 2759 Embroidery and art needlework; Commercial printing, nec

(G-15736)
VEON INC
Also Called: Adaptive Mobility Solutions
601 W 5th St (27889-4301)
PHONE..................252 623-2102
Michael Harragin, *Pr*
EMP: 10 **EST:** 2016
SQ FT: 1,500
SALES (est): 1.03MM **Privately Held**
Web: www.amslifts.com
SIC: 5047 3448 3536 3842 Medical equipment and supplies; Ramps, prefabricated metal; Boat lifts; Personal safety equipment

(G-15737)
VT HACKNEY INC
Also Called: Hackney A Div VT Spclzed Vhcle
400 Hackney Ave (27889-4726)
P.O. Box 880 (27889-0880)
PHONE..................252 946-6521
Michael Tucker, *Brnch Mgr*
EMP: 99
Web: www.hackneyusa.com
SIC: 3713 Truck bodies (motor vehicles)
HQ: Transportation Technologies, Inc.
911 W 5th St
Washington NC 27889
252 946-6521

(G-15738)
WASHINGTON CABINET COMPANY
4799 Voa Rd (27889-7997)
PHONE..................252 946-3457
Alan Peele, *Pt*
Wayne Jackson, *Pt*
EMP: 5 **EST:** 1987
SQ FT: 1,200
SALES (est): 353.87K **Privately Held**
Web: www.wcabinet.com
SIC: 2541 5712 1751 Cabinets, except refrigerated: show, display, etc.: wood; Cabinet work, custom; Cabinet and finish carpentry

(G-15739)
WASHINGTON NEWS PUBLISHING CO
Also Called: Washington Daily News
217 N Market St (27889-4949)
P.O. Box 1788 (27889-1788)
PHONE..................252 946-2144
Ashley B Futrell Junior, *Pr*
Susan B Futrell, *
Rachel Futrell, *
Ashley B Futrell Senior, *Ch Bd*
EMP: 17 **EST:** 1909
SQ FT: 15,000
SALES (est): 576.23K **Privately Held**
Web: www.thewashingtondailynews.com
SIC: 2711 Newspapers, publishing and printing

(G-15740)
WOODWORKING AT DINAHS LANDING
90 Dinahs Landing Rd (27889-7279)
PHONE..................252 402-2248
Kevin Newman, *Prin*
EMP: 5 **EST:** 2018
SALES (est): 100.5K **Privately Held**
SIC: 2431 Millwork

(G-15741)
WORMFARMER
859 Betsy Elbow Rd (27889-8319)
PHONE..................252 944-1012
Rodney Alligood, *Prin*
EMP: 5 **EST:** 2018
SALES (est): 74.42K **Privately Held**
SIC: 2875 Compost

Watha
Pender County

(G-15742)
UPPER ROOM
1166 Anderson Rd (28478-9282)
PHONE..................910 540-7719
Bonnie Ezzell, *Prin*
EMP: 4 **EST:** 2017
SALES (est): 45.36K **Privately Held**
Web: www.urcoffee.org
SIC: 3131 Footwear cut stock

Waxhaw
Union County

(G-15743)
ABBOTT LABORATORIES
9108 Kingsmead Ln (28173-9075)
P.O. Box 75896 (28275-0896)
PHONE..................704 243-1832
EMP: 4
SALES (corp-wide): 40.11B **Publicly Held**
Web: www.abbott.com
SIC: 2834 Pharmaceutical preparations
PA: Abbott Laboratories
100 Abbott Park Rd
Abbott Park IL 60064
224 667-6100

(G-15744)
AEROPLANTATION
630 Baron Rd (28173-9382)
PHONE..................704 843-2223

GEOGRAPHIC SECTION

Waxhaw - Union County (G-15774)

Peter Balletta, *CEO*
EMP: 5 **EST:** 2016
SALES (est): 74.73K **Privately Held**
SIC: 2721   Periodicals

(G-15745)
BIRCH BROS SOUTHERN INC
9510 New Town Rd   (28173-8574)
P.O. Box 70   (28173-1038)
PHONE..................................704 843-2111
Steven W Birch, *Pr*
EMP: 27 **EST:** 1883
SQ FT: 36,000
SALES (est): 5.56MM **Privately Held**
Web: www.birchbrothers.com
SIC: 5084 3559   Industrial machinery and equipment; Ammunition and explosives, loading machinery

(G-15746)
BRAND FUEL PROMOTIONS
400 N Broome St Ste 203   (28173-7033)
PHONE..................................704 256-4057
Steve Walker, *Mgr*
EMP: 7 **EST:** 2010
SALES (est): 119.48K **Privately Held**
SIC: 2752   Commercial printing, lithographic

(G-15747)
BRANDON HILBERT
Also Called: Waxhaw Cabinet Company
10704 Lancaster Hwy   (28173-9156)
PHONE..................................704 243-5593
Brandon Hilbert, *Owner*
EMP: 10 **EST:** 2015
SQ FT: 1,800
SALES (est): 475.62K **Privately Held**
SIC: 2434   Wood kitchen cabinets

(G-15748)
CAPTIVE-AIRE SYSTEMS INC
516 Wyndham Ln   (28173-6632)
PHONE..................................704 843-7215
Robert Ludley, *Pr*
EMP: 9
SALES (corp-wide): 485.13MM **Privately Held**
Web: www.captiveaire.com
SIC: 3444   Restaurant sheet metalwork
PA: Captive-Aire Systems, Inc.
    4641 Paragon Park Rd # 104
    Raleigh NC 27616
    919 882-2410

(G-15749)
CAROLINA BUSINESS AND
2436 Logan Field Dr   (28173-6862)
PHONE..................................704 826-7099
Jack Sluiter, *Pr*
EMP: 6 **EST:** 2014
SALES (est): 112.64K **Privately Held**
SIC: 2741   Miscellaneous publishing

(G-15750)
CAROLINA CUSTOM CABINETRY
6823 Davis Rd   (28173-8410)
PHONE..................................704 808-1225
EMP: 4 **EST:** 2013
SALES (est): 176.09K **Privately Held**
SIC: 2434   Wood kitchen cabinets

(G-15751)
DELLINGER WOODWORKS LLC
1806 Crestgate Dr   (28173-6734)
PHONE..................................980 245-6086
Jeremy Dellinger, *Prin*
EMP: 6 **EST:** 2017
SALES (est): 78.6K **Privately Held**
Web: www.dellingerwoodworks.com
SIC: 2431   Millwork

(G-15752)
DEMILO BROS NC LLC
Also Called: Demilo Bros.
1807 Palazzo Dr   (28173-0033)
PHONE..................................704 771-0762
Robert Demilo, *Managing Member*
EMP: 5 **EST:** 2017
SALES (est): 700K **Privately Held**
Web: www.demilobros.com
SIC: 1771 3251   Concrete work; Paving brick, clay

(G-15753)
DREAMWEAVERS BREWERY LLC
115 E North Main St   (28173-6029)
PHONE..................................704 507-7773
Anita Gimon, *Pr*
EMP: 4 **EST:** 2014
SQ FT: 4,900
SALES (est): 254.38K **Privately Held**
Web: www.dreamchasersbrewery.com
SIC: 2082   Beer (alcoholic beverage)

(G-15754)
DUBOSE NATIONAL ENRGY SVCS INC
103 Waxhaw Professional Park Dr Ste D   (28173-5022)
PHONE..................................704 295-1060
Sam Lambert, *Mgr*
EMP: 9
SALES (corp-wide): 14.81B **Publicly Held**
Web: www.dubosenes.com
SIC: 3965   Fasteners
HQ: Dubose National Energy Services, Inc.
    900 Industrial Dr
    Clinton NC 28328

(G-15755)
DUVALL TIMBER LLC
1223 Dobson Dr   (28173-7975)
PHONE..................................704 236-2211
EMP: 5 **EST:** 2018
SALES (est): 101.57K **Privately Held**
SIC: 2411   Logging

(G-15756)
FAHMAR INC
501 Running Horse Ln   (28173-7248)
PHONE..................................704 843-1872
Celedoio Marcos, *Prin*
EMP: 5 **EST:** 2010
SALES (est): 71.1K **Privately Held**
SIC: 3499   Machine bases, metal

(G-15757)
FLORES CRANE SERVICES LLC
8705 Kentucky Derby Dr   (28173-6592)
PHONE..................................704 243-4347
Maria Del Carmen Flores, *Admn*
EMP: 11 **EST:** 2014
SALES (est): 1.01MM **Privately Held**
SIC: 3531 7389   Crane carriers; Crane and aerial lift service

(G-15758)
FRONTIER MEAT PROCESSING INC
8303 Lancaster Hwy   (28173-9102)
PHONE..................................704 843-3921
Dale Walkup, *Pr*
Tim D Walkup, *VP*
Patty Liles, *Sec*
EMP: 7 **EST:** 1975
SQ FT: 1,500
SALES (est): 498.75K **Privately Held**
Web: www.frontiermeatswaxhawnc.com
SIC: 2011   Meat packing plants

(G-15759)
HAWK MANUFACTURING INC
3004 Arsdale Rd   (28173-7151)
PHONE..................................803 802-9777
Anthony F Domian, *Pr*
Debbie Domian, *Sec*
EMP: 9 **EST:** 2008
SALES (est): 608.49K **Privately Held**
Web: www.hawkmachineshop.com
SIC: 3599   Machine shop, jobbing and repair

(G-15760)
HITORK USA LLC
8311 Hampton Fare Ln   (28173-6994)
PHONE..................................803 446-7513
Vidhya Bangalore, *Mgr*
EMP: 5 **EST:** 2016
SALES (est): 107.44K **Privately Held**
SIC: 3569   Jack screws

(G-15761)
IN YOUR BUSINESS INC
4820 Pimlico Ln   (28173-7216)
PHONE..................................704 443-1330
Elizabeth Thomas-hollier, *Prin*
EMP: 5 **EST:** 2016
SALES (est): 50.81K **Privately Held**
SIC: 2741   Miscellaneous publishing

(G-15762)
INK CITY SCREEN PRINTING LLC
610 Cavendish Ln   (28173-7240)
PHONE..................................347 729-5870
Peter J Mancato, *Pr*
EMP: 5 **EST:** 2016
SALES (est): 92.3K **Privately Held**
SIC: 2752   Commercial printing, lithographic

(G-15763)
KBC OF NC LLC
4114 Western Union School Rd   (28173-9211)
PHONE..................................704 589-3711
EMP: 6 **EST:** 2014
SALES (est): 516.43K **Privately Held**
SIC: 3272   Slabs, crossing: concrete

(G-15764)
KEYPOINT LLC
Also Called: Keypoint Fabrication
8002 New Town Rd   (28173-9398)
PHONE..................................704 962-8110
EMP: 10 **EST:** 2012
SALES (est): 572.21K **Privately Held**
Web: www.keypointfab.com
SIC: 3449   Miscellaneous metalwork

(G-15765)
KLEIBERIT ADHESIVES USA INC
109b Howie Mine Rd   (28173-6873)
P.O. Box 1319   (28173-1013)
PHONE..................................704 843-3339
Klause Becker Weimann, *Pr*
◆ **EMP:** 15 **EST:** 1996
SQ FT: 1,200
SALES (est): 16.58MM
SALES (corp-wide): 25.84MM **Privately Held**
Web: www.kleiberit.com
SIC: 2891   Adhesives
PA: Kleiberit Se & Co. Kg
    Max-Becker-Str. 4
    Weingarten (Baden) BW 76356
    7244620

(G-15766)
MONO SYSTEMS INC
1506 Niall Ln   (28173-7989)
PHONE..................................914 934-2075
EMP: 5 **EST:** 2017

SALES (est): 90.88K **Privately Held**
SIC: 3443   Cable trays, metal plate

(G-15767)
MONOGRAM WHIMSY
1901 Crestgate Dr   (28173-6735)
PHONE..................................704 904-1476
Dana Wilson, *Prin*
EMP: 5 **EST:** 2010
SALES (est): 61.1K **Privately Held**
Web: www.monogramwhimsy.com
SIC: 2395   Embroidery and art needlework

(G-15768)
OASIS AKHAL-TEKES
6528 Rehobeth Rd   (28173-7603)
PHONE..................................704 843-3139
EMP: 4 **EST:** 2016
SALES (est): 105.37K **Privately Held**
Web: www.oasisakhal-tekes.com
SIC: 7372   Prepackaged software

(G-15769)
PRECISION WLDG FBRICATION SVCS
7105 Tirzah Church Rd   (28173-7635)
PHONE..................................704 243-1929
Kyle Norwood, *Prin*
EMP: 5 **EST:** 2018
SALES (est): 144.99K **Privately Held**
SIC: 7692   Welding repair

(G-15770)
PRESSURE WASHING NEAR ME LLC
Also Called: Mulch Magicians
10002 King George Ln   (28173-6816)
PHONE..................................704 280-0351
EMP: 5 **EST:** 2020
SALES (est): 187K **Privately Held**
SIC: 2821   Plastics materials and resins

(G-15771)
QUALITY CUSTOM WOODWORKS INC
5019 Pleasant Springs Rd   (28173-9785)
PHONE..................................704 843-1584
John Kronberger, *Pr*
EMP: 5 **EST:** 1993
SALES (est): 301.88K **Privately Held**
Web: www.qualitycustomwoodworks.com
SIC: 5712 2517   Cabinet work, custom; Wood television and radio cabinets

(G-15772)
R3CYCLE INDUSTRIES LLC
4417 Helms Rd   (28173-8884)
PHONE..................................404 754-4499
Julian Ochoa, *Owner*
EMP: 11 **EST:** 2018
SALES (est): 500.06K **Privately Held**
SIC: 3999   Manufacturing industries, nec

(G-15773)
RUTH HICKS ENTERPRISE INC
9417 Marvin School Rd   (28173-8594)
PHONE..................................704 469-4741
Ruth Hicks, *Pr*
Ruth C Hicks, *Pr*
Elbert Glenn Hicks Junior, *VP*
▼ **EMP:** 11 **EST:** 2007
SALES (est): 1MM **Privately Held**
Web: www.ruthhicksenterprises.com
SIC: 3999   Hair, dressing of, for the trade

(G-15774)
SERUM SOURCE INTERNATIONAL INC
406 Belvedere Ln   (28173-6581)
PHONE..................................704 588-6607

Waxhaw - Union County (G-15775)

Maranda E Swoyer, Pr
EMP: 10 **EST:** 2006
SALES (est): 364.66K **Privately Held**
Web: www.serumsourceintl.com
SIC: 2836 Biological products, except diagnostic

(G-15775)
SIRIUS TACTICAL ENTPS LLC
679 Brandy Ct (28173-9326)
PHONE..............................704 256-3660
EMP: 5 **EST:** 2012
SALES (est): 72.03K **Privately Held**
SIC: 3482 Small arms ammunition

(G-15776)
SOUTHERN PNT POWDR COATING CO
7110 Davis Rd (28173-8413)
PHONE..............................704 843-5505
EMP: 6 **EST:** 1998
SALES (est): 123.16K **Privately Held**
Web: www.sppcinc.com
SIC: 3479 Coating of metals and formed products

(G-15777)
STACKS KITCHEN MATTHEWS
1315 N Broome St (28173-9380)
PHONE..............................704 243-2024
EMP: 32
SALES (corp-wide): 248.61K **Privately Held**
Web: www.stackskitchen.com
SIC: 3421 Table and food cutlery, including butchers'
PA: Stacks Kitchen Matthews
11100 Monroe Rd
Matthews NC 28105
704 841-2025

(G-15778)
TANGLES KNITTING ON MAIN LLC
200 W North Main St (28173-6012)
PHONE..............................704 243-7150
EMP: 5 **EST:** 2009
SALES (est): 138.15K **Privately Held**
Web: www.tanglesyarn.com
SIC: 2284 Thread mills

(G-15779)
TAR HEEL STATE TITLE LLC
1737 Ridge Haven Rd (28173-7086)
PHONE..............................704 256-4965
David M Hoechster, Admn
EMP: 6 **EST:** 2012
SALES (est): 246K **Privately Held**
Web: www.tarheelstatetitle.com
SIC: 2865 Tar

(G-15780)
TECHSCAN INDUSTRIES LLC (PA)
4008 Hermes Ln (28173-7859)
PHONE..............................704 843-4518
Bryan E Scheuhing, Prin
EMP: 6 **EST:** 2007
SALES (est): 218.76K
SALES (corp-wide): 218.76K **Privately Held**
Web: www.techscanindustries.com
SIC: 3999 Framed artwork

(G-15781)
THERMODYNAMX LLC
Also Called: Thermodynamx
514 King St (28173-8950)
PHONE..............................704 622-1086
EMP: 4 **EST:** 2000
SQ FT: 2,300
SALES (est): 240.14K **Privately Held**

SIC: 3089 Thermoformed finished plastics products, nec

(G-15782)
TOMMY SIGNS
8716 Maggie Robinson Rd (28173-7681)
PHONE..............................704 877-1234
Tommy Williams, Prin
EMP: 5 **EST:** 2011
SALES (est): 172.27K **Privately Held**
SIC: 3993 Signs and advertising specialties

(G-15783)
TOTAL SPORTS ENTERPRISES
9624 Belloak Ln (28173-6767)
PHONE..............................704 237-3930
EMP: 5 **EST:** 2018
SALES (est): 194.8K **Privately Held**
Web: www.tseshop.com
SIC: 3949 Sporting and athletic goods, nec

(G-15784)
TRUSSES R US INC
200 S High St (28173-8819)
P.O. Box 1037 (28173-1009)
PHONE..............................704 361-7004
Eric Dvorak, Mgr
EMP: 8 **EST:** 2005
SALES (est): 24.73K **Privately Held**
SIC: 2439 Structural wood members, nec

(G-15785)
UNIQUE 3D PRINTING LLC
4423 Bigham Rd (28173-9569)
PHONE..............................704 843-7367
Lisa Gragson, Prin
EMP: 4 **EST:** 2018
SALES (est): 92.3K **Privately Held**
Web: www.3dprintingindustry.com
SIC: 2752 Commercial printing, lithographic

(G-15786)
UNMDENI PRESS LLC
2105 Glenhaven Dr (28173-0114)
PHONE..............................209 598-1581
EMP: 4 **EST:** 2021
SALES (est): 87.92K **Privately Held**
SIC: 2741 Miscellaneous publishing

(G-15787)
V & B CONSTRUCTION SVCS INC
8413 Walkup Rd (28173-8613)
P.O. Box 77415 (28271-7009)
PHONE..............................704 641-9936
Gayla Haag, Admn
EMP: 6 **EST:** 2019
SALES (est): 541.89K **Privately Held**
SIC: 1799 1389 Construction site cleanup; Construction, repair, and dismantling services

(G-15788)
VOCO AMERICA INC
1104 Real Quiet Ln (28173-6586)
PHONE..............................917 923-7698
EMP: 6 **EST:** 2018
SALES (est): 135.74K **Privately Held**
SIC: 3843 Dental equipment and supplies

(G-15789)
WAXHAW CREAMERY LLC
109 E North Main St (28173-6029)
PHONE..............................704 843-7927
Richard Geist, Managing Member
EMP: 13 **EST:** 2013
SALES (est): 880.04K **Privately Held**
Web: www.visitwaxhaw.com
SIC: 2021 Creamery butter

(G-15790)
WISHES FULFILLED
5504 Birchfield Cir (28173-7110)
P.O. Box 633 (28173-1002)
PHONE..............................704 905-8228
Mary Benson, Owner
EMP: 4 **EST:** 2015
SALES (est): 80.52K **Privately Held**
SIC: 3269 Art and ornamental ware, pottery

Waynesville
Haywood County

(G-15791)
A TO Z SIGNS & ENGRAVING INC
87 Willow Rd Apt B5 (28786-5579)
PHONE..............................828 456-6337
Joan L Barnes, Prin
EMP: 4 **EST:** 2009
SALES (est): 16.28K **Privately Held**
Web: www.signsandengraving.net
SIC: 3993 Signs and advertising specialties

(G-15792)
ALP SYSTEMS INC
Also Called: Lightning Protection
46 Allegiance Ln (28786-0460)
PHONE..............................828 454-5164
Stacy Bean, Pr
EMP: 15 **EST:** 2006
SQ FT: 2,000
SALES (est): 1.32MM **Privately Held**
Web: www.alpsystemsinc.com
SIC: 1799 3643 Lightning conductor erection; Lightning arrestors and coils

(G-15793)
AQUA DOC POOL SPARKLING S
30a Shamrock Ln (28786-8197)
PHONE..............................828 231-9398
Larry Herr, Owner
EMP: 5 **EST:** 2010
SALES (est): 130.48K **Privately Held**
Web: www.aquadocwnc.com
SIC: 3999 Hot tubs

(G-15794)
B & C WINERY
1141 Rockmont Rd (28785-2712)
PHONE..............................828 550-3610
EMP: 4 **EST:** 2014
SALES (est): 165.75K **Privately Held**
Web: www.bcwinerync.com
SIC: 2084 Wines

(G-15795)
BLUE RIDGE PAPER PRODUCTS LLC
Also Called: Evergreen Packaging
81 Old Howell Mill Rd (28786-0339)
PHONE..............................828 452-0834
Allen Denney, Mgr
EMP: 180
SQ FT: 27,666
Web: www.pactivevergreen.com
SIC: 2672 2621 Coated paper, except photographic, carbon, or abrasive; Paper mills
HQ: Blue Ridge Paper Products Llc
41 Main St
Canton NC 28716
828 454-0676

(G-15796)
CARAUSTAR INDUSTRIES INC
5095 Old River Rd (28786-7581)
PHONE..............................828 246-7234
EMP: 5
SALES (corp-wide): 5.22B **Publicly Held**
Web: www.greif.com

SIC: 2655 Tubes, fiber or paper: made from purchased material
HQ: Caraustar Industries, Inc.
5000 Astell Pwdr Sprng Rd
Austell GA 30106
770 948-3101

(G-15797)
CEDAR HILL STUDIO & GALLERY
Also Called: Sonshine Promises
196 N Main St (28786-3810)
P.O. Box 328 (28786-0328)
PHONE..............................828 456-6344
Gretchen Clasby, Owner
Mark B Clasby, Owner
EMP: 8 **EST:** 1972
SQ FT: 17,500
SALES (est): 876.21K **Privately Held**
Web: www.cedarhillstudio.com
SIC: 5199 2741 Art goods; Art copy and poster publishing

(G-15798)
CLASSY GLASS INC
12 Cougar Ct (28786-1817)
PHONE..............................828 452-2242
TOLL FREE: 877
EMP: 7 **EST:** 1995
SQ FT: 1,200
SALES (est): 595.87K **Privately Held**
Web: www.pelucida.com
SIC: 3231 5999 5231 Ornamental glass: cut, engraved or otherwise decorated; Trophies and plaques; Glass, leaded or stained

(G-15799)
CMT METAL FINISHES
1570 S Main St (28786-2155)
PHONE..............................828 400-0626
EMP: 4 **EST:** 2019
SALES (est): 97.35K **Privately Held**
SIC: 3479 Coating of metals and formed products

(G-15800)
CORNER STATION OLIVE OIL CO
224 Branner Ave (28786-3289)
PHONE..............................828 246-0218
EMP: 4 **EST:** 2018
SALES (est): 91.38K **Privately Held**
SIC: 2079 Olive oil

(G-15801)
DECEMBER DIAMONDS INC
3425 Dellwood Rd (28786-6218)
P.O. Box 1419 (28751-1419)
PHONE..............................828 926-3308
Scott Nielsen, Pr
▲ **EMP:** 4 **EST:** 1999
SALES (est): 369.97K **Privately Held**
Web: www.decemberdiamonds.com
SIC: 3961 Ornaments, costume, except precious metal and gems

(G-15802)
DISTINCTIVE BLDG & DESIGN INC
24 Chloe Ln (28786-0799)
P.O. Box 600 (28786-0600)
PHONE..............................828 456-4730
Tom Hines, Pr
EMP: 4 **EST:** 2000
SQ FT: 1,675
SALES (est): 560.91K **Privately Held**
Web: www.distinctivecustomhomes.com
SIC: 2452 1521 Log cabins, prefabricated, wood; Single-family housing construction

(G-15803)
EDGE BROADBAND SOLUTIONS LLC

Also Called: Gogofiber
244 Lea Plant Rd (28786-4984)
PHONE..................828 785-1420
Alan Gauvreau, *Managing Member*
Edward A Donnahoe, *Managing Member*
EMP: 20 EST: 2013
SALES (est): 5.82MM Privately Held
Web: www.edge-bbs.com
SIC: 7629 3661 3663 Telecommunication equipment repair (except telephones); Fiber optics communications equipment; Cable television equipment

(G-15804)
ELEMENT ARBOR INC
417 Sunny Dr (28786-7586)
PHONE..................828 550-2250
Nicholas P Johnson, *Owner*
EMP: 6 EST: 2015
SALES (est): 966.08K Privately Held
Web: www.elementarbor.com
SIC: 2819 Elements

(G-15805)
GILES CHEMICAL CORPORATION
75 Giles Pl (28786-1938)
PHONE..................828 452-4784
Richard N Nwrenn Junior, *Pr*
EMP: 4
SALES (corp-wide): 335.68MM Privately Held
Web: www.premiermagnesia.com
SIC: 2819 2899 Magnesium compounds or salts, inorganic; Salt
HQ: Giles Chemical Corporation
102 Commerce St
Waynesville NC 28786
828 452-4784

(G-15806)
GILES CHEMICAL CORPORATION (HQ)
Also Called: Giles Chemical Industries
102 Commerce St (28786-5739)
P.O. Box 370 (28786-0370)
PHONE..................828 452-4784
Richard N Wrenn Junior, *Pr*
Darrell H Clark, *Sec*
▲ EMP: 22 EST: 1950
SQ FT: 33,013
SALES (est): 44.58MM
SALES (corp-wide): 335.68MM Privately Held
Web: www.premiermagnesia.com
SIC: 2819 2899 Magnesium compounds or salts, inorganic; Salt
PA: Premier Magnesia, Llc
75 Giles Pl
Waynesville NC 28786
828 452-4784

(G-15807)
HI-TECH SCREENS INC
364 Lea Plant Rd (28786-0010)
PHONE..................828 452-5151
Chris Hartley, *Pr*
Wallace Foutch Ii, *CEO*
EMP: 10 EST: 2000
SQ FT: 15,000
SALES (est): 345.24K Privately Held
Web: www.hitechscreens.com
SIC: 2396 Screen printing on fabric articles

(G-15808)
JOHN LAUGHTER JEWELRY INC
146 N Main St (28786-3810)
PHONE..................828 456-4772
Tammy Mosely, *Mgr*
EMP: 6
SALES (corp-wide): 1.29MM Privately Held
Web: www.grantljewelry.com
SIC: 5944 3911 7631 Jewelry, precious stones and precious metals; Jewelry, precious metal; Jewelry repair services
PA: John Laughter Jewelry, Inc.
1800 Hendersonville Rd # 2
Asheville NC 28803
828 274-5770

(G-15809)
LILY BELLES
305 Castle Creek Dr (28786-6848)
PHONE..................828 246-0894
Lily Belles, *Prin*
EMP: 6 EST: 2010
SALES (est): 76.77K Privately Held
Web: www.lilybellesonline.com
SIC: 3552 Embroidery machines

(G-15810)
METZGERS BURL WOOD GALLERY
101 N Main St (28786-3809)
PHONE..................828 452-2550
Janet L Metzger, *Prin*
EMP: 4 EST: 2016
SALES (est): 90.51K Privately Held
Web: www.burlgallery.com
SIC: 2431 Millwork

(G-15811)
MOUNTAINEER INC
220 N Main St (28786-3812)
P.O. Box 129 (28786-0129)
PHONE..................828 452-0661
Jonathan Key, *Pr*
Jeff Schumacher, *
EMP: 10 EST: 1887
SALES (est): 229.53K Privately Held
Web: www.themountaineer.com
SIC: 2759 2752 2711 Newspapers: printing, nsk; Commercial printing, lithographic; Newspapers

(G-15812)
OAKS UNLIMITED INC (PA)
3530 Jonathan Creek Rd (28785-9864)
P.O. Box 1070 (28201-1070)
PHONE..................828 926-1621
Joe Pryor Ii, *Pr*
Trent Thomas, *
Nancy Pryor, *
▼ EMP: 25 EST: 1979
SALES (est): 5.69MM
SALES (corp-wide): 5.69MM Privately Held
Web: www.oaksunlimited.com
SIC: 2421 5031 Lumber: rough, sawed, or planed; Lumber: rough, dressed, and finished

(G-15813)
OLD STYLE PRINTING
1046 Sulphur Springs Rd (28786-4247)
PHONE..................828 452-1122
J Lloyd Allen, *Owner*
EMP: 5 EST: 1992
SALES (est): 193.76K Privately Held
SIC: 2752 Offset printing

(G-15814)
PERUSI WOODCARVING
103 Waldonpond Pl (28786-6258)
PHONE..................828 734-6121
Ronald Perusi, *Prin*
EMP: 5 EST: 2019
SALES (est): 79.78K Privately Held
Web: www.perusiwoodcarving.com
SIC: 2431 Millwork

(G-15815)
POWELL INDUSTRIES INC (PA)
Also Called: Powell Wholesale Lumber
4595 Jonathan Creek Rd (28785-8302)
P.O. Box 65 (28786-0065)
PHONE..................828 926-9114
Carl B Powell Junior, *Pr*
George G Powell, *
James M Powell, *
EMP: 55 EST: 1958
SQ FT: 20,000
SALES (est): 7.82MM
SALES (corp-wide): 7.82MM Privately Held
Web: www.powellind.com
SIC: 2426 5211 2421 Dimension, hardwood; Flooring, wood; Wood chips, produced at mill

(G-15816)
PREMIER MAGNESIA LLC (PA)
75 Giles Pl (28786-1938)
P.O. Box 370 (28786-0370)
PHONE..................828 452-4784
John Gehret, *CEO*
Rick Wrenn Junior, *Pr*
◆ EMP: 20 EST: 2001
SALES (est): 335.68MM
SALES (corp-wide): 335.68MM Privately Held
Web: www.premiermagnesia.com
SIC: 3295 Minerals, ground or treated

(G-15817)
PRINT HAUS INC
641 N Main St (28786-3819)
PHONE..................828 456-8622
Jeffrey Kuhlman, *CEO*
EMP: 7 EST: 1982
SQ FT: 3,500
SALES (est): 582.13K Privately Held
Web: www.theprinthaus.com
SIC: 2752 7334 2761 2759 Offset printing; Photocopying and duplicating services; Manifold business forms; Commercial printing, nec

(G-15818)
RIKKI TIKKI TEES
Also Called: Thomas Enterprises
764 S Haywood St (28786-4360)
PHONE..................828 454-0515
Richard Thomas, *Owner*
EMP: 5 EST: 1990
SALES (est): 249.1K Privately Held
Web: www.rikkitikkitees.com
SIC: 2759 2741 Screen printing; Miscellaneous publishing

(G-15819)
ROC-N-SOC INC
151 Kelly Park Ln (28786-2738)
PHONE..................828 452-1736
Steven Mcintosh, *Pr*
◆ EMP: 9 EST: 1990
SQ FT: 3,500
SALES (est): 638.66K Privately Held
Web: www.rocnsoc.com
SIC: 3931 Drums, parts, and accessories (musical instruments)

(G-15820)
SANDERS INDUSTRIES INC
Also Called: CMC
559 Bow And Arrow Cv (28785-0210)
PHONE..................410 277-8565
William Sanders, *Pr*
William N Sanders, *Pr*
W Scott Sanders, *VP*
Carolyn Sanders, *VP*
▲ EMP: 9 EST: 1967
SALES (est): 641.43K Privately Held
SIC: 2392 5023 2369 5136 Tablecloths: made from purchased materials; Linens, table; Children's robes and housecoats; Robes, men's and boys'

(G-15821)
SBG DIGITAL INC
Also Called: Satellite & Cellular
1562 S Main St (28786-2155)
PHONE..................828 476-0030
Sherry Garnes, *Pr*
EMP: 5 EST: 2001
SALES (est): 490.44K Privately Held
SIC: 3663 Satellites, communications

(G-15822)
SERIO SELF DEFENSE SCHOOL OF
38 Church St (28786-5709)
PHONE..................225 245-0693
Jillian Serio, *Prin*
EMP: 6 EST: 2017
SALES (est): 118.35K Privately Held
SIC: 3812 Defense systems and equipment

(G-15823)
SMITHS GARAGE AND MACHINE SHOP
710 Hyatt Creek Rd (28786-6107)
PHONE..................828 452-1664
Jimmy Smith, *Prin*
EMP: 4 EST: 2011
SALES (est): 95K Privately Held
SIC: 3599 Machine shop, jobbing and repair

(G-15824)
SMOKY MOUNTAIN NEWS INC (PA)
144 Montgomery St (28786-3720)
P.O. Box 629 (28786-0629)
PHONE..................828 452-4251
Scott Mccleod, *Prin*
Scott Mccloud, *Pr*
Greg Boothroyd, *VP*
EMP: 12 EST: 1999
SALES (est): 1.35MM
SALES (corp-wide): 1.35MM Privately Held
Web: www.smokymountainnews.com
SIC: 2711 Newspapers: publishing only, not printed on site

(G-15825)
SORRELLS SHEREE WHITE (PA)
Also Called: Whitewoven Handweaving Studio
1834 Cove Creek Rd (28785-2766)
PHONE..................828 452-4864
Sheree White Sorrells, *Owner*
EMP: 4 EST: 1981
SALES (est): 286.27K Privately Held
Web: www.rugweaver.com
SIC: 2231 2273 Weaving mill, broadwoven fabrics: wool or similar fabric; Rugs, hand and machine made

(G-15826)
SOUTHERN CONCRETE MTLS INC
201 Boundary St (28786-5754)
PHONE..................828 456-9048
Ronald Mahaley, *Mgr*
EMP: 20
SALES (corp-wide): 238.17MM Privately Held
Web: www.scmusa.com
SIC: 3273 Ready-mixed concrete
HQ: Southern Concrete Materials, Inc.
35 Meadow Rd
Asheville NC 28803
828 253-6421

Waynesville - Haywood County (G-15827)

(G-15827)
SPARKSMITH LLC
60 Communications Dr (28786-9743)
PHONE................................828 266-0152
EMP: 5 EST: 2018
SALES (est): 133.05K Privately Held
Web: www.sparksmith.com
SIC: 5531 3641 Automotive parts; Electric lamp (bulb) parts

(G-15828)
THB LEISURE LLC
1478 Dellwood Rd (28786-6914)
PHONE................................828 926-8484
EMP: 7 EST: 2016
SALES (est): 943.15K Privately Held
SIC: 2253 Lounge, bed, and leisurewear

(G-15829)
TOP NOTCH LOG HOMES INC
3517 Jonathan Creek Rd (28785-9864)
PHONE................................828 926-4300
EMP: 7 EST: 1996
SALES (est): 167.23K Privately Held
SIC: 2411 Logging

(G-15830)
TOWN OF WAYNESVILLE
Also Called: Water Treatment Department
341 Rocky Branch Rd (28786-1850)
PHONE................................828 456-8497
Kyle Cooke, Dir
EMP: 8
Web: www.waynesvillenc.gov
SIC: 3589 Water treatment equipment, industrial
PA: Town Of Waynesville
16 S Main St
Waynesville NC 28786
828 456-2491

(G-15831)
VICINITUS LLC
Also Called: Positively Haywood
788 Springbrook Farm Rd (28786-1879)
PHONE................................828 476-6055
Carol Adams, Prin
EMP: 5 EST: 2015
SALES (est): 67.13K Privately Held
Web: www.vicinitus.com
SIC: 2741 Miscellaneous publishing

(G-15832)
WAYNESVILLE SODA JERKS LLC
Also Called: Waynesville Soda Jerks
35 Bridges St (28786-8890)
PHONE................................828 278-8589
Christopher Allen, Owner
◆ EMP: 4 EST: 2013
SALES (est): 236.7K Privately Held
Web: www.waynesvillesodajerks.com
SIC: 2086 Carbonated beverages, nonalcoholic; pkged. in cans, bottles

(G-15833)
WINCHESTER WOODWORKS
168 Foothill Ln (28786-0110)
PHONE................................828 421-2693
Allen Davis, Prin
EMP: 4 EST: 2010
SALES (est): 69.68K Privately Held
Web: www.winchesterwoodworks.net
SIC: 2431 Millwork

(G-15834)
WMXF AM 1400
Also Called: Clear Channel Communications
54 N Main St (28786-3949)
PHONE................................828 456-8661
EMP: 55
SALES (est): 2.19MM Privately Held
SIC: 2731 Book publishing

(G-15835)
WNC CABINETRY LLC
730 N Main St (28786-3822)
PHONE................................828 400-6492
Ashley Mullis, Prin
EMP: 6 EST: 2015
SALES (est): 187.88K Privately Held
Web: www.wnccabinetry.com
SIC: 2434 Wood kitchen cabinets

Weaverville
Buncombe County

(G-15836)
ABB MOTORS AND MECHANICAL INC
Also Called: Baldor Dodge Reliance
70 Reems Creek Rd (28787-9211)
PHONE................................828 645-1706
EMP: 157
Web: www.dodge.com
SIC: 5511 3566 3463 3366 Automobiles, new and used; Speed changers, drives, and gears; Pump, compressor, turbine, and engine forgings, except auto; Bushings and bearings
HQ: Abb Motors And Mechanical Inc.
5711 Rs Boreham Jr St
Fort Smith AR 72901
479 646-4711

(G-15837)
B V HEDRICK GRAVEL & SAND CO
Also Called: North Buncombe Quarry
100 Gold View Rd (28787)
P.O. Box 610 (28787-0610)
PHONE................................828 645-5560
J V Goodman, Pr
EMP: 39
SALES (corp-wide): 238.17MM Privately Held
Web: www.hedrickind.com
SIC: 3281 1442 Stone, quarrying and processing of own stone products; Construction sand and gravel
PA: B. V. Hedrick Gravel & Sand Company
120 1/2 N Church St
Salisbury NC 28144
704 633-5982

(G-15838)
BALCRANK CORPORATION
90 Monticello Rd (28787-9441)
PHONE................................800 747-5300
◆ EMP: 25 EST: 2009
SQ FT: 130,000
SALES (est): 7.7MM Privately Held
Web: www.balcrank.com
SIC: 3569 3586 3429 3089 Lubricating equipment; Gasoline pumps, measuring or dispensing; Hardware, nec; Handles, brush or tool: plastics
HQ: Linter, North America Corporation
48 Patton Ave
Asheville NC 28801

(G-15839)
BARKLEYS MILL ON SOUTHERN CRO
6 Barkley Pl (28787-8234)
PHONE................................828 626-3344
Micah Stowe, Genl Mgr
EMP: 6 EST: 2013
SQ FT: 2,800
SALES (est): 236.1K Privately Held
SIC: 0139 2046 Broomcorn farm; Corn milling by-products

(G-15840)
BROOKSTONE BAPTIST CHURCH
Also Called: Southern Baptist Church
90 Griffee Rd (28787-9619)
PHONE................................828 658-9443
EMP: 23 EST: 1974
SQ FT: 5,400
SALES (est): 913.14K Privately Held
Web: www.brookstonechurch.org
SIC: 8661 7372 Baptist Church; Application computer software

(G-15841)
CLASSIC SCENT
72 Hillcrest Dr (28787-8921)
PHONE................................828 645-5171
Denise Peters, Owner
EMP: 6 EST: 1989
SALES (est): 238.14K Privately Held
Web: www.theclassicscent.com
SIC: 3999 Handles, handbag and luggage

(G-15842)
CONRAD EMBROIDERY COMPANY LLC
Also Called: C E C
22 A B Emblem Dr (28787-0258)
P.O. Box 695 (28787-0695)
PHONE................................828 645-3015
Paul Conrad, Managing Member
EMP: 46 EST: 2013
SALES (est): 5.29MM
SALES (corp-wide): 21.44MM Privately Held
Web: www.abemblem.com
SIC: 2395 Emblems, embroidered
PA: Conrad Industries, Inc.
22 A B Emblem Dr
Weaverville NC 28787
828 645-3015

(G-15843)
CONRAD INDUSTRIES INC (PA)
Also Called: A-B Emblem
22 A B Emblem Dr (28787-0258)
P.O. Box 695 (28787-0695)
PHONE................................828 645-3015
Bernhard Conrad, Pr
Jerry Williams, *
▲ EMP: 41 EST: 1944
SQ FT: 140,000
SALES (est): 21.44MM
SALES (corp-wide): 21.44MM Privately Held
Web: www.conrad-industries.com
SIC: 2395 Emblems, embroidered

(G-15844)
CORMARK INTERNATIONAL LLC
179 Reems Creek Rd (28787-8204)
PHONE................................828 658-8455
Massimo Corte, Prin
▲ EMP: 9 EST: 2004
SALES (est): 1.03MM Privately Held
Web: www.cormarkint.com
SIC: 2499 Decorative wood and woodwork

(G-15845)
CREEK INDUSTRIES INC
87 Island In The Sky Trl (28787-0379)
PHONE................................828 319-7490
Robert Breining, Prin
EMP: 11 EST: 2017
SALES (est): 433.23K Privately Held
SIC: 3999 Manufacturing industries, nec

(G-15846)
FILLAUER NORTH CAROLINA INC
220 Merrimon Ave Ste A (28787-9113)
PHONE................................828 658-8330
Richard Anderson, Pr
EMP: 25 EST: 1979
SQ FT: 35,000
SALES (est): 3.6MM Privately Held
Web: www.fillauer.com
SIC: 3842 5047 Orthopedic appliances; Orthopedic equipment and supplies
PA: Fillauer, Inc.
2710 Amnicola Hwy
Chattanooga TN 37406

(G-15847)
FOUR JAKS
25 Salem Acres Rd (28787-9419)
PHONE................................828 484-9545
Doug Leavitt, Owner
EMP: 5 EST: 2007
SALES (est): 212.83K Privately Held
SIC: 2421 3211 3272 5031 Building and structural materials, wood; Construction glass; Concrete structural support and building material; Building materials, exterior

(G-15848)
HIGH FIVE ENTERPRISES INC
Also Called: Wnc Homes & Realstate
12 Strawberry Ln (28787-9270)
P.O. Box 8683 (28814-8683)
PHONE................................828 279-5962
Alan Sheppard, Pr
EMP: 4 EST: 2012
SALES (est): 390.7K Privately Held
Web: www.rewnc.com
SIC: 2731 7389 Book publishing; Business services, nec

(G-15849)
J STAHL SALES & SOURCING INC (PA)
81 Monticello Rd (28787-9441)
P.O. Box 1673 (28787-1673)
PHONE................................828 645-3005
John Stahl, CEO
John Stahl, Pr
James Stahl, VP Sls
Elizabeth Stahl, Sec
▲ EMP: 23 EST: 1978
SQ FT: 15,000
SALES (est): 2.33MM
SALES (corp-wide): 2.33MM Privately Held
Web: www.stahlsac.com
SIC: 2393 3949 Canvas bags; Skin diving equipment, scuba type

(G-15850)
KRW PACKAGING MACHINERY INC
81 Monticello Rd (28787-9441)
PHONE................................828 658-0912
Kenneth Wilkes, Ofcr
EMP: 10 EST: 2011
SALES (est): 1.12MM Privately Held
Web: www.smartbottleinc.com
SIC: 3565 Packaging machinery

(G-15851)
LASER PRECISION CUTTING INC
181 Reems Creek Rd Ste 3 (28787-8229)
P.O. Box 1654 (28787-1654)
PHONE................................828 658-0644
Joseph Karpen, Pr
▲ EMP: 8 EST: 1990
SQ FT: 15,000
SALES (est): 987.72K Privately Held
Web: www.lpcutting.com

GEOGRAPHIC SECTION

SIC: 3599 Machine shop, jobbing and repair

(G-15852)
MOUNTAIN HOMES OF WNC LLC
12 White Walnut Dr (28787-8259)
PHONE..................................828 216-2546
Jeffrey Allen, *Managing Member*
EMP: 10 EST: 2019
SALES (est): 968.92K **Privately Held**
Web: www.mountainhomesofwestnc.com
SIC: 1389 7389 Construction, repair, and dismantling services; Business Activities at Non-Commercial Site

(G-15853)
MS WHLCHAIR N CA AM STATE COOR
61 Cheek Rd (28787-9635)
PHONE..................................828 230-1129
Brandee Ponder, *Prin*
EMP: 6 EST: 2011
SALES (est): 183.9K **Privately Held**
SIC: 3842 Wheelchairs

(G-15854)
MULTI-COLOR CORPORATION
15 Conrad Industrial Dr (28787-5505)
PHONE..................................828 658-6800
East Mark, *Brnch Mgr*
EMP: 29
SALES (corp-wide): 13.94B **Privately Held**
Web: www.mcclabel.com
SIC: 2759 Labels and seals: printing, nsk
HQ: Multi-Color Corporation
    4053 Clough Woods Dr
    Batavia OH 45103
    513 381-1480

(G-15855)
MYRICKS CUSTOM FAB INC
181 Reems Creek Rd Ste 2 (28787-8229)
PHONE..................................828 645-5800
Anthony Myricks, *Pr*
EMP: 4 EST: 2005
SALES (est): 349.11K **Privately Held**
SIC: 3499 Fabricated metal products, nec

(G-15856)
NO EVIL FOODS LLC
108 Monticello Rd Ste 2000 (28634)
P.O. Box 1199 (28787-1199)
PHONE..................................828 367-1536
Michael Woliansky, *CEO*
EMP: 70 EST: 2014
SALES (est): 5.88MM **Privately Held**
Web: www.noevilfoods.com
SIC: 2099 Food preparations, nec

(G-15857)
NORTH BUNCOMBE SMALL ENGINES
187 Dula Springs Rd (28787-9337)
PHONE..................................828 707-4874
EMP: 5 EST: 2012
SALES (est): 65K **Privately Held**
SIC: 3599 Machine shop, jobbing and repair

(G-15858)
PAYNE LEATHER AND TOOL LLC
179 Monticello Rd (28787-9324)
PHONE..................................336 391-8964
EMP: 5 EST: 2019
SALES (est): 112.38K **Privately Held**
SIC: 3999 Manufacturing industries, nec

(G-15859)
RENEW PROTECT LLC
127 Windago Rd (28787-8751)
PHONE..................................828 318-5654
EMP: 6 EST: 2017

SALES (est): 248.59K **Privately Held**
Web: www.renewprotect.com
SIC: 3999 Manufacturing industries, nec

(G-15860)
ROCKWELL AUTOMATION INC
70 Reems Creek Rd (28787-9211)
PHONE..................................828 645-4235
James Chlopek, *Mgr*
EMP: 19
Web: www.rockwellautomation.com
SIC: 3625 Relays and industrial controls
PA: Rockwell Automation, Inc.
    1201 S 2nd St
    Milwaukee WI 53204

(G-15861)
SAMOA CORPORATION
90 Monticello Rd (28787-9441)
PHONE..................................828 645-2290
Vicki O'shields, *Pr*
EMP: 30 EST: 2015
SQ FT: 90,000
SALES (est): 4.23MM **Privately Held**
Web: www.samoaindustrial.com
SIC: 3586 Oil pumps, measuring or dispensing

(G-15862)
SAMPLE GROUP INC (PA)
179 Merrimon Ave Ste 100 (28787-9675)
PHONE..................................828 658-9040
Gary Gottdiener, *Pr*
Pat Manente, *
▲ EMP: 350 EST: 1999
SQ FT: 160,000
SALES (est): 23.9MM
SALES (corp-wide): 23.9MM **Privately Held**
Web: www.thesamplegroup.com
SIC: 2299 Batting, wadding, padding and fillings

(G-15863)
SOUTHERN MADE CANDLES LLC
39 Salem Rd (28787-9417)
PHONE..................................704 740-7748
EMP: 4 EST: 2018
SALES (est): 39.69K **Privately Held**
SIC: 3999 Candles

(G-15864)
STAMPCO METAL PRODUCTS INC
108 Herron Cove Rd (28787-9221)
P.O. Box 8189 (28814-8189)
PHONE..................................828 645-4271
Marvin Eckerich, *Pr*
EMP: 32 EST: 1969
SQ FT: 23,000
SALES (est): 1.11MM **Privately Held**
Web: www.stampcometal.com
SIC: 3544 Special dies and tools

(G-15865)
THERMO FSHER SCNTFIC ASHVLLE L
220 Merrimon Ave Ste A (28787-9113)
PHONE..................................828 658-2711
EMP: 289
SALES (corp-wide): 44.91B **Publicly Held**
Web: www.thermofisher.com
SIC: 3826 Analytical instruments
HQ: Thermo Fisher Scientific (Asheville) Llc
    275 Aiken Rd
    Asheville NC 28804
    828 658-2711

(G-15866)
URBAN ORCHARD CIDER COMPANY
207 Monticello Rd (28787-9325)

PHONE..................................828 779-6372
Thomas Miller, *Pr*
Lori Miller, *CFO*
Josie Mielkey, *VP*
EMP: 8 EST: 2013
SQ FT: 3,800
SALES (est): 492.05K **Privately Held**
Web: www.urbanorchardcider.com
SIC: 2099 5921 Cider, nonalcoholic; Wine and beer

(G-15867)
VORTANT TECHNOLOGIES LLC
88 High Country Rd (28787-9374)
PHONE..................................828 645-1026
Phil Schaefer, *Pr*
EMP: 7 EST: 1999
SALES (est): 339.65K **Privately Held**
Web: www.vortant.com
SIC: 8731 7371 8711 3845 Engineering laboratory, except testing; Computer software development and applications; Electrical or electronic engineering; Electromedical apparatus

(G-15868)
WATERCOLORS BY MISTA
75 Church St (28787-9420)
PHONE..................................828 775-7751
Mista Whitson, *Prin*
EMP: 5 EST: 2010
SALES (est): 72.12K **Privately Held**
SIC: 3999 Framed artwork

(G-15869)
WNC MATERIAL SALES
351 Flat Creek Church Rd (28787-8519)
PHONE..................................828 658-8368
EMP: 7 EST: 2017
SALES (est): 209.65K **Privately Held**
Web: www.scmusa.com
SIC: 3273 Ready-mixed concrete

(G-15870)
WNC REFAB INC
125 Old Homestead Trl (28787-8757)
PHONE..................................828 658-8368
Steven Boone, *Pr*
EMP: 4 EST: 2013
SALES (est): 531.8K **Privately Held**
Web: www.wncrefab.com
SIC: 3441 5051 Fabricated structural metal; Nonferrous metal sheets, bars, rods, etc., nec

Welcome
Davidson County

(G-15871)
ATRIUM EXTRUSION SYSTEMS INC
300 Welcome Center Blvd (27374)
PHONE..................................336 764-6400
Gregory T Faherty, *CEO*
EMP: 23 EST: 1993
SALES (est): 684.97K **Privately Held**
Web: www.atrium.com
SIC: 3442 Window and door frames

(G-15872)
AURORA PLASTICS INC
Also Called: Aurora Plastics, Inc.
180 Welcome Center Blvd (27374)
P.O. Box 849 (27374-0849)
PHONE..................................336 775-2640
Larry Medford, *Mgr*
EMP: 10
Web: www.auroramaterialsolutions.com
SIC: 2821 Plastics materials and resins
HQ: Aurora Plastics, Llc

9280 Jefferson St
Streetsboro OH 44241

(G-15873)
MORTON METALCRAFT COMPANY N
P.O. Box 729 (27374-0729)
PHONE..................................336 731-5700
Charles Crump, *Pr*
EMP: 9 EST: 2008
SALES (est): 329.82K **Privately Held**
SIC: 3399 Primary metal products

(G-15874)
RICHARD CHLDRESS RACG ENTPS IN
236 Industrial Dr (27374)
P.O. Box 1189 (27374-1189)
PHONE..................................336 731-3334
Richard R Childress, *Pr*
EMP: 22
SALES (corp-wide): 45.88MM **Privately Held**
Web: www.rcrracing.com
SIC: 7549 3711 High performance auto repair and service; Automobile assembly, including specialty automobiles
PA: Richard Childress Racing Enterprises, Inc.
    425 Industrial Dr
    Welcome NC 27374
    336 731-3334

(G-15875)
RICHARD CHLDRESS RACG ENTPS IN (PA)
425 Industrial Dr (27374)
P.O. Box 1189 (27374-1189)
PHONE..................................336 731-3334
Richard Childress, *Pr*
Jean Wilson, *
Bill Patterson, *
▲ EMP: 475 EST: 1978
SQ FT: 83,000
SALES (est): 45.88MM
SALES (corp-wide): 45.88MM **Privately Held**
Web: www.rcrracing.com
SIC: 7549 7941 3711 High performance auto repair and service; Sports clubs, managers, and promoters; Automobile assembly, including specialty automobiles

(G-15876)
SUMMER INDUSTRIES LLC
Also Called: Summer Industries
262 Welcome Center Court (27374)
P.O. Box 789 (27374-0789)
PHONE..................................336 731-9217
▲ EMP: 106
Web: www.summerindustries.net
SIC: 3554 2655 Paper industries machinery; Tubes, fiber or paper: made from purchased material

(G-15877)
TUBULAR TEXTILE LLC
4157 Old Highway 52 (27374)
PHONE..................................336 731-2860
EMP: 7 EST: 2004
SQ FT: 10,000
SALES (est): 268.39K **Privately Held**
SIC: 3441 Fabricated structural metal

(G-15878)
WOOTEN GRAPHICS INC
172 Hinkle Ln (27374)
P.O. Box 819 (27374-0819)
PHONE..................................336 731-4650
James Wooten, *
Jewel Wooten, *

Jordan Wooten, *
EMP: 12 **EST:** 1977
SQ FT: 30,000
SALES (est): 489.11K **Privately Held**
Web: www.wootengraphics.com
SIC: 2759 2396 Screen printing; Automotive and apparel trimmings

---

Weldon
Halifax County

(G-15879)
AGNATURAL LLC
802 Julian R Allsbrook Hwy (27890-1166)
PHONE......................252 536-0322
Michael Dunlow, *Prin*
EMP: 6 **EST:** 2010
SALES (est): 178.33K **Privately Held**
SIC: 2074 Cottonseed oil, cake or meal

(G-15880)
BLAQ BEAUTY NATURALZ INC
Also Called: Blaq Beauty Naturalz
307 Woodlawn Ave (27890-1843)
PHONE......................252 326-5621
Zeandra M Jones, *CEO*
EMP: 9 **EST:** 2017
SALES (est): 52.36K **Privately Held**
Web: www.blaqbeautynaturalz.com
SIC: 2844 5999 Hair preparations, including shampoos; Miscellaneous retail stores, nec

(G-15881)
CHARTREUSE SHEPHERD
200 Mill St (27890-1358)
PHONE......................252 532-2708
Cheryl Thiel, *Mgr*
EMP: 5 **EST:** 2011
SALES (est): 73.25K **Privately Held**
Web: www.proteangraphics.com
SIC: 3499 Picture frames, metal

(G-15882)
HOOVER TREATED WOOD PDTS INC
1772 Trueblood Rd (27890-2000)
PHONE......................866 587-8761
Rick Farnsam, *Brnch Mgr*
EMP: 23
SALES (corp-wide): 4.41B **Publicly Held**
Web: www.frtw.com
SIC: 2491 5031 Structural lumber and timber, treated wood; Lumber: rough, dressed, and finished
HQ: Hoover Treated Wood Products, Inc.
154 Wire Rd
Thomson GA 30824
706 595-5058

(G-15883)
JBB PACKAGING LLC
100 Grace Dr (27890-1200)
PHONE......................201 470-8501
Brendan Barba, *Managing Member*
Robert George Runz, *Contrlr*
EMP: 10 **EST:** 2018
SALES (est): 1.21MM **Privately Held**
Web: www.jbbpkg.com
SIC: 2671 Plastic film, coated or laminated for packaging

(G-15884)
KENNAMETAL INC
100 Kennametal Dr (27890-1174)
PHONE......................252 536-5209
Glenn Faylor, *Brnch Mgr*
EMP: 77
SQ FT: 60,000
SALES (corp-wide): 2.08B **Publicly Held**
Web: www.kennametal.com
SIC: 3545 Cutting tools for machine tools
PA: Kennametal Inc.
525 William Penn Pl # 3300
Pittsburgh PA 15219
412 248-8000

(G-15885)
MEHERRIN RIVER FOREST PDTS INC
1478 Trueblood Rd (27890-2040)
P.O. Box 100 (23821-0100)
PHONE......................252 558-4238
Don Bright, *Pr*
EMP: 56
SALES (corp-wide): 1.62MM **Privately Held**
Web: www.meherrinriver.com
SIC: 2421 Sawmills and planing mills, general
PA: Meherrin River Forest Products, Inc.
71 N Oak St
Alberta VA 23821
434 949-7707

(G-15886)
NAES-OMS
1200 Julian R Allsbrook Hwy (27890-1170)
PHONE......................252 536-4525
Edward Hardwell, *Prin*
EMP: 6 **EST:** 2011
SALES (est): 134.4K **Privately Held**
Web: www.naes.com
SIC: 3443 Boiler shop products: boilers, smokestacks, steel tanks

(G-15887)
PATCH RUBBER COMPANY
Also Called: Advanced Traffic Marking
100 Patch Rubber Rd (27890-1220)
P.O. Box H (27870-8082)
PHONE......................252 536-2574
Stephen E Myers, *Pr*
John Orr, *
◆ **EMP:** 150 **EST:** 1947
SQ FT: 172,000
SALES (est): 40.29MM
SALES (corp-wide): 813.07MM **Publicly Held**
Web: www.patchrubber.com
SIC: 3069 Molded rubber products
PA: Myers Industries, Inc.
1293 S Main St
Akron OH 44301
330 253-5592

(G-15888)
ROANOKE VALLEY STEEL CORP
101 Kennametal Dr (27890-1175)
P.O. Box 661 (27890-0661)
PHONE......................252 530-4137
William K Neal Junior, *Pr*
EMP: 22 **EST:** 2001
SQ FT: 2,000
SALES (est): 768.94K **Privately Held**
Web: www.roanokevalleysteel.com
SIC: 3441 Fabricated structural metal

(G-15889)
WELDON MILLS DISTILLERY LLC (PA)
Also Called: Weldon Mills Distillery
200 Rock Fish Dr (27890-2106)
PHONE......................252 220-4235
Bruce Tyler, *Prin*
Michael Hinderliter, *Prin*
EMP: 5 **EST:** 2019
SALES (est): 524.19K
SALES (corp-wide): 524.19K **Privately Held**
Web: www.weldonmills.com
SIC: 2085 Distilled and blended liquors

(G-15890)
WELDON STEEL CORPORATION
101 Kennametal Dr (27890-1175)
P.O. Box 226 (27890-0226)
PHONE......................252 536-2113
William K Neal Junior, *Pr*
EMP: 44 **EST:** 1988
SQ FT: 50,000
SALES (est): 10.05MM **Privately Held**
Web: www.weldonsteel.com
SIC: 3441 Fabricated structural metal

Wendell
Wake County

(G-15891)
AAA LOUVERS INC
7328 Siemens Rd (27591-8315)
P.O. Box 721 (27591-0721)
PHONE......................919 365-7220
Larry Gower, *Pr*
EMP: 11 **EST:** 1988
SQ FT: 10,000
SALES (est): 1.65MM **Privately Held**
Web: www.aaalouvers.com
SIC: 2431 Doors and door parts and trim, wood

(G-15892)
BIG BUTTED WOMAN MUSIC LLC
7232 Beau View Dr (27591-0017)
PHONE......................919 720-3340
Kimberly J Jones, *Owner*
EMP: 5 **EST:** 2017
SALES (est): 49.63K **Privately Held**
SIC: 2741 Miscellaneous publishing

(G-15893)
BROACH CUSTOM SIGNS NC LLC
Also Called: Broach Custom Signs
3040 Wendell Blvd (27591-5902)
P.O. Box 2065 (27591-2065)
PHONE......................919 876-8380
EMP: 6 **EST:** 2006
SALES (est): 219.12K **Privately Held**
SIC: 3993 Electric signs

(G-15894)
CAPITAL CY ROOFG & SHTMTL LLC
601 Cook St (27591-9071)
P.O. Box 725 (27591-0725)
PHONE......................919 366-1850
Brooks Davis, *Pr*
EMP: 11 **EST:** 2020
SALES (est): 1.6MM **Privately Held**
SIC: 3444 Sheet metalwork

(G-15895)
CMS ASSOCIATES INC
7308 Siemens Rd Ste D (27591-6000)
P.O. Box 2139 (27591-2139)
PHONE......................919 365-0881
EMP: 7 **EST:** 1994
SQ FT: 6,000
SALES (est): 812K **Privately Held**
Web: www.cms-associates.com
SIC: 3679 Electronic circuits

(G-15896)
DAVE MULHOLLEM LOGGING INC
8853 Covered Bridge Rd (27591-8528)
PHONE......................919 796-8994
EMP: 7 **EST:** 2017
SALES (est): 304.33K **Privately Held**
SIC: 2411 Logging camps and contractors

(G-15897)
DOGWOOD PRINT
400 Big Branch Ln (27591-6860)
PHONE......................919 906-0617
Jonathan Priest, *Prin*
EMP: 4 **EST:** 2016
SALES (est): 85.35K **Privately Held**
Web: www.dogwoodprint.com
SIC: 2752 Commercial printing, lithographic

(G-15898)
DOUGLAS FABRICATION & MCH INC
430 Industrial Dr (27591-7714)
PHONE......................919 365-7553
Sharon Douglas, *Pr*
Thomas Douglas, *Sec*
EMP: 11 **EST:** 1986
SQ FT: 30,000
SALES (est): 2.49MM **Privately Held**
Web: www.douglasfab.com
SIC: 3089 3599 Thermoformed finished plastics products, nec; Machine shop, jobbing and repair

(G-15899)
E C L INC
485-1 Old Wilson Rd (27591-6302)
P.O. Box 120 (27591-0120)
PHONE......................919 365-7101
Tamatha Thompson, *Pr*
Al Lucas Junior, *VP*
EMP: 9 **EST:** 1999
SQ FT: 20,000
SALES (est): 453.55K **Privately Held**
SIC: 3444 Restaurant sheet metalwork

(G-15900)
EAGLE SPORTSWEAR LLC
Also Called: Eagle USA
4251 Wendell Blvd (27591-8412)
P.O. Box 127 (27591-0127)
PHONE......................919 365-9805
Brian Morrel, *Pr*
EMP: 10 **EST:** 2013
SALES (est): 133.12K **Privately Held**
SIC: 2389 Men's miscellaneous accessories

(G-15901)
ELECTRONIC PRODUCTS DESIGN INC
Also Called: E P D
2554 Lake Wendell Rd (27591-7164)
P.O. Box 1569 (27591-1569)
PHONE......................919 365-9199
Devera Eggimann, *Pr*
Peter Eggimann, *VP*
Michelle Glidewell, *Com Operations Vice President*
EMP: 9 **EST:** 1983
SQ FT: 12,000
SALES (est): 935.37K **Privately Held**
Web: www.epd-inc.com
SIC: 3677 Coil windings, electronic

(G-15902)
FORTRANS INC
7400 Siemens Rd Ste B (27591-8317)
P.O. Box 40 (27591-0040)
PHONE......................919 365-8004
Robert Cooke, *Pr*
Steven V Fiano, *CEO*
EMP: 4 **EST:** 1996
SQ FT: 5,000
SALES (est): 1.01MM **Privately Held**
Web: www.fortransinc.com
SIC: 5169 2819 Industrial chemicals; Industrial inorganic chemicals, nec

GEOGRAPHIC SECTION
Wendell - Wake County (G-15926)

(G-15903)
GRAFIX UNLIMITED LLC
497 Barrette Ln (27591-6103)
PHONE..................919 291-9035
Bradley Mccaskill, *Prin*
EMP: 4 **EST:** 2018
SALES (est): 180.03K **Privately Held**
SIC: 3993 Signs and advertising specialties

(G-15904)
HENRY & RYE INCORPORATED
485 Old Wilson Rd Ste 1 (27591-6302)
PHONE..................919 365-7045
Al Wayne Lucas, *Pr*
Al Wayne Lucas Senior, *Pr*
EMP: 14 **EST:** 1954
SQ FT: 20,000
SALES (est): 379.55K **Privately Held**
SIC: 3469 Kitchen fixtures and equipment: metal, except cast aluminum

(G-15905)
HIS GLORY CREATIONS PUBG LLC
4595 Wendell Blvd (27591-6921)
PHONE..................919 618-0262
EMP: 4 **EST:** 2017
SALES (est): 83.5K **Privately Held**
SIC: 2741 Miscellaneous publishing

(G-15906)
JUMBO CO
7301 Indian Rock Rd (27591-7663)
P.O. Box 1111 (27591-1111)
PHONE..................919 637-0313
Johnny Hendren, *Owner*
EMP: 4 **EST:** 2015
SALES (est): 154.08K **Privately Held**
Web: www.jumboco.com
SIC: 2759 Screen printing

(G-15907)
MAGNIFICENT CONCESSIONS LLC
Also Called: Food Industry
106 Northwinds North Dr (27591-7757)
PHONE..................919 413-1558
Shaunetta Burk, *CEO*
EMP: 20 **EST:** 2019
SALES (est): 626.21K **Privately Held**
Web: www.magnificentconcessions.com
SIC: 2599 Food wagons, restaurant

(G-15908)
MOBILE MINI INC
2231 Lake Wendell Rd #c (27591-7161)
PHONE..................919 365-3057
Mark Ayers, *Brnch Mgr*
EMP: 7
SALES (corp-wide): 2.36B **Publicly Held**
Web: www.mobilemini.com
SIC: 3448 Buildings, portable: prefabricated metal
HQ: Mobile Mini, Inc.
4646 E Van Buren St # 400
Phoenix AZ 85008
480 894-6171

(G-15909)
MODERN TOOL SERVICE
Also Called: Ideas Aesthetech
100 Walnut St (27591)
P.O. Box 220 (27591-0220)
PHONE..................919 365-7470
Larry Liles, *Owner*
EMP: 10 **EST:** 1960
SQ FT: 3,600
SALES (est): 435.21K **Privately Held**
SIC: 3545 Measuring tools and machines, machinists' metalworking type

(G-15910)
ONE PACKAGING EXCEL INC
6446 Stag Trl (27591-9272)
PHONE..................919 268-9330
Kevin J Martinez-avila, *Pr*
EMP: 5 **EST:** 2019
SALES (est): 253.75K **Privately Held**
Web: www.onepackagingexcel.com
SIC: 3999 Manufacturing industries, nec

(G-15911)
POWER CHEM INC
7316b Siemens Rd (27591-8315)
PHONE..................919 365-3400
Lawrence L Leonard, *Pr*
EMP: 6 **EST:** 1984
SALES (est): 463K **Privately Held**
SIC: 2833 Medicinals and botanicals

(G-15912)
PRECISION STAMPERS INC
Also Called: Stamp-Tech
480 Old Wilson Rd (27591-9355)
P.O. Box 1840 (27591-1840)
PHONE..................919 366-3333
Douglas Parrish, *Pr*
Terry King, *VP*
EMP: 6 **EST:** 1999
SQ FT: 4,000
SALES (est): 982.97K **Privately Held**
Web: www.stamptechinc.com
SIC: 3469 Stamping metal for the trade

(G-15913)
R J REYNOLDS TOBACCO COMPANY
7408 Siemens Rd Ste D (27591-8317)
PHONE..................919 366-0220
Joe Dilger, *Prin*
EMP: 86
Web: www.rjrt.com
SIC: 2111 Cigarettes
HQ: R. J. Reynolds Tobacco Company
401 N Main St
Winston Salem NC 27101
336 741-5000

(G-15914)
RICHARDS WLDG MET FBRCTION LLC
7324 Siemens Rd (27591-8315)
PHONE..................919 626-0134
Terry Richards, *Pr*
EMP: 16 **EST:** 2016
SALES (est): 1.77MM **Privately Held**
Web: www.richardsmetalfabrication.com
SIC: 7692 Welding repair

(G-15915)
RLS COMMERCIAL INTERIORS INC
7212 Siemens Rd (27591-8313)
PHONE..................919 365-4086
Robert L Stout, *Pr*
Deborah Y Stout, *Sec*
EMP: 6 **EST:** 1983
SQ FT: 10,000
SALES (est): 765.33K **Privately Held**
Web: www.millcaseinteriors.com
SIC: 2431 Doors, wood

(G-15916)
SIEMENS ENERGY INC
7000 Siemens Rd (27591-8309)
PHONE..................919 365-2200
Smith Macintosh, *Pr*
EMP: 166
SALES (corp-wide): 33.81B **Privately Held**
Web: new.siemens.com
SIC: 3621 Electric motor and generator parts
HQ: Siemens Energy, Inc.
4400 N Alafaya Trl
Orlando FL 32826
407 736-2000

(G-15917)
SIEMENS INDUSTRY INC
Engineered Products Division
7000 Siemens Rd (27591-8309)
PHONE..................919 365-2200
Terry Royer, *Brnch Mgr*
EMP: 106
SQ FT: 35,000
SALES (corp-wide): 84.48B **Privately Held**
Web: new.siemens.com
SIC: 3625 3566 Motor control centers; Speed changers, drives, and gears
HQ: Siemens Industry, Inc.
100 Technology Dr
Alpharetta GA 30005
847 215-1000

(G-15918)
SOUTHAG MFG INC
2023 Wendell Blvd (27591-6965)
PHONE..................919 365-5111
Bill Thornton, *Pr*
▲ **EMP:** 17 **EST:** 1985
SQ FT: 17,000
SALES (est): 763.33K **Privately Held**
SIC: 3792 5084 5083 Trailer coaches, automobile; Trailers, industrial; Lawn and garden machinery and equipment

(G-15919)
SPC MECHANICAL CORPORATION (PA)
Also Called: Spc Heating & Cooling
1500 Wendell Rd (27591-7374)
P.O. Box 3006 (27895-3006)
PHONE..................252 237-9035
S Christopher Williford, *Pr*
Peggy Williford, *
Larry Bissette, *
George Dail, *
Mark Williford, *
EMP: 235 **EST:** 1970
SALES (est): 117.47MM
SALES (corp-wide): 117.47MM **Privately Held**
Web: www.spcmechanical.com
SIC: 3494 1711 3444 Valves and pipe fittings, nec; Plumbing contractors; Sheet metalwork

(G-15920)
THIRD STREET SCREEN PRINT INC
115 E Third St (27591-9791)
PHONE..................919 365-2725
Eward Morrell, *Pr*
Kerry O'steen, *Sec*
EMP: 8 **EST:** 2014
SQ FT: 130,000
SALES (est): 420.94K **Privately Held**
Web: www.thirdstreetscreen.com
SIC: 2759 Screen printing

(G-15921)
TREE FROG INDUSTRIES LLC
246 Dogwood Trl (27591-9411)
PHONE..................919 986-2229
Michael Firstbrook, *Admn*
EMP: 5 **EST:** 2016
SALES (est): 70.75K **Privately Held**
SIC: 3999 Manufacturing industries, nec

(G-15922)
VENDELAY INDUSTRIES LLC
1941 Stagecoach Trl (27591-9871)
PHONE..................440 879-8363
Michael Bogomolny, *Prin*
EMP: 5 **EST:** 2015
SALES (est): 114.45K **Privately Held**
SIC: 3599 Industrial machinery, nec

(G-15923)
VISHAY MEASUREMENTS GROUP INC (HQ)
Also Called: Micro Measurements
951 Wendell Blvd (27591-9515)
P.O. Box 27777 (27611-7777)
PHONE..................919 365-3800
William M Clancy, *CEO*
Thomas P Kieffer, *Pr*
Steven Klausner, *Treas*
Jeffrey King, *Sec*
◆ **EMP:** 5 **EST:** 1962
SQ FT: 127,000
SALES (est): 43.42MM
SALES (corp-wide): 355.05MM **Publicly Held**
Web: www.micro-measurements.com
SIC: 3829 5065 Stress, strain, and flaw detecting/measuring equipment; Electronic parts and equipment, nec
PA: Vishay Precision Group, Inc.
3 Great Valley Pkwy # 150
Malvern PA 19355
484 321-5300

(G-15924)
VISHAY TRANSDUCERS LTD (HQ)
Also Called: Stress-Tek
951 Wendell Blvd (27591-9515)
PHONE..................919 365-3800
Ziv Shoshani, *CEO*
Keith Reichow, *
▲ **EMP:** 31 **EST:** 1978
SQ FT: 35,000
SALES (est): 4.88MM
SALES (corp-wide): 355.05MM **Publicly Held**
SIC: 3545 3679 3596 Scales, measuring (machinists' precision tools); Loads, electronic; Scales and balances, except laboratory
PA: Vishay Precision Group, Inc.
3 Great Valley Pkwy # 150
Malvern PA 19355
484 321-5300

(G-15925)
YATS STONE MASONRY LLC
7425 Buck Rd (27591-8227)
PHONE..................919 841-2297
Daniel Yat Pacheco, *Prin*
EMP: 5 **EST:** 2019
SALES (est): 89.11K **Privately Held**
SIC: 2024 Yogurt desserts, frozen

(G-15926)
YUKON INC
Also Called: Unique Concepts
485 Old Wilson Rd Ste 8 (27591-6302)
P.O. Box 56 (27591-0056)
PHONE..................919 366-2001
Fred Leach, *Pr*
David Curry, *VP*
Lynne Leach, *Treas*
Greg Taylor, *Stockholder*
EMP: 21 **EST:** 1994
SQ FT: 10,000
SALES (est): 1.65MM **Privately Held**
Web: www.uniqueconcepts.com
SIC: 2511 5712 Wood household furniture; Furniture stores

West End
Moore County

(G-15927)
J ALI CANDLES
172 Tanner Ln (27376-9177)
PHONE...............................910 603-2997
Jan Moss, *Prin*
EMP: 4 EST: 2018
SALES (est): 59.62K **Privately Held**
SIC: 3999 Candles

(G-15928)
JUBILEE SCREEN PRINTING INC
314 Grant St Ste F (27376-8388)
P.O. Box 485 (27376-0485)
PHONE...............................910 673-4240
EMP: 5 EST: 1991
SALES (est): 397.45K **Privately Held**
Web: www.jubileescreenprint.com
SIC: 7389 2759 Textile designers; Screen printing

(G-15929)
LONGLEAF TRUSS COMPANY
4476 Nc Highway 211 (27376-8382)
P.O. Box 225 (27376-0225)
PHONE...............................910 673-4711
Frederick L Taylor Ii, *VP*
Robert Gravely, *
Ann Gravely, *
EMP: 28 EST: 2000
SQ FT: 10,000
SALES (est): 3.97MM **Privately Held**
SIC: 2439 Trusses, wooden roof

(G-15930)
MILITARY PRODUCTS INC
Also Called: TAC Shield
5425 Nc Highway 211 (27376-9248)
P.O. Box 4613 (28374-4613)
PHONE...............................910 637-0315
David Nau, *CEO*
Barry Bond, *VP*
▲ **EMP:** 9 **EST:** 2010
SALES (est): 929.06K **Privately Held**
Web: www.tacshield.com
SIC: 2389 2387 2311 Men's miscellaneous accessories; Apparel belts; Military uniforms, men's and youths': purchased materials

(G-15931)
SANDHLLS FBRCTORS CRANE SVCS I
6536 7 Lakes Vlg (27376-9314)
PHONE...............................910 673-4573
Cliff Baldwin, *Pr*
EMP: 10 EST: 2005
SALES (est): 977.68K **Privately Held**
SIC: 3699 3599 Electrical equipment and supplies, nec; Machine shop, jobbing and repair

(G-15932)
SEVEN LAKES NEWS CORPORATION
Also Called: Carthage Gazette
2033 7 Lks S (27376-9609)
PHONE...............................910 685-0320
Victoria Levinger, *Prin*
Brandon Levinger, *Prin*
EMP: 4 EST: 2017
SALES (est): 231.32K **Privately Held**
Web: www.sevenlakesnews.com
SIC: 2711 Newspapers, publishing and printing

(G-15933)
SYLVESTER ARTSAN WOODWORKS LLC
751 7 Lks N (27376-9606)
PHONE...............................989 529-3573
Robert E Sylvester, *Owner*
EMP: 5 EST: 2017
SALES (est): 85.29K **Privately Held**
SIC: 2431 Millwork

(G-15934)
THOMPSON APPAREL INC
3061 7 Lks W (27376-9315)
PHONE...............................910 673-4560
Dolores B Thompson, *Pr*
EMP: 8 EST: 1996
SALES (est): 107.81K **Privately Held**
SIC: 2326 Men's and boy's work clothing

(G-15935)
WILSON MACHINE SHO
333 Hoffman Rd (27376-9025)
P.O. Box 685 (27376-0685)
PHONE...............................910 673-3505
EMP: 5 EST: 2013
SALES (est): 139.48K **Privately Held**
SIC: 3599 Machine shop, jobbing and repair

West Jefferson
Ashe County

(G-15936)
CAROLINA TIMBERWORKS LLC
210 Industrial Park Way (28694-7641)
PHONE...............................828 266-9663
Craig Kitson, *Prin*
EMP: 12 EST: 2003
SALES (est): 959.67K **Privately Held**
Web: www.carolinatimberworks.com
SIC: 8712 2421 Architectural services; Sawmills and planing mills, general

(G-15937)
COBBLE CREEK LUMBER LLC
225 Hice Ave (28694-7059)
P.O. Box 1848 (28694-1848)
PHONE...............................336 844-2620
EMP: 11 EST: 2017
SALES (est): 4.75MM **Privately Held**
Web: www.cobblecreeklumber.com
SIC: 2421 Sawmills and planing mills, general

(G-15938)
CREATIVE PRINTERS INC
4 N 6th Ave (28694-9522)
P.O. Box 53 (28694-0053)
PHONE...............................336 246-7746
EMP: 5 EST: 1993
SQ FT: 1,600
SALES (est): 486.81K **Privately Held**
Web: www.cpiprintgroup.com
SIC: 2752 2759 7389 Offset printing; Screen printing; Sign painting and lettering shop

(G-15939)
DR PPPER BTLG W JFFRSON NC IN
Also Called: Dr Pepper
109 W 3rd St (28694-9157)
P.O. Box 34 (28694-0034)
PHONE...............................336 846-2433
Michael Vannoy, *VP*
EMP: 42
SALES (corp-wide): 10MM **Privately Held**
Web: www.drpepper.com
SIC: 2086 Soft drinks: packaged in cans, bottles, etc.
PA: Dr. Pepper Bottling Company Of West Jefferson, North Carolina, Incorporated
2614 Nc Highway 163
West Jefferson NC
336 246-4591

(G-15940)
GLOBAL MANUFACTURING SVCS INC
Also Called: Global
140 Industrial Park Way (28694-7525)
PHONE...............................336 846-1674
Arlie Keith, *CEO*
Henry Doss, *Pr*
Lynna Greer, *CFO*
Andria Morgan, *VP*
EMP: 35 EST: 2002
SQ FT: 20,000
SALES (est): 5.3MM **Privately Held**
Web: www.gmsww.com
SIC: 3672 3675 Wiring boards; Electronic capacitors

(G-15941)
K & K STITCH & SCREEN
240 Helen Blevins Rd Unit 1 (28694-8465)
PHONE...............................336 246-5477
Kevin Hardy, *Owner*
EMP: 5 EST: 2003
SALES (est): 229.73K **Privately Held**
Web: www.explorations-unlimited.com
SIC: 2759 Screen printing

(G-15942)
LEVITON MANUFACTURING CO INC
618 S Jefferson Ave (28694-9739)
PHONE...............................336 846-3246
Van Shatley, *Mgr*
EMP: 5
SALES (corp-wide): 1.46B **Privately Held**
Web: www.leviton.com
SIC: 3643 3674 Plugs, electric; Diodes, solid state (germanium, silicon, etc.)
PA: Leviton Manufacturing Co., Inc.
201 N Service Rd
Melville NY 11747
800 323-8920

(G-15943)
LEVITON TOWN PLANT
618 S Jefferson Ave (28694-9739)
PHONE...............................336 846-3246
EMP: 6 EST: 2002
SALES (est): 218.83K **Privately Held**
SIC: 3643 Current-carrying wiring services

(G-15944)
MENDOZAS POWDER COATING LLC
189 Von Turner Rd (28694-7187)
PHONE...............................336 877-0783
EMP: 4 EST: 2021
SALES (est): 70.03K **Privately Held**
Web: mendozas-powder-coating.business.site
SIC: 3479 Coating of metals and formed products

(G-15945)
MOUNTAIN TIMES INC
Also Called: Sundown Times
7 W Main St (28694)
PHONE...............................336 246-6397
EMP: 4 EST: 1993
SALES (est): 220.88K **Privately Held**
Web: www.ashepostandtimes.com
SIC: 2711 Newspapers, publishing and printing

(G-15946)
MOUNTAIN TOP WOODWORKING
816 Old Obids Rd (28694-8204)
PHONE...............................336 982-4059
Alvin Day, *Owner*
EMP: 4 EST: 2005
SALES (est): 206.21K **Privately Held**
Web: www.mountaintopwoodworkingshop.com
SIC: 2431 Millwork

(G-15947)
PATRICK
348 Old Buffalo Rd (28694-8166)
PHONE...............................336 846-4759
Kenneth D Patrick, *Prin*
EMP: 5 EST: 2011
SALES (est): 143.96K **Privately Held**
SIC: 3531 Backhoes

(G-15948)
SCREEN SPECIALTY SHOP INC
8406 Nc Highway 163 (28694-8128)
PHONE...............................336 982-4135
Gary C Prange, *Pr*
Debra Lynn Prange, *VP*
EMP: 8 EST: 1990
SALES (est): 363.09K **Privately Held**
Web: www.sssink.com
SIC: 2759 Screen printing

(G-15949)
TOP DAWG LANDSCAPE INC
605 S Jefferson Ave # 1 (28694)
P.O. Box 326 (28694-0326)
PHONE...............................336 877-7519
Robert Hodges, *Pr*
EMP: 4 EST: 2012
SALES (est): 456K **Privately Held**
Web: www.topdawgnc.com
SIC: 3271 3645 0782 Blocks, concrete: landscape or retaining wall; Garden, patio, walkway and yard lighting fixtures: electric; Lawn and garden services

Westfield
Surry County

(G-15950)
B & L CUSTOM CABINETS INC
7165 Nc 89 Hwy W (27053-8324)
PHONE...............................704 857-1940
Brandon Black, *Pr*
EMP: 12 EST: 1987
SALES (est): 479.73K **Privately Held**
Web: www.becustomcabinets.com
SIC: 2541 2511 2434 1799 Bar fixtures, wood ; Bookcases, household: wood; Vanities, bathroom: wood; Kitchen cabinet installation

(G-15951)
CHARLOTTE SHUTTER AND SHADES
1825 Pell Rd (27053-7555)
PHONE...............................336 351-3391
Richard Pell, *Prin*
EMP: 5 EST: 2016
SALES (est): 78.13K **Privately Held**
SIC: 3442 Shutters, door or window: metal

(G-15952)
JPS ELSTMERICS WESTFIELD PLANT
1535 Elastic Plant Rd (27053-8242)
PHONE...............................336 351-0938
Marvin Conner, *Pr*
EMP: 6 EST: 2011
SALES (est): 64.55K **Privately Held**

SIC: 2211 Broadwoven fabric mills, cotton

Whispering Pines
Moore County

(G-15953)
CHRISTINE N HONEYWELL PT
76 Pine Lake Dr (28327-9373)
PHONE...................802 496-6509
Christine N Honeywell, *Prin*
EMP: 5 **EST:** 2011
SALES (est): 97.13K **Privately Held**
SIC: 3724 Aircraft engines and engine parts

(G-15954)
FRAMERS COTTAGE
58 Pine Ridge Dr (28327-9476)
PHONE...................910 638-0100
EMP: 4 **EST:** 2017
SALES (est): 67.43K **Privately Held**
SIC: 2711 Newspapers, publishing and printing

(G-15955)
PINE STATE WELDING
3 New Day Way (28327-6090)
PHONE...................910 639-3631
Chris Kelso, *Prin*
EMP: 5 **EST:** 2017
SALES (est): 121.72K **Privately Held**
SIC: 7692 Welding repair

Whitakers
Nash County

(G-15956)
CONSOLIDATED DIESEL INC
9377 N Us Highway 301 (27891-8621)
P.O. Box 670 (27891-0670)
PHONE...................252 437-6611
◆ **EMP:** 1400 **EST:** 1980
SALES (est): 101.25MM
SALES (corp-wide): 34.06B **Publicly Held**
SIC: 3519 Engines, diesel and semi-diesel or dual-fuel
PA: Cummins Inc.
500 Jackson St
Columbus IN 47201
812 377-5000

(G-15957)
TIPPETT LOGGING LLC
208 Marks St (27891-0016)
PHONE...................252 301-3170
Tim Tippett, *Owner*
EMP: 5 **EST:** 2020
SALES (est): 163.21K **Privately Held**
SIC: 2411 Logging camps and contractors

White Oak
Bladen County

(G-15958)
WOOD LOGGING
361 Gum Spring Rd (28399-9407)
P.O. Box 143 (28399-0143)
PHONE...................910 866-4018
Mickey Wood, *Owner*
EMP: 7 **EST:** 1992
SALES (est): 738.46K **Privately Held**
SIC: 2411 Logging camps and contractors

Whiteville
Columbus County

(G-15959)
BALDWIN SIGN & AWNING
2 Whiteville Mini Mall (28472-2105)
PHONE...................910 642-8812
Eric Baldwin, *Owner*
EMP: 4 **EST:** 2005
SALES (est): 236.16K **Privately Held**
Web: www.baldwinsigns.net
SIC: 3993 Signs and advertising specialties

(G-15960)
BUDGET PRINTING CO
1424 S Jk Powell Blvd Ste B (28472-9145)
P.O. Box 1175 (28472-1175)
PHONE...................910 642-7306
Lynn Packer, *Pr*
Jimmy Packer, *VP*
EMP: 4 **EST:** 1980
SALES (est): 313.86K **Privately Held**
SIC: 2752 Offset printing

(G-15961)
CAROLINA RETREAD LLC
30 Bitmore Rd (28472-4928)
P.O. Box 919 (28472-0919)
PHONE...................910 642-4123
Ricky Benton, *Pr*
EMP: 10 **EST:** 2010
SALES (est): 298.45K **Privately Held**
SIC: 7534 Rebuilding and retreading tires

(G-15962)
DONUT SHOP
1602 S Madison St (28472-4947)
PHONE...................910 640-3317
Mary Harrelson, *Pt*
Elizabeth Kasitati, *Pt*
EMP: 8 **EST:** 1995
SALES (est): 506.47K **Privately Held**
Web: www.donutshopdiner.com
SIC: 2051 5812 Doughnuts, except frozen; Eating places

(G-15963)
GEORGIA-PACIFIC LLC
Also Called: Plywood Plant
1980 Georgia Pacific Rd (28472-3026)
PHONE...................910 642-5041
Norman Haris, *Brnch Mgr*
EMP: 45
SALES (corp-wide): 36.93B **Privately Held**
Web: www.gp.com
SIC: 2435 Plywood, hardwood or hardwood faced
HQ: Georgia-Pacific Llc
133 Peachtree St Nw
Atlanta GA 30303
404 652-4000

(G-15964)
GORE S TRLR MANUFACTURER S INC
305 Gores Trailer Rd (28472-7541)
PHONE...................910 642-2246
Daniel Jackson Gore, *Pr*
Janice Gore, *VP*
EMP: 14 **EST:** 1972
SQ FT: 49,019
SALES (est): 2.34MM **Privately Held**
Web: www.goretrailers.com
SIC: 5599 3799 Utility trailers; Horse trailers, except fifth-wheel type

(G-15965)
H CLYDE MOORE JR
Also Called: Clyde Moore Logging
790 Honey Field Rd (28472-7952)
PHONE...................910 642-3507
H Clyde Moore Junior, *Owner*
EMP: 5 **EST:** 1983
SALES (est): 99.77K **Privately Held**
SIC: 2411 Logging camps and contractors

(G-15966)
HIGHCORP INCORPORATED
Also Called: News Reporter
127 W Columbus St (28472-4023)
P.O. Box 707 (28472-0707)
PHONE...................910 642-4104
James C High, *Pr*
Stuart High Nance, *
Leslie T High, *
EMP: 50 **EST:** 1896
SQ FT: 20,000
SALES (est): 2.09MM **Privately Held**
Web: www.nrcolumbus.com
SIC: 2711 Newspapers, publishing and printing

(G-15967)
J L POWELL & CO INC (PA)
Also Called: Cinema III Theaters
135 E Main St (28472-4131)
PHONE...................910 642-8989
Jesse C Fisher Junior, *Pr*
EMP: 8 **EST:** 1876
SALES (est): 1.01MM
SALES (corp-wide): 1.01MM **Privately Held**
Web: www.7-eleven.com
SIC: 6512 6513 2426 5411 Commercial and industrial building operation; Apartment building operators; Flooring, hardwood; Convenience stores

(G-15968)
JACKIE LEWIS PHOTOGRAPHY AKA
2458 Union Valley Rd (28472-5473)
PHONE...................910 640-1550
Jackie Lewis, *Owner*
EMP: 5 **EST:** 2016
SALES (est): 65.16K **Privately Held**
SIC: 2741 Miscellaneous publishing

(G-15969)
JACKS MOTOR PARTS INC
Hwy 701 (28472)
P.O. Box 338 (28472-0338)
PHONE...................910 642-4077
Yvonne Ellis, *Pr*
Keith Ellis, *VP*
EMP: 5 **EST:** 1963
SQ FT: 1,800
SALES (est): 470.48K **Privately Held**
SIC: 7538 3599 Engine repair, except diesel: automotive; Machine shop, jobbing and repair

(G-15970)
MAXPRO MANUFACTURING LLC
31 Industrial Blvd (28472-3867)
P.O. Box 567 (28472-0567)
PHONE...................910 640-5505
Joe Cobbe, *Pr*
Ron Foley, *Sr VP*
Elizabeth Dillon, *Marketing*
Mike Newman, *VP Mfg*
Renee Mullins, *International Sales Vice President*
EMP: 11 **EST:** 2012
SALES (est): 1.03MM **Privately Held**
Web: www.maxprofilms.com
SIC: 3578 Accounting machines and cash registers

(G-15971)
METAL ARC
5547 James B White Hwy S (28472-6515)
PHONE...................910 770-1180
EMP: 4 **EST:** 2018
SALES (est): 77.33K **Privately Held**
Web: metal-arc.business.site
SIC: 7692 Welding repair

(G-15972)
NATIONAL SPINNING CO INC
Hwy 130 240 Spinning Rd (28472)
P.O. Box 547 (28472-0547)
PHONE...................910 642-4181
Rick Barton, *Brnch Mgr*
EMP: 101
SALES (corp-wide): 102.19MM **Privately Held**
Web: www.natspin.com
SIC: 2281 Knitting yarn, spun
PA: National Spinning Co., Inc.
1481 W 2nd St Ste 103
Washington NC 27889
252 975-7111

(G-15973)
NICE BLENDS CORP
222 Industrial Blvd (28472-5417)
PHONE...................910 640-1000
Barrie Nadi, *Pr*
EMP: 54 **EST:** 1993
SQ FT: 24,000
SALES (est): 3.86MM **Privately Held**
Web: www.niceblends.com
SIC: 2099 2037 Spices, including grinding; Frozen fruits and vegetables

(G-15974)
NORTH CAROLINA PLYWOOD LLC
512 E Main St (28472-4309)
P.O. Box 458 (32331-0458)
PHONE...................850 948-2211
John Maultsby, *Managing Member*
John P Maultsby, *Managing Member*
EMP: 8 **EST:** 2013
SQ FT: 100,000
SALES (est): 982.89K **Privately Held**
Web: www.ncplywood.com
SIC: 2435 Plywood, hardwood or hardwood faced

(G-15975)
PRIDGEN WOODWORK INC
910 Jefferson St (28472-3701)
PHONE...................910 642-7175
Linnwood Pridgen, *VP*
A Rudolph Pridgen, *
EMP: 31 **EST:** 1947
SQ FT: 50,200
SALES (est): 2.96MM **Privately Held**
Web: www.pridgenwoodwork.com
SIC: 2431 2521 Doors and door parts and trim, wood; Cabinets, office: wood

(G-15976)
SHODJA TEXTILES INC
Also Called: Whiteville Fabrick
68 Industrial Dr (28472-4545)
P.O. Box 3 (28472-0003)
PHONE...................910 914-0456
Mohammad Shodja, *Pr*
Cameron Shodja, *VP*
EMP: 9 **EST:** 1972
SALES (est): 483.54K **Privately Held**
SIC: 2258 Lace and warp knit fabric mills

(G-15977)
WHITEVILLE AG
3654 James B White Hwy S (28472-8684)
PHONE...................910 914-0007

Whiteville - Columbus County (G-15978)

Timothy J Rausch Senior, *Prin*
EMP: 6 EST: 2012
SALES (est): 94.24K **Privately Held**
Web: www.whitevillenc.gov
SIC: 2711 Newspapers

(G-15978)
WHITEVILLE FABRICS LLC (PA)
68 Industrial Dr (28472-4545)
P.O. Box 3 (28472-0003)
PHONE..................910 914-0456
Cameron Shodja, *Managing Member*
▲ EMP: 17 EST: 2000
SALES (est): 2.94MM **Privately Held**
SIC: 2258 Warp and flat knit products

(G-15979)
WHITEVILLE FABRICS LLC
68 Industrial Blvd (28472-3867)
PHONE..................910 639-4444
Cameron Shodja, *Mgr*
EMP: 18
SIC: 2258 Warp and flat knit products
PA: Whiteville Fabrics, L.L.C.
  68 Industrial Dr
  Whiteville NC 28472

(G-15980)
WHITEVILLE FORKLIFT & EQP
Also Called: Whiteville Rentals
344 Vinson Blvd (28472-4999)
PHONE..................910 642-6642
EMP: 6 EST: 1991
SQ FT: 2,000
SALES (est): 826.45K **Privately Held**
Web: www.whitevillerentals.com
SIC: 3537 7699 Forklift trucks; Industrial truck repair

(G-15981)
WHITEVILLE PLYWOOD INC
500 E Main St (28472-4309)
P.O. Box 722 (28472-0722)
PHONE..................910 642-7114
EMP: 10 EST: 1958
SALES (est): 313.68K **Privately Held**
Web: www.ncplywood.com
SIC: 3089 2435 Panels, building: plastics, nec; Plywood, hardwood or hardwood faced

Whitsett
Guilford County

(G-15982)
ASCENDING IRON LLC
6504 Burlington Rd (27377-9200)
PHONE..................336 266-6462
EMP: 18 EST: 2019
SALES (est): 514.41K **Privately Held**
SIC: 3441 Fabricated structural metal

(G-15983)
BARNHARDTS WOODWORKING CO
1576 Nc Highway 61 (27377-9111)
PHONE..................336 449-5564
Harold J Barnhardt, *Prin*
EMP: 6 EST: 2010
SALES (est): 98.82K **Privately Held**
SIC: 2431 Millwork

(G-15984)
BOXMOOR TRUCK BEDLINERS & ACC
1900 Buckminster Dr (27377-9331)
PHONE..................336 447-4621
EMP: 7 EST: 2011
SALES (est): 293.7K **Privately Held**
SIC: 3714 Pickup truck bed liners

(G-15985)
CAROLINA BIOLOGICAL SUPPLY CO
6537 Judge Adams Rd (27377-9718)
PHONE..................336 446-7600
Ronald Simpson, *Mgr*
EMP: 150
SQ FT: 214,253
SALES (corp-wide): 82.68MM **Privately Held**
Web: www.carolina.com
SIC: 2836 5049 Biological products, except diagnostic; Laboratory equipment, except medical or dental
PA: Carolina Biological Supply Company
  2700 York Rd
  Burlington NC 27215
  336 584-0381

(G-15986)
CLAPP FERTILIZER AND TRCKG INC
2225 Herron Rd (27377-9801)
PHONE..................336 449-6103
Wendell G Clapp, *CEO*
EMP: 8 EST: 1948
SQ FT: 11,520
SALES (est): 2.11MM **Privately Held**
Web: www.kzootms.com
SIC: 5191 2873 5153 Fertilizer and fertilizer materials; Nitrogenous fertilizers; Grains

(G-15987)
CROSS TECHNOLOGIES INC
Cross Precision Measurement
6541c Franz Warner Pkwy (27377-9215)
PHONE..................336 292-0511
Dave Thornhill, *Brnch Mgr*
EMP: 60
SALES (corp-wide): 50MM **Privately Held**
Web: www.crossco.com
SIC: 5084 3492 Industrial machinery and equipment; Fluid power valves and hose fittings
HQ: Cross Technologies, Inc.
  4400 Piedmont Pkwy
  Greensboro NC 27410
  800 327-7727

(G-15988)
DREW ROBERTS LLC
Also Called: Can-Do Handyman Services
6627 Barton Creek Dr (27377-9277)
PHONE..................336 497-1679
EMP: 7 EST: 2013
SALES (est): 579.85K **Privately Held**
Web: www.newnusedoutlet.com
SIC: 8741 3955 5734 5731 Management services; Print cartridges for laser and other computer printers; Modems, monitors, terminals, and disk drives. computers; Consumer electronic equipment, nec

(G-15989)
ENGINEERED CONTROLS INTL LLC
Also Called: Ecii
1239 Rock Creek Dairy Rd (27377-9116)
PHONE..................336 449-7706
EMP: 200
SALES (corp-wide): 8.44B **Publicly Held**
Web: www.regoproducts.com
SIC: 3491 3494 Industrial valves; Valves and pipe fittings, nec
HQ: Engineered Controls International, Llc
  100 Rego Dr
  Elon NC 27244

(G-15990)
FOCKE & CO INC
5730 Millstream Rd (27377-9789)
PHONE..................336 449-7200
Juergen Focke, *Pr*
Johann Betschart, *

▲ EMP: 68 EST: 1989
SQ FT: 100,000
SALES (est): 17.6MM
SALES (corp-wide): 407.93MM **Privately Held**
Web: www.focke.com
SIC: 3565 Packaging machinery
PA: Focke & Co. (Gmbh & Co. Kg)
  Siemensstr. 10
  Verden (Aller) NI 27283
  42318910

(G-15991)
GALVANIZING CONSULTANTS INC
687 Winners Pt (27377-8720)
PHONE..................336 603-4218
John F Malone, *Pr*
Leana Malone, *VP*
Donald Wetzel, *Ex VP*
EMP: 5 EST: 1986
SALES (est): 365.14K **Privately Held**
Web: www.galvanizingconsulting.com
SIC: 3479 Coating of metals and formed products

(G-15992)
HARRELL PROPER TRANSPORT LLC
205 Boling Springs Ct (27377-9828)
PHONE..................336 202-7135
EMP: 6 EST: 2020
SALES (est): 486.21K **Privately Held**
SIC: 3537 Trucks: freight, baggage, etc.: industrial, except mining

(G-15993)
ICA MID-ATLANTIC INC
Also Called: Integrted Cble Assmbly Hldings
6532 Judge Adams Rd (27377-9835)
PHONE..................336 447-4546
Jim Laird, *Mgr*
Jim Laird, *VP*
Mehdi Ali Junior, *Mgr*
Jesus Maldonado, *
▲ EMP: 125 EST: 2002
SQ FT: 70,000
SALES (est): 25.33MM
SALES (corp-wide): 12.55B **Publicly Held**
Web: www.icaholdings.com
SIC: 3496 Miscellaneous fabricated wire products
HQ: Integrated Cable Assembly Holdings, Inc.
  6401 S Country Club Rd # 101
  Tucson AZ 85706
  520 290-9987

(G-15994)
J & W SERVICE INCORPORATED
7471 Danford Rd (27377)
P.O. Box 194 (27377-0194)
PHONE..................336 449-4584
Jerry L Small, *Pr*
Wanda Small, *VP*
EMP: 6 EST: 1984
SALES (est): 468.44K **Privately Held**
Web: www.jandwservice.com
SIC: 7699 1711 1521 8711 Mobile home repair; Heating systems repair and maintenance; Mobile home repair, on site; Heating and ventilation engineering

(G-15995)
LINDE GAS & EQUIPMENT INC
Also Called: Linde Gas North America
1304 Roosevelt Ct (27377-9121)
PHONE..................866 543-3427
Timothy Allen, *Brnch Mgr*
EMP: 14
Web: www.lindedirect.com
SIC: 2813 Nitrogen
HQ: Linde Gas & Equipment Inc.

10 Riverview Dr
Danbury CT 06810
844 445-4633

(G-15996)
MACHINE SPECIALTIES LLC
6511 Franz Warner Pkwy (27377-9215)
PHONE..................336 603-1919
Robert Simmons, *CEO*
Brent Allen, *
EMP: 160 EST: 1969
SQ FT: 150,000
SALES (est): 47.96MM
SALES (corp-wide): 47.96MM **Privately Held**
Web: www.machspec.com
SIC: 3599 Machine shop, jobbing and repair
PA: Calvert Street Capital Partners, Inc.
  2330 W Joppa Rd Ste 320
  Lutherville Timonium MD 21093
  443 573-3700

(G-15997)
MARK/TRECE INC
6799 Leaf Crest Dr Apt 2c (27377-8740)
PHONE..................336 292-3424
Bob Bauses, *Genl Mgr*
EMP: 20
SALES (corp-wide): 24.32MM **Privately Held**
Web: www.marktrece.com
SIC: 3555 7336 2796 Printing plates; Graphic arts and related design; Platemaking services
PA: Mark/Trece, Inc.
  2001 Stockton Rd
  Joppa MD 21085
  410 879-0060

(G-15998)
PAPERWORKS INDUSTRIES INC
6530 Franz Warner Pkwy (27377-9215)
PHONE..................336 447-7278
EMP: 112
Web: www.onepaperworks.com
SIC: 2653 Boxes, corrugated: made from purchased materials
PA: Paperworks Industries, Inc.
  1300 Virginia Dr Ste 220
  Fort Washington PA 19034

(G-15999)
PREPAC MANUFACTURING US LLC
3031 Hendren Rd (27377-9144)
PHONE..................800 665-1266
Michelle Mackinnon, *VP*
EMP: 15 EST: 2020
SALES (est): 8.26MM
SALES (corp-wide): 13.89MM **Privately Held**
SIC: 5021 2511 Furniture; Unassembled or unfinished furniture, household: wood
PA: Prepac Manufacturing Ltd.
  6705 Dennett Pl
  Delta BC V4G 1
  604 940-2300

(G-16000)
QUALICAPS INC (DH)
6505 Franz Warner Pkwy (27377-9215)
PHONE..................336 449-3900
Yogi Date, *Pr*
Paul J Verchick, *
◆ EMP: 175 EST: 1992
SQ FT: 94,000
SALES (est): 42.05MM
SALES (corp-wide): 3.03B **Privately Held**
Web: www.qualicaps.com
SIC: 2834 Pharmaceutical preparations
HQ: Qualicaps Co., Ltd.
  321-5, Ikezawacho

Yamatokoriyama NAR 639-1

(G-16001)
ROTRON INCORPORATED
Also Called: Ametek Rtron Technical Mtr Div
1210 Nc Highway 61 (27377-9114)
PHONE.................................336 449-3400
Jim Liddle, *Genl Mgr*
EMP: 120
SQ FT: 104,467
SALES (corp-wide): 6.6B **Publicly Held**
Web: www.rotron.com
SIC: 3564 5063 3621 Blowers and fans; Electrical apparatus and equipment; Motors and generators
HQ: Rotron Incorporated
55 Hasbrouck Ln
Woodstock NY 12498
845 679-2401

(G-16002)
SOUTHLAND LOG HOMES INC
5692 Millstream Rd (27377-9724)
PHONE.................................336 449-5388
Stacey Steelman, *Mgr*
EMP: 6
SQ FT: 4,173
SALES (corp-wide): 23.66MM **Privately Held**
Web: www.southlandloghomes.com
SIC: 2452 Log cabins, prefabricated, wood
PA: Southland Log Homes, Inc.
7521 Broad River Rd
Irmo SC 29063
803 781-5100

(G-16003)
THOMAS FERGUS
600 Walnut Crossing Dr (27377-9308)
PHONE.................................336 447-4289
Thomas Fergus, *Prin*
EMP: 5 **EST:** 2008
SALES (est): 87.56K **Privately Held**
SIC: 7372 Prepackaged software

(G-16004)
TRUSSWAY MANUFACTURING INC
Also Called: Trussway
940 Golf House Rd W Ste 201 (27377-9299)
PHONE.................................336 883-6966
Greg Ausderher, *Mgr*
EMP: 19
SALES (corp-wide): 17.1B **Publicly Held**
Web: www.bldr.com
SIC: 2439 Trusses, wooden roof
HQ: Trussway Manufacturing, Llc
9411 Alcorn St
Houston TX 77093

(G-16005)
ZINK HOLDINGS LLC
6900 Konica Dr (27377-9787)
PHONE.................................336 449-8000
Rick Lewis, *Brnch Mgr*
EMP: 85
SALES (corp-wide): 22.6MM **Privately Held**
Web: www.zink.com
SIC: 3861 Photographic equipment and supplies
PA: Zink Holdings Llc
114 Tived Ln E
Edison NJ 08837
781 761-5400

(G-16006)
ZINK IMAGING INC
Also Called: Zink
6900 Konica Dr (27377-9787)
PHONE.................................336 449-8000
Mary Jeffries, *CEO*
Paul Baker, *
Stephen R Herchen, *
Gary Lortie, *
Scott Wicker, *
EMP: 49 **EST:** 2005
SALES (est): 10.72MM
SALES (corp-wide): 22.6MM **Privately Held**
SIC: 3861 Photographic equipment and supplies
PA: Zink Holdings Llc
114 Tived Ln E
Edison NJ 08837
781 761-5400

Whittier
Jackson County

(G-16007)
JAMES KEITH NATIONS
Also Called: Keith Nations Log Company
69 Thomas Valley Rd (28789-9198)
PHONE.................................828 421-5391
James Keith Nations, *Prin*
EMP: 8 **EST:** 2012
SALES (est): 345.37K **Privately Held**
SIC: 2411 Logging

(G-16008)
KITUWAH INDUSTRIES LLC
1158 Seven Clans Ln (28789-0749)
PHONE.................................828 477-4616
Terry Mogensen, *Prin*
Jessica Myers, *Prin*
EMP: 6 **EST:** 2021
SALES (est): 99.8K **Privately Held**
Web: www.kituwahbuilders.com
SIC: 3999 Manufacturing industries, nec

(G-16009)
NEW ENGLAND WOOD WORKS
152 Four Wheel Dr (28789-8057)
PHONE.................................706 491-5885
Charles Coleman, *Prin*
EMP: 4 **EST:** 2017
SALES (est): 65.8K **Privately Held**
SIC: 2431 Millwork

(G-16010)
PEPSI-COLA BTLG HICKRY NC INC
Also Called: Pepsi-Cola
1060 Gateway Rd (28789-7640)
P.O. Box 1545 (28789-1545)
PHONE.................................828 497-1235
Teresa Leatherwood, *Off Mgr*
EMP: 20
SALES (corp-wide): 50.09MM **Privately Held**
Web: www.pepsihky.com
SIC: 2086 Bottled and canned soft drinks
PA: Pepsi-Cola Bottling Company Of Hickory, N.C., Inc.
2401 14th Avenue Cir Nw
Hickory NC 28601
828 322-8090

Wilkesboro
Wilkes County

(G-16011)
A D SERVICES
402 S Cherry St (28697-2823)
PHONE.................................336 667-8190
EMP: 5 **EST:** 2018
SALES (est): 80.05K **Privately Held**
SIC: 2711 Newspapers: publishing only, not printed on site

(G-16012)
ACTION INSTALLS LLC
1202 Industrial Park Rd (28697-8490)
PHONE.................................704 787-3828
Michael Kerhoulas, *Prin*
EMP: 6 **EST:** 2013
SALES (est): 186.72K **Privately Held**
Web: www.actionsign.com
SIC: 3993 Signs and advertising specialties

(G-16013)
APPALACHIAN LUMBER COMPANY INC (PA)
Also Called: Appalachian Lumber
5879 W Us Highway 421 (28697-7905)
PHONE.................................336 973-7205
William B Church Junior, *Pr*
Robin Church, *
▲ **EMP:** 32 **EST:** 1988
SQ FT: 64,000
SALES (est): 6.11MM
SALES (corp-wide): 6.11MM **Privately Held**
Web: www.appalachianlumber.net
SIC: 2431 2426 Panel work, wood; Furniture stock and parts, hardwood

(G-16014)
BEST IMAGE SIGNS LLC
Also Called: Best Image Signs and Graphics
178 Nicholas Landing Dr (28697-7169)
P.O. Box 296 (28651-0296)
PHONE.................................336 973-7445
EMP: 5 **EST:** 2005
SALES (est): 373.19K **Privately Held**
Web: www.bestimagesigns.com
SIC: 3993 Signs, not made in custom sign painting shops

(G-16015)
CALL FAMILY DISTILLERS LLC
1611 Industrial Dr (28697-7344)
PHONE.................................336 990-0708
EMP: 6 **EST:** 2015
SALES (est): 242.27K **Privately Held**
Web: www.callfamilydistillers.com
SIC: 2085 Distilled and blended liquors

(G-16016)
CHURCH & CHURCH LUMBER LLC
Brown Ford Rd (28697)
PHONE.................................336 973-4297
Mark Church, *Mgr*
EMP: 53
SALES (corp-wide): 15.41MM **Privately Held**
Web: www.churchandchurchlumber.com
SIC: 5031 2426 Lumber, plywood, and millwork; Hardwood dimension and flooring mills
PA: Church & Church Lumber, Llc
863 New Browns Ford Rd
Wilkesboro NC 28697
336 973-5700

(G-16017)
CHURCH & CHURCH LUMBER LLC (PA)
863 New Browns Ford Rd (28697-7365)
P.O. Box 619 (28651-0619)
PHONE.................................336 973-5700
Bruce Church, *
Ken Church, *
Cindy Holcombe, *
EMP: 90 **EST:** 1979
SALES (est): 15.41MM
SALES (corp-wide): 15.41MM **Privately Held**
Web: www.churchandchurchlumber.com

SIC: 2426 2421 Dimension, hardwood; Sawmills and planing mills, general

(G-16018)
CJ PARTNERS LLC
1702 W Us Highway 421 P (28697-2377)
PHONE.................................336 838-3080
C James, *Dir*
EMP: 8 **EST:** 2007
SALES (est): 122.95K **Privately Held**
SIC: 3721 Aircraft

(G-16019)
DYER PUBLISHING LLC
872 S Recreation Rd (28697-9152)
PHONE.................................336 452-2275
James Dyer, *Prin*
EMP: 5 **EST:** 2016
SALES (est): 45.48K **Privately Held**
SIC: 2741 Miscellaneous publishing

(G-16020)
EXTERIOR VINYL WHOLESALE
1808 Industrial Dr (28697-7346)
PHONE.................................336 838-7772
Patty Wells, *Pt*
James Brennan, *Pt*
Philip Brennan, *Pt*
Sergio Pezzotti, *Pt*
EMP: 5 **EST:** 1990
SQ FT: 11,000
SALES (est): 605.56K **Privately Held**
Web: www.exteriorvinyl.com
SIC: 3292 3441 Tile, vinyl asbestos; Fabricated structural metal

(G-16021)
FIRST PRRITY EMRGNCY VHCLES IN
1208 School St (28697-2625)
PHONE.................................908 645-0788
EMP: 27
SALES (corp-wide): 14.69MM **Privately Held**
Web: www.1fpg.com
SIC: 3711 Ambulances (motor vehicles), assembly of
HQ: First Priority Emergency Vehicles, Inc.
2444 Ridgeway Blvd # 500
Manchester NJ 08759
973 347-4321

(G-16022)
FLOWERS BAKING CO NEWTON LLC
802 N Moravian St (28697-2338)
PHONE.................................336 903-1345
John Johnston, *Mgr*
EMP: 9
SALES (corp-wide): 5.09B **Publicly Held**
SIC: 2051 Bread, cake, and related products
HQ: Flowers Baking Co. Of Newton, Llc
801 W Main St
Jamestown NC 27282
336 841-8840

(G-16023)
HAYES PRINT-STAMP CO INC
1150 Foster St (28697-8432)
PHONE.................................336 667-1116
David Eller, *Pr*
Teresa H Bowman, *Sec*
EMP: 6 **EST:** 1968
SQ FT: 6,000
SALES (est): 488.69K **Privately Held**
Web: www.hayesprint.net
SIC: 2752 3953 Offset printing; Time stamps, hand: rubber or metal

Wilkesboro - Wilkes County (G-16024)

(G-16024)
HERBAL INNOVATIONS LLC
Also Called: Herbal Ingenuity
151 Herbal Ingenuity Way (28697-8868)
PHONE.............................336 818-2332
Rich Ahren, *
Daniel Dickers, *
◆ **EMP:** 30 **EST:** 2015
SALES (est): 3.02MM **Privately Held**
Web: www.herbalingenuity.com
SIC: 5191 5499 1541 2099 Herbicides; Spices and herbs; Food products manufacturing or packing plant construction; Almond pastes

(G-16025)
INDUSTRIAL PRCESS SLUTIONS INC
915 Germantown Rd (28697-8843)
P.O. Box 1391 (28659-1391)
PHONE.............................336 926-1511
Sherman Aaron, *CEO*
Sherman Aaron, *Pr*
Theresa Aaron, *CFO*
▲ **EMP:** 4 **EST:** 2003
SALES (est): 326.85K **Privately Held**
Web: www.industrialprocesssolutionsinc.com
SIC: 3567 3398 Industrial furnaces and ovens; Metal heat treating

(G-16026)
INTERCONNECT PRODUCTS AND SERVICES INC (PA)
1206 Industrial Park Rd (28697-8490)
P.O. Box 55 (28697-0055)
PHONE.............................336 667-3356
EMP: 23 **EST:** 1982
SALES (est): 5.04MM
SALES (corp-wide): 5.04MM **Privately Held**
Web: www.interconnect-inc.com
SIC: 3679 4813 5045 5065 Harness assemblies, for electronic use: wire or cable; Telephone cable service, land or submarine; Computers, peripherals, and software; Electronic parts and equipment, nec

(G-16027)
INTERFLEX ACQUISITION CO LLC
Also Called: Carolina Printing & Converting
3200 W Nc Highway 268 (28697-7459)
PHONE.............................336 921-3505
Jeff Zeber, *Mgr*
EMP: 207
Web: www.interflexgroup.com
SIC: 2752 2759 Commercial printing, lithographic; Commercial printing, nec
HQ: Interflex Acquisition Company, Llc
   3200 W Nc Highway 268
   Wilkesboro NC 28697
   336 921-3505

(G-16028)
INTERFLEX ACQUISITION CO LLC
3200 Hwy 268 W (28697)
PHONE.............................336 921-3505
EMP: 194
Web: www.interflexgroup.com
SIC: 2752 3081 2759 2671 Commercial printing, lithographic; Unsupported plastics film and sheet; Commercial printing, nec; Paper; coated and laminated packaging
HQ: Interflex Acquisition Company, Llc
   3200 W Nc Highway 268
   Wilkesboro NC 28697
   336 921-3505

(G-16029)
INTERFLEX ACQUISITION CO LLC (HQ)
Also Called: Interflex Group
3200 W Nc Highway 268 (28697-7459)
PHONE.............................336 921-3505
EMP: 143 **EST:** 2012
SALES (est): 52.3MM **Privately Held**
Web: www.interflexgroup.com
SIC: 2752 Photolithographic printing
PA: Toppan Holdings Inc.
   1-3-3, Suido
   Bunkyo-Ku TKY 112-0

(G-16030)
INTERFLEX ACQUISITION CO LLC
251 Industrial Dr Ext (28697-7576)
PHONE.............................336 921-3505
EMP: 81
Web: www.interflexgroup.com
SIC: 3053 Gaskets; packing and sealing devices
HQ: Interflex Acquisition Company, Llc
   3200 W Nc Highway 268
   Wilkesboro NC 28697
   336 921-3505

(G-16031)
INTERFLEX ACQUISITION CO LLC
3200 W Nc Highway 268 (28697-7459)
PHONE.............................336 921-3505
Stephen Doyle, *Brnch Mgr*
EMP: 200
Web: www.interflexgroup.com
SIC: 3053 Packing materials
HQ: Interflex Acquisition Company, Llc
   3200 W Nc Highway 268
   Wilkesboro NC 28697
   336 921-3505

(G-16032)
JENKINS MILLWORK LLC
1603 Industrial Dr (28697-7344)
PHONE.............................336 667-3344
James Carter, *Managing Member*
▲ **EMP:** 27 **EST:** 2012
SALES (est): 1.03MM
SALES (corp-wide): 8.64MM **Privately Held**
Web: www.jenkinsmillworkllc.com
SIC: 2431 Millwork
PA: Millwork Products, L.L.C.
   1003 Monroe St
   Paducah KY 42001
   270 442-5481

(G-16033)
JERRY HUFFMAN SAWMILL
Also Called: Jerry Huffman Sawmill & Log
287 Cactus Ln (28697-8136)
PHONE.............................336 973-3606
Jerry Huffman, *Owner*
EMP: 8 **EST:** 1970
SALES (est): 543.09K **Privately Held**
SIC: 2421 Sawmills and planing mills, general

(G-16034)
KEITH LAWS
1001 N Marley Ford Rd (28697-8183)
PHONE.............................336 973-7220
Keith Laws, *Prin*
EMP: 5 **EST:** 2013
SALES (est): 126.69K **Privately Held**
SIC: 2411 Logging

(G-16035)
KEY CITY FURNITURE COMPANY INC
1804 River St (28697-7657)
P.O. Box 680 (28697-0680)
PHONE.............................336 818-1161
▲ **EMP:** 105
Web: www.keycityfurn.com
SIC: 2512 Living room furniture: upholstered on wood frames

(G-16036)
KOTOHIRA
1206 River St (28697-2138)
PHONE.............................336 667-0150
EMP: 6 **EST:** 2010
SALES (est): 94.05K **Privately Held**
SIC: 3421 Table and food cutlery, including butchers'

(G-16037)
OLLIS ENTERPRISES INC
Also Called: Precision Printing
1613 Industrial Dr (28697-7344)
PHONE.............................828 265-0004
Paul Ollis, *Pr*
EMP: 20 **EST:** 1983
SALES (est): 1.8MM **Privately Held**
SIC: 2752 2791 2789 Offset printing; Typesetting; Bookbinding and related work

(G-16038)
RANDY D MILLER LUMBER CO INC
538 Hwy 16 N (28697)
P.O. Box 1515 (28651-1515)
PHONE.............................336 973-7515
Randy D Miller, *Pr*
Janet Miller, *
EMP: 26 **EST:** 1983
SQ FT: 22,000
SALES (est): 6MM **Privately Held**
SIC: 2421 Lumber: rough, sawed, or planed

(G-16039)
SCREEN PRINTERS UNLIMITED LLC
331 E Main St Ste 1 (28697-2529)
PHONE.............................336 667-8737
Herbert Boehm, *Managing Member*
EMP: 4 **EST:** 1994
SQ FT: 12,000
SALES (est): 326.06K **Privately Held**
Web: www.shirtsandsigns.com
SIC: 2759 7389 Screen printing; Embroidery advertising

(G-16040)
SEASONS INSPIRATIONS
113 W Main St (28697-2422)
PHONE.............................336 990-0072
EMP: 5 **EST:** 2017
SALES (est): 51.38K **Privately Held**
Web: www.seasonsinspirations.com
SIC: 2284 Thread mills

(G-16041)
SIGNFACTORY DIRECT INC
1202 Industrial Park Rd (28697-8490)
PHONE.............................336 903-0300
Mike Kerhoulas, *Owner*
EMP: 8 **EST:** 1992
SALES (est): 747.72K **Privately Held**
Web: www.esignz.com
SIC: 3993 Signs and advertising specialties

(G-16042)
SPECIALTY FABRICATORS INC
1806 Industrial Dr (28697-7346)
P.O. Box 1384 (28697-1384)
PHONE.............................336 838-7704
Jody Caudill, *Sec*
EMP: 5 **EST:** 2001
SALES (est): 374.3K **Privately Held**
SIC: 3441 Fabricated structural metal

(G-16043)
SUN OVENS INTERNATIONAL INC
Also Called: Sun Oven
418 Wilkesboro Blvd Unit 1 (28697-2530)
PHONE.............................630 208-7273
Forrest Garvin, *CEO*
George C Critz Iii, *Pr*
EMP: 6 **EST:** 1998
SQ FT: 10,000
SALES (est): 2.31MM **Privately Held**
Web: www.sunoven.com
SIC: 3634 Ovens, portable: household
PA: Virexit Technologies, Inc.
   6428 W Wilkinson Blvd
   Belmont NC 28012

(G-16044)
SUNCREST FARMS CNTRY HAMS INC
Also Called: Junior Johnson Country Hams
1148 Foster St (28697-8432)
P.O. Box 634 (28697-0634)
PHONE.............................336 667-4441
EMP: 38 **EST:** 1995
SALES (est): 8.91MM **Privately Held**
Web: www.suncrestham.com
SIC: 2013 5421 Prepared pork products, from purchased pork; Meat markets, including freezer provisioners

(G-16045)
THE INTERFLEX GROUP INC
3200 W Nc Highway 268 (28697-7459)
PHONE.............................336 921-3505
▲ **EMP:** 205
SIC: 3053 Packing materials

(G-16046)
TYSON FOODS INC
Also Called: Tyson
1600 River St (28697-7630)
PHONE.............................336 838-0083
Lani Stevens, *Mgr*
EMP: 6
SALES (corp-wide): 52.88B **Publicly Held**
Web: www.tysonfoods.com
SIC: 2011 Meat packing plants
PA: Tyson Foods, Inc.
   2200 W Don Tyson Pkwy
   Springdale AR 72762
   479 290-4000

(G-16047)
TYSON FOODS INC
Also Called: Tyson
115 Factory St (28697-2896)
PHONE.............................336 838-2171
Kirk Church, *Prin*
EMP: 2400
SALES (corp-wide): 52.88B **Publicly Held**
Web: www.tysonfoods.com
SIC: 2011 Meat packing plants
PA: Tyson Foods, Inc.
   2200 W Don Tyson Pkwy
   Springdale AR 72762
   479 290-4000

(G-16048)
TYSON FOODS INC
Also Called: Tyson
901 Wilkes St (28697-2889)
PHONE.............................336 838-2171
Molly Adams, *Mgr*
EMP: 17
SALES (corp-wide): 52.88B **Publicly Held**
Web: www.tysonfoods.com
SIC: 2015 Poultry slaughtering and processing
PA: Tyson Foods, Inc.
   2200 W Don Tyson Pkwy
   Springdale AR 72762
   479 290-4000

GEOGRAPHIC SECTION

Williamston - Martin County (G-16074)

(G-16049)
TYSON FOODS INC
Tyson
706 Factory St (28697-2935)
PHONE...................336 838-2171
Kirk Church, *Mgr*
EMP: 123
SALES (corp-wide): 52.88B **Publicly Held**
Web: www.tysonfoods.com
SIC: 2015 2011 Poultry, slaughtered and dressed; Meat packing plants
PA: Tyson Foods, Inc.
2200 W Don Tyson Pkwy
Springdale AR 72762
479 290-4000

(G-16050)
US CHEMICAL STORAGE LLC
1806 River St (28697-7633)
PHONE...................828 264-6032
Mark Mcelhinny, *CEO*
EMP: 50 **EST:** 1998
SALES (est): 12.07MM
SALES (corp-wide): 500.07MM **Privately Held**
Web: www.uschemicalstorage.com
SIC: 3448 Buildings, portable: prefabricated metal
PA: Justrite Manufacturing Company, L.L.C.
3921 Dewitt Ave
Mattoon IL 61938
217 234-7486

(G-16051)
WELDING COMPANY
646 Old Us 421 Rd (28697-8214)
P.O. Box 1798 (28659-1798)
PHONE...................336 667-0265
Clifford Kemp, *Owner*
EMP: 5 **EST:** 1992
SQ FT: 1,200
SALES (est): 461.22K **Privately Held**
Web: www.welding.com
SIC: 7692 Welding repair

(G-16052)
WORLDWIDE PROTECTIVE PDTS LLC (DH)
Also Called: Worldwide Protective Products
1409 World Wide Ln (28697-2270)
PHONE...................877 678-4568
▲ **EMP:** 33 **EST:** 2004
SALES (est): 41.28MM
SALES (corp-wide): 2.8B **Privately Held**
Web: www.pipglobal.com
SIC: 2381 Fabric dress and work gloves
HQ: Protective Industrial Products, Inc.
25 British American Blvd
Latham NY 12110
518 861-0133

(G-16053)
WORLDWIDE PROTECTIVE PDTS LLC
1404 River St (28697-2108)
PHONE...................336 933-8035
EMP: 77
SALES (corp-wide): 2.8B **Privately Held**
SIC: 2381 Fabric dress and work gloves
HQ: Worldwide Protective Products Llc
1409 World Wide Ln
Wilkesboro NC 28697
877 678-4568

Willard
Pender County

(G-16054)
DAVID WEST
9090 Us Hwy 117 N (28478-8462)
PHONE...................910 271-0757
David West, *Admn*
EMP: 6 **EST:** 2017
SALES (est): 235.44K **Privately Held**
SIC: 7692 Welding repair

(G-16055)
P & S WELDING INC
8414 Us Hwy 117 N (28478-8450)
PHONE...................910 285-3126
Fred Simpson, *Pr*
Dale Simpson, *Sec*
EMP: 7 **EST:** 1980
SQ FT: 1,800
SALES (est): 756.95K **Privately Held**
SIC: 3312 Structural shapes and pilings, steel

Williamston
Martin County

(G-16056)
ABB LOGGING LLC
24815 Us Highway 64 (27892-7734)
PHONE...................252 809-0180
Ana Luz Gomez-paramo, *Prin*
EMP: 6 **EST:** 2019
SALES (est): 249.83K **Privately Held**
SIC: 2411 Logging

(G-16057)
ARGOS USA LLC
Also Called: Ready Mixed Concrete
741 Warren St (27892-2747)
P.O. Box 682 (27892-0682)
PHONE...................252 792-3148
Michael Odom, *Mgr*
EMP: 7
Web: www.argos-us.com
SIC: 3273 Ready-mixed concrete
HQ: Argos Usa Llc
3015 Windward Plz Ste 300
Alpharetta GA 30005
678 368-4300

(G-16058)
BY FAITH LOGGING INC
1046 Cedar Hill Dr (27892-8689)
PHONE...................252 792-0019
EMP: 6 **EST:** 2010
SALES (est): 392.72K **Privately Held**
Web: www.horiuchianddamicodds.com
SIC: 2411 Logging camps and contractors

(G-16059)
COX NRTH CRLINA PBLCATIONS INC
Also Called: Enterprise, The
106 W Main St (27892-2471)
P.O. Box 387 (27892-0387)
PHONE...................252 792-1181
EMP: 74
SALES (corp-wide): 2.85B **Privately Held**
Web: www.reflector.com
SIC: 2711 Newspapers, publishing and printing
HQ: Cox North Carolina Publications, Inc.
1150 Sugg Pkwy
Greenville NC 27834
252 329-9643

(G-16060)
FRONT PRCH CSTM FRMNG WODWORKS
1043 Zeke Rhodes Ln (27892-8303)
PHONE...................252 717-2868
EMP: 4 **EST:** 2018
SALES (est): 54.13K **Privately Held**
SIC: 2431 Millwork

(G-16061)
GRAVES INC
1909 W Main St (27892-7611)
P.O. Box 71 (27892-0071)
PHONE...................252 792-1191
C Swanson Graves Iii, *Pr*
Lind C Graves, *
Jane C Griffin, *
Linda C Graves, *
EMP: 25 **EST:** 1965
SQ FT: 20,000
SALES (est): 2.28MM **Privately Held**
Web: www.reddickequipment.com
SIC: 3523 3563 Sprayers and spraying machines, agricultural; Spraying outfits: metals, paints, and chemicals (compressor)

(G-16062)
GRIFFN S BRBCUE WLLIAMSTON INC
5362 Fire Dept Rd (27892-7910)
PHONE...................252 792-4887
Andy Griffin, *Pr*
EMP: 6 **EST:** 1956
SALES (est): 443.04K **Privately Held**
SIC: 2013 Sausages and other prepared meats

(G-16063)
HTM CONCEPTS MARTIN ENTPS LLC
23366 Nc Highway 125 (27892)
P.O. Box 1084 (27892-1084)
PHONE...................252 789-0508
Becky Wrenn, *Dir*
EMP: 5 **EST:** 2014
SALES (est): 227.34K **Privately Held**
Web: www.htmconcepts.com
SIC: 2759 Promotional printing

(G-16064)
KEN WOOD CORP
1660 Arthur Corey Rd (27892-8731)
PHONE...................252 792-6481
S Ken Wilson Iii, *Pr*
Ann Wilson, *VP*
EMP: 9 **EST:** 1987
SALES (est): 1.04MM **Privately Held**
SIC: 2411 Logging camps and contractors

(G-16065)
MAELLE KIDS INC
252 W Pine St (27892-1663)
PHONE...................252 799-7312
EMP: 5 **EST:** 2019
SALES (est): 65.51K **Privately Held**
SIC: 2721 Magazines: publishing only, not printed on site

(G-16066)
MCCLURE METAL SPECIALTIES INC
308 E Franklin St (27892-1811)
PHONE...................252 792-8624
EMP: 4 **EST:** 2019
SALES (est): 118.53K **Privately Held**
SIC: 3444 Sheet metalwork

(G-16067)
MILLERS SPORTS AND TROPHIES
101 Washington St (27892-2491)
P.O. Box 501 (27892-0501)
PHONE...................252 792-2050
Walter H Miller, *Pt*
John Miller Iii, *Pt*
EMP: 4 **EST:** 1937
SQ FT: 6,000
SALES (est): 397.29K **Privately Held**
SIC: 5941 2395 Specialty sport supplies, nec ; Embroidery and art needlework

(G-16068)
REDDICK EQUIPMENT CO NC LLC
1909 W Main St (27892-7611)
P.O. Box 71 (27892-0071)
PHONE...................252 792-1191
Victor Lilley, *Managing Member*
EMP: 8 **EST:** 2012
SQ FT: 1,500
SALES (est): 210.56K **Privately Held**
Web: www.reddickequipment.com
SIC: 3523 3563 Farm machinery and equipment; Air and gas compressors

(G-16069)
ROBERSON LOGGING LLC
1834 Holly Springs Church Rd (27892-8156)
PHONE...................252 799-7076
EMP: 10 **EST:** 2017
SALES (est): 880.56K **Privately Held**
SIC: 2411 Logging

(G-16070)
SOMETHING FOR YOUTH
503 E Main St (27892-2531)
P.O. Box 213 (27892-0213)
PHONE...................252 799-8837
EMP: 10
SALES (est): 308.24K **Privately Held**
SIC: 2531 Public building and related furniture

(G-16071)
STEVE EVANS LOGGING INC
7096 Us Highway 17 (27892-7953)
PHONE...................252 792-1836
Steve Evans, *Pr*
EMP: 5 **EST:** 1983
SALES (est): 603.88K **Privately Held**
SIC: 2411 Logging camps and contractors

(G-16072)
VINCENT L TAYLOR
3930 Bear Grass Rd (27892-7226)
PHONE...................252 792-2987
Vincent L Taylor, *Prin*
EMP: 8 **EST:** 2005
SALES (est): 258.47K **Privately Held**
SIC: 2411 Logging

(G-16073)
W AND W TRUSS BUILDERS INC
424 Railroad St (27892-2334)
PHONE...................252 792-1051
Don H Whitley, *Pr*
EMP: 10 **EST:** 1983
SQ FT: 40,000
SALES (est): 857.51K **Privately Held**
Web: www.wwtbi.com
SIC: 2439 Trusses, wooden roof

(G-16074)
WOLF TIMBER LLC
1040 David Rogerson Rd (27892-8081)
PHONE...................252 799-0495
Hugh B Kennedy, *Prin*
EMP: 5 **EST:** 2019
SALES (est): 68.85K **Privately Held**
SIC: 2411 Logging

Willow Spring
Wake County

(G-16075)
BAKERS QUALITY TRIM INC
1616 Kendall Hill Rd (27592-9069)
PHONE..............................919 552-3621
Joseph Baker, *Pr*
Lori Baker, *Sec*
EMP: 4 EST: 1991
SALES (est): 266.35K **Privately Held**
SIC: 2431 Interior and ornamental woodwork and trim

(G-16076)
C & M WELDING INSPECTIONS INC
7225 Blannie Farms Ln (27592-9077)
PHONE..............................919 762-7345
Joshua Minton, *Prin*
EMP: 5 EST: 2016
SALES (est): 42.72K **Privately Held**
SIC: 7692 Welding repair

(G-16077)
CABINETRY SQUARED
7309 Trouble Rd (27592-8070)
PHONE..............................919 589-7253
EMP: 4 EST: 2019
SALES (est): 58.05K **Privately Held**
Web: cabinetry-squared.business.site
SIC: 2434 Wood kitchen cabinets

(G-16078)
CANDY CANE COATINGS
7421 Blannie Farms Ln (27592-9082)
PHONE..............................919 605-6997
Justin Main, *Prin*
EMP: 5 EST: 2017
SALES (est): 60.05K **Privately Held**
SIC: 3479 Metal coating and allied services

(G-16079)
JOHNSON CONCRETE COMPANY
Johnson Concrete Products
1401 Nc 42 Hwy (27592-7879)
P.O. Box 188 (27592-0188)
PHONE..............................704 636-5231
Rich Curney, *Mgr*
EMP: 34
SALES (corp-wide): 24.37MM **Privately Held**
Web: www.johnsonproductsusa.com
SIC: 3271 3272 Blocks, concrete or cinder: standard; Pipe, concrete or lined with concrete
PA: Johnson Concrete Company
217 Klumac Rd
Salisbury NC 28144
704 636-5231

(G-16080)
KENS CANDLES AND SOAPS
1302 Old Fairground Rd (27592-9687)
PHONE..............................919 207-2880
Kenneth Lawrence, *Prin*
EMP: 5 EST: 2016
SALES (est): 39.69K **Privately Held**
SIC: 3999 Candles

(G-16081)
NC SAND AND ROCK INC
9520 Kennebec Rd (27592-9415)
PHONE..............................919 538-9001
Valerie Gonzalez, *Prin*
EMP: 8 EST: 2018
SALES (est): 872.13K **Privately Held**
SIC: 1442 Construction sand and gravel

(G-16082)
RICHARD WILCOX
1400 Struble Cir (27592-7678)
P.O. Box 201 (27592-0201)
PHONE..............................919 218-5907
Richard Wilcox, *Owner*
EMP: 7 EST: 2015
SALES (est): 208.84K **Privately Held**
SIC: 2741 Miscellaneous publishing

(G-16083)
SKEETER BEATERS
3021 Jackson King Rd (27592-7936)
PHONE..............................919 285-6054
Colby A Trice, *Prin*
EMP: 4 EST: 2019
SALES (est): 78.21K **Privately Held**
Web: www.theskeeterbeater.com
SIC: 3999 Manufacturing industries, nec

(G-16084)
WHITLEY METALS INC
769 Mount Pleasant Rd (27592-8000)
PHONE..............................919 894-3326
EMP: 5 EST: 1996
SALES (est): 810.13K **Privately Held**
Web: www.whitleymetal.com
SIC: 3441 Fabricated structural metal

(G-16085)
YOUNG LOGGING COMPANY INC
1517 Clayton Rd (27592-9351)
PHONE..............................919 552-9753
EMP: 7 EST: 1978
SALES (est): 601.58K **Privately Held**
SIC: 2411 Logging

Wilmington
New Hanover County

(G-16086)
1 CLICK WEB SOLUTIONS LLC
3333 Wrightsville Ave M (28403-4115)
PHONE..............................910 790-9330
EMP: 50 EST: 1996
SQ FT: 5,000
SALES (est): 2.16MM **Privately Held**
SIC: 2741 Telephone and other directory publishing

(G-16087)
123 PRECIOUS METAL REF LLC (PA)
Also Called: Www 123 Precious Metal Com
609a Piner Rd Ste 303 (28409-4201)
PHONE..............................910 228-5403
Pricilla Olivolo, *Managing Member*
Alford Olivolo, *Managing Member*
EMP: 4 EST: 2004
SALES (est): 300.57K
SALES (corp-wide): 300.57K **Privately Held**
Web: www.123preciousmetal.com
SIC: 3911 Jewelry, precious metal

(G-16088)
A SIGN FROM ABOVE INC
4515 Cedar Ave (28403-4357)
PHONE..............................910 352-0897
Pete Hancock, *Prin*
EMP: 6 EST: 2010
SALES (est): 223.64K **Privately Held**
Web: www.signcompanywilmingtonnc.com
SIC: 3993 Signs, not made in custom sign painting shops

(G-16089)
A&M SCREEN PRINTING NC INC
6404 Amsterdam Way Unit 4 (28405-2568)
PHONE..............................910 792-1111
Tony Delcotto, *Pr*
EMP: 4 EST: 1998
SALES (est): 293.69K **Privately Held**
SIC: 2396 Screen printing on fabric articles

(G-16090)
A1 BIOCHEM LABS LLC
5598 Marvin K Moss Ln Ste 2017 (28409-3702)
P.O. Box 11337 (13218-1337)
PHONE..............................315 299-4775
Rajendra Gadikota, *Managing Member*
◆ EMP: 5 EST: 2014
SALES (est): 2.1MM **Privately Held**
Web: www.a1biochemlabs.com
SIC: 2834 Pharmaceutical preparations

(G-16091)
AA CERAMICS
2002 Eastwood Rd (28403-7218)
PHONE..............................910 632-3053
EMP: 5 EST: 2013
SALES (est): 115.53K **Privately Held**
SIC: 3269 Pottery products, nec

(G-16092)
ACCELERATED PRESS INC
616 Windchime Dr (28412-7521)
PHONE..............................248 524-1850
Gaylord Vince, *Pr*
EMP: 7
SALES (est): 750.88K **Privately Held**
Web: www.acceleratedpress.com
SIC: 2752 7334 Offset printing; Photocopying and duplicating services

(G-16093)
ACTIVE HATS AND THINGS SUITE
2201 Inkberry Ct (28411-6502)
PHONE..............................888 352-9292
EMP: 4 EST: 2016
SALES (est): 84.69K **Privately Held**
SIC: 2353 Hats, caps, and millinery

(G-16094)
ADVANCE PRINTING SOLUTIONS
338 Aldrich Ln (28411-9660)
PHONE..............................301 919-7868
Charles Holden, *Prin*
EMP: 5 EST: 2010
SALES (est): 147.34K **Privately Held**
SIC: 2752 Commercial printing, lithographic

(G-16095)
ADVANCED MARKETING INTERNATIONAL INC
Also Called: Admark
211 Racine Dr Ste 202 (28403-8842)
PHONE..............................910 392-0508
◆ EMP: 12 EST: 1989
SALES (est): 2.83MM **Privately Held**
Web: www.admarkintl.com
SIC: 5169 5162 2819 Chemicals, industrial and heavy; Plastics materials, nec; Catalysts, chemical

(G-16096)
AESCO INC
Also Called: Cape Fear Graphics
1405 S 5th Ave (28401-6263)
PHONE..............................910 763-6612
Albert E Sikes, *Pr*
Tina Sikes, *Sec*
EMP: 6 EST: 1974
SQ FT: 9,600
SALES (est): 358.81K **Privately Held**
SIC: 2752 Offset printing

(G-16097)
AHLBERG CAMERAS INC
Also Called: Ahlberg Cameras
432 Landmark Dr Ste 3 (28412-6310)
PHONE..............................910 523-5876
Ulf Ahlberg, *CEO*
EMP: 17 EST: 2009
SALES (est): 967.01K
SALES (corp-wide): 7.13B **Privately Held**
Web: www.ahlbergcameras.com
SIC: 7389 3861 Design services; Cameras and related equipment
HQ: Ahlberg Cameras Ab
Gosvagen 22
NorrtAlje 761 4
176205500

(G-16098)
AIRGAS USA LLC
Also Called: Airgas National Welders
2824 Carolina Beach Rd (28412-1810)
PHONE..............................910 392-2711
Aaron Wescott, *Brnch Mgr*
EMP: 10
SQ FT: 9,360
SALES (corp-wide): 101.26MM **Privately Held**
Web: www.airgas.com
SIC: 5084 2813 Welding machinery and equipment; Industrial gases
HQ: Airgas Usa, Llc
259 N Radnor Chester Rd
Radnor PA 19087
216 642-6600

(G-16099)
ALBANY TOOL & DIE INC
315 Van Dyke Dr Ste A (28405-3765)
PHONE..............................910 392-1207
Andrew Kerekes, *Pr*
Andrew Kerekes Senior, *VP*
EMP: 14 EST: 1951
SQ FT: 4,000
SALES (est): 477.83K **Privately Held**
Web: www.albanytool.com
SIC: 3599 Machine shop, jobbing and repair

(G-16100)
ALCAMI CAROLINAS CORPORATION
Also Called: Alcami
1726 N 23rd St (28405-1822)
PHONE..............................910 254-7000
Stephan Kutzer, *CEO*
EMP: 11
SALES (corp-wide): 418.48MM **Privately Held**
Web: www.alcami.com
SIC: 8071 2834 Medical laboratories; Pharmaceutical preparations
HQ: Alcami Carolinas Corporation
2320 Scientific Park Dr
Wilmington NC 28405

(G-16101)
ALCAMI CAROLINAS CORPORATION
Also Called: Alcami
1206 N 23rd St (28405-1810)
PHONE..............................910 254-7000
Stephan Kutzer, *Brnch Mgr*
EMP: 8
SALES (corp-wide): 418.48MM **Privately Held**
Web: www.alcami.com
SIC: 2834 8731 Pharmaceutical preparations; Medical research, commercial
HQ: Alcami Carolinas Corporation
2320 Scientific Park Dr
Wilmington NC 28405

GEOGRAPHIC SECTION
Wilmington - New Hanover County (G-16125)

(G-16102)
ALCAMI CAROLINAS CORPORATION
1519 N 23rd St (28405-1827)
PHONE...................910 254-7000
Stephan Kutzer, *CEO*
EMP: 8
SALES (corp-wide): 418.48MM **Privately Held**
Web: www.alcami.com
SIC: 2834 8731 Pharmaceutical preparations; Medical research, commercial
HQ: Alcami Carolinas Corporation
2320 Scientific Park Dr
Wilmington NC 28405

(G-16103)
ALCAMI CAROLINAS CORPORATION (HQ)
Also Called: Alcami
2320 Scientific Park Dr (28405-1800)
PHONE...................910 254-7000
Patrick Walsh, *CEO*
Adam Lauber, *
Scott Warner, *Corporate Secretary*
Ken Morgan, *
Burton Ely, *
EMP: 463 **EST:** 2009
SALES (est): 224.79MM
SALES (corp-wide): 418.48MM **Privately Held**
Web: www.alcami.com
SIC: 2834 8731 8734 Drugs affecting neoplasms and endrocrine systems; Biological research; Product testing laboratories
PA: Alcami Corporation
2320 Scientific Park Dr
Wilmington NC 28405
910 254-7000

(G-16104)
ALCAMI CORPORATION (PA)
2320 Scientific Park Dr (28405-1800)
PHONE...................910 254-7000
Stephan Kutzer, *CEO*
Syed Hyusain, *
Adam Lauber, *
Ted Dolan, *
Scott Warner, *
EMP: 600 **EST:** 2009
SQ FT: 100,000
SALES (est): 418.48MM
SALES (corp-wide): 418.48MM **Privately Held**
Web: www.alcami.com
SIC: 2834 Pharmaceutical preparations

(G-16105)
ALCAMI HOLDINGS LLC
2320 Scientific Park Dr (28405-1800)
PHONE...................910 254-7000
Stephan Kutzer, *CEO*
EMP: 1038 **EST:** 2012
Web: www.alcaminow.com
SIC: 6719 2834 Investment holding companies, except banks; Pharmaceutical preparations

(G-16106)
ALLEN FACE & COMPANY LLC
2725 Old Wrightsboro Rd Ste 12-5 (28405-8013)
PHONE...................910 763-4501
EMP: 7 **EST:** 1993
SALES (est): 489.63K **Privately Held**
Web: www.allenface.com
SIC: 3825 Internal combustion engine analyzers, to test electronics

(G-16107)
ALLEN-GODWIN CONCRETE INC
8871 Sidbury Rd (28411-7923)
P.O. Box 11120 (28404-1120)
PHONE...................910 686-4890
John D Allen, *Pr*
Janet B Allen, *
Ebew Godwin, *
EMP: 18 **EST:** 2004
SQ FT: 4,000
SALES (est): 2.13MM **Privately Held**
SIC: 3273 Ready-mixed concrete

(G-16108)
ALPEK POLYESTER USA LLC
Also Called: Cape Fear Plant
1430 Commonwealth Dr (28403-0351)
P.O. Box 2042 (28402-2042)
PHONE...................910 371-4000
Leroy Butler, *Brnch Mgr*
EMP: 292
Web: www.alpekpolyester.com
SIC: 2821 2284 2824 Polyethylene resins; Thread mills; Polyester fibers
HQ: Alpek Polyester Usa, Llc
7621 Little Ave Ste 500
Charlotte NC 28226
704 940-7500

(G-16109)
AMERICAN MATERIALS COMPANY LLC (HQ)
Also Called: Summit Materials
1410 Commonwealth Dr Ste 201 (28403)
PHONE...................910 799-1411
Gary Bizzell, *Pr*
Daniel Roy, *Finance*
EMP: 18 **EST:** 1999
SQ FT: 2,500
SALES (est): 86.49MM
SALES (corp-wide): 2.62B **Publicly Held**
Web: www.americanmaterialsco.com
SIC: 1442 Construction sand and gravel
PA: Summit Materials, Inc.
1801 Calif St Ste 3500
Denver CO 80202
303 893-0012

(G-16110)
AMERICAN SPORTS LIGHTING INC
8713 Champion Hills Dr (28411-8105)
PHONE...................910 520-1074
Virginia Teachey, *Prin*
EMP: 6 **EST:** 2011
SALES (est): 176.38K **Privately Held**
Web: www.amsportslighting.com
SIC: 3648 Lighting equipment, nec

(G-16111)
ANCHORED HOME INC
1930 Oleander Dr (28403-2335)
PHONE...................910 769-7092
EMP: 6 **EST:** 2019
SALES (est): 136.37K **Privately Held**
Web: www.anchoredhomeilm.com
SIC: 2273 Carpets and rugs

(G-16112)
APPLE BRANCH COMPANY
6029 Inland Greens Dr (28405-3875)
PHONE...................910 859-8549
Linda Chewning, *Prin*
EMP: 6 **EST:** 2014
SALES (est): 98K **Privately Held**
SIC: 3571 Electronic computers

(G-16113)
AR CORP
7639 Myrtle Grove Rd (28409-4923)
P.O. Box 2555 (28402-2555)
PHONE...................910 763-8530
Elizabeth Ann Ross, *Pr*
◆ **EMP:** 4 **EST:** 1985
SALES (est): 472.09K **Privately Held**
Web: www.qisglass.com
SIC: 2835 Diagnostic substances

(G-16114)
AREA 51 POWDER COATING INC
2721 Old Wrightsboro Rd (28405-8036)
PHONE...................910 769-1724
Brett D Lenz, *Owner*
EMP: 11 **EST:** 2008
SALES (est): 773.61K **Privately Held**
Web: www.area51powdercoating.com
SIC: 3479 Coating of metals and formed products

(G-16115)
ARGOS USA LLC
Also Called: Argos Ready Mix
8871 Sidbury Rd (28411-7923)
PHONE...................910 686-4890
EMP: 4
Web: www.argos-us.com
SIC: 3273 Ready-mixed concrete
HQ: Argos Usa Llc
3015 Windward Plz Ste 300
Alpharetta GA 30005
678 368-4300

(G-16116)
ARGOS USA LLC
Also Called: Argos Ready Mix
800 Sunnyvale Dr (28412-7031)
PHONE...................910 796-3469
EMP: 34
Web: www.argos-us.com
SIC: 3273 Ready-mixed concrete
HQ: Argos Usa Llc
3015 Windward Plz Ste 300
Alpharetta GA 30005
678 368-4300

(G-16117)
ARMA CO LLC
Also Called: Ripoff Holsters
4557 Technology Dr Ste 4 (28405-2145)
PHONE...................717 295-6805
EMP: 10 **EST:** 2004
SALES (est): 485K **Privately Held**
SIC: 3842 Bulletproof vests

(G-16118)
ARW OPTICAL CORP
2021 Capital Dr (28405-6463)
PHONE...................910 452-7373
Gunter Wolff, *Pr*
EMP: 9 **EST:** 1980
SQ FT: 8,700
SALES (est): 939.53K **Privately Held**
Web: www.arwoptical.com
SIC: 3827 Optical instruments and apparatus

(G-16119)
ATHENIAN PRESS AND WORKSHOPS
701 N 23rd St (28405-2811)
PHONE...................919 961-5071
Lori Wilson, *Prin*
EMP: 5 **EST:** 2017
SALES (est): 59.23K **Privately Held**
SIC: 2741 Miscellaneous publishing

(G-16120)
ATLANTIC CARIBBEAN LLC
806 N 23rd St (28405-1802)
PHONE...................910 343-0624
EMP: 10 **EST:** 2006
SALES (est): 243.47K **Privately Held**
Web: www.atlanticpkg.com
SIC: 6799 2679 Investors, nec; Book covers, paper

(G-16121)
ATLANTIC CORP WILMINGTON INC (PA)
Also Called: Atlantic
806 N 23rd St (28405-1802)
PHONE...................910 343-0624
Russell Carter, *Pr*
Livingston Sheats, *VP*
Henry Boon, *VP*
Roger Teague, *Sec*
Susan Carter, *Treas*
◆ **EMP:** 95 **EST:** 1946
SQ FT: 100,000
SALES (est): 448MM
SALES (corp-wide): 448MM **Privately Held**
Web: www.atlanticpkg.com
SIC: 5113 2621 2679 Industrial and personal service paper; Paper mills; Paper products, converted, nec

(G-16122)
ATLANTIC CORPORATION (HQ)
Also Called: Packaging and Supply Solutions
806 N 23rd St (28405-1802)
PHONE...................910 343-0624
Steven C Quidley, *Pr*
◆ **EMP:** 63 **EST:** 1946
SALES (est): 150.96MM
SALES (corp-wide): 448MM **Privately Held**
Web: www.atlanticpkg.com
SIC: 2671 Paper, coated or laminated for packaging
PA: Atlantic Corporation Of Wilmington Inc.
806 N 23rd St
Wilmington NC 28405
910 343-0624

(G-16123)
ATLANTIC SOFTWARE CO
607 S 13th St (28401-5410)
PHONE...................910 763-3907
Richard Irving, *Owner*
EMP: 4 **EST:** 2002
SALES (est): 35K **Privately Held**
SIC: 7372 Prepackaged software

(G-16124)
ATMAX ENGINEERING
806 Morris Ct (28405-2626)
PHONE...................910 233-4881
Andrew Allen, *Owner*
EMP: 9 **EST:** 1995
SQ FT: 10,000
SALES (est): 247.53K **Privately Held**
SIC: 1442 Construction sand and gravel

(G-16125)
AVAIL FORENSICS LLC
Also Called: Avail Forensics
4022 Shipyard Blvd Fl 2 (28403-6190)
PHONE...................877 888-5895
Troy Vasos, *Pr*
Troy Vasos, *Managing Member*
EMP: 14 **EST:** 2018
SQ FT: 650
SALES (est): 4.4MM **Privately Held**
Web: www.availforensics.com
SIC: 5065 7373 8748 3577 Modems, computer; Systems engineering, computer related; Systems engineering consultant, ex. computer or professional; Data conversion equipment, media-to-media: computer

Wilmington - New Hanover County (G-16126)   GEOGRAPHIC SECTION

(G-16126)
AVIAN CETACEAN PRESS
1616 Jettys Reach (28409-4514)
P.O. Box 15643 (28408-5643)
PHONE..................................910 392-5537
EMP: 4 EST: 1990
SALES (est): 159.47K Privately Held
Web: www.aviancetaceanpress.com
SIC: 2741 Miscellaneous publishing

(G-16127)
AWC SIGN & LIGHT INC
6705 Spearow Ln (28411-7413)
P.O. Box 12783 (28405-0138)
PHONE..................................910 279-0493
Christopher Coleman, Prin
EMP: 5 EST: 2016
SALES (est): 287.36K Privately Held
Web: www.awcsignandlight.com
SIC: 3993 Signs and advertising specialties

(G-16128)
AXON SYSTEMS LLC
1985 Eastwood Rd Ste 204b (28403-7208)
PHONE..................................910 796-7872
Randall Willard, Owner
EMP: 5 EST: 2014
SALES (est): 42.01K Privately Held
SIC: 3577 Computer peripheral equipment, nec

(G-16129)
AZTECH PRODUCTS INC (PA)
Also Called: New Hanover Printing & Pubg
2145 Wrightsville Ave (28403-0270)
PHONE..................................910 763-5599
EMP: 6 EST: 1997
SALES (est): 846.52K
SALES (corp-wide): 846.52K Privately Held
SIC: 2752 Offset printing

(G-16130)
B&LK ENTERPRISES
Also Called: Southern Screen Printers
409 Oakland Dr (28405-3829)
PHONE..................................910 395-5151
Larry G Knowles, Pr
Becky Knowles, VP
EMP: 5 EST: 1979
SQ FT: 1,800
SALES (est): 270K Privately Held
SIC: 3953 3552 2396 2395 Screens, textile printing; Embroidery machines; Automotive and apparel trimmings; Pleating and stitching

(G-16131)
BACKWATER GUNS LLC
1024 S Kerr Ave (28403-4313)
PHONE..................................910 399-1451
Marlon Kirk Andrews, Prin
EMP: 11 EST: 2009
SALES (est): 829.51K Privately Held
Web: www.backwaterguns.com
SIC: 7699 5099 3489 Gun services; Machine guns; Guns or gun parts, over 30 mm.

(G-16132)
BALDINI FOR MEN
1125 Military Cutoff Rd Ste H (28405-3652)
PHONE..................................910 239-9150
EMP: 4
SALES (est): 67.05K Privately Held
Web: www.baldiniformen.com
SIC: 2329 Men's and boy's clothing, nec

(G-16133)
BATCHLERS LLC
211 Hervey Ln (28411-9655)
PHONE..................................910 619-4042
Eric Batchler, Prin
EMP: 5 EST: 2018
SALES (est): 161.54K Privately Held
Web: www.coffeaseeds.com
SIC: 3537 Trucks: freight, baggage, etc.: industrial, except mining

(G-16134)
BELOCAL PUBLISHING LLC
5051 New Centre Dr (28403-1623)
PHONE..................................910 202-1917
EMP: 6 EST: 2016
SALES (est): 83.84K Privately Held
Web: www.belocalpub.com
SIC: 2741 Miscellaneous publishing

(G-16135)
BENNETT BROTHERS YACHTS INC
1701 Jel Wade Dr Ste 16 (28401-2826)
PHONE..................................910 772-9277
Patricia Bennett, Pr
EMP: 30 EST: 1986
SQ FT: 15,000
SALES (est): 2.43MM Privately Held
Web: www.bbyachts.com
SIC: 3732 7389 Yachts, building and repairing; Yacht brokers

(G-16136)
BENTONS WLDG REPR & SVCS INC
1206 S 3rd St (28401-6108)
PHONE..................................910 343-8322
James A Tew, Pr
Amy Tew, Sec
EMP: 6 EST: 1975
SQ FT: 1,200
SALES (est): 479.56K Privately Held
SIC: 7692 Welding repair

(G-16137)
BEST SOLUTION CARGO LLC
3600 S College Rd Ste E359 (28412-5240)
PHONE..................................407 810-5559
Maryna Gologura, Prin
EMP: 5 EST: 2015
SALES (est): 115.77K Privately Held
SIC: 3537 4789 Trucks, tractors, loaders, carriers, and similar equipment; Cargo loading and unloading services

(G-16138)
BIG NICS LURES LLC
3705 New Colony Dr (28412-2045)
PHONE..................................910 805-1360
EMP: 4 EST: 2015
SALES (est): 144.77K Privately Held
Web: www.bignicfishing.com
SIC: 3949 Lures, fishing: artificial

(G-16139)
BLUE STALLION WOODWORKS
9106 Salem Ct (28411-6726)
PHONE..................................919 766-2865
EMP: 4 EST: 2018
SALES (est): 54.13K Privately Held
SIC: 2431 Millwork

(G-16140)
BMT MICRO INC
5019 Carolina Beach Rd (28412-7841)
P.O. Box 15016 (28408-5016)
PHONE..................................910 792-9100
EMP: 7 EST: 1992
SALES (est): 1.88MM Privately Held
Web: www.bmtmicro.com
SIC: 7372 7371 Publisher's computer software; Custom computer programming services

(G-16141)
BONE TRED BEDS SMMIT WOODWORKS
617 Creekwood Rd (28411-7963)
PHONE..................................910 319-7583
EMP: 4 EST: 2012
SALES (est): 62.53K Privately Held
SIC: 2431 Millwork

(G-16142)
BOWIE MACHINE WORKS LLC
Also Called: Groundswell Renovation & Repr
232 N Channel Haven Dr (28409-3504)
PHONE..................................910 297-6014
EMP: 5 EST: 2011
SALES (est): 185.55K Privately Held
SIC: 3599 Machine shop, jobbing and repair

(G-16143)
BRILLIANT SOLE INC
1930 Senova Trce (28405-6226)
PHONE..................................339 222-8528
Jeffrey W Guard, CEO
Mike Bower, Prin
Andrew Keener, Prin
William Fleming, Prin
EMP: 4 EST: 2017
SALES (est): 238.48K Privately Held
Web: www.runonbrilliantsole.com
SIC: 3577 Computer peripheral equipment, nec

(G-16144)
BUILDERS FIRSTSOURCE - SE GRP
4151 Emerson St (28403-1414)
PHONE..................................910 313-3056
Matthew Willard, Brnch Mgr
EMP: 9
SALES (corp-wide): 17.1B Publicly Held
Web: www.bldr.com
SIC: 2431 5211 Doors and door parts and trim, wood; Millwork and lumber
HQ: Builders Firstsource - Southeast Group, Llc
     6031 Connection Dr # 400
     Irving TX 75039
     844 487-8625

(G-16145)
BUSINESS BROKERAGE PRESS INC
2726 Warlick Dr (28409-2077)
PHONE..................................800 239-5085
EMP: 8 EST: 2018
SALES (est): 41.35K Privately Held
Web: www.businessbrokeragepress.com
SIC: 2741 Miscellaneous publishing

(G-16146)
C YORK LAW PLLC
2030 Eastwood Rd Ste 2 (28403-7225)
PHONE..................................910 256-1235
Cindy York, Prin
EMP: 5 EST: 2011
SALES (est): 166.68K Privately Held
Web: www.cyorklaw.com
SIC: 2711 Newspapers, publishing and printing

(G-16147)
C2C PLASTICS INC
3024 Hall Watters Dr Ste 101 (28405-8717)
PHONE..................................910 338-5260
Mark Pandozzi, CEO
EMP: 4 EST: 2019
SALES (est): 492.14K Privately Held
SIC: 3089 Injection molding of plastics

(G-16148)
CAMAG SCIENTIFIC INC
515 Cornelius Harnett Dr (28401-2856)
PHONE..................................910 343-1830
Don Oates, VP
EMP: 8 EST: 1984
SQ FT: 3,000
SALES (est): 4.6MM Privately Held
Web: www.camag.com
SIC: 3826 Analytical instruments
HQ: Camag Chemie-Erzeugnisse Und
     Adsorptionstechnik Ag
     Sonnenmattstrasse 11
     Muttenz BL 4132

(G-16149)
CAPE FEAR CNSTR GROUP LLC
102 Autumn Hall Dr Ste 210 (28403-2056)
PHONE..................................910 344-1000
EMP: 6
SALES (est): 822.33K Privately Held
SIC: 1389 Construction, repair, and dismantling services

(G-16150)
CAPE FEAR PBLICATIONS DIST LLC
2204 Market St (28403-1132)
PHONE..................................910 762-3451
EMP: 6 EST: 2010
SALES (est): 216.48K Privately Held
Web: www.capefearpublicationsdistribution.com
SIC: 2741 Miscellaneous publishing

(G-16151)
CAPE FEAR YACHT WORKS LLC
111 Bryan Rd (28412-7033)
PHONE..................................910 540-1685
EMP: 10 EST: 2000
SQ FT: 7,000
SALES (est): 926.65K Privately Held
Web: www.capefearyachtworks.com
SIC: 3732 5551 Sailboats, building and repairing; Boat dealers

(G-16152)
CAPEFEAR SPORTSWEAR
901 Upper Reach Dr (28409-2660)
PHONE..................................910 620-7844
Dennis Smith, Owner
▲ EMP: 5 EST: 2008
SALES (est): 441.31K Privately Held
Web: www.capefearsportswear.com
SIC: 2329 Men's and boys' sportswear and athletic clothing

(G-16153)
CAPITAL VALUE CENTER SLS & SVC
5406 Market St (28405-3508)
PHONE..................................910 799-4060
Mark Newmoyer, Prin
EMP: 7 EST: 2014
SALES (est): 175.35K Privately Held
SIC: 7549 3751 High performance auto repair and service; Motorcycle accessories

(G-16154)
CAPITOL WOODWORKS
3911 Peachtree Ave (28403-6729)
PHONE..................................919 703-9293
Cameron Stephenson, Prin
EMP: 5 EST: 2017
SALES (est): 59.54K Privately Held
SIC: 2431 Millwork

(G-16155)
CAPRE OMNIMEDIA LLC
801 N 4th St Apt 404 (28401-3485)
PHONE..................................917 460-3572
Brian Klebash, Pr

GEOGRAPHIC SECTION — Wilmington - New Hanover County (G-16183)

EMP: 5 EST: 2010
SALES (est): 190.09K **Privately Held**
Web: www.shure.international
SIC: 7299 7319 8742 2721 Facility rental and party planning services; Media buying service; Marketing consulting services; Trade journals: publishing and printing

(G-16156)
CARDIOPHARMA INC
100-A Eastwood Center Dr Ste 117 (28403)
PHONE....................910 791-1361
Daniel Gregory, *Pr*
EMP: 10 EST: 2006
SALES (est): 580.67K **Privately Held**
Web: www.cardio-pharma.com
SIC: 2834 Pharmaceutical preparations

(G-16157)
CAROLINA COMMERCIAL COATINGS
20 Wrights Aly (28401-4991)
PHONE....................910 279-6045
Donald Lashley, *Owner*
EMP: 6 EST: 1993
SALES (est): 493.16K **Privately Held**
SIC: 2851 Paints and allied products

(G-16158)
CAROLINA SHOWER DOOR INC
1901 Blue Clay Rd Ste G1 (28405-8059)
P.O. Box 12577 (28405-0130)
PHONE....................910 343-0009
Greg Manis, *Pr*
EMP: 4 EST: 2006
SALES (est): 87.55K **Privately Held**
Web: www.carolinashowerdoor.com
SIC: 3431 Shower stalls, metal

(G-16159)
CASABLANCA 4 LLC
4805 Wrightsville Ave (28403-6918)
PHONE....................910 702-4399
Clayton Gsell, *Prin*
Bruce Brawley, *Prin*
Chris Nesselroade, *Prin*
Steve Cobb, *Prin*
EMP: 4 EST: 2021
SALES (est): 156.69K **Privately Held**
SIC: 2842 Polishes and sanitation goods

(G-16160)
CASEWORK ETC INC
3116 Kitty Hawk Rd (28405-8621)
PHONE....................910 763-7119
Mitchell Wayne Matthews, *Pr*
Claudia Matthews, *VP*
EMP: 7 EST: 2007
SQ FT: 12,000
SALES (est): 919.58K **Privately Held**
SIC: 2434 Wood kitchen cabinets

(G-16161)
CAVA DI PIETRA INC
1502 N 23rd St (28405-1816)
PHONE....................910 338-5024
Christopher Mitscherlich, *Prin*
EMP: 8 EST: 2015
SALES (est): 122.48K **Privately Held**
SIC: 3272 Silo staves, cast stone or concrete

(G-16162)
CBD OPEN WATER DIVING
262 Battleship Rd (28401-2533)
PHONE....................910 232-3692
Chip Taylor, *Prin*
EMP: 6 EST: 2017
SALES (est): 120.94K **Privately Held**
SIC: 3999

(G-16163)
CBR SIGNS LLC
Also Called: Souther Signs Company
5649 Carolina Beach Rd (28412-2609)
PHONE....................910 794-8243
Andrea Wilson, *Managing Member*
EMP: 8 EST: 2015
SALES (est): 392.89K **Privately Held**
Web: www.southernsigncompany.com
SIC: 3993 Signs and advertising specialties

(G-16164)
CE KITCHEN INC
306 Old Dairy Rd (28405-3766)
PHONE....................910 399-2334
Jason Nista, *CEO*
Evonne Varady, *
Samuel B Potter, *
EMP: 100 EST: 2017
SALES (est): 7.42MM **Privately Held**
Web: www.cleaneatzkitchen.com
SIC: 2038 Dinners, frozen and packaged

(G-16165)
CELANESE
4600 Us Highway 421 N (28401-2225)
PHONE....................910 343-5000
EMP: 22 EST: 2019
SALES (est): 3.82MM **Privately Held**
SIC: 2819 Industrial inorganic chemicals, nec

(G-16166)
CELLAR
12 Nun St (28401-5016)
PHONE....................910 399-2997
EMP: 5 EST: 2010
SALES (est): 80.39K **Privately Held**
SIC: 2084 Wines

(G-16167)
CERES TURF INC
Also Called: CTI
2312 N 23rd St (28401-8812)
P.O. Box 12447 (28405-0119)
PHONE....................910 256-8974
◆ EMP: 4 EST: 2007
SQ FT: 15,000
SALES (est): 497.78K **Privately Held**
Web: www.ceresturf.com
SIC: 3523 Turf equipment, commercial

(G-16168)
CHADSWORTH INCORPORATED
Also Called: Polystone Columns
420 Raleigh St Ste A (28412-6335)
P.O. Box 2618 (28402-2618)
PHONE....................910 763-7600
Jeff L Davis, *CEO*
◆ EMP: 24 EST: 1987
SALES (est): 1.16MM **Privately Held**
Web: www.columns.com
SIC: 2431 3089 3281 Interior and ornamental woodwork and trim; Plastics hardware and building products; Cut stone and stone products

(G-16169)
CHARNEL INC
Also Called: Dock Street Printing Co
110 Dock St (28401-4433)
PHONE....................910 763-8476
William Goodwyn, *Owner*
EMP: 7 EST: 1973
SQ FT: 3,500
SALES (est): 234.83K **Privately Held**
Web: www.dockstreetprinting.com
SIC: 2752 Offset printing

(G-16170)
CHIC MONOGRAM
1222 Columbus Cir Apt C (28403-3927)
PHONE....................910 431-8704
EMP: 4 EST: 2018
SALES (est): 67.95K **Privately Held**
SIC: 2395 Embroidery and art needlework

(G-16171)
COASTAL FABRICA TION
1409 Audubon Blvd (28403-6749)
PHONE....................910 399-4460
EMP: 5 EST: 2018
SALES (est): 115.23K **Privately Held**
SIC: 3441 Fabricated structural metal

(G-16172)
COASTAL MILLWORK SUPPLY CO
1301 S 13th St (28401-6404)
PHONE....................910 763-3300
Jim Risley, *Pr*
Bob Padul, *
EMP: 30 EST: 2005
SALES (est): 3.87MM **Privately Held**
Web: www.coastalmillworksupply.com
SIC: 2431 Millwork

(G-16173)
COASTAL PRECAST SYSTEMS LLC
5125 Us Highway 421 N (28401-2251)
PHONE....................910 444-4682
Paul F Ogorchock, *Managing Member*
EMP: 143
Web: www.cpsprecast.com
SIC: 3272 Concrete products, precast, nec
PA: Coastal Precast Systems, Llc
1316 Yacht Dr Ste 307
Chesapeake VA 23320

(G-16174)
COASTAL TIDES SOAP CANDLES LLC
5305 Lord Tennyson Dr (28405-1522)
PHONE....................910 833-2132
Brandon Mschmude, *VP*
EMP: 4 EST: 2015
SALES (est): 85.27K **Privately Held**
Web: www.coastaltidessoap.com
SIC: 3999 Candles

(G-16175)
COLUMBIA SILICA SAND LLC
Also Called: American Materials Company
1410 Commonwealth Dr Ste 201 (28403)
PHONE....................803 755-1036
Sophie Sagrera, *Pr*
Jean Toal, *Sec*
Lilla Hoefer Ii, *Treas*
EMP: 10 EST: 1990
SALES (est): 1.04MM **Privately Held**
SIC: 1442 Common sand mining

(G-16176)
COMMON SCENTS SOLUTIONS
705 Glenarthur Dr (28412-3040)
PHONE....................812 344-4312
EMP: 4 EST: 2015
SALES (est): 84.98K **Privately Held**
SIC: 2844 Perfumes, cosmetics and other toilet preparations

(G-16177)
CONNECTIVITY GROUP LLC
Also Called: Apple Annie's Bake Shop
837 S Kerr Ave (28403-8427)
PHONE....................910 799-9023
Robert Cooley Junior, *Managing Member*
Frank Lewis, *
EMP: 35 EST: 1999
SALES (est): 1.64MM **Privately Held**
SIC: 2051 Bakery: wholesale or wholesale/retail combined

(G-16178)
CONROLL CORPORATION
3302 Kitty Hawk Rd Ste 100 (28405-8772)
PHONE....................910 202-4292
▲ EMP: 10
SIC: 3535 Conveyors and conveying equipment

(G-16179)
CONTAINER PRODUCTS CORPORATION (PA)
112 N College Rd (28405-3514)
P.O. Box 3767 (28406-0767)
PHONE....................910 392-6100
Dwight Campbell, *Pr*
C S Johnston, *Pr*
Jeff Kahle, *Ex VP*
EMP: 65 EST: 1981
SQ FT: 52,000
SALES (est): 18.69MM
SALES (corp-wide): 18.69MM **Privately Held**
Web: www.c-p-c.net
SIC: 3411 3443 3354 Metal cans; Industrial vessels, tanks, and containers; Aluminum extruded products

(G-16180)
CONTAINER TECHNOLOGY INC
Also Called: Container Technology
430 Raleigh St (28412-6367)
PHONE....................910 350-1303
EMP: 6 EST: 1994
SALES (est): 803.66K **Privately Held**
Web: www.containertechnology.com
SIC: 7692 7538 Welding repair; General truck repair

(G-16181)
CONVERT-A-STAIR LLC
3013 Hall Watters Dr Ste C (28405-8790)
PHONE....................888 908-5657
Brian Estes, *Pr*
Frank Everett, *Managing Member*
EMP: 4 EST: 2014
SALES (est): 264.05K **Privately Held**
Web: www.convertastair.com
SIC: 2431 Staircases and stairs, wood

(G-16182)
COPYCAT PRINT SHOP INC
637 S Kerr Ave (28403-8423)
P.O. Box 3347 (28406-0347)
PHONE....................910 799-1500
Betsy L Kahn, *Pr*
Marie S Kahn, *VP*
Max Kahn, *Treas*
EMP: 17 EST: 1970
SALES (est): 2.25MM **Privately Held**
Web: www.copycatprintshop.net
SIC: 7334 2752 Photocopying and duplicating services; Offset printing

(G-16183)
CORBETT PACKAGE COMPANY
1200 Castle Hayne Rd (28401-8885)
P.O. Box 210 (28402-0210)
PHONE....................910 763-9991
Edward M Corbett, *Pr*
James W Corbett, *Pt*
EMP: 55 EST: 2019
SALES (est): 5.07MM **Privately Held**
Web: www.thecorbettcompanies.com
SIC: 2435 Veneer stock, hardwood

Wilmington - New Hanover County (G-16184)   GEOGRAPHIC SECTION

(G-16184)
CORNING INCORPORATED
Also Called: Corning
310 N College Rd (28405-3590)
PHONE..................................910 784-7200
Thomas Nettleman, *Brnch Mgr*
EMP: 75
SALES (corp-wide): 12.59B **Publicly Held**
Web: www.corning.com
SIC: **3827** 3229 Optical instruments and lenses; Fiber optics strands
PA: Corning Incorporated
1 Riverfront Plz
Corning NY 14831
607 974-9000

(G-16185)
CREATIVE CUSTOM WDWKG LLC
Also Called: C C W
2150 Wrightsville Ave (28403-0271)
PHONE..................................910 431-8544
EMP: 5 EST: 2013
SALES (est): 233.93K **Privately Held**
Web: www.wilmingtoncustomcabinet.com
SIC: **2431** Millwork

(G-16186)
CREATIVE CUSTOM WOODWORKS INC
1290 S 15th St B (28401-6410)
PHONE..................................910 431-8544
John Andrew Salley, *Prin*
EMP: 8 EST: 2002
SALES (est): 400.5K **Privately Held**
Web: www.wilmingtoncustomcabinet.com
SIC: **2431** Millwork

(G-16187)
CREATIVE SIGNS INC
Also Called: Fastsigns
4305 Oleander Dr (28403-5007)
PHONE..................................910 395-0100
Pete Spadafora, *Pr*
EMP: 6 EST: 2014
SALES (est): 700K **Privately Held**
Web: www.fastsigns.com
SIC: **3993** Signs and advertising specialties

(G-16188)
CREATIVEWOODWORKS WILMINGTON
6708 Dorrington Dr (28412-3091)
PHONE..................................910 233-3042
Simon Sanders-vi, *Owner*
EMP: 5 EST: 2007
SALES (est): 59.93K **Privately Held**
SIC: **2431** Millwork

(G-16189)
CRETE SOLUTIONS LLC
2005 Eastwood Rd Ste 200 (28403-7233)
PHONE..................................910 726-1686
Harry M Shaw, *Managing Member*
EMP: 26 EST: 2017
SALES (est): 9.2MM **Privately Held**
Web: www.cretesolutionsllc.com
SIC: **3273** Ready-mixed concrete

(G-16190)
CRS/LAS INC
Also Called: All Ways Graphics
120 Racine Dr Ste 3 (28403-8836)
PHONE..................................910 392-0883
Charles R Stone Junior, *Pr*
EMP: 23 EST: 1991
SQ FT: 5,800
SALES (est): 1.73MM **Privately Held**
Web: www.allwaysgraphics.com

SIC: **2752** Offset printing

(G-16191)
CRYOSTOP INTERNATIONAL
105 Oxmoor Pl (28403-0136)
PHONE..................................910 452-5556
Michael Ingram, *Pr*
Sheila Ingram, *VP*
EMP: 5 EST: 2001
SALES (est): 406.34K **Privately Held**
Web: www.cryostop.com
SIC: **3399** Cryogenic treatment of metal

(G-16192)
CUSTOM REHABILITATION SPC INC
7225 Anaca Point Rd (28411-9501)
PHONE..................................910 471-2962
William D Eno, *Pr*
Carl Thompson, *VP*
EMP: 4 EST: 1994
SALES (est): 399.38K **Privately Held**
SIC: **5999** 3842 Medical apparatus and supplies; Orthopedic appliances

(G-16193)
CUSTOM SPT & IMPRINTABLES LLC
207 Antilles Ct Ste B (28405-4776)
PHONE..................................910 799-9914
EMP: 12 EST: 2007
SALES (est): 714.76K **Privately Held**
SIC: **2329** Men's and boys' sportswear and athletic clothing

(G-16194)
DARIUS ALL ACCESS LLC
Also Called: Darius All Access
1013 Glenlea Dr (28405-2203)
P.O. Box 105 (28402-0105)
PHONE..................................910 262-8567
Darius Brunson, *CEO*
EMP: 20 EST: 2020
SALES (est): 768.49K **Privately Held**
Web: www.dariusallaccess.com
SIC: **7299** 7349 3524 Handyman service; Cleaning service, industrial or commercial; Lawnmowers, residential: hand or power

(G-16195)
DAVIS NEWELL COMPANY INC
2962 N Kerr Ave (28405-8677)
PHONE..................................910 762-3500
Teresa Mcgee, *Pr*
Robert Mcgee, *VP*
▲ EMP: 17 EST: 1997
SQ FT: 15,000
SALES (est): 2.46MM **Privately Held**
Web: www.newelldavis.com
SIC: **3496** Woven wire products, nec

(G-16196)
DAZTECH INC
Also Called: Daztech Promotions
214 Walnut St (28401-3931)
P.O. Box 156 (28402-0156)
PHONE..................................800 862-6360
Kathy Bowen, *Pr*
Jon Spetrino, *VP*
▲ EMP: 4 EST: 1992
SQ FT: 4,000
SALES (est): 317.27K **Privately Held**
SIC: **2261** 5199 Screen printing of cotton broadwoven fabrics; Advertising specialties

(G-16197)
DDM INC
Also Called: Diversified Disposables Mfg
210 Sea Shell Ln (28411-7645)
PHONE..................................910 686-1481
W Harley Ford, *Pr*
EMP: 7 EST: 1976

SQ FT: 5,000
SALES (est): 389.36K **Privately Held**
SIC: **2389** 5047 Disposable garments and accessories; Medical and hospital equipment

(G-16198)
DECKLE PAPERBOARD SALES INC
256 Osprey Pl (28411-6895)
PHONE..................................910 686-9145
William F Lee, *Prin*
EMP: 7 EST: 2015
SALES (est): 236.62K **Privately Held**
SIC: **2631** Paperboard mills

(G-16199)
DERMASWEET LLC
817 Town Center Dr Ste 125- (28405-8340)
PHONE..................................843 834-1413
EMP: 4 EST: 2017
SALES (est): 55.89K **Privately Held**
Web: www.dermasweetnc.com
SIC: **2061** Raw cane sugar

(G-16200)
DIANE BRITT
Also Called: Design Workshop, The
3205 Kitty Hawk Rd Ste 1 (28405-8630)
PHONE..................................910 763-9600
Diane Britt, *Owner*
EMP: 4 EST: 1985
SQ FT: 2,500
SALES (est): 243.44K **Privately Held**
Web: www.pendercreek.com
SIC: **2391** 2392 Draperies, plastic and textile: from purchased materials; Bedspreads and bed sets: made from purchased materials

(G-16201)
DIGITAL PRINT & IMAGING INC
3001 Wrightsville Ave Ste C (28403-4189)
PHONE..................................910 341-3005
Brian Carter, *Pr*
Matt Carter, *VP*
EMP: 7 EST: 2002
SALES (est): 374.82K **Privately Held**
SIC: **2759** 5112 5044 Screen printing; Stationery and office supplies; Office equipment

(G-16202)
DIGITAURUS INC
4605 Wrightsville Ave (28403-6914)
PHONE..................................910 794-9243
Lisa Zupan, *Pr*
EMP: 4 EST: 1994
SQ FT: 3,000
SALES (est): 485.86K **Privately Held**
Web: www.digitaurus.com
SIC: **2759** Screen printing

(G-16203)
DIGITAURUS EMB SCREEN PRTG INC
6100 Chilcot Ln (28409-2064)
PHONE..................................910 794-3275
Jack Britt, *Pr*
EMP: 6 EST: 2015
SALES (est): 92.3K **Privately Held**
Web: www.digitaurus.com
SIC: **2759** Screen printing

(G-16204)
DORIAN CORPORATION
Also Called: Musicmedic.com
901 Martin St (28401-7827)
PHONE..................................910 352-6939
EMP: 10 EST: 2009
SALES (est): 763.89K **Privately Held**

Web: www.musicmedic.com
SIC: **5736** 3999 Musical instrument stores; Advertising curtains

(G-16205)
DR PEPPER CO OF WILMINGTON
Also Called: Dr Pepper
415 Landmark Dr (28412-6303)
PHONE..................................910 792-5400
Terry Dolwling, *Owner*
EMP: 7 EST: 2011
SALES (est): 81.6K **Privately Held**
Web: www.drpepper.com
SIC: **2086** Soft drinks: packaged in cans, bottles, etc.

(G-16206)
DRW RENOVATIONS & CUSTOM WDWKG
11 Robert E Lee Dr (28412-6723)
P.O. Box 7904 (28406-7904)
PHONE..................................910 471-9367
EMP: 4 EST: 2019
SALES (est): 54.13K **Privately Held**
Web: www.drwrenovationsnc.com
SIC: **2431** Millwork

(G-16207)
DUSTCONTROL INC
6720 Amsterdam Way Ste 400 (28405-3777)
PHONE..................................910 395-1808
▲ EMP: 16 EST: 2006
SQ FT: 15,302
SALES (est): 7.17MM **Privately Held**
Web: www.dustcontrol.us
SIC: **3564** 1796 3589 Purification and dust collection equipment; Machinery installation ; Vacuum cleaners and sweepers, electric: industrial
HQ: Dustcontrol Ab
Kumla Gardsvag 14
Norsborg 145 6
853194000

(G-16208)
E W GODWIN S SONS INC (PA)
1207 Castle Hayne Rd (28401-8886)
P.O. Box 1806 (28402-1806)
PHONE..................................910 762-7747
TOLL FREE: 800
James Z Godwin Ii, *Pr*
EMP: 22 EST: 1909
SQ FT: 6,400
SALES (est): 4.74MM
SALES (corp-wide): 4.74MM **Privately Held**
Web: www.ewgodwinlumber.com
SIC: **2421** 5211 Sawmills and planing mills, general; Lumber and other building materials

(G-16209)
EAGLE EYES CRRCLUM EDTRIAL SVC
114 Red Fox Rd (28409-3171)
PHONE..................................910 399-7445
Adelaide Mcculloch, *Prin*
EMP: 5 EST: 2018
SALES (est): 68.06K **Privately Held**
SIC: **2741** Miscellaneous publishing

(G-16210)
ELITE BUSINESS SOLUTIONS LLC
Also Called: Elite Business Technologies
420 Darlington Ave (28403-1353)
PHONE..................................910 713-9350
Quintabitha Mitchell, *Managing Member*
EMP: 6 EST: 2008
SALES (est): 82K **Privately Held**

GEOGRAPHIC SECTION

SIC: 7372 Prepackaged software

(G-16211)
END OF DAYS DISTILLERY
1815 Castle St (28403-2103)
PHONE....................910 399-1133
EMP: 11 EST: 2020
SALES (est): 1.85MM **Privately Held**
Web: www.eoddistillery.com
SIC: 2085 Distilled and blended liquors

(G-16212)
ERIC LEFFINGWELL
2925 Boundary St Ste 21 (28405-8076)
PHONE....................910 367-1928
Eric Leffingwell, *Prin*
EMP: 5 EST: 2013
SALES (est): 180.47K **Privately Held**
SIC: 2431 Millwork

(G-16213)
EVERGREEN FOREST PRODUCTS INC
2605 Blue Clay Rd (28405-8613)
PHONE....................910 762-9156
Brian Benford, *Pr*
Cheryl Benford, *Sec*
EMP: 5 EST: 1998
SALES (est): 828.54K **Privately Held**
Web: www.evergreennc.us
SIC: 2411 Logging camps and contractors

(G-16214)
EXPOGO INC
Also Called: Expogo Displays & Graphics
411 Landmark Dr (28412-6303)
PHONE....................910 452-3976
Wallace T Carter, *Pr*
▲ **EMP: 8 EST:** 1988
SALES (est): 948K **Privately Held**
Web: www.expogo.com
SIC: 3993 Signs and advertising specialties

(G-16215)
F & M STEEL PRODUCTS INC
3314 Enterprise Dr (28405-2120)
PHONE....................910 793-1345
Nathan Edwards, *Pr*
Floyd Knowles, *Pr*
Maggie Knowles, *VP*
Chris Banks, *VP*
EMP: 9 EST: 1996
SALES (est): 1.67MM **Privately Held**
Web: www.wilmingtongrill.com
SIC: 3444 Sheet metalwork

(G-16216)
FAC ETTE MANUFACTURING
208 Beech St (28405-4120)
PHONE....................910 599-7352
EMP: 4 EST: 2018
SALES (est): 62.97K **Privately Held**
SIC: 3999 Manufacturing industries, nec

(G-16217)
FATHOM OFFSHORE HOLDINGS LLC
Also Called: Fathom Offshore
3018 N Kerr Ave Ste A (28405-8679)
PHONE....................910 399-6882
Andrew I Holcomb, *Managing Member*
▲ **EMP: 9 EST:** 2006
SQ FT: 10,000
SALES (est): 444.48K **Privately Held**
Web: www.fathomoffshore.com
SIC: 3949 5941 5091 Fishing equipment; Fishing equipment; Fishing equipment and supplies

(G-16218)
FLOAT LIFTS OF CAROLINAS LLC
8012 Yellow Daisy Dr (28412-3275)
PHONE....................919 972-1082
Tim Holloway, *Brnch Mgr*
EMP: 6
SALES (corp-wide): 743.57K **Privately Held**
Web: www.floatlifts.com
SIC: 3536 Boat lifts
PA: Float Lifts Of The Carolinas, Llc
2527 Hoot Owl Dr
Hillsborough NC

(G-16219)
FLOYD S BRACES AND LIMBS INC
709 Parkway Blvd (28412-6556)
PHONE....................910 763-0821
Michael Floyd, *Pr*
Nancy Floyd, *Prin*
EMP: 6 EST: 1953
SALES (est): 605.45K **Privately Held**
SIC: 3842 Limbs, artificial

(G-16220)
FORTRON INDUSTRIES LLC
4600 Us Highway 421 N (28401-2225)
P.O. Box 327 (28402-0327)
PHONE....................910 343-5000
Ashish Kulkarni, *
▲ **EMP: 45 EST:** 2006
SALES (est): 4.63MM **Privately Held**
SIC: 3089 Plastics processing

(G-16221)
FRANCIS SIMPLY PUBLISHING CO
P.O. Box 329 (28480-0329)
PHONE....................910 399-2508
Frank Amoroso, *Owner*
EMP: 5 EST: 2013
SALES (est): 84.26K **Privately Held**
Web: www.behindeverygreatfortune.com
SIC: 2741 Miscellaneous publishing

(G-16222)
FRANK UNCLE PRODUCTIONS LLC
3719 Carolina Beach Rd (28412-1907)
PHONE....................910 769-2729
EMP: 4 EST: 2019
SALES (est): 49.15K **Privately Held**
SIC: 3861 Motion picture film

(G-16223)
FRITO-LAY NORTH AMERICA INC
3215 Kitty Hawk Rd (28405-8620)
PHONE....................980 224-3730
Sidney Bletcher, *Mgr*
EMP: 4
SALES (corp-wide): 86.39B **Publicly Held**
SIC: 2086 Carbonated soft drinks, bottled and canned
HQ: Frito-Lay North America, Inc.
7701 Legacy Dr
Plano TX 75024

(G-16224)
FTM ENTERPRISES INC
301 N Green Meadows Dr (28405-4041)
PHONE....................910 798-2045
Dennis Shaw, *Pr*
EMP: 10 EST: 2005
SALES (est): 1.43MM **Privately Held**
SIC: 3281 Cut stone and stone products

(G-16225)
FURNITURE COMPANY
822 Santa Maria Ave (28411-7641)
PHONE....................910 686-1937
EMP: 4 EST: 2011
SALES (est): 130K **Privately Held**

SIC: 2511 Wood household furniture

(G-16226)
G & E SOFTWARE INC
1410 Commonwealth Dr Ste 102b (28403)
PHONE....................910 762-5608
EMP: 10 EST: 2015
SALES (est): 539.32K **Privately Held**
SIC: 7372 Prepackaged software

(G-16227)
GASSER AND SONS
5102 Old Myrtle Grove Rd (28409-4122)
PHONE....................910 471-6907
EMP: 6 EST: 2017
SALES (est): 47.82K **Privately Held**
SIC: 3469 Stamping metal for the trade

(G-16228)
GE-HITCHI NCLEAR ENRGY INTL LL (HQ)
Also Called: Nuclear Energy Ne US
3901 Castle Hayne Rd (28402)
PHONE....................518 433-4338
Mark R Sweeney, *
EMP: 35 EST: 2007
SALES (est): 48.6MM
SALES (corp-wide): 67.95B **Publicly Held**
Web: www.gevernova.com
SIC: 2819 Nuclear fuel and cores, inorganic
PA: General Electric Company
1 Financial Ctr Ste 3700
Boston MA 02111
617 443-3000

(G-16229)
GELARTO INC
18 S Water St (28401-4477)
PHONE....................646 795-3505
Sandy Auriti, *Genl Mgr*
EMP: 10 EST: 2016
SALES (est): 903.81K **Privately Held**
Web: www.gelarto.com
SIC: 2024 Ice cream and frozen deserts

(G-16230)
GENERAL ELECTRIC COMPANY
GE
3901 Castle Hayne Rd (28401)
PHONE....................910 675-5000
Andrew White, *Brnch Mgr*
EMP: 2436
SALES (corp-wide): 67.95B **Publicly Held**
Web: www.ge.com
SIC: 2819 3519 3812 3728 Nuclear fuels, uranium slug (radioactive); Jet propulsion engines; Search and navigation equipment; Aircraft parts and equipment, nec
PA: General Electric Company
1 Financial Ctr Ste 3700
Boston MA 02111
617 443-3000

(G-16231)
GENERAL SHALE BRICK INC
Also Called: General Shale Brick
3750 Us Highway 421 N (28401-9022)
PHONE....................910 452-3498
Terry Wright, *Mgr*
EMP: 9
SALES (corp-wide): 5.17B **Privately Held**
Web: www.generalshale.com
SIC: 3251 5032 Brick clay: common face, glazed, vitrified, or hollow; Brick, stone, and related material
HQ: General Shale Brick, Inc.
3015 Bristol Hwy
Johnson City TN 37601
423 282-4661

(G-16232)
GLOBAL NUCLEAR FUEL LLC
3901 Castle Hayne Rd (28401)
PHONE....................910 819-6181
EMP: 17 EST: 1999
SALES (est): 2.38MM **Privately Held**
Web: www.gevernova.com
SIC: 2819 Nuclear fuel and cores, inorganic

(G-16233)
GLOBAL RESOURCE NC INC
Also Called: Sign-A-Rama
1001 Broomsedge Ter (28412-1054)
PHONE....................910 793-4770
Rebecca Kronfeld, *Pr*
EMP: 4 EST: 2001
SALES (est): 499.57K **Privately Held**
Web: www.signarama.com
SIC: 3993 Signs and advertising specialties

(G-16234)
GO ENERGIES LLC
1410 Commonwealth Dr Ste 102b (28403)
PHONE....................877 712-5999
EMP: 15 EST: 2010
SQ FT: 6,000
SALES (est): 4.99MM
SALES (corp-wide): 7.78MM **Privately Held**
Web: www.goenergies.com
SIC: 5983 7372 8742 Fuel oil dealers; Prepackaged software; Management consulting services
PA: Go Energies Holdings, Inc.
1410 Commwl Dr Ste 102b
Wilmington NC 28403
910 762-5802

(G-16235)
GO ENERGIES HOLDINGS INC (PA)
1410 Commonwealth Dr Ste 102b (28403)
PHONE....................910 762-5802
James Phillip Dorroll Ii, *Pr*
EMP: 9 EST: 2009
SALES (est): 7.78MM
SALES (corp-wide): 7.78MM **Privately Held**
Web: www.goenergies.com
SIC: 8742 7372 5983 Management consulting services; Prepackaged software; Fuel oil dealers

(G-16236)
GOLFWORKS
102 Old Eastwood Rd Ste C2 (28403)
PHONE....................910 796-3160
EMP: 4
SALES (est): 52.3K **Privately Held**
Web: www.golfworks.com
SIC: 3961 Costume jewelry

(G-16237)
GORE S MAR MET FABRICATION INC
302 N Channel Haven Dr (28409-3506)
PHONE....................910 763-6066
Danny Gore, *Pr*
David Gore, *VP*
EMP: 5 EST: 1985
SALES (est): 502.7K **Privately Held**
Web: www.goremarineinc.com
SIC: 3441 7692 Boat and barge sections, prefabricated metal; Welding repair

(G-16238)
GRACIE GOODNESS INC
113 Portwatch Way Ste 101 (28412-7056)
P.O. Box 7701 (28406-7701)
PHONE....................910 792-0800
Carter Price, *Pr*
Sallie Price, *VP*

Wilmington - New Hanover County (G-16239) — GEOGRAPHIC SECTION

EMP: 5 **EST:** 1995
SALES (est): 254.59K **Privately Held**
Web: www.goodnessgracie.com
SIC: 2052 Cookies

(G-16239)
GRAPHIC IMAGE OF CAPE FEAR INC
Also Called: Graphic Image
2840 S College Rd (28412-6827)
PHONE..................910 313-6768
Calvin Barnes, *Pr*
Demetrius Barnes, *Sec*
EMP: 4 **EST:** 1987
SQ FT: 1,500
SALES (est): 478.56K **Privately Held**
Web: www.mailroomshipandprint.com
SIC: 2759 7336 Commercial printing, nec; Graphic arts and related design

(G-16240)
GREATER WILMINGTON BUSINESS
101 N 3rd St (28401-4034)
PHONE..................910 343-8600
Joy B Allen, *Owner*
EMP: 5 **EST:** 2005
SALES (est): 394.17K **Privately Held**
Web: www.wilmingtonbiz.com
SIC: 2721 Magazines: publishing and printing

(G-16241)
GREENFIELD PRINTING CO
1536 S Front St (28401-6120)
PHONE..................910 763-0647
Hales Keith, *Prin*
EMP: 9 **EST:** 1994
SQ FT: 5,480
SALES (est): 165.87K **Privately Held**
Web: www.livenation.com
SIC: 2759 Commercial printing, nec

(G-16242)
GRIND ATHLETICS LLC
8119 Yellow Daisy Dr (28412-3269)
PHONE..................910 228-0035
Timothy Banford, *Prin*
EMP: 5 **EST:** 2016
SALES (est): 223.13K **Privately Held**
SIC: 3599 Grinding castings for the trade

(G-16243)
GUILFORD MILLS LLC
1001 Military Cutoff Rd Ste 300 (28405-4376)
PHONE..................910 794-5810
◆ **EMP:** 2600
SIC: 2258 2399 Cloth, warp knit; Automotive covers, except seat and tire covers

(G-16244)
HANOVER ELECTRIC MOTOR SVC INC
Also Called: Hanover Electric Motors & Sups
602 Wellington Ave (28401-7614)
PHONE..................910 762-3702
Bradley E Dunn, *Pr*
Bradley Dunn, *Pr*
Richard A Wingo, *VP*
Misty Dunn, *Treas*
EMP: 9 **EST:** 1960
SQ FT: 4,100
SALES (est): 2.06MM **Privately Held**
Web: www.hanoverelectric.com
SIC: 5063 7694 Motors, electric; Electric motor repair

(G-16245)
HANOVER IRON WORKS INC
2602 Park Ave (28403-4027)
P.O. Box 7155 (28406-7155)
PHONE..................910 763-7318
Horace T King Iii, *Pr*
Horace T King Iv, *VP*
William F King, *
EMP: 25 **EST:** 1903
SQ FT: 23,000
SALES (est): 682.43K **Privately Held**
Web: www.hiwsheetmetal.com
SIC: 3444 Sheet metalwork

(G-16246)
HANOVER IRON WORKS SHTMTL INC
Also Called: Cnc Laser Shop
1861 Dawson St (28403-2328)
PHONE..................910 399-1146
Thompson King, *Pr*
EMP: 7 **EST:** 2008
SALES (est): 711.15K **Privately Held**
SIC: 3444 Sheet metalwork

(G-16247)
HARBOR LINES LLC
127 Northern Blvd (28401-6731)
P.O. Box 2151 (28402-2151)
PHONE..................910 279-3796
EMP: 5 **EST:** 1987
SALES (est): 470.02K **Privately Held**
Web: www.harborlines.com
SIC: 3731 7389 Shipbuilding and repairing; Courier or messenger service

(G-16248)
HARTLEY LOUDSPEAKERS INC
Also Called: The Audio Lab
5732 Oleander Dr (28403-4714)
PHONE..................910 392-1200
Richard Schmetterer, *Pr*
▲ **EMP:** 18 **EST:** 1951
SALES (est): 455.69K **Privately Held**
Web: www.audiolab1.com
SIC: 3651 Speaker systems

(G-16249)
HARTLEY PRODUCTS CORP
5732 Oleander Dr (28403-4714)
PHONE..................910 392-0500
Richard Schmetterer, *Prin*
EMP: 6 **EST:** 2016
SALES (est): 61.69K **Privately Held**
SIC: 3651 Household audio and video equipment

(G-16250)
HERAEUS QUARTZ NORTH AMER LLC
Also Called: Wholesale Glass Fabricators
3016 Boundary St (28405-8619)
PHONE..................910 799-6230
Greg Little, *Mgr*
EMP: 28
SALES (corp-wide): 2.67MM **Privately Held**
SIC: 3231 3229 Products of purchased glass; Pressed and blown glass, nec
HQ: Heraeus Quartz North America Llc
100 Heraeus Blvd
Buford GA 30518
770 945-2275

(G-16251)
HERFF JONES
105 Portwatch Way Ste C (28412-7082)
PHONE..................910 399-2740
EMP: 5 **EST:** 2015
SALES (est): 192.5K **Privately Held**
SIC: 2752 Commercial printing, lithographic

(G-16252)
HIGH COTTON FABRICATION LLC
3126 Kitty Hawk Rd Ste 5 (28405-8625)
PHONE..................910 408-6961
EMP: 5 **EST:** 2018
SALES (est): 88.25K **Privately Held**
SIC: 7692 Welding repair

(G-16253)
HIGH SPEED WELDING LLC
1536 Castle Hayne Rd 6 (28405)
PHONE..................910 632-4427
Staurt A Foreman, *Managing Member*
EMP: 11 **EST:** 2006
SALES (est): 413.18K **Privately Held**
Web: www.highspeedweld.com
SIC: 7692 Welding repair

(G-16254)
HIGH TIDE CANVAS & UPHL INC
311 Judges Rd Ste 12a (28405-3647)
PHONE..................910 409-5903
EMP: 5 **EST:** 2018
SALES (est): 226.05K **Privately Held**
Web: www.hightidecanvas.com
SIC: 2211 Canvas

(G-16255)
HIS COMPANY INC
All-Spec
2516 Independence Blvd Ste 201 (28412-7161)
PHONE..................800 537-0351
Robert Dill, *Pr*
EMP: 6
SALES (corp-wide): 417.73MM **Publicly Held**
Web: www.hisco.com
SIC: 2891 5063 5065 Adhesives and sealants; Electrical apparatus and equipment; Electronic parts and equipment, nec
HQ: His Company, Inc.
6650 Concord Park Dr
Houston TX 77040
713 934-1600

(G-16256)
HOMESTEAD COUNTRY BUILT FURN (PA)
4942 Tanbark Dr (28412-7718)
PHONE..................910 799-6489
Russell L Hill, *Owner*
EMP: 5 **EST:** 1985
SALES (est): 321.92K **Privately Held**
SIC: 2511 Wood bedroom furniture

(G-16257)
HORIZON VISION RESEARCH INC
1717 Shipyard Blvd Ste 140 (28403-8023)
PHONE..................910 796-8600
Tara Tatum, *Contrlr*
EMP: 10 **EST:** 2002
SALES (est): 159.6K **Privately Held**
Web: www.damsickles.com
SIC: 3841 Surgical and medical instruments

(G-16258)
HOSMER WOODWORKS
321 E Renovah Cir (28403-1225)
PHONE..................415 730-5401
Matthew Hosmer, *Prin*
EMP: 5 **EST:** 2015
SALES (est): 59K **Privately Held**
SIC: 2431 Millwork

(G-16259)
HOUSE OF RAEFORD FARMS INC
118 Cardinal Drive Ext Ste 102 (28405-2482)
PHONE..................910 763-0475
Ron Carlos, *Owner*
EMP: 651
SALES (corp-wide): 1.79B **Privately Held**
Web: www.houseofraeford.com
SIC: 2015 Poultry slaughtering and processing
HQ: House Of Raeford Farms, Inc.
3333 S Us Highway 117
Rose Hill NC 28458
912 222-4090

(G-16260)
HUFF MJ LLC
5617 Carolina Beach Rd (28412-3376)
PHONE..................910 313-3133
Ronnie Hufstedler, *Prin*
EMP: 9 **EST:** 2013
SALES (est): 485.39K **Privately Held**
SIC: 2024 Ice cream and frozen deserts

(G-16261)
ICE COMPANIES INC (PA)
Also Called: Industrial Cleaning Eqp Co
2820 Carolina Beach Rd (28412-1810)
P.O. Box 66 (28402-0066)
PHONE..................910 791-1970
Frances C Gay, *CEO*
Larry Gay, *Pr*
Frances C Gay, *Treas*
Wayne Gay, *VP*
EMP: 8 **EST:** 1974
SQ FT: 18,800
SALES (est): 1.32MM
SALES (corp-wide): 1.32MM **Privately Held**
Web: www.icenc.com
SIC: 2842 5087 Cleaning or polishing preparations, nec; Cleaning and maintenance equipment and supplies

(G-16262)
ICE CUBE RECORDING STUDIOS ✺
801 Greenfield St (28401-7916)
PHONE..................910 260-7616
Laterria Davis, *Owner*
EMP: 4 **EST:** 2023
SALES (est): 125.39K **Privately Held**
SIC: 2097 Ice cubes

(G-16263)
ICON COOLERS LLC
7213 Ogden Business Ln (28411-7456)
PHONE..................855 525-4266
Ian Titley, *Admn*
EMP: 5 **EST:** 2017
SALES (est): 217.3K **Privately Held**
Web: www.iconcoolers.com
SIC: 3949 Sporting and athletic goods, nec

(G-16264)
IKA-WORKS INC (HQ)
Also Called: Ika
2635 Northchase Pkwy Se (28405-7419)
PHONE..................910 452-7059
Sarah Angel, *CEO*
Rene Stiegelmann, *
Michael Janssen, *
◆ **EMP:** 85 **EST:** 1985
SQ FT: 33,000
SALES (est): 26.02MM
SALES (corp-wide): 195.9MM **Privately Held**
Web: www.ikaprocess.com
SIC: 3821 Laboratory apparatus and furniture
PA: Ika-Werke Gmbh & Co. Kg
Janke-Und-Kunkel-Str. 10
Staufen Im Breisgau BW 79219
76338310

(G-16265)
IMS USA LLC
Also Called: Wood Tooling Shop
110 Portwatch Way Ste 103 (28412-7008)

GEOGRAPHIC SECTION
Wilmington - New Hanover County (G-16291)

PHONE.....................910 796-2040
Emanuele Porro, *Ofcr*
▲ **EMP:** 5 **EST:** 2010
SALES (est): 2.11MM
SALES (corp-wide): 666.25K **Privately Held**
Web: www.imsusanc.com
SIC: 3451 Screw machine products
PA: I.M.S. Industrial Management Services Spa
Via Antonio Tolomeo Trivulzio 1
Milano MI 20146

(G-16266)
INDUSTRIAL MACHINE & WLDG INC
1918 Castle Hayne Rd (28401-2766)
PHONE.....................910 251-1393
EMP: 6 **EST:** 1992
SQ FT: 9,000
SALES (est): 984.27K **Privately Held**
Web: www.industrialmachineandwelding.com
SIC: 3599 Machine shop, jobbing and repair

(G-16267)
INDUSTRIAL RLBLITY SPCLSTS INC
Also Called: MSI
2629 Blue Clay Rd (28405-8613)
PHONE.....................513 652-9337
Mackenzie Tackett, *Prin*
EMP: 20
SALES (corp-wide): 266.24K **Privately Held**
SIC: 3542 Arbor presses
PA: Industrial Reliability Specialists, Inc.
370 Douglas Ave
Chillicothe OH 45601
800 800-6345

(G-16268)
INMAN SEPTIC TANK SERVICE INC
2631 Blue Clay Rd (28405-8613)
PHONE.....................910 763-1146
William Inman, *Pr*
Michelle Inman, *Sec*
David Inman, *VP*
EMP: 6 **EST:** 1964
SQ FT: 6,218
SALES (est): 613.84K **Privately Held**
Web: www.mbty555.vip
SIC: 1711 7699 3272 Septic system construction; Septic tank cleaning service; Septic tanks, concrete

(G-16269)
INSPIRE CREATIVE STUDIOS INC
Also Called: Port City Films
720 N 3rd St Ste 101 (28401-3474)
P.O. Box 1849 (28402-1849)
PHONE.....................910 395-0200
Jonathan Medford, *Pr*
Curtis Thieman, *Prin*
EMP: 6 **EST:** 2005
SALES (est): 818.35K **Privately Held**
Web: www.inspirecreativestudios.com
SIC: 7311 7371 7812 8743 Advertising consultant; Computer software development and applications; Video production; Public relations services

(G-16270)
INTERNATIONAL WOOD SVCS INC
330 Shipyard Blvd Ste D (28412-1837)
PHONE.....................910 549-8142
EMP: 6 **EST:** 2013
SALES (est): 335.57K **Privately Held**
Web: www.internationalwoodservices.com
SIC: 2421 Building and structural materials, wood

(G-16271)
INTERROLL CORPORATION
3000 Corporate Dr (28405-7422)
PHONE.....................910 799-1100
Paul Zumbuhl, *CEO*
▲ **EMP:** 110 **EST:** 2002
SQ FT: 210,000
SALES (est): 42.49MM **Privately Held**
Web: www.interroll.com
SIC: 3535 Conveyors and conveying equipment
PA: Interroll Holding Ag
Via Gorelle 3
S. Antonino TI

(G-16272)
INTERROLL USA HOLDING LLC
3000 Corporate Dr (28405-7422)
PHONE.....................910 799-1100
EMP: 75 **EST:** 1996
Web: www.interroll.com
SIC: 6719 3535 Investment holding companies, except banks; Conveyors and conveying equipment
PA: Interroll Holding Ag
Via Gorelle 3
S. Antonino TI

(G-16273)
INVISTA CAPITAL MANAGEMENT LLC
Also Called: Kosa
4600 Us Highway 421 N (28401-2225)
P.O. Box 327 (28402-0327)
PHONE.....................316 828-1000
Billy King, *Brnch Mgr*
EMP: 1175
SALES (corp-wide): 36.93B **Privately Held**
Web: www.invista.com
SIC: 2821 2819 Plastics materials and resins ; Industrial inorganic chemicals, nec
HQ: Invista Capital Management, Llc
2801 Centerville Rd
Wilmington DE 19808
302 683-3000

(G-16274)
J B I CUSTOM CABINETS
4619 Filmore Dr Apt B (28403-2957)
PHONE.....................910 538-3831
David Urena Lorenzana, *Owner*
EMP: 6 **EST:** 2014
SALES (est): 137.33K **Privately Held**
SIC: 2434 Wood kitchen cabinets

(G-16275)
J&J PRECISION SERVICES LLC
1817 Brierwood Rd (28405-8411)
PHONE.....................970 412-4683
Jacob Yaden, *Prin*
EMP: 4 **EST:** 2018
SALES (est): 103.91K **Privately Held**
Web: www.jandjprecision.com
SIC: 3599 Machine shop, jobbing and repair

(G-16276)
J&R SERVICES/J&R LUMBER CO
1319 Military Cutoff Rd Ste Cc Pmb 173 (28405-3174)
PHONE.....................956 778-7005
John Vento, *Owner*
EMP: 4 **EST:** 2013
SALES (est): 310.93K **Privately Held**
SIC: 2449 5032 Berry crates, wood wirebound; Brick, stone, and related material

(G-16277)
JCV COMMUNICATIONS INC (PA)
Also Called: Jcv Communications
4563 Technology Dr Ste 7 (28405-2174)
PHONE.....................844 399-8282
EMP: 10 **EST:** 2001
SALES (est): 2.28MM **Privately Held**
Web: www.jcvcommunications.com
SIC: 3825 1731 Network analyzers; Cable television installation

(G-16278)
JDG WOODWORKS INC
1002 Shakespeare Dr (28405-2634)
PHONE.....................910 367-8806
Jeremy D Gary, *Pr*
EMP: 8 **EST:** 2006
SALES (est): 280.93K **Privately Held**
SIC: 2431 Millwork

(G-16279)
JEPP INDUSTRIES INC
6644 Shire Ln (28411-7057)
PHONE.....................910 232-8715
Jefferson Smith, *Prin*
EMP: 5 **EST:** 2010
SALES (est): 106.27K **Privately Held**
SIC: 3999 Manufacturing industries, nec

(G-16280)
JIMMY KEITH SURFBOARDS INC
453 Shipyard Blvd (28412-1840)
PHONE.....................910 297-9719
James L Keith, *Pr*
EMP: 4 **EST:** 2018
SALES (est): 72.21K **Privately Held**
Web: www.jimmykeithsurfboards.com
SIC: 3949 Surfboards

(G-16281)
JOHNSON CONTROLS INC
Also Called: Johnson Controls
395 N Green Meadows Dr (28405-3749)
PHONE.....................910 392-2372
Sheldon Utz, *Mgr*
EMP: 30
Web: www.johnsoncontrols.com
SIC: 2531 Seats, automobile
HQ: Johnson Controls, Inc.
5757 N Green Bay Ave
Milwaukee WI 53209
920 245-6409

(G-16282)
JOHNSON CUSTOM BOATS INC
6820a Market St (28405-9723)
PHONE.....................910 232-4594
Richard Johnson, *Pr*
EMP: 4 **EST:** 2011
SALES (est): 255.08K **Privately Held**
Web: www.johnsoncustomboats.com
SIC: 3732 Boatbuilding and repairing

(G-16283)
JONNIE CHARDONN
6027 Mount Carmel Parke (28412-5004)
PHONE.....................910 471-0418
Jonnie' Chardonn, *Prin*
EMP: 4 **EST:** 2016
SALES (est): 57.95K **Privately Held**
SIC: 2741 Miscellaneous publishing

(G-16284)
JUSTICE
3500 Oleander Dr Ste 1054 (28403-0854)
PHONE.....................910 392-1581
EMP: 33 **EST:** 2019
SALES (est): 114.16K **Privately Held**
Web: www.justice.gov
SIC: 2361 Girl's and children's dresses, blouses

(G-16285)
JW WRAPS LLC
4511 Staffordshire Dr Apt 2 (28412-1029)
PHONE.....................614 401-9164
Joe Ward, *Mgr*
EMP: 5 **EST:** 2021
SALES (est): 83.67K **Privately Held**
SIC: 2672 Glazed paper, except photographic, carbon, or abrasive

(G-16286)
KCI
2611 Hidden Pointe Dr (28411-7166)
PHONE.....................910 612-4914
EMP: 8 **EST:** 2018
SALES (est): 144.01K **Privately Held**
Web: www.kci.com
SIC: 2599 Hospital beds

(G-16287)
KENNETH MOORE SIGNS
Also Called: Moore Signs
6220 Riverwoods Dr Apt 103 (28412-2882)
PHONE.....................910 458-6428
EMP: 4 **EST:** 1995
SALES (est): 306.81K **Privately Held**
Web: www.kennethmooresigns.com
SIC: 3993 5046 2499 Signs and advertising specialties; Signs, electrical; Signboards, wood

(G-16288)
KENNY FOWLER HEATING AND A INC (PA)
Also Called: Honeywell Authorized Dealer
711 Wellington Ave (28401-7615)
PHONE.....................910 508-4553
Kenny Fowler, *Pr*
James Lewis, *Sls Mgr*
Debra Fowler, *VP*
EMP: 5 **EST:** 2009
SQ FT: 1,600
SALES (est): 948.95K
SALES (corp-wide): 948.95K **Privately Held**
Web: www.hvacwilmingtonnc.com
SIC: 1711 3585 5075 Heating systems repair and maintenance; Heating and air conditioning combination units; Warm air heating and air conditioning

(G-16289)
KESSEBOHMER USA INC
106 Market St # 300 (28401-4442)
PHONE.....................910 338-5080
◆ **EMP:** 10 **EST:** 2007
SALES (est): 2.8MM
SALES (corp-wide): 563.1MM **Privately Held**
Web: www.cleverstorage.com
SIC: 3469 Household cooking and kitchen utensils, metal
HQ: Kessebohmer Gmbh
Mindener Str. 208
Bad Essen NI 49152

(G-16290)
KNIGHT SAFETY COATINGS CO INC
201 Beval Rd (28401-9071)
PHONE.....................910 458-3145
EMP: 16 **EST:** 1996
SQ FT: 7,000
SALES (est): 242.06K **Privately Held**
SIC: 2891 Adhesives and sealants

(G-16291)
KWIATEK INNOVATIONS LLC
108 La Salle St (28411-6800)
PHONE.....................919 455-8295
EMP: 4 **EST:** 2019

Wilmington - New Hanover County (G-16292)   GEOGRAPHIC SECTION

SALES (est): 39.69K **Privately Held**
SIC: **3999** Manufacturing industries, nec

(G-16292)
L TS GAS AND SNAKS
2461 Carolina Beach Rd (28401-7656)
PHONE..................910 762-7130
David Spaller, *Owner*
EMP: 5 EST: 2017
SALES (est): 210.71K **Privately Held**
SIC: **1311** Crude petroleum and natural gas

(G-16293)
LABORIE SONS CSTM WODWORKS LLC
Also Called: Ls Woodworks
315 Van Dyke Dr (28405-4801)
PHONE..................910 769-2524
David E Laborie, *Managing Member*
EMP: 6 EST: 2014
SALES (est): 259.53K **Privately Held**
SIC: **2431** 2434 Millwork; Wood kitchen cabinets

(G-16294)
LEAR CORPORATION
Also Called: Guilford Performance Textiles
1001 Military Cutoff Rd Ste 300 (28405-4376)
PHONE..................910 794-5810
EMP: 2600
SALES (corp-wide): 23.47B **Publicly Held**
Web: www.lear.com
SIC: **2258** 2399 Cloth, warp knit; Automotive covers, except seat and tire covers
PA: Lear Corporation
  21557 Telegraph Rd
  Southfield MI 48033
  248 447-1500

(G-16295)
LEES TACKLE INC
5316 Us Highway 421 N (28401-2254)
P.O. Box 2478 (28402-2478)
PHONE..................910 386-5100
Roswell E Lee Junior, *Pr*
Brian Lee, *
▲ EMP: 24 EST: 1920
SQ FT: 40,000
SALES (est): 509.43K **Privately Held**
Web: www.leetackle.com
SIC: **3949** Rods and rod parts, fishing

(G-16296)
LEGACY KNITTING LLC
3310 Kitty Hawk Rd Ste 100 (28405-8637)
PHONE..................844 762-2678
EMP: 7 EST: 2020
SALES (est): 639.42K **Privately Held**
Web: www.legacyknitting.com
SIC: **2252** Socks

(G-16297)
LEGIONS STADIUM
2221 Carolina Beach Rd (28401-7237)
PHONE..................910 341-4604
Bruce Cavenaugh, *Owner*
EMP: 5 EST: 2004
SALES (est): 127.38K **Privately Held**
SIC: **2531** Stadium seating

(G-16298)
LENNOX STORES (PARTSPLUS)
3826 Us Highway 421 N Ste 160 (28401-9060)
PHONE..................910 660-7070
EMP: 5 EST: 2019
SALES (est): 105.37K **Privately Held**
Web: www.lennoxpros.com

SIC: **3585** Refrigeration and heating equipment

(G-16299)
LEONARD ALUM UTLITY BLDNGS INC
Also Called: Leonard Building & Trck Cover
5705 Market St (28405-3501)
PHONE..................910 392-4921
John Coiro, *Mgr*
EMP: 4
SALES (corp-wide): 98.91MM **Privately Held**
Web: www.leonardusa.com
SIC: **3448** 3713 3089 3714 Prefabricated metal buildings; Truck tops; Molding primary plastics; Motor vehicle parts and accessories
PA: Leonard Aluminum Utility Buildings, Inc.
  630 W Indpndnce Blvd
  Mount Airy NC 27030
  336 789-5018

(G-16300)
LICENSE PLATE AGENCY
2390 Carolina Beach Rd (28401-7647)
PHONE..................910 763-7076
Betty Smithson, *Owner*
EMP: 7 EST: 2012
SALES (est): 130.9K **Privately Held**
SIC: **3469** Automobile license tags, stamped metal

(G-16301)
LIMITLESS PRFMCE FBRICATION LL
4921 Berry Ct (28412-2400)
PHONE..................910 799-5441
Christopher Dallmer, *Prin*
EMP: 4 EST: 2016
SALES (est): 45.77K **Privately Held**
SIC: **3999** Manufacturing industries, nec

(G-16302)
LINDE INC
Also Called: Praxair
Hwy 421 N (28405)
P.O. Box 1169 (28402-1169)
PHONE..................910 343-0241
Vincent R Gutierrez, *Brnch Mgr*
EMP: 5
Web: www.lindeus.com
SIC: **2813** Nitrogen
HQ: Linde Inc.
  10 Riverview Dr
  Danbury CT 06810
  203 837-2000

(G-16303)
LINPRINT COMPANY
3405 Market St Unit 2 (28403-1321)
PHONE..................910 763-5103
Bradley G Donnell, *Pr*
Brenda Donnell, *Sec*
EMP: 19 EST: 1947
SQ FT: 11,500
SALES (est): 2.45MM **Privately Held**
Web: www.linprint.com
SIC: **2752** 2754 Lithographing on metal; Commercial printing, gravure

(G-16304)
LOGIC HYDRAULIC CONTROLS INC
6616 Windmill Way (28405-3745)
P.O. Box 11059 (28404-1059)
PHONE..................910 791-9293
Michael Van Vekoven, *Pr*
Rodney Matthews, *
Lorraine Van Vekoven, *
Andrew Vankoven, *
EMP: 27 EST: 1983

SQ FT: 30,000
SALES (est): 2.78MM **Privately Held**
Web: www.logichyd.com
SIC: **3492** 3728 3594 Control valves, fluid power: hydraulic and pneumatic; Aircraft parts and equipment, nec; Fluid power pumps and motors

(G-16305)
LOGICBAY CORP
2002 Eastwood Rd Ste 306 (28403-7202)
PHONE..................888 301-0751
John Panaccione, *CEO*
Christopher Franklin, *CFO*
Michael Shaughnessy, *COO*
Dave Goulet, *VP*
EMP: 10 EST: 2003
SALES (est): 411.66K **Privately Held**
SIC: **7372** Business oriented computer software

(G-16306)
LOGICOM COMPUTER SYSTEMS INC
1121 Military Cutoff Rd Ste C (28405-3968)
PHONE..................910 256-5916
Donald G Parrish, *Pr*
EMP: 6 EST: 2004
SALES (est): 287.78K **Privately Held**
Web: www.logicomcomputers.com
SIC: **7372** Prepackaged software

(G-16307)
LOGOSDIRECT LLC
6303 Oleander Dr Ste 102b (28403-3577)
PHONE..................866 273-2335
John Denison, *Managing Member*
EMP: 10 EST: 2007
SALES (est): 1.27MM **Privately Held**
Web: www.logosdirect.com
SIC: **2395** Embroidery and art needlework

(G-16308)
LOOKING GLASS TECHNOLOGY LLC
1901 Edgemont Ln (28405-4154)
PHONE..................910 679-8060
EMP: 4 EST: 2016
SALES (est): 152.31K **Privately Held**
SIC: **7372** Prepackaged software

(G-16309)
LUMINA NEWS
7232 Wrightsville Ave (28403-7223)
PHONE..................910 256-6569
Pat Lowe, *Owner*
EMP: 6 EST: 2006
SALES (est): 317.75K **Privately Held**
Web: www.luminanews.com
SIC: **2711** Newspapers, publishing and printing

(G-16310)
LUMSDEN WELDING COMPANY
Also Called: Lumsden Steel
6736 Carolina Beach Rd (28412-3006)
PHONE..................910 791-6336
Ricky Moore, *Pr*
Margaret Moore, *VP*
EMP: 8 EST: 1950
SQ FT: 4,000
SALES (est): 540K **Privately Held**
Web: www.lumsdenwelding.com
SIC: **7692** 1799 Welding repair; Sandblasting of building exteriors

(G-16311)
M & G POLYMERS USA LLC
1979 Eastwood Rd (28403-7214)
PHONE..................910 509-4414
EMP: 4

SALES (est): 383.1K **Privately Held**
SIC: **2819** Industrial inorganic chemicals, nec

(G-16312)
M J E J INC
3310 Kitty Hawk Rd Ste 100 (28405-8637)
PHONE..................910 399-3795
Jonathan Carne, *Pr*
▲ EMP: 16 EST: 2010
SALES (est): 844.96K **Privately Held**
SIC: **2211** Apparel and outerwear fabrics, cotton

(G-16313)
M&N CONSTRUCTION SUPPLY INC
323 Eastwood Rd Ste A (28403-1738)
P.O. Box 2046 (28402-2046)
PHONE..................910 791-0908
Sean Block, *Brnch Mgr*
EMP: 10
SALES (corp-wide): 5.05MM **Privately Held**
Web: www.mnconstructionsupply.com
SIC: **3441** Fabricated structural metal
PA: M&N Construction Supply, Inc.
  323 Eastwood Rd
  Wilmington NC 28403
  910 791-0908

(G-16314)
MARKRAFT CABINETS DIRECT SALES
2422 Castle Hayne Rd (28401-2677)
PHONE..................910 762-1986
EMP: 6 EST: 2019
SALES (est): 221.73K **Privately Held**
Web: www.markraft.com
SIC: **2434** Wood kitchen cabinets

(G-16315)
MARPAC LLC (PA)
Also Called: Yogasleep
3870 Us Highway 421 N (28401-9024)
PHONE..................910 602-1421
James Sllan, *
Gordon Wallace, *
◆ EMP: 60 EST: 1962
SALES (est): 9.79MM
SALES (corp-wide): 9.79MM **Privately Held**
Web: www.yogasleep.com
SIC: **3699** Sound signaling devices, electrical

(G-16316)
MASON INLET DISTILLERY LLC
611 Everbreeze Ln (28411-6104)
PHONE..................910 200-4584
Christopher Burney Smith, *Owner*
EMP: 5 EST: 2018
SALES (est): 233.66K **Privately Held**
Web: www.masoninlet.com
SIC: **2085** Distilled and blended liquors

(G-16317)
MCCARTHY TIRE SERVICE COMPANY
118 Portwatch Way (28412-7010)
PHONE..................910 791-0132
Kelly Mccarthy, *Prin*
EMP: 4
SALES (corp-wide): 339.82MM **Privately Held**
Web: www.mccarthytire.com
SIC: **7534** 5531 Tire retreading and repair shops; Automotive tires
PA: Mccarthy Tire Service Company Inc
  340 Kidder St
  City Of Wilkes Barre PA 18702
  570 822-3151

Wilmington - New Hanover County (G-16344)

(G-16318)
MCNAUGHTON-MCKAY SOUTHEAST INC
6719 Amsterdam Way (28405-3778)
P.O. Box 10400 (28404-0400)
PHONE.................................910 392-0940
Tim Curtis, *Brnch Mgr*
EMP: 10
SALES (corp-wide): 2.19B **Privately Held**
SIC: 5063 3625 Electrical supplies, nec; Motor control accessories, including overload relays
HQ: Mcnaughton-Mckay Southeast, Inc.
 6685 Best Friend Rd
 Norcross GA 30071
 770 825-8600

(G-16319)
MEDIA WILMINGTON CO
Also Called: Ad Pak, The
6700 Netherlands Dr Unit A (28405-4771)
P.O. Box 12430 (28405-0119)
PHONE.................................910 791-0688
Jeff Phenicie, *Pt*
Boykin Wright, *Pt*
EMP: 9 **EST:** 1990
SALES (est): 223.78K **Privately Held**
SIC: 2711 Newspapers, publishing and printing

(G-16320)
MERLINS MACHINE SHOP
4301 Deer Creek Ln (28405-2273)
PHONE.................................910 399-3677
EMP: 4 **EST:** 2019
SALES (est): 81.49K **Privately Held**
SIC: 3599 Machine shop, jobbing and repair

(G-16321)
METAL-CAD STL FRMNG SYSTEMS IN
Also Called: Custom Metal Products
150 Division Dr (28401-8849)
PHONE.................................910 343-3338
Larry W Prewitt, *Pr*
Ellen T Prewitt, *
EMP: 71 **EST:** 2000
SALES (est): 12.78MM **Privately Held**
Web: www.custommetalproductsnc.com
SIC: 3499 Aerosol valves, metal

(G-16322)
MEYER DECORATIVE SURFACES
3002 Corporate Dr (28405-7422)
PHONE.................................910 794-7225
Vickie Wiggins, *Brnch Mgr*
EMP: 5 **EST:** 2019
SALES (est): 77.45K **Privately Held**
Web: www.meyerdeco.com
SIC: 3083 Laminated plastics plate and sheet

(G-16323)
MICRONOVA SYSTEMS INC
Also Called: Multi Form
2038 Oleander Dr (28403-2336)
PHONE.................................910 202-0564
Lee Furr, *Pr*
Gene Burleson, *Dir*
EMP: 11 **EST:** 1980
SQ FT: 2,000
SALES (est): 280.63K **Privately Held**
Web: www.micronova.de
SIC: 7372 Home entertainment computer software

(G-16324)
MIKE POWELL INC
Also Called: Coastal Cabinets
3407a Enterprise Dr (28405-6406)
PHONE.................................910 792-6152
Danny Michael Powell, *Pr*
EMP: 16 **EST:** 1983
SQ FT: 4,000
SALES (est): 2.45MM **Privately Held**
Web: www.coastalcabinets.com
SIC: 1521 2431 2434 New construction, single-family houses; Millwork; Vanities, bathroom: wood

(G-16325)
MKC85 INC (PA)
2705 Castle Creek Ln (28401-2689)
PHONE.................................910 762-1986
Joe Jacobus, *CEO*
Grover C Edwards, *Pr*
Steve Ezzel, *CFO*
EMP: 15 **EST:** 1985
SQ FT: 3,500
SALES (est): 24.83MM
SALES (corp-wide): 24.83MM **Privately Held**
Web: www.markraft.com
SIC: 5211 2541 Cabinets, kitchen; Table or counter tops, plastic laminated

(G-16326)
MONKEY JCT MULCH & STONE INC
6512 Carolina Beach Rd (28412-3002)
PHONE.................................910 793-9111
EMP: 10 **EST:** 2002
SALES (est): 107.69K **Privately Held**
Web: www.mikesmulchandstone.com
SIC: 1411 Dimension stone

(G-16327)
MOSLEY
4917 Gate Post Ln (28412-8319)
P.O. Box 12897 (28405-0132)
PHONE.................................910 409-5814
EMP: 6 **EST:** 2017
SALES (est): 77.11K **Privately Held**
Web: cramosley.nhcs.net
SIC: 3569 Baling machines, for scrap metal, paper, or similar material

(G-16328)
MOUNTAIN VISTA EXTRACTS LLC
824 Inlet View Dr (28409-2106)
PHONE.................................910 489-3948
EMP: 5 **EST:** 2018
SALES (est): 242.7K **Privately Held**
SIC: 2836 Extracts

(G-16329)
MOXIE
2030 Eastwood Rd Ste 1 (28403-7225)
PHONE.................................646 481-7807
Chase Gobble, *Prin*
EMP: 5 **EST:** 2017
SALES (est): 78.46K **Privately Held**
Web: www.moxie.team
SIC: 7372 Business oriented computer software

(G-16330)
N2 COMPANY (PA)
Also Called: N2 Publishing
5051 New Centre Dr (28403-1623)
P.O. Box 10916 (28404-0916)
PHONE.................................910 202-0917
Duane Hixon, *CEO*
EMP: 13 **EST:** 2006
SQ FT: 1,000
SALES (est): 6.8MM **Privately Held**
Web: www.strollmag.com
SIC: 2741 Miscellaneous publishing

(G-16331)
NAILS SPARTY LLC
3224 N College Rd Ste D (28405-8626)
PHONE.................................910 794-5406
Ben Venh, *Owner*
EMP: 5 **EST:** 2008
SALES (est): 80.57K **Privately Held**
SIC: 2844 Manicure preparations

(G-16332)
NATURAL ADHESIVE LLC
9106 Booth Bay Ct (28411-6829)
PHONE.................................616 217-8392
Christopher Telman, *Prin*
EMP: 5 **EST:** 2016
SALES (est): 162.19K **Privately Held**
SIC: 2891 Adhesives

(G-16333)
NCINO INC (PA)
Also Called: Ncino
6770 Parker Farm Dr Ste 100 (28405-3184)
PHONE.................................888 676-2466
Pierre Naude, *Ch Bd*
Joshua Glover, *CRO*
David Rudow, *CFO*
Sean Desmond, *CUSTOMER SUCCESS*
Greg Orenstein, *CORP Development*
EMP: 115 **EST:** 2011
SQ FT: 57,000
SALES (est): 408.31MM
SALES (corp-wide): 408.31MM **Publicly Held**
SIC: 7372 Prepackaged software

(G-16334)
NCINO OPCO INC (HQ)
6770 Parker Farm Dr Ste 200 (28405-3183)
PHONE.................................888 676-2466
Pierre Naude, *CEO*
David Rudow, *CFO*
April Rieger, *
EMP: 770 **EST:** 2011
SQ FT: 57,000
SALES (est): 204.29MM
SALES (corp-wide): 408.31MM **Publicly Held**
Web: www.ncino.com
SIC: 7372 Prepackaged software
PA: Ncino, Inc.
 6770 Parker Farm Dr # 100
 Wilmington NC 28405
 888 676-2466

(G-16335)
NCR LCAL - OHIO DTROIT ALOHA P
306 RI Honeycutt Dr (28412-7172)
PHONE.................................440 202-3068
EMP: 4 **EST:** 2018
SALES (est): 209.24K **Privately Held**
SIC: 7372 Prepackaged software

(G-16336)
NEW HANOVER PRINTING AND PUBG
Also Called: New Hanover Printing
2145 Wrightsville Ave (28403-0270)
PHONE.................................910 520-7173
Cynthia Howell, *Pr*
Claude Howell, *Sec*
Charles Howell, *Prin*
EMP: 5 **EST:** 2015
SALES (est): 262.46K **Privately Held**
Web: www.newhanoverprinting.com
SIC: 2752 Offset printing

(G-16337)
NOBLE CUSTOM COATINGS LLC
2725 Old Wrightsboro Rd Ste 15-3 (28405-8066)
PHONE.................................910 228-6216
Christopher Shane Noble, *Admn*
EMP: 5 **EST:** 2013
SALES (est): 82.52K **Privately Held**
Web: www.noblecustomcoatings.com
SIC: 3479 Metal coating and allied services

(G-16338)
NONI BACCA WINERY
420 Eastwood Rd (28403-1869)
PHONE.................................910 397-7617
EMP: 4 **EST:** 2007
SALES (est): 392.95K **Privately Held**
Web: www.nbwinery.com
SIC: 2084 Wines

(G-16339)
NORDIC CUSTOM WOODWORKS
616 Windchime Dr (28412-7521)
PHONE.................................203 209-5854
Christian Michaelson, *Prin*
EMP: 5 **EST:** 2017
SALES (est): 54.13K **Privately Held**
SIC: 2431 Millwork

(G-16340)
NORMANDIE BAKERY INC
7316 Market St (28411-8807)
PHONE.................................910 686-1372
Phillippe Blondel, *Pr*
Bev Shuette, *VP*
Annette Blondel, *Sec*
Art Shuette, *Treas*
EMP: 6 **EST:** 1991
SALES (est): 305.51K **Privately Held**
SIC: 5461 2051 Retail bakeries; Bakery: wholesale or wholesale/retail combined

(G-16341)
NORMTEX INCORPORATED
1700 Verrazzano Pl (28405-4040)
P.O. Box 12 (28650-0012)
PHONE.................................828 428-3363
Henry T Lilly, *Pr*
Kathleen Lilly, *Sec*
◆ **EMP:** 9 **EST:** 1965
SQ FT: 114,644
SALES (est): 928.58K **Privately Held**
SIC: 2281 5199 Yarn spinning mills; Yarns, nec

(G-16342)
OAK-BARK CORPORATION (PA)
514 Wayne Dr (28403-1255)
▼ **EMP:** 10 **EST:** 1959
SQ FT: 4,500
SALES (est): 8.63MM
SALES (corp-wide): 8.63MM **Privately Held**
Web: www.oakbark12.com
SIC: 2869 Formaldehyde (formalin)

(G-16343)
OLD GROWTH RIVERWOOD INC
1407b Castle Hayne Rd (28401-8890)
PHONE.................................910 762-4077
Chris Metz, *Pr*
Terrie Metz, *VP*
EMP: 5 **EST:** 2007
SQ FT: 3,500
SALES (est): 497.86K **Privately Held**
Web: www.oldgrowthriverwood.com
SIC: 2511 2426 Camp furniture: wood; Flooring, hardwood

(G-16344)
ONE ON ONE PRESS LLC
616 Princess St (28401-4133)
PHONE.................................910 228-8821
Karen Doniere, *CEO*
EMP: 5 **EST:** 2019
SALES (est): 119.72K **Privately Held**
SIC: 2741 Miscellaneous publishing

Wilmington - New Hanover County (G-16345)   GEOGRAPHIC SECTION

(G-16345)
ORACLE HEARING GROUP
1016 Striking Island Dr (28403-4381)
PHONE 732 349-6804
EMP: 6 EST: 2013
SALES (est): 117.72K **Privately Held**
SIC: 7372 Prepackaged software

(G-16346)
ORBITA CORPORATION
6740 Netherlands Dr Ste D (28405-4702)
PHONE 910 256-5300
Charles Agnoff, *Pr*
Karen Lampkin, *
Mark Lampkin, *
Evelyn Agnoff, *
◆ EMP: 25 EST: 1997
SQ FT: 8,000
SALES (est): 4.65MM **Privately Held**
Web: www.orbita.com
SIC: 3873 Watches and parts, except crystals and jewels

(G-16347)
OUTER BANKS HAMMOCKS INC
7228 Wrightsville Ave (28403-7223)
PHONE 910 256-4001
Clark Helton, *Pr*
Sharon Helton, *Sec*
EMP: 10 EST: 1972
SQ FT: 1,000
SALES (est): 603.75K **Privately Held**
Web: www.obxhammocks.com
SIC: 2514 5021 5712 Hammocks: metal or fabric and metal combination; Outdoor and lawn furniture, nec; Outdoor and garden furniture

(G-16348)
PARADIGM SOLUTIONS INC
1213 Culbreth Dr (28405-3639)
PHONE 910 392-2611
Frank E Gensemer Senior, *Prin*
EMP: 9 EST: 2006
SALES (est): 567.6K **Privately Held**
SIC: 2759 Screen printing

(G-16349)
PATTERSON CUSTOM DRAPERY
4315 Deer Creek Ln (28405-2273)
PHONE 910 791-4332
Donna Patterson, *Pr*
Christopher Patterson, *Sec*
EMP: 8 EST: 2005
SALES (est): 457.82K **Privately Held**
Web: www.pattersoncustomdrapery.com
SIC: 2391 5023 Draperies, plastic and textile: from purchased materials; Window furnishings

(G-16350)
PENCO PRECISION LLC
Also Called: Machine Shop
1901 Blue Clay Rd Ste I (28405-8082)
PHONE 910 292-6542
EMP: 7 EST: 2019
SALES (est): 296.82K **Privately Held**
Web: www.pencoprecision.net
SIC: 3545 Precision tools, machinists'

(G-16351)
PEPSI BOTTLING VENTURES LLC
Also Called: Pepsi-Cola
415 Landmark Dr (28412-6303)
PHONE 910 792-5400
Randy Kennedy, *Mgr*
EMP: 98
SQ FT: 45,872
Web: www.pepsico.com
SIC: 2086 5149 Soft drinks: packaged in cans, bottles, etc.; Groceries and related products, nec
HQ: Pepsi Bottling Ventures Llc
4141 Parklake Ave Ste 600
Raleigh NC 27612
919 865-2300

(G-16352)
PG TECHNICHIANS
4106 Kettering Pl (28412-5112)
PHONE 910 742-1017
Larry Robichaux, *Mgr*
EMP: 5 EST: 2014
SALES (est): 83.95K **Privately Held**
SIC: 7692 Welding repair

(G-16353)
PHARMASONE LLC
1800 Sir Tyler Dr (28405-8305)
PHONE 910 679-8364
Colin Gray, *Prin*
Douglas Rupp, *Prin*
EMP: 5 EST: 2019
SALES (est): 444.69K **Privately Held**
SIC: 2834 Pharmaceutical preparations

(G-16354)
PHARMGATE ANIMAL HEALTH LLC
1800 Sir Tyler Dr (28405-8305)
PHONE 910 679-8364
Colin Gray, *Managing Member*
▲ EMP: 7 EST: 2010
SQ FT: 2,000
SALES (est): 1.41MM **Privately Held**
Web: www.pharmgate.com
SIC: 2834 Veterinary pharmaceutical preparations

(G-16355)
PHARMGATE INC (HQ)
1800 Sir Tyler Dr (28405-8305)
PHONE 910 679-8364
Colin Gray, *CEO*
▲ EMP: 10 EST: 2008
SALES (est): 30.24MM **Privately Held**
Web: www.pharmgate.com
SIC: 2834 Veterinary pharmaceutical preparations
PA: Jinhe Biotechnology Co., Ltd.
No.71, Xinping Road, Tuoketuo County
Hohhot NM 01020

(G-16356)
PLANET LOGO INC
23 N Front St # 3 (28401-4483)
PHONE 910 763-2554
EMP: 8 EST: 2006
SQ FT: 3,000
SALES (est): 1.36MM **Privately Held**
Web: www.planetlogoinc.com
SIC: 7311 3993 Advertising agencies; Signs and advertising specialties

(G-16357)
PLASTIC MOLDING CONNECTION
4164 Breezewood Dr # 102 (28412-2563)
PHONE 910 512-0834
George Millington, *Prin*
EMP: 5 EST: 2018
SALES (est): 87.47K **Privately Held**
SIC: 3089 Injection molding of plastics

(G-16358)
POLLY & CRACKERS LLC
520 Dock St (28401-4628)
PHONE 716 680-2456
Derek Wragge, *Prin*
EMP: 4 EST: 2016
SALES (est): 197.39K **Privately Held**
Web: www.pollyandcrackers.com
SIC: 2323 Men's and boy's neckwear

(G-16359)
POLLY AND ASSOCIATES LLC
7426 Janice Ln (28411-9658)
PHONE 910 319-7564
Elizabeth Simpson, *Prin*
EMP: 6 EST: 2016
SALES (est): 89.96K **Privately Held**
SIC: 2752 Commercial printing, lithographic

(G-16360)
POLYHOSE INCORPORATED
353 Acme Way (28401-2306)
PHONE 732 512-9141
Fatema Mohammed, *Prin*
EMP: 13 EST: 2007
SALES (est): 1MM **Privately Held**
Web: www.polyhose.com
SIC: 5661 3052 3492 Shoe stores; Air line or air brake hose, rubber or rubberized fabric; Fluid power valves and hose fittings

(G-16361)
POLYQUEST INCORPORATED (PA)
1979 Eastwood Rd Ste 201 (28403-7272)
PHONE 910 342-9554
John Marinelli, *CEO*
Thomas Durst, *Pr*
Brad Dutton, *VP*
Randy Bragg, *Treas*
Ryan Nettles, *Sr VP*
▲ EMP: 11 EST: 2000
SQ FT: 220,000
SALES (est): 94.5MM
SALES (corp-wide): 94.5MM **Privately Held**
Web: www.polyquest.com
SIC: 2821 Plastics materials and resins

(G-16362)
PORT CITY SIGNS & GRAPHICS INC
4011 Oleander Dr (28403-6816)
P.O. Box 4053 (28406-1053)
PHONE 910 350-8242
Fred Maurer, *Prin*
EMP: 6 EST: 2008
SALES (est): 653.77K **Privately Held**
Web: www.portcitysigns.com
SIC: 3993 Signs and advertising specialties

(G-16363)
PORT CITY WOOD WORKS INC
122 Country Place Rd (28409-4410)
PHONE 910 398-8274
Michael D Broach, *Pr*
EMP: 6 EST: 2010
SALES (est): 243.49K **Privately Held**
SIC: 2431 Millwork

(G-16364)
POWERS BOATWORKS
2725 Old Wrightsboro Rd Unit 8a (28405-8066)
PHONE 910 762-3636
Chris Powers, *Owner*
EMP: 6 EST: 2005
SALES (est): 370.41K **Privately Held**
SIC: 3732 Boatbuilding and repairing

(G-16365)
POWERSIGNS INC
3617 1/2 Market St (28403-1325)
PHONE 910 343-1789
Mark P Hicks, *Pr*
EMP: 7 EST: 2008
SALES (est): 204.55K **Privately Held**
Web: www.powersignsinc.com
SIC: 3993 Electric signs

(G-16366)
PPD INC (HQ)
Also Called: Ppd
929 N Front St (28401-3331)
PHONE 910 251-0081
David Simmons, *CEO*
William J Sharbaugh, *COO*
Glen Donovan, *CAO*
Christopher G Scully, *Ex VP*
B Judd Hartman, *Ex VP*
EMP: 237 EST: 2017
SQ FT: 395,000
SALES (est): 4.68B
SALES (corp-wide): 44.91B **Publicly Held**
Web: www.ppd.com
SIC: 8731 2834 Commercial physical research; Pharmaceutical preparations
PA: Thermo Fisher Scientific Inc.
168 3rd Ave
Waltham MA 02451
781 622-1000

(G-16367)
PPD INTERNATIONAL HOLDINGS LLC (DH)
929 N Front St (28401-3331)
PHONE 910 251-0081
Frederick Frank, *CEO*
EMP: 5 EST: 1990
SALES (est): 64.69MM
SALES (corp-wide): 44.91B **Publicly Held**
Web: www.ppd.com
SIC: 2834 Pharmaceutical preparations
HQ: Ppd, Inc.
929 N Front St
Wilmington NC 28401
910 251-0081

(G-16368)
PPG INDUSTRIES INC
Also Called: PPG 4434
4125 Oleander Dr (28403-6821)
PHONE 910 452-3289
Saul Matus, *Brnch Mgr*
EMP: 4
SALES (corp-wide): 17.65B **Publicly Held**
Web: www.ppgpaints.com
SIC: 2851 Paints and allied products
PA: Ppg Industries, Inc.
1 Ppg Pl
Pittsburgh PA 15272
412 434-3131

(G-16369)
PQ RECYCLING LLC (HQ)
1979 Eastwood Rd Ste 201 (28403-7272)
PHONE 910 342-9554
EMP: 25 EST: 2013
SQ FT: 5,000
SALES (est): 7MM
SALES (corp-wide): 94.5MM **Privately Held**
Web: www.polyquest.com
SIC: 2821 Plastics materials and resins
PA: Polyquest, Incorporated
1979 Eastwood Rd Ste 201
Wilmington NC 28403
910 342-9554

(G-16370)
PREMIER PRINTING & APPAREL
1939 Kent St (28403-2350)
PHONE 910 805-0545
EMP: 4 EST: 2018
SALES (est): 154.91K **Privately Held**
Web: www.printingandapparel.com
SIC: 2759 Screen printing

GEOGRAPHIC SECTION

Wilmington - New Hanover County (G-16398)

(G-16371)
PROFORM FINISHING PRODUCTS LLC
Also Called: National Gypsum Comp
838 Sunnyvale Dr (28412-7031)
PHONE..............................910 799-3954
Steve Lepage, *Mgr*
EMP: 49
SALES (corp-wide): 795.88MM **Privately Held**
Web: www.nationalgypsum.com
SIC: 3275 Wallboard, gypsum
HQ: Proform Finishing Products, Llc
   2001 Rexford Rd
   Charlotte NC 28211

(G-16372)
PROFORMA TIERNEY PRINTING
1213 Culbreth Dr (28405-3639)
PHONE..............................910 392-2611
EMP: 4 **EST:** 2012
SALES (est): 527.6K **Privately Held**
Web: www.tierneyscreenprinting.com
SIC: 2752 Commercial printing, lithographic

(G-16373)
QUEENSBORO INDUSTRIES INC
Also Called: Queensboro Shirt Company
1400 Marstellar St (28401-6067)
PHONE..............................910 251-1251
Fred Meyers, *Pr*
Jonathan Downy, *
Fabrivio Parella, *Information Technology Officer**
▲ **EMP:** 120 **EST:** 1982
SQ FT: 80,000
SALES (est): 16.92MM **Privately Held**
Web: www.queensboro.com
SIC: 2759 Screen printing

(G-16374)
QUINLAN PUBLISHING COMPANY
Also Called: Edge of The Carolinas Magazine
2102 Pender Ave (28403-1140)
PHONE..............................229 886-7995
EMP: 5 **EST:** 2011
SALES (est): 94.99K **Privately Held**
Web: www.edgeofthecarolinas.com
SIC: 2741 7389 Miscellaneous publishing; Business Activities at Non-Commercial Site

(G-16375)
R RABBIT INC
604 Woodland Forest Ct (28403-8831)
PHONE..............................910 297-6764
Roberta B Bennett, *Pr*
EMP: 5 **EST:** 2016
SALES (est): 86.05K **Privately Held**
Web: www.wabbitwiki.com
SIC: 2741 Miscellaneous publishing

(G-16376)
RAGS SIGNS + GRAPHICS LLC
102 Portwatch Way Ste C (28412-7085)
PHONE..............................910 793-9087
EMP: 4 **EST:** 2019
SALES (est): 25.81K **Privately Held**
Web: www.ragsigns.com
SIC: 3993 Signs and advertising specialties

(G-16377)
RALEIGH VENTURES INC
Also Called: Wilmington Record Center
6725 Amsterdam Way (28403-3778)
P.O. Box 1575 (28480-1575)
PHONE..............................910 350-0036
James K Wright Senior, *Pr*
James K Wright, *Pr*
James Wright Junior, *VP*
EMP: 5 **EST:** 1994
SQ FT: 14,160
SALES (est): 673.76K **Privately Held**
Web: www.pepsibottlingventures.com
SIC: 7374 3572 2086 Data processing service; Computer storage devices; Carbonated soft drinks, bottled and canned

(G-16378)
RAPID RESPONSE TECHNOLOGY LLC
1900 Eastwood Rd Ste 27 (28403-7205)
PHONE..............................910 763-3856
EMP: 5 **EST:** 2008
SALES (est): 222.34K **Privately Held**
SIC: 3799 3732 5088 All terrain vehicles (ATV); Motorboats, inboard or outboard: building and repairing; Boats, non-recreational

(G-16379)
REDRUM PRESS
3128 Kitty Hawk Rd (28405-8627)
PHONE..............................910 399-1334
EMP: 4 **EST:** 2018
SALES (est): 87.44K **Privately Held**
Web: redrum-press.business.site
SIC: 2741 Miscellaneous publishing

(G-16380)
REDRUM PRESS
414 S 5th Ave (28401-5110)
PHONE..............................866 374-7881
EMP: 6 **EST:** 2007
SALES (est): 106.06K **Privately Held**
Web: redrum-press.business.site
SIC: 2741 Miscellaneous publishing

(G-16381)
REGIONAL TRUCKNG COMPANY LLC
389 Darlington Ave # 102 (28403-1462)
PHONE..............................910 228-0245
Keyana C Lemon, *CEO*
EMP: 5 **EST:** 2015
SALES (est): 105.14K **Privately Held**
SIC: 3537 Trucks, tractors, loaders, carriers, and similar equipment

(G-16382)
RICHARD SCHWARTZ
322 S College Rd (28403-1632)
PHONE..............................914 358-4518
Richard Schwartz, *Prin*
EMP: 5 **EST:** 2015
SALES (est): 87.06K **Privately Held**
SIC: 2741 Miscellaneous publishing

(G-16383)
RICKY LOCKLAIR & RANDY LOCKLAI
619 Kelly Rd (28409-3164)
PHONE..............................910 470-3222
Rick Locklair, *Prin*
EMP: 5 **EST:** 2010
SALES (est): 164.72K **Privately Held**
SIC: 3993 Signs and advertising specialties

(G-16384)
RIVERSIDE ADVENTURE COMPANY
Also Called: Riverside
5 S Water St (28401-4447)
P.O. Box 864 (28402-0864)
PHONE..............................910 457-4944
Jack Jackson, *Genl Mgr*
EMP: 12 **EST:** 2010
SALES (est): 1.37MM **Privately Held**
Web: www.riversideadventure.com
SIC: 2326 Men's and boy's work clothing

(G-16385)
ROBERT CITRANO
Also Called: Cape Fear Designs
1710 Dawson St Ste C (28403-2327)
P.O. Box 2283 (28428-2283)
PHONE..............................910 264-7746
Robert Citrano, *Owner*
EMP: 5 **EST:** 2001
SQ FT: 1,500
SALES (est): 211.2K **Privately Held**
SIC: 2395 Embroidery and art needlework

(G-16386)
RODERICK MCH ERECTORS WLDG INC
Also Called: Seaport Crane
2701 Blue Clay Rd (28405-8615)
PHONE..............................910 343-0381
David Roderick, *Pr*
Constance Roderick, *VP*
James Roderick Junior, *VP*
EMP: 4 **EST:** 1967
SQ FT: 10,000
SALES (est): 410.43K **Privately Held**
SIC: 3441 7699 7692 1791 Fabricated structural metal; Industrial machinery and equipment repair; Welding repair; Structural steel erection

(G-16387)
ROSE ICE & COAL COMPANY
1202 Market St (28401-4344)
P.O. Box 41 (22842-0041)
PHONE..............................910 762-2464
TOLL FREE: 800
Archie L Harris, *Pr*
Sallyann Harris, *VP*
Clyde Roberts, *Genl Mgr*
EMP: 10 **EST:** 1933
SQ FT: 13,000
SALES (est): 501.9K **Privately Held**
Web: www.roseiceandcoal.com
SIC: 2097 5411 Manufactured ice; Convenience stores, independent

(G-16388)
ROYCE COMPANY LLC
6500 Windmill Way (28405-3743)
PHONE..............................910 395-0046
EMP: 9 **EST:** 2016
SALES (est): 187.06K **Privately Held**
SIC: 3499 Fabricated metal products, nec

(G-16389)
RUSS SIMMONS
Also Called: Simmons Scientific Products
414 Biscayne Dr (28411-9427)
P.O. Box 527 (27376-0527)
PHONE..............................910 686-1656
Russ Simmons, *Owner*
EMP: 4 **EST:** 1990
SALES (est): 282.59K **Privately Held**
Web: www.simmonsscientificproducts.com
SIC: 3829 Geophysical and meteorological testing equipment

(G-16390)
RUTH ARNOLD GRAPHICS & SIGNS
Also Called: R A G S
102 Portwatch Way Ste C (28412-7085)
PHONE..............................910 793-9087
Ruth Arnold, *Owner*
EMP: 6 **EST:** 1981
SALES (est): 250K **Privately Held**
Web: www.ragsigns.com
SIC: 3993 Advertising artwork

(G-16391)
S T WOOTEN CORPORATION
Also Called: Wilmington Concrete Plant
220 Sutton Lake Rd (28401-9000)
PHONE..............................910 762-1940
Scott Wooten, *Pr*
EMP: 22
SALES (corp-wide): 319.83MM **Privately Held**
Web: www.stwcorp.com
SIC: 3531 Concrete plants
PA: S. T. Wooten Corporation
   3801 Black Creek Rd Se
   Wilson NC 27893
   252 291-5165

(G-16392)
SAM SOFTWARE CORP
103 Oxmoor Pl (28403-0136)
PHONE..............................910 233-9924
Ralph L Brock, *Prin*
EMP: 5 **EST:** 2011
SALES (est): 102.13K **Privately Held**
SIC: 7372 Prepackaged software

(G-16393)
SAWMILL CATERING LLC
2528 Castle Hayne Rd (28401-2692)
PHONE..............................910 769-7455
EMP: 13 **EST:** 2017
SALES (est): 247.81K **Privately Held**
Web: www.sawmillcafeandcatering.com
SIC: 5812 2421 Caterers; Sawmills and planing mills, general

(G-16394)
SAYBOLT LP
2321 Burnett Blvd (28401-7003)
PHONE..............................910 763-8444
Bruce Bullard, *Mgr*
EMP: 6
SIC: 1389 Oil field services, nec
HQ: Saybolt Lp
   6316 Windfern Rd
   Houston TX 77040
   713 328-2673

(G-16395)
SEA & TEE RSORT RSDNTIAL PRPTS
922 Shelton Ct (28412-2532)
PHONE..............................910 231-8212
EMP: 4 **EST:** 2019
SALES (est): 183.59K **Privately Held**
SIC: 2759 Screen printing

(G-16396)
SEAGATE TECHNOLOGY LLC
7211 Ogden Business Ln Ste 201 (28411)
PHONE..............................910 821-8310
EMP: 11
Web: www.seagate.com
SIC: 3572 Computer storage devices
HQ: Seagate Technology Llc
   47488 Kato Rd
   Fremont CA 94538
   800 732-4283

(G-16397)
SEAWARD ACTION INC
219 Oakcrest Dr (28403-4502)
PHONE..............................252 671-1684
EMP: 6 **EST:** 2007
SALES (est): 86K **Privately Held**
Web: www.seawardaction.com
SIC: 3993 Signs and advertising specialties

(G-16398)
SECURED TRAFFIC CONTROL LLC
Also Called: Ironbound Waste Management
2801 Bloomfield Ln (28412-6648)

Wilmington - New Hanover County (G-16399)

PHONE.....................910 233-8148
EMP: 7 EST: 2016
SALES (est): 535.54K **Privately Held**
Web: www.thesaferoad.com
SIC: 3669 Communications equipment, nec

(G-16399)
SEPTEMBER SIGNS & GRAPHICS LLC
6731 Amsterdam Way Ste 4 (28405-4043)
PHONE.....................910 791-9084
EMP: 7 EST: 2001
SALES (est): 498.72K **Privately Held**
Web: www.septembersigns.com
SIC: 3993 Electric signs

(G-16400)
SERVICE ROFG SHTMTL WLMNGTON I
4838 Us Highway 421 N (28401-2244)
P.O. Box 1915 (28402-1915)
PHONE.....................910 343-9860
Paul G Davis, *Mgr*
Paul Davis, *Pr*
Harry Esbenshade Iii, *CEO*
EMP: 16 EST: 1999
SALES (est): 4.99MM
SALES (corp-wide): 109.23MM **Privately Held**
Web: www.tri-stateservicegroup.com
SIC: 3444 1761 Sheet metalwork; Roofing contractor
HQ: The Cypress Mountain Company
107 Staton Ct
Greenville NC 27834
252 758-2179

(G-16401)
SGL INC
8215 Mainsail Ln (28412-3218)
PHONE.....................910 790-3631
EMP: 4 EST: 2017
SALES (est): 52.4K **Privately Held**
SIC: 3624 Carbon and graphite products

(G-16402)
SHELFGENIE COASTAL CAROLINAS
Also Called: Shelf Genie
4144 Pine Hollow Dr (28412-1033)
PHONE.....................910 547-9595
Kelly Barefoot, *Prin*
EMP: 6 EST: 2018
SALES (est): 127.51K **Privately Held**
Web: www.shelfgenie.com
SIC: 2511 Wood household furniture

(G-16403)
SHERRI GOSSETT
Also Called: American Trayd
801 Bragg Dr (28409-6901)
PHONE.....................910 367-0099
Sherri Gossett, *Owner*
EMP: 4 EST: 2002
SALES (est): 20K **Privately Held**
SIC: 3089 Trays, plastics

(G-16404)
SIDEBOARD
4107 Oleander Dr Ste C (28403-6854)
PHONE.....................910 612-4398
EMP: 4 EST: 2019
SALES (est): 86.34K **Privately Held**
Web: www.hyportdigital.com
SIC: 2099 Food preparations, nec

(G-16405)
SIGN COMPANY OF WILMINGTON INC
428 Landmark Dr (28412-6336)
PHONE.....................910 392-1414
Richard Centiempo, *Pr*
Berkley Blackwell, *VP*
EMP: 10 EST: 2004
SQ FT: 12,500
SALES (est): 994.57K **Privately Held**
Web: www.tscwilm.com
SIC: 3993 Signs and advertising specialties

(G-16406)
SIZEMORE PRINTING
1547 Cameron Ct (28401-7900)
PHONE.....................910 228-8749
William Kinyoun, *Prin*
EMP: 4 EST: 2016
SALES (est): 83.91K **Privately Held**
SIC: 2752 Commercial printing, lithographic

(G-16407)
SOUND HEAVY MACHINERY INC (PA)
Also Called: Sound Parts & Service
1809 Blue Clay Rd (28405-8058)
PHONE.....................910 782-2477
Mark Bobo, *Pr*
▼ EMP: 4 EST: 2010
SALES (est): 5.17MM
SALES (corp-wide): 5.17MM **Privately Held**
Web: www.soundheavymachinery.com
SIC: 5084 3532 3537 3523 Engines and parts, diesel; Crushing, pulverizing, and screening equipment; Trucks, tractors, loaders, carriers, and similar equipment; Farm machinery and equipment

(G-16408)
SOUTH ATLANTIC LLC (DH)
Also Called: South Atlantic Galvanizing
1907 S 17th St Ste 2 (28401-6680)
P.O. Box 890425 (28289-0425)
PHONE.....................910 332-1900
Cary Peterson, *Managing Member*
◆ EMP: 10 EST: 1996
SQ FT: 5,000
SALES (est): 81.53MM
SALES (corp-wide): 336.48MM **Privately Held**
Web: www.southatlanticllc.com
SIC: 3479 Galvanizing of iron, steel, or end-formed products
HQ: Wedge Inc.
1907 S 17th St Ste 2
Wilmington NC 28401

(G-16409)
SOUTH-TEK SYSTEMS LLC
3700 Us Highway 421 N (28401-9022)
PHONE.....................910 332-4173
Ken Hessevick, *
Brad Jernigan, *
▼ EMP: 60 EST: 2004
SQ FT: 20,000
SALES (est): 19.57MM **Privately Held**
Web: www.southteksystems.com
SIC: 3569 Gas producers, generators, and other gas related equipment
PA: Pfingsten Partners, L.L.C.
151 N Franklin St # 2150
Chicago IL 60606

(G-16410)
SOUTHEASTERN MCH & WLDG CO INC
142 Shipyard Blvd (28412-6226)
P.O. Box 3383 (28406-0383)
PHONE.....................910 791-6661
R Jim Edens Iii, *Pr*
Bobby G Benson, *Sec*
EMP: 20 EST: 1965
SQ FT: 32,000
SALES (est): 2.28MM **Privately Held**
SIC: 3443 7692 3599 Fabricated plate work (boiler shop); Welding repair; Machine shop, jobbing and repair

(G-16411)
SOUTHERN STATES CHEMICAL INC
4600 Us Highway 421 N (28401-2225)
PHONE.....................910 762-5054
EMP: 20
SQ FT: 19,542
SALES (corp-wide): 107.46MM **Privately Held**
Web: www.sschemical.com
SIC: 2819 Sulfuric acid, oleum
HQ: Southern States Chemical, Inc.
118 E 35th St
Savannah GA 31401
912 944-3740

(G-16412)
SOUTHLAND AMUSEMENTS VEND INC (PA)
1611 Castle Hayne Rd Ste D3 (28401-8822)
P.O. Box 749 (28480-0749)
PHONE.....................910 343-1809
Robert Huckabee, *Pr*
Susan Schley, *
EMP: 30 EST: 1982
SQ FT: 10,000
SALES (est): 3MM **Privately Held**
Web: www.southlandentertainment.com
SIC: 7993 3999 Coin-operated amusement devices; Coin-operated amusement machines

(G-16413)
SPANGLERCV INC
3111 Kitty Hawk Rd Ste 2 (28405-8622)
P.O. Box 12901 (28405-0132)
PHONE.....................910 794-5547
▲ EMP: 6 EST: 2003
SALES (est): 1.01MM **Privately Held**
Web: www.wafercheck.com
SIC: 3491 Industrial valves

(G-16414)
SPARK716 LLC
Also Called: Tru Colors Brewing
6779 Gordon Rd (28411-8465)
PHONE.....................704 439-6864
George Taylor, *Prin*
EMP: 9 EST: 2020
SALES (est): 595.59K **Privately Held**
SIC: 2082 Beer (alcoholic beverage)

(G-16415)
SPECIALTY BOATWORKS INC
262 Battleship Rd (28401-2533)
PHONE.....................910 251-5219
EMP: 6 EST: 2019
SALES (est): 131.46K **Privately Held**
Web: www.specialtyboatworks.com
SIC: 3732 Boatbuilding and repairing

(G-16416)
ST JOHNS MUSEUM OF ART
114 Orange St (28401-4421)
PHONE.....................910 763-0281
Richard Sceiford, *Prin*
EMP: 4 EST: 2016
SALES (est): 55.85K **Privately Held**
SIC: 2711 Newspapers

(G-16417)
STEVEN SMOAKES
595 Sharease Cir (28405-3354)
PHONE.....................910 352-4287
Steven Smoakes, *Owner*
EMP: 6

SALES (est): 173.37K **Privately Held**
SIC: 3915 Jewelers' castings

(G-16418)
STITCH MORE BIG
6626 Gordon Rd Ste E (28411-8424)
PHONE.....................910 799-8992
EMP: 4 EST: 2013
SALES (est): 49.47K **Privately Held**
SIC: 2395 Embroidery and art needlework

(G-16419)
STRATTON PUBLISHING & MKTG INC
1457 Quadrant Cir (28405-4220)
P.O. Box 13133 (22312-9133)
PHONE.....................703 914-9200
Debra Stratton, *Pr*
EMP: 7 EST: 1991
SQ FT: 2,000
SALES (est): 565.72K **Privately Held**
SIC: 2721 8748 Magazines: publishing only, not printed on site; Publishing consultant

(G-16420)
STURDY CORPORATION
Also Called: Sturdy Control Div
1822 Carolina Beach Rd (28401-6504)
PHONE.....................910 763-2500
▲ EMP: 155 EST: 1971
SALES (est): 39.07MM **Privately Held**
Web: www.sturdycorp.com
SIC: 3714 3531 Governors, motor vehicle; Marine related equipment

(G-16421)
STURDY POWER CORPORATION LLC
1822 Carolina Beach Rd (28401-6504)
PHONE.....................910 763-2500
David R Sturdy, *Managing Member*
EMP: 17 EST: 2000
SALES (est): 655.37K **Privately Held**
Web: www.sturdycorp.com
SIC: 3629 Power conversion units, a.c. to d.c.: static-electric

(G-16422)
SURGILUM LLC
2 N Front St Ste 5 (28401-8407)
PHONE.....................910 202-2202
EMP: 7 EST: 2015
SQ FT: 2,000
SALES (est): 824.64K **Privately Held**
Web: www.surgilum.com
SIC: 3841 Surgical and medical instruments

(G-16423)
SWANSON CUSTOM WOOD WORKIN
611 Ann St (28401-4623)
PHONE.....................910 465-3199
Jeffrey Swanson, *Owner*
EMP: 5 EST: 2008
SALES (est): 72.96K **Privately Held**
SIC: 2431 Millwork

(G-16424)
SWEETTADER CUSTOM COMPOSITES
8118 Market St (28411-9386)
PHONE.....................910 262-6650
EMP: 4 EST: 2018
SALES (est): 151.34K **Privately Held**
SIC: 3599 Machine shop, jobbing and repair

(G-16425)
SYNOPTIX COMPANIES LLC
Also Called: Budget Blinds
130 Cinema Dr (28403-1490)
PHONE.....................910 790-3630

▲ = Import ▼ = Export
◆ = Import/Export

GEOGRAPHIC SECTION
Wilmington - New Hanover County (G-16450)

Brett Christmas, *Managing Member*
EMP: 13 **EST:** 2015
SALES (est): 884.84K **Privately Held**
Web: www.budgetblinds.com
SIC: 2591 Window blinds

(G-16426)
TARHEEL MONITORING LLC
709 Princess St (28401-4146)
PHONE.................................910 763-1490
EMP: 6 **EST:** 2009
SALES (est): 971.2K **Privately Held**
Web: www.tarheelmonitoring.com
SIC: 7359 8322 3663 Electronic equipment rental, except computers; Offender self-help agency; Global positioning systems (GPS) equipment

(G-16427)
TARHEEL WOOD DESIGNS INC
Also Called: Tarheel Solid Surfaces
6609b Windmill Way (28405-3746)
P.O. Box 10638 (28404-0638)
PHONE.................................910 395-2226
Earl Lee, *Pr*
Pamela Lee, *Sec*
EMP: 9 **EST:** 1987
SQ FT: 5,000
SALES (est): 985.86K **Privately Held**
Web: www.tarheelsolidsurfaces.com
SIC: 2434 Wood kitchen cabinets

(G-16428)
TEXLON INDUSTRIES LLC
4910 Pompano Ct (28403-6448)
PHONE.................................252 292-6590
David Sarmiento, *Prin*
EMP: 4 **EST:** 2019
SALES (est): 66.23K **Privately Held**
Web: www.texlonindustries.com
SIC: 3999 Manufacturing industries, nec

(G-16429)
TIMBERLAKE VENTURES INC
Also Called: Toxplanet
1908 Eastwood Rd Ste 327 (28403-7235)
P.O. Box 1603 (28031-1603)
PHONE.................................704 896-7499
Matthias Timberlake, *Pr*
EMP: 5 **EST:** 2015
SALES (est): 313.32K **Privately Held**
Web: www.enhesa.com
SIC: 2741 Internet publishing and broadcasting

(G-16430)
TOTE GLASS INC
621 N 4th St (28401-3413)
P.O. Box 1924 (28402-1924)
PHONE.................................910 515-4187
Dennis Walsak, *Pr*
EMP: 6 **EST:** 2011
SALES (est): 247.89K **Privately Held**
Web: www.toteglass.com
SIC: 3221 Bottles for packing, bottling, and canning: glass

(G-16431)
TRAVIS HARRELL
2936 Orville Wright Way Unit 1 (28405)
PHONE.................................828 279-2937
Travis Harrell, *Prin*
EMP: 6 **EST:** 2019
SALES (est): 119.2K **Privately Held**
SIC: 2431 Millwork

(G-16432)
TRAVISTEES
609 Piner Rd Ste A602 (28409-4201)
PHONE.................................910 506-8827
EMP: 4 **EST:** 2018
SALES (est): 148.82K **Privately Held**
Web: www.travistees.biz
SIC: 2759 Screen printing

(G-16433)
TRIDENT LURE
2153 Harrison St (28401-6921)
PHONE.................................910 520-4659
Marshall Davis, *Prin*
EMP: 4 **EST:** 2016
SALES (est): 78.49K **Privately Held**
SIC: 3949 Sporting and athletic goods, nec

(G-16434)
TRUELOVE FABRICATIONS INC
1319 S 4th St (28401-6203)
P.O. Box 4084 (28406-1084)
PHONE.................................910 343-0195
Leroy Truelove Iii, *Pr*
Wilma Truelove, *Sec*
EMP: 8 **EST:** 1988
SALES (est): 305.61K **Privately Held**
SIC: 3499 Aquarium accessories, metal

(G-16435)
TRUNK PUMP
6620 Gordon Rd Ste J (28411-8413)
PHONE.................................910 463-1282
Doug, Mcfarland, *Owner*
EMP: 6 **EST:** 2009
SALES (est): 96.14K **Privately Held**
Web: www.trunkpump.com
SIC: 3161 Trunks

(G-16436)
TWO FIFTY CLEANERS
Also Called: 250 Cyrstal Cleaner
5601 Carolina Beach Rd Ste C (28412-3695)
PHONE.................................910 397-0071
Sek Seo, *Pr*
EMP: 10 **EST:** 2000
SALES (est): 627.22K **Privately Held**
SIC: 3582 Drycleaning equipment and machinery, commercial, nec

(G-16437)
TWO24 DIGITAL LLC
Also Called: Two24 Digital Marketing
1325 Middle Sound Loop Rd (28411-7807)
PHONE.................................910 475-7555
Michael Moran, *Managing Member*
EMP: 7 **EST:** 2018
SALES (est): 329.51K **Privately Held**
Web: www.two24digital.com
SIC: 8742 2741 7311 7389 Marketing consulting services; Internet publishing and broadcasting; Advertising agencies; Advertising, promotional, and trade show services

(G-16438)
UNDER PRESSURE WILMINGTON LLC
Also Called: Pirtek Wilmington
119e Harley Rd (28405-3605)
PHONE.................................910 409-0194
EMP: 6 **EST:** 2021
SALES (est): 166.2K **Privately Held**
Web: www.cleanwilmingtonnc.com
SIC: 7699 3052 Cleaning services; Air line or air brake hose, rubber or rubberized fabric

(G-16439)
US PROTOTYPE INC
Also Called: Rapid Cut
341 S College Rd Ste 11 Pmb 3004 (28403-1622)
P.O. Box 609 (28443-0609)
PHONE.................................866 239-2848
Peter Lamporte, *Pr*
EMP: 20 **EST:** 2009
SQ FT: 2,500
SALES (est): 2.29MM **Privately Held**
Web: www.rapidcut.com
SIC: 3812 3714 3845 3679 Acceleration indicators and systems components, aerospace; Motor vehicle engines and parts; Electrocardiographs; Electronic loads and power supplies

(G-16440)
VAUGHN METALS INC
1314 S 12th St (28401-5946)
PHONE.................................910 791-6576
EMP: 5 **EST:** 2020
SALES (est): 185.87K **Privately Held**
SIC: 3441 Fabricated structural metal

(G-16441)
VILLARI FOOD GROUP LLC (PA)
1015 Ashes Dr Ste 102 (28405-8338)
P.O. Box 485 (28398-0485)
PHONE.................................910 293-2157
Salvatore Villari, *Managing Member*
Joseph P Villari, *Managing Member*
Rocco Villari, *Managing Member*
EMP: 39 **EST:** 2010
SQ FT: 35,000
SALES (est): 48.3MM
SALES (corp-wide): 48.3MM **Privately Held**
Web: www.villarifood.com
SIC: 2011 Meat packing plants

(G-16442)
WIELAND ELECTRIC INC (DH)
Also Called: Wieland
8207 Market St Ste P10680 (28404-0509)
PHONE.................................910 259-5050
Mark Matheny, *Pr*
Nicholas Fleming, *Pr*
Hana Radomil, *VP Fin*
▲ **EMP:** 10 **EST:** 1910
SQ FT: 200,000
SALES (est): 10.18MM
SALES (corp-wide): 414.21MM **Privately Held**
Web: www.wieland-americas.com
SIC: 5063 3496 3679 5065 Wire and cable; Miscellaneous fabricated wire products; Electronic circuits; Electronic parts and equipment, nec
HQ: Wieland Electric Gmbh
Brennerstr. 10-14
Bamberg BY 96052
95193240

(G-16443)
WILD CHILD CUSTOM GRAPHICS LLC
3126 Kitty Hawk Rd Ste 1 (28405-8625)
PHONE.................................910 762-5335
Chris Prince, *Owner*
EMP: 5 **EST:** 2007
SALES (est): 86K **Privately Held**
SIC: 3993 5099 7336 7389 Signs and advertising specialties; Signs, except electric; Graphic arts and related design; Design, commercial and industrial

(G-16444)
WILMINGTON CAMERA SERVICE LLC
905 N 23rd St (28405-1803)
PHONE.................................910 343-1089
EMP: 8 **EST:** 2008
SALES (est): 702.21K **Privately Held**
Web: www.wilmingtoncamera.com
SIC: 3861 Cameras and related equipment

(G-16445)
WILMINGTON COMPOST COMPANY LLC
1800 Eastwood Rd Apt 232 (28403-3664)
PHONE.................................910 839-3011
Riley Alber, *Prin*
EMP: 8 **EST:** 2018
SALES (est): 654.23K **Privately Held**
Web: www.wilmingtoncompostcompany.com
SIC: 2875 Compost

(G-16446)
WILMINGTON JOURNAL COMPANY
Also Called: Wilmington Journal, The
412 S 7th St (28401-5214)
P.O. Box 1020 (28402-1020)
PHONE.................................910 762-5502
Willy E Jervay, *Pr*
EMP: 8 **EST:** 1927
SALES (est): 695.17K **Privately Held**
Web: www.wilmingtonjournal.com
SIC: 2711 Newspapers, publishing and printing

(G-16447)
WILMINGTON MACHINE WORKS INC
Also Called: Ackermann Tool & Machine Co
3416 Enterprise Dr (28405-8893)
PHONE.................................910 343-8111
Kendall Wade Mccall, *Pr*
EMP: 16 **EST:** 1980
SQ FT: 9,700
SALES (est): 255.38K **Privately Held**
SIC: 3599 3544 Machine shop, jobbing and repair; Special dies, tools, jigs, and fixtures

(G-16448)
WILMINGTON MACHINERY INC
4628 Northchase Pkwy Ne (28405-7487)
P.O. Box 7308 (28406-7308)
PHONE.................................910 452-5090
Russell J La Belle, *Pr*
Susan Bino, *
Jeff Newman, *
▲ **EMP:** 25 **EST:** 1973
SQ FT: 60,000
SALES (est): 5.07MM **Privately Held**
Web: www.wilmingtonmachinery.com
SIC: 3599 Machine shop, jobbing and repair

(G-16449)
WILMINGTON MORTUARY SVC INC
Also Called: Wilmington Funeral & Cremation
1535 41st St (28403-7302)
PHONE.................................910 791-9099
John D Bevell Junior, *Pr*
EMP: 15 **EST:** 2005
SALES (est): 789.65K **Privately Held**
Web: www.wilmingtoncares.com
SIC: 3272 7261 Burial vaults, concrete or precast terrazzo; Crematory

(G-16450)
WILMINGTON RBR & GASKET CO INC
321 Raleigh St (28412-6307)
P.O. Box 15249 (28408-5249)
PHONE.................................910 762-4262
Howard Russell, *Pr*
EMP: 15 **EST:** 1985
SQ FT: 25,000
SALES (est): 2.39MM **Privately Held**
Web: www.wilmingtonrubber.com
SIC: 5085 3429 3053 Rubber goods, mechanical; Hardware, nec; Gaskets; packing and sealing devices

Wilmington - New Hanover County (G-16451) — GEOGRAPHIC SECTION

(G-16451)
WILMINGTON SCENTIFIC PUBLR LLC
890 S Kerr Ave Ste 1 (28403-8453)
PHONE.....................910 228-1974
EMP: 4 **EST:** 2010
SALES (est): 68.67K **Privately Held**
SIC: 2741 Miscellaneous publishing

(G-16452)
WILMINGTON STAR-NEWS INC (HQ)
Also Called: Lakeland Ledger Publishing
1003 S 17th St Ste 112 (28401-8038)
P.O. Box 840 (28402-0840)
PHONE.....................910 343-2000
Robert Gruber, *Pr*
EMP: 100 **EST:** 1896
SQ FT: 48,000
SALES (est): 21.34MM
SALES (corp-wide): 295.49MM **Privately Held**
Web: www.starnewsonline.com
SIC: 2752 2711 Commercial printing, lithographic; Newspapers, publishing and printing
PA: Halifax Media Holdings, Llc
901 6th St
Daytona Beach FL 32117
386 681-2404

(G-16453)
WILMINGTON TODAY LLC
1213 Culbreth Dr (28405-3639)
PHONE.....................910 509-7195
▲ **EMP:** 6 **EST:** 2006
SALES (est): 320.18K **Privately Held**
Web: www.wilmingtontoday.com
SIC: 2721 Magazines: publishing only, not printed on site

(G-16454)
WILMINGTON WINE LLC
605 Castle St (28401-5223)
PHONE.....................910 202-4749
EMP: 6 **EST:** 2016
SALES (est): 111.26K **Privately Held**
Web: www.wilmingtonwineshop.com
SIC: 2084 Wines, brandy, and brandy spirits

(G-16455)
WILMONGTON TRFFIC NEIGHBORHOOD
206 Operation Center Dr (28412-1943)
PHONE.....................910 341-7888
Jim Flechtner, *Mgr*
EMP: 6 **EST:** 2002
SALES (est): 170.17K **Privately Held**
SIC: 3669 Traffic signals, electric

(G-16456)
WORDEN BROTHERS INC
Also Called: Tc2000.com
6315 Boathouse Rd (28403-3576)
PHONE.....................919 202-8555
Christopher D Worden, *Pr*
Peter F Worden, *
Jon A Worden, *
EMP: 80 **EST:** 1988
SQ FT: 5,400
SALES (est): 6.72MM **Privately Held**
Web: www.worden.com
SIC: 7373 2731 Systems software development services; Books, publishing only

(G-16457)
XPERTEES PRFMCE SCREEN PRTG
1406 Castle Hayne Rd Ste 2 (28401-8889)
PHONE.....................910 763-7703
Rick Stefanick, *Pr*
EMP: 5 **EST:** 2005
SALES (est): 367.14K **Privately Held**
Web: www.xpertees.com
SIC: 2759 Screen printing

(G-16458)
YILDIZ ENTEGRE USA INC
1715 Woodbine St (28401)
PHONE.....................910 763-4733
Fehmi Yildiz, *Pr*
Ismail Hakki Yildiz, *VP*
Taner Basaga, *Sec*
▼ **EMP:** 9 **EST:** 2011
SALES (est): 836.8K **Privately Held**
Web: www.yildizentegre.com
SIC: 2421 Wood chips, produced at mill

(G-16459)
YP ADVRTISING PUBG LLC NOT LLC
Also Called: BellSouth
2250 Shipyard Blvd (28403-8024)
PHONE.....................910 794-5151
Jackie Hooks, *Brnch Mgr*
EMP: 125
SALES (corp-wide): 916.96MM **Publicly Held**
SIC: 2741 Miscellaneous publishing
HQ: Yp Advertising & Publishing Llc (Not Llc)
2247 Northlake Pkwy
Tucker GA 30084

(G-16460)
ZESKP LLC
Also Called: EZ Beverage Company
Wilmington
2027 Capital Dr (28405-6463)
PHONE.....................910 762-8300
Steven W Crouch, *CEO*
Ryan Tilworth, *Mgr*
EMP: 6 **EST:** 2010
SQ FT: 12,000
SALES (est): 660K **Privately Held**
SIC: 2086 5149 Water, natural: packaged in cans, bottles, etc.; Soft drinks

Wilson
Wilson County

(G-16461)
3C STORE FIXTURES INC
Also Called: 3 C
3363 Us Highway 301 N (27893-7990)
P.O. Box 219 (27894-0219)
PHONE.....................252 291-5181
Carolyn B Daniel, *CEO*
Michael Jones, *
▲ **EMP:** 81 **EST:** 1975
SQ FT: 400,000
SALES (est): 23.28MM **Privately Held**
Web: www.3cstorefixtures.com
SIC: 2521 2541 Cabinets, office: wood; Wood partitions and fixtures

(G-16462)
A & B SCREEN PRTG & EMB LLC
5515 Shepherd Rd (27893-7787)
PHONE.....................252 245-0573
Miroslava Tirado, *Prin*
EMP: 5 **EST:** 2017
SALES (est): 83.91K **Privately Held**
SIC: 2752 Commercial printing, lithographic

(G-16463)
A PLUS GRAPHICS INC
3101 Ward Blvd (27893-1729)
PHONE.....................252 243-0404
Bruce Jackson, *Pr*
Belinda Jackson, *VP*
EMP: 7 **EST:** 1991
SQ FT: 1,200
SALES (est): 855.32K **Privately Held**
Web: www.apluswilson.com
SIC: 2752 7336 Offset printing; Graphic arts and related design

(G-16464)
ADVANCED BRACE & LIMB
2693 Forest Hills Rd Sw (27893-8611)
PHONE.....................252 991-6109
EMP: 5 **EST:** 2014
SALES (est): 99.03K **Privately Held**
Web: www.advancedbraceandlimb.com
SIC: 3842 Limbs, artificial

(G-16465)
ANITAS MARKETING CONCEPTS INC
437 Ward Blvd Unit B (27893-1750)
P.O. Box 2821 (27894-2821)
PHONE.....................252 243-3993
Anita Jones, *Pr*
EMP: 4 **EST:** 2009
SALES (est): 354.15K **Privately Held**
Web: www.anitasmarketing.com
SIC: 7389 2752 Advertising, promotional, and trade show services; Offset printing

(G-16466)
AOA SIGNS INC
Also Called: A O A Signs
2707 Wooten Blvd Sw (27893-4483)
P.O. Box 83 (27055-0083)
PHONE.....................336 679-3344
Joy A Kay, *Pr*
Wadonna Poindexter Managing, *Prin*
EMP: 8 **EST:** 1971
SALES (est): 907.01K **Privately Held**
Web: www.aoasigns.com
SIC: 3993 Electric signs

(G-16467)
AQWA INC
2604 Willis Ct N (27896-8962)
PHONE.....................252 243-7693
Steven M Barry, *Pr*
James M Barry, *VP*
EMP: 6 **EST:** 2002
SQ FT: 30,000
SALES (est): 990.86K **Privately Held**
Web: www.aqwa.net
SIC: 3589 Sewage and water treatment equipment

(G-16468)
ARTISAN LEAF LLC
2231 Nash St Nw Ste E (27896-1712)
P.O. Box 1731 (27894-1731)
PHONE.....................252 674-1223
▼ **EMP:** 5 **EST:** 2014
SQ FT: 800
SALES (est): 365.35K **Privately Held**
Web: www.artisanleaf.com
SIC: 2541 Bar fixtures, wood

(G-16469)
ATLANTIC BEARING CO INC
321 Herring Ave Ne Bldg A (27893-4197)
P.O. Box 83 (27894-0083)
PHONE.....................252 243-0233
J Douglas Lamm, *Pr*
Wanda Lamm, *Sec*
EMP: 6 **EST:** 1987
SALES (est): 498.28K **Privately Held**
Web: www.atlantic-bearing.com
SIC: 3562 Ball and roller bearings

(G-16470)
AUTOMATED PRINTING SERVICES
431 Ward Blvd (27893-1750)
P.O. Box 307 (27894-0307)
PHONE.....................252 243-3993
Wesley Turnage, *Owner*
EMP: 10 **EST:** 1982
SQ FT: 6,300
SALES (est): 827.99K **Privately Held**
SIC: 2752 Offset printing

(G-16471)
AVERIX BIO LLC
3040 Black Creek Rd S (27893-9526)
PHONE.....................919 614-7600
Miles Wright, *CEO*
EMP: 20 **EST:** 2019
SALES (est): 2.53MM **Privately Held**
Web: www.averixbio.com
SIC: 2833 Medicinals and botanicals

(G-16472)
BAILEY FOODS LLC
Also Called: Bailey Slaughter House
2500 Nash St N Ste E (27896-1394)
PHONE.....................252 235-3558
R C Hunt, *Managing Member*
EMP: 21 **EST:** 1961
SALES (est): 654.61K **Privately Held**
SIC: 2011 0751 Meat packing plants; Slaughtering: custom livestock services

(G-16473)
BALLISTICS TECHNOLOGY INTL LTD
511 Goldsboro St Ne (27893-4044)
P.O. Box 4763 (27893-0763)
PHONE.....................252 360-1650
Tyron Sutton, *Brnch Mgr*
EMP: 8
SALES (corp-wide): 831.17K **Privately Held**
SIC: 3272 Concrete products, precast, nec
PA: Ballistics Technology International Ltd.
2207 Concord Pike 657
Wilmington DE 19803
877 291-1111

(G-16474)
BARRETTS PRINTING HOUSE INC
409 Goldsboro St S (27893-4923)
P.O. Box 305 (27894-0305)
PHONE.....................252 243-2820
Childs D Barrett, *Pr*
Margaret Ward, *Sec*
EMP: 6 **EST:** 1896
SQ FT: 2,800
SALES (est): 650.25K **Privately Held**
Web: www.barrettsprinting.com
SIC: 2752 Offset printing

(G-16475)
BB&P EMBROIDERY LLC
2801 Ward Blvd (27893-1733)
PHONE.....................252 206-1929
EMP: 5 **EST:** 2013
SALES (est): 230.21K **Privately Held**
SIC: 2395 Embroidery and art needlework

(G-16476)
BIG FISH DIGITAL SIGNS LLC
4222 Georgetown Dr N (27896-9505)
PHONE.....................252 363-1600
Michael G Mcharg, *Admn*
EMP: 5 **EST:** 2017
SALES (est): 89.53K **Privately Held**
Web: www.bigfishdigitalsigns.com
SIC: 3993 Signs and advertising specialties

(G-16477)
BLUE DOG GRAPHICS INC
619 Park Ave W (27893-3632)
PHONE.....................252 291-9191
Jerry Glenn Taylor Junior, *Prin*

GEOGRAPHIC SECTION
Wilson - Wilson County (G-16504)

EMP: 6 **EST:** 2014
SALES (est): 214.6K **Privately Held**
Web: www.bluedogusa.com
SIC: 7336 2396 Commercial art and graphic design; Fabric printing and stamping

(G-16478)
BRETT MCHENRY LOGGING LLC
3204 Nash St N Ste C (27896-3002)
PHONE.................................252 243-7285
Brett Mchenry, *Prin*
EMP: 10 **EST:** 2015
SALES (est): 845.9K **Privately Held**
SIC: 2411 Logging

(G-16479)
BREWMASTERS INC
2117 Forest Hills Rd W (27893)
PHONE.................................252 991-6035
Youssef Robert Morkos, *Prin*
EMP: 10 **EST:** 2013
SALES (est): 491.92K **Privately Held**
Web: www.brewmastersnc.com
SIC: 2082 Malt beverages

(G-16480)
BRIDGESTONE RET OPERATIONS LLC
Also Called: Firestone
1401 Ward Blvd (27893-3598)
P.O. Box 4 (27894-0004)
PHONE.................................252 243-5189
Reginald Reid, *Mgr*
EMP: 9
Web: www.bridgestoneamericas.com
SIC: 5531 7534 Automotive tires; Rebuilding and retreading tires
HQ: Bridgestone Retail Operations, Llc
333 E Lake St Ste 300
Bloomingdale IL 60108
630 259-9000

(G-16481)
BRUNSON MARINE GROUP LLC
4155 Dixie Inn Rd (27893-9000)
PHONE.................................252 291-0271
Robert R Brunson, *Managing Member*
EMP: 30 **EST:** 2014
SALES (est): 10MM **Privately Held**
Web: www.kencraftboats.com
SIC: 3089 Plastics boats and other marine equipment

(G-16482)
BUY SMART INC
Also Called: First Choice
1109 Brookside Dr Nw (27896-2134)
PHONE.................................252 293-4700
Pieter Van Den Berg, *Pr*
▲ **EMP:** 9 **EST:** 1999
SALES (est): 1.52MM **Privately Held**
Web: www.buysmartnc.com
SIC: 5083 3599 Agricultural machinery, nec; Amusement park equipment

(G-16483)
CAROLINA CLASSIC MANUFACTURING INC
510 Jones St S (27893-5032)
P.O. Box 159 (27894-0159)
PHONE.................................252 237-9105
EMP: 94
SIC: 3088 Tubs (bath, shower, and laundry), plastics

(G-16484)
CAROLINA KELLER LLC
2401 Stantonsburg Rd Se (27893-8414)
P.O. Box 370 (27894-0370)
PHONE.................................252 237-8181
▲ **EMP:** 150
SIC: 3566 Gears, power transmission, except auto

(G-16485)
CAROLINA PUBLISHING COMPANY
Also Called: North Carolina Sportsman Mag
1131 Anderson St Nw (27893-2463)
PHONE.................................252 206-1633
Tony Taylor, *Pr*
EMP: 7 **EST:** 1995
SALES (est): 82.49K **Privately Held**
SIC: 2721 Magazines: publishing and printing

(G-16486)
CARRAWAYS SIGN & WD CRAFTS LLC
1303 Gold St N (27893-2301)
PHONE.................................252 292-7141
EMP: 4 **EST:** 2021
SALES (est): 54.13K **Privately Held**
SIC: 2431 Woodwork, interior and ornamental, nec

(G-16487)
CEMEX MATERIALS LLC
1600 Thorne Ave S (27893-6043)
PHONE.................................252 243-6153
Ted Price, *Mgr*
EMP: 93
SIC: 3273 Ready-mixed concrete
HQ: Cemex Materials Llc
1720 Centrepark Dr E # 100
West Palm Beach FL 33401
561 833-5555

(G-16488)
CLOTHES CLEANING SYSTEM LLC
4475 Technology Dr Nw (27896-8686)
PHONE.................................252 243-3752
EMP: 5 **EST:** 2007
SQ FT: 20,000
SALES (est): 436.02K **Privately Held**
Web: www.clothescleaningsystems.com
SIC: 3441 Fabricated structural metal

(G-16489)
COMPASS GROUP USA INC
2102 Industrial Park Dr Se (27893-9300)
PHONE.................................252 291-7733
EMP: 40
SALES (corp-wide): 39.16B **Privately Held**
Web: www.compass-usa.com
SIC: 5962 2099 Food vending machines; Food preparations, nec
HQ: Compass Group Usa, Inc.
2400 Yorkmont Rd
Charlotte NC 28217

(G-16490)
CRAFT WOODWORK INC
4205 Craft Ln (27893-8565)
P.O. Box 3411 (27895-3411)
PHONE.................................252 237-7581
David Craft, *Pr*
David Scott Craft, *Pr*
EMP: 8 **EST:** 1974
SALES (est): 421.38K **Privately Held**
Web: www.craftwoodwork.com
SIC: 2434 2541 Wood kitchen cabinets; Wood partitions and fixtures

(G-16491)
CREEKSIDE CREATIVE DESIGN INC
206 Goldsboro St Sw (27893-4907)
PHONE.................................252 243-6272
Jimmy Sink, *Pr*
Alfred Sink, *Sec*
EMP: 9 **EST:** 1997
SQ FT: 16,000
SALES (est): 892.83K **Privately Held**
Web: www.creeksidecreativedesigns.com
SIC: 3446 Architectural metalwork

(G-16492)
DEGESCH AMERICA INC
1810 Firestone Pkwy Ne (27893-7991)
PHONE.................................800 548-2778
Chris Corvello, *Prin*
EMP: 26
SALES (corp-wide): 3.08MM **Privately Held**
Web: www.degeschamerica.com
SIC: 2879 Agricultural disinfectants
HQ: Degesch America, Inc.
153 Triangle Dr
Weyers Cave VA 24486
540 234-9281

(G-16493)
DOWN EAST OFFROAD INC
1425 Thorne Ave S (27893-6040)
PHONE.................................252 246-9440
Robert Bass, *Pr*
EMP: 10 **EST:** 1997
SQ FT: 8,000
SALES (est): 998.68K **Privately Held**
Web: www.downeastoffroad.com
SIC: 3799 5531 Off-road automobiles, except recreational vehicles; Automotive accessories

(G-16494)
EASTERN CABINET COMPANY INC
3100 Meteor Dr (27893-9029)
PHONE.................................252 237-5245
Troy Rouse, *Pr*
Thomas E Davis Junior, *Sec*
EMP: 5 **EST:** 1993
SQ FT: 4,000
SALES (est): 480.29K **Privately Held**
SIC: 2434 Wood kitchen cabinets

(G-16495)
EASTERN CAROLINA VAULT CO INC
1214 Queen St E (27893-5317)
P.O. Box 4202 (27893-0202)
PHONE.................................252 243-5614
Louis Hall, *Owner*
EMP: 4 **EST:** 1950
SALES (est): 406.79K **Privately Held**
SIC: 3272 Burial vaults, concrete or precast terrazzo

(G-16496)
ENGINEERED PROCESSING EQP LLC
5036 Country Club Dr N (27896-9122)
P.O. Box 12322 (27709-2322)
PHONE.................................919 321-6891
EMP: 8 **EST:** 2003
SALES (est): 480.42K **Privately Held**
Web: www.epei.us
SIC: 2834 Pharmaceutical preparations

(G-16497)
EON LABS INC
4700 Sandoz Dr N (27893-8143)
PHONE.................................252 234-2222
William F Holt, *VP*
▲ **EMP:** 333
Web: www.eonlabs.com
SIC: 2834 Pharmaceutical preparations
HQ: Eon Labs, Inc.
1999 Marcus Ave Ste 300
New Hyde Park NY 11042

(G-16498)
EVANS MACHINERY INC
5123 Ivy Ct (27893-7572)
P.O. Box 3408 (27895-3408)
PHONE.................................252 243-4006
Donald Evans, *Pr*
Bobby Evans, *
Charles Evans, *
Thomas Jackson, *SALES**
◆ **EMP:** 56 **EST:** 1979
SQ FT: 135,000
SALES (est): 9.71MM **Privately Held**
Web: www.evansmachinery.com
SIC: 3523 3441 Farm machinery and equipment; Fabricated structural metal

(G-16499)
FRESENIUS KABI USA LLC
5200 Corporate Pkwy (27893-9412)
PHONE.................................252 991-2692
EMP: 477
SALES (corp-wide): 42.42B **Privately Held**
Web: www.fresenius-kabi.com
SIC: 2834 Pharmaceutical preparations
HQ: Fresenius Kabi Usa, Llc
3 Corporate Dr
Lake Zurich IL 60047
847 550-2300

(G-16500)
FULFORDS RESTORATIONS (PA)
320 Barnes St S (27893-5002)
PHONE.................................252 243-7727
Edward Fulford Junior, *Owner*
▲ **EMP:** 5 **EST:** 1983
SQ FT: 70,000
SALES (est): 838.42K **Privately Held**
Web: www.fulfords.us
SIC: 2511 7641 Wood household furniture; Antique furniture repair and restoration

(G-16501)
GODS SON PLUMBING INC
Also Called: God's Son Plumbing Repair
1711 Roxbury Dr (27893-1859)
P.O. Box 571 (27894-0571)
PHONE.................................252 299-0983
William Pickett, *Prin*
EMP: 5 **EST:** 2007
SALES (est): 419.2K **Privately Held**
SIC: 3432 Plastic plumbing fixture fittings, assembly

(G-16502)
JAMES BUNN
4167 Black Creek Rd S (27893-9125)
PHONE.................................252 293-4867
James Bunn, *Owner*
EMP: 4 **EST:** 2016
SALES (est): 210.01K **Privately Held**
SIC: 3489 Ordnance and accessories, nec

(G-16503)
JUPITER BATHWARE INC
510 Jones St S (27893-5032)
P.O. Box 159 (27894-0159)
PHONE.................................800 343-8295
Hp Mc Coy, *Pr*
Brooks Davis, *Stockholder**
EMP: 19 **EST:** 2005
SQ FT: 115,000
SALES (est): 963.65K **Privately Held**
SIC: 3088 Plastics plumbing fixtures

(G-16504)
KATCHI TEES INCORPORATED
1108 Gold St N (27893-2514)
PHONE.................................252 315-4691
Teresa Jones, *CEO*
EMP: 4 **EST:** 2014

Wilson - Wilson County (G-16505)

GEOGRAPHIC SECTION

SALES (est): 261.06K **Privately Held**
SIC: 2759 7291 7389 5947 Screen printing; Tax return preparation services; Financial services; Gift baskets

(G-16505)
KENCRAFT MANUFACTURING INC
4078 Us Highway 117 (27893-0915)
PHONE..........................252 291-0271
Kenneth D Vick, *Pr*
EMP: 11 **EST**: 1975
SQ FT: 60,000
SALES (est): 459.85K **Privately Held**
Web: www.kencraftboats.com
SIC: 3732 5551 Boats, fiberglass: building and repairing; Boat dealers

(G-16506)
KIDDE TECHNOLOGIES INC
Kidde Dual Spectrum
4200 Airport Dr Nw (27896-8630)
PHONE..........................252 237-7004
EMP: 67
SALES (corp-wide): 22.1B **Publicly Held**
Web: www.kiddetechnologies.com
SIC: 3728 3674 Aircraft parts and equipment, nec; Semiconductors and related devices
HQ: Kidde Technologies Inc.
   4200 Airport Dr Nw
   Wilson NC 27896

(G-16507)
KIDDE TECHNOLOGIES INC
4200 Airport Dr Nw (27896-8630)
PHONE..........................252 237-7004
Brent Ehmke, *Brnch Mgr*
EMP: 325
SQ FT: 71,000
SALES (corp-wide): 22.1B **Publicly Held**
Web: www.kiddetechnologies.com
SIC: 3812 8611 Search and navigation equipment; Business associations
HQ: Kidde Technologies Inc.
   4200 Airport Dr Nw
   Wilson NC 27896

(G-16508)
KIDDE TECHNOLOGIES INC (DH)
Also Called: Fenwal Safety Systems
4200 Airport Dr Nw (27896-8630)
PHONE..........................252 237-7004
Terry Hayden, *Pr*
Brent Ehmke, *
W Thomas Ramsey, *
John F Hannon, *
▼ **EMP**: 285 **EST**: 1935
SQ FT: 71,000
SALES (est): 101.99MM
SALES (corp-wide): 22.1B **Publicly Held**
Web: www.kiddetechnologies.com
SIC: 3669 Fire alarm apparatus, electric
HQ: Kidde Fire Protection Inc.
   350 E Union St
   West Chester PA 19382

(G-16509)
LA PALMAS TORTILLERIA Y TAQUER
900 Goldsboro St Sw (27893-4950)
PHONE..........................252 206-1683
Gregorio Cuadra, *Prin*
EMP: 6 **EST**: 2007
SALES (est): 83.16K **Privately Held**
SIC: 2099 Tortillas, fresh or refrigerated

(G-16510)
LELY MANUFACTURING INC
4608 Lely Rd (27893-8111)
P.O. Box 789 (27894-0789)
PHONE..........................252 291-7050
Brian Taylor, *Pr*

Peter Langebeeke, *Dir*
▼ **EMP**: 15 **EST**: 1975
SALES (est): 2.19MM **Privately Held**
SIC: 3589 Sewage and water treatment equipment

(G-16511)
LINAMAR FORGINGS CAROLINA INC
2401 Old Stantonsburg Rd (27894)
P.O. Box 370 (27894-0370)
PHONE..........................252 237-8181
Jim Jarrell, *Pr*
Linda Hasenfratz, *VP*
Mark Stoddart, *VP*
Roger Fulton, *Sec*
Dale Schneider, *Treas*
▲ **EMP**: 100 **EST**: 2014
SQ FT: 245,000
SALES (est): 34.34MM
SALES (corp-wide): 5.89B **Privately Held**
SIC: 3562 3566 3462 Ball bearings and parts; Gears, power transmission, except auto; Iron and steel forgings
HQ: Linamar Holding Nevada, Inc.
   32233 8 Mile Rd
   Livonia MI 48152
   248 477-6240

(G-16512)
LINKONE SRC LLC
2018 Beeler Rd S (27893-9591)
PHONE..........................252 206-0960
Melanie Foster, *Managing Member*
EMP: 10 **EST**: 1994
SALES (est): 193.64K **Privately Held**
Web: www.sunriverservice.com
SIC: 2048 Prepared feeds, nec

(G-16513)
LIVEDO USA INC
4925 Livedo Dr (27893-9403)
PHONE..........................252 237-1373
Tadashi Hoshikawa, *Pr*
Keiichi Ishikawa, *VP*
◆ **EMP**: 55 **EST**: 2004
SALES (est): 19.5MM **Privately Held**
Web: www.livedousa.com
SIC: 2676 Sanitary paper products
PA: Livedo Corporation
   45-2, Otsu, Kanadachohanda
   Shikokuchuo EHM 799-0

(G-16514)
MCS OF FAYETTEVILLE
2810 Contentnea Rd S (27893-8501)
PHONE..........................252 234-6001
Jonathon Mclaurin, *Pr*
EMP: 5 **EST**: 2016
SALES (est): 60.84K **Privately Held**
Web: www.mcsoffayettevilleinc.com
SIC: 7692 Welding repair

(G-16515)
MERCK SHARP & DOHME LLC
Merck
4633 Merck Rd W (27893-9633)
PHONE..........................252 243-2011
Ken Jones, *Brnch Mgr*
EMP: 285
SALES (corp-wide): 60.12B **Publicly Held**
Web: www.merck.com
SIC: 2834 Pharmaceutical preparations
PA: Merck & Co., Inc.
   126 E Lincoln Ave
   Rahway NJ 07065
   908 740-4000

(G-16516)
MORTON BUILDINGS INC
3042 Forest Hills Rd Sw Ste C (27893-9294)

PHONE..........................252 291-1300
EMP: 9
SALES (corp-wide): 213.04MM **Privately Held**
Web: www.mortonbuildings.com
SIC: 3448 Prefabricated metal buildings and components
PA: Morton Buildings, Inc.
   252 W Adams St
   Morton IL 61550
   800 447-7436

(G-16517)
NASHVILLE WLDG & MCH WORKS INC
2356 Firestone Pkwy Ne (27893-7736)
PHONE..........................252 243-0113
Oscar Ellis Junior, *Pr*
Janice Boone, *Off Mgr*
EMP: 20 **EST**: 1974
SQ FT: 15,000
SALES (est): 2.76MM **Privately Held**
Web: www.nashvillewelding.com
SIC: 7692 7389 3599 Welding repair; Crane and aerial lift service; Machine shop, jobbing and repair

(G-16518)
NEOPAC US INC
4940 Lamm Rd (27893-9693)
PHONE..........................908 342-0990
EMP: 6 **EST**: 2019
SALES (est): 3.17MM **Privately Held**
Web: www.neopac.com
SIC: 2671 Plastic film, coated or laminated for packaging
HQ: Hoffmann Neopac Beteiligungen Ag
   Eisenbahnstrasse 71
   Thun BE 3645

(G-16519)
NIGOCHE WELDING SERVICES LLC
5608 Raccoon Ct Nw (27896-8787)
PHONE..........................252 373-8306
Freddy Jacobo Nigoche, *Owner*
EMP: 6 **EST**: 2017
SALES (est): 104.7K **Privately Held**
Web: nigoche-welding-services.business.site
SIC: 7692 Welding repair

(G-16520)
OBRIAN TARPING SYSTEMS INC
110 Beacon St W (27893-3646)
PHONE..........................252 291-6710
Sean O'brian, *Prin*
EMP: 14
SALES (corp-wide): 2.6MM **Privately Held**
Web: www.obriantarping.com
SIC: 2394 Canvas and related products
PA: O'brian Tarping Systems, Inc.
   2330 Womble Brooks Rd E
   Wilson NC 27893
   252 291-2141

(G-16521)
OBRIAN TARPING SYSTEMS INC (PA)
2330 Womble Brooks Rd E (27893-7947)
PHONE..........................252 291-2141
Woody V O'brian, *Pr*
Winnie O'brian, *Sec*
▼ **EMP**: 11 **EST**: 1961
SQ FT: 9,000
SALES (est): 2.6MM
SALES (corp-wide): 2.6MM **Privately Held**
Web: www.obriantarping.com
SIC: 2394 Tarpaulins, fabric: made from purchased materials

(G-16522)
PEAK DEMAND INC
605 Tarboro Street Anx Sw (27893-4849)
P.O. Box 1668 (27894-1668)
PHONE..........................252 360-2777
Scott Bargoil, *CFO*
EMP: 11 **EST**: 2016
SALES (est): 2.43MM **Privately Held**
Web: www.peakdemand.com
SIC: 3677 Electronic coils and transformers

(G-16523)
PRIDGEN-LUCAS LATISHA
Also Called: Bellalou Designs
3712 Stonehenge Ln W (27893-7791)
PHONE..........................252 360-7866
Latisha Pridgen-lucas, *Owner*
EMP: 6 **EST**: 2020
SALES (est): 144.59K **Privately Held**
SIC: 3944 Craft and hobby kits and sets

(G-16524)
PROTEIN FOR PETS OPCO LLC
Also Called: Sun River Service Company
2018 Beeler Rd S (27893-9591)
PHONE..........................252 206-0960
Jeff Ross, *Pr*
Watson Ross, *
Melanie Foster, *
▲ **EMP**: 29 **EST**: 2016
SQ FT: 15,000
SALES (est): 5.27MM **Privately Held**
Web: www.sunriverservice.com
SIC: 2048 Meat meal and tankage, prepared as animal feed

(G-16525)
PURDUE PHARMACEUTICALS LP
4701 International Blvd (27893-9664)
PHONE..........................252 265-1900
Edward Mahony, *Ex VP*
Stuart D Baker, *Ex VP*
David Long, *Sr VP*
Saeed Motahari, *Sr VP*
EMP: 11 **EST**: 1998
SALES (est): 21.99MM
SALES (corp-wide): 790.3MM **Privately Held**
Web: www.purduepharma.com
SIC: 5122 2834 Pharmaceuticals; Pharmaceutical preparations
HQ: Purdue Pharma L.P.
   201 Tresser Blvd Fl 1
   Stamford CT 06901

(G-16526)
Q T CORPORATION
2700 Forest Hills Rd Sw (27893)
PHONE..........................252 399-7600
EMP: 7 **EST**: 1993
SQ FT: 3,500
SALES (est): 1.08MM **Privately Held**
Web: www.qt-corporation.com
SIC: 3625 7373 8742 Relays and industrial controls; Computer integrated systems design; Industrial consultant

(G-16527)
R J REYNOLDS TOBACCO COMPANY
1500 Charleston St Se (27893-9035)
P.O. Box 636 (27894-0636)
PHONE..........................252 291-4700
Randy F Harris, *Mgr*
EMP: 121
Web: www.rjrt.com
SIC: 2141 Tobacco stemming and redrying
HQ: R. J. Reynolds Tobacco Company
   401 N Main St
   Winston Salem NC 27101
   336 741-5000

GEOGRAPHIC SECTION
Wilson - Wilson County (G-16550)

(G-16528)
R R DONNELLEY & SONS COMPANY
Also Called: R R Donnelley
1900 Charleston St Se (27893-9032)
PHONE..................................252 243-0337
Bret Beach, *Brnch Mgr*
EMP: 63
SALES (corp-wide): 15B **Privately Held**
Web: www.rrd.com
SIC: 2759 2671 Screen printing; Paper; coated and laminated packaging
HQ: R. R. Donnelley & Sons Company
35 W Wacker Dr
Chicago IL 60601
800 782-4892

(G-16529)
RECON USA LLC
4744 Potato House Ct (27893-8592)
P.O. Box 498 (27813-0498)
PHONE..................................252 206-1391
EMP: 5 **EST:** 2010
SALES (est): 446.54K **Privately Held**
SIC: 2141 Tobacco stemming

(G-16530)
REFRESCO BEVERAGES US INC
Also Called: Refresco Wilson
4843 International Blvd (27893-9673)
PHONE..................................252 234-0493
Joyce August, *Off Mgr*
EMP: 48
Web: www.refresco-na.com
SIC: 2086 Carbonated beverages, nonalcoholic: pkged. in cans, bottles
HQ: Refresco Beverages Us Inc.
8112 Woodland Center Blvd
Tampa FL 33614

(G-16531)
REFRESCO BEVERAGES US INC
1805 Purina Cir S (27893-9590)
PHONE..................................252 234-0493
EMP: 18
SIC: 2086 Soft drinks: packaged in cans, bottles, etc.
HQ: Refresco Beverages Us Inc.
8112 Woodland Center Blvd
Tampa FL 33614

(G-16532)
RHYNO ENTERPRISES
Also Called: Wilson Trophy & Hayes EMB
709 Tarboro St Sw (27893-4850)
P.O. Box 6170 (27894-6170)
PHONE..................................252 291-6700
Michael Hicks, *Owner*
EMP: 4 **EST:** 1994
SALES (est): 206.26K **Privately Held**
SIC: 2395 Embroidery and art needlework

(G-16533)
ROBERT RAPER WELDING INC
5326 Evansdale Rd (27893-8057)
P.O. Box 67 (27813-0067)
PHONE..................................252 399-0598
Robert K Raper, *Pr*
EMP: 5 **EST:** 2010
SALES (est): 313.4K **Privately Held**
SIC: 7692 Welding repair

(G-16534)
ROOFING TOOLS AND EQP INC (PA)
3710 Weaver Rd (27893-9441)
P.O. Box 126 (27894-0126)
PHONE..................................252 291-1800
John E Kent Junior, *Pr*
Elizabeth Kent Watson, *VP*
EMP: 9 **EST:** 1937
SQ FT: 36,000
SALES (est): 8.61MM
SALES (corp-wide): 8.61MM **Privately Held**
Web: www.roofingtool.com
SIC: 5033 5074 5075 3531 Roofing, asphalt and sheet metal; Heating equipment (hydronic); Air conditioning equipment, except room units, nec; Roofing equipment

(G-16535)
S K BOWLING INC
4475 Technology Dr Nw (27896-8686)
P.O. Box 8 (27894-0008)
PHONE..................................252 243-1803
Sam Bowling, *Pr*
Phil Sharitz, *VP*
EMP: 11 **EST:** 1984
SQ FT: 10,000
SALES (est): 1.65MM **Privately Held**
Web: www.skbowling.com
SIC: 3444 Sheet metal specialties, not stamped

(G-16536)
S STRICKLAND DIESEL SVC INC
5451 Old Raleigh Rd (27893-8322)
PHONE..................................252 291-6999
Brenda F Strickland, *Pr*
Kelly Strickland, *VP*
EMP: 7 **EST:** 1973
SQ FT: 9,600
SALES (est): 619.62K **Privately Held**
Web: www.stricklandsdieselservice.com
SIC: 7538 3599 5084 Diesel engine repair: automotive; Machine shop, jobbing and repair; Engines and parts, diesel

(G-16537)
S T WOOTEN CORPORATION
Also Called: Wilson Concrete Plant
2710 Commerce Rd S (27893-8122)
PHONE..................................252 291-5165
Scott Wooten, *Pr*
EMP: 22
SALES (corp-wide): 319.83MM **Privately Held**
Web: www.stwcorp.com
SIC: 3531 Concrete plants
PA: S. T. Wooten Corporation
3801 Black Creek Rd Se
Wilson NC 27893
252 291-5165

(G-16538)
S T WOOTEN CORPORATION (PA)
Also Called: S. T. Wooten
3801 Black Creek Rd Se (27893-9568)
P.O. Box 2408 (27894-2408)
PHONE..................................252 291-5165
Christopher Wooten, *Pr*
Nancy W Hammock, *
Keith H Merrick, *
George R Stickland, *
Gregory N Nelson, *
EMP: 45 **EST:** 1956
SQ FT: 15,000
SALES (est): 319.83MM
SALES (corp-wide): 319.83MM **Privately Held**
Web: www.stwcorp.com
SIC: 1611 3273 1623 General contractor, highway and street construction; Ready-mixed concrete; Water main construction

(G-16539)
SANDOZ INC
4700 Sandoz Dr (27893-8143)
PHONE..................................252 234-2222
Bill Coneber, *Mgr*
EMP: 305
Web: us.sandoz.com
SIC: 2834 Pharmaceutical preparations
HQ: Sandoz Inc.
100 College Rd W
Princeton NJ 08540
609 627-8500

(G-16540)
SCENTUAL CANDLES
1011 Tarboro St Sw (27893-4755)
PHONE..................................252 281-4919
Ivy Williams, *Owner*
EMP: 4 **EST:** 2016
SALES (est): 61.41K **Privately Held**
SIC: 3999 Candles

(G-16541)
SCHWEITZER-MAUDUIT INTL INC
Also Called: Swm Intl
2711 Commerce Rd S (27893-8122)
PHONE..................................252 360-4666
Jeffrey Kramer, *Brnch Mgr*
EMP: 5
Web: www.mativ.com
SIC: 3081 Unsupported plastics film and sheet
PA: Mativ Holdings, Inc.
100 Kimball Pl Ste 600
Alpharetta GA 30009

(G-16542)
SOUTH EAST MANUFACTURING CO
Also Called: Barnes Metalcrafters
113 Walnut St W (27893-3628)
P.O. Box 2492 (27894-2492)
PHONE..................................252 291-0925
EMP: 10 **EST:** 1996
SQ FT: 7,000
SALES (est): 1.94MM **Privately Held**
Web: www.barnesmetal.com
SIC: 3599 Machine shop, jobbing and repair

(G-16543)
STEPHENSON MILLWORK CO INC
210 Harper St Ne (27893-3307)
P.O. Box 699 (27894-0699)
PHONE..................................252 237-1141
Russell L Stephenson Junior, *Pr*
Russell L Stephenson Junior, *CEO*
Russell L Stephenson Iii, *Pr*
Lee Stephenson, *
EMP: 118 **EST:** 1945
SQ FT: 123,700
SALES (est): 22.52MM **Privately Held**
Web: www.stephensonmillwork.com
SIC: 2431 Millwork

(G-16544)
SUPREME MURPHY TRCK BODIES INC
4000 Airport Dr Nw (27896-8648)
P.O. Box 463 (46527-0463)
PHONE..................................252 291-2191
Omer G Kropf, *Pr*
Herbert M Gardner, *
William J Barrett, *
Robert W Wilson, *
EMP: 104 **EST:** 1935
SQ FT: 120,000
SALES (est): 25.43MM
SALES (corp-wide): 2.54B **Publicly Held**
SIC: 3713 3711 3585 Truck bodies (motor vehicles); Motor vehicles and car bodies; Refrigeration and heating equipment
HQ: Supreme Corporation
2581 Kercher Rd
Goshen IN 46528
574 642-4888

(G-16545)
SWOFFORD INC
Also Called: Montrose Hanger Co
301 Railroad St S (27893-5135)
P.O. Box 1149 (27894-1149)
PHONE..................................252 478-5969
Faye Swofford, *Mgr*
EMP: 6
SQ FT: 125,000
SALES (corp-wide): 1.5MM **Privately Held**
SIC: 2499 Washboards, wood and part wood
PA: Swofford, Inc.
6 Wisteria Ln
Bluffton SC 29909
843 379-8805

(G-16546)
THW OF WILSON INC
2515 Airport Blvd Nw Ste F (27896)
PHONE..................................252 237-7100
EMP: 7 **EST:** 2007
SALES (est): 220.51K **Privately Held**
SIC: 2836 Culture media

(G-16547)
TOBACCO RAG PROCESSORS INC (PA)
Also Called: T R P
4737 Yank Rd (27893-8528)
P.O. Box 498 (27813-0498)
PHONE..................................252 265-0081
T Davis Miller, *CEO*
Bobby Joe Johnson, *
Brian Tascher, *
◆ **EMP:** 33 **EST:** 2000
SALES (est): 24.18MM
SALES (corp-wide): 24.18MM **Privately Held**
Web: www.tobaccorag.com
SIC: 2141 2131 Tobacco stemming and redrying; Chewing and smoking tobacco

(G-16548)
TOBACCO RAG PROCESSORS INC
4744 Potato House Ct (27893-8592)
PHONE..................................252 265-0081
EMP: 21
SALES (corp-wide): 24.18MM **Privately Held**
Web: www.tobaccorag.com
SIC: 2131 2141 Chewing and smoking tobacco; Tobacco stemming and redrying
PA: Tobacco Rag Processors, Inc.
4737 Yank Rd
Wilson NC 27893
252 265-0081

(G-16549)
TOBACCO RAG PROCESSORS INC
2105 Black Creek Rd Se Bldg 6 (27893-9536)
PHONE..................................252 237-8180
EMP: 21
SALES (corp-wide): 24.18MM **Privately Held**
Web: www.tobaccorag.com
SIC: 2131 2141 Chewing and smoking tobacco; Tobacco stemming and redrying
PA: Tobacco Rag Processors, Inc.
4737 Yank Rd
Wilson NC 27893
252 265-0081

(G-16550)
TREGO INNOVATIONS LLC
2301 Wilco Blvd S (27893-9015)
PHONE..................................919 374-0089
Patrick Shelton, *Managing Member*
EMP: 5 **EST:** 2020
SALES (est): 262.05K **Privately Held**
Web: tregopartners.wordpress.com

SIC: 3086 Plastics foam products

(G-16551)
TRIAGA INC
1900 Stantonsburg Rd Se (27893-8406)
PHONE..........................919 412-6019
Darlene Quashie Henry, *Prin*
EMP: 9 EST: 2021
SALES (est): 3.37MM
SALES (corp-wide): 35.17B **Publicly Held**
Web: www.jobsinwilsonnc.com
SIC: 2111 Cigarettes
PA: Philip Morris International Inc.
     677 Wshngton Blvd Ste 110
     Stamford CT 06901
     203 905-2410

(G-16552)
TYLER WALSTON
3904 Airport Dr Nw Ste A (27896-8040)
PHONE..........................919 269-9300
Tyler Walston, *Owner*
EMP: 4 EST: 2018
SALES (est): 92.36K **Privately Held**
SIC: 7692 Welding repair

(G-16553)
UNDER COVERS PUBLISHING
703 Glendale Dr W (27893-2707)
PHONE..........................704 965-8744
David Hager, *Prin*
EMP: 5 EST: 2018
SALES (est): 119.38K **Privately Held**
SIC: 2741 Miscellaneous publishing

(G-16554)
UPPER COASTL PLAIN BUS DEV CTR
121 Nash St W (27893-4012)
PHONE..........................252 234-5900
Greg Goddard, *Dir*
EMP: 17 EST: 2007
SALES (est): 98.26K **Privately Held**
Web: www.ucpcog.org
SIC: 3523 Incubators and brooders, farm

(G-16555)
VOITH FABRICS INC
3040 Black Creek Rd S (27893-9526)
P.O. Box 1411 (27894-1411)
PHONE..........................252 291-3800
▲ EMP: 350
SIC: 2231 Broadwoven fabric mills, wool

(G-16556)
WAINWRIGHT WAREHOUSE
2427 Us Highway 301 S (27893-6893)
P.O. Box 249 (27880-0249)
PHONE..........................252 237-5121
Donald Windbourne, *Owner*
EMP: 5 EST: 1930
SALES (est): 483.42K **Privately Held**
SIC: 2111 0191 Cigarettes; General farms, primarily crop

(G-16557)
WAKE SUPPLY COMPANY
3200 Turnage Rd (27893-7580)
PHONE..........................252 234-6012
Anthony Beedie, *Brnch Mgr*
EMP: 7
SALES (corp-wide): 17.51MM **Privately Held**
Web: www.wakesupply.com
SIC: 2952 5033 Siding materials; Siding, except wood
PA: Wake Supply Company
     658 Maywood Ave Ste A
     Raleigh NC 27603
     252 234-6012

(G-16558)
WEENER PLASTICS INC
2201 Stantonsburg Rd Se (27893-8408)
P.O. Box 2165 (27894-2165)
PHONE..........................252 206-1400
Louis Meszaros, *Pr*
Angela Parnell, *
◆ EMP: 63 EST: 2006
SQ FT: 50,000
SALES (est): 23.35MM
SALES (corp-wide): 355.83K **Privately Held**
Web: www.wppg.com
SIC: 3082 3949 Unsupported plastics profile shapes; Sporting and athletic goods, nec
HQ: Weener Plastik Beteiligungs Gmbh
     Industriestr. 1
     Weener NI 26826
     49513060

(G-16559)
WHITE S TIRE SVC WILSON INC
501 Goldsboro St S (27893-4924)
P.O. Box 1469 (27894-1469)
PHONE..........................252 237-0770
Robert W White, *VP*
EMP: 8
SALES (corp-wide): 23.66MM **Privately Held**
Web: www.whitestireservice.com
SIC: 5531 7534 3011 5014 Automotive tires; Tire recapping; Tread rubber, camelback for tire retreading; Automobile tires and tubes
PA: White S Tire Service Of Wilson, Inc.
     701 Hines St S
     Wilson NC 27893
     252 237-5426

(G-16560)
WHITE S TIRE SVC WILSON INC (PA)
701 Hines St S (27893-5149)
P.O. Box 1469 (27894-1469)
PHONE..........................252 237-5426
James E White, *CEO*
Robert W White, *
EMP: 70 EST: 1951
SQ FT: 200,000
SALES (est): 23.66MM
SALES (corp-wide): 23.66MM **Privately Held**
Web: www.whitestireservice.com
SIC: 5531 7534 3011 5014 Automotive tires; Tire recapping; Tread rubber, camelback for tire retreading; Automobile tires and tubes

(G-16561)
WILSON DAILY TIMES INC
126 Nash St. W (27893)
P.O. Box 2447 (27894-2447)
PHONE..........................252 243-5151
Morgan Dickerman, *Pr*
Margaret Dickerman, *
EMP: 78 EST: 1900
SQ FT: 30,000
SALES (est): 8.16MM **Privately Held**
Web: www.restorationnewsmedia.com
SIC: 2711 Commercial printing and newspaper publishing combined

(G-16562)
WILSON MOLD & MACHINE CORP
2131 Nc Highway 42 E (27893-8812)
PHONE..........................252 243-1831
Terry Dobbins, *Pr*
▲ EMP: 85 EST: 1989
SALES (est): 9.92MM **Privately Held**
Web: www.wilsonmoldandmachine.com
SIC: 3599 7692 Machine shop, jobbing and repair; Welding repair

(G-16563)
WILSON OUTPATIENT IMAGING
1711 Medical Park Dr W (27893-2788)
PHONE..........................252 399-7430
EMP: 7 EST: 2019
SALES (est): 231.86K **Privately Held**
Web: www.wilsonmedical.com
SIC: 3841 Surgical and medical instruments

Windsor
Bertie County

(G-16564)
DELBERT WHITE LOGGING INC
452 White Oak Rd (27983-8006)
PHONE..........................252 209-4779
Delbert White, *Pr*
EMP: 7 EST: 1990
SALES (est): 635.87K **Privately Held**
SIC: 2411 Logging camps and contractors

(G-16565)
EAST COAST LOGGING INC
128 Mizelle Ln (27983-7228)
PHONE..........................252 794-4054
Neal Smith, *Owner*
EMP: 5 EST: 2002
SALES (est): 431.89K **Privately Held**
SIC: 2411 Logging camps and contractors

(G-16566)
EMANUEL HOGGARD
Also Called: Emanuel Hoggard Logging
837 Askewville Rd (27983-7967)
PHONE..........................252 794-3724
Emanuel Hoggard, *Owner*
EMP: 18 EST: 1996
SALES (est): 997.75K **Privately Held**
SIC: 2411 5812 Logging; Eating places

(G-16567)
MORVEN PARTNERS LP
Gillam Brothers Peanut Sheller
406 Spring St (27983-6843)
P.O. Box 550 (27983-0550)
PHONE..........................252 794-3435
EMP: 23
SIC: 2068 Salted and roasted nuts and seeds
PA: Morven Partners, L.P.
     11 Leigh Fisher Blvd
     El Paso TX 79906

(G-16568)
POWELL & STOKES INC
Also Called: Bertie County Peanuts
217 Us Highway 13 N (27983-8097)
PHONE..........................252 794-2138
EMP: 9 EST: 1919
SALES (est): 2.39MM **Privately Held**
Web: www.pnuts.net
SIC: 5159 5999 2068 Peanuts (bulk), unroasted; Feed and farm supply; Nuts: dried, dehydrated, salted or roasted

(G-16569)
S & K LOGGING INC
1408 S King St (27983-9665)
PHONE..........................252 794-2045
Kenneth S White Senior, *Pr*
Kenneth S White Junior, *VP*
Jason White, *VP*
Katherine White, *Sec*
EMP: 12 EST: 1993
SALES (est): 490.16K **Privately Held**
SIC: 2411 Logging camps and contractors

(G-16570)
SQUEAKS LOGGING INC
139 Republican Rd (27983-7501)
PHONE..........................252 794-1531
William Capehart, *Prin*
EMP: 6 EST: 2015
SALES (est): 247.78K **Privately Held**
SIC: 2411 Logging camps and contractors

(G-16571)
W & T LOGGING LLC
118 Conner Ln (27983-9584)
PHONE..........................252 209-4351
Tonyia Foy, *Prin*
EMP: 6 EST: 2013
SALES (est): 656.35K **Privately Held**
SIC: 2411 Logging camps and contractors

(G-16572)
W R WHITE INC
152 W Askewville St (27983-7238)
PHONE..........................252 794-6577
William R White, *Pr*
Steve M White, *VP*
Connie S Cowan, *Sec*
William D White, *VP*
EMP: 13 EST: 2001
SALES (est): 953.83K **Privately Held**
SIC: 2411 Logging camps and contractors

(G-16573)
WILLARD RODNEY WHITE
142 E Askewville St (27983-9560)
PHONE..........................252 794-3245
Willie R White, *Prin*
EMP: 6 EST: 2010
SALES (est): 151.64K **Privately Held**
SIC: 2741 Miscellaneous publishing

Wingate
Union County

(G-16574)
EBONY & IVORYS UNIQUE BTQ LLC
214 Glencroft Dr (28174-7808)
PHONE..........................704 324-4035
EMP: 5 EST: 2020
SALES (est): 241.73K **Privately Held**
SIC: 5621 3999 5699 Boutiques; Advertising display products; Customized clothing and apparel

(G-16575)
H & H WOOD PRODUCTS INC
3349 Us Hwy 74 E (28174)
P.O. Box 185 (28174-0185)
PHONE..........................704 233-4148
Richard Herring, *Pr*
EMP: 4 EST: 1947
SQ FT: 30,000
SALES (est): 307.1K **Privately Held**
SIC: 2431 Moldings, wood: unfinished and prefinished

(G-16576)
MAIN STREET MONOGRAMS
411 Maye St (28174-6732)
PHONE..........................704 233-5393
EMP: 4 EST: 2013
SALES (est): 61.17K **Privately Held**
SIC: 2395 Embroidery products, except Schiffli machine

(G-16577)
PILGRIMS PRIDE CORPORATION
Pilgrim's Pride Feed Mills Div
205 Edgewood Dr (28174-6700)
P.O. Box 668 (28103-0668)

GEOGRAPHIC SECTION
Winston Salem - Forsyth County (G-16603)

PHONE..............................704 233-4047
Tommy Long, *Mgr*
EMP: 104
Web: www.pilgrims.com
SIC: 2015 Chicken, slaughtered and dressed
HQ: Pilgrim's Pride Corporation
1770 Promontory Cir
Greeley CO 80634
970 506-8000

(G-16578)
SIGNS PLUS
6106 Olive Branch Rd (28174-8284)
PHONE..............................704 219-0290
Jeff Anderson, *Prin*
EMP: 5 **EST:** 2010
SALES (est): 55.33K **Privately Held**
SIC: 3993 Signs and advertising specialties

(G-16579)
THREE GYPSIES LLC
3918 Belk Mill Rd (28174-8761)
PHONE..............................843 337-7799
Melinda C Cato, *Prin*
EMP: 5 **EST:** 2018
SALES (est): 103.91K **Privately Held**
SIC: 3993 Signs and advertising specialties

Winnabow
Brunswick County

(G-16580)
EVERY DAY CARRY LLC
Also Called: Sporting Goods
4716 Black Pine Ct (28479-0501)
PHONE..............................203 231-0256
Marc Workiewicz, *Managing Member*
EMP: 10 **EST:** 2021
SALES (est): 317.26K **Privately Held**
SIC: 7389 3482 3484 5091 Business Activities at Non-Commercial Site; Small arms ammunition; Small arms; Firearms, sporting

(G-16581)
JLMADE LLC
2226 Jasper Forest Trl (28479-4401)
PHONE..............................252 515-2195
Jacob Yount, *Managing Member*
EMP: 6 **EST:** 2012
SALES (est): 234.56K **Privately Held**
SIC: 3089 Injection molding of plastics

(G-16582)
KITCHEN MAN INC
6361 Ocean Hwy E Ste 1 (28479-5757)
PHONE..............................910 408-1322
Chris Dabideen, *Pr*
EMP: 10 **EST:** 2015
SALES (est): 1.7MM **Privately Held**
Web: www.kitchenmannc.com
SIC: 3281 1799 Granite, cut and shaped; Counter top installation

(G-16583)
PORT CITY CABINETS LLC
109 S Palm Dr (28479-5187)
PHONE..............................910 622-0375
Richard Beighle, *Owner*
EMP: 4 **EST:** 2015
SALES (est): 166.79K **Privately Held**
Web: www.portcitycabinets.com
SIC: 2434 Wood kitchen cabinets

Winston Salem
Forsyth County

(G-16584)
1A SMART START LLC
2453 Spaugh Industrial Dr (27103-6498)
PHONE..............................336 765-7001
EMP: 7
Web: www.smartstartinc.com
SIC: 3694 Engine electrical equipment
PA: 1a Smart Start Llc
500 E Dallas Rd Ste 100
Grapevine TX 76051

(G-16585)
3 D SEWING CONTRACTORS
559 Sun Creek Dr (27104-2460)
PHONE..............................336 499-1619
EMP: 5 **EST:** 2019
SALES (est): 22.98K **Privately Held**
Web: www.hairworkscompany.com
SIC: 7694 Armature rewinding shops

(G-16586)
4TOPPS LLC
3135 Indiana Ave (27105-4343)
PHONE..............................704 281-8451
EMP: 6 **EST:** 2011
SALES (est): 935.89K **Privately Held**
SIC: 2531 Stadium seating

(G-16587)
A L BECK & SONS INC
505 Jones Rd (27107-9406)
PHONE..............................336 788-1896
Larry Beck, *CEO*
Steve Beck, *Sec*
EMP: 11 **EST:** 1973
SQ FT: 8,888
SALES (est): 998.1K **Privately Held**
SIC: 2011 Meat packing plants

(G-16588)
ACCUSPORT INTERNATIONAL INC (PA)
4310 Enterprise Dr Ste C (27106-3260)
PHONE..............................336 759-3300
Randall Tuttle, *CEO*
Don Thoruk, *Pr*
James Kluttz, *Ch*
▲ **EMP:** 15 **EST:** 1989
SQ FT: 8,000
SALES (est): 2.32MM **Privately Held**
Web: www.accusport.com
SIC: 3829 Measuring and controlling devices, nec

(G-16589)
ADELE KNITS INC
3304 Old Lexington Rd (27107-4119)
PHONE..............................336 499-6010
Henry A Brown Junior, *Ch Bd*
Bruce T Brown, *
Patricia Brown, *
EMP: 150 **EST:** 1970
SQ FT: 160,000
SALES (est): 43.55MM **Privately Held**
Web: www.adeleknitsinc.com
SIC: 5131 2259 Piece goods and notions; Bags and bagging, knit

(G-16590)
ADSIGN CORP
6100 Gun Club Rd (27103-9716)
P.O. Box 280 (27012-0280)
PHONE..............................336 766-3000
R Jack Perkins, *Pr*
Sue Perkins, *VP*
EMP: 8 **EST:** 1978
SQ FT: 5,500
SALES (est): 502.24K **Privately Held**
Web: www.adsigncorp.com
SIC: 3993 Signs, not made in custom sign painting shops

(G-16591)
ADVANCED DRAINAGE SYSTEMS INC
Foltz Concrete Pipe
11875 N Nc Highway 150 (27127-9182)
PHONE..............................336 764-0341
EMP: 21
SALES (corp-wide): 3.07B **Publicly Held**
Web: www.adspipe.com
SIC: 3272 Pipe, concrete or lined with concrete
PA: Advanced Drainage Systems, Inc.
4640 Trueman Blvd
Hilliard OH 43026
614 658-0050

(G-16592)
AERO 8 INC
3820 N Liberty St (27105-3911)
P.O. Box 11508 (27116-1508)
PHONE..............................336 776-9165
Thomas W Ferrell, *CEO*
Barry J Orell, *Pr*
Ricky N Parnell, *VP*
Gordon H T Sheeran, *VP*
EMP: 11 **EST:** 2007
SQ FT: 800
SALES (est): 5.3MM **Privately Held**
Web: www.aero8.net
SIC: 3724 Aircraft engines and engine parts

(G-16593)
AFE VICTORY INC
3779 Champion Blvd (27105-2667)
PHONE..............................856 428-4200
▲ **EMP:** 108
SIC: 3585 Refrigeration equipment, complete

(G-16594)
ALDERS POINT
590 Mock St (27127-2162)
PHONE..............................336 725-9021
Darrell Hill, *Prin*
EMP: 4 **EST:** 2006
SALES (est): 262.55K **Privately Held**
SIC: 3553 Furniture makers machinery, woodworking

(G-16595)
ALEXANDERS CBINETS COUNTERTOPS
4735 Kester Mill Rd (27103-1212)
P.O. Box 25445 (27114-5445)
PHONE..............................336 774-2966
Crystal Cramer, *CEO*
EMP: 4 **EST:** 2006
SALES (est): 389.46K **Privately Held**
SIC: 2434 Wood kitchen cabinets

(G-16596)
ALI GROUP NORTH AMERICA CORP
Also Called: Champion Industries
3765 Champion Blvd (27105-2667)
PHONE..............................336 661-1556
EMP: 100
SALES (corp-wide): 2.67MM **Privately Held**
Web: www.aligroup.com
SIC: 3589 Dishwashing machines, commercial
HQ: Ali Group North America Corporation
101 Corporate Woods Pkwy
Vernon Hills IL 60061
847 215-6565

(G-16597)
ALL OCCASION PRINTING
2408 Gardenia Rd (27107-2522)
PHONE..............................336 926-7766
EMP: 4 **EST:** 2013
SALES (est): 56.97K **Privately Held**
SIC: 2752 Commercial printing, lithographic

(G-16598)
ALL STICK LABEL LLC
3929 Westpoint Blvd Ste B (27103-6761)
PHONE..............................336 659-4660
EMP: 7 **EST:** 1997
SQ FT: 6,000
SALES (est): 474.3K **Privately Held**
Web: www.aslprintfx.com
SIC: 2759 Labels and seals: printing, nsk

(G-16599)
ALLIANCE ASSESSMENTS LLC
200 Northgate Park Dr (27106-3480)
PHONE..............................336 283-9246
Kenneth Dutton, *Prin*
EMP: 4 **EST:** 2012
SALES (est): 231.39K **Privately Held**
Web: www.allianceassessments.com
SIC: 2899 Drug testing kits, blood and urine

(G-16600)
ALPHA ALUMINUM LLC
Also Called: Phoenix Aluminum
1300 Cunningham Ave (27107-2203)
PHONE..............................336 777-5658
EMP: 7 **EST:** 2014
SALES (est): 382.49K **Privately Held**
Web: www.alphaaluminum.net
SIC: 3353 Aluminum sheet, plate, and foil

(G-16601)
ALPHAGRAPHICS
8100 N Point Blvd Ste A (27105-2561)
P.O. Box 11643 (27116-1643)
PHONE..............................336 759-8000
James Carpenter, *Pr*
EMP: 8 **EST:** 1998
SQ FT: 4,000
SALES (est): 719.19K **Privately Held**
Web: www.alphagraphics.com
SIC: 2752 Commercial printing, lithographic

(G-16602)
AMARR COMPANY (DH)
Also Called: Amarr Garage Doors
165 Carriage Ct (27105-1326)
PHONE..............................336 744-5100
Richard A Brenner, *Ch Bd*
Jeffrey D Mick, *
Richard S Sears, *
Matthew S Hukill, *
Stephen R Crawford, *
◆ **EMP:** 113 **EST:** 1951
SALES (est): 243.28MM
SALES (corp-wide): 11.51B **Privately Held**
Web: www.amarr.com
SIC: 5211 3442 2431 5031 Garage doors, sale and installation; Garage doors, overhead: metal; Garage doors, overhead, wood; Doors, garage
HQ: Assa Abloy Inc.
110 Sargent Dr
New Haven CT 06511

(G-16603)
AMERICAN SNUFF COMPANY LLC
Taylor Brothers
2415 S Stratford Rd (27103-6225)
P.O. Box 597 (27102-0597)
PHONE..............................336 768-4630
Gregory Sawyers, *Genl Mgr*
EMP: 212

Winston Salem - Forsyth County (G-16604)

GEOGRAPHIC SECTION

Web: www.americansnuffco.com
SIC: 2131 Chewing tobacco
HQ: American Snuff Company, Llc
5106 Tradeport Dr
Memphis TN 38141
901 761-2050

(G-16604)
AMERICAN WEBBING FITTINGS INC
4959 Home Rd (27106-2802)
PHONE.................................336 767-9390
Steve Schroeder, *Pr*
Steve Stewart, *Treas*
EMP: 18 EST: 1981
SALES (est): 2.44MM **Privately Held**
Web: www.americanwebbing.com
SIC: 2241 Narrow fabric mills

(G-16605)
ANNES BOOKS AND PAPERS
632 Laurel St (27101-5139)
PHONE.................................336 608-8612
Anne Murray, *Prin*
EMP: 4 EST: 2017
SALES (est): 87.14K **Privately Held**
SIC: 2621 Book paper

(G-16606)
APPLIED CATHETER TECH INC
113 Thomas St (27101-3628)
PHONE.................................336 817-1005
Jon S Wilson, *CEO*
EMP: 4 EST: 2008
SQ FT: 12,000
SALES (est): 177.77K **Privately Held**
Web: www.appliedcatheter.com
SIC: 3841 Surgical and medical instruments

(G-16607)
ARCHER BOX COMPANY
685 Kingsbury Cir (27106-5711)
PHONE.................................336 788-1910
James E Archer, *Pr*
Judy Archer, *Sec*
EMP: 14 EST: 1985
SQ FT: 27,000
SALES (est): 469.92K **Privately Held**
SIC: 2653 Boxes, corrugated: made from purchased materials

(G-16608)
ARGOS USA
1590 Williamson St (27107-1240)
PHONE.................................336 784-5181
EMP: 11
SALES (est): 343.87K **Privately Held**
Web: www.argos-us.com
SIC: 3273 Ready-mixed concrete

(G-16609)
ARGOS USA LLC
Also Called: Redi-Mix Concrete
1590 Williamson St (27107-1240)
PHONE.................................336 784-4888
Amy Radcliffe, *Brnch Mgr*
EMP: 59
Web: www.argos-us.com
SIC: 3273 Ready-mixed concrete
HQ: Argos Usa Llc
3015 Windward Plz Ste 300
Alpharetta GA 30005
678 368-4300

(G-16610)
ARMORED SELF DEFENSE LLC
519 Culpepper Ct (27104-3456)
PHONE.................................336 749-7556
EMP: 5 EST: 2018
SALES (est): 153.8K **Privately Held**
Web: www.armoredselfdefense.com

SIC: 3812 Defense systems and equipment

(G-16611)
ASCEND RESEARCH CORP
2150 Country Club Rd Ste 205 (27104-4241)
PHONE.................................336 710-5793
Janice W Lundmark, *Prin*
EMP: 4 EST: 2013
SALES (est): 224.19K **Privately Held**
Web: www.ascendresearchcorp.com
SIC: 2834 Pharmaceutical preparations

(G-16612)
B/E AEROSPACE INC
Also Called: Collins Aerospace
4965 Indiana Ave (27106-2826)
PHONE.................................336 692-8940
Brad Doss, *Logistics Leader*
EMP: 12
SALES (corp-wide): 68.92B **Publicly Held**
SIC: 2531 3728 3647 Public building and related furniture; Aircraft parts and equipment, nec; Vehicular lighting equipment
HQ: B/E Aerospace, Inc.
150 Oak Plaza Blvd # 200
Winston Salem NC 27105
336 747-5000

(G-16613)
B/E AEROSPACE INC (DH)
Also Called: Rockwell Collins
150 Oak Plaza Blvd Ste 200 (27105-1482)
PHONE.................................336 747-5000
Stephen Timm, *Pr*
Tatum Buse, *Finance**
▲ EMP: 30 EST: 1987
SQ FT: 31,300
SALES (est): 1.67B
SALES (corp-wide): 68.92B **Publicly Held**
Web: www.collinsaerospace.com
SIC: 2531 3728 3647 Seats, aircraft; Aircraft parts and equipment, nec; Aircraft lighting fixtures
HQ: Rockwell Collins, Inc.
400 Collins Rd Ne
Cedar Rapids IA 52498

(G-16614)
B/E AEROSPACE INC
175 Oak Plaza Blvd (27105-1471)
PHONE.................................336 293-1823
Steve Franke, *Brnch Mgr*
▲ EMP: 8
SALES (corp-wide): 67.07B **Publicly Held**
Web: www.collinsaerospace.com
SIC: 3728 Aircraft parts and equipment, nec
HQ: B/E Aerospace, Inc.
150 Oak Plaza Blvd # 200
Winston Salem NC 27105
336 747-5000

(G-16615)
B/E AEROSPACE INC
2598 Empire Dr (27103-6762)
PHONE.................................336 293-1823
Steve Franke, *Mgr*
▲ EMP: 9
SALES (corp-wide): 68.92B **Publicly Held**
Web: www.collinsaerospace.com
SIC: 3728 Aircraft parts and equipment, nec
HQ: B/E Aerospace, Inc.
150 Oak Plaza Blvd # 200
Winston Salem NC 27105
336 747-5000

(G-16616)
B/E AEROSPACE INC
190 Oak Plaza Blvd (27105-1470)
PHONE.................................336 744-6914

Alexander Pozzi, *Brnch Mgr*
EMP: 35
SALES (corp-wide): 67.07B **Publicly Held**
Web: www.collinsaerospace.com
SIC: 3728 Aircraft parts and equipment, nec
HQ: B/E Aerospace, Inc.
150 Oak Plaza Blvd # 200
Winston Salem NC 27105
336 747-5000

(G-16617)
B/E AEROSPACE INC
Also Called: Collins Aerospace
150 Oak Plz Blvd Bldg 2 (27105-1482)
PHONE.................................336 767-2000
EMP: 50
SALES (corp-wide): 68.92B **Publicly Held**
Web: www.collinsaerospace.com
SIC: 3728 Aircraft parts and equipment, nec
HQ: B/E Aerospace, Inc.
150 Oak Plaza Blvd # 200
Winston Salem NC 27105
336 747-5000

(G-16618)
B/E AEROSPACE INC
1455 Fairchild Rd # 1 (27105-4500)
PHONE.................................520 733-1719
Doug Rasnussen, *Brnch Mgr*
EMP: 100
SALES (corp-wide): 68.92B **Publicly Held**
Web: www.collinsaerospace.com
SIC: 3728 Aircraft parts and equipment, nec
HQ: B/E Aerospace, Inc.
150 Oak Plaza Blvd # 200
Winston Salem NC 27105
336 747-5000

(G-16619)
B/E AEROSPACE INC
B/E Arspace Seating Pdts Group
2599 Empire Dr (27103-6709)
PHONE.................................336 776-3500
Liam O'boyle, *Mgr*
EMP: 167
SALES (corp-wide): 68.92B **Publicly Held**
Web: www.collinsaerospace.com
SIC: 3728 Aircraft parts and equipment, nec
HQ: B/E Aerospace, Inc.
150 Oak Plaza Blvd # 200
Winston Salem NC 27105
336 747-5000

(G-16620)
B/E AEROSPACE INC
Also Called: Be Aerospace
1455 Fairchild Rd (27105-4500)
PHONE.................................336 767-2000
Michael Baughns, *Brnch Mgr*
EMP: 235
SALES (corp-wide): 67.07B **Publicly Held**
Web: www.collinsaerospace.com
SIC: 3728 Aircraft parts and equipment, nec
HQ: B/E Aerospace, Inc.
150 Oak Plaza Blvd # 200
Winston Salem NC 27105
336 747-5000

(G-16621)
BA INTERNATIONAL LLC
1000 E Hanes Mill Rd (27105-1384)
PHONE.................................336 519-8080
EMP: 24 EST: 2019
SALES (est): 1.72MM **Publicly Held**
SIC: 2253 T-shirts and tops, knit
PA: Hanesbrands Inc.
1000 E Hanes Mill Rd
Winston Salem NC 27105

(G-16622)
BAICY COMMUNICATIONS INC
Also Called: Immedia Print
1411 S Main St (27127-2705)
P.O. Box 26014 (27114-6014)
PHONE.................................336 722-7768
John Baicy, *Pr*
Elizabeth Baicy, *Sec*
EMP: 7 EST: 1988
SQ FT: 6,000
SALES (est): 771.47K **Privately Held**
Web: www.immediaprint.com
SIC: 2752 2791 Offset printing; Hand composition typesetting

(G-16623)
BE HOUSE PUBLISHING LLC
400 Barnes Rd (27107-6860)
PHONE.................................336 529-6143
Bridget Elam, *Owner*
EMP: 5 EST: 2018
SALES (est): 116.6K **Privately Held**
SIC: 2741 Miscellaneous publishing

(G-16624)
BEKAERT TEXTILES USA INC
200 Business Park Dr (27107-6538)
PHONE.................................336 769-4300
Dirk Vandeplancke, *Pr*
Michael Myers, *
Brandon Wells, *
Jetze Bouma, *
◆ EMP: 190 EST: 1991
SQ FT: 182,000
SALES (est): 44.17MM
SALES (corp-wide): 4.39B **Privately Held**
SIC: 2211 5021 Tickings; Mattresses
HQ: Bekaertdeslee
Deerlijkseweg 22
Waregem 8790
56624111

(G-16625)
BEKAERTDESLEE USA INC
200 Business Park Dr (27107-6538)
PHONE.................................336 747-4900
Rafael Rodriguez, *Pr*
Sam Sabbe, *
Dirk Verly, *Chief Human Resources Officer**
Jos Deslee, *Chief Strategic Officer**
EMP: 500 EST: 2002
SALES (est): 50.35MM
SALES (corp-wide): 4.39B **Privately Held**
Web: www.bekaertdeslee.com
SIC: 2211 5021 Tickings; Mattresses
HQ: Bekaertdeslee Holding
Deerlijkseweg 22
Waregem 8790

(G-16626)
BEKAERTDESLEE USA INC
Business Park Dr 240 (27107-6538)
PHONE.................................336 769-4300
Frederic Beucher, *CEO*
EMP: 39 EST: 2002
SALES (est): 3.77MM
SALES (corp-wide): 4.39B **Privately Held**
Web: www.bekaertdeslee.com
SIC: 2515 Mattresses, containing felt, foam rubber, urethane, etc.
HQ: Bekaertdeslee
Deerlijkseweg 22
Waregem 8790
56624111

(G-16627)
BETTER SOLUTIONS TECHNOLOGIES
6060 Providence Church Rd (27105-9740)
PHONE.................................704 227-7424
Ryan Strickland, *Owner*

GEOGRAPHIC SECTION
Winston Salem - Forsyth County (G-16653)

EMP: 4 **EST:** 2017
SALES (est): 75.95K **Privately Held**
SIC: 7372 Prepackaged software

(G-16628)
BEVERAGE-AIR CORPORATION (DH)
3779 Champion Blvd (27105-2667)
PHONE..................................336 245-6400
Filippo Berti, *CEO*
Oscar Villa, *
◆ **EMP:** 50 **EST:** 2008
SALES (est): 97.44MM
SALES (corp-wide): 2.67MM **Privately Held**
Web: www.beverage-air.com
SIC: 3585 Refrigeration and heating equipment
HQ: Ali Group North America Corporation
101 Corporate Woods Pkwy
Vernon Hills IL 60061
847 215-6565

(G-16629)
BG-CNC
309 Rainy Day Dr (27107-6018)
PHONE..................................336 596-3400
Bryan Gaviria, *Prin*
EMP: 6 **EST:** 2015
SALES (est): 162.81K **Privately Held**
SIC: 3441 Fabricated structural metal

(G-16630)
BIO-TECH PROSTHETICS
1728 S Hawthorne Rd (27103-4016)
PHONE..................................336 768-3666
EMP: 9
SALES (corp-wide): 1.12B **Privately Held**
Web: www.hangerclinic.com
SIC: 3842 5999 Prosthetic appliances; Orthopedic and prosthesis applications
HQ: Bio-Tech Prosthetics And Orthotics, Inc.
2301 N Church St
Greensboro NC 27405

(G-16631)
BIRTH TISSUE RECOVERY LLC (PA)
3051 Trenwest Dr Ste A (27103-3230)
PHONE..................................336 448-1910
Kurt R Weber, *CEO*
Kurt R Weber, *Pr*
Leah A Weber Vp Tissue, *Bank Operations*
Anna Tirrell, *Quality Assurance Vice President*
EMP: 21 **EST:** 2011
SQ FT: 6,000
SALES (est): 3.54MM
SALES (corp-wide): 3.54MM **Privately Held**
Web: www.birthtissuerecovery.com
SIC: 8099 8731 3841 Organ bank; Medical research, commercial; Surgical and medical instruments

(G-16632)
BLACK SAND COMPANY INC
745 W Clemmonsville Rd (27127-5000)
PHONE..................................336 788-6411
Cynthia Black Shoaf, *Pr*
Mark Shoaf, *VP*
EMP: 5 **EST:** 1927
SALES (est): 828.33K **Privately Held**
Web: www.blacksandco.com
SIC: 1442 Construction sand and gravel

(G-16633)
BLOOMDAY GRANITE & MARBLE INC
3810 Indiana Ave (27105-3409)
P.O. Box 11906 (27116-1906)
PHONE..................................336 724-0300
Frederick Cooke Junior, *CEO*
EMP: 26 **EST:** 1998
SALES (est): 4.99MM **Privately Held**
Web: www.bloomdaygranite.com
SIC: 5032 3281 Granite building stone; Granite, cut and shaped

(G-16634)
BLUE LIGHT WELDING OF TRIAD
2328 Pebble Creek Rd (27107-7602)
PHONE..................................336 442-9140
Redi Lambert, *Owner*
EMP: 5 **EST:** 2013
SALES (est): 55.72K **Privately Held**
SIC: 7692 Welding repair

(G-16635)
BRAND ART MANUFACTURING LLC
4991 Robinhood Rd (27106-4245)
PHONE..................................704 241-1104
Dennis D Becker, *Admn*
EMP: 5 **EST:** 2013
SALES (est): 229.09K **Privately Held**
Web: www.brandartmfg.com
SIC: 3999 Manufacturing industries, nec

(G-16636)
BRIDGESTONE RET OPERATIONS LLC
Also Called: Firestone
2743 Reynolda Rd (27106-3871)
PHONE..................................336 725-1580
David Bordeaux, *Mgr*
EMP: 8
SQ FT: 6,676
Web: www.bridgestoneamericas.com
SIC: 5531 7534 Automotive tires; Rebuilding and retreading tires
HQ: Bridgestone Retail Operations, Llc
333 E Lake St Ste 300
Bloomingdale IL 60108
630 259-9000

(G-16637)
BROAD BRANCH DISTILLERY LLC
2403 Buena Vista Rd (27104-2101)
PHONE..................................336 207-7855
EMP: 4 **EST:** 2014
SALES (est): 111.3K **Privately Held**
Web: www.broadbranchdistillery.com
SIC: 3556 Distillery machinery

(G-16638)
BROAD BRANCH DISTILLERY LLC
Also Called: Broad Branch Distillery
756 N Trade St (27101-1431)
PHONE..................................336 602-2824
EMP: 4 **EST:** 2015
SALES (est): 237.24K **Privately Held**
Web: www.broadbranchdistillery.com
SIC: 2085 Distilled and blended liquors

(G-16639)
BRUSHY MOUNTAIN BEE FARM INC (PA)
101 S Stratford Rd Ste 210 (27104)
PHONE..................................336 921-3640
Steve Forrest, *Pr*
Sandra Forrest, *
◆ **EMP:** 45 **EST:** 1977
SALES (est): 9.86MM
SALES (corp-wide): 9.86MM **Privately Held**
Web: www.brushymountainbeefarm.com
SIC: 2499 5191 2326 Beekeeping supplies, wood; Beekeeping supplies (non-durable); Men's and boy's work clothing

(G-16640)
BURKE MILL
3130 Burke Mill Ct (27105-5733)
PHONE..................................336 774-2952
EMP: 5 **EST:** 2010
SALES (est): 83K **Privately Held**
SIC: 2711 Newspapers, publishing and printing

(G-16641)
BUTTERCREME BAKERY INC
895 W Northwest Blvd (27101-1213)
PHONE..................................336 722-1022
Loland R Borton, *Pr*
EMP: 7 **EST:** 1977
SALES (est): 374.66K **Privately Held**
Web: www.rrpinsurance.com
SIC: 2051 Bread, cake, and related products

(G-16642)
BUZZISPACE INC (DH)
2880 Ridgewood Park Dr (27107-4581)
P.O. Box 2690 (27261-2690)
PHONE..................................336 821-3150
Thomas J Van Dessel, *CEO*
▲ **EMP:** 8 **EST:** 2012
SALES (est): 5.88MM **Privately Held**
Web: www.buzzi.space
SIC: 2522 Office furniture, except wood
HQ: Buzzispace Group
Italielei 8
Antwerpen 2000
32573234

(G-16643)
C&J PUBLISHING
948 Sportsmans Dr (27101-6305)
PHONE..................................336 722-8005
EMP: 4 **EST:** 2014
SALES (est): 44.94K **Privately Held**
SIC: 2741 Miscellaneous publishing

(G-16644)
CAROLINA CUSTOM DRAPERIES INC
5723 Country Club Rd Ste D (27104-3385)
PHONE..................................336 945-5190
Sylvia G Marvelli, *Pr*
Marshall Marvelli, *Sec*
EMP: 7 **EST:** 1977
SALES (est): 280K **Privately Held**
Web: www.carolinacustomdraperies.com
SIC: 2391 7389 Draperies, plastic and textile: from purchased materials; Interior designer

(G-16645)
CAROLINA MFG GROUP LLC
7840 N Point Blvd Unit 11031 (27116-0801)
PHONE..................................336 413-8335
Douglas Foley, *Prin*
EMP: 4 **EST:** 2016
SALES (est): 63.47K **Privately Held**
SIC: 3999 Manufacturing industries, nec

(G-16646)
CAROLINA NARROW FABRIC COMPANY
1100 N Patterson Ave (27101-1530)
P.O. Box 1485 (27102-1485)
PHONE..................................336 631-3000
Horace L Freeman Junior, *CEO*
Jeffrey Freeman, *Pr*
Lee Laughlin, *CFO*
▲ **EMP:** 125 **EST:** 1928
SQ FT: 135,000
SALES (est): 22.24MM **Privately Held**
Web: www.carolinanarrowfabric.com
SIC: 2241 Fabric tapes

(G-16647)
CAROLINA RUBBER & SPC INC
4301 Idlewild Industrial Dr (27105-2659)
PHONE..................................336 744-5111
EMP: 6 **EST:** 1994
SALES (est): 1.03MM **Privately Held**
Web: www.carolinarubber.com
SIC: 5085 3492 Hose, belting, and packing; Hose and tube fittings and assemblies, hydraulic/pneumatic

(G-16648)
CAROLINA SCREW PRODUCTS
P.O. Box 24154 (27114-4154)
PHONE..................................336 760-7400
Tom Hicks, *Prin*
EMP: 5 **EST:** 2008
SALES (est): 163.83K **Privately Held**
SIC: 3451 Screw machine products

(G-16649)
CATHTEK LLC
3825 Reidsville Rd (27101-2166)
PHONE..................................336 748-0686
Mark Martel, *Pr*
Todd Cassidy, *VP*
▲ **EMP:** 6 **EST:** 2000
SQ FT: 2,500
SALES (est): 1.85MM **Privately Held**
Web: www.cathtek.com
SIC: 5047 3842 Medical equipment and supplies; Abdominal supporters, braces, and trusses

(G-16650)
CHAMPION INDUSTRIES INC
3765 Champion Blvd (27105-2667)
PHONE..................................336 661-1556
▲ **EMP:** 100
Web: www.championindustries.com
SIC: 3589 Dishwashing machines, commercial

(G-16651)
CHARTER MEDICAL LTD
3948 Westpoint Blvd Ste A (27103-6770)
PHONE..................................336 768-6447
Gael Peron, *Pr*
Peter V Ferris, *
Paul G Igoe, *
◆ **EMP:** 90 **EST:** 1998
SALES (est): 23.97MM
SALES (corp-wide): 1.05B **Privately Held**
Web: www.chartermedical.com
SIC: 3841 Blood transfusion equipment
HQ: Fenner, Inc.
187 W Airport Rd
Lititz PA 17543
717 665-2421

(G-16652)
CHECK PRINTERS INC
2709 Boulder Park Ct (27101-4776)
PHONE..................................336 724-5980
EMP: 5 **EST:** 2019
SALES (est): 83.91K **Privately Held**
SIC: 2752 Commercial printing, lithographic

(G-16653)
CJR PRODUCTS INC
6206 Hacker Bend Ct (27103-9771)
PHONE..................................336 766-2710
John R Grayson, *Pr*
Jennie Grayson, *Owner*
EMP: 6 **EST:** 1988
SQ FT: 20,000
SALES (est): 479.25K **Privately Held**
Web: www.cjrproducts.com
SIC: 3714 Power steering equipment, motor vehicle

Winston Salem - Forsyth County (G-16654)

(G-16654)
CLEMMONS HARDWOODS CABINET SP
790 E 21st St (27105-5300)
PHONE.....................336 773-0551
Hubert Stanbery, *Mgr*
Jay Fomer, *Genl Mgr*
EMP: 5 **EST:** 1993
SALES (est): 64.61K **Privately Held**
SIC: 2434 Wood kitchen cabinets

(G-16655)
CLOVERLEAF MIXING INC
Also Called: Yadkin Valley Paving
121 Cloverleaf Dr (27103-6715)
PHONE.....................336 765-7900
EMP: 8 **EST:** 1997
SALES (est): 987.81K **Privately Held**
SIC: 2951 Asphalt and asphaltic paving mixtures (not from refineries)

(G-16656)
CML MICRO CIRCUIT USA
486 N Patterson Ave Ste 301 (27101-4261)
PHONE.....................336 744-5050
George Gurry, *Ch Bd*
Mark Gunyuzlu, *Pr*
Nigel Clark, *Treas*
▲ **EMP:** 20 **EST:** 1980
SQ FT: 27,500
SALES (est): 5.01MM
SALES (corp-wide): 24.81MM **Privately Held**
Web: www.cmlmicro.com
SIC: 3674 3672 Microcircuits, integrated (semiconductor); Printed circuit boards
PA: Cml Microsystems Plc
Oval Park
Maldon CM9 6
162 187-5500

(G-16657)
COLOR SPOT
6220 Hacker Bend Ct Ste A (27103-9778)
PHONE.....................336 778-3982
EMP: 6 **EST:** 2019
SALES (est): 181.64K **Privately Held**
Web: www.tcs.ink
SIC: 3993 Signs and advertising specialties

(G-16658)
COOK & BOARDMAN GROUP LLC (HQ)
3064 Salem Industrial Dr (27127-8854)
PHONE.....................336 768-8872
Darrin Anderson, *CEO*
David Eisner, *
Lance Simpson, *
EMP: 82 **EST:** 2010
SQ FT: 24,000
SALES (est): 477.92MM **Privately Held**
Web: www.cookandboardman.com
SIC: 2431 Door frames, wood
PA: Platinum Equity, Llc
360 N Crescent Dr Bldg S
Beverly Hills CA 90210

(G-16659)
COOK & BOARDMAN NC LLC
3916 Westpoint Blvd (27103-6719)
PHONE.....................336 768-8872
Tim Hutchen, *Mgr*
EMP: 20
Web: www.cookandboardman.com
SIC: 2431 Millwork
HQ: Cook & Boardman Nc, Llc
9347 D Ducks Ln Ste A
Charlotte NC 28273
704 334-8683

(G-16660)
COOK GROUP INC
Also Called: Cook Medical Endoscopy Div
5941 Grassy Creek Blvd (27105-1206)
PHONE.....................336 744-0157
Bill Gibbons, *Prin*
EMP: 16 **EST:** 2010
SALES (est): 1.74MM **Privately Held**
Web: www.cookmedical.com
SIC: 3841 Surgical and medical instruments

(G-16661)
COOK INCORPORATED
Also Called: Wilson-Cook Medical Inc.
4900 Bethania Station Rd (27105-1203)
PHONE.....................336 744-0157
Tamisha Clark, *Genl Mgr*
EMP: 560
SALES (corp-wide): 1.61B **Privately Held**
Web: www.cookmedical.com
SIC: 3841 Catheters
HQ: Cook Incorporated
750 N Daniels Way
Bloomington IN 47404
812 339-2235

(G-16662)
CORNING INCORPORATED
Also Called: Corning
3180 Centre Park Blvd (27107-4574)
PHONE.....................336 771-8000
Sandy Lion, *CEO*
EMP: 13
SALES (corp-wide): 12.59B **Publicly Held**
Web: www.corning.com
SIC: 3229 Glass fiber products
PA: Corning Incorporated
1 Riverfront Plz
Corning NY 14831
607 974-9000

(G-16663)
CORNING OPTCAL CMMNCATIONS LLC
Also Called: Corning
3180 Centre Park Blvd (27107-4574)
PHONE.....................336 771-8000
Sandy Lion, *Brnch Mgr*
EMP: 655
SALES (corp-wide): 12.59B **Publicly Held**
Web: www.corning.com
SIC: 3229 Pressed and blown glass, nec
HQ: Corning Optical Communications Llc
4200 Corning Pl
Charlotte NC 28216
828 901-5000

(G-16664)
COVILLE INC (PA)
8065 N Point Blvd Ste O (27106-3287)
P.O. Box 728 (27371-0728)
PHONE.....................336 759-0115
Don Trexler, *Pr*
Laurie Trexler, *VP*
EMP: 13 **EST:** 1975
SQ FT: 4,000
SALES (est): 25.44MM
SALES (corp-wide): 25.44MM **Privately Held**
Web: www.covilleinc.com
SIC: 2259 Bags and bagging, knit

(G-16665)
CRANIAL TECHNOLOGIES INC
1590 Westbrook Plaza Dr (27103-2965)
PHONE.....................336 760-5530
EMP: 5
Web: www.cranialtech.com
SIC: 3842 Surgical appliances and supplies
PA: Cranial Technologies, Inc.
1405 W Auto Dr Ste 201
Tempe AZ 85284

(G-16666)
CSC AWNINGS INC
3950 N Liberty St (27105-3810)
P.O. Box 21207 (27120-1207)
PHONE.....................336 744-5006
Eric Gerhardt, *Pr*
EMP: 5 **EST:** 1999
SQ FT: 2,000
SALES (est): 939.37K
SALES (corp-wide): 35.89MM **Privately Held**
Web: www.cscawnings.com
SIC: 2394 Awnings, fabric: made from purchased materials
PA: Bulldog Group, Inc.
758 Park Centre Dr
Kernersville NC 27284
336 724-2727

(G-16667)
D2H ADVANCED COMPOSITES INC
6210 Hacker Bend Ct Ste G (27103-9501)
PHONE.....................336 239-9637
EMP: 4 **EST:** 2020
SALES (est): 88.41K **Privately Held**
SIC: 2821 Plastics materials and resins

(G-16668)
D3 SOFTWARE INC
8411 N Nc Highway 109 (27107-9261)
PHONE.....................336 776-0202
EMP: 4 **EST:** 2017
SALES (est): 73.05K **Privately Held**
SIC: 7372 Prepackaged software

(G-16669)
DA WELDING LLC
1645 S Martin Luther King Jr Dr (27107-1310)
PHONE.....................336 231-7691
EMP: 5 **EST:** 2021
SALES (est): 25.09K **Privately Held**
SIC: 7692 Welding repair

(G-16670)
DALTONS METAL WORKS INC
Also Called: Daltons Metal Works
2411 Gumtree Rd (27107-9325)
P.O. Box 1683 (27374-1683)
PHONE.....................336 731-1442
Jack Dalton, *Owner*
Jack Dalton, *Pr*
Debbie Dalton, *VP*
EMP: 8 **EST:** 1991
SALES (est): 748.15K **Privately Held**
SIC: 3441 Fabricated structural metal

(G-16671)
DAVIDSON STEEL SERVICES LLC
11075 Old Us Highway 52 # 100 (27107-9840)
PHONE.....................336 775-1234
Sheryl Waddell Whicker, *Managing Member*
EMP: 5 **EST:** 2004
SQ FT: 1,800
SALES (est): 439.05K **Privately Held**
Web: www.davidsonsteel.com
SIC: 3441 Fabricated structural metal

(G-16672)
DAVIS SIGN COMPANY INC
208 Regent Dr (27103-6718)
P.O. Box 24264 (27114-4264)
PHONE.....................336 765-2990
William Davis Junior, *Pr*
William C Davis Senior, *Pr*
William C Davis Junior, *Pr*
Lee Hendrix, *Off Mgr*
EMP: 13 **EST:** 1986
SQ FT: 5,000
SALES (est): 970.89K **Privately Held**
Web: www.davissigncompany.com
SIC: 3993 Signs, not made in custom sign painting shops

(G-16673)
DAYTECH SOLUTIONS LLC
101 N Chestnut St Ste 211 (27101-4046)
PHONE.....................336 918-4122
EMP: 5
SALES (est): 549.6K **Privately Held**
Web: www.daytechsolutions.com
SIC: 3083 Thermoplastics laminates: rods, tubes, plates, and sheet

(G-16674)
DB CUSTOM CRAFTS LLC ○
267 Kendall Farms Ct (27107-6894)
PHONE.....................336 791-0940
EMP: 11 **EST:** 2022
SALES (est): 599.51K **Privately Held**
SIC: 2759 7389 Screen printing; Business Activities at Non-Commercial Site

(G-16675)
DESIGN ENGNRED FBRICATIONS INC
2461 Spaugh Industrial Dr (27103-6498)
PHONE.....................336 768-8260
M Glenn Wells, *Pr*
Sheryl Wells, *
EMP: 25 **EST:** 1991
SQ FT: 15,000
SALES (est): 3.87MM **Privately Held**
Web: www.def-inc.com
SIC: 3444 3531 Sheet metalwork; Construction machinery

(G-16676)
DEVORA DESIGNS INC
Also Called: Papersassy Boutique
1315 Creekshire Way Apt 312 (27103-3088)
PHONE.....................336 782-0964
EMP: 8 **EST:** 2006
SQ FT: 1,400
SALES (est): 475.84K **Privately Held**
Web: www.lavenderbelledesign.com
SIC: 5943 5112 2678 Stationery stores; Stationery; Stationery products

(G-16677)
DEWEY S BAKERY INC (PA)
Also Called: Salem Baking Company
3840 Kimwell Dr (27103-6720)
PHONE.....................336 748-0230
Scott Livengood, *CEO*
Elizabeth Spencer Hood, *CFO*
EMP: 10 **EST:** 1930
SQ FT: 50,000
SALES (est): 45.42MM
SALES (corp-wide): 45.42MM **Privately Held**
Web: www.deweys.com
SIC: 2052 5461 5451 2051 Cookies and crackers; Retail bakeries; Dairy products stores; Bagels, fresh or frozen

(G-16678)
DIGITAL DESIGN & MODELING LLC
6201 Hacker Bend Ct (27103-9771)
PHONE.....................336 766-2155
Tom Mcguire, *Pr*
EMP: 9 **EST:** 1999
SALES (est): 1.05MM **Privately Held**
SIC: 3544 Special dies, tools, jigs, and fixtures

GEOGRAPHIC SECTION

Winston Salem - Forsyth County (G-16706)

(G-16679)
DIGITAL LOG CABIN PRESS
2432 Fairway Dr (27103-3509)
PHONE.................................336 287-7265
David Bergstone, *Prin*
EMP: 4 **EST:** 2017
SALES (est): 59.23K **Privately Held**
Web: www.logcabinpress.com
SIC: 2741 Miscellaneous publishing

(G-16680)
DIGITS
306 S Stratford Rd (27103-1820)
PHONE.................................336 721-0209
Huong Nguyen, *Owner*
EMP: 4 **EST:** 2000
SALES (est): 91.42K **Privately Held**
SIC: 7299 2844 Tanning salon; Manicure preparations

(G-16681)
DIME EMB LLC
Also Called: Embroidery Store, The
3929 Westpoint Blvd Ste A (27103-6761)
PHONE.................................336 765-0910
William Fenimore Iii, *Brnch Mgr*
EMP: 10
SALES (corp-wide): 5.03MM **Privately Held**
Web: www.embstore.com
SIC: 2759 Commercial printing, nec
PA: Dime Emb Llc
　10495 Olympic Dr Ste 100
　Dallas TX 75220
　888 739-0555

(G-16682)
DIVISION 5 LLC
Also Called: Structural Steel of Carolina
1725 Vargrave St (27103-2205)
PHONE.................................336 725-0521
James Brewer, *Brnch Mgr*
EMP: 120
SALES (corp-wide): 31.95MM **Privately Held**
Web: www.division5inc.com
SIC: 3441 Fabricated structural metal
PA: Division 5, Llc
　2650 Strawn Rd
　Winston GA 30187
　770 577-0355

(G-16683)
DIXIE DECOYS LLC
119 Tucker Ave (27104-3727)
PHONE.................................703 554-9478
Brandon Causey, *Admn*
EMP: 5 **EST:** 2017
SALES (est): 139.65K **Privately Held**
Web: www.dixiedecoys.com
SIC: 3949 Sporting and athletic goods, nec

(G-16684)
DIZE COMPANY
Also Called: Dize Awning and Tent Company
1512 S Main St (27127-2707)
P.O. Box 937 (27102-0937)
PHONE.................................336 722-5181
TOLL FREE: 800
C R Skidmore Junior, *Pr*
Wanda Smith, *
▲ **EMP:** 60 **EST:** 1997
SQ FT: 80,000
SALES (est): 9.57MM **Privately Held**
Web: www.dizecompany.com
SIC: 2394 5023 3993 2591 Tarpaulins, fabric: made from purchased materials; Window furnishings; Signs and advertising specialties; Drapery hardware and window blinds and shades

(G-16685)
DMD LOGISTICS LLC
2124 Craver Meadows Ct (27127-8920)
PHONE.................................336 480-8149
EMP: 5
SALES (est): 271.59K **Privately Held**
SIC: 1389 7389 4789 Hot shot service; Business Activities at Non-Commercial Site ; Transportation services, nec

(G-16686)
DNB HUMIDIFIER MFG INC
175 Dixie Club Rd (27107-9136)
PHONE.................................336 764-2076
James T Donley, *Pr*
T Craig Donley, *VP*
Nancy Donley, *Sec*
Marc Davis, *Genl Mgr*
EMP: 12 **EST:** 1987
SQ FT: 40,000
SALES (est): 2.21MM **Privately Held**
Web: www.dnbhumidifier.com
SIC: 3634 5999 Humidifiers, electric: household; Alcoholic beverage making equipment and supplies

(G-16687)
DOUGLAS BATTERY MFG CO
500 Battery Dr (27107-4137)
PHONE.................................336 650-7000
EMP: 5 **EST:** 2020
SALES (est): 195.17K **Privately Held**
SIC: 3999 Manufacturing industries, nec

(G-16688)
EAST COAST ROADSTER
5401 Kingsbridge Rd (27103-5995)
PHONE.................................336 624-5083
Tom Lorick, *Prin*
EMP: 4 **EST:** 2010
SALES (est): 190.04K **Privately Held**
Web: www.eastcoastroadster.com
SIC: 3714 Motor vehicle parts and accessories

(G-16689)
EAST PENN MANUFACTURING CO
Also Called: Deka Batteries & Cables
3117 Starlight Dr Ste 200 (27107)
PHONE.................................336 771-1380
Michelle Allred, *Brnch Mgr*
EMP: 11
SQ FT: 12,500
SALES (corp-wide): 3.51B **Privately Held**
Web: www.eastpennmanufacturing.com
SIC: 3691 Storage batteries
PA: East Penn Manufacturing Co.
　102 Deka Rd
　Lyon Station PA 19536
　610 682-6361

(G-16690)
EASTERN CABINET INSTALLERS INC
4735 Kester Mill Rd (27103-1212)
PHONE.................................336 774-2966
Crystal Cramer, *Owner*
EMP: 4 **EST:** 2007
SALES (est): 328.78K **Privately Held**
Web: www.acceci.com
SIC: 2434 Wood kitchen cabinets

(G-16691)
ECOLAB INC
Ecolab Kay Chemical Co
90 Piedmont Industrial Dr Ste 400 (27107-6876)
PHONE.................................336 931-2237
EMP: 30
SALES (corp-wide): 15.32B **Publicly Held**
Web: www.ecolab.com

SIC: 2841 Soap and other detergents
PA: Ecolab Inc.
　1 Ecolab Pl
　Saint Paul MN 55102
　800 232-6522

(G-16692)
EI LLC
Also Called: Ei Solution Works
380 Knollwood St Ste 700 (27103-1862)
PHONE.................................704 857-0707
▲ **EMP:** 300
Web: www.eisolutionworks.com
SIC: 2834 2844 Pharmaceutical preparations ; Cosmetic preparations

(G-16693)
EL COMAL INC
2390 E Sprague St (27107-2441)
PHONE.................................336 788-8110
Guillarmo Mendoza, *Owner*
EMP: 8 **EST:** 1999
SALES (est): 336.45K **Privately Held**
Web: www.elcomal.com
SIC: 2099 Tortillas, fresh or refrigerated

(G-16694)
ELEPHANTS CORNER WINES LLC
550 Peters Creek Pkwy Unit No1640 (27101-4931)
PHONE.................................336 782-7084
Clint Saint, *Prin*
EMP: 6 **EST:** 2020
SALES (est): 218.72K **Privately Held**
Web: www.elephantscornerwines.com
SIC: 2084 Wines

(G-16695)
ELI COMPANY
79 Luzelle Dr (27103-6481)
PHONE.................................908 242-3497
Elisha Palomares, *Prin*
EMP: 4 **EST:** 2017
SALES (est): 47.1K **Privately Held**
SIC: 2834 Pharmaceutical preparations

(G-16696)
ENCORE GROUP INC
Also Called: Xpress Line
111 Cloverleaf Dr (27103-6715)
PHONE.................................336 768-7859
Lou Valente, *CFO*
EMP: 183
Web: www.encorecapital.com
SIC: 3999 3555 Novelties, bric-a-brac, and hobby kits; Printing trades machinery
PA: The Encore Group Inc
　80 E State Rt 4 Ste 290
　Paramus NJ

(G-16697)
ENGINEERED ATTACHMENTS LLC
Also Called: North American Attachments
200 Kapp St (27105-2641)
PHONE.................................336 703-5266
Mike Miller, *Managing Member*
▼ **EMP:** 6 **EST:** 2002
SALES (est): 1.15MM **Privately Held**
Web: www.na-attachments.com
SIC: 3531 Construction machinery

(G-16698)
ENVISION GLASS INC
3950 N Liberty St (27105-3810)
PHONE.................................336 283-9701
Craig Simmons, *Pr*
EMP: 10 **EST:** 2012
SALES (est): 438.02K **Privately Held**
Web: www.envisionglassinc.com

SIC: 3231 3444 Doors, glass: made from purchased glass; Door hoods, aluminum

(G-16699)
ERICSON FOODS INC
4143 Wycliff Dr (27106-2949)
PHONE.................................336 317-2199
Fred H Nelson, *Prin*
EMP: 10 **EST:** 2003
SALES (est): 590K **Privately Held**
SIC: 2099 Food preparations, nec

(G-16700)
EVERHART PRINTINC CO
241 Jefferson Ave (27107-9495)
PHONE.................................336 764-3978
Winfred E Everhart, *Owner*
EMP: 5 **EST:** 2014
SALES (est): 101.53K **Privately Held**
SIC: 2752 Commercial printing, lithographic

(G-16701)
EVERKEM DIVERSIFIED PDTS INC
120 Regent Dr (27103-6711)
PHONE.................................336 661-7801
EMP: 15 **EST:** 2011
SALES (est): 4.21MM **Privately Held**
Web: www.everkemproducts.com
SIC: 2891 3423 Adhesives; Caulking tools, hand

(G-16702)
EVERYTHING INDUSTRIAL SUPPLY
164 N Hawthorne Rd (27104-4356)
P.O. Box 1476 (27012-1476)
PHONE.................................743 333-2222
Austin York, *Managing Member*
EMP: 6 **EST:** 2018
SALES (est): 503.45K **Privately Held**
SIC: 3562 3052 3496 3621 Ball and roller bearings; V-belts, rubber; Conveyor belts; Inverters, rotating: electrical

(G-16703)
EXCEL SIGNS AND LIGHTING
5526 Germanton Rd (27105-1404)
PHONE.................................336 257-9225
John Wood, *Prin*
EMP: 4 **EST:** 2018
SALES (est): 69.15K **Privately Held**
SIC: 3993 Signs and advertising specialties

(G-16704)
EXP PHARMACEUTICALS INC
635 Vine St (27101-4185)
PHONE.................................336 631-2893
Jeffrey Apepperworth, *Pr*
EMP: 10 **EST:** 2017
SALES (est): 176.75K **Privately Held**
SIC: 2834 Pharmaceutical preparations

(G-16705)
FAIN ENTERPRISES INC
309 Deerglade Rd (27104-1860)
PHONE.................................336 724-0417
David Fain, *Pr*
Sherrie W Fain, *VP*
EMP: 12 **EST:** 1967
SQ FT: 8,000
SALES (est): 424K **Privately Held**
Web: www.fainenterprises.com
SIC: 2761 5112 Manifold business forms; Office supplies, nec

(G-16706)
FAIRCHILD INDUSTRIAL PDTS CO (DH)
3920 Westpoint Blvd (27103-6727)
PHONE.................................336 659-3400
Alan G Paine, *Pr*

Winston Salem - Forsyth County (G-16707)

David C Velten, *
▲ EMP: 94 EST: 1955
SQ FT: 88,000
SALES (est): 20.73MM
SALES (corp-wide): 772.72MM Privately Held
Web: www.fairchildproducts.com
SIC: 3823 3568 Process control instruments; Power transmission equipment, nec
HQ: Rotork Instruments Limited
Rotork House
Bath
122 573-3419

(G-16707)
FAIRCLOTH MACHINE SHOP INC
2355 Farrington Point Dr (27107-2453)
PHONE.....................336 777-1529
Loris Pannell, Prin
Loris Pannell, Pr
David Pannell, VP
Judy Pannell, Sec
EMP: 13 EST: 1965
SALES (est): 2.19MM Privately Held
Web: www.fairclothmachine.com
SIC: 3599 Machine shop, jobbing and repair

(G-16708)
FALLS AUTOMOTIVE SERVICE INC
Also Called: Falls Automotive & Tire Svc
1548 S Main St (27127-2707)
PHONE.....................336 723-0521
Tim Falls, Pr
Debbie Falls, VP
EMP: 5 EST: 1958
SQ FT: 6,500
SALES (est): 430.35K Privately Held
Web: falls-automotive.business.site
SIC: 7538 7534 General automotive repair shops; Tire retreading and repair shops

(G-16709)
FERGUSON MANUFACTURING COMPANY
6275 Raven Forest Ct (27105-8747)
P.O. Box 16044 (27115-6044)
PHONE.....................336 661-1116
Donald Ferguson, Pr
Donald B Ferguson, Pr
EMP: 11 EST: 1971
SQ FT: 40,000
SALES (est): 453.97K Privately Held
SIC: 3679 8711 3672 Electronic circuits; Engineering services; Printed circuit boards

(G-16710)
FIDDLIN FISH BREWING CO
Also Called: Fiddlin' Fish Brewing Company
772 N Trade St (27101-1431)
PHONE.....................336 999-8945
Stuart Barnhart, Pr
EMP: 15 EST: 2017
SALES (est): 549.33K Privately Held
Web: www.fiddlinfish.com
SIC: 2082 Malt beverages

(G-16711)
FIRESTOPPING PRODUCTS INC
Also Called: Flane Tech
120 Regent Dr (27103-6711)
PHONE.....................336 661-0102
Chin Chui Lin, Pr
Jason Lynch, VP
EMP: 10 EST: 1998
SALES (est): 970.75K Privately Held
Web: www.everkemproducts.com
SIC: 2891 Caulking compounds

(G-16712)
FISHEL STEEL COMPANY
760 Palmer Ln (27107-5297)
PHONE.....................336 788-2880
Roger Amstrong, Pr
EMP: 9 EST: 1930
SQ FT: 17,000
SALES (est): 2.07MM Privately Held
Web: www.fishelsteelws.com
SIC: 3315 4225 Wire and fabricated wire products; General warehousing and storage

(G-16713)
FLAME TECH INC
120 Regent Dr (27103-6711)
PHONE.....................336 661-7801
Jason C Lynch, Pr
Chin C Lin, VP
EMP: 20 EST: 2002
SALES (est): 531.82K Privately Held
Web: www.everkemproducts.com
SIC: 2421 Building and structural materials, wood

(G-16714)
FLORIDA FIRE SUPPLY
Also Called: Viking Fire Protection
3645 Reed St (27107-5428)
P.O. Box 527 (27261-0527)
PHONE.....................336 885-5007
Joseph G Collins, CEO
EMP: 36 EST: 1957
SALES (est): 4.28MM
SALES (corp-wide): 4.28MM Privately Held
Web: www.eaglefire.com
SIC: 3321 3498 Cast iron pipe and fittings; Pipe fittings, fabricated from purchased pipe
PA: Viking Fire Protection, Inc. Of The Southeast
3645 Reed St
Winston Salem NC 27107
336 885-5007

(G-16715)
FLOWERS BAKERY OF WINSTON-SALEM LLC
315 Cassell St (27107-4131)
PHONE.....................336 785-8700
▼ EMP: 190
SIC: 2051 2052 Cakes, bakery: except frozen ; Cookies and crackers

(G-16716)
FLOWERS BKG CO JAMESTOWN LLC
Also Called: Flowers Bakery Outlet
5610 Shattalon Dr (27105-1331)
PHONE.....................336 744-3525
EMP: 44
SALES (corp-wide): 5.09B Publicly Held
SIC: 2051 Bread, cake, and related products
HQ: Flowers Baking Co. Of Newton, Llc
801 W Main St
Jamestown NC 27282
336 841-8840

(G-16717)
FOOTHILLS BREWING
3800 Kimwell Dr (27103-6708)
PHONE.....................336 997-9484
James Bartholomaus, Pr
▲ EMP: 7 EST: 2011
SALES (est): 974.95K Privately Held
Web: www.foothillsbrewing.com
SIC: 2082 Ale (alcoholic beverage)

(G-16718)
FREEDOM MAILING & MKTG INC
Also Called: Freedom Creative Solutions
427 W End Blvd (27101-1120)
P.O. Box 1464 (27051-1464)
PHONE.....................336 595-6300
Daniel Baird, Pr
EMP: 4 EST: 2000
SQ FT: 4,800
SALES (est): 411.55K Privately Held
Web: www.freedomcreativesolutions.com
SIC: 2752 Offset printing

(G-16719)
GARDNER ASPHALT CO
Also Called: Gardner Gibson
1664 S Martin Luther King Jr Dr (27107-1311)
PHONE.....................336 784-8924
Raymond T Hyer, Ch Bd
Chris Fontana, Mgr
EMP: 10 EST: 1973
SQ FT: 5,000
SALES (est): 4.9MM
SALES (corp-wide): 923.49MM Privately Held
Web: www.gardner-gibson.com
SIC: 2951 Asphalt paving mixtures and blocks
HQ: Gardner-Gibson, Incorporated
4161 E 7th Ave
Tampa FL 33605
813 248-2101

(G-16720)
GFSI HOLDINGS LLC (HQ)
9700 Commerce Pkwy (27105)
PHONE.....................336 519-8080
Robert M Wolff, Ch
Robert G Shaw, VP Fin
Larry D Graveel, Pr
Michael H Gary, VP Sls
Jim Keaton, Pers/VP
EMP: 600 EST: 1996
SQ FT: 250,000
SALES (est): 160MM Publicly Held
SIC: 2339 2329 Sportswear, women's; Men's and boys' sportswear and athletic clothing
PA: Hanesbrands Inc.
1000 E Hanes Mill Rd
Winston Salem NC 27105

(G-16721)
GIVE YOU HOPE INDUSTRIES INC
2840 Kensington Rd (27106-5710)
PHONE.....................336 608-2774
EMP: 4 EST: 2015
SALES (est): 56.43K Privately Held
SIC: 3999 Manufacturing industries, nec

(G-16722)
GLG CORPORATION (PA)
Also Called: South Side Bargain Center
3410 Thomasville Rd (27107-5439)
Rural Route 4011 (27115)
PHONE.....................336 784-0396
Gordon L Greene, Pr
Edward F Greene, Sec
Jonathan Greene, VP
Evelyn Arndt Stcklhdr, Prin
▲ EMP: 16 EST: 1967
SQ FT: 100,000
SALES (est): 7.5MM
SALES (corp-wide): 7.5MM Privately Held
Web: www.southsidebargaincenter.com
SIC: 5211 1521 6162 2431 Lumber and other building materials; Single-family housing construction; Mortgage bankers and loan correspondents; Millwork

(G-16723)
GOLDING FARMS FOODS INC (PA)
Also Called: Golding Farms
6061 Gun Club Rd (27103-9727)
PHONE.....................336 766-6161
John Frostad, CEO
Violet Golding, *
▲ EMP: 58 EST: 1955
SQ FT: 40,000
SALES (est): 84.18MM
SALES (corp-wide): 84.18MM Privately Held
Web: www.goldingblends.com
SIC: 2099 2035 2061 Honey, strained and bottled; Seasonings and sauces, except tomato and dry; Raw cane sugar

(G-16724)
GOODYEAR TIRE & RUBBER COMPANY
Also Called: Goodyear
130 Country Club Ln (27104-3786)
PHONE.....................336 794-0035
EMP: 4
SALES (corp-wide): 20.07MM Publicly Held
Web: www.goodyear.com
SIC: 5531 3011 Automotive tires; Inner tubes, all types
PA: The Goodyear Tire & Rubber Company
200 E Innovation Way
Akron OH 44316
330 796-2121

(G-16725)
GOSLEN PRINTING COMPANY
Also Called: Blums Almanac
3250 Healy Dr (27103-1436)
PHONE.....................336 768-5775
Mark A Goslen, Pr
Robyn Goslen, Treas
EMP: 13 EST: 1872
SALES (est): 1.05MM Privately Held
Web: www.allegramarketingprint.com
SIC: 2752 2732 Offset printing; Book printing

(G-16726)
GRACE AND COMPANY LLC
183 Wayside Dr (27107-1751)
PHONE.....................336 893-7511
John Hedrick, Prin
EMP: 4 EST: 2017
SALES (est): 83.8K Privately Held
Web: www.grace.com
SIC: 2819 Industrial inorganic chemicals, nec

(G-16727)
GRANDMAS SUGAR SHACK
209 S Gordon Dr (27104-3711)
PHONE.....................336 760-8822
EMP: 4 EST: 2011
SALES (est): 169.53K Privately Held
SIC: 2052 Cookies and crackers

(G-16728)
GRAPHIC PACKAGING INTL LLC
320 W Hanes Mill Rd (27105-9626)
PHONE.....................336 744-1222
James Kleinfield, Genl Mgr
EMP: 53
Web: www.americraft.com
SIC: 2657 Folding paperboard boxes
HQ: Graphic Packaging International, Llc
1500 Riveredge Pkwy # 100
Atlanta GA 30328

(G-16729)
GRAPHIC PRODUCTIONS INC
Also Called: Express Graphics
301 N Main St Ste 2104 (27101-3836)
PHONE.....................336 765-9335
Mitchell Termotto, CEO
Scott Dahlin, Sec
EMP: 4 EST: 1987

GEOGRAPHIC SECTION

Winston Salem - Forsyth County (G-16753)

SQ FT: 8,500
SALES (est): 481.14K **Privately Held**
Web: www.exgraphics.com
SIC: 3993 Signs and advertising specialties

(G-16730)
GRINS ENTERPRISES LLC
Also Called: Grins Beverages
1051 Arbor Rd (27104-1101)
PHONE.................................336 831-0534
EMP: 5 EST: 2011
SALES (est): 214K **Privately Held**
Web: www.grinsbev.com
SIC: 2086 Carbonated beverages, nonalcoholic: pkged. in cans, bottles

(G-16731)
HAECO CABIN SOLUTIONS LLC
Also Called: Haeco Americas Cabin Solutions
5568 Gumtree Rd (27107-9583)
PHONE.................................336 464-0122
Mark Lunsford, *Brnch Mgr*
EMP: 537
SALES (corp-wide): 17.24B **Privately Held**
Web: www.haeco.aero
SIC: 2531 Seats, aircraft
HQ: Haeco Cabin Solutions, Llc
8010 Piedmont Triad Pkwy
Greensboro NC 27409

(G-16732)
HANES COMPANIES INC (HQ)
Also Called: Hanes Industries
815 Buxton St (27101-1310)
P.O. Box 202 (27102-0202)
PHONE.................................336 747-1600
Jerry W Greene Junior, *Pr*
Michael S Walters, *
Earnest Jett, *
Kenneth W Purser, *
Charles P Hutchins, *
◆ EMP: 160 EST: 1986
SQ FT: 709,921
SALES (est): 368.82MM
SALES (corp-wide): 5.15B **Publicly Held**
Web: www.hanesgeo.com
SIC: 2262 2261 2297 Dyeing: manmade fiber and silk broadwoven fabrics; Dyeing cotton broadwoven fabrics; Nonwoven fabrics
PA: Leggett & Platt, Incorporated
1 Leggett Rd
Carthage MO 64836
417 358-8131

(G-16733)
HANESBRANDS EXPORT CANADA LLC
1000 E Hanes Mill Rd (27105-1383)
PHONE.................................336 519-8080
Richard Noll, *CEO*
▼ EMP: 8 EST: 2013
SALES (est): 1.32MM **Publicly Held**
Web: ir.hanesbrands.com
SIC: 2389 Men's miscellaneous accessories
PA: Hanesbrands Inc.
1000 E Hanes Mill Rd
Winston Salem NC 27105

(G-16734)
HANESBRANDS INC (PA)
Also Called: Hanes
1000 E Hanes Mill Rd (27105-1383)
PHONE.................................336 519-8080
Stephen B Bratspies, *CEO*
Ronald L Nelson, *Ch Bd*
Tracy M Preston, *Legal*
Kristin L Oliver, *Chief Human Resources Officer*
Scott A Pleiman, *STRAT TRANS*
EMP: 1800 EST: 1901
SQ FT: 470,000
SALES (est): 5.64B **Publicly Held**
Web: www.hanes.com
SIC: 2253 2322 2342 2341 T-shirts and tops, knit; Underwear, men's and boys': made from purchased materials; Bras, girdles, and allied garments; Panties: women's, misses', children's, and infants'

(G-16735)
HARCO PRINTING INCORPORATED
130 Back Forty Dr (27127-7404)
PHONE.................................336 771-0234
Ricky Corn, *Pr*
Lester Hargett, *Sec*
EMP: 4 EST: 1998
SALES (est): 499.69K **Privately Held**
Web: www.harcoprinting.com
SIC: 2752 Offset printing

(G-16736)
HARI KRUPA OIL AND GAS LLC
6031 Claudius Ln Apt 201 (27103-7178)
PHONE.................................860 805-1704
Ripal Patel, *Owner*
EMP: 6 EST: 2017
SALES (est): 226.93K **Privately Held**
SIC: 1389 Oil and gas field services, nec

(G-16737)
HARTLEY READY MIX CON MFG INC (PA)
3510 Rothrock St (27107-5224)
P.O. Box 1719 (27374-1719)
PHONE.................................336 788-3928
Chad Hartley, *Pr*
EMP: 18 EST: 1950
SQ FT: 1,500
SALES (est): 6.36MM
SALES (corp-wide): 6.36MM **Privately Held**
Web: www.hartleyreadymix.com
SIC: 3273 Ready-mixed concrete

(G-16738)
HAUSER HVAC INSTALLATION
480 S Peace Haven Rd (27103-5973)
PHONE.................................336 416-2173
Darrell Hauser, *Owner*
EMP: 5 EST: 2015
SALES (est): 95.76K **Privately Held**
SIC: 1711 3272 Plumbing, heating, air-conditioning; Chimney caps, concrete

(G-16739)
HBI SOURCING LLC (HQ)
1000 E Hanes Mill Rd (27105-1384)
PHONE.................................336 519-8080
EMP: 11 EST: 2019
SALES (est): 8.66MM **Publicly Held**
Web: ir.hanesbrands.com
SIC: 2253 T-shirts and tops, knit
PA: Hanesbrands Inc.
1000 E Hanes Mill Rd
Winston Salem NC 27105

(G-16740)
HBI WH MINORITY HOLDINGS LLC ✪
1000 E Hanes Mill Rd (27105-1384)
PHONE.................................336 519-8080
EMP: 10 EST: 2022
SALES (est): 2.18MM **Publicly Held**
SIC: 2253 2342 T-shirts and tops, knit; Bras, girdles, and allied garments
PA: Hanesbrands Inc.
1000 E Hanes Mill Rd
Winston Salem NC 27105

(G-16741)
HEAVENLY CHEESECAKES
11040 Old Us Highway 52 (27107-9840)
PHONE.................................336 577-9390
Becky Brown, *Owner*
EMP: 8 EST: 1999
SALES (est): 424.55K **Privately Held**
SIC: 2051 Cakes, bakery: except frozen

(G-16742)
HEAVY METAL FABRICATION LLC
1382 Turkey Hill Rd (27106-3279)
PHONE.................................919 656-2717
EMP: 5 EST: 2018
SALES (est): 235.09K **Privately Held**
SIC: 3499 Fabricated metal products, nec

(G-16743)
HENSEL WOOD PRODUCTS CORP
2924 Buena Vista Rd (27106-5725)
PHONE.................................336 725-7568
Richard Hensel, *Owner*
Richard D Hensel Senior, *Pr*
Richard D Hensel Junior, *VP*
Aaron B Shough, *
Steven B Shough, *
EMP: 9 EST: 1956
SALES (est): 340.65K **Privately Held**
SIC: 2449 Tobacco hogsheads

(G-16744)
HERBALIFE MANUFACTURING LLC
3200 Temple School Rd (27103-3628)
PHONE.................................336 970-6400
EMP: 13
Web: www.herbalife.com
SIC: 2087 2023 Beverage bases, concentrates, syrups, powders and mixes; Dietary supplements, dairy and non-dairy based
HQ: Herbalife Manufacturing Llc
800 W Olympic Blvd Ste 40
Los Angeles CA 90015

(G-16745)
HHH TEMPERING RESOURCES INC
5901 Gun Club Rd (27103-9732)
PHONE.................................336 201-5396
Mike Synon, *Pr*
EMP: 10 EST: 2019
SALES (est): 2.43MM
SALES (corp-wide): 30.43MM **Privately Held**
Web: www.hhhglassequipment.com
SIC: 3398 Tempering of metal
PA: Salem Fabrication Technologies Group, Inc.
5901 Gun Club Rd
Winston Salem NC 27103
800 234-1982

(G-16746)
HILLSHIRE BRANDS COMPANY
Also Called: Sara Lee
470 W Hanes Mill Rd Frnt Frnt (27105-9102)
P.O. Box 2760 (27102-2760)
PHONE.................................336 519-8080
Mike Gannaway, *Mgr*
EMP: 6
SALES (corp-wide): 52.88B **Publicly Held**
Web: www.tysonfoods.com
SIC: 2252 2254 2253 Hosiery, nec; Underwear, knit; Knit outerwear mills
HQ: The Hillshire Brands Company
400 S Jefferson St Ste 1n
Chicago IL 60607
312 614-6000

(G-16747)
HOH CORPORATION
Also Called: Carolina Pumps Instrumentation
1701 Vargrave St (27107-2205)
PHONE.................................336 723-9274
David A Bryant, *Pr*
▼ EMP: 10 EST: 1991
SALES (est): 2.35MM **Privately Held**
Web: www.hohcorp.com
SIC: 4953 3589 Nonhazardous waste disposal sites; Water treatment equipment, industrial

(G-16748)
HOOD CONTAINER CORPORATION
555 Aureole St (27107-3201)
PHONE.................................336 784-0445
Greg Hall, *Brnch Mgr*
EMP: 1200
Web: www.hoodcontainer.com
SIC: 3086 Packaging and shipping materials, foamed plastics
HQ: Hood Container Corporation
2727 Paces Ferry Rd Se 1-1850
Atlanta GA 30339
855 605-6317

(G-16749)
HPFABRICS INC
Also Called: HP Textile
3821 Kimwell Dr (27103-6707)
PHONE.................................336 231-0278
Todd Lane, *Pr*
EMP: 8 EST: 2017
SALES (est): 234.38K **Privately Held**
SIC: 2211 2231 Upholstery, tapestry and wall coverings: cotton; Felts, blanketing and upholstery fabrics: wool

(G-16750)
HUGHES PRODUCTS CO INC
241 Emily Ann Dr (27107-8687)
P.O. Box 606 (27373-0606)
PHONE.................................336 769-3788
Jeffrey T Hughes, *Pr*
Lori Hughes, *Sec*
EMP: 8 EST: 1990
SQ FT: 11,475
SALES (est): 778.54K **Privately Held**
Web: www.hughesproductsco.com
SIC: 3949 Hunting equipment

(G-16751)
HUGHES PRODUCTS CO INC
4422 Wallburg Rd (27107-9268)
PHONE.................................336 475-0091
Jeffrey Hughes, *Contrlr*
EMP: 4 EST: 2018
SALES (est): 39.69K **Privately Held**
Web: www.hughesproductsco.com
SIC: 3999 Manufacturing industries, nec

(G-16752)
HYMAN FURNITURE WAREHOUSE LLC
Also Called: Hyman Furniture Warehouse
1901 Margaret St (27103-3001)
PHONE.................................336 528-4950
EMP: 4
SALES (est): 55.04K **Privately Held**
Web: www.hymanfurniture.com
SIC: 2426 1541 Furniture stock and parts, hardwood; Warehouse construction

(G-16753)
I-LUMENATE LLC
353 Jonestown Rd (27104-4620)
PHONE.................................336 448-0356
EMP: 4 EST: 2013
SALES (est): 256K **Privately Held**

Winston Salem - Forsyth County (G-16754) GEOGRAPHIC SECTION

SIC: 3949 Sporting and athletic goods, nec

(G-16754)
ICA(USA)INC
1728 Jonestown Rd (27103-6908)
PHONE..................704 798-3488
Dale Hiatt, *Pr*
EMP: 7 EST: 2019
SALES (est): 67.51K **Privately Held**
SIC: 3724 7389 Research and development on aircraft engines and parts; Business services, nec

(G-16755)
IN STITCHES CUSTOM EMB LLC
6011 Rollingreen Dr (27103-9793)
PHONE..................336 655-3498
EMP: 4 EST: 2019
SALES (est): 31.29K **Privately Held**
SIC: 2395 Embroidery products, except Schiffli machine

(G-16756)
IN STYLE KITCHEN CABINETRY
8570 N Nc Highway 109 (27107-8400)
PHONE..................336 769-9605
Harold Nash, *Prin*
EMP: 4 EST: 2011
SALES (est): 245.56K **Privately Held**
Web: www.instlyekitchens.com
SIC: 2434 Wood kitchen cabinets

(G-16757)
INDEPENDENCE PRINTING
130 Back Forty Dr (27127-7404)
PHONE..................336 771-0234
Ricky Corn, *Owner*
EMP: 4 EST: 1993
SQ FT: 1,000
SALES (est): 211.01K **Privately Held**
SIC: 2752 Offset printing

(G-16758)
INDUSTRIAL CONTROL PANELS INC
Also Called: ICP
152 Capp St Ste A (27105)
PHONE..................336 661-3037
EMP: 8 EST: 1995
SQ FT: 5,160
SALES (est): 959.74K **Privately Held**
Web: www.icppanelshop.com
SIC: 3613 Control panels, electric

(G-16759)
INDUSTRIAL LUBRICANTS INC
Also Called: Pro-Blend Chemical Co
1110 Fairchild Rd (27105-4528)
P.O. Box 17171 (27116-7171)
PHONE..................336 767-0013
F Gaither Jenkins, *Pr*
EMP: 34 EST: 1981
SQ FT: 23,000
SALES (est): 951.79K **Privately Held**
SIC: 2869 Industrial organic chemicals, nec

(G-16760)
INGREDION INCORPORATED
Corn Prdcts-Wnston Salem Plant
4501 Overdale Rd (27107-6145)
P.O. Box 12939 (27117-2939)
PHONE..................336 785-0100
Tony Kantor, *Mgr*
EMP: 100
SALES (corp-wide): 8.16B **Publicly Held**
Web: www.ingredion.com
SIC: 2046 Corn sugars and syrups
PA: Ingredion Incorporated
   5 Westbrook Corporate Ctr
   Westchester IL 60154
   708 551-2600

(G-16761)
INK WELL
Also Called: Ink Well
1650 Hutton St (27127-3704)
PHONE..................336 727-9750
EMP: 8 EST: 1996
SALES (est): 462.97K **Privately Held**
Web: www.theinkwellusa.com
SIC: 2752 Offset printing

(G-16762)
INSURRECTION INDUSTRIES LLC
4112 Glencove Ct (27106-4782)
PHONE..................443 801-7356
EMP: 5 EST: 2017
SALES (est): 85.02K **Privately Held**
SIC: 3999 Manufacturing industries, nec

(G-16763)
INTERNATIONAL MCHY SLS INC
Also Called: IMS
8065 N Point Blvd Ste J (27106-3287)
P.O. Box 11276 (27116-1276)
PHONE..................336 759-9548
Nicholas Sear, *Pr*
▲ EMP: 6 EST: 1977
SQ FT: 2,200
SALES (est): 460.1K **Privately Held**
SIC: 3552 Textile machinery

(G-16764)
INTERNATIONAL MINUTE PRESS
3490 Reynolda Rd (27106-3063)
PHONE..................336 231-3178
EMP: 6 EST: 1975
SALES (est): 41.35K **Privately Held**
Web: winstonsalem-nc.intlminutepress.com
SIC: 2752 Commercial printing, lithographic

(G-16765)
J C ENTERPRISES
936 Washington Ave (27101-5753)
P.O. Box 11483 (27116-1483)
PHONE..................336 986-1688
EMP: 5 EST: 2016
SALES (est): 81.4K **Privately Held**
SIC: 2672 Paper; coated and laminated, nec

(G-16766)
J&J MILLWORKS INC
3528 Thomasville Rd (27107-5441)
PHONE..................336 252-2868
EMP: 4 EST: 2020
SALES (est): 85.29K **Privately Held**
Web: www.alpha-omegainc.com
SIC: 2431 Millwork

(G-16767)
J6 & COMPANY LLC
5077 Bismark St (27105-3148)
PHONE..................336 997-4497
Jocelyn Dunston, *Managing Member*
EMP: 14 EST: 2016
SALES (est): 474.78K **Privately Held**
SIC: 7389 1389 Business Activities at Non-Commercial Site; Construction, repair, and dismantling services

(G-16768)
JABEC ENTERPRISE INC (PA)
5224 Mountain View Rd (27104-5116)
PHONE..................336 655-8441
Jeffrey Trinh, *Prin*
EMP: 5 EST: 2015
SALES (est): 740.9K
SALES (corp-wide): 740.9K **Privately Held**
SIC: 3732 Boatbuilding and repairing

(G-16769)
JENNIFER MOWRER
Also Called: Painpathways Magazine
150 Kimel Park Dr Ste 100 (27103-6992)
PHONE..................336 714-6462
Jennifer Mowrer, *Owner*
EMP: 6 EST: 2013
SALES (est): 241.55K **Privately Held**
SIC: 2721 7389 Magazines: publishing only, not printed on site; Business services, nec

(G-16770)
JESUS DAILY GROUP LLC
726 Morris Rd (27101-6419)
PHONE..................336 727-4781
Suzanne S Tabor, *Owner*
EMP: 6 EST: 2011
SALES (est): 6.18K **Privately Held**
SIC: 2711 Newspapers, publishing and printing

(G-16771)
JMEDIC INC
160 Hanes Mall Cir (27103-3094)
PHONE..................336 744-4444
Randy Davis, *Prin*
EMP: 8 EST: 2009
SALES (est): 268.34K **Privately Held**
Web: www.jmedic.com
SIC: 3694 Automotive electrical equipment, nec

(G-16772)
JOSEPH HALKER
Also Called: Al-Rite Manufacturing
481 Shady Grove Church Rd (27107-9665)
PHONE..................336 769-4734
Joseph Halker, *Owner*
EMP: 4 EST: 1979
SQ FT: 4,800
SALES (est): 161.63K **Privately Held**
SIC: 2512 Couches, sofas, and davenports: upholstered on wood frames

(G-16773)
JOSTENS INC
Also Called: Jostens
2505 Empire Dr (27103-6709)
PHONE..................336 765-0070
Ron Sisk, *Brnch Mgr*
EMP: 350
SQ FT: 123,700
SALES (corp-wide): 1.39B **Privately Held**
Web: maintenance.jostens.com
SIC: 3911 Rings, finger: precious metal
HQ: Jostens, Inc.
   7760 France Ave S Ste 400
   Minneapolis MN 55435
   952 830-3300

(G-16774)
JUAN PINO SIGNS INC
2041 Gumtree Rd (27107-9444)
PHONE..................336 764-4422
Juan Pino, *Pr*
EMP: 4 EST: 1978
SQ FT: 5,000
SALES (est): 300K **Privately Held**
Web: www.juanpinosignsinc.com
SIC: 3993 Signs, not made in custom sign painting shops

(G-16775)
KABA ILCO CORP
Also Called: Kaba Access Control
2941 Indiana Ave (27105-4425)
PHONE..................336 725-1331
Michael Kincaid, *Mgr*
EMP: 325
Web: www.ilco.us

SIC: 3499 3429 Locks, safe and vault: metal; Hardware, nec
HQ: Kaba Ilco Corp.
   400 Jeffreys Rd
   Rocky Mount NC 27804
   252 446-3321

(G-16776)
KEITHS CLEANING LLC
54 Hoskins Dr (27105-2508)
PHONE..................336 701-0185
EMP: 7
SALES (est): 79.3K **Privately Held**
SIC: 3471 7389 Cleaning, polishing, and finishing; Business services, nec

(G-16777)
KELLY PRINTING LLC
3490 Reynolda Rd (27106-3063)
PHONE..................336 760-0505
Kelly Boviall, *Prin*
EMP: 5 EST: 2011
SALES (est): 190.24K **Privately Held**
SIC: 2752 Offset printing

(G-16778)
KERANETICS LLC
200 E 1st St Box 4 (27101-4165)
PHONE..................336 725-0621
Luke Burnett, *CEO*
Rick Blank, *Ch Bd*
EMP: 17 EST: 2008
SALES (est): 2.05MM **Privately Held**
Web: www.keranetics.com
SIC: 2834 2836 Pharmaceutical preparations; Biological products, except diagnostic

(G-16779)
KRISPY KREME DOUGHNUT CORP
Also Called: Krispy Kreme
259 S Stratford Rd (27103-1817)
PHONE..................336 733-3780
Kevin Hoeing, *Mgr*
EMP: 29
SQ FT: 4,137
SALES (corp-wide): 1.69B **Publicly Held**
Web: www.krispykreme.com
SIC: 5461 2051 Doughnuts; Doughnuts, except frozen
HQ: Krispy Kreme Doughnut Corp
   2116 Hawkins St Ste 102
   Charlotte NC 28203
   980 270-7117

(G-16780)
KRISPY KREME DOUGHNUT CORP
3190 Centre Park Blvd (27107-4574)
P.O. Box B (27102)
PHONE..................336 726-8908
Patrick Cepson, *Brnch Mgr*
EMP: 22
SQ FT: 109,113
SALES (corp-wide): 1.69B **Publicly Held**
Web: www.krispykreme.com
SIC: 5461 3556 Doughnuts; Food products machinery
HQ: Krispy Kreme Doughnut Corp
   2116 Hawkins St Ste 102
   Charlotte NC 28203
   980 270-7117

(G-16781)
KRISPY KREME DOUGHNUTS INC (HQ)
Also Called: Krispy Kreme
370 Knollwood St (27103-1835)
P.O. Box 83 (27102-0083)
PHONE..................336 725-2981
G Price Cooper, *Ex VP*
◆ EMP: 200 EST: 1937
SQ FT: 86,000

GEOGRAPHIC SECTION
Winston Salem - Forsyth County (G-16807)

SALES (est): 1.3B
SALES (corp-wide): 1.69B **Publicly Held**
Web: www.krispykreme.com
SIC: 5461 5149 2051 Doughnuts; Bakery products; Doughnuts, except frozen
PA: Krispy Kreme, Inc.
2116 Hawkins St
Charlotte NC 28203
800 457-4779

(G-16782)
LA TORTILLERIA LLC
Also Called: La Tortilleria
2900 Lowery St (27101-6126)
PHONE.................336 773-0010
Daniel Calhoun, *Pr*
Nathaniel Calhoun, *Stockholder**
J Phillip Calhoun, *Stockholder**
▲ **EMP:** 190 **EST:** 1995
SQ FT: 100,000
SALES (est): 110MM **Privately Held**
Web: www.purplecrow.com
SIC: 2099 5141 Tortillas, fresh or refrigerated ; Food brokers

(G-16783)
LABEL PRINTING SYSTEMS INC
Also Called: Lps Tag & Label
3937 Westpoint Blvd (27101-6721)
PHONE.................336 760-3271
Richard Ebert, *Ch*
Greg Ebert, *Pr*
EMP: 20 **EST:** 1990
SQ FT: 25,000
SALES (est): 4.62MM **Privately Held**
Web: www.lpslabels.net
SIC: 2679 2759 Labels, paper: made from purchased material; Commercial printing, nec

(G-16784)
LATINO COMMUNICATIONS INC (PA)
Also Called: Que Pasa
3067 Waughtown St (27107-1634)
P.O. Box 12876 (27117-2876)
PHONE.................336 714-2823
Jose Isasi, *Pr*
Flora Isasi, ***
EMP: 55 **EST:** 1993
SALES (est): 4.65MM
SALES (corp-wide): 4.65MM **Privately Held**
Web: www.quepasamedia.com
SIC: 4832 2711 Radio broadcasting stations; Newspapers

(G-16785)
LEGACY VULCAN LLC
Mideast Division
4401 N Patterson Ave (27105-1638)
P.O. Box 4239 (27115-4239)
PHONE.................336 767-0911
Gray Kimel Junior, *Pr*
EMP: 16
Web: www.vulcanmaterials.com
SIC: 3273 Ready-mixed concrete
HQ: Legacy Vulcan, Llc
1200 Urban Center Dr
Vestavia AL 35242
205 298-3000

(G-16786)
LEONARD BLOCK COMPANY
2390 Midway School Rd (27107-8701)
PHONE.................336 764-0607
B Leonard, *Pr*
EMP: 16 **EST:** 1981
SQ FT: 5,000
SALES (est): 2.33MM **Privately Held**
Web: www.leonardblockcompany.com
SIC: 3271 5211 Blocks, concrete or cinder: standard; Masonry materials and supplies

(G-16787)
LEXINGTON ROAD PROPERTIES INC
500 Battery Dr (27107-4137)
PHONE.................336 650-7209
▲ **EMP:** 125
SIC: 3691 3692 Storage batteries; Primary batteries, dry and wet

(G-16788)
LINOR TECHNOLOGY INC
4741 S Main St (27127-7427)
PHONE.................336 485-6199
Gary Nalven, *CEO*
EMP: 15 **EST:** 2012
SALES (est): 1.35MM **Privately Held**
Web: www.linortek.com
SIC: 5084 3625 3823 3651 Instruments and control equipment; Relays and industrial controls; Data loggers, industrial process type; Audio electronic systems

(G-16789)
LIONSTAR TRANSPORT LLC
2597 Landmark Dr (27103-6717)
PHONE.................336 448-0166
EMP: 4
SALES (est): 182.43K **Privately Held**
SIC: 3799 Transportation equipment, nec

(G-16790)
LJ CBG ACQUISITION COMPANY
3916 Westpoint Blvd (27101-6719)
PHONE.................336 768-8872
Darrin Anderson, *CEO*
EMP: 2176 **EST:** 2018
SALES (est): 141.01MM **Privately Held**
SIC: 2431 Door frames, wood

(G-16791)
LLFLEX LLC
Also Called: Oracle Packaging
220 Polo Rd (27105-3441)
PHONE.................336 777-5000
EMP: 120
Web: www.llflex.com
SIC: 2672 Paper; coated and laminated, nec
HQ: Llflex, Llc
1225 W Burnett Ave
Louisville KY 40210
502 636-8400

(G-16792)
LORILLARD LLC (DH)
401 N Main St (27101-3804)
PHONE.................336 741-2000
Murray S Kessler, *Pr*
David H Taylor, *Ex VP*
Ronald S Milstein, *Ex VP*
Anthony B Petitt, *CAO*
EMP: 40 **EST:** 1997
SALES (est): 50.24MM **Privately Held**
Web: www.rjrt.com
SIC: 2111 Cigarettes
HQ: Reynolds American Inc.
401 N Main St
Winston Salem NC 27101
336 741-2000

(G-16793)
LOW COUNTRY STEEL SC LLC (PA)
2529 Viceroy Dr (27103-6713)
PHONE.................336 283-9611
Bradley Mcmurray, *Pr*
EMP: 32 **EST:** 2011
SALES (est): 4.54MM
SALES (corp-wide): 4.54MM **Privately Held**
SIC: 3449 Bars, concrete reinforcing: fabricated steel

(G-16794)
LULULEMON
312 S Stratford Rd (27103-1820)
PHONE.................336 723-3002
EMP: 7 **EST:** 1998
SALES (est): 42.55K **Privately Held**
SIC: 2389 Apparel and accessories, nec

(G-16795)
LYNDON STEEL COMPANY LLC (DH)
1947 Union Cross Rd (27107-6448)
PHONE.................336 785-0848
David R Morgan, *Pr*
Sam Winters, ***
Mike Carcieri, ***
EMP: 150 **EST:** 1977
SQ FT: 53,000
SALES (est): 43.73MM
SALES (corp-wide): 1.04B **Privately Held**
Web: www.lyndonsteel.com
SIC: 3441 Fabricated structural metal
HQ: Fabsouth Llc
721 Ne 44th St
Oakland Park FL 33334
954 938-5800

(G-16796)
MAD RUSH MEDIA
208 Oakwood Ct (27103-1955)
PHONE.................336 816-3972
Dave Laster, *Owner*
EMP: 4 **EST:** 2017
SALES (est): 106.78K **Privately Held**
Web: www.madrushmedia.com
SIC: 2741 Miscellaneous publishing

(G-16797)
MADISON AVE CASES
1005 Deepwood Ct (27104-1109)
PHONE.................843 214-0476
Madison Wallace, *Prin*
EMP: 5 **EST:** 2016
SALES (est): 130.19K **Privately Held**
SIC: 3523 Farm machinery and equipment

(G-16798)
MAPLEWOOD IMAGING CTR
3155 Maplewood Ave (27103-3903)
PHONE.................336 397-6000
Stephen Bower, *Prin*
EMP: 10 **EST:** 2002
SALES (est): 354.67K **Privately Held**
SIC: 3861 Film, sensitized motion picture, X-ray, still camera, etc.

(G-16799)
MARANZ INC
Also Called: Archer Advanced Rbr Components
2860 Lowery St (27101-6128)
PHONE.................336 996-7776
George Halages, *Pr*
George Halages, *Pr*
Alyssa White, ***
▲ **EMP:** 85 **EST:** 1997
SQ FT: 22,500
SALES (est): 16.95MM **Privately Held**
Web: www.archerseal.com
SIC: 3069 Rubber automotive products

(G-16800)
MARIE SHARPS USA LLC
1976 Runnymede Rd (27104-3112)
PHONE.................336 701-0377
Sonia Schilling, *CEO*
Michael Touby, *Pr*
EMP: 15 **EST:** 2017
SALES (est): 1.07MM **Privately Held**
Web: www.mariesharpsusa.com
SIC: 2033 Canned fruits and specialties

(G-16801)
MARSH FURNITURE COMPANY
Also Called: Marsh Kitchens
420 Jonestown Rd Ste D (27104-4771)
PHONE.................336 765-7832
Steve Schedt, *Mgr*
EMP: 5
SALES (corp-wide): 43.2MM **Privately Held**
Web: www.marshkb.com
SIC: 1751 1799 2434 Cabinet building and installation; Kitchen and bathroom remodeling; Wood kitchen cabinets
PA: Marsh Furniture Company
1001 S Centennial St
High Point NC 27260
336 884-7363

(G-16802)
MARTIN OBRIEN CABINETMAKER
1940 Brantley St (27103-3712)
PHONE.................336 773-1334
Martin Obrien, *Owner*
EMP: 5 **EST:** 2010
SALES (est): 190.25K **Privately Held**
Web: www.martinobriencabinetmaker.com
SIC: 2511 Wood household furniture

(G-16803)
MAYO RESOURCES INC
2860 Lowery St (27101-6128)
PHONE.................336 996-7776
EMP: 50
SALES (est): 3.67MM **Privately Held**
SIC: 5085 3053 Rubber goods, mechanical; Gaskets; packing and sealing devices

(G-16804)
MCDOWELLS MCH FABRICATION INC
2312a Cragmore Rd (27107-2458)
P.O. Box 12542 (27117-2542)
PHONE.................336 720-9944
Rick Mcdowell, *Pr*
EMP: 5 **EST:** 1998
SALES (est): 440.04K **Privately Held**
SIC: 3599 Machine shop, jobbing and repair

(G-16805)
MEL SCHLESINGER
1001 S Marshall St # 290 (27101-5852)
PHONE.................336 525-6357
Mel Schlesinger, *Prin*
EMP: 5 **EST:** 2015
SALES (est): 55.05K **Privately Held**
Web: melschlesinger.medium.com
SIC: 2741 Miscellaneous publishing

(G-16806)
MG FOODS INC
3195 Centre Park Blvd (27107-4575)
PHONE.................336 724-6327
EMP: 11 **EST:** 2008
SALES (est): 299.57K **Privately Held**
SIC: 2099 Food preparations, nec

(G-16807)
MHS LTD
Also Called: Wear-Flex Slings
4961 Home Rd Ste A (27106-2802)
PHONE.................336 767-2641
Earl Johnson, *Brnch Mgr*
EMP: 7
SALES (corp-wide): 2.44MM **Privately Held**

Winston Salem - Forsyth County (G-16808)

Web: www.wear-flex.com
SIC: 2298 Cordage and twine
PA: Mhs Ltd.
4959 Home Rd
Winston Salem NC 27106
336 767-2641

(G-16808)
MHS LTD (PA)
Also Called: Wear-Flex Slings
4959 Home Rd (27106-2802)
P.O. Box 2379 (27021-2379)
PHONE.................................336 767-2641
Steve Schroeder, *Pr*
Steve Stewart, *Sec*
EMP: 10 EST: 1958
SQ FT: 6,000
SALES (est): 2.44MM
SALES (corp-wide): 2.44MM **Privately Held**
Web: www.wear-flex.com
SIC: 2298 Nets, seines, slings and insulator pads

(G-16809)
MICROFINE INC
Also Called: Poochpad Products
100 Cloverleaf Dr (27103-6714)
P.O. Box 516 (27040-0516)
PHONE.................................336 768-1480
John Martin, *Pr*
◆ EMP: 5 EST: 2000
SALES (est): 779.55K **Privately Held**
Web: www.poochpad.com
SIC: 3999 5199 Pet supplies; Pet supplies

(G-16810)
MID-ATLANTIC CONCRETE PDTS INC
2460 Armstrong Dr (27103-6809)
PHONE.................................336 774-6544
Kenneth Armistead, *Pr*
EMP: 7 EST: 2005
SALES (est): 2.44MM **Privately Held**
Web: www.midatlanticcp.com
SIC: 3272 Concrete products, nec

(G-16811)
MINAS EQUITY PARTNERS LLC
2710 Boulder Park Ct (27101-4776)
PHONE.................................336 724-5152
EMP: 15 EST: 2020
SALES (est): 917.9K **Privately Held**
SIC: 3599 Machine shop, jobbing and repair

(G-16812)
MOCK TIRE & AUTOMOTIVE INC
834 S Stratford Rd (27103-3202)
PHONE.................................336 774-0081
EMP: 36
SALES (corp-wide): 18.02MM **Privately Held**
Web: www.mockberothtire.com
SIC: 5531 7539 7534 Automotive tires; Auto front end repair; Tire repair shop
PA: Mock Tire & Automotive Inc
4752 Country Club Rd
Winston Salem NC 27104
336 768-1010

(G-16813)
MOCK TIRE & AUTOMOTIVE INC (PA)
4752 Country Club Rd (27104-3599)
PHONE.................................336 768-1010
Carey W Mock, *VP*
Cecil G Mock, *
▲ EMP: 40 EST: 1973
SQ FT: 7,500
SALES (est): 18.02MM
SALES (corp-wide): 18.02MM **Privately Held**
Web: www.mockberothtire.com

SIC: 5531 7539 7534 Automotive tires; Auto front end repair; Tire repair shop

(G-16814)
MODERN MACHINE AND METAL FABRICATORS INC
3201 Centre Park Blvd (27107-4570)
PHONE.................................336 993-4808
EMP: 100 EST: 1966
SALES (est): 18.21MM **Privately Held**
SIC: 3444 3599 7692 Sheet metalwork; Machine shop, jobbing and repair; Welding repair

(G-16815)
MODORAL BRANDS INC
Also Called: Zonnic
401 N Main St (27101-3804)
P.O. Box 3000 (27102-3000)
PHONE.................................336 741-7230
EMP: 5 EST: 2010
SALES (est): 2.93MM **Privately Held**
Web: www.reynoldsamerican.com
SIC: 5912 8093 2111 2121 Drug stores; Drug clinic, outpatient; Cigarettes; Cigars
HQ: Reynolds American Inc.
401 N Main St
Winston Salem NC 27101
336 741-2000

(G-16816)
MOE JT ENTERPRISES INC ✪
Also Called: Paul Davis Restoration
130 Back Forty Dr (27127-7404)
PHONE.................................423 512-1427
Jeffrey Thomas Moe, *CEO*
EMP: 16 EST: 2022
SALES (est): 1.22MM **Privately Held**
Web: www.pauldavis.com
SIC: 2899 Water treating compounds

(G-16817)
MONOGRAMS ETC
1056 N Peace Haven Rd (27104-1318)
PHONE.................................336 769-8358
Elizabeth S Alderman, *Prin*
EMP: 4 EST: 2014
SALES (est): 64.62K **Privately Held**
Web: www.monogramsetc.com
SIC: 2395 Embroidery and art needlework

(G-16818)
MOTSINGER BLOCK PLANT INC
199 Disher Rd (27107-8872)
PHONE.................................336 764-0350
F Smith Motsinger, *Pr*
Neal Motsinger, *VP*
EMP: 8 EST: 1953
SQ FT: 10,000
SALES (est): 948.93K **Privately Held**
SIC: 3271 5032 Blocks, concrete or cinder: standard; Masons' materials

(G-16819)
NEW DAIRY OPCO LLC
Also Called: Dairy Fresh
800 E 21st St (27105-5354)
PHONE.................................336 725-8141
Larry Hughes, *Prin*
EMP: 38
SALES (corp-wide): 447.94MM **Privately Held**
SIC: 2026 Fluid milk
PA: New Dairy Opco, Llc
12400 Coit Rd Ste 200
Dallas TX 75251
214 258-1200

(G-16820)
NEW VISION INVESTMENTS INC
4310 Enterprise Dr Ste I (27106-3260)
PHONE.................................336 757-1120
Chad Trater, *Pr*
Billie Litwin, *VP*
EMP: 7 EST: 2001
SALES (est): 632.75K **Privately Held**
SIC: 3827 Optical instruments and lenses

(G-16821)
NONE
1411 Plaza West Rd (27103-1482)
PHONE.................................336 408-6008
EMP: 8 EST: 2019
SALES (est): 123.22K **Privately Held**
Web: www.sanofi.com
SIC: 2834 Pharmaceutical preparations

(G-16822)
NORTHSTAR TRAVEL MEDIA
Also Called: Weissmann Travel Reports
331 High St (27101-5234)
PHONE.................................336 714-3328
David C Cox, *CEO*
Carolyn Wall, *
Arnie Weissmann, *
Frederick Moses, *
William Busch Junior, *Sec*
EMP: 23 EST: 1986
SALES (est): 648.87K **Privately Held**
Web: www.northstartravelgroup.com
SIC: 2721 Trade journals: publishing only, not printed on site

(G-16823)
NOVAKON
2169 Griffith Rd (27103-6407)
PHONE.................................336 813-2309
John Sandstrom, *Pr*
EMP: 5 EST: 2016
SALES (est): 92.46K **Privately Held**
Web: www.novakon.net
SIC: 3599 Machine shop, jobbing and repair

(G-16824)
NOVEX INNOVATIONS LLC
101 N Chestnut St Ste 303 (27101-4046)
PHONE.................................336 231-6693
EMP: 6 EST: 2014
SQ FT: 8,200
SALES (est): 1.42MM **Privately Held**
Web: www.novexinnovations.com
SIC: 3842 8731 Implants, surgical; Biotechnical research, commercial

(G-16825)
NU-TECH ENTERPRISES INC
305 Junia Ave (27127-3113)
PHONE.................................336 725-1691
James Inman, *Pr*
EMP: 23 EST: 2001
SQ FT: 7,000
SALES (est): 585.63K **Privately Held**
Web: www.nu-tech.us
SIC: 3069 3599 Molded rubber products; Machine and other job shop work
PA: Cross Technology, Inc.
340 E Nc 67 Highway Byp
East Bend NC 27018

(G-16826)
ODIGIA INC
300 S Liberty St Ste 210 (27101-5201)
PHONE.................................336 462-8056
Joshua Moe, *Pr*
EMP: 5 EST: 2010
SALES (est): 460.18K **Privately Held**
Web: www.odigia.com

SIC: 7372 Educational computer software

(G-16827)
OLD HOMEPLACE VINEYARD LLC
623 Mcgee Rd (27107-8710)
PHONE.................................336 399-7293
David E Stone, *Admn*
EMP: 4 EST: 2016
SALES (est): 73.85K **Privately Held**
Web: www.oldhomeplacevineyard.com
SIC: 2084 Wines

(G-16828)
OLD SALEM INCORPORATED
Also Called: Old Salem Town Merchant
730 S Poplar St (27101-5834)
P.O. Box 10400 (27108)
PHONE.................................336 721-7305
Skeebo Loveren, *Bmch Mgr*
EMP: 6
SALES (corp-wide): 6.55MM **Privately Held**
Web: www.oldsalem.org
SIC: 5961 2052 2051 2022 Catalog and mail-order houses; Cookies and crackers; Bread, cake, and related products; Cheese; natural and processed
PA: Old Salem, Incorporated
600 S Main St
Winston Salem NC 27101
336 721-7300

(G-16829)
OLIVERS DRIVE SHAFT REPAIR
707 E 12 1/2 St (27101-1641)
PHONE.................................719 539-1823
EMP: 4 EST: 2019
SALES (est): 87.26K **Privately Held**
Web: www.oliversdriveshaft.com
SIC: 3714 Motor vehicle parts and accessories

(G-16830)
OMNI MOLD & DIE LLC
2710 Boulder Park Ct (27101-4776)
PHONE.................................336 724-5152
EMP: 16 EST: 2013
SQ FT: 18,000
SALES (est): 1.61MM **Privately Held**
Web: www.omnimoldnc.com
SIC: 3544 Forms (molds), for foundry and plastics working machinery

(G-16831)
ORACLE FLEXIBLE PACKAGING INC
220 Polo Rd (27105-3441)
P.O. Box 11137 (27116-1137)
PHONE.................................336 777-5000
◆ EMP: 285
SIC: 2672 Paper; coated and laminated, nec

(G-16832)
ORGANIZER LLC
274 Glen Eagles Dr (27104-5318)
PHONE.................................336 391-7591
EMP: 6 EST: 2019
SALES (est): 90K **Privately Held**
SIC: 2842 Cleaning or polishing preparations, nec

(G-16833)
ORTHOPEDIC SERVICES
3303 Healy Dr (27103-1498)
PHONE.................................336 716-3349
Jim Butts, *Pr*
EMP: 7 EST: 1964
SQ FT: 1,200
SALES (est): 507.67K **Privately Held**

GEOGRAPHIC SECTION

Winston Salem - Forsyth County (G-16857)

SIC: **3842** 8011 Orthopedic appliances; Offices and clinics of medical doctors

(G-16834)
PAGES SCREEN PRINTING LLC
4110 Cherry St (27105-2536)
P.O. Box 11196 (27116-1196)
PHONE...................................336 759-7979
Julia Page, *Sec*
EMP: 6 **EST:** 1983
SQ FT: 5,000
SALES (est): 550.96K **Privately Held**
Web: www.pagesscreenprinting.com
SIC: 2759 Screen printing

(G-16835)
PANEL WHOLESALERS INCORPORATED
Also Called: P W I Computer Accessories
3841 Kimwell Dr (27103-6707)
PHONE...................................336 765-4040
Stephen W Harper, *Pr*
Lars Harper, *VP*
Sally Harper, *Sec*
EMP: 10 **EST:** 1960
SQ FT: 35,000
SALES (est): 929.61K **Privately Held**
Web: www.pwistratform.com
SIC: 3089 Thermoformed finished plastics products, nec

(G-16836)
PARRISH TIRE COMPANY (PA)
Also Called: Ptc
5130 Indiana Ave (27106-2822)
PHONE...................................800 849-8473
Logan Jackson, *Pr*
Bill Jackson, *
Michael Everhart, *
Charles Everhart, *
◆ **EMP:** 65 **EST:** 1946
SQ FT: 115,000
SALES (est): 378.88MM
SALES (corp-wide): 378.88MM **Privately Held**
Web: www.parrishtire.com
SIC: 5014 5531 7534 Automobile tires and tubes; Automotive tires; Tire recapping

(G-16837)
PATRIA VINEYARD LLC
Also Called: Patria Vineyard
550 Peters Creek Pkwy Unit 1409 (27101-4931)
PHONE...................................336 407-8254
Kelia Dawn Coffey, *Pr*
EMP: 6 **EST:** 2012
SALES (est): 176.36K **Privately Held**
SIC: 2084 Wines

(G-16838)
PATTERSON MARQUE
3919 Waddill St (27105-3534)
PHONE...................................336 661-7520
Marque Patterson, *CEO*
EMP: 4 **EST:** 2010
SALES (est): 97.62K **Privately Held**
SIC: 2051 Cakes, pies, and pastries

(G-16839)
PENN ENGINEERING & MFG CORP
Pennengineering
2400 Lowery St (27101-4725)
PHONE...................................336 631-8741
Bob Gentile, *Mgr*
EMP: 250
SQ FT: 133,396
Web: www.pemnet.com
SIC: 3429 Metal fasteners

HQ: Penn Engineering & Manufacturing Corp.
5190 Old Easton Rd
Danboro PA 18916
800 237-4736

(G-16840)
PEPSI BOTTLING VENTURES LLC
Also Called: Pepsi-Cola
295 Business Park Dr (27107-6537)
PHONE...................................336 464-9227
EMP: 5
Web: www.pepsico.com
SIC: 2086 Carbonated soft drinks, bottled and canned
HQ: Pepsi Bottling Ventures Llc
4141 Parklake Ave Ste 600
Raleigh NC 27612
919 865-2300

(G-16841)
PEPSI BOTTLING VENTURES LLC
Also Called: Pepsi-Cola Bottler
390 Business Park Dr (27107-6547)
PHONE...................................336 464-9227
Dan Stone, *Unit Manager*
EMP: 50
Web: www.pepsibottlingventures.com
SIC: 2086 Carbonated soft drinks, bottled and canned
HQ: Pepsi Bottling Ventures Llc
4141 Parklake Ave Ste 600
Raleigh NC 27612
919 865-2300

(G-16842)
PEPSI BOTTLING VENTURES LLC
Also Called: Pepsi-Cola
3425 Myer Lee Dr (27101-6209)
PHONE...................................336 724-4800
Jimmy Burns, *Mgr*
EMP: 200
Web: www.pepsico.com
SIC: 2086 5149 Soft drinks: packaged in cans, bottles, etc.; Soft drinks
HQ: Pepsi Bottling Ventures Llc
4141 Parklake Ave Ste 600
Raleigh NC 27612
919 865-2300

(G-16843)
PEPSI-COLA METRO BTLG CO INC
Also Called: Pepsi-Cola
1100 Reynolds Blvd (27105-3400)
P.O. Box 10 (27102-0010)
PHONE...................................336 896-4000
Miah Gaudet, *Mgr*
EMP: 700
SALES (corp-wide): 86.39B **Publicly Held**
Web: www.pepsico.com
SIC: 2086 5149 Carbonated soft drinks, bottled and canned; Groceries and related products, nec
HQ: Pepsi-Cola Metropolitan Bottling Company, Inc.
700 Anderson Hill Rd
Purchase NY 10577
914 767-6000

(G-16844)
PEPSICO INC
Also Called: Pepsico
P.O. Box 1800 (27102-1800)
PHONE...................................914 253-2000
EMP: 8
SALES (corp-wide): 86.39B **Publicly Held**
Web: www.pepsico.com
SIC: 2086 Carbonated soft drinks, bottled and canned
PA: Pepsico, Inc.
700 Anderson Hill Rd

Purchase NY 10577
914 253-2000

(G-16845)
PERDUE FARMS INC
Also Called: Perdue Farms
7996 N Point Blvd (27106-3265)
PHONE...................................336 896-9121
EMP: 24
SALES (corp-wide): 1.24B **Privately Held**
Web: www.perdue.com
SIC: 2015 Poultry slaughtering and processing
PA: Perdue Farms Incorporated
31149 Old Ocean City Rd
Salisbury MD 21804
800 473-7383

(G-16846)
PERSONAL COMMUNICATION SYSTEMS INC
Also Called: P C S
301 N Main St (27101-3836)
PHONE...................................336 722-4917
▲ **EMP:** 58
Web: www.televox.com
SIC: 3661 Telephone and telegraph apparatus

(G-16847)
PETNET SOLUTIONS INC
3908 Westpoint Blvd Ste E (27103-6757)
PHONE...................................865 218-2000
EMP: 4
SALES (corp-wide): 84.48B **Privately Held**
Web: www.siemens.com
SIC: 2835 Radioactive diagnostic substances
HQ: Petnet Solutions, Inc.
810 Innovation Dr
Knoxville TN 37932
865 218-2000

(G-16848)
PHARMACEUTIC LITHO LABEL INC
3360 Old Lexington Rd (27107-4119)
PHONE...................................336 785-4000
James Ladd, *Mgr*
EMP: 20
SALES (corp-wide): 9.51MM **Privately Held**
Web: www.resourcelabel.com
SIC: 2759 2752 Letterpress printing; Commercial printing, lithographic
PA: Pharmaceutic Litho & Label Company, Inc.
450 North Ave E
Cranford NJ 07016
336 785-4000

(G-16849)
PHILIP MORRIS USA INC
Also Called: Philip Morris
4338 Grove Ave (27105-2841)
PHONE...................................336 744-4401
Ceazer Swazay, *Brnch Mgr*
EMP: 99
SALES (corp-wide): 24.48B **Publicly Held**
Web: www.philipmorrisusa.com
SIC: 2111 Cigarettes
HQ: Philip Morris Usa Inc.
6601 W Brd St
Richmond VA 23230
804 274-2000

(G-16850)
PHOENIX PACKAGING INC
111 E 10th St (27101-1509)
P.O. Box 15091 (27113-0091)
PHONE...................................336 724-1978
Tom Skinner, *Pr*
EMP: 25 **EST:** 1983

SALES (est): 2.08MM **Privately Held**
Web: www.purplepackaging.com
SIC: 2631 2653 Container, packaging, and boxboard; Corrugated boxes, partitions, display items, sheets, and pad

(G-16851)
PHOTO EMBLEM INCORPORATED
5010 S Main St (27105-6818)
PHONE...................................336 784-4000
Sherman Richardson, *Pr*
▲ **EMP:** 8 **EST:** 1978
SALES (est): 403.01K **Privately Held**
Web: www.photoemblem.com
SIC: 2399 Emblems, badges, and insignia: from purchased materials

(G-16852)
PIEDMONT FLIGHT INC
Also Called: Piedmont Flight Training
3789 N Liberty St (27105-3908)
PHONE...................................336 776-6070
F Houston Symmes, *Pr*
Sandra Symmes, *VP*
David Mount, *Prin*
Tara Connell, *Prin*
Kyle Mounts, *Prin*
EMP: 22 **EST:** 1991
SALES (est): 1.61MM **Privately Held**
Web: www.flypft.com
SIC: 3728 8748 Link trainers (aircraft training mechanisms); Business consulting, nec

(G-16853)
PIEDMONT HOIST AND CRANE INC (PA)
3350 Temple School Rd (27107-3735)
PHONE...................................336 992-1355
EMP: 24 **EST:** 1992
SALES (est): 12.03MM **Privately Held**
Web: www.piedmonthoist.com
SIC: 3536 Hoists, cranes, and monorails

(G-16854)
PIEDMONT INDUS COATINGS INC
160 University Center Dr (27105-1395)
PHONE...................................336 377-3399
EMP: 6 **EST:** 1994
SQ FT: 1,200
SALES (est): 484.76K **Privately Held**
Web: www.piedmontcoatings.com
SIC: 2851 Paints and allied products

(G-16855)
PIEDMONT PUBLISHING
418 N Marshall St (27101-2932)
PHONE...................................336 727-4099
Randy Noftle, *Prin*
EMP: 10 **EST:** 2005
SALES (est): 260.4K **Privately Held**
Web: www.wsjournal.com
SIC: 2741 2759 Miscellaneous publishing; Publication printing

(G-16856)
PINE CREEK PRODUCTS LLC
2856 Country Club Rd (27104-3014)
PHONE...................................336 399-8806
EMP: 10 **EST:** 2017
SALES (est): 500.06K **Privately Held**
SIC: 2431 Millwork

(G-16857)
PINE HALL BRICK CO INC (PA)
Also Called: Riverside Brick & Supply
2701 Shorefair Dr (27105-4235)
P.O. Box 11044 (27116-1044)
PHONE...................................336 721-7500
Fletcher Steele Junior, *Pr*
Flake F Steele Junior, *Pr*

Winston Salem - Forsyth County (G-16858)

Ed Harrell, *CFO*
William P Steele Senior, *Sec*
Hugh Dowdle Junior, *VP Mfg*
◆ **EMP:** 25 **EST:** 1907
SQ FT: 10,000
SALES (est): 79.78MM
SALES (corp-wide): 79.78MM **Privately Held**
Web: www.pinehallbrick.com
SIC: 3251 5032 Brick and structural clay tile; Brick, except refractory

(G-16858)
PLAYTEX DORADO LLC
1000 E Hanes Mill Rd (27105-1384)
PHONE.................336 519-8080
EMP: 19 **EST:** 1975
SALES (est): 2.1MM **Publicly Held**
SIC: 2253 T-shirts and tops, knit
PA: Hanesbrands Inc.
   1000 E Hanes Mill Rd
   Winston Salem NC 27105

(G-16859)
PLM INC
Also Called: Private Label Manufacturing
2371 Farrington Point Dr (27107-2453)
PHONE.................336 788-7529
Dale Traxler, *Pr*
Kathy Traxler, *Sec*
EMP: 7 **EST:** 1985
SQ FT: 8,000
SALES (est): 740.46K **Privately Held**
SIC: 2844 Perfumes, cosmetics and other toilet preparations

(G-16860)
POLYVLIES USA INC
260 Business Park Dr (27107-6538)
PHONE.................336 769-0206
Gunnar Beyer, *CEO*
▲ **EMP:** 25 **EST:** 2014
SALES (est): 5.91MM
SALES (corp-wide): 128.39K **Privately Held**
SIC: 2297 2299 5131 Nonwoven fabrics; Batting, wadding, padding and fillings; Synthetic fabrics, nec
HQ: Polyvlies Franz Beyer Gmbh
   Rodder Str. 52
   Horstel NW 48477
   545993100

(G-16861)
POWERLAB INC
3352 Old Lexington Rd Bldg 43 (27107-4119)
PHONE.................336 650-0706
EMP: 21
SALES (corp-wide): 9.5MM **Privately Held**
Web: www.powerlabinc.com
SIC: 3356 2816 Nonferrous rolling and drawing, nec; Lead pigments: white lead, lead oxides, lead sulfate
PA: Powerlab, Inc.
   1145 Highway 34 S
   Terrell TX 75160
   972 563-1477

(G-16862)
PPG INDUSTRIES INC
Also Called: PPG 9490
1455 Trademart Blvd (27127-5645)
PHONE.................336 771-8878
Mark Cummings, *Mgr*
EMP: 4
SALES (corp-wide): 17.65B **Publicly Held**
Web: www.ppg.com
SIC: 2851 Paints and allied products
PA: Ppg Industries, Inc.
   1 Ppg Pl
   Pittsburgh PA 15272
   412 434-3131

(G-16863)
PRECISION CONCEPTS GROUP LLC
2701 Boulder Park Ct (27101-4776)
PHONE.................336 761-8572
Vincent C Marino, *
▲ **EMP:** 310 **EST:** 2002
SQ FT: 33,000
SALES (est): 51.09MM **Privately Held**
Web: www.precisionconcepts.com
SIC: 8711 3841 3089 3469 Engineering services; Surgical and medical instruments; Injection molding of plastics; Stamping metal for the trade

(G-16864)
PRECISION PART SYSTEMS WNSTN-S
Also Called: Precision Part Systems
1035 W Northwest Blvd (27101-1104)
P.O. Box 5565 (27113-5565)
PHONE.................336 723-5210
Nick Doumas, *Pr*
Klaul Hinrichsen, *
Tom Mc Caffrey, *
Rita Gallos, *
EMP: 27 **EST:** 1983
SALES (est): 1.46MM **Privately Held**
Web: www.precisionpartsystems.com
SIC: 3423 Hand and edge tools, nec

(G-16865)
PRESS 53 LLC
560 N Trade St Ste 103 (27101-2937)
P.O. Box 30314 (27130-0314)
PHONE.................336 414-5599
Kevin Watson, *Prin*
EMP: 7 **EST:** 2006
SALES (est): 181.28K **Privately Held**
Web: www.press53.com
SIC: 2741 Miscellaneous publishing

(G-16866)
PRIME SOURCE OPC LLC
320 Perimeter Point Blvd (27105-3542)
PHONE.................336 661-3300
EMP: 35 **EST:** 2009
SALES (est): 4.95MM **Privately Held**
Web: www.primesourceopc.com
SIC: 2752 Offset printing

(G-16867)
PRIMESOURCE CORPORATION
320a Perimeter Point Blvd (27105-3542)
PHONE.................336 661-3300
Richard B Trout, *Pr*
Diane Trout, *Sec*
EMP: 23 **EST:** 1984
SALES (est): 1.78MM **Privately Held**
Web: www.primesourceopc.com
SIC: 3577 Printers and plotters

(G-16868)
PRINT MINE TEES
4604 Oak Ridge Dr (27105-3133)
PHONE.................336 972-1245
EMP: 4 **EST:** 2018
SALES (est): 83.91K **Privately Held**
SIC: 2752 Commercial printing, lithographic

(G-16869)
PRODUCT QUEST MANUFACTURING INC
380 Knollwood St Ste 700 (27103-1862)
PHONE.................386 239-8787
EMP: 120
SIC: 2844 Face creams or lotions

(G-16870)
PRODUCT QUEST MANUFACTURING LLC
380 Knollwood St Ste 700 (27103-1862)
PHONE.................386 239-8787
▲ **EMP:** 425
SIC: 2844 Face creams or lotions

(G-16871)
PRODUCT QUEST MFG LLC
380 Knollwood St Ste 700 (27103-1862)
PHONE.................321 255-3250
EMP: 8 **EST:** 2015
SALES (est): 654.82K **Privately Held**
SIC: 3999 Manufacturing industries, nec

(G-16872)
PROKIDNEY LLC
3929 Westpoint Blvd Ste G (27103-6761)
PHONE.................336 448-2857
Depak Jain, *COO*
EMP: 20 **EST:** 2015
SALES (est): 3.52MM **Privately Held**
Web: www.prokidney.com
SIC: 2836 Biological products, except diagnostic

(G-16873)
PROKIDNEY CORP
2000 Frontis Plaza Blvd Ste 250 (27103-5616)
PHONE.................336 999-7028
Tim Bertram, *CEO*
Pablo Legorreta, *
James Coulston, *CFO*
Deepak Jain, *COO*
Libbie P Mckenzie, *CMO*
EMP: 59 **EST:** 2018
SQ FT: 38,400
SIC: 2836 Biological products, except diagnostic

(G-16874)
PROMOS INC
1316 Westgate Center Dr (27103-2933)
PHONE.................336 251-1134
Lori White, *Pr*
EMP: 4 **EST:** 2018
SALES (est): 31.29K **Privately Held**
SIC: 2395 Pleating and stitching

(G-16875)
PROSPECTIVE COMMUNICATIONS LLC
1959 N Peace Haven Rd (27106-4850)
PHONE.................336 287-5535
EMP: 4 **EST:** 2017
SALES (est): 41.35K **Privately Held**
SIC: 2741 Miscellaneous publishing

(G-16876)
R J REYNOLDS TOBACCO COMPANY
950 Reynolds Blvd Bldg 605-12 (27105-3450)
PHONE.................336 741-2132
C Tinsley, *Brnch Mgr*
EMP: 155
Web: www.rjrt.com
SIC: 2111 2131 Cigarettes; Smoking tobacco
HQ: R. J. Reynolds Tobacco Company
   401 N Main St
   Winston Salem NC 27101
   336 741-5000

(G-16877)
R J REYNOLDS TOBACCO COMPANY (DH)
401 N Main St (27101-3804)
P.O. Box 2959 (27102-2959)
PHONE.................336 741-5000
◆ **EMP:** 100 **EST:** 2004
SALES (est): 1.36B **Privately Held**
Web: www.rjrt.com
SIC: 2131 Smoking tobacco
HQ: R. J. Reynolds Tobacco Holdings, Inc.
   401 N Main St
   Winston Salem NC 27101
   336 741-5000

(G-16878)
R J RYNOLDS TOB HOLDINGS INC (DH)
401 N Main St (27101-3804)
P.O. Box 2990 (27102-2990)
PHONE.................336 741-5000
Susan Ivey, *Pr*
Dianne M Neal, *Ex VP*
Tommy J Payne, *EXTERNAL Relations*
◆ **EMP:** 100 **EST:** 1875
SQ FT: 86,000
SALES (est): 1.85B **Privately Held**
Web: www.rjrt.com
SIC: 2111 Cigarettes
HQ: Reynolds American Inc.
   401 N Main St
   Winston Salem NC 27101
   336 741-2000

(G-16879)
RAI SERVICES COMPANY
401 N Main St (27101-3804)
PHONE.................336 741-6774
Luis Davila, *Pr*
EMP: 11 **EST:** 2009
SALES (est): 11.25MM **Privately Held**
Web: www.rjrt.com
SIC: 2111 Cigarettes
HQ: Reynolds American Inc.
   401 N Main St
   Winston Salem NC 27101
   336 741-2000

(G-16880)
RAY PUBLISHING
2360 Darwick Rd (27127-8779)
PHONE.................336 407-4843
Scott Ray, *Prin*
EMP: 4 **EST:** 2018
SALES (est): 94.43K **Privately Held**
Web: www.triadfamilynetwork.org
SIC: 2741 Miscellaneous publishing

(G-16881)
RAYLEN VINEYARDS INC
3055 Heather Meadow Dr (27106-5814)
PHONE.................336 998-3100
Steve Shepard, *VP*
Joe Neely, *Pr*
EMP: 8 **EST:** 1999
SALES (est): 800.89K **Privately Held**
Web: www.raylenvineyards.com
SIC: 2084 Wines

(G-16882)
RED PEPPER SALSA
336 Cheltenham Dr (27103-6134)
PHONE.................503 799-9170
Chris Haveman, *Owner*
EMP: 5 **EST:** 2015
SALES (est): 72.86K **Privately Held**
SIC: 2099 Dips, except cheese and sour cream based

(G-16883)
RENAISSANCE FIBER LLC
500 W 5th St Ste 400 (27101-2799)
PHONE.................860 857-5987
Daniel Yohannes Ph.d. Mba, *CEO*
Andrew Hume, *CSO*

GEOGRAPHIC SECTION

Winston Salem - Forsyth County (G-16907)

Bruce Maxwell, *CFO*
EMP: 7 **EST:** 2018
SALES (est): 253.79K **Privately Held**
Web: www.renaissance-fiber.com
SIC: 2299 Hemp yarn, thread, roving, and textiles

(G-16884)
REYNOLDS AMERICAN INC (HQ)
401 N Main St (27101-3804)
P.O. Box 2990 (27102-2990)
PHONE..............................336 741-2000
Ricardo Oberlander, *Pr*
Tony Hayward, *
Jeff Raborn, *
Priscilla Samuel, *SCIENTIFIC Research & Development**
Jonathan Reed, *Chief Commercial Officer**
◆ **EMP:** 39 **EST:** 2004
SALES (est): 2.77B **Privately Held**
Web: www.reynoldsamerican.com
SIC: 2111 2121 2131 Cigarettes; Cigars; Smoking tobacco
PA: British American Tobacco P.L.C.
Globe House
London WC2R

(G-16885)
RITE INSTANT PRINTING INC
Also Called: PIP Printing
1011 Burke St (27101-2412)
PHONE..............................336 768-5061
Charles Morgan, *Pr*
Kathy Morgan, *VP*
EMP: 7 **EST:** 1975
SALES (est): 501.89K **Privately Held**
Web: www.pip.com
SIC: 2752 7334 Offset printing; Photocopying and duplicating services

(G-16886)
ROCKWELL COLLINS INC
Also Called: Collins Aerospace
190 Oak Plaza Blvd (27105-1470)
PHONE..............................336 744-3288
EMP: 5
SALES (corp-wide): 68.92B **Publicly Held**
Web: www.rockwellcollins.com
SIC: 3728 Aircraft parts and equipment, nec
HQ: Rockwell Collins, Inc.
400 Collins Rd Ne
Cedar Rapids IA 52498

(G-16887)
ROCKWELL COLLINS INC
2599 Empire Dr (27103-6709)
PHONE..............................336 776-3444
EMP: 4
SALES (corp-wide): 68.92B **Publicly Held**
Web: www.rockwellcollins.com
SIC: 3812 Search and navigation equipment
HQ: Rockwell Collins, Inc.
400 Collins Rd Ne
Cedar Rapids IA 52498

(G-16888)
ROCKWELL COLLINS INC
Also Called: Collins Aerospace
1455 Fairchild Rd (27105-4549)
PHONE..............................336 744-1097
EMP: 6
SALES (corp-wide): 68.92B **Publicly Held**
Web: www.rockwellcollins.com
SIC: 3812 Search and navigation equipment
HQ: Rockwell Collins, Inc.
400 Collins Rd Ne
Cedar Rapids IA 52498

(G-16889)
ROOTS ORIGINALS LLC
4451 Cheyenne Ct (27106-4589)
PHONE..............................573 673-1669
Michael Haggas, *Prin*
EMP: 5 **EST:** 2017
SALES (est): 53.83K **Privately Held**
SIC: 2431 Millwork

(G-16890)
ROTORK-FAIRCHILD INDUS PDTS CO
3920 Westpoint Blvd (27103-6719)
PHONE..............................336 659-3400
Alan G Paine, *Prin*
EMP: 11 **EST:** 2013
SALES (est): 1.88MM **Privately Held**
Web: www.fairchildproducts.com
SIC: 3823 Process control instruments

(G-16891)
ROYCE TOO LLC (HQ)
3330 Healy Dr Ste 200 (27103-2024)
P.O. Box 497 (25402-0497)
PHONE..............................212 356-1627
Bob Boglioli, *Pr*
Ben Carson, *
◆ **EMP:** 30 **EST:** 2004
SQ FT: 200,000
SALES (est): 23.16MM **Privately Held**
Web: www.roycesocks.com
SIC: 7389 2252 Packaging and labeling services; Socks
PA: Okamoto Corporation
1-11-9, Nishihonmachi, Nishi-Ku
Osaka OSK 550-0

(G-16892)
SAFE RIDE WHEELCHAIR TRAN
P.O. Box 11841 (27116-1841)
PHONE..............................336 995-7529
Kenard Carter, *Prin*
EMP: 5 **EST:** 2009
SALES (est): 240.36K **Privately Held**
Web: www.saferidenc.com
SIC: 3842 Wheelchairs

(G-16893)
SALEM ONE INC (PA)
Also Called: Salem Printing
5670 Shattalon Dr (27105-1331)
PHONE..............................336 744-9990
Philip Kelley Junior, *Pr*
Philip Kelley, *
Steve Yarbraugh, *
EMP: 127 **EST:** 1973
SQ FT: 45,500
SALES (est): 25.3MM
SALES (corp-wide): 25.3MM **Privately Held**
Web: www.salem-one.com
SIC: 7389 2752 2759 Packaging and labeling services; Commercial printing, lithographic; Commercial printing, nec

(G-16894)
SALEM SPORTS INC (PA)
1519 S Martin Luther King Jr Dr (27107-1308)
PHONE..............................336 722-2444
John Sullivan, *Pr*
Judith Sullivan, *Sec*
Jeff M Ickes, *Pr*
Kim G Ickes, *Sec*
▼ **EMP:** 4 **EST:** 1992
SQ FT: 14,000
SALES (est): 4.07MM
SALES (corp-wide): 4.07MM **Privately Held**
Web: www.salemsports.com

SIC: 3993 Signs and advertising specialties

(G-16895)
SALEM TECHNOLOGIES INC
Also Called: S T I
2580 Salem Point Ct (27103-6729)
PHONE..............................336 777-3652
Robert Tribble, *Pr*
Robert O Bridges, *VP*
EMP: 17 **EST:** 1989
SQ FT: 15,300
SALES (est): 4.61MM **Privately Held**
Web: www.salemtechnologies.com
SIC: 3089 3699 3571 Plastics processing; Electrical equipment and supplies, nec; Electronic computers

(G-16896)
SALEM WOODWORKING COMPANY
4849 Kester Mill Rd (27103-1214)
PHONE..............................336 768-7443
EMP: 6 **EST:** 1980
SQ FT: 10,500
SALES (est): 493K **Privately Held**
Web: www.winstonsalemwoodworking.com
SIC: 2431 Millwork

(G-16897)
SAMSWOODWORKS
2648 Fairlawn Dr (27106-3802)
PHONE..............................336 893-5499
Samuel Alvarez, *Prin*
EMP: 5 **EST:** 2013
SALES (est): 134.61K **Privately Held**
SIC: 2431 Millwork

(G-16898)
SANTA FE NATURAL TOBACCO COMPANY FOUNDATION (DH)
Also Called: Santa Fe Natural Tobacco
401 N Main St (27101-3804)
P.O. Box 2990 (87504-2990)
PHONE..............................800 332-5595
▲ **EMP:** 150 **EST:** 1982
SALES (est): 397.84K **Privately Held**
SIC: 2131 Smoking tobacco
HQ: Reynolds American Inc.
401 N Main St
Winston Salem NC 27101
336 741-2000

(G-16899)
SCHOENBERG SALT CO
4927 Home Rd (27106-2802)
P.O. Box 791 (27012-0791)
PHONE..............................336 766-0600
▼ **EMP:** 12 **EST:** 2010
SALES (est): 977.3K **Privately Held**
Web: www.gosalt.com
SIC: 2899 Salt

(G-16900)
SE LOGO WEAR
303 S Broad St (27101-5022)
PHONE..............................336 748-1735
EMP: 11 **EST:** 2018
SALES (est): 491.1K **Privately Held**
Web: www.selogowear.com
SIC: 2396 Automotive and apparel trimmings

(G-16901)
SELS SMART ERA LTG SYSTEMS
2995 Starlight Dr (27107-4103)
PHONE..............................336 661-8031
EMP: 5 **EST:** 2018
SALES (est): 154.47K **Privately Held**
Web: www.selsled.com
SIC: 3648 Lighting equipment, nec

(G-16902)
SFD INDUSTRIES INC
2358 Motsinger Rd (27107-9769)
P.O. Box 596 (27373-0596)
PHONE..............................336 829-5796
EMP: 4 **EST:** 2020
SALES (est): 56.03K **Privately Held**
Web: www.riderowdy.com
SIC: 3999 Manufacturing industries, nec

(G-16903)
SG-CLW INC
Also Called: Smithgroup
1700 N Liberty St (27105-6186)
P.O. Box 20741 (27120-0741)
PHONE..............................336 865-4980
Darius Smith, *CEO*
EMP: 10 **EST:** 2020
SALES (est): 999.53K **Privately Held**
SIC: 5172 2911 7389 1311 Petroleum brokers; Petroleum refining; Business Activities at Non-Commercial Site; Crude petroleum and natural gas

(G-16904)
SHARP STONE SUPPLY INC
126 Griffith Plaza Dr (27103-6826)
PHONE..............................336 659-7777
Robert Fulton, *Prin*
EMP: 11 **EST:** 2002
SALES (est): 603.52K **Privately Held**
Web: www.sharpstonesupply.com
SIC: 3281 Cut stone and stone products

(G-16905)
SHARPE CO (PA)
230 Charlois Blvd (27103-1508)
P.O. Box 5716 (27113-5716)
PHONE..............................336 724-2871
David G Sharpe, *Pr*
Buddy Sharpe Junior, *VP*
Burke Wilson Iii, *Treas*
Terri Sealey, *
▲ **EMP:** 30 **EST:** 1956
SQ FT: 38,000
SALES (est): 10.58MM **Privately Held**
Web: www.sharpeco.net
SIC: 2754 7359 Commercial printing, gravure ; Equipment rental and leasing, nec

(G-16906)
SHARPE IMAGES PROPERTIES INC (PA)
Also Called: Sharpe Images
230 Charlois Blvd (27103-1508)
P.O. Box 5716 (27113-5716)
PHONE..............................336 724-2871
David Gregory Sharpe, *Pr*
B R Buddy Sharpe Junior, *VP*
Terri Sealey, *
Burke Wilson Iii, *Treas*
EMP: 29 **EST:** 1956
SQ FT: 11,000
SALES (est): 2.38MM
SALES (corp-wide): 2.38MM **Privately Held**
Web: www.sharpeco.net
SIC: 5999 5049 7334 7384 Architectural supplies; Engineers' equipment and supplies, nec; Photocopying and duplicating services; Photofinish laboratories

(G-16907)
SHEETS SMITH WEALTH MGT INC
120 Club Oaks Ct Ste 200 (27104-4769)
PHONE..............................336 765-2020
John R Sheets, *Pr*
William G Smith, *Pt*
Dave Gilbert, *Ex VP*
EMP: 25 **EST:** 1982

Winston Salem - Forsyth County (G-16908)

SALES (est): 5.66MM **Privately Held**
Web: www.sheetssmith.com
SIC: 6282 2541 Investment counselors; Wood partitions and fixtures

(G-16908)
SIGNCASTER CORPORATION
6210 Hacker Bend Ct Ste B (27103-9501)
PHONE..................................336 712-2525
Don Shaw, *Brnch Mgr*
EMP: 6
SALES (corp-wide): 91.84MM **Privately Held**
SIC: 7389 5087 2796 Engraving service; Engraving equipment and supplies; Engraving on copper, steel, wood, or rubber: printing plates
HQ: Signcaster Corporation
    12450 Oliver Ave S # 100
    Burnsville MN 55337
    800 869-7800

(G-16909)
SIGNS ETC
2432 Cherokee Ln (27103-4832)
PHONE..................................336 722-9341
Susan B Davis, *Owner*
Shannon Davis, *Off Mgr*
EMP: 4 EST: 1984
SQ FT: 13,000
SALES (est): 435.45K **Privately Held**
Web: www.signsetcofcharlotte.com
SIC: 7389 7336 3993 Sign painting and lettering shop; Graphic arts and related design; Signs and advertising specialties

(G-16910)
SIKORA AEROSPACE TECH INC
219 Lucerne Ln (27104-2916)
PHONE..................................336 870-6351
Frank Sikora, *Prin*
EMP: 5 EST: 2016
SALES (est): 110.91K **Privately Held**
SIC: 3721 Aircraft

(G-16911)
SKETTIS WOODWORKS
2225 Sedgemont Dr (27103-9745)
PHONE..................................336 671-9866
Steve Spinetti, *Prin*
EMP: 5 EST: 2016
SALES (est): 58.29K **Privately Held**
SIC: 2431 Millwork

(G-16912)
SNOW ELECTRIC CO INC
428 Brookstown Ave (27101-5026)
PHONE..................................336 723-2092
Homer I Snow Junior, *Pr*
James R Snow, *Sec*
EMP: 7 EST: 1925
SQ FT: 20,000
SALES (est): 1.09MM **Privately Held**
SIC: 5063 7694 Motors, electric; Armature rewinding shops

(G-16913)
SPORTSMANS SUPPLY COMPANY INC
2287 Cloverdale Ave (27103-2301)
PHONE..................................336 725-8791
Thomas Clary, *Ch*
EMP: 7 EST: 2017
SALES (est): 127.43K **Privately Held**
SIC: 2899 Chemical preparations, nec

(G-16914)
SRB TECHNOLOGIES INC (PA)
2580 Landmark Dr (27103-6716)
P.O. Box 25267 (27114-5267)
PHONE..................................336 659-2610
Brian Tullen, *Pr*
Michael Dougan, *
Stephane Levesque, *
EMP: 33 EST: 1979
SQ FT: 6,000
SALES (est): 4.85MM
SALES (corp-wide): 4.85MM **Privately Held**
Web: www.srbt.com
SIC: 3648 3993 Lighting equipment, nec; Signs and advertising specialties

(G-16915)
STAR READY-MIX INC
2865 Lowery St (27101-6127)
PHONE..................................336 725-9401
Joe Wolfe, *CEO*
EMP: 15 EST: 2004
SALES (est): 239.72K **Privately Held**
SIC: 3273 Ready-mixed concrete

(G-16916)
STARDUST CELLARS LLC (PA)
Also Called: Stardust Cellars
1764 Camden Rd (27103-4510)
PHONE..................................336 466-4454
Nicolas Von Cosmos, *CEO*
EMP: 4 EST: 2018
SALES (est): 478.25K
SALES (corp-wide): 478.25K **Privately Held**
Web: www.stardustcellars.com
SIC: 2084 5813 Wines; Tavern (drinking places)

(G-16917)
STATE OF ARC WELDING
4632 Stanley Ct (27101-2336)
PHONE..................................336 341-9780
Matthew Tilley, *Prin*
EMP: 5 EST: 2017
SALES (est): 58.23K **Privately Held**
SIC: 7692 Welding repair

(G-16918)
STOROPACK INC
2598 Empire Dr Ste G (27103-6763)
PHONE..................................800 827-7225
EMP: 4
SALES (corp-wide): 635.28MM **Privately Held**
Web: www.storopack.us
SIC: 5199 3086 2671 Packaging materials; Packaging and shipping materials, foamed plastics; Paper; coated and laminated packaging
HQ: Storopack, Inc.
    4758 Devitt Dr
    West Chester OH 45246
    513 874-0314

(G-16919)
STRATFORD DIE CASTING INC
1665 S Martin Luther King Jr Dr Ste A (27107-1335)
PHONE..................................336 784-0100
Norman Wallace, *Pr*
G Scott Wallace, *VP*
Virginia Lawson, *Sec*
EMP: 15 EST: 1980
SALES (est): 463.71K **Privately Held**
SIC: 3364 Zinc and zinc-base alloy die-castings

(G-16920)
STRATFORD METALFINISHING INC
1681 S Martin Luther King Jr Dr (27107-1310)
PHONE..................................336 723-7946
Scott Wallace, *Pr*
EMP: 48 EST: 1964
SALES (est): 6.87MM **Privately Held**
Web: www.stratfordmetal.com
SIC: 3471 Electroplating of metals or formed products

(G-16921)
STRATFORD TOOL & DIE CO INC
3841 Kimwell Dr (27103-6707)
PHONE..................................336 765-2030
Stephen W Harper, *Pr*
Keith Smith, *VP*
Sally Harper, *Sec*
EMP: 14 EST: 1965
SQ FT: 31,200
SALES (est): 872.94K **Privately Held**
Web: www.stratfordtoolanddie.com
SIC: 3544 Special dies and tools

(G-16922)
STROUPE MIRROR CO
2661 Reynolds Dr (27104-1927)
PHONE..................................336 475-2181
EMP: 7 EST: 1947
SALES (est): 65K **Privately Held**
Web: www.stroupemirror.com
SIC: 3231 Products of purchased glass

(G-16923)
SUN PRINTING COMPANY INC
956 Kenleigh Cir (27106-5605)
PHONE..................................336 773-1346
Greg Russ, *Prin*
Henry L Russ Junior, *Sec*
Ed Blazer, *VP*
EMP: 5 EST: 1929
SQ FT: 5,000
SALES (est): 234.81K **Privately Held**
Web: www.sunpco.com
SIC: 2759 5099 2752 5199 Letterpress printing; Rubber stamps; Offset printing; Advertising specialties

(G-16924)
SUNTEX INDUSTRIES
5000 S Main St (27107-6818)
PHONE..................................336 784-1000
Tom Ahn, *Owner*
EMP: 10 EST: 2016
SALES (est): 978.71K **Privately Held**
Web: www.suntexindustries.com
SIC: 3999 Manufacturing industries, nec

(G-16925)
SUPERIOR MANUFACTURING COMPANY
4102 Indiana Ave (27105-3415)
P.O. Box 4048 (27115-4048)
PHONE..................................336 661-1200
Bryan Peterson, *CEO*
Bryan S Peterson, *
Joe Brewster, *
Patricia Peterson, *
▲ EMP: 60 EST: 1945
SQ FT: 80,000
SALES (est): 8.84MM **Privately Held**
Web: www.superiormanufacturing.com
SIC: 3441 Fabricated structural metal

(G-16926)
SUTLERS SPIRIT COMPANY
840 Mill Works St (27101-1243)
PHONE..................................336 565-6006
EMP: 5 EST: 2017
SALES (est): 117.92K **Privately Held**
Web: www.sutlersspiritco.com
SIC: 2085 Distilled and blended liquors

(G-16927)
SWAIM ORNAMENTAL IRON WORKS
2570 Landmark Dr (27103-6716)
PHONE..................................336 765-5271
Don L Swaim, *Pr*
Gretchen Swaim, *Sec*
Trent Swaim, *VP*
EMP: 19 EST: 1951
SQ FT: 11,100
SALES (est): 2.26MM **Privately Held**
Web: www.swaimornamentalnc.com
SIC: 3446 Railings, banisters, guards, etc: made from metal pipe

(G-16928)
SWEET TREATS BY TREAT LADY LLC
650 Rugby Row Apt H (27106-5342)
PHONE..................................336 831-3282
EMP: 5 EST: 2021
SALES (est): 62.38K **Privately Held**
SIC: 2099 7389 Desserts, ready-to-mix; Business Activities at Non-Commercial Site

(G-16929)
T W GARNER FOOD COMPANY
600 Northgate Park Dr (27106-3429)
PHONE..................................336 661-1550
Ann Garner Riddle, *Brnch Mgr*
EMP: 4
SALES (corp-wide): 25.93MM **Privately Held**
Web: www.garnerfoods.com
SIC: 2033 Barbecue sauce: packaged in cans, jars, etc.
PA: T W Garner Food Company
    614 W 4th St
    Winston Salem NC 27101
    336 661-1550

(G-16930)
T W GARNER FOOD COMPANY (PA)
614 W 4th St (27101-2730)
PHONE..................................336 661-1550
Ann Garner, *Pr*
Harold H Garner Junior, *Sec*
◆ EMP: 48 EST: 1929
SQ FT: 75,000
SALES (est): 25.93MM
SALES (corp-wide): 25.93MM **Privately Held**
Web: www.garnerfoods.com
SIC: 2033 2035 Barbecue sauce: packaged in cans, jars, etc.; Pickles, sauces, and salad dressings

(G-16931)
T W GARNER FOOD COMPANY
4045 Indiana Ave (27105-3412)
PHONE..................................336 661-1550
Ann Garner Riddle, *Pr*
EMP: 4
SALES (corp-wide): 25.93MM **Privately Held**
Web: www.garnerfoods.com
SIC: 2033 Chili sauce, tomato: packaged in cans, jars, etc.
PA: T W Garner Food Company
    614 W 4th St
    Winston Salem NC 27101
    336 661-1550

(G-16932)
TAR HEEL MINI MOTORING CLUB
380 Knollwood St Ste H129 (27103-1884)
PHONE..................................336 391-8084
EMP: 6 EST: 2010
SALES (est): 150K **Privately Held**
SIC: 2865 Tar

GEOGRAPHIC SECTION
Winston Salem - Forsyth County (G-16960)

(G-16933)
TE CONNECTIVITY
3700 Reidsville Rd (27101-2165)
PHONE..................336 727-5295
EMP: 38 EST: 2014
SALES (est): 9.31MM Privately Held
SIC: 3678 Electronic connectors

(G-16934)
TE CONNECTIVITY CORPORATION
3900 Reidsville Rd (27101-2167)
PHONE..................336 664-7000
Randy Smith, Brnch Mgr
EMP: 49
Web: www.te.com
SIC: 3678 3643 Electronic connectors;
  Current-carrying wiring services
HQ: Te Connectivity Corporation
  1050 Westlakes Dr
  Berwyn PA 19312
  610 893-9800

(G-16935)
TE CONNECTIVITY CORPORATION
3800 Reidsville Rd (27101-2166)
PHONE..................336 727-5122
Larry Novotny, Mgr
EMP: 165
Web: www.te.com
SIC: 3678 8748 Electronic connectors;
  Testing services
HQ: Te Connectivity Corporation
  1050 Westlakes Dr
  Berwyn PA 19312
  610 893-9800

(G-16936)
TEAM CONNECTION
2508 Griffith Meadows Dr (27103-6329)
PHONE..................336 287-3892
Charmeka Foster, Prin
EMP: 8 EST: 2010
SALES (est): 114.72K Privately Held
SIC: 2759 Screen printing

(G-16937)
TEDDY SOFT PAPER PRODUCTS INC
535 E Clemmonsville Rd Ste A
(27107-5204)
PHONE..................336 784-5887
Sam Liontis, Pr
Bobby Laloudis, Prin
George Laloudis, Prin
EMP: 5 EST: 2015
SQ FT: 75,000
SALES (est): 630.59K Privately Held
Web: www.teddysoftpaper.com
SIC: 2621 Paper mills

(G-16938)
TENGION INC
Also Called: Tengion
3929 Westpoint Blvd Ste G (27103-6761)
PHONE..................336 722-5855
EMP: 27
Web: www.tengion.com
SIC: 2836 8731 Biological products, except
  diagnostic; Biotechnical research,
  commercial

(G-16939)
TGI INCORPORATED
3570 Vest Mill Rd Ste F (27103-2963)
PHONE..................336 768-0139
Christian F Stone, Pr
EMP: 5 EST: 2010
SALES (est): 93.82K Privately Held
SIC: 1389 Oil field services, nec

(G-16940)
THE COMPUTER SOLUTION COMPANY
Also Called: Tcsc
102 W 3rd St Ste 750 (27101-3902)
PHONE..................336 409-0782
Blaire Robinson, Pr
EMP: 13 EST: 1985
SALES (est): 1.38MM Privately Held
SIC: 7372 7379 Business oriented computer
  software; Computer related consulting
  services

(G-16941)
THERMCRAFT HOLDING CO LLC
3950 Overdale Rd (27107-6106)
PHONE..................336 784-4800
Lee Watson, CEO
EMP: 65 EST: 2021
SALES (est): 13.69MM
SALES (corp-wide): 25.17MM Privately
Held
Web: www.thermcraftinc.com
SIC: 3567 Heating units and devices,
  industrial: electric
PA: The Alloy Engineering Company
  844 Thacker St
  Berea OH 44017
  440 243-6800

(G-16942)
THREE FIFTY SIX INC
Also Called: Salem Stitches
832 S Main St (27101-5333)
P.O. Box 20155 (27120-0155)
PHONE..................336 631-5356
Kathleen Quirk-keyser, Pr
EMP: 5 EST: 2016
SALES (est): 103.31K Privately Held
Web: threefiftysixinc.godaddysites.com
SIC: 2741 Miscellaneous publishing

(G-16943)
TO THE POINT INC
130 Stratford Ct Ste E (27103-1852)
PHONE..................336 725-5303
Kevin Cope, Pr
Janice Stevens, VP
EMP: 8 EST: 1996
SQ FT: 5,000
SALES (est): 996.28K Privately Held
Web: www.ttpoint.com
SIC: 2395 Embroidery products, except
  Schiffli machine

(G-16944)
TOO HOTT CUSTOMS LLC
1249 W Academy St (27103-3812)
PHONE..................336 722-4919
Scott Walker, Owner
EMP: 7 EST: 2006
SALES (est): 717.09K Privately Held
Web: www.toohottcustoms.com
SIC: 3011 Tires and inner tubes

(G-16945)
TOOLMARX LLC
408 Ricks Dr (27103-1717)
PHONE..................919 725-0122
James Swing, Prin
EMP: 5 EST: 2018
SALES (est): 72.95K Privately Held
Web: www.toolmarx.com
SIC: 3999 Manufacturing industries, nec

(G-16946)
TRASH MASHER LLC
Also Called: Waste Smasher
1045 Burke St (27101-2412)
PHONE..................786 357-2697
Paul Chyrsson, Pr
Norman Thomas, *
EMP: 30 EST: 2015
SQ FT: 2,200
SALES (est): 2.7MM Privately Held
SIC: 3639 Trash compactors, household

(G-16947)
TRIAD AUTOMATION GROUP INC
Also Called: Triad Automation Group
4994 Indiana Ave Ste F (27106-2810)
P.O. Box 1065 (27012-1065)
PHONE..................336 767-1379
Joe Collins, Pr
Jon Freeman, VP
EMP: 22 EST: 2000
SQ FT: 12,000
SALES (est): 4.72MM Privately Held
Web: www.triadautomationgroup.com
SIC: 3823 Industrial process measurement
  equipment

(G-16948)
TRIAD SEMICONDUCTOR INC
1760 Jonestown Rd Ste 100 (27103-6993)
PHONE..................336 774-2150
Lynn Hayden, Pr
David Bell, *
James Kemerling, VP
John Goode, CFO
EMP: 54 EST: 2002
SQ FT: 5,800
SALES (est): 10.98MM Privately Held
Web: www.triadsemi.com
SIC: 3674 Integrated circuits, semiconductor
  networks, etc.

(G-16949)
TRIAD SMOOTHIES LLC
2541 Bitting Rd (27104-4101)
PHONE..................336 972-1130
Paul Harrison, Admn
EMP: 6 EST: 2012
SALES (est): 189.72K Privately Held
SIC: 2037 Frozen fruits and vegetables

(G-16950)
TRIAD-FIT
5677 Harrington Village Dr (27105-9140)
PHONE..................336 409-3818
Cory Silva, Owner
EMP: 5 EST: 2014
SALES (est): 44.88K Privately Held
Web: www.triad-fit.com
SIC: 2741 Miscellaneous publishing

(G-16951)
TRIANGLE BODY WORKS INC
2014 Waughtown St (27107-2498)
PHONE..................336 788-0631
Ronnie Lee Senior, Pr
EMP: 11 EST: 1927
SQ FT: 9,000
SALES (est): 722.76K Privately Held
Web: www.trianglebodyworks.com
SIC: 3713 7532 Truck bodies (motor
  vehicles); Body shop, trucks

(G-16952)
TRIMANTEC
4994 Indiana Ave (27106-2810)
PHONE..................336 767-1379
Joe Collins, Pr
Jon Freeman, VP
EMP: 20 EST: 2019
SALES (est): 5.05MM Privately Held
Web: www.trimantec.com
SIC: 3355 3613 Aluminum wire and cable;
  Power switching equipment

(G-16953)
TRIVIUM PACKAGING USA INC
Also Called: Ardagh
4000 Old Milwaukee Ln (27107-6103)
PHONE..................336 785-8500
Jerry Hubert, Brnch Mgr
EMP: 269
SALES (corp-wide): 1.42B Privately Held
Web: www.ardaghgroup.com
SIC: 3411 Aluminum cans
HQ: Trivium Packaging Usa Inc.
  10255 W Higgins Rd # 100
  Rosemont IL 60018

(G-16954)
TRUELOOK INC
575 E 4th St (27101-4113)
PHONE..................833 878-3566
Roger Yarrow, COO
EMP: 5 EST: 2000
SALES (est): 3.54MM Privately Held
Web: www.truelook.com
SIC: 3861 Cameras and related equipment

(G-16955)
TS KRUPA LLC
194 Briarcreek Dr (27107-9514)
PHONE..................336 782-1515
Brian Shollenberger, Prin
EMP: 5 EST: 2014
SALES (est): 135.11K Privately Held
Web: www.tskrupa.com
SIC: 2741 Miscellaneous publishing

(G-16956)
TSQUARED CABINETS
118 Griffith Plaza Dr (27103-6824)
PHONE..................336 655-0208
Troy Trinkle, Prin
EMP: 7 EST: 2013
SALES (est): 240.5K Privately Held
Web: www.t-squared-cabinets.com
SIC: 2434 Wood kitchen cabinets

(G-16957)
TWIN CITY CUSTOM CABINETS
1310 N Liberty St (27105-6626)
PHONE..................336 773-7200
Steven Womble, Prin
EMP: 4 EST: 2007
SALES (est): 351.15K Privately Held
SIC: 2434 Wood kitchen cabinets

(G-16958)
TWIN CITY SPORTS LLC
Also Called: Jersey City Sports
4836 Country Club Rd (27104-4504)
PHONE..................336 765-5070
EMP: 4 EST: 2017
SALES (est): 245.8K Privately Held
Web: www.jerseycitysports.net
SIC: 2759 Screen printing

(G-16959)
TWIN CY KWNIS FNDTION WNSTN-SL
1 W 4th St (27101-3972)
PHONE..................336 784-1649
EMP: 7 EST: 2011
SALES (est): 39.12K Privately Held
SIC: 2711 Newspapers, publishing and
  printing

(G-16960)
UPEL INC
1000 E Hanes Mill Rd (27105-1384)
PHONE..................336 519-8080
Gerald W Evans Junior, CEO
EMP: 26 EST: 1997
SALES (est): 2.74MM Publicly Held

Winston Salem - Forsyth County (G-16961)

SIC: **2253** 2342 2341 2322 T-shirts and tops, knit; Bras, girdles, and allied garments; Panties: women's, misses', children's, and infants'; Underwear, men's and boys': made from purchased materials
PA: Hanesbrands Inc.
  1000 E Hanes Mill Rd
  Winston Salem NC 27105

(G-16961)
UPPER SOUTH STUDIO INC
330 S Main St (27101-5217)
PHONE................................336 724-5480
Susan Rosen, *Pr*
Lawrence Rosen, *VP*
EMP: 12 **EST:** 1980
SQ FT: 7,000
SALES (est): 930.65K **Privately Held**
Web: www.uppersouthstudio.com
SIC: **2262** Dyeing: manmade fiber and silk broadwoven fabrics

(G-16962)
VILLAGE PRODUCE & CNTRY STR IN
Also Called: Ogburn Village Solutions
4219 N Liberty St (27105-2817)
PHONE................................336 661-8685
EMP: 4 **EST:** 2010
SALES (est): 298.74K **Privately Held**
SIC: **3429** 5399 Hardware, nec; Country general stores

(G-16963)
VIRTUE LABS LLC
95 W 32nd St (27105-3615)
PHONE................................781 316-5437
EMP: 47
SALES (corp-wide): 11.23MM **Privately Held**
Web: www.virtuelabs.com
SIC: **2844** Perfumes, cosmetics and other toilet preparations
PA: Virtue Labs, Llc
  426 S Dawson St
  Raleigh NC 27601
  844 782-4247

(G-16964)
VISE & CO LLC
5063 Ramillie Run (27106-9641)
PHONE................................336 354-3702
EMP: 5 **EST:** 2018
SALES (est): 64.54K **Privately Held**
SIC: **3949** Sporting and athletic goods, nec

(G-16965)
VULCAN CONSTRUCTION MTLS LLC
3651 Penn Ave (27105-3760)
P.O. Box 4007 (27115-4007)
PHONE................................336 767-1201
Walter Speas, *Mgr*
EMP: 4
Web: www.vulcanmaterials.com
SIC: **3273** Ready-mixed concrete
HQ: Vulcan Construction Materials, Llc
  1200 Urban Center Dr
  Vestavia AL 35242
  205 298-3000

(G-16966)
VULCAN CONSTRUCTION MTLS LLC
4401 N Patterson Ave (27105-1638)
PHONE................................336 767-0911
Brad Ratledge, *Brnch Mgr*
EMP: 21
Web: www.vulcanmaterials.com
SIC: **3273** Ready-mixed concrete
HQ: Vulcan Construction Materials, Llc
  1200 Urban Center Dr
  Vestavia AL 35242
  205 298-3000

(G-16967)
W GAMBY C O HANES DYE & FINISH
600 W Northwest Blvd (27101-1210)
PHONE................................336 724-9020
EMP: 26 **EST:** 2002
SALES (est): 82.38K **Privately Held**
SIC: **3999** Manufacturing industries, nec

(G-16968)
WEBER AND WEBER INC (PA)
Also Called: Sir Speedy
1011 Burke St (27101-2412)
PHONE................................336 722-4109
Arthur G Weber, *Pr*
Jody Weber Shaw, *VP*
J Dwight Shaw, *VP*
Susanne Weber, *Sec*
EMP: 18 **EST:** 1974
SQ FT: 6,000
SALES (est): 4.56MM
SALES (corp-wide): 4.56MM **Privately Held**
Web: www.sirspeedy.com
SIC: **2752** 7334 2791 2789 Commercial printing, lithographic; Photocopying and duplicating services; Typesetting; Bookbinding and related work

(G-16969)
WERSUNSLLC ◊
615 Saint George Sq Ct (27103-1356)
PHONE................................857 209-8701
Michael Paolillo, *Pr*
EMP: 6 **EST:** 2023
SALES (est): 253.2K **Privately Held**
SIC: **5999** 1795 6531 1531 Miscellaneous retail stores, nec; Demolition, buildings and other structures; Real estate leasing and rentals; Condominium developers

(G-16970)
WESTBEND VINEYARDS INC
599 S Stratford Rd (27103-1806)
PHONE................................336 768-7520
Jack Kroustalis, *Pr*
Lilian Kroustalis, *Sec*
EMP: 8 **EST:** 1987
SQ FT: 49,000
SALES (est): 584.51K **Privately Held**
SIC: **2084** Wine cellars, bonded: engaged in blending wines

(G-16971)
WESTROCK COMPANY
8080 N Point Blvd (27106-3204)
PHONE................................770 448-2193
EMP: 5
SALES (corp-wide): 20.31B **Publicly Held**
Web: www.westrock:com
SIC: **2899** 2631 Chemical preparations, nec; Paperboard mills
PA: Westrock Company
  1000 Abernathy Rd
  Atlanta GA 30328
  770 448-2193

(G-16972)
WESTROCK CONVERTING LLC
Also Called: Rock-Tenn Converting
5900 Grassy Creek Blvd (27105-1205)
PHONE................................336 661-1700
EMP: 7
SALES (corp-wide): 20.31B **Publicly Held**
Web: www.westrock.com
SIC: **2653** Boxes, corrugated: made from purchased materials
HQ: Westrock Converting, Llc
  1000 Abernathy Rd Ste 125
  Atlanta GA 30328
  770 448-2193

(G-16973)
WESTROCK RKT LLC
Also Called: Westrock Merchandising Disp
5930 Grassy Creek Blvd (27105-1205)
PHONE................................336 661-1700
EMP: 43
SALES (corp-wide): 20.31B **Publicly Held**
Web: www.westrock.com
SIC: **2653** Boxes, corrugated: made from purchased materials
HQ: Westrock Rkt, Llc
  1000 Abernathy Rd Ste 125
  Atlanta GA 30328
  770 448-2193

(G-16974)
WESTROCK RKT LLC
Alliance Display & Packg Div
5900a Grassy Creek Blvd (27105-1205)
PHONE................................336 661-7180
EMP: 161
SALES (corp-wide): 20.31B **Publicly Held**
Web: www.westrock.com
SIC: **2653** Hampers, solid fiber: made from purchased materials
HQ: Westrock Rkt, Llc
  1000 Abernathy Rd Ste 125
  Atlanta GA 30328
  770 448-2193

(G-16975)
WHAM BAM MONOGRAM
4050 Dresden Dr (27104-1532)
PHONE................................336 712-5109
Kasey Odom, *Prin*
EMP: 4 **EST:** 2016
SALES (est): 46.3K **Privately Held**
SIC: **2395** Embroidery and art needlework

(G-16976)
WILSON-COOK MEDICAL INC
5941 Grassy Creek Blvd (27105-1206)
PHONE................................336 744-0157
William Gibbons, *Pr*
EMP: 6 **EST:** 2016
SALES (est): 472.8K **Privately Held**
Web: www.cookmedical.com
SIC: **3841** Surgical and medical instruments

(G-16977)
WILSON-COOK MEDICAL INC
Also Called: Cook Endoscopy
4900 Bethania Station Rd (27105-1203)
P.O. Box 489 (47402-0489)
PHONE................................336 744-0157
EMP: 261
SIC: **3841** Diagnostic apparatus, medical

(G-16978)
WINSTN-SLEM CHRONICLE PUBG INC
1300 E 5th St (27101-4329)
P.O. Box 1636 (27102-1636)
PHONE................................336 722-8624
Ernest H Pitt, *Pr*
Ndubrisi Egemonye, *Stockholder*
Elaine L Pitt, *Sec*
Mike Pitt, *Genl Mgr*
Kevin Walker, *Prin*
EMP: 15 **EST:** 1974
SALES (est): 493.36K **Privately Held**
SIC: **2711** Newspapers, publishing and printing

(G-16979)
WINSTN-SLEM INDS FOR BLIND INC (PA)
Also Called: Ifb Solutions
7730 N Point Blvd (27106-3310)
PHONE................................336 759-0551
David Horton, *Ex Dir*
Daniel Boucher, *
◆ **EMP:** 500 **EST:** 1963
SQ FT: 160,000
SALES (est): 11.16MM
SALES (corp-wide): 11.16MM **Privately Held**
Web: www.ifbsolutions.org
SIC: **2515** 3021 2392 2253 Mattresses, containing felt, foam rubber, urethane, etc.; Protective footwear, rubber or plastic; Bags, laundry: made from purchased materials; Shirts(outerwear), knit

(G-16980)
WINSTON PRINTING COMPANY (PA)
Also Called: Winston Packaging Division
8095 N Point Blvd (27106-3283)
P.O. Box 11026 (27116-1026)
PHONE................................336 896-7631
James A Gordon, *Pr*
John Moore, *
Wayne Byrum, *
EMP: 97 **EST:** 1911
SQ FT: 75,000
SALES (est): 10.02MM
SALES (corp-wide): 10.02MM **Privately Held**
Web: www.winstonpackaging.com
SIC: **2759** Commercial printing, nec

(G-16981)
WINSTON SALEM ENGRAVING CO
446 Brookstown Ave (27101-5026)
P.O. Box 20036 (27120-0036)
PHONE................................336 725-4268
Richard M Mills, *Pr*
Glenn Mills, *Treas*
Trudy Sizemore, *Sec*
Glenda Mills, *VP*
EMP: 10 **EST:** 1964
SQ FT: 10,000
SALES (est): 847K **Privately Held**
Web: www.wsengraving.com
SIC: **2796** Platemaking services

(G-16982)
WINSTON SALEM JOURNAL
418 N Marshall St (27101-2979)
PHONE................................336 727-7211
David Stanfield, *Prin*
◆ **EMP:** 35 **EST:** 1885
SALES (est): 7.62MM **Privately Held**
Web: www.journalnow.com
SIC: **2711** Newspapers, publishing and printing

(G-16983)
WINSTON STEEL STAIR CO
216 Junia Ave (27127-3021)
PHONE................................336 721-0020
Steve Darnell, *Pr*
Tom Craver, *Treas*
EMP: 4 **EST:** 2008
SALES (est): 234.82K **Privately Held**
SIC: **3441** 3549 Fabricated structural metal; Metalworking machinery, nec

(G-16984)
WINSTON-SALEM CASKET COMPANY
4340 Indiana Ave (27105-2512)
PHONE................................336 661-1695
A W Bunch Iii, *Pr*
A W Bill Bunch Junior, *Pr*
EMP: 5 **EST:** 1948
SQ FT: 15,000
SALES (est): 386.3K **Privately Held**
SIC: **3995** 5087 Grave vaults, metal; Caskets

GEOGRAPHIC SECTION

Winterville - Pitt County (G-17012)

(G-16985)
WORTHINGTON CYLINDER CORP
1690 Lowery St (27101-5603)
PHONE.................................336 777-8600
EMP: 50
SALES (corp-wide): 4.92B **Publicly Held**
Web: www.worthingtonenterprises.com
SIC: 3443 Containers, shipping (bombs, etc.): metal plate
HQ: Worthington Cylinder Corporation
   200 W Old Wlson Bridge Rd
   Worthington OH 43085
   614 840-3210

(G-16986)
WRKCO INC
8080 N Point Blvd (27106-3204)
PHONE.................................336 759-7501
EMP: 5
SALES (corp-wide): 20.31B **Publicly Held**
SIC: 2631 Paperboard mills
HQ: Wrkco Inc.
   1000 Abernathy Rd Ste 12
   Atlanta GA 30328
   770 448-2193

(G-16987)
WRKCO INC
5900 Grassy Creek Blvd (27105-1205)
PHONE.................................770 448-2193
EMP: 39
SALES (corp-wide): 20.31B **Publicly Held**
SIC: 2631 Paperboard mills
HQ: Wrkco Inc.
   1000 Abernathy Rd Ste 12
   Atlanta GA 30328
   770 448-2193

(G-16988)
WRKCO INC
3946 Westpoint Blvd (27103-6719)
PHONE.................................336 765-7004
EMP: 5
SALES (corp-wide): 20.31B **Publicly Held**
SIC: 2631 5113 Paperboard mills; Corrugated and solid fiber boxes
HQ: Wrkco Inc.
   1000 Abernathy Rd Ste 12
   Atlanta GA 30328
   770 448-2193

(G-16989)
XPRES LLC
111 Cloverleaf Dr (27103-6715)
PHONE.................................336 245-1596
Michael Wallach, *
◆ EMP: 40 EST: 2010
SQ FT: 30,000
SALES (est): 6.66MM **Privately Held**
Web: www.xpres.com
SIC: 2752 Commercial printing, lithographic

(G-16990)
YONTZ & SONS PAINTING INC
3803 S Main St (27127-6044)
P.O. Box 282 (27373-0282)
PHONE.................................336 784-7099
Paul Yontz Junior, *Pr*
EMP: 9 EST: 1970
SQ FT: 2,400
SALES (est): 270.76K **Privately Held**
SIC: 1721 3471 Commercial painting; Plating and polishing

(G-16991)
ZOES KITCHEN INC
205 S Stratford Rd (27103-1871)
PHONE.................................336 748-0587
EMP: 25
SALES (corp-wide): 728.7MM **Publicly Held**
Web: www.zoeskitchen.com
SIC: 5812 3841 Restaurant, family: independent; Catheters
HQ: Zoe's Kitchen, Inc.
   5760 State Highway 121 # 25
   Plano TX 75024

(G-16992)
ZOOM APPAREL INC (PA)
303 S Broad St (27101-5022)
PHONE.................................336 993-9666
Jeffrey Federico, *Pr*
Christine Federico, *VP*
EMP: 4 EST: 2006
SQ FT: 6,000
SALES (est): 1.04MM **Privately Held**
Web: www.zoomapparel.com
SIC: 2759 2395 Screen printing; Embroidery and art needlework

Winterville
Pitt County

(G-16993)
A1 AWARDS & PROMOTIONS INC
2580 Railroad St (28590-9720)
PHONE.................................252 321-7701
Timothy Avery, *Pr*
EMP: 6 EST: 2019
SALES (est): 207.26K **Privately Held**
SIC: 2759 Screen printing

(G-16994)
ANCHORED SCENTS LLC
2842 Cresset Dr (28590-6620)
PHONE.................................910 709-1582
Richard J Cox, *Owner*
EMP: 5 EST: 2016
SALES (est): 89.27K **Privately Held**
SIC: 3999 Candles

(G-16995)
BUCK SUPPLY COMPANY INC
Also Called: Buck Marine Diesel
3060 Old Highway 11 (28590)
PHONE.................................252 215-1252
Kenneth Buck, *Pr*
Cindy Buck, *Sec*
EMP: 6 EST: 1952
SQ FT: 14,000
SALES (est): 607.22K **Privately Held**
Web: www.buckdiesel.com
SIC: 3519 Engines, diesel and semi-diesel or dual-fuel

(G-16996)
CHARLES WHITE WOODWORKING
3024 Church Street Ext (28590-8715)
PHONE.................................252 714-9124
Charles White, *Owner*
EMP: 5 EST: 2008
SALES (est): 213.63K **Privately Held**
Web: www.whitewoodworking.com
SIC: 2431 Millwork

(G-16997)
CLARIOS LLC
Also Called: Johnson Controls
4125 Bayswater Rd (28590-9818)
PHONE.................................252 754-0782
EMP: 34
SALES (corp-wide): 4.48B **Privately Held**
Web: www.clarios.com
SIC: 2531 Seats, automobile
HQ: Clarios, Llc
   5757 N Green Bay Ave
   Milwaukee WI 53209

(G-16998)
DADDY MIKES LLC
1211 Fellowes Ct (28590-2302)
PHONE.................................252 327-1840
Michael Clark, *Managing Member*
EMP: 4 EST: 2021
SALES (est): 62.38K **Privately Held**
SIC: 2099 Food preparations, nec

(G-16999)
DOWNEAST CABINETS WILLIAM BRYA
2543 Circle Dr (28590-8876)
PHONE.................................252 414-7730
William Brya, *Prin*
EMP: 5 EST: 2013
SALES (est): 67.13K **Privately Held**
SIC: 2434 Wood kitchen cabinets

(G-17000)
EW PAINTING LLC
3808 E Vancroft Cir Unit M6 (28590-5858)
PHONE.................................252 375-1403
EMP: 4 EST: 2021
SALES (est): 45K **Privately Held**
SIC: 3479 Painting, coating, and hot dipping

(G-17001)
GREENVILLE READY MIX CONCRETE (PA)
Also Called: Greenville Rdymx Dpd Team Con
5039 Nc 11 S (28590-7764)
P.O. Box 1639 (28590-1639)
PHONE.................................252 756-0119
Derek P Dunn, *Pr*
Elizabeth K Dunn, *Sec*
Cindy H Rhue, *Sec*
EMP: 20 EST: 1982
SQ FT: 3,000
SALES (est): 18.38MM
SALES (corp-wide): 18.38MM **Privately Held**
SIC: 5032 3273 Concrete mixtures; Ready-mixed concrete

(G-17002)
HENDERSON & KIRKLAND INC
Also Called: Kitchen & Bath Decisions
223 Forlines Rd (28590-8509)
PHONE.................................252 355-0224
Kirk Copeland, *Pr*
Sid Copeland Junior, *VP*
EMP: 9 EST: 1988
SQ FT: 13,500
SALES (est): 327.16K **Privately Held**
Web: www.kitchenandbathdecisions.com
SIC: 5211 2434 2431 Cabinets, kitchen; Wood kitchen cabinets; Millwork

(G-17003)
HYDRA CUT LLC
4745 Reedy Branch Rd (28590-9080)
PHONE.................................252 814-1654
EMP: 6 EST: 2018
SALES (est): 475.51K **Privately Held**
Web: www.hydra-cut.com
SIC: 3599 Machine shop, jobbing and repair

(G-17004)
JBR PROPERTIES OF GREENVILLE INC
Also Called: Roberts Company, The
133 Forlines Rd (28590-8508)
PHONE.................................252 355-9353
▲ EMP: 730 EST: 1977
SALES (est): 47.21MM **Privately Held**
SIC: 1541 3443 Industrial buildings, new construction, nec; Fabricated plate work (boiler shop)

(G-17005)
LIGHTHOUSE LED
4776 Reedy Branch Rd (28590-9080)
PHONE.................................252 756-1158
EMP: 4 EST: 2015
SALES (est): 132.25K **Privately Held**
Web: www.thelighthouseled.com
SIC: 3993 Signs and advertising specialties

(G-17006)
MCCABES COSTUMES LLC
4054 S Memorial Dr Ste O (28590-8690)
P.O. Box 694 (28590-0694)
PHONE.................................252 295-7691
EMP: 5 EST: 2020
SALES (est): 42.55K **Privately Held**
Web: www.mccabescostumes.com
SIC: 2389 Costumes

(G-17007)
MIKE LUSZCZ
3424 Sagewood Ct (28590-5500)
PHONE.................................252 717-6282
Mike Luszcz, *Prin*
EMP: 5 EST: 2010
SALES (est): 73.46K **Privately Held**
Web: www.mlboatworksrc.com
SIC: 3732 Boatbuilding and repairing

(G-17008)
MORGAN PRINTERS INC
4120 Bayswater Rd (28590-9817)
P.O. Box 2126 (27836-0126)
PHONE.................................252 355-5588
Lydia Morgan, *CEO*
Jack Morgan, *Pr*
Parker Morgan, *Mgr*
EMP: 13 EST: 1964
SQ FT: 11,600
SALES (est): 2.38MM **Privately Held**
Web: www.morganprinters.com
SIC: 2752 Offset printing

(G-17009)
MR HOME GENIUS LLC
2072 Sinmar Ln (28590-8457)
PHONE.................................252 902-4663
EMP: 5 EST: 2020
SALES (est): 121.92K **Privately Held**
Web: www.mrhomegenius.com
SIC: 3732 Boatbuilding and repairing

(G-17010)
NOBLE BROTHERS LOGGING COMPANY
237 W Meath Dr (28590-9184)
PHONE.................................252 355-2587
Larry Noble, *Pr*
Roger Noble, *Prin*
EMP: 4 EST: 1985
SALES (est): 370.67K **Privately Held**
SIC: 2411 Logging camps and contractors

(G-17011)
PHOENIX SIGN PROS INC
4409 Corey Rd (28590-9269)
PHONE.................................252 756-5685
Edward Lee Thornton, *Owner*
EMP: 4 EST: 2017
SALES (est): 50.69K **Privately Held**
Web: www.phoenixsignpros.net
SIC: 3993 Signs and advertising specialties

(G-17012)
ROYALKIND LLC
2131 Jubilee Ln (28590-9706)
PHONE.................................252 355-7484
Julia Lewis Fagundus, *Prin*
EMP: 5 EST: 2018
SALES (est): 105.09K **Privately Held**

Winterville - Pitt County (G-17013) — GEOGRAPHIC SECTION

SIC: 2741 Miscellaneous publishing

(G-17013)
S & S REPAIR SERVICE INC
1196 Pocosin Rd (28590-7137)
P.O. Box 102 (28590-0102)
PHONE..................252 756-5989
George T Savage, *Pr*
Claudia Savage, *Prin*
EMP: 18 EST: 1969
SQ FT: 10,000
SALES (est): 528.87K **Privately Held**
Web: www.siteboxstorage.com
SIC: 7699 3599 Construction equipment repair; Machine shop, jobbing and repair

(G-17014)
STUART RYAN KENT & CO
223 Forlines Rd (28590-8509)
P.O. Box 3752 (27836-1752)
PHONE..................252 916-8226
Stuart Kent, *Owner*
EMP: 4 EST: 2015
SALES (est): 127.59K **Privately Held**
SIC: 5021 3999 Beds; Atomizers, toiletry

(G-17015)
TRC ACQUISITION LLC
133 Forlines Rd (28590-8508)
PHONE..................252 355-9353
D Chris Bailey, *Managing Member*
Doyal Lee Barnett, *
Monty Glover, *
EMP: 505 EST: 2008
SALES (est): 25.83MM **Privately Held**
SIC: 1541 3443 Industrial buildings, new construction, nec; Fabricated plate work (boiler shop)

(G-17016)
UPPER RM OUTREACH MINISTRY INC
169 Boyd St (28590-7041)
PHONE..................252 364-8756
EMP: 4 EST: 2010
SALES (est): 51K **Privately Held**
SIC: 3131 Uppers

(G-17017)
VIATICUS INC
4104 Sterling Trace Dr (28590-9321)
PHONE..................252 258-4679
Mark Weitzel, *Prin*
EMP: 7 EST: 2010
SALES (est): 153.84K **Privately Held**
Web: www.viaticuspublishing.com
SIC: 2741 Miscellaneous publishing

(G-17018)
WINTERVILLE MACHINE WORKS INC
Also Called: Wmw Marine
2672 Mill St (28590-9228)
P.O. Box 520 (28590-0520)
PHONE..................252 756-2130
John R Carroll, *Pr*
Ted Cox, *
Greis Lane, *
▲ EMP: 65 EST: 1957
SQ FT: 40,000
SALES (est): 9.04MM **Privately Held**
Web: www.wmwworks.com
SIC: 3429 3599 3732 Marine hardware; Machine shop, jobbing and repair; Boatbuilding and repairing

(G-17019)
WORKFLOWONE
3914 Sterling Pointe Dr Unit 1 (28590-9203)
PHONE..................252 215-8880
Ryan Stroupe, *Prin*
EMP: 5 EST: 2010
SALES (est): 98.59K **Privately Held**
SIC: 2759 Commercial printing, nec

Winton
Hertford County

(G-17020)
ALFINITI INC
600 N Metcalf St (27986)
PHONE..................252 358-5811
Jean Pare, *Pr*
Richard James, *
▲ EMP: 75 EST: 2006
SQ FT: 325,000
SALES (est): 29.95MM
SALES (corp-wide): 2.1MM **Privately Held**
Web: www.alfiniti.com
SIC: 3354 Aluminum extruded products
HQ: Spectube Inc.
1152 Rue De La Manic
Chicoutimi QC G7K 1
418 696-2545

(G-17021)
CRMP INC
115 Hwy 158 W (27986)
P.O. Box 189 (27986-0189)
PHONE..................252 358-5461
Charles Harrell, *Genl Mgr*
EMP: 9 EST: 2005
SALES (est): 821.5K **Privately Held**
Web: www.crmpinc.com
SIC: 3273 Ready-mixed concrete

Woodland
Northampton County

(G-17022)
L & B CUSTOM WOODWORKING
736 Nc Highway 35 (27897-9667)
PHONE..................252 578-8955
James Pulley, *Owner*
EMP: 5 EST: 2004
SALES (est): 70.47K **Privately Held**
SIC: 2431 Millwork

Woodleaf
Rowan County

(G-17023)
MARIETTA MARTIN MATERIALS INC
Also Called: Martin Marietta Aggregates
720 Quarry Rd (27054-9365)
PHONE..................704 278-2218
Mike Cameron, *Mgr*
EMP: 5
Web: www.martinmarietta.com
SIC: 1422 1423 Crushed and broken limestone; Crushed and broken granite
PA: Martin Marietta Materials Inc
4123 Parklake Ave
Raleigh NC 27612

(G-17024)
PIEDMONT PALLET & CONT INC
667 Hendrix Farm Circle Ln (27054)
P.O. Box 400 (27054-0400)
PHONE..................336 284-6302
Mark Lottes, *Pr*
Beverly Lottes, *VP*
EMP: 4 EST: 1995
SQ FT: 3,800
SALES (est): 487.2K **Privately Held**
SIC: 2448 Pallets, wood

Wrightsville Beach
New Hanover County

(G-17025)
GREENFIELD ENERGY LLC
213 Seacrest Dr (28480-1731)
PHONE..................910 509-1805
Robin H Spinks, *Managing Member*
EMP: 10 EST: 2007
SALES (est): 1.4MM **Privately Held**
Web: www.consultgreenfield.net
SIC: 3621 7389 Frequency converters (electric generators); Business Activities at Non-Commercial Site

(G-17026)
MARINEMAX OF NORTH CAROLINA
Also Called: Marinemax
130 Short St (28480-1764)
PHONE..................910 256-8100
Bill Mcgill, *Pr*
EMP: 22 EST: 1992
SQ FT: 5,000
SALES (est): 5.39MM
SALES (corp-wide): 2.39B **Publicly Held**
Web: www.marinemax.com
SIC: 5551 7699 3732 Motor boat dealers; Nautical repair services; Boatbuilding and repairing
PA: Marinemax, Inc.
2600 Mccormick Dr Ste 200
Clearwater FL 33759
727 531-1700

(G-17027)
PRECISION GENOMICS INC
812 Lumina Ave S (28480-3104)
PHONE..................843 737-1911
Ody Duea, *Prin*
EMP: 6 EST: 2018
SALES (est): 74.42K **Privately Held**
SIC: 2835 Microbiology and virology diagnostic products

(G-17028)
STUMP PRINTING CO INC
Also Called: Stump's
525 Lumina Ave S (28480-6101)
PHONE..................260 723-5171
N Shepard Moyle, *CEO*
Wendy Moyle, *
◆ EMP: 185 EST: 1926
SALES (est): 20.87MM **Privately Held**
SIC: 5199 2679 5961 2759 Novelties, paper; Novelties, paper: made from purchased material; Catalog sales; Commercial printing, nec

Yadkinville
Yadkin County

(G-17029)
ABBOTT PRODUCTS INC
1617 Fern Valley Rd (27055-6270)
PHONE..................336 463-3135
Fred Smith, *Pr*
Richard Jacobson, *Ch Bd*
Glen Jacobson, *VP*
EMP: 20 EST: 1951
SQ FT: 15,000
SALES (est): 1.79MM **Privately Held**
Web: www.abbottbingoproducts.com
SIC: 3451 Screw machine products

(G-17030)
ADVANTAGE MACHINERY SVCS INC (PA)
Also Called: McLoud Trucking & Rigging
1407 Us 601 Hwy (27055-6358)
P.O. Box 1848 (27055-1848)
PHONE..................336 463-4700
EMP: 32 EST: 1992
SALES (est): 8.49MM **Privately Held**
Web: www.amsrigging.com
SIC: 7699 4213 1799 1796 Industrial machinery and equipment repair; Heavy hauling, nec; Rigging and scaffolding; Machine moving and rigging

(G-17031)
AUSTIN COMPANY OF GREENSBORO
Also Called: Austin Company, The
2100 Hoots Rd (27055-6654)
P.O. Box 2320 (27055-2320)
PHONE..................336 468-2851
James R Austin Iii, *Pr*
Dwayne Hunt, *
G Kevin Austin, *
Robin E Ludlow, *
Kristie Urbine Stkldr, *Prin*
EMP: 145 EST: 1964
SQ FT: 6,000
SALES (est): 23.25MM **Privately Held**
Web: www.austinenclosures.com
SIC: 3699 3644 Electrical equipment and supplies, nec; Junction boxes, electric

(G-17032)
B&G FOODS INC
500 Nonnis Way (27055)
P.O. Box 1489 (27055-1489)
PHONE..................336 849-7000
Larry Fisk, *Mgr*
EMP: 50
SALES (corp-wide): 2.06B **Publicly Held**
Web: www.bgfoods.com
SIC: 2052 Cookies and crackers
PA: B&G Foods, Inc.
4 Gatehall Dr Ste 110
Parsippany NJ 07054
973 401-6500

(G-17033)
BLUE RIDGE LBR LOG & TIMBER CO
2854 Old Us 421 Hwy W (27055-7146)
P.O. Box 2374 (27055-2374)
PHONE..................336 961-5211
Thomas Perry, *Pr*
Dennis Billing, *Sec*
EMP: 17 EST: 1998
SALES (est): 474.36K **Privately Held**
SIC: 2491 5211 2426 2421 Structural lumber and timber, treated wood; Lumber products; Hardwood dimension and flooring mills; Sawmills and planing mills, general

(G-17034)
BRIGGS-SHAFFNER ACQUISITION CO (PA)
Also Called: Briggs-Shaffner Company
1448 Us 601 Hwy (27055-6358)
P.O. Box 67 (27055-0067)
PHONE..................336 463-4272
Emmitte Winslow, *Pr*
F John Mazur, *VP*
L Joe Bogan, *VP*
Carol M Winslow, *Sec*
◆ EMP: 10 EST: 1892
SQ FT: 80,000
SALES (est): 9.13MM **Privately Held**
Web: www.briggsbeams.com
SIC: 3552 3365 3599 7699 Textile machinery; Aluminum and aluminum-based alloy castings; Machine shop, jobbing and repair; Industrial machinery and equipment repair

GEOGRAPHIC SECTION

Yadkinville - Yadkin County (G-17060)

(G-17035)
CAROLINA POWDER COATING
3753 Deer Creek Ln (27055-5816)
PHONE.................................336 934-6102
Joseph Wooley, *Prin*
EMP: 5 **EST:** 2018
SALES (est): 148.12K **Privately Held**
Web: www.carolinapowdercoating.net
SIC: 3479 Coating of metals and formed products

(G-17036)
DAVIS CUSTOM CABINETS
2545 Union Cross Church Rd (27055-7315)
PHONE.................................336 961-2817
Dara Davis, *Owner*
EMP: 5 **EST:** 2009
SALES (est): 76.51K **Privately Held**
Web: www.daviscustomcabinets.com
SIC: 2434 Wood kitchen cabinets

(G-17037)
DIVERSIFIED FOAM INC (PA)
1813 Us 601 Hwy (27055-6347)
P.O. Box 1358 (27055-1358)
PHONE.................................336 463-5512
Brent Matthews, *Pr*
W Lawrence Green, *
Patricia Matthews, *
Bobby Holland, *
EMP: 34 **EST:** 1983
SQ FT: 5,400
SALES (est): 4.78MM
SALES (corp-wide): 4.78MM **Privately Held**
Web: www.diversifiedfoamusa.com
SIC: 3086 Packaging and shipping materials, foamed plastics

(G-17038)
DORSETT TECHNOLOGIES INC (PA)
100 Woodlyn Dr (27055-6673)
P.O. Box 1339 (27055-1339)
PHONE.................................855 387-2232
EMP: 43 **EST:** 1956
SALES (est): 12.51MM
SALES (corp-wide): 12.51MM **Privately Held**
Web: www.dorsett-tech.com
SIC: 3822 Air conditioning and refrigeration controls

(G-17039)
EVEREADY MIX CONCRETE CO INC
421 Old Hwy E (27055)
P.O. Box 577 (27055-0577)
PHONE.................................336 961-6688
David Adams, *Pr*
Charles Adams, *VP*
EMP: 8 **EST:** 1971
SQ FT: 400
SALES (est): 905.21K **Privately Held**
SIC: 3273 Ready-mixed concrete

(G-17040)
HIBCO PLASTICS INC
1820 Us 601 Hwy (27055-6347)
P.O. Box 157 (27055-0157)
PHONE.................................336 463-2391
Daniel S Pavlansky, *Ch*
Mark Pavlansky, *
Dan Pavlansky, *
Keith Pavlansky, *
Jon Pavlansky, *
▲ **EMP:** 45 **EST:** 1957
SQ FT: 120,000
SALES (est): 12.38MM **Privately Held**
Web: www.hibco.com

SIC: 3086 5199 2679 3053 Insulation or cushioning material, foamed plastics; Automobile fabrics; Building, insulating, and packaging paper; Gaskets; packing and sealing devices

(G-17041)
IF DISHER MEAT PROCESSING
Also Called: Disher Packing Co
1437 Old Stage Rd (27055-6730)
PHONE.................................336 463-2907
Ida Mae Disher, *Owner*
Chris Disher, *Sec*
EMP: 5 **EST:** 1970
SALES (est): 396.73K **Privately Held**
SIC: 2011 Meat packing plants

(G-17042)
J S MYERS CO INC
2129 Ray T Moore Rd (27055-6819)
PHONE.................................336 463-5572
Carolyn Myers, *Pr*
Johnny Myers, *Sec*
EMP: 10 **EST:** 1974
SQ FT: 4,320
SALES (est): 843.73K **Privately Held**
SIC: 4212 3273 1794 Dump truck haulage; Ready-mixed concrete; Excavation and grading, building construction

(G-17043)
LOFLIN HANDLE CO INC
2625 Courtney Huntsville Rd (27055-6618)
PHONE.................................336 463-2422
J H Loflin Junior, *Pr*
Elizabeth Gonzales, *VP*
EMP: 10 **EST:** 1960
SQ FT: 12,000
SALES (est): 230.32K **Privately Held**
SIC: 2499 0132 5085 Handles, wood; Tobacco; Tools, nec

(G-17044)
LYDALL INC
2029 Anna Dr (27055-5276)
PHONE.................................336 468-1323
EMP: 7
Web: www.lydall.com
SIC: 2297 Nonwoven fabrics
HQ: Lydall, Inc.
    1 Colonial Rd
    Manchester CT 06042
    860 646-1233

(G-17045)
MC CONTROLS LLC
100 Woodlyn Dr (27055-6673)
P.O. Box 1339 (27055-1339)
PHONE.................................336 518-1303
Mason Miller, *CEO*
EMP: 5 **EST:** 2019
SALES (est): 104.27K **Privately Held**
SIC: 3822 1711 1731 Environmental controls; Heating and air conditioning contractors; General electrical contractor

(G-17046)
PERDUE FARMS INC
Also Called: Perdue Farms
806 W Main St (27055-7806)
PHONE.................................336 679-7733
Clyde Weathers, *Brnch Mgr*
EMP: 82
SALES (corp-wide): 1.24B **Privately Held**
Web: www.perdue.com
SIC: 2015 Poultry slaughtering and processing
PA: Perdue Farms Incorporated
    31149 Old Ocean City Rd
    Salisbury MD 21804
    800 473-7383

(G-17047)
QUALITY STEEL FABRICATION INC
1301 Union Cross Church Rd (27055-7303)
P.O. Box 1902 (27055-1902)
PHONE.................................336 961-2670
EMP: 7 **EST:** 1985
SALES (est): 752.45K **Privately Held**
SIC: 3441 Fabricated structural metal

(G-17048)
REBB INDUSTRIES INC
1617 Fern Valley Rd (27055-6270)
PHONE.................................336 463-2311
Richard Jacobson, *Pr*
EMP: 25 **EST:** 1978
SQ FT: 32,000
SALES (est): 808.64K **Privately Held**
SIC: 3599 Machine shop, jobbing and repair
PA: Viewriver Machine Corporation
    1617 Fern Valley Rd
    Yadkinville NC 27055

(G-17049)
S H WOODWORKING
1316 Travis Rd (27055-6271)
PHONE.................................336 463-2885
Scott Holden, *Prin*
EMP: 5 **EST:** 2011
SALES (est): 63.16K **Privately Held**
SIC: 2431 Millwork

(G-17050)
SHALLOWFORD FARMS POPCORN INC
Also Called: Shallowford Farms Popcorn
3732 Hartman Rd (27055-5638)
PHONE.................................336 463-5938
Booe Caswell, *Prin*
EMP: 6 **EST:** 1989
SQ FT: 1,500
SALES (est): 498.57K **Privately Held**
Web: www.shallowfordfarmspopcorn.com
SIC: 5441 2099 2096 Popcorn, including caramel corn; Food preparations, nec; Potato chips and similar snacks

(G-17051)
STEELMAN MILLING COMPANY INC
1517 Us 601 Hwy (27055-6344)
PHONE.................................336 463-5586
Max B Steelman, *Pr*
Betty Steelman, *Sec*
EMP: 6 **EST:** 1953
SQ FT: 7,000
SALES (est): 630.25K **Privately Held**
Web: www.steelmanmill.com
SIC: 5999 2048 5251 Feed and farm supply; Prepared feeds, nec; Chainsaws

(G-17052)
STRAIGHTLINE WOODWORKS
2845 Mize Rd (27055-6304)
PHONE.................................336 469-7029
Jeffery Wagoner, *Prin*
EMP: 4 **EST:** 2018
SALES (est): 54.13K **Privately Held**
SIC: 2431 Millwork

(G-17053)
SWEET HME CAROLNA VINYRD & WIN
3429 Old Us 421 Hwy E (27055-8026)
PHONE.................................336 469-9905
John Koren, *Prin*
EMP: 4 **EST:** 2013
SALES (est): 92.36K **Privately Held**
Web: www.sweethomecarolinawinery.com
SIC: 2084 Wines

(G-17054)
SWEET HOME YADKIN INC
1024 Brookhaven Ln (27055-5179)
PHONE.................................336 414-9822
Maria G Calderon, *Prin*
EMP: 5 **EST:** 2014
SALES (est): 209.72K **Privately Held**
SIC: 2084 Wines

(G-17055)
TMP OF NC INC
1201 Old Stage Rd (27055-6728)
PHONE.................................336 463-3225
Randall Simmons, *Pr*
EMP: 6 **EST:** 2000
SQ FT: 6,000
SALES (est): 600K **Privately Held**
SIC: 3599 Machine shop, jobbing and repair

(G-17056)
TOMMAR PUBLISHING INC
2937 Lone Hickory Rd (27055-6254)
PHONE.................................336 463-2690
Myron Gough, *Prin*
EMP: 7 **EST:** 2010
SALES (est): 71K **Privately Held**
Web: www.hickorylivingmagazine.com
SIC: 2741 Miscellaneous publishing

(G-17057)
TRIAD PRINT PROMO LLC
5336 Courtney Huntsville Rd (27055-8636)
PHONE.................................336 416-3488
EMP: 4 **EST:** 2018
SALES (est): 129.62K **Privately Held**
SIC: 2752 Commercial printing, lithographic

(G-17058)
UNIFI INC
1032 Unifi Industrial Rd (27055)
P.O. Box 698 (27055-0698)
PHONE.................................336 679-3830
Robert Snider, *Mgr*
EMP: 160
SALES (corp-wide): 623.53MM **Publicly Held**
Web: www.unifi.com
SIC: 2282 2281 Textured yarn; Yarn spinning mills
PA: Unifi, Inc.
    7201 W Friendly Ave
    Greensboro NC 27410
    336 294-4410

(G-17059)
UNIFI MANUFACTURING INC
Warehouse 2
601 E Main St (27055-8136)
PHONE.................................336 427-1515
Larry Fisk, *Pr*
EMP: 1139
SALES (corp-wide): 623.53MM **Publicly Held**
Web: www.unifi.com
SIC: 2281 Yarn spinning mills
HQ: Unifi Manufacturing, Inc.
    7201 W Friendly Ave
    Greensboro NC 27410

(G-17060)
UNIFI MANUFACTURING INC
1032 Unifi Industrial Rd (27055)
PHONE.................................336 679-8891
Larry Fisk, *Pr*
EMP: 1139
SALES (corp-wide): 623.53MM **Publicly Held**
Web: www.unifi.com
SIC: 2281 Nylon yarn, spinning of staple
HQ: Unifi Manufacturing, Inc.

Yadkinville - Yadkin County (G-17061)

7201 W Friendly Ave
Greensboro NC 27410

(G-17061)
VIEWRIVER MACHINE CORPORATION (PA)
Also Called: R E B B Industries
1617 Fern Valley Rd (27055-6270)
PHONE.....................336 463-2311
Richard Jacobson, *Pr*
Lee Wilmath, *
EMP: 25 **EST:** 1978
SALES (est): 4.72MM **Privately Held**
Web: nc-yadkinville.pacifica.org.au
SIC: 3599 Machine shop, jobbing and repair

(G-17062)
WARDEN SIGNS & SERVICE LLC
2249 Neelie Rd (27055-6305)
PHONE.....................336 416-4029
EMP: 4 **EST:** 2016
SALES (est): 50.69K **Privately Held**
SIC: 3993 Signs and advertising specialties

(G-17063)
WILO INCORPORATED (DH)
350 W Maple St (27055-7700)
P.O. Box 309 (27055-0309)
PHONE.....................336 679-4440
John W Willingham, *Pr*
▲ **EMP:** 30 **EST:** 1922
SQ FT: 135,000
SALES (est): 10.22MM
SALES (corp-wide): 95.81MM **Privately Held**
Web: www.inderamills.com
SIC: 2322 2341 Men's and boy's underwear and nightwear; Women's and children's undergarments
HQ: Intradeco Apparel, Inc.
9500 Nw 108th Ave
Medley FL 33178
305 264-8888

(G-17064)
YADKIN LUMBER COMPANY INC
800 N State St (27055-5258)
P.O. Box 729 (27055-0729)
PHONE.....................336 679-2432
Charles H Dinkins, *Pr*
Carolyn Long, *Sec*
EMP: 16 **EST:** 1949
SQ FT: 7,500
SALES (est): 901.86K **Privately Held**
SIC: 5211 2421 Lumber and other building materials; Lumber: rough, sawed, or planed

---

Yanceyville
Caswell County

(G-17065)
ROYAL TEXTILE MILLS INC
Also Called: Duke Athletic Products
929 Firetower Rd (27379-9381)
P.O. Box 250 (27379-0250)
PHONE.....................336 694-4121
Mark V Atwater, *Pr*
W David Atwater, *
Jerry L Cole, *
EMP: 75 **EST:** 1948
SQ FT: 36,000
SALES (est): 8.56MM **Privately Held**
Web: www.dukeathletic-tactical.com
SIC: 2322 2253 3949 2321 Underwear, men's and boys': made from purchased materials; T-shirts and tops, knit; Protective sporting equipment; Men's and boy's furnishings

---

Youngsville
Franklin County

(G-17066)
AMCOR PHRM PACKG USA LLC
Also Called: Wheaton Plastic Operations
111 Wheaton Ave (27596-9415)
P.O. Box 579 (27596-0579)
PHONE.....................919 556-9715
Julian Stewart, *Mgr*
EMP: 52
SALES (corp-wide): 14.69B **Privately Held**
SIC: 3085 Plastics bottles
HQ: Amcor Pharmaceutical Packaging Usa, Llc
625 Sharp St N
Millville NJ 08332
856 327-1540

(G-17067)
ANDRITZ FABRICS AND ROLLS INC
51 Flex Way (27596-7848)
PHONE.....................919 556-7235
Thomas Gutierrez, *Brnch Mgr*
EMP: 13
SALES (corp-wide): 7.83B **Privately Held**
Web: www.andritz.com
SIC: 3069 Printers' rolls and blankets: rubber or rubberized fabric
HQ: Andritz Fabrics And Rolls Inc.
8521 Six Forks Rd
Raleigh NC 27615
919 526-1400

(G-17068)
ATLANTIC COAST CABINET DISTRS
Also Called: ACC Distributors
150 Weathers Ct (27596-7844)
P.O. Box 1257 (27596-1257)
PHONE.....................919 554-8165
William A Konkle Iii, *Pr*
William A Konkle Junior, *VP*
Michelle Konkle, *
EMP: 25 **EST:** 1991
SQ FT: 68,000
SALES (est): 4.13MM **Privately Held**
Web: www.atlanticcoastcabinets.com
SIC: 2434 Wood kitchen cabinets

(G-17069)
B2RV2WOODWORKS
30 Canter Gable Pl (27596-7747)
PHONE.....................304 578-9881
Richard Wells, *Prin*
EMP: 4 **EST:** 2018
SALES (est): 54.13K **Privately Held**
SIC: 2431 Millwork

(G-17070)
BACHSTEIN CONSULTING LLC
70 Mosswood Blvd Ste 200 (27596-7990)
PHONE.....................410 322-4917
EMP: 6 **EST:** 2017
SALES (est): 514.7K **Privately Held**
Web: www.bachsteinconsulting.com
SIC: 8711 8748 7373 3484 Consulting engineer; Systems engineering consultant, ex. computer or professional; Computer-aided engineering (CAE) systems service; Guns (firearms) or gun parts, 30 mm. and below

(G-17071)
BESI MACHINING LLC
95 Cypress Dr (27596-8795)
P.O. Box 40363 (27629-0363)
PHONE.....................919 218-9241
EMP: 10 **EST:** 2016
SALES (est): 668.89K **Privately Held**
Web: www.besimachining.com
SIC: 7699 3559 Industrial machinery and equipment repair; Special industry machinery, nec

(G-17072)
BUILDERS FIRSTSOURCE INC
45 Mosswood Blvd (27596-7802)
P.O. Box 1017 (27596-1017)
PHONE.....................919 562-6601
Craig Cornelius, *Genl Mgr*
EMP: 9
SALES (corp-wide): 17.1B **Publicly Held**
Web: www.bldr.com
SIC: 5211 2431 5031 Millwork and lumber; Millwork; Lumber, plywood, and millwork
PA: Builders Firstsource, Inc.
6031 Connection Dr # 400
Irving TX 75039
214 880-3500

(G-17073)
CANYON STONE INC
409 Northbrook Dr (27596-7662)
PHONE.....................919 880-3273
Canyon Stone, *Brnch Mgr*
EMP: 12
SALES (corp-wide): 4.9MM **Privately Held**
Web: www.estoneworks.com
SIC: 3272 Stone, cast concrete
PA: Canyon Stone, Inc.
550 E Old Highway 56 B
Olathe KS 66061
913 254-9300

(G-17074)
CAPTIVE-AIRE SYSTEMS INC
360 Northbrook Dr (27596-7853)
PHONE.....................919 887-2721
Robert Luddy, *Prin*
EMP: 139
SALES (corp-wide): 485.13MM **Privately Held**
Web: www.captiveaire.com
SIC: 3444 Restaurant sheet metalwork
PA: Captive-Aire Systems, Inc.
4641 Paragon Park Rd # 104
Raleigh NC 27616
919 882-2410

(G-17075)
CAROLINA MACHINING FABRICATION
Also Called: Cmfi
321 N Nassau St (27596-9209)
P.O. Box 1217 (27596-1217)
PHONE.....................919 554-9700
Muhammed Asim, *Pr*
EMP: 4 **EST:** 2009
SQ FT: 770
SALES (est): 759.8K **Privately Held**
SIC: 3441 7699 1761 Fabricated structural metal; Industrial machinery and equipment repair; Sheet metal work, nec

(G-17076)
CAROLINA RESOURCE CORP
850 Park Ave (27596-9472)
PHONE.....................919 562-0200
EMP: 16 **EST:** 1978
SALES (est): 2.32MM **Privately Held**
Web: www.carolinaresource.com
SIC: 3544 3599 Special dies, tools, jigs, and fixtures; Machine shop, jobbing and repair

(G-17077)
CIRCUIT BOARD ASSEMBLERS INC
130 Mosswood Blvd (27596-8680)
PHONE.....................919 556-7881
Tom Albright, *Pr*
Tom Albright, *Ch*
Carol Albright, *
E C Sykes, *
EMP: 160 **EST:** 1985
SQ FT: 15,000
SALES (est): 13.13MM **Privately Held**
SIC: 3672 Printed circuit boards

(G-17078)
DOWN RANGE ARMORY INC
5240 Nc 96 Hwy W Ste 104 (27596-7758)
PHONE.....................919 749-5820
EMP: 4 **EST:** 2018
SALES (est): 88.22K **Privately Held**
SIC: 3489 Ordnance and accessories, nec

(G-17079)
ETS
928 Nc 96 Hwy E (27596-8857)
PHONE.....................919 556-7899
Andy Mcgee, *Mgr*
EMP: 4 **EST:** 2018
SALES (est): 125.92K **Privately Held**
SIC: 1311 Crude petroleum and natural gas

(G-17080)
EZ SIGN SERVICE
941 Us 1 Hwy (27596-7862)
PHONE.....................919 554-4300
EMP: 4 **EST:** 2017
SALES (est): 95.97K **Privately Held**
Web: www.ezsignservice.com
SIC: 3993 Signs and advertising specialties

(G-17081)
FRANKLIN LOGISTICAL SERVICES INC
Also Called: Welsh Paper Company
112 Franklin Park Dr (27596-9400)
P.O. Box 1529 (27588-1529)
PHONE.....................919 556-6711
▲ **EMP:** 100
SIC: 5113 3086 Paper, wrapping or coarse, and products; Packaging and shipping materials, foamed plastics

(G-17082)
GLENN TORRANCE MODELS LLC
50 Ward Dr (27596-7633)
PHONE.....................919 761-1363
Glenn Torrance, *Prin*
EMP: 5 **EST:** 2013
SALES (est): 187.88K **Privately Held**
SIC: 3944 Games, toys, and children's vehicles

(G-17083)
GRADY DISTRIBUTING CO INC
Also Called: ABC Hosiery
640 Park Ave (27596-9468)
P.O. Box 218 (27596-0218)
PHONE.....................919 556-5630
Anthony Grady, *Pr*
Pam Grady, *VP*
EMP: 12 **EST:** 1991
SALES (est): 988.46K **Privately Held**
Web: www.abchosiery.com
SIC: 2252 Socks

(G-17084)
HVTE INC
90 Mosswood Blvd Ste 100 (27596-7804)
P.O. Box 1135 (27596-1135)
PHONE.....................919 274-8899
Alvin Kopp, *Prin*
EMP: 10 **EST:** 2006
SALES (est): 290.16K **Privately Held**
SIC: 3825 Electrical power measuring equipment

(G-17085)
IMERYS PERLITE USA INC
Also Called: Harborlite
100 Robert Blunt Dr (27596-8524)
P.O. Box 727 (27596-0727)
PHONE..................................919 562-0031
EMP: 10
SALES (corp-wide): 3.28MM **Privately Held**
SIC: 3295 Perlite, aggregate or expanded
HQ: Imerys Perlite Usa, Inc.
  1732 N 1st St Ste 450
  San Jose CA 95112

(G-17086)
INTEGRATED INFO SYSTEMS INC
460 Boardwalk Dr (27596-3318)
P.O. Box 219 (27525-0219)
PHONE..................................919 488-5000
Richard K Washington, *CEO*
Deborah Washington, *Treas*
EMP: 10 EST: 2002
SQ FT: 2,500
SALES (est): 1.46MM **Privately Held**
Web: www.iisysinc.com
SIC: 3651 7382 5999 Household audio and video equipment; Security systems services; Audio-visual equipment and supplies

(G-17087)
K-FLEX USA LLC
100 K Flex Way (27596-9105)
PHONE..................................919 556-3475
Giuseppe Guarino, *Managing Member*
Carlo Spinelli, *
◆ EMP: 259 EST: 2001
SALES (est): 105.37MM
SALES (corp-wide): 355.83K **Privately Held**
Web: www.kflexusa.com
SIC: 3069 Hard rubber and molded rubber products
HQ: L'isolante K-Flex Spa
  Via Don Giuseppe Locatelli 35
  Roncello MB 20877
  039 682-4337

(G-17088)
LAYER27
205 Blue Heron Dr (27596-7674)
PHONE..................................919 909-9088
James Pierce, *Prin*
EMP: 5 EST: 2018
SALES (est): 130.29K **Privately Held**
Web: www.layer27.com
SIC: 3822 Hardware for environmental regulators

(G-17089)
OMEGA PRECIOUS METALS
40 Shorrey Pl (27596-7017)
PHONE..................................269 903-9330
Thomas Manley, *Owner*
EMP: 5 EST: 2013
SALES (est): 82.99K **Privately Held**
SIC: 3339 Precious metals

(G-17090)
PARK AVENUE METALCRAFT INC
850 Park Ave (27596-9472)
PHONE..................................919 554-2233
Stan Brown, *CEO*
John Dubbioso, *VP*
Stan Brown, *Pr*
Charles Cutts, *Sec*
EMP: 19 EST: 2000
SALES (est): 259.49K **Privately Held**
SIC: 3441 3544 Fabricated structural metal; Welding positioners (jigs)

(G-17091)
PIEDMONT LOGGING LLC
870 Park Ave (27596-9472)
PHONE..................................919 562-1861
EMP: 5 EST: 2017
SALES (est): 167.57K **Privately Held**
SIC: 2411 Logging

(G-17092)
POWERGPU LLC
762 Park Ave (27596-9470)
PHONE..................................919 702-6757
Jese Martinez, *Managing Member*
Stephanie Ivette Martinez, *Managing Member*
EMP: 17 EST: 2019
SALES (est): 5.49MM **Privately Held**
Web: www.powergpu.com
SIC: 3629 Electronic generation equipment

(G-17093)
ROBLING MEDICAL LLC
Also Called: Robling Medical
90 Weathers Ct (27596-7801)
PHONE..................................919 570-9605
Brent D Robling, *Pr*
Jodi Robling, *
▲ EMP: 70 EST: 1992
SQ FT: 18,000
SALES (est): 14.24MM **Privately Held**
Web: www.roblingmedical.com
SIC: 3841 Catheters

(G-17094)
ROOTS RUN DEEP LLC
90 Oak Leaf Trl (27596-7404)
PHONE..................................919 909-9117
Yan Garner, *Prin*
EMP: 6 EST: 2018
SALES (est): 226.55K **Privately Held**
SIC: 2084 Wines

(G-17095)
SAND HAMMER FORGING INC
594 Bert Winston Rd (27596-8781)
PHONE..................................919 554-9554
Agnieszka Freer, *Admn*
Dustin Freer, *Pr*
Stan Wyrembak, *VP*
Agnieszka Freer, *Corporate Secretary*
Alica Wyrembak, *Treas*
EMP: 6 EST: 2017
SALES (est): 510.91K **Privately Held**
Web: www.sandhammerforging.com
SIC: 3484 Small arms

(G-17096)
SIGMA PM
30 Monarch Ct (27596-7007)
PHONE..................................269 903-9330
EMP: 4 EST: 2018
SALES (est): 158.05K **Privately Held**
SIC: 3339 Precious metals

(G-17097)
SILVERLINING SCREEN PRTRS INC
90 Mosswood Blvd Ste 600 (27596-7849)
PHONE..................................919 554-0340
Victoria Jaynes, *Pr*
Gabriel Schultz, *Sec*
EMP: 4 EST: 1981
SQ FT: 6,500
SALES (est): 438.41K **Privately Held**
Web: www.silverliningscreenprinters.com
SIC: 2759 2261 5199 Screen printing; Screen printing of cotton broadwoven fabrics; Advertising specialties

(G-17098)
SIRCHIE ACQUISITION CO LLC (PA)
Also Called: Sirchie Finger Print Labs
100 Hunter Pl (27596-9447)
PHONE..................................800 356-7311
Inez Neff, *Pr*
Gary L Monroe, *
Jennifer Walton, *
Anthony Saggiomo, *
◆ EMP: 113 EST: 1956
SQ FT: 172,978
SALES (est): 25MM
SALES (corp-wide): 25MM **Privately Held**
Web: www.sirchie.com
SIC: 2899 Chemical preparations, nec

(G-17099)
SOUTHERN LITHOPLATE INC (PA)
105 Jeffrey Way (27596-9759)
P.O. Box 9400 (27588-6400)
PHONE..................................919 556-9400
Edward A Casson Iii, *Ch Bd*
Clark A Casson, *
Ronalda A Casson, *
◆ EMP: 110 EST: 1981
SQ FT: 135,000
SALES (est): 43.04MM
SALES (corp-wide): 43.04MM **Privately Held**
Web: www.slp.com
SIC: 2796 Lithographic plates, positives or negatives

(G-17100)
SPECTRUM PRODUCTS INC
153 Mosswood Blvd (27596-8685)
P.O. Box 2075 (27588-2075)
PHONE..................................919 556-7797
Scott Cissel, *Pr*
EMP: 11 EST: 1991
SQ FT: 8,000
SALES (est): 1.47MM **Privately Held**
Web: www.treegator.com
SIC: 3523 Fertilizing, spraying, dusting, and irrigation machinery

(G-17101)
STOWE WOODWARD LLC
Also Called: Stove-Woodward Co
14101 Capital Blvd Ste 101 (27596-7854)
PHONE..................................360 636-0330
Robert L Deckon, *Mgr*
EMP: 34
SALES (corp-wide): 7.83B **Privately Held**
SIC: 3069 Roll coverings, rubber
HQ: Stowe Woodward Llc
  8537 Six Forks Rd Ste 300
  Raleigh NC 27615

(G-17102)
STOWE WOODWARD LLC
51 Flex Way (27596-7848)
PHONE..................................919 556-7235
Dave Pretty, *Pr*
EMP: 58
SALES (corp-wide): 7.83B **Privately Held**
SIC: 3069 Roll coverings, rubber
HQ: Stowe Woodward Llc
  8537 Six Forks Rd Ste 300
  Raleigh NC 27615

(G-17103)
SURETECH ASSEMBLY INC
150a Jeffrey Way (27596-9759)
P.O. Box 1218 (27596-1218)
PHONE..................................919 569-0346
Ronald Bowman, *CEO*
Jack Hayes, *
▲ EMP: 50 EST: 2000
SQ FT: 20,000
SALES (est): 10.46MM
SALES (corp-wide): 490.36MM **Privately Held**
Web: www.suretechassembly.com
SIC: 3643 3679 3199 3694 Current-carrying wiring services; Harness assemblies, for electronic use: wire or cable; Harness or harness parts; Harness wiring sets, internal combustion engines
PA: East West Manufacturing, Llc
  4170 Ashford Dnwody Rd St
  Brookhaven GA 30319
  404 252-9441

(G-17104)
TAR RIVER TRADING POST LLC
Also Called: Distributor
385 Fleming Rd (27596-9698)
PHONE..................................919 589-3618
EMP: 5 EST: 2014
SQ FT: 5,400
SALES (est): 300.51K **Privately Held**
Web: www.tarrivertradingpost.com
SIC: 5083 3089 Farm and garden machinery; Tubs, plastics (containers)

(G-17105)
TEAM MANUFACTURING - E W LLC
35 Weathers Ct (27596-7800)
P.O. Box 1218 (27596-1218)
PHONE..................................919 554-2442
EMP: 58
SALES (corp-wide): 490.36MM **Privately Held**
Web: www.ewmfg.com
SIC: 3629 Electronic generation equipment
HQ: Team Manufacturing - East West, Llc
  4170 Ashford Dnwody Rd St
  Brookhaven GA 30319
  919 554-2442

(G-17106)
TELECOMMUNICATIONS TECH INC
Also Called: TTI Wireless
14101 Capital Blvd Ste 201 (27596-0166)
PHONE..................................919 556-7100
Thomas G Albright, *Pr*
Dale Albright, *VP*
Carol Albright, *Sec*
EMP: 15 EST: 1989
SALES (est): 957.57K **Privately Held**
Web: www.ttiwasp.com
SIC: 3823 Computer interface equipment, for industrial process control

(G-17107)
TOTAL FIRE SYSTEMS INC
30 Weathers Ct (27596-7801)
P.O. Box 1408 (27588-1408)
PHONE..................................919 556-9161
Mike Rohlik, *Pr*
Paul Collins, *
▼ EMP: 27 EST: 1990
SQ FT: 7,500
SALES (est): 5.11MM **Privately Held**
Web: www.totalfirenc.com
SIC: 3699 Fire control or bombing equipment, electronic

(G-17108)
TRIANGLE KITCHEN SUPPLY
336 Bert Winston Rd (27596-8726)
PHONE..................................919 562-3888
Andrew Hinton, *Owner*
EMP: 8 EST: 1973
SQ FT: 8,750
SALES (est): 327.89K **Privately Held**
SIC: 2434 Wood kitchen cabinets

Youngsville - Franklin County (G-17109)

(G-17109)
TRIANGLE METALWORKS INC
100 Moores Pond Rd (27596-9663)
PHONE..............................919 556-7786
Robbie Tilley, *Pr*
Sherri Tilley, *Sec*
EMP: 9 **EST:** 1995
SALES (est): 906.75K **Privately Held**
Web: www.trianglemetalworks.com
SIC: 3441 Fabricated structural metal

(G-17110)
TRIMM INTERNATIONAL INC
Also Called: Trimm
112 Franklin Park Dr (27596-9400)
PHONE..............................847 362-3700
G William Newton, *Pr*
Ayako M Newton, *Sec*
EMP: 20 **EST:** 1922
SALES (est): 5.61MM **Privately Held**
SIC: 3661 Telephone and telegraph apparatus

(G-17111)
TRUE SOUTHERN TEES
166 Cooley Rd (27596-9516)
PHONE..............................919 604-6068
Rodney Caudle, *Owner*
EMP: 4 **EST:** 2016
SALES (est): 73.03K **Privately Held**
SIC: 2759 Screen printing

(G-17112)
VIA PRNTING GRAPHIC DESIGN INC
Also Called: Graphic Master
5841 Gentle Wind Dr (27596-8511)
PHONE..............................919 872-8688
Rodger Via, *Pt*
Chris Via, *Pt*
EMP: 5 **EST:** 1983
SQ FT: 1,697
SALES (est): 328.32K **Privately Held**
Web: www.graphicmaster.net
SIC: 2752 Offset printing

(G-17113)
WEAVEXX LLC
14101 Capital Blvd (27596-0166)
PHONE..............................919 556-7235
Stephen R Light, *CEO*
Miguel Quionez,
▲ **EMP:** 900 **EST:** 1890
SQ FT: 250,000
SALES (est): 49.11MM
SALES (corp-wide): 7.83B **Privately Held**
Web: www.andritz.com
SIC: 2221 Specialty broadwoven fabrics, including twisted weaves
HQ: Andritz Fabrics And Rolls Inc.
8521 Six Forks Rd
Raleigh NC 27615
919 526-1400

(G-17114)
WERYWIN CORPORATION
70 Mosswood Blvd Ste 300 (27596-7990)
PHONE..............................410 322-4917
EMP: 4 **EST:** 2021
SALES (est): 107.64K **Privately Held**
Web: www.werywin.com
SIC: 3484 Guns (firearms) or gun parts, 30 mm. and below

(G-17115)
WHITE STREET BREWING CO INC
400 Park Ave (27596-8688)
P.O. Box 2066 (27588-2066)
PHONE..............................919 647-9439
Dino Radosta, *Prin*
EMP: 24 **EST:** 2011
SALES (est): 681.94K **Privately Held**
Web: www.whitestreetbrewing.com
SIC: 5813 5181 2082 Bars and lounges; Beer and ale; Ale (alcoholic beverage)

(G-17116)
WOODMASTER CUSTOM CABINETS INC
436 Park Ave (27596-8688)
PHONE..............................919 554-3707
Angela Ling, *Pr*
EMP: 12 **EST:** 2014
SALES (est): 552.81K **Privately Held**
Web: www.woodmasterwoodworks.com
SIC: 2434 2431 Wood kitchen cabinets; Millwork

Zebulon
Wake County

(G-17117)
ADVANCED PLASTIFORM INC (PA)
535 Mack Todd Rd (27597-2550)
PHONE..............................919 404-2080
Chris Jolly, *Pr*
EMP: 65 **EST:** 1987
SQ FT: 120,000
SALES (est): 25.61MM
SALES (corp-wide): 25.61MM **Privately Held**
Web: www.advancedplastiform.com
SIC: 5162 3559 Plastics products, nec; Ammunition and explosives, loading machinery

(G-17118)
ADVANCED PLASTIFORM INC
113 Legacy Crest Ct (27597-9610)
PHONE..............................919 404-2080
EMP: 28
SALES (corp-wide): 25.61MM **Privately Held**
Web: www.advancedplastiform.com
SIC: 3089 Injection molding of plastics
PA: Advanced Plastiform, Inc.
535 Mack Todd Rd
Zebulon NC 27597
919 404-2080

(G-17119)
AIMET HOLDING INC
Also Called: Aimet Technologies
115 Legacy Crest Ct (27597-9610)
P.O. Box 1216 (27597-1216)
PHONE..............................919 887-5205
David Jackson, *Pr*
▲ **EMP:** 33 **EST:** 1993
SQ FT: 80,000
SALES (est): 1.96MM **Privately Held**
Web: www.aimet.com
SIC: 3089 Injection molding of plastics

(G-17120)
AIMET TECHNOLOGIES LLC
115 Legacy Crest Ct (27597-9610)
PHONE..............................919 887-5205
Tony Sturrus, *Prin*
EMP: 13 **EST:** 2014
SALES (est): 497.13K **Privately Held**
SIC: 3089 Injection molding of plastics

(G-17121)
ASP HOLDINGS INC
Also Called: Power Pros
1014 N Arendell Ave (27597-2351)
P.O. Box 1585 (27545-1585)
PHONE..............................888 330-2538
EMP: 4 **EST:** 1994
SALES (est): 592.18K **Privately Held**
Web: www.powerprosinc.com
SIC: 3679 Power supplies, all types: static

(G-17122)
BROOKS MACHINE & DESIGN INC
1424 Old Us Highway 264 (27597)
P.O. Box 65 (27597-0065)
PHONE..............................919 404-0901
EMP: 17 **EST:** 1994
SQ FT: 8,000
SALES (est): 4.79MM **Privately Held**
Web: www.brooksmachine.com
SIC: 3599 Machine shop, jobbing and repair

(G-17123)
CABINET GUY
94 Privette Way (27597-6320)
PHONE..............................919 375-4559
Donna L Smith, *Owner*
EMP: 5 **EST:** 2017
SALES (est): 160.84K **Privately Held**
SIC: 2434 Wood kitchen cabinets

(G-17124)
CABLENC LLC
8012 Spiderlily Ct (27597-8952)
PHONE..............................919 307-9065
Justin Soustek, *CEO*
EMP: 9 **EST:** 2017
SALES (est): 504.59K **Privately Held**
SIC: 3651 7389 Household audio and video equipment; Business services, nec

(G-17125)
DEVIL DOG MANUFACTURING CO INC
400 E Gannon Ave (27597-2708)
P.O. Box 69 (27597-0069)
PHONE..............................919 269-7485
Tony Shannahan, *Brnch Mgr*
EMP: 194
SALES (corp-wide): 9.29MM **Privately Held**
SIC: 2369 2361 2339 2325 Jeans: girls', children's, and infants'; Girl's and children's dresses, blouses; Women's and misses' outerwear, nec; Men's and boy's trousers and slacks
PA: Devil Dog Manufacturing Co., Inc.
23 Market St
Ellenville NY 12428
845 647-4411

(G-17126)
ELECTRO MAGNETIC RESEARCH INC
Also Called: EMR Electric
9576 Covered Bridge Rd (27597-7410)
PHONE..............................919 365-3723
Rommel Edwards, *CEO*
EMP: 4 **EST:** 1986
SALES (est): 291.37K **Privately Held**
Web: www.emrelectric.com
SIC: 3625 8711 Industrial controls: push button, selector switches, pilot; Engineering services

(G-17127)
FIRST CLASS RIDEZ LLC
472 Mallie Pearce Rd (27597-6177)
PHONE..............................919 610-6043
Jeromy Lockleair, *Owner*
EMP: 5 **EST:** 2010
SALES (est): 96.87K **Privately Held**
Web: www.firstclassridez.com
SIC: 2842 Automobile polish

(G-17128)
GENERAL FOODS DISTRIBUTORS
207 E Sycamore St (27597-2833)
PHONE..............................919 279-7236
Omar A Lopez V, *Prin*
EMP: 5 **EST:** 2012
SALES (est): 164.72K **Privately Held**
SIC: 2099 Food preparations, nec

(G-17129)
GLAXOSMITHKLINE LLC
Also Called: Glaxosmithkline
1011 N Arendell Ave (27597-2300)
P.O. Box 1217 (27597-1217)
PHONE..............................919 269-5000
Cliff Disbrow, *Genl Mgr*
EMP: 27
SALES (corp-wide): 35.31B **Privately Held**
Web: us.gsk.com
SIC: 2834 Pharmaceutical preparations
HQ: Glaxosmithkline Llc
2929 Walnut St Ste 1700
Philadelphia PA 19104
888 825-5249

(G-17130)
GREY AREA NEWS
70 Harrison St (27597-9307)
PHONE..............................919 637-6973
Carolyn Whatley, *Owner*
EMP: 5 **EST:** 2018
SALES (est): 74.87K **Privately Held**
Web: www.greyareanews.com
SIC: 2711 Newspapers, publishing and printing

(G-17131)
H BROTHERS FINE WDWKG LLC
1512 Earpsboro Rd (27597-7088)
PHONE..............................931 216-1955
EMP: 4 **EST:** 2019
SALES (est): 63.88K **Privately Held**
Web: www.millbrothersinc.com
SIC: 2434 Wood kitchen cabinets

(G-17132)
KAM TOOL & DIE INC
530 N Industrial Dr (27597-2748)
PHONE..............................919 269-5099
EMP: 21 **EST:** 1995
SQ FT: 15,000
SALES (est): 2.21MM **Privately Held**
Web: www.kamtool.net
SIC: 3544 Special dies and tools

(G-17133)
LITTLE RIVER NATURALS LLC
7408 Riley Hill Rd (27597-8757)
PHONE..............................919 760-3708
EMP: 4 **EST:** 2019
SALES (est): 103.91K **Privately Held**
Web: www.littlerivernaturalsnc.com
SIC: 2844 Perfumes, cosmetics and other toilet preparations

(G-17134)
LIZARD LICK BREWING & DIST LLC
Also Called: Lizard Lick Brewing and Dist
138 E Vance St (27597-2838)
PHONE..............................919 887-4369
EMP: 4 **EST:** 2020
SALES (est): 96.9K **Privately Held**
SIC: 2085 Distilled and blended liquors

(G-17135)
NOEL GROUP LLC (PA)
501 Innovative Way (27597-2661)
PHONE..............................919 269-6500
Marc Noel, *Managing Member*
EMP: 6 **EST:** 1996
SALES (est): 95.55MM
SALES (corp-wide): 95.55MM **Privately Held**

Web: www.noelgroup.net
SIC: 3086 Packaging and shipping materials, foamed plastics

(G-17136)
NOMACO INC (HQ)
501 Innovative Way (27597-2661)
PHONE..................919 269-6500
Lars Von Kantzow, *Pr*
Steven Thompson, *
◆ **EMP:** 308 **EST:** 1979
SQ FT: 205,000
SALES (est): 84.34MM
SALES (corp-wide): 95.55MM **Privately Held**
Web: www.nomaco.com
SIC: 3086 Plastics foam products
PA: Noel Group, Llc
 501 Innovative Way
 Zebulon NC 27597
 919 269-6500

(G-17137)
NOMACORC HOLDINGS LLC
400 Vintage Park Dr (27597-3803)
PHONE..................919 460-2200
Amy Bess Cook, *Prin*
EMP: 9 **EST:** 2014
SALES (est): 189.71K **Privately Held**
SIC: 2084 Wines

(G-17138)
OAK CITY METAL LLC
700 Pony Rd Ste C (27597-2656)
PHONE..................919 375-4535
Melvin Brent Sanders, *Managing Member*
EMP: 6 **EST:** 2018
SALES (est): 489.45K **Privately Held**
SIC: 3429 Metal fasteners

(G-17139)
PAUL CASPER INC
3533 Rosinburg Rd (27597-5300)
P.O. Box 9 (27597-0009)
PHONE..................919 269-5362
Paul M Casper Junior, *Pr*
EMP: 6 **EST:** 1989
SQ FT: 5,000
SALES (est): 464.56K **Privately Held**
SIC: 7692 3441 3444 Welding repair; Fabricated structural metal; Sheet metalwork

(G-17140)
PINE GLO PRODUCTS INC
115 Legacy Crest Ct (27597-9610)
PHONE..................919 556-7787
Matthew Diehl, *Pr*
Carolyn Diehl, *Sec*
◆ **EMP:** 19 **EST:** 1979
SALES (est): 4.38MM **Privately Held**
Web: www.pinegloproducts.com
SIC: 2842 2841 Polishes and sanitation goods; Soap and other detergents

(G-17141)
RTT MACHINE & WELDING SVC INC
12671 W Nc 97 (27597-6428)
PHONE..................919 269-6863
Rodney Massey, *Pr*
EMP: 22 **EST:** 1996
SALES (est): 988.12K **Privately Held**
Web: www.rttmachine.com
SIC: 3599 Machine shop, jobbing and repair

(G-17142)
SGR WELDING & FABRICATION LLC
4364 Massey Rd (27597-6438)
PHONE..................252 299-3629
Steven Rodriquez, *Prin*
EMP: 5 **EST:** 2019
SALES (est): 82.81K **Privately Held**
SIC: 7692 Welding repair

(G-17143)
THEO DAVIS SONS INCORPORATED
Also Called: Theo Davis Printing
1415 W Gannon Ave (27597-3306)
P.O. Box 277 (27597-0277)
PHONE..................919 269-7401
Kenneth Carter, *Pr*
EMP: 28 **EST:** 1945
SQ FT: 28,000
SALES (est): 4.62MM
SALES (corp-wide): 15B **Privately Held**
SIC: 2752 2759 Offset printing; Laser printing
HQ: Consolidated Graphics, Inc.
 5858 Westheimer Rd # 200
 Houston TX 77057

(G-17144)
TRADEWINDS COFFEE CO INC
6308 Mitchell Mill Rd (27597-8407)
PHONE..................919 556-1835
Art Watkins, *Pr*
Elaine Watkins, *VP*
EMP: 10 **EST:** 1987
SQ FT: 2,500
SALES (est): 1.39MM **Privately Held**
Web: www.tradewindscoffee.com
SIC: 5149 5499 2095 Coffee, green or roasted; Coffee; Coffee roasting (except by wholesale grocers)

(G-17145)
VINVENTIONS USA LLC
Closure Innovations
505 Innovative Way (27597-2661)
PHONE..................919 460-2200
Eric Dunkelberg, *Genl Mgr*
EMP: 170
SALES (corp-wide): 93.28MM **Privately Held**
Web: us.vinventions.com
SIC: 2499 Corks, bottle
PA: Vinventions Usa, Llc
 888 Prospect St
 La Jolla CA 92037
 919 460-2200

(G-17146)
WORLD WICKS CANDLES
357 Gourd St (27597-5537)
PHONE..................919 791-6123
Abby Hilyer, *Prin*
EMP: 4 **EST:** 2018
SALES (est): 182.83K **Privately Held**
SIC: 3999 Candles

(G-17147)
Z COLLECTION LLC
77 Gennessee Dr (27597-2164)
PHONE..................919 247-1513
Zakeya Caldwell, *Managing Member*
EMP: 4 **EST:** 2017
SALES (est): 233.44K **Privately Held**
SIC: 3999 7389 5999 Hair and hair-based products; Business Activities at Non-Commercial Site; Alarm and safety equipment stores

Zionville
Watauga County

(G-17148)
BROWN BROTHERS CONSTRUCTION CO
10801 Us Highway 421 N (28698-9024)
PHONE..................828 297-2131
EMP: 13 **EST:** 1948
SQ FT: 1,000
SALES (est): 505.5K **Privately Held**
SIC: 1611 1794 2951 General contractor, highway and street construction; Excavation work; Asphalt paving mixtures and blocks

(G-17149)
VITAL BEING
194 Clay Wilson Dr (28698-9700)
PHONE..................828 964-5853
Nia Dickens, *Owner*
EMP: 4 **EST:** 2010
SALES (est): 48.25K **Privately Held**
SIC: 8049 2899 7389 Massage Therapist; Oils and essential oils; Business Activities at Non-Commercial Site

Zirconia
Henderson County

(G-17150)
CAPPS NOBLE LOGGING
Bob's Creek Road (28790)
PHONE..................828 696-9690
Noble Capps Junior, *Owner*
EMP: 6 **EST:** 1986
SALES (est): 239.57K **Privately Held**
SIC: 2411 Logging camps and contractors

(G-17151)
CAROLINA PAPER TUBES INC
Also Called: C P T
3932 Old Us Highway 25 (28790-7907)
P.O. Box 219 (25423-0219)
PHONE..................828 692-9686
Jerry Melton, *Pr*
Pennie Melton, *
▼ **EMP:** 32 **EST:** 1978
SQ FT: 40,000
SALES (est): 3.11MM **Privately Held**
Web: www.oxindustries.com
SIC: 2655 Tubes, fiber or paper: made from purchased material

(G-17152)
CUSTOM DECKS AND WOODWORKING
2294 Old Us 25 Hwy (28790-7863)
PHONE..................828 699-2349
EMP: 4 **EST:** 2010
SALES (est): 83.39K **Privately Held**
SIC: 2431 Millwork

(G-17153)
GREEN RIVER RESOURCE MGT
Also Called: Whole Log Lumber
195 Blueberry Farm Rd (28790-0265)
PHONE..................828 697-0357
EMP: 10 **EST:** 1984
SALES (est): 1.64MM **Privately Held**
Web: www.wholeloglumber.com
SIC: 5211 5023 2426 Flooring, wood; Wood flooring; Flooring, hardwood

(G-17154)
MAYBIN EMERGENCY POWER INC
197 Mountain Valley Cemetery Rd (28790-6721)
PHONE..................828 697-1195
Jim Maybin, *Pr*
Jessica Cox, *VP*
EMP: 7 **EST:** 1996
SQ FT: 3,500
SALES (est): 481.29K **Privately Held**
SIC: 7694 Electric motor repair

(G-17155)
MOUNTAIN VALLEY LOGGING LLC
297 Fate Maybin Ln (28790-6824)
PHONE..................828 551-0861
Harley F Capps Iii, *Prin*
EMP: 7 **EST:** 2018
SALES (est): 222.63K **Privately Held**
SIC: 2411 Logging

(G-17156)
NORTHERN CRES IR / MATT WLDROP
16 Kay Rd (28790)
PHONE..................828 848-8884
Matt Waldrop, *Ofcr*
EMP: 6 **EST:** 2013
SALES (est): 447.24K **Privately Held**
Web: www.northerncrescentiron.com
SIC: 3462 Construction or mining equipment forgings, ferrous

SIC INDEX

Standard Industrial Classification Alphabetical Index

SIC NO	PRODUCT

A

3291 Abrasive products
8721 Accounting, auditing, and bookkeeping
2891 Adhesives and sealants
7311 Advertising agencies
7319 Advertising, nec
2879 Agricultural chemicals, nec
3563 Air and gas compressors
4513 Air courier services
4522 Air transportation, nonscheduled
4512 Air transportation, scheduled
3721 Aircraft
3724 Aircraft engines and engine parts
3728 Aircraft parts and equipment, nec
4581 Airports, flying fields, and services
2812 Alkalies and chlorine
3363 Aluminum die-castings
3354 Aluminum extruded products
3365 Aluminum foundries
3355 Aluminum rolling and drawing, nec
3353 Aluminum sheet, plate, and foil
3483 Ammunition, except for small arms, nec
7999 Amusement and recreation, nec
3826 Analytical instruments
2077 Animal and marine fats and oils
0279 Animal specialties, nec
0752 Animal specialty services
6513 Apartment building operators
2389 Apparel and accessories, nec
2387 Apparel belts
3446 Architectural metalwork
8712 Architectural services
7694 Armature rewinding shops
3292 Asbestos products
2952 Asphalt felts and coatings
2951 Asphalt paving mixtures and blocks
5531 Auto and home supply stores
3581 Automatic vending machines
7521 Automobile parking
5012 Automobiles and other motor vehicles
2396 Automotive and apparel trimmings
5599 Automotive dealers, nec
7536 Automotive glass replacement shops
7539 Automotive repair shops, nec
7549 Automotive services, nec
3465 Automotive stampings
7537 Automotive transmission repair shops

B

2673 Bags: plastic, laminated, and coated
2674 Bags: uncoated paper and multiwall
3562 Ball and roller bearings
7241 Barber shops
7231 Beauty shops
0212 Beef cattle, except feedlots
5181 Beer and ale
0171 Berry crops
2836 Biological products, except diagnostic
1221 Bituminous coal and lignite-surface mining
2782 Blankbooks and looseleaf binders
3312 Blast furnaces and steel mills
3564 Blowers and fans
5551 Boat dealers
3732 Boatbuilding and repairing
3452 Bolts, nuts, rivets, and washers
2732 Book printing
2731 Book publishing
5942 Book stores
2789 Bookbinding and related work
5192 Books, periodicals, and newspapers
2086 Bottled and canned soft drinks
2342 Bras, girdles, and allied garments
2051 Bread, cake, and related products
3251 Brick and structural clay tile
5032 Brick, stone, and related material
1622 Bridge, tunnel, and elevated highway

2211 Broadwoven fabric mills, cotton
2221 Broadwoven fabric mills, manmade
2231 Broadwoven fabric mills, wool
0251 Broiler, fryer, and roaster chickens
3991 Brooms and brushes
7349 Building maintenance services, nec
3995 Burial caskets
8611 Business associations
8748 Business consulting, nec
7389 Business services, nec

C

4841 Cable and other pay television services
3578 Calculating and accounting equipment
5946 Camera and photographic supply stores
2064 Candy and other confectionery products
5441 Candy, nut, and confectionery stores
2091 Canned and cured fish and seafoods
2033 Canned fruits and specialties
2032 Canned specialties
2394 Canvas and related products
3624 Carbon and graphite products
2895 Carbon black
3955 Carbon paper and inked ribbons
3592 Carburetors, pistons, rings, valves
1751 Carpentry work
7217 Carpet and upholstery cleaning
2273 Carpets and rugs
7542 Carwashes
0119 Cash grains, nec
5961 Catalog and mail-order houses
2823 Cellulosic manmade fibers
3241 Cement, hydraulic
3253 Ceramic wall and floor tile
2043 Cereal breakfast foods
2022 Cheese; natural and processed
1479 Chemical and fertilizer mining
2899 Chemical preparations, nec
5169 Chemicals and allied products, nec
2131 Chewing and smoking tobacco
0252 Chicken eggs
5641 Children's and infants' wear stores
2066 Chocolate and cocoa products
2111 Cigarettes
2121 Cigars
0174 Citrus fruits
1459 Clay and related minerals, nec
3255 Clay refractories
5052 Coal and other minerals and ores
1241 Coal mining services
2295 Coated fabrics, not rubberized
7993 Coin-operated amusement devices
7215 Coin-operated laundries and cleaning
3316 Cold finishing of steel shapes
8221 Colleges and universities
7336 Commercial art and graphic design
5046 Commercial equipment, nec
3582 Commercial laundry equipment
3646 Commercial lighting fixtures
8732 Commercial nonphysical research
7335 Commercial photography
8731 Commercial physical research
2754 Commercial printing, gravure
2752 Commercial printing, lithographic
2759 Commercial printing, nec
6221 Commodity contracts brokers, dealers
4899 Communication services, nec
3669 Communications equipment, nec
5734 Computer and software stores
7376 Computer facilities management
7373 Computer integrated systems design
7378 Computer maintenance and repair
3577 Computer peripheral equipment, nec
7379 Computer related services, nec
3572 Computer storage devices
3575 Computer terminals

5045 Computers, peripherals, and software
3271 Concrete block and brick
3272 Concrete products, nec
1771 Concrete work
5145 Confectionery
5082 Construction and mining machinery
3531 Construction machinery
5039 Construction materials, nec
1442 Construction sand and gravel
2679 Converted paper products, nec
3535 Conveyors and conveying equipment
2052 Cookies and crackers
3366 Copper foundries
1021 Copper ores
3351 Copper rolling and drawing
2298 Cordage and twine
9223 Correctional institutions
2653 Corrugated and solid fiber boxes
3961 Costume jewelry
0131 Cotton
0724 Cotton ginning
2074 Cottonseed oil mills
4215 Courier services, except by air
2021 Creamery butter
0721 Crop planting and protection
0723 Crop preparation services for market
3466 Crowns and closures
1311 Crude petroleum and natural gas
1423 Crushed and broken granite
1422 Crushed and broken limestone
1429 Crushed and broken stone, nec
3643 Current-carrying wiring devices
2391 Curtains and draperies
3087 Custom compound purchased resins
7371 Custom computer programming services
3281 Cut stone and stone products
3421 Cutlery
2865 Cyclic crudes and intermediates

D

0241 Dairy farms
5451 Dairy products stores
5143 Dairy products, except dried or canned
7374 Data processing and preparation
8243 Data processing schools
0175 Deciduous tree fruits
2034 Dehydrated fruits, vegetables, soups
3843 Dental equipment and supplies
8072 Dental laboratories
5311 Department stores
7381 Detective and armored car services
2835 Diagnostic substances
2675 Die-cut paper and board
1411 Dimension stone
7331 Direct mail advertising services
5963 Direct selling establishments
7342 Disinfecting and pest control services
2085 Distilled and blended liquors
2047 Dog and cat food
3942 Dolls and stuffed toys
5714 Drapery and upholstery stores
2591 Drapery hardware and blinds and shades
1381 Drilling oil and gas wells
5813 Drinking places
5912 Drug stores and proprietary stores
5122 Drugs, proprietaries, and sundries
2023 Dry, condensed, evaporated products
7216 Drycleaning plants, except rugs
5099 Durable goods, nec

E

5812 Eating places
2079 Edible fats and oils
4931 Electric and other services combined
3634 Electric housewares and fans
3641 Electric lamps

SIC INDEX

SIC NO	PRODUCT
4911	Electric services
5063	Electrical apparatus and equipment
5064	Electrical appliances, television and radio
3699	Electrical equipment and supplies, nec
3629	Electrical industrial apparatus
7629	Electrical repair shops
1731	Electrical work
3845	Electromedical equipment
3313	Electrometallurgical products
3671	Electron tubes
3675	Electronic capacitors
3677	Electronic coils and transformers
3679	Electronic components, nec
3571	Electronic computers
3678	Electronic connectors
5065	Electronic parts and equipment, nec
3676	Electronic resistors
8211	Elementary and secondary schools
3534	Elevators and moving stairways
3694	Engine electrical equipment
8711	Engineering services
7929	Entertainers and entertainment groups
2677	Envelopes
3822	Environmental controls
7359	Equipment rental and leasing, nec
1794	Excavation work
2892	Explosives

F

SIC NO	PRODUCT
2381	Fabric dress and work gloves
3499	Fabricated metal products, nec
3498	Fabricated pipe and fittings
3443	Fabricated plate work (boiler shop)
3069	Fabricated rubber products, nec
3441	Fabricated structural metal
2399	Fabricated textile products, nec
8744	Facilities support services
5651	Family clothing stores
5083	Farm and garden machinery
3523	Farm machinery and equipment
0762	Farm management services
4221	Farm product warehousing and storage
5191	Farm supplies
5159	Farm-product raw materials, nec
3965	Fasteners, buttons, needles, and pins
2875	Fertilizers, mixing only
2655	Fiber cans, drums, and similar products
0139	Field crops, except cash grain
9311	Finance, taxation, and monetary policy
2261	Finishing plants, cotton
2262	Finishing plants, manmade
2269	Finishing plants, nec
6331	Fire, marine, and casualty insurance
5146	Fish and seafoods
3211	Flat glass
2087	Flavoring extracts and syrups, nec
5713	Floor covering stores
1752	Floor laying and floor work, nec
5992	Florists
2041	Flour and other grain mill products
5193	Flowers and florists supplies
3824	Fluid meters and counting devices
2026	Fluid milk
3593	Fluid power cylinders and actuators
3594	Fluid power pumps and motors
3492	Fluid power valves and hose fittings
2657	Folding paperboard boxes
2099	Food preparations, nec
3556	Food products machinery
5139	Footwear
3131	Footwear cut stock
3149	Footwear, except rubber, nec
0831	Forest products
0851	Forestry services
4731	Freight transportation arrangement
5148	Fresh fruits and vegetables
2092	Fresh or frozen packaged fish
2053	Frozen bakery products, except bread
2037	Frozen fruits and vegetables
2038	Frozen specialties, nec
0179	Fruits and tree nuts, nec
5989	Fuel dealers, nec
5983	Fuel oil dealers
7261	Funeral service and crematories
2371	Fur goods
5021	Furniture
2599	Furniture and fixtures, nec
5712	Furniture stores

G

SIC NO	PRODUCT
3944	Games, toys, and children's vehicles
7212	Garment pressing and cleaners' agents
3053	Gaskets; packing and sealing devices
5541	Gasoline service stations
7538	General automotive repair shops
0191	General farms, primarily crop
3569	General industrial machinery,
8062	General medical and surgical hospitals
4225	General warehousing and storage
5947	Gift, novelty, and souvenir shop
2361	Girl's and children's dresses, blouses
2369	Girl's and children's outerwear, nec
1793	Glass and glazing work
3221	Glass containers
5153	Grain and field beans
0172	Grapes
3321	Gray and ductile iron foundries
2771	Greeting cards
5149	Groceries and related products, nec
5141	Groceries, general line
5411	Grocery stores
3761	Guided missiles and space vehicles
2861	Gum and wood chemicals
3275	Gypsum products

H

SIC NO	PRODUCT
3423	Hand and edge tools, nec
3996	Hard surface floor coverings, nec
5072	Hardware
5251	Hardware stores
3429	Hardware, nec
2426	Hardwood dimension and flooring mills
2435	Hardwood veneer and plywood
2353	Hats, caps, and millinery
8099	Health and allied services, nec
3433	Heating equipment, except electric
7353	Heavy construction equipment rental
1629	Heavy construction, nec
7363	Help supply services
1611	Highway and street construction
5945	Hobby, toy, and game shops
0213	Hogs
3536	Hoists, cranes, and monorails
6719	Holding companies, nec
8082	Home health care services
5023	Homefurnishings
2252	Hosiery, nec
7011	Hotels and motels
5722	Household appliance stores
3639	Household appliances, nec
3651	Household audio and video equipment
3631	Household cooking equipment
2392	Household furnishings, nec
2519	Household furniture, nec
3632	Household refrigerators and freezers
3635	Household vacuum cleaners

I

SIC NO	PRODUCT
2024	Ice cream and frozen deserts
8322	Individual and family services
5113	Industrial and personal service paper
1541	Industrial buildings and warehouses
3567	Industrial furnaces and ovens
2813	Industrial gases
2819	Industrial inorganic chemicals, nec
7218	Industrial launderers
5084	Industrial machinery and equipment
3599	Industrial machinery, nec
2869	Industrial organic chemicals, nec
3543	Industrial patterns
1446	Industrial sand
5085	Industrial supplies
3537	Industrial trucks and tractors
3491	Industrial valves
7375	Information retrieval services
2816	Inorganic pigments
4785	Inspection and fixed facilities
1796	Installing building equipment
3825	Instruments to measure electricity
6411	Insurance agents, brokers, and service
3519	Internal combustion engines, nec
6282	Investment advice
6799	Investors, nec
3462	Iron and steel forgings

J

SIC NO	PRODUCT
3915	Jewelers' materials and lapidary work
5094	Jewelry and precious stones
5944	Jewelry stores
3911	Jewelry, precious metal
8331	Job training and related services

K

SIC NO	PRODUCT
2253	Knit outerwear mills
2254	Knit underwear mills
2259	Knitting mills, nec

L

SIC NO	PRODUCT
3821	Laboratory apparatus and furniture
2258	Lace and warp knit fabric mills
3083	Laminated plastics plate and sheet
9512	Land, mineral, and wildlife conservation
0781	Landscape counseling and planning
7219	Laundry and garment services, nec
3524	Lawn and garden equipment
0782	Lawn and garden services
3952	Lead pencils and art goods
2386	Leather and sheep-lined clothing
3151	Leather gloves and mittens
3199	Leather goods, nec
3111	Leather tanning and finishing
6311	Life insurance
3648	Lighting equipment, nec
5984	Liquefied petroleum gas dealers
5921	Liquor stores
0751	Livestock services, except veterinary
4111	Local and suburban transit
4214	Local trucking with storage
4212	Local trucking, without storage
2411	Logging
2992	Lubricating oils and greases
3161	Luggage
5211	Lumber and other building materials
5031	Lumber, plywood, and millwork

M

SIC NO	PRODUCT
2098	Macaroni and spaghetti
3545	Machine tool accessories
3541	Machine tools, metal cutting type
3542	Machine tools, metal forming type
3695	Magnetic and optical recording media
2083	Malt
2082	Malt beverages
8742	Management consulting services
8741	Management services
2761	Manifold business forms
2097	Manufactured ice
3999	Manufacturing industries, nec
4493	Marinas
3953	Marking devices
1741	Masonry and other stonework
2515	Mattresses and bedsprings
3829	Measuring and controlling devices, nec
3586	Measuring and dispensing pumps
5421	Meat and fish markets
2011	Meat packing plants
5147	Meats and meat products
3061	Mechanical rubber goods
5047	Medical and hospital equipment
7352	Medical equipment rental
8071	Medical laboratories
2833	Medicinals and botanicals
8699	Membership organizations, nec
5136	Men's and boy's clothing
2329	Men's and boy's clothing, nec
2321	Men's and boy's furnishings

2024 Harris North Carolina Manufacturers Directory

SIC INDEX

SIC NO	PRODUCT
2323	Men's and boy's neckwear
2311	Men's and boy's suits and coats
2325	Men's and boy's trousers and slacks
2322	Men's and boy's underwear and nightwear
2326	Men's and boy's work clothing
5611	Men's and boys' clothing stores
3143	Men's footwear, except athletic
5962	Merchandising machine operators
3412	Metal barrels, drums, and pails
3411	Metal cans
3479	Metal coating and allied services
3442	Metal doors, sash, and trim
3497	Metal foil and leaf
3398	Metal heat treating
2514	Metal household furniture
1081	Metal mining services
1099	Metal ores, nec
3431	Metal sanitary ware
3469	Metal stampings, nec
5051	Metals service centers and offices
3549	Metalworking machinery, nec
2431	Millwork
3296	Mineral wool
3295	Minerals, ground or treated
3532	Mining machinery
5699	Miscellaneous apparel and accessories
6159	Miscellaneous business credit
3496	Miscellaneous fabricated wire products
5499	Miscellaneous food stores
5399	Miscellaneous general merchandise
5719	Miscellaneous homefurnishings
3449	Miscellaneous metalwork
1499	Miscellaneous nonmetallic mining
7299	Miscellaneous personal services
2741	Miscellaneous publishing
5999	Miscellaneous retail stores, nec
5271	Mobile home dealers
2451	Mobile homes
6162	Mortgage bankers and correspondents
7822	Motion picture and tape distribution
7812	Motion picture and video production
3716	Motor homes
3714	Motor vehicle parts and accessories
5015	Motor vehicle parts, used
5013	Motor vehicle supplies and new parts
3711	Motor vehicles and car bodies
5571	Motorcycle dealers
3751	Motorcycles, bicycles, and parts
3621	Motors and generators
8412	Museums and art galleries
5736	Musical instrument stores
3931	Musical instruments

N

SIC NO	PRODUCT
2441	Nailed wood boxes and shook
2241	Narrow fabric mills
9711	National security
4924	Natural gas distribution
1321	Natural gas liquids
4922	Natural gas transmission
5511	New and used car dealers
5994	News dealers and newsstands
2711	Newspapers
2873	Nitrogenous fertilizers
3297	Nonclay refractories
8733	Noncommercial research organizations
3644	Noncurrent-carrying wiring devices
5199	Nondurable goods, nec
3364	Nonferrous die-castings except aluminum
3463	Nonferrous forgings
3369	Nonferrous foundries, nec
3356	Nonferrous rolling and drawing, nec
3357	Nonferrous wiredrawing and insulating
3299	Nonmetallic mineral products,
1481	Nonmetallic mineral services
6512	Nonresidential building operators
1542	Nonresidential construction, nec
2297	Nonwoven fabrics

O

SIC NO	PRODUCT
5044	Office equipment
2522	Office furniture, except wood
3579	Office machines, nec
8021	Offices and clinics of dentists
8011	Offices and clinics of medical doctors
8042	Offices and clinics of optometrists
8049	Offices of health practitioner
1382	Oil and gas exploration services
3533	Oil and gas field machinery
1389	Oil and gas field services, nec
1531	Operative builders
3851	Ophthalmic goods
5995	Optical goods stores
3827	Optical instruments and lenses
3489	Ordnance and accessories, nec
2824	Organic fibers, noncellulosic
0181	Ornamental nursery products
0783	Ornamental shrub and tree services
7312	Outdoor advertising services

P

SIC NO	PRODUCT
5142	Packaged frozen goods
3565	Packaging machinery
4783	Packing and crating
5231	Paint, glass, and wallpaper stores
1721	Painting and paper hanging
2851	Paints and allied products
5198	Paints, varnishes, and supplies
3554	Paper industries machinery
2621	Paper mills
2671	Paper; coated and laminated packaging
2672	Paper; coated and laminated, nec
2631	Paperboard mills
2542	Partitions and fixtures, except wood
7515	Passenger car leasing
7514	Passenger car rental
6794	Patent owners and lessors
3951	Pens and mechanical pencils
2721	Periodicals
6141	Personal credit institutions
3172	Personal leather goods, nec
2999	Petroleum and coal products, nec
5171	Petroleum bulk stations and terminals
5172	Petroleum products, nec
2911	Petroleum refining
2834	Pharmaceutical preparations
1475	Phosphate rock
2874	Phosphatic fertilizers
7334	Photocopying and duplicating services
7384	Photofinish laboratories
3861	Photographic equipment and supplies
5043	Photographic equipment and supplies
7221	Photographic studios, portrait
7991	Physical fitness facilities
2035	Pickles, sauces, and salad dressings
5131	Piece goods and notions
1742	Plastering, drywall, and insulation
3085	Plastics bottles
3086	Plastics foam products
5162	Plastics materials and basic shapes
2821	Plastics materials and resins
3084	Plastics pipe
3088	Plastics plumbing fixtures
3089	Plastics products, nec
2796	Platemaking services
3471	Plating and polishing
2395	Pleating and stitching
5074	Plumbing and hydronic heating supplies
3432	Plumbing fixture fittings and trim
1711	Plumbing, heating, air-conditioning
2842	Polishes and sanitation goods
3264	Porcelain electrical supplies
1474	Potash, soda, and borate minerals
2096	Potato chips and similar snacks
3269	Pottery products, nec
5144	Poultry and poultry products
0254	Poultry hatcheries
2015	Poultry slaughtering and processing
3568	Power transmission equipment, nec
3546	Power-driven handtools
3448	Prefabricated metal buildings
2452	Prefabricated wood buildings
7372	Prepackaged software
2048	Prepared feeds, nec
2045	Prepared flour mixes and doughs
3652	Prerecorded records and tapes
3229	Pressed and blown glass, nec
3334	Primary aluminum
3692	Primary batteries, dry and wet
3331	Primary copper
3399	Primary metal products
3339	Primary nonferrous metals, nec
3672	Printed circuit boards
5111	Printing and writing paper
2893	Printing ink
3555	Printing trades machinery
3823	Process control instruments
3231	Products of purchased glass
5049	Professional equipment, nec
8621	Professional organizations
2531	Public building and related furniture
9229	Public order and safety, nec
8743	Public relations services
2611	Pulp mills
3561	Pumps and pumping equipment

R

SIC NO	PRODUCT
7948	Racing, including track operation
3663	Radio and t.v. communications equipment
7622	Radio and television repair
4832	Radio broadcasting stations
5731	Radio, television, and electronic stores
7313	Radio, television, publisher representatives
4812	Radiotelephone communication
3743	Railroad equipment
4011	Railroads, line-haul operating
2061	Raw cane sugar
3273	Ready-mixed concrete
6531	Real estate agents and managers
6798	Real estate investment trusts
2493	Reconstituted wood products
5735	Record and prerecorded tape stores
5561	Recreational vehicle dealers
4613	Refined petroleum pipelines
4222	Refrigerated warehousing and storage
3585	Refrigeration and heating equipment
5078	Refrigeration equipment and supplies
7623	Refrigeration service and repair
4953	Refuse systems
9621	Regulation, administration of transportation
3625	Relays and industrial controls
8661	Religious organizations
7699	Repair services, nec
8361	Residential care
1522	Residential construction, nec
3645	Residential lighting fixtures
5461	Retail bakeries
5261	Retail nurseries and garden stores
7641	Reupholstery and furniture repair
2095	Roasted coffee
2384	Robes and dressing gowns
3547	Rolling mill machinery
5033	Roofing, siding, and insulation
1761	Roofing, siding, and sheetmetal work
3021	Rubber and plastics footwear
3052	Rubber and plastics hose and beltings

S

SIC NO	PRODUCT
2068	Salted and roasted nuts and seeds
2656	Sanitary food containers
2676	Sanitary paper products
4959	Sanitary services, nec
2013	Sausages and other prepared meats
3425	Saw blades and handsaws
2421	Sawmills and planing mills, general
3596	Scales and balances, except laboratory
2397	Schiffli machine embroideries
4151	School buses
8299	Schools and educational services
5093	Scrap and waste materials
3451	Screw machine products
3812	Search and navigation equipment
3341	Secondary nonferrous metals
7338	Secretarial and court reporting
6211	Security brokers and dealers
7382	Security systems services

SIC INDEX

SIC NO	PRODUCT
3674	Semiconductors and related devices
3263	Semivitreous table and kitchenware
5087	Service establishment equipment
3589	Service industry machinery, nec
7819	Services allied to motion pictures
8999	Services, nec
2652	Setup paperboard boxes
4952	Sewerage systems
5949	Sewing, needlework, and piece goods
3444	Sheet metalwork
0913	Shellfish
3731	Shipbuilding and repairing
5661	Shoe stores
6153	Short-term business credit
3993	Signs and advertising specialties
3914	Silverware and plated ware
1521	Single-family housing construction
3484	Small arms
3482	Small arms ammunition
2841	Soap and other detergents
8399	Social services, nec
2436	Softwood veneer and plywood
0711	Soil preparation services
2075	Soybean oil mills
3764	Space propulsion units and parts
3769	Space vehicle equipment, nec
3544	Special dies, tools, jigs, and fixtures
3559	Special industry machinery, nec
2429	Special product sawmills, nec
1799	Special trade contractors, nec
4226	Special warehousing and storage, nec
8093	Specialty outpatient clinics, nec
3566	Speed changers, drives, and gears
3949	Sporting and athletic goods, nec
5091	Sporting and recreation goods
5941	Sporting goods and bicycle shops
7941	Sports clubs, managers, and promoters
5112	Stationery and office supplies
2678	Stationery products
5943	Stationery stores
3325	Steel foundries, nec
3324	Steel investment foundries
3317	Steel pipe and tubes
3493	Steel springs, except wire
3315	Steel wire and related products
3691	Storage batteries
3259	Structural clay products, nec
1791	Structural steel erection
2439	Structural wood members, nec
6552	Subdividers and developers, nec
2843	Surface active agents
3841	Surgical and medical instruments
3842	Surgical appliances and supplies
8713	Surveying services
3613	Switchgear and switchboard apparatus
2822	Synthetic rubber

T

SIC NO	PRODUCT
3795	Tanks and tank components
7291	Tax return preparation services
4822	Telegraph and other communications
3661	Telephone and telegraph apparatus
4813	Telephone communication, except radio
4833	Television broadcasting stations
1743	Terrazzo, tile, marble, mosaic work
8734	Testing laboratories
2393	Textile bags
2299	Textile goods, nec
3552	Textile machinery
7922	Theatrical producers and services
2284	Thread mills
2282	Throwing and winding mills
0811	Timber tracts
2296	Tire cord and fabrics
7534	Tire retreading and repair shops
3011	Tires and inner tubes
5014	Tires and tubes
0132	Tobacco
5194	Tobacco and tobacco products
2141	Tobacco stemming and redrying
5993	Tobacco stores and stands
2844	Toilet preparations
7532	Top and body repair and paint shops
5092	Toys and hobby goods and supplies
7033	Trailer parks and campsites
3612	Transformers, except electric
5088	Transportation equipment and supplies
3799	Transportation equipment, nec
4789	Transportation services, nec
3792	Travel trailers and campers
3713	Truck and bus bodies
7513	Truck rental and leasing, without drivers
3715	Truck trailers
4213	Trucking, except local
6733	Trusts, nec
3511	Turbines and turbine generator sets
0253	Turkeys and turkey eggs
2791	Typesetting

U

SIC NO	PRODUCT
3081	Unsupported plastics film and sheet
3082	Unsupported plastics profile shapes
2512	Upholstered household furniture
5521	Used car dealers
5932	Used merchandise stores
7519	Utility trailer rental

V

SIC NO	PRODUCT
3494	Valves and pipe fittings, nec
5331	Variety stores
0161	Vegetables and melons
3647	Vehicular lighting equipment
7841	Video tape rental
3261	Vitreous plumbing fixtures
8249	Vocational schools, nec

W

SIC NO	PRODUCT
5075	Warm air heating and air conditioning
7631	Watch, clock, and jewelry repair
3873	Watches, clocks, watchcases, and parts
4489	Water passenger transportation
4941	Water supply
4449	Water transportation of freight
1781	Water well drilling
1623	Water, sewer, and utility lines
2385	Waterproof outerwear
2257	Weft knit fabric mills
3548	Welding apparatus
7692	Welding repair
2046	Wet corn milling
5182	Wine and distilled beverages
2084	Wines, brandy, and brandy spirits
3495	Wire springs
5632	Women's accessory and specialty stores
5137	Women's and children's clothing
2341	Women's and children's underwear
2331	Women's and misses' blouses and shirts
2339	Women's and misses' outerwear, nec
2337	Women's and misses' suits and coats
5621	Women's clothing stores
3144	Women's footwear, except athletic
3171	Women's handbags and purses
2251	Women's hosiery, except socks
2335	Women's, junior's, and misses' dresses
2449	Wood containers, nec
2511	Wood household furniture
2434	Wood kitchen cabinets
2521	Wood office furniture
2448	Wood pallets and skids
2541	Wood partitions and fixtures
2491	Wood preserving
2499	Wood products, nec
2517	Wood television and radio cabinets
3553	Woodworking machinery
1795	Wrecking and demolition work

X

SIC NO	PRODUCT
3844	X-ray apparatus and tubes

Y

SIC NO	PRODUCT
2281	Yarn spinning mills

SIC INDEX

Standard Industrial Classification Numerical Index

SIC NO	PRODUCT

01 agricultural production - crops
0119 Cash grains, nec
0131 Cotton
0132 Tobacco
0139 Field crops, except cash grain
0161 Vegetables and melons
0171 Berry crops
0172 Grapes
0174 Citrus fruits
0175 Deciduous tree fruits
0179 Fruits and tree nuts, nec
0181 Ornamental nursery products
0191 General farms, primarily crop

02 agricultural production - livestock and animal specialties
0212 Beef cattle, except feedlots
0213 Hogs
0241 Dairy farms
0251 Broiler, fryer, and roaster chickens
0252 Chicken eggs
0253 Turkeys and turkey eggs
0254 Poultry hatcheries
0279 Animal specialties, nec

07 agricultural services
0711 Soil preparation services
0721 Crop planting and protection
0723 Crop preparation services for market
0724 Cotton ginning
0751 Livestock services, except veterinary
0752 Animal specialty services
0762 Farm management services
0781 Landscape counseling and planning
0782 Lawn and garden services
0783 Ornamental shrub and tree services

08 forestry
0811 Timber tracts
0831 Forest products
0851 Forestry services

09 fishing, hunting and trapping
0913 Shellfish

10 metal mining
1021 Copper ores
1081 Metal mining services
1099 Metal ores, nec

12 coal mining
1221 Bituminous coal and lignite-surface mining
1241 Coal mining services

13 oil and gas extraction
1311 Crude petroleum and natural gas
1321 Natural gas liquids
1381 Drilling oil and gas wells
1382 Oil and gas exploration services
1389 Oil and gas field services, nec

14 mining and quarrying of nonmetallic minerals, except fuels
1411 Dimension stone
1422 Crushed and broken limestone
1423 Crushed and broken granite
1429 Crushed and broken stone, nec
1442 Construction sand and gravel
1446 Industrial sand
1459 Clay and related minerals, nec
1474 Potash, soda, and borate minerals
1475 Phosphate rock
1479 Chemical and fertilizer mining
1481 Nonmetallic mineral services
1499 Miscellaneous nonmetallic mining

15 construction - general contractors & operative builders
1521 Single-family housing construction
1522 Residential construction, nec
1531 Operative builders
1541 Industrial buildings and warehouses
1542 Nonresidential construction, nec

16 heamy construction, except building construction, contractor
1611 Highway and street construction
1622 Bridge, tunnel, and elevated highway
1623 Water, sewer, and utility lines
1629 Heavy construction, nec

17 construction - special trade contractors
1711 Plumbing, heating, air-conditioning
1721 Painting and paper hanging
1731 Electrical work
1741 Masonry and other stonework
1742 Plastering, drywall, and insulation
1743 Terrazzo, tile, marble, mosaic work
1751 Carpentry work
1752 Floor laying and floor work, nec
1761 Roofing, siding, and sheetmetal work
1771 Concrete work
1781 Water well drilling
1791 Structural steel erection
1793 Glass and glazing work
1794 Excavation work
1795 Wrecking and demolition work
1796 Installing building equipment
1799 Special trade contractors, nec

20 food and kindred products
2011 Meat packing plants
2013 Sausages and other prepared meats
2015 Poultry slaughtering and processing
2021 Creamery butter
2022 Cheese; natural and processed
2023 Dry, condensed, evaporated products
2024 Ice cream and frozen deserts
2026 Fluid milk
2032 Canned specialties
2033 Canned fruits and specialties
2034 Dehydrated fruits, vegetables, soups
2035 Pickles, sauces, and salad dressings
2037 Frozen fruits and vegetables
2038 Frozen specialties, nec
2041 Flour and other grain mill products
2043 Cereal breakfast foods
2045 Prepared flour mixes and doughs
2046 Wet corn milling
2047 Dog and cat food
2048 Prepared feeds, nec
2051 Bread, cake, and related products
2052 Cookies and crackers
2053 Frozen bakery products, except bread
2061 Raw cane sugar
2064 Candy and other confectionery products
2066 Chocolate and cocoa products
2068 Salted and roasted nuts and seeds
2074 Cottonseed oil mills
2075 Soybean oil mills
2077 Animal and marine fats and oils
2079 Edible fats and oils
2082 Malt beverages
2083 Malt
2084 Wines, brandy, and brandy spirits
2085 Distilled and blended liquors
2086 Bottled and canned soft drinks
2087 Flavoring extracts and syrups, nec
2091 Canned and cured fish and seafoods
2092 Fresh or frozen packaged fish
2095 Roasted coffee
2096 Potato chips and similar snacks
2097 Manufactured ice
2098 Macaroni and spaghetti
2099 Food preparations, nec

21 tobacco products
2111 Cigarettes
2121 Cigars
2131 Chewing and smoking tobacco
2141 Tobacco stemming and redrying

22 textile mill products
2211 Broadwoven fabric mills, cotton
2221 Broadwoven fabric mills, manmade
2231 Broadwoven fabric mills, wool
2241 Narrow fabric mills
2251 Women's hosiery, except socks
2252 Hosiery, nec
2253 Knit outerwear mills
2254 Knit underwear mills
2257 Weft knit fabric mills
2258 Lace and warp knit fabric mills
2259 Knitting mills, nec
2261 Finishing plants, cotton
2262 Finishing plants, manmade
2269 Finishing plants, nec
2273 Carpets and rugs
2281 Yarn spinning mills
2282 Throwing and winding mills
2284 Thread mills
2295 Coated fabrics, not rubberized
2296 Tire cord and fabrics
2297 Nonwoven fabrics
2298 Cordage and twine
2299 Textile goods, nec

23 apparel, finished products from fabrics & similar materials
2311 Men's and boy's suits and coats
2321 Men's and boy's furnishings
2322 Men's and boy's underwear and nightwear
2323 Men's and boy's neckwear
2325 Men's and boy's trousers and slacks
2326 Men's and boy's work clothing
2329 Men's and boy's clothing, nec
2331 Women's and misses' blouses and shirts
2335 Women's, junior's, and misses' dresses
2337 Women's and misses' suits and coats
2339 Women's and misses' outerwear, nec
2341 Women's and children's underwear
2342 Bras, girdles, and allied garments
2353 Hats, caps, and millinery
2361 Girl's and children's dresses, blouses
2369 Girl's and children's outerwear, nec
2371 Fur goods
2381 Fabric dress and work gloves
2384 Robes and dressing gowns
2385 Waterproof outerwear
2386 Leather and sheep-lined clothing
2387 Apparel belts
2389 Apparel and accessories, nec
2391 Curtains and draperies
2392 Household furnishings, nec
2393 Textile bags
2394 Canvas and related products
2395 Pleating and stitching
2396 Automotive and apparel trimmings
2397 Schiffli machine embroideries
2399 Fabricated textile products, nec

24 lumber and wood products, except furniture
2411 Logging
2421 Sawmills and planing mills, general
2426 Hardwood dimension and flooring mills
2429 Special product sawmills, nec

SIC INDEX

SIC NO	PRODUCT
2431	Millwork
2434	Wood kitchen cabinets
2435	Hardwood veneer and plywood
2436	Softwood veneer and plywood
2439	Structural wood members, nec
2441	Nailed wood boxes and shook
2448	Wood pallets and skids
2449	Wood containers, nec
2451	Mobile homes
2452	Prefabricated wood buildings
2491	Wood preserving
2493	Reconstituted wood products
2499	Wood products, nec

25 furniture and fixtures

SIC NO	PRODUCT
2511	Wood household furniture
2512	Upholstered household furniture
2514	Metal household furniture
2515	Mattresses and bedsprings
2517	Wood television and radio cabinets
2519	Household furniture, nec
2521	Wood office furniture
2522	Office furniture, except wood
2531	Public building and related furniture
2541	Wood partitions and fixtures
2542	Partitions and fixtures, except wood
2591	Drapery hardware and blinds and shades
2599	Furniture and fixtures, nec

26 paper and allied products

SIC NO	PRODUCT
2611	Pulp mills
2621	Paper mills
2631	Paperboard mills
2652	Setup paperboard boxes
2653	Corrugated and solid fiber boxes
2655	Fiber cans, drums, and similar products
2656	Sanitary food containers
2657	Folding paperboard boxes
2671	Paper; coated and laminated packaging
2672	Paper; coated and laminated, nec
2673	Bags: plastic, laminated, and coated
2674	Bags: uncoated paper and multiwall
2675	Die-cut paper and board
2676	Sanitary paper products
2677	Envelopes
2678	Stationery products
2679	Converted paper products, nec

27 printing, publishing and allied industries

SIC NO	PRODUCT
2711	Newspapers
2721	Periodicals
2731	Book publishing
2732	Book printing
2741	Miscellaneous publishing
2752	Commercial printing, lithographic
2754	Commercial printing, gravure
2759	Commercial printing, nec
2761	Manifold business forms
2771	Greeting cards
2782	Blankbooks and looseleaf binders
2789	Bookbinding and related work
2791	Typesetting
2796	Platemaking services

28 chemicals and allied products

SIC NO	PRODUCT
2812	Alkalies and chlorine
2813	Industrial gases
2816	Inorganic pigments
2819	Industrial inorganic chemicals, nec
2821	Plastics materials and resins
2822	Synthetic rubber
2823	Cellulosic manmade fibers
2824	Organic fibers, noncellulosic
2833	Medicinals and botanicals
2834	Pharmaceutical preparations
2835	Diagnostic substances
2836	Biological products, except diagnostic
2841	Soap and other detergents
2842	Polishes and sanitation goods
2843	Surface active agents
2844	Toilet preparations
2851	Paints and allied products
2861	Gum and wood chemicals
2865	Cyclic crudes and intermediates
2869	Industrial organic chemicals, nec
2873	Nitrogenous fertilizers
2874	Phosphatic fertilizers
2875	Fertilizers, mixing only
2879	Agricultural chemicals, nec
2891	Adhesives and sealants
2892	Explosives
2893	Printing ink
2895	Carbon black
2899	Chemical preparations, nec

29 petroleum refining and related industries

SIC NO	PRODUCT
2911	Petroleum refining
2951	Asphalt paving mixtures and blocks
2952	Asphalt felts and coatings
2992	Lubricating oils and greases
2999	Petroleum and coal products, nec

30 rubber and miscellaneous plastic products

SIC NO	PRODUCT
3011	Tires and inner tubes
3021	Rubber and plastics footwear
3052	Rubber and plastics hose and beltings
3053	Gaskets; packing and sealing devices
3061	Mechanical rubber goods
3069	Fabricated rubber products, nec
3081	Unsupported plastics film and sheet
3082	Unsupported plastics profile shapes
3083	Laminated plastics plate and sheet
3084	Plastics pipe
3085	Plastics bottles
3086	Plastics foam products
3087	Custom compound purchased resins
3088	Plastics plumbing fixtures
3089	Plastics products, nec

31 leather and leather products

SIC NO	PRODUCT
3111	Leather tanning and finishing
3131	Footwear cut stock
3143	Men's footwear, except athletic
3144	Women's footwear, except athletic
3149	Footwear, except rubber, nec
3151	Leather gloves and mittens
3161	Luggage
3171	Women's handbags and purses
3172	Personal leather goods, nec
3199	Leather goods, nec

32 stone, clay, glass, and concrete products

SIC NO	PRODUCT
3211	Flat glass
3221	Glass containers
3229	Pressed and blown glass, nec
3231	Products of purchased glass
3241	Cement, hydraulic
3251	Brick and structural clay tile
3253	Ceramic wall and floor tile
3255	Clay refractories
3259	Structural clay products, nec
3261	Vitreous plumbing fixtures
3263	Semivitreous table and kitchenware
3264	Porcelain electrical supplies
3269	Pottery products, nec
3271	Concrete block and brick
3272	Concrete products, nec
3273	Ready-mixed concrete
3275	Gypsum products
3281	Cut stone and stone products
3291	Abrasive products
3292	Asbestos products
3295	Minerals, ground or treated
3296	Mineral wool
3297	Nonclay refractories
3299	Nonmetallic mineral products,

33 primary metal industries

SIC NO	PRODUCT
3312	Blast furnaces and steel mills
3313	Electrometallurgical products
3315	Steel wire and related products
3316	Cold finishing of steel shapes
3317	Steel pipe and tubes
3321	Gray and ductile iron foundries
3324	Steel investment foundries
3325	Steel foundries, nec
3331	Primary copper
3334	Primary aluminum
3339	Primary nonferrous metals, nec
3341	Secondary nonferrous metals
3351	Copper rolling and drawing
3353	Aluminum sheet, plate, and foil
3354	Aluminum extruded products
3355	Aluminum rolling and drawing, nec
3356	Nonferrous rolling and drawing, nec
3357	Nonferrous wiredrawing and insulating
3363	Aluminum die-castings
3364	Nonferrous die-castings except aluminum
3365	Aluminum foundries
3366	Copper foundries
3369	Nonferrous foundries, nec
3398	Metal heat treating
3399	Primary metal products

34 fabricated metal products

SIC NO	PRODUCT
3411	Metal cans
3412	Metal barrels, drums, and pails
3421	Cutlery
3423	Hand and edge tools, nec
3425	Saw blades and handsaws
3429	Hardware, nec
3431	Metal sanitary ware
3432	Plumbing fixture fittings and trim
3433	Heating equipment, except electric
3441	Fabricated structural metal
3442	Metal doors, sash, and trim
3443	Fabricated plate work (boiler shop)
3444	Sheet metalwork
3446	Architectural metalwork
3448	Prefabricated metal buildings
3449	Miscellaneous metalwork
3451	Screw machine products
3452	Bolts, nuts, rivets, and washers
3462	Iron and steel forgings
3463	Nonferrous forgings
3465	Automotive stampings
3466	Crowns and closures
3469	Metal stampings, nec
3471	Plating and polishing
3479	Metal coating and allied services
3482	Small arms ammunition
3483	Ammunition, except for small arms, nec
3484	Small arms
3489	Ordnance and accessories, nec
3491	Industrial valves
3492	Fluid power valves and hose fittings
3493	Steel springs, except wire
3494	Valves and pipe fittings, nec
3495	Wire springs
3496	Miscellaneous fabricated wire products
3497	Metal foil and leaf
3498	Fabricated pipe and fittings
3499	Fabricated metal products, nec

35 industrial and commercial machinery and computer equipment

SIC NO	PRODUCT
3511	Turbines and turbine generator sets
3519	Internal combustion engines, nec
3523	Farm machinery and equipment
3524	Lawn and garden equipment
3531	Construction machinery
3532	Mining machinery
3533	Oil and gas field machinery
3534	Elevators and moving stairways
3535	Conveyors and conveying equipment
3536	Hoists, cranes, and monorails
3537	Industrial trucks and tractors
3541	Machine tools, metal cutting type
3542	Machine tools, metal forming type
3543	Industrial patterns
3544	Special dies, tools, jigs, and fixtures
3545	Machine tool accessories
3546	Power-driven handtools
3547	Rolling mill machinery
3548	Welding apparatus
3549	Metalworking machinery, nec

SIC INDEX

SIC NO	PRODUCT
3552	Textile machinery
3553	Woodworking machinery
3554	Paper industries machinery
3555	Printing trades machinery
3556	Food products machinery
3559	Special industry machinery, nec
3561	Pumps and pumping equipment
3562	Ball and roller bearings
3563	Air and gas compressors
3564	Blowers and fans
3565	Packaging machinery
3566	Speed changers, drives, and gears
3567	Industrial furnaces and ovens
3568	Power transmission equipment, nec
3569	General industrial machinery,
3571	Electronic computers
3572	Computer storage devices
3575	Computer terminals
3577	Computer peripheral equipment, nec
3578	Calculating and accounting equipment
3579	Office machines, nec
3581	Automatic vending machines
3582	Commercial laundry equipment
3585	Refrigeration and heating equipment
3586	Measuring and dispensing pumps
3589	Service industry machinery, nec
3592	Carburetors, pistons, rings, valves
3593	Fluid power cylinders and actuators
3594	Fluid power pumps and motors
3596	Scales and balances, except laboratory
3599	Industrial machinery, nec

36 electronic & other electrical equipment & components

SIC NO	PRODUCT
3612	Transformers, except electric
3613	Switchgear and switchboard apparatus
3621	Motors and generators
3624	Carbon and graphite products
3625	Relays and industrial controls
3629	Electrical industrial apparatus
3631	Household cooking equipment
3632	Household refrigerators and freezers
3634	Electric housewares and fans
3635	Household vacuum cleaners
3639	Household appliances, nec
3641	Electric lamps
3643	Current-carrying wiring devices
3644	Noncurrent-carrying wiring devices
3645	Residential lighting fixtures
3646	Commercial lighting fixtures
3647	Vehicular lighting equipment
3648	Lighting equipment, nec
3651	Household audio and video equipment
3652	Prerecorded records and tapes
3661	Telephone and telegraph apparatus
3663	Radio and t.v. communications equipment
3669	Communications equipment, nec
3671	Electron tubes
3672	Printed circuit boards
3674	Semiconductors and related devices
3675	Electronic capacitors
3676	Electronic resistors
3677	Electronic coils and transformers
3678	Electronic connectors
3679	Electronic components, nec
3691	Storage batteries
3692	Primary batteries, dry and wet
3694	Engine electrical equipment
3695	Magnetic and optical recording media
3699	Electrical equipment and supplies, nec

37 transportation equipment

SIC NO	PRODUCT
3711	Motor vehicles and car bodies
3713	Truck and bus bodies
3714	Motor vehicle parts and accessories
3715	Truck trailers
3716	Motor homes
3721	Aircraft
3724	Aircraft engines and engine parts
3728	Aircraft parts and equipment, nec
3731	Shipbuilding and repairing
3732	Boatbuilding and repairing
3743	Railroad equipment
3751	Motorcycles, bicycles, and parts
3761	Guided missiles and space vehicles
3764	Space propulsion units and parts
3769	Space vehicle equipment, nec
3792	Travel trailers and campers
3795	Tanks and tank components
3799	Transportation equipment, nec

38 measuring, photographic, medical, & optical goods, & clocks

SIC NO	PRODUCT
3812	Search and navigation equipment
3821	Laboratory apparatus and furniture
3822	Environmental controls
3823	Process control instruments
3824	Fluid meters and counting devices
3825	Instruments to measure electricity
3826	Analytical instruments
3827	Optical instruments and lenses
3829	Measuring and controlling devices, nec
3841	Surgical and medical instruments
3842	Surgical appliances and supplies
3843	Dental equipment and supplies
3844	X-ray apparatus and tubes
3845	Electromedical equipment
3851	Ophthalmic goods
3861	Photographic equipment and supplies
3873	Watches, clocks, watchcases, and parts

39 miscellaneous manufacturing industries

SIC NO	PRODUCT
3911	Jewelry, precious metal
3914	Silverware and plated ware
3915	Jewelers' materials and lapidary work
3931	Musical instruments
3942	Dolls and stuffed toys
3944	Games, toys, and children's vehicles
3949	Sporting and athletic goods, nec
3951	Pens and mechanical pencils
3952	Lead pencils and art goods
3953	Marking devices
3955	Carbon paper and inked ribbons
3961	Costume jewelry
3965	Fasteners, buttons, needles, and pins
3991	Brooms and brushes
3993	Signs and advertising specialties
3995	Burial caskets
3996	Hard surface floor coverings, nec
3999	Manufacturing industries, nec

40 railroad transportation

SIC NO	PRODUCT
4011	Railroads, line-haul operating

41 local & suburban transit & interurban highway transportation

SIC NO	PRODUCT
4111	Local and suburban transit
4151	School buses

42 motor freight transportation

SIC NO	PRODUCT
4212	Local trucking, without storage
4213	Trucking, except local
4214	Local trucking with storage
4215	Courier services, except by air
4221	Farm product warehousing and storage
4222	Refrigerated warehousing and storage
4225	General warehousing and storage
4226	Special warehousing and storage, nec

44 water transportation

SIC NO	PRODUCT
4449	Water transportation of freight
4489	Water passenger transportation
4493	Marinas

45 transportation by air

SIC NO	PRODUCT
4512	Air transportation, scheduled
4513	Air courier services
4522	Air transportation, nonscheduled
4581	Airports, flying fields, and services

46 pipelines, except natural gas

SIC NO	PRODUCT
4613	Refined petroleum pipelines

47 transportation services

SIC NO	PRODUCT
4731	Freight transportation arrangement
4783	Packing and crating
4785	Inspection and fixed facilities
4789	Transportation services, nec

48 communications

SIC NO	PRODUCT
4812	Radiotelephone communication
4813	Telephone communication, except radio
4822	Telegraph and other communications
4832	Radio broadcasting stations
4833	Television broadcasting stations
4841	Cable and other pay television services
4899	Communication services, nec

49 electric, gas and sanitary services

SIC NO	PRODUCT
4911	Electric services
4922	Natural gas transmission
4924	Natural gas distribution
4931	Electric and other services combined
4941	Water supply
4952	Sewerage systems
4953	Refuse systems
4959	Sanitary services, nec

50 wholesale trade - durable goods

SIC NO	PRODUCT
5012	Automobiles and other motor vehicles
5013	Motor vehicle supplies and new parts
5014	Tires and tubes
5015	Motor vehicle parts, used
5021	Furniture
5023	Homefurnishings
5031	Lumber, plywood, and millwork
5032	Brick, stone, and related material
5033	Roofing, siding, and insulation
5039	Construction materials, nec
5043	Photographic equipment and supplies
5044	Office equipment
5045	Computers, peripherals, and software
5046	Commercial equipment, nec
5047	Medical and hospital equipment
5049	Professional equipment, nec
5051	Metals service centers and offices
5052	Coal and other minerals and ores
5063	Electrical apparatus and equipment
5064	Electrical appliances, television and radio
5065	Electronic parts and equipment, nec
5072	Hardware
5074	Plumbing and hydronic heating supplies
5075	Warm air heating and air conditioning
5078	Refrigeration equipment and supplies
5082	Construction and mining machinery
5083	Farm and garden machinery
5084	Industrial machinery and equipment
5085	Industrial supplies
5087	Service establishment equipment
5088	Transportation equipment and supplies
5091	Sporting and recreation goods
5092	Toys and hobby goods and supplies
5093	Scrap and waste materials
5094	Jewelry and precious stones
5099	Durable goods, nec

51 wholesale trade - nondurable goods

SIC NO	PRODUCT
5111	Printing and writing paper
5112	Stationery and office supplies
5113	Industrial and personal service paper
5122	Drugs, proprietaries, and sundries
5131	Piece goods and notions
5136	Men's and boy's clothing
5137	Women's and children's clothing
5139	Footwear
5141	Groceries, general line
5142	Packaged frozen goods
5143	Dairy products, except dried or canned
5144	Poultry and poultry products
5145	Confectionery
5146	Fish and seafoods
5147	Meats and meat products
5148	Fresh fruits and vegetables
5149	Groceries and related products, nec
5153	Grain and field beans
5159	Farm-product raw materials, nec
5162	Plastics materials and basic shapes

SIC INDEX

SIC NO	PRODUCT
5169	Chemicals and allied products, nec
5171	Petroleum bulk stations and terminals
5172	Petroleum products, nec
5181	Beer and ale
5182	Wine and distilled beverages
5191	Farm supplies
5192	Books, periodicals, and newspapers
5193	Flowers and florists supplies
5194	Tobacco and tobacco products
5198	Paints, varnishes, and supplies
5199	Nondurable goods, nec

52 building materials, hardware, garden supplies & mobile homes

5211	Lumber and other building materials
5231	Paint, glass, and wallpaper stores
5251	Hardware stores
5261	Retail nurseries and garden stores
5271	Mobile home dealers

53 general merchandise stores

5311	Department stores
5331	Variety stores
5399	Miscellaneous general merchandise

54 food stores

5411	Grocery stores
5421	Meat and fish markets
5441	Candy, nut, and confectionery stores
5451	Dairy products stores
5461	Retail bakeries
5499	Miscellaneous food stores

55 automotive dealers and gasoline service stations

5511	New and used car dealers
5521	Used car dealers
5531	Auto and home supply stores
5541	Gasoline service stations
5551	Boat dealers
5561	Recreational vehicle dealers
5571	Motorcycle dealers
5599	Automotive dealers, nec

56 apparel and accessory stores

5611	Men's and boys' clothing stores
5621	Women's clothing stores
5632	Women's accessory and specialty stores
5641	Children's and infants' wear stores
5651	Family clothing stores
5661	Shoe stores
5699	Miscellaneous apparel and accessories

57 home furniture, furnishings and equipment stores

5712	Furniture stores
5713	Floor covering stores
5714	Drapery and upholstery stores
5719	Miscellaneous homefurnishings
5722	Household appliance stores
5731	Radio, television, and electronic stores
5734	Computer and software stores
5735	Record and prerecorded tape stores
5736	Musical instrument stores

58 eating and drinking places

5812	Eating places
5813	Drinking places

59 miscellaneous retail

5912	Drug stores and proprietary stores
5921	Liquor stores
5932	Used merchandise stores
5941	Sporting goods and bicycle shops
5942	Book stores
5943	Stationery stores
5944	Jewelry stores
5945	Hobby, toy, and game shops
5946	Camera and photographic supply stores
5947	Gift, novelty, and souvenir shop
5949	Sewing, needlework, and piece goods
5961	Catalog and mail-order houses
5962	Merchandising machine operators
5963	Direct selling establishments

SIC NO	PRODUCT
5983	Fuel oil dealers
5984	Liquefied petroleum gas dealers
5989	Fuel dealers, nec
5992	Florists
5993	Tobacco stores and stands
5994	News dealers and newsstands
5995	Optical goods stores
5999	Miscellaneous retail stores, nec

61 nondepository credit institutions

6141	Personal credit institutions
6153	Short-term business credit
6159	Miscellaneous business credit
6162	Mortgage bankers and correspondents

62 security & commodity brokers, dealers, exchanges & services

6211	Security brokers and dealers
6221	Commodity contracts brokers, dealers
6282	Investment advice

63 insurance carriers

6311	Life insurance
6331	Fire, marine, and casualty insurance

64 insurance agents, brokers and service

6411	Insurance agents, brokers, and service

65 real estate

6512	Nonresidential building operators
6513	Apartment building operators
6531	Real estate agents and managers
6552	Subdividers and developers, nec

67 holding and other investment offices

6719	Holding companies, nec
6733	Trusts, nec
6794	Patent owners and lessors
6798	Real estate investment trusts
6799	Investors, nec

70 hotels, rooming houses, camps, and other lodging places

7011	Hotels and motels
7033	Trailer parks and campsites

72 personal services

7212	Garment pressing and cleaners' agents
7215	Coin-operated laundries and cleaning
7216	Drycleaning plants, except rugs
7217	Carpet and upholstery cleaning
7218	Industrial launderers
7219	Laundry and garment services, nec
7221	Photographic studios, portrait
7231	Beauty shops
7241	Barber shops
7261	Funeral service and crematories
7291	Tax return preparation services
7299	Miscellaneous personal services

73 business services

7311	Advertising agencies
7312	Outdoor advertising services
7313	Radio, television, publisher representatives
7319	Advertising, nec
7331	Direct mail advertising services
7334	Photocopying and duplicating services
7335	Commercial photography
7336	Commercial art and graphic design
7338	Secretarial and court reporting
7342	Disinfecting and pest control services
7349	Building maintenance services, nec
7352	Medical equipment rental
7353	Heavy construction equipment rental
7359	Equipment rental and leasing, nec
7363	Help supply services
7371	Custom computer programming services
7372	Prepackaged software
7373	Computer integrated systems design
7374	Data processing and preparation
7375	Information retrieval services
7376	Computer facilities management

SIC NO	PRODUCT
7378	Computer maintenance and repair
7379	Computer related services, nec
7381	Detective and armored car services
7382	Security systems services
7384	Photofinish laboratories
7389	Business services, nec

75 automotive repair, services and parking

7513	Truck rental and leasing, without drivers
7514	Passenger car rental
7515	Passenger car leasing
7519	Utility trailer rental
7521	Automobile parking
7532	Top and body repair and paint shops
7534	Tire retreading and repair shops
7536	Automotive glass replacement shops
7537	Automotive transmission repair shops
7538	General automotive repair shops
7539	Automotive repair shops, nec
7542	Carwashes
7549	Automotive services, nec

76 miscellaneous repair services

7622	Radio and television repair
7623	Refrigeration service and repair
7629	Electrical repair shops
7631	Watch, clock, and jewelry repair
7641	Reupholstery and furniture repair
7692	Welding repair
7694	Armature rewinding shops
7699	Repair services, nec

78 motion pictures

7812	Motion picture and video production
7819	Services allied to motion pictures
7822	Motion picture and tape distribution
7841	Video tape rental

79 amusement and recreation services

7922	Theatrical producers and services
7929	Entertainers and entertainment groups
7941	Sports clubs, managers, and promoters
7948	Racing, including track operation
7991	Physical fitness facilities
7993	Coin-operated amusement devices
7999	Amusement and recreation, nec

80 health services

8011	Offices and clinics of medical doctors
8021	Offices and clinics of dentists
8042	Offices and clinics of optometrists
8049	Offices of health practitioner
8062	General medical and surgical hospitals
8071	Medical laboratories
8072	Dental laboratories
8082	Home health care services
8093	Specialty outpatient clinics, nec
8099	Health and allied services, nec

82 educational services

8211	Elementary and secondary schools
8221	Colleges and universities
8243	Data processing schools
8249	Vocational schools, nec
8299	Schools and educational services

83 social services

8322	Individual and family services
8331	Job training and related services
8361	Residential care
8399	Social services, nec

84 museums, art galleries and botanical and zoological gardens

8412	Museums and art galleries

86 membership organizations

8611	Business associations
8621	Professional organizations
8661	Religious organizations
8699	Membership organizations, nec

SIC INDEX

SIC NO	PRODUCT

87 engineering, accounting, research, and management services
8711 Engineering services
8712 Architectural services
8713 Surveying services
8721 Accounting, auditing, and bookkeeping
8731 Commercial physical research
8732 Commercial nonphysical research
8733 Noncommercial research organizations
8734 Testing laboratories
8741 Management services
8742 Management consulting services
8743 Public relations services
8744 Facilities support services
8748 Business consulting, nec

89 services, not elsewhere classified
8999 Services, nec

92 justice, public order and safety
9223 Correctional institutions
9229 Public order and safety, nec

93 public finance, taxation and monetary policy
9311 Finance, taxation, and monetary policy

95 administration of environmental quality and housing programs
9512 Land, mineral, and wildlife conservation

96 administration of economic programs
9621 Regulation, administration of transportation

97 national security and international affairs
9711 National security

SIC SECTION

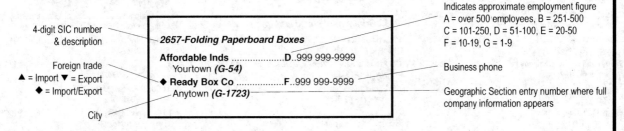

See footnotes for symbols and codes identification.
- The SIC codes in this section are from the latest Standard Industrial Classification manual published by the U.S. Government's Office of Management and Budget. For more information regarding SICs, see the Explanatory Notes.
- Companies may be listed under multiple classifications.

01 AGRICULTURAL PRODUCTION - CROPS

0119 Cash grains, nec
Cogent Dynamics Inc........................... G 828 628-9025
　Fletcher *(G-5995)*

0131 Cotton
Barnhardt Manufacturing Co................... C 704 331-0657
　Charlotte *(G-2282)*

0132 Tobacco
Loflin Handle Co Inc............................ F 336 463-2422
　Yadkinville *(G-17043)*
Top Tobacco LP................................. C 910 646-3014
　Lake Waccamaw *(G-9449)*

0139 Field crops, except cash grain
Barkleys Mill On Southern Cro.............. G 828 626-3344
　Weaverville *(G-15839)*
Fosterscape LLP................................ G 910 401-7638
　Fayetteville *(G-5827)*
Founders Hemp LLC........................... G 888 334-4367
　Asheboro *(G-436)*
Thompson Sunny Acres Inc................. G 910 206-1801
　Rockingham *(G-13644)*

0161 Vegetables and melons
◆ Dole Food Company Inc....................E 818 874-4000
　Charlotte *(G-2650)*

0171 Berry crops
McClellan Patric Michael..................... G 336 385-1878
　Creston *(G-4623)*

0172 Grapes
Hinnant Farms Vineyard LLC................ F 919 965-3350
　Pine Level *(G-12210)*
Shelton Vineyards Inc......................... E 336 366-4818
　Dobson *(G-4831)*

0174 Citrus fruits
◆ Dole Food Company Inc....................E 818 874-4000
　Charlotte *(G-2650)*

0175 Deciduous tree fruits
◆ Dole Food Company Inc....................E 818 874-4000
　Charlotte *(G-2650)*
McClellan Patric Michael..................... G 336 385-1878
　Creston *(G-4623)*

0179 Fruits and tree nuts, nec
◆ Dole Food Company Inc....................E 818 874-4000
　Charlotte *(G-2650)*

0181 Ornamental nursery products
Southern States Coop Inc.................... G 336 246-3201
　Creedmoor *(G-4620)*
Southern States Coop Inc.................... E 336 786-7545
　Mount Airy *(G-11575)*
Southern States Coop Inc.................... E 919 658-5061
　Mount Olive *(G-11669)*
Southern States Coop Inc.................... E 704 872-6364
　Statesville *(G-14896)*
Southern States Coop Inc.................... F 910 285-8213
　Wallace *(G-15628)*
Taylco Inc... E 910 739-0405
　Lumberton *(G-10057)*

0191 General farms, primarily crop
Boggs Farm Center Inc........................ G 704 538-7176
　Fallston *(G-5728)*
Catawba Farms Enterprises LLC........... F 828 464-5780
　Newton *(G-11917)*
Cauley Construction Company.............. G 252 522-1078
　Kinston *(G-9353)*
Fading D Farm LLC............................. G 704 633-3888
　Salisbury *(G-13962)*
Mystic Farm & Distillery....................... G 336 409-0131
　Durham *(G-5233)*
Wainwright Warehouse......................... G 252 237-5121
　Wilson *(G-16556)*

02 AGRICULTURAL PRODUCTION - LIVESTOCK AND ANIMAL SPECIALTIES

0212 Beef cattle, except feedlots
Boggs Farm Center Inc........................ G 704 538-7176
　Fallston *(G-5728)*
Cauley Construction Company.............. G 252 522-1078
　Kinston *(G-9353)*

0213 Hogs
Futrell Precasting LLC........................ G 252 568-3481
　Deep Run *(G-4716)*
◆ Hog Slat Incorporated....................... B 800 949-4647
　Newton Grove *(G-11988)*
Murphy-Brown LLC.............................. C 910 282-4264
　Rose Hill *(G-13780)*

▲ Murphy-Brown LLC............................ D 910 293-3434
　Warsaw *(G-15671)*

0241 Dairy farms
Buffalo Creek Farm & Crmry LLC.......... G 336 969-5698
　Germanton *(G-6552)*
Fading D Farm LLC............................. G 704 633-3888
　Salisbury *(G-13962)*

0251 Broiler, fryer, and roaster chickens
◆ Johnson Nash & Sons Farms Inc........ B 910 289-3113
　Rose Hill *(G-13778)*

0252 Chicken eggs
Pilgrims Pride Corporation.................... B 704 624-2171
　Marshville *(G-10222)*

0253 Turkeys and turkey eggs
◆ Johnson Nash & Sons Farms Inc........ B 910 289-3113
　Rose Hill *(G-13778)*
Sleepy Creek Turkeys LLC................... C 919 778-3130
　Goldsboro *(G-6657)*

0254 Poultry hatcheries
◆ Johnson Nash & Sons Farms Inc........ B 910 289-3113
　Rose Hill *(G-13778)*
Pilgrims Pride Corporation.................... B 704 624-2171
　Marshville *(G-10222)*

0279 Animal specialties, nec
Archie Supply LLC............................... G 336 987-0895
　Greensboro *(G-6813)*
Fosterscape LLP................................ G 910 401-7638
　Fayetteville *(G-5827)*

07 AGRICULTURAL SERVICES

0711 Soil preparation services
Carolina Golfco Inc.............................. G 704 525-7846
　Charlotte *(G-2397)*
Carolina Stalite Co Ltd Partnr............... E 704 279-2166
　Gold Hill *(G-6580)*
Carolina Stalite Co Ltd Partnr............... F 704 637-1515
　Salisbury *(G-13937)*

0721 Crop planting and protection
CPM of Nc Inc.................................... G 704 467-5819
　Concord *(G-4246)*

0723 Crop preparation services for market
Communitys Kitchen L3c...................... G 828 817-2308
　Tryon *(G-15423)*

07 AGRICULTURAL SERVICES

Garland Farm Supply Inc .... F 910 529-9731
   Garland *(G-6244)*
Mineral Springs Fertilizer Inc .... G 704 843-2683
   Mineral Springs *(G-10518)*
Renwood Mills LLC .... D 828 465-0302
   Newton *(G-11963)*
Sandy Land Peanut Company Inc .... F 252 356-2679
   Harrellsville *(G-7698)*

0724 Cotton ginning

Boggs Farm Center Inc .... G 704 538-7176
   Fallston *(G-5728)*
Coastal Carolina Gin LLC .... F 252 943-6990
   Pantego *(G-12162)*
Sampson Gin Company Inc .... F 910 567-5111
   Newton Grove *(G-11992)*

0751 Livestock services, except veterinary

Bailey Foods LLC .... E 252 235-3558
   Wilson *(G-16472)*
Mitchells Meat Processing .... F 336 591-7420
   Walnut Cove *(G-15633)*
▼ Parks Family Meats LLC .... F 217 446-4600
   Warsaw *(G-15672)*
Thomas Brothers Slaughter Hse .... G 336 667-1346
   North Wilkesboro *(G-12035)*

0752 Animal specialty services

Farm Services Inc .... G 336 226-7381
   Graham *(G-6689)*

0762 Farm management services

Sanders Ridge Inc .... G 336 677-1700
   Boonville *(G-1256)*

0781 Landscape counseling and planning

Butler Trieu Inc .... G 910 346-4929
   Jacksonville *(G-8992)*
Carolina Lawnscape Inc .... G 803 230-5570
   Charlotte *(G-2398)*
M & M Stone Sculpting & Engrv .... G 336 877-3842
   Todd *(G-15323)*
Native Naturalz Inc .... F 336 334-2984
   Greensboro *(G-7213)*
Southern Elements Hardscapes .... G 240 626-1586
   Sanford *(G-14188)*
Triple M Consolidated Inc .... G 910 484-1303
   Fayetteville *(G-5933)*

0782 Lawn and garden services

Bemis Manufacturing Company .... C 828 754-1086
   Lenoir *(G-9581)*
Butler Trieu Inc .... G 910 346-4929
   Jacksonville *(G-8992)*
Carlton Enterprizes LLC .... G 919 534-5424
   Rocky Point *(G-13743)*
Carolina Lawnscape Inc .... G 803 230-5570
   Charlotte *(G-2398)*
Classic Cleaning LLC .... E 800 220-7101
   Raleigh *(G-12626)*
Day 3 Lwncare Ldscpg Prfctnist .... G 910 574-8422
   Fayetteville *(G-5806)*
McKinney Lwncare Grbage Svc LL ...... G 828 766-9490
   Spruce Pine *(G-14649)*
Quality Turf Hauling LLC .... F 336 516-1156
   Haw River *(G-7756)*
RDc Debris Removal Cnstr LLC .... E 323 614-2353
   Smithfield *(G-14479)*
Southern Elements Hardscapes .... G 240 626-1586
   Sanford *(G-14188)*
Taylco Inc .... E 910 739-0405
   Lumberton *(G-10057)*

Top Dawg Landscape Inc .... G 336 877-7519
   West Jefferson *(G-15949)*

0783 Ornamental shrub and tree services

Bickerstaff Trees Inc .... G 336 372-8866
   Sparta *(G-14589)*
CTI Property Services Inc .... E 919 787-3789
   Raleigh *(G-12659)*
NBC Enterprises Inc .... F 910 705-5781
   Fayetteville *(G-5880)*

08 FORESTRY

0811 Timber tracts

Lane Land & Timber Inc .... G 252 443-1151
   Battleboro *(G-923)*

0831 Forest products

G & G Forest Products .... G 704 539-5110
   Union Grove *(G-15437)*
◆ Ivp Forest Products LLC .... F 252 241-8126
   Morehead City *(G-11177)*

0851 Forestry services

M & R Forestry Service Inc .... G 980 439-1261
   Albemarle *(G-96)*

09 FISHING, HUNTING AND TRAPPING

0913 Shellfish

Lloyds Oyster House Inc .... E 910 754-6958
   Shallotte *(G-14276)*

10 METAL MINING

1021 Copper ores

Ames Copper Group LLC .... F 860 622-7626
   Shelby *(G-14286)*

1081 Metal mining services

Charah LLC .... C 704 731-2300
   Charlotte *(G-2447)*
Charah LLC .... C 502 873-6993
   Mount Holly *(G-11626)*
Iperionx Technology LLC .... E 704 578-3217
   Charlotte *(G-2994)*
RDc Debris Removal Cnstr LLC .... E 323 614-2353
   Smithfield *(G-14479)*

1099 Metal ores, nec

Iperionx Limited .... E 704 578-3217
   Charlotte *(G-2993)*

12 COAL MINING

1221 Bituminous coal and lignite-surface mining

Florida Progress Corporation .... C 704 382-3853
   Raleigh *(G-12775)*

1241 Coal mining services

Aurum Capital Ventures Inc .... F 877 467-7780
   Cary *(G-1695)*
▲ Cowee Mountain Ruby Mine .... G 828 369-5271
   Franklin *(G-6123)*

13 OIL AND GAS EXTRACTION

1311 Crude petroleum and natural gas

Bretagne LLC .... G 336 299-8729
   Greensboro *(G-6850)*
City of Lexington .... E 336 248-3945
   Lexington *(G-9695)*
City of Shelby .... E 704 484-6840
   Shelby *(G-14295)*
Ets .... G 919 556-7899
   Youngsville *(G-17079)*
First Coast Energy LLP .... G 828 667-0625
   Asheville *(G-621)*
L TS Gas and Snaks .... G 910 762-7130
   Wilmington *(G-16292)*
Refinery 56 LLC .... G 910 215-0596
   Pinehurst *(G-12233)*
Renewco-Meadow Branch LLC .... G 404 584-3552
   Wake Forest *(G-15583)*
Sg-Clw Inc .... F 336 865-4980
   Winston Salem *(G-16903)*
Srng-Liberty LLC .... G 248 212-7209
   Charlotte *(G-3613)*
SRNg-T&w LLC .... G 704 271-9889
   Charlotte *(G-3614)*
Trans-Tech Energy LLC .... G 254 840-3355
   Rocky Mount *(G-13675)*
Warren Oil Co Inc Louisburg .... G 252 764-2171
   Swansboro *(G-15049)*

1321 Natural gas liquids

Bi County Gas Producers LLC .... G 704 844-8990
   Charlotte *(G-2307)*
Diversified Energy LLC .... G 828 266-9800
   Boone *(G-1194)*
Euliss Oil Company Inc .... G 336 622-3055
   Liberty *(G-9813)*
Green Power Producers .... G 704 844-8990
   Charlotte *(G-2863)*
Landfill Gas Producers .... F 704 844-8990
   Charlotte *(G-3072)*
Panenergy Corp .... F 704 594-6200
   Charlotte *(G-3310)*
Renewable Power Producers LLC .... G 704 844-8990
   Charlotte *(G-3433)*
South Central Oil and Prpn Inc .... G 704 982-2173
   Albemarle *(G-106)*

1381 Drilling oil and gas wells

4d Directional Boring LLC .... G 614 348-1339
   Elizabeth City *(G-5529)*
Bobby Benton .... G 252 527-7023
   Kinston *(G-9346)*
Carlson Environmental Cons PC .... D 704 283-9765
   Monroe *(G-10673)*
Earth Matters Inc .... G 410 747-4400
   Denver *(G-4775)*
NBC Enterprises Inc .... F 910 705-5781
   Fayetteville *(G-5880)*
Oilkleen Inc .... G 480 650-8711
   Mooresville *(G-11041)*
Tim Hlley Excvtg Drctnal Drlg .... G 336 595-3320
   Walkertown *(G-15617)*
Upfront Well of The Carolinas .... G 919 415-6000
   Raleigh *(G-13384)*
Vision Directional Drilling .... G 336 570-4621
   Burlington *(G-1514)*

1382 Oil and gas exploration services

3d Oil Inc .... G 609 408-9159
   Swansboro *(G-15041)*
Blackhawk Diversified Svcs Inc .... G 919 279-5679
   Raleigh *(G-12562)*
BP Oil Corp Distributors .... G 828 264-8516
   Boone *(G-1181)*

Citi Energy LLC .... F 336 379-0800
  Greensboro *(G-6910)*
▲ Das Oil Werks LLC .... G 919 267-5781
  New Hill *(G-11860)*
Energy and Entropy Inc .... G 919 933-1365
  Chapel Hill *(G-2013)*
EP Nisbet Company .... F 704 332-7755
  Charlotte *(G-2720)*
Funston Company .... G 910 383-1425
  Leland *(G-9544)*
Maverick Biofuels .... G 919 931-1434
  Durham *(G-5211)*
Mpv Morganton Pressu .... F 828 652-3704
  Marion *(G-10167)*
Onward Energy Holdings LLC .... G 980 294-0204
  Charlotte *(G-3304)*
Speer Oil Company LLC .... G 910 947-5494
  Carthage *(G-1667)*
Wr Allen LLC .... G 704 390-4032
  Charlotte *(G-3829)*

1389 Oil and gas field services, nec

Agility Fuel Systems LLC .... G 704 870-3520
  Salisbury *(G-13915)*
All In 1 Home Improvement .... G 252 725-4560
  Vanceboro *(G-15475)*
American Rnovation Systems LLC .... G 336 313-6210
  Thomasville *(G-15185)*
AMP Agency .... G 704 430-2313
  Harrisburg *(G-7701)*
Anew Look Homes LLC .... F 800 796-5152
  Hickory *(G-7935)*
Apergy Artfl Lift Intl LLC .... F 919 934-1533
  Smithfield *(G-14449)*
Atmox Inc .... F 704 248-2858
  Charlotte *(G-2237)*
Bailey Sales and Service LLC .... G 910 876-1103
  Elizabethtown *(G-5585)*
Bcp East Land LLC .... G 704 248-2000
  Charlotte *(G-2289)*
Bennett Elec Maint & Cnstr LLC .... G 910 231-0300
  Raeford *(G-12414)*
Betts Construction United Inc .... E 252 203-2849
  Grandy *(G-6718)*
Brown Building Corporation .... F 919 782-1800
  Morrisville *(G-11308)*
Cape Fear Cnstr Group LLC .... G 910 344-1000
  Wilmington *(G-16149)*
Carlton Enterprizes LLC .... G 919 534-5424
  Rocky Point *(G-13743)*
Carolina Siteworks Inc .... E 704 855-7483
  China Grove *(G-3881)*
Central Site Group LLC .... G 336 380-4121
  Ocean Isle Beach *(G-12088)*
CPM of Nc Inc .... G 704 467-5819
  Concord *(G-4246)*
Danisson USA Trading Ltd LLC .... G 704 965-8317
  Kernersville *(G-9188)*
Davie Property Restoration LLC .... G 336 923-4018
  Advance *(G-40)*
DMD Logistics LLC .... G 336 480-8149
  Winston Salem *(G-16685)*
Doble Engineering Company .... G 919 380-7461
  Morrisville *(G-11333)*
Duke Energy Center .... E 919 464-0960
  Raleigh *(G-12708)*
Edwin Reaves .... G 901 326-6382
  Fayetteville *(G-5818)*
Elevated Cnstr Renovations LLC .... G 910 301-4243
  Red Springs *(G-13500)*
Enrg Brand LLC .... G 980 298-8519
  Charlotte *(G-2714)*

Extensive Builders LLC .... G 980 621-3793
  Salisbury *(G-13960)*
Filter Srvcng of Chrltte 135 .... G 704 619-3768
  Charlotte *(G-2761)*
Fixed-NC LLC .... G 252 751-1911
  Greenville *(G-7526)*
GP Technology LLC .... G 919 876-3666
  Raleigh *(G-12811)*
Gt Rhyno Construction LLC .... G 919 737-3620
  Raleigh *(G-12824)*
Hari Krupa Oil and Gas LLC .... G 860 805-1704
  Winston Salem *(G-16736)*
Heath and Sons MGT Svcs LLC .... F 910 679-6142
  Rocky Point *(G-13747)*
Hensel Phelps .... G 828 585-4689
  Fletcher *(G-6011)*
Homeserve NC LLC .... G 740 552-8497
  Pittsboro *(G-12342)*
Hot Shot Services LLC .... G 336 244-0331
  State Road *(G-14727)*
Interntnal Instlltion Group LL .... F 704 231-1868
  Sparta *(G-14595)*
J & W Service Incorporated .... G 336 449-4584
  Whitsett *(G-15994)*
J &D Contractor Service Inc .... G 919 427-0218
  Angier *(G-142)*
J6 & Company LLC .... F 336 997-4497
  Winston Salem *(G-16767)*
Jim Hammonds Enterprises LLC .... G 828 775-8805
  Mars Hill *(G-10196)*
Johnson Controls Inc .... G 866 285-8345
  Morrisville *(G-11363)*
Jordan Piping Inc .... G 336 818-9252
  North Wilkesboro *(G-12019)*
K9 Installs Inc .... G 743 207-1507
  Clemmons *(G-4051)*
Kcs Imprv & Cnstr Co Inc .... G 336 288-3865
  Greensboro *(G-7147)*
Livengood Innovations LLC .... G 336 925-7604
  Linwood *(G-9946)*
M and M Docks LLC .... F 336 537-0092
  Lexington *(G-9753)*
M D Prevatt Inc .... F 919 796-4944
  Clayton *(G-3994)*
M&S Enterprises Inc .... G 910 259-1763
  Burgaw *(G-1345)*
Malinda Rackley .... G 252 886-3315
  Rocky Mount *(G-13709)*
McLean Sbsrface Utlity Engrg L .... F 336 340-0024
  Greensboro *(G-7194)*
Mountain Homes of Wnc LLC .... F 828 216-2546
  Weaverville *(G-15852)*
National Tank Monitor Inc .... F 704 335-8265
  Charlotte *(G-3237)*
Parker Oil Inc .... G 828 253-7265
  Asheville *(G-722)*
Petra Technologies Inc .... G 704 577-0687
  Indian Trail *(G-8956)*
Phyllis Pulling .... G 336 643-8201
  Oak Ridge *(G-12065)*
Prestige Cleaning Incorporated .... F 704 752-7747
  Charlotte *(G-3375)*
Quick N Easy 12 Nc739 .... G 336 824-3832
  Ramseur *(G-13449)*
RE Shads Group LLC .... G 704 299-8972
  Charlotte *(G-3417)*
Reservoir Group LLC .... G 610 764-0269
  Charlotte *(G-3437)*
Saybolt LP .... G 910 763-8444
  Wilmington *(G-16394)*
Serenity Home Services LLC .... G 910 233-8733
  Troutman *(G-15393)*

Simmie Bullard .... G 910 600-3191
  Pembroke *(G-12183)*
Southern Estates Metal Roofing .... G 704 245-2023
  Locust *(G-9971)*
Surface Buff LLC .... G 919 341-2873
  Cary *(G-1906)*
Surface Renewal Systems LLC .... G 704 207-3596
  Matthews *(G-10348)*
Ten Nails Construction Inc .... G 910 232-4883
  Hampstead *(G-7659)*
Tgi Incorporated .... G 336 768-0139
  Winston Salem *(G-16939)*
◆ Trans-Tech Energy Inc .... G 252 446-4357
  Rocky Mount *(G-13674)*
TransMontaigne Terminaling Inc .... F 303 626-8200
  Selma *(G-14262)*
Ultimate Cleaning Servces Dean .... G 865 382-2433
  Old Fort *(G-12106)*
Under Gods Authority .... G 910 891-1789
  Angier *(G-151)*
United Visions Corp .... G 704 953-4555
  Davidson *(G-4705)*
V & B Construction Svcs Inc .... G 704 641-9936
  Waxhaw *(G-15787)*
Victory Infrstrcture Cnstr LLC .... G 704 572-8247
  Marshville *(G-10227)*
Well Doctor LLC .... G 704 909-9258
  Charlotte *(G-3803)*
Wewoka Gas Producers LLC .... G 704 844-8990
  Charlotte *(G-3807)*
William Brantley .... G 910 627-7286
  Raeford *(G-12445)*
With Purpose Pressure Wshg LLC .... G 336 965-9473
  Greensboro *(G-7463)*
WW&s Construction Inc .... G 217 620-4042
  Dallas *(G-4661)*
Zoetic Digital Development .... G 919 720-5945
  Raleigh *(G-13437)*

14 MINING AND QUARRYING OF NONMETALLIC MINERALS, EXCEPT FUELS

1411 Dimension stone

Carolina Quarries Inc .... D 704 633-0201
  Salisbury *(G-13936)*
▲ Carolina Sunrock LLC .... E 919 575-4502
  Butner *(G-1543)*
Jacobs Creek Stone Company Inc .... F 336 857-2602
  Denton *(G-4738)*
Lbm Industries Inc .... G 828 631-1227
  Sylva *(G-15062)*
Lbm Industries Inc .... F 828 966-4270
  Sapphire *(G-14214)*
McNeely Trucking Co .... E 828 966-4270
  Sapphire *(G-14215)*
Monkey Jct Mulch & Stone Inc .... F 910 793-9111
  Wilmington *(G-16326)*
Nantahala Talc & Limestone Co .... F 828 321-4239
  Topton *(G-15326)*
Rouse Custom Stone .... G 336 655-1613
  Lewisville *(G-9672)*
Sunrock Group Holdings Corp .... D 919 747-6400
  Raleigh *(G-13315)*
Tarheel Sand & Stone Inc .... G 336 468-4003
  Hamptonville *(G-7679)*
Waycaster Nick Stone Co .... G 828 756-4011
  Marion *(G-10185)*
Wilson Grading LLC .... F 919 778-1580
  Goldsboro *(G-6671)*

14 MINING AND QUARRYING OF NONMETALLIC MINERALS, EXCEPT FUELS

Worldgranite & Stoneart Inc............... G..... 919 871-0078
 Raleigh *(G-13428)*

1422 Crushed and broken limestone

Boyd Stone & Quarries...................... G..... 828 659-6862
 Marion *(G-10144)*
Buffalo Crushed Stone Inc................. F..... 919 688-6881
 Durham *(G-4985)*
Bwi Etn LLC....................................... G..... 828 682-2645
 Burnsville *(G-1525)*
Heidelberg Mtls Sthast Agg LLC........ E..... 919 936-4221
 Princeton *(G-12400)*
Limestone Products Inc..................... G..... 704 283-9492
 Monroe *(G-10758)*
Marietta Martin Materials Inc............. D..... 704 525-7740
 Charlotte *(G-3125)*
Marietta Martin Materials Inc............. F..... 252 749-2641
 Fountain *(G-6095)*
Marietta Martin Materials Inc............. E..... 919 772-3563
 Garner *(G-6283)*
Marietta Martin Materials Inc............. F..... 336 668-3253
 Greensboro *(G-7180)*
Marietta Martin Materials Inc............. G..... 828 322-8386
 Hickory *(G-8091)*
Marietta Martin Materials Inc............. G..... 336 886-5015
 Jamestown *(G-9060)*
Marietta Martin Materials Inc............. G..... 336 769-3803
 Kernersville *(G-9213)*
Marietta Martin Materials Inc............. G..... 704 739-4761
 Kings Mountain *(G-9317)*
Marietta Martin Materials Inc............. G..... 910 743-6471
 Maysville *(G-10374)*
Marietta Martin Materials Inc............. G..... 704 283-4915
 Monroe *(G-10765)*
Marietta Martin Materials Inc............. F..... 919 788-4392
 Raleigh *(G-12994)*
Marietta Martin Materials Inc............. G..... 336 349-3333
 Reidsville *(G-13530)*
Marietta Martin Materials Inc............. F..... 704 636-6372
 Salisbury *(G-14009)*
Marietta Martin Materials Inc............. G..... 704 873-8191
 Statesville *(G-14839)*
Marietta Martin Materials Inc............. G..... 336 475-9134
 Thomasville *(G-15245)*
Marietta Martin Materials Inc............. G..... 704 278-2218
 Woodleaf *(G-17023)*
Martin Marietta Materia...................... G..... 336 372-6311
 Sparta *(G-14596)*
Martin Marietta Materials Inc............. G..... 919 894-2003
 Benson *(G-1039)*
Martin Marietta Materials Inc............. G..... 336 584-8875
 Burlington *(G-1455)*
Martin Marietta Materials Inc............. G..... 910 675-2283
 Castle Hayne *(G-1953)*
Martin Marietta Materials Inc............. G..... 704 547-9775
 Charlotte *(G-3131)*
Martin Marietta Materials Inc............. G..... 704 588-1471
 Charlotte *(G-3132)*
Martin Marietta Materials Inc............. G..... 704 932-4377
 China Grove *(G-3885)*
Martin Marietta Materials Inc............. G..... 704 786-8415
 Concord *(G-4309)*
Martin Marietta Materials Inc............. G..... 336 375-7584
 Greensboro *(G-7184)*
Martin Marietta Materials Inc............. G..... 336 674-0836
 Greensboro *(G-7185)*
Martin Marietta Materials Inc............. G..... 910 371-3848
 Leland *(G-9555)*
Martin Marietta Materials Inc............. F..... 828 754-3077
 Lenoir *(G-9633)*
Martin Marietta Materials Inc............. G..... 704 847-3087
 Matthews *(G-10267)*
Martin Marietta Materials Inc............. G..... 252 633-5308
 New Bern *(G-11820)*
Martin Marietta Materials Inc............. F..... 360 424-3441
 Raleigh *(G-12999)*
Martin Marietta Materials Inc............. G..... 336 672-1501
 Randleman *(G-13477)*
Martin Marietta Materials Inc............. G..... 336 672-1501
 Randleman *(G-13478)*
Martin Marietta Materials Inc............. G..... 919 788-4391
 Sanford *(G-14149)*
◆ Martin Marietta Materials Inc......... C..... 919 781-4550
 Raleigh *(G-13001)*
Quarries Petroleum............................ G..... 919 387-0986
 Apex *(G-236)*
Radford Quarries Inc......................... F..... 828 264-7008
 Boone *(G-1231)*

1423 Crushed and broken granite

Alamo North Texas Railroad Co........ G..... 919 787-9504
 Raleigh *(G-12485)*
Blue Rock Materials LLC................... F..... 828 479-3581
 Robbinsville *(G-13605)*
▲ Charlotte Instyle Inc....................... E..... 704 665-8880
 Charlotte *(G-2452)*
Georgia-Carolina Quarries Inc........... E..... 336 786-6978
 Mount Airy *(G-11511)*
Heidelberg Mtls Sthast Agg LLC........ E..... 910 893-8308
 Bunnlevel *(G-1330)*
Heidelberg Mtls Sthast Agg LLC........ E..... 910 893-2111
 Lillington *(G-9852)*
Heidelberg Mtls Sthast Agg LLC........ G..... 252 222-0812
 Morehead City *(G-11174)*
Legacy Vulcan LLC............................ G..... 704 788-7833
 Concord *(G-4301)*
Legacy Vulcan LLC............................ G..... 828 255-8561
 Enka *(G-5683)*
Luck Stone Corporation..................... E..... 336 786-4693
 Mount Airy *(G-11541)*
Marietta Martin Materials Inc............. G..... 704 278-2218
 Woodleaf *(G-17023)*
Martin Marietta Materials Inc............. G..... 336 584-8875
 Burlington *(G-1455)*
Martin Marietta Materials Inc............. G..... 919 863-4305
 Raleigh *(G-13000)*
◆ Martin Marietta Materials Inc......... C..... 919 781-4550
 Raleigh *(G-13001)*
Meridian Granite Company................ E..... 919 781-4550
 Raleigh *(G-13018)*
Wake Stone Corp............................... F..... 252 985-4411
 Battleboro *(G-931)*
Wake Stone Corporation................... E..... 919 775-7349
 Moncure *(G-10629)*

1429 Crushed and broken stone, nec

B V Hedrick Gravel & Sand Co.......... C..... 828 686-3844
 Swannanoa *(G-15020)*
Cardinal Stone Company Inc............. E..... 336 846-7191
 Jefferson *(G-9087)*
▲ Carolina Sunrock LLC..................... E..... 919 575-4502
 Butner *(G-1543)*
Heidelberg Mtls Sthast Agg LLC........ F..... 252 235-4162
 Bailey *(G-874)*
Heidelberg Mtls Sthast Agg LLC........ E..... 919 787-0613
 Raleigh *(G-12836)*
Luck Stone Corporation..................... E..... 919 545-0027
 Moncure *(G-10625)*
Mafic USA LLC................................... F..... 704 967-8006
 Shelby *(G-14343)*
Sunrock Group Holdings Corp........... D..... 919 747-6400
 Raleigh *(G-13315)*
Wake Stone Corp............................... F..... 252 985-4411
 Battleboro *(G-931)*

Yancey Stone Inc............................... F..... 828 682-2645
 Burnsville *(G-1537)*
Yancey Stone Inc............................... G..... 828 684-5522
 Fletcher *(G-6054)*

1442 Construction sand and gravel

A-1 Sandrock Inc............................... E..... 336 855-8195
 Greensboro *(G-6770)*
American Materials Company LLC.... G..... 252 752-2124
 Greenville *(G-7481)*
American Materials Company LLC.... E..... 910 532-6070
 Ivanhoe *(G-8979)*
American Materials Company LLC.... F..... 910 799-1411
 Wilmington *(G-16109)*
Aquadale Query.................................. G..... 704 474-3165
 Norwood *(G-12036)*
Ashley Taylor..................................... G..... 828 230-2953
 Candler *(G-1569)*
Atmax Engineering............................ G..... 910 233-4881
 Wilmington *(G-16124)*
B E R Trucking and Gravel................ G..... 919 738-5928
 Mount Olive *(G-11654)*
B V Hedrick Gravel & Sand Co.......... G..... 336 337-0706
 Asheville *(G-555)*
B V Hedrick Gravel & Sand Co.......... G..... 828 738-0332
 Marion *(G-10140)*
B V Hedrick Gravel & Sand Co.......... C..... 704 827-8114
 Stanley *(G-14686)*
B V Hedrick Gravel & Sand Co.......... C..... 828 686-3844
 Swannanoa *(G-15020)*
B V Hedrick Gravel & Sand Co.......... E..... 828 645-5560
 Weaverville *(G-15837)*
B V Hedrick Gravel & Sand Co.......... E..... 704 633-5982
 Salisbury *(G-13928)*
Beazer East Inc.................................. F..... 919 567-9512
 Holly Springs *(G-8688)*
Black Sand Company Inc................... G..... 336 788-6411
 Winston Salem *(G-16632)*
Blue Ridge Quarry............................. G..... 828 693-0025
 Flat Rock *(G-5960)*
Blue Rock Materials LLC................... F..... 828 479-3581
 Robbinsville *(G-13605)*
Bob Harrington Assoc........................ G..... 336 855-7252
 Greensboro *(G-6846)*
Bobby Cahoon Construction Inc........ E..... 252 249-1617
 Grantsboro *(G-6763)*
◆ Bonsal American Inc....................... D..... 704 525-1621
 Charlotte *(G-2334)*
Bulk Transport Service Inc................ G..... 910 329-0555
 Holly Ridge *(G-8680)*
Carolina Stone LLC............................ F..... 252 208-1633
 Dover *(G-4834)*
Clifford W Estes Co Inc..................... E..... 336 622-6410
 Staley *(G-14664)*
Columbia Silica Sand LLC................. F..... 803 755-1036
 Wilmington *(G-16175)*
Crowder Trucking LLC....................... G..... 910 797-4163
 Fayetteville *(G-5800)*
Cumberland Grav & Sand Min Co..... F..... 828 686-3844
 Swannanoa *(G-15024)*
Cumberland Gravel & Sand Co......... F..... 704 633-4241
 Salisbury *(G-13949)*
Cumberland Sand and Gravel............ G..... 704 474-3165
 Norwood *(G-12038)*
D&J Sand & Gravel............................. F..... 919 584-8267
 Goldsboro *(G-6606)*
G S Materials Inc............................... E..... 336 584-1745
 Burlington *(G-1418)*
Garland Langley Gravel..................... G..... 252 450-9022
 Rocky Mount *(G-13699)*
Garland Langley Sand and Grav....... G..... 252 235-2812
 Bailey *(G-873)*

15 CONSTRUCTION - GENERAL CONTRACTORS & OPERATIVE BUILDERS

Glover Materials Inc................................. G..... 252 536-2660
  Pleasant Hill *(G-12364)*

Gravel Monkey Geodes LLC................... G..... 224 848-0401
  Dunn *(G-4871)*

Grits and Gravel Services LLC............... G..... 919 758-8975
  Apex *(G-199)*

Harrins Sand & Gravel Inc...................... G..... 828 254-2744
  Asheville *(G-648)*

Hedrick B V Gravel & Sand Co................ E..... 704 848-4165
  Lilesville *(G-9837)*

Jason Culbertson..................................... G..... 910 733-6794
  Maxton *(G-10357)*

Landsdown Mining Corporation.............. F..... 704 753-5400
  Monroe *(G-10755)*

Long Branch Partners LLC...................... G..... 828 837-1400
  Brasstown *(G-1267)*

Long J E & Sons Grading Inc.................. F..... 336 228-9706
  Burlington *(G-1452)*

Martin Marietta Materials Inc.................. F..... 360 424-3441
  Raleigh *(G-12999)*

◆ Martin Marietta Materials Inc............... C..... 919 781-4550
  Raleigh *(G-13001)*

Mother Sand Fathers Black Sons........... G..... 919 301-8161
  Garner *(G-6293)*

Mugo Gravel & Grading Inc.................... E..... 704 782-3478
  Concord *(G-4320)*

NC Sand and Rock Inc............................. G..... 919 538-9001
  Willow Spring *(G-16081)*

Parrish Contracting LLC......................... G..... 828 524-9100
  Franklin *(G-6141)*

Prize Management LLC........................... G..... 252 532-1939
  Garysburg *(G-6329)*

Rogers Group Inc.................................... G..... 828 657-9331
  Mooresboro *(G-10840)*

S & K Sand LLC.. G..... 252 964-3144
  Bath *(G-916)*

Soundside Recycling & Mtls Inc............. G..... 252 491-8666
  Jarvisburg *(G-9086)*

Southside Materials LLC......................... G..... 336 388-5613
  Pelham *(G-12178)*

Tar Heel Enddntic Edctl Fndtio................ G..... 207 843-6703
  Raleigh *(G-13328)*

Tarheel Sand & Stone Inc........................ G..... 336 468-4003
  Hamptonville *(G-7679)*

Thrills Hauling LLC.................................. F..... 407 383-3483
  Arden *(G-383)*

Triple M Consolidated Inc...................... G..... 910 484-1303
  Fayetteville *(G-5933)*

Welbuilt Homes Inc................................. F..... 910 323-0098
  Fayetteville *(G-5952)*

1446 Industrial sand

Covia Holdings Corporation................... G..... 828 688-2169
  Bakersville *(G-882)*

Covia Holdings Corporation................... G..... 980 495-2092
  Huntersville *(G-8807)*

Covia Holdings Corporation................... G..... 828 765-4823
  Spruce Pine *(G-14634)*

Covia Holdings LLC................................. G..... 828 688-2169
  Bakersville *(G-883)*

Covia Holdings LLC................................. G..... 828 765-1215
  Spruce Pine *(G-14635)*

Covia Holdings LLC................................. G..... 828 765-4251
  Spruce Pine *(G-14636)*

Covia Holdings LLC................................. G..... 828 765-1114
  Spruce Pine *(G-14638)*

Hammill Construction Co Inc.................. F..... 704 279-5309
  Gold Hill *(G-6582)*

Next Generation Plastics Inc.................. G..... 828 453-0221
  Ellenboro *(G-5636)*

North Carolina Industrial Sand............... G..... 910 205-8535
  Rockingham *(G-13636)*

Taylor Timber Transport Inc................... G..... 252 943-1550
  Chocowinity *(G-3898)*

1459 Clay and related minerals, nec

Covia Holdings LLC................................. E..... 828 765-4283
  Spruce Pine *(G-14637)*

Profile Products LLC............................... E..... 828 327-4165
  Conover *(G-4489)*

Quartz Corp USA...................................... C..... 828 765-8950
  Spruce Pine *(G-14653)*

1474 Potash, soda, and borate minerals

Pcs Phosphate Company Inc.................. E..... 252 322-4111
  Aurora *(G-838)*

1475 Phosphate rock

Lbm Industries Inc................................... F..... 828 966-4270
  Sapphire *(G-14213)*

Pcs Phosphate... G..... 252 402-5779
  New Bern *(G-11833)*

Pcs Phosphate Company Inc.................. E..... 252 322-4111
  Aurora *(G-838)*

1479 Chemical and fertilizer mining

Piedmont Lithium Inc.............................. G..... 704 461-8000
  Belmont *(G-1003)*

Verdesian Life Science US LLC.............. E..... 919 825-1901
  Cary *(G-1919)*

1481 Nonmetallic mineral services

Powersnds Ppeline Partners LLC........... G..... 980 237-8900
  Charlotte *(G-3362)*

Proash LLC... G..... 336 597-8734
  Semora *(G-14264)*

Triple B Stone LLC................................... G..... 704 663-5860
  Terrell *(G-15180)*

1499 Miscellaneous nonmetallic mining

▲ Buchanan Gem Stone Mines Inc......... F..... 828 765-6130
  Spruce Pine *(G-14632)*

Classic Industrial Services..................... E..... 919 209-0909
  Smithfield *(G-14455)*

Comset Management Group................... G..... 910 574-6007
  Hope Mills *(G-8736)*

Emerald Village Inc................................. F..... 828 765-6463
  Little Switzerland *(G-9948)*

Fsc II LLC... F..... 919 783-5700
  Raleigh *(G-12785)*

Hiddenite Gems Inc................................. G..... 828 632-3394
  Hiddenite *(G-8219)*

◆ Iluka Resources Inc.............................. C..... 904 284-9832
  Raleigh *(G-12878)*

Johnson Paving Company Inc................ F..... 828 652-4911
  Marion *(G-10154)*

National Gypsum Services Co................ F..... 704 365-7300
  Charlotte *(G-3236)*

Oceans Flavor.. G..... 828 277-7564
  Asheville *(G-715)*

Sibelco North America Inc...................... D..... 828 766-6050
  Spruce Pine *(G-14657)*

Throwin Stones LLC................................ G..... 828 280-7870
  Asheville *(G-799)*

Vanderbilt Minerals LLC......................... E..... 910 948-2266
  Robbins *(G-13603)*

Zemex Industrial Minerals Inc................ G..... 828 765-5500
  Spruce Pine *(G-14662)*

15 CONSTRUCTION - GENERAL CONTRACTORS & OPERATIVE BUILDERS

1521 Single-family housing construction

Alamance Iron Works Inc....................... G..... 336 852-5940
  Greensboro *(G-6788)*

Around House Improvement LLC........... G..... 919 496-7029
  Bunn *(G-1327)*

Bennett Elec Maint & Cnstr LLC............. G..... 910 231-0300
  Raeford *(G-12414)*

Bridgport Restoration Svcs Inc.............. F..... 336 996-1212
  Kernersville *(G-9169)*

Brown Building Corporation................... F..... 919 782-1800
  Morrisville *(G-11308)*

Carolina Home Exteriors LLC................. F..... 252 637-6599
  New Bern *(G-11786)*

Champion Home Builders Inc................. C..... 910 893-5713
  Lillington *(G-9848)*

Distinctive Bldg & Design Inc................. G..... 828 456-4730
  Waynesville *(G-15802)*

◆ Downtown Graphics Network Inc....... G..... 704 637-0855
  Salisbury *(G-13954)*

E A Duncan Cnstr Co Inc........................ G..... 910 653-3535
  Tabor City *(G-15081)*

Fixed-NC LLC... G..... 252 751-1911
  Greenville *(G-7526)*

G A Lankford Construction..................... G..... 828 254-2467
  Alexander *(G-118)*

▲ GLG Corporation.................................. F..... 336 784-0396
  Winston Salem *(G-16722)*

Goembel Inc.. F..... 919 303-0485
  Apex *(G-196)*

Hamrick Fence Company........................ F..... 704 434-5011
  Boiling Springs *(G-1160)*

Heidelberg Mtls Ssthast Agg LLC........... E..... 919 936-4221
  Princeton *(G-12400)*

High Cntry Tmbrframe Gllery WD........... G..... 828 264-8971
  Boone *(G-1204)*

Hope Renovations..................................... F..... 919 960-1957
  Chapel Hill *(G-2024)*

J & W Service Incorporated.................... G..... 336 449-4584
  Whitsett *(G-15994)*

J &D Contractor Service Inc.................... G..... 919 427-0218
  Angier *(G-142)*

Kcs Imprv & Cnstr Co Inc....................... G..... 336 288-3865
  Greensboro *(G-7147)*

Khi LLC... G..... 828 654-9916
  Arden *(G-345)*

▲ Lewtak Pipe Organ Builders Inc......... G..... 336 554-2251
  Mocksville *(G-10585)*

Lowder Steel Inc..................................... E..... 336 431-9000
  Archdale *(G-293)*

Marsh Furniture Company...................... F..... 336 273-8196
  Greensboro *(G-7182)*

McDaniel Awning Co................................ G..... 704 636-8503
  Salisbury *(G-14010)*

Merhi Glass Inc.. G..... 919 961-5930
  Raleigh *(G-13017)*

Midway Blind & Awning Co Inc.............. G..... 336 226-4532
  Burlington *(G-1461)*

Mike Powell Inc.. F..... 910 792-6152
  Wilmington *(G-16324)*

Mill Creek Post & Beam Co..................... G..... 828 749-8000
  Saluda *(G-14072)*

Neals Carpentry & Cnstr......................... G..... 910 346-6154
  Jacksonville *(G-9017)*

Noble Bros Cabinets Mllwk LLC............. G..... 252 335-1213
  Elizabeth City *(G-5559)*

Noble Bros Cabinets Mllwk LLC............. G..... 252 482-9100
  Edenton *(G-5520)*

Nobscot Construction Co Inc................. G..... 919 929-2075
  Chapel Hill *(G-2048)*

Nuworks.. G..... 919 223-2587
  Goldsboro *(G-6640)*

15 CONSTRUCTION - GENERAL CONTRACTORS & OPERATIVE BUILDERS

Nvr Inc .... D 704 484-7170
Kings Mountain *(G-9320)*

Old Hickory Log Homes Inc .... G 704 489-8989
Denver *(G-4791)*

Pro Choice Contractors Corp .... F 919 696-7383
Raleigh *(G-13146)*

RDc Debris Removal Cnstr LLC .... E 323 614-2353
Smithfield *(G-14479)*

Robbinsville Cstm Molding Inc .... F 828 479-2317
Robbinsville *(G-13610)*

Rogers Manufacturing Company ..... G 910 259-9898
Burgaw *(G-1349)*

Safe Home Pro Inc .... F 704 662-2299
Cornelius *(G-4585)*

Selectbuild Construction Inc .... E 208 331-4300
Raleigh *(G-13244)*

Ten Nails Construction Inc .... G 910 232-4883
Hampstead *(G-7659)*

▼ Value Clothing Inc .... E 704 638-6111
Salisbury *(G-14061)*

W T Humphrey Inc .... D 910 455-3555
Jacksonville *(G-9044)*

With Purpose Pressure Wshg LLC ... G 336 965-9473
Greensboro *(G-7463)*

Zoetic Digital Development .... G 919 720-5945
Raleigh *(G-13437)*

1522 Residential construction, nec

Atlantic Group Usa Inc .... F 919 623-7824
Raleigh *(G-12530)*

Merhi Glass Inc .... G 919 961-5930
Raleigh *(G-13017)*

Seashore Builders Inc .... E 910 259-3404
Maple Hill *(G-10132)*

Thompson Millwork LLC .... D 919 596-8236
Mebane *(G-10433)*

United Visions Corp .... G 704 953-4555
Davidson *(G-4705)*

Zoetic Digital Development .... G 919 720-5945
Raleigh *(G-13437)*

1531 Operative builders

Competitive Edge Inc .... G 704 881-4157
Statesville *(G-14777)*

Medaccess Inc .... G 828 264-4085
Robbinsville *(G-13609)*

Smith Companies Lexington Inc ...... G 336 249-4941
Lexington *(G-9781)*

Wersunsllc .... G 857 209-8701
Winston Salem *(G-16969)*

▲ Williams Industries Inc .... C 919 604-1746
Raleigh *(G-13423)*

1541 Industrial buildings and warehouses

A R Byrd Company Inc .... G 704 732-5675
Lincolnton *(G-9864)*

Ansgar Industrial LLC .... A 704 962-5249
Charlotte *(G-2196)*

B V Hedrick Gravel & Sand Co .... E 704 633-5982
Salisbury *(G-13928)*

Bwxt Investment Company .... E 704 625-4900
Charlotte *(G-2369)*

▲ Central Steel Buildings Inc .... F 336 789-7896
Mount Airy *(G-11496)*

▲ Cornerstone Bldg Brands Inc .... B 281 897-7788
Cary *(G-1736)*

Eagle Carports Inc .... E 800 579-8589
Mount Airy *(G-11503)*

♦ Herbal Innovations LLC .... E 336 818-2332
Wilkesboro *(G-16024)*

Hyman Furniture Warehouse LLC ... G 336 528-4950
Winston Salem *(G-16752)*

▲ Jbr Properties of Greenville Inc .... A 252 355-9353
Winterville *(G-17004)*

▼ Millennium Mfg Structures LLC .... F 828 265-3737
Boone *(G-1222)*

Seashore Builders Inc .... E 910 259-3404
Maple Hill *(G-10132)*

Sonaron LLC .... G 808 232-6168
Fayetteville *(G-5919)*

TRC Acquisition LLC .... A 252 355-9353
Winterville *(G-17015)*

▲ Williams Industries Inc .... C 919 604-1746
Raleigh *(G-13423)*

1542 Nonresidential construction, nec

A R Byrd Company Inc .... G 704 732-5675
Lincolnton *(G-9864)*

American Builders Anson Inc .... E 704 272-7655
Polkton *(G-12383)*

Atlantic Group Usa Inc .... F 919 623-7824
Raleigh *(G-12530)*

B V Hedrick Gravel & Sand Co .... E 704 633-5982
Salisbury *(G-13928)*

▲ Cornerstone Bldg Brands Inc .... B 281 897-7788
Cary *(G-1736)*

Exteriors Inc Ltd .... G 919 325-2251
Spring Lake *(G-14625)*

♦ Hog Slat Incorporated .... B 800 949-4647
Newton Grove *(G-11988)*

International Tela-Com Inc .... F 828 651-9801
Fletcher *(G-6013)*

J &D Contractor Service Inc .... G 919 427-0218
Angier *(G-142)*

▲ Lock Drives Inc .... G 704 588-1844
Pineville *(G-12281)*

M F C Inc .... E 252 322-5004
Aurora *(G-836)*

Pro Choice Contractors Corp .... F 919 696-7383
Raleigh *(G-13146)*

Reliable Construction Co Inc .... E 704 289-1501
Monroe *(G-10795)*

Retail Installation Svcs LLC .... G 336 818-1333
Millers Creek *(G-10495)*

Robinsons Welding Service .... G 336 622-3150
Liberty *(G-9828)*

Seashore Builders Inc .... E 910 259-3404
Maple Hill *(G-10132)*

Sterling Cleora Corporation .... E 919 563-5800
Durham *(G-5374)*

Ten Nails Construction Inc .... G 910 232-4883
Hampstead *(G-7659)*

Tigerswan LLC .... C 919 439-7110
Apex *(G-248)*

United Visions Corp .... G 704 953-4555
Davidson *(G-4705)*

W T Humphrey Inc .... D 910 455-3555
Jacksonville *(G-9044)*

16 HEAMY CONSTRUCTION, EXCEPT BUILDING CONSTRUCTION, CONTRACTOR

1611 Highway and street construction

Apac-Atlantic Inc .... D 336 412-6800
Raleigh *(G-12512)*

Asheville Contracting Co Inc .... E 828 665-8900
Candler *(G-1567)*

Barnhill Contracting Company .... G 704 721-7500
Concord *(G-4204)*

Barnhill Contracting Company .... D 910 488-1319
Fayetteville *(G-5769)*

Barnhill Contracting Company .... E 252 752-7608
Greenville *(G-7493)*

Barnhill Contracting Company .... F 252 527-8021
Kinston *(G-9344)*

Batista Grading Inc .... F 919 359-3449
Clayton *(G-3958)*

Blythe Construction Inc .... G 336 854-9003
Greensboro *(G-6845)*

▲ Blythe Construction Inc .... B 704 375-8474
Charlotte *(G-2325)*

Brown Brothers Construction Co ..... F 828 297-2131
Zionville *(G-17148)*

Brown Building Corporation .... F 919 782-1800
Morrisville *(G-11308)*

Carlton Enterprizes LLC .... G 919 534-5424
Rocky Point *(G-13743)*

Carolina Paving Hickory Inc .... E 828 328-3909
Hickory *(G-7964)*

Carolina Paving Hickory Inc .... F 828 322-1706
Hickory *(G-7965)*

Chandler Concrete Inc .... F 919 598-1424
Durham *(G-5012)*

Cjc Enterprises .... E 919 266-3158
Wake Forest *(G-15541)*

Crowder Trucking LLC .... G 910 797-4163
Fayetteville *(G-5800)*

Dan Moore Inc .... G 336 475-8350
Thomasville *(G-15210)*

Dickerson Group Inc .... G 704 289-3111
Charlotte *(G-2631)*

Ferebee Corporation .... G 704 509-2586
Charlotte *(G-2751)*

Garris Grading and Paving Inc .... F 252 749-1101
Farmville *(G-5736)*

Gelder & Associates Inc .... C 919 772-6895
Raleigh *(G-12792)*

Haulco LLC .... G 336 781-0468
Trinity *(G-15344)*

Heath and Sons MGT Svcs LLC ..... F 910 679-6142
Rocky Point *(G-13747)*

Highland Paving Co LLC .... D 910 482-0080
Fayetteville *(G-5839)*

Hudson Paving Inc .... D 910 895-5910
Rockingham *(G-13630)*

Johnson Paving Company Inc .... F 828 652-4911
Marion *(G-10154)*

Lane Construction Corporation .... B 919 876-4550
Raleigh *(G-12956)*

Long Asp Pav Trckg of Grnsburg .... F 336 643-4121
Summerfield *(G-14986)*

Macleod Construction Inc .... C 704 483-3580
Charlotte *(G-3116)*

Mass Connection Inc .... G 910 424-0940
Fayetteville *(G-5868)*

Moretz & Sipe Inc .... G 828 327-8661
Hickory *(G-8098)*

Reliable Woodworks Inc .... G 704 785-9663
Concord *(G-4349)*

Russell Standard Corporation .... G 336 292-6875
Greensboro *(G-7320)*

S T Wooten Corporation .... G 919 965-9880
Princeton *(G-12404)*

S T Wooten Corporation .... E 252 291-5165
Wilson *(G-16538)*

Stone Supply Inc .... G 828 678-9966
Burnsville *(G-1534)*

Young & McQueen Grading Co Inc .... D 828 682-7714
Burnsville *(G-1539)*

1622 Bridge, tunnel, and elevated highway

▲ Blythe Construction Inc .... B 704 375-8474
Charlotte *(G-2325)*

SIC SECTION

17 CONSTRUCTION - SPECIAL TRADE CONTRACTORS

1623 Water, sewer, and utility lines

1st Choice Service Inc.................................... F 704 913-7485
  Cherryville *(G-3861)*

Agility Fuel Systems LLC........................... G 704 870-3520
  Salisbury *(G-13915)*

Batista Grading Inc..................................... F 919 359-3449
  Clayton *(G-3958)*

Carlson Environmental Cons PC................ D 704 283-9765
  Monroe *(G-10673)*

Cjc Enterprises.. E 919 266-3158
  Wake Forest *(G-15541)*

Davis Mechanical Inc.................................. F 704 272-9366
  Peachland *(G-12173)*

Ferebee Corporation................................... C 704 509-2586
  Charlotte *(G-2751)*

Hyper Networks LLC................................... F 704 837-8411
  Pineville *(G-12274)*

McLean Sbsrface Utlity Engrg L................. F 336 340-0024
  Greensboro *(G-7194)*

Merrill Resources Inc.................................. F 828 877-4450
  Penrose *(G-12186)*

NBC Enterprises Inc.................................... F 910 705-5781
  Fayetteville *(G-5880)*

Pipeline Plastics LLC................................... G 817 693-4100
  Fair Bluff *(G-5699)*

Quantico Water & Sewer LLC.................... G 336 528-9299
  Clemmons *(G-4057)*

S T Wooten Corporation............................. E 252 291-5165
  Wilson *(G-16538)*

▲ Spectrasite Communications LLC........... E 919 468-0112
  Cary *(G-1900)*

Vision Directional Drilling........................... G 336 570-4621
  Burlington *(G-1514)*

Wirenet Inc... E 513 774-7759
  Huntersville *(G-8906)*

Wnc White Corporation............................... E 828 477-4895
  Sylva *(G-15076)*

Zoetic Digital Development........................ G 919 720-5945
  Raleigh *(G-13437)*

1629 Heavy construction, nec

A-1 Sandrock Inc... E 336 855-8195
  Greensboro *(G-6770)*

Barnhill Contracting Company.................... D 910 488-1319
  Fayetteville *(G-5769)*

Bobby Cahoon Construction Inc................ E 252 249-1467
  Grantsboro *(G-6763)*

Bwxt Investment Company........................ E 704 625-4900
  Charlotte *(G-2369)*

Component Sourcing Intl LLC.................... E 704 843-9292
  Charlotte *(G-2534)*

Dagenhart Pallet Inc................................... F 828 241-2374
  Catawba *(G-1964)*

Daly Company Inc....................................... G 919 751-3625
  Goldsboro *(G-6607)*

Harsco Rail LLC.. G 980 960-2624
  Charlotte *(G-2893)*

Heath and Sons MGT Svcs LLC................ F 910 679-6142
  Rocky Point *(G-13747)*

High Rise Service Company Inc................. E 910 371-2325
  Leland *(G-9548)*

JM Williams Timber Company.................... G 919 362-1333
  Apex *(G-209)*

NBC Enterprises Inc.................................... F 910 705-5781
  Fayetteville *(G-5880)*

Soundside Recycling & Mtls Inc................. G 252 491-8666
  Jarvisburg *(G-9086)*

Stone Supply Inc... G 828 678-9966
  Burnsville *(G-1534)*

TNT Services Inc... F 252 261-3073
  Kitty Hawk *(G-9408)*

Trademark Landscape Group Inc............... F 910 253-0560
  Supply *(G-15013)*

Triton Marine Services Inc.......................... G 252 728-9958
  Beaufort *(G-969)*

United Visions Corp..................................... G 704 953-4555
  Davidson *(G-4705)*

Wnc White Corporation............................... E 828 477-4895
  Sylva *(G-15076)*

Young & McQueen Grading Co Inc............ D 828 682-7714
  Burnsville *(G-1539)*

17 CONSTRUCTION - SPECIAL TRADE CONTRACTORS

1711 Plumbing, heating, air-conditioning

▲ AC Corporation.. B 336 273-4472
  Greensboro *(G-6775)*

Affordable Septic Tank................................ G 910 417-9537
  Hamlet *(G-7615)*

Airboss Heating and Coolg Inc................... G 252 586-0500
  Littleton *(G-9950)*

Allen Kelly & Co Inc..................................... D 919 779-4197
  Raleigh *(G-12490)*

Ansonville Piping & Fabg Inc...................... G 704 826-8403
  Ansonville *(G-152)*

▲ Attic Tent Inc.. G 704 892-5399
  Mooresville *(G-10864)*

Bahnson Holdings Inc................................. D 336 760-3111
  Clemmons *(G-4029)*

Carolina Fire Protection Inc........................ E 910 892-1700
  Dunn *(G-4854)*

Chichibone Inc... G 919 785-0090
  Morrisville *(G-11321)*

Comfort Engineers Inc................................ E 919 383-0158
  Durham *(G-5027)*

Commercial Flter Svc of Triad.................... G 336 272-1443
  Greensboro *(G-6924)*

DCE Solar Service Inc................................ G 704 659-7474
  Cornelius *(G-4539)*

Dusty Rhoads Hvac Inc.............................. G 252 261-5892
  Kitty Hawk *(G-9403)*

Edwards Electronic Systems Inc................ E 919 359-2239
  Clayton *(G-3976)*

Ellenburg Sheet Metal................................. G 704 872-2089
  Statesville *(G-14794)*

Entropy Solar Integrators LLC.................... G 704 936-5018
  Charlotte *(G-2716)*

Envirnmntal Cmfort Sltions Inc................... E 980 272-7327
  Kannapolis *(G-9119)*

Enviro-Companies LLC.............................. G 919 758-6246
  Raleigh *(G-12741)*

Fixed-NC LLC.. G 252 751-1911
  Greenville *(G-7526)*

Franklin Sheet Metal Shop Inc.................... F 828 524-2821
  Franklin *(G-6130)*

Freedom Industries Inc............................... C 252 984-0007
  Rocky Mount *(G-13698)*

General Refrigeration Company................. G 919 661-4727
  Garner *(G-6273)*

Go Green Services LLC............................. D 336 252-2999
  Greensboro *(G-7048)*

Harco Air LLC.. G 252 491-5220
  Powells Point *(G-12397)*

Hauser Hvac Installation............................. G 336 416-2173
  Winston Salem *(G-16738)*

Heath and Sons MGT Svcs LLC................ F 910 679-6142
  Rocky Point *(G-13747)*

Hicks Wterstoves Solar Systems............... F 336 789-4977
  Mount Airy *(G-11518)*

Hollingsworth Heating Air Cond.................. G 252 824-0355
  Tarboro *(G-15108)*

Industrial Air Inc... C 336 292-1030
  Greensboro *(G-7113)*

Industrial Mechanical Services................... G 828 397-3231
  Hildebran *(G-8625)*

Inman Septic Tank Service Inc................... G 910 763-1146
  Wilmington *(G-16268)*

J & W Service Incorporated....................... G 336 449-4584
  Whitsett *(G-15994)*

Jenkins Services Group LLC...................... G 704 881-3210
  Catawba *(G-1965)*

Johnson Controls Inc.................................. E 704 521-8889
  Charlotte *(G-3030)*

Kenny Fowler Heating and A Inc................ G 910 508-4553
  Wilmington *(G-16288)*

Kinetic Systems Inc..................................... D 919 322-7200
  Durham *(G-5181)*

Leonard McSwain Sptic Tank Svc.............. G 704 482-1380
  Shelby *(G-14337)*

Lunar International Tech LLC..................... F 800 975-7153
  Charlotte *(G-3109)*

Mc Controls LLC.. G 336 518-1303
  Yadkinville *(G-17045)*

Mechanical Maintenance Inc...................... F 336 676-7133
  Climax *(G-4087)*

Miller Sheet Metal Co Inc........................... G 336 751-2304
  Mocksville *(G-10590)*

Muriel Harris Investments Inc..................... F 800 932-3191
  Fayetteville *(G-5879)*

NC Solar Now Inc.. F 919 833-9096
  Raleigh *(G-13058)*

O R Prdgen Sons Sptic Tank I.................... G 252 442-3338
  Rocky Mount *(G-13717)*

Pamlico Air Inc... F 252 995-6267
  Washington *(G-15724)*

Prestige Cleaning Incorporated.................. F 704 752-7747
  Charlotte *(G-3375)*

Prime Water Services Inc........................... G 919 504-1020
  Raleigh *(G-13140)*

◆ Progress Solar Solutions LLC................. F 919 363-3738
  Raleigh *(G-13150)*

Raleigh Mechanical & Mtls Inc................... F 919 598-4601
  Raleigh *(G-13179)*

Riley Power Group LLC.............................. C 910 420-6999
  Pinehurst *(G-12234)*

▲ Saab Barracuda LLC............................... E 910 814-3088
  Lillington *(G-9859)*

Southern Comfort A Systems LLC............. G 919 324-6336
  Morrisville *(G-11432)*

Southern Pdmont Pping Fbrction................ F 704 272-7936
  Peachland *(G-12176)*

Spc Mechanical Corporation...................... C 252 237-9035
  Wendell *(G-15919)*

Taylco Inc... E 910 739-0405
  Lumberton *(G-10057)*

TNT Services Inc... F 252 261-3073
  Kitty Hawk *(G-9408)*

Tony D Hildreth.. F 910 276-1803
  Laurel Hill *(G-9465)*

Trane US Inc.. F 704 697-9006
  Charlotte *(G-3715)*

Tri-City Mechanical Contrs Inc................... D 336 272-9495
  Greensboro *(G-7410)*

Triad Sheet Metal & Mech Inc.................... F 336 379-9891
  Greensboro *(G-7417)*

W T Humphrey Inc....................................... D 910 455-3555
  Jacksonville *(G-9044)*

Wen Bray Heating & AC.............................. G 828 267-0635
  Hickory *(G-8209)*

1721 Painting and paper hanging

Auto Parts Fayetteville LLC........................ G 910 889-4026
  Fayetteville *(G-5766)*

17 CONSTRUCTION - SPECIAL TRADE CONTRACTORS

Carlton Enterprizes LLC .... G 919 534-5424
  Rocky Point (G-13743)
CTI Property Services Inc .... E 919 787-3789
  Raleigh (G-12659)
Custom Steel Boats Inc .... F 252 745-7447
  Merritt (G-10439)
Hemco Wire Products Inc .... F 336 454-7280
  Jamestown (G-9052)
High Rise Service Company Inc .... E 910 371-2325
  Leland (G-9548)
Painting By Colors LLC .... G 919 963-2300
  Clayton (G-4005)
Parrish Contracting LLC .... G 828 524-9100
  Franklin (G-6141)
Patricia Hall .... G 704 729-6133
  Bessemer City (G-1077)
Peaches Enterprises Inc .... G 910 868-5800
  Fayetteville (G-5895)
Surface Renewal Systems LLC .... G 704 207-3596
  Matthews (G-10348)
Yontz & Sons Painting Inc .... G 336 784-7099
  Winston Salem (G-16990)

1731 Electrical work

Absolute Security & Lock Inc .... G 336 322-4598
  Roxboro (G-13792)
▲ AC Corporation .... B 336 273-4472
  Greensboro (G-6775)
Allen Kelly & Co Inc .... D 919 779-4197
  Raleigh (G-12490)
Amplified Elctronic Design Inc .... F 336 223-4811
  Greensboro (G-6806)
Atcom Inc .... F 704 357-7900
  Charlotte (G-2230)
Audio Vdeo Concepts Design Inc .... G 704 821-2823
  Indian Trail (G-8921)
Automated Controls LLC .... F 704 724-7625
  Huntersville (G-8796)
Belham Management Ind LLC .... G 704 815-4246
  Charlotte (G-2297)
Bennett Elec Maint & Cnstr LLC .... G 910 231-0300
  Raeford (G-12414)
Carolina Time Equipment Co Inc .... E 704 536-2700
  Charlotte (G-2409)
Cemco Electric Inc .... F 704 504-0294
  Charlotte (G-2441)
Commscope Inc North Carolina .... A 828 459-5000
  Claremont (G-3910)
Comp Environmental Inc .... F 919 316-1321
  Durham (G-5028)
Custom Controls Unlimited LLC .... F 919 812-6553
  Raleigh (G-12664)
Custom Light and Sound Inc .... E 919 286-1122
  Durham (G-5040)
Diebold Nixdorf Incorporated .... F 704 599-3100
  Charlotte (G-2632)
DMC LLC .... E 980 352-9806
  Concord (G-4254)
Edwards Electronic Systems Inc .... E 919 359-2239
  Clayton (G-3976)
Fieldsway Solutions LLC .... G 984 920-7791
  Four Oaks (G-6104)
Fixtures & More .... G 828 855-9093
  Hickory (G-8026)
Freedom Industries Inc .... C 252 984-0007
  Rocky Mount (G-13698)
Glh Systems & Controls Inc .... G 980 581-1304
  Stanfield (G-14679)
Integrated Roe Security LLC .... G 919 297-2036
  Raleigh (G-12896)
International Tela-Com Inc .... G 828 651-9801
  Fletcher (G-6013)

JA Smith Inc .... G 704 860-4910
  Lawndale (G-9500)
Jared Munday Electric Inc .... G 828 355-9024
  Boone (G-1210)
Jcv Communications Inc .... F 844 399-8282
  Wilmington (G-16277)
Lighting .... G 919 828-0351
  Raleigh (G-12970)
M & M Electric Service Inc .... E 704 867-0221
  Gastonia (G-6448)
M2 Optics Inc .... G 919 342-5619
  Raleigh (G-12985)
Mc Controls LLC .... G 336 518-1303
  Yadkinville (G-17045)
Moss Sign Company Inc .... G 828 299-7766
  Asheville (G-706)
NBC Enterprises Inc .... F 910 705-5781
  Fayetteville (G-5880)
Nkt Inc .... G 919 601-1970
  Cary (G-1832)
Pike Electric LLC .... B 336 316-7068
  Greensboro (G-7263)
Power Integrity Corp .... E 336 379-9773
  Greensboro (G-7269)
Presley Group Ltd .... D 828 254-9971
  Asheville (G-741)
Service Electric and Control .... G 704 888-5100
  Locust (G-9970)
◆ Southern Elc & Automtn Corp .... F 919 718-0122
  Sanford (G-14187)
Telecmmnctons Resource MGT Inc .... F 919 779-0776
  Raleigh (G-13336)
Total Controls Inc .... G 704 821-6341
  Matthews (G-10295)
▲ Unitape (usa) Inc .... F 828 464-5695
  Conover (G-4507)
Watson Electrical Cnstr Co LLC .... D 252 756-4550
  Greenville (G-7597)

1741 Masonry and other stonework

John J Morton Company Inc .... F 704 332-6633
  Charlotte (G-3028)
M & M Stone Sculpting & Engrv .... G 336 877-3842
  Todd (G-15323)
◆ Stonemaster Inc .... E 704 333-0353
  Charlotte (G-3638)
Taylco Inc .... E 910 739-0405
  Lumberton (G-10057)
Vega Construction Company Inc .... E 336 756-3477
  Pilot Mountain (G-12204)

1742 Plastering, drywall, and insulation

ABS Southeast LLC .... F 919 329-0014
  Raleigh (G-12464)
▲ Attic Tent Inc .... G 704 892-5399
  Mooresville (G-10864)
Delkote Machine Finishing Inc .... G 828 253-1023
  Asheville (G-606)
▲ Delve Interiors LLC .... C 336 274-4661
  Greensboro (G-6968)
Heed Group Inc .... G 877 938-8853
  Stanley (G-14696)
Precision Walls Inc .... G 336 852-7710
  Greensboro (G-7276)
◆ Sika Corporation .... E 704 810-0500
  Gastonia (G-6510)
Taylor Interiors LLC .... F 980 207-3160
  Charlotte (G-3674)

1743 Terrazzo, tile, marble, mosaic work

Apex Marble and Granite Inc .... E 919 462-9202
  Morrisville (G-11289)

▲ David Allen Company Inc .... C 919 821-7100
  Raleigh (G-12675)
▲ Grancreations Inc .... G 704 332-7625
  Charlotte (G-2852)
Precision Walls Inc .... G 336 852-7710
  Greensboro (G-7276)
Sare Granite & Tile .... G 828 676-2666
  Arden (G-374)

1751 Carpentry work

Alcorns Custom Woodworking Inc .... G 336 342-0908
  Reidsville (G-13505)
Amarr Company .... G 336 936-0010
  Mocksville (G-10553)
Andronics Construction Inc .... E 704 400-9562
  Indian Trail (G-8920)
Artistic Southern Inc .... D 919 861-4695
  Charlotte (G-2222)
Athol Arbor Corporation .... F 919 643-1100
  Hillsborough (G-8636)
Cabinet Solutions Usa Inc .... E 828 358-2349
  Hickory (G-7959)
Classic Cleaning LLC .... E 800 220-7101
  Raleigh (G-12626)
Comm-Kab Inc .... F 336 873-8787
  Asheboro (G-417)
Distinctive Cabinets Inc .... F 704 529-6234
  Charlotte (G-2642)
H & H Woodworking Inc .... G 336 884-5848
  High Point (G-8374)
▲ Idx Impressions LLC .... C 703 550-6902
  Washington (G-15711)
Interior Trim Creations Inc .... G 704 821-1470
  Charlotte (G-2981)
Jewers Doors Us Inc .... E 888 510-5331
  Greensboro (G-7136)
Marsh Furniture Company .... F 336 273-8196
  Greensboro (G-7182)
Marsh Furniture Company .... G 336 765-7832
  Winston Salem (G-16801)
Mountain Showcase Group Inc .... E 828 692-9494
  Hendersonville (G-7881)
Neals Carpentry & Cnstr .... G 910 346-6154
  Jacksonville (G-9017)
Riddley Retail Fixtures Inc .... E 704 435-8829
  Kings Mountain (G-9329)
Seashore Builders Inc .... E 910 259-3404
  Maple Hill (G-10132)
Selectbuild Construction Inc .... E 208 331-4300
  Raleigh (G-13244)
Ullman Group LLC .... F 704 246-7333
  Charlotte (G-3747)
Vaughn Woodworking Inc .... G 828 963-6858
  Banner Elk (G-905)
Washington Cabinet Company .... G 252 946-3457
  Washington (G-15738)
White Robert Custom Wdwkg .... G 704 489-2005
  Denver (G-4814)
Wildwood Studios Inc .... G 828 299-8696
  Asheville (G-822)

1752 Floor laying and floor work, nec

Creative Stone Fyetteville Inc .... F 910 491-1225
  Fayetteville (G-5799)

1761 Roofing, siding, and sheetmetal work

Allens Gutter Service .... G 910 738-9509
  Lumberton (G-10025)
ARS Extreme Construction Inc .... E 919 331-8024
  Angier (G-131)
Atlantic Coastal Enterprises .... G 910 478-0777
  Jacksonville (G-8988)

17 CONSTRUCTION - SPECIAL TRADE CONTRACTORS

Budd-Piper Roofing Company .... F 919 682-2121
   Durham *(G-4984)*

Carolina Custom Exteriors Inc .... F 828 232-0402
   Asheville *(G-581)*

Carolina Machining Fabrication .... G 919 554-9700
   Youngsville *(G-17075)*

Cypress Mountain Company .... G 252 758-2179
   Greenville *(G-7512)*

Dimensional Metals Inc .... G 704 279-9691
   Salisbury *(G-13953)*

Exteriors Inc Ltd .... G 919 325-2251
   Spring Lake *(G-14625)*

Herman Reeves Tex Shtmtl Inc .... E 704 865-2231
   Gastonia *(G-6415)*

Hughs Sheet Mtal Sttsvlle LLC .... F 704 872-4621
   Statesville *(G-14818)*

J T Metals LLC .... G 336 737-4189
   Goldston *(G-6675)*

Larry Bissette Inc .... F 919 773-2140
   Apex *(G-212)*

Metal Roofing Systems LLC .... E 704 820-3110
   Stanley *(G-14702)*

Midway Blind & Awning Co Inc .... G 336 226-4532
   Burlington *(G-1461)*

Muriel Harris Investments Inc .... F 800 932-3191
   Fayetteville *(G-5879)*

Oak Ridge Industries LLC .... E 252 833-4061
   Washington *(G-15720)*

On Time Metal LLC .... G 828 635-1001
   Hiddenite *(G-8224)*

▲ Owens Crning Nn-Woven Tech LLC .. F 740 321-6131
   Dallas *(G-4650)*

R E Bengel Sheet Metal Co .... E 252 637-3404
   New Bern *(G-11839)*

Raleigh Mechanical & Mtls Inc .... F 919 598-4601
   Raleigh *(G-13179)*

Ramsey Industries Inc .... E 704 827-3560
   Belmont *(G-1005)*

Ray Roofing Company Inc .... E 704 372-0100
   Charlotte *(G-3414)*

Service Rofg Shtmtl Wlmngton I .... F 910 343-9860
   Wilmington *(G-16400)*

Service Roofing and Shtmtl Co .... D 252 758-2179
   Greenville *(G-7582)*

Southern Estates Metal Roofing .... G 704 245-2023
   Locust *(G-9971)*

Taylorsville Precast Molds Inc .... E 828 632-4608
   Taylorsville *(G-15171)*

Triangle Installation Svc Inc .... G 919 363-7637
   Apex *(G-252)*

Vinyl Windows & Doors Corp .... F 910 944-2100
   Aberdeen *(G-35)*

1771 Concrete work

Apac-Atlantic Inc .... D 336 412-6800
   Raleigh *(G-12512)*

Barnhill Contracting Company .... F 336 584-1306
   Burlington *(G-1375)*

Barnhill Contracting Company .... D 910 488-1319
   Fayetteville *(G-5769)*

Barnhill Contracting Company .... F 252 527-8021
   Kinston *(G-9344)*

Chandler Concrete Inc .... D 704 636-4711
   Salisbury *(G-13939)*

Commercial Ready Mix Pdts Inc .... G 252 332-3590
   Ahoskie *(G-58)*

Concrete Service Company .... G 910 590-0035
   Clinton *(G-4093)*

Demilo Bros NC LLC .... G 704 771-0762
   Waxhaw *(G-15752)*

▲ Due Process Stable Trdg Co LLC ...... E 910 608-0284
   Lumberton *(G-10032)*

E & M Concrete Inc .... E 919 235-7221
   Fuquay Varina *(G-6197)*

Ferebee Corporation .... C 704 509-2586
   Charlotte *(G-2751)*

Garris Grading and Paving Inc .... F 252 749-1101
   Farmville *(G-5736)*

Heath and Sons MGT Svcs LLC .... F 910 679-6142
   Rocky Point *(G-13747)*

Hudson Paving Inc .... D 910 895-5910
   Rockingham *(G-13630)*

Long Asp Pav Trckg of Grnsburg .... F 336 643-4121
   Summerfield *(G-14986)*

RDc Debris Removal Cnstr LLC .... E 323 614-2353
   Smithfield *(G-14479)*

Selectbuild Construction Inc .... E 208 331-4300
   Raleigh *(G-13244)*

Solid Holdings LLC .... F 704 423-0260
   Charlotte *(G-3578)*

Southern Concrete Mtls Inc .... F 828 524-3555
   Franklin *(G-6144)*

Southern Concrete Mtls Inc .... F 877 788-3001
   Salisbury *(G-14045)*

TNT Services Inc .... F 252 261-3073
   Kitty Hawk *(G-9408)*

Vivet Inc .... G 909 390-1039
   Greensboro *(G-7444)*

Young & McQueen Grading Co Inc .... D 828 682-7714
   Burnsville *(G-1539)*

1781 Water well drilling

Camp S Well and Pump Co Inc .... G 828 453-7322
   Ellenboro *(G-5634)*

Merrill Resources Inc .... F 828 877-4450
   Penrose *(G-12186)*

Raymond Brown Well Company Inc ...... G 336 374-4999
   Danbury *(G-4663)*

1791 Structural steel erection

Ansonville Piping & Fabg Inc .... G 704 826-8403
   Ansonville *(G-152)*

Apex Steel Corp .... E 919 362-6611
   Raleigh *(G-12514)*

Asheville Maintenance and .... E 828 687-8110
   Arden *(G-312)*

Burton Steel Company .... F 910 675-9241
   Castle Hayne *(G-1944)*

Canalta Enterprises LLC .... E 919 615-1570
   Raleigh *(G-12586)*

Garden Metalwork .... G 828 733-1077
   Newland *(G-11887)*

King Stone Innovation LLC .... G 704 352-1134
   Charlotte *(G-3056)*

Oldcastle Infrastructure Inc .... E 919 772-6269
   Raleigh *(G-13082)*

Roderick Mch Erectors Wldg Inc .... G 910 343-0381
   Wilmington *(G-16386)*

Steel Supply and Erection Co .... F 336 625-4830
   Asheboro *(G-487)*

Watson Steel & Iron Works LLC .... E 704 821-7140
   Matthews *(G-10350)*

▲ Williams Industries Inc .... C 919 604-1746
   Raleigh *(G-13423)*

1793 Glass and glazing work

A R Perry Corporation .... F 252 492-6181
   Henderson *(G-7774)*

Albemarle Glass Company Inc .... G 704 982-3323
   Albemarle *(G-70)*

Building Envlope Erction Svcs .... F 252 747-2015
   Snow Hill *(G-14499)*

Orare Inc .... G 919 742-1003
   Siler City *(G-14429)*

Rice S Glass Company Inc .... E 919 967-9214
   Carrboro *(G-1655)*

▲ Sid Jenkins Inc .... G 336 632-0707
   Greensboro *(G-7337)*

Triangle Glass Service Inc .... G 919 477-9508
   Durham *(G-5408)*

1794 Excavation work

Bobby Cahoon Construction Inc .... E 252 249-1617
   Grantsboro *(G-6763)*

Brown Brothers Construction Co .... F 828 297-2131
   Zionville *(G-17148)*

Garris Grading and Paving Inc .... F 252 749-1101
   Farmville *(G-5736)*

J & L Bckh/Nvrnmental Svcs Inc .... G 910 237-7351
   Eastover *(G-5481)*

J S Myers Co Inc .... F 336 463-5572
   Yadkinville *(G-17042)*

Mugo Gravel & Grading Inc .... E 704 782-3478
   Concord *(G-4320)*

Privette Enterprises Inc .... E 704 634-3291
   Monroe *(G-10789)*

S T Wooten Corporation .... E 919 965-9880
   Princeton *(G-12404)*

Young & McQueen Grading Co Inc .... D 828 682-7714
   Burnsville *(G-1539)*

1795 Wrecking and demolition work

Batista Grading Inc .... F 919 359-3449
   Clayton *(G-3958)*

Bobby Cahoon Construction Inc .... E 252 249-1617
   Grantsboro *(G-6763)*

J & L Bckh/Nvrnmental Svcs Inc .... G 910 237-7351
   Eastover *(G-5481)*

Noble Oil Services Inc .... C 919 774-8180
   Sanford *(G-14159)*

Soundside Recycling & Mtls Inc .... G 252 491-8666
   Jarvisburg *(G-9086)*

Wersunsllc .... G 857 209-8701
   Winston Salem *(G-16969)*

1796 Installing building equipment

Advantage Machinery Svcs Inc .... E 336 463-4700
   Yadkinville *(G-17030)*

Alpha 3d LLC .... G 704 277-6300
   Charlotte *(G-2166)*

Asheville Maintenance and .... E 828 687-8110
   Arden *(G-312)*

◆ Assa Abloy Entrnce Systems US .... C 704 357-9924
   Monroe *(G-10655)*

▲ Cyrco Inc .... E 336 668-0977
   Greensboro *(G-6954)*

▲ Dustcontrol Inc .... F 910 395-1808
   Wilmington *(G-16207)*

Home Elevators & Lift Pdts LLC .... E 910 427-0006
   Sunset Beach *(G-14999)*

Johnson Industrial Mchy Svcs .... E 252 239-1944
   Lucama *(G-10017)*

Ken Staley Co Inc .... G 336 685-4294
   Franklinville *(G-6169)*

▲ Mantissa Corporation .... E 704 525-1749
   Charlotte *(G-3122)*

▲ Nederman Corporation .... F 704 399-7441
   Charlotte *(G-3244)*

Otis Elevator Company .... G 828 251-1248
   Asheville *(G-718)*

Otis Elevator Company .... C 704 519-0100
   Charlotte *(G-3306)*

Park Manufacturing Company .... F 704 869-6128
   Gastonia *(G-6483)*

Poehler Enterprises Inc .... G 704 239-1166
   Midland *(G-10475)*

17 CONSTRUCTION - SPECIAL TRADE CONTRACTORS

Precision Fabricators Inc .... G 336 835-4763
  Ronda *(G-13768)*
RPM Plastics LLC .... E 704 871-0518
  Statesville *(G-14881)*
Southeastern Elevator LLC .... G 252 726-9983
  Morehead City *(G-11192)*
Steel City Services LLC .... F 919 698-2407
  Durham *(G-5373)*
Thomas M Brown Inc .... F 704 597-0246
  Charlotte *(G-3690)*

1799 Special trade contractors, nec

Accel Wldg & Fabrication LLC .... G 980 722-7198
  Stanley *(G-14683)*
Accent Awnings Inc .... F 828 321-4517
  Andrews *(G-123)*
▲ Acme Stone Company Inc .... E 336 786-6978
  Mount Airy *(G-11472)*
Advance Signs & Service Inc .... E 919 639-4666
  Angier *(G-130)*
Advantage Machinery Svcs Inc .... E 336 463-4700
  Yadkinville *(G-17030)*
Afsc LLC .... D 704 523-4936
  Charlotte *(G-2142)*
Alamance Iron Works Inc .... G 336 852-5940
  Greensboro *(G-6788)*
Allens Environmental Cnstr LLC .... G 407 774-7100
  Brevard *(G-1269)*
Alp Systems Inc .... F 828 454-5164
  Waynesville *(G-15792)*
American Stainless Tubing LLC .... C 704 878-8823
  Troutman *(G-15366)*
AP Granite Installation LLC .... G 919 215-1795
  Clayton *(G-3954)*
Apergy Artfl Lift Intl LLC .... F 919 934-1533
  Smithfield *(G-14449)*
Apex Steel Corp .... E 919 362-6611
  Raleigh *(G-12514)*
Asheville Contracting Co Inc .... E 828 665-8900
  Candler *(G-1567)*
▲ Atlantic Hydraulics Svcs LLC .... E 919 542-2985
  Sanford *(G-14091)*
Automated Controls LLC .... F 704 724-7625
  Huntersville *(G-8796)*
Avery Machine & Welding Co .... G 828 733-4944
  Fayetteville *(G-5767)*
B & L Custom Cabinets Inc .... F 704 857-1940
  Westfield *(G-15950)*
Blue Mountain Metalworks Inc .... G 828 898-8582
  Banner Elk *(G-894)*
◆ Bradford Products LLC .... D 910 791-2202
  Leland *(G-9529)*
Bridgport Restoration Svcs Inc .... F 336 996-1212
  Kernersville *(G-9169)*
Burchette Sign Company Inc .... F 336 996-6501
  Colfax *(G-4143)*
Burkett Welding Services Inc .... F 252 635-2814
  New Bern *(G-11782)*
Cabinet Solutions Usa Inc .... E 828 358-2349
  Hickory *(G-7959)*
Carlton Enterprizes LLC .... G 919 534-5424
  Rocky Point *(G-13743)*
Carolina Marble & Granite .... G 704 523-2112
  Charlotte *(G-2399)*
Carolina Sgns Grphic Dsgns Inc .... G 919 383-3344
  Durham *(G-5004)*
Carolina Solar Structures Inc .... E 828 684-9900
  Asheville *(G-583)*
Clark Art Shop Inc .... G 919 832-8319
  Raleigh *(G-12625)*
Classic Cleaning LLC .... E 800 220-7101
  Raleigh *(G-12626)*

Closets By Design .... D 704 361-6424
  Charlotte *(G-2498)*
Collins Fabrication & Wldg LLC .... G 704 861-9326
  Gastonia *(G-6380)*
Connected 2k LLC .... G 910 321-7446
  Fayetteville *(G-5795)*
Core Technology Molding Corp .... E 336 294-2018
  Greensboro *(G-6937)*
Custom Steel Boats Inc .... F 252 745-7447
  Merritt *(G-10439)*
Cymbal LLC .... G 877 365-9622
  Cary *(G-1744)*
Digger Specialties Inc .... G 336 495-1517
  Randleman *(G-13464)*
Dimill Enterprises LLC .... G 919 629-2011
  Raleigh *(G-12684)*
Dna Services Inc .... G 910 279-2775
  Kure Beach *(G-9437)*
▲ Drydog Barriers LLC .... G 704 334-8222
  Indian Trail *(G-8930)*
Ebert Sign Company Inc .... G 336 768-2867
  Lexington *(G-9711)*
Englishs All Wood Homes Inc .... F 252 524-5000
  Grifton *(G-7600)*
Everglow Na Inc .... E 704 841-2580
  Matthews *(G-10247)*
▼ Filtration Technology Inc .... G 336 294-5655
  Greensboro *(G-7014)*
Fitch Sign Company Inc .... G 704 482-2916
  Shelby *(G-14317)*
Four Points Recycling LLC .... G 910 333-5961
  Jacksonville *(G-9000)*
▲ Gainsborough Baths LLC .... F 336 357-0797
  Lexington *(G-9722)*
Gastonia Ornamental Wldg Inc .... F 704 827-1146
  Mount Holly *(G-11635)*
Gillespies Fbrction Design Inc .... G 704 636-2349
  Salisbury *(G-13969)*
▲ Grancreations Inc .... G 704 332-7625
  Charlotte *(G-2852)*
Guerrero Enterprises Inc .... G 828 286-4900
  Rutherfordton *(G-13875)*
Guest Interiors .... G 828 244-5738
  Hickory *(G-8035)*
Hamrick Fence Company .... F 704 434-5011
  Boiling Springs *(G-1160)*
Harrison Fence Inc .... G 919 244-6908
  Apex *(G-200)*
Haulco LLC .... G 336 781-0468
  Trinity *(G-15344)*
High Rise Service Company Inc .... E 910 371-2325
  Leland *(G-9548)*
Ie Furniture Inc .... E 336 475-5050
  Archdale *(G-284)*
Interstate Sign Company Inc .... E 336 789-3069
  Mount Airy *(G-11524)*
Invisible Fencing of Mtn Reg .... G 828 667-8847
  Candler *(G-1584)*
Isana LLC .... G 704 439-6761
  Charlotte *(G-2997)*
Ivey Ln Inc .... G 336 230-0062
  Greensboro *(G-7129)*
J &D Contractor Service Inc .... G 919 427-0218
  Angier *(G-142)*
J T Metals LLC .... G 336 737-4189
  Goldston *(G-6675)*
J&P Metal Arts Inc .... G 704 684-5140
  Monroe *(G-10745)*
James Iron & Steel Inc .... E 704 283-2299
  Monroe *(G-10746)*
Kberg Productions LLC .... G 910 232-0342
  Raleigh *(G-12932)*

King Stone Innovation LLC .... G 704 352-1134
  Charlotte *(G-3056)*
Kitchen Man Inc .... F 910 408-1322
  Winnabow *(G-16582)*
Limitless Wldg Fabrication LLC .... G 252 753-0660
  Farmville *(G-5739)*
Lockwood Identity Inc .... C 704 597-9801
  Charlotte *(G-3099)*
Lumsden Welding Company .... G 910 791-6336
  Wilmington *(G-16310)*
M & M Stone Sculpting & Engrv .... G 336 877-3842
  Todd *(G-15323)*
Marsh Furniture Company .... F 336 273-8196
  Greensboro *(G-7182)*
Marsh Furniture Company .... G 336 765-7832
  Winston Salem *(G-16801)*
Maynard S Fabricators Inc .... G 336 230-1048
  Greensboro *(G-7191)*
McCorkle Sign Company Inc .... E 919 687-7080
  Durham *(G-5212)*
Mechanical Maintenance Inc .... F 336 676-7133
  Climax *(G-4087)*
Merhi Glass Inc .... G 919 961-5930
  Raleigh *(G-13017)*
Milligan House Movers Inc .... G 910 653-2272
  Tabor City *(G-15084)*
Moores Fiberglass Inc .... F 252 753-2583
  Walstonburg *(G-15640)*
Mundy Machine Co Inc .... G 704 922-8663
  Dallas *(G-4648)*
Murdock Building Company .... G 919 669-1859
  Rolesville *(G-13758)*
Noble Oil Services Inc .... C 919 774-8180
  Sanford *(G-14159)*
Nova Enterprises Inc .... E 828 687-8770
  Arden *(G-357)*
Parish Sign & Service Inc .... G 910 875-6121
  Raeford *(G-12430)*
Parrish Contracting LLC .... G 828 524-9100
  Franklin *(G-6141)*
Piedmont Weld & Pipe Inc .... G 704 782-7774
  Concord *(G-4332)*
Piedmont Well Covers Inc .... F 704 664-8488
  Mount Ulla *(G-11685)*
Pro Choice Contractors Corp .... G 919 696-7383
  Raleigh *(G-13146)*
Prp Ventures Inc .... F 919 554-8734
  Wake Forest *(G-15577)*
Retail Installation Svcs LLC .... G 336 818-1333
  Millers Creek *(G-10495)*
◆ S Kivett Inc .... E 910 592-0161
  Clinton *(G-4106)*
Sare Granite & Tile .... G 828 676-2666
  Arden *(G-374)*
Satco Truck Equipment Inc .... F 919 383-5547
  Durham *(G-5340)*
Sawyers Sign Service Inc .... F
  Mount Airy *(G-11571)*
Sign & Awning Systems Inc .... F 919 892-5900
  Dunn *(G-4883)*
Sign Connection Inc .... E 704 868-4500
  Gastonia *(G-6507)*
Sign Systems Inc .... F 828 322-5622
  Hickory *(G-8155)*
Sign World Inc .... F 704 529-4440
  Charlotte *(G-3550)*
Signal Signs of Ga Inc .... G 828 494-4913
  Murphy *(G-11716)*
Specialty Welding & Mch Inc .... G 828 464-1104
  Newton *(G-11972)*
Stamper Sheet Metal Inc .... G 336 476-5145
  Thomasville *(G-15282)*

20 FOOD AND KINDRED PRODUCTS

Stewarts Garage and Welding Co............ G..... 336 983-5563
  Tobaccoville *(G-15321)*

Sunqest Inc... G..... 828 325-4910
  Newton *(G-11975)*

Surface Renewal Systems LLC................. G..... 704 207-3596
  Matthews *(G-10348)*

Thomas Lcklars Cbnets Lrnburg............... G..... 910 369-2094
  Laurinburg *(G-9499)*

Tice Kitchens & Interiors LLC................... F..... 919 366-4117
  Raleigh *(G-13350)*

Tint Plus... G..... 910 229-5303
  Fayetteville *(G-5930)*

Tony D Hildreth.. F..... 910 276-1803
  Laurel Hill *(G-9465)*

Unique Office Solutions Inc..................... F..... 336 854-0900
  Greensboro *(G-7430)*

V & B Construction Svcs Inc..................... G..... 704 641-9936
  Waxhaw *(G-15787)*

Viktors Gran MBL Kit Cnter Top................ F..... 828 681-0713
  Arden *(G-389)*

Volta Group Corporation LLC................... E..... 919 637-0273
  Raleigh *(G-13408)*

Waldenwood Group Inc............................ F..... 704 313-8004
  Charlotte *(G-3790)*

Warsaw Welding Service Inc.................... F..... 910 293-4261
  Warsaw *(G-15676)*

Welcome Industrial Corp.......................... D..... 336 329-9640
  Burlington *(G-1517)*

With Purpose Pressure Wshg LLC............ G..... 336 965-9473
  Greensboro *(G-7463)*

20 FOOD AND KINDRED PRODUCTS

2011 Meat packing plants

A L Beck & Sons Inc................................. F..... 336 788-1896
  Winston Salem *(G-16587)*

Acre Station Meat Farm Inc..................... F..... 252 927-3700
  Pinetown *(G-12243)*

Advancepierre Foods Inc......................... A..... 828 459-7626
  Claremont *(G-3900)*

Alexanders Ham Company Inc................ F..... 704 857-9222
  Mooresville *(G-10853)*

B & B Distributing Inc.............................. G..... 336 592-5665
  Roxboro *(G-13794)*

Bailey Foods LLC...................................... E..... 252 235-3558
  Wilson *(G-16472)*

Bass Farms Inc... E..... 252 478-4147
  Spring Hope *(G-14613)*

C B Bunting & Sons Inc........................... G..... 252 813-4237
  Pinetops *(G-12241)*

Caldwells Mt Process Abattoirs................ G..... 828 428-8833
  Maiden *(G-10101)*

Carolina Packers Inc................................ D..... 919 934-2181
  Smithfield *(G-14453)*

Chaudhry Meat Company......................... F..... 919 742-9292
  Staley *(G-14663)*

Curtis Packing Company........................... D..... 336 275-7684
  Greensboro *(G-6947)*

D & M Packing Company.......................... F..... 704 982-3716
  Albemarle *(G-80)*

Flowers Slaughterhouse LLC.................... F..... 252 235-4106
  Sims *(G-14442)*

Foothills Sug Cured Cntry Hams............... F..... 336 835-2411
  Jonesville *(G-9096)*

Freirich Foods Inc..................................... C..... 704 636-2621
  Salisbury *(G-13966)*

Frontier Meat Processing Inc.................... G..... 704 843-3921
  Waxhaw *(G-15758)*

Ham Wayco Company............................... E..... 919 735-3962
  Goldsboro *(G-6623)*

Hobes Country Hams Inc......................... E..... 336 670-3401
  North Wilkesboro *(G-12015)*

Huffman Sales and Service LLC............... G..... 828 234-0693
  Burlington *(G-1431)*

If Disher Meat Processing........................ G..... 336 463-2907
  Yadkinville *(G-17041)*

Jbs USA LLC... F..... 828 855-9571
  Hickory *(G-8072)*

▲ Jbs USA LLC... F..... 828 725-7000
  Lenoir *(G-9622)*

Jdh Capital LLC.. F..... 704 357-1220
  Charlotte *(G-3016)*

Julian Freirich Food Products................... E..... 704 636-2621
  Salisbury *(G-13997)*

Key Packing Company Inc........................ G..... 910 464-5054
  Robbins *(G-13599)*

MCI Packing Company LLC...................... G..... 910 464-3507
  Robbins *(G-13600)*

Meatinternational LLC............................. G..... 910 628-8267
  Fairmont *(G-5704)*

Miller Meat Processing LLC..................... G..... 252 589-0004
  Seaboard *(G-14229)*

Mitchells Meat Processing....................... F..... 336 591-7420
  Walnut Cove *(G-15633)*

Mt Airy Meat Center Inc........................... F..... 336 786-2023
  Mount Airy *(G-11548)*

▲ Murphy-Brown LLC............................... D..... 910 293-3434
  Warsaw *(G-15671)*

▼ Parks Family Meats LLC...................... F..... 217 446-4600
  Warsaw *(G-15672)*

Piedmont Custom Meats Inc.................... E..... 336 628-4949
  Asheboro *(G-462)*

▲ Pork Company..................................... C..... 910 293-2157
  Warsaw *(G-15673)*

R D Jones Packing Co Inc........................ G..... 910 267-2846
  Faison *(G-5725)*

Randolph Packing Company..................... D..... 336 672-1470
  Asheboro *(G-472)*

S & S Deer Processing............................. G..... 704 827-6884
  Mount Holly *(G-11651)*

Sandy Ridge Pork..................................... G..... 919 989-8878
  Smithfield *(G-14481)*

Smithfeld Fresh Meats Sls Corp................ B..... 910 862-7675
  Tar Heel *(G-15090)*

Smithfield Foods Inc................................. C..... 910 299-3009
  Clinton *(G-4110)*

Smithfield Foods Inc................................. F..... 704 298-0936
  Kannapolis *(G-9133)*

Smithfield Foods Inc................................. D..... 252 208-4700
  Kinston *(G-9384)*

Smithfield Foods Inc................................. E..... 910 241-2022
  Tar Heel *(G-15091)*

Smithfield Foods Inc................................. C..... 910 862-7675
  Tar Heel *(G-15092)*

Smithfield Packing Company Inc.............. F..... 910 592-2104
  Clinton *(G-4111)*

Stevens Packing Inc................................. G..... 336 274-6033
  Greensboro *(G-7371)*

Thomas Brothers Slaughter Hse............... G..... 336 667-1346
  North Wilkesboro *(G-12035)*

Tyson Foods Inc....................................... G..... 336 838-0083
  Wilkesboro *(G-16046)*

Tyson Foods Inc....................................... A..... 336 838-2171
  Wilkesboro *(G-16047)*

Tyson Foods Inc....................................... C..... 336 838-2171
  Wilkesboro *(G-16049)*

Villari Bros Foods LLC.............................. E..... 910 293-2157
  Warsaw *(G-15675)*

Villari Food Group LLC............................. E..... 910 293-2157
  Wilmington *(G-16441)*

Wells Jnkins Wells Mt Proc Inc................. G..... 828 245-5554
  Forest City *(G-6086)*

Wells Pork and Beef Pdts Inc.................... F..... 910 259-2523
  Burgaw *(G-1357)*

White Bros Packing Co LLC...................... G..... 252 331-9253
  Elizabeth City *(G-5582)*

White Packing Co Inc -Va......................... G..... 540 373-9883
  Raleigh *(G-13422)*

2013 Sausages and other prepared meats

Advancepierre Foods Inc......................... A..... 828 459-7626
  Claremont *(G-3900)*

Alexanders Ham Company Inc................ F..... 704 857-9222
  Mooresville *(G-10853)*

American Skin Food Group LLC............... E..... 910 259-2232
  Burgaw *(G-1332)*

Ashe Hams Inc... E..... 828 259-9426
  Asheville *(G-530)*

▲ Bakkavor Foods Usa Inc...................... C..... 704 522-1977
  Charlotte *(G-2270)*

Bar-S Foods Co... E..... 847 652-3238
  Raleigh *(G-12544)*

Bass Farms Inc... E..... 252 478-4147
  Spring Hope *(G-14613)*

Bunge Oils Inc.. E..... 910 293-7917
  Warsaw *(G-15665)*

Cangilosi Spcialty Sausage Inc................. G..... 336 665-5775
  Greensboro *(G-6877)*

Carolina Packers Inc................................ D..... 919 934-2181
  Smithfield *(G-14453)*

Chandler Foods Inc.................................. E..... 336 299-1934
  Greensboro *(G-6903)*

Foell Packing Company of NC.................. F..... 919 776-0592
  Sanford *(G-14119)*

Freirich Foods Inc..................................... C..... 704 636-2621
  Salisbury *(G-13966)*

Goodnight Brothers Prod Co Inc............... E..... 828 264-8892
  Boone *(G-1201)*

Griffn S Brbcue Wlliamston Inc................ G..... 252 792-4887
  Williamston *(G-16062)*

Ham Wayco Company............................... E..... 919 735-3962
  Goldsboro *(G-6623)*

Harris-Robinette Inc................................. G..... 252 813-5794
  Pinetops *(G-12242)*

Hobes Country Hams Inc......................... E..... 336 670-3401
  North Wilkesboro *(G-12015)*

Hormel Foods Corp Svcs LLC................... F..... 704 527-1535
  Charlotte *(G-2922)*

Hunter Liver Mush Inc.............................. G..... 828 652-7902
  Marion *(G-10151)*

Jenkins Foods Inc.................................... E..... 704 434-2347
  Shelby *(G-14332)*

Jerky Man Inc.. G..... 828 749-3685
  Saluda *(G-14071)*

Jerky Outpost.. G..... 828 260-6221
  Banner Elk *(G-900)*

Julian Freirich Company Inc.................... E..... 704 636-2621
  Salisbury *(G-13996)*

Julian Freirich Food Products................... E..... 704 636-2621
  Salisbury *(G-13997)*

Kansas City Sausage Co LLC................... G..... 910 567-5604
  Godwin *(G-6578)*

Larry S Sausage Company........................ E..... 910 483-5148
  Fayetteville *(G-5859)*

Lmb Corp.. G..... 704 547-8886
  Charlotte *(G-3098)*

Mack S Liver Mush Inc............................. F..... 704 434-6188
  Shelby *(G-14341)*

Macs Farms Sausage Co Inc.................... G..... 910 594-0095
  Newton Grove *(G-11990)*

McLaughlin Farmhouse............................. G..... 704 660-0971
  Mooresville *(G-11019)*

▲ Monogram Food Solutions LLC............. E..... 901 685-7167
  Charlotte *(G-3200)*

20 FOOD AND KINDRED PRODUCTS

Patriot Jerky LLC .... G 828 850-9160
 Conover *(G-4479)*
Shanes Carolina Jerky LLC .... G 336 653-3673
 Thomasville *(G-15276)*
Shiners Stash Jerky .... G 828 302-6359
 Taylorsville *(G-15166)*
Skin Boys LLC .... E 910 259-2232
 Burgaw *(G-1350)*
Smithfield Foods Inc .... C 910 299-3009
 Clinton *(G-4110)*
Smithfield Foods Inc .... D 252 208-4700
 Kinston *(G-9384)*
Stevens Packing Inc .... G 336 274-6033
 Greensboro *(G-7371)*
Suncrest Farms Cntry Hams Inc .... E 336 667-4441
 Wilkesboro *(G-16044)*
Thomas Brothers Foods LLC .... F 336 672-0337
 Asheboro *(G-498)*
White Packing Co Inc -Va .... G 540 373-9883
 Raleigh *(G-13422)*
Williams Skin Co .... F 910 323-2628
 Fayetteville *(G-5954)*

2015 Poultry slaughtering and processing

Advancepierre Foods Inc .... A 828 459-7626
 Claremont *(G-3900)*
Basic American Foods .... G 336 887-3930
 High Point *(G-8267)*
Broomes Poultry Inc .... G 704 983-0965
 Albemarle *(G-75)*
Butterball LLC .... D 919 658-6743
 Goldsboro *(G-6598)*
Butterball LLC .... D 919 658-6743
 Mount Olive *(G-11657)*
Butterball LLC .... B 910 875-8711
 Raeford *(G-12415)*
▼ Butterball LLC .... E 919 255-7900
 Garner *(G-6258)*
Calvin C Mooney Poultry .... G 336 374-6690
 Ararat *(G-264)*
Carolina Egg Companies Inc .... D 252 459-2143
 Nashville *(G-11739)*
Carrol Poultry LLC .... G 347 203-9637
 Bladenboro *(G-1145)*
Case Farms LLC .... D 919 735-5010
 Dudley *(G-4841)*
Case Farms LLC .... E 919 658-2252
 Goldsboro *(G-6599)*
Case Farms LLC .... D 919 635-2390
 Mount Olive *(G-11659)*
Case Farms LLC .... F 704 528-4501
 Troutman *(G-15370)*
◆ Case Farms Processing Inc .... E 704 528-4501
 Troutman *(G-15371)*
Case Foods Inc .... C 919 736-4498
 Goldsboro *(G-6600)*
▼ Case Foods Inc .... F 704 528-4501
 Troutman *(G-15372)*
▲ Charles Craft Inc .... G 910 844-3521
 Laurinburg *(G-9474)*
Filet of Chicken .... E 336 751-4752
 Mocksville *(G-10571)*
Game Processing Leonards Wild .... G 980 429-7042
 Lincolnton *(G-9894)*
Hopkins Poultry Company .... F 336 656-3361
 Browns Summit *(G-1308)*
House of Raeford Farms Inc .... A 910 289-3191
 Raeford *(G-12423)*
House of Raeford Farms Inc .... A 910 763-0475
 Wilmington *(G-16259)*
◆ House of Raeford Farms Inc .... A 912 222-4090
 Rose Hill *(G-13777)*

House of Raeford Farms La LLC .... C 336 751-4752
 Mocksville *(G-10580)*
Integra Foods LLC .... F 910 984-2007
 Bladenboro *(G-1149)*
◆ Johnson Nash & Sons Farms Inc .... B 910 289-3113
 Rose Hill *(G-13778)*
Keystone Foods LLC .... C 336 342-6601
 Reidsville *(G-13529)*
Mountaire Farms LLC .... C 910 843-5942
 Lumber Bridge *(G-10020)*
Mountaire Farms LLC .... C 910 843-3332
 Lumber Bridge *(G-10021)*
Mountaire Farms LLC .... C 919 663-1768
 Siler City *(G-14424)*
Mountaire Farms Inc .... A 910 843-5942
 Lumber Bridge *(G-10022)*
Mountaire Farms Inc .... B 919 663-0848
 Siler City *(G-14425)*
Mountaire Farms Inc .... F 704 978-3055
 Statesville *(G-14848)*
Perdue Farms Inc .... E 252 348-4287
 Ahoskie *(G-64)*
Perdue Farms Inc .... D 910 673-4148
 Candor *(G-1597)*
Perdue Farms Inc .... E 704 278-2228
 Cleveland *(G-4078)*
Perdue Farms Inc .... B 252 358-8245
 Cofield *(G-4137)*
Perdue Farms Inc .... A 704 789-2400
 Concord *(G-4331)*
Perdue Farms Inc .... E 252 338-1543
 Elizabeth City *(G-5562)*
Perdue Farms Inc .... D 336 366-2591
 Elkin *(G-5628)*
Perdue Farms Inc .... C 252 758-2141
 Greenville *(G-7571)*
Perdue Farms Inc .... E 252 583-5731
 Halifax *(G-7610)*
Perdue Farms Inc .... D 919 284-2033
 Kenly *(G-9154)*
Perdue Farms Inc .... A 252 348-4200
 Lewiston Woodville *(G-9662)*
Perdue Farms Inc .... E 910 738-8581
 Lumberton *(G-10048)*
Perdue Farms Inc .... E 252 398-5112
 Murfreesboro *(G-11701)*
Perdue Farms Inc .... C 252 459-9763
 Nashville *(G-11748)*
Perdue Farms Inc .... E 336 896-9121
 Winston Salem *(G-16845)*
Perdue Farms Inc .... D 336 679-7733
 Yadkinville *(G-17046)*
Perdue Farms Incorporated .... A 910 997-8600
 Rockingham *(G-13638)*
Pilgrim LLC .... G 980 224-9567
 Charlotte *(G-3343)*
Pilgrims Pride Corporation .... E 704 721-3585
 Concord *(G-4333)*
Pilgrims Pride Corporation .... B 704 624-2171
 Marshville *(G-10222)*
Pilgrims Pride Corporation .... E 919 774-7333
 Sanford *(G-14171)*
Pilgrims Pride Corporation .... E 336 622-4251
 Staley *(G-14669)*
Pilgrims Pride Corporation .... C 704 233-4047
 Wingate *(G-16577)*
▼ Prestage Foods Inc .... B 910 865-6611
 Saint Pauls *(G-13908)*
Prestige Farms Inc .... E 919 861-8867
 Raleigh *(G-13139)*
Sanderson Farms Inc .... E 252 208-0036
 Kinston *(G-9383)*

Sanderson Farms LLC Proc Div .... A 910 274-0220
 Saint Pauls *(G-13909)*
Tyson Foods Inc .... F 910 483-3282
 Eastover *(G-5483)*
Tyson Foods Inc .... G 704 283-7571
 Monroe *(G-10826)*
Tyson Foods Inc .... F 336 838-2171
 Wilkesboro *(G-16048)*
Tyson Foods Inc .... C 336 838-2171
 Wilkesboro *(G-16049)*
Wayne Farms LLC .... A 336 386-8151
 Dobson *(G-4833)*
Wayne Farms LLC .... B 336 366-4413
 Elkin *(G-5632)*
Wayne Farms LLC .... F 770 538-2120
 Newton *(G-11984)*

2021 Creamery butter

Michaels Creamery Inc .... G 910 292-4172
 Fayetteville *(G-5873)*
Village Creamery & Caf Inc .... G 336 447-4726
 Elon *(G-5663)*
Waxhaw Creamery LLC .... F 704 843-7927
 Waxhaw *(G-15789)*

2022 Cheese; natural and processed

Buffalo Creek Farm & Crmry LLC .... G 336 969-5698
 Germanton *(G-6552)*
Celebrity Dairy LLC .... G 919 742-4931
 Siler City *(G-14404)*
Ethnicraft Usa LLC .... F 336 885-2055
 High Point *(G-8346)*
Fading D Farm LLC .... G 704 633-3888
 Salisbury *(G-13962)*
Kraft Cabin LLc .... G 224 409-4374
 Raleigh *(G-12946)*
▲ Looking Glass Creamery LLC .... G 828 458-0088
 Columbus *(G-4177)*
Old Salem Incorporated .... G 336 721-7305
 Winston Salem *(G-16828)*
Our Pride Foods Roxboro Inc .... G 336 597-4978
 Roxboro *(G-13813)*
Saputo Cheese USA Inc .... C 847 267-1100
 Troy *(G-15414)*
Stans Quality Foods Inc .... G 336 570-2572
 Burlington *(G-1500)*
Tin Can Ventures LLC .... G 919 732-9078
 Cedar Grove *(G-1973)*

2023 Dry, condensed, evaporated products

Arms Race Nutrition LLC .... G 888 978-2332
 Statesville *(G-14753)*
Bestco LLC .... E 704 664-4300
 Mooresville *(G-10875)*
Bionutra Life Sciences LLC .... G 828 572-2838
 Lenoir *(G-9590)*
Blue Ridge Silver Inc .... G 828 729-8610
 Boone *(G-1177)*
BNC Nutrition LLC .... G 336 567-0104
 Burlington *(G-1376)*
Body Engineering Inc .... G 704 650-3434
 Matthews *(G-10234)*
Chef Martini LLC .... A 919 327-3183
 Raleigh *(G-12618)*
Disruptive Enterprises LLC .... F 336 567-0104
 Burlington *(G-1407)*
Gold Star .... G 704 651-8186
 Mooresville *(G-10961)*
Herbalife Manufacturing LLC .... F 336 970-6400
 Winston Salem *(G-16744)*
Ka-Ex LLC .... G 704 343-5143
 Charlotte *(G-3042)*

SIC SECTION
20 FOOD AND KINDRED PRODUCTS

merica Labz LLC .... G 844 445-5335
  Statesville *(G-14842)*

Muscadine Naturals Inc .... G 888 628-5898
  Clemmons *(G-4053)*

NPC Corporation .... F 336 998-2386
  Mocksville *(G-10595)*

Pave Wellness LLC .... G 919 335-3575
  Durham *(G-5275)*

Rainforest Nutritionals Inc .... G 919 847-2221
  Raleigh *(G-13171)*

Sapphire Innvtive Thrapies LLC .... G 877 402-4325
  Chapel Hill *(G-2067)*

2024 Ice cream and frozen deserts

▼ Alamance Foods Inc .... C 336 226-6392
  Burlington *(G-1362)*

Antkar LLC .... G 919 322-4100
  Raleigh *(G-12509)*

Bignisha Rgrts Chill Cream LLC .... G 910 528-8966
  Fayetteville *(G-5770)*

Bilcat Inc .... E 828 295-3088
  Blowing Rock *(G-1154)*

Brick & Mortar Grill .... G 919 639-9700
  Angier *(G-133)*

Brick Mason Masonry .... G 704 502-4907
  Charlotte *(G-2354)*

Cintoms Inc .... G 828 684-1317
  Asheville *(G-593)*

Day & Nght Creal Bar Clmbia SC .... F 719 323-8265
  Fayetteville *(G-5805)*

▲ Delizza LLC .... F 252 442-0270
  Battleboro *(G-919)*

Dream Kreams LLC .... G 919 491-1984
  Kernersville *(G-9193)*

Frozen Dessert Specialists LLC .... G 336 362-8707
  Randleman *(G-13470)*

Gabden LLC .... G 704 451-8646
  Statesville *(G-14803)*

Gelarto Inc .... F 646 795-3505
  Wilmington *(G-16229)*

Goodberry Creamery Inc .... G 919 878-8870
  Wake Forest *(G-15562)*

Homeland Creamery LLC .... G 336 685-6455
  Julian *(G-9105)*

Huff Mj LLC .... G 910 313-3133
  Wilmington *(G-16260)*

Hunter Farms .... C 336 822-2300
  High Point *(G-8403)*

J & S Parkside LLC .... G 919 434-1293
  Cary *(G-1795)*

Je Freeze LLC .... G 980 231-5365
  Davidson *(G-4684)*

Jls Masonry Inc .... G 704 307-1219
  Monroe *(G-10750)*

M and H Masonry .... G 704 858-7230
  Monroe *(G-10762)*

Maola Milk and Ice Cream Co .... E 252 756-3160
  Greenville *(G-7557)*

Maple View Ice Cream .... F 919 960-5535
  Hillsborough *(G-8661)*

Meadows Frozen Custar .... G 336 298-7246
  Oak Ridge *(G-12060)*

▲ Mooresville Ice Cream Com .... E 704 664-5456
  Mooresville *(G-11024)*

Mountain Snow LLC .... G 828 403-7535
  Marion *(G-10166)*

North Carolina State Univ .... G 919 515-2760
  Raleigh *(G-13070)*

Paletria La Mnrca McHacana LLC .... G 919 803-0636
  Raleigh *(G-13095)*

R & A Masonry LLC .... G 919 672-6253
  Durham *(G-5315)*

Raleigh Rolls .... G 919 559-0451
  Raleigh *(G-13183)*

Seemingly Overzealous LLC .... G 770 634-7653
  Charlotte *(G-3523)*

Simply Natural Creamery LLC .... F 252 746-3334
  Ayden *(G-858)*

▲ Tony S Ice Cream Company Inc .... F 704 867-7085
  Gastonia *(G-6528)*

Tonys Ice Cream Co Inc .... G 704 853-0018
  Gastonia *(G-6529)*

Twisted Infusionz LLC .... G 252 432-4215
  Raleigh *(G-13372)*

Yats Stone Masonry Llc .... G 919 841-2297
  Wendell *(G-15925)*

Yo Zone .... G 336 270-5262
  Burlington *(G-1520)*

Yummy Tummy Ga LLC .... E 704 658-0445
  Mooresville *(G-11138)*

2026 Fluid milk

▼ Alamance Foods Inc .... C 336 226-6392
  Burlington *(G-1362)*

Carolina Dairy LLC .... F 910 569-7070
  Biscoe *(G-1105)*

Carolina Yogurt Inc .... G 828 754-9685
  Lenoir *(G-9596)*

Dfa Dairy Brands Fluid LLC .... G 704 341-2794
  Charlotte *(G-2625)*

Dfa Dairy Brands Fluid LLC .... G 336 714-9032
  Tarboro *(G-15101)*

Feeneys .... G 336 617-5874
  Greensboro *(G-7011)*

Maola Milk and Ice Cream Co .... E 252 756-3160
  Greenville *(G-7557)*

Maola Milk and Ice Cream Co .... E 844 287-1970
  New Bern *(G-11817)*

Milkco Inc .... B 828 254-8428
  Asheville *(G-702)*

New Dairy Opco LLC .... E 336 725-8141
  Winston Salem *(G-16819)*

▲ Origin Food Group LLC .... E 704 768-9000
  Statesville *(G-14855)*

Saputo Cheese USA Inc .... F 910 569-7070
  Biscoe *(G-1115)*

Victoria Sweet LLC .... G 336 474-8008
  Thomasville *(G-15299)*

2032 Canned specialties

▲ Atlantic Natural Foods LLC .... D 888 491-0524
  Nashville *(G-11734)*

Atlantis Foods Inc .... E 336 768-6101
  Clemmons *(G-4027)*

Bost Distributing Company Inc .... E 919 775-5931
  Sanford *(G-14095)*

Chandler Foods Inc .... E 336 299-1934
  Greensboro *(G-6903)*

Papa Parusos Foods Inc .... F 910 484-8801
  Fayetteville *(G-5893)*

Plantation House Foods Inc .... G 919 381-5495
  Durham *(G-5291)*

Ritas One Inc .... G 919 650-2415
  Cary *(G-1871)*

Soup Maven LLC .... G 727 919-5242
  Asheville *(G-781)*

Stevens Foodservice .... G 919 322-5470
  Raleigh *(G-13304)*

Tortilleria Duvy LLC .... G 336 497-1510
  Kernersville *(G-9246)*

Tyson Mexican Original Inc .... D 919 777-9428
  Sanford *(G-14201)*

2033 Canned fruits and specialties

Arcadia Beverage LLC .... G 828 684-3556
  Arden *(G-310)*

Arcadia Farms LLC .... D 828 684-3556
  Arden *(G-311)*

Baileys Sauces Inc .... G 252 756-7179
  Greenville *(G-7491)*

Bevs & Bites LLC .... G 704 247-7573
  Charlotte *(G-2305)*

Big Show Foods Inc .... F 919 920-1888
  Fremont *(G-6172)*

Blue Ridge Jams .... G 828 685-1783
  Hendersonville *(G-7826)*

Bobbos Stuff LLC .... G 828 883-8545
  Brevard *(G-1271)*

Brookwood Farms Inc .... D 919 663-3612
  Siler City *(G-14401)*

Cardinal Foods LLC .... E 910 259-9407
  Burgaw *(G-1334)*

Carolina Canners Inc .... D 843 537-5281
  Southern Pines *(G-14530)*

Clement Pappas Nc LLC .... G 856 455-1000
  Hendersonville *(G-7838)*

Dfa Dairy Brands Fluid LLC .... G 704 341-2794
  Charlotte *(G-2625)*

◆ Dole Food Company Inc .... E 818 874-4000
  Charlotte *(G-2650)*

Dunbar Foods Corporation .... D 910 892-3175
  Dunn *(G-4863)*

▲ Dutch Kettle LLC .... G 336 468-8422
  Hamptonville *(G-7669)*

DVine Foods .... G 910 862-2576
  Elizabethtown *(G-5594)*

Girlie Jams .... G 704 575-5815
  Cornelius *(G-4549)*

Goodstuff Juices LLC .... G 252 347-2341
  Greenville *(G-7532)*

Goshen House & Trading LLC .... G 832 407-8153
  Cary *(G-1776)*

Kraft Heinz Foods Company .... G 704 565-5500
  Charlotte *(G-3060)*

Lc Foods LLC .... G 919 510-6688
  Raleigh *(G-12961)*

Marie Sharps Usa LLC .... F 336 701-0377
  Winston Salem *(G-16800)*

McF Operating LLC .... E 828 685-8821
  Hendersonville *(G-7878)*

Mike DS Bbq LLC .... G 866 960-8652
  Durham *(G-5225)*

Miss Kllys Jllies Jams Such LL .... G 910 988-8042
  Southern Pines *(G-14542)*

Palace Green LLC .... G 919 827-7950
  Raleigh *(G-13094)*

Pamela Stoeppelwerth .... G 828 837-7293
  Marble *(G-10133)*

Papa Lonnies Inc .... G 336 573-9313
  Stoneville *(G-14964)*

T W Garner Food Company .... G 336 661-1550
  Winston Salem *(G-16929)*

T W Garner Food Company .... G 336 661-1550
  Winston Salem *(G-16931)*

◆ T W Garner Food Company .... E 336 661-1550
  Winston Salem *(G-16930)*

Tina M Jones .... G 828 685-2937
  Hendersonville *(G-7907)*

Welchs Recycling Inc .... G 336 638-9601
  Greensboro *(G-7455)*

Yamco LLC .... G 252 747-9267
  Snow Hill *(G-14511)*

2034 Dehydrated fruits, vegetables, soups

Anns House of Nuts .... G 252 795-6500
  Robersonville *(G-13614)*

20 FOOD AND KINDRED PRODUCTS

Berry Cold LLC .... G 910 267-4531
  Faison (G-5722)
Carolina Innvtive Fd Ingrdnts .... G 804 359-9311
  Nashville (G-11740)
Dehydration LLC .... G 252 747-8200
  Snow Hill (G-14502)
Interntnal Agrclture Group LLC .... F 908 323-3246
  Mooresville (G-10983)
Naturesrules Inc .... G 336 427-2526
  Madison (G-10081)

2035 Pickles, sauces, and salad dressings

3peter LLC .... F 919 475-2334
  Hillsborough (G-8631)
3peter LLC .... G 919 475-2334
  Hillsborough (G-8630)
Bevs & Bites LLC .... F 704 247-7573
  Charlotte (G-2305)
Chef Martini LLC .... A 919 327-3183
  Raleigh (G-12618)
D C Thomas Group Inc .... E 252 433-0132
  Henderson (G-7780)
D C Thomas Group Inc .... G 336 299-6263
  Greensboro (G-6956)
Dana Fancy Foods .... G 828 685-2937
  Hendersonville (G-7843)
DJS Pickles LLC .... G 828 647-0357
  Asheville (G-610)
Georges Sauces LLC .... G 252 459-3084
  Nashville (G-11745)
▲ Golding Farms Foods Inc .... D 336 766-6161
  Winston Salem (G-16723)
Jenkins Foods Inc .... E 704 434-2347
  Shelby (G-14332)
Jhonny Delgado .... G 704 218-9424
  Charlotte (G-3021)
Lusty Monk LLC .... G 828 645-5056
  Asheville (G-692)
Mount Olive Pickle Company .... G 704 867-5585
  Gastonia (G-6472)
Mount Olive Pickle Company Inc .... F 704 867-5585
  Gastonia (G-6473)
◆ Mount Olive Pickle Company Inc .... B 919 658-2535
  Mount Olive (G-11666)
Pop Products LLC .... G 336 263-1884
  Burlington (G-1476)
Posh Pickle Company LLC .... G 336 870-6712
  Greensboro (G-7268)
Schott Ventures LLC .... G 252 813-9660
  Charlotte (G-3508)
◆ T W Garner Food Company .... F 336 661-1550
  Winston Salem (G-16930)
Tracys Gourmet LLC .... G 919 672-1731
  Asheville (G-804)

2037 Frozen fruits and vegetables

▲ Alphin Brothers Inc .... E 910 892-8751
  Dunn (G-4850)
Caseiro International LLC .... G 919 530-8333
  Durham (G-5007)
Goodstuff Juices LLC .... G 252 347-2341
  Greenville (G-7532)
Milkco Inc .... B 828 254-8428
  Asheville (G-702)
Neighborhood Smoothie LLC .... G 919 845-5513
  Raleigh (G-13061)
Nice Blends Corp .... D 910 640-1000
  Whiteville (G-15973)
Seal Seasons Inc .... F 919 245-3535
  Durham (G-5347)
Smoothie Fabrication LLC .... G 704 291-7728
  Monroe (G-10809)

Smoothiesorg Inc .... G 704 906-4121
  Charlotte (G-3568)
Southport Smoothies LLC .... G 910 363-4526
  Southport (G-14582)
Triad Smoothies LLC .... G 336 972-1130
  Winston Salem (G-16949)
Tropical Fruit Juice Bar .... G 910 426-5842
  Fayetteville (G-5935)

2038 Frozen specialties, nec

Advancepierre Foods Inc .... A 828 459-7626
  Claremont (G-3900)
B Roberts Foods LLC .... E 704 522-1977
  Charlotte (G-2253)
Ce Kitchen Inc .... D 910 399-2334
  Wilmington (G-16164)
Chandler Foods Inc .... E 336 299-1934
  Greensboro (G-6903)
ICEE Company .... G 910 346-3937
  Jacksonville (G-9008)
James Fods Frnchise Corp Amer .... G 336 437-0393
  Graham (G-6694)
Kalo Foods LLC .... G 336 949-4802
  Stokesdale (G-14944)
McDonalds .... F 910 295-1112
  Pinehurst (G-12229)
Orange Bakery Inc .... E 704 875-3003
  Huntersville (G-8872)
▲ Poppies International I Inc .... D 252 442-4016
  Battleboro (G-930)
Ricewrap Foods Corporation .... F 919 614-1179
  Butner (G-1549)
▼ Stefano Foods Inc .... C 704 399-3935
  Charlotte (G-3628)

2041 Flour and other grain mill products

Archer-Daniels-Midland Company .... E 704 332-3165
  Charlotte (G-2210)
Archer-Daniels-Midland Company .... C 910 457-5011
  Southport (G-14565)
▲ Atkinson Milling Company .... D 919 965-3547
  Selma (G-14253)
Bartlett Milling Company LP .... D 704 872-9581
  Statesville (G-14759)
Bay State Milling Company .... E 704 664-4873
  Mooresville (G-10870)
Beaver Tooth Milling Inc .... G 910 262-4438
  Bolivia (G-1162)
Boonville Flour Feed Mill Inc .... G 336 367-7541
  Boonville (G-1253)
Buffaloe Milling Company Inc .... E 252 438-8637
  Kittrell (G-9394)
◆ Colony Gums LLC .... E 704 226-9666
  Monroe (G-10689)
House-Autry Mills Inc .... E 919 963-6200
  Four Oaks (G-6107)
Lakeside Mills Inc .... F 828 286-4866
  Spindale (G-14607)
Lindley Mills Inc .... F 336 376-6190
  Graham (G-6697)
Midstate Mills Inc .... C 828 464-1611
  Newton (G-11953)
Old School Mill Inc .... G 704 781-5451
  Stanfield (G-14681)
Proximity Foods Corporation .... G 336 691-1700
  Greensboro (G-7290)
Renwood Mills LLC .... D 828 465-0302
  Newton (G-11963)
Romanos Pizza .... G 704 782-5020
  Concord (G-4352)
Smith Milling Company .... G 336 957-8108
  Roaring River (G-13595)

Whitehat Seed Farms Inc .... G 252 264-2427
  Hertford (G-7925)

2043 Cereal breakfast foods

Bakeboxx Company .... F 336 861-1212
  High Point (G-8262)
Kellanova .... G 704 370-1658
  Huntersville (G-8843)
Kellanova .... G 704 241-6977
  Monroe (G-10752)
Lrw Holdings Inc .... G 919 609-4172
  Durham (G-5196)
Post Consumer Brands LLC .... G 336 672-0124
  Asheboro (G-464)

2045 Prepared flour mixes and doughs

Julias Southern Foods LLC .... G 919 609-6745
  Raleigh (G-12927)
Lovegrass Kitchen Inc .... G 919 234-7541
  Fuquay Varina (G-6210)

2046 Wet corn milling

Barkleys Mill On Southern Cro .... G 828 626-3344
  Weaverville (G-15839)
Ingredion Incorporated .... D 336 785-0100
  Winston Salem (G-16760)
Lc Foods LLC .... G 919 510-6688
  Raleigh (G-12961)
Pbrandecom .... G 336 294-9771
  Greensboro (G-7249)
Western Technology Inc .... F 336 361-0402
  Reidsville (G-13545)

2047 Dog and cat food

Barbaras Canine Catering Inc .... G 704 588-3647
  Charlotte (G-2277)
Braswell Milling Company .... E 252 459-2143
  Nashville (G-11736)
Carolina By-Products Co .... G 336 333-3030
  Greensboro (G-6882)
▲ Carolina Prime Pet Inc .... E 888 370-2360
  Lenoir (G-9595)
Crump Group USA Inc .... F 936 465-5870
  Nashville (G-11742)
Mars Petcare Us Inc .... D 252 438-1600
  Henderson (G-7798)
Nestle Purina Petcare Company .... E 314 982-1000
  Eden (G-5498)

2048 Prepared feeds, nec

A & B Milling Company .... E 252 445-3161
  Enfield (G-5673)
Apc LLC .... E 919 965-2051
  Selma (G-14252)
Bartlett Milling Company LP .... E 704 487-5061
  Shelby (G-14288)
Bartlett Milling Company LP .... D 704 872-9581
  Statesville (G-14759)
Bay State Milling Company .... E 704 664-4873
  Mooresville (G-10870)
Boggs Farm Center Inc .... G 704 538-7176
  Fallston (G-5728)
Boonville Flour Feed Mill Inc .... G 336 367-7541
  Boonville (G-1253)
Braswell Milling Company .... E 252 459-2143
  Nashville (G-11736)
Cargill Incorporated .... C 704 523-0414
  Charlotte (G-2388)
Cargill Incorporated .... G 704 278-2941
  Cleveland (G-4069)
Cargill Incorporated .... E 252 752-1879
  Greenville (G-7496)

20 FOOD AND KINDRED PRODUCTS

Coker Feed Mill Inc .... F 919 778-3491
  Goldsboro *(G-6602)*

Darling Ingredients Inc .... F 910 483-0473
  Fayetteville *(G-5804)*

Darling Ingredients Inc .... F 704 864-9941
  Gastonia *(G-6395)*

Darling Ingredients Inc .... F 704 694-3701
  Wadesboro *(G-15509)*

Deal-Rite Feeds Inc .... E 704 873-8646
  Statesville *(G-14785)*

G & M Milling Co Inc .... E 704 873-5758
  Statesville *(G-14802)*

Garland Farm Supply Inc .... F 910 529-9731
  Garland *(G-6244)*

Goldsboro Milling Company .... C 252 753-5371
  Farmville *(G-5737)*

Goldsboro Milling Company .... C 919 778-3130
  Goldsboro *(G-6618)*

Griffin Industries LLC .... E 704 624-9140
  Marshville *(G-10217)*

Hodge Farms LLC .... G 704 278-2684
  Mount Ulla *(G-11683)*

Ifta Usa Inc .... G 919 659-8393
  Durham *(G-5147)*

◆ Johnson Nash & Sons Farms Inc ...... B 910 289-3113
  Rose Hill *(G-13778)*

Linkone Src LLC .... F 252 206-0960
  Wilson *(G-16512)*

Midstate Mills Inc .... C 828 464-1611
  Newton *(G-11953)*

Monitor Roller Mill Inc .... G 336 591-4126
  Walnut Cove *(G-15634)*

Mountaire Farms LLC .... B 910 974-3232
  Candor *(G-1596)*

Mountaire Farms LLC .... C 704 978-3055
  Statesville *(G-14847)*

Mountaire Farms Inc .... D 910 844-3126
  Maxton *(G-10361)*

Murphy-Brown LLC .... D 910 277-8999
  Laurinburg *(G-9490)*

Murphy-Brown LLC .... D 910 293-3434
  Rose Hill *(G-13779)*

Murphy-Brown LLC .... D 910 282-4264
  Rose Hill *(G-13780)*

Nutrien AG Solutions Inc .... F 252 977-2025
  Rocky Mount *(G-13670)*

Nutrotonic LLC .... F 855 948-0008
  Charlotte *(G-3285)*

Pilgrims Pride Corporation .... B 704 624-2171
  Marshville *(G-10222)*

▲ Protein For Pets Opco LLC .... E 252 206-0960
  Wilson *(G-16524)*

Purina Mills LLC .... D 704 872-0456
  Statesville *(G-14873)*

▼ S P Co Inc .... G 919 848-3599
  Raleigh *(G-13222)*

Southeastern Minerals Inc .... E 252 492-0831
  Henderson *(G-7811)*

Southern States Coop Inc .... G 336 629-3977
  Asheboro *(G-484)*

Southern States Coop Inc .... G 336 246-3201
  Creedmoor *(G-4620)*

Southern States Coop Inc .... E 919 528-1516
  Creedmoor *(G-4621)*

Southern States Coop Inc .... G 336 786-7545
  Mount Airy *(G-11575)*

Southern States Coop Inc .... E 919 658-5061
  Mount Olive *(G-11669)*

Southern States Coop Inc .... E 919 693-6136
  Oxford *(G-12157)*

Southern States Coop Inc .... G 252 823-2520
  Princeville *(G-12406)*

Southern States Coop Inc .... F 336 599-2185
  Roxboro *(G-13824)*

Southern States Coop Inc .... E 704 872-6364
  Statesville *(G-14896)*

Southern States Coop Inc .... F 910 285-8213
  Wallace *(G-15628)*

▼ Springmill Products Inc .... G 336 406-9050
  Lawsonville *(G-9504)*

Star Milling Company .... G 704 873-9561
  Statesville *(G-14900)*

Steelman Milling Company Inc .... G 336 463-5586
  Yadkinville *(G-17051)*

Two Percent LLC .... G 301 401-2750
  Lincolnton *(G-9930)*

Valley Proteins (de) Inc .... C 336 333-3030
  Greensboro *(G-7435)*

2051 Bread, cake, and related products

A Taste of Heavenly Sweetness .... G 336 825-7321
  Greensboro *(G-6768)*

Accidental Baker .... G 919 732-6777
  Hillsborough *(G-8632)*

All Baked Out Company .... F 336 861-1212
  High Point *(G-8241)*

Apple Baking Company Inc .... E 704 637-6800
  Salisbury *(G-13922)*

Artesias Swets Bnged By Dior L .... G 704 794-3792
  Concord *(G-4198)*

Bakkavor Foods Usa Inc .... B 704 522-1977
  Charlotte *(G-2269)*

▲ Bakkavor Foods Usa Inc .... C 704 522-1977
  Charlotte *(G-2270)*

Bimbo Bakeries Usa Inc .... A 252 641-2200
  Tarboro *(G-15096)*

Bluebird Cupcakes .... G 919 616-7347
  Raleigh *(G-12565)*

Burney Sweets & More Inc .... G 910 862-2099
  Elizabethtown *(G-5587)*

Buttercreme Bakery Inc .... G 336 722-1022
  Winston Salem *(G-16641)*

▲ Carolina Foods LLC .... B 704 333-9812
  Charlotte *(G-2395)*

Casa Di Cupcakes .... G 919 255-9994
  Raleigh *(G-12609)*

Connectivity Group LLC .... E 910 799-9023
  Wilmington *(G-16177)*

Cupcake A La Mo LLC .... G 919 322-8824
  Raleigh *(G-12660)*

Cupcake Bar .... G 919 816-2905
  Durham *(G-5039)*

Cupcake Stop Shop LLC .... G 919 457-7900
  Raleigh *(G-12661)*

Delish Cakery Co .... G 704 724-7743
  Charlotte *(G-2613)*

Depalo Foods Inc .... E 704 827-0245
  Belmont *(G-983)*

Dewey S Bakery Inc .... F 336 748-0230
  Winston Salem *(G-16677)*

Donut Shop .... G 910 640-3317
  Whiteville *(G-15962)*

Dunkin Donuts .... F 919 217-9603
  Knightdale *(G-9417)*

Evelyn T Burney .... G 336 473-9794
  Rocky Mount *(G-13697)*

Event Extravaganza LLC .... F 252 679-7004
  Elizabeth City *(G-5544)*

Five Points Baking Company LLC .... G 919 349-2033
  Raleigh *(G-12771)*

▼ Flowers Bakery of Winston .... C 336 785-8700
  Winston Salem *(G-16715)*

Flowers Baking Co Newton LLC .... G 336 903-1345
  Wilkesboro *(G-16022)*

Flowers Baking Co Newton LLC .... D 336 841-8840
  Jamestown *(G-9049)*

Flowers Bkg Co Jamestown LLC .... G 252 492-1519
  Henderson *(G-7784)*

Flowers Bkg Co Jamestown LLC .... G 704 296-1000
  Monroe *(G-10720)*

Flowers Bkg Co Jamestown LLC .... E 919 776-8932
  Sanford *(G-14118)*

Flowers Bkg Co Jamestown LLC .... E 336 744-3525
  Winston Salem *(G-16716)*

Franklin Baking Company LLC .... F 252 752-4600
  Greenville *(G-7529)*

Franklin Baking Company LLC .... F 910 425-5090
  Hope Mills *(G-8737)*

Franklin Baking Company LLC .... G 919 832-7942
  Raleigh *(G-12780)*

Franklin Baking Company LLC .... F 252 410-0255
  Roanoke Rapids *(G-13574)*

Franklin Baking Company LLC .... G 252 946-3340
  Washington *(G-15705)*

▲ Franklin Baking Company LLC .... B 919 735-0344
  Goldsboro *(G-6614)*

Fuquay-Varina Baking Co Inc .... G 919 557-2237
  Fuquay Varina *(G-6201)*

Harris Teeter LLC .... D 704 846-7117
  Matthews *(G-10252)*

Harris Teeter LLC .... D 919 859-0110
  Raleigh *(G-12831)*

Harvest Time Bread Company .... D
  Mount Airy *(G-11517)*

Heavenly Cheesecakes .... G 336 577-9390
  Winston Salem *(G-16741)*

Ingles Markets Incorporated .... D 704 434-0096
  Boiling Springs *(G-1161)*

Jps Cupcakery LLC .... F 919 894-5000
  Benson *(G-1038)*

Kelley G Cupcakes .... G 314 368-5316
  Durham *(G-5179)*

Krispy Kreme Doughnut Corp .... E 919 669-6151
  Gastonia *(G-6440)*

Krispy Kreme Doughnut Corp .... E 336 854-8275
  Greensboro *(G-7158)*

Krispy Kreme Doughnut Corp .... E 336 733-3780
  Winston Salem *(G-16779)*

◆ Krispy Kreme Doughnut Corp .... C 980 270-7117
  Charlotte *(G-3062)*

◆ Krispy Kreme Doughnuts Inc .... C 336 725-2981
  Winston Salem *(G-16781)*

La Estrella Inc .... G 919 639-6559
  Angier *(G-144)*

La Farm Inc .... E 919 657-0657
  Cary *(G-1805)*

Lc Foods LLC .... G 919 510-6688
  Raleigh *(G-12961)*

Martins Fmous Pstry Shoppe Inc .... G 800 548-1200
  Charlotte *(G-3134)*

Martins Fmous Pstry Shoppe Inc .... G 800 548-1200
  Fayetteville *(G-5867)*

Martins Fmous Pstry Shoppe Inc .... G 800 548-1200
  Kernersville *(G-9214)*

Mennel Mil & Bky Mix NC LLC .... G 828 468-6015
  Newton *(G-11952)*

Mon Macaron LLC .... G 984 200-1387
  Raleigh *(G-13038)*

Neomonde Baking Company .... E 919 469-8009
  Morrisville *(G-11393)*

Normandie Bakery Inc .... G 910 686-1372
  Wilmington *(G-16340)*

Northeast Foods Inc .... F 919 585-5178
  Clayton *(G-4002)*

Novas Bakery Inc .... F 704 333-5566
  Charlotte *(G-3275)*

20 FOOD AND KINDRED PRODUCTS

Old Salem Incorporated .... G 336 721-7305
   Winston Salem *(G-16828)*

Orange Bakery Inc .... E 704 875-3003
   Huntersville *(G-8872)*

Patterson Marque .... G 336 661-7520
   Winston Salem *(G-16838)*

Patty Cakes .... G 828 696-8240
   Hendersonville *(G-7890)*

Picassomoesllc .... G 216 703-4547
   Hillsborough *(G-8665)*

Premier Cakes LLC .... G 919 274-8511
   Raleigh *(G-13137)*

Queen City Pastry Llc .... E 704 660-5706
   Mooresville *(G-11066)*

Retail Market Place .... G 984 201-1948
   Smithfield *(G-14480)*

▲ Scotts & Associates Inc .... F 336 581-3141
   Bear Creek *(G-942)*

Simple Baking .... G 704 523-4962
   Charlotte *(G-3555)*

Simple Supplies LLC .... G 336 358-7704
   Greensboro *(G-7341)*

Sls Baking Company .... G 704 421-2763
   Charlotte *(G-3564)*

SMA Enterprise LLC .... G 980 616-0140
   Concord *(G-4360)*

Spoons Bowls N Baking Pans LLC ... G 919 662-0494
   Raleigh *(G-13293)*

Sprinkle of Sugar LLC .... G 336 474-8620
   Thomasville *(G-15281)*

Suarez Bakery Inc .... F 704 525-0145
   Charlotte *(G-3644)*

Sunninghill Jill Baking Co LLC .... G 704 894-9901
   Cornelius *(G-4590)*

Sweet Room LLC .... G 336 567-1620
   High Point *(G-8560)*

Swirl Oakhurst LLC .... G 704 258-1209
   Charlotte *(G-3662)*

Underground Baking Co LLC .... G 828 674-7494
   Hendersonville *(G-7910)*

Wildflour Bakery Inc .... G 828 749-9224
   Saluda *(G-14075)*

2052 Cookies and crackers

B&G Foods Inc .... E 336 849-7000
   Yadkinville *(G-17032)*

Burney Sweets & More Inc .... G 910 862-2099
   Elizabethtown *(G-5587)*

Chestnut Land Company .... G 828 299-9108
   Asheville *(G-590)*

Dewey S Bakery Inc .... F 336 748-0230
   Winston Salem *(G-16677)*

Divine South Baking Co LLC .... G 828 421-2042
   Highlands *(G-8615)*

Evelyn T Burney .... G 336 473-9794
   Rocky Mount *(G-13697)*

▼ Flowers Bakery of Winston .... C 336 785-8700
   Winston Salem *(G-16715)*

Gracie Goodness Inc .... G 910 792-0800
   Wilmington *(G-16238)*

Graham Cracker LLC .... F 336 288-4440
   Greensboro *(G-7056)*

Grandmas Sugar Shack .... G 336 760-8822
   Winston Salem *(G-16727)*

Imperial Falcon Group Inc .... G 646 717-1128
   Charlotte *(G-2953)*

Kalo Foods LLC .... G 336 949-4802
   Stokesdale *(G-14944)*

Keebler Company .... D 919 774-6431
   Sanford *(G-14143)*

Lotus Bakeries Us LLC .... G 415 956-8956
   Mebane *(G-10417)*

Old Salem Incorporated .... G 336 721-7305
   Winston Salem *(G-16828)*

▼ S-L Snacks National LLC .... E 704 554-1421
   Charlotte *(G-3480)*

S-L Snacks Pa LLC .... C 704 554-1421
   Charlotte *(G-3481)*

♦ Scotts & Associates Inc .... F 336 581-3141
   Bear Creek *(G-942)*

SE Co-Brand Ventures LLC .... G 704 598-9322
   Charlotte *(G-3514)*

♦ Snyders-Lance Inc .... G 704 557-8013
   Charlotte *(G-3573)*

Snyders-Lance Inc .... A 704 554-1421
   Charlotte *(G-3574)*

Steven-Robert Originals LLC .... C 910 521-0199
   Pembroke *(G-12184)*

2053 Frozen bakery products, except bread

Big Bundts .... G 919 448-4184
   Chapel Hill *(G-1990)*

Bimbo Bakeries Usa Inc .... A 252 641-2200
   Tarboro *(G-15096)*

Hais Kookies & More .... G 980 819-8256
   Charlotte *(G-2880)*

Kalo Foods LLC .... G 336 949-4802
   Stokesdale *(G-14944)*

Orange Bakery Inc .... E 704 875-3003
   Huntersville *(G-8872)*

▼ Stefano Foods Inc .... C 704 399-3935
   Charlotte *(G-3628)*

2061 Raw cane sugar

Dermasweet LLC .... G 843 834-1413
   Wilmington *(G-16199)*

▲ Golding Farms Foods Inc .... D 336 766-6161
   Winston Salem *(G-16723)*

2064 Candy and other confectionery products

American Sprinkle Co Inc .... E 800 408-6708
   Pineville *(G-12253)*

Bakeboxx Company .... F 336 861-1212
   High Point *(G-8262)*

Best Bar Ever Inc .... G 910 508-3628
   Raleigh *(G-12552)*

♦ Bestco Holdings Inc .... B 704 664-4300
   Mooresville *(G-10874)*

Bilcat Inc .... E 828 295-3088
   Blowing Rock *(G-1154)*

Butterfields Candy LLC .... G 252 459-2577
   Nashville *(G-11738)*

Carolina Chocolatiers Inc .... G 828 652-4496
   Marion *(G-10146)*

Chocolate Fetish LLC .... G 828 258-2353
   Asheville *(G-592)*

Foiled Agin Choclat Coins LLC .... G 919 342-4601
   Sanford *(G-14120)*

French Broad Chocolates LLC .... G 828 252-4181
   Asheville *(G-629)*

Fudgeboat Inc .... G 910 617-9793
   Carolina Beach *(G-1638)*

Green Karma Labs LLC .... G 704 746-2363
   Statesville *(G-14807)*

Hershey Company .... F 919 284-0272
   Kenly *(G-9153)*

Hospitality Mints LLC .... E 828 262-0950
   Boone *(G-1208)*

▲ KLb Enterprises Incorporated .... F 336 605-0773
   Greensboro *(G-7153)*

Lollipop Cenral .... G 704 934-0015
   Kannapolis *(G-9126)*

Lovegrass Kitchen Inc .... G 919 234-7541
   Fuquay Varina *(G-6210)*

▲ Lucky Country USA LLC .... E 828 428-8313
   Lincolnton *(G-9903)*

Mast General Store Inc .... G 423 895-1632
   Boone *(G-1218)*

▲ Morinaga America Foods Inc ..... E 919 643-2439
   Mebane *(G-10420)*

Mr Bs Fun Foods Inc .... E 828 879-1901
   Connelly Springs *(G-4406)*

New Boston Fruit Slice & Confe ..... E 919 775-2471
   Sanford *(G-14158)*

▲ Piedmont Candy Company .... D 336 248-2477
   Lexington *(G-9770)*

Snyders-Lance Inc .... A 704 554-1421
   Charlotte *(G-3574)*

Tastebuds LLC .... G 704 461-8755
   Belmont *(G-1014)*

Tinas Fabulous Fudge LLC .... G 919 606-2616
   Hillsborough *(G-8669)*

Tnw Ventures Inc .... G 828 216-4089
   Pisgah Forest *(G-12328)*

2066 Chocolate and cocoa products

Barry Callebaut USA LLC .... D 828 685-2443
   Hendersonville *(G-7823)*

Celestial Cocoa Co .... G 704 871-2495
   Statesville *(G-14775)*

Chocolate Fetish LLC .... G 828 258-2353
   Asheville *(G-592)*

Chocolate Heaven Company .... G 828 421-2042
   Highlands *(G-8614)*

Chocolate Smiles Village LLC .... G 919 469-5282
   Cary *(G-1729)*

Escazu Artisan Chocolate LLC .... F 919 832-3433
   Raleigh *(G-12745)*

Mountain Bear & Co Inc .... G 828 631-0156
   Dillsboro *(G-4817)*

♦ Nutkao USA Inc .... E 252 595-1000
   Battleboro *(G-926)*

2068 Salted and roasted nuts and seeds

▼ Big Spoon Roasters LLC .... F 919 309-9100
   Hillsborough *(G-8638)*

Carolina Nut Inc .... F 910 293-4209
   Mount Olive *(G-11658)*

Innovative Business Growth LLC ... E 888 334-4367
   Asheboro *(G-445)*

Morven Partners LP .... E 252 794-3435
   Windsor *(G-16567)*

▼ Northampton Peanut Company ... D 252 585-0916
   Severn *(G-14268)*

Powell & Stokes Inc .... G 252 794-2138
   Windsor *(G-16568)*

Sachs Peanuts LLC .... F 910 647-4711
   Clarkton *(G-3948)*

Sandy Land Peanut Company Inc .. F 252 356-2679
   Harrellsville *(G-7698)*

See Clearly Inc .... G 929 464-6887
   Greensboro *(G-7330)*

Snyders-Lance Inc .... A 704 554-1421
   Charlotte *(G-3574)*

♦ Tropical Nut & Fruit Co .... C 800 438-4470
   Charlotte *(G-3731)*

Universal Blanchers LLC .... D 252 482-2112
   Edenton *(G-5522)*

2074 Cottonseed oil mills

Agnatural LLC .... G 252 536-0322
   Weldon *(G-15879)*

Oil Mill Salvage Recyclers Inc .... G 910 268-2111
   Gibson *(G-6555)*

Renew Life Formulas LLC .... D 727 450-1061
  Durham *(G-5325)*

2075 Soybean oil mills

Cargill Incorporated .... D 800 227-4455
  Fayetteville *(G-5783)*
Whitehat Seed Farms Inc .... G 252 264-2427
  Hertford *(G-7925)*

2077 Animal and marine fats and oils

Carolina By-Products Co .... G 336 333-3030
  Greensboro *(G-6882)*
Coastal Protein Products Inc .... G 910 567-6102
  Godwin *(G-6577)*
Darling Ingredients Inc .... F 910 483-0473
  Fayetteville *(G-5804)*
Darling Ingredients Inc .... F 704 864-9941
  Gastonia *(G-6395)*
Darling Ingredients Inc .... G 910 289-2083
  Rose Hill *(G-13775)*
Darling Ingredients Inc .... F 704 694-3701
  Wadesboro *(G-15509)*
Enterprise Rendering Company .... G 704 485-3018
  Oakboro *(G-12073)*
Neptune Hlth Wllness Innvtion .... C 888 664-9166
  Conover *(G-4475)*
Odens Fish & Oil Co Inc .... G 252 588-0036
  Ocracoke *(G-12097)*
Valley Proteins .... F 252 348-4200
  Lewiston Woodville *(G-9663)*
Valley Proteins (de) Inc .... C 336 333-3030
  Greensboro *(G-7435)*
Valley Proteins (de) Inc .... C 540 877-2533
  Oakboro *(G-12084)*

2079 Edible fats and oils

American Cltvtion Extrction Sv .... G 336 544-1072
  Greensboro *(G-6798)*
Arba LLC .... G 302 946-0079
  Charlotte *(G-2208)*
Bunge Oils Inc .... E 910 293-7917
  Warsaw *(G-15665)*
Corner Station Olive Oil Co .... G 828 246-0218
  Waynesville *(G-15800)*
Green Gate Olive Oils Inc .... G 910 986-0880
  Pinehurst *(G-12225)*
▲ Herbs Gaia Inc .... D 828 884-4242
  Brevard *(G-1276)*
Olive Beaufort Oil Company .... G 252 504-2474
  Beaufort *(G-962)*
Olive Beaufort Oil Company .... G 910 325-1556
  Swansboro *(G-15047)*
Olive Euro Oil LLC .... G 336 310-4624
  Kernersville *(G-9222)*
Olive Pinehurst Oil Co .... G 910 315-9923
  Aberdeen *(G-19)*
Olive Wagon LLC .... G 919 559-0845
  Raleigh *(G-13083)*
Oliventures Inc .... G 800 231-2619
  Raleigh *(G-13084)*
Outer Banks Olive Oil Company .... G 252 449-8229
  Kill Devil Hills *(G-9260)*
Whole Harvest Foods LLC .... E 910 293-7917
  Warsaw *(G-15677)*

2082 Malt beverages

6 Brothers LLC .... G 706 662-2232
  Charlotte *(G-2110)*
760 Craft Works LLC .... F 704 274-5216
  Huntersville *(G-8785)*
Adam Dalton Distillery LLC .... G 828 785-1499
  Asheville *(G-514)*

Anheuser-Busch LLC .... F 704 321-9319
  Charlotte *(G-2194)*
Aviator Brewing Company Inc .... G 919 601-5497
  Holly Springs *(G-8687)*
Bearwaters Brewing Company .... F 828 237-4200
  Canton *(G-1599)*
Beer Study .... G 919 240-5423
  Chapel Hill *(G-1989)*
Beverage Innovation Corp .... F 425 222-4900
  Concord *(G-4208)*
Bite My Cookies Brewing Co Inc .... G 919 602-7636
  Pittsboro *(G-12332)*
Bombshell Beer Company LLC .... F 919 823-1933
  Holly Springs *(G-8691)*
Brew Masters of Goldsboro .... G 919 288-2014
  Goldsboro *(G-6596)*
Brew Publik Incorporated .... G 704 231-2703
  Charlotte *(G-2352)*
Brewmasters Inc .... F 252 991-6035
  Wilson *(G-16479)*
Bull Durham Beer Co LLC .... G 919 744-3568
  Durham *(G-4990)*
Cabarrus Brewing Company LLC .... E 704 490-4487
  Concord *(G-4216)*
▲ Carolina Beverage Group LLC .... E 704 799-2337
  Mooresville *(G-10896)*
Craft Brew Alliance Inc .... G 828 263-1111
  Boone *(G-1188)*
Craft Revolution LLC .... F 347 924-7540
  Charlotte *(G-2568)*
Creative Brewing Company LLC .... G 919 297-8182
  Smithfield *(G-14458)*
Dreamweavers Brewery LLC .... G 704 507-7773
  Waxhaw *(G-15753)*
Duck-Rabbit Craft Brewery Inc .... G 252 753-7745
  Farmville *(G-5734)*
Ekos Brewmaster LLC .... G 704 973-5640
  Charlotte *(G-2688)*
Eurisko Beer Company .... G 828 774-5055
  Asheville *(G-618)*
Fiddlin Fish Brewing Co .... F 336 999-8945
  Winston Salem *(G-16710)*
▲ Foothills Brewing .... G 336 997-9484
  Winston Salem *(G-16717)*
Gingers Revenge LLC .... F 828 505-2462
  Asheville *(G-634)*
Glass Jug .... F 919 818-6907
  Durham *(G-5116)*
Glass Jug LLC .... F 919 813-0135
  Durham *(G-5117)*
Good Bros Ginger Brew LLC .... G 828 279-2512
  Mars Hill *(G-10195)*
Goose and Monkey Brewhouse LLC .... F 336 239-0206
  Lexington *(G-9724)*
Haw River Farmhouse Ales LLC .... G 336 525-9270
  Saxapahaw *(G-14217)*
Heckler Brewing Company .... G 910 748-0085
  Fayetteville *(G-5835)*
Heist Brewing Company LLC .... G 603 969-8012
  Charlotte *(G-2900)*
High Branch Brewing Co LLC .... G 704 706-3807
  Concord *(G-4279)*
▲ Highland Brewing Company Inc .... F 828 299-3370
  Asheville *(G-652)*
Hootenanny Brewing Company LLC .... G 704 254-6190
  Mooresville *(G-10976)*
House of Hops .... G 919 819-0704
  Raleigh *(G-12863)*
Hugger Mugger LLC .... F 910 585-2749
  Sanford *(G-14134)*
Innovation Brewing LLC .... G 828 586-9678
  Sylva *(G-15058)*

Koi Pond Brewing Company LLC .... G 252 231-1660
  Rocky Mount *(G-13706)*
Koolabrew LLC .... G 910 579-6711
  Shallotte *(G-14275)*
◆ Lake Norman Industries LLC .... G 704 987-9048
  Cornelius *(G-4565)*
Monster Brewing Company LLC .... D 828 883-2337
  Brevard *(G-1280)*
Mordecai Beverage Co .... G 919 831-9125
  Raleigh *(G-13042)*
▲ Mother Earth Brewing LLC .... G 252 208-2437
  Kinston *(G-9377)*
Nachos & Beer LLC .... G 828 298-2280
  Asheville *(G-709)*
New Sarum Brewing Co LLC .... G 704 310-5048
  Salisbury *(G-14018)*
Newgrass Brewing Company LLC .... G 704 477-2795
  Shelby *(G-14352)*
Next Generation Beer Co .... G 828 989-7662
  Asheville *(G-712)*
Ponysaurus Brewing LLC .... E 919 455-3737
  Durham *(G-5295)*
Preyer Brewing Company LLC .... G 336 420-0902
  Greensboro *(G-7282)*
Resident Culture Brewing LLC .... E 704 333-1862
  Charlotte *(G-3438)*
Salty Turtle Beer Company .... E 910 803-2019
  Surf City *(G-15016)*
Salud LLC .... E 980 495-6612
  Charlotte *(G-3485)*
Shortway Brewing Company LLC .... G 252 777-3065
  Newport *(G-11907)*
Side Hustle Ventures LLC .... G 919 816-2324
  Raleigh *(G-13253)*
Southern Range Brewing LLC .... G 704 289-4049
  Monroe *(G-10810)*
Southern Wicked Distillery Inc .... G 919 539-1620
  Raleigh *(G-13284)*
Spark716 LLC .... G 704 439-6864
  Wilmington *(G-16414)*
▲ Stout Beverages LLC .... E 704 293-7640
  Kings Mountain *(G-9334)*
▲ Stout Brands LLC .... E 704 293-7640
  Kings Mountain *(G-9335)*
Sugar Creek Brewing Co LLC .... E 704 521-3333
  Charlotte *(G-3646)*
Sunstead Brewing LLC .... G 980 949-6200
  Charlotte *(G-3655)*
Sweet Taters LLC .... G 252 969-0229
  Rocky Mount *(G-13736)*
Sycamore Brewing LLC .... G 704 910-3821
  Charlotte *(G-3664)*
▲ Triple C Brewing Company LLC .... F 704 372-3212
  Charlotte *(G-3729)*
Trophy On Maywood LLC .... F 919 803-1333
  Raleigh *(G-13367)*
Wedge Brewing Co .... F 828 505-2792
  Asheville *(G-817)*
Weeping Radish Farm Brewry LLC .... F 252 491-5205
  Grandy *(G-6719)*
White Street Brewing Co Inc .... E 919 647-9439
  Youngsville *(G-17115)*
Wnc Craft Beer Export LLC .... G 828 407-9444
  Asheville *(G-823)*

2083 Malt

Whitehat Seed Farms Inc .... G 252 264-2427
  Hertford *(G-7925)*

2084 Wines, brandy, and brandy spirits

Adagio Vineyards .... G 336 258-2333
  Elkin *(G-5609)*

20 FOOD AND KINDRED PRODUCTS

Adams Beverages NC LLC .... D 910 763-6216
Leland *(G-9525)*

Adams Beverages NC LLC .... D 910 738-8165
Lumberton *(G-10023)*

Adams Beverages NC LLC .... F 704 509-3000
Charlotte *(G-2134)*

Aek Inc .... G 704 864-7968
Gastonia *(G-6337)*

Alexander Crush Inc .... G 828 635-7136
Taylorsville *(G-15128)*

American Alcohollery LLC .... G 704 960-7243
Moravian Falls *(G-11141)*

Asheville Meadery LLC .... G 828 454-6188
Asheville *(G-538)*

Autumn Creek Vineyards Inc .... G 336 548-9463
Greensboro *(G-6823)*

B & C Winery .... G 828 550-3610
Waynesville *(G-15794)*

B C Winery .... G 828 550-3610
Maggie Valley *(G-10093)*

Banner Elk Winery Inc .... G 828 898-9090
Banner Elk *(G-892)*

Banner Elk Winery Inc .... G 828 260-1790
Banner Elk *(G-893)*

Battle Fermentables LLC .... G 336 225-4585
Durham *(G-4947)*

Belews Creek Vineyard .... G 904 345-1466
Kernersville *(G-9168)*

▲ Biltmore Estate Wine Co LLC .... C 828 225-6776
Asheville *(G-560)*

Black Rock Landscaping LLC .... G 910 295-4470
Carthage *(G-1661)*

Black Rock Winery LLC .... G 910 295-9511
Carthage *(G-1662)*

Blue Zephyr Vineyard .... G 336 366-5066
Dobson *(G-4820)*

Botanist and Barrel .... G 919 644-7777
Cedar Grove *(G-1970)*

Burntshirt Vineyards LLC .... F 828 685-2402
Hendersonville *(G-7830)*

Cabo Winery LLC .... G 704 785-9463
Concord *(G-4220)*

Cape Fear Vineyard Winery LLC .... G 844 846-3386
Elizabethtown *(G-5589)*

Cape Fear Vinyrd & Winery LLC .... G 910 645-4292
Elizabethtown *(G-5590)*

Carolina Coast Vineyard .... G 910 707-1777
Carolina Beach *(G-1634)*

Carolina Heritg Vinyrd Winery .... G 336 448-4781
Elkin *(G-5613)*

Catawba Farms Enterprises LLC .... F 828 464-5780
Newton *(G-11917)*

Cellar .... G 910 399-2997
Wilmington *(G-16166)*

Cellar 4201 LLC .... G 336 699-6030
East Bend *(G-5464)*

Chateau Jourdain LLC .... G 786 273-2869
Jonesville *(G-9094)*

Chestnut Trail Vineyard LLC .... G 336 655-4755
Mocksville *(G-10563)*

▲ Childress Vineyards LLC .... E 336 236-9463
Lexington *(G-9692)*

▲ Childress Winery LLC .... G 336 775-0522
Lexington *(G-9693)*

Cider Bros LLC .... F 919 943-9692
Lexington *(G-9694)*

Coastal Carolina Winery .... G 843 443-9463
Cornelius *(G-4536)*

Cougar Run Winery .... F 704 788-2746
Concord *(G-4245)*

Cypress Bend Vineyards Inc .... G 910 369-0411
Wagram *(G-15522)*

Davidson Wine Co LLC .... G 614 738-0051
Davidson *(G-4671)*

Deep Creek Winery .... G 828 341-0592
Bryson City *(G-1323)*

Divine Llama Vineyards LLC .... G 336 699-2525
East Bend *(G-5466)*

Dove Vine LLC .... G 336 751-3794
Mocksville *(G-10566)*

Doyles Vineyard .... G 919 544-6291
Durham *(G-5061)*

Drink A Bull LLC .... G 919 818-3321
Durham *(G-5065)*

Duplin Wine Cellars Inc .... E 910 289-3888
Rose Hill *(G-13776)*

Ebhc LLC .... G 704 733-9427
Charlotte *(G-2681)*

Elephants Corner Wines LLC .... G 336 782-7084
Winston Salem *(G-16694)*

Elkin Creek Vineyard LLC .... G 336 526-5119
Elkin *(G-5618)*

Far Niente LLC .... G 252 715-0154
Kitty Hawk *(G-9404)*

First Miracle Vine & Wine LLC .... G 910 990-5681
Garland *(G-6242)*

Grandfather Vinyrd Winery LLC .... G 828 963-2400
Banner Elk *(G-898)*

Grassy Creek Vineyard & Winery ...... G 336 835-2458
State Road *(G-14726)*

Green Creek Winery LLC .... G 828 863-4136
Columbus *(G-4174)*

Gregory Vineyards .... G 919 427-9409
Angier *(G-139)*

Grimes Mill LLC .... G 336 470-6864
Lexington *(G-9725)*

Haw River Valley Entps LLC .... G 336 584-4060
Gibsonville *(G-6562)*

Haze Gray Vineyards LLC .... G 610 247-9387
Dobson *(G-4824)*

Hertford ABC Board .... G 252 426-5290
Hertford *(G-7921)*

Hilton Vineyards LLC .... G 704 776-9656
Monroe *(G-10731)*

Hinnant Farms Vineyard LLC .... F 919 965-3350
Pine Level *(G-12210)*

Honeygirl Meadery LLC .... G 919 399-3056
Durham *(G-5139)*

Hooks Vineyard .... G 919 917-5658
Raleigh *(G-12858)*

Hutton Vineyards LLC .... G 336 374-2321
Dobson *(G-4827)*

Jackson Wine .... G 828 508-9292
Brevard *(G-1277)*

James Michael Vineyards LLC .... G 704 539-4749
Harmony *(G-7687)*

Jolo Winery & Vineyards LLC .... F 954 816-5649
Pilot Mountain *(G-12199)*

Jones Vondrehle Vineyards LLC .... F 336 874-2800
Thurmond *(G-15310)*

Kefi Winery Inc .... G 704 591-5791
Monroe *(G-10751)*

Ladybug Vineyard LLC .... G 336 366-4701
Dobson *(G-4828)*

◆ Lake Norman Industries LLC .... G 704 987-9048
Cornelius *(G-4565)*

Laurel Gray Vineyards Inc .... G 336 468-9463
Hamptonville *(G-7673)*

Linville Falls Winery .... G 828 733-9021
Newland *(G-11889)*

Longleaf Vineyard .... G 828 435-3555
Marshall *(G-10204)*

Lucky Tusk .... G 704 985-1127
Albemarle *(G-95)*

Maia LLC .... G 828 612-6109
Morganton *(G-11230)*

McRitchie Wine Company LLC .... G 336 874-3003
Thurmond *(G-15312)*

Medaloni Cellars LLC .... G 336 398-7818
Greensboro *(G-7196)*

Medaloni Cellars LLC .... G 305 509-2004
Lewisville *(G-9669)*

Melissae Meadery & Winery LLC ...... G 336 207-7097
Marion *(G-10165)*

Midnight Mndance Vineyards LLC .... G 336 835-6681
Jonesville *(G-9100)*

Mill Camp Wines & Ciders LLC .... G 810 923-7339
Boone *(G-1221)*

Mill Camp Wines & Ciders LLC .... G 810 923-7339
Boone *(G-1220)*

My Wine Saver LLC .... G 828 595-2632
Hendersonville *(G-7883)*

Nomacorc Holdings LLC .... G 919 460-2200
Zebulon *(G-17137)*

Noni Bacca Winery .... G 910 397-7617
Wilmington *(G-16338)*

Oklawaha Brewing Company LLC ..... F 828 595-9956
Hendersonville *(G-7888)*

Old Homeplace Vineyard LLC .... G 336 399-7293
Winston Salem *(G-16827)*

Old North State Winery Inc .... F 336 789-9463
Mount Airy *(G-11554)*

Parker-Binns Vineyard LLC .... G 828 894-0154
Mill Spring *(G-10490)*

Parkway Vineyard & Winery LLC ...... G 828 765-1400
Newland *(G-11892)*

Patria Vineyard LLC .... G 336 407-8254
Winston Salem *(G-16837)*

Pharmdawg Vineyards LLC .... G 770 596-0960
State Road *(G-14728)*

Piccione Vinyards .... G 312 342-0181
Ronda *(G-13767)*

Pilot Mountain Vineyards LLC .... G 828 400-9533
Pinnacle *(G-12322)*

Pleb Urban Winery .... G 828 767-6445
Asheville *(G-736)*

Priscllas Crystal Cast Wnes In .... G 252 422-8336
Newport *(G-11904)*

Queen of Wines LLC .... F 919 348-6630
Durham *(G-5314)*

▲ Raffaldini Vneyards Winery LLC ... F 336 835-9463
Ronda *(G-13769)*

Raylen Vineyards Inc .... G 336 998-3100
Winston Salem *(G-16881)*

Retro Meadery LLC .... G 910 622-7098
Burgaw *(G-1348)*

Rickety Bridge Winery Inc USA .... G 336 781-0645
High Point *(G-8510)*

Rise Over Run Inc .... G 303 819-1566
Swannanoa *(G-15034)*

Rock Ages Winery & Vineyard .... G 336 364-7625
Hendersonville *(G-7896)*

Rock Ages Winery & Vinyrd Inc .... G 336 364-7625
Hurdle Mills *(G-8914)*

Rockfish Creek Winery LLC .... G 910 729-0648
Raeford *(G-12436)*

Rocky River Vineyards LLC .... G 704 781-5035
Midland *(G-10478)*

Roots Run Deep LLC .... G 919 909-9117
Youngsville *(G-17094)*

Round Peak Vineyards LLC .... G 336 352-5595
Mount Airy *(G-11568)*

Russian Chapel Hills Winery .... G 828 863-0541
Columbus *(G-4180)*

Rustic Grape LLC .... G 828 319-7939
Asheville *(G-761)*

SIC SECTION

20 FOOD AND KINDRED PRODUCTS

Saint Paul Mountain Vineyards .... F 828 685-4002
   Hendersonville *(G-7897)*

Sanctuary Vineyards .... G 252 491-2387
   Jarvisburg *(G-9085)*

Sanders Ridge Inc .... G 336 677-1700
   Boonville *(G-1256)*

Seven Pines Vineyard Inc .... G 252 717-2283
   Fountain *(G-6097)*

Shadow Line Vineyard LLC .... G 828 234-5773
   Granite Falls *(G-6756)*

Shadow Springs Vineyard Inc .... G 336 998-6598
   Advance *(G-50)*

Shelton Vineyards Inc .... E 336 366-4818
   Dobson *(G-4831)*

Six Waterpots Vinyrd & Winery .... G 828 728-5099
   Hudson *(G-8780)*

Sommerville Enterprises LLC .... F 919 924-1594
   Hillsborough *(G-8668)*

Souther Williams Vineyard LLC .... G 828 651-8011
   Fletcher *(G-6042)*

Southern Range Brewing LLC .... G 704 289-4049
   Monroe *(G-10810)*

Stardust Cellars LLC .... G 336 466-4454
   Winston Salem *(G-16916)*

Starrlight Mead .... G 919 533-6314
   Pittsboro *(G-12351)*

Starrlight Mead LLC .... G 919 672-1469
   Durham *(G-5371)*

Stonefield Cellars LLC .... G 336 632-2391
   Stokesdale *(G-14951)*

◆ Suntory International .... F 917 756-2747
   Raleigh *(G-13316)*

Sweet Hme Carolna Vinyrd & Win .... G 336 469-9905
   Yadkinville *(G-17053)*

Sweet Home Yadkin Inc .... G 336 414-9822
   Yadkinville *(G-17054)*

Thistle Meadow Winery Inc .... G 800 233-1505
   Laurel Springs *(G-9467)*

Tom Burgiss .... G 336 359-2995
   Laurel Springs *(G-9468)*

Tunnel Creek Venues LLC .... G 336 322-3600
   Roxboro *(G-13828)*

Urban Orchard Cider Company .... F 252 904-5135
   Asheville *(G-811)*

Village At Duplin Winery LLC .... G 910 285-6814
   Wallace *(G-15629)*

Vineyard Bluffton LLC .... G 704 307-2737
   Charlotte *(G-3778)*

Vineyard Hill Distributing LLC .... G 828 684-5113
   Fletcher *(G-6049)*

Vineyards On Scuppernong LLC .... G 252 796-4727
   Columbia *(G-4170)*

Vintners Hill .... G 704 737-8023
   Mint Hill *(G-10547)*

Weathervane Winery Inc .... G 336 793-3366
   Lexington *(G-9802)*

Westbend Vineyards Inc .... G 336 768-7520
   Winston Salem *(G-16970)*

Whitefin Vineyards LLC .... G 219 902-6647
   Apex *(G-259)*

Williamson Mead & Brewing LLC .... F 661 827-7290
   Glade Valley *(G-6573)*

Willowcroft .... F 704 540-0367
   Charlotte *(G-3815)*

Wilmington Wine LLC .... G 910 202-4749
   Wilmington *(G-16454)*

Windsor Run Cellars Inc .... G 336 998-6598
   Advance *(G-53)*

Winery Assoc Southeast Inc .... G 919 219-1929
   Cary *(G-1927)*

Woodmill Winery Inc .... G 704 276-9911
   Vale *(G-15473)*

Yadkin Valley Herbs Inc .... G 336 468-4062
   Hamptonville *(G-7681)*

Yadkin Valley Wine Company .... G 336 467-0257
   Hamptonville *(G-7682)*

2085 Distilled and blended liquors

78c Spirits .... G 919 615-0839
   Raleigh *(G-12449)*

Asheville Distilling Company .... F 828 575-2000
   Asheville *(G-535)*

◆ Azure Skye Beverages Inc .... G 704 909-7394
   Charlotte *(G-2251)*

Blu Distilling Company LLC .... E 919 999-6736
   Durham *(G-4965)*

Blu Distilling Company LLC .... G 919 999-6736
   Raleigh *(G-12563)*

Blue Ridge Distilling Co Inc .... G 828 245-2041
   Bostic *(G-1260)*

Blue Seas LLC .... G 828 245-2041
   Bostic *(G-1261)*

Bogue Sound Distillery Inc .... G 252 241-1606
   Newport *(G-11898)*

▲ Bold Rock Partners LP .... F 828 595-9940
   Mills River *(G-10501)*

Broad Branch Distillery LLC .... G 336 602-2824
   Winston Salem *(G-16638)*

Buffalo City Distillery LLC .... G 252 256-1477
   Point Harbor *(G-12380)*

Call Family Distillers LLC .... G 336 990-0708
   Wilkesboro *(G-16015)*

Chemist .... G 828 505-8778
   Asheville *(G-589)*

Chopin Vodka .... G 336 707-8305
   Greensboro *(G-6908)*

Copper Barrel Distillery LLC .... G 336 262-6500
   North Wilkesboro *(G-12003)*

Dark Moon Distileries LLC .... G 704 222-8063
   Banner Elk *(G-895)*

Diablo Distilleries LLC .... G 910 467-5017
   Jacksonville *(G-8998)*

Doodle Sasser Distilling LLC .... G 704 806-6594
   Indian Trail *(G-8929)*

Durham Distillery Llc .... G 919 937-2121
   Durham *(G-5072)*

End of Days Distillery .... F 910 399-1133
   Wilmington *(G-16211)*

Fainting Goat Spirits LLC .... G 336 273-6221
   Greensboro *(G-7010)*

Foothills Distillery LLC .... G 704 462-1055
   Conover *(G-4455)*

Founding Fathers Distillery .... G 336 434-0149
   High Point *(G-8357)*

Four Hounds Distilling LLC .... G 757 717-9393
   Carolina Beach *(G-1637)*

Graybeard Distillery Inc .... F 919 361-9980
   Durham *(G-5126)*

Great Wagon Road Distlg Co LLC .... G 704 246-8740
   Charlotte *(G-2860)*

Great Wagon Road Distlg Co LLC .... G 704 469-9330
   Charlotte *(G-2861)*

Greensboro Distilling LLC .... G 336 273-6221
   Greensboro *(G-7062)*

H&H Distillery LLC .... G 828 338-9779
   Asheville *(G-646)*

Howling Moon Distillery Inc .... G 828 208-1469
   Asheville *(G-655)*

◆ Lake Norman Industries LLC .... G 704 987-9048
   Cornelius *(G-4565)*

Lassiter Distilling Company .... G 919 295-0111
   Knightdale *(G-9419)*

Laws Distillery Inc .... G 828 726-3663
   Lenoir *(G-9623)*

Lizard Lick Brewing & Dist LLC .... G 919 887-4369
   Zebulon *(G-17134)*

Loud Lemon Beverage LLC .... G 919 949-7649
   Bahama *(G-865)*

Mason Inlet Distillery LLC .... G 910 200-4584
   Wilmington *(G-16316)*

Mayberry Distillery .... G 336 719-6860
   Mount Airy *(G-11544)*

Muddy River Distillery LLC .... G 336 516-4190
   Belmont *(G-995)*

Mystic Farm & Distillery .... G 336 409-0131
   Durham *(G-5233)*

New River Distilling Co LLC .... G 732 673-4852
   Deep Gap *(G-4710)*

Oak & Bull Distilling LLC .... G 978 732-4531
   Raleigh *(G-13076)*

Oak & Grist Distilling Co LLC .... G 914 450-0589
   Asheville *(G-713)*

Oak & Grist Distilling Co LLC .... F 828 357-5750
   Black Mountain *(G-1131)*

Oak City Distilling Inc .... G 919 520-4102
   Raleigh *(G-13079)*

Outer Banks Craft Distlg LLC .... G 252 423-3011
   Manteo *(G-10128)*

Piedmont Distillers Inc .... D 336 445-0055
   Madison *(G-10082)*

Pine Top Distillery LLC .... G 888 261-5287
   Raleigh *(G-13110)*

Pinnix Distillery Inc .... G 828 412-5441
   Asheville *(G-733)*

Seventy Eight C Inc .... G 919 602-0677
   Raleigh *(G-13245)*

Shipwreck Rum Inc .... G 215 896-6172
   Clayton *(G-4008)*

Southern Distilling Co LLC .... G 704 677-4069
   Statesville *(G-14891)*

▲ Stout Brewing Company LLC .... G 704 288-4042
   Kings Mountain *(G-9336)*

Sutlers Spirit Company .... G 336 565-6006
   Winston Salem *(G-16926)*

Three Stacks Distilling Co LLC .... G 252 468-0779
   Kinston *(G-9388)*

Two Trees Distilling Co LLC .... G 803 767-1322
   Fletcher *(G-6046)*

Waltons Distillery Inc .... G 910 347-7770
   Jacksonville *(G-9045)*

Warehouse Distillery LLC .... G 828 464-5183
   Newton *(G-11983)*

Weldon Mills Distillery LLC .... G 252 220-4235
   Weldon *(G-15889)*

Wyoming Whiskey Inc .... G 561 573-5605
   Mooresville *(G-11132)*

2086 Bottled and canned soft drinks

Aberdeen Coca-Cola Btlg Co Inc .... E 910 944-2305
   Aberdeen *(G-1)*

▼ Alamance Foods Inc .... C 336 226-6392
   Burlington *(G-1362)*

Asheville Kombucha Mamas LLC .... E 828 595-4340
   Asheville *(G-537)*

Asheville Kombucha Mamas LLC .... F 828 394-2360
   Marshall *(G-10199)*

▼ Bebida Beverage Company .... E 704 660-0226
   Statesville *(G-14760)*

Brewitt & Dreenkupp Inc .... G 704 525-3366
   Charlotte *(G-2353)*

Carolina Beverage Corporation .... E 704 636-2191
   Salisbury *(G-13932)*

Carolina Bottling Company .... D 704 637-5869
   Salisbury *(G-13933)*

Ccbcc Inc .... A 704 557-4000
   Charlotte *(G-2425)*

20 FOOD AND KINDRED PRODUCTS

Ccbcc Operations LLC .... E 704 557-4038
  Charlotte (G-2426)
Ccbcc Operations LLC .... E 910 582-3543
  Hamlet (G-7619)
Ccbcc Operations LLC .... E 704 872-3634
  Statesville (G-14774)
Ccbcc Operations LLC .... D 828 687-1300
  Arden (G-319)
Ccbcc Operations LLC .... D 828 297-2141
  Boone (G-1185)
Ccbcc Operations LLC .... E 828 488-2874
  Bryson City (G-1321)
Ccbcc Operations LLC .... F 704 359-5600
  Charlotte (G-2427)
Ccbcc Operations LLC .... E 704 399-6043
  Charlotte (G-2429)
Ccbcc Operations LLC .... C 980 321-3226
  Charlotte (G-2430)
Ccbcc Operations LLC .... D 919 359-2966
  Clayton (G-3964)
Ccbcc Operations LLC .... E 910 483-6158
  Fayetteville (G-5787)
Ccbcc Operations LLC .... D 336 664-1116
  Greensboro (G-6896)
Ccbcc Operations LLC .... D 828 322-5097
  Hickory (G-7972)
Ccbcc Operations LLC .... D 704 225-1973
  Monroe (G-10678)
Ccbcc Operations LLC .... E 336 789-7111
  Mount Airy (G-11494)
Ccbcc Operations LLC .... E 704 364-8728
  Charlotte (G-2428)
Central Carolina Btlg Co Inc .... G 919 542-3226
  Bear Creek (G-937)
Choice USA Beverage Inc .... E 704 861-1029
  Gastonia (G-6377)
Choice USA Beverage Inc .... G 704 487-6951
  Shelby (G-14294)
Choice USA Beverage Inc .... D 704 823-1651
  Lowell (G-10007)
Coca Cola Bottling Co .... G 704 509-1812
  Charlotte (G-2516)
Coca-Cola Consolidated Inc .... G 704 398-2252
  Charlotte (G-2517)
Coca-Cola Consolidated Inc .... D 980 321-3001
  Charlotte (G-2518)
Coca-Cola Consolidated Inc .... C 919 550-0611
  Clayton (G-3968)
Coca-Cola Consolidated Inc .... D 252 334-1820
  Elizabeth City (G-5535)
Coca-Cola Consolidated Inc .... E 704 551-4500
  Kinston (G-9354)
Coca-Cola Consolidated Inc .... G 919 763-3172
  Leland (G-9538)
Coca-Cola Consolidated Inc .... E 828 322-5096
  Newton (G-11920)
▲ Coca-Cola Consolidated Inc .... A 704 557-4400
  Charlotte (G-2519)
Divine Lemonades LLC .... G 336 255-0739
  Reidsville (G-13517)
Dr Pepper Co of Wilmington .... G 910 792-5400
  Wilmington (G-16205)
Dr Pepper/Seven-Up Bottling .... F 828 322-8090
  Hickory (G-8012)
Dr Ppper Btlg W Jffrson NC In .... E 336 846-2433
  West Jefferson (G-15939)
Durham Coca-Cola Bottling Co .... G 919 510-0574
  Raleigh (G-12711)
Durham Coca-Cola Bottling Company .... C 919 383-1451
  Durham (G-5071)
Frito-Lay North America Inc .... G 980 224-3730
  Wilmington (G-16223)

Ginger Supreme Inc .... G 919 812-8986
  Apex (G-195)
Grins Enterprises LLC .... G 336 831-0534
  Winston Salem (G-16730)
Ice River Springs Usa Inc .... F 519 925-2929
  Morganton (G-11222)
ICEE Company .... G 704 357-6865
  Charlotte (G-2946)
◆ Independent Beverage Co LLC .... F 704 399-2504
  Charlotte (G-2959)
Le Bleu Corporation .... G 828 254-5105
  Arden (G-346)
Mae Rodgers Cola .... G 252 797-4253
  Creswell (G-4626)
McPherson Beverages Inc .... E 252 537-3571
  Roanoke Rapids (G-13579)
Midas Spring Water Btlg Co LLC .... G 704 392-2150
  Davidson (G-4685)
Midland Bottling LLC .... G 919 865-2300
  Raleigh (G-13031)
Milkco Inc .... B 828 254-8428
  Asheville (G-702)
Minges Bottling Group .... F 252 636-5898
  New Bern (G-11823)
Niagara Bottling LLC .... G 909 815-6310
  Mooresville (G-11036)
Old Saratoga Inc .... E 252 238-2175
  Saratoga (G-14216)
Original New York Seltzer LLC .... E 323 500-0757
  Cornelius (G-4573)
◆ Packo Bottling Inc .... E 919 496-4286
  Louisburg (G-9995)
Pepsi Bottling Group .... G 828 286-4406
  Rutherfordton (G-13884)
Pepsi Bottling Group Inc .... E 704 507-4031
  Midland (G-10473)
Pepsi Bottling Ventures LLC .... G 800 879-8884
  Cary (G-1849)
Pepsi Bottling Ventures LLC .... E 828 264-7702
  Deep Gap (G-4711)
Pepsi Bottling Ventures LLC .... E 252 335-4355
  Elizabeth City (G-5561)
Pepsi Bottling Ventures LLC .... C 919 863-4000
  Garner (G-6301)
Pepsi Bottling Ventures LLC .... D 919 865-2388
  Garner (G-6302)
Pepsi Bottling Ventures LLC .... D 919 778-8300
  Goldsboro (G-6644)
Pepsi Bottling Ventures LLC .... C 704 455-0800
  Harrisburg (G-7720)
Pepsi Bottling Ventures LLC .... E 252 451-1811
  Rocky Mount (G-13719)
Pepsi Bottling Ventures LLC .... E 910 865-1600
  Saint Pauls (G-13907)
Pepsi Bottling Ventures LLC .... E 704 873-0249
  Statesville (G-14858)
Pepsi Bottling Ventures LLC .... D 910 792-5400
  Wilmington (G-16351)
Pepsi Bottling Ventures LLC .... G 336 464-9227
  Winston Salem (G-16840)
Pepsi Bottling Ventures LLC .... E 336 464-9227
  Winston Salem (G-16841)
Pepsi Bottling Ventures LLC .... C 336 724-4800
  Winston Salem (G-16842)
▲ Pepsi Bottling Ventures LLC .... D 919 865-2300
  Raleigh (G-13107)
Pepsi Cola Bottling Co .... E 828 650-7800
  Fletcher (G-6031)
Pepsi Cola Co .... G 704 357-9166
  Charlotte (G-3328)
Pepsi-Cola Btlg Hickry NC Inc .... G 828 322-8090
  Granite Falls (G-6749)

Pepsi-Cola Btlg Hickry NC Inc .... E 828 322-8090
  Hickory (G-8110)
Pepsi-Cola Btlg Hickry NC Inc .... E 828 497-1235
  Whittier (G-16010)
Pepsi-Cola Btlg Hickry NC Inc .... C 828 322-8090
  Hickory (G-8111)
Pepsi-Cola Btlg New Bern Inc .... E 252 522-0232
  New Bern (G-11834)
Pepsi-Cola Metro Btlg Co Inc .... G 980 581-1099
  Charlotte (G-3329)
Pepsi-Cola Metro Btlg Co Inc .... E 704 736-2640
  Cherryville (G-3874)
Pepsi-Cola Metro Btlg Co Inc .... G 252 446-7181
  Rocky Mount (G-13720)
Pepsi-Cola Metro Btlg Co Inc .... A 336 896-4000
  Winston Salem (G-16843)
Pepsico Inc .... G 828 756-4662
  Marion (G-10171)
Pepsico Inc .... G 914 253-2000
  Winston Salem (G-16844)
Piedmont Cheerwine Bottling Co .... D 336 993-7733
  Colfax (G-4158)
Piedmont Coca-Cola Btlg Partnr .... C 252 752-2446
  Greenville (G-7574)
Piedmont Coca-Cola Btlg Partnr .... D 252 536-3611
  Halifax (G-7611)
Piedmont Coca-Cola Btlg Partnr .... C 252 637-3157
  New Bern (G-11836)
Piedmont Coca-Cola Btlg Partnr .... E 704 551-4400
  Charlotte (G-3339)
Pure Water Innovations Inc .... G 919 301-8189
  Spring Hope (G-14620)
Quality Beverage LLC .... E 910 371-3596
  Belville (G-1025)
Quality Beverage LLC .... G 704 637-5881
  Salisbury (G-14034)
Raleigh Ventures Inc .... G 910 350-0036
  Wilmington (G-16377)
Red Bull Distribution Co Inc .... F 910 500-1566
  Havelock (G-7745)
Redux Beverages LLC .... G 951 304-1144
  Hillsborough (G-8666)
Refresco Beverages US Inc .... E 252 234-0493
  Wilson (G-16530)
Refresco Beverages US Inc .... F 252 234-0493
  Wilson (G-16531)
◆ S & D Coffee Inc .... A 704 782-3121
  Concord (G-4355)
Sanford Coca-Cola Bottling Co .... E 919 774-4111
  Sanford (G-14180)
Summit Seltzer Company LLC .... G 980 819-6416
  Charlotte (G-3648)
Sun-Drop Btlg Rocky Mt NC Inc .... F 252 977-4586
  Rocky Mount (G-13735)
◆ Suntory International .... F 917 756-2747
  Raleigh (G-13316)
Unix Packaging LLC .... E 310 877-7979
  Morganton (G-11263)
◆ USa Wholesale and Distrg Inc .... F 888 484-6872
  Fayetteville (G-5945)
Vortex Bottle Shop LLC .... F 980 258-0827
  Harrisburg (G-7734)
Waynesville Soda Jerks LLC .... G 828 278-8589
  Waynesville (G-15832)
Zeskp LLC .... G 910 762-8300
  Wilmington (G-16460)

2087 Flavoring extracts and syrups, nec

Alternative Ingredients Inc .... G 336 378-5368
  Greensboro (G-6794)
▼ Blue Mountain Enterprises Inc .... E 252 522-1544
  Kinston (G-9345)

SIC SECTION

20 FOOD AND KINDRED PRODUCTS

Bunge Oils Inc .... E 910 293-7917
  Warsaw *(G-15665)*
Choice USA Beverage Inc .... D 704 823-1651
  Lowell *(G-10007)*
Crude LLC .... G 919 391-8185
  Raleigh *(G-12657)*
Flavor Sciences Inc .... E 828 758-2525
  Taylorsville *(G-15142)*
▲ Freedom Beverage Company .... G 336 316-1260
  Greensboro *(G-7022)*
Fuji Foods Inc .... E 336 897-3373
  Browns Summit *(G-1304)*
Fuji Foods Inc .... G 336 226-8817
  Burlington *(G-1416)*
▲ Fuji Foods Inc .... E 336 375-3111
  Browns Summit *(G-1305)*
GNT Usa LLC .... E 914 524-0600
  Dallas *(G-4643)*
▲ Great Eastern Sun Trdg Co Inc .... F 828 665-7790
  Asheville *(G-642)*
Herbalife Manufacturing LLC .... F 336 970-6400
  Winston Salem *(G-16744)*
▲ Larrys Beans Inc .... E 919 828-1234
  Raleigh *(G-12958)*
Little Beekeeper LLC .... G 704 215-9690
  Lincolnton *(G-9902)*
▲ Mary Macks Inc .... G 770 234-6333
  Clinton *(G-4097)*
Mother Murphys Labs Inc .... E 336 273-1737
  Greensboro *(G-7205)*
Mother Murphys Labs Inc .... D 336 273-1737
  Greensboro *(G-7206)*
Only Bitters .... G 617 413-6571
  Raleigh *(G-13085)*
Prime Beverage Group LLC .... C 704 385-5451
  Concord *(G-4339)*
Prime Beverage Group LLC .... G 704 385-5450
  Concord *(G-4338)*
Sakun Inc .... G 919 255-2994
  Cary *(G-1878)*
▲ Specialty Products Intl Ltd .... G 910 897-4706
  Erwin *(G-5688)*
Speed Energy Drink LLC .... F 704 949-1255
  Concord *(G-4364)*

2091 Canned and cured fish and seafoods

Avon Seafood .... G 252 995-4553
  Avon *(G-843)*
Bay Breeze Seafood Rest Inc .... E 828 697-7106
  Hendersonville *(G-7824)*
Bay City Crab Inc .... G 252 322-5291
  Aurora *(G-832)*
Capt Neills Seafood Inc .... C 252 796-0795
  Columbia *(G-4166)*
Carolina Seafood Company Inc .... G 252 322-5455
  Aurora *(G-833)*
◆ Classic Seafood Group Inc .... C 252 746-2818
  Ayden *(G-849)*
Lloyds Oyster House Inc .... E 910 754-6958
  Shallotte *(G-14276)*
Mattamuskeet Seafood Inc .... D 252 926-2431
  Swanquarter *(G-15039)*
Pamlico Packing Co Inc .... F 252 745-3688
  Vandemere *(G-15489)*
Pamlico Packing Co Inc .... F 252 745-3688
  Grantsboro *(G-6765)*
▲ Quality Foods From Sea Inc .... D 252 338-5455
  Elizabeth City *(G-5565)*
Quality Seafood Co Inc .... F 252 338-2800
  Elizabeth City *(G-5566)*
Queens Creek Seafood .... G 910 326-4801
  Hubert *(G-8752)*

Steve S Seafood Inc .... G 910 279-5711
  Leland *(G-9560)*

2092 Fresh or frozen packaged fish

▲ Alphin Brothers Inc .... E 910 892-8751
  Dunn *(G-4850)*
Aurora Packing Co Inc .... G 252 322-5232
  Aurora *(G-831)*
B & J Seafood Co Inc .... E 252 637-0483
  New Bern *(G-11775)*
▲ Bakkavor Foods Usa Inc .... C 704 522-1977
  Charlotte *(G-2270)*
Bay City Crab Inc .... G 252 322-5291
  Aurora *(G-832)*
Capt Charlies Seafood Inc .... E 252 796-7278
  Columbia *(G-4165)*
Capt Neills Seafood Inc .... C 252 796-0795
  Columbia *(G-4166)*
Carolina Catch Inc .... D 252 946-5796
  Washington *(G-15686)*
Carolina Seafood Company Inc .... G 252 322-5455
  Aurora *(G-833)*
Crazy Pig Inc .... G 704 997-2320
  Davidson *(G-4668)*
Fish Sticks LLC .... G 336 984-1791
  North Wilkesboro *(G-12007)*
Fishsticks .... G 919 900-8998
  Raleigh *(G-12769)*
Hare Asian Trading Company LLC .... E 910 524-4667
  Burgaw *(G-1340)*
Janet W Whitbeck Inc .... G 252 986-2800
  Hatteras *(G-7737)*
Lowland Seafood Inc .... G 252 745-3751
  Lowland *(G-10014)*
Pamlico Packing Co Inc .... F 252 745-3688
  Vandemere *(G-15489)*
Pamlico Packing Co Inc .... F 252 745-3688
  Grantsboro *(G-6765)*
Quality Seafood Co Inc .... F 252 338-2800
  Elizabeth City *(G-5566)*
Ricewrap Foods Corporation .... F 919 614-1179
  Butner *(G-1549)*
Salty Landing .... G 404 245-5699
  Etowah *(G-5693)*
Sea Supreme Inc .... G 919 556-1188
  Wake Forest *(G-15590)*
Toms Robinson Seafood Inc .... G 919 942-1221
  Carrboro *(G-1658)*
Williams Seafood Arapahoe Inc .... D 252 249-0594
  Arapahoe *(G-262)*

2095 Roasted coffee

AC Imports LLC .... G 919 229-6650
  Durham *(G-4898)*
Alamance Kaffee Werks LLC .... F 662 617-4573
  Burlington *(G-1363)*
Anchor Coffee Co Inc .... G 336 265-7458
  North Wilkesboro *(G-11997)*
Crane Coffee Roasters LLC .... G 443 960-0654
  Fuquay Varina *(G-6192)*
Five Star Coffee Roasters LLC .... G 919 671-0645
  Holly Springs *(G-8699)*
Fryeday Coffee Roasters LLC .... G 704 879-9083
  Lowell *(G-10008)*
High Noon Coffee Roasters LLC .... G 770 851-7004
  Asheville *(G-651)*
▲ Larrys Beans Inc .... E 919 828-1234
  Raleigh *(G-12958)*
Muddy Dog LLC .... G 919 371-2818
  Cary *(G-1828)*
Royal Cup Inc .... F 704 597-5756
  Charlotte *(G-3463)*

◆ S & D Coffee Inc .... A 704 782-3121
  Concord *(G-4355)*
Sharewell Coffee Company LLC .... G 828 290-8188
  Hendersonville *(G-7899)*
Tce Coffee LLC .... G 910 336-3439
  Fayetteville *(G-5927)*
Tradewinds Coffee Co Inc .... F 919 556-1835
  Zebulon *(G-17144)*
▼ Wallingford Coffee Mills Inc .... D 513 771-3131
  Concord *(G-4387)*
Well-Bean Coffee & Crumbs LLC .... G 833 777-2326
  Wake Forest *(G-15612)*

2096 Potato chips and similar snacks

American Skin Food Group LLC .... E 910 259-2232
  Burgaw *(G-1332)*
Bakers Southern Traditions Inc .... G 252 344-2120
  Roxobel *(G-13829)*
Blazing Foods LLC .... G 336 865-2933
  Charlotte *(G-2320)*
Frito-Lay North America Inc .... C 704 588-4150
  Charlotte *(G-2798)*
Ginny O s Inc .... F 919 816-7276
  Warsaw *(G-15668)*
Golden Pop Shop LLC .... G 704 236-9455
  Charlotte *(G-2844)*
Gruma Corporation .... E 919 778-5553
  Goldsboro *(G-6622)*
▲ Igh Enterprises Inc .... E 704 372-6744
  Charlotte *(G-2949)*
Julias Southern Foods LLC .... G 919 609-6745
  Raleigh *(G-12927)*
▲ KLb Enterprises Incorporated .... F 336 605-0773
  Greensboro *(G-7153)*
▲ Lc America Inc .... F 336 676-5129
  Colfax *(G-4153)*
Mr Bs Fun Foods Inc .... E 828 879-1901
  Connelly Springs *(G-4406)*
R W Garcia Co Inc .... E 828 428-0115
  Lincolnton *(G-9914)*
Ripe Revival Produce LLC .... G 252 567-8305
  Rocky Mount *(G-13728)*
S-L Snacks Pa LLC .... C 704 554-1421
  Charlotte *(G-3481)*
Salty Dog Snacks Inc .... G 252 532-2109
  La Grange *(G-9445)*
Shallowford Farms Popcorn Inc .... G 336 463-5938
  Yadkinville *(G-17050)*
Skin Boys LLC .... E 910 259-2232
  Burgaw *(G-1350)*
Snyders-Lance Inc .... A 704 554-1421
  Charlotte *(G-3574)*
Stormberg Foods LLC .... E 919 947-6011
  Goldsboro *(G-6662)*
Tyson Mexican Original Inc .... D 919 777-9428
  Sanford *(G-14201)*

2097 Manufactured ice

Carolina Ice Inc .... E 252 527-3178
  Kinston *(G-9351)*
Dfa Dairy Brands Fluid LLC .... G 704 341-2794
  Charlotte *(G-2625)*
Herrin Bros Coal & Ice Co .... G 704 332-2193
  Charlotte *(G-2906)*
Hickman Oil & Ice Co Inc .... G 910 576-2501
  Troy *(G-15406)*
Ice Cube Recording Studios .... G 910 260-7616
  Wilmington *(G-16262)*
Reddy Ice Group Inc .... D 704 824-4611
  Gastonia *(G-6502)*
Robert D Starr .... G 336 697-0286
  Greensboro *(G-7313)*

20 FOOD AND KINDRED PRODUCTS

Rose Ice & Coal Company .... F 910 762-2464
  Wilmington (G-16387)
Taylor Products Inc .... G 910 862-2576
  Elizabethtown (G-5606)
Zippy Ice Inc .... E 980 355-9851
  Charlotte (G-3852)

2098 Macaroni and spaghetti

▲ First Noodle Co Inc .... G 704 393-3238
  Charlotte (G-2766)

2099 Food preparations, nec

Advancepierre Foods Inc .... A 828 459-7626
  Claremont (G-3900)
Ajinomoto Hlth Ntrtn N Amer In .... C 919 231-0100
  Raleigh (G-12484)
Alta Foods llc .... D 919 734-0233
  Goldsboro (G-6588)
American Miso Company Inc .... F 828 287-2940
  Rutherfordton (G-13863)
Apex Salsa Company .... G 919 363-1486
  Apex (G-162)
Atkins Unlimited LLC .... G 704 984-8595
  Sanford (G-14090)
▲ Avoca LLC .... D 252 482-2133
  Merry Hill (G-10440)
Bay Valley Foods LLC .... D 715 366-4511
  Albertson (G-114)
▲ Bay Valley Foods LLC .... E 910 267-4711
  Faison (G-5721)
Bay Valley Foods LLC .... E 704 476-7141
  Kings Mountain (G-9294)
Big Show Foods Inc .... F 919 242-7769
  Wake Forest (G-15531)
Bost Distributing Company Inc .... E 919 775-5931
  Sanford (G-14095)
Cargill Incorporated .... D 800 227-4455
  Fayetteville (G-5783)
Carolina Innvtive Fd Ingrdnts .... G 804 359-9311
  Nashville (G-11740)
Cary Keisler Inc .... G 336 586-9333
  Burlington (G-1389)
Chandler Foods Inc .... E 336 299-1934
  Greensboro (G-6903)
Clay County Food Pantry Inc .... E 828 389-1657
  Hayesville (G-7761)
Clean Catch Fish Market LLC .... G 704 333-1212
  Charlotte (G-2494)
Communitys Kitchen L3c .... G 828 817-2308
  Tryon (G-15423)
Compass Group Usa Inc .... A 704 398-6515
  Charlotte (G-2532)
Compass Group Usa Inc .... B 919 381-9577
  Garner (G-6267)
Compass Group Usa Inc .... E 252 291-7733
  Wilson (G-16489)
Cool Runnings Jamaican LLC .... G 919 818-9220
  Raleigh (G-12645)
Culture Cuisine LLC .... G 347 278-3210
  Charlotte (G-2583)
Daddy Mikes LLC .... G 252 327-1840
  Winterville (G-16998)
Dover Foods Inc .... E 800 348-7416
  Mills River (G-10502)
▲ Drake S Fresh Pasta Company .... E 336 861-5454
  High Point (G-8330)
E2m Kitchen LLC .... E 704 985-5903
  Charlotte (G-2672)
El Comal Inc .... G 336 788-8110
  Winston Salem (G-16693)
Elizondo LLC .... G 910 590-6550
  Saint Pauls (G-13905)

Ely Tortilleria LLC .... G 704 886-8501
  Charlotte (G-2702)
Equinom Enterprises LLC .... G 704 817-8489
  Charlotte (G-2725)
Ericson Foods Inc .... F 336 317-2199
  Winston Salem (G-16699)
Flavor Seed LLC .... G 704 401-9319
  Charlotte (G-2772)
Foell Packing Company of NC .... F 919 776-0592
  Sanford (G-14119)
Fosterscape LLP .... G 910 401-7638
  Fayetteville (G-5827)
Frito-Lay North America Inc .... C 704 588-4150
  Charlotte (G-2798)
Fuji Foods Inc .... G 336 226-8817
  Burlington (G-1416)
▲ Fuji Foods Inc .... E 336 375-3111
  Browns Summit (G-1305)
Gallo Lea Organics LLC .... G 828 337-1037
  Asheville (G-630)
General Foods Distributors .... G 919 279-7236
  Zebulon (G-17128)
▲ Golding Farms Foods Inc .... D 336 766-6161
  Winston Salem (G-16723)
Gourmet Foods USA LLC .... G 704 248-1724
  Cornelius (G-4552)
▲ Great Eastern Sun Trdg Co Inc .... F 828 665-7790
  Asheville (G-642)
Hanor Co Inc .... G 252 977-0035
  Battleboro (G-921)
Harmony House Foods Inc .... G 800 696-1395
  Franklin (G-6132)
Hemp and Tea Company LLC .... G 704 248-8657
  Huntersville (G-8829)
◆ Herbal Innovations LLC .... E 336 818-2332
  Wilkesboro (G-16024)
Horballs Inc .... G 919 925-0483
  Raleigh (G-12859)
▲ Igh Enterprises Inc .... E 704 372-6744
  Charlotte (G-2949)
Improved Nature LLC .... D 919 588-2299
  Garner (G-6277)
Indulgent Essential Spices LLC .... G 919 973-3069
  Franklinton (G-6155)
Isabellas Fine Olive Oils & Vl .... G 704 237-4949
  Huntersville (G-8839)
James Foods Inc .... E 336 437-0393
  Graham (G-6695)
Jenkins Foods Inc .... E 704 434-2347
  Shelby (G-14332)
Johnson Harn Vngar Gee GL Pllc .... G 919 213-6163
  Raleigh (G-12921)
Julias Southern Foods LLC .... G 919 609-6745
  Raleigh (G-12927)
Kimbees Inc .... G 336 323-8773
  Greensboro (G-7150)
Kloud Hemp Co .... G 336 740-2528
  Greensboro (G-7154)
La Palmas Tortilleria Y Taquer .... G 252 206-1683
  Wilson (G-16509)
▲ La Tortilleria LLC .... C 336 773-0010
  Winston Salem (G-16782)
Ladybugs Medibles LLC .... G 704 635-7596
  Monroe (G-10754)
Landshire Inc .... G 919 650-3544
  Morrisville (G-11372)
Lc Foods LLC .... G 919 510-6688
  Raleigh (G-12961)
◆ LCI Corporation International .... E 704 399-7441
  Charlotte (G-3076)
Lucy In Rye LLC .... G 828 586-4601
  Sylva (G-15063)

Ludlam Family Foods LLC .... G 919 805-6061
  Durham (G-5197)
Ludlam Family Foods LLC .... G 919 805-6061
  Chapel Hill (G-2035)
▼ Mana Nutritive Aid Pdts Inc .... G 855 438-6262
  Matthews (G-10266)
McF Operating LLC .... E 828 685-8821
  Hendersonville (G-7878)
Mg Foods Inc .... F 336 724-6327
  Winston Salem (G-16806)
▲ Miss Tortillas Inc .... G 919 598-8646
  Durham (G-5228)
Morven Partners LP .... E 252 482-2193
  Edenton (G-5519)
Mre-Star .... G 407 403-3889
  Arden (G-354)
My Threesons Gourmet .... G 336 324-5638
  Reidsville (G-13535)
Nafshi Enterprises LLC .... G 910 986-9888
  Aberdeen (G-17)
Natures Cup LLC .... G 910 795-2700
  Raeford (G-12427)
Neu Spice and Seasonings Llc .... G 252 378-7912
  Washington (G-15719)
Next Generation Snacks Inc .... G 919 797-9623
  Morrisville (G-11395)
Nice Blends Corp .... D 910 640-1000
  Whiteville (G-15973)
No Evil Foods LLC .... D 828 367-1536
  Weaverville (G-15856)
Ocracoke Sauce Company LLC .... G 443 904-7972
  Ocracoke (G-12096)
Oil and Vinegar Market Inc .... G 919 491-9225
  Durham (G-5253)
Ole Mexican Foods Inc .... G 704 587-1763
  Charlotte (G-3293)
Over Rainbow Inc .... F 704 332-5521
  Charlotte (G-3307)
Palmetto and Associate LLC .... G 336 382-7432
  Greensboro (G-7242)
Panaceutics Nutrition Inc .... F 919 797-9623
  Durham (G-5269)
Peanut Butter Fingers LLC .... G 704 997-5787
  Cornelius (G-4574)
Peanut Butter Project .... G 704 654-0212
  Charlotte (G-3324)
Peanut Processors Inc .... F 910 862-2136
  Dublin (G-4838)
Peanut Processors Sherman Inc .... G 910 862-2136
  Dublin (G-4839)
Penny Connected Cafe LLC .... G 984 214-2131
  Pittsboro (G-12344)
Pickles Manufacturing LLC .... C 910 267-4711
  Faison (G-5724)
Poppy Handcrafted Popcorn Inc .... F 828 552-3149
  Black Mountain (G-1136)
Poppy Handcrafted Popcorn LLC .... F 828 552-3149
  Old Fort (G-12105)
◆ Pregel America Inc .... G 704 707-0300
  Concord (G-4336)
Red Clay Ciderworks .... G 980 498-0676
  Charlotte (G-3421)
Red Pepper Salsa .... G 503 799-9170
  Winston Salem (G-16882)
Rocco Inc .... G 252 634-1642
  Havelock (G-7746)
▲ Rolls Enterprises Inc .... G 919 545-9401
  Pittsboro (G-12348)
Rositas Tortillas Inc .... G 910 944-0577
  Aberdeen (G-26)
Sage Mule .... G 336 209-9183
  Greensboro (G-7323)

Salsa Greensboro .... G 781 648-4140
  Greensboro (G-7324)
Sarahs Salsa Inc .... G 336 508-3033
  Greensboro (G-7325)
▲ Scotts & Associates Inc .... F 336 581-3141
  Bear Creek (G-942)
Shallowford Farms Popcorn Inc .... G 336 463-5938
  Yadkinville (G-17050)
Sideboard .... G 910 612-4398
  Wilmington (G-16404)
Signature Seasonings LLC .... G 252 746-1001
  Ayden (G-856)
Sinnovita Inc .... G 919 694-0974
  Raleigh (G-13265)
Sistas 4 Life Food Svcs LLC .... G 704 957-6437
  Charlotte (G-3557)
Sizzlewich LLC .... G 980 299-1389
  Charlotte (G-3558)
Smiling Hara LLC .... G 828 545-4150
  Barnardsville (G-913)
Solo Foods LLC .... F 910 259-9407
  Burgaw (G-1351)
▼ Star Food Products Inc .... D 336 227-4079
  Burlington (G-1501)
◆ Star Snax LLC .... D 828 261-0255
  Conover (G-4500)
▼ Stefano Foods Inc .... C 704 399-3935
  Charlotte (G-3628)
Still There .... G 704 728-1888
  Charlotte (G-3633)
Stony Gap Wholesale Co Inc .... G 704 982-5360
  Albemarle (G-109)
Sweet Treats By Treat Lady LLC .... G 336 831-3482
  Winston Salem (G-16928)
Sweeteasy LLC .... G 252 698-0109
  Elizabeth City (G-5573)
Sweets Syrup LLC .... G 704 989-2156
  Charlotte (G-3660)
Syrup and More LLC .... G 781 548-1346
  Greensboro (G-7384)
Tate & Lyle Solutions USA LLC .... E 252 482-0402
  Merry Hill (G-10441)
Ted Wheeler .... G 252 438-0820
  Oxford (G-12159)
Tortillas San Antonio Inc .... G 252 459-5459
  Nashville (G-11752)
Tortilleria La Favorita .... G 910 892-0302
  Dunn (G-4886)
Tortilleria Los Paisanos .... G 704 283-8508
  Monroe (G-10822)
Tortilleria Los Remnedios II .... G 919 658-1714
  Mount Olive (G-11671)
◆ Tropical Nut & Fruit Co .... G 800 438-4470
  Charlotte (G-3731)
Tyson Mexican Original Inc .... D 919 777-9428
  Sanford (G-14201)
Universal Blanchers LLC .... D 252 482-2112
  Edenton (G-5522)
Urban Orchard Cider Company .... G 828 779-6372
  Weaverville (G-15866)
Urban Spiced LLC .... G 704 741-1174
  Charlotte (G-3759)
Vanguard Culinary Group Ltd .... D 910 484-8999
  Fayetteville (G-5947)
Vintage South Inc .... G 919 362-4079
  Apex (G-253)
Violet Sanford Holdings LLC .... E 919 775-5931
  Sanford (G-14203)
Virgilios Premium Vinegars .... G 919 717-3373
  Wake Forest (G-15610)
Vista Horticultural Group Inc .... F 828 633-6338
  Arden (G-390)

Wagco Oil and Vinegar Taproom .... G 919 295-6134
  Knightdale (G-9433)
▼ Wallingford Coffee Mills Inc .... D 513 771-3131
  Concord (G-4387)
Williams Skin Co .... F 910 323-2628
  Fayetteville (G-5954)

21 TOBACCO PRODUCTS

2111 Cigarettes

A W Spears Research Ctr .... G 336 335-6724
  Greensboro (G-6769)
◆ Alternative Brands Inc .... B 336 751-4818
  Mocksville (G-10552)
Commonwealth Brands Inc .... C 336 634-4200
  Greensboro (G-6925)
▲ Fontem Us Inc .... G 888 207-4588
  Charlotte (G-2784)
Happy Shack Smoke Shop .... G 980 833-8053
  Gastonia (G-6414)
Itg Brands .... D 336 335-6600
  Greensboro (G-7124)
Itg Brands .... D 919 366-0220
  Raleigh (G-12904)
Itg Brands LLC .... D 336 335-7000
  Greensboro (G-7125)
▲ Liggett Group LLC .... B 919 304-7700
  Mebane (G-10416)
Lorillard LLC .... E 336 741-2000
  Winston Salem (G-16792)
Lorillard Q-Tech Inc .... G 877 703-0386
  Greensboro (G-7169)
◆ Lorillard Tobacco Company LLC .... A 336 335-6600
  Greensboro (G-7170)
Medallion Company Inc .... C 919 990-3500
  Timberlake (G-15315)
Modoral Brands Inc .... G 336 741-7230
  Winston Salem (G-16815)
Mr Tobacco .... G 919 747-9052
  Raleigh (G-13047)
On Demand Hemp Company LLC .... G 336 757-0320
  Tobaccoville (G-15318)
Philip Morris USA Inc .... D 336 744-4401
  Winston Salem (G-16849)
R J Reynolds Tobacco Company .... D 919 366-0220
  Wendell (G-15913)
R J Reynolds Tobacco Company .... C 336 741-2132
  Winston Salem (G-16876)
◆ R J Rynolds Tob Holdings Inc .... D 336 741-5000
  Winston Salem (G-16878)
Rai Services Company .... F 336 741-6774
  Winston Salem (G-16879)
◆ Reynolds American Inc .... E 336 741-2000
  Winston Salem (G-16884)
Santa Fe Ntural Tob Foundation .... C 919 690-0880
  Oxford (G-12154)
Triaga Inc .... G 919 412-6019
  Wilson (G-16551)
◆ US Tobacco Cooperative Inc .... D 919 821-4560
  Raleigh (G-13386)
Vector Tobacco Inc .... E 919 990-3500
  Morrisville (G-11463)
Wainwright Warehouse .... G 252 237-5121
  Wilson (G-16556)

2121 Cigars

Modoral Brands Inc .... G 336 741-7230
  Winston Salem (G-16815)
North Carolina Tobacco Mfg LLC .... F 252 238-6514
  Stantonsburg (G-14712)
◆ Reynolds American Inc .... E 336 741-2000
  Winston Salem (G-16884)

Santa Fe Natural Tob Co Inc .... F 919 690-1905
  Oxford (G-12153)

2131 Chewing and smoking tobacco

Alnamer Inc .... G 252 215-0323
  Greenville (G-7479)
American Snuff Company LLC .... C 336 768-4630
  Winston Salem (G-16603)
▲ Cres Tobacco Company LLC .... E 336 983-7727
  King (G-9268)
▲ Ioto Usa LLC .... F 252 413-7343
  Greenville (G-7545)
Itg Holdings USA Inc .... E 954 772-9000
  Greensboro (G-7127)
Modoral Brands Inc .... G 336 741-7230
  Winston Salem (G-16815)
R J Reynolds Tobacco Company .... D 336 741-0400
  Tobaccoville (G-15319)
R J Reynolds Tobacco Company .... C 336 741-2132
  Winston Salem (G-16876)
◆ R J Reynolds Tobacco Company .... D 336 741-5000
  Winston Salem (G-16877)
◆ Reynolds American Inc .... E 336 741-2000
  Winston Salem (G-16884)
▲ Santa Fe Natural Tobacco .... C 800 332-5595
  Winston Salem (G-16898)
Tobacco Rag Processors Inc .... E 252 265-0081
  Wilson (G-16548)
Tobacco Rag Processors Inc .... E 252 237-8180
  Wilson (G-16549)
◆ Tobacco Rag Processors Inc .... E 252 265-0081
  Wilson (G-16547)
Top Tobacco LP .... C 910 646-3014
  Lake Waccamaw (G-9449)

2141 Tobacco stemming and redrying

Pyxus International Inc .... C 252 753-8000
  Farmville (G-5742)
R J Reynolds Tobacco Company .... C 252 291-4700
  Wilson (G-16527)
Recon Usa LLC .... G 252 206-1391
  Wilson (G-16529)
Tobacco Rag Processors Inc .... E 252 265-0081
  Wilson (G-16548)
Tobacco Rag Processors Inc .... E 252 237-8180
  Wilson (G-16549)
◆ Tobacco Rag Processors Inc .... E 252 265-0081
  Wilson (G-16547)
Top Tobacco LP .... C 910 646-3014
  Lake Waccamaw (G-9449)

22 TEXTILE MILL PRODUCTS

2211 Broadwoven fabric mills, cotton

◆ Alamac American Knits LLC .... C 910 618-2248
  Lumberton (G-10024)
▲ American Fiber & Finishing Inc .... E 704 984-9256
  Albemarle (G-73)
◆ American Silk Mills LLC .... F 570 822-7147
  High Point (G-8248)
▲ Amerifab International Inc .... E 336 882-9010
  High Point (G-8249)
Amys Custom Canvas .... G 910 713-8481
  Southport (G-14564)
At The Lake Canvas and Covers .... G 704 966-1586
  Sherrills Ford (G-14383)
Atlantic Trading LLC .... F
  Charlotte (G-2233)
◆ Barnhardt Manufacturing Company ..... C 800 277-0377
  Charlotte (G-2283)
◆ Bekaert Textiles USA Inc .... C 336 769-4300
  Winston Salem (G-16624)

Employee Codes: A=Over 500 employees, B=251-500
C=101-250, D=51-100, E=20-50, F=10-19, G=1-9

22 TEXTILE MILL PRODUCTS

Bekaertdeslee USA Inc .... B 336 747-4900
  Winston Salem *(G-16625)*
Belk Department Stores LP .... C 704 357-4000
  Charlotte *(G-2298)*
Beverly Knits Inc .... G 704 964-0835
  Gastonia *(G-6354)*
▲ Beverly Knits Inc .... D 704 861-1536
  Gastonia *(G-6355)*
Burlington House LLC .... D 336 379-6220
  Greensboro *(G-6863)*
◆ Burlington Industries LLC .... C 336 379-6220
  Greensboro *(G-6865)*
C Murrells Event Planning LLC .... G 910 382-2742
  Maysville *(G-10370)*
Canvas Beauty Bar LLC .... F 828 355-9688
  Boone *(G-1183)*
Canvas of Flesh .... G 980 234-5957
  Salisbury *(G-13931)*
◆ Carolina Mills Incorporated .... B 828 428-9911
  Maiden *(G-10102)*
▲ Champion Thread Company .... G 704 867-6611
  Gastonia *(G-6375)*
Chaos Worldwide LLC .... G 336 558-5654
  Greensboro *(G-6904)*
Circa 1801 .... E 828 397-7003
  Connelly Springs *(G-4399)*
Cloth Barn Inc .... F 919 735-3643
  Goldsboro *(G-6601)*
◆ Cone Denim LLC .... D 336 379-6165
  Greensboro *(G-6928)*
▲ Cone Jacquards LLC .... E 336 379-6220
  Greensboro *(G-6929)*
◆ Copland Industries Inc .... B 336 226-0272
  Burlington *(G-1400)*
Courtesy of Kamdyn LLC .... G 706 831-5395
  Charlotte *(G-2563)*
Creative Conquest LLC .... G 720 481-4372
  Shelby *(G-14304)*
◆ Creative Fabric Services LLC .... G 704 861-8383
  Gastonia *(G-6387)*
Creativemark Canvas LLC .... G 919 267-4660
  Apex *(G-178)*
◆ Ct-Nassau Ticking LLC .... E 336 570-0091
  Burlington *(G-1403)*
Culp Inc .... E 662 844-7144
  Burlington *(G-1404)*
Culp Inc .... C 336 643-7751
  Stokesdale *(G-14941)*
Custom Canvas Inc 2 .... G 252 633-0754
  New Bern *(G-11794)*
Custom Marine Canvas .... G 252 482-0675
  Edenton *(G-5511)*
◆ Cv Industries Inc .... G 828 328-1851
  Hickory *(G-8001)*
Downeast Marine Canvas LLC .... G 252 495-2631
  Washington *(G-15697)*
Elevate Textiles Inc .... G 910 997-5001
  Cordova *(G-4517)*
◆ Elevate Textiles Inc .... F 336 379-6220
  Charlotte *(G-2693)*
Elevate Textiles Holding Corp .... G 336 379-6220
  Charlotte *(G-2694)*
Faizon Global Inc .... G 704 774-1141
  Monroe *(G-10718)*
▲ Ferncrest Fashions Inc .... D 704 283-6422
  Monroe *(G-10719)*
Flint Spinning LLC .... G 336 665-3000
  Greensboro *(G-7018)*
◆ Glen Raven Inc .... C 336 227-6211
  Burlington *(G-1423)*
Gracefully Broken LLC .... G 980 474-0309
  Charlotte *(G-2851)*

Hackner Home LLC .... G 980 552-9573
  Shelby *(G-14323)*
Heritage Classic Wovens LLC .... F 828 247-6010
  Forest City *(G-6070)*
Heritage Knitting Co LLC .... E 704 872-7653
  Statesville *(G-14812)*
High Tide Canvas & Uphl Inc .... G 910 409-5903
  Wilmington *(G-16254)*
Highland Composites .... G 704 924-3090
  Greensboro *(G-7089)*
Hpfabrics Inc .... G 336 231-0278
  Winston Salem *(G-16749)*
Industrial Opportunities Inc .... B 828 321-4754
  Andrews *(G-126)*
Interrs-Exteriors Asheboro Inc .... F 336 629-2148
  Asheboro *(G-446)*
◆ Itg Holdings Inc .... A 336 379-6220
  Greensboro *(G-7126)*
Ivy Brand LLC .... G 980 225-7866
  Charlotte *(G-3001)*
JPS Elstmerics Westfield Plant .... G 336 351-0938
  Westfield *(G-15952)*
Kimmys Customs LLC .... G 904 699-2933
  Rural Hall *(G-13845)*
Lanart International Inc .... G 704 875-1972
  Huntersville *(G-8848)*
▲ Lantal Textiles Inc .... C 336 969-9551
  Rural Hall *(G-13847)*
Le Soigneur Canvas LLC .... G 910 670-3620
  Raleigh *(G-12962)*
Lillys Interiors Cstm Quilting .... G 336 475-1421
  Thomasville *(G-15242)*
Little Blank Canvas LLC .... G 336 887-6133
  High Point *(G-8432)*
Luray Textiles Inc .... E 336 670-3725
  North Wilkesboro *(G-12025)*
▲ M J E J Inc .... F 910 399-3795
  Wilmington *(G-16312)*
Manning Fabrics Inc .... E 910 295-1970
  Pinebluff *(G-12215)*
Manning Fabrics Inc .... G 910 295-1970
  Pinehurst *(G-12228)*
▲ Marlatex Corporation .... E 704 829-7797
  Charlotte *(G-3127)*
Mdkscrubs LLC .... G 980 250-4708
  Charlotte *(G-3156)*
▼ Mfi Products Inc .... F 910 944-2128
  Aberdeen *(G-15)*
Milliken & Company .... E 828 247-4300
  Bostic *(G-1265)*
Modena Southern Dyeing Corp .... G 704 866-9156
  Gastonia *(G-6468)*
New River Fabrics Inc .... G 704 462-1401
  Lawndale *(G-9502)*
Oakdale Cotton Mills .... G 336 454-1144
  Jamestown *(G-9064)*
Ofm Inc .... G 919 303-6389
  Apex *(G-221)*
Painted Canvas .... G 770 331-2462
  Fayetteville *(G-5892)*
▲ Perfect Fit Industries LLC .... C 800 864-7618
  Charlotte *(G-3330)*
Pro-Fit Boat Canvas LLC .... G 704 340-7733
  Mooresville *(G-11062)*
▲ Pure Country Inc .... D 828 859-9916
  Lynn *(G-10063)*
Raleigh Workshop Inc .... E 919 917-8969
  Raleigh *(G-13188)*
Ribbon Enterprises Inc .... G 828 264-6444
  Boone *(G-1234)*
▼ Riddle & Company LLC .... E 336 229-1856
  Burlington *(G-1485)*

Ripstop By Roll LLC .... F 877 525-7210
  Durham *(G-5332)*
Salt Life Canvas LLC .... G 252 722-2314
  Aydlett *(G-861)*
Sampson Gin Company Inc .... F 910 567-5111
  Newton Grove *(G-11992)*
◆ Sattler Corp .... D 828 759-2100
  Hudson *(G-8778)*
Skeen Decorative Fabrics Inc .... F 336 884-4044
  High Point *(G-8535)*
Star Wipers Inc .... E 888 511-2656
  Gastonia *(G-6515)*
Swatch Works Inc .... G 336 626-9971
  Asheboro *(G-489)*
Swatchworks Inc .... G 336 626-9971
  Asheboro *(G-490)*
▲ Textile-Based Delivery Inc .... E 866 256-8420
  Conover *(G-4504)*
Textum Opco LLC .... E 704 822-2400
  Belmont *(G-1016)*
Theodore Alexander Uphl LLC .... G 336 472-7540
  Thomasville *(G-15288)*
▲ Trelleborg Ctd Systems US Inc .... C 828 286-9126
  Rutherfordton *(G-13896)*
Valdese Textiles Inc .... F 828 874-4216
  Valdese *(G-15458)*
▲ Valdese Weavers LLC .... G 828 874-2181
  Valdese *(G-15459)*
Valdese Weavers LLC .... A 828 874-2181
  Valdese *(G-15460)*
▼ Value Clothing Inc .... E 704 638-6111
  Salisbury *(G-14061)*
VF Corporation .... G 336 424-6000
  Greensboro *(G-7438)*
VF Corporation .... F 336 424-6000
  Greensboro *(G-7439)*
Vlr LLC .... E 252 355-4610
  Morganton *(G-11265)*
Wade Manufacturing Company .... E 910 895-0276
  Rockingham *(G-13646)*
▲ Wade Manufacturing Company .... C 704 694-2131
  Wadesboro *(G-15519)*
Weather Marine Canvas LLC .... G 336 764-4015
  Lexington *(G-9801)*
Westpoint Home Inc .... B 910 369-2231
  Wagram *(G-15524)*
Wine and Canvas Studio .... G 251 591-7219
  Charlotte *(G-3816)*

2221 Broadwoven fabric mills, manmade

▲ Abercrombie Textiles I LLC .... F 704 487-1245
  Shelby *(G-14282)*
Admiral Marine Pdts & Svcs Inc .... G 704 489-8771
  Denver *(G-4758)*
American Olympus Fibrgls Corp .... G 828 459-0444
  Claremont *(G-3901)*
◆ American Silk Mills LLC .... F 570 822-7147
  High Point *(G-8248)*
American Tchncal Solutions Inc .... D 336 595-2763
  Walkertown *(G-15613)*
American Yarn LLC .... F 919 614-1542
  Burlington *(G-1365)*
Amesbury Group Inc .... D 704 978-2883
  Statesville *(G-14748)*
Amesbury Group Inc .... E 704 924-7694
  Statesville *(G-14749)*
Andritz Fabrics and Rolls Inc .... G 919 526-1400
  Raleigh *(G-12506)*
Asheboro Elastics Corp .... G 336 629-2626
  Asheboro *(G-404)*
◆ Asheboro Elastics Corp .... D 336 629-2626
  Asheboro *(G-403)*

SIC SECTION
22 TEXTILE MILL PRODUCTS

Ashfar Enterprises Inc......................... F 704 462-4672
  Newton (G-11913)
Barcovvsion LLC.................................. F 704 392-9371
  Charlotte (G-2279)
Bettys Drapery Design Workroom........... G 828 264-2392
  Boone (G-1176)
◆ Burlington Industries LLC................... C 336 379-6220
  Greensboro (G-6865)
◆ Carolina Mills Incorporated................ B 828 428-9911
  Maiden (G-10102)
◆ Carriff Corporation Inc....................... G 704 888-3330
  Midland (G-10459)
Classical Elements............................... G 828 575-9145
  Asheville (G-595)
▲ Composite Fabrics America LLC......... G 828 632-5220
  Taylorsville (G-15135)
▲ Cone Jacquards LLC......................... E 336 379-6220
  Greensboro (G-6929)
Copland Fabrics Inc............................. B 336 226-0272
  Burlington (G-1399)
◆ Copland Industries Inc....................... B 336 226-0272
  Burlington (G-1400)
Crypton Mills LLC................................. E 828 202-5875
  Cliffside (G-4085)
◆ Ct-Nassau Ticking LLC..................... E 336 570-0091
  Burlington (G-1403)
Culp Inc.. F 336 889-5161
  High Point (G-8310)
David Rothschild Co Inc....................... D 336 342-0035
  Reidsville (G-13516)
Design Concepts Incorporated.............. F 336 887-1932
  High Point (G-8321)
◆ Dicey Mills Inc.................................. F 704 487-6324
  Shelby (G-14312)
▼ Efa Inc... C 336 378-2603
  Greensboro (G-6990)
▼ Efa Inc... C 336 275-9401
  Greensboro (G-6991)
Elevate Textiles Inc............................. G 336 379-6220
  Burlington (G-1410)
◆ Elevate Textiles Inc........................... F 336 379-6220
  Charlotte (G-2693)
Elevate Textiles Holding Corp............... D 336 379-6220
  Charlotte (G-2694)
▲ Feinberg Enterprises Inc.................... F 704 822-2400
  Belmont (G-988)
Fiber Company..................................... G 336 725-5277
  Lewisville (G-9666)
Fibrix LLC... E 704 878-0027
  Statesville (G-14797)
▲ Filtex Inc... D 828 874-2100
  Rutherford College (G-13859)
◆ Flynt/Amtex Inc................................ E 336 226-0621
  Burlington (G-1414)
Freudenberg Prfmce Mtls LP................. C 828 665-5000
  Candler (G-1579)
▲ Gale Pacific Usa Inc.......................... F 407 772-7900
  Charlotte (G-2804)
Glen Raven Custom Fabrics LLC........... C 828 682-2142
  Burnsville (G-1526)
◆ Glen Raven Inc................................. C 336 227-6211
  Burlington (G-1423)
Glen Rven Tchnical Fabrics LLC............ C 336 229-5576
  Burlington (G-1425)
Glen Rven Tchnical Fabrics LLC............ E 336 227-6211
  Burlington (G-1424)
Hanes Companies Inc.......................... B 828 464-4673
  Conover (G-4460)
Hickory Heritage of Falling Creek Inc..... E
  Hickory (G-8048)
Highland Industries Inc........................ E 336 855-0625
  Greensboro (G-7090)

Highland Industries Inc........................ E 336 547-1600
  Greensboro (G-7091)
▲ Hyosung Holdings Usa Inc................. G 704 790-6134
  Charlotte (G-2942)
◆ Hyosung Usa Inc.............................. E 704 790-6100
  Charlotte (G-2943)
Interface Fabrics Group........................ G 336 526-0407
  Elkin (G-5620)
◆ Itg Holdings Inc................................ A 336 379-6220
  Greensboro (G-7126)
Ivy Brand LLC..................................... G 980 225-7866
  Charlotte (G-3001)
◆ Kings Plush Inc................................ C 704 739-9931
  Kings Mountain (G-9314)
Kontoor Brands Inc.............................. D 336 332-3577
  Greensboro (G-7157)
Langenthal Corporation......................... F 336 969-9551
  Rural Hall (G-13846)
Ledford Upholstery............................... G 704 732-0233
  Lincolnton (G-9899)
Liberty Street LLC................................ G 828 247-6010
  Forest City (G-6075)
Metyx USA Inc..................................... D 704 824-1030
  Gastonia (G-6464)
Moire Creations America LLC................ E 704 482-9860
  Shelby (G-14349)
Newgard Industries Inc......................... F 704 283-6011
  Monroe (G-10779)
Nouveau Verre Holdings Inc.................. F 336 545-0011
  Greensboro (G-7224)
Nvh Inc... G 336 545-0011
  Greensboro (G-7228)
▲ P&A Indstrial Fabrications LLC........... E 336 322-1766
  Roxboro (G-13815)
Patricia Hall....................................... G 704 729-6133
  Bessemer City (G-1077)
Performance Fibers............................... F 704 947-7193
  Huntersville (G-8874)
Piedmont Cmposites Tooling LLC........... D 828 632-8883
  Taylorsville (G-15156)
Plush Comforts.................................... G 336 882-9185
  High Point (G-8487)
Point Blank Enterprises Inc................... D 910 893-2071
  Lillington (G-9858)
◆ Precision Fabrics Group Inc................ E 336 281-3049
  Greensboro (G-7274)
Premier Quilting Corporation................. F 919 693-1151
  Oxford (G-12146)
▲ Quantum Materials LLC..................... F 336 605-9002
  Colfax (G-4159)
Schneider Mills Inc.............................. F 828 632-8181
  Taylorsville (G-15165)
▲ Seiren North America LLC.................. F 828 430-3456
  Morganton (G-11250)
◆ Shuford Mills LLC............................. G 828 324-4265
  Hickory (G-8150)
Simplifyber Inc.................................... G 919 396-8355
  Raleigh (G-13263)
Southline Converting LLC..................... G 828 781-6414
  Conover (G-4498)
Stowe Woodward Licensco LLC.............. G 919 526-1400
  Raleigh (G-13306)
Style Upholstering Inc.......................... G 828 322-4882
  Hickory (G-8171)
▲ Sunrise Development LLC................... F 828 453-0590
  Mooresboro (G-10841)
Svcm.. G 305 767-3595
  Lincolnton (G-9924)
▲ Tapestries Ltd.................................. G 336 883-9864
  Greensboro (G-7389)
Texinnovate Inc................................... E 336 279-7800
  Greensboro (G-7396)

▲ Trelleborg Ctd Systems US Inc............ C 828 286-9126
  Rutherfordton (G-13896)
◆ Unifi Inc.. D 336 294-4410
  Greensboro (G-7427)
Uniquetex LLC..................................... E 704 457-3003
  Grover (G-7609)
Valdese Textiles Inc............................. F 828 874-4216
  Valdese (G-15458)
Valdese Weavers LLC........................... A 828 874-2181
  Valdese (G-15460)
◆ Valdese Weavers LLC......................... B 828 874-2181
  Valdese (G-15461)
Wade Manufacturing Company............... E 910 895-0276
  Rockingham (G-13646)
▲ Wade Manufacturing Company............ C 704 694-2131
  Wadesboro (G-15519)
▲ Weavexx LLC.................................... A 919 556-7235
  Youngsville (G-17113)
Windsor Fiberglass Inc......................... F 910 259-0057
  Burgaw (G-1359)

2231 Broadwoven fabric mills, wool

Alpaca.. G 919 628-9686
  Sanford (G-14085)
Alpacadabra... G 336 429-0124
  Dobson (G-4818)
Altus Finishing LLC.............................. E 704 861-1536
  Gastonia (G-6341)
▲ Barrday Corp.................................... G 704 395-0311
  Charlotte (G-2284)
Burlington Industries III LLC................. G 336 379-2000
  Greensboro (G-6864)
◆ Burlington Industries LLC................... C 336 379-6220
  Greensboro (G-6865)
Burlington Intl Svcs Co......................... G 336 379-2000
  Greensboro (G-6866)
Burlington Investment II Inc.................. G 336 379-2000
  Greensboro (G-6867)
Burlington Worsteds Inc........................ G 336 379-2000
  Greensboro (G-6868)
Carlisle Finishing LLC........................... D 864 466-4173
  Greensboro (G-6880)
Circa 1801.. E 828 397-7003
  Connelly Springs (G-4399)
Cleos Alpacas Inc................................ G 704 663-9785
  Mooresville (G-10907)
◆ Elevate Textiles Inc........................... F 336 379-6220
  Charlotte (G-2693)
Elevate Textiles Holding Corp............... D 336 379-6220
  Charlotte (G-2694)
▲ Finishing Partners Inc....................... G 704 583-7322
  Charlotte (G-2762)
Hat Creek Alpacas................................ G 336 552-2284
  Reidsville (G-13525)
Hpfabrics Inc....................................... G 336 231-0278
  Winston Salem (G-16749)
I T G Raeford...................................... G 910 875-3736
  Raeford (G-12424)
Intertape Polymer Corp......................... E 704 279-3011
  Salisbury (G-13988)
◆ Itg Holdings Inc................................ A 336 379-6220
  Greensboro (G-7126)
Ivy Brand LLC..................................... G 980 225-7866
  Charlotte (G-3001)
Kitten Kaboodle Alpacas....................... G 252 289-5654
  Plymouth (G-12375)
Lake Country Alpacas........................... G 252 430-0963
  Henderson (G-7793)
▲ Lantal Textiles Inc............................ C 336 969-9551
  Rural Hall (G-13847)
Lustar Dyeing and Finshg Inc................ G 828 274-2440
  Asheville (G-691)

22 TEXTILE MILL PRODUCTS

Michelson Enterprises Inc .... G 828 693-5500
   Hendersonville *(G-7880)*
Milliken & Company .... E 828 247-4300
   Bostic *(G-1265)*
National Spinning Co Inc .... C 910 298-3131
   Beulaville *(G-1097)*
Sorrells Sheree White .... G 828 452-4864
   Waynesville *(G-15825)*
Trelleborg Ctd Systems US Inc .... C 864 576-1210
   Rutherfordton *(G-13894)*
▲ Voith Fabrics Inc .... B 252 291-3800
   Wilson *(G-16555)*
▲ Xtinguish LLC .... F 704 868-9500
   Charlotte *(G-3838)*

2241 Narrow fabric mills

All American Braids Inc .... E 704 852-4380
   Gastonia *(G-6339)*
American Webbing Fittings Inc .... F 336 767-9390
   Winston Salem *(G-16604)*
Asheboro Elastics Corp .... G 336 629-2626
   Asheboro *(G-404)*
◆ Asheboro Elastics Corp .... D 336 629-2626
   Asheboro *(G-403)*
▲ Carolina Narrow Fabric Company .... C 336 631-3000
   Winston Salem *(G-16646)*
Circa 1801 .... E 828 397-7003
   Connelly Springs *(G-4399)*
▲ Coats & Clark Inc .... D 704 542-5959
   Charlotte *(G-2512)*
▲ Coats N Amer De Rpblica Dmncan ..... C 800 242-8095
   Charlotte *(G-2515)*
◆ Continental Ticking Corp Amer .... D 336 570-0091
   Alamance *(G-68)*
◆ Ct-Nassau Tape LLC .... D 336 570-0091
   Alamance *(G-69)*
▲ Custom Fabric Samples Inc .... G 336 472-1854
   Thomasville *(G-15209)*
Datamark Graphics Inc .... E 336 629-0267
   Asheboro *(G-422)*
◆ Dunn Manufacturing Corp .... C 704 283-2147
   Monroe *(G-10709)*
▼ Efa Inc .... F 336 275-9401
   Greensboro *(G-6991)*
General Elastic Corporation .... F 336 431-8714
   High Point *(G-8364)*
◆ Hickory Brands Inc .... D 828 322-2600
   Hickory *(G-8044)*
Hickory Springs Mfg Co .... F 336 491-4131
   High Point *(G-8386)*
▲ Interstate Narrow Fabrics Inc .... D 336 578-1037
   Haw River *(G-7753)*
McMichael Mills Inc .... E 336 584-0134
   Burlington *(G-1459)*
◆ McMichael Mills Inc .... C 336 548-4242
   Mayodan *(G-10365)*
Minnewawa Inc .... F 865 522-8103
   Thomasville *(G-15252)*
Murdock Webbing Company Inc .... E 252 823-1131
   Tarboro *(G-15117)*
National Foam Inc .... C 919 639-6151
   Angier *(G-148)*
Newgard Industries Inc .... F 704 283-6011
   Monroe *(G-10779)*
Nouveau Verre Holdings Inc .... F 336 545-0011
   Greensboro *(G-7224)*
Nvh Inc .... G 336 545-0011
   Greensboro *(G-7228)*
◆ Parkdale Mills Incorporated .... D 704 874-5000
   Gastonia *(G-6486)*
Parker-Hannifin Corporation .... F 336 373-1761
   Greensboro *(G-7245)*

Quiknit Crafting Inc .... F 704 861-1030
   Gastonia *(G-6499)*
▲ Ramseur Inter-Lock Knitting Co .... G 336 824-2427
   Asheboro *(G-470)*
◆ Spanset Inc .... E 919 774-6316
   Sanford *(G-14189)*
▲ Spt Technology Inc .... F 612 332-1880
   Monroe *(G-10811)*
◆ Spuntech Industries Inc .... C 336 330-9000
   Roxboro *(G-13825)*
Standard Tytape Company Inc .... F 828 693-6594
   Hendersonville *(G-7906)*
◆ Supreme Elastic Corporation .... E 828 302-3836
   Conover *(G-4502)*
Tcu Industries Inc 602 369-7270
   Harrisburg *(G-7730)*
◆ US Cotton LLC .... C 216 676-6400
   Gastonia *(G-6535)*
US Label Corporation .... E 336 332-7000
   Greensboro *(G-7434)*
World Elastic Corporation .... E 704 786-9508
   Concord *(G-4391)*
▲ Wright of Thomasville Inc .... F 336 472-4200
   Thomasville *(G-15305)*
◆ Zimmermann - Dynayarn Usa LLC ..... E 336 222-8129
   Graham *(G-6717)*

2251 Women's hosiery, except socks

Acme - McCrary Corporation .... F 336 625-2161
   Siler City *(G-14395)*
Acme-Mccrary Corporation .... C 336 625-2161
   Asheboro *(G-398)*
Acme-Mccrary Corporation .... C 919 663-2200
   Siler City *(G-14396)*
▲ Acme-Mccrary Corporation .... B 336 625-2161
   Asheboro *(G-399)*
Bossong Corporation .... G 336 625-2175
   Asheboro *(G-410)*
▲ Cajah Corporation .... C 828 728-7300
   Hudson *(G-8764)*
Catawba Valley Finishing LLC .... E 828 464-2252
   Newton *(G-11918)*
▲ Central Carolina Hosiery Inc .... E 910 428-9688
   Biscoe *(G-1106)*
▲ Commonwealth Hosiery Mills Inc ...... D 336 498-2621
   Randleman *(G-13459)*
Concord Trading Inc .... E 704 375-3333
   Concord *(G-4241)*
▲ Crawford Knitting Company Inc .... D 336 824-1065
   Ramseur *(G-13442)*
De Feet International Inc .... E 828 397-7025
   Hildebran *(G-8621)*
Felice Hosiery Co Inc .... E 336 996-2371
   Kernersville *(G-9200)*
◆ Fine Line Hosiery Inc .... F 336 498-8022
   Asheboro *(G-435)*
Fine Sheer Industries Inc .... B 704 375-3333
   Concord *(G-4265)*
Glen Raven Inc .... G 336 227-6211
   Altamahaw *(G-122)*
◆ Goldtoemoretz LLC .... B 828 464-0751
   Newton *(G-11937)*
Hanesbrands Inc .... G 336 789-6118
   Mount Airy *(G-11515)*
Hanesbrands Inc .... A 336 519-8080
   Winston Salem *(G-16734)*
◆ Huffman Finishing Company Inc .... C 828 396-1741
   Granite Falls *(G-6739)*
◆ Kayser-Roth Corporation .... C 336 852-2030
   Greensboro *(G-7145)*
Mas Acme USA .... G 336 625-2161
   Asheboro *(G-456)*

▲ Mayo Knitting Mill Inc .... C 252 823-3101
   Tarboro *(G-15114)*
Neat Feet Hosiery Inc .... G 336 573-2177
   Stoneville *(G-14962)*
North Carolina Sock Inc .... G 828 327-4664
   Hickory *(G-8104)*
Rogers Knitting Inc .... G 336 789-4155
   Mount Airy *(G-11567)*
▲ Royal Hosiery Company Inc .... G 828 496-2200
   Granite Falls *(G-6755)*
Simmons Hosiery Mill Inc .... G 828 327-4890
   Hickory *(G-8157)*
▲ Slane Hosiery Mills Inc .... C 336 883-4136
   High Point *(G-8538)*
Special T Hosiery Mills Inc .... G 336 227-2858
   Burlington *(G-1499)*
▲ Star America Inc .... C 704 788-4700
   Concord *(G-4367)*
Sue-Lynn Textiles Inc .... C 336 578-0871
   Haw River *(G-7757)*
Surratt Hosiery Mill Inc .... F 336 859-4583
   Denton *(G-4751)*
Teamwork Inc .... G 336 578-3456
   Elon *(G-5662)*
Thorneburg Hosiery Mills Inc .... E 704 279-7247
   Rockwell *(G-13661)*
Thorneburg Hosiery Mills Inc .... E 704 838-6329
   Statesville *(G-14913)*
Upel Inc .... E 336 519-8080
   Winston Salem *(G-16960)*
◆ Ward Hosiery Company Inc .... G 828 381-2346
   Hickory *(G-8206)*
◆ Zimmermann - Dynayarn Usa LLC ..... E 336 222-8129
   Graham *(G-6717)*

2252 Hosiery, nec

B & B Hosiery Mill .... G 336 368-4849
   Pinnacle *(G-12319)*
B & M Wholesale Inc .... G 336 789-3916
   Mount Airy *(G-11479)*
Beard Hosiery Co .... D 828 758-1942
   Lenoir *(G-9580)*
▲ Bossong Hosiery Mills Inc .... C 336 625-2175
   Asheboro *(G-411)*
Cabarrus Hosiery Dist Inc .... G 704 436-3575
   Mount Pleasant *(G-11672)*
Carolina Hosiery Mills Inc .... G 336 226-5581
   Burlington *(G-1386)*
Carolina Hosiery Mills Inc .... G 336 226-5581
   Burlington *(G-1387)*
▲ Carolina Hosiery Mills Inc .... E 336 570-2129
   Burlington *(G-1388)*
Catawba Valley Finishing LLC .... E 828 464-2252
   Newton *(G-11918)*
Cedar Valley Hosiery Mill Inc .... G 828 396-1804
   Hudson *(G-8768)*
▲ Central Carolina Hosiery Inc .... E 910 428-9688
   Biscoe *(G-1106)*
Charlotte Sock Basket .... C 704 910-2388
   Charlotte *(G-2463)*
▲ Commonwealth Hosiery Mills Inc ...... D 336 498-2621
   Randleman *(G-13459)*
Concord Trading Inc .... E 704 375-3333
   Concord *(G-4241)*
▲ Crawford Knitting Company Inc .... D 336 824-1065
   Ramseur *(G-13442)*
Custom Socks Ink Inc .... E 828 695-9869
   Newton *(G-11929)*
De Feet International Inc .... E 828 397-7025
   Hildebran *(G-8621)*
▲ Devmir Legwear Inc .... G 919 545-5500
   Pittsboro *(G-12338)*

SIC SECTION
22 TEXTILE MILL PRODUCTS

Diabetic Sock Club .... G 800 214-0218
   Belmont *(G-984)*

Elder Hosiery Mills Inc .... F 336 226-0673
   Burlington *(G-1409)*

Farr Knitting Company Inc .... G 336 625-5561
   Asheboro *(G-433)*

Felice Hosiery Co Inc .... E 336 996-2371
   Kernersville *(G-9200)*

Fine Sheer Industries Inc .... B 704 375-3333
   Concord *(G-4265)*

◆ Gold Toe Stores Inc .... G 828 464-0751
   Newton *(G-11936)*

◆ Goldtoemoretz LLC .... B 828 464-0751
   Newton *(G-11937)*

Grady Distributing Co Inc .... F 919 556-5630
   Youngsville *(G-17083)*

◆ Graham Dyeing & Finishing Inc .... D 336 228-9981
   Burlington *(G-1426)*

Hanesbrands Inc .... G 336 789-6118
   Mount Airy *(G-11515)*

Hanesbrands Inc .... C 336 519-8080
   Rural Hall *(G-13843)*

Hanesbrands Inc .... A 336 519-8080
   Winston Salem *(G-16734)*

Harriss & Covington Hsy Mills .... G 336 882-6811
   High Point *(G-8376)*

◆ Harriss Cvington Hsy Mills Inc .... C 336 882-6811
   High Point *(G-8377)*

▼ Hill Hosiery Mill Inc .... F 336 472-7908
   Thomasville *(G-15230)*

Hillshire Brands Company .... G 336 519-8080
   Winston Salem *(G-16746)*

◆ Holt Hosiery Mills Inc .... C 336 227-1431
   Burlington *(G-1428)*

▲ Huffman Finishing Company Inc .... C 828 396-1741
   Granite Falls *(G-6739)*

Huitt Mills Inc .... E 828 322-8628
   Hildebran *(G-8624)*

Implus LLC .... F 828 485-3318
   Hickory *(G-8064)*

▲ Iq Brands Inc .... F 336 751-0040
   Advance *(G-44)*

J R B and J Knitting Inc .... G 910 439-4242
   Mount Gilead *(G-11601)*

▲ Jefferies Socks LLC .... E 336 226-7316
   Burlington *(G-1440)*

▲ JI Hosiery LLC .... F 910 974-7156
   Candor *(G-1593)*

Just Sayin Socks LLC .... G 828 513-1517
   Flat Rock *(G-5966)*

◆ Kayser-Roth Corporation .... C 336 852-2030
   Greensboro *(G-7145)*

▲ Kayser-Roth Hosiery Inc .... E 336 229-2269
   Graham *(G-6696)*

Kayser-Roth Hosiery Inc .... E 336 852-2030
   Greensboro *(G-7146)*

KB Socks Inc .... E 336 719-8000
   Mount Airy *(G-11529)*

Kelly Hosiery Mill Inc .... G 828 324-6456
   Hickory *(G-8073)*

Knit Tech Inc .... G 336 584-8999
   Elon College *(G-5665)*

L & R Knitting Inc .... G 828 874-2960
   Hickory *(G-8081)*

Lakeside Dyeing & Finshg Inc .... G 336 229-0064
   Burlington *(G-1448)*

Legacy Knitting LLC .... G 844 762-2678
   Wilmington *(G-16296)*

Legend Compression Wear .... G 877 711-5343
   Denton *(G-4742)*

▲ Lyons Hosiery Inc .... F 336 789-2651
   Mount Airy *(G-11542)*

M Davis and Associates LLC .... G 336 337-7089
   Greensboro *(G-7172)*

Marcott Hosiery LLC .... E 704 485-8702
   Oakboro *(G-12077)*

▲ Mayo Knitting Mill Inc .... C 252 823-3101
   Tarboro *(G-15114)*

Michael Tate .... G 336 374-4695
   Mount Airy *(G-11546)*

Midpines Hosiery Inc .... G 919 774-3888
   Sanford *(G-14153)*

NC Quality Sales LLC .... F 336 786-7211
   Mount Airy *(G-11550)*

Neat Feet Hosiery Inc .... G 336 573-2177
   Stoneville *(G-14962)*

Nester Hosiery Inc .... D 336 789-0026
   Mount Airy *(G-11552)*

▲ Nester Hosiery LLC .... E 336 789-0026
   Mount Airy *(G-11553)*

North Carolina Sock Inc .... G 828 327-4664
   Hickory *(G-8104)*

O P S Holding Company LLC .... G 361 446-8376
   Pineville *(G-12286)*

Odd Sock Inc .... G 704 451-4298
   Davidson *(G-4689)*

On Foot Innovations LLC .... G 336 301-3732
   Charlotte *(G-3295)*

One Black Sock LLC .... G 919 967-6855
   Carrboro *(G-1652)*

◆ Parker Hosiery Company Inc .... E 828 668-7628
   Old Fort *(G-12104)*

Pickett Hosiery Mills Inc .... E 336 227-2716
   Burlington *(G-1472)*

R Evans Hosiery LLC .... E 828 397-3715
   Connelly Springs *(G-4408)*

Renfro LLC .... D 336 719-8290
   Mount Airy *(G-11562)*

Renfro LLC .... E 336 786-3000
   Mount Airy *(G-11564)*

◆ Renfro LLC .... B 336 719-8000
   Mount Airy *(G-11563)*

Renfro Mexico Holdings LLC .... F 336 786-3501
   Mount Airy *(G-11565)*

Riverside Knitting Dept .... G 336 719-8252
   Mount Airy *(G-11566)*

Robinson Hosiery Mill Inc .... F 828 874-2228
   Valdese *(G-15453)*

▲ Robinwood Enterprises .... G 910 571-0145
   Troy *(G-15412)*

▲ Royal Hosiery Company Inc .... G 828 496-2200
   Granite Falls *(G-6755)*

Royal Textile Mills Inc .... D 336 694-4121
   Yanceyville *(G-17065)*

◆ Royce Too LLC .... E 212 356-1627
   Winston Salem *(G-16891)*

Russell-Fshion Foot Hsy Mlls I .... G 336 299-0741
   Troy *(G-15413)*

Sara Lee Socks .... G 336 789-6118
   Mount Airy *(G-11570)*

School Team Socks .... G 704 500-1738
   Charlotte *(G-3507)*

Serving Our Cmnty Kids Scks SC ...... G 704 814-4704
   Charlotte *(G-3530)*

Simmons Hosiery Mill Inc .... G 828 327-4890
   Hickory *(G-8157)*

◆ Slane Hosiery Mills Inc .... C 336 883-4136
   High Point *(G-8538)*

So & So Socks .... G 919 437-6458
   Raleigh *(G-13274)*

Sock Basket LLC .... G 828 251-7072
   Asheville *(G-779)*

Sock Factory Inc .... E 828 328-5207
   Hickory *(G-8161)*

Sock Inc .... G 561 254-2223
   Charlotte *(G-3576)*

Socks and Other Things LLC .... G 704 904-2472
   Charlotte *(G-3577)*

Socks Vterinary Hse Calls Pllc .... G 919 244-2826
   Cary *(G-1898)*

Special T Hosiery Mills Inc .... G 336 227-2858
   Burlington *(G-1499)*

Sports Solutions Inc .... F 336 368-1100
   Pilot Mountain *(G-12202)*

▲ Star America Inc .... C 704 788-4700
   Concord *(G-4367)*

Step In Sock .... G 704 508-9966
   Belmont *(G-1011)*

Surratt Hosiery Mill Inc .... F 336 859-4583
   Denton *(G-4751)*

Teamwork Inc .... G 336 578-3456
   Elon *(G-5662)*

Thorneburg Hosiery Mills Inc .... E 704 279-7247
   Rockwell *(G-13661)*

Thorneburg Hosiery Mills Inc .... E 704 872-6522
   Statesville *(G-14911)*

Thorneburg Hosiery Mills Inc .... E 704 838-6329
   Statesville *(G-14913)*

◆ Thorneburg Hosiery Mills Inc .... C 704 872-6522
   Statesville *(G-14912)*

Trimfit Inc .... C 336 476-6154
   Thomasville *(G-15296)*

Trinity Sock Group LLC .... G 336 226-0237
   Burlington *(G-1508)*

Tysinger Hosiery Mill Inc .... F 336 472-2148
   Lexington *(G-9798)*

Upel Inc .... E 336 519-8080
   Winston Salem *(G-16960)*

US Custom Socks Co LLC .... G 336 549-1088
   Greensboro *(G-7433)*

◆ Ward Hosiery Company Inc .... G 828 381-2346
   Hickory *(G-8206)*

◆ Wells Hosiery Mills Inc .... C 336 633-4881
   Asheboro *(G-510)*

▲ Wilson Brown Inc .... F 336 226-0237
   Burlington *(G-1518)*

Woodland Hosiery Inc .... G 910 439-4843
   Mount Gilead *(G-11616)*

2253 Knit outerwear mills

Associated Distributors Inc .... G 910 895-5800
   Hamlet *(G-7616)*

B & J Knits Inc .... G 704 876-1498
   Statesville *(G-14756)*

Ba International LLC .... E 336 519-8080
   Winston Salem *(G-16621)*

Belevation LLC .... F 803 517-9030
   Biscoe *(G-1104)*

Blue Bay Distributing Inc .... G 919 957-1300
   Durham *(G-4966)*

Blue Lagoon Inc .... G 828 324-2333
   Hickory *(G-7951)*

C & L Manufacturing .... G 336 957-8359
   Hays *(G-7773)*

◆ Charlotte Trimming Company Inc .. D 704 529-8427
   Charlotte *(G-2465)*

Contempora Fabrics Inc .... C 910 345-0150
   Lumberton *(G-10030)*

Diamond Apparel .... G 866 578-9708
   Advance *(G-41)*

▲ Gerbings LLC .... D 800 646-5916
   Greensboro *(G-7039)*

Hanesbrands Inc .... G 910 462-2001
   Laurel Hill *(G-9460)*

Hanesbrands Inc .... A 336 519-8080
   Winston Salem *(G-16734)*

22 TEXTILE MILL PRODUCTS

Hbi Sourcing LLC .... F 336 519-8080
  Winston Salem (G-16739)
Hbi Wh Minority Holdings LLC .... F 336 519-8080
  Winston Salem (G-16740)
Hillshire Brands Company .... G 336 519-8080
  Winston Salem (G-16746)
Hugger Inc .... C 704 735-7422
  Lincolnton (G-9895)
Innovaknits LLC .... G 828 536-9348
  Conover (G-4467)
◆ Kamp Usa Inc .... F 336 668-1169
  High Point (G-8421)
Knitwear America Inc .... G 704 396-1193
  Granite Falls (G-6741)
◆ L C Industries Inc .... C 919 596-8277
  Durham (G-5185)
Mitt S Nitts Inc .... E 919 596-6793
  Durham (G-5229)
Noble Wholesalers Inc .... G 409 739-3803
  Clayton (G-4001)
▲ Park Shirt Company .... F 931 879-5894
  Fayetteville (G-5894)
Pitman Knits Inc .... G 704 276-3262
  Vale (G-15470)
Playtex Dorado LLC .... F 336 519-8080
  Winston Salem (G-16858)
Royal Textile Mills Inc .... D 336 694-4121
  Yanceyville (G-17065)
Slum Dog Head Gear LLC .... F 704 713-8125
  Charlotte (G-3565)
Textile Piece Dyeing Co Inc .... C 704 732-4200
  Lincolnton (G-9927)
Thb Leisure LLC .... G 828 926-8484
  Waynesville (G-15828)
Upel Inc .... E 336 519-8080
  Winston Salem (G-16960)
Wings Store 765 .... F 910 458-0278
  Carolina Beach (G-1642)
◆ Winstn-Slem Inds For Blind Inc .... B 336 759-0551
  Winston Salem (G-16979)
▲ Xtinguish LLC .... F 704 868-9500
  Charlotte (G-3838)

2254 Knit underwear mills

Hillshire Brands Company .... G 336 519-8080
  Winston Salem (G-16746)
Verena Designs Inc .... E 336 869-8235
  High Point (G-8593)

2257 Weft knit fabric mills

◆ Carolina Mills Incorporated .... B 828 428-9911
  Maiden (G-10102)
Century Textile Mfg Inc .... F 704 869-6660
  Gastonia (G-6373)
Contempora Fabrics Inc .... G 910 345-0150
  Lumberton (G-10030)
Early Bird Hosiery Mills Inc .... F 828 324-6745
  Hickory (G-8015)
Heritage Knitting Co LLC .... E 704 872-7653
  Statesville (G-14812)
◆ Innofa Usa LLC .... E 336 635-2900
  Eden (G-5492)
Innovaknits LLC .... G 828 536-9348
  Conover (G-4467)
Innovative Knitting LLC .... E 336 350-8122
  Burlington (G-1438)
Knit-Wear Fabrics Inc .... F 336 226-4342
  Burlington (G-1444)
Luray Textiles Inc .... E 336 670-3725
  North Wilkesboro (G-12025)
▲ McMurray Fabrics Inc .... C 910 944-2128
  Aberdeen (G-11)

Mocaro Dyeing & Finishing Inc .... D 704 878-6645
  Statesville (G-14844)
Mocaro Industries Inc .... E 704 878-6645
  Statesville (G-14845)
New River Fabrics Inc .... G 704 462-1401
  Lawndale (G-9502)
▲ Ramseur Inter-Lock Knitting Co .... F 336 824-2427
  Asheboro (G-470)
Russ Knits Inc .... F 910 974-4114
  Candor (G-1598)
Sdfc LLC .... F 704 878-6645
  Monroe (G-10804)
South Fork Industries Inc .... D 828 428-9921
  Maiden (G-10117)
Tommys Tubing & Stockenettes .... F 336 449-6461
  Gibsonville (G-6572)
Toms Knit Fabrics .... G 704 867-4236
  Gastonia (G-6527)
Unifour Finishers Inc .... E 828 322-9435
  Hickory (G-8194)
Unifour Finishers Inc .... E 828 322-9435
  Hickory (G-8193)

2258 Lace and warp knit fabric mills

◆ Gildan Activewear (eden) Inc .... C 336 623-9555
  Eden (G-5491)
◆ Guilford Mills LLC .... A 910 794-5810
  Wilmington (G-16243)
Hornwood Inc .... E 704 694-3009
  Wadesboro (G-15512)
◆ Hornwood Inc .... B 704 848-4121
  Lilesville (G-9838)
Innovaknits LLC .... G 828 536-9348
  Conover (G-4467)
Knit-Wear Fabrics Inc .... F 336 226-4342
  Burlington (G-1444)
Lear Corporation .... E 910 296-8671
  Kenansville (G-9144)
Lear Corporation .... A 910 794-5810
  Wilmington (G-16294)
▼ McComb Industries Lllp .... D 336 229-9139
  Burlington (G-1458)
▼ Mohican Mills Inc .... B 704 735-3343
  Lincolnton (G-9908)
Shodja Textiles Inc .... G 910 914-0456
  Whiteville (G-15976)
▲ Supertex Inc .... E 336 622-1000
  Liberty (G-9833)
▲ Uwharrie Knits Inc .... F 704 474-4123
  Norwood (G-12047)
Warp Technologies Inc .... C 919 552-2311
  Holly Springs (G-8726)
Whiteville Fabrics LLC .... F 910 639-4444
  Whiteville (G-15979)
▲ Whiteville Fabrics LLC .... F 910 914-0456
  Whiteville (G-15978)

2259 Knitting mills, nec

Adele Knits Inc .... C 336 499-6010
  Winston Salem (G-16589)
Brookline Inc .... G 704 824-1390
  Cramerton (G-4600)
Compton Tape & Label Inc .... F 336 548-4400
  Madison (G-10070)
Coville Inc .... F 336 759-0115
  Winston Salem (G-16664)
▲ Gloves-Online Inc .... G 919 468-4244
  Cary (G-1775)
Griffin Tubing Company Inc .... G 336 449-4822
  Gibsonville (G-6560)
Mitt S Nitts Inc .... E 919 596-6793
  Durham (G-5229)

▲ Paceline Inc .... E 704 290-5007
  Matthews (G-10280)
Shelby Elastics of North Carolina LLC ..... D 704 487-4301
  Shelby (G-14364)
Tommys Tubing & Stockenettes .... F 336 449-6461
  Gibsonville (G-6572)
◆ United Glove Inc .... E 828 464-2510
  Newton (G-11981)

2261 Finishing plants, cotton

▲ Advanced Digital Textiles LLC .... E 704 226-9600
  Monroe (G-10636)
Barron Legacy Mgmt Group LLC .... G 301 367-4735
  Charlotte (G-2285)
Bread & Butter Custom Scrn Prt .... G 919 942-3198
  Chapel Hill (G-1995)
◆ Burlington Industries LLC .... C 336 379-6220
  Greensboro (G-6865)
Century Textile Mfg Inc .... F 704 869-6660
  Gastonia (G-6373)
Dawn Processing Company Inc .... G 704 629-5321
  Bessemer City (G-1062)
▲ Daztech Inc .... G 800 862-6360
  Wilmington (G-16196)
▲ Deep Rver Mlls Ctd Fabrics Inc .... F 910 464-3135
  Greensboro (G-6964)
Gaston Screen Printing Inc .... F 704 399-0459
  Charlotte (G-2810)
◆ Glen Raven Inc .... G 336 227-6211
  Burlington (G-1423)
Glen Rven Tchnical Fabrics LLC .... C 336 229-5576
  Burlington (G-1425)
▼ Graphic Attack Inc .... G 252 491-2174
  Harbinger (G-7683)
◆ Hanes Companies Inc .... C 336 747-1600
  Winston Salem (G-16732)
◆ Holt Sublimation Prtg Pdts Inc .... G 336 222-3600
  Burlington (G-1429)
▲ Huffman Finishing Company Inc .... C 828 396-1741
  Granite Falls (G-6739)
◆ Hydromer Inc .... E 908 526-2828
  Concord (G-4282)
◆ Itg Holdings Inc .... A 336 379-6220
  Greensboro (G-7126)
K Formula Enterprises Inc .... G 910 323-3315
  Fayetteville (G-5853)
Lakeside Dyeing & Finshg Inc .... G 336 229-0064
  Burlington (G-1448)
Marvin Bailey Screen Printing .... G 252 335-1554
  Elizabeth City (G-5556)
McMurray Fabrics Inc .... D 704 732-9613
  Lincolnton (G-9906)
Moire Creations America LLC .... E 704 482-9860
  Shelby (G-14349)
Mojo Sportswear Inc .... G 252 758-4176
  Greenville (G-7562)
One Hundred Ten Percent Screen .... G 252 728-3848
  Beaufort (G-963)
Raleigh Tees .... G 919 850-3378
  Raleigh (G-13187)
Richard E Page .... G 704 988-7090
  Charlotte (G-3450)
S & L Creations Inc .... G 704 824-1930
  Lowell (G-10011)
Screen Master .... G 252 492-8407
  Henderson (G-7810)
Silverlining Screen Prtrs Inc .... G 919 554-0340
  Youngsville (G-17097)
South Fork Industries Inc .... D 828 428-9921
  Maiden (G-10117)
T & R Signs .... G 919 779-1185
  Garner (G-6317)

SIC SECTION

22 TEXTILE MILL PRODUCTS

Tex-Tech Coatings LLC .... F 336 992-7500
  Kernersville (G-9243)
Thermal Control Products Inc .... E 704 454-7605
  Concord (G-4376)
Travis L Bunker .... G 336 352-3289
  Mount Airy (G-11589)
Trelleborg Ctd Systems US Inc .... C 864 576-1210
  Rutherfordton (G-13894)
Tryon Finishing Corporation .... F 828 859-5891
  Tryon (G-15429)
Tsg Finishing LLC .... E 828 328-5522
  Hickory (G-8188)
Tsg Finishing LLC .... D 828 328-5535
  Hickory (G-8189)
▲ Ultimate Textile Inc .... E 828 286-8880
  Rutherfordton (G-13898)
Unifour Finishers Inc .... E 828 322-9435
  Hickory (G-8194)
Unifour Finishers Inc .... E 828 322-9435
  Hickory (G-8193)
◆ Ward Hosiery Company Inc .... G 828 381-2346
  Hickory (G-8206)
▲ Xtinguish LLC .... F 704 868-9500
  Charlotte (G-3838)

2262 Finishing plants, manmade

▲ Advanced Digital Textiles LLC ..... E 704 226-9600
  Monroe (G-10636)
◆ Burlington Industries LLC .... C 336 379-6220
  Greensboro (G-6865)
Cedar Valley Finishing Co Inc .... F 704 289-9546
  Monroe (G-10679)
◆ Commercial Seaming Co Inc .... F 252 492-6178
  Henderson (G-7779)
Custom Screens Inc .... E 336 427-0265
  Madison (G-10071)
Gaston Screen Printing Inc .... F 704 399-0459
  Charlotte (G-2810)
◆ Hanes Companies Inc .... C 336 747-1600
  Winston Salem (G-16732)
◆ Holt Sublimation Prtg Pdts Inc ..... F 336 222-3600
  Burlington (G-1429)
▲ Huffman Finishing Company Inc .. C 828 396-1741
  Granite Falls (G-6739)
◆ Itg Holdings Inc .... A 336 379-6220
  Greensboro (G-7126)
McMurray Fabrics Inc .... D 704 732-9613
  Lincolnton (G-9906)
Moire Creations America LLC .... E 704 482-9860
  Shelby (G-14349)
◆ Precision Fabrics Group Inc .... E 336 281-3049
  Greensboro (G-7274)
Printology Signs Graphics LLC ...... G 843 473-4984
  Davidson (G-4691)
▲ Spoonflower Inc .... D 919 886-7885
  Durham (G-5370)
Upper South Studio Inc .... F 336 724-5480
  Winston Salem (G-16961)
Visigraphix Inc .... G 336 882-1935
  Colfax (G-4162)
Weaveup Inc .... G 443 540-4201
  Durham (G-5439)

2269 Finishing plants, nec

▲ Advanced Digital Textiles LLC ..... E 704 226-9600
  Monroe (G-10636)
Beth Wiseman .... G 704 735-4469
  Lincolnton (G-9875)
Bridgport Restoration Svcs Inc .... F 336 996-1212
  Kernersville (G-9169)
Carolina Dyeing and Finshg LLC .... E 336 227-2770
  Burlington (G-1385)

Carolina Yarn Processors Inc .... C 828 859-5891
  Tryon (G-15422)
Celand Yarn Dyers Inc .... G 336 472-4400
  Thomasville (G-15201)
Creative Label Solutions Inc .... G 828 320-5389
  Hickory (G-7999)
D & F Consolidated Inc .... G 704 664-6660
  Statesville (G-14781)
Dale Advertising Inc .... G 704 484-0971
  Shelby (G-14310)
Dawn Processing Company Inc ..... G 704 629-5321
  Bessemer City (G-1062)
Glen Rven Tchnical Fabrics LLC .... C 336 229-5576
  Burlington (G-1425)
▲ Grover Industries Inc .... F 828 859-9125
  Grover (G-7608)
▲ Insect Shield LLC .... E 336 272-4157
  Greensboro (G-7118)
Lakeside Dyeing & Finshg Inc .... G 336 229-0064
  Burlington (G-1448)
Minnewawa Inc .... F 865 522-8103
  Thomasville (G-15252)
Mocaro Industries Inc .... E 704 878-6645
  Statesville (G-14845)
Moire Creations America LLC .... E 704 482-9860
  Shelby (G-14349)
South Fork Industries Inc .... D 828 428-9921
  Maiden (G-10117)
▲ Spartan Dyers Inc .... D 704 829-0467
  Belmont (G-1009)
Tsg Finishing LLC .... D 828 328-5535
  Hickory (G-8189)
▲ Ultimate Textile Inc .... E 828 286-8880
  Rutherfordton (G-13898)
Unifi Inc .... D 336 348-6539
  Reidsville (G-13544)
US Label Corporation .... E 336 332-7000
  Greensboro (G-7434)
Westpoint Home Inc .... B 910 369-2231
  Wagram (G-15524)

2273 Carpets and rugs

Aladdin Manufacturing Corp .... A 336 623-6000
  Eden (G-5485)
Anchored Home Inc .... G 910 769-7092
  Wilmington (G-16111)
▲ Bellaire Dynamik LLC .... G 704 779-3755
  Charlotte (G-2299)
◆ Burlington Industries LLC .... C 336 379-6220
  Greensboro (G-6865)
◆ Capel Incorporated .... D 910 572-7000
  Troy (G-15402)
Colonial Braided Rug Co NC .... G 704 538-1824
  Shelby (G-14300)
Columbia Forest Products Inc .... G 336 605-0429
  Greensboro (G-6920)
Country Heart Braiding .... G 828 245-0562
  Rutherfordton (G-13870)
▲ Davis Rug Company .... G 704 434-7231
  Shelby (G-14311)
▲ Due Process Stable Trdg Co LLC . E 910 608-0284
  Lumberton (G-10032)
◆ Elevate Textiles Inc .... F 336 379-6220
  Charlotte (G-2693)
Elevate Textiles Holding Corp .... D 336 379-6220
  Charlotte (G-2694)
Flint Hill Textiles Inc .... G 704 434-9331
  Shelby (G-14318)
Furniture Fair Inc .... E 910 455-4044
  Jacksonville (G-9001)
◆ Glenoit Universal Ltd .... C 919 735-7111
  Goldsboro (G-6616)

▲ Grund America LLC .... E 704 287-1805
  Matthews (G-10319)
▲ Hampton Capital Partners LLC .... A
  Aberdeen (G-6)
Horizon Home Imports Inc .... G 704 859-5133
  Clemmons (G-4046)
◆ Itg Holdings Inc .... A 336 379-6220
  Greensboro (G-7126)
Karastan .... G 336 627-7200
  Eden (G-5493)
▲ Michaelian & Kohlberg Inc .... G 828 891-8511
  Horse Shoe (G-8741)
Mohawk Industries Inc .... G 919 609-4759
  Garner (G-6289)
Mohawk Industries Inc .... F 919 661-5590
  Garner (G-6290)
Pasb Inc .... G 704 490-2556
  Kannapolis (G-9129)
Raleigh Area Masters .... G 919 233-6713
  Raleigh (G-13173)
Royal Textile Mills Inc .... D 336 694-4121
  Yanceyville (G-17065)
Rug & Home Inc .... G 828 785-4480
  Asheville (G-760)
Shaw Industries Inc .... B 828 369-1701
  Franklin (G-6143)
Shaw Industries Group Inc .... E 877 996-5942
  Charlotte (G-3536)
Shaw Industries Group Inc .... E 877 996-5942
  Charlotte (G-3537)
Sorrells Sheree White .... G 828 452-4864
  Waynesville (G-15825)
▲ White Oak Carpet Mills Inc .... G 828 287-8892
  Spindale (G-14611)

2281 Yarn spinning mills

American & Efird LLC .... F 704 864-0977
  Gastonia (G-6343)
American & Efird LLC .... F 828 754-9066
  Lenoir (G-9572)
◆ Aquafil OMara Inc .... C 828 874-2100
  Rutherford College (G-13858)
◆ Carolina Mills Incorporated .... B 828 428-9911
  Maiden (G-10102)
Carolina Mills Warehouse .... G 828 428-9911
  Maiden (G-10103)
▲ Charles Craft Inc .... G 910 844-3521
  Laurinburg (G-9474)
◆ Coats & Clark Inc .... D 704 542-5959
  Charlotte (G-2512)
▲ Coats HP Inc .... B 704 824-9904
  Mc Adenville (G-10377)
Coats HP Inc .... E 704 329-5800
  Charlotte (G-2514)
▲ Coats N Amer De Rpblica Dmncan.. C 800 242-8095
  Charlotte (G-2515)
◆ Cs Carolina Inc .... G 336 578-0110
  Burlington (G-1402)
Cumins Machinery Corp .... G 336 622-1000
  Liberty (G-9809)
Dawn Processing Company Inc ..... G 704 629-5321
  Bessemer City (G-1062)
Fiber-Line LLC .... D 828 326-8700
  Hickory (G-8023)
▲ Filtec Precise Inc .... E 910 653-5200
  Tabor City (G-15082)
Frontier Yarns Inc .... D 919 776-9940
  Sanford (G-14122)
Frontier Yarns Inc .... E 919 776-9940
  Sanford (G-14121)
◆ Fsm Liquidation Corp .... A 919 776-9940
  Sanford (G-14123)

22 TEXTILE MILL PRODUCTS

◆ Gildan Yarns LLC .... G 704 633-5133
Salisbury *(G-13968)*

◆ Glen Raven Inc .... C 336 227-6211
Burlington *(G-1423)*

Glen Rven Tchnical Fabrics LLC .... C 336 229-5576
Burlington *(G-1425)*

Grateful Union Family Inc .... F 828 622-3258
Asheville *(G-640)*

Grp Inc .... G 919 776-9940
Sanford *(G-14128)*

▲ Hampton Art Inc .... C 252 975-7207
Washington *(G-15709)*

▲ Hickory Dyg & Winding Co Inc .... F 828 322-1550
Hickory *(G-8047)*

◆ Hickory Throwing Company .... E 828 322-1158
Hickory *(G-8055)*

Invista Capital Management LLC .... D 704 636-6000
Salisbury *(G-13989)*

Kordsa Inc .... C 910 462-2051
Laurel Hill *(G-9462)*

Krodsa USA Inc .... A 910 462-2041
Laurel Hill *(G-9463)*

Mannington Mills Inc .... E 704 824-3551
Mc Adenville *(G-10379)*

Marilyn Cook .... G 704 735-4414
Lincolnton *(G-9905)*

Meridian Industries Inc .... E 704 824-7880
Gastonia *(G-6460)*

Milliken & Company .... E 828 247-4300
Bostic *(G-1265)*

Milliken & Company .... F 336 548-5680
Mayodan *(G-10366)*

National Spinning Co Inc .... C 910 298-3131
Beulaville *(G-1097)*

National Spinning Co Inc .... C 336 226-0141
Burlington *(G-1467)*

National Spinning Co Inc .... C 910 642-4181
Whiteville *(G-15972)*

◆ National Spinning Co Inc .... C 252 975-7111
Washington *(G-15717)*

▲ National Spnning Oprations LLC .... F 252 975-7111
Washington *(G-15718)*

◆ Normtex Incorporated .... G 828 428-3363
Wilmington *(G-16341)*

▲ North Crlina Spnning Mills Inc .... E 704 732-1171
Lincolnton *(G-9911)*

Oakdale Cotton Mills .... G 336 454-1144
Jamestown *(G-9065)*

◆ Parkdale Incorporated .... C 704 874-5000
Gastonia *(G-6484)*

Parkdale America LLC .... E 704 739-7411
Kings Mountain *(G-9321)*

◆ Parkdale America LLC .... A 704 874-5000
Gastonia *(G-6485)*

Parkdale Mills Incorporated .... E 704 825-5324
Belmont *(G-998)*

Parkdale Mills Incorporated .... D 704 913-3917
Belmont *(G-999)*

Parkdale Mills Incorporated .... F 704 825-2529
Belmont *(G-1000)*

Parkdale Mills Incorporated .... E 704 739-7411
Kings Mountain *(G-9322)*

Parkdale Mills Incorporated .... E 704 855-3164
Landis *(G-9452)*

Parkdale Mills Incorporated .... E 336 243-2141
Lexington *(G-9768)*

Parkdale Mills Incorporated .... E 704 292-1255
Mineral Springs *(G-10519)*

Parkdale Mills Incorporated .... E 704 822-0778
Mount Holly *(G-11646)*

Parkdale Mills Incorporated .... D 919 774-7401
Sanford *(G-14163)*

Parkdale Mills Incorporated .... D 336 476-3181
Thomasville *(G-15261)*

Parkdale Mills Incorporated .... D 336 591-4644
Walnut Cove *(G-15635)*

◆ Parkdale Mills Incorporated .... D 704 874-5000
Gastonia *(G-6486)*

Parkdale Mills Inc .... E 704 857-3456
Landis *(G-9453)*

◆ Patrick Yarn Mill Inc .... C 704 739-4119
Kings Mountain *(G-9324)*

Pearson Textiles Inc .... G 919 776-8730
Sanford *(G-14165)*

Pharr McAdenville Corporation .... D 704 824-3551
Mc Adenville *(G-10380)*

▲ Richmond Specialty Yarns LLC .... C 910 652-5554
Ellerbe *(G-5643)*

Robinson Manufacturing Company .... E 252 335-2985
Elizabeth City *(G-5568)*

Rocky Mount Mill LLC .... F 919 890-6000
Raleigh *(G-13213)*

Sgrtex LLC .... D 336 635-9420
Eden *(G-5502)*

Shuford Yarns LLC .... C 828 396-2342
Granite Falls *(G-6757)*

▲ Shuford Yarns LLC .... D 828 324-4265
Hickory *(G-8151)*

Shuford Yarns Management Inc .... G 828 324-4265
Hickory *(G-8152)*

Spinrite Yarns LP .... A 252 833-4970
Washington *(G-15732)*

Summit Yarn LLC .... A 704 874-5000
Gastonia *(G-6517)*

◆ Supreme Elastic Corporation .... E 828 302-3836
Conover *(G-4502)*

◆ Tuscarora Yarns Inc .... B 704 436-6527
Mount Pleasant *(G-11680)*

Unifi Inc .... C 336 427-1890
Madison *(G-10090)*

Unifi Inc .... D 336 348-6539
Reidsville *(G-13544)*

Unifi Inc .... G 919 774-7401
Sanford *(G-14202)*

Unifi Inc .... C 336 679-3830
Yadkinville *(G-17058)*

◆ Unifi Inc .... D 336 294-4410
Greensboro *(G-7427)*

Unifi Manufacturing Inc .... A 336 427-1515
Yadkinville *(G-17059)*

Unifi Manufacturing Inc .... A 336 679-8891
Yadkinville *(G-17060)*

◆ Unifi Manufacturing Inc .... C 336 294-4410
Greensboro *(G-7428)*

Universal Fibers Inc .... A 336 672-2600
Asheboro *(G-503)*

▲ World Elastic Corporation .... E 704 786-9508
Concord *(G-4391)*

World Fibers Inc .... G 704 788-3017
Concord *(G-4392)*

World Fibers Inc .... G 704 788-3017
Concord *(G-4393)*

◆ Zimmermann - Dynayarn Usa LLC ..... E 336 222-8129
Graham *(G-6717)*

2282 Throwing and winding mills

◆ Aquafil OMara Inc .... C 828 874-2100
Rutherford College *(G-13858)*

BA Robbins Company LLC .... G 828 466-3900
Newton *(G-11914)*

◆ C S America Inc .... E
Burlington *(G-1382)*

▲ Coats HP Inc .... B 704 824-9904
Mc Adenville *(G-10377)*

Coats HP Inc .... E 704 329-5800
Charlotte *(G-2514)*

Glen Raven Inc .... G 336 227-6211
Altamahaw *(G-122)*

▲ Hickory Dyg & Winding Co Inc .... F 828 322-1550
Hickory *(G-8047)*

◆ Hickory Throwing Company .... E 828 322-1158
Hickory *(G-8055)*

◆ J Charles Saunders Co Inc .... E 704 866-9156
Gastonia *(G-6432)*

Keel Labs Inc .... G 917 848-9066
Morrisville *(G-11365)*

Lear Corporation .... E 910 296-8671
Kenansville *(G-9144)*

Marilyn Cook .... G 704 735-4414
Lincolnton *(G-9905)*

Material Return LLC .... G 828 234-5368
Morganton *(G-11231)*

◆ Meridian Spcalty Yrn Group Inc .... B 828 874-2151
Valdese *(G-15450)*

National Spinning Co Inc .... C 910 298-3131
Beulaville *(G-1097)*

New Generation Yarn Corp .... F 336 449-5607
Gibsonville *(G-6568)*

▲ Owens Crning Nn-Woven Tech LLC .. F 740 321-6131
Dallas *(G-4650)*

Parkdale Mills Incorporated .... F 704 825-2529
Belmont *(G-1000)*

Pharr McAdenville Corporation .... D 704 824-3551
Mc Adenville *(G-10380)*

▲ Polyspintex Inc .... G 704 523-4382
Charlotte *(G-3355)*

◆ Premiere Fibers LLC .... C 704 826-8321
Ansonville *(G-155)*

Sack-UPS Corporation .... F 828 584-4579
Morganton *(G-11249)*

Sam M Butler Inc .... E 704 364-8647
Charlotte *(G-3487)*

Sam M Butler Inc .... E 910 276-2360
Laurinburg *(G-9494)*

Sapona Manufacturing Co Inc .... C 336 873-8700
Asheboro *(G-476)*

◆ Sapona Manufacturing Co Inc .... E 336 625-2727
Cedar Falls *(G-1969)*

Unifi Inc .... C 336 679-3830
Yadkinville *(G-17058)*

◆ Unifi Inc .... D 336 294-4410
Greensboro *(G-7427)*

2284 Thread mills

Alpek Polyester Usa LLC .... B 910 371-4000
Wilmington *(G-16108)*

American & Efird Global LLC .... E 704 827-4311
Mount Holly *(G-11617)*

American & Efird LLC .... F 704 864-0977
Gastonia *(G-6343)*

American & Efird LLC .... F 704 867-3664
Gastonia *(G-6344)*

American & Efird LLC .... F 828 754-9066
Lenoir *(G-9572)*

American & Efird LLC .... F 704 827-4311
Mount Holly *(G-11618)*

American & Efird LLC .... F 704 823-2501
Mount Holly *(G-11620)*

▲ American & Efird LLC .... C 704 827-4311
Mount Holly *(G-11619)*

◆ Coats & Clark Inc .... D 704 542-5959
Charlotte *(G-2512)*

▲ Coats American Inc .... C 800 242-8095
Charlotte *(G-2513)*

▲ Coats N Amer De Rpblica Dmncan ... C 800 242-8095
Charlotte *(G-2515)*

Ctc Holdings LLC.................................... G 704 867-6611
Gastonia *(G-6390)*

Invista Capital Management LLC................ D 704 636-6000
Salisbury *(G-13989)*

◆ J Charles Saunders Co Inc........................E 704 866-9156
Gastonia *(G-6432)*

Ruddick Operating Company LLC................ A 704 372-5404
Charlotte *(G-3472)*

Sam M Butler Inc... E 704 364-8647
Charlotte *(G-3487)*

◆ Sam M Butler Inc...E 910 277-7456
Laurinburg *(G-9495)*

◆ Sans Technical Fibers LLC.........................E 704 869-8311
Gastonia *(G-6505)*

Seasons Inspirations .... G 336 990-0072
Wilkesboro *(G-16040)*

◆ Supreme Elastic Corporation........................ E 828 302-3836
Conover *(G-4502)*

Tangles Knitting On Main LLC..................... G 704 243-7150
Waxhaw *(G-15778)*

2295 Coated fabrics, not rubberized

▲ Athol Manufacturing Corp............................ F 919 575-6523
Butner *(G-1540)*

◆ Carlisle Corporation...................................... G..... 704 501-1100
Charlotte *(G-2390)*

Chase Laminating Inc................................... F 828 632-6666
Taylorsville *(G-15134)*

CMI Enterprises... G 305 685-9651
Forest City *(G-6064)*

◆ Compmillennia LLC......................................F 252 628-8065
Washington *(G-15693)*

Creative Dyeing & Finshg LLC..................... F 704 983-5555
Albemarle *(G-77)*

▲ Engineered Recycling Comp........................ E 704 358-6700
Charlotte *(G-2712)*

Fiber-Line LLC... D 828 326-8700
Hickory *(G-8023)*

Fs LLC.. E 919 309-9727
Durham *(G-5106)*

▲ Morbern USA Inc... E 336 883-4332
High Point *(G-8459)*

Nouveau Verre Holdings Inc........................ F 336 545-0011
Greensboro *(G-7224)*

Nvh Inc .... G 336 545-0011
Greensboro *(G-7228)*

Omnia LLC... G..... 919 696-2193
Oxford *(G-12138)*

▲ Parker Medical Associates LLC................. F 704 344-9998
Charlotte *(G-3313)*

Precision Textiles LLC.................................. C 336 861-0168
High Point *(G-8494)*

◆ Sam M Butler Inc..E 910 277-7456
Laurinburg *(G-9495)*

Shawmut Corporation.................................... F 336 229-5576
Burlington *(G-1493)*

Taylor Interiors LLC..................................... F 980 207-3160
Charlotte *(G-3674)*

Tosaf Aw Inc... D 980 533-3000
Bessemer City *(G-1088)*

Trelleborg Ctd Systems US Inc .... E 828 286-9126
Rutherfordton *(G-13895)*

▲ Trelleborg Ctd Systems US Inc .... C 828 286-9126
Rutherfordton *(G-13896)*

◆ Uretek LLC..E 203 468-0342
Rutherfordton *(G-13899)*

▲ Vescom America Inc .... E 252 431-6200
Henderson *(G-7816)*

2296 Tire cord and fabrics

◆ Burlan Manufacturing LLC..........................C 704 349-0000
Gastonia *(G-6362)*

▲ Hyosung Holdings Usa Inc.......................... G 704 790-6134
Charlotte *(G-2942)*

◆ Hyosung Usa Inc..E 704 790-6100
Charlotte *(G-2943)*

Tex-Tech Coatings LLC.............................. D 336 992-7500
Kernersville *(G-9242)*

Tex-Tech Coatings LLC.............................. F 336 992-7500
Kernersville *(G-9243)*

2297 Nonwoven fabrics

Advantage Nn-Wvens Cnvrting LL............ G 828 635-1880
Taylorsville *(G-15127)*

Allyn International Trdg Corp..................... G 877 858-2482
Marshville *(G-10210)*

◆ Avgol America Inc..C 336 936-2500
Mocksville *(G-10556)*

◆ Avintiv Inc...C 704 697-5100
Charlotte *(G-2249)*

Avintiv Specialty Mtls Inc........................... D 704 660-6242
Mooresville *(G-10867)*

◆ Avintiv Specialty Mtls Inc........................... A 704 697-5100
Charlotte *(G-2250)*

Berry Global Inc.. A 704 697-5100
Charlotte *(G-2302)*

▲ Carolina Nonwovens LLC........................... F 704 735-5600
Maiden *(G-10104)*

Chicopee Inc... G 919 894-4111
Benson *(G-1032)*

◆ Chicopee Inc...E 704 697-5100
Charlotte *(G-2476)*

Cumulus Fibres Inc...................................... B 704 394-2111
Charlotte *(G-2586)*

Dalco GF Technologies LLC...................... D 828 459-2577
Conover *(G-4445)*

◆ Dalco Gft Nonwovens LLC......................... D 828 459-2577
Conover *(G-4446)*

◆ Fiber Dynamics Inc...................................... D 336 886-7111
High Point *(G-8353)*

Fibrix LLC .... E 704 394-2111
Charlotte *(G-2758)*

Fibrix LLC... E 704 872-5223
Statesville *(G-14796)*

Fibrix LLC... E 704 878-0027
Statesville *(G-14797)*

▲ Freudenberg Nonwovens Lim..................... A 919 620-3900
Durham *(G-5103)*

Freudenberg Prfmce Mtls LP...................... C 828 665-5000
Candler *(G-1579)*

◆ Freudenberg Prfmce Mtls LP......................D 919 479-7443
Durham *(G-5104)*

▲ Glatfelter Inds Asheville Inc....................... D 828 670-0041
Candler *(G-1580)*

Glatflter Sntara Old Hckry Inc.................... F 615 526-2100
Charlotte *(G-2832)*

◆ Hanes Companies Inc..................................C 336 747-1600
Winston Salem *(G-16732)*

▲ Hendrix Batting Company............................ C 336 431-1181
High Point *(G-8382)*

Kem-Wove Inc.. E 704 588-0080
Charlotte *(G-3049)*

Lydall Inc... G 336 468-8522
Hamptonville *(G-7674)*

Lydall Inc... G 336 468-1323
Yadkinville *(G-17044)*

Mitt S Nitts Inc.. E 919 596-6793
Durham *(G-5229)*

Mountain International LLC......................... E 828 606-0194
Brevard *(G-1282)*

◆ Nutex Concepts NC Corp............................E 828 726-8801
Lenoir *(G-9643)*

◆ Pgi Polymer Inc...A 704 697-5100
Charlotte *(G-3336)*

◆ Polyvlies Usa Inc..E 336 769-0206
Winston Salem *(G-16860)*

◆ Printcraft Company Inc................................E 336 248-2544
Lexington *(G-9773)*

▲ Providencia Usa Inc..................................... D 704 881-2837
Statesville *(G-14872)*

◆ Saertex Usa LLC..E 704 464-5998
Huntersville *(G-8893)*

◆ Scorpio Acquisition Corp.............................E 704 697-5100
Charlotte *(G-3511)*

▲ Shalag US Inc.. D 919 690-0250
Oxford *(G-12155)*

◆ Tenowo Inc...F 704 732-3525
Lincolnton *(G-9925)*

◆ Twe Nonwovens Us Inc...............................E 336 431-7187
High Point *(G-8581)*

▲ Vitaflex LLC.. F 888 616-8848
Burlington *(G-1515)*

Warm Products Inc....................................... F 425 248-2424
Hendersonville *(G-7913)*

Westpoint Home Inc..................................... B 910 369-2231
Wagram *(G-15524)*

▲ Yanjan USA LLC.. C 704 380-6230
Statesville *(G-14931)*

2298 Cordage and twine

◆ Ace Marine Rigging & Supply Inc................F 252 726-6620
Morehead City *(G-11148)*

All American Braids Inc............................... E 704 852-4380
Gastonia *(G-6339)*

Apex Skip-Its LLC... G 919 270-1752
Apex *(G-163)*

Dayton Bag & Burlap Co.............................. G 704 873-7271
Statesville *(G-14783)*

Energy Management Insulation.................... F 828 894-3635
Columbus *(G-4173)*

Fusion Fiber Optics LLC.............................. G 252 933-5244
Kinston *(G-9367)*

◆ Hatteras Hammocks Inc...............................C 252 758-0641
Greenville *(G-7537)*

Jhrg Manufacturing LLC.............................. G 252 478-4977
Spring Hope *(G-14619)*

Ls Cable & System USA Inc....................... C 252 824-3553
Tarboro *(G-15112)*

MHS Ltd... G 336 767-2641
Winston Salem *(G-16807)*

MHS Ltd... F 336 767-2641
Winston Salem *(G-16808)*

Mills Manufacturing Corp............................ C 828 645-3061
Asheville *(G-703)*

Moon Audio.. G 919 649-5018
Cary *(G-1826)*

Oakdale Cotton Mills..................................... G 336 454-1144
Jamestown *(G-9065)*

Ravenox Rope... G 336 226-5260
Burlington *(G-1482)*

▲ Rocky Mount Cord Company...................... D 252 977-9130
Rocky Mount *(G-13731)*

Sackner Products Inc.................................. G 704 873-1086
Statesville *(G-14883)*

Sgb13 LLC.. F 844 627-5381
Burlington *(G-1492)*

Standard Tytape Company Inc................... F 828 693-6594
Hendersonville *(G-7906)*

▲ Yale Rope Technologies Inc....................... G 704 630-0331
Salisbury *(G-14068)*

2299 Textile goods, nec

▲ A Land of Furniture Inc............................... G 336 882-3866
High Point *(G-8229)*

▲ Azusa International Inc............................... G 704 879-4464
Gastonia *(G-6350)*

22 TEXTILE MILL PRODUCTS

◆ Barnhardt Manufacturing Company....C 800 277-0377
   Charlotte *(G-2283)*

Brandspeed..G 410 204-1032
   Mooresville *(G-10885)*

◆ Burke Mills Inc.......................................E 828 874-6341
   Valdese *(G-15442)*

Carbon Market Exchange LLC..................G 828 545-0140
   Asheville *(G-580)*

Creative Textiles Inc................................G 919 693-4427
   Oxford *(G-12123)*

Cumulus Fibres Inc....................................B 704 394-2111
   Charlotte *(G-2586)*

Custom Gears Inc.....................................G 704 735-6883
   Lincolnton *(G-9888)*

D2 Government Solutions LLC................E 662 655-4554
   New Bern *(G-11797)*

Dayton Bag & Burlap Co...........................G 704 873-7271
   Statesville *(G-14783)*

E By Design LLC......................................G 980 231-5483
   Cornelius *(G-4542)*

Everest Textile Usa LLC..........................E 828 245-2696
   Forest City *(G-6067)*

Fibrix LLC..E 704 394-2111
   Charlotte *(G-2758)*

Fibrix LLC..E 704 878-0027
   Statesville *(G-14797)*

Fimia Inc...G 828 697-8447
   Hendersonville *(G-7848)*

◆ Firestone Fibers Textiles LLC...............A 704 734-2110
   Kings Mountain *(G-9308)*

Global Products & Mfg Svcs Inc..............G 360 870-9876
   Charlotte *(G-2834)*

◆ Global Textile Alliance Inc....................G 336 217-1300
   Reidsville *(G-13520)*

▲ Hendrix Batting Company.....................C 336 431-1181
   High Point *(G-8382)*

▲ Hickory Business Furniture LLC..........B 828 328-2064
   Hickory *(G-8045)*

▼ High Point Fibers Inc............................E 336 887-8771
   High Point *(G-8390)*

▼ J E Herndon Company..........................E 704 739-4711
   Kings Mountain *(G-9310)*

Kem-Wove Inc..E 704 588-0080
   Charlotte *(G-3049)*

Kemmler Products Inc..............................G 704 663-5678
   Mooresville *(G-10995)*

Kids Playhouse LLC..................................G 704 299-4449
   Charlotte *(G-3053)*

Kimmys Customs LLC...............................G 904 699-2933
   Rural Hall *(G-13845)*

Kings Queens Plus Size Fashion.............G 704 223-4377
   Mooresville *(G-10999)*

Kloud Hemp Co..G 336 740-2528
   Greensboro *(G-7154)*

Legalize Pot Belly Pigs Co LLC................G 828 505-7053
   Asheville *(G-682)*

Leighdeux LLC...G 704 965-4889
   Charlotte *(G-3082)*

Northeast Textiles.....................................G 704 799-2235
   Mooresville *(G-11040)*

▲ Oakhurst Textiles Inc............................E 336 668-0733
   Greensboro *(G-7229)*

Opulence of Southern Pine......................G 919 467-1781
   Raleigh *(G-13088)*

Pearl Black Fashion Inc...........................G 252 689-6799
   Greenville *(G-7569)*

Performance Goods LLC..........................G 704 361-8600
   Harrisburg *(G-7721)*

▲ Polyspintex Inc......................................G 704 523-4382
   Charlotte *(G-3355)*

▲ Polyvlies Usa Inc...................................E 336 769-0206
   Winston Salem *(G-16860)*

Prime Syntex LLC......................................E 828 324-5496
   Thomasville *(G-15266)*

Regency Fibers LLC.................................E 828 459-7645
   Claremont *(G-3936)*

Renaissance Fiber LLC............................G 860 857-5987
   Winston Salem *(G-16883)*

S & S Samples Inc....................................G 336 472-0402
   Thomasville *(G-15273)*

Saluda Yarn Co Inc...................................F 828 749-2861
   Saluda *(G-14073)*

▲ Sample Group Inc..................................B 828 658-9040
   Weaverville *(G-15862)*

◆ Skeen Textiles Inc..................................F 336 884-4044
   High Point *(G-8536)*

Skeen Txtiles Auto Fabrics Inc................G 336 884-4044
   High Point *(G-8537)*

South Point Hospitality Inc......................F 704 542-2304
   Charlotte *(G-3586)*

Specialty Textiles Inc...............................G 704 710-8657
   Kings Mountain *(G-9332)*

Specialty Textiles Inc...............................C 704 739-4503
   Kings Mountain *(G-9333)*

▲ Spt Technology Inc...............................F 612 332-1880
   Monroe *(G-10811)*

◆ Spuntech Industries Inc........................C 336 330-9000
   Roxboro *(G-13825)*

▲ Sunrise Development LLC....................F 828 453-0590
   Mooresboro *(G-10841)*

Svcm... 305 767-3595
   Lincolnton *(G-9924)*

▲ Tex-Tech Industries Inc........................E 207 756-8606
   Kernersville *(G-9245)*

Textile Intl Entps LLC...............................G 336 545-0146
   Greensboro *(G-7397)*

◆ Vmod Fiber LLC......................................F 704 525-6851
   Charlotte *(G-3780)*

Wellington Leisure Products....................G 336 342-4701
   Pilot Mountain *(G-12205)*

William Barnet & Son LLC........................C 252 522-2418
   Kinston *(G-9393)*

Wind Defender LLC...................................G 410 913-4660
   Statesville *(G-14926)*

◆ World Fibers Inc.....................................G 704 786-9508
   Concord *(G-4394)*

Zonkd LLC..E 919 977-6463
   Raleigh *(G-13438)*

23 APPAREL, FINISHED PRODUCTS FROM FABRICS & SIMILAR MATERIALS

2311 Men's and boy's suits and coats

▼ American Safety Utility Corp................E 704 482-0601
   Shelby *(G-14285)*

Centric Brands LLC..................................C 646 582-6000
   Greensboro *(G-6900)*

Greene Mountain Outdoors LLC..............F 336 670-2186
   North Wilkesboro *(G-12011)*

Hawk Distributors Inc..............................G 888 334-1307
   Sanford *(G-14129)*

Lelantos Group Inc...................................D 704 780-4127
   Mooresville *(G-11005)*

London Garment Mfg LLC........................G 336 573-9300
   Stoneville *(G-14961)*

McDaniel Delmar..E 336 284-6377
   Mocksville *(G-10586)*

▲ Military Products Inc.............................G 910 637-0315
   West End *(G-15930)*

Nbn Sports Inc...G 919 824-5143
   Durham *(G-5240)*

Safety & Security Intl Inc.........................G 336 285-8673
   Greensboro *(G-7322)*

Salute Industries Inc................................E 844 937-2588
   Archdale *(G-298)*

Tailored Designs LLC...............................G 919 605-6349
   Charlotte *(G-3671)*

Tresmc LLC..G 919 900-0868
   Knightdale *(G-9432)*

Trotters Sewing Company Inc.................D 336 629-4550
   Asheboro *(G-501)*

US Patriot LLC...F 803 787-9398
   Fort Bragg *(G-6091)*

2321 Men's and boy's furnishings

◆ Century Place II LLC.............................E 704 790-0970
   Charlotte *(G-2443)*

Custom Ink...E 704 935-5604
   Charlotte *(G-2591)*

Devil Dog Manufacturing Co Inc.............C 919 269-7485
   Zebulon *(G-17125)*

Fun-Tees Inc..G 704 788-3003
   Concord *(G-4269)*

◆ Fun-Tees Inc...G 704 788-3003
   Concord *(G-4270)*

▼ Granite Knitwear Inc.............................E 704 279-5526
   Granite Quarry *(G-6760)*

◆ JD Apparel Inc..E 704 289-5600
   Monroe *(G-10748)*

Jensen Activewear.....................................G 704 982-3005
   Albemarle *(G-91)*

◆ M J Soffe Co..A 910 435-3138
   Fayetteville *(G-5863)*

MJ Soffe LLC...E 910 422-9002
   Rowland *(G-13791)*

Royal Textile Mills Inc..............................D 336 694-4121
   Yanceyville *(G-17065)*

Wrangler Apparel Corp.............................B 336 332-3400
   Greensboro *(G-7468)*

2322 Men's and boy's underwear and nightwear

▼ Carolina Apparel Group Inc..................D 704 694-6544
   Wadesboro *(G-15506)*

▲ Carolina International Inc.....................E 336 472-7788
   Thomasville *(G-15197)*

◆ Carolina Underwear Company..............E 336 472-7788
   Thomasville *(G-15200)*

Hanesbrands Inc..A 336 519-8080
   Winston Salem *(G-16734)*

Longworth Industries Inc.........................D 910 974-3068
   Candor *(G-1595)*

▼ Longworth Industries Inc.....................F 910 673-5290
   Southern Pines *(G-14539)*

Royal Textile Mills Inc..............................D 336 694-4121
   Yanceyville *(G-17065)*

Upel Inc..E 336 519-8080
   Winston Salem *(G-16960)*

Vanceboro Apparel Inc.............................G 252 244-2780
   Vanceboro *(G-15484)*

▲ Wilo Incorporated..................................E 336 679-4440
   Yadkinville *(G-17063)*

2323 Men's and boy's neckwear

316 Print Company LLC...........................G 919 454-6906
   Clayton *(G-3949)*

Angunique..G 336 392-5866
   Greensboro *(G-6808)*

Bigred Krafts LLC......................................G 919 480-2388
   Garner *(G-6257)*

▲ Brown & Church Neck Wear Co...........E 336 368-5502
   Pilot Mountain *(G-12196)*

23 APPAREL, FINISHED PRODUCTS FROM FABRICS & SIMILAR MATERIALS

Hbb Global LLC .... G 615 306-1270
  Apex *(G-201)*

HL James LLC .... G 516 398-3311
  Durham *(G-5138)*

Lizzys Logos Inc .... G 704 321-2588
  Matthews *(G-10263)*

Logothreads Inc .... G 704 892-9433
  Cornelius *(G-4569)*

MEI Tai Baby LLC .... G 919 260-4022
  Chapel Hill *(G-2038)*

Mudgear LLC .... G 347 674-9102
  Charlotte *(G-3212)*

On The Inside LLC .... G 828 606-8483
  Asheville *(G-716)*

Polly & Crackers LLC .... G 716 680-2456
  Wilmington *(G-16358)*

Refined Outdoors LLC .... G 704 634-4027
  Monroe *(G-10794)*

▲ Salem Neckwear Corporation .... G 336 498-2022
  Randleman *(G-13490)*

▲ Trueflies LLC .... G 828 337-9716
  Biltmore Lake *(G-1102)*

Venture Shades LLC .... G 804 240-2854
  Raleigh *(G-13396)*

Vf Jeanswear Inc .... F 336 332-3400
  Greensboro *(G-7441)*

Wicked Oceans .... G 252 269-0488
  Nags Head *(G-11729)*

2325 Men's and boy's trousers and slacks

Brilliant You LLC .... G 336 343-5535
  Greensboro *(G-6855)*

Centric Brands LLC .... C 646 582-6000
  Greensboro *(G-6900)*

Devil Dog Manufacturing Co Inc .... C 919 269-7485
  Zebulon *(G-17125)*

Fox Apparel Inc .... C 336 629-7641
  Asheboro *(G-437)*

Kontoor Brands Inc .... D 336 332-3586
  Greensboro *(G-7155)*

Lee Apparel Company Inc .... B 336 332-3400
  Greensboro *(G-7163)*

Ralph Lauren Corporation .... G 336 632-5000
  Greensboro *(G-7302)*

VF Corporation .... G 336 332-3400
  Greensboro *(G-7440)*

Vf Receivables LP .... F 336 424-6000
  Greensboro *(G-7442)*

Wrangler Apparel Corp .... B 336 332-3400
  Greensboro *(G-7468)*

2326 Men's and boy's work clothing

Aj & Raine Scrubs & More LLC .... G 646 374-5198
  Charlotte *(G-2149)*

American Plush Tex Mills LLC .... F 765 609-0456
  Red Springs *(G-13495)*

▼ American Safety Utility Corp .... E 704 482-0601
  Shelby *(G-14285)*

▲ Belvoir Manufacturing Corp .... D 252 746-1274
  Greenville *(G-7494)*

◆ Bennett Uniform Mfg Inc .... F 336 232-5772
  Greensboro *(G-6835)*

Brands Fashion US Inc .... G 704 953-8246
  Charlotte *(G-2348)*

◆ Brushy Mountain Bee Farm Inc ...... E 336 921-3640
  Winston Salem *(G-16639)*

▲ Causa LLC .... G 866 695-7022
  Charlotte *(G-2421)*

Creighton Ab Inc .... G 336 349-8275
  Reidsville *(G-13515)*

▲ Criticore Inc .... F 704 542-6876
  Charlotte *(G-2570)*

Dmg Manufacturing LLC .... E 828 855-1997
  Hickory *(G-8011)*

Evans and McClain LLC .... G 919 374-5578
  Raleigh *(G-12750)*

Excelsior Sewing LLC .... F 828 398-8056
  Fletcher *(G-6002)*

Garland Apparel Group LLC .... E 646 647-2790
  Garland *(G-6243)*

Hawk Distributors Inc .... G 888 334-1307
  Sanford *(G-14129)*

High Ground Incorporated .... G 704 372-6620
  Charlotte *(G-2910)*

Home T LLC .... F 646 797-4768
  Charlotte *(G-2917)*

Ican Clothes Company .... F 910 670-1494
  Fayetteville *(G-5840)*

▲ Ics North America Corp .... E 704 794-6620
  Concord *(G-4283)*

Intersport Group Inc .... G 814 968-3085
  Vilas *(G-15496)*

Keani Furniture Inc .... E 336 303-5484
  Asheboro *(G-448)*

Kontoor Brands Inc .... C 336 332-3400
  Greensboro *(G-7156)*

McDaniel Delmar .... E 336 284-6377
  Mocksville *(G-10586)*

Riverside Adventure Company .... F 910 457-4944
  Wilmington *(G-16384)*

S Loflin Enterprises Inc .... F 704 633-1159
  Salisbury *(G-14039)*

Seafarer LLC .... G 704 624-3200
  Marshville *(G-10224)*

Smissons Inc .... G 660 537-3219
  Clayton *(G-4009)*

Tafford Uniforms LLC .... D 888 823-3673
  Charlotte *(G-3670)*

Thompson Apparel Inc .... G 910 673-4560
  West End *(G-15934)*

Tillery Accessories Inc .... G 704 474-3013
  Norwood *(G-12046)*

Vanceboro Apparel Inc .... G 252 244-2780
  Vanceboro *(G-15484)*

White Knght Engneered Pdts Inc ...... E 828 687-0940
  Asheville *(G-820)*

Workwear Outfitters LLC .... D 877 824-0613
  Greensboro *(G-7467)*

2329 Men's and boy's clothing, nec

◆ Alleson of Rochester Inc .... D 585 272-0606
  Statesville *(G-14744)*

▲ Badger Sportswear LLC .... C 704 871-0990
  Statesville *(G-14758)*

Baldini For Men .... G 910 239-9150
  Wilmington *(G-16132)*

Brand New Life Clothing LLC .... G 980 266-4788
  Charlotte *(G-2345)*

▲ Capefear Sportswear .... G 910 620-7844
  Wilmington *(G-16152)*

▼ Capstar Corporation .... C 704 878-2007
  Statesville *(G-14770)*

Carolina Shirt Company Inc .... G 910 575-4447
  Calabash *(G-1552)*

Castle Hayne Hardware LLC .... F 910 675-9205
  Castle Hayne *(G-1945)*

Custom Spt & Imprintables LLC .... F 910 799-9914
  Wilmington *(G-16193)*

Eatumup Lure Company Inc .... G 336 218-0896
  Greensboro *(G-6988)*

Evolution of Style LLC .... G 914 329-3078
  Charlotte *(G-2735)*

Fox Apparel Inc .... C 336 629-7641
  Asheboro *(G-437)*

Gfsi Holdings LLC .... A 336 519-8080
  Winston Salem *(G-16720)*

Hudson Overall Company Inc .... G 336 314-5024
  Greensboro *(G-7104)*

Ican Clothes Company .... F 910 670-1494
  Fayetteville *(G-5840)*

▲ Ics North America Corp .... E 704 794-6620
  Concord *(G-4283)*

Levi Strauss International .... G 828 665-2417
  Asheville *(G-683)*

◆ M J Soffe Co .... A 910 435-3138
  Fayetteville *(G-5863)*

MJ Soffe LLC .... E 910 422-9002
  Rowland *(G-13791)*

Mk Global Holdings LLC .... E 704 334-1904
  Charlotte *(G-3190)*

Mulberry Street Inc .... G 252 638-3195
  New Bern *(G-11827)*

Professional Image .... G 336 294-6200
  Greensboro *(G-7288)*

Ralph Lauren Corporation .... G 336 632-5000
  High Point *(G-8504)*

Ramco .... G 704 794-6620
  Concord *(G-4347)*

Riley Jaron .... G 929 462-8300
  Greensboro *(G-7311)*

Salute Industries Inc .... E 844 937-2588
  Archdale *(G-298)*

Soma Intimates LLC .... G 704 365-1153
  Charlotte *(G-3579)*

Walter Reynolds .... G 704 735-6050
  Lincolnton *(G-9935)*

Wrangler Apparel Corp .... B 336 332-3400
  Greensboro *(G-7468)*

2331 Women's and misses' blouses and shirts

▲ Bon Worth Inc .... E 800 355-5131
  Hendersonville *(G-7829)*

Custom Ink .... E 704 935-5604
  Charlotte *(G-2591)*

◆ Fun-Tees Inc .... D 704 788-3003
  Concord *(G-4270)*

Grateful Union Family Inc .... F 828 622-3258
  Asheville *(G-640)*

Kontoor Brands Inc .... D 336 332-3586
  Greensboro *(G-7155)*

Patti Boo Inc .... G 828 648-6495
  Canton *(G-1621)*

Royce Apparel Inc .... E 704 933-6000
  Salisbury *(G-14038)*

Wrangler Apparel Corp .... B 336 332-3400
  Greensboro *(G-7468)*

2335 Women's, junior's, and misses' dresses

▲ Bon Worth Inc .... E 800 355-5131
  Hendersonville *(G-7829)*

Crt Inc .... G 704 905-9748
  Charlotte *(G-2575)*

Front Street Vlg Mstr Assn Inc .... G 252 838-1524
  Beaufort *(G-957)*

Gerson & Gerson Inc .... E 252 235-2441
  Middlesex *(G-10450)*

▼ Granite Knitwear Inc .... E 704 279-5526
  Granite Quarry *(G-6760)*

Hugger Inc .... C 704 735-7422
  Lincolnton *(G-9895)*

Jestines Jewels Inc .... G 704 904-0191
  Salisbury *(G-13991)*

Patti Boo Inc .... G 828 648-6495
  Canton *(G-1621)*

23 APPAREL, FINISHED PRODUCTS FROM FABRICS & SIMILAR MATERIALS

Weddings To Remember .... G 704 608-1181
Charlotte *(G-3801)*

2337 Women's and misses' suits and coats

◆ Bennett Uniform Mfg Inc .... F 336 232-5772
Greensboro *(G-6835)*

▲ Bon Worth Inc .... E 800 355-5131
Hendersonville *(G-7829)*

Centric Brands LLC .... C 646 582-6000
Greensboro *(G-6900)*

Formark Corporation .... F 704 922-9516
Charlotte *(G-2789)*

Fox Apparel Inc .... C 336 629-7641
Asheboro *(G-437)*

Hawk Distributors Inc .... G 888 334-1307
Sanford *(G-14129)*

Salute Industries Inc .... E 844 937-2588
Archdale *(G-298)*

2339 Women's and misses' outerwear, nec

◆ Alleson of Rochester Inc .... D 585 272-0606
Statesville *(G-14744)*

Apparel USA Inc .... E 212 869-5495
Fairmont *(G-5700)*

Badger Sportswear LLC .... D 704 871-0990
Statesville *(G-14757)*

▲ Badger Sportswear LLC .... C 704 871-0990
Statesville *(G-14758)*

▲ Belvoir Manufacturing Corp .... D 252 746-1274
Greenville *(G-7494)*

◆ Bennett Uniform Mfg Inc .... F 336 232-5772
Greensboro *(G-6835)*

Blacqueladi Styles LLC .... G 877 977-7798
Cary *(G-1707)*

▲ Bon Worth Inc .... E 800 355-5131
Hendersonville *(G-7829)*

Brilliant You LLC .... G 336 343-5535
Greensboro *(G-6855)*

Burlington Outlet .... G 910 278-3442
Oak Island *(G-12048)*

▼ Capstar Corporation .... C 704 878-2007
Statesville *(G-14770)*

Centric Brands LLC .... C 646 582-6000
Greensboro *(G-6900)*

Clar-Mar Inc .... D 704 435-9776
Cherryville *(G-3864)*

Devil Dog Manufacturing Co Inc .... C 919 269-7485
Zebulon *(G-17125)*

Divine Creations .... G 704 364-5844
Morehead City *(G-11168)*

Eagle Sportswear LLC .... G 252 235-4082
Middlesex *(G-10446)*

Eatumup Lure Company Inc .... G 336 218-0896
Greensboro *(G-6988)*

Formark Corporation .... F 704 922-9516
Charlotte *(G-2789)*

Fox Apparel Inc .... C 336 629-7641
Asheboro *(G-437)*

Gfsi Holdings LLC .... A 336 519-8080
Winston Salem *(G-16720)*

▼ Granite Knitwear Inc .... E 704 279-5526
Granite Quarry *(G-6760)*

Headbands of Hope LLC .... G 919 323-4140
Denver *(G-4780)*

Ican Clothes Company .... F 910 670-1494
Fayetteville *(G-5840)*

J C Custom Sewing Inc .... G 336 449-4586
Gibsonville *(G-6563)*

Junk Food Clothing Inc .... C 910 483-2500
Fayetteville *(G-5851)*

Kayla Jonise Bernhardt Crutch .... G 252 457-5367
Elizabeth City *(G-5552)*

Kontoor Brands Inc .... C 336 332-3400
Greensboro *(G-7156)*

Lee Apparel Company Inc .... B 336 332-3400
Greensboro *(G-7163)*

Levi Strauss International .... G 828 665-2417
Asheville *(G-683)*

Live It Boutique LLC .... G 704 492-2402
Charlotte *(G-3095)*

Lm Shea LLC .... G 919 608-1901
Raleigh *(G-12977)*

◆ M J Soffe Co .... A 910 435-3138
Fayetteville *(G-5863)*

McDaniel Delmar .... E 336 284-6377
Mocksville *(G-10586)*

Mitt S Nitts Inc .... E 919 596-6793
Durham *(G-5229)*

MJ Soffe LLC .... E 910 422-9002
Rowland *(G-13791)*

Mk Global Holdings LLC .... E 704 334-1904
Charlotte *(G-3190)*

MSE Beautyshapewear LLC .... G 910 500-0179
Fayetteville *(G-5878)*

Old Dell Designs .... G 910 532-6066
Magnolia *(G-10098)*

Patti Boo Inc .... G 828 648-6495
Canton *(G-1621)*

▲ Performance Apparel LLC .... F 805 541-0989
Southern Pines *(G-14544)*

Seafarer LLC .... G 704 624-3200
Marshville *(G-10224)*

▲ Sorbe Ltd .... G 704 562-2991
Matthews *(G-10344)*

Vanceboro Apparel Inc .... G 252 244-2780
Vanceboro *(G-15484)*

Walter Reynolds .... G 704 735-6050
Lincolnton *(G-9935)*

Wrangler Apparel Corp .... B 336 332-3400
Greensboro *(G-7468)*

2341 Women's and children's underwear

▲ Carolina International Inc .... E 336 472-7788
Thomasville *(G-15197)*

◆ Carolina Underwear Company .... E 336 472-7788
Thomasville *(G-15200)*

Hanesbrands Inc .... A 336 519-8080
Winston Salem *(G-16734)*

Longworth Industries Inc .... D 910 974-3068
Candor *(G-1595)*

▼ Longworth Industries Inc .... F 910 673-5290
Southern Pines *(G-14539)*

◆ Spencers Inc Mount Airy N C .... C 336 789-9111
Mount Airy *(G-11577)*

The Madison Manufacturing Inc .... E 336 548-9624
Madison *(G-10088)*

Upel Inc .... E 336 519-8080
Winston Salem *(G-16960)*

Vanceboro Apparel Inc .... G 252 244-2780
Vanceboro *(G-15484)*

Verena Designs Inc .... E 336 869-8235
High Point *(G-8593)*

▲ Wilo Incorporated .... E 336 679-4440
Yadkinville *(G-17063)*

2342 Bras, girdles, and allied garments

Hanesbrands Inc .... A 336 519-8080
Winston Salem *(G-16734)*

Hbi Wh Minority Holdings LLC .... G 336 519-8080
Winston Salem *(G-16740)*

In Pink .... G 919 380-1487
Cary *(G-1786)*

Remington 1816 Foundation .... G 866 686-7778
Charlotte *(G-3430)*

Upel Inc .... E 336 519-8080
Winston Salem *(G-16960)*

2353 Hats, caps, and millinery

Active Hats and Things Suite .... G 888 352-9292
Wilmington *(G-16093)*

▲ Americap Co Inc .... E 252 445-2388
Enfield *(G-5675)*

Custom Patch Hats LLC .... G 919 424-7723
Raleigh *(G-12666)*

Jadas Hats .... G 919 561-4373
Raleigh *(G-12911)*

2361 Girl's and children's dresses, blouses

▲ Cannon & Daughters Inc .... D 828 254-9236
Asheville *(G-579)*

Devil Dog Manufacturing Co Inc .... C 919 269-7485
Zebulon *(G-17125)*

◆ Fun-Tees Inc .... D 704 788-3003
Concord *(G-4270)*

Justice .... E 910 392-1581
Wilmington *(G-16284)*

Mulberry Street Inc .... G 252 638-3195
New Bern *(G-11827)*

Salon Couture .... G 910 693-1611
Southern Pines *(G-14552)*

Tiara Inc .... G 828 484-8236
Asheville *(G-800)*

2369 Girl's and children's outerwear, nec

Bonaventure Co LLC .... F 336 584-7530
Burlington *(G-1378)*

Devil Dog Manufacturing Co Inc .... C 919 269-7485
Zebulon *(G-17125)*

◆ M J Soffe Co .... A 910 435-3138
Fayetteville *(G-5863)*

Mulberry Street Inc .... G 252 638-3195
New Bern *(G-11827)*

▲ Sanders Industries Inc .... G 410 277-8565
Waynesville *(G-15820)*

Vanceboro Apparel Inc .... G 252 244-2780
Vanceboro *(G-15484)*

2371 Fur goods

Jones Fabricare Inc .... G 336 272-7261
Greensboro *(G-7139)*

2381 Fabric dress and work gloves

American Made Products Inc .... F 252 747-2010
Hookerton *(G-8728)*

▲ Carolina Glove Company .... E 828 464-1132
Conover *(G-4432)*

Magna Ready LLC .... G 617 909-4166
Raleigh *(G-12988)*

Mitt S Nitts Inc .... E 919 596-6793
Durham *(G-5229)*

◆ Southern Glove Inc .... B 828 464-4884
Newton *(G-11970)*

Sugarcane Studios LLC .... E 828 785-3167
Asheville *(G-789)*

◆ United Glove Inc .... E 828 464-2510
Newton *(G-11981)*

Worldwide Protective Pdts LLC .... D 336 933-8035
Wilkesboro *(G-16053)*

▲ Worldwide Protective Pdts LLC .... E 877 678-4568
Wilkesboro *(G-16052)*

2384 Robes and dressing gowns

Jocephus Originals Inc .... F 336 229-9600
Haw River *(G-7754)*

▲ Sanders Industries Inc .... G 410 277-8565
Waynesville *(G-15820)*

23 APPAREL, FINISHED PRODUCTS FROM FABRICS & SIMILAR MATERIALS

2385 Waterproof outerwear
▲ Drydog Barriers LLC.................................. G 704 334-8222
   Indian Trail *(G-8930)*

2386 Leather and sheep-lined clothing
Belt Shop Inc... F 704 865-3636
   Gastonia *(G-6352)*
▲ Gerbings LLC... D 800 646-5916
   Greensboro *(G-7039)*
Inspiration Leather Design Inc................... G 336 420-2265
   Jamestown *(G-9058)*
▲ JP Leather Company Inc........................... G 828 396-7728
   Hudson *(G-8771)*
▲ Madison Company Inc............................... E 336 548-9624
   Madison *(G-10079)*
Rmg Leather Usa LLC................................. F 828 466-5489
   Conover *(G-4492)*

2387 Apparel belts
Belt Shop Inc... F 704 865-3636
   Gastonia *(G-6352)*
Centric Brands LLC..................................... C 646 582-6000
   Greensboro *(G-6900)*
Hawk Distributors Inc................................. G 888 334-1307
   Sanford *(G-14129)*
▲ Madison Company Inc............................... E 336 548-9624
   Madison *(G-10079)*
▲ Military Products Inc.................................. G 910 637-0315
   West End *(G-15930)*
Point Blank Enterprises Inc........................ D 910 893-2071
   Lillington *(G-9858)*
The Madison Company Inc........................ E 336 548-9624
   Madison *(G-10088)*
▲ Wentworth Corporation.............................. F 336 548-1802
   Madison *(G-10091)*

2389 Apparel and accessories, nec
Apparel USA Inc.. E 212 869-5495
   Fairmont *(G-5700)*
Atlantic Trading LLC.................................... F
   Charlotte *(G-2233)*
▲ Belvoir Manufacturing Corp...................... D 252 746-1274
   Greenville *(G-7494)*
Burlington Coat Fctry Whse Cor................ E 919 468-9312
   Cary *(G-1718)*
Carolina Yarn Processors Inc.................... C 828 859-5891
   Tryon *(G-15422)*
Craftex Rework Inc..................................... G 252 239-0123
   Lucama *(G-10016)*
Custom Ink... E 704 935-5604
   Charlotte *(G-2591)*
Custom Patch Hats LLC............................. G 919 424-7723
   Raleigh *(G-12666)*
Ddm Inc.. G 910 686-1481
   Wilmington *(G-16197)*
Diamondback Armor.................................... G 828 288-6680
   Spindale *(G-14606)*
Dollar Eddie Rev.. G 919 596-7564
   Durham *(G-5059)*
Duck Head LLC... F 855 457-1865
   Greensboro *(G-6983)*
Eagle Sportswear LLC................................ F 919 365-9805
   Wendell *(G-15900)*
Fresh LLC.. G 919 592-7255
   Raleigh *(G-12782)*
Gerald Fisheries LLC.................................. G 907 518-0004
   New Bern *(G-11807)*
▼ Hanesbrands Export Canada LLC........... G 336 519-8080
   Winston Salem *(G-16733)*
Healing Crafter.. G 336 567-1620
   High Point *(G-8380)*
Health Supply Us LLC................................. F 888 408-1694
   Mooresville *(G-10971)*
Hinsons Typing & Printing.......................... G 919 934-9036
   Smithfield *(G-14462)*
Jestines Jewels Inc.................................... G 704 904-0191
   Salisbury *(G-13991)*
Kayser-Roth Hosiery Inc............................ E 336 852-2030
   Greensboro *(G-7146)*
La Sky Creations LLC................................. G 516 996-1231
   Fayetteville *(G-5858)*
Lebos Shoe Store Inc................................. F 704 987-6540
   Cornelius *(G-4567)*
Lululemon... G 336 723-3002
   Winston Salem *(G-16794)*
▲ Madison Company Inc............................... E 336 548-9624
   Madison *(G-10079)*
McCabes Costumes LLC........................... G 252 295-7691
   Winterville *(G-17006)*
▲ Military Products Inc.................................. G 910 637-0315
   West End *(G-15930)*
Mischief Makers Local 816 LLC................ E 336 763-2003
   Greensboro *(G-7202)*
MJ Soffe LLC... G 910 422-9002
   Rowland *(G-13791)*
▲ Morris Family Theatrical Inc..................... E 704 332-3304
   Charlotte *(G-3203)*
◆ Pearl River Group LLC............................... G 704 283-4667
   Monroe *(G-10785)*
Player Made LLC.. G 704 303-6926
   Charlotte *(G-3349)*
Powerhouse Dugout................................... G 704 215-6604
   Gastonia *(G-6492)*
▲ Precept Medical Products Inc.................. F 828 681-0209
   Arden *(G-365)*
Remington 1816 Foundation...................... G 866 686-7778
   Charlotte *(G-3430)*
◆ Royal Park Uniforms Inc........................... E 336 562-3345
   Prospect Hill *(G-12408)*
Snipes Group LLC...................................... G 757 266-0488
   Pittsboro *(G-12350)*
▼ Spiritus Systems Company....................... E 910 637-0196
   Aberdeen *(G-30)*
Tees Footwear Inc...................................... G 704 628-0376
   Indian Trail *(G-8967)*
The Madison Company Inc....................... E 336 548-9624
   Madison *(G-10088)*
The McQuackins Company LLC............... G 980 254-2309
   Gastonia *(G-6525)*
Vanceboro Apparel Inc.............................. G 252 244-2780
   Vanceboro *(G-15484)*
Whitewood Contracts LLC........................ E 336 885-9300
   High Point *(G-8603)*
Zoeys Btq Style Spclty Trats..................... G 910 808-1778
   Lillington *(G-9862)*

2391 Curtains and draperies
▲ A Window Treatment Co Inc..................... F 919 934-7100
   Smithfield *(G-14447)*
Atlantic Window Coverings Inc................. E 704 392-0043
   Charlotte *(G-2234)*
Carolina Custom Draperies Inc................ G 336 945-5190
   Winston Salem *(G-16644)*
Chf Industries Inc....................................... E 212 951-7800
   Charlotte *(G-2473)*
Diane Britt... G 910 763-9600
   Wilmington *(G-16200)*
▲ Ferncrest Fashions Inc............................. D 704 283-6422
   Monroe *(G-10719)*
Guest Interiors... G 828 244-5738
   Hickory *(G-8035)*
Lichtenberg Inc... G 336 949-9438
   Madison *(G-10078)*
National Mastercraft Inds Inc.................... F 919 896-8858
   Raleigh *(G-13055)*
Patterson Custom Drapery........................ G 910 791-4332
   Wilmington *(G-16349)*
Smith Draperies Inc................................... E 336 226-2183
   Burlington *(G-1496)*
▲ Stage Decoration and Sups Inc.............. F 336 621-5454
   Greensboro *(G-7364)*
Textile Products Inc................................... E 704 636-6221
   Salisbury *(G-14051)*
Walker Draperies Inc................................. F 919 220-1424
   Durham *(G-5437)*
▲ Wildcat Territory Inc................................. F 718 361-6726
   Thomasville *(G-15301)*

2392 Household furnishings, nec
▲ American Fiber & Finishing Inc.............. E 704 984-9256
   Albemarle *(G-73)*
Arden Companies LLC.............................. E 919 258-3081
   Sanford *(G-14087)*
Arden Companies LLC.............................. D 919 258-3081
   Sanford *(G-14088)*
Artisans Guild Incorporated..................... G 336 841-4140
   High Point *(G-8256)*
◆ Avintiv Specialty Mtls Inc........................ A 704 697-5100
   Charlotte *(G-2250)*
◆ Babine Lake Corporation......................... E 910 285-7955
   Hampstead *(G-7639)*
Bed In A Box.. G 800 588-5720
   Mount Airy *(G-11482)*
Berry Global Inc.. A 704 697-5100
   Charlotte *(G-2302)*
Blue Ridge Products Co Inc..................... E 828 322-7990
   Hickory *(G-7952)*
◆ Bob Barker Company Inc........................ C 800 334-9880
   Fuquay Varina *(G-6184)*
Carolina Fairway Cushions LLC............... G 336 434-4292
   Thomasville *(G-15196)*
Carpenter Co.. E 828 632-7061
   Taylorsville *(G-15133)*
Chf Industries Inc....................................... E 212 951-7800
   Charlotte *(G-2473)*
Creative Textiles Inc.................................. G 919 693-4427
   Oxford *(G-12123)*
Dale Ray Fabrics LLC............................... G 704 932-6411
   Kannapolis *(G-9116)*
Deep River Fabricators Inc...................... E 336 824-8881
   Franklinville *(G-6168)*
▲ Dewoolfson Down Intl Inc....................... G 828 963-2750
   Banner Elk *(G-896)*
Diane Britt... G 910 763-9600
   Wilmington *(G-16200)*
Discover Night LLC.................................... F 888 825-6282
   Raleigh *(G-12687)*
◆ E T C of Henderson N C Inc................... G 252 492-4033
   Henderson *(G-7781)*
Fiber Cushioning Inc................................. F 336 887-4782
   High Point *(G-8352)*
▲ Fiber Cushioning Inc................................ F 336 629-8442
   Asheboro *(G-434)*
◆ Glenoit Universal Ltd............................... C 919 735-7111
   Goldsboro *(G-6616)*
◆ Hardin Manufacturing Co........................ G 828 685-2008
   Hendersonville *(G-7858)*
Hickory Springs Mfg Co........................... D 336 861-4195
   High Point *(G-8385)*
Image Matters Inc..................................... G 336 940-3000
   Clemmons *(G-4047)*
Innovative Cushions LLC......................... F 336 861-2060
   Archdale *(G-285)*
J C Custom Sewing Inc........................... G 336 449-4586
   Gibsonville *(G-6563)*

Employee Codes: A=Over 500 employees, B=251-500
C=101-250, D=51-100, E=20-50, F=10-19, G=1-9

2024 Harris North Carolina Manufacturers Directory

23 APPAREL, FINISHED PRODUCTS FROM FABRICS & SIMILAR MATERIALS

◆ Jbs2 Inc..D 828 236-1300
　Swannanoa *(G-15027)*

◆ Js Fiber Co Inc....................................D 704 871-1582
　Statesville *(G-14828)*

Js Linens and Curtain Outlet................F 704 871-1582
　Statesville *(G-14829)*

▲ Js Royal Home Usa Inc......................E 704 542-2304
　Charlotte *(G-3038)*

L C Industries Inc..................................C 919 596-8277
　Durham *(G-5185)*

Leggett & Platt Incorporated................G 704 380-6208
　Statesville *(G-14835)*

Lions Services Inc................................B 704 921-1527
　Charlotte *(G-3091)*

▲ Lomar Specialty Advg Inc..................F 704 788-4380
　Concord *(G-4307)*

◆ Manual Woodworkers Weavers Inc..C 828 692-7333
　Hendersonville *(G-7876)*

Newell & Sons Inc................................F 336 597-2248
　Roxboro *(G-13807)*

◆ North Carolina Lumber Company.....F 336 498-6600
　Randleman *(G-13481)*

Owens Quilting Inc................................G 828 695-1495
　Newton *(G-11956)*

Pacific Coast Feather LLC...................G 252 492-0051
　Henderson *(G-7801)*

Party Tables Land Co LLC....................F 919 596-3521
　Durham *(G-5272)*

▲ Perfect Fit Industries LLC.................C 800 864-7618
　Charlotte *(G-3330)*

◆ Pgi Polymer Inc..................................A 704 697-5100
　Charlotte *(G-3336)*

Premium Cushion Inc............................E 828 464-4783
　Conover *(G-4487)*

▲ Pure Country Inc...............................D 828 859-9916
　Lynn *(G-10063)*

◆ Q C Apparel Inc.................................E 828 586-5663
　Sylva *(G-15065)*

Quality Home Fashions Inc...................G 704 983-5906
　Albemarle *(G-100)*

Quickie Manufacturing Corp.................C 910 737-6500
　Lumberton *(G-10049)*

R & D Weaving Inc.................................F 828 248-1910
　Ellenboro *(G-5638)*

Richard Shew..F 828 781-3294
　Conover *(G-4491)*

▼ Riddle & Company LLC.....................E 336 229-1856
　Burlington *(G-1485)*

Royale Comfort Seating Inc..................D 828 352-9021
　Taylorsville *(G-15162)*

▲ Sanders Industries Inc......................G 410 277-8565
　Waynesville *(G-15820)*

Signature Seating Inc............................E 828 325-0174
　Hickory *(G-8156)*

Smith Draperies Inc...............................E 336 226-2183
　Burlington *(G-1496)*

Snyder Paper Corporation....................F 336 884-1172
　High Point *(G-8539)*

Snyder Paper Corporation....................G 828 464-1189
　Newton *(G-11969)*

Stn Cushion Company...........................D 336 476-9100
　Thomasville *(G-15284)*

▲ Sunrise Development LLC................F 828 453-0590
　Mooresboro *(G-10841)*

▲ Tempo Products LLC........................E 336 434-8649
　High Point *(G-8565)*

Tempur Sealy International Inc.............E 336 861-2900
　Trinity *(G-15361)*

Textile Products Inc...............................E 704 636-6221
　Salisbury *(G-14051)*

◆ Trtl Inc...G 844 811-5816
　Raleigh *(G-13368)*

Velco Inc..F 828 324-5440
　Hickory *(G-8202)*

▲ Watson Party Tables Inc...................F 919 294-9153
　Durham *(G-5438)*

▲ Wayne Industries Inc........................E 336 434-5017
　Archdale *(G-304)*

Westpoint Home Inc..............................B 910 369-2231
　Wagram *(G-15524)*

▲ Wildcat Territory Inc..........................F 718 361-6726
　Thomasville *(G-15301)*

◆ Winstn-Slem Inds For Blind Inc........B 336 759-0551
　Winston Salem *(G-16979)*

2393 Textile bags

▲ American Pride Inc...........................E 828 697-8847
　Hendersonville *(G-7818)*

Camoteck LLC.......................................G 910 590-3213
　Clinton *(G-4089)*

◆ Cekal Specialties Inc........................E 704 822-6206
　Mount Holly *(G-11625)*

Cross Canvas Company Inc..................E 828 252-0440
　Asheville *(G-599)*

Cushion Manufacturing Inc...................G 828 324-9555
　Hickory *(G-8000)*

Dayton Bag & Burlap Co.......................G 704 873-7271
　Statesville *(G-14783)*

▲ East Coast Umbrella Inc..................E 910 462-2500
　Laurel Hill *(G-9459)*

Fisher Athletic Equipment Inc...............F 704 636-5713
　Salisbury *(G-13965)*

Fuller Specialty Company Inc...............F 336 226-3446
　Burlington *(G-1417)*

Hdb Inc...G 800 403-2247
　Greensboro *(G-7080)*

J C Custom Sewing Inc.........................F 336 449-4586
　Gibsonville *(G-6563)*

▲ J Stahl Sales & Sourcing Inc............E 828 645-3005
　Weaverville *(G-15849)*

▲ Lomar Specialty Advg Inc................F 704 788-4380
　Concord *(G-4307)*

Mountain International LLC...................E 828 606-0194
　Brevard *(G-1282)*

Nyp Corp Frmrly New Yrkr-Pters..........F 910 739-4403
　Lumberton *(G-10047)*

2394 Canvas and related products

A & J Canvas Inc....................................E 252 244-1509
　Vanceboro *(G-15474)*

Accent Awnings Inc...............................F 828 321-4517
　Andrews *(G-123)*

Agricltral-Industrial Fabr Inc..................G 336 591-3690
　Walnut Cove *(G-15630)*

Allison Sails and Canvas LLC...............G 910 515-1381
　Carolina Beach *(G-1631)*

Alpha Canvas and Awning Co Inc........F 704 333-1581
　Charlotte *(G-2167)*

Camoteck LLC.......................................G 910 590-3213
　Clinton *(G-4089)*

Canvasmasters LLC..............................G 828 369-0406
　Franklin *(G-6118)*

Cape Lookout Canvas & Customs........G 252 726-3751
　Morehead City *(G-11157)*

Carol Williams..G 252 883-7968
　Rocky Mount *(G-13687)*

Carteret Canvas Company....................G 252 247-9588
　Atlantic Beach *(G-828)*

◆ Cdv LLC..F 919 674-3460
　Morrisville *(G-11316)*

Clark Art Shop Inc.................................G 919 832-8319
　Raleigh *(G-12625)*

Coastal Awnings Inc..............................F 252 222-0707
　Morehead City *(G-11162)*

Coastal Canvas Mfg Inc........................G 252 728-4946
　Beaufort *(G-950)*

▼ Colored Metal Products Inc..............F 704 482-1407
　Shelby *(G-14301)*

Cross Canvas Company Inc..................E 828 252-0440
　Asheville *(G-599)*

CSC Awnings Inc...................................G 336 744-5006
　Winston Salem *(G-16666)*

Custom Canvas Works Inc....................F 919 662-4800
　Garner *(G-6270)*

◆ Custom Golf Car Supply Inc.............C 704 855-1130
　Salisbury *(G-13952)*

▲ Diamond Brand Gear Company........E 828 684-9848
　Fletcher *(G-5998)*

▲ Dize Company....................................D 336 722-5181
　Winston Salem *(G-16684)*

DLM Sales Inc.......................................F 704 399-2776
　Charlotte *(G-2647)*

◆ Dunn Manufacturing Corp................C 704 283-2147
　Monroe *(G-10709)*

Ernies Boat Canvas & Awning C..........E 252 491-8279
　Jarvisburg *(G-9084)*

◆ Hatteras Hammocks Inc....................C 252 758-0641
　Greenville *(G-7537)*

Howell & Sons Canvas Repairs............G 704 892-7913
　Cornelius *(G-4556)*

M & M Signs and Awnings Inc.............F 336 352-4300
　Mount Airy *(G-11543)*

OBrian Tarping Systems Inc.................F 252 291-6710
　Wilson *(G-16520)*

▼ OBrian Tarping Systems Inc............F 252 291-2141
　Wilson *(G-16521)*

▲ Prem Corp...E 704 921-1799
　Charlotte *(G-3373)*

Red Sky Shelters LLC...........................G 828 258-8417
　Asheville *(G-754)*

Ricks Custom Marine Canvas...............G 937 623-1672
　Cornelius *(G-4583)*

Rocky Mount Awning & Tent Co..........F 252 442-0184
　Rocky Mount *(G-13730)*

Sawyers Sign Service Inc.....................F
　Mount Airy *(G-11571)*

Sign & Awning Systems Inc.................F 919 892-5900
　Dunn *(G-4883)*

▲ Southbridge Inc.................................G 828 350-9112
　Asheville *(G-782)*

▲ Trelleborg Ctd Systems US Inc........C 828 286-9126
　Rutherfordton *(G-13896)*

Trimaco Inc..G 919 674-3460
　Morrisville *(G-11455)*

Trivantage..G 800 438-1061
　Statesville *(G-14918)*

◆ Trivantage LLC..................................D 800 786-1876
　Burlington *(G-1510)*

Watkins Custom Sewing Inc.................G 252 996-0642
　Wanchese *(G-15652)*

▲ WC&r Interests LLC..........................C 828 684-9848
　Fletcher *(G-6050)*

◆ Winstn-Slem Inds For Blind Inc........B 336 759-0551
　Winston Salem *(G-16979)*

2395 Pleating and stitching

1st Place Embroidery Inc......................G 704 239-8844
　Kannapolis *(G-9110)*

822tees Inc..G 910 822-8337
　Fayetteville *(G-5748)*

A Stitch To Remember..........................G 336 202-0026
　Summerfield *(G-14974)*

American Embroidery LLC....................G 910 229-3837
　Fayetteville *(G-5759)*

Amy Smith..G 828 352-1001
　Burnsville *(G-1522)*

23 APPAREL, FINISHED PRODUCTS FROM FABRICS & SIMILAR MATERIALS

Apex Embroidery Inc .... G 919 793-6083
  Apex (G-160)

Artex Group Inc .... G 866 845-1042
  Fairview (G-5706)

Artist S Needle Inc .... G 336 294-5884
  Greensboro (G-6817)

Artwear Embroidery Inc .... E 336 992-2166
  Kernersville (G-9165)

B&Lk Enterprises .... G 910 395-5151
  Wilmington (G-16130)

B6usa Inc .... F 919 833-3851
  Raleigh (G-12541)

▲ Baysix USA .... F 919 833-3851
  Raleigh (G-12547)

BB&p Embroidery LLC .... G 252 206-1929
  Wilson (G-16475)

Belle Embroidery LLC .... G 704 436-6895
  Concord (G-4207)

Biancas Stitch Works LLC .... G 828 505-0686
  Asheville (G-558)

Biltmore Embroiderers Inc .... G 828 298-7403
  Asheville (G-559)

Bnb Designs Inc .... G 919 587-9800
  Goldsboro (G-6593)

Body Billboards Inc .... G 919 544-4540
  Durham (G-4969)

Bradleys Inc .... E 704 484-2077
  Shelby (G-14289)

Busy BS Monogramming LLC .... G 919 870-6106
  Raleigh (G-12580)

Cali Stitches .... G 336 895-4714
  Greensboro (G-6875)

Carolina Embroidery Kenly Inc .... G 919 279-2356
  Kenly (G-9146)

Carolina Monogram Company .... G 919 285-3091
  Fuquay Varina (G-6186)

Carolina Patch & Leather LLC .... G 704 880-7724
  Statesville (G-14772)

Catawba Valley Quilters Guild .... G 828 322-4517
  Hickory (G-7970)

Chic Monogram .... G 910 431-8704
  Wilmington (G-16170)

Cintas Corporation No 2 .... D 336 632-4412
  Greensboro (G-6909)

▲ Colonial LLC .... E 336 434-5600
  High Point (G-8299)

Combintons Screen Prtg EMB Inc .... G 336 472-4420
  Thomasville (G-15204)

Conrad Embroidery Company LLC .... E 828 645-3015
  Weaverville (G-15842)

▲ Conrad Industries Inc .... E 828 645-3015
  Weaverville (G-15843)

Consumer Concepts .... F 252 247-7000
  Morehead City (G-11164)

Cook Group Inc .... G 336 605-5557
  Mooresville (G-10911)

▼ Crawford Industries Inc .... F 336 884-8822
  High Point (G-8306)

Crazy Ink Stitches .... G 910 964-2889
  Fayetteville (G-5798)

Creative Caps Inc .... G 919 701-1175
  Dunn (G-4859)

D&M Embroidery LLC .... G 910 467-3586
  Jacksonville (G-8996)

Dale Advertising Inc .... G 704 484-0971
  Shelby (G-14310)

Dons Stitches .... G 336 554-6697
  Mc Leansville (G-10389)

Durkee Embroidery Inc .... G 980 689-2684
  Cornelius (G-4541)

Emb Inc .... G 336 945-0759
  High Point (G-8342)

Embroid It .... G 704 617-0357
  Charlotte (G-2704)

Embroidery Corner .... G 910 817-7586
  Rockingham (G-13626)

Embroidery Nurse LLC .... G 919 630-5261
  Raleigh (G-12734)

▲ Fabric Services Hickory Inc .... F 828 397-7331
  Hildebran (G-8622)

Farmhouse Stitching .... G 910 308-7308
  Stedman (G-14935)

Fines and Carriel Inc .... G 919 929-0702
  Chapel Hill (G-2018)

Freeman Screen Printers Inc .... G 704 521-9148
  Charlotte (G-2795)

Fully Promoted Durham .... G 919 316-1538
  Durham (G-5108)

Fully Promoted Fuquay-Varina .... G 919 346-8955
  Fuquay Varina (G-6200)

Funny Bone EMB & Screening .... G 704 663-4711
  Mooresville (G-10951)

Gaston Screen Printing Inc .... F 704 399-0459
  Charlotte (G-2810)

Grace Apparel Company Inc .... G 828 242-8172
  Arden (G-335)

Grace Southern Embroidery .... G 336 254-5585
  Gibsonville (G-6559)

Graceful Stitching .... G 704 964-2121
  Gastonia (G-6409)

▼ High Point Quilting Inc .... F 336 861-4180
  High Point (G-8393)

Home Team Athletics Inc .... G 910 938-0862
  Jacksonville (G-9007)

Hometown Sports Inc .... G 919 732-7090
  Hillsborough (G-8655)

House of Stitches .... G 570 768-6930
  Dobson (G-4826)

Ibeny Embroidering LLC .... G 347 286-1299
  Charlotte (G-2945)

In Stitches Custom EMB LLC .... G 336 655-3498
  Winston Salem (G-16755)

Industrial Opportunities Inc .... B 828 321-4754
  Andrews (G-126)

Ink n Stitches LLC .... G 336 633-3898
  Asheboro (G-444)

Ink Pallets & Stitches LLC .... G 239 826-4772
  Hubert (G-8749)

International Embroidery .... G 704 792-0641
  Concord (G-4287)

Ivars Sportswear Inc .... G 336 227-9683
  Graham (G-6693)

Jalilud Embroidery LLC .... G 704 425-3492
  Charlotte (G-3008)

James Embroidery Company .... G 704 467-1224
  Mooresville (G-10986)

Just Stitchin Quilts LLc .... G 828 644-3368
  Hayesville (G-7767)

Kelleys Sports and Awards Inc .... G 828 728-4600
  Hudson (G-8772)

Kellys Embroidery .... G 919 738-5072
  Mount Olive (G-11664)

Khi LLC .... G 828 654-9916
  Arden (G-345)

Kraken-Skulls .... F 910 500-9100
  Fayetteville (G-5855)

La T Da Btq Monogramming .... G 336 457-9831
  Greensboro (G-7161)

Lake Norman EMB & Monogramming .... G 704 892-8450
  Cornelius (G-4564)

Lee Marks .... G 919 493-2208
  Durham (G-5188)

Liberty Embroidery Inc .... A 336 548-1802
  Madison (G-10077)

Logosdirect LLC .... F 866 273-2335
  Wilmington (G-16307)

Logowear .... G 336 969-0444
  Rural Hall (G-13849)

Louise L Nona L C .... G 704 242-0929
  Locust (G-9963)

Lumina Embroidery LLC .... G 910 371-1384
  Leland (G-9553)

M-Prints Inc .... G 828 265-4929
  Boone (G-1216)

Main Street Monograms .... G 704 233-5393
  Wingate (G-16576)

Manna Corp North Carolina .... G 828 696-3642
  Hendersonville (G-7875)

Melodia Goods and Embroidery .... G 910 674-3934
  Lumberton (G-10044)

Memories In Stitches .... G 910 725-0512
  Southern Pines (G-14541)

Millers Sports and Trophies .... G 252 792-2050
  Williamston (G-16067)

Minnie ME Monograms Inc .... G 919 243-8367
  Clayton (G-3996)

Mobay Sportswear Embroidery .... G 704 262-7783
  Concord (G-4317)

Mojo Sportswear Inc .... G 252 758-4176
  Greenville (G-7562)

Monogram Asheville .... G 828 707-8110
  Asheville (G-704)

Monogram Asheville LLC .... G 828 545-5367
  Fairview (G-5716)

Monogram This .... G 336 528-9980
  Mocksville (G-10592)

Monogram Whimsy .... G 704 904-1476
  Waxhaw (G-15767)

Monograms Etc .... G 336 769-8358
  Winston Salem (G-16817)

Moving Screens Incorporated .... G 336 364-9259
  Rougemont (G-13787)

NC Patches .... G 703 314-3428
  High Point (G-8464)

OH So Nice .... G 704 263-2668
  Stanley (G-14704)

Old South Monograms & EMB LLC .... G 704 921-8115
  Concord (G-4325)

Pacific Coast Feather LLC .... G 252 492-0051
  Henderson (G-7801)

Pammyts Monogram Gifts .... G 252 363-6331
  Bailey (G-877)

Pine State Corporate AP LLC .... F 336 789-9437
  Mount Airy (G-11557)

Popembroiderydesigns .... G 828 575-4252
  Leicester (G-9517)

Professnal Alterations EMB Inc .... G 910 577-8484
  Jacksonville (G-9022)

Promos Inc .... G 336 251-1134
  Winston Salem (G-16874)

Quilt Lizzy .... G 252 257-3800
  Ayden (G-853)

Rhyno Enterprises .... G 252 291-6700
  Wilson (G-16532)

Robert Citrano .... G 910 264-7746
  Wilmington (G-16385)

Rogers Screenprinting EMB Inc .... G 910 628-1983
  Fairmont (G-5705)

Sassy Stitches-N-Such Inc .... G 919 658-6105
  Mount Olive (G-11667)

Screen and Embroidery .... G 919 557-3151
  Fuquay Varina (G-6228)

Sew Blessed Embroidery .... G 704 840-7571
  Monroe (G-10806)

Southern Roots Monogramming .... G 706 599-5383
  Cleveland (G-4081)

23 APPAREL, FINISHED PRODUCTS FROM FABRICS & SIMILAR MATERIALS

◆ Ss Handcrafted Art LLC.................................. G 704 664-2544
    Mooresville *(G-11098)*

Stanley E Dixon Jr Inc................................... G 252 332-5004
    Ahoskie *(G-66)*

Steelcity LLC.. E 336 434-7000
    Archdale *(G-299)*

Stitch 2 Fit... G 704 677-4842
    Mooresville *(G-11102)*

Stitch 98 Inc... F 704 235-5783
    Mooresville *(G-11103)*

Stitch Barn.. G 252 717-1262
    Greenville *(G-7587)*

Stitch In Time Inc... G 910 497-4171
    Spring Lake *(G-14628)*

Stitch More Big... G 910 799-8992
    Wilmington *(G-16418)*

Stitch of Royalty... G 336 457-1888
    Greensboro *(G-7372)*

Stitch X Stitch LLC....................................... G 704 970-0667
    Charlotte *(G-3634)*

Stitch-A-Doozy... G 336 573-2339
    Stoneville *(G-14968)*

Stitch-N-Sassy.. G 704 491-8274
    Huntersville *(G-8901)*

Stitchcrafters Incorporated......................... G 828 397-7656
    Hickory *(G-8169)*

Stitchery Inc... G 336 248-5604
    Lexington *(G-9785)*

Stitches In Grove.. G 704 791-2402
    China Grove *(G-3890)*

Stitches of Thread.. G 704 840-7215
    Charlotte *(G-3635)*

Stitches On Critter Pond.............................. G 919 624-5886
    Wake Forest *(G-15599)*

Stitchinwright.. G 704 219-0697
    Charlotte *(G-3636)*

Stitchmaster LLC... G 336 852-6448
    Greensboro *(G-7373)*

STS Screen Printing Inc.............................. G 704 821-8488
    Matthews *(G-10347)*

Studio Stitch LLC... G 336 288-9200
    Greensboro *(G-7377)*

Sugarshack Bakery and EMB..................... G 803 920-3311
    Troy *(G-15417)*

Super Stitchy LLC.. G 919 762-0626
    Holly Springs *(G-8719)*

Three Wishes Monogramming..................... G 980 298-2981
    Harrisburg *(G-7731)*

To Knit and Stitch.. G 704 493-2523
    Charlotte *(G-3701)*

To The Point Inc.. G 336 725-5303
    Winston Salem *(G-16943)*

Topsail Sportswear Inc................................ G 910 270-4903
    Hampstead *(G-7661)*

Twg Inc... G 336 998-9731
    Advance *(G-52)*

Uniforms Galore... G 252 975-5878
    Washington *(G-15735)*

Vocatnal Sltons Hndrson Cnty I................. E 828 692-9626
    East Flat Rock *(G-5479)*

WB Embroidery Inc...................................... G 828 432-0076
    Morganton *(G-11268)*

Wendys Embrdred Spc Screen Prt........... F 704 982-5978
    Albemarle *(G-113)*

Wham Bam Monogram................................ G 336 712-5109
    Winston Salem *(G-16975)*

Zoom Apparel Inc.. G 336 993-9666
    Winston Salem *(G-16992)*

2396 Automotive and apparel trimmings

A&M Screen Printing NC Inc....................... G 910 792-1111
    Wilmington *(G-16089)*

Amy Smith... G 828 352-1001
    Burnsville *(G-1522)*

B&Lk Enterprises... G 910 395-5151
    Wilmington *(G-16130)*

Blue Dog Graphics Inc............................... G 252 291-9191
    Wilson *(G-16477)*

Boardwalk Inc.. G 252 240-1095
    Morehead City *(G-11155)*

Body Billboards Inc..................................... G 919 544-4540
    Durham *(G-4969)*

Brandrpm LLC.. D 704 225-1800
    Charlotte *(G-2347)*

Broome Sign Company................................ G 704 782-0422
    Concord *(G-4215)*

◆ Charlotte Trimming Company Inc............. D 704 529-8427
    Charlotte *(G-2465)*

Combintons Screen Prtg EMB Inc.............. G 336 472-4420
    Thomasville *(G-15204)*

Consumer Concepts..................................... F 252 247-7000
    Morehead City *(G-11164)*

Contagious Graphics Inc........................... E 704 529-5600
    Charlotte *(G-2543)*

Crystal Impressions Ltd.............................. F 252 821-7678
    Indian Trail *(G-8928)*

Culp Inc.. C 336 643-7751
    Stokesdale *(G-14941)*

Custom Screens Inc.................................... E 336 427-0265
    Madison *(G-10071)*

Dale Advertising Inc.................................... G 704 484-0971
    Shelby *(G-14310)*

Dayton Bag & Burlap Co............................ G 704 873-7271
    Statesville *(G-14783)*

Dicks Store... G 336 548-9358
    Madison *(G-10073)*

Domestic Fabrics Blankets Corp................ E 252 523-7948
    Kinston *(G-9359)*

Expressive Screen Printing......................... G 910 739-3221
    Lumberton *(G-10035)*

F & H Print Sign Design LLC..................... G 252 335-0181
    Elizabeth City *(G-5545)*

◆ Finch Industries Incorporated................... D 336 472-4499
    Thomasville *(G-15221)*

◆ Fms Enterprises Usa Inc........................... D 704 735-4249
    Lincolnton *(G-9893)*

Freeman Screen Printers Inc..................... G 704 521-9148
    Charlotte *(G-2795)*

G & G Enterprises....................................... G 336 764-2493
    Clemmons *(G-4041)*

Gaston Screen Printing Inc........................ F 704 399-0459
    Charlotte *(G-2810)*

Glen Rven Tchnical Fabrics LLC............... C 336 229-5576
    Burlington *(G-1425)*

Grace Apparel Company Inc...................... G 828 242-8172
    Arden *(G-335)*

◆ Haeco Americas LLC................................. A 336 668-4410
    Greensboro *(G-7073)*

Hi-Tech Screens Inc.................................... F 828 452-5151
    Waynesville *(G-15807)*

International Foam Pdts Inc....................... G 704 588-0080
    Charlotte *(G-2982)*

Island Xprtees of Oter Bnks In.................. E 252 480-3990
    Nags Head *(G-11720)*

Keiths Kustomz LLC.................................... G 704 524-8684
    Gastonia *(G-6438)*

Kelleys Sports and Awards Inc.................. G 828 728-4600
    Hudson *(G-8772)*

▲ King International Corporation................. E 336 983-5171
    King *(G-9274)*

Lee County Industries Inc......................... E 919 775-3439
    Sanford *(G-14148)*

Lee Marks.. G 919 493-2208
    Durham *(G-5188)*

Line Drive Sports Center Inc..................... G 336 824-1692
    Ramseur *(G-13446)*

M-Prints Inc.. G 828 265-4929
    Boone *(G-1216)*

Manna Corp North Carolina........................ G 828 696-3642
    Hendersonville *(G-7875)*

Marketing One Sportswear Inc................... G 704 334-9333
    Charlotte *(G-3126)*

Marvin Bailey Screen Printing.................... G 252 335-1554
    Elizabeth City *(G-5556)*

Motorsports Designs Inc............................ E 336 454-1181
    High Point *(G-8460)*

Patti Boo Inc.. G 828 648-6495
    Canton *(G-1621)*

Premium Fabricators LLC.......................... E 828 464-3818
    Conover *(G-4488)*

Pro-System Inc.. F 704 799-8100
    Mooresville *(G-11064)*

PSM Enterprises Inc................................... F 336 789-8888
    Mount Airy *(G-11561)*

Qst Industries Inc....................................... G 336 751-1000
    Mocksville *(G-10600)*

R & S Sporting Goods Ctr Inc................... G 336 599-0248
    Roxboro *(G-13820)*

Regimental Flag & T Shirts........................ G 919 496-2888
    Louisburg *(G-9999)*

Rogers Screenprinting EMB Inc................ G 910 628-1983
    Fairmont *(G-5705)*

SE Logo Wear.. F 336 748-1735
    Winston Salem *(G-16900)*

Simple & Sentimental LLC.......................... G 252 320-9458
    Ayden *(G-857)*

Soisa Inc.. G 336 940-4006
    Mocksville *(G-10604)*

Standard Tytape Company Inc................... F 828 693-6594
    Hendersonville *(G-7906)*

Stitchcrafters Incorporated......................... G 828 397-7656
    Hickory *(G-8169)*

T T S D Productions LLC............................ G 704 829-6666
    Belmont *(G-1013)*

Tapped Tees LLC.. G 919 943-9692
    Durham *(G-5386)*

Tarason Label Inc.. G 828 464-4743
    Hickory *(G-8174)*

TEC Graphics Inc.. F 919 567-2077
    Fuquay Varina *(G-6232)*

▲ Textile Printing Inc................................... G 704 521-8099
    Charlotte *(G-3683)*

Torches Design Studio Inc......................... G 704 966-4000
    Denver *(G-4808)*

▲ Trelleborg Ctd Systems US Inc................ C 828 286-9126
    Rutherfordton *(G-13896)*

Vocatnal Sltons Hndrson Cnty I................ E 828 692-9626
    East Flat Rock *(G-5479)*

Weaveup Inc... G 443 540-4201
    Durham *(G-5439)*

Wooten Graphics Inc................................... F 336 731-4650
    Welcome *(G-15878)*

2397 Schiffli machine embroideries

Collegiate Clors Christn Colors.................. G 919 536-8179
    Durham *(G-5024)*

Perfectly Threaded LLC.............................. G 336 229-0152
    Gibsonville *(G-6569)*

2399 Fabricated textile products, nec

▲ Aircraft Belts Inc....................................... E 919 956-4395
    Creedmoor *(G-4601)*

All-State Industries Inc............................... G 704 588-4081
    Charlotte *(G-2157)*

▲ Ballistic Recovery Systems Inc............... E 651 457-7491
    Pinebluff *(G-12213)*

SIC SECTION

24 LUMBER AND WOOD PRODUCTS, EXCEPT FURNITURE

◆ Beocare Group Inc.................................C..... 828 728-7300
  Hudson (G-8763)
Bhaki Bullies LLC....................................G..... 646 387-3974
  Knightdale (G-9413)
Bymonetcrochet..G..... 443 613-1736
  Charlotte (G-2371)
Crochet By Sue..G..... 201 723-4906
  Salisbury (G-13948)
Cw Media Inc...G..... 910 302-3066
  Raeford (G-12419)
Dickson Elberton Mill Inc........................G..... 336 226-3556
  Burlington (G-1406)
◆ Downtown Graphics Network Inc........G..... 704 637-0855
  Salisbury (G-13954)
◆ Dunn Manufacturing Corp..................C..... 704 283-2147
  Monroe (G-10709)
▲ Fex Straw Manufacturing Inc..............G..... 910 671-4141
  Lumberton (G-10037)
Flexi North America LLC........................G..... 704 588-0785
  Charlotte (G-2774)
Flint Hill Textiles Inc.............................G..... 704 434-9331
  Shelby (G-14318)
Game Day Crochet...................................G..... 704 635-7557
  Indian Trail (G-8936)
◆ Guilford Mills LLC...............................A..... 910 794-5810
  Wilmington (G-16243)
Harvey & Sons Net & Twine....................G..... 252 729-1731
  Davis (G-4707)
◆ Hatteras Hammocks Inc......................C..... 252 758-0641
  Greenville (G-7537)
◆ Hickory Springs Manufactu.................D..... 828 328-2201
  Hickory (G-8052)
Hook-It-Up..G..... 980 253-4542
  Charlotte (G-2920)
▲ Horseware Triple Crown Blanket........F..... 252 208-0080
  Raleigh (G-12862)
International Pet ACC LLC......................G..... 919 964-0738
  Raleigh (G-12900)
Lear Corporation.....................................A..... 910 794-5810
  Wilmington (G-16294)
▲ Lomar Specialty Advg Inc...................G..... 704 788-4380
  Concord (G-4307)
M & M Entps Banner Elk Inc..................G..... 828 898-2401
  Banner Elk (G-902)
Mills Manufacturing Corp.......................C..... 828 645-3061
  Asheville (G-703)
Nags Head Hammocks LLC.....................G..... 252 441-6115
  Nags Head (G-11724)
North Amercn Aerodynamics Inc...........D..... 336 599-9266
  Roxboro (G-13809)
Oleksynprannyk LLC..............................F..... 704 450-0182
  Mooresville (G-11043)
▲ Photo Emblem Incorporated...............G..... 336 784-4000
  Winston Salem (G-16851)
Piedmont Parachute Inc.........................G..... 336 597-2225
  Roxboro (G-13819)
R/W Connection Inc...............................G..... 252 446-0114
  Rocky Mount (G-13726)
Red Oak Sales Company.........................G..... 704 483-8464
  Denver (G-4798)
S & S Trawl Shop Inc.............................G..... 910 842-9197
  Supply (G-15010)
S Loflin Enterprises Inc.........................F..... 704 633-1159
  Salisbury (G-14039)
▲ Saab Barracuda LLC...........................E..... 910 814-3088
  Lillington (G-9859)
Sew Trendy...G..... 252 240-9796
  Morehead City (G-11188)
Spc-Usa Inc..G..... 910 875-9002
  Raeford (G-12440)
Thin Line Saddle Pads Inc.....................G..... 919 680-6803
  Durham (G-5400)

Tonyas Crocheted Creations..................G..... 704 421-2143
  Charlotte (G-3708)
Treklite Inc..G..... 919 610-1788
  Raleigh (G-13358)
Triangle Hrse Blanket Svcs LLC............G..... 919 945-9560
  Stem (G-14939)
Wovenart Inc..F..... 828 859-6349
  Tryon (G-15432)
▲ Yellow Dog Design Inc........................F..... 336 553-2172
  Greensboro (G-7472)

24 LUMBER AND WOOD PRODUCTS, EXCEPT FURNITURE

2411 Logging

3 D Footprints Logging Inc...................G..... 910 521-2640
  Maxton (G-10353)
360 Forest Products Inc........................G..... 910 285-5838
  Wallace (G-15618)
A & S Logging LLC.................................G..... 336 879-4364
  Seagrove (G-14232)
A and J Ta Logging................................G..... 919 663-1110
  Siler City (G-14394)
ABB Logging LLC....................................G..... 252 809-0180
  Williamston (G-16056)
Afsc LLC...D..... 704 523-4936
  Charlotte (G-2142)
Alan Walsh Logging LLC........................G..... 828 234-7500
  Lenoir (G-9570)
Allen Brothers Timber Company............E..... 910 997-6412
  Rockingham (G-13619)
Allen R Goodson Logging Co.................G..... 910 455-4177
  Jacksonville (G-8987)
Alligood Brothers Logging.....................G..... 252 927-2358
  Washington (G-15680)
Allsbrook Logging LLC...........................G..... 252 567-1085
  Enfield (G-5674)
Alpha Logging Inc..................................G..... 252 568-2727
  Deep Run (G-4715)
Anson Wood Products............................G..... 704 694-5390
  Wadesboro (G-15501)
Anthony B Andrews Logging Inc............G..... 252 448-8901
  Trenton (G-15332)
Appalachian Timber Company...............G..... 828 507-6505
  Sylva (G-15052)
Arauco - NA..G..... 910 569-7020
  Biscoe (G-1103)
Arcola Logging Co Inc...........................F..... 252 257-3205
  Macon (G-10068)
Arrants Logging Inc..............................F..... 252 792-1889
  Jamesville (G-9077)
Asheville Contracting Co Inc.................E..... 828 665-8900
  Candler (G-1567)
Ashworth Logging..................................G..... 910 464-2136
  Carthage (G-1659)
Associated Artists Southport.................G..... 910 457-5450
  Southport (G-14566)
Atlantic Logging Inc..............................F..... 252 229-9997
  New Bern (G-11772)
Autry Logging Inc..................................G..... 910 303-4943
  Stedman (G-14933)
Backwoods Logging LLC........................G..... 910 298-3786
  Pink Hill (G-12314)
Backwoods Logging Pink Hl Inc............G..... 910 298-1284
  Pink Hill (G-12315)
Barnes Logging Co Inc..........................F..... 252 799-6016
  Plymouth (G-12365)
Barry Lane Perry....................................G..... 252 799-4334
  Jamesville (G-9078)
Bateman Logging Co Inc.......................F..... 252 482-8959
  Edenton (G-5508)

Baur Logging LLC...................................G..... 757 535-5693
  Gatesville (G-6547)
Bh Logging...G..... 980 330-0229
  Statesville (G-14763)
Bill Ratliff Jr Logging I..........................G..... 704 694-5403
  Wadesboro (G-15502)
Billy Harrell Logging Inc.......................F..... 252 221-4995
  Tyner (G-15433)
Billy Harrell Logging Inc.......................G..... 252 426-1362
  Hertford (G-7916)
Black River Logging Inc........................G..... 910 669-2850
  Ivanhoe (G-8980)
Blankenship Logging..............................G..... 828 652-2250
  Nebo (G-11759)
Bobby A Herring Logging......................G..... 919 658-9768
  Mount Olive (G-11656)
Boone Logging Company Inc.................G..... 252 443-7641
  Elm City (G-5647)
Boyles Logging LLC................................G..... 910 206-7086
  Ellerbe (G-5641)
Bracey Bros Logging LLC......................G..... 910 231-9543
  Delco (G-4719)
Bradley Todd Baugus..............................G..... 252 665-4901
  Maysville (G-10369)
Brett McHenry Logging LLC..................F..... 252 243-7285
  Wilson (G-16478)
Broadway Logging Co Inc......................E..... 252 633-2693
  New Bern (G-11778)
Brown Brothers Lumber.........................G..... 828 632-6486
  Taylorsville (G-15132)
Brown Creek Timber Company Inc........G..... 704 694-3529
  Wadesboro (G-15504)
Bruce Stanley..G..... 828 683-1265
  Leicester (G-9508)
Buck Lucas Logging Companies............G..... 252 410-0160
  Roanoke Rapids (G-13568)
Buds Logging and Trucking...................G..... 704 465-8016
  Wadesboro (G-15505)
Bundy Logging Company Inc.................F..... 252 357-0191
  Gatesville (G-6548)
Burgess Duke Hward Ktrina Kner.........G..... 704 732-0547
  Lincolnton (G-9877)
By Faith Logging Inc.............................G..... 252 792-0019
  Williamston (G-16058)
Cahoon Brothers Logging LLC...............F..... 252 943-9901
  Pinetown (G-12245)
Cahoon Logging Company Inc..............G..... 252 943-6805
  Pinetown (G-12246)
Calvin Laws Jay.....................................G..... 336 973-4318
  Ferguson (G-5956)
Capps Noble Logging............................G..... 828 696-9690
  Zirconia (G-17150)
Caraway Logging Inc............................G..... 252 633-1230
  New Bern (G-11783)
Carolina East Timber Inc......................G..... 252 638-1914
  New Bern (G-11784)
Carter Thomas Wayne Sr.....................G..... 336 623-2177
  Reidsville (G-13513)
Cauley Construction Company..............G..... 252 522-1078
  Kinston (G-9353)
Cbr Logging LLC....................................G..... 252 791-0494
  Plymouth (G-12368)
Chapman Brothers Logging LLC...........G..... 828 437-6498
  Connelly Springs (G-4398)
Charles Ferguson Logging....................G..... 336 921-3126
  Moravian Falls (G-11144)
CJ Stallings Logging Inc.......................F..... 252 297-2272
  Belvidere (G-1021)
Cjc Enterprises......................................E..... 919 266-3158
  Wake Forest (G-15541)
Claybourn Walters Log Co Inc..............F..... 910 628-7075
  Fairmont (G-5701)

Employee Codes: A=Over 500 employees, B=251-500
C=101-250, D=51-100, E=20-50, F=10-19, G=1-9

24 LUMBER AND WOOD PRODUCTS, EXCEPT FURNITURE

Coastal Carolina Loggin .... G 252 474-2165
   Ernul *(G-5686)*
▲ Columbia West Virginia Corp .... E 336 605-0429
   Greensboro *(G-6921)*
Conetoe Land & Timber LLC .... F 252 717-4648
   Goldsboro *(G-6603)*
Corbett Timber Company .... G 910 406-1129
   Hampstead *(G-7644)*
Country Roads Logging LLC .... G 252 578-8191
   Margarettsville *(G-10136)*
Country Roads Logging LLC .... G 252 398-4770
   Como *(G-4183)*
Cutting Up Logging LLC .... G 910 389-3539
   Maysville *(G-10371)*
Cypress Creek Harvesting Inc .... G 805 462-9412
   Garland *(G-6241)*
D & M Logging of Wnc LLC .... G 828 648-4366
   Canton *(G-1612)*
D & W Logging Inc .... F 919 820-0826
   Four Oaks *(G-6102)*
D J Logging Inc .... G 919 219-6853
   Raleigh *(G-12669)*
D T Bracy Logging Inc .... G 252 332-8332
   Ahoskie *(G-59)*
Dan Morton Logging .... G 919 693-1898
   Oxford *(G-12126)*
Daniel A Malpass Logging .... G 910 669-2823
   Kelly *(G-9137)*
Dannies Logging Inc .... G 919 528-2370
   Creedmoor *(G-4612)*
Danny Huffman Logging LLC .... G 336 973-0555
   Purlear *(G-12410)*
Darrell T Bracy .... G 252 358-1432
   Ahoskie *(G-60)*
Dave Mulhollem Logging Inc .... G 919 796-8994
   Wendell *(G-15896)*
David E Meiggs .... G 252 340-1640
   Hertford *(G-7919)*
David J Spain .... G 252 902-6900
   Washington *(G-15694)*
David Miller Logging LLC .... G 336 831-4052
   Boonville *(G-1254)*
David Raynor Logging Inc .... E 910 980-0129
   Linden *(G-9939)*
Deberry Land & Timber Inc .... G 910 572-2698
   Troy *(G-15403)*
Delbert White Logging Inc .... G 252 209-4779
   Windsor *(G-16564)*
Derick Cordon Logging Inc .... F 252 964-2009
   Bath *(G-915)*
Dockery Logging .... G 828 557-9149
   Murphy *(G-11708)*
Donald R Young Logging Inc .... G 910 934-6769
   Lillington *(G-9850)*
Douglas Temple & Son Inc .... G 252 771-5676
   Elizabeth City *(G-5541)*
Down South Logging LLC .... G 843 333-1649
   Tabor City *(G-15080)*
Dr Logging LLC .... G 910 417-9643
   Hamlet *(G-7620)*
Duncan Junior D .... G 336 871-3599
   Sandy Ridge *(G-14078)*
Duplin Forest Products Inc .... F 910 285-5381
   Wallace *(G-15621)*
Dustin Ellis Logging .... G 704 732-6027
   Lincolnton *(G-9891)*
Dustin Lynn Sink .... G 336 442-5602
   Trinity *(G-15340)*
Duvall Timber LLC .... G 704 236-2211
   Waxhaw *(G-15755)*
E JS Logging Inc .... G 252 927-3539
   Pinetown *(G-12248)*

E Z Stop Number Two .... G 828 627-9081
   Clyde *(G-4124)*
East Coast Log & Timber Inc .... G 252 568-4344
   Albertson *(G-115)*
East Coast Logging Inc .... G 252 794-4054
   Windsor *(G-16565)*
Eddie Ta Mendenhall Logging .... G 919 718-9293
   Moncure *(G-10620)*
Edsel G Barnes Jr Inc .... G 252 793-4170
   Plymouth *(G-12372)*
Edwards Logging Inc .... G 336 783-0833
   Mount Airy *(G-11506)*
Emanuel Hoggard .... F 252 794-3724
   Windsor *(G-16566)*
Enterprise Loggers Company Inc .... F 252 586-4805
   Littleton *(G-9951)*
Eric Martin Jermey .... G 704 692-0389
   Bostic *(G-1262)*
Evans Logging Inc .... F 252 792-3865
   Jamesville *(G-9080)*
Evergreen Forest Products Inc .... G 910 762-9156
   Wilmington *(G-16213)*
Evergreen Logging LLC .... F 910 654-1662
   Evergreen *(G-5697)*
Faith Logging .... G 828 446-5671
   Lenoir *(G-9611)*
Foster Jackson & Sons LLC .... G 828 674-7941
   Saluda *(G-14070)*
Frankie York Logging Co .... G 252 633-4825
   New Bern *(G-11804)*
Fred R Harrris Logging Inc .... G 919 853-2266
   Louisburg *(G-9989)*
Freeman Transport and Logging .... G 910 220-5358
   Star *(G-14715)*
Fuqua Logging Company Inc .... F 336 562-5178
   Leasburg *(G-9505)*
G & G Logging .... G 336 352-5586
   Lowgap *(G-10013)*
G & H Broadway Logging Inc .... G 252 229-4594
   New Bern *(G-11805)*
G&N Logging LLC .... G 919 524-1555
   Middlesex *(G-10449)*
General Wood Preserving Co .... G 910 371-3131
   Leland *(G-9546)*
George P Gatling Logging .... G 252 465-8983
   Sunbury *(G-14996)*
Glacier Forestry Inc .... G 704 902-2594
   Mooresville *(G-10959)*
Gladsons Logging LLC .... F 252 670-8813
   Aurora *(G-835)*
Glenn Trexler & Sons Log Inc .... F 704 694-5644
   Wadesboro *(G-15510)*
Gmd Logging Inc .... G 704 985-5460
   Albemarle *(G-87)*
Gold Creek Inc .... G 336 468-4495
   Hamptonville *(G-7670)*
Goodson S All Terrain Log Inc .... F 910 347-7919
   Jacksonville *(G-9004)*
Goodsons All Terrain Log .... G 910 934-8451
   Jacksonville *(G-9005)*
Gouge Logging .... G 828 675-9216
   Burnsville *(G-1527)*
Grady & Son Atkins Logging .... G 919 934-7785
   Four Oaks *(G-6106)*
Grassy Ridge Logging Co .... G 919 935-5355
   Robbins *(G-13598)*
Greene Logging .... G 336 667-6960
   Purlear *(G-12412)*
Greenes Logging .... G 910 533-2021
   Roseboro *(G-13785)*
H & H Login .... G 704 272-8763
   Polkton *(G-12387)*

H & L Logging Inc .... F 252 793-2778
   Plymouth *(G-12374)*
H Clyde Moore Jr .... G 910 642-3507
   Whiteville *(G-15965)*
H&R Transport LLC .... G 910 588-4410
   Garland *(G-6245)*
Hardister Logging .... G 336 857-2397
   Denton *(G-4736)*
Harris Logging LLC .... G 336 859-2786
   Denton *(G-4737)*
Hofler Logging Inc .... G 252 465-8921
   Sunbury *(G-14998)*
Holmes Logging - Wallace LLC .... F 910 271-1216
   Wallace *(G-15623)*
Htc Logging Inc .... G 828 625-1601
   Mill Spring *(G-10487)*
Hunt Logging Co .... G 919 853-2850
   Louisburg *(G-9991)*
I I G Logging Inc .... G 704 984-3175
   Morven *(G-11471)*
Ivey Icenhour DBA .... G 704 786-0676
   Mount Pleasant *(G-11674)*
◆ Ivp Forest Products LLC .... F 252 241-8126
   Morehead City *(G-11177)*
J & J Logging Inc .... E 252 430-1110
   Henderson *(G-7790)*
J E Carpenter Logging Co Inc .... F 252 633-0037
   Trent Woods *(G-15328)*
J E Kerr Timber Co Corp .... G 252 537-0544
   Roanoke Rapids *(G-13576)*
J&D Logging Inc .... G 910 271-0750
   Warsaw *(G-15670)*
J&R Cohoon Logging & Tidewater .... F 252 943-6300
   Pantego *(G-12165)*
Jackson Logging .... G 919 658-2757
   Mount Olive *(G-11663)*
James Keith Nations .... G 828 421-5391
   Whittier *(G-16007)*
James L Johnson .... G 704 694-0103
   Wadesboro *(G-15514)*
James Moore & Son Logging .... G 336 656-9858
   Browns Summit *(G-1309)*
Jared Sasnett Logging Co Inc .... G 252 939-6289
   Kinston *(G-9370)*
Jds Logging LLC .... G 910 713-5980
   Ash *(G-395)*
Jeff Weaver Logging .... G 864 909-1758
   Columbus *(G-4175)*
Jeffers Logging Inc .... G 919 708-2193
   Sanford *(G-14139)*
Jennifer Niten Logging .... G 336 428-6245
   Elkin *(G-5621)*
Jerry Cox Logging .... G 919 742-6089
   Ramseur *(G-13443)*
Jh Logging .... G 336 599-0278
   Roxboro *(G-13805)*
Jif Logging Inc .... G 252 398-2249
   Murfreesboro *(G-11699)*
Jimmie A Hogan .... G 910 428-2535
   Biscoe *(G-1112)*
Jimmy D Nelms Logging Inc .... F 919 853-2597
   Louisburg *(G-9993)*
Jj Hernandez Logging LLC .... G 919 742-3381
   Siler City *(G-14418)*
Jk Logging LLC .... G 910 648-5471
   Evergreen *(G-5698)*
JM Williams Timber Company .... G 919 362-1333
   Apex *(G-209)*
Jmw Logging LLC .... G 919 934-4115
   Smithfield *(G-14466)*
Johnny Daniel .... G 336 859-2480
   Denton *(G-4739)*

24 LUMBER AND WOOD PRODUCTS, EXCEPT FURNITURE

Joseph and Jerry Curtis .... G 704 663-4811
　Mooresville *(G-10988)*
Josh Lane Logging LLC .... G 828 289-4052
　Union Mills *(G-15441)*
Jph III Logging Inc .... G 910 610-9338
　Laurinburg *(G-9482)*
Jrt Logging Inc .... G 704 322-0458
　Polkton *(G-12388)*
Juan J Hernandez .... G 919 742-3381
　Siler City *(G-14419)*
Justin Moretz & Greg Moretz Db ..... G 828 263-8668
　Deep Gap *(G-4709)*
K & J Ashworth Logging LLC .... G 336 879-2388
　Seagrove *(G-14242)*
K L Butler Logging Inc .... G 910 648-6016
　Bladenboro *(G-1150)*
Keck Logging & Chipping Inc .... G 336 538-6903
　Gibsonville *(G-6564)*
Keck Logging Company .... G 336 538-6903
　Gibsonville *(G-6565)*
Keith Call Logging LLC .... G 336 262-3681
　Millers Creek *(G-10493)*
Keith Laws .... G 336 973-7220
　Wilkesboro *(G-16034)*
Ken Horton Logging LLC .... G 336 789-2849
　Mount Airy *(G-11530)*
Ken Wood Corp .... G 252 792-6481
　Williamston *(G-16064)*
Kenneth Perkins .... G 919 267-9396
　Holly Springs *(G-8704)*
Kornegay Logging & Timber Co ...... G 919 658-5716
　Mount Olive *(G-11665)*
Laceys Tree Service .... G 910 330-2868
　Jacksonville *(G-9012)*
Lake Creek Logging & Trckg Inc .... F 910 532-2041
　Harrells *(G-7693)*
Lane Land & Timber Inc .... G 252 443-1151
　Battleboro *(G-923)*
Lannings Farming and Logging ...... G 828 246-8938
　Clyde *(G-4125)*
Laws Logging .... G 336 973-4318
　Ferguson *(G-5958)*
Ledford Logging Co Inc .... G 828 644-5410
　Murphy *(G-11711)*
Lees Logging Company .... F 910 385-7201
　Harrells *(G-7694)*
Leonard Logging Co .... G 336 857-2776
　Denton *(G-4743)*
Lite Logging LLC .... G 252 560-8131
　La Grange *(G-9442)*
Little Logging Inc .... F 704 201-8185
　Oakboro *(G-12076)*
Log Home Builders Inc .... G 704 638-0677
　Salisbury *(G-14007)*
Logger Head Logging .... G 919 842-0249
　New Hill *(G-11862)*
Luxury Escapes LLC .... F 706 373-8500
　Raleigh *(G-12983)*
Lyon Logging .... G 336 957-3131
　Thurmond *(G-15311)*
M & K Logging LLC .... G 252 349-8975
　New Bern *(G-11816)*
M M & D Harvesting Inc .... G 252 793-4074
　Plymouth *(G-12376)*
Mark III Logging Inc .... G 910 862-4820
　Tar Heel *(G-15089)*
Mark Lindsay Looper .... G 828 234-5453
　Lenoir *(G-9630)*
Matthew Johnson Logging .... G 919 291-0197
　Sanford *(G-14150)*
McKay Logging Inc .... G 910 334-3448
　Rockingham *(G-13634)*

McKeel & Sons Logging Inc .... G 252 244-3903
　Vanceboro *(G-15480)*
McKenzies Tree Service & Log .... G 910 995-1576
　Hamlet *(G-7627)*
McKoys Logging Company Inc .... G 910 862-2706
　Elizabethtown *(G-5598)*
McLendon Logging Incorporated ... G 910 439-6223
　Mount Gilead *(G-11604)*
McNeely Accounting & Tax Svc ...... G 828 652-7405
　Marion *(G-10164)*
Meacham Logging Inc .... G 910 652-2794
　Ellerbe *(G-5642)*
Mendoza Logging Inc .... G 252 935-5560
　Pantego *(G-12168)*
Merritt Logging & Chipping Co ...... F 910 862-4905
　Elizabethtown *(G-5599)*
Michael L Goodson Logging Inc .... G 910 346-8399
　Jacksonville *(G-9013)*
Micheal Langdon Logging Inc .... G 910 890-5295
　Erwin *(G-5687)*
Mickey Blanton Logging .... G 828 289-9344
　Mooresboro *(G-10839)*
Mike Atkins & Son Logging Inc ...... G 919 965-8002
　Selma *(G-14258)*
Mike Goodwin Logging .... G 704 848-8222
　Lilesville *(G-9840)*
Miller Logging Co Inc .... G 252 229-9860
　Vanceboro *(G-15481)*
Mini Semi Logging .... G 828 284-1360
　Burnsville *(G-1529)*
MN Logging LLC .... G 828 286-9262
　Rutherfordton *(G-13880)*
Montgomery Logging Inc .... G 910 572-2806
　Troy *(G-15409)*
Morgan & Son Logging .... G 828 389-9618
　Hayesville *(G-7769)*
Mountain Valley Logging LLC .... G 828 551-0861
　Zirconia *(G-17155)*
Mud Duck Operations .... G 910 253-7669
　Bolivia *(G-1165)*
Myers Brothers Logging LLC .... G 828 432-9738
　Morganton *(G-11237)*
Myers Logging LLC .... G 919 496-0379
　Castalia *(G-1940)*
Nat Black Logging Inc .... F 704 826-8834
　Ansonville *(G-153)*
Nathan Beiler .... G 252 935-5141
　Pantego *(G-12169)*
NC Logging & Clearing LLC .... G 919 524-4878
　Sanford *(G-14157)*
New Vision Logging LLC .... G 910 594-0571
　Newton Grove *(G-11991)*
Noble Brothers Logging Company .. G 252 355-2587
　Winterville *(G-17010)*
Noralex Inc .... G 252 974-1253
　Vanceboro *(G-15482)*
North Cape Fear Logging LLC .... G 910 876-3197
　Harrells *(G-7695)*
Nrfp Logging LLC .... G 919 738-0989
　Goldsboro *(G-6639)*
OBrien Logging Co .... G 910 655-3830
　Delco *(G-4723)*
OLT Logging Inc .... G 919 894-4506
　Smithfield *(G-14473)*
One More Cast .... G 252 995-6026
　Avon *(G-846)*
Outkast Timber Harvesting LLC ..... G 336 906-0962
　Randleman *(G-13482)*
P & C Logging LLC .... G 919 552-3420
　Fuquay Varina *(G-6221)*
Pack Brothers Logging .... G 828 894-2191
　Mill Spring *(G-10489)*

Phillip Dunn Logging Co Inc .... F 252 633-4577
　New Bern *(G-11835)*
Piedmont Logging LLC .... G 919 562-1861
　Youngsville *(G-17091)*
Plan B Chipping and Logging .... G 336 942-2692
　Sophia *(G-14520)*
Potter Logging .... G 704 483-2738
　Denver *(G-4795)*
Potts Logging Inc .... G 704 463-7549
　New London *(G-11875)*
Precision Log & Chipping LLC .... G 828 446-1592
　Taylorsville *(G-15158)*
Preferred Logging .... G 910 471-4011
　Delco *(G-4724)*
Price Logging Inc .... G 252 792-5687
　Jamesville *(G-9081)*
Pritchard Logging LLC .... G 828 447-4354
　Rutherfordton *(G-13885)*
Puett Trucking & Logging .... G 919 853-2071
　Louisburg *(G-9997)*
R & R Logging Inc .... G 704 483-5733
　Iron Station *(G-8976)*
R & S Logging Inc .... G 252 426-5880
　Hertford *(G-7923)*
R R Mickey Logging Inc .... G 910 205-0525
　Hamlet *(G-7631)*
R W Britt Logging Inc .... G 252 799-7682
　Pinetown *(G-12249)*
Rabbit Bottom Logging Co Inc .... F 252 257-3585
　Warrenton *(G-15660)*
Randolph Goodson Logging Inc ..... G 910 347-5117
　Jacksonville *(G-9025)*
Randy Chappell Logging LLC .... G 910 439-6690
　Mount Gilead *(G-11612)*
Randy Smith and Sons Logging ..... G 828 263-0574
　Deep Gap *(G-4712)*
Red Maple Logging Company Inc ... G 704 279-6379
　Rockwell *(G-13657)*
Richard C Jones .... G 919 853-2096
　Louisburg *(G-10000)*
Richard Lewis Von .... G 910 628-9292
　Orrum *(G-12117)*
Ricky Don Thornton .... G 910 271-2989
　Teachey *(G-15178)*
Ricky Wyatt Logging .... G 336 984-3145
　North Wilkesboro *(G-12032)*
Roberson Logging LLC .... F 252 799-7076
　Williamston *(G-16069)*
Robert L Rich Tmber Hrvstg Inc ..... G 910 529-7321
　Garland *(G-6246)*
Roland Brothers LLC .... G 336 385-9013
　Warrensville *(G-15653)*
Rondol Cordon Logging Inc .... G 252 944-9220
　Washington *(G-15729)*
Ronnie A Mabe .... G 336 994-2257
　King *(G-9280)*
Ronnie Boyds Logging LLC .... G 336 613-0229
　Eden *(G-5501)*
Ronnie Garrett Logging .... G 828 894-8413
　Columbus *(G-4179)*
Ronnie L Poole .... G 336 657-3956
　Ennice *(G-5685)*
Ross Phelps Logging Co Inc .... F 252 356-2560
　Colerain *(G-4140)*
Rotens Logging LLC .... G 336 981-7019
　North Wilkesboro *(G-12033)*
Roundwood Logging Inc .... G 252 230-9980
　Sims *(G-14444)*
Rudys Logging LLC .... G 910 918-2993
　Leland *(G-9559)*
Russell Loudermilk Logging .... G 828 632-4968
　Taylorsville *(G-15164)*

Employee Codes: A=Over 500 employees, B=251-500
C=101-250, D=51-100, E=20-50, F=10-19, G=1-9

24 LUMBER AND WOOD PRODUCTS, EXCEPT FURNITURE

S & K Logging Inc................................... F 252 794-2045
  Windsor *(G-16569)*

Shelton Logging & Chipping Inc............ G 336 548-3860
  Stoneville *(G-14966)*

Shepherd Family Logging LLC.............. G 910 572-4098
  Troy *(G-15415)*

Simmons Logging & Trucking Inc.......... F 910 287-6344
  Ash *(G-396)*

Skj Moore Logging LLC.......................... G 910 642-5724
  Nakina *(G-11731)*

Smith Brothers Logging........................... G 828 265-1506
  Deep Gap *(G-4713)*

Smiths Logging.. G 910 653-4422
  Tabor City *(G-15086)*

Snowbird Logging LLC............................ G 828 479-6635
  Robbinsville *(G-13613)*

▲ Southeast Wood Products Inc.............. F 910 285-4359
  Wallace *(G-15627)*

Southern Logging Inc.............................. F 336 859-5057
  Denton *(G-4748)*

Southern Style Logging LLC................... G 910 259-9897
  Rocky Point *(G-13750)*

Spencer Logging..................................... G 910 638-4899
  Southern Pines *(G-14557)*

Squeaks Logging Inc.............................. G 252 794-1531
  Windsor *(G-16570)*

SSS Logging Inc..................................... G 828 467-1155
  Marion *(G-10180)*

Stafford Logging LLC.............................. G 828 635-8584
  Moravian Falls *(G-11147)*

Steve & Ray Banks Logging Inc............. G 910 743-3051
  Maysville *(G-10376)*

Steve Evans Logging Inc........................ G 252 792-1836
  Williamston *(G-16071)*

Steve Whiteside Logging LLC................. G 828 287-5862
  Rutherfordton *(G-13891)*

Steven C Haddock DBA Haddock........... G 252 714-2431
  Vanceboro *(G-15483)*

Stone House Creek Logging................... G 252 586-4477
  Littleton *(G-9953)*

Stroud Logging....................................... G 828 541-2721
  Marble *(G-10134)*

Stump Logging.. G 910 620-7000
  Supply *(G-15012)*

Sugg Logging LLC.................................. G 910 995-5728
  Ellerbe *(G-5645)*

Summit Logging LLC.............................. G 910 734-8787
  Lumberton *(G-10056)*

Swain & Temple Inc................................ E 252 771-8147
  South Mills *(G-14525)*

SWB Logging LLC.................................. G 704 485-3411
  Oakboro *(G-12082)*

T and T Timber.. G 252 799-6077
  Roper *(G-13771)*

T E Garner Logging................................. G 252 678-3836
  Gaston *(G-6332)*

T W Hathcock Logging Inc...................... G 704 485-9457
  Locust *(G-9974)*

T&L Nursery and Logging LLC................ G 828 387-0448
  Newland *(G-11895)*

TA Logging LLC...................................... G 704 485-8337
  Oakboro *(G-12083)*

Tar River Thinning Inc............................. F 919 497-1647
  Louisburg *(G-10004)*

Taylor Timber Co LLC............................. G 910 588-6214
  Harrells *(G-7696)*

Ted M Hart Logging Inc.......................... G 919 776-7237
  Sanford *(G-14195)*

Terry Leggett Logging Co Inc.................. E 252 927-4671
  Pinetown *(G-12250)*

Terry Logging Company.......................... G 919 477-9170
  Bahama *(G-867)*

Thomas Gary Helton................................ G 828 726-3694
  Lenoir *(G-9656)*

Thomas Timber Inc.................................. F 910 532-4542
  Harrells *(G-7697)*

Thompson Timber Harvest LLC.............. G 919 632-4326
  Franklinton *(G-6166)*

Tim Con Wood Products Inc................... E 252 793-4819
  Roper *(G-13772)*

Timber Harvester Inc............................... G 910 346-9754
  Jacksonville *(G-9042)*

Timber Specialists Inc............................. G 704 902-5146
  Statesville *(G-14914)*

Timber Specialists LLC........................... F 704 873-5756
  Statesville *(G-14915)*

Timber Stand Improvements Inc............. G 910 439-6121
  Mount Gilead *(G-11613)*

Timothy Kornegay................................... G 919 222-3184
  Albertson *(G-116)*

Tippett Logging LLC................................ G 252 301-3170
  Whitakers *(G-15957)*

Top Notch Log Homes Inc....................... G 828 926-4300
  Waynesville *(G-15829)*

Trexler Logging Inc.................................. G 704 694-5272
  Wadesboro *(G-15517)*

Triple E Equipment LLC.......................... G 252 448-1002
  Trenton *(G-15336)*

Tucker Logging....................................... G 336 857-2674
  Denton *(G-4753)*

Tysinger Logging Inc............................... G 910 220-5053
  Star *(G-14724)*

Vincent L Taylor..................................... G 252 792-2987
  Williamston *(G-16072)*

Vultare Logging LLC............................... G 252 578-0377
  Roanoke Rapids *(G-13584)*

W & T Logging LLC................................ G 252 209-4351
  Windsor *(G-16571)*

W H Bunting Thinning............................. G 252 826-4025
  Scotland Neck *(G-14223)*

W R White Inc.. F 252 794-6577
  Windsor *(G-16572)*

Wade Biggs Logging Inc......................... F 252 927-4470
  Pinetown *(G-12251)*

Walker Logging....................................... G 336 964-1380
  Denton *(G-4755)*

Wayne Dunn Logging LLC...................... G 910 439-5478
  Mount Gilead *(G-11615)*

Wayne Lamb Logging Co........................ G 910 529-1115
  Garland *(G-6247)*

Wetherington Logging Inc....................... G 252 393-8435
  Stella *(G-14938)*

Whitener Sales Company........................ G 828 253-0518
  Asheville *(G-821)*

William Shawn Staley.............................. G 336 838-9193
  Millers Creek *(G-10496)*

Williams & Son Logging LLC................... G 252 533-9201
  Roanoke Rapids *(G-13590)*

Williams Logging Inc............................... G 919 542-2740
  Moncure *(G-10630)*

Wilson Bros Logging Inc......................... F 252 445-5317
  Enfield *(G-5682)*

Wilson Logging Nc LLC.......................... G 336 280-8648
  Summerfield *(G-14994)*

Wolf Timber LLC..................................... G 252 799-0495
  Williamston *(G-16074)*

Wood Logging.. G 910 866-4018
  White Oak *(G-15958)*

Wright & Hobbs Inc................................. E 252 537-5817
  Roanoke Rapids *(G-13591)*

Wst Logging LLC.................................... G 336 857-0147
  Denton *(G-4756)*

Young Logging Company Inc.................. G 919 552-9753
  Willow Spring *(G-16085)*

2421 Sawmills and planing mills, general

Alan Kimzey.. G 828 891-8720
  Mills River *(G-10498)*

Appalachian Getaways........................... G 828 243-3105
  Asheville *(G-521)*

Arcola Lumber Company Inc................... E 252 257-4923
  Warrenton *(G-15655)*

Arcola Sawmill.. G 252 257-1139
  Warrenton *(G-15656)*

Ashton Lewis Lumber Co Inc.................. D 252 357-0050
  Gatesville *(G-6546)*

Beasley Flooring Products Inc................ E 828 524-3248
  Bryson City *(G-1320)*

Big Pine Log and Lumber Inc.................. G 828 656-2754
  Marshall *(G-10200)*

Binderholz Enfield LLC........................... E 770 362-0558
  Enfield *(G-5676)*

Blue Ridge Lbr Log & Timber Co............ F 336 961-5211
  Yadkinville *(G-17033)*

Boones Sawmill Inc................................ G 828 287-8774
  Rutherfordton *(G-13867)*

Braxton Sawmill Inc................................ F 336 376-6798
  Graham *(G-6680)*

Bruce Trull Sawing Mill............................ G 828 667-1148
  Candler *(G-1572)*

Builders Firstsource Inc.......................... G 336 884-5454
  Greensboro *(G-6860)*

C & C Chipping Inc................................. F 252 249-1617
  Grantsboro *(G-6764)*

C & J Crosspieces LLC........................... F 910 652-4955
  Star *(G-14714)*

Cagle Sawmill Inc.................................... F 336 857-2274
  Denton *(G-4728)*

Canton Dry Kilns LLC............................. G 828 492-0715
  Canton *(G-1606)*

Canton Hardwood Company................... E 828 492-0715
  Canton *(G-1607)*

Capital Wood Products Inc...................... G 704 982-2417
  New London *(G-11867)*

Carolina Timberworks LLC..................... F 828 266-9663
  West Jefferson *(G-15936)*

Church & Church Lumber LLC................ F 336 838-1256
  Millers Creek *(G-10492)*

Church & Church Lumber LLC................ D 336 973-5700
  Wilkesboro *(G-16017)*

Clary Lumber Company.......................... D 252 537-2558
  Gaston *(G-6330)*

Cobble Creek Lumber LLC..................... F 336 844-2620
  West Jefferson *(G-15937)*

◆ Coco Lumber Company LLC................. G 336 906-3754
  Charlotte *(G-2520)*

Conover Lumber Company Inc............... F 828 464-4591
  Conover *(G-4438)*

Cook Brothers Lumber Co Inc................ F 828 524-4857
  Franklin *(G-6122)*

Creedmoor Forest Products.................... E 919 529-1779
  Creedmoor *(G-4611)*

Crossties Plus LLC................................. F 252 943-7437
  Plymouth *(G-12369)*

D C Custom Freight LLC......................... E 843 658-6484
  Marshville *(G-10213)*

Dagenhart Pallet Inc............................... F 828 241-2374
  Catawba *(G-1964)*

Daniels Lumber Sales Inc....................... F 336 622-5486
  Liberty *(G-9810)*

David Raynor Logging Inc...................... E 910 980-0129
  Linden *(G-9939)*

Delzer Construction................................ G 919 625-0755
  Cary *(G-1748)*

Domtar Paper Company LLC.................. B 252 793-8111
  Plymouth *(G-12371)*

SIC SECTION
24 LUMBER AND WOOD PRODUCTS, EXCEPT FURNITURE

Donald Henley & Sons Sawmill................G..... 336 625-5665
  Asheboro (G-424)
Duplin Forest Products Inc......................F..... 910 285-5381
  Wallace (G-15621)
E W Godwin S Sons Inc..........................E..... 910 762-7747
  Wilmington (G-16208)
East Coast Firewood LLC.........................F..... 919 542-0792
  Moncure (G-10619)
Edwards Timber Company Inc...................G..... 704 624-5098
  Marshville (G-10215)
Edwards Wood Pdts Inc/Woodlawn............G..... 828 756-4758
  Marion (G-10149)
Edwards Wood Products Inc....................D..... 704 624-5098
  Liberty (G-9811)
Edwards Wood Products Inc....................D..... 336 622-7537
  Liberty (G-9812)
◆ Edwards Wood Products Inc..................C..... 704 624-3624
  Marshville (G-10216)
Edwards Wood Products Inc....................D..... 910 276-6870
  Laurinburg (G-9477)
Elkins Sawmill Inc..................................E..... 919 362-1235
  Moncure (G-10621)
Ellis Lumber Company Inc.......................F..... 704 482-1414
  Shelby (G-14315)
F L Turlington Lumber Co Inc...................E..... 910 592-7197
  Clinton (G-4095)
Felts Lumber Co Inc..............................G..... 336 368-5667
  Pinnacle (G-12321)
Ferguson Lumber Inc.............................G..... 336 871-2591
  Sandy Ridge (G-14079)
Flame Tech Inc....................................E..... 336 661-7801
  Winston Salem (G-16713)
Four Jaks..G..... 828 484-9545
  Weaverville (G-15847)
Fraser West Inc...................................E..... 910 655-4106
  Riegelwood (G-13558)
Fred Winfield Lumber Co Inc....................E..... 828 648-3414
  Canton (G-1617)
Friddles Custom Sawing..........................G..... 336 210-0144
  Stokesdale (G-14942)
Fulp Lumber Company Inc.......................F..... 336 573-3113
  Stoneville (G-14957)
G & G Forest Products............................G..... 704 539-5110
  Union Grove (G-15437)
G & G Lumber Company Inc....................E..... 704 539-5110
  Harmony (G-7686)
Gates Custom Milling Inc........................E..... 252 357-0116
  Gatesville (G-6549)
Gilkey Lumber Co Inc.............................G..... 828 286-9069
  Rutherfordton (G-13872)
Glenn Lumber Company Inc....................E..... 704 434-7873
  Shelby (G-14320)
Glenn Lumber Company Inc....................E..... 704 434-9661
  Boiling Springs (G-1159)
▲ Godfrey Lumber Company Inc...............F..... 704 872-6366
  Statesville (G-14804)
Grubb & Son Sawmill Inc........................G..... 336 241-2252
  Trinity (G-15343)
H Parsons Incorporated.........................E..... 828 757-9191
  Lenoir (G-9616)
H W Culp Lumber Company....................D..... 704 463-7311
  New London (G-11871)
Harris Lumber Company Inc....................E..... 828 245-2664
  Rutherfordton (G-13877)
Hartley Brothers Sawmill Inc....................G..... 336 921-2955
  Boomer (G-1171)
Hedrick Brothers Lumber Co Inc...............F..... 336 746-5885
  Lexington (G-9729)
Hewlin Brothers Lumber Co.....................G..... 252 586-6473
  Enfield (G-5679)
High and High Inc.................................F..... 252 257-2390
  Henderson (G-7787)

Hofler H S & Sons Lumber Co..................F..... 252 465-8603
  Sunbury (G-14997)
Hostetler Sawmill.................................G..... 336 468-1800
  Hamptonville (G-7671)
Howard Brothers Mfg LLC......................G..... 919 772-4800
  Garner (G-6275)
Hull Brothers Lumber Co Inc...................E..... 336 789-5252
  Mount Airy (G-11519)
Ibx Lumber LLC...................................F..... 252 935-4050
  Pantego (G-12164)
Idaho Timber NC LLC............................D..... 252 430-0030
  Henderson (G-7789)
Independence Lumber............................G..... 336 366-3400
  Elkin (G-5619)
Independence Lumber Inc......................D..... 276 773-3744
  Davidson (G-4678)
▲ Industrial Wood Products Inc................D..... 336 333-5959
  Climax (G-4086)
International Wood Svcs Inc....................G..... 910 549-8142
  Wilmington (G-16270)
Itl Corp...F..... 828 659-9663
  Marion (G-10152)
▼ J & B Logging and Timber Co................E..... 919 934-4115
  Smithfield (G-14463)
J & D Wood Inc...................................F..... 910 628-9000
  Fairmont (G-5703)
J E Jones Lumber Company....................E..... 336 472-3478
  Lexington (G-9732)
▼ J W Jones Lumber Company Inc............D..... 252 771-2497
  Elizabeth City (G-5551)
Jeld-Wen Inc......................................C..... 336 838-0292
  North Wilkesboro (G-12016)
◆ Jeld-Wen Inc...................................B..... 800 535-3936
  Charlotte (G-3018)
Jerry G Williams & Sons Inc...................E..... 919 934-4115
  Smithfield (G-14464)
Jerry Huffman Sawmill..........................G..... 336 973-3606
  Wilkesboro (G-16033)
Jerry Williams & Son Inc.......................D..... 919 934-4115
  Smithfield (G-14465)
John K Chenausky................................G..... 336 427-2495
  Mayodan (G-10364)
Jordan Lumber & Supply Inc..................C..... 910 439-6121
  Mount Gilead (G-11602)
Jordan Lumber & Supply Inc..................C..... 910 428-9048
  Star (G-14717)
Jordan Lumber & Supply Inc..................C..... 910 439-6121
  Mount Gilead (G-11603)
Jordan-Holman Lumber Co Inc................D..... 828 396-3101
  Granite Falls (G-6740)
Josey Lumber Company Inc...................E..... 252 826-5614
  Scotland Neck (G-14219)
Kamlar Corporation..............................E..... 252 443-2576
  Rocky Mount (G-13705)
Katesville Pallet Mill Inc........................E..... 919 496-3162
  Franklinton (G-6156)
Keener Lumber Company Inc..................D..... 919 934-1087
  Smithfield (G-14467)
Keener Wood Products Inc.....................G..... 828 428-1562
  Maiden (G-10111)
Keller Companies Inc............................G..... 919 776-4641
  Sanford (G-14144)
Kepley-Frank Hardwood Co Inc...............E..... 336 746-5419
  Lexington (G-9740)
Kiln-Directcom....................................G..... 910 259-9794
  Burgaw (G-1343)
L F Delp Lumber Co Inc........................F..... 336 359-8202
  Laurel Springs (G-9466)
Lampe & Malphrus Lumber Co...............F..... 919 934-6152
  Smithfield (G-14469)
Lampe & Malphrus Lumber Co...............F..... 919 934-1124
  Smithfield (G-14471)

▼ Lampe & Malphrus Lumber Co.............D..... 919 934-6152
  Smithfield (G-14470)
Legacy Pre-Finishing Inc.......................F..... 704 528-7136
  Troutman (G-15385)
Liberty Dry Kiln Corp............................G..... 336 622-5490
  Liberty (G-9820)
Liberty Lumber Company........................F..... 336 622-4901
  Liberty (G-9821)
▲ Marsh Furniture Company...................B..... 336 884-7363
  High Point (G-8444)
◆ McCreary Modern Inc........................B..... 828 464-6465
  Newton (G-11951)
Megawood Inc....................................F..... 910 572-3796
  Mount Gilead (G-11607)
Meherrin River Forest Pdts Inc................D..... 252 558-4238
  Weldon (G-15885)
Miller Brothers Lumber Co Inc................E..... 336 366-3400
  Elkin (G-5626)
Mixon Mills Inc....................................G..... 828 297-5431
  Vilas (G-15497)
Myers Forest Products Inc......................E..... 704 278-4532
  Cleveland (G-4077)
Nelson Logging Company Inc..................E..... 919 849-2547
  Oxford (G-12136)
New South Lumber Company Inc............C..... 336 376-3130
  Graham (G-6705)
▼ Oaks Unlimited Inc............................E..... 828 926-1621
  Waynesville (G-15812)
Ossiriand Inc......................................G..... 336 385-1100
  Creston (G-4625)
Palletone North Carolina Inc..................D..... 704 462-1882
  Siler City (G-14430)
▼ Parton Forest Products Inc..................G..... 828 287-4257
  Rutherfordton (G-13882)
▼ Parton Lumber Company Inc...............D..... 828 287-4257
  Rutherfordton (G-13883)
Peachtree Lumber Company Inc.............E..... 828 837-0118
  Brasstown (G-1268)
Piedmont Hardwood Lbr Co Inc..............E..... 704 436-9311
  Mount Pleasant (G-11676)
Pine Log Co Inc..................................E..... 336 366-2770
  State Road (G-14729)
Pleasant Garden Dry Kiln......................G..... 336 674-2863
  Pleasant Garden (G-12359)
Polk Sawmill LLC................................G..... 828 863-0436
  Tryon (G-15427)
Powell Industries Inc............................D..... 828 926-9114
  Waynesville (G-15815)
Price Logging Inc................................G..... 252 792-5687
  Jamesville (G-9081)
Randy D Miller Lumber Co Inc................E..... 336 973-7515
  Wilkesboro (G-16038)
Robert L Rich Tmber Hrvstg Inc..............G..... 910 529-7321
  Garland (G-6246)
Ronald Lee Fulbright Lbr Inc..................F..... 704 462-1421
  Vale (G-15471)
Ross Phelps Logging Co Inc..................F..... 252 356-2560
  Colerain (G-4140)
S & L Sawmill Inc...............................E..... 704 483-3264
  Denver (G-4799)
Sawmill Catering LLC..........................F..... 910 769-7455
  Wilmington (G-16393)
Sawmill Opration Solutions LLC.............G..... 828 442-5907
  Black Mountain (G-1138)
Shaver Wood Products Inc....................D..... 704 278-1482
  Cleveland (G-4080)
Sipe Lumber Company Inc....................E..... 828 632-4679
  Taylorsville (G-15167)
Smoke House Lumber Company.............E..... 252 257-3303
  Warrenton (G-15662)
Somers Lumber and Mfg Inc..................F
  Harmony (G-7690)

24 LUMBER AND WOOD PRODUCTS, EXCEPT FURNITURE

Southeastern Hardwoods Inc .... G 828 581-0197
  Swannanoa (G-15037)
Southern Woods Lumber Inc .... F 919 963-2233
  Four Oaks (G-6112)
Southmark Forest Products .... G 919 300-1596
  Smithfield (G-14485)
Stephen P Wolfe .... G 252 792-3001
  Jamesville (G-9082)
Stoneville Lumber Company Inc .... F 336 623-4311
  Stoneville (G-14969)
Sunrise Sawmill Inc .... G 828 277-0120
  Asheville (G-791)
T & S Hardwoods Inc .... D 828 586-4044
  Sylva (G-15072)
T E Johnson Lumber Co Inc .... F 919 963-2233
  Four Oaks (G-6113)
T H Blue Inc .... E 910 673-3033
  Eagle Springs (G-5461)
Tabor City Lumber Company .... E 910 653-3162
  Tabor City (G-15087)
Thomas Lee Fortner Sawmill .... G 828 632-9525
  Taylorsville (G-15174)
Thomas Timber Inc .... F 910 532-4542
  Harrells (G-7697)
Toney Lumber Company Inc .... D 919 496-5711
  Louisburg (G-10005)
◆ Unilin Flooring Nc LLC .... C 336 313-4000
  Thomasville (G-15297)
United Visions Corp .... G 704 953-4555
  Davidson (G-4705)
Uwharrie Lumber Co .... E 910 572-3731
  Troy (G-15419)
Valwood Corporation .... F 828 321-4717
  Marble (G-10135)
▲ Veneer Technologies Inc .... C 252 223-5500
  Newport (G-11910)
Vida Wood Us Inc .... G 919 934-9904
  Smithfield (G-14487)
▲ W M Cramer Lumber Co .... D 828 397-7481
  Connelly Springs (G-4411)
W N C Pallet Forest Pdts Inc .... E 828 667-5426
  Candler (G-1591)
▼ Warmack Lumber Co Inc .... F 252 638-1435
  Cove City (G-4598)
Watts Bumgarner & Brown Inc .... F 828 632-4797
  Taylorsville (G-15176)
West Fraser Inc .... C 252 589-2011
  Seaboard (G-14230)
Weyerhaeuser Company .... F 252 746-7200
  Grifton (G-7603)
Weyerhaeuser Company .... F 252 791-3200
  Plymouth (G-12379)
Weyerhaeuser Company .... E 252 633-7100
  Vanceboro (G-15485)
Weyerhaeuser Nr Company .... D 252 633-7100
  Vanceboro (G-15487)
Wnc Dry Kiln Inc .... F 828 652-0050
  Marion (G-10188)
World Wood Company .... D 252 523-0021
  Cove City (G-4599)
Wrenn Brothers Inc .... G 919 742-3329
  Siler City (G-14435)
Wrenn Brothers Inc .... G 919 742-3717
  Siler City (G-14436)
Wright & Hobbs Inc .... E 252 537-5817
  Roanoke Rapids (G-13591)
Yadkin Lumber Company Inc .... F 336 679-2432
  Yadkinville (G-17064)
▼ Yildiz Entegre Usa Inc .... G 910 763-4733
  Wilmington (G-16458)

2426 Hardwood dimension and flooring mills

A C Furniture Company Inc .... B 336 623-3430
  Eden (G-5484)
▲ Adams Wood Turning Inc .... G 336 882-0196
  High Point (G-8232)
Ana Muf Corporation .... G 336 653-3509
  Ramseur (G-13439)
▲ Appalachian Lumber Company Inc .... E 336 973-7205
  Wilkesboro (G-16013)
Arcola Sawmill .... G 252 257-1139
  Warrenton (G-15656)
▲ Ariston Hospitality Inc .... E 626 458-8668
  High Point (G-8254)
▲ Associated Hardwoods Inc .... E 828 396-3321
  Granite Falls (G-6722)
B & E Woodturning Inc .... F 828 758-2843
  Lenoir (G-9577)
Bartimaeus By Design Inc .... C 336 475-4346
  Thomasville (G-15188)
Beasley Flooring Products Inc .... E 828 349-7000
  Franklin (G-6116)
Blue Ridge Lbr Log & Timber Co .... F 336 961-5211
  Yadkinville (G-17033)
Blue Ridge Products Co Inc .... E 828 322-7990
  Hickory (G-7952)
Bona USA .... F 704 220-6943
  Monroe (G-10666)
Braxton Sawmill Inc .... F 336 376-6798
  Graham (G-6680)
Bruex Inc .... E 828 754-1186
  Lenoir (G-9592)
Bull City Designs LLC .... F 919 908-6252
  Durham (G-4986)
C & B Frame Co Inc .... F 336 475-0194
  Thomasville (G-15192)
C & S Woodworking .... G 828 437-5024
  Valdese (G-15444)
Cagle Frames LLC .... F 910 464-1170
  Seagrove (G-14233)
Cagle Sawmill Inc .... F 336 857-2274
  Denton (G-4728)
Caldwell WD Carving Turning Co .... G 828 758-0186
  Lenoir (G-9593)
Carolina Leg Supply LLC .... G 828 446-6838
  Lenoir (G-9594)
Carrington Court Inc .... E 828 396-1049
  Granite Falls (G-6727)
Catawba Frames Inc .... G 828 459-7717
  Claremont (G-3904)
Cecil-Johnson Mfg Inc .... F 336 431-5233
  High Point (G-8291)
Chris Isom Inc .... F 336 629-0240
  Asheboro (G-415)
Church & Church Lumber LLC .... F 336 838-1256
  Millers Creek (G-10492)
Church & Church Lumber LLC .... D 336 973-4297
  Wilkesboro (G-16016)
Church & Church Lumber LLC .... D 336 973-5700
  Wilkesboro (G-16017)
Clary Lumber Company .... D 252 537-2558
  Gaston (G-6330)
Cleveland Lumber Company .... E 704 487-5263
  Shelby (G-14298)
Columbia Flooring .... G 304 239-2633
  Garner (G-6264)
Columbia Forest Products Inc .... G 336 605-0429
  Greensboro (G-6920)
Columbia Plywood Corporation .... B 828 724-4191
  Old Fort (G-12100)
Contemporary Furnishings Corp .... G 336 857-2988
  Denton (G-4730)
Curved Plywood Inc .... F 336 249-6901
  Lexington (G-9703)

D & S Frames Inc .... G 828 241-5962
  Claremont (G-3918)
▲ Danbartex LLC .... G 704 323-8728
  Mooresville (G-10923)
Daniels Woodcarving Co Inc .... F 828 632-7336
  Taylorsville (G-15140)
David Raynor Logging Inc .... E 910 980-0129
  Linden (G-9939)
▲ Delve Interiors LLC .... C 336 274-4661
  Greensboro (G-6968)
Designs In Wood .... G 336 372-8995
  Sparta (G-14593)
Df Framing LLC .... F 919 368-7903
  Siler City (G-14408)
Dimension Milling Co Inc .... G 336 983-2820
  Denton (G-4734)
Dimension Wood Products Inc .... F 828 459-9891
  Claremont (G-3920)
Drum Beat Fishing LLC .... G 252 455-5114
  Kitty Hawk (G-9402)
E Z Frames .... G 910 464-1813
  Seagrove (G-14237)
◆ Edwards Wood Products Inc .... C 704 624-3624
  Marshville (G-10216)
Eekkohart Floors & Lbr Co Inc .... G 336 409-2672
  Mocksville (G-10569)
Elite Wood Products .... G 828 994-4446
  Newton (G-11930)
Eskimo 7 Limited .... E 252 726-8181
  Morehead City (G-11171)
Ethan Allen Retail Inc .... E 828 428-9361
  Maiden (G-10107)
F L Turlington Lumber Co Inc .... E 910 592-7197
  Clinton (G-4095)
Fairgrove Furniture Co Inc .... G 828 322-8570
  Hickory (G-8021)
Fortner Lumber Inc .... F 704 585-2383
  Hiddenite (G-8216)
Framewright Inc .... F 828 459-2284
  Conover (G-4457)
Franklin Veneers Inc .... E 919 494-2284
  Franklinton (G-6154)
Gates Custom Milling Inc .... E 252 357-0116
  Gatesville (G-6549)
Glenn Lumber Company Inc .... E 704 434-7873
  Shelby (G-14320)
Green River Resource MGT .... F 828 697-0357
  Zirconia (G-17153)
Gregory Hill Frame .... F 828 428-0007
  Maiden (G-10109)
H T Jones Lumber Company .... F 252 332-4135
  Ahoskie (G-63)
Hfi Wind Down Inc .... C 828 438-5767
  Morganton (G-11220)
HM Frame Company Inc .... E 828 428-3354
  Newton (G-11940)
Hofler H S & Sons Lumber Co .... F 252 465-8603
  Sunbury (G-14997)
Horizon Forest Products Co LP .... G 336 993-9663
  Colfax (G-4151)
Horizon Frest Pdts Wlmngton LP .... D 919 424-8265
  Raleigh (G-12860)
◆ Hughes Furniture Inds Inc .... C 336 498-8700
  Randleman (G-13473)
Hull Brothers Lumber Co Inc .... E 336 789-5252
  Mount Airy (G-11519)
Hyman Furniture Warehouse LLC .... G 336 528-4950
  Winston Salem (G-16752)
▲ Ideaitlia Cntmporary Furn Corp .... C 828 464-1000
  Conover (G-4466)
Ideal Liquidation Inc .... F 828 632-3771
  Taylorsville (G-15148)

24 LUMBER AND WOOD PRODUCTS, EXCEPT FURNITURE

J & B Hardwood Inc .... G 828 226-2326
  Canton *(G-1619)*
J & D Wood Inc .... F 910 628-9000
  Fairmont *(G-5703)*
J L Frame Shop Inc .... G 828 256-6290
  Conover *(G-4469)*
J L Powell & Co Inc .... G 910 642-8989
  Whiteville *(G-15967)*
◆ JE Ekornes Usa Inc .... D 828 764-4001
  Morganton *(G-11226)*
Jerry Blevins .... G 336 384-3726
  Lansing *(G-9455)*
Jones Frame Inc .... E 336 434-2531
  High Point *(G-8417)*
Josey Lumber Company Inc .... E 252 826-5614
  Scotland Neck *(G-14219)*
L F Delp Lumber Co Inc .... F 336 359-8202
  Laurel Springs *(G-9466)*
La Barge Inc .... F 336 812-2400
  High Point *(G-8427)*
▲ Lambeth Dimension Inc .... G 336 629-3838
  Asheboro *(G-451)*
Lambeth Frames Inc .... G 336 953-9805
  Asheboro *(G-452)*
Latham Inc .... G 336 857-3702
  Denton *(G-4741)*
Lee Roys Frame Co Inc .... F 828 241-2513
  Catawba *(G-1966)*
Leisure Craft Holdings LLC .... D 828 693-8241
  Flat Rock *(G-5967)*
Leisure Craft Inc .... C 828 693-8241
  Flat Rock *(G-5968)*
Lines Unlimited Inc .... G 336 996-6603
  Walnut Cove *(G-15632)*
M & M Frame Company Inc .... G 336 859-8166
  Denton *(G-4745)*
◆ M & S Warehouse Inc .... E 828 728-3733
  Lenoir *(G-9628)*
Mac-Vann Inc .... G 919 577-0746
  Fuquay Varina *(G-6211)*
Mannington Mills Inc .... F 336 884-5600
  High Point *(G-8438)*
Maynard Frame Shop Inc .... F 910 428-2033
  Star *(G-14720)*
Mc Gees Crating Inc .... E 828 758-4660
  Lenoir *(G-9635)*
McNeill Frame Inc .... E 336 873-7934
  Seagrove *(G-14244)*
Mr Hardwood Floors Inc .... G 919 369-8027
  Raleigh *(G-13046)*
Murdock Building Company .... G 919 669-1859
  Rolesville *(G-13758)*
◆ North Carolina Lumber Company .... F 336 498-6600
  Randleman *(G-13481)*
Oceania Hardwoods LLC .... G 910 862-4447
  Elizabethtown *(G-5601)*
Old Growth Riverwood Inc .... G 910 762-4077
  Wilmington *(G-16343)*
Palletone North Carolina Inc .... D 704 462-1882
  Siler City *(G-14430)*
▼ Parton Lumber Company Inc .... D 828 287-4257
  Rutherfordton *(G-13883)*
Paul P Poovey Jr .... G 828 465-2975
  Newton *(G-11958)*
Perrys Frame Inc .... F 828 327-4681
  Newton *(G-11959)*
Piedmont Hardwood Lbr Co Inc .... E 704 436-9311
  Mount Pleasant *(G-11676)*
Pilot View Wood Works Inc .... F 336 883-2511
  High Point *(G-8484)*
Powell Industries Inc .... D 828 926-9114
  Waynesville *(G-15815)*

Price Logging Inc .... G 252 792-5687
  Jamesville *(G-9081)*
Quality Fabricators .... G 336 622-3402
  Staley *(G-14670)*
Ralph S Frame Works Inc .... D 336 431-2168
  High Point *(G-8505)*
Redi-Frame Inc .... E 828 322-4227
  Hickory *(G-8134)*
Rhf Investments Inc .... G 828 632-7070
  Taylorsville *(G-15161)*
Ritch Face Veneer Company .... E 336 883-4184
  High Point *(G-8512)*
▲ Robert St Clair Co Inc .... F 919 847-8611
  Raleigh *(G-13211)*
Robertsons Woodworking .... G 336 841-7221
  High Point *(G-8514)*
Ross Phelps Logging Co Inc .... F 252 356-2560
  Colerain *(G-4140)*
Rudisill Frame Shop Inc .... E 828 464-7020
  Newton *(G-11965)*
Ruskin Inc .... F 828 324-6500
  Hickory *(G-8143)*
S E Board Inc .... G 336 885-7230
  High Point *(G-8518)*
Select Frame Shop Inc .... D 910 428-1225
  Biscoe *(G-1116)*
Shaver Wood Products Inc .... D 704 278-1482
  Cleveland *(G-4080)*
Sipes Carving Shop Inc .... G 828 327-3077
  Hickory *(G-8158)*
Solid Frames Inc .... G 336 882-5082
  High Point *(G-8541)*
Southill Industrial Carving .... G 336 472-5311
  Thomasville *(G-15280)*
▲ Southwood Furniture Corp .... D 828 465-1776
  Hickory *(G-8165)*
Sure Wood Products Inc .... F 828 261-0004
  Hickory *(G-8172)*
T & S Hardwoods Inc .... D 828 586-4044
  Sylva *(G-15072)*
Textram Inc .... G 704 527-7557
  Charlotte *(G-3684)*
Timothy Lee Blacjmon .... G 336 481-9038
  Thomasville *(G-15290)*
Traditions Wood Carving & Frms .... G 828 322-5625
  Hickory *(G-8184)*
◆ Turn Bull Lumber Company .... E 910 862-4447
  Elizabethtown *(G-5607)*
Ufp Site Built LLC .... F 910 590-3220
  Clinton *(G-4117)*
◆ Unilin Flooring Nc LLC .... C 336 313-4000
  Thomasville *(G-15297)*
Unique Carving Inc .... G 336 472-6215
  Trinity *(G-15362)*
▲ United Finishers Intl Inc .... G 336 883-3901
  High Point *(G-8585)*
Universal Forest Products Inc .... F 252 338-0319
  Elizabeth City *(G-5580)*
Uwharrie Frames Mfg LLC .... E 336 626-6649
  Asheboro *(G-504)*
Uwharrie Lumber Co .... E 910 572-3731
  Troy *(G-15419)*
▲ Valendrawers Inc .... E 336 956-2118
  Lexington *(G-9799)*
▲ Veneer Technologies Inc .... C 252 223-5600
  Newport *(G-11910)*
Vivet Inc .... G 909 390-1039
  Greensboro *(G-7444)*
W & S Frame Company Inc .... F 828 728-6078
  Granite Falls *(G-6759)*
▲ W M Cramer Lumber Co .... D 828 397-7481
  Connelly Springs *(G-4411)*

Walton Lumber Co .... G 919 563-6565
  Mebane *(G-10436)*
Weyerhaeuser Company .... F 252 746-7200
  Grifton *(G-7603)*
Woodline Inc .... G 336 476-7100
  Thomasville *(G-15304)*
Woodwright of Wilson Co Inc .... G 252 243-9663
  Elm City *(G-5655)*
Wright & Hobbs Inc .... E 252 537-5817
  Roanoke Rapids *(G-13591)*
Zenecar LLC .... G 919 518-0464
  Raleigh *(G-13436)*
Zickgraf Enterprises Inc .... G 704 369-1200
  Franklin *(G-6150)*

2429 Special product sawmills, nec

Champion Burley .... G 919 693-6285
  Oxford *(G-12121)*
Southern Distilling Co LLC .... G 704 677-4069
  Statesville *(G-14891)*
Tru Luck Woodworks .... G 910 642-2753
  Nakina *(G-11732)*
Tws Specialty Woodworking .... G 315 492-1697
  Stanley *(G-14709)*

2431 Millwork

648 Woodworks LLC .... G 910 603-6286
  Fuquay Varina *(G-6177)*
AAA Louvers Inc .... F 919 365-7220
  Wendell *(G-15891)*
Acorn Woodworks NC LLC .... G 828 361-9953
  Murphy *(G-11704)*
Against Grain Woodworking Inc .... G 704 309-5750
  Charlotte *(G-2143)*
Against The Grain Woodworking .... G 704 969-5837
  Gastonia *(G-6338)*
Ajs Dezigns Inc .... G 828 652-6304
  Marion *(G-10138)*
Amarr Company .... G 704 599-5858
  Charlotte *(G-2178)*
Amarr Company .... G 336 936-0010
  Mocksville *(G-10553)*
◆ Amarr Company .... C 336 744-5100
  Winston Salem *(G-16602)*
Ambiance Doors LLC .... G 919 855-9220
  Raleigh *(G-12498)*
American Wdwrkery Bnjmn Htchi .... G 910 302-5678
  Fayetteville *(G-5762)*
American Woodmark Corporation .... E 704 947-3280
  Huntersville *(G-8790)*
American Woodworkery Inc .... G 910 916-8098
  Fayetteville *(G-5763)*
Andrew Bates .... G 252 413-6988
  Greenville *(G-7482)*
Andronics Construction Inc .... E 704 400-9562
  Indian Trail *(G-8920)*
Antler and Oak Joinery LLC .... G 845 505-6185
  Raleigh *(G-12510)*
▲ Appalachian Lumber Company Inc .... E 336 973-7205
  Wilkesboro *(G-16013)*
ARC Woodworking .... G 828 863-4994
  Tryon *(G-15421)*
Archdale Millworks Inc .... G 336 431-9019
  Archdale *(G-268)*
Around House Improvement LLC .... G 919 496-7029
  Bunn *(G-1327)*
Arthur Woodworking .... G 919 381-0329
  Durham *(G-4926)*
Artistic Southern Inc .... D 919 861-4695
  Charlotte *(G-2222)*
Artistic Woodworks Inc .... G 828 459-0178
  Claremont *(G-3902)*

24 LUMBER AND WOOD PRODUCTS, EXCEPT FURNITURE

Asheville Woodworks .... G 828 734-0536
Asheville *(G-543)*

Aspire Woodworks .... G 828 855-6811
Hickory *(G-7945)*

Athol Arbor Corporation .... F 919 643-1100
Hillsborough *(G-8636)*

Atlantic Woodworking .... G 704 680-8802
Mooresville *(G-10863)*

AZ Faux .... G 704 279-0114
Salisbury *(G-13926)*

B & B Wood Shop & Bldg Contrs .... G 828 488-2078
Bryson City *(G-1319)*

B&H Millwork and Fixtures Inc .... E 336 431-0068
High Point *(G-8260)*

B2rv2woodworks .... G 304 578-9881
Youngsville *(G-17069)*

Bakers Quality Trim Inc .... G 919 552-3621
Willow Spring *(G-16075)*

Baldwin Wood Works LLC .... G 828 974-2716
Mills River *(G-10499)*

Ballash Woodworks LLC .... G 910 709-0717
Fayetteville *(G-5768)*

Barber Furniture & Supply .... F 704 278-9367
Cleveland *(G-4068)*

Barewoodworking Inc .... F 828 758-0694
Lenoir *(G-9578)*

Barnhardts Woodworking Co .... G 336 449-5564
Whitsett *(G-15983)*

Beach Craft Woodworking LLC .... G 919 624-4463
Cary *(G-1700)*

Bedard Custom Woodworks .... G 828 432-6556
Morganton *(G-11200)*

Bent Creek Studio LLC .... G 336 692-6477
Clemmons *(G-4032)*

▲ Bfs Asset Holdings LLC .... C 303 784-4288
Raleigh *(G-12554)*

▲ Bfs Operations LLC .... A 919 431-1000
Raleigh *(G-12555)*

Bg Woodworks .... G 919 656-2529
Cary *(G-1702)*

Black River Woodwork LLC .... G 919 757-4559
Angier *(G-132)*

Black Wolf Custom Woodworks .... G 828 925-0399
Asheville *(G-562)*

Blinds Plus Inc .... G 910 487-5196
Fayetteville *(G-5773)*

Blue Heaven Woodworks .... G 704 743-6648
Concord *(G-4210)*

Blue Stallion Woodworks .... G 919 766-2865
Wilmington *(G-16139)*

Bo Taylor Custom Wdwkg LLC .... G 919 839-7175
Raleigh *(G-12567)*

Bob Callahan LLC .... G 828 620-9730
Asheville *(G-568)*

Bobby Barns Woodworking .... G 336 824-2821
Ramseur *(G-13441)*

Bonakemi Usa Incorporated .... C 704 218-3917
Monroe *(G-10667)*

Bone Tred Beds Smmit Woodworks .... G 910 319-7583
Wilmington *(G-16141)*

Born In A Barn Inc .... G 828 635-5808
Taylorsville *(G-15131)*

Branched Out Wood Works LLC .... G 828 515-0377
Leicester *(G-9507)*

Brookshire Woodworking Inc .... D 828 779-2119
Barnardsville *(G-906)*

Brookshire Woodworking Inc .... G 828 779-2119
Asheville *(G-574)*

Browns Woodworking LLC .... G 704 983-5917
Albemarle *(G-76)*

Brun Millworks LLC .... G 704 989-3145
Midland *(G-10458)*

Brushy Mtn Cstm Woodworks Inc .... G 336 921-3510
Moravian Falls *(G-11143)*

Bucks Woodworks LLC .... G 336 764-3979
Clemmons *(G-4033)*

Buffingtons Commercial Trim .... G 919 244-8848
Cary *(G-1715)*

Builders Firstsource Inc .... G 336 884-5454
Greensboro *(G-6860)*

Builders Firstsource Inc .... G 919 562-6601
Youngsville *(G-17072)*

Builders Firstsource - SE Grp .... G 910 313-3056
Wilmington *(G-16144)*

Builders Frstsrce - Sthast Gro .... D 910 944-2516
Aberdeen *(G-2)*

Building Center Inc .... D 704 889-8182
Pineville *(G-12257)*

Burdetts Custom Woodworks Inc .... G 919 592-9903
Cary *(G-1717)*

Burris Woodworks .... G 336 746-5286
Lexington *(G-9687)*

C&M Woodworks .... G 919 280-9896
Raleigh *(G-12582)*

Capitol Woodworks .... G 919 703-9293
Wilmington *(G-16154)*

Cardinal Millwork & Supply Inc .... E 336 665-9811
Greensboro *(G-6878)*

Carolina Building Services Inc .... F 704 664-7110
Mooresville *(G-10897)*

Carolina Sheds LLC .... G 336 623-7433
Eden *(G-5487)*

Carolina Stairs Inc .... F 704 664-5032
Mount Ulla *(G-11681)*

Carolina Urban Lumber .... G 704 755-5110
Pineville *(G-12260)*

Carolina Woodwork & Stair Inc .... G 704 363-5114
Charlotte *(G-2412)*

Carolina Woodworks Trim of NC .... G 252 492-9259
Henderson *(G-7778)*

Carpathian Woodworks Inc .... G 919 669-7546
Clayton *(G-3962)*

Carraways Sign & WD Crafts LLC .... G 252 292-7141
Wilson *(G-16486)*

Carter Millwork Inc .... D 800 861-0734
Lexington *(G-9690)*

Cedar Fork Woodworks LLC .... G 910 340-0821
Beulaville *(G-1092)*

◆ Chadsworth Incorporated .... E 910 763-7600
Wilmington *(G-16168)*

Charles White Woodworking .... G 252 714-9124
Winterville *(G-16996)*

Charlott Custom Woodworks .... G 704 634-0863
Cornelius *(G-4535)*

Chesnick Corporation .... F 919 231-2899
Raleigh *(G-12619)*

Clark Co Cstm Trim & Wdwkg Inc .... G 704 905-7131
Midland *(G-10462)*

Cleveland Lumber Company .... E 704 487-5263
Shelby *(G-14298)*

Coastal Custom Wood Works LLC .... G 252 675-8732
New Bern *(G-11790)*

Coastal Millwork Supply Co .... E 910 763-3300
Wilmington *(G-16172)*

Coastal Woodworking .... G 910 477-1330
Bolivia *(G-1163)*

Compass Woodworks Co .... G 704 232-0272
Salisbury *(G-13944)*

Contemporary Design Co LLC .... F 704 375-6030
Gastonia *(G-6386)*

Convert-A-Stair LLC .... G 888 908-5657
Wilmington *(G-16181)*

Cook & Boardman Group LLC .... D 336 768-8872
Winston Salem *(G-16658)*

Cook & Boardman Nc LLC .... E 336 768-8872
Winston Salem *(G-16659)*

Cornerstone Woodworks LLC .... G 908 343-3708
Charlotte *(G-2555)*

Craft Doors Usa LLC .... F 828 469-7029
Newton *(G-11927)*

Crafted Hart Hand .... G 704 539-4808
Union Grove *(G-15435)*

Creative Custom Wdwkg LLC .... G 910 431-8544
Wilmington *(G-16185)*

Creative Custom Woodworks Inc .... G 910 431-8544
Wilmington *(G-16186)*

Creative Woodworks .... G 910 233-3042
Hampstead *(G-7645)*

Creativewoodworks Wilmington .... G 910 233-3042
Wilmington *(G-16188)*

Credle Woodworks LLC .... G 919 353-4298
Hillsborough *(G-8647)*

Cris Bifaro Woodworks Inc .... G 828 776-2453
Asheville *(G-598)*

Crown Heritage Inc .... E 336 835-1424
Elkin *(G-5616)*

Crowntown Tinker LLC .... G 843 614-9566
Charlotte *(G-2574)*

Currier Woodworks Inc .... G 252 725-4233
Beaufort *(G-954)*

Curvemakers Inc .... G 919 690-1121
Oxford *(G-12125)*

Curvemakers Inc .... G 919 821-5792
Raleigh *(G-12662)*

Custom Decks and Woodworking .... G 828 699-2349
Zirconia *(G-17152)*

▲ Custom Doors Incorporated .... F 704 982-2885
Albemarle *(G-79)*

Custom Wood Creations .... G 252 341-7923
Greenville *(G-7511)*

Custom Wood Creations .... G 910 367-8747
Leland *(G-9539)*

◆ Dac Products Inc .... E 336 969-9786
Rural Hall *(G-13839)*

Dan Forrest Woodworks Wrap Up .... G 919 532-9190
Raleigh *(G-12672)*

Daughtrys Creations LLC .... G 704 929-8717
Newland *(G-11884)*

Davis Cabinet Co Wilson Inc .... F 252 291-9052
Sims *(G-14441)*

Davis Mechanical Inc .... F 704 272-9366
Peachland *(G-12173)*

Decarlo Woodworks .... G 919 327-3647
Apex *(G-181)*

Decicco Woodshop LLC .... G 914 213-8553
Cary *(G-1745)*

Decore-Ative Spc NC LLC .... C 704 291-9669
Monroe *(G-10704)*

Dellinger Woodworks LLC .... G 980 245-6086
Waxhaw *(G-15751)*

Distinctive Millworks LLC .... G 919 263-4337
Wake Forest *(G-15547)*

Division Six Incorporated .... G 910 420-3305
New Bern *(G-11801)*

DN Yager Woodworks .... G 704 236-3481
Matthews *(G-10312)*

▲ Door Store of America Inc .... F 919 781-3200
Raleigh *(G-12696)*

Door Works Huntersville LLC .... E 704 947-1900
Huntersville *(G-8809)*

Double Hung LLC .... E 888 235-8956
Greensboro *(G-6976)*

Douglas Duane Sniffen .... G 919 924-8337
Garner *(G-6271)*

Downsouth Wood Working LLC .... G 910 259-4617
Burgaw *(G-1337)*

SIC SECTION
24 LUMBER AND WOOD PRODUCTS, EXCEPT FURNITURE

Dragonfly Studios .... G 704 706-2910
  Concord *(G-4258)*
Drw Renovations & Custom Wdwkg ..... G 910 471-9367
  Wilmington *(G-16206)*
Dwelling NC Inc .... G 252 619-0226
  Edenton *(G-5513)*
East Bay Woodworks .... G 503 313-4079
  Mooresville *(G-10935)*
East Coast Door & Hardware Inc .... G 704 791-4128
  Concord *(G-4259)*
East End Mllwk DBA Avvento Inc .... G 516 313-7739
  Ocean Isle Beach *(G-12090)*
Eastern Cornerstone Cnstr LLC .... G 919 702-3583
  Louisburg *(G-9986)*
Ecmd Inc .... C 336 835-1182
  Elkin *(G-5617)*
▲ Ecmd Inc .... D 336 667-5976
  North Wilkesboro *(G-12006)*
Edwards Mountain Woodworks LLC ..... G 919 932-6050
  Chapel Hill *(G-2012)*
Elite Wood Classics Inc .... G 910 454-8745
  Oak Island *(G-12049)*
Endgrain Woodworks LLC .... G 980 237-2612
  Charlotte *(G-2711)*
Eric Leffingwell .... G 910 367-1928
  Wilmington *(G-16212)*
Ervin Woodworks LLC .... G 919 451-0652
  Efland *(G-5527)*
Exley Custom Woodwork Inc .... G 910 763-5445
  Castle Hayne *(G-1946)*
Extreme Scenes Inc .... F 336 687-3369
  High Point *(G-8348)*
Finely Finished Wdwkg LLC .... G 828 553-9549
  Hendersonville *(G-7849)*
Flat Iron Mill Works LLC .... G 828 768-7770
  Leicester *(G-9511)*
Fleming Wood & Rod LLC .... G 828 278-9194
  Vilas *(G-15495)*
Forest Millwork Inc .... F 828 251-5264
  Asheville *(G-624)*
Forged Timber Company .... G 704 351-7712
  Mooresville *(G-10948)*
Foundation Woodworks LLC .... G 828 713-9665
  Asheville *(G-625)*
Fox Briar Furniture & Wdwkg .... G 980 254-8433
  Mocksville *(G-10572)*
Frank Ficca Woodworking .... G 336 937-2985
  Summerfield *(G-14982)*
Franken Woodworking .... G 910 488-6931
  Fayetteville *(G-5828)*
Franklin Forest Products LLC .... G 336 982-5550
  Jefferson *(G-9088)*
Frederick and Frederick Entp .... F 252 235-4849
  Middlesex *(G-10448)*
Freedom Enterprise LLC .... G 502 510-7296
  Shallotte *(G-14273)*
Front Prch Cstm Frmng Wodworks .... G 252 717-2868
  Williamston *(G-16060)*
Funder America Inc .... F 336 751-3501
  Mocksville *(G-10575)*
◆ Funder America Inc .... C 336 751-3501
  Mocksville *(G-10574)*
Garner Woodworks LLC .... G 828 775-1790
  Swannanoa *(G-15026)*
Gary Forte Woodworking Inc .... G 704 780-0095
  Monroe *(G-10722)*
Gates Custom Milling Inc .... E 252 357-0116
  Gatesville *(G-6549)*
General Painting & Woodwork .... G 828 318-1252
  Asheville *(G-633)*
Ggs Woodworking .... G 704 279-5482
  Salisbury *(G-13967)*

Giving Tree Woodworks LLc .... G 704 930-5847
  Mount Holly *(G-11636)*
▲ GLG Corporation .... F 336 784-0396
  Winston Salem *(G-16722)*
Goodman Millwork Inc .... E 704 633-2421
  Salisbury *(G-13972)*
Grey Star Woodworks .... G 919 903-8471
  Moncure *(G-10623)*
Griggs Custom Woodwork .... G 828 719-1503
  Banner Elk *(G-899)*
GTW Woodworks .... G 704 640-5402
  Cleveland *(G-4072)*
Guyclee Millwork .... F 919 202-5738
  Selma *(G-14256)*
H & H Wood Products Inc .... G 704 233-4148
  Wingate *(G-16575)*
H & H Woodworking LLC .... G 336 676-6524
  Mc Leansville *(G-10392)*
H & H Woodworking Inc .... G 336 884-5848
  High Point *(G-8374)*
H and H Woodworking .... G 704 827-4506
  Stanley *(G-14695)*
H T Jones Lumber Company .... F 252 332-4135
  Ahoskie *(G-63)*
H&M Woodworks Inc .... F 919 496-5993
  Louisburg *(G-9990)*
Hammer & Shaw Woodworks .... G 336 339-4829
  Greensboro *(G-7076)*
Harley S Woodworks Inc .... G 828 776-0120
  Barnardsville *(G-911)*
Harrison Woodworks Inc .... G 919 632-3703
  Durham *(G-5132)*
Hedrick Construction .... G 336 362-3443
  Kernersville *(G-9204)*
Henderson & Kirkland Inc .... G 252 355-0224
  Winterville *(G-17002)*
Herd Woodworking LLC .... G 704 778-0556
  New London *(G-11873)*
Heritage Woodworks LLC .... G 919 774-1554
  Sanford *(G-14132)*
High Creek Woodworks .... G 919 418-1210
  Hillsborough *(G-8653)*
Hos Woodworking Inc .... G 712 298-1985
  Monroe *(G-10733)*
Hosmer Woodworks .... G 415 730-5401
  Wilmington *(G-16258)*
Hunter Innovations Ltd .... G 919 848-8814
  Raleigh *(G-12869)*
Hunter Millwork Inc .... F 704 821-0144
  Matthews *(G-10321)*
Idaho Wood Inc .... F 208 263-9521
  Oxford *(G-12132)*
▲ Idx Impressions LLC .... C 703 550-6902
  Washington *(G-15711)*
Interior Trim Creations Inc .... G 704 821-1470
  Charlotte *(G-2981)*
Interior Wood Works LLC .... G 910 754-3987
  Bolivia *(G-1164)*
Intracoastal Woodworks LLC .... G 910 270-5515
  Hampstead *(G-7649)*
Iron Forged Woodworks .... G 910 581-6574
  Jacksonville *(G-9009)*
Itc Millwork LLC .... D 704 821-1470
  Matthews *(G-10323)*
▲ J & M Woodworking Inc .... F 828 728-3253
  Hudson *(G-8770)*
J&J Millworks Inc .... G 336 252-2868
  Winston Salem *(G-16766)*
J&J Woodworking LLC .... G 704 941-9537
  Matthews *(G-10325)*
Jala Woodshop LLC .... G 704 439-6913
  Cornelius *(G-4563)*

JDG Woodworks Inc .... G 910 367-8806
  Wilmington *(G-16278)*
Jeld-Wen Inc .... D 828 724-9511
  Marion *(G-10153)*
Jeld-Wen Inc .... C 336 838-0292
  North Wilkesboro *(G-12016)*
▲ Jeld-Wen Holding Inc .... B 704 378-5700
  Charlotte *(G-3019)*
▲ Jenkins Millwork LLC .... E 336 667-3344
  Wilkesboro *(G-16032)*
Jhons Wood Work LLC .... G 828 231-6240
  Leicester *(G-9514)*
Jody Stowe .... G 704 519-6560
  Matthews *(G-10256)*
Joel Moretz .... G 828 355-9936
  Boone *(G-1211)*
Joeys Woodworking Gifts .... G 336 427-5263
  Madison *(G-10075)*
John H Peterson Jr .... G 910 762-9957
  Rocky Point *(G-13748)*
John Lindenberger .... G 919 337-6741
  Raleigh *(G-12918)*
Joines Custom Woodwork .... G 336 984-7237
  Moravian Falls *(G-11145)*
Jones Doors & Windows Inc .... F 336 998-8624
  Mocksville *(G-10582)*
Jr S Custom Woodworks .... G 336 643-1524
  Stokesdale *(G-14943)*
K&S Custom LLC .... G 336 861-1607
  Sophia *(G-14519)*
K&S Rustic Woodworks .... G 336 504-6988
  High Point *(G-8420)*
Kabinet Werks LLC .... G 704 359-7311
  Harrisburg *(G-7715)*
Kauffman & Co .... G 716 969-2005
  Charlotte *(G-3044)*
Keglers Woodworks LLC .... G 919 608-7220
  Raleigh *(G-12934)*
Kennedy Woodworking LLC .... G 704 278-9444
  Mount Ulla *(G-11684)*
Kettu Woodworks .... G 919 699-4173
  Wake Forest *(G-15568)*
Kevs Woodworking LLC .... G 850 559-3228
  Hubert *(G-8750)*
Kingdom Woodworks Inc .... G 704 678-8134
  Kings Mountain *(G-9312)*
Knowlton Woodworking LLC .... G 336 588-3502
  Seagrove *(G-14243)*
Kotek Holdings Inc .... E 919 643-1100
  Hillsborough *(G-8659)*
KS Custom Woodworks Inc .... G 252 714-3957
  Walstonburg *(G-15639)*
L & B Custom Woodworking .... G 252 578-8955
  Woodland *(G-17022)*
L & W GL Mirror & WD Works LLC .... G 336 562-2155
  Prospect Hill *(G-12407)*
Laborie Sons Cstm Wodworks LLC ...... G 910 769-2524
  Wilmington *(G-16293)*
Lee Builder Mart Inc .... E
  Sanford *(G-14147)*
Lets Build It Woodworking .... G 704 352-7131
  Concord *(G-4303)*
Libasci Woodworks Inc .... G 828 524-7073
  Franklin *(G-6135)*
Liberty Wood Products Inc .... F 828 524-7958
  Franklin *(G-6136)*
Linkous Carpentry & Wdwkg LLC .... G 828 460-5610
  Swannanoa *(G-15028)*
Lj Cbg Acquisition Company .... A 336 768-8872
  Winston Salem *(G-16790)*
Ln Woodworks .... G 509 480-0263
  Fayetteville *(G-5861)*

Employee Codes: A=Over 500 employees, B=251-500
C=101-250, D=51-100, E=20-50, F=10-19, G=1-9

24 LUMBER AND WOOD PRODUCTS, EXCEPT FURNITURE

Lookout Boat Window Frames LLC......... G..... 252 723-2222
  Morehead City *(G-11182)*

Louisiana-Pacific Corporation............... C..... 336 599-8080
  Roxboro *(G-13806)*

Madison Woodworking............................ G..... 704 634-1143
  Charlotte *(G-3118)*

Maines Woodworks Cstm Mil LLC.......... G..... 336 263-0799
  Hurdle Mills *(G-8910)*

Manhattan Woodworking Inc.................. G..... 704 528-5733
  Statesville *(G-14838)*

Mark L Wood.. G..... 919 977-6507
  Raleigh *(G-12997)*

Mark T Galvin... G..... 828 627-0823
  Clyde *(G-4126)*

Markham Woodworks LLC..................... G..... 252 492-5823
  Henderson *(G-7797)*

Martin Wood Products Inc..................... G..... 336 548-3470
  Madison *(G-10080)*

Martins Woodworking LLC..................... F..... 704 473-7617
  Lattimore *(G-9458)*

Marvida Acres LLC................................. G..... 336 392-0414
  Greensboro *(G-7187)*

Masonite International Corp.................. E..... 919 575-3700
  Butner *(G-1545)*

Master Kraft Inc..................................... E..... 704 234-2673
  Matthews *(G-10332)*

Masterpiece Staircase LLC.................... G..... 704 806-2894
  Matthews *(G-10333)*

Masters Craftsman................................. G..... 919 800-0096
  Raleigh *(G-13005)*

▲ Masterwrap Inc................................... E..... 336 243-4515
  Lexington *(G-9755)*

Matthews Building Supply Co................ E..... 704 847-2106
  Matthews *(G-10268)*

Matthews Millwork Inc........................... G..... 704 821-4499
  Monroe *(G-10767)*

Max Woodworks Inc............................... G..... 786 286-2668
  Black Mountain *(G-1129)*

Mesa Quality Fenestration Inc.............. G..... 828 393-0132
  Hendersonville *(G-7879)*

Metal Crafters of Goldsboro NC............ F..... 919 778-7200
  Goldsboro *(G-6635)*

Metalfab of North Carolina LLC............. C..... 704 841-1090
  Matthews *(G-10271)*

Metrolina Woodworks Inc...................... F..... 704 821-9095
  Stallings *(G-14672)*

Metropolitan Woodworks Inc................. G..... 704 215-5018
  Gastonia *(G-6463)*

Metzgers Burl Wood Gallery.................. G..... 828 452-2550
  Waynesville *(G-15810)*

Mh Libman Woodturning........................ G..... 828 360-5530
  Asheville *(G-701)*

Mike Powell Inc...................................... F..... 910 792-6152
  Wilmington *(G-16324)*

Miter Point LLC...................................... G..... 910 864-3645
  Fayetteville *(G-5876)*

Miters Touch Inc.................................... G..... 828 963-4445
  Banner Elk *(G-903)*

Modern Workbench LLC......................... G..... 828 845-4466
  Horse Shoe *(G-8742)*

Moretz Bldg & Woodworks LLC............. G..... 828 406-4672
  Fleetwood *(G-5976)*

Morrison Mill Work................................. G..... 828 774-5415
  Asheville *(G-705)*

▲ Moulding Millwork LLC....................... G..... 704 504-9880
  Charlotte *(G-3207)*

Moulding Source Incorporated.............. G..... 704 658-1111
  Mooresville *(G-11031)*

Mountain Top Woodworking.................. G..... 336 982-4059
  West Jefferson *(G-15946)*

Muddy Creek Mill Works Inc.................. G..... 828 659-5558
  Nebo *(G-11762)*

Mullis Millwork Inc................................ F..... 919 496-5993
  New Bern *(G-11828)*

Narron Woodworks................................. G..... 252 258-2151
  Kinston *(G-9378)*

New England Wood Works...................... G..... 706 491-5885
  Whittier *(G-16009)*

Nordic Custom Woodworks.................... G..... 203 209-5854
  Wilmington *(G-16339)*

Normac Kitchens Inc............................. F..... 704 485-1911
  Oakboro *(G-12079)*

North State Millwork.............................. G..... 252 442-9090
  Rocky Mount *(G-13715)*

Northside Millwork Inc.......................... E..... 919 732-6100
  Hillsborough *(G-8664)*

Oak & Axe Custom Woodworking........... G..... 919 434-1939
  Cary *(G-1835)*

Oak City Artisans LLC............................ G..... 347 738-1228
  Raleigh *(G-13077)*

Oak City Woodshop LLC........................ G..... 937 830-0808
  Cary *(G-1836)*

Oak City Woodworks.............................. G..... 919 247-5984
  Knightdale *(G-9424)*

Old Mill Precision Gun Works &............ G..... 704 284-2832
  Bessemer City *(G-1076)*

Olde Lexington Products Inc................. G..... 336 956-2355
  Linwood *(G-9947)*

Ole Pelicans Custom Wdwkg.................. G..... 252 808-7633
  Newport *(G-11903)*

Onsite Woodwork Corporation............... F..... 704 523-1380
  Charlotte *(G-3302)*

Orion Manufacturing LLC...................... G..... 714 633-5850
  Richfield *(G-13553)*

▲ Ornamental Mouldings LLC................ F..... 336 431-9120
  Archdale *(G-295)*

Osceola Custom Woodworks.................. G..... 336 514-3720
  Reidsville *(G-13537)*

Overman Cabinet & Supply LLC............ F..... 336 584-1349
  Burlington *(G-1469)*

Oyama Cabinet Inc................................ G..... 828 327-2668
  Conover *(G-4477)*

P & P Distributing Company.................. F..... 910 582-1968
  Hamlet *(G-7628)*

P R Sparks Enterprises Inc................... G..... 336 272-7200
  Greensboro *(G-7238)*

Pauls Custom Woodworking Inc............ G..... 828 712-6234
  Black Mountain *(G-1134)*

Pegasus Builders Supply LLC................ F..... 919 244-1586
  Durham *(G-5279)*

Perusi Woodcarving............................... G..... 828 734-6121
  Waynesville *(G-15814)*

Phillip Rice Woodworking LLC............... G..... 919 339-4543
  Oxford *(G-12141)*

Piedmont Stairworks LLC...................... E..... 704 483-3721
  Denver *(G-4794)*

Piedmont Stairworks LLC...................... G..... 704 697-0259
  Charlotte *(G-3341)*

Piedmont Turning & Wdwkg Co............. G..... 336 475-7161
  Thomasville *(G-15264)*

Piedmont Wood Products Inc................ F..... 828 632-4077
  Taylorsville *(G-15157)*

Pine Creek Products LLC....................... G..... 336 399-8806
  Winston Salem *(G-16856)*

Pitch & Burl LLC.................................... G..... 512 653-9413
  Charlotte *(G-3345)*

Pk Woodworks... G..... 828 284-4570
  Burnsville *(G-1531)*

Ply Gem Holdings Inc............................ D..... 919 677-3900
  Cary *(G-1852)*

Ply Gem Industries Inc......................... D..... 919 677-3900
  Cary *(G-1853)*

Port City Wood Works Inc..................... G..... 910 398-8274
  Wilmington *(G-16363)*

Porters Tavern Wood Works.................. G..... 910 639-4519
  Robbins *(G-13602)*

Prestige Millwork Inc............................ F..... 910 428-2360
  Star *(G-14722)*

Pridgen Woodwork Inc........................... E..... 910 642-7175
  Whiteville *(G-15975)*

Pro-Kay Supply Inc................................ F..... 910 628-0882
  Orrum *(G-12116)*

▲ Profilform Us Inc................................ E..... 252 430-0392
  Henderson *(G-7803)*

R L Roten Woodworking LLC................. G..... 336 982-3830
  Crumpler *(G-4630)*

Rabbit Town Molding & Trim LLC......... G..... 336 688-2162
  Trinity *(G-15354)*

Raleigh Custom Woodwork Inc.............. G..... 919 522-6621
  Raleigh *(G-13175)*

Raw Design Woodworks LLC................. G..... 516 477-1963
  Indian Trail *(G-8960)*

Red Shed Woodworks Inc...................... G..... 828 768-3854
  Marshall *(G-10207)*

Reeb Millwork Corporation.................... G..... 336 751-4650
  Mocksville *(G-10601)*

Refab Wood LLC.................................... G..... 919 272-2589
  Raleigh *(G-13203)*

Reliable Construction Co Inc................. E..... 704 289-1501
  Monroe *(G-10795)*

Rescued Wood Rehab LLC..................... G..... 984 500-7904
  Fuquay Varina *(G-6225)*

Richmond Millwork LLC......................... G..... 910 331-1009
  Rockingham *(G-13641)*

Ritchie Woodworks................................. G..... 980 322-7779
  China Grove *(G-3887)*

Ritenis Woodworks................................. G..... 336 643-6426
  Summerfield *(G-14991)*

Rivers Edge Woodworkers LLC............. G..... 252 443-5099
  Rocky Mount *(G-13729)*

Rls Commercial Interiors Inc................ G..... 919 365-4086
  Wendell *(G-15915)*

Robbinsville Cstm Molding Inc.............. F..... 828 479-2317
  Robbinsville *(G-13610)*

Robert Wiggins Wood Work LLC............ G..... 828 254-5644
  Asheville *(G-758)*

Roots Originals LLC.............................. G..... 573 673-1669
  Winston Salem *(G-16889)*

Rowland Woodworking Inc..................... E..... 336 887-0700
  High Point *(G-8516)*

Royal Impressions LLC......................... G..... 910 340-5955
  Greensboro *(G-7319)*

Royal Oak Stairs Inc............................. F..... 919 855-8988
  Raleigh *(G-13216)*

Rustic Innovations LLC......................... G..... 804 822-2492
  Raleigh *(G-13219)*

S Banner Cabinets Incorporated........... E..... 828 733-2031
  Newland *(G-11893)*

S H Woodworking.................................. G..... 336 463-2885
  Yadkinville *(G-17049)*

Sal and Sons Woodworking LLC............ G..... 910 489-5373
  Raeford *(G-12437)*

Salem Woodworking Company............... G..... 336 768-7443
  Winston Salem *(G-16896)*

Salisbury Millwork Inc.......................... G..... 704 603-4501
  Salisbury *(G-14040)*

Samswoodworks..................................... G..... 336 893-5499
  Winston Salem *(G-16897)*

Sandy Creek Woodworks....................... G..... 919 853-3415
  Louisburg *(G-10001)*

Sauder Woodworking Co........................ G..... 704 799-6782
  Mooresville *(G-11079)*

Scott Meek Woodworks.......................... G..... 828 283-0796
  Asheville *(G-765)*

Scott Woodworking................................. G..... 828 550-4742
  Asheville *(G-766)*

SIC SECTION
24 LUMBER AND WOOD PRODUCTS, EXCEPT FURNITURE

Seaside Woodworks .... G 910 523-1377
   Bolivia *(G-1166)*

▲ Select Stainless Products LLC .... E 888 843-2345
   Charlotte *(G-3524)*

Selectbuild Construction Inc .... E 208 331-4300
   Raleigh *(G-13244)*

Shaw Fine Woodworking .... G 336 529-4080
   Sparta *(G-14599)*

Shep Berryhill Woodworking .... G 828 242-3227
   Asheville *(G-769)*

Shower Glass LLC .... G 980 785-4030
   Indian Trail *(G-8962)*

Shutter Production Inc .... G 910 289-2620
   Rose Hill *(G-13781)*

Signature Custom Wdwkg Inc .... G 336 983-9905
   King *(G-9282)*

Simpson Sawmill LLC .... G 704 485-8814
   Oakboro *(G-12081)*

Skettis Woodworks .... G 336 671-9866
   Winston Salem *(G-16911)*

Skin Wellness By Patricia Inc .... G 704 634-6635
   Mooresville *(G-11089)*

Smith Companies Lexington Inc .... G 336 249-4941
   Lexington *(G-9781)*

Smith Creations LLC .... G 704 771-6749
   Swannanoa *(G-15036)*

▲ Smith Millwork Inc .... E 800 222-8498
   Lexington *(G-9782)*

Smith Woodworks Inc .... G 910 890-2923
   Dunn *(G-4884)*

Smokey Mountain Lumber Inc .... G 828 298-3958
   Asheville *(G-775)*

Snyder Custom Creations LLC .... G 704 743-3386
   Mooresville *(G-11092)*

Solid Woodworker .... G 336 786-7385
   Mount Airy *(G-11573)*

Solutions In Wood .... G 828 696-2996
   Hendersonville *(G-7901)*

Sornig Cstm Wdwrks Thmas Srnig .... G 734 925-3905
   Advance *(G-51)*

Southern Classic Stairs Inc .... G 828 285-9828
   Alexander *(G-120)*

Southern Custom Doors James NA ...... G 919 986-6943
   Raleigh *(G-13282)*

Southern Custom Doors LLC .... G 919 889-5404
   Raleigh *(G-13283)*

Southern Mllwk By Design Inc .... G 704 309-8854
   Matthews *(G-10345)*

Southern Pine Woodworking LLC .... G 910 690-9800
   Southern Pines *(G-14554)*

Southern Roots Millwork .... G 336 736-8812
   Asheboro *(G-483)*

Southern Staircase Inc .... G 704 363-2123
   Charlotte *(G-3596)*

Southern Staircase Inc .... D 704 357-1221
   Charlotte *(G-3597)*

Southern Woodcraft Design LLC .... G 919 693-8995
   Oxford *(G-12158)*

Southern Woodworking Inc .... G 336 693-5892
   Burlington *(G-1497)*

Southwood Doors LLC .... F 704 625-2578
   Conover *(G-4499)*

Sparks Mill Works LLC .... G 512 779-5837
   Asheville *(G-785)*

▲ Spartacraft Inc .... E 828 397-4630
   Connelly Springs *(G-4409)*

Spring Valley Carving Svcs LLC .... G 919 553-7906
   Clayton *(G-4012)*

Square One Woodworking .... G 828 277-5164
   Asheville *(G-786)*

St Lucie Woodworks Inc .... G 772 626-4778
   Raeford *(G-12441)*

Stairways From Heaven Inc .... G 828 627-3860
   Clyde *(G-4128)*

Stanleys Woodworking .... G 828 612-4286
   Newton *(G-11973)*

Stephenson Millwork Co Inc .... C 252 237-1141
   Wilson *(G-16543)*

Steve Noggle Turned Wood .... G 828 437-8017
   Morganton *(G-11257)*

Stevens Mill Woodworks LLC .... G 919 440-8834
   Goldsboro *(G-6661)*

Stevenson Woodworking .... G 919 362-9121
   Apex *(G-245)*

Stickler Woodworking Inc .... G 336 302-0683
   Asheboro *(G-488)*

▲ Stock Building Supply Hol .... A 919 431-1000
   Raleigh *(G-13305)*

Straight Edge Woodworks LLC .... G 704 456-7046
   Harrisburg *(G-7729)*

Straightline Woodworks .... G 336 469-7029
   Yadkinville *(G-17052)*

Strandh Woodworks LLC .... G 919 703-8056
   New Hill *(G-11865)*

Sugar Mountain Woodworks Inc .... G 423 292-6245
   Newland *(G-11894)*

Summit Peak Pens and WD Works .... G 336 404-8312
   Liberty *(G-9832)*

Susan Link Woodworks LLC .... G 828 492-8026
   Canton *(G-1627)*

Swanson Custom Wood Workin .... G 910 465-3199
   Wilmington *(G-16423)*

Swanson Custom Woodworking Inc ..... G 910 465-3199
   Southport *(G-14585)*

Sylvester Artsan Woodworks LLC .... G 989 529-3573
   West End *(G-15933)*

T J S Woodworks .... G 336 299-5913
   Greensboro *(G-7386)*

Ta Lost Pines Woodwork .... G 828 367-7517
   Asheville *(G-794)*

Tailored Visionz & Dreamz LLC .... G 919 340-3613
   Hollister *(G-8677)*

Tallent Wood Works .... G 704 592-2013
   Statesville *(G-14910)*

Thompson Joinery LLC .... G 919 672-2770
   Durham *(G-5401)*

Thompson Millwork LLC .... D 919 596-8236
   Mebane *(G-10433)*

▲ Tiger Mountain Woodworks Inc .... E 828 526-5577
   Highlands *(G-8618)*

Timber Wolf Forest Products .... F 828 728-7500
   Hudson *(G-8783)*

Timber Wolf Wood Creations Inc .... G 704 309-5118
   Charlotte *(G-3694)*

Tivoli Woodworks LLC .... G 336 602-3512
   Salisbury *(G-14053)*

Todrin Fine Woodwork Llc .... G 413 478-2818
   Chapel Hill *(G-2080)*

Tom Marsh Jr DBA Tm Woodworks ...... G 910 376-2760
   Hampstead *(G-7660)*

Travis Harrell .... G 828 279-2937
   Wilmington *(G-16431)*

Triad Prefinish & Lbr Sls Inc .... G 336 375-4849
   Greensboro *(G-7415)*

Triangle Custom Woodworks LLC .... G 919 637-8857
   Fuquay Varina *(G-6234)*

Triangle Woodworks Inc .... G 919 570-0337
   Wake Forest *(G-15605)*

Trim Inc .... F 336 751-3591
   Mocksville *(G-10609)*

Trimsters Inc .... F 919 639-3126
   Angier *(G-150)*

Trimworks Inc .... G 704 753-4149
   Monroe *(G-10823)*

Trinity Woodworks LLC .... G 980 938-4765
   Gold Hill *(G-6586)*

True Blue Wdcrfting Lser Etchi .... G 609 784-2431
   Clayton *(G-4019)*

TS Woodworks & RAD Design Inc .... F 704 238-1015
   Monroe *(G-10824)*

Tuckers Farm Inc .... G 704 375-8199
   Charlotte *(G-3737)*

Two Green Thumbs and More Inc .... G 704 614-8703
   Hickory *(G-8192)*

▲ United Finishers Intl Inc .... G 336 883-3901
   High Point *(G-8585)*

United Wood Products Inc .... G 336 626-2281
   Asheboro *(G-502)*

Van Duyn Woodwork .... G 919 760-0327
   Raleigh *(G-13391)*

Ventura Systems Inc .... F 704 712-8630
   Dallas *(G-4660)*

Vision Woodworks LLC .... G 704 779-0734
   Huntersville *(G-8905)*

Visions Stairways and Millwork .... E 919 878-5622
   Raleigh *(G-13406)*

Walnut Woodworks .... G 828 290-6438
   Flat Rock *(G-5973)*

Waterdog Wood Works LLC .... G 252 808-7978
   Oriental *(G-12114)*

Wayne Woodworks .... G 910 298-5669
   Pink Hill *(G-12318)*

Wells Woodworks Gary Wells .... G 828 553-0177
   Brevard *(G-1292)*

Western Crlina Cstm Cswork Inc .... F 828 669-0459
   Black Mountain *(G-1141)*

Wheelhouse Builders LLC .... G 828 553-7519
   Brevard *(G-1293)*

Whitaker Mill Works LLC .... G 919 772-3030
   Raleigh *(G-13421)*

Wigal Wood Works .... G 580 890-9723
   Fayetteville *(G-5953)*

Williamsburg Woodcraft Inc .... F 919 965-3363
   Selma *(G-14263)*

Willow Oak Woodworks .... G 919 906-1232
   Hurdle Mills *(G-8915)*

Winchester Woodworks .... G 828 421-2693
   Waynesville *(G-15833)*

Windsor Window Company .... G 704 283-7459
   Monroe *(G-10835)*

Windsor Window Company .... C 704 283-7459
   Monroe *(G-10836)*

Winfield Woodworks .... G 828 808-9727
   Fletcher *(G-6053)*

Witherspoon Woodworks LLC .... G 919 669-9103
   Raleigh *(G-13425)*

Wizards Wood Werks .... G 252 813-3929
   Macclesfield *(G-10067)*

Wolphs Wood Works Ltd .... G 719 629-6350
   Trenton *(G-15337)*

Wood Barn Inc .... F 252 826-5538
   Scotland Neck *(G-14225)*

Wood Barn Inc .... E 919 496-6714
   Louisburg *(G-10006)*

Wood Creations NC Inc .... F 704 865-1822
   Gastonia *(G-6542)*

Wood Surgeon .... G 252 728-5767
   Beaufort *(G-971)*

Wood Works .... G 336 580-4134
   Greensboro *(G-7466)*

Wood Works .... G 910 579-1487
   Sunset Beach *(G-15004)*

Wood Works of Ahoskie LLC .... G 252 287-7396
   Ahoskie *(G-67)*

Woodlake Wood Works .... G 919 972-1000
   Durham *(G-5446)*

24 LUMBER AND WOOD PRODUCTS, EXCEPT FURNITURE

Woodmaster Custom Cabinets Inc......... F 919 554-3707
  Youngsville *(G-17116)*
Woodtech/Interiors Inc..................... G 704 332-7215
  Charlotte *(G-3820)*
Woodwizards Inc............................. G 336 427-7698
  Stokesdale *(G-14952)*
Woodworking At Dinahs Landing......... G 252 402-2248
  Washington *(G-15740)*
Woodworking By Robt Wadde............. G 704 236-0883
  Matthews *(G-10352)*
Woodworking Unlimited Inc................ G 704 903-8080
  Olin *(G-12108)*
Work Custom LLC............................. G 704 488-3113
  Charlotte *(G-3821)*
Wurtz Woodworks Llc....................... G 704 657-6584
  Troutman *(G-15399)*
Wyatt Woodworks............................ G 919 619-8593
  Fuquay Varina *(G-6239)*
XI Paws Woodworking LLC................. G 336 309-1173
  Cameron *(G-1565)*
Young Wood Works LLC..................... G 704 654-1722
  Charlotte *(G-3845)*

2434 Wood kitchen cabinets

A Plus Kitchen Bath Cabinets............. G 919 622-0515
  Raleigh *(G-12452)*
ABC Cabinetry LLc............................ G 704 307-8310
  Monroe *(G-10633)*
Advance Cabinetry Inc...................... G 828 676-3550
  Fletcher *(G-5982)*
Alco Custom Cabinets Inc.................. G 919 363-9480
  Cary *(G-1678)*
Alexanders Cbinets Countertops......... G 336 774-2966
  Winston Salem *(G-16595)*
Allen & Son S Cabinet Shop Inc.......... G 919 963-2196
  Four Oaks *(G-6099)*
American Cabinetry......................... G 704 502-4450
  Huntersville *(G-8789)*
American Wood Reface Inc................ G 704 577-2948
  Monroe *(G-10645)*
American Wood Reface of Triad......... G 336 345-2837
  Kernersville *(G-9164)*
American Woodmark Corporation........ G 540 665-9100
  Stoneville *(G-14953)*
Anders Custom Cabinetry.................. G 828 342-4222
  Franklin *(G-6115)*
Angell Crafted Cabinetry................... G 336 655-7735
  Germanton *(G-6550)*
Artistic Kitchens & Baths LLC............. G 910 692-4000
  Southern Pines *(G-14527)*
Asheville Custom Closets................... G 828 337-7539
  Asheville *(G-534)*
Ashleys Kit Bath Dsign Stdio L........... F 828 669-5281
  Black Mountain *(G-1119)*
Aspen Cabinetry Inc......................... G 828 466-0216
  Conover *(G-4419)*
Atlantic Coast Cabinet Distrs.............. E 919 554-8165
  Youngsville *(G-17068)*
B & L Custom Cabinets Inc................. F 704 857-1940
  Westfield *(G-15950)*
Barber Furniture & Supply................. F 704 278-9367
  Cleveland *(G-4068)*
Bcac Holdings LLC........................... G 910 754-5689
  Supply *(G-15006)*
Belvedere Cabinets Inc..................... G 919 949-2005
  Cary *(G-1701)*
Bill Truitt Wood Works Inc................. G 704 398-8499
  Charlotte *(G-2311)*
Black Rock Granite & Cabinetry.......... G 828 787-1100
  Highlands *(G-8612)*
Blue Ridge Cab Connection LLC.......... G 828 891-2281
  Mills River *(G-10500)*

Brandon Hilbert.............................. F 704 243-5593
  Waxhaw *(G-15747)*
Brown Cabinet Co............................ G 704 933-2731
  Kannapolis *(G-9113)*
Burlington Distributing Co.................. G 336 292-1415
  Greensboro *(G-6862)*
Busbin Cabinetry............................. G 704 560-4485
  Belmont *(G-976)*
C & F Custom Cabinets Inc................ E 910 424-7475
  Hope Mills *(G-8733)*
C and L Cabinets LLC....................... G 828 550-9820
  Canton *(G-1604)*
Cabinet Connection of NC Inc............. G 919 653-1300
  Apex *(G-175)*
Cabinet Creations Inc....................... G 919 542-3722
  Moncure *(G-10616)*
Cabinet Door World LLC.................... F 877 929-2750
  Hickory *(G-7958)*
Cabinet Doors For Less..................... G 828 351-3510
  Conover *(G-4428)*
Cabinet Guy................................... G 919 375-4559
  Zebulon *(G-17123)*
Cabinet King Refinishing................... G 704 241-6405
  Mint Hill *(G-10525)*
Cabinet Makers Inc.......................... E 704 876-2808
  Statesville *(G-14769)*
Cabinet Man Cabinetry...................... G 336 382-0879
  Denton *(G-4727)*
Cabinet Masters and More LLC........... G 828 396-1881
  Granite Falls *(G-6725)*
Cabinet Plus................................... G 917 698-7708
  Huntersville *(G-8799)*
Cabinet Sales LLC............................ G 919 604-9536
  Raleigh *(G-12583)*
Cabinet Shop Inc............................. G 252 726-6965
  Morehead City *(G-11156)*
Cabinet Solutions Usa Inc.................. E 828 358-2349
  Hickory *(G-7959)*
Cabinet Transitions Inc..................... G 336 382-7154
  Greensboro *(G-6874)*
Cabinetry Squared........................... G 919 589-7253
  Willow Spring *(G-16077)*
Cabinets 4 U LLC............................. G 919 291-4617
  Hillsborough *(G-8641)*
Cabinets and Things......................... G 828 652-1734
  Union Mills *(G-15439)*
Cabinets Plus Inc............................. G 718 213-3300
  Charlotte *(G-2373)*
Cabinets Trim and More.................... G 704 680-7076
  Concord *(G-4219)*
Cabinetworks Group Mich LLC............ E 803 984-2285
  Charlotte *(G-2374)*
Cabinetworks Group Mich LLC............ E 919 868-8174
  Raleigh *(G-12584)*
Caldwell Cabinets NC LLC.................. E 828 212-0000
  Hudson *(G-8765)*
Cape Fear Cabinet Co Inc.................. F 910 703-8760
  Fayetteville *(G-5778)*
Capefear Woodworks........................ G 910 988-3306
  Leland *(G-9533)*
Cardinal Cabinetworks Inc................. G 919 829-3634
  Raleigh *(G-12594)*
Carocraft Cabinets Inc...................... E 704 376-0022
  Charlotte *(G-2391)*
Carolina Cab Specialist LLC................ G 919 818-4375
  Cary *(G-1724)*
Carolina Cabinets of Cedar Pt............. G 252 393-6236
  Swansboro *(G-15042)*
Carolina Creative Cabinets Inc............ G 919 842-2060
  Sanford *(G-14097)*
Carolina Custom Cabinetry................. G 704 808-1225
  Waxhaw *(G-15750)*

Carolina Custom Cabinets.................. G 910 525-3096
  Roseboro *(G-13783)*
Carolina Custom Cabinets Inc............. G 252 491-5475
  Powells Point *(G-12396)*
Carolina Surfaces LLC....................... G 910 874-1335
  Elizabethtown *(G-5591)*
Carolinas Top Shelf Cust Cabn............ G 704 376-5844
  Charlotte *(G-2414)*
Case Green Cabinetry....................... G 828 620-9730
  Asheville *(G-585)*
Casework Etc Inc............................. G 910 763-7119
  Wilmington *(G-16160)*
Charlotte Cabinetry LLC..................... G 704 966-2500
  Gastonia *(G-6376)*
Chesnick Corporation........................ F 919 231-2899
  Raleigh *(G-12619)*
Clemmons Hardwoods Cabinet Sp....... G 336 773-0551
  Winston Salem *(G-16654)*
Coastal Cabinetry Inc....................... G 910 367-8864
  Shallotte *(G-14271)*
Coastal Cabinets & Granite LLC.......... G 252 717-0611
  Simpson *(G-14437)*
Coastal Cabinets of New Bern............ G 252 514-5030
  New Bern *(G-11789)*
Cold Mtn Cabinetry.......................... G 828 577-8582
  Horse Shoe *(G-8739)*
Colonial Cabinets LLC....................... G 910 579-2954
  Calabash *(G-1553)*
Comm-Kab Inc................................ F 336 873-8787
  Asheboro *(G-417)*
Commercial Property LLC................... E 336 818-1078
  North Wilkesboro *(G-12002)*
Concord Custom Cabinets.................. G 704 773-0081
  Concord *(G-4239)*
Conestoga Wood Spc Corp................. D 919 284-2258
  Kenly *(G-9148)*
▲ Corilam Fabricating Co.................. E 336 993-2371
  Kernersville *(G-9182)*
Cornerstone Kitchens Inc.................. G 919 510-4200
  Raleigh *(G-12648)*
Cotner Cabinet................................ G 336 498-6199
  Randleman *(G-13460)*
Cotner Cabinet................................ G 336 672-1560
  Sophia *(G-14514)*
Covenantmade LLC.......................... F 336 434-4725
  Archdale *(G-275)*
Craft Woodwork Inc......................... G 252 237-7581
  Wilson *(G-16490)*
Craigscabinet................................. G 919 219-3970
  Clayton *(G-3970)*
Creations Cabinetry Design LLC.......... G 919 865-5979
  Raleigh *(G-12653)*
Creative Closets and Cabinetry........... G 570 952-1702
  Ocean Isle Beach *(G-12089)*
Creative Woodcrafters Inc................. G 828 252-9663
  Leicester *(G-9509)*
CTS Custom Cabinets........................ G 704 376-5844
  Charlotte *(G-2582)*
Custom Cabinet Works....................... G 828 396-6348
  Granite Falls *(G-6730)*
Custom Cabinets & Rmdlg Inc............. G 828 264-1806
  Boone *(G-1191)*
Custom Cabinets By Livengood........... G 704 279-3031
  Salisbury *(G-13950)*
Custom Marble Corporation................ G 910 215-0679
  Pinehurst *(G-12219)*
Custom Surfaces Corporation.............. G 252 638-3800
  New Bern *(G-11796)*
Cut Above Construction..................... G 828 758-8557
  Lenoir *(G-9602)*
Cynthia Saar.................................. G 910 480-2523
  Stedman *(G-14934)*

24 LUMBER AND WOOD PRODUCTS, EXCEPT FURNITURE

D & L Cabinets Inc .... F 336 376-6009
   Graham *(G-6687)*

Dante Cabinets .... G 919 306-3261
   Durham *(G-5046)*

Darrell Scott Carriker .... G 704 201-7465
   Midland *(G-10466)*

Dash Cabinet Company LLC .... G 704 746-7382
   Cornelius *(G-4538)*

Davis Cabinet Co Wilson Inc .... F 252 291-9052
   Sims *(G-14441)*

Davis Custom Cabinets .... G 336 961-2817
   Yadkinville *(G-17036)*

De Little Cabinet Inc .... G 704 888-5994
   Stanfield *(G-14677)*

Decima Corporation LLC .... E 734 516-1535
   Charlotte *(G-2610)*

Designer Woodwork .... G 910 521-1252
   Pembroke *(G-12182)*

Distinctive Cabinets Inc .... F 704 529-6234
   Charlotte *(G-2642)*

Doin It Rght Cbnetry More LLC .... G 980 297-3116
   Denver *(G-4774)*

Downeast Cabinets William Brya .... G 252 414-7730
   Winterville *(G-16999)*

Dublin Woodwork Shop .... G 910 862-2289
   Dublin *(G-4837)*

Duocraft Cabinets & Dist Co .... G 252 240-1476
   Morehead City *(G-11169)*

Eastcarolinacustomcabinets .... G 757 450-7385
   Moyock *(G-11696)*

Eastern Cabinet Company Inc .... G 252 237-5245
   Wilson *(G-16494)*

Eastern Cabinet Installers Inc .... G 336 774-2966
   Winston Salem *(G-16690)*

Eno Mt Cabinets James Ray .... G 919 644-1981
   Hillsborough *(G-8649)*

Eudys Cabinet Manufacturing .... E 704 888-4454
   Stanfield *(G-14678)*

Expressions Cabinetry LLC .... G 828 278-7999
   Fletcher *(G-6003)*

Ferguson Cabinet Works .... G 828 433-8710
   Morganton *(G-11213)*

Firehouse Cabinets .... G 704 689-5243
   Belmont *(G-990)*

▲ Gate City Kitchens LLC .... G 336 378-0870
   Greensboro *(G-7031)*

Gentrys Cabnt Doors .... G 336 957-8787
   Roaring River *(G-13593)*

Goembel Inc .... F 919 303-0485
   Apex *(G-196)*

Gonzalez Cab Installers LLC .... G 336 897-1046
   Greensboro *(G-7052)*

Grove Cabinet LLC .... G 828 575-4463
   Fairview *(G-5711)*

H Brothers Fine Wdwkg LLC .... G 931 216-1955
   Zebulon *(G-17131)*

Hager Cabinet Works John E Hag .... G 704 799-8113
   Mooresville *(G-10969)*

Hans Krug .... E 704 370-0809
   Charlotte *(G-2884)*

Hargenrader Cstm Woodcraft LLC .... G 828 896-7182
   Hickory *(G-8038)*

Harris Custom Cabinetry LLC .... G 828 289-5620
   Rutherfordton *(G-13876)*

Henderson & Kirkland Inc .... G 252 355-0224
   Winterville *(G-17002)*

Heritage Cabinet Company Inc .... F 252 648-8151
   Morehead City *(G-11176)*

Hester Cabinets .... G 336 376-0186
   Graham *(G-6691)*

Hollingsworth Custom Shop .... G 910 251-8849
   Castle Hayne *(G-1951)*

Hollingswrth Cbnets Intrors LL .... F 910 251-1490
   Castle Hayne *(G-1952)*

Home Imprv Solutions NC LLC .... G 919 876-3230
   Raleigh *(G-12856)*

Hometown Cabinets Inc .... G 919 245-3554
   Hillsborough *(G-8654)*

Honeycutt Custom Cabinets Inc .... E 910 567-6766
   Autryville *(G-841)*

▲ Idx Impressions LLC .... C 703 550-6902
   Washington *(G-15711)*

In Style Kitchen Cabinetry .... G 336 769-9605
   Winston Salem *(G-16756)*

Innovative Custom Cabinets Inc .... G 813 748-0655
   Kannapolis *(G-9124)*

Innovative Kitchens Baths Inc .... G 336 279-1188
   Greensboro *(G-7117)*

International Cabinetry Inc .... G 828 393-7998
   Hendersonville *(G-7866)*

Island Wood Crafts Ltd .... G 252 473-5363
   Wanchese *(G-15648)*

J & M Cabinet Installers LLC .... G 336 500-7148
   Greensboro *(G-7130)*

J B I Custom Cabinets .... G 910 538-3831
   Wilmington *(G-16274)*

Johnson Cabinet Co .... G 252 714-2051
   Simpson *(G-14438)*

Jon Mitchell Cabinets .... G 336 229-6261
   Burlington *(G-1442)*

Junes Craftmanship Inc .... G 704 230-0901
   Mooresville *(G-10992)*

Kay & Sons Woodworks Inc .... F 919 556-1060
   Wake Forest *(G-15566)*

KBK Cabinetry Inc .... G 704 506-0088
   Indian Trail *(G-8940)*

Kc Stone Enterprise Inc .... G 704 907-1361
   Indian Trail *(G-8941)*

Kc Stone Inc .... G 704 907-1361
   Matthews *(G-10327)*

Kd Cabinets Inc .... G 828 689-3848
   Marshall *(G-10203)*

Keep Stanly Beautiful Corp .... G 704 982-2649
   Albemarle *(G-92)*

Kens Custom Cabinets Inc .... G 252 637-3378
   New Bern *(G-11815)*

▲ Kitchen Cabinet Designers LLC .... C 919 833-6532
   Raleigh *(G-12943)*

Kitchen Cabinets and Design .... G 828 779-4453
   Asheville *(G-676)*

Kitchen Cabinets of Raleigh .... G 919 291-4397
   Wake Forest *(G-15569)*

Kitchen Masters Charlotte LLC .... F 704 375-3320
   Salisbury *(G-14000)*

Kkb Biltmore Inc .... G 828 274-6711
   Asheville *(G-677)*

Kohnle Cabinetry .... G 828 640-2498
   Hickory *(G-8079)*

Krieger Cabinets Dewayne .... G 704 630-0609
   Salisbury *(G-14002)*

Laborie Sons Cstm Wodworks LLC ...... G 910 769-2524
   Wilmington *(G-16293)*

Lakeshore Cabinet .... G 847 508-3594
   Huntersville *(G-8847)*

Larry S Cabinet Shop Inc .... G 252 442-4330
   Rocky Mount *(G-13707)*

Luxemark Company .... G 919 863-0101
   Raleigh *(G-12982)*

Markraft Cabinets Direct Sales .... G 910 762-1986
   Wilmington *(G-16314)*

Marsh Furniture Company .... F 336 229-5122
   Graham *(G-6700)*

Marsh Furniture Company .... F 336 273-8196
   Greensboro *(G-7182)*

Marsh Furniture Company .... F 336 884-7393
   High Point *(G-8443)*

Marsh Furniture Company .... G 336 765-7832
   Winston Salem *(G-16801)*

▲ Marsh Furniture Company .... B 336 884-7363
   High Point *(G-8444)*

Masterbrand Cabinets Inc .... D 252 523-4131
   Kinston *(G-9376)*

Masterbrand Cabinets Inc .... E 765 491-2385
   Lexington *(G-9754)*

McClellan Patric Michael .... G 336 385-1878
   Creston *(G-4623)*

McDowell County Millwork LLC .... F 828 682-6215
   Marion *(G-10162)*

McFarlin Cabinets .... G 828 310-9906
   Maiden *(G-10113)*

McLean Precision Cabinetry Inc .... G 910 327-9217
   Sneads Ferry *(G-14492)*

MDN Cabinets Inc .... G 919 662-1090
   Garner *(G-6285)*

Metro Woodcrafter of Nc Inc .... E 704 394-9622
   Charlotte *(G-3169)*

Mid Carolina Cabinets Inc .... G 704 358-9950
   Matthews *(G-10273)*

Mike Powell Inc .... F 910 792-6152
   Wilmington *(G-16324)*

Mike S Custom Cabinets Inc .... G 252 224-5351
   Pollocksville *(G-12394)*

Mint Hill Cabinet Shop Inc .... E 704 821-9373
   Monroe *(G-10770)*

Miters Touch Inc .... G 828 963-4445
   Banner Elk *(G-903)*

Morgans Cabinets Inc .... F 704 485-8693
   Oakboro *(G-12078)*

Mountain Cabinetry Closets LLC .... G 828 966-9000
   Brevard *(G-1281)*

Mountain Showcase Group Inc .... E 828 692-9494
   Hendersonville *(G-7881)*

Murphy S Custom Cabinetry Inc .... G 828 891-3050
   Hendersonville *(G-7882)*

Myricks Cabinet Shop Inc .... G 919 266-3720
   Knightdale *(G-9423)*

Nico Solid Maple Cabinets LLC .... G 602 319-2758
   Greensboro *(G-7220)*

Noble Bros Cabinets Mllwk LLC .... G 252 335-1213
   Elizabeth City *(G-5559)*

Noble Bros Cabinets Mllwk LLC .... G 252 482-9100
   Edenton *(G-5520)*

Noles Cabinets Inc .... F 919 552-4257
   Fuquay Varina *(G-6217)*

Norcraft Companies LP .... C 336 622-4281
   Liberty *(G-9825)*

Normac Kitchens Inc .... F 704 485-1911
   Oakboro *(G-12079)*

Norman Lake Cabinet Company .... G 704 498-6647
   Davidson *(G-4688)*

Nuworks .... G 919 223-2587
   Goldsboro *(G-6640)*

Odell Custom Cabinets .... G 704 201-6975
   Monroe *(G-10782)*

▲ Organized Cabinet LLC .... G 517 402-8639
   Morrisville *(G-11404)*

Oyama Cabinet Inc .... G 828 327-2668
   Conover *(G-4477)*

P R Sparks Enterprises Inc .... G 336 272-7200
   Greensboro *(G-7238)*

Pacific Cabinets .... G 919 695-3640
   Durham *(G-5267)*

Pb & J Industries Inc .... F 919 661-2738
   Raleigh *(G-13103)*

Pioneer Cabinets Inc .... G 828 688-2642
   Bakersville *(G-887)*

24 LUMBER AND WOOD PRODUCTS, EXCEPT FURNITURE

Port City Cabinets LLC .... G 910 622-0375
  Winnabow *(G-16583)*
Precision Cabinetry Inc .... G 828 465-3341
  Newton *(G-11962)*
Precision Cabinets Inc .... G 828 262-5080
  Boone *(G-1228)*
Premier Kit & Cabinetry Design .... G 910 224-5018
  Aberdeen *(G-22)*
Prestige Millwork Inc .... F 910 428-2360
  Star *(G-14722)*
Provision Cabinetry .... G 336 442-3537
  Archdale *(G-296)*
Quality Cabinets Woodworks .... G 252 536-0568
  Halifax *(G-7612)*
Raleigh Cabinet Works .... G 919 412-7750
  Raleigh *(G-13174)*
Red House Cabinets LLC .... G 919 201-2101
  Raleigh *(G-13198)*
Riverview Cabinet & Supply Inc .... G 336 228-1486
  Burlington *(G-1486)*
Robbinsville Cstm Molding Inc .... F 828 479-2317
  Robbinsville *(G-13610)*
Rowan Custom Cabinets Inc .... G 704 855-4778
  China Grove *(G-3888)*
Royal Maple LLC .... G 704 900-5086
  Charlotte *(G-3464)*
Rugby Acquisition LLC .... D 336 993-8686
  Kernersville *(G-9229)*
S Banner Cabinets Incorporated .... E 828 733-2031
  Newland *(G-11893)*
S Eudy Cabinet Shop Inc .... E 704 888-4454
  Stanfield *(G-14682)*
S Shelton Inc .... G 336 643-5916
  Stokesdale *(G-14948)*
S Zaytoun Custom Cabinets Inc .... F 252 638-8390
  New Bern *(G-11843)*
Sanford Kitchen & Bath Inc .... G 919 708-9080
  Sanford *(G-14181)*
Scotts Cabinet Store LLC .... G 919 725-2530
  Wake Forest *(G-15589)*
Seema Intl Custom Cabinetry .... G 917 703-0820
  Wake Forest *(G-15591)*
▲ Selpro LLC .... F 336 513-0550
  Greensboro *(G-7332)*
Signature Custom Cabinets LLC .... G 704 753-4874
  Monroe *(G-10807)*
Simmons Cstm Cbnetry Mllwk Inc .... G 252 240-1020
  Morehead City *(G-11190)*
Sjr Incorporated .... E 828 254-8966
  Asheville *(G-773)*
Smiths Custom Kitchen Inc .... G 828 652-9033
  Marion *(G-10177)*
Sorrells Cabinet Co Inc .... G 919 639-4320
  Lillington *(G-9860)*
Southern Cabinet Co Inc .... F 704 373-2299
  Matthews *(G-10291)*
Southern Design Cabinetry LLC .... F 919 340-1858
  Wake Forest *(G-15594)*
Stallings Cabinets Inc .... G 252 338-6747
  Elizabeth City *(G-5571)*
Stella Cabinet Works .... G 910 358-4248
  Maysville *(G-10375)*
Steves Cabinets Plus Inc .... G 919 351-0454
  Princeton *(G-12405)*
Stone Mountain Cabinetary .... G 828 676-3600
  Arden *(G-381)*
Sundance Cstm Painted Cabinets .... G 704 500-3732
  Cornelius *(G-4589)*
Sunhs Warehouse LLC .... G 919 908-1523
  Durham *(G-5380)*
Superior Custom Cabinets LLC .... G 919 778-1845
  Goldsboro *(G-6664)*

Tarheel Wood Designs Inc .... G 910 395-2226
  Wilmington *(G-16427)*
Tarheel Woodcrafters Inc .... G 252 432-3035
  Henderson *(G-7813)*
Tarlton Cabinet Shop .... G 704 573-7064
  Mint Hill *(G-10545)*
Team Triangle Cabinets .... G 919 609-1332
  Raleigh *(G-13332)*
Thomas Lcklars Cbnets Lrnburg .... G 910 369-2094
  Laurinburg *(G-9499)*
Tice Kitchens & Interiors LLC .... F 919 366-4117
  Raleigh *(G-13350)*
Tombogancraftsman Com .... G 919 932-9878
  Chapel Hill *(G-2081)*
Tommy W Smith Inc .... G 704 436-6616
  Mount Pleasant *(G-11678)*
Tonys Cabinets .... G 910 592-2028
  Clinton *(G-4115)*
Topline Cabinet Co Inc .... G 919 762-0045
  Holly Springs *(G-8722)*
Travis Alfrey Woodworking Inc .... G 910 639-3553
  Aberdeen *(G-33)*
Triangle Cabinet Company .... G 336 869-6401
  High Point *(G-8576)*
Triangle Kitchen Supply .... G 919 562-3888
  Youngsville *(G-17108)*
True Cabinet LLC .... F 828 855-9200
  Hickory *(G-8185)*
TS Woodworks & RAD Design Inc .... F 704 238-1015
  Monroe *(G-10824)*
Tsquared Cabinets .... G 336 655-0208
  Winston Salem *(G-16956)*
Twin City Custom Cabinets .... G 336 773-7200
  Winston Salem *(G-16957)*
U S Cabinets Express LLC .... G 336 875-4011
  High Point *(G-8582)*
US Precision Cabinetry LLC .... D 828 351-2020
  Rutherfordton *(G-13900)*
V/N Woodwork .... G 704 277-6336
  Indian Trail *(G-8969)*
Verona Cabinets & Surfaces LLC .... G 704 755-5259
  Charlotte *(G-3773)*
Vine & Branch Woodworks LLC .... G 704 663-0077
  Mooresville *(G-11120)*
Vivas Custom Cabinets LLC .... G 252 650-1103
  Elm City *(G-5654)*
Walker Woodworking Inc .... E 704 434-0823
  Shelby *(G-14381)*
Watkins Cabinets LLC .... G 704 634-1724
  Matthews *(G-10299)*
Windsors Cbnetry For Kit Baths .... G 336 275-0190
  Greensboro *(G-7462)*
Winstons Woodworks .... G 919 693-4120
  Oxford *(G-12161)*
Wnc Cabinetry LLC .... G 828 400-6492
  Waynesville *(G-15835)*
Wood Done Right Inc .... G 919 623-4557
  Chapel Hill *(G-2099)*
Wood Technology Inc .... E 828 464-8049
  Conover *(G-4515)*
Woodmaster Custom Cabinets Inc .... F 919 554-3707
  Youngsville *(G-17116)*
Woodmasters Woodworking Inc .... G 336 985-4000
  King *(G-9287)*
Woods Cabinet Company Inc .... G 919 207-1663
  Benson *(G-1046)*
Woods End LLC .... G 910 470-0389
  Castle Hayne *(G-1962)*
Woodworking Unlimited .... G 252 235-5285
  Bailey *(G-879)*
Xylem Inc .... G 919 772-4126
  Garner *(G-6328)*

Yadkin Valley Cabinet Co Inc .... G 336 786-9860
  Mount Airy *(G-11598)*
Your Cabinet Connection Inc .... G 919 641-2877
  Morrisville *(G-11468)*

2435 Hardwood veneer and plywood

A-1 Face Inc .... F 336 248-5555
  Lexington *(G-9677)*
▲ Adwood Corporation .... E 336 884-1846
  High Point *(G-8235)*
▼ Atlantic Veneer Company LLC .... C 252 728-3169
  Beaufort *(G-943)*
▲ Autumn House Inc .... D 828 728-1121
  Granite Falls *(G-6724)*
Burke Veneers Inc .... E 828 437-8510
  Morganton *(G-11203)*
Capitol Funds Inc .... D 704 482-0645
  Shelby *(G-14292)*
Chesterfield Wood Products Inc .... F 828 433-0042
  Morganton *(G-11204)*
Columbia Panel Mfg Co Inc .... G 336 861-4100
  High Point *(G-8300)*
Columbia Plywood Corporation .... B 828 724-4191
  Old Fort *(G-12100)*
Corbett Package Company .... D 910 763-9991
  Wilmington *(G-16183)*
David R Webb Company Inc .... G 336 605-3355
  Greensboro *(G-6960)*
▲ Diply LLC .... G 828 495-4352
  Hickory *(G-8010)*
Esco Industries Inc .... F 336 495-3772
  Randleman *(G-13469)*
Franklin Veneers Inc .... E 919 494-2284
  Franklinton *(G-6154)*
G & G Lumber Company Inc .... E 704 539-5110
  Harmony *(G-7686)*
Gates Custom Milling Inc .... E 252 357-0116
  Gatesville *(G-6549)*
Georgia-Pacific LLC .... D 919 580-1078
  Dudley *(G-4843)*
Georgia-Pacific LLC .... E 910 642-5041
  Whiteville *(G-15963)*
HM Frame Company Inc .... E 828 428-3354
  Newton *(G-11940)*
Mannington Mills Inc .... F 336 884-5600
  High Point *(G-8438)*
North Carolina Plywood LLC .... G 850 948-2211
  Whiteville *(G-15974)*
Ritch Face Veneer Company .... E 336 883-4184
  High Point *(G-8512)*
Robbinsville Cstm Molding Inc .... F 828 479-2317
  Robbinsville *(G-13610)*
▲ Sauers & Company Inc .... F 336 956-1200
  Lexington *(G-9776)*
Southern Vneer Spclty Pdts LLC .... F 919 642-7004
  Moncure *(G-10626)*
Superior Veneers Inc .... F 828 433-6986
  Morganton *(G-11258)*
Tailor Cut Wood Products Inc .... F 828 632-2808
  Taylorsville *(G-15169)*
Tramway Veneers Inc .... E 919 776-7606
  Sanford *(G-14198)*
Ufp New London LLC .... E 704 463-1400
  New London *(G-11880)*
▲ Veneer Technologies Inc .... C 252 223-5600
  Newport *(G-11910)*
Whiteville Plywood Inc .... F 910 642-7114
  Whiteville *(G-15981)*

2436 Softwood veneer and plywood

A-1 Face Inc .... F 336 248-5555
  Lexington *(G-9677)*

◆ Baltek Inc.....................................C.....336 398-1900
　Colfax (G-4141)
David R Webb Company Inc...............G.....336 605-3355
　Greensboro (G-6960)
Faces South Inc...............................F.....336 883-0647
　High Point (G-8350)
Georgia-Pacific LLC..........................G.....919 580-1078
　Dudley (G-4843)
Quality Veneer Company..................F.....336 622-2211
　Liberty (G-9827)
Ufp New London LLC......................E.....704 463-1400
　New London (G-11880)
Ven-Ply Incorporated.......................F.....336 841-4858
　High Point (G-8591)
Weyerhaeuser Company..................E.....336 835-5100
　Elkin (G-5633)

2439 Structural wood members, nec

Anderson Truss Company Inc..........F.....252 746-7726
　Ayden (G-847)
Andrews Truss Inc...........................E.....828 321-3105
　Andrews (G-124)
▲ Bfs Asset Holdings LLC...................C.....303 784-4288
　Raleigh (G-12554)
Blue Ridge Bldg Components Inc......G.....828 685-0452
　Dana (G-4662)
Builders Frstsrce - Rleigh LLC............D.....919 363-4956
　Apex (G-174)
C & C Chipping Inc..........................F.....252 249-1617
　Grantsboro (G-6764)
C & R Building Supply Inc................E.....910 567-6293
　Autryville (G-840)
Capitol Funds Inc.............................F.....910 439-5275
　Mount Gilead (G-11599)
Capitol Funds Inc.............................D.....704 482-0645
　Shelby (G-14292)
Capitol Funds Inc.............................E.....704 487-8547
　Shelby (G-14291)
Carolina Custom Exteriors Inc..........F.....828 232-0402
　Asheville (G-581)
Fast Arch of Carolinas Inc................G.....336 431-2724
　Archdale (G-279)
General Wholesale Bldg Sup Co.......D.....252 638-5861
　New Bern (G-11806)
High Cntry Tmbrframe Gllery WD.....G.....828 264-8971
　Boone (G-1204)
Idaho Timber NC LLC......................D.....252 430-0030
　Henderson (G-7789)
Log Home Builders Inc....................G.....704 638-0677
　Salisbury (G-14007)
Longleaf Truss Company.................E.....910 673-4711
　West End (G-15929)
Nvr Inc..D.....704 484-7170
　Kings Mountain (G-9320)
Peak Truss Builders LLC..................G.....919 552-5933
　Holly Springs (G-8710)
Rafters and Walls LLC.....................E.....980 404-0209
　Shelby (G-14359)
Roanoke Truss Inc...........................G.....252 537-0012
　Roanoke Rapids (G-13581)
Scotland Neck Heart Pine Inc..........G.....252 826-2755
　Scotland Neck (G-14220)
Smokey Mountain Lumber Inc.........G.....828 298-3958
　Asheville (G-775)
Smoky Mountain Timberwrights......F.....828 252-4205
　Asheville (G-777)
Truss Buildings LLC.........................G.....919 377-0217
　Cary (G-1915)
Truss Shop Inc.................................E.....336 372-6260
　Sparta (G-14600)
Trusses R US Inc..............................G.....704 361-7004
　Waxhaw (G-15784)

Trussway Manufacturing Inc............F.....336 883-6966
　Whitsett (G-16004)
▲ Truswood Inc..................................E.....800 473-8787
　Raleigh (G-13369)
Ufp New London LLC......................E.....704 463-1400
　New London (G-11880)
Ufp Site Built LLC............................D.....704 781-2520
　Locust (G-9976)
Universal Forest Products Inc..........G.....252 338-0319
　Elizabeth City (G-5580)
US Lbm Operating Co 2009 LLC......C.....910 864-8787
　Fayetteville (G-5943)
W and W Truss Builders Inc............G.....252 792-1051
　Williamston (G-16073)

2441 Nailed wood boxes and shook

A McGee Wood Products Inc...........F.....828 212-1700
　Granite Falls (G-6721)
Arcola Lumber Company Inc...........E.....252 257-4923
　Warrenton (G-15655)
Arcola Sawmill.................................G.....252 257-1139
　Warrenton (G-15656)
Carolina Crate & Pallet Inc..............E.....910 245-4001
　Vass (G-15491)
Carolina Crating Inc........................E.....910 276-7170
　Laurinburg (G-9472)
Carolina WD Pdts Mrshville Inc........D.....704 624-2119
　Marshville (G-10211)
Clemmons Pallet Skid Works Inc.....E.....336 766-5462
　Clemmons (G-4034)
Freedom Enterprise LLC..................G.....502 510-7296
　Shallotte (G-14273)
▲ Kontane Logistics Inc......................G.....828 397-5501
　Hickory (G-8080)
Mc Gees Crating Inc........................E.....828 758-4660
　Lenoir (G-9635)
▲ Spartacraft Inc.................................E.....828 397-4630
　Connelly Springs (G-4409)
Timberline Acquisition LLC..............E.....252 492-6144
　Henderson (G-7814)
Universal Forest Products Inc..........G.....252 338-0319
　Elizabeth City (G-5580)

2448 Wood pallets and skids

48forty Solutions LLC.....................A.....910 891-1534
　Dunn (G-4846)
A & J Pallets Inc..............................G.....336 969-0265
　Rural Hall (G-13832)
Alan Kimzey....................................G.....828 891-8720
　Mills River (G-10498)
Amware Pallet Services LLC...........F.....919 207-2403
　Benson (G-1030)
Atlas Box and Crating Co Inc..........G.....919 941-1023
　Durham (G-4934)
Bastrop Skid Company...................G.....252 793-6600
　Plymouth (G-12366)
Blue Stone Industries Ltd...............G.....919 379-3986
　Cary (G-1709)
Bluewater Pallet Solutions..............G.....336 697-9109
　Mc Leansville (G-10385)
Bolivia Lumber Company LLC.........F.....910 371-2515
　Leland (G-9528)
▲ Cargomovement International........G.....704 688-9720
　Charlotte (G-2389)
Carolina Base - Pac Corp................E.....828 728-7304
　Hudson (G-8766)
Carolina Crate & Pallet Inc..............E.....910 245-4001
　Vass (G-15491)
Carolina Crating Inc........................E.....910 276-7170
　Laurinburg (G-9472)
Carolina Mat Incorporated..............F.....252 793-1111
　Plymouth (G-12367)

Carolina Pallet Recycling Inc...........F.....828 652-6818
　Marion (G-10147)
Carolina WD Pdts Mrshville Inc........D.....704 624-2119
　Marshville (G-10211)
Carpenter Design Inc......................F.....828 248-9070
　Rutherfordton (G-13869)
Chep Recycled Pallet Solu...............G.....704 718-8199
　Charlotte (G-2472)
Clary Lumber Company..................D.....252 537-2558
　Gaston (G-6330)
Clemmons Pallet Skid Works Inc.....E.....336 766-5462
　Clemmons (G-4034)
Columbus Pallet Company Inc........G.....910 655-4513
　Delco (G-4720)
Convenient Pallets LLc...................G.....919 648-3396
　Seven Springs (G-14266)
CP Liquidation Inc...........................D.....704 921-1100
　Charlotte (G-2565)
Dagenhart Pallet Inc.......................F.....828 241-2374
　Catawba (G-1964)
Dails Pallet & Produce Inc...............G.....252 717-1338
　Kinston (G-9356)
Direct Wood Products.....................G.....336 238-2516
　Lexington (G-9709)
Discount Box & Pallet Inc................E.....336 272-2220
　Staley (G-14665)
Diversified Wood Products Inc........F.....252 793-6600
　Plymouth (G-12370)
Dusty Pallet....................................G.....828 524-5676
　Franklin (G-6127)
East Industries Inc...........................D.....252 442-9662
　Rocky Mount (G-13693)
Eds Pallet World Inc........................F.....828 453-8986
　Ellenboro (G-5635)
◆ Edwards Wood Products Inc...........C.....704 624-3624
　Marshville (G-10216)
Evergreen Pallets LLC.....................E.....828 313-0050
　Granite Falls (G-6732)
First Alance Logistics MGT LLC.......F.....704 522-0233
　Charlotte (G-2764)
Forest City Pallett Co Inc................G.....828 652-8432
　Nebo (G-11760)
Gamble Associates Inc...................F.....704 375-9301
　Charlotte (G-2806)
Glenn Lumber Company Inc...........E.....704 434-7873
　Shelby (G-14320)
Glenn Lumber Company Inc...........E.....704 434-9661
　Boiling Springs (G-1159)
Granville Pallet Co Inc.....................D.....919 528-2347
　Oxford (G-12131)
Gregory Pallet Co............................G.....336 349-2212
　Reidsville (G-13523)
Gregory Pallet Co LLC.....................G.....336 342-3590
　Elon (G-5658)
H Parsons Incorporated..................E.....828 757-9191
　Lenoir (G-9616)
Hildreth Wood Products Inc............G.....704 826-8326
　Wadesboro (G-15511)
Industrial Recycling Services...........G.....704 462-1882
　Newton (G-11943)
Jeld-Wen Inc...................................C.....336 838-0292
　North Wilkesboro (G-12016)
Johnston County Industries Inc.......C.....919 743-8700
　Selma (G-14257)
Lagael Manufacturing LLC..............G.....910 428-9383
　Star (G-14718)
Lucky Landports..............................G.....704 399-9880
　Charlotte (G-3107)
MAC Grading Co.............................F.....910 531-4642
　Autryville (G-842)
Mc Gees Crating Inc........................E.....828 758-4660
　Lenoir (G-9635)

24 LUMBER AND WOOD PRODUCTS, EXCEPT FURNITURE

McBride Lumber Co Partnr LLC............................ F 910 428-2747
   Star *(G-14721)*

Millwood Inc.. E 704 817-7541
   Charlotte *(G-3183)*

Myers Forest Products Inc................................... E 704 278-4532
   Cleveland *(G-4077)*

National Wden Pllet Cont Assoc.......................... F 919 837-2105
   Siler City *(G-14427)*

Neal S Pallet Company Inc................................... E 704 393-8568
   Charlotte *(G-3242)*

Neals Pallet Co Inc No 2...................................... G 704 393-0308
   Charlotte *(G-3243)*

Nicholsons Pallet Services Inc............................ G 704 826-8405
   Ansonville *(G-154)*

P1 Catawba Development Co LLC...................... G 704 462-1882
   Newton *(G-11957)*

Pallet Alliance Inc... F 919 442-1400
   Durham *(G-5268)*

Pallet Express Inc... C 336 621-2266
   Liberty *(G-9826)*

Pallet Plus Inc.. G 336 887-1810
   Trinity *(G-15353)*

Pallet Rack World.. G 336 253-8766
   Greensboro *(G-7241)*

Pallet Resource of NC Inc.................................... D 336 731-8338
   Lexington *(G-9766)*

Pallet World... G 919 800-1113
   Dunn *(G-4878)*

Pallet World USA Inc.. G 828 298-7270
   Asheville *(G-719)*

Palletone North Carolina Inc............................... D 919 575-6491
   Butner *(G-1547)*

Palletone North Carolina Inc............................... D 336 492-5565
   Mocksville *(G-10597)*

Palletone North Carolina Inc............................... D 704 462-1882
   Siler City *(G-14430)*

Pallets and More... G 919 815-6134
   Franklinton *(G-6162)*

Piedmont Pallet & Cont Inc.................................. G 336 284-6302
   Woodleaf *(G-17024)*

Precision Pallet LLC... F 252 935-5355
   Pantego *(G-12170)*

Pro Pallet South Inc... C 910 576-4902
   Troy *(G-15411)*

Propak Logistics... G 704 471-1070
   Shelby *(G-14358)*

Purely Pallets.. G 336 676-7107
   Greensboro *(G-7292)*

Reeder Pallet Company Inc.................................. F 336 879-3095
   Seagrove *(G-14245)*

Richard West Co Inc... G 252 793-4440
   Plymouth *(G-12377)*

Ross Skid Products Inc....................................... E 828 652-7450
   Marion *(G-10175)*

Ross Woodworking Inc.. G 704 629-4551
   Bessemer City *(G-1081)*

Ross Woodworking Inc.. G 704 629-4551
   Bessemer City *(G-1082)*

Sandhills Cnsld Svcs Inc..................................... G 919 718-7909
   Sanford *(G-14179)*

Somers Lumber and Mfg Inc............................... F
   Harmony *(G-7690)*

Starnes Pallet Service Inc................................... E 704 596-9006
   Charlotte *(G-3624)*

Statesville Pallet Company Inc........................... F 828 632-0268
   Hiddenite *(G-8227)*

Steelman Lumber & Pallet LLC........................... F 336 468-2757
   Hamptonville *(G-7678)*

Sunny View Pallet Company................................ G 828 625-9907
   Mill Spring *(G-10491)*

T P Supply Co Inc... E 336 789-2337
   Mount Airy *(G-11585)*

Timberline Acquisition LLC.................................. E 252 492-6144
   Henderson *(G-7814)*

Tree Brand Packaging Inc.................................... D 704 483-0719
   Denver *(G-4809)*

Tri-County Industries Inc.................................... C 252 977-3800
   Rocky Mount *(G-13676)*

Triple C Companies LLC...................................... F 704 966-1999
   Denver *(G-4811)*

Unified Pallets Inc.. G 910 891-2571
   Dunn *(G-4889)*

United Lumber Inc.. G 919 575-6491
   Butner *(G-1551)*

United Pallets & Truckin...................................... G 704 493-1636
   Charlotte *(G-3751)*

Universal Forest Products Inc............................. F 252 338-0319
   Elizabeth City *(G-5580)*

W N C Pallet Forest Pdts Inc................................ E 828 667-5426
   Candler *(G-1591)*

Walker Pallet Company Inc.................................. F 910 259-2235
   Burgaw *(G-1356)*

Wheeler Industries Inc... F 919 736-4256
   Pikeville *(G-12195)*

2449 Wood containers, nec

Arcola Hardwood Company Inc........................... F 252 257-4484
   Warrenton *(G-15654)*

Arcola Lumber Company Inc............................... E 252 257-4923
   Warrenton *(G-15655)*

Arcola Sawmill... G 252 257-1139
   Warrenton *(G-15656)*

Carolina Crate & Pallet Inc.................................. E 910 245-4001
   Vass *(G-15491)*

Carolina WD Pdts Mrshville Inc........................... D 704 624-2119
   Marshville *(G-10211)*

Case Specialists.. G 919 818-4476
   Raleigh *(G-12611)*

Container Systems Incorporated......................... D 919 496-6133
   Franklinton *(G-6153)*

Craftwood Veneers Inc... G 336 434-2158
   High Point *(G-8304)*

▼ Custom Air Trays Inc.. F 336 889-8729
   High Point *(G-8311)*

♦ Dac Products Inc... E 336 969-9786
   Rural Hall *(G-13839)*

Elberta Crate & Box Co....................................... C 252 257-4659
   Warrenton *(G-15658)*

Hensel Wood Products Corp............................... G 336 725-7568
   Winston Salem *(G-16743)*

Hildreth Wood Products Inc................................ G 704 826-8326
   Wadesboro *(G-15511)*

J & R Sales Inc... G 828 632-7402
   Hiddenite *(G-8221)*

J&R SERvices/J&r Lumber Co............................. G 956 778-7005
   Wilmington *(G-16276)*

▲ Kontane Logistics Inc...................................... G 828 397-5501
   Hickory *(G-8080)*

Lee County Industries Inc................................... E 919 775-3439
   Sanford *(G-14148)*

M O Deviney Lumber Co Inc............................... G 704 538-9071
   Casar *(G-1934)*

McBride Lumber Co Partnr LLC.......................... F 910 428-2747
   Star *(G-14721)*

Moorecraft Wood Proucts Inc............................. G 252 823-2510
   Tarboro *(G-15116)*

NC Backyard Coops.. G 336 250-0838
   Gold Hill *(G-6585)*

Pro Choice Contractors Corp............................... F 919 696-7383
   Raleigh *(G-13146)*

Raleigh Road Box Corporation............................ G 252 438-7401
   Henderson *(G-7806)*

2451 Mobile homes

Alan Lane Wesley.. G 704 433-8338
   Salisbury *(G-13917)*

Brig Homes NC... G 252 459-7026
   Nashville *(G-11737)*

Cavalier Home Builders LLC................................ C 252 459-7026
   Nashville *(G-11741)*

Champion Home Builders Inc.............................. G 910 893-5713
   Lillington *(G-9848)*

Clayton Homes Inc.. G 828 667-8701
   Candler *(G-1575)*

Clayton Homes Inc.. G 828 684-1550
   Fletcher *(G-5994)*

CMH Manufacturing Inc....................................... A 704 279-4659
   Rockwell *(G-13649)*

Conway Entps Carteret Cnty LLC....................... G 252 504-3518
   Beaufort *(G-951)*

Crest Capital LLC.. F 336 664-2400
   Greensboro *(G-6939)*

Daly Company Inc... G 919 751-3625
   Goldsboro *(G-6607)*

Eco Modern Homes LLC....................................... G 252 833-4335
   Chocowinity *(G-3894)*

▲ Elite Access International Inc......................... G 336 327-8096
   Greensboro *(G-6993)*

Elite Mountain Business LLC............................... G 828 349-0403
   Franklin *(G-6128)*

Esco Industries Inc... F 336 495-3772
   Randleman *(G-13469)*

Home City Ltd... G 910 428-2196
   Biscoe *(G-1111)*

Phillips Mobile Home Vlg LLC............................. G 704 298-4648
   Kannapolis *(G-9130)*

▲ Platipus Anchors Ltd....................................... G 919 662-0900
   Garner *(G-6303)*

R-Anell Custom Homes Inc.................................. E 704 483-5511
   Denver *(G-4797)*

R-Anell Housing Group LLC................................. D 704 445-9610
   Crouse *(G-4627)*

Readilite & Barricade Inc..................................... F 919 231-8309
   Raleigh *(G-13194)*

Sunshine Mnfctred Strctres Inc........................... E 704 279-6600
   Rockwell *(G-13659)*

Two Brothers NC LLC... G 336 516-5181
   Burlington *(G-1511)*

Wetherington S Mobile Home.............................. G 910 347-3664
   Jacksonville *(G-9046)*

2452 Prefabricated wood buildings

Bear Creek Log Tmber Homes LLC..................... G 336 751-6180
   Mocksville *(G-10557)*

Braswell Realty... G 828 733-5800
   Newland *(G-11882)*

Cavco Industries Inc.. D 910 410-5050
   Hamlet *(G-7618)*

▼ Deltec Homes Inc... E 828 253-0483
   Asheville *(G-607)*

Dex n Dox.. G 910 576-4644
   Troy *(G-15404)*

Distinctive Bldg & Design Inc............................. G 828 456-4730
   Waynesville *(G-15802)*

Enertia Building Systems Inc.............................. G 919 556-2391
   Wake Forest *(G-15553)*

Fascoe Realty... G 828 963-7600
   Boone *(G-1198)*

Glennstone Field Office....................................... G 919 680-8700
   Durham *(G-5124)*

Gray Wolf Log Homes Inc..................................... G 828 586-4662
   Sylva *(G-15057)*

Hope Renovations... F 919 960-1957
   Chapel Hill *(G-2024)*

Johnston County Industries Inc........................... C 919 743-8700
   Selma *(G-14257)*

24 LUMBER AND WOOD PRODUCTS, EXCEPT FURNITURE

Log Cabin Homes Ltd............................. G 252 454-1548
  Battleboro (G-924)
◆ Log Cabin Homes Ltd........................... D 252 454-1500
  Rocky Mount (G-13708)
Manning Building Products LLC............ G 919 662-9894
  Garner (G-6282)
Mast Woodworks.. F 336 468-1194
  Hamptonville (G-7677)
Mill Creek Post & Beam Co..................... G 828 749-8000
  Saluda (G-14072)
Mountain Rcrtion Log Cbins LLC............ G 828 387-6688
  Newland (G-11890)
Old Hickory Log Homes Inc................... G 704 489-8989
  Denver (G-4791)
Outlaw Step Co.. G 252 568-4384
  Deep Run (G-4717)
Piedmont Sales & Rentals LLC.............. G 919 499-9888
  Sanford (G-14170)
Quality Housing Corporation................. F 336 274-2622
  Greensboro (G-7300)
R-Anell Custom Homes Inc..................... E 704 483-5511
  Denver (G-4797)
Rclgh Inc... G 828 707-4383
  Asheville (G-753)
Salt Wood Products Inc............................. G 252 830-8875
  Greenville (G-7581)
Seashore Builders Inc............................... E 910 259-3404
  Maple Hill (G-10132)
South-East Lumber Company.................. E 336 996-5322
  Kernersville (G-9236)
Southland Log Homes Inc......................... G 336 449-5388
  Whitsett (G-16002)
Sunshine Mnfctred Strctres Inc............... E 704 279-6600
  Rockwell (G-13659)
▼ Topsider Building Systems Inc............. G 336 766-9300
  Clemmons (G-4062)
Tree Craft Log Homes Inc........................ G 828 689-2240
  Mars Hill (G-10197)
Tuff Shed Inc.. G 919 413-2494
  Morrisville (G-11458)
Ufp New London LLC............................... E 704 463-1400
  New London (G-11880)
▲ Web-Don Incorporated........................ E 800 532-0434
  Charlotte (G-3800)
▲ Wood Right Lumber Company............ G 910 576-4642
  Troy (G-15420)

2491 Wood preserving

Albemarle Wood Prsv Plant Inc.............. G 704 982-2516
  Albemarle (G-72)
Atlantic Wood & Timber LLC................... F 704 390-7479
  Charlotte (G-2235)
Blue Ridge Lbr Log & Timber Co............ F 336 961-5211
  Yadkinville (G-17033)
Boise Cascade Wood Pdts LLC............... G 336 598-3001
  Roxboro (G-13795)
Carolina Square Inc.................................. G 336 793-3222
  Mocksville (G-10562)
Coastal Treated Products LLC................ E 252 410-0180
  Roanoke Rapids (G-13571)
Culpeper Roanoke Rapids LLC............... G 252 678-3804
  Roanoke Rapids (G-13572)
Durable Wood Preservers Inc.................. G 704 537-3113
  Charlotte (G-2658)
Fiberon.. G 704 463-2955
  Concord (G-4264)
Fortress Wood Products Inc.................... F 336 854-5121
  High Point (G-8356)
General Wood Preserving Co Inc............ F 910 371-3131
  Leland (G-9546)
Gum Ridge Milling Company................... G 336 877-8894
  Fleetwood (G-5975)

Hoover Treated Wood Pdts Inc................ E 866 587-8761
  Weldon (G-15882)
Jak Moulding & Supply Inc...................... F 252 753-5546
  Walstonburg (G-15638)
Shenandoah Wood Preservers Inc......... E 252 826-4151
  Scotland Neck (G-14221)
Soha Holdings LLC.................................... E 828 264-2314
  Boone (G-1236)
Tarheel Wood Treating Company........... F 919 467-9176
  Morrisville (G-11438)
Tom Kleeberg... G 336 516-2363
  High Point (G-8572)
Tri-H Molding Co.. G 252 491-8530
  Harbinger (G-7684)
Ufp Biscoe LLC... F 910 294-8179
  Biscoe (G-1117)
Ufp Rockwell LLC..................................... G 704 279-0744
  Rockwell (G-13662)
Ufp Salisbury LLC.................................... B 704 855-1600
  Salisbury (G-14057)
Ufp Salisbury LLC.................................... F 704 855-1600
  Salisbury (G-14058)
Universal Forest Products Inc................. F 252 338-0319
  Elizabeth City (G-5580)
Wood-N-Boats Etc Inc............................... G 828 682-7470
  Burnsville (G-1536)
Woodline Inc... G 336 476-7100
  Thomasville (G-15304)
Woodtreaters Inc....................................... G 910 675-0038
  Rocky Point (G-13755)

2493 Reconstituted wood products

◆ Aconcagua Timber Corp....................... B 919 542-2128
  Moncure (G-10612)
Arauco - NA.. G 910 569-7020
  Biscoe (G-1103)
Arauco North America Inc....................... D 919 542-2128
  Moncure (G-10613)
Atc Panels... G 888 200-7955
  Moncure (G-10615)
◆ Atc Panels Inc....................................... F 919 653-6053
  Morrisville (G-11295)
▲ Attic Tent Inc.. G 704 892-5399
  Mooresville (G-10864)
Cottonwood Manufacturing Inc.............. G 704 504-0374
  Charlotte (G-2561)
Custom Finishers Inc............................... E 336 431-7141
  High Point (G-8313)
Egger Wood Products LLC....................... B 336 843-7000
  Linwood (G-9943)
▲ Flakeboard America Limited............. G 910 569-7010
  Biscoe (G-1109)
Georgia-Pacific LLC.................................. D 919 580-1078
  Dudley (G-4843)
◆ Huber Engineered Woods LLC........... E 800 933-9220
  Charlotte (G-2930)
Industrial Timber LLC.............................. D 704 919-1215
  Hiddenite (G-8220)
▲ Industrial Timber LLC........................ D 704 919-1215
  Charlotte (G-2966)
J R Craver & Associates Inc................... E 336 769-3330
  Clemmons (G-4049)
LL Cultured Marble Inc............................ F 336 789-3908
  Mount Airy (G-11539)
Louisiana-Pacific Corporation................ C 336 696-2751
  North Wilkesboro (G-12024)
Louisiana-Pacific Corporation................ G 336 696-2751
  Roaring River (G-13594)
Louisiana-Pacific Corporation................ C 336 599-8080
  Roxboro (G-13806)
Mohawk Industries Inc............................. C 910 439-6959
  Mount Gilead (G-11609)

Olon Industries Inc (us)............................ F 630 232-4705
  Mocksville (G-10596)
Quality Insulation Company.................... G 252 438-3711
  Henderson (G-7804)
◆ Uniboard USA LLC............................... C 919 542-2128
  Moncure (G-10628)
Weyerhaeuser Company.......................... E 336 835-5100
  Elkin (G-5633)

2499 Wood products, nec

1st Time Contracting................................ G 774 289-3321
  Clemmons (G-4023)
4 Home Products Inc................................ G 888 609-8222
  North Wilkesboro (G-11996)
A & J Pallets Inc....................................... G 336 969-0265
  Rural Hall (G-13832)
▲ A M Moore and Company Inc........... G 336 294-6994
  Greensboro (G-6767)
A-1 Face Inc... F 336 248-5555
  Lexington (G-9677)
Albright Qulty WD Turning Inc................ G 336 475-1434
  Thomasville (G-15182)
Alcorns Custom Woodworking Inc........ G 336 342-0908
  Reidsville (G-13505)
American Soil and Mulch Inc.................. F 919 460-1349
  Raleigh (G-12499)
▲ Apollo Designs LLC............................ E 336 886-0260
  High Point (G-8250)
Archdale Millworks Inc............................. G 336 431-9019
  Archdale (G-268)
Blind Nail and Company Inc................... G 919 967-0388
  Chapel Hill (G-1992)
Boards and Bowls LLC............................. G 704 293-2004
  Mooresville (G-10883)
◆ Brushy Mountain Bee Farm Inc......... E 336 921-3640
  Winston Salem (G-16639)
C & D Woodworking Inc........................... G 336 476-8722
  Thomasville (G-15193)
Cape Fear Coffee LLC............................. G 910 383-2429
  Leland (G-9532)
Carolina Bark Products LLC................... G 252 589-1324
  Seaboard (G-14227)
Carolina Crate & Pallet Inc..................... E 910 245-4001
  Vass (G-15491)
Carolina Stake and WD Pdts Inc............. G 704 545-7774
  Mint Hill (G-10527)
Chesterfield Wood Products Inc............ F 828 433-0042
  Morganton (G-11204)
Clausen Craftworks LLC.......................... G 704 252-5048
  Charlotte (G-2493)
◆ Cormark International LLC................ G 828 658-8455
  Weaverville (G-15844)
Cranberry Wood Works Inc..................... G 336 877-8771
  Fleetwood (G-5974)
Cw Media Inc.. G 910 302-3066
  Raeford (G-12419)
D C Custom Freight LLC.......................... E 843 658-6484
  Marshville (G-10213)
◆ Daramic LLC... D 704 587-8599
  Charlotte (G-2603)
Dean Company of North Carolina........... F 910 622-1012
  Holly Ridge (G-8681)
▲ Design Surfaces Inc........................... F 919 781-0310
  Raleigh (G-12679)
Dilworth Custom Framing....................... G 704 370-7660
  Charlotte (G-2637)
Ellismorris LLC.. G 646 538-1870
  Apex (G-189)
Fairview Woodcarving Inc....................... G 828 428-9491
  Maiden (G-10108)
Farleys Custom Carving Inc.................... G 828 256-9124
  Conover (G-4453)

24 LUMBER AND WOOD PRODUCTS, EXCEPT FURNITURE

Four Corners Frmng Gallery Inc............... G 704 662-7154
   Mooresville *(G-10949)*

G & G Management LLC....................... F 336 444-6271
   Greensboro *(G-7027)*

▲ G & G Moulding Inc............................ E 828 438-1112
   Morganton *(G-11214)*

Garick LLC....................................... G 704 455-6418
   Harrisburg *(G-7712)*

Gates Custom Milling Inc...................... E 252 357-0116
   Gatesville *(G-6549)*

George R Hardie................................ G 336 263-7920
   Liberty *(G-9815)*

▲ Ges Industries................................ E 252 430-8851
   Kittrell *(G-9396)*

Gilbert Hardwoods Inc......................... F 336 431-2127
   Trinity *(G-15342)*

◆ Graphik Dimensions Limited................. D 800 332-8884
   High Point *(G-8371)*

Greenville Wood Renewal Inc................. G 828 894-5376
   Mill Spring *(G-10485)*

H & P Wood Turnings Inc...................... G 910 675-2784
   Rocky Point *(G-13746)*

▼ Heartwood Pine Floors Inc.................. G 919 542-4394
   Moncure *(G-10624)*

Heartwood Refuge.............................. G 828 513-5016
   Hendersonville *(G-7860)*

Hefner Reels LLC............................... E 828 632-5717
   Taylorsville *(G-15146)*

Highland Craftsmen Inc........................ F 828 765-9010
   Spruce Pine *(G-14642)*

Hollywood Fit LLC............................... G 704 879-7426
   Gastonia *(G-6417)*

Huneywood Inc.................................. G 704 385-9785
   Monroe *(G-10735)*

Joey Manic Inc.................................. G 919 772-7756
   Oxford *(G-12134)*

Johnson Lumber Products Inc................ G 910 532-4201
   Ivanhoe *(G-8981)*

Jordan Group Corporation..................... G 803 309-9988
   Charlotte *(G-3034)*

JRs Custom Framing............................ G 704 449-2830
   Charlotte *(G-3037)*

Kamlar Corporation............................. E 252 443-2576
   Rocky Mount *(G-13705)*

Keener Wood Products Inc.................... G 828 428-1562
   Maiden *(G-10111)*

Kendall E Krause................................ G 910 690-4119
   Vass *(G-15492)*

Kenneth Moore Signs........................... G 910 458-6428
   Wilmington *(G-16287)*

◆ L G Sourcing Inc.............................. E 704 758-1000
   Mooresville *(G-11001)*

Legends Countertops LLC..................... G 980 230-4501
   Concord *(G-4302)*

Leist Studios Inc................................ G 828 262-5912
   Boone *(G-1214)*

Loflin Handle Co Inc............................ F 336 463-2422
   Yadkinville *(G-17043)*

Lynn Ladder Scaffolding Co Inc............... G 301 336-4700
   Charlotte *(G-3111)*

Madem-Moorecraft Reels USA Inc........... C 252 823-2510
   Tarboro *(G-15113)*

Marlinwoodworks LLC.......................... G 919 343-2605
   Lillington *(G-9856)*

Martin Lumber & Mulch LLC................... F 252 935-5294
   Pantego *(G-12167)*

McCrorie Group LLC............................ G 828 328-4538
   Hickory *(G-8093)*

Megawood Holdings Inc........................ G 910 439-2124
   Mount Gilead *(G-11608)*

Midwood Barkery LLC.......................... G 980 395-0498
   Charlotte *(G-3176)*

Miller Bee Supply Inc........................... F 336 670-2249
   North Wilkesboro *(G-12029)*

Minelli Usa LLC.................................. F 828 578-6734
   Hickory *(G-8095)*

Mirrormate LLC.................................. F 704 390-7377
   Charlotte *(G-3187)*

Moorecraft Reels Inc........................... D 252 823-2510
   Tarboro *(G-15115)*

Mulch Masters of NC Inc....................... F 919 676-0031
   Raleigh *(G-13050)*

Mulch Solutions LLC............................ G 704 893-5302
   Indian Trail *(G-8950)*

National Salvage & Svc Corp.................. E 919 739-5633
   Dudley *(G-4845)*

NC Moulding Acquisition LLC.................. F 336 249-7309
   Lexington *(G-9760)*

North Carolina Mulch Inc....................... G 252 478-4609
   Middlesex *(G-10452)*

Pamlico Shores Inc............................. E 252 926-0011
   Swanquarter *(G-15040)*

Phelps Wood Products LLC.................... F 336 284-2149
   Cleveland *(G-4079)*

Privette Enterprises Inc........................ G 704 634-3291
   Monroe *(G-10789)*

Pro Custom Cabinets LLC..................... G 704 239-6054
   Salisbury *(G-14031)*

Quantico Tactical Incorporated............... E 910 944-5800
   Aberdeen *(G-23)*

Ramons Custom Framing LLC................ G 252 208-8093
   Macclesfield *(G-10066)*

Reel Solutions Inc.............................. G 910 947-3117
   Carthage *(G-1665)*

Reliable Woodworks Inc........................ G 704 785-9663
   Concord *(G-4349)*

▲ Renner Usa Corp............................. G 704 527-9261
   Charlotte *(G-3435)*

Robert Hamms LLC............................. G 704 605-8057
   Monroe *(G-10797)*

Rodney S Cstm Cut Sign Co Inc.............. E 919 362-9669
   Holly Springs *(G-8712)*

RTO Services LLC............................... G 919 596-5406
   Durham *(G-5335)*

S Loflin Enterprises Inc......................... F 704 633-1159
   Salisbury *(G-14039)*

Salazar Custom Framing LLC................. G 919 349-0830
   Dunn *(G-4882)*

Saluda Mountain Products Inc................ F 828 696-2296
   Flat Rock *(G-5971)*

Sandalwood Healing Center Inc.............. G 828 228-4517
   Kernersville *(G-9232)*

Savvy Millwork LLC............................. G 919 625-5387
   Raleigh *(G-13233)*

Soundside Recycling & Mtls Inc............... G 252 491-8666
   Jarvisburg *(G-9086)*

◆ Southern Finishing Company Inc........... F 336 573-3741
   Stoneville *(G-14967)*

Square Peg Construction Inc.................. G 828 277-5164
   Asheville *(G-787)*

State of Art Custom Framing.................. G 336 629-7377
   Asheboro *(G-486)*

Swofford Inc..................................... G 252 478-5969
   Wilson *(G-16545)*

T Distribution NC Inc........................... E 828 438-1112
   Morganton *(G-11259)*

Tarheel Custom Woodworking Inc............ G 336 237-9344
   Lexington *(G-9789)*

Taylor Stave LLC................................ G 828 659-8880
   Nebo *(G-11764)*

Tea Dogu... G 818 404-6523
   Mebane *(G-10431)*

Traditions Wood Carving & Frms.............. G 828 322-5625
   Hickory *(G-8184)*

▼ Treeforms Inc.................................. E 336 292-8998
   Greensboro *(G-7409)*

◆ Turn Bull Lumber Company.................. E 910 862-4447
   Elizabethtown *(G-5607)*

Twin Oaks Gallery & Frmng LLC.............. G 704 466-3889
   Shelby *(G-14377)*

Universal Forest Products Inc................. F 252 338-0319
   Elizabeth City *(G-5580)*

Vaughn Woodworking Inc...................... G 828 963-6858
   Banner Elk *(G-905)*

▲ Vintage Editions Inc.......................... F 828 632-4185
   Taylorsville *(G-15175)*

Vinventions Usa LLC........................... C 919 460-2200
   Zebulon *(G-17145)*

White Robert Custom Wdwkg.................. G 704 489-2005
   Denver *(G-4814)*

▲ Whitley Holding Company.................... G 704 888-2625
   Midland *(G-10481)*

◆ Whitley/Monahan Handle LLC.............. E 704 888-2625
   Midland *(G-10482)*

▲ William L Day Companies Inc............... G 828 693-1333
   Tryon *(G-15431)*

Woodlawn Quality Plus......................... G 828 659-7721
   Marion *(G-10189)*

Woodley Enterprises LLC...................... G 828 944-0653
   Maggie Valley *(G-10097)*

Woods At Grove Park........................... G 336 226-6171
   Burlington *(G-1519)*

Woods At Lower River LLC..................... G 919 544-8044
   Durham *(G-5447)*

Woodteks LLC................................... G 336 244-1718
   Jonesville *(G-9103)*

Working Widget Technology LLC.............. G 704 684-6277
   Charlotte *(G-3822)*

World Art Gallery Incorporated................ G 910 989-0203
   Jacksonville *(G-9047)*

Worthyware Dsgns By D McHlle L............ E 803 565-0615
   Charlotte *(G-3828)*

Z-Bake Custom Picture Framing.............. G 919 848-4931
   Raleigh *(G-13435)*

25 FURNITURE AND FIXTURES

2511 Wood household furniture

A C Furniture Company Inc.................... B 336 623-3430
   Eden *(G-5484)*

A E Nesbitt Woodwork.......................... G 828 625-2428
   Black Mountain *(G-1118)*

Abbey Robert Inc................................ G 336 883-1078
   High Point *(G-8230)*

Affordable Beds & Furniture.................... G 336 988-1520
   Greensboro *(G-6785)*

Aidleyco LLC..................................... G 704 782-0648
   Mooresville *(G-10851)*

▲ Apollo Designs LLC........................... E 336 886-0260
   High Point *(G-8250)*

Artisans Guild Incorporated.................... G 336 841-4140
   High Point *(G-8256)*

Ashley Furniture Inds LLC..................... D 336 998-1066
   Advance *(G-37)*

B & L Custom Cabinets Inc.................... F 704 857-1940
   Westfield *(G-15950)*

Baker Interiors Furniture Co................... G 336 431-9115
   High Point *(G-8263)*

◆ Baker Interiors Furniture Co................. C 336 431-9115
   Connelly Springs *(G-4397)*

Barber Furniture & Supply..................... F 704 278-9367
   Cleveland *(G-4068)*

Barker and Martin Inc.......................... G 336 275-5056
   Greensboro *(G-6831)*

Bassett Furniture Direct Inc................... F 704 979-5700
   Concord *(G-4205)*

25 FURNITURE AND FIXTURES

Bernhardt Furniture Company............ F..... 828 759-6652
  Lenoir *(G-9584)*

Bernhardt Furniture Company............ F..... 828 758-9811
  Lenoir *(G-9585)*

Bernhardt Furniture Company............ F..... 828 759-6205
  Lenoir *(G-9587)*

◆ Bernhardt Furniture Company............C..... 828 758-9811
  Lenoir *(G-9586)*

◆ Bernhardt Industries Inc......................C..... 828 758-9811
  Lenoir *(G-9588)*

▲ Boggs Collective Inc............................ G..... 828 398-9701
  Asheville *(G-569)*

Bookcase Shop.. G..... 919 683-1922
  Durham *(G-4972)*

Bradington-Young LLC............................ C..... 276 656-3335
  Cherryville *(G-3862)*

Brown Cabinet Co.................................. G..... 704 933-2731
  Kannapolis *(G-9113)*

Cabinet Makers Inc............................... E..... 704 876-2808
  Statesville *(G-14769)*

▲ Carolina Business Furn Inc................. A..... 336 431-9400
  Archdale *(G-272)*

Carolina Csual Otdoor Furn Inc............. F..... 252 491-5171
  Jarvisburg *(G-9083)*

Carolina Farmstead LLC........................ G..... 800 822-6219
  Snow Hill *(G-14500)*

Carolina Furniture Mfrs Inc.................... G..... 336 873-7455
  Seagrove *(G-14236)*

◆ Carolina Mills Incorporated................. B..... 828 428-9911
  Maiden *(G-10102)*

Carolina Woodcraft LLC......................... G..... 919 585-2563
  Clayton *(G-3961)*

Carrington Court Inc............................. G..... 828 396-1049
  Granite Falls *(G-6727)*

Carroll Russell Mfg Inc.......................... E..... 919 779-2273
  Raleigh *(G-12604)*

Cashman Inc... G..... 252 995-4319
  Frisco *(G-6176)*

Century Furniture LLC............................ D..... 828 326-8410
  Hickory *(G-7975)*

Century Furniture LLC............................ C..... 828 326-8201
  Hickory *(G-7976)*

Century Furniture LLC............................ D..... 828 326-8535
  Hickory *(G-7977)*

Century Furniture LLC............................ C..... 828 326-8458
  Hickory *(G-7978)*

Century Furniture LLC............................ G..... 828 326-8300
  Hickory *(G-7981)*

Century Furniture LLC............................ G..... 336 889-8286
  High Point *(G-8292)*

Chf Industries Inc.................................. E..... 212 951-7800
  Charlotte *(G-2473)*

Chris Isom Inc.. F..... 336 629-0240
  Asheboro *(G-415)*

▲ Classic Leather Inc............................ B..... 828 328-2046
  Conover *(G-4436)*

Closets By Design.................................. D..... 704 361-6424
  Charlotte *(G-2498)*

Coastal Wood Products Inc.................... G..... 252 943-6650
  Pinetown *(G-12247)*

▲ Councill Company LLC....................... C..... 336 859-2155
  Denton *(G-4731)*

Craftmaster Furniture Inc..................... A..... 828 632-8127
  Hiddenite *(G-8215)*

Cranberry Wood Works Inc................... G..... 336 877-8771
  Fleetwood *(G-5974)*

◆ Cv Industries Inc................................ G..... 828 328-1851
  Hickory *(G-8001)*

◆ Davis Furniture Industries Inc........... C..... 336 889-2009
  High Point *(G-8319)*

◆ Dedon Inc.. F..... 336 790-1070
  Greensboro *(G-6963)*

◆ Design Workshop Incorporated......... F..... 910 293-7329
  Warsaw *(G-15666)*

▲ Designmaster Furniture Inc............... E..... 828 324-7992
  Hickory *(G-8008)*

Drexel Heritage Furnishings................... G..... 828 391-6400
  Lenoir *(G-9605)*

Ducduc LLC... G..... 212 226-1868
  Raleigh *(G-12707)*

◆ E J Victor Inc...................................... C..... 828 437-1991
  Morganton *(G-11210)*

▲ Easyglass Inc..................................... E..... 336 786-1800
  Mount Airy *(G-11505)*

Ethan Allen Retail Inc........................... E..... 828 428-9361
  Maiden *(G-10107)*

Fairfield Chair Company........................ E..... 828 785-5571
  Lenoir *(G-9609)*

◆ Fairfield Chair Company.................... C..... 828 758-5571
  Lenoir *(G-9610)*

▲ Fulfords Restorations........................ G..... 252 243-7727
  Wilson *(G-16500)*

Furniture Company.................................. G..... 910 686-1937
  Wilmington *(G-16225)*

Furniture Concepts................................. F..... 828 323-1590
  Hickory *(G-8029)*

G A Lankford Construction..................... G..... 828 254-2467
  Alexander *(G-118)*

Goodson Enterprises Inc........................ G..... 410 303-5053
  Candler *(G-1581)*

Gram Furniture.. G..... 828 241-2836
  Claremont *(G-3928)*

Guy Chaddock and Company LLC......... E..... 828 584-0664
  Morganton *(G-11217)*

H & H Furniture Mfrs Inc....................... C..... 336 873-7245
  Seagrove *(G-14239)*

Hancock & Moore LLC............................ C..... 828 495-8235
  Taylorsville *(G-15145)*

Hdm Furniture Industries Inc................ A..... 800 349-4579
  Hickory *(G-8039)*

Hdm Furniture Industries Inc................ C..... 336 882-8135
  Hickory *(G-8040)*

Hfi Wind Down Inc................................ C..... 828 430-3355
  Morganton *(G-11221)*

◆ Hickory Chair Company..................... D..... 800 225-0265
  Hickory *(G-8046)*

HM Frame Company Inc....................... E..... 828 428-3354
  Newton *(G-11940)*

Hollingswrth Cbnets Intrors LL............. F..... 910 251-1490
  Castle Hayne *(G-1952)*

Home Meridian Group LLC.................... D..... 336 819-7200
  High Point *(G-8399)*

▲ Home Meridian Holdings Inc............. C..... 336 887-1985
  High Point *(G-8400)*

Homestead Country Built Furn............. G..... 910 799-6489
  Wilmington *(G-16256)*

Hooker Furniture Corporation................ C..... 336 819-7200
  High Point *(G-8401)*

Ibolili Natural Fibers............................... G..... 866 834-9857
  Greensboro *(G-7109)*

Jalco Inc... G..... 336 434-5909
  Trinity *(G-15347)*

▼ Johnston Casuals Furniture Inc........ D..... 336 838-5178
  North Wilkesboro *(G-12018)*

Jones Frame Inc................................... E..... 336 434-2531
  High Point *(G-8417)*

Kenzie Layne Company......................... G..... 704 485-2282
  Locust *(G-9961)*

▲ Kincaid Furniture Company Inc......... D..... 828 728-3261
  Hudson *(G-8773)*

Kn Furniture Inc................................... E..... 336 953-3259
  Ramseur *(G-13444)*

Kolcraft Enterprises Inc........................ C..... 910 944-9325
  Aberdeen *(G-10)*

Kustom Kraft Wdwrks Mt Airy In............ G..... 336 786-2831
  Mount Airy *(G-11533)*

◆ Lacquer Craft Hospitality Inc............ C..... 336 822-8086
  High Point *(G-8428)*

Lambeth Frames Inc............................. G..... 336 953-9805
  Asheboro *(G-452)*

▲ Lea Industries Inc............................. C..... 336 294-5233
  Hudson *(G-8774)*

Leisure Craft Holdings LLC.................... D..... 828 693-8241
  Flat Rock *(G-5967)*

Leisure Craft Inc................................... C..... 828 693-8241
  Flat Rock *(G-5968)*

Liberty Hse Utility Buildings.................. G..... 828 209-3390
  Horse Shoe *(G-8740)*

▼ Linwood Inc.. F..... 336 300-8307
  Lexington *(G-9750)*

Magnussen Home Furnishings Inc......... G..... 336 841-4424
  Greensboro *(G-7178)*

Martin Obrien Cabinetmaker.................. G..... 336 773-1334
  Winston Salem *(G-16802)*

Maynard Frame Shop Inc...................... F..... 910 428-2033
  Star *(G-14720)*

Michael Parker Cabinetry...................... G..... 919 833-5117
  Raleigh *(G-13024)*

Murrah Woodcraft LLC.......................... G..... 919 302-3661
  Bahama *(G-866)*

Nobscot Construction Co Inc................ G..... 919 929-2075
  Chapel Hill *(G-2048)*

Ofs Brands Inc...................................... F..... 800 763-0212
  High Point *(G-8470)*

Old Growth Riverwood Inc................... G..... 910 762-4077
  Wilmington *(G-16343)*

One Furniture Group Corp.................... G..... 336 235-0221
  Greensboro *(G-7232)*

P R Sparks Enterprises Inc................... G..... 336 272-7200
  Greensboro *(G-7238)*

Philip Brady... G..... 336 581-3999
  Bennett *(G-1027)*

◆ Phoenix Home Furnishings Inc.......... C
  High Point *(G-8480)*

Precast Terrazzo Entps Inc.................. E..... 919 231-6200
  Raleigh *(G-13132)*

Precision Materials LLC........................ F..... 828 632-8851
  Taylorsville *(G-15159)*

Prepac Manufacturing US LLC.............. F..... 800 665-1266
  Whitsett *(G-15999)*

Pricely Inc... E..... 336 431-2055
  High Point *(G-8497)*

Progressive Furniture Inc..................... C..... 828 459-2151
  Claremont *(G-3935)*

Quality Contemporary Furniture............ G..... 919 758-7277
  Raleigh *(G-13163)*

Riverview Cabinet & Supply Inc........... G..... 336 228-1486
  Burlington *(G-1486)*

Robert Bergelin Company...................... E..... 828 437-6409
  Morganton *(G-11246)*

Royal Colony Furniture Inc................... G..... 336 472-8833
  Thomasville *(G-15272)*

Ruskin Inc... F..... 828 324-6500
  Hickory *(G-8143)*

Seagrove Lumber LLC............................ F..... 910 428-9663
  Seagrove *(G-14248)*

Shelfgenie... G..... 704 705-0005
  Charlotte *(G-3540)*

Shelfgenie Coastal Carolinas................ G..... 910 547-9595
  Wilmington *(G-16402)*

◆ Sherrill Furniture Company............... B..... 828 322-2640
  Hickory *(G-8149)*

South Mountain Crafts.......................... G..... 828 433-2607
  Morganton *(G-11255)*

◆ Southern Finishing Company Inc...... F..... 336 573-3741
  Stoneville *(G-14967)*

Employee Codes: A=Over 500 employees, B=251-500
C=101-250, D=51-100, E=20-50, F=10-19, G=1-9

25 FURNITURE AND FIXTURES

▲ Southwood Furniture Corp............. D..... 828 465-1776
  Hickory *(G-8165)*

Stanley Furniture Company LLC........... C..... 336 884-7700
  High Point *(G-8550)*

Stellar Innovations Inc................. G..... 704 746-2886
  Cornelius *(G-4588)*

▲ Stone Marble Co Inc................... G..... 773 227-1161
  Thomasville *(G-15285)*

▲ Storagemotion Inc..................... G..... 704 746-3700
  Mooresville *(G-11105)*

Stowed LLC............................. F..... 203 346-5687
  High Point *(G-8555)*

Style Upholstering Inc................. G..... 828 322-4882
  Hickory *(G-8171)*

Sullivan Workshop LLC.................. G..... 704 560-9900
  Charlotte *(G-3647)*

Superior Wood Products Inc............. F..... 336 472-2237
  Thomasville *(G-15286)*

▲ Sutter Street Manufacturing........... C..... 828 459-5598
  Claremont *(G-3940)*

Tatum Galleries Inc.................... G..... 828 963-6466
  Banner Elk *(G-904)*

◆ Thayer Coggin Inc.....................D..... 336 841-6000
  High Point *(G-8566)*

Thayer Coggin Furniture................ G..... 336 841-6000
  High Point *(G-8567)*

▲ Tiger Mountain Woodworks Inc.......... E..... 828 526-5577
  Highlands *(G-8618)*

▼ Treeforms Inc......................... E..... 336 292-8998
  Greensboro *(G-7409)*

Troutman Careconnect Corp.............. F..... 704 838-9389
  Troutman *(G-15394)*

▲ Troutman Chair Company LLC............ E..... 704 872-7625
  Troutman *(G-15395)*

▲ Tsai Winddown Inc..................... E..... 704 873-3106
  Statesville *(G-14919)*

Turning Pges Pctrial Heirlooms......... G..... 704 634-2911
  Charlotte *(G-3740)*

◆ Unigel Inc............................ G..... 828 228-2095
  Hickory *(G-8195)*

Universal Furniture Intl Inc........... G..... 828 241-3191
  Claremont *(G-3941)*

Universal Furniture Intl Inc........... C..... 828 464-0311
  Conover *(G-4509)*

◆ Universal Furniture Limited...........D..... 336 822-8888
  High Point *(G-8586)*

Uwharrie Chair Company LLC............. G..... 336 431-2055
  High Point *(G-8587)*

Vaughan-Bassett Furn Co Inc............ A..... 336 835-2670
  Elkin *(G-5631)*

Vaughan-Bassett Furn Co Inc............ A..... 336 889-9111
  High Point *(G-8589)*

WB Frames Inc.......................... G..... 828 459-2147
  Hickory *(G-8207)*

◆ Wdm Inc...............................E..... 704 283-7508
  Monroe *(G-10831)*

We Organize You LLC.................... G..... 919 773-8990
  Apex *(G-258)*

Weathercraft Outdoor Furn Inc.......... G..... 336 629-3939
  Asheboro *(G-508)*

◆ Whitewood Industries Inc..............D..... 336 472-0303
  Thomasville *(G-15300)*

Willow Creek Furniture Inc............. G..... 336 889-0076
  High Point *(G-8604)*

Winston Concept Furniture.............. G..... 336 472-7839
  Thomasville *(G-15302)*

Wise Living Inc........................ F..... 336 991-5346
  High Point *(G-8606)*

Wood Country Creations LLC............. G..... 704 545-5966
  Mint Hill *(G-10549)*

Wood N Things.......................... G..... 910 990-4448
  Clinton *(G-4119)*

Wood Technology Inc.................... E..... 828 464-8049
  Conover *(G-4515)*

Woodsmiths Company..................... F..... 406 626-3102
  Lenoir *(G-9661)*

Woodys Chair Shop...................... G..... 828 765-9277
  Spruce Pine *(G-14661)*

Xylem Inc.............................. G..... 919 772-4126
  Garner *(G-6328)*

▲ Yorkshire House Inc................... G..... 336 869-9714
  High Point *(G-8609)*

Yukon Inc.............................. E..... 919 366-2001
  Wendell *(G-15926)*

2512 Upholstered household furniture

▼ 4 Seasons Furniture Indust LLC........ F..... 336 873-7245
  Seagrove *(G-14231)*

A C Furniture Company Inc.............. B..... 336 623-3430
  Eden *(G-5484)*

▲ AB New Beginnings Inc................. D..... 828 465-6953
  Conover *(G-4412)*

American of High Point Inc............. E..... 336 431-1513
  High Point *(G-8247)*

Amor Furniture and Bedding LLC......... F..... 336 795-0044
  Liberty *(G-9806)*

Archdale Furniture Distributor......... G..... 336 431-1081
  Archdale *(G-267)*

▲ Aria Designs LLC...................... G..... 828 572-4303
  Lenoir *(G-9575)*

Baker Interiors Furniture Co........... G..... 336 431-9115
  High Point *(G-8263)*

Bassett Furniture Inds Inc............. G..... 828 465-7700
  Newton *(G-11915)*

Berkeley Home Furniture LLC............ G..... 336 882-0012
  High Point *(G-8271)*

Bernhardt Furniture Company............ F..... 828 572-4664
  Lenoir *(G-9582)*

Bernhardt Furniture Company............ F..... 828 759-6652
  Lenoir *(G-9584)*

Bernhardt Furniture Company............ F..... 828 758-9811
  Lenoir *(G-9585)*

Bernhardt Furniture Company............ F..... 828 759-6205
  Lenoir *(G-9587)*

◆ Bernhardt Furniture Company...........C..... 828 758-9811
  Lenoir *(G-9586)*

◆ Bernhardt Industries Inc..............C..... 828 758-9811
  Lenoir *(G-9588)*

Blackstone Furniture Inds Inc.......... F..... 910 428-2833
  Ether *(G-5690)*

Bradington-Young LLC................... C..... 276 656-3335
  Cherryville *(G-3862)*

▲ Bradington-Young LLC.................. C..... 704 435-5881
  Hickory *(G-7953)*

Brookline Furniture Co Inc............. D..... 336 841-8503
  Archdale *(G-270)*

Burrough Furniture..................... G..... 336 841-3129
  Archdale *(G-271)*

▲ C R Laine Furniture Co Inc............ C..... 828 328-1831
  Hickory *(G-7957)*

Cargill & Pendleton Inc................ E..... 336 882-5510
  High Point *(G-8283)*

Carolina Chair Inc..................... F..... 828 459-1330
  Conover *(G-4430)*

◆ Carolina Mills Incorporated...........B..... 828 428-9911
  Maiden *(G-10102)*

◆ Carolina Tape & Supply Corp...........E..... 828 322-3991
  Hickory *(G-7968)*

Carrington Court Inc................... G..... 828 396-1049
  Granite Falls *(G-6727)*

Cedar Rock Home Furnishings............ G..... 828 396-2361
  Hudson *(G-8767)*

Century Furniture LLC.................. C..... 828 326-8201
  Hickory *(G-7976)*

Century Furniture LLC.................. C..... 828 326-8458
  Hickory *(G-7978)*

Century Furniture LLC.................. E..... 828 326-8410
  Hickory *(G-7979)*

Century Furniture LLC.................. E..... 828 326-8650
  Hickory *(G-7980)*

Century Furniture LLC.................. E..... 828 326-8300
  Hickory *(G-7981)*

Century Furniture LLC.................. F..... 828 326-8495
  Hickory *(G-7982)*

Chair Man.............................. G..... 610 809-0871
  Manteo *(G-10127)*

Charles Stewart Co..................... C..... 828 322-9464
  Hickory *(G-7984)*

◆ Chateau DAx USA Ltd................... G..... 336 885-9777
  High Point *(G-8294)*

▲ Classic Leather Inc................... B..... 828 328-2046
  Conover *(G-4436)*

◆ Contemporary Furnishings Corp.........D..... 704 633-8000
  Salisbury *(G-13946)*

Contract Seating Inc................... G..... 828 322-6662
  Hickory *(G-7994)*

Cotton Belt Inc........................ D..... 252 689-6847
  Greenville *(G-7509)*

▲ Councill Company LLC.................. C..... 336 859-2155
  Denton *(G-4731)*

Country At Home Furniture Inc.......... F..... 828 464-7498
  Newton *(G-11926)*

▲ Cox Manufacturing Company Inc......... E..... 828 397-4123
  Hickory *(G-7997)*

Craftmaster Furniture Inc.............. A..... 828 632-8127
  Hiddenite *(G-8215)*

◆ Craftmaster Furniture Inc.............B..... 828 632-9786
  Hiddenite *(G-8214)*

Craymer McElwee Holdings Inc........... F..... 828 326-6100
  Hickory *(G-7998)*

Creations By Taylor.................... G..... 410 269-6430
  Mount Pleasant *(G-11673)*

◆ Custom Contract Furn LLC..............G..... 336 882-8565
  High Point *(G-8312)*

Custom Designs and Upholstery.......... F..... 336 882-1516
  Thomasville *(G-15208)*

◆ Cv Industries Inc..................... G..... 828 328-1851
  Hickory *(G-8001)*

▲ D R Kincaid Chair Co Inc.............. E..... 828 754-0255
  Lenoir *(G-9603)*

Dal Leather Inc........................ G..... 828 302-1667
  Conover *(G-4444)*

Daniels Woodcarving Co Inc............. F..... 828 632-7336
  Taylorsville *(G-15140)*

Design Theory LLC...................... F..... 336 912-0155
  High Point *(G-8322)*

Dexter Inc............................. G..... 828 459-7904
  Claremont *(G-3919)*

Dexter Inc............................. G..... 919 510-5050
  Raleigh *(G-12681)*

▲ Dfp Inc............................... D..... 336 841-3028
  High Point *(G-8323)*

Directional Buying Group Inc........... E..... 336 472-6187
  Thomasville *(G-15214)*

Distinctive Furniture Inc.............. G..... 828 754-3947
  Lenoir *(G-9604)*

Domenicks Furniture Mfr LLC............ E..... 336 442-3348
  High Point *(G-8329)*

◆ E J Victor Inc........................C..... 828 437-1991
  Morganton *(G-11210)*

Elite Furniture Mfg Inc................ G..... 336 882-0406
  High Point *(G-8340)*

England Inc............................ E..... 336 861-5266
  High Point *(G-8345)*

Fairfield Chair Company................ E..... 828 785-5571
  Lenoir *(G-9609)*

SIC SECTION

25 FURNITURE AND FIXTURES

◆ Fairfield Chair Company .... C 828 758-5571
  Lenoir *(G-9610)*
Framewright Inc .... F 828 459-2284
  Conover *(G-4457)*
Friendship Upholstery Co Inc .... E 828 632-9836
  Taylorsville *(G-15143)*
Furniture Concepts .... F 828 323-1590
  Hickory *(G-8029)*
Geiger International Inc .... F 828 324-6500
  Hildebran *(G-8623)*
Golden Rctangle Enteprises Inc .... G 828 389-3336
  Hayesville *(G-7766)*
Grand Manor Furniture Inc .... D 828 758-5521
  Lenoir *(G-9613)*
▲ H W S Company Inc .... B 828 322-8624
  Hickory *(G-8037)*
Hancock & Moore LLC .... C 828 495-8235
  Taylorsville *(G-15145)*
Hancock & Moore LLC .... D 828 495-8235
  Taylorsville *(G-15144)*
Hdm Furniture Industries Inc .... A 800 349-4579
  Hickory *(G-8039)*
Hdm Furniture Industries Inc .... E 336 812-4434
  High Point *(G-8379)*
Hester Enterprises Inc .... E 704 865-4480
  Gastonia *(G-6416)*
Hfi Wind Down Inc .... C 828 438-5767
  Morganton *(G-11220)*
HM Frame Company Inc .... E 828 428-3354
  Newton *(G-11940)*
HM Liquidation Inc .... G 828 495-8235
  Hickory *(G-8058)*
▲ Huddle Furniture Inc .... E 828 874-8888
  Valdese *(G-15448)*
◆ Hughes Furniture Inds Inc .... C 336 498-8700
  Randleman *(G-13473)*
Huntington House Inc .... E 828 495-4400
  Taylorsville *(G-15147)*
▲ Huntington House Inc .... C 828 495-4400
  Hickory *(G-8060)*
▲ Images of America Inc .... D 336 475-7106
  Thomasville *(G-15237)*
▲ Indiana Chair Frame Company .... E 574 825-9355
  Liberty *(G-9817)*
▲ Intensa Inc .... F 336 884-4003
  High Point *(G-8412)*
International Furnishings Inc .... G 336 472-8422
  Thomasville *(G-15238)*
▲ Isenhour Furniture Company .... D 828 632-8849
  Taylorsville *(G-15149)*
▲ Jack Cartwright Incorporated .... E 336 889-9400
  High Point *(G-8414)*
▼ Jarrett Brothers .... G 828 433-8036
  Morganton *(G-11225)*
▲ Jessica Charles LLC .... D 336 434-2124
  High Point *(G-8416)*
Joerns Healthcare Parent LLC .... B 800 966-6662
  Charlotte *(G-3027)*
Joseph Halker .... G 336 769-4734
  Winston Salem *(G-16772)*
Keani Furniture Inc .... E 336 303-5484
  Asheboro *(G-448)*
Kellex Corp .... C 828 874-0389
  Valdese *(G-15449)*
▲ Key City Furniture Company Inc .... C 336 818-1161
  Wilkesboro *(G-16035)*
▲ Kincaid Furniture Company Inc .... D 828 728-3261
  Hudson *(G-8773)*
King Hickory Furniture Company .... G 828 324-0472
  Hickory *(G-8075)*
King Hickory Furniture Company .... G 336 841-6140
  High Point *(G-8424)*

▲ King Hickory Furniture Company ...... C 828 322-6025
  Hickory *(G-8076)*
Kn Furniture Inc .... E 336 953-3259
  Ramseur *(G-13444)*
Kolcraft Enterprises Inc .... C 910 944-9345
  Aberdeen *(G-10)*
Lancer Incorporated .... C 910 428-2181
  Star *(G-14719)*
◆ Lazar Industries LLC .... C 919 742-9303
  Siler City *(G-14420)*
Lazar Industries East Inc .... F 919 742-9303
  Siler City *(G-14421)*
Lee Industries LLC .... C 828 464-8318
  Newton *(G-11947)*
Lee Industries LLC .... C 828 464-8318
  Newton *(G-11948)*
◆ Lee Industries LLC .... B 828 464-8318
  Conover *(G-4470)*
◆ Lexington Furniture Inds Inc .... C 336 474-5300
  Thomasville *(G-15241)*
Linrene Furniture Inc .... G 919 742-9391
  Siler City *(G-14422)*
◆ LLC Ferguson Copeland .... C 828 584-0664
  Morganton *(G-11229)*
▲ Lloyds Chatham Ltd Partnership ...... F 919 742-4692
  High Point *(G-8433)*
Lodging By Liberty Inc .... C 336 622-2201
  Siler City *(G-14423)*
M & M Frame Company Inc .... G 336 859-8166
  Denton *(G-4745)*
◆ March Furniture Manufacturing Inc ... C 336 824-4413
  Ramseur *(G-13447)*
▲ Marquis Contract Corporation .... E 336 884-8200
  High Point *(G-8442)*
Mastercraft Lamp Intl Furn .... G 336 882-1535
  High Point *(G-8449)*
Masterfield Furniture Co Inc .... E 828 632-8535
  Taylorsville *(G-15151)*
◆ McCreary Modern Inc .... B 828 464-6465
  Newton *(G-11951)*
◆ McKinley Leather Hickory Inc .... E 828 459-2884
  Claremont *(G-3931)*
McNeillys Inc .... E 704 300-1712
  Lawndale *(G-9501)*
◆ Minhas Furniture House Inc .... E 910 898-0808
  Robbins *(G-13601)*
Mitchell Gold Co LLC .... D 828 632-7916
  Taylorsville *(G-15152)*
◆ Mitchell Gold Co LLC C
  Taylorsville *(G-15153)*
Moores Upholstering Interiors .... G 704 240-8393
  Lincolnton *(G-9909)*
N Style Living Inc .... G 336 938-4014
  High Point *(G-8461)*
NC Custom Leather Inc .... F 828 404-2973
  Conover *(G-4474)*
Nobscot Construction Co Inc .... G 919 929-2075
  Chapel Hill *(G-2048)*
◆ North Carolina Lumber Company ...... F 336 498-6600
  Randleman *(G-13481)*
O Henry House Ltd .... E 336 431-5350
  Archdale *(G-294)*
▲ Old Hickory Tannery Inc .... E 828 465-6599
  Newton *(G-11955)*
◆ Paladin Industries Inc .... D 828 635-0448
  Hiddenite *(G-8225)*
Parker Southern Inc .... F 828 428-3506
  Maiden *(G-10115)*
◆ Paul Robert Chair Inc .... D 828 632-7021
  Taylorsville *(G-15155)*
Plat LLC .... F 828 358-4564
  Granite Falls *(G-6750)*

Prominence Furniture Inc .... E 336 475-6505
  Thomasville *(G-15267)*
R & D Weaving Inc .... F 828 248-1910
  Ellenboro *(G-5638)*
Rbc Inc .... G 336 889-7573
  High Point *(G-8506)*
◆ Rbc Inc .... C 336 889-7333
  Sophia *(G-14521)*
Restaurant Furniture Inc .... F 828 459-9992
  Claremont *(G-3937)*
Rhf Investments Inc .... G 828 326-8350
  Hickory *(G-8135)*
Richard Shew .... F 828 781-3294
  Conover *(G-4491)*
Rowes .... G 828 241-2609
  Catawba *(G-1967)*
Rufco Inc .... G 919 829-1332
  Wake Forest *(G-15585)*
S Dorsett Upholstery Inc .... G 336 472-7076
  Thomasville *(G-15275)*
◆ Schnadig Corporation .... E 336 389-5200
  Greensboro *(G-7327)*
Seam-Craft Inc .... F 336 861-4156
  High Point *(G-8521)*
Select Furniture Company Inc .... F 336 886-3572
  High Point *(G-8522)*
Sherrill Furniture Company .... G 828 322-8624
  Hickory *(G-8147)*
Sherrill Furniture Company .... F 828 328-5241
  Hickory *(G-8148)*
Sherrill Furniture Company .... G 336 884-0974
  High Point *(G-8523)*
Sherrill Furniture Company .... F 828 437-2256
  Morganton *(G-11252)*
Sherrill Furniture Company .... D 828 465-0844
  Newton *(G-11967)*
◆ Sherrill Furniture Company .... B 828 322-2640
  Hickory *(G-8149)*
Sides Furniture Inc .... G 336 869-5509
  High Point *(G-8524)*
Simplicity Sofas Inc .... G 800 813-2889
  High Point *(G-8531)*
Smith Novelty Company Inc .... G 704 982-7413
  Albemarle *(G-105)*
Southandenglish LLC .... G 336 888-8333
  High Point *(G-8543)*
Southfield Ltd .... F 336 434-6220
  High Point *(G-8546)*
▲ Southwood Furniture Corp .... D 828 465-1776
  Hickory *(G-8165)*
▲ Stone Marble Co Inc .... G 773 227-1161
  Thomasville *(G-15285)*
Style Upholstering Inc .... G 828 322-4882
  Hickory *(G-8171)*
Superior Wood Products Inc .... F 336 472-2237
  Thomasville *(G-15286)*
◆ Swaim Inc .... C 336 885-6131
  High Point *(G-8559)*
▲ Taylor King Furniture Inc .... C 828 632-7731
  Taylorsville *(G-15170)*
Tb Arhaus LLC .... C 828 465-6953
  Conover *(G-4503)*
TCS Designs Inc .... F 828 324-9944
  Hickory *(G-8175)*
Temple Inc .... D 828 428-8031
  Maiden *(G-10119)*
Theodore Alexander .... G 336 689-4178
  Greensboro *(G-7400)*
Thomasville Upholstery Inc .... C 828 345-6225
  Hickory *(G-8180)*
▲ Tomlinson/Erwin-Lambeth Inc .... D 336 472-5005
  Thomasville *(G-15293)*

25 FURNITURE AND FIXTURES

Universal Furniture Intl Inc .... G 828 241-3191
  Claremont (G-3941)
Universal Furniture Intl Inc .... C 828 464-0311
  Conover (G-4509)
◆ Universal Furniture Limited .... D 336 822-8888
  High Point (G-8586)
Upholstery Designs Hickory Inc .... E 828 324-2002
  Hickory (G-8196)
◆ Vanguard Furniture Co Inc .... B 828 328-5601
  Conover (G-4510)
Vaughan-Bassett Furn Co Inc .... A 336 835-2670
  Elkin (G-5631)
◆ Verellen Inc .... D 336 889-7379
  High Point (G-8592)
Violino USA Ltd .... E 336 889-6623
  High Point (G-8594)
▲ Watauga Creek LLC .... G 828 369-7881
  Franklin (G-6147)
Whitewood Contracts LLC .... E 336 885-9300
  High Point (G-8603)
Wise Living Inc .... F 336 991-5346
  High Point (G-8606)
▲ Woodmark Originals Inc .... G 336 841-6409
  High Point (G-8607)

2514 Metal household furniture

Biologics Inc .... G 919 546-9810
  Raleigh (G-12558)
Bull City Designs LLC .... E 919 908-6252
  Durham (G-4986)
Conestoga Wood Spc Corp .... D 919 284-2258
  Kenly (G-9148)
Creative Metal and Wood Inc .... F 336 475-9400
  Colfax (G-4145)
Dorel Ecommerce Inc .... F 828 378-0092
  Asheville (G-611)
Four Corners Home Inc .... G 828 398-4187
  Asheville (G-626)
Greg Price .... G 847 778-4426
  Hampstead (G-7648)
◆ Hickory Springs Manufactu .... D 828 328-2201
  Hickory (G-8052)
Leggett & Platt Incorporated .... G 704 380-6208
  Statesville (G-14835)
Leisure Craft Holdings LLC .... D 828 693-8241
  Flat Rock (G-5967)
Leisure Craft Inc .... C 828 693-8241
  Flat Rock (G-5968)
Mlf Company LLC .... F 919 231-9401
  Raleigh (G-13037)
Outer Banks Hammocks Inc .... F 910 256-4001
  Wilmington (G-16347)
Powder River Technologies Inc .... G 828 465-2894
  Newton (G-11961)
▲ Stiles Mfg Co Inc .... G 910 592-6344
  Clinton (G-4113)
◆ Swaim Inc .... C 336 885-6131
  High Point (G-8559)
Timmerman Manufacturing Inc .... F 828 464-1778
  Conover (G-4505)
Tube Enterprises Incorporated .... F 941 629-9267
  Shelby (G-14376)

2515 Mattresses and bedsprings

Affordable Bedding Inc .... G 828 254-5555
  Asheville (G-516)
Arden Companies LLC .... D 919 258-3081
  Sanford (G-14088)
Bedex LLC .... E 336 617-6755
  High Point (G-8269)
Bekaertdeslee USA Inc .... E 336 769-4300
  Winston Salem (G-16626)

Bemco Sleep Products Inc .... E 910 892-3107
  Dunn (G-4853)
Bjmf Inc .... E 704 554-6333
  Charlotte (G-2318)
Blue Ridge Products Co Inc .... E 828 322-7990
  Hickory (G-7952)
▲ Carolina Mattress Guild Inc .... D 336 841-8529
  Thomasville (G-15198)
Caudle Bedding Supplies .... G 336 498-2600
  Randleman (G-13458)
Comfort Bay Home Fashions Inc .... G 843 442-7477
  Hickory (G-7988)
Comfort Sleep LLC .... F 336 267-5853
  Thomasville (G-15205)
Cotton Belt Inc .... D 252 689-6847
  Greenville (G-7509)
Culp Inc .... E 336 885-2800
  Stokesdale (G-14940)
Dilworth Mattress Company Inc .... G 704 333-6564
  Charlotte (G-2638)
Elborn Holdings LLC .... E 919 917-1419
  Davidson (G-4673)
Hill-Rom Inc .... B 919 854-3600
  Cary (G-1784)
▲ Iredell Fiber Inc .... D 704 878-0884
  Statesville (G-14822)
Jones Frame Inc .... E 336 434-2531
  High Point (G-8417)
◆ Kingsdown Incorporated .... E 919 563-3531
  Mebane (G-10415)
L C Industries Inc .... C 919 596-8277
  Fayetteville (G-5857)
◆ L C Industries Inc .... C 919 596-8277
  Durham (G-5185)
Larlin Cushion Company .... F 828 465-5599
  Hickory (G-8083)
Leggett & Platt .... E 336 357-3641
  Lexington (G-9746)
Leggett & Platt Incorporated .... C 336 379-7777
  Greensboro (G-7166)
Leggett & Platt Incorporated .... D 336 884-4306
  High Point (G-8429)
Leggett & Platt Incorporated .... F 336 622-0121
  Liberty (G-9819)
Leggett & Platt Incorporated .... G 704 380-6208
  Statesville (G-14835)
Leggett & Platt Incorporated .... D 828 322-6855
  Conover (G-4471)
Leggett & Platt Incorporated .... D 336 889-2600
  High Point (G-8430)
Lin Wggins Mem Schlarship Fund ...... G 919 749-2340
  Fuquay Varina (G-6209)
Mattress Firm .... G 910 868-0950
  Fayetteville (G-5870)
Mattress Firm .... G 252 443-1259
  Rocky Mount (G-13711)
Mattress Warehouse .... G 919 463-0329
  Cary (G-1821)
◆ Ohio Mat Lcnsing Cmpnnts Group .. G 336 861-3500
  Trinity (G-15349)
Ohio-Sealy Mattress Mfg Co .... G 336 861-3500
  Trinity (G-15350)
Reliable Bedding Company .... E 336 883-0648
  Archdale (G-297)
Reliable Bedding Company .... G 336 886-7036
  High Point (G-8508)
Reliable Quilting Company .... G 336 886-7036
  High Point (G-8509)
Riverside Mattress Co Inc .... E 910 483-0461
  Fayetteville (G-5906)
Roadmster Trck Conversions Inc .... G 252 412-3980
  Grifton (G-7602)

Royale Komfort Bedding Inc .... F 828 632-5631
  Taylorsville (G-15163)
◆ Sealy Corporation .... C 336 861-3500
  Trinity (G-15355)
Sealy Mattress Co SW Virginia .... G 336 861-3500
  Trinity (G-15356)
◆ Sealy Mattress Company .... C 336 861-3500
  Trinity (G-15357)
Sealy Mattress Mfg Co LLC .... C 336 861-2900
  Trinity (G-15358)
Spring Air Mattress Corp .... D 336 272-1141
  Greensboro (G-7359)
Ssb Manufacturing Company .... D 704 596-4935
  Charlotte (G-3615)
Stn Cushion Company .... D 336 476-9100
  Thomasville (G-15284)
Studio 180 .... G 570 998-8746
  Cedar Grove (G-1972)
Tempur Sealy International Inc .... E 336 861-2900
  Trinity (G-15361)
Tender Care Products Inc .... F 828 726-8241
  Hickory (G-8177)
▼ Timeless Bedding Inc .... G 336 472-6603
  Lexington (G-9794)
Vaughan-Bassett Furn Co Inc .... A 336 835-2670
  Elkin (G-5631)
◆ Winstn-Slem Inds For Blind Inc .... B 336 759-0551
  Winston Salem (G-16979)

2517 Wood television and radio cabinets

American Tops Inc .... G 828 397-4910
  Hildebran (G-8619)
Distinctive Cabinets Inc .... F 704 529-6234
  Charlotte (G-2642)
Mountain Showcase Group Inc .... E 828 692-9494
  Hendersonville (G-7881)
Ocean Woodworking Inc .... G 910 579-2233
  Ocean Isle Beach (G-12094)
Philip Brady .... G 336 581-3999
  Bennett (G-1027)
Quality Custom Woodworks Inc .... G 704 843-1584
  Waxhaw (G-15771)
Sycamore Cabinetry Inc .... G 704 375-1617
  Dallas (G-4659)
Wood Technology Inc .... E 828 464-8049
  Conover (G-4515)

2519 Household furniture, nec

A N E Services LLC .... G 704 882-1117
  Charlotte (G-2117)
AAA Glass Company .... G 252 946-2396
  Washington (G-15678)
▲ Acacia Home & Garden Inc .... F 828 465-1700
  Conover (G-4413)
Arden Companies LLC .... D 919 258-3081
  Sanford (G-14088)
Arnold B Cochrane Inc .... G 336 294-8038
  Greensboro (G-6815)
Built To Last NC LLC .... F 252 232-0055
  Moyock (G-11693)
Bull City Designs LLC .... E 919 908-6252
  Durham (G-4986)
▲ Consumer Specialty Inc .... G 828 396-2195
  Hudson (G-8769)
Council Trnsp & Logistics LLC .... G 910 322-7588
  Fayetteville (G-5797)
Creative Metal and Wood Inc .... F 336 475-9400
  Colfax (G-4145)
▲ French Heritage Inc .... F 336 882-3565
  High Point (G-8358)
Joseph Sotanski .... E 407 324-6187
  Marion (G-10155)

SIC SECTION 25 FURNITURE AND FIXTURES

Keter Us Inc.. D..... 704 263-1967
  Stanley *(G-14699)*

▲ Looc Studio Inc... G..... 336 472-6877
  Newton *(G-11950)*

Market of Raleigh LLC.................................. G..... 919 212-2100
  Raleigh *(G-12998)*

Masters Moving Services Inc........................ G..... 919 523-9836
  Raleigh *(G-13006)*

▲ Millenia Usa LLC... F
  Hickory *(G-8094)*

Otto and Moore Inc....................................... F..... 336 887-0017
  High Point *(G-8472)*

◆ Rbc Inc.. C..... 336 889-7333
  Sophia *(G-14521)*

Riverwood Inc... E..... 336 956-3034
  Lexington *(G-9774)*

Selenis North America LLC......................... G..... 210 380-2723
  Fayetteville *(G-5914)*

Stephanie Baxter.. G..... 803 203-8467
  Lincolnton *(G-9922)*

Stephanies Mattress LLC............................. G..... 704 763-0705
  Charlotte *(G-3630)*

Suncast Corporation..................................... E..... 704 274-5394
  Huntersville *(G-8902)*

Val-U-King Group Inc................................... G..... 980 306-5342
  Gastonia *(G-6536)*

Whippoorwill Hills Inc................................... G..... 252 537-2765
  Roanoke Rapids *(G-13588)*

2521 Wood office furniture

▲ 3c Store Fixtures Inc................................... D..... 252 291-5181
  Wilson *(G-16461)*

A C Furniture Company Inc......................... B..... 336 623-3430
  Eden *(G-5484)*

A R Byrd Company Inc................................. G..... 704 732-5675
  Lincolnton *(G-9864)*

Amcase Inc... E..... 336 784-5992
  High Point *(G-8244)*

Appalachian Cabinet Inc.............................. G..... 828 265-0830
  Deep Gap *(G-4708)*

B&H Millwork and Fixtures Inc..................... E..... 336 431-0068
  High Point *(G-8260)*

Baypointe Partners LLC............................... G..... 336 882-5200
  Archdale *(G-269)*

Bernhardt Furniture Company...................... F..... 828 759-6245
  Lenoir *(G-9583)*

Bernhardt Furniture Company...................... F..... 828 758-9811
  Lenoir *(G-9585)*

Bernhardt Furniture Company...................... F..... 828 759-6205
  Lenoir *(G-9587)*

◆ Bernhardt Furniture Company..................... C..... 828 758-9811
  Lenoir *(G-9586)*

◆ Bernhardt Industries Inc............................... C..... 828 758-9811
  Lenoir *(G-9588)*

Boss Design US Inc..................................... G..... 844 353-7834
  High Point *(G-8275)*

Bull City Designs LLC.................................. E..... 919 908-6252
  Durham *(G-4986)*

Carolina Furniture Mfrs Inc........................... G..... 336 873-7355
  Seagrove *(G-14236)*

▲ Carolina House Furniture Inc....................... E..... 828 459-7400
  Claremont *(G-3903)*

◆ Century Furniture LLC................................. C..... 828 267-8739
  Hickory *(G-7983)*

▲ Classic Leather Inc..................................... B..... 828 328-2046
  Conover *(G-4436)*

Comm-Kab Inc.. F..... 336 873-8787
  Asheboro *(G-417)*

▲ Corilam Fabricating Co................................ E..... 336 993-2371
  Kernersville *(G-9182)*

Custom Cabinets By Livengood................... G..... 704 279-3031
  Salisbury *(G-13950)*

Cynthia Saar... G..... 910 480-2523
  Stedman *(G-14934)*

Darran Furniture Inds Inc............................. C..... 336 861-2400
  High Point *(G-8318)*

◆ Davis Furniture Industries Inc...................... C..... 336 889-2009
  High Point *(G-8319)*

▲ Delve Interiors LLC...................................... C..... 336 274-4661
  Greensboro *(G-6968)*

Dp Woodworks Inc.. G..... 704 821-7799
  Monroe *(G-10707)*

▲ Element Designs Inc.................................... D..... 704 332-3114
  Charlotte *(G-2691)*

Evelyn T Burney.. G..... 336 473-9794
  Rocky Mount *(G-13697)*

Geiger International Inc................................ F..... 828 324-6500
  Hildebran *(G-8623)*

Groupe Lacasse LLC.................................... E..... 336 778-2098
  Clemmons *(G-4042)*

Hancock & Moore LLC................................. C..... 828 495-8235
  Taylorsville *(G-15145)*

Harris House Furn Inds Inc.......................... E..... 336 431-2802
  Archdale *(G-282)*

Haworth Inc.. G..... 828 328-5600
  Conover *(G-4461)*

Haworth Inc.. G..... 336 885-4021
  High Point *(G-8378)*

Haworth Health Environments LLC............. E..... 828 328-5600
  Conover *(G-4462)*

▲ Hickory Business Furniture LLC.................. B..... 828 328-2064
  Hickory *(G-8045)*

▲ High Point Furniture Inds Inc....................... D..... 336 431-7101
  High Point *(G-8391)*

▲ Idx Impressions LLC................................... C..... 703 550-6902
  Washington *(G-15711)*

Ie Furniture Inc... E..... 336 475-5050
  Archdale *(G-284)*

Jasper Seating Company Inc....................... C..... 704 528-4506
  Troutman *(G-15384)*

▲ Looc Studio Inc... G..... 336 472-6877
  Newton *(G-11950)*

Michael Parker Cabinetry............................. G..... 919 833-5117
  Raleigh *(G-13024)*

Ocean Woodworking Inc.............................. G..... 910 579-2233
  Ocean Isle Beach *(G-12094)*

▲ Ofm LLC.. D..... 919 303-6389
  Holly Springs *(G-8709)*

Parker Southern Inc..................................... F..... 828 428-3506
  Maiden *(G-10115)*

Precision Materials LLC............................... F..... 828 632-8851
  Taylorsville *(G-15159)*

Precision Mtls - Blue Rdge LLC................... G..... 828 322-7990
  Hickory *(G-8119)*

Prestige Millwork Inc.................................... F..... 910 428-2360
  Star *(G-14722)*

Pridgen Woodwork Inc................................. E..... 910 642-7175
  Whiteville *(G-15975)*

Professinal Sales Associates....................... F..... 336 210-2756
  High Point *(G-8500)*

Rcws Inc... F..... 919 680-2655
  Durham *(G-5320)*

▲ Sbfi-North America Inc................................ F..... 828 236-3993
  Asheville *(G-764)*

Sdv Office Systems LLC............................. F..... 844 968-9500
  Fletcher *(G-6037)*

Sdv Office Systems LLC............................. G..... 844 968-9500
  Asheville *(G-767)*

Thomasville Upholstery Inc.......................... C..... 828 345-6225
  Hickory *(G-8180)*

Triune Business Furniture Inc...................... G..... 336 884-8341
  High Point *(G-8578)*

Ullmanique Inc.. G..... 336 885-5111
  High Point *(G-8583)*

Upholstery Designs Hickory Inc................... E..... 828 324-2002
  Hickory *(G-8196)*

Wood Country Creations LLC...................... G..... 704 545-5966
  Mint Hill *(G-10549)*

Woodsmiths Company................................. F..... 406 626-3102
  Lenoir *(G-9661)*

Xylem Inc.. G..... 919 772-4126
  Garner *(G-6328)*

2522 Office furniture, except wood

A C Furniture Company Inc......................... B..... 336 623-3430
  Eden *(G-5484)*

A R Byrd Company Inc................................ G..... 704 732-5675
  Lincolnton *(G-9864)*

▲ Abercrombie Textiles I LLC......................... F..... 704 487-1245
  Shelby *(G-14282)*

Baypointe Partners LLC............................... G..... 336 882-5200
  Archdale *(G-269)*

Bernhardt Furniture Company...................... F..... 828 759-6245
  Lenoir *(G-9583)*

Bernhardt Furniture Company...................... F..... 828 759-6205
  Lenoir *(G-9587)*

◆ Bernhardt Furniture Company..................... C..... 828 758-9811
  Lenoir *(G-9586)*

◆ Bernhardt Industries Inc............................... C..... 828 758-9811
  Lenoir *(G-9588)*

Blue-Hen Inc... G..... 407 322-2262
  Asheville *(G-567)*

▲ Buzzispace Inc... G..... 336 821-3150
  Winston Salem *(G-16642)*

Con-Tab Inc.. F..... 336 476-0104
  Thomasville *(G-15206)*

Coriander Designs.. G..... 425 402-8001
  Lincolnton *(G-9884)*

Davidson House Inc..................................... F..... 704 791-0171
  Davidson *(G-4670)*

◆ Davis Furniture Industries Inc...................... C..... 336 889-2009
  High Point *(G-8319)*

▲ Delve Interiors LLC...................................... C..... 336 274-4661
  Greensboro *(G-6968)*

Desmond Office Furniture Inc...................... F..... 828 235-9400
  Canton *(G-1613)*

Frazier Holdings LLC................................... G..... 919 868-8651
  Clayton *(G-3978)*

Haworth Inc.. E..... 828 328-5600
  Conover *(G-4461)*

HM Liquidation Inc....................................... G..... 828 495-8235
  Hickory *(G-8058)*

▲ Images of America Inc................................. D..... 336 475-7106
  Thomasville *(G-15237)*

▲ Intensa Inc... F..... 336 884-4003
  High Point *(G-8412)*

Kn Furniture Inc.. E..... 336 953-3259
  Ramseur *(G-13444)*

▲ L B Plastics Incorporated............................ D..... 704 663-1543
  Mooresville *(G-11000)*

▲ Old Hickory Tannery Inc.............................. E..... 828 465-6599
  Newton *(G-11955)*

◆ Portable Displays LLC................................. E..... 919 544-6504
  Cary *(G-1855)*

▲ Sbfi-North America Inc................................ F..... 828 236-3993
  Asheville *(G-764)*

Sdv Office Systems LLC............................. F..... 844 968-9500
  Fletcher *(G-6037)*

Sdv Office Systems LLC............................. G..... 844 968-9500
  Asheville *(G-767)*

▲ Studio Tk LLC.. E..... 919 464-2920
  Clayton *(G-4014)*

T & J Panel Systems Inc.............................. G..... 704 924-8600
  Statesville *(G-14909)*

Unique Office Solutions Inc.......................... F..... 336 854-0900
  Greensboro *(G-7430)*

25 FURNITURE AND FIXTURES

▲ Wheatstone Corporation .... D 252 638-7000
New Bern *(G-11855)*

2531 Public building and related furniture

4topps LLC .... G 704 281-8451
Winston Salem *(G-16586)*

A C Furniture Company Inc .... B 336 623-3430
Eden *(G-5484)*

Amcase Inc .... E 336 784-5992
High Point *(G-8244)*

Artisan LLC .... G 855 582-3539
Concord *(G-4199)*

Artisans Guild Incorporated .... G 336 841-4140
High Point *(G-8256)*

B/E Aerospace Inc .... E 336 692-8940
Winston Salem *(G-16612)*

▲ B/E Aerospace Inc .... E 336 747-5000
Winston Salem *(G-16613)*

◆ Beaufurn LLC .... E 336 768-2544
Advance *(G-38)*

Carolina Furniture Mfrs Inc .... G 336 873-7455
Seagrove *(G-14236)*

Clarios LLC .... E 866 589-8883
Charlotte *(G-2492)*

Clarios LLC .... E 336 884-5832
High Point *(G-8296)*

Clarios LLC .... B 336 761-1550
Kernersville *(G-9180)*

Clarios LLC .... E 252 754-0782
Winterville *(G-16997)*

▲ Corilam Fabricating Co .... E 336 993-2371
Kernersville *(G-9182)*

Custom Educational Furn LLC .... F 800 255-9189
Taylorsville *(G-15137)*

▲ Custom Products Inc .... D 704 663-4159
Mooresville *(G-10920)*

◆ Davis Furniture Industries Inc .... C 336 889-2009
High Point *(G-8319)*

▲ Dfp Inc .... D 336 841-3028
High Point *(G-8323)*

Gram Furniture .... G 828 241-2836
Claremont *(G-3928)*

Graphical Creations Inc .... F 704 888-8870
Stanfield *(G-14680)*

H & T Chair Co Inc .... G 828 264-7742
Boone *(G-1203)*

Haeco Cabin Solutions LLC .... A 336 464-0122
Winston Salem *(G-16731)*

Haeco Cabin Solutions LLC .... D 336 862-1418
Greensboro *(G-7074)*

Harris House Furn Inds Inc .... E 336 431-2802
Archdale *(G-282)*

Haworth Inc .... G 336 885-4021
High Point *(G-8378)*

Indiana Mills & Manufacturing .... C 336 862-7519
High Point *(G-8407)*

Interior Wood Specialties Inc .... E 336 431-0068
High Point *(G-8413)*

Jka Idustries .... G 980 225-5350
Salisbury *(G-13992)*

Johnson Controls Inc .... F 828 225-3200
Asheville *(G-673)*

Johnson Controls Inc .... F 919 905-5745
Durham *(G-5172)*

Johnson Controls Inc .... D 919 743-3500
Raleigh *(G-12920)*

Johnson Controls Inc .... E 910 392-2372
Wilmington *(G-16281)*

Johnson Controls Inc .... E 704 521-8889
Charlotte *(G-3031)*

Joie of Seating Inc .... F 704 795-7474
Concord *(G-4295)*

Ken Staley Co Inc .... G 336 685-4294
Franklinville *(G-6169)*

Krueger International Inc .... E 336 434-5011
High Point *(G-8426)*

L & R Installations Inc .... G 336 547-8998
Greensboro *(G-7159)*

Legions Stadium .... G 910 341-4604
Wilmington *(G-16297)*

Leisure Craft Holdings LLC .... D 828 693-8241
Flat Rock *(G-5967)*

Leisure Craft Inc .... C 828 693-8241
Flat Rock *(G-5968)*

Liat LLC .... D 704 528-4506
Troutman *(G-15386)*

Marshall Group of NC Inc .... G 252 638-8585
New Bern *(G-11819)*

Precision Materials LLC .... F 828 632-8851
Taylorsville *(G-15159)*

◆ S Kivett Inc .... E 910 592-0161
Clinton *(G-4106)*

Sedia Systems Inc .... F 336 887-3818
Asheboro *(G-479)*

Something For Youth .... F 252 799-8837
Williamston *(G-16070)*

Southern Classic Seating LLC .... F 336 498-3130
Sophia *(G-14522)*

Superior Wood Products Inc .... F 336 472-2237
Thomasville *(G-15286)*

◆ Syntec Inc .... D 336 861-9023
High Point *(G-8561)*

Toddler Tables .... G 919 772-4765
Ayden *(G-860)*

▼ Vaughan Enterprises Inc .... G 919 772-4765
Raleigh *(G-13394)*

2541 Wood partitions and fixtures

▲ 3c Store Fixtures Inc .... D 252 291-5181
Wilson *(G-16461)*

Ajs Dezigns Inc .... G 828 652-6304
Marion *(G-10138)*

Amcase Inc .... E 336 784-5992
High Point *(G-8244)*

AP Granite Installation LLC .... G 919 215-1795
Clayton *(G-3954)*

Appalachian Cabinet Inc .... G 828 265-0830
Deep Gap *(G-4708)*

▼ Artisan Leaf LLC .... G 252 674-1223
Wilson *(G-16468)*

B & L Custom Cabinets Inc .... F 704 857-1940
Westfield *(G-15950)*

Buffalo Inv Group NC LLC .... G 252 522-0050
Kinston *(G-9348)*

Carolina Cab Specialist LLC .... G 919 818-4375
Cary *(G-1724)*

Carolina Countertops of Garner ...... F 919 832-3335
Raleigh *(G-12595)*

Carolina Store Fixtures LLC .... G 252 508-0110
Jamesville *(G-9079)*

Carolinas Top Shelf Cust Cabn .... F 704 376-5844
Charlotte *(G-2414)*

▲ Corilam Fabricating Co .... E 336 993-2371
Kernersville *(G-9182)*

Craft Woodwork Inc .... G 252 237-7581
Wilson *(G-16490)*

Cub Creek Kitchens & Baths Inc ...... F 336 651-8983
North Wilkesboro *(G-12004)*

Custom Educational Furn LLC .... F 800 255-9189
Taylorsville *(G-15137)*

Custom Surfaces Corporation .... G 252 638-3800
New Bern *(G-11796)*

Cutting Edge Stoneworks Inc .... G 704 799-1227
Mooresville *(G-10921)*

D & B Concepts Inc .... F 336 885-8292
High Point *(G-8315)*

◆ D & D Displays Inc .... E 336 667-8765
North Wilkesboro *(G-12005)*

◆ Dac Products Inc .... E 336 969-9786
Rural Hall *(G-13839)*

Dale Reynolds Cabinets Inc .... G 704 890-5962
Charlotte *(G-2601)*

Davis Cabinet Co Wilson Inc .... F 252 291-9052
Sims *(G-14441)*

Display Options Woodwork Inc .... G 704 599-6525
Belmont *(G-985)*

E T Sales Inc .... E 704 888-4010
Midland *(G-10467)*

Endeavour Fbrication Group Inc ...... G 919 479-1453
Durham *(G-5086)*

Grice Showcase Display Mfg Inc ..... G 704 423-8888
Charlotte *(G-2868)*

▼ Hardwood Store of NC Inc .... F 336 449-9627
Gibsonville *(G-6561)*

Hargrove Countertops & ACC Inc ... E 919 981-0163
Raleigh *(G-12830)*

Harris Wood Products Inc .... G 704 550-5494
New London *(G-11872)*

Hollingswrth Cbnets Intrors LL .... F 910 251-1490
Castle Hayne *(G-1952)*

Holt Group Inc .... F 336 668-2770
High Point *(G-8398)*

▲ Idx Impressions LLC .... C 703 550-6902
Washington *(G-15711)*

◆ Interlam Corporation .... E 336 786-6254
Mount Airy *(G-11523)*

◆ Intermarket Technology Inc .... E 252 623-2199
Washington *(G-15713)*

Ivars Display .... E 909 923-2761
Shelby *(G-14331)*

Ivey Fixture & Design Inc .... G 704 283-4398
Monroe *(G-10742)*

Marsh Furniture Company .... F 336 273-8196
Greensboro *(G-7182)*

McAd Inc .... E 336 299-3030
Greensboro *(G-7193)*

Medals To Honor Inc .... G 910 326-4275
Hubert *(G-8751)*

Michael Parker Cabinetry .... G 919 833-5117
Raleigh *(G-13024)*

Mkc85 Inc .... F 910 762-1986
Wilmington *(G-16325)*

Normac Kitchens Inc .... F 704 485-1911
Oakboro *(G-12079)*

Old Castle Service Inc .... G 336 992-1601
Kernersville *(G-9221)*

Oyama Cabinet Inc .... G 828 327-2668
Conover *(G-4477)*

Panels By Paith Inc .... G 336 599-3437
Roxboro *(G-13816)*

Prp Ventures Inc .... F 919 554-8734
Wake Forest *(G-15577)*

Reliable Construction Co Inc .... F 704 289-1501
Monroe *(G-10795)*

Relic Wood LLC .... G 828 855-8924
Taylorsville *(G-15160)*

Riddley Retail Fixtures Inc .... E 704 435-8829
Kings Mountain *(G-9329)*

Rowland Woodworking Inc .... E 336 887-0700
High Point *(G-8516)*

RPM Installations Inc .... G 704 907-0868
Cornelius *(G-4584)*

Rugby Acquisition LLC .... D 336 993-8686
Kernersville *(G-9229)*

Rusco Fixture Company Inc .... E 704 474-3184
Norwood *(G-12043)*

SIC SECTION
25 FURNITURE AND FIXTURES

S Zaytoun Custom Cabinets Inc.............F 252 638-8390
  New Bern *(G-11843)*

Saluda Mountain Products Inc................F 828 696-2296
  Flat Rock *(G-5971)*

Sare Granite & Tile.....................................G 828 676-2666
  Arden *(G-374)*

Sheets Smith Wealth MGT Inc..................E 336 765-2020
  Winston Salem *(G-16907)*

▲ Spartacraft Inc...E 828 397-4630
  Connelly Springs *(G-4409)*

Stanly Fixs Acquisition LLC......................E 704 474-3184
  Norwood *(G-12044)*

Sterling Cleora Corporation......................E 919 563-5800
  Durham *(G-5374)*

Stonery LLC...G 704 662-8702
  Mooresville *(G-11104)*

Thompson Millwork LLC...........................D 919 596-8236
  Mebane *(G-10433)*

▼ Treeforms Inc..E 336 292-8998
  Greensboro *(G-7409)*

Triangle Custom Cabinets Inc..................G 919 387-1133
  Apex *(G-251)*

TS Woodworks & RAD Design Inc............F 704 238-1015
  Monroe *(G-10824)*

Ullman Group LLC....................................F 704 246-7333
  Charlotte *(G-3747)*

Washington Cabinet Company..................G 252 946-3457
  Washington *(G-15738)*

Wildwood Studios Inc...............................G 828 299-8696
  Asheville *(G-822)*

▲ William Stone & Tile Inc........................G 910 353-0914
  Hubert *(G-8757)*

Wilsonart LLC..G 866 267-7360
  Fletcher *(G-6052)*

2542 Partitions and fixtures, except wood

Amcase Inc..E 336 784-5992
  High Point *(G-8244)*

B&H Millwork and Fixtures Inc.................E 336 431-0068
  High Point *(G-8260)*

Cemco Partitions Inc................................G 336 643-6316
  Summerfield *(G-14978)*

Chatsworth Products Inc..........................C 252 514-2779
  New Bern *(G-11788)*

◆ Coregrp LLC...F 845 876-5109
  Mooresville *(G-10914)*

Cub Creek Kitchens & Baths Inc...............F 336 651-8983
  North Wilkesboro *(G-12004)*

Ds Smith PLC..E 919 557-3148
  Holly Springs *(G-8696)*

E G A Products Inc....................................F 704 664-1221
  Mooresville *(G-10932)*

▲ Elite Displays & Design Inc..................D 336 472-8200
  Thomasville *(G-15218)*

Endless Plastics LLC................................F 336 346-1839
  Greensboro *(G-6998)*

Forbes Custom Cabinets LLC...................E 919 362-4277
  Apex *(G-192)*

▼ Friedrich Metal Pdts Co Inc..................E 336 375-3067
  Browns Summit *(G-1303)*

Grice Showcase Display Mfg Inc...............G 704 423-8888
  Charlotte *(G-2868)*

Hemco Wire Products Inc.........................F 336 454-7280
  Jamestown *(G-9052)*

Idx Corporation...C 252 948-2048
  Washington *(G-15710)*

Innovative Design Tech LLC.....................G 919 331-0204
  Angier *(G-141)*

Jka Idustries...G 980 225-5350
  Salisbury *(G-13992)*

Leggett & Platt Incorporated....................G 704 380-6208
  Statesville *(G-14835)*

Leisure Craft Holdings LLC......................D 828 693-8241
  Flat Rock *(G-5967)*

Leisure Craft Inc.......................................C 828 693-8241
  Flat Rock *(G-5968)*

Madix..G 804 456-3007
  Raleigh *(G-12986)*

◆ Master Displays Inc..............................D 336 884-5575
  High Point *(G-8448)*

▲ McIntyre Manufacturing Group Inc......G 336 476-3646
  Thomasville *(G-15246)*

Mijo Enterprises Inc.................................G 252 442-6806
  Rocky Mount *(G-13712)*

Oro Manufacturing Company....................E 704 283-2186
  Monroe *(G-10783)*

Parker Brothers Incorporated..................G 910 564-4132
  Clinton *(G-4100)*

◆ Penco Products Inc..............................E 252 917-5287
  Greenville *(G-7570)*

▲ Sid Jenkins Inc......................................G 336 632-0707
  Greensboro *(G-7337)*

Stanly Fixtures Company Inc....................F 704 474-3184
  Norwood *(G-12045)*

Sterling Rack Inc......................................F 704 866-9131
  Gastonia *(G-6516)*

◆ Technibilt Ltd...E 828 464-7388
  Newton *(G-11976)*

Thomasvlle Mtal Fbricators Inc................E 336 248-4992
  Lexington *(G-9792)*

▼ Treeforms Inc..E 336 292-8998
  Greensboro *(G-7409)*

▼ Wireway/Husky Corp.............................C 704 483-1135
  Denver *(G-4815)*

2591 Drapery hardware and blinds and shades

▲ A Window Treatment Co Inc.................F 919 934-7100
  Smithfield *(G-14447)*

Bridgewater Blinds Interi.........................G 910 408-1900
  Leland *(G-9530)*

Carolina Blind Outlet Inc.........................G 828 697-8525
  Hendersonville *(G-7834)*

Decolux USA...G 704 340-3532
  Charlotte *(G-2611)*

▲ Dize Company.......................................D 336 722-5181
  Winston Salem *(G-16684)*

Elite Textiles Fabrication Inc...................F 888 337-0977
  High Point *(G-8341)*

Empire Carpet & Blinds Inc.....................F 704 541-3988
  Charlotte *(G-2709)*

Erics Cheesecakes LLC............................G 336 264-4303
  Burlington *(G-1412)*

First Rate Blinds......................................G 800 655-1080
  Cornelius *(G-4547)*

H2h Blinds..F 704 628-5084
  Matthews *(G-10250)*

James Iron & Steel Inc............................G 704 309-8507
  Oak Island *(G-12051)*

Locklear Cabinets Wdwrk Sp Inc..............G 910 521-4463
  Rowland *(G-13790)*

Mountaintop Cheesecakes LLC................G 336 391-9127
  Mocksville *(G-10593)*

My Favorite Cheesecake..........................G 919 824-0782
  Durham *(G-5232)*

Newell Brands Inc....................................G 336 812-8181
  High Point *(G-8466)*

Nova Wildcat Drapery Hdwr LLC..............E 704 696-5110
  Huntersville *(G-8862)*

Penrock LLC...E 704 800-6722
  Mooresville *(G-11049)*

Raven Rock Manufacturing Inc................G 910 308-8430
  Dunn *(G-4880)*

Rollease Acmeda Inc................................D 800 552-5100
  Conover *(G-4493)*

Royal Cheesecake Varieties LLC..............G 919 670-8766
  Raleigh *(G-13215)*

Royal Textile Products Sw LLC................G 602 276-4598
  Charlotte *(G-3465)*

◆ Selective Enterprises Inc.....................C 704 588-3310
  Charlotte *(G-3525)*

Synoptix Companies LLC.........................F 910 790-3630
  Wilmington *(G-16425)*

Turnage Blind Co......................................G 919 736-1809
  Goldsboro *(G-6666)*

USA Blind Inc...G 704 309-5171
  Charlotte *(G-3761)*

Vertical Solutions of NC Inc....................F 919 285-2251
  Holly Springs *(G-8724)*

Vista Products Inc...................................D 910 582-0130
  Hamlet *(G-7634)*

◆ Wichard Inc...G 704 597-1502
  Charlotte *(G-3811)*

2599 Furniture and fixtures, nec

Alexanders..G 910 938-0013
  Jacksonville *(G-8986)*

Alligood Cabinet Shop..............................G 252 927-3201
  Washington *(G-15681)*

Amcase Inc..E 336 784-5992
  High Point *(G-8244)*

AMG Casework LLC..................................F 919 462-9203
  Morrisville *(G-11286)*

Appalachian Cabinet Inc..........................G 828 265-0830
  Deep Gap *(G-4708)*

▲ Ariston Hospitality Inc.........................E 626 458-8668
  High Point *(G-8254)*

▲ Arper USA...G 336 434-2376
  High Point *(G-8255)*

Atelier Maison and Co LLC......................F 828 277-7202
  Asheville *(G-548)*

Baypointe Partners LLC...........................G 336 882-5200
  Archdale *(G-269)*

◆ Beaufurn LLC..E 336 768-2544
  Advance *(G-38)*

Bones Grill LLC..G 252 827-0454
  Tarboro *(G-15097)*

Bud Baumgarner.......................................G 828 256-6230
  Hickory *(G-7954)*

C R Laine Furniture Co Inc......................G 336 841-5337
  High Point *(G-8280)*

Capital City Cuisine LLC..........................G 919 432-2126
  Raleigh *(G-12588)*

▲ Carolina Business Furn Inc..................A 336 431-9400
  Archdale *(G-272)*

Contemporary Design Co LLC..................F 704 375-6030
  Gastonia *(G-6386)*

◆ Contemporary Furnishings Corp..........D 704 633-8000
  Salisbury *(G-13946)*

Distinction Hospitality Inc.......................F 336 875-3043
  High Point *(G-8325)*

Distinctive Soul Creations LLC................G 704 299-3269
  Charlotte *(G-2643)*

Drews Cabinets and Cases.......................G 919 796-3985
  Selma *(G-14254)*

Drexel Heritage Home Furnsngs..............G 336 812-4430
  High Point *(G-8331)*

Epsilon Holdings LLC...............................G 336 763-6147
  Greensboro *(G-7003)*

Government Sales LLC.............................G 252 726-6315
  Morehead City *(G-11172)*

▲ Hightower Group LLC...........................F 816 286-1051
  High Point *(G-8394)*

Holders Restaurant Furniture..................G 828 754-8383
  Lenoir *(G-9620)*

25 FURNITURE AND FIXTURES

Iv-S Metal Stamping Inc .... E 336 861-2100
  Archdale *(G-286)*

J E Ingram LLC .... G 770 354-5599
  Raleigh *(G-12908)*

Kci .... G 910 612-4914
  Wilmington *(G-16286)*

Kewaunee Scientific Corp .... A 704 873-7202
  Statesville *(G-14831)*

Kuntrys Soul-Food & Bbq LLC .... G 910 797-0766
  Fayetteville *(G-5856)*

Lakou LLC .... G 704 780-5129
  Charlotte *(G-3071)*

◆ Lee Industries LLC .... B 828 464-8318
  Conover *(G-4470)*

Magnificent Concessions LLC .... E 919 413-1558
  Wendell *(G-15907)*

Mariscos Nayarit Corp Inc .... E 919 615-4347
  Raleigh *(G-12995)*

Melt Your Heart LLC .... G 828 989-6749
  Leicester *(G-9515)*

Neil Allen Industries Inc .... G 336 887-6500
  High Point *(G-8465)*

On The Spot Grilling LLC .... G 704 963-4105
  Charlotte *(G-3297)*

Penco Products Inc .... C 252 798-4000
  Hamilton *(G-7614)*

◆ Penco Products Inc .... E 252 917-5287
  Greenville *(G-7570)*

▲ Pinnacle Furnishings Inc .... E 910 944-0908
  Aberdeen *(G-21)*

Rapp Productions Inc .... F 919 913-0270
  Carrboro *(G-1654)*

Restaurant Furniture Inc .... F 828 459-9992
  Claremont *(G-3937)*

Solace Healthcare Furn LLC .... F 336 884-0046
  High Point *(G-8540)*

Southern Traditions Two Inc .... G 919 742-4692
  Siler City *(G-14431)*

Statesman Furniture .... G 828 431-2146
  Conover *(G-4501)*

Sturgeon Creek Home LLC .... G 336 843-1403
  Lexington *(G-9787)*

Tameka Burros .... G 330 338-8941
  Concord *(G-4369)*

Tice Kitchens & Interiors LLC .... F 919 366-4117
  Raleigh *(G-13350)*

Tomlinson of Orlando Inc .... F 336 475-8000
  Thomasville *(G-15292)*

Touch Up Solutions Inc .... E 828 428-9094
  Maiden *(G-10120)*

Walnut Cove Furniture Inc .... G 336 591-8008
  Walnut Cove *(G-15636)*

Wangs and Thangs LLC .... G 980 925-7010
  Gastonia *(G-6539)*

Whatz Cookin LLC .... G 336 353-0227
  Mount Airy *(G-11594)*

Woodsmiths Company .... F 406 626-3102
  Lenoir *(G-9661)*

26 PAPER AND ALLIED PRODUCTS

2611 Pulp mills

Arauco - NA .... G 910 569-7020
  Biscoe *(G-1103)*

▲ Bft Lumberton Ops Corp .... E 910 737-3200
  Lumberton *(G-10027)*

Blue Ridge Paper Products Inc .... A 828 646-2000
  Canton *(G-1600)*

Broad River Forest Products .... G 828 287-8003
  Rutherfordton *(G-13868)*

Buckeye Technologies Inc .... C 704 822-6400
  Mount Holly *(G-11623)*

Clear Path Recycling LLC .... G 877 387-3738
  Fayetteville *(G-5792)*

Collins Banks Investments Inc .... G 252 439-1200
  Greenville *(G-7504)*

Everyday Fix Cyclery .... G 828 855-9989
  Hickory *(G-8020)*

◆ Glatfelter Mt Holly LLC .... D 704 812-2299
  Mount Holly *(G-11637)*

Glycotech Inc .... F 910 371-2234
  Leland *(G-9547)*

Ingram Woodyards Inc .... F 910 556-1250
  Sanford *(G-14138)*

International Paper Company .... G 704 334-5222
  Charlotte *(G-2986)*

Martin Materials Inc .... G 336 697-1800
  Greensboro *(G-7186)*

North Carolina Converting LLC .... F 704 871-2912
  Statesville *(G-14851)*

Old School Crushing Co Inc .... G 919 661-0011
  Garner *(G-6298)*

Person County Recycle Center .... G 336 597-4437
  Roxboro *(G-13817)*

Profile Products LLC .... E 828 327-4165
  Conover *(G-4489)*

Todco Inc .... F 336 248-2001
  Lexington *(G-9795)*

Westrock Mwv LLC .... G 919 334-3200
  Raleigh *(G-13419)*

Westrock Paper and Packg LLC ..... B 252 533-6000
  Roanoke Rapids *(G-13587)*

Weyerhaeuser Company .... E 252 633-7100
  Vanceboro *(G-15485)*

Weyerhaeuser Nr Co .... G 252 633-7252
  Vanceboro *(G-15488)*

2621 Paper mills

4 Love and Art .... G 210 838-4288
  Fayetteville *(G-5746)*

Abzorbit Inc .... F 828 464-9944
  Newton *(G-11911)*

Andrea L Grizzle .... G 252 202-3278
  Moyock *(G-11691)*

Annes Books and Papers .... G 336 608-8612
  Winston Salem *(G-16605)*

Arauco - NA .... G 910 569-7020
  Biscoe *(G-1103)*

Atlantic Corp Wilmington Inc .... E 910 259-3600
  Burgaw *(G-1333)*

◆ Atlantic Corp Wilmington Inc .... D 910 343-0624
  Wilmington *(G-16121)*

Attindas Hygiene Partners Inc .... D 252 752-1100
  Greenville *(G-7489)*

Attindas Hygiene Partners Inc .... G 919 237-4000
  Raleigh *(G-12533)*

Blue Ridge Paper Products Inc .... A 828 646-2000
  Canton *(G-1600)*

Blue Ridge Paper Products LLC ..... C 828 235-3023
  Canton *(G-1602)*

Blue Ridge Paper Products LLC ..... C 828 452-0834
  Waynesville *(G-15795)*

◆ Blue Ridge Paper Products LLC ...D 828 454-0676
  Canton *(G-1601)*

Blue Ridge Tube & Core LLC .... G 704 530-4311
  Conover *(G-4426)*

Buckeye Technologies Inc .... C 704 822-6400
  Mount Holly *(G-11623)*

Carolina Paper Guys LLC .... G 704 980-3112
  Charlotte *(G-2401)*

Cascades Moulded Pulp Inc .... E 910 997-2775
  Rockingham *(G-13621)*

◆ Cascades Tissue Group - NC Inc ...C 910 895-4033
  Rockingham *(G-13622)*

Cascades Tssue Group - Ore Inc ... D 503 397-2900
  Wagram *(G-15521)*

◆ Cdv LLC .... F 919 674-3460
  Morrisville *(G-11316)*

Clearwater Paper Shelby LLC .... B 704 476-3802
  Shelby *(G-14296)*

Competitive Edge Inc .... G 704 881-4157
  Statesville *(G-14777)*

CT Commercial Paper LLC .... D 704 485-3212
  Oakboro *(G-12071)*

Domtar Paper Company LLC .... D 252 752-1100
  Greenville *(G-7515)*

Domtar Paper Company LLC .... B 252 793-8111
  Plymouth *(G-12371)*

Ds Smith Packaging and Paper ...... G 336 668-0871
  Greensboro *(G-6980)*

▲ Encertec Inc .... G 336 288-7226
  Greensboro *(G-6997)*

Enriched Abundance Entp LLC ...... F 704 369-6363
  Charlotte *(G-2715)*

Evergreen Packaging LLC .... B 828 454-0676
  Canton *(G-1615)*

Evergreen Packaging LLC .... D 919 828-9134
  Raleigh *(G-12751)*

Filtrona Filters Inc .... D 336 362-1333
  Greensboro *(G-7015)*

Firm Ascend LLC .... G 704 464-3024
  Charlotte *(G-2763)*

Geami Ltd .... E 919 654-7700
  Raleigh *(G-12791)*

Georgia-Pacific LLC .... D 919 736-2722
  Dudley *(G-4844)*

Georgia-Pacific LLC .... C 252 438-2238
  Middleburg *(G-10443)*

Glatfelter Corporation .... G 828 877-2110
  Pisgah Forest *(G-12323)*

Glatfelter Corporation .... A 704 885-2555
  Charlotte *(G-2831)*

Gold Bond Building Pdts LLC .... G 704 365-7300
  Charlotte *(G-2843)*

▲ H & V Processing Inc .... F 336 224-2985
  Lexington *(G-9726)*

Hollingsworth & Vose Company ...... G 704 708-5913
  Matthews *(G-10254)*

International Paper Com .... G 828 200-9284
  Asheville *(G-663)*

International Paper Company .... G 910 259-1723
  Burgaw *(G-1341)*

International Paper Company .... G 704 393-8210
  Charlotte *(G-2983)*

International Paper Company .... G 704 588-8522
  Charlotte *(G-2984)*

International Paper Company .... C 704 398-8354
  Charlotte *(G-2985)*

International Paper Company .... G 704 334-5222
  Charlotte *(G-2986)*

International Paper Company .... G 910 738-8930
  Lumberton *(G-10040)*

International Paper Company .... D 828 464-3841
  Newton *(G-11946)*

International Paper Company .... G 919 831-4764
  Raleigh *(G-12899)*

International Paper Company .... G 910 655-2211
  Riegelwood *(G-13559)*

International Paper Company .... G 910 362-4900
  Riegelwood *(G-13560)*

International Paper Company .... D 704 872-6541
  Statesville *(G-14820)*

International Paper Company .... D 252 633-7509
  Vanceboro *(G-15479)*

26 PAPER AND ALLIED PRODUCTS

▲ Jackson Paper Manufacturing Co..... D 828 586-5534
  Sylva (G-15060)
Kimberly-Clark Corporation................ C 828 698-5230
  Hendersonville (G-7869)
◆ Laurel Hill Paper Co............................. E 910 997-4526
  Cordova (G-4518)
Leapfrog Document Services Inc....... F 704 372-1078
  Charlotte (G-3077)
M Davis and Associates LLC............... G 336 337-7089
  Greensboro (G-7172)
Morrisette Paper Company Inc........... G 336 342-5570
  Reidsville (G-13533)
Nakos Paper Products Inc.................. G 704 238-0717
  Charlotte (G-3229)
Paper Perfector LLC............................. G 910 695-1092
  Pinehurst (G-12230)
▼ Poly Packaging Systems Inc............ D 336 889-8334
  High Point (G-8489)
Pregis LLC... D 828 396-2373
  Granite Falls (G-6752)
Ranpak Corp.. G 919 790-8225
  Raleigh (G-13190)
Reynolds Consumer Products Inc...... A 704 371-5550
  Huntersville (G-8885)
Simply Btiful Events Decor LLC.......... G 252 375-3839
  Greenville (G-7585)
Snyder Paper Corporation.................. G 800 222-8562
  Asheville (G-778)
STS Packaging Charlotte LLC............ D 980 259-2290
  Charlotte (G-3642)
Synthomer Inc....................................... D 704 225-1872
  Monroe (G-10819)
Teddy Soft Paper Products Inc........... G 336 784-5887
  Winston Salem (G-16937)
▲ Transcontinental AC US LLC........... F 704 847-9171
  Matthews (G-10296)
Triangle Converting Corp.................... E 919 596-6656
  Durham (G-5407)
▲ Twisted Paper Products Inc........... E 336 393-0273
  Greensboro (G-7421)
Westrock Kraft Paper LLC.................. G 252 533-6000
  Roanoke Rapids (G-13586)
Westrock Paper and Packg LLC........ B 252 533-6000
  Roanoke Rapids (G-13587)
Westrock Shared Services LLC......... A 336 642-4165
  Rural Hall (G-13855)
Weyerhaeuser Company..................... E 252 633-7100
  Vanceboro (G-15485)

2631 Paperboard mills

Blue Ridge Paper Products Inc........... A 828 646-2000
  Canton (G-1600)
Box Company of America LLC........... E 910 582-0100
  Hamlet (G-7617)
Caraustar Brlngton Rgid Box In.......... E 336 226-1616
  Burlington (G-1383)
Caraustar Industries Inc...................... F 704 333-5488
  Charlotte (G-2385)
Caraustar Industries Inc...................... C 704 554-5796
  Charlotte (G-2386)
Caraustar Industries Inc...................... F 336 498-2631
  Randleman (G-13456)
Dbt Coatings LLC................................ G 336 834-9700
  Greensboro (G-6961)
Deckle Paperboard Sales Inc.............. G 910 686-9145
  Wilmington (G-16198)
Domtar Paper Company LLC............. B 252 793-8111
  Plymouth (G-12371)
◆ Edwards Wood Products Inc.......... C 704 624-3624
  Marshville (G-10216)
Graphic Packaging Intl LLC................ C 704 588-1750
  Charlotte (G-2856)

International Paper Company.............. C 910 362-4900
  Riegelwood (G-13560)
Kme Consolidated Inc......................... E 704 847-9888
  Matthews (G-10260)
Morrisette Paper Company Inc........... G 336 342-5570
  Reidsville (G-13533)
▲ Napco Inc.. C 336 372-5214
  Sparta (G-14597)
Option 1 Distribution LLC................... G 704 325-3001
  Conover (G-4476)
Packaging Services.............................. G 919 630-4145
  Raleigh (G-13093)
Pactiv LLC... D 252 527-6300
  Kinston (G-9380)
Parkwood Corporation......................... G 910 815-4300
  Oak Island (G-12053)
Phoenix Packaging Inc........................ E 336 724-1978
  Winston Salem (G-16850)
Pratt (jet Corr) Inc................................ A 704 878-6615
  Statesville (G-14865)
Precision Packaging Services I........... F 919 806-8152
  Durham (G-5303)
Precision Walls Inc.............................. G 336 852-7710
  Greensboro (G-7276)
Printing & Packaging Inc..................... E 704 482-3866
  Shelby (G-14357)
Schubert Packaging Systems LLC..... G 941 757-8380
  Charlotte (G-3509)
Sonoco Products Company................ E 828 648-1987
  Canton (G-1626)
Sonoco Products Company................ G 910 455-6903
  Jacksonville (G-9034)
Sonoco Products Company................ G 919 556-1504
  Wake Forest (G-15593)
▲ Southcorr LLC................................. D 336 498-1700
  Asheboro (G-482)
Southeastern Corrugated LLC............ G 980 224-9551
  Charlotte (G-3588)
Supplyone Rockwell Inc...................... C 704 279-5650
  Rockwell (G-13660)
▲ Transcontinental AC US LLC......... F 704 847-9171
  Matthews (G-10296)
Westrock Company............................. G 770 448-2193
  Winston Salem (G-16971)
Westrock Mwv LLC............................. G 919 334-3200
  Raleigh (G-13419)
Westrock Paper and Packg LLC........ B 252 533-6000
  Roanoke Rapids (G-13587)
Westrock Rkt LLC............................... E 704 662-8494
  Mooresville (G-11129)
Westrock Shared Services LLC......... A 336 642-4165
  Rural Hall (G-13855)
Weyerhaeuser New Bern.................... E 252 633-7100
  Vanceboro (G-15486)
Wrkco Inc.. G 828 692-6254
  East Flat Rock (G-5480)
Wrkco Inc.. G 919 304-0300
  Mebane (G-10438)
Wrkco Inc.. G 336 759-7501
  Winston Salem (G-16986)
Wrkco Inc.. E 770 448-2193
  Winston Salem (G-16987)
Wrkco Inc.. G 336 765-7004
  Winston Salem (G-16988)

2652 Setup paperboard boxes

A Klein & Co Inc.................................. C 828 459-9261
  Claremont (G-3899)
Caraustar Cstm Packg Group Inc...... C 336 498-2631
  Randleman (G-13455)
Caraustar Industries Inc...................... F 336 498-2631
  Randleman (G-13456)

▲ Eastcoast Packaging Inc................ E 919 562-6060
  Middlesex (G-10447)
Transylvnia Vcational Svcs Inc........... D 828 884-1548
  Fletcher (G-6045)
Transylvnia Vcational Svcs Inc........... C 828 884-3195
  Brevard (G-1291)
Westrock Rkt LLC............................... C 828 459-8006
  Claremont (G-3944)
Westrock Rkt LLC............................... E 704 662-8494
  Mooresville (G-11129)

2653 Corrugated and solid fiber boxes

3d Packaging LLC................................ F 336 625-0652
  Asheboro (G-397)
Archer Box Company.......................... F 336 788-1910
  Winston Salem (G-16607)
Axis Corrugated Container LLC......... F 919 575-0500
  Butner (G-1541)
C L Rabb Inc.. E 704 865-0295
  Gastonia (G-6365)
Caraustar Brlngton Rgid Box In.......... E 336 226-1616
  Burlington (G-1383)
▲ Cardinal Container Svcs Inc........... D 336 249-6816
  Lexington (G-9689)
◆ Carolina Container Company.........D 336 883-7146
  High Point (G-8284)
Carolina Container LLC....................... F 828 322-3380
  Hickory (G-7963)
Carolina Container LLC....................... F 910 277-0400
  Laurinburg (G-9471)
Carolina Core Solutions LLC.............. G 704 900-4208
  Conover (G-4431)
Carolina Packaging & Sup Inc............ D 919 201-5592
  Raleigh (G-12600)
Corney Transportation Inc.................. E 800 354-9111
  Saint Pauls (G-13904)
Custom Corrugated Cntrs Inc............ C 704 588-0371
  Charlotte (G-2589)
Custom Packaging Inc........................ C 828 684-5060
  Arden (G-323)
Ds Smith PLC...................................... E 919 557-3148
  Holly Springs (G-8696)
Ferguson & Company LLC................ G 704 332-4396
  Charlotte (G-2752)
Ferguson Box...................................... E 704 597-0310
  Charlotte (G-2753)
Ferguson Supply and Box Mfg Co..... D 704 597-0310
  Charlotte (G-2754)
Freeman Container Company Inc...... G 704 922-7972
  Dallas (G-4641)
Gbc Construction Gbc Cons.............. G 704 500-9232
  Conover (G-4458)
Gbc Distribution LLC........................... G 704 341-8473
  Charlotte (G-2811)
Georgia Pratt Box Inc.......................... C 919 872-3007
  Raleigh (G-12796)
Georgia-Pacific LLC............................ C 336 629-2151
  Asheboro (G-440)
Goodwill Employment & Training....... G 704 873-5005
  Statesville (G-14805)
Highland Containers Inc..................... C 336 887-5400
  Jamestown (G-9054)
▲ Highland Containers Inc................ C 336 887-5400
  Jamestown (G-9053)
Hood Container Corporation............... E 336 887-5400
  Jamestown (G-9055)
Industrial Container Corp.................... F 336 886-7031
  High Point (G-8408)
Industrial Container Inc....................... F 336 882-1310
  High Point (G-8409)
▲ Inter-Continental Corporation........ D 828 464-8250
  Newton (G-11945)

Employee Codes: A=Over 500 employees, B=251-500
C=101-250, D=51-100, E=20-50, F=10-19, G=1-9

26 PAPER AND ALLIED PRODUCTS

◆ Intermarket Technology Inc............. E..... 252 623-2199
  Washington (G-15713)
International Paper Company................ G..... 704 588-8522
  Charlotte (G-2987)
International Paper Company................ D..... 910 738-6214
  Lumberton (G-10041)
International Paper Company................ G..... 252 456-3111
  Manson (G-10124)
International Paper Company................ G..... 252 633-7407
  New Bern (G-11811)
Jackson Corrugated LLC..................... D..... 828 608-0931
  Morganton (G-11223)
Lls Investments Inc........................ F..... 919 662-7283
  Raleigh (G-12976)
Lone Star Container Sales Corp............. D..... 704 588-1737
  Charlotte (G-3102)
Michigan Packaging Company................. E..... 704 455-4206
  Concord (G-4314)
Package Craft LLC.......................... E..... 252 825-0111
  Bethel (G-1090)
Package Crafters Incorporated.............. D..... 336 431-9700
  High Point (G-8473)
Packaging Corporation America.............. G..... 252 753-8450
  Farmville (G-5741)
Packaging Corporation America.............. G..... 336 434-0600
  Goldsboro (G-6642)
Packaging Corporation America.............. F..... 704 664-5010
  Mooresville (G-11046)
Packaging Corporation America.............. D..... 828 584-1511
  Morganton (G-11241)
Packaging Corporation America.............. E..... 828 286-9156
  Rutherfordton (G-13881)
Packaging Corporation America.............. D..... 704 633-3611
  Salisbury (G-14023)
Packaging Corporation America.............. G..... 336 434-0600
  Trinity (G-15352)
▲ Packaging Unlimited NC Inc.............. D..... 704 732-7100
  Lincolnton (G-9912)
Paperworks Industries Inc.................. C..... 910 439-6137
  Mount Gilead (G-11611)
Paperworks Industries Inc.................. C..... 336 447-7278
  Whitsett (G-15998)
Phoenix Packaging Inc...................... E..... 336 724-1978
  Winston Salem (G-16850)
Piedmont Corrugated Specialty.............. D..... 828 874-1153
  Valdese (G-15452)
Piedmont Packaging Inc..................... G..... 336 886-5043
  High Point (G-8482)
Piranha Industries Inc..................... G..... 704 248-7843
  Charlotte (G-3344)
Pratt (jet Corr) Inc....................... A..... 704 878-6615
  Statesville (G-14865)
Pratt Industries........................... F..... 704 864-4022
  Gastonia (G-6494)
Pratt Industries Inc....................... D..... 919 334-7400
  Raleigh (G-13131)
Pratt Industries Inc....................... B..... 704 878-6615
  Statesville (G-14866)
RLM/Universal Packaging Inc................ F..... 336 644-6161
  Greensboro (G-7312)
Rocktenn In-Store Solutions Inc............ B..... 828 245-9871
  Forest City (G-6080)
Sonoco Products Company.................... E..... 704 875-2685
  Charlotte (G-3581)
Stronghaven Incorporated................... D..... 770 739-6080
  Matthews (G-10294)
Sumter Packaging Corporation............... G..... 704 873-0583
  Statesville (G-14908)
Sun & Surf Containers Inc.................. G..... 910 754-9600
  Shallotte (G-14279)
Supplyone Rockwell Inc..................... C..... 704 279-5650
  Rockwell (G-13660)

Thomco Inc................................. G..... 336 292-3300
  Greensboro (G-7401)
Westrock - Southern Cont LLC............... D..... 704 662-8496
  Mooresville (G-11128)
Westrock Company........................... G..... 470 484-1183
  Claremont (G-3943)
Westrock Company........................... G..... 828 248-4815
  Forest City (G-6087)
Westrock Converting LLC.................... B..... 828 245-9871
  Forest City (G-6088)
Westrock Converting LLC.................... G..... 336 661-1700
  Winston Salem (G-16972)
Westrock Paper and Packg LLC............... C..... 919 463-3100
  Morrisville (G-11466)
Westrock Rkt LLC........................... G..... 828 655-1303
  Marion (G-10186)
Westrock Rkt LLC........................... E..... 704 662-8494
  Mooresville (G-11129)
Westrock Rkt LLC........................... E..... 336 661-1700
  Winston Salem (G-16973)
Westrock Rkt LLC........................... C..... 336 661-7180
  Winston Salem (G-16974)
Weyerhaeuser Co............................ F..... 828 464-3841
  Newton (G-11985)
Weyerhaeuser Company....................... G..... 253 924-2345
  Charlotte (G-3808)
Wilmington Box Company..................... E..... 910 259-0402
  Burgaw (G-1358)
Wrkco Inc.................................. G..... 828 287-9430
  Rutherfordton (G-13903)

2655 Fiber cans, drums, and similar products

Atlantic Custom Container Inc.............. G..... 336 437-9302
  Graham (G-6678)
▲ Axjo America Inc........................ E..... 828 322-6046
  Conover (G-4420)
C L Rabb Inc............................... E..... 704 865-0295
  Gastonia (G-6365)
Caraustar Indus Cnsmr Pdts Gro............. G..... 336 564-2163
  Kernersville (G-9170)
Caraustar Indus Cnsmr Pdts Gro............. E..... 336 996-4165
  Kernersville (G-9171)
Caraustar Industries Inc................... E..... 336 992-1053
  Kernersville (G-9172)
Caraustar Industries Inc................... F..... 336 498-2631
  Randleman (G-13456)
Caraustar Industries Inc................... G..... 828 246-7234
  Waynesville (G-15796)
Carolina Carton............................ G..... 704 554-5796
  Pineville (G-12259)
▼ Carolina Paper Tubes Inc................ E..... 828 692-9686
  Zirconia (G-17151)
◆ Conitex Sonoco Usa Inc.................. C..... 704 864-5406
  Gastonia (G-6384)
Greif Inc.................................. D..... 704 588-3895
  Charlotte (G-2867)
Mauser Usa LLC............................. C..... 704 625-0737
  Charlotte (G-3145)
Mm Clayton LLC............................. B..... 919 553-4113
  Clayton (G-3997)
Sonoco Products Company.................... E..... 336 449-7731
  Elon College (G-5667)
Sonoco Products Company.................... F..... 828 322-8844
  Hickory (G-8164)
▲ Summer Industries LLC................... C..... 336 731-9217
  Welcome (G-15876)
Tex-Tech Engnred Cmposites LLC............. C..... 207 756-8606
  Kernersville (G-9244)
Thomasville-Dexel Incorporated............. E..... 336 819-5550
  High Point (G-8571)
Trident Fibers Inc......................... G..... 336 605-9002
  Greensboro (G-7419)

2656 Sanitary food containers

Candies Italian ICEE LLC................... G..... 980 475-7429
  Charlotte (G-2382)
Caraustar Industries Inc................... F..... 336 498-2631
  Randleman (G-13456)
CKS Packaging Inc.......................... E..... 704 663-6510
  Mooresville (G-10905)
Richards Southern Soul Fd LLC.............. G..... 919 210-8275
  Raleigh (G-13207)
Thomco Inc................................. G..... 336 292-3300
  Greensboro (G-7401)

2657 Folding paperboard boxes

A Klein & Co Inc........................... C..... 828 459-9261
  Claremont (G-3899)
Caraustar Brlngton Rgid Box In............. E..... 336 226-1616
  Burlington (G-1383)
Caraustar Cstm Packg Group Inc............. C..... 336 498-2631
  Randleman (G-13455)
Container Systems Incorporated............. D..... 919 496-6133
  Franklinton (G-6153)
Graphic Packaging Intl LLC................. C..... 704 588-1750
  Charlotte (G-2856)
Graphic Packaging Intl LLC................. D..... 336 744-1222
  Winston Salem (G-16728)
Kme Consolidated Inc....................... E..... 704 847-9888
  Matthews (G-10260)
Max Solutions Inc.......................... E..... 203 683-8094
  Concord (G-4311)
Pactiv LLC................................. G..... 910 944-1800
  Aberdeen (G-20)
Pactiv LLC................................. D..... 252 527-6300
  Kinston (G-9380)
Snyder Packaging Inc....................... D..... 704 786-3111
  Concord (G-4361)
Specialized Packaging Radisson LLC......... D..... 336 574-1513
  Greensboro (G-7357)
Thomco Inc................................. G..... 336 292-3300
  Greensboro (G-7401)
Westrock Rkt LLC........................... C..... 828 459-8006
  Claremont (G-3944)
Westrock Rkt LLC........................... C..... 828 464-5560
  Conover (G-4512)
Westrock Rkt LLC........................... B..... 770 448-2193
  Marion (G-10187)

2671 Paper; coated and laminated packaging

Abx Innvtive Pckg Slutions LLC............. D..... 980 443-1100
  Charlotte (G-2126)
◆ Atlantic Corporation.................... D..... 910 343-0624
  Wilmington (G-16122)
◆ Automated Solutions LLC................. F..... 828 396-9900
  Granite Falls (G-6723)
▲ Box Board Products Inc.................. C..... 336 668-3347
  Greensboro (G-6849)
Box Company of America LLC................. E..... 910 582-0100
  Hamlet (G-7617)
Challnge Prtg of Crlnas Inc Th............. G..... 919 777-2820
  Sanford (G-14101)
Datamark Graphics Inc...................... E..... 336 629-0267
  Asheboro (G-422)
De Luxe Packaging Corp..................... E..... 800 845-6051
  Charlotte (G-2608)
Ds Smith PLC............................... E..... 919 557-3148
  Holly Springs (G-8696)
◆ Dubose Strapping Inc.................... D..... 910 590-1020
  Clinton (G-4094)
▲ Eastcoast Packaging Inc................. E..... 919 562-6060
  Middlesex (G-10447)
Graphic Packaging Intl LLC................. C..... 704 588-1750
  Charlotte (G-2856)

SIC SECTION

26 PAPER AND ALLIED PRODUCTS

Induspac USA... G 919 484-9484
  Durham *(G-5151)*

Interflex Acquisition Co LLC..................... C 336 921-3505
  Wilkesboro *(G-16028)*

▲ Interntnal Tray Pads Packg Inc............... E 910 944-1800
  Aberdeen *(G-8)*

Jbb Packaging LLC..................................... F 201 470-8501
  Weldon *(G-15883)*

Jd2 Company LLC....................................... G 800 811-6441
  Denver *(G-4786)*

Jerseybincom.. G 828 545-0445
  Asheville *(G-670)*

Label Line Ltd... D 336 857-3115
  Asheboro *(G-450)*

Multi Packaging Solutions.......................... A 336 855-7142
  Greensboro *(G-7207)*

Neopac Us Inc.. G 908 342-0990
  Wilson *(G-16518)*

Npx One LLC... C 910 997-2217
  Rockingham *(G-13637)*

NS Packaging LLC.. F 800 688-7391
  Greensboro *(G-7226)*

Pactiv LLC... D 252 527-6300
  Kinston *(G-9380)*

Paragon Films Inc.. F 828 632-5552
  Taylorsville *(G-15154)*

▼ Poly Packaging Systems Inc................... D 336 889-8334
  High Point *(G-8489)*

Pregis Innovative Packg LLC..................... E 847 597-2200
  Granite Falls *(G-6751)*

◆ Printcraft Company Inc........................... E 336 248-2544
  Lexington *(G-9773)*

Quality Packaging Corp.............................. G 336 881-5300
  High Point *(G-8502)*

R R Donnelley & Sons Company............... D 252 243-0437
  Wilson *(G-16528)*

▲ Rgees LLC... G 828 708-7178
  Arden *(G-372)*

Sealed Air Corporation (us)....................... A 201 791-7600
  Charlotte *(G-3518)*

Shurtech Brands LLC.................................. G 704 799-0779
  Mooresville *(G-11086)*

Sonoco Hickory Inc..................................... C 828 286-1356
  Forest City *(G-6081)*

▲ St Johns Packaging Usa LLC................... C 336 292-9911
  Greensboro *(G-7362)*

Storopack Inc... G 800 827-7225
  Winston Salem *(G-16918)*

Tarason Label Inc... G 828 464-4743
  Hickory *(G-8174)*

▼ Valdese Packaging & Label Inc.............. E 828 879-9772
  Valdese *(G-15456)*

Westrock Mwv LLC..................................... G 919 334-3200
  Raleigh *(G-13419)*

2672 Paper; coated and laminated, nec

Achem Industry America Inc..................... G 704 283-6144
  Monroe *(G-10634)*

◆ Acucote Inc... C 336 578-1800
  Graham *(G-6677)*

Avery Dennison Corporation..................... D 336 621-2570
  Greensboro *(G-6824)*

Avery Dennison Corporation..................... G 336 553-2436
  Greensboro *(G-6825)*

Avery Dennison Corporation..................... G 336 856-8235
  Greensboro *(G-6826)*

Avery Dennison Corporation..................... G 864 938-1400
  Greensboro *(G-6827)*

Avery Dennison Corporation..................... F 336 665-6481
  Greensboro *(G-6828)*

Avery Dennison Rfid Company.................. F 626 304-2000
  Greensboro *(G-6829)*

Bay Tech Label Inc....................................... G 828 296-8900
  Asheville *(G-557)*

Blue Ridge Paper Products LLC................ C 828 452-0834
  Waynesville *(G-15795)*

Carolina Container LLC.............................. F 336 883-7146
  Thomasville *(G-15195)*

◆ Cdv LLC.. F 919 674-3460
  Morrisville *(G-11316)*

Datamark Graphics Inc............................... E 336 629-0267
  Asheboro *(G-422)*

Draft DOT International LLC..................... G 336 775-0525
  Lexington *(G-9710)*

▲ Gaston Systems Inc................................... F 704 263-6000
  Stanley *(G-14694)*

Granite Tape Co... G 828 396-5614
  Granite Falls *(G-6735)*

Intertape Polymer Corp.............................. D 980 907-4871
  Midland *(G-10469)*

J C Enterprises.. G 336 986-1688
  Winston Salem *(G-16765)*

JW Wraps LLC... G 614 401-9164
  Wilmington *(G-16285)*

Label Line Ltd... D 336 857-3115
  Asheboro *(G-450)*

Lakebrook Corporation............................... G 207 947-4051
  Oak Island *(G-12052)*

LIflex LLC.. C 336 777-5000
  Winston Salem *(G-16791)*

Loparex LLC.. C 336 635-0192
  Eden *(G-5496)*

◆ Loparex LLC... D 919 678-7700
  Cary *(G-1814)*

Marsh-Armfield Incorporated................... E 336 882-4175
  High Point *(G-8445)*

▲ Maxim Label Packg High Pt Inc............... F 336 861-1666
  High Point *(G-8451)*

Neptco Incorporated.................................. C 828 313-0149
  Granite Falls *(G-6747)*

Neptco Incorporated.................................. G 828 728-5951
  Lenoir *(G-9639)*

◆ Oracle Flexible Packaging Inc................. B 336 777-5000
  Winston Salem *(G-16831)*

▼ Pocono Coated Products LLC................. G 704 445-7891
  Cherryville *(G-3875)*

▲ Polymask Corporation............................. C 828 465-3053
  Conover *(G-4484)*

R T Barbee Company Inc........................... F 704 375-4421
  Charlotte *(G-3406)*

Shurtape Technologies LLC....................... G 704 553-9441
  Charlotte *(G-3543)*

Shurtape Technologies LLC....................... G 828 304-8302
  Hickory *(G-8153)*

Shurtape Technologies LLC....................... G 828 322-2700
  Hickory *(G-8154)*

◆ Stm Industries Inc.................................... E 828 322-2700
  Hickory *(G-8170)*

▲ T - Square Enterprises Inc...................... G 704 846-8233
  Charlotte *(G-3667)*

◆ Tailored Chemical Products Inc............. D 828 322-6512
  Hickory *(G-8173)*

TEC Graphics Inc.. F 919 567-2077
  Fuquay Varina *(G-6232)*

◆ Technical Coating Intl Inc....................... E 910 371-0860
  Belville *(G-1026)*

◆ Tesa Tape Inc.. D 704 554-0707
  Charlotte *(G-3682)*

Upm Raflatac Inc... F 828 335-3289
  Fletcher *(G-6047)*

Upm Raflatac Inc... F 828 651-4800
  Fletcher *(G-6048)*

◆ Upm Raflatac Inc...................................... B 828 651-4800
  Mills River *(G-10512)*

2673 Bags: plastic, laminated, and coated

Berry Global Films LLC............................... C 704 821-2316
  Matthews *(G-10304)*

▲ Bioselect Inc... G 704 521-8585
  Charlotte *(G-2315)*

Bulk Sak International Inc.......................... E 704 833-1361
  Gastonia *(G-6361)*

▲ Classic Packaging Company................... D 336 922-4224
  Pfafftown *(G-12187)*

Cryovac Leasing Corporation.................... E 980 430-7000
  Charlotte *(G-2578)*

Dayton Bag & Burlap Co............................. G 704 873-7271
  Statesville *(G-14783)*

Hood Packaging Corporation..................... C 910 582-1842
  Hamlet *(G-7623)*

▼ Ice Box Company Inc................................. F 910 579-3273
  Ocean Isle Beach *(G-12092)*

Imaflex Usa Inc.. E 336 885-8131
  Thomasville *(G-15235)*

◆ Liqui-Box Corporation.............................. D 804 325-1400
  Charlotte *(G-3092)*

Novolex Holdings LLC................................ D 980 498-4082
  Charlotte *(G-3277)*

▼ Poly Plastic Products NC Inc................... D 704 624-2555
  Marshville *(G-10223)*

Printpack Inc... C 828 693-1723
  Hendersonville *(G-7892)*

Reynolds Consumer Products Inc............. A 704 371-5550
  Huntersville *(G-8885)*

▲ Rgees LLC... G 828 708-7178
  Arden *(G-372)*

◆ Rubbermaid Commercial Pdts LLC........ A 540 667-8700
  Huntersville *(G-8888)*

Sealed Air Corporation............................... D 828 728-6610
  Hudson *(G-8779)*

Sealed Air Corporation (us)....................... A 201 791-7600
  Charlotte *(G-3518)*

Sealed Air LLC.. F 980 430-7000
  Charlotte *(G-3520)*

Shades and Shelves LLC............................. G 910 603-4906
  Pinehurst *(G-12236)*

Sonoco Hickory Inc..................................... C 828 286-1356
  Forest City *(G-6081)*

Transcontinental Tvl LLC........................... D 336 476-3131
  Thomasville *(G-15294)*

▲ Wastezero Inc.. E 919 322-1208
  Raleigh *(G-13413)*

2674 Bags: uncoated paper and multiwall

◆ Automated Solutions LLC....................... F 828 396-9900
  Granite Falls *(G-6723)*

▲ Cardinal Bag & Envelope Co Inc............ E 704 225-9636
  Monroe *(G-10672)*

Dayton Bag & Burlap Co............................. G 704 873-7271
  Statesville *(G-14783)*

◆ Downtown Graphics Network Inc......... G 704 637-0855
  Salisbury *(G-13954)*

Eagle Products Inc...................................... F 336 886-5688
  High Point *(G-8334)*

Hood Packaging Corporation..................... C 910 582-1842
  Hamlet *(G-7623)*

Novolex Holdings LLC................................ D 980 498-4082
  Charlotte *(G-3277)*

Pro Choice Contractors Corp..................... F 919 696-7383
  Raleigh *(G-13146)*

Sealed Air Corporation............................... D 828 728-6610
  Hudson *(G-8779)*

Southern Bag Corporation Ltd.................. G 910 582-1842
  Hamlet *(G-7632)*

Tsg2 Inc... G 704 347-4484
  Charlotte *(G-3733)*

26 PAPER AND ALLIED PRODUCTS

2675 Die-cut paper and board

Boingo Graphics Inc .... E 704 527-4963
Charlotte *(G-2331)*

Box Company of America LLC .... E 910 582-0100
Hamlet *(G-7617)*

▲ **Eastcoast Packaging Inc** .... E 919 562-6060
Middlesex *(G-10447)*

L C Industries Inc .... C 919 596-8277
Fayetteville *(G-5857)*

◆ **L C Industries Inc** .... C 919 596-8277
Durham *(G-5185)*

Lakebrook Corporation .... G 207 947-4051
Oak Island *(G-12052)*

Morrisette Paper Company Inc .... G 336 342-5570
Reidsville *(G-13533)*

◆ **Mueller Die Cut Solutions Inc** .... E 704 588-3900
Charlotte *(G-3213)*

Paper Specialties Inc .... G 919 431-0028
Raleigh *(G-13099)*

Snyder Packaging Inc .... D 704 786-3111
Concord *(G-4361)*

Triangle Converting Corp .... E 919 596-6656
Durham *(G-5407)*

◆ **Valdese Weavers LLC** .... B 828 874-2181
Valdese *(G-15461)*

2676 Sanitary paper products

▲ **Associated Hygienic Pdts LLC** .... D 770 497-9800
Greenville *(G-7487)*

Attends Healthcare Pdts Inc .... G 252 752-1100
Greenville *(G-7488)*

◆ **Attends Healthcare Products Inc** .... B 800 428-8363
Raleigh *(G-12532)*

Cardinal Tissue LLC .... D 815 503-2096
Spindale *(G-14605)*

◆ **Cascades Tissue Group - NC Inc** .... C 910 895-4033
Rockingham *(G-13622)*

Edtech Systems LLC .... G 919 341-0613
Raleigh *(G-12727)*

Hygiene Systems Inc .... G 910 462-2661
Laurel Hill *(G-9461)*

Kimberly-Clark Corporation .... C 828 698-5230
Hendersonville *(G-7869)*

◆ **L C Industries Inc** .... C 919 596-8277
Durham *(G-5185)*

◆ **Livedo Usa Inc** .... D 252 237-1373
Wilson *(G-16513)*

Marcal Paper Mills LLC .... B 828 322-1805
Hickory *(G-8090)*

◆ **Merfin Systems LLC** .... D 800 874-6373
King *(G-9276)*

Ontex Operations Usa LLC .... D 770 346-9250
Stokesdale *(G-14947)*

▲ **Pacon Manufacturing Corp LLC** .... C 732 764-9070
Navassa *(G-11758)*

Procter & Gamble Mfg Co .... D 336 954-0000
Greensboro *(G-7287)*

Sealed Air Corporation .... D 828 728-6610
Hudson *(G-8779)*

Shower ME With Love LLC .... F 704 302-1555
Charlotte *(G-3542)*

Top Tier Paper Products Inc .... G 828 994-2222
Conover *(G-4506)*

2677 Envelopes

Blue Ridge Paper Products Inc .... A 828 646-2000
Canton *(G-1600)*

S Ruppe Inc .... E 828 287-4936
Rutherfordton *(G-13889)*

Westrock Mwv LLC .... G 919 334-3200
Raleigh *(G-13419)*

2678 Stationery products

Blue Ridge Paper Products Inc .... A 828 646-2000
Canton *(G-1600)*

Devora Designs Inc .... G 336 782-0964
Winston Salem *(G-16676)*

Godglamit LLC .... G 336 558-1097
Charlotte *(G-2841)*

Kimberly Gordon Studios Inc .... E 980 287-6420
Charlotte *(G-3054)*

Texpack USA Inc .... E 704 864-5406
Gastonia *(G-6523)*

Westrock Mwv LLC .... G 919 334-3200
Raleigh *(G-13419)*

2679 Converted paper products, nec

◆ **3a Composites USA Inc** .... C 704 872-8974
Statesville *(G-14732)*

Abx Innvtive Pckg Slutions LLC .... D 980 443-1100
Charlotte *(G-2126)*

◆ **Acucote Inc** .... C 336 578-1800
Graham *(G-6677)*

American Converting Co Ltd LLC .... E 704 479-5025
Lincolnton *(G-9871)*

Atlantic Caribbean LLC .... F 910 343-0624
Wilmington *(G-16120)*

Atlantic Corp Wilmington Inc .... E 910 259-3600
Burgaw *(G-1333)*

◆ **Atlantic Corp Wilmington Inc** .... D 910 343-0624
Wilmington *(G-16121)*

Bay Tech Label Inc .... G 828 296-8900
Asheville *(G-557)*

Box Company of America LLC .... E 910 582-0100
Hamlet *(G-7617)*

Caraustar Industries Inc .... F 336 498-2631
Randleman *(G-13456)*

◆ **Carolina Container Company** .... D 336 883-7146
High Point *(G-8284)*

Carolina Precision Fibers Inc .... E 336 527-4140
Ronda *(G-13764)*

Carpet Rentals Inc .... E 704 872-4461
Statesville *(G-14773)*

◆ **Cdv LLC** .... F 919 674-3460
Morrisville *(G-11316)*

Genie Trcking Sltons Lbels LLC .... G 919 201-2600
Clayton *(G-3981)*

Grand Encore Charlotte LLC .... E 513 482-7500
Charlotte *(G-2854)*

Graphic Finshg Solutions LLC .... G 336 255-7857
Greensboro *(G-7058)*

▲ **Hibco Plastics Inc** .... E 336 463-2391
Yadkinville *(G-17040)*

Hill-Pak Inc .... G 336 431-3833
High Point *(G-8395)*

J R Cole Industries Inc .... D 704 523-6622
Charlotte *(G-3005)*

Label & Printing Solutions Inc .... G 919 782-1242
Raleigh *(G-12950)*

Label Line Ltd .... D 336 857-3115
Asheboro *(G-450)*

Label Printing Systems Inc .... E 336 760-3271
Winston Salem *(G-16783)*

Lpm Inc .... G 704 922-6137
Gastonia *(G-6444)*

National Gyps Receivables LLC .... E 704 365-7300
Charlotte *(G-3235)*

Ng Corporate LLC .... E 704 365-7300
Charlotte *(G-3259)*

Ng Operations LLC .... E 704 365-7300
Charlotte *(G-3260)*

Nonwovens of America Inc .... F 828 236-1300
Swannanoa *(G-15031)*

NPS Holdings LLC .... E 828 757-7501
Lenoir *(G-9642)*

Pactiv LLC .... E 336 292-2796
Greensboro *(G-7240)*

Paperworks .... G 704 548-9057
Charlotte *(G-3311)*

◆ **Proform Finishing Products LLC** .... B 704 365-7300
Charlotte *(G-3392)*

Quality Packaging Corp .... G 336 881-5300
High Point *(G-8502)*

Rapid Response Inc .... G 704 588-8890
Charlotte *(G-3409)*

Reliable Wallcovering LLC .... G 980 565-5224
Concord *(G-4348)*

▲ **Rgees LLC** .... G 828 708-7178
Arden *(G-372)*

◆ **Stump Printing Co Inc** .... C 260 723-5171
Wrightsville Beach *(G-17028)*

Tarason Label Inc .... G 828 464-4743
Hickory *(G-8174)*

◆ **Technical Coating Intl Inc** .... E 910 371-0860
Belville *(G-1026)*

Triangle Converting Corp .... E 919 596-6656
Durham *(G-5407)*

Veritiv Operating Company .... E 336 834-3488
Greensboro *(G-7437)*

▲ **W R Rayson Export Ltd** .... E 910 686-5802
Burgaw *(G-1355)*

Wallworx .... G 919 422-8604
Apex *(G-257)*

▲ **Welsh Cstm Sltting Rwnding LLC** .... E 336 665-6481
Greensboro *(G-7456)*

▼ **Winter Bell Company** .... G 336 887-2651
High Point *(G-8605)*

▲ **Wright of Thomasville Inc** .... F 336 472-4200
Thomasville *(G-15305)*

27 PRINTING, PUBLISHING AND ALLIED INDUSTRIES

2711 Newspapers

A D Services .... G 336 667-8190
Wilkesboro *(G-16011)*

ACC Sports Journal .... F 919 846-7502
Raleigh *(G-12466)*

Acento Latino .... G 910 486-2760
Fayetteville *(G-5750)*

Advantage Newspaper .... E 910 323-0349
Fayetteville *(G-5753)*

Advertising For You Now Inc .... G 704 706-9423
Concord *(G-4188)*

Alameen A Haqq .... G 336 965-8339
Greensboro *(G-6789)*

American City Bus Journals Inc .... C 336 271-6539
Greensboro *(G-6797)*

▲ **American City Bus Journals Inc** .... B 704 973-1000
Charlotte *(G-2181)*

Annette Cameron .... G 828 505-0404
Asheville *(G-520)*

Anson Express .... G 704 694-2480
Wadesboro *(G-15500)*

Apg/East LLC .... C 252 329-9500
Greenville *(G-7484)*

APS Hickory .... G 828 323-1010
Hickory *(G-7938)*

Asheville Citizen-Times .... G 828 252-5611
Asheville *(G-532)*

Asheville Global Report .... G 828 236-3103
Asheville *(G-536)*

Asian (korean) Herald Inc .... G 704 332-5656
Charlotte *(G-2227)*

SIC SECTION

27 PRINTING, PUBLISHING AND ALLIED INDUSTRIES

Automail LLC .... F 704 677-0152
   Mooresville *(G-10865)*

Ballpointe Pubg & Design LLC .... G 919 453-0449
   Wake Forest *(G-15530)*

Benmot Publishing Company Inc .... G 919 658-9456
   Mount Olive *(G-11655)*

Black Mountain News Inc .... G 828 669-8727
   Black Mountain *(G-1120)*

Blue Ridge Sun Inc .... G 336 372-5490
   Sparta *(G-14590)*

Boone Newspapers Inc .... E 252 332-2123
   Ahoskie *(G-56)*

Bridgetower Media LLC .... E 612 317-9420
   Greensboro *(G-6854)*

Brunswick Beacon Inc .... F 910 754-6890
   Shallotte *(G-14270)*

Burke Mill .... G 336 774-2952
   Winston Salem *(G-16640)*

Business Journals .... D 704 371-3248
   Charlotte *(G-2365)*

C Alan Publications LLC .... G 336 272-3920
   Greensboro *(G-6870)*

C York Law Pllc .... G 910 256-1235
   Wilmington *(G-16146)*

Camp Lejeune Globe .... G 910 939-0705
   Jacksonville *(G-8993)*

Cape Fear Newspapers Inc .... G 910 285-2178
   Wallace *(G-15620)*

Carolina Blue Publishing LLC .... G 704 628-6290
   Indian Trail *(G-8926)*

Carolina Newspapers Inc .... G 336 274-7829
   Greensboro *(G-6890)*

Carolina Trader .... G 910 433-2229
   Fayetteville *(G-5785)*

Carolina Weekly Newspaper Grou .... F 704 849-2261
   Charlotte *(G-2411)*

Carolinian Pubg Group LLC .... G 919 834-5558
   Raleigh *(G-12602)*

Carter Publishing Company Inc .... F 336 993-2161
   Kernersville *(G-9174)*

Carter-Hubbard Publishing Co .... F 336 838-4117
   North Wilkesboro *(G-12000)*

Carteret Publishing Company .... G 910 326-5066
   Swansboro *(G-15043)*

Carteret Publishing Company .... D 252 726-7081
   Morehead City *(G-11159)*

Catawba Vly Youth Soccer Assoc .... G 828 234-7082
   Hickory *(G-7971)*

Catholic News and Herald .... G 704 370-3333
   Charlotte *(G-2420)*

Champion Media LLC .... C 910 506-3021
   Laurinburg *(G-9473)*

Charlotte Observer .... E 704 358-5000
   Charlotte *(G-2453)*

Charlotte Observer Pubg Co .... E 704 987-3660
   Charlotte *(G-2454)*

Charlotte Observer Pubg Co .... E 704 572-0747
   Charlotte *(G-2455)*

Charlotte Observer Pubg Co .... E 704 358-6020
   Matthews *(G-10241)*

Charlotte Observer Pubg Co .... A 704 358-5000
   Charlotte *(G-2456)*

Charlotte Post Pubg Co Inc .... F 704 376-0496
   Charlotte *(G-2461)*

Charlotte Publishing Company .... E 704 547-0900
   Charlotte *(G-2462)*

Charlotte Weekly .... G 704 849-2261
   Charlotte *(G-2466)*

Charltte McKInburg Dream Ctr I .... G 704 421-4440
   Charlotte *(G-2467)*

Chatham News Publishing Co .... G 919 663-4042
   Siler City *(G-14406)*

Chronicle Mill Land LLC .... G 704 527-3227
   Gastonia *(G-6378)*

Chronicle Research Inc .... G 919 259-0970
   Morrisville *(G-11322)*

Chronicles .... G 252 617-1774
   Jacksonville *(G-8995)*

Citizen Media Inc .... G 704 363-6062
   Huntersville *(G-8803)*

Coman Publishing Co Inc .... F 919 688-0218
   Durham *(G-5026)*

Community First Media Inc .... G 704 482-4142
   Shelby *(G-14302)*

Community Newspapers Inc .... G 828 743-5101
   Cashiers *(G-1935)*

Community Newspapers Inc .... G 828 369-3430
   Franklin *(G-6121)*

Community Newspapers Inc .... G 828 389-8431
   Hayesville *(G-7763)*

Community Newspapers Inc .... G 828 479-3383
   Robbinsville *(G-13606)*

Community Newspapers Inc .... G 828 765-7169
   Spruce Pine *(G-14633)*

Cooke Communications NC LLC .... F 252 329-9500
   Greenville *(G-7506)*

County Press Inc .... G 919 894-2112
   Benson *(G-1033)*

Cox Nrth Crlina Pblcations Inc .... G 252 482-4418
   Edenton *(G-5510)*

Cox Nrth Crlina Pblcations Inc .... C 252 335-0841
   Elizabeth City *(G-5538)*

Cox Nrth Crlina Pblcations Inc .... G 910 296-0239
   Kenansville *(G-9142)*

Cox Nrth Crlina Pblcations Inc .... D 252 792-1181
   Williamston *(G-16059)*

Cox Nrth Crlina Pblcations Inc .... C 252 329-9643
   Greenville *(G-7510)*

Cryotherapy of Pines LLC .... G 910 988-0357
   Southern Pines *(G-14532)*

Cynthia Drew .... G 828 301-8697
   Barnardsville *(G-907)*

Daily Courier .... E 828 245-6431
   Rutherfordton *(G-13871)*

Daily Living Solutions Inc .... G 704 614-0977
   Charlotte *(G-2599)*

Daily N-Gine LLC .... G 336 285-8042
   Greensboro *(G-6957)*

Daily Victories Inc .... G 704 982-1341
   Albemarle *(G-81)*

Davie County Publishing Co .... F 336 751-2120
   Mocksville *(G-10565)*

Davie Paper Co .... G 425 941-1994
   Durham *(G-5050)*

Db North Carolina Holdings Inc .... E 910 323-4848
   Fayetteville *(G-5808)*

Defy Hickory .... G 828 222-4144
   Hickory *(G-8005)*

Democracy Greensboro .... G 336 635-7016
   Greensboro *(G-6969)*

Denton Orator .... G 336 859-3131
   Denton *(G-4732)*

Dolan LLC .... G 919 829-9333
   Raleigh *(G-12694)*

Dth Publishing Inc .... C 919 962-1163
   Chapel Hill *(G-2010)*

Duke Student Publishing Co Inc .... G 919 684-3811
   Durham *(G-5067)*

El Valle of Lake Norman Inc .... G 704 658-0212
   Mooresville *(G-10938)*

Ellis Publishing Company Inc .... F 252 444-1999
   New Bern *(G-11803)*

▲ Epi Group Llc .... B 843 577-7111
   Durham *(G-5091)*

Epoch Times Nc Inc .... G 919 649-6014
   Cary *(G-1760)*

F B Publications Inc .... F 910 484-6200
   Fayetteville *(G-5822)*

Fairfax Digital LLC .... F 407 822-2918
   Charlotte *(G-2745)*

Fairview Town Crier .... G 828 628-4547
   Fairview *(G-5710)*

▲ Fayetteville Publishing Co .... D 910 323-4848
   Fayetteville *(G-5824)*

Foundry A Print Cmmnctions LLC .... G 703 329-3300
   Apex *(G-193)*

Framers Cottage .... G 910 638-0100
   Whispering Pines *(G-15954)*

Franklin County Newspapers Inc .... F 919 496-6503
   Louisburg *(G-9988)*

Fun Publications Inc .... G 919 847-5263
   Raleigh *(G-12786)*

Future Endeavors Hickory LLC .... G 828 256-5488
   Hickory *(G-8030)*

Gannett Media Corp .... G 828 649-1075
   Marshall *(G-10202)*

Gannett Media Corp .... F 919 467-1402
   Morrisville *(G-11346)*

Gaston Gazette LLP .... A 704 869-1700
   Gastonia *(G-6405)*

Gastonia .... G 704 377-3687
   Gastonia *(G-6406)*

Gatehouse Media LLC .... F 336 626-6103
   Asheboro *(G-439)*

Good News Iphc Ministries Inc .... G 919 906-2104
   Jacksonville *(G-9003)*

Granville Publishing Co Inc .... G 919 528-2393
   Creedmoor *(G-4614)*

Green Line Media Inc .... E 828 251-1333
   Asheville *(G-643)*

Greensboro Drifters Inc .... G 336 375-6743
   Greensboro *(G-7063)*

Greensboro News & Record LLC .... A 336 373-7000
   Greensboro *(G-7064)*

Greensboro Voice .... F 336 255-1006
   Greensboro *(G-7067)*

Grey Area News .... G 919 637-6973
   Zebulon *(G-17130)*

Gulfstream Publications Inc .... G 252 449-2222
   Kitty Hawk *(G-9406)*

Halifax Media Group .... F 704 869-1700
   Gastonia *(G-6411)*

Halifax Media Holdings LLC .... G 828 692-5763
   Hendersonville *(G-7857)*

Harley Owners Group Sttsvlle I .... G 704 872-3883
   Statesville *(G-14808)*

Hendersnvlle Affrdbl Hsing Cor .... F 828 692-6175
   Hendersonville *(G-7862)*

Henderson Newspapers Inc .... D 252 436-2700
   Henderson *(G-7786)*

Herald A Pierre LLC .... G 919 730-2965
   Fairmont *(G-5702)*

Herald Huntersville .... G 704 766-2100
   Huntersville *(G-8830)*

Herald Printing Co Inc .... E 252 537-2505
   Roanoke Rapids *(G-13575)*

Herald Sanford Inc .... D 919 708-9000
   Sanford *(G-14130)*

Hickory Publishing Co Inc .... E 828 322-4510
   Hickory *(G-8049)*

Hickory Youth Sports Inc .... G 828 327-9550
   Hickory *(G-8057)*

High Country Media LLC .... G 828 733-2448
   Newland *(G-11888)*

High Country News Inc .... F 828 264-2262
   Boone *(G-1205)*

Employee Codes: A=Over 500 employees, B=251-500
C=101-250, D=51-100, E=20-50, F=10-19, G=1-9

27 PRINTING, PUBLISHING AND ALLIED INDUSTRIES

Company	Code	Phone
High Point Enterprise Inc — High Point (G-8387)	G	336 434-2716
High Point Enterprise Inc — High Point (G-8388)	F	336 883-2839
High Point Enterprise Inc — Thomasville (G-15229)	F	336 472-9500
High Point Enterprise Inc — High Point (G-8389)	C	336 888-3500
Highcorp Incorporated — Whiteville (G-15966)	E	910 642-4104
Hope Counseling Ctr — Sneads Ferry (G-14491)	G	910 741-0538
Horizon Publications Inc — Newton (G-11941)	F	828 464-0221
Hpt Hitoms LLC — Greensboro (G-7102)	G	336 541-8093
Hush Greensboro — Greensboro (G-7106)	G	336 676-6133
Indy Week — Raleigh (G-12886)	G	919 832-8774
Iodine Poetry Journal — Charlotte (G-2991)	G	704 595-9526
Iredell Holding LLC — Claremont (G-3930)	G	828 506-2555
Iwanna — Asheville (G-665)	G	828 505-7319
Jamestown News — Jamestown (G-9059)	G	336 841-4933
Jesus Daily Group LLC — Winston Salem (G-16770)	G	336 727-4781
Jim John — Mount Airy (G-11526)	G	336 352-4650
Jones Media — Boone (G-1212)	F	828 264-3612
Journal Doctors Inc — Cary (G-1799)	G	919 469-1438
Journal Vacuum Science & Tech — Cary (G-1800)	G	919 361-2787
JR Mooresville Inc — Statesville (G-14827)	G	973 434-6453
Kinston Free Press Company — Kinston (G-9371)	C	252 527-3191
Lantern of Hendersonville LLC — Hendersonville (G-7872)	G	828 513-5033
Latino Communications Inc — Charlotte (G-3073)	F	704 319-5044
Latino Communications Inc — Raleigh (G-12959)	F	919 645-1680
Latino Communications Inc — Winston Salem (G-16784)	D	336 714-2823
Ledger Publishing Company — Oxford (G-12135)	F	919 693-2646
Lincoln Herald LLC — Lincolnton (G-9901)	G	704 735-3620
Lumina News — Wilmington (G-16309)	G	910 256-6569
Magic Mile Media Inc — Kinston (G-9375)	F	252 572-1330
Mc Clatchy Interactive USA — Raleigh (G-13011)	F	919 861-1200
McDowell Pressure Washing — Marion (G-10163)	G	828 620-2141
McLoud Media — Murphy (G-11712)	G	828 837-9539
Media Wilimington Co — Wilmington (G-16319)	G	910 791-0688
Mid South Management NC Inc — Elkin (G-5625)	E	336 835-1513
Minuteman Provision Co LLC — Reidsville (G-13531)	G	252 996-0856
Montgomery Herald — Troy (G-15408)	G	910 576-6051
Mooresville NC — Mooresville (G-11025)	G	704 909-6459
Mooresville Parlor LLC — Mooresville (G-11026)	G	704 450-1836
Mooresville Tax Service Inc — Mooresville (G-11027)	G	704 360-1040
Mooresville Tribune — Hickory (G-8097)	G	704 872-0148
Mooresvlle Blue Dvil Band Bste — Mooresville (G-11028)	G	704 787-2994
Morganton Service League Inc — Morganton (G-11235)	G	828 439-9525
Mountain Area Info Netwrk — Asheville (G-707)	F	828 255-0182
Mountain Times Inc — West Jefferson (G-15945)	G	336 246-6397
Mountaineer Enterprise — Biltmore Lake (G-1101)	G	828 670-5425
Mountaineer Inc — Waynesville (G-15811)	F	828 452-0661
Mullen Publications Inc — Charlotte (G-3214)	F	704 527-5111
Nasaspaceflight LLC — Charlotte (G-3231)	G	980 430-9535
Nash County Newspapers Inc — Nashville (G-11747)	F	252 459-7101
Near Urban LLC — Sylva (G-15064)	G	828 631-6213
New Bern Craven Co Bd of Educ — New Bern (G-11829)	G	252 635-1822
News & Record — Reidsville (G-13536)	F	336 627-1781
News & Record Commercial Prtg — Greensboro (G-7217)	E	336 373-7300
News 14 Carolina — Charlotte (G-3253)	F	704 973-5700
News and Observer Pubg Co — Benson (G-1040)	F	919 894-4170
News and Observer Pubg Co — Durham (G-5245)	F	919 419-6500
News and Observer Pubg Co — Garner (G-6296)	F	919 829-8903
▲ News and Observer Pubg Co — Raleigh (G-13063)	A	919 829-4500
Next Magazine — Fayetteville (G-5882)	G	910 609-0638
Norman E Clark — Stoneville (G-14963)	G	336 573-9629
Norman Lake High — Mooresville (G-11039)	G	336 971-7348
Observer News Enterprise Inc — Newton (G-11954)	E	828 464-0221
Old-Time Music Group Inc — Durham (G-5256)	G	919 286-2041
Ottaway Associates LLC — Apex (G-223)	G	919 467-9988
Our Daily Living — Durham (G-5265)	G	919 220-8160
Owner Tryon Backdoor Dist — Tryon (G-15426)	G	864 237-1667
Paxton Media Group — Monroe (G-10784)	F	704 289-1541
Perfect Square Music Inc — Arden (G-363)	G	478 718-5702
Pflag Hickory — Hickory (G-8113)	G	828 244-5578
Philantrophy Journal — Raleigh (G-13109)	G	919 890-6240
Pilot LLC — Southern Pines (G-14545)	G	864 430-6337
Pilot LLC — Southern Pines (G-14546)	D	910 692-7271
Pinball Literary — Chapel Hill (G-2053)	G	919 240-4012
PMG Acquisition Corp — Lenoir (G-9647)	D	828 758-7381
PMG-DH Company — Durham (G-5292)	C	919 419-6500
Ponderosa News LLC — Fayetteville (G-5898)	G	910 867-6571
Post Publishing Company — Salisbury (G-14026)	D	704 633-8950
Post Voice LLC — Burgaw (G-1347)	G	910 259-9111
Pride Publishing & Typsg Inc — Charlotte (G-3380)	G	704 531-9988
Raleigh Downtowner — Raleigh (G-13176)	G	919 821-9000
Raysweathercom Inc — Boone (G-1233)	G	828 264-2030
Record Publishing Company — Dunn (G-4881)	E	910 230-1948
Rennasentient Inc — Cary (G-1868)	F	919 233-7710
Rhinoceros Times — Greensboro (G-7310)	F	336 763-4170
Richard D Stewart — Kenly (G-9156)	G	919 284-2295
Richmond Observer LLP — Rockingham (G-13642)	G	910 817-3169
Robert Laskowski — New Bern (G-11840)	G	203 732-0846
Rockingham Now — Reidsville (G-13538)	G	336 349-4331
Rotary Club Statesville — Statesville (G-14878)	F	704 872-6851
Ryjak Enterprises LLC — Southern Pines (G-14551)	F	910 638-0716
Sampson Weekly Inc — Clinton (G-4108)	G	910 590-2102
Sandhills Sentinel Inc — Aberdeen (G-28)	G	910 944-0992
Seaside Press Co Inc — Carolina Beach (G-1641)	G	910 458-8156
Sentinel Newspapers — Hayesville (G-7771)	F	828 389-8338
Seven Lakes News Corporation — West End (G-15932)	G	910 685-0320
Shelby Freedom Star Inc — Shelby (G-14365)	C	704 484-7000
Shopper — New Bern (G-11845)	G	252 633-1153
Silver Miller Holdings Llc — Marion (G-10176)	G	828 652-6677
Sk Publishing LLC — High Point (G-8534)	G	336 885-3637
Slam Publications LLC — Nags Head (G-11726)	F	252 480-2234
Smoky Mountain News Inc — Waynesville (G-15824)	F	828 452-4251
Snap Publications LLC — Greensboro (G-7346)	F	336 274-8531
Spectacular Publishing Inc — Durham (G-5366)	G	919 672-0289
Spring Hope Enterprise Inc — Spring Hope (G-14622)	G	252 478-3651
St Johns Museum of Art — Wilmington (G-16416)	G	910 763-0281
St of Greensboro LLC — Greensboro (G-7363)	G	336 851-1600
Statesville High — Statesville (G-14902)	F	704 873-3491
Statesville LLC — Statesville (G-14903)	G	704 872-3303

27 PRINTING, PUBLISHING AND ALLIED INDUSTRIES

Statesville Sandlot Basbal Inc .... G 704 880-1334
   Statesville *(G-14905)*

Sudanese Cmnty Schl Greensboro .... G 336 763-7761
   Greensboro *(G-7378)*

Sun-Journal Incorporated .... E 252 638-8101
   New Bern *(G-11848)*

Sundown Times Inc .... F 828 264-1881
   Boone *(G-1240)*

Surry Scene .... G 336 786-4141
   Mount Airy *(G-11583)*

Sylva Herald and Ruralite .... E 828 586-2611
   Sylva *(G-15070)*

Sylva Herald Pubg Co Incthe .... F 828 586-2611
   Sylva *(G-15071)*

Tallahassee Democrat .... G 919 832-9430
   Raleigh *(G-13326)*

Taylorsville Times .... F 828 632-2532
   Taylorsville *(G-15172)*

Times Journal Inc .... G 828 682-4067
   Burnsville *(G-1535)*

▲ Times News Publishing Company ..... E 336 226-4414
   Burlington *(G-1506)*

Times Printing Company .... E 252 473-2105
   Manteo *(G-10130)*

Times Printing Company Inc .... G 252 441-2223
   Kill Devil Hills *(G-9263)*

Topsail Voice LLC .... G 910 270-2944
   Hampstead *(G-7662)*

Triangle Tribune .... G 704 376-0496
   Durham *(G-5411)*

Tribune Papers Inc .... G 828 606-5050
   Asheville *(G-806)*

Trinicor Technology Incorporat .... G 866 848-1232
   Charlotte *(G-3728)*

Tryon Newsmedia LLC .... F 828 859-9151
   Tryon *(G-15430)*

Tucker Production Incorporated .... G 828 322-1036
   Hickory *(G-8190)*

Twin Cy Kwnis Fndtion Wnstn-SL .... G 336 784-1649
   Winston Salem *(G-16959)*

Up & Coming Magazine .... F 910 391-3859
   Fayetteville *(G-5941)*

Up and Coming Weekly .... E 910 484-6200
   Fayetteville *(G-5942)*

Urban News .... G 828 253-5585
   Asheville *(G-810)*

Virginn-Plot Mdia Cmpanies LLC .... G 252 441-3628
   Nags Head *(G-11728)*

Wake Forest Gazette .... G 919 556-3409
   Wake Forest *(G-15611)*

Want of ADS of Greensboro .... G 336 297-4300
   Greensboro *(G-7454)*

Washington Cnty Newspapers Inc .... G 252 793-2123
   Plymouth *(G-12378)*

Washington News Publishing Co .... F 252 946-2144
   Washington *(G-15739)*

▲ Wayne Printing Company Inc .... E 919 778-2211
   Goldsboro *(G-6669)*

Wen Biz Journal .... G 509 663-6730
   Marshall *(G-10208)*

West Stkes Wldcat Grdron CLB I .... G 336 985-6152
   King *(G-9284)*

Whiteville AG .... G 910 914-0007
   Whiteville *(G-15977)*

Wick Communications Co .... E 252 537-2505
   Roanoke Rapids *(G-13589)*

Wilmington Journal Company .... G 910 762-5502
   Wilmington *(G-16446)*

Wilmington Star-News Inc .... D 910 343-2000
   Wilmington *(G-16452)*

Wilson Daily Times Inc .... D 252 243-5151
   Wilson *(G-16561)*

Winstn-Slem Chronicle Pubg Inc .... F 336 722-8624
   Winston Salem *(G-16978)*

◆ Winston Salem Journal .... E 336 727-7211
   Winston Salem *(G-16982)*

Womack Newspaper Inc .... G 336 316-1231
   Greensboro *(G-7465)*

Womack Publishing Co Inc .... G 919 732-2171
   Hillsborough *(G-8673)*

Womack Publishing Co Inc .... G 252 586-2700
   Littleton *(G-9954)*

Womack Publishing Co Inc .... G 919 563-3555
   Mebane *(G-10437)*

Womack Publishing Co Inc .... F 704 660-5520
   Mooresville *(G-11131)*

Womack Publishing Co Inc .... D 252 480-2234
   Nags Head *(G-11730)*

Womack Publishing Co Inc .... G 252 257-3341
   Warrenton *(G-15663)*

▲ World Newspaper Publishing .... G 704 548-1737
   Charlotte *(G-3824)*

Wtvd Television LLC .... C 919 683-1111
   Durham *(G-5451)*

Yancy Common Times Journal .... G 828 682-2120
   Burnsville *(G-1538)*

2721 Periodicals

Academy Association Inc .... F 919 544-0835
   Durham *(G-4899)*

Aeroplantation .... G 704 843-2223
   Waxhaw *(G-15744)*

American City Bus Journals Inc .... G 704 973-1100
   Charlotte *(G-2182)*

▲ American City Bus Journals Inc .... B 704 973-1000
   Charlotte *(G-2181)*

▲ American Inst Crtif Pub Accntn .... B 919 402-0682
   Durham *(G-4915)*

Asssction Intl Crtif Prof Accn .... A 919 402-4500
   Durham *(G-4930)*

Biosupplynet Inc .... F 919 659-2121
   Morrisville *(G-11304)*

Business To Business Inc .... G 919 872-7077
   Raleigh *(G-12579)*

Capre Omnimedia LLC .... G 917 460-3572
   Wilmington *(G-16155)*

Carolina Bargain Trader Inc .... G 252 756-1500
   Greenville *(G-7498)*

Carolina Home Garden .... G 828 692-3230
   Hendersonville *(G-7835)*

Carolina Parenting Inc .... F 704 344-1980
   Charlotte *(G-2402)*

Carolina Publishing Company .... G 252 206-1633
   Wilson *(G-16485)*

Carolina Woman Inc .... G 919 869-8200
   Chapel Hill *(G-1998)*

Ceco Publishing Inc .... G 828 253-2047
   Asheville *(G-586)*

Cherokee Publishing Co Inc .... E 919 674-6020
   Cary *(G-1728)*

Christian Focus Magazine .... G 252 240-1656
   Morehead City *(G-11161)*

Cityview Publishing LLC .... F 910 423-6500
   Fayetteville *(G-5790)*

Cline Printing Inc .... G 704 394-8144
   Charlotte *(G-2496)*

Cmm Quarterly Inc .... G 704 995-3007
   Charlotte *(G-2506)*

Colefields Publishing Inc .... G 704 661-1599
   Charlotte *(G-2523)*

Duke University .... D 919 687-3600
   Durham *(G-5068)*

Education Center LLC .... E 336 854-0392
   Oak Ridge *(G-12059)*

Flamingo Group LLC .... G 910 478-9987
   Jacksonville *(G-8999)*

Forrentcom .... G 336 420-9562
   High Point *(G-8355)*

Forsyth Family Magazine Inc .... F 336 782-0331
   Clemmons *(G-4038)*

Ft Media Holdings LLC .... F 336 605-0121
   Greensboro *(G-7024)*

Furniture Tday Media Group LLC .... D 336 605-0121
   Greensboro *(G-7025)*

Grace Communion International .... E 626 650-2300
   Charlotte *(G-2849)*

Greater Wilmington Business .... G 910 343-8600
   Wilmington *(G-16240)*

Hearst Corporation .... F 704 348-8000
   Charlotte *(G-2898)*

Hearst Corporation .... F 704 348-8000
   Charlotte *(G-2899)*

Hemispheres Magazine .... E 336 255-0195
   Greensboro *(G-7086)*

Ifpo - Ifmo/American Image Inc .... G 336 945-9867
   Hamptonville *(G-7672)*

International Society Automtn .... E 919 206-4176
   Durham *(G-5162)*

ISA .... D 919 549-8411
   Durham *(G-5167)*

Jennifer Mowrer .... G 336 714-6462
   Winston Salem *(G-16769)*

Jo Mangum .... G 919 271-8822
   Asheville *(G-672)*

Jobs Magazine LLC .... G 919 319-6816
   Cary *(G-1797)*

Knight Communications Inc .... F 704 568-7804
   Indian Trail *(G-8943)*

Lafauci .... G 919 244-5912
   Holly Springs *(G-8705)*

Lift Equipment Inc .... G 704 799-3355
   Mooresville *(G-11009)*

▲ M&J Oldco Inc .... D 336 854-0309
   Greensboro *(G-7175)*

Maelle Kids Inc .... G 252 799-7312
   Williamston *(G-16065)*

Magazine Nakia Lashawn .... G 919 875-1156
   Raleigh *(G-12987)*

Mann Media Inc .... E 336 286-0600
   Greensboro *(G-7179)*

Mathisen Ventures Inc .... G 212 986-1025
   Charlotte *(G-3141)*

Mb-F Inc .... D 336 379-9352
   Greensboro *(G-7192)*

Ncoast Communications .... F 252 247-7442
   Morehead City *(G-11183)*

New Bern Magazine .... G 252 626-5812
   New Bern *(G-11830)*

▲ News and Observer Pubg Co .... A 919 829-4500
   Raleigh *(G-13063)*

Northstar Travel Media .... E 336 714-3328
   Winston Salem *(G-16822)*

Oasis Magazine LLC .... G 888 559-7549
   Huntersville *(G-8868)*

▲ Pace Communications Inc .... C 336 378-6065
   Greensboro *(G-7239)*

Pride Communications Inc .... G 704 375-9553
   Charlotte *(G-3379)*

Prism Publishing Inc .... F 919 319-6816
   Cary *(G-1860)*

Raleigh Magazine .... G 919 307-3047
   Raleigh *(G-13178)*

Randall-Reilly LLC .... C 704 814-1390
   Charlotte *(G-3408)*

Rapid River Magazine .... G 828 646-0071
   Canton *(G-1624)*

27 PRINTING, PUBLISHING AND ALLIED INDUSTRIES

Rapport Magazine Inc .... G 919 435-7690
  Southport *(G-14577)*
Rated Best of Charlotte .... G 704 309-3810
  Charlotte *(G-3411)*
Rbi .... G 336 605-0121
  Greensboro *(G-7304)*
Red Hand Media LLC .... F 704 523-6987
  Charlotte *(G-3422)*
Rose Media Inc .... F 919 736-1154
  Goldsboro *(G-6651)*
Scalawag .... G 917 671-7240
  Durham *(G-5342)*
Shannon Media Inc .... F 919 933-1551
  Chapel Hill *(G-2071)*
Sigma Xi Scntfic RES Hnor Soc .... G 919 549-4691
  Durham *(G-5356)*
Southern Trade Publications Co .... G 336 454-3516
  Greensboro *(G-7356)*
Spectrum News .... F 919 882-4009
  Raleigh *(G-13288)*
Stratton Publishing & Mktg Inc .... G 703 914-9200
  Wilmington *(G-16419)*
Success Publishing Inc .... C 919 807-1100
  Raleigh *(G-13312)*
Techjournal South .... G 919 832-1858
  Raleigh *(G-13334)*
Tobacco Mrchnts Assn of US Inc .... F 919 872-5040
  Raleigh *(G-13351)*
Todays Charlotte Woman .... G 704 521-6872
  Charlotte *(G-3703)*
Tourist Baseball Inc .... E 828 258-0428
  Asheville *(G-803)*
▲ Triple D Publishing Inc .... F 704 482-9673
  Shelby *(G-14375)*
Ty Brown .... G 828 264-6865
  Boone *(G-1244)*
Up & Coming Magazine .... F 910 391-3859
  Fayetteville *(G-5941)*
▲ Wilmington Today LLC .... G 910 509-7195
  Wilmington *(G-16453)*

2731 Book publishing

Ambassador Services Inc .... C 800 576-8627
  Gastonia *(G-6342)*
Andrea Hurst and Assoc LLC .... G 916 743-1846
  Garner *(G-6254)*
Anthology of Poetry Inc .... F 336 626-7762
  Asheboro *(G-402)*
Asheville Guidebook .... G 828 779-1569
  Fairview *(G-5707)*
Baker Taylor Investments I LLC .... F 704 998-3100
  Charlotte *(G-2267)*
▲ Bhaktivedanta Archives .... G 336 871-3636
  Sandy Ridge *(G-14076)*
Blue/Gray Books .... G 828 254-3972
  Alexander *(G-117)*
◆ C D Stampley Enterprises Inc .... F 704 333-6631
  Charlotte *(G-2372)*
Carlina Shotwell LLC .... G 252 417-8688
  Greenville *(G-7497)*
Carolina Wren Press Inc .... G 919 560-2738
  Durham *(G-5005)*
◆ Carson-Dellosa Publishing LLC .... D 336 632-0084
  Greensboro *(G-6893)*
▲ Celtic Ocean International Inc .... E 828 299-9005
  Arden *(G-320)*
Center for Creative Leadership .... B 336 288-7210
  Greensboro *(G-6898)*
Cherokee Publications .... G 828 627-2424
  Cherokee *(G-3854)*
Church Initiative Inc .... E 919 562-2112
  Wake Forest *(G-15540)*
Coding Institute LLC .... E 239 280-2300
  Durham *(G-5023)*
Comfort Publishing Svcs LLC .... G 704 907-7848
  Concord *(G-4236)*
Contemporary Concepts Inc .... E 704 864-9572
  Gastonia *(G-6385)*
Contemporary Publishing Co .... G 919 834-4432
  Raleigh *(G-12643)*
Dex Media East LLC .... D 919 297-1600
  Cary *(G-1750)*
Duke University .... D 919 687-3600
  Durham *(G-5068)*
Fidelity Associates Inc .... E 704 864-3766
  Gastonia *(G-6402)*
Foundry A Print Cmmnctions LLC .... G 703 329-3300
  Apex *(G-193)*
▲ Good Will Publishers Inc .... D 704 853-3237
  Gastonia *(G-6408)*
Graedon Enterprises Inc .... G 919 493-0448
  Durham *(G-5125)*
Grateful Steps Foundation .... G 828 277-0998
  Asheville *(G-639)*
▲ Gryphon House Inc .... E 800 638-0928
  Lewisville *(G-9667)*
Hatrack River Enterprises Inc .... G 336 282-9848
  Greensboro *(G-7078)*
High Five Enterprises Inc .... G 828 279-5962
  Weaverville *(G-15848)*
How Great Thou Art Publication .... G 704 851-3117
  Mc Farlan *(G-10381)*
International Society Automtn .... E 919 206-4176
  Durham *(G-5162)*
ISA .... D 919 549-8411
  Durham *(G-5167)*
JFK Conferences LLC .... E 980 255-3336
  Fayetteville *(G-5849)*
Jfl Enterprises Inc .... G 704 786-7838
  Concord *(G-4293)*
Joseph Decicco .... G 910 262-9701
  Hampstead *(G-7650)*
Kr Publications .... G 910 852-1525
  Lumberton *(G-10043)*
Landmark Music Group Inc .... G 919 800-7277
  Garner *(G-6280)*
▲ Light-Beams Publishing .... F 603 659-1300
  Carolina Beach *(G-1639)*
▼ Longleaf Services Inc .... F 800 848-6224
  Chapel Hill *(G-2033)*
Lulu Technology Circus Inc .... G 919 459-5858
  Morrisville *(G-11385)*
Mable Mullen .... G 252 599-1181
  Elizabeth City *(G-5555)*
Marco Products Inc .... F 215 956-0313
  New Bern *(G-11818)*
Mathisen Ventures Inc .... G 212 986-1025
  Charlotte *(G-3141)*
Mc Farland & Company Inc .... E 336 246-4460
  Jefferson *(G-9091)*
One Library At A Time Inc .... G 704 578-1812
  Charlotte *(G-3298)*
Payload Media Inc .... G 919 367-2969
  Cary *(G-1844)*
Phoenix St Claire Pubg LLC .... G 919 303-3223
  Cary *(G-1851)*
Plan Nine Publishing Inc .... G 336 454-7766
  High Point *(G-8486)*
Positive Prints Prof Svcs LLC .... G 336 701-2330
  Durham *(G-4913)*
Readable Communications Inc .... G 919 876-5260
  Raleigh *(G-13193)*
Royal Faires Inc .... F 704 896-5555
  Huntersville *(G-8887)*
S&R Investments LLC .... G 408 597-7007
  Charlotte *(G-3479)*
Sighttech LLC .... G 855 997-4448
  Charlotte *(G-3549)*
Sticker Farm LLC .... G 919 332-1342
  Charlotte *(G-3632)*
▲ Tan Books and Publishers Inc .... G 704 731-0651
  Charlotte *(G-3672)*
Technica Editorial Services .... G 919 918-3991
  Carrboro *(G-1657)*
Tower House Publishing LLC .... G 917 284-0619
  Sanford *(G-14197)*
Two of A Kind Publishing LLC .... G 704 497-2879
  Charlotte *(G-3742)*
University NC At Chapel Hl .... G 919 962-0369
  Chapel Hill *(G-2089)*
▲ University NC Press Inc .... E 919 966-3561
  Chapel Hill *(G-2090)*
Wisdom For Heart .... F 866 482-4253
  Cary *(G-1928)*
Wisdom House Books Inc .... G 919 883-4669
  Chapel Hill *(G-2098)*
Wlc LLC .... G 336 852-6422
  Greensboro *(G-7464)*
Wmxf AM 1400 .... D 828 456-8661
  Waynesville *(G-15834)*
Worden Brothers Inc .... D 919 202-8555
  Wilmington *(G-16456)*
Workman Publishing Co Inc .... G 919 967-0108
  Chapel Hill *(G-2100)*

2732 Book printing

Goslen Printing Company .... F 336 768-5775
  Winston Salem *(G-16725)*
Herff Jones LLC .... G 704 845-3355
  Charlotte *(G-2903)*
Hf Group LLC .... F 336 931-0800
  Greensboro *(G-7088)*
Lsc Communications Inc .... F 704 889-5800
  Pineville *(G-12282)*
New Journey Now .... G 336 234-1534
  Greensboro *(G-7216)*
Rose Reprographics .... G 336 222-0727
  Burlington *(G-1487)*
▲ Tan Books and Publishers Inc .... G 704 731-0651
  Charlotte *(G-3672)*

2741 Miscellaneous publishing

1 Click Web Solutions LLC .... E 910 790-9330
  Wilmington *(G-16086)*
3 Hungry Guys LLC .... G 408 644-3119
  Chapel Hill *(G-1980)*
6ehouseprodxions LLC .... G 704 334-7741
  Charlotte *(G-2111)*
A+ Custom Cut Print Press LLC .... G 910 337-1033
  Roseboro *(G-13782)*
ABC Publication .... G 919 614-3451
  Raleigh *(G-12462)*
Alamo Publishing Services .... G 252 269-1513
  New Bern *(G-11766)*
All American Pumpkin Patch LLC .... G 980 201-9104
  Charlotte *(G-2154)*
All of F-Words .... G 561 232-5824
  Charlotte *(G-2155)*
Alphamed Company Inc .... G 919 680-0011
  Durham *(G-4912)*
Ambcopy LLC .... G 919 308-1033
  Durham *(G-4913)*
Amber Brooks Publishing LLC .... G 704 582-1035
  Raleigh *(G-12497)*
American Image Press .... G 336 468-2796
  Hamptonville *(G-7666)*

27 PRINTING, PUBLISHING AND ALLIED INDUSTRIES

Amethyst Pencil LLC .... G 919 280-9025
   Cary *(G-1680)*

Amko Express Inc .... G 336 434-7192
   Archdale *(G-266)*

Angel Kardees Publishing .... G 336 983-0600
   Tobaccoville *(G-15316)*

Angel Tree Publishing .... G 704 454-7604
   Harrisburg *(G-7702)*

Annaline LLC .... G 828 505-7115
   Asheville *(G-519)*

Apex Publishing LLC .... G 919 886-7153
   Raleigh *(G-12513)*

Appalachian Pubg Group Inc .... G 828 505-3643
   Asheville *(G-522)*

Appalachian State University .... F 828 262-2047
   Boone *(G-1174)*

Aqua Analytica Press Inc .... G 336 263-6612
   Durham *(G-4922)*

Artist Studio Project Pubg LLC .... G 919 233-3873
   Raleigh *(G-12525)*

Ascend Essences LLC .... G 828 575-2502
   Asheville *(G-529)*

Ashville Postage Express .... G 828 255-9250
   Asheville *(G-545)*

Assurance Publications Inc .... G 423 473-3000
   Swannanoa *(G-15018)*

Athenian Press and Workshops .... G 919 961-5071
   Wilmington *(G-16119)*

Athens Publishing Company .... G 828 774-5270
   Asheville *(G-549)*

Autosound 2000 Inc .... G 336 227-3434
   Burlington *(G-1373)*

Avian Cetacean Press .... G 910 392-5537
   Wilmington *(G-16126)*

Aviary Publishers Inc .... G 919 331-0003
   Hillsborough *(G-8637)*

Azalea Art Press .... G 510 919-6117
   Southern Pines *(G-14528)*

B-Light Publishing LLC .... G 919 957-8997
   Morrisville *(G-11298)*

Backstreets Publishing .... G 919 968-9466
   Carrboro *(G-1645)*

Bad Cat Press LLC .... G 919 870-4908
   Raleigh *(G-12542)*

Barsina Publishing .... G 336 869-2849
   High Point *(G-8265)*

Bat Publishing .... G 828 754-2216
   Lenoir *(G-9579)*

Be House Publishing LLC .... G 336 529-6143
   Winston Salem *(G-16623)*

Beckett Media LP .... F 800 508-2582
   Durham *(G-4951)*

Belocal Publishing LLC .... G 910 202-1917
   Wilmington *(G-16134)*

Bermlord LLC .... G 704 631-4304
   Charlotte *(G-2301)*

Better Publishing Inc .... G 828 688-9188
   Bakersville *(G-880)*

Beyond Normal Media LLC .... G 980 263-9921
   Charlotte *(G-2306)*

▲ Bhaktivedanta Archives .... G 336 871-3636
   Sandy Ridge *(G-14076)*

Big Butted Woman Music LLC .... G 919 720-3340
   Wendell *(G-15892)*

Big Chair Publishing LLC .... G 336 207-4139
   Summerfield *(G-14976)*

Black Business Universe LLC .... G 215 279-1509
   Louisburg *(G-9980)*

Blair .... G 919 682-0555
   Chapel Hill *(G-1991)*

Blf Press LLC .... G 706 442-1154
   Clayton *(G-3960)*

Blossom Cotton Press LLC .... G 828 407-0467
   Hendersonville *(G-7825)*

Blue Unicorn LLC .... G 704 748-4832
   Charlotte *(G-2322)*

Bold Life Publication .... G 828 692-3230
   Hendersonville *(G-7828)*

Brickstone Publishing .... G 919 522-4052
   Holly Springs *(G-8692)*

Brightfish Press .... G 919 452-5737
   Durham *(G-4979)*

Brown Lady Publishing LLC .... G 980 833-0398
   Charlotte *(G-2358)*

Brushy Mountain Publishing .... G 828 298-6687
   Swannanoa *(G-15021)*

Buddy Book Publishing .... G 704 657-6909
   Mooresville *(G-10892)*

Bull City Press LLC .... G 919 883-5585
   Durham *(G-4987)*

Business Brokerage Press Inc .... G 800 239-5085
   Wilmington *(G-16145)*

C&J Publishing .... G 336 722-8005
   Winston Salem *(G-16643)*

Caky-Q .... G 215 287-9145
   Concord *(G-4221)*

Camp Publications LLC .... G 252 908-3684
   Tarboro *(G-15099)*

Cape Fear Pblications Dist LLC .... G 910 762-3451
   Wilmington *(G-16150)*

Cape Fear Press .... G 910 458-4647
   Carolina Beach *(G-1633)*

Carolina Academic Press LLC .... E 919 489-7486
   Durham *(G-4999)*

Carolina Ad Group .... G 919 628-0549
   Cary *(G-1723)*

Carolina Business and .... G 704 826-7099
   Waxhaw *(G-15749)*

Carson Dellosa Publishing Co .... G 336 294-8176
   Jamestown *(G-9048)*

Carson-Dellosa Publishing LLC .... E 336 632-0084
   Greensboro *(G-6894)*

Carypress Publishing .... G 919 346-4907
   Raleigh *(G-12607)*

Catawampus Press LLC .... G 201 572-3990
   Durham *(G-5009)*

CCM Press LLC .... G 704 825-9995
   Charlotte *(G-2432)*

Cedar Hill Studio & Gallery .... G 828 456-6344
   Waynesville *(G-15797)*

Celestial Publishing .... G 704 701-2027
   Concord *(G-4229)*

CFS Press Slim Ray .... G 828 505-1030
   Asheville *(G-587)*

Ch Publishing .... G 336 886-1984
   High Point *(G-8293)*

Chained Dragon LLC .... G 919 243-0974
   Clayton *(G-3966)*

Chaotic Terrain Press .... G 828 575-7300
   Asheville *(G-588)*

Charlotte Observer Pubg Co .... E 704 358-6020
   Matthews *(G-10241)*

Cherokee Publications Inc .... G 828 627-2424
   Clyde *(G-4121)*

Cherryrich Publishing LLC .... G 336 587-0805
   Greensboro *(G-6907)*

Chief Corporation .... F 704 916-4521
   Charlotte *(G-2477)*

China Free Press Inc .... G 919 308-9826
   Durham *(G-5017)*

Chiron Publications LLC .... G 828 285-0838
   Asheville *(G-591)*

Chronicle-Of-Victoriacom .... G 336 258-2022
   Jonesville *(G-9095)*

Church Initiative Inc .... E 919 562-2112
   Wake Forest *(G-15540)*

Ckke Publishing .... G 704 236-5981
   Charlotte *(G-2488)*

Clean Press 4 Less .... G 919 942-4141
   Chapel Hill *(G-2003)*

Clinton Press Inc .... F 336 275-8491
   Greensboro *(G-6917)*

Cog Glbal Media/Consulting LLC .... E 980 239-8042
   Matthews *(G-10244)*

Cold Off Press LLC .... G 984 444-9006
   Raleigh *(G-12633)*

Coman Publishing Co Inc .... F 919 688-0218
   Durham *(G-5026)*

Consolidated Press .... G 704 283-0776
   Monroe *(G-10694)*

Countync News LLC .... G 919 650-2767
   Cary *(G-1738)*

Crawlspace Press LLC .... G 919 645-7075
   Raleigh *(G-12652)*

Creative Documents .... G 704 674-5230
   Bessemer City *(G-1058)*

Crest Publications .... G 704 277-7194
   Charlotte *(G-2569)*

Crossroad Press .... G 252 340-3952
   Hertford *(G-7917)*

Daniels House Publications .... G 919 328-0709
   Durham *(G-5045)*

Datanyze LLC .... E 866 408-1633
   Durham *(G-5049)*

Davis Publishing Group In .... G 919 894-4170
   Benson *(G-1034)*

Deep River Press Inc .... G 910 249-9552
   Morehead City *(G-11167)*

Deverger Systems Inc .... G 828 253-2255
   Asheville *(G-608)*

Dex One Corporation .... A 919 297-1600
   Cary *(G-1751)*

Digital Log Cabin Press .... G 336 287-7265
   Winston Salem *(G-16679)*

Direct Legal Mail LLC .... G 919 353-9158
   Raleigh *(G-12685)*

Discovery Map .... G 435 901-1027
   Kitty Hawk *(G-9400)*

Discovery Map .... G 910 315-1155
   Pinehurst *(G-12220)*

Divine Connection .... G 252 975-1320
   Washington *(G-15695)*

Dlp Publishing LLC .... G 336 803-2188
   High Point *(G-8328)*

Document Imaging Systems Inc .... G 919 460-9440
   Raleigh *(G-12693)*

Domco Technology LLC .... G 888 834-8541
   Barnardsville *(G-908)*

Dream Doers Publishing LLC .... G 336 413-7101
   Tobaccoville *(G-15317)*

Dreamcatchers Publishing .... G 336 441-2255
   Raleigh *(G-12700)*

Dreamflyer Publications .... G 919 596-1906
   Durham *(G-5064)*

Dsd Press .... G 919 606-9923
   Cullowhee *(G-4631)*

Dskow Publishing LLC .... G 321 506-0004
   Raleigh *(G-12705)*

Dvd Rulers .... G 336 270-9269
   Greensboro *(G-6984)*

Dw Beam Publishing .... G 336 813-2451
   King *(G-9270)*

Dyer Publishing LLC .... G 336 452-2275
   Wilkesboro *(G-16019)*

E and J Publishing LLC .... G 877 882-2138
   Charlotte *(G-2669)*

Employee Codes: A=Over 500 employees, B=251-500
C=101-250, D=51-100, E=20-50, F=10-19, G=1-9

27 PRINTING, PUBLISHING AND ALLIED INDUSTRIES

Eagle Eyes Crrclum Edtrial Svc .... G 910 399-7445
  Wilmington *(G-16209)*
Eastonsweb Multimedia .... G 704 607-0941
  Charlotte *(G-2675)*
Edit Plus .... G 336 775-2764
  Clemmons *(G-4037)*
Edward & Lamar Publishing .... G 919 433-6625
  Durham *(G-5077)*
Eighty Orchard Publishing Inc .... G 980 689-5406
  Huntersville *(G-8814)*
Elizabeth S Java Express .... G 919 777-5282
  Sanford *(G-14115)*
Escapist .... G 919 806-4448
  Durham *(G-5093)*
Eventide Solutions LLC .... G 828 855-0448
  Hickory *(G-8018)*
Extra-Dimensional Pubg LLC .... G 704 574-4652
  Mc Adenville *(G-10378)*
Factor Inc .... G 919 358-0004
  Durham *(G-5095)*
Fastrack Publishing Co Inc .... G 828 294-0544
  Hickory *(G-8022)*
Find Your Voice LLC .... G 301 922-0978
  Mint Hill *(G-10532)*
Finley Enterprises LLC .... G 910 747-6679
  Durham *(G-5096)*
Firehouse Publications .... G 609 298-3742
  Raleigh *(G-12768)*
Fit1media LLC .... G 919 925-2200
  Raleigh *(G-12770)*
Foothold Publications Inc .... G 770 891-3423
  Raleigh *(G-12778)*
Francis Simply Publishing Co .... G 910 399-2508
  Wilmington *(G-16221)*
Frank Peterson .... G 910 892-6496
  Dunn *(G-4868)*
Franklin / Kerr Press LLC .... G 828 216-3021
  Concord *(G-4267)*
Free Will Bptst Press Fndtion .... F 252 746-6128
  Ayden *(G-852)*
Ft Media Holdings LLC .... F 336 605-0121
  Greensboro *(G-7024)*
Funny Girl Press .... G 919 247-8861
  Raleigh *(G-12787)*
Future Energy Svc Publishing .... G 336 298-8036
  Summerfield *(G-14984)*
Fyi Press Inc .... G 336 254-3452
  Greensboro *(G-7026)*
Galde Press Inc .... G 612 965-5515
  Hendersonville *(G-7854)*
Gathering Place Pubg Co LLC .... G 919 742-5850
  Siler City *(G-14413)*
Gem Publishing LLC .... G 828 885-5272
  Balsam Grove *(G-891)*
Glyphus LLC .... G 336 973-4793
  Purlear *(G-12411)*
Gold Boy Music Publicatio .... G 919 500-3023
  Chapel Hill *(G-2022)*
Gold Leaf Literary Svcs LLC .... G 864 915-0226
  Asheville *(G-636)*
Grace Press LLC .... G 704 277-4007
  Charlotte *(G-2850)*
Grace-Everett Press .... G 828 768-7366
  Arden *(G-336)*
Great-R Good Publishing Inc .... G 919 812-1555
  Cary *(G-1777)*
Green Line Media Inc .... E 828 251-1333
  Asheville *(G-643)*
Grenade Mentality Pubg Co .... G 704 865-7786
  Gastonia *(G-6410)*
Grey House Publishing Inc .... G 704 784-0051
  Concord *(G-4276)*

Gulfstream Publications Inc .... G 252 449-2222
  Kitty Hawk *(G-9406)*
Haines Corporation .... G 704 545-4361
  Matthews *(G-10251)*
Hardwood Publishing Co Inc .... G 704 543-4408
  Charlotte *(G-2888)*
Healey Publishing .... G 919 614-6685
  Cary *(G-1781)*
Health Educator Publications .... G 919 243-1299
  Clayton *(G-3987)*
Health Wyze Media .... G 336 528-4120
  Mocksville *(G-10579)*
Hearsay Guides LLC .... G 336 584-1440
  Elon *(G-5659)*
Heartland Publications .... G 910 592-8137
  Clinton *(G-4096)*
Heat Press Unlimited LLC .... G 910 273-6831
  Fayetteville *(G-5834)*
Heaven & Earth Works .... G 845 797-0902
  Brevard *(G-1275)*
Hello PHD LLC .... G 919 414-3215
  Hillsborough *(G-8652)*
Herff Jones Inc .... G 704 845-3355
  Charlotte *(G-2903)*
Hermit Feathers Press LLC .... G 336 404-8229
  Clemmons *(G-4045)*
Hidden Path Publication Inc .... G 704 878-6986
  Statesville *(G-14815)*
Hiddenite Conference Ctr LLC .... F 828 352-9200
  Hiddenite *(G-8218)*
High Falls Publishing .... G 904 234-0015
  Arden *(G-338)*
Hill-Publications LLC .... G 704 399-7002
  Charlotte *(G-2911)*
His Glory Creations Pubg LLC .... G 919 618-0262
  Wendell *(G-15905)*
HK Publishing Inc .... G 727 459-7724
  Asheville *(G-654)*
Holy Cow Publications LLC .... G 704 900-5779
  Charlotte *(G-2916)*
Hook Publications .... G 219 808-3989
  Bahama *(G-863)*
Hoover Bb Inc .... G 615 872-4510
  Gastonia *(G-6419)*
Hope Tree Publishing LLC .... G 336 858-5301
  High Point *(G-8402)*
Hopewriters LLC .... E 317 414-3342
  Monroe *(G-10732)*
Hunt Kendall Publishing .... G 919 510-0160
  Raleigh *(G-12868)*
Imprint Publishing LLC .... G 678 650-1140
  Charlotte *(G-2955)*
In Your Business Inc .... G 704 443-1330
  Waxhaw *(G-15761)*
Indie Publishing .... G 919 435-6215
  Raleigh *(G-12881)*
Indie Services .... G 336 524-6966
  Burlington *(G-1435)*
Information Age Publishing Inc .... G 704 752-9125
  Charlotte *(G-2972)*
Innerer Klang Letter Press .... G 828 253-3711
  Black Mountain *(G-1126)*
▲ Intereco USA Belt Filter Press .... G 919 349-6041
  Raleigh *(G-12898)*
International Minute Press .... G 336 854-1589
  Greensboro *(G-7119)*
International Minute Press .... G 910 725-1148
  Southern Pines *(G-14537)*
Investorcookbookscom .... G 919 280-8600
  Cary *(G-1793)*
Island Timez .... G 919 351-0346
  Goldsboro *(G-6627)*

SIC SECTION

Jack M Jarrett .... G 336 772-4108
  Greensboro *(G-7132)*
Jack Stevens Inc .... G 919 363-8589
  Apex *(G-208)*
Jackie Lewis Photography Aka .... G 910 640-1550
  Whiteville *(G-15968)*
Jacody Publishing .... G 336 438-1579
  Elon *(G-5660)*
Jarrett Press Publications .... G 919 862-0551
  Raleigh *(G-12914)*
Joken Publications .... G 704 957-7030
  Charlotte *(G-3033)*
Jonathan Holt LLC .... G 919 391-7062
  Chapel Hill *(G-2027)*
Jonnie Chardonn .... G 910 471-0418
  Wilmington *(G-16283)*
Journalistic Inc .... E 919 945-0700
  Chapel Hill *(G-2028)*
Julia Lipscomb .... G 919 528-1800
  Creedmoor *(G-4617)*
Keowee Publishing Co Inc .... G 828 877-4742
  Pisgah Forest *(G-12325)*
Keytune Mus Pubg Wrld Wide LLC .... G 910 286-7868
  Fayetteville *(G-5854)*
Kildaire Regency Publishing .... G 919 469-5851
  Cary *(G-1802)*
▲ Kindermusik International Inc .... E 800 628-5687
  Greensboro *(G-7151)*
Klazzy Magazine Inc .... G 704 293-8321
  Charlotte *(G-3057)*
Koi Fish Publishing House LLC .... G 704 540-8805
  Charlotte *(G-3059)*
Konptec Publishing LLC .... G 704 873-4262
  Statesville *(G-14832)*
Land and Loft LLC .... G 315 560-7060
  Raleigh *(G-12953)*
▲ Laser Ink Corporation .... E 919 361-5822
  Durham *(G-5186)*
Lawing Advg Mktg & Pubg LLC .... G 704 364-8649
  Charlotte *(G-3074)*
Lea Street Press LLC .... G 336 514-2351
  Blanch *(G-1152)*
Liberty Press .... G 336 996-3667
  Kernersville *(G-9208)*
Life Stories and Beyond .... G 704 579-7161
  Charlotte *(G-3085)*
Life Style Publishing Inc .... G 828 507-2209
  Cashiers *(G-1936)*
Lifestory Publishing LLC .... G 601 594-0018
  Asheville *(G-684)*
Lighthouse Press Inc .... G 919 371-8640
  Cary *(G-1810)*
Lighthouse Press Inc .... G 919 371-8640
  Apex *(G-214)*
Likeable Press LLC .... G 844 882-8340
  Charlotte *(G-3089)*
Lillianonline LLC .... G 919 850-4594
  Raleigh *(G-12972)*
Lin-Ink Publishing LLC .... G 704 485-5823
  Oakboro *(G-12075)*
Lines and Lineage LLC .... G 919 783-7517
  Raleigh *(G-12973)*
Little Leaps Press Inc .... G 404 664-1842
  Asheville *(G-688)*
Lookwhatqmade LLC .... G 980 330-1995
  Charlotte *(G-3103)*
Lovekin & Young PC .... G 828 322-5435
  Hickory *(G-8088)*
Lowman Publications .... G 919 929-7829
  Chapel Hill *(G-2034)*
Lulu Press Inc .... D 919 447-3290
  Durham *(G-5198)*

27 PRINTING, PUBLISHING AND ALLIED INDUSTRIES

M Press Inc .... G 336 292-5005
   Greensboro *(G-7174)*

Mad Rush Media .... G 336 816-3972
   Winston Salem *(G-16796)*

Main Street Rag Publishing Co .... G 704 573-2516
   Mint Hill *(G-10538)*

Mama Neds Subscription Box LLC .... G 954 703-9308
   Franklin *(G-6138)*

Map Shop LLC .... G 704 332-5557
   Charlotte *(G-3123)*

Map Supply Inc .... G 336 731-3230
   Flat Rock *(G-5969)*

Marathon Publications Inc .... G 651 341-4202
   Hendersonville *(G-7877)*

Marching Orders Incorporated .... G 336 497-4251
   Kernersville *(G-9212)*

Markets Global Publishing .... G 828 783-0599
   Spruce Pine *(G-14645)*

Mathisen Ventures Inc .... G 212 986-1025
   Charlotte *(G-3141)*

McBryde Publishing LLC .... G 252 638-8094
   Trent Woods *(G-15330)*

McGill Advsory Pblications Inc .... F 866 727-6100
   Charlotte *(G-3150)*

Media Publishing LLC .... G 919 273-0488
   Goldsboro *(G-6634)*

Medical Missionary Press .... G 828 649-3976
   Marshall *(G-10205)*

Meerkat Press LLC .... G 678 984-5489
   Asheville *(G-698)*

Mel Schlesinger .... G 336 525-6357
   Winston Salem *(G-16805)*

Memere Publishing .... G 704 597-9160
   Charlotte *(G-3163)*

Men With Wings Press .... G 828 989-6124
   Asheville *(G-699)*

Mesurio Inc .... G 919 633-8773
   Chapel Hill *(G-2042)*

Michael Edits .... G 704 737-5220
   Charlotte *(G-3174)*

Middle of Nowhere Music LLC .... G 301 237-7290
   Carrboro *(G-1651)*

Midnight Publishing Group Inc .... G 919 809-4277
   Cary *(G-1824)*

Milton Gorham .... G 919 816-8348
   Cary *(G-1825)*

Mind Flow Pubg & Prod LLC .... G 910 339-0005
   Fayetteville *(G-5875)*

Minor Press .... G 919 628-3044
   Charlotte *(G-3185)*

Mirror Image Publishing LLC .... G 336 643-7638
   Stokesdale *(G-14946)*

Mocha Memoir Press .... G 336 404-7445
   Kernersville *(G-9218)*

Monarch Educational Svcs LLC .... G 910 785-4087
   Clayton *(G-3998)*

Money 4 Lyfe .... G 704 606-8671
   Charlotte *(G-3199)*

Month9 Books LLC .... G 919 645-5786
   Raleigh *(G-13039)*

Moonshine Press .... G 828 371-8519
   Franklin *(G-6139)*

Mountain Intaglio LLC .... G 713 725-7926
   Asheville *(G-708)*

Mra Services Inc .... F 704 933-4300
   Kannapolis *(G-9127)*

▲ Music Matters Inc .... G 336 272-5303
   Greensboro *(G-7210)*

Musicland Express .... G 828 627-9431
   Clyde *(G-4127)*

My Alabaster Box LLC .... G 919 873-1442
   Raleigh *(G-13051)*

N2 Company .... F 910 202-0917
   Wilmington *(G-16330)*

N2 Everything LLC .... G 704 232-1407
   Rockwell *(G-13656)*

N2 Publishing .... G 336 293-3845
   Advance *(G-47)*

N2 Publishing .... G 828 337-9380
   Cary *(G-1829)*

N2 Publishing .... G 910 363-6919
   Castle Hayne *(G-1956)*

N2 Publishing .... G 704 492-7206
   Charlotte *(G-3225)*

N2 Publishing .... G 704 497-7087
   Charlotte *(G-3226)*

N2 Publishing .... G 919 795-6347
   Durham *(G-5234)*

N2 Publishing .... G 919 280-9566
   Durham *(G-5235)*

N2 Publishing .... G 410 370-5530
   Mount Holly *(G-11644)*

Nane Publishing LLC .... G 704 477-3462
   Shelby *(G-14351)*

▲ News and Observer Pubg Co .... A 919 829-4500
   Raleigh *(G-13063)*

News From An Angel .... G 336 456-5429
   Greensboro *(G-7218)*

Norsan Media LLC .... E 704 494-7181
   Charlotte *(G-3268)*

Novasearch Cons & Pubg LLC .... G 828 788-2332
   Bryson City *(G-1324)*

Olive Press LLC .... G 910 622-6718
   Sunset Beach *(G-15002)*

One On One Press LLC .... G 910 228-8821
   Wilmington *(G-16344)*

One Valley Studios LLC .... G 980 938-0465
   Charlotte *(G-3299)*

Online Memorial Services LLC .... G 914 471-6852
   Durham *(G-5258)*

Opportunity Knocks Twice Inc .... E 919 672-5374
   Durham *(G-5259)*

Oslo Press Inc .... G 919 606-2028
   Raleigh *(G-13092)*

Otter Publications .... G 336 643-5387
   Oak Ridge *(G-12063)*

Outdoor Paths LLC .... G 828 669-1526
   Black Mountain *(G-1132)*

Outer Banks Internet Inc .... G 252 441-6698
   Kill Devil Hills *(G-9259)*

Over Rainbow Publishing .... G 704 360-4075
   Mooresville *(G-11045)*

Oxford University Press LLC .... B 919 677-0977
   Cary *(G-1840)*

Paintbox Press LLC .... G 919 969-7512
   Chapel Hill *(G-2051)*

Paperwhites Press .... G 855 348-9848
   Apex *(G-225)*

Parchment Press .... G 931 347-2393
   Hiddenite *(G-8226)*

Parker Editing LLC .... G 919 544-8557
   Durham *(G-5271)*

Patricia Schaefer .... G 919 302-2726
   Apex *(G-227)*

Paws and Claws Publishing LLC .... G 336 541-3997
   High Point *(G-8478)*

Pdf and Associates .... G 252 332-7749
   Colerain *(G-4139)*

Peaberry Press LLC .... G 828 773-1489
   Asheville *(G-725)*

Peace of Mind Publications .... G 919 308-5137
   Durham *(G-5278)*

Pet Love Publishing LLC .... G 252 489-3832
   Kill Devil Hills *(G-9261)*

Phoenix Rising Press LLC .... G 480 284-1250
   Asheville *(G-728)*

Piedmont Publishing .... F 336 727-4099
   Winston Salem *(G-16855)*

Pilot Press LLC .... G 910 692-8366
   Southern Pines *(G-14547)*

Pine Tree Poetry .... G 336 584-0631
   Burlington *(G-1474)*

Pinecone Publishing LLC .... G 252 649-0973
   New Bern *(G-11837)*

Pirate Press LLC .... G 919 720-2736
   Apex *(G-231)*

Pisgah It Company LLC .... G 828 884-5290
   Brevard *(G-1285)*

Polished Pen .... G 704 451-4077
   Mooresville *(G-11054)*

Postal Express Plus .... G 336 626-0162
   Asheboro *(G-465)*

Precocious Pen LLC .... G 706 338-0010
   Charlotte *(G-3372)*

Press .... G 336 516-6074
   Burlington *(G-1478)*

Press 53 LLC .... G 336 414-5599
   Winston Salem *(G-16865)*

Press Air LLC .... G 240 313-6832
   Greenville *(G-7576)*

Press Coffee+crepes .... G 336 263-1180
   Graham *(G-6708)*

Press Flex LLC .... G 919 636-4551
   Carrboro *(G-1653)*

Press Ganey Associates Inc .... E 800 232-8032
   Charlotte *(G-3374)*

Press Play Counseling Pllc .... G 336 223-4234
   Greensboro *(G-7279)*

Prime Credit LLC .... G 704 729-7000
   Mooresville *(G-11060)*

Princeton Information .... G 980 224-7114
   Charlotte *(G-3382)*

Printworks Inc .... G 919 649-1547
   Raleigh *(G-13144)*

Production Media Inc .... F 919 325-0120
   Raleigh *(G-13149)*

Prospective Communications LLC .... G 336 287-5535
   Winston Salem *(G-16875)*

Prs Dunn LLC .... G 828 736-4907
   Asheville *(G-747)*

Prs Group LLC .... G 910 550-0088
   Sanford *(G-14172)*

Psalm 32 Publishing LLC .... G 704 799-7637
   Mooresville *(G-11065)*

Publishing Group Inc .... G 704 847-7150
   Matthews *(G-10283)*

Publishing Your Story LLC .... G 704 543-6555
   Charlotte *(G-3396)*

Qde Press .... G 256 390-4668
   Goldsboro *(G-6648)*

Quality Information Publs Inc .... G 919 593-4715
   Leicester *(G-9518)*

Quillsedge Press Inc .... G 410 207-0841
   Apex *(G-237)*

Quinlan Publishing Company .... G 229 886-7995
   Wilmington *(G-16374)*

Quinn Publishing Company .... G 828 668-4622
   Asheville *(G-749)*

R Rabbit Inc .... G 910 297-6764
   Wilmington *(G-16375)*

RA Fountain LLC .... G 252 749-3228
   Fountain *(G-6096)*

Rabbit Press LLC .... G 919 703-8206
   Raleigh *(G-13168)*

Rancho Park Publishing Inc .... G 919 942-9493
   Pittsboro *(G-12346)*

27 PRINTING, PUBLISHING AND ALLIED INDUSTRIES

Raven Sinclaire LLC.................................... G..... 828 423-3819
   Asheville *(G-752)*
Ray Publishing.. G..... 336 407-4843
   Winston Salem *(G-16880)*
RC Boldt Publishing LLC............................ G..... 904 624-0033
   Southport *(G-14578)*
RC Boldt Publishing LLC............................ G..... 904 624-0033
   Oak Island *(G-12054)*
Readers Publishing LLC............................. G..... 910 728-2911
   Parkton *(G-12171)*
Red Adept Publishing LLC......................... G..... 919 798-7410
   Garner *(G-6308)*
Red Dog Publications Inc........................... G..... 919 782-4422
   Raleigh *(G-13195)*
Redhawk Publishing.................................... G..... 919 274-6477
   Raleigh *(G-13201)*
Redrum Press... G..... 910 399-1334
   Wilmington *(G-16379)*
Redrum Press... G..... 866 374-7881
   Wilmington *(G-16380)*
Rehab Solutions Inc................................... G..... 800 273-3418
   Matthews *(G-10285)*
Reid For Read Publishing LLC................... G..... 910 263-8090
   Fayetteville *(G-5905)*
Rent Path Inc.. G..... 919 567-8166
   Fuquay Varina *(G-6224)*
Research Triangle Software Inc................. G..... 919 233-8796
   Cary *(G-1869)*
Research Trngle Edtrial Sltons.................... G..... 919 808-2719
   Durham *(G-5328)*
Rhd Service LLC.. E..... 919 297-1600
   Cary *(G-1870)*
Richard Schwartz....................................... G..... 914 358-4518
   Wilmington *(G-16382)*
Richard Wilcox.. G..... 919 218-5907
   Willow Spring *(G-16082)*
Riddle Inc... G..... 919 724-3272
   Raleigh *(G-13208)*
Rikki Tikki Tees.. G..... 828 454-0515
   Waynesville *(G-15818)*
Riptide Publishing LLC.............................. G..... 908 295-4517
   Burnsville *(G-1532)*
Riteway Express Inc of NC........................ G..... 828 966-4822
   Brevard *(G-1287)*
▲ Roadrnner Mtrcycle Turing Trvl............ G..... 336 765-7780
   Clemmons *(G-4059)*
Roaring Lion Publishing............................ G..... 828 350-1454
   Asheville *(G-757)*
Robar Rpp LLC... G..... 860 480-6498
   Chapel Hill *(G-2064)*
Rod Jahner.. G..... 919 435-7580
   Sunset Beach *(G-15003)*
Rogers Express Lube LLC........................ G..... 828 648-7772
   Canton *(G-1625)*
Ron Clearfield... G..... 828 683-4425
   Leicester *(G-9519)*
Roosterfish Media LLC............................. G..... 980 722-7454
   Mooresville *(G-11072)*
Rose Publishing.. G..... 828 669-1629
   Black Mountain *(G-1137)*
Rowlett Publishing LLC............................ G..... 828 285-2351
   Asheville *(G-759)*
Royalkind LLC.. G..... 252 355-7484
   Winterville *(G-17012)*
Rpj Honeycutt MBL Detail Press.............. G..... 704 640-5987
   China Grove *(G-3889)*
S & A Cherokee LLC............................... E..... 919 674-6020
   Cary *(G-1876)*
S and D Publishing Corporation.............. G..... 301 642-6425
   Burlington *(G-1490)*
▲ Saint Benedict Press LLC.................... E..... 704 731-0651
   Charlotte *(G-3482)*

Savage Pros LLC...................................... G..... 919 971-3153
   Raleigh *(G-13231)*
Savvy - Discountscom News Ltr............... F..... 252 729-8691
   Smyrna *(G-14490)*
Savvy Parrot Partners............................... G..... 919 417-8865
   Raleigh *(G-13234)*
School Directorease LLC......................... G..... 240 206-6273
   Charlotte *(G-3505)*
SCM Publishing LLC................................ G..... 252 456-2132
   Manson *(G-10125)*
Scott Foresman Publishers...................... G..... 252 946-7488
   Chocowinity *(G-3897)*
Seamare Press LLC................................. G..... 919 846-3540
   Raleigh *(G-13241)*
Seas Publications..................................... G..... 919 266-0035
   Raleigh *(G-13242)*
Security Self Storage................................ G..... 919 544-3969
   Durham *(G-5348)*
Seldon Cele... G..... 910 274-8070
   Oak Island *(G-12055)*
Seven Thunders Publishing Inc............... G..... 828 236-0221
   Leicester *(G-9520)*
Share Adventures Pubg Inc..................... G..... 919 973-1299
   Raleigh *(G-13246)*
Sharkflight Publishing LLC...................... G..... 919 744-5997
   Durham *(G-5351)*
Sillaman & Sons Inc................................. G..... 919 774-6324
   Sanford *(G-14184)*
▲ Silver Ink Publishing Inc..................... G..... 704 473-0192
   Shelby *(G-14367)*
Skc1 LLC... G..... 937 620-5187
   Cornelius *(G-4586)*
Sml Raleigh LLC...................................... G..... 919 585-0100
   Clayton *(G-4010)*
Sola Publishing....................................... F..... 336 226-8240
   Graham *(G-6710)*
Soulshine Publishing Co LLC................. G..... 336 688-4612
   Asheboro *(G-481)*
Spider Press Inc..................................... G..... 919 302-2726
   Apex *(G-243)*
Spring Creek Press................................. G..... 828 337-8296
   Hendersonville *(G-7904)*
Springlight Creative LLC......................... G..... 336 383-8076
   Greensboro *(G-7361)*
Spunky Sports LLC................................. G..... 919 435-0198
   Wake Forest *(G-15597)*
SRI Ventures Inc..................................... G..... 919 427-1681
   Sanford *(G-14190)*
Stackhouse Publishing Inc..................... G..... 203 699-6571
   Boone *(G-1239)*
Stan Bunn 1856 Pubg Co LLC............... G..... 980 613-0633
   Charlotte *(G-3620)*
Starfangled Press................................... G..... 804 338-9972
   Brevard *(G-1290)*
Stegall Petroleum Inc............................. G..... 704 283-5058
   Monroe *(G-10815)*
Stephen J McCusker.............................. G..... 336 884-1916
   High Point *(G-8551)*
Sterling Publications LLC....................... G..... 919 656-5042
   Raleigh *(G-13302)*
Stork News Tm of America..................... F..... 910 868-3065
   Fayetteville *(G-5923)*
Strawbridge Studios Inc......................... D..... 919 286-9512
   Durham *(G-5377)*
Stuart Dischell.. G..... 336 334-4695
   Greensboro *(G-7376)*
Studio Griffin LLC................................... G..... 919 661-9634
   Garner *(G-6316)*
Sun Publishing Company........................ F..... 919 942-5282
   Chapel Hill *(G-2075)*
Sunjune Ltrary Cllborative LLC.............. G..... 502 767-2867
   Asheville *(G-790)*

Sweet Sssfrass Publications Inc............. G..... 704 340-3862
   Charlotte *(G-3659)*
Swiner Publishing Company Inc............. G..... 919 599-3441
   Durham *(G-5382)*
Tarheel Publishing Co............................ F..... 919 553-9042
   Clayton *(G-4016)*
Teabar Publishing Inc............................ G..... 252 764-2453
   Emerald Isle *(G-5672)*
Tenpenny Press...................................... G..... 828 423-0799
   Asheville *(G-796)*
Thatcher Forest Publishing.................... G..... 919 402-9245
   Durham *(G-5397)*
Thinking Maps Inc.................................. G..... 919 678-8778
   Cary *(G-1908)*
Three Fifty Six Inc.................................. G..... 336 631-5356
   Winston Salem *(G-16942)*
Timberlake Ventures Inc........................ G..... 704 896-7499
   Wilmington *(G-16429)*
Tokyos Express...................................... G..... 910 735-0412
   Lumberton *(G-10059)*
Tom Hedrick Express............................. G..... 336 798-1293
   Lexington *(G-9796)*
Tommar Publishing Inc.......................... G..... 336 463-2690
   Yadkinville *(G-17056)*
Toplink Publishing................................. G..... 888 375-9818
   Kelly *(G-9139)*
Training Grund Pblications LLC............ G..... 252 568-3922
   Pink Hill *(G-12317)*
Training Industry Inc............................. D..... 919 653-4990
   Raleigh *(G-13356)*
Triad Hosting Inc................................... G..... 336 497-1932
   Summerfield *(G-14992)*
Triad-Fit... G..... 336 409-3818
   Winston Salem *(G-16950)*
Triangle Pointer Inc............................... G..... 919 968-4801
   Chapel Hill *(G-2083)*
Triangle Regulatory Pubg LLC............. G..... 919 886-4587
   Raleigh *(G-13362)*
TS Krupa LLC....................................... G..... 336 782-1515
   Winston Salem *(G-16955)*
Tudg Multimedia Firm........................... G..... 704 916-9819
   Huntersville *(G-8904)*
Turnberry Press.................................... G..... 860 670-4892
   Southern Pines *(G-14559)*
Turtle Dove Publications...................... G..... 828 337-4057
   Black Mountain *(G-1140)*
Twin Attic Publishing Hse Inc.............. G..... 919 426-0322
   Wake Forest *(G-15607)*
Two24 Digital LLC............................... G..... 910 475-7555
   Wilmington *(G-16437)*
Uai Technology Inc.............................. G..... 919 541-9339
   Durham *(G-5418)*
Under Covers Publishing..................... G..... 704 965-8744
   Wilson *(G-16553)*
Under One Crown Publishing LLC...... G..... 919 812-4930
   Raleigh *(G-13380)*
United House Publishing..................... G..... 248 605-3787
   Concord *(G-4383)*
United Writers Press........................... G..... 828 505-1037
   Asheville *(G-809)*
University Directories LLC.................. D..... 800 743-5556
   Durham *(G-5424)*
Unmdeni Press LLC............................ G..... 209 598-1581
   Waxhaw *(G-15786)*
Unruly Mutt Publishing LLC............... G..... 828 478-9097
   Sherrills Ford *(G-14390)*
Uptown Publishing Inc....................... G..... 704 543-0690
   Charlotte *(G-3758)*
Vasiliy Yavdoshnyak........................... G..... 919 995-9469
   Wake Forest *(G-15609)*
Venture Publishing............................. G..... 910 670-0552
   Fayetteville *(G-5948)*

27 PRINTING, PUBLISHING AND ALLIED INDUSTRIES

Verity Yacht Publications .... G 760 803-2550
 Fuquay Varina *(G-6235)*

Viaticus Inc .... G 252 258-4679
 Winterville *(G-17017)*

Vicinitus LLC .... G 828 476-6055
 Waynesville *(G-15831)*

Video Optimize LLC .... G 818 421-1489
 Castle Hayne *(G-1960)*

Violet Studio Games LLC .... G 919 785-1989
 Raleigh *(G-13402)*

Vista Tranquila Publishers LLC .... G 828 586-8401
 Sylva *(G-15073)*

Vm Publishing .... G 704 547-4322
 Mooresville *(G-11121)*

Wake Cross Roads Express LLC .... G 919 266-7966
 Raleigh *(G-13411)*

Warming Sun Music Publishing .... G 714 390-8010
 Pittsboro *(G-12354)*

◆ Webster Fine Art Limited .... G 919 349-8455
 Morrisville *(G-11465)*

Wedpics .... G 919 699-5676
 Raleigh *(G-13417)*

West Express .... G 704 276-9001
 Vale *(G-15472)*

White Picket Media Inc .... G 773 769-8400
 Cornelius *(G-4594)*

White Wolf Press LLC .... G 828 288-2077
 Rutherfordton *(G-13902)*

Willard Rodney White .... G 252 794-3245
 Windsor *(G-16573)*

Wilmington Scentific Publr LLC .... G 910 228-1974
 Wilmington *(G-16451)*

Wingfield House of Peace .... G 719 251-0618
 Nashville *(G-11756)*

Wood Tone Music Publishing .... G 704 659-1064
 Statesville *(G-14928)*

Woodies Sun Express .... G 704 332-7262
 Charlotte *(G-3819)*

Workcom Inc .... E 310 586-4000
 Cary *(G-1931)*

Writ Press Inc .... G 815 988-7074
 Durham *(G-5449)*

Write Good Stuff LLC .... G 704 522-8242
 Charlotte *(G-3830)*

Write Way Publishing Co LLC .... G 919 606-2681
 Clayton *(G-4022)*

Writing Penn LLC .... G 301 529-5324
 Durham *(G-5450)*

Wunderkind Press LLC .... G 919 381-0713
 Durham *(G-5452)*

Xarm Publishing Inc .... G 888 717-3591
 Charlotte *(G-3832)*

Yackety Yack Publishing Inc .... G 919 843-5092
 Chapel Hill *(G-2103)*

Yeeka LLC .... G 919 308-9826
 Durham *(G-5457)*

Yp Advrtising Pubg LLC Not LLC .... C 704 522-5500
 Charlotte *(G-3847)*

Yp Advrtising Pubg LLC Not LLC .... C 910 794-5151
 Wilmington *(G-16459)*

2752 Commercial printing, lithographic

3 Kids Screen Printing .... G 910 212-0672
 Evergreen *(G-5696)*

3 Star Enterprises LLC .... E 704 821-7503
 Indian Trail *(G-8917)*

3d Print Lodge LLC .... G 804 309-6028
 Roanoke Rapids *(G-13564)*

3d Upfitters LLC .... G 336 355-8673
 Greensboro *(G-6766)*

4 Over LLC .... F 919 875-3187
 Raleigh *(G-12447)*

828 Custom Printing LLC .... G 828 586-1828
 Sylva *(G-15051)*

A & B Screen Prtg & EMB LLC .... G 252 245-0573
 Wilson *(G-16462)*

A & M Paper and Printing .... G 919 813-7852
 Durham *(G-4895)*

A Better Image Printing Inc .... F 919 967-0319
 Durham *(G-4896)*

A Forbes Company .... F
 Lenoir *(G-9566)*

A Plus Graphics Inc .... G 252 243-0404
 Wilson *(G-16463)*

A-I Vnyl Grphics Prtg Slutions .... G 910 436-4880
 Spring Lake *(G-14624)*

A&R Printing LLC .... G 336 971-7677
 Clemmons *(G-4024)*

Able Graphics Company LLC .... G 336 753-1812
 Mocksville *(G-10551)*

Abolder Image .... G 336 856-1300
 Greensboro *(G-6774)*

Accelerated Press Inc .... G 248 524-1850
 Wilmington *(G-16092)*

ACe Cstm Kicks N Prints LLC .... G 336 457-9059
 Greensboro *(G-6777)*

Acme Sample Books Inc .... E 336 883-4336
 High Point *(G-8231)*

Acta Print & Marketing LLC .... G 704 773-1493
 Stanfield *(G-14673)*

Ad Spice Marketing LLC .... G 919 286-7110
 Durham *(G-4902)*

Additive Prtg & Robotics Inc .... G 704 375-6788
 Charlotte *(G-2136)*

Adpress Printing Incorporated .... G 336 294-2244
 Summerfield *(G-14975)*

ADS Printing Co Inc .... G 919 834-0579
 Raleigh *(G-12477)*

Advance Printing Solutions .... G 301 919-7868
 Wilmington *(G-16094)*

Advanced Teo Corp .... G 305 278-4474
 Charlotte *(G-2139)*

Advantage Printing Inc .... F 828 252-7667
 Arden *(G-307)*

Advantage Printing & Design .... G 252 523-8133
 Kinston *(G-9341)*

AEC Imaging & Graphics LLC .... G 910 693-1034
 Hope Mills *(G-8730)*

AEL Services LLC .... E 704 525-3710
 Charlotte *(G-2140)*

Aesco Inc .... G 910 763-6612
 Wilmington *(G-16096)*

Alexander Press Inc .... G 336 884-8063
 High Point *(G-8239)*

All In One Printing .... G 919 360-8092
 Raleigh *(G-12489)*

All Occasion Printing .... G 336 926-7766
 Winston Salem *(G-16597)*

All Star Printing .... G 252 689-6464
 Greenville *(G-7478)*

Allegra Marketing Print Mail .... G 828 698-7622
 Hendersonville *(G-7817)*

Allegra Marketing Print Mail .... G 919 373-0531
 Knightdale *(G-9410)*

Alpha and Omega Printing Inc .... G 336 778-1400
 Clemmons *(G-4025)*

Alpha Printing & Mailing .... G 704 751-4930
 Shelby *(G-14284)*

AlphaGraphics .... G 704 887-3430
 Charlotte *(G-2171)*

AlphaGraphics .... G 336 759-8000
 Winston Salem *(G-16601)*

AlphaGraphics Downtown Raleigh .... F 919 832-2828
 Garner *(G-6252)*

AlphaGraphics North Raleigh .... G 919 322-2257
 Raleigh *(G-12493)*

AlphaGraphics Pineville .... F 704 541-3678
 Charlotte *(G-2172)*

America Printer .... G 336 465-0269
 Randleman *(G-13452)*

American Indian Printing Inc .... G 336 230-1551
 Greensboro *(G-6800)*

American Indian Printing Inc .... G 336 884-5442
 High Point *(G-8245)*

American Lgacy Timeline Prints .... G 252 514-0225
 New Bern *(G-11769)*

American Multimedia Inc .... D 336 229-7101
 Burlington *(G-1364)*

American Printers Inc .... G 252 977-7468
 Rocky Mount *(G-13681)*

American Printing Co Inc .... G 336 852-9894
 Greensboro *(G-6801)*

American Printing Services .... G 336 465-0199
 Asheboro *(G-401)*

American Speedy Printing Ctrs .... G 828 322-3981
 Hickory *(G-7934)*

AMP Pros LLC .... G 910 315-1620
 Southern Pines *(G-14526)*

Anav Yofi Inc .... G 828 217-7746
 Charlotte *(G-2193)*

Andrews Graphics LLC .... G 252 633-3199
 New Bern *(G-11771)*

Anitas Marketing Concepts Inc .... G 252 243-3993
 Wilson *(G-16465)*

Anthony Alexander Prints Inc .... G 704 870-7213
 Charlotte *(G-2197)*

Apex Printing Company .... G 919 362-9856
 Apex *(G-161)*

Apidae Prints .... G 413 320-3839
 Durham *(G-4920)*

Appalachian State University .... F 828 262-2047
 Boone *(G-1174)*

Archdale Printing Company Inc .... G 336 884-5312
 High Point *(G-8251)*

Arrowhead Graphics Inc .... G 336 274-2419
 Greensboro *(G-6816)*

Artcraft Press Inc .... F 828 397-8612
 Icard *(G-8916)*

Artech Graphics Inc .... G 704 545-9804
 New London *(G-11866)*

Artesian Future Technology LLC .... F 919 904-4940
 Chapel Hill *(G-1987)*

Arthur Demarest .... G 252 473-1449
 Manteo *(G-10126)*

Arzberger Engravers Inc .... E 704 376-1151
 Charlotte *(G-2224)*

Asheboro Piedmont Printing Inc .... F 336 899-7910
 Asheboro *(G-406)*

Asheville Print Shop .... G 828 214-5286
 Asheville *(G-541)*

Asheville Quickprint .... G 828 252-7667
 Fletcher *(G-5984)*

Associated Printing & Svcs Inc .... F 828 286-9064
 Rutherfordton *(G-13864)*

Atlantis Graphics Inc .... E 919 361-5809
 Durham *(G-4933)*

Austin Printing Company Inc .... G 704 289-1445
 Monroe *(G-10658)*

Auten Reporting .... G 828 230-5035
 Asheville *(G-550)*

Automated Printing Services .... F 252 243-3993
 Wilson *(G-16470)*

Aztech Products Inc .... G 910 763-5599
 Wilmington *(G-16129)*

B F I Industries Inc .... G 919 229-4509
 Wake Forest *(G-15529)*

27 PRINTING, PUBLISHING AND ALLIED INDUSTRIES

SIC SECTION

B P Printing and Copying Inc .... G 704 821-8219
Matthews *(G-10303)*

Babusci Crtive Prtg Imging LLC .... G 704 423-9864
Charlotte *(G-2260)*

Baicy Communications Inc .... G 336 722-7768
Winston Salem *(G-16622)*

Baileys Quick Copy Shop Inc .... F 704 637-2020
Salisbury *(G-13929)*

Bakeshot Prtg & Graphics LLC .... G 704 532-9326
Charlotte *(G-2268)*

Ballantyne One .... G 704 926-7009
Charlotte *(G-2272)*

Barefoot Press Inc .... G 919 283-6396
Raleigh *(G-12545)*

Barretts Printing House Inc .... G 252 243-2820
Wilson *(G-16474)*

Baseline Screen Printing .... G 336 857-0101
Denton *(G-4726)*

Bbf Printing Solutions .... G 336 969-2323
Rural Hall *(G-13833)*

BEC-Car Printing Co Inc .... F 704 873-1911
Statesville *(G-14761)*

Bennett & Associates Inc .... G 919 477-7362
Durham *(G-4955)*

Better Business Printing Inc .... G 704 867-3366
Gastonia *(G-6353)*

Binders of Jhc LLC .... G 980 875-9274
Charlotte *(G-2313)*

Blackleys Printing Co .... G 919 553-6813
Clayton *(G-3959)*

Blue Ridge Printing Co Inc .... D 828 254-1000
Asheville *(G-566)*

Blue Ridge Quick Print Inc .... G 828 883-2420
Brevard *(G-1270)*

Boingo Graphics Inc .... E 704 527-4963
Charlotte *(G-2331)*

Boundless Inc .... G 919 622-9051
Four Oaks *(G-6101)*

BP Solutions Group Inc .... E 828 252-4476
Asheville *(G-570)*

Brand Fuel Promotions .... G 704 256-4057
Waxhaw *(G-15746)*

Brandilly of Nc Inc .... F 919 278-7896
Raleigh *(G-12572)*

Brevard Business Ctr .... G 828 883-4363
Brevard *(G-1272)*

Brian Allen Artisan Printer .... G 919 609-8992
Durham *(G-4976)*

Brickfields Incorporated .... G 704 351-1524
Charlotte *(G-2355)*

Brodie-Jones Printing Co Inc .... G 252 438-7992
Louisburg *(G-9981)*

Brown Printing Inc .... G 704 849-9292
Charlotte *(G-2360)*

Budget Printing Co .... G 910 642-7306
Whiteville *(G-15960)*

Bull Cy Arts Collaborative LLC .... G 919 949-4847
Durham *(G-4989)*

Burco International Inc .... F 828 252-4481
Asheville *(G-575)*

Burco Promotional Printing Inc .... G 864 546-3443
Asheville *(G-576)*

Burrow Family Corporation .... D 336 887-3173
High Point *(G-8279)*

C B C Printing .... G 828 497-5510
Cherokee *(G-3853)*

C D J & P Inc .... G 252 446-3611
Rocky Mount *(G-13686)*

Call Printing & Copying .... G 704 821-6554
Indian Trail *(G-8925)*

Canvas Giclee Printing .... G 910 458-4229
Carolina Beach *(G-1632)*

Carden Printing Company .... G 336 364-2923
Timberlake *(G-15313)*

Cardinal Graphics Inc .... G 704 545-4144
Mint Hill *(G-10526)*

Carolina Copy Services Inc .... F 704 375-9099
Cornelius *(G-4533)*

Carolina Graphic Services LLC .... G 336 668-0871
Greensboro *(G-6885)*

Carolina Newspapers Inc .... G 336 274-7829
Greensboro *(G-6890)*

Carolina Print Mill .... G 919 607-9452
Cary *(G-1725)*

Carolina Printing Associates .... G 704 477-0626
Shelby *(G-14293)*

Carolina Printing Co .... G 919 834-0433
Princeton *(G-12399)*

Carolina Prtg Wilmington Inc .... G 910 762-2453
Supply *(G-15007)*

Carolina Vinyl Printing .... G 910 603-3036
Pinehurst *(G-12218)*

▲ Carolina Warp Prints Inc .... F 704 866-4763
Gastonia *(G-6370)*

Carroll Signs & Advertising .... G 336 983-3415
King *(G-9267)*

Carter Printing .... G 919 373-0531
Knightdale *(G-9415)*

Carter Printing & Graphics Inc .... E 919 266-5280
Knightdale *(G-9416)*

Carter-Hubbard Publishing Co .... G 336 838-4117
North Wilkesboro *(G-12000)*

Cary Printing .... G 919 266-9005
Raleigh *(G-12606)*

Cascadas Nye Corporation .... F 919 834-8128
Raleigh *(G-12610)*

Cashiers Printing Inc .... G 828 787-1324
Highlands *(G-8613)*

◆ Causekeepers Inc .... E 336 824-2518
Franklinville *(G-6167)*

Cavu Printing Inc .... G 336 818-9790
Elkin *(G-5614)*

Celestial Products Inc .... G 540 338-4040
Huntersville *(G-8801)*

Central Carolina Printing LLC .... G 910 572-3344
Asheboro *(G-413)*

Ceprint Solutions Inc .... E 336 956-6327
Lexington *(G-9691)*

Chanmala Gallery Fine Art Prtg .... G 704 975-7695
Wake Forest *(G-15539)*

Charlotte Printing Company Inc .... F 704 888-5181
Concord *(G-4231)*

Charnel Inc .... G 910 763-8476
Wilmington *(G-16169)*

Check Printers Inc .... G 336 724-5980
Winston Salem *(G-16652)*

Choice Printing LLC .... G 919 790-0680
Raleigh *(G-12620)*

City Graphics Inc .... G 704 529-6448
Charlotte *(G-2486)*

City Prints LLC .... G 404 273-5741
Matthews *(G-10242)*

Cjk Custom Printing and D .... G 910 488-1288
Fayetteville *(G-5791)*

Clarks Printing Service Inc .... E 828 254-1432
Asheville *(G-594)*

Cline Printing Inc .... G 704 394-8144
Charlotte *(G-2496)*

Clinton Press Inc .... F 336 275-8491
Greensboro *(G-6917)*

Clondalkin Pharma & Healthcare .... F 336 292-4555
Greensboro *(G-6918)*

Coastal Fish Prints LLC .... G 910 200-7005
Hampstead *(G-7643)*

Coastal Impressions Inc .... G 252 480-1717
Nags Head *(G-11719)*

Coastal Press Inc .... G 252 726-1549
Morehead City *(G-11163)*

Coble Printing Co Inc .... G 919 693-4622
Oxford *(G-12122)*

Coleys Printing .... G 704 785-8837
Concord *(G-4235)*

Commercial Enterprises NC Inc .... G 910 592-8163
Clinton *(G-4091)*

Commercial Printing Company .... E 919 832-2828
Garner *(G-6265)*

Commercial Prtg Co of Clinton .... G 910 592-8163
Clinton *(G-4092)*

◆ Commercial Prtg Lincolnton NC .... G 704 735-6831
Lincolnton *(G-9883)*

Commercial Prtg Solututions .... G 828 764-4137
Morganton *(G-11206)*

Concord Printing Company Inc .... F 704 786-3717
Concord *(G-4240)*

Connected 2k LLC .... G 910 321-7446
Fayetteville *(G-5795)*

▼ Consolidated Press Inc .... G 704 372-6785
Charlotte *(G-2541)*

Cooper Thomas & Benton Prtg Co .... G 336 698-0951
Mc Leansville *(G-10387)*

Copy Cat Instant Prtg Chrltte .... G 704 529-6606
Charlotte *(G-2550)*

Copy Express Charlotte Inc .... G 704 527-1750
Charlotte *(G-2551)*

Copy King Inc .... G 336 333-9900
Greensboro *(G-6936)*

Copy That Business Services .... G 980 297-7088
Charlotte *(G-2552)*

Copy Works .... G 828 698-7622
Hendersonville *(G-7840)*

Copycat Print Shop Inc .... F 910 799-1500
Wilmington *(G-16182)*

Copymasters Printing Svcs Inc .... G 828 324-0532
Hickory *(G-7995)*

Copymatic United Cerebral .... F 252 695-6155
Greenville *(G-7507)*

Cornerstone Custom Printi .... G 919 524-7420
Clayton *(G-3969)*

▲ CPS Resources Inc .... E 704 628-7678
Monroe *(G-10697)*

Craig S Printing LLC .... G 336 786-2327
Dobson *(G-4822)*

CRC Printing Co Inc .... G 704 875-1804
Huntersville *(G-8808)*

Creative Printers Inc .... G 336 246-7746
West Jefferson *(G-15938)*

Creative Printers & Brks Inc .... G 828 321-4663
Andrews *(G-125)*

Creative Printing Stanley Inc .... G 704 732-6398
Lincolnton *(G-9887)*

Creative Prtg Intrnet Svcs LLC .... G 828 265-2800
Boone *(G-1190)*

Crisp Printers Inc .... G 704 867-6663
Gastonia *(G-6388)*

CRS/Las Inc .... E 910 392-0883
Wilmington *(G-16190)*

Currie Motorsports Inc .... G 910 580-1765
Raeford *(G-12418)*

Custom Marking & Printing Inc .... G 704 866-8245
Gastonia *(G-6392)*

Custom Printing Solutions Inc .... F 336 992-1161
Kernersville *(G-9186)*

D & B Printing Co .... G 919 876-3530
Raleigh *(G-12668)*

Dancing Moon Print Sltions Inc .... G 828 689-9353
Mars Hill *(G-10194)*

27 PRINTING, PUBLISHING AND ALLIED INDUSTRIES

Daniels Business Services Inc............ E 828 277-8250
 Asheville *(G-602)*
Darla Ward.. G 252 340-1895
 Elizabeth City *(G-5540)*
Davidson Printing Inc........................... G 336 357-0555
 Lexington *(G-9704)*
Davidson Printing & Machinery........... G 202 558-2055
 Stantonsburg *(G-14711)*
Dbw Print & Promo................................ G 704 906-8551
 Concord *(G-4252)*
Ddi Print.. G 919 829-8810
 Raleigh *(G-12676)*
▲ Decal Source Inc................................. E 336 574-3141
 Mc Leansville *(G-10388)*
Del-Mark Inc... F 828 322-6180
 Hickory *(G-8006)*
Delfortgroup Printing Services............ G 336 272-9344
 Greensboro *(G-6965)*
Deluxe Printing Co Inc.......................... E 828 322-1329
 Hickory *(G-8007)*
Design Printing Inc................................ G 336 472-3333
 Thomasville *(G-15212)*
▼ Dew Group Enterprises Inc.............. E 919 585-0100
 Clayton *(G-3974)*
Dg Printing Solutions............................ G 919 779-0225
 Raleigh *(G-12682)*
Dg Solutions LLC................................... G 864 605-3223
 Arden *(G-324)*
DH Screen Print Plus............................. G 704 609-4823
 Charlotte *(G-2626)*
Digital AP Prtg DBA F4mily Mtt............ G 980 939-8066
 Charlotte *(G-2633)*
Digital Ink Technology Inc.................... G 603 707-7843
 Charlotte *(G-2635)*
Digital Printing....................................... G 336 430-8011
 Colfax *(G-4148)*
Discount Printing Inc............................. G 704 365-3665
 Charlotte *(G-2641)*
Distributech... G 800 742-0141
 Cary *(G-1752)*
Dma Design Print................................... G 336 877-0068
 Lansing *(G-9454)*
Docu Source of NC................................ F 919 459-5900
 Morrisville *(G-11334)*
Dogwood Print....................................... G 919 906-0617
 Wendell *(G-15897)*
Dokja Inc... G 336 852-5190
 Greensboro *(G-6975)*
Dorsett Printing Company.................... G 910 895-3520
 Rockingham *(G-13624)*
Dove Communications Inc................... G 336 855-5491
 Greensboro *(G-6977)*
Down East Screen Printing LLC........... G 252 808-7742
 Beaufort *(G-955)*
Downtown Raleigh................................. G 919 821-7897
 Raleigh *(G-12698)*
Drake Enterprises Ltd........................... G 828 524-7045
 Franklin *(G-6124)*
▼ Dtbtla Inc... E 336 769-0000
 Greensboro *(G-6981)*
Duncan-Parnell Inc................................ G 252 977-7832
 Rocky Mount *(G-13692)*
E C U Univ Prtg & Graphics.................. F 252 737-1301
 Greenville *(G-7520)*
Earth Dog Enterprises LLC................... G 919 876-7768
 Raleigh *(G-12715)*
East Coast Digital Prtg Inc................... G 919 465-3799
 Cary *(G-1754)*
Eastern Offset Printing Co.................... G 252 247-6791
 Atlantic Beach *(G-829)*
Ed Kemp Associates Inc....................... G 336 869-2155
 High Point *(G-8336)*

EDM Technology Inc.............................. E 336 882-8115
 High Point *(G-8337)*
Elledge Family Inc................................. F 919 876-2300
 Raleigh *(G-12731)*
Emerald Printing Inc.............................. G 336 325-3522
 Pinnacle *(G-12320)*
Enterprint Corp...................................... G 919 821-7897
 Raleigh *(G-12740)*
Erleclair Inc.. E 919 233-7710
 Cary *(G-1761)*
Everhart Printinc Co.............................. G 336 764-3978
 Winston Salem *(G-16700)*
Fairway Printing Inc.............................. G 919 779-4797
 Raleigh *(G-12760)*
Fast Pro Media LLC............................... G 704 799-8040
 Cornelius *(G-4545)*
Fast Pro Media LLC............................... G 704 799-8040
 Cornelius *(G-4546)*
▲ Fayetteville Publishing Co................ D 910 323-4848
 Fayetteville *(G-5824)*
Fieldproof Prints LLC............................ G 270 313-8439
 Fayetteville *(G-5825)*
First Due Prints Inc............................... G 704 320-1251
 Indian Trail *(G-8935)*
Flanagan Printing Company Inc........... G 828 693-7380
 Hendersonville *(G-7851)*
Flash Printing Company Inc................. E 704 375-2474
 Charlotte *(G-2769)*
Fletcher Printville................................. G 828 348-5126
 Fletcher *(G-6006)*
Forsyth Printing Company Inc............. G 336 969-0383
 Rural Hall *(G-13840)*
Forward Design & Print Co Inc............. G 704 776-9304
 Monroe *(G-10721)*
Foxfire Printing..................................... G 252 329-8181
 Greenville *(G-7528)*
Free Will Bptst Press Fndtion.............. F 252 746-6128
 Ayden *(G-852)*
Freedom Mailing & Mktg Inc................ G 336 595-6300
 Winston Salem *(G-16718)*
Fully Involved Printing LLC.................. G 980 521-2670
 Concord *(G-4268)*
Future Prints Inc................................... G 704 241-4164
 Charlotte *(G-2801)*
Galaxy Graphics Inc.............................. G 704 724-9057
 Matthews *(G-10249)*
Gaston Printing and Signs LLC............ G 702 267-5633
 Belmont *(G-991)*
Geo-Lin Inc... G 336 884-0648
 Jamestown *(G-9050)*
Get Custom Print................................... G 336 682-3891
 Kernersville *(G-9202)*
Gibraltar Packaging Inc........................ C 910 439-6137
 Mount Gilead *(G-11600)*
Gik Inc... F 919 872-9498
 Raleigh *(G-12800)*
◆ Gilbarco Inc... A 336 547-5000
 Greensboro *(G-7043)*
Gilley Printers Inc................................. G 910 295-6317
 Pinehurst *(G-12223)*
Gilmore Globl Lgstics Svcs Inc............ D 919 277-2700
 Morrisville *(G-11347)*
Ginas Processing & Prtg Ctr................ G 910 476-0037
 Raeford *(G-12422)*
Ginkgo Print Studio LLC....................... G 828 275-6300
 Asheville *(G-635)*
Glover Corporation Inc......................... E 919 821-5535
 Raleigh *(G-12807)*
Goffstar Inc.. G 704 895-3878
 Charlotte *(G-2842)*
◆ Golf Associates Advertising Co....... E 828 252-6544
 Asheville *(G-637)*

Goslen Printing Company..................... F 336 768-5775
 Winston Salem *(G-16725)*
Graphic Finshg Solutions LLC.............. G 336 255-7857
 Greensboro *(G-7058)*
Graphic Impressions Inc...................... E 704 596-4921
 Charlotte *(G-2855)*
Graphic Products Inc............................ G 919 894-3661
 Benson *(G-1035)*
Graphic Rewards Inc............................. G 336 969-2733
 Rural Hall *(G-13842)*
Graphx Printing Inc............................... G 828 475-4970
 Morganton *(G-11216)*
Greensboro News & Record LLC......... A 336 373-7000
 Greensboro *(G-7064)*
Greybeard Printing Inc......................... G 828 252-3082
 Asheville *(G-644)*
Greyberry Printing................................ G 919 649-3187
 Raleigh *(G-12819)*
▲ Griffin Printing Inc............................. G 919 832-6931
 Raleigh *(G-12820)*
Gso Printing... G 336 292-1601
 Greensboro *(G-7069)*
Gso Printing Inc..................................... G 336 288-5778
 Greensboro *(G-7070)*
Haley Promotions Inc............................ G 336 402-7450
 Raleigh *(G-12827)*
Harco Printing Incorporated................ G 336 771-0234
 Winston Salem *(G-16735)*
Harrison Martha Print Studio............... G 949 290-8630
 Claremont *(G-3929)*
Hashtag Screen Printing...................... G 980 429-5447
 Vale *(G-15468)*
Hasty Print Works.................................. G 704 964-6401
 Mooresville *(G-10970)*
Hayes Print-Stamp Co Inc.................... G 336 667-1116
 Wilkesboro *(G-16023)*
Heated Bed Printing LLC...................... G 860 230-6142
 Durham *(G-5133)*
Henco North.. G 828 552-3671
 Asheville *(G-650)*
Herald Printing Inc............................... G 252 726-3534
 Morehead City *(G-11175)*
Herff Jones... G 910 399-2740
 Wilmington *(G-16251)*
Heritage Prtg & Graphics Inc............... G 704 551-0700
 Charlotte *(G-2905)*
Hickory Printing Group Inc H................ F 828 465-3431
 Conover *(G-4463)*
Hickory Printing Solutions LLC........... C 828 465-3431
 Conover *(G-4464)*
High Concepts LLC................................ G 704 377-3467
 Denver *(G-4781)*
Hill Printing Company........................... G 919 833-5934
 Raleigh *(G-12845)*
Hinson Industries Inc............................ G 252 937-7171
 Rocky Mount *(G-13700)*
Hinsons Typing & Printing.................... G 919 934-9036
 Smithfield *(G-14462)*
Hollands Floor Covering LLC............... G 602 703-1951
 New Bern *(G-11809)*
Holy Mountain Printing......................... G 801 634-3462
 Raleigh *(G-12855)*
Hunsucker Printing Co Inc................... G 336 629-9125
 Asheboro *(G-441)*
Huntpack Inc.. G 704 986-0684
 Albemarle *(G-90)*
Ideal Printing... G 336 754-4050
 Walkertown *(G-15614)*
Ideal Printing Services Inc.................. G 336 784-0074
 Kernersville *(G-9205)*
Image 420 Screenprinting Inc............. G 828 253-9420
 Asheville *(G-659)*

Employee Codes: A=Over 500 employees, B=251-500
C=101-250, D=51-100, E=20-50, F=10-19, G=1-9

27 PRINTING, PUBLISHING AND ALLIED INDUSTRIES

Image Solutions .... G 336 769-8403
　Pilot Mountain *(G-12197)*
▲ Image Works Inc .... G 336 668-3338
　Jamestown *(G-9056)*
Imagemark Business Svcs Inc .... G 704 865-4912
　Gastonia *(G-6423)*
Impact Digital Printing Inc .... G 704 609-7638
　Cornelius *(G-4560)*
Impact Printing and Design LLC .... G 919 377-9747
　Fuquay Varina *(G-6203)*
Imperial Printing Pdts Co Inc .... E 704 554-1188
　Lowell *(G-10009)*
Independence Printing .... G 336 771-0234
　Winston Salem *(G-16757)*
Industrial Motions Inc .... G 734 284-8944
　Apex *(G-205)*
▲ Industrial Sign & Graphics Inc .... E 704 371-4985
　Charlotte *(G-2965)*
Infinity S End Inc .... F 704 900-8355
　Charlotte *(G-2968)*
Ingalls Alton .... G 252 975-2056
　Washington *(G-15712)*
Ink City Screen Printing LLC .... G 347 729-5870
　Waxhaw *(G-15762)*
Ink Well .... G 336 727-9750
　Winston Salem *(G-16761)*
Ink Well Inc .... G 919 682-8279
　Durham *(G-5156)*
Ink Well Tatoo .... G 919 682-8279
　Durham *(G-5157)*
Inkwell .... G 919 433-7539
　Fayetteville *(G-5843)*
Inprimo Solutions Inc .... G 919 390-7776
　Raleigh *(G-12891)*
Insta Copy Shop Ltd .... F 704 376-1350
　Charlotte *(G-2977)*
Instant Imprints .... G 704 864-1510
　Gastonia *(G-6429)*
Instant Imprints .... G 919 468-9808
　Morrisville *(G-11360)*
Instant Imprints Greenville .... G 252 364-3254
　Greenville *(G-7543)*
Integrated Print Services Inc .... G 704 307-4495
　Charlotte *(G-2978)*
Interflex Acquisition Co LLC .... C 336 921-3505
　Wilkesboro *(G-16027)*
Interflex Acquisition Co LLC .... C 336 921-3505
　Wilkesboro *(G-16028)*
Interflex Acquisition Co LLC .... C 336 921-3505
　Wilkesboro *(G-16029)*
International Minute Press .... G 919 762-0054
　Fuquay Varina *(G-6205)*
International Minute Press .... G 704 827-7173
　Huntersville *(G-8836)*
International Minute Press .... G 704 246-3758
　Matthews *(G-10255)*
International Minute Press .... G 336 231-3178
　Winston Salem *(G-16764)*
Inventive Graphics Inc .... G 704 814-4900
　Charlotte *(G-2989)*
Itek Graphics LLC .... E 704 357-6002
　Concord *(G-4291)*
Its Your Time Business Center .... G 336 754-4456
　Walkertown *(G-15615)*
J & E Digital Printing Inc .... G 919 803-8913
　Raleigh *(G-12906)*
J R Cole Industries Inc .... F 704 523-6622
　Charlotte *(G-3006)*
Jag Graphics Inc .... G 828 259-9020
　Asheville *(G-668)*
James G Gouge .... G 336 854-1551
　High Point *(G-8415)*

JB II Printing LLC .... E 336 222-0717
　Burlington *(G-1439)*
Jeans Printshop LLC .... G 704 564-4348
　Charlotte *(G-3017)*
JM Graphics Inc .... G 704 375-1147
　Charlotte *(G-3024)*
Jofra Graphics Inc .... G 910 259-1717
　Burgaw *(G-1342)*
Jones Media .... F 828 264-3612
　Boone *(G-1212)*
Jones Printing Company Inc .... F 919 774-9442
　Sanford *(G-14141)*
Joseph C Woodard Prtg Co Inc .... F 919 829-0634
　Raleigh *(G-12922)*
Js Printing LLC .... G 919 773-1103
　Raleigh *(G-12925)*
Kathie S Mc Daniel .... G 336 835-1544
　Elkin *(G-5622)*
Keller Cres U To Be Phrmgraphi .... F 336 851-1150
　Greensboro *(G-7148)*
Kelly Printing LLC .... G 336 760-0505
　Winston Salem *(G-16777)*
Key Printing Inc .... F 252 459-4783
　Nashville *(G-11746)*
Kieffer Starlite Company .... G 800 659-2493
　Mount Airy *(G-11531)*
▲ King International Corporation .... E 336 983-5171
　King *(G-9274)*
Kingdom Prints LLC .... G 828 894-8851
　Columbus *(G-4176)*
Kinston Office Supply Co Inc .... E 252 523-7654
　Kinston *(G-9373)*
Kolb Boyette & Assoc Inc .... E 919 544-7839
　Durham *(G-5182)*
Kreber .... D 336 861-2700
　High Point *(G-8425)*
Kristen Screen Printing & EMB .... G 980 256-4561
　Charlotte *(G-3063)*
Kudzu Printing Company Inc .... G 828 330-4887
　Black Mountain *(G-1128)*
Kwik Kopy Business .... G 704 987-0111
　Huntersville *(G-8846)*
Label & Printing Solutions Inc .... G 919 782-1242
　Raleigh *(G-12950)*
Lad Ways of Printing Inc .... G 252 814-9559
　Fountain *(G-6094)*
Landmark Printing Inc .... G 919 833-5151
　Raleigh *(G-12954)*
Landmark Printing Co Inc .... G 919 833-5151
　Raleigh *(G-12955)*
▲ Laser Ink Corporation .... E 919 361-5822
　Durham *(G-5186)*
Legacy Graphics Inc .... E 919 741-6262
　Garner *(G-6281)*
Lenoir Printing Inc .... G 828 758-7260
　Lenoir *(G-9627)*
Linprint Company .... F 910 763-5103
　Wilmington *(G-16303)*
Litho Priting Inc .... G 919 755-9542
　Raleigh *(G-12975)*
Little Stitches EMB & Prtg LLC .... G 828 352-7550
　Taylorsville *(G-15150)*
Local Print .... G 919 620-9050
　Bahama *(G-864)*
Loftin & Company Inc .... E 704 393-9393
　Charlotte *(G-3100)*
Lynchs Office Supply Co Inc .... F 252 537-6041
　Roanoke Rapids *(G-13578)*
M & S Systems Inc .... G 336 996-7118
　Kernersville *(G-9211)*
M C C of Laurinburg Inc .... G 910 276-0519
　Laurinburg *(G-9486)*

Mail Management Services LLC .... F 828 236-0076
　Asheville *(G-693)*
Markell Publishing Company Inc .... G 336 226-7148
　Burlington *(G-1454)*
Master Marketing Group LLC .... G 870 932-4491
　Raleigh *(G-13004)*
Masters Hand Print Works Inc .... G 828 652-5833
　Marion *(G-10159)*
▲ Maxim Label Packg High Pt Inc .... F 336 861-1666
　High Point *(G-8451)*
Mb-F Inc .... D 336 379-9352
　Greensboro *(G-7192)*
Mc Stitch & Print .... G 336 263-3677
　Graham *(G-6701)*
◆ McGrann Paper Corporation .... E 800 240-9455
　Charlotte *(G-3151)*
Measurement Incorporated .... C 919 683-2413
　Durham *(G-5213)*
Medlit Solutions .... G 919 878-6789
　Garner *(G-6286)*
▲ Medlit Solutions LLC .... D 919 878-6789
　Garner *(G-6287)*
Mellineum Printing .... G 919 267-5752
　Apex *(G-217)*
Meredith - Webb Prtg Co Inc .... D 336 228-8378
　Burlington *(G-1460)*
Metro Productions Inc .... F 919 851-6420
　Raleigh *(G-13022)*
Minges Printing & Advg Co .... G 704 867-6791
　Gastonia *(G-6466)*
Minuteman Press .... G 336 270-4426
　Graham *(G-6704)*
Minuteman Press of Gastonia .... G 704 867-3366
　Gastonia *(G-6467)*
Minuteman Quick Copy Svc Inc .... G 910 455-5353
　Jacksonville *(G-9014)*
Mj Printing .... G 336 992-3828
　Kernersville *(G-9217)*
Mjt Us Inc .... G 704 826-7828
　Charlotte *(G-3189)*
Mlb Screen Printing .... G 704 363-6124
　Huntersville *(G-8856)*
Modern Information Svcs Inc .... G 704 872-1020
　Statesville *(G-14846)*
Monarch Printers .... F 704 376-1533
　Charlotte *(G-3198)*
Monk Lekeisha .... G 910 385-0361
　Goldsboro *(G-6637)*
Monte Enterprises Inc .... G 252 637-5803
　New Bern *(G-11825)*
Moore Printing & Graphics Inc .... E 919 821-3293
　Raleigh *(G-13041)*
Moores Printing .... G 336 856-0540
　Greensboro *(G-7204)*
More Than Billboards Inc .... E 336 723-1018
　Kernersville *(G-9219)*
Morgan Printers Inc .... F 252 355-5588
　Winterville *(G-17008)*
Motorsports Designs Inc .... E 336 454-1181
　High Point *(G-8460)*
Mountaineer Inc .... F 828 452-0661
　Waynesville *(G-15811)*
Mpressive Shirt Works LLC .... G 919 395-8295
　Raleigh *(G-13045)*
Multi Packaging Solutions .... A 336 855-7142
　Greensboro *(G-7207)*
Murphy Printing & Vinyl LLC .... G 828 835-4848
　Murphy *(G-11714)*
N2god Print Center LLC .... G 910 318-4259
　Laurinburg *(G-9491)*
Natel Inc .... G 336 227-1227
　Burlington *(G-1466)*

SIC SECTION
27 PRINTING, PUBLISHING AND ALLIED INDUSTRIES

▲ National Print Services Inc .... G 704 892-9209
Mooresville *(G-11033)*

NC Imprints Inc .... G 336 790-4546
Lexington *(G-9759)*

NC Printing LLC .... G 828 393-4615
Hendersonville *(G-7885)*

Nerdpopprints .... G 910 514-2279
Lillington *(G-9857)*

Nerdy Llama LLC .... G 571 431-8933
Lenoir *(G-9640)*

New Hanover Printing and Pubg .... G 910 520-7173
Wilmington *(G-16336)*

▲ News and Observer Pubg Co .... A 919 829-4500
Raleigh *(G-13063)*

Nine Thirteen LLC .... G 919 876-8070
Raleigh *(G-13064)*

Noble Printers .... G 877 786-6253
Raleigh *(G-13065)*

Norman Lake Graphics Inc .... G 704 896-8444
Huntersville *(G-8861)*

Notepad Enterprises LLC .... G 704 377-3467
Charlotte *(G-3271)*

Nrs Printing & Displays LLC .... G 704 907-2887
Charlotte *(G-3278)*

Observer News Enterprise Inc .... E 828 464-0221
Newton *(G-11954)*

Occasions Group Inc .... G 919 751-2400
Goldsboro *(G-6641)*

Occasions Group Inc .... E 252 321-5805
Greenville *(G-7566)*

Office Sup Svcs Inc Charlotte .... E 704 786-4677
Concord *(G-4323)*

Old Style Printing .... G 828 452-1122
Waynesville *(G-15813)*

Ollis Enterprises Inc .... E 828 265-0004
Wilkesboro *(G-16037)*

Omega Studios Inc .... G 704 889-5800
Pineville *(G-12287)*

On Demand Screen Printing LLC .... G 704 661-0788
Concord *(G-4327)*

One Stop Shipg & Prtg Etc LLC .... G 910 745-9733
Fayetteville *(G-5888)*

Os Press LLC .... G 910 485-7955
Fayetteville *(G-5890)*

Owen G Dunn Co Inc .... G 252 633-3197
New Bern *(G-11832)*

Pamela A Adams .... G 919 876-5949
Raleigh *(G-13096)*

Pamlico Screen Printing Inc .... G 252 944-6001
Washington *(G-15725)*

Pamor Fine Print .... G 919 559-2846
Raleigh *(G-13097)*

PBM Graphics Inc .... C 919 544-6222
Durham *(G-5276)*

PBM Graphics Inc .... C 336 664-5800
Greensboro *(G-7248)*

◆ PBM Graphics Inc .... C 919 544-6222
Durham *(G-5277)*

Perfect Cube LLC .... G 970 481-5745
Raleigh *(G-13108)*

Performance Print Services LLC .... G 919 957-9995
Durham *(G-5280)*

Perlman Inc .... F 704 332-1164
Charlotte *(G-3332)*

Person Printing Company Inc .... E 336 599-2146
Roxboro *(G-13818)*

Pharmaceutic Litho Label Inc .... E 336 785-4000
Winston Salem *(G-16848)*

Pics and Prints LLC .... G 917 753-3542
Harrisburg *(G-7722)*

Piedmont Business Forms Inc .... F 828 464-0010
Newton *(G-11960)*

◆ Piedmont Graphics Inc .... E 336 230-0040
Greensboro *(G-7257)*

Piedmont Triad Printing Inc .... G 336 235-3080
Greensboro *(G-7261)*

Pilgrim Tract Society Inc .... G 336 495-1241
Randleman *(G-13483)*

Pilot LLC .... D 910 692-7271
Southern Pines *(G-14546)*

Pioneer Printing Company Inc .... G 336 789-4011
Mount Airy *(G-11558)*

PIP Printing & Document Servic .... G 336 222-0717
Burlington *(G-1475)*

Platesetterscom .... G 888 380-7483
Greensboro *(G-7267)*

Plum Print Inc .... F 828 633-5535
Asheville *(G-737)*

PMG Acquisition Corp .... D 828 758-7381
Lenoir *(G-9647)*

Polly and Associates LLC .... G 910 319-7564
Wilmington *(G-16359)*

Polyprint Usa Inc .... G 888 389-8618
Charlotte *(G-3354)*

Poole Printing Company Inc .... G 919 876-5260
Raleigh *(G-13120)*

Pope Printing & Design Inc .... G 828 274-5945
Asheville *(G-738)*

Postal Instant Press .... F 336 222-0717
Burlington *(G-1477)*

Powell Ink Inc .... F 828 253-6886
Asheville *(G-739)*

Power Business Products LLC .... G 704 604-2844
Matthews *(G-10281)*

Precision Printing .... G 252 338-2450
Elizabeth City *(G-5564)*

Precision Printing .... G 336 273-5794
Greensboro *(G-7275)*

Preiss Paper & Printing .... G 919 325-3790
Raleigh *(G-13136)*

Pressed Design & Printing Llc .... G 252 314-6036
Rocky Mount *(G-13723)*

Prime Source Opc LLC .... E 336 661-3300
Winston Salem *(G-16866)*

▼ Primo Inc .... G 888 822-5815
Cornelius *(G-4578)*

Print & Pack Sense LLC .... G 336 394-6930
Eden *(G-5500)*

Print 4 ME Inc .... G 336 854-1589
Greensboro *(G-7283)*

Print Advisors LLC .... G 704 385-4315
Huntersville *(G-8882)*

Print Charlotte Inc .... G 704 488-5896
Charlotte *(G-3383)*

Print Doc Pack and .... G 910 454-9104
Southport *(G-14576)*

Print Express Enterprises Inc .... G 336 765-5505
Clemmons *(G-4055)*

Print Express Inc .... F 910 455-4554
Jacksonville *(G-9021)*

Print Express Plus .... G 252 541-4444
Roanoke Rapids *(G-13580)*

Print Haus Inc .... G 828 456-8622
Waynesville *(G-15817)*

Print Magic Transfers Llc .... G 848 250-9906
Charlotte *(G-3384)*

Print Management Group LLC .... F 704 821-0114
Charlotte *(G-3385)*

Print Media Associates Inc .... G 704 529-0555
Charlotte *(G-3386)*

Print Mine Tees .... G 336 972-1245
Winston Salem *(G-16868)*

Print Path .... G 843 615-7882
Hickory *(G-8123)*

Print Path LLC .... G 828 855-9966
Hickory *(G-8124)*

Print Professionals .... G 607 279-3335
Pinehurst *(G-12231)*

Print Shoppe of Rocky Mt Inc .... F 252 442-9912
Rocky Mount *(G-13724)*

Print Social .... G 980 430-4483
Huntersville *(G-8883)*

Print Usa Inc .... G 910 485-2254
Fayetteville *(G-5901)*

Print Works Fayetteville Inc .... G 910 864-8100
Fayetteville *(G-5902)*

Printcrafters Incorporated .... G 704 873-7387
Statesville *(G-14869)*

Printer Solutions Inc .... G 919 592-1077
Raleigh *(G-13142)*

Printery .... F 336 852-9774
Greensboro *(G-7284)*

Printing .... G 770 815-7367
Asheville *(G-742)*

Printing & Packaging Inc .... E 704 482-3866
Shelby *(G-14357)*

Printing Partners Inc .... G 336 996-2268
Kernersville *(G-9225)*

Printing Press .... G 828 299-1234
Asheville *(G-743)*

Printing Pro .... G 704 748-9396
Iron Station *(G-8975)*

Printing Svcs Greensboro Inc .... F 336 274-7663
Greensboro *(G-7285)*

Printlogic Inc .... E 336 626-6680
Asheboro *(G-468)*

Printmarketing LLC .... G 828 261-0063
Hickory *(G-8125)*

Prints On Parade LLC .... G 713 387-9061
Julian *(G-9107)*

Prints Plus .... G 828 389-7190
Hayesville *(G-7770)*

Printsurge Incorporated .... G 919 854-4376
Raleigh *(G-13143)*

Printville .... G 828 225-3777
Asheville *(G-744)*

Priority Prtg Charlotte Inc .... G 802 374-8360
Charlotte *(G-3389)*

Prism Printing & Design Inc .... G 919 706-5977
Cary *(G-1859)*

Private Label Digital Prtg LLC .... G 919 929-6053
Chapel Hill *(G-2057)*

Pro Cal Prof Decals Inc .... F 704 795-6090
Concord *(G-4340)*

Professional Bus Systems Inc .... G 704 333-2444
Charlotte *(G-3391)*

Professional Laminating LLC .... G 919 465-0400
Cary *(G-1861)*

Proforma Print Source .... G 919 383-2070
Durham *(G-5306)*

Proforma Tierney Printing .... G 910 392-2611
Wilmington *(G-16372)*

▲ Promographix Inc .... F 919 846-1379
Carolina Beach *(G-1640)*

Prostar Printing Prom Pro .... G 704 839-0253
Matthews *(G-10341)*

Quad/Graphics Inc .... E 706 648-5456
Charlotte *(G-3399)*

Quailwood Screen Prtg & EMB .... G 704 910-2385
Mint Hill *(G-10543)*

Quality Instant Printing Inc .... F 919 544-1777
Durham *(G-5313)*

Quality Printing Solutions Inc .... G 919 261-9527
Raleigh *(G-13165)*

Quality Prtg Cartridge Fctry .... G 336 852-2505
Greensboro *(G-7301)*

27 PRINTING, PUBLISHING AND ALLIED INDUSTRIES

Quick Color Solutions.................................. G 336 698-0951
  Mc Leansville *(G-10395)*
Quick Color Solutions Inc .... G 336 282-3900
  Chapel Hill *(G-2060)*
Quick Print of Concord .... G 704 782-6634
  Salisbury *(G-14035)*
Quik Print Inc .... G 910 738-6775
  Lumberton *(G-10050)*
R & D Label LLC .... G 336 889-2900
  Jamestown *(G-9068)*
R L Lasater Printing .... G 919 639-6662
  Angier *(G-149)*
R R Donnelley & Sons Company .... G 704 864-5717
  Gastonia *(G-6501)*
R T Barbee Company Inc .... F 704 375-4421
  Charlotte *(G-3406)*
Raleigh .... G 919 306-3208
  Raleigh *(G-13172)*
Raleigh Printing & Typing Inc .... G 919 662-8001
  Raleigh *(G-13181)*
Raleigh Screen Print Inc .... G 919 662-0358
  Aberdeen *(G-24)*
Randall Printing Inc .... G 336 272-3333
  Greensboro *(G-7303)*
Readable Communications Inc .... G 919 876-5260
  Raleigh *(G-13193)*
Red 5 Printing LLC .... G 704 996-3848
  Cornelius *(G-4581)*
Redbird Screen Printing LLC .... G 919 946-0005
  Raleigh *(G-13199)*
Revolution Screen Printing LLC .... G 704 340-4406
  Charlotte *(G-3441)*
Rgf Printing .... G 201 832-5233
  Snow Camp *(G-14497)*
Richa Inc .... G 704 944-0230
  Charlotte *(G-3448)*
Richa Inc .... F 704 331-9744
  Charlotte *(G-3449)*
Rite Instant Printing Inc .... G 336 768-5061
  Winston Salem *(G-16885)*
Riverbank Screen Printing Co .... G 910 248-4647
  Lumberton *(G-10052)*
Roark Printing Inc .... G 704 889-5544
  Pineville *(G-12295)*
Rocco Marie Ventures LLC .... G 704 341-8800
  Pineville *(G-12296)*
Rodney Tyler .... G 336 629-0951
  Asheboro *(G-475)*
Roi Sales Solutions Inc .... G 704 564-9748
  Charlotte *(G-3458)*
Ronald .... G 828 433-1377
  Morganton *(G-11247)*
Rose of City Prints .... G 980 201-9133
  Charlotte *(G-3460)*
Roz Inc .... G 704 737-7940
  Monroe *(G-10799)*
Russell Printing Inc .... G 404 366-0552
  Burlington *(G-1489)*
S Chamblee Incorporated .... E 919 833-7561
  Raleigh *(G-13221)*
S Ruppe Inc .... E 828 287-4936
  Rutherfordton *(G-13889)*
S&A Marketing Inc .... G 704 376-0938
  Charlotte *(G-3478)*
Salem One Inc .... F 336 722-2886
  Kernersville *(G-9231)*
Salem One Inc .... C 336 744-9990
  Winston Salem *(G-16893)*
Scriptorium Pubg Svcs Inc .... G 919 481-2701
  Durham *(G-5346)*
Sdp Impress ME .... G 919 947-1197
  Goldsboro *(G-6655)*

Seaside Press Co Inc .... G 910 458-8156
  Carolina Beach *(G-1641)*
Seaway Printing Company .... G 910 457-6158
  Southport *(G-14579)*
Secure Bag Custom Prints .... G 856 834-9037
  Concord *(G-4357)*
Sennett Security Products LLC .... D 336 375-1134
  Browns Summit *(G-1315)*
Shelby Business Cards .... G 704 481-8341
  Shelby *(G-14363)*
Sign and Print Shop .... G 919 542-0727
  Pittsboro *(G-12349)*
Signature Mailings .... G 919 981-5736
  New Hill *(G-11864)*
Sillaman & Sons Inc .... G 919 774-6324
  Sanford *(G-14184)*
Simple & Sentimental LLC .... G 252 320-9458
  Ayden *(G-857)*
Simple Graphx LLC .... G 828 428-1567
  Maiden *(G-10116)*
Sir Speedy Printing .... G 704 664-1911
  Mooresville *(G-11088)*
Sire Tees .... G 919 787-6843
  Raleigh *(G-13268)*
Sizemore Custom Jewelry Repair .... G 336 633-8979
  Pleasant Garden *(G-12360)*
Sizemore Printing .... G 910 228-8749
  Wilmington *(G-16406)*
Smith & Fox Inc .... G 828 684-4512
  Arden *(G-377)*
Smith Family Screen Printing .... G 336 317-4849
  Pleasant Garden *(G-12361)*
Smith Printing Company LLC .... G 704 575-9235
  Charlotte *(G-3567)*
SOS Printing Inc .... F 828 264-4262
  Boone *(G-1237)*
Southern Printing Company Inc .... G 910 259-4807
  Burgaw *(G-1352)*
Southport Graphics LLC .... G 919 650-3822
  Morrisville *(G-11433)*
Spee Dee Que Instant Prtg Inc .... G 919 683-1307
  Durham *(G-5367)*
SpeeDee Prints LLC .... G 704 366-1405
  Charlotte *(G-3601)*
Speediprint Inc .... F 910 483-2553
  Fayetteville *(G-5921)*
Stanfast .... G 336 841-7700
  High Point *(G-8549)*
Stein-Palmer Printing Co .... G 740 633-3894
  Mooresville *(G-11101)*
Stewart Screen Printing Inc .... G 336 451-9636
  High Point *(G-8553)*
Succession Solutions Inc .... F 704 631-9004
  Pineville *(G-12311)*
Sun Printing Company Inc .... G 336 773-1346
  Winston Salem *(G-16923)*
Sundrop Printing .... G 704 960-1592
  Kannapolis *(G-9135)*
Super G Print Lab LLC .... G 919 864-9351
  Durham *(G-5381)*
Sweetgran Prints .... G 919 387-0711
  Apex *(G-247)*
Sylva Herald and Ruralite .... E 828 586-2611
  Sylva *(G-15070)*
Systel Business Eqp Co Inc .... E 336 808-8000
  Greensboro *(G-7385)*
T & R Signs .... G 919 779-1185
  Garner *(G-6317)*
Table Rock Printers LLC .... G 828 433-1377
  Morganton *(G-11260)*
Tag-M Prints .... G 919 615-4222
  Raleigh *(G-13324)*

Tarason Label Inc .... G 828 464-4743
  Hickory *(G-8174)*
Taylor Business Forms Inc .... G 336 667-0300
  North Wilkesboro *(G-12034)*
Teeshizzle Printing .... G 336 715-1113
  Clemmons *(G-4061)*
Telepathic Graphics Inc .... F 919 342-4603
  Rocky Mount *(G-13672)*
Theo Davis Sons Incorporated .... E 919 269-7401
  Zebulon *(G-17143)*
Thompson Printing & Packg Inc .... G 704 313-7323
  Mooresboro *(G-10842)*
Time Warner Cable Inc .... G 704 751-5207
  Shelby *(G-14373)*
Tm15 Printing Services .... G 704 606-0112
  Charlotte *(G-3699)*
Total Print Solutions .... G 336 841-5292
  High Point *(G-8573)*
Treva Mason LLC .... G 704 566-7973
  Charlotte *(G-3721)*
Triad Business Card Assoc .... G 336 706-2729
  Greensboro *(G-7413)*
Triad Print Promo LLC .... G 336 416-3488
  Yadkinville *(G-17057)*
Triangle Solutions Inc .... G 919 481-1235
  Cary *(G-1912)*
Tryon Newsmedia LLC .... F 828 859-9151
  Tryon *(G-15430)*
Twigs Screen Printing .... G 910 770-1605
  Tabor City *(G-15088)*
Twyford Printing Company Inc .... G 910 892-3271
  Dunn *(G-4888)*
Unique 3d Printing LLC .... G 704 843-7367
  Waxhaw *(G-15785)*
Unique Printer Solutions LLC .... G 704 544-4822
  Charlotte *(G-3749)*
Unlimted Potential Sanford Inc .... E 919 852-1117
  Morrisville *(G-11460)*
Valassis Communications Inc .... D 919 544-4511
  Durham *(G-5429)*
Valassis Communications Inc .... D 919 361-7900
  Durham *(G-5430)*
Valdese Packaging & Label Inc .... F 828 879-9772
  Valdese *(G-15457)*
▼ Valdese Packaging & Label Inc .... E 828 879-9772
  Valdese *(G-15456)*
Value Printing Inc .... G 919 380-9883
  Cary *(G-1916)*
Vanilla Print Inc .... G 919 637-0745
  Cary *(G-1917)*
Via Prnting Graphic Design Inc .... G 919 872-8688
  Youngsville *(G-17112)*
Victory Press LLC .... G 704 660-0348
  Mooresville *(G-11119)*
Village Graphics .... G 252 745-4600
  Oriental *(G-12113)*
Village Instant Printing Inc .... G 919 968-0000
  Chapel Hill *(G-2094)*
Village Printing Co .... F 336 629-0951
  Asheboro *(G-505)*
Viovio Inc .... G 919 827-1932
  Raleigh *(G-13403)*
VIP Print and Signs .... G 919 968-0000
  Chapel Hill *(G-2095)*
Vista Print .... G 919 400-2736
  Raleigh *(G-13407)*
W B Mason Co Inc .... E 888 926-2766
  Charlotte *(G-3787)*
Wallace Printing Inc .... F 828 466-3300
  Newton *(G-11982)*
Walter Printing Company Inc .... F 704 982-8899
  Albemarle *(G-112)*

SIC SECTION
27 PRINTING, PUBLISHING AND ALLIED INDUSTRIES

Wayne Trademark Prtg Packg LLC .... E 336 887-3173
  Asheboro *(G-507)*

Weathervane Creative Inc .... G 828 542-0136
  Hickory *(G-8208)*

Weber & Weber Inc .... G 336 889-6322
  High Point *(G-8602)*

Weber and Weber Inc .... F 336 722-4109
  Winston Salem *(G-16968)*

Welloyt Enterprises Inc .... G 919 821-7897
  Raleigh *(G-13418)*

West Pointe Printing .... G 704 806-3670
  Charlotte *(G-3805)*

Westrock - Graphics Inc .... F 610 392-0416
  Charlotte *(G-3806)*

Westrock Rkt LLC .... B 770 448-2193
  Marion *(G-10187)*

Whatever You Need Screen Print .... G 704 287-8603
  Concord *(G-4388)*

Whimsical Prints Paper & Gifts .... G 919 544-8491
  Durham *(G-5440)*

▲ Whistle Stop Press Inc .... F 910 695-1403
  Southern Pines *(G-14560)*

Whitney Screen Printing .... G 910 673-0309
  Eagle Springs *(G-5463)*

Wick Communications Co .... E 252 537-2505
  Roanoke Rapids *(G-13589)*

▲ William George Printing LLC .... E 910 221-2700
  Hope Mills *(G-8738)*

Williams Printing Inc .... G 336 969-2733
  Rural Hall *(G-13856)*

Williams Printing Inc .... G 336 969-2733
  Rural Hall *(G-13857)*

Wilmington Star-News Inc .... D 910 343-2000
  Wilmington *(G-16452)*

Wilsonepes Printing .... G 252 224-0248
  New Bern *(G-11858)*

Wilsons Planning & Consulting .... G 919 592-0935
  Garner *(G-6326)*

Wright Printing Service Inc .... G 336 427-4768
  Madison *(G-10092)*

◆ Xpres LLC .... E 336 245-1596
  Winston Salem *(G-16989)*

Xtreme Postcard Profits System .... G 919 894-8886
  Benson *(G-1047)*

Young Graphics Inc .... G 336 249-3148
  Lexington *(G-9803)*

Your Source For Printing .... G 704 957-5922
  Charlotte *(G-3846)*

Zebra Communications Inc .... E 919 314-3700
  Morrisville *(G-11469)*

Zeri Consulting Inc .... G 412 512-2027
  Sneads Ferry *(G-14494)*

2754 Commercial printing, gravure

AEL Services LLC .... E 704 525-3710
  Charlotte *(G-2140)*

Amber Alert International Tm .... G 919 641-8773
  Raleigh *(G-12496)*

Appalachian State University .... G 828 262-7497
  Boone *(G-1175)*

Arzberger Engravers Inc .... E 704 376-1151
  Charlotte *(G-2224)*

Big Fish Dpi .... G 704 545-8112
  Mint Hill *(G-10522)*

Business Wise Inc .... G 704 554-4112
  Charlotte *(G-2367)*

Cottage .... G 919 872-1441
  Raleigh *(G-12649)*

Executive Promotions Inc .... F 704 663-4000
  Mooresville *(G-10940)*

Huntpack Inc .... G 704 986-0684
  Albemarle *(G-90)*

Linprint Company .... F 910 763-5103
  Wilmington *(G-16303)*

▲ Master Screens South LLC .... G 704 226-9600
  Monroe *(G-10766)*

◆ Shamrock Corporation .... C 336 574-4200
  Greensboro *(G-7334)*

▲ Sharpe Co .... E 336 724-2871
  Winston Salem *(G-16905)*

Synthomer Inc .... D 704 225-1872
  Monroe *(G-10819)*

2759 Commercial printing, nec

2 Wishes Tees LLC .... G 919 621-1401
  Cary *(G-1669)*

3d Maternitees LLC .... G 704 778-0633
  Huntersville *(G-8784)*

822tees Inc .... G 910 822-8337
  Fayetteville *(G-5748)*

A A Logo Gear .... G 704 795-7100
  Concord *(G-4185)*

A B C Screenprinting and EMB .... G 704 937-3452
  Grover *(G-7605)*

A Create Card Inc .... G 631 584-2273
  Charlotte *(G-2114)*

A1 Awards & Promotions Inc .... G 252 321-7701
  Winterville *(G-16993)*

Aardvark Screen Printing .... G 919 829-9058
  Raleigh *(G-12454)*

ABC Tees Stuff .... G 828 287-7843
  Forest City *(G-6056)*

Abe Entercom Holdings LLC .... E 336 691-4337
  Greensboro *(G-6773)*

AC Valor Reyes LLC .... G 910 431-3256
  Castle Hayne *(G-1941)*

Acorn Printing .... G 704 868-4522
  Bessemer City *(G-1048)*

Action Specialties LLC .... G 704 865-6699
  Gastonia *(G-6336)*

ADS N Art Screenprinting & EMB .... G 919 453-0400
  Wake Forest *(G-15525)*

Advantage Marketing .... G 919 872-8610
  Louisburg *(G-9978)*

AEL Services LLC .... E 704 525-3710
  Charlotte *(G-2140)*

All Stick Label LLC .... G 336 659-4660
  Winston Salem *(G-16598)*

Ambrose Signs Inc .... G 252 338-8522
  Camden *(G-1555)*

American Label Tech Inc .... F 984 269-5078
  Garner *(G-6253)*

American Multimedia Inc .... D 336 229-7101
  Burlington *(G-1364)*

American Solutions For Bu .... G 919 848-2442
  Raleigh *(G-12500)*

Amped Events LLC .... F 888 683-4386
  Gastonia *(G-6348)*

▲ Anilox Roll Company Inc .... G 704 588-1809
  Charlotte *(G-2195)*

Appalachian State University .... F 828 262-2047
  Boone *(G-1174)*

Aquarius Designs & Logo Wear .... G 919 821-4646
  Raleigh *(G-12515)*

Arden Engraving US Inc .... G 704 547-4581
  Charlotte *(G-2213)*

Armac Inc .... E 919 878-9836
  Raleigh *(G-12524)*

Arrowhead Graphics Inc .... G 336 274-2419
  Greensboro *(G-6816)*

Art Enterprises Inc .... G 828 277-1211
  Asheville *(G-528)*

Art House .... G 919 552-7367
  Fuquay Varina *(G-6181)*

Artcraft Press Inc .... F 828 397-8612
  Icard *(G-8916)*

Arzberger Engravers Inc .... E 704 376-1151
  Charlotte *(G-2224)*

Asheville Color & Imaging Inc .... G 828 774-5040
  Asheville *(G-533)*

Asheville Promo LLC .... G 828 575-2767
  Asheville *(G-542)*

Ashton LLC .... F 336 447-4951
  Gibsonville *(G-6556)*

Atlantic Coast Screen Prtg LLC .... G 910 200-0818
  Burlington *(G-1368)*

Aunt Tee LLC .... G 336 269-9466
  Burlington *(G-1371)*

Austin Business Forms Inc .... F 704 821-6165
  Indian Trail *(G-8922)*

Avant Publications LLC .... G 704 897-6048
  Mooresville *(G-10866)*

▲ Banknote Corp America Inc .... C 336 375-1134
  Browns Summit *(G-1300)*

Beach House Publications LLC .... E 252 504-2344
  Beaufort *(G-945)*

Beacon Thermography Inc .... G 727 470-1694
  Hampstead *(G-7640)*

Benchmark Screen Ptg Design .... G 704 785-7826
  Midland *(G-10457)*

Bender Apparel & Signs Inc .... G 252 636-8337
  New Bern *(G-11777)*

Blp Products and Services Inc .... G 704 899-5505
  Pineville *(G-12256)*

Blue Lzard Cstm Scrnprnting In .... G 919 296-9041
  Durham *(G-4967)*

Body Billboards Inc .... G 919 544-4540
  Durham *(G-4969)*

Bradleys Inc .... E 704 484-2077
  Shelby *(G-14289)*

Brunswick Screen Prtg & EMB .... F 910 579-1234
  Ocean Isle Beach *(G-12087)*

Bryan Austin .... F 336 841-6573
  High Point *(G-8276)*

Burlow Promotions Inc .... G 336 856-0500
  Greensboro *(G-6869)*

Business Mogul LLC .... G 919 605-2165
  Raleigh *(G-12578)*

C & M Enterprise Inc .... G 704 545-1180
  Mint Hill *(G-10524)*

Carolina Classifiedscom LLC .... D 704 246-0900
  Monroe *(G-10675)*

Carolina Printing Co .... G 919 834-0433
  Princeton *(G-12399)*

Carolina Sgns Grphic Dsgns Inc .... G 919 383-3344
  Durham *(G-5004)*

Carolina Tailors Inc .... F 252 247-6469
  Newport *(G-11899)*

Carolina Vinyl Shack LLC .... G 704 788-9493
  Concord *(G-4226)*

Carter Publishing Company Inc .... F 336 993-2161
  Kernersville *(G-9174)*

▲ Castle Shirt Company LLC .... F 336 992-7727
  Kernersville *(G-9175)*

◆ Causekeepers Inc .... E 336 824-2518
  Franklinville *(G-6167)*

▲ CCL Label .... F 919 713-0388
  Raleigh *(G-12613)*

CCL Label Inc .... C 704 714-4800
  Charlotte *(G-2431)*

CCL Label Inc .... E 919 713-0388
  Raleigh *(G-12614)*

Center For Ecozoic Studies .... G 919 929-4116
  Chapel Hill *(G-2002)*

Chesapeake Graphics Inc .... G 704 827-7172
  Stanley *(G-14688)*

27 PRINTING, PUBLISHING AND ALLIED INDUSTRIES

Circle Graphics Inc .... C 919 864-4518
  Raleigh *(G-12623)*

Coastal Press Inc .... G 252 726-1549
  Morehead City *(G-11163)*

Comedycd .... G 336 273-0077
  Greensboro *(G-6923)*

Commonwealth Graphics Inc .... G 704 997-8501
  Mooresville *(G-10909)*

Concord Printing Company Inc .... F 704 786-3717
  Concord *(G-4240)*

Consoldted Grphics - PBM Grphi .... G 919 544-6222
  Durham *(G-5031)*

Consumer Concepts .... F 252 247-7000
  Morehead City *(G-11164)*

Contagious Graphics Inc .... E 704 529-5600
  Charlotte *(G-2543)*

Contract Printing & Graphics .... G 919 832-7178
  Raleigh *(G-12644)*

Cork Tee .... G 919 536-3200
  Durham *(G-5033)*

Cranford Silk Screen Prcess In .... F 336 434-6544
  Archdale *(G-276)*

Crazie Tees .... G 704 898-2272
  Mount Holly *(G-11629)*

Creative Label Solutions .... G 828 315-9500
  Newton *(G-11928)*

Creative Label Solutions Inc .... G 828 320-5389
  Hickory *(G-7999)*

Creative Printers Inc .... G 336 246-7746
  West Jefferson *(G-15938)*

Creative Screening .... G 919 467-5081
  Cary *(G-1740)*

Creative T-Shirts Imaging LLC .... G 919 828-0204
  Raleigh *(G-12654)*

Creative Tees .... G 919 828-0204
  Raleigh *(G-12655)*

Crystal Clear Images Inc .... G 704 708-5420
  Charlotte *(G-2579)*

Crystal Impressions Ltd .... F 704 821-7678
  Indian Trail *(G-8928)*

Custom Creations By Ellen .... G 509 480-0263
  Fayetteville *(G-5802)*

Custom Express .... G 704 845-0900
  Matthews *(G-10245)*

Custom Tees Lab .... G 704 804-8706
  Charlotte *(G-2596)*

Dale Advertising Inc .... G 704 484-0971
  Shelby *(G-14310)*

Daniels Business Services Inc .... E 828 277-8250
  Asheville *(G-602)*

Daryl Duff Lockyer .... G 704 658-0695
  Mooresville *(G-10925)*

Datamark Graphics Inc .... E 336 629-0267
  Asheboro *(G-422)*

David Presnell .... G 336 372-5989
  Sparta *(G-14592)*

Davis Vogler Enterprises LLC .... G 402 257-7188
  Charlotte *(G-2607)*

DB CUSTOM CRAFTS LLC .... F 336 791-0940
  Winston Salem *(G-16674)*

Dbt Coatings LLC .... G 336 834-9700
  Greensboro *(G-6961)*

▲ Deep South Holding Company Inc .... D 336 427-0265
  Madison *(G-10072)*

Dia-Be-Tees LLC .... G 330 687-7792
  Mint Hill *(G-10529)*

Digital Print & Imaging Inc .... G 910 341-3005
  Wilmington *(G-16201)*

Digital Printing Systems Inc .... E 704 525-0190
  Charlotte *(G-2636)*

Digitaurus Inc .... G 910 794-9243
  Wilmington *(G-16202)*

Digitaurus EMB Screen Prtg Inc .... G 910 794-3275
  Wilmington *(G-16203)*

Dillon L Colter L C .... G 828 242-7750
  Chapel Hill *(G-2008)*

Dime EMB LLC .... F 336 765-0910
  Winston Salem *(G-16681)*

Dirty Dog Threads LLC .... G 704 240-3668
  Lincolnton *(G-9890)*

Document Directs Inc .... G 919 829-8810
  Raleigh *(G-12692)*

Docusource North Carolina LLC .... E 919 459-5900
  Morrisville *(G-11335)*

Draft DOT International LLC .... G 336 775-0525
  Lexington *(G-9710)*

▼ Dtbtla Inc .... E 336 769-0000
  Greensboro *(G-6981)*

Dynagraphics Screenprintng .... G 919 212-2898
  Holly Springs *(G-8697)*

E R W Printing .... G 704 201-5642
  Charlotte *(G-2671)*

East Coast Designs LLC .... G 910 865-1070
  Fayetteville *(G-5816)*

Easter Seals Ucp NC & VA Inc .... D 919 856-0250
  Raleigh *(G-12717)*

Eatumup Lure Company Inc .... G 336 218-0896
  Greensboro *(G-6988)*

Edge Promo Team LLC .... F 919 946-4218
  Clayton *(G-3975)*

EDM Technology Inc .... E 336 882-8115
  High Point *(G-8337)*

Egads Printing Co .... G 252 335-1554
  Elizabeth City *(G-5542)*

Electronic Imaging Svcs Inc .... F 704 587-3323
  Charlotte *(G-2690)*

Embroidme Lake Norman .... G 704 987-9630
  Cornelius *(G-4543)*

Endaxi Company Inc .... E 919 467-8895
  Morrisville *(G-11338)*

Epic Apparel .... G 980 335-0463
  Charlotte *(G-2722)*

Expressive Screen Printing .... G 910 739-3221
  Lumberton *(G-10035)*

EZ Custom Screen Printing .... E 704 821-8488
  Matthews *(G-10314)*

EZ Custom Scrnprinting EMB Inc .... G 704 821-9641
  Matthews *(G-10315)*

F C C LLC .... G 336 883-7314
  High Point *(G-8349)*

Fabrix Inc .... G 704 953-1239
  Charlotte *(G-2743)*

Fantasy Sports Breaks LLC .... G 276 233-5204
  Dobson *(G-4823)*

▲ Fayetteville Publishing Co .... D 910 323-4848
  Fayetteville *(G-5824)*

◆ Finch Industries Incorporated .... D 336 472-4499
  Thomasville *(G-15221)*

First Impressions Ltd .... F 704 536-3622
  Charlotte *(G-2765)*

Flexo Factor .... G 704 962-5404
  Charlotte *(G-2775)*

Flint Group US LLC .... G 828 687-2485
  Arden *(G-332)*

Flutterby Embroidery .... G 980 225-6053
  Harrisburg *(G-7709)*

Funny Bone EMB & Screening .... G 704 663-4711
  Mooresville *(G-10951)*

Galloreecom .... G 704 644-0978
  Charlotte *(G-2805)*

Geographics Screenprinting Inc .... G 704 357-3300
  Charlotte *(G-2825)*

Get Stuck Inc .... G 336 698-3277
  Greensboro *(G-7040)*

Ggs Technical Publications .... G 336 256-9600
  Greensboro *(G-7041)*

Gibraltar Packaging Inc .... C 910 439-6137
  Mount Gilead *(G-11600)*

Gilmore Globl Lgstics Svcs Inc .... D 919 277-2700
  Morrisville *(G-11347)*

Gmg Group LLC .... G 252 441-8374
  Kill Devil Hills *(G-9258)*

Go Postal In Boone Inc .... F 828 262-0027
  Boone *(G-1200)*

◆ Golf Associates Advertising Co .... E 828 252-6544
  Asheville *(G-637)*

Graphic Image of Cape Fear Inc .... G 910 313-6768
  Wilmington *(G-16239)*

Graphixx Screen Printing Inc .... G 919 736-3995
  Goldsboro *(G-6621)*

Graveoke Inc .... E 704 534-3480
  Charlotte *(G-2857)*

Greenfield Printing Co .... G 910 763-0647
  Wilmington *(G-16241)*

Happiteescom .... G 704 965-2507
  Charlotte *(G-2885)*

Have A Shirt Made .... G 910 201-9911
  Oak Island *(G-12050)*

Herald Printing Inc .... G 252 726-3534
  Morehead City *(G-11175)*

Hickory Printing Solutions LLC .... C 828 465-3431
  Conover *(G-4464)*

High Cotton Screenprinting .... G 704 872-7630
  Statesville *(G-14816)*

High Performance Marketing Inc .... G 919 870-9915
  Raleigh *(G-12843)*

Home Team Athletics Inc .... G 910 938-0862
  Jacksonville *(G-9007)*

Htm Concepts Martin Entps LLC .... G 252 789-0508
  Williamston *(G-16063)*

Humbly Made Brand .... G 740 506-1554
  Raleigh *(G-12866)*

Hunsucker Printing Co Inc .... G 336 629-9125
  Asheboro *(G-441)*

I Print Ttees LLC .... G 336 202-8148
  Greensboro *(G-7108)*

▲ Ics North America Corp .... E 704 794-6620
  Concord *(G-4283)*

ID Images LLC .... G 704 494-0444
  Charlotte *(G-2948)*

Identify Yourself LLC .... F 252 202-1452
  Kitty Hawk *(G-9407)*

If Tees Could Talk LLC .... G 919 938-8031
  Clayton *(G-3989)*

Image 420 Screenprinting Inc .... G 828 253-9420
  Asheville *(G-659)*

Image Designs Ink LLC .... G 252 235-1964
  Bailey *(G-875)*

Imagemark Business Svcs Inc .... G 704 865-4912
  Gastonia *(G-6423)*

Imprinting Systems Spcalty Inc .... G 704 527-4545
  Charlotte *(G-2956)*

Indestructible LLC .... G 804 601-4097
  Charlotte *(G-2960)*

Infinity S End Inc .... F 704 900-8355
  Charlotte *(G-2968)*

Ingalls Alton .... G 252 975-2056
  Washington *(G-15712)*

Ink n Stitches LLC .... G 336 633-3898
  Asheboro *(G-444)*

Inniah Production Incorporated .... G 828 765-6800
  Spruce Pine *(G-14644)*

Inspire Creative Studios Inc .... G 910 395-0200
  Wilmington *(G-16269)*

Interflex Acquisition Co LLC .... C 336 921-3505
  Wilkesboro *(G-16027)*

27 PRINTING, PUBLISHING AND ALLIED INDUSTRIES

Interflex Acquisition Co LLC............ C 336 921-3505
   Wilkesboro *(G-16028)*
Invitation Duck LLC............................ G 919 341-3739
   Cary *(G-1794)*
Iwanna... G 828 505-7319
   Asheville *(G-665)*
J C Lawrence Co.................................. G 919 553-3044
   Oriental *(G-12110)*
Jamn Tees.. G 336 444-4327
   Pilot Mountain *(G-12198)*
Jax Brothers Inc.................................. G 704 732-3351
   Lincolnton *(G-9897)*
Jtc Awards and Printing.................... G 910 346-9522
   Jacksonville *(G-9011)*
Jubilee Screen Printing Inc............... G 910 673-4240
   West End *(G-15928)*
Jumbo Co... G 919 637-0313
   Wendell *(G-15906)*
K & K Stitch & Screen......................... G 336 246-5477
   West Jefferson *(G-15941)*
Kahne Screen Print LLC.................... G 704 662-8549
   Mooresville *(G-10994)*
▲ Kalajdzic Inc..................................... F 855 465-4225
   Clemmons *(G-4052)*
Kannapolis Awards and Graphics.... G 704 224-3695
   Kannapolis *(G-9125)*
Katchi Tees Incorporated.................. G 252 315-4691
   Wilson *(G-16504)*
Kathie S Mc Daniel............................. G 336 835-1544
   Elkin *(G-5622)*
Kdm Enterprise LLC........................... G 919 689-9720
   Goldsboro *(G-6628)*
Kelleys Sports and Awards Inc........ G 828 728-4600
   Hudson *(G-8772)*
▲ Kerr Lake Cornhole & Printing..... G 252 430-7144
   Henderson *(G-7792)*
Kessel Development LLC.................. G 704 752-4282
   Charlotte *(G-3051)*
Kimballs Screen Print Inc................. G 704 636-0488
   Salisbury *(G-13999)*
King Business Service Inc................ G 910 610-1030
   Laurinburg *(G-9483)*
Kna.. F 704 847-4280
   Charlotte *(G-3058)*
Kraftsman Tactical Inc...................... G 336 465-3576
   Albemarle *(G-93)*
Kraken-Skulls....................................... F 910 500-9100
   Fayetteville *(G-5855)*
L & B Monograms Plus...................... G 336 229-0152
   Burlington *(G-1445)*
Label & Printing Solutions Inc........ G 919 782-1242
   Raleigh *(G-12950)*
Label Printing Systems Inc.............. E 336 760-3271
   Winston Salem *(G-16783)*
Label Southeast LLC.......................... G 518 796-6320
   Charlotte *(G-3068)*
Labels Tags & Inserts Inc................. F 336 227-8485
   Burlington *(G-1447)*
Lake Norman EMB & Monogramming.. G 704 892-8450
   Cornelius *(G-4564)*
Lake Nrman Screen Prtg Fctry L..... G 704 664-8337
   Mooresville *(G-11003)*
Lakeside Cstm Tees & Embroider... G 704 274-3730
   Cornelius *(G-4566)*
Laniers Screen Printing..................... G 336 857-2699
   Denton *(G-4740)*
Laru Industries Inc............................. F 704 821-7503
   Indian Trail *(G-8944)*
▲ Laser Ink Corporation..................... E 919 361-5822
   Durham *(G-5186)*
Laurel of Asheville LLC..................... F 828 670-7503
   Asheville *(G-681)*

LDR Designs... G 252 375-4484
   Greenville *(G-7555)*
Legend-Tees.. G 828 585-2066
   Arden *(G-348)*
Living Intntionally For Excell........... E 810 600-3425
   Cary *(G-1813)*
Logo Dogz... G 888 827-8866
   Monroe *(G-10760)*
Logo Label Printing Company......... G 919 309-0007
   Durham *(G-5195)*
Logo Wear Graphics LLC.................. F 336 382-0455
   Summerfield *(G-14985)*
Logonation Inc..................................... E 704 799-0612
   Mooresville *(G-11011)*
Lots of Labels..................................... G 252 410-1611
   Roanoke Rapids *(G-13577)*
Lsg LLC... E 919 878-5500
   Wallace *(G-15624)*
M D C Graphics LLC........................... G 336 454-6467
   High Point *(G-8434)*
M-Prints Inc.. G 828 265-4929
   Boone *(G-1216)*
Magnet America Intl Inc................... E 336 985-0320
   King *(G-9275)*
Magnet Guys... G 816 259-5201
   Durham *(G-5203)*
Make An Impression Inc................... G 919 557-7400
   Holly Springs *(G-8707)*
Mass Connection Inc......................... G 910 424-0940
   Fayetteville *(G-5868)*
Masters Hand Print Works Inc........ G 828 652-5833
   Marion *(G-10159)*
Masters Imaging Screen PR............. G 704 500-1039
   Mooresville *(G-11016)*
Max B Smith Jr..................................... G 828 434-0238
   Boone *(G-1219)*
▲ Maxim Label Packg High Pt Inc... F 336 861-1666
   High Point *(G-8451)*
Mb-F Inc... D 336 379-9352
   Greensboro *(G-7192)*
McLamb Group Inc............................. G 704 333-1171
   Charlotte *(G-3153)*
Measurement Incorporated............. C 919 683-2413
   Durham *(G-5213)*
▲ Medlit Solutions LLC...................... D 919 878-6789
   Garner *(G-6287)*
Memories of Orangeburg Inc.......... G 803 533-0035
   Mooresville *(G-11020)*
Merch Inc... G 919 933-6037
   Carrboro *(G-1650)*
Merch Connect Studios Inc............. G 336 501-6722
   Greensboro *(G-7198)*
MI Screen Printing Inc...................... G 704 500-1039
   Mooresville *(G-11022)*
Michael D Pressley.............................. G 828 652-8292
   Nebo *(G-11761)*
Miller Products Inc............................. E 704 587-1870
   Charlotte *(G-3182)*
Motorsports Designs Inc.................. E 336 454-1181
   High Point *(G-8460)*
Mountaineer Inc.................................. F 828 452-0661
   Waynesville *(G-15811)*
Moving Screens Incorporated........ G 336 364-9259
   Rougemont *(G-13787)*
Mrs GS Tees.. G 704 372-0610
   Charlotte *(G-3211)*
Mrschis Sticker N Tees...................... G 919 606-1940
   Clayton *(G-3999)*
Multi Packaging Solutions............... A 336 855-7142
   Greensboro *(G-7207)*
Multi-Color Corporation................... E 828 658-6800
   Weaverville *(G-15854)*

Mundo Uniformes LLC....................... G 704 287-1527
   Charlotte *(G-3218)*
Napoleon James................................... G 413 331-9560
   Charlotte *(G-3230)*
National Sign & Decal Inc................. G 828 478-2123
   Sherrills Ford *(G-14388)*
Nclogowearcom................................... G 919 821-4646
   Raleigh *(G-13060)*
Need T-Shirts Now.............................. G 910 644-0455
   Fayetteville *(G-5881)*
New Directions Enterprises Inc...... G 980 428-1866
   Charlotte *(G-3249)*
New Directions Screen Prtrs Inc.... G 704 393-1769
   Charlotte *(G-3250)*
News & Record Commercial Prtg... E 336 373-7300
   Greensboro *(G-7217)*
Nvizion Inc.. F 336 985-3862
   King *(G-9278)*
Omega Tees + Screen Prtg LLC....... G 828 268-0600
   Boone *(G-1226)*
Onc Tees.. G 252 671-7576
   Oriental *(G-12112)*
One Source Document Solutions... G 336 482-2360
   Greensboro *(G-7233)*
Orlandos Cstm Design T-Shirts...... G 919 220-5515
   Durham *(G-5264)*
Owen G Dunn Co Inc.......................... G 252 633-3197
   New Bern *(G-11832)*
Pages Screen Printing LLC.............. G 336 759-7979
   Winston Salem *(G-16834)*
Paraclete Xp Sky Venture LLC........ F 910 848-2600
   Raeford *(G-12428)*
Paraclete Xp Skyventure LLC......... E 910 904-0027
   Raeford *(G-12429)*
Paradigm Solutions Inc.................... G 910 392-2611
   Wilmington *(G-16348)*
Paradise Printers................................ G 336 570-2922
   Burlington *(G-1471)*
Park Communications LLC.............. G 919 852-1117
   Morrisville *(G-11405)*
Party Time Inc..................................... G 910 454-4577
   Southport *(G-14575)*
Patti Boo Designs Inc....................... G 828 648-6495
   Canton *(G-1622)*
Pharmaceutic Litho Label Inc......... E 336 785-4000
   Winston Salem *(G-16848)*
Piedmont Business Forms Inc........ F 828 464-0010
   Newton *(G-11960)*
Piedmont Publishing.......................... F 336 727-4099
   Winston Salem *(G-16855)*
Pinkston Properties LLC................... F 828 252-9867
   Asheville *(G-732)*
Plasticard Products Inc.................... G 828 665-7774
   Asheville *(G-734)*
Poole Printing Company Inc............ G 919 876-5260
   Raleigh *(G-13120)*
Pop Designs Mktg Solutions LLC... G 336 444-4033
   Mount Airy *(G-11559)*
Poppies LLC.. G 704 896-3433
   Huntersville *(G-8879)*
Poteet Printing Systems LLC.......... D 704 588-0005
   Charlotte *(G-3357)*
Pre Flight Inc.. G 828 758-1138
   Lenoir *(G-9649)*
Premier Printing & Apparel.............. G 910 805-0545
   Wilmington *(G-16370)*
Prince Manufacturing Corp.............. C 828 681-8860
   Mills River *(G-10510)*
Print Express Inc................................. F 910 455-4554
   Jacksonville *(G-9021)*
Print Haus Inc...................................... G 828 456-8622
   Waynesville *(G-15817)*

Employee Codes: A=Over 500 employees, B=251-500
C=101-250, D=51-100, E=20-50, F=10-19, G=1-9

27 PRINTING, PUBLISHING AND ALLIED INDUSTRIES

Print Zilla LLC .... G 800 340-6120
  Charlotte *(G-3387)*
Printcraft Company Inc .... D 336 248-2544
  Lexington *(G-9772)*
◆ Printcraft Company Inc .... E 336 248-2544
  Lexington *(G-9773)*
Printful Inc .... F 818 351-7181
  Charlotte *(G-3388)*
Printing Press .... G 828 299-1234
  Asheville *(G-743)*
Printing Svcs Greensboro Inc .... F 336 274-7663
  Greensboro *(G-7285)*
Pro Cal Prof Decals Inc .... F 704 795-6090
  Concord *(G-4340)*
Product Identification Inc .... E 919 544-4136
  Durham *(G-5305)*
Professional Laminating LLC .... G 919 465-0400
  Cary *(G-1862)*
Proforma Hanson Branding .... G 210 437-3061
  High Point *(G-8501)*
Promothreads Inc .... G 704 248-0942
  Cornelius *(G-4579)*
▲ Queensboro Industries Inc .... C 910 251-1251
  Wilmington *(G-16373)*
Quik Print Inc .... G 910 738-6775
  Lumberton *(G-10050)*
R R Donnelley & Sons Company .... E 919 596-8942
  Durham *(G-5316)*
R R Donnelley & Sons Company .... D 252 243-0337
  Wilson *(G-16528)*
R&R Custom Embroidery LLC .... G 336 693-5029
  Hurdle Mills *(G-8912)*
Ragg Co Inc .... G 336 838-4895
  North Wilkesboro *(G-12031)*
Raleigh Engraving Co .... G 919 832-5557
  Raleigh *(G-13177)*
Raleigh Shirt Printer .... G 919 261-6628
  Raleigh *(G-13185)*
Rdu Print Studio LLC .... G 919 260-0173
  Durham *(G-5321)*
Reliance Management Group Inc .... F 704 282-2255
  Monroe *(G-10796)*
Rikki Tikki Tees .... G 828 454-0515
  Waynesville *(G-15818)*
Rogers Screenprinting EMB Inc .... G 910 738-6208
  Lumberton *(G-10054)*
RTS Screen Printing .... G 252 972-3599
  Nashville *(G-11749)*
Russell Printing Inc .... G 404 366-0552
  Burlington *(G-1489)*
S & S Screenprinters LLC .... G 704 707-5497
  Charlotte *(G-3476)*
Salem One Inc .... C 336 744-9990
  Winston Salem *(G-16893)*
Sato Inc .... G 980 613-2022
  Mooresville *(G-11078)*
Screen It .... G 919 581-9981
  Goldsboro *(G-6654)*
Screen Printers Unlimited LLC .... G 336 667-8737
  Wilkesboro *(G-16039)*
Screen Specialty Shop Inc .... G 336 982-4135
  West Jefferson *(G-15948)*
Screens Stitches & Stones LLC .... G 704 622-1660
  Mooresville *(G-11081)*
Sea & Tee Rsort Rsdntial Prpts .... G 910 231-8212
  Wilmington *(G-16395)*
Serigraph Techniques Inc .... G 336 454-5066
  Jamestown *(G-9072)*
Sewing Plus LLC .... G 704 616-1750
  Bessemer City *(G-1083)*
Shannon Media Inc .... G 919 933-1551
  Chapel Hill *(G-2070)*

Sharpe Images Properties Inc .... E 336 724-2871
  Winston Salem *(G-16906)*
Shirtails .... G 910 277-0960
  Laurinburg *(G-9496)*
Silkscreen Specialists .... G 910 353-8859
  Jacksonville *(G-9030)*
Silverlining Screen Prtrs Inc .... G 919 554-0340
  Youngsville *(G-17097)*
Simply TS Inc .... G 828 586-1113
  Sylva *(G-15068)*
Skipper Graphics .... G 910 754-8729
  Shallotte *(G-14278)*
▲ Smart Play USA .... G 252 747-2587
  Snow Hill *(G-14508)*
Sml Raleigh LLC .... G 919 585-0100
  Clayton *(G-4010)*
SOS Printing Inc .... F 828 264-4262
  Boone *(G-1237)*
Southern Engraving Company .... G 336 656-0084
  High Point *(G-8544)*
Southstern Edctl Toy Bk Dstrs .... E 919 954-0140
  Raleigh *(G-13285)*
Spectrum Screen Prtg Svc Inc .... F 919 481-9905
  Cary *(G-1901)*
Spiral Graphics Inc .... G 919 571-3371
  Raleigh *(G-13290)*
Squeegee Tees & More Inc .... G 704 888-0336
  Midland *(G-10480)*
▲ St Johns Packaging Usa LLC .... C 336 292-9911
  Greensboro *(G-7362)*
Steeds Service Co .... G 336 748-1587
  Thomasville *(G-15283)*
Steves TS & Uniforms Inc .... G 919 554-4221
  Wake Forest *(G-15598)*
Stewart Sreen Printing .... G 336 434-4444
  Trinity *(G-15360)*
Sticky Fingers Vinyl .... G 336 859-0262
  Denton *(G-4749)*
STS Screen Printing Inc .... G 704 821-8488
  Matthews *(G-10347)*
◆ Stump Printing Co Inc .... C 260 723-5171
  Wrightsville Beach *(G-17028)*
Substance Incorporated .... F 800 985-9485
  Claremont *(G-3939)*
Sun Printing Company Inc .... G 336 773-1346
  Winston Salem *(G-16923)*
Supreme T-Shirts & Apparel .... F 919 772-9040
  Raleigh *(G-13317)*
Sweet Tees Screen Printing LLC .... G 919 497-0500
  Louisburg *(G-10003)*
T S Designs Incorporated .... E 336 226-5694
  Burlington *(G-1504)*
T Shirt More .... G 828 389-3200
  Hayesville *(G-7772)*
T T S D Productions LLC .... G 704 829-6666
  Belmont *(G-1013)*
▲ Tannis Root Productions Inc .... G 919 832-8552
  Raleigh *(G-13327)*
Tarason Label Inc .... G 828 464-4743
  Hickory *(G-8174)*
Team Connection .... G 336 287-3892
  Winston Salem *(G-16936)*
TEC Graphics Inc .... F 919 567-2077
  Fuquay Varina *(G-6232)*
Tees Pretty Things .... G 704 674-0982
  Gastonia *(G-6521)*
Tef Inc .... G 704 786-9577
  Concord *(G-4375)*
Telepathic Graphics Inc .... E 919 342-4603
  Raleigh *(G-13337)*
Tennessee Nedgraphics Inc .... F 704 414-4224
  Charlotte *(G-3681)*

Theo Davis Sons Incorporated .... E 919 269-7401
  Zebulon *(G-17143)*
Third Street Screen Print Inc .... G 919 365-2725
  Wendell *(G-15920)*
Thomco Inc .... G 336 292-3300
  Greensboro *(G-7401)*
Threesixty Graphix Inc .... G 704 960-4467
  Salisbury *(G-14052)*
Thunderbolt Tees .... G 828 855-1124
  Hickory *(G-8181)*
Tickets Plus Inc .... E 616 222-4000
  Morrisville *(G-11448)*
▲ Timeplanner Calendars Inc .... C 704 377-0024
  Charlotte *(G-3695)*
Times Printing Company Inc .... G 252 441-2223
  Kill Devil Hills *(G-9263)*
TLC Enterprises .... G 336 454-4981
  Jamestown *(G-9075)*
TNT Web & Grafix LLC .... G 252 289-8846
  Nashville *(G-11751)*
Touch Tone Tees LLC .... G 919 358-5536
  Raleigh *(G-13354)*
Transformational Bible Inst .... G 702 218-3528
  Elizabeth City *(G-5578)*
Travistees .... G 910 506-8827
  Wilmington *(G-16432)*
Triad Printing NC Inc .... G 336 422-8752
  Greensboro *(G-7416)*
Trin-I-Tee Designz LLC .... G 910 520-2032
  Rocky Point *(G-13754)*
True Southern Tees .... G 919 604-6068
  Youngsville *(G-17111)*
Tshirts Made By U .... G 980 309-9749
  Charlotte *(G-3734)*
Twin City Sports LLC .... G 336 765-5070
  Winston Salem *(G-16958)*
Two Engravers LLC .... G 919 526-0102
  Raleigh *(G-13373)*
Two Little Birds Screen Ptg .... G 336 988-7488
  Greensboro *(G-7422)*
Twyford Printing Company Inc .... G 910 892-3271
  Dunn *(G-4888)*
Underground Printing .... G 919 525-2029
  Chapel Hill *(G-2088)*
Uniforms Galore .... G 252 975-5878
  Washington *(G-15735)*
Unique Impressions .... G 704 873-3241
  Statesville *(G-14921)*
Valassis Communications Inc .... D 919 544-4511
  Durham *(G-5429)*
Valassis Communications Inc .... D 919 361-7900
  Durham *(G-5430)*
Valdese Packaging & Label Inc .... F 828 879-9772
  Valdese *(G-15457)*
▼ Valdese Packaging & Label Inc .... E 828 879-9772
  Valdese *(G-15456)*
Visigraphix Inc .... G 336 882-1935
  Colfax *(G-4162)*
Vision Envelope Inc .... F 704 392-9090
  Charlotte *(G-3779)*
Walgreen Co .... F 704 525-2628
  Charlotte *(G-3792)*
Walk In Faith LLC .... G 704 660-8337
  Mooresville *(G-11122)*
We Print T-Shirts Inc .... G 910 822-8337
  Fayetteville *(G-5951)*
Weathervane Creative Inc .... G 828 542-0136
  Hickory *(G-8208)*
Western Roto Engravers Incorporated ...... E 336 275-9821
  Greensboro *(G-7457)*
Westmoreland Printers Inc .... F 704 482-9100
  Shelby *(G-14382)*

27 PRINTING, PUBLISHING AND ALLIED INDUSTRIES

Winso Dsgns Screenprinting LLC .... G 704 967-5776
  Charlotte *(G-3817)*
Winston Printing Company .... D 336 896-7631
  Winston Salem *(G-16980)*
Wooten Graphics Inc .... F 336 731-4650
  Welcome *(G-15878)*
Workflowone .... G 252 215-8880
  Winterville *(G-17019)*
▲ Wright of Thomasville Inc .... F 336 472-4200
  Thomasville *(G-15305)*
Xpertees Prfmce Screen Prtg .... G 910 763-7703
  Wilmington *(G-16457)*
Yourlogowear .... G 704 664-1290
  Cornelius *(G-4595)*
Zoom Apparel Inc .... G 336 993-9666
  Winston Salem *(G-16992)*

2761 Manifold business forms

▲ American Forms Mfg Inc .... E 704 866-9139
  Gastonia *(G-6345)*
Apperson Inc .... E 704 399-2571
  Charlotte *(G-2203)*
Fain Enterprises Inc .... F 336 724-0417
  Winston Salem *(G-16705)*
◆ Golf Associates Advertising Co ..... E 828 252-6544
  Asheville *(G-637)*
Holley Selinda .... G 919 351-9466
  Raleigh *(G-12851)*
Print Haus Inc .... G 828 456-8622
  Waynesville *(G-15817)*
R R Donnelley & Sons Company .... G 704 864-5717
  Gastonia *(G-6501)*
Reynolds and Reynolds Company ...... G 321 287-3939
  Charlotte *(G-3445)*
S Ruppe Inc .... E 828 287-4936
  Rutherfordton *(G-13889)*
Taylor Communications Inc .... F 336 841-7700
  High Point *(G-8564)*
Taylor Communications Inc .... E 704 282-0989
  Monroe *(G-10820)*

2771 Greeting cards

Walgreen Co .... G 704 525-2628
  Charlotte *(G-3792)*
Wit & Whistle .... G 919 609-5309
  Cary *(G-1930)*

2782 Blankbooks and looseleaf binders

Alpha Mailing Service Inc .... E 704 484-1711
  Shelby *(G-14283)*
American Sample House Inc .... G 704 276-1970
  Vale *(G-15463)*
Binders Incorporated .... F 704 377-9704
  Charlotte *(G-2312)*
Blissfull Memories .... G 336 903-1835
  North Wilkesboro *(G-11999)*
Carolina Swatching Inc .... F 828 327-9499
  Hickory *(G-7967)*
Clarke Harland Corp .... G 210 697-8888
  High Point *(G-8297)*
Custom Sample Service Inc .... G 336 861-2010
  Archdale *(G-277)*
Deluxe Corp .... G 704 969-5200
  Charlotte *(G-2616)*
Deluxe Corporation .... F 336 851-4600
  Greensboro *(G-6967)*
Design Concepts Incorporated .... F 336 887-1932
  High Point *(G-8321)*
▲ E Feibusch Company Inc .... E 336 434-5095
  High Point *(G-8333)*
Focusales Inc .... F 919 614-3076
  Raleigh *(G-12777)*

▲ Napco Inc .... C 336 372-5214
  Sparta *(G-14597)*
Premedia Group LLC .... F 336 274-2421
  Greensboro *(G-7278)*
Printing Press .... G 828 299-1234
  Asheville *(G-743)*
Sample House Inc .... F 828 327-4786
  Hickory *(G-8145)*
Stamping & Scrapbooking Rm Inc ..... G 336 389-9538
  Greensboro *(G-7365)*
Swatchworks Inc .... G 336 626-9971
  Asheboro *(G-490)*
Synq Marketing Group LLC .... F 800 380-6360
  Charlotte *(G-3665)*
Visual Products Inc .... F 336 883-0156
  High Point *(G-8596)*

2789 Bookbinding and related work

Adpress Printing Incorporated .... G 336 294-2244
  Summerfield *(G-14975)*
American Multimedia Inc .... D 336 229-7101
  Burlington *(G-1364)*
American Sample House Inc .... G 704 276-1970
  Vale *(G-15463)*
Appalachian State University .... F 828 262-2047
  Boone *(G-1174)*
Arzberger Engravers Inc .... E 704 376-1851
  Charlotte *(G-2224)*
Asheboro Piedmont Printing Inc .... F 336 899-7910
  Asheboro *(G-406)*
Associated Printing & Svcs Inc .... F 828 286-9064
  Rutherfordton *(G-13864)*
Atlantis Graphics Inc .... E 919 361-5809
  Durham *(G-4933)*
Azalea Bindery LLC .... G 828 545-6219
  Asheville *(G-554)*
Bennett & Associates Inc .... G 919 477-7362
  Durham *(G-4955)*
Boingo Graphics Inc .... E 704 527-4963
  Charlotte *(G-2331)*
Book Lover Search .... G 336 889-6127
  High Point *(G-8274)*
BP Solutions Group Inc .... E 828 252-4476
  Asheville *(G-570)*
Carolina Swatching Inc .... F 828 327-9499
  Hickory *(G-7967)*
Carter-Hubbard Publishing Co .... F 336 838-4117
  North Wilkesboro *(G-12000)*
Coastal Press Inc .... G 252 726-1549
  Morehead City *(G-11163)*
Creative Services Usa Inc .... G 336 887-1958
  High Point *(G-8307)*
Custom Sample Service Inc .... G 336 861-2010
  Archdale *(G-277)*
David Presnell .... G 336 372-5989
  Sparta *(G-14592)*
DEA Sasso Light of Day .... G 828 258-0141
  Asheville *(G-605)*
Docusource North Carolina LLC .... E 919 459-5900
  Morrisville *(G-11335)*
Dokja Inc .... G 336 852-5190
  Greensboro *(G-6975)*
▲ E Feibusch Company Inc .... E 336 434-5095
  High Point *(G-8333)*
Etherngton Cnservation Ctr Inc .... D 336 665-1317
  Greensboro *(G-7004)*
Flash Printing Company Inc .... E 704 375-2474
  Charlotte *(G-2769)*
Flex Finishing Inc .... G 704 342-3600
  Charlotte *(G-2773)*
Free Will Bptst Press Fndtion .... F 252 746-6128
  Ayden *(G-852)*

Gik Inc .... F 919 872-9498
  Raleigh *(G-12800)*
Hickory Printing Solutions LLC .... C 828 465-3431
  Conover *(G-4464)*
◆ Holt Sublimation Prtg Pdts Inc .... C 336 222-3600
  Burlington *(G-1429)*
Itek Graphics LLC .... E 704 357-6002
  Concord *(G-4291)*
Jag Graphics Inc .... G 828 259-9020
  Asheville *(G-668)*
Joseph C Woodard Prtg Co Inc .... F 919 829-0634
  Raleigh *(G-12922)*
Kreber .... D 336 861-2700
  High Point *(G-8425)*
Leatherbound Book Works .... F 919 448-7847
  Durham *(G-5187)*
Lee County Industries Inc .... E 919 775-3439
  Sanford *(G-14148)*
Loftin & Company Inc .... E 919 393-9393
  Charlotte *(G-3100)*
Measurement Incorporated .... C 919 683-2413
  Durham *(G-5213)*
▲ Medlit Solutions LLC .... D 919 878-6789
  Garner *(G-6287)*
Occasions Group Inc .... E 252 321-5805
  Greenville *(G-7566)*
Ollis Enterprises Inc .... E 828 265-0004
  Wilkesboro *(G-16037)*
Owen G Dunn Co Inc .... G 252 633-3197
  New Bern *(G-11832)*
Pamela A Adams .... G 919 876-5949
  Raleigh *(G-13096)*
Person Printing Company Inc .... E 336 599-2146
  Roxboro *(G-13818)*
Piedmont Business Forms Inc .... F 828 464-0010
  Newton *(G-11960)*
Postal Instant Press .... F 336 222-0717
  Burlington *(G-1477)*
Powell Ink Inc .... F 828 253-6886
  Asheville *(G-739)*
Printing Svcs Greensboro Inc .... F 336 274-7663
  Greensboro *(G-7285)*
Quality Prtg Cartridge Fctry .... G 336 852-2505
  Greensboro *(G-7301)*
S Chamblee Incorporated .... E 919 833-7561
  Raleigh *(G-13221)*
S Ruppe Inc .... E 828 287-4936
  Rutherfordton *(G-13889)*
▲ Sampletech Inc .... F 336 882-1717
  High Point *(G-8519)*
Swatchcraft .... G 336 841-7113
  Jamestown *(G-9073)*
Three Trees Bindery .... G 704 724-9409
  Charlotte *(G-3692)*
▲ Unique Collating & Bindery Svc ..... E 336 664-0960
  Greensboro *(G-7429)*
Weber and Weber Inc .... F 336 722-4109
  Winston Salem *(G-16968)*

2791 Typesetting

Advertising Design Systems Inc .... G 828 264-8060
  Boone *(G-1172)*
American Multimedia Inc .... D 336 229-7101
  Burlington *(G-1364)*
Appalachian State University .... F 828 262-2047
  Boone *(G-1174)*
Asheboro Piedmont Printing Inc .... F 336 899-7910
  Asheboro *(G-406)*
Atlantis Graphics Inc .... E 919 361-5809
  Durham *(G-4933)*
Austin Printing Company Inc .... G 704 289-1445
  Monroe *(G-10658)*

27 PRINTING, PUBLISHING AND ALLIED INDUSTRIES

Baicy Communications Inc............................. G 336 722-7768
Winston Salem *(G-16622)*

Bennett & Associates Inc............................... G 919 477-7362
Durham *(G-4955)*

Boingo Graphics Inc..................................... E 704 527-4963
Charlotte *(G-2331)*

BP Solutions Group Inc................................. E 828 252-4476
Asheville *(G-570)*

Carter-Hubbard Publishing Co........................ F 336 838-4117
North Wilkesboro *(G-12000)*

Coastal Press Inc.. G 252 726-1549
Morehead City *(G-11163)*

▲ CPS Resources Inc................................... E 704 628-7678
Monroe *(G-10697)*

Creative Printing Inc..................................... E 828 265-2800
Boone *(G-1189)*

Dokja Inc.. G 336 852-5190
Greensboro *(G-6975)*

F C C LLC... G 336 883-7314
High Point *(G-8349)*

▲ Fayetteville Publishing Co......................... D 910 323-4848
Fayetteville *(G-5824)*

Flash Printing Company Inc........................... E 704 375-2474
Charlotte *(G-2769)*

Free Will Bptst Press Fndtion......................... F 252 746-6128
Ayden *(G-852)*

Gik Inc.. F 919 872-9498
Raleigh *(G-12800)*

Greensboro News & Record LLC..................... A 336 373-7000
Greensboro *(G-7064)*

Hickory Printing Solutions LLC........................ C 828 465-3431
Conover *(G-4464)*

Ips... G 704 788-3327
Concord *(G-4289)*

Jag Graphics Inc... G 828 259-9020
Asheville *(G-668)*

Jones Media... F 828 264-3612
Boone *(G-1212)*

Joseph C Woodard Prtg Co Inc........................ F 919 829-0634
Raleigh *(G-12922)*

Kathie S Mc Daniel....................................... G 336 835-1544
Elkin *(G-5622)*

Loftin & Company Inc.................................... E 704 393-9393
Charlotte *(G-3100)*

Measurement Incorporated............................ C 919 683-2413
Durham *(G-5213)*

▲ Medlit Solutions LLC................................ D 919 878-6789
Garner *(G-6287)*

Ollis Enterprises Inc..................................... E 828 265-0004
Wilkesboro *(G-16037)*

Owen G Dunn Co Inc..................................... G 252 633-3197
New Bern *(G-11832)*

Pamela A Adams... G 919 876-5949
Raleigh *(G-13096)*

Person Printing Company Inc......................... E 336 599-2146
Roxboro *(G-13818)*

Pilot LLC... D 910 692-7271
Southern Pines *(G-14546)*

Powell Ink Inc... F 828 253-6886
Asheville *(G-739)*

Printery.. F 336 852-9774
Greensboro *(G-7284)*

Printing & Packaging Inc................................ E 704 482-3866
Shelby *(G-14357)*

Printing Partners Inc.................................... G 336 996-2268
Kernersville *(G-9225)*

Printing Svcs Greensboro Inc......................... F 336 274-7663
Greensboro *(G-7285)*

Quality Prtg Cartridge Fctry........................... G 336 852-2505
Greensboro *(G-7301)*

Raleigh Engraving Co.................................... G 919 832-5557
Raleigh *(G-13177)*

Richard D Stewart... G 919 284-2295
Kenly *(G-9156)*

S Chamblee Incorporated.............................. E 919 833-7561
Raleigh *(G-13221)*

S Ruppe Inc... E 828 287-4936
Rutherfordton *(G-13889)*

Tseng Information Systems Inc...................... G 919 682-9197
Durham *(G-5414)*

Weber and Weber Inc.................................... F 336 722-4109
Winston Salem *(G-16968)*

2796 Platemaking services

Carter-Hubbard Publishing Co........................ F 336 838-4117
North Wilkesboro *(G-12000)*

Container Graphics Corp................................ E 704 588-7230
Pineville *(G-12261)*

Docusource North Carolina LLC...................... E 919 459-5900
Morrisville *(G-11335)*

Dtp Inc... G 336 272-5122
Greensboro *(G-6982)*

F C C LLC... G 336 883-7314
High Point *(G-8349)*

GA Communications Inc................................ G 336 360-1860
Mooresville *(G-10953)*

Greensboro News & Record LLC..................... A 336 373-7000
Greensboro *(G-7064)*

Image Matters Inc.. G 336 940-3000
Clemmons *(G-4047)*

Jones Media... F 828 264-3612
Boone *(G-1212)*

Lee County Industries Inc.............................. E 919 775-3439
Sanford *(G-14148)*

Mark/Trece Inc.. E 336 292-3424
Whitsett *(G-15997)*

Motor Vhcles Lcense Plate Agcy..................... G 252 338-6965
Elizabeth City *(G-5558)*

Pre Flight Inc... G 828 758-1138
Lenoir *(G-9649)*

Roto-Plate Inc.. F 336 226-4965
Burlington *(G-1488)*

Signcaster Corporation.................................. G 336 712-2525
Winston Salem *(G-16908)*

◆ Southern Lithoplate Inc............................. C 919 556-9400
Youngsville *(G-17099)*

Winston Salem Engraving Co........................ F 336 725-4268
Winston Salem *(G-16981)*

Xsys North America Corporation.................... E 828 654-6805
Arden *(G-393)*

Xsys North America Corporation.................... F 704 504-2626
Charlotte *(G-3837)*

28 CHEMICALS AND ALLIED PRODUCTS

2812 Alkalies and chlorine

▼ Albemarle Corporation............................... A 980 299-5700
Charlotte *(G-2152)*

Buckeye International Inc.............................. G 704 523-9400
Charlotte *(G-2363)*

Global Ecosciences Inc.................................. G 252 631-6266
Wake Forest *(G-15560)*

Jci Jones Chemicals Inc................................. G 704 392-9767
Charlotte *(G-3014)*

Occidental Chemical Corp............................... G 910 675-7200
Castle Hayne *(G-1958)*

▲ Pavco Inc.. E 704 496-6800
Charlotte *(G-3321)*

PPG Industries Inc.. G 919 772-3093
Greensboro *(G-7272)*

2813 Industrial gases

Airgas Usa LLC.. F 704 394-1420
Charlotte *(G-2147)*

Airgas Usa LLC.. F 704 333-5475
Charlotte *(G-2148)*

Airgas Usa LLC.. G 919 544-1056
Durham *(G-4908)*

Airgas Usa LLC.. G 919 544-3773
Durham *(G-4909)*

Airgas Usa LLC.. G 919 735-5276
Goldsboro *(G-6587)*

Airgas Usa LLC.. F 910 392-2711
Wilmington *(G-16098)*

Ambro-Sol Usa LLC...................................... G 844 824-6959
Rutherfordton *(G-13862)*

Andy-OXY Co Inc.. E 828 258-0271
Asheville *(G-518)*

Arc3 Gases Inc... F 336 275-3333
Greensboro *(G-6812)*

Arc3 Gases Inc... F 704 220-1029
Monroe *(G-10650)*

Arc3 Gases Inc... G 910 892-4016
Dunn *(G-4851)*

Artcraft Tumblers... G 704 798-6115
Salisbury *(G-13923)*

Bar Argon... G 704 574-9486
Charlotte *(G-2276)*

Dark Hydrogen LLC....................................... G 530 360-8660
Concord *(G-4251)*

East Coast Oxygen Inc................................... G 828 252-7770
Asheville *(G-613)*

Helium Agency LLC....................................... G 919 833-1358
Raleigh *(G-12837)*

Helium Brands LLC....................................... F 561 350-1328
Cary *(G-1783)*

James Oxygen and Supply Co......................... E 704 322-5438
Hickory *(G-8071)*

Legacy Biogas LLC.. G 713 253-9013
Goldsboro *(G-6629)*

Linde Gas & Equipment Inc........................... F 919 380-7411
Cary *(G-1811)*

Linde Gas & Equipment Inc........................... F 704 587-7096
Charlotte *(G-3090)*

Linde Gas & Equipment Inc........................... D 919 549-0633
Durham *(G-5190)*

Linde Gas & Equipment Inc........................... F 866 543-3427
Whitsett *(G-15995)*

Linde Inc... G 910 343-0241
Wilmington *(G-16302)*

Matheson Tri-Gas Inc.................................... F 919 556-6461
Wake Forest *(G-15571)*

Messer LLC.. E 704 583-0313
Charlotte *(G-3167)*

Neon Rooster LLC.. G 330 806-7291
Aberdeen *(G-18)*

Panenergy Corp.. F 704 594-6200
Charlotte *(G-3310)*

2816 Inorganic pigments

Americhem Inc... E 704 782-6411
Concord *(G-4195)*

Avient Colorants USA LLC.............................. D 704 331-7000
Charlotte *(G-2248)*

Powerlab Inc.. E 336 650-0706
Winston Salem *(G-16861)*

Ultra Coatings Incorporated.......................... E 336 883-8853
High Point *(G-8584)*

2819 Industrial inorganic chemicals, nec

8th Element Cndtning Prfmce LLC.................. G 828 298-1290
Asheville *(G-512)*

Access Technologies LLC............................... G 574 286-1255
Mooresville *(G-10847)*

28 CHEMICALS AND ALLIED PRODUCTS

◆ Advanced Marketing International Inc F 910 392-0508
   Wilmington *(G-16095)*

Airgas Usa LLC .... F 704 394-1420
   Charlotte *(G-2147)*

Airgas Usa LLC .... G 919 544-3773
   Durham *(G-4909)*

Airgas Usa LLC .... G 919 735-5276
   Goldsboro *(G-6587)*

Al-Tex Dyes Co LLC .... G 704 849-9727
   Matthews *(G-10232)*

Albemarle Corporation .... C 704 739-2501
   Kings Mountain *(G-9290)*

▼ Albemarle Corporation .... A 980 299-5700
   Charlotte *(G-2152)*

◆ Albemarle US Inc .... C 704 739-2501
   Kings Mountain *(G-9291)*

All Elements Incorporated .... G 919 641-9576
   Cary *(G-1679)*

▼ American Ripener LLC .... G 704 527-8813
   Charlotte *(G-2183)*

◆ Apollo Chemical Corp .... D 336 226-1161
   Burlington *(G-1366)*

Applied Nano Solutions Inc .... G 336 687-6517
   Trinity *(G-15338)*

◆ Archroma US Inc .... E 704 353-4100
   Charlotte *(G-2211)*

Arkema Inc .... D 919 469-6700
   Cary *(G-1688)*

▲ Baikowski International Corp .... F 704 587-7100
   Charlotte *(G-2265)*

Beauty Elements LLC .... G 910 333-9957
   Jacksonville *(G-8990)*

Blue Nano Inc .... F 888 508-6266
   Cornelius *(G-4527)*

Bluestone Metals & Chem LLC .... G 704 662-8632
   Cornelius *(G-4528)*

Bluestone Specialty Chem LLC .... F 704 662-8632
   Cornelius *(G-4529)*

Borden Chemical .... G 828 584-3800
   Morganton *(G-11202)*

Bryson Industries Inc .... F 336 931-0026
   Thomasville *(G-15191)*

Carus LLC .... E 704 822-1441
   Belmont *(G-977)*

Celanese .... E 910 343-5000
   Wilmington *(G-16165)*

Chemol Company Inc .... E 336 333-3050
   Greensboro *(G-6906)*

Chemtrade Logistics (us) Inc .... E 773 646-2500
   Charlotte *(G-2471)*

◆ Clariant Corporation .... D 704 331-7000
   Charlotte *(G-2491)*

Clift Industries Inc .... G 704 752-0031
   Mount Holly *(G-11628)*

Coalogix Inc .... C 704 827-8933
   Charlotte *(G-2510)*

Conference Inc .... G 704 349-0203
   Gastonia *(G-6383)*

Corrtrac Systems Corporation .... G 252 232-3975
   Currituck *(G-4633)*

Dupont Specialty Pdts USA LLC .... E 919 248-5109
   Durham *(G-5070)*

◆ Dystar LP .... E 704 561-3000
   Charlotte *(G-2668)*

Eidp Inc .... D 910 483-4681
   Fayetteville *(G-5819)*

Eidp Inc .... D 252 522-6111
   Grifton *(G-7599)*

Eidp Inc .... D 910 371-4000
   Leland *(G-9540)*

Element Arbor Inc .... G 828 550-2250
   Waynesville *(G-15804)*

Element Countertops Inc .... G 704 641-7145
   Monroe *(G-10712)*

Element Strategy LLC .... G 704 997-5627
   Davidson *(G-4674)*

Element West LLC .... G 336 853-6118
   Lexington *(G-9713)*

Elemental Bee .... G 336 471-9085
   High Point *(G-8339)*

Elements Brands LLC .... F 503 230-8008
   Charlotte *(G-2692)*

Elements Imaging LLC .... F 504 258-3317
   Candler *(G-1578)*

Elements In Focus LLC .... G 561 289-8641
   Cary *(G-1756)*

Fil-Chem Inc .... G 919 878-1270
   Raleigh *(G-12766)*

FMC Corporation .... E 704 868-5300
   Bessemer City *(G-1067)*

FMC Corporation .... B 704 426-5336
   Bessemer City *(G-1068)*

Fortrans Inc .... G 919 365-8004
   Wendell *(G-15902)*

Fuji Silysia Chemical Ltd .... F 919 484-4158
   Greenville *(G-7530)*

▲ Fuji Silysia Chemical USA Ltd .... E 252 413-0003
   Greenville *(G-7531)*

◆ Ge-Hitchi Nclear Enrgy Amrcas .... A 910 819-5073
   Castle Hayne *(G-1948)*

Ge-Hitchi Nclear Enrgy Intl LL .... E 518 433-4338
   Wilmington *(G-16228)*

General Electric Company .... A 910 675-5000
   Wilmington *(G-16230)*

Geo Specialty Chemicals Inc .... G 252 793-2121
   Plymouth *(G-12373)*

Giles Chemical Corporation .... G 828 452-4784
   Waynesville *(G-15805)*

▲ Giles Chemical Corporation .... E 828 452-4784
   Waynesville *(G-15806)*

Global Laser Enrichment LLC .... E 910 819-7255
   Castle Hayne *(G-1949)*

Global Nuclear Fuel LLC .... F 910 819-6181
   Wilmington *(G-16232)*

◆ Global Nuclear Fuel-Americas LLC .... E 910 819-5950
   Castle Hayne *(G-1950)*

Grace and Company LLC .... G 336 893-7511
   Winston Salem *(G-16726)*

Gresco Manufacturing Inc .... G 336 475-8101
   Thomasville *(G-15228)*

◆ Hemo Bioscience Inc .... G 919 313-2888
   Durham *(G-5135)*

Highland International .... G 828 265-2513
   Boone *(G-1206)*

◆ Industrial and Agricultur .... E 910 843-2121
   Red Springs *(G-13501)*

◆ Innospec Inc .... E 704 633-8028
   Salisbury *(G-13985)*

Innospec Inc .... E 704 633-8028
   Salisbury *(G-13986)*

Invista Capital Management LLC .... A 316 828-1000
   Wilmington *(G-16273)*

Leke LLC .... E 704 523-1452
   Pineville *(G-12280)*

M & G Polymers Usa LLC .... G 910 509-4414
   Wilmington *(G-16311)*

Marlowe-Van Loan Corporation .... E 336 886-7126
   High Point *(G-8440)*

Metallix Refining Inc .... E 252 413-0346
   Greenville *(G-7559)*

▲ Microban Products Company .... D 704 766-4267
   Huntersville *(G-8854)*

Mount Vernon Chemicals LLC .... D 336 226-1161
   Burlington *(G-1463)*

Mount Vernon Mills Inc .... B 336 226-1161
   Burlington *(G-1464)*

Natural Elements Bath and Body .... G 828 226-0853
   Brevard *(G-1283)*

▲ Netqem LLC .... G 919 544-4122
   Durham *(G-5243)*

New Element .... G 704 890-7292
   Charlotte *(G-3251)*

▼ Novalent Ltd .... F 336 375-7555
   Greensboro *(G-7225)*

Olin Black Enterprise LLC .... G 704 363-5675
   Midland *(G-10472)*

Oneh2 Inc .... E 844 996-6342
   Hickory *(G-8107)*

▲ Pavco Inc .... E 704 496-6800
   Charlotte *(G-3321)*

Pcs Phosphate Company Inc .... E 252 322-4111
   Aurora *(G-838)*

Pencco Inc .... F 252 235-5300
   Middlesex *(G-10453)*

Piedmont Lithium Carolinas Inc .... F 434 664-7643
   Belmont *(G-1002)*

Pretinned Carbide Co Inc .... F 704 871-9644
   Statesville *(G-14868)*

◆ Qc LLC .... E 800 883-0010
   Cary *(G-1864)*

Rockwood Lithium .... F 704 739-2501
   Kings Mountain *(G-9330)*

Sciepharm LLC .... C 307 352-9559
   Durham *(G-5343)*

Sciteck Diagnostics Inc .... G 828 650-0409
   Fletcher *(G-6036)*

Sibelco .... E 828 765-1114
   Spruce Pine *(G-14655)*

Solvay USA Inc .... C 919 786-4555
   Raleigh *(G-13280)*

▲ Sostram Corporation .... G 919 226-1195
   Durham *(G-5364)*

Southern States Chemical Inc .... E 910 762-5054
   Wilmington *(G-16411)*

Steag SCR-Tech Inc .... E 704 827-8933
   Charlotte *(G-3626)*

Synnovator Inc .... G 919 360-0518
   Durham *(G-5384)*

Tecgrachem Inc .... G 336 993-6785
   Kernersville *(G-9241)*

▲ Techmet Carbides Inc .... D 828 624-0222
   Hickory *(G-8176)*

Tutcu-Farnam Custom Products .... E 828 684-3766
   Arden *(G-388)*

◆ Unichem IV Ltd .... F 336 578-5476
   Haw River *(G-7758)*

Venator Chemicals LLC .... D 704 454-4811
   Harrisburg *(G-7733)*

2821 Plastics materials and resins

3a Composites Holding Inc .... E 704 658-3527
   Davidson *(G-4664)*

◆ Abt Inc .... E 704 528-9806
   Troutman *(G-15364)*

Albemarle Corporation .... G 252 482-7423
   Edenton *(G-5506)*

▼ Albemarle Corporation .... A 980 299-5700
   Charlotte *(G-2152)*

Allotropica Technologies Inc .... G 919 522-4374
   Chapel Hill *(G-1982)*

Alpek Polyester Miss Inc .... C 228 533-4000
   Charlotte *(G-2164)*

Alpek Polyester Usa LLC .... C 910 433-8200
   Fayetteville *(G-5758)*

Alpek Polyester Usa LLC .... B 910 371-4000
   Wilmington *(G-16108)*

28 CHEMICALS AND ALLIED PRODUCTS

◆ Alpek Polyester Usa LLC................D.....704 940-7500
  Charlotte *(G-2165)*

American Durafilm Co Inc...............G.....704 895-7701
  Mooresville *(G-10856)*

◆ Aqua Plastics Inc.........................E.....828 324-6284
  Hickory *(G-7939)*

Arclin USA LLC..............................G.....919 542-2526
  Moncure *(G-10614)*

◆ Auriga Polymers Inc....................C.....864 579-5570
  Charlotte *(G-2239)*

Aurora Plastics Inc.........................F.....336 775-2640
  Welcome *(G-15872)*

◆ Avient Protective Mtls LLC............D.....252 707-2547
  Greenville *(G-7490)*

Bio-TEC Environmental LLC...........G.....505 629-1777
  Charlotte *(G-2314)*

Bluesky Polymers LLC....................G.....919 522-4374
  Cary *(G-1710)*

Calsak Plastics Inc.........................G.....704 597-8555
  Charlotte *(G-2377)*

Carpenter Co................................D.....828 464-9470
  Conover *(G-4433)*

Carpenter Co................................E.....828 322-6545
  Hickory *(G-7969)*

Carpenter Co................................D.....336 861-5730
  High Point *(G-8286)*

Carpenter Co................................E.....828 632-7061
  Taylorsville *(G-15133)*

Celanese Intl Corp.........................F.....704 480-5798
  Grover *(G-7606)*

Celgard LLC..................................D.....704 588-5310
  Charlotte *(G-2439)*

Celgard LLC..................................D.....704 720-5200
  Concord *(G-4230)*

◆ Celgard LLC...............................C.....800 235-4273
  Charlotte *(G-2440)*

Chase Corporation.........................G.....828 855-9316
  Hickory *(G-7985)*

Chase Corporation.........................G.....828 649-5578
  Hickory *(G-7986)*

Chroma Color Corporation..............D.....336 629-9184
  Asheboro *(G-416)*

Chroma Color Corporation..............C.....704 637-7000
  Salisbury *(G-13941)*

Coates Designers & Crafstmen......G.....828 349-9700
  Franklin *(G-6120)*

Consolidated Pipe & Sup Co Inc....F.....336 294-8577
  Greensboro *(G-6930)*

Cs Systems Company Inc...............F.....800 525-9878
  Candler *(G-1576)*

◆ Custom Polymers Inc..................F.....704 332-6070
  Charlotte *(G-2593)*

▲ Custom Polymers Pet LLC............E.....866 717-0716
  Charlotte *(G-2594)*

D2h Advanced Composites Inc......G.....336 239-9637
  Winston Salem *(G-16667)*

◆ Darnel Inc..................................G.....704 625-9869
  Monroe *(G-10703)*

Ddp Spclty Elctrnic Mtls US 9........D.....336 547-7112
  Greensboro *(G-6962)*

Delcor Polymers Inc.......................G.....704 847-0640
  Matthews *(G-10246)*

Dow Silicones Corporation.............D.....336 547-7100
  Greensboro *(G-6978)*

Dupont Teijin Films........................G.....910 433-8200
  Fayetteville *(G-5813)*

▲ Eastern Plastics Company...........G.....704 542-7786
  Charlotte *(G-2673)*

Eidp Inc..G.....252 522-6286
  Kinston *(G-9362)*

Essay Operations Inc.....................G.....252 443-6010
  Rocky Mount *(G-13696)*

Evonik Superabsorber LLC.............C.....336 333-7540
  Greensboro *(G-7007)*

Freudenberg Prfmce Mtls LP..........F.....919 620-3900
  Durham *(G-5105)*

Future Foam Inc............................D.....336 885-4121
  High Point *(G-8361)*

Genpak LLC..................................D.....704 588-6202
  Charlotte *(G-2822)*

Gersan Industries Incorporated......G.....336 886-5455
  High Point *(G-8365)*

Hanwha Advanced Mtls Amer LLC..E.....704 434-2271
  Shelby *(G-14325)*

Hexion Inc....................................E.....910 483-1311
  Fayetteville *(G-5838)*

Hexion Inc....................................D.....336 884-8918
  High Point *(G-8384)*

Hexion Inc....................................E.....828 584-3800
  Morganton *(G-11219)*

Huntsman Corporation....................F.....706 272-4020
  Charlotte *(G-2933)*

Huntsman International LLC...........E.....704 588-6082
  Charlotte *(G-2934)*

▲ Huntsman Textile Effects.............E.....704 587-5000
  Charlotte *(G-2935)*

Imaflex Usa Inc.............................E.....336 474-1190
  Thomasville *(G-15236)*

◆ Indorama Ventures USA Inc..........C.....336 672-0101
  Asheboro *(G-443)*

Ineo Usa Inc.................................G.....919 467-2199
  Cary *(G-1788)*

Intertape Polymer Corp..................D.....252 792-2083
  Everetts *(G-5695)*

Intrinsic Advanced Mtls LLC...........G.....704 874-5000
  Gastonia *(G-6430)*

Invista Capital Management LLC....D.....704 636-6000
  Salisbury *(G-13989)*

Invista Capital Management LLC....A.....316 828-1000
  Wilmington *(G-16273)*

J-M Manufacturing Company Inc....D.....919 575-6515
  Creedmoor *(G-4615)*

Jpi Coastal..................................F.....704 310-5867
  Salisbury *(G-13995)*

JPS Composite Materials Corp.......C.....704 872-9831
  Statesville *(G-14826)*

▲ Kattermann Ventures Inc............E.....828 651-8737
  Fletcher *(G-6015)*

Kestrel I Acquisition Corporation....A.....919 990-7500
  Durham *(G-5180)*

Kilop USA Inc................................G.....336 297-4999
  Greensboro *(G-7149)*

Lanxess Corporation......................G.....704 923-0121
  Dallas *(G-4647)*

Lanxess Corporation......................F.....704 868-7200
  Gastonia *(G-6443)*

◆ Liquidating Reichhold Inc............A.....919 990-7500
  Durham *(G-5191)*

Lkf Inc..F.....336 475-7400
  Thomasville *(G-15243)*

Mallard Creek Polymers LLC..........G.....877 240-0171
  Charlotte *(G-3119)*

Mallard Creek Polymers LLC..........G.....704 547-0622
  Charlotte *(G-3120)*

Mallard Creek Polymers LLC..........G.....704 547-0622
  Harrisburg *(G-7716)*

◆ Mallard Creek Polymers LLC.......E.....704 547-0622
  Charlotte *(G-3121)*

Mdt Bromley LLC...........................E.....828 651-8737
  Fletcher *(G-6021)*

Mexichem Spcalty Compounds Inc..D.....704 889-7821
  Pineville *(G-12283)*

▲ Microban Products Company........D.....704 766-4267
  Huntersville *(G-8854)*

Modern Densifying Inc...................F.....704 434-8335
  Shelby *(G-14348)*

Modern Polymers Inc.....................G.....704 435-5825
  Cherryville *(G-3872)*

▼ Modern Polymers Inc..................E.....704 435-5825
  Cherryville *(G-3873)*

Norell Inc......................................G.....828 584-2600
  Morganton *(G-11239)*

Olympic Products LLC....................D.....336 378-9620
  Greensboro *(G-7231)*

Olympic Products LLC....................D.....336 378-9620
  Greensboro *(G-7230)*

Peninsula Polymers........................G.....336 885-8185
  High Point *(G-8479)*

◆ Performance Additives LLC.........F.....215 321-4388
  Southern Pines *(G-14543)*

Phase II Creations Inc...................G.....336 249-0673
  Lexington *(G-9769)*

Plaskolite LLC...............................C.....704 588-3800
  Charlotte *(G-3347)*

Plastic Products Inc......................E.....704 739-7463
  Bessemer City *(G-1078)*

Plastic Solutions Inc.....................F.....678 353-2100
  Ellenboro *(G-5637)*

Poly One Distribution.....................G.....704 872-8168
  Statesville *(G-14863)*

▲ Polychem Alloy Inc.....................E.....828 754-7570
  Lenoir *(G-9648)*

◆ Polygal Inc.................................F.....704 588-3800
  Charlotte *(G-3351)*

Polyone Corporation......................G.....704 838-0457
  Statesville *(G-14864)*

Polyone Distribution.......................G.....919 413-4547
  Rolesville *(G-13759)*

▲ Polyquest Incorporated..............F.....910 342-9554
  Wilmington *(G-16361)*

Poole Company LLC......................G.....828 275-0460
  Fairview *(G-5717)*

◆ Poppelmann Plastics USA LLC...E.....828 466-9500
  Claremont *(G-3933)*

PPG Industries Inc........................G.....919 772-3093
  Greensboro *(G-7272)*

PQ Recycling LLC..........................E.....910 342-9554
  Wilmington *(G-16369)*

Pressure Washing Near Me LLC....C.....704 280-0351
  Waxhaw *(G-15770)*

Prototech Manufacturing Inc..........F.....508 646-8849
  Washington *(G-15728)*

◆ Reichhold Holdings Us Inc..........A.....919 990-7500
  Durham *(G-5323)*

Resinall Corp................................C.....252 585-1445
  Severn *(G-14269)*

▲ Robix America Inc......................C.....336 668-9555
  Greensboro *(G-7314)*

Rugby Acquisition LLC...................D.....336 993-8686
  Kernersville *(G-9229)*

◆ Rutland Group Inc.....................C.....704 553-0046
  Pineville *(G-12300)*

◆ Rutland Holdings LLC.................E.....704 553-0046
  Pineville *(G-12301)*

Samos Polymers Corporation.........F.....704 241-2065
  Stanley *(G-14706)*

Sanctuary Systems LLC................D.....305 989-0953
  Fremont *(G-6173)*

▲ Scentair Technologies LLC..........D.....704 504-2320
  Charlotte *(G-3498)*

▲ Schlaadt Plastics Limited............F.....252 634-9494
  New Bern *(G-11844)*

Sealed Air Corporation..................A.....980 221-3235
  Charlotte *(G-3517)*

▲ Spt Technology Inc.....................F.....612 332-1880
  Monroe *(G-10811)*

SIC SECTION
28 CHEMICALS AND ALLIED PRODUCTS

Spt Technology Inc .... G 704 290-5007
  Monroe *(G-10812)*

Ssd Designs LLC .... F 980 245-2988
  Charlotte *(G-3616)*

▲ Starpet Inc .... C 336 672-0101
  Asheboro *(G-485)*

Superskinsystems Inc .... G 336 601-6005
  Greensboro *(G-7380)*

▲ Syncot Plastics Inc .... D 704 967-0010
  Belmont *(G-1012)*

◆ Tailored Chemical Products Inc .... D 828 322-6512
  Hickory *(G-8173)*

Tosaf Inc .... G 704 396-7097
  Bessemer City *(G-1086)*

◆ Tosaf Inc .... F 980 533-3000
  Bessemer City *(G-1087)*

◆ Toter LLC .... D 800 424-0422
  Statesville *(G-14916)*

▲ Unifi Kinston LLC .... E 252 522-6518
  Kinston *(G-9389)*

▲ W M Plastics Inc .... F 704 599-0511
  Charlotte *(G-3789)*

▼ Wp Reidsville LLC .... C 336 342-1200
  Reidsville *(G-13547)*

2822 Synthetic rubber

Axchem Solutions Inc .... G 919 742-9810
  Siler City *(G-14398)*

◆ Custom Polymers Inc .... F 704 332-6070
  Charlotte *(G-2593)*

Dupont Electronic Polymers L P .... F 919 248-5135
  Durham *(G-5069)*

ERA Polymers Corporation .... F 704 931-3675
  Stanley *(G-14693)*

Fibex LLC .... E 336 358-5014
  Greensboro *(G-7012)*

▲ Fibex LLC .... E 336 605-9002
  Colfax *(G-4150)*

▲ Indulor America LP .... E 336 578-6855
  Graham *(G-6692)*

Kestrel I Acquisition Corporation .... A 919 990-7500
  Durham *(G-5180)*

Lanxess Corporation .... F 704 868-7200
  Gastonia *(G-6443)*

◆ Liquidating Reichhold Inc .... A 919 990-7500
  Durham *(G-5191)*

◆ M & P Polymers Inc .... G 910 246-6585
  Pinehurst *(G-12227)*

◆ Reichhold Holdings Us Inc .... A 919 990-7500
  Durham *(G-5323)*

Seal It Services Inc .... F 919 777-0374
  Sanford *(G-14183)*

Sunray Inc .... E 828 287-7030
  Rutherfordton *(G-13892)*

Tethis Inc .... E 919 808-2866
  Raleigh *(G-13340)*

Wellco Two Inc .... G 828 667-4662
  Asheville *(G-818)*

2823 Cellulosic manmade fibers

Additive America Inc .... G 252 549-0247
  Kinston *(G-9340)*

Carolina Prcsion Fbers Spv LLC .... E 336 527-4140
  Ronda *(G-13763)*

Invista Capital Management LLC .... D 704 636-6000
  Salisbury *(G-13989)*

Neptco Incorporated .... C 828 313-0149
  Granite Falls *(G-6747)*

Profile Products LLC .... E 828 327-4165
  Conover *(G-4489)*

▼ Thanet Inc .... E 704 483-4175
  Denver *(G-4807)*

2824 Organic fibers, noncellulosic

Alpek Polyester Usa LLC .... B 910 371-4000
  Wilmington *(G-16108)*

◆ Auriga Polymers Inc .... C 864 579-5570
  Charlotte *(G-2239)*

▼ Basofil Fibers LLC .... E 828 304-2307
  Charlotte *(G-2287)*

▲ Coats HP Inc .... B 704 824-9904
  Mc Adenville *(G-10377)*

Coats HP Inc .... E 704 329-5800
  Charlotte *(G-2514)*

Durafiber Technologies .... A 704 912-3700
  Huntersville *(G-8810)*

▲ Durafiber Technologies (dft) Inc .... A 704 912-3700
  Huntersville *(G-8811)*

▲ Durafiber Technologies (d .... A 704 912-3770
  Huntersville *(G-8812)*

Durafiber Technologies DFT Inc .... G 704 639-2722
  Salisbury *(G-13956)*

Durafiber Technologies DFT Inc .... G 919 356-3824
  Sanford *(G-14111)*

Fibrix LLC .... E 704 878-0027
  Statesville *(G-14797)*

◆ Fibrix LLC .... E 828 459-7064
  Conover *(G-4454)*

High Speed Gear Inc .... F 910 325-1000
  Swansboro *(G-15045)*

◆ Innofa Usa LLC .... E 336 635-2900
  Eden *(G-5492)*

Mannington Mills Inc .... E 704 824-3551
  Mc Adenville *(G-10379)*

Military Wraps Inc .... F 910 671-0008
  Lumberton *(G-10045)*

Morbern LLC .... E 336 883-4332
  High Point *(G-8458)*

Omnia Products LLC .... G 919 514-3977
  Oxford *(G-12139)*

◆ Pbi Performance Products Inc .... D 704 554-3378
  Charlotte *(G-3322)*

Pharr McAdenville Corporation .... D 704 824-3551
  Mc Adenville *(G-10380)*

▼ Polycor Holdings Inc .... D 828 459-7064
  Conover *(G-4483)*

◆ Snp Inc .... E 919 598-0400
  Durham *(G-5361)*

▼ Southern Fiber Inc .... E 704 736-0011
  Lincolnton *(G-9919)*

Stein Fibers Ltd .... E 704 599-2804
  Charlotte *(G-3629)*

Trelleborg Ctd Systems US Inc .... C 828 286-9126
  Rutherfordton *(G-13897)*

Warp Technologies Inc .... C 919 552-2311
  Holly Springs *(G-8726)*

2833 Medicinals and botanicals

A House of Hemp LLC .... G 910 984-1441
  Linden *(G-9938)*

Alternative Health Dist LLC .... G 336 465-6618
  Mooresville *(G-10854)*

Averix Bio LLC .... E 919 614-7600
  Wilson *(G-16471)*

Cbdmd Inc .... F 704 445-3060
  Charlotte *(G-2422)*

Direct Digital LLC .... E 704 557-0987
  Charlotte *(G-2640)*

Ehs Retail LLC .... F 336 629-4367
  Asheboro *(G-428)*

Emergo Therapeutics Inc .... F 919 649-5544
  Durham *(G-5083)*

Fosterscape LLP .... G 910 401-7638
  Fayetteville *(G-5827)*

Founders Hemp LLC .... G 888 334-4367
  Asheboro *(G-436)*

Healing Springs Farmacy .... G 336 549-6159
  Greensboro *(G-7081)*

▲ Herbs Gaia Inc .... D 828 884-4242
  Brevard *(G-1276)*

Inneroptic Technology Inc .... G 919 732-2090
  Hillsborough *(G-8656)*

Interntnal Agrclture Group LLC .... F 908 323-3246
  Mooresville *(G-10983)*

Mallinckrodt LLC .... G 919 878-2900
  Raleigh *(G-12992)*

Medkoo Inc .... G 919 636-5577
  Durham *(G-5215)*

Natsol LLC .... F 704 302-1246
  Matthews *(G-10275)*

▲ Pisgah Laboratories Inc .... E 828 884-2789
  Pisgah Forest *(G-12327)*

Power Chem Inc .... G 919 365-3400
  Wendell *(G-15911)*

White Stone Labs Inc .... G 704 775-5274
  Mooresville *(G-11130)*

2834 Pharmaceutical preparations

◆ A1 Biochem Labs LLC .... G 315 299-4775
  Wilmington *(G-16090)*

▼ A2a Integrated Logistics Inc .... G 800 493-3736
  Fayetteville *(G-5749)*

Abbott Enterprises .... G 252 757-1298
  Greenville *(G-7477)*

Abbott Laboratories .... G 704 243-1832
  Waxhaw *(G-15743)*

Abbott Sales LLC .... G 919 523-5478
  Raleigh *(G-12460)*

▼ Accord Healthcare Inc .... E 919 941-7878
  Raleigh *(G-12467)*

Aceragen Inc .... F 919 271-1032
  Durham *(G-4900)*

Achelios Therapeutics LLC .... G 919 354-6233
  Durham *(G-4901)*

Aerami Therapeutics Inc .... F 650 773-5926
  Durham *(G-4905)*

Aerami Thrpeutics Holdings Inc .... G 919 589-7495
  Durham *(G-4906)*

Aerie Pharmaceuticals Inc .... G 919 237-5300
  Durham *(G-4907)*

▼ Albemarle Corporation .... A 980 299-5700
  Charlotte *(G-2152)*

Albion Medical Holdings Inc .... F 800 378-3906
  Lenoir *(G-9571)*

Alcami Carolinas Corporation .... G 919 957-5500
  Durham *(G-4911)*

Alcami Carolinas Corporation .... G 910 619-3952
  Garner *(G-6251)*

Alcami Carolinas Corporation .... G 910 254-7000
  Morrisville *(G-11281)*

Alcami Carolinas Corporation .... G 910 254-7000
  Morrisville *(G-11282)*

Alcami Carolinas Corporation .... G 910 254-7000
  Morrisville *(G-11283)*

Alcami Carolinas Corporation .... F 910 254-7000
  Wilmington *(G-16100)*

Alcami Carolinas Corporation .... G 910 254-7000
  Wilmington *(G-16101)*

Alcami Carolinas Corporation .... G 910 254-7000
  Wilmington *(G-16102)*

Alcami Carolinas Corporation .... B 910 254-7000
  Wilmington *(G-16103)*

Alcami Corporation .... A 910 254-7000
  Wilmington *(G-16104)*

Alcami Holdings LLC .... A 910 254-7000
  Wilmington *(G-16105)*

28 CHEMICALS AND ALLIED PRODUCTS

Allergan Inc .... G 704 301-7790
  Raleigh (G-12491)
American Pharmaceutical Svcs .... G 828 328-1816
  Hickory (G-7933)
Anelleo Inc .... G 919 448-4008
  Chapel Hill (G-1984)
Arbor Organic Technologies LLC .... E 704 276-7100
  Lincolnton (G-9874)
Arbor Pharmaceuticals Inc .... G 919 792-1700
  Raleigh (G-12517)
Areteia Therapeutics Inc .... F 973 985-0597
  Chapel Hill (G-1985)
Aristos Pharmaceuticals Inc .... F 919 678-6592
  Cary (G-1687)
Array Biopharma Inc .... D 303 381-6600
  Morrisville (G-11291)
Arrivo Management LLC .... G 919 460-9500
  Morrisville (G-11292)
Ascend Research Corp .... G 336 710-5793
  Winston Salem (G-16611)
Askbio .... G 336 407-6217
  Durham (G-4929)
Asklepios Bopharmaceutical Inc .... C 919 561-6210
  Morrisville (G-11294)
Astrazeneca Pharmaceuticals LP .... D 919 647-4990
  Durham (G-4931)
Atsena Therapeutics Inc .... E 352 273-9342
  Durham (G-4935)
Aurobindo Pharma USA Inc .... E 732 839-9400
  Durham (G-4936)
Aurolife Pharma LLC .... E 732 839-9408
  Durham (G-4937)
Avadim Holdings Inc .... E 877 677-2723
  Asheville (G-551)
Avadim Holdings Inc .... E 877 677-2723
  Charlotte (G-2244)
Avadim Holdings Inc .... E 877 677-2723
  Swannanoa (G-15019)
Avient Protective Mtls LLC .... D 704 862-5100
  Stanley (G-14684)
Avior Inc .... G 919 234-0068
  Cary (G-1697)
Avista Pharma Solutions Inc .... E 919 544-8600
  Durham (G-4939)
Axitare Corporation .... G 919 256-8196
  Raleigh (G-12537)
B3 Bio Inc .... G 919 226-3079
  Durham (G-4940)
Balanced Pharma Incorporated .... G 704 278-7054
  Cornelius (G-4525)
Banner Life Sciences LLC .... E 336 812-8700
  High Point (G-8264)
Battery Watering Systems LLC .... G 336 714-0448
  Clemmons (G-4030)
Bausch Health Americas Inc .... F 949 461-6000
  Durham (G-4948)
Baxter Healthcare Corporation .... B 828 756-6600
  Marion (G-10142)
Baxter Healthcare Corporation .... F 828 756-6623
  Marion (G-10143)
Bayer Corp .... E 704 373-0991
  Charlotte (G-2288)
Bayer Corporation .... E 800 242-5897
  Durham (G-4949)
◆ Bayer Cropscience Inc .... D 412 777-2000
  Durham (G-4950)
Bayer Healthcare LLC .... E 919 461-6525
  Morrisville (G-11300)
Bayer Hlthcare Pharmaceuticals .... G 602 469-6846
  Raleigh (G-12546)
▲ Be Pharmaceuticals Inc .... G 704 560-1444
  Cary (G-1699)

Beaker Inc .... F 919 803-7422
  Raleigh (G-12549)
Bestco LLC .... E 704 664-4300
  Mooresville (G-10876)
Bestco LLC .... C 704 664-4300
  Mooresville (G-10877)
Bestco LLC .... C 704 664-4300
  Mooresville (G-10878)
◆ Bestco LLC .... C 704 664-4300
  Mooresville (G-10879)
▲ Biocryst Pharmaceuticals Inc .... B 919 859-1302
  Durham (G-4958)
Biogen MA Inc .... G 919 941-1100
  Durham (G-4959)
Biogen Pharma .... G 919 993-1100
  Morrisville (G-11303)
Biolex Therapeutics Inc .... E 919 542-9901
  Pittsboro (G-12331)
Biomontr Labs .... G 919 650-1185
  Cary (G-1704)
Bioresource International Inc .... G 919 267-3758
  Apex (G-171)
Bpc Plasma Inc .... F 910 463-2603
  Jacksonville (G-8991)
Bpl Usa LLC .... F 919 354-8405
  Durham (G-4975)
Bright Path Laboratories Inc .... G 858 281-8121
  Kannapolis (G-9112)
Brii Biosciences Inc .... F 919 240-5605
  Durham (G-4980)
Bristol-Myers Squibb Company .... G 800 321-1335
  Charlotte (G-2357)
Bristol-Myers Squibb Company .... B 336 855-5500
  Greensboro (G-6857)
Camargo Phrm Svcs LLC .... G 513 618-0325
  Durham (G-4995)
Cambrex High Point Inc .... D 336 841-5250
  High Point (G-8281)
Capnostics LLC .... F 610 442-1363
  Concord (G-4223)
Cardiac Wllness Spplements LLC .... F 252 757-3939
  Greenville (G-7495)
Cardinal Health 414 LLC .... G 704 644-7989
  Charlotte (G-2387)
Cardiopharma Inc .... F 910 791-1361
  Wilmington (G-16156)
Cardioxyl Pharmaceuticals Inc .... G 919 869-8586
  Chapel Hill (G-1997)
Carolinas Cord Blood Bank .... G 919 668-1102
  Durham (G-5006)
Catalent Greenville Inc .... E 732 537-6200
  Greenville (G-7499)
Catalent Greenville Inc .... D 252 752-3800
  Greenville (G-7500)
Catalent Pharma Solutions LLC .... F 919 481-4855
  Morrisville (G-11313)
Catalent Pharma Solutions LLC .... C 919 481-4855
  Morrisville (G-11314)
Catalent Pharma Solutions Inc .... F 919 465-8206
  Durham (G-5008)
Catalent Pharma Solutions Inc .... F 919 481-2614
  Morrisville (G-11315)
Cell Microsystems Inc .... G 919 608-2035
  Durham (G-5010)
Cem-102 Pharmaceuticals Inc .... G 919 576-2306
  Chapel Hill (G-2000)
Cempra Pharmaceuticals Inc .... F 919 803-6882
  Chapel Hill (G-2001)
Cenerx Biopharma Inc .... G 919 234-4072
  Cary (G-1727)
Certirx Corporation .... G 919 354-1029
  Rtp (G-13830)

Chemogenics Biopharma LLC .... G 919 323-8133
  Durham (G-5015)
Chimerix Inc .... E 919 806-1074
  Durham (G-5016)
Civentichem Usa LLC .... G 919 672-8865
  Cary (G-1731)
Cleveland Compounding Inc .... C 704 487-1971
  Shelby (G-14297)
Closure Medical Corporation .... C 919 876-7800
  Raleigh (G-12630)
Cloud Pharmaceuticals Inc .... G 919 558-1254
  Durham (G-5021)
Cmp Pharma Inc .... E 252 753-7111
  Farmville (G-5732)
Cornerstone Biopharma Inc .... F 919 678-6507
  Cary (G-1735)
Cosette Pharmaceuticals Inc .... C 704 735-5700
  Lincolnton (G-9885)
▲ Cosette Phrmctcals NC Labs LLC ..... C 908 753-2000
  Lincolnton (G-9886)
Daily Manufacturing Inc .... F 704 782-0700
  Rockwell (G-13651)
Dataspectrum .... G 919 341-3300
  Raleigh (G-12673)
Davospharma .... G 919 662-8432
  Apex (G-180)
Debmed Usa LLC .... F 704 263-4240
  Charlotte (G-2609)
Delarrivo Inc .... G 919 460-9500
  Morrisville (G-11330)
Diagnostic Devices .... G 704 599-5908
  Charlotte (G-2627)
Dignify Inc .... G 336 500-8668
  Greensboro (G-6971)
Dignify Therapeutics LLC .... G 919 371-8138
  Durham (G-5052)
Diomorph Pharmaceuticals LP .... F 919 354-6233
  Chapel Hill (G-2009)
Docent Pharma Services LLC .... G 229 310-0111
  Apex (G-183)
Dova Pharmaceuticals Inc .... F 919 748-5975
  Durham (G-5060)
Dpi Newco LLC .... A 252 758-3436
  Greenville (G-7516)
Dsk Biopharma Inc .... G 919 465-9104
  Morrisville (G-11336)
DSM .... G 408 582-2610
  Greenville (G-7517)
Dsm Inc .... F 919 876-2802
  Raleigh (G-12706)
▲ DSM Pharmaceuticals Inc .... E 252 758-3436
  Greenville (G-7518)
▲ DSM Pharmaceuticals Inc .... A 252 758-3436
  Greenville (G-7519)
Dynamic Nutraceuticals LLC .... E 704 380-2324
  Statesville (G-14791)
East Coast Biologics .... G 717 919-9980
  Fayetteville (G-5815)
▲ Ei LLC .... B 704 857-0707
  Winston Salem (G-16692)
Eisai Inc .... F 919 941-6920
  Raleigh (G-12728)
Elanco US Inc .... F 812 230-2745
  Greensboro (G-6992)
Eli Company .... G 908 242-3497
  Winston Salem (G-16695)
Eli Lilly and Company .... F 317 296-1226
  Durham (G-5078)
Embrex Poultry Health LLC .... F 910 844-5566
  Maxton (G-10355)
Encube Ethicals Inc .... F 984 439-2761
  Durham (G-5085)

SIC SECTION
28 CHEMICALS AND ALLIED PRODUCTS

Engineered Processing Eqp LLC .... G 919 321-6891
  Wilson *(G-16496)*
▲ Environmental Science US LLC .... F 800 331-2867
  Cary *(G-1759)*
Envisia Therapeutics Inc .... E 919 973-1440
  Durham *(G-5090)*
▲ Eon Labs Inc .... B 252 234-2222
  Wilson *(G-16497)*
Eppin Pharma Inc .... G 919 608-2984
  Chapel Hill *(G-2017)*
Esc Brands LLC .... G 888 331-8332
  Lexington *(G-9717)*
Evoqua Water Technologies LLC .... F 919 477-2161
  Durham *(G-5094)*
Exela Drug Substance LLC .... E 828 758-5474
  Lenoir *(G-9607)*
Exela Pharma Sciences LLC .... E 828 758-5474
  Lenoir *(G-9608)*
Exp Pharmaceuticals Inc .... F 336 631-2893
  Winston Salem *(G-16704)*
Fervent Pharmaceuticals LLC .... G 252 558-9700
  Greenville *(G-7525)*
Fidelity Pharmaceuticals LLC .... G 704 274-3192
  Huntersville *(G-8819)*
Fortovia Therapeutics Inc .... G 919 872-5578
  Raleigh *(G-12779)*
Fortrea Holdings Inc .... E 877 495-0816
  Durham *(G-5102)*
Fresenius Kabi Usa LLC .... B 252 991-2692
  Wilson *(G-16499)*
Fsc Therapeutics LLC .... F 704 941-2500
  Charlotte *(G-2799)*
Fujifilm Diosynth Biotechnolog .... G 919 337-4400
  Durham *(G-5107)*
Fujifilm Dsynth Btchnlgies USA .... C 919 337-4400
  Morrisville *(G-11343)*
Furiex Pharmaceuticals LLC .... E 919 456-7800
  Morrisville *(G-11344)*
G1 Therapeutics Inc .... C 919 213-9835
  Durham *(G-5110)*
Gale Global Research Inc .... G 910 795-8595
  Leland *(G-9545)*
▲ Gb Biosciences LLC .... D 336 632-6000
  Greensboro *(G-7032)*
Generics Bidco II LLC .... C 980 389-2501
  Charlotte *(G-2819)*
◆ Generics Bidco II LLC .... E 704 612-8830
  Charlotte *(G-2820)*
Genixus Corp .... G 877 436-4987
  Concord *(G-4272)*
Genixus Corp .... F 877 436-4987
  Kannapolis *(G-9120)*
George Clinical Inc .... G 919 789-2022
  Raleigh *(G-12795)*
Gilead Sciences Inc .... G 650 574-3000
  Raleigh *(G-12801)*
Gingras Sleep Medicine PA .... G 704 944-0562
  Charlotte *(G-2829)*
Glaxosmithkline 69 Pharma .... G 612 719-4438
  Durham *(G-5118)*
Glaxosmithkline LLC .... G 704 962-5786
  Cornelius *(G-4550)*
Glaxosmithkline LLC .... E 919 483-5302
  Durham *(G-5119)*
Glaxosmithkline LLC .... E 919 483-2100
  Durham *(G-5120)*
Glaxosmithkline LLC .... G 252 315-9774
  Durham *(G-5121)*
Glaxosmithkline LLC .... F 919 483-2100
  Durham *(G-5122)*
Glaxosmithkline LLC .... G 336 392-3058
  Greensboro *(G-7045)*

Glaxosmithkline LLC .... G 919 628-3630
  Morrisville *(G-11348)*
Glaxosmithkline LLC .... E 919 483-5006
  Research Triangle Pa *(G-13551)*
Glaxosmithkline LLC .... E 919 269-5000
  Zebulon *(G-17129)*
Glaxosmithkline Services Inc .... B 919 483-2100
  Durham *(G-5123)*
Glenmark Phrmceuticals Inc USA .... D 704 218-2600
  Monroe *(G-10723)*
Glycyx Pharmaceuticals Ltd .... G 919 862-1097
  Raleigh *(G-12808)*
GNH Pharmaceuticals USA LLC .... G 919 820-3077
  Charlotte *(G-2838)*
Gracili Therapeutics Inc .... G 617 331-4110
  Rtp *(G-13831)*
▲ Greer Laboratories Inc .... C 828 754-5327
  Lenoir *(G-9615)*
Grifols Inc .... D 919 553-5011
  Clayton *(G-3983)*
Grifols Therapeutics LLC .... D 919 359-7069
  Clayton *(G-3984)*
Grifols Therapeutics LLC .... G 919 553-0172
  Clayton *(G-3985)*
Grifols Therapeutics LLC .... D 919 316-6668
  Durham *(G-5128)*
▲ Grifols Therapeutics LLC .... B 919 316-6300
  Durham *(G-5127)*
Hammock Pharmaceuticals Inc .... G 704 727-7926
  Charlotte *(G-2883)*
Happy Jack Incorporated .... G 252 747-2911
  Snow Hill *(G-14503)*
Hdh Pharma Inc .... G 919 462-1494
  Cary *(G-1780)*
Health Choice Pharmacy .... G 281 741-8358
  Arden *(G-337)*
Hendersonville Phrm RES .... G 828 696-2483
  Hendersonville *(G-7863)*
High Point Pharmaceuticals LLC .... F 336 841-0300
  High Point *(G-8392)*
Hipra Scientific USA .... F 919 605-8256
  Raleigh *(G-12846)*
Hospira Inc .... E 252 977-5111
  Battleboro *(G-922)*
Hospira Inc .... F 704 335-1300
  Charlotte *(G-2923)*
Hospira Inc .... B 919 553-3831
  Clayton *(G-3988)*
Hospira Inc .... C 252 977-5500
  Rocky Mount *(G-13669)*
Hospira Inc .... A 252 977-5111
  Rocky Mount *(G-13702)*
Huvepharma Inc .... F 910 506-4649
  Maxton *(G-10356)*
Icagen LLC .... D 919 941-5206
  Durham *(G-5144)*
Idexx Pharmaceuticals Inc .... E 336 834-6500
  Greensboro *(G-7112)*
Imbrium Therapeutics LP .... F 984 439-1075
  Morrisville *(G-11358)*
In Acorda Therapeutics .... G 914 347-4300
  Raleigh *(G-12880)*
Indapharma LLC .... G 919 968-4500
  Chapel Hill *(G-2025)*
Indivior Manufacturing LLC .... D 804 594-0974
  Raleigh *(G-12882)*
Inhalon Biopharma Inc .... G 650 439-0110
  Durham *(G-5155)*
▲ Innobioactives LLC .... G 336 235-0838
  Greensboro *(G-7116)*
Innocrin Pharmaceuticals Inc .... G 919 467-8539
  Fuquay Varina *(G-6204)*

Inpernum Pharma Solutions LLC .... G 919 599-5501
  Durham *(G-5159)*
Intas Pharmaceuticals Limited .... D 919 941-7878
  Raleigh *(G-12895)*
Interpace Pharma Solutions Inc .... G 919 678-7024
  Morrisville *(G-11361)*
▲ Ioto Usa LLC .... F 252 413-7343
  Greenville *(G-7545)*
Iqvia Pharma Inc .... D 919 998-2000
  Durham *(G-5166)*
Ixc Discovery Inc .... E 919 941-5206
  Durham *(G-5169)*
Kbi Biopharma Inc .... G 919 479-9898
  Durham *(G-5178)*
Kbi Biopharma Inc .... G 919 479-9898
  Durham *(G-5177)*
Keranetics LLC .... F 336 725-0621
  Winston Salem *(G-16778)*
King Bio Inc .... D 828 255-0201
  Asheville *(G-675)*
King Phrmceuticals RES Dev LLC .... B 919 653-7001
  Cary *(G-1803)*
Kintor Pharmaceuticals Inc .... G 984 208-1255
  Chapel Hill *(G-2029)*
Kowa Research Institute Inc .... E 919 433-1600
  Morrisville *(G-11368)*
Krenitsky Pharmaceuticals Inc .... G 919 493-4631
  Chapel Hill *(G-2030)*
Krigen Pharmaceuticals LLC .... G 919 523-7530
  Lillington *(G-9854)*
Krigen Pharmaceuticals LLC .... G 919 961-3751
  Lillington *(G-9855)*
Ksep Systems LLC .... F 919 339-1850
  Morrisville *(G-11369)*
Lexitas Pharma Services Inc .... D 919 205-0012
  Durham *(G-5189)*
Lick er Lips Lip Balm LLC .... G 702 355-5433
  Charlotte *(G-3084)*
Lonza Rtp .... G 800 748-8979
  Morrisville *(G-11382)*
Lq3 Pharmaceuticals Inc .... G 919 794-7391
  Morrisville *(G-11383)*
M&M Bioplastic LLC .... Gb 877 366-5227
  Mill Spring *(G-10488)*
Majorpharma US Inc .... G 919 799-2010
  Raleigh *(G-12989)*
Mallinckrodt LLC .... F 919 878-2800
  Raleigh *(G-12991)*
Mallinckrodt LLC .... G 919 878-2900
  Raleigh *(G-12992)*
Mayne Pharma Commercial LLC .... B 984 242-1400
  Raleigh *(G-13009)*
Mayne Pharma Ventures LLC .... G 252 752-3800
  Raleigh *(G-13010)*
Melinta Therapeutics Inc .... G 919 313-6601
  Chapel Hill *(G-2039)*
Merck .... G 919 423-4328
  Chapel Hill *(G-2040)*
Merck & Co Inc .... E 908 423-3000
  Charlotte *(G-3166)*
Merck Sharp & Dohme LLC .... G 919 425-4000
  Durham *(G-5219)*
Merck Sharp & Dohme LLC .... B 252 243-2011
  Wilson *(G-16515)*
Merck Teknika LLC .... E 919 620-7200
  Durham *(G-5220)*
▲ Merz Incorporated .... C 919 582-8196
  Raleigh *(G-13019)*
Merz North America Inc .... F 919 582-8000
  Raleigh *(G-13020)*
▲ Merz Pharmaceuticals LLC .... D 919 582-8000
  Raleigh *(G-13021)*

Employee Codes: A=Over 500 employees, B=251-500
C=101-250, D=51-100, E=20-50, F=10-19, G=1-9

28 CHEMICALS AND ALLIED PRODUCTS

Millennium Pharmaceuticals Inc .... D 866 466-7779
  Charlotte *(G-3180)*

Mixx-Point 5 Project LLC .... G 858 298-4625
  Swannanoa *(G-15029)*

Musa Gold LLC .... F 704 579-7894
  Charlotte *(G-3223)*

Mylan Pharmaceuticals Inc .... E 336 271-6571
  Greensboro *(G-7211)*

Nationwide Analgesics LLC .... G 704 651-5551
  Matthews *(G-10274)*

Natures Pharmacy Inc .... G 828 251-0094
  Asheville *(G-710)*

Nautilus Holdco Inc .... G 919 859-1302
  Durham *(G-5239)*

Neptune Hlth Wllness Innvtion .... C 888 664-9166
  Conover *(G-4475)*

Neuronex Inc .... G 919 460-9500
  Morrisville *(G-11394)*

Neurotronik Inc .... F 919 883-4155
  Durham *(G-5244)*

New Life Medicals Inc .... G 610 615-1483
  Garner *(G-6295)*

New Paradigm Therapeutics Inc .... G 919 259-0026
  Chapel Hill *(G-2047)*

Niras Inc .... G 919 439-4562
  Cary *(G-1831)*

None .... G 336 408-6008
  Winston Salem *(G-16821)*

Nontoxic Pthgen Erdction Cons .... G 800 308-1094
  Matthews *(G-10276)*

Nortria Inc .... F 919 440-3253
  Raleigh *(G-13073)*

▲ Novartis Vccnes Dagnostics Inc .... B 617 871-7000
  Holly Springs *(G-8708)*

Novo Nordisk Phrm Inds LP .... D 919 820-9985
  Clayton *(G-4003)*

Novo Nordisk Phrm Inds LP .... B 919 820-9985
  Clayton *(G-4004)*

Novo Nordisk Phrm Inds LP .... E 919 550-2200
  Durham *(G-5250)*

Nutra-Pharma Mfg Corp NC .... D 631 846-2500
  Lexington *(G-9764)*

Nutraceutical Lf Sciences Inc .... B 336 956-0800
  Lexington *(G-9765)*

Nvn Liquidation Inc .... G 919 485-8080
  Pittsboro *(G-12343)*

Oncoceutics Inc .... F 678 897-0563
  Durham *(G-5257)*

OnTarget Labs Inc .... G 919 846-3877
  Raleigh *(G-13086)*

Oriel Therapeutics Inc .... E 919 313-1290
  Durham *(G-5263)*

Patheon Calculus Merger LLC .... G 919 226-3200
  Morrisville *(G-11406)*

Patheon Inc .... G 919 226-3200
  Durham *(G-5273)*

Patheon Inc .... A 919 226-3200
  Durham *(G-5274)*

▲ Patheon Manufacturing Svcs LLC .... D 252 758-3436
  Greenville *(G-7568)*

Patheon Pharmaceuticals Inc .... A 866 728-4366
  High Point *(G-8475)*

◆ Patheon Pharmaceuticals Inc .... D 919 226-3200
  Morrisville *(G-11407)*

Patheon Phrmceuticals Svcs Inc .... E 919 226-3200
  Morrisville *(G-11408)*

Patheon Softgels Inc .... F 336 812-8700
  Greensboro *(G-7247)*

◆ Patheon Softgels Inc .... D 336 812-8700
  High Point *(G-8476)*

Paw Pharma Services LLC .... G 919 367-0413
  Cary *(G-1843)*

Pfizer Inc .... G 252 382-3309
  Battleboro *(G-928)*

Pfizer Inc .... F 919 941-5185
  Durham *(G-5284)*

Pfizer Inc .... E 252 977-5111
  Rocky Mount *(G-13721)*

Pfizer Inc .... C 919 775-7100
  Sanford *(G-14168)*

▲ Pharmaceutical Dimensions .... G 336 297-4851
  Greensboro *(G-7252)*

Pharmaceutical Equipment Svcs .... G 239 699-9120
  Asheville *(G-727)*

Pharmacutical Dimension .... G 336 664-5287
  Greensboro *(G-7253)*

Pharmagra Holding Company LLC .... E 828 884-8656
  Brevard *(G-1284)*

Pharmasone LLC .... G 910 679-8364
  Wilmington *(G-16353)*

▲ Pharmgate Animal Health LLC .... G 910 679-8364
  Wilmington *(G-16354)*

▲ Pharmgate Inc .... F 910 679-8364
  Wilmington *(G-16355)*

Piedmont Animal Health Inc .... E 336 544-0320
  Greensboro *(G-7254)*

Pozen Inc .... F 919 913-1030
  Raleigh *(G-13125)*

Ppd Inc .... C 910 251-0081
  Wilmington *(G-16366)*

Ppd International Holdings LLC .... G 910 251-0081
  Wilmington *(G-16367)*

Praetego Inc .... G 919 237-7969
  Durham *(G-5301)*

◆ Premex Inc .... F 561 962-4128
  Durham *(G-5304)*

Promethera Biosciences LLC .... D 919 354-1930
  Durham *(G-5307)*

Promethera Biosciences LLC .... G 919 354-1933
  Raleigh *(G-13151)*

Propella Therapeutics Inc .... G 703 631-7523
  Pittsboro *(G-12345)*

PSI Pharma Support America Inc .... E 919 249-2660
  Durham *(G-5308)*

Purdue Pharmaceuticals LP .... F 252 265-1900
  Wilson *(G-16525)*

◆ Qualicaps Inc .... C 336 449-3900
  Whitsett *(G-16000)*

Quatrobio LLC .... G 919 460-9500
  Morrisville *(G-11414)*

Rainforest Nutritionals Inc .... G 919 847-2221
  Raleigh *(G-13171)*

Raybow Usa Inc .... F 828 884-8656
  Brevard *(G-1286)*

Recipharm Laboratories Inc .... E 919 884-2064
  Morrisville *(G-11416)*

Redhill Biopharma Inc .... D 984 444-7010
  Raleigh *(G-13202)*

Sagent Pharmaceuticals Inc .... C 919 327-5500
  Raleigh *(G-13227)*

Salubrent Phrma Solutions Corp .... G 301 980-7224
  Kannapolis *(G-9131)*

Sandoz Inc .... B 252 234-2222
  Wilson *(G-16539)*

Santarus Inc .... B 919 862-1000
  Raleigh *(G-13228)*

Satsuma Pharmaceuticals Inc .... G 650 410-3200
  Durham *(G-5341)*

Scipher Medicine Corporation .... G 781 755-2063
  Durham *(G-5344)*

Scorpius Holdings Inc .... E 919 240-7133
  Morrisville *(G-11423)*

Sobi Inc .... G 844 506-3682
  Durham *(G-5362)*

Solvekta LLC .... G 336 944-4677
  Greensboro *(G-7348)*

Specgx LLC .... C 919 878-4706
  Raleigh *(G-13286)*

Sprout Pharmaceuticals Inc .... F 919 882-0850
  Raleigh *(G-13294)*

Sterling Pharma Usa LLC .... E 919 678-0702
  Cary *(G-1904)*

Stiefel Laboratories Inc .... C 888 784-3335
  Durham *(G-5376)*

Stiefel Laboratories Inc .... E 888 784-3335
  Durham *(G-5375)*

Sunstar Network LLC .... G 828 684-3571
  Arden *(G-382)*

Superior Cabling Solutions LLC .... G 704 736-9017
  Lincolnton *(G-9923)*

Syneos Health Consulting Inc .... D 866 462-7373
  Morrisville *(G-11436)*

Synereca Pharmaceuticals Inc .... G 919 966-3929
  Chapel Hill *(G-2077)*

Synthon Pharmaceuticals Inc .... E 919 493-6006
  Durham *(G-5385)*

Synthonix Inc .... G 919 875-9277
  Wake Forest *(G-15601)*

Tarheel Solutions LLC .... G 336 420-9265
  Pleasant Garden *(G-12362)*

Tavros Therapeutics Inc .... E 919 602-2631
  Durham *(G-5387)*

Tergus Pharma LLC .... E 919 549-9700
  Durham *(G-5396)*

Tg Therapeutics Inc .... D 212 554-4484
  Morrisville *(G-11446)*

Therapeutics .... G 919 695-7291
  Raleigh *(G-13343)*

Transtech Pharma LLC .... C 336 841-0300
  High Point *(G-8575)*

Tripharm Services Inc .... F 984 243-0800
  Morrisville *(G-11457)*

Turbomed LLC .... F 973 527-5299
  Fayetteville *(G-5936)*

Umethod Health Inc .... F 984 232-6699
  Raleigh *(G-13378)*

United Therapeutics Corp .... F 919 246-9389
  Durham *(G-5422)*

United Therapeutics Corp .... G 919 361-6141
  Durham *(G-5423)*

◆ Universal Preservachem Inc .... D 732 568-1266
  Mebane *(G-10434)*

Urovant Sciences Inc .... F 919 323-8528
  Durham *(G-5428)*

V1 Pharma LLC .... G 919 338-5744
  Raleigh *(G-13388)*

Vascular Pharmaceuticals Inc .... G 919 345-7933
  Chapel Hill *(G-2092)*

Vast Therapeutics Inc .... G 919 321-1403
  Morrisville *(G-11462)*

Viiv Healthcare Company .... G 919 445-2770
  Chapel Hill *(G-2093)*

Viiv Healthcare Company .... A 919 483-2100
  Durham *(G-5434)*

Vogenx Inc .... G 919 659-5677
  Durham *(G-5435)*

Vtv Therapeutics Inc .... E 336 841-0300
  High Point *(G-8598)*

Vtv Therapeutics LLC .... E 336 841-0300
  High Point *(G-8599)*

Ward Specialty Pharmacy LLC .... G 252 459-5544
  Rocky Mount *(G-13739)*

West Pharmaceutical Svcs Inc .... G 252 522-8956
  Kinston *(G-9392)*

Wholesale Kennel Supply Co .... G 919 742-2515
  Siler City *(G-14434)*

28 CHEMICALS AND ALLIED PRODUCTS

Wyeth Holdings LLC .... A 919 775-7100
  Sanford *(G-14210)*
Zoetis Inc .... C 919 941-5185
  Durham *(G-5460)*
Zoetis Products LLC .... G 336 333-9356
  Greensboro *(G-7476)*

2835 Diagnostic substances

◆ AR Corp .... G 910 763-8530
  Wilmington *(G-16113)*
Baebies Inc .... D 919 891-0432
  Durham *(G-4942)*
Cardinal Health 414 LLC .... G 704 644-7989
  Charlotte *(G-2387)*
Celplor LLC .... G 919 961-1961
  Cary *(G-1726)*
Gateway Campus .... G 919 833-0096
  Raleigh *(G-12790)*
Gbf Inc .... D 336 665-0205
  High Point *(G-8363)*
Liebel-Flarsheim Company LLC .... C 919 878-2930
  Raleigh *(G-12969)*
Liposcience Inc .... C 919 212-1999
  Morrisville *(G-11381)*
Molecular Toxicology Inc .... F 828 264-9099
  Boone *(G-1223)*
Multigen Diagnostics LLC .... G 336 510-1120
  Greensboro *(G-7208)*
North Carolina Department of A .... G 828 684-8188
  Arden *(G-356)*
▲ Novartis Vccnes Dagnostics Inc ..... B 617 871-7000
  Holly Springs *(G-8708)*
Petnet Solutions Inc .... G 919 572-5544
  Durham *(G-5283)*
Petnet Solutions Inc .... G 865 218-2000
  Winston Salem *(G-16847)*
Precision Genomics Inc .... G 843 737-1911
  Wrightsville Beach *(G-17027)*
Pregnancy Support Services .... G 919 490-0203
  Chapel Hill *(G-2056)*
Sapere Bio Inc .... G 919 260-2565
  Durham *(G-5337)*
Sciteck Diagnostics Inc .... G 828 650-0409
  Fletcher *(G-6036)*
Thurston Genomics LLC .... G 980 237-7547
  Charlotte *(G-3693)*
Triangle Prcsion Dgnostics Inc .... G 919 345-0110
  Durham *(G-5409)*
◆ Tripath Imaging Inc .... D 336 222-9707
  Burlington *(G-1509)*
Your Choice Pregnancy Clinic .... G 919 577-9050
  Fuquay Varina *(G-6240)*

2836 Biological products, except diagnostic

Albion Medical Holdings Inc .... F 800 378-3906
  Lenoir *(G-9571)*
Anatech Ltd .... F 704 489-1488
  Denver *(G-4761)*
Astellas Gene Therapies Inc .... G 415 638-4561
  Sanford *(G-14089)*
Avp Vaccines LLC .... G 704 799-0161
  Mooresville *(G-10868)*
Biologix of The Triangle Inc .... G 919 696-4544
  Cary *(G-1703)*
Boehrnger Inglheim Anmal Hlth .... D 919 577-9020
  Fuquay Varina *(G-6185)*
Bonap Inc .... G 919 967-6240
  Chapel Hill *(G-1994)*
Business Mogul LLC .... G 919 605-2165
  Raleigh *(G-12578)*
Carolina Biological Supply Co .... C 336 446-7600
  Whitsett *(G-15985)*
◆ Carolina Biological Supply Company . C 336 584-0381
  Burlington *(G-1384)*
Cedarlane Laboratories USA .... E 336 513-5135
  Burlington *(G-1391)*
Chelsea Therapeutics International Ltd . C 704 341-1516
  Charlotte *(G-2469)*
Cytonet LLC .... F
  Durham *(G-5044)*
▲ Embrex LLC .... C 919 941-5185
  Durham *(G-5080)*
Engaged Media Inc .... E 239 280-4202
  Durham *(G-5087)*
Epicypher Inc .... F 855 374-2461
  Durham *(G-5092)*
Genotech Inc .... G 919 369-4947
  Cary *(G-1773)*
Greer Laboratories Inc .... E 828 758-2388
  Lenoir *(G-9614)*
▲ Greer Laboratories Inc .... C 828 754-5327
  Lenoir *(G-9615)*
Grifols Therapeutics LLC .... F 919 316-6214
  Durham *(G-5129)*
Grifols Therapeutics LLC .... A 919 316-6612
  Raleigh *(G-12821)*
▲ Grifols Therapeutics LLC .... B 919 316-6300
  Durham *(G-5127)*
Immunotek Bio Centers LLC .... E 828 569-6264
  Hickory *(G-8063)*
Immunotek Bio Centers LLC .... E 336 781-4901
  High Point *(G-8406)*
International Ptnrshp For Vacc .... G 919 367-0379
  Cary *(G-1792)*
Jts Venom Performance .... G 704 214-7849
  Maiden *(G-10110)*
Kdr Visuality LLC .... G 704 451-1290
  Charlotte *(G-3046)*
Kedplasma .... G 704 691-3287
  Gastonia *(G-6437)*
Keranetics LLC .... F 336 725-0621
  Winston Salem *(G-16778)*
▲ Microban Products Company .... D 704 766-4267
  Huntersville *(G-8854)*
Molecular Toxicology Inc .... F 828 264-9099
  Boone *(G-1223)*
Mountain Vista Extracts LLC .... G 910 489-3948
  Wilmington *(G-16328)*
NC Carolina Venom .... G 704 635-8696
  Indian Trail *(G-8951)*
▲ Novartis Vccnes Dagnostics Inc ..... B 617 871-7000
  Holly Springs *(G-8708)*
Passport Health Triangle .... F 919 781-0053
  Cary *(G-1842)*
Pfizer Inc .... C 919 775-7100
  Sanford *(G-14168)*
Plasma Games .... G 252 721-3294
  Raleigh *(G-13113)*
Plasma Games Inc .... E 919 627-1252
  Raleigh *(G-13114)*
Plasma Surgical .... G 704 608-6756
  Huntersville *(G-8875)*
Plasma Web Services Inc .... G 561 703-0485
  Charlotte *(G-3348)*
Prokidney LLC .... E 336 448-2857
  Winston Salem *(G-16872)*
Prokidney Corp .... D 336 999-7028
  Winston Salem *(G-16873)*
Quo Vademus LLC .... G 910 296-1632
  Kenansville *(G-9145)*
Seqirus Inc .... F 919 577-5000
  Holly Springs *(G-8715)*
Serum Source International Inc .... F 704 588-6607
  Waxhaw *(G-15774)*
Sheffibilt Inc .... G 336 963-0086
  Asheboro *(G-480)*
Shoe Venom .... G 919 763-4512
  Raleigh *(G-13249)*
Sir Plasma .... G 919 232-1961
  Raleigh *(G-13267)*
Tengion Inc .... E 336 722-5855
  Winston Salem *(G-16938)*
Thw of Wilson Inc .... G 252 237-7100
  Wilson *(G-16546)*
Venom Stars Inc .... G 828 256-8621
  Hickory *(G-8203)*
Wildcraft Extracts LLC .... G 828 273-8173
  Sylva *(G-15075)*

2841 Soap and other detergents

222 Dream Co LLC .... G 919 803-9741
  Fayetteville *(G-5745)*
Ada Marketing Inc .... E 910 221-2189
  Dunn *(G-4848)*
▲ AG Provision LLC .... E 910 296-0302
  Kenansville *(G-9140)*
Anders Natural Soap Co Inc .... G 919 678-9393
  Cary *(G-1682)*
Bottom Line Technologies Inc .... F 919 472-0541
  Durham *(G-4974)*
Buckeye International Inc .... G 704 523-9400
  Charlotte *(G-2363)*
C & C Chemical Company Inc .... F 828 255-7639
  Asheville *(G-577)*
Carden Farms Soap Inc .... G 919 570-0745
  Franklinton *(G-6152)*
Controlled Release Tech Inc .... G 704 487-0878
  Shelby *(G-14303)*
Country Lotus Soaps LLC .... G 786 384-4174
  Charlotte *(G-2562)*
CTS Cleaning Systems Inc .... G 910 483-5349
  Fayetteville *(G-5801)*
Ecolab Inc .... E 336 931-2237
  Winston Salem *(G-16691)*
Essential Soap Co .... G 704 737-2385
  Charlotte *(G-2729)*
▼ Greenology Products LLC .... E 877 473-3650
  Raleigh *(G-12815)*
Greenwich Bay Trading Co Inc .... E 919 781-5008
  Raleigh *(G-12816)*
▲ Innovasource LLC .... F 704 584-0072
  Huntersville *(G-8834)*
Lathers Skin Essentials .... G 828 449-9244
  Hickory *(G-8084)*
Marlin Company Inc .... G 828 758-9999
  Lenoir *(G-9631)*
◆ Marlin Company Inc .... F 828 754-0980
  Lenoir *(G-9632)*
Naturally ME Boutique Inc .... G 919 519-0783
  Durham *(G-5238)*
Old Town Soap Co .... F 704 796-8775
  China Grove *(G-3886)*
Orianna Naturals LLC .... G 336 877-1560
  Todd *(G-15324)*
◆ Pine Glo Products Inc .... F 919 556-7787
  Zebulon *(G-17140)*
Pretty Baby Herbal Soaps .... G 704 209-0669
  Salisbury *(G-14030)*
Procter & Gamble Mfg Co .... D 336 954-0000
  Greensboro *(G-7287)*
▲ Qualpak LLC .... E 910 610-1213
  Laurinburg *(G-9493)*
Rachel Dubois .... G 919 870-8063
  Raleigh *(G-13169)*
SC Johnson Prof USA Inc .... D 704 263-4240
  Greensboro *(G-7326)*

28 CHEMICALS AND ALLIED PRODUCTS

◆ SC Johnson Professional..................D ... 704 263-4240
   Stanley *(G-14708)*

Sheets Laundry Club Inc.......................F ... 704 662-8696
   Mooresville *(G-11083)*

▲ Showline Inc......................................F ... 919 255-9160
   Raleigh *(G-13250)*

Showline Automotive Pdts Inc............G ... 919 255-9160
   Raleigh *(G-13251)*

South / Win LLC..................................D ... 336 398-5650
   Greensboro *(G-7350)*

Specialty National Inc.........................E ... 336 996-8783
   Kernersville *(G-9238)*

◆ Spuntech Industries Inc....................C ... 336 330-9000
   Roxboro *(G-13825)*

◆ Surry Chemicals Incorporated..........E ... 336 786-4607
   Mount Airy *(G-11580)*

◆ Syntha Group Inc..............................D ... 336 885-5131
   High Point *(G-8562)*

Unx Industries Inc...............................G ... 252 355-8433
   Greenville *(G-7593)*

Unx-Christeyns LLC............................E ... 252 756-8616
   Greenville *(G-7595)*

Whispering Willow Soap Co LLC........G ... 828 455-0322
   Denver *(G-4813)*

2842 Polishes and sanitation goods

A & B Chem-Dry...................................F ... 919 878-0288
   Raleigh *(G-12451)*

A Cleaner Tomorrow Dry Clg LLC........G ... 919 639-6396
   Dunn *(G-4847)*

Abzorbit Inc..F ... 828 464-9944
   Newton *(G-11911)*

Ace Industries Inc................................G ... 336 427-5316
   Madison *(G-10069)*

AEC Consumer Products LLC.............F ... 704 904-0578
   Fayetteville *(G-5754)*

◆ Amano Pioneer Eclipse Corp..........D ... 336 372-8080
   Sparta *(G-14588)*

Annihilare Medical Systems Inc..........F ... 855 545-5677
   Lincolnton *(G-9872)*

◆ Autec Inc..E ... 704 871-9141
   Statesville *(G-14755)*

Awesome Products Inc........................G ... 336 374-5900
   Mount Airy *(G-11478)*

Buckeye International Inc.....................G ... 704 523-9400
   Charlotte *(G-2363)*

Busch Enterprises Inc..........................G ... 704 878-2067
   Statesville *(G-14768)*

Cali Metal Polish..................................G ... 704 788-2466
   Concord *(G-4222)*

Casablanca 4 LLC...............................G ... 910 702-4399
   Wilmington *(G-16159)*

Chem-Tech Solutions Inc.....................E ... 704 829-9202
   Belmont *(G-980)*

Cherryville Distrg Co Inc......................G ... 704 435-9692
   Cherryville *(G-3863)*

Chrome Bubbles By Maurice................G ... 704 224-8866
   Charlotte *(G-2479)*

Controlled Release Tech Inc................G ... 704 487-0878
   Shelby *(G-14303)*

Dewill Inc...G ... 919 426-9550
   Cary *(G-1749)*

Dings Etc...G ... 252 933-0208
   Kinston *(G-9357)*

Easy Fresh Products...........................G ... 704 216-4111
   Fountain *(G-6093)*

Ecolab Inc...G ... 704 527-5912
   Charlotte *(G-2683)*

Ecolab Inc...E ... 336 931-2289
   Greensboro *(G-6989)*

Economy Clrs Lillington LLC................G ... 910 893-3927
   Coats *(G-4129)*

Elevate Cleaning Service....................G ... 347 928-4030
   Fayetteville *(G-5820)*

Elsco Inc...G ... 509 885-4525
   Seaboard *(G-14228)*

Eminess Technologies Inc..................E ... 704 283-2600
   Monroe *(G-10713)*

Enc Industrial Supply..........................G ... 252 862-8300
   Ahoskie *(G-62)*

Entrust Services LLC..........................F ... 336 274-5175
   Greensboro *(G-7002)*

First Class Ridez LLC.........................G ... 919 610-6043
   Zebulon *(G-17127)*

Fresh As A Daisy Inc..........................G ... 336 869-3002
   High Point *(G-8359)*

Fresh-N-Mobile LLC............................G ... 704 251-4643
   Charlotte *(G-2797)*

Global Ecosciences Inc.......................G ... 252 631-6266
   Wake Forest *(G-15560)*

H & H Products Incorporated..............G ... 910 891-4276
   Dunn *(G-4873)*

◆ Harper Corporation of America........C ... 704 588-3371
   Charlotte *(G-2890)*

Heed Group Inc..................................G ... 877 938-8853
   Stanley *(G-14696)*

◆ Hickory Brands Inc..........................D ... 828 322-2600
   Hickory *(G-8044)*

Ice Companies Inc..............................G ... 910 791-1970
   Wilmington *(G-16261)*

Illinois Tool Works Inc.........................C ... 336 996-7046
   Kernersville *(G-9206)*

Isana LLC...G ... 704 439-6761
   Charlotte *(G-2997)*

Jci Jones Chemicals Inc.....................E ... 704 392-9767
   Charlotte *(G-3014)*

◆ Kay Chemical Company..................A ... 336 668-7290
   Greensboro *(G-7144)*

M and R Inc...G ... 704 332-5999
   Charlotte *(G-3114)*

▲ Microban Products Company...........D ... 704 766-4267
   Huntersville *(G-8854)*

Mill-Chem Manufacturing Inc..............E ... 336 889-8038
   Thomasville *(G-15251)*

Mooresvlle Pub Wrks Snttion De.........G ... 704 664-4278
   Mooresville *(G-11029)*

▼ Novalent Ltd.....................................F ... 336 375-7555
   Greensboro *(G-7225)*

Organizer Llc......................................G ... 336 391-7591
   Winston Salem *(G-16832)*

Patel Deepal......................................G ... 704 634-5141
   Concord *(G-4330)*

Piece of Pie LLC.................................F ... 919 286-7421
   Durham *(G-5289)*

◆ Pine Glo Products Inc.....................F ... 919 556-7787
   Zebulon *(G-17140)*

Procter & Gamble Mfg Co..................D ... 336 954-0000
   Greensboro *(G-7287)*

Public Health Corps Inc......................G ... 336 545-2999
   Greensboro *(G-7291)*

Pureon Inc..D ... 480 505-3409
   Monroe *(G-10790)*

Quail Dry Cleaning.............................G ... 704 947-7335
   Charlotte *(G-3401)*

Remodeez LLC...................................F ... 704 428-9050
   Charlotte *(G-3431)*

Rga Enterprises Inc............................D ... 704 398-0487
   Charlotte *(G-3447)*

Solo Solutions Corporation.................G ... 336 992-2585
   Kernersville *(G-9235)*

Speed Brite Inc...................................G ... 704 639-9771
   Salisbury *(G-14046)*

Sun Cleaners & Laundry Inc..............G ... 704 325-3722
   Newton *(G-11974)*

Superior Envmtl Svcs LLC..................G ... 919 717-1199
   Knightdale *(G-9429)*

Unx Industries Inc...............................G ... 252 355-8433
   Greenville *(G-7593)*

Unx Industries Inc...............................D ... 252 756-8616
   Greenville *(G-7594)*

W G of Southwest Raleigh Inc............G ... 919 629-7327
   Holly Springs *(G-8725)*

◆ Walex Products Company Inc.........F ... 910 371-2242
   Leland *(G-9565)*

2843 Surface active agents

Arrochem Inc.......................................F ... 704 827-0216
   Mount Holly *(G-11621)*

◆ Cht R Beitlich Corporation................E ... 704 523-4242
   Charlotte *(G-2481)*

Cross-Link Inc.....................................G ... 828 657-4477
   Cliffside *(G-4084)*

Diarkis LLC..G ... 704 888-5244
   Locust *(G-9957)*

◆ Fine Line Hosiery Inc.......................F ... 336 498-8022
   Asheboro *(G-435)*

Henkel Corporation..............................D ... 704 633-1731
   Salisbury *(G-13976)*

▼ Lindley Laboratories Inc....................F ... 336 449-7521
   Gibsonville *(G-6567)*

◆ Surry Chemicals Incorporated.........E ... 336 786-4607
   Mount Airy *(G-11580)*

◆ Syntha Group Inc.............................D ... 336 885-5131
   High Point *(G-8562)*

2844 Toilet preparations

▲ 3rd Phaze Bdy Oils Urban Lnks........G ... 704 344-1138
   Charlotte *(G-2109)*

A M P Laboratories Ltd........................G ... 704 894-9721
   Cornelius *(G-4519)*

A Matter of Scents...............................G ... 980 939-3285
   Charlotte *(G-2116)*

Active Concepts...................................G ... 704 276-7386
   Lincolnton *(G-9866)*

Active Concepts LLC...........................G ... 704 276-7372
   Lincolnton *(G-9867)*

▲ Active Concepts LLC........................E ... 704 276-7100
   Lincolnton *(G-9868)*

Adora..G ... 336 880-0342
   High Point *(G-8233)*

Adoratherapy Inc..................................F ... 917 297-8904
   Asheville *(G-515)*

◆ Albaad Usa Inc.................................B ... 336 634-0091
   Reidsville *(G-13504)*

Alywillow..G ... 919 454-4826
   Raleigh *(G-12495)*

▲ American Fiber & Finishing Inc........E ... 704 984-9256
   Albemarle *(G-73)*

Aprinnova LLC.....................................G ... 910 371-2234
   Leland *(G-9526)*

Armorri Cosmetics LLC.......................G ... 910 352-6209
   Durham *(G-4924)*

Artisan Aromatics................................G ... 800 456-6675
   Burnsville *(G-1523)*

Beauty 4 Love LLC..............................G ... 704 802-2844
   Charlotte *(G-2294)*

Blaq Beauty Naturalz Inc....................G ... 252 326-5621
   Weldon *(G-15880)*

Body Butter Blends LLC......................G ... 704 307-9200
   Charlotte *(G-2329)*

◆ Body Shop Inc..................................C ... 919 554-4900
   Wake Forest *(G-15534)*

Burts Bees Inc.....................................B ... 919 998-5200
   Durham *(G-4994)*

Burts Bees Inc.....................................B ... 919 238-6450
   Morrisville *(G-11310)*

28 CHEMICALS AND ALLIED PRODUCTS

◆ Burts Bees Inc .... C 919 998-5200
    Durham *(G-4993)*
Carolina Perfumer Inc .... G 910 295-5600
    Pinehurst *(G-12217)*
Cheeky Lather LLC .... G 919 672-8071
    Efland *(G-5525)*
Cindys Souther Scents .... G 828 492-0562
    Canton *(G-1609)*
Clover Garden Soaps .... G 828 970-7289
    Maiden *(G-10105)*
Clutch Inc .... F 919 448-8654
    Durham *(G-5022)*
Common Scents .... G 704 780-2230
    Charlotte *(G-2530)*
Common Scents Solutions .... G 812 344-4312
    Wilmington *(G-16176)*
Conopco Inc .... B 910 875-4121
    Raeford *(G-12416)*
Coty Inc .... D 919 895-5000
    Sanford *(G-14105)*
Coty US LLC .... A 919 895-5374
    Sanford *(G-14106)*
Cryogen LLC .... F 919 649-7027
    Raleigh *(G-12658)*
Deb SBS Inc .... F 704 263-4240
    Stanley *(G-14690)*
Dexios Services LLC .... G 704 946-5101
    Cornelius *(G-4540)*
Digits .... G 336 721-0209
    Winston Salem *(G-16680)*
Domimex .... G 919 602-3921
    Raleigh *(G-12695)*
Don Koons Inc .... E 919 603-0948
    Oxford *(G-12128)*
Eb5 Corporation .... G 503 230-8008
    Charlotte *(G-2680)*
▲ Ei LLC .... B 704 857-0707
    Winston Salem *(G-16692)*
Emage Medical LLC .... G 704 904-1873
    Charlotte *(G-2703)*
Erythis Inc .... G 704 644-0963
    Huntersville *(G-8816)*
Filltech Inc .... F 704 279-4300
    Rockwell *(G-13652)*
Filltech USA LLC .... E 704 279-4300
    Rockwell *(G-13653)*
Floraleads Group .... G 919 303-1420
    Raleigh *(G-12773)*
Gent of Scent .... G 980 505-9903
    Charlotte *(G-2824)*
Giddy LLC .... G 813 767-1344
    Chapel Hill *(G-2021)*
Go Green Miracle Balm .... G 630 209-0226
    Cornelius *(G-4551)*
Greenwich Bay Trading Co Inc .... E 919 781-5008
    Raleigh *(G-12816)*
Haircutters of Raleigh Inc .... G 919 781-3465
    Raleigh *(G-12826)*
HFC Prestige Products Inc .... G 919 895-5300
    Sanford *(G-14133)*
Humble Tree Naturals .... G 704 770-1007
    Charlotte *(G-2931)*
Hummingbird Naturals LLC .... G 774 276-0889
    Knightdale *(G-9418)*
Johnny Slicks Inc .... G 910 803-2159
    Holly Ridge *(G-8683)*
Karess Krafters .... G 919 961-5575
    Holly Springs *(G-8703)*
Keller Cosmetics Inc .... G 704 399-2226
    Monroe *(G-10753)*
Koru Naturals LLC .... G 800 253-7011
    Hillsborough *(G-8658)*

Lash Out Inc .... G 919 342-0221
    Clayton *(G-3992)*
Lipstick Chatter LLC .... G 919 285-3439
    Holly Springs *(G-8706)*
Lipstick Ministries Inc .... G 910 228-0097
    Raleigh *(G-12974)*
Litex Industries Inc .... G 704 799-3758
    Mooresville *(G-11010)*
Little River Naturals LLC .... G 919 760-3708
    Zebulon *(G-17133)*
Lo & Behold LLC .... G 336 988-0589
    Durham *(G-5193)*
Love Thy Skin LLC .... G 910 703-2321
    Coats *(G-4133)*
Luxebright Skin Care LLC .... G 877 614-9128
    Matthews *(G-10264)*
Luxuriously Natural Products .... G 919 345-9050
    Franklinton *(G-6158)*
Michelles Scrubs and More .... G 980 215-9461
    Stanley *(G-14703)*
Mommi & ME Kozmeticz LLC .... G 704 620-0082
    Charlotte *(G-3195)*
Nails Sparty LLC .... G 910 794-5406
    Wilmington *(G-16331)*
Naturally ME Boutique Inc .... G 919 519-0783
    Durham *(G-5238)*
Neet Scrubs .... G 704 431-5019
    Salisbury *(G-14017)*
▲ O Grayson Company .... E 704 932-6195
    Kannapolis *(G-9128)*
Oakstone Associates LLC .... F 704 946-5101
    Cornelius *(G-4571)*
Onixx Manufacturing LLC .... G 828 298-4625
    Swannanoa *(G-15032)*
Pampering Moms Ntral Skin Care .... G 706 490-3083
    Raleigh *(G-13098)*
◆ Parkdale Mills Incorporated .... D 704 874-5000
    Gastonia *(G-6486)*
Peculiar Roots LLC .... G 845 379-4039
    Greensboro *(G-7250)*
Perfect 10 Brands LLC .... G 702 738-0183
    Cary *(G-1850)*
▲ Philosophy Inc .... E 602 794-8701
    Sanford *(G-14169)*
Plm Inc .... G 336 788-7529
    Winston Salem *(G-16859)*
Procter & Gamble Mfg Co .... A 336 954-0000
    Browns Summit *(G-1314)*
Procter & Gamble Mfg Co .... D 336 954-0000
    Greensboro *(G-7287)*
Product Quest Manufacturing Inc .... C 386 239-8787
    Winston Salem *(G-16869)*
▲ Product Quest Manufacturing LLC .... B 386 239-8787
    Winston Salem *(G-16870)*
Pure Soy Scents .... G 980 722-1483
    Mount Holly *(G-11649)*
Raw Elements .... G 704 307-8025
    Charlotte *(G-3413)*
Rebecca Trickey .... G 910 584-5549
    Raeford *(G-12435)*
Revlon Inc .... C 919 603-2782
    Oxford *(G-12148)*
Revlon Inc .... E 919 603-2000
    Oxford *(G-12149)*
Revlon Consumer Products Corp .... D 919 603-2000
    Oxford *(G-12150)*
S & B Scents Inc .... G 828 287-9410
    Rutherfordton *(G-13888)*
Salonexclusive Beauty LLC .... G 704 488-3909
    Charlotte *(G-3484)*
Sawyer Creek Soaps LLC .... G 910 231-5013
    Wallace *(G-15626)*

SC Johnson Prof USA Inc .... D 704 263-4240
    Stanley *(G-14707)*
◆ SC Johnson Prof USA Inc .... C 443 521-1606
    Charlotte *(G-3496)*
▲ Scentair Technologies LLC .... D 704 504-2320
    Charlotte *(G-3498)*
Sephora Inside Jcpenney .... G 919 778-4800
    Goldsboro *(G-6656)*
Skin So Soft Spa Inc .... G 800 674-7554
    Charlotte *(G-3560)*
Sklar Bov Solutions Inc .... F 704 872-7277
    Statesville *(G-14886)*
Sleepy Bee Worx LLC .... G 336 824-6998
    Franklinville *(G-6170)*
Southern Scents .... G 910 431-6492
    Hampstead *(G-7656)*
Suds ME Up Buttercup .... G 704 419-2075
    Kings Mountain *(G-9337)*
Taltic Properties LLC .... G 731 656-2735
    Mooresville *(G-11109)*
Tea and Honey Blends LLC .... G 919 673-4273
    Raleigh *(G-13331)*
That Make Scents LLC .... G 919 283-0237
    Clayton *(G-4018)*
Traceymack Products .... G 919 499-8459
    Cameron *(G-1564)*
UGLy Essentials LLC .... F 910 319-9945
    Raleigh *(G-13376)*
Unilever .... G 910 988-1054
    Raeford *(G-12444)*
Unique Body Blends Inc .... G 910 302-5484
    Fayetteville *(G-5938)*
◆ Universal Preservachem Inc .... D 732 568-1266
    Mebane *(G-10434)*
Up On Hill .... G 704 664-7971
    Troutman *(G-15397)*
◆ US Cotton LLC .... C 216 676-6400
    Gastonia *(G-6535)*
Virtue Labs LLC .... E 781 316-5437
    Winston Salem *(G-16963)*
Virtue Labs LLC .... G 844 782-4247
    Raleigh *(G-13404)*
◆ Walex Products Company Inc .... F 910 371-2242
    Leland *(G-9565)*
Yentiyahs Naturals LLC .... G 919 295-4279
    Raleigh *(G-13434)*

2851 Paints and allied products

ACC Coatings LLC .... F 336 701-0080
    Elkin *(G-5608)*
Actega North America Inc .... G 704 736-9389
    Iron Station *(G-8973)*
Akzo Nobel Coatings Inc .... F 704 366-8435
    Charlotte *(G-2150)*
Akzo Nobel Coatings Inc .... G 336 665-9897
    Greensboro *(G-6787)*
Akzo Nobel Coatings Inc .... E 336 841-5111
    High Point *(G-8237)*
◆ Alberdingk Boley Inc .... D 336 454-5000
    Greensboro *(G-6790)*
▲ Aldo Products Company Inc .... G 704 932-3054
    Salisbury *(G-13918)*
▼ Allied Pressroom Products Inc .... E 954 920-0909
    Monroe *(G-10641)*
Americhem Inc .... E 704 782-6411
    Concord *(G-4195)*
Atec Coatings LLC .... G 336 753-8888
    Mocksville *(G-10554)*
Atec Wind Energy Products LLC .... G 336 753-8888
    Mocksville *(G-10555)*
Auto Parts Fayetteville LLC .... G 910 889-4026
    Fayetteville *(G-5766)*

28 CHEMICALS AND ALLIED PRODUCTS

Axalta Coating Systems LLC .... F 855 629-2582
  Concord (G-4202)
Axalta Coating Systems Ltd .... G 336 802-5701
  High Point (G-8257)
Axalta Coating Systems Ltd .... E 336 802-4392
  High Point (G-8258)
Bay Painting Contractors .... G 252 435-5374
  Moyock (G-11692)
Carolina Commercial Coatings .... G 910 279-6045
  Wilmington (G-16157)
Cast Iron Elegance Inc .... F 919 662-8777
  Raleigh (G-12612)
◆ Cdv LLC .... F 919 674-3460
  Morrisville (G-11316)
Compass Color & Coating LLC .... G 704 393-6745
  Charlotte (G-2531)
▲ Crossroads Coatings Inc .... F 704 873-2244
  Statesville (G-14779)
Delta Contractors Inc .... F 817 410-9481
  Linden (G-9940)
Electric Glass Fiber Amer LLC .... C 336 357-8151
  Lexington (G-9712)
▲ Electric Glass Fiber Amer LLC .... B 704 434-2261
  Shelby (G-14313)
Ennis-Flint .... G 336 477-8439
  Thomasville (G-15219)
Ennis-Flint Inc .... G 800 331-8118
  Thomasville (G-15220)
◆ Ennis-Flint Inc .... F 800 331-8118
  Greensboro (G-7000)
Eoncoat LLC .... G 941 928-9401
  Fuquay Varina (G-6198)
Fixxus Indus Holdings Co LLC .... E 336 674-3088
  Archdale (G-280)
Flint Acquisition Corp .... D 336 475-6600
  Thomasville (G-15222)
Flint Ennis Inc .... G 800 331-8118
  High Point (G-8354)
Flint Trading Inc .... F 336 308-3770
  Thomasville (G-15223)
Highland International LLC .... F 828 265-2513
  Boone (G-1207)
◆ IGM Resins USA Inc .... D 704 588-2500
  Charlotte (G-2950)
Igm Specialties Holding Inc .... F 704 945-8702
  Charlotte (G-2951)
J T Metals LLC .... G 336 737-4189
  Goldston (G-6675)
◆ Keim Mineral Coatings Amer Inc .... F 704 588-4811
  Charlotte (G-3048)
Kestrel I Acquisition Corporation .... A 919 990-7500
  Durham (G-5180)
◆ Liquidating Reichhold Inc .... A 919 990-7500
  Durham (G-5191)
◆ Lord Corporation .... B 919 468-5979
  Cary (G-1817)
Lord Far East Inc .... E 919 468-5979
  Cary (G-1819)
Lubrizol Global Management Inc .... D 704 865-7451
  Gastonia (G-6447)
▲ Matlab Inc .... F 336 629-4161
  Asheboro (G-457)
◆ Meridian Zero Degrees LLC .... E 866 454-6757
  Aberdeen (G-12)
Modern Recreational Tech .... E 847 272-2278
  Hickory (G-8096)
New Finish Inc .... E 704 474-4116
  Norwood (G-12041)
Northwest Coatings Systems Inc .... G 336 924-1459
  Pfafftown (G-12188)
Oerlikon AM US Inc .... E 980 260-2827
  Huntersville (G-8870)

Paint Company of NC .... G 336 764-1648
  Clemmons (G-4054)
Piedmont Indus Coatings Inc .... G 336 377-3399
  Winston Salem (G-16854)
PMG SM Holdings LLC .... F 336 548-3250
  Madison (G-10084)
PPG Architectural Finishes Inc .... G 910 484-5161
  Fayetteville (G-5899)
PPG Architectural Finishes Inc .... G 704 864-6783
  Gastonia (G-6493)
PPG Architectural Finishes Inc .... G 336 273-9761
  Greensboro (G-7271)
PPG Architectural Finishes Inc .... G 704 847-7251
  Matthews (G-10282)
PPG Architectural Finishes Inc .... G 704 658-9250
  Mooresville (G-11056)
PPG Architectural Finishes Inc .... G 828 438-9210
  Morganton (G-11242)
PPG Architectural Finishes Inc .... G 919 981-0600
  Raleigh (G-13126)
PPG Architectural Finishes Inc .... G 919 872-6500
  Raleigh (G-13127)
PPG Architectural Finishes Inc .... G 919 779-5400
  Raleigh (G-13128)
PPG Architectural Finishes Inc .... G 704 633-0673
  Salisbury (G-14028)
PPG Industries Inc .... G 919 319-0113
  Cary (G-1857)
PPG Industries Inc .... G 704 542-8880
  Charlotte (G-3364)
PPG Industries Inc .... G 704 523-0888
  Charlotte (G-3365)
PPG Industries Inc .... G 919 382-3100
  Durham (G-5300)
PPG Industries Inc .... G 919 772-3093
  Greensboro (G-7272)
PPG Industries Inc .... C 336 856-9280
  Greensboro (G-7273)
PPG Industries Inc .... G 252 480-1970
  Kill Devil Hills (G-9262)
PPG Industries Inc .... G 704 658-9250
  Mooresville (G-11057)
PPG Industries Inc .... G 919 981-0600
  Raleigh (G-13129)
PPG Industries Inc .... G 910 452-3289
  Wilmington (G-16368)
PPG Industries Inc .... G 336 771-8878
  Winston Salem (G-16862)
Rack Works Inc .... E 336 368-1302
  Pilot Mountain (G-12201)
Renaissance Innovations LLC .... E 774 901-4642
  Durham (G-5324)
Renaissance Innovations LLC .... G 844 473-7246
  Apex (G-239)
Renner Wood Companies .... F 704 527-9261
  Charlotte (G-3436)
Road Infrstrcture Inv Hldngs I .... E 336 475-6600
  Thomasville (G-15271)
RPM Wood Finishes Group Inc .... D 828 261-0325
  Hickory (G-8141)
RPM Wood Finishes Group Inc .... G 828 261-0325
  Hickory (G-8142)
RPM Wood Finishes Group Inc .... D 828 728-8266
  Hudson (G-8777)
▲ RPM Wood Finishes Group Inc .... B 828 261-0325
  Hickory (G-8140)
Rust-Oleum Corporation .... G 704 662-7730
  Mooresville (G-11077)
S Choice Baker Inc .... G 919 556-1188
  Wake Forest (G-15586)
◆ S&F Products .... G 714 412-1298
  Holly Springs (G-8714)

Sherwin-Williams Company .... D 704 548-2820
  Charlotte (G-3541)
Sherwin-Williams Company .... E 336 292-3000
  Greensboro (G-7335)
Sherwin-Williams Company .... G 919 436-2460
  Raleigh (G-13248)
Sherwin-Williams Company .... E 704 881-0245
  Statesville (G-14885)
Sibelco North America Inc .... D 828 766-6050
  Spruce Pine (G-14656)
Valspar Corporation .... G 704 897-5700
  Davidson (G-4706)
Verylak Inc .... F 812 442-7281
  Lewisville (G-9675)

2861 Gum and wood chemicals

Monticello Labs Inc .... G 919 623-6390
  Hurdle Mills (G-8911)
Soto Industries LLC .... E 706 643-5011
  Charlotte (G-3582)
Westrock Mwv LLC .... E 919 334-3200
  Raleigh (G-13419)

2865 Cyclic crudes and intermediates

Americhem Inc .... E 704 782-6411
  Concord (G-4195)
◆ Burlington Chemical Co LLC .... G 336 584-0111
  Greensboro (G-6861)
Clariant Corporation .... D 704 331-7000
  Charlotte (G-2489)
Dystar Americas Holding Corp .... G 704 561-3000
  Charlotte (G-2666)
Dystar Carolina Chemical Corp .... D 704 391-6322
  Charlotte (G-2667)
Dystar LP .... D 336 342-6631
  Reidsville (G-13518)
◆ Dystar LP .... G 704 561-3000
  Charlotte (G-2668)
Heubach Colorants USA LLC .... E 408 686-2935
  Charlotte (G-2908)
Marlowe-Van Loan Corporation .... E 336 886-7126
  High Point (G-8440)
▲ Melatex Incorporated .... F 704 332-5046
  Charlotte (G-3162)
Tar Heel Credit Counciling .... G 336 254-0348
  Greensboro (G-7390)
Tar Heel Cuisine Inc .... G 704 435-6979
  Cherryville (G-3877)
Tar Heel Fence & Vinyl .... G 336 465-1297
  Sophia (G-14523)
Tar Heel Grnd Cmmndery Order K .... G 910 867-6764
  Fayetteville (G-5926)
Tar Heel Landworks LLC .... F 336 941-3009
  Mocksville (G-10607)
Tar Heel Materials & Hdlg LLC .... G 704 659-5143
  Cleveland (G-4082)
Tar Heel Metal Structures .... G 252 208-7171
  Kinston (G-9387)
Tar Heel Mini Motoring Club .... G 336 391-8084
  Winston Salem (G-16932)
Tar Heel State Title LLC .... G 704 256-4965
  Waxhaw (G-15779)
Tar River Mining Inc .... G 252 753-3447
  Fountain (G-6098)
Tarheel Air & Lube Inc .... F 704 469-1075
  Concord (G-4370)
Tarheel State Restorations .... G 980 621-3196
  Concord (G-4371)

2869 Industrial organic chemicals, nec

▼ Albemarle Corporation .... A 980 299-5700
  Charlotte (G-2152)

SIC SECTION

28 CHEMICALS AND ALLIED PRODUCTS

Alltech Inc .... E 336 635-5190
  Eden (G-5486)
Altech-Eco Corporation .... F 828 654-8300
  Arden (G-308)
Archer-Daniels-Midland Company .... C 910 457-5011
  Southport (G-14565)
Aurorium LLC .... D 336 292-1781
  Greensboro (G-6822)
BASF .... G 919 731-1700
  Pikeville (G-12191)
BASF Corporation .... C 704 588-5280
  Charlotte (G-2286)
BASF Corporation .... D 919 433-6773
  Durham (G-4944)
BASF Corporation .... A 919 547-2000
  Durham (G-4945)
BASF Corporation .... E 919 461-6500
  Morrisville (G-11299)
BASF Plant Science LP .... D 919 547-2000
  Durham (G-4946)
◆ Boehme-Filatex Inc .... C 336 342-4507
  Reidsville (G-13510)
Carbon Conversion Systems LLC .... G 919 883-4238
  Chapel Hill (G-1996)
Chemol Company Inc .... E 336 333-3050
  Greensboro (G-6906)
Chemtech Industrial Inc .... G 919 400-5743
  Louisburg (G-9983)
Chirazyme Labs Inc .... G 252 717-1112
  Washington (G-15687)
Clariant Corporation .... D 704 371-3272
  Charlotte (G-2490)
Clariant Corporation .... E 704 235-5700
  Mooresville (G-10906)
Clariant Corporation .... E 704 822-2100
  Mount Holly (G-11627)
◆ Clariant Corporation .... D 704 331-7000
  Charlotte (G-2491)
Compagnie Parento Inc .... G 828 758-2525
  Lenoir (G-9600)
Custom Nano Inc .... G 919 608-3540
  Raleigh (G-12665)
Ddp Spclty Elctrnic Mtls US 9 .... D 336 547-7112
  Greensboro (G-6962)
◆ Dystar LP .... E 704 561-3000
  Charlotte (G-2668)
Eastern Fuel Procurement Inc .... G 252 523-2799
  Kinston (G-9360)
Enzyme Customs .... G 704 888-8278
  Locust (G-9959)
Evonik Corporation .... D 336 333-3565
  Greensboro (G-7006)
FCC Butner .... G 919 575-3900
  Butner (G-1544)
Fishkillerdaves LLC .... G 252 441-7703
  Kill Devil Hills (G-9257)
Fuel Doc 16 .... G 919 284-5400
  Kenly (G-9152)
Gee Spot Mobile Bar LLC .... G 910 581-1786
  Jacksonville (G-9002)
Hexion Inc .... E 910 483-1311
  Fayetteville (G-5838)
Hospira Inc .... B 919 553-3831
  Clayton (G-3988)
Imperial Falcon Group Inc .... G 646 717-1128
  Charlotte (G-2953)
Industrial Lubricants Inc .... E 336 767-0013
  Winston Salem (G-16759)
Innospec Active Chemicals LLC .... E 704 633-8028
  Salisbury (G-13984)
▲ Innospec Active Chemicals LLC .... D 336 882-3308
  High Point (G-8410)

KAO Specialties Americas LLC .... C 336 884-2214
  High Point (G-8422)
Kestrel I Acquisition Corporation ...... A 919 990-7500
  Durham (G-5180)
Leke LLC .... E 704 523-1452
  Pineville (G-12280)
▼ Lindley Laboratories Inc .... F 336 449-7521
  Gibsonville (G-6567)
◆ Liquidating Reichhold Inc .... A 919 990-7500
  Durham (G-5191)
Litholyte Corporation LLC .... G 252 671-2032
  Trent Woods (G-15329)
Marlowe-Van Loan Corporation .... E 336 886-7126
  High Point (G-8440)
Mary Bogest Impressions .... G 336 848-0910
  High Point (G-8447)
Maverick Biofeuls .... G 919 749-8717
  Durham (G-5210)
Mid Town Dixie Express Fuel .... G 336 318-1200
  Asheboro (G-458)
▲ Mirror Tech Inc .... G 336 342-6041
  Reidsville (G-13532)
Momentive Performance Mtls Inc .... C 704 805-6252
  Charlotte (G-3193)
Momentive Performance Mtls Inc .... D 704 805-6200
  Huntersville (G-8857)
N-Zyme Specialist LLC .... G 919 349-2429
  Wake Forest (G-15573)
▼ Norag Technology LLC .... G 336 316-0417
  Pelham (G-12177)
North Amercn Bio-Energies LLC ...... G 828 759-7101
  Lenoir (G-9641)
Novozymes Inc .... D 919 494-3950
  Franklinton (G-6159)
Novozymes North America Inc .... E 919 494-3220
  Morrisville (G-11399)
◆ Novozymes North America Inc ..... D 919 494-2014
  Franklinton (G-6160)
Oak-Bark Corporation .... E 910 655-2263
  Riegelwood (G-13561)
▼ Oak-Bark Corporation .... F
  Wilmington (G-16342)
▼ Piedmont Chemical Inds I LLC ..... D 336 885-5131
  High Point (G-8481)
▲ Pisgah Laboratories Inc .... E 828 884-2789
  Pisgah Forest (G-12327)
Seacon Corp .... G 704 331-3920
  Charlotte (G-3515)
◆ Silar LLC .... E 910 655-4212
  Riegelwood (G-13563)
▲ Silicones Inc .... F 336 886-5018
  High Point (G-8529)
Silicones Inc .... G 336 886-5018
  High Point (G-8530)
Sovereign Technologies LLC .... F 828 358-5355
  Hickory (G-8166)
▲ Stewart Superabsorbents LLC ..... G 828 855-9316
  Hickory (G-8168)
Transeco Energy Corporation .... G 828 684-6400
  Arden (G-384)
Triangle Chemical Company .... G 919 942-3237
  Chapel Hill (G-2082)
◆ Trinity Manufacturing Inc .... D 910 582-5650
  Hamlet (G-7633)
Tyton NC Biofuels LLC .... E 910 878-7820
  Raeford (G-12443)
Video Fuel .... G 919 676-9940
  High Point (G-13399)
◆ Vpm Liquidating Inc .... F 336 292-1781
  Greensboro (G-7451)
Wpt LLC .... G 704 770-1311
  Monroe (G-10837)

Wright Chemicals LLC .... G 919 296-1771
  Durham (G-5448)
Xona Microfluidics Inc .... G 951 553-6400
  Durham (G-5456)

2873 Nitrogenous fertilizers

Acton Corporation .... G 434 728-4491
  Greensboro (G-6778)
Carolina Eastern Inc .... G 252 795-3128
  Robersonville (G-13615)
Clapp Fertilizer and Trckg Inc .... G 336 449-6103
  Whitsett (G-15986)
▲ Farm Chemicals Inc .... F 910 875-4277
  Raeford (G-12420)
Harvey Fertilizer and Gas Co .... E 919 731-2474
  Goldsboro (G-6624)
Harvey Fertilizer and Gas Co .... F 252 523-9090
  Kinston (G-9368)
▲ Harvey Fertilizer and Gas Co ..... E 252 526-4150
  Kinston (G-9369)
Helena Agri-Enterprises LLC .... F 910 422-8901
  Rowland (G-13789)
Kamlar Corporation .... E 252 443-2576
  Rocky Mount (G-13705)
Mineral Springs Fertilizer Inc .... G 704 843-2683
  Mineral Springs (G-10518)
Nutrien AG Solutions Inc .... A 252 322-4111
  Aurora (G-837)
Nutrien AG Solutions Inc .... G 252 235-4161
  Bailey (G-876)
Scotts Company LLC .... F 704 663-6088
  Mooresville (G-11080)
Southern States Coop Inc .... G 336 246-3201
  Creedmoor (G-4620)
Southern States Coop Inc .... E 336 786-7545
  Mount Airy (G-11575)
Southern States Coop Inc .... E 919 658-5061
  Mount Olive (G-11669)
Southern States Coop Inc .... E 704 872-6364
  Statesville (G-14896)
Southern States Coop Inc .... F 910 285-8213
  Wallace (G-15628)

2874 Phosphatic fertilizers

Nutrien AG Solutions Inc .... F 252 977-2025
  Rocky Mount (G-13670)
Pcs Phosphate Company Inc .... E 252 322-4111
  Aurora (G-838)
Potash Corp Saskatchewan Inc .... D 252 322-4111
  Aurora (G-839)
Scotts Company LLC .... F 704 663-6088
  Mooresville (G-11080)
Southern States Coop Inc .... G 336 246-3201
  Creedmoor (G-4620)
Southern States Coop Inc .... E 336 786-7545
  Mount Airy (G-11575)
Southern States Coop Inc .... E 919 658-5061
  Mount Olive (G-11669)
Southern States Coop Inc .... E 704 872-6364
  Statesville (G-14896)
Southern States Coop Inc .... F 910 285-8213
  Wallace (G-15628)

2875 Fertilizers, mixing only

Brandt Consolidated Inc .... G 910 567-2965
  Godwin (G-6575)
C A Perry & Son Inc .... G 252 330-2323
  Elizabeth City (G-5532)
C A Perry & Son Inc .... E 252 221-4463
  Hobbsville (G-8675)
Camp Chemical Corporation .... F 336 597-2214
  Roxboro (G-13797)

28 CHEMICALS AND ALLIED PRODUCTS

Carolina Compost .... G 252 202-6602
   Camden *(G-1556)*

Charles Hill Enterprises .... F 828 665-2116
   Candler *(G-1573)*

Cmd Land Services LLC .... G 919 554-2281
   Wake Forest *(G-15543)*

Crown Town Compost LLC .... G 704 654-5689
   Charlotte *(G-2573)*

Daddy Petes Plant Pleaser .... G 704 585-2355
   Stony Point *(G-14971)*

Eastern Compost LLC .... G 252 446-3636
   Elm City *(G-5649)*

Harvey Fertilizer and Gas Co .... E 919 731-2474
   Goldsboro *(G-6624)*

Harvey Fertilizer and Gas Co .... G 252 523-9090
   Kinston *(G-9368)*

▲ Harvey Fertilizer and Gas Co .... E 252 526-4150
   Kinston *(G-9369)*

Northwest AG Product .... G 509 547-8234
   Cary *(G-1833)*

Nutrien AG Solutions Inc .... G 252 585-0282
   Conway *(G-4516)*

Nutrien AG Solutions Inc .... F 252 977-2025
   Rocky Mount *(G-13670)*

Southern AG Insecticides Inc .... E 828 692-2233
   Hendersonville *(G-7902)*

Southern States Coop Inc .... E 704 872-6364
   Statesville *(G-14896)*

T H Blue Inc .... G 910 673-3033
   Eagle Springs *(G-5461)*

Tarheel Enviromental LLC .... G 910 425-4939
   Stedman *(G-14937)*

Tryon Equine Compost LLC .... G 914 774-7486
   Columbus *(G-4181)*

Wilmington Compost Company LLC ... G 910 839-3011
   Wilmington *(G-16445)*

Wormfarmer .... G 252 944-1012
   Washington *(G-15741)*

2879 Agricultural chemicals, nec

AG Chemical .... G 561 886-0919
   Cary *(G-1676)*

Amika LLC .... G 984 664-9804
   Cary *(G-1681)*

Aqua 10 Corporation .... G 252 726-5421
   Morehead City *(G-11149)*

Arysta Lifescience Inc .... D 919 678-4900
   Cary *(G-1690)*

▲ Arysta Lifescience N Amer LLC ..... E 919 678-4900
   Cary *(G-1691)*

Atticus LLC .... E 984 465-4754
   Cary *(G-1694)*

Cape Fear Chemicals Inc .... G 910 862-3139
   Elizabethtown *(G-5588)*

Chemours Company .... E 910 483-4681
   Fayetteville *(G-5788)*

Chemours Company Fc LLC .... C 910 678-1314
   Fayetteville *(G-5789)*

Degesch America Inc .... E 800 548-2778
   Wilson *(G-16492)*

Dupont .... G 919 414-0089
   Raleigh *(G-12710)*

E I Du Pont De Nemours .... G 919 518-1332
   Raleigh *(G-12712)*

Fair Products Inc .... G 919 467-1599
   Cary *(G-1767)*

▲ Gb Biosciences LLC .... D 336 632-6000
   Greensboro *(G-7032)*

Harvey Fertilizer and Gas Co .... E 252 753-2063
   Farmville *(G-5738)*

Helena Agri-Enterprises LLC .... G 828 685-1182
   Hendersonville *(G-7861)*

▲ I Must Garden LLC .... G 919 929-2299
   Raleigh *(G-12872)*

Jabb of Carolinas Inc .... G 919 965-9007
   Pine Level *(G-12211)*

Lanxess Corporation .... F 704 868-7200
   Gastonia *(G-6443)*

▲ Makhteshim Agan North Amer Inc .. E 919 256-9300
   Raleigh *(G-12990)*

◆ Mey Corporation .... G 919 932-5800
   Chapel Hill *(G-2043)*

Monsanto Company .... G 252 212-5421
   Battleboro *(G-925)*

Privette Enterprises Inc .... E 704 634-3291
   Monroe *(G-10789)*

▲ Pro Farm Group Inc .... D 530 750-2800
   Raleigh *(G-13147)*

Scotts Company LLC .... E 704 663-6088
   Mooresville *(G-11080)*

Southeastern Minerals Inc .... E 252 492-0831
   Henderson *(G-7811)*

Southern AG Insecticides Inc .... E 828 264-8843
   Boone *(G-1238)*

Southern AG Insecticides Inc .... E 828 692-2233
   Hendersonville *(G-7902)*

▲ Summit Agro Usa LLC .... G 984 260-0407
   Durham *(G-5379)*

◆ Trinity Manufacturing Inc .... D 910 582-5650
   Hamlet *(G-7633)*

Tyratech Inc .... E 919 415-4275
   Morrisville *(G-11459)*

▲ Upl NA Inc .... E 610 491-2800
   Durham *(G-5426)*

Vestaron Corporation .... D 919 694-1022
   Durham *(G-5432)*

◆ Vpm Liquidating Inc .... F 336 292-1781
   Greensboro *(G-7451)*

2891 Adhesives and sealants

Aggressive Adhesives Inc .... G 910 270-3282
   Hampstead *(G-7635)*

▲ Aldo Products Company Inc .... G 704 932-3054
   Salisbury *(G-13918)*

American Acrylic Adhesives .... G 520 954-1700
   Mooresville *(G-10855)*

Arclin USA LLC .... G 919 542-2526
   Moncure *(G-10614)*

Avanti Coatings Inc .... G 908 723-4596
   Hendersonville *(G-7822)*

▲ Beardowadams Inc .... F 704 359-8443
   Charlotte *(G-2292)*

Bonding Materials LLC .... G 704 277-6697
   Charlotte *(G-2332)*

Capital City Sealants LLC .... G 919 427-4077
   Raleigh *(G-12589)*

Carolina Solvents Inc .... E 828 322-1920
   Hickory *(G-7966)*

Carroll-Baccari Inc .... G 561 585-2227
   Flat Rock *(G-5962)*

◆ Coatings and Adhesives Corp .... C 910 371-3184
   Leland *(G-9537)*

Cohera Medical Inc .... G 800 641-7458
   Raleigh *(G-12632)*

Colquimica Adhesives Inc .... E 704 318-4750
   Charlotte *(G-2525)*

Dap Products Inc .... F 704 799-9640
   Mooresville *(G-10924)*

Daystar Materials Inc .... G 919 734-0460
   Goldsboro *(G-6609)*

Dbt Coatings LLC .... G 336 834-9700
   Greensboro *(G-6961)*

Ddp Spclty Elctrnic Mtls US 9 .... D 336 547-7112
   Greensboro *(G-6962)*

Everkem Diversified Pdts Inc .... F 336 661-7801
   Winston Salem *(G-16701)*

Firestopping Products Inc .... F 336 661-0102
   Winston Salem *(G-16711)*

GLS Products LLC .... G 704 334-2425
   Charlotte *(G-2836)*

◆ Harper-Love Adhesives Corp .... D 704 588-4395
   Charlotte *(G-2891)*

HB Fuller Co .... G 415 878-7202
   Morrisville *(G-11353)*

HB Fuller Company .... G 336 294-5939
   Greensboro *(G-7079)*

Henkel US Operations Corp .... G 704 799-0385
   Mooresville *(G-10972)*

Henkel US Operations Corp .... E 704 647-3500
   Salisbury *(G-13977)*

Hexion Inc .... G 336 884-8918
   High Point *(G-8384)*

◆ Hexpol Compounding NC Inc .... A 704 872-1585
   Statesville *(G-14813)*

Hickory Adchem Inc .... G 828 327-0936
   Hickory *(G-8043)*

His Company Inc .... G 800 537-0351
   Wilmington *(G-16255)*

Impact Technologies LLC .... G 704 400-5364
   Concord *(G-4284)*

Ips Corporation .... E 919 598-2400
   Durham *(G-5164)*

Ips Structural Adhesives Inc .... E 919 598-2400
   Durham *(G-5165)*

Jowat Corporation .... G 336 434-9356
   Archdale *(G-288)*

◆ Jowat Corporation .... D 336 434-9000
   Archdale *(G-289)*

Jowat International Corp .... E 336 434-9000
   Archdale *(G-290)*

Jowat Properties Corp .... F 336 434-9000
   Archdale *(G-291)*

Kestrel I Acquisition Corporation .... A 919 990-7500
   Durham *(G-5180)*

◆ Kleiberit Adhesives USA Inc .... F 704 843-3339
   Waxhaw *(G-15765)*

Knight Safety Coatings Co Inc .... F 910 458-3145
   Wilmington *(G-16290)*

Laticrete International Inc .... G 910 582-2252
   Hamlet *(G-7626)*

LD Davis Industries Inc .... E 704 289-4551
   Monroe *(G-10756)*

◆ Liquidating Reichhold Inc .... A 919 990-7500
   Durham *(G-5191)*

▲ Loba-Wakol LLC .... E 704 527-5919
   Wadesboro *(G-15515)*

Lord Corporation .... D 919 469-2500
   Cary *(G-1818)*

◆ Lord Corporation .... B 919 468-5979
   Cary *(G-1817)*

Lord Far East Inc .... E 919 468-5979
   Cary *(G-1819)*

Manning Fabrics Inc .... G 910 295-1970
   Pinehurst *(G-12228)*

Marlin Company Inc .... G 828 758-9999
   Lenoir *(G-9631)*

◆ Marlin Company Inc .... F 828 754-0980
   Lenoir *(G-9632)*

Natural Adhesive LLC .... G 616 217-8392
   Wilmington *(G-16332)*

◆ Phoenix Tapes Usa LLC .... G 704 588-3090
   Charlotte *(G-3338)*

Power Adhesives Ltd .... G 704 578-9984
   Charlotte *(G-3358)*

Pregis LLC .... E 828 465-9197
   Conover *(G-4486)*

SIC SECTION
28 CHEMICALS AND ALLIED PRODUCTS

Psa Incorporated............................... F 910 371-1115
 Belville *(G-1024)*
Pyramid Cement Products Inc............ F 704 373-2529
 Pineville *(G-12292)*
◆ Reichhold Holdings Us Inc................ A 919 990-7500
 Durham *(G-5323)*
▲ Robix America Inc............................ C 336 668-9555
 Greensboro *(G-7314)*
Rutland Fire Clay Company................ G 802 775-5519
 Chapel Hill *(G-2066)*
Scott Bader Inc.................................. F 330 920-4410
 Mocksville *(G-10602)*
Sensus USA Inc................................. C 919 576-6185
 Morrisville *(G-11426)*
◆ Sensus USA Inc................................. E 919 845-4000
 Morrisville *(G-11425)*
◆ Sika Corporation................................ E 704 810-0500
 Gastonia *(G-6510)*
Slade Operating Company LLC......... E 704 873-1366
 Statesville *(G-14887)*
Southern Resin Inc............................. E 336 475-1348
 Thomasville *(G-15279)*
Spectrum Adhesives Inc..................... G 828 396-4200
 Granite Falls *(G-6758)*
▲ STI Polymer Inc................................. E 800 874-5878
 Sanford *(G-14194)*
◆ Tailored Chemical Products Inc......... D 828 322-6512
 Hickory *(G-8173)*
Textile Rubber and Chem Co Inc........ G 704 376-3582
 Indian Trail *(G-8968)*
◆ Tosaf Inc... F 980 533-3000
 Bessemer City *(G-1087)*
Udm Systems LLC............................. G 919 789-0777
 Raleigh *(G-13374)*
▲ Udm Systems LLC............................. G 919 789-0777
 Raleigh *(G-13375)*
Unecol Adhesives N Amer LLC.......... G 888 963-8879
 Durham *(G-5419)*
▲ Web-Don Incorporated...................... E 800 532-0434
 Charlotte *(G-3800)*
▲ Weiss USA LLC................................. G 704 282-4496
 Monroe *(G-10832)*
Wholeseal International...................... G 919 346-0788
 Pittsboro *(G-12355)*

2892 Explosives

Austin Powder Company..................... F 828 645-4291
 Denton *(G-4725)*
Dyno Nobel Explosive Blasting........... G 919 771-1522
 Garner *(G-6272)*
Gunpowder Creek Distillers LLC........ G 828 851-0799
 Hickory *(G-8036)*
K2 Solutions Inc................................. B 910 692-6898
 Southern Pines *(G-14538)*
◆ Maxam North America Inc................. F 214 736-8100
 Mooresville *(G-11018)*

2893 Printing ink

▲ Actega Wit Inc................................... C 704 735-8282
 Lincolnton *(G-9865)*
▼ Allied Pressroom Products Inc.......... E 954 920-0909
 Monroe *(G-10641)*
▲ American Water Graphics Inc........... F 828 247-0700
 Forest City *(G-6058)*
Archie Supply LLC............................. G 336 987-0895
 Greensboro *(G-6813)*
Arpro M-Tec LLC............................... F 828 433-0699
 Morganton *(G-11198)*
Crossroads Fuel Service Inc............... E 252 426-5216
 Hertford *(G-7918)*
Doris E Inc... G 919 858-5419
 Raleigh *(G-12697)*

DSM Desotech Inc............................. G 704 862-5000
 Stanley *(G-14691)*
▲ Environmental Inks and Co................ C 828 433-1922
 Morganton *(G-11212)*
Flint Group Inc.................................. F 828 687-4363
 Arden *(G-330)*
Flint Group US LLC........................... G 828 687-4309
 Arden *(G-331)*
Flint Group US LLC........................... G 704 504-2626
 Charlotte *(G-2779)*
▲ GSE Dispensing................................ G 704 509-2651
 Charlotte *(G-2873)*
Hoffman Steinberg.............................. G 336 292-5501
 Greensboro *(G-7095)*
Hubergroup Usa Inc........................... F 336 292-5501
 Greensboro *(G-7103)*
▲ Ink Tec Inc.. F 828 465-6411
 Newton *(G-11944)*
INX International Ink Co..................... F 704 372-2080
 Charlotte *(G-2990)*
Mirchandani Inc.................................. G 919 872-8871
 Raleigh *(G-13034)*
◆ Mitsubishi Chemical Amer Inc............ D 980 580-2839
 Charlotte *(G-3188)*
◆ Monarch Color Corporation................ E 704 394-4626
 Charlotte *(G-3196)*
RPM Wood Finishes Group Inc......... D 828 261-0325
 Hickory *(G-8141)*
RPM Wood Finishes Group Inc......... D 828 728-8266
 Hudson *(G-8777)*
Rutland Group Inc.............................. G 704 553-0046
 Charlotte *(G-3474)*
▲ Siegwerk Eic LLC.............................. F 800 368-4657
 Morganton *(G-11253)*
Sun Chemical Corporation................. E 704 587-4531
 Charlotte *(G-3650)*
Wikoff Color Corporation.................... E 704 392-4657
 Charlotte *(G-3813)*
Wikoff Color Corporation.................... E 336 668-3423
 Greensboro *(G-7460)*
Xsys North America Corporation........ E 828 687-2485
 Arden *(G-394)*

2895 Carbon black

Etmo TEC LLC................................... G 704 878-9979
 Statesville *(G-14795)*

2899 Chemical preparations, nec

Accurate Fabrications Inc................... G 910 383-2140
 Leland *(G-9524)*
Ae Technology Inc.............................. F 704 528-2000
 Troutman *(G-15365)*
▼ Alamance Foods Inc.......................... C 336 226-6392
 Burlington *(G-1362)*
▼ Albemarle Corporation....................... A 980 299-5700
 Charlotte *(G-2152)*
Alliance Assessments LLC................ G 336 283-9246
 Winston Salem *(G-16599)*
American Chrome & Chem NA Inc..... G 910 675-7200
 Castle Hayne *(G-1942)*
American Phoenix Inc......................... C 910 484-4007
 Fayetteville *(G-5760)*
Attl Products Inc................................ G 336 475-8101
 Thomasville *(G-15187)*
▲ Barker Industries Inc......................... G 704 391-1023
 Charlotte *(G-2281)*
Blast Off Intl Chem & Mfg Co............ G 509 885-4525
 Seaboard *(G-14226)*
Bnnano Inc... F 844 926-6266
 Burlington *(G-1377)*
◆ Bonsal American Inc.......................... D 704 525-1621
 Charlotte *(G-2334)*

Buckeye International Inc.................... G 704 523-9400
 Charlotte *(G-2363)*
◆ Burlington Chemical Co LLC.............. G 336 584-0111
 Greensboro *(G-6861)*
Camco Manufacturing Inc................... G 336 348-6609
 Reidsville *(G-13511)*
◆ Camco Manufacturing LLC................ C 800 334-2004
 Greensboro *(G-6876)*
Camerins Pixel Flare.......................... G 704 502-6922
 Charlotte *(G-2379)*
◆ Carlisle Corporation........................... G 704 501-1100
 Charlotte *(G-2390)*
Carolina Bottle Mfr LLC...................... G 704 635-8759
 Monroe *(G-10674)*
Carolina Connections Inc................... G 336 786-7030
 Mount Airy *(G-11488)*
Carolina Flare Sportfishng LLC.......... G 252 205-5563
 Sims *(G-14440)*
Celcore Inc... G 828 669-4875
 Black Mountain *(G-1122)*
Championx LLC.................................. G 704 506-4830
 Belmont *(G-979)*
Chem-Tech Solutions Inc.................... E 704 829-9202
 Belmont *(G-980)*
▲ Chem-Tex Laboratories Inc................ E 706 602-8600
 Concord *(G-4232)*
Chemtech North Carolina LLC........... E 910 514-9575
 Lillington *(G-9849)*
Clariant Corporation........................... D 704 331-7000
 Charlotte *(G-2489)*
Clean Solutions LLC.......................... G 919 391-8047
 Charlotte *(G-2495)*
Continental Manufacturing Co............ G 336 697-2591
 Mc Leansville *(G-10386)*
Copia Labs Inc................................... G 910 904-1000
 Raeford *(G-12417)*
Dst Manufacturing LLC...................... G 336 676-6096
 Randleman *(G-13465)*
Emerald Carolina Chemical LLC........ D 704 393-0089
 Charlotte *(G-2706)*
Enviroserve Chemicals Inc................. F 910 892-1791
 Dunn *(G-4865)*
Eoncoat LLC...................................... G 941 928-9401
 Lenoir *(G-9606)*
Euclid Chemical Company.................. G 704 283-2544
 Monroe *(G-10717)*
◆ Fiber Composites LLC....................... B 704 463-7120
 New London *(G-11870)*
Fire Retardant Chem Tech LLC......... G 980 253-8880
 Matthews *(G-10316)*
Flare Dichiaro.................................... G 336 500-5160
 Greensboro *(G-7017)*
FMC Corporation................................ E 704 868-5300
 Bessemer City *(G-1067)*
FMC Corporation................................ B 704 426-5336
 Bessemer City *(G-1068)*
Freudenberg Prfmce Mtls LP............. C 828 665-5000
 Candler *(G-1579)*
▲ Gb Biosciences LLC.......................... G 336 632-6000
 Greensboro *(G-7032)*
Gbf Inc... D 336 665-0205
 High Point *(G-8363)*
Giles Chemical Corporation................ G 828 452-4784
 Waynesville *(G-15805)*
▲ Giles Chemical Corporation................ E 828 452-4784
 Waynesville *(G-15806)*
Global Bioprotect LLC........................ F 336 861-0162
 High Point *(G-8367)*
◆ Goulston Technologies Inc................. E 704 289-6464
 Monroe *(G-10727)*
Gtg Engineering Inc........................... G 877 569-8572
 Clarendon *(G-3946)*

28 CHEMICALS AND ALLIED PRODUCTS

Gtg Engineering Inc .... G ... 910 457-0068
  Southport (G-14571)

◆ Gtg Engineering Inc .... G ... 877 569-8572
  Clarendon (G-3947)

Hexion Inc .... E ... 910 483-1311
  Fayetteville (G-5838)

Hospira Inc .... B ... 919 553-3831
  Clayton (G-3988)

Hydrotex Usa Inc .... G ... 919 876-4170
  Raleigh (G-12870)

Hzo Inc .... D ... 919 439-0505
  Morrisville (G-11355)

Ifs Industries Inc .... E ... 919 234-1397
  Morrisville (G-11357)

▲ Info-Gel LLC .... G ... 704 599-5770
  Charlotte (G-2970)

Ivm Chemicals Inc .... E ... 407 506-4913
  Charlotte (G-3000)

Jci Jones Chemicals Inc .... E ... 704 392-9767
  Charlotte (G-3014)

Jeskri Associates Inc .... G ... 704 291-9991
  Monroe (G-10749)

Kberg Productions LLC .... G ... 910 232-0342
  Raleigh (G-12932)

Kestrel I Acquisition Corporation .... A ... 919 990-7500
  Durham (G-5180)

Keystone Powdered Metal Co .... E ... 704 730-8805
  Kings Mountain (G-9311)

Lanxess Corporation .... F ... 704 868-7200
  Gastonia (G-6443)

Laticrete International Inc .... F ... 910 582-2252
  Hamlet (G-7626)

◆ LCI Corporation International .... E ... 704 399-7441
  Charlotte (G-3076)

Lime-Chem Inc .... G ... 910 843-2121
  Rockwell (G-13655)

Liquid Ice Corporation .... F ... 704 882-3505
  Matthews (G-10328)

◆ Liquidating Reichhold Inc .... A ... 919 990-7500
  Durham (G-5191)

Lord Corporation .... D ... 919 342-3380
  Cary (G-1816)

Loy & Loy Inc .... G ... 919 942-6356
  Graham (G-6699)

Lubrizol Global Management Inc .... D ... 704 865-7451
  Gastonia (G-6447)

M Davis and Associates LLC .... G ... 336 337-7089
  Greensboro (G-7172)

Marlowe-Van Loan Sales Co .... F ... 336 882-3351
  High Point (G-8441)

Matchem Inc .... G ... 336 886-5000
  High Point (G-8450)

Metal & Materials Proc LLC .... G ... 260 438-8901
  Aberdeen (G-13)

▲ Microban Products Company .... D ... 704 766-4267
  Huntersville (G-8854)

Moe Jt Enterprises Inc .... F ... 423 512-1427
  Winston Salem (G-16816)

Molecular Toxicology Inc .... F ... 828 264-9099
  Boone (G-1223)

◆ National Foam Inc .... G ... 919 639-6100
  Angier (G-147)

▲ Nitta Gelatin Usa Inc .... E ... 910 484-0457
  Fayetteville (G-5883)

▼ Novalent Ltd .... F ... 336 375-7555
  Greensboro (G-7225)

Nsi Lab Solutions Inc .... F ... 919 789-3000
  Raleigh (G-13075)

Old Belt Extracts LLC .... G ... 336 530-5784
  Roxboro (G-13811)

Opw Fueling Components Inc .... E ... 919 464-4569
  Smithfield (G-14475)

▲ Pavco Inc .... E ... 704 496-6800
  Charlotte (G-3321)

Pencco Inc .... F ... 252 235-5300
  Middlesex (G-10453)

▲ Polytec Inc .... E ... 704 277-3960
  Mooresville (G-11055)

Protek Services LLC .... G ... 910 556-4121
  Cameron (G-1562)

◆ Radiator Specialty Company .... D ... 704 688-2302
  Indian Trail (G-8959)

Riba Fairfield .... G ... 919 294-4819
  Durham (G-5330)

RSC Bio Solutions LLC .... G ... 800 661-3558
  Charlotte (G-3467)

RSC Chemical Solutions LLC .... E ... 704 821-7643
  Indian Trail (G-8961)

Rust911 Inc .... G ... 607 425-2882
  Hickory (G-8144)

S A L T Soak Away Lfes Trubles .... G ... 910 238-2695
  Jacksonville (G-9027)

▼ Schoenberg Salt Co .... F ... 336 766-0600
  Winston Salem (G-16899)

▲ Seacon Corporation .... G ... 704 333-6000
  Charlotte (G-3516)

Second Earth Inc .... G ... 336 740-9333
  Greensboro (G-7329)

Shadow Creek Consulting Inc .... E ... 716 860-7397
  Statesville (G-14884)

Silver Moon Nutraceuticals LLC .... G ... 828 698-5795
  Fletcher (G-6039)

◆ Sirchie Acquisition Co LLC .... C ... 800 356-7311
  Youngsville (G-17098)

Soto Industries LLC .... E ... 706 643-5011
  Charlotte (G-3582)

Specgx LLC .... C ... 919 878-4706
  Raleigh (G-13286)

Sportsmans Supply Company Inc .... G ... 336 725-8791
  Winston Salem (G-16913)

◆ Surry Chemicals Incorporated .... E ... 336 786-4607
  Mount Airy (G-11580)

◆ Tailored Chemical Products Inc .... D ... 828 322-6512
  Hickory (G-8173)

Tribodyn Technologies Inc .... F ... 859 750-6299
  Mooresville (G-11115)

◆ Unitex Chemical Corp .... F ... 336 378-0965
  Greensboro (G-7432)

Venator Chemicals LLC .... D ... 704 454-4811
  Harrisburg (G-7733)

Vital Being .... G ... 828 964-5853
  Zionville (G-17149)

Westrock Company .... G ... 770 448-2193
  Winston Salem (G-16971)

William Bostic .... G ... 336 629-5243
  Asheboro (G-511)

Winton Products Company .... F ... 704 399-5151
  Charlotte (G-3818)

Xelera Inc .... G ... 855 493-5372
  Charlotte (G-3833)

Xelera Inc .... G ... 540 915-6181
  Denver (G-4816)

Xylem Water Solutions USA Inc .... E ... 704 409-9700
  Charlotte (G-3841)

29 PETROLEUM REFINING AND RELATED INDUSTRIES

2911 Petroleum refining

Agrofuel LLC .... G ... 704 876-6667
  Statesville (G-14741)

Balanced Health Plus LLC .... F ... 704 604-9524
  Charlotte (G-2271)

Carolina Bg .... G ... 704 847-8840
  Matthews (G-10236)

Carolina Wood Residuals LLC .... G ... 252 633-3374
  Cove City (G-4597)

Gsam Residuals LLC .... G ... 704 200-2634
  Charlotte (G-2872)

Harvey Fertilizer and Gas Co .... E ... 919 731-2474
  Goldsboro (G-6624)

Murphy USA Inc .... E ... 828 758-7055
  Lenoir (G-9638)

Native Naturalz Inc .... F ... 336 334-2984
  Greensboro (G-7213)

▲ Parker Gas Company Inc .... F ... 800 354-7250
  Clinton (G-4101)

Pbf LLC .... G ... 828 252-1742
  Asheville (G-724)

Pitt Road LLC .... G ... 252 331-5818
  Elizabeth City (G-5563)

Qualice LLC .... F ... 910 419-6589
  Hamlet (G-7630)

Sg-Clw Inc .... F ... 336 865-4980
  Winston Salem (G-16903)

Sinowest Mfg LLC .... G ... 919 289-9337
  Raleigh (G-13266)

Stop N Go LLC .... F ... 919 523-7355
  Morrisville (G-11434)

Volta Group Corporation LLC .... E ... 919 637-0273
  Raleigh (G-13408)

▼ Warren Oil Company LLC .... D ... 910 892-6456
  Dunn (G-4890)

Yanek LLC .... G ... 252 558-3757
  Snow Hill (G-14512)

2951 Asphalt paving mixtures and blocks

Barnhill Contracting Company .... F ... 336 584-1306
  Burlington (G-1375)

Barnhill Contracting Company .... G ... 704 721-7500
  Concord (G-4204)

Barnhill Contracting Company .... D ... 910 488-1319
  Fayetteville (G-5769)

Barnhill Contracting Company .... E ... 252 752-7608
  Greenville (G-7493)

Blythe Construction Inc .... G ... 704 788-9733
  Concord (G-4211)

Blythe Construction Inc .... E ... 336 854-9003
  Greensboro (G-6845)

▲ Blythe Construction Inc .... B ... 704 375-8474
  Charlotte (G-2325)

Boggs Materials Inc .... G ... 704 289-8482
  Monroe (G-10664)

Boggs Transport Inc .... E ... 704 289-8482
  Monroe (G-10665)

Brown Brothers Construction Co .... F ... 828 297-2131
  Zionville (G-17148)

▲ Carolina Sunrock LLC .... E ... 919 575-4502
  Butner (G-1543)

Cloverleaf Mixing Inc .... G ... 336 765-7900
  Winston Salem (G-16655)

Custom Brick Company Inc .... E ... 919 832-2804
  Raleigh (G-12663)

D&S Asphalt Materials Inc .... G ... 828 894-2778
  Tryon (G-15424)

Dickerson Group Inc .... G ... 704 289-3111
  Charlotte (G-2631)

Fibrecrete Pprsrvtion Tech Inc .... G ... 336 789-7259
  Mount Airy (G-11509)

Fsc Holdings Inc .... G ... 919 782-1247
  Raleigh (G-12784)

Gardner Asphalt Co .... F ... 336 784-8924
  Winston Salem (G-16719)

Garris Grading and Paving Inc .... F ... 252 749-1101
  Farmville (G-5736)

SIC SECTION

30 RUBBER AND MISCELLANEOUS PLASTIC PRODUCTS

Gelder & Associates Inc .... C 919 772-6895
  Raleigh *(G-12792)*
Gem Asset Acquisition LLC .... E 919 851-0799
  Cary *(G-1772)*
Gem Asset Acquisition LLC .... E 704 697-9577
  Charlotte *(G-2815)*
Gem Asset Acquisition LLC .... G 336 854-8200
  Greensboro *(G-7033)*
Gem Asset Acquisition LLC .... G 704 225-3321
  Charlotte *(G-2814)*
Haulco LLC .... G 336 781-0468
  Trinity *(G-15344)*
Highland Paving Co LLC .... D 910 482-0080
  Fayetteville *(G-5839)*
Highway Maintenance Ofc .... G 252 534-4031
  Jackson *(G-8982)*
Hudson Paving Inc .... D 910 895-5910
  Rockingham *(G-13630)*
Johnson Paving Company Inc .... F 828 652-4911
  Marion *(G-10154)*
Krebs Corporation .... G 336 548-3250
  Madison *(G-10076)*
Lane Construction Corporation .... B 919 876-4550
  Raleigh *(G-12956)*
Long Asp Pav Trckg of Grnsburg .... F 336 643-4121
  Summerfield *(G-14986)*
Maymead Materials .... G 828 758-9299
  Lenoir *(G-9634)*
Russell Standard Corporation .... G 336 292-6875
  Greensboro *(G-7320)*
Russell Standard Nc LLC .... C 336 292-6875
  Greensboro *(G-7321)*
S T Wooten Corporation .... E 919 965-9880
  Princeton *(G-12404)*
Sunrock Group Holdings Corp .... D 919 747-6400
  Raleigh *(G-13315)*
Thorworks Industries Inc .... G 919 852-3714
  Raleigh *(G-13348)*
Vulcan Materials Company .... G 704 545-5687
  Charlotte *(G-3784)*

2952 Asphalt felts and coatings

Actega North America Inc .... G 704 736-9389
  Iron Station *(G-8973)*
Axalta Coating Systems USA LLC .... F 336 802-5701
  High Point *(G-8259)*
C3 Sealcoating LLC .... G 919 880-5515
  Wake Forest *(G-15537)*
◆ Carlisle Corporation .... G 704 501-1100
  Charlotte *(G-2390)*
Carolina Solvents Inc .... E 828 322-1920
  Hickory *(G-7966)*
Certainteed LLC .... C 919 603-1971
  Oxford *(G-12120)*
Metal Roofing Systems LLC .... E 704 820-3110
  Stanley *(G-14702)*
Ply Gem Holdings Inc .... D 919 677-3900
  Cary *(G-1852)*
Plycem Usa LLC .... D 336 696-2007
  North Wilkesboro *(G-12030)*
Rgpack Concrete LLC .... G 919 561-0855
  Chinquapin *(G-3893)*
Solid Holdings LLC .... F 704 423-0260
  Charlotte *(G-3578)*
Texture Plus Inc .... E 631 218-9200
  Lincolnton *(G-9928)*
Triad Corrugated Metal Inc .... E 336 625-9727
  Asheboro *(G-499)*
Wake Supply Company .... G 252 234-6012
  Wilson *(G-16557)*

2992 Lubricating oils and greases

Blumenthal Holdings LLC .... G 704 688-2302
  Charlotte *(G-2324)*
Citgo Quik Lube of Clayton .... G 919 550-0935
  Clayton *(G-3967)*
Lockrey Company LLC .... G 856 665-4794
  Salisbury *(G-14005)*
Lord Corporation .... D 919 342-3380
  Cary *(G-1816)*
▲ Lubrimetal Corporation .... F 828 212-1083
  Granite Falls *(G-6742)*
Mil-Comm Products Inc .... G 704 450-6415
  Statesville *(G-14843)*
▼ Moroil Corp .... F 704 795-9595
  Concord *(G-4319)*
Noble Oil Services Inc .... C 919 774-8180
  Sanford *(G-14159)*
Power Coolant & Chemical LLC .... G 704 759-3435
  Southern Pines *(G-14549)*
Revoultion Oil Inc .... G 704 577-2546
  Mooresville *(G-11068)*
▲ Sanford Transition Company Inc .... E 919 775-4989
  Sanford *(G-14182)*

2999 Petroleum and coal products, nec

Carolina Golfco Inc .... G 704 525-7846
  Charlotte *(G-2397)*

30 RUBBER AND MISCELLANEOUS PLASTIC PRODUCTS

3011 Tires and inner tubes

▲ Airboss Rbr Compounding NC LLC .... E 252 826-4919
  Scotland Neck *(G-14218)*
▲ Black Tire Service Inc .... G 919 908-6347
  Durham *(G-4964)*
◆ Carlisle Corporation .... G 704 501-1100
  Charlotte *(G-2390)*
Carolina Giant Tires Inc .... F 919 609-9077
  Henderson *(G-7777)*
Derrow Enterprises Inc .... G 252 635-3375
  New Bern *(G-11800)*
Diagnostic Shop Inc .... G 704 933-3435
  Kannapolis *(G-9117)*
Gerrard Family LLC .... G 704 545-5117
  Mint Hill *(G-10534)*
Goodyear Tire & Rubber Company .... D 910 488-9295
  Fayetteville *(G-5830)*
Goodyear Tire & Rubber Company .... G 919 552-9340
  Holly Springs *(G-8700)*
Goodyear Tire & Rubber Company .... G 336 794-0035
  Winston Salem *(G-16724)*
Mr Tire Inc .... G 704 735-8024
  Lincolnton *(G-9910)*
Oliver Rubber Company LLC .... B 336 629-1436
  Asheboro *(G-459)*
◆ Roll-Tech Molding Products LLC .... E 828 431-4515
  Hickory *(G-8139)*
Smart Cast Group .... F 855 971-2287
  Raleigh *(G-13272)*
Too Hott Customs LLC .... G 336 722-4919
  Winston Salem *(G-16944)*
Tyrata Inc .... F 919 210-8992
  Durham *(G-5417)*
White S Tire Svc Wilson Inc .... G 252 237-0770
  Wilson *(G-16559)*
White S Tire Svc Wilson Inc .... D 252 237-5426
  Wilson *(G-16560)*
Wmb of Wake County Inc .... F 919 782-0419
  Raleigh *(G-13426)*

3021 Rubber and plastics footwear

▲ CBA Productions Inc .... G 703 568-4758
  Fayetteville *(G-5786)*
McRae Industries Inc .... C 910 439-6149
  Mount Gilead *(G-11605)*
Vans Inc .... G 704 364-3811
  Charlotte *(G-3766)*
Vans Inc .... G 919 792-2555
  Raleigh *(G-13393)*
◆ Winstn-Slem Inds For Blind Inc .... B 336 759-0551
  Winston Salem *(G-16979)*

3052 Rubber and plastics hose and beltings

▲ Alliance Hose & Tube Works Inc .... G 336 378-9736
  Greensboro *(G-6793)*
Belt Shop Inc .... F 704 865-3636
  Gastonia *(G-6352)*
Beltservice Corporation .... E 704 947-2264
  Huntersville *(G-8797)*
Dayco Products LLC .... D 910 843-1024
  Red Springs *(G-13497)*
Eaton Corporation .... D 828 286-4157
  Forest City *(G-6066)*
Everything Industrial Supply .... G 743 333-2222
  Winston Salem *(G-16702)*
Flextrol Corporation .... F 704 888-1120
  Locust *(G-9960)*
Forbo Belting .... E 704 948-0800
  Huntersville *(G-8822)*
Forbo Siegling LLC .... G 704 948-0800
  Huntersville *(G-8823)*
Forbo Siegling LLC .... G 704 948-0800
  Huntersville *(G-8824)*
▲ Forbo Siegling LLC .... B 704 948-0800
  Huntersville *(G-8825)*
Forming Belt Service LLC .... G 828 465-0001
  Newton *(G-11932)*
▼ Industrial Power Inc .... G 910 483-4230
  Fayetteville *(G-5841)*
▲ Mmb One Inc .... F 704 523-8163
  Charlotte *(G-3191)*
National Foam Inc .... C 919 639-6151
  Angier *(G-148)*
Plastiflex North Carolina LLC .... D 704 871-8448
  Statesville *(G-14862)*
Polyhose Incorporated .... F 732 512-9141
  Wilmington *(G-16360)*
Sesame Technologies Inc .... F 252 964-2205
  Washington *(G-15730)*
◆ Steele Rubber Products Inc .... D 704 483-9343
  Denver *(G-4803)*
▲ Superior Fire Hose Corp .... E 704 643-5888
  Pineville *(G-12312)*
Titeflex Corporation .... G 647 638-7160
  Charlotte *(G-3697)*
Transtex Belting .... G 704 334-5353
  Charlotte *(G-3718)*
Triangle Indus Sup Hldings LLC .... G 704 395-0600
  Charlotte *(G-3725)*
Under Pressure Wilmington LLC .... G 910 409-0194
  Wilmington *(G-16438)*

3053 Gaskets; packing and sealing devices

Amesbury Group Inc .... E 704 924-7694
  Statesville *(G-14749)*
Carolina Components Group Inc .... E 919 635-8438
  Durham *(G-5001)*
◆ CGR Products Inc .... D 336 621-4568
  Greensboro *(G-6901)*
Charlotte Compressor Llc .... F 704 399-9993
  Charlotte *(G-2451)*
▲ Coltec Industries Inc .... A 704 731-1500
  Charlotte *(G-2527)*

30 RUBBER AND MISCELLANEOUS PLASTIC PRODUCTS

◆ Enpro Industries Inc .... C 704 731-1500
  Charlotte *(G-2713)*

▲ Henniges Automotive N Amer Inc ...... D 336 342-9300
  Reidsville *(G-13526)*

▲ Hibco Plastics Inc .... E 336 463-2391
  Yadkinville *(G-17040)*

Interflex Acquisition Co LLC .... D 336 921-3505
  Wilkesboro *(G-16030)*

Interflex Acquisition Co LLC .... C 336 921-3505
  Wilkesboro *(G-16031)*

Mayo Resources Inc .... E 336 996-7776
  Winston Salem *(G-16803)*

Michael Simmons .... G 704 298-1103
  Concord *(G-4313)*

◆ Mueller Die Cut Solutions Inc .... E 704 588-3900
  Charlotte *(G-3213)*

Packaging Plus North Carolina .... F 336 643-4097
  Summerfield *(G-14990)*

▲ Pfaff Molds Ltd Partnership .... F 704 423-9484
  Charlotte *(G-3334)*

Qualiseal Technology LLC .... G 704 731-1522
  Charlotte *(G-3402)*

Rempac LLC .... E 910 737-6557
  Lumberton *(G-10051)*

Rubber Mill Inc .... G 336 622-1680
  Conover *(G-4494)*

▲ Rubber Mill Inc .... E 336 622-1680
  Liberty *(G-9830)*

▲ SAS Industries Inc .... F 631 727-1441
  Elizabeth City *(G-5570)*

Slade Operating Company LLC .... E 704 873-1366
  Statesville *(G-14887)*

Southern Rubber Company Inc .... E 336 299-2456
  Greensboro *(G-7355)*

T & N Manufacturing Co Inc .... G 704 788-1418
  Davidson *(G-4698)*

▲ The Interflex Group Inc .... C 336 921-3505
  Wilkesboro *(G-16045)*

▲ Tim P Krahulec .... G 919 554-1331
  Wake Forest *(G-15603)*

▲ Universal Rubber Products Inc .... G 704 483-1249
  Denver *(G-4812)*

Victaulic Company .... E 910 371-5588
  Leland *(G-9564)*

Wilmington Rbr & Gasket Co Inc .... F 910 762-4262
  Wilmington *(G-16450)*

3061 Mechanical rubber goods

Carolina Custom Rubber Inc .... G 704 636-6989
  Salisbury *(G-13934)*

Cinters Inc .... G 336 267-3051
  Raleigh *(G-12622)*

Easth20 Holdings Llc .... G 919 313-2100
  Greensboro *(G-6987)*

Essay Operations Inc .... G 252 443-6010
  Rocky Mount *(G-13696)*

▲ Novaflex Hose Inc .... D 336 578-2161
  Haw River *(G-7755)*

Oliver Rubber Company LLC .... B 336 629-1436
  Asheboro *(G-459)*

Surgical Guide Systems LLC .... G 919 244-4463
  Chapel Hill *(G-2076)*

3069 Fabricated rubber products, nec

American Phoenix Inc .... C 910 484-4007
  Fayetteville *(G-5760)*

Andritz Fabrics and Rolls Inc .... F 919 556-7235
  Youngsville *(G-17067)*

Andritz Fabrics and Rolls Inc .... D 919 526-1400
  Raleigh *(G-12506)*

Bear Pages .... G 828 837-0785
  Murphy *(G-11706)*

▲ Blachford Rbr Acquisition Corp .... E 704 730-1005
  Kings Mountain *(G-9295)*

▲ Bsci Inc .... G 704 664-3005
  Mooresville *(G-10890)*

C & M Industrial Supply Co .... G 704 483-4001
  Mill Spring *(G-10484)*

Carolina Custom Rubber Inc .... G 704 636-6989
  Salisbury *(G-13934)*

Catawba Valley Fabrication Inc .... E 828 459-1191
  Conover *(G-4435)*

Comfort Tech Inc .... F 910 428-1779
  Biscoe *(G-1108)*

Contour Enterprises LLC .... D 828 328-1550
  Hildebran *(G-8620)*

Cooper Crouse-Hinds LLC .... E 252 566-3014
  La Grange *(G-9439)*

Core Technology Molding Corp .... E 336 294-2018
  Greensboro *(G-6937)*

Craftsman Foam Fabricators Inc .... F 336 476-5655
  Thomasville *(G-15207)*

Custom Assemblies Inc .... E 919 202-4533
  Pine Level *(G-12207)*

Custom Marking & Printing Inc .... G 704 866-8245
  Gastonia *(G-6392)*

◆ Daramic LLC .... D 704 587-8599
  Charlotte *(G-2603)*

Daughters & Ryan Inc .... G 919 284-0153
  Kenly *(G-9151)*

Dove Medical Supply LLC .... G 336 643-9367
  Summerfield *(G-14980)*

Earth Edge LLC .... F 828 624-0252
  Hickory *(G-8016)*

East West Manufacturing LLC .... G 704 663-5975
  Mooresville *(G-10936)*

Eastern Crlina Vctonal Ctr Inc .... D 252 758-4188
  Greenville *(G-7521)*

Easth20 Holdings Llc .... G 919 313-2100
  Greensboro *(G-6987)*

Eaton Corporation .... C 910 695-2900
  Pinehurst *(G-12221)*

Elite Comfort Solutions LLC .... C 828 328-2201
  Conover *(G-4450)*

Ena Advanced Rubber Tech .... G 919 235-0245
  Raleigh *(G-12737)*

Flint Group US LLC .... G 828 687-2485
  Arden *(G-332)*

Fort Bragg Surplus .... G 828 351-4195
  Canton *(G-1616)*

Frenzelit Inc .... E 336 814-4317
  Lexington *(G-9721)*

◆ Fusion Incorporated .... E 252 244-4300
  Vanceboro *(G-15477)*

GP Foam Fabricators Inc .... E 336 434-3600
  High Point *(G-8370)*

◆ Hexpol Compounding NC Inc .... A 704 872-1585
  Statesville *(G-14813)*

▲ Hickory Springs Manufactu .... D 828 328-2201
  Hickory *(G-8052)*

Hickory Springs Mfg Co .... G 828 322-7994
  Hickory *(G-8053)*

Hickory Springs Mfg Co .... G 828 728-9274
  Lenoir *(G-9619)*

Highland Foam Inc .... F 828 327-0400
  Conover *(G-4465)*

Hilliard Fabricators LLC .... E 336 861-8833
  Thomasville *(G-15231)*

Hygeia Corporation .... G 704 933-5190
  Kannapolis *(G-9122)*

Hygeia Marketing Corporation .... F 704 933-5190
  Kannapolis *(G-9123)*

▲ Interstate Foam & Supply Inc .... C 828 459-9700
  Conover *(G-4468)*

◆ K-Flex USA LLC .... B 919 556-3475
  Youngsville *(G-17087)*

▲ L B Plastics Incorporated .... D 704 663-1543
  Mooresville *(G-11000)*

▼ Lgc Consulting Inc .... E 704 216-0171
  Salisbury *(G-14003)*

▲ Longwood Industries Inc .... F 336 272-3710
  Greensboro *(G-7168)*

▲ Maranz Inc .... D 336 996-7776
  Winston Salem *(G-16799)*

Marx Industries Incorporated .... E 828 396-6700
  Hudson *(G-8775)*

▲ Maxime Knitting International .... G 803 627-2768
  Charlotte *(G-3146)*

Medaccess Inc .... G 828 264-4085
  Robbinsville *(G-13609)*

▲ Mount Hope Machinery Co .... F
  Charlotte *(G-3208)*

▲ Mustang Reproductions Inc .... F 704 786-0990
  Concord *(G-4321)*

Nu-Tech Enterprises Inc .... F 336 725-1691
  Winston Salem *(G-16825)*

Ohio Foam Corporation .... F 704 883-8402
  Statesville *(G-14854)*

◆ Patch Rubber Company .... C 252 536-2574
  Weldon *(G-15887)*

◆ Perma Flex Roller Technology .... E 704 633-1201
  Salisbury *(G-14024)*

◆ Perma-Flex Rollers Inc .... E 704 633-1201
  Salisbury *(G-14025)*

▲ Perrycraft Inc .... F 336 372-2545
  Sparta *(G-14598)*

Prototech Manufacturing Inc .... F 508 646-8849
  Washington *(G-15728)*

▲ Qrmc Ltd .... E 828 696-2000
  Hendersonville *(G-7893)*

Rempac LLC .... E 910 737-6557
  Lumberton *(G-10051)*

▲ Rp Fletcher Machine Co Inc .... D 336 249-6101
  Lexington *(G-9775)*

Rubber Mill Inc .... G 336 622-1680
  Conover *(G-4494)*

▲ Rubber Mill Inc .... E 336 622-1680
  Liberty *(G-9830)*

▲ Savatech Corp .... G 386 760-0706
  Rutherfordton *(G-13890)*

Skelly Inc .... F 828 433-7070
  Morganton *(G-11254)*

▲ Spota LLC .... F 919 569-6765
  Wake Forest *(G-15596)*

Stowe Woodward LLC .... E 360 636-0330
  Youngsville *(G-17101)*

Stowe Woodward LLC .... G 919 556-7235
  Youngsville *(G-17102)*

Sun Fabricators Inc .... E 336 885-0095
  High Point *(G-8556)*

Tekni-Plex Inc .... D 919 553-4151
  Clayton *(G-4017)*

Trelleborg Ctd Systems US Inc .... C 828 286-9126
  Rutherfordton *(G-13897)*

Water Treatment Facility .... G 919 742-2939
  Siler City *(G-14433)*

▲ William Goodyear Co .... F 704 283-7824
  Monroe *(G-10833)*

Wright Roller Company .... F 336 852-8393
  Greensboro *(G-7469)*

3081 Unsupported plastics film and sheet

◆ 3a Composites USA Inc .... C 704 872-8974
  Statesville *(G-14732)*

Abx Innvtive Pckg Slutions LLC .... D 980 443-1100
  Charlotte *(G-2126)*

SIC SECTION

30 RUBBER AND MISCELLANEOUS PLASTIC PRODUCTS

◆ Aqua Plastics Inc .... E 828 324-6284
   Hickory (G-7939)
Berry Global Inc .... G 336 841-1723
   High Point (G-8272)
Berry Global Inc .... C 704 289-1526
   Monroe (G-10661)
Berry Global Films LLC .... C 704 821-2316
   Matthews (G-10304)
◆ Bonset America Corporation .... C 336 375-0234
   Browns Summit (G-1301)
Bright View Technologies Corp .... E 919 228-4370
   Durham (G-4978)
Cardinal Plastics Inc .... G 704 739-9420
   Kings Mountain (G-9298)
◆ Celgard LLC .... C 800 235-4273
   Charlotte (G-2440)
Clear Defense LLC .... E 336 370-1699
   Greensboro (G-6916)
Daliah Plastics Corp .... E 336 629-0551
   Asheboro (G-421)
Desco Industries Inc .... F 919 718-0000
   Sanford (G-14107)
◆ Dymetrol Company Inc .... F 866 964-8632
   Bladenboro (G-1148)
Gaylord Inc .... D 704 694-2434
   Mint Hill (G-10533)
▲ Geocomp Inc .... F 704 480-7688
   Shelby (G-14319)
Icons America LLC .... E 704 922-0041
   Dallas (G-4645)
Inteplast Group Corporation .... E 704 504-3200
   Charlotte (G-2979)
Interflex Acquisition Co LLC .... C 336 921-3505
   Wilkesboro (G-16028)
Krs Plastics Inc .... F 910 653-3602
   Tabor City (G-15083)
◆ Liqui-Box Corporation .... D 804 325-1400
   Charlotte (G-3092)
▲ Longwood Industries Inc .... F 336 272-3710
   Greensboro (G-7168)
Marine & Industrial Plastics .... G 252 224-1000
   Pollocksville (G-12393)
Mikron Industries Inc .... D 713 961-4600
   Durham (G-5227)
Olon Industries Inc (us) .... F 630 232-4705
   Mocksville (G-10596)
Pacrim Inc .... E 919 363-7711
   Apex (G-224)
Paragon Films Inc .... F 828 632-5552
   Taylorsville (G-15154)
◆ Piedmont Plastics Inc .... D 704 597-8200
   Charlotte (G-3340)
Plastic Ingenuity Inc .... D 919 693-2009
   Oxford (G-12143)
Printpack Inc .... C 828 649-3800
   Marshall (G-10206)
Rays Classic Vinyl Repair Inc .... G 910 520-1626
   Hampstead (G-7654)
Ready Solutions Inc .... G 704 534-9221
   Davidson (G-4693)
◆ Roechling Indus Gastonia LP .... C 704 922-7814
   Dallas (G-4655)
Schweitzer-Mauduit Intl Inc .... G 252 360-4666
   Wilson (G-16541)
Southern Film Extruders Inc .... C 336 885-8091
   High Point (G-8545)
Southern Prestige Intl LLC .... F 704 872-9524
   Statesville (G-14894)
Specialty Perf LLC .... G 704 872-9980
   Statesville (G-14897)

3082 Unsupported plastics profile shapes

American Extruded Plastics Inc .... E 336 274-1131
   Greensboro (G-6799)
Boramed Inc .... G 919 419-9518
   Durham (G-4973)
M2 Optics Inc .... G 919 342-5619
   Raleigh (G-12985)
◆ Piedmont Plastics Inc .... D 704 597-8200
   Charlotte (G-3340)
Plastic Technology Inc .... E 828 328-8570
   Conover (G-4481)
Plastic Technology Inc .... F 828 328-2201
   Hickory (G-8116)
Precise Technology Inc .... G 704 576-9527
   Charlotte (G-3368)
▲ Robetex Inc .... F 910 671-8787
   Lumberton (G-10053)
◆ Roechling Indus Gastonia LP .... C 704 922-7814
   Dallas (G-4655)
▲ United Plastics Corporation .... C 336 786-2127
   Mount Airy (G-11592)
◆ Weener Plastics Inc .... D 252 206-1400
   Wilson (G-16558)

3083 Laminated plastics plate and sheet

Bemis Manufacturing Company .... C 828 754-1086
   Lenoir (G-9581)
Clear Defense LLC .... E 336 370-1699
   Greensboro (G-6916)
Crawford Composites LLC .... E 704 483-4175
   Denver (G-4768)
Daytech Solutions LLC .... G 336 918-4122
   Winston Salem (G-16673)
▲ Dynacast LLC .... E 704 927-2790
   Charlotte (G-2662)
Innovative Laminations Company .... F 252 745-8133
   New Bern (G-11810)
Manning Fabrics Inc .... G 910 295-1970
   Pinehurst (G-12228)
Meyer Decorative Surfaces .... G 910 794-7225
   Wilmington (G-16322)
▲ Ram Industries Inc .... F 704 982-4015
   Albemarle (G-102)
▲ Rk Enterprises LLC .... G 910 481-0777
   Fayetteville (G-5908)
▲ Robetex Inc .... F 910 671-8787
   Lumberton (G-10053)
Tech Medical Plastics Inc .... F 919 563-9272
   Mebane (G-10432)
Tekni-Plex Inc .... D 919 553-4151
   Clayton (G-4017)
Unilin North America LLC .... E 919 773-5900
   Garner (G-6321)
◆ Upm Raflatac Inc .... B 828 651-4800
   Mills River (G-10512)

3084 Plastics pipe

Advanced Drainage Systems Inc .... E 704 629-4151
   Bessemer City (G-1050)
Charlotte Pipe and Foundry Co .... B 704 348-5416
   Charlotte (G-2458)
Charlotte Pipe and Foundry Co .... A 704 372-3650
   Monroe (G-10680)
Charlotte Pipe and Foundry Co .... A 704 887-8015
   Oakboro (G-12069)
◆ Charlotte Pipe and Foundry Co .... C 704 372-5030
   Charlotte (G-2457)
Charlotte Pipe and Foundry Com .... F 704 379-0700
   Charlotte (G-2459)
Charlotte Pipe Inc .... E 704 291-3269
   Monroe (G-10681)
Consolidated Pipe & Sup Co Inc .... F 336 294-8577
   Greensboro (G-6930)

▼ Crumpler Plastic Pipe Inc .... D 910 525-4046
   Roseboro (G-13784)
Fitt Usa Inc .... F 866 348-8872
   Mooresville (G-10946)
Ipex USA LLC .... F 704 889-2431
   Pineville (G-12276)
◆ Ipex USA LLC .... C 704 889-2431
   Pineville (G-12275)
J-M Manufacturing Company Inc .... D 919 575-6515
   Creedmoor (G-4615)
National Pipe & Plastics Inc .... C 336 996-2711
   Colfax (G-4155)
◆ Opw Fling Cntnment Systems Inc .... E 919 209-2280
   Smithfield (G-14474)
Performance Plastics Pdts Inc .... D 336 454-0350
   Jamestown (G-9066)
◆ Silver-Line Plastics LLC .... C 828 252-8755
   Asheville (G-771)
Southern Pipe Inc .... F 704 550-5935
   Albemarle (G-108)
▼ Southern Pipe Inc .... E 704 463-5202
   New London (G-11878)
Teknor Apex Company .... E 401 642-3598
   Jamestown (G-9074)

3085 Plastics bottles

Amcor Phrm Packg USA LLC .... D 919 556-9715
   Youngsville (G-17066)
CKS Packaging Inc .... D 336 578-5800
   Graham (G-6685)
Intertech Corporation .... D 336 621-1891
   Greensboro (G-7120)
Mesa International .... G 207 774-5946
   Thomasville (G-15247)
Precision Concepts Intl LLC .... G 704 360-8923
   Mooresville (G-11058)
Sonoco Products Company .... G 910 455-6903
   Jacksonville (G-9034)
◆ Southeastern Container Inc .... C 828 350-7200
   Enka (G-5684)
Vav Plastics Nc LLC .... G 704 325-9332
   Charlotte (G-3767)

3086 Plastics foam products

A Plus Service Inc .... G 828 324-4397
   Hickory (G-7927)
ABT Foam LLC .... F 704 508-1010
   Statesville (G-14735)
Amesbury Group Inc .... D 704 978-2883
   Statesville (G-14748)
Amesbury Group Inc .... E 704 924-7694
   Statesville (G-14749)
▲ Apex Packaging Corporation LLC .... E 704 847-7274
   Charlotte (G-2200)
Armacell LLC .... D 828 464-5880
   Conover (G-4417)
◆ Armacell LLC .... C 919 913-0555
   Chapel Hill (G-1986)
Armacell US Holdings LLC .... C 919 304-3846
   Mebane (G-10399)
Barnhardt Manufacturing Co .... C 704 331-0657
   Charlotte (G-2282)
Barnhardt Manufacturing Co .... C 336 789-9161
   Mount Airy (G-11481)
◆ Barnhardt Manufacturing Company .. C 800 277-0377
   Charlotte (G-2283)
Blue Stone Industries Ltd .... G 919 379-3986
   Cary (G-1709)
Bunting Equipment Company Inc .... F 336 626-7300
   Sophia (G-14513)
Bwh Foam and Fiber Inc .... F 336 498-6949
   Randleman (G-13454)

Employee Codes: A=Over 500 employees, B=251-500
C=101-250, D=51-100, E=20-50, F=10-19, G=1-9

30 RUBBER AND MISCELLANEOUS PLASTIC PRODUCTS

Carolina Energy Concepts LLC .... G 910 833-4203
 Hampstead *(G-7642)*
Carpenter Co .... E 828 322-6545
 Hickory *(G-7969)*
Carpenter Co .... D 336 861-5730
 High Point *(G-8286)*
Carpenter Co .... E 828 632-7061
 Taylorsville *(G-15133)*
▲ Classic Packaging Company .... D 336 922-4224
 Pfafftown *(G-12187)*
Crown Foam Products Inc .... F 336 434-4024
 High Point *(G-8309)*
▲ Cryovac LLC .... A 980 430-7000
 Charlotte *(G-2576)*
Cryovac Intl Holdings Inc .... E 980 430-7000
 Charlotte *(G-2577)*
Dart Container Corp Georgia .... C 336 495-1101
 Randleman *(G-13463)*
Deep River Fabricators Inc .... E 336 824-8881
 Franklinville *(G-6168)*
Diversified Foam Inc .... E 336 463-5512
 Yadkinville *(G-17037)*
▲ Dynamic Systems Inc .... E 828 683-3523
 Leicester *(G-9510)*
Enginred Plstic Components Inc .... C 919 663-3141
 Siler City *(G-14410)*
◆ Ffnc Inc .... D 336 885-4121
 High Point *(G-8351)*
▲ Franklin Logistical Services Inc .... D 919 556-6711
 Youngsville *(G-17081)*
Frisby Technologies Inc .... F 336 998-6652
 Advance *(G-42)*
Future Foam Inc .... E 336 861-8095
 Archdale *(G-281)*
Future Foam Inc .... D 336 885-4121
 High Point *(G-8361)*
Fxi Inc .... D 336 431-1171
 High Point *(G-8362)*
Gaylord Inc .... D 704 694-2434
 Mint Hill *(G-10533)*
▲ Guilford Fabricators Inc .... F 336 434-3163
 High Point *(G-8372)*
▲ Hibco Plastics Inc .... E 336 463-2391
 Yadkinville *(G-17040)*
▲ Hickory Springs California LLC .... A 828 328-2201
 Hickory *(G-8051)*
Hickory Springs Mfg Co .... E 828 632-9733
 Hiddenite *(G-8217)*
Hickory Springs Mfg Co .... D 336 861-4195
 High Point *(G-8385)*
Hood Container Corporation .... A 336 784-0445
 Winston Salem *(G-16748)*
Independence Holdings Inc .... G 704 588-6202
 Charlotte *(G-2958)*
Janesville LLC .... C 828 668-9251
 Old Fort *(G-12102)*
▲ Kidkusion Inc .... F 252 946-7162
 Washington *(G-15714)*
Marves Industries Inc .... D 828 397-4400
 Hildebran *(G-8627)*
Marx LLC .... D 828 396-6700
 Granite Falls *(G-6743)*
Marx Industries Incorporated .... E 828 396-6700
 Hudson *(G-8775)*
◆ Ncfi Polyurethanes .... C 336 789-9161
 Mount Airy *(G-11551)*
▼ Ngx .... E 866 782-7749
 Tarboro *(G-15119)*
Noel Group LLC .... G 919 269-6500
 Zebulon *(G-17135)*
◆ Nomaco Inc .... B 919 269-6500
 Zebulon *(G-17136)*

Npx One LLC .... C 910 997-2217
 Rockingham *(G-13637)*
Pactiv LLC .... G 828 396-2373
 Granite Falls *(G-6748)*
Pactiv LLC .... F 828 758-7580
 Lenoir *(G-9645)*
Pak-Lite Inc .... E 919 563-1097
 Mebane *(G-10422)*
▲ Palziv North America Inc .... G 919 497-0010
 Louisburg *(G-9996)*
Piranha Industries Inc .... G 704 248-7843
 Charlotte *(G-3344)*
▼ Poly Packaging Systems Inc .... D 336 889-8334
 High Point *(G-8489)*
Prestige Fabricators Inc .... B 336 626-4595
 Asheboro *(G-467)*
Prototech Manufacturing Inc .... F 508 646-8849
 Washington *(G-15728)*
▼ Reedy International Corp .... F 980 819-6930
 Charlotte *(G-3424)*
Ritchie Foam Company Inc .... G 704 663-2533
 Mooresville *(G-11070)*
Sealed Air Corporation .... E 336 883-9184
 High Point *(G-8520)*
Sealed Air Corporation .... D 828 728-6610
 Hudson *(G-8779)*
Sealed Air Corporation .... C 828 726-2100
 Lenoir *(G-9652)*
Sealed Air Corporation (us) .... A 201 791-7600
 Charlotte *(G-3518)*
Sealed Air Intl Holdings LLC .... C 980 221-3235
 Charlotte *(G-3519)*
Shaw Industries Group Inc .... E 877 996-5942
 Charlotte *(G-3536)*
Storopack Inc .... G 800 827-7225
 Winston Salem *(G-16918)*
Swimways .... F 252 563-1101
 Tarboro *(G-15123)*
T Renee Severt LLC .... G 248 540-3741
 Chapel Hill *(G-2078)*
Technicon Industries Inc .... G 704 788-1131
 Concord *(G-4373)*
Thompson Printing & Packg Inc .... G 704 313-7323
 Mooresboro *(G-10842)*
Trego Innovations LLC .... G 919 374-0089
 Wilson *(G-16550)*
Unified2 Globl Packg Group LLC .... C 774 696-3643
 Durham *(G-5420)*
Vpc Foam USA Inc .... D 704 622-0552
 Conover *(G-4511)*
Watauga Opportunities Inc .... E 828 264-5009
 Boone *(G-1247)*
Wood Products Packg Intl Inc .... G 704 279-3011
 Faith *(G-5726)*

3087 Custom compound purchased resins

Avient Colorants USA LLC .... D 704 331-7000
 Charlotte *(G-2248)*
Borealis Compounds Inc .... E 908 798-7497
 Taylorsville *(G-15130)*
Crp Usa LLC .... G 704 660-0258
 Mooresville *(G-10918)*
◆ Hexpol Compounding NC Inc .... A 704 872-1585
 Statesville *(G-14813)*
Lubrizol Global Management Inc .... D 704 865-7451
 Gastonia *(G-6447)*
Phoenix Epoxy Systems LLC .... G 252 747-3735
 Hookerton *(G-8729)*
Premix North Carolina LLC .... G 704 412-7922
 Belmont *(G-1004)*
◆ Rutland Group Inc .... C 704 553-0046
 Pineville *(G-12300)*

◆ Rutland Holdings LLC .... E 704 553-0046
 Pineville *(G-12301)*
Sealed Air Corporation .... D 828 728-6610
 Hudson *(G-8779)*
Sealed Air Corporation (us) .... A 201 791-7600
 Charlotte *(G-3518)*
Teknor Apex Company .... E 401 642-3598
 Jamestown *(G-9074)*
Tru-Contour Inc .... F 704 455-8700
 Concord *(G-4379)*
▲ Zeon Technologies Inc .... G 704 680-9160
 Salisbury *(G-14069)*

3088 Plastics plumbing fixtures

Carolina Classic Manufacturing Inc .... D 252 237-9105
 Wilson *(G-16483)*
Creekraft Cultured Marble Inc .... F 252 636-5488
 New Bern *(G-11793)*
Custom Marble Corporation .... G 910 215-0679
 Pinehurst *(G-12219)*
Fiberglass Fabrication Inc .... E 828 685-0940
 Hendersonville *(G-7847)*
▲ Gainsborough Baths LLC .... F 336 357-0797
 Lexington *(G-9722)*
Jupiter Bathware Inc .... F 800 343-8295
 Wilson *(G-16503)*
LL Cultured Marble Inc .... F 336 789-3908
 Mount Airy *(G-11539)*
Marion Cultured Marble Inc .... F 828 724-4782
 Marion *(G-10157)*
Moen Incorporated .... E 252 638-3300
 New Bern *(G-11824)*
Moores Fiberglass Inc .... F 252 753-2583
 Walstonburg *(G-15640)*
Plastic Oddities Inc .... E 704 484-1830
 Shelby *(G-14355)*

3089 Plastics products, nec

ABS Southeast LLC .... F 919 329-0014
 Raleigh *(G-12464)*
▲ Accu-Form Polymers Inc .... E 910 293-6961
 Warsaw *(G-15664)*
◆ Accuma Corporation .... C 704 873-1488
 Statesville *(G-14738)*
Ace Plastics Inc .... G 704 527-5752
 Charlotte *(G-2127)*
Acme Nameplate & Mfg Inc .... E 704 283-8175
 Monroe *(G-10635)*
Advanced Drainage Systems .... F 704 629-4151
 Bessemer City *(G-1049)*
Advanced Plastic Extrusion LLC .... G 252 224-1444
 Pollocksville *(G-12391)*
Advanced Plastiform Inc .... F 919 404-2080
 Zebulon *(G-17118)*
Afsc LLC .... D 704 523-4936
 Charlotte *(G-2142)*
Aim LLC .... G 980 333-0008
 Charlotte *(G-2144)*
Aim Molding & Door LLC .... G 704 913-7211
 Charlotte *(G-2145)*
▲ Aimet Holding Inc .... E 919 887-5205
 Zebulon *(G-17119)*
Aimet Technologies LLC .... F 919 887-5205
 Zebulon *(G-17120)*
▼ All Source Security Cont Cal .... F 704 504-9908
 Charlotte *(G-2156)*
Allstar Waste Systems Inc .... G 252 343-5156
 Rocky Mount *(G-13680)*
Altium Packaging LLC .... F 704 873-6729
 Statesville *(G-14746)*
Altium Packaging LLC .... D 336 472-1500
 Thomasville *(G-15183)*

SIC SECTION 30 RUBBER AND MISCELLANEOUS PLASTIC PRODUCTS

Altium Packaging LP................................ D 336 342-4749
 Reidsville (G-13506)
◆ Amcor Tob Packg Americas Inc......... A 828 274-1611
 Asheville (G-517)
American Composites Engrg.................. F 252 641-9866
 Tarboro (G-15095)
American Plastic Inc................................ G 828 652-3511
 Marion (G-10139)
▼ American Wick Drain Corp................. E 704 296-5801
 Monroe (G-10644)
Amesbury Group Inc................................ D 704 978-2883
 Statesville (G-14748)
Amesbury Group Inc................................ E 704 924-7694
 Statesville (G-14749)
Applied Plastic Services Inc................... E 910 655-2156
 Bolton (G-1167)
◆ Aqua Plastics Inc................................. E 828 324-6284
 Hickory (G-7939)
Asheville Thermoform Plas Inc................ F 828 684-8440
 Fletcher (G-5985)
▲ Ashland Products Inc.......................... C 815 266-0250
 Huntersville (G-8794)
▲ Asmo North America LLC................... A 704 872-2319
 Statesville (G-14754)
▲ Atlantic Automotive Entps LLC........... F 910 377-4108
 Tabor City (G-15077)
Auto Parts Fayetteville LLC..................... G 910 889-4026
 Fayetteville (G-5766)
AWC Holding Company........................... F ... 919 677-3900
 Cary (G-1698)
Baily Enterprises LLC.............................. F 704 587-0109
 Charlotte (G-2266)
◆ Balcrank Corporation........................... E 800 747-5300
 Weaverville (G-15838)
Bandera Us LLC....................................... G 224 250-6559
 Charlotte (G-2274)
Beacon Roofing Supply Inc..................... G 704 886-1555
 Charlotte (G-2291)
Beaufort Composite Tech Inc.................. F 252 728-1547
 Beaufort (G-946)
Berry Global Inc....................................... E 252 332-7270
 Ahoskie (G-55)
Berry Global Inc....................................... G 252 984-4100
 Battleboro (G-918)
Berry Global Inc....................................... E 919 207-3202
 Benson (G-1031)
Berry Global Inc....................................... G 336 841-1723
 High Point (G-8272)
Berry Global Inc....................................... C 704 289-1526
 Monroe (G-10661)
Berry Global Inc....................................... C 704 664-3733
 Mooresville (G-10873)
Berry Global Inc....................................... D 252 984-4104
 Rocky Mount (G-13664)
Best Machine & Fabrication Inc.............. G 919 731-7101
 Dudley (G-4840)
Biomerics LLC.. G 336 810-7178
 Mebane (G-10400)
▲ Bioselect Inc... G 704 521-8585
 Charlotte (G-2315)
Blue Ridge... F 828 325-4705
 Conover (G-4424)
Blue Ridge Molding LLC.......................... D 828 485-2017
 Conover (G-4425)
▼ Bms Investment Holdings LLC........... E 336 949-4107
 Mayodan (G-10263)
▲ Borgwarner Turbo Systems LLC........ D 828 650-7515
 Arden (G-315)
Borneo Inc... F 252 398-3100
 Murfreesboro (G-11698)
Boyd Gmn Inc... C 206 284-2200
 Monroe (G-10668)

◆ Braiform Enterprises Inc..................... C 828 277-6420
 Asheville (G-571)
▲ Brispa Investments Inc....................... C 336 668-3636
 Greensboro (G-6856)
Brunson Marine Group LLC.................... E 252 291-0271
 Wilson (G-16481)
▲ Bull Engineered Products Inc............ D 704 504-0300
 Charlotte (G-2364)
C&K Plastics Nc LLC............................... F 833 232-4848
 Mooresville (G-10893)
C2c Plastics Inc....................................... G 910 338-5260
 Wilmington (G-16147)
Cabarrus Plastics Inc.............................. C 704 784-2100
 Concord (G-4218)
Cardinal Plastics Sales Inc..................... G 336 540-9013
 Greensboro (G-6879)
◆ Carlisle Corporation............................ G 704 501-1100
 Charlotte (G-2390)
Caro-Polymers Inc................................... F 704 629-5319
 Bessemer City (G-1055)
Carolina Base - Pac Corp........................ E 828 728-7304
 Hudson (G-8766)
◆ Carolina Extruded Plastics Inc.......... E 336 272-1191
 Greensboro (G-6884)
Carolina Home Exteriors LLC................. F 252 637-6599
 New Bern (G-11786)
Carolina Moldings Inc............................. F 704 523-7471
 Charlotte (G-2400)
Carolina Precision Plas LLC................... D 336 283-4700
 Mocksville (G-10561)
◆ Carolina Precision Plastics L............. D 336 498-2654
 Asheboro (G-412)
▲ Carolina Print Works Inc.................... F 704 637-6902
 Salisbury (G-13935)
Central Carolina Products Inc................ C 336 226-1449
 Burlington (G-1392)
Central Carolina Products Inc................ D 336 226-0005
 Burlington (G-1393)
Centro Inc... E 319 626-3200
 Claremont (G-3905)
Certainteed LLC....................................... C 828 459-0556
 Claremont (G-3906)
◆ Chadsworth Incorporated................... E 910 763-7600
 Wilmington (G-16168)
◆ Charlotte Pipe and Foundry Co......... C 704 372-5030
 Charlotte (G-2457)
Cks Packaging... E 704 663-6510
 Mooresville (G-10904)
CKS Packaging Inc.................................. D 336 578-5800
 Graham (G-6685)
CKS Packaging Inc.................................. E 704 663-6510
 Mooresville (G-10905)
Clt 2016 Inc.. D 704 886-1555
 Charlotte (G-2501)
CMI Plastics Inc....................................... E 252 746-2171
 Ayden (G-850)
◆ Coats & Clark Inc................................. D 704 542-5959
 Charlotte (G-2512)
▲ Coats N Amer De Rpblica Dmncan... C 800 242-8095
 Charlotte (G-2515)
Coeur Inc... G 252 946-1963
 Washington (G-15692)
▲ Coltec Industries Inc........................... A 704 731-1500
 Charlotte (G-2527)
Concept Plastics Inc............................... C 336 889-2001
 High Point (G-8303)
Consolidated Metco Inc.......................... D 360 828-2689
 Arden (G-322)
Consolidated Models Inc........................ E 252 746-2171
 Ayden (G-851)
Corner Stone Plastics Inc....................... G 336 629-1828
 Asheboro (G-418)

County of Alexander................................ E 828 632-1101
 Taylorsville (G-15136)
▲ CPS Resources Inc............................. E 704 628-7678
 Monroe (G-10697)
Creative Liquid Coatings Inc.................. D 336 415-6214
 Mount Airy (G-11498)
Cross Technology Inc............................. E 336 725-4700
 East Bend (G-5465)
CT Commercial Paper LLC...................... D 704 485-3212
 Oakboro (G-12071)
Custom Extrusion Inc.............................. G 336 495-7070
 Asheboro (G-420)
▼ Debotech Inc... C 704 664-1361
 Mooresville (G-10927)
Decorative Plastics LLC.......................... G 252 638-6684
 New Bern (G-11799)
◆ Delta Mold Inc...................................... D 704 588-6600
 Charlotte (G-2615)
Dexterity LLC... F 919 524-7732
 Greenville (G-7514)
Digger Specialties Inc............................. F 919 255-2533
 Fuquay Varina (G-6196)
Digger Specialties Inc............................. G 336 495-1517
 Randleman (G-13464)
▲ Diverse Corporate Tech Inc................ E 828 245-3717
 Forest City (G-6065)
Dons Disposal... G 919 542-2208
 Pittsboro (G-12341)
Double O Plastics Inc.............................. E 704 788-8517
 Concord (G-4256)
Douglas Fabrication & Mch Inc.............. F 919 365-7553
 Wendell (G-15898)
◆ Dps Molding Inc................................... F 732 763-4811
 Vanceboro (G-15476)
Dunstone Company Inc........................... F 704 841-1380
 Charlotte (G-2657)
Duramax Holdings LLC........................... C 704 588-9191
 Charlotte (G-2659)
▲ Dynacast LLC...................................... E 704 927-2790
 Charlotte (G-2662)
Easth20 Holdings Llc............................... G 919 313-2100
 Greensboro (G-6987)
◆ Elkamet Inc... C 828 233-4001
 East Flat Rock (G-5474)
Enginred Plstic Components Inc........... C 919 663-3141
 Siler City (G-14410)
Englishs All Wood Homes Inc................ F 252 524-5000
 Grifton (G-7600)
◆ Enpro Industries Inc............................ C 704 731-1500
 Charlotte (G-2713)
▲ Etimex USA Inc.................................... D 704 583-0002
 Charlotte (G-2732)
Exlon Extrusion Inc................................. F 336 621-1295
 Asheboro (G-432)
Fawn Industries Inc................................. D 252 462-4700
 Nashville (G-11744)
Fiber Composites LLC............................ D 704 463-7118
 New London (G-11869)
Fiberglass Fabrication Inc...................... G 828 685-0940
 Hendersonville (G-7847)
Fibreworks Composites LLC.................. E 704 696-1084
 Mooresville (G-10944)
Fineline Prototyping Inc.......................... D 919 781-7702
 Morrisville (G-11340)
▲ Fortron Industries LLC....................... E 910 343-5000
 Wilmington (G-16220)
Fourshare LLC... F 336 714-0448
 Clemmons (G-4039)
◆ Genpak LLC... E 800 626-6695
 Charlotte (G-2823)
▲ Gentry Plastics Inc.............................. E 704 864-4300
 Gastonia (G-6407)

Employee Codes: A=Over 500 employees, B=251-500
C=101-250, D=51-100, E=20-50, F=10-19, G=1-9

30 RUBBER AND MISCELLANEOUS PLASTIC PRODUCTS

Glenn Mauser Company Inc .... F 828 464-8996
  Newton *(G-11935)*
Global Packaging Inc .... D 610 666-1608
  Hamlet *(G-7622)*
▲ Gloves-Online Inc .... G 919 468-4244
  Cary *(G-1775)*
▲ Great Pacific Entps US Inc .... E 980 256-7729
  Charlotte *(G-2859)*
Hayward Industries Inc .... C 336 712-9900
  Clemmons *(G-4043)*
◆ Hayward Industries Inc .... B 908 351-5400
  Charlotte *(G-2894)*
Hoffman Plasti-Form Company .... G 336 431-2934
  High Point *(G-8396)*
Hornet Capital LLC .... G 252 641-8000
  Tarboro *(G-15109)*
▲ Hughes Sup of Thomasville Inc .... D 336 475-8146
  Thomasville *(G-15232)*
Hydroeye Marine Group LLC .... G 828 394-4406
  Connelly Springs *(G-4404)*
Identigraph Signs & Awnings .... G 704 635-7911
  Monroe *(G-10736)*
Impact Plastics Inc .... F 910 205-1493
  Hamlet *(G-7624)*
Injection Technology Corporation .... C 828 684-1362
  Arden *(G-341)*
▲ Inplac North America Inc .... G 704 587-1151
  Charlotte *(G-2976)*
Integrity Plastics .... G 828 247-8801
  Forest City *(G-6071)*
Intertech Corporation .... D 336 621-1891
  Greensboro *(G-7120)*
Janco LLC .... F 919 847-8816
  Raleigh *(G-12912)*
Jeld-Wen Inc .... C 336 838-0292
  North Wilkesboro *(G-12016)*
JImade LLC .... G 252 515-2195
  Winnabow *(G-16581)*
▲ L B Plastics Incorporated .... D 704 663-1543
  Mooresville *(G-11000)*
Laird Plastics Inc .... G 704 597-8555
  Charlotte *(G-3070)*
Lamco Machine Tool Inc .... F 252 247-4360
  Morehead City *(G-11181)*
Lamination Services Inc .... E 336 643-7369
  Stokesdale *(G-14945)*
Lathamscu .... G 336 477-5008
  Mocksville *(G-10584)*
Leonard Alum Utlity Bldngs Inc .... G 919 872-4442
  Raleigh *(G-12968)*
Leonard Alum Utlity Bldngs Inc .... G 910 392-4921
  Wilmington *(G-16299)*
◆ Liqui-Box Corporation .... D 804 325-1400
  Charlotte *(G-3092)*
▲ Locust Plastics Inc .... D 704 636-2742
  Salisbury *(G-14006)*
Machinery Sales .... G 704 822-0110
  Stanley *(G-14701)*
Mack Molding Company Inc .... C 704 878-9641
  Statesville *(G-14837)*
Manning Fabrics Inc .... G 910 295-1970
  Pinehurst *(G-12228)*
Manufacturing Services Inc .... E 704 629-4163
  Bessemer City *(G-1074)*
Marine & Industrial Plastics .... G 252 224-1000
  Pollocksville *(G-12393)*
Medical Cable Specialists Inc .... E 828 890-2888
  Mills River *(G-10507)*
Micro Lens Technology Inc .... G 704 893-2109
  Indian Trail *(G-8949)*
▲ Micro Lens Technology Inc .... G 704 847-9234
  Matthews *(G-10272)*

Mikron Industries Inc .... D 713 961-4600
  Durham *(G-5227)*
Millar Industries Inc .... E 828 687-0639
  Arden *(G-351)*
Molded Fibr GL Cmpny/Nrth Crli .... C 828 584-4974
  Morganton *(G-11234)*
▲ Mpe Usa Inc .... E 704 340-4910
  Pineville *(G-12284)*
▲ New Innovative Products Inc .... G 919 631-6759
  Pine Level *(G-12212)*
Newell Brands Distribution LLC .... D 770 418-7000
  Gastonia *(G-6478)*
Newell Brands Inc .... E 704 987-4760
  Huntersville *(G-8858)*
Newell Brands Inc .... G 704 895-8082
  Huntersville *(G-8859)*
▲ Nypro Asheville Inc .... C 828 684-3141
  Arden *(G-358)*
Nypro Inc .... A 919 304-1400
  Mebane *(G-10421)*
▲ Nypro Oregon Inc .... A 541 753-4700
  Arden *(G-359)*
Oneida Molded Plastics LLC .... F 919 663-3141
  Siler City *(G-14428)*
◆ Opw Fling Cntnment Systems Inc .... E 919 209-2280
  Smithfield *(G-14474)*
Overkill Fabrication .... G 336 480-1787
  Boonville *(G-1255)*
▲ Pam Trading Corporation .... F 336 668-0901
  Kernersville *(G-9224)*
Panel Wholesalers Incorporated .... F 336 765-4040
  Winston Salem *(G-16835)*
Parkway Products LLC .... C 828 684-1362
  Arden *(G-360)*
Pbs Ventures Inc .... G 252 235-2001
  Bailey *(G-878)*
PCI of North Carolina LLC .... E 919 467-5151
  Cary *(G-1845)*
◆ Pen-Cell Plastics Inc .... E 252 467-2210
  Rocky Mount *(G-13718)*
Penn Compression Moulding Inc .... G 919 934-5144
  Smithfield *(G-14476)*
Performance Plastics Pdts Inc .... D 336 454-0350
  Jamestown *(G-9066)*
Pipeline Plastics LLC .... G 817 693-4100
  Fair Bluff *(G-5699)*
Plasgad Usa LLC .... E 704 775-6461
  Statesville *(G-14861)*
Plastek Group .... G 910 895-2089
  Rockingham *(G-13639)*
Plastek Industries Inc .... C 814 878-4457
  Hamlet *(G-7629)*
Plastic Ingenuity Inc .... G 919 693-2009
  Oxford *(G-12143)*
Plastic Molding Connection .... G 910 512-0834
  Wilmington *(G-16357)*
Plastic Products Inc .... F 704 739-7463
  Kings Mountain *(G-9326)*
Plastics Mlding Dsgn Plus LLC .... F 828 459-7853
  Conover *(G-4482)*
Poly-Tech Industrial Inc .... G 704 992-8100
  Huntersville *(G-8877)*
Poly-Tech Industrial Inc .... E 704 948-8055
  Huntersville *(G-8878)*
◆ Polymer Concepts Inc .... F 336 495-7713
  Randleman *(G-13484)*
◆ Poppelmann Properties USA LLC ... G 828 466-9500
  Claremont *(G-3934)*
▲ Post EC Holdings Inc .... E 919 989-0175
  Smithfield *(G-14477)*
Precise Technology Inc .... G 704 576-9527
  Charlotte *(G-3368)*

▲ Precision Concepts Group LLC .... B 336 761-8572
  Winston Salem *(G-16863)*
▲ Precision Concepts Mebane LLC ..... D 919 563-9292
  Mebane *(G-10425)*
Pretium Packaging LLC .... E 336 621-1891
  Greensboro *(G-7280)*
Prime Mill LLC .... F 336 819-4300
  High Point *(G-8498)*
Product Finishing Solutions Co .... G 704 785-8941
  Concord *(G-4341)*
Proto Labs Inc .... C 833 245-8827
  Morrisville *(G-11413)*
◆ Pucuda Inc .... F 860 526-8004
  New Bern *(G-11838)*
▲ R&D Plastics of Hickory Ltd .... E 828 431-4660
  Hickory *(G-8133)*
Ramsey Industries Inc .... E 704 827-3560
  Belmont *(G-1005)*
Rcnc Inc .... G 919 728-6691
  Wake Forest *(G-15581)*
◆ Reichhold Holdings Us Inc .... A 919 990-7500
  Durham *(G-5323)*
Resinart East Inc .... F 828 687-0215
  Fletcher *(G-6034)*
Revolution Pd LLC .... G 919 949-0241
  Pittsboro *(G-12347)*
▲ Rexam Beauty and Closures Inc ..... A 704 551-1500
  Charlotte *(G-3442)*
Reynolds Consumer Products Inc ...... G 704 371-5550
  Huntersville *(G-8885)*
Rmi Plastic .... G 704 995-9489
  Mooresville *(G-11071)*
Robbins Beane Inc .... G 336 953-5919
  Asheboro *(G-474)*
▲ Robetex Inc .... F 910 671-8787
  Lumberton *(G-10053)*
Rowmark LLC .... G 252 448-9900
  Trenton *(G-15334)*
Royale Comfort Seating Inc .... D 828 352-9021
  Taylorsville *(G-15162)*
RPM Plastics Inc .... F 704 871-0518
  Statesville *(G-14880)*
RPM Plastics LLC .... E 704 871-0518
  Statesville *(G-14881)*
RPM Products Inc .... F 704 871-0518
  Statesville *(G-14882)*
Rpp Acquisition LLC .... E 919 248-9001
  Kenly *(G-9157)*
Rs Industries Inc .... G 704 289-2734
  Monroe *(G-10800)*
◆ Rubbermaid Commercial Pdts LLC . A 540 667-8700
  Huntersville *(G-8888)*
Rubbermaid Incorporated .... A 888 859-8294
  Huntersville *(G-8889)*
Rubbermaid Incorporated .... A 704 987-4339
  Huntersville *(G-8890)*
Saint-Gobain Vetrotex Amer Inc .... C 704 895-5906
  Huntersville *(G-8894)*
Salem Technologies Inc .... F 336 777-3652
  Winston Salem *(G-16895)*
Sapona Manufacturing Co Inc .... C 336 873-8700
  Asheboro *(G-476)*
Sapona Plastic LLC .... G 336 873-7201
  Seagrove *(G-14247)*
▲ Sapona Plastics LLC .... D 336 873-8700
  Asheboro *(G-478)*
◆ Schaefer Systems International Inc . C 704 944-4500
  Charlotte *(G-3499)*
Schaefer Systems Intnl Inc .... G 704 944-4500
  Charlotte *(G-3500)*
Schaefer Systems Intnl Inc .... G 704 944-4550
  Charlotte *(G-3501)*

31 LEATHER AND LEATHER PRODUCTS

Sealed Air Corporation .... D 828 728-6610
　Hudson *(G-8779)*

Sealed Air Corporation (us) .... A 201 791-7600
　Charlotte *(G-3518)*

Senox Corporation .... G 704 371-5043
　Charlotte *(G-3526)*

Sherri Gossett .... G 910 367-0099
　Wilmington *(G-16403)*

Sigma Plastics Group .... E 336 885-8091
　High Point *(G-8525)*

Skyline Plastic Systems Inc .... F 828 891-2515
　Mills River *(G-10511)*

◆ Sonoco Hickory Inc .... D 828 328-2466
　Hickory *(G-8163)*

Sonoco Products Company .... D 828 245-0118
　Forest City *(G-6082)*

Southeaster Plastic Inc .... F 336 275-6616
　Greensboro *(G-7351)*

Southern Vinyl Mfg Inc .... F 252 523-2520
　Kinston *(G-9385)*

▲ Spnc Associates Inc .... D 919 467-5151
　Cary *(G-1902)*

▲ Sspc Inc .... E
　Charlotte *(G-3617)*

Stanford Manufacturing LLC .... F 336 999-8799
　Clemmons *(G-4060)*

Stephen P Wolfe .... G 252 792-3001
　Jamesville *(G-9082)*

Sunray Inc .... E 828 287-7030
　Rutherfordton *(G-13892)*

▲ Superior Plastics Inc .... F 704 864-5472
　Gastonia *(G-6518)*

▲ Surteco USA Inc .... E 336 668-9555
　Greensboro *(G-7381)*

Sysmetric USA .... G 704 522-8778
　Mooresville *(G-11108)*

Tar River Trading Post LLC .... G 919 589-3618
　Youngsville *(G-17104)*

Tarheel Plastics LLC .... E
　Lexington *(G-9790)*

Team Gsg LLC .... G 252 830-1032
　Greenville *(G-7588)*

Tech Medical Plastics Inc .... F 919 563-9272
　Mebane *(G-10432)*

◆ Technical Coating Intl Inc .... E 910 371-0860
　Belville *(G-1026)*

Technimark .... G 336 736-9366
　Randleman *(G-13493)*

Technimark LLC .... G 336 498-4171
　Asheboro *(G-491)*

Technimark LLC .... G 336 498-4171
　Asheboro *(G-492)*

◆ Technimark LLC .... B 336 498-4171
　Asheboro *(G-493)*

Technimark Reynosa LLC .... G 336 498-4171
　Asheboro *(G-494)*

▲ Technimark Reynosa LLC .... B 336 498-4171
　Asheboro *(G-495)*

Teijin Automotive Tech Inc .... G 828 757-8313
　Lenoir *(G-9654)*

Teijin Automotive Tech Inc .... B 704 797-8744
　Salisbury *(G-14049)*

Tenn-Tex Plastics Inc .... E 336 931-1100
　Colfax *(G-4161)*

Texlon Plastics Corp .... E 704 866-8785
　Gastonia *(G-6522)*

TFS Management Group LLC .... G 704 399-3999
　Charlotte *(G-3685)*

▼ Thanet Inc .... E 704 483-4175
　Denver *(G-4807)*

▼ THEM International Inc .... G 336 855-7880
　Greensboro *(G-7399)*

Thermodynamx LLC .... G 704 622-1086
　Waxhaw *(G-15781)*

Thomson Plastics Inc .... D 336 843-4255
　Lexington *(G-9793)*

Thundrbird Mlding Grnsboro LLC .... D 336 668-3636
　Greensboro *(G-7403)*

◆ Tosaf Inc .... F 980 533-3000
　Bessemer City *(G-1087)*

Total Solution Industries Inc .... F 919 900-8801
　Raleigh *(G-13353)*

Toter LLC .... E 704 936-5610
　Charlotte *(G-3711)*

Toter LLC .... D 800 424-0422
　Statesville *(G-14916)*

Trac Plastics Inc .... F 704 864-9140
　Gastonia *(G-6531)*

Treg Tool Inc .... G 828 676-0035
　Arden *(G-385)*

◆ Trelleborg Salisbury Inc .... E 704 797-8030
　Salisbury *(G-14055)*

Tri-Star Plastics Corp .... E 704 598-2800
　Denver *(G-4810)*

◆ Triangle Plastics Inc .... G 919 598-8839
　Raleigh *(G-13361)*

United Decorative Plas NC Inc .... G 252 637-1803
　Trent Woods *(G-15331)*

▲ United Southern Industries Inc .... D 866 273-1810
　Forest City *(G-6085)*

Universal Plastic Products Inc .... G 336 856-0882
　Jamestown *(G-9076)*

US Drainage Systems LLC .... G 828 855-1906
　Hickory *(G-8199)*

US One DOT Com Inc .... G 704 587-0678
　Charlotte *(G-3760)*

US Plastic Moldings .... G 800 262-2111
　Statesville *(G-14922)*

▲ V and E Components Inc .... F 336 884-0088
　High Point *(G-8588)*

Variform Inc .... D 828 277-6420
　Asheville *(G-813)*

Vault LLC .... F 336 698-3796
　High Point *(G-8590)*

Veka East Inc .... B 800 654-5589
　Morganton *(G-11264)*

Volex Inc .... E 828 485-4500
　Hickory *(G-8204)*

Volex Inc .... E 828 485-4500
　Hickory *(G-8205)*

Wambam Fence Inc .... F 877 778-5733
　Charlotte *(G-3794)*

Warren Plastics Inc .... G 704 827-9887
　Mount Holly *(G-11652)*

Whiteville Plywood Inc .... F 910 642-7114
　Whiteville *(G-15981)*

▲ Wilbert Inc .... E 704 247-3850
　Belmont *(G-1018)*

Wilbert Plastic Services Inc .... F 866 273-1810
　Belmont *(G-1019)*

▲ Wilbert Plstic Svcs Acqstion L .... E 704 455-5191
　Harrisburg *(G-7735)*

▲ Wilbert Plstic Svcs Acqstion L .... G 704 822-1423
　Belmont *(G-1020)*

◆ Wirthwein New Bern Corp .... C 252 634-2871
　New Bern *(G-11859)*

▲ Xceldyne Group LLC .... D 336 472-2242
　Thomasville *(G-15307)*

31 LEATHER AND LEATHER PRODUCTS

3111 Leather tanning and finishing

▲ Arcona Leather Company LLC .... G 828 396-7728
　Hudson *(G-8761)*

◆ Automated Solutions LLC .... F 828 396-9900
　Granite Falls *(G-6723)*

▲ Carolina Fur Dressing Company .... E 919 231-0086
　Raleigh *(G-12598)*

Carroll Companies Inc .... F 828 466-5489
　Conover *(G-4434)*

Coast To Coast Lea & Vinyl Inc .... G 336 886-5050
　High Point *(G-8298)*

▲ Dani Leather USA Inc .... G 973 598-0890
　High Point *(G-8317)*

Distinction Leather Company .... G
　Conover *(G-4448)*

Greene Mountain Outdoors LLC .... F 336 670-2186
　North Wilkesboro *(G-12011)*

Inspiration Leather Design Inc .... G 336 420-2265
　Jamestown *(G-9058)*

◆ Leather Miracles LLC .... D 828 464-7448
　Hickory *(G-8086)*

Raxter Custom Bags .... G 864 421-5181
　Wake Forest *(G-15579)*

Tasman Industries Inc .... G 502 587-0701
　High Point *(G-8563)*

▲ Willow Tex LLC .... E 336 789-1009
　Mount Airy *(G-11595)*

3131 Footwear cut stock

A Bean Counter Inc .... G 919 359-9586
　Garner *(G-6250)*

Barlin Ranch & Pets Inc .... G 910 814-1930
　Lillington *(G-9843)*

Better Burger Group LLC .... G 704 662-9152
　Charlotte *(G-2304)*

Bricks & Quarters LLC .... G 704 321-0124
　Matthews *(G-10305)*

Candace Rand .... G 336 643-7082
　Summerfield *(G-14977)*

Counter Effect .... G 252 636-0080
　New Bern *(G-11791)*

Direct Action K-9 LLC .... G 910 246-0806
　Southern Pines *(G-14533)*

Green Bean Counters LLC .... G 919 545-2324
　Chapel Hill *(G-2023)*

Mqh LLC .... G 570 417-3165
　Reidsville *(G-13534)*

Quarter Turn LLC .... G 336 712-0811
　Clemmons *(G-4058)*

Rand Ange Enterprises Inc .... G 336 472-7313
　Thomasville *(G-15270)*

Rod Rand Inc .... G 336 565-4874
　Liberty *(G-9829)*

Upper Deck Company .... G 760 496-9149
　Durham *(G-5427)*

Upper Rm Outreach Ministry Inc .... G 252 364-8756
　Winterville *(G-17016)*

Upper Room .... G 910 540-7719
　Watha *(G-15742)*

3143 Men's footwear, except athletic

Allbirds Inc .... F 980 296-0006
　Charlotte *(G-2158)*

Century Hosiery Inc .... C 336 859-3806
　Denton *(G-4729)*

▲ McRae Industries Inc .... E 910 439-6147
　Mount Gilead *(G-11606)*

3144 Women's footwear, except athletic

Century Hosiery Inc .... C 336 859-3806
　Denton *(G-4729)*

▲ McRae Industries Inc .... E 910 439-6147
　Mount Gilead *(G-11606)*

31 LEATHER AND LEATHER PRODUCTS

Unplugged Incorporated .... G 704 726-0614
   Charlotte *(G-3756)*

3149 Footwear, except rubber, nec

Century Hosiery Inc .... C 336 859-3806
   Denton *(G-4729)*

3151 Leather gloves and mittens

▲ Gloves-Online Inc .... G 919 468-4244
   Cary *(G-1775)*

3161 Luggage

Birddog Outdoor Co Inc .... G 919 604-8134
   Cary *(G-1706)*
Bratz Playground LLC .... F 704 858-1934
   Charlotte *(G-2349)*
Case Smith Inc .... F 336 969-9786
   Rural Hall *(G-13836)*
Conn-Selmer Inc .... D 704 289-6459
   Monroe *(G-10690)*
Cross Canvas Company Inc .... E 828 252-0440
   Asheville *(G-599)*
Glaser Designs Inc .... G 415 552-3188
   Raleigh *(G-12803)*
Highiq LLC .... G 704 956-8716
   Concord *(G-4280)*
Kute N Klassy By Jen LLc .... G 828 755-5613
   Forest City *(G-6074)*
Lilas Trunk .... G 919 548-0784
   Bear Creek *(G-939)*
New Media Golf Inc .... F 828 533-9954
   Highlands *(G-8616)*
Paulas Pretty Things Inc .... G 919 656-1163
   Pikeville *(G-12193)*
Picassomoesllc .... G 216 703-4547
   Hillsborough *(G-8665)*
Random & Kind LLC .... G 919 249-8809
   Durham *(G-5319)*
Saundra D Hall .... G 828 251-9859
   Asheville *(G-763)*
Trinket Trunk .... G 910 483-2292
   Fayetteville *(G-5932)*
Trunk Pump .... G 910 463-1282
   Wilmington *(G-16435)*
Tumi Store - Chrltte Dglas Int .... E 704 359-8771
   Charlotte *(G-3738)*
Tumi Store - Streets South Pt .... G 919 224-1028
   Durham *(G-5415)*

3171 Women's handbags and purses

Blacqueladi Styles LLC .... G 877 977-7798
   Cary *(G-1707)*
Glaser Designs Inc .... F 415 552-3188
   Raleigh *(G-12803)*
▲ Grace & Glory Goods LLC .... G 828 575-2166
   Asheville *(G-638)*
R Riveter LLC .... G 406 321-2315
   Southern Pines *(G-14550)*

3172 Personal leather goods, nec

Glaser Designs Inc .... F 415 552-3188
   Raleigh *(G-12803)*
Kyson Leather Incorporated .... G 919 245-0053
   Hurdle Mills *(G-8909)*
◆ McKinley Leather Hickory Inc .... E 828 459-2884
   Claremont *(G-3931)*
Pioneer Square Brands Inc .... G 360 733-5608
   High Point *(G-8485)*
Point Blank Enterprises Inc .... D 910 893-2071
   Lillington *(G-9858)*
Wallets For Water .... G 704 564-0763
   Charlotte *(G-3793)*

Wobo Wallet LLC .... G 704 604-6041
   Harrisburg *(G-7736)*

3199 Leather goods, nec

AC Valor Reyes LLC .... G 910 431-3256
   Castle Hayne *(G-1941)*
B & B Leather Co Inc .... F 704 598-9080
   Charlotte *(G-2252)*
◆ Carroll Companies Inc .... E 828 264-2521
   Boone *(G-1184)*
Coast To Coast Lea & Vinyl Inc .... G 336 886-5050
   High Point *(G-8298)*
Colsenkeane Leather LLC .... G 704 750-9887
   Charlotte *(G-2526)*
Doggies r US .... G 336 455-1113
   Greensboro *(G-6974)*
Ellison Company Inc .... G 704 889-7518
   Charlotte *(G-2698)*
Fully Invlved Leatherworks LLC .... G 704 799-9938
   Troutman *(G-15378)*
Fully Involved Leatherworks .... G 704 799-9938
   Statesville *(G-14801)*
Gene Leather Mean .... G 910 325-7098
   Hubert *(G-8748)*
Greene Mountain Outdoors LLC .... F 336 670-2186
   North Wilkesboro *(G-12011)*
In Blue Handmade Inc .... G 828 774-5094
   Asheville *(G-660)*
Kishwa Leather LLC .... G 828 234-4592
   Hickory *(G-8077)*
Kiss Manufacturing Co Inc .... G 828 524-6293
   Franklin *(G-6134)*
Mva Leatherwood LLC .... G 704 519-4200
   Charlotte *(G-3224)*
Oleksynprannyk LLC .... F 704 450-0182
   Mooresville *(G-11043)*
Point Blank Enterprises Inc .... D 910 893-2071
   Lillington *(G-9858)*
Ralph Harris Leather Inc .... G 336 874-2100
   State Road *(G-14730)*
Red Aamerosa Leatherworks LLC .... G 717 991-0308
   Locust *(G-9968)*
Rmb Custom Leather LLC .... G 704 762-1614
   Oakboro *(G-12080)*
Stikeleather Inc .... G 828 352-9095
   Taylorsville *(G-15168)*
▲ Suretech Assembly Inc .... E 919 569-0346
   Youngsville *(G-17103)*
Taylor Made Cases Inc .... F 919 209-0555
   Benson *(G-1043)*
Thin Line Saddle Pads Inc .... G 919 680-6803
   Durham *(G-5400)*
▲ VH Industries Inc .... E 704 743-2400
   Concord *(G-4385)*
Voltage LLC .... F 919 391-9405
   Chapel Hill *(G-2096)*

32 STONE, CLAY, GLASS, AND CONCRETE PRODUCTS

3211 Flat glass

A R Perry Corporation .... F 252 492-6181
   Henderson *(G-7774)*
Cardinal CT Company .... C 336 719-6857
   Mount Airy *(G-11487)*
Cardinal Glass Industries Inc .... C 704 660-0900
   Mooresville *(G-10895)*
Corning Incorporated .... D 704 569-6000
   Midland *(G-10464)*
Counter Art .... G 704 658-0312
   Mooresville *(G-10915)*

Four Jaks .... G 828 484-9545
   Weaverville *(G-15847)*
Grace Construction & Glass .... G 919 805-8380
   Clayton *(G-3982)*
▲ Industrial Glass Tech LLC .... F 704 853-2429
   Gastonia *(G-6426)*
James E Latta .... G 919 682-5793
   Durham *(G-5170)*
Optometric Eyecare Center Inc .... G 910 326-3050
   Swansboro *(G-15048)*
Pilkington .... G 828 357-8043
   Black Mountain *(G-1135)*
Pilkington Group Inc .... G 336 545-0425
   Greensboro *(G-7264)*
Pilkington North America Inc .... E 910 276-5630
   Laurinburg *(G-9492)*
PPG Industries Inc .... G 919 772-3093
   Greensboro *(G-7272)*
Tint Plus .... G 910 229-5303
   Fayetteville *(G-5930)*

3221 Glass containers

Carolina Copacking LLC .... E 252 433-0130
   Henderson *(G-7776)*
CHI Resources .... G 828 835-7878
   Murphy *(G-11707)*
Gerresheimer Glass Inc .... F 828 433-5000
   Morganton *(G-11215)*
Jennifer E Smith ND .... G 704 871-1229
   Statesville *(G-14824)*
King Bio Inc .... E 828 398-6058
   Asheville *(G-674)*
Precision Concepts Intl LLC .... G 704 360-8923
   Mooresville *(G-11058)*
Tote Glass Inc .... G 910 515-4187
   Wilmington *(G-16430)*
Zoallc .... G 910 215-0235
   Aberdeen *(G-36)*

3229 Pressed and blown glass, nec

Bright Angle LLC .... G 828 771-6966
   Asheville *(G-573)*
Carolina York LLC .... F 704 237-0873
   Charlotte *(G-2413)*
Connexion Technologies .... F 919 674-0036
   Cary *(G-1732)*
Corning Incorporated .... F 828 465-0016
   Newton *(G-11925)*
Corning Incorporated .... F 252 316-4500
   Tarboro *(G-15100)*
Corning Incorporated .... D 910 784-7200
   Wilmington *(G-16184)*
Corning Incorporated .... F 336 771-8000
   Winston Salem *(G-16662)*
Corning Optcal Cmmncations LLC .... A 336 771-8000
   Winston Salem *(G-16663)*
▲ Easyglass Inc .... E 336 786-1800
   Mount Airy *(G-11505)*
Heraeus Quartz North Amer LLC .... E 910 799-6230
   Wilmington *(G-16250)*
Incantare Art By Marilyn LLC .... F 704 713-8846
   Charlotte *(G-2957)*
M 5 Scentific Glassblowing Inc .... G 704 663-0101
   Mooresville *(G-11012)*
M2 Optics Inc .... G 919 342-5619
   Raleigh *(G-12985)*
Mateenbar USA Inc .... E 704 662-2005
   Concord *(G-4310)*
Nippon Electric Glass Co Ltd .... G 336 357-8151
   Lexington *(G-9761)*
Opticoncepts Inc .... G 828 874-0667
   Morganton *(G-11240)*

32 STONE, CLAY, GLASS, AND CONCRETE PRODUCTS

Piedmont Well Covers Inc .... F 704 664-8488
   Mount Ulla *(G-11685)*

PPG Industries Inc .... G 919 772-3093
   Greensboro *(G-7272)*

▲ PPG-Devold LLC .... E 704 434-2261
   Shelby *(G-14356)*

Preformed Line Products Co .... C 704 983-6161
   Albemarle *(G-99)*

Roblon US Inc .... D 828 396-2121
   Granite Falls *(G-6754)*

San Kawa LLC .... G 704 982-4527
   Albemarle *(G-103)*

◆ Slane O W Glass Co Inc .... F 704 872-4291
   Statesville *(G-14888)*

◆ Spruce Pine Batch Inc .... G 828 765-9876
   Spruce Pine *(G-14658)*

▲ Spt Technology Inc .... F 612 332-1880
   Monroe *(G-10811)*

3231 Products of purchased glass

A R Perry Corporation .... F 252 492-6181
   Henderson *(G-7774)*

Albemarle Glass Company Inc .... G 704 982-3323
   Albemarle *(G-70)*

All Glass Inc .... G 828 324-8609
   Hickory *(G-7931)*

Cgi Inc .... F 704 932-1820
   Kannapolis *(G-9115)*

Cgmi Acquisition Company LLC .... F 919 533-6123
   Kernersville *(G-9176)*

Classy Glass Inc .... G 828 452-2242
   Waynesville *(G-15798)*

Creativeminds Design LLC .... G 678 457-6148
   Monroe *(G-10698)*

Custom Glass Works Inc .... G 704 597-0290
   Charlotte *(G-2590)*

Done-Gone Adios Inc .... F 336 993-7300
   Kernersville *(G-9192)*

Eastern Band Cherokee Indians .... E 828 497-6824
   Cherokee *(G-3856)*

▲ Easyglass Inc .... E 336 786-1800
   Mount Airy *(G-11505)*

Envision Glass Inc .... F 336 283-9701
   Winston Salem *(G-16698)*

◆ Finch Industries Incorporated .... D 336 472-4499
   Thomasville *(G-15221)*

◆ Florida Marine Tanks Inc .... F 305 620-9030
   Henderson *(G-7783)*

Gardner Glass Products Inc .... F 336 838-2151
   North Wilkesboro *(G-12009)*

◆ Gardner Glass Products Inc .... C 336 651-9300
   North Wilkesboro *(G-12010)*

Gerresheimer Glass Inc .... F 828 433-5000
   Morganton *(G-11215)*

Ggi Glass Distributors Corp .... E 910 895-2022
   Rockingham *(G-13627)*

▲ Glass Unlimited High Point Inc .... D 336 889-4551
   High Point *(G-8366)*

Glass Works of Hickory Inc .... G 828 322-2122
   Hickory *(G-8033)*

Heraeus Quartz North Amer LLC .... E 910 799-6230
   Wilmington *(G-16250)*

Jackson Arts Market LLC .... G 415 659-0710
   Sylva *(G-15059)*

James Lammers .... G 252 491-2303
   Powells Point *(G-12398)*

▲ Lenoir Mirror Company .... C 828 728-3271
   Lenoir *(G-9626)*

M 5 Scientific Glassblowing Inc .... G 704 663-0101
   Mooresville *(G-11012)*

Merge Scientific Solutions LLC .... G 919 346-0999
   Fuquay Varina *(G-6215)*

Miller Glass .... F 828 681-8083
   Arden *(G-352)*

Norell Inc .... G 828 584-2600
   Morganton *(G-11239)*

Orare Inc .... G 919 742-1003
   Siler City *(G-14429)*

PPG Industries Inc .... G 919 772-3093
   Greensboro *(G-7272)*

▲ Press Glass Inc .... D 336 573-2393
   Stoneville *(G-14965)*

▲ Prism Research Glass Inc .... F 919 571-0078
   Raleigh *(G-13145)*

Shed Brand Inc .... G 704 523-0096
   Charlotte *(G-3538)*

Shed Brand Studios LLC .... G 704 523-0096
   Charlotte *(G-3539)*

▲ Sid Jenkins Inc .... G 336 632-0707
   Greensboro *(G-7337)*

◆ Slane O W Glass Co Inc .... F 704 872-4291
   Statesville *(G-14888)*

Stroupe Mirror Co .... G 336 475-2181
   Winston Salem *(G-16922)*

Triangle Glass Service Inc .... G 919 477-9508
   Durham *(G-5408)*

Triton Glass LLC .... G 704 982-4333
   Albemarle *(G-111)*

US Mirrors .... G 919 561-6800
   Raleigh *(G-13385)*

◆ Van Wingerden Grnhse Co Inc .... E 828 891-7389
   Mills River *(G-10513)*

Windsor Window Company .... C 704 283-7459
   Monroe *(G-10836)*

3241 Cement, hydraulic

Argos USA LLC .... G 919 942-0381
   Carrboro *(G-1644)*

Beazer East Inc .... F 919 567-9512
   Holly Springs *(G-8688)*

Bonsal American Inc .... G 704 848-4141
   Lilesville *(G-9835)*

Giant Cement Co .... G 704 583-1568
   Charlotte *(G-2828)*

Vega Construction Company Inc .... E 336 756-3477
   Pilot Mountain *(G-12204)*

3251 Brick and structural clay tile

▲ Clay Taylor Products Inc .... D 704 636-2411
   Salisbury *(G-13942)*

Cunningham Brick Company .... C 336 248-8541
   Lexington *(G-9702)*

Demilo Bros NC LLC .... G 704 771-0762
   Waxhaw *(G-15752)*

Dudley Inc .... G 704 636-8850
   Salisbury *(G-13955)*

▲ Forterra Brick LLC .... C 704 341-8750
   Charlotte *(G-2791)*

General Shale Brick Inc .... F 704 937-7431
   Grover *(G-7607)*

General Shale Brick Inc .... E 919 775-2121
   Moncure *(G-10622)*

General Shale Brick Inc .... G 919 828-0541
   Raleigh *(G-12793)*

General Shale Brick Inc .... G 919 775-2121
   Sanford *(G-14124)*

General Shale Brick Inc .... G 910 452-3498
   Wilmington *(G-16231)*

J L Anderson Co Inc .... G 704 289-9599
   Monroe *(G-10744)*

Meridian Brick LLC .... D 704 636-0131
   Salisbury *(G-14013)*

Nash Brick Company .... E 252 443-9665
   Enfield *(G-5680)*

Pine Hall Brick Co Inc .... E 336 721-7500
   Winston Salem *(G-16857)*

Statesville Brick Company .... D 704 872-4123
   Statesville *(G-14901)*

Triangle Brick Company .... D 919 387-9257
   Moncure *(G-10627)*

Triangle Brick Company .... E 704 695-1420
   Wadesboro *(G-15518)*

▲ Triangle Brick Company .... E 919 544-1796
   Durham *(G-5406)*

3253 Ceramic wall and floor tile

◆ Bonsal American Inc .... D 704 525-1621
   Charlotte *(G-2334)*

Floorazzo .... G 919 663-1684
   Siler City *(G-14411)*

Gray Ox Inc .... F 704 662-8247
   Mooresville *(G-10963)*

Mohawk Industries Inc .... G 336 313-4156
   Thomasville *(G-15253)*

Precast Terrazzo Entps Inc .... E 919 231-6200
   Raleigh *(G-13132)*

Viktors Gran MBL Kit Cnter Top .... F 828 681-0713
   Arden *(G-389)*

3255 Clay refractories

Harbisonwalker Intl Inc .... G 704 599-6540
   Charlotte *(G-2887)*

Oldcastle Retail Inc .... B 704 799-8083
   Cornelius *(G-4572)*

Pyrotek Incorporated .... E 704 642-1993
   Salisbury *(G-14033)*

Resco Products Inc .... F 336 299-1441
   Greensboro *(G-7306)*

Resco Products Inc .... G 336 299-1441
   Greensboro *(G-7307)*

Vesuvius Penn Corporation .... F 724 535-4374
   Charlotte *(G-3774)*

3259 Structural clay products, nec

Allfuel Hst Inc .... F 919 868-9410
   Hampstead *(G-7636)*

Exteriors Inc Ltd .... G 919 325-2251
   Spring Lake *(G-14625)*

Hearth & Home Technologies LLC .... C 336 274-1663
   Greensboro *(G-7082)*

Lee Brick & Tile Company .... D 919 774-4800
   Sanford *(G-14146)*

Pine Hall Brick Co Inc .... F 336 721-7500
   Madison *(G-10083)*

3261 Vitreous plumbing fixtures

As America Inc .... E 704 398-4602
   Charlotte *(G-2225)*

Athena Marble Incorporated .... F 704 636-7810
   Salisbury *(G-13924)*

Custom Marble Corporation .... G 910 215-0679
   Pinehurst *(G-12219)*

Division Eight Inc .... F 336 852-1275
   Greensboro *(G-6973)*

R Jacobs Fine Plbg & Hdwr Inc .... F 919 720-4202
   Raleigh *(G-13167)*

▲ Tileware Global LLC .... G 828 322-9273
   Hickory *(G-8183)*

Welcome Industrial Corp .... D 336 329-9640
   Burlington *(G-1517)*

3263 Semivitreous table and kitchenware

▲ Swiss Made Brands USA Inc .... F 704 900-6622
   Charlotte *(G-3663)*

3264 Porcelain electrical supplies

32 STONE, CLAY, GLASS, AND CONCRETE PRODUCTS

Duco-SCI Inc .... E 704 289-9502
   Monroe *(G-10708)*

Greenleaf Corporation .... E 828 693-0461
   East Flat Rock *(G-5476)*

♦ Hitachi Metals NC Ltd .... C 704 855-2800
   China Grove *(G-3884)*

Pyrotek Incorporated .... E 704 642-1993
   Salisbury *(G-14033)*

▲ Reuel Inc .... E 919 734-0460
   Goldsboro *(G-6650)*

The Tarheel Electric Memb .... F 919 876-4603
   Raleigh *(G-13342)*

3269 Pottery products, nec

AA Ceramics .... G 910 632-3053
   Wilmington *(G-16091)*

♦ Border Concepts Inc .... G 704 541-5509
   Charlotte *(G-2335)*

Buffer Zone Ceramics .... G 828 863-2000
   Columbus *(G-4172)*

Cairn Studio Ltd .... E 704 664-7128
   Mooresville *(G-10894)*

Ceder Creek Gallery & Pottery .... G 919 528-1041
   Creedmoor *(G-4610)*

Celtic Ceramics .... G 919 510-6817
   Raleigh *(G-12615)*

Clay Kinnakeet Inc .... G 252 995-0101
   Avon *(G-844)*

♦ Daramic LLC .... D 704 587-8599
   Charlotte *(G-2603)*

East Fork Pottery LLC .... G 828 237-7200
   Asheville *(G-614)*

East Fork Pottery LLC .... F 828 237-7200
   Asheville *(G-615)*

Haand .... F 336 350-7597
   Burlington *(G-1427)*

Jamie M Dollahan .... G 571 435-2060
   Maysville *(G-10373)*

Jugtown Pottery .... G 910 464-3266
   Seagrove *(G-14241)*

Laura Cooke Ceramics .... G 336 580-4308
   Asheville *(G-680)*

Lucy V Dierks Ceramics Inc .... G 757 692-5145
   Asheville *(G-690)*

♦ Selee Corporation .... C 828 693-0256
   Hendersonville *(G-7898)*

Shed Brand Inc .... G 704 523-0096
   Charlotte *(G-3538)*

Strassberg Ceramics .... G 704 315-2034
   Davidson *(G-4697)*

Studio Touya .... G 910 464-3116
   Seagrove *(G-14249)*

Wishes Fulfilled .... G 704 905-8228
   Waxhaw *(G-15790)*

3271 Concrete block and brick

▲ Adams Products Company .... C 919 467-2218
   Morrisville *(G-11278)*

Argos USA LLC .... C 704 872-9566
   Statesville *(G-14752)*

Carolina Lawnscape Inc .... G 803 230-5570
   Charlotte *(G-2398)*

CTI Property Services Inc .... E 919 787-3789
   Raleigh *(G-12659)*

Custom Brick Company Inc .... E 919 832-2804
   Raleigh *(G-12663)*

DnI Services LLC .... G 910 689-8759
   Harrells *(G-7692)*

East Fork Pottery LLC .... G 828 575-2150
   Asheville *(G-616)*

▼ Fayblock Materials Inc .... D 910 323-9198
   Fayetteville *(G-5823)*

▲ Focal Point Products Inc .... D 252 824-0015
   Tarboro *(G-15104)*

General Shale Brick Inc .... E 919 775-2121
   Moncure *(G-10622)*

Global Stone Impex LLC .... G 336 609-1113
   Greensboro *(G-7047)*

Good Earth Ministries .... G 828 287-9826
   Rutherfordton *(G-13873)*

Greystone Concrete Pdts Inc .... E 252 438-5144
   Henderson *(G-7785)*

Hefty Concrete Inc .... G 910 483-1598
   Fayetteville *(G-5836)*

Helping Hands Concrete Llc .... G 828 817-1288
   Mill Spring *(G-10486)*

Johnson Concrete Company .... G 704 786-4204
   Concord *(G-4294)*

Johnson Concrete Company .... E 336 248-2918
   Lexington *(G-9736)*

Johnson Concrete Company .... E 704 636-5231
   Willow Spring *(G-16079)*

♦ Johnson Concrete Company .... E 704 636-5231
   Salisbury *(G-13993)*

Landsman Forest Lawn Guard .... G 828 898-3433
   Banner Elk *(G-901)*

Leonard Block Company .... F 336 764-0607
   Winston Salem *(G-16786)*

Motsinger Block Plant Inc .... G 336 764-0350
   Winston Salem *(G-16818)*

▲ Mystic Lifestyle Inc .... F 704 960-4530
   Concord *(G-4322)*

Old Castle Apg South Inc .... G 919 383-2521
   Durham *(G-5255)*

Oldcastle Adams .... F 336 310-0542
   Colfax *(G-4156)*

Oldcastle Retail Inc .... B 704 799-8083
   Cornelius *(G-4572)*

Southeastern Concrete Pdts Co .... D 704 873-2226
   Statesville *(G-14890)*

Southern Block Company .... F 910 293-7844
   Warsaw *(G-15674)*

Southern Elements Hardscapes .... G 240 626-1586
   Sanford *(G-14188)*

Southern Hardscape Pdts Inc .... G 704 528-6726
   Statesville *(G-14892)*

Taylco Inc .... E 910 739-0405
   Lumberton *(G-10057)*

Top Dawg Landscape Inc .... G 336 877-7519
   West Jefferson *(G-15949)*

Trademark Landscape Group Inc .... F 910 253-0560
   Supply *(G-15013)*

Union Masonry Inc .... G 919 217-7806
   Raleigh *(G-13382)*

3272 Concrete products, nec

360 Ballistics LLC .... G 919 883-8338
   Cary *(G-1670)*

A & D Precast Inc .... G 704 735-3337
   Lincolnton *(G-9863)*

Abt Inc .... G 314 610-8798
   Troutman *(G-15363)*

♦ Abt Inc .... G 704 528-9806
   Troutman *(G-15364)*

▲ Adams Products Company .... C 919 467-2218
   Morrisville *(G-11278)*

Advanced Drainage Systems Inc .... E 336 764-0341
   Winston Salem *(G-16591)*

Affordable Septic Tank .... G 910 417-9537
   Hamlet *(G-7615)*

Amesbury Industries Inc .... E 919 978-3250
   Statesville *(G-14750)*

▲ Apollo Designs LLC .... E 336 886-0260
   High Point *(G-8250)*

Argos USA LLC .... C 704 872-9566
   Statesville *(G-14752)*

Arnold-Wilbert Corporation .... D 919 735-5008
   Goldsboro *(G-6592)*

Asheville Vault Service Inc .... E 828 665-6799
   Candler *(G-1568)*

Autry Con Pdts & Bldrs Sup Co .... G 704 504-8830
   Charlotte *(G-2242)*

B & C Concrete Products Inc .... G 336 838-4201
   North Wilkesboro *(G-11998)*

Ballistics Technology Intl Ltd .... G 252 360-1650
   Wilson *(G-16473)*

Beazer East Inc .... G 919 380-2610
   Morrisville *(G-11301)*

Best Workers Company .... G 336 665-0076
   Riegelwood *(G-13557)*

Blue Rdge Elc Mmbers Fndtion I .... D 828 754-9071
   Lenoir *(G-9591)*

Bonsal American Inc .... G 336 854-8200
   Greensboro *(G-6847)*

Bonsal American Inc .... G 704 848-4141
   Lilesville *(G-9835)*

♦ Bonsal American Inc .... G 704 525-1621
   Charlotte *(G-2334)*

Brant & Lassiter Septic Tank .... G 252 587-4321
   Potecasi *(G-12395)*

Bryant Grant Mutual Burial Asn .... G 828 524-2411
   Franklin *(G-6117)*

Canyon Stone Inc .... F 919 880-3273
   Youngsville *(G-17073)*

Carolina Cemetery Park Corp .... G 704 528-5543
   Troutman *(G-15369)*

Carolina Precast Concrete .... F 910 230-0028
   Dunn *(G-4855)*

Carolina Traffic Devices Inc .... F 704 588-7055
   Charlotte *(G-2410)*

Carr Precast Concrete Inc .... E 910 892-1151
   Dunn *(G-4856)*

Cast First Stone Ministry .... G 704 437-1053
   Troutman *(G-15373)*

Cast Stone Systems Inc .... E 252 257-1599
   Warrenton *(G-15657)*

Cava Di Pietra Inc .... G 910 338-5024
   Wilmington *(G-16161)*

Cherry Contracting Inc .... D 336 969-1825
   Rural Hall *(G-13838)*

Coastal Precast Systems LLC .... C 910 444-4682
   Wilmington *(G-16173)*

Column & Post Inc .... E 919 255-1533
   Fuquay Varina *(G-6191)*

Concrete Pipe & Precast LLC .... E 910 892-6411
   Dunn *(G-4858)*

Concrete Pipe & Precast LLC .... E 704 485-4614
   Oakboro *(G-12070)*

Continental Stone Company .... G 336 951-2945
   Reidsville *(G-13514)*

Craven Tire Inc .... G 252 633-0200
   New Bern *(G-11792)*

Custom Brick Company Inc .... E 919 832-2804
   Raleigh *(G-12663)*

▲ David Allen Company Inc .... C 919 821-7100
   Raleigh *(G-12675)*

Decocrete .... G 910 358-4175
   Jacksonville *(G-8997)*

Dellinger Precast Inc .... E 704 483-2868
   Denver *(G-4771)*

Eastern Carolina Vault Co Inc .... G 252 243-5614
   Wilson *(G-16495)*

Easy Stones Corp .... G 980 201-9506
   Charlotte *(G-2677)*

Erader Mills Septic Tank Inc .... F 252 478-5960
   Spring Hope *(G-14617)*

32 STONE, CLAY, GLASS, AND CONCRETE PRODUCTS

▼ Fayblock Materials Inc .... D 910 323-9198
   Fayetteville *(G-5823)*

Fletcher Limestone Company Inc .... F 828 684-6701
   Fletcher *(G-6005)*

Floorazzo Tile LLC .... F 919 663-1684
   Siler City *(G-14412)*

Forterra Pipe & Precast LLC .... G 910 892-6411
   Dunn *(G-4867)*

Four Jaks .... G 828 484-9545
   Weaverville *(G-15847)*

Futrell Precasting LLC .... G 252 568-3481
   Deep Run *(G-4716)*

Garners Septic Tank Inc .... G 919 718-5181
   Raeford *(G-12421)*

Gate Precast Company .... C 919 603-1633
   Oxford *(G-12129)*

Greystone Concrete Pdts Inc .... E 252 438-5144
   Henderson *(G-7785)*

Hairfield Wilbert Burial Vlt .... E 828 437-4319
   Morganton *(G-11218)*

Hauser Hvac Installation .... G 336 416-2173
   Winston Salem *(G-16738)*

Henson Family Investments LLC .... E 910 817-9450
   Rockingham *(G-13628)*

High Point Precast Pdts Inc .... G 336 434-1815
   Lexington *(G-9730)*

◆ Hog Slat Incorporated .... B 800 949-4647
   Newton Grove *(G-11988)*

Ideal Precast Inc .... F 919 801-8287
   Durham *(G-5146)*

Imagine That Creations LLC .... F 480 528-6775
   Black Mountain *(G-1125)*

Imperial Vault Company .... E 336 983-6343
   King *(G-9273)*

Inman Septic Tank Service Inc .... G 910 763-1146
   Wilmington *(G-16268)*

▲ International Precast Inc .... E 919 742-4241
   Siler City *(G-14416)*

International Vault Inc .... E 919 742-3132
   Siler City *(G-14417)*

Johnson Concrete Company .... E 704 636-5231
   Willow Spring *(G-16079)*

◆ Johnson Concrete Company .... E 704 636-5231
   Salisbury *(G-13993)*

Jones Ornamental Concrete .... F 828 685-3740
   Hendersonville *(G-7867)*

Kbc of Nc LLC .... G 704 589-3711
   Waxhaw *(G-15763)*

Leonard McSwain Sptic Tank Svc .... G 704 482-1380
   Shelby *(G-14337)*

Lindsay Precast Inc .... E 919 494-7600
   Franklinton *(G-6157)*

Lucas Concrete Products Inc .... E 704 525-9622
   Charlotte *(G-3106)*

Mack Industries .... G 252 977-3733
   Elm City *(G-5651)*

▲ Manhattan Amrcn Terrazzo Strip .... C 336 622-4247
   Staley *(G-14667)*

MC Precast Concrete Inc .... D 919 367-3636
   Apex *(G-216)*

Merchants Metals Inc .... G 704 921-9192
   Charlotte *(G-3165)*

Merritts Pottery Inc .... F 910 862-3774
   Elizabethtown *(G-5600)*

Metromont Materials Corp .... G 828 253-9383
   Asheville *(G-700)*

Mid-Atlantic Concrete Pdts Inc .... G 336 774-6654
   Winston Salem *(G-16810)*

Mitchell Concrete Products Inc .... G 919 934-4333
   Smithfield *(G-14472)*

Moretz & Sipe Inc .... G 828 327-8661
   Hickory *(G-8098)*

Neighborhood Union Burial Soc .... G 252 448-0581
   Trenton *(G-15333)*

Northeastern Ready Mix .... G 252 335-1931
   Elizabeth City *(G-5560)*

O R Prdgen Sons Sptic Tank I .... G 252 442-3338
   Rocky Mount *(G-13717)*

Oak City Columns LLC .... G 919 848-8814
   Raleigh *(G-13078)*

Old Castle Apg South Inc .... G 919 383-2521
   Durham *(G-5255)*

Oldcastle Infrastructure Inc .... E 704 788-4050
   Concord *(G-4326)*

Oldcastle Infrastructure Inc .... F 910 433-2931
   Fayetteville *(G-5887)*

Oldcastle Infrastructure Inc .... E 919 552-2252
   Fuquay Varina *(G-6219)*

Oldcastle Infrastructure Inc .... G 919 552-5715
   Fuquay Varina *(G-6220)*

Oldcastle Infrastructure Inc .... E 919 772-6269
   Raleigh *(G-13082)*

Oldcastle Retail Inc .... B 704 799-8083
   Cornelius *(G-4572)*

◆ Oldcastle Retail Inc .... F 704 525-1621
   Charlotte *(G-3292)*

P & D Archtectural Precast Inc .... F 252 566-9811
   La Grange *(G-9444)*

Piedmont Surfaces of Triad LLC .... E 336 627-7790
   Eden *(G-5499)*

Pipe Bridge Products Inc .... G 919 786-4499
   Raleigh *(G-13111)*

▲ Precast Solutions Inc .... F 336 656-7991
   Browns Summit *(G-1313)*

Precast Supply Company Inc .... F 704 784-2000
   Concord *(G-4335)*

Precast Terrazzo Entps Inc .... E 919 231-6200
   Raleigh *(G-13132)*

Prestress of Carolinas LLC .... F 704 587-4273
   Charlotte *(G-3376)*

Quality Precast Inc .... G 919 497-0660
   Louisburg *(G-9998)*

Quikrete Companies LLC .... E 704 272-7677
   Peachland *(G-12175)*

Rowan Monuments LLC .... G 704 905-6651
   Salisbury *(G-14037)*

S T Wooten Corporation .... F 919 783-5507
   Raleigh *(G-13223)*

Sentry Vault Service Inc .... G 252 243-2241
   Elm City *(G-5653)*

Shoaf Precast Septic Tank Inc .... G 336 787-5826
   Lexington *(G-9778)*

Smith-Carolina Corporation .... E 336 349-2905
   Reidsville *(G-13540)*

Southeastern Concrete Pdts Co .... D 704 873-2226
   Statesville *(G-14890)*

Southern Block Company .... F 910 293-7844
   Warsaw *(G-15674)*

Speer Concrete Inc .... E 910 947-3144
   Carthage *(G-1666)*

Stay-Right Pre-Cast Concrete Inc .... D 919 494-7600
   Franklinton *(G-6164)*

Techo-Bloc .... G 336 431-4133
   Archdale *(G-300)*

TNT Services Inc .... F 252 261-3073
   Kitty Hawk *(G-9408)*

Troy Ready - Mix Inc .... G 910 572-1011
   Troy *(G-15418)*

Tru-Contour Inc .... F 704 455-8700
   Concord *(G-4379)*

Utility Precast Inc .... E 704 721-0106
   Concord *(G-4384)*

Vim Products Inc .... G 919 277-0267
   Raleigh *(G-13401)*

Watson Concrete Pipe Company .... G 828 754-6476
   Lenoir *(G-9660)*

Western Crlina Mutl Brial Assn .... G 828 837-2577
   Murphy *(G-11718)*

Wilbert Burial Vault Company .... E 910 739-7276
   Lumberton *(G-10060)*

Wilbert Funeral Services Inc .... E 800 828-5879
   Greensboro *(G-7461)*

Wilbert Yates Vault Co Inc .... F 704 399-8453
   Charlotte *(G-3814)*

Wilmington Mortuary Svc Inc .... F 910 791-9099
   Wilmington *(G-16449)*

WP Simmons Inc .... F 336 789-3114
   Mount Airy *(G-11597)*

Yates Wilbert Vault LLC .... F 704 399-8453
   Charlotte *(G-3843)*

3273 Ready-mixed concrete

Abhw Concrete Co .... G 252 940-1002
   Washington *(G-15679)*

Adams Oldcastle .... G 980 229-7678
   Charlotte *(G-2135)*

Allen-Godwin Concrete Inc .... F 910 686-4890
   Wilmington *(G-16107)*

Allie M Powell III .... G 252 535-9717
   Roanoke Rapids *(G-13565)*

Ameri-Con Materials Inc .... F 828 863-0444
   Mill Spring *(G-10483)*

Argos Ready Mix (carolinas) Corp .... B 919 790-1520
   Raleigh *(G-12519)*

Argos USA .... F 336 784-5181
   Winston Salem *(G-16608)*

Argos USA LLC .... E 910 675-1262
   Castle Hayne *(G-1943)*

Argos USA LLC .... G 704 679-9431
   Charlotte *(G-2214)*

Argos USA LLC .... E 910 299-5046
   Clinton *(G-4088)*

Argos USA LLC .... F 704 483-4013
   Denver *(G-4763)*

Argos USA LLC .... G 910 892-3188
   Dunn *(G-4852)*

Argos USA LLC .... G 919 552-2294
   Fuquay Varina *(G-6180)*

Argos USA LLC .... E 919 772-4188
   Garner *(G-6255)*

Argos USA LLC .... E 828 322-9325
   Hickory *(G-7941)*

Argos USA LLC .... E 336 841-3379
   High Point *(G-8253)*

Argos USA LLC .... G 919 732-7509
   Hillsborough *(G-8634)*

Argos USA LLC .... E 252 527-8008
   Kinston *(G-9343)*

Argos USA LLC .... G 704 872-9566
   Mooresville *(G-10862)*

Argos USA LLC .... G 252 223-4348
   Newport *(G-11897)*

Argos USA LLC .... F 919 828-3695
   Raleigh *(G-12520)*

Argos USA LLC .... F 919 775-5441
   Raleigh *(G-12521)*

Argos USA LLC .... E 919 790-1520
   Raleigh *(G-12522)*

Argos USA LLC .... G 252 443-5046
   Roanoke Rapids *(G-13566)*

Argos USA LLC .... G 252 291-8888
   Sims *(G-14439)*

Argos USA LLC .... C 704 872-9566
   Statesville *(G-14752)*

Argos USA LLC .... E 919 554-2087
   Wake Forest *(G-15528)*

32 STONE, CLAY, GLASS, AND CONCRETE PRODUCTS — SIC SECTION

Company	Code	Phone
Argos USA LLC — Washington (G-15682)	G	252 946-4704
Argos USA LLC — Williamston (G-16057)	G	252 792-3148
Argos USA LLC — Wilmington (G-16115)	G	910 686-4890
Argos USA LLC — Wilmington (G-16116)	E	910 796-3469
Argos USA LLC — Winston Salem (G-16609)	D	336 784-4888
Asheboro Ready-Mix Inc — Asheboro (G-407)	E	336 672-0957
B V Hedrick Gravel & Sand Co — Salisbury (G-13928)	E	704 633-5982
Black Concrete Inc — Lexington (G-9685)	F	336 243-1388
Blue DOT Readi-Mix LLC — Mint Hill (G-10523)	F	704 971-7676
Cabarrus Concrete Co — Concord (G-4217)	F	704 788-3000
Capital Rdymx Pittsboro LLC — Moncure (G-10617)	F	919 217-0222
Capital Ready Mix Concrete LLC — Knightdale (G-9414)	E	919 217-0222
Capitol Funds Inc — Mount Gilead (G-11599)	F	910 439-5275
Capitol Funds Inc — Shelby (G-14291)	E	704 487-8547
Carolina Concrete Inc — Charlotte (G-2393)	F	704 596-6511
Carolina Concrete Inc — Matthews (G-10237)	E	704 821-7645
Carolina Concrete Materials — Swannanoa (G-15022)	G	828 686-3040
Carolina Ready Mix & Build — Swannanoa (G-15023)	G	828 686-3041
Carolina Ready-Mix LLC — Monroe (G-10677)	G	704 225-1112
Carolina Sunrock LLC — Creedmoor (G-4609)	G	919 201-4201
Carolina Sunrock LLC — Kittrell (G-9395)	E	252 433-4617
Carolina Sunrock LLC — Raleigh (G-12601)	E	919 861-1860
Carolina Sunrock LLC — Wake Forest (G-15538)	E	919 554-0500
▲ Carolina Sunrock LLC — Butner (G-1543)	E	919 575-4502
Cemex Cnstr Mtls ATL LLC — Statesville (G-14776)	G	704 873-3263
Cemex Materials LLC — Harrisburg (G-7704)	C	704 455-1100
Cemex Materials LLC — Thomasville (G-15202)	D	800 627-2986
Cemex Materials LLC — Wilson (G-16487)	D	252 243-6153
Central Carolina Concrete LLC — Greensboro (G-6899)	E	336 315-0785
CFI Ready Mix LLC — Lillington (G-9847)	G	910 814-4238
Chandler Con Pdts of Chrstnber — Burlington (G-1394)	G	336 226-1181
Chandler Concrete Co — Siler City (G-14405)	G	919 742-2627
Chandler Concrete Co Inc — Biscoe (G-1107)	G	910 974-4744
Chandler Concrete Co Inc — Burlington (G-1395)	D	336 272-6127
Chandler Concrete High Co — Boone (G-1187)	F	828 264-8694
Chandler Concrete Inc — Asheboro (G-414)	F	336 625-1070
Chandler Concrete Inc — Crumpler (G-4628)	G	336 982-8760
Chandler Concrete Inc — Durham (G-5012)	F	919 598-1424
Chandler Concrete Inc — Eden (G-5488)	G	336 342-5771
Chandler Concrete Inc — Graham (G-6683)	G	336 222-9716
Chandler Concrete Inc — Greensboro (G-6902)	F	336 297-1179
Chandler Concrete Inc — Hillsborough (G-8644)	G	919 644-1058
Chandler Concrete Inc — Pittsboro (G-12336)	G	919 542-4242
Chandler Concrete Inc — Roxboro (G-13799)	F	336 599-8343
Chandler Concrete Inc — Salisbury (G-13939)	D	704 636-4711
Chandler Concrete Inc — Sparta (G-14591)	G	336 372-4348
Charlotte Block Inc — Charlotte (G-2450)	G	704 399-4526
Childers Concrete Company — High Point (G-8295)	F	336 841-3111
Commercial Ready Mix Pdts Inc — Ahoskie (G-58)	G	252 332-3590
Commercial Ready Mix Pdts Inc — Elizabeth City (G-5536)	F	252 335-9740
Commercial Ready Mix Pdts Inc — Moyock (G-11695)	F	252 232-1250
Commercial Ready Mix Pdts Inc — Pendleton (G-12185)	F	252 585-1777
Commercial Spclty Trck Hldngs — Burlington (G-1398)	C	859 234-1100
Concrete Service Co Inc — Fayetteville (G-5794)	E	910 483-0396
Concrete Service Company — Clinton (G-4093)	G	910 590-0035
Concrete Supply Co LLC — Charlotte (G-2537)	G	864 517-4055
Concrete Supply Holdings Inc — Charlotte (G-2538)	B	704 372-2930
Crete Solutions LLC — Wilmington (G-16189)	E	910 726-1686
Crh Americas Inc — Monroe (G-10699)	C	704 282-8443
Crmp Inc — Winton (G-17021)	G	252 358-5461
Dean S Ready Mixed Inc — Albemarle (G-82)	E	704 982-5520
DOT Blue Readi-Mix LLC — Charlotte (G-2652)	E	704 391-3000
DOT Blue Readi-Mix LLC — Harrisburg (G-7707)	E	704 247-2778
DOT Blue Readi-Mix LLC — Monroe (G-10706)	E	704 247-2777
DOT Blue Readi-Mix LLC — Statesville (G-14790)	E	704 978-2331
E & M Concrete Inc — Fuquay Varina (G-6197)	E	919 235-7221
Eagle Rock Concrete LLC — Apex (G-186)	E	919 596-7077
Eagle Rock Concrete LLC — Raleigh (G-12714)	E	919 281-0120
Eagle Rock Concrete LLC — Raleigh (G-12713)	E	919 781-3744
Eveready Mix Concrete Co Inc — Yadkinville (G-17039)	G	336 961-6688
Explosives Supply Company — Spruce Pine (G-14640)	F	828 765-2762
Forsyth Redi-Mix Inc — Rural Hall (G-13841)	F	336 969-0446
Greenville Ready Mix Concrete — Winterville (G-17001)	E	252 756-0119
Greystone Concrete Pdts Inc — Henderson (G-7785)	E	252 438-5144
Hamby Brother S Incorporated — North Wilkesboro (G-12013)	F	336 667-1154
Hamby Brothers Concrete Inc — Lenoir (G-9618)	E	828 754-2176
Hamrick Precast LLC — Shelby (G-14324)	G	704 434-6551
Hartley Ready Mix Con Mfg Inc — Greensboro (G-7077)	G	336 294-5995
Hartley Ready Mix Con Mfg Inc — Winston Salem (G-16737)	F	336 788-3928
Heidelberg Materials Us Inc — Sims (G-14443)	E	252 235-4162
Heidelberg Mtls Sthast Agg LLC — Wake Forest (G-15564)	E	919 556-4011
Heidelberg Mtls US Cem LLC — Durham (G-5134)	E	919 682-5791
Heritage Concrete Service Corp — Dunn (G-4875)	G	910 892-4445
Heritage Concrete Service Corp — Sanford (G-14131)	E	919 775-5014
Hildreth Ready Mix LLC — Rockingham (G-13629)	G	704 694-2034
I Mix 4 U LLC — Thomasville (G-15234)	G	336 307-6297
J S Myers Co Inc — Yadkinville (G-17042)	F	336 463-5572
Jab-C LLC — Mineral Springs (G-10517)	G	704 507-6196
Kerrs Hickry Ready-Mixed Con — Hickory (G-8074)	E	828 322-3157
Legacy Vulcan LLC — Boone (G-1213)	G	828 963-7100
Legacy Vulcan LLC — Concord (G-4301)	G	704 788-7833
Legacy Vulcan LLC — Elizabeth City (G-5554)	G	252 338-2201
Legacy Vulcan LLC — Elkin (G-5624)	G	336 835-1439
Legacy Vulcan LLC — Enka (G-5683)	G	828 255-8561
Legacy Vulcan LLC — Gold Hill (G-6583)	G	704 279-5566
Legacy Vulcan LLC — Henderson (G-7794)	G	252 438-3161
Legacy Vulcan LLC — Hendersonville (G-7873)	G	828 692-0254
Legacy Vulcan LLC — Lenoir (G-9624)	G	828 754-5348
Legacy Vulcan LLC — Morganton (G-11227)	G	828 437-2616
Legacy Vulcan LLC — North Wilkesboro (G-12021)	G	336 838-8072
Legacy Vulcan LLC — Rockingham (G-13633)	G	910 895-2415
Legacy Vulcan LLC — Winston Salem (G-16785)	F	336 767-0911
Lenoir Concrete Cnstr Co — Lenoir (G-9625)	G	828 759-0449
Loflin Concrete Co Inc — Kernersville (G-9209)	E	336 904-2788
Loflin Materials Inc — Kernersville (G-9210)	G	336 993-2432
Loven Ready Mix LLC — Boone (G-1215)	G	828 265-4671
Macleod Construction Inc — Charlotte (G-3116)	C	704 483-3580
Martin Marietta Materials Inc — Castle Hayne (G-1954)	G	910 602-6058

32 STONE, CLAY, GLASS, AND CONCRETE PRODUCTS

Martin Marietta Materials Inc .... G 919 929-7131
  Chapel Hill *(G-2036)*

Martin Marietta Materials Inc .... G 704 392-1333
  Charlotte *(G-3130)*

Martin Marietta Materials Inc .... F 919 557-7412
  Fuquay Varina *(G-6213)*

Martin Marietta Materials Inc .... F 704 932-4379
  Landis *(G-9451)*

Martin Marietta Materials Inc .... G 919 664-1700
  Raleigh *(G-13002)*

Martin Marietta Materials Inc .... G 910 324-7430
  Richlands *(G-13556)*

Massey Ready-Mix Concrete Inc .... G 336 221-8100
  Burlington *(G-1457)*

McDowell Cement Products Co .... G 828 765-2762
  Spruce Pine *(G-14646)*

McDowell Cement Products Co .... F 828 652-5721
  Marion *(G-10161)*

Monsted Mix Inc .... G 704 979-6911
  Charlotte *(G-3201)*

Mulls Con & Septic Tanks Inc .... G 828 437-0959
  Morganton *(G-11236)*

Northeastern Ready Mix .... G 252 335-1931
  Elizabeth City *(G-5560)*

Oldcastle Retail Inc .... B 704 799-8083
  Cornelius *(G-4572)*

Quality Concrete Co Inc .... F 910 483-7155
  Fayetteville *(G-5903)*

Quikrete Companies LLC .... E 704 272-7677
  Peachland *(G-12175)*

Ready Mix of Carolinas Inc .... E 704 888-3027
  Locust *(G-9967)*

Ready Mixed Concrete .... G 252 758-1181
  Ayden *(G-854)*

Ready When You Are .... G 828 243-7514
  Arden *(G-370)*

Redy Mix of Carolinas Inc .... G 704 888-2224
  Locust *(G-9969)*

Rinker Materials .... F 704 455-1100
  Harrisburg *(G-7724)*

Rinker Materials .... G 704 827-8175
  Mount Holly *(G-11650)*

Riverside Cement Co .... G 760 245-5321
  Raleigh *(G-13209)*

Roanoke Chowan Ready Mix Inc .... G 252 332-7995
  Ahoskie *(G-65)*

Robert S Concrete Service Inc .... G 910 391-3973
  Fayetteville *(G-5909)*

S & W Ready Mix Con Co LLC .... F 910 592-2191
  Clinton *(G-4105)*

S & W Ready Mix Con Co LLC .... G 910 645-6868
  Elizabethtown *(G-5603)*

S & W Ready Mix Con Co LLC .... G 910 864-0939
  Fayetteville *(G-5911)*

S & W Ready Mix Con Co LLC .... F 919 751-1796
  Goldsboro *(G-6653)*

S & W Ready Mix Con Co LLC .... F 910 329-1201
  Holly Ridge *(G-8685)*

S & W Ready Mix Con Co LLC .... F 252 527-1881
  Kinston *(G-9382)*

S & W Ready Mix Con Co LLC .... F 252 726-2566
  Morehead City *(G-11186)*

S & W Ready Mix Con Co LLC .... F 252 633-2115
  New Bern *(G-11841)*

S & W Ready Mix Con Co LLC .... F 910 496-3232
  Spring Lake *(G-14627)*

S & W Ready Mix Con Co LLC .... F 910 285-2191
  Wallace *(G-15625)*

S & W Ready Mix Con Co LLC .... G 910 592-1733
  Clinton *(G-4104)*

S T Wooten Corporation .... E 252 291-5165
  Wilson *(G-16538)*

Smyrna Ready Mix Concrete LLC .... G 252 447-5356
  Havelock *(G-7747)*

Smyrna Ready Mix Concrete LLC .... F 252 637-4155
  New Bern *(G-11847)*

Southern Concrete Incorporated .... F 919 906-4069
  Broadway *(G-1297)*

Southern Concrete Materials .... G 704 641-9604
  Concord *(G-4363)*

Southern Concrete Materials Inc .... C 828 253-6421
  Asheville *(G-783)*

Southern Concrete Mtls Inc .... E 828 684-3636
  Arden *(G-378)*

Southern Concrete Mtls Inc .... E 828 670-6450
  Asheville *(G-784)*

Southern Concrete Mtls Inc .... E 828 682-2298
  Burnsville *(G-1533)*

Southern Concrete Mtls Inc .... F 704 394-2346
  Charlotte *(G-3591)*

Southern Concrete Mtls Inc .... E 704 394-2344
  Charlotte *(G-3592)*

Southern Concrete Mtls Inc .... G 828 681-5178
  Fletcher *(G-6043)*

Southern Concrete Mtls Inc .... F 828 524-3555
  Franklin *(G-6144)*

Southern Concrete Mtls Inc .... E 828 692-6517
  Hendersonville *(G-7903)*

Southern Concrete Mtls Inc .... F 877 788-3001
  Salisbury *(G-14045)*

Southern Concrete Mtls Inc .... F 828 586-5280
  Sylva *(G-15069)*

Southern Concrete Mtls Inc .... G 828 456-9048
  Waynesville *(G-15826)*

Southern Hldings Goldsboro Inc .... F 919 920-6998
  Goldsboro *(G-6658)*

Southern Ready Mix LLC .... G 919 988-8448
  Goldsboro *(G-6659)*

Speer Concrete Inc .... E 910 947-3144
  Carthage *(G-1666)*

Star Ready-Mix Inc .... F 336 725-9401
  Winston Salem *(G-16915)*

Sunrock Group Holdings Corp .... D 919 747-6400
  Raleigh *(G-13315)*

Thomas Concrete Carolina .... G 919 828-6923
  Raleigh *(G-13346)*

Thomas Concrete Carolina Inc .... F 704 333-0390
  Charlotte *(G-3688)*

Thomas Concrete Carolina Inc .... F 919 557-3144
  Fuquay Varina *(G-6233)*

Thomas Concrete Carolina Inc .... F 919 460-5317
  Morrisville *(G-11447)*

Thomas Concrete Carolina Inc .... F 919 832-0451
  Raleigh *(G-13347)*

Thomas Concrete SC Inc .... F 704 868-4545
  Gastonia *(G-6526)*

Three Sisters Ready Mix LLC .... F 919 217-0222
  Knightdale *(G-9430)*

Titan America LLC .... G 336 754-0143
  Belews Creek *(G-973)*

TNT Services Inc .... F 252 261-3073
  Kitty Hawk *(G-9408)*

Toxaway Concrete Inc .... F 828 966-4270
  Cashiers *(G-1938)*

Tri City Concrete Co LLC .... E 828 245-2011
  Forest City *(G-6084)*

Tri-City Concrete LLC .... G 704 372-2930
  Charlotte *(G-3723)*

Triangle Ready Mix LLC .... E 919 859-4190
  Morrisville *(G-11454)*

Tyrrell Ready Mix Inc .... G 252 796-0265
  Columbia *(G-4169)*

Vulcan Construction Mtls LLC .... F 828 754-3200
  Lenoir *(G-9658)*

Vulcan Construction Mtls LLC .... G 336 767-1201
  Winston Salem *(G-16965)*

Vulcan Construction Mtls LLC .... E 336 767-0911
  Winston Salem *(G-16966)*

Vulcan Materials Company .... G 828 963-7100
  Boone *(G-1246)*

Vulcan Materials Company .... G 704 545-5687
  Charlotte *(G-3784)*

Vulcan Materials Company .... G 704 549-1540
  Charlotte *(G-3785)*

Vulcan Materials Company .... G 828 692-0039
  Hendersonville *(G-7912)*

Vulcan Materials Company .... G 336 869-2148
  Kernersville *(G-9252)*

Watauga Ready Mixed .... G 336 246-6441
  Boone *(G-1248)*

White Cap LP .... G 704 921-4420
  Charlotte *(G-3810)*

Williams Ready Mix Pdts Inc .... F 704 283-1137
  Monroe *(G-10834)*

Wnc Material Sales .... G 828 658-8368
  Weaverville *(G-15869)*

3275 Gypsum products

Esco Industries Inc .... F 336 495-3772
  Randleman *(G-13469)*

Mbp Acquisition LLC .... F 704 349-5055
  Monroe *(G-10768)*

Ng Operations LLC .... D 704 916-2082
  Charlotte *(G-3261)*

Precision Walls Inc .... G 336 852-7710
  Greensboro *(G-7276)*

Proform Finishing Products LLC .... E 704 398-3900
  Mount Holly *(G-11648)*

Proform Finishing Products LLC .... E 910 799-3954
  Wilmington *(G-16371)*

◆ Proform Finishing Products LLC .... B 704 365-7300
  Charlotte *(G-3392)*

United States Gypsum Company .... F 828 765-9481
  Spruce Pine *(G-14660)*

3281 Cut stone and stone products

▲ Acme Stone Company Inc .... E 336 786-6978
  Mount Airy *(G-11472)*

Amanzi Marble & Granite LLC .... G 336 993-9998
  Kernersville *(G-9162)*

American Stone Company .... D 919 929-7131
  Chapel Hill *(G-1983)*

Apex Marble and Granite Inc .... E 919 462-9202
  Morrisville *(G-11289)*

Armen Stone LLC .... G 743 228-3901
  Burlington *(G-1367)*

Asp Distribution Inc .... F 336 375-5672
  Greensboro *(G-6820)*

Athena Marble Incorporated .... F 704 636-7810
  Salisbury *(G-13924)*

B V Hedrick Gravel & Sand Co .... E 828 645-5560
  Weaverville *(G-15837)*

Beautimar Manufactured MBL Inc .... F 919 779-1181
  Raleigh *(G-12550)*

Bloomday Granite & Marble Inc .... E 336 724-0300
  Winston Salem *(G-16633)*

Boone-Woody Mining Company Inc ..... G 828 675-5188
  Micaville *(G-10442)*

Buechel Stone Corp .... D 800 236-4474
  Marion *(G-10145)*

▲ Caesarstone Tech USA Inc .... G 818 779-0999
  Charlotte *(G-2376)*

Capital Marble Creations Inc .... F 910 893-2462
  Lillington *(G-9845)*

Carolina Marble & Granite .... G 704 523-2112
  Charlotte *(G-2399)*

32 STONE, CLAY, GLASS, AND CONCRETE PRODUCTS

Carolina Marble Products Inc .... F 252 753-3020
   Farmville *(G-5731)*

◆ Carolina North Granite Corp .... D 336 719-2600
   Mount Airy *(G-11490)*

Carolina Quarries Inc .... D 704 633-0201
   Salisbury *(G-13936)*

Carolina Stalite Co Ltd Partnr .... E 704 279-2166
   Gold Hill *(G-6580)*

Carolina Stalite Co Ltd Partnr .... E 704 474-3165
   Norwood *(G-12037)*

Carolina Stalite Co Ltd Partnr .... F 704 637-1515
   Salisbury *(G-13937)*

Century Stone LLC .... G 919 774-3334
   Sanford *(G-14099)*

◆ Chadsworth Incorporated .... E 910 763-7600
   Wilmington *(G-16168)*

Clifford W Estes Co Inc .... E 336 622-6410
   Staley *(G-14664)*

Conway Development Inc .... F 252 756-2168
   Greenville *(G-7505)*

Creative Stone Fyetteville Inc .... F 910 491-1225
   Fayetteville *(G-5799)*

Custom Marble Corporation .... G 910 215-0679
   Pinehurst *(G-12219)*

E T Sales Inc .... E 704 888-4010
   Midland *(G-10467)*

Exquisite Granite and MBL Inc .... G 336 851-8890
   Greensboro *(G-7009)*

FTM Enterprises Inc .... F 910 798-2045
   Wilmington *(G-16224)*

Georgia-Carolina Quarries Inc .... E 336 786-6978
   Mount Airy *(G-11511)*

Ginkgo Stone LLC .... G 704 451-8678
   Charlotte *(G-2830)*

▲ Grancreations Inc .... G 704 332-7625
   Charlotte *(G-2852)*

Granite Memorials Inc .... G 336 786-6596
   Mount Airy *(G-11512)*

Heidelberg Mtls Sthast Agg LLC .... E 910 893-8308
   Bunnlevel *(G-1330)*

Ivey Ln Inc .... G 336 230-0062
   Greensboro *(G-7129)*

Jacobs Creek Stone Company Inc .... F 336 857-2602
   Denton *(G-4738)*

John J Morton Company Inc .... F 704 332-6633
   Charlotte *(G-3028)*

Ketchie Marble Co Inc .... G 704 279-8377
   Salisbury *(G-13998)*

King Stone Innovation LLC .... G 704 352-1134
   Charlotte *(G-3056)*

Kitchen Man Inc .... F 910 408-1322
   Winnabow *(G-16582)*

Lawing Marble Co Inc .... G 704 732-0360
   Lincolnton *(G-9898)*

Lbm Industries Inc .... F 828 966-4270
   Sapphire *(G-14213)*

Locust Monument LLC .... G 704 888-5600
   Locust *(G-9962)*

M & M Stone Sculpting & Engrv .... G 336 877-3842
   Todd *(G-15323)*

Mables Headstone & Monu Co LLP .... G 919 724-8705
   Creedmoor *(G-4618)*

Marion Cultured Marble Inc .... F 828 724-4782
   Marion *(G-10157)*

McAd Inc .... E 336 299-3030
   Greensboro *(G-7193)*

▲ Midcoastal Development Corp .... G 336 622-3091
   Staley *(G-14668)*

Modern Marble & Glass Inc .... G 336 668-4197
   Greensboro *(G-7203)*

Mongoose LLC .... F 919 400-0772
   Burlington *(G-1462)*

National Marble Products Inc .... G 910 326-3005
   Emerald Isle *(G-5670)*

▲ Natural Granite & Marble Inc .... G 919 872-1508
   Raleigh *(G-13056)*

Nova Enterprises Inc .... E 828 687-8770
   Arden *(G-357)*

Piedmont Marble Inc .... G 336 274-1800
   Oak Ridge *(G-12066)*

Quality Marble .... G 336 472-1000
   Thomasville *(G-15268)*

Royal Baths Manufacturing Co .... E 704 837-1701
   Charlotte *(G-3461)*

RSI Home Products Inc .... C 828 428-6300
   Lincolnton *(G-9917)*

Russell Custom Stone LLC .... G 336 859-5755
   New London *(G-11877)*

Sharp Stone Supply Inc .... F 336 659-7777
   Winston Salem *(G-16904)*

▲ Sid Jenkins Inc .... G 336 632-0707
   Greensboro *(G-7337)*

Southern Marble Co LLC .... G 704 982-4142
   Albemarle *(G-107)*

Southern Stone Cutting .... G 252 566-3116
   La Grange *(G-9446)*

◆ Stone Resource Inc .... E 336 889-7800
   High Point *(G-8554)*

▼ Stonemaster Inc .... F 704 333-0353
   Charlotte *(G-3638)*

Stoneworx Inc .... G 252 937-8080
   Rocky Mount *(G-13734)*

Tarheel Marble Company Inc .... F 704 888-6003
   Locust *(G-9975)*

▲ Trade Venture Stones LLC .... G 919 803-3923
   Knightdale *(G-9431)*

Tserings LLC .... G 704 283-8811
   Monroe *(G-10825)*

▲ Turmar Marble Inc .... F 704 391-1800
   Charlotte *(G-3739)*

Unique Stone Incorporated .... G 910 817-9450
   Rockingham *(G-13645)*

USA Dreamstone LLC .... G 919 615-4329
   Garner *(G-6323)*

Wake Monument Company Inc .... G 919 556-3422
   Rolesville *(G-13761)*

Wake Stone Corporation .... E 919 677-0050
   Cary *(G-1923)*

Wake Stone Corporation .... E 919 266-1100
   Knightdale *(G-9434)*

Waycaster Nick Stone Co .... G 828 756-4011
   Marion *(G-10185)*

▲ Web-Don Incorporated .... E 800 532-0434
   Charlotte *(G-3800)*

Wiggins North State Co Inc .... G 919 556-3231
   Rolesville *(G-13762)*

Winecoff Mmrals Sttesville Inc .... G 704 873-9661
   Statesville *(G-14927)*

Woodsmiths Company .... F 406 626-3102
   Lenoir *(G-9661)*

World Stone Fabricators Inc .... E 704 372-9968
   Charlotte *(G-3825)*

World Stone of Sanford LLC .... F 919 468-8450
   Sanford *(G-14209)*

WP Simmons Inc .... F 336 789-3114
   Mount Airy *(G-11597)*

3291 Abrasive products

Advanced Superabrasives Inc .... E 828 689-3200
   Mars Hill *(G-10191)*

◆ E T C of Henderson N C Inc .... G 252 492-4033
   Henderson *(G-7781)*

Eagle Superabrasives Inc .... F 828 261-7281
   Hickory *(G-8014)*

▲ Farris Belt & Saw Company .... F 704 527-6166
   Charlotte *(G-2748)*

▼ His Glassworks Inc .... G 828 254-2559
   Asheville *(G-653)*

Hones Enterprises .... G 336 378-9351
   Greensboro *(G-7100)*

Keselowski Advanced Mfg LLC .... E 704 799-0206
   Statesville *(G-14830)*

◆ Klingspor Abrasives Inc .... C 828 322-3030
   Hickory *(G-8078)*

▲ Sia Abrasives Inc USA .... D 704 587-7355
   Lincolnton *(G-9918)*

▲ Starcke Abrasives Usa Inc .... E 704 583-3338
   Charlotte *(G-3623)*

Sunbelt Abrasives Inc .... G 336 882-6837
   High Point *(G-8557)*

Syntech Abrasives Inc .... F 704 525-8030
   Charlotte *(G-3666)*

Tiger Steel Inc .... G 336 624-4481
   Mount Airy *(G-11588)*

W G Cannon Paint Co Inc .... G 828 754-5376
   Lenoir *(G-9659)*

3292 Asbestos products

Certainteed LLC .... F 336 696-2007
   North Wilkesboro *(G-12001)*

Contaminant Control .... G 704 886-0205
   Concord *(G-4242)*

Exterior Vinyl Wholesale .... G 336 838-7772
   Wilkesboro *(G-16020)*

Hydro Tube Enterprises Inc .... F 919 258-3070
   Sanford *(G-14136)*

Plycem Usa LLC .... D 336 696-2007
   North Wilkesboro *(G-12030)*

3295 Minerals, ground or treated

3M Company .... D 919 642-0006
   Moncure *(G-10611)*

Carolina Stalite Co Ltd Partnr .... E 704 279-2166
   Gold Hill *(G-6581)*

◆ Cormetech Inc .... C 919 620-3000
   Charlotte *(G-2554)*

Covia Holdings LLC .... E 828 765-4283
   Spruce Pine *(G-14637)*

Glendon Pyrophyllite Inc .... G 919 464-5243
   Sanford *(G-14125)*

Imerys Clays Inc .... G 828 648-2668
   Canton *(G-1618)*

◆ Imerys Mica Kings Mountain Inc .... E 704 739-3616
   Kings Mountain *(G-9309)*

Imerys Perlite Usa Inc .... F 919 562-0031
   Youngsville *(G-17085)*

Iperionx Limited .... E 704 578-3217
   Charlotte *(G-2993)*

◆ Martin Marietta Materials Inc .... C 919 781-4550
   Raleigh *(G-13001)*

Mathis Quarries Inc .... G 336 984-4010
   North Wilkesboro *(G-12026)*

◆ Premier Magnesia LLC .... E 828 452-4784
   Waynesville *(G-15816)*

Quartz Corp USA .... E 828 765-8950
   Spruce Pine *(G-14653)*

◆ Quartz Corp USA .... D 828 766-2104
   Spruce Pine *(G-14654)*

Southeastern Minerals Inc .... E 252 492-0831
   Henderson *(G-7811)*

Southern Products Company Inc .... E 910 281-3189
   Hoffman *(G-8676)*

Vanderbilt Minerals LLC .... E 910 948-2266
   Robbins *(G-13603)*

3296 Mineral wool

SIC SECTION

33 PRIMARY METAL INDUSTRIES

Bunting Equipment Company Inc........... F 336 626-7300
  Sophia (G-14513)
Freudenberg Prfmce Mtls LP.................. C 828 665-5000
  Candler (G-1579)
JPS Communications Inc...................... D 919 534-1168
  Raleigh (G-12923)
Mid-Atlantic Specialties Inc.................. G 919 212-1939
  Raleigh (G-13030)
▲ Owens Corning Glass Metal Svcs....... D 704 721-2000
  Concord (G-4328)
Sharp Fiberglass LLC............................ G 610 760-0638
  Kittrell (G-9398)
▼ Wwj LLC.. E 704 871-8500
  Statesville (G-14929)

3297 Nonclay refractories

◆ 3tex Inc.. E 919 481-2500
  Rutherfordton (G-13860)
General Electric Company...................... A 910 675-5000
  Wilmington (G-16230)
◆ Martin Marietta Materials Inc.............. C 919 781-4550
  Raleigh (G-13001)
PCC Airfoils LLC.................................... B 919 774-4300
  Sanford (G-14164)
Resco Products Inc............................... G 336 299-1441
  Greensboro (G-7307)
▲ Skamol Americas Inc.......................... G 704 544-1015
  Charlotte (G-3559)
◆ Vesuvius Nc LLC................................ D 336 578-7728
  Graham (G-6715)
◆ Vesuvius USA Corporation................. D 412 429-1800
  Charlotte (G-3775)
Virginia Carolina Refr Inc....................... G 704 216-0223
  Salisbury (G-14062)

3299 Nonmetallic mineral products,

B & B Stucco and Stone LLC................. F 704 524-1230
  Stanley (G-14685)
B&V Stucco LLC.................................... G 828 682-9700
  Burnsville (G-1524)
▲ Cairn Studio Ltd................................ G 704 892-3581
  Davidson (G-4667)
Carolina Specialties Inc......................... G 704 525-9499
  Charlotte (G-2406)
Clifford W Estes Co Inc.......................... E 336 622-6410
  Staley (G-14664)
Jacqueline Cole..................................... G 828 277-3566
  Asheville (G-667)
Jarrett Shane DBA Jarrett Stuc............. G 828 768-8385
  Asheville (G-669)
▲ Lab Designs LLC............................... G 336 429-4114
  Mount Airy (G-11534)
M & J Stucco LLC.................................. G 704 634-2249
  Monroe (G-10761)
Omega Products..................................... G 704 684-1920
  Indian Trail (G-8953)
Plastering.. G 336 402-0445
  Julian (G-9106)
Premier Stucco LLC............................... G 919 676-2306
  Raleigh (G-13138)
Ramirezstucco Company........................ G 828 458-8495
  Hendersonville (G-7894)
Sanher Stucco & Lather Inc.................. F 704 241-8517
  Charlotte (G-3488)
Treklite Inc.. G 919 610-1788
  Raleigh (G-13358)

33 PRIMARY METAL INDUSTRIES

3312 Blast furnaces and steel mills

ABB Installation Products Inc................ E 828 322-1855
  Hickory (G-7928)

AD Tubi Usa Inc.................................... E 919 930-3023
  Siler City (G-14397)
American Stainless Tubing LLC........... C 704 878-8823
  Troutman (G-15366)
▲ Bessemer City Machine Shop Inc..... E 704 629-4111
  Bessemer City (G-1053)
Brothers Metal Fab Inc......................... F 336 270-3761
  Burlington (G-1380)
Charlotte Pipe and Foundry Co............ B 704 348-5416
  Charlotte (G-2458)
Cleveland-Cliffs Plate LLC..................... A 828 464-9214
  Newton (G-11919)
Commercial Metals Company................ G 336 584-0333
  Burlington (G-1397)
Commercial Metals Company................ G 919 833-9737
  Gastonia (G-6381)
Competition Tooling Inc....................... G 336 887-4414
  High Point (G-8301)
Component Sourcing Intl LLC............... E 704 843-9292
  Charlotte (G-2534)
◆ Controls Southeast Inc..................... C 704 644-5000
  Pineville (G-12262)
Dallas Fabrication.................................. G 704 629-4000
  Bessemer City (G-1060)
Davis Equipment Handlers Inc.............. G 704 792-9176
  Charlotte (G-2606)
Eizi Group Llc....................................... G 919 397-3638
  Raleigh (G-12729)
Garage Guys... F 704 494-8841
  Charlotte (G-2807)
Gerdau Ameristeel US Inc.................... C 704 596-0361
  Charlotte (G-2827)
GKN Sinter Metals LLC........................ C 828 464-0642
  Conover (G-4459)
Greenbrook Tms Neurohealth Ctr......... G 855 910-4867
  Mooresville (G-10964)
Greene Precision Products Inc.............. G 828 262-0116
  Boone (G-1202)
▲ Interntonal Specialty Pdts Inc.......... G 828 326-9053
  Hickory (G-8067)
Kinetic Systems Inc............................. D 919 322-7200
  Durham (G-5181)
▲ Lee Controls LLC.............................. F 732 752-5200
  Southport (G-14572)
Lelantos Group Inc............................... D 704 780-4127
  Mooresville (G-11005)
Meritor Inc.. C 828 433-4600
  Morganton (G-11232)
Metallus Inc.. D 330 471-6293
  Columbus (G-4178)
Moes Hndy Svcs Fnce Instl Mno.......... G 910 712-1402
  Raeford (G-12426)
▲ Mount Hope Machinery Co............... F
  Charlotte (G-3208)
Muriel Harris Investments Inc.............. F 800 932-3191
  Fayetteville (G-5879)
Nucor Castrip Arkansas LLC................ G 704 366-7000
  Charlotte (G-3280)
Nucor Corporation................................ C 252 356-3700
  Cofield (G-4136)
◆ Nucor Corporation............................. C 704 366-7000
  Charlotte (G-3281)
Nucor Energy Holdings Inc................... F 704 366-7000
  Charlotte (G-3282)
Nucor Steel Sales Corporation............. F 302 622-4066
  Charlotte (G-3283)
▲ Okaya Shinnichi Corp America.......... E 704 588-3131
  Charlotte (G-3289)
Old Hickory Stainless Stl Inc................ G 910 567-6751
  Godwin (G-6579)
P & S Welding Inc................................ G 910 285-3126
  Willard (G-16055)

Performance Plastics Pdts Inc.............. D 336 454-0350
  Jamestown (G-9066)
Quality Mechanical Contrs LLC............ D 336 228-0638
  Burlington (G-1480)
Roberts Family Enterprises LLP........... G 919 785-3111
  Raleigh (G-13212)
Saertex Multicom LP............................ E 704 946-9229
  Huntersville (G-8892)
▲ Saertex Multicom LP........................ F 704 946-9229
  Huntersville (G-8891)
Solo Wheels and Accessories............... G 919 333-2945
  Dunn (G-4885)
Southeast Tubular Products Inc........... E 704 883-8883
  Statesville (G-14889)
Spantek Expanded Metal Inc................ E 704 479-6210
  Lincolnton (G-9920)
Stainless Steel Countertops NC........... G 919 935-0835
  Cameron (G-1563)
Steel City Services LLC....................... F 919 698-2407
  Durham (G-5373)
Steel Technologies LLC........................ D 910 592-1266
  Clinton (G-4112)
Structural Materials Inc....................... G 828 754-6413
  Lenoir (G-9653)
Te Wheel Inc.. G 336 376-1364
  Graham (G-6712)
Thermochem Recovery Intl................... F 919 606-3282
  Durham (G-5399)
Tms International LLC......................... F 704 604-0287
  Charlotte (G-3700)
Vulcraft Carrier Corp........................... F 704 367-8674
  Charlotte (G-3786)
Wagon Wheel... G 828 689-4755
  Mars Hill (G-10198)
Wheel City Wholesale Inc..................... F 828 665-2442
  Asheville (G-819)
Wheel Pros LLC.................................... G 336 851-6705
  Greensboro (G-7459)

3313 Electrometallurgical products

▲ Betek Tools Inc................................. F 980 498-2523
  Charlotte (G-2303)

3315 Steel wire and related products

▲ A B Carter Inc.................................. D 704 865-1201
  Gastonia (G-6334)
Afsc LLC... D 704 523-4936
  Charlotte (G-2142)
▲ Blue Ridge Metals Corporation......... C 828 687-2525
  Fletcher (G-5989)
▲ Cavert Wire Company Inc................ E 800 969-2601
  Rural Hall (G-13837)
Classic Cleaning LLC........................... E 800 220-7101
  Raleigh (G-12626)
Coleman Cable LLC.............................. E 828 389-8013
  Hayesville (G-7762)
◆ Draka Elevator Products Inc............. C 252 984-5100
  Rocky Mount (G-13690)
Fishel Steel Company.......................... G 336 788-2880
  Winston Salem (G-16712)
Granite Falls Furnaces LLC................. E 828 324-4394
  Granite Falls (G-6734)
Harrison Fence Inc............................... G 919 244-6908
  Apex (G-200)
▲ Haynes Wire Company...................... D 828 692-5791
  Mountain Home (G-11690)
◆ Insteel Wire Products Company........ C 336 719-9000
  Mount Airy (G-11521)
ISS.. G 919 317-8314
  Durham (G-5168)
Lee Spring Company LLC..................... E 336 275-3631
  Greensboro (G-7165)

33 PRIMARY METAL INDUSTRIES

Masonite Corporation .... B 704 599-0235
  Charlotte (G-3138)
Merchants Metals LLC .... D 704 878-8706
  Statesville (G-14841)
Rack Works Inc .... E 336 368-1302
  Pilot Mountain (G-12201)
◆ Sandvik Inc .... C 919 563-5008
  Mebane (G-10427)
Schafer Manufacturing Co LLC .... G 704 528-5321
  Troutman (G-15392)
Southern Steel and Wire Inc .... D 336 548-9611
  Madison (G-10087)
Specialty Nails Company .... G 336 883-0135
  High Point (G-8548)
▲ Torpedo Specialty Wire Inc .... D 252 977-3900
  Rocky Mount (G-13737)
Turner & Reeves Fence Co LLC .... G 910 671-8851
  Clayton (G-4020)
Van Blake Dixon .... F 336 282-1861
  Greensboro (G-7436)
▲ Williams Industries Inc .... C 919 604-1746
  Raleigh (G-13423)
▼ Wireway/Husky Corp .... C 704 483-1135
  Denver (G-4815)
Zndus Inc .... G 704 981-8660
  Statesville (G-14932)

3316 Cold finishing of steel shapes

▲ Manhattan Amrcn Terrazzo Strip .... C 336 622-4247
  Staley (G-14667)
◆ Sandvik Inc .... C 919 563-5008
  Mebane (G-10427)
Southern Metals Company .... E 704 394-3161
  Charlotte (G-3594)

3317 Steel pipe and tubes

▲ Alliance Hose & Tube Works Inc .... G 336 378-9736
  Greensboro (G-6793)
▲ Allrail Inc .... G 828 287-3747
  Rutherfordton (G-13861)
Appalachian Pipe Distrs LLC .... F 704 688-5703
  Charlotte (G-2202)
Blacksand Metal Works LLC .... F 703 489-8282
  Fayetteville (G-5771)
Border Concepts Inc .... C 336 248-2419
  Lexington (G-9686)
◆ Border Concepts Inc .... G 704 541-5509
  Charlotte (G-2335)
Buhlmann North America LP .... G 704 485-4144
  Oakboro (G-12068)
▲ East Coast Stl Fabrication Inc .... E 757 351-2601
  Hertford (G-7920)
▼ Fortiline LLC .... E 704 788-9800
  Concord (G-4266)
▲ Global Forming Tech Ltd .... G 919 234-1384
  Cary (G-1774)
▲ Heatmaster LLC .... E 919 639-4568
  Angier (G-140)
▼ Hlm Legacy Group Inc .... C 704 878-8423
  Troutman (G-15381)
Maysteel Porters LLC .... B 704 864-1313
  Gastonia (G-6459)
NC River Riders LLC .... G 336 244-6220
  Ronda (G-13766)
Piedmont Pipe Mfg LLC .... G 704 489-0911
  Denver (G-4793)
▲ Porters Group LLC .... B 704 864-1313
  Gastonia (G-6490)
Riley Power Group LLC .... C 910 420-6999
  Pinehurst (G-12234)
◆ Sandvik Inc .... C 919 563-5008
  Mebane (G-10427)

▲ Tricorn Usa Inc .... C 828 369-6682
  Franklin (G-6146)
Zekelman Industries Inc .... F 704 560-6768
  Mooresville (G-11139)

3321 Gray and ductile iron foundries

▲ ABT Foam Inc .... F 800 433-1119
  Statesville (G-14734)
◆ Charlotte Pipe and Foundry Co .... C 704 372-5030
  Charlotte (G-2457)
Ej Usa Inc .... G 919 362-7744
  Apex (G-188)
Florida Fire Supply .... E 336 885-5007
  Winston Salem (G-16714)
Humber Street Facility Inc .... E 919 775-3628
  Sanford (G-14135)
Modacam Incorporated .... G 704 489-8500
  Denver (G-4789)
Southern Cast Inc .... E 704 335-0692
  Charlotte (G-3590)
▲ Venture Products Intl Inc .... G 828 285-0495
  Asheville (G-814)

3324 Steel investment foundries

Cold Mountain Capital LLC .... F 828 210-8129
  Asheville (G-596)

3325 Steel foundries, nec

American Builders Anson Inc .... E 704 272-7655
  Polkton (G-12383)
Coder Foundry .... E 704 910-3077
  Charlotte (G-2521)
Harris Rebar Inc .... F 919 528-8333
  Benson (G-1037)
Norca Engineered Products LLC .... E 919 846-2010
  Raleigh (G-13067)
Nucor Corporation .... C 252 356-3700
  Cofield (G-4136)
▲ Rim-TEC Castings Eastern LLC .... E 336 302-0912
  Asheboro (G-473)
Seven Cast .... G 704 335-0692
  Charlotte (G-3532)

3331 Primary copper

◆ Imc-Metalsamerica LLC .... G 704 482-8200
  Shelby (G-14330)
Rfr Metal Fabrication Inc .... D 919 693-1354
  Oxford (G-12151)
▲ Stillwood Ammun Systems LLC .... G 919 721-9096
  Burlington (G-1502)

3334 Primary aluminum

◆ 3a Composites USA Inc .... C 704 872-8974
  Statesville (G-14732)
▲ AGM Carolina Inc .... G 336 431-4100
  High Point (G-8236)
Alcoa Power Generating Inc .... E 704 422-5691
  Badin (G-862)
Essex Group Inc .... G 704 921-9605
  Charlotte (G-2730)
Kymera International LLC .... F 919 544-8090
  Durham (G-5184)
Muriel Harris Investments Inc .... F 800 932-3191
  Fayetteville (G-5879)

3339 Primary nonferrous metals, nec

▲ Alloyworks LLC .... F 704 645-0511
  Salisbury (G-13920)
Cvmr (usa) Inc .... C 828 288-3768
  Union Mills (G-15440)
KS Precious Metals LLC .... G 910 687-0244
  Pinehurst (G-12226)

Metallix Refining Inc .... E 252 413-0346
  Greenville (G-7559)
▲ Metchem Inc .... G 910 944-1405
  Aberdeen (G-14)
Omega Precious Metals .... G 269 903-9330
  Youngsville (G-17089)
Parker-Hannifin Corporation .... G 704 662-3500
  Statesville (G-14856)
Sigma PM .... G 269 903-9330
  Youngsville (G-17096)
◆ Umicore USA Inc .... E 919 874-7171
  Raleigh (G-13379)

3341 Secondary nonferrous metals

◆ Elan Trading Inc .... C 704 342-1696
  Charlotte (G-2689)
Renew Recycling LLC .... D 919 550-8012
  Clayton (G-4007)
S Foil Incorporated .... F 704 455-5134
  Harrisburg (G-7725)

3351 Copper rolling and drawing

Essex Group Inc .... G 704 921-9605
  Charlotte (G-2730)
Hickory Wire Inc .... F 828 322-9473
  Hickory (G-8056)
▲ Manhattan Amrcn Terrazzo Strip .... C 336 622-4247
  Staley (G-14667)
▲ Torpedo Specialty Wire Inc .... D 252 977-3900
  Rocky Mount (G-13737)
▲ Wieland Copper Products LLC .... B 336 445-4500
  Pine Hall (G-12206)

3353 Aluminum sheet, plate, and foil

Alpha Aluminum LLC .... G 336 777-5658
  Winston Salem (G-16600)
▲ Aviation Metals NC Inc .... F 704 264-1647
  Charlotte (G-2246)
Bharat Forge Aluminum USA Inc .... C 585 576-7483
  Sanford (G-14093)
Central States Mfg Inc .... C 336 719-3280
  Mount Airy (G-11495)
Granges Americas Inc .... C 704 633-6020
  Salisbury (G-13973)
Howmet Aerospace Inc .... C 704 334-7276
  Charlotte (G-2926)
J&P Metal Arts Inc .... G 704 684-5140
  Monroe (G-10745)

3354 Aluminum extruded products

▲ Alfiniti Inc .... D 252 358-5811
  Winton (G-17020)
▲ Aviation Metals NC Inc .... F 704 264-1647
  Charlotte (G-2246)
◆ CCL Metal Science LLC .... D 910 299-0911
  Clinton (G-4090)
Container Products Corporation .... D 910 392-6100
  Wilmington (G-16179)
Hydro Extrusion Usa LLC .... D 336 227-8826
  Burlington (G-1433)
IPC Corporation .... F 704 821-7084
  Stallings (G-14671)
Metal Impact East LLC .... C 336 578-4515
  Graham (G-6702)
Owens Corning Sales LLC .... E 419 248-8000
  Roxboro (G-13814)
Pexco LLC .... D 336 493-7500
  Asheboro (G-461)
Seg Systems LLC .... F 704 579-5800
  Huntersville (G-8896)

3355 Aluminum rolling and drawing, nec

SIC SECTION

33 PRIMARY METAL INDUSTRIES

Design Specialties Inc........................... E 919 772-6955
   Raleigh *(G-12678)*

Mark Stoddard.. G 910 797-7214
   Fayetteville *(G-5866)*

◆ **Mitsubishi Chemical Amer Inc**............ D 980 580-2839
   Charlotte *(G-3188)*

Nkt Inc... G 919 601-1970
   Cary *(G-1832)*

Southwire Company LLC....................... F 704 379-9600
   Huntersville *(G-8898)*

Trimantec.. E 336 767-1379
   Winston Salem *(G-16952)*

3356 Nonferrous rolling and drawing, nec

Advanced Plating Technologies............. G 704 291-9325
   Monroe *(G-10637)*

Aseptia Inc.. C 678 373-6751
   Raleigh *(G-12528)*

ATI Allvac.. G 541 967-9000
   Monroe *(G-10657)*

▲ **Aviation Metals NC Inc**....................... F 704 264-1647
   Charlotte *(G-2246)*

Haynes International Inc....................... E 765 456-6000
   Mountain Home *(G-11689)*

Metal & Materials Proc LLC................... G 260 438-8901
   Aberdeen *(G-13)*

Metallix Refining Inc............................. E 252 413-0346
   Greenville *(G-7559)*

Mg12 LP.. G 828 440-1144
   Tryon *(G-15425)*

Peter J Hamann..................................... G 910 484-7877
   Fayetteville *(G-5897)*

Powerlab Inc.. E 336 650-0706
   Winston Salem *(G-16861)*

◆ **Sandvik Inc**.. C 919 563-5008
   Mebane *(G-10427)*

Southern Metals Company..................... E 704 394-3161
   Charlotte *(G-3594)*

▲ **Stainless & Nickel Alloys LLC**............. G 704 201-2898
   Charlotte *(G-3619)*

Tin Shed LLc.. G 919 928-0500
   Chapel Hill *(G-2079)*

▲ **Torpedo Specialty Wire Inc**................. D 252 977-3900
   Rocky Mount *(G-13737)*

Wanda Nickel.. G 828 265-3246
   Deep Gap *(G-4714)*

3357 Nonferrous wiredrawing and insulating

Abl Electronics Supply Inc.................... G 704 784-4225
   Concord *(G-4186)*

AFL Network Services Inc..................... E 704 289-5522
   Monroe *(G-10639)*

AFL Network Services Inc..................... E 919 658-2311
   Mount Olive *(G-11653)*

◆ **Arris Solutions LLC**............................ A 678 473-2000
   Hickory *(G-7943)*

Batt Fabricators Inc.............................. F 336 431-9334
   Trinity *(G-15339)*

C O Jelliff Corporation.......................... G 828 428-3672
   Maiden *(G-10100)*

CNA Technology LLC............................ G 954 312-1200
   Greenville *(G-7502)*

Coleman Cable LLC.............................. E 828 389-8013
   Hayesville *(G-7762)*

Commscope Inc North Carolina............ A 828 459-5000
   Claremont *(G-3910)*

◆ **Commscope Inc North Carolina**.......... D 828 324-2200
   Claremont *(G-3909)*

Commscope Technologies LLC............. A 828 324-2200
   Claremont *(G-3916)*

Commscope Technologies LLC............. F 919 934-9711
   Smithfield *(G-14457)*

◆ **Cordset Designs Inc**........................... E 252 568-4001
   Pink Hill *(G-12316)*

Corning Incorporated............................ D 704 569-6000
   Midland *(G-10464)*

Corning Incorporated............................ F 252 316-4500
   Tarboro *(G-15100)*

Corning Optcal Cmmncations LLC....... A 828 327-5290
   Hickory *(G-7996)*

Crww Specialty Composites Inc............ F 828 548-5002
   Claremont *(G-3917)*

▲ **Draka Communications Amer**............ B 828 459-8456
   Claremont *(G-3921)*

◆ **Draka Elevator Products Inc**.............. C 252 984-5100
   Rocky Mount *(G-13690)*

▲ **Draka Holdings Usa Inc**..................... A 828 383-0020
   Claremont *(G-3922)*

Draka Transport USA LLC..................... G 828 459-8895
   Claremont *(G-3923)*

Draka Usa Inc....................................... F 828 459-9787
   Claremont *(G-3924)*

Emtelle USA Inc.................................... E 828 707-9970
   Fletcher *(G-6000)*

Essex Group Inc................................... G 704 921-9605
   Charlotte *(G-2730)*

Frenzelit Inc.. E 336 814-4317
   Lexington *(G-9721)*

▲ **Huber + Suhner Inc**........................... E 704 790-7300
   Charlotte *(G-2928)*

▲ **Huber + Suhner North Amer Corp**...... D 704 790-7300
   Charlotte *(G-2929)*

Leviton Manufacturing Co Inc.............. E 828 584-1611
   Morganton *(G-11228)*

Ls Cable & System USA Inc................. C 252 824-3553
   Tarboro *(G-15112)*

Neptco Incorporated............................. C 828 728-5951
   Lenoir *(G-9639)*

◆ **Nexans USA Inc**................................. B 828 323-2660
   Hickory *(G-8102)*

Opticoncepts Inc................................... E 828 320-0138
   Hickory *(G-8108)*

Rave Networx Inc................................. G 910 808-9346
   Fuquay Varina *(G-6223)*

▼ **Sumitomo Elc Lightwave Corp**............ C 919 541-8100
   Raleigh *(G-13313)*

Superior Essex Inc................................ D 252 823-5111
   Tarboro *(G-15121)*

Superior Essex Intl LP.......................... C 252 823-5111
   Tarboro *(G-15122)*

Tensor Fiber Optics Tech..................... G 828 322-8224
   Hickory *(G-8178)*

Transcendent Technologies LLC........... G 704 334-1258
   Charlotte *(G-3717)*

Tyco Electronics Corporation................ G 717 986-5311
   Greensboro *(G-7423)*

▲ **Unitape (usa) Inc**............................... F 828 464-5695
   Conover *(G-4507)*

US Conec Ltd.. G 828 323-8883
   Hickory *(G-8197)*

US Conec Ltd.. D 828 323-8883
   Hickory *(G-8198)*

3363 Aluminum die-castings

Carolina Foundry Inc............................ F 704 376-3145
   Charlotte *(G-2396)*

Cascade Die Casting Group Inc............ C 336 882-0186
   High Point *(G-8289)*

Cs Alloys... G 704 675-5810
   Gastonia *(G-6389)*

▲ **Dynacast LLC**.................................... E 704 927-2790
   Charlotte *(G-2662)*

Dynacast International LLC.................. G 704 927-2790
   Charlotte *(G-2663)*

▲ **Ksm Castings USA Inc**...................... E 704 751-0559
   Shelby *(G-14335)*

Leggett & Platt Incorporated................ G 704 380-6208
   Statesville *(G-14835)*

Linamar Light Metal S-Mr LLC............. A 828 348-4010
   Mills River *(G-10506)*

RCM Industries Inc.............................. C 828 286-4003
   Rutherfordton *(G-13886)*

Sensus USA Inc.................................... C 919 576-6185
   Morrisville *(G-11426)*

◆ **Sensus USA Inc**................................. E 919 845-4000
   Morrisville *(G-11425)*

3364 Nonferrous die-castings except aluminum

Carolina Foundry Inc............................ F 704 376-3145
   Charlotte *(G-2396)*

Cascade Die Casting Group Inc............ C 336 882-0186
   High Point *(G-8289)*

◆ **Coats & Clark Inc**............................... D 704 542-5959
   Charlotte *(G-2512)*

▲ **Coats N Amer De Rpblica Dmncan**.... C 800 242-8095
   Charlotte *(G-2515)*

▲ **Dynacast LLC**.................................... E 704 927-2790
   Charlotte *(G-2662)*

Dynacast International LLC.................. G 704 927-2790
   Charlotte *(G-2663)*

Dynacast US Holdings Inc.................... E 704 927-2786
   Charlotte *(G-2664)*

Form Technologies Inc......................... E 704 927-2790
   Charlotte *(G-2788)*

Stratford Die Casting Inc..................... F 336 784-0100
   Winston Salem *(G-16919)*

3365 Aluminum foundries

Advanced Machine Services.................. G 910 410-0099
   Rockingham *(G-13617)*

◆ **Briggs-Shaffner Acquisition Co**.......... F 336 463-4272
   Yadkinville *(G-17034)*

Cascade Die Casting Group Inc............ C 336 882-0186
   High Point *(G-8289)*

CAT Logistics Inc................................. F 252 447-2490
   New Bern *(G-11787)*

Consolidated Metco Inc....................... F 704 289-6492
   Monroe *(G-10691)*

Consolidated Metco Inc....................... D 704 289-6491
   Monroe *(G-10692)*

▲ **Dynacast LLC**.................................... E 704 927-2790
   Charlotte *(G-2662)*

Maiden Casting Company..................... G 704 735-6812
   Maiden *(G-10112)*

RCM Industries Inc.............................. C 828 286-4003
   Rutherfordton *(G-13886)*

3366 Copper foundries

ABB Motors and Mechanical Inc........... C 828 645-1706
   Weaverville *(G-15836)*

Blue Ridge Propeller Repr LLC.............. G 276 340-1597
   Mc Leansville *(G-10384)*

Carolina Bronze Sculpture Inc.............. G 336 873-8291
   Seagrove *(G-14235)*

Foundry Commercial............................ F 704 348-6875
   Charlotte *(G-2792)*

▲ **Kayne & Son Custom Hdwr Inc**.......... G 828 665-1988
   Candler *(G-1585)*

Maiden Casting Company..................... G 704 735-6812
   Maiden *(G-10112)*

Matthews Industrial.............................. G 704 239-5925
   Spencer *(G-14601)*

▲ **Saueressig North America Inc**........... E 336 395-6200
   Burlington *(G-1491)*

33 PRIMARY METAL INDUSTRIES

Zwz Bearing USA Inc .... E 734 456-6206
  Lincolnton *(G-9937)*

3369 Nonferrous foundries, nec

Dynacast International LLC .... G 704 927-2790
  Charlotte *(G-2663)*
PCC Airfoils LLC .... B 919 774-4300
  Sanford *(G-14164)*
Rim-TEC Castings Eastern LLC .... G 336 302-0912
  Davidson *(G-4695)*
Tru-Cast Inc .... E 336 294-2370
  Greensboro *(G-7420)*
▲ United Brass Works Inc .... C 336 498-2661
  Randleman *(G-13494)*

3398 Metal heat treating

American Metallurgy Inc .... G 336 889-3277
  High Point *(G-8246)*
Atmo-TEC .... G 704 528-3935
  Troutman *(G-15367)*
Bodycote Thermal Proc Inc .... F 704 664-1808
  Mooresville *(G-10884)*
By-Design Black Oxide & TI LLC .... F 828 874-0610
  Valdese *(G-15443)*
East Crlina Metal Treating Inc .... E 919 834-2100
  Raleigh *(G-12716)*
Furnace Rebuilders Inc .... F 704 483-4025
  Denver *(G-4777)*
Hhh Tempering Resources Inc .... F 336 201-5396
  Winston Salem *(G-16745)*
▲ Industrial Prcess Slutions Inc .... G 336 926-1511
  Wilkesboro *(G-16025)*
J F Heat Treating Inc .... G 704 864-0998
  Gastonia *(G-6433)*
▲ M-B Industries Inc .... C 828 862-4201
  Rosman *(G-13786)*
Metal Improvement Company LLC ...... D 704 525-3818
  Charlotte *(G-3168)*
Metal Improvement Company LLC ...... G 414 536-1573
  Gastonia *(G-6461)*
National Peening Inc .... F 704 872-0113
  Statesville *(G-14850)*
▲ Powerlyte Paintball Game Pdts .... F 919 713-4317
  Raleigh *(G-13124)*
Thermal Metal Treating Inc .... E 910 944-3636
  Aberdeen *(G-32)*
Tuff Temp Corp .... F 252 398-3400
  Murfreesboro *(G-11703)*
United TI & Stamping Co NC Inc .... D 910 323-8588
  Fayetteville *(G-5939)*
Zion Industries Inc .... F 828 397-2701
  Hildebran *(G-8629)*

3399 Primary metal products

▲ Airspeed LLC .... E 919 644-1222
  Hillsborough *(G-8633)*
▲ Blue Ridge Metals Corporation .... C 828 687-2525
  Fletcher *(G-5989)*
Cross Technology Inc .... E 336 725-4700
  East Bend *(G-5465)*
Cryostop International .... G 910 452-5556
  Wilmington *(G-16191)*
D Block Metals LLC .... G 980 238-2600
  Lincolnton *(G-9889)*
▲ D Block Metals LLC .... F 704 705-5895
  Gastonia *(G-6393)*
Kendall E Krause .... G 910 690-4119
  Vass *(G-15492)*
Keystone Powdered Metal Co .... E 704 435-4036
  Cherryville *(G-3870)*
Kymera International LLC .... G 919 544-8090
  Durham *(G-5184)*

Metal Structures Plus LLC .... G 704 896-7155
  Mooresville *(G-11021)*
Morton Metalcraft Company N .... G 336 731-5700
  Welcome *(G-15873)*
NC Agriculture Teachers Assoc .... G 704 290-1513
  Monroe *(G-10778)*
Oerlikon Metco (us) Inc .... F 713 715-6300
  Huntersville *(G-8871)*
Piranha Nail and Staple Inc .... G 336 852-8358
  Greensboro *(G-7265)*
Quinn Powder Coating .... G 252 235-0200
  Middlesex *(G-10455)*
◆ SCM Metal Products Inc .... E 919 544-8090
  Durham *(G-5345)*
Timothy W Gillespie .... G 919 567-2687
  Holly Springs *(G-8721)*
Wurth Revcar Fasteners Inc .... E 919 772-9930
  Garner *(G-6327)*

34 FABRICATED METAL PRODUCTS

3411 Metal cans

Ball Metal Beverage Cont Corp .... C 336 342-4711
  Reidsville *(G-13507)*
Container Products Corporation .... D 910 392-6100
  Wilmington *(G-16179)*
▼ Fleetgenius of Nc Inc .... C 828 726-3001
  Lenoir *(G-9612)*
Leisure Craft Holdings LLC .... D 828 693-8241
  Flat Rock *(G-5967)*
Leisure Craft Inc .... C 828 693-8241
  Flat Rock *(G-5968)*
Tin Can Ventures LLC .... E 919 732-9078
  Cedar Grove *(G-1973)*
Tin Cans LLC .... F 910 322-2626
  Lillington *(G-9861)*
Trivium Packaging USA Inc .... B 336 785-8500
  Winston Salem *(G-16953)*
Waste Container Services LLC .... G 910 257-4474
  Fayetteville *(G-5950)*

3412 Metal barrels, drums, and pails

General Steel Drum LLC .... F 704 525-7160
  Charlotte *(G-2818)*
Greif Inc .... D 704 588-3895
  Charlotte *(G-2867)*
▲ Inter-Continental Corporation .... D 828 464-8250
  Newton *(G-11945)*
Lee County Industries Inc .... E 919 775-3439
  Sanford *(G-14148)*
Mauser Usa LLC .... E 704 398-2325
  Charlotte *(G-3144)*
Mauser Usa LLC .... C 704 625-0737
  Charlotte *(G-3145)*
Mauser Usa LLC .... D 704 455-2111
  Harrisburg *(G-7718)*
South Boulevard Associates Inc .... D 704 525-7160
  Charlotte *(G-3584)*
◆ Toter LLC .... D 800 424-0422
  Statesville *(G-14916)*
Waste Container Services LLC .... G 910 257-4474
  Fayetteville *(G-5950)*

3421 Cutlery

Bic Corporation .... D 704 598-7700
  Charlotte *(G-2308)*
Butchers Best Inc .... G 252 533-0961
  Roanoke Rapids *(G-13569)*
Cakerator Inc .... G 919 270-5899
  Raleigh *(G-12585)*

Daniel Winkler Knifemaker LLC .... G 828 262-3691
  Boone *(G-1192)*
Edge-Works Manufacturing Co .... G 910 455-9834
  Burgaw *(G-1339)*
Edgewell Per Care Brands LLC .... E 336 672-4500
  Asheboro *(G-425)*
Edgewell Per Care Brands LLC .... G 336 629-1581
  Asheboro *(G-426)*
Edgewell Per Care Brands LLC .... E 336 672-4500
  Asheboro *(G-427)*
▲ Forveson Corp .... G 336 292-6237
  Greensboro *(G-7019)*
◆ Fred Marvin and Associates Inc .... G 330 784-9211
  Greensboro *(G-7021)*
Generations L LLC .... G 336 835-3095
  Jonesville *(G-9097)*
Hao WEI Lai Inc .... G 336 789-9969
  Mount Airy *(G-11516)*
Heal .... G 828 287-8787
  Rutherfordton *(G-13878)*
◆ Irwin Industrial Tool Company .... C 704 987-4555
  Huntersville *(G-8838)*
▲ J Culpepper & Co .... G 828 524-6842
  Otto *(G-12118)*
Kotohira .... G 336 667-0150
  Wilkesboro *(G-16036)*
L Michelle LLC .... G 980 946-0204
  Mooresville *(G-11002)*
Mother of Pearl Co Inc .... G 828 524-6842
  Franklin *(G-6140)*
Pineland Cutlery Inc .... G 910 757-0035
  Southern Pines *(G-14548)*
Procter & Gamble Mfg Co .... D 336 954-0000
  Greensboro *(G-7287)*
Singsa .... G 336 882-9160
  High Point *(G-8533)*
Spartan Blades LLC .... G 910 757-0035
  Southern Pines *(G-14556)*
Stacks Kitchen Matthews .... E 704 243-2024
  Waxhaw *(G-15777)*
Sugar Pops .... G 704 799-0959
  Mooresville *(G-11107)*
Sweet Sanctions LLC .... F 717 222-1859
  Hampstead *(G-7657)*
Sword Conservatory Inc .... G 919 557-4465
  Holly Springs *(G-8720)*

3423 Hand and edge tools, nec

Allegion Access Tech LLC .... E 704 789-7000
  Concord *(G-4191)*
Apex Tool Group LLC .... D 410 773-7800
  Huntersville *(G-8792)*
▲ Asheville Bit & Steel Company .... F 828 274-3766
  Asheville *(G-531)*
Belkoz Inc .... G 919 703-0694
  Raleigh *(G-12551)*
Chester Lewis Newsome .... G 919 605-4887
  Greenville *(G-7501)*
Cleaver Returns Inc .... G 630 508-8062
  Fuquay Varina *(G-6189)*
Coconut Paradise Inc .... G 704 662-3443
  Mooresville *(G-10908)*
Contemporary Products Inc .... G 919 779-4228
  Garner *(G-6268)*
▲ Council Tool Company Inc .... E 910 646-3011
  Lake Waccamaw *(G-9448)*
DCS USA Corporation .... G 919 535-8000
  Morrisville *(G-11329)*
Equipment & Supply Inc .... E 704 289-6565
  Monroe *(G-10716)*
Everkem Diversified Pdts Inc .... F 336 661-7801
  Winston Salem *(G-16701)*

SIC SECTION
34 FABRICATED METAL PRODUCTS

Fiskars Brands Inc .... E 336 292-6237
  Greensboro *(G-7016)*

▲ Great Star Industrial Usa LLC .... G 704 892-4965
  Huntersville *(G-8827)*

◆ Greenworks North America LLC .... D 704 658-0539
  Mooresville *(G-10965)*

Hamilton Indus Grinding Inc .... E 828 253-6796
  Asheville *(G-647)*

Hayward Industries Inc .... C 336 712-9900
  Clemmons *(G-4043)*

◆ Hayward Industries Inc .... B 908 351-5400
  Charlotte *(G-2894)*

▲ Horizon Tool Inc .... C 336 299-4182
  Greensboro *(G-7101)*

Irwin .... G 704 987-4339
  Huntersville *(G-8837)*

◆ Irwin Industrial Tool Company .... C 704 987-4555
  Huntersville *(G-8838)*

Lidseen North Carolina Inc .... G 828 389-8082
  Hayesville *(G-7768)*

▲ Marbach America Inc .... E 704 644-4900
  Charlotte *(G-3124)*

Masonite Corporation .... B 704 599-0235
  Charlotte *(G-3138)*

▲ McKenzie Sports Products LLC .... C 704 279-7985
  Salisbury *(G-14011)*

Microtech Knives Inc .... D 828 684-4355
  Mills River *(G-10508)*

Mil3 Inc .... F 919 362-1217
  Apex *(G-219)*

Peco Inc .... E 828 684-1234
  Arden *(G-362)*

Precision Part Systems Wnstn-S .... E 336 723-5210
  Winston Salem *(G-16864)*

Robert Bosch Tool Corporation .... F 252 551-7512
  Greenville *(G-7580)*

Rush Masonry Management LLC .... G 910 787-9100
  Jacksonville *(G-9026)*

S Duff Fabricating Inc .... G 910 298-3060
  Beulaville *(G-1098)*

Shira Forge .... G 828 226-5687
  Sylva *(G-15067)*

Trane Technologies Company LLC .... C 910 692-8700
  Southern Pines *(G-14558)*

▲ United Southern Industries Inc .... D 866 273-1810
  Forest City *(G-6085)*

USA Made Blade .... G 704 798-6478
  Salisbury *(G-14060)*

3425 Saw blades and handsaws

Byrnes Enterprises .... G 919 876-3223
  Raleigh *(G-12581)*

▲ Grasche USA Inc .... E 828 322-1226
  Hickory *(G-8034)*

Leitz Tooling Systems LP .... G 336 861-3367
  Archdale *(G-292)*

Precision Saw Works Inc .... E 704 272-8326
  Polkton *(G-12389)*

Quality Saw Shop Inc .... G 336 882-1722
  High Point *(G-8503)*

▲ Raleigh Saw Co Inc .... G 919 832-2248
  Raleigh *(G-13184)*

Robert Bosch Tool Corporation .... E 704 735-7464
  Lincolnton *(G-9915)*

▲ Union Grove Saw & Knife Inc .... D 704 539-4442
  Union Grove *(G-15438)*

3429 Hardware, nec

Absolute Security & Lock Inc .... G 336 322-4598
  Roxboro *(G-13792)*

◆ Ace Marine Rigging & Supply Inc .... F 252 726-6620
  Morehead City *(G-11148)*

▲ Acme Rental Company .... F 704 873-3731
  Statesville *(G-14740)*

▲ ACS Advnced Clor Solutions Inc .... G 252 442-0098
  Rocky Mount *(G-13679)*

Alloy Fabricators Inc .... E 704 263-2281
  Alexis *(G-121)*

▲ Amerock LLC .... F 800 435-6959
  Huntersville *(G-8791)*

◆ Amesbury Acqstion Hldngs 2 Inc .... C 704 924-8586
  Statesville *(G-14747)*

Amesbury Group Inc .... E 704 924-7694
  Statesville *(G-14749)*

Apex Industrial Group LLC .... G 919 578-9039
  Sanford *(G-14086)*

▲ Appalachian Technology LLC .... E 828 210-8888
  Asheville *(G-524)*

▲ Appalchian Stove Fbrcators Inc .... F 828 253-0164
  Asheville *(G-525)*

◆ Assa Abloy ACC Door Cntrls Gro .... C 877 974-2255
  Monroe *(G-10653)*

Assa Abloy Accessories and .... B 704 233-4011
  Monroe *(G-10654)*

▲ Avanti Hearth Products LLC .... G 704 866-4342
  Belmont *(G-975)*

◆ Balcrank Corporation .... E 800 747-5300
  Weaverville *(G-15838)*

Belwith Products LLC .... G 336 841-3899
  High Point *(G-8270)*

Blue Ridge Global Inc .... G 828 252-5225
  Asheville *(G-565)*

Blum Inc .... G 919 345-6214
  Oak Ridge *(G-12058)*

◆ Blum Inc .... B 704 827-1345
  Stanley *(G-14687)*

Buie Manufacturing Company .... E 910 610-3504
  Laurinburg *(G-9470)*

Cabinet Solutions Usa Inc .... E 828 358-2349
  Hickory *(G-7959)*

▲ Carolina North Mfg Inc .... G 336 992-0082
  Kernersville *(G-9173)*

CSC Family Holdings Inc .... G 336 993-2680
  Colfax *(G-4147)*

▲ Custom Industries Inc .... E 336 299-2885
  Greensboro *(G-6950)*

Custom Seatings .... G 828 879-1964
  Valdese *(G-15447)*

Division 10 .... G 919 661-1101
  Raleigh *(G-12689)*

Division Eight Inc .... F 336 852-1275
  Greensboro *(G-6973)*

Easykeyscom Inc .... F 877 839-5397
  Charlotte *(G-2678)*

Endura Products LLC .... F 336 991-8818
  High Point *(G-8343)*

▲ Endura Products LLC .... B 336 668-2472
  Colfax *(G-4149)*

▼ Fireresq Incorporated .... F 888 975-0858
  Mooresville *(G-10945)*

Fix-A-Latch Usa LLC .... E 435 901-4146
  Chapel Hill *(G-2020)*

Fix-A-Latch Usa LLC .... G 435 901-4146
  Chapel Hill *(G-2019)*

Fortress International Corp NC .... G 336 645-9365
  Conover *(G-4456)*

◆ Grass America Inc .... C 336 996-4041
  Kernersville *(G-9203)*

Hardware Ventures Inc .... G 919 818-9039
  Clayton *(G-3986)*

Hearth & Home Technologies LLC .... C 336 274-1663
  Greensboro *(G-7082)*

▲ Hickory Springs California LLC .... A 828 328-2201
  Hickory *(G-8051)*

Hickory Springs Mfg Co .... D 828 328-2201
  Hickory *(G-8054)*

▲ Ilco Unican Holding Corp .... D 252 446-3321
  Rocky Mount *(G-13703)*

◆ Imperial Usa Ltd .... E 704 596-2444
  Charlotte *(G-2954)*

Industrial Metal Products of .... F 910 944-8110
  Aberdeen *(G-7)*

Ingersoll-Rand Indus US Inc .... D 704 896-4000
  Davidson *(G-4680)*

Jacob Holtz Company .... E 828 328-1003
  Hickory *(G-8070)*

Jtec Radiowave .... G 704 799-1658
  Mooresville *(G-10991)*

Kaba Ilco Corp .... B 336 725-1331
  Winston Salem *(G-16775)*

◆ Kaba Ilco Corp .... A 252 446-3321
  Rocky Mount *(G-13704)*

Kdy Automation Solutions Inc .... G 888 219-0049
  Morrisville *(G-11364)*

Kearfott Corporation .... B 828 350-5300
  Black Mountain *(G-1127)*

▲ Ketchie-Houston Inc .... E 704 786-5101
  Concord *(G-4300)*

Kitchen Bath Gllries N Hlls LL .... G 919 600-6200
  Raleigh *(G-12942)*

▲ Marcon International Inc .... E 704 455-9400
  Harrisburg *(G-7717)*

Marine Tooling Technology Inc .... G 336 887-9577
  High Point *(G-8439)*

Masonite Corporation .... B 704 599-0235
  Charlotte *(G-3138)*

▼ Mepla-Alfit Incorporated .... E 336 289-2300
  Kernersville *(G-9215)*

◆ Norton Door Controls .... E 704 233-4011
  Monroe *(G-10781)*

Nova Mobility Systems Inc .... G 800 797-9861
  Charlotte *(G-3272)*

Nuclamp System LLC .... G 336 643-1766
  Oak Ridge *(G-12061)*

Oak City Metal LLC .... G 919 375-4535
  Zebulon *(G-17138)*

Omnia Industries LLC .... G 704 707-6062
  Matthews *(G-10278)*

Parker-Hannifin Corporation .... G 704 664-1922
  Mooresville *(G-11047)*

Penn Engineering & Mfg Corp .... C 336 631-8741
  Winston Salem *(G-16839)*

▲ Perrycraft Inc .... F 336 372-2545
  Sparta *(G-14598)*

Restoration Hardware Inc .... F 919 544-4196
  Durham *(G-5329)*

Rize LLC .... G 910 487-9759
  Fayetteville *(G-5907)*

Royal Brass & Hose .... F 704 847-2156
  Charlotte *(G-3462)*

Seac Banche Usa Inc .... G 919 360-6442
  Chapel Hill *(G-2068)*

▲ Sentinel Door Controls LLC .... F 704 921-4627
  Charlotte *(G-3528)*

Sikorsky Aircraft Corporation .... G 252 447-5050
  New Bern *(G-11846)*

Skinner Company .... G 336 580-4716
  Greensboro *(G-7343)*

Stanley Black & Decker Inc .... G 704 509-0844
  Charlotte *(G-3621)*

Stephen P Wolfe .... G 252 792-3001
  Jamesville *(G-9082)*

Success In Marketplace LLC .... G 919 608-1259
  Raleigh *(G-13311)*

Sun Path Products Inc .... D 910 875-9002
  Raeford *(G-12442)*

34 FABRICATED METAL PRODUCTS

Sunray Inc .... E 828 287-7030
   Rutherfordton *(G-13892)*

Telecmmnctons Resource MGT Inc .... F 919 779-0776
   Raleigh *(G-13336)*

Triangle Biosystems Inc .... F 919 361-2663
   Durham *(G-5405)*

◆ Ultra-Mek Inc .... D 336 859-4552
   Denton *(G-4754)*

Village Produce & Cntry Str In .... G 336 661-8685
   Winston Salem *(G-16962)*

Volvo Group North America LLC .... A 731 968-0151
   Greensboro *(G-7448)*

WaveTherm Corporation .... E 919 307-8071
   Raleigh *(G-13415)*

Wilmington Rbr & Gasket Co Inc .... F 910 762-4262
   Wilmington *(G-16450)*

▲ Winterville Machine Works Inc .... D 252 756-2130
   Winterville *(G-17018)*

◆ Woodlane Envmtl Tech Inc .... E 828 894-8383
   Columbus *(G-4182)*

X-Jet Technologies Inc .... G 800 983-7467
   Raleigh *(G-13429)*

3431 Metal sanitary ware

Americh Corporation .... D 704 588-3075
   Charlotte *(G-2188)*

Capital Marble Creations Inc .... F 910 893-2462
   Lillington *(G-9845)*

Carolina Shower Door Inc .... G 910 343-0009
   Wilmington *(G-16158)*

Comer Sanitary Service Inc .... F 336 629-8311
   Lexington *(G-9697)*

Croscill Home LLC .... C 919 735-7111
   Oxford *(G-12124)*

Custom Marble Corporation .... G 910 215-0679
   Pinehurst *(G-12219)*

Elkay Ohio Plumbing Pdts Co .... A 910 739-8181
   Lumberton *(G-10034)*

▲ Grancreations Inc .... G 704 332-7625
   Charlotte *(G-2852)*

Metalfab of North Carolina LLC .... C 704 841-1090
   Matthews *(G-10271)*

Readilite & Barricade Inc .... F 919 231-8309
   Raleigh *(G-13194)*

▲ Select Stainless Products LLC .... E 888 843-2345
   Charlotte *(G-3524)*

◆ Thompson Traders Inc .... F 336 272-3003
   Greensboro *(G-7402)*

Tubs-Usa LLC .... F 336 884-5737
   High Point *(G-8580)*

3432 Plumbing fixture fittings and trim

American Backflow Technologies .... G 252 714-8378
   Greenville *(G-7480)*

B & B Building Maintenance LLC .... G 910 494-2715
   Bunnlevel *(G-1329)*

Brasscraft Manufacturing Co .... F 336 475-2131
   Thomasville *(G-15190)*

Clearwater Services LLC .... G 704 995-9260
   Concord *(G-4233)*

Enviro-Companies LLC .... G 919 758-6246
   Raleigh *(G-12741)*

▼ Flologic Inc .... G 919 878-1808
   Morrisville *(G-11342)*

Gods Son Plumbing Inc .... G 252 299-0983
   Wilson *(G-16501)*

H & H Representatives Inc .... G 704 596-6950
   Charlotte *(G-2877)*

▲ Key Gas Components Inc .... E 828 655-1700
   Marion *(G-10156)*

Masco Corporation .... G 704 658-9646
   Mooresville *(G-11015)*

Piedmont Well Covers Inc .... F 704 664-8488
   Mount Ulla *(G-11685)*

Romac Industries Inc .... D 704 915-3317
   Dallas *(G-4656)*

Royal Baths Manufacturing Co .... E 704 837-1701
   Charlotte *(G-3461)*

SL Liquidation LLC .... B 910 353-3666
   Jacksonville *(G-9033)*

Union Plastics Company .... G 704 624-2112
   Marshville *(G-10226)*

Victaulic Company .... E 910 371-5588
   Leland *(G-9564)*

◆ Watts Drainage Products Inc .... F 828 288-2179
   Spindale *(G-14609)*

3433 Heating equipment, except electric

▲ Appalchian Stove Fbrcators Inc .... F 828 253-0164
   Asheville *(G-525)*

DCE Solar Service Inc .... G 704 659-7474
   Cornelius *(G-4539)*

Dna Services Inc .... G 910 279-2775
   Kure Beach *(G-9437)*

Edco Products Inc .... E 828 264-1490
   Boone *(G-1197)*

Entropy Solar Integrators LLC .... G 704 936-5018
   Charlotte *(G-2716)*

◆ Flynn Burner Corporation .... E 704 660-1500
   Mooresville *(G-10947)*

◆ Gas-Fired Products Inc .... E 704 372-3485
   Charlotte *(G-2809)*

Green Quest Inc .... G 828 464-7336
   Newton *(G-11938)*

Hearth & Home Technologies LLC .... C 336 274-1663
   Greensboro *(G-7082)*

Heat Transfer Sales LLC .... E 800 842-3328
   Greensboro *(G-7083)*

Heat Transfer Sales LLC .... F 336 292-8777
   Greensboro *(G-7084)*

Heat Transfer Sales of Th .... E 336 294-3838
   Greensboro *(G-7085)*

Hicks Wterstoves Solar Systems .... F 336 789-4977
   Mount Airy *(G-11518)*

Low Impact Tech USA Inc .... G 828 428-6310
   Fletcher *(G-6019)*

Machining Technology Services .... G 704 282-1071
   Monroe *(G-10763)*

▲ Marley Company LLC .... C 704 752-4400
   Charlotte *(G-3128)*

Marley-Wylain Company .... C 336 627-6000
   Eden *(G-5497)*

Romac Industries Inc .... D 704 915-3317
   Dallas *(G-4656)*

▲ Smg Hearth and Home LLC .... F 919 973-4079
   Morrisville *(G-11430)*

Snap Rite Manufacturing Inc .... E 910 897-4080
   Coats *(G-4134)*

Solar Connection LLC .... G 828 484-9163
   Marion *(G-10178)*

Solar Hot Limited .... G 919 439-2387
   Raleigh *(G-13276)*

▲ Solarh2ot Ltd .... G 919 439-2387
   Raleigh *(G-13279)*

Sunqest Inc .... G 828 325-4910
   Newton *(G-11975)*

Sunstar Heating Products Inc .... E 704 372-3486
   Charlotte *(G-3654)*

Taylor Manufacturing Inc .... E 910 862-2576
   Elizabethtown *(G-5605)*

Thermo Products LLC .... E 800 348-5130
   Denton *(G-4752)*

3441 Fabricated structural metal

48 Customs Inc .... F 336 403-0731
   Mocksville *(G-10550)*

Accel Wldg & Fabrication LLC .... G 980 722-7198
   Stanley *(G-14683)*

Accelerated Media Technologies .... G 336 599-2070
   Roxboro *(G-13793)*

Ace Fabrication Inc .... F 919 934-3251
   Smithfield *(G-14448)*

Alamance Steel Fabricators .... G 336 887-3015
   High Point *(G-8238)*

▼ Alamo Distribution LLC .... C 704 398-5600
   Belmont *(G-974)*

Alco Metal Fabricators Inc .... F 704 739-1168
   Kings Mountain *(G-9292)*

Alliance Mch & Fabrication LLC .... G 704 629-5677
   Gastonia *(G-6340)*

American Trutzschler Inc .... E 704 399-4521
   Charlotte *(G-2186)*

Amt/Bcu Inc .... E 336 622-6200
   Liberty *(G-9807)*

Anthony Fabrication .... G 704 658-1519
   Mooresville *(G-10861)*

Ark Inc .... G 919 841-3637
   Raleigh *(G-12523)*

ARS Extreme Construction Inc .... E 919 331-8024
   Angier *(G-131)*

Ascending Iron LLC .... F 336 266-6462
   Whitsett *(G-15982)*

Asheville Maintenance and .... E 828 687-8110
   Arden *(G-312)*

Ashley Welding & Machine Co .... F 252 482-3321
   Edenton *(G-5507)*

Atwell Fabrication LLC .... G 704 763-9792
   Concord *(G-4201)*

▲ Babington Technology LLC .... E 252 984-0349
   Rocky Mount *(G-13682)*

Bakers Stnless Fabrication Inc .... G 919 934-2707
   Smithfield *(G-14450)*

Bartimaeus By Design Inc .... C 336 475-4346
   Thomasville *(G-15188)*

BB Metals Inc .... G 336 345-3430
   Lexington *(G-9684)*

Bear Creek Fabrication LLC .... F 919 837-2444
   Bear Creek *(G-936)*

Best Choice Met Structures LLC .... F 877 683-1168
   Elkin *(G-5611)*

Bet-Mac Wilson Steel Inc .... G 919 528-1540
   Creedmoor *(G-4606)*

Bg-Cnc .... G 336 596-3400
   Winston Salem *(G-16629)*

Biffle Steel Services LLC .... G 704 626-0909
   Mooresville *(G-10880)*

Bill S Iron Shop Inc .... G 919 596-8360
   Durham *(G-4956)*

Blacksand Metal Works LLC .... F 703 489-8282
   Fayetteville *(G-5771)*

◆ BMA America Inc .... F 970 353-3770
   Charlotte *(G-2326)*

◆ Bob Barker Company Inc .... C 800 334-9880
   Fuquay Varina *(G-6184)*

Bondo Innovations LLC .... G 704 888-9910
   Stanfield *(G-14676)*

Border Concepts Inc .... G 336 248-2419
   Lexington *(G-9686)*

BP Associates Inc .... C 704 833-1494
   Gastonia *(G-6359)*

◆ BP Associates Inc .... C 704 864-3032
   Gastonia *(G-6358)*

Bulldurhamfabrications Com .... G 919 479-1919
   Durham *(G-4991)*

Burkett Welding Services Inc .... F 252 635-2814
   New Bern *(G-11782)*

34 FABRICATED METAL PRODUCTS

Burton Steel Company .... F 910 675-9241
  Castle Hayne *(G-1944)*
Capitol Funds Inc .... D 704 482-0645
  Shelby *(G-14292)*
▲ Cardinal Metalworks LLC .... D 910 259-9990
  Burgaw *(G-1335)*
Carolina Custom Towers LLC .... G 252 671-3779
  Morehead City *(G-11158)*
Carolina Duct Fabrication Inc .... G 252 478-9955
  Spring Hope *(G-14616)*
Carolina Fab Inc .... F 704 820-8694
  Mount Holly *(G-11624)*
Carolina Fabricators LLC .... F 919 510-8410
  Raleigh *(G-12597)*
Carolina Machining Fabrication .... G 919 554-9700
  Youngsville *(G-17075)*
Chatsworth Products Inc .... C 252 514-2779
  New Bern *(G-11788)*
City Machine Company Inc .... E 828 754-9661
  Lenoir *(G-9599)*
Cives Corp .... G 919 518-2140
  Raleigh *(G-12624)*
Clothes Cleaning System LLC .... G 252 243-3752
  Wilson *(G-16488)*
▲ CMC Rebar .... G 704 865-8571
  Gastonia *(G-6379)*
Cmw Manufacturing LLC .... E 704 216-0171
  Salisbury *(G-13943)*
Coastal Fabrica Tion .... G 910 399-4460
  Wilmington *(G-16171)*
Cochrane Steel Industries Inc .... F 704 291-9330
  Monroe *(G-10686)*
Colliers Welding LLC .... G 910 818-5728
  Fayetteville *(G-5793)*
Collins Fabrication & Wldg LLC .... G 704 861-9326
  Gastonia *(G-6380)*
Columbus Industries LLC .... E 910 872-1625
  Bladenboro *(G-1146)*
Comfort Engineers Inc .... E 919 383-0158
  Durham *(G-5027)*
Commercial Fabricators Inc .... E 828 465-1010
  Newton *(G-11921)*
Commercial Metals Company .... E 704 375-5937
  Charlotte *(G-2528)*
Commercial Metals Company .... E 704 399-9020
  Charlotte *(G-2529)*
▲ Common Part Groupings LLC .... F 704 948-0097
  Huntersville *(G-8805)*
Concept Frames Inc .... D 828 465-2015
  Newton *(G-11924)*
Concept Steel Inc .... E 704 874-0414
  Gastonia *(G-6382)*
Confab Manufacturing Co LLC .... E 704 366-7140
  Charlotte *(G-2539)*
Conover Metal Products Inc .... E 828 464-9414
  Conover *(G-4439)*
Cooper B-Line Inc .... C 704 522-6272
  Charlotte *(G-2549)*
CP Components LLC .... G 330 715-1837
  Mooresville *(G-10916)*
Cricket Forge LLC .... G 919 680-3513
  Durham *(G-5036)*
CSC Family Holdings Inc .... G 336 993-2680
  Colfax *(G-4147)*
CSC Family Holdings Inc .... G 252 459-7416
  Nashville *(G-11743)*
CSC Family Holdings Inc .... E 336 275-9711
  Greensboro *(G-6945)*
▲ Custom Enterprises Inc .... G 336 226-8296
  Burlington *(G-1405)*
Custom Steel Incorporated .... G 919 383-9170
  Durham *(G-5042)*

Custom Steel Fabricators Inc .... E 336 498-5099
  Randleman *(G-13461)*
Cutworm Specialties Inc .... G 828 389-1999
  Hayesville *(G-7765)*
CWC Fabricating .... G 704 360-8264
  Mount Ulla *(G-11682)*
D M F Incorporated .... G 919 553-5191
  Clayton *(G-3971)*
Daltons Metal Works Inc .... G 336 731-1442
  Winston Salem *(G-16670)*
Dave Steel Company Inc .... F 828 252-2771
  Asheville *(G-603)*
Dave Steel Company Inc .... D 828 252-2771
  Asheville *(G-604)*
Davidson Steel Services LLC .... G 336 775-1234
  Winston Salem *(G-16671)*
Davis Steel and Iron Co Inc .... E 704 821-7676
  Matthews *(G-10311)*
Detmer Metals LLC .... G 704 997-6114
  Mooresville *(G-10929)*
Diamondback Industries LLC .... E 336 956-8871
  Lexington *(G-9707)*
Directus Holdings LLC .... G 919 510-8410
  Raleigh *(G-12686)*
Division 5 LLC .... C 336 725-0521
  Winston Salem *(G-16682)*
Dunavants Welding & Steel Inc .... G 252 338-6533
  Camden *(G-1557)*
Dwiggins Metal Masters Inc .... G 336 751-2379
  Mocksville *(G-10568)*
East Coast Fab LLC .... F 336 285-7444
  Randleman *(G-13468)*
▲ East Coast Stl Fabrication Inc .... E 757 351-2601
  Hertford *(G-7920)*
Edwards Unlimited Inc .... G 252 226-4583
  Henderson *(G-7782)*
Engineered Steel Products LLC .... E 336 495-5266
  Sophia *(G-14515)*
Engineered Steel Products Inc .... E 336 495-5266
  Sophia *(G-14516)*
▲ Equipment Dsign Fbrication Inc .... G 704 372-4513
  Gastonia *(G-6401)*
◆ Evans Machinery Inc .... D 252 243-4006
  Wilson *(G-16498)*
Ever Glo Sign Co Inc .... G 704 633-3324
  Salisbury *(G-13959)*
Everettes Industrial Repr Svc .... F 252 527-4269
  Goldsboro *(G-6613)*
Exterior Vinyl Wholesale .... G 336 838-7772
  Wilkesboro *(G-16020)*
Fab Designs Incorporated .... G 704 636-2349
  Salisbury *(G-13961)*
Fabco Industries .... G 919 481-3010
  Cary *(G-1765)*
Fabricated Solutions LLC .... G 704 982-7789
  Albemarle *(G-84)*
Fabrication Associates Inc .... D 704 535-8050
  Charlotte *(G-2742)*
Fabrication Automation LLC .... G 704 785-2120
  Concord *(G-4261)*
Fabricted Parts Assemblies LLC .... G 704 784-3376
  Concord *(G-4262)*
Fabrineering LLC .... G 704 999-9906
  Mooresville *(G-10941)*
Fabrineering LLC .... G 704 661-4877
  Mooresville *(G-10942)*
Farris Fab & Machine Inc .... G 704 629-4879
  Bessemer City *(G-1065)*
Farris Fab & Machine Inc .... C 704 629-4879
  Bessemer City *(G-1066)*
▲ Farris Fab & Machine Inc .... D 704 629-4879
  Cherryville *(G-3868)*

Fe26 LLC .... G 980 875-0170
  Charlotte *(G-2750)*
▲ Ferrofab Inc .... E 910 557-5624
  Hamlet *(G-7621)*
Forma-Fab Metals Inc .... E 919 563-5630
  Mebane *(G-10409)*
Freedom Metals Inc .... F 704 333-1214
  Charlotte *(G-2794)*
Fuller Wldg & Fabricators Inc .... E 336 751-3712
  Mocksville *(G-10573)*
Gb Industries .... G 828 692-9163
  East Flat Rock *(G-5475)*
Gerdau Ameristeel US Inc .... E 919 833-9737
  Raleigh *(G-12798)*
Glovers Welding LLC .... F 252 586-7692
  Littleton *(G-9952)*
Gore S Mar Met Fabrication Inc .... G 910 763-6066
  Wilmington *(G-16237)*
GP Fabrication Inc .... E 336 361-0410
  Reidsville *(G-13521)*
H T Wade Enterprises Inc .... F 336 375-8900
  Browns Summit *(G-1307)*
Ham Brothers Inc .... F 704 827-1303
  Gastonia *(G-6412)*
Harris Rebar Inc .... F 919 528-8333
  Benson *(G-1037)*
Heat Transfer Sales of Th .... E 336 294-3838
  Greensboro *(G-7085)*
Heavy Metal Supply .... G 919 625-3508
  Raleigh *(G-12835)*
Heavy Metal Supply LLC .... G 919 625-3508
  Cary *(G-1782)*
Hercules Steel Company Inc .... E 910 488-5110
  Fayetteville *(G-5837)*
Heyel Custom Metal .... G 919 957-8442
  Raleigh *(G-12840)*
Heyel Custom Metal Inc .... G 919 957-8442
  Raleigh *(G-12841)*
Hicks Wterstoves Solar Systems .... F 336 789-4977
  Mount Airy *(G-11518)*
High-Tech Fabrications Inc .... F 336 871-2990
  Lawsonville *(G-9503)*
Hirschfeld Industries Brdg LLC .... A 336 271-8252
  Greensboro *(G-7093)*
Hovis Metal Fabricating Inc .... F 704 922-5293
  Dallas *(G-4644)*
Howard Steel Inc .... F 704 376-9631
  Charlotte *(G-2925)*
Hubbard Iron Inc .... G 828 776-7168
  Gastonia *(G-6420)*
Hughes Metal Works LLC .... E 336 297-0808
  Greensboro *(G-7105)*
Hughs Sheet Mtal Sttsvlle LLC .... F 704 872-4621
  Statesville *(G-14818)*
Ifab Corp .... G 704 864-3032
  Gastonia *(G-6422)*
Industrial Mechanical Services .... G 828 397-3231
  Hildebran *(G-8625)*
Industrial Mechatronics Inc .... G 704 900-2407
  Charlotte *(G-2962)*
Industrial Metal Products of .... F 910 944-8110
  Aberdeen *(G-7)*
◆ Insteel Industries Inc .... C 336 786-2141
  Mount Airy *(G-11520)*
Ipd Co .... F 704 999-4484
  Charlotte *(G-2992)*
J & S Fab Inc .... G 704 528-4251
  Troutman *(G-15383)*
J & W Steel Inc .... F 980 579-0452
  Charlotte *(G-3003)*
JD Steel LLC .... G 843 367-7456
  Pineville *(G-12277)*

34 FABRICATED METAL PRODUCTS

John Jenkins Company .... E 336 375-3717
  Browns Summit *(G-1311)*
Jordan Innvtive Fbrication LLC .... E 910 428-2368
  Biscoe *(G-1113)*
◆ K & S Tool & Manufacturing Co .... E 336 410-7260
  High Point *(G-8419)*
Kbb Towers LLC .... G 828 243-1812
  Fletcher *(G-6016)*
Kisner Corporation .... F 919 510-8410
  Raleigh *(G-12941)*
Lavender Inc .... E 704 481-8327
  Shelby *(G-14336)*
Limitless Wldg Fabrication LLC .... G 252 753-0660
  Farmville *(G-5739)*
Llewellyn Mtal Fabricators Inc .... F 704 283-4816
  Monroe *(G-10759)*
Luna Metal Buildings and Con .... G 336 628-0273
  Asheboro *(G-455)*
Lydall Thermal/Acoustical Inc .... A 336 468-8522
  Hamptonville *(G-7676)*
▲ Lydall Thermal/Acoustical Inc .... D 336 468-8522
  Hamptonville *(G-7675)*
Lyerlys Wldg & Fabrication Inc .... G 704 680-2317
  Gold Hill *(G-6584)*
Lyndon Steel Company LLC .... C 336 785-0848
  Winston Salem *(G-16795)*
M F C Inc .... E 252 322-5004
  Aurora *(G-836)*
M&N Construction Supply Inc .... F 910 791-0908
  Wilmington *(G-16313)*
Maco Inc .... E 704 434-6800
  Shelby *(G-14342)*
Manufacturing Methods LLC .... E 910 371-1700
  Leland *(G-9554)*
Mark W McKenzie .... G 860 529-2476
  Bostic *(G-1264)*
Martinez Wldg Fabrication Corp .... F 919 957-8904
  Raleigh *(G-13003)*
▲ Master Form Inc .... E 704 292-1041
  Matthews *(G-10331)*
Maysteel Porters LLC .... B 704 864-1313
  Gastonia *(G-6459)*
McCabes Indus Mllwrght Mfg Inc .... E 910 843-8699
  Red Springs *(G-13502)*
McCombs Steel .... G 828 572-7600
  Lenoir *(G-9636)*
McCombs Steel Company Inc .... E 704 873-7563
  Statesville *(G-14840)*
McCune Technology Inc .... F 910 424-2978
  Fayetteville *(G-5871)*
▼ McGee Corporation .... D 704 882-1500
  Matthews *(G-10270)*
▲ Metal Tech Murfreesboro Inc .... E 252 398-4041
  Murfreesboro *(G-11700)*
Metal Works Mfg Co .... D 704 482-1399
  Shelby *(G-14347)*
Metalcraft Fabricating Company .... F 919 477-2117
  Durham *(G-5222)*
Mikes Welding & Fabrication .... G 336 472-5804
  Thomasville *(G-15250)*
▼ Millennium Mfg Structures LLC .... F 828 265-3737
  Boone *(G-1222)*
Minda North America LLC .... E 828 313-0092
  Granite Falls *(G-6746)*
Mmdi Inc .... D 704 882-4550
  Matthews *(G-10336)*
Modern Structure Solutions LLC .... G 984 286-2447
  Hudson *(G-8776)*
▲ MTS Holdings Corp Inc .... E 336 227-0151
  Burlington *(G-1465)*
Mundy Machine Co Inc .... G 704 922-8663
  Dallas *(G-4648)*

Myers Quality Machine Co Inc .... F 336 498-4187
  Randleman *(G-13480)*
NC Steel Services Inc .... F 252 393-7888
  Swansboro *(G-15046)*
New South Fabricator LLC .... G 704 922-2072
  Dallas *(G-4649)*
North State Steel Inc .... F 919 496-2506
  Louisburg *(G-9994)*
North State Steel Inc .... E 252 830-8884
  Greenville *(G-7565)*
◆ Nucor Corporation .... C 704 366-7000
  Charlotte *(G-3281)*
Nucor Harris Rebar NC Inc .... C 910 739-9747
  Lumberton *(G-10046)*
Ottenweller Co Inc .... F 336 783-6959
  Mount Airy *(G-11555)*
Packiq LLC .... E 910 964-4331
  Fayetteville *(G-5891)*
Park Avenue Metalcraft Inc .... F 919 554-2233
  Youngsville *(G-17090)*
Parsons Metal Fabricators Inc .... F 828 758-7521
  Lenoir *(G-9646)*
Paul Casper Inc .... G 919 269-5362
  Zebulon *(G-17139)*
Peachland Dsign Fbrication LLC .... F 704 272-9296
  Peachland *(G-12174)*
Peak Steel LLC .... F 919 362-5955
  Apex *(G-229)*
Performnce Strl Con Sltons LLC .... G 980 333-6414
  Davidson *(G-4690)*
Piedmont Fabrication .... G 336 634-0096
  Greensboro *(G-7256)*
Piedmont Metals Burlington Inc .... E 336 584-7742
  Burlington *(G-1473)*
Piedmont Metalworks LLC .... G 919 598-6500
  Mebane *(G-10424)*
Piedmont Steel Company LLC .... F 336 875-5133
  High Point *(G-8483)*
Pilot Rack Company .... G 336 351-5851
  Mount Airy *(G-11556)*
▲ Porters Group LLC .... B 704 864-1313
  Gastonia *(G-6490)*
Precision Fabrication Inc .... F 336 885-6091
  High Point *(G-8492)*
Precision Steel Works LLC .... G 252 467-0338
  Rocky Mount *(G-13671)*
Production Wldg Fbrication Inc .... E 828 687-7466
  Arden *(G-369)*
Protech Fabrication Inc .... E 704 663-1721
  Mount Ulla *(G-11686)*
Quality Steel Fabrication Inc .... G 336 961-2670
  Yadkinville *(G-17047)*
Quality Steel Structure LLC .... G 910 975-3409
  Boone *(G-1229)*
R & R Ironworks Inc .... F 828 448-0524
  Morganton *(G-11243)*
Reaper Custom Fabrication LLC .... G 336 972-4065
  Tobaccoville *(G-15320)*
Richmond Steel Welding .... G 910 582-4026
  Rockingham *(G-13643)*
Riddley Metals Inc .... F 704 435-8829
  Shelby *(G-14360)*
Roanoke Valley Steel Corp .... E 252 538-4137
  Weldon *(G-15888)*
Robinson Mch & Cutter Grinding .... G 704 629-5591
  Bessemer City *(G-1080)*
Roderick Mch Erectors Wldg Inc .... G 910 343-0381
  Wilmington *(G-16386)*
Rovertym .... G 704 635-7305
  Monroe *(G-10798)*
Royal Welding Inc .... F 704 750-9353
  Pineville *(G-12297)*

Rugged Metal Designs Inc .... G 336 352-5150
  Dobson *(G-4830)*
Ruhl Inc .... G 910 497-3172
  Spring Lake *(G-14626)*
S&S Metal Structures LLC .... G 336 466-7929
  Mount Airy *(G-11569)*
Salisbury Mtal Fabrication LLC .... G 704 278-0785
  Salisbury *(G-14041)*
Sanford Steel Corporation .... F 919 898-4799
  Goldston *(G-6676)*
Sieber Industrial Inc .... F 252 746-2003
  Ayden *(G-855)*
Smith Architectural Metals LLC .... E 336 273-1970
  Greensboro *(G-7345)*
Southco Industries Inc .... C 704 482-1477
  Shelby *(G-14369)*
Southeastern Steel Cnstr Inc .... F 910 346-4462
  Jacksonville *(G-9036)*
◆ Southeastern Tool & Die Inc .... D 910 944-7677
  Aberdeen *(G-29)*
Southern Steelworks LLC .... E 828 548-3660
  Highlands *(G-8617)*
Specialty Fabricators Inc .... G 336 838-7704
  Wilkesboro *(G-16042)*
◆ Specialty Manufacturing Inc .... C 704 247-9300
  Charlotte *(G-3598)*
Specialty Welding & Mch Inc .... G 828 464-1104
  Newton *(G-11972)*
Stainless Steel Spc Inc .... G 919 779-4290
  Raleigh *(G-13297)*
Stainless Stl Fabricators Inc .... F 919 833-3520
  Raleigh *(G-13298)*
Steel and Pipe Corporation .... E 919 776-0751
  Sanford *(G-14193)*
Steel Construct Systems LLC .... E 704 781-5575
  Locust *(G-9972)*
Steel Fab .... G 980 721-8969
  Mooresville *(G-11100)*
Steel Specialty Co Belmont Inc .... E 704 825-4745
  Belmont *(G-1010)*
Steel Technology Inc .... G 252 937-7122
  Rocky Mount *(G-13733)*
Steelco Inc .... F 704 896-1207
  Matthews *(G-10346)*
Steelcraft Structures LLC .... G 980 434-5400
  Statesville *(G-14906)*
Steelfab Inc .... B 704 394-5376
  Charlotte *(G-3627)*
Steelfab of Virginia Inc .... E 919 828-9545
  Raleigh *(G-13301)*
▲ Stiles Mfg Co Inc .... G 910 592-6344
  Clinton *(G-4113)*
Structural Planners Inc .... F 919 848-8964
  Raleigh *(G-13309)*
Structural Steel Products Corp .... D 919 359-2811
  Clayton *(G-4013)*
▲ Superior Manufacturing Company ..... D 336 661-1200
  Winston Salem *(G-16925)*
T Cs Services Inc .... G 910 655-2796
  Bolton *(G-1168)*
Tab Steel & Fabricating Inc .... E 828 323-8300
  Hildebran *(G-8628)*
Tank Fab Inc .... F 910 675-8999
  Rocky Point *(G-13753)*
Tce Manufacturing LLC .... G 252 330-9919
  Elizabeth City *(G-5574)*
Thieman Manufacturing Tech LLC .... F 828 453-1866
  Ellenboro *(G-5640)*
Thomasvlle Mtal Fbricators Inc .... E 336 248-4992
  Lexington *(G-9792)*
Timmons Fabrications Inc .... F 919 688-8998
  Durham *(G-5403)*

SIC SECTION

34 FABRICATED METAL PRODUCTS

Tower Engrg Professionals Inc............ C 919 661-6351
   Raleigh *(G-13355)*

Towerco LLC.. F 919 653-5700
   Cary *(G-1911)*

Trane Technologies Company LLC........ B 336 751-3561
   Mocksville *(G-10608)*

Tri-City Mechanical Contrs Inc............. D 336 272-9495
   Greensboro *(G-7410)*

Tri-Steel Fabricators Inc..................... E 252 291-7900
   Sims *(G-14445)*

Triad Stainless Inc............................... G 336 315-5515
   Greensboro *(G-7418)*

Triangle Metalworks Inc....................... G 919 556-7786
   Youngsville *(G-17109)*

Triangle Steel Systems LLC................. G 919 615-0282
   Garner *(G-6318)*

Truefab LLC.. F 919 620-8158
   Durham *(G-5413)*

Tubular Textile LLC.............................. G 336 731-2860
   Welcome *(G-15877)*

United Machine & Metal Fab Inc.......... E 828 464-5167
   Conover *(G-4508)*

Universal Steel NC LLC........................ G 336 476-3105
   Thomasville *(G-15298)*

▼ US Buildings LLC............................. D 828 264-6198
   Boone *(G-1245)*

US Metal Crafters LLC......................... E 336 861-2100
   Archdale *(G-301)*

USA Metal Structure LLP..................... G 336 717-2884
   Dobson *(G-4832)*

Vann S Wldg & Orna Works Inc........... F 704 289-6056
   Monroe *(G-10829)*

Vaughn Metals Inc............................... G 910 791-6576
   Wilmington *(G-16440)*

Versatile Machine Fab.......................... G 336 699-8271
   East Bend *(G-5471)*

W&W-Afco Steel LLC........................... D 336 993-2680
   Colfax *(G-4164)*

W&W-Afco Steel LLC........................... E 336 275-9711
   Greensboro *(G-7453)*

W&W-Afco Steel LLC........................... E 252 459-7116
   Nashville *(G-11753)*

Waldenwood Group Inc....................... F 704 313-8004
   Charlotte *(G-3790)*

Waldenwood Group LLC..................... F 704 331-8004
   Charlotte *(G-3791)*

Wallace Welding Inc............................ F 919 934-2488
   Smithfield *(G-14488)*

Ward & Son Inc................................... G 252 338-6589
   Elizabeth City *(G-5581)*

Waters Brothers Contrs Inc.................. F 252 446-7141
   Rocky Mount *(G-13740)*

Watson Metals Co................................ G 336 366-4500
   State Road *(G-14731)*

Wede Corporation................................ F 704 864-1313
   Kings Mountain *(G-9338)*

Welding Solutions LLC........................ E 828 665-4363
   Fletcher *(G-6051)*

Weldon Steel Corporation.................... E 252 536-2113
   Weldon *(G-15890)*

Whitley Metals Inc............................... G 919 894-3326
   Willow Spring *(G-16084)*

Wicked Fab-Worx LLC.......................... G 828 492-0112
   Canton *(G-1629)*

▲ Williams Industries Inc..................... C 919 604-1746
   Raleigh *(G-13423)*

Winston Steel Stair Co......................... G 336 721-0020
   Winston Salem *(G-16983)*

Wirenet Inc.. E 513 774-7759
   Huntersville *(G-8906)*

Wnc Refab Inc..................................... G 828 658-8368
   Weaverville *(G-15870)*

◆ Zarges Inc....................................... F 704 357-6285
   Charlotte *(G-3848)*

3442 Metal doors, sash, and trim

A R Perry Corporation......................... F 252 492-6181
   Henderson *(G-7774)*

▲ Airspeed LLC.................................. E 919 644-1222
   Hillsborough *(G-8633)*

Alside Window Co................................ G 407 293-9010
   Kinston *(G-9342)*

Amarr Company................................... G 704 599-5858
   Charlotte *(G-2178)*

Amarr Company................................... G 336 936-0010
   Mocksville *(G-10553)*

◆ Amarr Company............................... C 336 744-5100
   Winston Salem *(G-16602)*

Amesbury Group Inc............................ D 704 978-2883
   Statesville *(G-14748)*

Amesbury Group Inc............................ E 704 924-7694
   Statesville *(G-14749)*

◆ Assa Abloy Entrnce Systems US...... C 704 357-9924
   Monroe *(G-10655)*

Atlantic Coastal Shutters LLC............. G 252 441-4358
   Kill Devil Hills *(G-9254)*

Atrium Extrusion Systems Inc............. E 336 764-6400
   Welcome *(G-15871)*

Building Envlope Erction Svcs............. F 252 747-2015
   Snow Hill *(G-14499)*

Champion Win Co of Charlotte............ F 704 398-0085
   Charlotte *(G-2446)*

Charlotte Shutter and Shades.............. G 336 351-3391
   Westfield *(G-15951)*

Coastal Awnings Inc............................ F 252 222-0707
   Morehead City *(G-11162)*

▲ Cornerstone Bldg Brands Inc........... B 281 897-7788
   Cary *(G-1736)*

◆ Dac Products Inc............................. E 336 969-9786
   Rural Hall *(G-13839)*

Door Screen.. G 406 531-4516
   Kitty Hawk *(G-9401)*

East Coast Hurricane Shutters.............. G 910 352-5717
   Burgaw *(G-1338)*

Energy Svers Windows Doors Inc......... G 252 758-8700
   Greenville *(G-7523)*

Envirnmental Win Solutions LLC........... G 704 200-2001
   Charlotte *(G-2717)*

Garden Metalwork................................ G 828 733-1077
   Newland *(G-11887)*

Godwin Door & Hardware Inc.............. E 919 580-0543
   Goldsboro *(G-6617)*

Him Inc.. F 336 409-7795
   King *(G-9272)*

Jeld-Wen Inc....................................... C 336 838-0292
   North Wilkesboro *(G-12016)*

◆ Jeld-Wen Inc................................... B 800 535-3936
   Charlotte *(G-3018)*

▲ Jeld-Wen Holding Inc..................... B 704 378-5700
   Charlotte *(G-3019)*

Jewers Doors Us Inc............................ E 888 510-5331
   Greensboro *(G-7136)*

Jus Doors Inc...................................... F 888 510-5331
   Greensboro *(G-7142)*

Kindred Rolling Doors LLC................... G 704 905-3806
   Gastonia *(G-6439)*

McDaniel Awning Co............................ G 704 636-8503
   Salisbury *(G-14010)*

Merhi Glass Inc.................................... G 919 961-5930
   Raleigh *(G-13017)*

Moss Supply Company......................... G 704 596-8717
   Charlotte *(G-3205)*

Ora Inc.. G 540 903-7177
   Marion *(G-10170)*

Owens Corning Sales LLC................... E 419 248-8000
   Roxboro *(G-13814)*

Panels By Paith Inc.............................. G 336 599-3437
   Roxboro *(G-13816)*

Peelle Company................................... G 631 231-6000
   Monroe *(G-10786)*

Plantation Shutter Pros Inc.................. E 843 591-6834
   Midland *(G-10474)*

Ramsey Industries Inc......................... E 704 827-3560
   Belmont *(G-1005)*

Reynaers Inc....................................... E 480 272-9688
   Charlotte *(G-3443)*

Reynolds Advanced Mtls Inc................ E 704 357-0600
   Charlotte *(G-3444)*

Rice S Glass Company Inc................... E 919 967-9214
   Carrboro *(G-1655)*

Shutter Factory Inc.............................. G 252 974-2795
   Washington *(G-15731)*

Shutterhutch....................................... G 704 918-7852
   Charlotte *(G-3544)*

Sonaron LLC.. G 808 232-6168
   Fayetteville *(G-5919)*

Tompkins Industries Inc....................... C 828 254-2351
   Asheville *(G-802)*

Trim Inc... F 336 751-3591
   Mocksville *(G-10609)*

▲ Ultimate Products Inc...................... F 919 836-1627
   Raleigh *(G-13377)*

Vinyl Windows & Doors Corp............... F 910 944-2100
   Aberdeen *(G-35)*

YKK AP America Inc............................ F 336 665-1963
   Greensboro *(G-7474)*

3443 Fabricated plate work (boiler shop)

A O Smith Water Products Co............. F 704 597-8910
   Charlotte *(G-2118)*

Abernethy Welding & Repair Inc.......... G 828 324-7361
   Vale *(G-15462)*

Adamson Global Technology Corp....... G 252 523-5200
   Kinston *(G-9339)*

Agility Fuel Systems LLC.................... G 704 870-3520
   Salisbury *(G-13915)*

◆ Akg North America Inc.................... E 919 563-4286
   Mebane *(G-10396)*

◆ Akg Nrth Amercn Operations Inc..... F 919 563-4286
   Mebane *(G-10397)*

◆ Akg of America Inc......................... E 919 563-4286
   Mebane *(G-10398)*

▼ Alamo Distribution LLC.................... C 704 398-5600
   Belmont *(G-974)*

Alloy Fabricators Inc........................... E 704 263-2281
   Alexis *(G-121)*

American Metal Fabricators Inc............ E 704 824-8585
   Gastonia *(G-6347)*

▲ Applied Medical Tech Inc................ E 919 255-3220
   Creedmoor *(G-4605)*

B&B Cap Liners LLC............................ G 585 598-1828
   Raleigh *(G-12539)*

Bendel Tank Heat Exchanger LLC........ F 704 596-5112
   Charlotte *(G-2300)*

◆ Bfs Industries LLC.......................... E 919 575-6711
   Butner *(G-1542)*

◆ BMA America Inc............................ F 970 353-3770
   Charlotte *(G-2326)*

Bthec Inc... E 704 596-5112
   Charlotte *(G-2362)*

Bwxt Mpower Inc................................. E 980 365-4000
   Charlotte *(G-2370)*

◆ Canvas Sx LLC................................ C 980 474-3700
   Charlotte *(G-2384)*

Carolina Piping Services Inc................. G 704 405-0297
   Kings Mountain *(G-9300)*

34 FABRICATED METAL PRODUCTS

Carolina Products Inc .... E 704 364-9029
  Charlotte (G-2403)
Cherokee Transfer Station .... G 828 497-4519
  Cherokee (G-3855)
Chicago Tube and Iron Company .... D 704 781-2060
  Locust (G-9956)
Classic Car Metal & Parts LLC .... G 919 567-0693
  Fuquay Varina (G-6187)
Columbiana Hi Tech LLC .... D 336 497-3600
  Kernersville (G-9181)
Commscope Technologies LLC .... F 919 934-9711
  Smithfield (G-14457)
Container Products Corporation .... D 910 392-6100
  Wilmington (G-16179)
Contech Engnered Solutions LLC .... E 704 596-4226
  Charlotte (G-2545)
Contech Engnered Solutions LLC .... G 919 858-7820
  Raleigh (G-12640)
Contech Engnered Solutions LLC .... G 919 851-2880
  Raleigh (G-12641)
Crown Case Co .... G 704 453-1542
  Charlotte (G-2572)
Cybermatrix Inc .... G 910 292-9370
  Fayetteville (G-5803)
Dumpster Mate LLC .... G 919 303-7402
  Apex (G-184)
Fabrication Associates Inc .... D 704 535-8050
  Charlotte (G-2742)
Fiberglass Fabrication Inc .... G 828 685-0940
  Hendersonville (G-7847)
▼ Fleetgenius of Nc Inc .... C 828 726-3001
  Lenoir (G-9612)
◆ Florida Marine Tanks Inc .... F 305 620-9030
  Henderson (G-7783)
▼ Friedrich Metal Pdts Co Inc .... E 336 375-3067
  Browns Summit (G-1303)
▼ Gaston County Dyeing Mach .... D 704 822-5000
  Mount Holly (G-11634)
General Industries Inc .... E 919 751-1791
  Goldsboro (G-6615)
Highland Tank NC Inc .... C 336 218-0801
  Greensboro (G-7092)
Hockmeyer Equipment Corp .... D 252 338-4705
  Elizabeth City (G-5548)
Icon Boiler Inc .... E 844 562-4266
  Greensboro (G-7110)
Ind Fab Inc .... F 252 977-0811
  Elm City (G-5650)
Industrial Air Inc .... C 336 292-1030
  Greensboro (G-7113)
▲ Ips Perforating Inc .... F 704 881-0050
  Statesville (G-14821)
J & L Bckh/Nvrnmental Svcs Inc .... G 910 237-7351
  Eastover (G-5481)
▲ Jbr Properties of Greenville Inc .... A :.... 252 355-9353
  Winterville (G-17004)
Job Shop Fabricators Inc .... G 336 427-7300
  Madison (G-10074)
Kings Prtble Wldg Fbrction LLC .... G 336 789-2372
  Mount Airy (G-11532)
Kirk & Blum Manufacturing Co .... E 801 728-6533
  Greensboro (G-7152)
Lrs Technology Inc .... G 336 669-5982
  Lexington (G-9752)
M M M Inc .... G 252 527-0229
  La Grange (G-9443)
▲ Marley Company LLC .... C 704 752-4400
  Charlotte (G-3128)
McCune Technology Inc .... D 910 424-2978
  Fayetteville (G-5871)
Miller Dumpster Service LLC .... G 704 504-9300
  Charlotte (G-3181)

◆ Mitsubishi Chemical Amer Inc .... D 980 580-2839
  Charlotte (G-3188)
Mono Systems Inc .... G 914 934-2075
  Waxhaw (G-15766)
Moore Dumpster Service LLC .... G 704 560-4410
  Ocean Isle Beach (G-12093)
Mrr Southern LLC .... F 919 436-3571
  Raleigh (G-13049)
Naes-Oms .... G 252 536-4525
  Weldon (G-15886)
NC Diesel Performance LLC .... G 704 431-3257
  Salisbury (G-14016)
Nordfab LLC .... C 336 821-0829
  Thomasville (G-15258)
Piedmont Fiberglass Inc .... E 828 632-8883
  Statesville (G-14859)
Piedmont Well Covers Inc .... F 704 664-8488
  Mount Ulla (G-11685)
Poppe Inc .... F 828 345-6036
  Hickory (G-8117)
Purthermal LLC .... G 828 855-0108
  Hickory (G-8129)
Rack Works Inc .... G 336 368-1302
  Pilot Mountain (G-12201)
Royall Development Co Inc .... C 336 889-2569
  High Point (G-8517)
Second Green Holdings Inc .... F 336 996-6073
  Colfax (G-4160)
Southeastern Mch & Wldg Co Inc .... E 910 791-6661
  Wilmington (G-16410)
SPX Cooling Tech LLC .... E 630 881-9777
  Charlotte (G-3606)
SPX Corporation .... G 336 627-6020
  Eden (G-5503)
SPX Flow Us LLC .... C 919 735-4570
  Goldsboro (G-6660)
Tank Fab Inc .... F 910 675-8999
  Rocky Point (G-13753)
Thieman Manufacturing Tech LLC .... F 828 453-1866
  Ellenboro (G-5640)
▼ Tower Components Inc .... D 336 824-2102
  Ramseur (G-13450)
TRC Acquisition LLC .... A 252 355-9353
  Winterville (G-17015)
Turner Equipment Company Inc .... E 919 734-8328
  Goldsboro (G-6667)
▲ Ward Vessel and Exchanger Corp .... D 704 568-3001
  Charlotte (G-3795)
Waste Container Repair Svcs .... G 910 257-4474
  Fayetteville (G-5949)
Waste Industries Usa LLC .... D 919 325-3000
  Raleigh (G-13412)
◆ Wastequip LLC .... F 704 366-7140
  Charlotte (G-3796)
◆ Wastequip Manufacturing Co LLC ... Jr..... 704 504-7597
  Charlotte (G-3797)
We Partners LLC .... G 360 750-3500
  Raleigh (G-13416)
Wiggins Design Fabrication Inc .... G 252 826-5239
  Scotland Neck (G-14224)
▼ Wind Shear Inc .... F 704 788-9463
  Concord (G-4390)
Wnc White Corporation .... E 828 477-4895
  Sylva (G-15076)
Worthington Cylinder Corp .... E 336 777-8600
  Winston Salem (G-16985)
▲ Ziehl-Abegg Inc .... E 336 834-9339
  Greensboro (G-7475)

3444 Sheet metalwork

A B Metals of Polkton LLC .... G 704 694-6635
  Polkton (G-12382)

SIC SECTION

A C S Enterprises NC Inc .... F 704 226-9898
  Monroe (G-10631)
A Plus Carports .... G 336 367-1261
  Boonville (G-1252)
Abco Automation Inc .... C 336 375-6400
  Browns Summit (G-1298)
Able Metal Fabricators Inc .... E 704 394-8972
  Charlotte (G-2124)
Acm Panels .... G 704 839-0104
  Matthews (G-10300)
Advanced Mfg Solutions NC Inc .... E 828 633-2633
  Candler (G-1566)
▼ Afi Capital Inc .... C 919 212-6400
  Raleigh (G-12481)
Air Control Inc .... E 252 492-2300
  Henderson (G-7775)
▼ Alamo Distribution LLC .... C 704 398-5600
  Belmont (G-974)
Alert Metal Works Inc .... E 704 922-3152
  Dallas (G-4634)
Allen Kelly & Co Inc .... D 919 779-4197
  Raleigh (G-12490)
Allens Gutter Service .... G 910 738-9509
  Lumberton (G-10025)
Allied Sheet Metal Works Inc .... F 704 376-8469
  Charlotte (G-2161)
Allied Tool and Machine Co .... G 336 993-2131
  Kernersville (G-9160)
Alloy Fabricators Inc .... E 704 263-2281
  Alexis (G-121)
America Sheet Metal Inc .... E 980 318-7749
  Harrisburg (G-7700)
▼ American Wick Drain Corp .... E 704 296-5801
  Monroe (G-10644)
APT Industries Inc .... F 704 598-9100
  Charlotte (G-2206)
Axccellus LLC .... F 919 589-9800
  Apex (G-169)
Beacon Roofing Supply Inc .... G 704 886-1555
  Charlotte (G-2291)
Benton & Sons Fabrication Inc .... E 919 734-1700
  Pikeville (G-12192)
Budd-Piper Roofing Company .... F 919 682-2121
  Durham (G-4984)
Bull City Sheet Metal LLC .... F 919 354-0993
  Durham (G-4988)
▲ Byers Prcision Fabricators Inc .... E 828 693-4088
  Hendersonville (G-7831)
C P Eakes Company .... F 336 574-1800
  Greensboro (G-6873)
Calco Enterprises Inc .... F 910 695-0089
  Aberdeen (G-3)
Camco Manufacturing Inc .... G 336 348-6609
  Reidsville (G-13511)
Capital Cy Roofg & Shtmtl LLC .... F 919 366-1850
  Wendell (G-15894)
Captive-Aire Systems Inc .... G 704 843-7215
  Waxhaw (G-15748)
Captive-Aire Systems Inc .... C 919 887-2721
  Youngsville (G-17074)
◆ Captive-Aire Systems Inc .... C 919 882-2410
  Raleigh (G-12593)
◆ Carolina Custom Booth Co LLC ...... E 336 886-3127
  High Point (G-8285)
Carolina Spral Duct Fbrction L .... F 704 395-3289
  Charlotte (G-2407)
Carolina-Virginia Mfg Co Inc .... G 336 623-1307
  Stoneville (G-14954)
Centurion Industries Inc .... C 704 867-2304
  Gastonia (G-6372)
Champion Win Co of Charlotte .... F 704 398-0085
  Charlotte (G-2446)

34 FABRICATED METAL PRODUCTS

Chatsworth Products Inc .... C 252 514-2779
  New Bern (G-11788)
Clt 2016 Inc .... D 704 886-1555
  Charlotte (G-2501)
Collins Fabrication & Wldg LLC .... G 704 861-9326
  Gastonia (G-6380)
▼ Colored Metal Products Inc .... F 704 482-1407
  Shelby (G-14301)
Comfort Engineers Inc .... E 919 383-0158
  Durham (G-5027)
Construction Metal Pdts Inc .... E 704 871-8704
  Statesville (G-14778)
Copper Line Custom .... G 704 956-0734
  Mooresville (G-10912)
▲ Cornerstone Bldg Brands Inc .... B 281 897-7788
  Cary (G-1736)
Cox Machine Co Inc .... F 704 296-0118
  Monroe (G-10696)
CPI Satcom & Antenna Tech Inc ...... C 704 462-7330
  Conover (G-4440)
▲ CSC Sheet Metal Inc .... F 919 544-8887
  Durham (G-5038)
▲ Custom Industries Inc .... E 336 299-2885
  Greensboro (G-6950)
Custom Metal Creation LLC .... G 828 302-0623
  Vale (G-15464)
Custom Sheetmetal Services Inc ..... G 919 282-1088
  Durham (G-5041)
Cypress Mountain Company .... G 252 758-2179
  Greenville (G-7512)
Dantherm Filtration Inc .... F 336 889-5599
  Thomasville (G-15211)
Dayton Metals .... G 937 615-9812
  Fayetteville (G-5807)
Design Engnred Fbrications Inc .... E 336 768-8260
  Winston Salem (G-16675)
DOT Blue Services Inc .... F 704 342-2970
  Charlotte (G-2653)
Dunavants Welding & Steel Inc .... G 252 338-6533
  Camden (G-1557)
Dusty Rhoads Hvac Inc .... G 252 261-5892
  Kitty Hawk (G-9403)
Dwiggins Metal Masters Inc .... G 336 751-2379
  Mocksville (G-10568)
E C L Inc .... G 919 365-7101
  Wendell (G-15899)
▲ Effikal LLC .... G 252 522-3031
  Kinston (G-9361)
Ellenburg Sheet Metal .... G 704 872-2089
  Statesville (G-14794)
Envision Glass Inc .... F 336 283-9701
  Winston Salem (G-16698)
Erdle Perforating Holdings Inc .... G 704 588-4380
  Charlotte (G-2726)
F & M Steel Products Inc .... G 910 793-1345
  Wilmington (G-16215)
Fabrication Associates Inc .... D 704 535-8050
  Charlotte (G-2742)
▲ Field Controls LLC .... D 252 208-7300
  Kinston (G-9366)
Form Tech Concrete Forms Inc .... F 704 395-9910
  Charlotte (G-2787)
Franklin Sheet Metal Shop Inc .... F 828 524-2821
  Franklin (G-6130)
Garnett Component Sales Inc .... G 919 562-5158
  Wake Forest (G-15558)
General Metals Inc .... E 919 202-0100
  Pine Level (G-12209)
Gibbs Machine Company Incorporated. E 336 856-1907
  Greensboro (G-7042)
Gray Flex Systems Inc .... D 910 897-3539
  Coats (G-4130)

Gray Metal South Inc .... C 910 892-2119
  Dunn (G-4872)
Griffiths Corporation .... D 704 554-5657
  Pineville (G-12272)
H&S Autoshot LLC .... E 847 662-8500
  Mooresville (G-10968)
Hamlin Sheet Metal Company Inc ... D 919 894-2224
  Benson (G-1036)
◆ Hamlin Sheet Metal Compan .... E 919 772-8780
  Garner (G-6274)
Hanover Iron Works Inc .... E 910 763-7318
  Wilmington (G-16245)
Hanover Iron Works Shtmtl Inc .... G 910 399-1146
  Wilmington (G-16246)
Harco Air LLC .... G 252 491-5220
  Powells Point (G-12397)
Herman Reeves Tex Shtmtl Inc .... E 704 865-2231
  Gastonia (G-6415)
▲ Hi-Tech Fabrication Inc .... C 919 781-6150
  Raleigh (G-12842)
Hughs Sheet Mtal Sttsvlle LLC .... F 704 872-4621
  Statesville (G-14818)
Industrial Metal Craft Inc .... F 704 864-3416
  Gastonia (G-6427)
Industrial Metal Products of .... F 910 944-8110
  Aberdeen (G-7)
Industrial Sheet Metal Works .... G 828 654-9655
  Arden (G-340)
Ism Inc .... E
  Arden (G-342)
Iv-S Metal Stamping Inc .... E 336 861-2100
  Archdale (G-286)
Jacksonville Metal Mfg Inc .... G 910 938-7635
  Jacksonville (G-9010)
Joe and La Inc .... F 336 585-0313
  Burlington (G-1441)
John Jenkins Company .... E 336 375-3717
  Browns Summit (G-1311)
Joseph F Decker .... G 704 335-0021
  Charlotte (G-3035)
K&H Acquisition Company LLC .... G 704 788-1128
  Concord (G-4297)
K&M Sheet Metal LLC .... F 919 544-8887
  Durham (G-5175)
Kcp Inc .... G 919 854-7824
  Raleigh (G-12933)
Kevins Sheet Metal .... G 910 253-6203
  Leland (G-9550)
Kirk & Blum Manufacturing Co .... E 801 728-6533
  Greensboro (G-7152)
Knuckleheadz Kustomz Inc .... G 252 646-3354
  Morehead City (G-11180)
L6 Realty LLC .... G 704 654-3000
  Charlotte (G-3067)
Larry Bissette Inc .... F 919 773-2140
  Apex (G-212)
Len Corporation .... F 919 876-2964
  Knightdale (G-9420)
▲ Loflin Fabrication LLC .... E 336 859-4333
  Denton (G-4744)
Lyon Roofing Inc .... F 828 397-2301
  Hildebran (G-8626)
M & W Industries Inc .... E 704 837-0331
  Charlotte (G-3113)
M&N Construction Supply Inc .... G 336 996-7740
  Colfax (G-4154)
Mac/Fab Company Inc .... E 704 822-1103
  Mount Holly (G-11641)
▲ Master Form Inc .... E 704 292-1041
  Matthews (G-10331)
McClure Metal Specialties Inc .... G 252 792-8654
  Williamston (G-16066)

McCune Technology Inc .... F 910 424-2978
  Fayetteville (G-5871)
McDaniel Awning Co .... G 704 636-8503
  Salisbury (G-14010)
▼ McGee Corporation .... D 704 882-1500
  Matthews (G-10270)
McGill Corporation .... G 919 467-1993
  Cary (G-1822)
Metal Inc Triad .... G 980 429-2278
  Lincolnton (G-9907)
Metal Roofing Systems LLC .... E 704 820-3110
  Stanley (G-14702)
Metal Sales Manufacturing Corp ..... E 704 859-0550
  Mocksville (G-10589)
Metal Structures Plus LLC .... G 704 896-7155
  Mooresville (G-11021)
Midway Blind & Awning Co Inc .... G 336 226-4532
  Burlington (G-1461)
Mincar Group Inc .... G 919 772-7170
  Raleigh (G-13033)
Mitchell Welding Inc .... E 828 765-2620
  Spruce Pine (G-14651)
◆ Mitsubishi Chemical Amer Inc ..... D 980 580-2839
  Charlotte (G-3188)
Modern Machine and Metal .... D 336 993-4808
  Winston Salem (G-16814)
▼ Monroe Metal Manufacturing Inc ... D 800 366-1391
  Monroe (G-10775)
▲ MTS Holdings Corp Inc .... E 336 227-0151
  Burlington (G-1465)
Muriel Harris Investments Inc .... F 800 932-3191
  Fayetteville (G-5879)
My County Metal Operations LLC ... G 828 765-5265
  Spruce Pine (G-14652)
NC Metal Crafters Inc .... G 336 425-9727
  High Point (G-8463)
▲ Nederman Corporation .... F 704 399-7441
  Charlotte (G-3244)
▲ New Peco Inc .... E 828 684-1234
  Arden (G-355)
Nitro Manufacturing Inc .... F 704 663-3155
  Mooresville (G-11038)
Nordfab Ducting .... G 336 821-0840
  Charlotte (G-3267)
Northeast Tool and Mfg Company ... E 704 882-1187
  Matthews (G-10337)
Northern Star Technologies Inc .... G 516 353-3333
  Indian Trail (G-8952)
Oak Ridge Industries LLC .... E 252 833-4061
  Washington (G-15720)
Obx Metalworks LLC .... G 757 434-0211
  Knotts Island (G-9435)
On Time Metal LLC .... G 828 635-1001
  Hiddenite (G-8224)
Oro Manufacturing Company .... E 704 283-2186
  Monroe (G-10783)
Owens Corning Sales LLC .... E 419 248-8000
  Roxboro (G-13814)
P&S Machining Fabrication LLC ...... E 336 227-0151
  Burlington (G-1470)
Paul Casper Inc .... G 919 269-5362
  Zebulon (G-17139)
Penco Products Inc .... C 252 798-4000
  Hamilton (G-7614)
Peter J Hamann .... G 910 484-7877
  Fayetteville (G-5897)
Powerfab .... G 336 674-0624
  Randleman (G-13485)
Precise Sheet Metal Mech LLC .... G 336 693-3246
  Raeford (G-12432)
Precision Fabricators Inc .... G 336 835-4763
  Ronda (G-13768)

34 FABRICATED METAL PRODUCTS

Precision Machine Products Inc .... D 704 865-7490
Gastonia (G-6496)

▲ Precision Mch Fabrication Inc .... D 919 231-8648
Raleigh (G-13134)

▲ Production Systems Inc .... E 336 886-7161
High Point (G-8499)

Professional Sheet Metal LLC .... G 336 755-3794
Mount Airy (G-11560)

▲ QMF Mtal Elctrnic Slutions Inc .... D 336 992-8002
Kernersville (G-9227)

R E Bengel Sheet Metal Co .... E 252 637-3404
New Bern (G-11839)

Raleigh Mechanical & Mtls Inc .... F 919 598-4601
Raleigh (G-13179)

Ray Roofing Company Inc .... E 704 372-0100
Charlotte (G-3414)

Reagan Enterprises LLC .... G 704 564-7588
Statesville (G-14875)

Rfr Metal Fabrication Inc .... D 919 693-1354
Oxford (G-12151)

Robinson Mch & Cutter Grinding .... G 704 629-5591
Bessemer City (G-1080)

Rocky Mount Awning & Tent Co .... F 252 442-0184
Rocky Mount (G-13730)

Rpac Racing LLC .... D 704 696-8650
Statesville (G-14879)

S and R Sheet Metal Inc .... G 336 476-1069
Thomasville (G-15274)

S Duff Fabricating Inc .... G 910 298-3060
Beulaville (G-1098)

S K Bowling Inc .... F 252 243-1803
Wilson (G-16535)

Schwartz Steel Service Inc .... E 704 865-9576
Gastonia (G-6506)

Service Rofg Shtmtl Wlmngton I .... F 910 343-9860
Wilmington (G-16400)

Service Roofing and Shtmtl Co .... D 252 758-2179
Greenville (G-7582)

Sheet Metal Duct Suppliers LLC .... G 919 732-4362
Hillsborough (G-8667)

Sheet Metal Products Inc .... G 919 954-9950
Raleigh (G-13247)

Simon Industries Inc .... E 919 469-2004
Raleigh (G-13262)

Smith Fabrication Inc .... G 704 660-5170
Mooresville (G-11090)

Smt Inc .... D 919 782-4804
Raleigh (G-13273)

Southern Comfort A Systems LLC .... G 919 324-6336
Morrisville (G-11432)

▲ Southern Fabricators Inc .... D 704 272-7615
Polkton (G-12390)

Southern Pdmont Pping Fbrction .... F 704 272-7936
Peachland (G-12176)

Spc Mechanical Corporation .... C 252 237-9035
Wendell (G-15919)

◆ Specialty Manufacturing Inc .... C 704 247-9300
Charlotte (G-3598)

Specified Metals Inc .... G 336 786-6254
Mount Airy (G-11576)

Stainless Supply Inc .... F 704 635-2064
Monroe (G-10814)

Stamper Sheet Metal Inc .... G 336 476-5145
Thomasville (G-15282)

◆ Standard Tools and Eqp Co .... E 336 697-7177
Greensboro (G-7366)

Steven Meseroll .... G 850 264-6079
Matthews (G-10293)

Superior Finishing Systems LLC .... G 336 956-2000
Lexington (G-9788)

Superior Machine Co SC Inc .... E 828 652-6141
Marion (G-10181)

Suppliers To Wholesalers Inc .... F 704 375-7406
Charlotte (G-3656)

Swanson Sheetmetal Inc .... F 704 283-3955
Monroe (G-10818)

Taylorsville Precast Molds Inc .... G 828 632-4608
Taylorsville (G-15171)

Tfam Solutions LLC .... G 910 637-0266
Aberdeen (G-31)

Thieman Manufacturing Tech LLC .... F 828 453-1866
Ellenboro (G-5640)

Thomasvlle Mtal Fbricators Inc .... E 336 248-4992
Lexington (G-9792)

Tin Man Customs North Carolina .... G 828 391-8080
Valdese (G-15455)

Triad Corrugated Metal Inc .... F 919 775-1663
Sanford (G-14200)

Triad Corrugated Metal Inc .... E 336 625-9727
Asheboro (G-499)

Triad Fabrication and Mch Inc .... F 336 993-6042
Kernersville (G-9247)

Triad Sheet Metal & Mech Inc .... F 336 379-9891
Greensboro (G-7417)

Triad Welding Contractors Inc .... G 336 882-3902
Clemmons (G-4063)

Triangle Installation Svc Inc .... G 919 363-7637
Apex (G-252)

Triangle Stainless Inc .... G 919 596-1335
Butner (G-1550)

◆ Union Corrugating Company .... G 910 483-0479
Fayetteville (G-5937)

Universal Steel NC LLC .... E 336 476-3105
Thomasville (G-15298)

US Metal Crafters LLC .... E 336 861-2100
Archdale (G-301)

USA Dutch Inc .... E 336 227-8600
Graham (G-6713)

USA Dutch Inc .... E 919 732-6956
Efland (G-5528)

▼ Ventilation Direct .... G 919 573-1522
Raleigh (G-13395)

W H Rgers Shtmtl Ir Wrks Inc .... E 704 394-2191
Charlotte (G-3788)

W T Humphrey Inc .... D 910 455-3555
Jacksonville (G-9044)

Waste Container Services LLC .... G 910 257-4474
Fayetteville (G-5950)

Wede Corporation .... F 704 864-1313
Kings Mountain (G-9338)

▼ Wph Ventures Inc .... E 828 676-1700
Arden (G-392)

WV Holdings Inc .... G 704 853-8338
Gastonia (G-6544)

3446 Architectural metalwork

◆ Advanced Technology Inc .... E 336 668-0488
Greensboro (G-6783)

Afsc LLC .... D 704 523-4936
Charlotte (G-2142)

Alamance Iron Works Inc .... G 336 852-5940
Greensboro (G-6788)

Alamance Steel Fabricators .... G 336 887-3015
High Point (G-8238)

▼ Alamo Distribution LLC .... C 704 398-5600
Belmont (G-974)

Apex Steel Corp .... E 919 362-6611
Raleigh (G-12514)

Automated Controls LLC .... F 704 724-7625
Huntersville (G-8796)

Bargainstairpartscom LLC .... G 214 883-9524
Asheboro (G-408)

Bill Slate Grating .... G 336 591-8607
Walnut Cove (G-15631)

◆ Border Concepts Inc .... G 704 541-5509
Charlotte (G-2335)

Burlington Msclineous Mtls LLC .... F 336 376-1264
Graham (G-6682)

C P Eakes Company .... F 336 574-1800
Greensboro (G-6873)

Carolina Time Equipment Co Inc .... E 704 536-2700
Charlotte (G-2409)

Cast Iron Elegance Inc .... F 919 662-8777
Raleigh (G-12612)

Commercial Fabricators Inc .... E 828 465-1010
Newton (G-11921)

Concept Fusion LLC .... G 252 406-7052
Middlesex (G-10445)

Creekside Creative Design Inc .... G 252 243-6272
Wilson (G-16491)

Dakota Fab & Welding Inc .... G 919 881-0027
Siler City (G-14407)

Davis Steel and Iron Co Inc .... E 704 821-7676
Matthews (G-10311)

Dlss Manufacturing LLC .... G 919 619-7594
Pittsboro (G-12339)

Dudleys Fence Company .... G 252 566-5759
La Grange (G-9440)

Dwiggins Metal Masters Inc .... G 336 751-2379
Mocksville (G-10568)

Eaton-Schultz Inc .... F 704 331-8004
Charlotte (G-2679)

Esher LLC .... G 704 975-1463
Huntersville (G-8817)

Garden Gate Ornamental Iron In .... G 704 922-1635
Dallas (G-4642)

◆ Grady F Smith & Co Inc .... F 866 900-0983
Greenville (G-7533)

Hotchkis Performance Mfg Inc .... G 704 660-3060
Mooresville (G-10978)

Hurleys Ornamental Iron .... G 910 576-4731
Troy (G-15407)

Interstate Fabrications LLC .... G 704 209-0263
Salisbury (G-13987)

Iron-Crete Designs .... G 919 738-2803
Goldsboro (G-6626)

Ism Inc .... E
Arden (G-342)

J C Stair Erectors .... G 336 240-0560
Randleman (G-13475)

J4 Construction LLC .... G 704 550-7970
Wadesboro (G-15513)

James Cotter Ironworks .... F 919 644-2664
Cedar Grove (G-1971)

James Iron & Steel Inc .... E 704 283-2299
Monroe (G-10746)

Janellco Products Inc .... G 704 896-1415
Davidson (G-4683)

Joseph F Decker .... G 704 335-0021
Charlotte (G-3035)

Kens Trim & Stairs Ken Swarey .... G 336 835-4298
Elkin (G-5623)

Ladder & Things .... G 704 779-7211
Charlotte (G-3069)

Leo Gaev Metalworks Inc .... F 919 883-4666
Chapel Hill (G-2031)

Little River Metalworks LLC .... G 919 920-0292
Goldsboro (G-6631)

Marine Systems Inc .... F 828 254-5354
Asheville (G-695)

McDaniel Awning Co .... G 704 636-8503
Salisbury (G-14010)

Metal Works .... G 828 898-8582
Granite Falls (G-6745)

Mlf Company LLC .... F 919 231-9401
Raleigh (G-13037)

SIC SECTION

34 FABRICATED METAL PRODUCTS

NC Stairs and Rails Inc.................................G..... 336 460-5687
  Ramseur (G-13448)

Nci Group Inc..G..... 919 926-4800
  Raleigh (G-13059)

Oldcastle Buildingenvelope Inc.....................F..... 704 504-0345
  Charlotte (G-3291)

Ornamental Specialties Inc..........................F..... 704 821-9154
  Matthews (G-10339)

Poehler Enterprises Inc................................G..... 704 239-1166
  Midland (G-10475)

Power-Utility Products Company...................F..... 704 375-0776
  Charlotte (G-3361)

Protech Metals LLC.....................................E..... 910 295-6905
  Pinehurst (G-12232)

Rocket Installation LLC................................G..... 704 657-9492
  Troutman (G-15391)

Southern Staircase Inc................................D..... 704 357-1221
  Charlotte (G-3597)

Steel Smart Incorporated............................E..... 919 736-0681
  Pikeville (G-12194)

Steel Specialty Co Belmont Inc....................E..... 704 825-4745
  Belmont (G-1010)

▲ Stiles Mfg Co Inc.....................................G..... 910 592-6344
  Clinton (G-4113)

Stony Knoll Forge..G..... 704 507-0179
  Marshville (G-10225)

Swaim Ornamental Iron Works.....................F..... 336 765-5271
  Winston Salem (G-16927)

Tampco Inc..D..... 336 835-1895
  Elkin (G-5629)

Timmerman Manufacturing Inc....................F..... 828 464-1778
  Conover (G-4505)

Vann S Wldg & Orna Works Inc...................F..... 704 289-6056
  Monroe (G-10829)

Watson Steel & Iron Works LLC..................E..... 704 821-7140
  Matthews (G-10350)

Zack Noble Metalworks LLC........................G..... 828 688-3468
  Asheville (G-824)

3448 Prefabricated metal buildings

A Plus Carports..G..... 336 367-1261
  Boonville (G-1252)

Alaska Structures Inc..................................D..... 910 323-0562
  Fayetteville (G-5756)

American Carports Structures......................G..... 336 710-1091
  Mount Airy (G-11476)

American Carports Stuctures.......................G..... 844 628-4973
  Mount Airy (G-11477)

Amt/Bcu Inc...E..... 336 622-6200
  Liberty (G-9807)

Arboles NC Incorporated..............................F..... 828 675-4882
  Clayton (G-3955)

Atlantic Coastal Enterprises.........................G..... 910 478-0777
  Jacksonville (G-8988)

Barnyard Utlity Bldngs-Strg/Tl......................G..... 704 867-4700
  Gastonia (G-6351)

Barnyard Utlity Bldngs-Strg/Tl......................G..... 704 226-9454
  Monroe (G-10660)

Bennett Buildings of Conover.......................G..... 828 465-6117
  Conover (G-4422)

◆ Betco Inc..D..... 704 872-2999
  Statesville (G-14762)

Bluescope Buildings N Amer Inc..................C..... 336 996-4801
  Greensboro (G-6843)

Bonitz Inc...E..... 803 799-0181
  Concord (G-4213)

Boondock S Manufacturing Inc....................G..... 828 891-4242
  Etowah (G-5691)

Boxman Studios LLC...................................G..... 704 333-3733
  Charlotte (G-2342)

Buildings R US...G..... 828 382-0167
  Forest City (G-6062)

Buildings R US...G..... 704 482-3166
  Shelby (G-14290)

Camelot Rturn Intrmdate Hldngs..................D..... 866 419-0042
  Cary (G-1721)

Cardinal Buildings LLC................................G..... 919 422-5670
  Garner (G-6261)

◆ Carolina Carports Inc...............................D..... 336 367-6400
  Dobson (G-4821)

Carolina Greenhouse Plants Inc..................F..... 252 523-9300
  Kinston (G-9350)

Carolina Solar Structures Inc.......................E..... 828 684-9900
  Asheville (G-583)

Carport Central Inc......................................D..... 980 321-9898
  Mount Airy (G-11491)

Carport Commander LLC............................G..... 800 688-6151
  Mount Airy (G-11492)

Carport Direct Inc..G..... 336 715-8217
  Mount Airy (G-11493)

Central States Mfg Inc.................................C..... 336 719-3280
  Mount Airy (G-11495)

▲ Central Steel Buildings Inc......................F..... 336 789-7896
  Mount Airy (G-11496)

CF Steel LLC...G..... 704 516-1750
  Midland (G-10460)

Classic Steel Buildings Inc..........................G..... 252 465-4184
  Sunbury (G-14995)

Coast To Coast Carports Inc.......................E..... 336 783-3015
  Mount Airy (G-11497)

Coastal Machine & Welding Inc...................G..... 910 754-6476
  Shallotte (G-14272)

Component Sourcing Intl LLC......................E..... 704 843-9292
  Charlotte (G-2534)

▲ Cornerstone Bldg Brands Inc..................B..... 281 897-7788
  Cary (G-1736)

Direct Discount Carports.............................G..... 888 642-1910
  Mount Airy (G-11502)

E A Duncan Cnstr Co Inc............................G..... 910 653-3535
  Tabor City (G-15081)

Eagle Carports Inc......................................E..... 800 579-8589
  Mount Airy (G-11503)

Eastcoast Carports......................................G..... 336 755-3409
  Mount Airy (G-11504)

Express Carport LLC...................................G..... 888 389-2485
  Asheville (G-619)

▼ Friedrich Metal Pdts Co Inc.....................E..... 336 375-3067
  Browns Summit (G-1303)

Go Ask Erin LLC...G..... 336 747-3777
  Roxboro (G-13804)

Harvest Homes and Handi Houses..............G..... 704 637-3878
  Salisbury (G-13975)

Harvest Homes and Handi Houses..............G..... 336 243-2382
  Lexington (G-9728)

Heritage Building Company LLC.................F..... 704 431-4494
  Statesville (G-14811)

Heritage Steel LLC......................................F..... 704 431-4097
  Salisbury (G-13978)

Innovative Awngs & Screens LLC................F..... 833 337-4233
  Cornelius (G-4561)

J&J Outdoor Accessories............................G..... 910 742-1969
  Delco (G-4721)

Lear Metal Carports LLC.............................G..... 877 219-4677
  Mount Airy (G-11537)

Lees Screen Enclosures & More..................G..... 843 283-7227
  Sunset Beach (G-15000)

Leonard Alum Utility Bldngs Inc...................G..... 336 226-9410
  Burlington (G-1450)

Leonard Alum Utility Bldngs Inc...................G..... 919 872-4442
  Raleigh (G-12968)

Leonard Alum Utility Bldngs Inc...................G..... 910 392-4921
  Wilmington (G-16299)

Leonard Alum Utility Bldngs Inc...................D..... 336 789-5018
  Mount Airy (G-11538)

◆ Lock Drives Inc...G..... 704 588-1844
  Pineville (G-12281)

M & R Forestry Service Inc..........................G..... 980 439-1261
  Albemarle (G-96)

Manufacturing Structures LLC.....................G..... 828 264-6198
  Boone (G-1217)

Mast Woodworks..F..... 336 468-1194
  Hamptonville (G-7677)

Mayse Manufacturing Co Inc.......................G..... 828 245-1891
  Forest City (G-6076)

McGee Corporation......................................E..... 980 721-1911
  Matthews (G-10269)

▼ McGee Corporation..................................D..... 704 882-1500
  Matthews (G-10270)

Metal Buildings Charlotte.............................G..... 980 365-6583
  Midland (G-10471)

Metallum Structures Inc...............................G..... 877 517-4422
  Mount Airy (G-11545)

Millennium Buildings Inc..............................G..... 866 216-8499
  Dobson (G-4829)

▼ Millennium Mfg Structures LLC................F..... 828 265-3737
  Boone (G-1222)

Milligan House Movers Inc..........................G..... 910 653-2272
  Tabor City (G-15084)

Mobile Mini - Stor Tanks Pumps..................G..... 919 365-0377
  Knightdale (G-9421)

Mobile Mini Inc...G..... 480 894-6311
  Knightdale (G-9422)

Mobile Mini Inc...G..... 919 365-3057
  Wendell (G-15908)

Morton Buildings Inc....................................G..... 252 291-1300
  Wilson (G-16516)

Nash Building Systems Inc..........................F..... 252 823-1905
  Tarboro (G-15118)

Nci Group Inc...G..... 919 926-4800
  Raleigh (G-13059)

Neals Carpentry & Cnstr..............................G..... 910 346-6154
  Jacksonville (G-9017)

Norwood Manufacturing Inc.........................E..... 704 474-0505
  Norwood (G-12042)

◆ Nucor Corporation....................................C..... 704 366-7000
  Charlotte (G-3281)

OSteel Buildings Inc....................................F..... 704 824-6061
  Gastonia (G-6481)

Pine View Buildings LLC.............................D..... 704 876-1501
  Statesville (G-14860)

▲ Remedios LLC..G..... 203 453-6000
  Charlotte (G-3429)

Richfeld Prtable Buildings Inc......................G..... 704 463-1802
  Richfield (G-13554)

RMC Advanced Technologies Inc................D..... 704 325-7100
  Newton (G-11964)

▲ Robco Manufacturing Inc.........................E..... 252 438-7399
  Henderson (G-7807)

Rogers Manufacturing Company..................G..... 910 259-9898
  Burgaw (G-1349)

Simonton Windows & Doors Inc..................D..... 919 677-3938
  Cary (G-1890)

Southeastern Outdoor Pdts Inc....................E..... 910 608-0015
  Lumberton (G-10055)

Southern Leisure Builders Inc......................G..... 910 381-0426
  Jacksonville (G-9037)

Storage System Solutions Inc......................G..... 336 710-5600
  Mount Airy (G-11578)

Sunshine Mnfctred Strctres Inc....................E..... 704 279-6600
  Rockwell (G-13659)

T-N-T Carports Inc......................................G..... 336 789-3818
  Mount Airy (G-11586)

▼ T-N-T Carports Inc..................................E..... 336 789-3818
  Mount Airy (G-11587)

Toza Truss LLC...G..... 336 301-6338
  Bennett (G-1028)

34 FABRICATED METAL PRODUCTS

Tri-State Carports Inc .... G 276 755-2081
  Mount Airy *(G-11590)*
Triton Industries LLC .... F 336 816-3794
  Mount Airy *(G-11591)*
Turner Equipment Company Inc .... E 919 734-8328
  Goldsboro *(G-6667)*
Twin Carports LLC .... F 336 790-8284
  East Bend *(G-5470)*
Twin Carports LLC .... G 866 486-3924
  Pilot Mountain *(G-12203)*
Unrivaled Metal Buildings LLC .... G 844 848-8676
  Maiden *(G-10121)*
US Chemical Storage LLC .... E 828 264-6032
  Wilkesboro *(G-16050)*
◆ Van Wingerden Grnhse Co Inc .... E 828 891-7389
  Mills River *(G-10513)*
Veon Inc .... F 252 623-2102
  Washington *(G-15736)*
Viking Steel Structures LLC .... G 877 623-7549
  Boonville *(G-1258)*
Vinyl Structures LLC .... G 336 468-4311
  Hamptonville *(G-7680)*
Wholesale Direct Carports .... G 336 399-3221
  King *(G-9285)*
▲ Williamson Greenhouses Inc .... F 910 592-7072
  Clinton *(G-4118)*

3449 Miscellaneous metalwork

◆ 3a Composites USA Inc .... C 704 872-8974
  Statesville *(G-14732)*
Blue Mountain Metalworks Inc .... G 828 898-8582
  Banner Elk *(G-894)*
Canalta Enterprises LLC .... E 919 615-1570
  Raleigh *(G-12586)*
Composite Factory LLC .... F 484 264-3306
  Mooresville *(G-10910)*
Concept Steel Inc .... G 704 874-0414
  Gastonia *(G-6382)*
Custom Design Inc .... G 704 637-7110
  Salisbury *(G-13951)*
Dave Steel Company Inc .... F 828 252-2771
  Asheville *(G-603)*
Dave Steel Company Inc .... D 828 252-2771
  Asheville *(G-604)*
Davis Steel and Iron Co Inc .... E 704 821-7676
  Matthews *(G-10311)*
Dwiggins Metal Masters Inc .... G 336 751-2379
  Mocksville *(G-10568)*
Eland Industries Inc .... E 910 304-5353
  Hampstead *(G-7646)*
Freedom Industries Inc .... C 252 984-0007
  Rocky Mount *(G-13698)*
Gastonia Ornamental Wldg Inc .... F 704 827-1146
  Mount Holly *(G-11635)*
Gerdau Ameristeel US Inc .... E 919 833-9737
  Raleigh *(G-12798)*
Gorilla Offroad Company .... G 815 715-6003
  Rolesville *(G-13757)*
J F Fabricators LLC .... G 704 454-7224
  Harrisburg *(G-7713)*
Keypoint LLC .... F 704 962-8110
  Waxhaw *(G-15764)*
Low Country Steel SC LLC .... E 336 283-9611
  Winston Salem *(G-16793)*
Lowder Steel Inc .... E 336 431-9000
  Archdale *(G-293)*
Paul Charles Englert .... G 704 824-2102
  Gastonia *(G-6487)*
Pigeon Rver Cstm Mtalworks LLC .... G 828 619-0559
  Canton *(G-1623)*
Protech Metals LLC .... E 910 295-6905
  Pinehurst *(G-12232)*

Queen City Engrg & Design .... G 704 918-5851
  Concord *(G-4344)*
Simpson Strong-Tie Company Inc .... E 336 841-1338
  High Point *(G-8532)*
Steel Smart Incorporated .... E 919 736-0681
  Pikeville *(G-12194)*
Steelfab Inc .... B 704 394-5376
  Charlotte *(G-3627)*
Steelfab of Virginia Inc .... E 919 828-9545
  Raleigh *(G-13301)*
Umi Company Inc .... G 704 479-6210
  Lincolnton *(G-9932)*
Underbrinks LLC .... G 866 495-4465
  Salisbury *(G-14059)*
Universal Steel NC LLC .... E 336 476-3105
  Thomasville *(G-15298)*

3451 Screw machine products

Abbott Products Inc .... E 336 463-3135
  Yadkinville *(G-17029)*
Accuking Inc .... G 252 649-2323
  New Bern *(G-11765)*
Angels Path Ventures Inc .... G 828 654-9530
  Arden *(G-309)*
B & Y Machining Co Inc .... G 252 235-2180
  Bailey *(G-868)*
Barefoot Cnc Inc .... G 828 438-5038
  Morganton *(G-11199)*
Black Mtn Mch Fabrication Inc .... E 828 669-9557
  Black Mountain *(G-1121)*
Bravo Team LLC .... E 704 309-1918
  Mooresville *(G-10887)*
Carolina Screw Products .... G 336 760-7400
  Winston Salem *(G-16648)*
Conner Brothers Machine Co Inc .... D 704 864-6084
  Bessemer City *(G-1056)*
Curtis L Maclean L C .... G 704 940-5531
  Mooresville *(G-10919)*
Edward Heil Screw Products .... G 828 345-6140
  Conover *(G-4449)*
Ellison Technologies Inc .... D 704 545-7362
  Charlotte *(G-2699)*
Gary J Younts Machine Company .... F 336 476-7930
  Thomasville *(G-15227)*
Griffiths Corporation .... G 704 554-5657
  Pineville *(G-12272)*
▲ IMS Usa LLC .... G 910 796-2040
  Wilmington *(G-16265)*
M & W Industries Inc .... E 704 837-0331
  Charlotte *(G-3113)*
Manufacturing Services Inc .... E 704 629-4163
  Bessemer City *(G-1074)*
Tomarjo Corp .... G 336 762-0065
  Thomasville *(G-15291)*
West Side Industries LLC .... G 980 223-8665
  Statesville *(G-14924)*

3452 Bolts, nuts, rivets, and washers

Acument Global Technologies .... G 704 598-3539
  Charlotte *(G-2132)*
▲ Avdel USA LLC .... E 704 888-7100
  Stanfield *(G-14675)*
Belwith Products LLC .... G 336 841-3899
  High Point *(G-8270)*
▲ C E Smith Co Inc .... E 336 273-0166
  Greensboro *(G-6872)*
Cardinal America Inc .... G 704 810-1620
  Statesville *(G-14771)*
Derita Precision Mch Co Inc .... F 704 392-7285
  Charlotte *(G-2620)*
Gesipa Fasteners Usa Inc .... E 336 751-1855
  Mocksville *(G-10577)*

Lightning Bolt Ink LLC .... G 828 281-1274
  Asheville *(G-686)*
Masonite Corporation .... B 704 599-0235
  Charlotte *(G-3138)*
McJast Inc .... F 828 884-4809
  Pisgah Forest *(G-12326)*
Metal Processors Inc .... F 336 993-2181
  Kernersville *(G-9216)*
Moore S Welding Service Inc .... G 919 837-5769
  Bear Creek *(G-940)*
◆ Pan American Screw LLC .... D 828 466-0060
  Conover *(G-4478)*
Pins and Needles .... G 910 639-9662
  Pinebluff *(G-12216)*
Power Washer Pros .... G 252 446-4643
  Rocky Mount *(G-13722)*

3462 Iron and steel forgings

Altra Industrial Motion Corp .... D 704 588-5610
  Charlotte *(G-2173)*
Artistic Ironworks LLC .... G 919 908-6888
  Durham *(G-4927)*
Authentic Iron LLC .... G 910 648-6989
  Bladenboro *(G-1143)*
Blue Horseshoe .... G 980 312-8202
  Charlotte *(G-2321)*
Carroll Co .... F 919 779-1900
  Garner *(G-6262)*
Chatham Steel Corporation .... E 912 233-4182
  Durham *(G-5013)*
Consolidated Pipe & Sup Co Inc .... F 336 294-8577
  Greensboro *(G-6930)*
◆ GKN Driveline Newton LLC .... A 828 428-3711
  Newton *(G-11933)*
H Horseshoe .... G 336 853-5913
  Lexington *(G-9727)*
▲ Ketchie-Houston Inc .... E 704 786-5101
  Concord *(G-4300)*
▲ Liechti America .... G 704 948-1277
  Huntersville *(G-8852)*
▲ Linamar Forgings Carolina Inc .... D 252 237-8181
  Wilson *(G-16511)*
Minute-Man Products Inc .... E 828 692-0256
  East Flat Rock *(G-5477)*
Northern Cres Ir / Matt Wldrop .... E 828 848-8884
  Zirconia *(G-17156)*
Pierce Farrier Supply Inc .... G 704 753-4358
  Indian Trail *(G-8957)*
Roush & Yates Racing Engs LLC .... D 704 799-6216
  Mooresville *(G-11073)*
▲ Roush & Yates Racing Engs LLC .... C 704 799-6216
  Mooresville *(G-11074)*
S Duff Fabricating Inc .... G 910 298-3060
  Beulaville *(G-1098)*
Sona Autocomp USA LLC .... C 919 965-5555
  Selma *(G-14260)*
◆ Sona Blw Precision Forge Inc .... C 919 828-3375
  Selma *(G-14261)*
◆ Tim Conner Enterprises Inc .... E 704 629-4327
  Bessemer City *(G-1085)*
Victory 1 Performance Inc .... F 704 799-1955
  Mooresville *(G-11118)*
Volvo Motor Graders Inc .... D 704 609-3604
  Charlotte *(G-3782)*
Yates Precision Machining LLC .... F 704 662-7165
  Mooresville *(G-11136)*

3463 Nonferrous forgings

ABB Motors and Mechanical Inc .... C 828 645-1706
  Weaverville *(G-15836)*
Accudyne Industries LLC .... E 469 518-4777
  Davidson *(G-4665)*

SIC SECTION
34 FABRICATED METAL PRODUCTS

Emmco Sport LLC .... G 336 354-7244
   Kernersville *(G-9196)*

Entrust Services LLC .... F 336 274-5175
   Greensboro *(G-7002)*

3465 Automotive stampings

919 Motoring LLC .... G 919 872-4996
   Raleigh *(G-12450)*

AMF-NC Enterprise Company LLC .... F 704 489-2206
   Denver *(G-4760)*

Belwith Products LLC .... G 336 841-3899
   High Point *(G-8270)*

▲ Borgwarner Turbo Systems LLC .... D 828 650-7515
   Arden *(G-315)*

Continental Auto Systems Inc .... B 828 654-2000
   Fletcher *(G-5996)*

Coopers Fayetteville Inc .... F 910 483-0606
   Fayetteville *(G-5796)*

Dutch Miller Charlotte Inc .... E 704 522-8422
   Charlotte *(G-2660)*

Gray Manufacturing Tech LLC .... G 704 489-2206
   Denver *(G-4778)*

Harrah Enterprise Ltd .... G 336 253-3963
   Cornelius *(G-4554)*

▲ Irvan-Smith Inc .... F 704 788-2554
   Concord *(G-4290)*

Off Road Addiction .... G 910 620-4675
   Fayetteville *(G-5885)*

Performance Entps & Parts Inc .... G 336 621-6572
   Greensboro *(G-7251)*

Revmax Performance LLC .... F 877 780-4334
   Charlotte *(G-3440)*

Revolution Pd LLC .... G 919 949-0241
   Pittsboro *(G-12347)*

Shiloh Products Inc .... G 336 548-6035
   Mayodan *(G-10367)*

Vibration Solutions LLC .... G 704 896-7535
   Charlotte *(G-3776)*

3466 Crowns and closures

Aquahut .... G 704 335-8554
   Charlotte *(G-2207)*

◆ Assa Abloy ACC Door Cntrls Gro .... C 877 974-2255
   Monroe *(G-10653)*

3469 Metal stampings, nec

ABT Manufacturing LLC .... E 704 847-9188
   Statesville *(G-14736)*

Acme Aerofab LLC .... G 704 806-3582
   Charlotte *(G-2129)*

Alleghany Garbage Service Inc .... G 336 372-4413
   Sparta *(G-14587)*

Allied Tool and Machine Co .... G 336 993-2131
   Kernersville *(G-9160)*

Allred Metal Stamping Works Inc .... E 336 886-5221
   High Point *(G-8242)*

Ashdan Enterprises .... G 336 375-9698
   Greensboro *(G-6818)*

Atlantic Tool & Die Co Inc .... G 910 270-2888
   Hampstead *(G-7638)*

Belwith Products LLC .... G 336 841-3899
   High Point *(G-8270)*

Bnp Inc .... F 919 775-7070
   Sanford *(G-14094)*

Border Concepts Inc .... G 336 248-2419
   Lexington *(G-9686)*

Burris Machine Company Inc .... G 828 322-6914
   Hickory *(G-7955)*

C E Smith Co Inc .... E 336 273-0166
   Greensboro *(G-6871)*

▲ C E Smith Co Inc .... E 336 273-0166
   Greensboro *(G-6872)*

Carolina Metals Inc .... E 828 667-0876
   Asheville *(G-582)*

Carolina Stamping Company .... D 704 637-0260
   Salisbury *(G-13938)*

◆ Ceramco Incorporated .... E 704 588-4814
   Charlotte *(G-2444)*

City of Graham .... F 336 570-6811
   Graham *(G-6684)*

CMS Tool and Die Inc .... F 910 458-3322
   Carolina Beach *(G-1636)*

Col-Eve Metal Products Co .... G 336 472-7039
   Lexington *(G-9696)*

Component Sourcing Intl LLC .... E 704 843-9292
   Charlotte *(G-2534)*

Curleys Plumbing .... G 252 578-8666
   Roanoke Rapids *(G-13573)*

▲ Custom Cnverting Solutions Inc .... E 336 292-2616
   Greensboro *(G-6949)*

Derita Precision Mch Co Inc .... F 704 392-7285
   Charlotte *(G-2620)*

DMV Commissioners Office .... G 704 679-3914
   Charlotte *(G-2649)*

Dynamic Stampings of NC I .... G 704 864-1572
   Gastonia *(G-6399)*

Erdle Perforating Holdings Inc .... F 704 588-4380
   Charlotte *(G-2726)*

▼ Friedrich Metal Pdts Co Inc .... E 336 375-3067
   Browns Summit *(G-1303)*

Furniture At Work .... F 336 472-6619
   Trinity *(G-15341)*

Gasser and Sons .... G 910 471-6907
   Wilmington *(G-16227)*

Gerald Hartsoe .... G 336 498-3233
   Randleman *(G-13471)*

Gold Medal North Carolina II .... G 336 665-4997
   Greensboro *(G-7050)*

Griffiths Corporation .... D 704 552-6793
   Pineville *(G-12271)*

Griffiths Corporation .... D 704 554-5657
   Pineville *(G-12272)*

Henry & Rye Incorporated .... F 919 365-7045
   Wendell *(G-15904)*

▲ Hi-Tech Fabrication Inc .... C 919 781-6150
   Raleigh *(G-12842)*

▲ Home Impressions Inc .... B 828 328-1142
   Hickory *(G-8059)*

▲ Hunt Country Component LLC .... G 336 475-7000
   Thomasville *(G-15233)*

Innovative Mfg Solutions Inc .... G 919 219-2424
   Apex *(G-207)*

▲ Interactive Safety Pdts Inc .... E 704 664-7377
   Huntersville *(G-8835)*

Iv-S Metal Stamping Inc .... E 336 861-2100
   Archdale *(G-286)*

Jacob Holtz Company .... E 828 328-1003
   Hickory *(G-8070)*

◆ K & S Tool & Manufacturing Co .... E 336 410-7260
   High Point *(G-8419)*

◆ Kessebohmer USA Inc .... F 910 338-5080
   Wilmington *(G-16289)*

License Plate Agency .... G 910 763-7076
   Wilmington *(G-16300)*

Lidseen North Carolina Inc .... G 828 389-8082
   Hayesville *(G-7768)*

▲ M-B Industries Inc .... C 828 862-4201
   Rosman *(G-13786)*

Mac/Fab Company Inc .... E 704 822-1103
   Mount Holly *(G-11641)*

Matt Bieneman Enterprises LLC .... G 704 856-0200
   Mooresville *(G-11017)*

McJast Inc .... F 828 884-4809
   Pisgah Forest *(G-12326)*

Metal Works High Point Inc .... D 336 886-4612
   High Point *(G-8453)*

Metalfab of North Carolina LLC .... C 704 841-1090
   Matthews *(G-10271)*

▲ Moores Mch Co Fayetteville Inc .... D 919 837-5354
   Bear Creek *(G-941)*

NC License Plate .... G 336 889-8247
   High Point *(G-8462)*

NC License Plate Agency .... G 910 347-1000
   Jacksonville *(G-9016)*

NC Motor Vhcl Lcnse Plate Agcy .... G 336 228-7152
   Burlington *(G-1468)*

▲ Nederman Corporation .... F 704 399-7441
   Charlotte *(G-3244)*

New Can Company Inc .... G 704 853-3711
   Gastonia *(G-6476)*

New Standard Corporation .... C 252 446-5481
   Rocky Mount *(G-13714)*

North Carolina Dept Trnsp .... E 704 633-5873
   Salisbury *(G-14020)*

North Crlina Lcense Plate Agcy .... G 910 485-1590
   Fayetteville *(G-5884)*

Parker Industries Inc .... D 828 437-7779
   Connelly Springs *(G-4407)*

▲ Precision Concepts Group LLC .... B 336 761-8572
   Winston Salem *(G-16863)*

Precision Partners LLC .... E 800 545-3121
   Charlotte *(G-3370)*

Precision Stampers Inc .... G 919 366-3333
   Wendell *(G-15912)*

Precision Tool & Stamping Inc .... E 910 592-0174
   Clinton *(G-4102)*

▲ RC Investment Company .... E 336 226-5511
   Burlington *(G-1483)*

Rfr Metal Fabrication Inc .... D 919 693-1354
   Oxford *(G-12151)*

Robinson Mch & Cutter Grinding .... G 704 629-5591
   Bessemer City *(G-1080)*

▲ Select Stainless Products LLC .... E 888 843-2345
   Charlotte *(G-3524)*

Singer Equipment Company Inc .... E 910 484-1128
   Fayetteville *(G-5918)*

SMC Holdco Inc .... G 910 844-3956
   Laurinburg *(G-9498)*

Southern Spring & Stamping .... F 336 548-3520
   Stokesdale *(G-14949)*

Spruce Pine Mica Company .... F 828 765-4241
   Spruce Pine *(G-14659)*

Stamping School LLC .... G 407 435-3135
   Hendersonville *(G-7905)*

Stroup Machine & Mfg Inc .... G 704 394-0023
   Charlotte *(G-3641)*

Team 21st .... F 910 826-3676
   Fayetteville *(G-5928)*

Thompson & Little Inc .... E 910 484-1128
   Fayetteville *(G-5929)*

Toner Machining Tech Inc .... D 828 432-8007
   Morganton *(G-11261)*

Toolcraft Inc North Carolina .... F 828 659-7379
   Marion *(G-10183)*

◆ Toter LLC .... D 800 424-0422
   Statesville *(G-14916)*

Umi Company Inc .... G 704 479-6210
   Lincolnton *(G-9932)*

United TI & Stamping Co NC Inc .... D 910 323-8588
   Fayetteville *(G-5939)*

◆ Vrush Industries Inc .... F 336 886-7700
   High Point *(G-8597)*

Wolverine Mtal Stmping Sltons .... E 919 774-4729
   Sanford *(G-14208)*

Youngs Welding & Machine Svcs .... G 910 488-1190
   Fayetteville *(G-5955)*

Employee Codes: A=Over 500 employees, B=251-500
C=101-250, D=51-100, E=20-50, F=10-19, G=1-9

34 FABRICATED METAL PRODUCTS

3471 Plating and polishing

Advanced Motor Sports Coatings.......... G 336 472-5518
   Thomasville *(G-15181)*

Advanced Plating Technologies .... G 704 291-9325
   Monroe *(G-10637)*

Advplating LLC .... G 704 291-9325
   Monroe *(G-10638)*

Allied Metal Finishing Inc .... E 704 347-1477
   Charlotte *(G-2159)*

Allied Plating Finishing LLC .... G 704 347-1477
   Charlotte *(G-2160)*

Amplate Inc .... E 704 607-0191
   Charlotte *(G-2189)*

Asheville Metal Finishing Inc .... E 828 253-1476
   Asheville *(G-539)*

Blue Ridge Plating Company .... G 828 274-1795
   Hendersonville *(G-7827)*

C & R Hard Chrome Service Inc .... G 704 861-8831
   Gastonia *(G-6364)*

Capitol Bumper .... G 919 772-7330
   Fayetteville *(G-5782)*

Capitol Bumper .... G 919 772-7330
   Fayetteville *(G-5781)*

Carolina Finshg & Coating Inc .... F 704 730-8233
   Kings Mountain *(G-9299)*

Charlotte Metal Finishing Inc .... G 704 732-7570
   Lincolnton *(G-9881)*

Charlotte Plating Inc .... G 704 552-2100
   Charlotte *(G-2460)*

Chrome Man... G 704 550-6423
   Midland *(G-10461)*

Custom Metal Finishing .... G 704 445-1710
   Cherryville *(G-3866)*

Dave Steel Company Inc .... D 828 252-2771
   Asheville *(G-604)*

Fairmont Metal Finishing Inc .... G 336 434-4188
   Archdale *(G-278)*

Far From A Maid LLC .... G 803 610-1727
   Charlotte *(G-2747)*

Greensboro Platers .... G 336 274-7654
   Greensboro *(G-7065)*

H & H Polishing Inc................................. E 704 393-8728
   Charlotte *(G-2876)*

Hi-TEC Plating Inc................................. F 704 872-8969
   Statesville *(G-14814)*

▲ Hi-Tech Fabrication Inc...................... C 919 781-6150
   Raleigh *(G-12842)*

Industrial Anodizing .... F 336 434-2110
   Trinity *(G-15346)*

Industrial Elcpltg Co Inc .... G 704 867-4547
   Gastonia *(G-6424)*

Industrial Elcpltg Co Inc .... D 704 867-4547
   Gastonia *(G-6425)*

▲ Kayne & Son Custom Hdwr Inc.......... G 828 665-1988
   Candler *(G-1585)*

Keiths Cleaning LLC................................ G 336 701-0185
   Winston Salem *(G-16776)*

♦ Kings Mountain Intl Inc....................... D 704 739-4227
   Kings Mountain *(G-9313)*

L F T Inc .... G 828 253-6830
   Asheville *(G-678)*

Lees Polishing & Powdercoatin............... G 704 827-4309
   Stanley *(G-14700)*

Malcolms Metal & More .... G 828 286-1419
   Bostic *(G-1263)*

Marc Staples Sculpture .... G 919 475-9633
   Durham *(G-5208)*

▲ Master Form Inc .... E 704 292-1041
   Matthews *(G-10331)*

Nb Corporation.. F 336 852-8786
   Greensboro *(G-7214)*

Nb Corporation.. E 336 274-7654
   Greensboro *(G-7215)*

▲ Paragon Navigator Inc........................ G 336 316-1206
   Greensboro *(G-7243)*

Parker Metal Finishing Company............ F 336 275-9657
   Greensboro *(G-7244)*

Phillips Plating Co Inc .... G 252 637-2695
   Bridgeton *(G-1295)*

Piedmont Plating Corporation .... E 336 272-2311
   Greensboro *(G-7260)*

Precision Alloys Inc .... F 919 231-6329
   Raleigh *(G-13133)*

Precision Metal Finishing Inc.................. G 704 799-0250
   Mooresville *(G-11059)*

Prince Group LLC .... E 828 681-8860
   Mills River *(G-10509)*

Rodeco Company .... F 919 775-7149
   Sanford *(G-14175)*

Scrappys Metal LLC............................... G 828 557-5861
   Murphy *(G-11715)*

▼ Short Run Pro LLC.............................. F 704 825-1599
   Belmont *(G-1007)*

Sterling Rack Inc..................................... F 704 866-9131
   Gastonia *(G-6516)*

Stratford Metalfinishing Inc .... E 336 723-7946
   Winston Salem *(G-16920)*

Surtronics Inc.. E 919 834-8027
   Raleigh *(G-13318)*

Te Connectivity Corporation .... C 336 665-4400
   Greensboro *(G-7394)*

Tico Polishing .... G 704 788-2466
   Concord *(G-4377)*

Triad Anodizing & Plating Inc................. G 336 292-7028
   Greensboro *(G-7412)*

United Mtal Fnshg Inc Grnsboro............ E 336 272-8107
   Greensboro *(G-7431)*

United TI & Stamping Co NC Inc............ D 910 323-8588
   Fayetteville *(G-5939)*

Universal Black Oxide Inc .... G 704 867-1772
   Gastonia *(G-6534)*

Williams Plating Company Inc................ F 828 681-0301
   Arden *(G-391)*

▲ Xceldyne Group LLC .... D 336 472-2242
   Thomasville *(G-15307)*

Yontz & Sons Painting Inc .... G 336 784-7099
   Winston Salem *(G-16990)*

3479 Metal coating and allied services

A-1 Coatings... G 704 790-9528
   Salisbury *(G-13911)*

A1 Powder Coating LLC......................... G 704 394-0705
   Charlotte *(G-2120)*

Abcor Supply Inc.................................... F 919 468-0856
   Chapel Hill *(G-1981)*

Acme Nameplate & Mfg Inc.................... G 704 283-8175
   Monroe *(G-10635)*

Anatech Ltd.. F 704 489-1488
   Denver *(G-4761)*

Area 51 Powder Coating Inc................... F 910 769-1724
   Wilmington *(G-16114)*

As Inc.. G 704 225-1700
   Monroe *(G-10651)*

Auto Parts Fayetteville LLC.................... G 910 889-4026
   Fayetteville *(G-5766)*

Big Oak Coatings LLC............................. G 919 771-8470
   Raleigh *(G-12556)*

Boyd Gmn Inc... C 206 284-2200
   Monroe *(G-10668)*

C&V Powder Coating .... G 910 228-1173
   Leland *(G-9531)*

Calico Technologies Inc .... E 704 483-2202
   Denver *(G-4767)*

Candy Cane Coatings............................. G 919 605-6997
   Willow Spring *(G-16078)*

Carolina Coastal Coatings .... F 910 346-9607
   Jacksonville *(G-8994)*

Carolina Coastal Coatings Inc .... F 910 346-9607
   Maple Hill *(G-10131)*

Carolina Custom Coating .... G 704 224-1503
   Rockwell *(G-13647)*

Carolina Powder Coating .... G 336 934-6102
   Yadkinville *(G-17035)*

Champion Powdercoating Inc .... G 704 866-8148
   Gastonia *(G-6374)*

Cincinnati Thermal Spray Inc .... E 910 675-2909
   Rocky Point *(G-13744)*

Clear Stone Coating Inc......................... G 424 543-0811
   Wake Forest *(G-15542)*

Cloud9 Coatings LLc.............................. G 704 252-0287
   Charlotte *(G-2499)*

Cmt Metal Finishes .... G 828 400-0626
   Waynesville *(G-15799)*

Coating Concepts Inc............................ G 704 391-0499
   Charlotte *(G-2511)*

Coatings Technologies Inc .... F 704 821-8231
   Indian Trail *(G-8927)*

CRC... G 704 664-1242
   Mooresville *(G-10917)*

Crown Trophy Inc.................................... G 336 851-1011
   Greensboro *(G-6944)*

Cryptic Coatings .... G 828 994-4474
   Conover *(G-4443)*

Cryptic Coatings Ltd............................... G 704 966-1617
   Denver *(G-4770)*

Custom Chrome & Coatings Inc .... G 704 226-6808
   Charlotte *(G-2588)*

Custom Powder Worx.............................. G 828 310-1373
   Taylorsville *(G-15138)*

Dannys Sandblasting.............................. G 910 876-4596
   Bladenboro *(G-1147)*

Dj Powdercoating Ironwork LLC............. G 336 310-4725
   Kernersville *(G-9191)*

Dotson Metal Finishing Inc..................... F 828 298-9844
   Asheville *(G-612)*

Eric Arnold Klein..................................... F 828 464-0001
   Newton *(G-11931)*

Ew Painting LLC..................................... E 252 375-1403
   Winterville *(G-17000)*

Exotics Power Coat................................. G 336 831-3865
   Kernersville *(G-9199)*

♦ Galvan Industries Inc......................... C 704 455-5102
   Harrisburg *(G-7711)*

Galvanizing Consultants Inc.................. G 336 603-4218
   Whitsett *(G-15991)*

Greg Price.. G 847 778-4426
   Hampstead *(G-7648)*

▲ H M Elliott Inc..................................... F 704 663-8226
   Mooresville *(G-10967)*

Hemco Wire Products Inc .... F 336 454-7280
   Jamestown *(G-9052)*

▲ Hi-Tech Fabrication Inc...................... C 919 781-6150
   Raleigh *(G-12842)*

HMS Protec Inc.. G 954 803-2319
   Maggie Valley *(G-10095)*

Hot Box Power Coating Inc.................... G 704 398-8224
   Charlotte *(G-2924)*

Industrial Cting Solutions Inc................ G 910 398-7556
   Leland *(G-9549)*

JC Powder Coating LLC.......................... G 919 362-9311
   New Hill *(G-11861)*

Jimmys Coating Unlimited Inc............... G 704 915-2420
   Gastonia *(G-6435)*

Jonathan Stamey..................................... G 828 577-0450
   Pisgah Forest *(G-12324)*

34 FABRICATED METAL PRODUCTS

Kelleys Sports and Awards Inc .... G 828 728-4600
  Hudson (G-8772)
Landmark Coatings LLC .... G 336 492-2492
  Mocksville (G-10583)
Made By Custom LLC .... G 704 980-9840
  Charlotte (G-3117)
Mendozas Powder Coating LLC .... G 336 877-0783
  West Jefferson (G-15944)
National Carton and Coating Co .... G 704 647-0705
  Salisbury (G-14015)
NC Graphic Pros LLC .... G 252 492-7326
  Kittrell (G-9397)
Noble Custom Coatings LLC .... G 910 228-6216
  Wilmington (G-16337)
Oerlikon Metco (us) Inc .... F 713 715-6300
  Huntersville (G-8871)
Ontario Spcialty Coatings Corp .... G 980 207-3944
  Charlotte (G-3303)
Pages Hydro Dipping Coatings .... G 910 322-2077
  Linden (G-9941)
Piedmont Lminating Coating Inc .... F 336 272-1600
  Greensboro (G-7258)
Powder Coat USA .... G 919 954-7170
  Raleigh (G-13121)
Powder Coating By 3 S X .... G 704 784-3724
  Concord (G-4334)
Powder Coating Services Inc .... E 704 349-4100
  Gastonia (G-6491)
Powder Systems Inc .... F 336 885-1352
  High Point (G-8490)
Powder Works Inc .... F 336 475-7715
  Thomasville (G-15265)
Powdertek .... G 828 225-3250
  Arden (G-364)
Premier Powder Coating Inc .... G 336 672-3828
  Asheboro (G-466)
Prime Coatings .... G 828 217-8287
  Hickory (G-8121)
Prime Coatings LLC .... G 828 855-1136
  Hickory (G-8122)
Prince Group LLC .... E 828 681-8860
  Mills River (G-10509)
Prince Manufacturing Corp .... C 828 681-8860
  Mills River (G-10510)
Procoaters Inc .... F 336 992-0012
  Kernersville (G-9226)
Product Finishing Solutions Co .... G 704 785-8941
  Concord (G-4341)
Product Identification Inc .... E 919 544-4136
  Durham (G-5305)
Professional Laminating LLC .... G 919 465-0400
  Cary (G-1862)
Protech Metals LLC .... E 910 295-6905
  Pinehurst (G-12232)
Purthermal LLC .... G 828 855-0108
  Hickory (G-8129)
Quad City High Prfmce Coatings .... F 937 623-2282
  Leland (G-9557)
R & R Powder Coating Inc .... F 704 853-0727
  Dallas (G-4653)
Raleigh Powder Coating Co .... G 919 301-8065
  Raleigh (G-13180)
Randolph Machine Inc .... G 336 799-1039
  Randleman (G-13487)
Roadrunner Powder Coating .... G 919 749-5290
  Benson (G-1042)
Rogue Custom Kote LLC .... G 919 498-5000
  Sanford (G-14177)
RPM Wood Finishes Group Inc .... D 828 261-0325
  Hickory (G-8141)
RPM Wood Finishes Group Inc .... D 828 728-8266
  Hudson (G-8777)

RR Powder Coatings .... G 704 240-3266
  Lincolnton (G-9916)
Russell T Bundy Associates Inc .... F 704 523-6132
  Charlotte (G-3473)
South Atlantic LLC .... F 336 376-0410
  Graham (G-6711)
◆ South Atlantic LLC .... F 910 332-1900
  Wilmington (G-16408)
Southeast Blastg & Coating LLC .... G 252 725-0010
  Morehead City (G-11191)
Southern Pnt Powdr Coating Co .... G 704 843-5505
  Waxhaw (G-15776)
Southland Coatings Tech LLC .... G 336 644-8919
  Oak Ridge (G-12067)
Southside Protective Coatings .... G 757 938-9188
  Gates (G-6545)
Structral Catings Hertford LLC .... F 919 553-3034
  Cofield (G-4138)
Superior Powder Coating LLC .... G 704 869-0004
  Gastonia (G-6519)
Tactical Coatings Inc .... G 704 692-4511
  Shelby (G-14371)
▲ TEC Coat .... E 412 215-0152
  Charlotte (G-3676)
Triangle Coatings Inc .... G 919 781-6108
  Morrisville (G-11451)
▲ Turbocoating Corp .... E 828 328-8726
  Hickory (G-8191)
Ultra Coatings Incorporated .... E 336 883-8853
  High Point (G-8584)
United TI & Stamping Co NC Inc .... D 910 323-8588
  Fayetteville (G-5939)
Universal Black Oxide Inc .... G 704 867-1772
  Gastonia (G-6534)
Waste Container Repair Svcs .... G 910 257-4474
  Fayetteville (G-5949)
Weapon Works LLC .... G 800 556-9498
  Burlington (G-1516)

3482 Small arms ammunition

Canis Lupus Enterprises LLC .... G 828 450-2074
  Hendersonville (G-7832)
Easy E Enterprises LLC .... G 704 763-7906
  Durham (G-5075)
Every Day Carry LLc .... F 203 231-0256
  Winnabow (G-16580)
Global Synergy Group Inc .... G 704 254-9886
  Matthews (G-10318)
Gridlock Enterprises LLC .... G 910 939-4867
  Jacksonville (G-9006)
Interordnance Amer Ltd Partnr .... G 321 212-7801
  Monroe (G-10740)
Michael Ray McKinney .... G 828 765-7001
  Spruce Pine (G-14650)
North American Trade LLC .... G 828 712-3004
  Fletcher (G-6030)
R & S Precision Customs LLC .... G 704 984-3480
  Albemarle (G-101)
Riley Defense Inc .... G 704 507-9224
  Hickory (G-8136)
Sirius Tactical Entps LLC .... G 704 256-3660
  Waxhaw (G-15775)
SRI Gear LLC .... G 704 910-2751
  Charlotte (G-3612)
▲ Stillwood Ammun Systems LLC .... G 919 721-9096
  Burlington (G-1502)

3483 Ammunition, except for small arms, nec

Custom Armor Group Inc .... G 336 617-4667
  Greensboro (G-6948)
Gitsum Precision LLC .... G 336 453-3998
  Stoneville (G-14958)

North American Trade LLC .... G 828 712-3004
  Fletcher (G-6030)
War Sport LLC .... G 910 948-2237
  Eagle Springs (G-5462)

3484 Small arms

Aboard Trade LLC .... G 919 341-7045
  Southport (G-14563)
◆ Alotech Inc .... E 919 774-1297
  Goldston (G-6672)
Arisaka LLC .... F 919 601-5625
  Apex (G-165)
Bachstein Consulting LLC .... G 410 322-4917
  Youngsville (G-17070)
Every Day Carry LLc .... F 203 231-0256
  Winnabow (G-16580)
Gitsum Precision LLC .... G 336 453-3998
  Stoneville (G-14958)
Grip Pod Systems Intl LLC .... G 239 233-3694
  Raleigh (G-12822)
Holsters For Life LLC .... G 704 862-0212
  Gastonia (G-6418)
Kart Precision Barrel Corp .... G 910 754-5212
  Shallotte (G-14274)
Manroy Usa LLC .... G 828 286-9725
  Spindale (G-14608)
Microtech Defense Inds Inc .... G 828 684-4355
  Fletcher (G-6026)
Remington Arms Company LLC .... B 800 544-8892
  Madison (G-10085)
Remington Arms Company LLC .... C 800 544-8892
  Madison (G-10086)
Riley Defense Inc .... G 704 507-9224
  Hickory (G-8136)
Sand Hammer Forging Inc .... G 919 554-9554
  Youngsville (G-17095)
Urban Tactical and Cstm Armory ...... G 252 686-0122
  Kinston (G-9390)
US Arms & Ammunition LLC .... G 252 652-7400
  New Bern (G-11854)
Weapon Works LLC .... G 800 556-9498
  Burlington (G-1516)
Werywin Corporation .... G 410 322-4917
  Youngsville (G-17114)

3489 Ordnance and accessories, nec

Advanced Non-Lethal Tech Inc .... G 847 812-6450
  Raleigh (G-12479)
Agile Ventures LLC .... G 202 716-7958
  East Flat Rock (G-5472)
Appalachian Arms Inc .... G 828 332-1900
  Hayesville (G-7760)
Armament Chimera .... G 336 893-5639
  Clemmons (G-4026)
Backwater Guns LLC .... F 910 399-1451
  Wilmington (G-16131)
Down Range Armory Inc .... G 919 749-5820
  Youngsville (G-17078)
Heavy Armor Division LLC .... G 980 328-8883
  Indian Trail (G-8938)
House of Guns Inc .... G 910 381-0732
  Richlands (G-13555)
James Bunn .... G 252 293-4867
  Wilson (G-16502)
Jbs Ordnance Inc .... G 980 722-3659
  Charlotte (G-3010)
Loading Republic Inc .... G 704 561-1077
  Concord (G-4306)
RTD Precision LLC .... G 910 624-2624
  Fayetteville (G-5910)
Sturm Ruger & Company Inc .... B 336 427-0286
  Mayodan (G-10368)

34 FABRICATED METAL PRODUCTS

Wolfpit Tactical .... G 828 234-1279
  Morganton (G-11269)

3491 Industrial valves

ADC Industries Inc .... G 919 550-9515
  Clayton (G-3952)
Asco LP .... G 919 460-5200
  Cary (G-1692)
▲ Bonomi North America Inc .... F 704 412-9031
  Charlotte (G-2333)
▲ Brasscraft .... C 336 475-2131
  Thomasville (G-15189)
Burkert USA Corporation .... C 800 325-1405
  Huntersville (G-8798)
▲ Carolina Conveying Inc .... G 828 235-1005
  Canton (G-1608)
Celeros Flow Technology LLC .... D 704 752-3100
  Charlotte (G-2438)
Circor Pumps North America LLC ..... C 877 853-7867
  Monroe (G-10684)
Curtiss-Wright Corporation .... G 704 481-1150
  Shelby (G-14307)
Curtiss-Wright Corporation .... B 704 869-4600
  Davidson (G-4669)
David Conrad .... G 336 253-6966
  Greensboro (G-6958)
Eizi Group Llc .... G 919 397-3638
  Raleigh (G-12729)
Engineered Controls Intl LLC .... C 336 226-3244
  Burlington (G-1411)
Engineered Controls Intl LLC .... C 828 466-2153
  Conover (G-4451)
Engineered Controls Intl LLC .... C 336 449-7706
  Whitsett (G-15989)
▲ Engineered Controls Intl LLC .... C 336 449-7707
  Elon (G-5657)
Engineering Mfg Svcs Co .... F 704 821-7325
  Monroe (G-10714)
Equilibar LLC .... E 828 650-6590
  Fletcher (G-6001)
▲ General Control Equipment Co ...... F 704 588-0484
  Charlotte (G-2816)
Hersey Meters Co LLC .... E 704 278-2221
  Cleveland (G-4073)
▲ Huber Technology Inc .... E 704 949-1010
  Denver (G-4782)
Hydrant Mechanics .... G 919 922-3829
  Princeton (G-12401)
▲ Key Gas Components Inc .... E 828 655-1700
  Marion (G-10156)
▲ Mpv Mrgnton Prssure Vssels NC ... C 828 652-3704
  Marion (G-10168)
◆ Mueller Steam Specialty .... D 910 865-8241
  Saint Pauls (G-13906)
Parker-Hannifin Corporation .... E 828 245-3233
  Forest City (G-6079)
▲ Robert H Wager Company Inc .... F 336 969-6909
  Rural Hall (G-13851)
Romac Industries Inc .... D 704 915-3317
  Dallas (G-4656)
Sensus USA Inc .... C 919 576-6185
  Morrisville (G-11426)
◆ Sensus USA Inc .... E 919 845-4000
  Morrisville (G-11425)
▲ Spanglercv Inc .... G 910 794-5547
  Wilmington (G-16413)
SPX Flow Inc .... C 704 752-4400
  Charlotte (G-3607)
▲ Tvl International LLC .... G 704 814-0930
  Matthews (G-10297)
▲ United Brass Works Inc .... C 336 498-2661
  Randleman (G-13494)

Watts Regulator .... G 978 689-6066
  Saint Pauls (G-13910)
Watts Regulator Co .... A 828 286-4151
  Spindale (G-14610)
Zurn Elkay Wtr Solutions Corp .... F 910 501-1853
  Lumberton (G-10062)
Zurn Elkay Wtr Solutions Corp .... G 855 663-9876
  Sanford (G-14211)

3492 Fluid power valves and hose fittings

Anchor Coupling Inc .... B 919 739-8000
  Goldsboro (G-6590)
Bmrs Management Services Inc .... G 704 793-4319
  Concord (G-4212)
Bulldog Hose Company LLC .... E 919 639-6151
  Angier (G-134)
Carolina Components Group Inc .... E 919 635-8438
  Durham (G-5001)
Carolina Rubber & Spc Inc .... G 336 744-5111
  Winston Salem (G-16647)
Cross Technologies Inc .... G 336 370-4673
  Greensboro (G-6943)
Cross Technologies Inc .... D 336 292-0511
  Whitsett (G-15987)
Cross Technologies Inc .... E 800 327-7727
  Greensboro (G-6942)
▲ Custom Hydraulics & Design .... F 704 347-0023
  Cherryville (G-3865)
▲ Deetag USA Inc .... G 828 465-2644
  Conover (G-4447)
Dickie Jones .... G 828 733-5084
  Newland (G-11885)
▲ Dixon Valve & Coupling Co LLC .... F 704 334-9175
  Dallas (G-4637)
Eagle Assembly Unlimited Inc .... G 252 462-0408
  Castalia (G-1939)
Eaton Corporation .... D 828 286-4157
  Forest City (G-6066)
Engineered Controls Intl LLC .... C 828 466-2153
  Conover (G-4451)
▲ Flo-Tite Inc Valves & Contrls .... E 910 738-8904
  Lumberton (G-10038)
▼ George W Dahl Company Inc .... E 336 668-4444
  Greensboro (G-7038)
▲ Hawe North America Inc .... F 704 509-1599
  Huntersville (G-8828)
Hydac Technology Corp .... D 610 266-0100
  Denver (G-4783)
Hydraulic Hose Depot Inc .... G 252 356-1862
  Cofield (G-4135)
Logic Hydraulic Controls Inc .... E 910 791-9293
  Wilmington (G-16304)
McC Holdings Inc .... C 828 724-4000
  Marion (G-10160)
Metrohose Incorporated .... G 252 329-9891
  Greenville (G-7560)
On-Site Hose Inc .... G 919 303-3840
  Apex (G-222)
Polyhose Incorporated .... F 732 512-9141
  Wilmington (G-16360)
Romac Industries Inc .... D 704 915-3317
  Dallas (G-4656)
SCI Sharp Controls Inc .... G 704 394-1395
  Pineville (G-12304)
▲ Stanadyne Intrmdate Hldngs LLC ... C 860 525-0821
  Jacksonville (G-9038)
▲ Talladega Mchy & Sup Co NC .... G 256 362-4124
  Fayetteville (G-5925)

3493 Steel springs, except wire

Lee Spring Company LLC .... E 336 275-3631
  Greensboro (G-7165)

SIC SECTION

Matthew Warren Inc .... E 704 837-0331
  Charlotte (G-3143)
Southern ATL Spring Mfg Sls LL .... E 704 279-1331
  Granite Quarry (G-6762)
◆ Stabilus Inc .... D 704 865-7444
  Gastonia (G-6513)
Stable Holdco Inc .... B 704 866-7140
  Gastonia (G-6514)

3494 Valves and pipe fittings, nec

◆ Aalberts Integrated Pipin .... E 704 841-6000
  Charlotte (G-2121)
▲ American Valve Inc .... D 336 668-0554
  Greensboro (G-6802)
Appalachian Pipe Distrs LLC .... F 704 688-5703
  Charlotte (G-2202)
Atlantic Tube & Fitting LLC .... G 704 545-6166
  Mint Hill (G-10520)
▲ Bonomi North America Inc .... F 704 412-9031
  Charlotte (G-2333)
◆ Controls Southeast Inc .... C 704 644-5000
  Pineville (G-12262)
Engineered Controls Intl LLC .... C 336 226-3244
  Burlington (G-1411)
Engineered Controls Intl LLC .... C 828 466-2153
  Conover (G-4451)
Engineered Controls Intl LLC .... C 336 449-7706
  Whitsett (G-15989)
General Refrigeration Company .... G 919 661-4727
  Garner (G-6273)
Hayward Industries Inc .... C 336 712-9900
  Clemmons (G-4043)
◆ Hayward Industries Inc .... B 908 351-5400
  Charlotte (G-2894)
Industrial Mgmt of Materials .... F 704 359-9928
  Charlotte (G-2963)
James M Pleasants Company Inc ..... F 888 902-8324
  Greensboro (G-7134)
James M Pleasants Company Inc ..... E 336 275-3152
  Greensboro (G-7133)
▲ Key Gas Components Inc .... E 828 655-1700
  Marion (G-10156)
Mid-Atlantic Drainage Inc .... F 828 324-0808
  Conover (G-4472)
Mosack Group LLC .... D 888 229-2874
  Mint Hill (G-10541)
National Foam Inc .... C 919 639-6151
  Angier (G-148)
Romac Industries Inc .... D 704 915-3317
  Dallas (G-4656)
SCI Sharp Controls Inc .... G 704 394-1395
  Pineville (G-12304)
Spc Mechanical Corporation .... C 252 237-9035
  Wendell (G-15919)
Thomas Mfg Co Inc Thomasville .... G 336 474-6030
  Thomasville (G-15289)
◆ Titan Flow Control Inc .... E 910 735-0000
  Lumberton (G-10058)
▲ Tlv Corporation .... E 704 597-9070
  Charlotte (G-3698)
Triangle Pipe Ftting Sltons In .... G 919 696-8635
  Morrisville (G-11453)
▲ United Brass Works Inc .... C 336 498-2661
  Randleman (G-13494)
Victaulic Company .... E 910 371-5588
  Leland (G-9564)

3495 Wire springs

▲ Cox Precision Springs Inc .... F 336 629-8500
  Asheboro (G-419)
◆ Hickory Springs Manufactu .... D 828 328-2201
  Hickory (G-8052)

Lee Spring Company......................... G 336 275-3631
  Greensboro *(G-7164)*
Lee Spring Company LLC.................. E 336 275-3631
  Greensboro *(G-7165)*
Leggett & Platt Incorporated............. G 704 380-6208
  Statesville *(G-14835)*
Leggett & Platt Incorporated.............. D 336 889-2600
  High Point *(G-8431)*
▲ M-B Industries Inc........................... C 828 862-4201
  Rosman *(G-13786)*
Magnarep Incorporated..................... G 919 949-5488
  Durham *(G-5202)*
N C Coil Inc..................................... G 336 983-4440
  King *(G-9277)*
Newcomb Spring Corp........................ E 704 588-2043
  Gastonia *(G-6477)*
Northeast Tool and Mfg Company........ E 704 882-1187
  Matthews *(G-10337)*
Piedmont Springs Company Inc............ F 828 322-5347
  Hickory *(G-8115)*
▲ Southern Precision Spring Inc............. E 704 392-4393
  Charlotte *(G-3595)*

3496 Miscellaneous fabricated wire products

Aluminum Screen Manufacturing......... G 336 605-8080
  Greensboro *(G-6795)*
American Fabricators......................... G 252 637-2600
  New Bern *(G-11768)*
Ashley Sling Inc................................ E 704 347-0071
  Charlotte *(G-2226)*
◆ Automated Solutions LLC.................. F 828 396-9900
  Granite Falls *(G-6723)*
▲ Belt Concepts America Inc................ F 888 598-2358
  Spring Hope *(G-14614)*
Belt Shop Inc.................................... F 704 865-3636
  Gastonia *(G-6352)*
Carolina Material Handling Inc............ F 336 294-2346
  Greensboro *(G-6889)*
▲ Cavert Wire Company Inc.................. E 800 969-2601
  Rural Hall *(G-13837)*
Ceramawire...................................... G 252 335-7411
  Elizabeth City *(G-5533)*
Chatsworth Products Inc.................... C 252 514-2779
  New Bern *(G-11788)*
Coleman Cable LLC.......................... E 828 389-8013
  Hayesville *(G-7762)*
▲ Davis Newell Company Inc................ F 910 762-3500
  Wilmington *(G-16195)*
▲ Dradura USA Corp........................... D 252 637-9660
  New Bern *(G-11802)*
Eastern Wholesale Fence LLC.............. D 631 698-0975
  Salisbury *(G-13957)*
◆ Elevate Textiles Inc........................... F 336 379-6220
  Charlotte *(G-2693)*
Elevate Textiles Holding Corp.............. G 336 379-6220
  Charlotte *(G-2694)*
Essex Group Inc................................ G 704 921-9605
  Charlotte *(G-2730)*
Everything Industrial Supply................ G 743 333-2222
  Winston Salem *(G-16702)*
Express Wire Services Inc.................. G 704 393-5156
  Charlotte *(G-2739)*
◆ Forbo Movement Systems.................. E 704 334-5353
  Charlotte *(G-2786)*
Fuller Specialty Company Inc............. F 336 226-3446
  Burlington *(G-1417)*
Hemco Wire Products Inc.................. F 336 454-7280
  Jamestown *(G-9052)*
I & I Sling Inc.................................. G 336 323-1532
  Greensboro *(G-7107)*
▲ Ica Mid-Atlantic Inc.......................... C 336 447-4546
  Whitsett *(G-15993)*

Intercontinental Metals Corp................ D 336 786-2141
  Mount Airy *(G-11522)*
Leggett & Platt Incorporated............... D 336 889-2600
  High Point *(G-8431)*
▲ M-B Industries Inc........................... C 828 862-4201
  Rosman *(G-13786)*
▲ Masonry Reinforcing Corp Amer......... C 704 525-5554
  Charlotte *(G-3139)*
▲ McIntyre Manufacturing Group Inc..... D 336 476-3646
  Thomasville *(G-15246)*
McJast Inc....................................... F 828 884-4809
  Pisgah Forest *(G-12326)*
Merchants Metals LLC........................ G 919 598-8471
  Raleigh *(G-13015)*
Merchants Metals LLC........................ D 704 878-8706
  Statesville *(G-14841)*
Preformed Line Products Co................ C 704 983-6161
  Albemarle *(G-99)*
Prysmian Cbles Systems USA LLC........ E 828 322-9473
  Hickory *(G-8128)*
Rack Works Inc................................. E 336 368-1302
  Pilot Mountain *(G-12201)*
Redtail Group LLC............................. G 828 539-4700
  Swannanoa *(G-15033)*
◆ Rolf Koerner LLC.............................. G 704 714-8866
  Charlotte *(G-3459)*
Royal Wire Products Inc.................... E 704 596-2110
  Charlotte *(G-3466)*
▲ Sid Jenkins Inc................................. G 336 632-0707
  Greensboro *(G-7337)*
Sunbelt Enterprises Inc....................... F 704 788-4749
  Concord *(G-4368)*
◆ Technibilt Ltd.................................. E 828 464-7388
  Newton *(G-11976)*
◆ Unified Scrning Crshing - NC I .... G 336 824-2151
  Ramseur *(G-13451)*
Voltage LLC...................................... F 919 391-9405
  Chapel Hill *(G-2096)*
◆ Wieland Electric Inc.......................... F 910 259-5050
  Wilmington *(G-16442)*
▼ Wireway/Husky Corp......................... C 704 483-1135
  Denver *(G-4815)*

3497 Metal foil and leaf

▲ Acme Liquidating Company LLC........ E 704 873-3711
  Statesville *(G-14739)*
De Luxe Packaging Corp..................... E 800 845-6051
  Charlotte *(G-2608)*
Granges Americas Inc........................ C 704 633-6020
  Salisbury *(G-13973)*
Kurz Transfer Products LP.................. D 336 764-4128
  Lexington *(G-9742)*
▲ Kurz Transfer Products LP.................. D 704 927-3700
  Huntersville *(G-8845)*
Reynolds Consumer Products Inc.......... A 704 371-5550
  Huntersville *(G-8885)*

3498 Fabricated pipe and fittings

Advanced Systems Intgrtion LLC........... G 260 447-5555
  Wake Forest *(G-15526)*
Ansgar Industrial LLC........................ A 704 962-5249
  Charlotte *(G-2196)*
Charlotte Pipe and Foundry Co............ B 704 348-5416
  Charlotte *(G-2458)*
Chicago Tube and Iron Company......... D 704 781-2060
  Locust *(G-9956)*
Coil Masters LLC............................... G 704 500-8341
  Mocksville *(G-10564)*
◆ Controls Southeast Inc...................... C 704 644-5000
  Pineville *(G-12262)*
▲ Custom Enterprises Inc..................... G 336 226-8296
  Burlington *(G-1405)*

Erdle Perforating Holdings Inc.............. F 704 588-4380
  Charlotte *(G-2726)*
Florida Fire Supply............................. E 336 885-5007
  Winston Salem *(G-16714)*
Hydro Tube South LLC....................... F 919 258-3070
  Sanford *(G-14137)*
Ipex USA LLC................................... F 704 889-2431
  Charlotte *(G-2995)*
Ipex USA LLC................................... F 704 889-2431
  Pineville *(G-12276)*
Jim Fab of North Carolina Inc............. E 704 278-1000
  Cleveland *(G-4074)*
Kds Fabricating and Mch Sp LLC......... F 828 632-5091
  Hiddenite *(G-8222)*
▲ Key Gas Components Inc.................. E 828 655-1700
  Marion *(G-10156)*
▲ Kooks Custom Headers Inc................ E 704 768-2288
  Statesville *(G-14834)*
North Star Fbrication Repr Inc............. G 704 393-5243
  Charlotte *(G-3269)*
Performance Plastics Pdts Inc.............. D 336 454-0350
  Jamestown *(G-9066)*
Protech Fabrication Inc...................... F 704 663-1721
  Mount Ulla *(G-11686)*
Purthermal LLC................................. G 828 855-0108
  Hickory *(G-8129)*
Tube Specialties Co Inc..................... C 704 818-8933
  Statesville *(G-14920)*
US Industrial Piping Inc.................... D 336 993-9505
  Kernersville *(G-9249)*
Victaulic Company............................. E 910 371-5588
  Leland *(G-9564)*
Waggoner Manufacturing Co............... E 704 278-2000
  Mount Ulla *(G-11687)*

3499 Fabricated metal products, nec

Advanced Metal Supply....................... G 336 883-7135
  High Point *(G-8234)*
Alco Metal Fabricato.......................... G 704 739-1168
  Bessemer City *(G-1051)*
Allan Fitch....................................... G 919 834-2593
  Knightdale *(G-9409)*
◆ AP&t North America Inc................... F 704 292-2900
  Monroe *(G-10648)*
ARC Steel Fabrication LLC................. F 980 533-8302
  Bessemer City *(G-1052)*
Artistic Ironworks LLC....................... G 919 908-6888
  Durham *(G-4927)*
Avl Custom Fabrication...................... G 828 713-0333
  Asheville *(G-552)*
Babco Inc.. G 888 376-5083
  Ayden *(G-848)*
Barden Metal Fabrication LLC.............. G 252 772-5984
  Havelock *(G-7740)*
Barnhill Metal Fabrication................... G 252 236-5114
  Elm City *(G-5646)*
Barrier1 Systems Inc.......................... F 336 617-8478
  Greensboro *(G-6832)*
Black Mtn Mch Fabrication Inc............ E 828 669-9557
  Black Mountain *(G-1121)*
Blue Mountain Metalworks Inc............ G 828 898-8582
  Banner Elk *(G-894)*
C & D Fabrications Inc...................... F 919 639-2489
  Angier *(G-135)*
Chartreuse Shepherd.......................... G 252 532-2708
  Weldon *(G-15881)*
Chatsworth Products Inc.................... C 252 514-2779
  New Bern *(G-11788)*
▲ Colonial Tin Works Inc..................... E 336 668-4126
  Greensboro *(G-6919)*
Concierge Transit LLC........................ G 704 778-0755
  Charlotte *(G-2536)*

Employee Codes: A=Over 500 employees, B=251-500
C=101-250, D=51-100, E=20-50, F=10-19, G=1-9

34 FABRICATED METAL PRODUCTS

Contemporary Products Inc............... G 919 779-4228
  Garner *(G-6268)*

Control and Barricade LLC............... G 704 315-2138
  Durham *(G-5032)*

Custom Cnc LLC............................... G 828 734-8293
  Clyde *(G-4122)*

▲ Cyrco Inc.. E 336 668-0977
  Greensboro *(G-6954)*

Davis Brothers Roofing..................... G 828 578-8561
  Hickory *(G-8002)*

Diversfied Holdings Dallas Inc........... F 704 922-5293
  Mount Holly *(G-11631)*

▲ Docmagnet Inc............................... G 919 788-7999
  Raleigh *(G-12691)*

♦ Dubose Strapping Inc..................... D 910 590-1020
  Clinton *(G-4094)*

Em2 Machine Corporation................. G 336 707-8409
  Greensboro *(G-6996)*

▲ Epic Enterprises Inc...................... E 910 692-5750
  Southern Pines *(G-14535)*

Fahmar Inc.. G 704 843-1872
  Waxhaw *(G-15756)*

Forged Cstm Met Fbrication LLC...... G 910 274-8300
  Castle Hayne *(G-1947)*

Four Corners Frmng Gallery Inc....... G 704 662-7154
  Mooresville *(G-10949)*

♦ Graphik Dimensions Limited........... D 800 332-8884
  High Point *(G-8371)*

Gray Manufacturing Co..................... F 615 841-3066
  Charlotte *(G-2858)*

Heavy Metal Fabrication LLC............ G 919 656-2717
  Winston Salem *(G-16742)*

Hinson Metal Fabrication................... G 828 944-0908
  Maggie Valley *(G-10094)*

International Vault Inc....................... E 919 742-3132
  Siler City *(G-14417)*

Ism Inc.. E
  Arden *(G-342)*

Iv-S Metal Stamping Inc.................... E 336 861-2100
  Archdale *(G-286)*

J & J Metal Fabrication LLC.............. G 704 746-5279
  Troutman *(G-15382)*

Jeffrey Sheffer................................... G 919 861-9126
  Raleigh *(G-12915)*

Kaba Ilco Corp................................... B 336 725-1331
  Winston Salem *(G-16775)*

M & M Frame Company Inc.............. G 336 859-8166
  Denton *(G-4745)*

Marc Staples Sculpture..................... G 919 475-9633
  Durham *(G-5208)*

Mecha Inc.. F 919 858-0372
  Raleigh *(G-13012)*

Merchant 1 Manufacturing LLC......... G 336 617-3008
  Summerfield *(G-14989)*

Metal Works High Point Inc.............. D 336 886-4612
  High Point *(G-8453)*

Metal-Cad Stl Frmng Systems In...... D 910 343-3338
  Wilmington *(G-16321)*

Mma Manufacturing Inc..................... E 828 692-0256
  East Flat Rock *(G-5478)*

Myricks Custom Fab Inc.................... G 828 645-5800
  Weaverville *(G-15855)*

North Star Fbrication Repr Inc........... G 704 393-5243
  Charlotte *(G-3269)*

Northsouth Biomagnetics Inc............. G 828 478-2277
  Sherrills Ford *(G-14389)*

Oro Manufacturing Company............ E 704 283-2186
  Monroe *(G-10783)*

Pauls Cstm Fbrication Mch LLC........ G 757 746-2743
  Camden *(G-1558)*

Pedal 2 Metal LLP............................. G 910 723-2289
  Fayetteville *(G-5896)*

Penco Products Inc........................... C 252 798-4000
  Hamilton *(G-7614)*

Precision Partners LLC..................... G 704 560-6442
  Charlotte *(G-3369)*

Prezioso Ventures LLC..................... G 704 793-1602
  Concord *(G-4337)*

▼ Problem Solver Inc......................... F 919 596-5555
  Raleigh *(G-13148)*

♦ Ramsey Products Corporation......... D 704 394-0322
  Belmont *(G-1006)*

Royce Company LLC......................... G 910 395-0046
  Wilmington *(G-16388)*

Sinnovatek Inc.................................... G 919 694-0974
  Raleigh *(G-13264)*

Spraying Systems Co........................ G 704 357-6499
  Charlotte *(G-3605)*

Stair Tamer LLC................................ G 252 336-4437
  Shiloh *(G-14393)*

Thomas & Gendics Inc...................... G 919 842-7860
  Sanford *(G-14196)*

Timmerman Manufacturing Inc.......... F 828 464-1778
  Conover *(G-4505)*

Truefab LLC....................................... F 919 620-8158
  Durham *(G-5413)*

Truelove Fabrications Inc.................. G 910 343-0195
  Wilmington *(G-16434)*

Twisted Metal Fabrication.................. G 704 915-1023
  Gastonia *(G-6533)*

♦ Usw-Menard Inc.............................. G 910 371-1899
  Leland *(G-9563)*

Vault of Forsyth Inc........................... G 336 996-2044
  Kernersville *(G-9250)*

Waldos Wldg Met Fbrication LLC...... G 704 638-0462
  Salisbury *(G-14064)*

Welding On Wheels........................... G 704 239-7831
  Salisbury *(G-14065)*

Werner Co.. G 704 235-5660
  Mooresville *(G-11126)*

West Side Industries LLC.................. G 980 223-8665
  Statesville *(G-14924)*

Zurn Industries LLC........................... E 919 775-2255
  Sanford *(G-14212)*

35 INDUSTRIAL AND COMMERCIAL MACHINERY AND COMPUTER EQUIPMENT

3511 Turbines and turbine generator sets

Abb Inc... E 704 587-1362
  Charlotte *(G-2122)*

♦ ABB Inc... C 919 856-2360
  Cary *(G-1674)*

Babcock Wlcox Eqity Invstmnts......... E 704 625-4900
  Charlotte *(G-2258)*

Babcock Wlcox Intl Sls Svc Cor......... F 704 625-4900
  Charlotte *(G-2259)*

Bwxt Investment Company................ E 704 625-4900
  Charlotte *(G-2369)*

Caterpillar Inc.................................... D 919 777-2000
  Sanford *(G-14098)*

Diamond Power Intl LLC.................... F 704 625-4900
  Charlotte *(G-2628)*

Diamond Pwr Astrlia Hldngs Inc........ G 704 625-4900
  Charlotte *(G-2629)*

Diamond Pwr Eqity Invstmnts In....... G 704 625-4900
  Charlotte *(G-2630)*

Grand Coulee Consortium................. G 704 943-4343
  Charlotte *(G-2853)*

♦ Industrial Sup Solutions Inc............. E 704 636-4241
  Salisbury *(G-13983)*

▲ Leistriz Advanced Turbine.............. C 336 969-1352
  Rural Hall *(G-13848)*

Megtec India Holdings LLC............... G 704 625-4900
  Charlotte *(G-3160)*

Megtec Turbosonic Tech Inc............. F 704 625-4900
  Charlotte *(G-3161)*

Powermolekul Inc.............................. G 919 264-8487
  Cary *(G-1856)*

Revloc Reclamation Service Inc........ G 704 625-4900
  Charlotte *(G-3439)*

Siemens Energy Inc........................... C 704 551-5100
  Charlotte *(G-3547)*

Siemens Energy Inc........................... C 336 969-1351
  Rural Hall *(G-13853)*

Waterwheel Factory........................... G 828 369-5928
  Franklin *(G-6148)*

Windlift Inc... G 919 490-8575
  Durham *(G-5442)*

▲ Xylem Lnc...................................... E 704 409-9700
  Charlotte *(G-3839)*

3519 Internal combustion engines, nec

Blue Gas Marine Inc.......................... F 919 238-3427
  Apex *(G-172)*

Buck Supply Company Inc................ G 252 215-1252
  Winterville *(G-16995)*

Caterpillar Inc.................................... D 919 777-2000
  Sanford *(G-14098)*

▲ Coltec Industries Inc...................... A 704 731-1500
  Charlotte *(G-2527)*

♦ Consolidated Diesel Inc.................. A 252 437-6611
  Whitakers *(G-15956)*

Cummins Atlantic LLC....................... E 704 596-7690
  Charlotte *(G-2584)*

Cummins Atlantic LLC....................... D 336 275-4531
  Greensboro *(G-6946)*

Cummins Atlantic LLC....................... E 919 284-9111
  Kenly *(G-9149)*

▲ Cummins Atlantic LLC................... E 704 588-1240
  Charlotte *(G-2585)*

Cummins Inc...................................... G 704 588-1240
  Pineville *(G-12264)*

Custom Engines Ltd.......................... G 910 532-4114
  Harrells *(G-7691)*

Daimler Truck North Amer LLC......... A 704 645-5000
  Cleveland *(G-4071)*

♦ Engine Systems Inc........................ D 252 977-2720
  Rocky Mount *(G-13695)*

♦ Enpro Industries Inc....................... C 704 731-1500
  Charlotte *(G-2713)*

Farm Services Inc............................. G 336 226-7381
  Graham *(G-6689)*

General Electric Company................. A 910 675-5000
  Wilmington *(G-16230)*

Griffin Automotive Marine Inc............ G 252 940-0714
  Washington *(G-15706)*

▲ Holman & Moody Inc...................... G 704 394-4141
  Charlotte *(G-2914)*

Holman Automotive Inc..................... G 704 583-2888
  Charlotte *(G-2915)*

▲ Ilmor Marine LLC........................... E 704 360-1901
  Mooresville *(G-10981)*

Jasper Penske Engines..................... F 704 788-8996
  Concord *(G-4292)*

John R Bell....................................... G 252 297-2499
  Belvidere *(G-1022)*

Jones Marine Inc............................... G 704 639-0173
  Salisbury *(G-13994)*

Lehr LLC.. F 704 827-9368
  Huntersville *(G-8849)*

NC Diesel Performance LLC............. G 704 431-3257
  Salisbury *(G-14016)*

SIC SECTION
35 INDUSTRIAL AND COMMERCIAL MACHINERY AND COMPUTER EQUIPMENT

Outlet Marine Engines Inc .... G 919 279-3338
   Cary *(G-1839)*

Patricks Small Engines .... G 910 653-2061
   Tabor City *(G-15085)*

Pcai Inc .... D 704 588-1240
   Charlotte *(G-3323)*

Southport NC .... G 910 524-7425
   Southport *(G-14581)*

Trane Technologies Company LLC .... C 910 692-8700
   Southern Pines *(G-14558)*

Waterboxer Inc .... G 919 279-3338
   Cary *(G-1924)*

White River Marine Group LLC .... C 252 633-3101
   New Bern *(G-11856)*

Xre Performance Engines LLC .... G 704 663-3505
   Mooresville *(G-11133)*

3523 Farm machinery and equipment

Airborn Industries Inc .... E 704 483-5000
   Lincolnton *(G-9869)*

American Urns .... G 828 994-4239
   Conover *(G-4414)*

◆ Befco Inc .... E 252 977-9920
   Rocky Mount *(G-13684)*

Carolina Golfco Inc .... G 704 525-7846
   Charlotte *(G-2397)*

Case & Bear Great Homes LLC .... G 704 595-3832
   Charlotte *(G-2417)*

Case Basket Creations .... G 828 381-4908
   Granite Falls *(G-6728)*

Case By Case LLC .... G 910 814-3288
   Lillington *(G-9846)*

Case-Closed Investigations .... G 336 794-2274
   Morehead City *(G-11160)*

Cases For A Cause .... G 704 239-3269
   Rockwell *(G-13648)*

◆ Ceres Turf Inc .... G 910 256-8974
   Wilmington *(G-16167)*

Coastal Agrobusiness Inc .... G 828 697-2220
   Flat Rock *(G-5963)*

Coastal Agrobusiness Inc .... G 252 798-3481
   Hamilton *(G-7613)*

◆ Coastal Agrobusiness Inc .... D 252 238-7391
   Greenville *(G-7503)*

Dairy Services .... G 919 303-2442
   Raleigh *(G-12670)*

Daughtridge Enterprises Inc .... G 252 977-7775
   Rocky Mount *(G-13665)*

Deere & Company .... B 919 567-6400
   Fuquay Varina *(G-6195)*

Deere & Company .... G 336 996-8100
   Kernersville *(G-9189)*

◆ Evans Machinery Inc .... D 252 243-4000
   Wilson *(G-16498)*

◆ Gas-Fired Products Inc .... E 704 372-3485
   Charlotte *(G-2809)*

General Fertilizer Eqp Inc .... F 336 299-4711
   Greensboro *(G-7035)*

▲ Granville Equipment LLC .... G 919 693-1425
   Oxford *(G-12130)*

Graves Inc .... E 252 792-1191
   Williamston *(G-16061)*

Gum Drop Cases LLC .... G 206 805-0818
   High Point *(G-8373)*

H & H Farm Machine Co Inc .... E 704 753-1555
   Monroe *(G-10729)*

Hog Slat Incorporated .... E 252 209-0092
   Aulander *(G-830)*

Hog Slat Incorporated .... G 910 862-7081
   Elizabethtown *(G-5596)*

Hog Slat Incorporated .... E 800 949-4647
   Newton Grove *(G-11989)*

Hog Slat Incorporated .... E 919 663-3321
   Siler City *(G-14414)*

◆ Hog Slat Incorporated .... B 800 949-4647
   Newton Grove *(G-11988)*

James River Equipment .... E 704 821-7399
   Monroe *(G-10747)*

JM Innovations LLC .... G 704 495-4841
   Charlotte *(G-3025)*

Jo-Mar Group LLC .... E
   Belmont *(G-993)*

Johnson Industrial Mchy Svcs .... E 252 239-1944
   Lucama *(G-10017)*

▲ Lock Drives Inc .... G 704 588-1844
   Pineville *(G-12281)*

Madison Ave Cases .... G 843 214-0476
   Winston Salem *(G-16797)*

North American Implements Inc .... G 336 476-2904
   Thomasville *(G-15259)*

▲ Pasture Management Systems Inc .... F 704 436-6401
   Mount Pleasant *(G-11675)*

Reddick & Reddick LLC .... G 919 845-7333
   Raleigh *(G-13200)*

Reddick Equipment Co NC LLC .... G 252 792-1191
   Williamston *(G-16068)*

Sides Spreader and Eqp Co Inc .... F 336 978-6732
   Lexington *(G-9779)*

Sleepy Creek Turkeys LLC .... C 919 778-3130
   Goldsboro *(G-6657)*

Smoky Mtn Nativ Plant Assn .... G 828 479-8788
   Robbinsville *(G-13612)*

▼ Sound Heavy Machinery Inc .... G 910 782-2477
   Wilmington *(G-16407)*

Spectrum Products Inc .... F 919 556-7797
   Youngsville *(G-17100)*

Stanly Tractor Company .... G 704 983-1106
   New London *(G-11879)*

STI Turf Equipment LLC .... D 704 393-8873
   Charlotte *(G-3631)*

▲ Stiles Mfg Co Inc .... G 910 592-6344
   Clinton *(G-4113)*

Stone Equipment Company Inc .... C 980 202-4448
   Lexington *(G-9786)*

Strickland Bros Entps Inc .... F 252 478-3058
   Spring Hope *(G-14623)*

Taylor Manufacturing Inc .... E 910 862-2576
   Elizabethtown *(G-5605)*

Tetac .... G 919 369-9106
   Franklinton *(G-6165)*

Tractor Country Inc .... F 252 523-3007
   Dover *(G-4835)*

Tri-W Farms Inc .... G 910 533-3596
   Clinton *(G-4116)*

Upper Coastl Plain Bus Dev Ctr .... F 252 234-5900
   Wilson *(G-16554)*

3524 Lawn and garden equipment

American Honda Motor Co Inc .... B 336 578-6300
   Swepsonville *(G-15050)*

◆ Befco Inc .... E 252 977-9920
   Rocky Mount *(G-13684)*

▲ Bosmere Inc .... F 704 784-1608
   Salisbury *(G-13930)*

CAM Enterprises Inc .... F 252 946-4877
   Washington *(G-15684)*

Certified Lawnmower Inc .... G 704 527-2765
   Belmont *(G-978)*

D D Lawncare Service .... G 336 895-3353
   Gibsonville *(G-6558)*

Daphne Lawson Espino .... G 910 290-2762
   Beulaville *(G-1093)*

Darius All Access LLC .... E 910 262-8567
   Wilmington *(G-16194)*

Day 3 Lwncare Ldscpg Prfctnist .... G 910 574-8422
   Fayetteville *(G-5806)*

Deere & Company .... B 919 567-6400
   Fuquay Varina *(G-6195)*

Green Pastures Lawn Care .... G 828 758-9265
   Boomer *(G-1170)*

Ground Control Landscape MGT .... G 704 472-3448
   Shelby *(G-14322)*

Group 6 Holdings Inc .... F 888 804-5008
   Denver *(G-4779)*

H & H Farm Machine Co Inc .... E 704 753-1555
   Monroe *(G-10729)*

Husqvrna Cnsmr Otdoor Pdts NA .... A 704 597-5000
   Charlotte *(G-2937)*

Husqvrna Cnsmr Otdoor Pdts NA .... A 704 494-4810
   Charlotte *(G-2938)*

◆ Husqvrna Cnsmr Otdoor Pdts NA .... D 704 597-5000
   Charlotte *(G-2936)*

John Deere Consumer Pdts Inc .... C 919 804-2000
   Cary *(G-1798)*

Jrm Inc .... E 888 576-7007
   Clemmons *(G-4050)*

Miller Saws & Supplies Inc .... G 252 636-3347
   New Bern *(G-11822)*

▲ New Peco Inc .... E 828 684-1234
   Arden *(G-355)*

Peco Inc .... E 828 684-1234
   Arden *(G-362)*

▼ Root Spring Scraper Co .... F 269 382-2025
   Pinehurst *(G-12235)*

S Duff Fabricating Inc .... G 910 298-3060
   Beulaville *(G-1098)*

Sunseeker US Inc .... G 443 253-1546
   Indian Trail *(G-8966)*

Swell Home Solutions Inc .... G 919 440-4692
   Mount Olive *(G-11670)*

▲ United Southern Industries Inc .... D 866 273-1810
   Forest City *(G-6085)*

▲ Vegherb LLC .... F 800 914-9835
   Erwin *(G-5689)*

3531 Construction machinery

A-1 Concrete & Cnstr LLC .... G 828 712-1160
   Arden *(G-306)*

AAA Paver Care Inc .... G 828 687-1669
   Fletcher *(G-5979)*

Advanced Grading & Excvtg LLC .... G 828 320-7465
   Newton *(G-11912)*

Advantage Machinery Svcs Inc .... E 336 463-4700
   Yadkinville *(G-17030)*

Allied Marine Contractors LLC .... G 910 367-2159
   Hampstead *(G-7637)*

Altec Industries Inc .... D 828 678-5500
   Burnsville *(G-1521)*

Altec Industries Inc .... B 919 528-2535
   Creedmoor *(G-4603)*

Altec Industries Inc .... F 336 786-3623
   Mount Airy *(G-11475)*

▲ Altec Northeast LLC .... D 508 320-9041
   Creedmoor *(G-4604)*

American Attachments Inc .... G 336 859-2002
   Lexington *(G-9679)*

Ampac Machinery LLC .... F 919 596-5320
   Durham *(G-4917)*

Apac-Atlantic Inc .... D 336 412-6800
   Raleigh *(G-12512)*

Arrow Equipment LLC .... G 803 765-2040
   Charlotte *(G-2218)*

Asphalt Emulsion Inds LLC .... G 252 726-0653
   Morehead City *(G-11150)*

Automated Designs Inc .... F 828 696-9625
   Flat Rock *(G-5959)*

35 INDUSTRIAL AND COMMERCIAL MACHINERY AND COMPUTER EQUIPMENT

Bakchoe Services .... G 828 321-3360
  Topton *(G-15325)*

Bares Backhoe & Septic System .... G 336 352-3951
  Mount Airy *(G-11480)*

Barnhill Contracting Company .... F 252 527-8021
  Kinston *(G-9344)*

Bartleys Backhoe Service .... G 910 918-1384
  Chadbourn *(G-1974)*

Beasley Contracting .... G 828 479-3775
  Robbinsville *(G-13604)*

◆ Befco Inc .... E 252 977-9920
  Rocky Mount *(G-13684)*

Berco of America Inc .... E 336 931-1415
  Greensboro *(G-6836)*

Bgi Recovery Llc .... G 336 429-6976
  Mount Airy *(G-11483)*

Bobcat of Mount Airy .... G 336 459-3844
  Mount Airy *(G-11484)*

◆ Bromma Inc .... E 919 620-8039
  Durham *(G-4982)*

Cardinal Stone Company Inc .... E 336 846-7191
  Jefferson *(G-9087)*

Carolina Paving Hickory Inc .... G 828 328-3909
  Hickory *(G-7964)*

Carolina Paving Hickory Inc .... F 828 322-1706
  Hickory *(G-7965)*

Caterpillar Inc .... D 919 550-1100
  Clayton *(G-3963)*

Caterpillar Inc .... D 919 777-2000
  Sanford *(G-14098)*

Champion LLC .... F 704 392-1038
  Charlotte *(G-2445)*

Conjet Inc .... G 636 485-4724
  Charlotte *(G-2540)*

▲ Construction Attachments Inc .... D 828 758-2674
  Lenoir *(G-9601)*

◆ Cutting Systems Inc .... D 704 592-2451
  Union Grove *(G-15436)*

Dan Moore Inc .... G 336 475-8350
  Thomasville *(G-15210)*

Darren Moretz Backhoe Ser .... G 828 964-1006
  Boone *(G-1193)*

Design Engnred Fbrications Inc .... E 336 768-8260
  Winston Salem *(G-16675)*

Dimensional Metals Inc .... G 704 279-9691
  Salisbury *(G-13953)*

East Cast Trckg Bckhoe Svcs LL .... G 919 209-0198
  Smithfield *(G-14459)*

Edd Loftis Backhoe Servic .... G 919 971-5740
  Ocean Isle Beach *(G-12091)*

Ellis Backhoe Service Inc .... G 336 451-6265
  Greensboro *(G-6994)*

Engcon North America .... E 203 691-5920
  High Point *(G-8344)*

▼ Engineered Attachments LLC .... G 336 703-5266
  Winston Salem *(G-16697)*

Everything Attachments .... G 828 464-0161
  Conover *(G-4452)*

Ferebee Corporation .... C 704 509-2586
  Charlotte *(G-2751)*

Ferguson Highway Products Inc .... F 704 320-3087
  Indian Trail *(G-8934)*

Flores Crane Services LLC .... F 704 243-4347
  Waxhaw *(G-15757)*

Four Points Recycling LLC .... F 910 333-5961
  Jacksonville *(G-9000)*

General Fertilizer Eqp Inc .... F 336 299-4711
  Greensboro *(G-7035)*

Harsco Metro Rail LLC .... G 980 960-2624
  Charlotte *(G-2892)*

Harsco Rail LLC .... G 980 960-2624
  Charlotte *(G-2893)*

Hills Machinery Company LLC .... G 828 820-5265
  Mills River *(G-10504)*

Hockmeyer Equipment Corp .... D 252 338-4705
  Elizabeth City *(G-5548)*

Holder Backhoe & Hauling Inc .... F 336 622-7388
  Liberty *(G-9816)*

Hyper Networks LLC .... F 704 837-8411
  Pineville *(G-12274)*

Ingersoll-Rand Indus US Inc .... D 704 896-4000
  Davidson *(G-4680)*

Ingersoll-Rand Intl Holdg .... B 704 655-4000
  Davidson *(G-4681)*

▲ Instrotek Inc .... E 919 875-8371
  Durham *(G-5160)*

◆ International Cnstr Eqp Inc .... E 704 821-8200
  Matthews *(G-10322)*

J & M Pavers LLC .... E 704 776-6613
  Monroe *(G-10743)*

▲ John Deere Kernersville LLC .... A 336 996-8100
  Kernersville *(G-9207)*

Ken Garner Mfg - RHO Inc .... E 336 969-0416
  Rural Hall *(G-13844)*

Kevins Backhoe Service .... G 336 591-7751
  Germanton *(G-6554)*

Linder Industrial Machinery Co .... G 980 777-8345
  Concord *(G-4304)*

▲ Loflin Fabrication LLC .... E 336 859-4333
  Denton *(G-4744)*

Long Life Lighting Inc .... E 919 833-1292
  Raleigh *(G-12979)*

Man Lift Mfg Co .... E 414 486-1760
  Shelby *(G-14344)*

▼ Meadows Mills Inc .... E 336 838-2282
  North Wilkesboro *(G-12027)*

Melton Backhoe Service Inc .... G 828 779-6728
  Black Mountain *(G-1130)*

Metal Roofing Systems LLC .... G 704 820-3110
  Stanley *(G-14702)*

▲ Mid-Atlantic Crane and Eqp Co .... E 919 790-3535
  Raleigh *(G-13029)*

North American Implements Inc .... G 336 476-2904
  Thomasville *(G-15259)*

Paladin Custom Works .... F 336 996-2796
  Kernersville *(G-9223)*

Patrick .... G 336 846-4759
  West Jefferson *(G-15947)*

Peco Inc .... E 828 684-1234
  Arden *(G-362)*

Pittmanbac .... G 252 430-4745
  Henderson *(G-7802)*

◆ Power Curbers Inc .... D 704 636-5871
  Salisbury *(G-14027)*

Redi-Mix LP .... E 704 596-6511
  Charlotte *(G-3423)*

Roadsafe Traffic Systems Inc .... G 919 772-9401
  High Point *(G-8513)*

Robs Backhoe Service .... G 910 295-3317
  Aberdeen *(G-25)*

Rocky Springs Applicator .... G 704 546-7560
  Harmony *(G-7688)*

Rol-Mol Inc .... G 828 328-1210
  Hickory *(G-8138)*

Ronny D Phelps .... G 828 206-6339
  Hot Springs *(G-8746)*

Roofing Supply .... G 919 779-6223
  Garner *(G-6310)*

Roofing Tools and Eqp Inc .... F 252 291-1800
  Wilson *(G-16534)*

▼ Root Spring Scraper Co .... F 269 382-2025
  Pinehurst *(G-12235)*

Rut Manufacturing Inc .... F 336 859-0328
  Denton *(G-4747)*

S T Wooten Corporation .... E 919 363-3141
  Apex *(G-240)*

S T Wooten Corporation .... E 919 562-1851
  Franklinton *(G-6163)*

S T Wooten Corporation .... E 919 772-7991
  Fuquay Varina *(G-6227)*

S T Wooten Corporation .... E 252 393-2206
  Garner *(G-6312)*

S T Wooten Corporation .... E 919 779-6089
  Garner *(G-6313)*

S T Wooten Corporation .... E 919 779-7589
  Garner *(G-6314)*

S T Wooten Corporation .... E 252 636-2568
  New Bern *(G-11842)*

S T Wooten Corporation .... E 919 965-7176
  Princeton *(G-12403)*

S T Wooten Corporation .... E 252 291-5165
  Raleigh *(G-13224)*

S T Wooten Corporation .... E 919 776-2736
  Sanford *(G-14178)*

S T Wooten Corporation .... E 910 762-1940
  Wilmington *(G-16391)*

S T Wooten Corporation .... E 252 291-5165
  Wilson *(G-16537)*

Sain Grading & Backhoe .... G 704 481-9179
  Shelby *(G-14362)*

Sides Spreader and Eqp Co Inc .... F 336 978-6732
  Lexington *(G-9779)*

Smart Cast Group .... E 855 971-2287
  Raleigh *(G-13272)*

Southern Trucking & Backhoe .... G 919 548-9723
  Siler City *(G-14432)*

St Engineering Leeboy Inc .... G 704 966-3300
  Lincolnton *(G-9921)*

Stone Supply Inc .... G 828 678-9966
  Burnsville *(G-1534)*

Strickland Backhoe .... G 910 893-5274
  Bunnlevel *(G-1331)*

▲ Sturdy Corporation .... C 910 763-2500
  Wilmington *(G-16420)*

Superior Dry Kilns Inc .... E 828 754-7001
  Hudson *(G-8782)*

Surface Buff LLC .... G 919 341-2873
  Cary *(G-1906)*

T Simmons Backhoe .... G 336 295-3100
  Browns Summit *(G-1317)*

T T Beckham Backhoe Service .... G 252 438-7620
  Henderson *(G-7812)*

Tandemloc Inc .... D 252 447-7155
  Havelock *(G-7748)*

Tcom Ground Systems LP .... F 252 338-3200
  Elizabeth City *(G-5576)*

Tim Hlley Excvtg Drctnal Drlg .... G 336 595-3320
  Walkertown *(G-15617)*

Tom Rochester & Associates Inc .... G 704 896-5805
  Charlotte *(G-3706)*

Top Hat Bbcat Backhoe Svcs Inc .... G 336 382-0068
  Madison *(G-10089)*

▼ USA Attachments Inc .... E 336 983-0763
  King *(G-9283)*

Vermeer Manufacturing Company .... F 410 285-0200
  Charlotte *(G-3772)*

◆ VT Leeboy Inc .... C 704 966-3300
  Lincolnton *(G-9934)*

▲ W R Long Inc .... E 252 823-4570
  Tarboro *(G-15125)*

Ward Backhoe Bulldozer Svc LLC .... G 252 446-5878
  Battleboro *(G-932)*

Woodland Logging Inc .... G 910 298-3350
  Beulaville *(G-1099)*

Young & McQueen Grading Co Inc .... D 828 682-7714
  Burnsville *(G-1539)*

SIC SECTION
35 INDUSTRIAL AND COMMERCIAL MACHINERY AND COMPUTER EQUIPMENT

3532 Mining machinery

80 Acres Urban Agriculture Inc............... G..... 704 437-6115
 Granite Falls *(G-6720)*
Batista Grading Inc................................ F..... 919 359-3449
 Clayton *(G-3958)*
Brunner & Lay Inc................................. G..... 828 274-2770
 Flat Rock *(G-5961)*
Junaluska Mill Engineering..................... G..... 828 321-3693
 Andrews *(G-127)*
Omni Group LLC.................................... G..... 828 404-3104
 Hickory *(G-8106)*
Paschal Associates Ltd........................... F..... 336 625-2535
 Raleigh *(G-13100)*
▼ Sound Heavy Machinery Inc................. G..... 910 782-2477
 Wilmington *(G-16407)*
Stone Supply Inc.................................... G..... 828 678-9966
 Burnsville *(G-1534)*

3533 Oil and gas field machinery

Lintons Gas Piping & Service................. F..... 828 734-6259
 Canton *(G-1620)*
Patty Knio... G..... 919 995-2670
 Raleigh *(G-13102)*
◆ Sandvik Inc.. C..... 919 563-5008
 Mebane *(G-10427)*

3534 Elevators and moving stairways

Citilift Company..................................... G..... 704 241-6477
 Charlotte *(G-2483)*
Crockers Inc... F..... 336 366-2005
 Elkin *(G-5615)*
Eastern Elevator Inc............................... G..... 877 840-2638
 Raleigh *(G-12718)*
Ecs Group-NC LLC................................ G..... 919 830-1171
 Wake Forest *(G-15550)*
Home Elevators & Lift Pdts LLC............. E..... 910 427-0006
 Sunset Beach *(G-14999)*
▲ Nussbaum Auto Solutions LP.............. F..... 704 864-2470
 Gastonia *(G-6480)*
Otis Elevator Company.......................... G..... 828 251-1248
 Asheville *(G-718)*
Otis Elevator Company.......................... C..... 704 519-0100
 Charlotte *(G-3306)*
Park Manufacturing Company................ F..... 704 869-6128
 Gastonia *(G-6483)*
Poehler Enterprises Inc.......................... G..... 704 239-1166
 Midland *(G-10475)*
Port City Elevator Inc............................. E..... 910 790-9300
 Castle Hayne *(G-1959)*
Rs Bostic Service Inc............................. G..... 252 527-4781
 Kinston *(G-9381)*
Schindler Elevator Corporation............... F..... 910 590-5590
 Clinton *(G-4109)*
Southeastern Elevator LLC.................... G..... 252 726-9983
 Morehead City *(G-11192)*
Vertical Access LLC............................... G..... 800 325-1116
 Snow Hill *(G-14509)*

3535 Conveyors and conveying equipment

▲ AC Corporation................................... B..... 336 273-4472
 Greensboro *(G-6775)*
Advance Conveying Tech LLC............... E..... 704 710-4001
 Kings Mountain *(G-9289)*
Altec Industries Inc................................ B..... 919 528-2535
 Creedmoor *(G-4603)*
Automated Lumber Handling Inc............ G..... 828 754-4662
 Lenoir *(G-9576)*
▲ Basic Machinery Company Inc........... D..... 919 663-2244
 Siler City *(G-14399)*
▲ Belt Concepts America Inc................. F..... 888 598-2358
 Spring Hope *(G-14614)*

Beltservice Corporation.......................... E..... 704 947-2264
 Huntersville *(G-8797)*
▲ Conroll Corporation............................. F..... 910 202-4292
 Wilmington *(G-16178)*
Conveying Solutions LLC....................... F..... 704 636-4241
 Salisbury *(G-13947)*
◆ Conveyor Tech LLC............................. C..... 919 776-7227
 Goldston *(G-6674)*
Conveyor Technologies Inc.................... G..... 919 732-8291
 Efland *(G-5526)*
◆ Conveyor Technologies of .... D..... 919 776-7227
 Sanford *(G-14103)*
Davis Conveyor Components................. G..... 704 557-1742
 Charlotte *(G-2605)*
Esco Group LLC..................................... G..... 919 900-8226
 Raleigh *(G-12746)*
◆ Forbo Movement Systems.................. E..... 704 334-5353
 Charlotte *(G-2786)*
▲ Forbo Siegling LLC............................. B..... 704 948-0800
 Huntersville *(G-8825)*
Gardner Machinery Corporation............. F..... 704 372-3890
 Charlotte *(G-2808)*
Goals In Service LLC............................. G..... 919 440-2656
 Seven Springs *(G-14267)*
▲ Gough Econ Inc................................... E..... 704 399-4501
 Charlotte *(G-2848)*
Greenline Corporation............................ G..... 704 333-3377
 Charlotte *(G-2866)*
◆ Industrial Sup Solutions Inc................ E..... 704 636-4241
 Salisbury *(G-13983)*
▲ Interroll Corporation............................ F..... 910 799-1100
 Wilmington *(G-16271)*
Interroll USA Holding LLC...................... D..... 910 799-1100
 Wilmington *(G-16272)*
Ism Inc.. E
 Arden *(G-342)*
▲ Jayson Concepts Inc........................... E..... 828 654-8900
 Arden *(G-344)*
▲ Lns Turbo Inc...................................... D..... 704 739-7111
 Kings Mountain *(G-9316)*
Machinex Technologies Inc.................... E..... 773 867-8801
 High Point *(G-8437)*
▲ Mantissa Corporation.......................... E..... 704 525-1749
 Charlotte *(G-3122)*
Material Handling Technologies Inc........ D..... 919 388-0050
 Morrisville *(G-11388)*
Memios LLC.. D..... 336 664-5256
 Greensboro *(G-7197)*
Movex Usa Inc.. G..... 434 616-2590
 Raleigh *(G-13044)*
▲ National Conveyors Company Inc....... G..... 860 325-4011
 Charlotte *(G-3234)*
Niels Jorgensen Company Inc................ G..... 910 259-1624
 Burgaw *(G-1346)*
Nunn Probst Installations Inc................. G..... 704 822-9443
 Belmont *(G-997)*
Process Automation Tech Inc................. F..... 828 298-1055
 Asheville *(G-745)*
▲ Production Systems Inc...................... E..... 336 886-7161
 High Point *(G-8499)*
▲ Pteris Global (usa) Inc........................ F..... 980 253-3267
 Charlotte *(G-3395)*
Qcs Acquisition Corporation................... G..... 252 446-5000
 Rocky Mount *(G-13725)*
RSI Leasing Inc NS Tbt......................... G..... 704 587-9300
 Charlotte *(G-3468)*
Sherrill Contract Mfg Inc........................ F..... 704 922-7871
 Dallas *(G-4657)*
Southco Industries Inc............................ C..... 704 482-1477
 Shelby *(G-14369)*
Sunco Powder Systems Inc.................... E..... 704 545-3922
 Charlotte *(G-3651)*

Superior Finishing Systems LLC............ G..... 336 956-2000
 Lexington *(G-9788)*
▲ Transbotics Corporation...................... E..... 704 362-1115
 Charlotte *(G-3716)*

3536 Hoists, cranes, and monorails

Altec Industries Inc................................ B..... 919 528-2535
 Creedmoor *(G-4603)*
▲ Altec Northeast LLC............................ D..... 508 320-9041
 Creedmoor *(G-4604)*
▲ Boat Lift US Inc................................... G..... 239 283-9040
 Leland *(G-9527)*
▼ Boat Lift Warehouse LLC.................... G..... 877 468-5438
 Snow Hill *(G-14498)*
Columbus McKinnon Corporation........... D..... 704 694-2156
 Wadesboro *(G-15507)*
◆ Duff-Norton Company Inc................... G..... 704 588-0510
 Charlotte *(G-2656)*
Float Lifts of Carolinas LLC.................... G..... 919 972-1082
 Wilmington *(G-16218)*
HI & Dri Boat Lift Systems Inc............... G..... 704 663-5438
 Mooresville *(G-10973)*
Hydrohoist of North Carolina.................. G..... 704 799-1910
 Mooresville *(G-10979)*
▲ Kuenz America Inc.............................. F..... 984 255-1018
 Raleigh *(G-12948)*
▲ Mias Inc... G..... 704 665-1098
 Charlotte *(G-3173)*
Piedmont Hoist and Crane Inc................ E..... 336 992-1355
 Winston Salem *(G-16853)*
Service and Equipment Company........... G..... 910 545-5886
 Jacksonville *(G-9029)*
Thomas M Brown Inc.............................. F..... 704 597-0246
 Charlotte *(G-3690)*
◆ Toter LLC... D..... 800 424-0422
 Statesville *(G-14916)*
Veon Inc... F..... 252 623-2102
 Washington *(G-15736)*

3537 Industrial trucks and tractors

A+ Pro Transport Inc.............................. G..... 980 215-8694
 Charlotte *(G-2119)*
Altec Industries Inc................................ B..... 919 528-2535
 Creedmoor *(G-4603)*
Arbon Equipment Corporation................ F..... 414 355-2600
 Charlotte *(G-2209)*
At Your Service Express LLC................. E..... 704 270-9918
 Charlotte *(G-2229)*
▲ Basic Machinery Company Inc........... D..... 919 663-2244
 Siler City *(G-14399)*
Batchlers LLC... G..... 910 619-4042
 Wilmington *(G-16133)*
Best Solution Cargo LLC........................ G..... 407 810-5559
 Wilmington *(G-16137)*
Bethlehem Manufacturing Co.................. F..... 828 495-7731
 Hickory *(G-7949)*
Bottomley Enterprises Inc...................... D..... 336 657-6400
 Mount Airy *(G-11485)*
◆ Bromma Inc.. E..... 919 620-8039
 Durham *(G-4982)*
Buck Racing Engines Inc....................... G..... 336 983-6562
 King *(G-9265)*
Butler Trailer Mfg Co Inc........................ F..... 336 674-8850
 Randleman *(G-13453)*
C&A Hockaday Transport LLC................ G..... 252 676-5956
 Roanoke Rapids *(G-13570)*
Carolina Expediters LLC......................... G..... 888 537-5330
 Mount Airy *(G-11489)*
Carolina Material Handling Inc............... F..... 336 294-2346
 Greensboro *(G-6889)*
Caterpillar Inc... D..... 919 777-2000
 Sanford *(G-14098)*

Employee Codes: A=Over 500 employees, B=251-500
C=101-250, D=51-100, E=20-50, F=10-19, G=1-9

35 INDUSTRIAL AND COMMERCIAL MACHINERY AND COMPUTER EQUIPMENT

Cbj Transit LLC .... D 252 417-9972
  Garner (G-6263)
Central Carolina Forklift LLC .... G 919 545-9749
  Moncure (G-10618)
▲ Combilift USA LLC .... F 336 378-8884
  Greensboro (G-6922)
Crown Equipment Corporation .... E 336 291-2500
  Colfax (G-4146)
Crown Equipment Corporation .... D 704 721-4000
  Concord (G-4247)
Crown Equipment Corporation .... E 919 773-4160
  Garner (G-6269)
Crown Equipment Corporation .... B 252 522-3088
  Kinston (G-9355)
CSM Logistics LLC .... G 980 800-2621
  Charlotte (G-2581)
▲ Cutting Systems Inc .... D 704 592-2451
  Union Grove (G-15436)
D&E Freight LLC .... F 704 977-4847
  Charlotte (G-2597)
Daimler Truck North Amer LLC .... A 704 645-5000
  Cleveland (G-4071)
Discount Pallet Services LLC .... G 910 892-3760
  Dunn (G-4862)
DOWns&moss A1 Trucking LLC .... G 704 981-0880
  Mint Hill (G-10530)
Driveco Inc .... G 704 615-2111
  Charlotte (G-2654)
Drs Transportation Inc .... G 919 215-2770
  Raleigh (G-12704)
E-Z Dumper Products LLC .... F 717 762-8432
  Southern Pines (G-14534)
Elektrikredd LLC .... G 704 805-0110
  Matthews (G-10313)
Elite Forestry Solutions LLC .... G 757 777-2729
  Charlotte (G-2696)
Fastlife Transport LLC .... G 484 350-6754
  Charlotte (G-2749)
Fleet Fixers Inc .... G 704 986-0066
  Albemarle (G-85)
Forklift Network .... G 877 327-7260
  Cornelius (G-4548)
◆ Forklift Pro Inc .... F 704 716-3636
  Pineville (G-12269)
Forward Dsptching Lgistics LLC .... G 252 907-9797
  Greenville (G-7527)
Fuller Dynasty Brand LLC .... G 336 847-3875
  Eden (G-5490)
General Electric Company .... F 919 563-7445
  Mebane (G-10410)
General Electric Company .... B 919 563-5561
  Mebane (G-10411)
Go For Green Fleet Svcs LLC .... G 803 306-3683
  Charlotte (G-2840)
Good Grief Marketing LLC .... G 336 989-1984
  Greensboro (G-7053)
Gregory Poole Equipment Co .... G 252 931-5100
  Greenville (G-7535)
Hanging C Farms .... F 704 239-6691
  Kannapolis (G-9121)
Harrell Proper Transport LLC .... G 336 202-7135
  Whitsett (G-15992)
Hc Forklift America Corp .... F 980 888-8335
  Charlotte (G-2895)
Hyster-Yale Group Inc .... E 252 931-5100
  Greenville (G-7540)
Hyster-Yale Group Inc .... F 252 931-5100
  Greenville (G-7541)
◆ Hyster-Yale Group Inc .... G 252 931-5100
  Greenville (G-7542)
Jhrg Manufacturing LLC .... G 252 478-4977
  Spring Hope (G-14619)

Just n Tyme Trucking LLC .... G 704 804-9519
  Charlotte (G-3039)
▼ Kaufman Trailers Inc .... E 336 790-6800
  Lexington (G-9739)
◆ Kinston Neuse Corporation .... C 252 522-3088
  Kinston (G-9372)
Ksw Logistics & Transport LLC .... G 919 578-5788
  Raleigh (G-12947)
▲ Master Tow Inc .... E 910 630-2000
  Fayetteville (G-5869)
Maxson & Associates .... G 336 632-0524
  Greensboro (G-7190)
▲ McIntyre Manufacturing Group Inc .... D 336 476-3646
  Thomasville (G-15246)
Mjpc Transport LLC .... G 877 590-9512
  Raleigh (G-13036)
Mlg Trnscndent Trckg Trnsp Svc .... G 336 905-1192
  High Point (G-8457)
MMS Logistics Incorporated .... G 336 214-3552
  Mc Leansville (G-10394)
Moon N Sea Nc LLC .... G 704 588-1963
  Charlotte (G-3202)
▼ Multi-Shifter Inc .... F 704 588-9611
  Charlotte (G-3215)
New Vision Momentum Entp LLC .... G 800 575-1244
  Charlotte (G-3252)
Nexxt Level Trucking LLC .... G 980 205-4425
  Charlotte (G-3256)
Nmhg 252 229-0071
  Greenville (G-7564)
No1 Can Do It Betta Trckg LLC .... G 336 858-7693
  High Point (G-8467)
Nolan Manufacturing LLC .... G 336 490-0086
  Denton (G-4746)
North American Implements .... E 336 476-2904
  Lexington (G-9762)
Paper Route Transportation LLC .... G 919 478-6615
  Sanford (G-14162)
Parkers Equipment Company .... G 252 560-0088
  Snow Hill (G-14506)
Port City Elevator Inc .... E 910 790-9300
  Castle Hayne (G-1959)
Prevette & Sons Hauling LLC .... G 336 909-2717
  Mocksville (G-10598)
Propane Trucks & Tanks Inc .... G 919 362-5000
  Apex (G-234)
Rainey and Wilson Logistics .... G 910 736-8540
  Raeford (G-12434)
Rapid Run Transport LLC .... F 704 615-3458
  Charlotte (G-3410)
Reginald DWayne Dillard .... G 980 254-5505
  Charlotte (G-3427)
Regional Truckng Company LLC .... G 910 228-0245
  Wilmington (G-16381)
RSI Leasing Inc NS Tbt .... G 704 587-9300
  Charlotte (G-3468)
Rucker Intrgrted Logistics LLC .... G 704 352-2018
  Charlotte (G-3471)
S & S Trucking Company .... G 910 843-6264
  Red Springs (G-13503)
Scootatrailertm .... G 336 671-0444
  Lexington (G-9777)
Smithway Inc .... G 828 628-1756
  Fairview (G-5718)
Sml Transportation LLC .... G 704 402-6744
  Harmony (G-7689)
▼ Sound Heavy Machinery Inc .... G 910 782-2477
  Wilmington (G-16407)
Sterling Rack Inc .... F 704 866-9131
  Gastonia (G-6516)
Superior Dry Kilns Inc .... E 828 754-7001
  Hudson (G-8782)

Swing Kurve Logistic Trckg LLC .... G 704 506-7371
  Charlotte (G-3661)
▼ TCI Mobility Inc .... F 704 867-8331
  Gastonia (G-6520)
Tcom Limited Partnership .... B 252 330-5555
  Elizabeth City (G-5575)
Three Ladies and A Male LLC .... G 704 287-1584
  Charlotte (G-3691)
Triple H Hauling LLC .... G 984 220-4676
  Elizabeth City (G-5579)
Trunorth Wrrnty Plans N Amer L .... E 800 903-7489
  Huntersville (G-8903)
V M Trucking Inc .... G 984 239-4853
  Morehead City (G-11195)
◆ Wastequip .... G 704 366-7140
  Charlotte (G-3796)
Webbs Logistics LLC .... F 919 591-4308
  Garner (G-6325)
Westlift LLC .... F 919 242-4379
  Goldsboro (G-6670)
Whiteville Forklift & Eqp .... G 910 642-6642
  Whiteville (G-15980)
Wlc Forklift Services LLC .... G 336 345-2571
  Reidsville (G-13546)

3541 Machine tools, metal cutting type

Accurate Fabrications Inc .... G 910 383-2140
  Leland (G-9524)
Achilli USA Inc .... G 704 940-0115
  Raleigh (G-12470)
Amada America Inc .... G 877 262-3287
  High Point (G-8243)
▲ Atlantic Hydraulics Svcs LLC .... E 919 542-2985
  Sanford (G-14091)
Belkoz Inc .... G 919 703-0694
  Raleigh (G-12551)
▲ Betek Tools Inc .... F 980 498-2523
  Charlotte (G-2303)
Blue Inc Usa LLC .... E 828 346-8660
  Conover (G-4423)
Brown Equipment and Capitl Inc .... F 704 921-4644
  Monroe (G-10670)
C & J Machine Company Inc .... G 704 922-5913
  Dallas (G-4636)
▲ Casetec Precision Machine LLC .... G 704 663-6043
  Mooresville (G-10899)
Central Tool & Mfg Co Inc .... G 828 328-2383
  Hickory (G-7974)
Circor Precision Metering LLC .... A 919 774-7667
  Sanford (G-14102)
Delta Phoenix Inc .... E 336 621-3960
  Greensboro (G-6966)
Drill & Fill Mfg LLC .... G 252 937-4555
  Rocky Mount (G-13691)
▲ Efco USA Inc .... G 800 332-6872
  Charlotte (G-2686)
Exact Cut Inc .... F 336 207-4022
  Greensboro (G-7008)
▲ Grindtec Enterprises Corp .... G 704 636-1825
  Salisbury (G-13974)
Hamilton Indus Grinding Inc .... E 828 253-6796
  Asheville (G-647)
▼ His Glassworks Inc .... G 828 254-2559
  Asheville (G-653)
J & B Tool Making Inc .... G 704 827-4805
  Mount Holly (G-11639)
▲ Kyocera Precision Tools Inc .... G 800 823-7284
  Hendersonville (G-7870)
L & R Specialties Inc .... F 704 853-3296
  Gastonia (G-6441)
Lynn Electronics Corporation .... G 704 369-0093
  Concord (G-4308)

SIC SECTION

35 INDUSTRIAL AND COMMERCIAL MACHINERY AND COMPUTER EQUIPMENT

▲ Machine Tool Components LLC .... G 866 466-0120
Indian Trail (G-8948)

▲ Matcor Mtal Fbrction Wlcome In .... C 336 731-5700
Lexington (G-9756)

Motion Control Integration .... G 704 608-1279
Charlotte (G-3206)

◆ Normac Incorporated .... E 828 209-9000
Hendersonville (G-7886)

Northeast Tool and Mfg Company .... E 704 882-1187
Matthews (G-10337)

▲ Okuma America Corporation .... C 704 588-7000
Charlotte (G-3290)

Precision Industries Inc .... F 828 465-3418
Conover (G-4485)

▲ Putsch & Company Inc .... E 828 684-0671
Fletcher (G-6033)

Sandvik Tooling .... G 919 563-5008
Mebane (G-10429)

▲ Schelling America Inc .... E 919 544-0430
Morrisville (G-11418)

Schenck USA Corp .... G 704 529-5300
Conover (G-4495)

Slack & Parr International .... G 704 527-2975
Dallas (G-4658)

Staunton Saw Service .... G 919 471-3883
Durham (G-5372)

Superior Dry Kilns Inc .... E 828 754-7001
Hudson (G-8782)

Surry Logistix LLC .... G 336 710-3446
Mount Airy (G-11582)

Tactile Workshop LLC .... G 919 738-9924
Raleigh (G-13323)

▲ Tigra Usa Inc .... G 828 324-8227
Hickory (G-8182)

Triad Cutting Tools Inc .... G 336 873-8708
Asheboro (G-500)

U Tech Cnc Se LLC .... G 980 500-8263
Charlotte (G-3745)

▲ Union Grove Saw & Knife Inc .... D 704 539-4442
Union Grove (G-15438)

▼ Whiteside Mch & Repr Co Inc .... E 828 459-2141
Claremont (G-3945)

▲ Wieland Electric Inc .... F 910 259-5050
Wilmington (G-16442)

Willis Manufacturing Inc .... E 828 244-0435
Conover (G-4513)

Windco LLC .... G 704 846-6029
Indian Trail (G-8971)

3542 Machine tools, metal forming type

American Racg Hders Exhust Inc .... E 631 608-1986
Stanfield (G-14674)

Arnold S Welding Service Inc .... E 910 323-3822
Fayetteville (G-5764)

CPM Wolverine Proctor LLC .... F 336 479-2983
Lexington (G-9699)

CPM Wolverine Proctor LLC .... D 336 248-5181
Lexington (G-9700)

◆ Cyril Bath Company .... F 704 289-8531
Monroe (G-10701)

Delta Phoenix Inc .... E 336 621-3960
Greensboro (G-6966)

E G A Products Inc .... F 704 664-1221
Mooresville (G-10932)

◆ Emery Corporation .... D 828 433-1536
Morganton (G-11211)

Gesipa Fasteners Usa Inc .... E 336 751-1555
Mocksville (G-10577)

◆ Gesipa Fasteners Usa Inc .... F 609 208-1740
Mocksville (G-10578)

▼ Grey Holdings Inc .... E 828 862-4772
Brevard (G-1274)

Industrial Rlblity Spclsts Inc .... E 513 652-9337
Wilmington (G-16267)

▲ Legacy Mechanical .... F 704 225-8558
Monroe (G-10757)

Linde Advanced Mtl Tech Inc .... D 828 862-4772
Brevard (G-1278)

▲ M & A Equipment Inc .... G 704 703-9400
Charlotte (G-3112)

◆ Moores Mch Co Fayetteville Inc ...... G 919 837-5354
Bear Creek (G-941)

◆ Murata Machinery Usa Inc .... C 704 875-9280
Charlotte (G-3219)

◆ Murata McHy USA Holdings Inc ...... F 704 394-8331
Charlotte (G-3220)

Ora Inc .... G 540 903-7177
Marion (G-10170)

Prattgears .... G 414 704-3912
Salisbury (G-14029)

Price Metal Spinning Inc .... G 704 922-3195
Dallas (G-4652)

◆ Schunk Intec Inc .... D 919 572-2705
Morrisville (G-11420)

Sona Autocomp USA LLC .... C 919 965-5555
Selma (G-14260)

◆ Sona Blw Precision Forge Inc .... C 919 828-3375
Selma (G-14261)

Surry Logistix LLC .... G 336 710-3446
Mount Airy (G-11582)

Ultra Machine & Fabrication Inc .... C 704 482-1399
Shelby (G-14379)

Wuko Inc .... G 980 938-0512
Greensboro (G-7470)

Wysong and Miles Company .... E 336 621-3960
Greensboro (G-7471)

3543 Industrial patterns

Lampe & Malphrus Lumber Co .... F 919 934-1124
Smithfield (G-14471)

Pattern Box .... G 704 535-8743
Charlotte (G-3318)

Sweet Tea Girls Patterns .... G 843 907-2727
Clayton (G-4015)

3544 Special dies, tools, jigs, and fixtures

A & M Tool Inc .... F 828 891-9990
Mills River (G-10497)

ABT Manufacturing LLC .... E 704 847-9188
Statesville (G-14736)

Acme Die & Machine Corporation .... F 704 864-8426
Gastonia (G-6335)

American Artworks .... G 910 803-2525
Holly Ridge (G-8679)

Ameritech Die & Mold Inc .... E 704 664-0801
Mooresville (G-10857)

Ameritech Die & Mold South Inc .... F 704 664-0801
Mooresville (G-10858)

Ameritek Inc .... E 336 292-1165
Greensboro (G-6803)

Ameritek Lasercut Dies Inc .... E 336 292-1165
Greensboro (G-6805)

Atlantic Mold Inc .... G 919 832-8151
Fuquay Varina (G-6182)

Atlantic Tool & Die Co Inc .... G 910 270-2888
Hampstead (G-7638)

Bethlehem Manufacturing Co .... F 828 495-7731
Hickory (G-7949)

Bnp Inc .... F 919 775-7070
Sanford (G-14094)

Brooks of Dallas Inc .... G 704 922-5219
Dallas (G-4635)

Brooks Tool Inc .... G 704 283-0110
Monroe (G-10669)

Cairn Studio Ltd .... E 704 664-7128
Mooresville (G-10894)

Capital of Garner .... G 919 582-0202
Garner (G-6260)

Carolina Resource Corp .... F 919 562-0200
Youngsville (G-17076)

Cascade Die Casting Group Inc .... E 336 882-0186
High Point (G-8290)

Container Graphics Corp .... E 704 588-7230
Pineville (G-12261)

▲ Container Graphics Corp .... F 919 481-4200
Cary (G-1733)

Continental Tool Works Inc .... G 828 692-2578
Hendersonville (G-7839)

Converting Technology Inc .... G 336 333-2386
Greensboro (G-6934)

Cross Technology Inc .... E 336 725-4700
East Bend (G-5465)

DEB Manufacturing Inc .... G 704 703-6618
Concord (G-4253)

Die-Tech Inc .... F 336 475-9186
Thomasville (G-15213)

Digital Design & Modeling LLC .... G 336 766-2155
Winston Salem (G-16678)

Douglas Wolcott .... G 336 475-0052
Thomasville (G-15215)

Dura-Craft Die Inc .... G 828 632-1944
Taylorsville (G-15141)

Dwd Industries LLC .... E 336 498-6327
Randleman (G-13466)

▲ Dynacast US Holdings Inc .... G 704 927-2790
Charlotte (G-2665)

Elizabeth Carbide Die Co Inc .... D 336 472-5555
Lexington (G-9714)

Elizabeth Carbide NC Inc .... E 336 472-5555
Lexington (G-9715)

▲ Emerald Tool and Mold Inc .... F 336 996-6445
Kernersville (G-9195)

◆ Emery Corporation .... D 828 433-1536
Morganton (G-11211)

Enplas Life Tech Inc .... G 828 633-2250
Asheville (G-617)

Fisk Tool Company .... G 828 684-5454
Arden (G-329)

Flat Rock Tool & Mold Inc .... G 828 692-2578
Hendersonville (G-7852)

Foot To Die For .... G 704 577-2822
Charlotte (G-2785)

Gerald Hartsoe .... G 336 498-3233
Randleman (G-13471)

Goodyear Tire & Rubber Company .... D 704 928-4500
Statesville (G-14806)

Griffiths Corporation .... D 704 554-5657
Pineville (G-12272)

▲ H + M USA Management Co Inc .... E 704 599-9325
Charlotte (G-2878)

▲ Hasco America Inc .... G 828 650-2631
Fletcher (G-6010)

Industrial Metal Products of .... F 910 944-8110
Aberdeen (G-7)

Industrial Mtal Flame Spryers .... G 919 596-9381
Durham (G-5152)

Its A Snap .... G 828 254-3456
Asheville (G-664)

Jmk Tool & Die Inc .... G 910 897-6373
Coats (G-4131)

KAM Tool & Die Inc .... E 919 269-5099
Zebulon (G-17132)

▲ Madern Usa Inc .... E 919 363-4248
Apex (G-215)

Marine Systems Inc .... F 828 254-5354
Asheville (G-695)

35 INDUSTRIAL AND COMMERCIAL MACHINERY AND COMPUTER EQUIPMENT — SIC SECTION

▲ Meusburger Us Inc .... F 704 526-0330
  Mint Hill (G-10539)
Millar Industries Inc .... E 828 687-0639
  Arden (G-351)
Modern Mold & Tool Company .... G 704 377-2300
  Mount Holly (G-11643)
Mold Trans LLC .... G 828 356-5181
  Fletcher (G-6027)
Northeast Tool and Mfg Company .... E 704 882-1187
  Matthews (G-10337)
Omni Mold & Die LLC .... F 336 724-5152
  Winston Salem (G-16830)
Palmer Senn .... G 704 451-3971
  Charlotte (G-3309)
Park Avenue Metalcraft Inc .... F 919 554-2233
  Youngsville (G-17090)
Parker Industries Inc .... D 828 437-7779
  Connelly Springs (G-4407)
Piedmont Fiberglass Inc .... E 828 632-8883
  Statesville (G-14859)
Precision Partners LLC .... G 800 545-3121
  Charlotte (G-3370)
Precision Tool & Stamping Inc .... G 910 592-0174
  Clinton (G-4102)
Precision Tool Dye and Mold .... F 828 687-2990
  Arden (G-368)
Progressive Service Die Co .... F 910 353-4836
  Jacksonville (G-9023)
Progressive Tool & Mfg Inc .... F 336 664-1130
  Greensboro (G-7289)
Prototype Tooling Co .... G 704 864-7777
  Gastonia (G-6498)
Pyrotek Incorporated .... E 704 642-1993
  Salisbury (G-14033)
▲ Qrmc Ltd .... E 828 696-2000
  Hendersonville (G-7893)
▼ R A Serafini Inc .... E 704 864-6763
  Gastonia (G-6500)
▲ Rp Fletcher Machine Co Inc .... D 336 249-6101
  Lexington (G-9775)
◆ Schunk Intec Inc .... D 919 572-2705
  Morrisville (G-11420)
▲ Select Mold Service Inc .... F 910 323-1287
  Fayetteville (G-5913)
Southeastern Die of NC .... E 336 275-5212
  Greensboro (G-7352)
◆ Southeastern Tool & Die Inc .... D 910 944-7677
  Aberdeen (G-29)
Southern Steel and Wire Inc .... D 336 548-9611
  Madison (G-10087)
Speciality Cox Mfg LLC .... G 828 684-5762
  Arden (G-379)
Specialty Machine Co Inc .... E 704 853-2102
  Gastonia (G-6511)
▲ Spnc Associates Inc .... D 919 467-5151
  Cary (G-1902)
Stafford Cutting Dies Inc .... D 704 821-6330
  Indian Trail (G-8965)
Stampco Metal Products Inc .... E 828 645-4271
  Weaverville (G-15864)
Stratford Tool & Die Co Inc .... F 336 765-2030
  Winston Salem (G-16921)
Superior Tooling Inc .... F 919 570-9762
  Wake Forest (G-15600)
T D M Corporation .... E
  Fletcher (G-6044)
Tgr Enterprises Incorporated .... G 828 665-4427
  Candler (G-1590)
Toner Machining Tech Inc .... D 828 432-8007
  Morganton (G-11261)
Valmet Inc .... C 704 541-1453
  Charlotte (G-3763)

Western Crlina TI Mold Corp In .... E 828 890-4448
  Mills River (G-10514)
Wilmington Machine Works Inc .... F 910 343-8111
  Wilmington (G-16447)
Wirtz Wire Edm LLC .... F 828 696-0830
  Hendersonville (G-7915)
Worth Products LLC .... F 252 747-9994
  Snow Hill (G-14510)
◆ Wright Machine & Tool Co Inc .... E 828 298-8440
  Swannanoa (G-15038)

3545 Machine tool accessories

21st Century Tech of Amer .... F 910 826-3676
  Fayetteville (G-5744)
Advanced Superabrasives Inc .... G 828 689-3200
  Mars Hill (G-10191)
Alternative Cutting Tools LLC .... G 484 684-9924
  Ocean Isle Beach (G-12086)
Arrowood Mechanical Design LLC .... G 828 989-1605
  Hendersonville (G-7821)
Burris Machine Company Inc .... G 828 322-6914
  Hickory (G-7955)
C & C Precision Machine Inc .... G 704 739-0505
  Kings Mountain (G-9297)
▲ C R Onsrud Inc .... E 704 508-7000
  Troutman (G-15368)
Calco Enterprises Inc .... F 910 695-0089
  Aberdeen (G-3)
◆ Canvas Sx LLC .... C 980 474-3700
  Charlotte (G-2384)
Carbo-Cut Inc .... G 828 685-7890
  Hendersonville (G-7833)
Carolina Components Group Inc .... E 919 635-8438
  Durham (G-5001)
Central Tool & Mfg Co Inc .... G 828 328-2383
  Hickory (G-7974)
Cooper Bussmann LLC .... C 252 566-0278
  La Grange (G-9438)
▲ Creative Tooling Solutions Inc .... G 704 504-5415
  Pineville (G-12263)
Croft Precision Tools Inc .... G 704 399-4124
  Charlotte (G-2571)
Cross Technology Inc .... E 336 725-4700
  East Bend (G-5465)
◆ Diamond Dog Tools Inc .... D 828 687-3686
  Arden (G-325)
Disston Co Inc .... G 336 547-6300
  Greensboro (G-6972)
◆ Dormer Pramet LLC .... B 800 877-3745
  Mebane (G-10407)
Em2 Machine Corp .... G 336 297-4110
  Summerfield (G-14981)
◆ Emery Corporation .... D 828 433-1536
  Morganton (G-11211)
Eversharp Saw & Tool Inc .... G 828 345-1200
  Hickory (G-8019)
Fisk Tool Company .... G 828 684-5454
  Arden (G-329)
Frank G Shumate .... G 336 784-0828
  Kernersville (G-9201)
◆ Freud America Inc .... C 800 334-4107
  High Point (G-8360)
Greenleaf Corporation .... E 828 693-0461
  East Flat Rock (G-5476)
▲ Hickory Saw & Tool Inc .... E 828 324-5585
  Hickory (G-8050)
I G P .... G 828 728-5338
  Lenoir (G-9621)
If Armor International LLC .... C 704 482-1399
  Shelby (G-14329)
◆ Irwin Industrial Tool Company .... C 704 987-4555
  Huntersville (G-8838)

Kenmar Inc .... F 336 884-8722
  High Point (G-8423)
Kennametal Inc .... D 336 672-3313
  Asheboro (G-449)
Kennametal Inc .... G 704 588-4777
  Charlotte (G-3050)
Kennametal Inc .... D 252 492-4163
  Henderson (G-7791)
Kennametal Inc .... D 252 536-5209
  Weldon (G-15884)
▲ Kyocera Precision Tools Inc .... G 800 823-7284
  Hendersonville (G-7870)
▲ Linamar North Carolina Inc .... F 828 348-5343
  Arden (G-349)
Lns Turbo North America .... G 704 435-6376
  Cherryville (G-3871)
LS Starrett Company .... E 336 789-5141
  Mount Airy (G-11540)
Mitsubishi Materials USA Corp .... E 980 312-3100
  Mooresville (G-11023)
Modern Tool Service .... F 919 365-7470
  Wendell (G-15909)
North Carolina Mfg Inc .... E 919 734-1115
  Goldsboro (G-6638)
Packet Pushers Interactive LLC .... G 928 793-2450
  Sanford (G-14161)
Penco Precision LLC .... G 910 292-6542
  Wilmington (G-16350)
Pie Pushers .... G 919 901-0743
  Durham (G-5288)
Premier Tool LLC .... G 704 895-8223
  Cornelius (G-4577)
Production Tool and Die Co Inc .... F 704 525-0498
  Charlotte (G-3390)
▲ Putsch & Company Inc .... E 828 684-0671
  Fletcher (G-6033)
Robert Bosch Tool Corporation .... E 252 551-7512
  Greenville (G-7580)
Rock-Weld Industries Inc .... G 336 375-6862
  Greensboro (G-7315)
▲ Rp Fletcher Machine Co Inc .... D 336 249-6101
  Lexington (G-9775)
Rymon Company Inc .... G 704 519-5310
  Charlotte (G-3475)
◆ Salice America Inc .... E 704 841-7810
  Charlotte (G-3483)
◆ Sandvik Inc .... C 919 563-5008
  Mebane (G-10427)
Sandvik McHning Sltons USA LLC .... F 919 563-5008
  Mebane (G-10428)
Smith Setzer and Sons Inc .... E 828 241-3161
  Catawba (G-1968)
Speedwell Machine Works Inc .... F 704 866-7418
  Gastonia (G-6512)
Stanley Black & Decker Inc .... G 704 293-9392
  Huntersville (G-8900)
Stanly Tractor Company .... G 704 983-1106
  New London (G-11879)
Tar Heel Tling Prcsion McHning .... E 919 965-6160
  Smithfield (G-14486)
▲ Techsouth Inc .... E 704 334-1100
  Matthews (G-10349)
Tfam Solutions LLC .... G 910 637-0266
  Aberdeen (G-31)
Toner Machining Tech Inc .... D 828 432-8007
  Morganton (G-11261)
Toolcraft Inc North Carolina .... F 828 659-7379
  Marion (G-10183)
Unique Tool and Mfg Co .... E 336 498-2614
  Franklinville (G-6171)
United Machine & Metal Fab Inc .... E 828 464-5167
  Conover (G-4508)

35 INDUSTRIAL AND COMMERCIAL MACHINERY AND COMPUTER EQUIPMENT

▲ Vishay Transducers Ltd.................... E 919 365-3800
   Wendell *(G-15924)*

W D Lee & Company............................. E 704 864-0346
   Gastonia *(G-6537)*

W T Mander & Son Inc......................... G 336 562-5755
   Prospect Hill *(G-12409)*

Wise Storage Solutions LLC............... E 336 789-5141
   Mount Airy *(G-11596)*

Yat Usa Inc.. G 480 584-4096
   Huntersville *(G-8908)*

▲ Yg-1 America Inc................................ E 980 318-5348
   Charlotte *(G-3844)*

3546 Power-driven handtools

Apex Tool Group LLC......................... C 919 387-0099
   Apex *(G-164)*

Black & Decker (us) Inc...................... G 336 852-1300
   Greensboro *(G-6840)*

Black & Decker Corporation................ G 803 396-3700
   Charlotte *(G-2319)*

Black & Decker Corporation................ G 704 799-3929
   Mooresville *(G-10882)*

Black & Decker Corporation................ G 919 878-0357
   Raleigh *(G-12561)*

Bolton Investors Inc............................ G 919 471-1197
   Durham *(G-4971)*

Chicago Pneumatic Tool Co LLC......... F 704 504-6937
   Charlotte *(G-2475)*

Controlled Rock Drilling & Bl............... G 704 876-9004
   Olin *(G-12107)*

◆ Denver Global Products Inc................C 704 665-1800
   Charlotte *(G-2619)*

▲ Efco USA Inc...................................... G 800 332-6872
   Charlotte *(G-2686)*

Farm Services Inc............................... G 336 226-7381
   Graham *(G-6689)*

◆ Freud America Inc...............................C 800 334-4107
   High Point *(G-8360)*

Ingersoll-Rand Indus US Inc............... D 704 896-4000
   Davidson *(G-4680)*

John Deere Consumer Pdts Inc........... C 919 804-2000
   Cary *(G-1798)*

Ledger Hardware Inc.......................... G 828 688-4798
   Bakersville *(G-885)*

Leitz Tooling Systems LP.................... G 336 861-3367
   Archdale *(G-292)*

Masonite Corporation.......................... B 704 599-0235
   Charlotte *(G-3138)*

Quality Equipment LLC....................... G 919 493-3545
   Durham *(G-5312)*

◆ Snap-On Power Tools Inc....................C 828 835-4400
   Murphy *(G-11717)*

Stanley Black & Decker....................... E 704 987-2271
   Huntersville *(G-8899)*

Stanley Customer Support Divis.......... G 704 789-7000
   Concord *(G-4366)*

Trane Technologies Company LLC..... C 910 692-8700
   Southern Pines *(G-14558)*

Weber Screwdriving Systems Inc........ E 704 360-5820
   Mooresville *(G-11124)*

Wto Inc.. F 704 714-7765
   Charlotte *(G-3831)*

3547 Rolling mill machinery

Ew Jackson Transportation LLC.......... G 919 586-2514
   Holly Springs *(G-8698)*

South Atlantic LLC.............................. F 336 376-0410
   Graham *(G-6711)*

3548 Welding apparatus

American Welding & Gas Inc.............. G 984 222-2600
   Raleigh *(G-12501)*

▲ Burco Welding & Cutng Pdts Inc......... G 336 887-6100
   High Point *(G-8278)*

Fanuc America Corporation................. G 704 596-5121
   Huntersville *(G-8818)*

Hanson Systems Inc........................... G 828 687-3701
   Fletcher *(G-6009)*

▲ Kincol Industries Incorporated............ G 704 372-8435
   Charlotte *(G-3055)*

▲ Liburdi Dimetrics Corporation............. E 704 230-2510
   Mooresville *(G-11007)*

Modlins Anonized Aluminum Wldg...... G 252 753-7274
   Farmville *(G-5740)*

Qws LLC.. E 252 723-2106
   Morehead City *(G-11185)*

U S Alloy Co... F 888 522-8296
   Lowell *(G-10012)*

Van Welder LLC................................... G 919 495-2902
   Graham *(G-6714)*

3549 Metalworking machinery, nec

▲ Atlantic Hydraulics Svcs LLC.............. E 919 542-2985
   Sanford *(G-14091)*

DCS USA Corporation......................... G 919 535-8000
   Morrisville *(G-11329)*

East West Manufacturing LLC............. G 704 663-5975
   Mooresville *(G-10936)*

▲ Efco USA Inc...................................... G 800 332-6872
   Charlotte *(G-2686)*

Feeder Innovations Corporation.......... G 910 276-3511
   Laurinburg *(G-9480)*

G T Racing Heads Inc......................... G 336 905-7988
   Sophia *(G-14517)*

Gerringer Enterprises.......................... G 336 227-6535
   Burlington *(G-1420)*

H C Production Co............................... G 910 483-5267
   Fayetteville *(G-5832)*

High Definition Tool Corp.................... E 828 397-2467
   Connelly Springs *(G-4403)*

IMS Fabrication Inc............................. E 704 216-0255
   Salisbury *(G-13982)*

J Wise Inc.. E 828 202-5563
   Lincolnton *(G-9896)*

Joe and La Inc..................................... F 336 585-0313
   Burlington *(G-1441)*

Kds Fabricating and Mch Sp LLC......... F 828 632-5091
   Hiddenite *(G-8222)*

Manufacturing Methods LLC................ E 910 371-1700
   Leland *(G-9554)*

Nine-Ai Inc... F 781 825-3267
   Davidson *(G-4687)*

Obi Machine & Tool Inc....................... G 252 946-1580
   Chocowinity *(G-3896)*

Petty Machine Company Inc................ E 704 864-3254
   Gastonia *(G-6488)*

▲ Rosendahl Nextrom USA Inc.............. F 828 464-2543
   Claremont *(G-3938)*

Scott Systems Intl Inc.......................... F 704 362-1115
   Charlotte *(G-3512)*

▲ Techmet Carbides Inc........................ D 828 624-0222
   Hickory *(G-8176)*

Winston Steel Stair Co......................... G 336 721-0020
   Winston Salem *(G-16983)*

3552 Textile machinery

▲ A B Carter Inc..................................... D 704 865-1201
   Gastonia *(G-6334)*

Abercrombie Textiles Inc..................... G 704 487-0935
   Shelby *(G-14281)*

▼ Alandale Industries Inc....................... G 910 576-1291
   Troy *(G-15400)*

◆ American Linc Corporation.................E 704 861-9242
   Gastonia *(G-6346)*

▲ American Trutzschler Inc.................... D 704 399-4521
   Charlotte *(G-2187)*

Another Creation By Lady J................. G 919 334-9797
   Raleigh *(G-12508)*

B&Lk Enterprises................................. G 910 395-5151
   Wilmington *(G-16130)*

Barudan America Inc........................... G 800 627-4776
   High Point *(G-8266)*

▲ Belmont Textile Machinery Co............ E 704 827-5836
   Mount Holly *(G-11622)*

▲ Bgm Inc... G 704 776-4086
   Monroe *(G-10662)*

▲ Bowman-Hollis Manufacturing Co...... E 704 374-1500
   Charlotte *(G-2341)*

◆ Briggs-Shaffner Acquisition Co...........F 336 463-4272
   Yadkinville *(G-17034)*

Burnett Machine Company Inc............ F 704 867-7786
   Gastonia *(G-6363)*

C & J Machine Company Inc............... G 704 922-5913
   Dallas *(G-4636)*

Carolina Loom Reed Company Inc..... F 336 274-7631
   Greensboro *(G-6887)*

Carolina Tex Sls Gastonia Inc............. F 704 739-1646
   Kings Mountain *(G-9301)*

Carolina Textile Services Inc................ G 910 843-3033
   Red Springs *(G-13496)*

▲ Custom Enterprises Inc...................... G 336 226-8296
   Burlington *(G-1405)*

Custom Industries Inc.......................... F 704 825-3346
   Belmont *(G-981)*

▲ Custom Industries Inc........................ G 336 299-2885
   Greensboro *(G-6950)*

◆ D & S International Inc........................F 336 578-3800
   Mebane *(G-10406)*

▲ D M & E Corporation.......................... E 704 482-8876
   Shelby *(G-14309)*

Diversified Textile Mchy Corp.............. G 704 739-2121
   Kings Mountain *(G-9304)*

Ellerre Tech Inc.................................... E 704 524-9096
   Dallas *(G-4638)*

▼ Excel Inc... F 704 735-6535
   Lincolnton *(G-9892)*

Fab-Con Machinery Dev Corp............. E 516 883-3999
   Harrisburg *(G-7708)*

◆ Fab-Con Machinery Dev Corp............D 704 486-7120
   Oakboro *(G-12074)*

▲ Ferguson Companies......................... G
   Linwood *(G-9945)*

◆ Fletcher Industries Inc........................E 910 692-7133
   Southern Pines *(G-14536)*

Flint Group US LLC............................. G 828 687-4291
   Arden *(G-333)*

French Apron Manufacturing Co......... G 704 865-7666
   Gastonia *(G-6403)*

Gastex LLC.. G 704 824-9861
   Gastonia *(G-6404)*

▼ Gaston County Dyeing Mach.............. D 704 822-5000
   Mount Holly *(G-11634)*

Imperial Machine Company Inc........... E 704 739-8038
   Bessemer City *(G-1071)*

▲ International McHy Sls Inc.................. G 336 759-9548
   Winston Salem *(G-16763)*

◆ Itm Ltd South.......................................G 336 883-2400
   Greensboro *(G-7128)*

▲ J & P Entrprses of Crlinas Inc............ E 704 861-1867
   Gastonia *(G-6431)*

J J Jenkins Incorporated..................... E 704 821-6648
   Matthews *(G-10324)*

James T White Company..................... F 704 865-9811
   Gastonia *(G-6434)*

▲ Kern-Liebers USA Textile Inc............ E 704 329-7153
   Matthews *(G-10259)*

35 INDUSTRIAL AND COMMERCIAL MACHINERY AND COMPUTER EQUIPMENT — SIC SECTION

Lily Belles .... G 828 246-0894
   Waynesville *(G-15809)*

▼ Lincoln County Fabricators Inc .... E 704 735-1398
   Lincolnton *(G-9900)*

▲ M-B Industries Inc .... C 828 862-4201
   Rosman *(G-13786)*

Monarch Knitting McHy Corp .... E 704 283-8171
   Monroe *(G-10772)*

◆ Monarch Knitting McHy Corp .... F 704 291-3300
   Monroe *(G-10773)*

◆ Monarch Manufacturing Corp .... F 704 283-8171
   Monroe *(G-10774)*

◆ Mount Hope Machinery Co .... F
   Charlotte *(G-3208)*

◆ Murata McHy USA Holdings Inc .... F 704 394-8331
   Charlotte *(G-3220)*

Myers Quality Machine Co Inc .... F 336 498-4187
   Randleman *(G-13480)*

Old Made Quilts .... G 919 692-1060
   Oxford *(G-12137)*

▲ Parts and Systems Company Inc ...... F 828 684-7070
   Arden *(G-361)*

Petty Machine Company Inc .... E 704 864-3254
   Gastonia *(G-6488)*

▲ Pinco Usa Inc .... G 704 895-5766
   Cornelius *(G-4575)*

▲ Polyspintex Inc .... G 704 523-4382
   Charlotte *(G-3355)*

Precision Comb Works Inc .... G 704 864-2761
   Gastonia *(G-6495)*

Precision Machine Products Inc .... D 704 865-7490
   Gastonia *(G-6496)*

◆ Sam M Butler Inc .... E 910 277-7456
   Laurinburg *(G-9495)*

Sherrill Contract Mfg Inc .... F 704 922-7871
   Dallas *(G-4657)*

▲ Spgprints America Inc .... D 704 598-7171
   Charlotte *(G-3603)*

▲ Stork United Corporation .... A 704 598-7171
   Charlotte *(G-3639)*

▼ TCI Mobility Inc .... F 704 867-8331
   Gastonia *(G-6520)*

Textile Sales Intl Inc .... G 704 483-7966
   Denver *(G-4806)*

▲ Textrol Laboratories Inc .... E 704 764-3400
   Monroe *(G-10821)*

Tri State Plastics Inc .... G 704 865-7431
   Gastonia *(G-6532)*

Tsg Finishing LLC .... G 828 328-5522
   Hickory *(G-8186)*

Tsg Finishing LLC .... G 828 328-5541
   Hickory *(G-8187)*

Tsg Finishing LLC .... G 828 328-5522
   Hickory *(G-8188)*

▲ Tubular Textile Machinery .... G 336 956-6444
   Lexington *(G-9797)*

◆ Vanguard Pai Lung LLC .... G 704 283-8171
   Monroe *(G-10828)*

Woolfoam Corporation .... G 336 886-4964
   High Point *(G-8608)*

3553 Woodworking machinery

Alders Point .... G 336 725-9021
   Winston Salem *(G-16594)*

Atlantic Commercial Caseworks .... G 704 393-9500
   Charlotte *(G-2231)*

Automated Lumber Handling Inc .... G 828 754-4662
   Lenoir *(G-9576)*

▲ Bacci America Inc .... F 704 375-5044
   Charlotte *(G-2261)*

Bmi Wood Products Inc .... G 919 829-9505
   Raleigh *(G-12566)*

Carbide Saws Incorporated .... F 336 882-6835
   High Point *(G-8282)*

Caterpillar Inc .... D 919 550-1100
   Clayton *(G-3963)*

▲ Cefla North America Inc .... E 704 598-0020
   Charlotte *(G-2437)*

Dixon Custom Cabinetry LLC .... F 336 992-3306
   Kernersville *(G-9190)*

Edmiston Hydrlic Swmill Eqp In .... E 336 921-2304
   Boomer *(G-1169)*

▲ Etk International Inc .... G 704 819-1541
   Indian Trail *(G-8932)*

▲ Eurohansa Inc .... G 336 885-1010
   High Point *(G-8347)*

▲ Farris Belt & Saw Company .... F 704 527-6166
   Charlotte *(G-2748)*

Fletcher Machine Inds Inc .... D 336 249-6101
   Lexington *(G-9718)*

▲ Grecon Dimter Inc .... F 828 397-5139
   Connelly Springs *(G-4402)*

▲ Holz-Her Us Inc .... G 704 587-3400
   Mooresville *(G-10975)*

▲ Jly Invstmnts Inc Fka Nwman Mc ..... E 336 273-8261
   Browns Summit *(G-1310)*

▲ Karl Ogden Enterprises Inc .... G 704 845-2785
   Matthews *(G-10258)*

Khi LLC .... G 828 654-9916
   Arden *(G-345)*

Leitz Tooling Systems LP .... G 336 861-3367
   Archdale *(G-292)*

▲ Ligna Machinery Inc .... E 336 584-0030
   Burlington *(G-1451)*

▼ Meadows Mills Inc .... F 336 838-2282
   North Wilkesboro *(G-12027)*

Mill Art Wood .... G 919 828-7376
   Raleigh *(G-13032)*

Murrah Woodcraft .... G 919 302-3661
   Durham *(G-5231)*

Normac Kitchens Inc .... E 704 485-1911
   Locust *(G-9964)*

Ostwalt Leasing Co Inc .... G 704 528-4528
   Troutman *(G-15388)*

▲ Otb Machinery Inc .... G 336 323-1035
   Thomasville *(G-15260)*

Peco Inc .... E 828 684-1234
   Arden *(G-362)*

▼ Rfsprotech LLC .... E 704 845-2785
   Matthews *(G-10286)*

Router Bit Service Company Inc .... E 336 431-5535
   High Point *(G-8515)*

▲ Rp Fletcher Machine Co Inc .... D 336 249-6101
   Lexington *(G-9775)*

Singley Specialty Co Inc .... G 336 852-8581
   Greensboro *(G-7342)*

Smith Woodturning Inc .... G 828 464-2230
   Newton *(G-11968)*

Tawnico LLC .... G 704 606-2345
   Charlotte *(G-3673)*

Ventura Inc .... G 252 291-7125
   Fremont *(G-6174)*

Venture Cabinets .... G 252 299-0051
   Fremont *(G-6175)*

3554 Paper industries machinery

Ameritek Inc .... F 336 292-1165
   Greensboro *(G-6804)*

▲ Masterwork USA Inc .... G 704 288-9506
   Charlotte *(G-3140)*

Metso Outotec USA Inc .... E 877 677-2005
   Bessemer City *(G-1075)*

Steen Inc .... G 336 545-3328
   Greensboro *(G-7369)*

▲ Summer Industries LLC .... C 336 731-9217
   Welcome *(G-15876)*

◆ Triple Crown International LLC .... G 704 846-4983
   Charlotte *(G-3730)*

Valmet Inc .... G 803 289-4900
   Charlotte *(G-3764)*

W V Doyle Enterprises Inc .... G 336 885-2035
   High Point *(G-8600)*

3555 Printing trades machinery

▲ Anilox Roll Company Inc .... G 704 588-1809
   Charlotte *(G-2195)*

▲ Cary Manufacturing Corporation ...... G 704 527-4402
   Charlotte *(G-2416)*

Cogent Dynamics Inc .... G 828 628-9025
   Fletcher *(G-5995)*

▲ Container Graphics Corp .... F 919 481-4200
   Cary *(G-1733)*

Creative Printing Inc .... G 828 265-2800
   Boone *(G-1189)*

CTX Builders Supply .... G 704 983-6748
   Albemarle *(G-78)*

Diazit Company Inc .... G 919 556-5188
   Wake Forest *(G-15546)*

Digital Highpoint LLC .... C 336 883-7146
   High Point *(G-8324)*

▲ Diversfied Prtg Techniques Inc .... E 704 583-9433
   Charlotte *(G-2644)*

Encore Group Inc .... C 336 768-7859
   Winston Salem *(G-16696)*

Harper Companies Intl Inc .... G 800 438-3111
   Charlotte *(G-2889)*

◆ Harper Corporation of America .... C 704 588-3371
   Charlotte *(G-2890)*

Lazeredge LLC .... G 336 480-7934
   Mount Airy *(G-11535)*

Lazeredge LLC .... G 336 480-7934
   Mount Airy *(G-11536)*

Mark/Trece Inc .... F 973 884-1005
   Greensboro *(G-7181)*

Mark/Trece Inc .... E 336 292-3424
   Whitsett *(G-15997)*

National Color Graphics Inc .... G 704 263-3187
   Mount Holly *(G-11645)*

National Roller Supply Inc .... G 704 853-1174
   Gastonia *(G-6475)*

North Carolina Dept Pub Safety .... G 919 733-0867
   Raleigh *(G-13069)*

▲ Rotec North American .... G 828 681-0151
   Arden *(G-373)*

▲ Spgprints America Inc .... D 704 598-7171
   Charlotte *(G-3603)*

Trio Labs Inc .... F 919 818-9646
   Morrisville *(G-11456)*

3556 Food products machinery

A1gumballs .... G 919 494-1322
   Raleigh *(G-12453)*

▲ AC Corporation .... B 336 273-4472
   Greensboro *(G-6775)*

AMF Automation Tech LLC .... G 919 288-1523
   Goldsboro *(G-6589)*

▲ Are Management LLC .... E 336 855-7800
   High Point *(G-8252)*

Babington Technology Inc .... G 252 984-0349
   Rocky Mount *(G-13683)*

▲ Baker Thermal Solutions LLC .... E 919 674-3750
   Clayton *(G-3957)*

Booneshine Brewing Co Inc .... G 828 263-4305
   Boone *(G-1180)*

Broad Branch Distillery LLC .... G 336 207-7855
   Winston Salem *(G-16637)*

35 INDUSTRIAL AND COMMERCIAL MACHINERY AND COMPUTER EQUIPMENT

Buhler Inc... C 800 722-7483
  Cary *(G-1716)*

Carolina Packing House Sups................... G 910 653-3438
  Tabor City *(G-15079)*

Cates Mechanical Corporation.................. G 704 458-5163
  Charlotte *(G-2419)*

Community Brewing Ventures LLC........... G 800 579-6539
  Newton *(G-11923)*

Corporate Place LLC.................................. E 704 808-3848
  Charlotte *(G-2559)*

Dean St Processing LLC............................ G 252 235-0401
  Bailey *(G-871)*

Delaney Holdings Co................................. E 704 808-3848
  Charlotte *(G-2612)*

Designtek Fabrication Inc.......................... F 910 359-0130
  Red Springs *(G-13498)*

East Crlina Olseed Prcssors LL............... D 252 935-5553
  Pantego *(G-12163)*

▲ Embrex LLC.. C 919 941-5185
  Durham *(G-5080)*

Ezbrew Inc.. G 833 233-2739
  Cary *(G-1764)*

Flagstone Foods LLC................................. B 252 795-6500
  Robersonville *(G-13616)*

Fmp Equipment Corp................................. F 336 621-2882
  Browns Summit *(G-1302)*

▼ Friedrich Metal Pdts Co Inc..................... E 336 375-3067
  Browns Summit *(G-1303)*

▲ Gea Intec LLC.. E 919 433-0131
  Durham *(G-5112)*

Griffin Marketing Group.............................. G 336 558-5802
  Greensboro *(G-7068)*

Huo LI Juice & Co LLC............................... F 804 299-0806
  Huntersville *(G-8831)*

Induction Food Systems Inc..................... G 919 907-0179
  Raleigh *(G-12883)*

Jbt Aerotech Services................................ G 336 740-3737
  Greensboro *(G-7135)*

Krispy Kreme Doughnut Corp................... G 336 726-8908
  Winston Salem *(G-16780)*

M G Newell Corporation............................. D 336 393-0100
  Greensboro *(G-7173)*

Marshall Middleby Inc................................ D 919 762-1000
  Fuquay Varina *(G-6212)*

▼ Meadows Mills Inc..................................... E 336 838-2282
  North Wilkesboro *(G-12027)*

▲ Microthermics Inc....................................... F 919 878-8045
  Raleigh *(G-13028)*

◆ Middleby Marshall Inc................................ C 919 762-1000
  Fuquay Varina *(G-6216)*

Prima Elements LLC................................... G 910 483-8406
  Fayetteville *(G-5900)*

▲ Putsch & Company Inc.............................. E 828 684-0671
  Fletcher *(G-6033)*

Sinnovatek Inc... G 919 694-0974
  Raleigh *(G-13264)*

SPX Flow Inc.. C 704 752-4400
  Charlotte *(G-3607)*

SPX Flow Holdings Inc............................... E 704 808-3848
  Charlotte *(G-3608)*

SPX Flow Tech Systems Inc...................... A 704 752-4400
  Charlotte *(G-3609)*

SPX Flow Technology Usa Inc.................. D 704 808-3848
  Charlotte *(G-3610)*

SPX Latin America Corporation................ E 704 808-3848
  Charlotte *(G-3611)*

▲ Stanza Machinery Inc................................ E 704 599-0623
  Charlotte *(G-3622)*

▲ Stork United Corporation.......................... A 704 598-7171
  Charlotte *(G-3639)*

◆ Tipper Tie Inc.. C 919 362-8811
  Apex *(G-249)*

Utsey Duskie & Associates....................... G 704 663-0036
  Mooresville *(G-11117)*

Wins Smokehouse Services Ltd.............. G 828 884-7476
  Pisgah Forest *(G-12330)*

3559 Special industry machinery, nec

Advanced Plastiform Inc........................... D 919 404-2080
  Zebulon *(G-17117)*

Apb Wrecker Service LLC......................... G 704 400-0857
  Charlotte *(G-2199)*

Atmosphric Plsma Solutions Inc.............. G 919 341-8325
  Cary *(G-1693)*

◆ Autec Inc.. E 704 871-9141
  Statesville *(G-14755)*

Auto-Systems and Service Inc................. F 336 824-3580
  Ramseur *(G-13440)*

▲ Autopark Logistics LLC............................ G 704 365-3544
  Charlotte *(G-2241)*

Aylward Enterprises LLC.......................... E 252 639-9242
  New Bern *(G-11774)*

Bayatronics LLC.. F 980 432-0438
  Concord *(G-4206)*

▲ Besana-Lovati Inc....................................... F 336 768-6064
  Hamptonville *(G-7667)*

Besi Machining LLC................................... F 919 218-9241
  Youngsville *(G-17071)*

Biesse America Inc.................................... G 704 357-3131
  Charlotte *(G-2309)*

Birch Bros Southern Inc............................ E 704 843-2111
  Waxhaw *(G-15745)*

Brushy Mountain Dry Kilns LLC............... G 336 379-8314
  Greensboro *(G-6859)*

◆ Canvas Sx LLC... C 980 474-3700
  Charlotte *(G-2384)*

Carolina Mechanical Services Inc........... E 919 477-7100
  Durham *(G-5002)*

▲ Centor Inc.. F 704 896-7535
  Charlotte *(G-2442)*

Clean Green Inc.. G 919 596-3500
  Durham *(G-5020)*

Coastal Carolina Gin LLC.......................... F 252 943-6990
  Pantego *(G-12162)*

◆ Corob North America Inc.......................... F 704 588-8408
  Charlotte *(G-2558)*

Corporate Place LLC.................................. E 704 808-3848
  Charlotte *(G-2559)*

Courtney Martins Kiln................................ G 828 467-1414
  Bakersville *(G-881)*

Cox Machine Co Inc................................... F 704 296-0118
  Monroe *(G-10696)*

Cross Co... G 336 856-6110
  High Point *(G-8308)*

CVC Equipment Company......................... G 704 300-6242
  Cherryville *(G-3867)*

▲ D M & E Corporation.................................. E 704 482-8876
  Shelby *(G-14309)*

Delaney Holdings Co................................. E 704 808-3848
  Charlotte *(G-2612)*

Designtek Fabrication Inc.......................... F 910 359-0130
  Red Springs *(G-13498)*

◆ Dymetrol Company Inc.............................. F 866 964-8632
  Bladenboro *(G-1148)*

▲ Encertec Inc.. G 336 288-7226
  Greensboro *(G-6997)*

Enforge LLC... E 704 983-4146
  Albemarle *(G-83)*

Enplas Life Tech Inc................................... G 828 633-2250
  Asheville *(G-617)*

Envirotek Worldwide LLC.......................... F 704 285-6400
  Charlotte *(G-2719)*

Erlanger Auto Care Inc.............................. G 336 249-9674
  Lexington *(G-9716)*

Falls of Neuse Management LLC............. A 919 573-2900
  Raleigh *(G-12761)*

Fanuc America Corporation...................... G 704 596-5121
  Huntersville *(G-8818)*

Fil-Chem Inc.. G 919 878-1270
  Raleigh *(G-12766)*

Fireline Shields Llc.................................... G 704 948-3680
  Huntersville *(G-8821)*

G & E Investments Inc............................... F 704 395-2155
  Charlotte *(G-2802)*

Gardner Machinery Corporation.............. F 704 372-3890
  Charlotte *(G-2808)*

Gladiator Enterprises Inc......................... G 336 944-6932
  Greensboro *(G-7044)*

▲ Global Resource Corporation.................. G 919 972-7803
  Morrisville *(G-11349)*

Gold Refinery.. G 336 501-2977
  Browns Summit *(G-1306)*

Gold Refinery.. G 336 471-4817
  High Point *(G-8369)*

Hockmeyer Equipment Corp..................... D 252 338-4705
  Elizabeth City *(G-5548)*

▲ Ilsemann Corp.. G 610 323-4143
  Charlotte *(G-2952)*

Indian Tff-Tank Greensboro Inc............... G 336 625-2629
  Asheboro *(G-442)*

Industrial Metal Products of..................... F 910 944-8110
  Aberdeen *(G-7)*

Industry Choice Solutions LLC................ G 828 628-1991
  Fairview *(G-5714)*

▲ Kanthal Thermal Process Inc.................. D 704 784-3001
  Concord *(G-4298)*

Keffer Auto Huntersville LLC.................... G 877 260-4062
  Huntersville *(G-8842)*

▲ Kiln Drying Systems Cmpnnts In............ E 828 891-8115
  Etowah *(G-5692)*

LCI Corporation International................... G 704 399-7441
  Charlotte *(G-3075)*

◆ LCI Corporation International................... E 704 399-7441
  Charlotte *(G-3076)*

McDonald Services Inc.............................. E 704 597-0590
  Charlotte *(G-3149)*

McDonald Services Inc.............................. G 704 753-9669
  Monroe *(G-10769)*

Mdsi Inc.. G 919 783-8730
  Browns Summit *(G-1312)*

Merchant 1 Marketing LLC........................ G 888 853-9992
  Greensboro *(G-7199)*

Micropore Technologies Inc...................... F 984 344-7499
  Morrisville *(G-11390)*

Mono Plate Inc.. G 631 643-3100
  Apex *(G-220)*

◆ NGK Ceramics Usa Inc.............................. F 704 664-7000
  Mooresville *(G-11035)*

P P Kiln Erectors.. G 980 825-2263
  Salisbury *(G-14022)*

Petro Equipment Sls & Svc LLC............... G 828 492-0700
  Troutman *(G-15390)*

Petty Machine Company Inc..................... E 704 864-3254
  Gastonia *(G-6488)*

Power Components Inc............................. G 704 321-9481
  Charlotte *(G-3360)*

Powerhouse Resources Intl LLC............. D 919 291-1783
  Raleigh *(G-13123)*

Progressive Elc Greenville LLC............... F 252 413-6957
  Emerald Isle *(G-5671)*

▲ Psi-Polymer Systems Inc......................... E 828 468-2600
  Conover *(G-4490)*

Quarry & Kiln LLC...................................... F 704 888-0775
  Midland *(G-10477)*

Shred-Tech Usa LLC.................................. G 919 387-8220
  Raleigh *(G-13252)*

Employee Codes: A=Over 500 employees, B=251-500
C=101-250, D=51-100, E=20-50, F=10-19, G=1-9

2024 Harris North Carolina Manufacturers Directory

35 INDUSTRIAL AND COMMERCIAL MACHINERY AND COMPUTER EQUIPMENT — SIC SECTION

▲ Single Temperature Contrls Inc .... G 704 504-4800
Charlotte *(G-3556)*

SL - Laser Systems LLC .... G 704 561-9990
Charlotte *(G-3563)*

Southeastern Installation Inc .... E 704 352-7146
Lexington *(G-9783)*

SPX Flow Holdings Inc .... G 704 808-3848
Charlotte *(G-3608)*

SPX Flow Technology Usa Inc .... D 704 808-3848
Charlotte *(G-3610)*

SPX Latin America Corporation .... E 704 808-3848
Charlotte *(G-3611)*

Superior Dry Kilns Inc .... E 828 754-7001
Hudson *(G-8782)*

Texas Refinery .... G 704 213-4990
Salisbury *(G-14050)*

Ultraloop Technologies Inc .... G 919 636-2842
Chapel Hill *(G-2086)*

Wastequip .... F 800 255-4126
Statesville *(G-14923)*

Watson-Hegner Corporation .... G 704 922-9660
Gastonia *(G-6540)*

Wet Dog Glass LLC .... G 910 428-4111
Greensboro *(G-7458)*

▼ Wet Dog Glass LLC .... G 910 428-4111
Star *(G-14725)*

▲ Williams Performance Inc .... G 704 603-4431
Mount Ulla *(G-11608)*

Wispry Inc .... G 919 854-7500
Cary *(G-1929)*

3561 Pumps and pumping equipment

1st Choice Service Inc .... F 704 913-7685
Cherryville *(G-3861)*

Air Control Inc .... E 252 492-2300
Henderson *(G-7775)*

Allied/Carter Machining Inc .... G 704 784-1253
Concord *(G-4192)*

◆ Bfs Industries LLC .... E 919 575-6711
Butner *(G-1542)*

Bornemann Pumps Inc .... G 704 849-8636
Matthews *(G-10235)*

Camp S Well and Pump Co Inc .... G 828 453-7322
Ellenboro *(G-5634)*

Chichibone Inc .... G 919 785-0090
Morrisville *(G-11321)*

Chichibone Inc .... F 919 785-0090
Kernersville *(G-9177)*

Circor Precision Metering LLC .... A 919 774-7667
Sanford *(G-14102)*

▲ Circor Precision Metering LLC .... D 704 289-6511
Monroe *(G-10682)*

Circor Pumps North America LLC .... D 704 289-6511
Monroe *(G-10683)*

◆ Clyde Union (us) Inc .... C 704 808-3000
Charlotte *(G-2503)*

Clydeunion Pumps Inc .... E 704 808-3848
Charlotte *(G-2504)*

▲ Colfax Amrcas Engnered Systems ..... G 704 289-6511
Monroe *(G-10687)*

▲ Colfax Pump Group .... C 704 289-6511
Monroe *(G-10688)*

Dynisco Instruments LLC .... E 828 326-9888
Hickory *(G-8013)*

Enovis Corporation .... F 704 289-6511
Monroe *(G-10715)*

Fairbanks Nijhuis .... G 262 728-7449
Cary *(G-1768)*

Flowserve Corporation .... E 704 494-0497
Charlotte *(G-2782)*

Flowserve Corporation .... G 910 371-9011
Leland *(G-9543)*

Flowserve US Inc .... F 972 443-6500
Raleigh *(G-12776)*

◆ G Denver and Co LLC .... E 704 896-4000
Davidson *(G-4675)*

Haldex Inc .... C 828 652-9308
Marion *(G-10150)*

Hayward Industries Inc .... C 336 712-9900
Clemmons *(G-4043)*

Hayward Industries Inc .... A 336 712-9900
Clemmons *(G-4044)*

◆ Hayward Industries Inc .... B 908 351-5400
Charlotte *(G-2894)*

◆ Hurst Jaws of Life Inc .... C 704 487-6961
Shelby *(G-14328)*

IMO Industries Inc .... C 704 289-6511
Monroe *(G-10738)*

▲ IMO Industries Inc .... D 301 323-9000
Monroe *(G-10737)*

INGERSOLL RAND INC .... A 704 896-4000
Davidson *(G-4679)*

Ingersoll-Rand Company .... D 704 655-4836
Charlotte *(G-2974)*

Ingersoll-Rand Indus US Inc .... D 704 896-4000
Davidson *(G-4680)*

James M Pleasants Company Inc .... E 336 275-3152
Greensboro *(G-7133)*

▲ Kral USA Inc .... G 704 814-6164
Matthews *(G-10261)*

▲ Maag Reduction Inc .... E 704 716-9000
Charlotte *(G-3115)*

▲ Marley Company LLC .... C 704 752-4400
Charlotte *(G-3128)*

Merrill Resources Inc .... F 828 877-4450
Penrose *(G-12186)*

◆ Opw Fling Cntnment Systems Inc .... E 919 209-2280
Smithfield *(G-14474)*

Pentair Water Pool and Spa Inc .... F 919 463-4640
Cary *(G-1848)*

◆ Pentair Water Pool and Spa Inc .... A 919 566-8000
Sanford *(G-14166)*

◆ Primax Usa Inc .... C 704 587-3377
Charlotte *(G-3381)*

Raymond Brown Well Company Inc .... G 336 374-4999
Danbury *(G-4663)*

SL Liquidation LLC .... B 910 353-3666
Jacksonville *(G-9033)*

SPX Flow Inc .... C 704 752-4400
Charlotte *(G-3607)*

▲ Stockholm Corporation .... E 704 552-9314
Charlotte *(G-3637)*

Sundyne Corp .... F 303 249-5350
Charlotte *(G-3652)*

Trs-Sesco LLC .... D 336 996-2220
Kernersville *(G-9248)*

Vooner Flogard LLC .... G 980 225-3277
Charlotte *(G-3783)*

◆ Xaloy Extrusion LLC .... E 828 326-9888
Hickory *(G-8212)*

▲ Xylem Water Solutions USA Inc .... D 704 409-9700
Charlotte *(G-3840)*

3562 Ball and roller bearings

American Roller Bearing Inc .... C 828 624-1460
Hiddenite *(G-8213)*

American Roller Bearing Inc .... F 828 624-1460
Morganton *(G-11197)*

Atlantic Bearing Co Inc .... G 252 243-0233
Wilson *(G-16469)*

▲ Baldor Dodge Reliance .... F 828 652-0074
Marion *(G-10141)*

Coc USA Inc .... G 888 706-0059
Matthews *(G-10243)*

▲ Dersheng Usa Inc .... G 336 434-5055
High Point *(G-8320)*

Everything Industrial Supply .... G 743 333-2222
Winston Salem *(G-16702)*

Hpc NC .... G 704 978-0103
Statesville *(G-14817)*

Justice Bearing LLC .... G 800 355-2500
Mooresville *(G-10993)*

▲ Ketchie-Houston Inc .... E 704 786-5101
Concord *(G-4300)*

▲ Linamar Forgings Carolina Inc .... D 252 237-8181
Wilson *(G-16511)*

Lincolnton Bearing Plant .... G 704 794-5964
Iron Station *(G-8974)*

Lsrwm Corp .... G 704 866-8533
Gastonia *(G-6445)*

◆ Lsrwm Corp .... E 704 866-8533
Gastonia *(G-6446)*

Ltlb Holding Company .... D 704 585-2908
Hiddenite *(G-8223)*

▲ Ltlb Holding Company .... F 828 624-1460
Hickory *(G-8089)*

▲ Nn Inc .... G 980 264-4300
Charlotte *(G-3264)*

Pioneer Motor Bearing Company .... E 704 937-7000
Kings Mountain *(G-9325)*

▼ Problem Solver Inc .... F 919 596-5555
Raleigh *(G-13148)*

◆ Reich LLC .... C 828 651-9019
Arden *(G-371)*

Staunton Capital Inc .... E 704 866-8533
Greensboro *(G-7368)*

Timken Company .... C 704 736-2700
Iron Station *(G-8977)*

▲ Urethane Innovators Inc .... E 252 637-7110
New Bern *(G-11853)*

3563 Air and gas compressors

Air & Gas Solutions LLC .... E 704 897-2182
Charlotte *(G-2146)*

Atlas Copco Compressors LLC .... F 704 525-0124
Charlotte *(G-2236)*

Backyard Entps & Svcs LLC .... G 828 755-4960
Spindale *(G-14603)*

▲ Eagle Compressors Inc .... E 336 370-4159
Greensboro *(G-6985)*

Eagleair Inc .... G 336 398-8000
Greensboro *(G-6986)*

▲ Elgi Compressors USA Inc .... G 704 943-7966
Charlotte *(G-2695)*

Fresh Air Technologies LLC .... F 704 622-7877
Matthews *(G-10317)*

◆ G Denver and Co LLC .... E 704 896-4000
Davidson *(G-4675)*

Graves Inc .... E 252 792-1191
Williamston *(G-16061)*

Hayward Industries Inc .... A 336 712-9900
Clemmons *(G-4044)*

Hertz Kompressoren USA Inc .... G 704 579-5900
Charlotte *(G-2907)*

Ingersoll Rand Inc .... E 704 774-4290
Charlotte *(G-2973)*

INGERSOLL RAND INC .... A 704 896-4000
Davidson *(G-4679)*

Ingersoll-Rand Indus US Inc .... D 704 896-4000
Davidson *(G-4680)*

Metal Impact East LLC .... E 743 205-1900
Graham *(G-6703)*

Nordson Corporation .... G 724 656-5600
Hickory *(G-8103)*

▲ Pattons Medical LLC .... E 704 529-5442
Charlotte *(G-3319)*

35 INDUSTRIAL AND COMMERCIAL MACHINERY AND COMPUTER EQUIPMENT

Peco Inc .... E 828 684-1234
   Arden *(G-362)*

▲ Production Systems Inc .... E 336 886-7161
   High Point *(G-8499)*

Reddick Equipment Co NC LLC .... G 252 792-1191
   Williamston *(G-16068)*

Safe Air Systems Inc .... E 336 674-0749
   Randleman *(G-13489)*

▲ Schmalz Inc .... C 919 713-0880
   Raleigh *(G-13237)*

Sub-Aquatics Inc .... E 336 674-0749
   Randleman *(G-13492)*

Superior Finishing Systems LLC .... G 336 956-2000
   Lexington *(G-9788)*

Trane Technologies Company LLC .... B 336 751-3561
   Mocksville *(G-10608)*

Universal Air Products Corp .... G 704 374-0600
   Charlotte *(G-3755)*

3564 Blowers and fans

▲ Absolent Inc .... F 919 570-2862
   Raleigh *(G-12465)*

Acculabs Technologies Inc .... G 919 468-8780
   Morrisville *(G-11276)*

Air Control Inc .... E 252 492-2300
   Henderson *(G-7775)*

Air Craftsmen Inc .... F 336 248-5777
   Statesville *(G-14742)*

Air Purification Inc .... F 919 783-6161
   Raleigh *(G-12482)*

Air Systems Mfg of Lenoir Inc .... E 828 757-3500
   Lenoir *(G-9569)*

Airbox LLC .... G 855 927-1386
   Statesville *(G-14743)*

▲ Airflow Products Company Inc .... C 919 975-0240
   Selma *(G-14251)*

Associated Metal Works Inc .... E 704 546-7002
   Harmony *(G-7685)*

Bahnson Holdings Inc .... D 336 760-3111
   Clemmons *(G-4029)*

◆ Breezer Holdings LLC .... D 844 233-5673
   Charlotte *(G-2351)*

▲ Bruning and Federle Mfg Co .... E 704 873-7237
   Statesville *(G-14766)*

Bwxt Investment Company .... E 704 625-4900
   Charlotte *(G-2369)*

Camfil Usa Inc .... E 828 465-2880
   Conover *(G-4429)*

Camfil Usa Inc .... D 252 975-1141
   Washington *(G-15685)*

▲ Cleanaire Inc .... B 252 623-4010
   Washington *(G-15690)*

Commercial Flter Svc of Triad .... G 336 272-1443
   Greensboro *(G-6924)*

Cosatron .... F 704 785-8145
   Concord *(G-4244)*

D J Enviro Solutions .... G 828 495-7448
   Taylorsville *(G-15139)*

Dantherm Filtration Inc .... F 336 889-5599
   Thomasville *(G-15211)*

▲ Dustcontrol Inc .... F 910 395-1808
   Wilmington *(G-16207)*

Dynamic Air Engineering Inc .... E 714 540-1000
   Claremont *(G-3925)*

Eas Incorporated .... G 704 734-4945
   Kings Mountain *(G-9305)*

▲ Envirco Corporation .... E 919 775-2201
   Sanford *(G-14117)*

Environmental Specialties LLC .... D 919 829-9300
   Raleigh *(G-12742)*

Exquisite Air and Water .... G 919 524-4625
   Raleigh *(G-12757)*

Ffi Holdings III Corp .... E 800 690-3650
   Charlotte *(G-2755)*

▲ Field Controls LLC .... D 252 208-7300
   Kinston *(G-9366)*

Filtration Technology Inc .... G 336 509-9960
   Greensboro *(G-7013)*

▼ Filtration Technology Inc .... G 336 294-5655
   Greensboro *(G-7014)*

Firefly Balloons Inc .... G 704 878-9501
   Statesville *(G-14800)*

Flanders Corporation .... D 252 946-0744
   Washington *(G-15700)*

◆ Flanders Corporation .... F 252 946-8081
   Washington *(G-15699)*

◆ Flanders Filters Inc .... C 252 946-8081
   Washington *(G-15701)*

▲ Flanders/Csc LLC .... D 252 946-8081
   Washington *(G-15702)*

◆ G Denver and Co LLC .... E 704 896-4000
   Davidson *(G-4675)*

▲ Global Plasma Solutions Inc .... E 980 279-5622
   Charlotte *(G-2833)*

Greenheck Fan Co .... F 336 852-5788
   Greensboro *(G-7061)*

Greenheck Fan Corporation .... G 704 476-3700
   Shelby *(G-14321)*

Hughs Sheet Mtal Sttsvlle LLC .... F 704 872-4621
   Statesville *(G-14818)*

Hunter Fan Company .... G 704 896-9250
   Cornelius *(G-4558)*

Joe Armstrong .... G 336 207-6503
   Greensboro *(G-7138)*

Jorlink Usa Inc .... F 336 288-1613
   Greensboro *(G-7140)*

Kch Services Inc .... E 828 245-9836
   Forest City *(G-6073)*

Kirk & Blum Manufacturing Co .... E 801 728-6533
   Greensboro *(G-7152)*

Kitchen Vntilation Systems LLC .... G 704 476-3565
   Kings Mountain *(G-9315)*

▼ Meadows Mills Inc .... E 336 838-2282
   North Wilkesboro *(G-12027)*

◆ Mikropor America Inc .... F
   Charlotte *(G-3178)*

Mikropul LLC .... G 704 998-2600
   Charlotte *(G-3179)*

Miller Ctrl Mfg Inc Clinton NC .... G 910 592-5112
   Clinton *(G-4098)*

National Air Filters Inc .... F 919 231-8596
   Raleigh *(G-13053)*

◆ Nederman Inc .... D 336 821-0827
   Thomasville *(G-15255)*

▲ Nederman Corporation .... F 704 399-7441
   Charlotte *(G-3244)*

Nederman Mikropul LLC .... G 704 998-2600
   Charlotte *(G-3246)*

Novaerus US Inc .... G 813 304-2468
   Charlotte *(G-3273)*

P & G Manufacturing Wash Inc .... G 252 946-9110
   Washington *(G-15721)*

Pamlico Air Inc .... F 252 995-6267
   Washington *(G-15724)*

Patholdco Inc .... G 919 212-1300
   Morrisville *(G-11409)*

◆ Precisionaire Inc .... D 252 946-8081
   Washington *(G-15727)*

▲ Punker LLC .... F 828 322-1951
   Lincolnton *(G-9913)*

▲ Purolator Facet Inc .... E 336 668-4444
   Greensboro *(G-7293)*

▲ Ricura Corporation .... F 704 875-0366
   Huntersville *(G-8886)*

Rotron Incorporated .... C 336 449-3400
   Whitsett *(G-16001)*

Schletter NA Inc .... F 704 595-4200
   Charlotte *(G-3503)*

SCR-Tech LLC .... C 704 504-0191
   Charlotte *(G-3513)*

Select Air Systems Usa Inc .... E 704 289-1122
   Monroe *(G-10805)*

Staclean Diffuser Company LLC .... F 704 636-8697
   Salisbury *(G-14047)*

Sunco Powder Systems Inc .... E 704 545-3922
   Charlotte *(G-3651)*

◆ Trane Technologies Company LLC ... A 704 655-4000
   Davidson *(G-4702)*

◆ Trane US Inc .... A 704 655-4000
   Davidson *(G-4704)*

United Air Filter Company Corp .... E 704 334-5311
   Charlotte *(G-3750)*

Universal Air Products Corp .... G 704 374-0600
   Charlotte *(G-3755)*

WV Holdings Inc .... G 704 853-8338
   Gastonia *(G-6544)*

▲ Ziehl-Abegg Inc .... E 336 834-9339
   Greensboro *(G-7475)*

3565 Packaging machinery

A Hartness Inc .... G 704 351-2323
   Charlotte *(G-2115)*

Abco Automation Inc .... C 336 375-6400
   Browns Summit *(G-1298)*

◆ Alotech Inc .... E 919 774-1297
   Goldston *(G-6672)*

Automated Machine Technologies ..... G 919 361-0121
   Morrisville *(G-11297)*

Awcnc LLC .... E 252 633-5757
   New Bern *(G-11773)*

▲ Axon LLC .... E 919 772-8383
   Raleigh *(G-12538)*

Aylward Enterprises LLC .... E 252 639-9242
   New Bern *(G-11774)*

▲ Bamal Corporation .... F 980 225-7700
   Charlotte *(G-2273)*

Bunzl Processor Dist LLC .... G 910 738-8111
   Lumberton *(G-10028)*

Cates Mechanical Corporation .... G 704 458-5163
   Charlotte *(G-2419)*

Chase-Logeman Corporation .... F 336 665-0754
   Greensboro *(G-6905)*

▲ Chudy Group LLC .... D 262 279-5307
   Durham *(G-5018)*

Container Systems Incorporated .... D 919 496-6133
   Franklinton *(G-6153)*

Danby Barcoding LLC .... G 770 416-9845
   Kernersville *(G-9187)*

Direct Pack East LLC .... E 910 331-0071
   Rockingham *(G-13623)*

▲ Focke & Co Inc .... D 336 449-7200
   Whitsett *(G-15990)*

Gb Labs LLC .... G 919 606-7253
   Lexington *(G-9723)*

Groninger USA LLC .... E 704 588-3873
   Charlotte *(G-2871)*

Hycorr LLC .... G 216 570-7408
   Huntersville *(G-8832)*

▲ Keymac USA LLC .... F 704 877-5137
   Charlotte *(G-3052)*

Korber Medipak Systems NA Inc .... E 727 538-4644
   Cary *(G-1804)*

Korber Medipak Systems NA Inc .... E 727 538-4644
   Morrisville *(G-11367)*

Krw Packaging Machinery Inc .... F 828 658-0912
   Weaverville *(G-15850)*

Employee Codes: A=Over 500 employees, B=251-500
C=101-250, D=51-100, E=20-50, F=10-19, G=1-9

35 INDUSTRIAL AND COMMERCIAL MACHINERY AND COMPUTER EQUIPMENT SIC SECTION

Land of Sky Mobile Canning LLC............ G 303 880-1297
  Asheville *(G-679)*
▲ Ossid LLC.. D 252 446-6177
  Battleboro *(G-927)*
Petty Machine Company Inc................... E 704 864-3254
  Gastonia *(G-6488)*
◆ Roberts Polypro Inc............................. E 704 588-1794
  Charlotte *(G-3455)*
▲ Syntegon Technology Svcs LLC........... E 919 877-0886
  Raleigh *(G-13321)*
▲ U S Bottlers McHy Co Inc................... D 704 588-4750
  Charlotte *(G-3744)*
◆ Windak Inc... F 828 322-2292
  Conover *(G-4514)*

3566 Speed changers, drives, and gears

ABB Motors and Mechanical Inc............ C 828 645-1706
  Weaverville *(G-15836)*
▲ Abundant Manufacturing Inc............... E 704 871-9911
  Statesville *(G-14737)*
▲ Carolina Keller LLC............................ C 252 237-8181
  Wilson *(G-16484)*
Gefran Inc.. F 501 442-1521
  Charlotte *(G-2813)*
Hydreco Inc... F 704 295-7575
  Charlotte *(G-2941)*
It Is Sew.. G 252 531-7859
  Greenville *(G-7546)*
Joe and Kitty Brown Inc......................... E 704 629-4327
  Bessemer City *(G-1072)*
▲ Linamar Forgings Carolina Inc............ D 252 237-8181
  Wilson *(G-16511)*
Martin Sprocket & Gear Inc.................... F 817 258-3000
  Albemarle *(G-97)*
Martin Sprocket & Gear Inc.................... F 704 394-9111
  Charlotte *(G-3133)*
Nord Gear Corporation........................... G 888 314-6673
  Charlotte *(G-3266)*
Parker-Hannifin Corporation................... E 704 588-3246
  Charlotte *(G-3315)*
▲ Perfection Gear Inc............................ D 828 253-0000
  Asheville *(G-726)*
Regal Rexnord Corporation.................... F 800 825-6544
  Charlotte *(G-3426)*
▲ Shelby Kendrion Inc........................... C 704 482-9582
  Shelby *(G-14366)*
Siemens Industry Inc............................. C 919 365-2200
  Wendell *(G-15917)*

3567 Industrial furnaces and ovens

ABB Installation Products Inc................. E 828 322-1855
  Hickory *(G-7928)*
Billy Rice... G 828 691-4831
  Mars Hill *(G-10193)*
Buhler Inc.. C 800 722-7483
  Cary *(G-1716)*
Custom Electric Mfg LLC........................ E 248 305-7700
  Concord *(G-4249)*
Greenline... G 704 333-3477
  Charlotte *(G-2865)*
▲ Industrial Prcess Slutions Inc............. G 336 926-1511
  Wilkesboro *(G-16025)*
L F I Services Inc.................................. G 215 343-0411
  Sanford *(G-14145)*
▲ Lambda Technologies Inc.................. E 919 462-1919
  Morrisville *(G-11371)*
Nutec Inc... E 877 318-2430
  Huntersville *(G-8867)*
▲ Production Systems Inc..................... E 336 886-7161
  High Point *(G-8499)*
Radcon Inc.. G 919 806-5233
  Durham *(G-5318)*

Southeastern Installation Inc.................. E 704 352-7146
  Lexington *(G-9783)*
Superior Finishing Systems LLC............. G 336 956-2000
  Lexington *(G-9788)*
Thermcraft Holding Co LLC.................... D 336 784-4800
  Winston Salem *(G-16941)*
Tutco Inc... D 828 654-1665
  Arden *(G-387)*

3568 Power transmission equipment, nec

Altra Industrial Motion Corp................... G 704 588-5610
  Charlotte *(G-2174)*
Assa Abloy Inc....................................... F 704 776-8773
  Monroe *(G-10656)*
Boston Gear LLC................................... B 704 588-5610
  Charlotte *(G-2337)*
◆ Cavotec USA Inc................................ E 704 873-3009
  Mooresville *(G-10900)*
Component Technology Intl Inc.............. G 704 331-0888
  Charlotte *(G-2535)*
Eaton Corporation.................................. C 910 695-2900
  Pinehurst *(G-12221)*
▲ Emrise Corporation............................ C 408 200-3040
  Durham *(G-5084)*
◆ Fairchild Industrial Pdts Co................ D 336 659-3400
  Winston Salem *(G-16706)*
Flextrol Corporation................................ F 704 888-1120
  Locust *(G-9960)*
GKN Driveline North Amer Inc................ G 336 364-6200
  Timberlake *(G-15314)*
Haldex Inc... C 828 652-9308
  Marion *(G-10150)*
▲ Ketchie-Houston Inc.......................... E 704 786-5101
  Concord *(G-4300)*
Keystone Powdered Metal Co................. E 704 435-4036
  Cherryville *(G-3870)*
Martin Sprocket & Gear Inc.................... F 817 258-3000
  Albemarle *(G-97)*
Meritor Inc... D 910 844-9401
  Maxton *(G-10360)*
◆ Oiles America Corporation.................. F 704 784-4500
  Concord *(G-4324)*
Tb Woods Incorporated.......................... D 704 588-5610
  Charlotte *(G-3675)*

3569 General industrial machinery,

Abco Automation Inc............................. C 336 375-6400
  Browns Summit *(G-1298)*
Accurate Fabrications Inc...................... G 910 383-2140
  Leland *(G-9524)*
Aerospace Filtration Division.................. G 336 668-4444
  Greensboro *(G-6784)*
◆ Balcrank Corporation.......................... E 800 747-5300
  Weaverville *(G-15838)*
▼ Beacon Industrial Mfg LLC.................. A 704 399-7441
  Charlotte *(G-2290)*
Beco Holding Company Inc.................... C 800 826-3473
  Charlotte *(G-2295)*
◆ Bijur Delimon Intl Inc......................... E 919 465-4448
  Morrisville *(G-11302)*
◆ Buckeye Fire Equipment Company...... E 704 739-7415
  Kings Mountain *(G-9296)*
Carolina Fire Protection Inc.................... E 910 892-1700
  Dunn *(G-4854)*
Catamount Energy Corporation............... F 802 773-6684
  Charlotte *(G-2418)*
Cemco Electric Inc................................. F 704 504-0294
  Charlotte *(G-2441)*
City of Morganton.................................. F 828 584-1460
  Morganton *(G-11205)*
Ddp Spclty Elctrnic Mtls US 9................ D 336 547-7112
  Greensboro *(G-6962)*

Dellinger Enterprises Ltd....................... E 704 825-9687
  Belmont *(G-982)*
Descher LLC.. G 919 828-7708
  Raleigh *(G-12677)*
Deurotech America Inc.......................... F 980 272-6827
  Charlotte *(G-2623)*
Drum Filter Media Inc............................ G 336 434-4195
  High Point *(G-8332)*
◆ Duff-Norton Company Inc................... G 704 588-0510
  Charlotte *(G-2656)*
Elxsi Corporation.................................... B 407 849-1090
  Charlotte *(G-2701)*
Erdle Perforating Holdings Inc................ F 704 588-4380
  Charlotte *(G-2726)*
F-N-D Machinery Services Inc................ G 336 906-2817
  Denton *(G-4735)*
Fagus Grecon Inc................................... F 503 641-7731
  Charlotte *(G-2744)*
Fanuc America Corporation.................... G 704 596-5121
  Huntersville *(G-8818)*
Farval Lubrication Systems.................... E 252 527-6001
  Kinston *(G-9364)*
▲ Farval Lubrication Systems................ E 252 527-6001
  Kinston *(G-9365)*
Ffi Holdings III Corp.............................. E 800 690-3650
  Charlotte *(G-2755)*
▼ Fireresq Incorporated......................... F 888 975-0858
  Mooresville *(G-10945)*
Flameoff Coatings Inc............................ G 888 816-7468
  Raleigh *(G-12772)*
Flanders Corporation............................. G 919 934-3020
  Smithfield *(G-14460)*
Flanders Filters Inc............................... G 252 217-3978
  Smithfield *(G-14461)*
Flash Technology LLC............................ F 980 474-3700
  Charlotte *(G-2770)*
Foss Industrial Recycling LLC................ F 336 342-4812
  La Grange *(G-9441)*
Fuji America Inc..................................... G 704 527-3854
  Charlotte *(G-2800)*
Genesis Water Technologies Inc............. E 704 360-5165
  Charlotte *(G-2821)*
Gibson Accumulator LLC....................... F 336 449-4753
  Burlington *(G-1422)*
Global Filter Source LLC....................... G 919 571-4945
  Raleigh *(G-12804)*
GNB Ventures LLC................................ F 704 488-4468
  Charlotte *(G-2837)*
Gregory Poole Equipment Co.................. F 919 872-2691
  Raleigh *(G-12818)*
Hayward Industries Inc.......................... C 336 712-9900
  Clemmons *(G-4043)*
◆ Hayward Industries Inc...................... B 908 351-5400
  Charlotte *(G-2894)*
Hitork USA LLC..................................... G 803 446-7513
  Waxhaw *(G-15760)*
Hummingbird 3d Solutions LLC.............. G 336 792-6637
  Burlington *(G-1432)*
◆ Hurst Jaws of Life Inc........................ C 704 487-6961
  Shelby *(G-14328)*
Industrial Automation Company.............. F 877 727-8757
  Raleigh *(G-12884)*
▲ Industrial Piping Inc.......................... A 704 588-1100
  Charlotte *(G-2964)*
Ingersoll-Rand US Holdco Inc................. G 704 655-4000
  Davidson *(G-4682)*
Ipi Acquisition LLC................................ A 704 588-1100
  Charlotte *(G-2996)*
Irsi Automation Inc................................ G 336 303-5320
  Mc Leansville *(G-10393)*
Ism Inc.. E
  Arden *(G-342)*

SIC SECTION

35 INDUSTRIAL AND COMMERCIAL MACHINERY AND COMPUTER EQUIPMENT

Jack Pagan & Assoc Inc .... G 919 872-0159
  Raleigh *(G-12910)*

John W Foster Sales Inc .... G 704 821-3822
  Matthews *(G-10326)*

Keller Technology Corporation .... E 704 875-1605
  Huntersville *(G-8844)*

Kenmar Inc .... F 336 884-8722
  High Point *(G-8423)*

Lightning X Products Inc .... G 704 295-0299
  Charlotte *(G-3088)*

Linter North America Corp .... G 828 645-4261
  Asheville *(G-687)*

▼ Liquid Process Systems Inc .... G 704 821-1115
  Indian Trail *(G-8945)*

▲ Ltd Industries LLC .... E 704 897-2182
  Charlotte *(G-3105)*

Main Filter LLC .... E 704 735-0009
  Lincolnton *(G-9904)*

◆ Mann+hmmel Fltrtion Tech US LL ... C 704 869-3300
  Gastonia *(G-6452)*

Mann+hummel Filtration Technol .... G 704 869-3952
  Gastonia *(G-6455)*

Mann+hummel Filtration Technol .... D 704 869-3501
  Gastonia *(G-6456)*

Metro Fire Lifesafety LLC .... G 704 529-7348
  Gastonia *(G-6462)*

Mosley .... G 910 409-5814
  Wilmington *(G-16327)*

NAPA Filters .... G 704 864-6748
  Gastonia *(G-6474)*

◆ National Foam Inc .... E 919 639-6100
  Angier *(G-147)*

Ora Inc .... G 540 903-7177
  Marion *(G-10170)*

Peformance Chassis .... G 919 319-3484
  Cary *(G-1847)*

Pentair Water Pool and Spa Inc .... F 919 463-4640
  Cary *(G-1848)*

◆ Pentair Water Pool and Spa Inc ..... A 919 566-8000
  Sanford *(G-14166)*

Petroliance LLC .... C 336 472-3000
  Thomasville *(G-15263)*

Phoenix Assembly NC LLC .... G 252 801-4250
  Battleboro *(G-929)*

Pneumax Automation LLC .... G 704 215-6991
  Dallas *(G-4651)*

Ralph B Hall .... G 919 258-3634
  Sanford *(G-14173)*

Reclaim Filters and Systems .... G 919 528-1787
  Wake Forest *(G-15582)*

Recoupl Inc .... G 704 544-0202
  Charlotte *(G-3420)*

Rotating Machinery Analys .... G 512 743-1248
  Brevard *(G-1288)*

Rubber Mill Inc .... G 336 622-1680
  Conover *(G-4494)*

▲ Rubber Mill Inc .... E 336 622-1680
  Liberty *(G-9830)*

◆ Russell Finex Inc .... F 704 588-9808
  Pineville *(G-12299)*

Scott Technologies Inc .... B 704 291-8300
  Monroe *(G-10803)*

◆ Scott Technologies Inc .... E 704 291-8300
  Monroe *(G-10802)*

Sloop Pt Vlntr Fire Dept Inc .... G 910 270-3267
  Hampstead *(G-7655)*

Solara Solutions LLC .... F 919 534-1500
  Morrisville *(G-11431)*

▼ South-Tek Systems LLC .... D 910 332-4173
  Wilmington *(G-16409)*

Southern Machine Services .... G 919 658-9300
  Mount Olive *(G-11668)*

Southern Products Company Inc .... E 910 281-3189
  Hoffman *(G-8676)*

Superior Finishing Systems LLC .... G 336 956-2000
  Lexington *(G-9788)*

Supreme Sweepers LLC .... G 888 698-9996
  Charlotte *(G-3657)*

Surelift Inc .... G 828 963-6899
  Boone *(G-1241)*

Textile Parts and Mch Co Inc .... F 704 865-5003
  Gastonia *(G-6524)*

US Filter .... G 828 274-8282
  Asheville *(G-812)*

West Dynamics Us Inc .... E 704 735-0009
  Lincolnton *(G-9936)*

3571 Electronic computers

Albert E Mann .... G 919 497-0815
  Louisburg *(G-9979)*

Apple Branch Company .... G 910 859-8549
  Wilmington *(G-16112)*

Apple Inc .... F 516 318-6744
  Cary *(G-1685)*

Apple Valley Cabin LLC .... G 828 513-1911
  Hendersonville *(G-7820)*

Artibis Corporation .... G 919 592-4794
  Cary *(G-1689)*

Barcovvsion LLC .... F 704 392-9371
  Charlotte *(G-2279)*

Clean-Sweep Solutions Inc .... G 469 450-8317
  Raleigh *(G-12627)*

Digital Audio Corporation .... F 919 572-6767
  Hendersonville *(G-7844)*

Dimill Enterprises LLC .... G 919 629-2011
  Raleigh *(G-12684)*

Dramen of Raleigh LLC .... G 919 828-5464
  Raleigh *(G-12699)*

Fred L Brown .... G 336 643-7523
  Summerfield *(G-14983)*

General Dynmics Mssion Systems ...... F 910 497-7900
  Fort Bragg *(G-6089)*

Green Apple Studio .... G 919 377-2239
  Cary *(G-1778)*

HP Inc .... G 704 523-3548
  Charlotte *(G-2927)*

Hypernova Inc .... G 704 360-0096
  Charlotte *(G-2944)*

I2e Group LLC .... G 336 884-2014
  High Point *(G-8404)*

International Bus Mchs Corp .... B 919 543-6919
  Durham *(G-5161)*

Itron Inc .... D 919 876-2600
  Raleigh *(G-12905)*

K12 Computers .... G 336 754-6111
  Lexington *(G-9738)*

Karwin Technologies Inc .... G 919 612-3974
  Clayton *(G-3991)*

Lenovo (united States) Inc .... G 919 486-9627
  Morrisville *(G-11374)*

Lenovo (united States) Inc .... D 919 237-8389
  Morrisville *(G-11375)*

▲ Lenovo (united States) Inc .... A 855 253-6686
  Morrisville *(G-11376)*

Lenovo Holding Company Inc .... F 855 253-6686
  Morrisville *(G-11377)*

▲ Lenovo US Fulfillment Ctr LLC .... C 855 253-6686
  Morrisville *(G-11378)*

Litton Systems Inc .... G 704 588-2340
  Charlotte *(G-3094)*

Mason International .... G 704 921-3407
  Charlotte *(G-3137)*

McKelvey Fulks .... G 704 357-1550
  Charlotte *(G-3152)*

Monolith Corporation .... E 919 878-1900
  Wake Forest *(G-15572)*

Novant Health Appel .... G 704 316-5025
  Charlotte *(G-3274)*

Omnicell .... G 910 538-2141
  Hampstead *(G-7652)*

Original Image .... G 919 781-0064
  Raleigh *(G-13091)*

▲ Pro-Face America LLC .... E 734 477-0600
  Greensboro *(G-7286)*

Q-Edge Corporation .... G 919 935-8167
  Durham *(G-5310)*

Salem Technologies Inc .... F 336 777-3652
  Winston Salem *(G-16895)*

Selex Es LLC .... D 336 379-7135
  Greensboro *(G-7331)*

Serra Wireless Inc .... G 980 318-0873
  Charlotte *(G-3529)*

Shiftwizard Inc .... F 866 828-3318
  Morrisville *(G-11427)*

Steve Brooks .... G 919 248-1458
  Raleigh *(G-13303)*

▲ Teguar Corporation .... E 704 960-1761
  Charlotte *(G-3678)*

Teradata Corporation .... F 919 816-1900
  Raleigh *(G-13339)*

Usat LLC .... E 919 942-4214
  Chapel Hill *(G-2091)*

Utd Technology Corp .... G 704 612-0121
  Mint Hill *(G-10546)*

◆ Walker and Associates Inc .... C 336 731-6391
  Lexington *(G-9800)*

Zelaya Bros LLC .... G 980 833-0099
  Charlotte *(G-3850)*

3572 Computer storage devices

Boy Scout Troop .... G 704 643-8955
  Charlotte *(G-2343)*

Carolina Data Recovery LLC .... G 704 536-1717
  Charlotte *(G-2394)*

Christopher Ridley .... G 919 291-9999
  Raleigh *(G-12621)*

Consolidated EMC Inc .... G 980 245-2859
  Matthews *(G-10310)*

Digiton Corp .... G 919 601-4826
  Apex *(G-182)*

EMC Contractor LLC .... G 910 576-7101
  Troy *(G-15405)*

EMC Corporation .... G 720 341-3274
  Charlotte *(G-2705)*

EMC Corporation .... F 919 767-0641
  Durham *(G-5082)*

EMC Corporation .... F 919 851-3241
  Raleigh *(G-12735)*

Emergent Tech Solutions Inc .... G 704 777-1909
  Charlotte *(G-2707)*

Halifax EMC .... F 252 445-5111
  Enfield *(G-5678)*

Ict/Data On Cd Inc .... G 704 841-8404
  Charlotte *(G-2947)*

Inmylife Inc .... G 336 644-8856
  Greensboro *(G-7115)*

Jean Dupree .... G 919 821-4020
  Salisbury *(G-13990)*

Memoryc Inc .... G 980 224-2875
  Charlotte *(G-3164)*

Netapp Inc .... E 919 476-4571
  Durham *(G-5242)*

Quantum Insulation Inc .... G 252 752-7828
  Greenville *(G-7578)*

Quantum Newswire .... G 919 439-8800
  Raleigh *(G-13166)*

Employee Codes: A=Over 500 employees, B=251-500
C=101-250, D=51-100, E=20-50, F=10-19, G=1-9

35 INDUSTRIAL AND COMMERCIAL MACHINERY AND COMPUTER EQUIPMENT

Quantum Solutions............................F.....828 615-7500
  Hickory *(G-8130)*
Quantum Usa LLP..............................G.....919 704-8266
  Chapel Hill *(G-2059)*
Queen City Event Mgmt Cnsltng...........G.....704 780-7811
  Charlotte *(G-3404)*
Raleigh Ventures Inc..........................G.....910 350-0036
  Wilmington *(G-16377)*
Seagate Technology LLC....................F.....910 821-8310
  Wilmington *(G-16396)*
Verbatim Americas LLC......................G.....704 547-6551
  Charlotte *(G-3769)*
▲ Verbatim Americas LLC..................D.....704 547-6500
  Charlotte *(G-3770)*
◆ Verbatim Corporation.....................D.....704 547-6500
  Charlotte *(G-3771)*
◆ Walker and Associates Inc..............C.....336 731-6391
  Lexington *(G-9800)*

3575 Computer terminals

Apple Inc..F.....516 318-6744
  Cary *(G-1685)*
NCR Voyix Corporation.......................G.....937 445-5000
  Cary *(G-1830)*
Phynix Pc Inc....................................F.....503 890-1444
  Middlesex *(G-10454)*
▲ Pro-Face America LLC..................E.....734 477-0600
  Greensboro *(G-7286)*

3577 Computer peripheral equipment, nec

Adama US..G.....919 817-7103
  Durham *(G-4903)*
Altera Corporation...............................G.....919 852-1004
  Raleigh *(G-12494)*
Alterra Labs LLC................................G.....704 770-7695
  Morrisville *(G-11285)*
Amt Datasouth Corp............................E.....704 523-8500
  Charlotte *(G-2192)*
Apple Inc..F.....516 318-6744
  Cary *(G-1685)*
Avail Forensics LLC...........................F.....877 888-5895
  Wilmington *(G-16125)*
Axon Systems LLC.............................G.....910 796-7872
  Wilmington *(G-16128)*
Black Box Corporation........................G.....704 248-6430
  Pineville *(G-12255)*
Branch Office Solutions Inc................G.....800 743-1047
  Indian Trail *(G-8924)*
Brilliant Sole Inc.................................G.....339 222-8528
  Wilmington *(G-16143)*
▲ Cable Devices Incorporated...........C.....714 554-4370
  Hickory *(G-7960)*
◆ Carlisle Corporation......................G.....704 501-1100
  Charlotte *(G-2390)*
Cisco Systems Inc.............................G.....910 707-1052
  Carolina Beach *(G-1635)*
Cisco Systems Inc.............................G.....704 338-7350
  Charlotte *(G-2482)*
Cisco Systems Inc.............................F.....919 392-2000
  Morrisville *(G-11323)*
Cisco Systems Inc.............................A.....919 392-2000
  Morrisville *(G-11324)*
Coastal Office Eqp & Computers..........G.....252 335-9427
  Elizabeth City *(G-5534)*
Commscope Technologies LLC...........F.....919 934-9711
  Smithfield *(G-14457)*
Covington Barcoding Inc.....................G.....336 996-5759
  Kernersville *(G-9183)*
Ensinger Polytech Inc.........................G.....704 992-8100
  Huntersville *(G-8815)*
Faith Computer Repairs......................G.....910 730-1731
  Lumberton *(G-10036)*

Garrettcom Inc..................................D.....510 438-9071
  Mooresville *(G-10954)*
Hermes Medical Solutions Inc............G.....252 355-4373
  Greenville *(G-7539)*
International Bus Mchs Corp...............B.....919 543-6919
  Durham *(G-5161)*
JPS Communications Inc...................D.....919 534-1168
  Raleigh *(G-12923)*
Lea Aid Acquisition Company.............F.....919 872-6210
  Raleigh *(G-12963)*
Lynn Electronics Corporation..............G.....704 369-0093
  Concord *(G-4308)*
Monolith Corporation..........................E.....919 878-1900
  Wake Forest *(G-15572)*
NCR Voyix Corporation.......................G.....937 445-5000
  Cary *(G-1830)*
Oracle Corporation.............................D.....919 205-6000
  Morrisville *(G-11403)*
Pendulum Inc....................................G.....704 491-6320
  Charlotte *(G-3327)*
Primesource Corporation....................E.....336 661-3300
  Winston Salem *(G-16867)*
▲ Pro-Face America LLC..................E.....734 477-0600
  Greensboro *(G-7286)*
Revware Inc.......................................G.....919 790-0000
  Raleigh *(G-13205)*
Riverbed Technology LLC...................E.....415 247-8800
  Durham *(G-5333)*
Rsa Security LLC...............................E.....704 847-4725
  Matthews *(G-10287)*
Sato Global Solutions Inc...................F.....954 261-3279
  Charlotte *(G-3494)*
Savoye Solutions Inc.........................G.....919 466-9784
  Raleigh *(G-13232)*
Sighttech LLC....................................G.....855 997-4448
  Charlotte *(G-3549)*
Southern Data Systems Inc................F.....919 781-7603
  Oxford *(G-12156)*
St Investors Inc.................................D.....704 969-7500
  Charlotte *(G-3618)*
Strategic 3d Solutions Inc..................F.....919 451-5963
  Raleigh *(G-13307)*
Technology Partners LLC...................D.....704 553-1004
  Charlotte *(G-3677)*
▲ Terarecon Inc...............................D.....650 372-1100
  Durham *(G-5395)*
Thomco Inc.......................................G.....336 292-3300
  Greensboro *(G-7401)*
Toshiba Globl Cmmrce Sltons In.........E.....984 444-2767
  Durham *(G-5404)*
Vocollect Inc.....................................E.....980 279-4119
  Charlotte *(G-3781)*
Xerox Corporation..............................E.....919 428-9718
  Cary *(G-1932)*
Xeroxdata Center...............................G.....704 329-7245
  Charlotte *(G-3835)*
Zebra Technologies Corporation..........G.....704 517-5271
  Charlotte *(G-3849)*

3578 Calculating and accounting equipment

Add-On Technologies Inc....................F.....704 882-2227
  Indian Trail *(G-8918)*
Advanced Point SL Systems Inc.........G.....877 381-6100
  Charlotte *(G-2138)*
Atlantic Bankcard Center Inc..............G.....336 855-9250
  Greensboro *(G-6821)*
Buvic LLC..G.....910 302-7950
  Fayetteville *(G-5776)*
Cisco Systems Inc.............................F.....919 392-2000
  Morrisville *(G-11323)*
Diebold Nixdorf Incorporated...............F.....704 599-3100
  Charlotte *(G-2632)*

Express Yourself................................G.....919 526-0611
  Raleigh *(G-12755)*
Extron Electronics..............................G.....919 850-1000
  Raleigh *(G-12758)*
◆ Gilbarco Inc..................................A.....336 547-5000
  Greensboro *(G-7043)*
Maxpro Manufacturing LLC.................F.....910 640-5505
  Whiteville *(G-15970)*
Meridian Point of Sale Inc..................G.....336 315-9800
  Greensboro *(G-7200)*
NCR Voyix Corporation.......................G.....937 445-5000
  Cary *(G-1830)*
Noregon Systems Inc.........................G.....336 615-8555
  Greensboro *(G-7223)*
One Source SEC & Sound Inc............G.....281 850-9487
  Mooresville *(G-11044)*

3579 Office machines, nec

◆ Atrc Inc..D.....919 872-5800
  Raleigh *(G-12531)*
▲ Bell and Howell LLC.....................A.....919 767-4401
  Durham *(G-4953)*
Bell and Howell LLC..........................E.....919 767-6400
  Durham *(G-4954)*
Carolina Time Equipment Co Inc.........E.....704 536-2700
  Charlotte *(G-2409)*
Pitney Bowes Inc...............................F.....336 805-3320
  Greensboro *(G-7266)*
Pitney Bowes Inc...............................G.....919 785-3480
  Raleigh *(G-13112)*
Postal Liquidation Inc........................C
  Durham *(G-5298)*

3581 Automatic vending machines

Country Corner...................................G.....919 444-9663
  Pittsboro *(G-12337)*
Jb-Isecurity LLC................................G.....910 824-7601
  Fayetteville *(G-5847)*
Microtronic Us LLC............................F.....336 869-0429
  High Point *(G-8456)*

3582 Commercial laundry equipment

3dductcleaning LLC...........................G.....919 723-4512
  Selma *(G-14250)*
Hockmeyer Equipment Corp................D.....252 338-4705
  Elizabeth City *(G-5548)*
Laundry Svc Tech Ltd Lblty Co...........G.....908 327-1997
  Matthews *(G-10262)*
▼ Leonard Automatics Inc...............E.....704 483-9316
  Denver *(G-4788)*
Perfection Fabrics Inc........................G.....828 328-3322
  Hickory *(G-8112)*
◆ Talley Machinery Corporation........G.....336 664-0012
  Greensboro *(G-7388)*
Two Fifty Cleaners.............................F.....910 397-0071
  Wilmington *(G-16436)*

3585 Refrigeration and heating equipment

▲ Afe Victory Inc.............................C.....856 428-4200
  Winston Salem *(G-16593)*
Air System Components Inc...............G.....919 279-8868
  Sanford *(G-14083)*
Air System Components Inc...............D.....919 775-2201
  Sanford *(G-14084)*
Air System Components Inc...............D.....252 641-5900
  Tarboro *(G-15093)*
Air System Components Inc...............D.....252 641-0875
  Tarboro *(G-15094)*
Airboss Heating and Coolg Inc............G.....252 586-0500
  Littleton *(G-9950)*
▲ American Coil Inc.........................F.....310 515-1215
  Bostic *(G-1259)*

35 INDUSTRIAL AND COMMERCIAL MACHINERY AND COMPUTER EQUIPMENT

American Moistening Co Inc .... F 704 889-7281
  Pineville (G-12252)
▼ Aqua Logic Inc .... E 858 292-4773
  Monroe (G-10649)
◆ Arneg LLC .... D 336 956-5300
  Lexington (G-9680)
Bahnson Holdings Inc .... D 336 760-3111
  Clemmons (G-4029)
◆ Bally Refrigerated Boxes Inc .... C 252 240-2829
  Morehead City (G-11151)
◆ Beverage-Air Corporation .... E 336 245-6400
  Winston Salem (G-16628)
Boles Holding Inc .... G 828 264-4200
  Boone (G-1178)
Buhler Inc .... C 800 722-7483
  Cary (G-1716)
Carolina Products Inc .... E 704 364-9029
  Charlotte (G-2403)
Carrier Carolinas .... G 336 292-0909
  Greensboro (G-6892)
Carrier Corporation .... C 704 921-3800
  Charlotte (G-2415)
Carrier Corporation .... G 704 494-2600
  Morrisville (G-11312)
Cbg Draft Services Lc LLC .... G 704 727-3300
  Charlotte (G-2423)
Charlies Heating & Cooling LLC .... G 336 260-1973
  Snow Camp (G-14495)
Chichibone Inc .... F 919 785-0090
  Kernersville (G-9177)
City Compressor Rebuilders .... G 704 947-1811
  Charlotte (G-2485)
City Compressor Rebuilders .... E 704 947-1811
  Charlotte (G-2484)
Culligan Water Conditioning .... G 252 646-3800
  Morehead City (G-11166)
Daikin Applied Americas Inc .... G 704 588-0087
  Charlotte (G-2598)
▲ Dienes Apparatus Inc .... G 704 525-3770
  Pineville (G-12265)
Dynamic Air Engineering Inc .... E 714 540-1000
  Claremont (G-3925)
Eneco East Inc .... G 828 322-6008
  Hickory (G-8017)
Firstsource Distributors LLC .... G 704 553-8510
  Charlotte (G-2767)
Go Green Services LLC .... D 336 252-2999
  Greensboro (G-7048)
Heat Transfer Sales LLC .... F 336 292-8777
  Greensboro (G-7084)
J&R Precision Heating and Air .... G 910 480-8322
  Fayetteville (G-5844)
James M Pleasants Company Inc .... E 336 275-3152
  Greensboro (G-7133)
Jenkins Services Group LLC .... G 704 881-3210
  Catawba (G-1965)
Kenny Fowler Heating and A Inc .... G 910 508-4553
  Wilmington (G-16288)
Lennox International Inc .... E 828 633-4805
  Candler (G-1586)
Lennox Stores (partsplus) .... G 910 660-7070
  Wilmington (G-16298)
Lenox Birkdale LLC .... G 704 997-8116
  Huntersville (G-8850)
Lenox Land .... G 704 507-4877
  Huntersville (G-8851)
◆ Liqui-Box Corporation .... D 804 325-1400
  Charlotte (G-3092)
Man Around House .... G 919 625-5933
  Durham (G-5204)
◆ Middleby Marshall Inc .... C 919 762-1000
  Fuquay Varina (G-6216)

◆ Morris & Associates Inc .... D 919 582-9200
  Garner (G-6292)
NC Filtration of Florida LLC .... D 704 822-4444
  Belmont (G-996)
Nissens Cooling Solutions Inc .... F 704 696-8575
  Mooresville (G-11037)
▲ NSi Holdings Inc .... F 914 664-3542
  Huntersville (G-8864)
▼ Parameter Generation Ctrl Inc .... E 828 669-8717
  Black Mountain (G-1133)
Ppa Industries Inc .... E 828 328-1142
  Hickory (G-8118)
Pro Refrigeration Inc .... E 336 283-7281
  Mocksville (G-10599)
Rheem Manufacturing Company .... C 336 495-6800
  Randleman (G-13488)
Rifled Air Conditioning Inc .... E 800 627-1707
  High Point (G-8511)
Roctool Inc .... G 888 364-6321
  Sanford (G-14174)
Snap Rite Manufacturing Inc .... E 910 897-4080
  Coats (G-4134)
◆ Southeast Air Control Inc .... E 704 392-0149
  Charlotte (G-3587)
Supreme Murphy Trck Bodies Inc .... C 252 291-2191
  Wilson (G-16544)
Thermo King Corporation .... C 732 652-6774
  Davidson (G-4700)
Thermo Products LLC .... E 800 348-5130
  Denton (G-4752)
Tier 1 Heating and Air LLC .... F 910 556-1444
  Vass (G-15494)
▲ Trane Company .... E 704 398-4600
  Charlotte (G-3713)
Trane Export LLC .... E 608 788-0569
  Davidson (G-4701)
◆ Trane Technologies Company LLC .... A 704 655-4000
  Davidson (G-4702)
Trane Technologies Mfg LLC .... F 704 655-4000
  Davidson (G-4703)
Trane US Inc .... G 828 277-8664
  Asheville (G-805)
Trane US Inc .... D 704 525-9600
  Charlotte (G-3714)
Trane US Inc .... F 704 697-9006
  Charlotte (G-3715)
Trane US Inc .... G 336 273-6353
  Greensboro (G-7406)
Trane US Inc .... F 336 378-0670
  Greensboro (G-7407)
Trane US Inc .... G 336 387-1735
  Greensboro (G-7408)
Trane US Inc .... G 919 781-0458
  Morrisville (G-11449)
◆ Trane US Inc .... A 704 655-4000
  Davidson (G-4704)
Transarctic North Carolina Inc .... E 336 861-6116
  High Point (G-8574)
Trs-Sesco LLC .... D 336 996-2220
  Kernersville (G-9248)
United Air Filter Company Corp .... E 704 334-5311
  Charlotte (G-3750)
W A Brown & Son Incorporated .... E 704 636-5131
  Salisbury (G-14063)
Wen Bray Heating & AC .... G 828 267-0635
  Hickory (G-8209)
Work Well Hydrtion Systems LLC .... G 704 853-7788
  Gastonia (G-6543)
Xp Climate Control LLC .... G 828 266-2006
  Boone (G-1251)

3586 Measuring and dispensing pumps

Aptargroup Inc .... C 828 970-6300
  Lincolnton (G-9873)
◆ Balcrank Corporation .... E 800 747-5300
  Weaverville (G-15838)
Circor Precision Metering LLC .... A 919 774-7667
  Sanford (G-14102)
Gasboy International Inc .... G 336 547-5000
  Greensboro (G-7030)
◆ Gilbarco Inc .... A 336 547-5000
  Greensboro (G-7043)
▲ Marley Company LLC .... C 704 752-4400
  Charlotte (G-3128)
Nelson Holdings Nc Inc .... F 828 322-9226
  Hickory (G-8100)
Samoa Corporation .... E 828 645-2290
  Weaverville (G-15861)

3589 Service industry machinery, nec

A3-Usa Inc .... G 724 871-7170
  Chinquapin (G-3891)
Abernethy Welding & Repair Inc .... G 828 324-7361
  Vale (G-15462)
Adr Hydro-Cut Inc .... G 919 388-2251
  Morrisville (G-11279)
Ali Group North America Corp .... E 800 648-4389
  High Point (G-8240)
Ali Group North America Corp .... D 336 661-1556
  Winston Salem (G-16596)
Allens Environmental Cnstr LLC .... G 407 774-7100
  Brevard (G-1269)
Alpha-Advantage Inc .... G 252 441-3766
  Kitty Hawk (G-9399)
Amano Pioneer Eclipse Corp .... E 704 900-1352
  Charlotte (G-2177)
◆ Amano Pioneer Eclipse Corp .... D 336 372-8080
  Sparta (G-14588)
Amerochem Corporation .... E 252 634-9344
  New Bern (G-11770)
◆ Amiad Filtration Systems Ltd .... E 805 377-0288
  Mooresville (G-10859)
▲ Amiad USA Inc .... F 704 662-3133
  Mooresville (G-10860)
Anderson Living Center LLC .... G 828 229-3243
  Forest City (G-6059)
Aquapro Solutions LLC .... G 828 255-0772
  Asheville (G-527)
Aquatic Pressure Washing .... G 910 232-3273
  Raleigh (G-12516)
Aqwa Inc .... G 252 243-7693
  Wilson (G-16467)
B&C Xterior Cleaning Svc Inc .... G 919 779-7905
  Raleigh (G-12540)
Bk Seamless Gutters LLC .... G 252 955-5414
  Spring Hope (G-14615)
Butler Trieu Inc .... G 910 346-4929
  Jacksonville (G-8992)
Caldwells Water Conditioning .... G 828 253-6605
  Asheville (G-578)
Carolina Water Consultants LLC .... G 828 251-2420
  Fletcher (G-5992)
▲ Cary Manufacturing Corporation ...... G 704 527-4402
  Charlotte (G-2416)
Centaur Laboratories Inc .... F 919 249-5072
  Oxford (G-12119)
▲ Champion Industries Inc .... D 336 661-1556
  Winston Salem (G-16650)
City of Greensboro .... E 336 373-5855
  Greensboro (G-6911)
Columbus Industries LLC .... E 910 872-1625
  Bladenboro (G-1146)
County of Anson .... G 704 848-4849
  Lilesville (G-9836)

35 INDUSTRIAL AND COMMERCIAL MACHINERY AND COMPUTER EQUIPMENT

County of Dare .... C 252 475-5990
   Kill Devil Hills *(G-9255)*
Desco Equipment Company Inc .... G 704 873-2844
   Statesville *(G-14787)*
Drch Inc .... G 919 383-9421
   Durham *(G-5063)*
▲ Dustcontrol Inc .... F 910 395-1808
   Wilmington *(G-16207)*
Eizi Group Llc .... G 919 397-3638
   Raleigh *(G-12729)*
◆ Entex Technologies Inc .... F 919 933-1380
   Chapel Hill *(G-2016)*
Envirnmntal Prcess Systems Inc .... G 704 827-0740
   Mount Holly *(G-11632)*
Epsiusa .... G 704 827-0740
   Mount Holly *(G-11633)*
Ew2 Environmental Inc .... G 704 542-2444
   Charlotte *(G-2736)*
▲ Ferguson Companies .... G
   Linwood *(G-9945)*
Ferguson Waterworks .... G 704 540-7225
   Pineville *(G-12268)*
Galaxy Pressure Washing Inc .... G 888 299-3129
   Pineville *(G-12270)*
Gold Medal Products Co .... G 336 665-4997
   Greensboro *(G-7051)*
◆ Great Products Inc .... G 910 944-2020
   Aberdeen *(G-5)*
Green Waste Management LLC .... G 704 289-0720
   Charlotte *(G-2864)*
Greenstory Globl Gvrnment Mlta .... F 828 446-9278
   Terrell *(G-15179)*
Hayward Industries Inc .... C 336 712-9900
   Clemmons *(G-4043)*
Hayward Industries Inc .... A 336 712-9900
   Clemmons *(G-4044)*
◆ Hayward Industries Inc .... B 908 351-5400
   Charlotte *(G-2894)*
Hess Manufacturing Inc .... E 704 637-3300
   Salisbury *(G-13979)*
▼ Hoh Corporation .... F 336 723-9274
   Winston Salem *(G-16747)*
▲ Hydro Service & Supplies Inc .... E 919 544-3744
   Durham *(G-5142)*
I2m LLC .... G 984 202-0582
   Raleigh *(G-12873)*
Imagine One LLC .... G 828 324-6454
   Hickory *(G-8061)*
Imagine One Resources LLC .... G 828 328-1142
   Hickory *(G-8062)*
Jim Myers & Sons Inc .... D 704 554-8397
   Charlotte *(G-3022)*
Jq Pro Detailing LLC .... G 336 543-0663
   Greensboro *(G-7141)*
▲ Kuenz America Inc .... F 984 255-1018
   Raleigh *(G-12948)*
Legacy Commercial Service LLC .... G 757 831-5291
   Charlotte *(G-3080)*
▼ Lely Manufacturing Inc .... F 252 291-7050
   Wilson *(G-16510)*
Level Ten Facilities Svcs LLC .... G 704 759-6799
   Charlotte *(G-3083)*
Living Water Filter Co Inc .... G 252 438-6600
   Henderson *(G-7795)*
Majestic Xpress Handwash Inc .... G 919 440-7611
   Goldsboro *(G-6633)*
◆ Mann+hmmel Fltrtion Tech US LL .... C 704 869-3300
   Gastonia *(G-6452)*
▼ Marshall Air Systems Inc .... D 704 525-6230
   Charlotte *(G-3129)*
Marshall Middleby Inc .... D 919 762-1000
   Fuquay Varina *(G-6212)*

Meco Inc .... G 919 557-7330
   Fuquay Varina *(G-6214)*
Midsouth Power Eqp Co Inc .... F 336 389-0515
   Greensboro *(G-7201)*
◆ Mikropor America Inc .... F
   Charlotte *(G-3178)*
Miller S Utility MGT Inc .... G 910 298-3847
   Beulaville *(G-1096)*
Mt Press Services Inc .... G 647 979-8675
   Mint Hill *(G-10542)*
Nala Membranes Inc .... G 540 230-5606
   Durham *(G-5237)*
North Drham Wtr Rclmtion Fclty .... G 919 560-4384
   Durham *(G-5248)*
Nunnery-Freeman Inc .... F 252 438-3149
   Henderson *(G-7799)*
▲ Onyx Environmental Solutions Inc .... E 800 858-3533
   Stanley *(G-14705)*
Painting By Colors LLC .... G 919 963-2300
   Clayton *(G-4005)*
▲ Pauls Water Treatment LLC .... G 336 886-5600
   High Point *(G-8477)*
Pentair Water Pool and Spa Inc .... G 919 463-4640
   Cary *(G-1848)*
◆ Pentair Water Pool and Spa Inc .... A 919 566-8000
   Sanford *(G-14166)*
▲ Pep Filters Inc .... E 704 662-3133
   Mooresville *(G-11051)*
Piedmont Paper Stock LLC .... F 336 285-8592
   Greensboro *(G-7259)*
Protect Plus Pro LLC .... G 828 328-1142
   Hickory *(G-8126)*
Pure Flow Inc .... D 336 532-0300
   Graham *(G-6709)*
Quality Cleaning Services LLC .... F 919 638-4969
   Durham *(G-5311)*
Rasa Malaysia .... G 919 601-1765
   Chapel Hill *(G-2062)*
Resource Management Associates .... G 919 841-9642
   Raleigh *(G-13204)*
Scaltrol Inc .... G 678 990-0858
   Charlotte *(G-3497)*
Secured Shred .... G 443 288-6375
   Raleigh *(G-13243)*
Semper FI Water LLC .... G 910 381-3569
   Jacksonville *(G-9028)*
Sinnovatek Inc .... G 919 694-0974
   Raleigh *(G-13264)*
Skyview Commercial Cleaning .... G 704 858-0134
   Charlotte *(G-3562)*
Solarbrook Water and Pwr Corp .... G 919 231-3205
   Raleigh *(G-13278)*
Supreme Sweepers LLC .... G 888 698-9996
   Charlotte *(G-3657)*
Tempest Environmental Corp .... G 919 973-1609
   Durham *(G-5393)*
▼ Tempest Envmtl Systems Inc .... F 919 973-1609
   Durham *(G-5394)*
Town of Jonesville .... G 336 835-2250
   Jonesville *(G-9102)*
Town of Maggie Valley Inc .... F 828 926-0145
   Maggie Valley *(G-10096)*
Town of Tarboro .... E 252 641-4284
   Tarboro *(G-15124)*
Town of Waynesville .... G 828 456-8497
   Waynesville *(G-15830)*
Vacs America Inc .... G 910 259-9854
   Burgaw *(G-1354)*
▲ Water-Revolution LLC .... G 336 525-1015
   Blanch *(G-1153)*
▲ Wedeco Uv Technologies Inc .... G 704 716-7600
   Charlotte *(G-3802)*

◆ Wmf Americas Inc .... E 704 882-3898
   Indian Trail *(G-8972)*
Xelaqua Inc .... G 919 964-4181
   Raleigh *(G-13430)*

3592 Carburetors, pistons, rings, valves

Bill Pink Carburetors LLC .... G 704 575-1645
   Denver *(G-4765)*
Classic Carburetor Rebuilders .... G 336 613-5715
   Eden *(G-5489)*
Marvel-Schbler Arcft Crbrtors .... F 336 446-0002
   Burlington *(G-1456)*
Robert Blake .... G 704 720-9341
   Concord *(G-4351)*

3593 Fluid power cylinders and actuators

Allied Mobile Systems LLC .... G 888 503-1501
   Dunn *(G-4849)*
▲ Atlantic Hydraulics Svcs LLC .... E 919 542-2985
   Sanford *(G-14091)*
▲ Bonomi North America Inc .... F 704 412-9031
   Charlotte *(G-2333)*
Curtiss-Wright Controls Inc .... C 704 481-1150
   Shelby *(G-14306)*
◆ Duff-Norton Company Inc .... G 704 588-0510
   Charlotte *(G-2656)*
◆ Indian Head Industries Inc .... E 704 547-7411
   Charlotte *(G-2961)*
Lord Corporation .... D 919 342-3380
   Cary *(G-1816)*
Parmer International Inc .... G 704 374-0066
   Charlotte *(G-3316)*
▲ Shelby Kendrion Inc .... C 704 482-9582
   Shelby *(G-14366)*
▲ Triumph Actuation Systems LLC .... C 336 766-9036
   Clemmons *(G-4064)*

3594 Fluid power pumps and motors

▲ Asmo Greenville of North .... B 252 754-1000
   Greenville *(G-7486)*
▲ Atlantic Hydraulics Svcs LLC .... E 919 542-2985
   Sanford *(G-14091)*
Caterpillar Inc .... D 919 550-1100
   Clayton *(G-3963)*
Denso Manufacturing NC Inc .... B 252 754-1000
   Greenville *(G-7513)*
E-Z Dumper Products LLC .... F 717 762-8432
   Southern Pines *(G-14534)*
East West Manufacturing LLC .... G 704 663-5975
   Mooresville *(G-10936)*
◆ Hurst Jaws of Life Inc .... C 704 487-6961
   Shelby *(G-14328)*
▲ Hyde Park Partners Inc .... D 704 587-4819
   Charlotte *(G-2939)*
Hydralic Engnered Pdts Svc Inc .... G 704 374-1306
   Charlotte *(G-2940)*
Livingston & Haven LLC .... C 704 588-3670
   Charlotte *(G-3096)*
Logic Hydraulic Controls Inc .... E 910 791-9293
   Wilmington *(G-16304)*
Mro Stop LLC .... F 704 587-5429
   Charlotte *(G-3210)*
Parker-Hannifin Corporation .... B 704 739-9781
   Kings Mountain *(G-9323)*
◆ Schunk Intec Inc .... D 919 572-2705
   Morrisville *(G-11420)*
SCI Sharp Controls Inc .... G 704 394-1395
   Pineville *(G-12304)*

3596 Scales and balances, except laboratory

American Scale Company LLC .... F 704 921-4556
   Charlotte *(G-2184)*

35 INDUSTRIAL AND COMMERCIAL MACHINERY AND COMPUTER EQUIPMENT

Computerway Food Systems Inc............ E 336 841-7289
  High Point (G-8302)
True Portion Inc............................... F 336 362-6326
  High Point (G-8579)
▲ Vishay Transducers Ltd..................... E 919 365-3800
  Wendell (G-15924)
Vision Metals Inc.............................. F 336 622-7300
  Liberty (G-9834)

3599 Industrial machinery, nec

3d Quality LLC................................. G 201 580-0913
  Charlotte (G-2108)
3v Performance LLC........................... G 980 222-7230
  Denver (G-4757)
A & G Machining LLC......................... G 919 329-7207
  Garner (G-6249)
A & S Tool & Die Co Inc...................... G 336 993-3440
  Kernersville (G-9158)
AAA Machine Shop............................ G 704 989-1385
  Monroe (G-10632)
Abco Automation Inc.......................... C 336 375-6400
  Browns Summit (G-1298)
Accu-Tool LLC.................................. F 919 363-2600
  Apex (G-156)
Accurate Machine & Tool LLC................ F 919 212-0266
  Raleigh (G-12469)
Acme Die & Machine Corporation........... F 704 864-8426
  Gastonia (G-6335)
Acme Machine LLC............................ F 828 483-6440
  Fletcher (G-5981)
Advanced Cutting Tech Inc................... G 910 944-3028
  Maxton (G-10354)
Advanced Machining Tooling LLC........... G 704 633-8157
  Salisbury (G-13914)
Advanced Mch & Fabrication Inc............ G 704 489-0096
  Denver (G-4759)
Aero Precision Machine Inc................... F 336 685-0016
  Liberty (G-9805)
AES America Inc................................ G 847 879-1146
  Charlotte (G-2141)
Albany Tool & Die Inc......................... F 910 392-1207
  Wilmington (G-16099)
Allen Mch & Fabrication LLC................. F 336 521-4409
  Asheboro (G-400)
◆ Alotech Inc..................................... E 919 774-1297
  Goldston (G-6672)
Alotech North................................... G 919 774-1297
  Goldston (G-6673)
Alpha 3d LLC................................... G 704 277-6300
  Charlotte (G-2166)
Alphatech Inc................................... E 828 684-9709
  Fletcher (G-5983)
American Cylinder Products Inc............. F 336 993-7722
  Kernersville (G-9163)
◆ American Linc Corporation................. E 704 861-9242
  Gastonia (G-6346)
American Materials Company LLC.......... E 910 532-6659
  Rose Hill (G-13773)
American Rewinding Nc Inc.................. E 704 289-4177
  Monroe (G-10642)
Ana Gizzi.. G 908 334-8733
  Statesville (G-14751)
Angels Path Ventures Inc..................... G 828 654-9530
  Arden (G-309)
Annas Machine Shop Inc..................... G 828 754-4184
  Lenoir (G-9573)
Anson Machine Works Inc.................... G 704 272-7457
  Polkton (G-12384)
Anson Machine Works Inc.................... G 704 272-7457
  Polkton (G-12385)
Apjet Inc.. G 919 595-5538
  Morrisville (G-11290)

Appalachian Tool & Machine Inc............. E 828 669-0142
  Swannanoa (G-15017)
Asheboro Machine Shop Inc.................. G 336 625-6322
  Asheboro (G-405)
August Precision............................... G 919 830-6616
  Chapel Hill (G-1988)
Auto Machine Shop Inc....................... G 910 483-6016
  Fayetteville (G-5765)
Automated Machine Technologies........... G 919 361-0121
  Morrisville (G-11297)
Avail Forensics LLC............................ F 877 888-5895
  Wilmington (G-16125)
Avery Machine & Welding Co................. G 828 733-4944
  Fayetteville (G-5767)
Axccellus LLC................................... F 919 589-9800
  Apex (G-169)
B & B Industries Inc........................... E 704 882-4688
  Indian Trail (G-8923)
B & B Machine Co Inc......................... G 704 637-2356
  Salisbury (G-13927)
B & J Tool Inc................................... G 336 265-8306
  Greensboro (G-6830)
B&D Spindles LLC.............................. G 910 895-9769
  Rockingham (G-13620)
B+e Manufacturing Co Inc.................... E 704 236-8439
  Monroe (G-10659)
Bace LLC.. F 704 394-2230
  Charlotte (G-2262)
Ball S Machine & Mfg Co Inc................. F 828 667-0411
  Candler (G-1570)
Bannister Inc.................................... E 252 638-6611
  New Bern (G-11776)
Barbour S Marine Supply Co Inc............. F 252 728-2136
  Beaufort (G-944)
Barnes Precision Machine Inc................ F 919 362-6805
  Apex (G-170)
Benton & Sons Fabrication Inc............... E 919 734-1700
  Pikeville (G-12192)
▲ Bessemer City Machine Shop Inc......... E 704 629-4111
  Bessemer City (G-1053)
Betech Inc....................................... E 828 687-9917
  Fletcher (G-5987)
Bibey Machine Company Inc................. E 336 275-9421
  Greensboro (G-6838)
Bircher Incorporated........................... G 252 726-5470
  Morehead City (G-11153)
Black Mtn Mch Fabrication Inc............... E 828 669-9557
  Black Mountain (G-1121)
Blount Precision Machining Inc.............. G 252 825-3701
  Bethel (G-1089)
Blue Ridge Tool Inc............................ G 336 993-8111
  High Point (G-8273)
Blue Ridge Tool Inc............................ G 336 993-8111
  Colfax (G-4142)
Blue Steel Inc................................... G 704 864-2583
  Gastonia (G-6356)
Bob Martin...................................... G 910 245-3593
  Vass (G-15490)
Bob Peak Enterprises Inc..................... G 704 564-0711
  China Grove (G-3880)
Bond Technologies............................. G 919 866-0075
  Raleigh (G-12569)
Boone Iron Works Inc......................... G 828 264-5284
  Boone (G-1179)
Bowen Machine Company Inc............... F 704 629-9111
  Gastonia (G-6357)
Bowie Machine Works LLC.................... G 910 297-6014
  Wilmington (G-16142)
◆ Briggs-Shaffner Acquisition Co............. F 336 463-4272
  Yadkinville (G-17034)
▲ Broadsight Systems Inc..................... G 336 837-1272
  Mebane (G-10401)

▲ Broadwind Indus Solutions LLC............ E 919 777-2907
  Sanford (G-14096)
Brock and Triplett Machine Sp............... G 336 667-6951
  Moravian Falls (G-11142)
Brooks Machine & Design Inc................ F 919 404-0901
  Zebulon (G-17122)
Bulldog Machine Inc........................... G 704 200-7838
  Matthews (G-10306)
Bunting Equipment Company Inc............ F 336 626-7300
  Sophia (G-14513)
Burlington Machine Service................... G 336 228-6758
  Burlington (G-1381)
Burnett Machine Company Inc............... F 704 867-7786
  Gastonia (G-6363)
Burris Machine Company Inc................. G 828 322-6914
  Hickory (G-7956)
Busick Brothers Machine Inc.................. F 336 969-2717
  Rural Hall (G-13834)
▲ Buy Smart Inc................................. G 252 293-4700
  Wilson (G-16482)
C & B Salvage Company Inc.................. G 336 374-3946
  Ararat (G-263)
C & C Precision Machine Inc................. E 704 739-0505
  Kings Mountain (G-9297)
C & W Mch & Fabrication Inc................. G 252 522-5476
  Kinston (G-9349)
Campbell & Sons Machining Co.............. G 704 394-0291
  Lincolnton (G-9878)
◆ Canvas Sx LLC................................. C 980 474-3700
  Charlotte (G-2384)
Capper McCall Co.............................. G 919 270-8813
  Raleigh (G-12592)
Carnes-Miller Gear Company Inc............ F 704 888-4448
  Locust (G-9955)
Carolina... F 919 851-0906
  Cary (G-1722)
Carolina Core Machine LLC................... E 336 342-1141
  Reidsville (G-13512)
Carolina Laser Cutting Inc.................... E 336 292-1474
  Greensboro (G-6886)
Carolina Mch Fayetteville Inc................. F 910 425-9115
  Hope Mills (G-8734)
Carolina Prcsion Cmponents Inc............. E 828 496-1045
  Granite Falls (G-6726)
Carolina Prcsion Machining Inc.............. E 336 751-7788
  Mocksville (G-10559)
Carolina Precision Machining................. F 336 751-7788
  Mocksville (G-10560)
Carolina Resource Corp....................... F 919 562-0200
  Youngsville (G-17076)
Carolina Tex Sls Gastonia Inc................ F 704 739-1646
  Kings Mountain (G-9301)
Carr Mill Supplies Inc......................... G 336 883-0135
  High Point (G-8287)
Carters Machine Company Inc............... G 704 784-3106
  Concord (G-4227)
Cas Machine Design LLC...................... G 919 515-2834
  Raleigh (G-12608)
▲ Casetec Precision Machine LLC............. G 704 663-6043
  Mooresville (G-10899)
Centaur Laboratories Inc...................... F 919 249-5072
  Oxford (G-12119)
Central Carolina Products Inc................ D 336 226-0005
  Burlington (G-1393)
Central Machine Company.................... F 336 855-0022
  Archdale (G-273)
Certified Machining Inc....................... F 919 777-9608
  Sanford (G-14100)
Chapman Machine............................. G 704 739-1834
  Kings Mountain (G-9302)
Charter Dura-Bar Inc.......................... F 704 637-1906
  Salisbury (G-13940)

Employee Codes: A=Over 500 employees, B=251-500
C=101-250, D=51-100, E=20-50, F=10-19, G=1-9

35 INDUSTRIAL AND COMMERCIAL MACHINERY AND COMPUTER EQUIPMENT — SIC SECTION

▲ Chiron America Inc................................D..... 704 587-9526
Charlotte *(G-2478)*

Chrisco Machine Shop LLC....................G..... 828 428-9966
Lincolnton *(G-9882)*

City Machine Company Inc....................E..... 828 754-9661
Lenoir *(G-9599)*

Cjt Machine Inc.......................................G..... 828 376-3693
Hendersonville *(G-7837)*

Clt Machine LLc.....................................G..... 704 778-8305
Charlotte *(G-2502)*

CMS Tool and Die Inc............................F..... 910 458-3322
Carolina Beach *(G-1636)*

Cnc Performance Eng LLC....................G..... 704 599-2555
Charlotte *(G-2508)*

Cole Machine Inc....................................G..... 336 222-8381
Snow Camp *(G-14496)*

Compass Precision LLC.........................F..... 704 790-6764
Charlotte *(G-2533)*

Component Technology Intl Inc..............G..... 704 331-0888
Charlotte *(G-2535)*

Conner Brothers Machine Co Inc...........D..... 704 864-6084
Bessemer City *(G-1056)*

Conover Machine and Design Inc..........G..... 828 328-6737
Hickory *(G-7993)*

Consolidated Inspections Inc.................G..... 919 658-5800
Mount Olive *(G-11660)*

CRC Machine & Fabrication Inc.............F..... 980 522-1361
Bessemer City *(G-1057)*

CSM Manufacturing Inc..........................F..... 336 570-2282
Graham *(G-6686)*

Current Enterprises Inc..........................G..... 919 469-1227
Morrisville *(G-11326)*

Curti USA Corporation............................G..... 910 769-1977
Belville *(G-1023)*

Custom Automated Machines Inc..........G..... 704 289-7038
Monroe *(G-10700)*

Custom Industries Inc............................F..... 704 825-3346
Belmont *(G-981)*

▲ Custom Industries Inc.........................E..... 336 299-2885
Greensboro *(G-6950)*

Custom Machine Company Inc..............F..... 704 629-5326
Bessemer City *(G-1059)*

Custom Machining Inc............................G..... 336 996-0855
Kernersville *(G-9185)*

D & D Entps Greensboro Inc..................F..... 336 495-3407
Greensboro *(G-6955)*

D & D Entps Greensboro Inc..................E..... 336 495-3407
Randleman *(G-13462)*

D & D Machine Works Inc......................G..... 704 878-0117
Statesville *(G-14780)*

Daily Grind..G..... 919 864-8775
Morrisville *(G-11327)*

Daily Grind LLC......................................G..... 910 541-0471
Surf City *(G-15015)*

Dallas Machine and................................G..... 704 629-5611
Bessemer City *(G-1061)*

Damco Inc...F..... 252 633-1404
New Bern *(G-11798)*

Davis Davis Mch & Wldg Co Inc............F..... 252 443-2652
Rocky Mount *(G-13689)*

Davis Machine Co Inc.............................G..... 704 865-2863
Gastonia *(G-6396)*

Dayco Manufacturing Inc.......................F..... 919 989-1820
Clayton *(G-3973)*

♦ Daystar Machining Tech Inc................E..... 828 684-1316
Fletcher *(G-5997)*

Deal Machine Shop Inc..........................F..... 704 872-7618
Statesville *(G-14784)*

Deberry Precision Machine Inc..............G..... 704 422-3274
New London *(G-11868)*

Deep Creek Motors Inc..........................G..... 336 599-0000
Roxboro *(G-13800)*

Dellinger Enterprises Ltd........................E..... 704 825-9687
Belmont *(G-982)*

Denver Waterjet LLC..............................G..... 980 222-7447
Denver *(G-4772)*

Designcraft...G..... 919 903-5711
Chapel Hill *(G-2007)*

Diamond Enterprises..............................G..... 828 495-4448
Hickory *(G-8009)*

Diversfied McHning Cncepts Inc............G..... 828 665-2465
Candler *(G-1577)*

Diversified Specialties Inc......................E..... 704 825-3671
Belmont *(G-986)*

Dm2...G..... 336 362-3425
King *(G-9269)*

Dma Inc...G..... 704 527-0992
Charlotte *(G-2648)*

Douglas Fabrication & Mch Inc..............F..... 919 365-7553
Wendell *(G-15898)*

Dp Custom Works LLC...........................G..... 704 221-7291
Marshville *(G-10214)*

Dramar Machine Devices Inc.................E..... 704 866-0904
Gastonia *(G-6398)*

DSI Innovations LLC..............................E..... 336 893-8385
Thomasville *(G-15216)*

Dyna-Tech Manufacturing Inc................F..... 704 839-0203
Monroe *(G-10710)*

Dynamic Machine Works LLC................F..... 336 462-7370
Clemmons *(G-4036)*

Dynamic Machining X Mfg LLC..............E..... 336 362-3425
King *(G-9271)*

E F P Inc...F..... 336 498-4134
Randleman *(G-13467)*

Eagle Machining Usa Inc.......................F..... 717 235-9383
Huntersville *(G-8813)*

Eaglestone Technology Inc....................F..... 336 476-0244
High Point *(G-8335)*

Earls Precision Machining......................G..... 919 542-1869
Sanford *(G-14112)*

Economy Grinding Straightening............E..... 704 400-2500
Charlotte *(G-2684)*

Ecs Enterprises Inc................................D..... 704 786-1600
Kannapolis *(G-9118)*

Eddie Hsr S Prcsion McHning In............G..... 704 750-4244
Kings Mountain *(G-9307)*

Eddie S Mountain Machine Inc..............G..... 828 685-0733
Hendersonville *(G-7846)*

Edwards Unlimited Inc...........................G..... 252 226-4583
Henderson *(G-7782)*

▲ Electrical Apparatus & Mch Co...........F..... 704 333-2987
Gastonia *(G-6400)*

Elite Metal Performance LLC.................F..... 704 660-0006
Statesville *(G-14793)*

Elomi Inc...E..... 904 591-0095
Concord *(G-4260)*

Equipment Parts Inc...............................E..... 704 827-7545
Belmont *(G-987)*

Erecto Mch & Fabrication Inc.................G..... 704 922-8621
Dallas *(G-4639)*

Estes Machine Co..................................F..... 336 786-7680
Mount Airy *(G-11507)*

Everettes Company Inc..........................F..... 336 956-2097
Linwood *(G-9944)*

Everettes Industrial Repr Svc.................F..... 252 527-4269
Goldsboro *(G-6613)*

Extreme Tractor Parts LLC.....................G..... 919 605-6040
Fuquay Varina *(G-6199)*

Fab-Tec Inc...D..... 704 864-6872
Dallas *(G-4640)*

Faircloth Machine Shop Inc....................F..... 336 777-1529
Winston Salem *(G-16707)*

Falcon Industries LLC............................G..... 336 229-1048
Burlington *(G-1413)*

Farmer Machine Group LLC...................F..... 704 629-5133
Bessemer City *(G-1064)*

Farris Fab & Machine Inc.......................G..... 704 629-4879
Bessemer City *(G-1065)*

Farris Fab & Machine Inc.......................C..... 704 629-4879
Bessemer City *(G-1066)*

▲ Farris Fab & Machine Inc...................D..... 704 629-4879
Cherryville *(G-3868)*

Fieldco Machining Inc............................F..... 828 891-4100
Fletcher *(G-6004)*

Foo Machine & Tool Precision...............F..... 919 258-5099
Broadway *(G-1296)*

Foundry Group LLC...............................G..... 412 973-9762
Denver *(G-4776)*

Frances Machine Shop..........................G..... 910 653-3477
Chadbourn *(G-1975)*

Franklin Machine Company LLC............F..... 828 524-2313
Franklin *(G-6129)*

Fulton Technology Corporation..............G..... 828 657-1611
Mooresboro *(G-10838)*

G & J Machine Shop Inc........................E..... 336 668-0996
Greensboro *(G-7028)*

G T Racing Heads Inc............................G..... 336 905-7988
Sophia *(G-14517)*

G60 Cnc LLC..G..... 704 796-0478
Concord *(G-4271)*

Gaston Indus Machining LLC.................G..... 704 825-3346
Bessemer City *(G-1069)*

General Machining Inc...........................G..... 336 342-2759
Reidsville *(G-13519)*

General Mch Wldg of Burlington............G..... 336 227-5400
Burlington *(G-1419)*

General Precision Svc............................G..... 919 553-2604
Clayton *(G-3980)*

Gentle Machine and Tool Inc.................G..... 336 492-5055
Mocksville *(G-10576)*

Geonics..G..... 704 956-7999
Concord *(G-4273)*

Gesipa Fasteners Usa Inc.....................E..... 336 751-1555
Mocksville *(G-10577)*

♦ Gesipa Fasteners Usa Inc..................F..... 609 208-1740
Mocksville *(G-10578)*

GF Machining Solutions.........................F..... 704 927-8929
Huntersville *(G-8826)*

Gibbs Machine Company Incorporated.E..... 336 856-1907
Greensboro *(G-7042)*

Gillespies Fbrction Design Inc...............G..... 704 636-2349
Salisbury *(G-13969)*

Gordon Enterprises.................................G..... 919 776-8784
Sanford *(G-14127)*

Gormac Custom Mfg Inc........................G..... 828 891-9984
Arden *(G-334)*

Goshen Engineering Inc........................G..... 919 429-9798
Mount Olive *(G-11661)*

Grandeur Manufacturing Inc..................E..... 336 526-2468
Jonesville *(G-9098)*

Greens Machine & Tool Inc...................F..... 828 654-0042
Fletcher *(G-6008)*

Grind Athletics LLC................................G..... 910 228-0035
Wilmington *(G-16242)*

Gunmar Machine Corporation................F..... 910 738-6295
Lumberton *(G-10039)*

H & B Tool & Die Supply Co..................G..... 704 376-8531
Charlotte *(G-2874)*

H & R Mullis Machine Inc......................F..... 704 791-4149
Midland *(G-10468)*

Hamilton Machine Works LLC................G..... 919 779-6892
Raleigh *(G-12828)*

Hancock & Grandson Inc.......................G..... 252 728-2416
Beaufort *(G-959)*

Hawk Manufacturing Inc........................G..... 803 802-9777
Waxhaw *(G-15759)*

35 INDUSTRIAL AND COMMERCIAL MACHINERY AND COMPUTER EQUIPMENT

Heintz Bros Automotives Inc................ G 704 872-8081
  Statesville *(G-14809)*
Helms Machine Company...................... G 704 289-5571
  Monroe *(G-10730)*
Hi-TEC Machine Corp........................... E 828 652-1060
  Old Fort *(G-12101)*
Highland Tool and Gauge Inc................ F 828 891-8557
  Mills River *(G-10503)*
Hkb Enterprises LLC............................ G 704 831-0402
  Charlotte *(G-2912)*
Hmf Inc... G 704 821-6765
  Matthews *(G-10320)*
Hodges Precision Machine................... G 336 366-3024
  Dobson *(G-4825)*
Holder Machine & Mfg Co..................... G 828 479-8627
  Robbinsville *(G-13608)*
▲ Holman & Moody Inc........................ G 704 394-4141
  Charlotte *(G-2914)*
Hooks Inc Chris................................... G 704 516-1529
  Charlotte *(G-2921)*
Hoser Inc... F 704 989-7151
  Monroe *(G-10734)*
Hydra Cut LLC..................................... G 252 814-1654
  Winterville *(G-17003)*
Hydraulics Express.............................. G 828 251-2500
  Asheville *(G-656)*
I-40 Machine and Tool Inc.................... G 704 881-0242
  Statesville *(G-14819)*
I2e Group LLC..................................... G 336 884-2014
  High Point *(G-8404)*
Imperial Machine Company Inc............. E 704 739-8038
  Bessemer City *(G-1071)*
Indaux Usa Inc.................................... G 336 861-0740
  Advance *(G-43)*
Industrial Machine & Wldg Inc............... G 910 251-1393
  Wilmington *(G-16266)*
Industrial Machine Company................. F 704 922-9750
  Dallas *(G-4646)*
Industrial Metal Products of.................. F 910 944-8110
  Aberdeen *(G-7)*
Industrial Mtal Flame Spryers................ G 919 596-9381
  Durham *(G-5152)*
▲ Industrial Piping Inc........................ A 704 588-1100
  Charlotte *(G-2964)*
Industrial Tling Svcs Ashvlle................. G 828 683-4168
  Leicester *(G-9513)*
Ingram Machine & Balancing................ G 828 254-3420
  Asheville *(G-662)*
Intelligent Tool Corp............................ F 704 799-0449
  Concord *(G-4286)*
Ipi Acquisition LLC.............................. A 704 588-1100
  Charlotte *(G-2996)*
Island Machining LLC.......................... G 704 278-3553
  Mooresville *(G-10985)*
J & J Machine Works Inc..................... G 336 434-4081
  Archdale *(G-287)*
J & K Tools LLC................................. G 828 299-0589
  Asheville *(G-666)*
J & P Machine Works Inc.................... G 252 758-1719
  Greenville *(G-7547)*
J & S Tools Inc.................................. G 252 514-7805
  New Bern *(G-11812)*
J&J Precision Services LLC................. G 970 412-4683
  Wilmington *(G-16275)*
J&L Machine & Fabrication Inc............. E 704 755-5552
  Stanley *(G-14698)*
Jacks Motor Parts Inc.......................... G 910 642-4077
  Whiteville *(G-15969)*
Jaeco Precision Inc............................. G 336 633-1025
  Asheboro *(G-447)*
▲ James Tool Machine & Engrg Inc..... C 828 584-8722
  Morganton *(G-11224)*

Jimbuilt Machines Inc........................... G 828 874-3530
  Connelly Springs *(G-4405)*
Jmc Tool & Machine Co....................... E 919 775-7070
  Sanford *(G-14140)*
Joe and La Inc.................................... F 336 585-0313
  Burlington *(G-1441)*
John West Auto Service Inc.................. G 919 250-0825
  Raleigh *(G-12919)*
Johnson Cnc LLC................................ E 910 428-1245
  Star *(G-14716)*
Johnson Industrial Mchy Svcs............... E 252 239-1944
  Lucama *(G-10017)*
Johnson Machine Co Inc..................... G 252 638-2620
  New Bern *(G-11814)*
Johnston Knife and Tool Inc................. G 704 208-9191
  Mint Hill *(G-10537)*
K & C Machine Co Inc......................... F 336 373-0745
  Greensboro *(G-7143)*
K & S Tool & Manufacturing Co............. F 336 410-7260
  High Point *(G-8418)*
▲ K-M Machine Company Inc............. D 910 428-2368
  Biscoe *(G-1114)*
Kwg Music LLC................................... G 773 771-2017
  Durham *(G-5183)*
L & K Machining Inc............................ F 336 222-9444
  Burlington *(G-1446)*
L and L Machine Co Inc....................... F 704 864-5521
  Gastonia *(G-6442)*
Lacy J Miller Machine........................... G 336 764-0518
  Lexington *(G-9743)*
Laser Dynamics Inc............................. G 704 658-9769
  Mooresville *(G-11004)*
▲ Laser Precision Cutting Inc............. G 828 658-0644
  Weaverville *(G-15851)*
Latham-Hall Corporation....................... E 336 475-9723
  Thomasville *(G-15240)*
Laurinburg Machine Company............... G 910 276-0360
  Laurinburg *(G-9484)*
Lawrence Williams............................... G 910 462-2332
  Laurel Hill *(G-9464)*
Leland Machine Shop Inc..................... G 910 371-0360
  Leland *(G-9551)*
Levi Innovations Inc............................. F 828 684-6640
  Fletcher *(G-6018)*
Lewis Machine Company Inc................ G 828 668-7752
  Old Fort *(G-12103)*
Lightwave Fabrication Mch LLC............. G 252 927-1591
  Pantego *(G-12166)*
Ljm Machine Co Inc............................ F 336 764-0518
  Lexington *(G-9751)*
Logic Manufacturing Inc....................... E 704 821-0535
  Indian Trail *(G-8946)*
Lws Tools Inc.................................... G 919 247-1913
  Angier *(G-146)*
M S I Precision Machine Inc................. G 704 629-9375
  Bessemer City *(G-1073)*
▲ Mabry Industries Inc....................... E 336 584-1311
  Elon College *(G-5666)*
Mac/Fab Company Inc........................ E 704 822-1103
  Mount Holly *(G-11641)*
◆ Machine Builders & Design Inc......... E 704 482-3456
  Shelby *(G-14340)*
Machine Consulting Svcs Inc............... G 919 596-3033
  Durham *(G-5201)*
Machine Nunn Cnc Shop LLC.............. G 704 873-4931
  Statesville *(G-14836)*
Machine Shop..................................... G 910 246-0720
  Carthage *(G-1663)*
Machine Specialties LLC..................... C 336 603-1919
  Whitsett *(G-15996)*
Machinex.. G 336 665-5030
  High Point *(G-8436)*

Machining Solutions Inc....................... F 704 528-5436
  Troutman *(G-15387)*
Magna Machining Inc.......................... E 704 463-9904
  Richfield *(G-13552)*
Mammoth Machine and Design LLC...... G 704 727-3330
  Mooresville *(G-11014)*
Mang Systems Inc.............................. G 704 292-1041
  Matthews *(G-10330)*
Manufacturing Services Inc.................. E 704 629-4163
  Bessemer City *(G-1074)*
Marc Machine Works Inc..................... F 704 865-3625
  Gastonia *(G-6458)*
Marine Fabrications LLC...................... G 252 473-4767
  Wanchese *(G-15649)*
Marion Machine LLC............................ C 800 627-1639
  Marion *(G-10158)*
Mary Kay Inc...................................... G 336 998-1663
  Advance *(G-46)*
Master Machining Inc.......................... E 910 675-3660
  Castle Hayne *(G-1955)*
◆ Max Daetwyler Corp........................ E 704 875-1200
  Huntersville *(G-8853)*
McDowells Mch Fabrication Inc............ G 336 720-9944
  Winston Salem *(G-16804)*
McGee Brothers Machine & Wldg.......... G 828 766-9122
  Spruce Pine *(G-14647)*
McJast Inc... F 828 884-4809
  Pisgah Forest *(G-12326)*
▼ Meadows Mills Inc.......................... E 336 838-2282
  North Wilkesboro *(G-12027)*
Mebane Machine & Tool LLC............... G 919 597-1169
  Mebane *(G-10419)*
Mecha Inc.. F 919 858-0372
  Raleigh *(G-13012)*
Mechanical Specialty Inc..................... G 336 272-5606
  Greensboro *(G-7195)*
Mega Machine Shop Inc...................... G 336 492-2728
  Mocksville *(G-10587)*
Merlins Machine Shop......................... G 910 399-3677
  Wilmington *(G-16320)*
Mertek Solutions Inc........................... E 919 774-7827
  Sanford *(G-14152)*
Metalcraft Specialties Inc..................... G 828 779-2523
  Candler *(G-1587)*
Mid-Atlantic Tool and Die Inc............... F 252 946-2598
  Washington *(G-15715)*
Mik All Machine Co Inc....................... F 704 866-4302
  Gastonia *(G-6465)*
Minas Equity Partners LLC.................. F 336 724-5152
  Winston Salem *(G-16811)*
Mint Machining A North Car................. G 440 479-9074
  Charlotte *(G-3186)*
Mitchell Medlin Machine Shop.............. G 704 289-2840
  Monroe *(G-10771)*
Mmj Machining and Fabg Inc............... F 336 495-1029
  Randleman *(G-13479)*
Modern Machine and Metal.................. D 336 993-4808
  Winston Salem *(G-16814)*
Modern Machining Inc......................... G 919 775-7332
  Sanford *(G-14154)*
Moffitt Machine Company Inc............... G 910 485-2159
  Fayetteville *(G-5877)*
Moore Machine Products Inc................ G 910 592-2718
  Clinton *(G-4099)*
Morgan Tool & Die LLC....................... G 910 281-0201
  Aberdeen *(G-16)*
Morris Group...................................... G 973 713-2211
  New Bern *(G-11826)*
Morris Machine Company Inc............... G 704 824-4242
  Gastonia *(G-6470)*
Morris South LLC............................... D 704 523-6008
  Charlotte *(G-3204)*

Employee Codes: A=Over 500 employees, B=251-500
C=101-250, D=51-100, E=20-50, F=10-19, G=1-9

2024 Harris North Carolina
Manufacturers Directory

35 INDUSTRIAL AND COMMERCIAL MACHINERY AND COMPUTER EQUIPMENT — SIC SECTION

Motorsports Machining Tech LLC .... F 336 475-3742
  Thomasville *(G-15254)*
Mundy Machine Co Inc .... G 704 922-8663
  Dallas *(G-4648)*
Myers Tool and Machine Co Inc .... D 336 956-1324
  Lexington *(G-9758)*
▲ Nabell USA Corporation .... E 704 986-2455
  Albemarle *(G-98)*
Nashville Wldg & Mch Works Inc .... E 252 243-0113
  Wilson *(G-16517)*
Neff Tool and Machine LLC .... G 507 226-1708
  Chapel Hill *(G-2046)*
New World Technologies Inc .... F 828 652-8662
  Marion *(G-10169)*
▲ Newton Machine Co Inc .... G 704 394-2099
  Charlotte *(G-3254)*
Nolen Machine Co Inc .... G 704 867-7851
  Gastonia *(G-6479)*
North Buncombe Small Engines .... G 828 707-4874
  Weaverville *(G-15857)*
North Carolina Dept Labor .... F 919 807-2770
  Raleigh *(G-13068)*
North Carolina Mfg Inc .... E 919 734-1115
  Goldsboro *(G-6638)*
North Iredell Grinding Inc .... F 704 902-4771
  Statesville *(G-14852)*
North State Machine Inc .... F 336 956-1441
  Lexington *(G-9763)*
Novakon .... G 336 813-2309
  Winston Salem *(G-16823)*
Noxon Automation USA LLC .... G 919 390-1560
  Morrisville *(G-11400)*
Nu-Tech Enterprises Inc .... E 336 725-1691
  Winston Salem *(G-16825)*
Olivia Machine & Tool Inc .... F 919 499-6021
  Sanford *(G-14160)*
▲ Omega Manufacturing Corp .... F 704 597-0418
  Charlotte *(G-3294)*
Omninvest LLC .... G 336 623-1717
  Harrisburg *(G-7719)*
Ora Inc .... G 540 903-7177
  Marion *(G-10170)*
Ostec Industries Corp .... G 704 488-3841
  Denver *(G-4792)*
Ostwalt Machine Company Inc .... G 704 528-5730
  Troutman *(G-15389)*
Paul Norman Company Inc .... G 704 399-4221
  Charlotte *(G-3320)*
Pemmco Manufacturing Inc .... D 336 625-1122
  Asheboro *(G-460)*
Performance Machine & Fab Inc .... F 336 983-0414
  King *(G-9279)*
Petra Precision Machining .... G 919 751-3461
  Goldsboro *(G-6645)*
Petteway Body Shop Inc .... G 910 455-3272
  Jacksonville *(G-9020)*
Piedmont Precision Products .... F 828 304-0791
  Hickory *(G-8114)*
Piedmont Technical Services .... G 770 530-8313
  Charlotte *(G-3342)*
Pinnacle Converting Eqp & Svcs .... E 704 376-3855
  Pineville *(G-12290)*
Pinnacle Converting Eqp Inc .... E 704 376-3855
  Pineville *(G-12291)*
Pioneer Machine Works Inc .... G 704 864-5528
  Gastonia *(G-6489)*
Pleasant Gardens Machine Inc .... F 828 724-4173
  Marion *(G-10172)*
Poplin & Sons Machine Co Inc .... F 704 289-2079
  Monroe *(G-10788)*
Precision Design Machinery .... G 336 889-8157
  High Point *(G-8491)*

Precision Fabricators Inc .... G 336 835-4763
  Ronda *(G-13768)*
Precision Machine Tools Corp .... G 704 882-3700
  Matthews *(G-10340)*
▲ Precision Mch Components Inc .... G 704 201-8482
  Denver *(G-4796)*
▲ Precision Mch Fabrication Inc .... D 919 231-8648
  Raleigh *(G-13134)*
Precision Mindset Pllc .... G 704 508-1314
  Statesville *(G-14867)*
Precision Partners LLC .... E 800 545-3121
  Charlotte *(G-3370)*
Precision Pdts Asheville Inc .... E 828 684-4207
  Arden *(G-366)*
Precision Products Inc .... G 336 688-0298
  High Point *(G-8493)*
Precision Tool Dye and Mold .... F 828 687-2990
  Arden *(G-368)*
Precision Wldg Mch Charlotte .... G 704 357-1288
  Charlotte *(G-3371)*
Premier Mfg Co .... E 704 781-4001
  Midland *(G-10476)*
Pro Tool Company Inc .... F 336 998-9212
  Advance *(G-48)*
Production Wldg Fbrication Inc .... E 828 687-7466
  Arden *(G-369)*
Proedge Precision LLC .... E 704 872-3393
  Statesville *(G-14871)*
Promatic Automation Inc .... E 828 684-1700
  Fletcher *(G-6032)*
Prometals Inc .... G 919 693-8884
  Oxford *(G-12147)*
Protech Metals LLC .... G 910 295-6905
  Pinehurst *(G-12232)*
Prowl Precision and Power LLC .... G 336 580-1558
  Burlington *(G-1479)*
PSI Liquidating Inc .... G 704 888-9930
  Locust *(G-9966)*
Quality Machine & Tool .... G 336 769-9131
  Kernersville *(G-9228)*
Quality Mch & Fabrication Inc .... G 252 435-6041
  Moyock *(G-11697)*
Quartz Matrix LLC .... G 828 631-3207
  Sylva *(G-15066)*
Quilt Shop .... G 828 263-8691
  Boone *(G-1230)*
Quinnessential Tools Company .... G 540 623-7965
  Raeford *(G-12433)*
▲ R H Bolick & Company Inc .... G 828 322-7847
  Hickory *(G-8132)*
R&H Machining Fabrication Inc .... G 828 253-8930
  Asheville *(G-751)*
Ramco Machine & Pump Svc Inc .... G 910 371-3388
  Leland *(G-9558)*
Randolph Machine Inc .... G 336 625-0411
  Asheboro *(G-471)*
Rawco LLC .... G 908 832-7700
  Cornelius *(G-4580)*
Ray Houses Machine Shop .... G 919 553-1249
  Clayton *(G-4006)*
Rbi Manufacturing Inc .... F 252 977-6764
  Rocky Mount *(G-13727)*
Rbw LLC .... G 919 319-1289
  Cary *(G-1866)*
Rebb Industries Inc .... E 336 463-2311
  Yadkinville *(G-17048)*
Reel-Tex Inc .... G 704 868-4419
  Gastonia *(G-6503)*
Reynolda Mfg Solutions Inc .... F 336 699-4204
  East Bend *(G-5467)*
Reynolda Mfg Solutions Inc .... E 336 699-4204
  East Bend *(G-5468)*

Richardson Enterprises NC Inc .... G 704 675-8666
  Dallas *(G-4654)*
Riley Power Group LLC .... C 910 420-6999
  Pinehurst *(G-12234)*
Robinson & Son Machine Inc .... E 910 592-4779
  Clinton *(G-4103)*
Robinson Mch & Cutter Grinding .... G 704 629-5591
  Bessemer City *(G-1080)*
Rock Industrial Services Inc .... F 910 652-6267
  Ellerbe *(G-5644)*
Rowan Precision Machining Inc .... G 704 279-6092
  Granite Quarry *(G-6761)*
Rowdy Manufacturing LLC .... G 704 662-0000
  Mooresville *(G-11075)*
Roy Dunn .... G 919 963-3700
  Four Oaks *(G-6111)*
Rtp Machine Inc .... G 919 279-3338
  Cary *(G-1874)*
Rtt Machine & Welding Svc Inc .... E 919 269-6863
  Zebulon *(G-17141)*
Rufus N Ivie III .... G 704 482-2559
  Shelby *(G-14361)*
S & D Machine & Tool Inc .... G 919 479-8433
  Durham *(G-5336)*
S & S Repair Service Inc .... F 252 756-5989
  Winterville *(G-17013)*
S & W Metal Works Inc .... G 252 641-0912
  Tarboro *(G-15120)*
S Ernie Machine Co Inc .... F 336 852-6355
  Julian *(G-9108)*
S Oakley Machine Shop Inc .... G 336 599-6105
  Roxboro *(G-13822)*
S Strickland Diesel Svc Inc .... G 252 291-6999
  Wilson *(G-16536)*
Sanders Company Inc .... E 252 338-3995
  Elizabeth City *(G-5569)*
Sandhlls Fbrctors Crane Svcs I .... F 910 673-4573
  West End *(G-15931)*
Scoggins Industrial Inc .... F 252 977-9222
  Sharpsburg *(G-14280)*
Seymour Advanced Tech LLC .... G 704 709-9070
  Denver *(G-4800)*
Sloans Machine Shop .... G 919 499-5655
  Sanford *(G-14186)*
Smith Fabrication Inc .... G 704 660-5170
  Mooresville *(G-11090)*
Smiths Garage and Machine Shop .... G 828 452-1664
  Waynesville *(G-15823)*
▲ Smokey Mountain Amusements .... G 828 479-2814
  Robbinsville *(G-13611)*
Smoky Mountain Machining Inc .... D 828 665-1193
  Asheville *(G-776)*
Sniders Machine Shop Inc .... G 704 279-6129
  Rockwell *(G-13658)*
Social Grind Gourmet Cof LLC .... G 919 937-9503
  Durham *(G-5363)*
Solomon Engineering Inc .... E 828 855-1652
  Hickory *(G-8162)*
South East Manufacturing Co .... F 252 291-0925
  Wilson *(G-16542)*
Southeastern Enterprises .... F 704 373-1750
  Charlotte *(G-3589)*
Southeastern Mch & Wldg Co Inc .... E 910 791-6661
  Wilmington *(G-16410)*
◆ Southeastern Tool & Die Inc .... D 910 944-7677
  Aberdeen *(G-29)*
Southern Machine Services .... G 919 658-9300
  Mount Olive *(G-11668)*
Southern Prestige Industries Inc .... E 704 872-9524
  Statesville *(G-14893)*
Southern Prestige Intl LLC .... F 704 872-9524
  Statesville *(G-14894)*

36 ELECTRONIC & OTHER ELECTRICAL EQUIPMENT & COMPONENTS

Special Fab & Machine Inc.................... E 336 956-2121
   Lexington *(G-9784)*

Specialty Perf LLC.................................. G 704 872-9980
   Statesville *(G-14897)*

Speedwell Machine Works Inc............... E 704 866-7418
   Gastonia *(G-6512)*

Sphenodon Tool Co Inc.......................... G 252 757-3460
   Greenville *(G-7586)*

Spm Machine Works Inc........................ G 252 321-2134
   Ayden *(G-859)*

Square One Machine LLC....................... G 704 600-6296
   Shelby *(G-14370)*

Stine Gear & Machine Company............ F 704 445-1245
   Bessemer City *(G-1084)*

Stovers Precision Tooling Inc................ G 704 876-3673
   Statesville *(G-14907)*

Stump and Grind LLC............................. G 704 488-2271
   Charlotte *(G-3643)*

Sun Valley Stl Fabrication Inc............... F 704 289-5830
   Monroe *(G-10817)*

Superior Machine Co SC Inc.................. E 828 652-6141
   Marion *(G-10181)*

Superior Machine Shop Inc................... F 910 675-1336
   Rocky Point *(G-13752)*

Sweettader Custom Composites............ G 910 262-6650
   Wilmington *(G-16424)*

▲ Syntegon Technology Svcs LLC......... E 919 877-0886
   Raleigh *(G-13321)*

T D M Corporation................................... E
   Fletcher *(G-6044)*

T Hoff Manufacturing Corp.................... G 919 833-8671
   Raleigh *(G-13322)*

▲ T Precision Machining Inc.................. E 828 250-0993
   Asheville *(G-793)*

Tak Cnc LLC.. G 336 506-7775
   Elon *(G-5661)*

Tar Heel Tling Prcsion McHning............ E 919 965-6160
   Smithfield *(G-14486)*

Tarheel Tool & Gauge LLC..................... E 704 213-6924
   Salisbury *(G-14048)*

Taylor Manufacturing Inc...................... E 910 862-2576
   Elizabethtown *(G-5605)*

Tc Machine &REpair................................ G 336 468-4792
   Boonville *(G-1257)*

▲ Tdc International LLC........................ G 704 875-1198
   Concord *(G-4372)*

Team Industries Inc............................... C 828 837-5377
   Andrews *(G-128)*

Tech-Tool Inc... G 919 906-6229
   Hampstead *(G-7658)*

Textile Designed Machine Co................ F 704 664-1374
   Mooresville *(G-11110)*

Thornburg Machine & Sup Co Inc......... E 704 735-5421
   Lincolnton *(G-9929)*

Tiger Precision Products LLC............... G 714 360-4134
   Mooresville *(G-11113)*

Tigertek Industrial Svcs LLC................. E 336 623-1717
   Stoneville *(G-14970)*

Tilson Machine Inc.................................. D 828 668-4416
   Marion *(G-10182)*

Titeflex Corporation............................... G 647 638-7160
   Charlotte *(G-3697)*

Tmp of Nc Inc.. G 336 463-3225
   Yadkinville *(G-17055)*

Tobe Manufacturing Inc........................ F 910 439-6203
   Mount Gilead *(G-11614)*

Toner Machining Technologies.............. F 828 432-8007
   Morganton *(G-11262)*

Tony D Hildreth..................................... F 910 276-1803
   Laurel Hill *(G-9465)*

Tool Rental Depot LLC............................ G 704 636-6400
   Salisbury *(G-14054)*

Tri-TEC Ind Inc....................................... F 704 424-5995
   Charlotte *(G-3724)*

Triad Fabrication and Mch Inc.............. F 336 993-6042
   Kernersville *(G-9247)*

Triad Precision Products Inc................ F 336 474-0980
   Thomasville *(G-15295)*

Triplett & Coffey Inc............................... F 828 263-0561
   Boone *(G-1243)*

Triumph Tool Nc Inc.............................. E 828 676-3677
   Arden *(G-386)*

Tru-Cast Inc.. E 336 294-2370
   Greensboro *(G-7420)*

True Machine LLC................................... G 919 270-2552
   Oxford *(G-12160)*

Turnamics Inc... E 828 254-1059
   Asheville *(G-807)*

Turnkey Technologies Inc..................... G 704 245-6437
   Salisbury *(G-14056)*

Tyndall Machine Tool Inc...................... G 919 542-4014
   Pittsboro *(G-12352)*

Ultra Machine & Fabrication Inc........... C 704 482-1399
   Shelby *(G-14379)*

Unique Concepts................................... G 919 366-2001
   Garner *(G-6322)*

▲ Unique-Skill Precision Inc................. G 910 393-0090
   Ocean Isle Beach *(G-12095)*

United Machine Works Inc.................... E 252 752-7434
   Greenville *(G-7592)*

United Technical Services LLC............. F 980 237-1335
   Charlotte *(G-3753)*

Universal Machine and Tool Inc........... G 828 659-2002
   Marion *(G-10184)*

Upchurch Machine Co Inc..................... E 704 588-2895
   Charlotte *(G-3757)*

US Metal Crafters LLC........................... E 336 861-2100
   Archdale *(G-301)*

Vendelay Industries LLC....................... G 440 879-8363
   Wendell *(G-15922)*

Viewriver Machine Corporation............ E 336 463-2311
   Yadkinville *(G-17061)*

Vortex USA Inc....................................... F 972 410-3619
   Cornelius *(G-4593)*

W D Lee & Company............................. E 704 864-0346
   Gastonia *(G-6537)*

W H Rgers Shtmtl Ir Wrks Inc.............. E 704 394-2191
   Charlotte *(G-3788)*

Wallace Spencer.................................... G 704 865-1147
   Gastonia *(G-6538)*

Wallace Welding Inc............................. F 919 934-2488
   Smithfield *(G-14488)*

Weathers Machine Mfg Inc.................. F 919 552-5945
   Fuquay Varina *(G-6238)*

▼ West Side Prcsion Mch Pdts Inc...... F 908 647-4903
   Statesville *(G-14925)*

Wilkes Welding and Mch Co Inc........... G 336 670-2742
   Mc Grady *(G-10382)*

Wilmington Machine Works Inc........... F 910 343-8111
   Wilmington *(G-16447)*

▲ Wilmington Machinery Inc................ E 910 452-5090
   Wilmington *(G-16448)*

Wilson Iron Works Incorporated.......... D 252 291-4465
   Rocky Mount *(G-13677)*

Wilson Machine & Tool Inc................... G 919 776-0043
   Sanford *(G-14207)*

Wilson Machine Sho.............................. G 910 673-3505
   West End *(G-15935)*

▲ Wilson Mold & Machine Corp........... D 252 243-1831
   Wilson *(G-16562)*

Winston Tool Company Inc.................. G 336 983-3722
   King *(G-9286)*

▲ Winterville Machine Works Inc........ D 252 756-2130
   Winterville *(G-17018)*

Woempner Machine Company Inc....... G 336 475-2268
   Thomasville *(G-15303)*

Wood Machine Service Inc................... F 252 446-2142
   Rocky Mount *(G-13742)*

Wooten John.. G 828 322-4031
   Hickory *(G-8210)*

Worth Products LLC.............................. F 252 747-9994
   Snow Hill *(G-14510)*

◆ Wright Machine & Tool Co Inc......... E 828 298-8440
   Swannanoa *(G-15038)*

Wyrick Machine and Tool Co................ G 336 841-8261
   Pleasant Garden *(G-12363)*

▲ Xceldyne Group LLC.......................... D 336 472-2242
   Thomasville *(G-15307)*

Yates American Machine Company...... G 336 685-5118
   Julian *(G-9109)*

Zumco Inc.. F 828 891-3300
   Horse Shoe *(G-8743)*

36 ELECTRONIC & OTHER ELECTRICAL EQUIPMENT & COMPONENTS

3612 Transformers, except electric

Abb Inc.. E 704 587-1362
   Charlotte *(G-2122)*

ABB Enterprise Software Inc................ C 919 582-3283
   Raleigh *(G-12455)*

▲ ABB Holdings Inc................................ D 919 856-2360
   Cary *(G-1673)*

ABB Inc.. E 252 827-2121
   Pinetops *(G-12240)*

ABB Inc.. D 919 856-3920
   Raleigh *(G-12456)*

ABB Inc.. D 919 856-2360
   Raleigh *(G-12457)*

◆ ABB Inc... C 919 856-2360
   Cary *(G-1674)*

ABB Power Systems Inc........................ F 919 856-2389
   Raleigh *(G-12458)*

▼ ABB Power T & D Company Inc........ A 919 856-3806
   Raleigh *(G-12459)*

Abundant Power Solutions LLC............ F 704 271-9890
   Charlotte *(G-2125)*

Alk Investments LLC............................. G 984 233-5353
   Raleigh *(G-12488)*

Aprotech Powertrain LLC..................... E 828 253-1350
   Asheville *(G-526)*

Ced Incorporated................................... F 336 378-0044
   Greensboro *(G-6897)*

Eaton Corporation................................. B 828 684-2381
   Arden *(G-326)*

▲ Impulse NC LLC................................. E 919 658-2311
   Mount Olive *(G-11662)*

▲ Instrument Trans Eqp Corp.............. D 704 282-4331
   Monroe *(G-10739)*

Itec.. F 704 282-4331
   Monroe *(G-10741)*

▲ Liburdi Dimetrics Corporation.......... E 704 230-2510
   Mooresville *(G-11007)*

▲ Manufacturing Systems Eqp Inc....... F 704 283-2086
   Monroe *(G-10764)*

Nwl Inc.. E 252 747-5943
   Snow Hill *(G-14505)*

Pennsylvania Trans Tech Inc............... D 910 875-7600
   Raeford *(G-12431)*

Philpott Motors Ltd............................... F 704 566-2400
   Charlotte *(G-3337)*

Power Integrity Corp............................. E 336 379-9773
   Greensboro *(G-7269)*

Separation Technologies LLC............... C 336 597-9814
   Semora *(G-14265)*

36 ELECTRONIC & OTHER ELECTRICAL EQUIPMENT & COMPONENTS

◆ Smartrac Tech Fletcher Inc............C..... 828 651-6051
Fletcher (G-6041)

Trans East Inc............................D..... 910 892-1081
Dunn (G-4887)

Transformer Sales & Service............G..... 910 594-1495
Newton Grove (G-11994)

3613 Switchgear and switchboard apparatus

Abb Inc.....................................E..... 704 587-1362
Charlotte (G-2122)

ABB Enterprise Software Inc............C..... 919 582-3283
Raleigh (G-12455)

ABB Inc.....................................A..... 252 827-2121
Pinetops (G-12239)

ABB Inc.....................................D..... 919 856-2360
Raleigh (G-12457)

◆ ABB Inc..................................C..... 919 856-2360
Cary (G-1674)

Acroplis Cntrls Engineers Pllc..........F..... 919 275-3884
Raleigh (G-12473)

American Moistening Co Inc............F..... 704 889-7281
Pineville (G-12252)

Brooks Manufacturing Solutions........F..... 336 438-1280
Graham (G-6681)

Brooks Mfg Solutions Inc...............F..... 336 438-1280
Burlington (G-1379)

◆ Carolina Elctrnic Assmblers In......E..... 919 938-1086
Smithfield (G-14452)

Carolina Products Inc....................E..... 704 364-9029
Charlotte (G-2403)

Cooper Bussmann LLC..................C..... 252 566-0278
La Grange (G-9438)

▲ Dna Group Inc..........................E..... 919 881-0889
Raleigh (G-12690)

Eaton Corporation........................B..... 828 684-2381
Arden (G-326)

Electro Switch Corp......................C..... 919 833-0707
Raleigh (G-12730)

◆ Elster American Meter Company LLC.F..... 402 873-8200
Charlotte (G-2700)

Elster Solutions LLC.....................B..... 919 212-4819
Raleigh (G-12733)

Gasp Inc..................................G..... 828 891-1628
Fletcher (G-6007)

General Electric Company..............G..... 704 561-5700
Charlotte (G-2817)

General Electric Company..............B..... 919 563-5561
Mebane (G-10411)

Glh Systems & Controls Inc............G..... 980 581-1304
Stanfield (G-14679)

▲ Grecon Inc..............................F..... 503 641-7731
Charlotte (G-2862)

Industrial Cnnctons Sltons LLC........E..... 203 229-3932
Cary (G-1787)

Industrial Control Panels Inc...........G..... 336 661-3037
Winston Salem (G-16758)

Industrial Panel Company LLC........E..... 866 736-1290
Burlington (G-1437)

Industrial Panel Company LLC........G..... 866 736-1290
Burlington (G-1436)

Interstate All Batteries Ctr..............G..... 704 979-3430
Concord (G-4288)

JA Smith Inc..............................G..... 704 860-4910
Lawndale (G-9500)

▲ JMS Southeast Inc....................E..... 704 873-1835
Statesville (G-14825)

Miller Ctrl Mfg Inc Clinton NC..........G..... 910 592-5112
Clinton (G-4098)

▲ Precision Mch Fabrication Inc......D..... 919 231-8468
Raleigh (G-13134)

▲ Precision Time Systems Inc........F..... 910 253-9850
Supply (G-15008)

PSI Control Solutions LLC..............E..... 704 596-5617
Charlotte (G-3393)

R S Integrators Inc......................G..... 704 588-8288
Pineville (G-12294)

▲ Reuel Inc...............................E..... 919 734-0460
Goldsboro (G-6650)

Schneider Electric Usa Inc..............G..... 919 266-3671
Knightdale (G-9428)

Schneider Electric Usa Inc..............C..... 888 778-2733
Morrisville (G-11419)

▲ Shallco Inc.............................E..... 919 934-3135
Smithfield (G-14482)

▲ Shelby Kendrion Inc.................C..... 704 482-9582
Shelby (G-14366)

Short Circuit Audio LLC.................G..... 908 868-7077
Greensboro (G-7336)

▲ Siemens Power Transmissio.......A..... 919 463-8702
Cary (G-1888)

Southern Electrical Eqp Co Inc........G..... 704 392-1396
Indian Trail (G-8964)

Ssi Services Inc..........................G..... 919 867-1450
Raleigh (G-13295)

Tencarva Machinery Company LLC...F..... 336 665-1435
Greensboro (G-7395)

Trimantec..................................E..... 336 767-1379
Winston Salem (G-16952)

▲ Xylem Lnc...............................E..... 704 409-9700
Charlotte (G-3839)

3621 Motors and generators

057 Technology LLC.....................G..... 855 557-7057
Hickory (G-7926)

ABB Motors and Mechanical Inc......G..... 336 272-6104
Greensboro (G-6772)

ABB Motors and Mechanical Inc......B..... 704 734-2500
Kings Mountain (G-9288)

ABB Motors and Mechanical Inc......G..... 479 646-4711
Marion (G-10137)

Alk Investments LLC....................G..... 984 233-5353
Raleigh (G-12488)

Allan Drth Sons Gnrtor Sls Svc........G..... 828 526-9325
Highlands (G-8611)

Alternative Pwr Sls & Rent LLP.......G..... 919 467-8001
Morrisville (G-11284)

Altom Fuel Cells LLC....................G..... 828 231-6889
Leicester (G-9506)

Ao Smith Chatlotte......................G..... 704 597-8910
Charlotte (G-2198)

▲ Ashbran LLC............................G..... 919 215-3567
Clayton (G-3956)

▲ Asmo North America LLC...........A..... 704 872-2319
Statesville (G-14754)

Battlgrund Strter Gnerator Inc........G..... 336 685-4511
Julian (G-9104)

◆ Buehler Motor Inc.....................E..... 919 380-3333
Morrisville (G-11309)

Bwx Technologies Inc...................D..... 980 365-4000
Charlotte (G-2368)

Coastal Carolina Clean Pwr LLC......F..... 910 296-1909
Kenansville (G-9141)

Cummins Inc..............................G..... 704 588-1240
Pineville (G-12264)

Curtiss-Wright Corporation.............B..... 704 869-4600
Davidson (G-4669)

DCS USA Corporation...................G..... 919 535-8000
Morrisville (G-11329)

◆ Denso Manufacturing NC Inc......B..... 704 878-6663
Statesville (G-14786)

▲ Dna Group Inc..........................E..... 919 881-0889
Raleigh (G-12690)

Eaton Corporation........................B..... 828 684-2381
Arden (G-326)

Elnik Systems LLC.......................G..... 973 239-6066
Pineville (G-12267)

Emergency Energy Systems Inc......G..... 910 285-6400
Wallace (G-15622)

Everything Industrial Supply............G..... 743 333-2222
Winston Salem (G-16702)

GE Vernova International LLC.........F..... 704 587-1300
Charlotte (G-2812)

Genelect Services Inc...................G..... 828 255-7999
Asheville (G-632)

Generator Supercenter Raleigh.......G..... 919 925-3434
Raleigh (G-12794)

Global Emssons Systems Inc-USA..G..... 704 585-8490
Troutman (G-15380)

Goldsboro Strter Altrntor Svc.........G..... 919 735-6745
Goldsboro (G-6620)

Greenfield Energy LLC..................F..... 910 509-1805
Wrightsville Beach (G-17025)

Hitachi Energy USA Inc.................C..... 919 856-2360
Raleigh (G-12850)

Hlmf Logistics Inc.......................G..... 704 782-0356
Pineville (G-12273)

Ini Power Systems Inc..................F..... 919 677-7112
Morrisville (G-11359)

Josh Allred...............................G..... 336 873-1006
Seagrove (G-14240)

Lennox International Inc................E..... 828 633-4805
Candler (G-1586)

Li-Ion Motors Corp.......................G..... 704 662-0827
Mooresville (G-11006)

Mikes Core & Battery Inc...............G..... 910 920-4490
Fayetteville (G-5874)

Motor Rite Inc............................F..... 919 625-3653
Raleigh (G-13043)

◆ Ohio Electric Motors Inc.............D..... 828 626-2901
Barnardsville (G-912)

Petty Machine Company Inc..........E..... 704 864-3254
Gastonia (G-6488)

Pinnacle Converting Eqp Inc..........E..... 704 376-3855
Pineville (G-12291)

Powersecure Inc.........................G..... 919 818-8700
Princeton (G-12402)

◆ Powertec Industrial Motors Inc....F..... 704 227-1580
Charlotte (G-3363)

◆ Progress Solar Solutions LLC.....F..... 919 363-3738
Raleigh (G-13150)

R D Tillson & Associates Inc..........G..... 336 454-1410
Jamestown (G-9069)

Regal Rexnord Corporation............F..... 800 825-6544
Charlotte (G-3426)

Rotron Incorporated.....................C..... 336 449-3400
Whitsett (G-16001)

Sag Harbor Industries Inc..............E..... 252 753-7175
Farmville (G-5743)

SCR Controls Inc........................F..... 704 821-6651
Matthews (G-10342)

Siemens Energy Inc.....................C..... 336 969-1351
Rural Hall (G-13853)

Siemens Energy Inc.....................C..... 919 365-2200
Wendell (G-15916)

Siemens Med Solutions USA Inc.....E..... 919 468-7400
Cary (G-1887)

▼ Sirius Energies Corporation........G..... 704 425-6272
Concord (G-4359)

Trane Technologies Company LLC..B..... 336 751-3561
Mocksville (G-10608)

Xavier Power Systems..................F..... 910 734-7813
Lumberton (G-10061)

▲ Xylem Lnc...............................E..... 704 409-9700
Charlotte (G-3839)

3624 Carbon and graphite products

SIC SECTION
36 ELECTRONIC & OTHER ELECTRICAL EQUIPMENT & COMPONENTS

Asbury Graphite Mills............................ G 910 671-4141
 Lumberton (G-10026)
▼ Debotech Inc...................................... C 704 664-1361
 Mooresville (G-10927)
Energy Conversion Syste..................... G 910 892-8081
 Dunn (G-4864)
Morgan Advanced Mtls Tech Inc........... C 910 892-9677
 Dunn (G-4877)
Nouveau Verre Holdings Inc.................. F 336 545-0011
 Greensboro (G-7224)
Nvh Inc... G 336 545-0011
 Greensboro (G-7228)
◆ Pbi Performance Products Inc............D 704 554-3378
 Charlotte (G-3322)
Sgl Inc... G 910 790-3631
 Wilmington (G-16401)
Sgl Carbon LLC................................... G 828 437-3221
 Morganton (G-11251)
◆ Sgl Carbon LLC................................. E 704 593-5100
 Charlotte (G-3533)
Sgl Composites Inc............................... F 704 593-5100
 Charlotte (G-3534)
Sgl Technologies LLC.......................... G 704 593-5100
 Charlotte (G-3535)
Slade Operating Company LLC........... E 704 873-1366
 Statesville (G-14887)
▼ Thanet Inc.. E 704 483-4175
 Denver (G-4807)
Tokai Carbon GE LLC.......................... E 980 260-1130
 Charlotte (G-3705)

3625 Relays and industrial controls

2391 Eatons Ferry Rd Assoc LLC......... G 919 844-0565
 Raleigh (G-12446)
◆ Aalberts Integrated Pipin...................E 704 841-6000
 Charlotte (G-2121)
Abb Inc... E 704 587-1362
 Charlotte (G-2122)
ABB Enterprise Software Inc................. C 919 582-3283
 Raleigh (G-12455)
◆ ABB Inc..C 919 856-2360
 Cary (G-1674)
Abco Automation Inc............................. C 336 375-6400
 Browns Summit (G-1298)
Abco Controls and Eqp Inc................... G 704 394-2424
 Charlotte (G-2123)
▲ AC Corporation.................................. B 336 273-4472
 Greensboro (G-6775)
Aiken Development LLC...................... G 828 572-4040
 Lenoir (G-9568)
Alan R Williams Inc............................... E 704 372-8281
 Charlotte (G-2151)
Alcon Components Usa Inc.................. G 704 799-2723
 Mooresville (G-10852)
Ambient Noise Control LLC.................. G 919 477-6791
 Durham (G-4914)
▲ CMC Sencon Inc................................ E 919 938-3216
 Smithfield (G-14456)
Cross Technologies Inc........................ E 800 327-7467
 Greensboro (G-6942)
Curtiss-Wright Controls Inc................... E 704 869-2300
 Shelby (G-14305)
Custom Controls Unlimited LLC........... F 919 812-6553
 Raleigh (G-12664)
Dozier Industrial Electric Inc................. F 252 451-0020
 Rocky Mount (G-13666)
DSI Innovations LLC............................ E 336 893-8385
 Thomasville (G-15216)
◆ Duff-Norton Company Inc..................G 704 588-0510
 Charlotte (G-2656)
Eaton Corporation................................. B 828 684-2381
 Arden (G-326)

Eaton Corporation................................. B 910 677-5375
 Fayetteville (G-5817)
Eaton Corporation................................. C 919 870-3000
 Raleigh (G-12720)
Eaton Scientific Inc............................... G 919 855-9886
 Raleigh (G-12725)
Electro Magnetic Research Inc............. G 919 365-3723
 Zebulon (G-17126)
Envirnmntal Cmfort Sltions Inc.............. E 980 272-7327
 Kannapolis (G-9119)
Fortech Inc.. F 704 333-0621
 Charlotte (G-2790)
General Electric Company.................... F 919 563-7445
 Mebane (G-10410)
General Electric Company.................... B 919 563-5561
 Mebane (G-10411)
▲ Griffin Motion LLC............................. F 919 577-6333
 Apex (G-198)
Healthy Eaton LLC............................... G 980 207-3887
 Charlotte (G-2897)
Hitech Controls Inc............................... G 336 498-1534
 Randleman (G-13472)
◆ Hubbell Industrial Contrls Inc............C 336 434-2800
 Archdale (G-283)
I C E S Gaston County Inc................... G 704 263-1418
 Stanley (G-14697)
ITT LLC.. F 704 716-7600
 Charlotte (G-2999)
ITT LLC.. G 336 662-0113
 Colfax (G-4152)
J&L Manufacturing Inc........................... F 919 801-3219
 Fuquay Varina (G-6206)
JA Smith Inc.. G 704 860-4910
 Lawndale (G-9500)
Linor Technology Inc............................. F 336 485-6199
 Winston Salem (G-16788)
Lynn Electronics Corporation................ G 704 369-0093
 Concord (G-4308)
Masonite Corporation............................ B 704 599-0235
 Charlotte (G-3138)
McKenzie Supply Company.................. G 910 276-1691
 Laurinburg (G-9489)
McNaughton-Mckay Southeast Inc....... F 910 392-0940
 Wilmington (G-16318)
Melltronics Industrial Inc....................... G 704 821-6651
 Matthews (G-10335)
Middlesex Plant..................................... G 252 235-2121
 Middlesex (G-10451)
Miller Ctrl Mfg Inc Clinton NC............... G 910 592-5112
 Clinton (G-4098)
Moog Inc.. B 828 837-5115
 Murphy (G-11713)
Nexjen Systems LLC............................ E 704 969-7070
 Charlotte (G-3255)
Nsi Industries.. D 800 321-5847
 Huntersville (G-8865)
▲ Pro-Tech Inc....................................... G 704 872-6227
 Statesville (G-14870)
Q T Corporation.................................... G 252 399-7600
 Wilson (G-16526)
Rockwell Automation Inc...................... G 919 804-0200
 Cary (G-1872)
Rockwell Automation Inc...................... D 704 665-6000
 Charlotte (G-3456)
Rockwell Automation Inc...................... F 828 652-0074
 Marion (G-10174)
Rockwell Automation Inc...................... F 828 645-4235
 Weaverville (G-15860)
Schneider Electric Usa Inc................... C 919 266-3671
 Knightdale (G-9428)
▲ Shelby Kendrion Inc.......................... C 704 482-9582
 Shelby (G-14366)

◆ Shopbot Tools Inc............................. E 919 680-4800
 Durham (G-5354)
Siemens Industry Inc............................ C 919 365-2200
 Wendell (G-15917)
▲ Siemens Power Transmissio............ A 919 463-8702
 Cary (G-1888)
Silanna Semicdtr N Amer Inc............... D 984 444-6500
 Raleigh (G-13261)
Solvere LLC... E 704 829-1015
 Belmont (G-1008)
Southern Electrical Eqp Co Inc............. G 704 392-1396
 Indian Trail (G-8964)
◆ Southern Electrical Eqp Co Inc......... E 704 392-1396
 Charlotte (G-3593)
State Electric Supply Company............ F 336 855-8200
 Greensboro (G-7367)
▲ Stay Online LLC................................ E 888 346-4688
 Creedmoor (G-4622)
Strandberg Engrg Labs Inc................... F 336 274-3775
 Greensboro (G-7374)
Sure Trip Inc.. F 704 983-4651
 Albemarle (G-110)
Te Connectivity Corporation.................. G 828 338-1000
 Fairview (G-5720)
▲ Textrol Laboratories Inc.................... E 704 764-3400
 Monroe (G-10821)
Total Controls Inc.................................. G 704 821-6341
 Matthews (G-10295)
Trane Technologies Company LLC....... C 910 692-8700
 Southern Pines (G-14558)
Triac Corporation................................... F 336 297-1130
 Greensboro (G-7411)
Triangle Microsystems Inc.................... F 919 878-1880
 Raleigh (G-13359)
Unifour Tech Inc.................................... G 828 256-4962
 Newton (G-11980)
Vance Industrial Elec Inc...................... G 336 570-1992
 Burlington (G-1512)
Vic Panel Sales Division....................... G 336 861-2899
 Archdale (G-303)

3629 Electrical industrial apparatus

3M Company... G 919 774-3808
 Sanford (G-14080)
Ametek Electronics Systems................ E 800 645-9721
 Knightdale (G-9411)
Desco Industries Inc............................. E 919 718-0000
 Sanford (G-14108)
Eaton Corporation................................. D 864 433-1603
 Raleigh (G-12721)
Eaton Corporation................................. C 919 872-3020
 Raleigh (G-12722)
Eaton Power Quality Corp.................... C 919 872-3020
 Raleigh (G-12723)
▲ Eaton Power Quality Group Inc........ F 919 872-3020
 Raleigh (G-12724)
Ensales Electrical Assoc Inc................ F 910 298-3305
 Beulaville (G-1094)
Equagen Engineers Pllc....................... E 919 444-5442
 Raleigh (G-12744)
Exide Technologies LLC...................... G 704 521-8016
 Charlotte (G-2738)
Exide Technologies LLC...................... G 919 553-3578
 Clayton (G-3977)
H C Production Co................................ G 910 483-5267
 Fayetteville (G-5832)
▲ Ifanatic LLC....................................... G 919 387-6062
 Apex (G-203)
◆ Laird Thermal Systems Inc...............E 919 597-7300
 Morrisville (G-11370)
▲ Majorpower Corporation................... E 919 563-6610
 Mebane (G-10418)

Employee Codes: A=Over 500 employees, B=251-500
C=101-250, D=51-100, E=20-50, F=10-19, G=1-9

2024 Harris North Carolina
Manufacturers Directory

36 ELECTRONIC & OTHER ELECTRICAL EQUIPMENT & COMPONENTS

▲ North Fork Electric Inc.................... G..... 336 982-4020
 Crumpler *(G-4629)*

Nwl Inc... E..... 252 747-5943
 Snow Hill *(G-14505)*

Power Integrity Corp......................... E..... 336 379-9773
 Greensboro *(G-7269)*

Powergpu LLC.................................... F..... 919 702-6757
 Youngsville *(G-17092)*

▲ Powersecure International Inc......... A..... 919 556-3056
 Wake Forest *(G-15576)*

◆ Static Control Components Inc.......... A..... 919 774-3808
 Sanford *(G-14191)*

Static Control Ic-Disc Inc.................. E..... 919 774-3808
 Sanford *(G-14192)*

Sturdy Power Corporation LLC......... F..... 910 763-2500
 Wilmington *(G-16421)*

Team Manufacturing - E W LLC........ D..... 919 554-2442
 Youngsville *(G-17105)*

Xpc Corporation................................ F..... 919 210-1756
 Raleigh *(G-13432)*

Xpc Corporation................................ F..... 800 582-4524
 Raleigh *(G-13433)*

3631 Household cooking equipment

Bsh Home Appliances Corp............... E..... 252 636-4454
 New Bern *(G-11779)*

Electrolux Home Products Inc........... B..... 252 527-5100
 Kinston *(G-9363)*

Jebco Inc... E..... 919 557-2001
 Holly Springs *(G-8702)*

Marshall Middleby Inc....................... D..... 919 762-1000
 Fuquay Varina *(G-6212)*

◆ Middleby Marshall Inc....................... C..... 919 762-1000
 Fuquay Varina *(G-6216)*

Weber Stephen Products LLC............ F..... 704 662-0335
 Mooresville *(G-11125)*

Whaley Foodservice LLC................... D..... 704 529-6242
 Charlotte *(G-3809)*

3632 Household refrigerators and freezers

Bsh Home Appliances Corp............... B..... 252 672-9155
 New Bern *(G-11780)*

K2 Scientific LLC............................... F..... 800 218-7613
 Charlotte *(G-3041)*

3634 Electric housewares and fans

▲ Aeroquip Corp.................................. G..... 828 286-4157
 Forest City *(G-6057)*

Airbox LLC.. G..... 855 927-1386
 Statesville *(G-14743)*

Blossman Propane Gas & Appl.......... F..... 828 396-0144
 Hickory *(G-7950)*

Carolina Water Jets........................... G..... 704 853-3663
 Gastonia *(G-6371)*

CPM Acquisition Corp....................... F..... 972 243-8070
 Lexington *(G-9698)*

▲ Dampp-Chaser Electronics Corp....... E..... 828 692-8271
 Hendersonville *(G-7842)*

DNB Humidifier Mfg Inc.................... F..... 336 764-2076
 Winston Salem *(G-16686)*

Grizzly Cookware LLC....................... G..... 704 322-3521
 Charlotte *(G-2870)*

Hamilton Beach Brands Inc............... G..... 252 975-0444
 Washington *(G-15708)*

▲ Madison Manufacturing Company.... D..... 828 622-7500
 Hot Springs *(G-8745)*

▲ Marley Company LLC........................ C..... 704 752-4400
 Charlotte *(G-3128)*

Minka Lighting Inc............................. D..... 704 785-9200
 Concord *(G-4316)*

Puffing Monkey................................... G..... 919 556-7779
 Wake Forest *(G-15578)*

Royal Blunts Connections Inc........... G..... 919 961-4910
 Raleigh *(G-13214)*

Sculptural Arts Coating Inc.............. G..... 336 379-7651
 Greensboro *(G-7328)*

Sun Ovens International Inc............. G..... 630 208-7273
 Wilkesboro *(G-16043)*

▲ Trane US Inc..................................... A..... 704 655-4000
 Davidson *(G-4704)*

▲ Trick Tank Inc................................... G..... 980 406-3200
 Charlotte *(G-3726)*

TTI Floor Care North Amer Inc......... D..... 440 996-2000
 Charlotte *(G-3735)*

3635 Household vacuum cleaners

Clean and Vac................................... G..... 919 753-7951
 Fuquay Varina *(G-6188)*

▲ Vacuum Handling North Amer LLC... E..... 828 327-2290
 Hickory *(G-8201)*

3639 Household appliances, nec

Airborn Industries Inc....................... E..... 704 483-5000
 Lincolnton *(G-9869)*

Best Price Appliance LLC.................. G..... 336 662-3117
 Greensboro *(G-6837)*

Big Vac.. G..... 910 947-3654
 Carthage *(G-1660)*

Bsh Home Appls A Ltd Partnr........... B..... 252 636-4200
 New Bern *(G-11781)*

Crizaf Inc.. G..... 919 251-7661
 Durham *(G-5037)*

McKinney Lwncare Grbage Svc LL.... G..... 828 766-9490
 Spruce Pine *(G-14649)*

Mt Gilead Cut & Sew Inc.................. F..... 910 439-9909
 Mount Gilead *(G-11610)*

Prime Water Services Inc.................. G..... 919 504-1020
 Raleigh *(G-13140)*

Psnc Energy....................................... G..... 919 367-2735
 Apex *(G-235)*

Smartway of Carolinas LLC.............. F..... 704 900-7877
 Charlotte *(G-3566)*

State Industries Inc........................... G..... 704 597-8910
 Charlotte *(G-3625)*

Trash Masher LLC............................. E..... 786 357-2697
 Winston Salem *(G-16946)*

3641 Electric lamps

Acquionics Inc................................... F..... 980 256-5700
 Charlotte *(G-2130)*

▲ Adams Wood Turning Inc.................. G..... 336 882-0196
 High Point *(G-8232)*

Alk Investments LLC......................... G..... 984 233-5353
 Raleigh *(G-12488)*

▲ Arva LLC... G..... 803 336-2230
 Charlotte *(G-2223)*

▲ Fintronx LLC.................................... F..... 919 324-3960
 Raleigh *(G-12767)*

Fixtures & More................................ G..... 828 855-9093
 Hickory *(G-8026)*

Greenlights LLC................................ E..... 919 766-8900
 Cary *(G-1779)*

Hiviz Lighting Inc.............................. G..... 703 382-5675
 Hendersonville *(G-7865)*

Invictus Lighting LLC........................ G..... 828 855-9324
 Hickory *(G-8068)*

◆ Robert Abbey Inc.............................. C..... 828 322-3480
 Hickory *(G-8137)*

Sol-Rex Miniature Lamp Works......... G..... 845 292-1510
 Beaufort *(G-967)*

Sparksmith LLC................................ G..... 828 266-0152
 Waynesville *(G-15827)*

◆ Specialty Manufacturing Inc............. C..... 704 247-9300
 Charlotte *(G-3598)*

◆ Sunnex Inc.. F..... 800 445-7869
 Charlotte *(G-3653)*

Traxon Technologies LLC.................. E..... 201 508-1570
 Charlotte *(G-3719)*

U V Reptile Labs Inc......................... G..... 252 241-4584
 Hubert *(G-8753)*

Variety Consult LLC.......................... G..... 704 275-2284
 Shelby *(G-14380)*

3643 Current-carrying wiring devices

ABB Installation Products Inc........... E..... 828 322-1855
 Hickory *(G-7928)*

Alp Systems Inc................................. F..... 828 454-5164
 Waynesville *(G-15792)*

Amphenol Procom Inc....................... D..... 888 262-7542
 Conover *(G-4416)*

Anything Overstock........................... G..... 828 572-2157
 Lenoir *(G-9574)*

C-Tron Incorporated......................... F..... 919 494-7811
 Franklinton *(G-6151)*

Capital Lghtning Prtection Inc........... G..... 919 832-5574
 Raleigh *(G-12590)*

Coleman Cable LLC........................... E..... 828 389-8013
 Hayesville *(G-7762)*

Commscope Technologies LLC........... A..... 828 324-2200
 Claremont *(G-3916)*

Commscope Technologies LLC........... G..... 828 324-2200
 Hickory *(G-7992)*

Deringer-Ney Inc............................... E..... 828 649-3232
 Marshall *(G-10201)*

▲ Dna Group Inc.................................. E..... 919 881-0889
 Raleigh *(G-12690)*

Eaton Corporation............................. B..... 828 684-2381
 Arden *(G-326)*

Eaton Corporation............................. C..... 919 965-2341
 Selma *(G-14255)*

Erico International Corp.................... G..... 910 944-3355
 Aberdeen *(G-4)*

Hubbell Incorporated......................... E..... 828 687-8505
 Arden *(G-339)*

International Tela-Com Inc............... F..... 828 651-9801
 Fletcher *(G-6013)*

Kearfott Corporation.......................... B..... 828 350-5300
 Black Mountain *(G-1127)*

Leviton Manufacturing Co Inc........... E..... 828 584-1611
 Morganton *(G-11228)*

Leviton Manufacturing Co Inc........... G..... 336 846-3246
 West Jefferson *(G-15942)*

Leviton Town Plant........................... G..... 336 846-3246
 West Jefferson *(G-15943)*

Lightning Prtction Systems LLC........ D..... 252 213-9900
 Raleigh *(G-12971)*

M & M Electric Service Inc............... E..... 704 867-0221
 Gastonia *(G-6448)*

Modern Lightning Protection Co....... F..... 252 756-3006
 Greenville *(G-7561)*

Nsi Holdings Inc................................ F..... 704 439-2420
 Huntersville *(G-8863)*

▲ NSi Holdings Inc................................ F..... 914 664-3542
 Huntersville *(G-8864)*

◆ Nsi Industries LLC............................ D..... 800 321-5847
 Huntersville *(G-8866)*

Pass & Seymour Inc.......................... A..... 315 468-6211
 Concord *(G-4329)*

Preformed Line Products Co.............. C..... 704 983-6161
 Albemarle *(G-99)*

Quality Lghtning Prtection Inc.......... F..... 919 832-9399
 Raleigh *(G-13164)*

▲ Quiktron Inc..................................... F..... 828 327-6009
 Hickory *(G-8131)*

▲ Shelby Kendrion Inc........................... C..... 704 482-9582
 Shelby *(G-14366)*

36 ELECTRONIC & OTHER ELECTRICAL EQUIPMENT & COMPONENTS

Southern Devices Inc .... G 828 584-1611
 Morganton *(G-11256)*
▲ Stay Online LLC .... E 888 346-4688
 Creedmoor *(G-4622)*
▲ Suretech Assembly Inc .... E 919 569-0346
 Youngsville *(G-17103)*
Te Connectivity Corporation .... B 828 338-1000
 Fairview *(G-5719)*
Te Connectivity Corporation .... G 919 557-8425
 Fuquay Varina *(G-6230)*
Te Connectivity Corporation .... F 919 552-3811
 Fuquay Varina *(G-6231)*
Te Connectivity Corporation .... E 336 664-7000
 Winston Salem *(G-16934)*
TEC Graphics Inc .... F 919 567-2077
 Fuquay Varina *(G-6232)*
Tri-City Mechanical Contrs Inc .... D 336 272-9495
 Greensboro *(G-7410)*
Triad Power & Controls Inc .... G 336 375-9780
 Greensboro *(G-7414)*
Vision Technologies Inc .... F 919 387-7878
 Apex *(G-254)*
▲ Wieland Electric Inc .... F 910 259-5050
 Wilmington *(G-16442)*
Wright Electric Inc .... G 704 435-6988
 Cherryville *(G-3878)*

3644 Noncurrent-carrying wiring devices

Austin Company of Greensboro .... C 336 468-2851
 Yadkinville *(G-17031)*
Basalt Specialty Products Inc .... G 336 835-5153
 Elkin *(G-5610)*
Bear Creek Raceway Inc .... G 336 367-4264
 Dobson *(G-4819)*
Carolina Products Inc .... E 704 364-9029
 Charlotte *(G-2403)*
Chase Corporation .... G 828 396-2121
 Granite Falls *(G-6729)*
Chase Corporation .... G 828 726-6023
 Lenoir *(G-9598)*
DMC LLC .... E 980 352-9806
 Concord *(G-4254)*
Erico .... G 704 846-5743
 Charlotte *(G-2727)*
Essex Group Inc .... G 704 921-9605
 Charlotte *(G-2730)*
Hydro Extrusion Usa LLC .... D 336 227-8826
 Burlington *(G-1433)*
Motor Raceways Inc .... G 252 715-3990
 Nags Head *(G-11723)*
Pcore .... F 919 734-0460
 Goldsboro *(G-6643)*
Penn Compression Moulding Inc .... G 919 934-5144
 Smithfield *(G-14476)*
Preformed Line Products Co .... C 704 983-6161
 Albemarle *(G-99)*
Preformed Line Products Co .... G 336 461-3513
 New London *(G-11876)*
Sbrc Hobbies & Raceway LLC .... G 336 782-8420
 Rural Hall *(G-13852)*
▲ Sigma Engineered Solutions PC ..... D 919 773-0011
 Garner *(G-6315)*

3645 Residential lighting fixtures

▲ A M Moore and Company Inc .... G 336 294-6994
 Greensboro *(G-6767)*
▲ Adams Wood Turning Inc .... G 336 882-0196
 High Point *(G-8232)*
◆ Atlas Lighting Products Inc .... C 336 222-9258
 Burlington *(G-1370)*
▲ Clarolux Inc .... E 336 378-6800
 Greensboro *(G-6912)*

◆ Coast Lamp Manufacturing Inc ...... E 828 648-7876
 Canton *(G-1610)*
Doug Bowman Galleries .... G 704 662-5620
 Chimney Rock *(G-3879)*
Egi Associates Inc .... F 704 561-3337
 Charlotte *(G-2687)*
▲ Furnlite Inc .... E 704 538-3193
 Fallston *(G-5729)*
Kings Chandelier Company .... G 336 623-6188
 Eden *(G-5495)*
▲ Oakhurst Company Inc .... G 336 474-4600
 High Point *(G-8468)*
◆ Progress Solar Solutions LLC .... F 919 363-3738
 Raleigh *(G-13150)*
◆ Robert Abbey Inc .... C 828 322-3480
 Hickory *(G-8137)*
Sapps Ventures .... G 910 824-0762
 Raeford *(G-12438)*
Stevens Lighting Inc .... F 910 944-7187
 Carthage *(G-1668)*
◆ Sunnex Inc .... F 800 445-7869
 Charlotte *(G-3653)*
Top Dawg Landscape Inc .... G 336 877-7519
 West Jefferson *(G-15949)*
Ultimate Floor Cleaning .... G 704 912-8978
 Charlotte *(G-3748)*
▲ W F Harris Lighting Inc .... F 704 283-7477
 Monroe *(G-10830)*
◆ Wildwood Lamps & Accents Inc ... E 252 446-3266
 Rocky Mount *(G-13741)*

3646 Commercial lighting fixtures

▲ A M Moore and Company Inc .... G 336 294-6994
 Greensboro *(G-6767)*
▲ Arva LLC .... G 803 336-2230
 Charlotte *(G-2223)*
◆ Atlas Lighting Products Inc .... C 336 222-9258
 Burlington *(G-1370)*
Avcon Inc .... E 919 388-0203
 Cary *(G-1696)*
B&M Donnelly Inc .... G 704 358-9229
 Charlotte *(G-2256)*
Biologcal Innvtion Optmztion S .... F 321 260-2467
 Wake Forest *(G-15533)*
Conservation Station Inc .... G 919 932-9201
 Chapel Hill *(G-2005)*
Enttec Americas LLC .... F 919 200-6468
 Durham *(G-5088)*
Idaho Wood Inc .... F 208 263-9521
 Oxford *(G-12132)*
Invictus Lighting LLC .... G 828 855-9324
 Hickory *(G-8068)*
Kings Chandelier Company .... G 336 623-6188
 Eden *(G-5495)*
▲ Led Lighting Fixtures Inc .... G 919 991-0700
 Morrisville *(G-11373)*
Lighting .... G 919 828-0351
 Raleigh *(G-12970)*
Lumenfocus LLC .... F 252 430-6970
 Henderson *(G-7796)*
Optimum Lighting LLC .... E 508 646-6324
 Henderson *(G-7800)*
◆ Progress Solar Solutions LLC .... F 919 363-3738
 Raleigh *(G-13150)*
Rapid Connector .... G 843 315-4700
 Manteo *(G-10129)*
Rsf Solid State Lighting Inc .... G 252 478-9915
 Spring Hope *(G-14621)*
▲ Shat-R-Shield Lighting Inc .... D 800 223-0853
 Salisbury *(G-14042)*
Shield & Steel Enterprises LLC .... G 704 607-0869
 Salisbury *(G-14043)*

▲ Specialty Lighting LLC .... F 704 538-6522
 Fallston *(G-5730)*
Stevens Lighting Inc .... F 910 944-7187
 Carthage *(G-1668)*
▲ W F Harris Lighting Inc .... F 704 283-7477
 Monroe *(G-10830)*

3647 Vehicular lighting equipment

B/E Aerospace Inc .... F 336 692-8940
 Winston Salem *(G-16612)*
▲ B/E Aerospace Inc .... E 336 747-5000
 Winston Salem *(G-16613)*
Go Ev and Go Green Corp .... G 704 327-9040
 Charlotte *(G-2839)*
Three GS Enterprises Inc .... F 828 696-2060
 Flat Rock *(G-5972)*

3648 Lighting equipment, nec

American Sports Lighting Inc .... G 910 520-1074
 Wilmington *(G-16110)*
▲ Blue Sun Energy Inc .... G 336 218-6707
 Greensboro *(G-6842)*
▲ Busiapp Corporation .... F 877 558-2518
 Morrisville *(G-11311)*
Curlee Machinery Company .... G 919 467-9311
 Cary *(G-1743)*
Cyberlux Corporation .... F 984 363-6894
 Research Triangle Pa *(G-13549)*
Dandy Light Traps Inc .... G 980 223-2744
 Statesville *(G-14782)*
Energizer Holdings Inc .... E 336 672-3526
 Asheboro *(G-431)*
Enttec Americas LLC .... F 919 200-6468
 Durham *(G-5088)*
Epl & Solar Corp .... G 201 577-8966
 Wake Forest *(G-15554)*
Eye Dialogue .... F 704 567-7789
 Charlotte *(G-2740)*
▲ Fg Group Holdings Inc .... F 704 994-8279
 Charlotte *(G-2756)*
▲ Furnlite Inc .... E 704 538-3193
 Fallston *(G-5729)*
Led Integrations .... G 336 257-9935
 Burlington *(G-1449)*
Light Source Usa Inc .... F 704 504-8399
 Charlotte *(G-3087)*
Lightjunction .... G 919 607-9717
 Morrisville *(G-11380)*
▲ M-B Industries Inc .... C 828 862-4201
 Rosman *(G-13786)*
Nexxus Lighting Inc .... E 407 857-9900
 Charlotte *(G-3257)*
Parhelion Incorporated .... F 866 409-1839
 Apex *(G-226)*
PDM Lighting LLC .... G 919 771-3230
 Raleigh *(G-13104)*
Pelican Ventures LLC .... G 919 518-8203
 Raleigh *(G-13105)*
Pentair Water Pool and Spa Inc .... F 919 463-4640
 Cary *(G-1848)*
◆ Pentair Water Pool and Spa Inc ..... A 919 566-8000
 Sanford *(G-14166)*
Powertac Usa Inc .... G 919 239-4470
 Greensboro *(G-7270)*
◆ Progress Solar Solutions LLC .... F 919 363-3738
 Raleigh *(G-13150)*
S C I A Inc .... G 919 387-7000
 Cary *(G-1877)*
Sels Smart ERA Ltg Systems .... G 336 661-8031
 Winston Salem *(G-16901)*
Solacure LLC .... G 336 601-2868
 Browns Summit *(G-1316)*

36 ELECTRONIC & OTHER ELECTRICAL EQUIPMENT & COMPONENTS

◆ Specialty Manufacturing Inc .... C 704 247-9300
Charlotte *(G-3598)*

Srb Technologies Inc .... E 336 659-2610
Winston Salem *(G-16914)*

◆ Sunnex Inc .... F 800 445-7869
Charlotte *(G-3653)*

▲ W F Harris Lighting Inc .... F 704 283-7477
Monroe *(G-10830)*

3651 Household audio and video equipment

522 Flipper LLC .... G 919 785-3417
Raleigh *(G-12448)*

▲ Acoustic Image LLC .... G 919 785-1280
Raleigh *(G-12472)*

Advanced Tech Systems Inc .... F 336 299-6695
Greensboro *(G-6782)*

Anthony Demaria Labs Inc .... F 845 255-4695
Cary *(G-1683)*

Apple Inc .... F 516 318-6744
Cary *(G-1685)*

Cablenc LLC .... G 919 307-9065
Zebulon *(G-17124)*

Carolina Certif Mus Group LLC .... G 984 234-2073
Durham *(G-5000)*

Carr Amplifers .... G 919 545-0747
Pittsboro *(G-12334)*

Carr Amplifiers Inc .... G 919 545-0747
Pittsboro *(G-12335)*

▲ Cary Audio Design LLC .... E 919 355-0010
Raleigh *(G-12605)*

Cco Holdings LLC .... C 828 414-4238
Blowing Rock *(G-1155)*

Cco Holdings LLC .... C 828 355-4149
Boone *(G-1186)*

Cco Holdings LLC .... C 910 292-4083
Dunn *(G-4857)*

Cco Holdings LLC .... C 828 270-7016
Hickory *(G-7973)*

Cco Holdings LLC .... C 919 502-4007
Kenly *(G-9147)*

Cco Holdings LLC .... C 828 394-0635
Lenoir *(G-9597)*

Cco Holdings LLC .... C 704 308-3361
Lincolnton *(G-9880)*

Cco Holdings LLC .... C 828 528-4004
Newland *(G-11883)*

Cco Holdings LLC .... C 919 200-6260
Siler City *(G-14402)*

Cco Holdings LLC .... C 828 368-4161
Valdese *(G-15445)*

Cymbal LLC .... G 877 365-9622
Cary *(G-1744)*

East Coast Digital Inc .... F 919 304-1142
Mebane *(G-10408)*

Eastern Sun Communications Inc .... G 704 408-7668
Charlotte *(G-2674)*

▼ Evolution Technologies Inc .... G 919 544-3777
Raleigh *(G-12752)*

Fairfield Pro AV Inc .... F 214 375-8570
Charlotte *(G-2746)*

▲ Hartley Loudspeakers Inc .... F 910 392-1200
Wilmington *(G-16248)*

Hartley Products Corp .... G 910 392-0500
Wilmington *(G-16249)*

Integrated Info Systems Inc .... F 919 488-5000
Youngsville *(G-17086)*

JPS Communications Inc .... D 919 534-1168
Raleigh *(G-12923)*

Linor Technology Inc .... F 336 485-6199
Winston Salem *(G-16788)*

Moon Audio .... G 919 649-5018
Cary *(G-1826)*

▲ Multi Technical Services Inc .... G 919 553-2995
Clayton *(G-4000)*

Oberle Group .... G 336 399-6833
Pfafftown *(G-12189)*

Ocean 10 Security LLC .... F 828 484-1481
Asheville *(G-714)*

Palmer Senn .... G 704 451-3971
Charlotte *(G-3309)*

PC Satellite Solutions .... G 252 217-7237
Roper *(G-13770)*

Secure Canopy LLC .... G 980 322-0590
Albemarle *(G-104)*

Signal Path International LLC .... G 704 391-9337
Matthews *(G-10290)*

Unique Home Theater Inc .... G 704 787-3239
Concord *(G-4382)*

▲ Wheatstone Corporation .... D 252 638-7000
New Bern *(G-11855)*

Worldwide Entrmt Mltimedia LLC .... G 704 208-6113
Charlotte *(G-3826)*

3652 Prerecorded records and tapes

American Multimedia Inc .... G 336 229-7101
Burlington *(G-1364)*

▲ Cda Inc C
Charlotte *(G-2434)*

Digi Ronin Games LLC .... G 919 845-9960
Raleigh *(G-12683)*

Digital Recorders Inc .... C 919 361-2155
Morrisville *(G-11331)*

Merge Media Ltd .... F 919 688-9969
Chapel Hill *(G-2041)*

Operable Inc .... G 757 617-0935
Wake Forest *(G-15575)*

Puny Human LLC .... F 919 420-4538
Raleigh *(G-13158)*

Reel-Scout Inc .... G 704 348-1484
Charlotte *(G-3425)*

Robert Wrren MBL TV Prductions .... G 910 483-4777
Eastover *(G-5482)*

SMC Corporation of America .... F 704 947-7556
Huntersville *(G-8897)*

Snowman Software .... G 888 918-4384
Durham *(G-5360)*

Sony Music Holdings Inc .... G 336 886-1807
High Point *(G-8542)*

Talking Devices Company .... G 828 658-0660
Asheville *(G-795)*

Technolio Inc .... G 919 481-4454
Morrisville *(G-11440)*

Turnsmith LLC .... G 919 667-9804
Chapel Hill *(G-2085)*

Ultimix Records .... G 336 288-7566
Greensboro *(G-7426)*

Virscidian Inc .... G 919 809-7651
Cary *(G-1921)*

Xdri Inc .... G 919 361-2155
Durham *(G-5454)*

Yellow Rubber Ball LLC .... G 919 357-6307
Durham *(G-5458)*

3661 Telephone and telegraph apparatus

Abacon Telecommunications LLC .... E 336 855-1179
Greensboro *(G-6771)*

Alcatel Dunkermotoren .... G 704 782-0691
Concord *(G-4190)*

Amphenol Procom Inc .... D 888 262-7542
Conover *(G-4416)*

Andrea L Grizzle .... G 252 202-3278
Moyock *(G-11691)*

◆ Arris Solutions LLC .... A 678 473-2000
Hickory *(G-7943)*

Atcom Inc .... F 704 357-7900
Charlotte *(G-2230)*

Avaya LLC .... B 919 425-8268
Research Triangle Pa *(G-13548)*

Bluejay Enterprises Group Inc .... G 866 670-8811
Charlotte *(G-2323)*

Code LLC .... E 828 328-6004
Hickory *(G-7987)*

Commscope Technologies LLC .... A 828 324-2200
Claremont *(G-3916)*

◆ Conversant Products Inc .... F 919 465-3456
Cary *(G-1734)*

Corning Incorporated .... F 252 316-4500
Tarboro *(G-15100)*

Corning Optcal Cmmncations LLC .... C 828 901-5000
Charlotte *(G-2557)*

◆ Corning Optcal Cmmncations LLC .... A 828 901-5000
Charlotte *(G-2556)*

Edge Broadband Solutions LLC .... E 828 785-1420
Waynesville *(G-15803)*

▲ Emrise Corporation .... C 408 200-3040
Durham *(G-5084)*

◆ Extreme Networks Inc .... B 408 579-2800
Morrisville *(G-11339)*

Fiberlink .... F 901 826-8126
Troutman *(G-15376)*

Fiberlink Inc .... G 828 274-5629
Asheville *(G-620)*

▲ Hatteras Networks Inc .... E 919 991-5440
Morrisville *(G-11352)*

JPS Communications Inc .... D 919 534-1168
Raleigh *(G-12923)*

Lba Group Inc .... E 252 329-9243
Greenville *(G-7553)*

◆ Lba Technology Inc .... E 252 757-0279
Greenville *(G-7554)*

▲ Newton Instrument Company .... C 919 575-6426
Butner *(G-1546)*

◆ Nexans USA Inc .... B 828 323-2660
Hickory *(G-8102)*

Nvent Thermal LLC .... A 919 552-3811
Fuquay Varina *(G-6218)*

Pakaraima Fiber Optics Inc .... G 704 671-2229
Gastonia *(G-6482)*

▲ Personal Communication Sy .... D 336 722-4917
Winston Salem *(G-16846)*

Photon Energy Corp .... G 888 336-8128
Asheville *(G-729)*

Prime Wire and Cable .... G 704 799-6000
Mooresville *(G-11061)*

R E Mason Enterprises Inc .... G 910 483-5016
Fayetteville *(G-5904)*

Siemens Airport .... E 704 359-5551
Charlotte *(G-3546)*

Siemens Corporation .... G 919 465-1287
Cary *(G-1886)*

◆ Southern Elc & Automtn Corp .... F 919 718-0122
Sanford *(G-14187)*

▲ Spectrasite Communications LLC .... E 919 468-0112
Cary *(G-1900)*

▲ Tekelec Inc C
Morrisville *(G-11442)*

Tekelec Global Inc .... A 919 460-5500
Morrisville *(G-11443)*

Tellad Supply Company .... G 919 572-6700
Durham *(G-5392)*

Trimm International Inc .... E 847 362-3700
Youngsville *(G-17110)*

Usat LLC .... E 919 942-4214
Chapel Hill *(G-2091)*

Uteck .... F 910 483-5016
Fayetteville *(G-5946)*

36 ELECTRONIC & OTHER ELECTRICAL EQUIPMENT & COMPONENTS

3663 Radio and t.v. communications equipment

5 Star Satellite Inc .... G 910 584-4354
  Fayetteville (G-5747)
Advintech Inc .... G 336 327-2666
  Liberty (G-9804)
Akoustis Technologies Inc .... C 704 997-5735
  Huntersville (G-8787)
▲ Amphenol Antenna Solutions .... E 828 324-6971
  Conover (G-4415)
Apple Inc .... F 516 318-6744
  Cary (G-1685)
Arris Global Services Inc .... E 215 323-1000
  Hickory (G-7942)
◆ Arris Solutions LLC .... A 678 473-2000
  Hickory (G-7943)
Ascom (us) Inc .... C 877 712-7266
  Morrisville (G-11293)
Audio Advice Inc .... D 919 881-2005
  Raleigh (G-12534)
▲ Avl Technologies Inc .... D 828 250-9950
  Asheville (G-553)
Bae Systems Info Elctrnic Syst .... E 919 323-5800
  Durham (G-4941)
Bahakel Communications Ltd LLC .... B 704 372-4434
  Charlotte (G-2264)
Brandywine Communications .... G 770 853-1799
  Wake Forest (G-15535)
Cable Devices Incorporated .... F 704 588-0859
  Charlotte (G-2375)
Cable Devices Incorporated .... F 704 588-0859
  Pineville (G-12258)
Carolina Design & Mfg Inc .... G 919 554-1823
  Louisburg (G-9982)
Carolina Unplugged .... G 336 965-4443
  Greensboro (G-6891)
CBS Radio Holdings Inc .... E 704 319-9369
  Charlotte (G-2424)
Cco Holdings LLC .... C 828 414-4238
  Blowing Rock (G-1155)
Cco Holdings LLC .... C 828 355-4149
  Boone (G-1186)
Cco Holdings LLC .... C 910 292-4083
  Dunn (G-4857)
Cco Holdings LLC .... C 828 270-7016
  Hickory (G-7973)
Cco Holdings LLC .... C 919 502-4007
  Kenly (G-9147)
Cco Holdings LLC .... C 828 394-0635
  Lenoir (G-9597)
Cco Holdings LLC .... C 704 308-3361
  Lincolnton (G-9880)
Cco Holdings LLC .... C 828 528-4004
  Newland (G-11883)
Cco Holdings LLC .... C 919 200-6260
  Siler City (G-14402)
Cco Holdings LLC .... C 828 368-4161
  Valdese (G-15445)
Commscope Inc North Carolina .... G 828 459-5001
  Claremont (G-3908)
Commscope Inc North Carolina .... F 828 324-2200
  Hickory (G-7989)
Commscope Inc North Carolina .... F 828 466-8600
  Newton (G-11922)
◆ Commscope Inc North Carolina ...... D 828 324-2200
  Claremont (G-3909)
Commscope LLC .... C 828 324-2200
  Claremont (G-3911)
Commscope Cnnctvity Sltons LLC .... F 828 324-2200
  Hickory (G-7990)

Commscope Connectivity LLC .... E 828 324-2200
  Claremont (G-3912)
Commscope Dsl Systems LLC .... D 828 324-2200
  Hickory (G-7991)
Commscope Holding Company Inc ...... A 828 459-5000
  Claremont (G-3913)
Commscope Intl Holdings LLC .... E 828 324-2200
  Claremont (G-3914)
Commscope Technologies Fin LLC ..... F 828 323-4970
  Claremont (G-3915)
Commscope Technologies LLC .... F 919 329-8700
  Garner (G-6266)
Commscope Technologies LLC .... E 336 665-6000
  Greensboro (G-6926)
Commscope Technologies LLC .... F 919 934-9711
  Smithfield (G-14457)
Communications & Pwr Inds LLC .... G 828 241-5735
  Catawba (G-1963)
CPI Satcom & Antenna Tech Inc .... C 704 462-7330
  Conover (G-4440)
◆ CPI Satcom & Antenna Tech Inc ..... E 704 462-7330
  Conover (G-4441)
▲ Crest Electronics Inc .... F 336 855-6422
  Greensboro (G-6940)
Dexterity LLC .... F 919 524-7732
  Greenville (G-7514)
Edge Broadband Solutions LLC .... E 828 785-1420
  Waynesville (G-15803)
Flexview Systems LLC .... G 704 644-3079
  Charlotte (G-2778)
General Dynmics Mssion Systems ...... C 336 323-9752
  Greensboro (G-7034)
Gigabeam Corporation .... F 919 206-4426
  Durham (G-5114)
Golfstar Technology LLC .... G 910 420-3122
  Pinehurst (G-12224)
Gpx Intelligence Inc .... E 888 260-0706
  Greensboro (G-7055)
Itron Inc .... D 919 876-2600
  Raleigh (G-12905)
JPS Communications Inc .... D 919 534-1168
  Raleigh (G-12923)
JPS Intrprbility Solutions Inc .... F 919 332-5009
  Raleigh (G-12924)
Lba Group Inc .... E 252 329-9243
  Greenville (G-7553)
◆ Lba Technology Inc .... E 252 757-0279
  Greenville (G-7554)
Lcf Enterprise .... G 208 415-4300
  Hickory (G-8085)
Lea Aid Acquisition Company .... F 919 872-6210
  Raleigh (G-12963)
Lets Talk Some Shit .... G 704 264-6212
  Paw Creek (G-12172)
Little River Yachts LLC .... G 828 323-4955
  Hickory (G-8087)
Lunar International Tech LLC .... F 800 975-7153
  Charlotte (G-3109)
McShan Inc .... G 980 355-9790
  Charlotte (G-3154)
Motorola Mobility LLC .... E 919 294-1289
  Morrisville (G-11391)
▲ Multi Technical Services Inc .... G 919 553-2995
  Clayton (G-4000)
Ni4l Antennas and Elec LLC .... G 828 738-6445
  Moravian Falls (G-11146)
Pendulum Electromagnetics Inc .... F 919 571-9970
  Raleigh (G-13106)
Qualcomm Incorporated .... G 336 323-3300
  Clemmons (G-4056)
Qualia Networks Inc .... G 805 637-2083
  Raleigh (G-13162)

◆ Raven Antenna Systems Inc .... C 919 934-9711
  Smithfield (G-14478)
Rf Das Systems Inc .... G 980 279-2388
  Charlotte (G-3446)
Ruckus Wireless Inc .... B 919 677-0571
  Cary (G-1875)
Sbg Digital Inc .... G 828 476-0030
  Waynesville (G-15821)
Seamless Satellite Solutions .... E 828 421-8988
  Franklin (G-6142)
Serra Wireless Inc .... G 980 318-0873
  Charlotte (G-3529)
Shadowtrack 247 LLC .... F 828 398-0980
  Fletcher (G-6038)
Sierra Nevada Corporation .... E 910 307-0362
  Fayetteville (G-5915)
Swir Vision Systems Inc .... E 919 248-0032
  Durham (G-5383)
T-Metrics Inc .... E 704 523-9583
  Charlotte (G-3669)
Tabur Services .... G 704 483-1650
  Denver (G-4805)
Tarheel Monitoring LLC .... G 910 763-1490
  Wilmington (G-16426)
Teletec Corporation .... F 919 954-7300
  Raleigh (G-13338)
Thompson Sunny Acres Inc .... G 910 206-1801
  Rockingham (G-13644)
Triton Marine Services Inc .... G 252 728-9958
  Beaufort (G-969)
Universal Mania Inc .... G 866 903-0852
  Fayetteville (G-5940)
Vextra Technologies LLC .... G 828 464-4419
  Claremont (G-3942)
▲ Wheatstone Corporation .... D 252 638-7000
  New Bern (G-11855)
Wirenet Inc .... E 513 774-7759
  Huntersville (G-8906)

3669 Communications equipment, nec

3 Alarm Smoke Detector Svcs .... G 757 636-6773
  Currituck (G-4632)
Acn Opportunity Delaware LLC .... G 704 260-3000
  Concord (G-4187)
Acterna LLC .... F 919 388-5100
  Morrisville (G-11277)
Ademco Inc .... G 704 525-8899
  Charlotte (G-2137)
Ademco Inc .... G 336 668-3644
  Greensboro (G-6779)
Ademco Inc .... G 919 872-5556
  Raleigh (G-12476)
AFA Billing Services .... G 910 868-8324
  Fayetteville (G-5755)
Amplified Elctronic Design Inc .... F 336 223-4811
  Greensboro (G-6806)
▲ Argus Fire CONtrol-Pf&s Inc .... E 704 372-1228
  Charlotte (G-2215)
▲ C & S Antennas Inc .... F 828 324-2454
  Conover (G-4427)
Carolina Pwr Signalization LLC .... E 910 323-5589
  Fayetteville (G-5784)
Carrier Fire SEC Americas Corp .... E 919 563-5911
  Mebane (G-10404)
▲ Elk Products Inc .... E 828 397-4200
  Connelly Springs (G-4400)
Envision Inc .... G 919 832-8962
  Raleigh (G-12743)
Flat Water Corp .... G 704 584-7764
  Charlotte (G-2771)
Fulcher Elc Fayetteville Inc .... E 910 483-7772
  Fayetteville (G-5829)

36 ELECTRONIC & OTHER ELECTRICAL EQUIPMENT & COMPONENTS

General Dynmcs Mssion Systems............ C 336 698-8000
  Mc Leansville *(G-10391)*
Johnson Controls.. C 704 501-0500
  Charlotte *(G-3029)*
▼ Kidde Technologies Inc............................. B 252 237-7004
  Wilson *(G-16508)*
▲ New Innovative Products Inc..................... G 919 631-6759
  Pine Level *(G-12212)*
Pomdevices LLC... F 919 200-6538
  Durham *(G-5294)*
Preferred Communication Inc..................... G 919 575-4600
  Butner *(G-1548)*
R & J Road Service Inc.............................. C 252 239-1404
  Lucama *(G-10018)*
Roadmasters Traffic Ctrl LLC....................... G 704 585-9635
  Statesville *(G-14877)*
Romeo Six LLC.. F 919 589-7150
  Holly Springs *(G-8713)*
▲ Safe Fire Detection Inc............................. F 704 821-7920
  Monroe *(G-10801)*
Safeguard Medical Alarms Inc.................... G 312 506-2900
  Harrisburg *(G-7727)*
Seal Innovation Inc...................................... F 919 302-7870
  Raleigh *(G-13240)*
Secured Traffic Control LLC........................ G 910 233-8148
  Wilmington *(G-16398)*
Simplyhome LLC.. F 828 684-8441
  Arden *(G-376)*
Squarehead Technology LLC....................... G 571 299-4849
  Hickory *(G-8167)*
◆ Tektone Sound & Signal Mfg Inc............ D 828 524-9967
  Franklin *(G-6145)*
Telephonics Corporation............................. G 631 755-7446
  Elizabeth City *(G-5577)*
◆ Walter Kidde Portable Eqp Inc............... B 919 563-5911
  Mebane *(G-10435)*
Wilmington Trffic Neighborhood............... G 910 341-7888
  Wilmington *(G-16455)*

3671 Electron tubes

▲ Advanced Digital Cable Inc..................... E 828 389-1652
  Hayesville *(G-7759)*
Communications & Pwr Inds LLC................ E 650 846-2900
  Conover *(G-4437)*
Ecoatm LLC.. E 858 324-4111
  Boone *(G-1195)*
Electropin Technologies LLC....................... G 919 288-1203
  Goldsboro *(G-6612)*
Tactical Support Equipment Inc................... F 910 425-3360
  Fayetteville *(G-5924)*
Vintage Vacuum Tubes LLC........................ G 336 688-7443
  Burlington *(G-1513)*
Xintek Inc.. F 919 449-5799
  Chapel Hill *(G-2102)*

3672 Printed circuit boards

615 Alton Place LLC................................... G 336 431-4487
  High Point *(G-8228)*
American Circuits Inc................................. E 704 376-2800
  Charlotte *(G-2180)*
▲ Assembly Technologies Inc..................... F 704 596-3903
  Charlotte *(G-2228)*
BEC... G 919 244-0831
  Holly Springs *(G-8689)*
C-Tron Incorporated.................................. F 919 494-7811
  Franklinton *(G-6151)*
Circuit Board Assemblers Inc..................... C 919 556-7881
  Youngsville *(G-17077)*
▲ Cml Micro Circuit USA........................... E 336 744-5050
  Winston Salem *(G-16656)*
Ferguson Manufacturing Company............ F 336 661-1116
  Winston Salem *(G-16709)*

Flextronics Corporation.............................. G 704 598-3300
  Charlotte *(G-2776)*
Flextronics Intl USA Inc.............................. B 704 509-8700
  Charlotte *(G-2777)*
Flextronics Intl USA Inc.............................. C 919 998-4000
  Morrisville *(G-11341)*
Galaxy Electronics Inc............................... F 704 343-9881
  Charlotte *(G-2803)*
General McRocircuits - E W LLC................ C 704 663-5975
  Mooresville *(G-10956)*
General Microcircuits Inc........................... E 704 663-5975
  Mooresville *(G-10957)*
Global Manufacturing Svcs Inc.................. E 336 846-1674
  West Jefferson *(G-15940)*
▲ Grt Electronics LLC................................ F 919 821-1996
  Raleigh *(G-12823)*
Hitech Circuits Inc.................................... E 336 838-3420
  Indian Trail *(G-8939)*
Jabil Inc... E 828 684-3141
  Arden *(G-343)*
Jabil Inc... G 828 209-4202
  Mills River *(G-10505)*
▲ M & M Technology Inc......................... E 704 882-9432
  Indian Trail *(G-8947)*
▲ Mac Panel Company............................ E 336 861-3100
  High Point *(G-8435)*
Mathis Elec Sls & Svc Inc......................... F 828 274-5925
  Asheville *(G-696)*
Plexus Corp... D 919 807-8000
  Raleigh *(G-13116)*
Protronics Inc.. G 919 217-0007
  Knightdale *(G-9427)*
S M Company Inc..................................... F 828 274-0827
  Asheville *(G-762)*
SBS Diversified Tech Inc........................... F 336 884-5564
  Jamestown *(G-9071)*
Spectrum Integrity Inc.............................. F 805 426-4267
  Trinity *(G-15359)*
▲ Wolfspeed Inc..................................... C 919 407-5300
  Durham *(G-5444)*

3674 Semiconductors and related devices

510nano Inc... F 919 521-5982
  Durham *(G-4894)*
Advanced Micro Devices Inc..................... G 919 840-8080
  Morrisville *(G-11280)*
Agile Microwave Technology Inc............... G 984 228-8001
  Cary *(G-1677)*
Air Control Inc... E 252 492-2300
  Henderson *(G-7775)*
Akoustis Inc... E 704 997-5735
  Huntersville *(G-8786)*
Altera Corporation..................................... G 919 852-1004
  Raleigh *(G-12494)*
Amalfi Semiconductor Inc......................... G 336 664-1233
  Greensboro *(G-6796)*
Amkor Technology Inc.............................. G 919 248-1800
  Durham *(G-4916)*
AMS USA Inc.. E 919 755-2889
  Raleigh *(G-12502)*
Analog Devices Inc................................... G 336 202-6503
  Durham *(G-4918)*
Analog Devices Inc................................... E 336 668-9511
  Greensboro *(G-6807)*
Analog Devices Inc................................... G 919 831-2790
  Raleigh *(G-12504)*
▲ Arva LLC.. G 803 336-2230
  Charlotte *(G-2223)*
ATI Industrial Automation Inc.................... C 919 772-0115
  Apex *(G-167)*
Avago Technology..................................... G 704 887-7735
  Charlotte *(G-2245)*

Broadcom Corporation............................... D 919 865-2954
  Durham *(G-4981)*
▲ Brumley/South Inc................................ G 704 664-9251
  Mooresville *(G-10889)*
▲ Cml Micro Circuit USA........................... E 336 744-5050
  Winston Salem *(G-16656)*
Convergent Integration Inc........................ G 704 516-5922
  Charlotte *(G-2547)*
Corning Incorporated................................. F 252 316-4500
  Tarboro *(G-15100)*
Cortina Systems... G 919 226-1800
  Morrisville *(G-11325)*
Creeled Inc.. B 919 313-5330
  Durham *(G-5035)*
Disco Hi-TEC America Inc........................ G 919 468-6003
  Morrisville *(G-11332)*
Entropy Solar Integrators LLC................... G 704 936-5018
  Charlotte *(G-2716)*
Flexgen Power Systems Inc...................... G 855 327-5674
  Durham *(G-5100)*
Flexgen Power Systems Inc...................... F 855 327-5674
  Durham *(G-5101)*
Gainspan Corporation................................ D 408 627-6500
  Morrisville *(G-11345)*
Galaxy Electronics Inc.............................. F 704 343-9881
  Charlotte *(G-2803)*
Ghost Hawk Intel LLC............................... G 910 235-0323
  Pinehurst *(G-12222)*
Guerrilla Rf Inc.. D 336 510-7840
  Greensboro *(G-7071)*
Harris Solar Inc... G 704 490-8374
  Concord *(G-4277)*
▲ Hexatech Inc... F 919 481-4412
  Morrisville *(G-11354)*
Hexatech Inc... G 919 633-0583
  Raleigh *(G-12839)*
Hiviz Led Lighting LLC............................. F 703 662-3458
  Hendersonville *(G-7864)*
Hoffman Materials LLC............................. F 717 243-2011
  Granite Falls *(G-6736)*
Hoffman Materials LLC............................. F 828 212-1669
  Granite Falls *(G-6738)*
◆ Industrial Hard Carbon LLC.................. E 704 489-1488
  Denver *(G-4785)*
Iqe North Carolina LLC............................. G 336 609-6270
  Greensboro *(G-7121)*
Kidde Technologies Inc............................. D 252 237-7004
  Wilson *(G-16506)*
Kidsvidz Productions.................................. G 704 663-4487
  Mooresville *(G-10998)*
▼ Kyma Technologies Inc......................... F 919 789-8880
  Raleigh *(G-12949)*
Larry Shackelford...................................... G 919 467-8817
  Cary *(G-1807)*
Leviton Manufacturing Co Inc................... G 336 846-3246
  West Jefferson *(G-15942)*
Lullicoin LLC... G 336 955-1159
  Charlotte *(G-3108)*
Lumeova Inc.. G 908 229-4651
  Raleigh *(G-12981)*
Macom Technology Solutions Inc............. E 919 807-9100
  Morrisville *(G-11386)*
Marvell Semiconductor Inc........................ C 408 222-2500
  Morrisville *(G-11387)*
Maxtronic Technologies LLC..................... G 704 756-5354
  Charlotte *(G-3147)*
Memoryc Inc.. G 980 224-2875
  Charlotte *(G-3164)*
Memscap Inc... E 919 248-4102
  Durham *(G-5217)*
Micro-OHM Corporation............................ G 800 845-5167
  Raleigh *(G-13026)*

36 ELECTRONIC & OTHER ELECTRICAL EQUIPMENT & COMPONENTS

Microchip Technology Inc .... F 919 844-7510
   Raleigh *(G-13027)*

Micross Advnced Intrcnnect TEC .... E 919 248-1872
   Durham *(G-5224)*

Multisite Led LLC .... G 650 823-7247
   Charlotte *(G-3216)*

Nexperia USA Inc .... G 919 740-6235
   Durham *(G-5246)*

Nhanced Semiconductors Inc .... E 630 561-6813
   Morrisville *(G-11396)*

Nitronex LLC .... E 919 807-9100
   Morrisville *(G-11397)*

Nokia of America Corporation .... G 919 850-6000
   Raleigh *(G-13066)*

North Crlina Rnwable Prpts LLC .... G 407 536-5346
   Raleigh *(G-13071)*

Northrop Grmman Gdnce Elec Inc .... E 704 588-2340
   Charlotte *(G-3270)*

Northstar Computer Tech Inc .... G 980 272-1969
   Monroe *(G-10780)*

Nvidia Corporation .... F 408 486-2000
   Durham *(G-5252)*

Nxp Usa Inc .... G 919 468-3251
   Cary *(G-1834)*

▲ Phononic Inc .... C 919 908-6300
   Durham *(G-5286)*

Poweramerica Institute .... F 919 515-6013
   Raleigh *(G-13122)*

Powersecure Solar LLC .... B 919 213-0798
   Durham *(G-5299)*

Qorvo Inc .... B 336 664-1233
   Greensboro *(G-7294)*

Qorvo Inc .... A 336 664-1233
   Greensboro *(G-7295)*

Qorvo International Holdg Inc .... G 336 664-1233
   Greensboro *(G-7296)*

Qorvo International Svcs Inc .... E 336 664-1233
   Greensboro *(G-7297)*

Qorvo Us Inc .... G 336 662-1150
   Greensboro *(G-7298)*

Qorvo Us Inc .... D 336 931-8298
   Greensboro *(G-7299)*

Qorvo Us Inc .... G 503 615-9000
   Jamestown *(G-9067)*

Qualcomm Datacenter Tech Inc .... D 858 567-1121
   Raleigh *(G-13161)*

Qualia Networks Inc .... G 805 637-2083
   Raleigh *(G-13162)*

▲ Reuel Inc .... E 919 734-0460
   Goldsboro *(G-6650)*

▲ Rf Micro Devices Inc .... A 336 664-1233
   Greensboro *(G-7308)*

Rfhic US Corporation .... G 919 677-8780
   Morrisville *(G-11417)*

Rfmd LLC .... F 336 664-1233
   Greensboro *(G-7309)*

Rfmd Infrstrcture PDT Group In .... E 704 996-2997
   Raleigh *(G-13206)*

Rhino Networks LLC .... E 855 462-9434
   Asheville *(G-755)*

Rt Cardiac Systems Inc .... G 954 908-1074
   Raleigh *(G-13218)*

Samsung Semiconductor Inc .... G 919 380-8483
   Cary *(G-1879)*

Sarda Technologies Inc .... G 919 757-6825
   Durham *(G-5338)*

Silanna Semicdtr N Amer Inc .... D 984 444-6500
   Raleigh *(G-13261)*

♦ Skan US Inc .... F 919 354-6380
   Raleigh *(G-13270)*

Skyworks Solutions Inc .... E 336 291-4200
   Greensboro *(G-7344)*

Telit Wireless Solutions Inc .... D 919 439-7977
   Durham *(G-5391)*

Tfs Inc .... G 919 556-9161
   Wake Forest *(G-15602)*

Thunderbird Technologies Inc .... G 919 481-3239
   Raleigh *(G-13349)*

Triad Semiconductor Inc .... D 336 774-2150
   Winston Salem *(G-16948)*

Viavi Solutions Inc .... G 919 388-5100
   Morrisville *(G-11464)*

Vrg Components Inc .... F 980 244-3862
   Indian Trail *(G-8970)*

Wolfspeed Inc .... G 919 407-5300
   Durham *(G-5443)*

▲ Wolfspeed Inc .... C 919 407-5300
   Durham *(G-5444)*

Wolfspeed Employee Services Co .... F 919 313-5300
   Durham *(G-5445)*

X-Celeprint Inc .... F 919 248-0020
   Durham *(G-5453)*

Xilinx Inc .... F 919 846-3922
   Raleigh *(G-13431)*

▲ Xylem Lnc .... E 704 409-9700
   Charlotte *(G-3839)*

Ziptronix Inc .... F 919 459-2400
   Morrisville *(G-11470)*

3675 Electronic capacitors

ABB Inc .... D 919 856-2360
   Raleigh *(G-12457)*

Global Manufacturing Svcs Inc .... E 336 846-1674
   West Jefferson *(G-15940)*

Hitachi Energy USA Inc .... F 919 324-5403
   Raleigh *(G-12849)*

Hitachi Energy USA Inc .... C 919 856-2360
   Raleigh *(G-12850)*

Kemet Electronics Corporation .... E 864 963-6300
   Shelby *(G-14334)*

LLC Diamond Bell .... G 704 806-4705
   Charlotte *(G-3097)*

M2 Optics Inc .... G 919 342-5619
   Raleigh *(G-12985)*

Nwl Inc .... E 252 747-5943
   Snow Hill *(G-14505)*

▲ Reuel Inc .... E 919 734-0460
   Goldsboro *(G-6650)*

United Chemi-Con Inc .... B 336 384-6903
   Lansing *(G-9456)*

3676 Electronic resistors

Invisible Fencing of Mtn Reg .... G 828 667-8847
   Candler *(G-1584)*

K & L Resources .... G 910 494-3736
   Fayetteville *(G-5852)*

3677 Electronic coils and transformers

Albatross Supply LLC .... G 336 488-1128
   Hamptonville *(G-7665)*

♦ Amiad Filtration Systems Ltd .... E 805 377-0288
   Mooresville *(G-10859)*

Branford Filtration LLC .... D 704 394-2111
   Mooresville *(G-10886)*

Carolina Metals Inc .... E 828 667-0876
   Asheville *(G-582)*

Electronic Products Design Inc .... G 919 365-9199
   Wendell *(G-15901)*

Fueltec Systems LLC .... G 828 212-1141
   Granite Falls *(G-6733)*

Kwik Elc Mtr Sls & Svc Inc .... G 252 335-2524
   Elizabeth City *(G-5553)*

▼ Liquid Process Systems Inc .... G 704 821-1115
   Indian Trail *(G-8945)*

♦ Mann+hmmel Fltrtion Tech US LL ..... C 704 869-3300
   Gastonia *(G-6452)*

♦ Nederman Mikropul Canada Inc .... G 704 998-2606
   Charlotte *(G-3247)*

Peak Demand Inc .... F 252 360-2777
   Wilson *(G-16522)*

Prolec-GE Waukesha Inc .... B 919 734-8900
   Goldsboro *(G-6646)*

PSI Global USA .... C 704 544-1893
   Charlotte *(G-3394)*

▲ Purolator Facet Inc .... E 336 668-4444
   Greensboro *(G-7293)*

Smart Wires Inc .... D 919 294-3999
   Durham *(G-5359)*

3678 Electronic connectors

Amphenol Procom Inc .... D 888 262-7542
   Conover *(G-4416)*

▲ Appalachian Technology LLC .... E 828 210-8888
   Asheville *(G-524)*

Cla Properties LLC .... G 336 476-7828
   Thomasville *(G-15203)*

Coleman Cable LLC .... E 828 389-8013
   Hayesville *(G-7762)*

Crompton Instruments .... G 919 557-8698
   Fuquay Varina *(G-6193)*

Fusion Fiber Optics LLC .... G 252 933-5244
   Kinston *(G-9367)*

▲ Huber + Suhner Inc .... E 704 790-7300
   Charlotte *(G-2928)*

♦ Nexans USA Inc .... B 828 323-2660
   Hickory *(G-8102)*

▲ Southland Electrical Sup LLC .... C 336 227-1486
   Burlington *(G-1498)*

Te Connectivity .... E 336 727-5295
   Winston Salem *(G-16933)*

Te Connectivity Corporation .... B 828 338-1000
   Fairview *(G-5719)*

Te Connectivity Corporation .... G 919 552-3811
   Fuquay Varina *(G-6229)*

Te Connectivity Corporation .... G 919 557-8425
   Fuquay Varina *(G-6230)*

Te Connectivity Corporation .... F 919 552-3811
   Fuquay Varina *(G-6231)*

Te Connectivity Corporation .... E 336 664-7000
   Greensboro *(G-7393)*

Te Connectivity Corporation .... C 336 665-4400
   Greensboro *(G-7394)*

Te Connectivity Corporation .... E 336 664-7000
   Winston Salem *(G-16934)*

Te Connectivity Corporation .... C 336 727-5122
   Winston Salem *(G-16935)*

Tyco Electronics Corporation .... E 336 665-4562
   Greensboro *(G-7424)*

US Conec Ltd .... D 828 323-8883
   Hickory *(G-8198)*

3679 Electronic components, nec

Acterna LLC .... F 919 388-5100
   Morrisville *(G-11277)*

Advanced Substrate .... F 336 285-5955
   Greensboro *(G-6781)*

▲ Anuva Services Inc .... F 919 468-6441
   Morrisville *(G-11288)*

Applied Drives Inc .... G 704 573-2324
   Charlotte *(G-2204)*

▲ Ashbran LLC .... G 919 215-3567
   Clayton *(G-3956)*

Asp Holdings Inc .... G 888 330-2538
   Zebulon *(G-17121)*

♦ Carolina Elctrnic Assmblers In .... E 919 938-1086
   Smithfield *(G-14452)*

36 ELECTRONIC & OTHER ELECTRICAL EQUIPMENT & COMPONENTS

CCS International Circuits LLC .... G 704 907-1208
  Matthews *(G-10239)*
CD Snow Hill LLC .... D 252 747-5943
  Snow Hill *(G-14501)*
◆ Cem Corporation .... C 704 821-7015
  Matthews *(G-10307)*
Click Electronics LLC .... F 704 840-6855
  Raleigh *(G-12628)*
CMS Associates Inc .... G 919 365-0881
  Wendell *(G-15895)*
Cnc-Ke Inc .... D 704 333-0145
  Charlotte *(G-2509)*
◆ Commscope Inc North Carolina .... D 828 324-2200
  Claremont *(G-3909)*
Commscope Technologies LLC .... F 919 934-9711
  Smithfield *(G-14457)*
Communications & Pwr Inds LLC .... E 650 846-2900
  Conover *(G-4437)*
Cooper Crouse-Hinds LLC .... E 252 566-3014
  La Grange *(G-9439)*
Crackle Holdings LP .... A 704 927-7620
  Charlotte *(G-2567)*
Duotech Services Inc .... E 828 369-5411
  Franklin *(G-6126)*
Eclipse Composite Engineering .... E 801 601-8559
  Mooresville *(G-10937)*
Edc Inc .... D 336 993-0468
  Kernersville *(G-9194)*
▲ Emrise Corporation .... C 408 200-3040
  Durham *(G-5084)*
Entergy Group LLC .... G 866 988-8884
  Sanford *(G-14116)*
Ferguson Manufacturing Company .... F 336 661-1116
  Winston Salem *(G-16709)*
▲ Finnord North America Corp .... F 704 723-4913
  Huntersville *(G-8820)*
Geotrak Incorporated .... E 919 303-1467
  Apex *(G-194)*
Globalectronics Inc .... G 919 599-6680
  Raleigh *(G-12806)*
Gocaissoncom .... G 336 454-4610
  Jamestown *(G-9051)*
Hoffman Materials Inc .... E 717 243-2011
  Granite Falls *(G-6737)*
▲ Huber + Suhner Inc .... E 704 790-7300
  Charlotte *(G-2928)*
Innova-Con Incorporated .... E 919 303-1467
  Apex *(G-206)*
Interconnect Products and .... E 336 667-3356
  Wilkesboro *(G-16026)*
▲ Iron Box LLC .... E 919 890-0025
  Raleigh *(G-12901)*
James W McManus Inc .... G 828 688-2560
  Bakersville *(G-884)*
Kratos Antenna Solutions Corp .... G 919 934-9711
  Smithfield *(G-14468)*
▲ Lutze Inc .... E 704 504-0222
  Charlotte *(G-3110)*
▲ Lxd Research & Display LLC .... F 919 600-6440
  Raleigh *(G-12984)*
M2 Optics Inc .... G 919 342-5619
  Raleigh *(G-12985)*
Marmon Holdings Inc .... F 910 291-2571
  Laurinburg *(G-9488)*
▲ Matsusada Precision Inc .... G 704 496-2644
  Charlotte *(G-3142)*
Matthew Laws .... G 828 313-2204
  Granite Falls *(G-6744)*
MTS Systems Corporation .... C 919 677-2352
  Cary *(G-1827)*
Mystery Circuits LLC .... G 919 942-4992
  Chapel Hill *(G-2045)*
Nuvotronics Inc .... D 984 666-3543
  Durham *(G-5251)*
Parker-Hannifin Corporation .... E 704 588-3246
  Charlotte *(G-3315)*
Precision Graphics Inc .... G 252 917-3174
  Snow Hill *(G-14507)*
◆ Protechnologies Inc .... E 336 368-1375
  Pilot Mountain *(G-12200)*
Pt Marketing Incorporated .... E 412 471-8995
  Raleigh *(G-13157)*
◆ QMF Mtal Elctrnic Slutions Inc .... D 336 992-8002
  Kernersville *(G-9227)*
◆ Rostra Precision Controls Inc .... D 910 291-2502
  Aberdeen *(G-27)*
Scion International US .... G 919 570-9303
  Wake Forest *(G-15588)*
▲ Shallco Inc .... E 919 934-3135
  Smithfield *(G-14482)*
Silanna Semicdtr N Amer Inc .... D 984 444-6500
  Raleigh *(G-13261)*
▲ Smallhd LLC .... E 919 439-2166
  Cary *(G-1895)*
Smith Systems Inc .... E 828 884-3490
  Brevard *(G-1289)*
▲ Snap One LLC .... B 704 927-7620
  Charlotte *(G-3569)*
Snap One Holdings Corp .... D 704 927-7620
  Charlotte *(G-3570)*
Spruce Pine Mica Company .... F 828 765-4241
  Spruce Pine *(G-14659)*
▲ Suretech Assembly Inc .... E 919 569-0346
  Youngsville *(G-17103)*
Tecworks Inc .... G 704 829-9700
  Belmont *(G-1015)*
▲ Tresco .... C 361 985-3154
  Boone *(G-1242)*
US Microwave Inc .... G 520 891-2444
  Pittsboro *(G-12353)*
US Prototype Inc .... E 866 239-2848
  Wilmington *(G-16439)*
USA Dreamstone LLC .... G 919 615-4329
  Garner *(G-6323)*
◆ Utility Solutions Inc .... G 828 323-8914
  Hickory *(G-8200)*
▲ Vishay Transducers Ltd .... E 919 365-3800
  Wendell *(G-15924)*
▲ Wieland Electric Inc .... F 910 259-5050
  Wilmington *(G-16442)*

3691 Storage batteries

Associated Battery Company .... F 704 821-8311
  Matthews *(G-10301)*
Clarios LLC .... B 336 761-1550
  Kernersville *(G-9180)*
East Penn Manufacturing Co .... F 336 771-1380
  Winston Salem *(G-16689)*
Energizer Holdings Inc .... E 336 672-3526
  Asheboro *(G-431)*
Enerjali LLC .... G 336 451-6479
  Kernersville *(G-9197)*
Exide .... G 919 357-9845
  Charlotte *(G-2737)*
▲ Lexington Road Properties Inc .... C 336 650-7209
  Winston Salem *(G-16787)*
Magnevolt Inc .... F 919 553-2202
  Clayton *(G-3995)*
Polypore International LP .... D 704 587-8409
  Charlotte *(G-3353)*
Saft America Inc .... B 828 874-4111
  Valdese *(G-15454)*
Smith Utility Buildings .... G 336 957-8211
  Traphill *(G-15327)*

Spectrum Brands Inc .... G 704 658-2060
  Mooresville *(G-11095)*

3692 Primary batteries, dry and wet

Clarios LLC .... B 336 761-1550
  Kernersville *(G-9180)*
Edgewell Per Care Brands LLC .... G 336 672-4500
  Asheboro *(G-427)*
Himcen Battery Inc .... G 408 828-8744
  Apex *(G-202)*
L L C Batteries of N C .... G 919 331-0241
  Angier *(G-143)*
▲ Lexington Road Properties Inc .... C 336 650-7209
  Winston Salem *(G-16787)*
Saft America Inc .... B 828 874-4111
  Valdese *(G-15454)*
Spectrum Brands Inc .... G 800 854-3151
  Charlotte *(G-3599)*

3694 Engine electrical equipment

1a Smart Start LLC .... G 336 765-7001
  Winston Salem *(G-16584)*
Cummins Inc .... G 704 588-1240
  Pineville *(G-12264)*
GKN Driveline North Amer Inc .... C 336 364-6200
  Timberlake *(G-15314)*
Goldsboro Strter Altrntor Svc .... G 919 735-6745
  Goldsboro *(G-6620)*
Hemco Wire Products Inc .... F 336 454-7280
  Jamestown *(G-9052)*
Ineos Automotive Americas LLC .... G 404 513-8577
  Raleigh *(G-12887)*
Jmedic Inc .... G 336 744-4444
  Winston Salem *(G-16771)*
Johnston County Industries Inc .... C 919 743-8700
  Selma *(G-14257)*
Lmg Holdings Inc .... F 919 653-0910
  Durham *(G-5192)*
▲ Manufacturing Systems Eqp Inc .... F 704 283-2086
  Monroe *(G-10764)*
Mc Cullough Auto Elc & Assoc .... G 704 376-5388
  Charlotte *(G-3148)*
Pass & Seymour Inc .... A 315 468-6211
  Concord *(G-4329)*
▲ Reman Technologies Inc .... E 704 921-2293
  Charlotte *(G-3428)*
Scattered Wrenches Inc .... G 919 480-1605
  Raleigh *(G-13236)*
Smart Start Inc .... G 828 328-2822
  Hickory *(G-8159)*
▲ Suretech Assembly Inc .... E 919 569-0346
  Youngsville *(G-17103)*
Window Motor World Inc .... G 800 252-2649
  Boone *(G-1250)*
▲ Ziehl-Abegg Inc .... E 336 834-9339
  Greensboro *(G-7475)*

3695 Magnetic and optical recording media

▲ Assa Abloy AB .... D 704 283-2101
  Monroe *(G-10652)*
Consolidated Sciences Inc .... G 919 870-0344
  Raleigh *(G-12639)*
High Mobility Solutions Inc .... G 704 849-8242
  Matthews *(G-10253)*
Legalis Dms LLC .... F 919 741-8260
  Raleigh *(G-12965)*
Synchrono Group Inc .... E 888 389-0439
  Raleigh *(G-13320)*
Talking Devices Company .... G 828 658-0660
  Asheville *(G-795)*

3699 Electrical equipment and supplies, nec

SIC SECTION

37 TRANSPORTATION EQUIPMENT

A&B Integrators LLC .... F 919 371-0750
  Durham (G-4897)
Accurate Weld LLC .... G 828 310-1517
  Taylorsville (G-15126)
▲ Acw Technology Inc .... A
  Raleigh (G-12474)
▲ Advanced Electronic Svcs Inc .... D 336 789-0792
  Mount Airy (G-11473)
Aegis Power Systems Inc .... E 828 837-4029
  Murphy (G-11705)
Alert Protection Systems Inc .... G 919 467-4357
  Raleigh (G-12487)
American Physcl SEC Group LLC .... G 919 363-1894
  Apex (G-159)
Anndori Outdoor Art LLC .... E 336 202-8400
  Greensboro (G-6809)
Asco Power Technologies LP .... C 919 460-5200
  Apex (G-166)
Asco Power Technologies LP .... F 336 731-5000
  Lexington (G-9681)
Assa Abloy Accessories and .... B 704 233-4011
  Monroe (G-10654)
◆ Assa Abloy Entrnce Systems US .... C 704 357-9924
  Monroe (G-10655)
Atom Power Inc .... D 844 704-2866
  Huntersville (G-8795)
Audio Vdeo Concepts Design Inc .... G 704 821-2823
  Indian Trail (G-8921)
Austin Company of Greensboro .... C 336 468-2851
  Yadkinville (G-17031)
Automated Controls LLC .... F 704 724-7625
  Huntersville (G-8796)
Campus Safety Products LLC .... G 919 321-1477
  Durham (G-4996)
▲ Cargotec Port Security LLC .... G 919 620-1763
  Durham (G-4998)
Carolina Electric Mtr Repr LLC .... G 704 289-3732
  Monroe (G-10676)
Carolina Growler Inc .... E 910 948-2114
  Robbins (G-13597)
Carolina Tex Sls Gastonia Inc .... F 704 739-1646
  Kings Mountain (G-9301)
◆ Commscope Inc North Carolina .... D 828 324-2200
  Claremont (G-3909)
Communications & Pwr Inds LLC .... E 650 846-2900
  Conover (G-4437)
Consoldted Elctrnic Rsrces Inc .... G 919 321-0004
  Durham (G-5030)
Consolidated Elec Distrs Inc .... G 828 433-4689
  Morganton (G-11207)
◆ Consolidated Mfg Intl LLC .... G 919 781-3411
  Raleigh (G-12638)
Controlled Products Systems G .... G 704 392-2859
  Charlotte (G-2546)
▲ Cordset Designs Inc .... E 252 568-4001
  Pink Hill (G-12316)
Cortical Metrics LLC .... G 919 903-9943
  Carrboro (G-1646)
Crowdguard Inc .... G 919 605-1948
  Cary (G-1742)
Custom Light and Sound Inc .... E 919 286-1122
  Durham (G-5040)
Diverse Security Systems Inc .... G 919 848-9599
  Raleigh (G-12688)
Eaton Corporation .... B 828 684-2381
  Arden (G-326)
Eaton Corporation .... C 919 872-3020
  Raleigh (G-12722)
Edwards Electronic Systems Inc .... G 919 359-2239
  Clayton (G-3976)
◆ Feller LLC .... E 910 383-6920
  Leland (G-9541)

Hamrick Fence Company .... F 704 434-5011
  Boiling Springs (G-1160)
Hanson Systems Inc .... G 828 687-3701
  Fletcher (G-6009)
Hitachi Energy USA Inc .... C 919 856-2360
  Raleigh (G-12850)
Hollingsworth Heating Air Cond .... G 252 824-0355
  Tarboro (G-15108)
Infinite Controls Inc .... C 919 623-4818
  Chapel Hill (G-2026)
Integrated Roe Security LLC .... G 919 297-8036
  Raleigh (G-12896)
International Thermodyne Inc .... G 704 579-8218
  Charlotte (G-2988)
Jared Munday Electric Inc .... G 828 355-9024
  Boone (G-1210)
◆ Jenkins Electric Company .... D 800 438-3003
  Charlotte (G-3020)
Kuebler Inc .... F 704 705-4711
  Charlotte (G-3064)
L3harris Technologies Inc .... G 704 588-7126
  Charlotte (G-3066)
Leonine Protection Systems LLC .... G 704 296-2675
  Mount Holly (G-11640)
Little Reds Engraving LLC .... G 910 599-7747
  Burgaw (G-1344)
M2 Optics Inc .... G 919 342-5619
  Raleigh (G-12985)
Machine Control Company Inc .... G 704 708-5782
  Matthews (G-10265)
▲ Magnum Enterprize Inc .... G 252 524-5391
  Grifton (G-7601)
◆ Marpac LLC .... D 910 602-1421
  Wilmington (G-16315)
Memscap Inc .... C 919 248-1441
  Durham (G-5218)
NC Solar Now Inc .... F 919 833-9096
  Raleigh (G-13058)
Offshore Marine Elec LLC .... G 252 504-2624
  Newport (G-11902)
◆ Pace Incorporated .... E 910 695-7223
  Vass (G-15493)
Pathway Technologies Inc .... G 919 847-2680
  Raleigh (G-13101)
Pcx Holding LLC .... D 919 550-2800
  Knightdale (G-9425)
Pike Electric LLC .... B 336 316-7068
  Greensboro (G-7263)
Plan B Enterprises LLC .... G 919 387-4856
  New Hill (G-11863)
Posh Pad .... G 910 988-4800
  Stedman (G-14936)
Power and Ctrl Solutions LLC .... G 704 609-9623
  Charlotte (G-3359)
▲ Precision Drive Systems LLC .... G 704 922-1206
  Bessemer City (G-1079)
Process Electronics Corp .... F 704 827-9019
  Mount Holly (G-11647)
Public Safety UAS LLC .... G 336 601-7578
  Gibsonville (G-6570)
Raw Earth Energy Corporation .... G 704 492-0793
  Charlotte (G-3412)
RDM Industrial Electronics Inc .... D 828 652-8346
  Nebo (G-11763)
▲ Record Usa Inc .... E 704 289-9212
  Monroe (G-10793)
▲ Reuel Inc .... E 919 734-0460
  Goldsboro (G-6650)
Salem Technologies Inc .... F 336 777-3652
  Winston Salem (G-16895)
Sandhlls Fbrctors Crane Svcs I .... F 910 673-4573
  West End (G-15931)

Schneider Automation Inc .... C 919 855-1262
  Raleigh (G-13238)
Security Consult Inc .... G 704 531-8399
  Charlotte (G-3522)
▲ Sentinel Door Controls LLC .... F 704 921-4627
  Charlotte (G-3528)
Service Electric and Control .... G 704 888-5100
  Locust (G-9970)
Shipman Technologies Inc .... E 919 294-8405
  Durham (G-5353)
Sierra Nevada Corporation .... E 910 307-0362
  Fayetteville (G-5915)
Sine Wave Technologies Inc .... G 704 765-9636
  Davidson (G-4696)
Skyspy LLC .... G 703 472-4639
  Charlotte (G-3561)
▲ Smart Electric North Amer LLC .... G 828 323-1200
  Conover (G-4497)
Smithfield Ced .... G 919 934-5041
  Smithfield (G-14483)
Sonaspection International .... F 704 262-3384
  Concord (G-4362)
South Eastern Electric Whl .... G 252 826-0123
  Scotland Neck (G-14222)
Spartan Manufacturing Corp .... E 336 996-5585
  Kernersville (G-9237)
Spectra Integrated Systems Inc .... G 919 876-3666
  Raleigh (G-13287)
▼ TCI Mobility Inc .... F 704 867-8331
  Gastonia (G-6520)
▼ Total Fire Systems Inc .... E 919 556-9161
  Youngsville (G-17107)
Total Technologies LLC .... G 336 259-5541
  Gastonia (G-6530)
Turbomed LLC .... F 973 527-5299
  Fayetteville (G-5936)
◆ Utility Solutions Inc .... G 828 323-8914
  Hickory (G-8200)
Vortex-Cyclone Technologies .... F 919 225-1724
  Raleigh (G-13410)
Wahah Electric Supply .... G 717 208-2260
  Southport (G-14586)
Wilmore Electronics Company Inc .... D 919 732-9351
  Hillsborough (G-8672)
▲ Zibra LLC .... G 704 271-4503
  Mooresville (G-11140)

37 TRANSPORTATION EQUIPMENT

3711 Motor vehicles and car bodies

Air Speed Stock Car Fabricatio .... G 704 720-7245
  Concord (G-4189)
Allison Brothers Race Cars Inc .... F 704 278-0174
  Salisbury (G-13919)
Ashville Wrecker Service Inc .... G 828 252-2388
  Asheville (G-546)
B S R-Hess Race Cars Inc .... E 704 547-0901
  Charlotte (G-2254)
Brown Mitchell Hodges LLC .... G 800 477-8982
  Charlotte (G-2359)
◆ Bucher Municipal N Amer Inc .... E 704 658-1333
  Mooresville (G-10891)
Bus Safety Inc .... G 336 671-0838
  Mocksville (G-10558)
Can-AM Custom Trucks Inc .... G 704 334-0322
  Charlotte (G-2381)
▼ Carolina Movile Bus Systems .... G 336 475-0983
  Thomasville (G-15199)
▲ Cleveland Freightliner Truck .... E 704 645-5000
  Cleveland (G-4070)

Employee Codes: A=Over 500 employees, B=251-500
C=101-250, D=51-100, E=20-50, F=10-19, G=1-9

37 TRANSPORTATION EQUIPMENT

▼ Csi Armoring Inc .... G 336 313-8451
  Lexington (G-9701)
▲ Custom Cnverting Solutions Inc .... E 336 292-2616
  Greensboro (G-6949)
Daimler Truck North Amer LLC .... A 704 645-5000
  Cleveland (G-4071)
Dej Holdings LLC .... E 704 799-4800
  Mooresville (G-10928)
◆ Demmel Inc .... D 828 585-6600
  East Flat Rock (G-5473)
▲ Designline Corporation .... C 704 494-7800
  Charlotte (G-2621)
Designline Usa LLC .... E 704 494-7800
  Charlotte (G-2622)
◆ Direct Chassislink Inc .... E 704 594-3800
  Charlotte (G-2639)
E-N-G Mobile Systems LLC .... F 925 798-4060
  Fayetteville (G-5814)
Ecovehicle Enterprises Inc .... G 704 544-9907
  Charlotte (G-2685)
Elio Inc .... G 919 708-5554
  Sanford (G-14114)
Enc Conveyance LLC .... G 252 378-9990
  Rocky Mount (G-13667)
Epk LLC .... F 980 643-4787
  Salisbury (G-13958)
Epv Corporation .... G 704 494-7800
  Charlotte (G-2723)
Epv Corporation .... E 704 494-7800
  Charlotte (G-2724)
Ev Fleet Inc .... G 704 425-6272
  Charlotte (G-2734)
Exprolink Corp .... G 919 215-4675
  Raleigh (G-12756)
First Prrity Emrgncy Vhcles In .... E 908 645-0788
  Wilkesboro (G-16021)
Force Protection Inc .... F 336 597-2381
  Roxboro (G-13803)
Ford Division .... G 336 838-4155
  North Wilkesboro (G-12008)
Fortem Genus Inc .... G 910 574-5214
  Fayetteville (G-5826)
GM Defense LLC .... D 800 462-8782
  Concord (G-4275)
Go Green Racing .... G 916 295-2621
  Mooresville (G-10960)
Grahams Transportation LLC .... G 910 627-6880
  Fayetteville (G-5831)
Granite Tactical Vehicles Inc .... F 336 789-5555
  Mount Airy (G-11513)
Halcore Group Inc .... E 336 982-9824
  Jefferson (G-9089)
◆ Halcore Group Inc .... B 336 846-8010
  Jefferson (G-9090)
Hedgecock Racing Entps Inc .... F 336 887-4221
  High Point (G-8381)
Highline Performance Group .... E 704 799-3500
  Mooresville (G-10974)
Hollifield Enterprises .... G 828 766-7552
  Spruce Pine (G-14643)
Holman Automotive Inc .... G 704 583-2888
  Charlotte (G-2915)
▲ James Tool Machine & Engrg Inc .... C 828 584-8722
  Morganton (G-11224)
Jasper Engine Exchange Inc .... E 704 664-2300
  Mooresville (G-10987)
Jasper Penske Engines .... F 704 788-8996
  Concord (G-4292)
Jeff Anderson .... G 910 481-8923
  Fayetteville (G-5848)
Jem Acres Inc .... G 252 823-3483
  Tarboro (G-15110)

Labonte Racing Inc .... F 336 431-1004
  Trinity (G-15348)
Lelantos Group Inc .... D 704 780-4127
  Mooresville (G-11005)
Lynn Jones Race Cars .... G 252 522-0705
  Kinston (G-9374)
Mack Trucks Inc .... G 336 291-9064
  Greensboro (G-7176)
◆ Mack Trucks Inc .... A 336 291-9001
  Greensboro (G-7177)
Matthews Spcialty Vehicles Inc .... D 336 297-9600
  Greensboro (G-7189)
Maxxdrive LLC .... G 704 600-8684
  Shelby (G-14345)
▼ Mickey Truck Bodies Inc .... B 336 882-6806
  High Point (G-8455)
Navistar Inc .... G 704 596-3860
  Charlotte (G-3239)
North Crlina Dept Crime Ctrl P .... G 252 522-1511
  Kinston (G-9379)
North Crlina Dept Crime Ctrl P .... G 336 599-9233
  Roxboro (G-13810)
Operating Shelby LLC Tag .... E 704 482-1399
  Shelby (G-14354)
▲ Penske Racing South Inc .... C 704 664-2300
  Mooresville (G-11050)
Performance Racing Whse Inc .... G 704 838-1400
  Mooresville (G-11053)
Pratt Mller Engrg Fbrction LLC .... G 704 977-0642
  Huntersville (G-8881)
Prevost Car (us) Inc .... F 336 812-3504
  High Point (G-8496)
▲ Prevost Car (us) Inc .... E 908 222-7211
  Greensboro (G-7281)
Propane Trucks & Tanks Inc .... F 919 362-5000
  Apex (G-234)
Race Tech Race Cars Cmpnnts In .... G 336 538-4941
  Burlington (G-1481)
RFH Tactical Mobility Inc .... F 910 916-0284
  Milton (G-10516)
Richard Chldress Racg Entps In .... E 336 731-3334
  Welcome (G-15874)
▲ Richard Chldress Racg Entps In ..... B 336 731-3334
  Welcome (G-15875)
▲ Riley Technologies LLC .... E 704 663-6319
  Mooresville (G-11069)
Rowdy Manufacturing LLC .... G 704 662-0000
  Mooresville (G-11075)
Rp Motor Sports Inc .... E 704 720-4200
  Concord (G-4353)
Smith Fabrication Inc .... G 704 660-5170
  Mooresville (G-11090)
Solar Pack .... E 919 515-2194
  Raleigh (G-13277)
Southco Industries Inc .... C 704 482-1477
  Shelby (G-14369)
Spevco Inc .... D 336 924-8100
  Pfafftown (G-12190)
Streets Auto Sales & Four WD .... G 704 888-8686
  Locust (G-9973)
Subaru Folger Automotive .... E 704 531-8888
  Charlotte (G-3645)
Supreme Murphy Trck Bodies Inc .... C 252 291-2191
  Wilson (G-16544)
Thomas Built Buses Inc .... A 336 889-4871
  High Point (G-8569)
Thomas of High Point .... G 336 889-4871
  High Point (G-8570)
Tim Nicholson Race Cars LLC .... G 336 253-6767
  Reidsville (G-13541)
Toymakerz LLC .... F 843 267-3477
  Reidsville (G-13543)

Trenton Emergency Med Svcs Inc .... F 252 448-2646
  Trenton (G-15335)
Triple R MBL Cigr Lounge LLC .... G 252 281-7738
  Rocky Mount (G-13738)
◆ US Legend Cars Intl Inc .... E 704 455-3896
  Harrisburg (G-7732)
Vision Motor Cars Inc .... G 704 425-6271
  Concord (G-4386)
Your Fire Source Inc .... F 828 669-9000
  Black Mountain (G-1142)

3713 Truck and bus bodies

Abernethy Welding & Repair Inc .... G 828 324-7361
  Vale (G-15462)
Altec Industries Inc .... B 919 528-2535
  Creedmoor (G-4603)
▲ Altec Northeast LLC .... D 508 320-9041
  Creedmoor (G-4604)
AM Haire Mfg & Svc Corp .... C 336 472-4444
  Thomasville (G-15184)
Amrep Inc .... D 704 949-2595
  Salisbury (G-13921)
Amrep Inc .... E 909 923-0430
  Charlotte (G-2191)
Anchor-Richey Emergency Vehicl .... E 828 495-8145
  Taylorsville (G-15129)
Bucks Wrecker Service .... G 704 776-0899
  Statesville (G-14767)
Cabarrus Plastics Inc .... C 704 784-2100
  Concord (G-4218)
Can-AM Custom Trucks Inc .... G 704 334-0322
  Charlotte (G-2381)
Carroll Co .... F 919 779-1900
  Garner (G-6262)
Courtesy Ford Inc .... E 252 338-4783
  Elizabeth City (G-5537)
Daimler Truck North Amer LLC .... A 704 868-5700
  Gastonia (G-6394)
Designline Usa LLC .... E 704 494-7800
  Charlotte (G-2622)
Enterprise Twd .... G 704 822-6166
  Stanley (G-14692)
Epv Corporation .... G 704 494-7800
  Charlotte (G-2723)
Epv Corporation .... E 704 494-7800
  Charlotte (G-2724)
Fontaine Modification Company .... F 704 392-8502
  Charlotte (G-2783)
◆ Godwin Manufacturing Co Inc .... C 910 897-4995
  Dunn (G-4870)
Guy N Langley .... G 252 972-9875
  Rocky Mount (G-13668)
Hackney & Sons Midwest Inc .... G 252 946-6521
  Washington (G-15707)
Immixt LLC .... G 336 207-8679
  Siler City (G-14415)
John Jenkins Company .... E 336 375-3717
  Browns Summit (G-1311)
Johnie Gregory Trck Bodies Inc .... G 252 264-2626
  Hertford (G-7922)
Knapheide Trck Eqp Co Midsouth ...... E 910 484-0558
  Midland (G-10470)
Laurinburg Machine Company .... G 910 276-0360
  Laurinburg (G-9484)
Leonard Alum Utlity Bldngs Inc .... G 919 872-4442
  Raleigh (G-12968)
Leonard Alum Utlity Bldngs Inc .... G 910 392-4921
  Wilmington (G-16299)
Lift Bodies Inc .... G 336 667-2588
  North Wilkesboro (G-12023)
Matthews Spcialty Vehicles Inc .... D 336 297-9600
  Greensboro (G-7189)

37 TRANSPORTATION EQUIPMENT

Mdb Investors LLC .... F 704 507-6850
   Charlotte *(G-3155)*

Meritor Inc .... C 828 433-4600
   Morganton *(G-11232)*

Mickey Truck Bodies Inc .... G 336 882-6806
   High Point *(G-8454)*

Mickey Truck Bodies Inc .... G 336 882-6806
   Thomasville *(G-15248)*

▼ Mickey Truck Bodies Inc .... B 336 882-6806
   High Point *(G-8455)*

Osprea Logistics Usa LLC .... E 704 504-1677
   Charlotte *(G-3305)*

Petroleum Tank Corporation .... F 919 284-2418
   Kenly *(G-9155)*

▲ Prevost Car (us) Inc .... E 908 222-7211
   Greensboro *(G-7281)*

Propane Trucks & Tanks Inc .... F 919 362-5000
   Apex *(G-234)*

Quality Trck Bodies & Repr Inc .... E 252 245-5100
   Elm City *(G-5652)*

Quality Turf Hauling LLC .... F 336 516-1156
   Haw River *(G-7756)*

R J Yeller Distribution Inc .... G 800 944-2589
   Charlotte *(G-3405)*

Satco Truck Equipment Inc .... F 919 383-5547
   Durham *(G-5340)*

Smithway Inc .... G 828 628-1756
   Fairview *(G-5718)*

Southco Industries Inc .... C 704 482-1477
   Shelby *(G-14369)*

Supreme Murphy Trck Bodies Inc .... C 252 291-2191
   Wilson *(G-16544)*

Thomas Built Buses Inc .... A 336 889-4871
   High Point *(G-8569)*

▲ Transportation Tech Inc .... C 252 946-6521
   Washington *(G-15734)*

Triangle Body Works Inc .... F 336 788-0631
   Winston Salem *(G-16951)*

◆ Vna Holding Inc .... A 336 393-4890
   Greensboro *(G-7445)*

Volvo Group North America LLC .... A 336 393-2000
   Greensboro *(G-7447)*

◆ Volvo Group North America LLC .... A 336 393-2000
   Greensboro *(G-7446)*

◆ Volvo Logistics North America Inc .... C 336 393-4746
   Greensboro *(G-7449)*

◆ Volvo Trucks North America Inc .... A 336 393-2000
   Greensboro *(G-7450)*

VT Hackney Inc .... D 252 946-6521
   Washington *(G-15737)*

Waste Container Repair Svcs .... G 910 257-4474
   Fayetteville *(G-5949)*

3714 Motor vehicle parts and accessories

▲ Abundant Manufacturing Inc .... E 704 871-9911
   Statesville *(G-14737)*

Accuride Corporation .... G 336 393-0671
   Greensboro *(G-6776)*

Ae Wiring LLC .... F 252 749-0195
   Fountain *(G-6092)*

Aerofabb LLC .... G 919 793-8487
   Raleigh *(G-12480)*

Agve Inc .... G 704 243-8300
   Matthews *(G-10231)*

Aisin North Carolina Corp .... C 919 529-0951
   Creedmoor *(G-4602)*

◆ Aisin North Carolina Corp .... A 919 479-6400
   Durham *(G-4910)*

Altra Industrial Motion Corp .... D 704 588-5610
   Charlotte *(G-2173)*

American Racg Hders Exhust Inc .... E 631 608-1986
   Stanfield *(G-14674)*

Amsted Industries Incorporated .... G 704 226-5243
   Monroe *(G-10646)*

Amt .... G 617 549-4395
   Thomasville *(G-15186)*

Andreani USA Inc .... G 828 435-0125
   Hendersonville *(G-7819)*

Andrews Products Inc .... G 704 785-9715
   Concord *(G-4197)*

◆ AP Emissions Technologies LLC .... A 919 580-2000
   Goldsboro *(G-6591)*

Arrival Automotive USA Inc .... F 415 439-2002
   Charlotte *(G-2217)*

▲ Atkinson International Inc .... D 704 865-7750
   Gastonia *(G-6349)*

Auria Albemarle LLC .... B 704 983-5166
   Albemarle *(G-74)*

▲ Auria Old Fort LLC .... C 828 668-7601
   Old Fort *(G-12098)*

▲ Auria Old Fort II LLC .... D 828 668-3277
   Old Fort *(G-12099)*

Auria Troy LLC .... D 910 572-3721
   Troy *(G-15401)*

▼ Axle Holdings LLC .... E 800 895-3276
   Concord *(G-4203)*

▲ B & B Fabrication Inc .... F 623 581-7600
   Mooresville *(G-10869)*

Barrs Competition .... F 704 482-5169
   Shelby *(G-14287)*

Ben Huffman Enterprises LLC .... G 704 724-4705
   Mooresville *(G-10872)*

Beulaville Wstn Auto Value Inc .... F 910 298-4246
   Beulaville *(G-1091)*

Billet Speed Inc .... G 828 226-8127
   Sylva *(G-15054)*

Bordeaux Dynocams .... G 910 655-9482
   Delco *(G-4718)*

Borg-Warner Automotive Inc .... G 828 684-3501
   Fletcher *(G-5990)*

Borgwarner Arden LLC .... F 248 754-9200
   Arden *(G-313)*

Borgwarner Inc .... E 828 684-4000
   Arden *(G-314)*

▲ Bosch Rexroth Corporation .... E 704 583-4338
   Charlotte *(G-2336)*

Bostrom Seating Inc .... A 704 596-0040
   Charlotte *(G-2338)*

Boxmoor Truck Bedliners & ACC .... G 336 447-4621
   Whitsett *(G-15984)*

Br549 Enterprises LLC .... G 704 799-0955
   Sherrills Ford *(G-14384)*

Brembo North America Inc .... G 704 799-0530
   Concord *(G-4214)*

Brucato Power Inc .... G 919 234-1776
   Apex *(G-173)*

▲ BT America Inc .... G 704 434-8072
   Boiling Springs *(G-1158)*

CAM Craft LLC .... G 828 681-5183
   Arden *(G-316)*

Camco Manufacturing Inc .... G 336 348-6609
   Reidsville *(G-13511)*

Camcraft Performance Cams .... G 828 492-0950
   Canton *(G-1605)*

Can-AM Custom Trucks Inc .... G 704 334-0322
   Charlotte *(G-2381)*

Carbotech USA Inc .... G 704 481-8500
   Concord *(G-4224)*

Carolina Attachments LLC .... F 336 474-7309
   Thomasville *(G-15194)*

Carolina Cltch Brake Rbldrs In .... G 828 327-9358
   Hickory *(G-7962)*

▲ Cataler North America Corp .... C 828 970-0246
   Lincolnton *(G-9879)*

Catlow Inc .... G 336 894-3367
   Greensboro *(G-6895)*

Ceco Friction Products Inc .... F 704 857-1156
   Landis *(G-9450)*

Certification Services In .... G 828 458-1573
   Fletcher *(G-5993)*

Chromed Out Frame Covers Inc .... G 704 813-8811
   Charlotte *(G-2480)*

City of Charlotte-Atando .... F 704 336-2722
   Charlotte *(G-2487)*

Cjr Products Inc .... G 336 766-2710
   Winston Salem *(G-16653)*

◆ Clarcor Eng MBL Solutions LLC .... C 860 992-3496
   Washington *(G-15688)*

Classic Wood Manufacturing .... G 336 691-1344
   Greensboro *(G-6913)*

▲ Cleveland Yutaka Corporation .... D 704 480-9290
   Shelby *(G-14299)*

Coconut Paradise Inc .... G 704 662-3443
   Mooresville *(G-10908)*

Commercial Vehicle Group Inc .... E 704 886-6407
   Concord *(G-4238)*

Consolidated Metco Inc .... D 828 488-5126
   Bryson City *(G-1322)*

Consolidated Metco Inc .... C 828 488-5114
   Canton *(G-1611)*

Consolidated Metco Inc .... D 704 226-5246
   Monroe *(G-10693)*

Continental Auto Systems Inc .... B 828 654-2000
   Fletcher *(G-5996)*

Continental Auto Systems Inc .... B 828 584-4500
   Morganton *(G-11208)*

Continental Auto Systems Inc .... D 828 584-4500
   Valdese *(G-15446)*

Coolant & Cleaning Tech Inc .... G 704 753-1333
   Monroe *(G-10695)*

Cooper-Standard Automotive Inc .... D 919 735-5394
   Goldsboro *(G-6604)*

Corvac Inc .... G 772 692-5514
   Hayesville *(G-7764)*

Cox Machine Co Inc .... F 704 296-0118
   Monroe *(G-10696)*

Cummins Inc .... G 919 284-9111
   Kenly *(G-9150)*

Cummins Inc .... G 704 588-1240
   Pineville *(G-12264)*

Curtis L Maclean L C .... C 704 940-5531
   Mooresville *(G-10919)*

▲ Cycle Pro LLC .... F 704 662-6682
   Mooresville *(G-10922)*

Daimler Truck North Amer LLC .... A 704 868-5700
   Gastonia *(G-6394)*

Dambach Lagersysteme Inc .... G 704 421-6425
   Charlotte *(G-2602)*

David Vizard Motortec Features .... G 865 850-0666
   Mount Holly *(G-11630)*

◆ Dce Inc .... G 704 230-4649
   Mooresville *(G-10926)*

Deuces Custom .... G 704 658-1777
   Mooresville *(G-10930)*

Dhollandia Us Llc .... G 909 251-7979
   Bessemer City *(G-1063)*

▲ Diamondback Products Inc .... G 336 236-9800
   Lexington *(G-9708)*

▲ Dill Air Controls Products LLC .... C 919 692-2300
   Oxford *(G-12127)*

Dnj Engine Comp Onents .... G 704 855-5505
   China Grove *(G-3882)*

Doosan Bobcat North Amer Inc .... C 704 883-3500
   Statesville *(G-14789)*

Dover Power LLC .... G 704 485-2020
   Oakboro *(G-12072)*

37 TRANSPORTATION EQUIPMENT

Durham Racing Engines Inc............................ G..... 336 471-1830
  Thomasville *(G-15217)*

East Coast Roadster.. G..... 336 624-5083
  Winston Salem *(G-16688)*

Eaton Corporation.. C..... 704 937-7411
  Kings Mountain *(G-9306)*

Eaton Corporation.. B..... 336 322-0696
  Roxboro *(G-13801)*

Edelbrock LLC... D..... 919 718-9737
  Sanford *(G-14113)*

Elite Metal Performance LLC............................ F..... 704 660-0006
  Statesville *(G-14793)*

Epic Restorations LLC..................................... G..... 866 597-2733
  Roxboro *(G-13802)*

Esta Extraction USA LP................................... G..... 704 942-8844
  Charlotte *(G-2731)*

Fat Man Fabrications Inc................................. E..... 704 545-0369
  Mint Hill *(G-10531)*

▲ FCC (north Carolina) LLC............................ G..... 910 462-4465
  Laurinburg *(G-9479)*

Five Star Bodies.. G..... 262 325-9126
  Troutman *(G-15377)*

Fox Factory Inc... F..... 828 633-6840
  Asheville *(G-627)*

Fox Factory Inc... G..... 831 421-1791
  Mooresville *(G-10950)*

G-Loc Brakes LLC.. G..... 704 765-0213
  Mooresville *(G-10952)*

Gear Fx Driveline LLC..................................... G..... 704 799-9117
  Mooresville *(G-10955)*

GKN Dna Inc... G..... 919 304-7378
  Mebane *(G-10412)*

GKN Driveline Newton LLC.............................. E..... 828 428-5292
  Newton *(G-11934)*

◆ GKN Driveline Newton LLC.......................... A..... 828 428-3711
  Newton *(G-11933)*

GKN Driveline North Amer Inc......................... E..... 919 304-7252
  Mebane *(G-10413)*

GKN Driveline North Amer Inc......................... C..... 336 364-6200
  Timberlake *(G-15314)*

Global Products LLC....................................... G..... 336 227-7327
  Greensboro *(G-7046)*

GM Defense LLC... D..... 800 462-8782
  Concord *(G-4275)*

◆ Godwin Manufacturing Co Inc...................... C..... 910 897-4995
  Dunn *(G-4870)*

Goodyear Tire & Rubber Company.................. G..... 919 552-9340
  Holly Springs *(G-8700)*

Gracie & Lucas LLC.. G..... 704 707-3207
  Mooresville *(G-10962)*

Grede II LLC... B..... 910 428-2111
  Biscoe *(G-1110)*

Grimme Services LLC..................................... G..... 828 490-6366
  Asheville *(G-645)*

Guilford Performance Textiles......................... G..... 910 296-5362
  Kenansville *(G-9143)*

Haldex Inc.. C..... 828 652-9308
  Marion *(G-10150)*

Hamilton Sundstrand Corp............................... B..... 860 654-6000
  Charlotte *(G-2882)*

Hanak Enterprises.. G..... 704 315-5249
  Gastonia *(G-6413)*

Hanwha Advanced Mtls Amer LLC................... E..... 704 434-2271
  Shelby *(G-14325)*

▼ Hendrens Racg Engs Chassis Inc................. G..... 828 286-0780
  Rutherfordton *(G-13879)*

Hickory Springs Mfg Co................................... F..... 336 491-4131
  High Point *(G-8386)*

High Street Baptist Church.............................. G..... 336 234-0400
  Milton *(G-10515)*

Hitch Crafters LLC.. G..... 336 859-3257
  Lexington *(G-9731)*

▲ Holman & Moody Inc.................................. G..... 704 394-4141
  Charlotte *(G-2914)*

Holman Automotive Inc.................................. G..... 704 583-2888
  Charlotte *(G-2915)*

Hotchkis Bryde Incorporated.......................... G..... 704 660-3060
  Mooresville *(G-10977)*

Ignite Dirt Sports LLC..................................... G..... 704 770-7806
  Cornelius *(G-4559)*

Indian Head Industries Inc............................. D..... 704 547-7411
  Murphy *(G-11710)*

◆ Indian Head Industries Inc......................... E..... 704 547-7411
  Charlotte *(G-2961)*

◆ Inter-Continental Gear & Brake.................. G..... 704 599-3420
  Charlotte *(G-2980)*

Isometrics Inc.. F..... 336 342-4150
  Reidsville *(G-13527)*

◆ Isometrics Inc.. E..... 336 349-2329
  Reidsville *(G-13528)*

Jasper Engine Exchange Inc.......................... E..... 704 664-2300
  Mooresville *(G-10987)*

Jenkins Properties Inc.................................... E..... 336 667-4282
  North Wilkesboro *(G-12017)*

▲ Jri Development Group LLC....................... G..... 704 660-8346
  Mooresville *(G-10989)*

Jri Shocks LLC... F..... 704 660-8346
  Mooresville *(G-10990)*

▲ Kck Holding Corp....................................... E..... 336 513-0002
  Burlington *(G-1443)*

Kee Auto Top Manufacturing Co...................... G..... 704 332-8213
  Charlotte *(G-3047)*

Kessler Inc... G..... 248 717-0027
  Indian Trail *(G-8942)*

Kgt Enterprises Inc.. G..... 704 662-3272
  Mooresville *(G-10997)*

Kooks Custom Headers.................................. G..... 704 838-1110
  Statesville *(G-14833)*

Lake Shore Radiator Inc................................ F..... 336 271-2626
  Greensboro *(G-7162)*

Lear Corporation.. E..... 919 552-5667
  Fuquay Varina *(G-6208)*

Lear Enterprises Inc...................................... G..... 704 321-0027
  Charlotte *(G-3078)*

Leonard Alum Utlty Bldngs Inc....................... G..... 919 872-4442
  Raleigh *(G-12968)*

Leonard Alum Utlty Bldngs Inc....................... G..... 910 392-4921
  Wilmington *(G-16299)*

▲ Linnig Corporation..................................... D..... 704 482-9582
  Shelby *(G-14338)*

Longs Machine & Tool Inc.............................. E..... 336 625-3844
  Asheboro *(G-454)*

Lord Corporation... D..... 919 342-3380
  Cary *(G-1816)*

◆ Mack Trucks Inc.. A..... 336 291-9001
  Greensboro *(G-7177)*

▲ Magna Composites LLC............................. B..... 704 797-8744
  Salisbury *(G-14008)*

Mahle Motorsports Inc................................... F..... 888 255-1942
  Fletcher *(G-6020)*

▲ Mann+hmmel Fltrtion Tech Group.............. G..... 704 869-3300
  Gastonia *(G-6449)*

▼ Mann+hmmel Fltrtion Tech Intrm............... F..... 704 869-3300
  Gastonia *(G-6450)*

Mann+hmmel Fltrtion Tech US LL.................. D..... 704 869-3700
  Gastonia *(G-6451)*

Mann+hmmel Prlator Filters LLC.................... C..... 910 425-4181
  Fayetteville *(G-5865)*

Mann+hmmel Prlator Filters LLC.................... C..... 704 869-3441
  Gastonia *(G-6453)*

◆ Mann+hmmel Prlator Filters LLC................ E..... 910 425-4181
  Fayetteville *(G-5864)*

Mann+hummel Filtration Technol................... D..... 704 869-3500
  Gastonia *(G-6454)*

Mann+hummel Filtration Technol................... G..... 704 869-3952
  Gastonia *(G-6455)*

Mann+hummel Filtration Technol................... D..... 704 869-3501
  Gastonia *(G-6456)*

◆ Mann+hummel Filtration Te....................... A..... 704 869-3300
  Gastonia *(G-6457)*

Marmon Engine Controls LLC........................ E..... 843 701-5145
  Laurinburg *(G-9487)*

Marmon Holdings Inc.................................... F..... 910 291-2571
  Laurinburg *(G-9488)*

▲ Master Tow Inc.. E..... 910 630-2000
  Fayetteville *(G-5869)*

Mayflower Vehicle Systems LLC..................... D..... 704 937-4400
  Kings Mountain *(G-9318)*

▲ MB Marketing & Mfg Inc............................ G..... 828 285-0882
  Asheville *(G-697)*

McCoy Motorsports.. G..... 704 929-8802
  Cleveland *(G-4075)*

Meritor Inc... F..... 910 425-4181
  Fayetteville *(G-5872)*

Meritor Inc... F..... 828 687-2000
  Fletcher *(G-6023)*

Meritor Inc... F..... 828 687-2000
  Fletcher *(G-6024)*

Meritor Inc... D..... 828 247-0440
  Forest City *(G-6077)*

Meritor Inc... F..... 910 844-9401
  Maxton *(G-10359)*

Meritor Inc... F..... 910 844-9401
  Maxton *(G-10360)*

Meritor Inc... C..... 828 433-4600
  Morganton *(G-11232)*

Metalcraft & Mech Svc Inc............................. G..... 919 736-1029
  Goldsboro *(G-6636)*

▲ Moores Cylinder Heads LLC...................... E..... 704 786-8412
  Concord *(G-4318)*

▲ Moores Mch Co Fayetteville Inc................. D..... 919 837-5354
  Bear Creek *(G-941)*

Motoring Inc.. G..... 704 809-1265
  Mooresville *(G-11030)*

Motorsport Innovations Inc............................ G..... 704 728-7837
  Davidson *(G-4686)*

Motorsports Machining Tech LLC................... F..... 336 475-3742
  Thomasville *(G-15254)*

Mr Tire Inc.. F..... 828 322-8130
  Hickory *(G-8099)*

MSI Defense Solutions LLC........................... D..... 704 660-8348
  Mooresville *(G-11032)*

NC Saturn Parts LLC..................................... G..... 704 802-5277
  Charlotte *(G-3240)*

▲ Ohlins Usa Inc... E..... 828 692-4525
  Hendersonville *(G-7887)*

Oilkleen LLC.. F..... 480 650-8711
  Mooresville *(G-11042)*

Olivers Drive Shaft Repair............................. G..... 719 539-1823
  Winston Salem *(G-16829)*

On Point Mobile Detailing LLC....................... G..... 404 593-8882
  Charlotte *(G-3296)*

▲ Parker Gas Company Inc........................... F..... 800 354-7250
  Clinton *(G-4101)*

PCC Airfoils LLC.. B..... 919 774-4300
  Sanford *(G-14164)*

Poppelmann Plastics USA.............................. G..... 828 466-9500
  Claremont *(G-3932)*

Powerbrake Corporation................................ G..... 704 804-2438
  Huntersville *(G-8880)*

Precision Pdts Prfmce Ctr Inc....................... E..... 828 684-8569
  Arden *(G-367)*

Pro-Motor Engines Inc.................................. G..... 704 664-6800
  Mooresville *(G-11063)*

R M Gear Harness... G..... 336 498-1169
  Randleman *(G-13486)*

SIC SECTION
37 TRANSPORTATION EQUIPMENT

Race Technologies Concord NC .... G 704 799-0530
  Concord *(G-4346)*
Razor Motorsports .... G 704 517-0649
  Charlotte *(G-3415)*
Reuben James Auto Electric .... G 910 980-1056
  Falcon *(G-5727)*
Richardson Racing Products Inc .... G 704 784-2602
  Concord *(G-4350)*
Ripari Automotive LLC .... G 585 267-0228
  Charlotte *(G-3452)*
▲ Roadactive Suspension Inc .... G 704 523-2646
  Charlotte *(G-3454)*
▲ Rostra Precision Controls Inc .... D 910 291-2502
  Aberdeen *(G-27)*
Rp Motor Sports Inc .... E 704 720-4200
  Concord *(G-4353)*
RTC Ventures LLC .... G 704 247-9781
  Charlotte *(G-3470)*
Saf-Holland Inc .... G 336 310-4595
  Kernersville *(G-9230)*
Satco Truck Equipment Inc .... F 919 383-5547
  Durham *(G-5340)*
Save-A-Load Inc .... G 704 650-4947
  Charlotte *(G-3495)*
Schnitzer Group Usa Inc .... G 347 982-6880
  Charlotte *(G-3504)*
▲ Scorpion Products Inc .... G 336 813-3241
  King *(G-9281)*
Siebenwurst US Inc .... G 704 333-7790
  Charlotte *(G-3545)*
Simrek Corporation .... G 336 497-5331
  Kernersville *(G-9234)*
SL Liquidation LLC .... D 910 353-3666
  Jacksonville *(G-9031)*
SL Liquidation LLC .... B 910 353-3666
  Jacksonville *(G-9033)*
◆ SL Liquidation LLC .... B 860 525-0821
  Jacksonville *(G-9032)*
Spod Inc .... G 910 477-6297
  Southport *(G-14584)*
SRI Performance LLC .... E 704 662-6982
  Mooresville *(G-11097)*
▲ Stanadyne Intrmdate Hldngs LLC .... C 860 525-0821
  Jacksonville *(G-9038)*
Stanadyne Jacksonville LLC .... C 860 683-4553
  Jacksonville *(G-9039)*
Stanadyne Operating Co LLC .... D 910 353-3666
  Jacksonville *(G-9040)*
Studleys Independent Rods .... G 704 296-9036
  Monroe *(G-10816)*
▲ Sturdy Corporation .... C 910 763-2500
  Wilmington *(G-16420)*
Superfast Performance Pdts Inc .... G 828 980-8072
  Hudson *(G-8781)*
Suspensions LLC .... F 704 809-1269
  Denver *(G-4804)*
T & N Manufacturing Co Inc .... G 704 788-1418
  Davidson *(G-4698)*
Teijin Automotive Tech Inc .... C 828 754-8441
  Lenoir *(G-9655)*
Teijin Automotive Tech Inc .... D 828 466-7000
  Newton *(G-11977)*
Tenowo Inc .... A 704 732-3525
  Lincolnton *(G-9926)*
Thyssenkrupp Bilstein Amer Inc .... F 704 663-7563
  Mooresville *(G-11112)*
Tire Kountry LLC .... G 336 637-8320
  Reidsville *(G-13542)*
Trane Technologies Company LLC .... G 910 692-8700
  Southern Pines *(G-14558)*
Trend Performance Products .... G 828 862-8290
  Pisgah Forest *(G-12329)*

Trevira North America LLC .... G 704 910-0970
  Charlotte *(G-3722)*
Triangle Auto Components LLC .... F 704 848-4121
  Lilesville *(G-9841)*
Truck Parts Inc .... F 704 332-7909
  Charlotte *(G-3732)*
▲ Uchiyama Mfg Amer LLC .... B 919 731-2364
  Goldsboro *(G-6668)*
Ultimate Qm Inc .... G 704 500-9035
  Stanley *(G-14710)*
Unique Tool and Mfg Co .... E 336 498-2614
  Franklinville *(G-6171)*
◆ US Legend Cars Intl Inc .... E 704 455-3896
  Harrisburg *(G-7732)*
US Prototype Inc .... E 866 239-2848
  Wilmington *(G-16439)*
Visual Impact Prfmce Systems L .... G 704 278-3552
  Cleveland *(G-4083)*
Wenker Inc .... G 704 333-7790
  Charlotte *(G-3804)*
Wesley Leblanc Racing LLC .... G 336 560-7630
  Archdale *(G-305)*
Xceldyne LLC .... D 336 472-2242
  Thomasville *(G-15306)*
Xceldyne Technologies LLC .... D 336 475-0201
  Thomasville *(G-15308)*
Xtreme Fabrication Ltd .... F 336 472-4562
  Thomasville *(G-15309)*
Zeta Performance Vhcl Tech LLC .... G 804 690-8979
  Cornelius *(G-4596)*
ZF Chassis Components LLC .... C 828 468-3711
  Newton *(G-11986)*
Zingerle Group Usa Inc .... G 704 312-1600
  Charlotte *(G-3851)*

3715 Truck trailers

Accelrted Svcs Mooresville Inc .... G 704 658-6666
  Mooresville *(G-10845)*
Battle Trucking Inc .... G 919 708-2288
  Sanford *(G-14092)*
Bkc Industries Inc .... G 919 575-6699
  Creedmoor *(G-4607)*
Bucks Wrecker Service .... G 704 776-0899
  Statesville *(G-14767)*
Chimneyrock Storage .... G 828 685-2893
  Hendersonville *(G-7836)*
Daimler Truck North Amer LLC .... A 704 645-5000
  Cleveland *(G-4071)*
Ecovehicle Enterprises Inc .... G 704 544-9907
  Charlotte *(G-2685)*
Eugenes Trucking Inc .... G 910 267-0555
  Faison *(G-5723)*
F & C Repair and Sales LLC .... F 704 907-2461
  Charlotte *(G-2741)*
FEC Inc .... G 828 765-4599
  Spruce Pine *(G-14641)*
Gaines Motor Lines Inc .... C 828 322-2000
  Hickory *(G-8031)*
Kraftsman Inc .... D 336 824-1114
  Ramseur *(G-13445)*
L & S Automotive Inc .... G 704 391-7657
  Charlotte *(G-3065)*
Liberty Trailers LLC .... G 219 866-7141
  Liberty *(G-9822)*
Majic TNT Inc .... G 252 425-0489
  Liberty *(G-9824)*
▲ Master Tow Inc .... E 910 630-2000
  Fayetteville *(G-5869)*
▼ Mickey Truck Bodies Inc .... B 336 882-6806
  High Point *(G-8455)*
Payload Trailers Inc .... G 833 239-6565
  Thomasville *(G-15262)*

Road King Trailers Inc .... E 828 670-8012
  Candler *(G-1588)*
Smithway Inc .... G 828 628-1756
  Fairview *(G-5718)*
Speedway Link Inc .... F 704 338-2028
  Matthews *(G-10292)*
Spring Repair Service Inc .... F 336 299-5660
  Greensboro *(G-7360)*
Vision Metals Inc .... F 336 622-7300
  Liberty *(G-9834)*

3716 Motor homes

Hunckler Fabrication LLC .... F 336 753-0905
  Mocksville *(G-10581)*
Matthews Spcialty Vehicles Inc .... D 336 297-9600
  Greensboro *(G-7189)*
Van Products Inc .... E 919 878-7110
  Raleigh *(G-13392)*

3721 Aircraft

Adamantium Aerospace Inc .... G 252 444-6265
  Havelock *(G-7739)*
Anuma Aerospace LLC .... G 919 600-0142
  Raleigh *(G-12511)*
Atlas Aerospace Inc .... G 704 528-3356
  Cleveland *(G-4067)*
BEC-Faye LLC .... G 252 714-8700
  Grimesland *(G-7604)*
Birds Eye View Aerial Drone .... G 828 691-1550
  Candler *(G-1571)*
Blimp Works Inc .... F 704 876-2378
  Statesville *(G-14765)*
Boeing Arospc Operations Inc .... F 919 722-4351
  Goldsboro *(G-6594)*
Boeing Company .... G 704 572-8280
  Charlotte *(G-2330)*
Boeing Company .... G 919 722-1983
  Sjafb *(G-14446)*
Charter Jet Transport Inc .... G 704 359-8833
  Charlotte *(G-2468)*
CJ Partners LLC .... G 336 838-3080
  Wilkesboro *(G-16018)*
Cyberlux Corporation .... F 984 363-6894
  Research Triangle Pa *(G-13549)*
Fire Fly Ballons 2006 LLC .... F 704 878-9501
  Statesville *(G-14798)*
Firefly Balloons 2010 Inc .... G 704 878-9501
  Statesville *(G-14799)*
Franklin Aerospace Inc .... G 336 474-1960
  Thomasville *(G-15225)*
Gulfstream Plans & Design Inc .... G 704 641-2544
  Cornelius *(G-4553)*
Hawthorne Services .... F 910 436-9013
  Fayetteville *(G-5833)*
Highlander Unmanned Drone .... G 828 776-6061
  Fairview *(G-5713)*
Honda Aircraft Company LLC .... F 336 662-0246
  Greensboro *(G-7097)*
Honda Aircraft Company LLC .... F 336 662-0246
  Greensboro *(G-7098)*
◆ Honda Aircraft Company LLC .... B 336 662-0246
  Greensboro *(G-7099)*
Lulaza Aerospace LLC .... G 919 371-4240
  Morrisville *(G-11384)*
Marshall USA LLC .... G 301 481-1241
  Greensboro *(G-7183)*
Piedmont AVI Cmponent Svcs LLC .... C 336 423-5100
  Greensboro *(G-7255)*
Precision Arbatics USA Pty Ltd .... G 770 292-9122
  Chapel Hill *(G-2054)*
◆ Ride Best LLC .... G 252 489-2959
  Rodanthe *(G-13756)*

37 TRANSPORTATION EQUIPMENT

Signature Flight Air Inc .... E 919 840-4400
 Morrisville *(G-11429)*
Sikora Aerospace Tech Inc .... G 336 870-6351
 Winston Salem *(G-16910)*
Southern Aero LLC .... G 336 476-9094
 Thomasville *(G-15278)*
Spirit Aerosystems Inc .... A 252 208-4645
 Kinston *(G-9386)*
Summit Aviation Inc .... F 302 834-5400
 Greensboro *(G-7379)*
Tcom Limited Partnership .... B 252 330-5555
 Elizabeth City *(G-5575)*
Textron Aviation Inc .... C 336 605-7000
 Greensboro *(G-7398)*
United States Dept of Navy .... G 252 464-7228
 Cherry Point *(G-3860)*
USA Drones .... G 937 830-1856
 Belmont *(G-1017)*
Vicki Vermont Aircraft Sale .... G 828 225-6517
 Asheville *(G-815)*
Vx Aerospace Corporation .... F 828 433-5353
 Morganton *(G-11266)*
Vx Aerospace Holdings Inc .... F 828 433-5353
 Morganton *(G-11267)*
Wham Aviation LLC .... G 336 605-4663
 Summerfield *(G-14993)*

3724 Aircraft engines and engine parts

Aero 8 Inc .... F 336 776-9165
 Winston Salem *(G-16592)*
Carolina Precision Tech LLC .... E 215 675-4590
 Mooresville *(G-10898)*
Christine N Honeywell PT .... G 802 496-6509
 Whispering Pines *(G-15953)*
Circor Precision Metering LLC .... A 919 774-7667
 Sanford *(G-14102)*
Curtiss-Wright Controls Inc .... E 704 869-2300
 Shelby *(G-14305)*
Ek Air LLC .... G 704 881-1959
 Statesville *(G-14792)*
▲ GE Aircraft Engs Holdings Inc .... A 919 361-4400
 Durham *(G-5111)*
◆ Goodrich Corporation .... C 704 423-7000
 Charlotte *(G-2847)*
Hiab USA Inc .... F 704 896-9089
 Cornelius *(G-4555)*
Honda Aero Inc .... D 336 226-2376
 Burlington *(G-1430)*
Honeywell .... E 734 942-5823
 Charlotte *(G-2918)*
Honeywell International Inc .... G 910 436-5144
 Fort Bragg *(G-6090)*
Honeywell International Inc .... A 919 662-7539
 Raleigh *(G-12857)*
◆ Honeywell International Inc .... A 704 627-6200
 Charlotte *(G-2919)*
Ica(usa)inc .... G 704 798-3488
 Winston Salem *(G-16754)*
▲ James Tool Machine & Engrg Inc .. C 828 584-8722
 Morganton *(G-11224)*
◆ Lord Corporation .... B 919 468-5979
 Cary *(G-1817)*
Lord Far East Inc .... E 919 468-5979
 Cary *(G-1819)*
Pratt & Whitney Eng Svcs Inc .... G 860 565-4321
 Asheville *(G-740)*
Precision Metals LLC .... G 919 762-7481
 Benson *(G-1041)*
Smiths Aerospace Components ...... G 828 274-4540
 Asheville *(G-774)*
Thermal Pane Inc .... G 336 722-9977
 Lexington *(G-9791)*

Triad Engines Parts & Svcs Inc .... G 800 334-6437
 Burlington *(G-1507)*
Unique Tool and Mfg Co .... E 336 498-2614
 Franklinville *(G-6171)*

3728 Aircraft parts and equipment, nec

A & A Drone Service LLC .... G 704 928-5054
 Statesville *(G-14733)*
AAR Key Enterprises Inc .... G 919 337-9706
 Morrisville *(G-11275)*
Acme Aerofab LLC .... G 704 806-3582
 Charlotte *(G-2129)*
Air-We-Go LLC .... E 704 289-6565
 Monroe *(G-10640)*
Aircraft Parts Solutions LLC .... G 843 300-1725
 Apex *(G-157)*
AMF-NC Enterprise Company LLC ... F 704 489-2206
 Denver *(G-4760)*
Ark Aviation Inc .... G 336 379-0900
 Greensboro *(G-6814)*
ASAP Components .... G 919 258-2230
 Raleigh *(G-12526)*
B/E Aerospace Inc .... G 336 841-7698
 High Point *(G-8261)*
B/E Aerospace Inc .... F 336 692-8940
 Winston Salem *(G-16612)*
▲ B/E Aerospace Inc .... G 336 293-1823
 Winston Salem *(G-16614)*
▲ B/E Aerospace Inc .... G 336 293-1823
 Winston Salem *(G-16615)*
B/E Aerospace Inc .... G 336 744-6914
 Winston Salem *(G-16616)*
B/E Aerospace Inc .... E 336 767-2000
 Winston Salem *(G-16617)*
B/E Aerospace Inc .... D 520 733-1719
 Winston Salem *(G-16618)*
B/E Aerospace Inc .... G 336 776-3500
 Winston Salem *(G-16619)*
B/E Aerospace Inc .... C 336 767-2000
 Winston Salem *(G-16620)*
▲ B/E Aerospace Inc .... G 336 747-5000
 Winston Salem *(G-16613)*
▲ Ballistic Recovery Systems Inc ..... E 651 457-7491
 Pinebluff *(G-12213)*
▲ Beta Fueling Systems LLC .... D 336 342-0306
 Reidsville *(G-13509)*
Blanket Aero LLC .... F 704 591-2878
 Concord *(G-4209)*
Blue Force Technologies LLC .... D 919 443-1660
 Morrisville *(G-11305)*
▲ Brice Manufacturing Co Inc .... E 818 896-2938
 Greensboro *(G-6851)*
Carolina Ground Svc Eqp Inc .... F 252 565-0288
 New Bern *(G-11785)*
Carolina Metals Inc .... E 828 667-0876
 Asheville *(G-582)*
Circor Precision Metering LLC .... A 919 774-7667
 Sanford *(G-14102)*
Collins Aerospace .... F 704 423-7000
 Charlotte *(G-2524)*
Curtiss-Wright Controls Inc .... F 704 869-2320
 Gastonia *(G-6391)*
Curtiss-Wright Controls Inc .... E 704 869-2300
 Shelby *(G-14305)*
▲ Curtiss-Wright Controls Inc .... E 704 869-4600
 Charlotte *(G-2587)*
Cyberlux Corporation .... F 984 363-6894
 Research Triangle Pa *(G-13549)*
D2 Government Solutions LLC .... E 662 655-4554
 New Bern *(G-11797)*
DEB Manufacturing Inc .... G 704 703-6618
 Concord *(G-4253)*

Dronescape Pllc .... G 704 953-3798
 Charlotte *(G-2655)*
Dt Aerospace Inc .... G 919 417-1895
 Hillsborough *(G-8648)*
Equipment & Supply Inc .... E 704 289-6565
 Monroe *(G-10716)*
Esterline Technologies Corp .... G 910 814-1222
 Lillington *(G-9851)*
Firstmark Aerospace Corp .... G 919 956-4323
 Durham *(G-5098)*
Frisby Aerospace Inc .... G 336 712-8004
 Clemmons *(G-4040)*
GE Aviation Systems LLC .... C 828 210-5076
 Asheville *(G-631)*
General Electric Company .... A 910 675-5000
 Wilmington *(G-16230)*
Goaero LLC .... G 815 713-1190
 Greensboro *(G-7049)*
Goodrich Corporation .... G 704 282-2500
 Monroe *(G-10725)*
Goodrich Corporation .... G 704 282-2500
 Monroe *(G-10726)*
◆ Goodrich Corporation .... C 704 423-7000
 Charlotte *(G-2847)*
Gounmanned LLC .... G 919 835-2140
 Raleigh *(G-12810)*
Gray Manufacturing Tech LLC .... F 704 489-2206
 Denver *(G-4778)*
Honda Aircraft Company LLC .... F 336 662-0849
 Greensboro *(G-7096)*
Honeywell International Inc .... C 252 977-2100
 Rocky Mount *(G-13701)*
Isometrics Inc .... F 336 342-4150
 Reidsville *(G-13527)*
◆ Isometrics Inc .... E 336 349-2329
 Reidsville *(G-13528)*
▲ James Tool Machine & Engrg Inc .. C 828 584-8722
 Morganton *(G-11224)*
Kearfott Corporation .... B 828 350-5300
 Black Mountain *(G-1127)*
Kidde Technologies Inc .... D 252 237-7004
 Wilson *(G-16506)*
Legacy Aerospace and Def LLC .... G 828 398-0981
 Arden *(G-347)*
Logic Hydraulic Controls Inc .... E 910 791-9293
 Wilmington *(G-16304)*
◆ Lord Corporation .... B 919 468-5979
 Cary *(G-1817)*
Lord Far East Inc .... E 919 468-5979
 Cary *(G-1819)*
Ontic Engineering and Mfg Inc .... B 919 395-3908
 Creedmoor *(G-4619)*
Oro Manufacturing Company .... E 704 283-2186
 Monroe *(G-10783)*
PCC Airfoils LLC .... B 919 774-4300
 Sanford *(G-14164)*
Piedmont Flight Inc .... E 336 776-6070
 Winston Salem *(G-16852)*
Proedge Precision LLC .... E 704 872-3393
 Statesville *(G-14871)*
▲ Purolator Facet Inc .... E 336 668-4444
 Greensboro *(G-7293)*
R S Skillen .... G 828 433-5353
 Morganton *(G-11244)*
Rockwell Collins Inc .... G 336 744-3288
 Winston Salem *(G-16886)*
Safety & Security Intl Inc .... G 336 285-8673
 Greensboro *(G-7322)*
Sierra Nevada Corporation .... D 919 595-8551
 Durham *(G-5355)*
Soisa Inc .... G 336 940-4006
 Mocksville *(G-10604)*

Southern Prestige Intl LLC .... F 704 872-9524
  Statesville (G-14894)
Specialty Perf LLC .... G 704 872-9980
  Statesville (G-14897)
Spirit Aerosystems Inc .... A 252 208-4645
  Kinston (G-9386)
◆ Spirit Aerosystems NC Inc .... F 252 208-4645
  Raleigh (G-13292)
◆ Starhgen Arospc Components LLC ... F 704 660-1001
  Mooresville (G-11099)
T Air Inc .... D 980 595-2840
  Charlotte (G-3668)
Tcom Limited Partnership .... B 252 330-5555
  Elizabeth City (G-5575)
Telair US LLC .... C 919 705-2400
  Goldsboro (G-6665)
Tempest Aero Group .... F 336 449-5054
  Burlington (G-1505)
Tempest Aero Group .... E 336 449-5054
  Gibsonville (G-6571)
Tigerswan LLC .... C 919 439-7110
  Apex (G-248)
▲ Triumph Actuation Systems LLC ... C 336 766-9036
  Clemmons (G-4064)
◆ Unison Engine Components Inc ..... B 828 274-4540
  Asheville (G-808)
United States Dept of Navy .... E 252 466-4415
  Cherry Point (G-3858)
Vannoy Construction Arcft LLC .... G 336 846-7191
  Jefferson (G-9093)
Veritable Aerospace .... G 919 258-2230
  Raleigh (G-13398)
Vx Aerospace Corporation .... F 828 433-5353
  Morganton (G-11266)
▲ Weststar Precision Inc .... E 919 557-2820
  Cary (G-1926)
Wildcat Petroleum Service Inc .... F 704 379-0132
  Matthews (G-10351)

3731 Shipbuilding and repairing

Big Rock Industries Inc .... G 252 222-3618
  Morehead City (G-11152)
Edenton Boatworks LLC .... E 252 482-7600
  Edenton (G-5514)
Gallishaw Elite Rigging LLC .... G 757 240-8963
  Elizabeth City (G-5546)
Harbor Lines LLC .... G 910 279-3796
  Wilmington (G-16247)
International Bus Connection .... G 251 391-1158
  Cary (G-1791)
Lake Lure Marine .... G 828 200-5908
  Lake Lure (G-9447)
Lighthouse of Wayne County Inc ..... F 919 736-1313
  Goldsboro (G-6630)
M & J Marine LLC .... F 252 249-0522
  Oriental (G-12111)
Oilkleen Inc .... G 480 650-8711
  Mooresville (G-11041)
Oilkleen LLC .... F 480 650-8711
  Mooresville (G-11042)
Pilothouse Marine Services LLC .... G 252 732-6427
  Beaufort (G-965)
Riley Power Group LLC .... C 910 420-6999
  Pinehurst (G-12234)
Vigor LLC .... G 704 661-0891
  Matthews (G-10298)
Vigor LLC .... G 980 474-1124
  Charlotte (G-3777)
Waterline Systems Inc .... G 910 708-1000
  Hubert (G-8756)
Yang Ming America Corporation ...... G 704 357-3817
  Charlotte (G-3842)

3732 Boatbuilding and repairing

2nd Shift Cycles LLC .... G 336 462-3262
  Lexington (G-9676)
2topia Cycles Inc .... G 704 778-7849
  Charlotte (G-2106)
▲ 33rd Strike Group LLC .... G 910 371-9688
  Leland (G-9523)
A & J Canvas Inc .... E 252 244-1509
  Vanceboro (G-15474)
A Squared Pro Services LLC .... G 336 675-3546
  Burlington (G-1360)
▼ Alb Boats .... C 252 482-7600
  Edenton (G-5505)
Anglers Marine NC .... G 919 585-7900
  Clayton (G-3953)
B&S Shingle Savers Inc .... G 336 264-3898
  Burlington (G-1374)
Baja Marine Inc .... E 252 975-2000
  Washington (G-15683)
Barrs Competition .... F 704 482-5169
  Shelby (G-14287)
▲ Bayliss Boatworks Inc .... E 252 473-9797
  Wanchese (G-15641)
Bayliss Boatyard Inc .... F 252 473-9797
  Wanchese (G-15642)
Bennett Brothers Yachts Inc .... E 910 772-9277
  Wilmington (G-16135)
Bilge Masters Inc .... G 704 995-4293
  Charlotte (G-2310)
Black Oak Boat Works .... G 828 252-4997
  Asheville (G-561)
Blackbeards Boatworks .... G 252 726-6161
  Morehead City (G-11154)
◆ Briggs Boat Works Incorporated ... F 252 473-2393
  Wanchese (G-15643)
Brooks Boatworks Inc .... G 252 974-1005
  Bath (G-914)
Brp US Inc .... G 828 766-1164
  Spruce Pine (G-14630)
Brp US Inc .... D 828 766-1100
  Spruce Pine (G-14631)
Bryan Blake James .... G 252 729-8021
  Gloucester (G-6574)
Budsin Wood Craft .... G 252 729-1540
  Marshallberg (G-10209)
C E Hicks Enterprises Inc .... F 919 772-5131
  Garner (G-6259)
Cabarrus Cycling Company .... G 704 938-8735
  Kannapolis (G-9114)
Caison Yachts Inc .... G 910 270-6394
  Hampstead (G-7641)
Cape Fear Boat Works Inc .... F 910 371-3460
  Navassa (G-11757)
Cape Fear Yacht Works LLC .... G 910 540-1685
  Wilmington (G-16151)
▼ CC Boats Inc .... F 252 482-3699
  Edenton (G-5509)
Certified Fiberglass Inc .... G 252 241-9641
  Cape Carteret (G-1630)
Coastal Trimworks Inc .... G 910 231-8532
  Leland (G-9536)
Cote Timeworks LLC .... G 910 246-1767
  Southern Pines (G-14531)
Craig & Sandra Blackwell Inc .... G 252 473-1803
  Wanchese (G-15644)
Croswait Custom Composites Inc .... G 252 423-1245
  Wanchese (G-15645)
Crystal Coast Boatworks .... G 252 723-9370
  Beaufort (G-952)
Crystal Coast Composites Inc .... F 252 838-0025
  Beaufort (G-953)

Crystal Coast Composites Inc .... G 252 838-0025
  Morehead City (G-11165)
Custom Boatworks Inc .... G 252 235-2461
  Bailey (G-869)
Custom Fiberglass Products .... G 252 235-2461
  Bailey (G-870)
Custom Marine Fabrication Inc .... G 252 638-5422
  New Bern (G-11795)
Custom Steel Boats Inc .... F 252 745-7447
  Merritt (G-10439)
◆ Daedalus Composites LLC .... F 252 368-9000
  Edenton (G-5512)
Donzi Marine LLC .... F 252 975-2000
  Washington (G-15696)
▼ Egret Boats LLC .... G 252 948-0004
  Washington (G-15698)
Elite Marine LLC .... E 919 495-6388
  Four Oaks (G-6103)
Fiberglass Fabrication Inc .... G 828 685-0940
  Hendersonville (G-7847)
Fountain Powerboat Inds Inc .... C 252 975-2000
  Washington (G-15703)
Fountain Powerboats Inc .... D 252 975-2000
  Washington (G-15704)
French Broad Boatworks .... G 828 230-6600
  Asheville (G-628)
Gem Buoy Incorporated .... G 252 469-3680
  Tarboro (G-15105)
Giant Wake Forest LLC .... G 919 556-7433
  Wake Forest (G-15559)
Gillikin Marine Railways Inc .... G 252 726-7284
  Beaufort (G-958)
▼ Grady-White Boats Inc .... C 252 752-2111
  Greenville (G-7534)
◆ Gunboat International Ltd .... F 252 305-8700
  Wanchese (G-15646)
Gwg Boatworks LLC .... G 252 422-0757
  Morehead City (G-11173)
Harding Enterprise Inc .... G 252 725-9785
  Beaufort (G-960)
◆ Hatteras Yachts Inc .... A 252 633-3101
  New Bern (G-11808)
Hc Composites LLC .... C 252 641-8000
  Tarboro (G-15107)
Hermes Marine LLC .... E 252 368-9000
  Edenton (G-5515)
Hurricane Aqua Sports Inc .... G 910 293-2941
  Warsaw (G-15669)
Hysucat USA LLC .... G 919 345-0240
  Raleigh (G-12871)
Iconic Marine Group LLC .... D 252 975-2000
  Chocowinity (G-3895)
Jabec Enterprise Inc .... G 336 655-8441
  Winston Salem (G-16768)
Jarrett Bay Offshore .... G 919 803-1990
  Raleigh (G-12913)
JG Agnew Holdings Inc .... G 704 594-0900
  Harrisburg (G-7714)
John Glen Alexander Corp .... G 704 309-7258
  Huntersville (G-8841)
Johnson Custom Boats Inc .... G 910 232-4594
  Wilmington (G-16282)
Jones Brothers Marine Mfg Inc .... F 252 240-1995
  Morehead City (G-11178)
Jones Marine Inc .... G 704 639-0173
  Salisbury (G-13994)
Kencraft Manufacturing Inc .... F 252 291-0271
  Wilson (G-16505)
Kennys Fiberglass Restoration .... G 704 252-0979
  Mooresville (G-10996)
Knooosc Inc .... G 415 640-0080
  Morehead City (G-11179)

37 TRANSPORTATION EQUIPMENT

Lake House Enterprises Inc .... G 919 424-3780
　Raleigh *(G-12952)*
Laytons Custom Boatworks LLC .... G 252 482-1504
　Edenton *(G-5518)*
◆ Legacy Paddlesports LLC .... C 828 684-1933
　Fletcher *(G-6017)*
M & J Marine LLC .... F 252 249-0522
　Oriental *(G-12111)*
Mann Custom Boats Inc .... E 252 473-1716
　Manns Harbor *(G-10122)*
Marine Tooling Technology Inc .... G 336 887-9577
　High Point *(G-8439)*
Marinemax of North Carolina .... E 910 256-8100
　Wrightsville Beach *(G-17026)*
Mass Enterprises LLC .... F 443 585-0732
　New Bern *(G-11821)*
▼ May-Craft Fiberglass Pdts Inc .... E 919 934-3000
　Four Oaks *(G-6109)*
Mike Luszcz .... G 252 717-6282
　Winterville *(G-17007)*
Moores Marine Yacht Center Inc .... F 252 504-7060
　Beaufort *(G-961)*
Mr Home Genius LLC .... G 252 902-4663
　Winterville *(G-17009)*
Nomad Houseboats Inc .... G 252 288-5670
　New Bern *(G-11831)*
Obx Boatworks LLC .... G 336 878-9490
　High Point *(C-8469)*
Onslow Bay Boatworks & Marine .... G 910 270-3703
　Hampstead *(G-7653)*
Pacific Seacraft LLC .... G 252 948-1421
　Washington *(G-15722)*
Pair Marine Inc .... F 252 717-7009
　Washington *(G-15723)*
▼ Parker Marine Enterprises Inc .... D 252 728-5621
　Beaufort *(G-964)*
Powers Boatworks .... G 910 762-3636
　Wilmington *(G-16364)*
Rapid Response Technology LLC .... G 910 763-3856
　Wilmington *(G-16378)*
▼ Regulator Marine Inc .... D 252 482-3837
　Edenton *(G-5521)*
Rent A Guy Now LLC .... G 919 637-1104
　Garner *(G-6209)*
Richard Scarborough Boat Works .... G 252 473-3646
　Wanchese *(G-15650)*
Rings True LLC .... G 919 265-7600
　Carrboro *(G-1656)*
Salt Boatworks Inc .... G 919 394-3795
　Newport *(G-11906)*
Sea Mark Boats Inc .... G 910 675-1877
　Rocky Point *(G-13749)*
Shearline Boatworks LLC .... G 252 726-6916
　Morehead City *(G-11189)*
Shm Jarrett Bay Trs LLC .... G 972 488-1314
　Beaufort *(G-966)*
Smoky Mountain Jet Boats LLC .... F 828 488-0522
　Bryson City *(G-1325)*
Specialty Boatworks Inc .... G 910 251-5219
　Wilmington *(G-16415)*
Spencer Yachts Inc .... G 252 473-2660
　Manns Harbor *(G-10123)*
▼ Starflite Companies Inc .... C 252 728-2690
　Beaufort *(G-968)*
Stroudcraft Marine LLC .... F 910 623-4055
　Rocky Point *(G-13751)*
Sullivan Motorsports Inc .... G 252 923-2257
　Bath *(G-917)*
Taylor Boat Works .... G 252 726-6374
　Morehead City *(G-11194)*
Taylor Manufacturing Inc .... E 910 862-2576
　Elizabethtown *(G-5605)*

Todds Rv & Marine Inc .... F 828 651-0007
　Hendersonville *(G-7908)*
Trawler Incorporated .... G 252 745-3751
　Lowland *(G-10015)*
Triad Marine Center Inc .... G 252 634-1880
　New Bern *(G-11851)*
True World Marine LLC .... G 252 728-2541
　Beaufort *(G-970)*
Twin Troller Boats Inc .... G 919 207-2622
　Benson *(G-1044)*
U S Propeller Service Inc .... G 704 528-9515
　Troutman *(G-15396)*
Wanchese Dock and Haul LLC .... G 252 473-6424
　Wanchese *(G-15651)*
Warrior Boats .... G 336 885-2628
　High Point *(G-8601)*
White River Marine Group LLC .... C 252 633-3101
　New Bern *(G-11856)*
Williams United LLC .... G 336 251-7355
　Kernersville *(G-9253)*
Winter Custom Yachts Inc .... F 910 325-7583
　Hubert *(G-8758)*
▲ Winterville Machine Works Inc .... D 252 756-2130
　Winterville *(G-17018)*
Xcelerator Boatworks Inc .... G 704 622-8978
　Statesville *(G-14930)*

3743 Railroad equipment

▲ Dellner Inc .... E 704 527-2121
　Charlotte *(G-2614)*
Freightpal Inc .... G 704 971-8183
　Charlotte *(G-2796)*
Frit Car Inc .... E 252 638-2675
　Bridgeton *(G-1294)*
◆ Kck Holding Corp .... E 336 513-0002
　Burlington *(G-1443)*
Knorr Brake Truck Systems Co .... A 888 836-6922
　Salisbury *(G-14001)*
New York Air Brake LLC .... D 315 786-5200
　Salisbury *(G-14019)*
Ohilda Bombardier .... G 704 658-7134
　Locust *(G-9965)*
Power Logistixs LLC .... G 919 799-0303
　Selma *(G-14259)*
◆ Railroad Friction Pdts Corp .... C 910 844-9709
　Maxton *(G-10362)*
Twin Oaks Service South Inc .... G 704 914-7142
　Shelby *(G-14378)*

3751 Motorcycles, bicycles, and parts

B & B Welding Inc .... G 336 643-5702
　Oak Ridge *(G-12057)*
Barrs Competition .... F 704 482-5169
　Shelby *(G-14287)*
C & S Custom .... G 336 242-9730
　Lexington *(G-9688)*
▲ Cane Creek Cycling Cmpnnts Inc .... E 828 684-3551
　Fletcher *(G-5991)*
Capital Value Center Sls & Svc .... G 910 799-4060
　Wilmington *(G-16153)*
Choppers and Hotrods .... G 336 993-3939
　Kernersville *(G-9178)*
Club The Nantahala Bicycle Inc .... G 828 524-4900
　Franklin *(G-6119)*
Devils Kindred MC .... E 336 712-7689
　Swansboro *(G-15044)*
Driver Distribution Inc .... G 984 204-2929
　Raleigh *(G-12702)*
Driver Distribution Inc .... G 984 204-2929
　Maiden *(G-10106)*
Edelbrock LLC .... D 919 718-9737
　Sanford *(G-14113)*

Evil Swingarms 1 LLC .... G 336 847-2476
　Seagrove *(G-14238)*
Garys Garage .... G 828 513-5055
　Hendersonville *(G-7855)*
Hop A Chopper Inc .... G 704 624-6794
　Marshville *(G-10219)*
Huck Cycles Corporation .... G 704 275-1735
　Cornelius *(G-4557)*
Indian Motorcycle Company .... G 704 879-4560
　Lowell *(G-10010)*
▲ Industry Nine LLC .... G 828 210-5113
　Asheville *(G-661)*
Ironworks Motorcycles .... G 336 542-7868
　Greensboro *(G-7123)*
James King .... G 910 308-8818
　Fayetteville *(G-5845)*
John Jones DBA Grass Choppers .... G 336 413-6613
　Lewisville *(G-9668)*
Moto Group LLC .... F 828 350-7653
　Fletcher *(G-6028)*
▲ Next World Design Inc .... F 800 448-1223
　Thomasville *(G-15256)*
P P M Cycle and Custom .... G 336 434-5243
　Trinity *(G-15351)*
Performance Parts Intl LLC .... F 704 660-1084
　Mooresville *(G-11052)*
Rhoddie Bicycle Outfitters Inc .... G 828 414-9800
　Blowing Rock *(G-1156)*
Rinehart Racing Inc .... E 828 350-7653
　Fletcher *(G-6035)*
Suspension Experts LLC .... E 855 419-3072
　Roxboro *(G-13827)*
▲ Sv Plastics LLC .... G 336 472-2242
　Thomasville *(G-15287)*
Vexea Mx LLC .... G 910 787-9391
　Jacksonville *(G-9043)*

3761 Guided missiles and space vehicles

End Camp North .... G 980 337-4600
　Charlotte *(G-2710)*

3764 Space propulsion units and parts

▲ James Tool Machine & Engrg Inc .... C 828 584-8722
　Morganton *(G-11224)*

3769 Space vehicle equipment, nec

Carolina Metals Inc .... E 828 667-0876
　Asheville *(G-582)*
Firstmark Aerospace Corp .... D 919 956-4200
　Creedmoor *(G-4613)*
Kearfott Corporation .... B 828 350-5300
　Black Mountain *(G-1127)*

3792 Travel trailers and campers

Allison Globl Mnufacturing Inc .... F 704 392-7883
　Charlotte *(G-2162)*
Alossi Renewal Spa LLC .... G 406 338-7700
　Raleigh *(G-12492)*
Boondock S Manufacturing Inc .... G 828 891-4242
　Etowah *(G-5691)*
Cold Mountain Capital LLC .... F 828 210-8129
　Asheville *(G-596)*
Derrow Enterprises Inc .... G 252 635-3375
　New Bern *(G-11800)*
Elite Metal Performance LLC .... F 704 660-0006
　Statesville *(G-14793)*
Greene Mountain Outdoors LLC .... F 336 670-2186
　North Wilkesboro *(G-12011)*
Inka Outdoor LLC .... G 828 539-0842
　Gastonia *(G-6428)*
▲ Southag Mfg Inc .... F 919 365-5111
　Wendell *(G-15918)*

3795 Tanks and tank components

▲ Carolina Custom Tank LLC............... F 980 406-3200
  Gastonia *(G-6368)*
Crown Defense Ltd........................... G 202 800-8848
  Denver *(G-4769)*
▲ Parker Gas Company Inc................ F 800 354-7250
  Clinton *(G-4101)*

3799 Transportation equipment, nec

A-1 Hitch & Trailors Sales Inc........... F 910 755-6025
  Supply *(G-15005)*
American Growler Inc......................... E 352 671-5393
  Robbins *(G-13596)*
BOB Trailers Inc.............................. E 208 375-5171
  Charlotte *(G-2328)*
Brisk Transport 910 LLC..................... G 910 527-7398
  Cameron *(G-1560)*
Colfax Trailer & Repair LLC................ G 336 993-8511
  Colfax *(G-4144)*
Complete Trnsp & Dist Ctr Inc............ G 336 457-6960
  Greensboro *(G-6927)*
Crown Defense Ltd........................... G 202 800-8848
  Denver *(G-4769)*
Down East Offroad Inc....................... F 252 246-9440
  Wilson *(G-16493)*
Faith Farm Inc................................. G 704 431-4566
  Salisbury *(G-13963)*
Front Line Express LLC..................... G 800 260-1357
  Greensboro *(G-7023)*
Gore S Trlr Manufacturer S Inc.......... F 910 642-2246
  Whiteville *(G-15964)*
Heaths R&R Transport LLC................ G 252 558-5215
  Greenville *(G-7538)*
Jo-Natta Transportation LLC............... G 888 424-8789
  Fayetteville *(G-5850)*
▼ Kaufman Trailers Inc...................... E 336 790-6800
  Lexington *(G-9739)*
Kenn M LLC..................................... G 678 755-6607
  Raleigh *(G-12935)*
Libra Life Group Llc......................... G 910 550-8664
  Leland *(G-9552)*
Lionstar Transport LLC..................... G 336 448-0166
  Winston Salem *(G-16789)*
Long Trailer Co Inc........................... G 252 823-8828
  Tarboro *(G-15111)*
Naarva.. G 704 333-3070
  Charlotte *(G-3228)*
New Beginnings Trnsp LLC................ G 704 293-0493
  Charlotte *(G-3248)*
North Carolina Dept Trnsp................. G 828 733-9002
  Newland *(G-11891)*
Rapid Response Technology LLC....... G 910 763-3856
  Wilmington *(G-16378)*
Sanford S Atv Repair LLC.................. G 252 438-2730
  Henderson *(G-7809)*
Seans Transportation LLC.................. G 646 603-8128
  Charlotte *(G-3521)*
Speed Utv LLC................................. E 704 949-1255
  Concord *(G-4365)*
▲ Stiles Mfg Co Inc.......................... G 910 592-6344
  Clinton *(G-4113)*
◆ Technibilt Ltd............................... E 828 464-7388
  Newton *(G-11976)*
Trick Karts Inc................................. G 704 883-0089
  Statesville *(G-14917)*
Turner Boys Carrier Svc LLC.............. G 919 946-7553
  Raleigh *(G-13371)*
Williams Easy Hitch Inc..................... G 919 302-0062
  Durham *(G-5441)*
Xxxtreme Motorsport......................... G 704 663-1500
  Mooresville *(G-11135)*

38 MEASURING, PHOTOGRAPHIC, MEDICAL, & OPTICAL GOODS, & CLOCKS

3812 Search and navigation equipment

◆ Accurate Technology Inc................ G 828 654-7920
  Fletcher *(G-5980)*
Advanced Detection Tech LLC............ E 704 663-1949
  Mooresville *(G-10850)*
Airfield Solutions LLC........................ G 844 478-6929
  Hubert *(G-8747)*
Airfield Solutions LLC........................ G 919 348-4271
  Jacksonville *(G-8985)*
Armored Self Defense LLC................. G 336 749-7556
  Winston Salem *(G-16610)*
Assa Abloy Accessories and............... B 704 233-4011
  Monroe *(G-10654)*
Bae Systems Inc............................... D 855 223-8363
  Charlotte *(G-2263)*
Beyond Electronics Corp.................... G 919 231-8000
  Raleigh *(G-12553)*
Black Barrel Defense LLC................... G 336 468-8102
  Hamptonville *(G-7668)*
Blue Diamond Defense LLC................ G 334 905-0246
  Sylva *(G-15055)*
Blue Maiden Defense........................ G 678 292-8342
  Pinebluff *(G-12214)*
Blue Ridge Armor LLC....................... G 844 556-6855
  Rutherfordton *(G-13866)*
Btc Electronic Components LLC.......... E 919 229-2162
  Wake Forest *(G-15536)*
Chemring Snsors Elctrnic Syste.......... G 980 235-2200
  Charlotte *(G-2470)*
◆ Commscope Inc North Carolina....... D 828 324-2200
  Claremont *(G-3909)*
Commscope Technologies LLC............ F 919 934-9711
  Smithfield *(G-14457)*
Curtiss-Wright Controls Inc................ E 704 869-2300
  Shelby *(G-14305)*
Curtiss-Wright Corporation................. B 704 869-4600
  Davidson *(G-4669)*
Cyber Defense Advisors..................... G 336 899-6072
  Greensboro *(G-6952)*
Damsel Dedicated To Defense............ G 910 546-5603
  Southport *(G-14570)*
Damsel In Defense........................... E 919 362-5972
  Apex *(G-179)*
Damsel In Defense........................... F 919 744-8776
  Clayton *(G-3972)*
Damsel In Defense........................... G 919 901-9926
  Goldsboro *(G-6608)*
Dark City Defense............................. G 805 729-8800
  Black Mountain *(G-1123)*
Defense Logistics Services LLC.......... C 703 449-1620
  Fayetteville *(G-5809)*
Defense of Implicit........................... G 919 554-2735
  Louisburg *(G-9985)*
Dodson Defense LLC......................... G 336 421-9649
  Burlington *(G-1408)*
Dynamic Defense Tactics II LLC......... G 703 850-1103
  Canton *(G-1614)*
Eco Building Corporation................... G 910 736-1540
  Red Springs *(G-13499)*
Empowered Defense LLC................... G 919 624-1304
  Raleigh *(G-12736)*
Fil-Chem Inc................................... G 919 878-1270
  Raleigh *(G-12766)*
Firstmark Aerospace Corp.................. G 919 956-4200
  Creedmoor *(G-4613)*
Foothills Fire Defense LLC................. G 828 381-3988
  Hickory *(G-8027)*
Foothills Fire Defense LLC................. G 828 612-9575
  Hickory *(G-8028)*
Garmin International Inc.................... B 919 337-0116
  Cary *(G-1771)*
General Dynmics Mssion Systems...... C 336 698-8000
  Mc Leansville *(G-10391)*
General Electric Company.................. A 910 675-5000
  Wilmington *(G-16230)*
Green Line Defense LLC.................... G 828 707-5236
  Leicester *(G-9512)*
High Velocity Defense........................ G 704 738-3574
  Salisbury *(G-13980)*
Honeywell International Inc................ C 252 977-2100
  Rocky Mount *(G-13701)*
Ickler Manufacturing LLC................... G 704 658-1195
  Mooresville *(G-10980)*
James W McManus Inc..................... G 828 688-2560
  Bakersville *(G-884)*
▲ JMS Southeast Inc........................ E 704 873-1835
  Statesville *(G-14825)*
Kdh Defense Systems Inc.................. C 336 635-4158
  Eden *(G-5494)*
Kearfott Corporation.......................... B 828 350-5300
  Black Mountain *(G-1127)*
Kidde Technologies Inc...................... B 252 237-7004
  Wilson *(G-16507)*
Lynx Defense Corporation.................. G 919 701-9411
  Four Oaks *(G-6108)*
Mas Defense LLC.............................. G 980 265-1005
  Charlotte *(G-3136)*
Navelite LLC.................................... G 336 509-9924
  Jamestown *(G-9062)*
New Phoenix Aerospace Inc............... F 919 380-8500
  Raleigh *(G-13062)*
Northrop Grmman Gdnce Elec Inc...... E 704 588-2340
  Charlotte *(G-3270)*
Northrop Grmman Tchncal Svcs I...... E 252 447-7575
  Havelock *(G-7744)*
Northrop Grumman Systems Corp..... E 252 225-0911
  Atlantic *(G-827)*
Northrop Grumman Systems Corp..... D 252 447-7557
  Cherry Point *(G-3857)*
Northrop Grumman Systems Corp..... D 919 465-5020
  Morrisville *(G-11398)*
Northstar Computer Tech Inc.............. G 980 272-1969
  Monroe *(G-10780)*
Personal Defense Trainin.................... G 910 455-4473
  Jacksonville *(G-9019)*
Ping Gps Inc.................................... G 704 806-7945
  Cornelius *(G-4576)*
Plane Defense Ltd............................ G 828 254-6061
  Hendersonville *(G-7891)*
Qualia Networks Inc.......................... G 805 637-2083
  Raleigh *(G-13162)*
Rockwell Collins Inc.......................... G 336 776-3444
  Winston Salem *(G-16887)*
Rockwell Collins Inc.......................... G 336 744-1097
  Winston Salem *(G-16888)*
Roy Bridgmohan............................... G 804 426-9652
  Henderson *(G-7808)*
Sash and Saber Castings................... G 919 870-5513
  Raleigh *(G-13230)*
Sense and Defenseability LLC............ G 704 880-0165
  Stony Point *(G-14973)*
Serio Self Defense School of.............. G 225 245-0693
  Waynesville *(G-15822)*
Sierra Nevada Corporation................. D 919 595-8551
  Durham *(G-5355)*
Sierra Nevada Corporation................. E 910 307-0362
  Fayetteville *(G-5915)*

38 MEASURING, PHOTOGRAPHIC, MEDICAL, & OPTICAL GOODS, & CLOCKS

Sierra Nevada Corporation......................... F 775 331-0222
   Southern Pines *(G-14553)*

Soul Defense LLC.................................... G 704 726-7898
   Charlotte *(G-3583)*

Spatial Light LLC..................................... G 617 213-0314
   Cary *(G-1899)*

Tempest Aero Group................................ E 336 449-5054
   Gibsonville *(G-6571)*

Ultra Elec Ocean Systems Inc .... G 781 848-3400
   Wake Forest *(G-15608)*

United States Dept of Navy........................ G 252 466-4514
   Cherry Point *(G-3859)*

US Prototype Inc .... E 866 239-2848
   Wilmington *(G-16439)*

Usat LLC .... E 919 942-4214
   Chapel Hill *(G-2091)*

Willis Defense LLC................................... G 704 609-9953
   Iron Station *(G-8978)*

3821 Laboratory apparatus and furniture

Air Control Inc....................................... E 252 492-2300
   Henderson *(G-7775)*

Aisthesis Products Inc............................. G 828 627-6555
   Clyde *(G-4120)*

Biovind LLC.. G 512 217-3077
   Charlotte *(G-2317)*

◆ Carolina Biological Supply Company ....C 336 584-0381
   Burlington *(G-1384)*

Clinicians Advocacy Group Inc .... G 704 751-9515
   Charlotte *(G-2497)*

Cooper Technical Services Inc .... G 910 285-2925
   Rose Hill *(G-13774)*

▲ Corilam Fabricating Co......................... E 336 993-2371
   Kernersville *(G-9182)*

Corning Incorporated............................... C 919 620-6200
   Durham *(G-5034)*

Diversified Woodcrafts Inc........................ E 336 688-3114
   High Point *(G-8326)*

Dove Medical Supply LLC......................... E 336 643-9367
   Summerfield *(G-14980)*

Ecodyst Inc.. G 919 599-4963
   Apex *(G-187)*

Fisher Scientific Company LLC................. D 800 252-7100
   Asheville *(G-623)*

◆ Flow Sciences Inc............................... E 910 763-1717
   Leland *(G-9542)*

◆ Ika-Works Inc..................................... D 910 452-7059
   Wilmington *(G-16264)*

Intensa Inc... E 336 884-4096
   High Point *(G-8411)*

Kewaunee Scientific Corp......................... A 704 873-7202
   Statesville *(G-14831)*

▲ Pacon Manufacturing Corp LLC.............. C 732 764-9070
   Navassa *(G-11758)*

▼ Parameter Generation Ctrl Inc............... E 828 669-8717
   Black Mountain *(G-1133)*

Primevigilance Inc.................................. G 781 703-5540
   Raleigh *(G-13141)*

Research Instruments Inc........................ G 919 383-2775
   Durham *(G-5327)*

▲ Sarstedt Inc....................................... C 828 465-4000
   Newton *(G-11966)*

▲ Thermo Fsher Scntfc Ashvlle L............. B 828 658-2711
   Asheville *(G-798)*

Xona Microfluidics Inc............................. G 951 553-6400
   Durham *(G-5456)*

3822 Environmental controls

Ademco Inc... G 919 872-5556
   Raleigh *(G-12476)*

AMR Systems LLC.................................. G 704 980-9072
   Charlotte *(G-2190)*

Belham Management Ind LLC.................. G 704 815-4246
   Charlotte *(G-2297)*

Building Automation Svcs LLC.................. F 336 884-4026
   High Point *(G-8277)*

Camco Manufacturing Inc........................ G 336 348-6609
   Reidsville *(G-13511)*

Comp Environmental Inc.......................... F 919 316-1321
   Durham *(G-5028)*

Cooke Companies Intl .... F 919 968-0848
   Chapel Hill *(G-2006)*

▲ Dampp-Chaser Electronics Corp............ E 828 692-8271
   Hendersonville *(G-7842)*

Delkote Machine Finishing Inc.................. G 828 253-1023
   Asheville *(G-606)*

Ditex LLC .... G 919 215-3773
   Durham *(G-5054)*

▲ Dna Group Inc.................................... E 919 881-0889
   Raleigh *(G-12690)*

Dorsett Technologies Inc.......................... E 855 387-2232
   Yadkinville *(G-17038)*

Dynamac Corporation............................. G 919 544-6428
   Durham *(G-5073)*

▲ Effikal LLC... E 252 522-3031
   Kinston *(G-9361)*

Flame-Tec LLC....................................... F 844 352-6383
   Hendersonville *(G-7850)*

Global Envmtl Ctrl III Inc.......................... G 704 603-6155
   Salisbury *(G-13970)*

Green Stream Technologies Inc................. G 844 499-8880
   Wake Forest *(G-15563)*

Hoffman Building Tech Inc....................... C 336 292-8777
   Greensboro *(G-7094)*

Huber Usa Inc.. F 919 674-4266
   Raleigh *(G-12865)*

Icare Usa Inc... G 919 877-9607
   Raleigh *(G-12874)*

Industrial Heat LLC................................. G 919 743-5727
   Raleigh *(G-12885)*

▲ JMS Southeast Inc............................. E 704 873-1835
   Statesville *(G-14825)*

Johnson Controls Inc.............................. E 704 521-8889
   Charlotte *(G-3030)*

Johnson Global CmpInce Contrls............... G 704 552-1119
   Charlotte *(G-3032)*

Layer27.. F 919 909-9088
   Youngsville *(G-17088)*

Mc Controls LLC..................................... G 336 518-1303
   Yadkinville *(G-17045)*

Miller Ctrl Mfg Inc Clinton NC.................... G 910 592-5112
   Clinton *(G-4098)*

▲ Nascent Technology LLC..................... F 704 654-3035
   Charlotte *(G-3232)*

▼ Parameter Generation Ctrl Inc............... E 828 669-8717
   Black Mountain *(G-1133)*

▲ Pas USA Inc....................................... F 252 974-5500
   Washington *(G-15726)*

Qualia Networks Inc................................ G 805 637-2083
   Raleigh *(G-13162)*

Realxperience LLC.................................. G 512 775-4386
   Durham *(G-5322)*

Ruskin LLC.. G 919 583-5444
   Goldsboro *(G-6652)*

◆ Salice America Inc.............................. G 704 841-7810
   Charlotte *(G-3483)*

▲ Shelby Kendrion Inc........................... C 704 482-9582
   Shelby *(G-14366)*

Strandberg Engrg Labs Inc....................... F 336 274-3775
   Greensboro *(G-7374)*

Thermik Corporation............................... E 252 636-5720
   New Bern *(G-11850)*

◆ Trane US Inc...................................... A 704 655-4000
   Davidson *(G-4704)*

▲ TRf Manufacturing NC Inc.................... E 252 223-1112
   Newport *(G-11909)*

Ultratech Industries Inc........................... G 919 779-2004
   Benson *(G-1045)*

W A Brown & Son Incorporated................. E 704 636-5131
   Salisbury *(G-14063)*

3823 Process control instruments

▲ AC Corporation................................... B 336 273-4472
   Greensboro *(G-6775)*

Acucal Inc... G 252 337-9975
   Elizabeth City *(G-5530)*

Areva... F 704 805-2935
   Huntersville *(G-8793)*

Armtec Esterline Corp.............................. E 910 814-3029
   Lillington *(G-9842)*

ATI Industrial Automation Inc.................... C 919 772-0115
   Apex *(G-167)*

B G V Inc... E 704 588-3047
   Pineville *(G-12254)*

Barcovision LLC..................................... F 704 392-9371
   Charlotte *(G-2278)*

Biodot Inc... G 949 440-3685
   Hillsborough *(G-8639)*

Bluetick Inc... F 336 294-4102
   Greensboro *(G-6844)*

Centice Corporation................................ E 919 653-0424
   Raleigh *(G-12617)*

Cordex Instruments Inc........................... G 877 836-0764
   Charlotte *(G-2553)*

Czechmate Enterprises LLC..................... G 704 784-6547
   Concord *(G-4250)*

Dana Industries...................................... G 919 496-3262
   Louisburg *(G-9984)*

Delta Msrment Cmbstn Cntrls LL.............. E 919 623-7133
   Cary *(G-1747)*

Diverse Flooring Systems......................... G 910 425-8915
   Fayetteville *(G-5812)*

Electrical Panel & Contrls Inc.................... F 336 434-4445
   High Point *(G-8338)*

Emerson Electric Co................................ G 704 480-8519
   Shelby *(G-14316)*

Emerson Process Management................. F 704 357-0294
   Charlotte *(G-2708)*

Eng Solutions Inc................................... F 919 831-1830
   Chapel Hill *(G-2014)*

▲ Eno Scientific LLC.............................. G 910 778-2660
   Hillsborough *(G-8650)*

▲ Fairchild Industrial Pdts Co.................. D 336 659-3400
   Winston Salem *(G-16706)*

Gerald Hartsoe....................................... G 336 498-3233
   Randleman *(G-13471)*

▲ Global Sensors................................... G 704 827-4331
   Mount Holly *(G-11638)*

◆ Global Sensors LLC............................ G 704 827-4331
   Belmont *(G-992)*

Grover Gaming Inc.................................. D 252 329-7900
   Greenville *(G-7536)*

Hoffer Calibration Svcs LLC...................... G 252 338-6379
   Elizabeth City *(G-5549)*

▼ Hoffer Flow Controls Inc....................... D 252 331-1997
   Elizabeth City *(G-5550)*

▲ JMS Southeast Inc............................. E 704 873-1835
   Statesville *(G-14825)*

Kdy Automation Solutions Inc................... G 888 219-0049
   Morrisville *(G-11364)*

▲ Liburdi Turbine Services LLC................ E 704 230-2510
   Mooresville *(G-11008)*

Linor Technology Inc............................... F 336 485-6199
   Winston Salem *(G-16788)*

▲ Mac Panel Company............................ E 336 861-3100
   High Point *(G-8435)*

38 MEASURING, PHOTOGRAPHIC, MEDICAL, & OPTICAL GOODS, & CLOCKS

Motion Sensors Inc .... E 252 335-7294
 Elizabeth City *(G-5557)*
MTS Systems Corporation .... C 919 677-2352
 Cary *(G-1827)*
▲ Multi Technical Services Inc .... G 919 553-2995
 Clayton *(G-4000)*
Nexjen Systems LLC .... E 704 969-7070
 Charlotte *(G-3255)*
Oryx Systems Inc .... G 704 519-8803
 Indian Trail *(G-8955)*
▲ Palmer Instruments Inc .... E 828 658-3131
 Asheville *(G-720)*
▲ Palmer Wahl Instruments Inc .... E 828 658-3131
 Asheville *(G-721)*
Park Court Properties RE Inc .... F 919 304-3110
 Mebane *(G-10423)*
Progressive Intl Elec Inc .... G 919 266-4442
 Knightdale *(G-9426)*
QMAX Industries LLC .... G 704 643-7299
 Pineville *(G-12293)*
▲ Robert H Wager Company Inc .... F 336 969-6909
 Rural Hall *(G-13851)*
Rotork-Fairchild Indus Pdts Co .... G 336 659-3400
 Winston Salem *(G-16890)*
Rtst LLC .... G 704 999-9906
 Mooresville *(G-11076)*
Sapphire Tchncal Solutions LLC .... G 704 561-3100
 Pineville *(G-12302)*
Sgl Carbon LLC .... G 828 437-3221
 Morganton *(G-11251)*
Signalscape Inc .... E 919 859-4565
 Cary *(G-1889)*
Solarbrook Water and Pwr Corp .... G 919 231-3205
 Raleigh *(G-13278)*
Sota Vision Inc .... E 800 807-7187
 Midland *(G-10479)*
Southsern Prcess Eqp Cntrls I .... F 704 483-1141
 Denver *(G-4802)*
Strandberg Engrg Labs Inc .... F 336 274-3775
 Greensboro *(G-7374)*
Symbrium Inc .... F 919 879-2470
 Raleigh *(G-13319)*
Tarheel Waves LLC .... G 855 897-2327
 Greensboro *(G-7391)*
Tc2 Labs LLC .... G 919 380-2171
 Raleigh *(G-13329)*
Telecommunications Tech Inc .... F 919 556-7100
 Youngsville *(G-17106)*
Temposonics LLC .... G 470 380-5103
 Cary *(G-1907)*
Thermaco Incorporated .... G 336 629-4651
 Asheboro *(G-497)*
Trafag Inc .... G 704 343-6339
 Charlotte *(G-3712)*
Triad Automation Group Inc .... E 336 767-1379
 Winston Salem *(G-16947)*
Triangle Microsystems Inc .... F 919 878-1880
 Raleigh *(G-13359)*
▲ Troxler Electronic Labs Inc .... D 919 549-8661
 Durham *(G-5412)*
Vishay Precision Group Inc .... F 919 374-5555
 Raleigh *(G-13405)*
Water Tech Solutions Inc .... G 704 408-8391
 Mooresville *(G-11123)*
◆ Woodlane Envmtl Tech Inc .... E 828 894-8383
 Columbus *(G-4182)*

3824 Fluid meters and counting devices

Danaher Indus Sensors Contrls .... G 910 862-5426
 Elizabethtown *(G-5592)*
▲ Dynapar Corporation .... C 800 873-8731
 Elizabethtown *(G-5595)*

◆ Elster American Meter Company LLC .F 402 873-8200
 Charlotte *(G-2700)*
▲ Measurement Controls Inc .... F 704 921-1101
 Charlotte *(G-3157)*
▲ Mueller Systems LLC .... C 704 278-2221
 Cleveland *(G-4076)*
Nichols Spdmtr & Instr Co Inc .... G 336 273-2881
 Greensboro *(G-7219)*
Phitech Laboratories Inc .... G 910 420-1020
 Jackson Springs *(G-8983)*
Quantico Water & Sewer LLC .... G 336 528-9299
 Clemmons *(G-4057)*
Romac Industries Inc .... D 704 915-3317
 Dallas *(G-4656)*
Sensus .... F 919 376-2617
 Cary *(G-1885)*
Sensus USA Inc .... B 919 879-3200
 Morrisville *(G-11424)*
Sensus USA Inc .... C 919 576-6185
 Morrisville *(G-11426)*
◆ Sensus USA Inc .... E 919 845-4000
 Morrisville *(G-11425)*
Triangle Microsystems Inc .... G 919 878-1880
 Raleigh *(G-13359)*
Utility Metering Solutions Inc .... G 910 270-2885
 Hampstead *(G-7663)*
Vontier Corporation .... D 984 275-6000
 Raleigh *(G-13409)*

3825 Instruments to measure electricity

Acterna LLC .... F 919 388-5100
 Morrisville *(G-11277)*
Allen Face & Company LLC .... G 910 763-4501
 Wilmington *(G-16106)*
◆ Arris Technology Inc .... D 678 473-2907
 Hickory *(G-7944)*
Breezeplay LLC .... F 980 297-0885
 Charlotte *(G-2350)*
C O Jelliff Corporation .... G 828 428-3672
 Maiden *(G-10100)*
Comtech Group Inc .... G 919 313-4800
 Durham *(G-5029)*
Controls Instrumentation Inc .... F 704 786-1700
 Concord *(G-4243)*
Delta Msrment Cmbstn Cntrls LL .... E 919 623-7133
 Cary *(G-1747)*
Educated Design & Develop .... E 919 469-9434
 Cary *(G-1755)*
◆ Elster Solutions LLC .... B 919 212-4800
 Raleigh *(G-12732)*
▲ Emrise Corporation .... C 408 200-3040
 Durham *(G-5084)*
Firstmark Aerospace Corp .... D 919 956-4200
 Creedmoor *(G-4613)*
G B Technologies .... G 919 954-0721
 Raleigh *(G-12788)*
▲ Grecon Inc .... F 503 641-7731
 Charlotte *(G-2862)*
Hvte Inc .... F 919 274-8899
 Youngsville *(G-17084)*
Ideal Precision Meter Inc .... E 919 571-2000
 Raleigh *(G-12877)*
Infinity Communications LLC .... E 919 797-2334
 Durham *(G-5154)*
International Instrumentation .... G 919 496-4208
 Bunn *(G-1328)*
Jcv Communications Inc .... F 844 399-8282
 Wilmington *(G-16277)*
Joyce Heflin President .... G 919 451-0003
 Durham *(G-5173)*
Konica Mnlta Hlthcare Amrcas I .... E 919 792-6420
 Garner *(G-6278)*

Langley & Huther Rf Tech .... G 919 880-4968
 Raleigh *(G-12957)*
Linor Technology Inc .... F 336 485-6199
 Winston Salem *(G-16788)*
Lutheran Svcs For The Aging .... G 910 457-5604
 Southport *(G-14574)*
Minipro LLC .... G 844 517-4776
 Chapel Hill *(G-2044)*
MTS Systems Corporation .... C 919 677-2352
 Cary *(G-1827)*
▲ Multitrode Inc .... E 561 994-8090
 Charlotte *(G-3217)*
▲ Ndsl Inc .... F 919 790-7877
 Durham *(G-5241)*
Network Integrity Systems Inc .... G 828 322-2181
 Hickory *(G-8101)*
Nexjen Systems LLC .... E 704 969-7070
 Charlotte *(G-3255)*
Northline Nc LLC .... F 336 283-4811
 Rural Hall *(G-13850)*
▲ Palmer Instruments Inc .... E 828 658-3131
 Asheville *(G-720)*
Qorvo Inc .... A 336 664-1233
 Greensboro *(G-7295)*
Radon Control Inc .... G 828 265-9534
 Boone *(G-1232)*
Renewble Enrgy Intgrtion Group .... G 704 596-6186
 Charlotte *(G-3434)*
RNS International Inc .... E 704 329-0444
 Charlotte *(G-3453)*
◆ Southern Elc & Automtn Corp .... F 919 718-0122
 Sanford *(G-14187)*
▲ Tekelec Inc C
 Morrisville *(G-11442)*
Tekelec Global Inc .... A 919 460-5500
 Morrisville *(G-11443)*
Tektronix Inc .... G 704 527-5000
 Charlotte *(G-3679)*
Tektronix Inc .... G 919 233-9490
 Raleigh *(G-13335)*
▲ Todaytec LLC .... E 704 790-2440
 Charlotte *(G-3704)*
▲ Troxler Electronic Labs Inc .... D 919 549-8661
 Durham *(G-5412)*
◆ TTI Floor Care North Amer Inc .... B 440 996-2000
 Charlotte *(G-3736)*
Venable .... G 252 430-6208
 Henderson *(G-7815)*
Viztek LLC .... E 919 792-6420
 Garner *(G-6324)*

3826 Analytical instruments

Apex Waves LLC .... G 919 809-5227
 Cary *(G-1684)*
Atrium Hlth Bspcmen Repository .... G 704 863-4001
 Mint Hill *(G-10521)*
Autom8 LLC .... G 704 252-3425
 Charlotte *(G-2240)*
Biofluidica Inc .... G 858 535-6493
 Raleigh *(G-12557)*
▲ Biomerieux Inc .... B 919 620-2000
 Durham *(G-4960)*
Biorad .... G 919 463-7866
 Cary *(G-1705)*
Bmg Labtech Inc .... F 919 678-1633
 Cary *(G-1712)*
Box Scientific LLC .... G 408 361-8631
 Newton *(G-11916)*
Camag Scientific Inc .... G 910 343-1830
 Wilmington *(G-16148)*
◆ Carolina Biological Supply Company .C 336 584-0381
 Burlington *(G-1384)*

38 MEASURING, PHOTOGRAPHIC, MEDICAL, & OPTICAL GOODS, & CLOCKS

◆ Cem Corporation .... C 704 821-7015
Matthews *(G-10307)*

Cem Holdings Corporation .... E 704 821-7015
Matthews *(G-10308)*

Centice Corporation .... E 919 653-0424
Raleigh *(G-12617)*

Cooke Companies Intl .... F 919 968-0848
Chapel Hill *(G-2006)*

DOE & Ingalls Investors Inc .... E 919 598-1986
Durham *(G-5056)*

DOE & Ingalls Management LLC .... F 919 598-1986
Durham *(G-5057)*

▲ DOE & Inglls Nrth Crlina Oprti .... E 919 282-1792
Durham *(G-5058)*

Dog Black Services LLC .... G 336 266-0778
Graham *(G-6688)*

Environmental Specialties LLC .... D 919 829-9300
Raleigh *(G-12742)*

▲ Environmental Supply Co Inc .... F 919 956-9688
Durham *(G-5089)*

Fisher Scientific Company LLC .... D 800 252-7100
Asheville *(G-623)*

Green Stream Technologies Inc .... G 844 499-8880
Wake Forest *(G-15563)*

Hamilton .... G 704 896-1427
Davidson *(G-4676)*

Horiba Instruments Inc .... F 828 676-2801
Fletcher *(G-6012)*

Htx Technologies LLC .... F 919 928-5688
Carrboro *(G-1648)*

Institute For Resch Biotecnoly .... G 252 689-2205
Greenville *(G-7544)*

Kberg Productions LLC .... G 910 232-0342
Raleigh *(G-12932)*

Microsolv Technology Corp .... F 720 949-1302
Leland *(G-9556)*

Parata Systems LLC .... G 919 363-2454
Cary *(G-1841)*

Parata Systems LLC .... C 888 727-2821
Durham *(G-5270)*

Phitonex Inc 855 874-4866
Durham *(G-5285)*

Pine RES Instrumentation Inc .... F 919 782-8320
Durham *(G-5290)*

Practichem LLC .... G 919 714-8430
Morrisville *(G-11411)*

Precision Prtcle Msrements Inc .... G 919 667-6960
Mebane *(G-10426)*

Sapphire Tchncal Solutions LLC .... G 704 561-3100
Pineville *(G-12302)*

Sciteck Diagnostics Inc .... G 828 650-0409
Fletcher *(G-6036)*

Sensory Analytics LLC .... E 336 315-6090
Greensboro *(G-7333)*

Shimadzu Scientific Instrs Inc .... G 919 425-1010
Durham *(G-5352)*

Staclean Diffuser Company LLC .... F 704 636-8697
Salisbury *(G-14047)*

Thermo Elctron Scntfic Instrs .... G 828 281-2651
Asheville *(G-797)*

Thermo Fisher Scientific Inc .... G 800 955-6288
Durham *(G-5398)*

Thermo Fisher Scientific Inc .... F 252 707-7093
Greenville *(G-7589)*

Thermo Fisher Scientific Inc .... G 800 955-6288
High Point *(G-8568)*

Thermo Fisher Scientific Inc .... E 919 876-2352
Raleigh *(G-13344)*

Thermo Fsher Scntfic Ashvlle L .... B 828 658-2711
Weaverville *(G-15865)*

▲ Thermo Fsher Scntfic Ashvlle L ...... B 828 658-2711
Asheville *(G-798)*

Trajan Inc .... G 919 435-1105
Raleigh *(G-13357)*

▼ Warren Oil Company LLC .... D 910 892-6456
Dunn *(G-4890)*

Waters Corporation .... G 910 270-3137
Hampstead *(G-7664)*

Zysense LLC 215 485-1955
Chapel Hill *(G-2105)*

3827 Optical instruments and lenses

Advanced Photonic Crystals LLC .... G 803 547-0881
Cornelius *(G-4520)*

ARW Optical Corp .... G 910 452-7373
Wilmington *(G-16118)*

Corning Incorporated .... D 910 784-7200
Wilmington *(G-16184)*

Imagineoptix Corporation .... F 919 757-4945
Durham *(G-5149)*

Klearoptics Inc .... G 760 224-6770
Lattimore *(G-9457)*

Lightform Inc .... G 908 281-9098
Asheville *(G-685)*

M3 Products Com .... G 631 938-1245
Matthews *(G-10329)*

New Vision Investments Inc .... G 336 757-1120
Winston Salem *(G-16820)*

Optics Inc .... G 336 288-9504
Greensboro *(G-7236)*

Optics Inc .... G 336 884-5677
High Point *(G-8471)*

▲ Opto Alignment Technology Inc ..... E 704 893-0399
Indian Trail *(G-8954)*

Precision Optics LLC .... G 919 619-4468
Chapel Hill *(G-2055)*

▲ Rk Enterprises LLC .... G 910 481-0777
Fayetteville *(G-5908)*

Roger D Thomas .... G 919 258-3148
Sanford *(G-14176)*

US Optics .... F 828 874-2242
Connelly Springs *(G-4410)*

3829 Measuring and controlling devices, nec

▲ Accusport International Inc .... F 336 759-3300
Winston Salem *(G-16588)*

▲ Allied Manufacturing Tech Inc .... F 704 276-8192
Lincolnton *(G-9870)*

▲ Apex Instruments Incorporated ..... E 919 557-7300
Fuquay Varina *(G-6179)*

Bently Nevada LLC .... G 919 772-5530
Garner *(G-6256)*

Biomerieux Inc .... G 800 682-2666
Raleigh *(G-12559)*

▲ Biotage LLC .... D 704 654-4900
Charlotte *(G-2316)*

◆ Boon Edam Inc .... E 910 814-3800
Lillington *(G-9844)*

C W Lawley Incorporated .... G 919 467-7782
Cary *(G-1719)*

◆ Canvas Sx LLC .... C 980 474-3700
Charlotte *(G-2384)*

◆ Carolina Biological Supply Company C 336 584-0381
Burlington *(G-1384)*

Carolina Lasers .... G 919 872-8001
Raleigh *(G-12599)*

Ceast USA Inc .... G 704 423-0081
Charlotte *(G-2435)*

Cherokee Instruments Inc .... F 919 552-0554
Angier *(G-137)*

Circor Pumps North America LLC ..... D 704 289-6511
Monroe *(G-10683)*

Desco Industries Inc .... E 919 718-0000
Sanford *(G-14110)*

Dynisco Instruments LLC .... E 828 326-9888
Hickory *(G-8013)*

Educated Design & Develop .... E 919 469-9434
Cary *(G-1755)*

▲ Efco USA Inc .... G 800 332-6872
Charlotte *(G-2686)*

Elsag North America LLC .... E 336 379-7135
Greensboro *(G-6995)*

▲ Field Controls LLC .... D 252 208-7300
Kinston *(G-9366)*

Fisher Scientific Company LLC .... D 800 252-7100
Asheville *(G-623)*

Froehling & Robertson Inc .... E 804 264-2701
Raleigh *(G-12783)*

General Electric Company .... F 704 821-8260
Indian Trail *(G-8937)*

Geosonics Inc .... G 919 790-9500
Raleigh *(G-12797)*

Gom Americas Inc .... G 704 912-1600
Charlotte *(G-2846)*

Hap Innovations LLC .... E 919 650-6497
Morrisville *(G-11351)*

Hemosonics LLC .... G 800 280-5589
Durham *(G-5136)*

Hemosonics LLC .... D 800 280-5589
Durham *(G-5137)*

▲ IMO Industries Inc .... D 301 323-9000
Monroe *(G-10737)*

Inotec AMD Inc .... G 888 354-9772
Hickory *(G-8066)*

▲ James Tool Machine & Engrg Inc ... E 828 584-8722
Morganton *(G-11224)*

▲ JMS Southeast Inc .... E 704 873-1835
Statesville *(G-14825)*

K & M Products of NC Inc .... F 828 524-5905
Franklin *(G-6133)*

Lord Corporation .... E 877 275-5673
Cary *(G-1815)*

Los Vientos Windpower Ib LLC .... E 704 594-6200
Charlotte *(G-3104)*

Mallinckrodt LLC .... G 919 878-2900
Raleigh *(G-12992)*

▲ Micro Epsilon Amer Ltd Partnr .... G 919 787-9707
Raleigh *(G-13025)*

Milwaukee Instruments Inc .... G 252 443-3630
Rocky Mount *(G-13713)*

Mycoatingsolutions .... G 704 619-0308
Monroe *(G-10777)*

Orpak Usa Inc .... D 201 441-9820
Greensboro *(G-7237)*

Pace Scientific Inc .... G 704 799-0688
Boone *(G-1227)*

▲ Palmer Instruments Inc .... E 828 658-3131
Asheville *(G-720)*

▲ Pretoria Transit Interiors Inc .... E 615 867-8515
Charlotte *(G-3377)*

Qualitrol Company LLC .... G 704 587-9267
Charlotte *(G-3403)*

Revware Inc .... G 919 790-0000
Raleigh *(G-13205)*

RG Convergence Tech LLC .... G 336 953-2796
Burlington *(G-1484)*

RNS International Inc .... E 704 329-0444
Charlotte *(G-3453)*

Roehrig Engineering Inc .... E 336 956-3800
Greensboro *(G-7316)*

Russ Simmons .... G 910 686-1656
Wilmington *(G-16389)*

Sapphire Tchncal Solutions LLC .... G 704 561-3100
Pineville *(G-12302)*

Sentek Dynamics Inc .... G 980 556-7081
Kannapolis *(G-9132)*

Stellar Technology................................. G 716 250-1900
   Cary (G-1903)
Tcom Limited Partnership................... B 252 330-5555
   Elizabeth City (G-5575)
▲ Thermo Fsher Scntfic Ashvlle L....... B 828 658-2711
   Asheville (G-798)
Total Sono LLC...................................... G 908 349-8610
   Cary (G-1910)
Trafag Inc... G 704 343-6339
   Charlotte (G-3712)
▲ Troxler Electronic Labs Inc.............. D 919 549-8661
   Durham (G-5412)
Usat LLC.. E 919 942-4214
   Chapel Hill (G-2091)
Vinatoru Enterprises Inc...................... G 336 227-4300
   Graham (G-6716)
◆ Vishay Measurements Group Inc........G 919 365-3800
   Wendell (G-15923)
Windridge Sensors LLC....................... F 919 272-8714
   Holly Springs (G-8727)

3841 Surgical and medical instruments

3shape Inc... G 919 813-8694
   Morrisville (G-11271)
623 Medical LLC.................................. F 877 455-0112
   Morrisville (G-11272)
Accumed Corp....................................... D 800 278-6796
   Raleigh (G-12468)
Acme United Corporation..................... E 252 822-5051
   Rocky Mount (G-13663)
▲ Acw Technology Inc......................... A
   Raleigh (G-12474)
Adhezion Biomedical LLC................... G 828 728-6116
   Hudson (G-8760)
Advantage Fitness Products LLC........ G 336 643-8810
   Archdale (G-265)
Alcon... G 919 624-5868
   Raleigh (G-12486)
Alpha Medsource LLC.......................... G 704 408-8505
   Huntersville (G-8788)
Alveolus Inc... E 704 921-2215
   Charlotte (G-2175)
Andersen Energy Inc............................ G 336 376-0107
   Haw River (G-7749)
▼ Andersen Products Inc.................... E 336 376-3000
   Haw River (G-7750)
Andersen Sterilizers Inc....................... E 336 376-8622
   Haw River (G-7751)
Angstrom Medica Inc............................ F 781 933-6121
   Greenville (G-7483)
Applied Catheter Tech Inc.................... G 336 817-1005
   Winston Salem (G-16606)
Arcus Medical LLC............................... G 704 332-3424
   Charlotte (G-2212)
Aromatherapy By Irene LLC................ G 404 457-1871
   Marston (G-10229)
Ascepi Medical Group LLC................... G 919 336-4246
   Raleigh (G-12527)
Asensus Surgical Inc............................ G 919 765-8400
   Durham (G-4928)
▲ AVIOQ Inc.. E 919 314-5535
   Durham (G-4938)
Bariatric Partners Inc............................ G 704 542-2256
   Charlotte (G-2280)
Beacon Prosthetics & Orthotics............ G 919 231-6890
   Raleigh (G-12548)
Becton Dickinson and Company........... B 201 847-6800
   Durham (G-4952)
Becton Dickinson and Company........... E 919 963-1307
   Four Oaks (G-6100)
Biogeniv Inc... G 828 850-1007
   Lenoir (G-9589)

▲ Biomerieux Inc................................... B 919 620-2000
   Durham (G-4960)
Bioventus Inc... E 919 474-6700
   Durham (G-4962)
Birth Tissue Recovery LLC.................. E 336 448-1910
   Winston Salem (G-16631)
Brandel LLC... G 704 525-4548
   Charlotte (G-2346)
▲ Cancer Diagnostics Inc.................... E 877 846-5393
   Durham (G-4997)
Carefusion 303 Inc................................ E 919 528-5253
   Creedmoor (G-4608)
◆ Carolina Lquid Chmistries Corp........E 336 722-8910
   Greensboro (G-6888)
Carolina Precision Tech LLC................ F 215 675-4590
   Mooresville (G-10898)
◆ Charter Medical Ltd......................... D 336 768-6447
   Winston Salem (G-16651)
Colowrap LLC....................................... F 888 815-3376
   Durham (G-5025)
Contego Medical Inc............................. E 919 606-3917
   Raleigh (G-12642)
Convatec Inc.. C 336 855-5500
   Greensboro (G-6931)
Convatec Inc.. C 336 297-3021
   Greensboro (G-6932)
▲ Convatec Purchasing Department... G 336 297-3021
   Greensboro (G-6933)
Cook Group Inc..................................... F 336 744-0157
   Winston Salem (G-16660)
Cook Incorporated................................ A 336 744-0157
   Winston Salem (G-16661)
Core Sound Imaging Inc...................... E 919 277-0636
   Raleigh (G-12647)
Corning Incorporated............................ C 919 620-6200
   Durham (G-5034)
Covidien Holding Inc............................. C 919 878-2930
   Raleigh (G-12650)
Custom Assemblies Inc........................ E 919 202-4533
   Pine Level (G-12207)
D R Burton Healthcare LLC................. F 252 228-7038
   Farmville (G-5733)
Desco Industries Inc............................. F 919 718-0000
   Sanford (G-14109)
Diamond Orthopedic LLC..................... G 704 585-8258
   Gastonia (G-6397)
East West Manufacturing LLC............. G 704 663-5975
   Mooresville (G-10936)
Easy Light LLC..................................... G 972 313-5474
   Charlotte (G-2676)
Elite Metal Performance LLC............... F 704 660-0006
   Statesville (G-14793)
Emitbio Inc... G 919 321-1726
   Morrisville (G-11337)
Eye Glass Lady LLC............................. F 828 669-2154
   Black Mountain (G-1124)
Fertility Tech Resources Inc................ G 404 626-9786
   Murphy (G-11709)
Genco... G 919 963-4227
   Four Oaks (G-6105)
Gilero LLC.. C 919 595-8220
   Durham (G-5115)
Greg Goodwin PA.................................. G 828 657-5371
   Forest City (G-6069)
▲ Greiner Bio-One North Amer Inc..... B 704 261-7800
   Monroe (G-10728)
H W Andersen Products Inc................. G 336 376-3000
   Haw River (G-7752)
Health Supply Us LLC.......................... F 888 408-1694
   Mooresville (G-10971)
Healthlink Europe.................................. F 919 368-2187
   Raleigh (G-12832)

Healthlink Europe.................................. F 919 783-4142
   Raleigh (G-12833)
Healthlink International Inc................... F 877 324-2837
   Raleigh (G-12834)
Horizon Vision Research Inc............... F 910 796-8600
   Wilmington (G-16257)
Hyperbranch Medical Tech Inc............ F 919 433-3325
   Durham (G-5143)
Ickler Manufacturing LLC..................... G 704 658-1195
   Mooresville (G-10980)
Innavasc Medical Inc............................ F 813 902-2228
   Durham (G-5158)
Intelligent Endoscopy LLC................... E 336 608-4375
   Clemmons (G-4048)
Janus Development Group Inc............ F 252 551-9042
   Greenville (G-7548)
Karamedica Inc...................................... G 919 302-1325
   Raleigh (G-12930)
Kashif Mazhar....................................... G 919 314-2891
   Durham (G-5176)
▲ Kyocera Precision Tools Inc............ G 800 823-7284
   Hendersonville (G-7870)
Liebel-Flarsheim Company LLC.......... C 919 878-2930
   Raleigh (G-12969)
Logiksavvy Solutions LLC.................... G 336 392-6149
   Greensboro (G-7167)
Lucerno Dynamics LLC........................ G 317 294-1395
   Cary (G-1820)
Luxor Hydration LLC............................. F 919 568-5047
   Durham (G-5200)
Mallinckrodt LLC................................... F 919 878-2900
   Raleigh (G-12992)
Maplight Therapeutics Inc.................... G 603 553-9013
   Greenville (G-7558)
Martin Manufacturing Co LLC.............. G 919 741-5439
   Rocky Mount (G-13710)
Maximum Asp... G 919 544-7900
   Morrisville (G-11389)
Med Express/Medical Spc Inc.............. F 919 572-2568
   Durham (G-5214)
Medcor Inc... G 888 579-1050
   Lexington (G-9757)
◆ Medi Mall Inc................................... G 877 501-6334
   Fletcher (G-6022)
Medical Engineering Labs.................... G 704 487-0166
   Shelby (G-14346)
Micell Technologies Inc........................ E 919 313-2102
   Durham (G-5223)
Mission Srgcal Innovations LLC.......... G 810 965-7455
   Raleigh (G-13035)
MTI Medical Cables LLC...................... F 828 890-2888
   Fletcher (G-6029)
Multigen Diagnostics LLC..................... G 336 510-1120
   Greensboro (G-7208)
Murray Inc.. E 704 329-0400
   Charlotte (G-3221)
Murray Inc.. E 847 620-7990
   Charlotte (G-3222)
Ncontact Surgical LLC......................... E
   Morrisville (G-11392)
Next Safety Inc...................................... F 336 246-7700
   Jefferson (G-9092)
Nocturnal Product Dev LLC.................. F 919 321-1331
   Durham (G-5247)
Nuvasive Inc.. F 336 430-3169
   Greensboro (G-7227)
Odin Technologies LLC........................ G 408 309-1925
   Charlotte (G-3288)
Optopol Usa Inc.................................... G 833 678-6765
   Raleigh (G-13087)
▲ Oxlife of NC LLC.............................. G 828 684-7353
   Hendersonville (G-7889)

38 MEASURING, PHOTOGRAPHIC, MEDICAL, & OPTICAL GOODS, & CLOCKS

▲ Parker Medical Associates LLC...... F 704 344-9998
Charlotte (G-3314)

▲ Pattons Medical LLC...... E 704 529-5442
Charlotte (G-3319)

▲ Pelton & Crane Company...... B 704 588-2126
Charlotte (G-3326)

Perfusio Corp...... G 252 656-0404
Greenville (G-7572)

Perseus Intermediate Inc...... E 919 474-6700
Durham (G-5281)

Photonicare Inc...... E 866 411-3277
Durham (G-5287)

Pioneer Srgcal Orthblogics Inc...... F 252 355-4405
Greenville (G-7575)

Plexus Corp...... D 919 807-8000
Raleigh (G-13116)

Polyzen LLC...... D 919 319-9599
Apex (G-232)

Polyzen Inc...... F 919 319-9599
Cary (G-1854)

▲ Precision Concepts Group LLC...... B 336 761-8572
Winston Salem (G-16863)

Qatch Technologies LLC...... G 678 908-3112
Chapel Hill (G-2058)

Rdd Pharma Inc...... G 302 319-9970
Raleigh (G-13191)

React Innovations LLC...... G 704 773-1276
Charlotte (G-3418)

Retrofix Screws LLC...... G 980 432-8412
Salisbury (G-14036)

Retroject Inc...... G 919 619-3042
Chapel Hill (G-2063)

Rm Liquidation Inc...... D 828 274-7996
Asheville (G-756)

▲ Robling Medical LLC...... D 919 570-9605
Youngsville (G-17093)

Safeguard Medical...... D 855 428-6074
Harrisburg (G-7726)

Salem Professional Anesthesia...... G 336 998-3396
Advance (G-49)

Scinovia Corp...... F 703 957-0396
Raleigh (G-13239)

Sfp Research Inc...... G 336 622-5266
Liberty (G-9831)

Sicel Technologies Inc...... E 919 465-2236
Morrisville (G-11428)

Sonablate Corp...... F 888 874-4384
Charlotte (G-3580)

Staclear Inc...... G 919 838-2844
Raleigh (G-13296)

Statesville Med MGT Svcs LLC...... F 704 996-6748
Statesville (G-14904)

Strong Medical Partners LLC...... D 716 507-4476
Pineville (G-12309)

Strong Medical Partners LLC...... E 716 626-9400
Pineville (G-12308)

Stryker Corp...... G 919 455-6755
Raleigh (G-13310)

Stryker Corporation...... F 919 433-3325
Durham (G-5378)

▼ Suntech Medical Inc...... D 919 654-2300
Morrisville (G-11435)

Surgilum LLC...... G 910 202-2202
Wilmington (G-16422)

Technosoft Innovations Inc...... G 919 388-3360
Morrisville (G-11441)

Teleflex Incorporated...... G 919 433-2575
Durham (G-5388)

Teleflex Incorporated...... F 919 544-8000
Morrisville (G-11444)

Teleflex Medical Incorporated...... G 336 498-4153
Asheboro (G-496)

Teleflex Medical Incorporated...... G 919 544-8000
Durham (G-5390)

◆ Teleflex Medical Incorporated...... D 919 544-8000
Morrisville (G-11445)

◆ Touchamerica Inc...... F 919 732-6968
Hillsborough (G-8670)

◆ Transenterix Surgical Inc...... D 919 765-8400
Morrisville (G-11450)

Traumtic Drect Trnsfsion Dvcs...... G 423 364-5828
Apex (G-250)

Trimed LLC...... G 919 615-2784
Raleigh (G-13365)

◆ Tripath Imaging Inc...... D 336 222-9707
Burlington (G-1509)

Tryton Medical Inc...... G 919 226-1490
Raleigh (G-13370)

Valencell Inc...... G 919 747-3668
Raleigh (G-13390)

▼ Vasonova Inc...... F 650 327-1412
Morrisville (G-11461)

Visitech Systems Inc...... G 919 387-0524
Apex (G-255)

Webster Entps Jackson Cnty Inc...... E 828 586-8981
Sylva (G-15074)

Weslacova Corp...... G 704 607-1449
Mooresville (G-11127)

Wilson Outpatient Imaging...... G 252 399-7430
Wilson (G-16563)

Wilson-Cook Medical Inc...... G 336 744-0157
Winston Salem (G-16976)

Wilson-Cook Medical Inc...... B 336 744-0157
Winston Salem (G-16977)

▼ Wnyh LLC...... C 716 853-1800
Mocksville (G-10610)

Yukon Medical LLC...... G 919 595-8250
Durham (G-5459)

Zoes Kitchen Inc...... E 336 748-0587
Winston Salem (G-16991)

3842 Surgical appliances and supplies

410 Medical Inc...... F 919 241-7900
Durham (G-4893)

Ability Orthopedics...... G 704 630-6789
Salisbury (G-13912)

Adaptive Technologies LLC...... G 919 231-6890
Raleigh (G-12475)

Advanced Brace & Limb...... G 252 991-6109
Wilson (G-16464)

Advanced Brace & Limb Inc...... G 910 483-5737
Fayetteville (G-5751)

Advanced Brace & Limb Inc...... G 919 818-0359
Raleigh (G-12478)

Affordable Wheelchair Vans LLC...... G 910 443-6989
Greensboro (G-6786)

Albemrle Orthotics Prosthetics...... E 252 338-3002
Elizabeth City (G-5531)

Albemrle Orthotics Prosthetics...... G 252 332-4334
Ahoskie (G-54)

All 4 U Home Medical LLC...... G 828 437-0684
Morganton (G-11196)

Allyn International Trdg Corp...... G 877 858-2482
Marshville (G-10210)

Alternative Care Group LLC...... G 336 499-5644
Kernersville (G-9161)

▲ Ambra Le Roy LLC...... G 704 392-7080
Charlotte (G-2179)

▲ American Fiber & Finishing Inc...... E 704 984-9256
Albemarle (G-73)

American Prosthetics...... G 704 782-0908
Concord (G-4194)

▲ Amtai Medical Equipment Inc...... F 919 872-1803
Raleigh (G-12503)

▼ Andersen Products Inc...... E 336 376-3000
Haw River (G-7750)

Andersen Sterilizers Inc...... E 336 376-8622
Haw River (G-7751)

Arma Co LLC...... F 717 295-6805
Wilmington (G-16117)

Artificial Funhouse...... G 919 423-4103
Hillsborough (G-8635)

▲ Astral Buoyancy Company...... G 828 255-2638
Asheville (G-547)

Atlantic Prosthetics Orthtcs...... G 919 806-3260
Durham (G-4932)

Bar Squared Inc...... F 919 878-0578
Raleigh (G-12543)

Beacon Prosthetics & Orthotics...... G 919 231-6890
Raleigh (G-12548)

▲ Beocare Inc...... C 828 728-7300
Hudson (G-8762)

Bio-Tech Prosthetics...... G 336 768-3666
Winston Salem (G-16630)

Bio-Tech Prsthtics Orthtics In...... G 336 333-9081
Greensboro (G-6839)

Biologic Solutions LLC...... G 919 770-8266
Holly Springs (G-8690)

Biomedical Innovations Inc...... G 910 603-0267
Southern Pines (G-14529)

Biotech Prsthtics Orthtics Drh...... G 919 471-4994
Durham (G-4961)

◆ BSN Medical Inc...... C 704 554-9933
Charlotte (G-2361)

Cape Fear Orthtics Prsthtics I...... G 910 483-0933
Fayetteville (G-5780)

Carolina Ear Hring Aid Assoc L...... G 919 876-4327
Raleigh (G-12596)

Carolina Tarwheels Whlchair Bs...... G 704 791-5803
Concord (G-4225)

Carolina Whelchair Basktbal Co...... G 828 248-2055
Forest City (G-6063)

▲ Carolon Company...... D 336 969-6001
Rural Hall (G-13835)

Caromed International Inc...... F 919 878-0578
Raleigh (G-12603)

▲ Cathtek LLC...... G 336 748-0686
Winston Salem (G-16649)

Center For Orthotic & Prosthet...... D 919 585-4173
Clayton (G-3965)

Center For Orthtic Prsthtic CA...... E 919 797-1230
Durham (G-5011)

Coastal Machine & Welding Inc...... G 910 754-6476
Shallotte (G-14272)

◆ Comfortland International LLC...... F 866 277-3135
Mebane (G-10405)

Cranial Technologies Inc...... G 336 760-5530
Winston Salem (G-16665)

Creative Prosthetics and Ortho...... G 828 994-4808
Conover (G-4442)

▼ Custom Medical Specialties Inc...... F 919 202-8462
Pine Level (G-12208)

Custom Rehabilitation Spc Inc...... G 910 471-2962
Wilmington (G-16192)

Delaby Brace and Limb Co...... G 910 484-2509
Fayetteville (G-5810)

East Carolina Brace Limb Inc...... E 252 726-8068
Morehead City (G-11170)

◆ Elastic Therapy LLC...... D 336 625-0529
Asheboro (G-429)

Ethicon Inc...... G 919 234-2124
Cary (G-1762)

Faith Prsthtc-Rthotic Svcs Inc...... F 704 782-0908
Concord (G-4263)

Fillauer North Carolina Inc...... E 828 658-8330
Weaverville (G-15846)

SIC SECTION
38 MEASURING, PHOTOGRAPHIC, MEDICAL, & OPTICAL GOODS, & CLOCKS

Fla Orthopedics Inc .... D 800 327-4110
  Charlotte (G-2768)
Floyd S Braces and Limbs Inc .... G 910 763-0821
  Wilmington (G-16219)
▲ Gloves-Online Inc .... G 919 468-4244
  Cary (G-1775)
Greene Mountain Outdoors LLC .... F 336 670-2186
  North Wilkesboro (G-12011)
Guilford Orthtic Prothetic Inc .... G 336 676-5394
  Greensboro (G-7072)
Health Supply Us LLC .... F 888 408-1694
  Mooresville (G-10971)
Hollister Incorporated .... G 919 792-2095
  Raleigh (G-12852)
Hyperbranch Medical Tech Inc .... F 919 433-3325
  Durham (G-5143)
▲ Ing Source LLC .... F 828 855-0481
  Hickory (G-8065)
Ingle Protective Systems Inc .... F 704 788-3327
  Concord (G-4285)
Ipas .... C 919 967-7052
  Durham (G-5163)
Ironlungs Boxing & Personal .... G 919 332-8966
  Raleigh (G-12902)
Jackson Products Inc .... F 704 598-4949
  Wake Forest (G-15565)
Jhrg LLC .... G 252 478-4997
  Spring Hope (G-14618)
Jhrg Manufacturing LLC .... G 252 478-4977
  Spring Hope (G-14619)
◆ Kaye Products Inc .... E 919 732-6444
  Hillsborough (G-8657)
◆ Kayser-Roth Corporation .... C 336 852-2030
  Greensboro (G-7145)
Knit-Rite Inc .... C 910 557-5378
  Hamlet (G-7625)
Lifespan Incorporated .... D 336 838-2614
  North Wilkesboro (G-12022)
Lifespan Incorporated .... E 704 944-5100
  Charlotte (G-3086)
◆ Medical Action Industries Inc .... D
  Arden (G-350)
Medical Device Bus Svcs Inc .... F 704 423-0033
  Charlotte (G-3158)
Medical Spclties of Crlnas Inc .... G 910 575-4542
  Sunset Beach (G-15001)
Medical Specialties Inc .... G 704 694-2434
  Wadesboro (G-15516)
Medtrnic Sofamor Danek USA Inc .... G 919 457-9982
  Cary (G-1823)
Michael H Branch Inc .... G 252 532-0930
  Gaston (G-6331)
Mign Inc .... G 609 304-1617
  Charlotte (G-3177)
Mool Law Firm LLC .... G 217 496-3355
  Boone (G-1224)
Ms Whlchair N CA AM State Coor .... G 828 230-1129
  Weaverville (G-15853)
MSA Safety Sales LLC .... D 910 353-1540
  Jacksonville (G-9015)
Nonwoven Medical Tech LLC .... G 888 978-6199
  Charlotte (G-3265)
North Crlina Orthtics Prsthtic .... E 919 210-0906
  Wake Forest (G-15574)
North Crlina Soc For Rsprtory .... G 919 619-4206
  Hillsborough (G-8663)
Novex Innovations LLC .... G 336 231-6693
  Winston Salem (G-16824)
Nufabrx LLC .... G 888 683-2279
  Charlotte (G-3284)
Operation Wheelchair .... G 910 391-1945
  Fayetteville (G-5889)

Orthopedic Appliance Company .... E 828 254-6305
  Asheville (G-717)
Orthopedic Appliance Company .... G 828 348-1960
  Hickory (G-8109)
Orthopedic Services .... G 336 716-3349
  Winston Salem (G-16833)
Orthorx Inc .... G 919 929-5550
  Chapel Hill (G-2050)
▲ Oxlife of NC LLC .... G 828 684-7353
  Hendersonville (G-7889)
▲ Paceline Inc .... E 704 290-5007
  Matthews (G-10280)
▲ Pacon Manufacturing Corp LLC .... C 732 764-9070
  Navassa (G-11758)
Performance Orthotics .... G 704 945-7790
  Charlotte (G-3331)
▲ Precept Medical Products Inc .... F 828 681-0209
  Arden (G-365)
Premier Body Armor LLC .... F 704 750-3118
  Gastonia (G-6497)
▲ Project Bean LLC .... D 201 438-1598
  Harrisburg (G-7723)
Prophysics Innovations Inc .... F 919 245-0406
  Cary (G-1863)
▲ Protection Products Inc .... E 828 324-2173
  Hickory (G-8127)
▲ R82 Inc .... E 704 882-0668
  Matthews (G-10284)
Random Rues Botanical LLC .... G 252 214-2759
  Greenville (G-7579)
Rethink Technologies Inc .... F 980 250-4683
  Davidson (G-4694)
Royal Baths Manufacturing Co .... E 704 837-1701
  Charlotte (G-3461)
Safe Home Pro Inc .... F 704 662-2299
  Cornelius (G-4585)
Safe Ride Wheelchair Tran .... G 336 995-7529
  Winston Salem (G-16892)
Safety Wheelchair Company .... G 919 819-3775
  Raleigh (G-13226)
▲ Safewaze LLC .... D 704 262-7893
  Concord (G-4356)
▲ Scivolutions Inc .... E 704 853-0100
  Kings Mountain (G-9331)
Scott Technologies Inc .... B 704 291-8300
  Monroe (G-10803)
Skyland Prsthtics Orthtics Inc .... E 828 684-1644
  Fletcher (G-6040)
Soundside Orthtics Prsthtics L .... G 910 238-2026
  Jacksonville (G-9035)
▲ Spenco Medical Corporation .... E 919 544-7900
  Durham (G-5369)
Spintech LLC .... E 704 885-4758
  Statesville (G-14899)
Structure Medical LLC .... D 704 799-3450
  Mooresville (G-11106)
Stryker Corporation .... F 919 433-3225
  Durham (G-5378)
Suits Usa Inc .... G 336 786-8808
  Mount Airy (G-11579)
Surgical Center of Morehea .... F 252 247-0314
  Morehead City (G-11193)
Teleflex Incorporated .... G 919 433-2575
  Durham (G-5388)
Teleflex Incorporated .... G 919 433-2575
  Durham (G-5389)
Test ME Out Inc .... G 252 635-6770
  New Bern (G-11849)
The Wheelchair Place LLC .... G 828 855-9099
  Hickory (G-8179)
Trimed LLC .... G 919 615-2874
  Raleigh (G-13365)

U-Hear of Hickory .... G 704 434-2062
  Mooresboro (G-10843)
United Protective Tech LLC .... E 704 888-2470
  Locust (G-9977)
Veon Inc .... F 252 623-2102
  Washington (G-15736)
▲ VH Industries Inc .... E 704 743-2400
  Concord (G-4385)
Village Ceramics Inc .... G 828 685-9491
  Hendersonville (G-7911)
Walker Street LLC .... G 919 880-3959
  Fuquay Varina (G-6237)

3843 Dental equipment and supplies

Almore International Inc .... G 503 643-6633
  Hickory (G-7932)
◆ Amann Girrbach North Amer LP .... F 704 837-1404
  Charlotte (G-2176)
Anutra Medical Inc .... F 919 648-1215
  Morrisville (G-11287)
Aribex Inc .... E 866 340-5522
  Charlotte (G-2216)
Bioventus Inc .... E 919 474-6700
  Durham (G-4962)
▲ Cdb Corporation .... E 910 383-6464
  Leland (G-9534)
▲ Cefla Dental Group America .... F 704 731-5293
  Charlotte (G-2436)
Custom Smiles Inc .... F 919 331-2090
  Angier (G-138)
▲ Dental Equipment LLC .... B 704 588-2126
  Charlotte (G-2617)
▲ Dentonics Inc .... F 704 238-0245
  Monroe (G-10705)
◆ Dentsply Sirona Inc .... A 844 848-0137
  Charlotte (G-2618)
Kavo Kerr Group .... F 704 927-0617
  Charlotte (G-3045)
▲ Kyocera Precision Tools Inc .... G 800 823-7284
  Hendersonville (G-7870)
Nelson Rodriguez .... G 828 433-1223
  Morganton (G-11238)
Oasis Denistry .... G 704 332-8188
  Charlotte (G-3287)
▲ Pelton & Crane Company .... B 704 588-2126
  Charlotte (G-3326)
Preventive Technologies Inc .... G 704 684-1211
  Indian Trail (G-8958)
◆ Salvin Dental Specialties LLC .... D 704 442-5400
  Charlotte (G-3486)
Starlight Manufacturing Inc .... G 252 426-7867
  Hertford (G-7924)
Village Ceramics Inc .... G 828 685-9491
  Hendersonville (G-7911)
Voco America Inc .... G 917 923-7698
  Waxhaw (G-15788)

3844 X-ray apparatus and tubes

Digitome Corporation .... G 860 651-5560
  Davidson (G-4672)
▲ Flow X Ray Corporation .... D 631 242-9729
  Battleboro (G-920)
▲ Wolf X-Ray Corporation .... D 631 242-9729
  Battleboro (G-934)
Xinray Systems Inc .... F 919 701-4100
  Chapel Hill (G-2101)

3845 Electromedical equipment

Albemrle Orthotics Prosthetics .... G 252 332-4334
  Ahoskie (G-54)
Altaravision Inc .... G 919 342-5778
  Apex (G-158)

38 MEASURING, PHOTOGRAPHIC, MEDICAL, & OPTICAL GOODS, & CLOCKS

▲ Biomerieux Inc .... B 919 620-2000
   Durham *(G-4960)*

▲ Bioventus LLC .... D 800 396-4325
   Durham *(G-4963)*

Combat Medical Systems LLC .... E 704 705-1222
   Harrisburg *(G-7706)*

◆ Cyberbiota Incorporated .... G 919 308-3839
   Durham *(G-5043)*

Fernel Therapeutics Inc .... G 919 614-2375
   Apex *(G-191)*

Hemosonics LLC .... E 800 280-5589
   Durham *(G-5136)*

Hemosonics LLC .... D 800 280-5589
   Durham *(G-5137)*

Inneroptic Technology Inc .... G 919 732-2090
   Hillsborough *(G-8656)*

▲ Kyocera Precision Tools Inc .... G 800 823-7284
   Hendersonville *(G-7870)*

Lumedica Inc .... G 919 886-1863
   Durham *(G-5199)*

◆ Medi Mall Inc .... G 877 501-6334
   Fletcher *(G-6022)*

Mobius Imaging LLC .... E 704 773-7652
   Charlotte *(G-3192)*

Odin Technologies LLC .... G 408 309-1925
   Charlotte *(G-3288)*

Ori Diagnostic Instruments LLC .... G 919 864-8140
   Durham *(G-5262)*

▲ Oxlife of NC LLC .... G 828 684-7353
   Hendersonville *(G-7889)*

Polarean Inc .... F 919 206-7900
   Durham *(G-5293)*

Ribometrix .... G 919 744-9634
   Durham *(G-5331)*

Size Stream LLC .... G 919 355-5708
   Cary *(G-1893)*

▲ Tearscience Inc .... D 919 459-4880
   Morrisville *(G-11439)*

Telephys Inc .... G 312 625-9128
   Davidson *(G-4699)*

Thomas Mendolia MD .... G 336 835-5688
   Mooresville *(G-11111)*

Trackx Technology LLC .... F 888 787-2259
   Hillsborough *(G-8671)*

United Mobile Imaging Inc .... G 800 983-9840
   Clemmons *(G-4065)*

US Prototype Inc .... E 866 239-2848
   Wilmington *(G-16439)*

Vald Group Inc .... G 704 345-5145
   Charlotte *(G-3762)*

Volumetrics Med Systems LLC .... G 800 472-0900
   Durham *(G-5436)*

Vortant Technologies LLC .... G 828 645-1026
   Weaverville *(G-15867)*

3851 Ophthalmic goods

Chentech Corp .... G 919 749-8765
   Holly Springs *(G-8694)*

Clarity Vision of Smithfield .... G 919 938-6101
   Smithfield *(G-14454)*

Eye Glass Lady LLC .... F 828 669-2154
   Black Mountain *(G-1124)*

Herbal Spectacle Inc .... G 540 270-7543
   Candler *(G-1582)*

Luxottica of America Inc .... G 910 867-0200
   Fayetteville *(G-5862)*

Luxottica of America Inc .... G 919 778-5692
   Goldsboro *(G-6632)*

O D Eyecarecenter P A .... G 252 443-7011
   Rocky Mount *(G-13716)*

◆ Ocutech Inc .... G 919 967-6460
   Chapel Hill *(G-2049)*

Optical Place Inc .... E 336 274-1300
   Greensboro *(G-7235)*

Spectacle Envy .... G 336 231-3135
   Mocksville *(G-10605)*

◆ Winstn-Slem Inds For Blind Inc .... B 336 759-0551
   Winston Salem *(G-16979)*

3861 Photographic equipment and supplies

Above Topsail LLC .... G 910 803-1759
   Holly Ridge *(G-8678)*

Ahlberg Cameras Inc .... F 910 523-5876
   Wilmington *(G-16097)*

Applied Technologies Group .... G 618 977-9872
   Cornelius *(G-4521)*

Ball Photo Supply Inc .... G 828 252-2443
   Asheville *(G-556)*

Byron Dale Spivey .... G 910 653-3128
   Tabor City *(G-15078)*

Carolina Cartridge Systems Inc .... E 704 347-2447
   Charlotte *(G-2392)*

▲ Crest Electronics Inc .... F 336 855-6422
   Greensboro *(G-6940)*

Digital Progressions Inc .... F 336 676-6570
   Greensboro *(G-6970)*

Dmarcian .... E 828 767-7588
   Brevard *(G-1273)*

▲ Fg Group Holdings Inc .... E 704 994-8279
   Charlotte *(G-2756)*

Frank Uncle Productions LLC .... G 910 769-2729
   Wilmington *(G-16222)*

Geometry Workbook .... G 252 714-3327
   Charlotte *(G-2826)*

Jason Case Corp .... F 212 786-2288
   Durham *(G-5171)*

Kliersolutions .... G 919 806-1287
   Apex *(G-211)*

Kodak .... G 919 559-7232
   Morrisville *(G-11366)*

Laser Recharge Carolina Inc .... F 919 467-5902
   Cary *(G-1808)*

M T Industries Inc .... E 828 697-2864
   Hendersonville *(G-7874)*

Maplewood Imaging Ctr .... F 336 397-6000
   Winston Salem *(G-16798)*

Mark Johnson .... G 919 834-1157
   Raleigh *(G-12996)*

▲ Nabell USA Corporation .... E 704 986-2455
   Albemarle *(G-98)*

Phitech Laboratories Inc .... G 910 420-1020
   Jackson Springs *(G-8983)*

Rb3 Enterprises Inc .... G 919 795-5822
   Wake Forest *(G-15580)*

▲ Smallhd LLC .... E 919 439-2166
   Cary *(G-1895)*

Strong Global Entrmt Inc .... C 704 471-6784
   Charlotte *(G-3640)*

Subsea Video Systems Inc .... G 252 338-1001
   Elizabeth City *(G-5572)*

Tehan Company Inc .... G 800 283-7290
   Burgaw *(G-1353)*

Truelook Inc .... G 833 878-3566
   Winston Salem *(G-16954)*

Videndum Prod Solutions Inc .... G 919 244-0760
   Cary *(G-1920)*

Wilmington Camera Service LLC .... G 910 343-1089
   Wilmington *(G-16444)*

Zink Holdings LLC .... D 336 449-8000
   Whitsett *(G-16005)*

Zink Imaging Inc .... E 336 449-8000
   Whitsett *(G-16006)*

3873 Watches, clocks, watchcases, and parts

Ben Pushpa Inc .... F 828 428-8590
   Maiden *(G-10099)*

◆ Orbita Corporation .... E 910 256-5300
   Wilmington *(G-16346)*

Sealed Edge Cutting .... G 828 859-2840
   Tryon *(G-15428)*

Southern Digital Watch Repair .... G 336 299-6718
   Greensboro *(G-7353)*

39 MISCELLANEOUS MANUFACTURING INDUSTRIES

3911 Jewelry, precious metal

123 Precious Metal Ref LLC .... G 910 228-5403
   Wilmington *(G-16087)*

Acme General Design Group LLC .... G 843 466-6000
   Benson *(G-1029)*

Alex and Ani LLC .... G 704 366-6029
   Charlotte *(G-2153)*

Barnes Dmnd Gllery Jwly Mfrs I .... G 910 347-4300
   Jacksonville *(G-8989)*

Bejeweled Creations .... G 336 552-0841
   Reidsville *(G-13508)*

Blacqueladi Styles LLC .... G 877 977-7798
   Cary *(G-1707)*

Byrd Designs Inc .... G 828 628-0151
   Fairview *(G-5709)*

Calypso Cottage LLC .... G 252 728-4299
   Beaufort *(G-948)*

▲ Charles & Colvard Ltd .... F 919 468-0399
   Morrisville *(G-11318)*

Charmed Wright LLC .... G 704 850-8186
   Mooresville *(G-10902)*

Cindy Blackburn .... G 336 643-3822
   Kernersville *(G-9179)*

▲ Cygany Inc .... G 773 293-2999
   Greensboro *(G-6953)*

D C Crsman Mfr Fine Jwly Inc .... G 828 252-9891
   Asheville *(G-601)*

Dallas L Pridgen Inc .... G 919 732-4422
   Carrboro *(G-1647)*

David Yurman Enterprises LLC .... G 704 366-7259
   Charlotte *(G-2604)*

Diamond Outdoor Entps Inc .... G 336 857-1450
   Denton *(G-4733)*

Donald Haack Diamonds Inc .... G 704 365-4400
   Charlotte *(G-2651)*

Dons Fine Jewelry Inc .... G 336 724-7826
   Clemmons *(G-4035)*

Dreamseedscom Seeds of Light .... G 239 541-0501
   Fletcher *(G-5999)*

Duncan Design Ltd .... G 919 834-7713
   Raleigh *(G-12709)*

Engage2excel Inc .... D 704 872-5231
   Mooresville *(G-10939)*

Eurogold Art .... G 336 989-6205
   Kernersville *(G-9198)*

Faerie Star Forge .... G 910 743-2862
   Maysville *(G-10372)*

Gma Creative Inc .... G 919 435-6984
   Wake Forest *(G-15561)*

Goldsmith By Rudi Ltd .... G 828 693-1030
   Hendersonville *(G-7856)*

Herff Jones LLC .... G 704 962-1483
   Charlotte *(G-2902)*

Herff Jones LLC .... G 704 873-5563
   Statesville *(G-14810)*

Jewelry By Gail Inc .... G 252 441-5387
   Nags Head *(G-11721)*

Jewelry Spoken Here .... G 828 225-8464
   Asheville *(G-671)*

JkI Inc .... F 252 355-6714
  Greenville (G-7550)
John Laughter Jewelry Inc .... G 828 456-4772
  Waynesville (G-15808)
Jostens Inc .... B 336 765-0070
  Winston Salem (G-16773)
Michael S North Wilkesboro Inc .... G 336 838-5964
  North Wilkesboro (G-12028)
NCSMJ Inc .... F 704 544-1118
  Pineville (G-12285)
Nzuri Accessories & Co LLC .... G 980 333-9530
  Charlotte (G-3286)
R & B Partnership .... G 828 298-7988
  Asheville (G-750)
R Gregory Jewelers Inc .... F 704 872-6669
  Statesville (G-14874)
Soulku LLC .... F 828 273-4278
  Asheville (G-780)
▲ Starcraft Diamonds Inc .... F 252 717-2548
  Washington (G-15733)
Sumpters Jwly & Collectibles .... G 704 399-5348
  Charlotte (G-3649)
Thomas Jewelers .... G 252 756-1641
  Greenville (G-7590)
Vault of Forsyth Inc .... G 336 996-2044
  Kernersville (G-9250)
William Travis Jewelry Ltd .... G 919 968-0011
  Chapel Hill (G-2097)

3914 Silverware and plated ware

D Winchester Designs .... G 704 607-0678
  Monroe (G-10702)
◆ DWM INTERNATIONAL INC .... E 646 290-7448
  Charlotte (G-2661)
Trinkets and Whimsey .... G 919 368-6044
  Hendersonville (G-7909)

3915 Jewelers' materials and lapidary work

Alex and Ani LLC .... G 704 366-6029
  Charlotte (G-2153)
Bengal-Protea Ltd .... G 336 299-0299
  Greensboro (G-6834)
▲ Buchanan Gem Stone Mines Inc ... F 828 765-6130
  Spruce Pine (G-14632)
Charles & Colvard Direct LLC .... F 919 468-0399
  Morrisville (G-11319)
Charlesandcolvardcom LLC .... E 877 202-5467
  Morrisville (G-11320)
▲ Jewel Masters Inc .... F 336 243-2711
  Lexington (G-9734)
Moon and Lola Inc .... G 919 306-2257
  Raleigh (G-13040)
Steven Smoakes .... G 910 352-4287
  Wilmington (G-16417)
Stonehaven Jewelry Gallery Ltd .... G 919 462-8888
  Cary (G-1905)

3931 Musical instruments

Andrews Violinist .... G 910 458-1226
  Kure Beach (G-9436)
Appalachian Strings Inc .... G 828 712-8721
  Asheville (G-523)
C A Zimmer Inc .... G 704 483-4560
  Denver (G-4766)
Cape Fear Music Center LLC .... G 910 480-2362
  Fayetteville (G-5779)
Conn-Selmer Inc .... D 704 289-6459
  Monroe (G-10690)
DAngelico Guitars .... G 908 451-9606
  Lumberton (G-10031)
Engine Wellness Inc .... G 503 231-0495
  Chapel Hill (G-2015)

Epi Centre Sundries .... G 704 650-9575
  Charlotte (G-2721)
Fire Flutes .... G 321 230-3878
  Wake Forest (G-15556)
Heartland Harps .... G 828 329-6477
  Hendersonville (G-7859)
J L Smith & Co Inc .... F 704 521-1088
  Charlotte (G-3004)
Kelhorn Corporation .... G 828 837-5833
  Brasstown (G-1266)
Kurt Widenhouse Violins .... G 704 825-3289
  Belmont (G-994)
Leiva Strings Inc .... G 919 538-6269
  Raleigh (G-12966)
▲ Lewtak Pipe Organ Builders Inc .... G 336 554-2251
  Mocksville (G-10585)
▲ Lucky Man Inc .... E 828 251-0090
  Asheville (G-689)
Luthiers Workshop LLC .... G 919 241-4578
  Hillsborough (G-8660)
Music & Arts .... G 919 329-6069
  Garner (G-6294)
◆ MW Enterprises Inc .... G 828 963-7083
  Vilas (G-15498)
Ola Marimba Inc .... G 919 479-9995
  Durham (G-5254)
Oneaka Dance Company .... G 704 299-7432
  Charlotte (G-3300)
Raleigh Ringers Inc .... G 919 847-7574
  Raleigh (G-13182)
◆ ROC-N-Soc Inc .... G 828 452-1736
  Waynesville (G-15819)
Saraz Musical Instruments .... G 828 782-8896
  Swannanoa (G-15035)
School of Rock Charlotte .... G 704 842-3172
  Charlotte (G-3506)
Song of Wood Ltd .... G 828 669-7675
  Black Mountain (G-1139)
Southern Organ Services Ltd .... G 828 667-8230
  Candler (G-1589)

3942 Dolls and stuffed toys

A Stitch In Time .... G 828 274-5193
  Asheville (G-513)
PCS Collectibles LLC .... G 805 306-1140
  Huntersville (G-8873)

3944 Games, toys, and children's vehicles

All Signs & Graphics LLC .... G 910 323-3115
  Fayetteville (G-5757)
Banilla Games Inc .... G 252 329-7977
  Greenville (G-7492)
Bougiejones .... G 704 492-3029
  Charlotte (G-2340)
▲ Cannon & Daughters Inc .... D 828 254-9236
  Asheville (G-579)
Cog In Games LLP .... G 704 763-4609
  Charlotte (G-2522)
Curious Discoveries Inc .... G 336 643-0432
  Summerfield (G-14979)
▲ Epic Kites LLC .... G 203 209-6831
  Kill Devil Hills (G-9256)
Flying Smiles Inc .... G 252 255-3054
  Kitty Hawk (G-9405)
Game Box LLC .... G 866 241-1882
  Greensboro (G-7029)
Glenn Torrance Models LLC .... G 919 761-1363
  Youngsville (G-17082)
Gracefully Gifted Hands LLC .... G 845 248-8743
  Raleigh (G-12812)
Grailgame Inc .... G 804 517-3102
  Reidsville (G-13522)

Hartford Products Inc .... G 919 471-5937
  Hillsborough (G-8651)
Imperial Falcon Group Inc .... G 646 717-1128
  Charlotte (G-2953)
▲ Jasie Blanks LLC .... F 910 485-0016
  Fayetteville (G-5846)
Kenson Parenting Solutions .... G 919 637-1499
  Wake Forest (G-15567)
Kitty Hawk Kites Inc .... F 252 441-4124
  Nags Head (G-11722)
◆ Lionel LLC .... D 704 454-4200
  Concord (G-4305)
Personal Xpressionz LLC .... G 919 587-7462
  Durham (G-5282)
Pridgen-Lucas Latisha .... G 252 360-7866
  Wilson (G-16523)
Puzzle Piece LLC .... G 910 688-7119
  Carthage (G-1664)
Puzzles From Past LLC .... G 704 231-5878
  Huntersville (G-8884)
▲ Schleich USA Inc .... G 704 659-7997
  Charlotte (G-3502)
South Mountain Crafts .... G 828 433-2607
  Morganton (G-11255)
◆ US Legend Cars Intl Inc .... E 704 455-3896
  Harrisburg (G-7732)
Wersunsllc .... G 857 209-8701
  Winston Salem (G-16969)
World of RC Parts .... G 252 291-4088
  Lucama (G-10019)

3949 Sporting and athletic goods, nec

▲ ABC Fitness Products LLC .... G 704 649-0000
  Raleigh (G-12461)
Acorn Climbing LLC .... G 919 518-5022
  Raleigh (G-12471)
Advantage Fitness Products Inc .... F 336 643-8810
  Kernersville (G-9159)
▲ American Netting Corp .... F 919 567-3737
  Fuquay Varina (G-6178)
Archangel Arms LLC .... G 984 235-2536
  Raleigh (G-12518)
Arnold S Welding Service Inc .... E 910 323-3822
  Fayetteville (G-5764)
Bad Monkey Lures LLC .... G 910 433-5617
  Hope Mills (G-8732)
Barrys Custom Lures LLC .... G 828 256-1792
  Hickory (G-7948)
Beautiful Brains Inc .... G 828 244-5850
  Conover (G-4421)
Becwill Corp .... G 919 552-8266
  Fuquay Varina (G-6183)
Big Nics Lures LLC .... G 910 805-1360
  Wilmington (G-16138)
Bluff Mountain Outfitters Inc .... G 828 622-7162
  Hot Springs (G-8744)
Bommerang Imprints .... G 704 933-9075
  Kannapolis (G-9111)
Boomerang Foods LLC .... G 336 558-3798
  Greensboro (G-6848)
Bowed Up Lures .... G 757 376-7944
  Southern Shores (G-14561)
Brookhurst Associates .... G 919 792-0987
  Raleigh (G-12576)
Bumpkin Skateboards LLC .... G 919 821-2037
  Raleigh (G-12577)
▲ Carolina Gym Supply Corp .... G 919 732-6999
  Hillsborough (G-8642)
Charlotte Springfree Trmpoline .... G 704 312-1212
  Charlotte (G-2464)
Chicadoo .... G 704 562-8796
  Charlotte (G-2474)

39 MISCELLANEOUS MANUFACTURING INDUSTRIES

Claypro LLC .... G 828 301-6309
   Norlina *(G-11995)*

Cloud Nine Foods Inc .... G 817 909-8988
   Newport *(G-11900)*

Clutch Climbing Gear LLC .... G 336 262-9719
   Ferguson *(G-5957)*

▼ Colored Metal Products Inc .... F 704 482-1407
   Shelby *(G-14301)*

Competition Cages .... G 919 644-1334
   Hillsborough *(G-8646)*

◆ Custom Golf Car Supply Inc .... C 704 855-1130
   Salisbury *(G-13952)*

Db Power Sports .... G 828 324-1500
   Hickory *(G-8003)*

Deep Creek Lures Inc .... G 910 892-1791
   Dunn *(G-4861)*

Deerhunter Tree Stands Inc .... G 704 462-1116
   Hickory *(G-8004)*

Dissonant Skateboards .... G 607 793-8210
   Asheville *(G-609)*

Dix Enterprises Inc .... F 336 558-9512
   High Point *(G-8327)*

Dixie Decoys LLC .... G 703 554-9478
   Winston Salem *(G-16683)*

Dobbins Products .... G 919 580-0621
   Goldsboro *(G-6610)*

East Coast Bat Company Inc .... G 704 305-3649
   Locust *(G-9958)*

Essay Operations Inc .... G 252 443-6010
   Rocky Mount *(G-13696)*

Ethics Archery LLC .... G 980 429-2070
   Vale *(G-15465)*

Family Industries Inc .... F 919 875-4499
   Raleigh *(G-12762)*

▲ Fathom Offshore Holdings LLC .... G 910 399-6882
   Wilmington *(G-16217)*

First In Flght Skateboards LLC .... G 828 449-9150
   Hickory *(G-8025)*

Fish Getter Lure Co LLC .... G 704 538-9863
   Casar *(G-1933)*

Fisher Athletic Equipment Inc .... E 704 636-5713
   Salisbury *(G-13965)*

Frostie Bottom Tree Stand LLC .... G 828 466-1708
   Claremont *(G-3927)*

Gains Fitness Gear LLC .... G 800 403-2904
   Wake Forest *(G-15557)*

Geosurfaces Southeast Inc .... E 704 660-3000
   Mooresville *(G-10958)*

Gillespies Fbrction Design Inc .... G 704 636-2349
   Salisbury *(G-13969)*

Gladiator Enterprises Inc .... G 336 944-6932
   Greensboro *(G-7044)*

Golf Shop .... G 704 636-7070
   Salisbury *(G-13971)*

Graystone Manor Lake Lure LLC .... G 828 395-2099
   Rutherfordton *(G-13874)*

Greene Precision Products Inc .... G 828 262-0116
   Boone *(G-1202)*

Greene Products Inc .... G 336 670-2186
   North Wilkesboro *(G-12012)*

Greengate Skatepark LLC .... G 336 333-5800
   Greensboro *(G-7060)*

H & H Furniture Mfrs Inc .... C 336 873-7245
   Seagrove *(G-14239)*

▲ H-T-L Perma USA Ltd Partnr .... E 704 377-3100
   Charlotte *(G-2879)*

Hanks Game Calls .... G 336 317-3530
   Reidsville *(G-13524)*

Hanta Rods and Lures LLC .... G 919 480-5138
   Raleigh *(G-12829)*

Hawk Distributors Inc .... G 888 334-1307
   Sanford *(G-14129)*

Helmet Halo .... G 828 407-3742
   Asheville *(G-649)*

High Velocity Archery LLC .... G 910 620-5215
   Kelly *(G-9138)*

Hughes Products Co Inc .... G 336 769-3788
   Winston Salem *(G-16750)*

I-Lumenate .... G 704 966-1910
   Denver *(G-4784)*

I-Lumenate LLC .... G 336 448-0356
   Winston Salem *(G-16753)*

Icon Coolers LLC .... G 855 525-4266
   Wilmington *(G-16263)*

◆ Implus Footcare LLC .... B 800 446-7587
   Durham *(G-5150)*

▲ J Stahl Sales & Sourcing Inc .... E 828 645-3005
   Weaverville *(G-15849)*

Jab Lures .... G 860 885-9314
   South Mills *(G-14524)*

Jimmy Keith Surfboards Inc .... G 910 297-9719
   Wilmington *(G-16280)*

◆ Js Fiber Co Inc .... D 704 871-1582
   Statesville *(G-14828)*

Kask America Inc .... E 704 960-4851
   Charlotte *(G-3043)*

Kelken Enterprises LLC .... G 910 890-7211
   Lillington *(G-9853)*

Kol Incorporated .... G 919 872-2340
   Raleigh *(G-12945)*

Laceration Lures LLC .... G 919 612-3368
   Raleigh *(G-12951)*

▲ Lees Tackle Inc .... G 910 386-5100
   Wilmington *(G-16295)*

▲ Liberty Investment & MGT Corp .... F 919 544-0344
   Morrisville *(G-11379)*

Lures Galore LLC .... G 336 643-0948
   Summerfield *(G-14987)*

▲ McKenzie Sports Products LLC .... C 704 279-7985
   Salisbury *(G-14011)*

McNeely Motorsports Inc .... G 704 426-7430
   Matthews *(G-10334)*

▲ Mettech Inc .... G 919 833-9460
   Raleigh *(G-13023)*

Miracle Recreation Eqp Co .... B 704 875-6550
   Huntersville *(G-8855)*

NC Softball Sales .... G 704 663-2134
   Mooresville *(G-11034)*

North Sports Inc .... G 252 995-4970
   Avon *(G-845)*

Not Just Archery .... G 828 294-7727
   Hickory *(G-8105)*

Openfire Systems .... G 336 251-3991
   Millers Creek *(G-10494)*

Parker Athletic Products LLC .... G 704 370-0400
   Charlotte *(G-3312)*

▲ Parker Medical Associates LLC .... F 704 344-9998
   Charlotte *(G-3313)*

Peggs Recreation Inc .... G 704 660-0007
   Mooresville *(G-11048)*

Piedmont Fiberglass Inc .... E 828 632-8883
   Statesville *(G-14859)*

◆ Playpower Inc .... D 704 949-1600
   Huntersville *(G-8876)*

Pool Tables Plus .... G 704 535-8002
   Charlotte *(G-3356)*

Precision Sports Paintball .... G 828 212-0415
   Hickory *(G-8120)*

Precor Incorporated .... E 336 603-1000
   Greensboro *(G-7277)*

Protex Sport Products Inc .... F 336 956-2419
   Salisbury *(G-14032)*

▲ Revels Turf and Tractor LLC .... E 919 552-5697
   Fuquay Varina *(G-6226)*

▲ Rigem Right .... F 252 726-9508
   Newport *(G-11905)*

Ringneck and Lure LLC .... G 704 377-8581
   Charlotte *(G-3451)*

Roostem Hunting Products LLC .... G 919 693-3359
   Oxford *(G-12152)*

Royal Baths Manufacturing Co .... E 704 837-1701
   Charlotte *(G-3461)*

Royal Textile Mills Inc .... D 336 694-4121
   Yanceyville *(G-17065)*

▲ RSR Fitness Inc .... F 919 255-1233
   Raleigh *(G-13217)*

Ruffton Brewhouse .... G 828 289-8060
   Rutherfordton *(G-13887)*

Safariland Group .... G 919 779-6141
   Raleigh *(G-13225)*

◆ Sea Striker Inc .... E 252 247-4113
   Morehead City *(G-11187)*

▲ Secret Spot Inc .... G 252 441-4030
   Nags Head *(G-11725)*

Simpleshot Inc .... G 888 202-7475
   Asheville *(G-772)*

Smith Holdings .... G 704 472-4937
   Shelby *(G-14368)*

▲ Sports Products LLC .... G 919 562-4074
   Wake Forest *(G-15595)*

Sportsedge Inc .... F 704 528-0188
   Greensboro *(G-7358)*

Sportsfield Specialties Inc .... F 704 637-2140
   Mocksville *(G-10606)*

Surfline Inc .... G 252 715-1630
   Nags Head *(G-11727)*

Syntech of Burlington Inc .... E 336 570-2035
   Burlington *(G-1503)*

Thomas Golf Inc .... G 704 461-1342
   Charlotte *(G-3689)*

Thomson Plastics Inc .... D 336 843-4255
   Lexington *(G-9793)*

Thunder Alley Enterprises .... G 910 371-0119
   Leland *(G-9561)*

Timber Ninja Outdoors LLC .... G 828 380-1664
   Asheville *(G-801)*

Topgolf .... E 704 612-4745
   Charlotte *(G-3709)*

Total Limit Lures .... G 910 330-5786
   Concord *(G-4378)*

Total Sports Enterprises .... G 704 237-3930
   Waxhaw *(G-15783)*

Tradition Surfboards LLC .... G 404 229-4223
   Calabash *(G-1554)*

Treklite Inc .... G 919 610-1788
   Raleigh *(G-13358)*

Trident Lure .... G 910 520-4659
   Wilmington *(G-16433)*

▲ Triplette Fencing Supply Inc .... G 336 835-1205
   Elkin *(G-5630)*

◆ Ucs Inc .... D 704 732-9922
   Lincolnton *(G-9931)*

◆ United Canvas & Sling Inc .... E 704 732-9922
   Lincolnton *(G-9933)*

VA Composites Inc .... G 844 474-2387
   Aberdeen *(G-34)*

Vise & Co LLC .... G 336 354-3702
   Winston Salem *(G-16964)*

◆ Weener Plastics Inc .... D 252 206-1400
   Wilson *(G-16558)*

Wilder Tactical LLC .... G 704 750-7141
   Gastonia *(G-6541)*

Wolfe Products Inc .... G 919 645-7573
   Apex *(G-260)*

Young Bat Enterprises Inc .... G 828 376-3706
   Fletcher *(G-6055)*

39 MISCELLANEOUS MANUFACTURING INDUSTRIES

3951 Pens and mechanical pencils

Bic Corporation.. D 704 598-7700
  Charlotte *(G-2308)*
Coopercraft Pens... G 910 603-1191
  Raleigh *(G-12646)*
Industries of Blind Inc.................................... C 336 274-1591
  Greensboro *(G-7114)*

3952 Lead pencils and art goods

Designs By Rachel... G 828 783-0698
  Spruce Pine *(G-14639)*
Eco-Kids LLC.. G 207 899-2752
  Raleigh *(G-12726)*
Reissmann Entertainment Inc................... G 734 641-4434
  Statesville *(G-14876)*
◆ Speedball Art Products Co LLC............. D 800 898-7224
  Statesville *(G-14898)*

3953 Marking devices

B&Lk Enterprises... G 910 395-5151
  Wilmington *(G-16130)*
Bear Pages... G 828 837-0785
  Murphy *(G-11706)*
Ennis-Flint Inc.. G 800 331-8118
  Thomasville *(G-15220)*
◆ Emnis-Flint Inc... F 800 331-8118
  Greensboro *(G-7000)*
▲ Flint Trading Inc....................................... D 336 475-6600
  Thomasville *(G-15224)*
Hayes Print-Stamp Co Inc........................... G 336 667-1116
  Wilkesboro *(G-16023)*
Mass Connection Inc................................... G 910 424-0940
  Fayetteville *(G-5868)*
National Sign & Decal Inc............................ G 828 478-2123
  Sherrills Ford *(G-14388)*
Stamp Approval - Anita White.................... G 910 433-2279
  Fayetteville *(G-5922)*
▲ Trophy House Inc.................................... F 910 323-1791
  Fayetteville *(G-5934)*

3955 Carbon paper and inked ribbons

Ace Laser Recycling Inc............................... G 919 775-5521
  Sanford *(G-14081)*
Branch Office Solutions Inc........................ G 800 743-1047
  Indian Trail *(G-8924)*
Cartridge World.. G 336 885-0989
  High Point *(G-8288)*
Complete Comp St of Ralgh Inc................. E 919 828-5227
  Raleigh *(G-12635)*
Digital Highpoint LLC.................................... C 336 883-7146
  High Point *(G-8324)*
▲ Dnp Imagingcomm America Corp........ B 704 784-8100
  Concord *(G-4255)*
Drew Roberts LLC.. G 336 497-1679
  Whitsett *(G-15988)*
Duraline Imaging Inc.................................... G 828 692-1301
  Flat Rock *(G-5964)*
Filmon Process Corp................................... G 828 684-1360
  Arden *(G-328)*
▲ Image Industries NC Inc....................... F 828 464-8882
  Newton *(G-11942)*
New East Cartridge Inc................................ G 252 329-0837
  Greenville *(G-7563)*
Sato Global Solutions Inc........................... F 954 261-3279
  Charlotte *(G-3494)*
◆ Static Control Components Inc........... A 919 774-3808
  Sanford *(G-14191)*

3961 Costume jewelry

Bracelets and More....................................... G 419 236-4933
  Morrisville *(G-11306)*

Byrd Designs Inc.. G 828 628-0151
  Fairview *(G-5709)*
◆ Causekeepers Inc................................... E 336 824-2518
  Franklinville *(G-6167)*
▲ December Diamonds Inc....................... G 828 926-3308
  Waynesville *(G-15801)*
Golfworks.. G 910 796-3160
  Wilmington *(G-16236)*
Humility Bracelets.. G 704 277-5896
  Charlotte *(G-2932)*
Queen Wrist Bling Inc.................................. G 980 635-0287
  Concord *(G-4345)*

3965 Fasteners, buttons, needles, and pins

◆ Aplix Inc... B 704 588-1920
  Charlotte *(G-2201)*
▲ Avdel USA LLC.. E 704 888-7100
  Stanfield *(G-14675)*
◆ Coats & Clark Inc.................................... D 704 542-5959
  Charlotte *(G-2512)*
▲ Coats N Amer De Rpblica Dmncan..... C 800 242-8095
  Charlotte *(G-2515)*
Dubose National Enrgy Svcs Inc.............. G 704 295-1060
  Waxhaw *(G-15754)*
Gesipa Fasteners Usa Inc.......................... E 336 751-1555
  Mocksville *(G-10577)*
◆ Gesipa Fasteners Usa Inc.................... F 609 208-1740
  Mocksville *(G-10578)*
◆ Heico Fasteners Inc............................... E 828 261-0184
  Hickory *(G-8041)*
◆ Ideal Fastener Corporation.................. C 919 693-3115
  Oxford *(G-12133)*
ND Southeastern Fastener......................... G 704 329-0033
  Charlotte *(G-3241)*

3991 Brooms and brushes

▲ Carolina Brush Company...................... E 704 867-0286
  Gastonia *(G-6366)*
▲ Carolina Brush Mfg Co......................... E 704 867-0286
  Gastonia *(G-6367)*
▲ Newell Novelty Co Inc.......................... G 336 597-2246
  Roxboro *(G-13808)*
▲ P&A Indstrial Fabrications LLC........... E 336 322-1766
  Roxboro *(G-13815)*
Quickie Manufacturing Corp....................... C 910 737-6500
  Lumberton *(G-10049)*
Renaissance Innovations LLC.................. G 844 473-7246
  Apex *(G-239)*
Shur Line Inc.. E 317 442-8850
  Mooresville *(G-11085)*
Tarheel Pavement Clg Svcs Inc................ F 704 895-8015
  Cornelius *(G-4591)*
▲ Zibra LLC... G 704 271-4503
  Mooresville *(G-11140)*

3993 Signs and advertising specialties

310 Sign Company.. G 704 910-2242
  Charlotte *(G-2107)*
910 Sign Co LLC.. G 910 353-2298
  Jacksonville *(G-8984)*
A Greeting On Green LLC........................... G 919 607-0966
  Cary *(G-1671)*
A Sign From Above Inc................................ G 910 352-0897
  Wilmington *(G-16088)*
A To Z Signs & Engraving Inc.................... G 828 456-6337
  Waynesville *(G-15791)*
AAA Mobile Signs LLC................................. G 919 463-9768
  Morrisville *(G-11274)*
AAA Mobile Signs LLC................................. G 252 446-9777
  Rocky Mount *(G-13678)*
Aarons Quality Signs................................... G 704 841-7733
  Matthews *(G-10230)*

ABC Signs... G 252 223-5900
  Newport *(G-11896)*
ABC Signs and Graphics LLC.................... G 252 652-6620
  Havelock *(G-7738)*
Abee Custom Signs Inc............................... G 336 229-1554
  Burlington *(G-1361)*
Acsm Inc... G 704 910-0243
  Charlotte *(G-2131)*
Action Graphics and Signs Inc.................. G 919 690-1260
  Bullock *(G-1326)*
Action Installs LLC....................................... G 704 787-3828
  Wilkesboro *(G-16012)*
Action Sign Company Lenoir..................... F 828 754-4116
  Lenoir *(G-9567)*
Actionsigncom... G 828 572-2308
  Hudson *(G-8759)*
Ad Runner MBL Outdoor Advg Inc........... G 336 945-1190
  Lewisville *(G-9664)*
Ad-Art Signs Inc.. G 704 377-5369
  Charlotte *(G-2133)*
Aditi 108 Inc... G 704 763-3741
  Mooresville *(G-10849)*
Adsign Corp.. G 336 766-3000
  Winston Salem *(G-16590)*
Advance Signs & Service Inc.................... E 919 639-4666
  Angier *(G-130)*
Adventure Sign and Ltg LLC...................... G 336 401-3410
  Mount Airy *(G-11474)*
Affordable Signs & Awnings...................... G 910 237-1323
  Hope Mills *(G-8731)*
All Signs & Graphics LLC........................... G 910 323-3115
  Fayetteville *(G-5757)*
All Star Sign Company................................. G 214 862-6797
  Franklin *(G-6114)*
Allen Industries Inc...................................... C 336 294-4777
  Greensboro *(G-6792)*
▼ Allen Industries Inc................................ D 336 668-2791
  Greensboro *(G-6791)*
Alltech Sign Service LLC............................ G 803 548-9787
  Charlotte *(G-2163)*
Alpha Signs & Embroidery Inc.................. G 704 878-8870
  Statesville *(G-14745)*
Alpha Signs & Lighting Inc........................ F 910 567-5813
  Newton Grove *(G-11987)*
Altitude Sign Company LLC....................... G 980 339-8160
  Matthews *(G-10233)*
American Sign Shop Inc.............................. G 704 527-6100
  Charlotte *(G-2185)*
American Signs By Tomorrow................... G 910 484-2313
  Fayetteville *(G-5761)*
Ancient Mariner Inc..................................... F 704 635-7911
  Monroe *(G-10647)*
Andark Graphics Inc.................................... G 704 882-1400
  Indian Trail *(G-8919)*
Anderson Designs.. G 919 489-1514
  Durham *(G-4919)*
Anthem Displays LLC.................................. F 910 746-8988
  Elizabethtown *(G-5583)*
Anthem Displays LLC.................................. F 910 862-3550
  Elizabethtown *(G-5584)*
Aoa Signs Inc.. G 336 679-3344
  Wilson *(G-16466)*
Apple Rock Advg & Prom Inc..................... E 336 232-4800
  Greensboro *(G-6811)*
Art Sign Co... G 919 596-8681
  Durham *(G-4925)*
Artcraft Sign Co.. G 919 841-7686
  Spring Hope *(G-14612)*
Artisan Direct LLC.. G 704 655-9100
  Cornelius *(G-4523)*
▲ Artisan Signs and Graphics Inc.......... F 704 655-9100
  Cornelius *(G-4524)*

Employee Codes: A=Over 500 employees, B=251-500
C=101-250, D=51-100, E=20-50, F=10-19, G=1-9

39 MISCELLANEOUS MANUFACTURING INDUSTRIES

Artistic Images Inc .... G 704 332-6225
  Charlotte *(G-2221)*
AS Ignco .... G 828 466-1044
  Conover *(G-4418)*
Asi Signage Innovations .... G 336 508-4668
  Greensboro *(G-6819)*
Asi Signage North Carolina .... F 919 362-9669
  Holly Springs *(G-8686)*
Atlantic Pinstriping ATL Wraps .... G 704 201-4406
  Matthews *(G-10302)*
Atlantic Pnstriping Greensboro .... G 910 880-3717
  Charlotte *(G-2232)*
Atlantic Sign Media Inc .... F 336 584-1375
  Burlington *(G-1369)*
Atlas Sign Industries Nc LLC .... E 704 788-3733
  Concord *(G-4200)*
Atlas Signs .... G 919 238-5078
  Morrisville *(G-11296)*
Auto Trim Design .... G 336 747-3309
  Burlington *(G-1372)*
AWC Sign & Light Inc .... G 910 279-0493
  Wilmington *(G-16127)*
Awning Innovations .... G 336 831-8996
  Clemmons *(G-4028)*
B-Led Inc .... G 828 680-1444
  Mars Hill *(G-10192)*
B&P Enterprise NC Inc .... G 727 669-6877
  Hickory *(G-7947)*
Baac Business Solutions Inc .... G 704 333-4321
  Charlotte *(G-2257)*
Baldwin Sign & Awning .... G 910 642-8812
  Whiteville *(G-15959)*
Banner Signs Today Inc .... G 704 525-2241
  Charlotte *(G-2275)*
Barracuda Displays .... G 704 322-0971
  Midland *(G-10456)*
Beane Signs Inc .... G 336 629-6748
  Asheboro *(G-409)*
Beaty Corporation .... G 704 599-4949
  Charlotte *(G-2293)*
Beeson Sign Co Inc .... G 336 993-5617
  Kernersville *(G-9167)*
Belk Construction Inc .... G 704 507-6327
  Mooresville *(G-10871)*
Bender Signs .... G 252 631-5144
  Pollocksville *(G-12392)*
Best Image Signs LLC .... G 336 973-7445
  Wilkesboro *(G-16014)*
Big Fish Digital Signs LLC .... G 252 363-1600
  Wilson *(G-16476)*
Blashfield Sign Company Inc .... G 910 485-7200
  Fayetteville *(G-5772)*
Blue Light Images Company Inc .... E 336 983-4986
  King *(G-9264)*
Bordentown Highway Sign LLC .... G 919 870-8116
  Raleigh *(G-12570)*
Boyd Gmn Inc .... C 206 284-2200
  Monroe *(G-10668)*
Boyles Sign Shop Inc .... G 336 782-1189
  Germanton *(G-6551)*
BP Signs Inc .... G 704 531-8000
  Charlotte *(G-2344)*
Broach Custom Signs NC LLC .... G 919 876-8380
  Wendell *(G-15893)*
Burchette Services Corporation .... G 919 225-2890
  Durham *(G-4992)*
Burchette Sign Company Inc .... F 336 996-6501
  Colfax *(G-4143)*
Buzz Saw Inc .... G 910 321-7446
  Fayetteville *(G-5777)*
Camco Manufacturing Inc .... G 336 348-6609
  Reidsville *(G-13511)*

Capital Sign Solutions LLC .... E 919 789-1452
  Raleigh *(G-12591)*
Carmel By D3sign LLC .... G 336 617-6383
  Greensboro *(G-6881)*
Carolina Cstm Signs & Graphics .... G 336 681-4337
  Greensboro *(G-6883)*
Carolina Sgns Grphic Dsgns Inc .... G 919 383-3344
  Durham *(G-5004)*
Carolina Sign Co Inc .... G 704 399-3995
  Charlotte *(G-2404)*
Carolina Sign Svc .... G 919 247-0927
  Angier *(G-136)*
Carolina Signs .... G 704 622-1939
  Gastonia *(G-6369)*
Carolina Signs & Lighting Inc .... G 336 399-1400
  King *(G-9266)*
Carolina Signs and Wonders Inc .... F 704 286-1343
  Charlotte *(G-2405)*
Carolina Stickers & Signs LLC .... G 704 649-7318
  Charlotte *(G-2408)*
Casco Signs Inc .... E 704 788-9055
  Concord *(G-4228)*
Cbr Signs LLC .... G 910 794-8243
  Wilmington *(G-16163)*
Ccbs & Sign Shop Inc .... G 252 728-4866
  Beaufort *(G-949)*
CD Dickie & Associates Inc .... F 704 527-9102
  Charlotte *(G-2433)*
Chameleon Wraps & Designs .... G 910 544-9801
  Orrum *(G-12115)*
Charlotte Aarrow LLC .... G 704 909-7692
  Charlotte *(G-2449)*
Cheadles Auto Art & Sign .... G 828 254-2600
  Arden *(G-321)*
Choice Awards & Signs .... G 704 844-0860
  Matthews *(G-10309)*
Clark Sign Corporation .... G 336 431-4944
  Archdale *(G-274)*
Classic Address Signs .... G 919 734-4482
  Dudley *(G-4842)*
Classic Sign Services LLC .... G 704 401-1466
  Monroe *(G-10685)*
CMA Signs LLC .... F 919 245-8339
  Hillsborough *(G-8645)*
Coates Designers & Craftsmen .... G 828 349-9700
  Franklin *(G-6120)*
Cobb Clark Richard II .... G 704 274-5479
  Huntersville *(G-8804)*
Cobb Sign Company Incorporated .... F 336 227-0181
  Burlington *(G-1396)*
Color Spot .... G 336 778-3982
  Winston Salem *(G-16657)*
Connected 2k LLC .... G 910 321-7446
  Fayetteville *(G-5795)*
Consumer Concepts .... F 252 247-7000
  Morehead City *(G-11164)*
Contagious Graphics Inc .... E 704 529-5600
  Charlotte *(G-2543)*
Cook Group Inc .... G 336 605-5557
  Mooresville *(G-10911)*
Cornhole Stop .... G 704 728-1550
  Cornelius *(G-4537)*
Cranky Creative Group .... G 877 775-9727
  Raleigh *(G-12651)*
Craven Sign Services Inc .... G 336 883-7306
  High Point *(G-8305)*
Creative Images Inc .... G 919 467-2188
  Cary *(G-1739)*
Creative Signs Inc .... G 910 395-0100
  Wilmington *(G-16187)*
Creativeminds Design LLC .... G 678 457-6148
  Monroe *(G-10698)*

Custom Metal Creation LLC .... G 828 302-0623
  Vale *(G-15464)*
Custom Neon & Graphics Inc .... G 704 344-1715
  Charlotte *(G-2592)*
Custom Signage Company .... G 909 215-2404
  Charlotte *(G-2595)*
Custom Signs .... G 336 847-7700
  High Point *(G-8314)*
Darren Lee Depalo .... G 252 259-4515
  Havelock *(G-7741)*
Davcom Enterprises Inc .... G 919 872-9522
  Raleigh *(G-12674)*
Davis Sign Company Inc .... F 336 765-2990
  Winston Salem *(G-16672)*
Dem Party Gurls Entrmt LLC .... G 910 964-3599
  Fayetteville *(G-5811)*
Dert Sign Co .... G 336 225-1800
  Lexington *(G-9706)*
Desena Commercial Services LLC .... G 336 786-1111
  Mount Airy *(G-11500)*
Desena Commercial Svc .... G 336 786-1111
  Mount Airy *(G-11501)*
Designelement .... F 919 383-5561
  Raleigh *(G-12680)*
Digital Printing Systems Inc .... E 704 525-0190
  Charlotte *(G-2636)*
Direct Wholesale Signs LLC .... G 704 750-2842
  Kings Mountain *(G-9303)*
Display Techs LLC .... G 704 966-0679
  Denver *(G-4773)*
Display Your Graphics LLC .... G 828 489-2282
  Hendersonville *(G-7845)*
Diversified Signs & Graphics .... G 704 392-8165
  Charlotte *(G-2645)*
▲ Dize Company .... D 336 722-5181
  Winston Salem *(G-16684)*
East Coast Signs .... G 910 462-2632
  Laurinburg *(G-9475)*
Ebert Sign Company Inc .... G 336 768-2867
  Lexington *(G-9711)*
Ecs Enterprises Inc .... D 704 786-1600
  Kannapolis *(G-9118)*
Embroidme .... G 919 316-1538
  Durham *(G-5081)*
Embroidme Lake Norman .... G 704 987-9630
  Cornelius *(G-4543)*
Endless Plastics LLC .... F 336 346-1839
  Greensboro *(G-6998)*
Engaging Signs & Graphics .... G 919 371-0885
  Raleigh *(G-12739)*
Eternal Wraps .... G 704 756-1914
  Cornelius *(G-4544)*
Ever Glo Sign Co Inc .... G 704 633-3324
  Salisbury *(G-13959)*
Everglow Na Inc .... E 704 841-2580
  Matthews *(G-10247)*
Excel Signs and Lighting .... G 336 257-9225
  Winston Salem *(G-16703)*
Exhibit World Inc .... G 704 882-2272
  Indian Trail *(G-8933)*
▲ Expogo Inc .... G 910 452-3976
  Wilmington *(G-16214)*
EZ Sign Service .... G 919 604-3508
  Wake Forest *(G-15555)*
EZ Sign Service .... G 919 554-4300
  Youngsville *(G-17080)*
Fairway Outdoor Advg LLC .... F 919 755-1900
  Raleigh *(G-12759)*
Famous Amos Signs .... G 919 820-2211
  Dunn *(G-4866)*
Fast Lane Signs .... G 336 745-5257
  Mocksville *(G-10570)*

39 MISCELLANEOUS MANUFACTURING INDUSTRIES

Fastsigns... G 252 364-8745
   Greenville *(G-7524)*

Fastsigns... G 704 360-3805
   Mooresville *(G-10943)*

Ferguson Design Inc........................... E 704 394-0120
   Belmont *(G-989)*

Fines and Carriel Inc........................... G 919 929-0702
   Chapel Hill *(G-2018)*

Fisher Signs Murals & Frames............ G 919 286-0591
   Durham *(G-5099)*

Fitch Sign Company Inc....................... G 704 482-2916
   Shelby *(G-14317)*

Flat Rock Signs & Graphics................. G 828 693-0908
   Flat Rock *(G-5965)*

Foto Grafix.. G 336 570-1885
   Burlington *(G-1415)*

Franchise Signs International.............. G 704 209-1087
   Rockwell *(G-13654)*

Franken Signs.. G 704 339-0059
   Charlotte *(G-2793)*

Frazees Trophies.................................. G 910 892-6722
   Dunn *(G-4869)*

Furr Signs... G 704 455-5849
   Harrisburg *(G-7710)*

Global Resource NC Inc....................... G 910 793-4770
   Wilmington *(G-16233)*

Gmg Group LLC................................... G 252 441-8374
   Kill Devil Hills *(G-9258)*

Gogopanels... G 702 800-1941
   Raleigh *(G-12809)*

Goins Signs Inc.................................... G 336 427-5783
   Stoneville *(G-14959)*

Goldsboro Neon Sign Co Inc................ G 919 735-2035
   Goldsboro *(G-6619)*

Gooder Grafix Inc................................ G 828 349-4097
   Franklin *(G-6131)*

Grafix Unlimited LLC.......................... G 919 291-9035
   Wendell *(G-15903)*

▲ Grandwell Industries Inc................... E 919 557-1221
   Fuquay Varina *(G-6202)*

Graphic Components LLC................... E 336 542-2128
   Greensboro *(G-7057)*

Graphic Productions Inc...................... G 336 765-9335
   Winston Salem *(G-16729)*

▼ Graphic Systems Intl Inc.................. E 336 662-8686
   Greensboro *(G-7059)*

Graphical Creations Inc....................... F 704 888-8870
   Stanfield *(G-14680)*

Graphix Solution Inc............................ F 919 213-0371
   Apex *(G-197)*

Greene Imaging & Design Inc.............. G 919 787-3737
   Raleigh *(G-12814)*

Greer and Associates Inc..................... G 919 383-3500
   Raleigh *(G-12817)*

Guerrero Enterprises Inc..................... G 828 286-4900
   Rutherfordton *(G-13875)*

Hand 2 Hand Signs............................. G 919 401-2420
   Durham *(G-5130)*

Happy Sign Surprise LLC.................... G 704 341-3359
   Charlotte *(G-2886)*

Harwood Signs...................................... G 704 857-6203
   China Grove *(G-3883)*

Hatleys Signs & Service Inc................. G 704 723-4027
   Concord *(G-4278)*

Headrick Otdoor Mdia of Crlnas........... F 704 487-5971
   Shelby *(G-14326)*

Heed Group Inc................................... G 877 938-8453
   Stanley *(G-14696)*

Hello Signs LLC................................... G 704 572-4853
   Charlotte *(G-2901)*

Heritage Custom Signs & Disp............ F 704 655-1465
   Charlotte *(G-2904)*

Hertford Printing Signs....................... G 252 426-5505
   Elizabeth City *(G-5547)*

High Tech Signs Inc............................ G 919 859-3206
   Raleigh *(G-12844)*

Holland Sign Plus Engrv Sltons............ G 252 339-5389
   Edenton *(G-5516)*

Icon Sign Systems Inc......................... G 828 253-4266
   Asheville *(G-657)*

Identity Custom Signage Inc................ F 336 882-7446
   High Point *(G-8405)*

▲ Image Design..................................... F 910 862-8988
   Elizabethtown *(G-5597)*

Image Matters Inc............................... G 336 940-3000
   Clemmons *(G-4047)*

Image360 North Raleigh NC................ G 919 307-4119
   Raleigh *(G-12879)*

▲ Industrial Sign & Graphics Inc........... E 704 371-4985
   Charlotte *(G-2965)*

Infinity S End Inc................................ F 704 900-8355
   Charlotte *(G-2968)*

Interstate Sign Company Inc.............. E 336 789-3069
   Mount Airy *(G-11524)*

Island Xprtees of Oter Bnks In............ E 252 480-3990
   Nags Head *(G-11720)*

J & D Thorpe Enterprises Inc.............. G 919 553-0918
   Clayton *(G-3990)*

J Morgan Signs Inc............................. F 336 274-6509
   Greensboro *(G-7131)*

J R Craver & Associates Inc................ E 336 769-3330
   Clemmons *(G-4049)*

▲ J Signs and Graphics LLC................. G 910 315-2657
   Aberdeen *(G-9)*

Jantec Sign Group LLC....................... E 336 429-5010
   Mount Airy *(G-11525)*

Jaxonsigns.. G 910 467-3409
   Holly Ridge *(G-8682)*

JB II Printing LLC.............................. E 336 222-0717
   Burlington *(G-1439)*

JC Signs Inc.. G 704 995-0988
   Charlotte *(G-3011)*

JC Signs Charlotte............................... G 704 370-2725
   Charlotte *(G-3012)*

Jeremy Weitzel..................................... G 919 878-4474
   Raleigh *(G-12916)*

Jester-Crown Inc................................. G 919 872-1070
   Raleigh *(G-12917)*

Jgi Inc... E 704 522-8860
   Pineville *(G-12278)*

Jj Led Solution Inc.............................. G 704 261-4279
   Charlotte *(G-3023)*

Jka Idustries....................................... G 980 225-5350
   Salisbury *(G-13992)*

JKS Motorsports Inc........................... G 336 722-4129
   Lexington *(G-9735)*

Joesigns Inc... G 252 638-1622
   New Bern *(G-11813)*

Jones Sign.. G 828 478-4780
   Sherrills Ford *(G-14386)*

Jr Signs LLC.. G 980 255-3083
   Concord *(G-4296)*

Juan Pino Signs Inc............................. G 336 764-4422
   Winston Salem *(G-16774)*

K & D Signs LLC................................. F 336 786-1111
   Mount Airy *(G-11527)*

K&K Holdings Inc................................ G 704 341-5567
   Charlotte *(G-3040)*

Kat Designs Inc................................... G 336 789-7288
   Mount Airy *(G-11528)*

Kathys Signs For Less......................... G 910 840-1447
   Chadbourn *(G-1977)*

KB Sign Solutions LLC........................ G 217 474-5861
   Concord *(G-4299)*

Kelly Signs.. G 828 778-4146
   Hendersonville *(G-7868)*

Kenneth Moore Signs........................... G 910 458-6428
   Wilmington *(G-16287)*

Ki Agency LLC..................................... G 919 977-7075
   Raleigh *(G-12937)*

King Tutt Graphics.............................. G 919 977-6901
   Raleigh *(G-12938)*

King Tutt Graphics LLC..................... G 877 546-4888
   Raleigh *(G-12939)*

Kingtuttgraphics.................................. G 919 748-0843
   Raleigh *(G-12940)*

Kranken Signs Vehicle Wraps............. G 704 339-0059
   Pineville *(G-12279)*

La Signs Inc... G 919 779-1185
   Garner *(G-6279)*

Laws Sign Group LLC......................... G 919 755-3632
   Raleigh *(G-12960)*

Legacy Designs & Graphx LLC............ G 910 237-2916
   Angier *(G-145)*

Legacy National Installers LLC........... G 336 804-1990
   Pleasant Garden *(G-12357)*

Liberty Sign and Lighting LLC............ G 336 703-7465
   Lexington *(G-9749)*

Lighthouse Led..................................... G 252 756-1158
   Winterville *(G-17005)*

Lighthouse Led Inc.............................. G 252 916-0998
   Greenville *(G-7556)*

Lights-Lights LLC............................... G 919 798-2317
   Coats *(G-4132)*

Lockwood Identity Inc......................... C 704 597-9801
   Charlotte *(G-3099)*

Ls of Raleigh....................................... G 919 457-0340
   Raleigh *(G-12980)*

M & M Signs and Awnings Inc............ F 336 352-4300
   Mount Airy *(G-11543)*

Magna Sign Intl................................... G 813 727-0205
   Wake Forest *(G-15570)*

Main Street Vinyl LLC........................ G 336 585-3089
   Burlington *(G-1453)*

Major Display Inc................................ G 800 260-1067
   Franklin *(G-6137)*

Matthews Mobile Media LLC.............. G 336 303-4982
   Greensboro *(G-7188)*

McCorkle Sign Company Inc................ E 919 687-7080
   Durham *(G-5212)*

Melendez Signs LLC............................ G 980 298-4057
   Concord *(G-4312)*

Mercury Signs Inc............................... G 919 808-1205
   Apex *(G-218)*

Meredith Media Co............................... F 919 748-4808
   Durham *(G-5221)*

Merge LLC... G 919 832-3924
   Raleigh *(G-13016)*

Metro Print Inc.................................... F 704 827-3796
   Mount Holly *(G-11642)*

Metrolina Sign Co................................ G 704 343-0885
   Charlotte *(G-3170)*

Metrolina Sign Supply LLC................. G 704 343-0885
   Charlotte *(G-3171)*

Mistretta Laser Engraving.................. G 704 418-5786
   Forest City *(G-6078)*

Moretz Signs Inc.................................. G 828 387-4600
   Beech Mountain *(G-972)*

Morningstar Signs and Banners........... G 704 861-0020
   Gastonia *(G-6469)*

Moss Sign Company Inc....................... F 828 299-7766
   Asheville *(G-706)*

Motorsports Designs Inc...................... E 336 454-1181
   High Point *(G-8460)*

Mount Airy Signs & Letters Inc........... F 336 786-5777
   Mount Airy *(G-11547)*

39 MISCELLANEOUS MANUFACTURING INDUSTRIES

Mp Digital Print & Signs Inc .... G 571 315-1562
  Cornelius *(G-4570)*
NC Graphic Pros LLC .... G 252 492-7326
  Kittrell *(G-9397)*
NC Sign and Lighting Svc LLC .... F 586 764-0563
  Jamestown *(G-9063)*
Newton Sign Co Inc .... G 910 347-1661
  Jacksonville *(G-9018)*
Nomadic Display LLC .... F 800 336-5019
  Greensboro *(G-7221)*
▲ Nomadic North America LLC .... E 703 866-9200
  Greensboro *(G-7222)*
North State Signs Inc .... G 919 977-7053
  Raleigh *(G-13072)*
Oak City Sign Solutions Inc .... G 919 792-8077
  Raleigh *(G-13080)*
Ocean Road Graphics Signs .... G 919 404-1444
  Four Oaks *(G-6110)*
Onsight Inc .... G 704 747-4168
  Charlotte *(G-3301)*
Optimum Sign Age .... G 919 372-8018
  Cary *(G-1838)*
▲ Oramental Post .... F 704 376-8111
  Pineville *(G-12288)*
Outside Lines .... G 919 327-3041
  Garner *(G-6299)*
Overstreet Sign Contrs Inc .... G 919 596-7300
  Durham *(G-5266)*
Parish Sign & Service Inc .... E 910 875-6121
  Raeford *(G-12430)*
PC Signs & Graphics LLC .... G 919 661-5801
  Garner *(G-6300)*
Peaches Enterprises Inc .... G 910 868-5800
  Fayetteville *(G-5895)*
Pegasus Art and Signs LLC .... G 704 588-4948
  Charlotte *(G-3325)*
PFC Group LLC .... D 704 393-4040
  Charlotte *(G-3335)*
Phoenix Sign Pros Inc .... G 252 756-5685
  Winterville *(G-17011)*
Piedmont Directional Signs Inc .... G 704 607-6809
  Belmont *(G-1001)*
Piedmont Mediaworks Inc .... F 828 575-2250
  Asheville *(G-730)*
Piedmont Signs .... G 704 291-2345
  Monroe *(G-10787)*
Piranha Industries Inc .... G 704 248-7843
  Charlotte *(G-3344)*
Planet Logo Inc .... G 910 763-2554
  Wilmington *(G-16356)*
Plastic Art Design Inc .... G 919 878-1672
  Raleigh *(G-13115)*
Playrace Inc .... E 828 251-2211
  Asheville *(G-735)*
Poblocki Sign Company LLC .... D 919 354-3800
  Morrisville *(G-11410)*
Point Harbor Art .... G 804 852-3633
  Point Harbor *(G-12381)*
Port City Signs & Graphics Inc .... G 910 350-8242
  Wilmington *(G-16362)*
◆ Portable Displays LLC .... E 919 544-6504
  Cary *(G-1855)*
Powersigns Inc .... G 910 343-1789
  Wilmington *(G-16365)*
Precision Signs Inc .... G 919 615-0979
  Garner *(G-6305)*
Print Management Group LLC .... F 704 821-0114
  Charlotte *(G-3385)*
Printology Signs Graphics LLC .... G 843 473-4984
  Davidson *(G-4691)*
▲ Prismaflex Usa Inc .... F 910 862-3550
  Elizabethtown *(G-5602)*

Professional Bus Systems Inc .... G 704 333-2444
  Charlotte *(G-3391)*
Professional Laminating LLC .... G 919 465-0400
  Cary *(G-1862)*
▲ Promographix Inc .... F 919 846-1379
  Carolina Beach *(G-1640)*
Prosign .... G 919 222-6907
  Goldsboro *(G-6647)*
Proveer .... G 800 542-9941
  Raleigh *(G-13155)*
Purple Star Graphics Inc .... G 704 723-4020
  Concord *(G-4342)*
Qasioun LLC .... G 704 531-8000
  Charlotte *(G-3398)*
Qi Signs LLC .... G 336 625-0938
  Asheboro *(G-469)*
R and L Collision Center Inc .... F 704 739-2500
  Kings Mountain *(G-9328)*
R O Givens Signs Inc .... G 252 338-6578
  Elizabeth City *(G-5567)*
Ra Printing & Sign LLC .... G 704 393-0264
  Charlotte *(G-3407)*
Rags Signs + Graphics LLC .... G 910 793-9087
  Wilmington *(G-16376)*
Raleigh Sign Design .... G 919 244-1802
  Holly Springs *(G-8711)*
Raleigh Sign Solutions LLC .... G 919 578-7255
  Raleigh *(G-13186)*
Rama Sadri .... G 919 875-8088
  Raleigh *(G-13189)*
Readilite & Barricade Inc .... F 919 231-8309
  Raleigh *(G-13194)*
Rec Plus Inc .... E 704 375-9098
  Charlotte *(G-3419)*
Reese Sign Service Inc .... G 919 580-0705
  Goldsboro *(G-6649)*
Rena Sales .... G 704 364-3006
  Charlotte *(G-3432)*
Retail Installation Svcs LLC .... G 336 818-1333
  Millers Creek *(G-10495)*
Ricky Locklair & Randy Locklai .... G 910 470-3222
  Wilmington *(G-16383)*
RLM/Universal Packaging Inc .... F 336 644-6161
  Greensboro *(G-7312)*
Robbins Sign Supply Inc .... F 828 758-1954
  Lenoir *(G-9650)*
Rodney S Cstm Cut Sign Co Inc .... E 919 362-9669
  Holly Springs *(G-8712)*
Routh Sign Service .... G 336 272-0895
  Greensboro *(G-7318)*
Rustic Oak Sign Co .... G 919 619-4452
  Raleigh *(G-13220)*
Ruth Arnold Graphics & Signs .... G 910 793-9087
  Wilmington *(G-16390)*
S Tri Inc .... G 704 542-8186
  Charlotte *(G-3477)*
▼ Salem Sports Inc .... G 336 722-2444
  Winston Salem *(G-16894)*
Sawyers Sign Service Inc .... F
  Mount Airy *(G-11571)*
Seaward Action Inc .... G 252 671-1684
  Wilmington *(G-16397)*
Sensational Signs .... G 704 358-1099
  Charlotte *(G-3527)*
September Signs & Graphics LLC .... G 910 791-9084
  Wilmington *(G-16399)*
Shop Dawg Signs LLC .... G 919 556-2672
  Wake Forest *(G-15592)*
Shutterbug Grafix & Signs .... G 910 315-1556
  Pinehurst *(G-12237)*
Shytle Sign and Ltg Svcs LLC .... G 828 429-4120
  Ellenboro *(G-5639)*

Sidney Perry Cooper III .... G 252 257-3886
  Warrenton *(G-15661)*
Sign & Awning Systems Inc .... F 919 892-5900
  Dunn *(G-4883)*
Sign A Rama Inc .... G 336 893-8042
  Lewisville *(G-9673)*
Sign and Doodle .... G 704 763-7501
  Concord *(G-4358)*
Sign Company of Wilmington Inc .... F 910 392-1414
  Wilmington *(G-16405)*
Sign Connection Inc .... E 704 868-4500
  Gastonia *(G-6507)*
Sign Gypsies Hickory .... G 828 244-3085
  Conover *(G-4496)*
Sign Here of Lake Norman Inc .... G 704 483-6454
  Denver *(G-4801)*
▼ Sign Medic Inc .... G 336 789-5972
  Mount Airy *(G-11572)*
Sign Mine Inc .... G 336 884-5780
  High Point *(G-8526)*
Sign O Rama .... G 704 443-0092
  Matthews *(G-10289)*
Sign On Time .... G 704 507-2486
  Mooresville *(G-11087)*
Sign Resources of NC .... G 336 310-4611
  Kernersville *(G-9233)*
Sign Scientist LLC .... G 919 685-7641
  Raleigh *(G-13254)*
Sign Shop of The Triangle Inc .... G 919 363-3930
  Apex *(G-242)*
Sign Shoppe Inc .... G 910 754-5144
  Supply *(G-15011)*
Sign Solutions LLC .... G 828 687-9789
  Arden *(G-375)*
Sign Systems Inc .... F 828 322-5622
  Hickory *(G-8155)*
Sign Systems Inc .... G 828 785-1722
  Asheville *(G-770)*
Sign Technology Inc .... G 336 887-3211
  High Point *(G-8527)*
Sign With Anderson LLC .... G 704 599-6977
  Gastonia *(G-6508)*
Sign With Ease Inc .... G 919 285-3224
  Holly Springs *(G-8716)*
Sign World Inc .... F 704 529-4440
  Charlotte *(G-3550)*
Sign Worxpress .... G 336 437-9889
  Burlington *(G-1495)*
Sign-A-Rama .... G 919 383-5561
  Raleigh *(G-13255)*
Signage Innovations Group LLC .... G 704 392-8165
  Charlotte *(G-3551)*
Signal Signs of Ga Inc .... G 828 494-4913
  Murphy *(G-11716)*
Signarama of Roxboro .... G 336 322-1663
  Roxboro *(G-13823)*
Signarc of Matthews LLC .... G 704 209-4444
  Matthews *(G-10343)*
Signature Signs Inc .... G 336 431-2072
  High Point *(G-8528)*
Signergy LLC .... G 919 876-1370
  Raleigh *(G-13256)*
Signfactory Direct Inc .... G 336 903-0300
  Wilkesboro *(G-16041)*
Significant Others .... G 919 539-7551
  Raleigh *(G-13257)*
Signify It Inc .... F 910 678-8111
  Fayetteville *(G-5916)*
Signlite Services Inc .... G 336 751-9543
  Mocksville *(G-10603)*
Signlogic Inc .... G 910 862-8965
  Elizabethtown *(G-5604)*

39 MISCELLANEOUS MANUFACTURING INDUSTRIES

Signs By Design .... G 919 217-8000
   Raleigh *(G-13258)*

Signs By Design .... G 919 217-8000
   Raleigh *(G-13259)*

Signs By Tomorrow .... G 704 527-6100
   Charlotte *(G-3552)*

Signs Designed LLC .... G 704 332-4800
   Indian Trail *(G-8963)*

Signs Done Right .... G 910 384-2007
   Laurinburg *(G-9497)*

Signs Etc .... G 336 722-9341
   Winston Salem *(G-16909)*

Signs Etc of Charlotte .... E 704 522-8860
   Charlotte *(G-3554)*

Signs Etc of Charlotte .... F 704 522-8860
   Charlotte *(G-3553)*

Signs Now .... G 410 923-3534
   Fayetteville *(G-5917)*

Signs Now .... G 919 546-0006
   Raleigh *(G-13260)*

Signs Now 103 LLC .... G 252 355-0768
   Greenville *(G-7583)*

Signs Now Charlotte .... G 704 844-0552
   Pineville *(G-12306)*

Signs Now of Greenville .... G 252 382-0020
   Nashville *(G-11750)*

Signs Plus .... G 704 219-0290
   Wingate *(G-16578)*

Signs Sealed Delivered .... G 919 213-1280
   Durham *(G-5357)*

Signs Unlimited Inc .... F 919 596-7612
   Durham *(G-5358)*

Signsations Ltd .... G 571 340-3330
   Chapel Hill *(G-2072)*

Signsmith Custom Signs & Awnin .... F 252 752-4321
   Greenville *(G-7584)*

Signz Inc .... G 704 824-7446
   Gastonia *(G-6509)*

Siqnarama Pinevillw .... G 704 835-1123
   Pineville *(G-12307)*

Sitzer & Spuria Inc .... G 919 929-0299
   Chapel Hill *(G-2073)*

Skipper Graphics .... G 910 754-8729
   Shallotte *(G-14278)*

Southeastern Sign Works Inc .... F 336 789-5516
   Mount Airy *(G-11574)*

Southern Signworks .... G 828 683-8726
   Leicester *(G-9521)*

Speedcal Graphics Inc .... G 704 412-3321
   Charlotte *(G-3600)*

Speedgraphics Sign Design Inc .... G 828 771-0322
   Arden *(G-380)*

Speedpro Imaging .... G 704 321-1200
   Charlotte *(G-3602)*

Speedpro Imaging .... G 704 799-8040
   Cornelius *(G-4587)*

Speedpro Imaging .... G 704 495-6749
   Mooresville *(G-11096)*

Speedpro Imaging .... G 919 578-4338
   Raleigh *(G-13289)*

Speedpro Imaging Durham .... G 919 278-7964
   Durham *(G-5368)*

Srb Technologies Inc .... E 336 659-2610
   Winston Salem *(G-16914)*

Stay Alert Safety Services Inc .... E 919 828-5399
   Raleigh *(G-13300)*

Sterling Products Corporation .... G 646 423-3175
   Greensboro *(G-7370)*

Sticky Life .... G 910 817-4531
   Newton Grove *(G-11993)*

Stonetree Signs .... G 336 625-0938
   Denton *(G-4750)*

Studio Displays Inc .... F 704 588-6590
   Pineville *(G-12310)*

Superior Sign Company Inc .... G 336 454-2226
   High Point *(G-8558)*

Syd Inc .... G 336 294-8807
   Greensboro *(G-7383)*

Syntech of Burlington Inc .... E 336 570-2035
   Burlington *(G-1503)*

T & R Signs .... G 919 779-1185
   Garner *(G-6317)*

Talking Devices Company .... G 828 658-0660
   Asheville *(G-795)*

Tebo Displays LLC .... G 919 832-8525
   Raleigh *(G-13333)*

TEC Graphics Inc .... F 919 567-2077
   Fuquay Varina *(G-6232)*

Three Gypsies LLC .... G 843 337-7799
   Wingate *(G-16579)*

Tier 1 Graphics LLC .... G 704 625-6880
   Cornelius *(G-4592)*

TNT Signs & Graphics .... G 704 460-5050
   Shelby *(G-14374)*

Tommy Signs .... G 704 877-1234
   Waxhaw *(G-15782)*

Tomorrow Cell LLC .... G 704 378-8555
   Charlotte *(G-3707)*

Triangle Inner Vision Company .... G 919 460-6013
   Morrisville *(G-11452)*

Triangle Sign Solutions .... G 919 302-2482
   Wake Forest *(G-15604)*

Triangle Solutions Inc .... G 919 481-1235
   Cary *(G-1912)*

▲ Twinvision North America Inc .... C 919 361-2155
   Durham *(G-5416)*

United Group Graphics Inc .... G 919 596-3932
   Durham *(G-5421)*

US Logoworks LLC .... F 910 307-0312
   Fayetteville *(G-5944)*

Veteran Safety Solutions LLC .... G 980 339-2721
   Southmont *(G-14562)*

Vic Inc .... E 336 545-1124
   Greensboro *(G-7443)*

Victory Signs LLC .... G 919 642-3091
   Fuquay Varina *(G-6236)*

▲ Vintage Editions Inc .... F 828 632-4185
   Taylorsville *(G-15175)*

Vittro Sign Studio .... G 917 698-1594
   Apex *(G-256)*

Vivid Pro Signs .... G 919 352-8485
   Sanford *(G-14204)*

Warden Signs & Service LLC .... G 336 416-4029
   Yadkinville *(G-17062)*

Web 4 Half LLC .... E 855 762-4638
   Asheboro *(G-509)*

Webb of Wnc LLC .... G 828 648-2670
   Canton *(G-1628)*

Weddles Signs .... G 276 779-9218
   Mount Airy *(G-11593)*

Whats Your Sign LLC .... G 919 274-5703
   Raleigh *(G-13420)*

Wicked Rooster Signs Inc .... G 828 844-0404
   Hendersonville *(G-7914)*

Wild Child Custom Graphics LLC .... G 910 762-5335
   Wilmington *(G-16443)*

Williams Signs .... G 828 321-2338
   Andrews *(G-129)*

Wilson Billboard Advg Inc .... G 919 934-2421
   Smithfield *(G-14489)*

Wright Business Concepts Inc .... G 828 466-1044
   Hickory *(G-8211)*

Xo Signs .... G 919 328-9170
   Durham *(G-5455)*

Xtreme Graphix .... G 704 746-5744
   Mooresville *(G-11134)*

Yesco Sign Lighting Service .... G 336 285-0795
   Greensboro *(G-7473)*

3995 Burial caskets

Winston-Salem Casket Company .... G 336 661-1695
   Winston Salem *(G-16984)*

3996 Hard surface floor coverings, nec

Tarheel Mats Inc .... G 252 325-1903
   Camden *(G-1559)*

Unilin North America LLC .... E 919 773-6000
   Garner *(G-6320)*

Unilin North America LLC .... E 919 773-5900
   Garner *(G-6321)*

3999 Manufacturing industries, nec

131 Candle Co .... G 325 650-4903
   Durham *(G-4892)*

222 Dream Co LLC .... G 919 803-9741
   Fayetteville *(G-5745)*

26 Industries Inc .... G 704 839-3218
   Concord *(G-4184)*

3-Oceans Mfg Inc .... G 919 600-4500
   Garner *(G-6248)*

89 Industries .... G 303 681-3188
   Littleton *(G-9949)*

A Cleaner Tomorrow Dry Clg LLC .... G 919 639-6396
   Dunn *(G-4847)*

A Plus Five Star Trnsp LLC .... G 919 771-4820
   Clayton *(G-3950)*

▲ Access Manufacturing Tech LLC .... G 224 610-0171
   Mooresville *(G-10846)*

Acu Trol Inc .... G 919 566-8332
   Sanford *(G-14082)*

Addendum LLC .... G 704 664-9898
   Mooresville *(G-10848)*

AIM Industries Inc .... G 336 656-9990
   Browns Summit *(G-1299)*

Ajc Craftworks Inc .... G 919 279-1621
   Raleigh *(G-12483)*

American Eagle Mfg LLC .... G 252 633-0603
   New Bern *(G-11767)*

American Made Industries Inc .... G 650 218-7608
   Concord *(G-4193)*

Amish Lights Candles .... G 330 546-3900
   Concord *(G-4196)*

Anchored Scents LLC .... G 910 709-1582
   Winterville *(G-16994)*

Andrews Industries LLC .... G 919 266-9656
   Raleigh *(G-12505)*

Andy Maylish Fabrication Inc .... G 704 785-1491
   Denver *(G-4762)*

Angel Industries Inc .... G 919 264-0765
   Raleigh *(G-12507)*

Apollonias Candles Things LLC .... G 910 408-2508
   Durham *(G-4921)*

Applied Components Mfg LLC .... G 828 323-8915
   Hickory *(G-7936)*

Applied Components Mfg LLC .... G 828 322-6535
   Hickory *(G-7937)*

Aqua Blue Inc .... G 704 896-9007
   Cornelius *(G-4522)*

Aqua Doc Pool Sparkling S .... G 828 231-9398
   Waynesville *(G-15793)*

Arden Companies LLC .... E 919 258-3081
   Sanford *(G-14087)*

Asheville Pet Supply .... G 828 252-2054
   Asheville *(G-540)*

Ask Elevator Service Inc .... G 336 674-2715
   Pleasant Garden *(G-12356)*

39 MISCELLANEOUS MANUFACTURING INDUSTRIES

Asterra Labs LLC .... G 800 430-9074
  Nashville *(G-11733)*
Astroturf .... G 336 528-5496
  Lexington *(G-9682)*
Astroturf Corp .... G 336 238-9060
  Lexington *(G-9683)*
Atlantic Group Usa Inc .... F 919 623-7824
  Raleigh *(G-12530)*
Atlantic Manufacturing LLC ...... G 336 497-5500
  Kernersville *(G-9166)*
Atlantic Mfg & Fabrication Inc ... G 704 647-6200
  Salisbury *(G-13925)*
Auralites Inc .... G 828 687-7990
  Fletcher *(G-5986)*
▲ Autoverters Inc .... F 252 537-0426
  Roanoke Rapids *(G-13567)*
Ava Aliza Candle Co LLC .... G 704 906-4328
  Charlotte *(G-2243)*
Bark House Supply Company ..... G 828 765-9010
  Spruce Pine *(G-14629)*
Barrette Welch McFall Ms .... G 919 606-7537
  Durham *(G-4943)*
Barry Lowe Fabrication .... G 828 776-7354
  Fairview *(G-5708)*
Bass Fabrications LLC .... G 252 312-8937
  Hobbsville *(G-8674)*
Beachbub USA .... G 336 965-5941
  Greensboro *(G-6833)*
Beast Chains .... G 336 346-9081
  High Point *(G-8268)*
Beelite Inc .... G 828 584-1488
  Morganton *(G-11201)*
Belev En U Water Mfg Co .... G 704 620-0450
  Cornelius *(G-4526)*
Bell Book & Candle LLC .... G 336 480-1422
  Clemmons *(G-4031)*
Bethany Small .... G 910 409-2167
  Southport *(G-14567)*
▲ Bhaktivedanta Archives .... G 336 871-3636
  Sandy Ridge *(G-14076)*
Bickerstaff Trees Inc .... G 336 372-8866
  Sparta *(G-14589)*
Biganodes LLC .... G 828 245-1115
  Forest City *(G-6060)*
Blue Ridge Bracket Co .... G 828 242-8577
  Asheville *(G-563)*
Blue Ridge Bracket Inc .... G 828 808-3273
  Fletcher *(G-5988)*
Blur Development Group LLC .... E 919 701-4213
  Cary *(G-1711)*
Boka Industries LLC .... G 704 237-4692
  Cornelius *(G-4530)*
Boleef Industries .... G 336 330-0404
  Roxboro *(G-13796)*
Boles Industries LLC .... G 919 489-9254
  Durham *(G-4970)*
Bonaventure Group Inc .... F 919 781-6610
  Raleigh *(G-12568)*
Bordchek Industries LLC .... G 864 363-2117
  Cornelius *(G-4531)*
Borden Mfg Co Fund Inc .... G 919 734-4301
  Goldsboro *(G-6595)*
Bouncers and Slides Inc .... G 252 908-2292
  Nashville *(G-11735)*
Boyd Manufacturing Inc .... F 336 301-6433
  Siler City *(G-14400)*
BR Lee Industries Inc .... G 704 966-3317
  Lincolnton *(G-9876)*
◆ Bradford Products LLC .... D 910 791-2202
  Leland *(G-9529)*
Brand Art Manufacturing LLC .... G 704 241-1104
  Winston Salem *(G-16635)*

Brandy Thompson .... F 321 252-2911
  Fayetteville *(G-5774)*
Brett Salter .... G 828 252-4311
  Asheville *(G-572)*
Brew Candle Company .... G 980 275-9355
  Boone *(G-1182)*
Brian McGregor Enterprise .... G 919 732-2317
  Hillsborough *(G-8640)*
Brite Sky LLC .... G 757 589-4676
  Godwin *(G-6576)*
Brittany Smith .... G 912 313-0588
  Greensboro *(G-6858)*
Brooks Manufacturing Solutions .. F 336 438-1280
  Graham *(G-6681)*
Bryants Fire Extinguisher Co .... G 252 563-4111
  Tarboro *(G-15098)*
Buddy Cut Inc .... G 888 608-4701
  Pittsboro *(G-12333)*
C J Manufacturing Inc .... G 252 927-4913
  Pinetown *(G-12244)*
C6 Manufacturing .... G 704 896-3934
  Cornelius *(G-4532)*
Caldwell Hohl Artworks .... G 336 879-9090
  Seagrove *(G-14234)*
Cambbro Manufacturing Company . F 919 568-8506
  Mebane *(G-10402)*
Cambro .... G 919 563-0761
  Mebane *(G-10403)*
Camera To Candle .... G 339 224-1073
  Huntersville *(G-8800)*
Candle Bar .... G 704 497-6099
  Charlotte *(G-2383)*
Candypearls Hair LLC .... G 252 558-7202
  Raleigh *(G-12587)*
Carbon-Less Industries Inc ...... G 704 361-1231
  Harrisburg *(G-7703)*
Cardinal Creek Cndles Gfts LLC .. G 336 941-3158
  Advance *(G-39)*
Care A Lot Pet Supply .... G 757 457-9425
  Moyock *(G-11694)*
Caring For Body LLC .... G 706 897-9904
  Arden *(G-317)*
Carolina Candle .... G 336 835-6020
  Elkin *(G-5612)*
Carolina Gyps Reclamation LLC .. G 704 895-4506
  Cornelius *(G-4534)*
Carolina Mfg Group LLC .... G 336 413-8335
  Winston Salem *(G-16645)*
Carolina Mnufactured Homes LLC . G 910 374-6889
  Lumberton *(G-10029)*
Carolina Perfumer Inc .... G 910 295-5600
  Pinehurst *(G-12217)*
Cat Daddy Ventures LLC .... G 252 229-8617
  Arden *(G-318)*
CB Industries .... G 704 660-1955
  Mooresville *(G-10901)*
Cbd Open Water Diving .... G 910 232-3692
  Wilmington *(G-16162)*
CCI Hair Boutique LLC .... F 407 216-9213
  Hope Mills *(G-8735)*
Celebration Candles Inc .... G 610 360-1545
  Leland *(G-9535)*
Charming Pot Candle Co LLC ..... G 828 768-4827
  Candler *(G-1574)*
Chatter Free Tling Sltions Inc ... G 828 659-7379
  Marion *(G-10148)*
Cjm Industries LLC .... G 704 506-5926
  Mooresville *(G-10903)*
Claremont Products LLC .... G 704 325-3580
  Claremont *(G-3907)*
Classic Scent .... G 828 645-5171
  Weaverville *(G-15841)*

Classy Dolls Massage & Btq LLC . G 336 209-3933
  Greensboro *(G-6914)*
Clean As A Whistle .... G 919 949-7738
  Durham *(G-5019)*
Clean Green Sustainable Lf LLC .. F 855 946-8785
  Greensboro *(G-6915)*
Cmw Mfg LLC .... G 330 283-5551
  Charlotte *(G-2507)*
Cnc Creations .... G 704 508-2668
  Troutman *(G-15374)*
Coastal Tides Soap Candles LLC .. G 910 833-2132
  Wilmington *(G-16174)*
Coates Designers & Crafstmen ... G 828 349-9700
  Franklin *(G-6120)*
Collier Industries NC .... G 980 263-0510
  Stanley *(G-14689)*
Collin Manufacturing Inc .... G 919 917-5969
  Wake Forest *(G-15544)*
Collin Mfg Inc .... G 919 917-6264
  Oriental *(G-12109)*
Commdoor Inc .... G 800 565-1851
  Concord *(G-4237)*
Component Manufacturing & Mch . G 336 699-4204
  Lewisville *(G-9665)*
Concise Manufacturing Inc .... G 704 796-8419
  Salisbury *(G-13945)*
Conmech Industries LLC .... G 919 306-6228
  Apex *(G-177)*
Continental Manufacturing Co .... G 336 697-2591
  Mc Leansville *(G-10386)*
Cooper Industries LLC .... G 304 545-1482
  Greensboro *(G-6935)*
Coramdeo Lighting Industries ..... G 704 906-8864
  Mooresville *(G-10913)*
Core Beginnings .... G 614 551-1963
  Wadesboro *(G-15508)*
Core Grip LLC .... G 252 341-7783
  Greenville *(G-7508)*
Cornerstone Mfg Co LLC .... G 704 624-6145
  Marshville *(G-10212)*
Corsan LLC .... F 704 765-9979
  Huntersville *(G-8806)*
Cosmopros .... G 704 717-7420
  Charlotte *(G-2560)*
Cottage House Wreaths .... G 336 234-7079
  Blanch *(G-1151)*
CP Industries Inc .... G 704 816-0580
  Charlotte *(G-2564)*
Cr Appraisal Firm LLC .... G 704 344-0909
  Charlotte *(G-2566)*
Craig Hart .... G 269 365-5568
  Greensboro *(G-6938)*
Creative Fish Company Inc .... G 203 515-8631
  Kernersville *(G-9184)*
Creative Lights .... G 336 209-8209
  Stoneville *(G-14956)*
Creek Industries Inc .... F 828 319-7490
  Weaverville *(G-15845)*
Cristal Dragon Candle Company .. G 336 997-4210
  Sandy Ridge *(G-14077)*
Cross Manufacturing LLC .... G 336 269-6542
  Burlington *(G-1401)*
Cross Manufacturing LLC .... G 336 603-6926
  Gibsonville *(G-6557)*
Crown Town Industries LLC ...... G 704 579-0387
  Concord *(G-4248)*
Cs Manufacturing Cs Mfg .... G 704 837-1701
  Charlotte *(G-2580)*
Cutting Edge Industries .... G 336 937-2129
  Greensboro *(G-6951)*
Cv Industries .... G 919 778-7280
  Goldsboro *(G-6605)*

39 MISCELLANEOUS MANUFACTURING INDUSTRIES

D & D Industries .... G 252 331-2528
   Elizabeth City *(G-5539)*

D & T Soy Candles .... G 704 320-2804
   Polkton *(G-12386)*

Daisy Pink Co .... G 704 907-3526
   Charlotte *(G-2600)*

Dale Reynolds Cabinets Inc .... G 704 890-5962
   Charlotte *(G-2601)*

Dauntless Mfg Solutions LLC .... G 757 870-2173
   Asheboro *(G-423)*

David Oreck Candle .... F 336 375-8411
   Greensboro *(G-6959)*

▲ Daydream Education LLC .... G 800 591-6150
   Clyde *(G-4123)*

Denton Wreath Company .... G 828 479-4992
   Robbinsville *(G-13607)*

▲ Devan Us Inc .... G 704 365-7111
   Charlotte *(G-2624)*

Direct Distribution Inds Inc .... G 910 217-0000
   Wagram *(G-15523)*

DIss Mfg .... G 919 619-6184
   Pittsboro *(G-12340)*

Dorian Corporation .... F 910 352-6939
   Wilmington *(G-16204)*

Douglas Battery Mfg Co .... G 336 650-7000
   Winston Salem *(G-16687)*

Draxlor Industries Inc .... G 757 274-6771
   Durham *(G-5062)*

Dropping Gemz Nail Studio LLC .... G 919 440-4744
   Raleigh *(G-12703)*

Dynamic Mounting .... G 704 978-8723
   Mooresville *(G-10931)*

E Cache & Co LLC .... F 919 590-0779
   Charlotte *(G-2670)*

E-Liquid Brands LLC .... E 828 385-5090
   Mooresville *(G-10933)*

E&G Industries Inc .... G 347 665-3039
   Durham *(G-5074)*

Eagle Rock Industries LLC .... G 919 799-1021
   Siler City *(G-14409)*

Earnhardt Manufacturing .... G 910 738-9426
   Lumberton *(G-10033)*

Earth-Kind Inc .... G 701 751-4456
   Mooresville *(G-10934)*

▲ East Coast Umbrella Inc .... E 910 462-2500
   Laurel Hill *(G-9459)*

East West Diversified LLC .... G 919 671-0301
   Wake Forest *(G-15549)*

Eastern Carolina Mfg Co LLC .... G 252 824-3794
   Tarboro *(G-15102)*

Eastern Manufacturing LLC .... G 919 580-2058
   Goldsboro *(G-6611)*

Ebony & Ivorys Unique Btq LLC .... G 704 324-4035
   Wingate *(G-16574)*

Echo Industries Inc .... G 704 921-2293
   Charlotte *(G-2682)*

Element Tree Essentials LLC .... G 828 707-0407
   Arden *(G-327)*

Ella B Candles LLC .... E 980 339-8898
   Charlotte *(G-2697)*

Ellie Industries Inc .... G 828 626-3935
   Barnardsville *(G-909)*

Encore Group Inc .... C 336 768-7859
   Winston Salem *(G-16696)*

Enepay Corporation .... G 919 788-1454
   Raleigh *(G-12738)*

Energizer Battery Mfg .... G 336 736-7936
   Asheboro *(G-430)*

Enoco LLC .... G 336 398-5650
   Greensboro *(G-7001)*

Equagen Engineers Pllc .... E 919 444-5442
   Raleigh *(G-12744)*

Essence Candles .... G 980 785-4309
   Troutman *(G-15375)*

Essence Noire LLC .... G 704 351-8322
   Charlotte *(G-2728)*

Evergreen Silks NC Inc .... F 704 845-5577
   Matthews *(G-10248)*

Fac Ette Manufacturing .... G 910 599-7352
   Wilmington *(G-16216)*

Fee Kees Wreaths LLC .... G 704 636-1008
   Salisbury *(G-13964)*

Fiber Transport Systems Inc .... G 704 905-3549
   Charlotte *(G-2757)*

Fields Industries LLC .... G 704 264-3872
   Charlotte *(G-2760)*

Fifty Combs LLC .... G 252 406-6242
   Tarboro *(G-15103)*

▲ Fill Pac LLC .... F 828 322-1916
   Hickory *(G-8024)*

Filtrona Filters Inc .... D 336 362-1333
   Greensboro *(G-7015)*

Fisherman Creations Inc .... E 252 725-0138
   Beaufort *(G-956)*

Flow Fabrication .... G 704 376-8555
   Charlotte *(G-2780)*

Forage Soaps LLC .... G 828 737-9088
   Newland *(G-11886)*

▲ Fragrant Passage Candle Co LP .... E 336 375-8411
   Greensboro *(G-7020)*

Full Circle Grinding LLC .... G 919 879-9529
   Clayton *(G-3979)*

Furniture Mfrs Claring Hse Inc .... G 866 477-8468
   Thomasville *(G-15226)*

G H Group LLC .... G 919 264-0939
   Raleigh *(G-12789)*

Gallimore Fmly Investments Inc .... F 336 625-5138
   Asheboro *(G-438)*

General Foam Plastics Corp .... G 757 857-0153
   Tarboro *(G-15106)*

▲ Gentry Mills Inc .... D 704 983-5555
   Albemarle *(G-86)*

Get Wickd Candles .... G 704 437-9062
   Troutman *(G-15379)*

Gfm Industries LLC .... G 614 439-5349
   Burlington *(G-1421)*

Gifted Hands Styling Salon .... G 828 781-2781
   Hickory *(G-8032)*

Give You Hope Industries Inc .... G 336 608-2774
   Winston Salem *(G-16721)*

Glossy Wicks LLC .... G 980 349-5908
   Charlotte *(G-2835)*

GNB Ventures LLC .... F 704 488-4468
   Charlotte *(G-2837)*

Gold Canyon Candles .... G 828 358-5729
   Connelly Springs *(G-4401)*

Gratz Industries .... G 828 467-6380
   Asheville *(G-641)*

Griffin Manufacturing LLC .... G 704 984-2070
   Albemarle *(G-88)*

Grinding & Metals Inc .... G 704 588-5999
   Charlotte *(G-2869)*

Gw Industries LLC .... G 919 608-1911
   Raleigh *(G-12825)*

H&H Metal Fab .... G 828 757-3747
   Lenoir *(G-9617)*

Hair Socety Inc .... G 919 588-1453
   Morrisville *(G-11350)*

▲ Hanes Industries-Newton .... F 828 469-2000
   Newton *(G-11939)*

Happy Wax .... G 888 400-3053
   Durham *(G-5131)*

Harmony Farm Candles .... G 919 698-5200
   Mebane *(G-10414)*

Harris Industries LLC .... G 410 924-3894
   Mint Hill *(G-10536)*

Health At Home Inc .... F 850 543-4482
   Charlotte *(G-2896)*

Heed Group Inc .... G 877 938-8853
   Stanley *(G-14696)*

Heico Manufacturing Inc .... G 828 304-5499
   Hickory *(G-8042)*

Henry Williams Jr .... G 336 897-8714
   High Point *(G-8383)*

Hensley Corporation .... G 828 230-9447
   Fairview *(G-5712)*

Hershey Group LLC .... G 336 855-3888
   Greensboro *(G-7087)*

Highlight Industries Inc .... G 704 661-1734
   Concord *(G-4281)*

Historic Interpretations Inc .... G 919 339-1558
   Raleigh *(G-12847)*

Hodge Industries Inc .... G 704 491-0104
   Charlotte *(G-2913)*

Holten Industries LLC .... G 919 810-8467
   Raleigh *(G-12854)*

Hoodoo Honey LLC .... G 252 548-0697
   Durham *(G-5140)*

Hoppercleve Designs LLC .... G 919 721-4406
   Cameron *(G-1561)*

Hudson Industries LLC .... G 704 480-0014
   Shelby *(G-14327)*

▲ Hudson S Hardware Inc .... E 919 553-3030
   Garner *(G-6276)*

Hughes Products Co Inc .... G 336 475-0091
   Winston Salem *(G-16751)*

Humboldt Mfg Co Inc .... G 919 832-6509
   Raleigh *(G-12867)*

Idael Mfg Co .... G 919 480-1329
   Raleigh *(G-12875)*

▲ Impact Fulfillment Svcs LLC .... C 336 227-1130
   Burlington *(G-1434)*

IMS Intrnational Mfrs Showroom .... G 336 454-0388
   Jamestown *(G-9057)*

Innovative Technology Mfg LLC .... G 980 248-3731
   Mooresville *(G-10982)*

Inovative Vapes of Boone .... G 828 386-1041
   Boone *(G-1209)*

Insurrection Industries LLC .... G 443 801-7356
   Winston Salem *(G-16762)*

Ironmex Fabrication Inc .... G 336 937-1045
   Greensboro *(G-7122)*

Isabellas Oils LLC .... G 828 221-4274
   Hickory *(G-8069)*

J Ali Candles .... G 910 603-2997
   West End *(G-15927)*

Jacob Holm Industries Amer Inc .... G 828 490-6017
   Fletcher *(G-6014)*

Jag Industries LLC .... G 704 655-2507
   Huntersville *(G-8840)*

Jasmine Wade Co LLC .... G 704 345-8301
   Charlotte *(G-3009)*

JC Wicks LLC .... G 828 514-9788
   Charlotte *(G-3013)*

Jefferson Group Inc .... E 252 752-6195
   Greenville *(G-7549)*

Jepp Industries Inc .... G 910 232-8715
   Wilmington *(G-16279)*

Jhd Enterprise LLC .... G 919 612-1787
   Creedmoor *(G-4616)*

Joanna Division Ch F Inds .... G 704 522-5000
   Charlotte *(G-3026)*

Jochum Industries .... G 336 288-7975
   Greensboro *(G-7137)*

Johnny Slicks Inc .... G 910 803-2159
   Holly Ridge *(G-8683)*

Employee Codes: A=Over 500 employees, B=251-500
C=101-250, D=51-100, E=20-50, F=10-19, G=1-9

39 MISCELLANEOUS MANUFACTURING INDUSTRIES

Joseph Sotanski .... E 407 324-6187
  Marion *(G-10155)*
◆ Justneem LLC .... G 919 414-8826
  Apex *(G-210)*
Justrite Manufacturing .... G 336 990-0918
  North Wilkesboro *(G-12020)*
K & K Industries LLC .... G 336 689-4293
  Lexington *(G-9737)*
Karl RI Manufacturing .... G 919 846-3801
  Raleigh *(G-12931)*
◆ Kennel-Aire LLC .... E 704 459-0044
  Norwood *(G-12039)*
Kens Candles and Soaps .... G 919 207-2880
  Willow Spring *(G-16080)*
Kerdea Technologies Inc .... F 971 900-1113
  Greenville *(G-7552)*
Keryflex Podadvance Inc .... G 888 763-2382
  Raleigh *(G-12936)*
Kinetic Performance Llc .... G 910 248-2121
  Raeford *(G-12425)*
King Charles Industries LLC .... G 704 848-4121
  Lilesville *(G-9839)*
King Charles Industries LLC .... G 910 974-4114
  Candor *(G-1594)*
Kituwah Industries LLC .... G 828 477-4616
  Whittier *(G-16008)*
Koonts Manufacturing Inc .... G 336 300-8009
  Lexington *(G-9741)*
Kwiatek Innovations LLC .... G 919 455-8295
  Wilmington *(G-16291)*
L & B Jandrew Enterprises .... G 828 687-8927
  Hendersonville *(G-7871)*
La Oaxaquena .... G 336 274-0173
  Greensboro *(G-7160)*
LA West Inc .... G 704 685-2833
  Sherrills Ford *(G-14387)*
Ladder Carry LLC .... G 704 245-2359
  Cary *(G-1806)*
Lady C E Crews LLC .... G 703 565-3687
  Hickory *(G-8082)*
Lamberts Industries .... G 980 244-0898
  Albemarle *(G-94)*
Laura Gaskin .... G 828 628-5891
  Fairview *(G-5715)*
Lee Linear .... G 800 221-0811
  Southport *(G-14573)*
Lee Paving Solutions LLC .... G 828 302-0415
  Denver *(G-4787)*
Legacy River Company .... G 704 618-7260
  Charlotte *(G-3081)*
Let It Flo LLC .... G 717 421-3754
  Fayetteville *(G-5860)*
Lexington Home Brands Mfg .... G 336 243-5740
  Lexington *(G-9747)*
Limitless Prfmce Fbrication LL .... G 910 799-5441
  Wilmington *(G-16301)*
Litbywhit LLC .... G 704 293-5743
  Charlotte *(G-3093)*
Lizmere Cavaliers .... G 704 418-2543
  Shelby *(G-14339)*
LLC Stanton Gray .... G 704 975-9392
  Newton *(G-11949)*
Love Knot Candles .... G 336 456-1619
  Greensboro *(G-7171)*
Lr Manufacturing Inc .... G 910 399-1410
  Delco *(G-4722)*
Luxury Tresses Collection LLC .... G 910 501-4451
  Laurinburg *(G-9485)*
Mammoth Industries LLC .... G 919 749-8183
  Raleigh *(G-12993)*
Mammoth Machine and Design LLC .... G 704 727-3330
  Mooresville *(G-11014)*

Manda Pandas LLC .... G 919 452-7917
  Durham *(G-5205)*
Manufactur LLC .... G 919 937-2090
  Durham *(G-5206)*
Manufacturing Analysis Inc .... G 919 434-3005
  Carrboro *(G-1649)*
Manufacturing Strategies LLC .... G 828 758-9092
  Lenoir *(G-9629)*
Marties Miniatures .... G 336 869-5952
  High Point *(G-8446)*
Marvica McLendon LLC .... G 704 965-9408
  Charlotte *(G-3135)*
Marvin Saltzman .... G 919 942-7091
  Chapel Hill *(G-2037)*
Maximizer Systems Inc .... F 828 345-6036
  Hickory *(G-8092)*
McKenzie Industries Inc .... G 336 870-9229
  Jamestown *(G-9061)*
Mdi Solutions LLC .... F 845 721-6758
  Salisbury *(G-14012)*
Mdm Mfg LLC .... G 919 908-6574
  Hillsborough *(G-8662)*
Medallion Company Inc .... C 919 990-3500
  Timberlake *(G-15315)*
Meera Industries Usa LLC .... G 336 906-7570
  High Point *(G-8452)*
▲ Meghan Blake Industries Inc .... E 704 462-2988
  Vale *(G-15469)*
MGe Products LLC .... G 828 443-3214
  Morganton *(G-11233)*
Miahna Moon LLC .... G 704 449-9495
  Charlotte *(G-3172)*
◆ Microfine Inc .... G 336 768-1480
  Winston Salem *(G-16809)*
Mikron Industries .... G 253 398-1382
  Durham *(G-5226)*
Miller Bee Supply Inc .... F 336 670-2249
  North Wilkesboro *(G-12029)*
Minnewawa Inc .... G 865 522-8103
  Charlotte *(G-3184)*
Mint Hill Industries .... G 704 545-8852
  Mint Hill *(G-10540)*
Mizelle Industries LLC .... G 252 940-5506
  Washington *(G-15716)*
Mommamade Scents LLC .... G 704 458-5901
  Charlotte *(G-3194)*
Moose Candle Company .... G 828 244-1384
  Conover *(G-4473)*
Moose-Tek Industries Inc .... G 336 416-7034
  New London *(G-11874)*
Morgan Manufacturing .... G 336 497-5763
  Kernersville *(G-9220)*
Mountain Leisure Hot Tubs LLC .... F 828 649-7727
  Arden *(G-353)*
Moya Custom Designs LLC .... G 984 208-3118
  Siler City *(G-14426)*
Mpx Manufacturing Inc .... G 704 762-9207
  Salisbury *(G-14014)*
Mvp Group International Inc .... E 336 527-2238
  Mount Airy *(G-11549)*
◆ Mvp Group International Inc .... E 843 216-8380
  Elkin *(G-5627)*
Myfuturenc Inc .... F 919 649-7834
  Raleigh *(G-13052)*
N & N Industries Inc .... G 919 770-1311
  Sanford *(G-14156)*
Nacho Industries Inc .... G 919 937-9471
  Durham *(G-5236)*
Narricot Industries LLC .... G 215 322-3908
  Greensboro *(G-7212)*
National Container Group LLC .... G 704 393-9050
  Charlotte *(G-3233)*

National Ctr For Social Impact .... G 984 212-2285
  Raleigh *(G-13054)*
National Voctnl Tech Honor Soc .... G 828 698-8011
  Flat Rock *(G-5970)*
Natives Rest Candles .... G 828 774-9838
  Hendersonville *(G-7884)*
NC Pallet Manufacturer LLC .... G 910 576-4902
  Troy *(G-15410)*
Nederman Manufacturing .... F 704 898-7945
  Charlotte *(G-3245)*
Neptune Hlth Wllness Innvtion .... C 888 664-9166
  Conover *(G-4475)*
New Life Cbd .... G 828 545-7203
  Swannanoa *(G-15030)*
New River Mills .... G 336 385-1446
  Creston *(G-4624)*
Norcep Industries .... G 910 762-5933
  Castle Hayne *(G-1957)*
Norfield LLC .... G 530 879-3121
  Garner *(G-6297)*
Novak Industries LLC .... G 704 662-2982
  Maiden *(G-10114)*
Novem Industries Inc .... G 704 660-6460
  Charlotte *(G-3276)*
Oak Street Mfg .... G 877 465-4344
  Statesville *(G-14853)*
Obscura Mfg LLC .... G 336 419-5648
  Lenoir *(G-9644)*
Oleksynprannyk LLC .... F 704 450-0182
  Mooresville *(G-11043)*
One Packaging Excel Inc .... G 919 268-9330
  Wendell *(G-15910)*
Optimal Industries LLC .... G 601 530-5222
  Salisbury *(G-14021)*
Optomill Solutions LLC .... G 704 560-4037
  Matthews *(G-10338)*
P A Indl Fabrications .... D 252 329-8881
  Greenville *(G-7567)*
Pag Asb LLC .... G 336 883-4187
  High Point *(G-8474)*
Paps Performance & Machine LLC ...... G 336 225-1877
  Lexington *(G-9767)*
Pashes LLC .... G 704 682-6535
  Statesville *(G-14857)*
Pate Industries .... G 704 889-2376
  Pineville *(G-12289)*
◆ Paul Hoge Creations Inc .... F 704 624-6860
  Marshville *(G-10221)*
Payne Leather and Tool LLC .... G 336 391-8964
  Weaverville *(G-15858)*
Peak City Candles Inc .... G 919 601-8223
  Apex *(G-228)*
Peak Level Media Solutions LLC .... G 919 917-8002
  Cary *(G-1846)*
Pendergast Industries LLC .... G 919 636-1621
  Chapel Hill *(G-2052)*
Perfect Match Candles LLC .... G 919 482-6649
  Apex *(G-230)*
Phillips Corporation .... E 336 665-1080
  Colfax *(G-4157)*
PL&e Sales Inc .... G 704 561-9650
  Charlotte *(G-3346)*
Plantd Inc .... D 434 906-3445
  Oxford *(G-12142)*
Plushh LLC .... G 919 647-7911
  Raleigh *(G-13117)*
Pluto Labs LLC .... G 919 691-3550
  Oxford *(G-12144)*
Pma Industries Inc .... G 704 575-6200
  Charlotte *(G-3350)*
Pmb Industries Inc .... F 336 453-3121
  Lexington *(G-9771)*

39 MISCELLANEOUS MANUFACTURING INDUSTRIES

Pnb Manufacturing .... G 336 883-0021
  High Point (G-8488)
Polypore Inc .... D 704 587-8409
  Charlotte (G-3352)
Posh Industries LLC .... G 919 596-8434
  Durham (G-5296)
Potterwyx Scnted Candles Soaps .... G 336 245-8560
  Lewisville (G-9671)
Precision Boat Mfg .... G 336 395-8795
  Graham (G-6707)
Pretty Honest LLC .... G 804 837-1038
  Charlotte (G-3378)
Prezioso Ventures LLC .... G 704 793-1602
  Concord (G-4337)
Producers Gin Murfreesboro LLC ...... G 252 398-3762
  Murfreesboro (G-11702)
Product Quest Mfg LLC .... G 321 255-3250
  Winston Salem (G-16871)
Professional Laminating LLC .... G 919 465-0400
  Cary (G-1862)
Progressive Industries Inc .... G 919 267-6948
  Apex (G-233)
Protect Adoptable Labs .... G 253 383-2733
  Asheville (G-746)
Pullover Pal .... G 910 340-1801
  Jacksonville (G-9024)
Purilum LLC .... E 252 931-8020
  Greenville (G-7577)
Qspac Industries Inc .... E 704 635-7815
  Monroe (G-10791)
Quadalupe Industries Inc .... G 786 241-0315
  Asheville (G-748)
Quadsaw Usa LLC .... G 980 339-8554
  Charlotte (G-3400)
Quality Salvage Industries .... G 336 884-4433
  Thomasville (G-15269)
Qualtech Industries Inc .... G 704 734-0345
  Kings Mountain (G-9327)
R3cycle Industries LLC .... F 404 754-4499
  Waxhaw (G-15772)
Rail-Scale-Models .... G 248 421-6276
  Garner (G-6307)
Ratoon Agroprocessing LLC .... G 828 273-9114
  Marion (G-10173)
RC Industries .... G 828 693-1953
  Hendersonville (G-7895)
Re-Crtion Sstainable Wdwkg LLC ...... G 919 612-4791
  Raleigh (G-13192)
Red Wolfe Industries LLC .... G 336 570-2282
  Hurdle Mills (G-8913)
Reecewreathandcraftsetsycom .... G 828 252-6228
  Alexander (G-119)
Reeses Balloon Art .... G 919 303-2147
  Cary (G-1867)
Renew Protect LLC .... G 828 318-5654
  Weaverville (G-15859)
Replar Mfg Inc .... G 919 622-5942
  Durham (G-5326)
Resolute Fabricators LLC .... G 704 728-1249
  Cornelius (G-4582)
Ritter Fab LLC .... G 336 879-2428
  Seagrove (G-14246)
Rothrock Industries .... G 336 454-4549
  Jamestown (G-9070)
Rq Industries Inc .... G 704 701-1471
  Concord (G-4354)
Rsk Industries LLC .... G 216 905-4014
  Wake Forest (G-15584)
▼ Ruth Hicks Enterprise Inc .... G 704 469-4741
  Waxhaw (G-15773)
S Y Shop Inc .... G 704 545-7710
  Mint Hill (G-10544)

Salon & Spa Design Services .... G 919 556-6380
  Wake Forest (G-15587)
Sapona Manufacturing Co Inc .... G 336 625-2161
  Asheboro (G-477)
Sas Industries Company LLC .... G 704 323-9098
  Pineville (G-12303)
Sassy Queen Collection LLC .... G 919 949-0085
  Durham (G-5339)
Sawgrass Industries .... G 912 884-4008
  Saluda (G-14074)
Sbm Industries LLC .... G 919 625-3672
  Raleigh (G-13235)
Scentual Candles .... G 252 281-4919
  Wilson (G-16540)
Schueler Industries Inc .... G 847 613-0673
  Hickory (G-8146)
Sealco Manufacturing LLC .... G 704 662-2850
  Mooresville (G-11082)
Seneca Devices Inc .... G 301 412-3576
  Durham (G-5349)
Sesmfg LLC .... G 803 917-3248
  Charlotte (G-3531)
Sewerkote .... G 919 598-1974
  Chapel Hill (G-2069)
Sewerkote LLC .... G 919 602-8002
  Durham (G-5350)
Sfd Industries Inc .... G 336 829-5796
  Winston Salem (G-16902)
Shealy Designed Wood Pdts LLC .... G 704 308-9435
  Cherryville (G-3876)
Shelby Candles .... G 336 804-4182
  Thomasville (G-15277)
Shenk Industries Inc .... G 828 808-3327
  Asheville (G-768)
Shocktec Inc .... G 704 663-5678
  Mooresville (G-11084)
Shoffner Industries Inc .... G 336 226-9356
  Burlington (G-1494)
Shoreline Industries Inc .... G 910 571-0111
  Troy (G-15416)
Siggbey Industries LLC .... G 336 483-6035
  Greensboro (G-7339)
Simontic Composite Inc .... E 336 897-9885
  Greensboro (G-7340)
Sincere Scents Co LLC .... G 910 616-4697
  Southport (G-14580)
Sk Enterprises Mfg LLC .... G 919 721-1458
  Sanford (G-14185)
Skeeter Beaters .... G 919 285-6054
  Willow Spring (G-16083)
Ski Time Industries Inc .... G 704 455-3870
  Harrisburg (G-7728)
▲ Skidril Industries LLC .... F 800 843-3745
  Randleman (G-13491)
Sniff N Rescue Candles LLC .... G 704 909-9853
  Mooresville (G-11091)
Sniff To Remember LLC .... G 210 373-2115
  Charlotte (G-3572)
Snow On Go Trucking LLC .... G 980 892-1791
  Salisbury (G-14044)
Solara of Carolinas .... G 910 723-1270
  Linden (G-9942)
Southern Elegance Candle LLC .... G 706 825-7658
  Raeford (G-12439)
Southern Home Spa and Wtr Pdts ..... G 336 286-3564
  Greensboro (G-7354)
Southern Made Candles LLC .... G 704 740-7748
  Weaverotte (G-15863)
Southland Amusements Vend Inc ..... E 910 343-1809
  Wilmington (G-16412)
Southland Industries .... G 336 989-0904
  High Point (G-8547)

Soy Clever Candle Co LLC .... G 919 869-5360
  Clayton (G-4011)
Specialty Trnsp Systems Inc .... G 828 464-9738
  Newton (G-11971)
Spectre Custom Solutions LLC .... G 704 450-4428
  Mooresville (G-11094)
Speed King Manufacturing Inc .... G 910 457-1995
  Southport (G-14583)
Speer Operational Tech LLC .... G 864 631-2512
  Marion (G-10179)
Spire Industries Inc .... G 435 994-4756
  Raleigh (G-13291)
Spotless Industries LLC .... G 980 430-1560
  Charlotte (G-3604)
Spring Rock Farms Inc .... G 336 973-1447
  Purlear (G-12413)
Ss Manufacturing Inc .... G 770 317-8121
  Kannapolis (G-9134)
▲ Stage Decoration and Sups Inc ...... F 336 621-5454
  Greensboro (G-7364)
▲ Stansell Industries LLC .... G 864 371-2425
  Asheville (G-788)
Stellar Innovations Inc .... G 704 746-2886
  Cornelius (G-4588)
Steri-Air LLC .... G 336 434-1166
  High Point (G-8552)
Stick Candles .... G 315 369-0011
  Cashiers (G-1937)
Stiletto Manufacturing Inc .... G 252 564-4877
  Columbia (G-4168)
Stitchmaster LLC .... G 336 852-6448
  Greensboro (G-7373)
Stokes Mfg LLC .... G 336 270-8746
  Roxboro (G-13826)
Strike & Flame Candles .... G 336 207-4487
  Greensboro (G-7375)
Stuart Ryan Kent & Co .... G 252 916-8226
  Winterville (G-17014)
Sung Industries Inc .... G 919 387-8550
  Apex (G-246)
Suntex Industries .... F 336 784-1000
  Winston Salem (G-16924)
Susan Strazzella .... G 828 676-1162
  Asheville (G-792)
Sutton Scientifics Inc .... G 910 428-1600
  Star (G-14723)
Sweet Wick Candle Company LLC .... G 770 687-1519
  Kernersville (G-9240)
Tag Stringing Service Inc .... G 336 294-9394
  Greensboro (G-7387)
Tagtraum Industries Inc .... G 919 809-7797
  Raleigh (G-13325)
Tak Manufacturing LLC .... G 704 473-6391
  Shelby (G-14372)
Tarheel Old English Sheepdog .... G 336 499-6788
  Lewisville (G-9674)
Tcc Manufacturing .... G 828 970-7270
  Maiden (G-10118)
Techscan Industries LLC .... G 704 843-4518
  Waxhaw (G-15780)
Tethis Manufacturing LLC .... G 919 808-2866
  Raleigh (G-13341)
Texlon Industries LLC .... G 252 292-6590
  Wilmington (G-16428)
Textile Manufacturing Tech LLC .... G 828 632-3012
  Taylorsville (G-15173)
Thomas B Brugh Mfg Rep .... G 858 385-8987
  Charlotte (G-3687)
Tinman Candles .... G 828 329-1140
  Etowah (G-5694)
Titan Land Group LLC .... G 704 400-1842
  Charlotte (G-3696)

39 MISCELLANEOUS MANUFACTURING INDUSTRIES

Tk Elevator Corporation .... C 336 272-4563
Greensboro (G-7404)

Tmcm Services LLC .... G 336 609-4378
Greensboro (G-7405)

Tobacco Outlet Products LLC .... G 704 341-9388
Charlotte (G-3702)

Toolmarx LLC .... G 919 725-0122
Winston Salem (G-16945)

Toque Industries LLC .... G 704 640-6232
Charlotte (G-3710)

Tree Frog Industries LLC .... G 919 986-2229
Wendell (G-15921)

◆ Tree Masters Inc .... E 828 464-9443
Newton (G-11979)

Tri-Tech Forensics Inc .... D 910 457-6600
Leland (G-9562)

Triangle Trggr-Pint Thrapy Inc .... G 919 845-1818
Raleigh (G-13363)

Tribofilm Research Inc .... G 919 838-2844
Raleigh (G-13364)

Twisted Fire Industires LLC .... G 704 652-8559
Concord (G-4380)

Ubora Dens LLC .... G 704 425-3560
Concord (G-4381)

Uncle Browns Scented Candles .... G 704 993-0409
Monroe (G-10827)

Underground Renovations LLC .... G 202 316-9286
Raleigh (G-13381)

Unity Hlthcare Lab Billing LLP .... G 980 209-0402
Charlotte (G-3754)

Urban Industries Corp .... F 980 209-9471
Pineville (G-12313)

◆ USa Wholesale and Distrg Inc .... F 888 484-6872
Fayetteville (G-5945)

Useable Products .... G 919 870-6693
Raleigh (G-13387)

Vaibas Industries LLC .... G 919 749-4422
Raleigh (G-13389)

Vallee Industries Inc .... G 910 477-0092
Oak Island (G-12056)

Valley Run Candles LLC .... G 828 729-8652
Durham (G-5431)

Vandilay Industries LLC .... G 704 962-5140
Charlotte (G-3765)

◆ Vecoplan LLC .... E 336 861-6070
Archdale (G-302)

Velocita Inc .... G 336 764-8513
Clemmons (G-4066)

Veon Inc .... F 252 623-2102
Washington (G-15736)

Vermont Designs Unlimited LLC .... G 910 846-4477
Supply (G-15014)

Vibration Solutions .... G 704 754-3118
Troutman (G-15398)

Vision Contract Mfg LLC .... E 336 405-8784
High Point (G-8595)

W & F Manufacturing LLC .... G 336 665-4023
Colfax (G-4163)

W Gamby C O Hanes Dye & Finish .... E 336 724-9020
Winston Salem (G-16967)

W W Industries .... G 336 312-1806
Greensboro (G-7452)

Walco International .... G 704 624-2473
Marshville (G-10228)

Walflor Industries Inc .... G 360 899-8060
Candler (G-1592)

War Sport Manufacturing LLC .... G 252 220-6505
Nashville (G-11754)

Watercolors By Mista .... G 828 775-7751
Weaverville (G-15868)

Waxhaw Candle Company LLC .... G 980 245-2827
Charlotte (G-3798)

Wayne Trademark .... G 336 887-3173
Asheboro (G-506)

We Cbd LLC .... G 336 969-0400
Rural Hall (G-13854)

Wears Industries Inc .... G 828 575-9466
Asheville (G-816)

Weaver Fabrication .... G 336 877-3427
Fleetwood (G-5977)

Web 4 Half LLC .... E 855 762-4638
Asheboro (G-509)

West Side Industries LLC .... G 980 223-8665
Statesville (G-14924)

Whelan Industries LLC .... G 704 506-9515
Mint Hill (G-10548)

White Tiger Btq & Candle Co .... G 919 610-7244
Sanford (G-14205)

Wicked Calm Candles LLc .... G 856 343-2499
Clayton (G-4021)

Wildflwers Btq of Blowing Rock .... G 828 295-9655
Blowing Rock (G-1157)

Wind Chime Plaza .... G 919 848-9715
Raleigh (G-13424)

Wix By Mel .... G 973 479-0795
Carolina Beach (G-1643)

World Wicks Candles .... G 919 791-6123
Zebulon (G-17146)

Worsham Sprinkler Co Inc .... G 704 805-9700
Charlotte (G-3827)

Wreathsplusbylyn .... G 252 281-3674
Stantonsburg (G-14713)

Wright Industries LLC .... G 919 824-2936
Huntersville (G-8907)

Xtra Light Manufacturing .... G 919 422-7281
Apex (G-261)

Young & Son Mfg LLC .... G 704 799-1658
Mooresville (G-11137)

Z Collection LLC .... G 919 247-1513
Zebulon (G-17147)

Zeal Industries LLC .... G 828 575-9894
Asheville (G-825)

Zengerle Industries Inc .... G 919 240-5415
Chapel Hill (G-2104)

40 RAILROAD TRANSPORTATION

4011 Railroads, line-haul operating

Florida Progress Corporation .... C 704 382-3853
Raleigh (G-12775)

41 LOCAL & SUBURBAN TRANSIT & INTERURBAN HIGHWAY TRANSPORTATION

4111 Local and suburban transit

Concierge Transit LLC .... G 704 778-0755
Charlotte (G-2536)

4151 School buses

◆ Hickory Springs Manufactu .... D 828 328-2201
Hickory (G-8052)

42 MOTOR FREIGHT TRANSPORTATION

4212 Local trucking, without storage

A Plus Five Star Trnsp LLC .... G 919 771-4820
Clayton (G-3950)

Affordable Septic Tank .... G 910 417-9537
Hamlet (G-7615)

Bobby Cahoon Construction Inc .... E 252 249-1617
Grantsboro (G-6763)

Central Carolina Concrete LLC .... E 336 315-0785
Greensboro (G-6899)

Comer Sanitary Service Inc .... F 336 629-8311
Lexington (G-9697)

Crowder Trucking LLC .... G 910 797-4163
Fayetteville (G-5800)

▼ Fayblock Materials Inc .... D 910 323-9198
Fayetteville (G-5823)

Fresh-N-Mobile LLC .... G 704 251-4643
Charlotte (G-2797)

Hammill Construction Co Inc .... F 704 279-5309
Gold Hill (G-6582)

Haulco LLC .... G 336 781-0468
Trinity (G-15344)

J S Myers Co Inc .... F 336 463-5572
Yadkinville (G-17042)

Kendall E Krause .... G 910 690-4119
Vass (G-15492)

Kornegay Logging & Timber Co .... G 919 658-5716
Mount Olive (G-11665)

Long Asp Pav Trckg of Grnsburg .... F 336 643-4121
Summerfield (G-14986)

McLean Sbsrface Utlity Engrg L .... F 336 340-0024
Greensboro (G-7194)

Milligan House Movers Inc .... G 910 653-2272
Tabor City (G-15084)

New Finish Inc .... E 704 474-4116
Norwood (G-12041)

Privette Enterprises Inc .... E 704 634-3291
Monroe (G-10789)

Quality Turf Hauling LLC .... G 336 516-1156
Haw River (G-7756)

Raleigh Road Box Corporation .... G 252 438-7401
Henderson (G-7806)

Stone Supply Inc .... G 828 678-9966
Burnsville (G-1534)

T H Blue Inc .... E 910 673-3033
Eagle Springs (G-5461)

Triple H Hauling LLC .... G 984 220-4676
Elizabeth City (G-5579)

V M Trucking Inc .... G 984 239-4853
Morehead City (G-11195)

4213 Trucking, except local

Advantage Machinery Svcs Inc .... E 336 463-4700
Yadkinville (G-17030)

Bundy Logging Company Inc .... F 252 357-0191
Gatesville (G-6548)

Firm Ascend LLC .... G 704 464-3024
Charlotte (G-2763)

Fixtures & More .... G 828 855-9093
Hickory (G-8026)

J & L Bckh/Nvrnmental Svcs Inc .... G 910 237-7351
Eastover (G-5481)

RSI Leasing Inc NS Tbt .... G 704 587-9300
Charlotte (G-3468)

▲ Southeast Wood Products Inc .... F 910 285-4359
Wallace (G-15627)

T H Blue Inc .... E 910 673-3033
Eagle Springs (G-5461)

4214 Local trucking with storage

Bundy Logging Company Inc .... F 252 357-0191
Gatesville (G-6548)

Comer Sanitary Service Inc .... F 336 629-8311
Lexington (G-9697)

Elizabeth Logistic LLC .... D 803 920-3931
Indian Trail (G-8931)

Loflin Concrete Co Inc .... E 336 904-2788
Kernersville (G-9209)

SIC SECTION

48 COMMUNICATIONS

Lunar International Tech LLC......................F..... 800 975-7153
  Charlotte *(G-3109)*
Wheeler Industries Inc............................F..... 919 736-4256
  Pikeville *(G-12195)*

4215 Courier services, except by air
Go Postal In Boone Inc............................F..... 828 262-0027
  Boone *(G-1200)*
Rapid Run Transport LLC..........................F..... 704 615-3458
  Charlotte *(G-3410)*

4221 Farm product warehousing and storage
C A Perry & Son Inc.............................G..... 252 330-2323
  Elizabeth City *(G-5532)*
C A Perry & Son Inc.............................E..... 252 221-4463
  Hobbsville *(G-8675)*
High Rise Service Company Inc..................E..... 910 371-2325
  Leland *(G-9548)*

4222 Refrigerated warehousing and storage
Smith Utility Buildings..........................G..... 336 957-8211
  Traphill *(G-15327)*

4225 General warehousing and storage
▲ Airspeed LLC.................................E..... 919 644-1222
  Hillsborough *(G-8633)*
Ashley Furniture Inds LLC.......................D..... 336 998-1066
  Advance *(G-37)*
Buildings R US..................................G..... 704 482-3166
  Shelby *(G-14290)*
Fishel Steel Company............................G..... 336 788-2880
  Winston Salem *(G-16712)*
Metrohose Incorporated..........................G..... 252 329-9891
  Greenville *(G-7560)*
Pactiv LLC......................................G..... 828 396-2373
  Granite Falls *(G-6748)*
Parkdale Mills Incorporated.....................F..... 704 825-2529
  Belmont *(G-1000)*
Patheon Softgels Inc............................F..... 336 812-8700
  Greensboro *(G-7247)*
Phoenix Assembly NC LLC.........................G..... 252 801-4250
  Battleboro *(G-929)*
Warehouse Distillery LLC........................G..... 828 464-5183
  Newton *(G-11983)*

4226 Special warehousing and storage, nec
Cairn Studio Ltd................................E..... 704 664-7128
  Mooresville *(G-10894)*
▲ Ideaitlia Cntmporary Furn Corp................C..... 828 464-1000
  Conover *(G-4466)*
Legalis Dms LLC.................................F..... 919 741-8260
  Raleigh *(G-12965)*
Svcm..G..... 305 767-3595
  Lincolnton *(G-9924)*
Trimfit Inc.....................................C..... 336 476-6154
  Thomasville *(G-15296)*
Weyerhaeuser Company............................F..... 252 746-7200
  Grifton *(G-7603)*

44 WATER TRANSPORTATION

4449 Water transportation of freight
Florida Progress Corporation....................C..... 704 382-3853
  Raleigh *(G-12775)*

4489 Water passenger transportation
Amerochem Corporation...........................E..... 252 634-9444
  New Bern *(G-11770)*

4493 Marinas
Cape Fear Boat Works Inc........................F..... 910 371-3460
  Navassa *(G-11757)*

45 TRANSPORTATION BY AIR

4512 Air transportation, scheduled
Charter Jet Transport Inc.......................G..... 704 359-8833
  Charlotte *(G-2468)*
D2 Government Solutions LLC.....................E..... 662 655-4554
  New Bern *(G-11797)*
T Air Inc.......................................D..... 980 595-2840
  Charlotte *(G-3668)*

4513 Air courier services
Concierge Transit LLC...........................G..... 704 778-0755
  Charlotte *(G-2536)*
T Air Inc.......................................D..... 980 595-2840
  Charlotte *(G-3668)*

4522 Air transportation, nonscheduled
D2 Government Solutions LLC.....................E..... 662 655-4554
  New Bern *(G-11797)*

4581 Airports, flying fields, and services
D2 Government Solutions LLC.....................E..... 662 655-4554
  New Bern *(G-11797)*
◆ Haeco Americas LLC............................A..... 336 668-4410
  Greensboro *(G-7073)*
Haeco Cabin Solutions LLC.......................D..... 336 862-1418
  Greensboro *(G-7074)*
Piedmont AVI Cmponent Svcs LLC..................C..... 336 423-5100
  Greensboro *(G-7255)*
Powerhouse Resources Intl LLC...................D..... 919 291-1783
  Raleigh *(G-13123)*
Summit Aviation Inc.............................F..... 302 834-5400
  Greensboro *(G-7379)*
Textron Aviation Inc............................C..... 336 605-7000
  Greensboro *(G-7398)*

46 PIPELINES, EXCEPT NATURAL GAS

4613 Refined petroleum pipelines
Panenergy Corp..................................F..... 704 594-6200
  Charlotte *(G-3310)*

47 TRANSPORTATION SERVICES

4731 Freight transportation arrangement
AC Imports LLC..................................G..... 919 229-6650
  Durham *(G-4898)*
D C Custom Freight LLC..........................E..... 843 658-6484
  Marshville *(G-10213)*
Deliveright Logistics Inc.......................C..... 862 279-7332
  Lexington *(G-9705)*
Elizabeth Logistic LLC..........................D..... 803 920-3931
  Indian Trail *(G-8931)*
Gaines Motor Lines Inc..........................C..... 828 322-2000
  Hickory *(G-8031)*
Kendall E Krause................................G..... 910 690-4119
  Vass *(G-15492)*
Kenn M LLC......................................G..... 678 755-6607
  Raleigh *(G-12935)*
Lls Investments Inc.............................F..... 919 662-7283
  Raleigh *(G-12976)*
Phoenix Assembly NC LLC.........................G..... 252 801-4250
  Battleboro *(G-929)*
Rapid Run Transport LLC.........................F..... 704 615-3458
  Charlotte *(G-3410)*

4783 Packing and crating
▲ Broadwind Indus Solutions LLC.................E..... 919 777-2907
  Sanford *(G-14096)*

Hershey Group LLC...............................G..... 336 855-3888
  Greensboro *(G-7087)*
Lls Investments Inc.............................F..... 919 662-7283
  Raleigh *(G-12976)*
Ssi Services Inc................................G..... 919 867-1450
  Raleigh *(G-13295)*

4785 Inspection and fixed facilities
Surelift Inc....................................G..... 828 963-6899
  Boone *(G-1241)*

4789 Transportation services, nec
Accelrted Svcs Mooresville Inc..................G..... 704 658-6666
  Mooresville *(G-10845)*
At Your Service Express LLC.....................E..... 704 270-9918
  Charlotte *(G-2229)*
Best Solution Cargo LLC.........................G..... 407 810-5559
  Wilmington *(G-16137)*
Bucks Wrecker Service...........................G..... 704 776-0899
  Statesville *(G-14767)*
Carolina Expediters LLC.........................G..... 888 537-5330
  Mount Airy *(G-11489)*
Cymbal LLC......................................G..... 877 365-9622
  Cary *(G-1744)*
D&E Freight LLC.................................F..... 704 977-4847
  Charlotte *(G-2597)*
DMD Logistics LLC...............................G..... 336 480-8149
  Winston Salem *(G-16685)*
Harsco Rail LLC.................................G..... 980 960-2624
  Charlotte *(G-2893)*
Haulco LLC......................................G..... 336 781-0468
  Trinity *(G-15344)*
Level Ten Facilities Svcs LLC...................G..... 704 759-6799
  Charlotte *(G-3083)*
MMS Logistics Incorporated......................G..... 336 214-3552
  Mc Leansville *(G-10394)*
Speedway Link Inc...............................F..... 704 338-2028
  Matthews *(G-10292)*
Surry Logistix LLC..............................G..... 336 710-3446
  Mount Airy *(G-11582)*

48 COMMUNICATIONS

4812 Radiotelephone communication
Infinity Communications LLC.....................E..... 919 797-2334
  Durham *(G-5154)*
McShan Inc......................................G..... 980 355-9790
  Charlotte *(G-3154)*
▲ Spectrasite Communications LLC................E..... 919 468-0112
  Cary *(G-1900)*

4813 Telephone communication, except radio
Akoustis Inc....................................E..... 704 997-5735
  Huntersville *(G-8786)*
Cengage Learning Inc............................E..... 919 829-8181
  Raleigh *(G-12616)*
Charlotte Observer Pubg Co......................A..... 704 358-5000
  Charlotte *(G-2456)*
CNA Technology LLC..............................G..... 954 312-1200
  Greenville *(G-7502)*
Fastzone Dsl & Internet Servic..................G..... 828 963-1350
  Banner Elk *(G-897)*
Interconnect Products and.......................E..... 336 667-3356
  Wilkesboro *(G-16026)*
M I Connection..................................F..... 704 662-3255
  Mooresville *(G-11013)*
Mountain Area Info Netwrk.......................F..... 828 255-0182
  Asheville *(G-707)*
▲ Spectrasite Communications LLC................E..... 919 468-0112
  Cary *(G-1900)*
Telit Wireless Solutions Inc....................D..... 919 439-7977
  Durham *(G-5391)*

48 COMMUNICATIONS

◆ Walker and Associates Inc..........C 336 731-6391
  Lexington (G-9800)

4822 Telegraph and other communications

Everyday Fix Cyclery......................G 828 855-9989
  Hickory (G-8020)
King Business Service Inc..............G 910 610-1030
  Laurinburg (G-9483)

4832 Radio broadcasting stations

Latino Communications Inc............F 704 319-5044
  Charlotte (G-3073)
Latino Communications Inc............F 919 645-1680
  Raleigh (G-12959)
Latino Communications Inc............D 336 714-2823
  Winston Salem (G-16784)
National Ctr For Social Impact........G 984 212-2285
  Raleigh (G-13054)
Wtvd Television LLC......................C 919 683-1111
  Durham (G-5451)

4833 Television broadcasting stations

News 14 Carolina............................F 704 973-5700
  Charlotte (G-3253)
Robert Wrren MBL TV Prductions....G 910 483-4777
  Eastover (G-5482)
Wtvd Television LLC......................C 919 683-1111
  Durham (G-5451)

4841 Cable and other pay television services

Cco Holdings LLC..........................C 828 414-4238
  Blowing Rock (G-1155)
Cco Holdings LLC..........................C 828 355-4149
  Boone (G-1186)
Cco Holdings LLC..........................C 910 292-4083
  Dunn (G-4857)
Cco Holdings LLC..........................C 828 270-7016
  Hickory (G-7973)
Cco Holdings LLC..........................C 919 502-4007
  Kenly (G-9147)
Cco Holdings LLC..........................C 828 394-0635
  Lenoir (G-9597)
Cco Holdings LLC..........................C 704 308-3361
  Lincolnton (G-9880)
Cco Holdings LLC..........................C 828 528-4004
  Newland (G-11883)
Cco Holdings LLC..........................C 919 200-6260
  Siler City (G-14402)
Cco Holdings LLC..........................C 828 368-4161
  Valdese (G-15445)
Cog Glbal Media/Consulting LLC....E 980 239-8042
  Matthews (G-10244)
M I Connection..............................F 704 662-3255
  Mooresville (G-11013)

4899 Communication services, nec

Bluetick Inc....................................F 336 294-4102
  Greensboro (G-6844)
Commscope LLC............................C 828 324-2200
  Claremont (G-3911)
Commscope Holding Company Inc...A 828 459-5000
  Claremont (G-3913)
Fast Pro Media LLC........................G 704 799-8040
  Cornelius (G-4546)
Gpx Intelligence Inc........................E 888 260-0706
  Greensboro (G-7055)
▲ Spectrasite Communications LLC...E 919 468-0112
  Cary (G-1900)

49 ELECTRIC, GAS AND SANITARY SERVICES

4911 Electric services

Florida Progress Corporation..........C 704 382-3853
  Raleigh (G-12775)
Go Ev and Go Green Corp..............G 704 327-9040
  Charlotte (G-2839)
Johnson Controls Inc......................G 866 285-8345
  Morrisville (G-11363)
Livingston & Haven LLC................C 704 588-3670
  Charlotte (G-3096)
Panenergy Corp..............................F 704 594-6200
  Charlotte (G-3310)
Pike Electric LLC............................B 336 316-7068
  Greensboro (G-7263)

4922 Natural gas transmission

Panenergy Corp..............................F 704 594-6200
  Charlotte (G-3310)

4924 Natural gas distribution

Blue Gas Marine Inc........................F 919 238-3427
  Apex (G-172)

4931 Electric and other services combined

Flexgen Power Systems Inc............G 855 327-5674
  Durham (G-5100)
Flexgen Power Systems Inc............F 855 327-5674
  Durham (G-5101)
▲ Powersecure International Inc......A 919 556-3056
  Wake Forest (G-15576)

4941 Water supply

County of Anson..............................G 704 848-4849
  Lilesville (G-9836)
Prime Water Services Inc................G 919 504-1020
  Raleigh (G-13140)
Quantico Water & Sewer LLC........G 336 528-9299
  Clemmons (G-4057)
Tempest Environmental Corp..........G 919 973-1609
  Durham (G-5393)

4952 Sewerage systems

Quantico Water & Sewer LLC........G 336 528-9299
  Clemmons (G-4057)

4953 Refuse systems

A-1 Sandrock Inc............................E 336 855-8195
  Greensboro (G-6770)
Alleghany Garbage Service Inc......G 336 372-4413
  Sparta (G-14587)
Clean Green Inc..............................G 919 596-3500
  Durham (G-5020)
Crizaf Inc..G 919 251-7661
  Durham (G-5037)
◆ Custom Polymers Inc....................F 704 332-6070
  Charlotte (G-2593)
Duramax Holdings LLC..................C 704 588-9191
  Charlotte (G-2659)
Eastern Crlina Vctonal Ctr Inc........D 252 758-4188
  Greenville (G-7521)
◆ Elan Trading Inc............................E 704 342-1696
  Charlotte (G-2689)
Fiber Composites LLC....................D 704 463-7118
  New London (G-11869)
Global Ecosciences Inc..................G 252 631-6266
  Wake Forest (G-15560)
▼ Hoh Corporation............................F 336 723-9274
  Winston Salem (G-16747)
National Container Group LLC......G 704 393-9050
  Charlotte (G-3233)
Noble Oil Services Inc....................C 919 774-8180
  Sanford (G-14159)

SIC SECTION

Parkdale Mills Incorporated............F 704 825-2529
  Belmont (G-1000)
RDc Debris Removal Cnstr LLC....E 323 614-2353
  Smithfield (G-14479)
Soundside Recycling & Mtls Inc....G 252 491-8666
  Jarvisburg (G-9086)
Steelman Lumber & Pallet LLC......F 336 468-2757
  Hamptonville (G-7678)
Todco Inc..F 336 248-2001
  Lexington (G-9795)
Waste Industries Usa LLC..............D 919 325-3000
  Raleigh (G-13412)
▲ Wastezero Inc................................E 919 322-1208
  Raleigh (G-13413)

4959 Sanitary services, nec

Airfield Solutions LLC....................G 919 348-4271
  Jacksonville (G-8985)
Big Vac..G 910 947-3654
  Carthage (G-1660)
Butler Trieu Inc................................G 910 346-4929
  Jacksonville (G-8992)
Carlson Environmental Cons PC....D 704 283-9765
  Monroe (G-10673)
Global Ecosciences Inc..................G 252 631-6266
  Wake Forest (G-15560)
Noble Oil Services Inc....................C 919 774-8180
  Sanford (G-14159)
Protek Services LLC......................G 910 556-4121
  Cameron (G-1562)

50 WHOLESALE TRADE - DURABLE GOODS

5012 Automobiles and other motor vehicles

▼ Axle Holdings LLC........................E 800 895-3276
  Concord (G-4203)
Ironworks Motorcycles....................G 336 542-7868
  Greensboro (G-7123)
◆ Mack Trucks Inc............................A 336 291-9001
  Greensboro (G-7177)
◆ National Foam Inc..........................E 919 639-6100
  Angier (G-147)
Parker-Hannifin Corporation............G 704 664-1922
  Mooresville (G-11047)
Pro-System Inc................................F 704 799-8100
  Mooresville (G-11064)
Streets Auto Sales & Four WD........G 704 888-8686
  Locust (G-9973)
◆ Vna Holding Inc..............................A 336 393-4890
  Greensboro (G-7445)
Volvo Group North America LLC....A 336 393-2000
  Greensboro (G-7447)
◆ Volvo Group North America LLC....A 336 393-2000
  Greensboro (G-7446)
◆ Volvo Trucks North America Inc....A 336 393-2000
  Greensboro (G-7450)

5013 Motor vehicle supplies and new parts

A-1 Hitch & Trailors Sales Inc........F 910 755-6025
  Supply (G-15005)
Auto Machine Shop Inc..................G 910 483-6016
  Fayetteville (G-5765)
Camco Manufacturing Inc..............G 336 348-6609
  Reidsville (G-13511)
Capitol Bumper................................G 919 772-7330
  Fayetteville (G-5782)
Consolidated Truck Parts Inc..........G 704 279-5543
  Rockwell (G-13650)
Cummins Atlantic LLC....................D 336 275-4531
  Greensboro (G-6946)

Fontaine Modification Company .... F 704 392-8502
  Charlotte (G-2783)
Heintz Bros Automotives Inc .... G 704 872-8081
  Statesville (G-14809)
Johnson Machine Co Inc .... G 252 638-2620
  New Bern (G-11814)
Lake Shore Radiator Inc .... F 336 271-2626
  Greensboro (G-7162)
▲ Mann+hmmel Fltrtion Tech Group ..... G 704 869-3300
  Gastonia (G-6449)
Mc Cullough Auto Elc & Assoc .... G 704 376-5388
  Charlotte (G-3148)
Merchant 1 Marketing LLC .... G 888 853-9992
  Greensboro (G-7199)
▼ Mfi Products Inc .... F 910 944-2128
  Aberdeen (G-15)
Nichols Spdmtr & Instr Co Inc .... G 336 273-2881
  Greensboro (G-7219)
Oldcastle Infrastructure Inc .... E 919 772-6269
  Raleigh (G-13082)
Patty Knio .... G 919 995-2670
  Raleigh (G-13102)
Perry Brothers Tire Svc Inc .... F 919 693-2128
  Oxford (G-12140)
▲ Pfaff Molds Ltd Partnership .... F 704 423-9484
  Charlotte (G-3334)
▲ Prevost Car (us) Inc .... E 908 222-7211
  Greensboro (G-7281)
Pro-Motor Engines Inc .... G 704 664-6800
  Mooresville (G-11063)
RNS International Inc .... E 704 329-0444
  Charlotte (G-3453)
Robert Blake .... G 704 720-9341
  Concord (G-4351)
T & N Manufacturing Co Inc .... G 704 788-1418
  Davidson (G-4698)
Tri-City Mechanical Contrs Inc .... D 336 272-9495
  Greensboro (G-7410)
Truck Parts Inc .... F 704 332-7909
  Charlotte (G-3732)
▲ Venture Products Intl Inc .... E 828 285-0495
  Asheville (G-814)
◆ Vna Holding Inc .... A 336 393-4890
  Greensboro (G-7445)
Volvo Group North America LLC .... A 336 393-2000
  Greensboro (G-7447)
◆ Volvo Group North America LLC ...... A 336 393-2000
  Greensboro (G-7446)
◆ Volvo Trucks North America Inc .... A 336 393-2000
  Greensboro (G-7450)
Whitaker S Tire Service Inc .... F 704 786-6174
  Concord (G-4389)
Xtreme Fabrication Ltd .... F 336 472-4562
  Thomasville (G-15309)

5014 Tires and tubes

Cecil Budd Tire Company LLC .... F 919 742-2322
  Siler City (G-14403)
Derrow Enterprises Inc .... G 252 635-3375
  New Bern (G-11800)
◆ Dunlop Aircraft Tyres Inc .... E 336 283-0979
  Mocksville (G-10567)
Ed S Tire Laurinburg Inc .... G 910 277-0565
  Laurinburg (G-9476)
Haneys Tire Recapping Svc LLC .... G 910 276-2636
  Laurinburg (G-9481)
Johnnys Tire Sales and Svc Inc .... F 252 353-8473
  Greenville (G-7551)
M & R Retreading & Oil Co Inc .... F 704 474-4101
  Norwood (G-12040)
Moss Brothers Tires & Svc Inc .... G 910 895-4572
  Rockingham (G-13635)

Mr Tire Inc .... F 704 483-1500
  Denver (G-4790)
Mr Tire Inc .... F 828 322-8130
  Hickory (G-8099)
Mr Tire Inc .... G 704 739-6456
  Kings Mountain (G-9319)
Mr Tire Inc .... G 828 758-0047
  Lenoir (G-9637)
Mr Tire Inc .... G 704 735-8024
  Lincolnton (G-9910)
Mr Tire Inc .... G 704 484-0816
  Shelby (G-14350)
Mr Tire Inc .... G 704 872-4127
  Statesville (G-14849)
Oakie S Tire & Recapping Inc .... F 704 482-5629
  Shelby (G-14353)
Parrish Tire Company .... E 704 372-2013
  Charlotte (G-3317)
Parrish Tire Company .... E 704 872-6565
  Jonesville (G-9101)
◆ Parrish Tire Company .... D 800 849-8473
  Winston Salem (G-16836)
Perry Brothers Tire Svc Inc .... E 919 693-2128
  Oxford (G-12140)
Perry Brothers Tire Svc Inc .... E 919 775-7225
  Sanford (G-14167)
Piedmont Truck Tires Inc .... F 828 277-1549
  Asheville (G-731)
Piedmont Truck Tires Inc .... F 336 223-9412
  Graham (G-6706)
Piedmont Truck Tires Inc .... E 336 668-0091
  Greensboro (G-7262)
Towel City Tire & Wheel LLC .... G 704 933-2143
  Kannapolis (G-9136)
Whitaker S Tire Service Inc .... F 704 786-6174
  Concord (G-4389)
White S Tire Svc Wilson Inc .... G 252 237-0770
  Wilson (G-16559)
White S Tire Svc Wilson Inc .... D 252 237-5426
  Wilson (G-16560)
Whites Tire Svc New Bern Inc .... G 252 633-1670
  New Bern (G-11857)
Wmb of Wake County Inc .... F 919 782-0419
  Raleigh (G-13426)

5015 Motor vehicle parts, used

Auto Parts Fayetteville LLC .... F 910 889-4026
  Fayetteville (G-5766)
CAM Craft LLC .... G 828 681-5183
  Arden (G-316)
Tire Kountry LLC .... G 336 637-8320
  Reidsville (G-13542)

5021 Furniture

Affordable Bedding Inc .... G 828 254-5555
  Asheville (G-516)
Amor Furniture and Bedding LLC .... F 336 795-0044
  Liberty (G-9806)
▲ Apollo Designs LLC .... E 336 886-0260
  High Point (G-8250)
Ashley Furniture Inds LLC .... D 336 998-1066
  Advance (G-37)
◆ Beaufurn LLC .... E 336 768-2544
  Advance (G-38)
◆ Bekaert Textiles USA Inc .... C 336 769-4300
  Winston Salem (G-16624)
Bekaertdeslee USA Inc .... B 336 747-4900
  Winston Salem (G-16625)
Bookcase Shop .... G 919 683-1922
  Durham (G-4972)
Brookline Furniture Co Inc .... D 336 841-8503
  Archdale (G-270)

Carolina Csual Otdoor Furn Inc .... F 252 491-5171
  Jarvisburg (G-9083)
◆ Chateau DAx USA Ltd .... G 336 885-9777
  High Point (G-8294)
Con-Tab Inc .... F 336 476-0104
  Thomasville (G-15206)
▲ Consumer Specialty Inc .... G 828 396-2195
  Hudson (G-8769)
▲ Delve Interiors LLC .... C 336 274-4661
  Greensboro (G-6968)
▲ Designmaster Furniture Inc .... E 828 324-7992
  Hickory (G-8008)
Elite Furniture Mfg Inc .... G 336 882-0406
  High Point (G-8340)
▲ French Heritage Inc .... F 336 882-3565
  High Point (G-8358)
Funder America Inc .... F 336 751-3501
  Mocksville (G-10575)
Furniture At Work .... F 336 472-6619
  Trinity (G-15341)
Ie Furniture Inc .... E 336 475-5050
  Archdale (G-284)
Jerry Blevins .... G 336 384-3726
  Lansing (G-9455)
◆ Lexington Furniture Inds Inc .... C 336 474-5300
  Thomasville (G-15241)
Lodging By Liberty Inc .... C 336 622-2201
  Siler City (G-14423)
Magnussen Home Furnishings Inc ...... G 336 841-4424
  Greensboro (G-7178)
Mattress Firm .... G 910 868-0950
  Fayetteville (G-5870)
Mattress Firm .... G 252 443-1259
  Rocky Mount (G-13711)
◆ Minhas Furniture House Inc .... E 910 898-0808
  Robbins (G-13601)
Mongoose LLC .... F 919 400-0772
  Burlington (G-1462)
Office Sup Svcs Inc Charlotte .... E 704 786-4677
  Concord (G-4323)
Outer Banks Hammocks Inc .... F 910 256-4001
  Wilmington (G-16347)
Penco Products Inc .... C 252 798-4000
  Hamilton (G-7614)
Prepac Manufacturing US LLC .... F 800 665-1266
  Whitsett (G-15999)
Prime Mill LLC .... F 336 819-4300
  High Point (G-8498)
Professinal Sales Associates .... F 336 210-2756
  High Point (G-8500)
Rack Works Inc .... E 336 368-1302
  Pilot Mountain (G-12201)
◆ Rbc Inc .... C 336 889-7333
  Sophia (G-14521)
◆ Schnadig Corporation .... E 336 389-5200
  Greensboro (G-7327)
Simplicity Sofas Inc .... G 800 813-2889
  High Point (G-8531)
Southandenglish LLC .... G 336 888-8333
  High Point (G-8543)
▲ Stone Marble Co Inc .... G 773 227-1161
  Thomasville (G-15285)
Stuart Ryan Kent & Co .... G 252 916-8226
  Winterville (G-17014)
Unique Office Solutions Inc .... F 336 854-0900
  Greensboro (G-7430)
◆ Vrush Industries Inc .... F 336 886-7700
  High Point (G-8597)
▲ Watauga Creek LLC .... G 828 369-7881
  Franklin (G-6147)
Welcome Industrial Corp .... D 336 329-9640
  Burlington (G-1517)

50 WHOLESALE TRADE - DURABLE GOODS

◆ Whitewood Industries Inc .... D 336 472-0303
　Thomasville (G-15300)

Wood Technology Inc .... E 828 464-8049
　Conover (G-4515)

Woodwright of Wilson Co Inc .... G 252 243-9663
　Elm City (G-5655)

5023 Homefurnishings

▲ Appalchian Stove Fbrcators Inc .... F 828 253-0164
　Asheville (G-525)

Artisans Guild Incorporated .... G 336 841-4140
　High Point (G-8256)

Atlantic Window Coverings Inc .... E 704 392-0043
　Charlotte (G-2234)

▲ Avanti Hearth Products LLC .... G 704 866-4342
　Belmont (G-975)

Baypointe Partners LLC .... G 336 882-5200
　Archdale (G-269)

◆ Capel Incorporated .... D 910 572-7000
　Troy (G-15402)

◆ Century Furniture LLC .... C 828 267-8739
　Hickory (G-7983)

Chf Industries Inc .... E 212 951-7800
　Charlotte (G-2473)

▲ Colonial Tin Works Inc .... E 336 668-4126
　Greensboro (G-6919)

▲ Dize Company .... D 336 722-5181
　Winston Salem (G-16684)

Elevate Textiles Inc .... G 336 379-6220
　Burlington (G-1410)

Four Corners Frmng Gallery Inc .... G 704 662-7154
　Mooresville (G-10949)

▲ Freudenberg Nonwovens Lim .... A 919 620-3900
　Durham (G-5103)

▲ G & G Moulding Inc .... E 828 438-1112
　Morganton (G-11214)

Government Sales LLC .... G 252 726-6315
　Morehead City (G-11172)

Green River Resource MGT .... F 828 697-0357
　Zirconia (G-17153)

Ibolili Natural Fibers .... G 866 834-9857
　Greensboro (G-7109)

▲ Js Royal Home Usa Inc .... E 704 542-2304
　Charlotte (G-3038)

Kimmys Customs LLC .... G 904 699-2933
　Rural Hall (G-13845)

◆ Kingsdown Incorporated .... E 919 563-3531
　Mebane (G-10415)

◆ L G Sourcing Inc .... E 704 758-1000
　Mooresville (G-11001)

▲ Michaelian & Kohlberg Inc .... G 828 891-8511
　Horse Shoe (G-8741)

Mongoose LLC .... F 919 400-0772
　Burlington (G-1462)

Patterson Custom Drapery .... G 910 791-4332
　Wilmington (G-16349)

Rhf Investments Inc .... G 828 326-8350
　Hickory (G-8135)

Royal Textile Products Sw LLC .... G 602 276-4598
　Charlotte (G-3465)

▲ Sanders Industries Inc .... G 410 277-8565
　Waynesville (G-15820)

◆ Selective Enterprises Inc .... C 704 588-3310
　Charlotte (G-3525)

Shutter Factory Inc .... G 252 974-2795
　Washington (G-15731)

T Distribution NC Inc .... E 828 438-1112
　Morganton (G-11259)

▲ Tapestries Ltd .... G 336 883-9864
　Greensboro (G-7389)

◆ Vmod Fiber LLC .... F 704 525-6851
　Charlotte (G-3780)

◆ Wichard Inc .... G 704 597-1502
　Charlotte (G-3811)

5031 Lumber, plywood, and millwork

◆ Ace Marine Rigging & Supply Inc .... F 252 726-6620
　Morehead City (G-11148)

Albatross Supply LLC .... G 336 488-1128
　Hamptonville (G-7665)

Amarr Company .... G 336 936-0010
　Mocksville (G-10553)

◆ Amarr Company .... C 336 744-5100
　Winston Salem (G-16602)

Arbon Equipment Corporation .... F 414 355-2600
　Charlotte (G-2209)

▲ Associated Hardwoods Inc .... E 828 396-3321
　Granite Falls (G-6722)

Bastrop Skid Company .... G 252 793-6600
　Plymouth (G-12366)

Beacon Roofing Supply Inc .... G 704 886-1555
　Charlotte (G-2291)

◆ Bfs Asset Holdings LLC .... C 303 784-4288
　Raleigh (G-12554)

◆ Bfs Operations LLC .... A 919 431-1000
　Raleigh (G-12555)

Bolivia Lumber Company LLC .... F 910 371-2515
　Leland (G-9528)

Builders Firstsource Inc .... G 919 562-6601
　Youngsville (G-17072)

Building Center Inc .... D 704 889-8182
　Pineville (G-12257)

Butler Trailer Mfg Co Inc .... F 336 674-8850
　Randleman (G-13453)

Church & Church Lumber LLC .... D 336 973-4297
　Wilkesboro (G-16016)

Clt 2016 Inc .... D 704 886-1555
　Charlotte (G-2501)

Columbia Forest Products Inc .... G 336 605-0429
　Greensboro (G-6920)

Conover Lumber Company Inc .... F 828 464-4591
　Conover (G-4438)

Custom Marble Corporation .... G 910 215-0679
　Pinehurst (G-12219)

D & B Concepts Inc .... F 336 885-8292
　High Point (G-8315)

▲ Design Surfaces Inc .... F 919 781-0310
　Raleigh (G-12679)

Dex n Dox .... G 910 576-4644
　Troy (G-15404)

Discount Box & Pallet Inc .... E 336 272-2220
　Staley (G-14665)

Dixon Custom Cabinetry LLC .... F 336 992-3306
　Kernersville (G-9190)

Double Hung LLC .... G 888 235-8956
　Greensboro (G-6976)

Durable Wood Preservers Inc .... G 704 537-3113
　Charlotte (G-2658)

East Industries Inc .... D 252 442-9662
　Rocky Mount (G-13693)

▲ Ecmd Inc .... D 336 667-5976
　North Wilkesboro (G-12006)

Four Jaks .... G 828 484-9545
　Weaverville (G-15847)

Gilbert Hardwoods Inc .... F 336 431-2127
　Trinity (G-15342)

▲ Global Veneer Sales Inc .... G 336 885-5061
　High Point (G-8368)

Harris Wood Products Inc .... G 704 550-5494
　New London (G-11872)

Hoover Treated Wood Pdts Inc .... E 866 587-8761
　Weldon (G-15882)

Horizon Forest Products Co LP .... G 336 993-9663
　Colfax (G-4151)

Hunter Innovations Ltd .... G 919 848-8814
　Raleigh (G-12869)

Idaho Timber NC LLC .... D 252 430-0030
　Henderson (G-7789)

Industrial Timber LLC .... D 704 919-1215
　Hiddenite (G-8220)

▲ Industrial Timber LLC .... D 704 919-1215
　Charlotte (G-2966)

J E Jones Lumber Company .... E 336 472-3478
　Lexington (G-9732)

J E Kerr Timber Co Corp .... F 252 537-0544
　Roanoke Rapids (G-13576)

◆ Jeld-Wen Inc .... B 800 535-3936
　Charlotte (G-3018)

◆ L G Sourcing Inc .... E 704 758-1000
　Mooresville (G-11001)

Liberty Lumber Company .... E 336 622-4901
　Liberty (G-9821)

◆ Log Cabin Homes Ltd .... D 252 454-1500
　Rocky Mount (G-13708)

Lookout Boat Window Frames LLC .... G 252 723-2222
　Morehead City (G-11182)

M O Deviney Lumber Co Inc .... G 704 538-9071
　Casar (G-1934)

MAC Grading Co .... F 910 531-4642
　Autryville (G-842)

Martin Lumber & Mulch LLC .... F 252 935-5294
　Pantego (G-12167)

Mesa Quality Fenestration Inc .... G 828 393-0132
　Hendersonville (G-7879)

Mint Hill Cabinet Shop Inc .... E 704 821-9373
　Monroe (G-10770)

Moulding Source Incorporated .... G 704 658-1111
　Mooresville (G-11031)

Murphy S Custom Cabinetry Inc .... G 828 891-3050
　Hendersonville (G-7882)

New South Lumber Company Inc ..... C 336 376-3130
　Graham (G-6705)

Nova Enterprises Inc .... E 828 687-8770
　Arden (G-357)

▼ Oaks Unlimited Inc .... E 828 926-1621
　Waynesville (G-15812)

▲ Ornamental Mouldings LLC .... F 336 431-9120
　Archdale (G-295)

Overman Cabinet & Supply LLC .... G 336 584-1349
　Burlington (G-1469)

P & P Distributing Company .... F 910 582-1968
　Hamlet (G-7628)

Rafters and Walls LLC .... E 980 404-0209
　Shelby (G-14359)

Resinart East Inc .... F 828 687-0215
　Fletcher (G-6034)

RSI Home Products Inc .... E 828 428-6300
　Lincolnton (G-9917)

Rugby Acquisition LLC .... D 336 993-8686
　Kernersville (G-9229)

◆ S Kivett Inc .... E 910 592-0161
　Clinton (G-4106)

Salt Wood Products Inc .... G 252 830-8875
　Greenville (G-7581)

▲ Sauers & Company Inc .... F 336 956-1200
　Lexington (G-9776)

Selectbuild Construction Inc .... E 208 331-4300
　Raleigh (G-13244)

Sipe Lumber Company Inc .... E 828 632-4679
　Taylorsville (G-15167)

▲ Smith Millwork Inc .... E 800 222-8498
　Lexington (G-9782)

Somers Lumber and Mfg Inc .... F
　Harmony (G-7690)

South-East Lumber Company .... E 336 996-5322
　Kernersville (G-9236)

50 WHOLESALE TRADE - DURABLE GOODS

Southern Staircase Inc................................ D 704 357-1221
  Charlotte (G-3597)
Southern Vneer Spclty Pdts LLC................ F 919 642-7004
  Moncure (G-10626)
Southmark Forest Products......................... G 919 300-1596
  Smithfield (G-14485)
Steelman Lumber & Pallet LLC................... G 336 468-2757
  Hamptonville (G-7678)
▲ Stock Building Supply Hol...................... A 919 431-1000
  Raleigh (G-13305)
Tabor City Lumber Company....................... E 910 653-3162
  Tabor City (G-15087)
Tompkins Industries Inc.............................. C 828 254-2351
  Asheville (G-802)
Toney Lumber Company Inc....................... D 919 496-5711
  Louisburg (G-10005)
Triad Prefinish & Lbr Sls Inc....................... G 336 375-4849
  Greensboro (G-7415)
▲ Ultimate Products Inc............................. F 919 836-1627
  Raleigh (G-13377)
▲ United Finishers Intl Inc......................... G 336 883-3901
  High Point (G-8585)
Vinyl Windows & Doors Corp...................... F 910 944-2100
  Aberdeen (G-35)
▲ W M Cramer Lumber Co........................ D 828 397-7481
  Connelly Springs (G-4411)
W N C Pallet Forest Pdts Inc...................... E 828 667-5426
  Candler (G-1591)
Weyerhaeuser Company.............................. E 336 835-5100
  Elkin (G-5633)
Weyerhaeuser Company.............................. F 252 791-3200
  Plymouth (G-12379)
Wood Country Creations LLC...................... G 704 545-5966
  Mint Hill (G-10549)
▲ Wood Right Lumber Company............... G 910 576-4642
  Troy (G-15420)
World Wood Company.................................. D 252 523-0021
  Cove City (G-4599)

5032 Brick, stone, and related material

▲ Adams Products Company..................... C 919 467-2218
  Morrisville (G-11278)
Apac-Atlantic Inc... D 336 412-6800
  Raleigh (G-12512)
Asphalt Emulsion Inds LLC.......................... G 252 726-0653
  Morehead City (G-11150)
Barnhill Contracting Company..................... F 252 527-8021
  Kinston (G-9344)
Bloomday Granite & Marble Inc................. E 336 724-0300
  Winston Salem (G-16633)
Bright Angle LLC... G 828 771-6966
  Asheville (G-573)
Concrete Service Co Inc.............................. E 910 483-0396
  Fayetteville (G-5794)
Concrete Service Company........................ G 910 590-0035
  Clinton (G-4093)
Custom Brick Company Inc......................... E 919 832-2804
  Raleigh (G-12663)
D&S Asphalt Materials Inc........................... G 828 894-2778
  Tryon (G-15424)
Design Specialties Inc................................. E 919 772-6955
  Raleigh (G-12678)
Explosives Supply Company....................... F 828 765-2762
  Spruce Pine (G-14640)
Fletcher Limestone Company Inc............... F 828 684-6701
  Fletcher (G-6005)
Fsc II LLC.. F 919 783-5700
  Raleigh (G-12785)
General Shale Brick Inc.............................. G 919 828-0541
  Raleigh (G-12793)
General Shale Brick Inc.............................. G 919 775-2121
  Sanford (G-14124)
General Shale Brick Inc.............................. G 910 452-3498
  Wilmington (G-16231)
Greenville Ready Mix Concrete................. E 252 756-0119
  Winterville (G-17001)
Heidelberg Mtls Sthast Agg LLC................ E 910 893-8308
  Bunnlevel (G-1330)
J&R SERvices/J&r Lumber Co.................. G 956 778-7005
  Wilmington (G-16276)
Jones Ornamental Concrete...................... F 828 685-3740
  Hendersonville (G-7867)
Lbm Industries Inc....................................... F 828 966-4270
  Sapphire (G-14213)
Marietta Martin Materials Inc..................... G 336 769-3803
  Kernersville (G-9213)
Martin Marietta Materials Inc..................... G 336 674-0836
  Greensboro (G-7185)
Merchants Metals Inc.................................. G 704 921-9192
  Charlotte (G-3165)
Motsinger Block Plant Inc........................... G 336 764-0350
  Winston Salem (G-16818)
Old Castle Apg South Inc........................... G 919 383-2521
  Durham (G-5255)
Performnce Strl Con Sltons LLC............... G 980 333-6414
  Davidson (G-4690)
◆ Pine Hall Brick Co Inc............................. E 336 721-7500
  Winston Salem (G-16857)
Plycem Usa LLC.. D 336 696-2007
  North Wilkesboro (G-12030)
Radford Quarries Inc................................... F 828 264-7008
  Boone (G-1231)
▲ Sid Jenkins Inc... G 336 632-0707
  Greensboro (G-7337)
Southern Marble Co LLC............................ G 704 982-4142
  Albemarle (G-107)
Speer Concrete Inc..................................... E 910 947-3144
  Carthage (G-1666)
Surface Buff LLC.. G 919 341-2873
  Cary (G-1906)
Tarheel Marble Company Inc..................... F 704 888-6003
  Locust (G-9975)
▲ Trade Venture Stones LLC.................... G 919 803-3923
  Knightdale (G-9431)
Troy Ready - Mix Inc.................................... G 910 572-1011
  Troy (G-15418)
Viktors Gran MBL Kit Cnter Top................ F 828 681-0713
  Arden (G-389)
Wake Stone Corporation............................. E 919 775-7349
  Moncure (G-10629)
Welbuilt Homes Inc...................................... F 910 323-0098
  Fayetteville (G-5952)

5033 Roofing, siding, and insulation

Carolina Home Exteriors LLC..................... F 252 637-6599
  New Bern (G-11786)
Exteriors Inc Ltd... G 919 325-2251
  Spring Lake (G-14625)
Mid-Atlantic Specialties Inc........................ G 919 212-1939
  Raleigh (G-13030)
Roofing Tools and Eqp Inc......................... G 252 291-1800
  Wilson (G-16534)
Triad Corrugated Metal Inc........................ E 336 625-9727
  Asheboro (G-499)
◆ Union Corrugating Company.................. E 910 483-0479
  Fayetteville (G-5937)
Vinyl Windows & Doors Corp...................... F 910 944-2100
  Aberdeen (G-35)
Wake Supply Company................................ G 252 234-6012
  Wilson (G-16557)

5039 Construction materials, nec

1st Choice Service Inc................................. F 704 913-7685
  Cherryville (G-3861)
Afsc LLC.. D 704 523-4936
  Charlotte (G-2142)
Asheville Contracting Co Inc...................... E 828 665-8900
  Candler (G-1567)
Bobby Cahoon Construction Inc................ E 252 249-1617
  Grantsboro (G-6763)
Carolina Prcsion Fbers Spv LLC............... E 336 527-4140
  Ronda (G-13763)
Cymbal LLC.. G 877 365-9622
  Cary (G-1744)
Design Specialties Inc................................. E 919 772-6955
  Raleigh (G-12678)
Eastern Wholesale Fence LLC.................. D 631 698-0975
  Salisbury (G-13957)
Explosives Supply Company....................... F 828 765-2762
  Spruce Pine (G-14640)
Maxson & Associates................................... G 336 632-0524
  Greensboro (G-7190)
Outlaw Step Co... G 252 568-4384
  Deep Run (G-4717)
Southern Concrete Mtls Inc........................ G 828 681-5178
  Fletcher (G-6043)
Southern Concrete Mtls Inc........................ E 828 692-6517
  Hendersonville (G-7903)
Woodland Logging Inc................................. G 910 298-3350
  Beulaville (G-1099)

5043 Photographic equipment and supplies

Creative Conquest LLC............................... G 720 481-4372
  Shelby (G-14304)

5044 Office equipment

Branch Office Solutions Inc........................ G 800 743-1047
  Indian Trail (G-8924)
Bryan Austin... F 336 841-6573
  High Point (G-8276)
Digital Print & Imaging Inc......................... G 910 341-3005
  Wilmington (G-16201)
Systel Business Eqp Co Inc....................... E 336 808-8000
  Greensboro (G-7385)

5045 Computers, peripherals, and software

Amt Datasouth Corp..................................... E 704 523-8500
  Charlotte (G-2192)
Database Incorporated................................ G 202 684-6252
  Durham (G-5048)
Dimill Enterprises LLC................................ G 919 629-2011
  Raleigh (G-12684)
EMC Corporation.. G 720 341-3274
  Charlotte (G-2705)
Envirnmntal Systems RES Inst I................ E 704 541-9810
  Charlotte (G-2718)
Glover Corporation Inc................................ E 919 821-5535
  Raleigh (G-12807)
Interconnect Products and......................... E 336 667-3356
  Wilkesboro (G-16026)
Iqe North Carolina LLC............................... F 336 609-6270
  Greensboro (G-7121)
Logiksavvy Solutions LLC........................... G 336 392-6149
  Greensboro (G-7167)
McKelvey Fulks... G 704 357-1550
  Charlotte (G-3152)
Medicor Imaging Inc.................................... E 704 332-5532
  Charlotte (G-3159)
NCSMJ Inc... F 704 544-1118
  Pineville (G-12285)
Reynolds and Reynolds Company............ G 321 287-3939
  Charlotte (G-3445)
▲ Sato America LLC.................................... C 704 644-1650
  Charlotte (G-3493)
Sighttech LLC... G 855 997-4448
  Charlotte (G-3549)

50 WHOLESALE TRADE - DURABLE GOODS

Smartway of Carolinas LLC .... F 704 900-7877
  Charlotte *(G-3566)*
St Investors Inc .... D 704 969-7500
  Charlotte *(G-3618)*
▲ Teguar Corporation .... E 704 960-1761
  Charlotte *(G-3678)*
◆ Vrush Industries Inc .... F 336 886-7700
  High Point *(G-8597)*

5046 Commercial equipment, nec

Bunzl Processor Dist LLC .... G 910 738-8111
  Lumberton *(G-10028)*
Chef Martini LLC .... A 919 327-3183
  Raleigh *(G-12618)*
Custom Neon & Graphics Inc .... G 704 344-1715
  Charlotte *(G-2592)*
Dandy Light Traps Inc .... G 980 223-2744
  Statesville *(G-14782)*
Elxsi Corporation .... B 407 849-1090
  Charlotte *(G-2701)*
Gold Medal Products Co .... G 336 665-4997
  Greensboro *(G-7051)*
Government Sales LLC .... G 252 726-6315
  Morehead City *(G-11172)*
Heed Group Inc .... G 877 938-8853
  Stanley *(G-14696)*
Innovative Design Tech LLC .... G 919 331-0204
  Angier *(C-141)*
Kenneth Moore Signs .... G 910 458-6428
  Wilmington *(G-16287)*
Maxson & Associates .... G 336 632-0524
  Greensboro *(G-7190)*
Picassomoesllc .... G 216 703-4547
  Hillsborough *(G-8665)*
Precision Walls Inc .... G 336 852-7710
  Greensboro *(G-7276)*
Restaurant Furniture Inc .... F 828 459-9992
  Claremont *(G-3937)*
Riddley Retail Fixtures Inc .... E 704 435-8829
  Kings Mountain *(G-9329)*
Satco Truck Equipment Inc .... F 919 383-5547
  Durham *(G-5340)*
◆ Schaefer Systems International Inc .... C 704 944-4500
  Charlotte *(G-3499)*
Schaefer Systems Intl Inc .... G 704 944-4550
  Charlotte *(G-3501)*
Signature Signs Inc .... G 336 431-2072
  High Point *(G-8528)*
Singer Equipment Company Inc .... E 910 484-1128
  Fayetteville *(G-5918)*
Southeastern Sign Works Inc .... F 336 789-5516
  Mount Airy *(G-11574)*
◆ Technibilt Ltd .... E 828 464-7388
  Newton *(G-11976)*
Thompson & Little Inc .... E 910 484-1128
  Fayetteville *(G-5929)*
True Portion Inc .... F 336 362-6326
  High Point *(G-8579)*

5047 Medical and hospital equipment

Aj & Raine Scrubs & More LLC .... G 646 374-5198
  Charlotte *(G-2149)*
Albemrle Orthotics Prosthetics .... E 252 338-3002
  Elizabeth City *(G-5531)*
▲ Amtai Medical Equipment Inc .... F 919 872-1803
  Raleigh *(G-12503)*
▲ Cathtek LLC .... G 336 748-0686
  Winston Salem *(G-16649)*
Colowrap Inc .... F 888 815-3376
  Durham *(G-5025)*
Combat Medical Systems LLC .... E 704 705-1222
  Harrisburg *(G-7706)*

▲ Custom Industries Inc .... E 336 299-2885
  Greensboro *(G-6950)*
Ddm Inc .... G 910 686-1481
  Wilmington *(G-16197)*
▲ Dentonics Inc .... F 704 238-0245
  Monroe *(G-10705)*
Dove Medical Supply LLC .... F 336 643-9367
  Summerfield *(G-14980)*
Fidelity Pharmaceuticals LLC .... G 704 274-3192
  Huntersville *(G-8819)*
Fillauer North Carolina Inc .... E 828 658-8330
  Weaverville *(G-15846)*
Fla Orthopedics Inc .... D 800 327-4110
  Charlotte *(G-2768)*
GNB Ventures LLC .... F 704 488-4468
  Charlotte *(G-2837)*
▲ Greiner Bio-One North Amer Inc .... B 704 261-7800
  Monroe *(G-10728)*
Health Supply Us LLC .... F 888 408-1694
  Mooresville *(G-10971)*
Janus Development Group Inc .... F 252 551-9042
  Greenville *(G-7548)*
Joerns Healthcare Parent LLC .... B 800 966-6662
  Charlotte *(G-3027)*
Kberg Productions LLC .... G 910 232-0342
  Raleigh *(G-12932)*
Keani Furniture Inc .... E 336 303-5484
  Asheboro *(C-448)*
M Davis and Associates LLC .... G 336 337-7089
  Greensboro *(G-7172)*
Med Express/Medical Spc Inc .... F 919 572-2568
  Durham *(G-5214)*
Medcor Inc .... G 888 579-1050
  Lexington *(G-9757)*
◆ Medi Mall Inc .... G 877 501-6334
  Fletcher *(G-6022)*
Medtrnic Sofamor Danek USA Inc .... G 919 457-9982
  Cary *(G-1823)*
▲ Meghan Blake Industries Inc .... E 704 462-2988
  Vale *(G-15469)*
▲ Protection Products Inc .... E 828 324-2173
  Hickory *(G-8127)*
Rm Liquidation Inc .... D 828 274-7996
  Asheville *(G-756)*
RPM Products Inc .... F 704 871-0518
  Statesville *(G-14882)*
▲ Sarstedt Inc .... C 828 465-4000
  Newton *(G-11966)*
Sdv Office Systems LLC .... F 844 968-9500
  Fletcher *(G-6037)*
Sdv Office Systems LLC .... G 844 968-9500
  Asheville *(G-767)*
Sg-Clw Inc .... F 336 865-4980
  Winston Salem *(G-16903)*
Smissons Inc .... F 660 537-3219
  Clayton *(G-4009)*
Specialty Trnsp Systems Inc .... F 828 464-9738
  Newton *(G-11971)*
Speer Operational Tech LLC .... G 864 631-2512
  Marion *(G-10179)*
▼ Suntech Medical Inc .... F 919 654-2300
  Morrisville *(G-11435)*
Test ME Out Inc .... F 252 635-6770
  New Bern *(G-11849)*
◆ Tripath Imaging Inc .... D 336 222-9707
  Burlington *(G-1509)*
Turbomed LLC .... F 973 527-5299
  Fayetteville *(G-5936)*
United Mobile Imaging Inc .... G 800 983-9840
  Clemmons *(G-4065)*
Veon Inc .... F 252 623-2102
  Washington *(G-15736)*

Yukon Medical LLC .... G 919 595-8250
  Durham *(G-5459)*

5049 Professional equipment, nec

AEC Imaging & Graphics LLC .... G 910 693-1034
  Hope Mills *(G-8730)*
Biosupplynet Inc .... F 919 659-2121
  Morrisville *(G-11304)*
Carolina Biological Supply Co .... C 336 446-7600
  Whitsett *(G-15985)*
◆ Carolina Biological Supply Company .... C 336 584-0381
  Burlington *(G-1384)*
Centice Corporation .... E 919 653-0424
  Raleigh *(G-12617)*
◆ Diamond Dog Tools Inc .... D 828 687-3686
  Arden *(G-325)*
Diebold Nixdorf Incorporated .... F 704 599-3100
  Charlotte *(G-2632)*
Duncan-Parnell Inc .... G 252 977-7832
  Rocky Mount *(G-13692)*
Fisher Scientific Company LLC .... D 800 252-7100
  Asheville *(G-623)*
Lea Aid Acquisition Company .... F 919 872-6210
  Raleigh *(G-12963)*
Optical Place Inc .... E 336 274-1300
  Greensboro *(G-7235)*
Piranha Nail and Staple Inc .... G 336 852-8358
  Greensboro *(G-7265)*
Sharpe Images Properties Inc .... E 336 724-2871
  Winston Salem *(G-16906)*
Squarehead Technology LLC .... G 571 299-4849
  Hickory *(G-8167)*
Trafag Inc .... G 704 343-6339
  Charlotte *(G-3712)*
Tri-Tech Forensics Inc .... D 910 457-6600
  Leland *(G-9562)*
Turbomed LLC .... F 973 527-5299
  Fayetteville *(G-5936)*

5051 Metals service centers and offices

Advanced Drainage Systems Inc .... E 704 629-4151
  Bessemer City *(G-1050)*
▲ Airspeed LLC .... E 919 644-1222
  Hillsborough *(G-8633)*
▼ Alamo Distribution LLC .... C 704 398-5600
  Belmont *(G-974)*
Allens Gutter Service .... G 910 738-9509
  Lumberton *(G-10025)*
▲ Asheville Bit & Steel Company .... F 828 274-3766
  Asheville *(G-531)*
▲ Aviation Metals NC Inc .... F 704 264-1647
  Charlotte *(G-2246)*
▲ Bessemer City Machine Shop Inc .... F 704 629-4111
  Bessemer City *(G-1053)*
Biganodes LLC .... G 828 245-1115
  Forest City *(G-6060)*
C & B Salvage Company Inc .... G 336 374-3946
  Ararat *(G-263)*
Charter Dura-Bar Inc .... F 704 637-1906
  Salisbury *(G-13940)*
Chatham Steel Corporation .... E 912 233-4182
  Durham *(G-5013)*
Chicago Tube and Iron Company .... D 704 781-2060
  Locust *(G-9956)*
Component Sourcing Intl LLC .... E 704 843-9292
  Charlotte *(G-2534)*
Consolidated Pipe & Sup Co Inc .... F 336 294-8577
  Greensboro *(G-6930)*
Corsan LLC .... F 704 765-9979
  Huntersville *(G-8806)*
Dave Steel Company Inc .... F 828 252-2771
  Asheville *(G-603)*

50 WHOLESALE TRADE - DURABLE GOODS

Dave Steel Company Inc............................ D 828 252-2771
  Asheville *(G-604)*
Dunavants Welding & Steel Inc................ G 252 338-6533
  Camden *(G-1557)*
Freedom Metals Inc.................................. F 704 333-1214
  Charlotte *(G-2794)*
Harris Rebar Inc.. F 919 528-8333
  Benson *(G-1037)*
Hercules Steel Company Inc..................... E 910 488-5110
  Fayetteville *(G-5837)*
Howard Steel Inc....................................... F 704 376-9631
  Charlotte *(G-2925)*
IPC Corporation.. F 704 821-7084
  Stallings *(G-14671)*
▲ Iron Box LLC... F 919 890-0025
  Raleigh *(G-12901)*
McCombs Steel Company Inc................... E 704 873-7563
  Statesville *(G-14840)*
McCune Technology Inc............................ F 910 424-2978
  Fayetteville *(G-5871)*
▲ Pavco Inc.. E 704 496-6800
  Charlotte *(G-3321)*
Reynolds Advanced Mtls Inc..................... E 704 357-0600
  Charlotte *(G-3444)*
Sanders Company Inc............................... E 252 338-3995
  Elizabeth City *(G-5569)*
Schwartz Steel Service Inc........................ E 704 865-9576
  Gastonia *(G-6506)*
Steel and Pipe Corporation....................... E 919 776-0751
  Sanford *(G-14193)*
Sun Valley Stl Fabrication Inc.................... F 704 289-5830
  Monroe *(G-10817)*
Triad Sheet Metal & Mech Inc................... F 336 379-9891
  Greensboro *(G-7417)*
◆ Umicore USA Inc.................................. E 919 874-7171
  Raleigh *(G-13379)*
Wnc Refab Inc.. G 828 658-8368
  Weaverville *(G-15870)*

5052 Coal and other minerals and ores

Daystar Materials Inc................................ E 919 734-0460
  Goldsboro *(G-6609)*
◆ Umicore USA Inc.................................. E 919 874-7171
  Raleigh *(G-13379)*

5063 Electrical apparatus and equipment

Abb Inc... E 704 587-1362
  Charlotte *(G-2122)*
ABB Inc... A 252 827-2121
  Pinetops *(G-12239)*
◆ ABB Inc.. C 919 856-2360
  Cary *(G-1674)*
ABB Motors and Mechanical Inc............... G 336 272-6104
  Greensboro *(G-6772)*
Abl Electronics Supply Inc........................ G 704 784-4225
  Concord *(G-4186)*
Ademco Inc... G 704 525-8899
  Charlotte *(G-2137)*
Ademco Inc... G 336 668-3644
  Greensboro *(G-6779)*
Ademco Inc... G 919 872-5556
  Raleigh *(G-12476)*
Advance Stores Company Inc................... F 336 545-9091
  Greensboro *(G-6780)*
Alk Investments LLC................................ G 984 233-5353
  Raleigh *(G-12488)*
Automated Controls LLC........................... F 704 724-7625
  Huntersville *(G-8796)*
Blue Ridge Elc Mtr Repr Inc...................... G 828 258-0800
  Asheville *(G-564)*
▲ Blue Sun Energy Inc............................. G 336 218-6707
  Greensboro *(G-6842)*

Bolton Investors Inc.................................. G 919 471-1197
  Durham *(G-4971)*
Bowden Electric Motor Svc Inc................. G 252 446-4203
  Rocky Mount *(G-13685)*
Carolina Time Equipment Co Inc.............. E 704 536-2700
  Charlotte *(G-2409)*
Cemco Electric Inc.................................... F 704 504-0294
  Charlotte *(G-2441)*
▲ Clarolux Inc... E 336 378-6800
  Greensboro *(G-6912)*
Clayton Electric Mtr Repr Inc.................... F 336 584-3756
  Elon College *(G-5664)*
Code LLC.. E 828 328-6004
  Hickory *(G-7987)*
Conservation Station Inc........................... G 919 932-9201
  Chapel Hill *(G-2005)*
Cummins Atlantic LLC.............................. E 704 596-7690
  Charlotte *(G-2584)*
▲ Cummins Atlantic LLC......................... E 704 588-1240
  Charlotte *(G-2585)*
Dixie Electro Mech Svcs Inc..................... F 704 332-1116
  Charlotte *(G-2646)*
▲ Dna Group Inc...................................... G 919 881-0889
  Raleigh *(G-12690)*
Edgewell Per Care Brands LLC................. G 336 672-4500
  Asheboro *(G-427)*
Edwards Electronic Systems Inc.............. E 919 359-2239
  Clayton *(G-3976)*
Egi Associates Inc.................................... F 704 561-3337
  Charlotte *(G-2687)*
Eizi Group Llc... G 919 397-3638
  Raleigh *(G-12729)*
Electric Motor Service of Shelby Inc......... F 704 482-9979
  Shelby *(G-14314)*
Electric Motor Svc Ahoskie Inc................. G 252 332-4364
  Ahoskie *(G-61)*
Electric Mtr Sls Svc Pitt Cnty.................... G 252 752-3170
  Greenville *(G-7522)*
Electric Mtr Sp Wake Frest Inc.................. E 919 556-3229
  Wake Forest *(G-15552)*
Electrical Equipment Company................. E 910 276-2141
  Laurinburg *(G-9478)*
Elektran Inc... F 910 997-6640
  Rockingham *(G-13625)*
Envirnmntal Cmfort Sltions Inc................. G 980 272-7327
  Kannapolis *(G-9119)*
Epl & Solar Corp....................................... G 201 577-8966
  Wake Forest *(G-15554)*
Exide Technologies LLC........................... G 704 521-8016
  Charlotte *(G-2738)*
Exide Technologies LLC........................... G 919 553-3578
  Charlotte *(G-3977)*
▲ Fintronx LLC... F 919 324-3960
  Raleigh *(G-12767)*
General Motor Repair & Svc Inc................ G 336 292-1715
  Greensboro *(G-7036)*
Hammond Electric Motor Company........... F 704 983-3178
  Albemarle *(G-89)*
Hanover Electric Motor Svc Inc................. G 910 762-3702
  Wilmington *(G-16244)*
Hill & Ferencz Elc Mtr Co Inc.................... F 919 736-7373
  Goldsboro *(G-6625)*
His Company Inc....................................... G 800 537-0351
  Wilmington *(G-16255)*
Holland Supply Company.......................... E 252 492-7541
  Henderson *(G-7788)*
◆ Hubbell Industrial Contrls Inc............... C 336 434-2800
  Archdale *(G-283)*
Interstate All Batteries Ctr........................ G 704 979-3430
  Concord *(G-4288)*
▲ Iron Box LLC... E 919 890-0025
  Raleigh *(G-12901)*

JA Smith Inc... G 704 860-4910
  Lawndale *(G-9500)*
◆ Jenkins Electric Company..................... D 800 438-3003
  Charlotte *(G-3020)*
Johnson Controls Inc................................ E 704 521-8889
  Charlotte *(G-3030)*
L L C Batteries of N C............................... G 919 331-0241
  Angier *(G-143)*
Lingle Electric Repair Inc......................... F 704 636-5591
  Salisbury *(G-14004)*
Long Life Lighting Inc.............................. G 919 833-1292
  Raleigh *(G-12979)*
Ls Cable & System USA Inc..................... C 252 824-3553
  Tarboro *(G-15112)*
▲ Lutze Inc... E 704 504-0222
  Charlotte *(G-3110)*
▲ Manufacturing Systems Eqp Inc.......... F 704 283-2086
  Monroe *(G-10764)*
McKenzie Supply Company...................... G 910 276-1691
  Laurinburg *(G-9489)*
McKinney Electric & Mch Co Inc............... G 828 765-7910
  Spruce Pine *(G-14648)*
McNaughton-Mckay Southeast Inc........... F 910 392-0940
  Wilmington *(G-16318)*
Minka Lighting Inc.................................... D 704 785-9200
  Concord *(G-4316)*
Motor Shop Inc.. G 704 867-8488
  Gastonia *(G-6471)*
Ni4l Antennas and Elec LLC..................... G 828 738-6445
  Moravian Falls *(G-11146)*
Pcai Inc... D 704 588-1240
  Charlotte *(G-3323)*
Piedmont Elc Mtr Repr Inc Ashb................ F 336 495-0500
  Asheboro *(G-463)*
Power-Utility Products Company.............. F 704 375-0776
  Charlotte *(G-3361)*
Randall Supply Inc.................................... E 704 289-6479
  Monroe *(G-10792)*
Rocky Mount Electric Motor LLC.............. G 252 446-1510
  Rocky Mount *(G-13732)*
Rotron Incorporated.................................. C 336 449-3400
  Whitsett *(G-16001)*
Sanders Electric Motor Svc Inc................. E 828 754-0513
  Lenoir *(G-9651)*
▲ Sigma Engineered Solutions PC........... D 919 773-0011
  Garner *(G-6315)*
▲ Smart Electric North Amer LLC............ G 828 323-1200
  Conover *(G-4497)*
Snow Electric Co Inc................................ G 336 723-2092
  Winston Salem *(G-16912)*
Southern Electric Motor Co...................... G 919 688-7879
  Durham *(G-5365)*
▲ Southland Electrical Sup LLC............... C 336 227-1486
  Burlington *(G-1498)*
State Electric Supply Company................ F 336 855-8200
  Greensboro *(G-7367)*
Stone Cllins Mtr Rewinding Inc................ G 910 347-2775
  Jacksonville *(G-9041)*
Surry Elc Mtr & Contrls Inc....................... F 336 786-1717
  Mount Airy *(G-11581)*
Tencarva Machinery Company LLC.......... F 336 665-1435
  Greensboro *(G-7395)*
▲ Wieland Electric Inc............................. F 910 259-5050
  Wilmington *(G-16442)*

5064 Electrical appliances, television and radio

McKenzie Supply Company...................... G 910 276-1691
  Laurinburg *(G-9489)*
Psnc Energy.. G 919 367-2735
  Apex *(G-235)*

50 WHOLESALE TRADE - DURABLE GOODS

5065 Electronic parts and equipment, nec

A&B Integrators LLC .... F 919 371-0750
  Durham (G-4897)
Abacon Telecommunications LLC .... E 336 855-1179
  Greensboro (G-6771)
Acterna LLC .... F 919 388-5100
  Morrisville (G-11277)
Alert Protection Systems Inc .... G 919 467-4357
  Raleigh (G-12487)
Avail Forensics LLC .... F 877 888-5895
  Wilmington (G-16125)
Btc Electronic Components LLC .... E 919 229-2162
  Wake Forest (G-15536)
▲ Cargotec Port Security LLC .... G 919 620-1763
  Durham (G-4998)
Commscope Technologies LLC .... F 919 329-8700
  Garner (G-6266)
Custom Light and Sound Inc .... E 919 286-1122
  Durham (G-5040)
Disco Hi-TEC America Inc .... G 919 468-6003
  Morrisville (G-11332)
Dupont Specialty Pdts USA LLC .... E 919 248-5109
  Durham (G-5070)
East West Manufacturing LLC .... G 704 663-5975
  Mooresville (G-10936)
Edwards Electronic Systems Inc .... E 919 359-2239
  Clayton (G-3976)
Extron Electronics .... G 919 850-1000
  Raleigh (G-12758)
His Company Inc .... G 800 537-0351
  Wilmington (G-16255)
▲ Huber + Suhner Inc .... E 704 790-7300
  Charlotte (G-2928)
▲ Huber + Suhner North Amer Corp .... D 704 790-7300
  Charlotte (G-2929)
Interconnect Products and .... E 336 667-3356
  Wilkesboro (G-16026)
Kuebler Inc .... F 704 705-4711
  Charlotte (G-3064)
▲ Lutze Inc .... E 704 504-0222
  Charlotte (G-3110)
▲ Majorpower Corporation .... E 919 563-6610
  Mebane (G-10418)
◆ Murata McHy USA Holdings Inc .... F 704 394-8331
  Charlotte (G-3220)
Serra Wireless Inc .... G 980 318-0873
  Charlotte (G-3529)
Synopsys Inc .... G 919 941-6600
  Morrisville (G-11437)
Tactical Support Equipment Inc .... F 910 425-3360
  Fayetteville (G-5924)
Telecmmnctons Resource MGT Inc .... F 919 779-0776
  Raleigh (G-13336)
Tellad Supply Company .... G 919 572-6700
  Durham (G-5392)
Total Technologies LLC .... G 336 259-5541
  Gastonia (G-6530)
United Chemi-Con Inc .... B 336 384-6903
  Lansing (G-9456)
US Microwave Inc .... G 520 891-2444
  Pittsboro (G-12353)
◆ Vishay Measurements Group Inc .... G 919 365-3800
  Wendell (G-15923)
Vrg Components Inc .... F 980 244-8462
  Indian Trail (G-8970)
◆ Walker and Associates Inc .... C 336 731-6391
  Lexington (G-9800)
▲ Wieland Electric Inc .... F 910 259-5050
  Wilmington (G-16442)

5072 Hardware

A&B Integrators LLC .... F 919 371-0750
  Durham (G-4897)
▲ AGM Carolina Inc .... G 336 431-4100
  High Point (G-8236)
Allegion Access Tech LLC .... E 704 789-7000
  Concord (G-4191)
◆ Bamal Corporation .... G 980 225-7700
  Charlotte (G-2273)
Belwith Products LLC .... G 336 841-3899
  High Point (G-8270)
Con-Tab Inc .... F 336 476-0104
  Thomasville (G-15206)
◆ Freud America Inc .... C 800 334-4107
  High Point (G-8360)
Godwin Door & Hardware Inc .... E 919 580-0543
  Goldsboro (G-6617)
◆ Grass America Inc .... G 336 996-4041
  Kernersville (G-9203)
◆ Greenworks North America LLC .... D 704 658-0539
  Mooresville (G-10965)
◆ Hickory Springs Manufactu .... D 828 328-2201
  Hickory (G-8052)
◆ Imperial Usa Ltd .... E 704 596-2444
  Charlotte (G-2954)
Joe Armstrong .... G 336 207-6503
  Greensboro (G-7138)
Restoration Hardware Inc .... F 919 544-4196
  Durham (G-5329)
RPM Wood Finishes Group Inc .... D 828 261-0325
  Hickory (G-8142)
◆ Salice America Inc .... E 704 841-7810
  Charlotte (G-3483)
▲ Sentinel Door Controls LLC .... F 704 921-4627
  Charlotte (G-3528)
Total Technologies LLC .... G 336 259-5541
  Gastonia (G-6530)
Triangle Indus Sup Hldings LLC .... E 704 395-0600
  Charlotte (G-3725)
◆ TTI Floor Care North Amer Inc .... B 440 996-2000
  Charlotte (G-3736)
Vista Products Inc .... D 910 582-0130
  Hamlet (G-7634)
Yat Usa Inc .... G 480 584-4096
  Huntersville (G-8908)

5074 Plumbing and hydronic heating supplies

510nano Inc .... F 919 521-5982
  Durham (G-4894)
▲ American Valve Inc .... D 336 668-0554
  Greensboro (G-6802)
▲ Brasscraft .... C 336 475-2131
  Thomasville (G-15189)
CTS Cleaning Systems Inc .... G 910 483-5349
  Fayetteville (G-5801)
DCE Solar Service Inc .... G 704 659-7474
  Cornelius (G-4539)
Drch Inc .... G 919 383-9421
  Durham (G-5063)
Exquisite Air and Water .... G 919 524-4625
  Raleigh (G-12757)
Ffi Holdings III Corp .... E 800 690-3650
  Charlotte (G-2755)
▼ Flologic Inc .... E 919 878-1808
  Morrisville (G-11342)
Genesis Water Technologies Inc .... E 704 360-5165
  Charlotte (G-2821)
Heat Transfer Sales of Th .... E 336 294-3838
  Greensboro (G-7085)
High Point Precast Pdts Inc .... G 336 434-1815
  Lexington (G-9730)
Jim Fab of North Carolina Inc .... E 704 278-1000
  Cleveland (G-4074)
Johnson Controls Inc .... E 704 521-8889
  Charlotte (G-3030)
McKenzie Supply Company .... G 910 276-1691
  Laurinburg (G-9489)
Mid-Atlantic Drainage Inc .... F 828 324-0808
  Conover (G-4472)
Plastic Oddities Inc .... E 704 484-1830
  Shelby (G-14355)
R Jacobs Fine Plbg & Hdwr Inc .... F 919 720-4202
  Raleigh (G-13167)
Roofing Tools and Eqp Inc .... G 252 291-1800
  Wilson (G-16534)
Scaltrol Inc .... G 678 990-0858
  Charlotte (G-3497)
Solar Hot Limited .... G 919 439-2387
  Raleigh (G-13276)
Sunqest Inc .... G 828 325-4910
  Newton (G-11975)
Work Well Hydrtion Systems LLC .... G 704 853-7788
  Gastonia (G-6543)
Zurn Industries LLC .... E 919 775-2255
  Sanford (G-14212)

5075 Warm air heating and air conditioning

▲ Appalachian Stove Fbrcators Inc .... F 828 253-0164
  Asheville (G-525)
Boles Holding Inc .... G 828 264-4200
  Boone (G-1178)
Envirnmntal Cmfort Sltions Inc .... E 980 272-7327
  Kannapolis (G-9119)
Ffi Holdings III Corp .... E 800 690-3650
  Charlotte (G-2755)
▼ Filtration Technology Inc .... G 336 294-5655
  Greensboro (G-7014)
Heat Transfer Sales of Th .... E 336 294-3838
  Greensboro (G-7085)
James M Pleasants Company Inc .... E 336 275-3152
  Greensboro (G-7133)
Johnson Controls Inc .... E 704 521-8889
  Charlotte (G-3030)
Kenny Fowler Heating and A Inc .... G 910 508-4553
  Wilmington (G-16288)
Kirk & Blum Manufacturing Co .... E 801 728-6533
  Greensboro (G-7152)
Nederman Mikropul LLC .... G 704 998-2600
  Charlotte (G-3246)
Ppa Industries Inc .... E 828 328-1142
  Hickory (G-8118)
Rheem Manufacturing Company .... C 336 495-6800
  Randleman (G-13488)
▲ Ricura Corporation .... F 704 875-0366
  Huntersville (G-8886)
Roofing Tools and Eqp Inc .... G 252 291-1800
  Wilson (G-16534)
Tfam Solutions LLC .... G 910 637-0266
  Aberdeen (G-31)
▲ Ultimate Products Inc .... F 919 836-1627
  Raleigh (G-13377)

5078 Refrigeration equipment and supplies

◆ Bally Refrigerated Boxes Inc .... C 252 240-2829
  Morehead City (G-11151)
Metalfab of North Carolina LLC .... C 704 841-1090
  Matthews (G-10271)
▲ Select Stainless Products LLC .... E 888 843-2345
  Charlotte (G-3524)
▲ TRf Manufacturing NC Inc .... E 252 223-1112
  Newport (G-11909)
W A Brown & Son Incorporated .... E 704 636-5131
  Salisbury (G-14063)

5082 Construction and mining machinery

Berco of America Inc .... E 336 931-1415
  Greensboro (G-6836)
Carolina Traffic Devices Inc .... F 704 588-7055
  Charlotte (G-2410)
◆ Cavotec USA Inc .... E 704 873-3009
  Mooresville (G-10900)
Component Sourcing Intl LLC .... E 704 843-9292
  Charlotte (G-2534)
▲ Cutting Systems Inc .... D 704 592-2451
  Union Grove (G-15436)
Gregory Poole Equipment Co .... F 919 872-2691
  Raleigh (G-12818)
James River Equipment .... E 704 821-7399
  Monroe (G-10747)
Lynn Ladder Scaffolding Co Inc .... G 301 336-4700
  Charlotte (G-3111)
M&N Construction Supply Inc .... G 336 996-7740
  Colfax (G-4154)
Quality Equipment LLC .... G 919 493-3545
  Durham (G-5312)
▼ Sound Heavy Machinery Inc .... G 910 782-2477
  Wilmington (G-16407)

5083 Farm and garden machinery

▲ Buy Smart Inc .... G 252 293-4700
  Wilson (G-16482)
D D Lawncare Service .... G 336 895-3353
  Gibsonville (G-6558)
Farm Services Inc .... G 336 226-7381
  Graham (G-6689)
General Fertilizer Eqp Inc .... F 336 299-4711
  Greensboro (G-7035)
Griffin Industries LLC .... E 704 624-9140
  Marshville (G-10217)
Ground Control Landscape MGT .... G 704 472-3448
  Shelby (G-14322)
North American Implements Inc .... G 336 476-2904
  Thomasville (G-15259)
▲ Southag Mfg Inc .... F 919 365-5111
  Wendell (G-15918)
Tar River Trading Post LLC .... G 919 589-3618
  Youngsville (G-17104)

5084 Industrial machinery and equipment

▲ Adwood Corporation .... E 336 884-1846
  High Point (G-8235)
Airgas Usa LLC .... F 704 394-1420
  Charlotte (G-2147)
Airgas Usa LLC .... F 704 333-5475
  Charlotte (G-2148)
Airgas Usa LLC .... G 919 544-3773
  Durham (G-4909)
Airgas Usa LLC .... G 919 735-5276
  Goldsboro (G-6587)
Airgas Usa LLC .... G 704 636-5049
  Salisbury (G-13916)
Airgas Usa LLC .... F 910 392-2711
  Wilmington (G-16098)
▼ Alamo Distribution LLC .... C 704 398-5600
  Belmont (G-974)
Amada America Inc .... G 877 262-3287
  High Point (G-8243)
◆ American Linc Corporation .... E 704 861-9242
  Gastonia (G-6346)
▲ American Trutzschler Inc .... D 704 399-4521
  Charlotte (G-2187)
Andy-OXY Co Inc .... E 828 258-0271
  Asheville (G-518)
◆ AP&t North America Inc .... F 704 292-2900
  Monroe (G-10648)
Apex Industrial Group LLC .... G 919 578-9039
  Sanford (G-14086)
Arbon Equipment Corporation .... F 414 355-2600
  Charlotte (G-2209)
Arc3 Gases Inc .... F 704 220-1029
  Monroe (G-10650)
Arc3 Gases Inc .... E 910 892-4016
  Dunn (G-4851)
Arnold S Welding Service Inc .... E 910 323-3822
  Fayetteville (G-5764)
Ask Elevator Service Inc .... G 336 674-2715
  Pleasant Garden (G-12356)
Automated Machine Technologies .... G 919 361-0121
  Morrisville (G-11297)
Babington Technology Inc .... G 252 984-0349
  Rocky Mount (G-13683)
▲ Basic Machinery Company Inc .... D 919 663-2244
  Siler City (G-14399)
Bear Pages .... G 828 837-0785
  Murphy (G-11706)
Birch Bros Southern Inc .... E 704 843-2111
  Waxhaw (G-15745)
▲ Bosch Rexroth Corporation .... E 704 583-4338
  Charlotte (G-2336)
Bunzl Processor Dist LLC .... G 910 738-8111
  Lumberton (G-10028)
▲ Burco Welding & Cutng Pdts Inc .... G 336 887-6100
  High Point (G-8278)
Burris Machine Company Inc .... G 828 322-6914
  Hickory (G-7955)
▲ C R Onsrud Inc .... E 704 508-7000
  Troutman (G-15368)
Carolina Material Handling Inc .... F 336 294-2346
  Greensboro (G-6889)
Carolina Moldings Inc .... F 704 523-7471
  Charlotte (G-2400)
▲ Carotek Inc .... D 704 844-1100
  Matthews (G-10238)
▲ Cefla North America Inc .... E 704 598-0020
  Charlotte (G-2437)
Chase-Logeman Corporation .... F 336 665-0754
  Greensboro (G-6905)
▲ Chiron America Inc .... D 704 587-9526
  Charlotte (G-2478)
Cintas Corporation No 2 .... D 336 632-4412
  Greensboro (G-6909)
◆ Clyde Union (us) Inc .... C 704 808-3000
  Charlotte (G-2503)
Community Brewing Ventures LLC .... G 800 579-6539
  Newton (G-11923)
Container Graphics Corp .... E 704 588-7230
  Pineville (G-12261)
▲ Container Graphics Corp .... F 919 481-4200
  Cary (G-1733)
▲ CPS Resources Inc .... E 704 628-7678
  Monroe (G-10697)
Crizaf Inc .... G 919 251-7661
  Durham (G-5037)
Cross Technologies Inc .... D 336 292-0511
  Whitsett (G-15987)
Cross Technologies Inc .... E 800 327-7727
  Greensboro (G-6942)
Crown Equipment Corporation .... E 336 291-2500
  Colfax (G-4146)
Cumins Machinery Corp .... G 336 622-1000
  Liberty (G-9809)
Cummins Atlantic LLC .... E 704 596-7690
  Charlotte (G-2584)
Cummins Atlantic LLC .... E 336 275-4531
  Greensboro (G-6946)
Cummins Atlantic LLC .... E 919 284-9111
  Kenly (G-9149)
▲ Cummins Atlantic LLC .... E 704 588-1240
  Charlotte (G-2585)
▲ Custom Hydraulics & Design .... F 704 347-0023
  Cherryville (G-3865)
Custom Machine Company Inc .... F 704 629-5326
  Bessemer City (G-1059)
▲ Deetag USA Inc .... G 828 465-2644
  Conover (G-4447)
Deurotech America Inc .... F 980 272-6827
  Charlotte (G-2623)
Digital Highpoint LLC .... C 336 883-7146
  High Point (G-8324)
▲ Diversfied Prtg Techniques Inc .... E 704 583-9433
  Charlotte (G-2644)
Diversified Energy LLC .... G 828 266-9800
  Boone (G-1194)
Drum Filter Media Inc .... G 336 434-4195
  High Point (G-8332)
Dudleys Fence Company .... G 252 566-5759
  La Grange (G-9440)
Dwd Industries LLC .... E 336 498-6327
  Randleman (G-13466)
Ellison Technologies Inc .... D 704 545-7362
  Charlotte (G-2699)
▲ Encertec Inc .... G 336 288-7226
  Greensboro (G-6997)
◆ Engine Systems Inc .... D 252 977-2720
  Rocky Mount (G-13695)
▲ Epic Enterprises Inc .... E 910 692-5750
  Southern Pines (G-14535)
◆ Fab-Con Machinery Dev Corp .... D 704 486-7120
  Oakboro (G-12074)
▲ Flanders/Csc LLC .... D 252 946-8081
  Washington (G-15702)
Glover Corporation Inc .... E 919 821-5535
  Raleigh (G-12807)
▲ Grecon Dimter Inc .... F 828 397-5139
  Connelly Springs (G-4402)
▲ Grecon Inc .... F 503 641-7731
  Charlotte (G-2862)
Gregory Poole Equipment Co .... G 252 931-5100
  Greenville (G-7535)
Gregory Poole Equipment Co .... F 919 872-2691
  Raleigh (G-12818)
Hargrove Countertops & ACC Inc .... E 919 981-0163
  Raleigh (G-12830)
▲ Hawe North America Inc .... E 704 509-1599
  Huntersville (G-8828)
Heat Transfer Sales of Th .... E 336 294-3838
  Greensboro (G-7085)
Hester Enterprises Inc .... E 704 865-4480
  Gastonia (G-6416)
Hiab USA Inc .... F 704 896-9089
  Cornelius (G-4555)
▼ His Glassworks Inc .... G 828 254-2559
  Asheville (G-653)
▲ Huber Technology Inc .... E 704 949-1010
  Denver (G-4782)
Hunter Fan Company .... G 704 896-9250
  Cornelius (G-4558)
▲ Hyde Park Partners Inc .... D 704 587-4819
  Charlotte (G-2939)
Hydralic Engnered Pdts Svc Inc .... G 704 374-1306
  Charlotte (G-2940)
I C E S Gaston County Inc .... G 704 263-1418
  Stanley (G-14697)
IMO Industries Inc .... C 704 289-6511
  Monroe (G-10738)
◆ Industrial Sup Solutions Inc .... E 704 636-4241
  Salisbury (G-13983)
▲ J & P Entrprses of Crlinas Inc .... E 704 861-1867
  Gastonia (G-6431)

50 WHOLESALE TRADE - DURABLE GOODS

J J Jenkins Incorporated .... E 704 821-6648
Matthews *(G-10324)*

James Oxygen and Supply Co .... E 704 322-5438
Hickory *(G-8071)*

▼ Kaufman Trailers Inc .... E 336 790-6800
Lexington *(G-9739)*

◆ LCI Corporation International .... E 704 399-7441
Charlotte *(G-3076)*

Ledger Hardware Inc .... G 828 688-4798
Bakersville *(G-885)*

▲ Ligna Machinery Inc .... E 336 584-0030
Burlington *(G-1451)*

Linor Technology Inc .... F 336 485-6199
Winston Salem *(G-16788)*

Livingston & Haven LLC .... E 704 588-3670
Charlotte *(G-3096)*

▲ Lock Drives Inc .... G 704 588-1844
Pineville *(G-12281)*

▲ Maag Reduction Inc .... E 704 716-9000
Charlotte *(G-3115)*

▲ Machine Tool Components LLC .... G 866 466-0120
Indian Trail *(G-8948)*

Machinex .... G 336 665-5030
High Point *(G-8436)*

Machinex Technologies Inc .... E 773 867-8801
High Point *(G-8437)*

Mang Systems Inc .... G 704 292-1041
Matthews *(G-10330)*

Material Handling Technologies Inc .... D 919 388-0050
Morrisville *(G-11388)*

Matheson Tri-Gas Inc .... F 919 556-6461
Wake Forest *(G-15571)*

Maxson & Associates .... G 336 632-0524
Greensboro *(G-7190)*

McDonald Services Inc .... G 704 753-9669
Monroe *(G-10769)*

▲ Mid-Atlantic Crane and Eqp Co .... E 919 790-3535
Raleigh *(G-13029)*

Mixon Mills Inc .... G 828 297-5431
Vilas *(G-15497)*

Mmj Machining and Fabg Inc .... F 336 495-1029
Randleman *(G-13479)*

◆ Monarch Knitting McHy Corp .... F 704 291-3300
Monroe *(G-10773)*

Morris Machine Company Inc .... G 704 824-4242
Gastonia *(G-6470)*

▲ Mount Hope Machinery Co .... F
Charlotte *(G-3208)*

Mro Stop LLC .... F 704 587-5429
Charlotte *(G-3210)*

▲ Mueller Die Cut Solutions Inc .... E 704 588-3900
Charlotte *(G-3213)*

◆ Murata Machinery Usa Inc .... C 704 875-9280
Charlotte *(G-3219)*

◆ Nederman Inc .... D 336 821-0827
Thomasville *(G-15255)*

▲ Nederman Corporation .... F 704 399-7441
Charlotte *(G-3244)*

Northline Nc LLC .... F 336 283-4811
Rural Hall *(G-13850)*

Oerlikon AM US Inc .... E 980 260-2827
Huntersville *(G-8870)*

Oerlikon Metco (us) Inc .... F 713 715-6300
Huntersville *(G-8871)*

▲ Okuma America Corporation .... C 704 588-7000
Charlotte *(G-3290)*

Otis Elevator Company .... G 828 251-1248
Asheville *(G-718)*

Otis Elevator Company .... C 704 519-0100
Charlotte *(G-3306)*

▲ Palmer Wahl Instruments Inc .... E 828 658-3131
Asheville *(G-721)*

◆ Pam Trading Corporation .... E 336 668-0901
Kernersville *(G-9224)*

Parker-Hannifin Corporation .... E 828 245-3233
Forest City *(G-6079)*

▲ Pavco Inc .... E 704 496-6800
Charlotte *(G-3321)*

Pcai Inc .... E 704 588-1240
Charlotte *(G-3323)*

Petroleum Tank Corporation .... F 919 284-2418
Kenly *(G-9155)*

Pharmaceutical Equipment Svcs .... G 239 699-9120
Asheville *(G-727)*

Phillips Corporation .... E 336 665-1080
Colfax *(G-4157)*

Port City Elevator Inc .... E 910 790-9300
Castle Hayne *(G-1959)*

Print Management Group LLC .... F 704 821-0114
Charlotte *(G-3385)*

▲ Psi-Polymer Systems Inc .... E 828 468-2600
Conover *(G-4490)*

Rapid Response Inc .... G 704 588-8890
Charlotte *(G-3409)*

Rock-Weld Industries Inc .... G 336 375-6862
Greensboro *(G-7315)*

Rodeco Company .... F 919 775-7149
Sanford *(G-14175)*

Rose Welding & Crane Service I .... G 252 796-9171
Columbia *(G-4167)*

RPM Plastics LLC .... E 704 871-0518
Statesville *(G-14881)*

◆ Russell Finex Inc .... F 704 588-9808
Pineville *(G-12299)*

Rvb Systems Group Inc .... G 919 362-5211
Garner *(G-6311)*

S Strickland Diesel Svc Inc .... G 252 291-6999
Wilson *(G-16536)*

▲ Schaefer Systems International Inc .... C 704 944-4500
Charlotte *(G-3499)*

Schaefer Systems Intl Inc .... G 704 944-4550
Charlotte *(G-3501)*

▲ Schelling America Inc .... E 919 544-0430
Morrisville *(G-11418)*

▲ Schmalz Inc .... C 919 713-0880
Raleigh *(G-13237)*

◆ Schunk Intec Inc .... D 919 572-2705
Morrisville *(G-11420)*

Sinnovatek Inc .... G 919 694-0974
Raleigh *(G-13264)*

Slack & Parr International .... G 704 527-2975
Dallas *(G-4658)*

▼ Sound Heavy Machinery Inc .... G 910 782-2477
Wilmington *(G-16407)*

▲ Southag Mfg Inc .... F 919 365-5111
Wendell *(G-15918)*

▲ Stanza Machinery Inc .... E 704 599-0623
Charlotte *(G-3622)*

▲ Stork United Corporation .... A 704 598-7171
Charlotte *(G-3639)*

Svcm .... G 305 767-3595
Lincolnton *(G-9924)*

T P Supply Co Inc .... E 336 789-2337
Mount Airy *(G-11585)*

Talladega Mchy & Sup Co NC .... G 256 362-4124
Fayetteville *(G-5925)*

▼ TCI Mobility Inc .... F 704 867-8331
Gastonia *(G-6520)*

Thomas M Brown Inc .... F 704 597-0246
Charlotte *(G-3690)*

Tk Elevator Corporation .... C 336 272-4563
Greensboro *(G-7404)*

Triangle Glass Service Inc .... G 919 477-9508
Durham *(G-5408)*

▲ U S Bottlers McHy Co Inc .... D 704 588-4750
Charlotte *(G-3744)*

◆ Vanguard Pai Lung LLC .... G 704 283-8171
Monroe *(G-10828)*

Vrg Components Inc .... F 980 244-3862
Indian Trail *(G-8970)*

Waste Container Repair Svcs .... G 910 257-4474
Fayetteville *(G-5949)*

Weathers Machine Mfg Inc .... F 919 552-5945
Fuquay Varina *(G-6238)*

West Dynamics Us Inc .... E 704 735-0009
Lincolnton *(G-9936)*

◆ Xaloy Extrusion LLC .... E 828 326-9888
Hickory *(G-8212)*

5085 Industrial supplies

A R Perry Corporation .... F 252 492-6181
Henderson *(G-7774)*

Airgas Usa LLC .... F 704 394-1420
Charlotte *(G-2147)*

Airgas Usa LLC .... G 919 544-3773
Durham *(G-4909)*

Airgas Usa LLC .... G 919 735-5276
Goldsboro *(G-6587)*

Alan R Williams Inc .... E 704 372-8281
Charlotte *(G-2151)*

Allyn International Trdg Corp .... G 877 858-2482
Marshville *(G-10210)*

Altra Industrial Motion Corp .... E 704 588-5610
Charlotte *(G-2174)*

▲ Apex Packaging Corporation LLC .... E 704 847-7274
Charlotte *(G-2200)*

Automated Designs Inc .... F 828 696-9625
Flat Rock *(G-5959)*

B & M Wholesale Inc .... G 336 789-3916
Mount Airy *(G-11479)*

Biganodes LLC .... G 828 245-1115
Forest City *(G-6060)*

▲ Bonomi North America Inc .... F 704 412-9031
Charlotte *(G-2333)*

Boston Gear LLC .... B 704 588-5610
Charlotte *(G-2337)*

Boxman Studios LLC .... G 704 333-3733
Charlotte *(G-2342)*

▲ Carolina Brush Company .... E 704 867-0286
Gastonia *(G-6366)*

Carolina Rubber & Spc Inc .... G 336 744-5111
Winston Salem *(G-16647)*

Carr Mill Supplies Inc .... G 336 883-0135
High Point *(G-8287)*

Consolidated Pipe & Sup Co Inc .... F 336 294-8577
Greensboro *(G-6930)*

Cross Technologies Inc .... G 336 370-4673
Greensboro *(G-6943)*

▲ Custom Hydraulics & Design .... F 704 347-0023
Cherryville *(G-3865)*

▲ D M & E Corporation .... E 704 482-8876
Shelby *(G-14309)*

▲ Dixon Valve & Coupling Co LLC .... F 704 334-9175
Dallas *(G-4637)*

Easth20 Holdings Llc .... G 919 313-2100
Greensboro *(G-6987)*

▲ Flo-Tite Inc Valves & Contrls .... E 910 738-8904
Lumberton *(G-10038)*

▼ Fortiline LLC .... E 704 788-9800
Concord *(G-4266)*

▲ Grasche USA Inc .... E 828 322-1226
Hickory *(G-8034)*

◆ Great Products Inc .... G 910 944-2020
Aberdeen *(G-5)*

▲ H-T-L Perma USA Ltd Partnr .... E 704 377-3100
Charlotte *(G-2879)*

Hamilton Indus Grinding Inc................... E .... 828 253-6796 Asheville *(G-647)*	Southern Spring & Stamping.................... F .... 336 548-3520 Stokesdale *(G-14949)*	Foxster Opco LLC.................................. E .... 910 297-6996 Hampstead *(G-7647)*
Harbisonwalker Intl Inc........................ G ..... 704 599-6540 Charlotte *(G-2887)*	Structural Materials Inc......................... G .... 828 754-6413 Lenoir *(G-9653)*	◆ Haeco Americas LLC............................A .... 336 668-4410 Greensboro *(G-7073)*
▲ Hawe North America Inc...................... E .... 704 509-1599 Huntersville *(G-8828)*	T P Supply Co Inc................................. E .... 336 789-2337 Mount Airy *(G-11585)*	Harsco Rail LLC.................................... G .... 980 960-2624 Charlotte *(G-2893)*
Holland Supply Company....................... E .... 252 492-7541 Henderson *(G-7788)*	Talladega Mchy & Sup Co NC................. G .... 256 362-4124 Fayetteville *(G-5925)*	Jones Marine Inc................................... G .... 704 639-0173 Salisbury *(G-13994)*
◆ Ideal Fastener Corporation...................C .... 919 693-3115 Oxford *(G-12133)*	Triangle Indus Sup Hldings LLC.............. G .... 704 395-0600 Charlotte *(G-3725)*	▲ Kck Holding Corp.................................. E .... 336 513-0002 Burlington *(G-1443)*
◆ Industrial Sup Solutions Inc...................E .... 704 636-4241 Salisbury *(G-13983)*	▲ Uchiyama Mfg Amer LLC...................... B .... 919 731-2364 Goldsboro *(G-6668)*	Ontic Engineering and Mfg Inc............... B .... 919 395-3908 Creedmoor *(G-4619)*
Ips Corporation....................................... E .... 919 598-2400 Durham *(G-5164)*	Wilmington Rbr & Gasket Co Inc............. F .... 910 762-4262 Wilmington *(G-16450)*	Rapid Response Technology LLC........... G .... 910 763-3856 Wilmington *(G-16378)*
Justice Bearing LLC............................... G .... 800 355-2500 Mooresville *(G-10993)*	**5087 Service establishment equipment**	◆ Trivantage LLC.....................................D .... 800 786-1876 Burlington *(G-1510)*
Laurinburg Machine Company............... G .... 910 276-0460 Laurinburg *(G-9484)*	Ace Industries Inc................................. G .... 336 427-5316 Madison *(G-10069)*	**5091 Sporting and recreation goods**
Lee Spring Company LLC....................... E .... 336 275-3631 Greensboro *(G-7165)*	American Sample House Inc.................. G .... 704 276-1970 Vale *(G-15463)*	Aqua Blue Inc.. G .... 704 896-9007 Cornelius *(G-4522)*
Loflin Handle Co Inc.............................. F .... 336 463-2422 Yadkinville *(G-17043)*	Anderson Living Center LLC................... G .... 828 229-3243 Forest City *(G-6059)*	Bic Corporation..................................... D .... 704 598-7700 Charlotte *(G-2308)*
▲ Ltd Industries LLC................................ E .... 704 897-2182 Charlotte *(G-3105)*	Asheville Vault Service Inc.................... E .... 828 665-6799 Candler *(G-1568)*	Custom Marine Fabrication Inc............... G .... 252 638-5422 New Bern *(G-11795)*
▲ Machine Tool Components LLC.............. G .... 866 466-0120 Indian Trail *(G-8948)*	Beco Holding Company Inc....................C .... 800 826-3473 Charlotte *(G-2295)*	Every Day Carry LLc.............................. F .... 203 231-0256 Winnabow *(G-16580)*
Mayo Resources Inc.............................. E .... 336 996-7776 Winston Salem *(G-16803)*	◆ Burts Bees Inc......................................C .... 919 998-5200 Durham *(G-4993)*	▲ Fathom Offshore Holdings LLC............. G .... 910 399-6882 Wilmington *(G-16217)*
▲ Measurement Controls Inc.................... F .... 704 921-1101 Charlotte *(G-3157)*	Cherryville Distrg Co Inc....................... G .... 704 435-9692 Cherryville *(G-3863)*	Golfstar Technology LLC....................... G .... 910 420-3122 Pinehurst *(G-12224)*
▲ Mmb One Inc.. F .... 704 523-8163 Charlotte *(G-3191)*	Cosmopros.. G .... 704 717-7420 Charlotte *(G-2560)*	Iconic Marine Group LLC...................... D .... 252 975-2000 Chocowinity *(G-3895)*
▲ Mount Hope Machinery Co..................... F Charlotte *(G-3208)*	CTS Cleaning Systems Inc..................... G .... 910 483-5349 Fayetteville *(G-5801)*	▲ Mettech Inc... G .... 919 833-9460 Raleigh *(G-13023)*
◆ Murata Machinery Usa Inc....................C .... 704 875-9280 Charlotte *(G-3219)*	▼ Fireresq Incorporated.......................... F .... 888 975-0858 Mooresville *(G-10945)*	North American Trade LLC................... G .... 828 712-3004 Fletcher *(G-6030)*
National Container Group LLC.............. G .... 704 393-9050 Charlotte *(G-3233)*	Gardner Machinery Corporation............. F .... 704 372-3890 Charlotte *(G-2808)*	S & S Trawl Shop Inc............................ G .... 910 842-9197 Supply *(G-15010)*
▲ Novaflex Hose Inc................................. D .... 336 578-2161 Haw River *(G-7755)*	Ice Companies Inc................................ G .... 910 791-1970 Wilmington *(G-16261)*	Thomas Golf Inc.................................... G .... 704 461-1342 Charlotte *(G-3689)*
▲ Oiles America Corporation.................... F .... 704 784-4500 Concord *(G-4324)*	Imperial Vault Company......................... E .... 336 983-6343 King *(G-9273)*	▲ Triplette Fencing Supply Inc................. G .... 336 835-1205 Elkin *(G-5630)*
Parker-Hannifin Corporation................... F .... 336 373-1761 Greensboro *(G-7245)*	Johnny Slicks Inc.................................. G .... 910 803-2159 Holly Ridge *(G-8683)*	◆ Trivantage LLC.....................................D .... 800 786-1876 Burlington *(G-1510)*
Person Printing Company Inc................. E .... 336 599-2146 Roxboro *(G-13818)*	Jorlink Usa Inc..................................... F .... 336 288-1613 Greensboro *(G-7140)*	◆ US Legend Cars Intl Inc........................E .... 704 455-3896 Harrisburg *(G-7732)*
Pioneer Motor Bearing Company............ E .... 704 937-7000 Kings Mountain *(G-9325)*	King Business Service Inc..................... G .... 910 610-1030 Laurinburg *(G-9483)*	**5092 Toys and hobby goods and supplies**
▲ Purolator Facet Inc............................... E .... 336 668-4444 Greensboro *(G-7293)*	Laundry Svc Tech Ltd Lblty Co............... G .... 908 327-1997 Matthews *(G-10262)*	Gerald Fisheries LLC............................. G .... 907 518-0004 New Bern *(G-11807)*
Purser Centl Rewinding Co Inc.............. F .... 704 786-3131 Concord *(G-4343)*	Lightning X Products Inc....................... G .... 704 295-0299 Charlotte *(G-3088)*	Grateful Union Family Inc....................... F .... 828 622-3258 Asheville *(G-640)*
Ravenox Rope....................................... G .... 336 226-5260 Burlington *(G-1482)*	M Davis and Associates LLC................. G .... 336 337-7089 Greensboro *(G-7172)*	World of RC Parts.................................. G .... 252 291-4088 Lucama *(G-10019)*
Reclaim Filters and Systems................. G .... 919 528-1787 Wake Forest *(G-15582)*	National Foam Inc.................................C .... 919 639-6101 Angier *(G-148)*	**5093 Scrap and waste materials**
Robert Bosch Tool Corporation.............. E .... 704 735-7464 Lincolnton *(G-9915)*	Signcaster Corporation.......................... G .... 336 712-2525 Winston Salem *(G-16908)*	Allyn International Trdg Corp................. G .... 877 858-2482 Marshville *(G-10210)*
Rubber Mill Inc...................................... G .... 336 622-1680 Conover *(G-4494)*	◆ Talley Machinery Corporation................G .... 336 664-0012 Greensboro *(G-7388)*	◆ Elan Trading Inc....................................E .... 704 342-1696 Charlotte *(G-2689)*
▲ Rubber Mill Inc..................................... E .... 336 622-1680 Liberty *(G-9830)*	UGLy Essentials LLC............................. F .... 910 319-9945 Raleigh *(G-13376)*	Fisherman Creations Inc........................ E .... 252 725-0138 Beaufort *(G-956)*
Sanders Company Inc........................... E .... 252 338-3995 Elizabeth City *(G-5569)*	Winston-Salem Casket Company........... G .... 336 661-1695 Winston Salem *(G-16984)*	Piedmont Paper Stock LLC.................... F .... 336 285-8592 Greensboro *(G-7259)*
▲ SAS Industries Inc............................... F .... 631 727-1441 Elizabeth City *(G-5570)*	**5088 Transportation equipment and supplies**	Renew Recycling LLC............................ D .... 919 550-8012 Clayton *(G-4007)*
Service and Equipment Company........... G .... 910 545-5886 Jacksonville *(G-9029)*	At Your Service Express LLC................. E .... 704 270-9918 Charlotte *(G-2229)*	S Foil Incorporated................................ F .... 704 455-5134 Harrisburg *(G-7725)*
Sherrill Contract Mfg Inc........................ F .... 704 922-7871 Dallas *(G-4657)*	Barbour S Marine Supply Co Inc............ F .... 252 728-2136 Beaufort *(G-944)*	◆ Umicore USA Inc...................................E .... 919 874-7171 Raleigh *(G-13379)*
Southern Rubber Company Inc.............. E .... 336 299-2456 Greensboro *(G-7355)*	Carolina Ground Svc Eqp Inc................. F .... 252 565-0288 New Bern *(G-11785)*	Wnc Dry Kiln Inc................................... F .... 828 652-0050 Marion *(G-10188)*

50 WHOLESALE TRADE - DURABLE GOODS

5094 Jewelry and precious stones

Bengal-Protea Ltd................................. G 336 299-0299
  Greensboro *(G-6834)*
Duncan Design Ltd................................ G 919 834-7713
  Raleigh *(G-12709)*
Gma Creative Inc................................... G 919 435-6984
  Wake Forest *(G-15561)*
Made By Custom LLC............................. G 704 980-9840
  Charlotte *(G-3117)*
NCSMJ Inc... F 704 544-1118
  Pineville *(G-12285)*
Soulku LLC... F 828 273-4278
  Asheville *(G-780)*
Sumpters Jwly & Collectibles................. G 704 399-5348
  Charlotte *(G-3649)*
▲ Trophy House Inc............................... F 910 323-1791
  Fayetteville *(G-5934)*

5099 Durable goods, nec

Allyn International Trdg Corp................. G 877 858-2482
  Marshville *(G-10210)*
▼ American Safety Utility Corp.............. E 704 482-0601
  Shelby *(G-14285)*
B & M Wholesale Inc............................. G 336 789-3916
  Mount Airy *(G-11479)*
Backwater Guns LLC............................. F 910 399-1451
  Wilmington *(G-16131)*
Beco Holding Company Inc.................. C 800 826-3473
  Charlotte *(G-2295)*
▲ Cda Inc... C
  Charlotte *(G-2434)*
Consolidated Elec Distrs Inc................. G 828 433-4689
  Morganton *(G-11207)*
Conway Development Inc..................... F 252 756-2168
  Greenville *(G-7505)*
Darren Lee Depalo................................ G 252 259-4515
  Havelock *(G-7741)*
Deberry Land & Timber Inc.................. G 910 572-2698
  Troy *(G-15403)*
Decima Corporation LLC....................... E 734 516-1535
  Charlotte *(G-2610)*
Domtar Paper Company LLC................ D 252 752-1100
  Greenville *(G-7515)*
Frazees Trophies................................... G 910 892-6722
  Dunn *(G-4869)*
GNB Ventures LLC............................... F 704 488-4468
  Charlotte *(G-2837)*
▲ Home Impressions Inc...................... B 828 328-1142
  Hickory *(G-8059)*
J L Smith & Co Inc............................... F 704 521-1088
  Charlotte *(G-3004)*
Lea Aid Acquisition Company............... F 919 872-6210
  Raleigh *(G-12963)*
M Davis and Associates LLC............... G 336 337-7089
  Greensboro *(G-7172)*
Memories of Orangeburg Inc................ G 803 533-0035
  Mooresville *(G-11020)*
◆ Norton Door Controls........................ E 704 233-4011
  Monroe *(G-10781)*
◆ Schaefer Systems International Inc... C 704 944-4500
  Charlotte *(G-3499)*
Schaefer Systems Intl Inc.................... G 704 944-4550
  Charlotte *(G-3501)*
Signature Signs Inc.............................. G 336 431-2072
  High Point *(G-8528)*
Song of Wood Ltd................................ G 828 669-7675
  Black Mountain *(G-1139)*
Sony Music Holdings Inc..................... G 336 886-1807
  High Point *(G-8542)*
South Eastern Electric Whl................... G 252 826-0123
  Scotland Neck *(G-14222)*

Speer Operational Tech LLC................. G 864 631-2512
  Marion *(G-10179)*
Sun Printing Company Inc.................... G 336 773-1346
  Winston Salem *(G-16923)*
◆ Trivantage LLC..................................D 800 786-1876
  Burlington *(G-1510)*
▲ VH Industries Inc.............................. E 704 743-2400
  Concord *(G-4385)*
◆ Walter Kidde Portable Eqp Inc.........B 919 563-5911
  Mebane *(G-10435)*
Wild Child Custom Graphics LLC........... G 910 762-5335
  Wilmington *(G-16443)*

51 WHOLESALE TRADE - NONDURABLE GOODS

5111 Printing and writing paper

Archie Supply LLC................................ G 336 987-0895
  Greensboro *(G-6813)*
▲ Jasie Blanks LLC.............................. F 910 485-0016
  Fayetteville *(G-5846)*
◆ McGrann Paper Corporation.............E 800 240-9455
  Charlotte *(G-3151)*

5112 Stationery and office supplies

Acme United Corporation...................... E 252 822-5051
  Rocky Mount *(G-13663)*
Archie Supply LLC................................ G 336 987-0895
  Greensboro *(G-6813)*
◆ Atrc Inc..D 919 872-5800
  Raleigh *(G-12531)*
Austin Business Forms Inc................... F 704 821-6165
  Indian Trail *(G-8922)*
Bic Corporation..................................... D 704 598-7700
  Charlotte *(G-2308)*
Cartridge World..................................... G 336 885-0989
  High Point *(G-8288)*
▼ Consolidated Press Inc...................... G 704 372-6785
  Charlotte *(G-2541)*
Devora Designs Inc.............................. G 336 782-0964
  Winston Salem *(G-16676)*
Digital Print & Imaging Inc.................... G 910 341-3005
  Wilmington *(G-16201)*
Fain Enterprises Inc.............................. G 336 724-0417
  Winston Salem *(G-16705)*
Gbf Inc.. D 336 665-0205
  High Point *(G-8363)*
Laser Recharge Carolina Inc................ F 919 467-5902
  Cary *(G-1808)*
Person Printing Company Inc............... E 336 599-2146
  Roxboro *(G-13818)*
Printing Press....................................... G 828 299-1234
  Asheville *(G-743)*
S Ruppe Inc.. E 828 287-4936
  Rutherfordton *(G-13889)*
Sdv Office Systems LLC...................... F 844 968-9500
  Fletcher *(G-6037)*
Sdv Office Systems LLC...................... G 844 968-9500
  Asheville *(G-767)*
Taylor Business Forms Inc................... G 336 667-0300
  North Wilkesboro *(G-12034)*
Wit & Whistle.. G 919 609-5309
  Cary *(G-1930)*

5113 Industrial and personal service paper

3d Packaging LLC................................ F 336 625-0652
  Asheboro *(G-397)*
Anderson Living Center LLC................. G 828 229-3243
  Forest City *(G-6059)*
Atlantic Corp Wilmington Inc................ E 910 259-3600
  Burgaw *(G-1333)*

◆ Atlantic Corp Wilmington Inc............D 910 343-0624
  Wilmington *(G-16121)*
▲ Axjo America Inc............................... E 828 322-6046
  Conover *(G-4420)*
▲ Box Board Products Inc.................... C 336 668-3347
  Greensboro *(G-6849)*
Box Company of America LLC............. E 910 582-0100
  Hamlet *(G-7617)*
C L Rabb Inc.. E 704 865-0295
  Gastonia *(G-6365)*
◆ Carolina Tape & Supply Corp............E 828 322-3991
  Hickory *(G-7968)*
Custom Packaging Inc......................... C 828 684-5060
  Arden *(G-323)*
▲ Eastcoast Packaging Inc................... E 919 562-6060
  Middlesex *(G-10447)*
Ferguson Supply and Box Mfg Co........ D 704 597-0310
  Charlotte *(G-2754)*
▲ Franklin Logistical Services Inc........ D 919 556-6711
  Youngsville *(G-17081)*
Freeman Container Company Inc.......... G 704 922-7972
  Dallas *(G-4641)*
Genpak LLC.. D 704 588-6202
  Charlotte *(G-2822)*
Georgia-Pacific LLC.............................. C 336 629-2151
  Asheboro *(G-440)*
Gold Medal Products Co...................... G 336 665-4997
  Greensboro *(G-7051)*
▲ Inplac North America Inc.................. G 704 587-1151
  Charlotte *(G-2976)*
Lls Investments Inc.............................. F 919 662-7283
  Raleigh *(G-12976)*
Packaging Corporation America........... F 704 664-5010
  Mooresville *(G-11046)*
▲ Packaging Unlimited NC Inc............. D 704 732-7100
  Lincolnton *(G-9912)*
Pactiv LLC.. E 336 292-2796
  Greensboro *(G-7240)*
Pactiv LLC.. F 828 758-7580
  Lenoir *(G-9645)*
Pratt Industries Inc............................... D 919 334-7400
  Raleigh *(G-13131)*
RLM/Universal Packaging Inc............... F 336 644-6161
  Greensboro *(G-7312)*
Thomco Inc... G 336 292-3300
  Greensboro *(G-7401)*
Veritiv Operating Company................... E 336 834-3488
  Greensboro *(G-7437)*
Westrock Rkt LLC................................ C 828 464-5560
  Conover *(G-4512)*
Wrkco Inc.. G 336 765-7004
  Winston Salem *(G-16988)*

5122 Drugs, proprietaries, and sundries

A M P Laboratories Ltd........................ G 704 894-9721
  Cornelius *(G-4519)*
▲ Ambra Le Roy LLC........................... G 704 392-7080
  Charlotte *(G-2179)*
Bartlett Milling Company LP................. E 704 487-5061
  Shelby *(G-14288)*
▲ Bioventus LLC.................................. D 800 396-4325
  Durham *(G-4963)*
◆ Bob Barker Company Inc..................C 800 334-9880
  Fuquay Varina *(G-6184)*
Burts Bees Inc...................................... B 919 998-5200
  Durham *(G-4994)*
Burts Bees Inc...................................... B 919 238-6450
  Morrisville *(G-11310)*
◆ Burts Bees Inc..................................C 919 998-5200
  Durham *(G-4993)*
Fidelity Pharmaceuticals LLC................ G 704 274-3192
  Huntersville *(G-8819)*

51 WHOLESALE TRADE - NONDURABLE GOODS

Glaxosmithkline LLC .... G 252 315-9774
  Durham *(G-5121)*
Glaxosmithkline LLC .... F 919 483-2100
  Durham *(G-5122)*
Glenmark Phrmceuticals Inc USA ... D 704 218-2600
  Monroe *(G-10723)*
Interntnal Agrclture Group LLC ...... F 908 323-3246
  Mooresville *(G-10983)*
Karamedica Inc .... G 919 302-1325
  Raleigh *(G-12930)*
Keller Cosmetics Inc .... G 704 399-2226
  Monroe *(G-10753)*
King Bio Inc .... D 828 255-0201
  Asheville *(G-675)*
◆ Mvp Group International Inc .... E 843 216-8380
  Elkin *(G-5627)*
Old Town Soap Co .... F 704 796-8775
  China Grove *(G-3886)*
Pfizer Inc .... C 919 775-7100
  Sanford *(G-14168)*
Pharmacutical Dimension .... G 336 664-5287
  Greensboro *(G-7253)*
▲ Philosophy Inc .... E 602 794-8701
  Sanford *(G-14169)*
◆ Premex Inc .... F 561 962-4128
  Durham *(G-5304)*
Purdue Pharmaceuticals LP .... F 252 265-1900
  Wilson *(G-16525)*
Random Rues Botanical LLC .... G 252 214-2759
  Greenville *(G-7579)*
Revlon Inc .... E 919 603-2000
  Oxford *(G-12149)*
Stiefel Laboratories Inc .... C 888 784-3335
  Durham *(G-5376)*
Stiefel Laboratories Inc .... E 888 784-3335
  Durham *(G-5375)*
UGLy Essentials LLC .... F 910 319-9945
  Raleigh *(G-13376)*
V1 Pharma LLC .... G 919 338-5744
  Raleigh *(G-13388)*

5131 Piece goods and notions

Adele Knits Inc .... C 336 499-6010
  Winston Salem *(G-16589)*
◆ Bob Barker Company Inc .... C 800 334-9880
  Fuquay Varina *(G-6184)*
▲ Champion Thread Company .... G 704 867-6611
  Gastonia *(G-6375)*
Classical Elements .... G 828 575-9145
  Asheville *(G-595)*
Cloth Barn Inc .... F 919 735-3643
  Goldsboro *(G-6601)*
◆ Continental Ticking Corp Amer ..... D 336 570-0091
  Alamance *(G-68)*
◆ Copland Industries Inc .... B 336 226-0272
  Burlington *(G-1400)*
Culp Inc .... E 662 844-7144
  Burlington *(G-1404)*
D & F Consolidated Inc .... G 704 664-6660
  Statesville *(G-14781)*
Distinctive Furniture Inc .... G 828 754-3947
  Lenoir *(G-9604)*
Domestic Fabrics Blankets Corp ... E 252 523-7948
  Kinston *(G-9359)*
◆ Freudenberg Prfmce Mtls LP .... D 919 479-7443
  Durham *(G-5104)*
▲ Gentry Mills Inc .... G 704 983-5555
  Albemarle *(G-86)*
◆ Global Textile Alliance Inc .... G 336 217-1300
  Reidsville *(G-13520)*
Heritage Prtg & Graphics Inc .... G 704 551-0700
  Charlotte *(G-2905)*

Langenthal Corporation .... F 336 969-9551
  Rural Hall *(G-13846)*
▲ Lantal Textiles Inc .... C 336 969-9551
  Rural Hall *(G-13847)*
▲ Morbern USA Inc .... E 336 883-4332
  High Point *(G-8459)*
NC Graphic Pros LLC .... G 252 492-7326
  Kittrell *(G-9397)*
New River Fabrics Inc .... G 704 462-1401
  Lawndale *(G-9502)*
▲ Oakhurst Textiles Inc .... E 336 668-0733
  Greensboro *(G-7229)*
Omnia LLC .... G 919 696-2193
  Oxford *(G-12138)*
Pearson Textiles Inc .... G 919 776-8730
  Sanford *(G-14165)*
▲ Polyvlies Usa Inc .... E 336 769-0206
  Winston Salem *(G-16860)*
Ripstop By Roll LLC .... F 877 525-7210
  Durham *(G-5332)*
Sam M Butler Inc .... E 704 364-8647
  Charlotte *(G-3487)*
◆ Selective Enterprises Inc .... C 704 588-3310
  Charlotte *(G-3525)*
Sml Raleigh LLC .... G 919 585-0100
  Clayton *(G-4010)*
Svcm .... G 305 767-3595
  Lincolnton *(G-9924)*
Warm Products Inc .... F 425 248-2424
  Hendersonville *(G-7913)*
Wovenart Inc .... F 828 859-6349
  Tryon *(G-15432)*

5136 Men's and boy's clothing

Apparel USA Inc .... E 212 869-5495
  Fairmont *(G-5700)*
Associated Distributors Inc .... G 910 895-5800
  Hamlet *(G-7616)*
Badger Sportswear LLC .... D 704 871-0990
  Statesville *(G-14757)*
◆ Bob Barker Company Inc .... C 800 334-9880
  Fuquay Varina *(G-6184)*
Burlington Coat Fctry Whse Cor ... E 919 468-9312
  Cary *(G-1718)*
Carolina Tailors Inc .... F 252 247-6469
  Newport *(G-11899)*
Ehs Retail LLC .... F 336 629-4367
  Asheboro *(G-428)*
◆ Gildan Activewear (eden) Inc .... C 336 623-9555
  Eden *(G-5491)*
◆ Gold Toe Stores Inc .... G 828 464-0751
  Newton *(G-11936)*
Home T LLC .... F 646 797-4768
  Charlotte *(G-2917)*
▲ Ics North America Corp .... E 704 794-6620
  Concord *(G-4283)*
▲ Madison Company Inc .... E 336 548-9624
  Madison *(G-10079)*
Marketing One Sportswear Inc ..... G 704 334-9333
  Charlotte *(G-3126)*
◆ Raleigh Workshop Inc .... E 919 917-8969
  Raleigh *(G-13188)*
▲ Sanders Industries Inc .... G 410 277-8565
  Waynesville *(G-15820)*
Seafarer LLC .... G 704 624-3200
  Marshville *(G-10224)*
Simmons Hosiery Mill Inc .... G 828 327-4890
  Hickory *(G-8157)*
Walter Reynolds .... G 704 735-6050
  Lincolnton *(G-9935)*

5137 Women's and children's clothing

AC Valor Reyes LLC .... G 910 431-3256
  Castle Hayne *(G-1941)*
Apparel USA Inc .... E 212 869-5495
  Fairmont *(G-5700)*
Badger Sportswear LLC .... D 704 871-0990
  Statesville *(G-14757)*
Burlington Coat Fctry Whse Cor ... E 919 468-9312
  Cary *(G-1718)*
Ehs Retail LLC .... F 336 629-4367
  Asheboro *(G-428)*
Gerson & Gerson Inc .... E 252 235-2441
  Middlesex *(G-10450)*
▲ Ics North America Corp .... E 704 794-6620
  Concord *(G-4283)*
Marketing One Sportswear Inc ..... G 704 334-9333
  Charlotte *(G-3126)*
Moon and Lola Inc .... G 919 306-2257
  Raleigh *(G-13040)*
◆ Parker Hosiery Company Inc .... E 828 668-7628
  Old Fort *(G-12104)*
◆ Raleigh Workshop Inc .... E 919 917-8969
  Raleigh *(G-13188)*
▲ Sanders Industries Inc .... G 410 277-8565
  Waynesville *(G-15820)*
Seafarer LLC .... G 704 624-3200
  Marshville *(G-10224)*
Simmons Hosiery Mill Inc .... G 828 327-4890
  Hickory *(G-8157)*
▲ Sorbe Ltd .... G 704 562-2991
  Matthews *(G-10344)*
Sue-Lynn Textiles Inc .... C 336 578-0871
  Haw River *(G-7757)*
▲ Sunrise Development LLC .... F 828 453-0590
  Mooresboro *(G-10841)*
Tiara Inc .... G 828 484-8236
  Asheville *(G-800)*
Tresmc LLC .... G 919 900-0868
  Knightdale *(G-9432)*
Walter Reynolds .... G 704 735-6050
  Lincolnton *(G-9935)*

5139 Footwear

◆ Implus Footcare LLC .... B 800 446-7587
  Durham *(G-5150)*
McRae Industries Inc .... C 910 439-6149
  Mount Gilead *(G-11605)*
VF Corporation .... G 336 424-6000
  Greensboro *(G-7438)*
VF Corporation .... F 336 424-6000
  Greensboro *(G-7439)*

5141 Groceries, general line

Alta Foods llc .... D 919 734-0233
  Goldsboro *(G-6588)*
▲ La Tortilleria LLC .... C 336 773-0010
  Winston Salem *(G-16782)*
◆ USa Wholesale and Distrg Inc ..... F 888 484-6872
  Fayetteville *(G-5945)*
▼ Value Clothing Inc .... E 704 638-6111
  Salisbury *(G-14061)*

5142 Packaged frozen goods

Evelyn T Burney .... G 336 473-9794
  Rocky Mount *(G-13697)*
▲ Monogram Food Solutions LLC ... E 901 685-7167
  Charlotte *(G-3200)*
Thomas Brothers Foods LLC .... F 336 672-0337
  Asheboro *(G-498)*

5143 Dairy products, except dried or canned

Celebrity Dairy LLC .... G 919 742-4931
  Siler City *(G-14404)*

51 WHOLESALE TRADE - NONDURABLE GOODS

Dfa Dairy Brands Fluid LLC .... G 704 341-2794
  Charlotte (G-2625)
Hershey Company .... F 919 284-0272
  Kenly (G-9153)
Lc Foods LLC .... G 919 510-6688
  Raleigh (G-12961)
Queen City Pastry Llc .... E 704 660-5706
  Mooresville (G-11066)
Tonys Ice Cream Co Inc .... G 704 853-0018
  Gastonia (G-6529)

5144 Poultry and poultry products

Carolina Egg Companies Inc .... D 252 459-2143
  Nashville (G-11739)

5145 Confectionery

Bilcat Inc .... E 828 295-3088
  Blowing Rock (G-1154)
Gold Medal Products Co .... G 336 665-4997
  Greensboro (G-7051)
▲ Lc America Inc .... F 336 676-5129
  Colfax (G-4153)
Lotus Bakeries Us LLC .... G 415 956-8956
  Mebane (G-10417)
Lrw Holdings Inc .... G 919 609-4172
  Durham (G-5196)
Snyders-Lance Inc .... A 704 554-1421
  Charlotte (G-3574)
Tastebuds LLC .... G 704 461-8755
  Belmont (G-1014)
◆ Tropical Nut & Fruit Co .... C 800 438-4470
  Charlotte (G-3731)

5146 Fish and seafoods

Atlantis Foods Inc .... E 336 768-6101
  Clemmons (G-4027)
B & J Seafood Co Inc .... E 252 637-0483
  New Bern (G-11775)
Bay Breeze Seafood Rest Inc .... E 828 697-7106
  Hendersonville (G-7824)
Capt Charlies Seafood Inc .... E 252 796-7278
  Columbia (G-4165)
Carolina Seafood Company Inc .... G 252 322-5455
  Aurora (G-833)
◆ Classic Seafood Group Inc .... C 252 746-2818
  Ayden (G-849)
Gillikin Marine Railways Inc .... G 252 726-7284
  Beaufort (G-958)
Janet W Whitbeck Inc .... G 252 986-2800
  Hatteras (G-7737)
Lloyds Oyster House Inc .... E 910 754-6958
  Shallotte (G-14276)
Lowland Seafood Inc .... G 252 745-3751
  Lowland (G-10014)
Pamlico Packing Co Inc .... F 252 745-3688
  Vandemere (G-15489)
Pamlico Packing Co Inc .... F 252 745-3688
  Grantsboro (G-6765)
▲ Quality Foods From Sea Inc .... D 252 338-5455
  Elizabeth City (G-5565)
Quality Seafood Co Inc .... E 252 338-2800
  Elizabeth City (G-5566)

5147 Meats and meat products

Alexanders Ham Company Inc .... F 704 857-9222
  Mooresville (G-10853)
Bass Farms Inc .... E 252 478-4147
  Spring Hope (G-14613)
Goodnight Brothers Prod Co Inc .... E 828 264-8892
  Boone (G-1201)
Julian Freirich Food Products .... E 704 636-2621
  Salisbury (G-13997)

▲ Monogram Food Solutions LLC .... E 901 685-7167
  Charlotte (G-3200)
▼ Star Food Products Inc .... D 336 227-4079
  Burlington (G-1501)
Stevens Packing Inc .... G 336 274-6033
  Greensboro (G-7371)
Thomas Brothers Foods LLC .... F 336 672-0337
  Asheboro (G-498)

5148 Fresh fruits and vegetables

Aseptia Inc .... C 678 373-6751
  Raleigh (G-12528)
◆ Dole Food Company Inc .... E 818 874-4000
  Charlotte (G-2650)

5149 Groceries and related products, nec

◆ Azure Skye Beverages Inc .... G 704 909-7394
  Charlotte (G-2251)
Bakeboxx Company .... F 336 861-1212
  High Point (G-8262)
Bakers Southern Traditions Inc .... G 252 344-2120
  Roxobel (G-13829)
▲ Celtic Ocean International Inc .... E 828 299-9005
  Arden (G-320)
Chef Martini LLC .... A 919 327-3183
  Raleigh (G-12618)
Chocolate Fetish LLC .... G 828 258-2353
  Asheville (G-592)
Chocolate Smiles Village LLC .... G 919 469-5282
  Cary (G-1729)
Choice USA Beverage Inc .... G 704 487-6951
  Shelby (G-14294)
Clay County Food Pantry Inc .... G 828 389-1657
  Hayesville (G-7761)
Coca Cola Bottling Co .... G 704 509-1812
  Charlotte (G-2516)
Coca-Cola Consolidated Inc .... G 919 550-0611
  Clayton (G-3968)
Coca-Cola Consolidated Inc .... D 252 334-1820
  Elizabeth City (G-5535)
Dfa Dairy Brands Fluid LLC .... G 704 341-2794
  Charlotte (G-2625)
Escazu Artisan Chocolate LLC .... F 919 832-3433
  Raleigh (G-12745)
Fosterscape LLP .... G 910 401-7638
  Fayetteville (G-5827)
Gerald Fisheries LLC .... G 907 518-0004
  New Bern (G-11807)
▲ Great Eastern Sun Trdg Co Inc .... F 828 665-7790
  Asheville (G-642)
Hare Asian Trading Company LLC .... E 910 524-4667
  Burgaw (G-1340)
Interntnal Agrclture Group LLC .... F 908 323-3246
  Mooresville (G-10983)
◆ Krispy Kreme Doughnuts Inc .... C 336 725-2981
  Winston Salem (G-16781)
▲ Larrys Beans Inc .... E 919 828-1234
  Raleigh (G-12958)
◆ Liqui-Box Corporation .... D 804 325-1400
  Charlotte (G-3092)
Lotus Bakeries Us LLC .... G 415 956-8956
  Mebane (G-10417)
Novas Bakery Inc .... F 704 333-5566
  Charlotte (G-3275)
Pepsi Bottling Ventures LLC .... C 919 863-4000
  Garner (G-6301)
Pepsi Bottling Ventures LLC .... E 252 451-1811
  Rocky Mount (G-13719)
Pepsi Bottling Ventures LLC .... D 910 792-5400
  Wilmington (G-16351)
Pepsi Bottling Ventures LLC .... C 336 724-4800
  Winston Salem (G-16842)

Pepsi-Cola Btlg Hickry NC Inc .... G 828 322-8090
  Granite Falls (G-6749)
Pepsi-Cola Btlg Hickry NC Inc .... E 828 322-8090
  Hickory (G-8110)
Pepsi-Cola Btlg Hickry NC Inc .... C 828 322-8090
  Hickory (G-8111)
Pepsi-Cola Metro Btlg Co Inc .... A 336 896-4000
  Winston Salem (G-16843)
Random Rues Botanical LLC .... G 252 214-2759
  Greenville (G-7579)
Royal Cup Inc .... F 704 597-5756
  Charlotte (G-3463)
◆ S & D Coffee Inc .... A 704 782-3121
  Concord (G-4355)
Sistas 4 Life Food Svcs LLC .... G 704 957-6437
  Charlotte (G-3557)
Stony Gap Wholesale Co Inc .... G 704 982-5360
  Albemarle (G-109)
◆ Suntory International .... F 917 756-2747
  Raleigh (G-13316)
Tracys Gourmet LLC .... G 919 672-1731
  Asheville (G-804)
Tradewinds Coffee Co Inc .... F 919 556-1835
  Zebulon (G-17144)
◆ Tropical Nut & Fruit Co .... C 800 438-4470
  Charlotte (G-3731)
Vintage South Inc .... G 919 362-4079
  Apex (G-253)
Zeskp LLC .... G 910 762-8300
  Wilmington (G-16460)

5153 Grain and field beans

C A Perry & Son Inc .... G 252 330-2323
  Elizabeth City (G-5532)
C A Perry & Son Inc .... E 252 221-4463
  Hobbsville (G-8675)
Catawba Farms Enterprises LLC .... F 828 464-5780
  Newton (G-11917)
▲ Celtic Ocean International Inc .... E 828 299-9005
  Arden (G-320)
Clapp Fertilizer and Trckg Inc .... G 336 449-6103
  Whitsett (G-15986)
▲ Farm Chemicals Inc .... F 910 875-4277
  Raeford (G-12420)

5159 Farm-product raw materials, nec

C A Perry & Son Inc .... G 252 330-2323
  Elizabeth City (G-5532)
C A Perry & Son Inc .... E 252 221-4463
  Hobbsville (G-8675)
East Crlina Olseed Prcssors LL .... D 252 935-5553
  Pantego (G-12163)
▼ Northampton Peanut Company .... D 252 585-0916
  Severn (G-14268)
Pluto Labs LLC .... G 919 691-3550
  Oxford (G-12144)
Powell & Stokes Inc .... G 252 794-2138
  Windsor (G-16568)
Pyxus International Inc .... C 252 753-8000
  Farmville (G-5742)
◆ USa Wholesale and Distrg Inc .... F 888 484-6872
  Fayetteville (G-5945)

5162 Plastics materials and basic shapes

▲ Ace Plastics Inc .... G 704 527-5752
  Charlotte (G-2127)
◆ Advanced Marketing International Inc .... F 910 392-0508
  Wilmington (G-16095)
Advanced Plastiform Inc .... D 919 404-2080
  Zebulon (G-17117)
◆ Advanced Technology Inc .... E 336 668-0488
  Greensboro (G-6783)

SIC SECTION 51 WHOLESALE TRADE - NONDURABLE GOODS

Cardinal Plastics Inc .... G 704 739-9420
   Kings Mountain *(G-9298)*

Custom Extrusion Inc .... G 336 495-7070
   Asheboro *(G-420)*

Easth20 Holdings Llc .... G 919 313-2100
   Greensboro *(G-6987)*

Endless Plastics Inc .... F 336 346-1839
   Greensboro *(G-6998)*

◆ Interlam Corporation .... E 336 786-6254
   Mount Airy *(G-11523)*

Mdsi Inc .... G 919 783-8730
   Browns Summit *(G-1312)*

Mdt Bromley LLC .... E 828 651-8737
   Fletcher *(G-6021)*

▲ Mpe Usa Inc .... E 704 340-4910
   Pineville *(G-12284)*

◆ Piedmont Plastics Inc .... D 704 597-8200
   Charlotte *(G-3340)*

Poly-Tech Industrial Inc .... E 704 948-8055
   Huntersville *(G-8878)*

◆ Reichhold Holdings Us Inc .... A 919 990-7500
   Durham *(G-5323)*

Tri-Star Plastics Corp .... E 704 598-2800
   Denver *(G-4810)*

▲ United Plastics Corporation .... C 336 786-2127
   Mount Airy *(G-11592)*

▲ Wilbert Plstic Svcs Acqstion L .... E 704 455-5191
   Harrisburg *(G-7735)*

5169 Chemicals and allied products, nec

A House of Hemp LLC .... G 910 984-1441
   Linden *(G-9938)*

Access Technologies LLC .... G 574 286-1255
   Mooresville *(G-10847)*

Ada Marketing Inc .... E 910 221-2189
   Dunn *(G-4848)*

◆ Advanced Marketing International Inc .. F 910 392-0508
   Wilmington *(G-16095)*

Air & Gas Solutions LLC .... E 704 897-2182
   Charlotte *(G-2146)*

Airgas Usa LLC .... F 704 394-1420
   Charlotte *(G-2147)*

Airgas Usa LLC .... G 919 544-1056
   Durham *(G-4908)*

Airgas Usa LLC .... G 919 544-3773
   Durham *(G-4909)*

Airgas Usa LLC .... G 919 735-5276
   Goldsboro *(G-6587)*

American Chrome & Chem NA Inc .... G 910 675-7200
   Castle Hayne *(G-1942)*

Arc3 Gases Inc .... F 336 275-3333
   Greensboro *(G-6812)*

Arc3 Gases Inc .... F 704 220-1029
   Monroe *(G-10650)*

Arc3 Gases Inc .... E 910 892-4016
   Dunn *(G-4851)*

◆ Burlington Chemical Co LLC .... G 336 584-0111
   Greensboro *(G-6861)*

Carolina Bg .... G 704 847-8840
   Matthews *(G-10236)*

▲ Chem-Tex Laboratories Inc .... E 706 602-8600
   Concord *(G-4232)*

◆ Coatings and Adhesives Corp .... C 910 371-3184
   Leland *(G-9537)*

Custom Nano Inc .... G 919 608-3540
   Raleigh *(G-12665)*

Desco Equipment Company Inc .... G 704 873-2844
   Statesville *(G-14787)*

Eminess Technologies Inc .... E 704 283-2600
   Monroe *(G-10713)*

Explosives Supply Company .... F 828 765-2762
   Spruce Pine *(G-14640)*

▲ Fibex LLC .... G 336 605-9002
   Colfax *(G-4150)*

Fil-Chem Inc .... G 919 878-1270
   Raleigh *(G-12766)*

Fortrans Inc .... G 919 365-8004
   Wendell *(G-15902)*

▼ Greenology Products LLC .... E 877 473-3650
   Raleigh *(G-12815)*

James Oxygen and Supply Co .... E 704 322-5438
   Hickory *(G-8071)*

Jci Jones Chemicals Inc .... E 704 392-9767
   Charlotte *(G-3014)*

◆ Jowat Corporation .... D 336 434-9000
   Archdale *(G-289)*

Jowat International Corp .... E 336 434-9000
   Archdale *(G-290)*

▲ Kincol Industries Incorporated .... G 704 372-8435
   Charlotte *(G-3055)*

Kymera International LLC .... F 919 544-8090
   Durham *(G-5184)*

Lathers Skin Essentials .... G 828 449-9244
   Hickory *(G-8084)*

Leke LLC .... G 704 523-1452
   Pineville *(G-12280)*

Marlowe-Van Loan Sales Co .... F 336 882-3351
   High Point *(G-8441)*

◆ Maxam North America Inc .... F 214 736-8100
   Mooresville *(G-11018)*

▲ Melatex Incorporated .... F 704 332-5046
   Charlotte *(G-3162)*

◆ Newell Novelty Co Inc .... G 336 597-2246
   Roxboro *(G-13808)*

▲ Oxlife of NC LLC .... G 828 684-7353
   Hendersonville *(G-7889)*

▲ Pavco Inc .... E 704 496-6800
   Charlotte *(G-3321)*

Pencco Inc .... F 252 235-5300
   Middlesex *(G-10453)*

▲ Polytec Inc .... E 704 277-3960
   Mooresville *(G-11055)*

Qualice LLC .... F 910 419-6589
   Hamlet *(G-7630)*

▼ Reedy International Corp .... F 980 819-6930
   Charlotte *(G-3424)*

▲ Reichhold Holdings Us Inc .... A 919 990-7500
   Durham *(G-5323)*

▲ Sostram Corporation .... G 919 226-1195
   Durham *(G-5364)*

South / Win LLC .... D 336 398-5650
   Greensboro *(G-7350)*

▲ T - Square Enterprises Inc .... G 704 846-8233
   Charlotte *(G-3667)*

Textile Rubber and Chem Co Inc .... G 704 376-3582
   Indian Trail *(G-8968)*

◆ Umicore USA Inc .... E 919 874-7171
   Raleigh *(G-13379)*

◆ Universal Preservachem Inc .... D 732 568-1266
   Mebane *(G-10434)*

5171 Petroleum bulk stations and terminals

▼ Warren Oil Company LLC .... D 910 892-6456
   Dunn *(G-4890)*

5172 Petroleum products, nec

Apergy Artfl Lift Intl LLC .... F 919 934-1533
   Smithfield *(G-14449)*

Crossroads Fuel Service Inc .... E 252 426-5216
   Hertford *(G-7918)*

Danisson USA Trading Ltd LLC .... G 704 965-8317
   Kernersville *(G-9188)*

Euliss Oil Company Inc .... G 336 622-3055
   Liberty *(G-9813)*

Herrin Bros Coal & Ice Co .... G 704 332-2193
   Charlotte *(G-2906)*

▼ Moroil Corp .... F 704 795-9595
   Concord *(G-4319)*

Nelson Holdings Nc Inc .... F 828 322-9226
   Hickory *(G-8100)*

Panenergy Corp .... F 704 594-6200
   Charlotte *(G-3310)*

Sg-Clw Inc .... F 336 865-4980
   Winston Salem *(G-16903)*

South Central Oil and Prpn Inc .... G 704 982-2173
   Albemarle *(G-106)*

Southern States Coop Inc .... F 910 285-8213
   Wallace *(G-15628)*

Volta Group Corporation LLC .... G 919 637-0273
   Raleigh *(G-13408)*

▼ Warren Oil Company LLC .... D 910 892-6456
   Dunn *(G-4890)*

5181 Beer and ale

Glass Jug .... F 919 818-6907
   Durham *(G-5116)*

Glass Jug LLC .... F 919 813-0135
   Durham *(G-5117)*

Koi Pond Brewing Company LLC .... G 252 231-1660
   Rocky Mount *(G-13706)*

Salty Turtle Beer Company .... E 910 803-2019
   Surf City *(G-15016)*

White Street Brewing Co Inc .... E 919 647-9439
   Youngsville *(G-17115)*

5182 Wine and distilled beverages

Aviator Brewing Company Inc .... G 919 601-5497
   Holly Springs *(G-8687)*

Drink A Bull LLC .... G 919 818-3321
   Durham *(G-5065)*

Outer Banks Craft Distlg LLC .... G 252 423-3011
   Manteo *(G-10128)*

5191 Farm supplies

▲ AG Provision LLC .... E 910 296-0302
   Kenansville *(G-9140)*

Boggs Farm Center Inc .... G 704 538-7176
   Fallston *(G-5728)*

◆ Brushy Mountain Bee Farm Inc .... E 336 921-3640
   Winston Salem *(G-16639)*

C A Perry & Son Inc .... G 252 330-2323
   Elizabeth City *(G-5532)*

C A Perry & Son Inc .... E 252 221-4463
   Hobbsville *(G-8675)*

Camp Chemical Corporation .... F 336 597-2214
   Roxboro *(G-13797)*

Carolina Greenhouse Plants Inc .... F 252 523-9300
   Kinston *(G-9350)*

Clapp Fertilizer and Trckg Inc .... G 336 449-6103
   Whitsett *(G-15986)*

Coastal Agrobusiness Inc .... G 828 697-2220
   Flat Rock *(G-5963)*

Coastal Agrobusiness Inc .... G 252 798-3481
   Hamilton *(G-7613)*

◆ Coastal Agrobusiness Inc .... D 252 238-7391
   Greenville *(G-7503)*

G & M Milling Co Inc .... E 704 873-5758
   Statesville *(G-14802)*

Goodnight Brothers Prod Co Inc .... E 828 264-8892
   Boone *(G-1201)*

Harvey Fertilizer and Gas Co .... E 252 753-2063
   Farmville *(G-5738)*

Harvey Fertilizer and Gas Co .... F 252 523-9090
   Kinston *(G-9368)*

▲ Harvey Fertilizer and Gas Co .... E 252 526-4150
   Kinston *(G-9369)*

51 WHOLESALE TRADE - NONDURABLE GOODS

Helena Agri-Enterprises LLC .... G 828 685-1182
  Hendersonville *(G-7861)*
Helena Agri-Enterprises LLC .... F 910 422-8901
  Rowland *(G-13789)*
◆ Herbal Innovations LLC .... E 336 818-2332
  Wilkesboro *(G-16024)*
◆ Industrial and Agricultur .... E 910 843-2121
  Red Springs *(G-13501)*
Mountaire Farms LLC .... B 910 974-3232
  Candor *(G-1596)*
Mountaire Farms Inc .... D 910 844-3126
  Maxton *(G-10361)*
Nutrien AG Solutions Inc .... G 252 585-0282
  Conway *(G-4516)*
Nutrien AG Solutions Inc .... F 252 977-2025
  Rocky Mount *(G-13670)*
Southern AG Insecticides Inc .... E 828 264-8843
  Boone *(G-1238)*
Southern AG Insecticides Inc .... E 828 692-2233
  Hendersonville *(G-7902)*
Southern States Coop Inc .... E 704 872-6364
  Statesville *(G-14896)*
Southern States Coop Inc .... E 910 285-8213
  Wallace *(G-15628)*
Thompson Sunny Acres Inc .... G 910 206-1801
  Rockingham *(G-13644)*
▲ Upl NA Inc .... E 610 491-2800
  Durham *(G-5426)*

5192 Books, periodicals, and newspapers

Book Lover Search .... G 336 889-6127
  High Point *(G-8274)*
Cherokee Publications .... G 828 627-2424
  Cherokee *(G-3854)*
Comfort Publishing Svcs LLC .... G 704 907-7848
  Concord *(G-4236)*
▲ Gryphon House Inc .... E 800 638-0928
  Lewisville *(G-9667)*
Oxford University Press LLC .... B 919 677-0977
  Cary *(G-1840)*
Wisdom House Books Inc .... G 919 883-4669
  Chapel Hill *(G-2098)*

5193 Flowers and florists supplies

Government Sales LLC .... G 252 726-6315
  Morehead City *(G-11172)*
Jefferson Group Inc .... E 252 752-6195
  Greenville *(G-7549)*

5194 Tobacco and tobacco products

Mr Tobacco .... G 919 747-9052
  Raleigh *(G-13047)*
Royal Blunts Connections Inc .... G 919 961-4910
  Raleigh *(G-13214)*

5198 Paints, varnishes, and supplies

Akzo Nobel Coatings Inc .... G 336 665-9897
  Greensboro *(G-6787)*
Bonakemi Usa Incorporated .... C 704 218-3917
  Monroe *(G-10667)*
Controlled Release Tech Inc .... G 704 487-0878
  Shelby *(G-14303)*
Highland International LLC .... F 828 265-2513
  Boone *(G-1207)*
◆ Keim Mineral Coatings Amer Inc .... F 704 588-4811
  Charlotte *(G-3048)*
Renaissance Innovations LLC .... G 844 473-7246
  Apex *(G-239)*
Sherwin-Williams Company .... E 336 292-3000
  Greensboro *(G-7335)*
Sherwin-Williams Company .... G 919 436-2460
  Raleigh *(G-13248)*

5199 Nondurable goods, nec

3d Packaging LLC .... F 336 625-0652
  Asheboro *(G-397)*
American Plush Tex Mills LLC .... F 765 609-0456
  Red Springs *(G-13495)*
◆ Aquafil OMara Inc .... C 828 874-2100
  Rutherford College *(G-13858)*
▲ Arcona Leather Company LLC .... G 828 396-7728
  Hudson *(G-8761)*
Aseptia Inc .... G 678 373-6751
  Raleigh *(G-12528)*
B & B Leather Co Inc .... F 704 598-9080
  Charlotte *(G-2252)*
B F I Industries Inc .... G 919 229-4509
  Wake Forest *(G-15529)*
Badger Sportswear LLC .... D 704 871-0990
  Statesville *(G-14757)*
Bickerstaff Trees Inc .... G 336 372-8866
  Sparta *(G-14589)*
Blue Stone Industries Ltd .... G 919 379-3986
  Cary *(G-1709)*
Burlow Promotions Inc .... G 336 856-0500
  Greensboro *(G-6869)*
C & M Enterprise Inc .... G 704 545-1180
  Mint Hill *(G-10524)*
▲ Cardinal Container Svcs Inc .... D 336 249-6816
  Lexington *(G-9689)*
Carroll Companies Inc .... F 828 466-5489
  Conover *(G-4434)*
▲ Carroll Companies Inc .... E 828 264-2521
  Boone *(G-1184)*
Carroll Signs & Advertising .... G 336 983-3415
  King *(G-9267)*
◆ Causekeepers Inc .... E 336 824-2518
  Franklinville *(G-6167)*
Cedar Hill Studio & Gallery .... G 828 456-6344
  Waynesville *(G-15797)*
◆ Conitex Sonoco Usa Inc .... C 704 864-5406
  Gastonia *(G-6384)*
Consumer Concepts .... F 252 247-7000
  Morehead City *(G-11164)*
Crown Trophy Inc .... G 336 851-1011
  Greensboro *(G-6944)*
Dale Advertising Inc .... G 704 484-0971
  Shelby *(G-14310)*
▲ Daztech Inc .... G 800 862-6360
  Wilmington *(G-16196)*
Dicks Store .... G 336 548-9358
  Madison *(G-10073)*
Dobbins Products .... G 919 580-0621
  Goldsboro *(G-6610)*
▲ Fibex LLC .... G 336 605-9002
  Colfax *(G-4150)*
Freudenberg Prfmce Mtls LP .... C 828 665-5000
  Candler *(G-1579)*
Geami Ltd .... E 919 654-7700
  Raleigh *(G-12791)*
Global Packaging Inc .... D 610 666-1608
  Hamlet *(G-7622)*
Gourmet Foods USA LLC .... G 704 248-1724
  Cornelius *(G-4552)*
Heritage Prtg & Graphics Inc .... G 704 551-0700
  Charlotte *(G-2905)*
▲ Hibco Plastics Inc .... E 336 463-2391
  Yadkinville *(G-17040)*
▲ Hyosung Holdings Usa Inc .... G 704 790-6134
  Charlotte *(G-2942)*
▲ Hyosung Usa Inc .... E 704 790-6100
  Charlotte *(G-2943)*
Identify Yourself LLC .... F 252 202-1452
  Kitty Hawk *(G-9407)*

Ink n Stitches LLC .... G 336 633-3898
  Asheboro *(G-444)*
International Foam Pdts Inc .... G 704 588-0080
  Charlotte *(G-2982)*
International Pet ACC LLC .... G 919 964-0738
  Raleigh *(G-12900)*
▲ Interntnal Tray Pads Packg Inc .... E 910 944-1800
  Aberdeen *(G-8)*
▲ J & P Entrprses of Crlinas Inc .... E 704 861-1867
  Gastonia *(G-6431)*
J R Craver & Associates Inc .... E 336 769-3330
  Clemmons *(G-4049)*
Jenkins Properties Inc .... E 336 667-4282
  North Wilkesboro *(G-12017)*
◆ Leather Miracles LLC .... D 828 464-7448
  Hickory *(G-8086)*
Legacy River Company .... G 704 618-7260
  Charlotte *(G-3081)*
Loparex LLC .... C 336 635-0192
  Eden *(G-5496)*
Map Supply Inc .... G 336 731-3230
  Flat Rock *(G-5969)*
Markell Publishing Company Inc .... G 336 226-7148
  Burlington *(G-1454)*
Marketing One Sportswear Inc .... G 704 334-9333
  Charlotte *(G-3126)*
Memories of Orangeburg Inc .... G 803 533-0035
  Mooresville *(G-11020)*
◆ Microfine Inc .... G 336 768-1480
  Winston Salem *(G-16809)*
Mm Clayton LLC .... B 919 553-4113
  Clayton *(G-3997)*
◆ Normtex Incorporated .... G 828 428-3363
  Wilmington *(G-16341)*
Office Sup Svcs Inc Charlotte .... E 704 786-4677
  Concord *(G-4323)*
Olympic Products LLC .... D 336 378-9620
  Greensboro *(G-7231)*
▲ Packaging Unlimited NC Inc .... D 704 732-7100
  Lincolnton *(G-9912)*
Pactiv LLC .... G 910 944-1800
  Aberdeen *(G-20)*
▼ Poly Packaging Systems Inc .... D 336 889-8334
  High Point *(G-8489)*
Pregis Innovative Packg LLC .... E 847 597-2200
  Granite Falls *(G-6751)*
Pretium Packaging LLC .... E 336 621-1891
  Greensboro *(G-7280)*
▲ Project Bean LLC .... D 201 438-1598
  Harrisburg *(G-7723)*
PSM Enterprises Inc .... F 336 789-8888
  Mount Airy *(G-11561)*
Quiknit Crafting Inc .... G 704 861-1030
  Gastonia *(G-6499)*
Richa Inc .... G 704 944-0230
  Charlotte *(G-3448)*
Richa Inc .... F 704 331-9744
  Charlotte *(G-3449)*
RLM/Universal Packaging Inc .... F 336 644-6161
  Greensboro *(G-7312)*
Silverlining Screen Prtrs Inc .... G 919 554-0340
  Youngsville *(G-17097)*
Snyder Paper Corporation .... G 828 464-1189
  Newton *(G-11969)*
◆ Sonoco Hickory Inc .... D 828 328-2466
  Hickory *(G-8163)*
Storopack Inc .... G 800 827-7225
  Winston Salem *(G-16918)*
◆ Stump Printing Co Inc .... C 260 723-5171
  Wrightsville Beach *(G-17028)*
Sun Printing Company Inc .... G 336 773-1346
  Winston Salem *(G-16923)*

52 BUILDING MATERIALS, HARDWARE, GARDEN SUPPLIES & MOBILE HOMES

T & R Signs... G 919 779-1185
  Garner (G-6317)
▲ Tannis Root Productions Inc .... G 919 832-8552
  Raleigh (G-13327)
◆ Tesa Tape Inc .... D 704 554-0707
  Charlotte (G-3682)
Textile Manufacturing Tech LLC .... G 828 632-3012
  Taylorsville (G-15173)
Thompson Printing & Packg Inc .... G 704 313-7323
  Mooresboro (G-10842)
Tobacco Outlet Products LLC .... G 704 341-9388
  Charlotte (G-3702)
◆ Trivantage LLC .... D 800 786-1876
  Burlington (G-1510)
Unified2 Globl Packg Group LLC .... G 774 696-3643
  Durham (G-5420)
Unique Stone Incorporated .... G 910 817-9450
  Rockingham (G-13645)
Wholesale Kennel Supply Co .... G 919 742-2515
  Siler City (G-14434)

52 BUILDING MATERIALS, HARDWARE, GARDEN SUPPLIES & MOBILE HOMES

5211 Lumber and other building materials

All Glass Inc .... G 828 324-8609
  Hickory (G-7931)
Alligood Cabinet Shop .... G 252 927-3201
  Washington (G-15681)
◆ Amarr Company .... C 336 744-5100
  Winston Salem (G-16602)
Atlantic Coastal Enterprises .... G 910 478-0777
  Jacksonville (G-8988)
Authentic Iron LLC .... G 910 648-6989
  Bladenboro (G-1143)
Barber Furniture & Supply .... F 704 278-4367
  Cleveland (G-4068)
▲ Bfs Asset Holdings LLC .... C 303 784-4288
  Raleigh (G-12554)
▲ Bfs Operations LLC .... A 919 431-1000
  Raleigh (G-12555)
Big Pine Log and Lumber Inc .... G 828 656-2754
  Marshall (G-10200)
Blue Ridge Lbr Log & Timber Co .... F 336 961-5211
  Yadkinville (G-17033)
Builders Firstsource Inc .... G 336 884-5454
  Greensboro (G-6860)
Builders Firstsource Inc .... G 919 562-6601
  Youngsville (G-17072)
Builders Firstsource - SE Grp .... G 910 313-3056
  Wilmington (G-16144)
Builders Frstsrce - Rleigh LLC .... D 919 363-4956
  Apex (G-174)
Builders Frstsrce - Sthast Gro .... D 910 944-2516
  Aberdeen (G-2)
C & M Industrial Supply Co .... G 704 483-4001
  Mill Spring (G-10484)
C & R Building Supply Inc .... E 910 567-6293
  Autryville (G-840)
Carolina Cab Specialist LLC .... G 919 818-4375
  Cary (G-1724)
Carport Central Inc .... D 980 321-9898
  Mount Airy (G-11491)
Cleveland Lumber Company .... E 704 487-5263
  Shelby (G-14298)
Concrete Service Company .... G 910 590-0035
  Clinton (G-4093)
▲ Cummins Atlantic LLC .... E 704 588-1240
  Charlotte (G-2585)

▲ Design Surfaces Inc .... F 919 781-0310
  Raleigh (G-12679)
Division 10 .... G 919 661-1101
  Raleigh (G-12689)
E W Godwin S Sons Inc .... E 910 762-7747
  Wilmington (G-16208)
Energy Svers Windows Doors Inc .... G 252 758-8700
  Greenville (G-7523)
General Shale Brick Inc .... F 704 937-7431
  Grover (G-7607)
General Wholesale Bldg Sup Co .... D 252 638-5861
  New Bern (G-11806)
Glenn Lumber Company Inc .... E 704 434-7873
  Shelby (G-14320)
▲ GLG Corporation .... F 336 784-0396
  Winston Salem (G-16722)
Glover Materials Inc .... G 252 536-2660
  Pleasant Hill (G-12364)
Goodman Millwork Inc .... E 704 633-2421
  Salisbury (G-13972)
Green River Resource MGT .... F 828 697-0357
  Zirconia (G-17153)
▼ Hardwood Store of NC Inc .... F 336 449-9627
  Gibsonville (G-6561)
Hargrove Countertops & ACC Inc .... E 919 981-0163
  Raleigh (G-12830)
Henderson & Kirkland Inc .... G 252 355-0224
  Winterville (G-17002)
Hewlin Brothers Lumber Co .... G 252 586-6473
  Enfield (G-5679)
Hunter Millwork Inc .... F 704 821-0144
  Matthews (G-10321)
Interrs-Exteriors Asheboro Inc .... F 336 629-2148
  Asheboro (G-446)
Ivey Ln Inc .... G 336 230-0062
  Greensboro (G-7129)
Jak Moulding & Supply Inc .... F 252 753-5546
  Walstonburg (G-15638)
Lee Builder Mart Inc .... E
  Sanford (G-14147)
Leonard Block Company .... F 336 764-0607
  Winston Salem (G-16786)
M O Deviney Lumber Co Inc .... G 704 538-9071
  Casar (G-1934)
Marsh Furniture Company .... F 336 273-8196
  Greensboro (G-7182)
Matthews Building Supply Co .... E 704 847-2106
  Matthews (G-10268)
Maxson & Associates .... G 336 632-0524
  Greensboro (G-7190)
Mint Hill Cabinet Shop Inc .... E 704 821-9373
  Monroe (G-10770)
Mkc85 Inc .... F 910 762-1986
  Wilmington (G-16325)
Mountain Showcase Group Inc .... E 828 692-9494
  Hendersonville (G-7881)
Native Naturalz Inc .... F 336 334-2984
  Greensboro (G-7213)
Pine Hall Brick Co Inc .... F 336 721-7500
  Madison (G-10083)
Powell Industries Inc .... D 828 926-9114
  Waynesville (G-15815)
Precision Cabinets Inc .... G 828 262-5080
  Boone (G-1228)
Privette Enterprises Inc .... E 704 634-3291
  Monroe (G-10789)
Robbinsville Cstm Molding Inc .... F 828 479-2317
  Robbinsville (G-13610)
Ronald Lee Fulbright Lbr Inc .... F 704 462-1421
  Vale (G-15471)
Salt Wood Products Inc .... G 252 830-8875
  Greenville (G-7581)

Selectbuild Construction Inc .... E 208 331-4300
  Raleigh (G-13244)
Shutter Production Inc .... G 910 289-2620
  Rose Hill (G-13781)
Sipe Lumber Company Inc .... E 828 632-4679
  Taylorsville (G-15167)
Smith Companies Lexington Inc .... G 336 249-4941
  Lexington (G-9781)
Smokey Mountain Lumber Inc .... G 828 298-3958
  Asheville (G-775)
Sorrells Cabinet Co Inc .... G 919 639-4320
  Lillington (G-9860)
Southeastern Hardwoods Inc .... G 828 581-0197
  Swannanoa (G-15037)
Southern Concrete Materials Inc .... C 828 253-6421
  Asheville (G-783)
▲ Southland Electrical Sup LLC .... C 336 227-1486
  Burlington (G-1498)
▲ Stock Building Supply Hol .... A 919 431-1000
  Raleigh (G-13305)
T E Johnson Lumber Co Inc .... F 919 963-2233
  Four Oaks (G-6113)
Thomas Concrete SC Inc .... G 704 868-4545
  Gastonia (G-6526)
Tice Kitchens & Interiors LLC .... F 919 366-4117
  Raleigh (G-13350)
▲ TRf Manufacturing NC Inc .... E 252 223-1112
  Newport (G-11909)
Triad Corrugated Metal Inc .... E 336 625-9727
  Asheboro (G-499)
Triad Prefinish & Lbr Sls Inc .... G 336 375-4849
  Greensboro (G-7415)
Triangle Brick Company .... E 704 695-1420
  Wadesboro (G-15518)
▲ Triangle Brick Company .... E 919 544-1796
  Durham (G-5406)
Ufp Site Built LLC .... F 910 590-3220
  Clinton (G-4117)
Viktors Gran MBL Kit Cnter Top .... F 828 681-0713
  Arden (G-389)
Walton Lumber Co .... G 919 563-6565
  Mebane (G-10436)
▲ William Stone & Tile Inc .... G 910 353-0914
  Hubert (G-8757)
Yadkin Lumber Company Inc .... F 336 679-2432
  Yadkinville (G-17064)

5231 Paint, glass, and wallpaper stores

Capitol Funds Inc .... F 910 439-5275
  Mount Gilead (G-11599)
Capitol Funds Inc .... E 704 487-8547
  Shelby (G-14291)
Classy Glass Inc .... G 828 452-2242
  Waynesville (G-15798)
Cleveland Lumber Company .... E 704 487-5263
  Shelby (G-14298)
Done-Gone Adios Inc .... F 336 993-7300
  Kernersville (G-9192)
▲ Industrial Glass Tech LLC .... F 704 853-2429
  Gastonia (G-6426)
Lbm Industries Inc .... F 828 966-4270
  Sapphire (G-14214)
Ledger Hardware Inc .... G 828 688-4798
  Bakersville (G-885)
Orare Inc .... G 919 742-1003
  Siler City (G-14429)
Sherwin-Williams Company .... E 336 292-3000
  Greensboro (G-7335)
Triangle Glass Service Inc .... G 919 477-9508
  Durham (G-5408)
W G Cannon Paint Co Inc .... G 828 754-5376
  Lenoir (G-9659)

52 BUILDING MATERIALS, HARDWARE, GARDEN SUPPLIES & MOBILE HOMES

5251 Hardware stores

- ◆ Ace Marine Rigging & Supply Inc .... F 252 726-6620
  Morehead City *(G-11148)*
- ▲ AGM Carolina Inc .... G 336 431-4100
  High Point *(G-8236)*
- B&C Xterior Cleaning Svc Inc .... G 919 779-7905
  Raleigh *(G-12540)*
- ▲ Bfs Operations LLC .... A 919 431-1000
  Raleigh *(G-12555)*
- Bolton Investors Inc .... G 919 471-1197
  Durham *(G-4971)*
- C & M Industrial Supply Co .... G 704 483-4001
  Mill Spring *(G-10484)*
- Capitol Funds Inc .... F 910 439-5275
  Mount Gilead *(G-11599)*
- Capitol Funds Inc .... E 704 487-8547
  Shelby *(G-14291)*
- Castle Hayne Hardware LLC .... F 910 675-9205
  Castle Hayne *(G-1945)*
- Discount Pallet Services LLC .... G 910 892-3760
  Dunn *(G-4862)*
- ◆ Gesipa Fasteners Usa Inc .... F 609 208-1740
  Mocksville *(G-10578)*
- ▲ Hudson S Hardware Inc .... E 919 553-3030
  Garner *(G-6276)*
- Joe Armstrong .... G 336 207-6503
  Greensboro *(G-7138)*
- Ledger Hardware Inc .... G 828 688-4798
  Bakersville *(G-885)*
- Matthews Building Supply Co .... E 704 847-2106
  Matthews *(G-10268)*
- Merrill Resources Inc .... G 828 877-4450
  Penrose *(G-12186)*
- Quality Equipment LLC .... G 919 493-3545
  Durham *(G-5312)*
- ▲ Shopbot Tools Inc .... E 919 680-4800
  Durham *(G-5354)*
- ◆ Snap-On Power Tools Inc .... C 828 835-4400
  Murphy *(G-11717)*
- Steelman Milling Company Inc .... G 336 463-5586
  Yadkinville *(G-17051)*
- ▲ Stock Building Supply Hol .... A 919 431-1000
  Raleigh *(G-13305)*
- Triad Cutting Tools Inc .... G 336 873-8708
  Asheboro *(G-500)*
- W E Nixons Wldg & Hdwr Inc .... G 252 221-4348
  Edenton *(G-5523)*
- Yat Usa Inc .... G 480 584-4096
  Huntersville *(G-8908)*

5261 Retail nurseries and garden stores

- American Soil and Mulch Inc .... F 919 460-1349
  Raleigh *(G-12499)*
- Certified Lawnmower Inc .... G 704 527-2765
  Belmont *(G-978)*
- Farm Services Inc .... G 336 226-7381
  Graham *(G-6689)*
- ▲ I Must Garden LLC .... G 919 929-2299
  Raleigh *(G-12872)*
- Mineral Springs Fertilizer Inc .... G 704 843-2683
  Mineral Springs *(G-10518)*
- Quality Equipment LLC .... G 919 493-3545
  Durham *(G-5312)*
- R E Mason Enterprises Inc .... G 910 483-5016
  Fayetteville *(G-5904)*
- Southern States Coop Inc .... F 336 599-2185
  Roxboro *(G-13824)*
- Stanly Tractor Company .... G 704 983-1106
  New London *(G-11879)*
- ▲ Vegherb LLC .... G 800 914-9835
  Erwin *(G-5689)*

5271 Mobile home dealers

- ▲ Cutting Systems Inc .... D 704 592-2451
  Union Grove *(G-15436)*
- ▼ Deltec Homes Inc .... E 828 253-0483
  Asheville *(G-607)*
- Home City Ltd .... G 910 428-2196
  Biscoe *(G-1111)*

53 GENERAL MERCHANDISE STORES

5311 Department stores

- Belk Department Stores LP .... C 704 357-4000
  Charlotte *(G-2298)*
- Burlington Coat Fctry Whse Cor .... E 919 468-9312
  Cary *(G-1718)*
- ◆ Gildan Activewear (eden) Inc .... C 336 623-9555
  Eden *(G-5491)*
- Val-U-King Group Inc .... G 980 306-5342
  Gastonia *(G-6536)*

5331 Variety stores

- Atlantic Trading LLC .... F
  Charlotte *(G-2233)*
- Brasingtons Inc .... G 704 694-5191
  Wadesboro *(G-15503)*
- Infinity S End Inc .... F 704 900-8355
  Charlotte *(G-2968)*

5399 Miscellaneous general merchandise

- Village Produce & Cntry Str In .... G 336 661-8685
  Winston Salem *(G-16962)*

54 FOOD STORES

5411 Grocery stores

- Amko Express Inc .... G 336 434-7192
  Archdale *(G-266)*
- B & D Enterprises Inc .... F 704 739-2958
  Kings Mountain *(G-9293)*
- Bluff Mountain Outfitters Inc .... G 828 622-7162
  Hot Springs *(G-8744)*
- Cardinal Foods LLC .... E 910 259-9407
  Burgaw *(G-1334)*
- Clean Catch Fish Market LLC .... G 704 333-1212
  Charlotte *(G-2494)*
- Coker Feed Mill Inc .... F 919 778-3491
  Goldsboro *(G-6602)*
- Communitys Kitchen L3c .... G 828 817-2308
  Tryon *(G-15423)*
- Harris Teeter LLC .... D 704 846-7117
  Matthews *(G-10252)*
- Harris Teeter LLC .... D 919 859-0110
  Raleigh *(G-12831)*
- Ingles Markets Incorporated .... D 704 434-0096
  Boiling Springs *(G-1161)*
- J L Powell & Co Inc .... G 910 642-8989
  Whiteville *(G-15967)*
- James Fods Frnchise Corp Amer .... G 336 437-0393
  Graham *(G-6694)*
- Kol Incorporated .... G 919 872-2340
  Raleigh *(G-12945)*
- Rose Ice & Coal Company .... F 910 762-2464
  Wilmington *(G-16387)*
- Ruddick Operating Company LLC .... A 704 372-5404
  Charlotte *(G-3472)*
- Stevens Packing Inc .... G 336 274-6033
  Greensboro *(G-7371)*
- Whole Harvest Foods LLC .... E 910 293-7917
  Warsaw *(G-15677)*

5421 Meat and fish markets

- Acre Station Meat Farm Inc .... F 252 927-3700
  Pinetown *(G-12243)*
- Ashe Hams Inc .... G 828 259-9426
  Asheville *(G-530)*
- Clean Catch Fish Market LLC .... G 704 333-1212
  Charlotte *(G-2494)*
- Mitchells Meat Processing .... F 336 591-7420
  Walnut Cove *(G-15633)*
- Mt Airy Meat Center Inc .... F 336 786-2023
  Mount Airy *(G-11548)*
- Stevens Packing Inc .... G 336 274-6033
  Greensboro *(G-7371)*
- Suncrest Farms Cntry Hams Inc .... E 336 667-4441
  Wilkesboro *(G-16044)*
- Wells Jnkins Wells Mt Proc Inc .... G 828 245-5544
  Forest City *(G-6086)*

5441 Candy, nut, and confectionery stores

- Bilcat Inc .... E 828 295-3088
  Blowing Rock *(G-1154)*
- Butterfields Candy LLC .... G 252 459-2577
  Nashville *(G-11738)*
- Chocolate Fetish LLC .... G 828 258-2353
  Asheville *(G-592)*
- Chocolate Smiles Village LLC .... G 919 469-5282
  Cary *(G-1729)*
- French Broad Chocolates LLC .... G 828 252-4181
  Asheville *(G-629)*
- ▼ Northampton Peanut Company .... D 252 585-0916
  Severn *(G-14268)*
- Sachs Peanuts LLC .... F 910 647-4711
  Clarkton *(G-3948)*
- Shallowford Farms Popcorn Inc .... G 336 463-5938
  Yadkinville *(G-17050)*
- Sugar Pops .... G 704 799-0959
  Mooresville *(G-11107)*
- Tastebuds LLC .... G 704 461-8755
  Belmont *(G-1014)*

5451 Dairy products stores

- Bilcat Inc .... E 828 295-3088
  Blowing Rock *(G-1154)*
- Buffalo Creek Farm & Crmry LLC .... G 336 969-5698
  Germanton *(G-6552)*
- Dewey S Bakery Inc .... F 336 748-0230
  Winston Salem *(G-16677)*
- G & M Milling Co Inc .... E 704 873-5758
  Statesville *(G-14802)*
- Goodberry Creamery Inc .... F 919 878-8870
  Wake Forest *(G-15562)*
- ▲ Mooresville Ice Cream Com .... E 704 664-5456
  Mooresville *(G-11024)*
- Paletria La Mnrca McHacana LLC .... G 919 803-0636
  Raleigh *(G-13095)*
- ▲ Tony S Ice Cream Company Inc .... F 704 867-7085
  Gastonia *(G-6528)*

5461 Retail bakeries

- Bakeboxx Company .... F 336 861-1212
  High Point *(G-8262)*
- Chestnut Land Company .... G 828 299-9108
  Asheville *(G-590)*
- Dewey S Bakery Inc .... F 336 748-0230
  Winston Salem *(G-16677)*
- Dunkin Donuts .... F 919 217-9603
  Knightdale *(G-9417)*
- Ingles Markets Incorporated .... D 704 434-0096
  Boiling Springs *(G-1161)*
- Krispy Kreme Doughnut Corp .... E 919 669-6151
  Gastonia *(G-6440)*

SIC SECTION

55 AUTOMOTIVE DEALERS AND GASOLINE SERVICE STATIONS

Krispy Kreme Doughnut Corp............. E 336 854-8275
  Greensboro (G-7158)
Krispy Kreme Doughnut Corp............. E 336 733-3780
  Winston Salem (G-16779)
Krispy Kreme Doughnut Corp............. E 336 726-8908
  Winston Salem (G-16780)
◆ Krispy Kreme Doughnut Corp............ C 980 270-7117
  Charlotte (G-3062)
◆ Krispy Kreme Doughnuts Inc............. C 336 725-2981
  Winston Salem (G-16781)
Normandie Bakery Inc............. G 910 686-1372
  Wilmington (G-16340)
Novas Bakery Inc............. F 704 333-5566
  Charlotte (G-3275)
SE Co-Brand Ventures LLC............. G 704 598-9322
  Charlotte (G-3514)
Sprinkle of Sugar LLC............. G 336 474-8620
  Thomasville (G-15281)
Swirl Oakhurst LLC............. G 704 258-1209
  Charlotte (G-3662)
Wildflour Bakery Inc............. G 828 749-9224
  Saluda (G-14075)

5499 Miscellaneous food stores

▲ Atlantic Natural Foods LLC............. D 888 491-0524
  Nashville (G-11734)
Bakers Southern Traditions Inc............. G 252 344-2120
  Roxobel (G-13829)
Blazing Foods LLC............. G 336 865-2933
  Charlotte (G-2320)
Blue Ridge Jams............. G 828 685-1783
  Hendersonville (G-7826)
Daily Manufacturing Inc............. F 704 782-0700
  Rockwell (G-13651)
Goodstuff Juices LLC............. G 252 347-2341
  Greenville (G-7532)
◆ Herbal Innovations LLC............. E 336 818-2332
  Wilkesboro (G-16024)
Induction Food Systems Inc............. G 919 907-0179
  Raleigh (G-12883)
Lc Foods LLC............. G 919 510-6688
  Raleigh (G-12961)
Ludlam Family Foods LLC............. G 919 805-6061
  Chapel Hill (G-2035)
McDonalds............. F 910 295-1112
  Pinehurst (G-12229)
Natures Pharmacy Inc............. G 828 251-0094
  Asheville (G-710)
Nutrotonic LLC............. F 855 948-0008
  Charlotte (G-3285)
Random Rues Botanical LLC............. G 252 214-2759
  Greenville (G-7579)
Stormberg Foods LLC............. E 919 947-6011
  Goldsboro (G-6662)
◆ Suntory International............. F 917 756-2747
  Raleigh (G-13316)
Tradewinds Coffee Co Inc............. F 919 556-1835
  Zebulon (G-17144)
Well-Bean Coffee & Crumbs LLC............. G 833 777-2326
  Wake Forest (G-15612)

55 AUTOMOTIVE DEALERS AND GASOLINE SERVICE STATIONS

5511 New and used car dealers

ABB Motors and Mechanical Inc............. C 828 645-1706
  Weaverville (G-15836)
▼ Axle Holdings LLC............. E 800 895-3276
  Concord (G-4203)
Courtesy Ford Inc............. E 252 338-4783
  Elizabeth City (G-5537)
Daimler Truck North Amer LLC............. A 704 645-5000
  Cleveland (G-4071)
Dutch Miller Charlotte Inc............. E 704 522-8422
  Charlotte (G-2660)
▲ Saab Barracuda LLC............. E 910 814-3088
  Lillington (G-9859)
Streets Auto Sales & Four WD............. G 704 888-8686
  Locust (G-9973)
Subaru Folger Automotive............. E 704 531-8888
  Charlotte (G-3645)
Vestal Buick Gmc Inc............. D 336 310-0261
  Kernersville (G-9251)
◆ Volvo Trucks North America Inc............. A 336 393-2000
  Greensboro (G-7450)
Window Motor World Inc............. G 800 252-2649
  Boone (G-1250)

5521 Used car dealers

Courtesy Ford Inc............. E 252 338-4783
  Elizabeth City (G-5537)
G A Lankford Construction............. G 828 254-2467
  Alexander (G-118)
Quality Investments Inc............. E 252 492-8777
  Henderson (G-7805)

5531 Auto and home supply stores

A 1 Tire Service Inc............. G 828 684-1860
  Fletcher (G-5978)
Accel Discount Tire............. G 704 636-0323
  Salisbury (G-13913)
Advance Stores Company Inc............. F 336 545-9091
  Greensboro (G-6780)
Aiken-Black Tire Service Inc............. E 828 322-3736
  Hickory (G-7930)
Albemarle Tire Retreading Inc............. G 704 982-4113
  Albemarle (G-71)
Alk Investments LLC............. G 984 233-5353
  Raleigh (G-12488)
Avery County Recapping Co Inc............. E 828 733-0161
  Newland (G-11881)
Bill Martin Inc............. F 704 873-0241
  Statesville (G-14764)
Boondock S Manufacturing Inc............. G 828 891-4242
  Etowah (G-5691)
Bray S Recapping Service Inc............. E 336 786-6182
  Mount Airy (G-11486)
Bridgestone Ret Operations LLC............. G 919 471-4468
  Durham (G-4977)
Bridgestone Ret Operations LLC............. G 910 864-4106
  Fayetteville (G-5775)
Bridgestone Ret Operations LLC............. F 704 861-8146
  Gastonia (G-6360)
Bridgestone Ret Operations LLC............. G 919 778-0230
  Goldsboro (G-6597)
Bridgestone Ret Operations LLC............. G 336 282-6646
  Greensboro (G-6852)
Bridgestone Ret Operations LLC............. F 336 852-8524
  Greensboro (G-6853)
Bridgestone Ret Operations LLC............. G 252 522-5126
  Kinston (G-9347)
Bridgestone Ret Operations LLC............. G 919 872-6402
  Raleigh (G-12573)
Bridgestone Ret Operations LLC............. G 919 872-6566
  Raleigh (G-12574)
Bridgestone Ret Operations LLC............. G 252 243-5189
  Wilson (G-16480)
Bridgestone Ret Operations LLC............. G 336 725-1580
  Winston Salem (G-16636)
Cecil Budd Tire Company LLC............. F 919 742-2322
  Siler City (G-14403)
Claybrook Tire Inc............. F 336 573-3135
  Stoneville (G-14955)
Colony Tire Corporation............. G 252 973-0004
  Rocky Mount (G-13688)
Consolidated Truck Parts Inc............. G 704 279-5543
  Rockwell (G-13650)
Courtesy Ford Inc............. E 252 338-4783
  Elizabeth City (G-5537)
Crossroads Tire Store Inc............. G 704 888-2064
  Midland (G-10465)
Cummins Atlantic LLC............. D 336 275-4531
  Greensboro (G-6946)
Diagnostic Shop Inc............. G 704 933-3435
  Kannapolis (G-9117)
Down East Offroad Inc............. F 252 246-9440
  Wilson (G-16493)
Ed S Tire Laurinburg Inc............. G 910 277-0565
  Laurinburg (G-9476)
Enfield Tire Service Inc............. G 252 445-5016
  Enfield (G-5677)
Foster Tire Sales Inc............. G 336 248-6726
  Lexington (G-9719)
Goodyear Tire & Rubber Company............. G 919 552-9340
  Holly Springs (G-8700)
Goodyear Tire & Rubber Company............. G 336 794-0035
  Winston Salem (G-16724)
Greensboro Tire & Auto Service............. G 336 294-9495
  Greensboro (G-7066)
Hall Tire and Battery Co Inc............. F 336 275-3812
  Greensboro (G-7075)
Haneys Tire Recapping Svc LLC............. F 910 276-2636
  Laurinburg (G-9481)
Heintz Bros Automotives Inc............. G 704 872-8081
  Statesville (G-14809)
▲ Irvan-Smith Inc............. F 704 788-2554
  Concord (G-4290)
John Conrad Inc............. G 336 475-8144
  Thomasville (G-15239)
Johnnys Tire Sales and Svc Inc............. E 252 353-8473
  Greenville (G-7551)
Kerdea Technologies Inc............. F 971 900-1113
  Greenville (G-7552)
Kgt Enterprises Inc............. E 704 662-3272
  Mooresville (G-10997)
L L C Batteries of N C............. G 919 331-0241
  Angier (G-143)
Leonard Alum Utlty Bldngs Inc............. G 336 226-9410
  Burlington (G-1450)
Leonard Alum Utlty Bldngs Inc............. G 919 872-4442
  Raleigh (G-12968)
Leonard Alum Utlty Bldngs Inc............. D 336 789-5018
  Mount Airy (G-11538)
M & M Tire and Auto Inc............. G 336 643-7877
  Summerfield (G-14988)
M & R Retreading & Oil Co Inc............. F 704 474-4101
  Norwood (G-12040)
McCarthy Tire Service Company............. G 910 791-0132
  Wilmington (G-16317)
Merchants Inc............. G 252 447-2121
  Havelock (G-7743)
Mock Tire & Automotive Inc............. E 336 753-8473
  Mocksville (G-10591)
Mock Tire & Automotive Inc............. E 336 774-0081
  Winston Salem (G-16812)
▲ Mock Tire & Automotive Inc............. E 336 768-1010
  Winston Salem (G-16813)
Moss Brothers Tires & Svc Inc............. G 910 895-4572
  Rockingham (G-13635)
Mr Tire Inc............. G 828 262-3555
  Boone (G-1225)
Mr Tire Inc............. F 704 483-1500
  Denver (G-4790)
Mr Tire Inc............. F 828 322-8130
  Hickory (G-8099)

55 AUTOMOTIVE DEALERS AND GASOLINE SERVICE STATIONS

Mr Tire Inc..G.....704 739-6456
   Kings Mountain *(G-9319)*

Mr Tire Inc..G.....828 758-0047
   Lenoir *(G-9637)*

Mr Tire Inc..G.....704 735-8024
   Lincolnton *(G-9910)*

Mr Tire Inc..G.....704 484-0816
   Shelby *(G-14350)*

Mr Tire Inc..G.....704 872-4127
   Statesville *(G-14849)*

Oakie S Tire & Recapping Inc................F.....704 482-5629
   Shelby *(G-14353)*

Parrish Tire Company..............................E.....704 372-2013
   Charlotte *(G-3317)*

Parrish Tire Company..............................F.....336 334-9979
   Greensboro *(G-7246)*

Parrish Tire Company..............................E.....704 872-6565
   Jonesville *(G-9101)*

◆ Parrish Tire Company............................D.....800 849-8473
   Winston Salem *(G-16836)*

Perry Brothers Tire Svc Inc.....................F.....919 693-2128
   Oxford *(G-12140)*

Perry Brothers Tire Svc Inc.....................E.....919 775-7225
   Sanford *(G-14167)*

Phil S Tire Service Inc.............................G.....828 682-2421
   Burnsville *(G-1530)*

Piedmont Truck Tires Inc........................F.....828 277-1549
   Asheville *(G-731)*

Piedmont Truck Tires Inc........................F.....828 202-5337
   Conover *(G-4480)*

Piedmont Truck Tires Inc........................F.....336 223-9412
   Graham *(G-6706)*

Piedmont Truck Tires Inc........................E.....336 668-0091
   Greensboro *(G-7262)*

▲ Prem Corp..E.....704 921-1799
   Charlotte *(G-3373)*

Quality Investments Inc...........................E.....252 492-8777
   Henderson *(G-7805)*

Richmond Investment..............................E.....910 410-8200
   Rockingham *(G-13640)*

Roosevelt Tire Service Inc......................F.....704 864-5464
   Gastonia *(G-6504)*

Roy Dunn...G.....919 963-3700
   Four Oaks *(G-6111)*

Satco Truck Equipment Inc.....................F.....919 383-5547
   Durham *(G-5340)*

◆ Sika Corporation....................................E.....704 810-0500
   Gastonia *(G-6510)*

Small Brothers Tire Co Inc......................G.....704 289-3531
   Monroe *(G-10808)*

Snider Tire Inc..D.....704 373-2910
   Charlotte *(G-3571)*

Snider Tire Inc..F.....336 691-5480
   Greensboro *(G-7347)*

Snider Tire Inc..G.....828 324-9955
   Hickory *(G-8160)*

Sparksmith LLC..G.....828 266-0152
   Waynesville *(G-15827)*

Super Retread Center Inc.......................F.....919 734-0073
   Goldsboro *(G-6663)*

Team X-Treme LLC..................................G.....919 562-8100
   Rolesville *(G-13760)*

Thrifty Tire...G.....919 220-7800
   Durham *(G-5402)*

Tire Sls Svc Inc Fytteville NC.................E.....910 485-1121
   Fayetteville *(G-5931)*

Tires Incorporated of Clinton.................F.....910 592-4741
   Clinton *(G-4114)*

Towel City Tire & Wheel LLC..................G.....704 933-2143
   Kannapolis *(G-9136)*

Treadz LLC..G.....704 664-0995
   Mooresville *(G-11114)*

Trick Karts Inc..G.....704 883-0089
   Statesville *(G-14917)*

Turn Key Tire Service Inc.......................G.....919 836-8473
   Garner *(G-6319)*

Universal Tire Service Inc.......................G.....919 779-8798
   Raleigh *(G-13383)*

Van Products Inc......................................E.....919 878-7110
   Raleigh *(G-13392)*

Village Tire Center Inc............................G.....919 862-8500
   Raleigh *(G-13400)*

Whitaker S Tire Service Inc....................F.....704 786-6174
   Concord *(G-4389)*

White S Tire Svc Wilson Inc...................G.....252 237-0770
   Wilson *(G-16559)*

White S Tire Svc Wilson Inc...................D.....252 237-5426
   Wilson *(G-16560)*

Whites Tire Svc New Bern Inc...............G.....252 633-1170
   New Bern *(G-11857)*

Williams Electric Mtr Repr Inc...............G.....919 859-9790
   Sanford *(G-14206)*

Wilson Tire and Automotive Inc............G.....336 584-9638
   Elon College *(G-5668)*

5541 Gasoline service stations

City of Greensboro..................................E.....336 373-5855
   Greensboro *(G-6911)*

College Sun Do...G.....910 521-9189
   Pembroke *(G-12181)*

E Z Stop Number Two..............................G.....828 627-9081
   Clyde *(G-4124)*

Hardison Tire Co Inc................................F.....252 745-4561
   Bayboro *(G-935)*

Murphy USA Inc..E.....828 758-7055
   Lenoir *(G-9638)*

5551 Boat dealers

◆ Ace Marine Rigging & Supply Inc........F.....252 726-6620
   Morehead City *(G-11148)*

Anglers Marine NC..................................G.....919 585-7900
   Clayton *(G-3953)*

Barbour S Marine Supply Co Inc............F.....252 728-2136
   Beaufort *(G-944)*

Cape Fear Yacht Works LLC..................F.....910 540-1685
   Wilmington *(G-16151)*

Coastal Woodworking..............................G.....910 477-1330
   Bolivia *(G-1163)*

Jones Marine Inc.....................................G.....704 639-0173
   Salisbury *(G-13994)*

Kencraft Manufacturing Inc....................G.....252 291-0271
   Wilson *(G-16505)*

M & J Marine LLC...................................F.....252 249-0522
   Oriental *(G-12111)*

Mann Custom Boats Inc..........................E.....252 473-1716
   Manns Harbor *(G-10122)*

Marinemax of North Carolina.................E.....910 256-8100
   Wrightsville Beach *(G-17026)*

Nomad Houseboats Inc...........................G.....252 288-5670
   New Bern *(G-11831)*

Todds Rv & Marine Inc............................F.....828 651-0007
   Hendersonville *(G-7908)*

Triad Marine Center Inc.........................G.....252 634-1880
   New Bern *(G-11851)*

5561 Recreational vehicle dealers

Derrow Enterprises Inc..........................G.....252 635-3375
   New Bern *(G-11800)*

Todds Rv & Marine Inc............................F.....828 651-0007
   Hendersonville *(G-7908)*

5571 Motorcycle dealers

Barrs Competition....................................F.....704 482-5169
   Shelby *(G-14287)*

Ironworks Motorcycles............................G.....336 542-7868
   Greensboro *(G-7123)*

Smoky Mountain Machining Inc.............D.....828 665-1193
   Asheville *(G-776)*

5599 Automotive dealers, nec

A-1 Hitch & Trailors Sales Inc................F.....910 755-6025
   Supply *(G-15005)*

Gore S Trlr Manufacturer S Inc.............F.....910 642-2246
   Whiteville *(G-15964)*

▼ Kaufman Trailers Inc...........................E.....336 790-6800
   Lexington *(G-9739)*

Kraftsman Inc...D.....336 824-1114
   Ramseur *(G-13445)*

Leonard Alum Utility Bldngs Inc...........G.....919 872-4442
   Raleigh *(G-12968)*

Road King Trailers Inc...........................E.....828 670-8012
   Candler *(G-1588)*

56 APPAREL AND ACCESSORY STORES

5611 Men's and boys' clothing stores

Hudson Overall Company Inc................G.....336 314-5024
   Greensboro *(G-7104)*

5621 Women's clothing stores

Belevation LLC...F.....803 517-9030
   Biscoe *(G-1104)*

Ebony & Ivorys Unique Btq LLC...........G.....704 324-4035
   Wingate *(G-16574)*

G & G Enterprises...................................G.....336 764-2493
   Clemmons *(G-4041)*

▲ Grace & Glory Goods LLC.................G.....828 575-2166
   Asheville *(G-638)*

Grace Apparel Company Inc..................G.....828 242-8172
   Arden *(G-335)*

Hanesbrands Inc......................................G.....910 462-2001
   Laurel Hill *(G-9460)*

Jestines Jewels Inc................................G.....704 904-0191
   Salisbury *(G-13991)*

Live It Boutique LLC................................G.....704 492-2402
   Charlotte *(G-3095)*

Pine State Corporate AP LLC................F.....336 789-9437
   Mount Airy *(G-11557)*

R Riveter LLC...G.....406 321-2315
   Southern Pines *(G-14550)*

W E Nixons Wldg & Hdwr Inc.................G.....252 221-4348
   Edenton *(G-5523)*

5632 Women's accessory and specialty stores

◆ Fine Line Hosiery Inc..........................F.....336 498-8022
   Asheboro *(G-435)*

Jones Fabricare Inc................................G.....336 272-7261
   Greensboro *(G-7139)*

▲ Morris Family Theatrical Inc.............E.....704 332-3304
   Charlotte *(G-3203)*

Sweet Room LLC.....................................G.....336 567-1620
   High Point *(G-8560)*

Tafford Uniforms LLC..............................D.....888 823-3673
   Charlotte *(G-3670)*

Wings Store 765......................................G.....910 458-0278
   Carolina Beach *(G-1642)*

5641 Children's and infants' wear stores

Aidleyco LLC...G.....704 782-0648
   Mooresville *(G-10851)*

▲ Cannon & Daughters Inc....................D.....828 254-9236
   Asheville *(G-579)*

Pashes LLC .... G 704 682-6535
　Statesville (G-14857)

Stork News Tm of America .... F 910 868-3065
　Fayetteville (G-5923)

W E Nixons Wldg & Hdwr Inc .... G 252 221-4348
　Edenton (G-5523)

5651 Family clothing stores

Labonte Racing Inc .... F 336 431-1004
　Trinity (G-15348)

Pdf and Associates .... G 252 332-7749
　Colerain (G-4139)

◆ Raleigh Workshop Inc .... E 919 917-8969
　Raleigh (G-13188)

Ralph Lauren Corporation .... G 336 632-5000
　High Point (G-8504)

▲ Secret Spot Inc .... G 252 441-4030
　Nags Head (G-11725)

5661 Shoe stores

Bio-Tech Prsthtics Orthtics In .... G 336 333-9081
　Greensboro (G-6839)

Lebos Shoe Store Inc .... F 704 987-6540
　Cornelius (G-4567)

Polyhose Incorporated .... F 732 512-9141
　Wilmington (G-16360)

W E Nixons Wldg & Hdwr Inc .... G 252 221-4348
　Edenton (G-5523)

5699 Miscellaneous apparel and accessories

Acorn Printing .... G 704 868-4522
　Bessemer City (G-1048)

Brands Fashion US Inc .... G 704 953-8246
　Charlotte (G-2348)

Carolina Shirt Company Inc .... G 910 575-4447
　Calabash (G-1552)

Ebony & Ivorys Unique Btq LLC .... G 704 324-4035
　Wingate (G-16574)

Funny Bone EMB & Screening ...... G 704 663-4711
　Mooresville (G-10951)

Global Products & Mfg Svcs Inc .... G 360 870-9876
　Charlotte (G-2834)

Gmg Group LLC .... G 252 441-8374
　Kill Devil Hills (G-9258)

Happy Jack Incorporated .... G 252 747-2911
　Snow Hill (G-14503)

▲ Ics North America Corp .... E 704 794-6620
　Concord (G-4283)

K Formula Enterprises Inc .... G 910 323-3315
　Fayetteville (G-5853)

Kimmys Customs LLC .... G 904 699-2933
　Rural Hall (G-13845)

Kontoor Brands Inc .... C 336 332-3400
　Greensboro (G-7156)

Manna Corp North Carolina .... G 828 696-3642
　Hendersonville (G-7875)

McDaniel Delmar .... E 336 284-6377
　Mocksville (G-10586)

▲ Morris Family Theatrical Inc .... E 704 332-3304
　Charlotte (G-3203)

New Media Golf Inc .... F 828 533-9954
　Highlands (G-8616)

Plushh LLC .... G 919 647-7911
　Raleigh (G-13117)

Rec Plus Inc .... E 704 375-9098
　Charlotte (G-3419)

Screen Master .... G 252 492-8407
　Henderson (G-7810)

Tresmc LLC .... G 919 900-0868
　Knightdale (G-9432)

57 HOME FURNITURE, FURNISHINGS AND EQUIPMENT STORES

5712 Furniture stores

A R Byrd Company Inc .... G 704 732-5675
　Lincolnton (G-9864)

▲ Acacia Home & Garden Inc .... F 828 465-1700
　Conover (G-4413)

Alligood Cabinet Shop .... G 252 927-3201
　Washington (G-15681)

Archie Supply LLC .... G 336 987-0895
　Greensboro (G-6813)

▲ Aria Designs LLC .... F 828 572-4303
　Lenoir (G-9575)

B & B Wood Shop & Bldg Contrs ... G 828 488-2078
　Bryson City (G-1319)

Bassett Furniture Inds Inc .... D 828 465-7700
　Newton (G-11915)

Bernhardt Furniture Company .... F 828 759-6205
　Lenoir (G-9587)

Bjmf Inc .... E 704 554-6333
　Charlotte (G-2318)

Blue-Hen Inc .... G 407 322-2262
　Asheville (G-567)

Browns Woodworking LLC .... G 704 983-5917
　Albemarle (G-76)

Burrough Furniture .... G 336 841-3129
　Archdale (G-271)

Carolina Chair Inc .... F 828 459-1330
　Conover (G-4430)

Carrington Court Inc .... G 828 396-1049
　Granite Falls (G-6727)

Cedar Rock Home Furnishings ...... G 828 396-2361
　Hudson (G-8767)

Comm-Kab Inc .... F 336 873-8787
　Asheboro (G-417)

Cynthia Saar .... G 910 480-2523
　Stedman (G-14934)

◆ Dedon Inc .... F 336 790-1070
　Greensboro (G-6963)

Dexter Inc .... G 919 510-5050
　Raleigh (G-12681)

Digital Printing Systems Inc .... E 704 525-0190
　Charlotte (G-2636)

Dilworth Mattress Company Inc .... G 704 333-6564
　Charlotte (G-2638)

Distinctive Furniture Inc .... G 828 754-3947
　Lenoir (G-9604)

▲ East Coast Umbrella Inc .... E 910 462-2500
　Laurel Hill (G-9459)

Elite Wood Products .... G 828 994-4446
　Newton (G-11930)

Ethan Allen Retail Inc .... E 828 428-9361
　Maiden (G-10107)

Furniture Fair Inc .... E 910 455-4044
　Jacksonville (G-9001)

Hfi Wind Down Inc .... C 828 438-5767
　Morganton (G-11220)

▲ Ideaitlia Cntmporary Furn Corp ..... C 828 464-1000
　Conover (G-4466)

Innovative Awngs & Screens LLC .. F 833 337-4233
　Cornelius (G-4561)

Keani Furniture Inc .... E 336 303-5484
　Asheboro (G-448)

◆ Kingsdown Incorporated .... E 919 563-3531
　Mebane (G-10415)

Kinston Office Supply Co Inc .... E 252 523-7654
　Kinston (G-9373)

◆ Lexington Furniture Inds Inc .... C 336 474-5300
　Thomasville (G-15241)

Locklear Cabinets Wdwrk Sp Inc ... G 910 521-4463
　Rowland (G-13790)

◆ M & S Warehouse Inc .... E 828 728-3733
　Lenoir (G-9628)

M C C of Laurinburg Inc .... G 910 276-0519
　Laurinburg (G-9486)

▲ Marsh Furniture Company .... B 336 884-7363
　High Point (G-8444)

Mattress Firm .... G 910 868-0950
　Fayetteville (G-5870)

Mattress Firm .... G 252 443-1259
　Rocky Mount (G-13711)

McNeillys Inc .... E 704 300-1712
　Lawndale (G-9501)

◆ Mitchell Gold Co LLC C
　Taylorsville (G-15153)

Miters Touch Inc .... G 828 963-4445
　Banner Elk (G-903)

Murphy S Custom Cabinetry Inc .... G 828 891-3050
　Hendersonville (G-7882)

Nags Head Hammocks LLC .... G 252 441-6115
　Nags Head (G-11724)

Neil Allen Industries Inc .... G 336 887-6500
　High Point (G-8465)

Nobscot Construction Co Inc .... G 919 929-2075
　Chapel Hill (G-2048)

O Henry House Ltd .... E 336 431-5350
　Archdale (G-294)

Olde Lexington Products Inc .... G 336 956-2355
　Linwood (G-9947)

Outer Banks Hammocks Inc .... F 910 256-4001
　Wilmington (G-16347)

Panels By Paith Inc .... G 336 599-3437
　Roxboro (G-13816)

▲ Perfect Fit Industries LLC .... C 800 864-7618
　Charlotte (G-3330)

Plastic Art Design Inc .... G 919 878-1672
　Raleigh (G-13115)

Quality Custom Woodworks Inc .... G 704 843-1584
　Waxhaw (G-15771)

Reliable Bedding Company .... E 336 883-0648
　Archdale (G-297)

Royal Colony Furniture Inc .... G 336 472-8833
　Thomasville (G-15272)

S Banner Cabinets Incorporated .... E 828 733-2031
　Newland (G-11893)

Sides Furniture Inc .... G 336 869-5509
　High Point (G-8524)

Smartway of Carolinas LLC .... F 704 900-7877
　Charlotte (G-3566)

Stephanies Mattress LLC .... G 704 763-0705
　Charlotte (G-3630)

Tatum Galleries Inc .... G 828 963-6466
　Banner Elk (G-904)

▲ Tiger Mountain Woodworks Inc .... E 828 526-5577
　Highlands (G-8618)

Unique Office Solutions Inc .... F 336 854-0900
　Greensboro (G-7430)

◆ Verellen Inc .... D 336 889-7379
　High Point (G-8592)

◆ Vrush Industries Inc .... F 336 886-7700
　High Point (G-8597)

W B Mason Co Inc .... E 888 926-2766
　Charlotte (G-3787)

Washington Cabinet Company .... G 252 946-3457
　Washington (G-15738)

▲ Watauga Creek LLC .... G 828 369-7881
　Franklin (G-6147)

Weathercraft Outdoor Furn Inc ...... G 336 629-3939
　Asheboro (G-508)

Wildwood Studios Inc .... G 828 299-8696
　Asheville (G-822)

57 HOME FURNITURE, FURNISHINGS AND EQUIPMENT STORES

Woodwright of Wilson Co Inc .... G 252 243-9663
   Elm City *(G-5655)*
World Art Gallery Incorporated .... G 910 989-0203
   Jacksonville *(G-9047)*
Yukon Inc .... E 919 366-2001
   Wendell *(G-15926)*

5713 Floor covering stores

Anderson Living Center LLC .... G 828 229-3243
   Forest City *(G-6059)*
▲ Bfs Operations LLC .... A 919 431-1000
   Raleigh *(G-12555)*
Colonial Braided Rug Co NC .... G 704 538-1824
   Shelby *(G-14300)*
▼ Heartwood Pine Floors Inc .... G 919 542-4394
   Moncure *(G-10624)*
Interrs-Exteriors Asheboro Inc .... F 336 629-2148
   Asheboro *(G-446)*
Mongoose LLC .... F 919 400-0772
   Burlington *(G-1462)*
▲ Stock Building Supply Hol .... A 919 431-1000
   Raleigh *(G-13305)*

5714 Drapery and upholstery stores

Bettys Drapery Design Workroom .... G 828 264-2392
   Boone *(G-1176)*
Cloth Barn Inc .... F 919 735-3643
   Goldsboro *(G-6601)*
Dale Ray Fabrics LLC .... G 704 932-6411
   Kannapolis *(G-9116)*
Distinctive Furniture Inc .... G 828 754-3947
   Lenoir *(G-9604)*
Simplicity Sofas Inc .... G 800 813-2889
   High Point *(G-8531)*
Textile Products Inc .... E 704 636-6221
   Salisbury *(G-14051)*
Walker Draperies Inc .... F 919 220-1424
   Durham *(G-5437)*

5719 Miscellaneous homefurnishings

Ashdan Enterprises .... G 336 375-9698
   Greensboro *(G-6818)*
Blinds Plus Inc .... G 910 487-5196
   Fayetteville *(G-5773)*
Carolina Blind Outlet Inc .... G 828 697-8525
   Hendersonville *(G-7834)*
Ceder Creek Gallery & Pottery .... G 919 528-1041
   Creedmoor *(G-4610)*
Dale Ray Fabrics LLC .... G 704 932-6411
   Kannapolis *(G-9116)*
▲ Dewoolfson Down Intl Inc .... G 828 963-2750
   Banner Elk *(G-896)*
▲ Fintronx LLC .... F 919 324-3960
   Raleigh *(G-12767)*
▲ G & G Moulding Inc .... E 828 438-1112
   Morganton *(G-11214)*
Glass Works of Hickory Inc .... G 828 322-2122
   Hickory *(G-8033)*
Guest Interiors .... G 828 244-5738
   Hickory *(G-8035)*
Hunckler Fabrication LLC .... F 336 753-0905
   Mocksville *(G-10581)*
Interrs-Exteriors Asheboro Inc .... F 336 629-2148
   Asheboro *(G-446)*
Jugtown Pottery .... G 910 464-3266
   Seagrove *(G-14241)*
Lawing Marble Co Inc .... G 704 732-0360
   Lincolnton *(G-9898)*
Leighdeux LLC .... G 704 965-4889
   Charlotte *(G-3082)*
Lighting .... G 919 828-0351
   Raleigh *(G-12970)*

Southern Marble Co LLC .... G 704 982-4142
   Albemarle *(G-107)*

5722 Household appliance stores

Accel Discount Tire .... G 704 636-0323
   Salisbury *(G-13913)*
Best Price Appliance LLC .... G 336 662-3117
   Greensboro *(G-6837)*
Creative Stone Fyetteville Inc .... F 910 491-1225
   Fayetteville *(G-5799)*
Electrolux Home Products Inc .... B 252 527-5100
   Kinston *(G-9363)*
▲ Grancreations Inc .... G 704 332-7625
   Charlotte *(G-2852)*
Mr Tire Inc .... F 704 483-1500
   Denver *(G-4790)*
Mr Tire Inc .... G 704 739-6456
   Kings Mountain *(G-9319)*
Mr Tire Inc .... G 704 484-0816
   Shelby *(G-14350)*
Mr Tire Inc .... G 704 872-4127
   Statesville *(G-14849)*
Perry Brothers Tire Svc Inc .... E 919 775-7225
   Sanford *(G-14167)*
Psnc Energy .... G 919 367-2735
   Apex *(G-235)*
The Tarheel Electric Memb .... F 919 876-4603
   Raleigh *(G-13342)*
TTI Floor Care North Amer Inc .... D 440 996-2000
   Charlotte *(G-3735)*
Walnut Cove Furniture Inc .... G 336 591-8008
   Walnut Cove *(G-15636)*
▲ Web-Don Incorporated .... E 800 532-0434
   Charlotte *(G-3800)*
Wen Bray Heating & AC .... G 828 267-0635
   Hickory *(G-8209)*

5731 Radio, television, and electronic stores

▲ C & S Antennas Inc .... F 828 324-2454
   Conover *(G-4427)*
▲ Crest Electronics Inc .... F 336 855-6422
   Greensboro *(G-6940)*
Drew Roberts LLC .... G 336 497-1679
   Whitsett *(G-15988)*
Ni4l Antennas and Elec LLC .... G 828 738-6445
   Moravian Falls *(G-11146)*
Perry Brothers Tire Svc Inc .... F 919 693-2128
   Oxford *(G-12140)*
Perry Brothers Tire Svc Inc .... E 919 775-7225
   Sanford *(G-14167)*
Serra Wireless Inc .... G 980 318-0873
   Charlotte *(G-3529)*
Southern Printing Company Inc .... G 910 259-4807
   Burgaw *(G-1352)*

5734 Computer and software stores

Barefoot Cnc Inc .... G 828 438-5038
   Morganton *(G-11199)*
Branch Office Solutions Inc .... G 800 743-1047
   Indian Trail *(G-8924)*
Coastal Office Eqp & Computers .... G 252 335-9427
   Elizabeth City *(G-5534)*
Complete Comp St of Ralgh Inc .... E 919 828-5227
   Raleigh *(G-12635)*
Drew Roberts LLC .... G 336 497-1679
   Whitsett *(G-15988)*
Global Products & Mfg Svcs Inc .... G 360 870-9876
   Charlotte *(G-2834)*
Grover Gaming Inc .... D 252 329-7900
   Greenville *(G-7536)*
Ideacode Inc .... G 919 341-5170
   Greensboro *(G-7111)*

Infisoft Software .... G 704 307-2619
   Charlotte *(G-2969)*
Information Tech Works LLC .... F 919 232-5332
   Raleigh *(G-12888)*
Jtc Awards and Printing .... G 910 346-9522
   Jacksonville *(G-9011)*
Northstar Computer Tech Inc .... G 980 272-1969
   Monroe *(G-10780)*
Payload Media Inc .... G 919 367-2969
   Cary *(G-1844)*
Preferred Data Corporation .... G 336 886-3282
   High Point *(G-8495)*
▲ Terarecon Inc .... D 650 372-1100
   Durham *(G-5395)*

5735 Record and prerecorded tape stores

Davie County Publishing Co .... F 336 751-2120
   Mocksville *(G-10565)*
Dobbins Products .... G 919 580-0621
   Goldsboro *(G-6610)*
Mohawk Industries Inc .... G 919 609-4759
   Garner *(G-6289)*
Song of Wood Ltd .... G 828 669-7675
   Black Mountain *(G-1139)*
Ultimix Records .... G 336 288-7566
   Greensboro *(G-7426)*

5736 Musical instrument stores

Classical Elements .... G 828 575-9145
   Asheville *(G-595)*
Dorian Corporation .... F 910 352-6939
   Wilmington *(G-16204)*
J L Smith & Co Inc .... F 704 521-1088
   Charlotte *(G-3004)*
Kelhorn Corporation .... G 828 837-5833
   Brasstown *(G-1266)*
Music & Arts .... G 919 329-6069
   Garner *(G-6294)*
▲ Music Matters Inc .... G 336 272-5303
   Greensboro *(G-7210)*
◆ MW Enterprises Inc .... G 828 963-7083
   Vilas *(G-15498)*
Song of Wood Ltd .... G 828 669-7675
   Black Mountain *(G-1139)*

58 EATING AND DRINKING PLACES

5812 Eating places

Alamance Kaffee Werks LLC .... F 662 617-4573
   Burlington *(G-1363)*
Anchor Coffee Co Inc .... G 336 265-7458
   North Wilkesboro *(G-11997)*
Bilcat Inc .... E 828 295-3088
   Blowing Rock *(G-1154)*
Booneshine Brewing Co Inc .... G 828 263-4305
   Boone *(G-1180)*
Brewitt & Dreenkupp Inc .... G 704 525-3366
   Charlotte *(G-2353)*
Brick & Mortar Grill .... G 919 639-9700
   Angier *(G-133)*
Cabarrus Brewing Company LLC .... E 704 490-4487
   Concord *(G-4216)*
Carolina Yogurt Inc .... G 828 754-9685
   Lenoir *(G-9596)*
Chatham News Publishing Co .... G 919 663-4042
   Siler City *(G-14406)*
Cintoms Inc .... G 828 684-1317
   Asheville *(G-593)*
Cupcake Bar .... G 919 816-2905
   Durham *(G-5039)*

SIC SECTION

59 MISCELLANEOUS RETAIL

Donut Shop.. G 910 640-3317
   Whiteville *(G-15962)*

Dunkin Donuts... F 919 217-9603
   Knightdale *(G-9417)*

Elxsi Corporation... B 407 849-1090
   Charlotte *(G-2701)*

Emanuel Hoggard.. F 252 794-3724
   Windsor *(G-16566)*

Jebco Inc... E 919 557-2001
   Holly Springs *(G-8702)*

Lmb Corp... G 704 547-8886
   Charlotte *(G-3098)*

McDonalds... F 910 295-1112
   Pinehurst *(G-12229)*

Mike DS Bbq LLC.. G 866 960-8652
   Durham *(G-5225)*

Neomonde Baking Company....................... E 919 469-8009
   Morrisville *(G-11393)*

Nunnery-Freeman Inc.................................. F 252 438-3149
   Henderson *(G-7799)*

Over Rainbow Inc.. F 704 332-5521
   Charlotte *(G-3307)*

Sawmill Catering LLC.................................. F 910 769-7455
   Wilmington *(G-16393)*

Sistas 4 Life Food Svcs LLC....................... G 704 957-6437
   Charlotte *(G-3557)*

Sugar Creek Brewing Co LLC...................... E 704 521-3333
   Charlotte *(G-3646)*

◆ Suntory International................................. F 917 756-2747
   Raleigh *(G-13316)*

Sweet Room LLC... G 336 567-1620
   High Point *(G-8560)*

Swirl Oakhurst LLC...................................... G 704 258-1209
   Charlotte *(G-3662)*

Toms Robinson Seafood Inc....................... G 919 942-1221
   Carrboro *(G-1658)*

Tonys Ice Cream Co Inc............................. G 704 853-0018
   Gastonia *(G-6529)*

◆ USa Wholesale and Distrg Inc................. F 888 484-6872
   Fayetteville *(G-5945)*

Vortex Bottle Shop LLC.............................. F 980 258-0827
   Harrisburg *(G-7734)*

Wildflour Bakery Inc.................................... G 828 749-9224
   Saluda *(G-14175)*

Yummy Tummy Ga LLC.............................. E 704 658-0445
   Mooresville *(G-11138)*

Zoes Kitchen Inc... E 336 748-0587
   Winston Salem *(G-16991)*

5813 Drinking places

760 Craft Works LLC................................... F 704 274-5216
   Huntersville *(G-8785)*

Bearwaters Brewing Company.................... F 828 237-4200
   Canton *(G-1599)*

▲ Bold Rock Partners LP............................ F 828 595-9940
   Mills River *(G-10501)*

Bombshell Beer Company LLC................... F 919 823-1933
   Holly Springs *(G-8691)*

Booneshine Brewing Co Inc....................... G 828 263-4305
   Boone *(G-1180)*

Cabarrus Brewing Company LLC................ E 704 490-4487
   Concord *(G-4216)*

Ebhc LLC... G 704 733-9427
   Charlotte *(G-2681)*

Glass Jug.. F 919 818-6907
   Durham *(G-5116)*

Glass Jug LLC.. F 919 813-0135
   Durham *(G-5117)*

High Branch Brewing Co LLC..................... G 704 706-3807
   Concord *(G-4279)*

▲ Highland Brewing Company Inc............. F 828 299-3370
   Asheville *(G-652)*

Innovation Brewing LLC............................. G 828 586-9678
   Sylva *(G-15058)*

Koi Pond Brewing Company LLC................ G 252 231-1660
   Rocky Mount *(G-13706)*

McDonalds... F 910 295-1112
   Pinehurst *(G-12229)*

Oklawaha Brewing Company LLC............... F 828 595-9956
   Hendersonville *(G-7888)*

Resident Culture Brewing LLC.................... E 704 333-1862
   Charlotte *(G-3438)*

Salty Turtle Beer Company........................ E 910 803-2019
   Surf City *(G-15016)*

Shortway Brewing Company LLC............... G 252 777-3065
   Newport *(G-11907)*

Stardust Cellars LLC................................... G 336 466-4454
   Winston Salem *(G-16916)*

Sugar Creek Brewing Co LLC...................... E 704 521-3333
   Charlotte *(G-3646)*

Sweet Room LLC... G 336 567-1620
   High Point *(G-8560)*

Sycamore Brewing LLC.............................. E 704 910-3821
   Charlotte *(G-3664)*

▲ Triple C Brewing Company LLC............. F 704 372-3212
   Charlotte *(G-3729)*

White Street Brewing Co Inc..................... E 919 647-9439
   Youngsville *(G-17115)*

Williamson Mead & Brewing LLC............... F 661 827-7290
   Glade Valley *(G-6573)*

59 MISCELLANEOUS RETAIL

5912 Drug stores and proprietary stores

Bausch Health Americas Inc..................... F 949 461-6000
   Durham *(G-4948)*

Harris Teeter LLC.. D 704 846-7117
   Matthews *(G-10252)*

King Bio Inc... D 828 255-0201
   Asheville *(G-675)*

Modoral Brands Inc..................................... G 336 741-7230
   Winston Salem *(G-16815)*

Natures Pharmacy Inc................................. G 828 251-0094
   Asheville *(G-710)*

Walgreen Co.. F 704 525-2628
   Charlotte *(G-3792)*

5921 Liquor stores

Aviator Brewing Company Inc.................... G 919 601-5497
   Holly Springs *(G-8687)*

Drink A Bull LLC... G 919 818-3321
   Durham *(G-5065)*

First Miracle Vine & Wine LLC.................... G 910 990-5681
   Garland *(G-6242)*

Glass Jug.. F 919 818-6907
   Durham *(G-5116)*

Glass Jug LLC.. F 919 813-0135
   Durham *(G-5117)*

Jkl Inc.. F 252 355-6714
   Greenville *(G-7550)*

Koi Pond Brewing Company LLC................ G 252 231-1660
   Rocky Mount *(G-13706)*

Land of Sky Mobile Canning LLC............... G 303 880-1297
   Asheville *(G-679)*

Medaloni Cellars LLC................................. G 336 398-7818
   Greensboro *(G-7196)*

Sanders Ridge Inc....................................... G 336 677-1700
   Boonville *(G-1256)*

Urban Orchard Cider Company.................. G 828 779-6372
   Weaverville *(G-15866)*

5932 Used merchandise stores

Barker and Martin Inc................................. G 336 275-5056
   Greensboro *(G-6831)*

Etherngton Cnservation Ctr Inc................. D 336 665-1317
   Greensboro *(G-7004)*

J C Lawrence Co... G 919 553-3044
   Oriental *(G-12110)*

Microtronic Us LLC..................................... F 336 869-0429
   High Point *(G-8456)*

Sumpters Jwly & Collectibles................... G 704 399-5348
   Charlotte *(G-3649)*

5941 Sporting goods and bicycle shops

Brandrpm LLC.. D 704 225-1800
   Charlotte *(G-2347)*

▲ Cane Creek Cycling Cmpnnts Inc.......... E 828 684-3551
   Fletcher *(G-5991)*

▲ Carolina Gym Supply Corp..................... G 919 732-6999
   Hillsborough *(G-8642)*

Custom Marine Fabrication Inc................. G 252 638-5422
   New Bern *(G-11795)*

Dobbins Products.. G 919 580-0621
   Goldsboro *(G-6610)*

▲ Fathom Offshore Holdings LLC............ G 910 399-6882
   Wilmington *(G-16217)*

Fusion Sport Inc.. E 720 987-4403
   Durham *(G-5109)*

Gmg Group LLC... G 252 441-8374
   Kill Devil Hills *(G-9258)*

Home Team Athletics Inc........................... G 910 938-0862
   Jacksonville *(G-9007)*

▲ I Must Garden LLC.................................. G 919 929-2299
   Raleigh *(G-12872)*

Kelleys Sports and Awards Inc................. G 828 728-4600
   Hudson *(G-8772)*

Ken Staley Co Inc....................................... G 336 685-4294
   Franklinville *(G-6169)*

Land and Loft LLC...................................... G 315 560-7060
   Raleigh *(G-12953)*

Line Drive Sports Center Inc..................... G 336 824-1692
   Ramseur *(G-13446)*

▲ Mettech Inc.. G 919 833-9460
   Raleigh *(G-13023)*

Millers Sports and Trophies...................... G 252 792-2050
   Williamston *(G-16067)*

Mr Tire Inc... G 828 262-3555
   Boone *(G-1225)*

Mr Tire Inc... F 704 483-1500
   Denver *(G-4790)*

Mr Tire Inc... F 828 322-8130
   Hickory *(G-8099)*

Mr Tire Inc... G 704 739-6456
   Kings Mountain *(G-9319)*

Mr Tire Inc... G 828 758-0047
   Lenoir *(G-9637)*

Mr Tire Inc... G 704 735-8024
   Lincolnton *(G-9910)*

Mr Tire Inc... G 704 484-0816
   Shelby *(G-14350)*

Mr Tire Inc... G 704 872-4127
   Statesville *(G-14849)*

R & S Sporting Goods Ctr Inc................... G 336 599-0248
   Roxboro *(G-13820)*

Screen Master... G 252 492-8407
   Henderson *(G-7810)*

Sturm Ruger & Company Inc..................... B 336 427-0286
   Mayodan *(G-10368)*

▲ Triplette Fencing Supply Inc................. G 336 835-1205
   Elkin *(G-5630)*

5942 Book stores

Dobbins Products.. G 919 580-0621
   Goldsboro *(G-6610)*

Free Will Bptst Press Fndtion................... F 252 746-6128
   Ayden *(G-852)*

59 MISCELLANEOUS RETAIL

▲ Good Will Publishers Inc .... D 704 853-3237
  Gastonia (G-6408)
Grateful Steps Foundation .... G 828 277-0998
  Asheville (G-639)
Idea People Inc .... G 704 398-4437
  Huntersville (G-8833)
Kinston Office Supply Co Inc .... E 252 523-7654
  Kinston (G-9373)

5943 Stationery stores

▲ American Forms Mfg Inc .... E 704 866-9139
  Gastonia (G-6345)
◆ Carson-Dellosa Publishing LLC .... D 336 632-0084
  Greensboro (G-6893)
Carter Publishing Company Inc .... F 336 993-2161
  Kernersville (G-9174)
Coastal Press Inc .... G 252 726-1549
  Morehead City (G-11163)
Devora Designs Inc .... G 336 782-0964
  Winston Salem (G-16676)
Good Grief Marketing LLC .... G 336 989-1984
  Greensboro (G-7053)
Jofra Graphics Inc .... G 910 259-1717
  Burgaw (G-1342)
King Business Service Inc .... G 910 610-1030
  Laurinburg (G-9483)
L C Industries Inc .... C 919 596-8277
  Fayetteville (G-5857)
◆ L C Industries Inc .... C 919 596-8277
  Durham (G-5185)
Leapfrog Document Services Inc .... F 704 372-1078
  Charlotte (G-3077)
Lynchs Office Supply Co Inc .... F 252 537-6041
  Roanoke Rapids (G-13578)
M C C of Laurinburg Inc .... G 910 276-0519
  Laurinburg (G-9486)
Office Sup Svcs Inc Charlotte .... E 704 786-4677
  Concord (G-4323)
Owen G Dunn Co Inc .... G 252 633-3197
  New Bern (G-11832)
Print Management Group LLC .... F 704 821-0114
  Charlotte (G-3385)
Printing Press .... G 828 299-1234
  Asheville (G-743)
Southern Printing Company Inc .... G 910 259-4807
  Burgaw (G-1352)
Times Printing Company .... E 252 473-2105
  Manteo (G-10130)
Times Printing Company Inc .... G 252 441-2223
  Kill Devil Hills (G-9263)
W B Mason Co Inc .... E 888 926-2766
  Charlotte (G-3787)
Westmoreland Printers Inc .... F 704 482-9100
  Shelby (G-14382)
Wright Printing Service Inc .... G 336 427-4768
  Madison (G-10092)

5944 Jewelry stores

Barnes Dmnd Gllery Jwly Mfrs I .... G 910 347-4300
  Jacksonville (G-8989)
▲ Buchanan Gem Stone Mines Inc ..... F 828 765-6130
  Spruce Pine (G-14632)
Byrd Designs Inc .... G 828 628-0151
  Fairview (G-5709)
D C Crsman Mfr Fine Jwly Inc .... G 828 252-9891
  Asheville (G-601)
Donald Haack Diamonds Inc .... G 704 365-4400
  Charlotte (G-2651)
Dons Fine Jewelry Inc .... G 336 724-7826
  Clemmons (G-4035)
Duncan Design Ltd .... G 919 834-7713
  Raleigh (G-12709)

Gma Creative Inc .... G 919 435-6984
  Wake Forest (G-15561)
▲ Jewel Masters Inc .... F 336 243-2711
  Lexington (G-9734)
Jewelry By Gail Inc .... G 252 441-5387
  Nags Head (G-11721)
Jkl Inc .... F 252 355-6714
  Greenville (G-7550)
John Laughter Jewelry Inc .... G 828 456-4772
  Waynesville (G-15808)
Made By Custom LLC .... G 704 980-9840
  Charlotte (G-3117)
Michael S North Wilkesboro Inc .... G 336 838-5964
  North Wilkesboro (G-12028)
NCSMJ Inc .... G 704 544-1118
  Pineville (G-12285)
R & B Partnership .... G 828 298-7988
  Asheville (G-750)
R Gregory Jewelers Inc .... F 704 872-6669
  Statesville (G-14874)
Speed Brite Inc .... G 704 639-9771
  Salisbury (G-14046)
▲ Starcraft Diamonds Inc .... F 252 717-2548
  Washington (G-15733)
Thomas Jewelers .... G 252 756-1641
  Greenville (G-7590)
William Travis Jewelry Ltd .... G 919 968-0011
  Chapel Hill (G-2097)

5945 Hobby, toy, and game shops

Bear Pages .... G 828 837-0785
  Murphy (G-11706)
Bluff Mountain Outfitters Inc .... G 828 622-7162
  Hot Springs (G-8744)
Bright Angle LLC .... G 828 771-6966
  Asheville (G-573)
Burlington Outlet .... G 910 278-3442
  Oak Island (G-12048)
Grateful Union Family Inc .... F 828 622-3258
  Asheville (G-640)

5946 Camera and photographic supply stores

Ball Photo Supply Inc .... G 828 252-2443
  Asheville (G-556)

5947 Gift, novelty, and souvenir shop

A Stitch In Time .... G 828 274-5193
  Asheville (G-513)
Bakers Southern Traditions Inc .... G 252 344-2120
  Roxobel (G-13829)
Burlington Outlet .... G 910 278-3442
  Oak Island (G-12048)
Carolina Perfumer Inc .... G 910 295-5600
  Pinehurst (G-12217)
Ceder Creek Gallery & Pottery .... G 919 528-1041
  Creedmoor (G-4610)
▲ Colonial Tin Works Inc .... E 336 668-4126
  Greensboro (G-6919)
James Lammers .... G 252 491-2303
  Powells Point (G-12398)
Jkl Inc .... F 252 355-6714
  Greenville (G-7550)
Joie of Seating Inc .... F 704 795-7474
  Concord (G-4295)
Katchi Tees Incorporated .... G 252 315-4691
  Wilson (G-16504)
Michael S North Wilkesboro Inc .... G 336 838-5964
  North Wilkesboro (G-12028)
Oleksynprannyk LLC .... F 704 450-0182
  Mooresville (G-11043)

Party Time Inc .... G 910 454-4577
  Southport (G-14575)
Poppies LLC .... G 704 896-3433
  Huntersville (G-8879)
Simple & Sentimental LLC .... G 252 320-9458
  Ayden (G-857)
▼ Starflite Companies Inc .... C 252 728-2690
  Beaufort (G-968)
◆ USa Wholesale and Distrg Inc .... F 888 484-6872
  Fayetteville (G-5945)
Wings Store 765 .... G 910 458-0278
  Carolina Beach (G-1642)
Wit & Whistle .... G 919 609-5309
  Cary (G-1930)

5949 Sewing, needlework, and piece goods

Artist S Needle Inc .... G 336 294-5884
  Greensboro (G-6817)
Cloth Barn Inc .... F 919 735-3643
  Goldsboro (G-6601)
▲ Composite Fabrics America LLC ..... G 828 632-5220
  Taylorsville (G-15135)
Contempora Fabrics Inc .... C 910 345-0150
  Lumberton (G-10030)
Distinctive Furniture Inc .... G 828 754-3947
  Lenoir (G-9604)
Embroidme .... G 919 316-1538
  Durham (G-5081)
▲ Hampton Art Inc .... C 252 975-7207
  Washington (G-15709)
Innovaknits LLC .... G 828 536-9348
  Conover (G-4467)
Kessel Development LLC .... G 704 752-4282
  Charlotte (G-3051)
L & B Monograms Plus .... G 336 229-0152
  Burlington (G-1445)
Ledford Upholstery .... G 704 732-0233
  Lincolnton (G-9899)
▲ Mayo Knitting Mill Inc .... C 252 823-3101
  Tarboro (G-15114)
McMurray Fabrics Inc .... D 704 732-9613
  Lincolnton (G-9906)
◆ Meridian Spcalty Yrn Group Inc .... B 828 874-2151
  Valdese (G-15450)
Quilt Shop .... G 828 263-8691
  Boone (G-1230)
▲ Uwharrie Knits Inc .... F 704 474-4123
  Norwood (G-12047)

5961 Catalog and mail-order houses

Advantage Fitness Products LLC .... G 336 643-8810
  Archdale (G-265)
Apex Waves LLC .... G 919 809-5227
  Cary (G-1684)
Buddy Cut Inc .... G 888 608-4701
  Pittsboro (G-12333)
Cbdmd Inc .... F 704 445-3060
  Charlotte (G-2422)
▲ Celtic Ocean International Inc .... E 828 299-9005
  Arden (G-320)
Cherokee Publications .... G 828 627-2424
  Cherokee (G-3854)
Dallas L Pridgen Inc .... G 919 732-4422
  Carrboro (G-1647)
Eb5 Corporation .... G 503 230-8008
  Charlotte (G-2680)
▼ Fireresq Incorporated .... F 888 975-0858
  Mooresville (G-10945)
Glen Raven Custom Fabrics LLC .... C 828 682-2142
  Burnsville (G-1526)
Grailgame Inc .... G 804 517-3102
  Reidsville (G-13522)

SIC SECTION

59 MISCELLANEOUS RETAIL

Grateful Union Family Inc............... F 828 622-3258
  Asheville *(G-640)*

Hometown Sports Inc...................... G 919 732-7090
  Hillsborough *(G-8655)*

◆ Kayser-Roth Corporation............... C 336 852-2030
  Greensboro *(G-7145)*

Nutrotonic LLC................................. F 855 948-0008
  Charlotte *(G-3285)*

Old Salem Incorporated.................. G 336 721-7305
  Winston Salem *(G-16828)*

Owen G Dunn Co Inc........................ G 252 633-3197
  New Bern *(G-11832)*

Simple & Sentimental LLC............... G 252 320-9458
  Ayden *(G-857)*

Speed Utv LLC.................................. E 704 949-1255
  Concord *(G-4365)*

◆ Stump Printing Co Inc.................... C 260 723-5171
  Wrightsville Beach *(G-17028)*

▲ Trophy House Inc......................... F 910 323-1791
  Fayetteville *(G-5934)*

▲ William L Day Companies Inc....... F 828 693-1333
  Tryon *(G-15431)*

5962 Merchandising machine operators

Coca-Cola Consolidated Inc........... C 919 550-0611
  Clayton *(G-3968)*

Compass Group Usa Inc.................. A 704 398-6515
  Charlotte *(G-2532)*

Compass Group Usa Inc.................. B 919 381-9577
  Garner *(G-6267)*

Compass Group Usa Inc.................. E 252 291-7733
  Wilson *(G-16489)*

Durham Coca-Cola Bottling Company. C 919 383-1531
  Durham *(G-5071)*

5963 Direct selling establishments

Bakers Southern Traditions Inc....... G 252 344-2120
  Roxobel *(G-13829)*

Lotus Bakeries Us LLC...................... G 415 956-8956
  Mebane *(G-10417)*

Old Saratoga Inc.............................. E 252 238-2175
  Saratoga *(G-14216)*

Over Rainbow Inc............................. F 704 332-5521
  Charlotte *(G-3307)*

Picassomoesllc................................. G 216 703-4547
  Hillsborough *(G-8665)*

Random Rues Botanical LLC........... G 252 214-2759
  Greenville *(G-7579)*

5983 Fuel oil dealers

Euliss Oil Company Inc.................... G 336 622-3055
  Liberty *(G-9813)*

Go Energies LLC................................ F 877 712-5999
  Wilmington *(G-16234)*

Go Energies Holdings Inc................. G 910 762-5802
  Wilmington *(G-16235)*

Herrin Bros Coal & Ice Co................ G 704 332-2193
  Charlotte *(G-2906)*

Hickman Oil & Ice Co Inc................. G 910 576-2501
  Troy *(G-15406)*

M & R Retreading & Oil Co Inc........ F 704 474-4101
  Norwood *(G-12040)*

▲ Parker Gas Company Inc............. F 800 354-7250
  Clinton *(G-4101)*

▼ Starflite Companies Inc................ C 252 728-2690
  Beaufort *(G-968)*

5984 Liquefied petroleum gas dealers

Blossman Propane Gas & Appl...... F 828 396-0144
  Hickory *(G-7950)*

Euliss Oil Company Inc.................... G 336 622-3055
  Liberty *(G-9813)*

▲ Parker Gas Company Inc............. F 800 354-7250
  Clinton *(G-4101)*

5989 Fuel dealers, nec

Herrin Bros Coal & Ice Co................ G 704 332-2193
  Charlotte *(G-2906)*

5992 Florists

Harris Teeter LLC............................. D 704 846-7117
  Matthews *(G-10252)*

5993 Tobacco stores and stands

▲ Fontem Us Inc.............................. G 888 207-4588
  Charlotte *(G-2784)*

J Wise Inc... E 828 202-5563
  Lincolnton *(G-9896)*

Jim Fab of North Carolina Inc......... E 704 278-1000
  Cleveland *(G-4074)*

5994 News dealers and newsstands

Raleigh Downtowner....................... G 919 821-9000
  Raleigh *(G-13176)*

5995 Optical goods stores

Clarity Vision of Smithfield............. G 919 938-6101
  Smithfield *(G-14454)*

Luxottica of America Inc................. G 910 867-0200
  Fayetteville *(G-5862)*

Luxottica of America Inc................. G 919 778-5692
  Goldsboro *(G-6632)*

O D Eyecarecenter P A.................... G 252 443-7011
  Rocky Mount *(G-13716)*

Optical Place Inc.............................. E 336 274-1300
  Greensboro *(G-7235)*

Optics Inc.. G 336 288-9504
  Greensboro *(G-7236)*

5999 Miscellaneous retail stores, nec

A House of Hemp LLC..................... G 910 984-1441
  Linden *(G-9938)*

▲ Acme Stone Company Inc........... E 336 786-6978
  Mount Airy *(G-11472)*

Admiral Marine Pdts & Svcs Inc..... G 704 489-8771
  Denver *(G-4758)*

Aidleyco LLC.................................... G 704 782-0648
  Mooresville *(G-10851)*

Airgas Usa LLC................................. G 919 544-1056
  Durham *(G-4908)*

All 4 U Home Medical LLC.............. G 828 437-0684
  Morganton *(G-11196)*

All Glass Inc..................................... G 828 324-8609
  Hickory *(G-7931)*

Applied Drives Inc............................ G 704 573-2324
  Charlotte *(G-2204)*

Banner Signs Today Inc................... G 704 525-2241
  Charlotte *(G-2275)*

Bio-Tech Prosthetics........................ G 336 768-3666
  Winston Salem *(G-16630)*

Bio-Tech Prsthtics Orthtics In......... G 336 333-9081
  Greensboro *(G-6839)*

Blaq Beauty Naturalz Inc................ G 252 326-5621
  Weldon *(G-15880)*

Blue Ridge Elc Mtr Repr Inc............ G 828 258-0800
  Asheville *(G-564)*

Blue Ridge Quick Print Inc.............. G 828 883-2420
  Brevard *(G-1270)*

Boardwalk Inc................................... G 252 240-1095
  Morehead City *(G-11155)*

◆ Body Shop Inc............................... C 919 554-4900
  Wake Forest *(G-15534)*

Boonville Flour Feed Mill Inc.......... G 336 367-7541
  Boonville *(G-1253)*

Brigman Electric Motors Inc........... G 828 492-0568
  Canton *(G-1603)*

▲ Buchanan Gem Stone Mines Inc. F 828 765-6130
  Spruce Pine *(G-14632)*

Busch Enterprises Inc....................... G 704 878-2067
  Statesville *(G-14768)*

CAM Enterprises Inc........................ F 252 946-4877
  Washington *(G-15684)*

Camp Chemical Corporation.......... F 336 597-2214
  Roxboro *(G-13797)*

Canipe & Lynn Elc Mtr Repr Inc..... G 828 322-9052
  Hickory *(G-7961)*

Cape Fear Orthtics Prsthtics I........ G 910 483-0933
  Fayetteville *(G-5780)*

Carolina Container LLC................... F 336 883-7146
  Thomasville *(G-15195)*

Carolina Sgns Grphic Dsgns Inc..... G 919 383-3344
  Durham *(G-5004)*

Carolina Water Consultants LLC... G 828 251-2420
  Fletcher *(G-5992)*

Carpenter Co.................................... D 828 464-9470
  Conover *(G-4433)*

Classy Glass Inc............................... G 828 452-2242
  Waynesville *(G-15798)*

Connected 2k LLC............................. G 910 321-7446
  Fayetteville *(G-5795)*

Conway Development Inc............... F 252 756-2168
  Greenville *(G-7505)*

Craven Tire Co................................. G 252 633-0200
  New Bern *(G-11792)*

Crown Trophy Inc............................. G 336 851-1011
  Greensboro *(G-6944)*

▲ Cummins Atlantic LLC................. E 704 588-1240
  Charlotte *(G-2585)*

Custom Rehabilitation Spc Inc....... G 910 471-2962
  Wilmington *(G-16192)*

▲ Danbartex LLC.............................. G 704 323-8728
  Mooresville *(G-10923)*

Dixie Electro Mech Svcs Inc............ F 704 332-1116
  Charlotte *(G-2646)*

DLM Sales Inc................................... F 704 399-2776
  Charlotte *(G-2647)*

DNB Humidifier Mfg Inc.................. F 336 764-2076
  Winston Salem *(G-16686)*

Duncan-Parnell Inc.......................... G 252 977-7832
  Rocky Mount *(G-13692)*

Electric Motor Service of Shelby Inc. F 704 482-9979
  Shelby *(G-14314)*

Evoqua Water Technologies LLC... F 919 477-2161
  Durham *(G-5094)*

Faith Farm Inc.................................. G 704 431-4566
  Salisbury *(G-13963)*

Faith Prsthtc-Rthotic Svcs Inc........ F 704 782-0908
  Concord *(G-4263)*

Farm Services Inc............................. G 336 226-7381
  Graham *(G-6689)*

Fines and Carriel Inc....................... G 919 929-0702
  Chapel Hill *(G-2018)*

▼ Fireresq Incorporated.................. F 888 975-0858
  Mooresville *(G-10945)*

▼ Flologic Inc................................... G 919 878-1808
  Morrisville *(G-11342)*

Fosterscape LLP............................... G 910 401-7638
  Fayetteville *(G-5827)*

Founders Hemp LLC......................... G 888 334-4367
  Asheboro *(G-436)*

Four Corners Frmng Gallery Inc..... G 704 662-7154
  Mooresville *(G-10949)*

Frazees Trophies.............................. G 910 892-6722
  Dunn *(G-4869)*

Free Will Bptst Press Fndtion......... F 252 746-6128
  Ayden *(G-852)*

Employee Codes: A=Over 500 employees, B=251-500
C=101-250, D=51-100, E=20-50, F=10-19, G=1-9

2024 Harris North Carolina Manufacturers Directory

59 MISCELLANEOUS RETAIL

G & G Management LLC .... F 336 444-6271
  Greensboro (G-7027)
GNB Ventures LLC .... F 704 488-4468
  Charlotte (G-2837)
Granite Memorials Inc .... G 336 786-6596
  Mount Airy (G-11512)
▲ Guilford Fabricators Inc .... G 336 434-3163
  High Point (G-8372)
Harvest Homes and Handi Houses .... G 704 637-3878
  Salisbury (G-13975)
Heart Electric Motor Service .... G 704 922-4720
  Bessemer City (G-1070)
Heritage Prtg & Graphics Inc .... G 704 551-0700
  Charlotte (G-2905)
Herrin Bros Coal & Ice Co .... G 704 332-2193
  Charlotte (G-2906)
High Country Electric Mtrs LLC .... G 336 838-4808
  North Wilkesboro (G-12014)
Infinity S End Inc .... F 704 900-8355
  Charlotte (G-2968)
Innovative Awngs & Screens LLC .... F 833 337-4233
  Cornelius (G-4561)
Integrated Info Systems Inc .... F 919 488-5000
  Youngsville (G-17086)
J & D Thorpe Enterprises Inc .... G 919 553-0918
  Clayton (G-3990)
Johnny Slicks Inc .... G 910 803-2159
  Holly Ridge (G-8683)
Js Linens and Curtain Outlet .... F 704 871-1582
  Statesville (G-14829)
Jtc Awards and Printing .... G 910 346-9522
  Jacksonville (G-9011)
Kelleys Sports and Awards Inc .... G 828 728-4600
  Hudson (G-8772)
◆ Kennel-Aire LLC .... E 704 459-0044
  Norwood (G-12039)
Kloud Hemp Co .... G 336 740-2528
  Greensboro (G-7154)
Kwik Elc Mtr Sls & Svc Inc .... G 252 335-2524
  Elizabeth City (G-5553)
L & B Jandrew Enterprises .... G 828 687-8927
  Hendersonville (G-7871)
Learning Craftsmen Inc .... G 813 321-5003
  Apex (G-213)
Legend Compression Wear .... G 877 711-5343
  Denton (G-4742)
Luxebright Skin Care LLC .... G 877 614-9128
  Matthews (G-10264)
Lynchs Office Supply Co Inc .... F 252 537-6041
  Roanoke Rapids (G-13578)
M & S Systems Inc .... G 336 996-7118
  Kernersville (G-9211)
Mables Headstone & Monu Co LLP .... G 919 724-8705
  Creedmoor (G-4618)
McKinney Electric & Mch Co Inc .... G 828 765-7910
  Spruce Pine (G-14648)
Medaccess Inc .... G 828 264-4085
  Robbinsville (G-13609)
◆ Medi Mall Inc .... G 877 501-6334
  Fletcher (G-6022)
Mid-Atlantic Drainage Inc .... F 828 324-0808
  Conover (G-4472)
Mike DS Bbq LLC .... G 866 960-8652
  Durham (G-5225)
Mirrormate LLC .... F 704 390-7377
  Charlotte (G-3187)
Monitor Roller Mill Inc .... G 336 591-4126
  Walnut Cove (G-15634)
Moon Audio .... G 919 649-5018
  Cary (G-1826)
Morningstar Signs and Banners .... G 704 861-0020
  Gastonia (G-6469)

Motor Shop Inc .... G 704 867-8488
  Gastonia (G-6471)
NC Graphic Pros LLC .... G 252 492-7326
  Kittrell (G-9397)
Neptune Hlth Wllness Innvtion .... C 888 664-9166
  Conover (G-4475)
Orianna Naturals LLC .... G 336 877-1560
  Todd (G-15324)
Picassomoesllc .... G 216 703-4547
  Hillsborough (G-8665)
Piedmont Fiberglass Inc .... E 828 632-8883
  Statesville (G-14859)
Pilgrims Pride Corporation .... B 704 624-2171
  Marshville (G-10222)
Powell & Stokes Inc .... G 252 794-2138
  Windsor (G-16568)
Pregis LLC .... D 828 396-2373
  Granite Falls (G-6752)
▲ Prem Corp .... E 704 921-1799
  Charlotte (G-3373)
Rec Plus Inc .... E 704 375-9098
  Charlotte (G-3419)
Rm Liquidation Inc .... G 828 274-7996
  Asheville (G-756)
S & L Creations Inc .... G 704 824-1930
  Lowell (G-10011)
Safeguard Medical Alarms Inc .... F 312 506-2900
  Harrisburg (G-7727)
Sanders Electric Motor Svc Inc .... G 828 754-0513
  Lenoir (G-9651)
Scaltrol Inc .... G 678 990-0858
  Charlotte (G-3497)
Screen Master .... G 252 492-8407
  Henderson (G-7810)
Second Earth Inc .... G 336 740-9333
  Greensboro (G-7329)
Sharpe Images Properties Inc .... E 336 724-2871
  Winston Salem (G-16906)
Snipes Group LLC .... G 757 266-0488
  Pittsboro (G-12350)
Solarbrook Water and Pwr Corp .... G 919 231-3205
  Raleigh (G-13278)
South Mountain Crafts .... G 828 433-2607
  Morganton (G-11255)
Southern Electric Motor Co .... G 919 688-7879
  Durham (G-5365)
Southern States Coop Inc .... G 336 629-3977
  Asheboro (G-484)
Southern States Coop Inc .... E 919 528-1516
  Creedmoor (G-4621)
Southern States Coop Inc .... E 919 693-6136
  Oxford (G-12157)
Southern States Coop Inc .... G 252 823-2520
  Princeville (G-12406)
Speer Operational Tech LLC .... G 864 631-2512
  Marion (G-10179)
Steelman Milling Company Inc .... G 336 463-5586
  Yadkinville (G-17051)
Stellar Innovations Inc .... G 704 746-2886
  Cornelius (G-4588)
Surry Elc Mtr & Contrls Inc .... F 336 786-1717
  Mount Airy (G-11581)
Tekni-Plex Inc .... D 919 553-4151
  Clayton (G-4017)
Telecmmnctons Resource MGT Inc .... F 919 779-0776
  Raleigh (G-13336)
Tractor Country Inc .... F 252 523-3007
  Dover (G-4835)
▲ Trophy House Inc .... F 910 323-1791
  Fayetteville (G-5934)
United Mobile Imaging Inc .... G 800 983-9840
  Clemmons (G-4065)

Utd Technology Corp .... G 704 612-0121
  Mint Hill (G-10546)
Veon Inc .... F 252 623-2102
  Washington (G-15736)
W E Nixons Wldg & Hdwr Inc .... G 252 221-4348
  Edenton (G-5523)
Wake Monument Company Inc .... G 919 556-3422
  Rolesville (G-13761)
Walgreen Co .... F 704 525-2628
  Charlotte (G-3792)
Wersunsllc .... G 857 209-8701
  Winston Salem (G-16969)
Wholesale Kennel Supply Co .... G 919 742-2515
  Siler City (G-14434)
Wildflwers Btq of Blowing Rock .... G 828 295-9655
  Blowing Rock (G-1157)
Winecoff Mmrals Sttesville Inc .... G 704 873-9661
  Statesville (G-14927)
World Art Gallery Incorporated .... G 910 989-0203
  Jacksonville (G-9047)
Z Collection LLC .... G 919 247-1513
  Zebulon (G-17147)

61 NONDEPOSITORY CREDIT INSTITUTIONS

6141 Personal credit institutions

◆ Mack Trucks Inc .... A 336 291-9001
  Greensboro (G-7177)

6153 Short-term business credit

◆ Mack Trucks Inc .... A 336 291-9001
  Greensboro (G-7177)
McRae Industries Inc .... C 910 439-6149
  Mount Gilead (G-11605)

6159 Miscellaneous business credit

◆ Vna Holding Inc .... A 336 393-4890
  Greensboro (G-7445)

6162 Mortgage bankers and correspondents

▲ GLG Corporation .... F 336 784-0396
  Winston Salem (G-16722)
Ramsey Industries Inc .... E 704 827-3560
  Belmont (G-1005)

62 SECURITY & COMMODITY BROKERS, DEALERS, EXCHANGES & SERVICES

6211 Security brokers and dealers

Integrated Roe Security LLC .... G 919 297-8036
  Raleigh (G-12896)

6221 Commodity contracts brokers, dealers

Smissons Inc .... G 660 537-3219
  Clayton (G-4009)

6282 Investment advice

Sheets Smith Wealth MGT Inc .... E 336 765-2020
  Winston Salem (G-16907)

63 INSURANCE CARRIERS

6311 Life insurance

Western Crlina Mutl Brial Assn .... G 828 837-2577
  Murphy (G-11718)

6331 Fire, marine, and casualty insurance

SIC SECTION

64 INSURANCE AGENTS, BROKERS AND SERVICE

Discovery Insurance Company............ D 800 876-1492
Kinston *(G-9358)*

6411 Insurance agents, brokers, and service

Atlantic Group Usa Inc......................... F 919 623-7824
Raleigh *(G-12530)*

Donald Haack Diamonds Inc................ G 704 365-4400
Charlotte *(G-2651)*

Hinson Industries Inc........................... G 252 937-7171
Rocky Mount *(G-13700)*

Katchi Tees Incorporated...................... G 252 315-4691
Wilson *(G-16504)*

Motor Vhcles Lcense Plate Agcy........... G 252 338-6965
Elizabeth City *(G-5558)*

65 REAL ESTATE

6512 Nonresidential building operators

B V Hedrick Gravel & Sand Co............. E 704 633-5982
Salisbury *(G-13928)*

Cla Properties LLC.............................. G 336 476-7828
Thomasville *(G-15203)*

Industrial Container Inc........................ F 336 882-1310
High Point *(G-8409)*

J L Powell & Co Inc............................. G 910 642-8989
Whiteville *(G-15967)*

Jenkins Properties Inc......................... E 336 667-4282
North Wilkesboro *(G-12017)*

Moorecraft Wood Proucts Inc............... G 252 823-2510
Tarboro *(G-15116)*

Robert Wrren MBL TV Prductions......... G 910 483-4777
Eastover *(G-5482)*

6513 Apartment building operators

J L Powell & Co Inc............................. G 910 642-8989
Whiteville *(G-15967)*

6531 Real estate agents and managers

Anew Look Homes LLC....................... F 800 796-5152
Hickory *(G-7935)*

Braswell Realty.................................... G 828 733-5800
Newland *(G-11882)*

Brookhurst Associates......................... G 919 792-0987
Raleigh *(G-12576)*

Brunswick Beacon Inc.......................... F 910 754-6890
Shallotte *(G-14270)*

Fascoe Realty..................................... G 828 963-7600
Boone *(G-1198)*

Fathom Holdings Inc............................ E 888 455-6040
Cary *(G-1769)*

Green Waste Management LLC............ G 704 289-0720
Charlotte *(G-2864)*

Jdh Capital LLC.................................. F 704 357-1220
Charlotte *(G-3016)*

Joe Robin Darnell................................ G 704 482-1186
Shelby *(G-14333)*

L6 Realty LLC..................................... G 704 654-3000
Charlotte *(G-3067)*

▼ Lindley Laboratories Inc................... G 336 449-7521
Gibsonville *(G-6567)*

▲ Solarh2ot Ltd.................................. G 919 439-2387
Raleigh *(G-13279)*

Town of Maggie Valley Inc................... G 828 926-0145
Maggie Valley *(G-10096)*

Wersunsllc.. G 857 209-7601
Winston Salem *(G-16969)*

6552 Subdividers and developers, nec

Capitol Funds Inc................................ F 910 439-5275
Mount Gilead *(G-11599)*

Capitol Funds Inc................................ E 704 487-8547
Shelby *(G-14291)*

67 HOLDING AND OTHER INVESTMENT OFFICES

6719 Holding companies, nec

Alcami Holdings LLC........................... A 910 254-7000
Wilmington *(G-16105)*

Atticus LLC... E 984 465-4754
Cary *(G-1694)*

▼ Hlm Legacy Group Inc..................... C 704 878-8823
Troutman *(G-15381)*

Interroll USA Holding LLC.................... D 910 799-1100
Wilmington *(G-16272)*

Ipi Acquisition LLC.............................. A 704 588-1100
Charlotte *(G-2996)*

K&K Holdings Inc................................ G 704 341-5567
Charlotte *(G-3040)*

Pharr McAdenville Corporation............. D 704 824-3551
Mc Adenville *(G-10380)*

6733 Trusts, nec

Pinkston Properties LLC...................... F 828 252-9867
Asheville *(G-732)*

6794 Patent owners and lessors

◆ Body Shop Inc................................. C 919 554-4900
Wake Forest *(G-15534)*

◆ Ohio Mat Lcnsing Cmpnnts Group..... G 336 861-3500
Trinity *(G-15349)*

6798 Real estate investment trusts

Anew Look Homes LLC....................... F 800 796-5152
Hickory *(G-7935)*

6799 Investors, nec

Atlantic Caribbean LLC........................ F 910 343-0624
Wilmington *(G-16120)*

◆ Century Furniture LLC...................... C 828 267-8739
Hickory *(G-7983)*

Igm Specialties Holding Inc.................. F 704 945-8702
Charlotte *(G-2951)*

Lm Shea LLC...................................... G 919 608-1901
Raleigh *(G-12977)*

Rhf Investments Inc............................ G 828 326-8350
Hickory *(G-8135)*

Solarbrook Water and Pwr Corp........... G 919 231-3205
Raleigh *(G-13278)*

70 HOTELS, ROOMING HOUSES, CAMPS, AND OTHER LODGING PLACES

7011 Hotels and motels

Catawba Farms Enterprises LLC........... F 828 464-5870
Newton *(G-11917)*

Celebrity Dairy LLC............................. G 919 742-4931
Siler City *(G-14404)*

Tom Burgiss.. G 336 359-2995
Laurel Springs *(G-9468)*

7033 Trailer parks and campsites

B & D Enterprises Inc.......................... F 704 739-2958
Kings Mountain *(G-9293)*

72 PERSONAL SERVICES

7212 Garment pressing and cleaners' agents

A Cleaner Tomorrow Dry Clg LLC.......... G 919 639-6396
Dunn *(G-4847)*

7215 Coin-operated laundries and cleaning

A Cleaner Tomorrow Dry Clg LLC.......... G 919 639-6396
Dunn *(G-4847)*

Rachel Dubois..................................... G 919 870-8063
Raleigh *(G-13169)*

7216 Drycleaning plants, except rugs

A Cleaner Tomorrow Dry Clg LLC.......... G 919 639-6396
Dunn *(G-4847)*

Bridgport Restoration Svcs Inc............. F 336 996-1212
Kernersville *(G-9169)*

Stitch In Time Inc................................ G 910 497-4171
Spring Lake *(G-14628)*

7217 Carpet and upholstery cleaning

Bridgport Restoration Svcs Inc............. F 336 996-1212
Kernersville *(G-9169)*

7218 Industrial launderers

Ican Clothes Company......................... F 910 670-1494
Fayetteville *(G-5840)*

7219 Laundry and garment services, nec

A Stitch In Time.................................. G 828 274-5193
Asheville *(G-513)*

Howell & Sons Canvas Repairs............. G 704 892-7913
Cornelius *(G-4556)*

Jones Fabricare Inc............................. G 336 272-7261
Greensboro *(G-7139)*

Professnal Alterations EMB Inc............ G 910 577-8484
Jacksonville *(G-9022)*

7221 Photographic studios, portrait

David Presnell..................................... G 336 372-5989
Sparta *(G-14592)*

Strawbridge Studios Inc....................... D 919 286-9512
Durham *(G-5377)*

7231 Beauty shops

Brandy Thompson................................ F 321 252-2911
Fayetteville *(G-5774)*

Gifted Hands Styling Salon................... G 828 781-2781
Hickory *(G-8032)*

Haircutters of Raleigh Inc.................... G 919 781-3465
Raleigh *(G-12826)*

Katchi Tees Incorporated...................... G 252 315-4691
Wilson *(G-16504)*

7241 Barber shops

Executive Grooming LLC...................... G 919 706-5382
Raleigh *(G-12753)*

Kraken-Skulls..................................... F 910 500-9100
Fayetteville *(G-5855)*

7261 Funeral service and crematories

▼ Custom Air Trays Inc....................... F 336 889-8729
High Point *(G-8311)*

Gooder Grafix Inc................................ G 828 349-4097
Franklin *(G-6131)*

Wiggins North State Co Inc.................. G 919 556-3231
Rolesville *(G-13762)*

Wilmington Mortuary Svc Inc................ F 910 791-9099
Wilmington *(G-16449)*

7291 Tax return preparation services

Katchi Tees Incorporated...................... G 252 315-4691
Wilson *(G-16504)*

72 PERSONAL SERVICES

7299 Miscellaneous personal services

A Stitch In Time... G 828 274-5193
   Asheville *(G-513)*

Brandy Thompson.. F 321 252-2911
   Fayetteville *(G-5774)*

Capre Omnimedia LLC................................ G 917 460-3572
   Wilmington *(G-16155)*

Communitys Kitchen L3c........................... G 828 817-2308
   Tryon *(G-15423)*

Creative Stone Fyetteville Inc.................... G 910 491-1225
   Fayetteville *(G-5799)*

Darius All Access LLC............................... E 910 262-8567
   Wilmington *(G-16194)*

Digits.. G 336 721-0209
   Winston Salem *(G-16680)*

Fixed-NC LLC.. G 252 751-1911
   Greenville *(G-7526)*

Kraken-Skulls.. F 910 500-9100
   Fayetteville *(G-5855)*

Owens Quilting Inc.................................... G 828 695-1495
   Newton *(G-11956)*

Picassomoesllc... G 216 703-4547
   Hillsborough *(G-8665)*

Quilt Shop... G 828 263-8691
   Boone *(G-1230)*

Salon Couture... G 910 693-1611
   Southern Pines *(G-14552)*

Sugar Pops... G 704 799-0959
   Mooresville *(G-11107)*

Telephys Inc... G 312 625-9128
   Davidson *(G-4699)*

Triangle Trggr-Pint Thrapy Inc................... G 919 845-1818
   Raleigh *(G-13363)*

73 BUSINESS SERVICES

7311 Advertising agencies

822tees Inc... G 910 822-8337
   Fayetteville *(G-5748)*

Advertising Design Systems Inc................ G 828 264-8060
   Boone *(G-1172)*

B&P Enterprise NC Inc............................... G 727 669-6877
   Hickory *(G-7947)*

Clarks Printing Service Inc........................ E 828 254-1432
   Asheville *(G-594)*

Creative Conquest LLC.............................. G 720 481-4372
   Shelby *(G-14304)*

Dale Advertising Inc.................................. G 704 484-0971
   Shelby *(G-14310)*

Ed Kemp Associates Inc............................ G 336 869-2155
   High Point *(G-8336)*

Embroidme Lake Norman........................... G 704 987-9630
   Cornelius *(G-4543)*

Executive Promotions Inc.......................... F 704 663-4000
   Mooresville *(G-10940)*

Fit1media LLC... G 919 925-2200
   Raleigh *(G-12770)*

◆ Golf Associates Advertising Co............. E 828 252-6544
   Asheville *(G-637)*

Idea People Inc.. G 704 398-4437
   Huntersville *(G-8833)*

Ifpo - Ifmo/American Image Inc................ G 336 945-9867
   Hamptonville *(G-7672)*

Inspire Creative Studios Inc...................... G 910 395-0200
   Wilmington *(G-16269)*

JB II Printing LLC....................................... E 336 222-0717
   Burlington *(G-1439)*

▲ Lomar Specialty Advg Inc..................... F 704 788-4380
   Concord *(G-4307)*

Planet Logo Inc.. G 910 763-2554
   Wilmington *(G-16356)*

Shannon Media Inc..................................... F 919 933-1551
   Chapel Hill *(G-2071)*

Two24 Digital LLC...................................... G 910 475-7555
   Wilmington *(G-16437)*

Yp Advrtising Pubg LLC Not LLC............. C 704 522-5500
   Charlotte *(G-3847)*

7312 Outdoor advertising services

Action Sign Company Lenoir Inc............... F 828 754-4116
   Lenoir *(G-9567)*

Fairway Outdoor Advg LLC....................... F 919 755-1900
   Raleigh *(G-12759)*

Signlite Services Inc.................................. G 336 751-9543
   Mocksville *(G-10603)*

Sweatnet Inc... G 847 331-7287
   Charlotte *(G-3658)*

Wilson Billboard Advg Inc......................... G 919 934-2421
   Smithfield *(G-14489)*

7313 Radio, television, publisher representatives

Gatehouse Media LLC................................ F 336 626-6103
   Asheboro *(G-439)*

Iwanna.. G 828 505-7319
   Asheville *(G-665)*

Latino Communications Inc....................... F 919 645-1680
   Raleigh *(G-12959)*

Yp Advrtising Pubg LLC Not LLC............. C 704 522-5500
   Charlotte *(G-3847)*

7319 Advertising, nec

Apple Rock Advg & Prom Inc.................... E 336 232-4800
   Greensboro *(G-6811)*

Capre Omnimedia LLC................................ G 917 460-3572
   Wilmington *(G-16155)*

Dzone Inc.. F 919 678-0300
   Research Triangle Pa *(G-13550)*

Good Grief Marketing LLC......................... G 336 989-1984
   Greensboro *(G-7053)*

NC Diesel Performance LLC...................... G 704 431-3257
   Salisbury *(G-14016)*

RLM/Universal Packaging Inc.................... F 336 644-6161
   Greensboro *(G-7312)*

Two24 Digital LLC...................................... G 910 475-7555
   Wilmington *(G-16437)*

7331 Direct mail advertising services

Alpha Mailing Service Inc.......................... E 704 484-1711
   Shelby *(G-14283)*

Heritage Prtg & Graphics Inc.................... G 704 551-0700
   Charlotte *(G-2905)*

King Business Service Inc......................... G 910 610-1030
   Laurinburg *(G-9483)*

▲ Laser Ink Corporation............................ E 919 361-5822
   Durham *(G-5186)*

Mb-F Inc... D 336 379-9352
   Greensboro *(G-7192)*

Meredith - Webb Prtg Co Inc..................... D 336 228-8378
   Burlington *(G-1460)*

Metro Productions Inc............................... F 919 851-6420
   Raleigh *(G-13022)*

Mjt Us Inc... G 704 826-7828
   Charlotte *(G-3189)*

Professional Laminating LLC..................... G 919 465-0400
   Cary *(G-1862)*

Randall-Reilly LLC..................................... C 704 814-1390
   Charlotte *(G-3408)*

Salem One Inc.. F 336 722-2886
   Kernersville *(G-9231)*

▲ William George Printing LLC................ G 910 221-2700
   Hope Mills *(G-8738)*

Yp Advrtising Pubg LLC Not LLC............. C 704 522-5500
   Charlotte *(G-3847)*

7334 Photocopying and duplicating services

Accelerated Press Inc................................ G 248 524-1850
   Wilmington *(G-16092)*

AEC Imaging & Graphics LLC................... G 910 693-1034
   Hope Mills *(G-8730)*

Asheville Quickprint.................................. G 828 252-7667
   Fletcher *(G-5984)*

Better Business Printing Inc..................... G 704 867-3366
   Gastonia *(G-6353)*

Branch Office Solutions Inc...................... G 800 743-1047
   Indian Trail *(G-8924)*

Carolina Copy Services Inc....................... F 704 375-9099
   Cornelius *(G-4533)*

Copy King Inc... G 336 333-9900
   Greensboro *(G-6936)*

Copycat Print Shop Inc............................. F 910 799-1500
   Wilmington *(G-16182)*

Document Imaging Systems Inc................ G 919 460-9440
   Raleigh *(G-12693)*

Gik Inc.. F 919 872-9498
   Raleigh *(G-12800)*

Kathie S Mc Daniel.................................... G 336 835-1544
   Elkin *(G-5622)*

Legalis Dms LLC.. F 919 741-8260
   Raleigh *(G-12965)*

Make An Impression Inc............................ G 919 557-7400
   Holly Springs *(G-8707)*

Moore Printing & Graphics Inc.................. E 919 821-3293
   Raleigh *(G-13041)*

Occasions Group Inc.................................. G 919 751-2400
   Goldsboro *(G-6641)*

Occasions Group Inc.................................. E 252 321-5805
   Greenville *(G-7566)*

Print Express Inc....................................... F 910 455-4554
   Jacksonville *(G-9021)*

Print Haus Inc.. G 828 456-8622
   Waynesville *(G-15817)*

Printing Svcs Greensboro Inc.................... F 336 274-7663
   Greensboro *(G-7285)*

Quality Instant Printing Inc...................... F 919 544-1777
   Durham *(G-5313)*

Richa Inc... G 704 944-0230
   Charlotte *(G-3448)*

Richa Inc... F 704 331-9744
   Charlotte *(G-3449)*

Rite Instant Printing Inc........................... G 336 768-5061
   Winston Salem *(G-16885)*

Sharpe Images Properties Inc.................. E 336 724-2871
   Winston Salem *(G-16906)*

Sillaman & Sons Inc................................... G 919 774-6324
   Sanford *(G-14184)*

SOS Printing Inc.. F 828 264-4262
   Boone *(G-1237)*

Steeds Service Co...................................... G 336 748-1587
   Thomasville *(G-15283)*

Triangle Solutions Inc............................... G 919 481-1235
   Cary *(G-1912)*

Unlimted Potential Sanford Inc................. E 919 852-1117
   Morrisville *(G-11460)*

Village Instant Printing Inc....................... G 919 968-0000
   Chapel Hill *(G-2094)*

Weber and Weber Inc................................ F 336 722-4109
   Winston Salem *(G-16968)*

Zebra Communications Inc........................ E 919 314-3700
   Morrisville *(G-11469)*

7335 Commercial photography

Above Topsail LLC..................................... G 910 803-1759
   Holly Ridge *(G-8678)*

SIC SECTION
73 BUSINESS SERVICES

Advertising Design Systems Inc .... G 828 264-8060
  Boone *(G-1172)*
David Presnell .... G 336 372-5989
  Sparta *(G-14592)*
Kreber .... D 336 861-2700
  High Point *(G-8425)*

7336 Commercial art and graphic design

A Plus Graphics Inc .... G 252 243-0404
  Wilson *(G-16463)*
Advertising Design Systems Inc .... G 828 264-8060
  Boone *(G-1172)*
Barron Legacy Mgmt Group LLC .... G 301 367-4735
  Charlotte *(G-2285)*
Big Fish Dpi .... G 704 545-8112
  Mint Hill *(G-10522)*
Blue Dog Graphics Inc .... G 252 291-9191
  Wilson *(G-16477)*
Body Billboards Inc .... G 919 544-4540
  Durham *(G-4969)*
Boundless Inc .... G 919 622-9051
  Four Oaks *(G-6101)*
Brandilly of Nc Inc .... F 919 278-7896
  Raleigh *(G-12572)*
◆ Causekeepers Inc .... E 336 824-2518
  Franklinville *(G-6167)*
CD Dickie & Associates Inc .... F 704 527-9102
  Charlotte *(G-2433)*
Connected 2k LLC .... G 910 321-7446
  Fayetteville *(G-5795)*
Contract Printing & Graphics .... G 919 832-7178
  Raleigh *(G-12644)*
Creative Conquest LLC .... G 720 481-4372
  Shelby *(G-14304)*
Designs By Rachel .... G 828 783-0698
  Spruce Pine *(G-14639)*
◆ DWM INTERNATIONAL INC .... E 646 290-7448
  Charlotte *(G-2661)*
Embroidme Lake Norman .... G 704 987-9630
  Cornelius *(G-4543)*
Family Industries Inc .... F 919 875-4499
  Raleigh *(G-12762)*
Fast Pro Media LLC .... G 704 799-8040
  Cornelius *(G-4545)*
Fast Pro Media LLC .... G 704 799-8040
  Cornelius *(G-4546)*
Fiber Company .... G 336 725-5277
  Lewisville *(G-9666)*
Fieldsway Solutions LLC .... G 984 920-7791
  Four Oaks *(G-6104)*
Fiestic Inc .... F 888 935-3999
  Raleigh *(G-12765)*
Foundry A Print Cmmnctions LLC .... G 703 329-3300
  Apex *(G-193)*
Gmg Group LLC .... G 252 441-8374
  Kill Devil Hills *(G-9258)*
Graphic Components LLC .... E 336 542-2128
  Greensboro *(G-7057)*
Graphic Image of Cape Fear Inc .... G 910 313-6768
  Wilmington *(G-16239)*
Gulfstream Publications Inc .... G 252 449-2222
  Kitty Hawk *(G-9406)*
Heritage Prtg & Graphics Inc .... G 704 551-0700
  Charlotte *(G-2905)*
High Performance Marketing Inc .... G 919 870-9915
  Raleigh *(G-12843)*
▲ Idx Impressions LLC .... C 703 550-6902
  Washington *(G-15711)*
Kathie S Mc Daniel .... G 336 835-1544
  Elkin *(G-5622)*
Kreber .... D 336 861-2700
  High Point *(G-8425)*

LDR Designs .... G 252 375-4484
  Greenville *(G-7555)*
Logo Wear Graphics LLC .... F 336 382-0455
  Summerfield *(G-14985)*
Mark/Trece Inc .... E 336 292-3424
  Whitsett *(G-15997)*
Max B Smith Jr .... G 828 434-0238
  Boone *(G-1219)*
Merge LLC .... G 919 832-3924
  Raleigh *(G-13016)*
Metro Productions Inc .... F 919 851-6420
  Raleigh *(G-13022)*
Moving Screens Incorporated .... G 336 364-9259
  Rougemont *(G-13787)*
Multi Packaging Solutions .... A 336 855-7142
  Greensboro *(G-7207)*
NC Graphic Pros LLC .... G 252 492-7326
  Kittrell *(G-9397)*
Piranha Industries Inc .... G 704 248-7843
  Charlotte *(G-3344)*
Precision Concepts Intl LLC .... G 704 360-8923
  Mooresville *(G-11058)*
Prism Publishing Inc .... F 919 319-6816
  Cary *(G-1860)*
Rapp Productions Inc .... F 919 913-0270
  Carrboro *(G-1654)*
Signs Etc .... G 336 722-9341
  Winston Salem *(G-16909)*
Skipper Graphics .... G 910 754-8729
  Shallotte *(G-14278)*
▲ St Johns Packaging Usa LLC .... C 336 292-9911
  Greensboro *(G-7362)*
Studio Displays Inc .... F 704 588-6590
  Pineville *(G-12310)*
▲ Tannis Root Productions Inc .... G 919 832-8552
  Raleigh *(G-13327)*
Triangle Solutions Inc .... G 919 481-1235
  Cary *(G-1912)*
Village Graphics .... G 252 745-4600
  Oriental *(G-12113)*
Weathervane Creative Inc .... G 828 542-0136
  Hickory *(G-8208)*
Wild Child Custom Graphics LLC .... G 910 762-5335
  Wilmington *(G-16443)*
Zebra Communications Inc .... E 919 314-3700
  Morrisville *(G-11469)*

7338 Secretarial and court reporting

Carter-Hubbard Publishing Co .... F 336 838-4117
  North Wilkesboro *(G-12000)*
Dtp Inc .... G 336 272-5122
  Greensboro *(G-6982)*
Jones Media .... F 828 264-3612
  Boone *(G-1212)*
Raleigh Printing & Typing Inc .... G 919 662-8001
  Raleigh *(G-13181)*

7342 Disinfecting and pest control services

Bridgport Restoration Svcs Inc .... F 336 996-1212
  Kernersville *(G-9169)*

7349 Building maintenance services, nec

A & B Chem-Dry .... F 919 878-0288
  Raleigh *(G-12451)*
Abercrombie Textiles Inc .... G 704 487-0935
  Shelby *(G-14281)*
Asheville Maintenance and .... E 828 687-8110
  Arden *(G-312)*
Classic Cleaning LLC .... E 800 220-7101
  Raleigh *(G-12626)*
Cymbal LLC .... G 877 365-9622
  Cary *(G-1744)*

Darius All Access LLC .... E 910 262-8567
  Wilmington *(G-16194)*
Galaxy Pressure Washing Inc .... G 888 299-3129
  Pineville *(G-12270)*
Green Waste Management LLC .... G 704 289-0720
  Charlotte *(G-2864)*
Isana LLC .... G 704 439-6761
  Charlotte *(G-2997)*
K & L Resources .... G 910 494-3736
  Fayetteville *(G-5852)*
Patel Deepal .... G 704 634-5141
  Concord *(G-4330)*
Prestige Cleaning Incorporated .... F 704 752-7747
  Charlotte *(G-3375)*
Surface Buff LLC .... G 919 341-2873
  Cary *(G-1906)*
W G of Southwest Raleigh Inc .... G 919 629-7327
  Holly Springs *(G-8725)*

7352 Medical equipment rental

Medaccess Inc .... G 828 264-4085
  Robbinsville *(G-13609)*

7353 Heavy construction equipment rental

◆ International Cnstr Eqp Inc .... E 704 821-8200
  Matthews *(G-10322)*
Stanly Tractor Company .... G 704 983-1106
  New London *(G-11879)*

7359 Equipment rental and leasing, nec

Arc3 Gases Inc .... F 336 275-3333
  Greensboro *(G-6812)*
Arc3 Gases Inc .... F 704 220-1029
  Monroe *(G-10650)*
Arc3 Gases Inc .... E 910 892-4016
  Dunn *(G-4851)*
B V Hedrick Gravel & Sand Co .... E 704 633-5982
  Salisbury *(G-13928)*
Cherokee Instruments Inc .... F 919 552-0554
  Angier *(G-137)*
Classic Industrial Services .... E 919 209-0909
  Smithfield *(G-14455)*
Comer Sanitary Service Inc .... F 336 629-8311
  Lexington *(G-9697)*
Form Tech Concrete Forms Inc .... F 704 395-9910
  Charlotte *(G-2787)*
Gregory Poole Equipment Co .... F 919 872-2691
  Raleigh *(G-12818)*
Kids Playhouse LLC .... G 704 299-4449
  Charlotte *(G-3053)*
Lynn Ladder Scaffolding Co Inc .... G 301 336-4700
  Charlotte *(G-3111)*
M&N Construction Supply Inc .... G 336 996-7740
  Colfax *(G-4154)*
Medaccess Inc .... G 828 264-4085
  Robbinsville *(G-13609)*
R O Givens Signs Inc .... G 252 338-6578
  Elizabeth City *(G-5567)*
Readilite & Barricade Inc .... F 919 231-8309
  Raleigh *(G-13194)*
▲ Sharpe Co .... E 336 724-2871
  Winston Salem *(G-16905)*
Tarheel Monitoring LLC .... G 910 763-1490
  Wilmington *(G-16426)*
Ultimate Floor Cleaning .... G 704 912-8978
  Charlotte *(G-3748)*
▲ Watson Party Tables Inc .... F 919 294-9153
  Durham *(G-5438)*

7363 Help supply services

Delta Contractors Inc .... F 817 410-9481
  Linden *(G-9940)*

Employee Codes: A=Over 500 employees, B=251-500
C=101-250, D=51-100, E=20-50, F=10-19, G=1-9

73 BUSINESS SERVICES

7371 Custom computer programming services

27 Software US Inc.................................... F 704 968-2879
   Mooresville *(G-10844)*
Able Softsystems Corp........................... G 919 241-7907
   Raleigh *(G-12463)*
Add-On Technologies Inc...................... F 704 882-2227
   Indian Trail *(G-8918)*
Advanced Computer Lrng Co LLC......... E 910 779-2254
   Fayetteville *(G-5752)*
Advanced Digital Systems Inc............... F 919 485-4819
   Durham *(G-4904)*
Aiken Development LLC........................ G 828 572-4040
   Lenoir *(G-9568)*
Applied Strategies Inc........................... G 704 525-4478
   Charlotte *(G-2205)*
Artibis Corporation................................. G 919 592-4794
   Cary *(G-1689)*
Bae Systems Info Elctrnic Syst............. E 919 323-5800
   Durham *(G-4941)*
Bluetick Inc... F 336 294-4102
   Greensboro *(G-6844)*
Bmt Micro Inc... G 910 792-9100
   Wilmington *(G-16140)*
Bravo Team LLC.................................... E 704 309-1918
   Mooresville *(G-10887)*
Camelot Computers Inc......................... G 704 554-1670
   Charlotte *(G-2378)*
Cmisolutions Inc..................................... E 704 759-9950
   Charlotte *(G-2505)*
Comp Environmental Inc........................ F 919 316-1321
   Durham *(G-5028)*
Computational Engrg Intl Inc.................. G 919 363-0883
   Apex *(G-176)*
Computer Task Group Inc...................... G 919 677-1313
   Raleigh *(G-12636)*
Cyberlux Corporation.............................. F 984 363-6894
   Research Triangle Pa *(G-13549)*
Czechmate Enterprises LLC.................. G 704 784-6547
   Concord *(G-4250)*
Deverger Systems Inc............................ G 828 253-2255
   Asheville *(G-608)*
Digital Designs Inc.................................. E 704 790-7100
   Charlotte *(G-2634)*
Digital Turbine Media Inc........................ E 866 254-2453
   Durham *(G-5051)*
Dynamac Corporation............................. E 919 544-6428
   Durham *(G-5073)*
Fics America Inc..................................... D 704 329-7391
   Charlotte *(G-2759)*
Fiestic Inc... F 888 935-3999
   Raleigh *(G-12765)*
Firstreport Software Inc......................... G 828 441-0404
   Asheville *(G-622)*
Flameoff Coatings Inc............................ G 888 816-7468
   Raleigh *(G-12772)*
Goldmine Software................................. G 704 944-3579
   Charlotte *(G-2845)*
Horizon Lab Systems LLC..................... E 919 896-7737
   Raleigh *(G-12861)*
Ideacode Inc... G 919 341-5170
   Greensboro *(G-7111)*
Infisoft Software..................................... G 704 307-2619
   Charlotte *(G-2969)*
Infobelt LLC.. F 980 223-4000
   Charlotte *(G-2971)*
Information Tech Works LLC................. F 919 232-5332
   Raleigh *(G-12888)*
Innait Inc... G 406 241-5245
   Charlotte *(G-2975)*

Inneroptic Technology Inc..................... G 919 732-2090
   Hillsborough *(G-8656)*
Insightsoftware LLC............................... E 919 872-7800
   Raleigh *(G-12892)*
Inspectionxpert Corporation.................. F 919 249-6442
   Raleigh *(G-12893)*
Inspire Creative Studios Inc.................. G 910 395-0200
   Wilmington *(G-16269)*
Intelligent Apps LLC.............................. G 919 628-6256
   Raleigh *(G-12897)*
International Bus Mchs Corp................ B 919 543-6919
   Durham *(G-5161)*
Iqe North Carolina LLC......................... F 336 609-6270
   Greensboro *(G-7121)*
▲ Jasie Blanks LLC.............................. G 910 485-0016
   Fayetteville *(G-5846)*
Jctm LLC.. D 252 571-8678
   Charlotte *(G-3015)*
Kdy Automation Solutions Inc.............. G 888 219-0049
   Morrisville *(G-11364)*
▲ Lenovo (united States) Inc............... A 855 253-6686
   Morrisville *(G-11376)*
Logicbit Software LLC........................... E 888 366-2280
   Durham *(G-5194)*
Logiksavvy Solutions LLC..................... G 336 392-6149
   Greensboro *(G-7167)*
Medicor Imaging Inc.............................. E 704 332-5532
   Charlotte *(G-3159)*
Noregon Systems Inc............................ C 336 615-8555
   Greensboro *(G-7223)*
Novisystems Inc..................................... G 919 205-5005
   Raleigh *(G-13074)*
Onion Peel Software Inc........................ F 919 460-1789
   Morrisville *(G-11401)*
Openfire Systems................................... G 336 251-3991
   Millers Creek *(G-10494)*
Pai Services LLC.................................... .... 856 231-4667
   Charlotte *(G-3308)*
▲ Phononic Inc...................................... C 919 908-6300
   Durham *(G-5286)*
Pogo Software Inc.................................. F 407 267-4864
   Raleigh *(G-13118)*
Predatar Inc.. G 919 827-4516
   Raleigh *(G-13135)*
Preferred Data Corporation................... G 336 886-3282
   High Point *(G-8495)*
Proctorfree Inc....................................... F 704 759-6569
   Davidson *(G-4692)*
Qplot Corporation................................... G 949 302-7928
   Raleigh *(G-13160)*
Red Hat Inc... A 919 754-3700
   Raleigh *(G-13196)*
Red Hat SA I LLC................................... F 919 754-3700
   Raleigh *(G-13197)*
Rvb Systems Group Inc........................ G 919 362-5211
   Garner *(G-6311)*
S C I A Inc.. G 919 387-7000
   Cary *(G-1877)*
▲ Sas Institute Inc................................. A 919 677-8000
   Cary *(G-1884)*
Sato Global Solutions Inc..................... F 954 261-3279
   Charlotte *(G-3494)*
School Directorease LLC...................... G 240 206-6273
   Charlotte *(G-3505)*
Scriptorium Pubg Svcs Inc................... G 919 481-2701
   Durham *(G-5346)*
Signalscape Inc...................................... E 919 859-4565
   Cary *(G-1889)*
Splendidcrm Software Inc.................... G 919 604-1258
   Holly Springs *(G-8718)*
Synopsys Inc.. F 919 941-6600
   Morrisville *(G-11437)*

Tc2 Labs LLC... G 919 380-2171
   Raleigh *(G-13329)*
▲ Tekelec Inc... C
   Morrisville *(G-11442)*
Tekelec Global Inc.................................. A 919 460-5500
   Morrisville *(G-11443)*
Telephys Inc... .... 312 625-9128
   Davidson *(G-4699)*
Terida LLC... F 910 693-1633
   Pinehurst *(G-12238)*
Twork Technology Inc........................... F 704 218-9675
   Charlotte *(G-3743)*
USA Metal Structure LLP...................... G 336 717-2884
   Dobson *(G-4832)*
VA Claims LLC....................................... .... 305 984-0936
   Greenville *(G-7596)*
Vortant Technologies LLC..................... G 828 645-1026
   Weaverville *(G-15867)*
Vortex Bottle Shop LLC........................ F 980 258-0827
   Harrisburg *(G-7734)*
Web 4 Half LLC..................................... E 855 762-4638
   Asheboro *(G-509)*
Xsport Global Inc................................... F 212 541-6222
   Charlotte *(G-3836)*

7372 Prepackaged software

/N Software Inc....................................... F 919 544-7070
   Chapel Hill *(G-1978)*
27 Software US Inc................................ F 704 968-2879
   Mooresville *(G-10844)*
2u NC... G 919 525-5075
   Chapel Hill *(G-1979)*
6th Sense Analytics............................... G 919 439-4740
   Morrisville *(G-11273)*
A & A Financial Services LLC............... G 800 572-6684
   Charlotte *(G-2112)*
A4 Health Systems Inc.......................... B 919 851-6177
   Cary *(G-1672)*
Able Softsystems Corp.......................... G 919 241-7907
   Raleigh *(G-12463)*
Aceyus Inc.. E 704 443-7900
   Charlotte *(G-2128)*
Admissionpros LLC............................... F 919 256-3889
   Cary *(G-1675)*
Advanced Computer Lrng Co LLC........ E 910 779-2254
   Fayetteville *(G-5752)*
Advanced Digital Systems Inc.............. F 919 485-4819
   Durham *(G-4904)*
Alpha Theory LLC.................................. .... 212 235-2180
   Charlotte *(G-2168)*
Alpha Theory LLC.................................. G 704 844-1018
   Charlotte *(G-2170)*
Alpha Theory LLC.................................. .... 212 235-2180
   Charlotte *(G-2169)*
Altera Corporation.................................. G 919 852-1004
   Raleigh *(G-12494)*
AMS Software Inc.................................. F 919 570-6001
   Wake Forest *(G-15527)*
Apex Analytix LLC................................. C 336 272-4669
   Greensboro *(G-6810)*
Apple Inc... F 516 318-6744
   Cary *(G-1685)*
Applied Strategies Inc........................... G 704 525-4478
   Charlotte *(G-2205)*
Appsense Incorporated......................... C 919 666-0080
   Cary *(G-1686)*
Archivesocial Inc.................................... E 888 558-6032
   Durham *(G-4923)*
◆ Arris Technology Inc........................ D 678 473-2907
   Hickory *(G-7944)*
Arrow Educational Products Inc........... G 910 521-0840
   Pembroke *(G-12180)*

SIC SECTION
73 BUSINESS SERVICES

Artifex Inc .... G 704 773-6942
   Charlotte *(G-2220)*

Assyst Bullmer Inc .... G 919 467-2211
   Raleigh *(G-12529)*

Atlantic Software Co .... G 910 763-3907
   Wilmington *(G-16123)*

Attus Technologies Inc .... E 704 341-5750
   Charlotte *(G-2238)*

Avercast LLC .... E 208 538-5380
   Emerald Isle *(G-5669)*

Avidxchange Holdings Inc .... E 800 560-9305
   Charlotte *(G-2247)*

Axial Exchange Inc .... G 919 576-9988
   Raleigh *(G-12536)*

Beeline Global LLC .... G 704 562-8221
   Charlotte *(G-2296)*

Better Solutions Technologies .... G 704 227-7424
   Winston Salem *(G-16627)*

Biker Software .... G 919 761-1681
   Wake Forest *(G-15532)*

Bill Perfect Inc .... F 954 889-6699
   Denver *(G-4764)*

Billsoft Inc .... E 913 859-9674
   Durham *(G-4957)*

Biz Technology Solutions LLC .... E 704 658-1707
   Mooresville *(G-10881)*

Biznet Software Inc .... F 919 872-7800
   Raleigh *(G-12560)*

Blacktip Solutions .... G 336 303-1580
   Greensboro *(G-6841)*

Bloom Ai Inc .... G 704 620-2886
   Cary *(G-1708)*

Blue Crab Software LLC .... G 301 585-8187
   Chapel Hill *(G-1993)*

Blue Wolf Technologies LLP .... G 919 810-1508
   Raleigh *(G-12564)*

BMC Software Inc .... G 704 283-8179
   Monroe *(G-10663)*

BMC Solutions LLC .... G 704 386-0194
   Charlotte *(G-2327)*

BMC Studios .... G 443 547-7319
   Durham *(G-4968)*

Bmt Micro Inc .... G 910 792-9100
   Wilmington *(G-16140)*

Boss Key Productions Inc .... D 919 659-5704
   Raleigh *(G-12571)*

Bottomline Medical .... G 704 527-0919
   Charlotte *(G-2339)*

▲ Bravosolution Us Inc .... E 312 373-3100
   Morrisville *(G-11307)*

Brick City Gaming Inc .... F 919 297-2081
   Cary *(G-1713)*

Brightly Software Inc .... C 919 816-8237
   Cary *(G-1714)*

Brightwill Technologies LLC .... G 919 757-3176
   Raleigh *(G-12575)*

Brilliant Pos LLC .... G 704 315-2352
   Charlotte *(G-2356)*

Bronto Software LLC .... C 919 595-2500
   Durham *(G-4983)*

Brookstone Baptist Church .... E 828 658-9443
   Weaverville *(G-15840)*

Business Systems of America .... G 704 766-2755
   Charlotte *(G-2366)*

Cadence Design Systems Inc .... G 919 380-3900
   Cary *(G-1720)*

Camelot Computers Inc .... F 704 554-1670
   Charlotte *(G-2378)*

Camstar Systems Inc .... C 704 227-6600
   Charlotte *(G-2380)*

Carolina Road Media LLC .... G 844 222-7069
   Durham *(G-5003)*

CBA Software Inc .... F 919 289-9820
   Hillsborough *(G-8643)*

Cdata Software Inc .... E 919 928-5214
   Chapel Hill *(G-1999)*

Cdp Inc .... G 336 270-6151
   Burlington *(G-1390)*

Cengage Learning Inc .... E 919 829-8181
   Raleigh *(G-12616)*

Centeredge Software .... G 336 598-5934
   Roxboro *(G-13798)*

Channeladvisor Corporation .... D 919 228-4700
   Morrisville *(G-11317)*

Channeltivity LLC .... F 704 408-3560
   Matthews *(G-10240)*

Charge Onsite LLC .... G 888 343-2688
   Charlotte *(G-2448)*

Checkfree Services Corporation .... B 919 941-2640
   Durham *(G-5014)*

Cicero Inc .... G 919 380-5000
   Cary *(G-1730)*

Citrix System .... G 919 607-9973
   Holly Springs *(G-8695)*

Client Care Web Inc .... E 704 787-9901
   Concord *(G-4234)*

Clinetic Inc .... F 513 295-1332
   Raleigh *(G-12629)*

Cloud Sftwr Group Holdings Inc .... A 919 839-6139
   Raleigh *(G-12631)*

Cloud Software Group Inc .... G 919 969-6500
   Chapel Hill *(G-2004)*

Cloud Stream Systems LLC .... G 704 916-9664
   Harrisburg *(G-7705)*

Cloudgenera Inc .... E 980 332-4040
   Charlotte *(G-2500)*

Cmisolutions Inc .... E 704 759-9950
   Charlotte *(G-2505)*

Competitive Solutions Inc .... E 919 851-0058
   Raleigh *(G-12634)*

Computational Engrg Intl Inc .... E 919 363-0883
   Apex *(G-176)*

Computer Task Group Inc .... G 919 677-1313
   Raleigh *(G-12636)*

Connectmedia Ventures LLC .... G 773 551-7446
   Raleigh *(G-12637)*

Consultants In Data Proc Inc .... G 704 542-6339
   Charlotte *(G-2542)*

Contec LLC .... E 408 389-7206
   Charlotte *(G-2544)*

Conxit Technology Group Inc .... G 877 998-4227
   Charlotte *(G-2548)*

Cosync Inc .... G 919 523-8336
   Cary *(G-1737)*

Crestline Software LLC .... G 336 217-1005
   Greensboro *(G-6941)*

Crm A LLC .... G 888 600-7567
   Cary *(G-1741)*

Crmnext Inc .... E 415 424-4644
   Raleigh *(G-12656)*

Csit Group .... G 828 233-5750
   Asheville *(G-600)*

Cyber Imaging Systems Inc .... F 919 872-5179
   Raleigh *(G-12667)*

D3 Software Inc .... G 336 870-9138
   High Point *(G-8316)*

D3 Software Inc .... G 336 776-0202
   Winston Salem *(G-16668)*

Data443 Risk Mitigation Inc .... E 919 858-6542
   Durham *(G-5047)*

Database Incorporated .... G 202 684-6252
   Durham *(G-5048)*

Datascope North America Inc .... E 980 819-5244
   Mint Hill *(G-10528)*

Dauntless Discovery LLC .... C 610 909-7383
   Morrisville *(G-11328)*

Dealer Track Inc .... G 919 554-0972
   Wake Forest *(G-15545)*

Definitive Media Corp .... F 714 730-4958
   Cary *(G-1746)*

Deliveright Logistics Inc .... C 862 279-7332
   Lexington *(G-9705)*

Digital Audio Corporation .... F 919 572-6767
   Hendersonville *(G-7844)*

Digital Designs Inc .... E 704 790-7100
   Charlotte *(G-2634)*

Digital Printing Systems Inc .... E 704 525-0190
   Charlotte *(G-2636)*

Digital Turbine Media Inc .... E 866 254-2453
   Durham *(G-5051)*

Digitome Corporation .... G 860 651-5560
   Davidson *(G-4672)*

Dilisym Services Inc .... G 919 558-1323
   Durham *(G-5053)*

Discovery Insurance Company .... D 800 876-1492
   Kinston *(G-9358)*

DL Hopper & Associates Inc .... G 252 838-1062
   Newport *(G-11901)*

Docsite LLC .... F 866 823-3958
   Durham *(G-5055)*

Docurep LLC .... G 919 280-4723
   Wake Forest *(G-15548)*

Dp Solutions Inc .... F 336 854-7700
   Greensboro *(G-6979)*

Drake Software LLC .... B 828 524-2922
   Franklin *(G-6125)*

Dreamship Inc .... G 908 601-8152
   Raleigh *(G-12701)*

Drug Safety Navigator LLC .... F 919 885-0549
   Durham *(G-5066)*

Dzone Inc .... F 919 678-0300
   Research Triangle Pa *(G-13550)*

E&C Medical Intelligence Inc .... E 609 228-7898
   Cary *(G-1753)*

Easynotes LLC .... G 919 870-5228
   Raleigh *(G-12719)*

Eatclub Inc .... G 609 578-7942
   Chapel Hill *(G-2011)*

Eclipse Health Outcomes Inc .... G 706 589-4086
   Durham *(G-5076)*

◆ ECR Software Corporation .... E 828 265-2907
   Boone *(G-1196)*

Educatrx Inc .... G 980 328-0013
   Monroe *(G-10711)*

Elite Business Solutions LLC .... G 910 713-9350
   Wilmington *(G-16210)*

Elizabeth Logistic LLC .... D 803 920-3931
   Indian Trail *(G-8931)*

Emath360 LLC .... F 919 744-4944
   Cary *(G-1757)*

EMC Corporation .... G 720 341-3274
   Charlotte *(G-2705)*

Employus Inc .... F 919 706-4008
   Cary *(G-1758)*

En Fleur Corporation .... G 919 556-1623
   Louisburg *(G-9987)*

Engineered Software .... G 336 299-4843
   Greensboro *(G-6999)*

Envirnmntal Systems RES Inst I .... E 704 541-9810
   Charlotte *(G-2718)*

Esequence Inc .... G 919 831-1995
   Raleigh *(G-12747)*

Esymphony Software Solutions I .... G 919 293-0233
   Raleigh *(G-12748)*

Ethereon Software Corp .... G 919 510-5112
   Raleigh *(G-12749)*

73 BUSINESS SERVICES

Euclid Innovations Inc................................F.....877 382-5431
  Charlotte *(G-2733)*
Everview...G.....800 549-4722
  Mount Airy *(G-11508)*
Executive Grooming LLC...........................G.....919 706-5382
  Raleigh *(G-12753)*
Expersis Software Inc................................G.....919 874-0608
  Cary *(G-1763)*
Exposure Software LLC.............................F.....919 832-4124
  Raleigh *(G-12754)*
◆ Extreme Networks Inc.............................B.....408 579-2800
  Morrisville *(G-11339)*
Facilitydudecom Inc...................................F.....919 459-6430
  Cary *(G-1766)*
Faro10 LLC..G.....757 285-8069
  Apex *(G-190)*
Fastzone Dsl & Internet Servic..................G.....828 963-1350
  Banner Elk *(G-897)*
Fathom Holdings Inc..................................E.....888 455-6040
  Cary *(G-1769)*
Feedtrail Incorporated................................F.....757 618-7760
  Raleigh *(G-12763)*
Fics America Inc..D.....704 329-7391
  Charlotte *(G-2759)*
Fieldsway Solutions LLC...........................G.....984 920-7791
  Four Oaks *(G-6104)*
Fieldx Inc..G.....919 926-7001
  Raleigh *(G-12764)*
Fiestic Inc...F.....888 935-3999
  Raleigh *(G-12765)*
First Leads Inc...G.....919 672-5329
  Durham *(G-5097)*
Firstreport Software Inc.............................G.....828 441-0404
  Asheville *(G-622)*
Flow Rhythm Inc...G.....704 737-2178
  Charlotte *(G-2781)*
Fogle Computing Corporation...................G.....828 697-9080
  Hendersonville *(G-7853)*
Folkwear..G.....828 626-3100
  Barnardsville *(G-910)*
Foxster Opco LLC......................................E.....910 297-6996
  Hampstead *(G-7647)*
Fusion Sport Inc...E.....720 987-4403
  Durham *(G-5109)*
G & E Software Inc....................................F.....910 762-5608
  Wilmington *(G-16226)*
Galvix Inc..G.....925 434-6243
  Cary *(G-1770)*
Gayco..G.....252 753-4777
  Walstonburg *(G-15637)*
General Dynamics Corporation.................E.....336 698-8571
  Mc Leansville *(G-10390)*
Genesys Cloud Services Inc.....................E.....317 872-3000
  Durham *(G-5113)*
Genesys Technology Inc...........................F.....336 789-0763
  Mount Airy *(G-11510)*
Geneva Software Co Inc............................G.....336 275-8887
  Greensboro *(G-7037)*
Getbridge LLC..C.....919 645-2800
  Raleigh *(G-12799)*
◆ Gilbarco Inc...A.....336 547-5000
  Greensboro *(G-7043)*
GK Software Usa Inc.................................E.....984 255-7995
  Raleigh *(G-12802)*
Global Software LLC.................................G.....919 872-7800
  Raleigh *(G-12805)*
Global Software Labs LLC........................G.....404 550-4390
  Monroe *(G-10724)*
Go Energies LLC..F.....877 712-5999
  Wilmington *(G-16234)*
Go Energies Holdings Inc.........................G.....910 762-5802
  Wilmington *(G-16235)*

Goldmine Software.....................................G.....704 944-3579
  Charlotte *(G-2845)*
◆ Goodrich Corporation.............................C.....704 423-7000
  Charlotte *(G-2847)*
Granville Miller LLC..................................G.....919 865-0602
  Raleigh *(G-12813)*
Grid Research LLC....................................G.....704 345-9774
  Mint Hill *(G-10535)*
Halogen Software US Inc..........................G.....866 566-7778
  Charlotte *(G-2881)*
Healthline Info Systems Inc......................F.....704 655-0447
  Davidson *(G-4677)*
Help/Systems LLC.....................................G.....844 425-2966
  Raleigh *(G-12838)*
Hiatus Inc...F.....844 572-6185
  Charlotte *(G-2909)*
Hitachi Energy USA Inc.............................F.....919 649-7022
  Raleigh *(G-12848)*
Horizon Lab Systems LLC........................E.....919 896-7737
  Raleigh *(G-12861)*
Hortonworks Inc...G.....855 846-7866
  Durham *(G-5141)*
Hrtms Incorporated....................................G.....919 741-5099
  Raleigh *(G-12864)*
Hyper Analytical Software LLC.................G.....919 267-4897
  Cary *(G-1785)*
I-Leadr Inc..F.....910 431-5252
  Sherrills Ford *(G-14385)*
Icontact LLC...D.....919 957-6150
  Morrisville *(G-11356)*
ID Pros LLC..G.....904 887-6210
  Gastonia *(G-6421)*
Idea People Inc..G.....704 398-4437
  Huntersville *(G-8833)*
Idea Software Inc.......................................G.....407 453-3883
  Raleigh *(G-12876)*
Ideablock LLC..G.....919 551-5054
  Durham *(G-5145)*
Ideacode Inc...G.....919 341-5170
  Greensboro *(G-7111)*
Ientertainment Network Inc......................G.....919 238-4090
  Burnsville *(G-1528)*
Igniterate LLC...G.....919 473-9560
  Durham *(G-5148)*
Ilumivu Inc..G.....410 570-8846
  Asheville *(G-658)*
Inferensys Inc...G.....910 398-1200
  Durham *(G-5153)*
Infinite Software Resorces LLC................G.....704 509-0031
  Charlotte *(G-2967)*
Infinity Learning Solutions........................G.....828 665-8292
  Candler *(G-1583)*
Infisoft Software...G.....704 307-2619
  Charlotte *(G-2969)*
Infobelt LLC..F.....980 223-4000
  Charlotte *(G-2971)*
Information Tech Works LLC....................F.....919 232-5332
  Raleigh *(G-12888)*
Informtion Rtrval Cmpanies Inc................E.....919 460-7447
  Cary *(G-1789)*
Inn-Flow Inc..F.....919 277-9027
  Cary *(G-1790)*
Innait Inc...G.....406 241-5245
  Charlotte *(G-2975)*
Innovtive Msrment Slutions Inc................G.....757 560-0820
  Edenton *(G-5517)*
Innowera Ltd Liability Company...............G.....214 295-9508
  Raleigh *(G-12889)*
Innspector Software LLC..........................G.....828 712-7127
  Biltmore Lake *(G-1100)*
Inovaetion Inc..F.....919 651-1628
  Raleigh *(G-12890)*

Insightsoftware LLC..................................E.....919 872-7800
  Raleigh *(G-12892)*
Insource Sftwr Solutions Inc....................G.....704 895-1052
  Cornelius *(G-4562)*
Inspectionxpert Corporation.....................F.....919 249-6442
  Raleigh *(G-12893)*
Insurance Systems Group Inc..................F.....919 834-4907
  Raleigh *(G-12894)*
Intelligent Apps LLC..................................G.....919 628-6256
  Raleigh *(G-12897)*
Iqmetrix USA Inc..D.....704 987-9903
  Mooresville *(G-10984)*
Issuer Direct Corporation.........................D.....919 481-4000
  Raleigh *(G-12903)*
Itlaq Technologies.....................................G.....305 549-8561
  Charlotte *(G-2998)*
J M I Barcodes..G.....919 289-4125
  Raleigh *(G-12909)*
Jackway Software LLC.............................G.....919 747-1190
  Holly Springs *(G-8701)*
Jaggaer LLC...D.....919 659-2100
  Morrisville *(G-11362)*
Jctm LLC..D.....252 571-8678
  Charlotte *(G-3015)*
Jeffrey Ancheta..G.....919 552-0892
  Fuquay Varina *(G-6207)*
Jenesis Software Inc.................................G.....828 245-1171
  Forest City *(G-6072)*
Jfl Enterprises Inc.....................................G.....704 786-7838
  Concord *(G-4293)*
JMP Statistical Discovery Llc..................D.....877 594-6567
  Cary *(G-1796)*
Johnson Controls Inc................................G.....866 285-8345
  Morrisville *(G-11363)*
Jrg Technologies Corp..............................F.....850 362-4310
  Charlotte *(G-3036)*
Jsbd Software LLC....................................G.....919 841-1218
  Raleigh *(G-12926)*
Juniper Networks Inc................................F.....888 586-4737
  Raleigh *(G-12928)*
Just Black LLC...G.....252 204-5437
  Gastonia *(G-6436)*
Justenough Software Corp Inc.................G.....800 949-3432
  Durham *(G-5174)*
Justi LLC..G.....919 434-5002
  Cary *(G-1801)*
Kaleida Systems Inc..................................G.....704 814-4429
  Matthews *(G-10257)*
Kaleido Inc..F.....984 205-9436
  Raleigh *(G-12929)*
▼ Knowledge Management Asso...........G.....781 250-2001
  Raleigh *(G-12944)*
Laser Recharge Carolina Inc...................G.....919 467-5902
  Cary *(G-1808)*
Learning Craftsmen Inc............................G.....813 321-5003
  Apex *(G-213)*
Learningstationcom Inc............................F.....704 926-5400
  Charlotte *(G-3079)*
Learnplatform Inc......................................G.....919 247-5998
  Raleigh *(G-12964)*
Leoforce LLC..E.....919 539-5434
  Raleigh *(G-12967)*
Liferay Inc..G.....703 957-8542
  Cary *(G-1809)*
Liquidehr Inc..E.....866 618-1531
  Cary *(G-1812)*
Lkn Perform LLC..G.....704 215-4900
  Cornelius *(G-4568)*
Lobbyguard Solutions LLC......................F.....919 785-3301
  Raleigh *(G-12978)*
Logicbay Corp..F.....888 301-0751
  Wilmington *(G-16305)*

SIC SECTION — 73 BUSINESS SERVICES

Logicbit Software LLC .... E 888 366-2280
   Durham *(G-5194)*

Logicom Computer Systems Inc .... G 910 256-5916
   Wilmington *(G-16306)*

London Luxury LLC .... G 980 819-1966
   Charlotte *(G-3101)*

Looking Glass Technology LLC .... G 910 679-8060
   Wilmington *(G-16308)*

M I Connection .... F 704 662-3255
   Mooresville *(G-11013)*

M Vision Software Inc .... G 703 530-9900
   Southern Pines *(G-14540)*

Make Solutions Inc .... F 623 444-0098
   Asheville *(G-694)*

Mapjoy LLC .... G 919 450-8360
   Durham *(G-5207)*

Matrix Technologies Inc .... G 414 291-1000
   Raleigh *(G-13007)*

Medaptus Inc .... G 617 896-4000
   Raleigh *(G-13013)*

Medicor Imaging Inc .... E 704 332-5532
   Charlotte *(G-3159)*

Medlio Inc .... G 919 599-4870
   Durham *(G-5216)*

Medvertical LLC .... G 919 867-4268
   Raleigh *(G-13014)*

Micronova Systems Inc .... F 910 202-0564
   Wilmington *(G-16323)*

Microsoft Corporation .... A 704 527-2987
   Charlotte *(G-3175)*

Moduslink Corporation .... E 781 663-5000
   Garner *(G-6288)*

Monarch Medical Tech LLC .... F 704 335-1300
   Charlotte *(G-3197)*

Movers and Shakers LLC .... G 980 771-0505
   Charlotte *(G-3209)*

Moxie .... G 646 481-7807
   Wilmington *(G-16329)*

Mrf Technologies LLC .... G 919 714-2852
   Raleigh *(G-13048)*

Munibilling .... D 800 259-7020
   Greensboro *(G-7209)*

Murano Corporation .... F 919 294-8233
   Durham *(G-5230)*

N3xt Inc .... G 704 905-2209
   Charlotte *(G-3227)*

Navex Global Inc .... F 866 297-0224
   Charlotte *(G-3238)*

Navia Inc .... G 626 372-9791
   Raleigh *(G-13057)*

Ncino Inc .... C 888 676-2466
   Wilmington *(G-16333)*

Ncino Opco Inc .... A 888 676-2466
   Wilmington *(G-16334)*

NCR Lcal - Ohio Dtroit Aloha P .... G 440 202-3068
   Wilmington *(G-16335)*

Neurametrix Inc .... G 408 507-2366
   Asheville *(G-711)*

Nexxussoft Corporation .... G 561 352-5232
   Charlotte *(G-3258)*

Nite Crawlers LLC .... G 910 309-0543
   Charlotte *(G-3263)*

Nivedtech .... G 336 823-9501
   Thomasville *(G-15257)*

Notemeal Inc .... E 312 550-2049
   Durham *(G-5249)*

Noteworthy Software Inc .... G 828 604-1123
   Valdese *(G-15451)*

Novisystems Inc .... G 919 205-5005
   Raleigh *(G-13074)*

Oakbrook Solutions Inc .... E 336 714-0431
   Oak Ridge *(G-12062)*

Oasis Akhal-Tekes .... G 704 843-3139
   Waxhaw *(G-15768)*

Oasys Mobile Inc .... F 919 807-5600
   Cary *(G-1837)*

Objective Security Corporation .... F 415 997-9967
   Raleigh *(G-13081)*

Ocufii Inc .... G 804 874-4036
   Huntersville *(G-8869)*

Odigia Inc .... G 336 462-8056
   Winston Salem *(G-16826)*

Offerisor LLC .... G 704 970-9700
   Matthews *(G-10277)*

One Srce Dcument Solutions Inc .... E 800 401-9544
   Greensboro *(G-7234)*

Onion Peel Software Inc .... F 919 460-1789
   Morrisville *(G-11401)*

Oracle Corporation .... G 919 595-2500
   Morrisville *(G-11402)*

Oracle Corporation .... D 919 205-6000
   Morrisville *(G-11403)*

Oracle Hearing Group .... G 732 349-6804
   Wilmington *(G-16345)*

Oracle of God Ministries Nc .... G 919 522-2113
   Raleigh *(G-13089)*

Oracle Systems Corporation .... G 704 423-1426
   Matthews *(G-10279)*

Oracle Systems Corporation .... G 919 257-2300
   Raleigh *(G-13090)*

Orgbook Inc .... G 615 483-5410
   Durham *(G-5260)*

Orgspan Inc .... G 855 674-7726
   Durham *(G-5261)*

Pai Services LLC .... G 856 231-4667
   Charlotte *(G-3308)*

Payment Collect LLC .... G 828 214-5550
   Asheville *(G-723)*

Pf2 Eis LLC .... C 704 549-6931
   Charlotte *(G-3333)*

Phoenix Software Systems Inc .... G 252 756-6451
   Greenville *(G-7573)*

Pogo Software Inc .... F 407 267-4864
   Raleigh *(G-13118)*

Pogomaxy Inc .... G 919 623-0118
   Raleigh *(G-13119)*

Powersolve Corporation LLC .... F 919 662-8515
   Garner *(G-6304)*

▲ Practice Fusion Inc .... C 415 346-7700
   Raleigh *(G-13130)*

Practicepro Sftwr Systems Inc .... G 212 244-2100
   Charlotte *(G-3366)*

Pramana LLC .... G 910 233-5118
   Cary *(G-1858)*

Precision Fermentations Inc .... F 919 717-3983
   Durham *(G-5302)*

Predatar Inc .... G 919 827-4516
   Raleigh *(G-13135)*

Preferred Data Corporation .... G 336 886-3282
   High Point *(G-8495)*

Priority Backgrounds LLC .... G 919 557-3247
   Fuquay Varina *(G-6222)*

Proctorfree Inc .... F 704 759-6569
   Davidson *(G-4692)*

Progress Software Corp .... E 919 461-4200
   Morrisville *(G-11412)*

Prometheus Group Holdings LLC .... D 919 835-0810
   Raleigh *(G-13152)*

Propharma Group LLC .... D 888 242-0559
   Raleigh *(G-13153)*

Prosapient Inc .... F 984 282-2823
   Raleigh *(G-13154)*

Proximal Design Labs LLC .... G 919 599-5742
   Raleigh *(G-13156)*

Pyramid Software Inc .... G 336 209-2684
   Raleigh *(G-13159)*

Qplot Corporation .... G 949 302-7928
   Raleigh *(G-13160)*

Quest Software Inc .... G 919 337-4719
   Morrisville *(G-11415)*

Quinsite LLC Fka Mile 5 Anlyti .... F 317 313-5152
   Chapel Hill *(G-2061)*

R65 Labs Inc .... G 919 219-1983
   Durham *(G-5317)*

Rabid Games LLC .... F 704 754-6382
   Spencer *(G-14602)*

Rackwise Inc .... F 919 533-5533
   Raleigh *(G-13170)*

Rapidform Inc .... G 408 856-6200
   Cary *(G-1865)*

Red Hat Inc .... A 919 754-3700
   Raleigh *(G-13196)*

Red Hat SA I LLC .... E 919 754-3700
   Raleigh *(G-13197)*

Revware Inc .... G 919 790-0000
   Raleigh *(G-13205)*

Reynolds and Reynolds Company .... G 321 287-3939
   Charlotte *(G-3445)*

Ronak LLC .... G 781 589-1973
   Cary *(G-1873)*

Roobrik Inc .... G 919 667-7750
   Greensboro *(G-7317)*

Rssbus Inc .... F 919 969-7675
   Chapel Hill *(G-2065)*

Rstack Solutions LLC .... F 980 337-1295
   Charlotte *(G-3469)*

Rvb Systems Group Inc .... G 919 362-5211
   Garner *(G-6311)*

Sam Software Corp .... G 910 233-9924
   Wilmington *(G-16392)*

Sapiens Americas Corporation .... F 919 405-1500
   Raleigh *(G-13229)*

Sas Federal LLC .... G 919 531-7505
   Cary *(G-1880)*

Sas Institute Inc .... G 954 494-8189
   Cary *(G-1881)*

Sas Institute Inc .... G 919 677-8000
   Cary *(G-1882)*

Sas Institute Inc .... G 919 531-4153
   Cary *(G-1883)*

Sas Institute Inc .... G 704 831-5595
   Charlotte *(G-3489)*

Sas Institute Inc .... G 704 331-3956
   Charlotte *(G-3490)*

▲ Sas Institute Inc .... A 919 677-8000
   Cary *(G-1884)*

Sas of Carolinas LLC .... G 704 332-7165
   Charlotte *(G-3491)*

Sas R & D Services Inc .... G 954 432-2345
   Charlotte *(G-3492)*

Sas Solutions Inc .... G 919 369-4424
   Apex *(G-241)*

▲ Sato America LLC .... C 704 644-1650
   Charlotte *(G-3493)*

Scalable Software Inc .... G 713 316-4900
   Huntersville *(G-8895)*

◆ Schaefer Systems International Inc .... C 704 944-4500
   Charlotte *(G-3499)*

Science Applications Intl Corp .... G 910 822-2100
   Fayetteville *(G-5912)*

Scientigo Inc .... G 704 837-0500
   Charlotte *(G-3510)*

Sciquest Holdings Inc .... D 919 659-2100
   Morrisville *(G-11421)*

Sciquest Parent LLC .... F 919 659-2100
   Morrisville *(G-11422)*

Employee Codes: A=Over 500 employees, B=251-500
C=101-250, D=51-100, E=20-50, F=10-19, G=1-9

73 BUSINESS SERVICES

Scribbles Software LLC .... F 704 390-5690
   Pineville *(G-12305)*

Second Main Phase Slutions LLC .... G 704 303-0090
   Matthews *(G-10288)*

Siemens Industry Software Inc .... F 704 227-6600
   Charlotte *(G-3548)*

Sierra Software LLC .... F 877 285-2867
   Greensboro *(G-7338)*

Simplecertifiedmailcom LLC .... G 888 462-1750
   Cary *(G-1891)*

Simplicti Sftwr Solutions Inc .... F 919 858-8898
   Cary *(G-1892)*

Sitelink Software LLC .... D 919 865-0789
   Raleigh *(G-13269)*

Slickedit Inc .... E 919 473-0070
   Cary *(G-1894)*

Small Business Software LLC .... G 919 400-8298
   Raleigh *(G-13271)*

Smartlink Mobile Systems LLC .... F 919 674-8400
   Cary *(G-1896)*

Smartware Group Inc .... F 866 858-7800
   Cary *(G-1897)*

Snapz Software Inc .... G 302 234-0402
   Smithfield *(G-14484)*

Socialtopias LLC .... F 704 910-1713
   Charlotte *(G-3575)*

Software Goldsmith Inc .... G 919 346-0403
   Holly Springs *(G-8717)*

Software Professionals Inc .... G 503 860-4507
   Raleigh *(G-13275)*

Sofware LLC .... G 757 287-7409
   Hendersonville *(G-7900)*

Songs of Water LLC .... G 336 337-4674
   Greensboro *(G-7349)*

Southern Software Inc .... D 336 879-3350
   Southern Pines *(G-14555)*

Southern Software Inc .... G 910 638-8700
   Fayetteville *(G-5920)*

Splendidcrm Software Inc .... G 919 604-1258
   Holly Springs *(G-8718)*

Spranto America Inc .... G 919 741-5095
   Apex *(G-244)*

Starr Training .... G 336 644-0252
   Kernersville *(G-9239)*

Starta Development Inc .... G 919 865-7700
   Raleigh *(G-13299)*

Stronger By Science Tech LLC .... G 336 391-9377
   Raleigh *(G-13308)*

Sunday Drive Holdings Inc .... G 919 825-5613
   Raleigh *(G-13314)*

Sweatnet LLC .... G 847 331-7287
   Charlotte *(G-3658)*

Swk Technologies Inc .... F 336 230-0200
   Greensboro *(G-7382)*

Symbrium Inc .... F 919 879-2470
   Raleigh *(G-13319)*

Synergem Technologies Inc .... E 866 859-0911
   Mount Airy *(G-11584)*

Synopsys Inc .... F 919 941-6600
   Morrisville *(G-11437)*

Td Cloud Services .... G 518 258-6788
   Raleigh *(G-13330)*

Technology Partners LLC .... D 704 553-1004
   Charlotte *(G-3677)*

Telos Group LLC .... G 704 904-0599
   Charlotte *(G-3680)*

Temprano Techvestors Inc .... F 877 545-1509
   Newton *(G-11978)*

Terida LLC .... F 910 693-1633
   Pinehurst *(G-12238)*

The Computer Solution Company .... F 336 409-0782
   Winston Salem *(G-16940)*

Thirdparty Labs .... G 919 741-5118
   Raleigh *(G-13345)*

Thomas Fergus .... G 336 447-4289
   Whitsett *(G-16003)*

Thorco LLC .... F 919 363-6234
   Cary *(G-1909)*

Topquadrant Inc .... E 919 300-7945
   Raleigh *(G-13352)*

▲ Transbotics Corporation .... E 704 362-1115
   Charlotte *(G-3716)*

Transdata Solutions Inc .... G 919 770-9329
   Sanford *(G-14199)*

Tresata Inc .... E 980 224-2097
   Charlotte *(G-3720)*

Triangle Microworks Inc .... G 919 870-5101
   Raleigh *(G-13360)*

Triangle Systems Inc .... G 919 544-0090
   Durham *(G-5410)*

Triangle Systems Inc .... G 919 544-0090
   Chapel Hill *(G-2084)*

Triaxis Games LLC .... G 919 720-7804
   Holly Springs *(G-8723)*

Trickfit & Suepack Training .... G 919 737-2231
   Wake Forest *(G-15606)*

Triggermesh Inc .... F 919 228-8049
   Cary *(G-1913)*

Trimech Solutions LLC .... G 919 535-5662
   Cary *(G-1914)*

Trimech Solutions LLC .... G 704 503-6644
   Charlotte *(G-3727)*

Tritech Ventures Inc .... G 919 846-3415
   Raleigh *(G-13366)*

Tryhard Infinity LLC .... G 252 269-0985
   New Bern *(G-11852)*

Twork Technology Inc .... F 704 218-9675
   Charlotte *(G-3743)*

Udio Commercial LLC .... G 609 977-2700
   Hubert *(G-8754)*

Ukg Kronos Systems LLC .... G 800 225-1561
   Charlotte *(G-3746)*

Ukg Kronos Systems LLC .... G 800 225-1561
   Greensboro *(G-7425)*

UNC Campus Health Services .... D 919 966-2281
   Chapel Hill *(G-2087)*

Unspecified Inc .... G 919 907-2726
   Durham *(G-5425)*

Upull LLC .... G 609 977-2700
   Hubert *(G-8755)*

Usat LLC .... E 919 942-4214
   Chapel Hill *(G-2091)*

Utd Technology Corp .... G 704 612-0121
   Mint Hill *(G-10546)*

VA Claims LLC .... G 305 984-0936
   Greenville *(G-7596)*

Velocitor Solutions .... G 704 635-4293
   Charlotte *(G-3768)*

Vencedor Software Group Inc .... G 978 390-1187
   Cary *(G-1918)*

Veradigm LLC .... A 919 847-8102
   Raleigh *(G-13397)*

Verdante Bioenergy Svcs LLC .... G 828 394-1246
   Lenoir *(G-9657)*

Viasic Inc .... G 336 774-2150
   Durham *(G-5433)*

Virtus Entertainment Inc .... E 919 467-9700
   Cary *(G-1922)*

Visionair Inc .... A 910 675-9117
   Castle Hayne *(G-1961)*

Wave Front Computers LLC .... G 919 896-6121
   Raleigh *(G-13414)*

We Glowed Up LLC .... G 856 266-5000
   Charlotte *(G-3799)*

SIC SECTION

Wispry Inc .... G 919 854-7500
   Cary *(G-1929)*

Woodshed Software .... G 941 240-1780
   Salisbury *(G-14067)*

Workday Inc .... G 919 703-2559
   Raleigh *(G-13427)*

▲ World CAM LLC .... G 704 655-1018
   Charlotte *(G-3823)*

Xenial Inc .... E 800 253-8664
   Charlotte *(G-3834)*

Xschem Inc .... E 919 379-3500
   Morrisville *(G-11467)*

Xsport Global Inc .... F 212 541-6222
   Charlotte *(G-3836)*

Yepzy Inc .... F 855 461-2678
   Concord *(G-4395)*

Zagros Sadjadi Software .... G 336 848-8171
   High Point *(G-8610)*

Zealousweb .... G 619 354-3216
   Concord *(G-4396)*

7373 Computer integrated systems design

057 Technology LLC .... G 855 557-7057
   Hickory *(G-7926)*

Acroplis Cntrls Engineers Pllc .... F 919 275-3884
   Raleigh *(G-12473)*

Advanced Mfg Solutions NC Inc .... E 828 633-2633
   Candler *(G-1566)*

Avail Forensics LLC .... F 877 888-5895
   Wilmington *(G-16125)*

Bachstein Consulting LLC .... G 410 322-4917
   Youngsville *(G-17070)*

Billsoft Inc .... E 913 859-9674
   Durham *(G-4957)*

Blue Wolf Technologies LLP .... G 919 810-1508
   Raleigh *(G-12564)*

Cicero Inc .... G 919 380-5000
   Cary *(G-1730)*

Computerway Food Systems Inc .... E 336 841-7289
   High Point *(G-8302)*

Custom Controls Unlimited LLC .... F 919 812-6553
   Raleigh *(G-12664)*

Descher LLC .... G 919 828-7708
   Raleigh *(G-12677)*

Esequence Inc .... G 919 831-1995
   Raleigh *(G-12747)*

◆ Extreme Networks Inc .... B 408 579-2800
   Morrisville *(G-11339)*

Fieldsway Solutions LLC .... G 984 920-7791
   Four Oaks *(G-6104)*

General Dynmics Mssion Systems .... C 336 698-8000
   Mc Leansville *(G-10391)*

Infobelt LLC .... F 980 223-4000
   Charlotte *(G-2971)*

Innait Inc .... G 406 241-5245
   Charlotte *(G-2975)*

International Bus Mchs Corp .... B 919 543-6919
   Durham *(G-5161)*

Juniper Networks Inc .... F 888 586-4737
   Raleigh *(G-12928)*

Medicor Imaging Inc .... E 704 332-5532
   Charlotte *(G-3159)*

◆ Meridian Zero Degrees LLC .... E 866 454-6757
   Aberdeen *(G-12)*

Q T Corporation .... G 252 399-7600
   Wilson *(G-16526)*

Qplot Corporation .... G 949 302-7928
   Raleigh *(G-13160)*

Romeo Six LLC .... F 919 589-7150
   Holly Springs *(G-8713)*

S C I A Inc .... G 919 387-7000
   Cary *(G-1877)*

SIC SECTION
73 BUSINESS SERVICES

Sato Global Solutions Inc .... F 954 261-3279
  Charlotte (G-3494)
Science Applications Intl Corp .... G 910 822-2100
  Fayetteville (G-5912)
▲ Sostram Corporation .... G 919 226-1195
  Durham (G-5364)
St Investors Inc .... D 704 969-7500
  Charlotte (G-3618)
Trimech Solutions LLC .... G 704 503-6644
  Charlotte (G-3727)
Twork Technology Inc .... F 704 218-9675
  Charlotte (G-3743)
Utd Technology Corp .... G 704 612-0121
  Mint Hill (G-10546)
Worden Brothers Inc .... D 919 202-8555
  Wilmington (G-16456)

7374 Data processing and preparation

Big Fish Dpi .... G 704 545-8112
  Mint Hill (G-10522)
Checkfree Services Corporation .... B 919 941-2640
  Durham (G-5014)
Computer Task Group Inc .... G 919 677-1313
  Raleigh (G-12636)
Consultants In Data Proc Inc .... G 704 542-6339
  Charlotte (G-2542)
Infobelt LLC .... F 980 223-4000
  Charlotte (G-2971)
Innait Inc .... G 406 241-5245
  Charlotte (G-2975)
Legalis Dms LLC .... F 919 741-8260
  Raleigh (G-12965)
Line Drive Sports Center Inc .... G 336 824-1692
  Ramseur (G-13446)
Mjt Us Inc .... G 704 826-7828
  Charlotte (G-3189)
NCR Voyix Corporation .... G 937 445-5000
  Cary (G-1830)
Northrop Grumman Systems Corp .... E 252 225-0911
  Atlantic (G-827)
Outer Banks Internet Inc .... G 252 441-6698
  Kill Devil Hills (G-9259)
Quinsite LLC Fka Mile 5 Anlyti .... F 317 313-5152
  Chapel Hill (G-2061)
Raleigh Ventures Inc .... G 910 350-0036
  Wilmington (G-16377)
Richa Inc .... G 704 944-0230
  Charlotte (G-3448)
Richa Inc .... F 704 331-9744
  Charlotte (G-3449)
S & A Cherokee LLC .... E 919 674-6020
  Cary (G-1876)
Stitchmaster LLC .... G 336 852-6448
  Greensboro (G-7373)
Telepathic Graphics Inc .... E 919 342-4603
  Raleigh (G-13337)

7375 Information retrieval services

Bluetick Inc .... F 336 294-4102
  Greensboro (G-6844)
Carolina Connections Inc .... G 336 786-7030
  Mount Airy (G-11488)
ID Pros LLC .... G 904 887-6210
  Gastonia (G-6421)
Quinsite LLC Fka Mile 5 Anlyti .... F 317 313-5152
  Chapel Hill (G-2061)
◆ Vrush Industries Inc .... F 336 886-7700
  High Point (G-8597)

7376 Computer facilities management

Infobelt LLC .... F 980 223-4000
  Charlotte (G-2971)

7378 Computer maintenance and repair

Artesian Future Technology LLC .... F 919 904-4940
  Chapel Hill (G-1987)
Biz Technology Solutions LLC .... E 704 658-1707
  Mooresville (G-10881)
Carolina Cartridge Systems Inc .... E 704 347-2447
  Charlotte (G-2392)
Coastal Office Eqp & Computers .... G 252 335-9427
  Elizabeth City (G-5534)
Complete Comp St of Ralgh Inc .... E 919 828-5227
  Raleigh (G-12635)
Comtech Group Inc .... G 919 313-4800
  Durham (G-5029)
Innait Inc .... G 406 241-5245
  Charlotte (G-2975)
Northrop Grumman Systems Corp .... E 252 225-0911
  Atlantic (G-827)
St Investors Inc .... D 704 969-7500
  Charlotte (G-3618)

7379 Computer related services, nec

A4 Health Systems Inc .... B 919 851-6177
  Cary (G-1672)
Acterna LLC .... F 919 388-5100
  Morrisville (G-11277)
Blue Wolf Technologies LLP .... G 919 810-1508
  Raleigh (G-12564)
Bluetick Inc .... F 336 294-4102
  Greensboro (G-6844)
Computer Task Group Inc .... G 919 677-1313
  Raleigh (G-12636)
Comtech Group Inc .... G 919 313-4800
  Durham (G-5029)
Consultants In Data Proc Inc .... G 704 542-6339
  Charlotte (G-2542)
Datanyze LLC .... E 866 408-1633
  Durham (G-5049)
Digital Designs Inc .... E 704 790-7100
  Charlotte (G-2634)
Fred L Brown .... G 336 643-7523
  Summerfield (G-14983)
◆ Graphik Dimensions Limited .... D 800 332-8884
  High Point (G-8371)
Informtion Rtrval Cmpanies Inc .... E 919 460-7447
  Cary (G-1789)
LDR Designs .... G 252 375-4484
  Greenville (G-7555)
Learning Craftsmen Inc .... G 813 321-5003
  Apex (G-213)
Learnplatform Inc .... G 919 247-5998
  Raleigh (G-12964)
Logiksavvy Solutions LLC .... G 336 392-6149
  Greensboro (G-7167)
Magic Mile Media Inc .... F 252 572-1330
  Kinston (G-9375)
NCR Voyix Corporation .... G 937 445-5000
  Cary (G-1830)
Onion Peel Software Inc .... F 919 460-1789
  Morrisville (G-11401)
Romeo Six LLC .... F 919 589-7150
  Holly Springs (G-8713)
Sighttech LLC .... G 855 997-4448
  Charlotte (G-3549)
Southern Data Systems Inc .... F 919 781-7603
  Oxford (G-12156)
Succession Solutions Inc .... F 704 631-9004
  Pineville (G-12311)
Synergem Technologies Inc .... E 866 859-0911
  Mount Airy (G-11584)
Terida LLC .... F 910 693-1633
  Pinehurst (G-12238)

The Computer Solution Company .... F 336 409-0782
  Winston Salem (G-16940)
Thorco LLC .... F 919 363-6234
  Cary (G-1909)
Twork Technology Inc .... F 704 218-9675
  Charlotte (G-3743)
Usat LLC .... F 919 942-4214
  Chapel Hill (G-2091)
VA Claims LLC .... G 305 984-0936
  Greenville (G-7596)
Verdante Bioenergy Svcs LLC .... G 828 394-1246
  Lenoir (G-9657)
◆ Vrush Industries Inc .... F 336 886-7700
  High Point (G-8597)

7381 Detective and armored car services

A&B Integrators LLC .... F 919 371-0750
  Durham (G-4897)
Diebold Nixdorf Incorporated .... F 704 599-3100
  Charlotte (G-2632)

7382 Security systems services

A&B Integrators LLC .... F 919 371-0750
  Durham (G-4897)
Absolute Security & Lock Inc .... G 336 322-4598
  Roxboro (G-13792)
Advanced Detection Tech LLC .... E 704 663-1949
  Mooresville (G-10850)
American Physcl SEC Group LLC .... G 919 363-1894
  Apex (G-159)
Amplified Elctronic Design Inc .... F 336 223-4811
  Greensboro (G-6806)
Automated Controls LLC .... F 704 724-7625
  Huntersville (G-8796)
Campus Safety Products LLC .... G 919 321-1477
  Durham (G-4996)
▲ Crest Electronics Inc .... F 336 855-6422
  Greensboro (G-6940)
Diebold Nixdorf Incorporated .... F 704 599-3100
  Charlotte (G-2632)
GNB Ventures LLC .... F 704 488-4468
  Charlotte (G-2837)
Integrated Info Systems Inc .... F 919 488-5000
  Youngsville (G-17086)
Integrated Roe Security LLC .... G 919 297-8036
  Raleigh (G-12896)
Lelantos Group Inc .... D 704 780-4127
  Mooresville (G-11005)
Lunar International Tech LLC .... F 800 975-7153
  Charlotte (G-3109)
▲ Marcon International Inc .... E 704 455-9400
  Harrisburg (G-7717)
Modern Lightning Protection Co .... F 252 756-3006
  Greenville (G-7561)
One Source SEC & Sound Inc .... G 281 850-9487
  Mooresville (G-11044)
Security Consult Inc .... G 704 531-8399
  Charlotte (G-3522)
◆ Tektone Sound & Signal Mfg Inc .... D 828 524-9967
  Franklin (G-6145)
Teletec Corporation .... F 919 954-7300
  Raleigh (G-13338)

7384 Photofinish laboratories

Dtp Inc .... G 336 272-5122
  Greensboro (G-6982)
Sharpe Images Properties Inc .... E 336 724-2871
  Winston Salem (G-16906)

7389 Business services, nec

3dductcleaning LLC .... G 919 723-4512
  Selma (G-14250)

73 BUSINESS SERVICES

760 Craft Works LLC .... F 704 274-5216
  Huntersville *(G-8785)*

A Stitch In Time .... G 828 274-5193
  Asheville *(G-513)*

Abercrombie Textiles Inc .... G 704 487-0935
  Shelby *(G-14281)*

Accel Discount Tire .... G 704 636-0323
  Salisbury *(G-13913)*

Ad Spice Marketing LLC .... G 919 286-7110
  Durham *(G-4902)*

Adoratherapy Inc .... F 917 297-8904
  Asheville *(G-515)*

Advanced Non-Lethal Tech Inc .... G 847 812-6450
  Raleigh *(G-12479)*

Ahlberg Cameras Inc .... F 910 523-5876
  Wilmington *(G-16097)*

Airfield Solutions LLC .... G 919 348-4271
  Jacksonville *(G-8985)*

Aj & Raine Scrubs & More LLC .... G 646 374-5198
  Charlotte *(G-2149)*

Allfuel Hst Inc .... G 919 868-9410
  Hampstead *(G-7636)*

AlphaGraphics Pineville .... F 704 541-3678
  Charlotte *(G-2172)*

American Rnovation Systems LLC ..... G 336 313-6210
  Thomasville *(G-15185)*

AMP Agency .... G 704 430-2313
  Harrisburg *(G-7701)*

Amy Smith .... G 828 352-1001
  Burnsville *(G-1522)*

Anitas Marketing Concepts Inc .... G 252 243-3993
  Wilson *(G-16465)*

Apex Analytix LLC .... C 336 272-4669
  Greensboro *(G-6810)*

Appalachian Pipe Distrs LLC .... F 704 688-5703
  Charlotte *(G-2202)*

▲ Aria Designs LLC .... F 828 572-4303
  Lenoir *(G-9575)*

Arisaka LLC .... F 919 601-5625
  Apex *(G-165)*

Asheville Color & Imaging Inc .... G 828 774-5040
  Asheville *(G-533)*

Atlantic Bankcard Center Inc .... G 336 855-9250
  Greensboro *(G-6821)*

▲ Autoverters Inc .... F 252 537-0426
  Roanoke Rapids *(G-13567)*

Bailey Sales and Service LLC .... G 910 876-1103
  Elizabethtown *(G-5585)*

▲ Bamal Corporation .... F 980 225-7700
  Charlotte *(G-2273)*

Banner Signs Today Inc .... G 704 525-2241
  Charlotte *(G-2275)*

Bennett Brothers Yachts Inc .... E 910 772-9277
  Wilmington *(G-16135)*

Beyond Normal Media LLC .... G 980 263-9921
  Charlotte *(G-2306)*

Bloom Ai Inc .... G 704 620-2886
  Cary *(G-1708)*

Blue Ridge Quick Print Inc .... G 828 883-2420
  Brevard *(G-1270)*

Boramed Inc .... G 919 419-9518
  Durham *(G-4973)*

Brands Fashion US Inc .... G 704 953-8246
  Charlotte *(G-2348)*

Brite Sky LLC .... G 757 589-4676
  Godwin *(G-6576)*

Broome Sign Company .... G 704 782-0422
  Concord *(G-4215)*

Bryan Austin .... F 336 841-6573
  High Point *(G-8276)*

Bull City Designs LLC .... E 919 908-6252
  Durham *(G-4986)*

By-Design Black Oxide & TI LLC .... F 828 874-0610
  Valdese *(G-15443)*

C&A Hockaday Transport LLC .... G 252 676-5956
  Roanoke Rapids *(G-13570)*

Cablenc LLC .... G 919 307-9065
  Zebulon *(G-17124)*

Capital City Cuisine LLC .... G 919 432-2126
  Raleigh *(G-12588)*

Carlton Enterprizes LLC .... G 919 534-5424
  Rocky Point *(G-13743)*

Carolina Coastal Coatings Inc .... F 910 346-9607
  Maple Hill *(G-10131)*

Carolina Connections Inc .... G 336 786-7030
  Mount Airy *(G-11488)*

Carolina Custom Draperies Inc .... G 336 945-5190
  Winston Salem *(G-16644)*

CBS Radio Holdings Inc .... E 704 319-9369
  Charlotte *(G-2424)*

CD Dickie & Associates Inc .... F 704 527-9102
  Charlotte *(G-2433)*

▲ Champion Thread Company .... G 704 867-6611
  Gastonia *(G-6375)*

Charlies Heating & Cooling LLC .... G 336 260-1973
  Snow Camp *(G-14495)*

Chicopee Inc .... G 919 894-4111
  Benson *(G-1032)*

Coding Institute LLC .... E 239 280-2300
  Durham *(G-5023)*

Council Trnsp & Logistics LLC .... G 910 322-7588
  Fayetteville *(G-5797)*

Covington Barcoding Inc .... G 336 996-5759
  Kernersville *(G-9183)*

Crane Coffee Roasters LLC .... G 443 960-0654
  Fuquay Varina *(G-6192)*

Creative Brewing Company LLC .... G 919 297-8182
  Smithfield *(G-14458)*

Creative Printers Inc .... G 336 246-7746
  West Jefferson *(G-15938)*

Creative Printers & Brks Inc .... G 828 321-4663
  Andrews *(G-125)*

Crump Group USA Inc .... F 936 465-5870
  Nashville *(G-11742)*

Crypton Mills LLC .... E 828 202-5875
  Cliffside *(G-4085)*

Cupcake Stop Shop LLC .... G 919 457-7900
  Raleigh *(G-12661)*

◆ Custom Contract Furn LLC .... G 336 882-8565
  High Point *(G-8312)*

Custom Finishers Inc .... E 336 431-7141
  High Point *(G-8313)*

Custom Nano Inc .... G 919 608-3540
  Raleigh *(G-12665)*

CVC Equipment Company .... G 704 300-6242
  Cherryville *(G-3867)*

Cvmr (usa) Inc .... C 828 288-3768
  Union Mills *(G-15440)*

Danby Barcoding LLC .... G 770 416-9845
  Kernersville *(G-9187)*

Daniels Business Services Inc .... E 828 277-8250
  Asheville *(G-602)*

Davie Property Restoration LLC .... G 336 923-4018
  Advance *(G-40)*

Day 3 Lwncare Ldscpg Prfctnist .... G 910 574-8422
  Fayetteville *(G-5806)*

DB CUSTOM CRAFTS LLC .... F 336 791-0940
  Winston Salem *(G-16674)*

Decolux USA .... G 704 340-3532
  Charlotte *(G-2611)*

▲ Delve Interiors LLC .... C 336 274-4661
  Greensboro *(G-6968)*

Distinctive Furniture Inc .... G 828 754-3947
  Lenoir *(G-9604)*

Dix Enterprises Inc .... F 336 558-9512
  High Point *(G-8327)*

DMD Logistics LLC .... G 336 480-8149
  Winston Salem *(G-16685)*

Dreamship Inc .... G 908 601-8152
  Raleigh *(G-12701)*

Dronescape Pllc .... G 704 953-3798
  Charlotte *(G-2655)*

Drs Transportation Inc .... G 919 215-2770
  Raleigh *(G-12704)*

Eatclub Inc .... G 609 578-7942
  Chapel Hill *(G-2011)*

Educatrx Inc .... G 980 328-0013
  Monroe *(G-10711)*

Elevated Cnstr Renovations LLC .... G 910 301-4243
  Red Springs *(G-13500)*

Envirnmntal Cmfort Sltions Inc .... E 980 272-7327
  Kannapolis *(G-9119)*

▲ Environmental Supply Co Inc .... F 919 956-9688
  Durham *(G-5089)*

Esco Industries Inc .... F 336 495-3772
  Randleman *(G-13469)*

Esequence Inc .... G 919 831-1995
  Raleigh *(G-12747)*

Every Day Carry LLc .... F 203 231-0256
  Winnabow *(G-16580)*

Evolution of Style LLC .... G 914 329-3078
  Charlotte *(G-2735)*

Exhibit World Inc .... G 704 882-2272
  Indian Trail *(G-8933)*

Extensive Builders LLC .... G 980 621-3793
  Salisbury *(G-13960)*

Exteriors Inc Ltd .... G 919 325-2251
  Spring Lake *(G-14625)*

Fast Pro Media LLC .... G 704 799-8040
  Cornelius *(G-4545)*

Fast Pro Media LLC .... G 704 799-8040
  Cornelius *(G-4546)*

Fastzone Dsl & Internet Servic .... G 828 963-1350
  Banner Elk *(G-897)*

Fe26 LLC .... G 980 875-0170
  Charlotte *(G-2750)*

Fines and Carriel Inc .... G 919 929-0702
  Chapel Hill *(G-2018)*

Firm Ascend LLC .... G 704 464-3024
  Charlotte *(G-2763)*

Fitch Sign Company Inc .... G 704 482-2916
  Shelby *(G-14317)*

Flores Crane Services LLC .... F 704 243-4347
  Waxhaw *(G-15757)*

Forward Dsptching Lgistics LLC .... G 252 907-9797
  Greenville *(G-7527)*

Franks Millwright Services .... G 336 248-6692
  Lexington *(G-9720)*

Froehling & Robertson Inc .... E 804 264-2701
  Raleigh *(G-12783)*

Frostie Bottom Tree Stand LLC .... G 828 466-1708
  Claremont *(G-3927)*

Galaxy Pressure Washing Inc .... G 888 299-3129
  Pineville *(G-12270)*

Galvix Inc .... G 925 434-6243
  Cary *(G-1770)*

Gentrys Cabnt Doors .... G 336 957-8787
  Roaring River *(G-13593)*

Georges Sauces LLC .... G 252 459-3084
  Nashville *(G-11745)*

Gilmore Globl Lgstics Svcs Inc .... D 919 277-2700
  Morrisville *(G-11347)*

Go For Green Fleet Svcs LLC .... G 803 306-3683
  Charlotte *(G-2840)*

Goldsboro Neon Sign Co Inc .... G 919 735-2035
  Goldsboro *(G-6619)*

SIC SECTION
73 BUSINESS SERVICES

Gracefully Broken LLC.................................. G 980 474-0309
  Charlotte *(G-2851)*

Grahams Transportation LLC................... G 910 627-6880
  Fayetteville *(G-5831)*

Greenfield Energy LLC............................... F 910 509-1805
  Wrightsville Beach *(G-17025)*

Gt Rhyno Construction LLC....................... G 919 737-3620
  Raleigh *(G-12824)*

Harbor Lines LLC...................................... G 910 279-3796
  Wilmington *(G-16247)*

High Five Enterprises Inc........................... G 828 279-5962
  Weaverville *(G-15848)*

High Velocity Archery LLC......................... G 910 620-5215
  Kelly *(G-9138)*

Hrtms Incorporated.................................... G 919 741-5099
  Raleigh *(G-12864)*

Ica(usa)inc... G 704 798-3488
  Winston Salem *(G-16754)*

Imperial Falcon Group Inc......................... G 646 717-1128
  Charlotte *(G-2953)*

◆ Implus Footcare LLC.............................. B 800 446-7587
  Durham *(G-5150)*

Inspiration Leather Design Inc................... G 336 420-2265
  Jamestown *(G-9058)*

Intelligent Apps LLC.................................. G 919 628-6256
  Raleigh *(G-12897)*

Intelligent Tool Corp.................................. F 704 799-0449
  Concord *(G-4286)*

Intersport Group Inc.................................. G 814 968-3085
  Vilas *(G-15496)*

J &D Contractor Service Inc..................... G 919 427-0218
  Angier *(G-142)*

J R Cole Industries Inc.............................. D 704 523-6622
  Charlotte *(G-3005)*

J6 & Company LLC.................................... F 336 997-4497
  Winston Salem *(G-16767)*

Jalco Inc... G 336 434-5909
  Trinity *(G-15347)*

▲ Jasie Blanks LLC.................................. F 910 485-0016
  Fayetteville *(G-5846)*

Jeld-Wen Inc... C 336 838-0292
  North Wilkesboro *(G-12016)*

Jenkins Services Group LLC.................... G 704 881-3210
  Catawba *(G-1965)*

Jennifer Mowrer... G 336 714-6462
  Winston Salem *(G-16769)*

JFK Conferences LLC............................... E 980 255-3336
  Fayetteville *(G-5849)*

JKS Motorsports Inc.................................. G 336 722-4129
  Lexington *(G-9735)*

Joe Armstrong... G 336 207-6503
  Greensboro *(G-7138)*

Jubilee Screen Printing Inc....................... G 910 673-4240
  West End *(G-15928)*

Just Black LLC.. G 252 204-5437
  Gastonia *(G-6436)*

Just n Tyme Trucking LLC........................ G 704 804-9519
  Charlotte *(G-3039)*

Justice Bearing LLC.................................. G 800 355-2500
  Mooresville *(G-10993)*

▲ K-M Machine Company Inc................. D 910 428-2368
  Biscoe *(G-1114)*

K&K Holdings Inc...................................... G 704 341-5567
  Charlotte *(G-3040)*

Katchi Tees Incorporated.......................... G 252 315-4691
  Wilson *(G-16504)*

Keel Labs Inc.. G 917 848-9066
  Morrisville *(G-11365)*

Keiths Cleaning LLC.................................. G 336 701-0185
  Winston Salem *(G-16776)*

Kenn M LLC... G 678 755-6607
  Raleigh *(G-12935)*

King Business Service Inc........................ G 910 610-1030
  Laurinburg *(G-9483)*

Klearoptics Inc... G 760 224-6770
  Lattimore *(G-9457)*

Knight Communications Inc..................... F 704 568-7804
  Indian Trail *(G-8943)*

Knooosc Inc... G 415 640-0080
  Morehead City *(G-11179)*

Label & Printing Solutions Inc.................. G 919 782-1242
  Raleigh *(G-12950)*

LDR Designs.. G 252 375-4484
  Greenville *(G-7555)*

Learning Craftsmen Inc............................. G 813 321-5003
  Apex *(G-213)*

Legalis Dms LLC....................................... F 919 741-8260
  Raleigh *(G-12965)*

Lions Services Inc.................................... B 704 921-1527
  Charlotte *(G-3091)*

Little Reds Engraving LLC........................ G 910 599-7747
  Burgaw *(G-1344)*

Livengood Innovations LLC..................... G 336 925-7604
  Linwood *(G-9946)*

Livingston & Haven LLC........................... C 704 588-3670
  Charlotte *(G-3096)*

Lucerno Dynamics LLC............................. G 317 294-1395
  Cary *(G-1820)*

Luxor Hydration LLC................................. F 919 568-5047
  Durham *(G-5200)*

◆ M & S Warehouse Inc........................... E 828 728-3733
  Lenoir *(G-9628)*

M I Connection.. F 704 662-3255
  Mooresville *(G-11013)*

M&M Bioplastic LLC.................................. G 877 366-5227
  Mill Spring *(G-10488)*

Make Solutions Inc.................................... F 623 444-0098
  Asheville *(G-694)*

Mark Stoddard... G 910 797-7214
  Fayetteville *(G-5866)*

Marketing One Sportswear Inc................. G 704 334-9333
  Charlotte *(G-3126)*

Marvica McLendon LLC............................ G 704 965-9408
  Charlotte *(G-3135)*

Mdkscrubs LLC... G 980 250-4708
  Charlotte *(G-3156)*

Merchant 1 Manufacturing LLC................ G 336 617-3008
  Summerfield *(G-14989)*

Mijo Enterprises Inc.................................. G 252 442-6806
  Rocky Mount *(G-13712)*

Minges Printing & Advg Co...................... G 704 867-6791
  Gastonia *(G-6466)*

Mjt Us Inc.. G 704 826-7828
  Charlotte *(G-3189)*

Modern Structure Solutions LLC.............. G 984 286-2447
  Hudson *(G-8776)*

Monk Lekeisha.. G 910 385-0361
  Goldsboro *(G-6637)*

Montgomery Logging Inc......................... G 910 572-2806
  Troy *(G-15409)*

Moore S Welding Service Inc.................. G 919 837-5769
  Bear Creek *(G-940)*

Mountain Homes of Wnc LLC................... F 828 216-2546
  Weaverville *(G-15852)*

Moya Custom Designs LLC...................... G 984 208-3118
  Siler City *(G-14426)*

N3xt Inc... G 704 905-2209
  Charlotte *(G-3227)*

Nafshi Enterprises LLC............................. G 910 986-9888
  Aberdeen *(G-17)*

Nashville Wldg & Mch Works Inc............. E 252 243-0113
  Wilson *(G-16517)*

NC Diesel Performance LLC..................... G 704 431-3257
  Salisbury *(G-14016)*

Neurametrix Inc... G 408 507-2366
  Asheville *(G-711)*

▲ Next World Design Inc........................ F 800 448-1223
  Thomasville *(G-15256)*

Ni4I Antennas and Elec LLC..................... G 828 738-6445
  Moravian Falls *(G-11146)*

North American Trade LLC....................... G 828 712-3004
  Fletcher *(G-6030)*

Northern Star Technologies Inc................ G 516 353-3333
  Indian Trail *(G-8952)*

Northsouth Biomagnetics Inc.................. G 828 478-2277
  Sherrills Ford *(G-14389)*

Nutrotonic LLC.. F 855 948-0008
  Charlotte *(G-3285)*

Occasions Group Inc................................ E 252 321-5805
  Greenville *(G-7566)*

Ocufii Inc... G 804 874-4036
  Huntersville *(G-8869)*

On Point Mobile Detailing LLC................. G 404 593-8882
  Charlotte *(G-3296)*

Orlandos Cstm Design T-Shirts............... G 919 220-5515
  Durham *(G-5264)*

▲ Packaging Unlimited NC Inc................ D 704 732-7100
  Lincolnton *(G-9912)*

Pampering Moms Ntral Skin Care........... G 706 490-3083
  Raleigh *(G-13098)*

Panaceutics Nutrition Inc......................... F 919 797-9623
  Durham *(G-5269)*

Paper Route Transportation LLC............. G 919 478-6615
  Sanford *(G-14162)*

Patti Boo Inc... G 828 648-6495
  Canton *(G-1621)*

Patti Boo Designs Inc............................... G 828 648-6495
  Canton *(G-1622)*

PC Signs & Graphics LLC........................ G 919 661-5801
  Garner *(G-6300)*

Peak Level Media Solutions LLC............. G 919 917-8002
  Cary *(G-1846)*

▲ Performance Additives LLC................ F 215 321-4388
  Southern Pines *(G-14543)*

Performance Parts Intl LLC...................... F 704 660-1084
  Mooresville *(G-11052)*

Personal Xpressionz LLC......................... G 919 587-7462
  Durham *(G-5282)*

Phynix Pc Inc.. F 503 890-1444
  Middlesex *(G-10454)*

Piedmont Fiberglass Inc.......................... E 828 632-8883
  Statesville *(G-14859)*

Piranha Industries Inc.............................. G 704 248-7843
  Charlotte *(G-3344)*

Power and Ctrl Solutions LLC.................. G 704 609-9623
  Charlotte *(G-3359)*

▲ Powerlyte Paintball Game Pdts.......... F 919 713-4317
  Raleigh *(G-13124)*

Powermolekul Inc..................................... G 919 264-8487
  Cary *(G-1856)*

Pramana LLC.. G 910 233-5118
  Cary *(G-1858)*

Print Magic Transfers Llc......................... G 848 250-9906
  Charlotte *(G-3384)*

Production Media Inc............................... F 919 325-0120
  Raleigh *(G-13149)*

Professnal Alterations EMB Inc............... G 910 577-8484
  Jacksonville *(G-9022)*

▲ Promographix Inc................................. F 919 846-1379
  Carolina Beach *(G-1640)*

Prototech Manufacturing Inc................... F 508 646-8849
  Washington *(G-15728)*

Queen Wrist Bling Inc.............................. G 980 635-0287
  Concord *(G-4345)*

Quinlan Publishing Company.................. G 229 886-7995
  Wilmington *(G-16374)*

Employee Codes: A=Over 500 employees, B=251-500
C=101-250, D=51-100, E=20-50, F=10-19, G=1-9

73 BUSINESS SERVICES

Raleigh Tees .... G 919 850-3378
  Raleigh *(G-13187)*

Randall Printing Inc .... G 336 272-3333
  Greensboro *(G-7303)*

Random & Kind LLC .... G 919 249-8809
  Durham *(G-5319)*

Rebecca Trickey .... G 910 584-5549
  Raeford *(G-12435)*

Retroject Inc .... G 919 619-3042
  Chapel Hill *(G-2063)*

Richards Southern Soul Fd LLC .... G 919 210-8275
  Raleigh *(G-13207)*

▲ Riley Technologies LLC .... E 704 663-6319
  Mooresville *(G-11069)*

Roadmasters Traffic Ctrl LLC .... G 704 585-9635
  Statesville *(G-14877)*

Rogers Knitting Inc .... G 336 789-4155
  Mount Airy *(G-11567)*

Royal Textile Products Sw LLC .... G 602 276-4598
  Charlotte *(G-3465)*

◆ Royce Too LLC .... E 212 356-1627
  Winston Salem *(G-16891)*

Rucker Intrgrted Logistics LLC .... G 704 352-2018
  Charlotte *(G-3471)*

S C I A Inc .... G 919 387-7000
  Cary *(G-1877)*

▼ S P Co Inc .... G 919 848-3599
  Raleigh *(G-13222)*

Sakun Inc .... G 919 255-2994
  Cary *(G-1878)*

Salem One Inc .... G 336 744-9990
  Winston Salem *(G-16893)*

Salon & Spa Design Services .... G 919 556-6380
  Wake Forest *(G-15587)*

Salonexclusive Beauty LLC .... G 704 488-3909
  Charlotte *(G-3484)*

▲ Sanford Transition Company Inc .... E 919 775-4989
  Sanford *(G-14182)*

Scoggins Industrial Inc .... F 252 977-9222
  Sharpsburg *(G-14280)*

SCR-Tech LLC .... C 704 504-0191
  Charlotte *(G-3513)*

Screen Printers Unlimited LLC .... G 336 667-8737
  Wilkesboro *(G-16039)*

Secured Shred .... G 443 288-6375
  Raleigh *(G-13243)*

Serenity Home Services LLC .... G 910 233-8733
  Troutman *(G-15393)*

Service and Equipment Company .... G 910 545-5886
  Jacksonville *(G-9029)*

Sg-Clw Inc .... F 336 865-4980
  Winston Salem *(G-16903)*

Sign Shop of The Triangle Inc .... G 919 363-3930
  Apex *(G-242)*

Signcaster Corporation .... G 336 712-2525
  Winston Salem *(G-16908)*

Signs Etc .... G 336 722-9341
  Winston Salem *(G-16909)*

Sitzer & Spuria Inc .... G 919 929-0299
  Chapel Hill *(G-2073)*

Skyview Commercial Cleaning .... G 704 858-0134
  Charlotte *(G-3562)*

Smissons Inc .... G 660 537-3219
  Clayton *(G-4009)*

Sml Transportation LLC .... G 704 402-6744
  Harmony *(G-7689)*

Southill Industrial Carving .... G 336 472-5311
  Thomasville *(G-15280)*

Steel Supply and Erection Co .... F 336 625-4830
  Asheboro *(G-487)*

Stephanie Baxter .... G 803 203-8467
  Lincolnton *(G-9922)*

▲ Sv Plastics LLC .... G 336 472-2242
  Thomasville *(G-15287)*

Sweet Treats By Treat Lady LLC .... G 336 831-3282
  Winston Salem *(G-16928)*

Tailored Visionz & Dreamz LLC .... G 919 340-3613
  Hollister *(G-8677)*

Tatum Galleries Inc .... G 828 963-6466
  Banner Elk *(G-904)*

Tawnico LLC .... G 704 606-2345
  Charlotte *(G-3673)*

Taylor Interiors LLC .... F 980 207-3160
  Charlotte *(G-3674)*

Td Cloud Services .... G 518 258-6788
  Raleigh *(G-13330)*

Textile Products Inc .... E 704 636-6221
  Salisbury *(G-14051)*

The McQuackins Company LLC .... G 980 254-2309
  Gastonia *(G-6525)*

Thompson Printing & Packg Inc .... G 704 313-7323
  Mooresboro *(G-10842)*

Three Ladies and A Male LLC .... G 704 287-1584
  Charlotte *(G-3691)*

Tony D Hildreth .... F 910 276-1803
  Laurel Hill *(G-9465)*

Triangle Prcsion Dgnostics Inc .... G 919 345-0110
  Durham *(G-5409)*

◆ Triple Crown International LLC .... G 704 846-4983
  Charlotte *(G-3730)*

Tryhard Infinity LLC .... G 252 269-0985
  New Bern *(G-11852)*

Two24 Digital LLC .... G 910 475-7555
  Wilmington *(G-16437)*

UGLy Essentials LLC .... F 910 319-9945
  Raleigh *(G-13376)*

Ultimate Floor Cleaning .... G 704 912-8978
  Charlotte *(G-3748)*

US Logoworks LLC .... F 910 307-0312
  Fayetteville *(G-5944)*

Viiv Healthcare Company .... A 919 483-2100
  Durham *(G-5434)*

Vital Being .... G 828 964-5853
  Zionville *(G-17149)*

Watson Steel & Iron Works LLC .... E 704 821-7140
  Matthews *(G-10350)*

Weaveup Inc .... G 443 540-4201
  Durham *(G-5439)*

Whatz Cookin LLC .... G 336 353-0227
  Mount Airy *(G-11594)*

White Tiger Btq & Candle Co .... G 919 610-7244
  Sanford *(G-14205)*

Wild Child Custom Graphics LLC .... G 910 762-5335
  Wilmington *(G-16443)*

WW&s Construction Inc .... G 217 620-4042
  Dallas *(G-4661)*

Z Collection LLC .... G 919 247-1513
  Zebulon *(G-17147)*

Zelaya Bros LLC .... G 980 833-0099
  Charlotte *(G-3850)*

Zysense LLC .... G 215 485-1955
  Chapel Hill *(G-2105)*

75 AUTOMOTIVE REPAIR, SERVICES AND PARKING

7513 Truck rental and leasing, without drivers

Chimneyrock Storage .... G 828 685-2893
  Hendersonville *(G-7836)*

Dutchman Creek Self-Storage .... G 919 363-8878
  Apex *(G-185)*

Security Self Storage .... G 919 544-3969
  Durham *(G-5348)*

V M Trucking Inc .... G 984 239-4853
  Morehead City *(G-11195)*

7514 Passenger car rental

Van Products Inc .... E 919 878-7110
  Raleigh *(G-13392)*

7515 Passenger car leasing

Courtesy Ford Inc .... E 252 338-4783
  Elizabeth City *(G-5537)*

7519 Utility trailer rental

C & M Enterprise Inc .... G 704 545-1180
  Mint Hill *(G-10524)*

Readilite & Barricade Inc .... F 919 231-8309
  Raleigh *(G-13194)*

Spring Repair Service Inc .... F 336 299-5660
  Greensboro *(G-7360)*

7521 Automobile parking

▲ Custom Doors Incorporated .... F 704 982-2885
  Albemarle *(G-79)*

7532 Top and body repair and paint shops

Jenkins Properties Inc .... E 336 667-4282
  North Wilkesboro *(G-12017)*

▼ Mickey Truck Bodies Inc .... B 336 882-6806
  High Point *(G-8455)*

Quality Trck Bodies & Repr Inc .... E 252 245-5100
  Elm City *(G-5652)*

R and L Collision Center Inc .... F 704 739-2500
  Kings Mountain *(G-9328)*

Southern Classic Seating LLC .... F 336 498-3130
  Sophia *(G-14522)*

Triangle Body Works Inc .... F 336 788-0631
  Winston Salem *(G-16951)*

7534 Tire retreading and repair shops

A 1 Tire Service Inc .... G 828 684-1860
  Fletcher *(G-5978)*

Accel Discount Tire .... G 704 636-0323
  Salisbury *(G-13913)*

Advance Stores Company Inc .... F 336 545-9091
  Greensboro *(G-6780)*

Aiken-Black Tire Service Inc .... E 828 322-3736
  Hickory *(G-7930)*

Albemarle Tire Retreading Inc .... G 704 982-4113
  Albemarle *(G-71)*

Arenas Tires .... G 828 962-9422
  Hickory *(G-7940)*

Auto Care & Truck Wash LLC .... G 704 363-6341
  Raleigh *(G-12535)*

Autosmart Inc .... G 919 210-7936
  Apex *(G-168)*

Avery County Recapping Co Inc .... E 828 733-0161
  Newland *(G-11881)*

Big Tire Outfitters .... G 919 568-9605
  Mc Leansville *(G-10383)*

Bill Martin Inc .... F 704 873-0241
  Statesville *(G-14764)*

Bray S Recapping Service Inc .... E 336 786-6182
  Mount Airy *(G-11486)*

Bridgestone Ret Operations LLC .... G 919 471-4468
  Durham *(G-4977)*

Bridgestone Ret Operations LLC .... G 910 864-4106
  Fayetteville *(G-5775)*

Bridgestone Ret Operations LLC .... F 704 861-8146
  Gastonia *(G-6360)*

Bridgestone Ret Operations LLC .... G 919 778-0230
  Goldsboro *(G-6597)*

75 AUTOMOTIVE REPAIR, SERVICES AND PARKING

Bridgestone Ret Operations LLC .... G 336 282-6646
   Greensboro *(G-6852)*

Bridgestone Ret Operations LLC .... F 336 852-8524
   Greensboro *(G-6853)*

Bridgestone Ret Operations LLC .... G 252 522-5126
   Kinston *(G-9347)*

Bridgestone Ret Operations LLC .... G 919 872-6402
   Raleigh *(G-12573)*

Bridgestone Ret Operations LLC .... G 919 872-6566
   Raleigh *(G-12574)*

Bridgestone Ret Operations LLC .... G 252 243-5189
   Wilson *(G-16480)*

Bridgestone Ret Operations LLC .... G 336 725-1580
   Winston Salem *(G-16636)*

Burnett Darrill Stephen .... G 828 287-8778
   Spindale *(G-14604)*

Carolina Giant Tires Inc .... F 919 609-9077
   Henderson *(G-7777)*

Carolina Retread LLC .... F 910 642-4123
   Whiteville *(G-15961)*

Cecil Budd Tire Company LLC .... F 919 742-2322
   Siler City *(G-14403)*

Claybrook Tire Inc .... F 336 573-3135
   Stoneville *(G-14955)*

College Sun Do .... G 910 521-9189
   Pembroke *(G-12181)*

Colony Tire Corporation .... G 252 973-0004
   Rocky Mount *(G-13688)*

Crossroads Tire Store Inc .... G 704 888-2064
   Midland *(G-10465)*

◆ Dunlop Aircraft Tyres Inc .... E 336 283-0979
   Mocksville *(G-10567)*

Ed S Tire Laurinburg Inc .... G 910 277-0565
   Laurinburg *(G-9476)*

Elias Gonzalez .... G 910 271-9514
   Warsaw *(G-15667)*

Enfield Tire Service Inc .... G 252 445-5016
   Enfield *(G-5677)*

Falls Automotive Service Inc .... G 336 723-0521
   Winston Salem *(G-16708)*

Foster Tire Sales Inc .... G 336 248-6726
   Lexington *(G-9719)*

▲ Global Veneer Sales Inc .... G 336 885-5061
   High Point *(G-8368)*

Go Ev and Go Green Corp .... G 704 327-9040
   Charlotte *(G-2839)*

Greensboro Tire & Auto Service .... G 336 294-9495
   Greensboro *(G-7066)*

Hall Tire and Battery Co Inc .... F 336 275-3812
   Greensboro *(G-7075)*

Halls Auto Repair .... G 919 879-9946
   Dunn *(G-4874)*

Haneys Tire Recapping Svc LLC .... F 910 276-2636
   Laurinburg *(G-9481)*

Hardison Tire Co Inc .... F 252 745-4561
   Bayboro *(G-935)*

John Conrad Inc .... G 336 475-8144
   Thomasville *(G-15239)*

Johnnys Tire Sales and Svc Inc .... F 252 353-8473
   Greenville *(G-7551)*

Lewis Brothers Tire & Algnmt .... G 919 359-9050
   Clayton *(G-3993)*

Lexington Tire & Auto LLC .... G 336 249-2105
   Lexington *(G-9748)*

M & M Tire and Auto Inc .... G 336 643-7877
   Summerfield *(G-14988)*

M & R Retreading & Oil Co Inc .... F 704 474-4101
   Norwood *(G-12040)*

McCarthy Tire Service Company .... G 910 791-0432
   Wilmington *(G-16317)*

Merchants Inc .... G 252 447-2421
   Havelock *(G-7743)*

Mock Tire & Automotive Inc .... E 336 753-8473
   Mocksville *(G-10591)*

Mock Tire & Automotive Inc .... E 336 774-0081
   Winston Salem *(G-16812)*

▲ Mock Tire & Automotive Inc .... E 336 768-1010
   Winston Salem *(G-16813)*

Moss Brothers Tires & Svc Inc .... G 910 895-4572
   Rockingham *(G-13635)*

Mr Tire Inc .... G 828 262-3555
   Boone *(G-1225)*

Mr Tire Inc .... F 704 483-1500
   Denver *(G-4790)*

Mr Tire Inc .... F 828 322-8130
   Hickory *(G-8099)*

Mr Tire Inc .... G 704 739-6456
   Kings Mountain *(G-9319)*

Mr Tire Inc .... G 828 758-0047
   Lenoir *(G-9637)*

Mr Tire Inc .... G 704 735-8024
   Lincolnton *(G-9910)*

Mr Tire Inc .... G 704 484-0816
   Shelby *(G-14350)*

Mr Tire Inc .... G 704 872-4127
   Statesville *(G-14849)*

Newfound Tire & Quick Lube Inc .... G 828 683-3232
   Leicester *(G-9516)*

Oakie S Tire & Recapping Inc .... F 704 482-5629
   Shelby *(G-14353)*

Parrish Tire Company .... E 704 372-2013
   Charlotte *(G-3317)*

Parrish Tire Company .... F 336 334-9979
   Greensboro *(G-7246)*

Parrish Tire Company .... E 704 872-6565
   Jonesville *(G-9101)*

◆ Parrish Tire Company .... D 800 849-8473
   Winston Salem *(G-16836)*

Perry Brothers Tire Svc Inc .... F 919 693-2128
   Oxford *(G-12140)*

Perry Brothers Tire Svc Inc .... E 919 775-7225
   Sanford *(G-14167)*

Phil S Tire Service Inc .... G 828 682-2421
   Burnsville *(G-1530)*

Piedmont Truck Tires Inc .... F 828 277-1549
   Asheville *(G-731)*

Piedmont Truck Tires Inc .... F 828 202-5337
   Conover *(G-4480)*

Piedmont Truck Tires Inc .... F 336 223-9412
   Graham *(G-6706)*

Piedmont Truck Tires Inc .... E 336 668-0091
   Greensboro *(G-7262)*

Pumpkin Pacific LLC .... G 704 226-4176
   Charlotte *(G-3397)*

Quality Investments Inc .... E 252 492-8777
   Henderson *(G-7805)*

Richmond Investment .... E 910 410-8200
   Rockingham *(G-13640)*

Roosevelt Tire Service Inc .... F 704 864-5464
   Gastonia *(G-6504)*

Safe Tire & Autos LLC .... G 910 590-3101
   Clinton *(G-4107)*

Small Brothers Tire Co Inc .... G 704 289-3531
   Monroe *(G-10808)*

Snider Tire Inc .... D 704 373-2910
   Charlotte *(G-3571)*

Snider Tire Inc .... F 336 691-5480
   Greensboro *(G-7347)*

Snider Tire Inc .... G 828 324-9955
   Hickory *(G-8160)*

Stoltz Automotive Inc .... G 336 595-4218
   Walkertown *(G-15616)*

Super Retread Center Inc .... F 919 734-0073
   Goldsboro *(G-6663)*

Tbc Retail Group Inc .... G 336 540-8066
   Greensboro *(G-7392)*

Team X-Treme LLC .... G 919 562-8100
   Rolesville *(G-13760)*

Terrys Tires & Services LLC .... G 336 251-7366
   East Bend *(G-5469)*

Thrifty Tire .... G 919 220-7800
   Durham *(G-5402)*

Tire Sls Svc Inc Fytteville NC .... E 910 485-1121
   Fayetteville *(G-5931)*

Tires Incorporated of Clinton .... E 910 592-4741
   Clinton *(G-4114)*

To The Top Tires and Svc LLC .... G 252 886-3286
   Rocky Mount *(G-13673)*

Toe River Service Station LLC .... G 828 688-6385
   Bakersville *(G-890)*

Towel City Tire & Wheel LLC .... G 704 933-2143
   Kannapolis *(G-9136)*

Treadz LLC .... G 704 664-0995
   Mooresville *(G-11114)*

Turn Key Tire Service Inc .... G 919 836-8473
   Garner *(G-6319)*

Universal Tire Service Inc .... G 919 779-8798
   Raleigh *(G-13383)*

Vestal Buick Gmc Inc .... D 336 310-0261
   Kernersville *(G-9251)*

Village Tire Center Inc .... G 919 862-8500
   Raleigh *(G-13400)*

Whitaker S Tire Service Inc .... F 704 786-6174
   Concord *(G-4389)*

White S Tire Svc Wilson Inc .... G 252 237-0770
   Wilson *(G-16559)*

White S Tire Svc Wilson Inc .... D 252 237-5426
   Wilson *(G-16560)*

White Tire and Service LLC .... G 704 636-0323
   Salisbury *(G-14066)*

Whites Tire Svc New Bern Inc .... G 252 633-1170
   New Bern *(G-11857)*

Wilson Tire and Automotive Inc .... G 336 584-9638
   Elon College *(G-5668)*

Woodlawn Tire and Algnmt Inc .... G 828 756-4212
   Marion *(G-10190)*

7536 Automotive glass replacement shops

A R Perry Corporation .... F 252 492-6181
   Henderson *(G-7774)*

Orare Inc .... G 919 742-1003
   Siler City *(G-14429)*

Rice S Glass Company Inc .... E 919 967-9214
   Carrboro *(G-1655)*

7537 Automotive transmission repair shops

Parrish Tire Company .... F 336 334-9979
   Greensboro *(G-7246)*

7538 General automotive repair shops

Aiken-Black Tire Service Inc .... E 828 322-3736
   Hickory *(G-7930)*

B & B Welding Inc .... G 336 643-5702
   Oak Ridge *(G-12057)*

Barrs Competition .... F 704 482-5169
   Shelby *(G-14287)*

Container Technology Inc .... G 910 350-1303
   Wilmington *(G-16180)*

Courtesy Ford Inc .... E 252 338-4783
   Elizabeth City *(G-5537)*

Cummins Atlantic LLC .... E 704 596-7690
   Charlotte *(G-2584)*

▲ Cummins Atlantic LLC .... E 704 588-1240
   Charlotte *(G-2585)*

Diagnostic Shop Inc .... G 704 933-3435
   Kannapolis *(G-9117)*

75 AUTOMOTIVE REPAIR, SERVICES AND PARKING

F & C Repair and Sales LLC............................. F 704 907-2461
  Charlotte *(G-2741)*
Falls Automotive Service Inc............................ G 336 723-0521
  Winston Salem *(G-16708)*
Greensboro Tire & Auto Service....................... G 336 294-9495
  Greensboro *(G-7066)*
Griffin Automotive Marine Inc........................... G 252 940-0714
  Washington *(G-15706)*
Haneys Tire Recapping Svc LLC...................... F 910 276-2636
  Laurinburg *(G-9481)*
Jacks Motor Parts Inc..................................... G 910 642-4077
  Whiteville *(G-15969)*
John West Auto Service Inc............................. G 919 250-0825
  Raleigh *(G-12919)*
Johnson Machine Co Inc................................. G 252 638-2620
  New Bern *(G-11814)*
L & S Automotive Inc..................................... G 704 391-7657
  Charlotte *(G-3065)*
Lewis Brothers Tire & Algnmt........................... G 919 359-9050
  Clayton *(G-3993)*
◆ Mack Trucks Inc.. A 336 291-9001
  Greensboro *(G-7177)*
Mr Tire Inc.. G 828 262-3555
  Boone *(G-1225)*
Mr Tire Inc.. F 704 483-1500
  Denver *(G-4790)*
Mr Tire Inc.. F 828 322-8130
  Hickory *(G-8099)*
Mr Tire Inc.. G 704 739-6456
  Kings Mountain *(G-9319)*
Mr Tire Inc.. G 828 758-0047
  Lenoir *(G-9637)*
Mr Tire Inc.. G 704 735-8024
  Lincolnton *(G-9910)*
Mr Tire Inc.. G 704 484-0816
  Shelby *(G-14350)*
Mr Tire Inc.. G 704 872-4127
  Statesville *(G-14849)*
NC Diesel Performance LLC............................ G 704 431-3257
  Salisbury *(G-14016)*
Quality Investments Inc................................... E 252 492-8777
  Henderson *(G-7805)*
R & J Mechanical & Welding LLC..................... G 919 362-6630
  Apex *(G-238)*
S Strickland Diesel Svc Inc.............................. G 252 291-6999
  Wilson *(G-16536)*
Satco Truck Equipment Inc.............................. F 919 383-5547
  Durham *(G-5340)*
Snider Tire Inc.. F 336 691-5480
  Greensboro *(G-7347)*
Spring Repair Service Inc............................... F 336 299-5660
  Greensboro *(G-7360)*
Stoltz Automotive Inc..................................... G 336 595-4218
  Walkertown *(G-15616)*
Sullivan Motorsports Inc.................................. G 252 923-2257
  Bath *(G-917)*
Team X-Treme LLC....................................... G 919 562-8100
  Rolesville *(G-13760)*
Universal Tire Service Inc............................... G 919 779-8798
  Raleigh *(G-13383)*
Wooten John... G 828 322-4031
  Hickory *(G-8210)*
Zickgraf Enterprises Inc................................. G 828 524-2313
  Franklin *(G-6149)*

7539 Automotive repair shops, nec

A 1 Tire Service Inc....................................... G 828 684-1860
  Fletcher *(G-5978)*
Anglers Marine NC... G 919 585-7900
  Clayton *(G-3953)*
Avery County Recapping Co Inc....................... E 828 733-0161
  Newland *(G-11881)*
B S R-Hess Race Cars Inc............................... E 704 547-0901
  Charlotte *(G-2254)*
Bridgestone Ret Operations LLC...................... F 336 852-8524
  Greensboro *(G-6853)*
▲ Broadsight Systems Inc............................... G 336 837-1272
  Mebane *(G-10401)*
Carolina.. F 919 851-0906
  Cary *(G-1722)*
▲ Chiron America Inc................................... D 704 587-9526
  Charlotte *(G-2478)*
Claybrook Tire Inc... F 336 573-3135
  Stoneville *(G-14955)*
Colfax Trailer & Repair LLC............................ G 336 993-8511
  Colfax *(G-4144)*
Diagnostic Shop Inc...................................... G 704 933-3435
  Kannapolis *(G-9117)*
G T Racing Heads Inc................................... G 336 905-7988
  Sophia *(G-14517)*
Goldsboro Strter Altrntor Svc............................ G 919 735-6745
  Goldsboro *(G-6620)*
Hall Tire and Battery Co Inc............................. F 336 275-3812
  Greensboro *(G-7075)*
John Conrad Inc.. G 336 475-8144
  Thomasville *(G-15239)*
Mc Cullough Auto Elc & Assoc......................... G 704 376-5388
  Charlotte *(G-3148)*
Mock Tire & Automotive Inc............................. E 336 753-8473
  Mocksville *(G-10591)*
Mock Tire & Automotive Inc............................. E 336 774-0081
  Winston Salem *(G-16812)*
▲ Mock Tire & Automotive Inc........................ E 336 768-1010
  Winston Salem *(G-16813)*
Nichols Spdmtr & Instr Co Inc.......................... G 336 273-2881
  Greensboro *(G-7219)*
One Source SEC & Sound Inc.......................... G 281 850-9487
  Mooresville *(G-11044)*
Parrish Tire Company..................................... F 336 334-9979
  Greensboro *(G-7246)*
Performance Entps & Parts Inc......................... G 336 621-6572
  Greensboro *(G-7251)*
▲ Prevost Car (us) Inc................................... E 908 222-7211
  Greensboro *(G-7281)*
Pumpkin Pacific LLC...................................... G 704 226-4176
  Charlotte *(G-3397)*
R S Integrators Inc.. G 704 588-8288
  Pineville *(G-12294)*
Scattered Wrenches Inc.................................. G 919 480-1605
  Raleigh *(G-13236)*
Sonaron LLC... G 808 232-6168
  Fayetteville *(G-5919)*
Spring Repair Service Inc............................... F 336 299-5660
  Greensboro *(G-7360)*
Stoltz Automotive Inc..................................... G 336 595-4218
  Walkertown *(G-15616)*
Subaru Folger Automotive................................ E 704 531-8888
  Charlotte *(G-3645)*
Tbc Retail Group Inc..................................... G 336 540-8066
  Greensboro *(G-7392)*
Treadz LLC.. G 704 664-0995
  Mooresville *(G-11114)*
Whitaker S Tire Service Inc............................. F 704 786-6174
  Concord *(G-4389)*

7542 Carwashes

Auto Care & Truck Wash LLC.......................... G 704 363-6341
  Raleigh *(G-12535)*
B & D Enterprises Inc.................................... F 704 739-2958
  Kings Mountain *(G-9293)*
B&C Xterior Cleaning Svc Inc........................... G 919 779-7905
  Raleigh *(G-12540)*

7549 Automotive services, nec

Accelrted Svcs Mooresville Inc......................... G 704 658-6666
  Mooresville *(G-10845)*
Apb Wrecker Service LLC............................... G 704 400-0857
  Charlotte *(G-2199)*
Bucks Wrecker Service................................... G 704 776-0899
  Statesville *(G-14767)*
Capital Value Center Sls & Svc........................ G 910 799-4060
  Wilmington *(G-16153)*
Diagnostic Shop Inc...................................... G 704 933-3435
  Kannapolis *(G-9117)*
Mr Tire Inc.. G 828 758-0047
  Lenoir *(G-9637)*
Newfound Tire & Quick Lube Inc....................... G 828 683-3232
  Leicester *(G-9516)*
Orpak Usa Inc... D 201 441-9820
  Greensboro *(G-7237)*
Pro-Motor Engines Inc................................... G 704 664-6800
  Mooresville *(G-11063)*
Pumpkin Pacific LLC...................................... G 704 226-4176
  Charlotte *(G-3397)*
Richard Chldress Racg Entps In........................ E 336 731-3334
  Welcome *(G-15874)*
▲ Richard Chldress Racg Entps In................... B 336 731-3334
  Welcome *(G-15875)*
Specialty Trnsp Systems Inc............................. G 828 464-9738
  Newton *(G-11971)*
Tire Kountry LLC... G 336 637-8320
  Reidsville *(G-13542)*

76 MISCELLANEOUS REPAIR SERVICES

7622 Radio and television repair

Sonaron LLC... G 808 232-6168
  Fayetteville *(G-5919)*

7623 Refrigeration service and repair

Chichibone Inc.. F 919 785-0090
  Kernersville *(G-9177)*
Daikin Applied Americas Inc............................ G 704 588-0087
  Charlotte *(G-2598)*
Diagnostic Shop Inc...................................... G 704 933-3435
  Kannapolis *(G-9117)*
Environmental Specialties LLC......................... D 919 829-9300
  Raleigh *(G-12742)*
Johnson Controls Inc..................................... D 919 743-3500
  Raleigh *(G-12920)*
Trs-Sesco LLC.. D 336 996-2220
  Kernersville *(G-9248)*

7629 Electrical repair shops

A & W Electric Inc... E 704 333-4986
  Charlotte *(G-2113)*
▲ Advanced Electronic Svcs Inc...................... D 336 789-0792
  Mount Airy *(G-11473)*
Allan Drth Sons Gnrtor Sls Svc........................ G 828 526-9325
  Highlands *(G-8611)*
▲ Anuva Services Inc.................................... F 919 468-6441
  Morrisville *(G-11288)*
Applied Drives Inc.. G 704 573-2324
  Charlotte *(G-2204)*
Bsh Home Appliances Corp............................. B 252 672-9155
  New Bern *(G-11780)*
◆ Conversant Products Inc............................. F 919 465-3456
  Cary *(G-1734)*
Duotech Services Inc..................................... E 828 369-5411
  Franklin *(G-6126)*
Eaton Corporation.. D 864 433-1603
  Raleigh *(G-12721)*
Eaton Corporation.. C 919 872-3020
  Raleigh *(G-12722)*

76 MISCELLANEOUS REPAIR SERVICES

Eaton Power Quality Corp............................ C 919 872-3020
  Raleigh (G-12723)
▲ Eaton Power Quality Group Inc. .... F 919 872-3020
  Raleigh (G-12724)
Edge Broadband Solutions LLC.................... E 828 785-1420
  Waynesville (G-15803)
Electric Motor Service of Shelby Inc .... F 704 482-9979
  Shelby (G-14314)
Electrical Equipment Company................... E 910 276-2141
  Laurinburg (G-9478)
▲ Esco Electronic Services Inc.................. F 252 753-4433
  Farmville (G-5735)
Eversharp Saw & Tool Inc.......................... G 828 345-1200
  Hickory (G-8019)
GE Vernova International LLC.................... F 704 587-1300
  Charlotte (G-2812)
Genelect Services Inc .... F 828 255-7999
  Asheville (G-632)
Lighting.. G 919 828-0351
  Raleigh (G-12970)
Presley Group Ltd...................................... D 828 254-9971
  Asheville (G-741)
Protronics Inc.. F 919 217-0007
  Knightdale (G-9427)
SCR Controls Inc....................................... F 704 821-6651
  Matthews (G-10342)
Superior Machine Co SC Inc....................... E 828 652-6141
  Marion (G-10181)
Trans East Inc.. D 910 892-1081
  Dunn (G-4887)
Transformer Sales & Service...................... G 910 594-1495
  Newton Grove (G-11994)

7631 Watch, clock, and jewelry repair

D C Crsman Mfr Fine Jwly Inc.................... G 828 252-9891
  Asheville (G-601)
Donald Haack Diamonds Inc...................... G 704 365-4400
  Charlotte (G-2651)
Dons Fine Jewelry Inc................................ G 336 724-7826
  Clemmons (G-4035)
Jkl Inc... F 252 355-6714
  Greenville (G-7550)
John Laughter Jewelry Inc......................... G 828 456-4772
  Waynesville (G-15808)
Made By Custom LLC................................. G 704 980-9840
  Charlotte (G-3117)
R Gregory Jewelers Inc.............................. G 704 872-6669
  Statesville (G-14874)
Southern Digital Watch Repair................... G 336 299-6718
  Greensboro (G-7353)
Stonehaven Jewelry Gallery Ltd................. G 919 462-8888
  Cary (G-1905)
Sumpters Jwly & Collectibles..................... G 704 399-5348
  Charlotte (G-3649)

7641 Reupholstery and furniture repair

Barker and Martin Inc................................ G 336 275-5056
  Greensboro (G-6831)
Bedex LLC... E 336 617-6755
  High Point (G-8269)
▲ Brice Manufacturing Co Inc.................... E 818 896-2938
  Greensboro (G-6851)
Davidson House Inc................................... F 704 791-0171
  Davidson (G-4670)
Freedom Enterprise LLC............................ G 502 510-7296
  Shallotte (G-14273)
▲ Fulfords Restorations............................. G 252 243-7727
  Wilson (G-15052)
◆ Hughes Furniture Inds Inc...................... C 336 498-8700
  Randleman (G-13473)
Ledford Upholstery................................... G 704 732-0233
  Lincolnton (G-9899)

Moores Upholstering Interiors................... G 704 240-8393
  Lincolnton (G-9909)
Otto and Moore Inc................................... F 336 887-0017
  High Point (G-8472)
Rufco Inc... G 919 829-1332
  Wake Forest (G-15585)
S Dorsett Upholstery Inc........................... G 336 472-7076
  Thomasville (G-15275)
◆ S Kivett Inc... E 910 592-0161
  Clinton (G-4106)
▲ Stone Marble Co Inc.............................. G 773 227-1161
  Thomasville (G-15285)
Touch Up Solutions Inc.............................. E 828 428-9094
  Maiden (G-10120)
Unique Office Solutions Inc....................... F 336 854-0900
  Greensboro (G-7430)

7692 Welding repair

277 Metal Inc.. G 704 372-4513
  Gastonia (G-6333)
A&W Welding Inc....................................... G 252 482-3233
  Edenton (G-5504)
AA Welding and Fabricatio......................... G 919 272-5433
  Clayton (G-3951)
Acme Welding Co...................................... G 770 841-4335
  Harrisburg (G-7699)
Advanced Machine Services LLC................ G 910 410-0099
  Rockingham (G-13618)
Affordable Welding Specialists.................. G 828 446-4436
  Hickory (G-7929)
Airgas Usa LLC.. G 704 636-5049
  Salisbury (G-13916)
Alamance Electric & Wldg Inc.................... G 336 584-9339
  Elon (G-5656)
All Pro Fabrication & Wldg LLC.................. G 336 953-4082
  Lexington (G-9678)
Alloy Fabricators Inc.................................. E 704 263-2281
  Alexis (G-121)
Allsteel Welding LLC.................................. G 919 429-0468
  Middlesex (G-10444)
Aluminum Barges com LLC........................ G 239 272-4857
  Boone (G-1173)
Anchor Welding LLC................................... G 919 747-1926
  Knightdale (G-9412)
Ansonville Piping & Fabg Inc..................... G 704 826-8403
  Ansonville (G-152)
Arc3 Gases Inc.. F 336 275-3333
  Greensboro (G-6812)
Arc3 Gases Inc.. F 704 220-1029
  Monroe (G-10650)
Arc3 Gases Inc.. E 910 892-4016
  Dunn (G-4851)
Archie S Steel Service Inc......................... G 252 355-5007
  Greenville (G-7485)
Arrow Glazing Fabrication Inc.................... G 704 926-1509
  Charlotte (G-2219)
Asheville Prcsion Mch Rblding I................. G 828 254-0884
  Asheville (G-544)
Avery Machine & Welding Co..................... G 828 733-4944
  Fayetteville (G-5767)
B & D Enterprises Inc................................ F 704 739-2958
  Kings Mountain (G-9293)
B&A Welding Miscellaneous LLC................ G 980 287-9187
  Charlotte (G-2255)
Badger Welding Incorporated.................... G 828 863-2078
  Rutherfordton (G-13865)
Banks Welding... G 828 586-2258
  Sylva (G-15053)
Bentons Wldg Repr & Svcs Inc................... G 910 343-9322
  Wilmington (G-16136)
Black Rver Wldg Fbrication LLC................. G 910 471-7434
  Atkinson (G-826)

Blacksand Metal Works LLC....................... F 703 489-8282
  Fayetteville (G-5771)
Bladen Fabricators LLC.............................. G 910 866-5225
  Bladenboro (G-1144)
Blands Welding.. G 704 932-1864
  Davidson (G-4666)
Blue ARC Fabrication Mech LLC................. G 336 693-7878
  Graham (G-6679)
Blue Light Welding of Triad....................... G 336 442-9140
  Winston Salem (G-16634)
▲ Boyd Welding and Mfg Inc..................... F 828 247-0630
  Forest City (G-6061)
Brafford Welding....................................... G 336 318-5436
  Liberty (G-9808)
Brasingtons Inc... G 704 694-5191
  Wadesboro (G-15503)
Braswell Welding....................................... G 252 838-0089
  Beaufort (G-947)
Bright Fabrication LLC............................... G 704 660-3151
  Mooresville (G-10888)
Brightleaf Wldg & Mch Repr LLC................ G 919 934-3300
  Smithfield (G-14451)
Bumgarners Welding.................................. G 704 764-7041
  Monroe (G-10671)
Burnett Welding.. G 803 360-7406
  Elizabethtown (G-5586)
Burns Welding Services LLC...................... G 336 908-5716
  Germanton (G-6553)
C & B Welding & Fab Inc............................ G 704 435-6942
  Bessemer City (G-1054)
C & J Welding Inc...................................... G 919 552-0275
  Holly Springs (G-8693)
C & M Welding Inspections Inc.................. G 919 762-7345
  Willow Spring (G-16076)
C and D Welders LLC................................. G 910 552-3294
  Wallace (G-15619)
Calhoun Welding Inc.................................. G 252 281-1455
  Macclesfield (G-10064)
Carer Welding... G 336 558-3906
  Randleman (G-13457)
Carolina Tractor & Eqp Co......................... G 828 251-2500
  Asheville (G-584)
Carolina Welding & Cnstr.......................... G 252 814-8740
  Kinston (G-9352)
▲ Carotek Inc.. D 704 844-1100
  Matthews (G-10238)
Central ARC Wldg Solutions LLC................ G 704 858-1614
  Huntersville (G-8802)
Chapman Welding LLC............................... G 919 951-8131
  Efland (G-5524)
CJS Welding.. G 252 972-7511
  Elm City (G-5648)
Clayton Welding.. G 252 717-5909
  Washington (G-15689)
CM Welding... G 704 791-0572
  Midland (G-10463)
Coastal Machine & Welding Inc.................. G 910 754-6476
  Shallotte (G-14272)
Coastal Sales Inc....................................... G 252 717-3542
  Washington (G-15691)
Collins Fabrication & Wldg LLC.................. G 704 861-9326
  Gastonia (G-6380)
Colt Welding... G 361 244-2513
  Fuquay Varina (G-6190)
Combs Welding LLC................................... G 336 984-3832
  Roaring River (G-13592)
Combs Welding LLC................................... G 336 452-1386
  Ronda (G-13765)
Container Technology Inc.......................... G 910 350-1303
  Wilmington (G-16180)
Coomers Welding LLC................................ G 919 708-8087
  Sanford (G-14104)

76 MISCELLANEOUS REPAIR SERVICES

Costin Welding and Fabrication............. G..... 910 789-7961
  Burgaw (G-1336)
Crawfords Forge.................................... G..... 828 280-2555
  Hendersonville (G-7841)
Creasmans Welding................................ G..... 828 667-1875
  Asheville (G-597)
▲ Custom Enterprises Inc..................... G..... 336 226-8296
  Burlington (G-1405)
Custom Machine Company Inc............... F..... 704 629-5326
  Bessemer City (G-1059)
Cutting Edge Piping Svcs LLC................ G..... 704 419-3995
  Shelby (G-14308)
Cwi Services LLC.................................. G..... 704 560-9755
  Southport (G-14568)
D & D Welding & Repair LLC................. G..... 336 648-1393
  Mount Airy (G-11499)
Da Welding LLC..................................... G..... 336 231-7691
  Winston Salem (G-16669)
Dah Inc... G..... 910 887-3675
  Southport (G-14569)
Dales Welding Service........................... G..... 919 872-6969
  Raleigh (G-12671)
David Beasley.. G..... 910 891-2557
  Dunn (G-4860)
David Bennett.. F..... 919 798-3424
  Fuquay Varina (G-6194)
David West.. G..... 910 271-0757
  Willard (G-16054)
Davis Davis Mch & Wldg Co Inc.............. F..... 252 443-2652
  Rocky Mount (G-13689)
Delgados Welding Inc............................ G..... 910 588-4762
  Elizabethtown (G-5593)
Deohges Welding Service LLC................ G..... 828 396-2770
  Granite Falls (G-6731)
Diversified Welding and Steel................. G..... 704 504-1111
  Pineville (G-12266)
Donald Auton.. G..... 704 872-7528
  Statesville (G-14788)
Donalds Welding Inc.............................. F..... 910 298-5234
  Chinquapin (G-3892)
Double R Welding & Fabrication.............. G..... 704 340-5825
  Concord (G-4257)
Dunavants Welding & Steel Inc............... G..... 252 338-6533
  Camden (G-1557)
Duncan Joseph E & Duncan Billy............. G..... 828 299-8464
  Swannanoa (G-15205)
Dutchman Creek Self-Storage................ G..... 919 363-8878
  Apex (G-185)
Dynamic Fabrication & Wldg Inc............. G..... 828 390-8377
  Morganton (G-11209)
Ecomarc LLC.. G..... 828 226-4780
  Sylva (G-15056)
Ed Majka LLC....................................... G..... 570 985-9677
  Shiloh (G-14391)
Eddies Welding Inc............................... G..... 704 585-2024
  Stony Point (G-14972)
Edwards Lawnmower & Wldg Repr.......... G..... 919 235-7173
  Wake Forest (G-15551)
Elite Wldg & Fabrications LLC................ G..... 919 224-6007
  Warrenton (G-15659)
Elmore Welding Inc............................... G..... 919 584-7460
  Durham (G-5079)
Estes Machine Co................................. F..... 336 786-7680
  Mount Airy (G-11507)
Everettes Industrial Repr Svc................ F..... 252 527-4269
  Goldsboro (G-6613)
Evident Fab LLC................................... G..... 973 294-4507
  Havelock (G-7742)
Evolution Mobile Welding LLC................ G..... 336 383-9277
  Greensboro (G-7005)
Extreme Stud Welding LLC.................... G..... 828 217-2587
  Vale (G-15466)

EZ Fabrication Inc................................. G..... 828 674-0661
  Claremont (G-3926)
Fabrication Associates Inc..................... D..... 704 535-8050
  Charlotte (G-2742)
Filer Micro Welding............................... G..... 828 248-1813
  Forest City (G-6068)
Flores Welding Inc................................ F..... 919 838-1060
  Raleigh (G-12774)
Franklin Industrial Contrs Inc................ G..... 252 670-6682
  Aurora (G-834)
Franks Millwright Services..................... G..... 336 248-6692
  Lexington (G-9720)
Freedom Steel Welding LLC................... G..... 704 884-1277
  Cherryville (G-3869)
Freeman Custom Welding Inc................. G..... 919 210-6267
  Raleigh (G-12781)
Full Throttle Fabrication LLC.................. G..... 910 770-1180
  Chadbourn (G-1976)
Fusion Fabrication & Wldg LLC............... G..... 704 240-9416
  Vale (G-15467)
Fusion Welding..................................... G..... 508 320-3525
  Rocky Point (G-13745)
Garcia Brothers Welding LLC.................. G..... 919 207-8190
  Bailey (G-872)
Gary Tucker... G..... 919 837-5724
  Bear Creek (G-938)
General Mch Wldg of Burlington.............. G..... 336 227-5400
  Burlington (G-1419)
General Refrigeration Company.............. G..... 919 661-4727
  Garner (G-6273)
Genesis Wldg & Fabrication LLC............. G..... 336 622-9533
  Liberty (G-9814)
George F Wlson Wldg Fbrication............. G..... 828 262-1668
  Boone (G-1199)
Gibbs Machine Company Incorporated.... E..... 336 856-1907
  Greensboro (G-7042)
Gibbs Performance Spc Inc.................... G..... 704 746-2225
  Concord (G-4274)
Glovers Welding LLC............................. F..... 252 586-7692
  Littleton (G-9952)
Godfrey Industrial Welding..................... G..... 919 604-0498
  Sanford (G-14126)
Gonzalez Welding Inc............................ G..... 336 270-8179
  Graham (G-6690)
Gordon Wldg & Fabrication LLC.............. G..... 336 406-7471
  Greensboro (G-7054)
Gore S Mar Met Fabrication Inc.............. G..... 910 763-6066
  Wilmington (G-16237)
GS Fab Inc... G..... 704 799-1227
  Mooresville (G-10966)
Gunmar Machine Corporation................. F..... 910 738-6295
  Lumberton (G-10039)
Guns Welding LLC................................. G..... 336 786-1020
  Mount Airy (G-11514)
H & C Erectors and Welding LLC............. G..... 704 615-9849
  Charlotte (G-2875)
Hales Welding and Fabrication............... G..... 252 907-5508
  Macclesfield (G-10065)
Hancock & Grandson Inc....................... G..... 252 728-2416
  Beaufort (G-959)
Harbor Welding Inc............................... G..... 252 473-3777
  Wanchese (G-15647)
Harris Welding..................................... G..... 336 514-6640
  High Point (G-8375)
Hartman Welding.................................. G..... 336 372-2220
  Sparta (G-14594)
Hayes Welding..................................... G..... 336 989-6171
  Sophia (G-14518)
Heat Transfer Sales of Th...................... E..... 336 294-3838
  Greensboro (G-7085)
High Cotton Fabrication LLC.................. G..... 910 408-6961
  Wilmington (G-16252)

High Rise Service Company Inc.............. E..... 910 371-2325
  Leland (G-9548)
High Speed Welding LLC....................... F..... 910 632-4427
  Wilmington (G-16253)
Highs Welding Shop.............................. G..... 704 624-5707
  Marshville (G-10218)
Hillsville Welding.................................. G..... 336 861-0732
  Trinity (G-15345)
His Specialty Fab LLC........................... G..... 704 279-1638
  Salisbury (G-13981)
Hohn Welding Services LLC................... G..... 336 870-9617
  High Point (G-8397)
Holmes Welding LLC............................. G..... 919 779-8844
  Raleigh (G-12853)
Hughes Welding & Crane Svc LLC.......... G..... 910 895-9767
  Rockingham (G-13631)
Idustrial Burkett Services..................... F..... 252 244-0143
  Vanceboro (G-15478)
▼ Imagination Fabrication..................... G..... 919 280-4430
  Apex (G-204)
Industrial Metal Maint Inc...................... G..... 910 285-3240
  Teachey (G-15177)
Industrial Welding &............................. G..... 910 309-8540
  Fayetteville (G-5842)
Integrity Welding LLC........................... G..... 919 556-5144
  Louisburg (G-9992)
Iron Men Fabrication............................ G..... 336 929-6263
  Randleman (G-13474)
Iv-S Metal Stamping Inc....................... E..... 336 861-2100
  Archdale (G-286)
J & D Welding & Fabg Corp.................. G..... 704 393-9115
  Charlotte (G-3002)
J A King... F..... 800 327-7727
  Raleigh (G-12907)
J R Nixon Welding............................... G..... 252 221-4574
  Tyner (G-15434)
J&B Welding LLC................................. G..... 910 316-5838
  Lumberton (G-10042)
J&C Welding and Fabrication................ G..... 704 654-8253
  Charlotte (G-3007)
Jax Specialty Welding LLC................... G..... 704 380-3548
  Statesville (G-14823)
JC Welding and Machine LLC................ G..... 336 306-2026
  Lexington (G-9733)
Joe Robin Darnell............................... G..... 704 482-1186
  Shelby (G-14333)
Jones Fab LLC.................................... G..... 336 940-2769
  Advance (G-45)
Jones Welding.................................... G..... 828 508-0080
  Sylva (G-15061)
JP Mechanic & Welding Inc.................. G..... 919 650-7438
  Staley (G-14666)
K & W Welding LLC.............................. G..... 910 895-9220
  Rockingham (G-13632)
K & W Welding LLC.............................. G..... 910 844-2288
  Maxton (G-10358)
K P Welding Inc.................................. G..... 540 250-7187
  Jonesville (G-9099)
Kenny Robinson S Wldg Svc Inc............ G..... 760 213-6454
  Liberty (G-9818)
Kinetic Sltons Fabrication LLC.............. G..... 607 749-0946
  Holly Ridge (G-8684)
Kings Prtble Wldg Fbrction LLC............ G..... 336 789-2372
  Mount Airy (G-11532)
Krieg Corp... G..... 704 361-1223
  Charlotte (G-3061)
Kurrent Wldg & Fabrication Inc............. G..... 800 738-6114
  Stoneville (G-14960)
Larry D Troxler.................................. G..... 336 585-1141
  Gibsonville (G-6566)
Laying Dimes Welding & Fab LLC.......... G..... 704 677-5521
  Lexington (G-9745)

76 MISCELLANEOUS REPAIR SERVICES

Leons Welding & Decking LLC............ G 919 923-7327
 Chapel Hill *(G-2032)*
Liberty Welding............................... G 336 964-0640
 Liberty *(G-9823)*
Limitless Wldg Fabrication LLC........... G 252 753-0660
 Farmville *(G-5739)*
Lloyds Fabricating Solutions.............. G 336 250-0154
 Thomasville *(G-15244)*
Lowes Welding and Camper Repr....... G 336 214-9058
 Graham *(G-6698)*
Luck Fabrication Incorporated............ G 336 498-0905
 Randleman *(G-13476)*
Lumsden Welding Company............... G 910 791-6336
 Wilmington *(G-16310)*
Lyerlys Wldg & Fabrication Inc........... G 704 680-2317
 Gold Hill *(G-6584)*
Magnum Mobile Welding Wrap Up...... G 910 372-3380
 Beulaville *(G-1095)*
Marc Machine Works Inc................... F 704 865-3625
 Gastonia *(G-6458)*
Marine Fabrications LLC................... G 252 473-4767
 Wanchese *(G-15649)*
Marsh Welding................................ G 919 335-5332
 Durham *(G-5209)*
Martin Welding Inc........................... G 919 436-8805
 Garner *(G-6284)*
Matthews Welding Service................ G 828 862-4510
 Brevard *(G-1279)*
Maverick Metalworks LLC.................. G 919 609-1274
 Raleigh *(G-13008)*
Max Patterson................................. G 910 947-2524
 Sanford *(G-14151)*
Maynard S Fabricators Inc................. G 336 230-1048
 Greensboro *(G-7191)*
MCS of Fayetteville.......................... G 252 234-6001
 Wilson *(G-16514)*
Mechanical Maintenance Inc.............. F 336 676-7133
 Climax *(G-4087)*
Medley S Garage Welding.................. G 336 674-0422
 Pleasant Garden *(G-12358)*
Mendez Welding LLC........................ G 336 618-9337
 Mocksville *(G-10588)*
Metal ARC...................................... G 910 770-1180
 Whiteville *(G-15971)*
Metal Solutions LLC......................... G 252 702-7523
 Snow Hill *(G-14504)*
Micronics Tig-Welding...................... G 828 691-0755
 Fletcher *(G-6025)*
Mike Beasley Services Inc................. G 910 892-6216
 Dunn *(G-4876)*
Mikes Welding & Fabricating.............. G 336 472-5804
 Thomasville *(G-15249)*
Mikes Welding Service of Conc........... G 704 786-9795
 Concord *(G-4315)*
Miller Sheet Metal Co Inc.................. G 336 751-2304
 Mocksville *(G-10590)*
Mitchell Welding Inc......................... E 828 765-2620
 Spruce Pine *(G-14651)*
Modern Machine and Metal................ D 336 993-4808
 Winston Salem *(G-16814)*
Modlins Anonized Aluminum Wldg...... G 252 753-7274
 Farmville *(G-5740)*
Monical Enterprises Inc..................... G 757 692-1345
 Hampstead *(G-7651)*
Montys Welding & Fabrication............ G 919 337-7859
 Garner *(G-6291)*
Moore S Welding Service Inc.............. G 919 837-5769
 Bear Creek *(G-940)*
▲ Moores Mch Co Fayetteville Inc....... D 919 837-5354
 Bear Creek *(G-941)*
MR Fabrications LLC......................... G 980 785-3943
 Marshville *(G-10220)*

▲ MTS Holdings Corp Inc................... E 336 227-0151
 Burlington *(G-1465)*
Mtz Welding Inc............................... G 919 708-8288
 Sanford *(G-14155)*
Mullis Mechanical Inc....................... G 704 254-5229
 Monroe *(G-10776)*
Nashville Wldg & Mch Works Inc......... E 252 243-0113
 Wilson *(G-16517)*
Newriverwelding.............................. G 336 413-3040
 Mocksville *(G-10594)*
Nic Nac Welding Co.......................... G 704 502-5178
 Charlotte *(G-3262)*
Nigoche Welding Services LLC........... G 252 373-8306
 Wilson *(G-16519)*
Ninos Wldg & Cnstr Svcs LLC............. G 980 214-5804
 Huntersville *(G-8860)*
Nucon Welding Inc........................... G 980 253-9369
 Charlotte *(G-3279)*
OHerns Welding Inc......................... G 910 484-2087
 Fayetteville *(G-5886)*
Olive Hl Wldg Fabrication Inc............. E 336 597-0737
 Roxboro *(G-13812)*
Olympian Welding............................ G 919 608-3829
 Franklinton *(G-6161)*
Parrish Welding............................... G 336 707-3878
 Oak Ridge *(G-12064)*
Pats Mobile Welding......................... G 910 891-9581
 Dunn *(G-4879)*
Paul Casper Inc............................... G 919 269-5362
 Zebulon *(G-17139)*
Perkins Fabrications Inc.................... G 828 688-3157
 Bakersville *(G-886)*
Peter J Hamann............................... G 910 484-7877
 Fayetteville *(G-5897)*
Peterson Welding Inc........................ G 336 480-4152
 Lewisville *(G-9670)*
Pg Technichians............................... G 910 742-1017
 Wilmington *(G-16352)*
Piedmont Weld & Pipe Inc.................. G 704 782-7774
 Concord *(G-4332)*
Pine State Welding........................... G 910 639-3631
 Whispering Pines *(G-15955)*
Powell Welding Inc........................... G 828 433-0831
 Drexel *(G-4836)*
Precise Mobile Welding..................... G 980 785-7085
 Charlotte *(G-3367)*
Precision Fabricators Inc................... G 336 835-4763
 Ronda *(G-13768)*
Precision Welding Mntnc................... G 336 504-5894
 Oxford *(G-12145)*
Precision Wldg Fbrication Svcs........... G 704 243-1929
 Waxhaw *(G-15769)*
Quality Welding............................... G 910 754-3232
 Shallotte *(G-14277)*
Quillen Welding Services LLC............. G 252 269-4908
 Morehead City *(G-11184)*
Quilt Shop...................................... G 828 263-8691
 Boone *(G-1230)*
R & H Welding LLC........................... G 919 763-7955
 Boone *(G-6306)*
R & J Mechanical & Welding LLC......... G 919 362-6630
 Apex *(G-238)*
R Jones Fabrication LLC.................... G 937 779-0826
 Mooresville *(G-11067)*
R S Welding LLC.............................. G 828 437-0768
 Morganton *(G-11245)*
Ram Welding & Fabrication Inc........... G 704 985-8486
 Mount Pleasant *(G-11677)*
Rcr Welding LLC.............................. G 704 200-8527
 Charlotte *(G-3416)*
Recap Inc....................................... G 336 299-8794
 Greensboro *(G-7305)*

Reeves Indus Wldg Fabrication........... G 910 399-7127
 Riegelwood *(G-13562)*
Relentless Wldg & Fabrication............ G 336 402-3749
 High Point *(G-8507)*
Rhythms Welding LLC....................... G 910 477-7150
 Supply *(G-15009)*
Richards Welding and Repr Inc........... G 828 396-8705
 Granite Falls *(G-6753)*
Richards Wldg Met Fbrction LLC......... F 919 626-0134
 Wendell *(G-15914)*
Rickys Welding Inc........................... G 252 336-4437
 Shiloh *(G-14392)*
Riley Power Group LLC..................... C 910 420-6999
 Pinehurst *(G-12234)*
Robert Gregory................................ G 919 821-9188
 Raleigh *(G-13210)*
Robert Raper Welding Inc.................. G 252 399-0598
 Wilson *(G-16533)*
Robinson Mch & Cutter Grinding......... G 704 629-5591
 Bessemer City *(G-1080)*
Robinsons Welding Service................ G 336 622-3150
 Liberty *(G-9828)*
Rocas Welding LLC.......................... G 252 290-2233
 Durham *(G-5334)*
Rock Creek Welding Inc.................... G 828 385-1554
 Bakersville *(G-888)*
Roderick Mch Erectors Wldg Inc......... G 910 343-0381
 Wilmington *(G-16386)*
Rodriguez Welding LLC..................... G 980 299-9449
 Charlotte *(G-3457)*
Rose Welding & Crane Service I.......... G 252 796-9171
 Columbia *(G-4167)*
Roxboro Welding.............................. G 336 364-2307
 Roxboro *(G-13821)*
Royal Welding LLC........................... G 704 750-9353
 Pineville *(G-12298)*
Rugers Welding................................ G 919 471-8795
 Rougemont *(G-13788)*
Ruppards Welding Service LLC........... G 828 386-8191
 Boone *(G-1235)*
S Boyd Welding............................... G 336 349-8349
 Reidsville *(G-13539)*
S Oakley Machine Shop Inc................ G 336 599-6105
 Roxboro *(G-13822)*
S&S Welding................................... G 828 408-2794
 Morganton *(G-11248)*
Sgr Welding & Fabrication LLC........... G 252 299-3629
 Zebulon *(G-17142)*
Skyline Welding LLC......................... G 336 479-0166
 Lexington *(G-9780)*
Smiths Mower Marine & Wldg LLC....... G 919 729-0070
 Louisburg *(G-10002)*
South East Welding........................... G 980 428-0742
 Charlotte *(G-3585)*
Southeast Wldg Fabrication LLC......... G 828 385-1380
 Bakersville *(G-889)*
Southeastern MBL Wldg Repr LLC....... G 919 521-7039
 Raleigh *(G-13281)*
Southeastern Mch & Wldg Co Inc........ E 910 791-6661
 Wilmington *(G-16410)*
Southern Star Cstm Fbrction LL.......... G 704 880-8948
 Statesville *(G-14895)*
Sowers Welding Service..................... G 704 929-5617
 Mooresville *(G-11093)*
Specialty Welding............................. G 828 248-6229
 Forest City *(G-6083)*
Stackz Welding................................ G 336 564-5481
 Stokesdale *(G-14950)*
Stafford Welding.............................. G 704 774-1837
 Monroe *(G-10813)*
State of ARC Welding........................ G 336 341-9780
 Winston Salem *(G-16917)*

Employee Codes: A=Over 500 employees, B=251-500
C=101-250, D=51-100, E=20-50, F=10-19, G=1-9

2024 Harris North Carolina
Manufacturers Directory

76 MISCELLANEOUS REPAIR SERVICES

Steel Supply and Erection Co.............. F..... 336 625-4810
   Asheboro *(G-487)*

Stewarts Garage and Welding Co.......... G..... 336 983-5563
   Tobaccoville *(G-15321)*

Storybook Farm Metal Shop Inc............ G..... 919 967-9491
   Chapel Hill *(G-2074)*

Strickland Bros Entps Inc........................ F..... 252 478-3058
   Spring Hope *(G-14623)*

Tatums Trucking & Welding LLC......... G..... 919 697-6913
   Mebane *(G-10430)*

Technique Chassis LLC........................... E..... 517 819-3579
   Concord *(G-4374)*

That Welder Guy.. G..... 252 342-0391
   Newport *(G-11908)*

Think Welding.. G..... 980 230-2842
   Charlotte *(G-3686)*

Thompson Welding & Mechcl Svc......... G..... 252 536-9431
   Roanoke Rapids *(G-13582)*

Thompson Wldg & Mech Svc LLC.......... G..... 252 535-4269
   Roanoke Rapids *(G-13583)*

Thornburg Machine & Sup Co Inc........... E..... 704 735-5421
   Lincolnton *(G-9929)*

Thurman Toler... G..... 252 758-4082
   Greenville *(G-7591)*

Tobaccoville Welding LLC....................... G..... 336 287-7323
   Tobaccoville *(G-15322)*

▼ Tool-Weld LLC...................................... G..... 843 986-4931
   Rutherfordton *(G-13893)*

Trefena Welds.. G..... 203 551-1370
   Browns Summit *(G-1318)*

Trinweld Welding Services LLC.............. G..... 704 721-5944
   Mount Pleasant *(G-11679)*

Triplett & Coffey Inc................................. F..... 828 263-0561
   Boone *(G-1243)*

Tristate Welding & Fabrication............... G..... 336 899-5206
   High Point *(G-8577)*

Two Brothers Wldg Miscellaneous......... G..... 704 488-9845
   Charlotte *(G-3741)*

Tyler Walston... G..... 919 269-9300
   Wilson *(G-16552)*

United Services Group LLC.................... G..... 980 237-1335
   Charlotte *(G-3752)*

United Technical Services LLC............... F..... 980 237-1335
   Charlotte *(G-3753)*

United TI & Stamping Co NC Inc............ D..... 910 323-8588
   Fayetteville *(G-5939)*

United Welding and Iron Work................. G..... 704 281-3706
   Mooresville *(G-11116)*

Vernons Mobile Welding LLC.................. G..... 336 388-0415
   Pelham *(G-12179)*

Villabona Iron Works Inc.......................... F..... 252 522-4005
   Kinston *(G-9391)*

W D Lee & Company................................ E..... 704 864-0346
   Gastonia *(G-6537)*

W E Nixons Wldg & Hdwr Inc.................. G..... 252 221-4348
   Edenton *(G-5523)*

Wallace Welding Inc................................. F..... 919 934-2488
   Smithfield *(G-14488)*

Walrath Welding.. G..... 704 771-6640
   Sneads Ferry *(G-14493)*

Warsaw Welding Service Inc.................. F..... 910 293-4261
   Warsaw *(G-15676)*

Waste Container Repair Svcs................. G..... 910 257-4474
   Fayetteville *(G-5949)*

Watkins Wldg Fabrications LLC.............. G..... 828 429-2369
   Rutherfordton *(G-13901)*

Webb S Maint & Piping Inc...................... F..... 252 972-2616
   Battleboro *(G-933)*

Welders Log... G..... 919 473-3045
   Cary *(G-1925)*

Welding - Fbrcation - Repr Inc................ G..... 828 963-9372
   Boone *(G-1249)*

Welding Company..................................... G..... 336 667-0265
   Wilkesboro *(G-16051)*

Welding Needs.. G..... 252 902-4082
   Greenville *(G-7598)*

Welding Solutions LLC........................... E..... 828 665-4363
   Fletcher *(G-6051)*

Weldingart4u LLC..................................... G..... 252 220-0294
   Nashville *(G-11755)*

Wells Mechanical Services LLC............ G..... 252 532-2632
   Roanoke Rapids *(G-13585)*

Wells Welding Svc.................................... G..... 252 519-2808
   Enfield *(G-5681)*

West Stanly Fabrication Inc................... G..... 704 254-2967
   Oakboro *(G-12085)*

Wicked Welds LLC.................................. G..... 704 907-5531
   Charlotte *(G-3812)*

Wilkes Welding and Mch Co Inc............ G..... 336 670-2742
   Mc Grady *(G-10382)*

Williams Mech & Wldg Svcs LLC.......... G..... 919 820-5287
   Dunn *(G-4891)*

▲ Wilson Mold & Machine Corp............ D..... 252 243-1831
   Wilson *(G-16562)*

Wilson Wldg & Line Boring LLC........... G..... 828 406-2078
   Vilas *(G-15499)*

Wldg Honeycutt & Fabrication............... G..... 252 413-8754
   Columbia *(G-4171)*

Woodys Welding LLC............................... G..... 828 391-1484
   Morganton *(G-11270)*

Young Fabrication..................................... G..... 828 776-3203
   Leicester *(G-9522)*

Youngs Welding & Machine Svcs........... G..... 910 488-1190
   Fayetteville *(G-5955)*

Zickgraf Enterprises Inc......................... G..... 828 524-2313
   Franklin *(G-6149)*

7694 Armature rewinding shops

3 D Sewing Contractors.......................... G..... 336 499-1619
   Winston Salem *(G-16585)*

A & W Electric Inc.................................... E..... 704 333-4986
   Charlotte *(G-2113)*

American Rewinding Nc Inc.................. E..... 704 289-4177
   Monroe *(G-10642)*

American Rewinding of NC Inc.............. E..... 704 589-1020
   Monroe *(G-10643)*

Averitt Enterprises Inc........................... F..... 910 276-1294
   Laurinburg *(G-9469)*

▲ B & M Electric Motor Service............ G..... 828 267-0829
   Hickory *(G-7946)*

Blue Ridge Elc Mtr Repr Inc................... G..... 828 258-0800
   Asheville *(G-564)*

Bowden Electric Motor Svc Inc.............. G..... 252 446-4203
   Rocky Mount *(G-13685)*

Brigman Electric Motors Inc................... G..... 828 492-0568
   Canton *(G-1603)*

Brittenhams Rebuilding Service............. F..... 252 332-3181
   Ahoskie *(G-57)*

Canipe & Lynn Elc Mtr Repr Inc............ G..... 828 322-9052
   Hickory *(G-7961)*

Clayton Electric Mtr Repr Inc................. G..... 336 584-3756
   Elon College *(G-5664)*

Consolidated Truck Parts Inc................. G..... 704 279-5543
   Rockwell *(G-13650)*

▲ Custom Industries Inc...................... E..... 336 299-2885
   Greensboro *(G-6950)*

Dixie Electro Mech Svcs Inc................... F..... 704 332-1116
   Charlotte *(G-2646)*

Electric Motor Rewinding Inc................ G..... 252 338-8856
   Elizabeth City *(G-5543)*

Electric Motor Service of Shelby Inc...... G..... 704 482-9979
   Shelby *(G-14314)*

Electric Motor Svc Ahoskie Inc.............. G..... 252 332-4364
   Ahoskie *(G-61)*

Electric Mtr Sls Svc Pitt Cnty................. G..... 252 752-3170
   Greenville *(G-7522)*

Electric Mtr Sp Wake Frest Inc.............. E..... 252 446-4173
   Rocky Mount *(G-13694)*

Electric Mtr Sp Wake Frest Inc.............. E..... 919 556-3229
   Wake Forest *(G-15552)*

Electrical Equipment Company............... G..... 910 276-2141
   Laurinburg *(G-9478)*

Elektran Inc... F..... 910 997-6640
   Rockingham *(G-13625)*

Energetics Inc... G..... 910 483-2581
   Fayetteville *(G-5821)*

▲ Esco Electronic Services Inc.............. F..... 252 753-4433
   Farmville *(G-5735)*

GE Vernova International LLC................. F..... 704 587-1300
   Charlotte *(G-2812)*

General Motor Repair & Svc Inc............. G..... 336 292-1715
   Greensboro *(G-7036)*

Hammond Electric Motor Company....... F..... 704 983-3178
   Albemarle *(G-89)*

Hanover Electric Motor Svc Inc.............. G..... 910 762-3702
   Wilmington *(G-16244)*

Heart Electric Motor Service................... G..... 704 922-4720
   Bessemer City *(G-1070)*

High Country Electric Mtrs LLC............. G..... 336 838-4808
   North Wilkesboro *(G-12014)*

Hill & Ferencz Elc Mtr Co Inc.................. G..... 919 736-7373
   Goldsboro *(G-6625)*

Holland Supply Company......................... E..... 252 492-7541
   Henderson *(G-7788)*

◆ Jenkins Electric Company................... D..... 800 438-3003
   Charlotte *(G-3020)*

Jordan Electric Motors Inc..................... F..... 919 708-7010
   Sanford *(G-14142)*

Kwik Elc Mtr Sls & Svc Inc...................... G..... 252 335-2524
   Elizabeth City *(G-5553)*

Lake City Electric Motor Repr................. G..... 336 248-2377
   Lexington *(G-9744)*

Leonard Electric Mtr Repr Inc................. G..... 336 625-2375
   Asheboro *(G-453)*

Lingle Electric Repair Inc....................... F..... 704 636-5591
   Salisbury *(G-14004)*

Maybin Emergency Power Inc................ G..... 828 697-1195
   Zirconia *(G-17154)*

McKinney Electric & Mch Co Inc............ G..... 828 765-7910
   Spruce Pine *(G-14648)*

Motor Shop Inc... G..... 704 867-8488
   Gastonia *(G-6471)*

Omninvest LLC... G..... 336 623-1717
   Harrisburg *(G-7719)*

Piedmont Elc Mtr Repr Inc Ashb............ F..... 336 495-0500
   Asheboro *(G-463)*

Presley Group Ltd.................................... D..... 828 254-9971
   Asheville *(G-741)*

Pumps Blowers & Elc Mtrs LLC.............. G..... 919 286-4975
   Durham *(G-5309)*

Purser Centl Rewinding Co Inc.............. F..... 704 786-3131
   Concord *(G-4343)*

Randall Supply Inc.................................. E..... 704 289-6479
   Monroe *(G-10792)*

Rocky Mount Electric Motor LLC........... G..... 252 446-1510
   Rocky Mount *(G-13732)*

Sanders Electric Motor Svc Inc.............. E..... 828 754-0513
   Lenoir *(G-9651)*

Snow Electric Co Inc................................ G..... 336 723-2092
   Winston Salem *(G-16912)*

Southern Electric Motor Co..................... G..... 919 688-7879
   Durham *(G-5365)*

Stone Cllins Mtr Rewinding Inc.............. G..... 910 347-2775
   Jacksonville *(G-9041)*

Surry Elc Mtr & Contrls Inc..................... F..... 336 786-1717
   Mount Airy *(G-11581)*

76 MISCELLANEOUS REPAIR SERVICES

Tencarva Machinery Company LLC....... F 336 665-1435
  Greensboro *(G-7395)*
Tigertek Industrial Svcs LLC................... E 336 623-1717
  Stoneville *(G-14970)*
Watson Electrical Cnstr Co LLC............. D 252 756-4550
  Greenville *(G-7597)*
Williams Electric Mtr Repr Inc................ G 919 859-9790
  Sanford *(G-14206)*
XCEL Hrmetic Mtr Rewinding Inc............ G 704 694-6001
  Wadesboro *(G-15520)*

7699 Repair services, nec

Absolute Security & Lock Inc.................. G 336 322-4598
  Roxboro *(G-13792)*
Accel Wldg & Fabrication LLC................. G 980 722-7198
  Stanley *(G-14683)*
Admiral Marine Pdts & Svcs Inc.............. G 704 489-8771
  Denver *(G-4758)*
Advantage Machinery Svcs Inc................ E 336 463-4700
  Yadkinville *(G-17030)*
▲ Aircraft Belts Inc.................................... E 919 956-4395
  Creedmoor *(G-4601)*
Ashevlle Prcsion Mch Rblding I............... G 828 254-0884
  Asheville *(G-544)*
▲ Atlantic Hydraulics Svcs LLC................ G 919 542-2985
  Sanford *(G-14091)*
Auto Parts Fayetteville LLC..................... G 910 889-4026
  Fayetteville *(G-5766)*
Autry Con Pdts & Bldrs Sup Co................ G 704 504-8830
  Charlotte *(G-2242)*
B&C Xterior Cleaning Svc Inc................... G 919 779-7905
  Raleigh *(G-12540)*
Backwater Guns LLC................................. F 910 399-1451
  Wilmington *(G-16131)*
Barrs Competition..................................... F 704 482-5169
  Shelby *(G-14287)*
Besi Machining LLC.................................. F 919 218-9241
  Youngsville *(G-17071)*
Blinds Plus Inc... G 910 487-5196
  Fayetteville *(G-5773)*
▲ Bowman-Hollis Manufacturing Co....... E 704 374-1500
  Charlotte *(G-2341)*
Brant & Lassiter Septic Tank.................... G 252 587-4321
  Potecasi *(G-12395)*
◆ Briggs-Shaffner Acquisition Co............ F 336 463-4272
  Yadkinville *(G-17034)*
Bwxt Investment Company....................... E 704 625-4900
  Charlotte *(G-2369)*
Campbell & Sons Machining Co................ G 704 394-0291
  Lincolnton *(G-9878)*
Carbide Saws Incorporated..................... F 336 882-6835
  High Point *(G-8282)*
Carolina Electric Mtr Repr LLC................. G 704 289-3732
  Monroe *(G-10676)*
Carolina Machining Fabrication................ G 919 554-9700
  Youngsville *(G-17075)*
Carolina Textile Services Inc..................... G 910 843-3033
  Red Springs *(G-13496)*
Central Tool & Mfg Co Inc......................... G 828 328-2383
  Hickory *(G-7974)*
Certified Lawnmower Inc........................... G 704 527-2765
  Belmont *(G-978)*
Cherokee Instruments Inc......................... F 919 552-0554
  Angier *(G-137)*
Chicago Tube and Iron Company............... D 704 781-2060
  Locust *(G-9956)*
Classic Cleaning LLC................................ E 800 220-7101
  Raleigh *(G-12626)*
Dellinger Precast Inc................................ G 704 483-2868
  Denver *(G-4771)*
Dimill Enterprises LLC............................. G 919 629-2011
  Raleigh *(G-12684)*

Galaxy Pressure Washing Inc................... G 888 299-3129
  Pineville *(G-12270)*
Gamble Associates Inc............................ F 704 375-9301
  Charlotte *(G-2806)*
Gastex LLC... G 704 824-9861
  Gastonia *(G-6404)*
▲ GE Aircraft Engs Holdings Inc............... A 919 361-4400
  Durham *(G-5111)*
GE Vernova International LLC.................. G 704 587-1300
  Charlotte *(G-2812)*
▲ Grindtec Enterprises Corp..................... G 704 636-1825
  Salisbury *(G-13974)*
Hamilton Indus Grinding Inc..................... E 828 253-6796
  Asheville *(G-647)*
▲ Hickory Saw & Tool Inc......................... E 828 324-5585
  Hickory *(G-8050)*
High Rise Service Company Inc................ E 910 371-2325
  Leland *(G-9548)*
Hlmf Logistics Inc.................................... G 704 782-0356
  Pineville *(G-12273)*
Holder Machine & Mfg Co......................... G 828 479-8627
  Robbinsville *(G-13608)*
▲ Hydro Service & Supplies Inc.............. E 919 544-3744
  Durham *(G-5142)*
Indian Motorcycle Company..................... G 704 879-4560
  Lowell *(G-10010)*
Inman Septic Tank Service Inc................. G 910 763-1146
  Wilmington *(G-16268)*
Ironworks Motorcycles............................. G 336 542-7868
  Greensboro *(G-7123)*
Irsi Automation Inc.................................. G 336 303-5320
  Mc Leansville *(G-10393)*
J & W Service Incorporated..................... G 336 449-4584
  Whitsett *(G-15994)*
◆ Jly Invstmnts Inc Fka Nwman Mc........... E 336 273-8261
  Browns Summit *(G-1310)*
▲ Kayne & Son Custom Hdwr Inc.............. G 828 665-1988
  Candler *(G-1585)*
Limitless Wldg Fabrication LLC................ G 252 753-0660
  Farmville *(G-5739)*
M & J Marine LLC..................................... F 252 249-0522
  Oriental *(G-12111)*
MAC Grading Co.. F 910 531-4642
  Autryville *(G-842)*
Marinemax of North Carolina.................... E 910 256-8100
  Wrightsville Beach *(G-17026)*
Maxson & Associates.............................. G 336 632-0524
  Greensboro *(G-7190)*
McKinney Electric & Mch Co Inc............... G 828 765-7910
  Spruce Pine *(G-14648)*
▲ Measurement Controls Inc.................... F 704 921-1101
  Charlotte *(G-3157)*
Moes Hndy Svcs Fnce Instl Mno............... G 910 712-1402
  Raeford *(G-12426)*
Motor Shop Inc.. G 704 867-8488
  Gastonia *(G-6471)*
Mulls Con & Septic Tanks Inc.................... G 828 437-0959
  Morganton *(G-11236)*
National Container Group LLC................. G 704 393-9050
  Charlotte *(G-3233)*
Neal S Pallet Company Inc....................... E 704 393-8568
  Charlotte *(G-3242)*
Noble Oil Services Inc............................. C 919 774-8180
  Sanford *(G-14159)*
Not Just Archery...................................... G 828 294-7927
  Hickory *(G-8105)*
Petroleum Tank Corporation..................... F 919 284-2418
  Kenly *(G-9155)*
Precision Saw Works Inc......................... E 704 272-8326
  Polkton *(G-12389)*
▲ Prem Corp... E 704 921-1799
  Charlotte *(G-3373)*

Pro-Motor Engines Inc............................. G 704 664-6800
  Mooresville *(G-11063)*
Quality Equipment LLC............................ G 919 493-3545
  Durham *(G-5312)*
▲ Raleigh Saw Co Inc................................ G 919 832-2248
  Raleigh *(G-13184)*
▲ Rk Enterprises LLC.............................. G 910 481-0777
  Fayetteville *(G-5908)*
Robert Hamms LLC................................... G 704 605-8057
  Monroe *(G-10797)*
Roderick Mch Erectors Wldg Inc............... G 910 343-0381
  Wilmington *(G-16386)*
Router Bit Service Company Inc............... E 336 431-5535
  High Point *(G-8515)*
S & S Repair Service Inc........................... F 252 756-5989
  Winterville *(G-17013)*
Safe Air Systems Inc................................. E 336 674-0749
  Randleman *(G-13489)*
Scattered Wrenches Inc............................ G 919 480-1605
  Raleigh *(G-13236)*
Schindler Elevator Corporation................. F 910 590-5590
  Clinton *(G-4109)*
Sizemore Custom Jewelry Repair............. G 336 633-8979
  Pleasant Garden *(G-12360)*
▲ Smart Play USA...................................... G 252 747-2587
  Snow Hill *(G-14508)*
Spring Repair Service Inc........................ F 336 299-5660
  Greensboro *(G-7360)*
Storybook Farm Metal Shop Inc............... G 919 967-9491
  Chapel Hill *(G-2074)*
Sub-Aquatics Inc..................................... E 336 674-0749
  Randleman *(G-13492)*
T Air Inc.. D 980 595-2840
  Charlotte *(G-3668)*
▲ Techsouth Inc....................................... G 704 334-1100
  Matthews *(G-10349)*
Tk Elevator Corporation............................ C 336 272-4563
  Greensboro *(G-7404)*
Todds Rv & Marine Inc............................ F 828 651-0007
  Hendersonville *(G-7908)*
Tool Rental Depot LLC.............................. G 704 636-6400
  Salisbury *(G-14054)*
Tractor Country Inc................................. F 252 523-3007
  Dover *(G-4835)*
Treadz LLC.. G 704 664-0995
  Mooresville *(G-11114)*
Triad Cutting Tools Inc............................ G 336 873-8708
  Asheboro *(G-500)*
Triangle Glass Service Inc........................ G 919 477-9508
  Durham *(G-5408)*
Trimed LLC.. G 919 615-2784
  Raleigh *(G-13365)*
Triton Marine Services Inc........................ G 252 728-9958
  Beaufort *(G-969)*
Turbomed LLC... F 973 527-5299
  Fayetteville *(G-5936)*
U S Propeller Service Inc.......................... G 704 528-9515
  Troutman *(G-15396)*
Ultimate Floor Cleaning............................ G 704 912-8978
  Charlotte *(G-3748)*
Under Pressure Wilmington LLC............... G 910 409-0194
  Wilmington *(G-16438)*
▲ Union Grove Saw & Knife Inc............... D 704 539-4442
  Union Grove *(G-15438)*
Valley Proteins (de) Inc........................... C 336 333-3030
  Greensboro *(G-7435)*
Waggoner Manufacturing Co..................... E 704 278-2000
  Mount Ulla *(G-11687)*
Waste Container Repair Svcs................... G 910 257-4474
  Fayetteville *(G-5949)*
Welding - Fbrcation - Repr Inc.................. G 828 963-9372
  Boone *(G-1249)*

76 MISCELLANEOUS REPAIR SERVICES

Western Crlina Tl Mold Corp In................ E..... 828 890-4448
  Mills River *(G-10514)*
Westlift LLC... F..... 919 242-4379
  Goldsboro *(G-6670)*
Whaley Foodservice LLC....................... D..... 704 529-6242
  Charlotte *(G-3809)*
Whiteville Forklift & Eqp........................ G..... 910 642-6442
  Whiteville *(G-15980)*
Zickgraf Enterprises Inc........................ G..... 828 524-2313
  Franklin *(G-6149)*

78 MOTION PICTURES

7812 Motion picture and video production

Avcon Inc.. E..... 919 388-0203
  Cary *(G-1696)*
Cog Glbal Media/Consulting LLC........... E..... 980 239-8042
  Matthews *(G-10244)*
Inspire Creative Studios Inc.................. G..... 910 395-0200
  Wilmington *(G-16269)*
Metro Productions Inc........................... F..... 919 851-6420
  Raleigh *(G-13022)*
Palmer Senn.. G..... 704 451-3971
  Charlotte *(G-3309)*

7819 Services allied to motion pictures

American Multimedia Inc....................... D..... 336 229-7101
  Burlington *(G-1364)*
Robert Wrren MBL TV Prductions.......... G..... 910 483-4777
  Eastover *(G-5482)*

7822 Motion picture and tape distribution

AEC Consumer Products LLC................ F..... 704 904-0578
  Fayetteville *(G-5754)*
Pop Products LLC.................................. G..... 336 263-1884
  Burlington *(G-1476)*

7841 Video tape rental

Wen Bray Heating & AC......................... G..... 828 267-0635
  Hickory *(G-8209)*

79 AMUSEMENT AND RECREATION SERVICES

7922 Theatrical producers and services

Oneaka Dance Company....................... G..... 704 299-7432
  Charlotte *(G-3300)*
Robert Wrren MBL TV Prductions.......... G..... 910 483-4777
  Eastover *(G-5482)*
Royal Faires Inc..................................... F..... 704 896-5555
  Huntersville *(G-8887)*
▲ Stage Decoration and Sups Inc......... F..... 336 621-5454
  Greensboro *(G-7364)*
Toymakerz LLC....................................... F..... 843 267-3477
  Reidsville *(G-13543)*

7929 Entertainers and entertainment groups

Brown Mitchell Hodges LLC................... G..... 800 477-8982
  Charlotte *(G-2359)*
Gracefully Broken LLC........................... G..... 980 474-0309
  Charlotte *(G-2851)*
Oneaka Dance Company....................... G..... 704 299-7432
  Charlotte *(G-3300)*
School of Rock Charlotte........................ G..... 704 842-3172
  Charlotte *(G-3506)*

7941 Sports clubs, managers, and promoters

▲ Richard Chldress Racg Entps In........ B..... 336 731-3334
  Welcome *(G-15875)*
Tourist Baseball Inc............................... E..... 828 258-0428
  Asheville *(G-803)*

7948 Racing, including track operation

Fibreworks Composites LLC.................. E..... 704 696-1084
  Mooresville *(G-10944)*
Labonte Racing Inc................................ F..... 336 431-1004
  Trinity *(G-15348)*
▲ Penske Racing South Inc................... C..... 704 664-2300
  Mooresville *(G-11050)*
Rp Motor Sports Inc.............................. E..... 704 720-4200
  Concord *(G-4353)*
Rpac Racing LLC................................... D..... 704 696-8650
  Statesville *(G-14879)*

7991 Physical fitness facilities

Gladiator Enterprises Inc...................... G..... 336 944-6932
  Greensboro *(G-7044)*
Southern Home Spa and Wtr Pdts......... G..... 336 286-3564
  Greensboro *(G-7354)*
Trickfit & Suepack Training................... G..... 919 737-2231
  Wake Forest *(G-15606)*

7993 Coin-operated amusement devices

Brown Mitchell Hodges LLC................... G..... 800 477-8982
  Charlotte *(G-2359)*
Grover Gaming Inc................................ D..... 252 329-7900
  Greenville *(G-7536)*
Southland Amusements Vend Inc......... E..... 910 343-1809
  Wilmington *(G-16412)*

7999 Amusement and recreation, nec

Clark Art Shop Inc................................. G..... 919 832-8319
  Raleigh *(G-12625)*
Mb-F Inc... D..... 336 379-9352
  Greensboro *(G-7192)*
Mk Global Holdings LLC........................ E..... 704 334-1904
  Charlotte *(G-3190)*
New Media Golf Inc................................ F..... 828 533-9954
  Highlands *(G-8616)*
Paraclete Xp Sky Venture LLC............... F..... 910 848-2600
  Raeford *(G-12428)*
Paraclete Xp Skyventure LLC................ E..... 910 904-0027
  Raeford *(G-12429)*
Powerhouse Dugout............................... G..... 704 215-6604
  Gastonia *(G-6492)*
Prima Elernents LLC.............................. G..... 910 483-8406
  Fayetteville *(G-5900)*
Tickets Plus Inc..................................... E..... 616 222-4000
  Morrisville *(G-11448)*

80 HEALTH SERVICES

8011 Offices and clinics of medical doctors

▼ Accord Healthcare Inc....................... E..... 919 941-7878
  Raleigh *(G-12467)*
▲ Herbs Gaia Inc................................... D..... 828 884-4242
  Brevard *(G-1276)*
Novant Health Appel............................. G..... 704 316-5025
  Charlotte *(G-3274)*
Orthopedic Services............................. G..... 336 716-3349
  Winston Salem *(G-16833)*
Statesville Med MGT Svcs LLC.............. F..... 704 996-6748
  Statesville *(G-14904)*
Surgical Center of Morehea.................. F..... 252 247-0314
  Morehead City *(G-11193)*
Telephys Inc.. G..... 312 625-9128
  Davidson *(G-4699)*
Thomas Mendolia MD............................ G..... 336 835-5688
  Mooresville *(G-11111)*

8021 Offices and clinics of dentists

Fidelity Associates Inc.......................... E..... 704 864-3766
  Gastonia *(G-6402)*

Preventive Technologies Inc................. G..... 704 684-1211
  Indian Trail *(G-8958)*

8042 Offices and clinics of optometrists

O D Eyecarecenter P A........................... G..... 252 443-7011
  Rocky Mount *(G-13716)*
Optics Inc... G..... 336 288-9504
  Greensboro *(G-7236)*
Optics Inc... G..... 336 884-5677
  High Point *(G-8471)*

8049 Offices of health practitioner

Vital Being... G..... 828 964-5853
  Zionville *(G-17149)*

8062 General medical and surgical hospitals

Statesville Med MGT Svcs LLC.............. F..... 704 996-6748
  Statesville *(G-14904)*

8071 Medical laboratories

Alcami Carolinas Corporation................ F..... 910 254-7000
  Wilmington *(G-16100)*
▲ Biomerieux Inc................................... B..... 919 620-2000
  Durham *(G-4960)*
Liposcience Inc..................................... C..... 919 212-1999
  Morrisville *(G-11381)*
Neurametrix Inc..................................... G..... 408 507-2366
  Asheville *(G-711)*
Pregnancy Support Services................. G..... 919 490-0203
  Chapel Hill *(G-2056)*

8072 Dental laboratories

▲ Cdb Corporation................................ E..... 910 383-6464
  Leland *(G-9534)*
Village Ceramics Inc............................. G..... 828 685-9491
  Hendersonville *(G-7911)*

8082 Home health care services

Allotropica Technologies Inc................. G..... 919 522-4374
  Chapel Hill *(G-1982)*
Hap Innovations LLC............................. E..... 919 650-6497
  Morrisville *(G-11351)*

8093 Specialty outpatient clinics, nec

Cape Fear Orthtics Prsthtics I............... G..... 910 483-0933
  Fayetteville *(G-5780)*
Modoral Brands Inc............................... G..... 336 741-7230
  Winston Salem *(G-16815)*
Transylvnia Vcational Svcs Inc.............. D..... 828 884-1548
  Fletcher *(G-6045)*
Transylvnia Vcational Svcs Inc.............. C..... 828 884-3195
  Brevard *(G-1291)*
Unity Hlthcare Lab Billing LLP............... G..... 980 209-0402
  Charlotte *(G-3754)*

8099 Health and allied services, nec

Annihilare Medical Systems Inc............ F..... 855 545-5677
  Lincolnton *(G-9872)*
Birth Tissue Recovery LLC..................... E..... 336 448-1910
  Winston Salem *(G-16631)*
Health At Home Inc............................... F..... 850 543-4482
  Charlotte *(G-2896)*
Medaccess Inc....................................... G..... 828 264-4085
  Robbinsville *(G-13609)*
◆ Premex Inc... F..... 561 962-4128
  Durham *(G-5304)*
Unity Hlthcare Lab Billing LLP............... G..... 980 209-0402
  Charlotte *(G-3754)*

82 EDUCATIONAL SERVICES

8211 Elementary and secondary schools

SIC SECTION

87 ENGINEERING, ACCOUNTING, RESEARCH, AND MANAGEMENT SERVICES

Lifespan Incorporated.............................D 336 838-2614
  North Wilkesboro (G-12022)
Lifespan Incorporated.............................E 704 944-5100
  Charlotte (G-3086)

8221 Colleges and universities

Appalachian State University.................F 828 262-2047
  Boone (G-1174)
Appalachian State University.................G 828 262-7497
  Boone (G-1175)
North Carolina State Univ......................G 919 515-2760
  Raleigh (G-13070)
University NC At Chapel Hl....................G 919 962-0369
  Chapel Hill (G-2089)

8243 Data processing schools

Academy Association Inc.....................F 919 544-0835
  Durham (G-4899)
Applied Strategies Inc..........................G 704 525-4478
  Charlotte (G-2205)
Camstar Systems Inc............................C 704 227-6600
  Charlotte (G-2380)
Emath360 LLC..F 919 744-4944
  Cary (G-1757)
Ideacode Inc..G 919 341-5170
  Greensboro (G-7111)

8249 Vocational schools, nec

Hope Renovations..................................F 919 960-1957
  Chapel Hill (G-2024)
Training Industry Inc.............................D 919 653-4990
  Raleigh (G-13356)

8299 Schools and educational services

Advanced Computer Lrng Co LLC.........E 910 779-2254
  Fayetteville (G-5752)
▲ American Inst Crtif Pub Accntn............B 919 402-0682
  Durham (G-4915)
Assoction Intl Crtif Prof Accn..................A 919 402-4500
  Durham (G-4930)
Center for Creative Leadership..............B 336 288-7210
  Greensboro (G-6898)
Communitys Kitchen L3c.......................G 828 817-2308
  Tryon (G-15423)
Emath360 LLC..F 919 744-4944
  Cary (G-1757)
Jfl Enterprises Inc..................................G 704 786-7838
  Concord (G-4293)
▲ Kindermusik International Inc.............E 800 628-5687
  Greensboro (G-7151)
Lulu Technology Circus Inc...................E 919 459-5858
  Morrisville (G-11385)
Music & Arts..G 919 329-6069
  Garner (G-6294)
National Ctr For Social Impact...............G 984 212-2285
  Raleigh (G-13054)
Oberle Group..G 336 399-6833
  Pfafftown (G-12189)
Pdf and Associates................................G 252 332-7749
  Colerain (G-4139)
Prima Elements LLC..............................G 910 483-8406
  Fayetteville (G-5900)
RFH Tactical Mobility Inc.......................F 910 916-0284
  Milton (G-10516)
School of Rock Charlotte.......................G 704 842-3172
  Charlotte (G-3506)
Stamping & Scrapbooking Rm Inc........G 336 389-9538
  Greensboro (G-7365)
VA Claims LLC......................................G 305 984-0936
  Greenville (G-7596)

83 SOCIAL SERVICES

8322 Individual and family services

Clay County Food Pantry Inc................G 828 389-1657
  Hayesville (G-7761)
Fixed-NC LLC..G 252 751-1911
  Greenville (G-7526)
Hope Renovations..................................F 919 960-1957
  Chapel Hill (G-2024)
Infinity Communications LLC................E 919 797-2334
  Durham (G-5154)
Kenson Parenting Solutions..................G 919 637-1499
  Wake Forest (G-15567)
Lighthouse of Wayne County Inc..........F 919 736-1313
  Goldsboro (G-6630)
Oneaka Dance Company.......................G 704 299-7432
  Charlotte (G-3300)
Smart Start Inc.......................................G 828 328-2822
  Hickory (G-8159)
Tarheel Monitoring LLC........................G 910 763-1490
  Wilmington (G-16426)

8331 Job training and related services

Eastern Crlina Vctonal Ctr Inc...............D 252 758-4188
  Greenville (G-7521)
Hope Renovations..................................F 919 960-1957
  Chapel Hill (G-2024)
Industrial Opportunities Inc....................B 828 321-4754
  Andrews (G-126)
Lee County Industries Inc......................E 919 775-3439
  Sanford (G-14148)
Lions Services Inc..................................B 704 921-1527
  Charlotte (G-3091)
Sighttech LLC..G 855 997-4448
  Charlotte (G-3549)
Transylvnia Vcational Svcs Inc..............D 828 884-1548
  Fletcher (G-6045)
Transylvnia Vcational Svcs Inc..............C 828 884-3195
  Brevard (G-1291)
Tri-County Industries Inc.......................C 252 977-3800
  Rocky Mount (G-13676)
Vocatnal Sltons Hndrson Cnty I.............E 828 692-9626
  East Flat Rock (G-5479)
Watauga Opportunities Inc....................E 828 264-5009
  Boone (G-1247)
Webster Entps Jackson Cnty Inc..........E 828 586-8981
  Sylva (G-15074)

8361 Residential care

Gladiator Enterprises Inc......................G 336 944-6932
  Greensboro (G-7044)
Lifespan Incorporated.............................E 704 944-5100
  Charlotte (G-3086)
Watauga Opportunities Inc....................E 828 264-5009
  Boone (G-1247)

8399 Social services, nec

Ipas..C 919 967-7052
  Durham (G-5163)

84 MUSEUMS, ART GALLERIES AND BOTANICAL AND ZOOLOGICAL GARDENS

8412 Museums and art galleries

Doug Bowman Galleries.........................G 704 662-5620
  Chimney Rock (G-3879)
Emerald Village Inc................................F 828 765-6463
  Little Switzerland (G-9948)

86 MEMBERSHIP ORGANIZATIONS

8611 Business associations

Kidde Technologies Inc.........................B 252 237-7004
  Wilson (G-16507)
◆ US Tobacco Cooperative Inc.............D 919 821-4560
  Raleigh (G-13386)

8621 Professional organizations

▲ American Inst Crtif Pub Accntn............B 919 402-0682
  Durham (G-4915)
Assoction Intl Crtif Prof Accn..................A 919 402-4500
  Durham (G-4930)
International Society Automtn...............E 919 206-4176
  Durham (G-5162)

8661 Religious organizations

Brookstone Baptist Church....................E 828 658-9443
  Weaverville (G-15840)
Church Initiative Inc...............................E 919 562-2112
  Wake Forest (G-15540)
Grace Communion International............E 626 650-2300
  Charlotte (G-2849)
New Journey Now..................................G 336 234-1534
  Greensboro (G-7216)

8699 Membership organizations, nec

Oneaka Dance Company.......................G 704 299-7432
  Charlotte (G-3300)
Pregnancy Support Services.................G 919 490-0203
  Chapel Hill (G-2056)

87 ENGINEERING, ACCOUNTING, RESEARCH, AND MANAGEMENT SERVICES

8711 Engineering services

Abb Inc...E 704 587-1362
  Charlotte (G-2122)
ABB Enterprise Software Inc................C 919 582-3283
  Raleigh (G-12455)
◆ ABB Inc..C 919 856-2360
  Cary (G-1674)
Abco Automation Inc.............................C 336 375-6400
  Browns Summit (G-1298)
Acroplis Cntrls Engineers Pllc...............F 919 275-3884
  Raleigh (G-12473)
Advanced Computer Lrng Co LLC.........E 910 779-2254
  Fayetteville (G-5752)
▲ Airspeed LLC......................................E 919 644-1222
  Hillsborough (G-8633)
Automated Designs Inc.........................F 828 696-9625
  Flat Rock (G-5959)
Bachstein Consulting LLC......................G 410 322-4917
  Youngsville (G-17070)
Bahnson Holdings Inc...........................D 336 760-3111
  Clemmons (G-4029)
Belham Management Ind LLC..............G 704 815-4246
  Charlotte (G-2297)
Belkoz Inc..G 919 703-0694
  Raleigh (G-12551)
Big Rock Industries Inc.........................G 252 222-3618
  Morehead City (G-11152)
Boeing Arospc Operations Inc..............F 919 722-4351
  Goldsboro (G-6594)
Carlson Environmental Cons PC...........D 704 283-9765
  Monroe (G-10673)
Century Furniture LLC..........................D 828 326-8535
  Hickory (G-7977)
Cnc Performance Eng LLC...................G 704 599-2555
  Charlotte (G-2508)

Employee Codes: A=Over 500 employees, B=251-500
C=101-250, D=51-100, E=20-50, F=10-19, G=1-9

87 ENGINEERING, ACCOUNTING, RESEARCH, AND MANAGEMENT SERVICES

Coalogix Inc .... C 704 827-8933
   Charlotte *(G-2510)*

Collins Aerospace .... F 704 423-7000
   Charlotte *(G-2524)*

Comp Environmental Inc .... F 919 316-1321
   Durham *(G-5028)*

Cross Technology Inc .... E 336 725-4700
   East Bend *(G-5465)*

Custom Controls Unlimited LLC .... F 919 812-6553
   Raleigh *(G-12664)*

Descher LLC .... G 919 828-7708
   Raleigh *(G-12677)*

Doble Engineering Company .... G 919 380-7461
   Morrisville *(G-11333)*

Dronescape Pllc .... G 704 953-3798
   Charlotte *(G-2655)*

Electro Magnetic Research Inc .... G 919 365-3723
   Zebulon *(G-17126)*

Entropy Solar Integrators LLC .... G 704 936-5018
   Charlotte *(G-2716)*

Equagen Engineers Pllc .... E 919 444-5442
   Raleigh *(G-12744)*

Ferguson Manufacturing Company ..... F 336 661-1116
   Winston Salem *(G-16709)*

▲ Finnord North America Corp .... F 704 723-4913
   Huntersville *(G-8820)*

Flextronics Intl USA Inc .... C 919 998-4000
   Morrisville *(G-11341)*

Froehling & Robertson Inc .... E 804 264-2701
   Raleigh *(G-12783)*

General Dynmics Mssion Systems ..... C 336 698-8000
   Mc Leansville *(G-10391)*

Global Products & Mfg Svcs Inc .... G 360 870-9876
   Charlotte *(G-2834)*

Goshen Engineering Inc .... G 919 429-9798
   Mount Olive *(G-11661)*

Irsi Automation Inc .... G 336 303-5320
   Mc Leansville *(G-10393)*

J & W Service Incorporated .... G 336 449-4584
   Whitsett *(G-15994)*

J J Jenkins Incorporated .... E 704 821-6648
   Matthews *(G-10324)*

JA Smith Inc .... G 704 860-4910
   Lawndale *(G-9500)*

John Deere Consumer Pdts Inc .... C 919 804-2000
   Cary *(G-1798)*

Kdy Automation Solutions Inc .... G 888 219-0049
   Morrisville *(G-11364)*

Keller Technology Corporation .... E 704 875-1605
   Huntersville *(G-8844)*

Lba Group Inc .... E 252 329-9243
   Greenville *(G-7553)*

Man Lift Mfg Co .... E 414 486-1760
   Shelby *(G-14344)*

McLean Sbsrface Utlity Engrg L .... F 336 340-0024
   Greensboro *(G-7194)*

Motorsport Innovations Inc .... G 704 728-7837
   Davidson *(G-4686)*

Mra Services Inc .... F 704 933-4300
   Kannapolis *(G-9127)*

MSI Defense Solutions LLC .... D 704 660-8348
   Mooresville *(G-11032)*

▲ Multi Technical Services Inc .... G 919 553-2995
   Clayton *(G-4000)*

▲ Nederman Corporation .... F 704 399-7441
   Charlotte *(G-3244)*

▲ Penske Racing South Inc .... C 704 664-2300
   Mooresville *(G-11050)*

Plan B Enterprises LLC .... G 919 387-4856
   New Hill *(G-11863)*

Pratt Mller Engrg Fbrction LLC .... C 704 977-0642
   Huntersville *(G-8881)*

▲ Precision Concepts Group LLC .... B 336 761-8572
   Winston Salem *(G-16863)*

R D Tillson & Associates Inc .... G 336 454-1410
   Jamestown *(G-9069)*

Roehrig Engineering Inc .... E 336 956-3800
   Greensboro *(G-7316)*

SCR Controls Inc .... F 704 821-6651
   Matthews *(G-10342)*

Simon Industries Inc .... E 919 469-2004
   Raleigh *(G-13262)*

Sitzer & Spuria Inc .... G 919 929-0299
   Chapel Hill *(G-2073)*

Ssi Services Inc .... G 919 867-1450
   Raleigh *(G-13295)*

Subsea Video Systems Inc .... G 252 338-1001
   Elizabeth City *(G-5572)*

Sunqest Inc .... G 828 325-4910
   Newton *(G-11975)*

▲ Tdc International LLC .... G 704 875-1198
   Concord *(G-4372)*

Team Industries Inc .... C 828 837-5377
   Andrews *(G-128)*

▲ Textrol Laboratories Inc .... E 704 764-3400
   Monroe *(G-10821)*

Tower Engrg Professionals Inc .... C 919 661-6351
   Raleigh *(G-13355)*

VA Claims LLC .... G 305 984-0936
   Greenville *(G-7596)*

Volta Group Corporation LLC .... G 919 637-0273
   Raleigh *(G-13408)*

Vortant Technologies LLC .... G 828 645-1026
   Weaverville *(G-15867)*

◆ Walker and Associates Inc .... C 336 731-6391
   Lexington *(G-9800)*

Young & McQueen Grading Co Inc .... D 828 682-7714
   Burnsville *(G-1539)*

8712 Architectural services

American Physcl SEC Group LLC ...... G 919 363-1894
   Apex *(G-159)*

Carolina Timberworks LLC .... F 828 266-9663
   West Jefferson *(G-15936)*

Solid Holdings LLC .... F 704 423-0260
   Charlotte *(G-3578)*

Sterling Cleora Corporation .... E 919 563-5800
   Durham *(G-5374)*

8713 Surveying services

McLean Sbsrface Utlity Engrg L .... F 336 340-0024
   Greensboro *(G-7194)*

8721 Accounting, auditing, and bookkeeping

All Signs & Graphics LLC .... G 910 323-3115
   Fayetteville *(G-5757)*

Esequence Inc .... G 919 831-1995
   Raleigh *(G-12747)*

Oxford University Press LLC .... B 919 677-0977
   Cary *(G-1840)*

8731 Commercial physical research

Advanced Non-Lethal Tech Inc .... G 847 812-6450
   Raleigh *(G-12479)*

Alcami Carolinas Corporation .... G 910 619-3952
   Garner *(G-6251)*

Alcami Carolinas Corporation .... G 910 254-7000
   Morrisville *(G-11283)*

Alcami Carolinas Corporation .... G 910 254-7000
   Wilmington *(G-16101)*

Alcami Carolinas Corporation .... G 910 254-7000
   Wilmington *(G-16102)*

Alcami Carolinas Corporation .... B 910 254-7000
   Wilmington *(G-16103)*

▼ Andersen Products Inc .... E 336 376-3000
   Haw River *(G-7750)*

Birth Tissue Recovery LLC .... E 336 448-1910
   Winston Salem *(G-16631)*

Carolinas Cord Blood Bank .... G 919 668-1102
   Durham *(G-5006)*

Case Farms LLC .... D 919 735-5010
   Dudley *(G-4841)*

Case Farms LLC .... E 919 658-2252
   Goldsboro *(G-6599)*

Case Farms LLC .... F 704 528-4501
   Troutman *(G-15370)*

Cedarlane Laboratories USA .... E 336 513-5135
   Burlington *(G-1391)*

Centaur Laboratories Inc .... E 919 249-5072
   Oxford *(G-12119)*

Cisco Systems Inc .... A 919 392-2000
   Morrisville *(G-11324)*

Core Technology Molding Corp .... E 336 294-2018
   Greensboro *(G-6937)*

Epicypher Inc .... F 855 374-2461
   Durham *(G-5092)*

Gale Global Research Inc .... G 910 795-8595
   Leland *(G-9545)*

Greer Laboratories Inc .... E 828 758-2388
   Lenoir *(G-9614)*

Health Supply Us LLC .... F 888 408-1694
   Mooresville *(G-10971)*

◆ Hydromer Inc .... E 908 526-2828
   Concord *(G-4282)*

K2 Solutions Inc .... B 910 692-6898
   Southern Pines *(G-14538)*

King Phrmceuticals RES Dev LLC ...... B 919 653-7001
   Cary *(G-1803)*

Lexitas Pharma Services Inc .... D 919 205-0012
   Durham *(G-5189)*

Linde Gas & Equipment Inc .... D 919 549-0633
   Durham *(G-5190)*

Lord Corporation .... G 919 469-2500
   Cary *(G-1818)*

Neurametrix Inc .... G 408 507-2366
   Asheville *(G-711)*

Novex Innovations LLC .... G 336 231-6693
   Winston Salem *(G-16824)*

Nuvotronics Inc .... D 984 666-3543
   Durham *(G-5251)*

▲ Penske Racing South Inc .... C 704 664-2300
   Mooresville *(G-11050)*

Pharmagra Holding Company LLC .... E 828 884-8656
   Brevard *(G-1284)*

Ppd Inc .... C 910 251-0081
   Wilmington *(G-16366)*

Praetego Inc .... G 919 237-7969
   Durham *(G-5301)*

Propharma Group LLC .... D 888 242-0559
   Raleigh *(G-13153)*

Qatch Technologies LLC .... G 678 908-3112
   Chapel Hill *(G-2058)*

Raybow Usa Inc .... F 828 884-8656
   Brevard *(G-1286)*

▲ Scentair Technologies LLC .... C 704 504-2320
   Charlotte *(G-3498)*

Signalscape Inc .... E 919 859-4565
   Cary *(G-1889)*

Smoky Mtn Nativ Plant Assn .... G 828 479-8788
   Robbinsville *(G-13612)*

Squarehead Technology LLC .... G 571 299-4849
   Hickory *(G-8167)*

Tengion Inc .... E 336 722-5855
   Winston Salem *(G-16938)*

Textile Manufacturing Tech LLC .... G 828 632-3012
   Taylorsville *(G-15173)*

87 ENGINEERING, ACCOUNTING, RESEARCH, AND MANAGEMENT SERVICES

Triangle Biosystems Inc .... F 919 361-2663
 Durham *(G-5405)*

Tribofilm Research Inc .... G 919 838-2844
 Raleigh *(G-13364)*

▲ Troxler Electronic Labs Inc .... D 919 549-8661
 Durham *(G-5412)*

Vacs America Inc .... G 910 259-9854
 Burgaw *(G-1354)*

Venator Chemicals LLC .... D 704 454-4811
 Harrisburg *(G-7733)*

Verdante Bioenergy Svcs LLC .... G 828 394-1246
 Lenoir *(G-9657)*

Vortant Technologies LLC .... G 828 645-1026
 Weaverville *(G-15867)*

◆ Walker and Associates Inc .... C 336 731-6491
 Lexington *(G-9800)*

8732 Commercial nonphysical research

Dex One Corporation .... A 919 297-1600
 Cary *(G-1751)*

Fuji Silysia Chemical Ltd .... F 919 484-4158
 Greenville *(G-7530)*

Konica Mnlta Hlthcare Amrcas I .... E 919 792-6420
 Garner *(G-6278)*

Pro-Motor Engines Inc .... G 704 664-6800
 Mooresville *(G-11063)*

Sighttech LLC .... G 855 997-4448
 Charlotte *(G-3549)*

Viztek LLC .... E 919 792-6420
 Garner *(G-6324)*

8733 Noncommercial research organizations

Fire Retardant Chem Tech LLC .... G 980 253-8880
 Matthews *(G-10316)*

Kbi Biopharma Inc .... D 919 479-9898
 Durham *(G-5177)*

King Phrmceuticals RES Dev LLC .... B 919 653-7001
 Cary *(G-1803)*

Parata Systems LLC .... C 888 727-2821
 Durham *(G-5270)*

Sigma Xi Scntfic RES Hnor Soc .... E 919 549-4691
 Durham *(G-5356)*

8734 Testing laboratories

Acterna LLC .... F 919 388-5100
 Morrisville *(G-11277)*

Albion Medical Holdings Inc .... F 800 378-3906
 Lenoir *(G-9571)*

Alcami Carolinas Corporation .... G 910 619-3952
 Garner *(G-6251)*

Alcami Carolinas Corporation .... B 910 254-7000
 Wilmington *(G-16203)*

▼ American Safety Utility Corp .... E 704 482-0601
 Shelby *(G-14285)*

▲ Apex Instruments Incorporated .... E 919 557-7300
 Fuquay Varina *(G-6179)*

Avista Pharma Solutions Inc .... E 919 544-8600
 Durham *(G-4939)*

Bachstein Consulting LLC .... G 410 322-4917
 Youngsville *(G-17070)*

▲ Broadwind Indus Solutions LLC .... E 919 777-2907
 Sanford *(G-14096)*

Catalent Pharma Solutions LLC .... C 919 481-4855
 Morrisville *(G-11314)*

Cross Technologies Inc .... E 800 327-7727
 Greensboro *(G-6942)*

Dynisco Instruments LLC .... E 828 326-9888
 Hickory *(G-8013)*

Educated Design & Develop .... E 919 469-9434
 Cary *(G-1755)*

Froehling & Robertson Inc .... E 804 264-2701
 Raleigh *(G-12783)*

Greer Laboratories Inc .... E 828 758-2388
 Lenoir *(G-9614)*

▲ Greer Laboratories Inc .... C 828 754-5327
 Lenoir *(G-9615)*

Sapphire Tchncal Solutions LLC .... G 704 561-3100
 Pineville *(G-12302)*

SCR-Tech LLC .... C 704 504-0191
 Charlotte *(G-3513)*

Tergus Pharma LLC .... E 919 549-9700
 Durham *(G-5396)*

Unity Hlthcare Lab Billing LLP .... G 980 209-0402
 Charlotte *(G-3754)*

8741 Management services

Allyn International Trdg Corp .... G 877 858-2482
 Marshville *(G-10210)*

Bus Safety Inc .... G 336 671-0838
 Mocksville *(G-10558)*

Carlson Environmental Cons PC .... D 704 283-9765
 Monroe *(G-10673)*

Competitive Solutions Inc .... E 919 851-0058
 Raleigh *(G-12634)*

Drew Roberts LLC .... G 336 497-1679
 Whitsett *(G-15988)*

Equagen Engineers Pllc .... E 919 444-5442
 Raleigh *(G-12744)*

Jebco Inc .... E 919 557-2001
 Holly Springs *(G-8702)*

◆ Kayser-Roth Corporation .... C 336 852-2030
 Greensboro *(G-7145)*

Phoenix Assembly NC LLC .... G 252 801-4250
 Battleboro *(G-929)*

S & A Cherokee LLC .... E 919 674-6020
 Cary *(G-1876)*

Trademark Landscape Group Inc .... F 910 253-0560
 Supply *(G-15013)*

▲ Triangle Brick Company .... E 919 544-1796
 Durham *(G-5406)*

◆ Volvo Logistics North America Inc .... C 336 393-4746
 Greensboro *(G-7449)*

W T Humphrey Inc .... D 910 455-3555
 Jacksonville *(G-9044)*

Xenial Inc .... E 800 253-8664
 Charlotte *(G-3834)*

8742 Management consulting services

822tees Inc .... G 910 822-8337
 Fayetteville *(G-5748)*

Academy Association Inc .... F 919 544-0835
 Durham *(G-4899)*

Anew Look Homes LLC .... F 800 796-5152
 Hickory *(G-7935)*

Apex Analytix LLC .... C 336 272-4669
 Greensboro *(G-6810)*

Archie Supply LLC .... G 336 987-0895
 Greensboro *(G-6813)*

Barron Legacy Mgmt Group LLC .... G 301 367-4735
 Charlotte *(G-2285)*

Blue Ridge Quick Print Inc .... G 828 883-2420
 Brevard *(G-1270)*

▲ Broadwind Indus Solutions LLC .... E 919 777-2907
 Sanford *(G-14096)*

Camstar Systems Inc .... C 704 227-6600
 Charlotte *(G-2380)*

Capre Omnimedia LLC .... G 917 460-3572
 Wilmington *(G-16155)*

Carolina By-Products Co .... G 336 333-3030
 Greensboro *(G-6882)*

Competitive Solutions Inc .... E 919 851-0058
 Raleigh *(G-12634)*

DMC LLC .... E 980 352-9806
 Concord *(G-4254)*

Eco Building Corporation .... G 910 736-1540
 Red Springs *(G-13499)*

Educatrx Inc .... G 980 328-0013
 Monroe *(G-10711)*

Electronic Imaging Svcs Inc .... F 704 587-3323
 Charlotte *(G-2690)*

Emath360 LLC .... F 919 744-4944
 Cary *(G-1757)*

Esequence Inc .... G 919 831-1995
 Raleigh *(G-12747)*

Go Energies LLC .... F 877 712-5999
 Wilmington *(G-16234)*

Go Energies Holdings Inc .... G 910 762-5802
 Wilmington *(G-16235)*

Goshen Engineering Inc .... G 919 429-9798
 Mount Olive *(G-11661)*

Heed Group Inc .... G 877 938-8853
 Stanley *(G-14696)*

Hinsons Typing & Printing .... G 919 934-9036
 Smithfield *(G-14462)*

Intelligent Apps LLC .... G 919 628-6256
 Raleigh *(G-12897)*

Irsi Automation Inc .... G 336 303-5320
 Mc Leansville *(G-10393)*

Jestines Jewels Inc .... G 704 904-0191
 Salisbury *(G-13991)*

K2 Solutions Inc .... B 910 692-6898
 Southern Pines *(G-14538)*

LDR Designs .... G 252 375-4484
 Greenville *(G-7555)*

Logiksavvy Solutions LLC .... G 336 392-6149
 Greensboro *(G-7167)*

Make Solutions Inc .... F 623 444-0098
 Asheville *(G-694)*

▲ Microthermics Inc .... F 919 878-8045
 Raleigh *(G-13028)*

National Ctr For Social Impact .... G 984 212-2285
 Raleigh *(G-13054)*

Nexxt Level Trucking LLC .... G 980 205-4425
 Charlotte *(G-3256)*

Oberle Group .... G 336 399-6833
 Pfafftown *(G-12189)*

One Srce Dcument Solutions Inc .... E 800 401-9544
 Greensboro *(G-7234)*

▲ Pace Communications Inc .... C 336 378-6065
 Greensboro *(G-7239)*

Pashes LLC .... G 704 682-6535
 Statesville *(G-14857)*

◆ Portable Displays LLC .... E 919 544-6504
 Cary *(G-1855)*

Positive Prints Prof Svcs LLC .... G 336 701-2330
 Durham *(G-5297)*

Propharma Group LLC .... D 888 242-0559
 Raleigh *(G-13153)*

Q T Corporation .... G 252 399-7600
 Wilson *(G-16526)*

Red Oak Sales Company .... G 704 483-8464
 Denver *(G-4798)*

Rennasentient Inc .... F 919 233-7710
 Cary *(G-1868)*

Reynolds Consumer Products Inc .... A 704 371-5550
 Huntersville *(G-8885)*

Salem One Inc .... F 336 722-2886
 Kernersville *(G-9231)*

Scott Systems Intl Inc .... F 704 362-1115
 Charlotte *(G-3512)*

Sonaron LLC .... G 808 232-6168
 Fayetteville *(G-5919)*

◆ Syntec Inc .... D 336 861-9023
 High Point *(G-8561)*

Training Industry Inc .... D 919 653-4990
 Raleigh *(G-13356)*

87 ENGINEERING, ACCOUNTING, RESEARCH, AND MANAGEMENT SERVICES

◆ Triple Crown International LLC............. G 704 846-4983
  Charlotte *(G-3730)*

Two24 Digital LLC............................. G 910 475-7555
  Wilmington *(G-16437)*

UNC Campus Health Services................ D 919 966-2281
  Chapel Hill *(G-2087)*

Wirenet Inc.................................... E 513 774-7759
  Huntersville *(G-8906)*

8743 Public relations services

822tees Inc.................................... G 910 822-8337
  Fayetteville *(G-5748)*

Apple Rock Advg & Prom Inc................. E 336 232-4800
  Greensboro *(G-6811)*

Ed Kemp Associates Inc..................... G 336 869-2155
  High Point *(G-8336)*

Inspire Creative Studios Inc................. G 910 395-0200
  Wilmington *(G-16269)*

S & A Cherokee LLC.......................... E 919 674-6020
  Cary *(G-1876)*

UGLy Essentials LLC.......................... F 910 319-9945
  Raleigh *(G-13376)*

8744 Facilities support services

Tempest Environmental Corp................. G 919 973-1609
  Durham *(G-5393)*

8748 Business consulting, nec

Aceyus Inc..................................... E 704 443-7900
  Charlotte *(G-2128)*

Airfield Solutions LLC........................ G 919 348-4271
  Jacksonville *(G-8985)*

Alpha Theory LLC............................. G 212 235-2180
  Charlotte *(G-2168)*

Alpha Theory LLC............................. G 212 235-2180
  Charlotte *(G-2169)*

Amplified Elctronic Design Inc............... F 336 223-4811
  Greensboro *(G-6806)*

Atlantic Group Usa Inc........................ F 919 623-7824
  Raleigh *(G-12530)*

Avail Forensics LLC........................... F 877 888-5895
  Wilmington *(G-16125)*

Bachstein Consulting LLC.................... G 410 322-4917
  Youngsville *(G-17070)*

Brightly Software Inc......................... C 919 816-8237
  Cary *(G-1714)*

Camstar Systems Inc......................... C 704 227-6600
  Charlotte *(G-2380)*

Carlson Environmental Cons PC.............. D 704 283-9765
  Monroe *(G-10673)*

Carolina Signs................................ G 704 622-1939
  Gastonia *(G-6369)*

Carolina Textile Services Inc................ G 910 843-3033
  Red Springs *(G-13496)*

Cleveland Compounding Inc................. G 704 487-1971
  Shelby *(G-14297)*

Code LLC...................................... E 828 328-6004
  Hickory *(G-7987)*

Competitive Solutions Inc.................... E 919 851-0058
  Raleigh *(G-12634)*

▲ Cycle Pro LLC.............................. F 704 662-6682
  Mooresville *(G-10922)*

Easter Seals Ucp NC & VA Inc................ D 919 856-0250
  Raleigh *(G-12717)*

Emath360 LLC................................. F 919 744-4944
  Cary *(G-1757)*

Envirnmntal Cmfort Sltions Inc.............. E 980 272-7327
  Kannapolis *(G-9119)*

▲ Environmental Supply Co Inc............. F 919 956-9688
  Durham *(G-5089)*

I-Leadr Inc..................................... F 910 431-5252
  Sherrills Ford *(G-14385)*

Idea People Inc................................ G 704 398-4437
  Huntersville *(G-8833)*

Ideacode Inc.................................. G 919 341-5170
  Greensboro *(G-7111)*

▲ Impact Fulfillment Svcs LLC............... F 336 227-1130
  Burlington *(G-1434)*

Infinite Software Resorces LLC.............. G 704 509-0031
  Charlotte *(G-2967)*

Infinity Communications LLC................ E 919 797-2334
  Durham *(G-5154)*

James King.................................... G 910 308-8818
  Fayetteville *(G-5845)*

JPS Communications Inc..................... D 919 534-1168
  Raleigh *(G-12923)*

Kberg Productions LLC....................... G 910 232-0342
  Raleigh *(G-12932)*

L Michelle LLC................................ G 980 946-0204
  Mooresville *(G-11002)*

◆ Lake Norman Industries LLC............. G 704 987-9048
  Cornelius *(G-4565)*

Learning Craftsmen Inc...................... G 813 321-5003
  Apex *(G-213)*

Learnplatform Inc............................. G 919 247-5998
  Raleigh *(G-12964)*

Measurement Incorporated................... C 919 683-2413
  Durham *(G-5213)*

National Voctnl Tech Honor Soc............. G 828 698-8011
  Flat Rock *(G-5970)*

Native Naturalz Inc............................ F 336 334-2984
  Greensboro *(G-7213)*

Piedmont Flight Inc........................... E 336 776-6070
  Winston Salem *(G-16852)*

Qplot Corporation............................. G 949 302-7928
  Raleigh *(G-13160)*

Security Consult Inc.......................... G 704 531-8399
  Charlotte *(G-3522)*

▲ Spectrasite Communications LLC....... E 919 468-0112
  Cary *(G-1900)*

Stratton Publishing & Mktg Inc............... G 703 914-9200
  Wilmington *(G-16419)*

Sutton Scientifics Inc........................ G 910 428-1600
  Star *(G-14723)*

Te Connectivity Corporation................. G 336 727-5122
  Winston Salem *(G-16935)*

Teletec Corporation........................... F 919 954-7300
  Raleigh *(G-13338)*

Thinking Maps Inc............................. G 919 678-8778
  Cary *(G-1908)*

Triangle Regulatory Pubg LLC................ G 919 886-4587
  Raleigh *(G-13362)*

89 SERVICES, NOT ELSEWHERE CLASSIFIED

8999 Services, nec

Beth Wiseman................................. G 704 735-4469
  Lincolnton *(G-9875)*

Cmd Land Services LLC...................... G 919 554-2281
  Wake Forest *(G-15543)*

Commscope Technologies LLC.............. A 828 324-2200
  Claremont *(G-3916)*

Dimill Enterprises LLC........................ G 919 629-2011
  Raleigh *(G-12684)*

Geosonics Inc................................. G 919 790-9500
  Raleigh *(G-12797)*

Incantare Art By Marilyn LLC................. F 704 713-8846
  Charlotte *(G-2957)*

McLean Sbsrface Utlity Engrg L.............. F 336 340-0024
  Greensboro *(G-7194)*

Native Naturalz Inc............................ F 336 334-2984
  Greensboro *(G-7213)*

Prophysics Innovations Inc................... F 919 245-0406
  Cary *(G-1863)*

Qplot Corporation............................. G 949 302-7928
  Raleigh *(G-13160)*

Tempest Environmental Corp................. G 919 973-1609
  Durham *(G-5393)*

Xona Microfluidics Inc........................ G 951 553-6400
  Durham *(G-5456)*

92 JUSTICE, PUBLIC ORDER AND SAFETY

9223 Correctional institutions

North Carolina Dept Pub Safety.............. G 919 733-0867
  Raleigh *(G-13069)*

9229 Public order and safety, nec

North Crlina Dept Crime Ctrl P................ G 252 522-1511
  Kinston *(G-9379)*

North Crlina Dept Crime Ctrl P................ G 336 599-9233
  Roxboro *(G-13810)*

93 PUBLIC FINANCE, TAXATION AND MONETARY POLICY

9311 Finance, taxation, and monetary policy

North Carolina Dept Labor.................... F 919 807-2770
  Raleigh *(G-13068)*

95 ADMINISTRATION OF ENVIRONMENTAL QUALITY AND HOUSING PROGRAMS

9512 Land, mineral, and wildlife conservation

North Carolina Department of A.............. G 828 684-8188
  Arden *(G-356)*

96 ADMINISTRATION OF ECONOMIC PROGRAMS

9621 Regulation, administration of transportation

North Carolina Dept Trnsp.................... G 828 733-9002
  Newland *(G-11891)*

97 NATIONAL SECURITY AND INTERNATIONAL AFFAIRS

9711 National security

James King.................................... G 910 308-8818
  Fayetteville *(G-5845)*

United States Dept of Navy................... G 252 466-4514
  Cherry Point *(G-3859)*

United States Dept of Navy................... G 252 464-7228
  Cherry Point *(G-3860)*

ALPHABETIC SECTION

R & R Sealants (HQ)..999 999-9999
  651 Tally Blvd, Yourtown (99999) *(G-458)*
Ready Box Co...999 999-9999
  704 Lawrence Rd, Anytown (99999) *(G-1723)*
Rendall Mfg Inc, Anytown Also Called RMI *(G-1730)*

- Address, city & ZIP
- Designates this location as a headquarters
- Business phone
- Geographic Section entry number where full company information appears

See footnotes for symbols and codes identification.
- Companies listed alphabetically.
- Complete physical or mailing address.

(A Development Stage Company), Morrisville Also Called: Global Resource Corporation *(G-11349)*

/N Software Inc (PA)..919 544-7070
  101 Europa Dr Ste 150 Chapel Hill (27517) *(G-1978)*

057 Technology LLC..855 557-7057
  728 11th Street Pl Nw Hickory (28601) *(G-7926)*

079948726, Colfax Also Called: W&W-Afco Steel LLC *(G-4164)*

1 Click Web Solutions LLC................................910 790-9330
  3333 Wrightsville Ave M Wilmington (28403) *(G-16086)*

123 Precious Metal Ref LLC (PA)......................910 228-5403
  609a Piner Rd Ste 303 Wilmington (28409) *(G-16087)*

131 Candle Co..325 650-4903
  312 Wayne Cir Durham (27707) *(G-4892)*

18 Chestnuts, Asheville Also Called: Soup Maven LLC *(G-781)*

1816, Charlotte Also Called: Remington 1816 Foundation *(G-3430)*

1a Smart Start LLC..336 765-7001
  2453 Spaugh Industrial Dr Winston Salem (27103) *(G-16584)*

1st Choice Service Inc......................................704 913-7685
  3661 Eaker Rd Cherryville (28021) *(G-3861)*

1st Place Embroidery Inc..................................704 239-8844
  6749 Plyler Rd Kannapolis (28081) *(G-9110)*

1st Time Contracting...774 289-3321
  104 Western Villa Dr Clemmons (27012) *(G-4023)*

2 Wishes Tees LLC...919 621-1401
  109 Tavernelle Pl Cary (27519) *(G-1669)*

21st Century Hosiery, Haw River Also Called: Sue-Lynn Textiles Inc *(G-7757)*

21st Century Tech of Amer................................910 826-3676
  6316 Yadkin Rd Fayetteville (28303) *(G-5744)*

21st Century Technologies Amer, Fayetteville Also Called: 21st Century Tech of Amer *(G-5744)*

222 Dream Co LLC..919 803-9741
  627 Northampton Rd Fayetteville (28303) *(G-5745)*

2391 Eatons Ferry Rd Assoc LLC.....................919 844-0565
  7610 Six Forks Rd Ste 200 Raleigh (27615) *(G-12446)*

250 Cyrstal Cleaner, Wilmington Also Called: Two Fifty Cleaners *(G-16436)*

26 Industries Inc..704 839-3218
  337 Sunnyside Dr Se Concord (28025) *(G-4184)*

27 Software US Inc..704 968-2879
  153 Farm Knoll Way Mooresville (28117) *(G-10844)*

277 Metal Inc...704 372-4513
  201 Davis Heights Dr Gastonia (28052) *(G-6333)*

2nd Shift Cycles LLC...336 462-3262
  6670 Old Us Highway 52 Lexington (27295) *(G-9676)*

2topia Cycles Inc..704 778-7849
  1512 Southwood Ave Charlotte (28203) *(G-2106)*

2u NC...919 525-5075
  1210 Environ Way Chapel Hill (27517) *(G-1979)*

3 Alarm Smoke Detector Svcs..........................757 636-6773
  134 Laurel Woods Way Currituck (27929) *(G-4632)*

3 C, Wilson Also Called: 3c Store Fixtures Inc *(G-16461)*

3 D Footprints Logging Inc................................910 521-2640
  145 Cabinet Shop Rd Maxton (28364) *(G-10353)*

3 D Sewing Contractors....................................336 499-1619
  559 Sun Creek Dr Winston Salem (27104) *(G-16585)*

3 Hungry Guys LLC...408 644-3119
  220 Lake Manor Rd Chapel Hill (27516) *(G-1980)*

3 Kids Screen Printing......................................910 212-0672
  10860 Old Lumberton Rd Evergreen (28438) *(G-5696)*

3 Star Enterprises LLC......................................704 821-7503
  115 Business Park Dr Indian Trail (28079) *(G-8917)*

3-Oceans Mfg Inc..919 600-4500
  3301 Jones Sausage Rd Ste 121 Garner (27529) *(G-6248)*

310 Sign Company..704 910-2242
  4335 Taggart Creek Rd Ste C Charlotte (28208) *(G-2107)*

316 Print Company LLC....................................919 454-6906
  121 Palmer Dr Clayton (27527) *(G-3949)*

33rd Strike Group LLC......................................910 371-9688
  9101 Lackey Rd Ne Ste 4 Leland (28451) *(G-9523)*

360 Ballistics LLC...919 883-8338
  206 High House Rd Ste 102 Cary (27513) *(G-1670)*

360 Forest Products Inc....................................910 285-5838
  113 N Rockfish St Wallace (28466) *(G-15618)*

3a Composites Holding Inc...............................704 658-3527
  721 Jetton St Ste 325 Davidson (28036) *(G-4664)*

3a Composites USA Inc (HQ)...........................704 872-8974
  3480 Taylorsville Hwy Statesville (28625) *(G-14732)*

3c Packaging LLC, Clayton Also Called: Mm Clayton LLC *(G-3997)*

3c Store Fixtures Inc...252 291-5181
  3363 Us Highway 301 N Wilson (27893) *(G-16461)*

3d Maternitees LLC...704 778-0633
  9101 Torrence Creek Ct Huntersville (28078) *(G-8784)*

3d Oil Inc...609 408-9159
  316 Silver Creek Landing Rd Swansboro (28584) *(G-15041)*

3d Packaging LLC...336 625-0652
  451 Railroad St Asheboro (27203) *(G-397)*

3d Print Lodge LLC...804 309-6028
  620 E Littleton Rd Roanoke Rapids (27870) *(G-13564)*

3d Quality LLC..201 580-0913
  8021 Meadowdale Ln Charlotte (28212) *(G-2108)*

3d Upfitters LLC..336 355-8673
  1814 Swannanoa Dr Greensboro (27410) *(G-6766)*

3dductcleaning LLC..919 723-4512
  207 Merriman Dr Selma (27576) *(G-14250)*

3M, Sanford Also Called: 3M Company *(G-14080)*

3M Company..919 642-0006
  4191 Hwy 87 S Moncure (27559) *(G-10611)*

3M Company..919 774-3808
  3010 Lee Ave Sanford (27332) *(G-14080)*

3M Polymask, Conover Also Called: Polymask Corporation *(G-4484)*

3peter LLC (PA)...919 475-2334
  1621 Rosebriar Pl Hillsborough (27278) *(G-8630)*

3peter LLC...919 475-2334
  500 Valley Forge Rd Hillsborough (27278) *(G-8631)*

3rd Phaze Bdy Oils Urban Lnks........................704 344-1138
  3300 N Graham St Charlotte (28206) *(G-2109)*

(PA)=Parent Co (HQ)=Headquarters (DH)=Div Headquarters

ALPHABETIC SECTION

3shape Inc 919 813-8694
2800 Perimeter Park Dr Ste E Morrisville (27560) *(G-11271)*

3tex Inc 919 481-2500
208 Laurel Hill Dr Rutherfordton (28139) *(G-13860)*

3v Performance LLC 980 222-7230
7813 Commerce Dr Denver (28037) *(G-4757)*

4 Home Products Inc 888 609-8222
201 Elkin Hwy Ste I North Wilkesboro (28659) *(G-11996)*

4 Love and Art 210 838-4288
3701 Standard Dr Fayetteville (28306) *(G-5746)*

4 Over LLC 919 875-3187
5609 Departure Dr Raleigh (27616) *(G-12447)*

4 Seasons Furniture Indust LLC 336 873-7245
236 N Broad St Seagrove (27341) *(G-14231)*

4 Your Cause, Franklinville Also Called: Causekeepers Inc *(G-6167)*

410 Medical Inc 919 241-7900
68 Tw Alexander Dr Durham (27709) *(G-4893)*

48 Customs Inc 336 403-0731
896 Pine Ridge Rd Mocksville (27028) *(G-10550)*

48forty Solutions LLC 910 891-1534
2 Dinan Rd Dunn (28334) *(G-4846)*

4d Directional Boring LLC 614 348-1339
204 Ibis Way Elizabeth City (27909) *(G-5529)*

4topps LLC 704 281-8451
3135 Indiana Ave Winston Salem (27105) *(G-16586)*

5 Star Satellite Inc 910 584-4354
2537 Lull Water Dr Fayetteville (28306) *(G-5747)*

510nano Inc 919 521-5982
5441 Lumley Rd Ste 101 Durham (27703) *(G-4894)*

522 Flipper LLC 919 785-3417
4301 Worley Dr Raleigh (27613) *(G-12448)*

6 Brothers LLC 706 662-2232
2628 Tanbridge Rd Charlotte (28226) *(G-2110)*

600 Racing Service, Harrisburg Also Called: US Legend Cars Intl Inc *(G-7732)*

615 Alton Place LLC 336 431-4487
615 Alton Pl High Point (27263) *(G-8228)*

62 Woodworking, Thomasville Also Called: Timothy Lee Blacjmon *(G-15290)*

623 Medical, Morrisville Also Called: 623 Medical LLC *(G-11272)*

623 Medical LLC 877 455-0112
635 Davis Dr Ste 100 Morrisville (27560) *(G-11272)*

648 Woodworks LLC 910 603-6286
601 Sage Ct Fuquay Varina (27526) *(G-6177)*

6ehouseprodxions LLC 704 334-7741
1300 Baxter St Ste 100b Charlotte (28204) *(G-2111)*

6th Sense Analytics 919 439-4740
1 Copley Pkwy Ste 560 Morrisville (27560) *(G-11273)*

760 Craft Works LLC 704 274-5216
100 Gilead Rd Huntersville (28078) *(G-8785)*

78c Spirits 919 615-0839
2660 Discovery Dr Raleigh (27616) *(G-12449)*

80 Acres Urban Agriculture Inc 704 437-6115
4141 Yorkview Ct Granite Falls (28630) *(G-6720)*

822tees Inc 910 822-8337
2598 Raeford Rd Fayetteville (28305) *(G-5748)*

828 Custom Printing LLC 828 586-1828
321 Jackson Plz Ste B Sylva (28779) *(G-15051)*

89 Industries 303 681-3188
14711 Nc Highway 48 Littleton (27850) *(G-9949)*

8th Element, Asheville Also Called: 8th Elment Cndtning Prfmce LLC *(G-512)*

8th Elment Cndtning Prfmce LLC 828 298-1290
120 Elm Dr Asheville (28805) *(G-512)*

910 Sign Co LLC 910 353-2298
614 Richlands Hwy Jacksonville (28540) *(G-8984)*

919 Motoring LLC 919 872-4996
5540 Atlantic Springs Rd Ste 109 Raleigh (27616) *(G-12450)*

A & A Drone Service LLC 704 928-5054
166 Ralph Rd Statesville (28625) *(G-14733)*

A & A Financial Services LLC 800 572-6684
9716 Rea Rd Ste B538 Charlotte (28277) *(G-2112)*

A & B Chem-Dry 919 878-0288
4208 Bertram Dr Raleigh (27604) *(G-12451)*

A & B Milling Company 252 445-3161
200 Halifax St Enfield (27823) *(G-5673)*

A & B Screen Prtg & EMB LLC 252 245-0573
5515 Shepherd Rd Wilson (27893) *(G-16462)*

A & B Signs, Colfax Also Called: Burchette Sign Company Inc *(G-4143)*

A & D Precast Inc 704 735-3337
1032 N Flint St Lincolnton (28092) *(G-9863)*

A & G Machining LLC 919 329-7207
333 Technical Ct Ste 33 Garner (27529) *(G-6249)*

A & J Canvas Inc 252 244-1509
2450 Streets Ferry Rd Vanceboro (28586) *(G-15474)*

A & J Pallets Inc 336 969-0265
121 Anderson St Rural Hall (27045) *(G-13832)*

A & M Paper and Printing 919 813-7852
4122 Bennett Memorial Road Ste 108 Durham (27705) *(G-4895)*

A & M Tool Inc 828 891-9990
125 School House Rd Mills River (28759) *(G-10497)*

A & S Logging LLC 336 879-4364
4170 Maness Rd Seagrove (27341) *(G-14232)*

A & S Tool & Die Co Inc 336 993-3440
1510 Brookford Industrial Dr Kernersville (27284) *(G-9158)*

A & W Electric Inc 704 333-4986
127 W 28th St Charlotte (28206) *(G-2113)*

A 1 Tire Service Inc 828 684-1860
24 Cane Creek Rd Fletcher (28732) *(G-5978)*

A A Logo Gear 704 795-7100
310 Church St N Concord (28025) *(G-4185)*

A and J Ta Logging 919 663-1110
186 Epps Clark Rd Siler City (27344) *(G-14394)*

A B B Power Technolgies, Pinetops Also Called: ABB Inc *(G-12239)*

A B C Screenprinting and EMB 704 937-3452
106 Sprouse Ln Grover (28073) *(G-7605)*

A B Carter Inc (PA) 704 865-1201
4801 York Hwy Gastonia (28052) *(G-6334)*

A B I, Creedmoor Also Called: Aircraft Belts Inc *(G-4601)*

A B Metals of Polkton LLC 704 694-6635
6245 Us Highway 74 W Polkton (28135) *(G-12382)*

A B T, Statesville Also Called: ABT Foam LLC *(G-14735)*

A Balloon For You, Asheville Also Called: A Stitch In Time *(G-513)*

A Bean Counter Inc 919 359-9586
176 Foxglove Dr Garner (27529) *(G-6250)*

A Better Image Printing Inc 919 967-0319
4310 Garrett Rd Durham (27707) *(G-4896)*

A C Furniture Company Inc 336 623-3430
724 Riverside Dr Eden (27288) *(G-5484)*

A C S Enterprises NC Inc 704 226-9898
307 N Secrest Ave Monroe (28110) *(G-10631)*

A Cleaner Tomorrow and Laundry, Dunn Also Called: A Cleaner Tomorrow Dry Clg LLC *(G-4847)*

A Cleaner Tomorrow Dry Clg LLC (PA) 919 639-6396
102 S Wilson Ave Dunn (28334) *(G-4847)*

A Create Card Inc 631 584-2273
6409 Providence Farm Ln Apt 7401 Charlotte (28277) *(G-2114)*

A D Services 336 667-8190
402 S Cherry St Wilkesboro (28697) *(G-16011)*

A E Nesbitt Woodwork 828 625-2428
40 Bald Mountain Church Rd Black Mountain (28711) *(G-1118)*

A Foodtruckqueen, Charlotte Also Called: F & C Repair and Sales LLC *(G-2741)*

A Forbes Company
1035 Harper Ave Sw Lenoir (28645) *(G-9566)*

A Greeting On Green LLC 919 607-0966
3912 Overcup Oak Ln Cary (27519) *(G-1671)*

A Hartness Inc 704 351-2323
1143 Eastview Dr Charlotte (28211) *(G-2115)*

A House of Hemp LLC 910 984-1441
235 Shepard Dr Linden (28356) *(G-9938)*

A Klein & Co Inc 828 459-9261
1 Heart Dr Claremont (28610) *(G-3899)*

A L Beck & Sons Inc 336 788-1896
505 Jones Rd Winston Salem (27107) *(G-16587)*

A Land of Furniture Inc 336 882-3866
430 S Main St Ste 431 High Point (27260) *(G-8229)*

ALPHABETIC SECTION

A M Moore and Company Inc (PA) 336 294-6994
 1207 Park Ter Greensboro (27403) *(G-6767)*

A M P Laboratories Ltd 704 894-9721
 20905 Torrence Chapel Rd Ste 204 Cornelius (28031) *(G-4519)*

A Matter of Scents 980 939-3285
 5329 Providence Rd Charlotte (28226) *(G-2116)*

A McGee Wood Products Inc 828 212-1700
 171 N Main St Granite Falls (28630) *(G-6721)*

A N E Services LLC 704 882-1117
 1716 Garette Rd Charlotte (28218) *(G-2117)*

A New Gnrtion Entrmt MGT Cnslt, Garner Also Called: Landmark Music Group Inc *(G-6280)*

A O A Signs, Wilson Also Called: Aoa Signs Inc *(G-16466)*

A O Smith Water Products Co 704 597-8910
 4302 Raleigh St Charlotte (28213) *(G-2118)*

A Palletone Company, Newton Also Called: Industrial Recycling Services *(G-11943)*

A Place To Copy, Raleigh Also Called: Elledge Family Inc *(G-12731)*

A Plus Carports 336 367-1261
 6833 Us Highway 601 Boonville (27011) *(G-1252)*

A Plus Five Star Trnsp LLC 919 771-4820
 301 Mccarthy Dr Clayton (27527) *(G-3950)*

A Plus Graphics Inc 252 243-0404
 3101 Ward Blvd Wilson (27893) *(G-16463)*

A Plus Kitchen Bath Cabinets 919 622-0515
 120 Saint Albans Dr Apt 291 Raleigh (27609) *(G-12452)*

A Plus Service Inc 828 324-4397
 2233a Highland Ave Ne Hickory (28601) *(G-7927)*

A R Byrd Company, Lincolnton Also Called: A R Byrd Company Inc *(G-9864)*

A R Byrd Company Inc 704 732-5675
 171 Joshua Ct Lincolnton (28092) *(G-9864)*

A R Perry Corporation 252 492-6181
 220 Old Epsom Rd Henderson (27536) *(G-7774)*

A S I, Pineville Also Called: Leke LLC *(G-12280)*

A Sign Co, Hickory Also Called: Wright Business Concepts Inc *(G-8211)*

A Sign From Above Inc 910 352-0897
 4515 Cedar Ave Wilmington (28403) *(G-16088)*

A Squared Pro Services LLC 336 675-3546
 3441 Brookstone Dr Burlington (27215) *(G-1360)*

A Stitch In Time 828 274-5193
 1259 Sweeten Creek Rd 25a Asheville (28803) *(G-513)*

A Stitch To Remember 336 202-0026
 7621 Whitaker Dr Summerfield (27358) *(G-14974)*

A Taste of Heavenly Sweetness 336 825-7321
 4518 W Market St Greensboro (27407) *(G-6768)*

A To Z Signs & Engraving Inc 828 456-6337
 87 Willow Rd Apt B5 Waynesville (28786) *(G-15791)*

A W S, Fayetteville Also Called: Arnold S Welding Service Inc *(G-5764)*

A W Spears Research Ctr 336 335-6724
 420 N English St Greensboro (27405) *(G-6769)*

A Window Treatment Co Inc 919 934-7100
 525 S Brightleaf Blvd Smithfield (27577) *(G-14447)*

A-1 Coatings 704 790-9528
 525 Linda St Salisbury (28146) *(G-13911)*

A-1 Concrete & Cnstr LLC 828 712-1160
 42 Avery Creek Rd Arden (28704) *(G-306)*

A-1 Face Inc 336 248-5555
 480 Dixon St Ste C Lexington (27292) *(G-9677)*

A-1 Hitch & Trailors Sales Inc 910 755-6025
 360 Ocean Hwy E Supply (28462) *(G-15005)*

A-1 Sandrock Inc (PA) 336 855-8195
 2606 Phoenix Dr Ste 518 Greensboro (27406) *(G-6770)*

A-1 Trucking, Greensboro Also Called: A-1 Sandrock Inc *(G-6770)*

A-B Emblem, Weaverville Also Called: Conrad Industries Inc *(G-15843)*

A-I Vnyl Grphics Prtg Slutions 910 436-4880
 154 Rosebud St Spring Lake (28390) *(G-14624)*

A-Line, Concord Also Called: Prezioso Ventures LLC *(G-4337)*

A.E. Logging, Trenton Also Called: Triple E Equipment LLC *(G-15336)*

A&B Integrators LLC 919 371-0750
 2800 Meridian Pkwy Durham (27713) *(G-4897)*

A&M Screen Printing NC Inc 910 792-1111
 6404 Amsterdam Way Unit 4 Wilmington (28405) *(G-16089)*

A&R Printing LLC 336 971-7677
 3551 Glenfield Ln Clemmons (27012) *(G-4024)*

A&W Welding Inc 252 482-3233
 1106 Haughton Rd 37 Edenton (27932) *(G-5504)*

A+ Custom Cut Print Press LLC 910 337-1033
 708 N Broad St Roseboro (28382) *(G-13782)*

A+ Pro Transport Inc 980 215-8694
 6201 Fairview Rd Charlotte (28210) *(G-2119)*

A1 Awards & Promotions Inc 252 321-7701
 2580 Railroad St Winterville (28590) *(G-16993)*

A1 Biochem Labs LLC 315 299-4775
 5598 Marvin K Moss Ln Ste 2017 Wilmington (28409) *(G-16090)*

A1 Powder Coating LLC 704 394-0705
 8612 Wilkinson Blvd Charlotte (28214) *(G-2120)*

A1 Vending, Raleigh Also Called: A1gumballs *(G-12453)*

A1gumballs 919 494-1322
 316 W Millbrook Rd Ste 113 Raleigh (27609) *(G-12453)*

A2a Integrated Logistics Inc 800 493-3736
 1830 Owen Dr Ste 102 Fayetteville (28304) *(G-5749)*

A3-Usa Inc 724 871-7170
 1674 Fountaintown Rd Chinquapin (28521) *(G-3891)*

A4 Health Systems Inc 919 851-6177
 5501 Dillard Dr Cary (27518) *(G-1672)*

AA Ceramics 910 632-3053
 2002 Eastwood Rd Wilmington (28403) *(G-16091)*

AA Welding and Fabricatio 919 272-5433
 1012 Ridge Dr Clayton (27520) *(G-3951)*

AAA Glass Company 252 946-2396
 2513 W 5th St Washington (27889) *(G-15678)*

AAA Louvers Inc 919 365-7220
 7328 Siemens Rd Wendell (27591) *(G-15891)*

AAA Machine Shop 704 989-1385
 904 Clarence Secrest Rd Monroe (28110) *(G-10632)*

AAA Mobile Signs LLC 919 463-9768
 10404 Chapel Hill Rd Ste 110 Morrisville (27560) *(G-11274)*

AAA Mobile Signs LLC 252 446-9777
 106 Zebulon Ct Rocky Mount (27804) *(G-13678)*

AAA Paver Care Inc 828 687-1669
 124 Old Salem Ct Fletcher (28732) *(G-5979)*

AAF Flanders, Washington Also Called: Flanders Corporation *(G-15699)*

Aalberts Integrated Piping Systems Americas Inc (HQ) ... 704 841-6000
 10715 Sikes Pl Ste 200 Charlotte (28277) *(G-2121)*

Aallied Die Casting of N C, Rutherfordton Also Called: RCM Industries Inc *(G-13886)*

AAR Key Enterprises Inc 919 337-9706
 1209 Justice Walk Ave Morrisville (27560) *(G-11275)*

Aardvark Screen Printing 919 829-9058
 1600 Automotive Way Raleigh (27604) *(G-12454)*

Aarons Quality Signs 704 841-7733
 524 E Charles St Matthews (28105) *(G-10230)*

AB New Beginnings Inc 828 465-6953
 1211 Keisler Rd Se Conover (28613) *(G-4412)*

Abacon Telecommunications LLC (PA) 336 855-1179
 4388 Federal Dr Greensboro (27410) *(G-6771)*

Abb Inc 704 587-1362
 12037 Goodrich Dr Charlotte (28273) *(G-2122)*

ABB Enterprise Software Inc 919 582-3283
 1021 Main Campus Dr Raleigh (27606) *(G-12455)*

ABB Holdings Inc (DH) 919 856-2360
 305 Gregson Dr Cary (27511) *(G-1673)*

ABB Inc (DH) 919 856-2360
 305 Gregson Dr Cary (27511) *(G-1674)*

ABB Inc 252 827-2121
 3022 Nc 43 N Pinetops (27864) *(G-12239)*

ABB Inc 252 827-2121
 Us Hwy 43 Pinetops (27864) *(G-12240)*

ABB Inc 919 856-3920
 901 Main Campus Dr Ste 300 Raleigh (27606) *(G-12456)*

ABB Inc 919 856-2360
 1021 Main Campus Dr Raleigh (27606) *(G-12457)*

ABB Installation Products Inc 828 322-1855
 415 19th Street Dr Se Hickory (28602) *(G-7928)*

ABB Logging LLC — ALPHABETIC SECTION

ABB Logging LLC 252 809-0180
24815 Us Highway 64 Williamston (27892) *(G-16056)*

ABB Motors and Mechanical Inc 336 272-6104
1220 Rotherwood Rd Greensboro (27406) *(G-6772)*

ABB Motors and Mechanical Inc 704 734-2500
101 Reliance Rd Kings Mountain (28086) *(G-9288)*

ABB Motors and Mechanical Inc 479 646-4711
510 Rockwell Dr Marion (28752) *(G-10137)*

ABB Motors and Mechanical Inc 828 645-1706
70 Reems Creek Rd Weaverville (28787) *(G-15836)*

ABB Power Systems, Raleigh *Also Called: ABB Inc (G-12457)*

ABB Power Systems Inc 919 856-2389
901 Main Campus Dr Ste 300 Raleigh (27606) *(G-12458)*

ABB Power T & D Company Inc 919 856-3806
1021 Main Campus Dr Raleigh (27606) *(G-12459)*

Abb, Inc., Charlotte *Also Called: Abb Inc (G-2122)*

Abbey Robert Inc 336 883-1078
633 Huntington Dr High Point (27262) *(G-8230)*

Abbott Enterprises 252 757-1298
3383 Prescott Ln Greenville (27858) *(G-7477)*

Abbott Laboratories 704 243-1832
9108 Kingsmead Ln Waxhaw (28173) *(G-15743)*

Abbott Products Inc 336 463-3135
1617 Fern Valley Rd Yadkinville (27055) *(G-17029)*

Abbott Sales LLC 919 523-5478
1309 Hedgelawn Way Raleigh (27615) *(G-12460)*

ABC 11, Durham *Also Called: Wtvd Television LLC (G-5451)*

ABC Cabinetry LLc 704 307-8310
5600 Lander Benton Rd Monroe (28110) *(G-10633)*

ABC Fitness Products LLC (PA) 704 649-0000
8541 Glenwood Ave Raleigh (27612) *(G-12461)*

ABC Hosiery, Youngsville *Also Called: Grady Distributing Co Inc (G-17083)*

ABC Publication 919 614-3451
924 Blenheim Dr Raleigh (27612) *(G-12462)*

ABC Signs 252 223-5900
214 Roberts Rd Newport (28570) *(G-11896)*

ABC Signs and Graphics LLC 252 652-6620
160 Us Highway 70 W Havelock (28532) *(G-7738)*

ABC Tees Stuff 828 287-7843
289 Knollwood Dr Forest City (28043) *(G-6056)*

Abco Automation Inc 336 375-6400
6202 Technology Dr Browns Summit (27214) *(G-1298)*

Abco Controls and Eqp Inc 704 394-2424
4110 Monroe Rd Charlotte (28205) *(G-2123)*

Abcor Supply Inc (PA) 919 468-0856
811 Oxfordshire Ln Chapel Hill (27517) *(G-1981)*

Abe Entercom Holdings LLC 336 691-4337
100 N Greene St Ste M Greensboro (27401) *(G-6773)*

Abee Custom Signs Inc 336 229-1554
544 Chapel Hill Rd Burlington (27215) *(G-1361)*

Abercrombie Textiles Inc (PA) 704 487-0935
3051 River Rd Shelby (28152) *(G-14281)*

Abercrombie Textiles I LLC (PA) 704 487-1245
1322 Mount Sinai Church Rd Shelby (28152) *(G-14282)*

Aberdeen Coca-Cola Btlg Co Inc 910 944-2305
203 W South St Aberdeen (28315) *(G-1)*

Abernethy Welding & Repair Inc 828 324-7361
2267 Welding Shop Rd Vale (28168) *(G-15462)*

ABF Store, Greensboro *Also Called: Affordable Beds & Furniture (G-6785)*

Abhw Concrete Co 252 940-1002
347 S Wharton Station Rd Washington (27889) *(G-15679)*

Ability Orthopedics 704 630-6789
209 Statesville Blvd Salisbury (28144) *(G-13912)*

Abl Electronics Supply Inc 704 784-4225
1032 Central Dr Nw Ste A Concord (28027) *(G-4186)*

Able Graphics Company LLC 336 753-1812
126 Horn St Mocksville (27028) *(G-10551)*

Able Metal Fabricators Inc 704 394-8972
3441 Reno Ave Charlotte (28216) *(G-2124)*

Able Softsystems Corp 919 241-7907
1017 Main Campus Dr Ste 1501 Raleigh (27606) *(G-12463)*

Aboard Trade LLC 919 341-7045
4705 Southport Supply Rd Se Ste 208 Southport (28461) *(G-14563)*

Abolder Image 336 856-1300
205 Aloe Rd Greensboro (27409) *(G-6774)*

Above Topsail LLC 910 803-1759
301 Us Highway 17 S Holly Ridge (28445) *(G-8678)*

Abrasive Resource, Charlotte *Also Called: Starcke Abrasives Usa Inc (G-3623)*

Abrasives Industries AG, Lincolnton *Also Called: Sia Abrasives Inc USA (G-9918)*

ABS Southeast LLC (PA) 919 329-0014
5902 Fayetteville Rd Raleigh (27603) *(G-12464)*

Absolent Inc 919 570-2862
6541 Meridien Dr Ste 125 Raleigh (27616) *(G-12465)*

Absolute Security & Lock Inc 336 322-4598
216 S Main St Roxboro (27573) *(G-13792)*

ABT, Statesville *Also Called: ABT Manufacturing LLC (G-14736)*

Abt Inc 314 610-8798
259 Murdock Rd Troutman (28166) *(G-15363)*

Abt Inc (PA) 704 528-9806
259 Murdock Rd Troutman (28166) *(G-15364)*

ABT Foam Inc 800 433-1119
1405 Industrial Dr Statesville (28625) *(G-14734)*

ABT Foam LLC 704 508-1010
1405 Industrial Dr Statesville (28625) *(G-14735)*

ABT Manufacturing LLC 704 847-9188
1903 Weinig St Statesville (28677) *(G-14736)*

Abundant Manufacturing Inc 704 871-9911
820 Cochran St Statesville (28677) *(G-14737)*

Abundant Power Solutions LLC 704 271-9890
222 S Church St Ste 401 Charlotte (28202) *(G-2125)*

Abx Innvtive Pckg Slutions LLC (PA) 980 443-1100
3525 Whitehall Park Dr Ste 300 Charlotte (28273) *(G-2126)*

Abzorbit Inc 828 464-9944
2628 Northwest Blvd Newton (28658) *(G-11911)*

AC Corporation (DH) 336 273-4472
301 Creek Ridge Rd Greensboro (27406) *(G-6775)*

AC Corporation North Carolina, Greensboro *Also Called: AC Corporation (G-6775)*

AC Imports LLC 919 229-6650
6211 Cabin Branch Dr Durham (27712) *(G-4898)*

AC Valor Reyes LLC 910 431-3256
4610 College Rd N Castle Hayne (28429) *(G-1941)*

Acacia Home & Garden Inc 828 465-1700
101 N Mclin Creek Rd Conover (28613) *(G-4413)*

Academy Association Inc 919 544-0835
2222 Sedwick Rd Ste 101 Durham (27713) *(G-4899)*

Acadeus, Raleigh *Also Called: Propharma Group LLC (G-13153)*

ACC Coatings LLC 336 701-0080
620 E Main St Elkin (28621) *(G-5608)*

ACC Distributors, Youngsville *Also Called: Atlantic Coast Cabinet Distrs (G-17068)*

ACC Sports Journal 919 846-7502
3012 Highwoods Blvd Ste 200 Raleigh (27604) *(G-12466)*

Accel Discount Tire (PA) 704 636-0323
201 E Liberty St Salisbury (28144) *(G-13913)*

Accel Wldg & Fabrication LLC 980 722-7198
389 Glencrest Dr Stanley (28164) *(G-14683)*

Accelerated Media Technologies 336 599-2070
4400 Semora Rd Roxboro (27574) *(G-13793)*

Accelerated Press Inc 248 524-1850
616 Windchime Dr Wilmington (28412) *(G-16092)*

Accelrted Svcs Mooresville Inc 704 658-6666
107 Rinehardt Rd Mooresville (28115) *(G-10845)*

Accent Awnings Inc (PA) 828 321-4517
91 Morgan Rd Andrews (28901) *(G-123)*

Access Manufacturing Tech LLC 224 610-0171
163 Cooley Rd Mooresville (28117) *(G-10846)*

Access Technologies LLC 574 286-1255
163 Cooley Rd Mooresville (28117) *(G-10847)*

Accidental Baker 919 732-6777
115 Boone Square St Hillsborough (27278) *(G-8632)*

Accord Healthcare Inc (HQ) 919 941-7878
8041 Arco Corporate Dr Ste 200 Raleigh (27617) *(G-12467)*

Accord Ventilation Products, Greensboro *Also Called: American Valve Inc (G-6802)*

ALPHABETIC SECTION

Accounting Office, Mooresville *Also Called: Bestco LLC (G-10875)*

Accu-Form Polymers Inc 910 293-6961
170 Water Tank Rd Warsaw (28398) *(G-15664)*

Accu-Tool LLC 919 363-2600
2490 Reliance Ave Apex (27539) *(G-156)*

Accudyne Industries LLC (PA) 469 518-4777
800 Beaty St Ste A Davidson (28036) *(G-4665)*

Accuking Inc 252 649-2323
3458 Martin Dr New Bern (28562) *(G-11765)*

Acculabs Technologies Inc 919 468-8780
1018 Morrisville Pkwy Ste E Morrisville (27560) *(G-11276)*

Accuma Corporation (DH) 704 873-1488
133 Fanjoy Rd Statesville (28625) *(G-14738)*

Accumed Corp (HQ) 800 278-6796
160 Mine Lake Ct Ste 200 Raleigh (27615) *(G-12468)*

Accurate Fabrications Inc 910 383-2140
1987 Andrew Jackson Hwy Bldg B Leland (28451) *(G-9524)*

Accurate Machine & Tool LLC 919 212-0266
5124 Trademark Dr Raleigh (27610) *(G-12469)*

Accurate Technology Inc (PA) 828 654-7920
270 Rutledge Rd Fletcher (28732) *(G-5980)*

Accurate Weld LLC 828 310-1517
2374 Friendship Church Rd Taylorsville (28681) *(G-15126)*

Accuride Corporation 336 393-0671
7031 Albert Pick Rd Ste 305 Greensboro (27409) *(G-6776)*

Accusport International Inc (PA) 336 759-3300
4310 Enterprise Dr Ste C Winston Salem (27106) *(G-16588)*

Ace, Tarboro *Also Called: American Composites Engrg (G-15095)*

ACe Cstm Kicks N Prints LLC 336 457-9059
5939 W Friendly Ave Apt 26l Greensboro (27410) *(G-6777)*

Ace Fabrication Inc 919 934-3251
2880 Us Highway 70 Bus W Smithfield (27577) *(G-14448)*

Ace Hardware, Bakersville *Also Called: Ledger Hardware Inc (G-885)*

Ace Industries Inc 336 427-5316
213 Carlton Rd Madison (27025) *(G-10069)*

Ace Laser Recycling Inc 919 775-5521
1808 Rice Rd Sanford (27330) *(G-14081)*

Ace Marine Rigging & Supply Inc (PA) 252 726-6620
600 Arendell St Morehead City (28557) *(G-11148)*

Ace Plastics, Charlotte *Also Called: Ace Plastics Inc (G-2127)*

Ace Plastics Inc 704 527-5752
5130 Hovis Rd Ste A Charlotte (28208) *(G-2127)*

Acento Latino 910 486-2760
458 Whitfield St Fayetteville (28306) *(G-5750)*

Aceragen Inc 919 271-1032
15 Tw Alexander Dr 418 Durham (27709) *(G-4900)*

Acetrace, Greensboro *Also Called: Sierra Software LLC (G-7338)*

Aceyus Inc 704 443-7900
11111 Carmel Commons Blvd Ste 210 Charlotte (28226) *(G-2128)*

Achelios Therapeutics LLC 919 354-6233
4364 S Alston Ave Ste 300 Durham (27713) *(G-4901)*

Achem Industry America Inc 704 283-6144
2910 Stitt St Monroe (28110) *(G-10634)*

Achilli USA Inc 704 940-0715
4030 Wake Forest Rd Ste 349 Raleigh (27609) *(G-12470)*

Ackermann Tool & Machine Co, Wilmington *Also Called: Wilmington Machine Works Inc (G-16447)*

Aclc, Fayetteville *Also Called: Advanced Computer Lrng Co LLC (G-5752)*

Acm Panels 704 839-0104
708 Kelly Dr Matthews (28104) *(G-10300)*

Acme - McCrary Corporation 336 625-2161
1311 E 11th St Siler City (27344) *(G-14395)*

ACME - MCCRARY CORPORATION, Siler City *Also Called: Acme - McCrary Corporation (G-14395)*

Acme Aerofab LLC 704 806-3582
1907 Scott Futrell Dr Charlotte (28208) *(G-2129)*

Acme Die & Machine Corporation 704 864-8426
202 Trakas Blvd Gastonia (28052) *(G-6335)*

Acme General Design Group LLC 843 466-6000
101 N Market St Benson (27504) *(G-1029)*

Acme Liquidating Company LLC 704 873-3731
1784 Salisbury Rd Statesville (28677) *(G-14739)*

Acme Machine LLC 828 483-6440
101 Continuum Dr # 100 Fletcher (28732) *(G-5981)*

Acme Metal Products, Statesville *Also Called: Acme Liquidating Company LLC (G-14739)*

Acme Nameplate & Mfg Inc 704 283-8175
300 Acme Dr (Off Hwy 74 E) Monroe (28112) *(G-10635)*

Acme Rental Company 704 873-3731
1784 Salisbury Rd Statesville (28677) *(G-14740)*

Acme Sample Books, High Point *Also Called: Pag Asb LLC (G-8474)*

Acme Sample Books Inc 336 883-4336
603 Fraley Rd High Point (27263) *(G-8231)*

Acme Stone Company Inc 336 786-6978
1700 Fancy Gap Rd Mount Airy (27030) *(G-11472)*

Acme United Corporation 252 822-5051
2280 Tanner Rd Rocky Mount (27801) *(G-13663)*

Acme Welding Co 770 841-4335
7200 Robinson Church Rd Harrisburg (28075) *(G-7699)*

Acme-Mccrary Corporation 336 625-2161
159 North St Asheboro (27203) *(G-398)*

Acme-Mccrary Corporation (DH) 336 625-2161
162 N Cherry St Asheboro (27203) *(G-399)*

Acme-Mccrary Corporation 919 663-2200
1200 E 3rd St Siler City (27344) *(G-14396)*

Acn Opportunity Delaware LLC 704 260-3000
1000 Progress Pl Concord (28025) *(G-4187)*

Aconcagua Timber Corp 919 542-2128
985 Corinth Rd Moncure (27559) *(G-10612)*

Acorn Climbing LLC 919 518-5022
8309 Davishire Dr Raleigh (27615) *(G-12471)*

Acorn Printing 704 868-4522
4122 Kings Mountain Hwy Bessemer City (28016) *(G-1048)*

Acorn Woodworks NC LLC 828 361-9953
1221 Warren Dr Murphy (28906) *(G-11704)*

Acoustek Nonwovens, Statesville *Also Called: Wwj LLC (G-14929)*

Acoustic Image, Raleigh *Also Called: Acoustic Image LLC (G-12472)*

Acoustic Image LLC 919 785-1280
839 The Village Cir Raleigh (27615) *(G-12472)*

Acquionics Inc 980 256-5700
4215 Stuart Andrew Blvd Ste E Charlotte (28217) *(G-2130)*

Acre Station Meat Farm Inc 252 927-3700
17076 Nc Highway 32 N Pinetown (27865) *(G-12243)*

Acroplis Cntrls Engineers Pllc 919 275-3884
313 S Blount St Ste 200d Raleigh (27601) *(G-12473)*

Acroprint Time Recorders, Raleigh *Also Called: Atrc Inc (G-12531)*

ACS Advnced Clor Solutions Inc 252 442-0098
120 S Business Ct Rocky Mount (27804) *(G-13679)*

Acsm Inc 704 910-0243
113 Freeland Ln Charlotte (28217) *(G-2131)*

Acta Print & Marketing LLC 704 773-1493
224 Deerwood Ln Stanfield (28163) *(G-14673)*

Actega North America Inc 704 736-9389
3840 E Highway 27 Iron Station (28080) *(G-8973)*

Actega Wit, Iron Station *Also Called: Actega North America Inc (G-8973)*

Actega Wit Inc 704 735-8282
125 Technolgy Dr Lincolnton (28092) *(G-9865)*

Acterna LLC 919 388-5100
1100 Perimeter Park Dr Ste 101 Morrisville (27560) *(G-11277)*

Action Graphics, Charlotte *Also Called: Perlman Inc (G-3332)*

Action Graphics and Signs Inc 919 690-1260
8694b Us Hwy 15 Bullock (27507) *(G-1326)*

Action Installs LLC 704 787-3828
1202 Industrial Park Rd Wilkesboro (28697) *(G-16012)*

Action Sign Company Lenoir Inc 828 754-4116
511 Creekway Dr Nw Lenoir (28645) *(G-9567)*

Action Specialties LLC 704 865-6699
1916 S York Rd Gastonia (28052) *(G-6336)*

Actionsign Group, Lenoir *Also Called: Action Sign Company Lenoir Inc (G-9567)*

Actionsigncom 828 572-2308
2640 Hickory Blvd Hudson (28638) *(G-8759)*

Active Concepts 704 276-7386
109 Technolgy Dr Lincolnton (28092) *(G-9866)*

Active Concepts LLC 704 276-7372
110 Technolgy Dr Lincolnton (28092) *(G-9867)*

(PA)=Parent Co (HQ)=Headquarters (DH)=Div Headquarters

ALPHABETIC SECTION

Active Concepts LLC.. 704 276-7100
  107 Technolgy Dr Lincolnton (28092) *(G-9868)*

Active Hats and Things Suite.................................... 888 352-9292
  2201 Inkberry Ct Wilmington (28411) *(G-16093)*

Acton Corporation.. 434 728-4491
  1451 S Elm Eugene St Greensboro (27406) *(G-6778)*

Acu Trol Inc... 919 566-8332
  1620 Hawkins Ave Sanford (27330) *(G-14082)*

Acucal Inc... 252 337-9975
  108 Enterprise Dr Elizabeth City (27909) *(G-5530)*

Acucote, Graham Also Called: Acucote Inc *(G-6677)*

Acucote Inc (DH)... 336 578-1800
  910 E Elm St Graham (27253) *(G-6677)*

Acument Global Technologies................................... 704 598-3539
  3000 Crosspoint Center Ln Ste F Charlotte (28269) *(G-2132)*

Acw Technology Inc
  3725 Althorp Dr Raleigh (27616) *(G-12474)*

Ad Pak, The, Wilmington Also Called: Media Wilimington Co *(G-16319)*

Ad Press Printing, Summerfield Also Called: Adpress Printing Incorporated *(G-14975)*

Ad Runner MBL Outdoor Advg Inc............................ 336 945-1190
  2555 Williams Rd Lewisville (27023) *(G-9664)*

Ad Spice Marketing LLC... 919 286-7110
  4310 Garrett Rd Durham (27707) *(G-4902)*

AD Tubi Usa Inc... 919 930-3023
  3031 Hamp Stone Rd Siler City (27344) *(G-14397)*

Ad-Art Signs Inc.. 704 377-5369
  2613 Lucena St Charlotte (28206) *(G-2133)*

Ada Marketing Inc... 910 221-2189
  601 N Ashe Ave Dunn (28334) *(G-4848)*

Adagio Vineyards... 336 258-2333
  139 Benge Dr Elkin (28621) *(G-5609)*

Adam Dalton Distillery LLC....................................... 828 785-1499
  251 Biltmore Ave Asheville (28801) *(G-514)*

Adama US.. 919 817-7103
  4134 S Alston Ave Durham (27713) *(G-4903)*

Adama US, Raleigh Also Called: Makhteshim Agan North Amer Inc *(G-12990)*

Adamantium Aerospace Inc....................................... 252 444-6265
  412 Cherry Branch Dr Havelock (28532) *(G-7739)*

Adams 919 Plumbing, Raleigh Also Called: Enviro-Companies LLC *(G-12741)*

Adams Beverages Leland, Leland Also Called: Adams Beverages NC LLC *(G-9525)*

Adams Beverages Lumberton, Lumberton Also Called: Adams Beverages NC LLC *(G-10023)*

Adams Beverages NC LLC (PA)................................ 704 509-3000
  7505 Statesville Rd Charlotte (28269) *(G-2134)*

Adams Beverages NC LLC... 910 763-6216
  2265 Mercantile Dr Leland (28451) *(G-9525)*

Adams Beverages NC LLC... 910 738-8165
  797 Caton Rd Lumberton (28360) *(G-10023)*

Adams Handmade Soap, Dunn Also Called: Ada Marketing Inc *(G-4848)*

Adams Line Striping, Cornelius Also Called: Safe Home Pro Inc *(G-4585)*

Adams Oldcastle... 980 229-7678
  9968 Metromont Industrial Blvd Charlotte (28269) *(G-2135)*

Adams Products, Durham Also Called: Old Castle Apg South Inc *(G-5255)*

Adams Products Company... 919 467-2218
  5701 Mccrimmon Pkwy Ste 201 Morrisville (27560) *(G-11278)*

Adams Wood Turning Inc... 336 882-0196
  216 Woodbine St High Point (27260) *(G-8232)*

Adamson Global Technology Corp (PA).................. 252 523-5200
  2018 W Vernon Ave Kinston (28504) *(G-9339)*

Adaptive Health, Charlotte Also Called: Direct Digital LLC *(G-2640)*

Adaptive Mobility Solutions, Washington Also Called: Veon Inc *(G-15736)*

Adaptive Technologies LLC.. 919 231-6890
  3224 Lake Woodard Dr Ste 100 Raleigh (27604) *(G-12475)*

ADC, Hayesville Also Called: Advanced Digital Cable Inc *(G-7759)*

ADC Industries Inc.. 919 550-9515
  106 N Lombard St Clayton (27520) *(G-3952)*

Adcut, Maxton Also Called: Advanced Cutting Tech Inc *(G-10354)*

Add-On Technologies Inc... 704 882-2227
  7000 Stinson Hartis Rd Ste D Indian Trail (28079) *(G-8918)*

Addendum LLC.. 704 664-9898
  119 Sunhaven Ln Mooresville (28117) *(G-10848)*

Additive America Inc.. 252 549-0247
  300 N Herritage St Kinston (28501) *(G-9340)*

Additive Prtg & Robotics Inc..................................... 704 375-6788
  4601 Park Rd Ste 620 Charlotte (28209) *(G-2136)*

Adele Knits Inc.. 336 499-6010
  3304 Old Lexington Rd Winston Salem (27107) *(G-16589)*

Ademco Inc... 704 525-8899
  800 Clanton Rd Ste F Charlotte (28217) *(G-2137)*

Ademco Inc... 336 668-3644
  4500 Green Point Dr Greensboro (27410) *(G-6779)*

Ademco Inc... 919 872-5556
  2741 Noblin Rd Ste 101 Raleigh (27604) *(G-12476)*

Adhezion Biomedical LLC... 828 728-6116
  506 Pine Mountain Rd Hudson (28638) *(G-8760)*

ADI Global Distribution, Charlotte Also Called: Ademco Inc *(G-2137)*

ADI Global Distribution, Greensboro Also Called: Ademco Inc *(G-6779)*

ADI Global Distribution, Raleigh Also Called: Ademco Inc *(G-12476)*

ADI/PDM Trade Group, High Point Also Called: Precision Design Machinery *(G-8491)*

Adica Enterprises, Elizabeth City Also Called: Coastal Office Eqp & Computers *(G-5534)*

Aditi 108 Inc... 704 763-3741
  132 Joe Knox Ave Ste 111 Mooresville (28117) *(G-10849)*

ADM, Charlotte Also Called: Archer-Daniels-Midland Company *(G-2210)*

ADM, Southport Also Called: Archer-Daniels-Midland Company *(G-14565)*

Admark, Wilmington Also Called: Advanced Marketing International Inc *(G-16095)*

Admiral Marine Pdts & Svcs Inc............................... 704 489-8771
  770 Crosspoint Dr Denver (28037) *(G-4758)*

Admissionpros LLC.. 919 256-3889
  800 Pinner Weald Way Ste 101 Cary (27513) *(G-1675)*

Adora... 336 880-0342
  1245 Hickory Chapel Rd High Point (27260) *(G-8233)*

Adoratherapy Inc... 917 297-8904
  31 Mount Vernon Cir Asheville (28804) *(G-515)*

Adpress Printing Incorporated................................... 336 294-2244
  7000 Morganshire Ct Summerfield (27358) *(G-14975)*

Adr Hydro-Cut Inc.. 919 388-2251
  125 International Dr Ste E Morrisville (27560) *(G-11279)*

ADS, Bessemer City Also Called: Advanced Drainage Systems Inc *(G-1050)*

ADS Graphic Design, Boone Also Called: Advertising Design Systems Inc *(G-1172)*

ADS N Art Screenprinting & EMB............................ 919 453-0400
  929 Heritage Lake Rd Ste 400 Wake Forest (27587) *(G-15525)*

ADS Printing Co Inc... 919 834-0579
  733 W Hargett St Raleigh (27603) *(G-12477)*

Adsign Corp.. 336 766-3000
  6100 Gun Club Rd Winston Salem (27103) *(G-16590)*

Advance Auto Parts, Greensboro Also Called: Advance Stores Company Inc *(G-6780)*

Advance Cabinetry Inc... 828 676-3550
  15 Design Ave Unit 201 Fletcher (28732) *(G-5982)*

Advance Conveying Tech LLC.................................. 704 710-4001
  171 Kings Rd Kings Mountain (28086) *(G-9289)*

Advance Printing Solutions....................................... 301 919-7868
  338 Aldrich Ln Wilmington (28411) *(G-16094)*

Advance Signs & Service Inc.................................... 919 639-4666
  596 W Church St Angier (27501) *(G-130)*

Advance Stores Company Inc.................................... 336 545-9091
  2514 Battleground Ave Ste A Greensboro (27408) *(G-6780)*

Advanced Brace & Limb... 252 991-6109
  2693 Forest Hills Rd Sw Wilson (27893) *(G-16464)*

Advanced Brace & Limb Inc..................................... 910 483-5737
  4140 Ferncreek Dr Ste 803 Fayetteville (28314) *(G-5751)*

Advanced Brace & Limb Inc..................................... 919 818-0359
  3617 Nightfall Ct Raleigh (27607) *(G-12478)*

Advanced Brace and Limb, Fayetteville Also Called: Advanced Brace & Limb Inc *(G-5751)*

Advanced Computer Lrng Co LLC........................... 910 779-2254
  208 Hay St Ste 2c Fayetteville (28301) *(G-5752)*

Advanced Cutting Tech Inc....................................... 910 944-3028
  12760 Airport Rd Maxton (28364) *(G-10354)*

Advanced Detection Tech LLC.................................. 704 663-1949
  215 Overhill Dr 1 Mooresville (28117) *(G-10850)*

Advanced Digital Cable Inc (PA).............................. 828 389-1652
  94 Eagle Fork Rd Hayesville (28904) *(G-7759)*

ALPHABETIC SECTION

Advanced Digital Systems Inc.. 919 485-4819
4601 Creekstone Dr Ste 180 Durham (27703) *(G-4904)*

Advanced Digital Textiles LLC.. 704 226-9600
600 Broome St Monroe (28110) *(G-10636)*

Advanced Drainage Systems.. 704 629-4151
333 Southridge Pkwy Bessemer City (28016) *(G-1049)*

Advanced Drainage Systems Inc.. 704 629-4151
333 Southridge Pkwy Bessemer City (28016) *(G-1050)*

Advanced Drainage Systems Inc.. 336 764-0341
11875 N Nc Highway 150 Winston Salem (27127) *(G-16591)*

Advanced Electronic Svcs Inc (PA).. 336 789-0792
101 Technology Ln Mount Airy (27030) *(G-11473)*

Advanced Grading & Excvtg LLC.. 828 320-7465
4360 Caldwell Rd Newton (28658) *(G-11912)*

Advanced Machine Services.. 910 410-0099
835 N Us Highway 220 Rockingham (28379) *(G-13617)*

Advanced Machine Services LLC.. 910 410-0099
128 Industrial Park Dr Rockingham (28379) *(G-13618)*

Advanced Machining, Salisbury Also Called: Advanced Machining Tooling LLC *(G-13914)*

Advanced Machining Tooling LLC.. 704 633-8157
215 Forbes Ave Salisbury (28147) *(G-13914)*

Advanced Marketing International Inc.. 910 392-0508
211 Racine Dr Ste 202 Wilmington (28403) *(G-16095)*

Advanced Mch & Fabrication Inc.. 704 489-0096
7842 Commerce Dr Denver (28037) *(G-4759)*

Advanced Metal Supply.. 336 883-7135
5873 Parker St High Point (27263) *(G-8234)*

Advanced Mfg Solutions NC Inc.. 828 633-2633
53 Rutherford Rd Candler (28715) *(G-1566)*

Advanced Micro Devices Inc.. 919 840-8080
3000 Rdu Center Dr Ste 230 Morrisville (27560) *(G-11280)*

Advanced Motor Sports Coatings.. 336 472-5518
17 High Tech Blvd Thomasville (27360) *(G-15181)*

Advanced Non-Lethal Tech Inc.. 847 812-6450
8311 Brier Creek Pkwy Raleigh (27617) *(G-12479)*

Advanced Photonic Crystals LLC.. 803 547-0881
19825 North Cove Rd # 216 Cornelius (28031) *(G-4520)*

Advanced Plastic Extrusion LLC.. 252 224-1444
213 Sermon Rd Pollocksville (28573) *(G-12391)*

Advanced Plastiform Inc (PA).. 919 404-2080
535 Mack Todd Rd Zebulon (27597) *(G-17117)*

Advanced Plastiform Inc.. 919 404-2080
113 Legacy Crest Ct Zebulon (27597) *(G-17118)*

Advanced Plating Technologies.. 704 291-9325
2600 Stitt St Monroe (28110) *(G-10637)*

Advanced Point SL Systems Inc.. 877 381-6100
2800 Heathstead Pl Charlotte (28210) *(G-2138)*

Advanced Substrate.. 336 285-5955
7860 Thorndike Rd Greensboro (27409) *(G-6781)*

Advanced Superabrasives Inc.. 828 689-3200
1270 N Main St Mars Hill (28754) *(G-10191)*

Advanced Systems Intgrtion LLC (PA).. 260 447-5555
8512 Mangum Hollow Dr Wake Forest (27587) *(G-15526)*

Advanced Tech Systems Inc.. 336 299-6695
2606 Phoenix Dr Ste 602 Greensboro (27406) *(G-6782)*

Advanced Technology Inc.. 336 668-0488
6106 W Market St Greensboro (27409) *(G-6783)*

Advanced Teo Corp.. 305 278-4474
5707 Hornet Dr Charlotte (28216) *(G-2139)*

Advanced Traffic Marking, Weldon Also Called: Patch Rubber Company *(G-15887)*

Advancepierre Foods Inc.. 828 459-7626
3437 E Main St Claremont (28610) *(G-3900)*

Advantage Fitness Products, Archdale Also Called: Advantage Fitness Products LLC *(G-265)*

Advantage Fitness Products Inc.. 336 643-8810
115 Gralin St Kernersville (27284) *(G-9159)*

Advantage Fitness Products LLC.. 336 643-8810
3511 Garrell St Archdale (27263) *(G-265)*

Advantage Golf School, Highlands Also Called: New Media Golf Inc *(G-8616)*

Advantage Machinery Svcs Inc (PA).. 336 463-4700
1407 Us 601 Hwy Yadkinville (27055) *(G-17030)*

Advantage Marketing.. 919 872-8610
129 Bartholomew Rd Louisburg (27549) *(G-9978)*

Advantage Newspaper.. 910 323-0349
501 Executive Pl Ste B Fayetteville (28305) *(G-5753)*

Advantage Nn-Wvens Cnvrting LL.. 828 635-1880
173 Wittenburg Industrial Dr Taylorsville (28681) *(G-15127)*

Advantage Printing Inc.. 828 252-7667
1848 Brevard Rd Arden (28704) *(G-307)*

Advantage Printing & Design.. 252 523-8133
2425 N Herritage St Kinston (28501) *(G-9341)*

Adventure Sign and Ltg LLC.. 336 401-3410
473 Oak Ridge Dr Mount Airy (27030) *(G-11474)*

Advertising Design Systems Inc.. 828 264-8060
269 Grand Blvd Boone (28607) *(G-1172)*

Advertising For You Now Inc.. 704 706-9423
298 Church St N Concord (28025) *(G-4188)*

Advintech Inc.. 336 327-2666
2825 Nc Highway 62 E Liberty (27298) *(G-9804)*

Advplating LLC.. 704 291-9325
2600 Stitt St Monroe (28110) *(G-10638)*

Adwood Corporation.. 336 884-1846
260 Durand Ave High Point (27263) *(G-8235)*

Ae Technology Inc.. 704 528-2000
150 Ostwalt Amity Rd Troutman (28166) *(G-15365)*

Ae Wiring LLC.. 252 749-0195
5887 W Blount St Fountain (27829) *(G-6092)*

AEC Consumer Products, Fayetteville Also Called: AEC Consumer Products LLC *(G-5754)*

AEC Consumer Products LLC.. 704 904-0578
3005 Bankhead Dr Fayetteville (28306) *(G-5754)*

AEC Imaging & Graphics LLC (PA).. 910 693-1034
5755 Dove Dr Hope Mills (28348) *(G-8730)*

AEC Narrow Fabrics, Asheboro Also Called: Asheboro Elastics Corp *(G-403)*

AEC Narrow Fabrics, Asheboro Also Called: Asheboro Elastics Corp *(G-404)*

AEG International, Charlotte Also Called: Livingston & Haven LLC *(G-3096)*

Aegis Power Systems Inc.. 828 837-4029
805 Greenlawn Cemetery Rd Murphy (28906) *(G-11705)*

Aek Inc.. 704 864-7968
3705 Saint Regis Dr Gastonia (28056) *(G-6337)*

AEL Services LLC.. 704 525-3710
8200 Arrowridge Blvd Ste A Charlotte (28273) *(G-2140)*

Aerami Therapeutics Inc (PA).. 650 773-5926
600 Park Offices Dr Durham (27709) *(G-4905)*

Aerami Thrpeutics Holdings Inc.. 919 589-7495
2520 Meridian Pkwy Ste 400 Durham (27713) *(G-4906)*

Aerie Pharmaceuticals Inc (HQ).. 919 237-5300
4301 Emperor Blvd Ste 400 Durham (27703) *(G-4907)*

Aero 8 Inc.. 336 776-9165
3820 N Liberty St Winston Salem (27105) *(G-16592)*

Aero Precision Machine Inc.. 336 685-0016
6024 Smithwood Rd Liberty (27298) *(G-9805)*

Aerofabb LLC.. 919 793-8487
3312 Marcony Way Raleigh (27610) *(G-12480)*

Aeroplantation.. 704 843-2223
630 Baron Rd Waxhaw (28173) *(G-15744)*

Aeroquip Corp.. 828 286-4157
240 Daniel Rd Forest City (28043) *(G-6057)*

Aerospace Filtration Division.. 336 668-4444
8439 Triad Dr Greensboro (27409) *(G-6784)*

AES America Inc.. 847 879-1146
4508b Westinghouse Blvd Ste B Charlotte (28273) *(G-2141)*

Aesco Inc.. 910 763-6612
1405 S 5th Ave Wilmington (28401) *(G-16096)*

AF&f, Albemarle Also Called: American Fiber & Finishing Inc *(G-73)*

AFA Billing Services.. 910 868-8324
894 Elm St Ste D Fayetteville (28303) *(G-5755)*

Afe Victory Inc.. 856 428-4200
3779 Champion Blvd Winston Salem (27105) *(G-16593)*

Afex, Raleigh Also Called: Bonaventure Group Inc *(G-12568)*

Affordable Bedding Inc.. 828 254-5555
996 Patton Ave Ste A Asheville (28806) *(G-516)*

Affordable Beds & Furniture.. 336 988-1520
4607 W Gate City Blvd Greensboro (27407) *(G-6785)*

Affordable Septic Tank.. 910 417-9537
315 Fox Trot Rd Hamlet (28345) *(G-7615)*

Affordable Signs & Awnings ALPHABETIC SECTION

Affordable Signs & Awnings... 910 237-1323
  3959 Stone St Hope Mills (28348) *(G-8731)*

Affordable Welding Specialists.. 828 446-4436
  7460 Burke County Line Rd Hickory (28602) *(G-7929)*

Affordable Wheelchair Vans LLC..................................... 910 443-6989
  1304 Quail Dr Greensboro (27408) *(G-6786)*

Afi Capital Inc... 919 212-6400
  801 Beacon Lake Dr Raleigh (27610) *(G-12481)*

AFL Network Services Inc.. 704 289-5522
  2807 Gray Fox Rd Monroe (28110) *(G-10639)*

AFL Network Services Inc.. 919 658-2311
  100 Impulse Way Mount Olive (28365) *(G-11653)*

Afsc LLC... 704 523-4936
  3605 S Tryon St Charlotte (28217) *(G-2142)*

AG Chemical.. 561 886-0919
  140 Towerview Ct Cary (27513) *(G-1676)*

AG Provision LLC (PA).. 910 296-0302
  277 Faison W Mcgowan Rd Kenansville (28349) *(G-9140)*

Against Grain Woodworking Inc.................................... 704 309-5750
  1015 Seigle Ave Charlotte (28205) *(G-2143)*

Against The Grain Woodworking................................... 704 969-5837
  154 Superior Stainless Rd Gastonia (28052) *(G-6338)*

Agastat, Fairview *Also Called:* Te Connectivity Corporation *(G-5720)*

Agency Management Soluitons, Forest City *Also Called:* Jenesis Software Inc *(G-6072)*

Aggregates Div, Raleigh *Also Called:* Martin Marietta Materials Inc *(G-12999)*

Aggressive Adhesives Inc... 910 270-3282
  1971 Sloop Point Loop Rd Hampstead (28443) *(G-7635)*

Agile Microwave Technology Inc................................... 984 228-8001
  701 Cascade Pointe Ln Ste 101 Cary (27513) *(G-1677)*

Agile Mwt, Cary *Also Called:* Agile Microwave Technology Inc *(G-1677)*

Agile Ventures LLC... 202 716-7958
  2107 Spartanburg Hwy East Flat Rock (28726) *(G-5472)*

Agility Fuel Systems LLC.. 704 870-3520
  1010 Corporate Center Dr Salisbury (28146) *(G-13915)*

AGM Carolina Inc.. 336 431-4100
  1031 E Springfield Rd High Point (27263) *(G-8236)*

Agnatural LLC... 252 536-0322
  802 Julian R Allsbrook Hwy Weldon (27890) *(G-15879)*

Agricltral-Industrial Fabr Inc... 336 591-3690
  223 S Main St Walnut Cove (27052) *(G-15630)*

Agrofuel LLC... 704 876-6667
  964 Snow Creek Rd Statesville (28625) *(G-14741)*

Agve Inc.. 704 243-8300
  13029 Bleinheim Ln Ste B Matthews (28105) *(G-10231)*

Ahlberg Cameras, Wilmington *Also Called:* Ahlberg Cameras Inc *(G-16097)*

Ahlberg Cameras Inc.. 910 523-5876
  432 Landmark Dr Ste 3 Wilmington (28412) *(G-16097)*

Aidleyco LLC... 704 782-0648
  532 Patterson Ave # 220 Mooresville (28115) *(G-10851)*

Aie We Go, Monroe *Also Called:* Air-We-Go LLC *(G-10640)*

Aiken Development LLC... 828 572-4040
  1028 West Ave Nw Lenoir (28645) *(G-9568)*

Aiken-Black Tire Service Inc.. 828 322-3736
  823 1st Ave Nw Hickory (28601) *(G-7930)*

Aikencontrols, Lenoir *Also Called:* Aiken Development LLC *(G-9568)*

AIM Industries Inc.. 336 656-9990
  391 Brann Rd Browns Summit (27214) *(G-1299)*

Aim LLC... 980 333-0008
  4910 Lakeview Rd Charlotte (28216) *(G-2144)*

Aim Molding & Door LLC.. 704 913-7211
  5431 Starflower Dr Charlotte (28215) *(G-2145)*

Aimet Holding Inc... 919 887-5205
  115 Legacy Crest Ct Zebulon (27597) *(G-17119)*

Aimet Technologies, Zebulon *Also Called:* Aimet Holding Inc *(G-17119)*

Aimet Technologies LLC... 919 887-5205
  115 Legacy Crest Ct Zebulon (27597) *(G-17120)*

Air & Gas Solutions LLC... 704 897-2182
  5509 David Cox Rd Charlotte (28269) *(G-2146)*

Air Control Inc.. 252 492-2300
  237 Raleigh Rd Henderson (27536) *(G-7775)*

Air Controls Division, Roxboro *Also Called:* Eaton Corporation *(G-13801)*

Air Craftsmen Inc.. 336 248-5777
  2503 Northside Dr Statesville (28625) *(G-14742)*

Air Force Fleet Readiness Ctr, Cherry Point *Also Called:* United States Dept of Navy *(G-3860)*

Air Purification Inc (PA).. 919 783-6161
  8121 Ebenezer Church Rd Raleigh (27612) *(G-12482)*

Air Speed Stock Car Fabricatio.................................... 704 720-7245
  190b Pitts School Rd Nw Concord (28027) *(G-4189)*

Air System Components Inc.. 919 279-8868
  275 Pressly Foushee Rd Sanford (27330) *(G-14083)*

Air System Components Inc.. 919 775-2201
  101 Mcneill Rd Sanford (27330) *(G-14084)*

Air System Components Inc.. 252 641-5900
  3301 N Main St Tarboro (27886) *(G-15093)*

Air System Components Inc.. 252 641-0875
  3301 N Main St Tarboro (27886) *(G-15094)*

Air Systems Mfg of Lenoir Inc..................................... 828 757-3500
  2621 Hogan Dr Lenoir (28645) *(G-9569)*

Air-We-Go LLC... 704 289-6565
  4507 W Highway 74 Monroe (28110) *(G-10640)*

Airborn Industries Inc... 704 483-5000
  115 Industrial Park Rd Lincolnton (28092) *(G-9869)*

Airboss Heating and Coolg Inc.................................... 252 586-0500
  127 W South Main St Littleton (27850) *(G-9950)*

Airboss Rbr Compounding NC LLC............................ 252 826-4919
  500 Airboss Pkwy Scotland Neck (27874) *(G-14218)*

Airboss Rubber Solutions, Scotland Neck *Also Called:* Airboss Rbr Compounding NC LLC *(G-14218)*

Airbox LLC... 855 927-1386
  2668 Peachtree Rd Statesville (28625) *(G-14743)*

Airclean Systems, Creedmoor *Also Called:* Applied Medical Tech Inc *(G-4605)*

Aircraft Belts Inc (DH).. 919 956-4395
  1176 Telecom Dr Creedmoor (27522) *(G-4601)*

Aircraft Parts Solutions LLC.. 843 300-1725
  3378 Apex Peakway Apex (27502) *(G-157)*

Airdream.net, Davidson *Also Called:* Elborn Holdings LLC *(G-4673)*

Airfield Solutions LLC.. 844 478-6929
  142 Leslie Ct Hubert (28539) *(G-8747)*

Airfield Solutions LLC (PA).. 919 348-4271
  825 Gum Branch Rd Ste 102 Jacksonville (28540) *(G-8985)*

Airflow Products Company Inc.................................... 919 975-0240
  100 Oak Tree Dr Selma (27576) *(G-14251)*

Airgas, Durham *Also Called:* Airgas Usa LLC *(G-4908)*

Airgas, Salisbury *Also Called:* Airgas Usa LLC *(G-13916)*

Airgas National Carbonation, Charlotte *Also Called:* Airgas Usa LLC *(G-2147)*

Airgas National Welders, Wilmington *Also Called:* Airgas Usa LLC *(G-16098)*

Airgas Usa LLC.. 704 394-1420
  3101 Stafford Dr Charlotte (28208) *(G-2147)*

Airgas Usa LLC.. 704 333-5475
  5311 77 Center Dr Charlotte (28217) *(G-2148)*

Airgas Usa LLC.. 919 544-1056
  2810 S Miami Blvd Durham (27703) *(G-4908)*

Airgas Usa LLC.. 919 544-3773
  630 United Dr Durham (27713) *(G-4909)*

Airgas Usa LLC.. 919 735-5276
  109 Hinnant Rd Goldsboro (27530) *(G-6587)*

Airgas Usa LLC.. 704 636-5049
  1924 S Main St Salisbury (28144) *(G-13916)*

Airgas Usa LLC.. 910 392-2711
  2824 Carolina Beach Rd Wilmington (28412) *(G-16098)*

Airloom Furnishing, Bennett *Also Called:* Philip Brady *(G-1027)*

Airplus, Durham *Also Called:* Implus Footcare LLC *(G-5150)*

Airspeed LLC... 919 644-1222
  980 Corporate Dr Ste 200 Hillsborough (27278) *(G-8633)*

Airt, Charlotte *Also Called:* T Air Inc *(G-3668)*

Airtek, Goldsboro *Also Called:* AP Emissions Technologies LLC *(G-6591)*

Aisin North Carolina Corp... 919 529-0951
  1187 Telecom Dr Creedmoor (27522) *(G-4602)*

Aisin North Carolina Corp (DH).................................. 919 479-6400
  4112 Old Oxford Rd Durham (27712) *(G-4910)*

Aisthesis Products Inc.. 828 627-6555
  70 Brigadoon Dr Clyde (28721) *(G-4120)*

ALPHABETIC SECTION — Alco Metal Fabricato

Aj & Raine Scrubs & More LLC.. 646 374-5198
657 Fielding Rd Charlotte (28214) *(G-2149)*

Ajc Craftworks Inc... 919 279-1621
8900 Miranda Dr Raleigh (27617) *(G-12483)*

Ajinomoto, Raleigh *Also Called: Ajinomoto Hlth Ntrtn N Amer In (G-12484)*

Ajinomoto Hlth Ntrtn N Amer In.. 919 231-0100
4020 Ajinomoto Dr Raleigh (27610) *(G-12484)*

Ajs Dezigns Inc... 828 652-6304
Ashworth Rd Marion (28752) *(G-10138)*

Akg North America Inc.. 919 563-4286
7315 Oakwood Street Ext Mebane (27302) *(G-10396)*

Akg Nrth Amercn Operations Inc (DH)....................................... 919 563-4286
7315 Oakwood Street Ext Mebane (27302) *(G-10397)*

Akg of America Inc (DH).. 919 563-4286
7315 Oakwood Street Ext Mebane (27302) *(G-10398)*

Akoustis Inc (HQ).. 704 997-5735
9805 Northcross Center Ct Ste A Huntersville (28078) *(G-8786)*

Akoustis Technologies Inc (PA).. 704 997-5735
9805 Northcross Center Ct Ste A Huntersville (28078) *(G-8787)*

Akzo Nobel Coatings, High Point *Also Called: Akzo Nobel Coatings Inc (G-8237)*

Akzo Nobel Coatings Inc.. 704 366-8435
7506 E Independence Blvd Charlotte (28227) *(G-2150)*

Akzo Nobel Coatings Inc.. 336 665-9897
4500 Green Point Dr Ste 104 Greensboro (27410) *(G-6787)*

Akzo Nobel Coatings Inc.. 336 841-5111
1431 Progress Ave High Point (27260) *(G-8237)*

Al-Rite Manufacturing, Winston Salem *Also Called: Joseph Halker (G-16772)*

Al-Tex Dyes Co LLC.. 704 849-9727
1531 Wickerby Ct Matthews (28105) *(G-10232)*

Aladdin Manufacturing Corp.. 336 623-6000
712 Henry St Eden (27288) *(G-5485)*

Alamac American Knits LLC... 910 618-2248
1885 Alamac Rd Lumberton (28358) *(G-10024)*

Alamance Cabinets, Graham *Also Called: Marsh Furniture Company (G-6700)*

Alamance Electric & Wldg Inc.. 336 584-9339
3562 Stoney Creek Church Rd Elon (27244) *(G-5656)*

Alamance Facility, Mebane *Also Called: GKN Dna Inc (G-10412)*

Alamance Foods Inc (PA)... 336 226-6392
840 Plantation Dr Burlington (27215) *(G-1362)*

Alamance Iron Works Inc... 336 852-5940
3900 Patterson St Greensboro (27407) *(G-6788)*

Alamance Kaffee Werks LLC... 662 617-4573
3105 Midland Ct Burlington (27215) *(G-1363)*

Alamance Steel Fabricators... 336 887-3015
5926 Prospect St High Point (27263) *(G-8238)*

Alameen A Haqq.. 336 965-8339
4424 Gray Wolf Way Greensboro (27406) *(G-6789)*

Alamo Distribution LLC (DH)... 704 398-5600
2100 Oaks Pkwy Belmont (28012) *(G-974)*

Alamo Iron Works, Belmont *Also Called: Alamo Distribution LLC (G-974)*

Alamo North Texas Railroad Co.. 919 787-9504
2710 Wycliff Rd Raleigh (27607) *(G-12485)*

Alamo Publishing Services... 252 269-1513
316 Shoreline Dr New Bern (28562) *(G-11766)*

Alan Kimzey.. 828 891-8720
42 Sawmill Rd Mills River (28759) *(G-10498)*

Alan Lane Wesley... 704 433-8338
580 Daves Dr Salisbury (28146) *(G-13917)*

Alan R Williams Inc (HQ)... 704 372-8281
2318 Arty Ave Charlotte (28208) *(G-2151)*

Alan Walsh Logging, Lenoir *Also Called: Alan Walsh Logging LLC (G-9570)*

Alan Walsh Logging LLC.. 828 234-7500
2687 Nc Highway 268 Lenoir (28645) *(G-9570)*

Alandale Industries Inc.. 910 576-1291
208 Burnette St Troy (27371) *(G-15400)*

Alaska Structures Inc.. 910 323-0562
2545 Ravenhill Dr Ste 101 Fayetteville (28303) *(G-5756)*

ALASKA STRUCTURES, INC., Fayetteville *Also Called: Alaska Structures Inc (G-5756)*

Alb Boats.. 252 482-7600
140 Midway Dr Edenton (27932) *(G-5505)*

Albaad Fem US, Reidsville *Also Called: Albaad Usa Inc (G-13504)*

Albaad Usa Inc.. 336 634-0091
1900 Barnes St Reidsville (27320) *(G-13504)*

Albany Tool & Die Inc... 910 392-1207
315 Van Dyke Dr Ste A Wilmington (28405) *(G-16099)*

Albatross Steel Buildings, Hamptonville *Also Called: Albatross Supply LLC (G-7665)*

Albatross Supply LLC.. 336 488-1128
2851 Rocky Branch Rd Hamptonville (27020) *(G-7665)*

Albemarle, Charlotte *Also Called: Albemarle Corporation (G-2152)*

Albemarle Boats, Edenton *Also Called: Edenton Boatworks LLC (G-5514)*

Albemarle Corporation (PA).. 980 299-5700
4250 Congress St Ste 900 Charlotte (28209) *(G-2152)*

Albemarle Corporation.. 252 482-7423
140 Midway Dr Edenton (27932) *(G-5506)*

Albemarle Corporation.. 704 739-2501
348 Holiday Inn Dr Kings Mountain (28086) *(G-9290)*

Albemarle Glass and Stone, Albemarle *Also Called: Albemarle Glass Company Inc (G-70)*

Albemarle Glass Company Inc.. 704 982-3323
1217 Pee Dee Ave Albemarle (28001) *(G-70)*

Albemarle Tire Retreading Inc... 704 982-4113
542 W Main St Albemarle (28001) *(G-71)*

Albemarle US Inc (DH).. 704 739-2501
348 Holiday Inn Dr Kings Mountain (28086) *(G-9291)*

Albemarle Wood Prsv Plant Inc... 704 982-2516
1509 Snuggs Park Rd Albemarle (28001) *(G-72)*

Albemrle Orthotics Prosthetics (PA).. 252 332-4334
103 Nc Highway 42 W Ahoskie (27910) *(G-54)*

Albemrle Orthotics Prosthetics.. 252 338-3002
106 Medical Dr Elizabeth City (27909) *(G-5531)*

Alberdingk Boley Inc... 336 454-5000
6008 W Gate City Blvd Greensboro (27407) *(G-6790)*

Albert E Mann... 919 497-0815
106 Clifton Ridge Ct Louisburg (27549) *(G-9979)*

Albion Medical Holdings Inc (DH).. 800 378-3906
639 Nuway Cir Lenoir (28645) *(G-9571)*

Albright Qulty WD Turning Inc... 336 475-1434
193 Black Farm Rd Thomasville (27360) *(G-15182)*

Alcami, Durham *Also Called: Alcami Carolinas Corporation (G-4911)*

Alcami, Garner *Also Called: Alcami Carolinas Corporation (G-6251)*

Alcami, Wilmington *Also Called: Alcami Carolinas Corporation (G-16100)*

Alcami, Wilmington *Also Called: Alcami Carolinas Corporation (G-16101)*

Alcami, Wilmington *Also Called: Alcami Carolinas Corporation (G-16103)*

Alcami Carolinas Corporation.. 919 957-5500
4620 Creekstone Dr Ste 200 Durham (27703) *(G-4911)*

Alcami Carolinas Corporation.. 910 619-3952
5100 Jones Sausage Rd Ste 110 Garner (27529) *(G-6251)*

Alcami Carolinas Corporation.. 910 254-7000
627 Davis Dr Ste 100 Morrisville (27560) *(G-11281)*

Alcami Carolinas Corporation.. 910 254-7000
419 Davis Dr Ste 300 Morrisville (27560) *(G-11282)*

Alcami Carolinas Corporation.. 910 254-7000
200 Innovation Ave Ste 150 Morrisville (27560) *(G-11283)*

Alcami Carolinas Corporation.. 910 254-7000
1726 N 23rd St Wilmington (28405) *(G-16100)*

Alcami Carolinas Corporation.. 910 254-7000
1206 N 23rd St Wilmington (28405) *(G-16101)*

Alcami Carolinas Corporation.. 910 254-7000
1519 N 23rd St Wilmington (28405) *(G-16102)*

Alcami Carolinas Corporation (HQ).. 910 254-7000
2320 Scientific Park Dr Wilmington (28405) *(G-16103)*

Alcami Corporation (PA).. 910 254-7000
2320 Scientific Park Dr Wilmington (28405) *(G-16104)*

Alcami Holdings LLC.. 910 254-7000
2320 Scientific Park Dr Wilmington (28405) *(G-16105)*

Alcatel Dunkermotoren.. 704 782-0691
5850 Potomac Dr Nw Concord (28027) *(G-4190)*

Alcatel-Lucent USA, Raleigh *Also Called: Nokia of America Corporation (G-13066)*

Alco Custom Cabinets Inc.. 919 363-9480
103 Stagville Ct Cary (27519) *(G-1678)*

Alco Metal Fabricato... 704 739-1168
1111 Oates Rd Bessemer City (28016) *(G-1051)*

Alco Metal Fabricators Inc — 704 739-1168
307 S Cansler St Kings Mountain (28086) *(G-9292)*

Alcoa Badin Works, Badin *Also Called: Alcoa Power Generating Inc (G-862)*

Alcoa Power Generating Inc — 704 422-5691
293 Nc Hwy 740 Badin (28009) *(G-862)*

Alcon — 919 624-5868
6425 Belle Crest Dr Raleigh (27612) *(G-12486)*

Alcon Components, Mooresville *Also Called: Alcon Components Usa Inc (G-10852)*

Alcon Components Usa Inc — 704 799-2723
121 Oakpark Dr Mooresville (28115) *(G-10852)*

Alcorns Custom Woodworking Inc — 336 342-0908
941 Flat Rock Rd Reidsville (27320) *(G-13505)*

Alders Point — 336 725-9021
590 Mock St Winston Salem (27127) *(G-16594)*

Aldo Products Company Inc — 704 932-3054
1320 Litton Dr Salisbury (28147) *(G-13918)*

Alert Metal Works Inc — 704 922-3152
105 Yates St Dallas (28034) *(G-4634)*

Alert Protection Systems Inc — 919 467-4357
1401 Monkwood Pl Raleigh (27603) *(G-12487)*

Alex and Ani LLC — 704 366-6029
4400 Sharon Rd Ste 201 Charlotte (28211) *(G-2153)*

Alexander Crush Inc — 828 635-7136
452 Paynes Dairy Rd Taylorsville (28681) *(G-15128)*

Alexander Fabrics, Burlington *Also Called: McComb Industries Llp (G-1458)*

Alexander Press Inc — 336 884-8063
701 Greensboro Rd High Point (27260) *(G-8239)*

Alexanders — 910 938-0013
165 Blue Creek School Rd Jacksonville (28540) *(G-8986)*

Alexanders Cbinets Countertops — 336 774-2966
4735 Kester Mill Rd Winston Salem (27103) *(G-16595)*

Alexanders Ham Company Inc — 704 857-9222
5920 Highway 152 W Mooresville (28115) *(G-10853)*

Alf Sjoberg, Chapel Hill *Also Called: Blind Nail and Company Inc (G-1992)*

Alfiniti Inc — 252 358-5811
600 N Metcalf St Winton (27986) *(G-17020)*

Algonquin Books of Chapel Hill, Chapel Hill *Also Called: Workman Publishing Co Inc (G-2100)*

Ali Group North America Corp — 800 648-4389
738 Gallimore Dairy Rd Ste 113 High Point (27265) *(G-8240)*

Ali Group North America Corp — 336 661-1556
3765 Champion Blvd Winston Salem (27105) *(G-16596)*

Alk Investments LLC — 984 233-5353
6812 Glenwood Ave Ste 100 Raleigh (27612) *(G-12488)*

All 4 U Home Medical LLC — 828 437-0684
617 S Green St Ste 100 Morganton (28655) *(G-11196)*

All American Braids Inc — 704 852-4380
1613 Warren Ave Gastonia (28054) *(G-6339)*

All American Pumpkin Patch LLC — 980 201-9104
4456 Central Ave Charlotte (28205) *(G-2154)*

All Baked Out Company — 336 861-1212
629 Mcway Dr High Point (27263) *(G-8241)*

All Decked Out, Frisco *Also Called: Cashman Inc (G-6176)*

All Elements Incorporated — 919 641-9576
2010 Roland Glen Rd Cary (27519) *(G-1679)*

All Glass Inc — 828 324-8609
1125 S Center St Hickory (28602) *(G-7931)*

All In 1 Home Improvement — 252 725-4560
261 Streets Ferry Rd Vanceboro (28586) *(G-15475)*

All In One Printing — 919 360-8092
4607 Grinding Stone Dr Apt A Raleigh (27604) *(G-12489)*

All Occasion Printing — 336 926-7766
2408 Gardenia Rd Winston Salem (27107) *(G-16597)*

All of F-Words — 561 232-5824
7007 Gardner Pond Ct Charlotte (28270) *(G-2155)*

All Pro Fabrication & Wldg LLC — 336 953-4082
241 Arnold Rd Lexington (27295) *(G-9678)*

All Signs & Graphics LLC — 910 323-3115
301 Hope Mills Rd Fayetteville (28304) *(G-5757)*

All Source Security Cont Cal — 704 504-9908
1500 Continental Blvd Ste K Charlotte (28273) *(G-2156)*

All Star Marketing & Media Co, Franklin *Also Called: All Star Sign Company (G-6114)*

All Star Printing — 252 689-6464
903 Dickinson Ave Greenville (27834) *(G-7478)*

All Star Sign Company — 214 862-6797
20 Coddies Ter Franklin (28734) *(G-6114)*

All State Belting, Charlotte *Also Called: All-State Industries Inc (G-2157)*

All Stick Label LLC — 336 659-4660
3929 Westpoint Blvd Ste B Winston Salem (27103) *(G-16598)*

All Ways Graphics, Wilmington *Also Called: CRS/Las Inc (G-16190)*

All-State Industries Inc — 704 588-4081
1400 Westinghouse Blvd Ste 100 Charlotte (28273) *(G-2157)*

Allan Dearth and Sons, Highlands *Also Called: Allan Drth Sns Gnrtor Sls Svc (G-8611)*

Allan Drth Sons Gnrtor Sls Svc — 828 526-9325
11259 Buck Creek Rd Highlands (28741) *(G-8611)*

Allan Fitch — 919 834-2593
212 Dwelling Pl Knightdale (27545) *(G-9409)*

Allbirds Inc — 980 296-0006
100 W Worthington Ave Charlotte (28203) *(G-2158)*

ALLBIRDS, INC., Charlotte *Also Called: Allbirds Inc (G-2158)*

Alleghany Garbage Service, Sparta *Also Called: Alleghany Garbage Service Inc (G-14587)*

Alleghany Garbage Service Inc — 336 372-4413
453 N Main St Sparta (28675) *(G-14587)*

Allegion Access Tech LLC — 704 789-7000
1000 Stanley Dr Concord (28027) *(G-4191)*

Allegra Knightdale, Knightdale *Also Called: Allegra Marketing Print Mail (G-9410)*

Allegra Marketing, Asheville *Also Called: Mail Management Services LLC (G-693)*

Allegra Marketing Print Mail — 828 698-7622
348 7th Ave E Hendersonville (28792) *(G-7817)*

Allegra Marketing Print Mail — 919 373-0531
1009 Steeple Square Ct Knightdale (27545) *(G-9410)*

Allegra Print & Imaging, Asheville *Also Called: Powell Ink Inc (G-739)*

Allegra Print & Imaging, Fayetteville *Also Called: Print Works Fayetteville Inc (G-5902)*

Allegra Print & Imaging, Rocky Mount *Also Called: Hinson Industries Inc (G-13700)*

Allen & Son S Cabinet Shop Inc — 919 963-2196
5942 Us Highway 301 S Four Oaks (27524) *(G-6099)*

Allen Brothers Timber Company — 910 997-6412
723 N Us Highway 220 Rockingham (28379) *(G-13619)*

Allen Face & Company LLC — 910 763-4501
2725 Old Wrightsboro Rd Ste 12-5 Wilmington (28405) *(G-16106)*

Allen Goodson Logging Co, Jacksonville *Also Called: Allen R Goodson Logging Co (G-8987)*

Allen Industries Inc (PA) — 336 668-2791
6434 Burnt Poplar Rd Greensboro (27409) *(G-6791)*

Allen Industries Inc — 336 294-4777
4100 Sheraton Ct Greensboro (27410) *(G-6792)*

Allen Kelly & Co Inc — 919 779-4197
220 Tryon Rd Ste A Raleigh (27603) *(G-12490)*

Allen Mch & Fabrication LLC — 336 521-4409
420 Industrial Park Ave Asheboro (27205) *(G-400)*

Allen R Goodson Logging Co — 910 455-4177
1417 Kellum Loop Rd Jacksonville (28546) *(G-8987)*

Allen-Godwin Concrete Inc — 910 686-4890
8871 Sidbury Rd Wilmington (28411) *(G-16107)*

Allens Environmental Cnstr LLC — 407 774-7100
84 Greenfield Cir Brevard (28712) *(G-1269)*

Allens Gutter Service — 910 738-9509
209 T P Rd Lumberton (28358) *(G-10025)*

Allergan, Raleigh *Also Called: Allergan Inc (G-12491)*

Allergan Inc — 704 301-7790
7701 Umstead Forest Dr Raleigh (27612) *(G-12491)*

Alleson Athletic, Statesville *Also Called: Alleson of Rochester Inc (G-14744)*

Alleson of Rochester Inc (DH) — 585 272-0606
111 Badger Ln Statesville (28625) *(G-14744)*

Allfuel Hst Inc — 919 868-9410
109 W High Bluff Dr Hampstead (28443) *(G-7636)*

Alliance Assessments LLC — 336 283-9246
200 Northgate Park Dr Winston Salem (27106) *(G-16599)*

Alliance Hose & Tube Works Inc — 336 378-9736
3012 S Elm Eugene Street Ste F Greensboro (27406) *(G-6793)*

Alliance Mch & Fabrication LLC — 704 629-5677
3421 Fairview Dr Gastonia (28052) *(G-6340)*

ALPHABETIC SECTION

Alliance One International, King *Also Called: Cres Tobacco Company LLC* *(G-9268)*
Allie M Powell III.. 252 535-9717
   3692 Nc Highway 48 Roanoke Rapids (27870) *(G-13565)*
Allied Industrial, Marion *Also Called: Ajs Dezigns Inc* *(G-10138)*
Allied Manufacturing Tech Inc... 704 276-8192
   1477 Roseland Dr Lincolnton (28092) *(G-9870)*
Allied Marine Contractors LLC.. 910 367-2159
   92 Harold Ct Hampstead (28443) *(G-7637)*
Allied Metal Finishing Inc.. 704 347-1477
   2525 Lucena St Charlotte (28206) *(G-2159)*
Allied Mobile Systems LLC... 888 503-1501
   17665 Us 421 S Dunn (28334) *(G-4849)*
Allied Plating Finishing LLC.. 704 347-1477
   2525 Lucena St Charlotte (28206) *(G-2160)*
Allied Pressroom Products Inc (PA).................................... 954 920-0909
   4814 Persimmon Ct Monroe (28110) *(G-10641)*
Allied Sheet Metal Works Inc.. 704 376-8469
   612 Charles Ave Charlotte (28205) *(G-2161)*
Allied Tool and Machine Co (PA)... 336 993-2131
   115 Corum St Kernersville (27284) *(G-9160)*
Allied/Carter Machining Inc... 704 784-1253
   540 Lake Lynn Rd Concord (28025) *(G-4192)*
Alligood Brothers Logging... 252 927-2358
   436 Mill Hole Rd Washington (27889) *(G-15680)*
Alligood Cabinet Shop.. 252 927-3201
   121 Alligood Dr Washington (27889) *(G-15681)*
Alligood Cabinets, Washington *Also Called: Alligood Cabinet Shop* *(G-15681)*
Allison Brothers Race Cars Inc... 704 278-0174
   7920 Statesville Blvd Salisbury (28147) *(G-13919)*
Allison Globl Mnufacturing Inc.. 704 392-7883
   3900 Sam Wilson Rd Charlotte (28214) *(G-2162)*
Allison Sails and Canvas LLC... 910 515-1381
   915 Lake Park Blvd N Ste G Carolina Beach (28428) *(G-1631)*
Allkindsa Signs, Raleigh *Also Called: Jeremy Weitzel* *(G-12916)*
Allotropica Technologies Inc... 919 522-4374
   601 W Rosemary St Unit 503 Chapel Hill (27516) *(G-1982)*
Alloy Fabricators Inc... 704 263-2281
   334 Alexis High Shoals Rd Alexis (28006) *(G-121)*
Alloyworks LLC... 704 645-0511
   814 W Innes St Salisbury (28144) *(G-13920)*
Allrail Inc.. 828 287-3747
   289 Calton Hill Ln Rutherfordton (28139) *(G-13861)*
Allred Metal Stamping Works Inc.. 336 886-5221
   1305 Old Thomasville Rd High Point (27260) *(G-8242)*
Allsbrook Logging LLC.. 252 567-1085
   173 Pro House Dr Enfield (27823) *(G-5674)*
Allstar Waste Systems Inc.. 252 343-5156
   4270 S Browntown Rd Rocky Mount (27804) *(G-13680)*
Allsteel Welding LLC... 919 429-0468
   11936 W Nc 97 Middlesex (27557) *(G-10444)*
Alltech Inc.. 336 635-5190
   11761 Hwy 770 E Eden (27288) *(G-5486)*
Alltech Sign Service LLC.. 803 548-9787
   8334 Arrowridge Blvd Ste C Charlotte (28273) *(G-2163)*
Allyn International Trdg Corp (PA)...................................... 877 858-2482
   412 College St Marshville (28103) *(G-10210)*
Almore International Inc.. 503 643-6633
   441 19th St Se Hickory (28602) *(G-7932)*
Alnamer Inc.. 252 215-0323
   501 S Memorial Dr Greenville (27834) *(G-7479)*
Alossi Renewal Spa LLC.. 406 338-7700
   300 Okamato St Raleigh (27603) *(G-12492)*
Alotech Inc... 919 774-1297
   751 S Church St Goldston (27252) *(G-6672)*
Alotech North.. 919 774-1297
   751 S Church St Goldston (27252) *(G-6673)*
Alp Systems Inc.. 828 454-5164
   46 Allegiance Ln Waynesville (28786) *(G-15792)*
Alpaca.. 919 628-9686
   813 S Horner Blvd Sanford (27330) *(G-14085)*
Alpacadabra... 336 429-0124
   125 Rock Lane Dr Dobson (27017) *(G-4818)*

Alpek Polyester Miss Inc (DH).. 228 533-4000
   7621 Little Ave Ste 500 Charlotte (28226) *(G-2164)*
Alpek Polyester Usa LLC (DH).. 704 940-7500
   7621 Little Ave Ste 500 Charlotte (28226) *(G-2165)*
Alpek Polyester Usa LLC.. 910 433-8200
   3216 Cedar Creek Rd Fayetteville (28312) *(G-5758)*
Alpek Polyester Usa LLC.. 910 371-4000
   1430 Commonwealth Dr Wilmington (28403) *(G-16108)*
Alpha 3d LLC... 704 277-6300
   1141 Homestead Glen Blvd Charlotte (28214) *(G-2166)*
Alpha Aluminum LLC.. 336 777-5658
   1300 Cunningham Ave Winston Salem (27107) *(G-16600)*
Alpha and Omega Printing Inc.. 336 778-1400
   2554 Lewisville Clemmons Rd Clemmons (27012) *(G-4025)*
Alpha Canvas and Awning Co Inc....................................... 704 333-1581
   411 E 13th St Charlotte (28206) *(G-2167)*
Alpha Logging Inc... 252 568-2727
   3759 Live Oak Hog Co Road Deep Run (28525) *(G-4715)*
Alpha Mailing Service Inc... 704 484-1711
   501 N Washington St Shelby (28150) *(G-14283)*
Alpha Medsource LLC.. 704 408-8505
   14009 Island Dr Huntersville (28078) *(G-8788)*
Alpha Printing & Mailing.. 704 751-4930
   501 N Washington St Shelby (28150) *(G-14284)*
Alpha Signs & Embroidery Inc.. 704 878-8870
   321 S Tradd St Statesville (28677) *(G-14745)*
Alpha Signs & Lighting Inc.. 910 567-5813
   515 Old Crow Rd Newton Grove (28366) *(G-11987)*
Alpha Theory LLC... 212 235-2180
   3537 Keithcastle Ct Charlotte (28210) *(G-2168)*
Alpha Theory LLC (PA)... 212 235-2180
   5701 Westpark Dr Ste 105 Charlotte (28217) *(G-2169)*
Alpha Theory LLC... 704 844-1018
   2201 Coronation Blvd Ste 140 Charlotte (28227) *(G-2170)*
Alpha-Advantage Inc.. 252 441-3766
   891 Emeline Ln Kitty Hawk (27949) *(G-9399)*
Alphagraphcis of New Bern, New Bern *Also Called: Andrews Graphics LLC* *(G-11771)*
AlphaGraphics.. 704 887-3430
   13850 Ballantyne Corporate Pl Ste 500 Charlotte (28277) *(G-2171)*
AlphaGraphics.. 336 759-8000
   8100 N Point Blvd Ste A Winston Salem (27105) *(G-16601)*
AlphaGraphics, Cary *Also Called: Erleclair Inc* *(G-1761)*
AlphaGraphics, Cary *Also Called: Rennasentient Inc* *(G-1868)*
AlphaGraphics, Charlotte *Also Called: AlphaGraphics Pineville* *(G-2172)*
AlphaGraphics, Charlotte *Also Called: Brown Printing Inc* *(G-2360)*
AlphaGraphics, Charlotte *Also Called: Inventive Graphics Inc* *(G-2989)*
AlphaGraphics, Garner *Also Called: AlphaGraphics Downtown Raleigh* *(G-6252)*
AlphaGraphics, Raleigh *Also Called: AlphaGraphics North Raleigh* *(G-12493)*
AlphaGraphics Downtown Raleigh..................................... 919 832-2828
   3731 Centurion Dr Garner (27529) *(G-6252)*
AlphaGraphics North Raleigh.. 919 322-2257
   8321 Bandford Way Ste 1 Raleigh (27615) *(G-12493)*
AlphaGraphics Pineville.. 704 541-3678
   10100 Park Cedar Dr Ste 178 Charlotte (28210) *(G-2172)*
Alphamed Company Inc (PA).. 919 680-0011
   6100 Guess Rd Durham (27712) *(G-4912)*
Alphamed Press, Durham *Also Called: Alphamed Company Inc* *(G-4912)*
Alphatech Inc.. 828 684-9709
   388 Cane Creek Rd Fletcher (28732) *(G-5983)*
Alphin Brothers Inc... 910 892-8751
   2302 Us 301 S Dunn (28334) *(G-4850)*
Alside Window Co.. 407 293-9010
   3800 Window Way Kinston (28504) *(G-9342)*
Alta Foods llc... 919 734-0233
   105 Industry Ct Goldsboro (27530) *(G-6588)*
Altaravision Inc... 919 342-5778
   130 Salem Towne Ct Apex (27502) *(G-158)*
Altec Inds Mt Airy Operations, Mount Airy *Also Called: Altec Industries Inc* *(G-11475)*
Altec Industries Inc... 828 678-5500
   150 Altec Rd Burnsville (28714) *(G-1521)*

ALPHABETIC SECTION

Altec Industries Inc 919 528-2535
  1550 Aerial Ave Creedmoor (27522) *(G-4603)*
Altec Industries Inc 336 786-3623
  200 Altec Way Mount Airy (27030) *(G-11475)*
Altec Northeast LLC 508 320-9041
  1550 Aerial Ave Creedmoor (27522) *(G-4604)*
Altech-Eco Corporation 828 654-8300
  101 Fair Oaks Rd Arden (28704) *(G-308)*
Altera Corporation 919 852-1004
  5540 Centerview Dr Ste 318 Raleigh (27606) *(G-12494)*
Altered State Brewing Company, Raleigh *Also Called: Side Hustle Ventures LLC (G-13253)*
Alternative Brands Inc 336 751-4818
  321 Farmington Rd Mocksville (27028) *(G-10552)*
Alternative Care Group LLC 336 499-5644
  931 S Main St Ste A Kernersville (27284) *(G-9161)*
Alternative Cutting Tools LLC 484 684-9924
  1628 Waterway Cove Dr Sw Ocean Isle Beach (28469) *(G-12086)*
Alternative Energy Products, Charlotte *Also Called: Raw Earth Energy Corporation (G-3412)*
Alternative Health Dist LLC 336 465-6618
  106 N Commercial Dr Ste A Mooresville (28115) *(G-10854)*
Alternative Ingredients Inc 336 378-5368
  300 Dougherty St Greensboro (27406) *(G-6794)*
Alternative Pwr Sls & Rent LLP 919 467-8001
  1000 Northgate Ct Morrisville (27560) *(G-11284)*
Alterra Labs LLC 704 770-7695
  1316 Sorrel Park Dr Morrisville (27560) *(G-11285)*
Altior Industries, Monroe *Also Called: Pearl River Group LLC (G-10785)*
Altitude Sign Company LLC 980 339-8160
  900 Winter Wood Dr Matthews (28105) *(G-10233)*
Altium Packaging LLC 704 873-6729
  124 Commerce Blvd Statesville (28625) *(G-14746)*
Altium Packaging LLC 336 472-1500
  1408 Unity St Thomasville (27360) *(G-15183)*
Altium Packaging LP 336 342-4749
  606 Walters St Unit B Reidsville (27320) *(G-13506)*
Altom Fuel Cells LLC 828 231-6889
  117 Jones Rd Leicester (28748) *(G-9506)*
Altra Industrial Motion Corp 704 588-5610
  701 N I-85 Service Rd Charlotte (28216) *(G-2173)*
Altra Industrial Motion Corp 704 588-5610
  701 Carrier Dr Charlotte (28216) *(G-2174)*
Altus Finishing LLC 704 861-1536
  1711 Sparta Ct Gastonia (28052) *(G-6341)*
Alumadock Marine Structure, Henderson *Also Called: Robco Manufacturing Inc (G-7807)*
Aluminum Barges com LLC 239 272-4857
  154 Lilac Ln Boone (28607) *(G-1173)*
Aluminum Screen Manufacturing 336 605-8080
  4501 Green Point Dr Ste 104 Greensboro (27410) *(G-6795)*
Alveolus Inc 704 921-2215
  9013 Perimeter Woods Dr Ste B Charlotte (28216) *(G-2175)*
Alywillow 919 454-4826
  5301 Hillsborough St Ste 100 Raleigh (27606) *(G-12495)*
AM Haire Mfg & Svc Corp 336 472-4444
  516 Pineywood Rd Thomasville (27360) *(G-15184)*
Amada America Inc 877 262-3287
  109 Penny Rd High Point (27260) *(G-8243)*
Amalfi Semiconductor Inc 336 664-1233
  7628 Thorndike Rd Greensboro (27409) *(G-6796)*
Amann Girrbach North Amer LP 704 837-1404
  13900 S Lakes Dr Ste D Charlotte (28273) *(G-2176)*
Amann Girrbach North America, Charlotte *Also Called: Amann Girrbach North Amer LP (G-2176)*
Amano Pioneer Eclipse Corp 704 900-1352
  9013 Perimeter Woods Dr Ste A Charlotte (28216) *(G-2177)*
Amano Pioneer Eclipse Corp (DH) 336 372-8080
  1 Eclipse Rd Sparta (28675) *(G-14588)*
Amanzi Marble & Granite LLC 336 993-9998
  703 Park Lawn Ct Kernersville (27284) *(G-9162)*
Amarr Company 704 599-5858
  2801 Hutchison Mcdonald Rd Charlotte (28269) *(G-2178)*
Amarr Company 336 936-0010
  275 Enterprise Way Mocksville (27028) *(G-10553)*
Amarr Company (DH) 336 744-5100
  165 Carriage Ct Winston Salem (27105) *(G-16602)*
Amarr Garage Doors, Charlotte *Also Called: Amarr Company (G-2178)*
Amarr Garage Doors, Winston Salem *Also Called: Amarr Company (G-16602)*
Ambassador Services Inc 800 576-8627
  1520 S York Rd Gastonia (28052) *(G-6342)*
Ambcopy LLC 919 308-1033
  214 Crisp Rd Durham (27713) *(G-4913)*
Amber Alert International Tm (PA) 919 641-8773
  6537 English Oaks Dr Raleigh (27615) *(G-12496)*
Amber Brooks Publishing LLC 704 582-1035
  7233 Mine Shaft Rd Raleigh (27615) *(G-12497)*
Ambiance Doors LLC 919 855-9220
  3208 Wellington Ct Ste 109 Raleigh (27615) *(G-12498)*
Ambient Noise Control LLC 919 477-6791
  2903 Carver St Durham (27705) *(G-4914)*
Ambra Le Roy LLC 704 392-7080
  8541 Crown Crescent Ct Charlotte (28227) *(G-2179)*
Ambra Leroy Medical Products, Charlotte *Also Called: Ambra Le Roy LLC (G-2179)*
Ambro-Sol Usa LLC 844 824-6959
  286 Industrial Park Rd Rutherfordton (28139) *(G-13862)*
Ambrose Signs Inc 252 338-8522
  123 Sawyers Creek Rd Camden (27921) *(G-1555)*
AMC, Arden *Also Called: Asheville Maintenance and Construction Inc (G-312)*
Amcase Inc 336 784-5992
  2214 Shore St High Point (27263) *(G-8244)*
Amcor Phrm Packg USA LLC 919 556-9715
  111 Wheaton Ave Youngsville (27596) *(G-17066)*
Amcor Tob Packg Americas Inc 828 274-1611
  3055 Sweeten Creek Rd Asheville (28803) *(G-517)*
Ameri-Con Materials Inc 828 863-0444
  2554 Deep Gap Farm Rd Mill Spring (28756) *(G-10483)*
America Printer 336 465-0269
  5349 Racine Rd Randleman (27317) *(G-13452)*
America Sheet Metal Inc 980 318-7749
  5502 Roberta Rd Harrisburg (28075) *(G-7700)*
American & Efird 56, Gastonia *Also Called: American & Efird LLC (G-6343)*
American & Efird Global LLC (DH) 704 827-4311
  22 American St Mount Holly (28120) *(G-11617)*
American & Efird LLC 704 864-0977
  3200 York Hwy Gastonia (28056) *(G-6343)*
American & Efird LLC 704 867-3664
  401 Grover St Gastonia (28054) *(G-6344)*
American & Efird LLC 828 754-9066
  619 Connelly Springs Rd Sw Lenoir (28645) *(G-9572)*
American & Efird LLC 704 827-4311
  22 American St Mount Holly (28120) *(G-11618)*
American & Efird LLC (DH) 704 827-4311
  24 American St Mount Holly (28120) *(G-11619)*
American & Efird LLC 704 823-2501
  101 Mill St Mount Holly (28120) *(G-11620)*
American Acrylic Adhesives 520 954-1700
  111 Montrose Dr Mooresville (28115) *(G-10855)*
American Alcohollery LLC 704 960-7243
  385 Hose Rd Moravian Falls (28654) *(G-11141)*
American Artworks 910 803-2525
  714 E Ocean Rd Holly Ridge (28445) *(G-8679)*
American Attachments Inc 336 859-2002
  702 N Silver St Lexington (27292) *(G-9679)*
American Backflow Technologies 252 714-8378
  5414 Nc Highway 33 E Greenville (27858) *(G-7480)*
American Builders Anson Inc (PA) 704 272-7655
  8564 Hwy 74 W Polkton (28135) *(G-12383)*
American Cabinetry 704 502-4450
  7918 Leisure Ln Huntersville (28078) *(G-8789)*
American Carolina Lighting, Pisgah Forest *Also Called: McJast Inc (G-12326)*
American Carports Structures 336 710-1091
  152 Eastwind Ct Mount Airy (27030) *(G-11476)*
American Carports Stuctures 844 628-4973
  155 Mount View Dr Mount Airy (27030) *(G-11477)*
American Chrome & Chem NA Inc 910 675-7200
  5408 Holly Shelter Rd Castle Hayne (28429) *(G-1942)*

ALPHABETIC SECTION — American Snuff Company LLC

American Circuits Inc 704 376-2800
  10100 Sardis Crossing Dr Charlotte (28270) *(G-2180)*

American City Bus Journals Inc (HQ) 704 973-1000
  120 W Morehead St Ste 400 Charlotte (28202) *(G-2181)*

American City Bus Journals Inc 704 973-1100
  550 S Caldwell St Ste 910 Charlotte (28202) *(G-2182)*

American City Bus Journals Inc 336 271-6539
  101 S Elm St Ste 100 Greensboro (27401) *(G-6797)*

American Classic Furniture, Hudson Also Called: Consumer Specialty Inc *(G-8769)*

American Cltvtion Extrction Sv 336 544-1072
  245 E Friendly Ave Ste 100 Greensboro (27401) *(G-6798)*

American Coil Inc 310 515-1215
  157 N Main St Bostic (28018) *(G-1259)*

American Composites Engrg (HQ) 252 641-9866
  1090 W Saint James St Tarboro (27886) *(G-15095)*

American Converting Co Ltd LLC 704 479-5025
  1161 Burris Blvd Lincolnton (28092) *(G-9871)*

American Cylinder Products Inc 336 993-7722
  115 Furlong Industrial Dr Kernersville (27284) *(G-9163)*

American Durafilm Co Inc 704 895-7701
  117 Infield Ct Mooresville (28117) *(G-10856)*

American Eagle Mfg LLC 252 633-0603
  3280 Us Highway 70 E New Bern (28560) *(G-11767)*

American Embroidery LLC 910 229-3837
  424 Swan Island Ct Fayetteville (28311) *(G-5759)*

American Emergency Vehicles, Jefferson Also Called: Halcore Group Inc *(G-9090)*

American Extruded Plastics Inc 336 274-1131
  938 Reynolds Pl Greensboro (27403) *(G-6799)*

American Fabricators 252 637-2600
  4395 Us Highway 17 S New Bern (28562) *(G-11768)*

American Fence & Supply, Charlotte Also Called: Afsc LLC *(G-2142)*

American Fiber & Finishing Inc (PA) 704 984-9256
  225 N Depot St Albemarle (28001) *(G-73)*

American Forms Mfg Inc (PA) 704 866-9139
  170 Tarheel Dr Gastonia (28056) *(G-6345)*

American Growler Inc (PA) 352 671-5393
  121 N Green St Robbins (27325) *(G-13596)*

American Honda Motor Co Inc 336 578-6300
  3721 Nc Hwy 119 Swepsonville (27359) *(G-15050)*

American Image Press 336 468-2796
  5043 Highland Grove Pl Hamptonville (27020) *(G-7666)*

American Indian Printing Inc 336 230-1551
  1310 Beaman Pl Greensboro (27408) *(G-6800)*

American Indian Printing Inc 336 884-5442
  710 Dorado Cir High Point (27265) *(G-8245)*

American Inst Crtif Pub Accntn (PA) 919 402-0682
  220 Leigh Farm Rd Durham (27707) *(G-4915)*

American Institute of Cpas, Durham Also Called: American Inst Crtif Pub Accntn *(G-4915)*

American Label Tech Inc 984 269-5078
  343 Technology Dr Ste 2106 Garner (27529) *(G-6253)*

American Lgacy Timeline Prints 252 514-0225
  905 Coral Ct New Bern (28560) *(G-11769)*

American Linc Corporation 704 861-9242
  159 Wolfpack Rd Gastonia (28056) *(G-6346)*

American Made Industries Inc 650 218-7608
  4825 Chesney St Nw Concord (28027) *(G-4193)*

American Made Products Inc 252 747-2010
  606 5th St Hookerton (28538) *(G-8728)*

American Materials Company, Wilmington Also Called: Columbia Silica Sand LLC *(G-16175)*

American Materials Company LLC 252 752-2124
  2703 Nc Highway 222 Greenville (27834) *(G-7481)*

American Materials Company LLC 910 532-6070
  3596 Dr Kerr Rd Ivanhoe (28447) *(G-8979)*

American Materials Company LLC 910 532-6659
  9763 Taylors Bridge Hwy Rose Hill (28458) *(G-13773)*

American Materials Company LLC (HQ) 910 799-1411
  1410 Commonwealth Dr Ste 201 Wilmington (28403) *(G-16109)*

American Media International, Burlington Also Called: American Multimedia Inc *(G-1364)*

American Metal Fabricators Inc 704 824-8585
  2608 Lowell Rd Gastonia (28054) *(G-6347)*

American Metal Treating, High Point Also Called: American Metallurgy Inc *(G-8246)*

American Metallurgy Inc 336 889-3277
  505 Garrison St High Point (27260) *(G-8246)*

American Miso Company Inc 828 287-2940
  4225 Maple Creek Rd Rutherfordton (28139) *(G-13863)*

American Modular Technologies, Liberty Also Called: Amt/Bcu Inc *(G-9807)*

American Moistening Co Inc 704 889-7281
  10402 Rodney St Pineville (28134) *(G-12252)*

American Multimedia Inc (PA) 336 229-7101
  2609 Tucker St Burlington (27215) *(G-1364)*

American Netting Corp 919 567-3737
  3209 Air Park Rd Fuquay Varina (27526) *(G-6178)*

American of High Point Inc 336 431-1513
  2224 Shore St High Point (27263) *(G-8247)*

American Olympus Fibrgls Corp 828 459-0444
  3054 Kelly Blvd Claremont (28610) *(G-3901)*

American Pharmaceutical Svcs 828 328-1816
  1255 25th Street Pl Se Hickory (28602) *(G-7933)*

American Phoenix Inc 910 484-4007
  318 Blount St Fayetteville (28301) *(G-5760)*

American Physcl SEC Group LLC 919 363-1894
  1030 Goodworth Dr Apex (27539) *(G-159)*

American Plastic Inc 828 652-3511
  136 W Marion Business Park Marion (28752) *(G-10139)*

American Plush Tex Mills LLC 765 609-0456
  213 S Edinborough St Red Springs (28377) *(G-13495)*

American Power Products, Denver Also Called: Group 6 Holdings Inc *(G-4779)*

American Pride Inc 828 697-8847
  135 Sugarloaf Rd Hendersonville (28792) *(G-7818)*

American Printers Inc 252 977-7468
  120 Sorsbys Aly Rocky Mount (27804) *(G-13681)*

American Printing Co Inc 336 852-9894
  600c Edwardia Dr Greensboro (27409) *(G-6801)*

American Printing Services 336 465-0199
  3048 Whippoorwill Dr Asheboro (27205) *(G-401)*

American Prosthetics 704 782-0908
  Concord (28026) *(G-4194)*

American Quality Foods, Mills River Also Called: Dover Foods Inc *(G-10502)*

American Racg Hders Exhust Inc 631 608-1986
  120 Riverstone Dr Stanfield (28163) *(G-14674)*

American Rewinding Co, Monroe Also Called: American Rewinding Nc Inc *(G-10642)*

American Rewinding Nc Inc 704 289-4177
  1825 N Rocky River Rd Monroe (28110) *(G-10642)*

American Rewinding of NC Inc 704 589-1020
  1825 N Rocky River Rd Monroe (28110) *(G-10643)*

American Ripener LLC 704 527-8813
  803 Pressley Rd Ste 106 Charlotte (28217) *(G-2183)*

American Rnovation Systems LLC 336 313-6210
  208 Bell Dr Thomasville (27360) *(G-15185)*

American Roller Bearing Co, Hickory Also Called: Ltlb Holding Company *(G-8089)*

American Roller Bearing Inc 828 624-1460
  1095 Mcclain Rd Hiddenite (28636) *(G-8213)*

American Roller Bearing Inc (HQ) 828 624-1460
  307 Burke Dr Morganton (28655) *(G-11197)*

American Safety Utility Corp 704 482-0601
  529 Caleb Rd Shelby (28152) *(G-14285)*

American Sample House Inc 704 276-1970
  2105 Cat Square Rd Vale (28168) *(G-15463)*

American Scale Company LLC 704 921-4556
  7231 Covecreek Dr Charlotte (28215) *(G-2184)*

American Sign, Greensboro Also Called: Syd Inc *(G-7383)*

American Sign Shop, Charlotte Also Called: American Sign Shop Inc *(G-2185)*

American Sign Shop Inc 704 527-6100
  2440 Whitehall Park Dr Ste 100 Charlotte (28273) *(G-2185)*

American Signs By Tomorrow 910 484-2313
  425 W Russell St Fayetteville (28301) *(G-5761)*

American Silk Mills LLC (PA) 570 822-7147
  329 S Wrenn St Ste 101 High Point (27260) *(G-8248)*

American Skin, Burgaw Also Called: Skin Boys LLC *(G-1350)*

American Skin Food Group LLC 910 259-2232
  140 Industrial Dr Burgaw (28425) *(G-1332)*

American Snuff Company LLC 336 768-4630
  2415 S Stratford Rd Winston Salem (27103) *(G-16603)*

American Soil and Mulch Inc   **ALPHABETIC SECTION**

American Soil and Mulch Inc... 919 460-1349
   1109 Athens Dr Raleigh (27606) *(G-12499)*

American Solutions For Bu... 919 848-2442
   9201 Leesville Rd Ste 120 Raleigh (27613) *(G-12500)*

American Speedy Printing, Asheville *Also Called: Greybeard Printing Inc (G-644)*

American Speedy Printing, Hickory *Also Called: American Speedy Printing Ctrs (G-7934)*

American Speedy Printing Ctrs.. 828 322-3981
   337 Main Ave Ne Hickory (28601) *(G-7934)*

American Sports Lighting Inc... 910 520-1074
   8713 Champion Hills Dr Wilmington (28411) *(G-16110)*

American Sprinkle Co Inc.. 800 408-6708
   11240 Rivers Edge Rd Pineville (28134) *(G-12253)*

American Stainless Tubing LLC.. 704 878-8823
   129 Honeycutt Rd Troutman (28166) *(G-15366)*

American Stone Company... 919 929-7131
   1807 Nc Highway 54 W Chapel Hill (27516) *(G-1983)*

American Tchncal Solutions Inc... 336 595-2763
   4790 Walkertown Plaza Blvd Walkertown (27051) *(G-15613)*

American Tops Inc... 828 397-4910
   8968 Dietz Ave Hildebran (28637) *(G-8619)*

American Trayd, Wilmington *Also Called: Sherri Gossett (G-16403)*

American Truetzschler, Charlotte *Also Called: American Trutzschler Inc (G-2187)*

American Trutzschler Inc.. 704 399-4521
   5315 Heavy Equipment School Rd Charlotte (28214) *(G-2186)*

American Trutzschler Inc (PA)... 704 399-4521
   12300 Moores Chapel Rd Charlotte (28214) *(G-2187)*

American Urns.. 828 994-4239
   908 7th Ave Sw Conover (28613) *(G-4414)*

American Valve Inc (PA)... 336 668-0554
   4321 Piedmont Pkwy Greensboro (27410) *(G-6802)*

American Water Graphics Inc.. 828 247-0700
   317 Vance St Forest City (28043) *(G-6058)*

American Wdwrkery Bnjmin Htchi.. 910 302-5678
   3617 Clinton Rd Fayetteville (28312) *(G-5762)*

American Webbing Fittings Inc... 336 767-9390
   4959 Home Rd Winston Salem (27106) *(G-16604)*

American Welding & Gas Inc (PA)... 984 222-2600
   4900 Falls Of Neuse Rd Ste 150 Raleigh (27609) *(G-12501)*

American Wick Drain Corp.. 704 296-5801
   1209 Airport Rd Monroe (28110) *(G-10644)*

American Wood Reface Inc.. 704 577-2948
   509 Jim Parker Rd Monroe (28110) *(G-10645)*

American Wood Reface of Triad... 336 345-2837
   5339 Valleydale Rd Kernersville (27284) *(G-9164)*

American Woodmark Corporation.. 704 947-3280
   9825 Northcross Center Ct Ste N Huntersville (28078) *(G-8790)*

American Woodmark Corporation.. 540 665-9100
   300 S Henry St Stoneville (27048) *(G-14953)*

American Woodworkery Inc... 910 916-8098
   802 Bladen Cir Fayetteville (28312) *(G-5763)*

American Yarn LLC... 919 614-1542
   1305 Graham St Burlington (27217) *(G-1365)*

Americap Co Inc.. 252 445-2388
   276 Daniels Bridge Rd Enfield (27823) *(G-5675)*

Americh Corporation... 704 588-3075
   10700 John Price Rd Charlotte (28273) *(G-2188)*

Americhem Inc.. 704 782-6411
   723 Commerce Dr Concord (28025) *(G-4195)*

Amerifab International Inc... 336 882-9010
   203 Feld Ave High Point (27263) *(G-8249)*

Amerikrate, Lincolnton *Also Called: American Converting Co Ltd LLC (G-9871)*

Ameritech Die & Mold Inc.. 704 664-0801
   107 Knob Hill Rd Mooresville (28117) *(G-10857)*

Ameritech Die & Mold South Inc (PA).................................... 704 664-0801
   107 Knob Hill Rd Mooresville (28117) *(G-10858)*

Ameritek, Greensboro *Also Called: Ameritek Lasercut Dies Inc (G-6805)*

Ameritek Inc... 336 292-1165
   118 S Walnut Cir Greensboro (27409) *(G-6803)*

Ameritek Inc... 336 292-1165
   122 S Walnut Cir Ste B Greensboro (27409) *(G-6804)*

Ameritek Lasercut Dies Inc.. 336 292-1165
   122 S Walnut Cir Ste B Greensboro (27409) *(G-6805)*

Amerochem Corporation... 252 634-9344
   1885 Old Airport Rd New Bern (28562) *(G-11770)*

Amerock LLC (DH).. 800 435-6959
   10115 Kincey Ave Ste 210 Huntersville (28078) *(G-8791)*

Ames Copper Group LLC... 860 622-7626
   125 Old Boiling Springs Rd Shelby (28152) *(G-14286)*

Amesbury Acqstion Hldngs 2 Inc (HQ).................................... 704 924-8586
   2061 Sherrill Dr Statesville (28625) *(G-14747)*

Amesbury Group Inc... 704 978-2883
   125 Amesbury Truth Dr Statesville (28625) *(G-14748)*

Amesbury Group Inc... 704 924-7694
   1920 Flintstone Dr Statesville (28677) *(G-14749)*

Amesbury Industries Inc.. 704 978-3250
   125 Amesbury Truth Dr Statesville (28625) *(G-14750)*

Ametek Electronics Systems.. 800 645-9721
   8001 Knightdale Blvd Ste 121 Knightdale (27545) *(G-9411)*

Ametek Rtron Technical Mtr Div, Whitsett *Also Called: Rotron Incorporated (G-16001)*

Amethyst Pencil LLC.. 919 280-9025
   254 Northlands Dr Cary (27519) *(G-1680)*

AMF Automation Tech LLC... 919 288-1523
   2815 Carolina Commerce Dr Goldsboro (27530) *(G-6589)*

AMF Custom Upholstery, Lincolnton *Also Called: Moores Upholstering Interiors (G-9909)*

AMF-NC Enterprise Company LLC.. 704 489-2206
   3570 Denver Dr Denver (28037) *(G-4760)*

AMG Casework LLC... 919 462-9203
   10315 Chapel Hill Rd Morrisville (27560) *(G-11286)*

Amiad Filtration Systems Ltd (PA).. 805 377-0288
   120 Talbert Rd Ste J Mooresville (28117) *(G-10859)*

Amiad USA Inc (DH).. 704 662-3133
   120 Talbert Rd Ste J Mooresville (28117) *(G-10860)*

Amiad Water Systems, Mooresville *Also Called: Amiad Filtration Systems Ltd (G-10859)*

Amidon Ballistic Concrete, Cary *Also Called: 360 Ballistics LLC (G-1670)*

Amika LLC.. 984 664-9804
   5000 Centre Green Way Cary (27513) *(G-1681)*

Amish Barns, Durham *Also Called: RTO Services LLC (G-5335)*

Amish Lights Candles... 330 546-3900
   226 Kendra Dr Sw Concord (28025) *(G-4196)*

Amko Express Inc.. 336 434-7192
   10167 N Main St Archdale (27263) *(G-266)*

Amkor Technology Inc.. 919 248-1800
   3021 Cornwallis Rd Durham (27709) *(G-4916)*

Amoco, Pineville *Also Called: American Moistening Co Inc (G-12252)*

Amor Furniture, Liberty *Also Called: Amor Furniture and Bedding LLC (G-9806)*

Amor Furniture and Bedding LLC.. 336 795-0044
   143 S Asheboro St Liberty (27298) *(G-9806)*

AMP Agency.. 704 430-2313
   6220 Hudspeth Rd Harrisburg (28075) *(G-7701)*

AMP Pros LLC.. 910 315-1620
   105 Stornoway Dr Southern Pines (28387) *(G-14526)*

Amp-Cherokee Envmtl Solutions, Angier *Also Called: Cherokee Instruments Inc (G-137)*

Ampac Machinery LLC.. 919 596-5320
   319 Us 70 Service Rd Durham (27703) *(G-4917)*

Amped, Greensboro *Also Called: Amplified Elctronic Design Inc (G-6806)*

Amped Events LLC... 888 683-4386
   401 S Marietta St Gastonia (28052) *(G-6348)*

Amphenol Antenna Solutions... 828 324-6971
   1123 Industrial Dr Sw Conover (28613) *(G-4415)*

Amphenol Procom Inc... 888 262-7542
   1123 Industrial Dr Sw Conover (28613) *(G-4416)*

Amplate Inc... 704 607-0191
   7820 Tyner St Charlotte (28262) *(G-2189)*

Amplified Elctronic Design Inc... 336 223-4811
   7617 Boeing Dr Greensboro (27409) *(G-6806)*

AMR Systems LLC... 704 980-9072
   13850 Balntyn Corp Pl # 500 Charlotte (28277) *(G-2190)*

Amrep Inc (DH)... 909 923-0430
   6525 Morrison Blvd Ste 300 Charlotte (28211) *(G-2191)*

Amrep Inc.. 704 949-2595
   1405 Julian Rd Salisbury (28146) *(G-13921)*

AMS, Raleigh *Also Called: AMS USA Inc (G-12502)*

ALPHABETIC SECTION — Anns House of Nuts

AMS Software Inc 919 570-6001
2012 S Main St Wake Forest (27587) *(G-15527)*

AMS USA Inc 919 755-2889
353 E Six Forks Rd Ste 250 Raleigh (27609) *(G-12502)*

Amsted Industries Incorporated 704 226-5243
4515 Corporate Dr Monroe (28110) *(G-10646)*

Amt 617 549-4395
113 Sunrise Center Dr Thomasville (27360) *(G-15186)*

Amt Datasouth Corp 704 523-8500
5033 Sirona Dr Ste 800 Charlotte (28273) *(G-2192)*

Amt/Bcu Inc 336 622-6200
6306 Old 421 Rd Liberty (27298) *(G-9807)*

Amtai Medical Equipment Inc 919 872-1803
5605 Primavera Ct Raleigh (27616) *(G-12503)*

Amware Pallet Services LLC 919 207-2403
1700 Chicopee Rd Benson (27504) *(G-1030)*

Amy Smith 828 352-1001
100 Club Dr Ste 270 Burnsville (28714) *(G-1522)*

Amys Custom Canvas 910 713-8481
4677 Southgate Blvd Se Southport (28461) *(G-14564)*

Ana Gizzi 908 334-8733
124 Hatfield Rd Statesville (28625) *(G-14751)*

Ana Muf Corporation 336 653-3509
2530 Nc Highway 49 N Ramseur (27316) *(G-13439)*

Analog Devices Inc 336 202-6503
4001 Nc Hwy 54 Ste 3100 Durham (27709) *(G-4918)*

Analog Devices Inc 336 668-9511
7910 Triad Center Dr Greensboro (27409) *(G-6807)*

Analog Devices Inc 919 831-2790
223 S West St Ste 1400 Raleigh (27603) *(G-12504)*

Anatech, Durham *Also Called: Cancer Diagnostics Inc (G-4997)*

Anatech Ltd (PA) 704 489-1488
771 Crosspoint Dr Denver (28037) *(G-4761)*

Anav Yofi Inc 828 217-7746
1501 Majestic Meadow Dr Charlotte (28216) *(G-2193)*

Anchor Coffee Co Inc 336 265-7458
313b 9th St Ste 1 North Wilkesboro (28659) *(G-11997)*

Anchor Coffee Co., North Wilkesboro *Also Called: Anchor Coffee Co Inc (G-11997)*

Anchor Coupling Inc 919 739-8000
106 Industry Ct Goldsboro (27530) *(G-6590)*

Anchor Richey E V S, Taylorsville *Also Called: Anchor-Richey Emergency Vehicl (G-15129)*

Anchor Welding LLC 919 747-1926
1310 Bristoe Dr Apt 201 Knightdale (27545) *(G-9412)*

Anchor-Richey Emergency Vehicl 828 495-8145
241 Advent Church Rd Taylorsville (28681) *(G-15129)*

Anchored Home Inc 910 769-7092
1930 Oleander Dr Wilmington (28403) *(G-16111)*

Anchored Scents LLC 910 709-1582
2842 Cresset Dr Winterville (28590) *(G-16994)*

Ancient Mariner Inc 704 635-7911
1402 Walkup Ave Monroe (28110) *(G-10647)*

Andark Graphics Inc 704 882-1400
7204 Stinson Hartis Rd Ste A Indian Trail (28079) *(G-8919)*

Anders Custom Cabinetry 828 342-4222
540 Terrell Rd Franklin (28734) *(G-6115)*

Anders Natural Soap Co Inc 919 678-9393
1943 Evans Rd Cary (27513) *(G-1682)*

Andersen Energy Inc 336 376-0107
3151 Caroline Dr Haw River (27258) *(G-7749)*

Andersen Products, Haw River *Also Called: Andersen Sterilizers Inc (G-7751)*

Andersen Products Inc 336 376-3000
3202 Caroline Dr Haw River (27258) *(G-7750)*

Andersen Sterilizers Inc 336 376-8622
3202 Caroline Dr Haw River (27258) *(G-7751)*

Anderson Designs 919 489-1514
3406 Westover Rd Durham (27707) *(G-4919)*

Anderson Living Center LLC 828 229-3243
390 Hardin Rd Forest City (28043) *(G-6059)*

Anderson Truss Company Inc 252 746-7726
4825 Anderson Truss Rd Ayden (28513) *(G-847)*

Andrea Hurst and Assoc LLC 916 743-1846
1424 Cane Creek Dr Garner (27529) *(G-6254)*

Andrea L Grizzle 252 202-3278
101 Trinity Ln Box 751 Moyock (27958) *(G-11691)*

Andreani USA Inc 828 435-0125
137 E Central St Hendersonville (28792) *(G-7819)*

Andrew Bates 252 413-6988
3161 Mills Rd Greenville (27858) *(G-7482)*

Andrew Pearson Design, Mount Airy *Also Called: Easyglass Inc (G-11505)*

Andrews Graphics LLC 252 633-3199
3731 Trent Rd New Bern (28562) *(G-11771)*

Andrews Industries LLC 919 266-9656
1700 Rocky Falls Ct Raleigh (27610) *(G-12505)*

Andrews Products Inc 704 785-9715
7168 Weddington Rd Nw Concord (28027) *(G-4197)*

Andrews Truss Inc 828 321-3105
47 Mcclelland Creek Rd Andrews (28901) *(G-124)*

Andrews Violinist 910 458-1226
546 Anchor Way Kure Beach (28449) *(G-9436)*

Andritz Fabrics and Rolls Inc (HQ) 919 526-1400
8521 Six Forks Rd Raleigh (27615) *(G-12506)*

Andritz Fabrics and Rolls Inc 919 556-7235
51 Flex Way Youngsville (27596) *(G-17067)*

Andronics Construction Inc 704 400-9562
110 Business Park Dr Indian Trail (28079) *(G-8920)*

Andronx, Indian Trail *Also Called: Andronics Construction Inc (G-8920)*

Andy Maylish Fabrication Inc 704 785-1491
5384 Stone Henge Dr Denver (28037) *(G-4762)*

Andy-OXY Co Inc (PA) 828 258-0271
27 Heritage Dr Asheville (28806) *(G-518)*

Anelleo Inc 919 448-4008
519 Dairy Glen Rd Chapel Hill (27516) *(G-1984)*

Anew Look Homes LLC 800 796-5152
1717 Highland Ave Ne Ste 102 Hickory (28601) *(G-7935)*

Angel Industries Inc 919 264-0765
905 Capital Blvd Raleigh (27603) *(G-12507)*

Angel Kardees Publishing 336 983-0600
7509 Meadowgreen Ct Tobaccoville (27050) *(G-15316)*

Angel Tree Publishing 704 454-7604
8378 Pompano Rd Harrisburg (28075) *(G-7702)*

Angell Crafted Cabinetry 336 655-7735
1070 Reich Dr Germanton (27019) *(G-6550)*

Angels Path Ventures Inc 828 654-9530
21 Commerce Way Arden (28704) *(G-309)*

Anglers Marine NC 919 585-7900
13578 Us 70 Business Hwy W Clayton (27520) *(G-3953)*

Angstrom Medica Inc 781 933-6121
1800 N Greene St Ste A Greenville (27834) *(G-7483)*

Angunique 336 392-5866
6190 Pine Cove Ct Greensboro (27410) *(G-6808)*

Angus Fire, Angier *Also Called: National Foam Inc (G-147)*

Angus Fire, Angier *Also Called: National Foam Inc (G-148)*

Anheuser-Busch, Charlotte *Also Called: Anheuser-Busch LLC (G-2194)*

Anheuser-Busch LLC 704 321-9319
11325 N Community House Rd Charlotte (28277) *(G-2194)*

Anilox Roll Company Inc (PA) 704 588-1809
10955 Withers Cove Park Dr Charlotte (28278) *(G-2195)*

Animal Supply House, Hendersonville *Also Called: L & B Jandrew Enterprises (G-7871)*

Anitas Marketing Concepts Inc 252 243-3993
437 Ward Blvd Unit B Wilson (27893) *(G-16465)*

Annaline LLC 828 505-7115
12 White Ash Dr Asheville (28803) *(G-519)*

Annas Machine Shop Inc 828 754-4184
1751 Main St Nw Lenoir (28645) *(G-9573)*

Anndori Outdoor Art LLC 336 202-8400
4001 Hickory Tree Ln Greensboro (27405) *(G-6809)*

Annes Books and Papers 336 608-8612
632 Laurel St Winston Salem (27101) *(G-16605)*

Annette Cameron 828 505-0404
60 Holland St Asheville (28801) *(G-520)*

Annihilare Medical Systems Inc 855 545-5677
311 Motz Ave # E Lincolnton (28092) *(G-9872)*

Anns House of Nuts 252 795-6500
1159 Robersonville Products Rd Robersonville (27871) *(G-13614)*

ALPHABETIC SECTION

Another Creation By Lady J..919 334-9797
7636 Silver View Ln Raleigh (27613) *(G-12508)*

Ansgar Industrial LLC (PA)..704 962-5249
6000 Fairview Rd Ste 1200 Charlotte (28210) *(G-2196)*

Anson County Water Treatment, Lilesville *Also Called: County of Anson (G-9836)*

Anson Express..704 694-2480
205 W Morgan St Wadesboro (28170) *(G-15500)*

Anson Machine Works Inc..704 272-7657
505 Hwy 74 Polkton (28135) *(G-12384)*

Anson Machine Works Inc..704 272-7657
100 Efird Cir Polkton (28135) *(G-12385)*

Anson Wood Products..704 694-5390
Parsons St Wadesboro (28170) *(G-15501)*

Ansonville Piping & Fabg Inc..704 826-8403
122 Ansonville Polkton Rd Ansonville (28007) *(G-152)*

Anthem Displays LLC..910 746-8988
518 Ben Greene Industrial Park Rd Elizabethtown (28337) *(G-5583)*

Anthem Displays LLC..910 862-3550
113 W Broad St Elizabethtown (28337) *(G-5584)*

Anthology of Poetry Inc..336 626-7762
307 E Salisbury St Asheboro (27203) *(G-402)*

Anthony Alexander Prints Inc..704 870-7213
834 Harrier Rd Charlotte (28216) *(G-2197)*

Anthony B Andrews Logging Inc..252 448-8901
1000 Phillps Rd Trenton (28585) *(G-15332)*

Anthony Demaria Labs Inc..845 255-4695
122 Windbyrne Dr Cary (27513) *(G-1683)*

Anthony Fabrication..704 658-1519
254 Rolling Hill Rd Mooresville (28117) *(G-10861)*

Antkar LLC..919 322-4100
2831 Jones Franklin Rd Raleigh (27606) *(G-12509)*

Antler and Oak Joinery LLC..845 505-6185
6436 Cape Charles Dr Raleigh (27617) *(G-12510)*

Anuma Aerospace LLC..919 600-0142
720 Pebblebrook Dr Raleigh (27609) *(G-12511)*

Anutra Medical Inc..919 648-1215
1000 Perimeter Park Dr Ste E Morrisville (27560) *(G-11287)*

Anuva, Morrisville *Also Called: Anuva Services Inc (G-11288)*

Anuva Services Inc..919 468-6441
140 Southcenter Ct Ste 600 Morrisville (27560) *(G-11288)*

Anything Overstock..828 572-2157
2135 Arrowhead Ln Lenoir (28645) *(G-9574)*

Ao Smith Chatlotte..704 597-8910
4302 Raleigh St Charlotte (28213) *(G-2198)*

Aoa Signs Inc..336 679-3344
2707 Wooten Blvd Sw Wilson (27893) *(G-16466)*

AP Emissions Technologies LLC..919 580-2000
300 Dixie Trl Goldsboro (27530) *(G-6591)*

AP Granite Installation LLC..919 215-1795
2213 Stephanie Ln Clayton (27520) *(G-3954)*

AP Solutions, Cary *Also Called: Atmosphric Plsma Solutions Inc (G-1693)*

AP&t North America Inc..704 292-2900
4817 Persimmon Ct Monroe (28110) *(G-10648)*

APAC, Concord *Also Called: Barnhill Contracting Company (G-4204)*

APAC, Greenville *Also Called: Barnhill Contracting Company (G-7493)*

APAC, Raleigh *Also Called: Apac-Atlantic Inc (G-12512)*

Apac-Atlantic Inc (DH)..336 412-6800
2626 Glenwood Ave Ste 550 Raleigh (27608) *(G-12512)*

Apb Wrecker Service LLC..704 400-0857
114 E 28th St Charlotte (28206) *(G-2199)*

Apc LLC..919 965-2051
1451 W Noble St Selma (27576) *(G-14252)*

APD, Charlotte *Also Called: Appalachian Pipe Distrs LLC (G-2202)*

Apergy Artfl Lift Intl LLC..919 934-1533
3250 Us Highway 70 Bus E Smithfield (27577) *(G-14449)*

Apex, Pollocksville *Also Called: Advanced Plastic Extrusion LLC (G-12391)*

Apex Analytix LLC (HQ)..336 272-4669
1501 Highwoods Blvd Ste 200 Greensboro (27410) *(G-6810)*

Apex Embroidery Inc..919 793-6083
996 Ambergate Sta Apex (27502) *(G-160)*

Apex Facility and Dist Ctr, Apex *Also Called: Apex Tool Group LLC (G-164)*

Apex Industrial Group LLC..919 578-9039
2903 Lee Ave Sanford (27332) *(G-14086)*

Apex Instruments Incorporated..919 557-7300
204 Technology Park Ln Fuquay Varina (27526) *(G-6179)*

Apex Manufacturing Facility, Apex *Also Called: Bioresource International Inc (G-171)*

Apex Marble and Granite Inc..919 462-9202
10315b Chapel Hill Rd Morrisville (27560) *(G-11289)*

Apex Packaging Corporation LLC..704 847-7274
15105 John J Delaney Dr Charlotte (28277) *(G-2200)*

Apex Plant, Apex *Also Called: Eagle Rock Concrete LLC (G-186)*

Apex Printing Company..919 362-9856
514 E Williams St Apex (27502) *(G-161)*

Apex Publishing LLC..919 886-7153
3434 Edwards Mill Rd Ste 112 Raleigh (27612) *(G-12513)*

Apex Salsa Company..919 363-1486
912 N York Ct Apex (27502) *(G-162)*

Apex Skip-Its LLC..919 270-1752
1806 Keokuk Ct Apex (27523) *(G-163)*

Apex Steel Corp..919 362-6611
301 Petfinder Ln Raleigh (27603) *(G-12514)*

Apex Tool Group LLC..919 387-0099
1000 Lufkin Rd Apex (27539) *(G-164)*

Apex Tool Group LLC..410 773-7800
13620 Reese Blvrd Pkwy E Ste 410 Huntersville (28078) *(G-8792)*

Apex Waves LLC..919 809-5227
1624 Old Apex Rd Cary (27513) *(G-1684)*

Apex/Pittsboro Concrete Plant, Apex *Also Called: S T Wooten Corporation (G-240)*

Apg/East LLC..252 329-9500
1150 Sugg Pkwy Greenville (27834) *(G-7484)*

Apidae Prints..413 320-3839
601 Ramseur St Durham (27701) *(G-4920)*

Apjet Inc (PA)..919 595-5538
523 Davis Dr Ste 100 Morrisville (27560) *(G-11290)*

Aplix Inc (DH)..704 588-1920
12300 Steele Creek Rd Charlotte (28273) *(G-2201)*

Apollo By Mosack Group, Mint Hill *Also Called: Mosack Group LLC (G-10541)*

Apollo Chemical Corp..336 226-1161
2001 Willow Spring Ln Burlington (27215) *(G-1366)*

Apollo Designs, High Point *Also Called: Apollo Designs LLC (G-8250)*

Apollo Designs LLC (PA)..336 886-0260
2147 Brevard Rd High Point (27263) *(G-8250)*

Apollo Valves, Charlotte *Also Called: Aalberts Integrated Piping Systems Americas Inc (G-2121)*

Apollonias Candles Things LLC..910 408-2508
2112 Broad St Apt E8 Durham (27705) *(G-4921)*

Appalachian Arms Inc..828 332-1900
45 Davis Loop Hayesville (28904) *(G-7760)*

Appalachian Cabinet Inc..828 265-0830
7373 Old 421 S Deep Gap (28618) *(G-4708)*

Appalachian Getaways..828 243-3105
45 Pinedale Rd Asheville (28805) *(G-521)*

Appalachian Lumber, Wilkesboro *Also Called: Appalachian Lumber Company Inc (G-16013)*

Appalachian Lumber Company Inc (PA)..336 973-7205
5879 W Us Highway 421 Wilkesboro (28697) *(G-16013)*

Appalachian Mountain Brewery, Boone *Also Called: Craft Brew Alliance Inc (G-1188)*

Appalachian Pipe Distrs LLC..704 688-5703
828 East Blvd Charlotte (28203) *(G-2202)*

Appalachian Pubg Group Inc..828 505-3643
183 Edgewood Rd Asheville (28804) *(G-522)*

Appalachian State University..828 262-2047
169 Air Ln Boone (28608) *(G-1174)*

Appalachian State University..828 262-7497
525 Rivers St Rm 221 Boone (28608) *(G-1175)*

Appalachian Strings Inc..828 712-8721
1 Page Ave Ste 126 Asheville (28801) *(G-523)*

Appalachian Technology, Asheville *Also Called: Appalachian Technology LLC (G-524)*

Appalachian Technology LLC..828 210-8888
187 Elk Mountain Rd Asheville (28804) *(G-524)*

Appalachian Timber Company..828 507-6505
151 Posey Blanton Rd Sylva (28779) *(G-15052)*

Appalachian Tool & Machine Inc..828 669-0142
121 Lytle Cove Rd Swannanoa (28778) *(G-15017)*

ALPHABETIC SECTION

Appalachian Truss, Clayton *Also Called: Arboles NC Incorporated (G-3955)*

Appalchian Stove Fbrcators Inc.. 828 253-0164
329 Emma Rd Asheville (28806) *(G-525)*

Apparel USA Inc.. 212 869-5495
102 Trinity St Fairmont (28340) *(G-5700)*

Apperson Inc... 704 399-2571
2908 Stewart Creek Blvd Charlotte (28216) *(G-2203)*

Apple, Cary *Also Called: Apple Inc (G-1685)*

Apple Annie's Bake Shop, Wilmington *Also Called: Connectivity Group LLC (G-16177)*

Apple Baking Company Inc... 704 637-6800
4470 Hampton Rd Salisbury (28144) *(G-13922)*

Apple Branch Company... 910 859-8549
6029 Inland Greens Dr Wilmington (28405) *(G-16112)*

Apple Inc.. 516 318-6744
301 Metlife Way Cary (27513) *(G-1685)*

Apple Rock Advg & Prom Inc (PA)... 336 232-4800
7602 Business Park Dr Greensboro (27409) *(G-6811)*

Apple Rock Displays, Greensboro *Also Called: Apple Rock Advg & Prom Inc (G-6811)*

Apple Valley Cabin LLC... 828 513-1911
1609 Kanuga Rd Hendersonville (28739) *(G-7820)*

Applied Catheter Tech Inc... 336 817-1005
113 Thomas St Winston Salem (27101) *(G-16606)*

Applied Components Mfg LLC.. 828 323-8915
101 33rd Street Dr Se Hickory (28602) *(G-7936)*

Applied Components Mfg LLC.. 828 322-6535
415 19th St Sw Hickory (28602) *(G-7937)*

Applied Drives Inc.. 704 573-2324
11016 Tara Oaks Dr Charlotte (28227) *(G-2204)*

Applied Medical Tech Inc (PA)... 919 255-3220
1506 Ivac Way Creedmoor (27522) *(G-4605)*

Applied Nano Solutions Inc... 336 687-6517
106 Lake Dr Trinity (27370) *(G-15338)*

Applied Plastic Services Inc... 910 655-2156
5932 Old Lake Rd Bolton (28423) *(G-1167)*

Applied Strategies Inc.. 704 525-4478
1515 Mockingbird Ln Ste 700 Charlotte (28209) *(G-2205)*

Applied Technologies Group... 618 977-9872
19701 Bethel Church Rd Ste 103 Cornelius (28031) *(G-4521)*

Appointments, Tryon *Also Called: Tryon Newsmedia LLC (G-15430)*

Appsense, Cary *Also Called: Appsense Incorporated (G-1686)*

Appsense Incorporated... 919 666-0080
1100 Crescent Green Ste 206 Cary (27518) *(G-1686)*

Aprinnova LLC... 910 371-2234
2271 Andrew Jackson Hwy Ne Leland (28451) *(G-9526)*

Aprotech Powertrain LLC... 828 253-1350
31 Adams Hill Rd Asheville (28806) *(G-526)*

APS Hickory.. 828 323-1010
1257 25th Street Pl Se Hickory (28602) *(G-7938)*

APT Industries Inc... 704 598-9100
601 E Sugar Creek Rd Charlotte (28213) *(G-2206)*

Aptargroup Inc... 828 970-6300
3300 Finger Mill Rd Lincolnton (28092) *(G-9873)*

APV Heat Exchanger PDT Group, Goldsboro *Also Called: SPX Flow Us LLC (G-6660)*

Aqua 10 Corporation.. 252 726-5421
5112 Midyette Ave Morehead City (28557) *(G-11149)*

Aqua Analytica Press Inc... 336 263-6612
1024 Laceflower Dr Durham (27713) *(G-4922)*

Aqua Blue Inc.. 704 896-9007
9624 Bailey Rd Ste 270 Cornelius (28031) *(G-4522)*

Aqua Doc Pool Sparkling S... 828 231-9398
30a Shamrock Ln Waynesville (28786) *(G-15793)*

Aqua Logic Inc.. 858 292-4773
2806 Gray Fox Rd Monroe (28110) *(G-10649)*

Aqua Plastics Inc.. 828 324-6284
1474 17th St Ne Hickory (28601) *(G-7939)*

Aqua-Matic, Raleigh *Also Called: Captive-Aire Systems Inc (G-12593)*

Aquadale Query... 704 474-3165
12423 Old Aquadale Rd Norwood (28128) *(G-12036)*

Aquafil OMara Inc.. 828 874-2100
160 Fashion Ave Rutherford College (28671) *(G-13858)*

Aquahut.. 704 335-8554
600 Morris St Charlotte (28202) *(G-2207)*

Aquapro Solutions LLC... 828 255-0772
46 New Leicester Hwy Ste 102 Asheville (28806) *(G-527)*

Aquarius Designs & Logo Wear... 919 821-4646
4429 Beryl Rd Raleigh (27606) *(G-12515)*

Aquatic Pressure Washing.. 910 232-3273
6534 English Oaks Dr Raleigh (27615) *(G-12516)*

Aqwa Inc... 252 243-7693
2604 Willis Ct N Wilson (27896) *(G-16467)*

AR Corp.. 910 763-8530
7639 Myrtle Grove Rd Wilmington (28409) *(G-16113)*

AR Workshop Greensboro, Greensboro *Also Called: G & G Management LLC (G-7027)*

Arauco - NA... 910 569-7020
157 Atc Dr Biscoe (27209) *(G-1103)*

Arauco North America Inc.. 919 542-2128
985 Corinth Rd Moncure (27559) *(G-10613)*

Arba LLC... 302 946-0079
525 N Tryon St Ste 1600 Charlotte (28202) *(G-2208)*

Arboles NC Incorporated.. 828 675-4882
228 Sicily Dr Clayton (27527) *(G-3955)*

Arbon Equipment Corporation... 414 355-2600
14100 S Lakes Dr Charlotte (28273) *(G-2209)*

Arbor Organic Technologies LLC... 704 276-7100
107 Technolgy Dr Lincolnton (28092) *(G-9874)*

Arbor Pharmaceuticals Inc... 919 792-1700
5511 Capital Center Dr Ste 224 Raleigh (27606) *(G-12517)*

ARC Steel Fabrication LLC.. 980 533-8302
649 Bess Town Rd Bessemer City (28016) *(G-1052)*

ARC West, Charlotte *Also Called: Anilox Roll Company Inc (G-2195)*

ARC Woodworking.. 828 863-4994
84 Brewery Ln Tryon (28782) *(G-15421)*

Arc3 Gases Inc (PA).. 910 892-4016
1600 Us-301 S Dunn (28334) *(G-4851)*

Arc3 Gases Inc... 336 275-3333
810 Post St Greensboro (27405) *(G-6812)*

Arc3 Gases Inc... 704 220-1029
2411 Nelda Dr Monroe (28110) *(G-10650)*

Arcadia Beverage, Arden *Also Called: Arcadia Beverage LLC (G-310)*

Arcadia Beverage LLC (PA)... 828 684-3556
34 Arcadia Farms Rd Arden (28704) *(G-310)*

Arcadia Farms LLC.. 828 684-3556
34 Arcadia Farms Rd Arden (28704) *(G-311)*

Archangel Arms LLC.. 984 235-2536
3405 Banks Rd Raleigh (27603) *(G-12518)*

Archdale Furniture Distributor... 336 431-1081
112 Englewood Dr Archdale (27263) *(G-267)*

Archdale Millworks Inc.. 336 431-9019
1204 Corporation Dr Archdale (27263) *(G-268)*

Archdale Printing Company Inc... 336 884-5312
1316 Trinity Ave High Point (27260) *(G-8251)*

Archdale Trinity News, High Point *Also Called: High Point Enterprise Inc (G-8387)*

Archer Advanced Rbr Components, Winston Salem *Also Called: Maranz Inc (G-16799)*

Archer Box Company.. 336 788-1910
685 Kingsbury Cir Winston Salem (27106) *(G-16607)*

Archer-Daniels-Midland Company.. 704 332-3165
620 W 10th St Charlotte (28202) *(G-2210)*

Archer-Daniels-Midland Company.. 910 457-5011
1730 E Moore St Southport (28461) *(G-14565)*

Archie S Steel Service Inc... 252 355-5007
4575 Us Highway 13 S Greenville (27834) *(G-7485)*

Archie Supply LLC (PA)... 336 987-0895
5939 W Friendly Ave Apt 51k Greensboro (27410) *(G-6813)*

Archivesocial, Durham *Also Called: Archivesocial Inc (G-4923)*

Archivesocial Inc.. 888 558-6032
212 W Main St Ste 500 Durham (27701) *(G-4923)*

Archroma, Charlotte *Also Called: Archroma US Inc (G-2211)*

Archroma US Inc (DH)... 704 353-4100
5435 77 Center Dr Ste 10 Charlotte (28217) *(G-2211)*

Arclin USA LLC... 919 542-2526
790 Corinth Rd Moncure (27559) *(G-10614)*

Arcola Hardwood Company Inc.. 252 257-4484
2316 Nc Highway 43 Warrenton (27589) *(G-15654)*

Arcola Logging Co Inc 252 257-3205
134 Chip Capps Rd Macon (27551) *(G-10068)*

Arcola Lumber Company Inc 252 257-4923
2316 Nc Highway 43 Warrenton (27589) *(G-15655)*

Arcola Sawmill 252 257-1139
2316 Nc Highway 43 Warrenton (27589) *(G-15656)*

Arcona Leather Company LLC (PA) 828 396-7728
2615 Mission Rd Hudson (28638) *(G-8761)*

Arcright Welding Service, Fayetteville Also Called: Peter J Hamann *(G-5897)*

Arcus Medical LLC 704 332-3424
2401 Distribution St Ste B Charlotte (28203) *(G-2212)*

Ardagh, Winston Salem Also Called: Trivium Packaging USA Inc *(G-16953)*

Arden, Sanford Also Called: Arden Companies LLC *(G-14087)*

Arden Companies, Sanford Also Called: Arden Companies LLC *(G-14088)*

Arden Companies LLC 919 258-3081
1611 Broadway Rd Sanford (27332) *(G-14087)*

Arden Companies LLC 919 258-3081
1611 Broadway Rd Sanford (27332) *(G-14088)*

Arden Engraving US Inc 704 547-4581
100 Forsyth Hall Dr Charlotte (28273) *(G-2213)*

Are Management LLC 336 855-7800
1420 Lorraine Ave High Point (27263) *(G-8252)*

Area 51 Powder Coating Inc 910 769-1724
2721 Old Wrightsboro Rd Wilmington (28405) *(G-16114)*

Arenas Tires 828 962-9422
128 15th St Se Hickory (28602) *(G-7940)*

Areteia Therapeutics Inc 973 985-0597
101 Glen Lennox Dr Chapel Hill (27517) *(G-1985)*

Areva 704 805-2935
11515 Vanstory Dr Ste 140 Huntersville (28078) *(G-8793)*

Argos Ready Mix, Raleigh Also Called: Argos USA LLC *(G-12522)*

Argos Ready Mix, Wilmington Also Called: Argos USA LLC *(G-16115)*

Argos Ready Mix, Wilmington Also Called: Argos USA LLC *(G-16116)*

Argos Ready Mix (carolinas) Corp 919 790-1520
3610 Bush St Raleigh (27609) *(G-12519)*

Argos USA 336 784-5181
1590 Williamson St Winston Salem (27107) *(G-16608)*

Argos USA LLC 919 942-0381
219 Guthrie Ave Carrboro (27510) *(G-1644)*

Argos USA LLC 910 675-1262
5225 Holly Shelter Rd Castle Hayne (28429) *(G-1943)*

Argos USA LLC 704 679-9431
325 E Hebron St Charlotte (28273) *(G-2214)*

Argos USA LLC 910 299-5046
3095 Turkey Hwy Clinton (28328) *(G-4088)*

Argos USA LLC 704 483-4013
4451 N Nc 16 Business Hwy Denver (28037) *(G-4763)*

Argos USA LLC 910 892-3188
401 N Fayetteville Ave Dunn (28334) *(G-4852)*

Argos USA LLC 919 552-2294
1506 Holland Rd Fuquay Varina (27526) *(G-6180)*

Argos USA LLC 919 772-4188
1915 W Garner Rd Garner (27529) *(G-6255)*

Argos USA LLC 828 322-9325
2001 Main Ave Se Hickory (28602) *(G-7941)*

Argos USA LLC 336 841-3379
406 Tomlinson St High Point (27260) *(G-8253)*

Argos USA LLC 919 732-7509
411 Valley Forge Rd Hillsborough (27278) *(G-8634)*

Argos USA LLC 252 527-8008
3350 Nc Highway 11 N Kinston (28501) *(G-9343)*

Argos USA LLC 704 872-9566
Hwy 150 E Mooresville (28115) *(G-10862)*

Argos USA LLC 252 223-4348
247 Carl Garner Rd Newport (28570) *(G-11897)*

Argos USA LLC 919 828-3695
3200 Spring Forest Rd Ste 210 Raleigh (27616) *(G-12520)*

Argos USA LLC 919 775-5441
3200 Spring Forest Rd Ste 210 Raleigh (27616) *(G-12521)*

Argos USA LLC 919 790-1520
3200 Spring Forest Rd Ste 210 Raleigh (27616) *(G-12522)*

Argos USA LLC 252 443-5046
75 W 13th St Roanoke Rapids (27870) *(G-13566)*

Argos USA LLC 252 291-8888
6823 Bruce Rd Sims (27880) *(G-14439)*

Argos USA LLC 704 872-9566
2289 Salisbury Hwy Statesville (28677) *(G-14752)*

Argos USA LLC 919 554-2087
5025 Unicon Dr Wake Forest (27587) *(G-15528)*

Argos USA LLC 252 946-4704
1020 E 5th St Washington (27889) *(G-15682)*

Argos USA LLC 252 792-3148
741 Warren St Williamston (27892) *(G-16057)*

Argos USA LLC 910 686-4890
8871 Sidbury Rd Wilmington (28411) *(G-16115)*

Argos USA LLC 910 796-3469
800 Sunnyvale Dr Wilmington (28412) *(G-16116)*

Argos USA LLC 336 784-4888
1590 Williamson St Winston Salem (27107) *(G-16609)*

Argus Fire Control, Charlotte Also Called: Argus Fire CONtrol-Pf&s Inc *(G-2215)*

Argus Fire CONtrol-Pf&s Inc 704 372-1228
2723 Interstate St Charlotte (28208) *(G-2215)*

Arh, Stanfield Also Called: American Racg Hders Exhust Inc *(G-14674)*

Aria Designs LLC 828 572-4303
800 Hickory Blvd Sw Lenoir (28645) *(G-9575)*

Aribex Inc 866 340-5522
11727 Fruehauf Dr Charlotte (28273) *(G-2216)*

Arisaka, Apex Also Called: Arisaka LLC *(G-165)*

Arisaka LLC 919 601-5625
1600 Olive Chapel Rd Ste 260 Apex (27502) *(G-165)*

Ariston Hospitality Inc 626 458-8668
1581 Prospect St High Point (27260) *(G-8254)*

Aristos Pharmaceuticals Inc 919 678-6592
1255 Crescent Green Ste 250 Cary (27518) *(G-1687)*

Ark Inc 919 841-3637
555 Fayetteville St # 201 Raleigh (27601) *(G-12523)*

Ark Aviation Inc 336 379-0900
200 N Raleigh St Greensboro (27401) *(G-6814)*

Ark Shores, Raleigh Also Called: Ark Inc *(G-12523)*

Arkema Coating Resins, Cary Also Called: Arkema Inc *(G-1688)*

Arkema Inc 919 469-6700
410 Gregson Dr Cary (27511) *(G-1688)*

Arma Co LLC 717 295-6805
4557 Technology Dr Ste 4 Wilmington (28405) *(G-16117)*

Armac Inc 919 878-9836
4027 Atlantic Ave Raleigh (27604) *(G-12524)*

Armacell LLC (HQ) 919 913-0555
55 Vilcom Center Dr Ste 200 Chapel Hill (27514) *(G-1986)*

Armacell LLC 828 464-5880
1004 Keisler Rd Nw Conover (28613) *(G-4417)*

Armacell US Holdings LLC 919 304-3846
7600 Oakwood Street Ext Mebane (27302) *(G-10399)*

Armament Chimera 336 893-5639
6332 Cephis Dr Clemmons (27012) *(G-4026)*

Armen Stone LLC 743 228-3901
322 Fonville St Burlington (27217) *(G-1367)*

Armored Self Defense LLC 336 749-7556
519 Culpepper Ct Winston Salem (27104) *(G-16610)*

Armorri Cosmetics LLC 910 352-6209
5534 Sunlight Dr Apt 108 Durham (27707) *(G-4924)*

Arms & Hopie Dist & Sup, Greensboro Also Called: Joe Armstrong *(G-7138)*

Arms Race Nutrition LLC 888 978-2332
1415 Wilkesboro Hwy Statesville (28625) *(G-14753)*

Armtec Esterline Corp 910 814-3029
608 E Mcneill St Lillington (27546) *(G-9842)*

Arneg LLC 336 956-5300
750 Old Hargrave Rd Lexington (27295) *(G-9680)*

Arneg USA, Lexington Also Called: Arneg LLC *(G-9680)*

Arnold B Cochrane Inc 336 294-8038
3 Kenbridge Ct Greensboro (27410) *(G-6815)*

Arnold S Welding Service Inc (PA) 910 323-3822
1405 Waterless St Fayetteville (28306) *(G-5764)*

ALPHABETIC SECTION — Ascend Research Corp

Arnold-Wilbert Corporation (PA) 919 735-5008
1401 W Grantham St Goldsboro (27530) *(G-6592)*

Aromatherapy By Irene LLC 404 457-1871
27041 Hoffman Rd Marston (28363) *(G-10229)*

Around Campus Group, The, Durham Also Called: University Directories LLC *(G-5424)*

Around House Improvement LLC 919 496-7029
75 Gus Mcghee Rd Bunn (27508) *(G-1327)*

Arper USA (PA) 336 434-2376
660 Southwest St High Point (27260) *(G-8255)*

Arpro M-Tec LLC 828 433-0699
212 E Fleming Dr Morganton (28655) *(G-11198)*

Arrants Logging Inc 252 792-1889
3600 Jerden Thicket Rd Jamesville (27846) *(G-9077)*

Array Biopharma Inc 303 381-6600
3005 Carrington Mill Blvd Morrisville (27560) *(G-11291)*

Arris Global Services Inc 215 323-1000
1100 Commscope Pl Se Hickory (28602) *(G-7942)*

Arris Solutions LLC (DH) 678 473-2000
1100 Commscope Pl Se Hickory (28602) *(G-7943)*

Arris Solutions, Inc., Hickory Also Called: Arris Solutions LLC *(G-7943)*

Arris Technology Inc (DH) 678 473-2907
1100 Commscope Pl Se Hickory (28602) *(G-7944)*

Arrival Automotive USA Inc (DH) 415 439-2002
330 W Tremont Ave Charlotte (28203) *(G-2217)*

Arrivo Management LLC 919 460-9500
3000 Rdu Center Dr Morrisville (27560) *(G-11292)*

Arrochem Inc 704 827-0216
201 Westland Farm Rd Mount Holly (28120) *(G-11621)*

Arrow Educational Products Inc 910 521-0840
208 Union Chapel Rd 101 Pembroke (28372) *(G-12180)*

Arrow Equipment LLC (PA) 803 765-2040
9000 Statesville Rd Charlotte (28269) *(G-2218)*

Arrow Glazing Fabrication Inc 704 926-1509
6161 Mcdaniel Ln Charlotte (28213) *(G-2219)*

Arrowhead Graphics Inc 336 274-2419
508 Houston St Greensboro (27401) *(G-6816)*

Arrowood 3d Printing, Hendersonville Also Called: Arrowood Mechanical Design LLC *(G-7821)*

Arrowood Mechanical Design LLC 828 989-1605
104 Arrowood Ln Hendersonville (28791) *(G-7821)*

ARS Extreme Construction Inc 919 331-8024
175 Medical Dr Angier (27501) *(G-131)*

Art Enterprises Inc 828 277-1211
1156 Sweeten Creek Rd Asheville (28803) *(G-528)*

Art House 919 552-7327
3325 Air Park Rd Fuquay Varina (27526) *(G-6181)*

Art Press, Manteo Also Called: Arthur Demarest *(G-10126)*

Art Sign Co 919 596-8681
209 S Goley St Durham (27701) *(G-4925)*

Artcraft Press Inc 828 397-8612
7814 Old Hwy 10 Icard (28666) *(G-8916)*

Artcraft Sign Co 919 841-7686
205 N Louisburg Rd Spring Hope (27882) *(G-14612)*

Artcraft Tumblers 704 798-6115
3220 Old Union Church Rd Salisbury (28146) *(G-13923)*

Artech Graphics Inc 704 545-9804
176 Yadkin Falls Rd New London (28127) *(G-11866)*

Artesian Builds, Chapel Hill Also Called: Artesian Future Technology LLC *(G-1987)*

Artesian Future Technology LLC 919 904-4940
5801 Cascade Dr Chapel Hill (27514) *(G-1987)*

Artesias Swets Bnged By Dior L 704 794-3792
208 Church St Ne Ste 1 Concord (28025) *(G-4198)*

Artex Group Inc 866 845-1042
1004 Charlotte Hwy Fairview (28730) *(G-5706)*

Artful Shelter, Asheville Also Called: Southbridge Inc *(G-782)*

Arthur Demarest 252 473-1449
419 Skyco Rd Manteo (27954) *(G-10126)*

Arthur Woodworking 919 381-0329
1805 Vale St Durham (27703) *(G-4926)*

Artibis Corporation 919 592-4794
2474 Walnut St Ste 203 Cary (27518) *(G-1689)*

Artifex Inc 704 773-6942
3037 Silver Birch Dr Charlotte (28269) *(G-2220)*

Artificial Funhouse 919 423-4103
101 Cheshire Dr Hillsborough (27278) *(G-8635)*

Artisan LLC 855 582-3539
8620 Westmoreland Dr Nw Concord (28027) *(G-4199)*

Artisan Aromatics 800 456-6675
517 Jim Creek Rd Burnsville (28714) *(G-1523)*

Artisan Direct LLC 704 655-9100
18335 Old Statesville Rd Ste L Cornelius (28031) *(G-4523)*

Artisan Graphics, Cornelius Also Called: Artisan Signs and Graphics Inc *(G-4524)*

Artisan Leaf LLC 252 674-1223
2231 Nash St Nw Ste E Wilson (27896) *(G-16468)*

Artisan Signs and Graphics Inc 704 655-9100
18335 Old Statesville Rd Ste L Cornelius (28031) *(G-4524)*

Artisanal Brewing Ventures, Charlotte Also Called: Craft Revolution LLC *(G-2568)*

Artisans Guild Incorporated 336 841-4140
639 Mcway Dr Ste 101 High Point (27263) *(G-8256)*

Artist S Needle Inc 336 294-5884
2611 Phoenix Dr Greensboro (27406) *(G-6817)*

Artist Studio Project Pubg LLC 919 233-3873
5620 Millrace Trl Raleigh (27606) *(G-12525)*

Artistic Images Inc 704 332-6225
900 Remount Rd 920 Charlotte (28203) *(G-2221)*

Artistic Ironworks LLC 919 908-6888
700 E Club Blvd Ste B Durham (27704) *(G-4927)*

Artistic Kitchens & Baths LLC 910 692-4000
683 Sw Broad St Southern Pines (28387) *(G-14527)*

Artistic Quilting, High Point Also Called: Crawford Industries Inc *(G-8306)*

Artistic Southern Inc 919 861-4695
1108 Continental Blvd Charlotte (28273) *(G-2222)*

Artistic Woodworks Inc 828 459-0178
3748 Dericas Ct Claremont (28610) *(G-3902)*

Artwear Embroidery Inc (PA) 336 992-2166
621 Indeneer Dr Kernersville (27284) *(G-9165)*

Arva LLC 803 336-2230
9410 D Ducks Ln Charlotte (28273) *(G-2223)*

Arvinmeritor Automotive, Maxton Also Called: Meritor Inc *(G-10359)*

Arvinmeritor Hvy Vhcl Systems, Fletcher Also Called: Meritor Inc *(G-6024)*

ARW Optical Corp 910 452-7373
2021 Capital Dr Wilmington (28405) *(G-16118)*

Arysta Lifescience Inc 919 678-4900
15401 Weston Pkwy Ste 150 Cary (27513) *(G-1690)*

Arysta Lifescience N Amer LLC (HQ) 919 678-4900
15401 Weston Pkwy Ste 150 Cary (27513) *(G-1691)*

Arzberger Engravers Inc 704 376-1151
2518 Dunavant St Charlotte (28203) *(G-2224)*

As Inc 704 225-1700
1920 Tower Industrial Dr Monroe (28110) *(G-10651)*

As America Inc 704 398-4602
4500 Morris Field Dr Charlotte (28208) *(G-2225)*

AS Ignco 828 466-1044
1320 Fairgrove Church Rd Se Conover (28613) *(G-4418)*

Asamo Co, Greenville Also Called: Asmo Greenville of North Carolina Inc *(G-7486)*

ASAP Components 919 258-2230
410 Lord Berkley Rd Raleigh (27610) *(G-12526)*

ASAP Embroideries, Morehead City Also Called: Consumer Concepts *(G-11164)*

ASAP Marketing, Greenville Also Called: Carlina Shotwell LLC *(G-7497)*

ASAP Printing, Raleigh Also Called: 4 Over LLC *(G-12447)*

Asb Graphics, High Point Also Called: Acme Sample Books Inc *(G-8231)*

Asbury Graphite Mills 910 671-4141
191 Magna Blvd Lumberton (28360) *(G-10026)*

ASC, Sanford Also Called: Air System Components Inc *(G-14083)*

ASC, Tarboro Also Called: Air System Components Inc *(G-15093)*

ASC Distribution, Asheville Also Called: Appalachian Stove Fbrcators Inc *(G-525)*

Ascend Essences LLC 828 575-2502
6 N Kensington Rd Asheville (28804) *(G-529)*

Ascend Fitness, Asheville Also Called: Ascend Essences LLC *(G-529)*

Ascend Research Corp 336 710-5793
2150 Country Club Rd Ste 205 Winston Salem (27104) *(G-16611)*

Ascending Iron LLC — 336 266-6462
6504 Burlington Rd Whitsett (27377) *(G-15982)*

Ascepi Medical Group LLC — 919 336-4246
3344 Hillsborough St Ste 100 Raleigh (27607) *(G-12527)*

Asco LP — 919 460-5200
111 Corning Rd Ste 120 Cary (27518) *(G-1692)*

Asco Power Technologies LP — 919 460-5200
3412 Apex Peakway Apex (27502) *(G-166)*

Asco Power Technologies LP — 336 731-5000
325 Welcome Center Blvd Lexington (27295) *(G-9681)*

Ascom (us) Inc — 877 712-7266
300 Perimeter Park Dr Ste D Morrisville (27560) *(G-11293)*

Asensus Surgical Inc (PA) — 919 765-8400
1 Tw Alexander Dr Ste 160 Durham (27703) *(G-4928)*

Aseptia Inc — 678 373-6751
723 W Johnson St Ste 100 Raleigh (27603) *(G-12528)*

Ashbran LLC — 919 215-3567
700 Parkridge Dr Clayton (27527) *(G-3956)*

Ashdan Enterprises — 336 375-9698
608 Summit Ave Ste 201 Greensboro (27405) *(G-6818)*

Ashe Hams Inc — 828 259-9426
707 Merrimon Ave Asheville (28804) *(G-530)*

Asheboro Activewear, Asheboro *Also Called: Wells Hosiery Mills Inc (G-510)*

Asheboro Courrier Tribune, Asheboro *Also Called: Gatehouse Media LLC (G-439)*

Asheboro Elastics Corp (PA) — 336 629-2626
150 N Park St Asheboro (27203) *(G-403)*

Asheboro Elastics Corp — 336 629-2626
1947 N Fayetteville St Asheboro (27203) *(G-404)*

Asheboro Machine Shop Inc — 336 625-6322
3027 Us Business 220 S Asheboro (27204) *(G-405)*

Asheboro Maltomeal, Asheboro *Also Called: Post Consumer Brands LLC (G-464)*

Asheboro Piedmont Printing Inc — 336 899-7910
2753 Us Highway 220 Bus S Asheboro (27205) *(G-406)*

Asheboro Ready-Mix Inc — 336 672-0957
524 W Bailey St Asheboro (27203) *(G-407)*

Asheville Bit & Steel Company — 828 274-3766
111 Edgewood Rd S Asheville (28803) *(G-531)*

Asheville Citizen-Times — 828 252-5611
14 Ohenry Ave Asheville (28803) *(G-532)*

Asheville Color & Imaging Inc — 828 774-5040
611 Tunnel Rd Ste E Asheville (28805) *(G-533)*

Asheville Contracting Co Inc — 828 665-8900
1270 Smoky Park Hwy Candler (28715) *(G-1567)*

Asheville Custom Closets — 828 337-7539
20 Stone River Dr Asheville (28804) *(G-534)*

Asheville Distilling Company — 828 575-2000
45 S French Broad Ave Asheville (28801) *(G-535)*

Asheville Fence, Candler *Also Called: Asheville Contracting Co Inc (G-1567)*

Asheville Global Report — 828 236-3103
20 Battery Park Ave Asheville (28801) *(G-536)*

Asheville Guidebook — 828 779-1569
18 Garren Mountain Ln Fairview (28730) *(G-5707)*

Asheville Kombucha Mamas LLC — 828 595-4340
54 Chestnut Ter Asheville (28803) *(G-537)*

Asheville Kombucha Mamas LLC (PA) — 828 394-2360
242 Derringer Dr Marshall (28753) *(G-10199)*

Asheville Maintenance and Construction Inc — 828 687-8110
150 Glenn Bridge Rd Arden (28704) *(G-312)*

Asheville Meadery LLC — 828 454-6188
155 Johnston Blvd Asheville (28806) *(G-538)*

Asheville Metal Finishing Inc — 828 253-1476
178 Clingman Ave Asheville (28801) *(G-539)*

Asheville Paint & Powder Coat, Asheville *Also Called: Dotson Metal Finishing Inc (G-612)*

Asheville Pet Supply — 828 252-2054
1451 Merrimon Ave Asheville (28804) *(G-540)*

Asheville Print Shop — 828 214-5286
740 Haywood Rd Asheville (28806) *(G-541)*

Asheville Promo LLC — 828 575-2767
202 Asheland Ave Asheville (28801) *(G-542)*

Asheville Quickprint — 828 252-7667
8 Chanter Dr Fletcher (28732) *(G-5984)*

Asheville Thermoform Plas Inc — 828 684-8440
200 Cane Creek Industrial Park Rd Fletcher (28732) *(G-5985)*

Asheville Tourist Baseball, Asheville *Also Called: Tourist Baseball Inc (G-803)*

Asheville Vault Service Inc (PA) — 828 665-6799
2239 Smoky Park Hwy Candler (28715) *(G-1568)*

Asheville Wilbert Vault Svc, Candler *Also Called: Asheville Vault Service Inc (G-1568)*

Asheville Woodworks — 828 734-0536
31 Panola St Asheville (28801) *(G-543)*

Ashevlle Prcsion Mch Rblding I — 828 254-0884
51 Haywood Rd Asheville (28806) *(G-544)*

Ashfar Enterprises Inc — 704 462-4672
3772 Plateau Rd Newton (28658) *(G-11913)*

Ashland Hardware Systems, Huntersville *Also Called: Ashland Products Inc (G-8794)*

Ashland Products Inc — 815 266-0250
8936 N Exec Dr S 250 Huntersville (28078) *(G-8794)*

Ashley Furniture, Advance *Also Called: Ashley Furniture Inds LLC (G-37)*

Ashley Furniture Inds LLC — 336 998-1066
333 Ashley Furniture Way Advance (27006) *(G-37)*

Ashley Interiors, High Point *Also Called: Rbc Inc (G-8506)*

Ashley Sling Inc — 704 347-0071
2401 N Graham St Charlotte (28206) *(G-2226)*

ASHLEY SLING, INC., Charlotte *Also Called: Ashley Sling Inc (G-2226)*

Ashley Taylor — 828 230-2953
809 Case Cove Rd Candler (28715) *(G-1569)*

Ashley Welding & Machine Co — 252 482-3321
104 Tower Dr Edenton (27932) *(G-5507)*

Ashleys Kit Bath Dsign Stdio L — 828 669-5281
2950 Us 70 Hwy Black Mountain (28711) *(G-1119)*

Ashton Lewis Lumber Co Inc — 252 357-0050
96 Lewis Mill Rd Gatesville (27938) *(G-6546)*

Ashton LLC (PA) — 336 447-4951
309 Bethel St Gibsonville (27249) *(G-6556)*

Ashville Postage Express — 828 255-9250
22 New Leicester Hwy Ste C Asheville (28806) *(G-545)*

Ashville Wrecker Service Inc — 828 252-2388
80 Weaverville Rd Asheville (28804) *(G-546)*

Ashworth Logging — 910 464-2136
249 Hunter Ridge Ln Carthage (28327) *(G-1659)*

Asi Signage Innovations — 336 508-4668
4204 Hobbs Rd Greensboro (27410) *(G-6819)*

Asi Signage North Carolina — 919 362-9669
600 Irving Pkwy Holly Springs (27540) *(G-8686)*

Asian (korean) Herald Inc — 704 332-5656
1300 Baxter St Ste 155 Charlotte (28204) *(G-2227)*

Ask Elevator Service Inc — 336 674-2715
6000 Spring Forest Ct Pleasant Garden (27313) *(G-12356)*

Askbio — 336 407-6217
8 Davis Dr Durham (27709) *(G-4929)*

Askbio, Morrisville *Also Called: Asklepios Bopharmaceutical Inc (G-11294)*

Asklepios Bopharmaceutical Inc (HQ) — 919 561-6210
507 Airport Blvd Ste 111 Morrisville (27560) *(G-11294)*

Asmo Greenville of North Carolina Inc — 252 754-1000
1125 Sugg Pkwy Greenville (27834) *(G-7486)*

Asmo North America LLC — 704 872-2319
470 Crawford Rd Statesville (28625) *(G-14754)*

Asp Distribution Inc — 336 375-5672
100 Bonita Dr Greensboro (27405) *(G-6820)*

Asp Holdings Inc — 888 330-2538
1014 N Arendell Ave Zebulon (27597) *(G-17121)*

Aspen Cabinetry Inc — 828 466-0216
908 Industrial Dr Sw Conover (28613) *(G-4419)*

Asphalt Emulsion Inds LLC — 252 726-0653
107 Arendell St Morehead City (28557) *(G-11150)*

Asphalt Plant 1, Raleigh *Also Called: Fsc Holdings Inc (G-12784)*

Aspire Woodworks — 828 855-6811
4946 Alexander Pl Ne Hickory (28601) *(G-7945)*

Assa Abloy, Monroe *Also Called: Assa Abloy ACC Door Cntrls Gro (G-10653)*

Assa Abloy AB — 704 283-2101
1902 Airport Rd Monroe (28110) *(G-10652)*

Assa Abloy ACC Door Cntrls Gro (DH) — 877 974-2255
1902 Airport Rd Monroe (28110) *(G-10653)*

ALPHABETIC SECTION — Atlantic Sign Media Inc

Assa Abloy Accessories and 704 233-4011
3000 E Highway 74 Monroe (28112) *(G-10654)*

Assa Abloy Entrnce Systems US (DH) 704 357-9924
1900 Airport Rd Ste B Monroe (28110) *(G-10655)*

Assa Abloy Inc 704 776-8773
3000 E Highway 74 Monroe (28112) *(G-10656)*

Assembly Technologies Inc 704 596-3903
6716 Orr Rd Charlotte (28213) *(G-2228)*

Associated Artists Southport 910 457-5450
130 E West St Southport (28461) *(G-14566)*

Associated Battery Company 704 821-8311
3469 Gribble Rd Matthews (28104) *(G-10301)*

Associated Distributors Inc 910 895-5800
120 Doe Loop Hamlet (28345) *(G-7616)*

Associated Hardwoods Inc (PA) 828 396-3321
650 N Main St Granite Falls (28630) *(G-6722)*

Associated Hygienic Pdts LLC (PA) 770 497-9800
1029 Old Creek Rd Greenville (27834) *(G-7487)*

Associated Hygienic Products, Greenville Also Called: Associated Hygienic Pdts LLC *(G-7487)*

Associated Metal Works Inc 704 546-7002
137 E Memorial Hwy Harmony (28634) *(G-7685)*

Associated Posters, Kernersville Also Called: More Than Billboards Inc *(G-9219)*

Associated Printing & Svcs Inc 828 286-9064
905 N Main St Rutherfordton (28139) *(G-13864)*

Assoction Intl Crtif Prof Accn (PA) 919 402-4500
220 Leigh Farm Rd Durham (27707) *(G-4930)*

Assurance Publications Inc 423 473-3000
101 College Cir Swannanoa (28778) *(G-15018)*

Assyst Bullmer Inc 919 467-2211
3221 Durham Dr Ste 101 Raleigh (27603) *(G-12529)*

Astellas Gene Therapies Inc 415 638-6561
6074 Enterprise Park Dr Sanford (27330) *(G-14089)*

Asterra Labs LLC 800 430-9074
800 Cooke Rd Nashville (27856) *(G-11733)*

Astral Buoyancy Company 828 255-2638
347 Depot St # 201 Asheville (28801) *(G-547)*

Astral Designs, Asheville Also Called: Astral Buoyancy Company *(G-547)*

Astrazeneca Pharmaceuticals LP 919 647-4990
4222 Emperor Blvd Ste 560 Durham (27703) *(G-4931)*

Astroturf 336 528-5496
676 High Rock Shores Dr Lexington (27292) *(G-9682)*

Astroturf Corp 336 238-9060
176 Windchime Ct Lexington (27295) *(G-9683)*

At The Lake Canvas and Covers 704 966-1586
4059 Shasta Ln Sherrills Ford (28673) *(G-14383)*

At Your Service Express LLC 704 270-9918
101 N Tryon St Ste 112 Charlotte (28246) *(G-2229)*

Atc Conversions, Raleigh Also Called: Jeffrey Sheffer *(G-12915)*

Atc Panels 888 200-7955
985 Corinth Rd Moncure (27559) *(G-10615)*

Atc Panels Inc 919 653-6053
2000 Aerial Center Pkwy Ste 113 Morrisville (27560) *(G-11295)*

Atcom Bus Telecom Solutions, Charlotte Also Called: Atcom Inc *(G-2230)*

Atcom Inc 704 357-7900
3330 Oak Lake Blvd Charlotte (28208) *(G-2230)*

Atec, Mocksville Also Called: Atec Wind Energy Products LLC *(G-10555)*

Atec Coatings LLC 336 753-8888
111 Bailey St Mocksville (27028) *(G-10554)*

Atec Wind Energy Products LLC 336 753-8888
111 Bailey St Mocksville (27028) *(G-10555)*

Atelier Maison and Co LLC 828 277-7202
121 Sweeten Creek Rd Ste 50 Asheville (28803) *(G-548)*

Atg Division, Rutherfordton Also Called: Trelleborg Ctd Systems US Inc *(G-13894)*

Athena Marble Incorporated 704 636-7810
7400 Bringle Ferry Rd Salisbury (28146) *(G-13924)*

Athenian Press and Workshops 919 961-5071
701 N 23rd St Wilmington (28405) *(G-16119)*

Athens Publishing Company 828 774-5270
70 Woodfin Pl Asheville (28801) *(G-549)*

Athol Arbor Corporation 919 643-1100
511 Valley Forge Rd Hillsborough (27278) *(G-8636)*

Athol Manufacturing Corp 919 575-6523
100 22nd St Butner (27509) *(G-1540)*

ATI, Charlotte Also Called: Assembly Technologies Inc *(G-2228)*

ATI Allvac 541 967-9000
6400 Alloy Way Monroe (28110) *(G-10657)*

ATI Industrial Automation Inc (DH) 919 772-0115
1031 Goodworth Dr Apex (27539) *(G-167)*

ATI Laminates, Greensboro Also Called: Advanced Technology Inc *(G-6783)*

Atkins Unlimited LLC 704 984-8595
127 Atkins Ln Sanford (27330) *(G-14090)*

Atkins, Mike & Son Logging, Selma Also Called: Mike Atkins & Son Logging Inc *(G-14258)*

Atkinson International Inc 704 865-7750
3800 Little Mountain Rd Gastonia (28056) *(G-6349)*

Atkinson Milling Company 919 965-3547
95 Atkinson Mill Rd Intersection Hwy 42 & 39 Selma (27576) *(G-14253)*

Atkinson's Mill, Selma Also Called: Atkinson Milling Company *(G-14253)*

Atlantic, Wilmington Also Called: Atlantic Corp Wilmington Inc *(G-16121)*

Atlantic Automotive Entps LLC 910 377-4108
1007 Pireway Rd Ste B Tabor City (28463) *(G-15077)*

Atlantic Bankcard Center Inc 336 855-9250
2920 Manufacturers Rd Greensboro (27406) *(G-6821)*

Atlantic Bearing Co Inc 252 243-0233
321 Herring Ave Ne Bldg A Wilson (27893) *(G-16469)*

Atlantic Caribbean LLC 910 343-0624
806 N 23rd St Wilmington (28405) *(G-16120)*

Atlantic Coast Cabinet Distrs 919 554-8165
150 Weathers Ct Youngsville (27596) *(G-17068)*

Atlantic Coast Protein Co, Selma Also Called: Apc LLC *(G-14252)*

Atlantic Coast Screen Prtg LLC 910 200-0818
2312 Airpark Rd Burlington (27215) *(G-1368)*

Atlantic Coastal Enterprises 910 478-0777
300 New Bridge St Jacksonville (28540) *(G-8988)*

Atlantic Coastal Shutters LLC 252 441-4358
2701 N Croatan Hwy Kill Devil Hills (27948) *(G-9254)*

Atlantic Commercial Caseworks 704 393-9500
4700 Rozzelles Ferry Rd Charlotte (28216) *(G-2231)*

Atlantic Corp Wilmington Inc 910 259-3600
151 Industrial Dr Burgaw (28425) *(G-1333)*

Atlantic Corp Wilmington Inc (PA) 910 343-0624
806 N 23rd St Wilmington (28405) *(G-16121)*

Atlantic Corporation (HQ) 910 343-0624
806 N 23rd St Wilmington (28405) *(G-16122)*

Atlantic Counter Top & ACC, Raleigh Also Called: Hargrove Countertops & ACC Inc *(G-12830)*

Atlantic Custom Container Inc 336 437-9302
327 E Elm St Graham (27253) *(G-6678)*

Atlantic Division, High Point Also Called: Cascade Die Casting Group Inc *(G-8290)*

Atlantic Engineering, Troutman Also Called: Ae Technology Inc *(G-15365)*

Atlantic Enterprises, Tabor City Also Called: Atlantic Automotive Entps LLC *(G-15077)*

Atlantic Group Usa Inc (PA) 919 623-7824
3401 Gresham Lake Rd Ste 118 Raleigh (27615) *(G-12530)*

Atlantic Hydraulics Svcs LLC 919 542-2985
5225 Womack Rd Sanford (27330) *(G-14091)*

Atlantic Logging Inc 252 229-9997
232 Stony Branch Rd New Bern (28562) *(G-11772)*

Atlantic Manufacturing LLC 336 497-5500
1322 S Park Dr Kernersville (27284) *(G-9166)*

Atlantic Mfg & Fabrication Inc 704 647-6200
705 S Railroad St Unit 1 Salisbury (28144) *(G-13925)*

Atlantic Mold Inc 919 832-8151
1000 N Main St Ste 221 Fuquay Varina (27526) *(G-6182)*

Atlantic Natural Foods LLC 888 491-0524
110 Industry Ct Nashville (27856) *(G-11734)*

Atlantic Pinstriping ATL Wraps 704 201-4406
4108 Matthews Indian Trail Rd Matthews (28104) *(G-10302)*

Atlantic Pnstriping Greensboro 910 880-3717
5072 Ashford Crest Ln Charlotte (28226) *(G-2232)*

Atlantic Prosthetics Orthtcs 919 806-3260
6208 Fayetteville Rd # 101 Durham (27713) *(G-4932)*

Atlantic Screen Print, Elizabeth City Also Called: R O Givens Signs Inc *(G-5567)*

Atlantic Sign Media Inc 336 584-1375
111 Trail One Ste 101 Burlington (27215) *(G-1369)*

Atlantic Software Co 910 763-3907
607 S 13th St Wilmington (28401) *(G-16123)*

Atlantic Tool & Die Co Inc 910 270-2888
2363 Nc Highway 210 W Hampstead (28443) *(G-7638)*

Atlantic Trading LLC
307 Ridgewood Ave Charlotte (28209) *(G-2233)*

Atlantic Tube & Fitting LLC 704 545-6166
4475 Morris Park Dr Ste L Mint Hill (28227) *(G-10520)*

Atlantic Veneer Company LLC (HQ) 252 728-3169
2457 Lennoxville Rd Beaufort (28516) *(G-943)*

Atlantic Window Coverings Inc 704 392-0043
6150 Brookshire Blvd Ste D Charlotte (28216) *(G-2234)*

Atlantic Wood & Timber LLC 704 390-7479
2200 Border Dr Charlotte (28208) *(G-2235)*

Atlantic Woodworking 704 680-8802
154 Kiskadee Dr Mooresville (28117) *(G-10863)*

Atlantis Food Service, Clemmons *Also Called: Atlantis Foods Inc (G-4027)*

Atlantis Foods Inc 336 768-6101
4525 Hampton Rd Clemmons (27012) *(G-4027)*

Atlantis Graphics Inc (PA) 919 361-5809
2410 E Nc Highway 54 Durham (27713) *(G-4933)*

Atlas Aerospace Inc 704 528-3356
1536 Triplett Rd Cleveland (27013) *(G-4067)*

Atlas American Lighting, Burlington *Also Called: Atlas Lighting Products Inc (G-1370)*

Atlas Box and Crating Inc 919 941-1023
3829 S Miami Blvd Ste 100 Durham (27703) *(G-4934)*

Atlas Copco Compressors LLC 704 525-0124
2101 Westinghouse Blvd # D Charlotte (28273) *(G-2236)*

Atlas Lighting Products Inc 336 222-9258
1406 S Mebane St Burlington (27215) *(G-1370)*

Atlas Sign Industries, Concord *Also Called: Atlas Sign Industries Nc LLC (G-4200)*

Atlas Sign Industries Nc LLC 704 788-3733
707 Commerce Dr Concord (28025) *(G-4200)*

Atlas Signs 919 238-5078
951 Aviation Pkwy Ste 1000 Morrisville (27560) *(G-11296)*

Atmax Engineering 910 233-4881
806 Morris Ct Wilmington (28405) *(G-16124)*

Atmo-TEC 704 528-3935
130 Ostwalt Amity Rd Troutman (28166) *(G-15367)*

Atmosphric Plsma Solutions Inc 919 341-8325
11301 Penny Rd Ste D Cary (27518) *(G-1693)*

Atmox Inc 704 248-2858
10612d Providence Rd Ste 229 Charlotte (28277) *(G-2237)*

Atom Power, Huntersville *Also Called: Atom Power Inc (G-8795)*

Atom Power Inc 844 704-2866
13245 Reese Blvd W Ste 130 Huntersville (28078) *(G-8795)*

Atrc Inc 919 872-5800
1200 Melton Ct Raleigh (27615) *(G-12531)*

Atricure, Morrisville *Also Called: Ncontact Surgical LLC (G-11392)*

Atrium Extrusion Systems Inc 336 764-6400
300 Welcome Center Blvd Welcome (27374) *(G-15871)*

Atrium Hlth Bspcmen Repository 704 863-4001
10545 Blair Rd Ste 1001 Mint Hill (28227) *(G-10521)*

Atsena Therapeutics Inc 352 273-9342
280 S Mangum St Ste 350 Durham (27701) *(G-4935)*

Atsi, Walkertown *Also Called: American Tchncal Solutions Inc (G-15613)*

Attends Healthcare Pdts Inc 252 752-1100
1029 Old Creek Rd Greenville (27834) *(G-7488)*

Attends Healthcare Products Inc (PA) 800 428-8363
8020 Arco Corporate Dr Ste 200 Raleigh (27617) *(G-12532)*

Attic Tent Inc 704 892-5399
164 Mill Pond Ln Mooresville (28115) *(G-10864)*

Atticus LLC 984 465-4754
940 Nw Cary Pkwy Ste 200 Cary (27513) *(G-1694)*

Attindas Hygiene Partners Inc 252 752-1100
350 Industrial Blvd Greenville (27834) *(G-7489)*

Attindas Hygiene Partners Inc (PA) 919 237-4000
8020 Arco Corporate Dr Ste 200 Raleigh (27617) *(G-12533)*

Attl Products Inc 336 475-8101
216 E Holly Hill Rd Thomasville (27360) *(G-15187)*

Attus Technologies Inc 704 341-5750
13860 Ballantyne Corporate Pl Ste 200 Charlotte (28277) *(G-2238)*

Atwell Fabrication LLC 704 763-9792
4338 Motorsports Dr Sw Concord (28027) *(G-4201)*

Audio Advice Inc 919 881-2005
8621 Glenwood Ave Ste 117 Raleigh (27617) *(G-12534)*

Audio Vdeo Concepts Design Inc 704 821-2823
1409 Babbage Ln Ste B Indian Trail (28079) *(G-8921)*

August Precision 919 830-6616
1712 Farrington Point Rd Chapel Hill (27517) *(G-1988)*

Aunt Tee LLC 336 269-9466
1327 N Beaumont Ct Apt B Burlington (27217) *(G-1371)*

Auntie Anne's, Asheville *Also Called: Chestnut Land Company (G-590)*

Auntie Anne's, Charlotte *Also Called: SE Co-Brand Ventures LLC (G-3514)*

Auralites Inc 828 687-7990
9a National Ave Fletcher (28732) *(G-5986)*

Auria Albemarle LLC 704 983-5166
313 Bethany Rd Albemarle (28001) *(G-74)*

Auria Old Fort LLC (DH) 828 668-7601
1506 E Main St Old Fort (28762) *(G-12098)*

Auria Old Fort II LLC 828 668-3277
1542 E Main St Old Fort (28762) *(G-12099)*

Auria Troy LLC 910 572-3721
163 Glen Rd Troy (27371) *(G-15401)*

Auriga Polymers Inc (DH) 864 579-5570
4235 Southstream Blvd Ste 450 Charlotte (28217) *(G-2239)*

Aurobindo Pharma USA Inc 732 839-9400
2929 Weck Dr Durham (27709) *(G-4936)*

Aurolife Pharma LLC 732 839-9408
2929 Weck Dr Durham (27709) *(G-4937)*

Aurora Packing Co Inc 252 322-5232
655 Second St Aurora (27806) *(G-831)*

Aurora Plastics Inc 336 775-2640
180 Welcome Center Blvd Welcome (27374) *(G-15872)*

Aurora Plastics, Inc., Welcome *Also Called: Aurora Plastics Inc (G-15872)*

Aurorium, Greensboro *Also Called: Aurorium LLC (G-6822)*

Aurorium LLC 336 292-1781
2110 W Gate City Blvd Greensboro (27403) *(G-6822)*

Aurum Capital Ventures Inc 877 467-7780
270 Cornerstone Dr Ste 101c Cary (27519) *(G-1695)*

Austin Business Forms Inc 704 821-6165
241 Post Office Dr Ste A5 Indian Trail (28079) *(G-8922)*

Austin Company of Greensboro 336 468-2851
2100 Hoots Rd Yadkinville (27055) *(G-17031)*

Austin Company, The, Yadkinville *Also Called: Austin Company of Greensboro (G-17031)*

Austin Powder Company 828 645-4291
372 Ernest Smith Rd Denton (27239) *(G-4725)*

Austin Powder South East, Denton *Also Called: Austin Powder Company (G-4725)*

Austin Print Solutions, Indian Trail *Also Called: Austin Business Forms Inc (G-8922)*

Austin Printing Company Inc 704 289-1445
1823 Morgan Mill Rd Monroe (28110) *(G-10658)*

Austin Tarp & Cargo Control, Charlotte *Also Called: Prem Corp (G-3373)*

Autec Inc 704 871-9141
2500 W Front St Statesville (28677) *(G-14755)*

Auten Reporting 828 230-5035
9 W Chestnut Ridge Ave Asheville (28804) *(G-550)*

Authentic Iron LLC 910 648-6989
17838 Nc 131 Hwy Bladenboro (28320) *(G-1143)*

Auto Care & Truck Wash LLC 704 363-6341
1316 S Blount St Raleigh (27601) *(G-12535)*

Auto Machine Shop Inc 910 483-6016
309 Winslow St Fayetteville (28301) *(G-5765)*

Auto Marine Boat Repairs, Garner *Also Called: C E Hicks Enterprises Inc (G-6259)*

Auto Parts Fayetteville LLC 910 889-4026
929 Bragg Blvd Ste 2 Fayetteville (28301) *(G-5766)*

Auto Parts USA, Fayetteville *Also Called: Auto Parts Fayetteville LLC (G-5766)*

Auto Trim Design 336 747-3309
614 Chapel Hill Rd Burlington (27215) *(G-1372)*

Auto-Systems and Service Inc 336 824-3580
839 Crestwick Rd Ramseur (27316) *(G-13440)*

Autom8 LLC 704 252-3425
2925 Silverthorn Dr Charlotte (28273) *(G-2240)*

ALPHABETIC SECTION — Awnings Etc

Automail LLC..704 677-0152
2987 Charlotte Hwy Mooresville (28117) *(G-10865)*

Automated Controls LLC..704 724-7625
13416 S Old Statesville Rd Huntersville (28078) *(G-8796)*

Automated Designs Inc..828 696-9625
105 Education Dr Flat Rock (28731) *(G-5959)*

Automated Entrances, Clayton Also Called: ADC Industries Inc *(G-3952)*

Automated Lumber Handling Inc......................................828 754-4662
723 Virginia St Sw Lenoir (28645) *(G-9576)*

Automated Machine Technologies....................................919 361-0121
10404 Chapel Hill Rd Ste 100 Morrisville (27560) *(G-11297)*

Automated Printing Services..252 243-3993
431 Ward Blvd Wilson (27893) *(G-16470)*

Automated Solutions LLC (PA)...828 396-9900
4101 Us Highway 321a Granite Falls (28630) *(G-6723)*

Autopark Logistics LLC..704 365-3544
2703 Madison Oaks Ct Charlotte (28226) *(G-2241)*

Autosmart Inc..919 210-7936
510 Fairview Rd Apex (27502) *(G-168)*

Autosound 2000 Inc..336 227-3434
2557 Faucette Ln Burlington (27217) *(G-1373)*

Autoverters Inc..252 537-0426
2212 W 10th St Roanoke Rapids (27870) *(G-13567)*

Autry Con Pdts & Bldrs Sup Co..704 504-8830
8918 Byrum Dr Charlotte (28217) *(G-2242)*

Autry Con Pdts & Septic Svcs, Charlotte Also Called: Autry Con Pdts & Bldrs Sup Co *(G-2242)*

Autry Logging Inc..910 303-4943
824 Magnolia Church Rd Stedman (28391) *(G-14933)*

Autumn Creek Vineyards Inc..336 548-9463
2105 Lafayette Ave Greensboro (27408) *(G-6823)*

Autumn House Inc...828 728-1121
1206 Premier Rd Granite Falls (28630) *(G-6724)*

Autumn Wood Products, Granite Falls Also Called: Autumn House Inc *(G-6724)*

Ava Aliza Candle Co LLC...704 906-4328
9814 Park Springs Ct Charlotte (28210) *(G-2243)*

Avadim Health, Swannanoa Also Called: Avadim Holdings Inc *(G-15019)*

Avadim Holdings Inc..877 677-2723
600a Centrepark Dr Asheville (28805) *(G-551)*

Avadim Holdings Inc..877 677-2723
4944 Parkway Plaza Blvd Ste 480 Charlotte (28217) *(G-2244)*

Avadim Holdings Inc (PA)...877 677-2723
4 Old Patton Cove Rd Swannanoa (28778) *(G-15019)*

Avago Technology...704 887-7735
9815 David Taylor Dr Charlotte (28262) *(G-2245)*

Avail Forensics, Wilmington Also Called: Avail Forensics LLC *(G-16125)*

Avail Forensics LLC...877 888-5895
4022 Shipyard Blvd Fl 2 Wilmington (28403) *(G-16125)*

Avant Publications LLC..704 897-6048
116 Morlake Dr Ste 203 Mooresville (28117) *(G-10866)*

Avanti Coatings Inc..908 723-4596
26 P E M Dr Hendersonville (28792) *(G-7822)*

Avanti Hearth Products LLC...704 866-4342
110 Dorie Dr Belmont (28012) *(G-975)*

Avaya LLC...919 425-8268
4001 E Chapel Hl Research Triangle Pa (27709) *(G-13548)*

Avcon Inc..919 388-0203
101 Triangle Trade Dr Ste 101 Cary (27513) *(G-1696)*

Avdel USA LLC (HQ)...704 888-7100
614 Nc Hwy 200 S Stanfield (28163) *(G-14675)*

Avercast LLC...208 538-5380
8921 Crew Dr Emerald Isle (28594) *(G-5669)*

Averitt Electric Motor Repair, Laurinburg Also Called: Averitt Enterprises Inc *(G-9469)*

Averitt Enterprises Inc..910 276-1294
14121 Highland Rd Laurinburg (28352) *(G-9469)*

Averix Bio LLC...919 614-7600
3040 Black Creek Rd S Wilson (27893) *(G-16471)*

Avery County Recapping Co Inc......................................828 733-0161
405 Linville St Newland (28657) *(G-11881)*

Avery County Tire, Newland Also Called: Avery County Recapping Co Inc *(G-11881)*

Avery Dennison Corporation..336 621-2570
2100 Summit Ave Greensboro (27405) *(G-6824)*

Avery Dennison Corporation..336 553-2436
620 Green Valley Rd Ste 306 Greensboro (27408) *(G-6825)*

Avery Dennison Corporation..336 856-8235
1100 Revolution Mill Dr # 11 Greensboro (27405) *(G-6826)*

Avery Dennison Corporation..864 938-1400
1100 Revolution Mill Dr # 11 Greensboro (27405) *(G-6827)*

Avery Dennison Corporation..336 665-6481
200 Citation Ct Greensboro (27409) *(G-6828)*

Avery Dennison Rfid Company..626 304-2000
1100 Revolution Mill Dr # 11 Greensboro (27405) *(G-6829)*

Avery Journal Times, Newland Also Called: High Country Media LLC *(G-11888)*

Avery Machine & Welding Co..828 733-4944
1312 Longleaf Dr Fayetteville (28305) *(G-5767)*

Avgol America Inc...336 936-2500
178 Avgol Dr Mocksville (27028) *(G-10556)*

Avgol Nonwovens, Mocksville Also Called: Avgol America Inc *(G-10556)*

Avian Cetacean Press...910 392-5537
1616 Jettys Reach Wilmington (28409) *(G-16126)*

Aviary Publishers Inc...919 331-0003
221 Crawford Rd Hillsborough (27278) *(G-8637)*

AVIATION METALS, Charlotte Also Called: Aviation Metals NC Inc *(G-2246)*

Aviation Metals NC Inc..704 264-1647
1810 W Pointe Dr Ste D Charlotte (28214) *(G-2246)*

Aviator Brewing Company Inc..919 601-5497
5504 Caleb Knolls Dr Holly Springs (27540) *(G-8687)*

AVIDXCHANGE, Charlotte Also Called: Avidxchange Holdings Inc *(G-2247)*

Avidxchange Holdings Inc (PA)..800 560-9305
1210 Avid Xchange Ln Charlotte (28206) *(G-2247)*

Avient Colorants USA LLC...704 331-7000
4000 Monroe Rd Charlotte (28205) *(G-2248)*

Avient Protective Mtls LLC (HQ)......................................252 707-2547
5750 Martin Luther King Jr Hwy Greenville (27834) *(G-7490)*

Avient Protective Mtls LLC..704 862-5100
1101 S Highway 27 Stanley (28164) *(G-14684)*

Avintiv Inc (HQ)...704 697-5100
9335 Harris Corners Pkwy Ste 300 Charlotte (28269) *(G-2249)*

Avintiv Specialty Mtls Inc (HQ)..704 697-5100
9335 Harris Corners Pkwy Ste 300 Charlotte (28269) *(G-2250)*

Avintiv Specialty Mtls Inc..704 660-6242
111 Excellance Ln Mooresville (28115) *(G-10867)*

AVIOQ Inc...919 314-5535
76 Tw Alexander Dr Durham (27709) *(G-4938)*

Avior Inc...919 234-0068
221 James Jackson Ave Cary (27513) *(G-1697)*

Avior Bio, Cary Also Called: Avior Inc *(G-1697)*

Avista Pharma Solutions Inc (HQ)...................................919 544-8600
3501 Tricenter Blvd Ste C Durham (27713) *(G-4939)*

Avl Custom Fabrication...828 713-0333
250 Baird Cove Rd Asheville (28804) *(G-552)*

Avl Technologies, Asheville Also Called: Avl Technologies Inc *(G-553)*

Avl Technologies Inc...828 250-9950
15 N Merrimon Ave Asheville (28804) *(G-553)*

Avoca LLC (DH)..252 482-2133
841 Avoca Rd Merry Hill (27957) *(G-10440)*

Avon Seafood..252 995-4553
Harbor Rd Avon (27915) *(G-843)*

Avp Vaccines LLC...704 799-0161
112 Lightship Dr Mooresville (28117) *(G-10868)*

AWC, Charlotte Also Called: Atlantic Window Coverings Inc *(G-2234)*

AWC Holding Company...919 677-3900
5020 Weston Pkwy Ste 400 Cary (27513) *(G-1698)*

AWC Sign & Light Inc..910 279-0493
6705 Spearow Ln Wilmington (28411) *(G-16127)*

Awcnc LLC..252 633-5757
401 Industrial Dr New Bern (28562) *(G-11773)*

Awesome Products Inc..336 374-5900
1625 Sheep Farm Rd Mount Airy (27030) *(G-11478)*

Awning Innovations...336 831-8996
6325 Clementine Dr Clemmons (27012) *(G-4028)*

Awning Shop, Shelby Also Called: Colored Metal Products Inc *(G-14301)*

Awnings Etc, Garner Also Called: Custom Canvas Works Inc *(G-6270)*

Axalta Coating Systems LLC 855 629-2582
5388 Stowe Ln Concord (28027) *(G-4202)*

Axalta Coating Systems Ltd 336 802-5701
1717 W English Rd High Point (27262) *(G-8257)*

Axalta Coating Systems Ltd 336 802-4392
2137 Brevard Rd High Point (27263) *(G-8258)*

Axalta Coating Systems USA LLC 336 802-5701
1717 W English Rd High Point (27262) *(G-8259)*

Axccellus LLC 919 589-9800
2501 Schieffelin Rd Apex (27502) *(G-169)*

Axchem Solutions Inc 919 742-9810
1325 N 2nd Ave Siler City (27344) *(G-14398)*

Axial Exchange Inc 919 576-9988
1111 Haynes St Ste 113 Raleigh (27604) *(G-12536)*

Axis Corrugated Container LLC (HQ) 919 575-0500
201 Industrial Dr Butner (27509) *(G-1541)*

Axitare Corporation 919 256-8196
1717 Brassfield Rd Raleigh (27614) *(G-12537)*

Axjo America Inc 828 322-6046
221 S Mclin Creek Rd Ste A Conover (28613) *(G-4420)*

Axle Holdings LLC 800 895-3276
5051 Davidson Hwy Concord (28027) *(G-4203)*

Axon LLC 919 772-8383
3080 Business Park Dr Ste 103 Raleigh (27610) *(G-12538)*

Axon Styrotech, Raleigh *Also Called: Axon LLC (G-12538)*

Axon Systems LLC 910 796-7872
1985 Eastwood Rd Ste 204b Wilmington (28403) *(G-16128)*

Aylward Enterprises LLC (PA) 252 639-9242
401 Industrial Dr New Bern (28562) *(G-11774)*

AZ Faux 704 279-0114
1910 Saint Luke Church Rd Salisbury (28146) *(G-13926)*

Azalea Art Press 510 919-6117
210a S Valley Rd Southern Pines (28387) *(G-14528)*

Azalea Bindery LLC 828 545-6219
1 Brookgreen Pl Asheville (28804) *(G-554)*

Aztech Products Inc (PA) 910 763-5599
2145 Wrightsville Ave Wilmington (28403) *(G-16129)*

Azure Skye Beverages Inc 704 909-7394
5253 Old Dowd Rd Unit 3 Charlotte (28208) *(G-2251)*

Azusa International 704 879-4464
2510 N Chester St Gastonia (28052) *(G-6350)*

B & B Building Maintenance LLC 910 494-2715
5318 Hwy 210 S Bunnlevel (28323) *(G-1329)*

B & B Distributing Inc 336 592-5665
2888 Durham Rd Ste 102 Roxboro (27573) *(G-13794)*

B & B Fabrication Inc 623 581-7600
125 Infield Ct Mooresville (28117) *(G-10869)*

B & B Hosiery Mill 336 368-4849
3608 Volunteer Rd Pinnacle (27043) *(G-12319)*

B & B Industries Inc 704 882-4688
4824 Unionville Indian Trail Rd W Ste A Indian Trail (28079) *(G-8923)*

B & B Leather Co Inc 704 598-9080
5518 Nevin Rd Charlotte (28269) *(G-2252)*

B & B Machine Co Inc 704 637-2356
1890 Barringer Rd Salisbury (28147) *(G-13927)*

B & B Stucco and Stone LLC 704 524-1230
816 Joseph Antoon Cir Stanley (28164) *(G-14685)*

B & B Welding Inc 336 643-5702
2900 Oak Ridge Rd Oak Ridge (27310) *(G-12057)*

B & B Wood Shop & Bldg Contrs 828 488-2078
4829 Highway 19 W Bryson City (28713) *(G-1319)*

B & C Concrete Products Inc 336 838-4201
228 New Brickyard Rd North Wilkesboro (28659) *(G-11998)*

B & C Winery 828 550-3610
1141 Rockmont Rd Waynesville (28785) *(G-15794)*

B & D Enterprises Inc 704 739-2958
736 Stony Point Rd Kings Mountain (28086) *(G-9293)*

B & E Woodturning Inc 828 758-2843
2395 Howard Arnette Rd Lenoir (28645) *(G-9577)*

B & J Knits 704 876-1498
3492 Wilkesboro Hwy Statesville (28625) *(G-14756)*

B & J Seafood Co Inc 252 637-0483
1101 Us Highway 70 E New Bern (28560) *(G-11775)*

B & J Tool Inc 336 265-8306
4515 Pleasant Garden Rd Greensboro (27406) *(G-6830)*

B & L Custom Cabinets Inc 704 857-1940
7165 Nc 89 Hwy W Westfield (27053) *(G-15950)*

B & M Electric Motor Service 828 267-0829
20 17th Street Pl Nw Hickory (28601) *(G-7946)*

B & M Wholesale, Mount Airy *Also Called: B & M Wholesale Inc (G-11479)*

B & M Wholesale Inc 336 789-3916
1800 Sparger Rd Mount Airy (27030) *(G-11479)*

B & S Exterior Cleaning, Burlington *Also Called: B&S Shingle Savers Inc (G-1374)*

B & W Enterprises, Traphill *Also Called: Smith Utility Buildings (G-15327)*

B & W Stone Company, Micaville *Also Called: Boone-Woody Mining Company Inc (G-10442)*

B & Y Machining Co Inc 252 235-2180
4495 Us Highway 264a Bailey (27807) *(G-868)*

B A S F Colors & Colorants, Charlotte *Also Called: BASF Corporation (G-2286)*

B C D, Durham *Also Called: Bull City Designs LLC (G-4986)*

B C I, Charlotte *Also Called: Border Concepts Inc (G-2335)*

B C M Company, Etowah *Also Called: Boondock S Manufacturing Inc (G-5691)*

B C Winery 828 550-3610
2499 Soco Rd Maggie Valley (28751) *(G-10093)*

B E R Trucking and Gravel 919 738-5928
594 Pineview Cemetery Rd Mount Olive (28365) *(G-11654)*

B F I Industries Inc 919 229-4509
3650 Rogers Rd # 334 Wake Forest (27587) *(G-15529)*

B G V Inc 704 588-3047
12245 Nations Ford Rd Ste 503 Pineville (28134) *(G-12254)*

B J Logging, Louisburg *Also Called: Richard C Jones (G-10000)*

B P Printing and Copying Inc 704 821-8219
3756 Pleasant Plains Rd Matthews (28104) *(G-10303)*

B Roberts Foods LLC 704 522-1977
2700 Westinghouse Blvd Ste A Charlotte (28273) *(G-2253)*

B S R-Hess Race Cars Inc 704 547-0901
7701 N Tryon St Charlotte (28262) *(G-2254)*

B V Hedrick Gravel & Sand Co 336 337-0706
15 Yorkshire St Asheville (28803) *(G-555)*

B V Hedrick Gravel & Sand Co 828 738-0332
1182 Old Glenwood Rd Marion (28752) *(G-10140)*

B V Hedrick Gravel & Sand Co (PA) 704 633-5982
120 1/2 N Church St Salisbury (28144) *(G-13928)*

B V Hedrick Gravel & Sand Co 704 827-8114
6941 Quarry Ln Stanley (28164) *(G-14686)*

B V Hedrick Gravel & Sand Co 828 686-3844
Old Us 70 Swannanoa (28778) *(G-15020)*

B V Hedrick Gravel & Sand Co 828 645-5560
100 Gold View Rd Weaverville (28787) *(G-15837)*

B W Woodworks, Garner *Also Called: Douglas Duane Sniffen (G-6271)*

B-Led Inc 828 680-1444
400 Hickory Dr Mars Hill (28754) *(G-10192)*

B-Light Publishing LLC 919 957-8997
309 Durants Neck Ln Morrisville (27560) *(G-11298)*

B. Robert's Prepared Foods, Charlotte *Also Called: B Roberts Foods LLC (G-2253)*

B/E Aerospace Inc 336 841-7698
2376 Hickswood Rd Ste 106 High Point (27265) *(G-8261)*

B/E Aerospace Inc 336 692-8940
4965 Indiana Ave Winston Salem (27106) *(G-16612)*

B/E Aerospace Inc (DH) 336 747-5000
150 Oak Plaza Blvd Ste 200 Winston Salem (27105) *(G-16613)*

B/E Aerospace Inc 336 293-1823
175 Oak Plaza Blvd Winston Salem (27105) *(G-16614)*

B/E Aerospace Inc 336 293-1823
2598 Empire Dr Winston Salem (27103) *(G-16615)*

B/E Aerospace Inc 336 744-6914
190 Oak Plaza Blvd Winston Salem (27105) *(G-16616)*

B/E Aerospace Inc 336 767-2000
150 Oak Plz Blvd Bldg 2 Winston Salem (27105) *(G-16617)*

B/E Aerospace Inc 520 733-1719
1455 Fairchild Rd # 1 Winston Salem (27105) *(G-16618)*

B/E Aerospace Inc 336 776-3500
2599 Empire Dr Winston Salem (27103) *(G-16619)*

ALPHABETIC SECTION

B/E Aerospace Inc.. 336 767-2000
  1455 Fairchild Rd Winston Salem (27105) *(G-16620)*

B&A Welding Miscellaneous LLC... 980 287-9187
  8628 Catfish Dr Charlotte (28214) *(G-2255)*

B&B Cap Liners LLC.. 585 598-1828
  3208 Spottswood St Ste 115 Raleigh (27615) *(G-12539)*

B&B Wood Shop Showroom, Bryson City Also Called: B & B Wood Shop & Bldg Contrs *(G-1319)*

B&C Xterior Cleaning Svc Inc... 919 779-7905
  142 Annaron Ct Raleigh (27603) *(G-12540)*

B&D Spindles LLC... 910 895-9769
  216 Lakeshore Dr Rockingham (28379) *(G-13620)*

B&G Foods Inc.. 336 849-7000
  500 Nonnis Way Yadkinville (27055) *(G-17032)*

B&H Millwork and Fixtures Inc.. 336 431-0068
  1130 Bedford St High Point (27263) *(G-8260)*

B&Lk Enterprises... 910 395-5151
  409 Oakland Dr Wilmington (28405) *(G-16130)*

B&M Donnelly Inc.. 704 358-9229
  1230 W Morehead St Ste 108 Charlotte (28208) *(G-2256)*

B&P Enterprise NC Inc.. 727 669-6877
  4128 Icard Ridge Rd Hickory (28601) *(G-7947)*

B&S Shingle Savers Inc.. 336 264-3898
  4459 Bellemont Mount Hermon Rd Burlington (27215) *(G-1374)*

B&V Stucco LLC... 828 682-9700
  37 Harmony Rdg Burnsville (28714) *(G-1524)*

B&W, Charlotte Also Called: Bwxt Investment Company *(G-2369)*

B+e Manufacturing Co Inc.. 704 236-8439
  4811 Persimmon Ct Monroe (28110) *(G-10659)*

B2rv2woodworks... 304 578-9881
  30 Canter Gable Pl Youngsville (27596) *(G-17069)*

B3 Bio Inc.. 919 226-3079
  6 Davis Dr Durham (27709) *(G-4940)*

B6usa Inc.. 919 833-3851
  414 Dupont Cir Raleigh (27603) *(G-12541)*

Ba International LLC.. 336 519-8080
  1000 E Hanes Mill Rd Winston Salem (27105) *(G-16621)*

BA Robbins Company LLC... 828 466-3900
  110 E 15th St Newton (28658) *(G-11914)*

Baac Business Solutions Inc... 704 333-4321
  1701 South Blvd Charlotte (28203) *(G-2257)*

Babco Inc... 888 376-5083
  639 Sumrell Rd Ayden (28513) *(G-848)*

Babcock Wlcox Eqity Invstmnts.. 704 625-4900
  13024 Ballantyne Corporate Pl Ste 700 Charlotte (28277) *(G-2258)*

Babcock Wlcox Intl Sls Svc Cor.. 704 625-4900
  13024 Ballantyne Corporate Pl Ste 700 Charlotte (28277) *(G-2259)*

Babeegreens, Asheville Also Called: Tiara Inc *(G-800)*

Babine Lake Corporation (PA).. 910 285-7955
  113 Dogwood Cir Hampstead (28443) *(G-7639)*

Babington Technology LLC.. 252 984-0349
  159 Fabrication Way Rocky Mount (27804) *(G-13682)*

Babington Technology Inc (PA).. 252 984-0349
  159 Fabrication Way Rocky Mount (27804) *(G-13683)*

Babusci Crtive Prtg Imging LLC... 704 423-9864
  4115 Rose Lake Dr Ste A Charlotte (28217) *(G-2260)*

Bacci America Inc.. 704 375-5044
  1704 East Blvd Ste 101 Charlotte (28203) *(G-2261)*

Bace LLC.. 704 394-2230
  322 W 32nd St Charlotte (28206) *(G-2262)*

Bachstein Consulting LLC.. 410 322-4917
  70 Mosswood Blvd Ste 200 Youngsville (27596) *(G-17070)*

Backstreets Publishing... 919 968-9466
  200 N Greensboro St Ste D Carrboro (27510) *(G-1645)*

Backwater Guns LLC... 910 399-1451
  1024 S Kerr Ave Wilmington (28403) *(G-16131)*

Backwoods Logging LLC.. 910 298-3786
  1066 Sumner Rd Pink Hill (28572) *(G-12314)*

Backwoods Logging Pink Hl Inc.. 910 298-1284
  1066 Sumner Rd Pink Hill (28572) *(G-12315)*

Backyard Entps & Svcs LLC... 828 755-4960
  281 Spindale St Spindale (28160) *(G-14603)*

Bad Cat Press LLC... 919 870-4908
  13200 Strickland Rd Ste 114-215 Raleigh (27613) *(G-12542)*

Bad Monkey Lures LLC.. 910 433-5617
  835 Jack Pine St Hope Mills (28348) *(G-8732)*

Badger Sportswear LLC... 704 871-0990
  111 Badger Ln Statesville (28625) *(G-14757)*

Badger Sportswear LLC (HQ).. 704 871-0990
  111 Badger Ln Statesville (28625) *(G-14758)*

Badger Welding Incorporated.. 828 863-2078
  387 Creek Rd Rutherfordton (28139) *(G-13865)*

Bae Systems Inc... 855 223-8363
  11215 Rushmore Dr Charlotte (28277) *(G-2263)*

Bae Systems Info Elctrnic Syst.. 919 323-5800
  4721 Emperor Blvd Ste 330 Durham (27703) *(G-4941)*

BAE SYSTEMS INFORMATION AND ELECTRONIC SYSTEMS INTEGRATION INC., Durham Also Called: Bae Systems Info Elctrnic Syst *(G-4941)*

Baebies Inc.. 919 891-0432
  25 Alexandria Way Durham (27709) *(G-4942)*

Bahakel Communications Ltd LLC....................................... 704 372-4434
  701 Television Pl Charlotte (28205) *(G-2264)*

Bahnson Holdings Inc (HQ).. 336 760-3111
  4731 Commercial Park Ct Clemmons (27012) *(G-4029)*

Baicy Communications Inc... 336 722-7768
  1411 S Main St Winston Salem (27127) *(G-16622)*

Baikowski International Corp (HQ)....................................... 704 587-7100
  6601 Northpark Blvd Ste H Charlotte (28216) *(G-2265)*

Bailey Foods LLC.. 252 235-3558
  2500 Nash St N Ste E Wilson (27896) *(G-16472)*

Bailey Sales and Service LLC.. 910 876-1103
  1604 Suggs Taylor Rd Elizabethtown (28337) *(G-5585)*

Bailey Slaughter House, Wilson Also Called: Bailey Foods LLC *(G-16472)*

Baileys Quick Copy Shop Inc (PA)... 704 637-2020
  324 E Fisher St Salisbury (28144) *(G-13929)*

Baileys Sauces Inc... 252 756-7179
  3765 Mills Rd Greenville (27858) *(G-7491)*

Baily Enterprises LLC.. 704 587-0109
  12016 Steele Creek Rd Charlotte (28273) *(G-2266)*

Baja Marine Inc.. 252 975-2000
  1653 Whichards Beach Road Washington (27889) *(G-15683)*

Bakchoe Services... 828 321-3360
  545 Long Branch Rd Topton (28781) *(G-15325)*

Bakeboxx Company.. 336 861-1212
  629 Mcway Dr High Point (27263) *(G-8262)*

Baker Furniture, High Point Also Called: Baker Interiors Furniture Co *(G-8263)*

Baker Interiors Furniture Co (DH).. 336 431-9115
  1 Baker Way Connelly Springs (28612) *(G-4397)*

Baker Interiors Furniture Co.. 336 431-9115
  2219 Shore St High Point (27263) *(G-8263)*

Baker Taylor Investments I LLC... 704 998-3100
  2810 Clseum Cntre Dr 30 # 300 Charlotte (28217) *(G-2267)*

Baker Thermal Solutions LLC... 919 674-3750
  8182 Us 70 Bus Hwy W Clayton (27520) *(G-3957)*

Bakers Quality Trim Inc... 919 552-3621
  1616 Kendall Hill Rd Willow Spring (27592) *(G-16075)*

Bakers Southern Traditions Inc.. 252 344-2120
  704 E Church St Roxobel (27872) *(G-13829)*

Bakers Sthern Trdtions Peanuts, Roxobel Also Called: Bakers Southern Traditions Inc *(G-13829)*

Bakers Stnless Fabrication Inc... 919 934-2707
  1520 Freedom Rd Smithfield (27577) *(G-14450)*

Bakery Feeds, Marshville Also Called: Griffin Industries LLC *(G-10217)*

Bakeshot Prtg & Graphics LLC.. 704 532-9326
  121 Greenwich Rd Ste 101 Charlotte (28211) *(G-2268)*

Bakkavor Foods Usa Inc.. 704 522-1977
  10220 Western Ridge Rd Ste P Charlotte (28273) *(G-2269)*

Bakkavor Foods Usa Inc (DH).. 704 522-1977
  2700 Westinghouse Blvd Charlotte (28273) *(G-2270)*

Balance Systems, Statesville Also Called: Amesbury Acqstion Hldngs 2 Inc *(G-14747)*

Balanced Health Plus LLC.. 704 604-9524
  7804 Fairview Rd Box 275 Charlotte (28226) *(G-2271)*

Balanced Pharma Incorporated... 704 278-7054
  18204 Mainsail Pointe Dr Cornelius (28031) *(G-4525)*

Balcrank Corporation

ALPHABETIC SECTION

Balcrank Corporation.. 800 747-5300
  90 Monticello Rd Weaverville (28787) *(G-15838)*
Baldini For Men.. 910 239-9150
  1125 Military Cutoff Rd Ste H Wilmington (28405) *(G-16132)*
Baldor Dodge Reliance.. 828 652-0074
  510 Rockwell Dr Marion (28752) *(G-10141)*
Baldor Dodge Reliance, Weaverville Also Called: ABB Motors and Mechanical Inc *(G-15836)*
Baldor Motors & Drives, Greensboro Also Called: ABB Motors and Mechanical Inc *(G-6772)*
Baldwin Sign & Awning.. 910 642-8812
  2 Whiteville Mini Mall Whiteville (28472) *(G-15959)*
Baldwin Wood Works LLC.. 828 974-2716
  143 Knoll Ridge Rd Mills River (28759) *(G-10499)*
Ball Metal Beverage Cont Corp.. 336 342-4711
  1900 Barnes St Reidsville (27320) *(G-13507)*
Ball Metal Beverage Cont Div, Reidsville Also Called: Ball Metal Beverage Cont Corp *(G-13507)*
Ball Photo, Asheville Also Called: Ball Photo Supply Inc *(G-556)*
Ball Photo Supply Inc.. 828 252-2443
  85 Tunnel Rd Ste 8 Asheville (28805) *(G-556)*
Ball S Machine, Candler Also Called: Ball S Machine & Mfg Co Inc *(G-1570)*
Ball S Machine & Mfg Co Inc.. 828 667-0411
  2120 Smoky Park Hwy Candler (28715) *(G-1570)*
Ballabox, Matthews Also Called: Kme Consolidated Inc *(G-10260)*
Ballantyne One.. 704 926-7009
  15720 Brixham Hill Ave Ste 300 Charlotte (28277) *(G-2272)*
Ballash Woodworks LLC.. 910 709-0717
  701 Murray Hill Rd Fayetteville (28303) *(G-5768)*
Ballistic Recovery Systems Inc (PA)....................................... 651 457-7491
  41383 Us 1 Hwy Pinebluff (28373) *(G-12213)*
Ballistics Technology Intl Ltd... 252 360-1650
  511 Goldsboro St Ne Wilson (27893) *(G-16473)*
Ballpointe Pubg & Design LLC.. 919 453-0449
  1200 Crozier Ct Wake Forest (27587) *(G-15530)*
Bally Refrigerated Boxes Inc (PA).. 252 240-2829
  135 Little Nine Rd Morehead City (28557) *(G-11151)*
Baltek Inc (DH).. 336 398-1900
  5240 National Center Dr Colfax (27235) *(G-4141)*
Bamal Corporation (HQ)... 980 225-7700
  13725 S Point Blvd Charlotte (28273) *(G-2273)*
Bamal Fastener, Charlotte Also Called: Bamal Corporation *(G-2273)*
Bandera Us LLC.. 224 250-6559
  2120 Airport Flex Dr Charlotte (28208) *(G-2274)*
Banilla Games Inc... 252 329-7977
  3506 Greenville Blvd Ne Greenville (27834) *(G-7492)*
Banknote Corp America Inc.. 336 375-1134
  6109 Corporate Park Dr Browns Summit (27214) *(G-1300)*
Banknote Corporation America, Browns Summit Also Called: Sennett Security Products LLC *(G-1315)*
Banks Rd Concrete Plant, Fuquay Varina Also Called: S T Wooten Corporation *(G-6227)*
Banks Welding.. 828 586-2258
  465 Old Settlement Rd Sylva (28779) *(G-15053)*
Banks, Steve and Ray Logging, Maysville Also Called: Steve & Ray Banks Logging Inc *(G-10376)*
Banner Elk Winery & Villa, Banner Elk Also Called: Banner Elk Winery Inc *(G-893)*
Banner Elk Winery Inc.. 828 898-9090
  135 Deer Run Ln Banner Elk (28604) *(G-892)*
Banner Elk Winery Inc (PA).. 828 260-1790
  60 Deer Run Ln Banner Elk (28604) *(G-893)*
Banner Life Sciences LLC.. 336 812-8700
  3980 Premier Dr Ste 110 High Point (27265) *(G-8264)*
Banner Signs Today Inc... 704 525-2241
  2526 S Tryon St Charlotte (28203) *(G-2275)*
Bannister Inc.. 252 638-6611
  303 Crescent St New Bern (28560) *(G-11776)*
Bar Argon... 704 574-9486
  4544 South Blvd Ste H Charlotte (28209) *(G-2276)*
Bar Squared Inc... 919 878-0578
  5605 Spring Ct Raleigh (27616) *(G-12543)*
Bar-S Foods Co.. 847 652-3238
  2101 Westinghouse Blvd Ste 109 Raleigh (27604) *(G-12544)*
Barbaras Canine Catering Inc.. 704 588-3647
  1447 S Tryon St Ste 101 Charlotte (28203) *(G-2277)*

Barber Furniture & Supply.. 704 278-9367
  590 Mountain Rd Cleveland (27013) *(G-4068)*
Barber Shop AP Screen Prtg, Fayetteville Also Called: Kraken-Skulls *(G-5855)*
Barbour S Marine Supply Co Inc.. 252 728-2136
  410 Hedrick St Beaufort (28516) *(G-944)*
Barcovision LLC... 704 392-9371
  4420 Taggart Creek Rd Charlotte (28208) *(G-2278)*
Barcovvsion LLC (PA).. 704 392-9371
  4420 Taggart Creek Rd Ste 110 Charlotte (28208) *(G-2279)*
Barcy, D T Logging, Ahoskie Also Called: Darrell T Bracy *(G-60)*
Barden Metal Fabrication LLC.. 252 772-5984
  116 Elizabeth St Havelock (28532) *(G-7740)*
Barefoot Cnc Inc.. 828 438-5038
  333 Sanford Dr Morganton (28655) *(G-11199)*
Barefoot Press Inc.. 919 283-6396
  731 Pershing Rd Raleigh (27608) *(G-12545)*
Bares Backhoe & Septic System... 336 352-3951
  2020 Haystack Rd Mount Airy (27030) *(G-11480)*
Barewoodworking Inc.. 828 758-0694
  4400 Fox Rd Lenoir (28645) *(G-9578)*
Bargainstairpartscom LLC... 214 883-9524
  1525 Danny Bell Rd Asheboro (27205) *(G-408)*
Bariatric Partners Inc... 704 542-2256
  7401 Carmel Executive Park Dr Charlotte (28226) *(G-2280)*
Bark House Supply Company.. 828 765-9010
  534 Oak Ave Spruce Pine (28777) *(G-14629)*
Barker and Martin Inc... 336 275-5056
  1316 Headquarters Dr Greensboro (27405) *(G-6831)*
Barker Industries Inc (PA).. 704 391-1023
  220 Crompton St Charlotte (28273) *(G-2281)*
Barkleys Mill On Southern Cro.. 828 626-3344
  6 Barkley Pl Weaverville (28787) *(G-15839)*
Barlin Ranch & Pets Inc.. 910 814-1930
  390 D R Harvell Ln Lillington (27546) *(G-9843)*
Barnes Dmnd Gllery Jwly Mfrs I.. 910 347-4300
  120 College Plz Jacksonville (28546) *(G-8989)*
Barnes Logging Co Inc.. 252 799-6016
  308 Golf Rd Plymouth (27962) *(G-12365)*
Barnes Metalcrafters, Wilson Also Called: South East Manufacturing Co *(G-16542)*
Barnes Precision Machine Inc.. 919 362-6805
  1434 Farrington Rd Ste 300 Apex (27523) *(G-170)*
Barnhardt Manufacturing Co... 704 331-0657
  1300 Hawthorne Ln Charlotte (28205) *(G-2282)*
Barnhardt Manufacturing Co... 336 789-9161
  1515 Carter St Mount Airy (27030) *(G-11481)*
Barnhardt Manufacturing Company (PA)............................... 800 277-0377
  1100 Hawthorne Ln Charlotte (28205) *(G-2283)*
Barnhardts Woodworking Co.. 336 449-5564
  1576 Nc Highway 61 Whitsett (27377) *(G-15983)*
Barnhill Contracting Company.. 336 584-1306
  1858 Huffman Mill Rd Burlington (27215) *(G-1375)*
Barnhill Contracting Company.. 704 721-7500
  725 Derita Rd Concord (28027) *(G-4204)*
Barnhill Contracting Company.. 910 488-1319
  1100 Robeson St Fayetteville (28305) *(G-5769)*
Barnhill Contracting Company.. 252 752-7608
  562 Barrus Construction Rd Greenville (27834) *(G-7493)*
Barnhill Contracting Company.. 252 527-8021
  604 E New Bern Rd Kinston (28504) *(G-9344)*
Barnhill Metal Fabrication.. 252 236-5114
  6247 Webb Lake Rd Elm City (27822) *(G-5646)*
Barnyard Utility Bldngs-Strg/Tl... 704 867-4700
  1990 E Franklin Blvd Gastonia (28054) *(G-6351)*
Barnyard Utility Bldngs-Strg/Tl... 704 226-9454
  3906 W Highway 74 Monroe (28110) *(G-10660)*
Barracuda Displays... 704 322-0971
  3305 Muddy Creek Rd Midland (28107) *(G-10456)*
Barrday Corp (HQ).. 704 395-0311
  1450 W Pointe Dr Ste C Charlotte (28214) *(G-2284)*
Barrday Protective Solutions, Charlotte Also Called: Barrday Corp *(G-2284)*
Barrette Welch McFall Ms... 919 606-7537
  3705 Saint Marks Rd Durham (27707) *(G-4943)*

ALPHABETIC SECTION

Barretts Printing House Inc.. 252 243-2820
409 Goldsboro St S Wilson (27893) *(G-16474)*

Barrier1, Greensboro *Also Called: Barrier1 Systems Inc (G-6832)*

Barrier1 Systems Inc.. 336 617-8478
8015 Thorndike Rd Greensboro (27409) *(G-6832)*

Barron Legacy Mgmt Group LLC.. 301 367-4735
1737 Arbor Vista Dr Charlotte (28262) *(G-2285)*

Barrs Competition.. 704 482-5169
124 Drum Rd Shelby (28152) *(G-14287)*

Barry Callebaut USA LLC.. 828 685-2443
51 Saint Pauls Rd Hendersonville (28792) *(G-7823)*

Barry Lane Perry.. 252 799-4334
2465 Manning Rd Jamesville (27846) *(G-9078)*

Barry Lowe Fabrication.. 828 776-7354
1583 Charlotte Hwy Fairview (28730) *(G-5708)*

Barrys Custom Lures LLC.. 828 256-1792
3463 38th Street Dr Ne Hickory (28601) *(G-7948)*

Barsina Publishing.. 336 869-2849
3510 Pine Valley Rd High Point (27265) *(G-8265)*

Bartimaeus By Design Inc.. 336 475-4346
1010 Randolph St Thomasville (27360) *(G-15188)*

Bartlett Milling Company LP.. 704 487-5061
1101 Airport Rd Shelby (28150) *(G-14288)*

Bartlett Milling Company LP.. 704 872-9581
701 S Center St Statesville (28677) *(G-14759)*

Bartleys Backhoe Service.. 910 918-1384
5751 Peacock Rd Chadbourn (28431) *(G-1974)*

Barudan America Inc.. 800 627-4776
9826 Us Highway 311 Ste 4 High Point (27263) *(G-8266)*

Basalt Specialty Products Inc.. 336 835-5153
600 E Main St Elkin (28621) *(G-5610)*

Baseline Screen Printing.. 336 857-0101
7148 Charles Mountain Rd Denton (27239) *(G-4726)*

BASF.. 919 731-1700
703 Nor Am Rd Pikeville (27863) *(G-12191)*

BASF Corporation.. 704 588-5280
11501 Steele Creek Rd Charlotte (28273) *(G-2286)*

BASF Corporation.. 919 433-6773
2 Tw Alexander Dr Durham (27709) *(G-4944)*

BASF Corporation.. 919 547-2000
26 Davis Dr Durham (27709) *(G-4945)*

BASF Corporation.. 919 461-6500
3500 Paramount Pkwy Morrisville (27560) *(G-11299)*

BASF Plant Science LP.. 919 547-2000
26 Davis Dr Durham (27709) *(G-4946)*

Basic American Foods.. 336 887-3930
1560 N Main St Ste 101a High Point (27262) *(G-8267)*

Basic Group, The, Siler City *Also Called: Basic Machinery Company Inc (G-14399)*

Basic Machinery Company Inc.. 919 663-2244
1220 Harold Andrews Rd Siler City (27344) *(G-14399)*

Baskin-Robbins, Knightdale *Also Called: Dunkin Donuts (G-9417)*

Basofil Fibers LLC.. 828 304-2307
4824 Parkway Plaza Blvd Ste 250 Charlotte (28217) *(G-2287)*

Bass Fabrications LLC.. 252 312-8937
36 Keys Cross Rd Hobbsville (27946) *(G-8674)*

Bass Farm Sausage, Spring Hope *Also Called: Bass Farms Inc (G-14613)*

Bass Farms Inc.. 252 478-4147
6685 Highway 64 Alt East Spring Hope (27882) *(G-14613)*

Bassett Furniture Direct, Concord *Also Called: Bassett Furniture Direct Inc (G-4205)*

Bassett Furniture Direct Inc.. 704 979-5700
7830 Lyles Ln Nw Concord (28027) *(G-4205)*

Bassett Furniture Inds Inc.. 828 465-7700
111 E 20th St Newton (28658) *(G-11915)*

Bassett Upholstery Division, Newton *Also Called: Bassett Furniture Inds Inc (G-11915)*

Bastrop Skid Company (PA).. 252 793-6600
111 W Water St Plymouth (27962) *(G-12366)*

Bat Publishing.. 828 754-2216
3125 Auld Farm Dr Lenoir (28645) *(G-9579)*

Batca Fitness Systems, Raleigh *Also Called: RSR Fitness Inc (G-13217)*

Batchlers LLC.. 910 619-4042
211 Hervey Ln Wilmington (28411) *(G-16133)*

Bateman Logging Co Inc.. 252 482-8959
1531 Virginia Rd Edenton (27932) *(G-5508)*

Batista Grading Inc.. 919 359-3449
710 E Main St Clayton (27520) *(G-3958)*

Batt Fabricators Inc.. 336 431-9334
12957 Trinity Rd Trinity (27370) *(G-15339)*

Batteries Plus, Raleigh *Also Called: Alk Investments LLC (G-12488)*

Battery Watering Systems LLC.. 336 714-0448
6645 Holder Rd Clemmons (27012) *(G-4030)*

Battery Watering Technology, Clemmons *Also Called: Fourshare LLC (G-4039)*

Battle Fermentables LLC (PA).. 336 225-4585
1604 Lathrop St Durham (27703) *(G-4947)*

Battle Trucking Inc.. 919 708-2288
911 San Lee Dr Sanford (27330) *(G-14092)*

Battle Trucking Company, Sanford *Also Called: Battle Trucking Inc (G-14092)*

Battlgrund Strter Gnerator Inc.. 336 685-4511
4497 Folger Rd Julian (27283) *(G-9104)*

Baumgartner Associates, Navassa *Also Called: Pacon Manufacturing Corp LLC (G-11758)*

Baur Logging LLC.. 757 535-5693
613 Court St Gatesville (27938) *(G-6547)*

Bausch Health Americas Inc.. 949 461-6000
406 Blackwell St Ste 410 Durham (27701) *(G-4948)*

Baxter Healthcare Corporation.. 828 756-6600
65 Pitts Station Rd Marion (28752) *(G-10142)*

Baxter Healthcare Corporation.. 828 756-6623
65 Pitts Station Rd Marion (28752) *(G-10143)*

Baxter US, Marion *Also Called: Baxter Healthcare Corporation (G-10142)*

Bay Breeze Seafood, Hendersonville *Also Called: Bay Breeze Seafood Rest Inc (G-7824)*

Bay Breeze Seafood Rest Inc.. 828 697-7106
1830 Asheville Hwy Hendersonville (28791) *(G-7824)*

Bay City Crab Inc.. 252 322-5291
1131 Main Street Ext Aurora (27806) *(G-832)*

Bay Painting Contractors.. 252 435-5374
128 Bayside Dr Moyock (27958) *(G-11692)*

Bay Six, Raleigh *Also Called: B6usa Inc (G-12541)*

Bay State Milling Company.. 704 664-4873
448 N Main St Mooresville (28115) *(G-10870)*

Bay Tech Label Inc.. 828 296-8900
36 Old Charlotte Hwy Asheville (28803) *(G-557)*

Bay Valley Foods LLC.. 715 366-4511
2953 N Nc 111 903 Hwy Albertson (28508) *(G-114)*

Bay Valley Foods LLC.. 910 267-4711
354 N Faison Ave Faison (28341) *(G-5721)*

Bay Valley Foods LLC.. 704 476-7141
120 Woodlake Pkwy Kings Mountain (28086) *(G-9294)*

Bayatronics LLC.. 980 432-0438
7089 Weddington Rd Nw Concord (28027) *(G-4206)*

Bayer Agriculture, Durham *Also Called: Bayer Corporation (G-4949)*

Bayer Corp.. 704 373-0991
2332 Croydon Rd Charlotte (28207) *(G-2288)*

Bayer Corporation.. 800 242-5897
2 Tw Alexander Dr Durham (27709) *(G-4949)*

Bayer Cropscience, Cary *Also Called: Environmental Science US LLC (G-1759)*

Bayer Cropscience Inc.. 412 777-2000
2400 Ellis Rd Durham (27703) *(G-4950)*

Bayer Healthcare LLC.. 919 461-6525
3500 Paramount Pkwy Morrisville (27560) *(G-11300)*

Bayer Hlthcare Pharmaceuticals.. 602 469-6846
1820 Liatris Ln Raleigh (27613) *(G-12546)*

Bayer Technology and Services, Morrisville *Also Called: Bayer Healthcare LLC (G-11300)*

Bayliss Boatworks Inc.. 252 473-9797
600 Harbor Rd Wanchese (27981) *(G-15641)*

Bayliss Boatyard Inc.. 252 473-9797
600 Harbor Rd Wanchese (27981) *(G-15642)*

Baypointe Partners LLC.. 336 882-5200
403 Interstate Dr Archdale (27263) *(G-269)*

Baysix USA.. 919 833-3851
414 Dupont Cir Raleigh (27603) *(G-12547)*

BB Metals Inc.. 336 345-3430
148 Primrose Dr Lexington (27292) *(G-9684)*

BB&p Embroidery LLC 252 206-1929
2801 Ward Blvd Wilson (27893) *(G-16475)*

Bbf Printing Solutions 336 969-2323
1190 Old Beltway Rural Hall (27045) *(G-13833)*

BBT ARCHIVES, Sandy Ridge *Also Called: Bhaktivedanta Archives (G-14076)*

Bcac Holdings LLC 910 754-5689
674 Ocean Hwy W Supply (28462) *(G-15006)*

Bce South, Indian Trail *Also Called: 3 Star Enterprises LLC (G-8917)*

Bce South, Indian Trail *Also Called: Laru Industries Inc (G-8944)*

Bcp East Land LLC 704 248-2000
13860 Balntyn Corp Pl Charlotte (28277) *(G-2289)*

Bd Diagnostics Tripath, Burlington *Also Called: Tripath Imaging Inc (G-1509)*

Bd Medical Technology, Durham *Also Called: Becton Dickinson and Company (G-4952)*

Be Aerospace, Winston Salem *Also Called: B/E Aerospace Inc (G-16620)*

Be House Publishing LLC 336 529-6143
400 Barnes Rd Winston Salem (27107) *(G-16623)*

Be Pharmaceuticals Inc 704 560-1444
203 New Edition Ct Cary (27511) *(G-1699)*

Beach Craft Woodworking LLC 919 624-4463
100 Parkbow Ct Cary (27519) *(G-1700)*

Beach House Publications LLC 252 504-2344
2475 Hwy 70 Beaufort Beaufort (28516) *(G-945)*

Beachbub USA 336 965-5941
561 Pegg Rd Greensboro (27409) *(G-6833)*

Beacon Industrial Mfg LLC 704 399-7441
4404a Chesapeake Dr Charlotte (28216) *(G-2290)*

Beacon Prosthetics & Orthotics 919 231-6890
3224 Lake Woodard Dr Raleigh (27604) *(G-12548)*

Beacon Prosthetics & Orthotics, Raleigh *Also Called: Adaptive Technologies LLC (G-12475)*

Beacon Roofing Supply Inc 704 886-1555
1836 Equitable Pl Charlotte (28213) *(G-2291)*

Beacon Thermography Inc 727 470-1694
406 Adelaide Dr Hampstead (28443) *(G-7640)*

Beaker Inc 919 803-7422
700 Spring Forest Rd Ste 121 Raleigh (27609) *(G-12549)*

Beane Signs Inc 336 629-6748
218 Vista Pkwy Asheboro (27205) *(G-409)*

Bear Creek Fabrication LLC 919 837-2444
1930 Campbell Rd Bear Creek (27207) *(G-936)*

Bear Creek Log Tmber Homes LLC 336 751-6180
371 Valley Rd Mocksville (27028) *(G-10557)*

Bear Creek Raceway Inc 336 367-4264
8736 Us 601 Dobson (27017) *(G-4819)*

Bear Pages 828 837-0785
99 Smoke Rise Cir Murphy (28906) *(G-11706)*

Beard Hosiery Co 828 758-1942
652 Nuway Cir Lenoir (28645) *(G-9580)*

Beardowadams Inc 704 359-8443
3034 Horseshoe Ln Charlotte (28208) *(G-2292)*

Bearwaters Brewing Company 828 237-4200
101 Park St Canton (28716) *(G-1599)*

Beasley Contracting 828 479-3675
756 Gladdens Creek Rd Robbinsville (28771) *(G-13604)*

Beasley Flooring Products Inc 828 524-3248
77 Industrial Park Rd Bryson City (28713) *(G-1320)*

Beasley Flooring Products Inc 828 349-7000
41 Hardwood Dr Franklin (28734) *(G-6116)*

Beast Chains 336 346-9081
733 Spinning Wheel Pt High Point (27265) *(G-8268)*

Beaty Corporation 704 599-4949
7407 N Tryon St Charlotte (28262) *(G-2293)*

Beaufort Composite Tech Inc 252 728-1547
111 Safrit Dr Beaufort (28516) *(G-946)*

Beaufort Naval Armorers, Morehead City *Also Called: Bircher Incorporated (G-11153)*

Beaufurn, Advance *Also Called: Beaufurn LLC (G-38)*

Beaufurn LLC 336 768-2544
5269 Us Highway 158 Advance (27006) *(G-38)*

Beautiful Brains Inc 828 244-5850
508 4th Ave Ne Conover (28613) *(G-4421)*

Beautimar Manufactured MBL Inc 919 779-1181
1221 Home Ct Raleigh (27603) *(G-12550)*

Beauty 4 Love LLC 704 802-2844
1819 Sardis Rd N Ste 350 Charlotte (28270) *(G-2294)*

Beauty Elements LLC 910 333-9957
200 Doctors Dr Ste C Jacksonville (28546) *(G-8990)*

Beaver Tooth Milling Inc 910 262-4438
209 Midway Rd Se Bolivia (28422) *(G-1162)*

Beazer East Inc 919 567-9512
7000 Cass Holt Rd Holly Springs (27540) *(G-8688)*

Beazer East Inc 919 380-2610
3131 Rdu Center Dr Ste 220 Morrisville (27560) *(G-11301)*

Bebida Beverage Company 704 660-0226
1304 N Barkley Rd Statesville (28677) *(G-14760)*

BEC 919 244-0831
4908 Linksland Dr Holly Springs (27540) *(G-8689)*

BEC, Raleigh *Also Called: Beyond Electronics Corp (G-12553)*

BEC-Car Printing Co Inc (PA) 704 873-1911
970 Davie Ave Statesville (28677) *(G-14761)*

BEC-Faye LLC 252 714-8700
3393 Mobleys Bridge Rd Grimesland (27837) *(G-7604)*

Beckett Media LP 800 508-2582
2222 Sedwick Rd Ste 102 Durham (27713) *(G-4951)*

Beco Holding Company Inc (PA) 800 826-3473
10926 David Taylor Dr Ste 300 Charlotte (28262) *(G-2295)*

Becton Dickinson and Company 201 847-6800
21 Davis Dr Durham (27709) *(G-4952)*

Becton Dickinson and Company 919 963-1307
130 Four Oaks Pkwy Four Oaks (27524) *(G-6100)*

Becwill Corp 919 552-8266
3209 Air Park Rd Fuquay Varina (27526) *(G-6183)*

Bed In A Box 800 588-5720
199 Woltz St Mount Airy (27030) *(G-11482)*

Bedard Custom Woodworks 828 432-6556
1513 Southpointe Dr Morganton (28655) *(G-11200)*

Bedex LLC 336 617-6755
210 Swathmore Ave High Point (27263) *(G-8269)*

Bee Line Printing, Burgaw *Also Called: Jofra Graphics Inc (G-1342)*

Bee Tree Hardwoods, Swannanoa *Also Called: Southeastern Hardwoods Inc (G-15037)*

Beeline Global LLC 704 562-8221
5560 Holyoke Ln Charlotte (28226) *(G-2296)*

Beelite Inc 828 584-1488
3292 Norman Dr Morganton (28655) *(G-11201)*

Beer Study 919 240-5423
504 W Franklin St Chapel Hill (27516) *(G-1989)*

Beeson Sign Co Inc 336 993-5617
213 Berry Garden Rd Kernersville (27284) *(G-9167)*

Beet River Traders, Ramseur *Also Called: Line Drive Sports Center Inc (G-13446)*

Beewell, Raleigh *Also Called: Medvertical LLC (G-13014)*

Befco Inc 252 977-9920
1781 S Wesleyan Blvd Rocky Mount (27803) *(G-13684)*

Behappy.me, Charlotte *Also Called: Printful Inc (G-3388)*

Bejeweled Creations 336 552-0841
386 River Run Dr Reidsville (27320) *(G-13508)*

Bekaert Textiles USA Inc 336 769-4300
200 Business Park Dr Winston Salem (27107) *(G-16624)*

Bekaertdeslee USA Inc 336 747-4900
200 Business Park Dr Winston Salem (27107) *(G-16625)*

Bekaertdeslee USA Inc 336 769-4300
Business Park Dr 240 Winston Salem (27107) *(G-16626)*

Belev En U Water Mfg Co 704 620-0450
19600 W Catawba Ave Ste 201 Cornelius (28031) *(G-4526)*

Belevation LLC 803 517-9030
207 Shady Oak Dr Biscoe (27209) *(G-1104)*

Belews Creek Vineyard 904 345-1466
1952 Pondarosa Dr Kernersville (27284) *(G-9168)*

Belham Management Ind LLC 704 815-4246
9307 Monroe Rd Ste A Charlotte (28270) *(G-2297)*

Belk Construction Inc 704 507-6327
358 Montibello Dr Mooresville (28117) *(G-10871)*

Belk Department Stores LP 704 357-4000
2801 W Tyvola Rd Charlotte (28217) *(G-2298)*

Belkoz Inc 919 703-0694
4900 Thornton Rd Raleigh (27616) *(G-12551)*

ALPHABETIC SECTION

Bell and Howell LLC (PA)..919 767-4401
   3791 S Alston Ave Durham (27713) *(G-4953)*

Bell and Howell LLC..919 767-6400
   3791 S Alston Ave Durham (27713) *(G-4954)*

Bell Book & Candle LLC...336 480-1422
   1801 Curraghmore Rd Clemmons (27012) *(G-4031)*

Bellaire Dynamik LLC...704 779-3755
   4714 Stockholm Ct Charlotte (28273) *(G-2299)*

Bellalou Designs, Wilson *Also Called: Pridgen-Lucas Latisha (G-16523)*

Bellatony, Pineville *Also Called: Forklift Pro Inc (G-12269)*

Belle Embroidery LLC..704 436-6895
   6744 Cress Rd Concord (28025) *(G-4207)*

BellSouth, Charlotte *Also Called: Yp Advrtising Pubg LLC Not LLC (G-3847)*

BellSouth, Wilmington *Also Called: Yp Advrtising Pubg LLC Not LLC (G-16459)*

Belmont Textile Machinery Co..704 827-5836
   1212 W Catawba Ave Mount Holly (28120) *(G-11622)*

Belocal Publishing LLC..910 202-1917
   5051 New Centre Dr Wilmington (28403) *(G-16134)*

Belt Concepts America Inc..888 598-2358
   605 N Pine St Spring Hope (27882) *(G-14614)*

Belt Shop Inc...704 865-3636
   1941 Chespark Dr Gastonia (28052) *(G-6352)*

Beltservice Corporation...704 947-2264
   9540 Julian Clark Ave Huntersville (28078) *(G-8797)*

Belvedere Cabinets Inc..919 949-2005
   103 Parkspring Ct Cary (27519) *(G-1701)*

Belvoir Manufacturing Corp (PA)...252 746-1274
   4081 Nc Highway 33 W Greenville (27834) *(G-7494)*

Belwith Products LLC..336 841-3899
   1006 N Main St High Point (27262) *(G-8270)*

Bemco Sleep Products Inc..910 892-3107
   601 N Ashe Ave Dunn (28334) *(G-4853)*

Bemis Manufacturing Company...828 754-1086
   201 Industrial Ct Lenoir (28645) *(G-9581)*

Ben Huffman Enterprises LLC...704 724-4705
   516 River Hwy Ste D Mooresville (28117) *(G-10872)*

Ben Pushpa Inc..828 428-8590
   2896 E Maiden Rd Maiden (28650) *(G-10099)*

Benchmark Screen Ptg Design..704 785-7826
   12416 Pine Bluff Rd Midland (28107) *(G-10457)*

Bendel Tank Heat Exchanger LLC.....................................704 596-5112
   4823 N Graham St Charlotte (28269) *(G-2300)*

Bender Apparel & Signs Inc..252 636-8337
   1841 Old Airport Rd New Bern (28562) *(G-11777)*

Bender Signs..252 631-5144
   8400 Us Highway 17 Pollocksville (28573) *(G-12392)*

Bengal Protea, Greensboro *Also Called: Bengal-Protea Ltd (G-6834)*

Bengal-Protea Ltd...336 299-0299
   600 Green Valley Rd Ste 303 Greensboro (27408) *(G-6834)*

Benjamin Moore Authorized Ret, Shelby *Also Called: Cleveland Lumber Company (G-14298)*

Benmot Publishing Company Inc.......................................919 658-9456
   214 N Center St Mount Olive (28365) *(G-11655)*

Bennett & Associates Inc..919 477-7362
   3312 Guess Rd Durham (27705) *(G-4955)*

Bennett Brothers Yachts Inc..910 772-9277
   1701 Jel Wade Dr Ste 16 Wilmington (28401) *(G-16135)*

Bennett Buildings of Conover..828 465-6117
   920 Conover Blvd W Conover (28613) *(G-4422)*

Bennett Elec Maint & Cnstr LLC..910 231-0300
   586 Allegiance St Raeford (28376) *(G-12414)*

Bennett Uniform Mfg Inc (PA)...336 232-5772
   4377 Federal Dr Greensboro (27410) *(G-6835)*

Bent Creek Studio LLC...336 692-6477
   162 Washington Dr Clemmons (27012) *(G-4032)*

Bently Nevada LLC..919 772-5530
   1411 Kenbrook Dr Garner (27529) *(G-6256)*

Benton & Sons Fabrication Inc..919 734-1700
   1921 N Nc 581 Hwy Pikeville (27863) *(G-12192)*

Benton Card, Benson *Also Called: Graphic Products Inc (G-1035)*

Bentons Wldg Repr & Svcs Inc..910 343-8322
   1206 S 3rd St Wilmington (28401) *(G-16136)*

Benz Tling A Bus Unit Schnck U, Conover *Also Called: Schenck USA Corp (G-4495)*

Beocare Inc..828 728-7300
   1905 International Blvd Hudson (28638) *(G-8762)*

Beocare Group Inc (PA)...828 728-7300
   1905 International Blvd Hudson (28638) *(G-8763)*

Ber-Car Printing, Statesville *Also Called: BEC-Car Printing Co Inc (G-14761)*

Berco of America Inc..336 931-1415
   615 Pegg Rd Greensboro (27409) *(G-6836)*

Berenfield Containers, Harrisburg *Also Called: Mauser Usa LLC (G-7718)*

Berkeley Home Furniture LLC...336 882-0012
   2228 Shore St High Point (27263) *(G-8271)*

Bermlord LLC..704 631-4304
   8912 Windygap Rd Charlotte (28278) *(G-2301)*

Bernhardt Design Plant 3, Lenoir *Also Called: Bernhardt Furniture Company (G-9583)*

Bernhardt Design Plant 7, Lenoir *Also Called: Bernhardt Furniture Company (G-9587)*

Bernhardt Furniture Company..828 572-4664
   1814 Morganton Blvd Sw Lenoir (28645) *(G-9582)*

Bernhardt Furniture Company..828 759-6245
   1502 Morganton Blvd Sw Lenoir (28645) *(G-9583)*

Bernhardt Furniture Company..828 759-6652
   1828 Morganton Blvd Sw Lenoir (28645) *(G-9584)*

Bernhardt Furniture Company..828 758-9811
   1840 Morganton Blvd Sw Lenoir (28645) *(G-9585)*

Bernhardt Furniture Company (HQ)...................................828 758-9811
   1839 Morganton Blvd Sw Lenoir (28645) *(G-9586)*

Bernhardt Furniture Company..828 759-6205
   1402 Morganton Blvd Sw Lenoir (28645) *(G-9587)*

Bernhardt Furniture Company, Lenoir *Also Called: Bernhardt Industries Inc (G-9588)*

Bernhardt Industries Inc (PA)...828 758-9811
   1839 Morganton Blvd Sw Lenoir (28645) *(G-9588)*

Beroth Tire of Mocksville, Mocksville *Also Called: Mock Tire & Automotive Inc (G-10591)*

Berry Cold LLC...910 267-4531
   2488 W Nc 403 Hwy Faison (28341) *(G-5722)*

Berry Global Inc..252 332-7270
   228 Johnny Mitchell Rd Ahoskie (27910) *(G-55)*

Berry Global Inc..252 984-4100
   6941 Corporation Pkwy Battleboro (27809) *(G-918)*

Berry Global Inc..919 207-3202
   1203 Chicopee Rd Benson (27504) *(G-1031)*

Berry Global Inc..704 697-5100
   9335 Harris Corners Pkwy Ste 300 Charlotte (28269) *(G-2302)*

Berry Global Inc..336 841-1723
   314 Mandustry St High Point (27262) *(G-8272)*

Berry Global Inc..704 289-1526
   3414 Wesley Chapel Stouts Rd Monroe (28110) *(G-10661)*

Berry Global Inc..704 664-3733
   111 Excellance Ln Mooresville (28115) *(G-10873)*

Berry Global Inc..252 984-4104
   6941 Corporation Pkwy Rocky Mount (27801) *(G-13664)*

Berry Global Films LLC...704 821-2316
   303 Seaboard Dr Matthews (28104) *(G-10304)*

Berry Plastics, Ahoskie *Also Called: Berry Global Inc (G-55)*

Berry Plastics, Charlotte *Also Called: Berry Global Inc (G-2302)*

Berry Plastics, Mooresville *Also Called: Berry Global Inc (G-10873)*

Bertie County Peanuts, Windsor *Also Called: Powell & Stokes Inc (G-16568)*

Besam Entrance Solution, Monroe *Also Called: Assa Abloy Entmce Systems US (G-10655)*

Besana-Lovati Inc (PA)...336 768-6064
   4112 W Old Us 421 Hwy Hamptonville (27020) *(G-7667)*

Besi Machining LLC..919 218-9241
   95 Cypress Dr Youngsville (27596) *(G-17071)*

Bessemer City Machinery Sales, Bessemer City *Also Called: Bessemer City Machine Shop Inc (G-1053)*

Bessemer City Machine Shop Inc.....................................704 629-4111
   524 Bess Town Rd Bessemer City (28016) *(G-1053)*

Best Bar Ever Inc..910 508-3628
   Raleigh (27611) *(G-12552)*

Best Choice Met Structures LLC.......................................877 683-1168
   370 Standard St Elkin (28621) *(G-5611)*

Best Image Signs LLC..336 973-7445
   178 Nicholas Landing Dr Wilkesboro (28697) *(G-16014)*

ALPHABETIC SECTION

Best Image Signs and Graphics, Wilkesboro Also Called: Best Image Signs LLC *(G-16014)*
Best Kiteboarding, Rodanthe Also Called: Ride Best LLC *(G-13756)*
Best Machine & Fabrication Inc 919 731-7101
 117 Sleepy Creek Rd Dudley (28333) *(G-4840)*
Best Price Appliance LLC 336 662-3117
 2101 Patterson St Ste A Greensboro (27407) *(G-6837)*
Best Solution Cargo LLC 407 810-5559
 3600 S College Rd Ste E359 Wilmington (28412) *(G-16137)*
Best Vacuum Cleaners, Hayesville Also Called: Corvac Inc *(G-7764)*
Best Workers Company 336 665-0076
 5494 Port Royal Rd Ne Riegelwood (28456) *(G-13557)*
Bestco Holdings Inc 704 664-4300
 288 Mazeppa Rd Mooresville (28115) *(G-10874)*
Bestco LLC 704 664-4300
 137 Bestco Ln Mooresville (28115) *(G-10875)*
Bestco LLC 704 664-4300
 119 E Super Sport Dr Mooresville (28117) *(G-10876)*
Bestco LLC 704 664-4300
 139 Cam Ct Mooresville (28115) *(G-10877)*
Bestco LLC 704 664-4300
 208 Manufacturers Blvd Mooresville (28115) *(G-10878)*
Bestco LLC (PA) 704 664-4300
 288 Mazeppa Rd Mooresville (28115) *(G-10879)*
Bet-Mac Wilson Steel Inc 919 528-1540
 118 S Durham Ave (Hwy 15) Creedmoor (27522) *(G-4606)*
Beta Fluid Systems, Reidsville Also Called: Beta Fueling Systems LLC *(G-13509)*
Beta Fueling Systems LLC 336 342-0306
 1209 Freeway Dr Reidsville (27320) *(G-13509)*
Betco Inc (DH) 704 872-2999
 228 Commerce Blvd Statesville (28625) *(G-14762)*
Betech Inc 828 687-9917
 190 Continuum Dr Fletcher (28732) *(G-5987)*
Betek Tools Inc 980 498-2523
 8325 Arrowridge Blvd Ste A Charlotte (28273) *(G-2303)*
Beth Wiseman 704 735-4469
 224 Hollow Rd Lincolnton (28092) *(G-9875)*
Bethany Small 910 409-2167
 4353 Marsh Elder Ct Se Southport (28461) *(G-14567)*
Bethlehem Manufacturing Co (PA) 828 495-7731
 36 Bethlehem Manufacturing Ln Hickory (28601) *(G-7949)*
Better Burger Group LLC 704 662-9152
 4310 Sharon Rd Ste X05 Charlotte (28211) *(G-2304)*
Better Business Printing Inc 704 867-3366
 495 E Long Ave Gastonia (28054) *(G-6353)*
Better Publishing Inc 828 688-9188
 467 Byrd Rd Bakersville (28705) *(G-880)*
Better Solutions Technologies 704 227-7424
 6060 Providence Church Rd Winston Salem (27105) *(G-16627)*
Betts Construction United Inc 252 203-2849
 119 Edgewater Dr Grandy (27939) *(G-6718)*
Bettys Drapery Design Workroom 828 264-2392
 3207 Nc Highway 105 S Boone (28607) *(G-1176)*
Beulaville Wstn Auto Value Inc 910 298-4246
 516 W Main St Beulaville (28518) *(G-1091)*
Bevana, Newton Also Called: Community Brewing Ventures LLC *(G-11923)*
Beverage Innovation Corp 425 222-4900
 1858 Kannapolis Pkwy Concord (28027) *(G-4208)*
Beverage-Air Corporation (DH) 336 245-6400
 3779 Champion Blvd Winston Salem (27105) *(G-16628)*
Beverly Knits Inc 704 964-0835
 1640 Federal St Gastonia (28052) *(G-6354)*
Beverly Knits Inc (PA) 704 861-1536
 1675 Garfield Dr Gastonia (28052) *(G-6355)*
Bevs & Bites LLC 704 247-7573
 2913 Selwyn Ave Charlotte (28209) *(G-2305)*
Beyond Electronics Corp 919 231-8000
 12405 Cilcain Ct Raleigh (27614) *(G-12553)*
Beyond Normal Media LLC 980 263-9921
 13656 Meade Glen Ct Charlotte (28273) *(G-2306)*
Beyond This Day, Gastonia Also Called: Ambassador Services Inc *(G-6342)*
Bfc Plant 2, Lenoir Also Called: Bernhardt Furniture Company *(G-9584)*

Bfc Plant 5a, Lenoir Also Called: Bernhardt Furniture Company *(G-9582)*
Bfs Asset Holdings LLC (HQ) 303 784-4288
 4800 Falls Of Neuse Rd Ste 400 Raleigh (27609) *(G-12554)*
Bfs Industries LLC 919 575-6711
 200 Industrial Dr Butner (27509) *(G-1542)*
Bfs Operations LLC (HQ) 919 431-1000
 4800 Falls Of Neuse Rd Raleigh (27609) *(G-12555)*
Bft Lumberton, Lumberton Also Called: Bft Lumberton Ops Corp *(G-10027)*
Bft Lumberton Ops Corp 910 737-3200
 1000 Noir St Lumberton (28358) *(G-10027)*
Bg Woodworks 919 656-2529
 204 Lawrence Rd Cary (27511) *(G-1702)*
Bg-Cnc 336 596-3400
 309 Rainy Day Dr Winston Salem (27107) *(G-16629)*
Bgi Recovery Llc 336 429-6976
 127 Belvue Dr Mount Airy (27030) *(G-11483)*
Bgm Inc 704 776-4086
 2524 Old Charlotte Hwy Monroe (28110) *(G-10662)*
Bh Holdings, Durham Also Called: Bell and Howell LLC *(G-4954)*
Bh Logging 980 330-0229
 130 Hugo Ln Statesville (28677) *(G-14763)*
Bhaki Bullies LLC 646 387-3974
 1301 Cherry Hollow Way Knightdale (27545) *(G-9413)*
Bhaktivedanta Archives 336 871-3636
 1453 Tom Shelton Rd Sandy Ridge (27046) *(G-14076)*
Bharat Forge Aluminum USA Inc (DH) 585 576-7483
 777 Kalyani Way Sanford (27330) *(G-14093)*
Bi County Gas Producers LLC 704 844-8990
 10600 Nations Ford Rd Charlotte (28273) *(G-2307)*
Biancas Stitch Works LLC 828 505-0686
 122 Hudson St Asheville (28806) *(G-558)*
Bibey Machine Company Inc 336 275-9421
 642 S Spring St Greensboro (27406) *(G-6838)*
Bic Corporation 704 598-7700
 5900 Long Creek Park Dr Charlotte (28269) *(G-2308)*
Bickerstaff Trees Inc 336 372-8866
 866 Nc Highway 18 S Sparta (28675) *(G-14589)*
Biddeford Mill, Wagram Also Called: Westpoint Home Inc *(G-15524)*
Biesse America Inc 704 357-3131
 4110 Meadow Oak Dr Charlotte (28208) *(G-2309)*
Biffle Steel Services LLC 704 626-0909
 140 Pintail Run Ln Mooresville (28117) *(G-10880)*
Big Boss Baking Company, High Point Also Called: Bakeboxx Company *(G-8262)*
Big Bundts 919 448-4184
 500 Market St Chapel Hill (27516) *(G-1990)*
Big Butted Woman Music LLC 919 720-3340
 7232 Beau View Dr Wendell (27591) *(G-15892)*
Big Chair Publishing LLC 336 207-4139
 7902 Thoroughbred Dr Summerfield (27358) *(G-14976)*
Big Dipper, Asheboro Also Called: Thermaco Incorporated *(G-497)*
Big E'S Hauling, Roanoke Rapids Also Called: Vultare Logging LLC *(G-13584)*
Big Fish Digital Signs LLC 252 363-1600
 4222 Georgetown Dr N Wilson (27896) *(G-16476)*
Big Fish Dpi 704 545-8112
 9740 Lawyers Rd Mint Hill (28227) *(G-10522)*
Big Nics Lures LLC 910 805-1360
 3705 New Colony Dr Wilmington (28412) *(G-16138)*
Big Oak Coatings LLC 919 771-8470
 1148 Vannstone Dr Raleigh (27603) *(G-12556)*
Big Pine Log and Lumber Inc 828 656-2754
 14245 Us 25/70 Hwy Marshall (28753) *(G-10200)*
Big Rock Industries Inc 252 222-3618
 111 Turners Dairy Rd Ste A Morehead City (28557) *(G-11152)*
Big Rock Propellers, Morehead City Also Called: Big Rock Industries Inc *(G-11152)*
Big Show Foods Inc 919 920-1888
 588 Turner Swamp Rd Fremont (27830) *(G-6172)*
Big Show Foods Inc 919 242-7769
 3959 Hwy 39 S Wake Forest (27588) *(G-15531)*
Big Spoon Roasters LLC 919 309-9100
 500 Meadowlands Dr Hillsborough (27278) *(G-8638)*
Big Tire Outfitters 919 568-9605
 5210 Cragganmore Dr Mc Leansville (27301) *(G-10383)*

Big Vac.. 910 947-3654
551 Priest Hill Rd Carthage (28327) *(G-1660)*

Biganodes LLC... 828 245-1115
117 Westerly Hills Dr Forest City (28043) *(G-6060)*

Bignisha Rgrts Chill Cream LLC.. 910 528-8966
3547 Gainey Rd Fayetteville (28306) *(G-5770)*

Bigred Krafts LLC... 919 480-2388
5100 Solemn Grove Rd Garner (27529) *(G-6257)*

Bijur Delimon Intl Inc (DH).. 919 465-4448
1 Copley Pkwy Ste 104 Morrisville (27560) *(G-11302)*

Biker Software.. 919 761-1681
1165 Litchborough Way Wake Forest (27587) *(G-15532)*

Bilcat Inc (PA).. 828 295-3088
1103 Main St Blowing Rock (28605) *(G-1154)*

Bilge Masters Inc... 704 995-4293
6239 River Cabin Ln Charlotte (28278) *(G-2310)*

Bill Martin Inc.. 704 873-0241
106 Martin Ln Statesville (28625) *(G-14764)*

Bill Perfect Inc... 954 889-6699
4207 Burnwood Trl Denver (28037) *(G-4764)*

Bill Pink Carburetors LLC... 704 575-1645
6137 Denver Industrial Park Rd Ste A Denver (28037) *(G-4765)*

Bill Ratliff Jr Logging I... 704 694-5403
4437 Beck Rd Wadesboro (28170) *(G-15502)*

Bill S Iron Shop Inc... 919 596-8360
2243 Glover Rd Durham (27703) *(G-4956)*

Bill Slate Grating.. 336 591-8607
1045 Slate Farm Rd Walnut Cove (27052) *(G-15631)*

Bill Truitt Wood Works Inc.. 704 398-8499
3124 W Trade St # B Charlotte (28208) *(G-2311)*

Bill's Ornamental Iron Shop, Durham *Also Called: Bill S Iron Shop Inc (G-4956)*

Bill's Welding & Son, Statesville *Also Called: Donald Auton (G-14788)*

Billet Speed Inc.. 828 226-8127
488 Fairview Rd Sylva (28779) *(G-15054)*

Billsoft Inc.. 913 859-9674
512 S Mangum St Ste 100 Durham (27701) *(G-4957)*

Billy Boat Performance Exhaust, Mooresville *Also Called: B & B Fabrication Inc (G-10869)*

Billy Harrell Logging Inc.. 252 221-4995
152 County Line Rd Tyner (27980) *(G-15433)*

Billy Harrell Logging Inc.. 252 426-1362
108 Ililda Dr Hertford (27944) *(G-7916)*

Billy Rice.. 828 691-4831
365 Horace Rice Rd Mars Hill (28754) *(G-10193)*

Bilt USA Manufacturing, Charlotte *Also Called: Mdb Investors LLC (G-3155)*

Biltmore Embroiderers Inc.. 828 298-7403
448 Sondley Woods Pl Asheville (28805) *(G-559)*

Biltmore Estate Wine Co LLC.. 828 225-6776
1 N Pack Sq Ste 400 Asheville (28801) *(G-560)*

Bimbo Bakeries Usa Inc... 252 641-2200
110 Sara Lee Rd Tarboro (27886) *(G-15096)*

Binderholz Enfield LLC.. 770 362-0558
260 Piper Ln Enfield (27823) *(G-5676)*

Binders Incorporated.. 704 377-9704
1303 Upper Asbury Ave Charlotte (28206) *(G-2312)*

Binders of Jhc LLC... 980 875-9274
3322 Leamington Ln Charlotte (28226) *(G-2313)*

Bio Air, Greensboro *Also Called: Custom Industries Inc (G-6950)*

Bio D, Morehead City *Also Called: Aqua 10 Corporation (G-11149)*

Bio-TEC Environmental LLC... 505 629-1777
8910 Pioneer Ave Charlotte (28273) *(G-2314)*

Bio-Tech Prosthetics.. 336 768-3666
1728 S Hawthorne Rd Winston Salem (27103) *(G-16630)*

Bio-Tech Prsthtics Orthtics In (HQ)... 336 333-9081
2301 N Church St Greensboro (27405) *(G-6839)*

BIOCRYST, Durham *Also Called: Biocryst Pharmaceuticals Inc (G-4958)*

Biocryst Pharmaceuticals Inc (PA).. 919 859-1302
4505 Emperor Blvd Ste 200 Durham (27703) *(G-4958)*

Biodot Inc... 949 440-3685
2211 Leah Dr Hillsborough (27278) *(G-8639)*

Biofluidica Inc... 858 535-6493
176 Mine Lake Ct Raleigh (27615) *(G-12557)*

Biogen MA Inc... 919 941-1100
5000 Davis Dr Durham (27709) *(G-4959)*

Biogen Pharma.. 919 993-1100
3798 Hopson Rd Morrisville (27560) *(G-11303)*

Biogeniv Inc.. 828 850-1007
640 Nuway Cir Lenoir (28645) *(G-9589)*

Biolex Therapeutics Inc... 919 542-9901
158 Credle St Pittsboro (27312) *(G-12331)*

Biologcal Innvtion Optmztion S.. 321 260-2467
224 E Holding Ave # 2116 Wake Forest (27587) *(G-15533)*

Biologic Solutions LLC.. 919 770-8266
5004 Sadelia Pl Holly Springs (27540) *(G-8690)*

Biologics Inc.. 919 546-9810
625 Oberlin Rd Raleigh (27605) *(G-12558)*

Biologix of The Triangle Inc.. 919 696-4544
103 Hidden Rock Ct Cary (27513) *(G-1703)*

Biomedical Innovations Inc... 910 603-0267
410 N Bennett St Southern Pines (28387) *(G-14529)*

Biomerics LLC... 336 810-7178
1413 S Third St Mebane (27302) *(G-10400)*

Biomerieux Inc (DH).. 919 620-2000
100 Rodolphe St Durham (27712) *(G-4960)*

Biomerieux Inc.. 800 682-2666
3300 Tarheel Dr Raleigh (27609) *(G-12559)*

Biomontr Labs... 919 650-1185
15200 Weston Pkwy Ste 106 Cary (27513) *(G-1704)*

Bionutra Life Sciences LLC... 828 572-2838
2464 Norwood St Sw Lenoir (28645) *(G-9590)*

Biorad... 919 463-7866
202 Preston Arbor Ln Cary (27513) *(G-1705)*

Bioresource International Inc... 919 267-3758
2000 N Salem St Apex (27523) *(G-171)*

Bios Lighting, Wake Forest *Also Called: Biologcal Innvtion Optmztion S (G-15533)*

Bioselect Inc... 704 521-8585
4740 Dwight Evans Rd Charlotte (28217) *(G-2315)*

Biosupplynet Inc... 919 659-2121
3020 Carrington Mill Blvd Ste 100 Morrisville (27560) *(G-11304)*

Biotage LLC (HQ).. 704 654-4900
10430 Harris Oak Blvd Ste C Charlotte (28269) *(G-2316)*

Biotec, Charlotte *Also Called: Bio-TEC Environmental LLC (G-2314)*

Biotech Prsthtics Orthtics Drh... 919 471-4994
314 Crutchfield St Durham (27704) *(G-4961)*

Biotech Research Laboratories, Sanford *Also Called: Philosophy Inc (G-14169)*

BIOVENTUS, Durham *Also Called: Bioventus Inc (G-4962)*

Bioventus Inc (PA).. 919 474-6700
4721 Emperor Blvd Ste 100 Durham (27703) *(G-4962)*

Bioventus LLC (HQ).. 800 396-4325
4721 Emperor Blvd Ste 100 Durham (27703) *(G-4963)*

Biovind LLC... 512 217-3077
2219 Vail Ave Charlotte (28207) *(G-2317)*

Birch Bros Southern Inc.. 704 843-2111
9510 New Town Rd Waxhaw (28173) *(G-15745)*

Bircher Incorporated.. 252 726-5470
119 Industrial Dr Morehead City (28557) *(G-11153)*

Birddog Outdoor Co Inc... 919 604-8134
406 Crickentree Dr Cary (27518) *(G-1706)*

Birds Eye View Aerial Drone.. 828 691-1550
19 Westfield Way Candler (28715) *(G-1571)*

Birth Tissue Recovery LLC (PA).. 336 448-1910
3051 Trenwest Dr Ste A Winston Salem (27103) *(G-16631)*

Biscoe Foundry, Biscoe *Also Called: Grede II LLC (G-1110)*

Bite My Cookies Brewing Co Inc... 919 602-7636
213 Lorax Ln Pittsboro (27312) *(G-12332)*

Biz On Wheels, Charlotte *Also Called: R J Yeller Distribution Inc (G-3405)*

Biz Technology Solutions LLC... 704 658-1707
353 Oates Rd Mooresville (28117) *(G-10881)*

Biznet Software Inc... 919 872-7800
8529 Six Forks Rd Ste 400 Raleigh (27615) *(G-12560)*

BJ Williamson, Clinton *Also Called: Williamson Greenhouses Inc (G-4118)*

Bjmf Inc... 704 554-6333
8200 South Blvd Charlotte (28273) *(G-2318)*

ALPHABETIC SECTION

Bk Seamless Gutters, Spring Hope Also Called: Bk Seamless Gutters LLC *(G-14615)*
Bk Seamless Gutters LLC.. 252 955-5414
1705 Old Us 64 Spring Hope (27882) *(G-14615)*

Bkc Industries Inc.. 919 575-6699
2117 Will Suitt Rd Creedmoor (27522) *(G-4607)*

Blachford Rbr Acquisition Corp.. 704 730-1005
707 Broadview Dr Kings Mountain (28086) *(G-9295)*

Blachford Rp Corporation, Kings Mountain Also Called: Blachford Rbr Acquisition Corp *(G-9295)*

Black & Decker, Charlotte Also Called: Black & Decker Corporation *(G-2319)*

Black & Decker, Mooresville Also Called: Black & Decker Corporation *(G-10882)*

Black & Decker, Raleigh Also Called: Black & Decker Corporation *(G-12561)*

Black & Decker (us) Inc... 336 852-1300
4621 W Gate City Blvd Greensboro (27407) *(G-6840)*

Black & Decker Corporation.. 803 396-3700
15040 Choate Cir Charlotte (28273) *(G-2319)*

Black & Decker Corporation.. 704 799-3929
134 Talbert Pointe Dr Mooresville (28117) *(G-10882)*

Black & Decker Corporation.. 919 878-0357
2930 Capital Blvd Raleigh (27604) *(G-12561)*

Black Barrel Defense LLC... 336 468-8102
7541 Mayberry Mill Rd Hamptonville (27020) *(G-7668)*

Black Box Corporation... 704 248-6430
10817 Southern Loop Blvd Pineville (28134) *(G-12255)*

Black Business Universe LLC... 215 279-1509
113 Fox Park Rd Louisburg (27549) *(G-9980)*

Black Concrete Inc... 336 243-1388
705 Cotton Grove Rd Lexington (27292) *(G-9685)*

Black Mountain Machine & Tool, Black Mountain Also Called: Black Mtn Mch Fabrication Inc *(G-1121)*

Black Mountain News Inc.. 828 669-8727
111 Richardson Blvd Black Mountain (28711) *(G-1120)*

Black Mtn Mch Fabrication Inc... 828 669-9557
2988 Us 70 Hwy Black Mountain (28711) *(G-1121)*

Black Oak Boat Works.. 828 252-4997
23 Spring Cove Rd Asheville (28804) *(G-561)*

Black Ops, Elizabeth City Also Called: D & D Industries *(G-5539)*

Black River Logging Inc... 910 669-2850
20289 North Carolina Hwy 210 E Ivanhoe (28447) *(G-8980)*

Black River Woodwork LLC... 919 757-4559
574 N Broad St E Angier (27501) *(G-132)*

Black Rock Granite & Cabinetry...................................... 828 787-1100
2543 Cashiers Rd Highlands (28741) *(G-8612)*

Black Rock Landscaping LLC... 910 295-4470
6652 Us 15 501 Hwy Carthage (28327) *(G-1661)*

Black Rock Winery LLC.. 910 295-9511
6652 Us 15 501 Hwy Carthage (28327) *(G-1662)*

Black Rver Wldg Fbrication LLC....................................... 910 471-7434
127 Big Eagle Rd Atkinson (28421) *(G-826)*

Black Sand Company Inc.. 336 788-6411
745 W Clemmonsville Rd Winston Salem (27127) *(G-16632)*

Black Tire Service Inc.. 919 908-6347
1400 E Geer St Durham (27704) *(G-4964)*

Black Wolf Custom Woodworks....................................... 828 925-0399
48 Cris Ln Asheville (28806) *(G-562)*

Blackbeards Boatworks.. 252 726-6161
4531 Arendell St Morehead City (28557) *(G-11154)*

Blackhawk Diversified Svcs Inc....................................... 919 279-5679
5618 Deblyn Ave Raleigh (27612) *(G-12562)*

Blackleys Printing & Sign Shop, Clayton Also Called: Blackleys Printing Co *(G-3959)*

Blackleys Printing Co... 919 553-6813
229 E Main St Clayton (27520) *(G-3959)*

Blacksand Metal Works LLC... 703 489-8282
433 Delbert Dr Fayetteville (28306) *(G-5771)*

Blackstone Furniture Inds Inc.. 910 428-2833
624 Hogan Farm Rd Ether (27247) *(G-5690)*

Blacktip Solutions... 336 303-1580
3125 Kathleen Ave Ste 221 Greensboro (27408) *(G-6841)*

Blackwater, Concord Also Called: Loading Republic Inc *(G-4306)*

Blackwell Boatwork, Wanchese Also Called: Craig & Sandra Blackwell Inc *(G-15644)*

Blacqueladi Styles LLC.. 877 977-7798
5000 Centre Green Way Ste 500 Cary (27513) *(G-1707)*

Bladen Fabricators LLC.. 910 866-5225
2646 Old Hwy 41 Bladenboro (28320) *(G-1144)*

Blair.. 919 682-0555
421 Westwood Dr Chapel Hill (27516) *(G-1991)*

BLAIR, Durham Also Called: Carolina Wren Press Inc *(G-5005)*

Blake Boat Works, Gloucester Also Called: Bryan Blake James *(G-6574)*

Blake Enterprises, Concord Also Called: Robert Blake *(G-4351)*

Blands Welding.. 704 932-1864
6764 Dare Dr Davidson (28036) *(G-4666)*

Blankenship Logging.. 828 652-2250
397 Biggerstaff Loop Nebo (28761) *(G-11759)*

Blanket Aero LLC... 704 591-2878
9300 Aviation Blvd Nw Ste A Concord (28027) *(G-4209)*

Blaq Beauty Naturalz, Weldon Also Called: Blaq Beauty Naturalz Inc *(G-15880)*

Blaq Beauty Naturalz Inc.. 252 326-5621
307 Woodlawn Ave Weldon (27890) *(G-15880)*

Blashfield Sign Company Inc.. 910 485-7200
303 Williams St Fayetteville (28301) *(G-5772)*

Blast Off Intl Chem & Mfg Co... 509 885-4525
199 Crocker St Seaboard (27876) *(G-14226)*

Blast-It-All, Salisbury Also Called: Hess Manufacturing Inc *(G-13979)*

Blazing Foods LLC... 336 865-2933
1520 West Blvd Charlotte (28208) *(G-2320)*

Blf Press LLC... 706 442-1154
370 Sugarberry Ln Clayton (27527) *(G-3960)*

Blimp Works Inc.. 704 876-2378
156 Barnes Airship Dr Statesville (28625) *(G-14765)*

Blind Nail and Company Inc... 919 967-0388
3027 Blueberry Ln Chapel Hill (27516) *(G-1992)*

Blinds Plus Inc... 910 487-5196
5137 Raeford Rd Fayetteville (28304) *(G-5773)*

Blissfull Memories... 336 903-1835
101 6th St North Wilkesboro (28659) *(G-11999)*

Bloom Ai Inc.. 704 620-2886
101 S Devimy Ct Cary (27511) *(G-1708)*

Bloomday Granite & Marble Inc.. 336 724-0300
3810 Indiana Ave Winston Salem (27105) *(G-16633)*

Blossman Propane Gas & Appl... 828 396-0144
2315 Catawba Valley Blvd Se Hickory (28602) *(G-7950)*

Blossom Cotton Press LLC... 828 407-0467
100 Springhead Trl Hendersonville (28739) *(G-7825)*

Blount Precision Machining Inc....................................... 252 825-3701
155 Railroad St W Bethel (27812) *(G-1089)*

Blowing Rocket, Boone Also Called: Jones Media *(G-1212)*

Blp Logging Company, Jamesville Also Called: Barry Lane Perry *(G-9078)*

Blp Paper, Charlotte Also Called: Nakos Paper Products Inc *(G-3229)*

Blp Products and Services Inc... 704 899-5505
605 N Polk St Ste D Pineville (28134) *(G-12256)*

Blu Distilling Company LLC.. 919 999-6736
609 Foster St Durham (27701) *(G-4965)*

Blu Distilling Company LLC (PA)...................................... 919 999-6736
3420 Landor Rd Raleigh (27609) *(G-12563)*

Blu Ecigs, Charlotte Also Called: Fontem Us Inc *(G-2784)*

Blue ARC Fabrication Mech LLC....................................... 336 693-7878
2126 S Nc Highway 54 Graham (27253) *(G-6679)*

Blue Bay Distributing Inc.. 919 957-1300
3720 Appling Way Durham (27703) *(G-4966)*

Blue Crab Software LLC.. 301 585-8187
325 Bayberry Dr Chapel Hill (27517) *(G-1993)*

Blue Diamond Defense LLC... 334 905-0246
245 Old Indian Flatts Ln Sylva (28779) *(G-15055)*

Blue Dog Graphics Inc.. 252 291-9191
619 Park Ave W Wilson (27893) *(G-16477)*

Blue DOT Readi-Mix LLC (PA).. 704 971-7676
11330 Bain School Rd Mint Hill (28227) *(G-10523)*

Blue Force Technologies LLC... 919 443-1660
627 Distribution Dr Ste D Morrisville (27560) *(G-11305)*

Blue Gas Marine Inc... 919 238-3427
2528 Schieffelin Rd Apex (27502) *(G-172)*

Blue Heaven Woodworks.. 704 743-6648
5520 Old Monroe Cir Concord (28025) *(G-4210)*

ALPHABETIC SECTION — Blythe Construction Inc

Blue Horseshoe..980 312-8202
13024 Ballantyne Corporate Pl Charlotte (28277) *(G-2321)*

Blue Inc Usa LLC..828 346-8660
1808 Emmanuel Church Rd Conover (28613) *(G-4423)*

Blue Lagoon Inc...828 324-2333
1011 10th Street Blvd Nw Hickory (28601) *(G-7951)*

Blue Light Images Company Inc..............................336 983-4986
428 Newsome Rd King (27021) *(G-9264)*

Blue Light Welding of Triad.....................................336 442-9140
2328 Pebble Creek Rd Winston Salem (27107) *(G-16634)*

Blue Lzard Cstm Scrnprnting In..............................919 296-9041
2305 Orangewood Dr Ste 108 Durham (27705) *(G-4967)*

Blue Maiden Defense..678 292-8342
165 Laurel Oak Ln Pinebluff (28373) *(G-12214)*

Blue Mountain Enterprises Inc................................252 522-1544
4000 Commerce Dr Kinston (28504) *(G-9345)*

Blue Mountain Flavors, Kinston Also Called: Blue Mountain Enterprises Inc *(G-9345)*

Blue Mountain Metalworks Inc................................828 898-8582
567 Main St E Banner Elk (28604) *(G-894)*

Blue Nano Inc...888 508-6266
18946 Brigadoon Pl Cornelius (28031) *(G-4527)*

Blue Rdge Elc Mmbers Fndtion I............................828 754-9071
219 Nuway Cir Lenoir (28645) *(G-9591)*

Blue Ridge...828 325-4705
121 Fairgrove Church Rd Se Conover (28613) *(G-4424)*

Blue Ridge Armor LLC..844 556-6855
340 Industrial Park Rd Rutherfordton (28139) *(G-13866)*

Blue Ridge Bldg Components Inc...........................828 685-0452
208 Justice Hills Dr Dana (28724) *(G-4662)*

Blue Ridge Bracket Co..828 242-8577
5 Creekside Ct Asheville (28803) *(G-563)*

Blue Ridge Bracket Inc...828 808-3273
66 Fletcher Commercial Dr Fletcher (28732) *(G-5988)*

Blue Ridge Cab Connection LLC............................828 891-2281
7 Brandy Branch Rd Mills River (28759) *(G-10500)*

Blue Ridge Christian News, Spruce Pine Also Called: Inniah Production Incorporated *(G-14644)*

Blue Ridge Distilling Co Inc.....................................828 245-2041
228 Redbud Ln Bostic (28018) *(G-1260)*

Blue Ridge Elc Mtr Repr Inc....................................828 258-0800
629 Emma Rd Asheville (28806) *(G-564)*

BLUE RIDGE ELECTRIC MEMBERS FOUNDATION, INC., Lenoir Also Called: Blue Rdge Elc Mmbers Fndtion I *(G-9591)*

Blue Ridge Global Inc..828 252-5225
128 Bingham Rd Asheville (28806) *(G-565)*

Blue Ridge Jams..828 685-1783
75 Lytle Rd Hendersonville (28792) *(G-7826)*

Blue Ridge Lbr Log & Timber Co.............................336 961-5211
2854 Old Us 421 Hwy W Yadkinville (27055) *(G-17033)*

Blue Ridge Metals Corporation................................828 687-2525
180 Mills Gap Rd Fletcher (28732) *(G-5989)*

Blue Ridge Molding LLC..828 485-2017
121a Fairgrove Church Rd Se Conover (28613) *(G-4425)*

Blue Ridge Paper Products Inc................................828 646-2000
175 Main St Canton (28716) *(G-1600)*

BLUE RIDGE PAPER PRODUCTS INC., Canton Also Called: Blue Ridge Paper Products Inc *(G-1600)*

Blue Ridge Paper Products LLC (DH)....................828 454-0676
41 Main St Canton (28716) *(G-1601)*

Blue Ridge Paper Products LLC..............................828 235-3023
119 Park St Canton (28716) *(G-1602)*

Blue Ridge Paper Products LLC..............................828 452-0834
81 Old Howell Mill Rd Waynesville (28786) *(G-15795)*

Blue Ridge Plastic Molding, Conover Also Called: Blue Ridge Molding LLC *(G-4425)*

Blue Ridge Plating Company...................................828 274-1795
127 Foxwood Dr Hendersonville (28791) *(G-7827)*

Blue Ridge Printing Co Inc.......................................828 254-1000
544 Haywood Rd Asheville (28806) *(G-566)*

Blue Ridge Products Co Inc.....................................828 322-7990
3050 Main Ave Nw Hickory (28601) *(G-7952)*

Blue Ridge Propeller Repr LLC................................276 340-1597
5307 Verna Rd Mc Leansville (27301) *(G-10384)*

Blue Ridge Quarry...828 693-0025
3675 Spartanburg Hwy Flat Rock (28731) *(G-5960)*

Blue Ridge Quick Print Inc......................................828 883-2420
82 E French Broad St Brevard (28712) *(G-1270)*

Blue Ridge Silver Inc...828 729-8610
173 Marsh Lndg Boone (28607) *(G-1177)*

Blue Ridge Sun Inc..336 372-5490
32 W Whitehead St Sparta (28675) *(G-14590)*

Blue Ridge Tool Inc...336 993-8111
2546 Willard Dairy Rd High Point (27265) *(G-8273)*

Blue Ridge Tool Inc...336 993-8111
505 Lakedale Rd Colfax (27235) *(G-4142)*

Blue Ridge Tube & Core LLC..................................704 530-4311
1203 Farrington St Sw 2nd Fl Conover (28613) *(G-4426)*

Blue Rock Materials LLC..828 479-3581
750 Tallulah Rd Robbinsville (28771) *(G-13605)*

Blue Seas LLC...828 245-2041
228 Redbud Ln Bostic (28018) *(G-1261)*

Blue Stallion Woodworks..919 766-2865
9106 Salem Ct Wilmington (28411) *(G-16139)*

Blue Steel Inc..704 864-2583
4905 Sparrow Dairy Rd Gastonia (28056) *(G-6356)*

Blue Stone Block Supermarket, Burlington Also Called: Chandler Concrete Co Inc *(G-1395)*

Blue Stone Industries Ltd.......................................919 379-3986
10030 Green Level Church Rd Cary (27519) *(G-1709)*

Blue Sun Energy Inc..336 218-6707
408 Gallimore Dairy Rd Ste C Greensboro (27409) *(G-6842)*

Blue Unicorn LLC..704 748-4832
2724 Highworth Ln Charlotte (28214) *(G-2322)*

Blue Wolf Technologies LLP....................................919 810-1508
9650 Strickland Rd Ste 103 Raleigh (27615) *(G-12564)*

Blue Wtr Indstries-Yancey Quar, Burnsville Also Called: Bwi Etn LLC *(G-1525)*

Blue Zephry Vineyard..336 366-5066
6457 Haystack Rd Dobson (27017) *(G-4820)*

Blue-Hen Inc..407 322-2262
60 N Market St Ste C200 Asheville (28801) *(G-567)*

Blue/Gray Books..828 254-3972
804 Macedonia Rd Alexander (28701) *(G-117)*

Bluebird Cupcakes..919 616-7347
2524 Beech Gap Ct Raleigh (27603) *(G-12565)*

Bluejay Enterprises Group Inc................................866 670-8811
3721 Atmore St Charlotte (28205) *(G-2323)*

Bluescope Buildings N Amer Inc.............................336 996-4801
7031 Albert Pick Rd Ste 200 Greensboro (27409) *(G-6843)*

Bluesky Polymers LLC..919 522-4374
100 Woodsage Way Cary (27518) *(G-1710)*

Bluestone Metals & Chem LLC................................704 662-8632
19720 Jetton Rd Ste 101 Cornelius (28031) *(G-4528)*

Bluestone Specialty Chem LLC...............................704 662-8632
19720 Jetton Rd Ste 101 Cornelius (28031) *(G-4529)*

Bluetick Inc..336 294-4102
1501 Highwoods Blvd Ste 104 Greensboro (27410) *(G-6844)*

Bluetick Services, Greensboro Also Called: Bluetick Inc *(G-6844)*

Bluewater Pallet Solutions......................................336 697-9109
5517 Burlington Rd Mc Leansville (27301) *(G-10385)*

Bluff Mountain Outfitters Inc..................................828 622-7162
152 Bridge St Hot Springs (28743) *(G-8744)*

Blum Inc...919 345-6214
594 Carson Ridge Dr Oak Ridge (27310) *(G-12058)*

Blum Inc...704 827-1345
7733 Old Plank Rd Stanley (28164) *(G-14687)*

Blumenthal Holdings LLC (PA)................................704 688-2302
1355 Greenwood Clfs Ste 200 Charlotte (28204) *(G-2324)*

Blums Almanac, Winston Salem Also Called: Goslen Printing Company *(G-16725)*

Blur Development Group LLC..................................919 701-4213
170 Weston Oaks Ct Cary (27513) *(G-1711)*

Blur Product Development, Cary Also Called: Blur Development Group LLC *(G-1711)*

Blythe Construction, Concord Also Called: Blythe Construction Inc *(G-4211)*

Blythe Construction Inc (DH)..................................704 375-8474
2911 N Graham St Charlotte (28206) *(G-2325)*

Blythe Construction Inc..704 788-9733
7450 Poplar Tent Rd Concord (28027) *(G-4211)*

Blythe Construction Inc — ALPHABETIC SECTION

Blythe Construction Inc 336 854-9003
2606 Phoenix Dr Ste 502 Greensboro (27406) *(G-6845)*

BMA America Inc 970 353-3770
2020 Starita Rd Ste E Charlotte (28206) *(G-2326)*

BMC Brewing, Pittsboro Also Called: Bite My Cookies Brewing Co Inc *(G-12332)*

BMC Construction, Raleigh Also Called: Selectbuild Construction Inc *(G-13244)*

BMC Software, Monroe Also Called: BMC Software Inc *(G-10663)*

BMC Software Inc 704 283-8179
2980 Mason St Monroe (28110) *(G-10663)*

BMC Solutions LLC 704 386-0194
3119 Misty Creek Dr Charlotte (28269) *(G-2327)*

BMC Studios 443 547-7319
240 Erlwood Way Apt 204 Durham (27704) *(G-4968)*

Bmg Labtech Inc 919 678-1633
13000 Weston Pkwy Ste 109 Cary (27513) *(G-1712)*

Bmi Wood Products Inc 919 829-9505
2506 Yonkers Rd Raleigh (27604) *(G-12566)*

Bmrs Management Services Inc 704 793-4319
4005 Dearborn Pl Nw Concord (28027) *(G-4212)*

Bms Investment Holdings LLC 336 949-4107
225 Commerce Ln Mayodan (27027) *(G-10363)*

Bmt Micro Inc 910 792-9100
5019 Carolina Beach Rd Wilmington (28412) *(G-16140)*

Bnb Designs Inc 919 587-9800
601 N James St Ste A Goldsboro (27530) *(G-6593)*

BNC Nutrition LLC 336 567-0104
1452a Industry Dr Burlington (27215) *(G-1376)*

Bnnano Inc 844 926-6266
2119 W Webb Ave Burlington (27217) *(G-1377)*

Bnp Inc 919 775-7070
5910 Elwin Buchanan Dr Sanford (27330) *(G-14094)*

Bo Taylor Custom Wdwkg LLC 919 839-7175
417 Eby Dr Raleigh (27610) *(G-12567)*

Boards and Bowls LLC 704 293-2004
141 Brookleaf Ln Mooresville (28115) *(G-10883)*

Boardwalk Inc 252 240-1095
4911 Bridges St Ext # A Morehead City (28557) *(G-11155)*

Boat Lift US Inc 239 283-9040
2216 Mercantile Dr Leland (28451) *(G-9527)*

Boat Lift Warehouse LLC 877 468-5438
900 Hwy 258 S Snow Hill (28580) *(G-14498)*

Boats Unlimited, New Bern Also Called: Triad Marine Center Inc *(G-11851)*

Bob Barker Company Inc (PA) 800 334-9880
7925 Purfoy Rd Fuquay Varina (27526) *(G-6184)*

Bob Callahan LLC 828 620-9730
104 Lakeshore Dr Asheville (28804) *(G-568)*

Bob Harrington Assoc 336 855-7252
3411 N Rockingham Rd Greensboro (27407) *(G-6846)*

Bob Martin 910 245-3593
1248 Greenbriar Dr Vass (28394) *(G-15490)*

Bob Peak Enterprises Inc 704 564-0711
3550 Patterson Rd China Grove (28023) *(G-3880)*

BOB Trailers Inc 208 375-5171
13501 S Ridge Dr Charlotte (28273) *(G-2328)*

Bobbees Bottling, Louisburg Also Called: Packo Bottling Inc *(G-9995)*

Bobbos Stuff LLC 828 883-8545
550 Park Ave Brevard (28712) *(G-1271)*

Bobby A Herring Logging 919 658-9768
324 Alum Springs Rd Mount Olive (28365) *(G-11656)*

Bobby Barns Woodworking 336 824-2821
1337 Nc Hwy 22 S Ramseur (27316) *(G-13441)*

Bobby Benton 252 527-7023
396 Sandy Foundation Rd Kinston (28504) *(G-9346)*

Bobby Cahoon Construction Inc 252 249-1617
6003 Neuse Rd Grantsboro (28529) *(G-6763)*

Bobby Choon Mar Cnstr Land Dev, Grantsboro Also Called: Bobby Cahoon Construction Inc *(G-6763)*

Bobcat of Mount Airy 336 459-3844
825 W Lebanon St Ste 101 Mount Airy (27030) *(G-11484)*

Body Billboards Inc 919 544-4540
4905 S Alston Ave Durham (27713) *(G-4969)*

Body Butter Blends LLC 704 307-9200
10419 Hyndman Ct Charlotte (28214) *(G-2329)*

Body Engineering Inc 704 650-3434
701 Matthews Mint Hill Rd Matthews (28105) *(G-10234)*

Body Shop, Wake Forest Also Called: Body Shop Inc *(G-15534)*

Body Shop Inc (DH) 919 554-4900
5036 One World Way Wake Forest (27587) *(G-15534)*

Bodycote Thermal Proc Inc 704 664-1808
128 Speedway Ln Mooresville (28117) *(G-10884)*

Bodycote Thermal Processing, Mooresville Also Called: Bodycote Thermal Proc Inc *(G-10884)*

Boehme-Filatex Inc 336 342-4507
209 Watlington Industrial Dr Reidsville (27320) *(G-13510)*

Boehrnger Inglheim Anmal Hlth 919 577-9020
3225 Air Park Rd Fuquay Varina (27526) *(G-6185)*

Boeing, Charlotte Also Called: Boeing Company *(G-2330)*

Boeing, Goldsboro Also Called: Boeing Arospc Operations Inc *(G-6594)*

Boeing Arospc Operations Inc 919 722-4351
1950 Jabara Ave Bldg 4517 Goldsboro (27531) *(G-6594)*

Boeing Company 704 572-8280
4930 Minuteman Way Charlotte (28208) *(G-2330)*

Boeing Company 919 722-1983
1155 Blakeslee Ave Sjafb (27531) *(G-14446)*

Boggs Collective Inc 828 398-9701
239 Amboy Rd Asheville (28806) *(G-569)*

Boggs Farm Center Inc 704 538-7176
807 E Stagecoach Trl Fallston (28042) *(G-5728)*

Boggs Group, Monroe Also Called: Boggs Transport Inc *(G-10665)*

Boggs Materials Inc (PA) 704 289-8482
1613 W Roosevelt Blvd Monroe (28110) *(G-10664)*

Boggs Transport Inc 704 289-8482
2318 Concord Hwy Monroe (28110) *(G-10665)*

Bogue Sound Distillery Inc 252 241-1606
108 Bogue Commercial Dr Newport (28570) *(G-11898)*

Boingo Graphics Inc 704 527-4963
656 Michael Wylie Dr Charlotte (28217) *(G-2331)*

Boise Cascade Wood Pdts LLC 336 598-3001
1000 N Park Dr Roxboro (27573) *(G-13795)*

Boka Industries LLC 704 237-4692
19406 E Battery St Cornelius (28031) *(G-4530)*

Bold Life Publication 828 692-3230
105 S Main St Ste A Hendersonville (28792) *(G-7828)*

Bold Rock Hard Cider, Mills River Also Called: Bold Rock Partners LP *(G-10501)*

Bold Rock Partners LP 828 595-9940
72 School House Rd Mills River (28759) *(G-10501)*

Boldesigns, Hudson Also Called: Superior Dry Kilns Inc *(G-8782)*

Boleef Industries 336 330-0404
368 Nelson Loop Rd Roxboro (27574) *(G-13796)*

Boles Holding Inc 828 264-4200
2165 Highway 105 Boone (28607) *(G-1178)*

Boles Industries LLC 919 489-9254
112 Landsbury Dr Durham (27707) *(G-4970)*

Bolivia Lumber Company LLC (PA) 910 371-2515
405 Old Mill Rd Ne Leland (28451) *(G-9528)*

Bolton Investors Inc 919 471-1197
4914 N Roxboro St Ste 7 Durham (27704) *(G-4971)*

Bombshell Beer Company LLC 919 823-1933
120 Quantum St Holly Springs (27540) *(G-8691)*

Bommerang Imprints 704 933-9075
2305 Beaver Pond Rd Kannapolis (28083) *(G-9111)*

Bon Worth Inc (PA) 800 355-5131
219 Commercial Hill Dr Hendersonville (28792) *(G-7829)*

Bon Worth Factory Outlets, Hendersonville Also Called: Bon Worth Inc *(G-7829)*

Bona US, Monroe Also Called: Bonakemi Usa Incorporated *(G-10667)*

Bona USA 704 220-6943
4275 Corporate Center Dr Monroe (28110) *(G-10666)*

Bonakemi Usa Incorporated 704 218-3917
4275 Corporate Center Dr Monroe (28110) *(G-10667)*

Bonap Inc 919 967-6240
9319 Bracken Ln Chapel Hill (27516) *(G-1994)*

Bonaventure Co LLC 336 584-7530
1147 Saint Marks Church Rd Ste G Burlington (27215) *(G-1378)*

ALPHABETIC SECTION — Boxcarr Handmade Cheese

Bonaventure Group Inc.. 919 781-6610
  6031 Oak Forest Dr Raleigh (27616) *(G-12568)*
Bond Technologies.. 919 866-0075
  909 Walkertown Dr Raleigh (27614) *(G-12569)*
Bonding Materials LLC.. 704 277-6697
  809 Westmere Ave Ste C Charlotte (28208) *(G-2332)*
Bondo Innovations LLC... 704 888-9910
  14904 Barbee Rd Stanfield (28163) *(G-14676)*
Bone Tred Beds Smmit Woodworks............................ 910 319-7583
  617 Creekwood Rd Wilmington (28411) *(G-16141)*
Bones Grill LLC... 252 827-0454
  2404 Summerfield Dr Tarboro (27886) *(G-15097)*
Bonitz Inc... 803 799-0181
  4539 Enterprise Dr Nw Concord (28027) *(G-4213)*
Bonomi North America Inc... 704 412-9031
  306 Forsyth Hall Dr Charlotte (28273) *(G-2333)*
Bonsal American Inc (DH)... 704 525-1621
  625 Griffith Rd Ste 100 Charlotte (28217) *(G-2334)*
Bonsal American Inc... 336 854-8200
  139 S Walnut Cir Greensboro (27409) *(G-6847)*
Bonsal American Inc... 704 848-4141
  351 Haileys Ferry Rd Lilesville (28091) *(G-9835)*
Bonset America Corporation (PA)............................... 336 375-0234
  6107 Corporate Park Dr Browns Summit (27214) *(G-1301)*
Boogs Materials Plant 1, Monroe Also Called: Boggs Materials Inc *(G-10664)*
Book Lover Search.. 336 889-6127
  High Point (27261) *(G-8274)*
Bookcase Shop (PA)... 919 683-1922
  301 S Duke St Durham (27701) *(G-4972)*
Boomerang Foods LLC.. 336 558-3798
  2602 Lamroc Rd Greensboro (27407) *(G-6848)*
Boon Edam Inc (DH)... 910 814-3800
  402 Mckinney Pkwy Lillington (27546) *(G-9844)*
Boondock S Manufacturing Inc.................................... 828 891-4242
  6085 Brevard Rd Etowah (28729) *(G-5691)*
Boone Brands, Sanford Also Called: Violet Sanford Holdings LLC *(G-14203)*
Boone Iron Works Inc.. 828 264-5284
  253 Ray Brown Rd Boone (28607) *(G-1179)*
Boone Ironworks, Boone Also Called: Boone Iron Works Inc *(G-1179)*
Boone Logging Company Inc....................................... 252 443-7641
  1996 Vaughan Rd Elm City (27822) *(G-5647)*
Boone Newspapers Inc... 252 332-2123
  801 Parker Ave E Ste 803 Ahoskie (27910) *(G-56)*
Boone-Woody Mining Company Inc............................ 828 675-5188
  4456 E Us Hwy 19 E Micaville (28755) *(G-10442)*
Boones Sawmill Inc... 828 287-8774
  182 Goldfinch Ln Rutherfordton (28139) *(G-13867)*
Booneshine Brewing Co Inc... 828 263-4305
  465 Industrial Park Dr Boone (28607) *(G-1180)*
Boonville Flour Feed Mill Inc.. 336 367-7541
  203 S Caralino Ave Boonville (27011) *(G-1253)*
Boramed Inc.. 919 419-9518
  4800 Centerway Dr Durham (27705) *(G-4973)*
Bordchek Industries LLC.. 864 363-2117
  19701 Bethel Church Rd Ste 103-164 Cornelius (28031) *(G-4531)*
Bordeaux Dynocams... 910 655-9482
  Delco (28436) *(G-4718)*
Borden, Fayetteville Also Called: Hexion Inc *(G-5838)*
Borden, High Point Also Called: Hexion Inc *(G-8384)*
Borden, Morganton Also Called: Borden Chemical *(G-11202)*
Borden Chemical.. 828 584-3800
  114 Industrial Blvd Morganton (28655) *(G-11202)*
Borden Mfg Co Fund Inc... 919 734-4301
  1506 E Ash St Goldsboro (27530) *(G-6595)*
Bordentown Highway Sign LLC................................... 919 870-8116
  9921 Waterview Rd Raleigh (27615) *(G-12570)*
Border Concepts Inc (PA).. 704 541-5509
  15720 Brixham Hill Ave Charlotte (28277) *(G-2335)*
Border Concepts Inc... 336 248-2419
  115 Lexington Pkwy Lexington (27295) *(G-9686)*
Borealis Compounds Inc.. 908 798-7497
  401 We Baab Industrial Dr Taylorsville (28681) *(G-15130)*

Borg-Warner Automotive Inc.. 828 684-3501
  Cane Creek Ind Pk Fletcher (28732) *(G-5990)*
Borgwarner Arden LLC.. 248 754-9200
  1849 Brevard Rd Arden (28704) *(G-313)*
Borgwarner Inc... 828 684-4000
  1849 Brevard Rd Arden (28704) *(G-314)*
Borgwarner Turbo Systems LLC (DH)........................ 828 650-7515
  1849 Brevard Rd Arden (28704) *(G-315)*
Born In A Barn Inc... 828 635-5808
  1542 Rocky Face Church Rd Taylorsville (28681) *(G-15131)*
Bornemann Pumps Inc.. 704 849-8636
  901a Matthews Mint Hill Rd Matthews (28105) *(G-10235)*
Borneo Inc... 252 398-3100
  10 Commerce St Murfreesboro (27855) *(G-11698)*
Bosch Rexroth Corporation (DH)................................ 704 583-4338
  14001 S Lakes Dr South Point Business Park Charlotte (28273) *(G-2336)*
Bosmere Inc.. 704 784-1608
  2701 S Main St Salisbury (28147) *(G-13930)*
Boss Design US Inc... 844 353-7834
  2014 Chestnut Street Ext High Point (27262) *(G-8275)*
Boss Key Productions Inc.. 919 659-5704
  230 Fayetteville St Ste 300 Raleigh (27601) *(G-12571)*
Bossong Corporation.. 336 625-2175
  840 W Salisbury St Asheboro (27203) *(G-410)*
Bossong Hosiery Mills Inc (PA)................................... 336 625-2175
  840 W Salisbury St Asheboro (27203) *(G-411)*
Bost Distributing Company Inc.................................... 919 775-5931
  2209 Boone Trail Rd Sanford (27330) *(G-14095)*
Boston Fruit Slice & Conf, Sanford Also Called: New Boston Fruit Slice & Confe *(G-14158)*
Boston Gear, Charlotte Also Called: Altra Industrial Motion Corp *(G-2174)*
Boston Gear, Charlotte Also Called: Tb Woods Incorporated *(G-3675)*
Boston Gear LLC.. 704 588-5610
  701 Carrier Dr Charlotte (28216) *(G-2337)*
Bostrom Seating Inc.. 704 596-0040
  3000 Crosspoint Center Ln Ste P Charlotte (28269) *(G-2338)*
Botanist and Barrel.. 919 644-7777
  105 Persimmon Hill Ln Cedar Grove (27231) *(G-1970)*
Bottom Line Technologies Inc..................................... 919 472-0541
  1000 Parliament Ct # 310 Durham (27703) *(G-4974)*
Bottomley Enterprises Inc.. 336 657-6400
  452 Oak Grove Church Rd Mount Airy (27030) *(G-11485)*
Bottomline Medical.. 704 527-0919
  5200 Milford Rd Charlotte (28210) *(G-2339)*
Bougiejones.. 704 492-3029
  5212 Galway Dr Charlotte (28215) *(G-2340)*
Bouncers and Slides Inc... 252 908-2292
  2218 N Nc Highway 58 Nashville (27856) *(G-11735)*
Boundless Inc... 919 622-9051
  102 S Main St Four Oaks (27524) *(G-6101)*
Bov Solutions, Statesville Also Called: Sklar Bov Solutions Inc *(G-14886)*
Bowden Electric Motor Svc Inc.................................... 252 446-4203
  1681 S Wesleyan Blvd Rocky Mount (27803) *(G-13685)*
Bowed Up Lures... 757 376-7944
  25 12th Ave Southern Shores (27949) *(G-14561)*
Bowen Machine Company Inc...................................... 704 629-9111
  3421 Fairview Dr Gastonia (28052) *(G-6357)*
Bowie Machine Works LLC... 910 297-6014
  232 N Channel Haven Dr Wilmington (28409) *(G-16142)*
Bowman Distribution, Newland Also Called: Dickie Jones *(G-11885)*
Bowman-Hollis Manufacturing Co (PA)...................... 704 374-1500
  2925 Old Steele Creek Rd Charlotte (28208) *(G-2341)*
Box Board Products Inc... 336 668-3347
  8313 Triad Dr Greensboro (27409) *(G-6849)*
Box Company of America LLC..................................... 910 582-0100
  12 Ev Hogan Dr Hamlet (28345) *(G-7617)*
Box Drop Furniture Whl NC, Greensboro Also Called: Epsilon Holdings LLC *(G-7003)*
Box Scientific, Newton Also Called: Box Scientific LLC *(G-11916)*
Box Scientific LLC.. 408 361-8631
  2805 Rosewood Ln Newton (28658) *(G-11916)*
Box Shop, Thomasville Also Called: Carolina Container LLC *(G-15195)*
Boxcarr Handmade Cheese, Cedar Grove Also Called: Tin Can Ventures LLC *(G-1973)*

Boxman Studios LLC	704 333-3733
12140 Vance Davis Dr Charlotte (28269) *(G-2342)*	
Boxmoor Truck Bedliners & ACC	336 447-4621
1900 Buckminster Dr Whitsett (27377) *(G-15984)*	
Boy Scout Troop	704 643-8955
3000 Wamath Dr Charlotte (28210) *(G-2343)*	
Boyd Gmn Inc	206 284-2200
300 Acme Dr Monroe (28112) *(G-10668)*	
Boyd Manufacturing Inc	336 301-6433
222 W Raleigh St Siler City (27344) *(G-14400)*	
Boyd Stone & Quarries	828 659-6862
2207 Cannon Rd Marion (28752) *(G-10144)*	
Boyd Welding and Mfg Inc	828 247-0630
324 Pine St Forest City (28043) *(G-6061)*	
Boyd's Welding and Fabrication, Forest City Also Called: Boyd Welding and Mfg Inc *(G-6061)*	
Boyles Logging LLC	910 206-7086
496 Pleasant Hill Church Rd Ellerbe (28338) *(G-5641)*	
Boyles Sign Shop Inc	336 782-1189
4050 Stafford Mill Rd Germanton (27019) *(G-6551)*	
BP Associates Inc (PA)	704 864-3032
2408 Forbes Rd Gastonia (28056) *(G-6358)*	
BP Associates Inc	704 833-1494
105 Wolfpack Rd Gastonia (28056) *(G-6359)*	
BP Oil Corp Distributors	828 264-8516
585 E King St Boone (28607) *(G-1181)*	
BP Signs Inc	704 531-8000
4845 E Independence Blvd Unit B Charlotte (28212) *(G-2344)*	
BP Solutions Group Inc	828 252-4476
24 Wilmington St Asheville (28806) *(G-570)*	
Bpc Plasma Inc	910 463-2603
113 Yopp Rd Jacksonville (28540) *(G-8991)*	
Bpl Usa LLC	919 354-8405
302 E Pettigrew St Ste C190 Durham (27701) *(G-4975)*	
BR Lee Industries Inc	704 966-3317
500 Lincoln County Parkway Ext Lincolnton (28092) *(G-9876)*	
Br549 Enterprises LLC	704 799-0955
1558 Sherwood Ct Sherrills Ford (28673) *(G-14384)*	
Bracelets and More	419 236-4933
306 Millet Dr Morrisville (27560) *(G-11306)*	
Bracey Bros Logging LLC	910 231-9543
418 Lennon Rd Delco (28436) *(G-4719)*	
Bradford Products, Leland Also Called: Bradford Products LLC *(G-9529)*	
Bradford Products LLC (PA)	910 791-2202
2101 Enterprise Dr Ne Leland (28451) *(G-9529)*	
Bradington-Young LLC	276 656-3335
941 Tot Dellinger Rd Cherryville (28021) *(G-3862)*	
Bradington-Young LLC (HQ)	704 435-5881
4040 10th Avenue Dr Sw Hickory (28602) *(G-7953)*	
Bradley Screen Printing, Shelby Also Called: Bradleys Inc *(G-14289)*	
Bradley Todd Baugus	252 665-4901
6444 White Oak River Rd Maysville (28555) *(G-10369)*	
Bradleys Inc	704 484-2077
2522 W Dixon Blvd Shelby (28152) *(G-14289)*	
Brady's Baked Goods, Roxboro Also Called: B & B Distributing Inc *(G-13794)*	
Brafford Welding	336 318-5436
2262 Ramseur Julian Rd Liberty (27298) *(G-9808)*	
Braiform Enterprises Inc	828 277-6420
12 Gerber Rd Ste B Asheville (28803) *(G-571)*	
Branch 0457, Hope Mills Also Called: Franklin Baking Company LLC *(G-8737)*	
Branch Office Solutions Inc	800 743-1047
4391 Indian Trail Fairview Rd Ste A Indian Trail (28079) *(G-8924)*	
Branch Welding Greensville Co, Gaston Also Called: Michael H Branch Inc *(G-6331)*	
Branched Out Wood Works LLC	828 515-0377
42 Gillespie Dr Leicester (28748) *(G-9507)*	
Brand Art Manufacturing LLC	704 241-1104
4991 Robinhood Rd Winston Salem (27106) *(G-16635)*	
Brand Fuel Promotions	704 256-4057
400 N Broome St Ste 203 Waxhaw (28173) *(G-15746)*	
Brand New Life Clothing LLC	980 266-4788
1914 J N Pease Pl Charlotte (28262) *(G-2345)*	
Brandel LLC	704 525-4548
2909 Rockbrook Dr Charlotte (28211) *(G-2346)*	
Brandilly Marketing Creative, Raleigh Also Called: Brandilly of Nc Inc *(G-12572)*	
Brandilly of Nc Inc	919 278-7896
1053 E Whitaker Mill Rd Ste 115 Raleigh (27604) *(G-12572)*	
Brandon Hilbert	704 243-5593
10704 Lancaster Hwy Waxhaw (28173) *(G-15747)*	
Brandrpm, Charlotte Also Called: Brandrpm LLC *(G-2347)*	
Brandrpm LLC	704 225-1800
9555 Monroe Rd Charlotte (28270) *(G-2347)*	
Brands Fashion US Inc	704 953-8246
2600 Mcdonald Rd Charlotte (28269) *(G-2348)*	
Brandspeed	410 204-1032
915 River Hwy Mooresville (28117) *(G-10885)*	
Brandt Consolidated Inc	910 567-2965
2126 Old Wrench School Rd Godwin (28344) *(G-6575)*	
Brandy Thompson	321 252-2911
6712 Bone Creek Dr Apt A Fayetteville (28314) *(G-5774)*	
Brandywine Communications	770 853-1799
1204 Golden Star Way Wake Forest (27587) *(G-15535)*	
Branford Filtration LLC (PA)	704 394-2111
119 Poplar Pointe Dr Ste C Mooresville (28117) *(G-10886)*	
Brant & Lassiter Septic Tank	252 587-4321
Hwy 35 Potecasi (27867) *(G-12395)*	
Brasingtons Inc	704 694-5191
1515 Us Highway 74 W Wadesboro (28170) *(G-15503)*	
Brasscraft	336 475-2131
1024 Randolph St Thomasville (27360) *(G-15189)*	
Brasscraft Brownstown, Thomasville Also Called: Brasscraft Manufacturing Co *(G-15190)*	
Brasscraft Manufacturing Co	336 475-2131
1024 Randolph St Thomasville (27360) *(G-15190)*	
Braswell Foods, Nashville Also Called: Braswell Milling Company *(G-11736)*	
Braswell Milling Company (PA)	252 459-2143
105 E Cross St Nashville (27856) *(G-11736)*	
Braswell Realty	828 733-5800
320 Linville St Newland (28657) *(G-11882)*	
Braswell Welding	252 838-0089
502 Perkins Rd Beaufort (28516) *(G-947)*	
Bratz Playground LLC	704 858-1934
9501 Lucy Jane Ln Apt 310 Charlotte (28270) *(G-2349)*	
Bravo Team LLC	704 309-1918
603 N Church St Mooresville (28115) *(G-10887)*	
Bravosolution Us Inc (DH)	312 373-3100
3020 Carrington Mill Blvd Ste 100 Morrisville (27560) *(G-11307)*	
Braxton Culler, Sophia Also Called: Rbc Inc *(G-14521)*	
Braxton Sawmill Inc	336 376-6798
7519 Lindley Mill Rd Lot D Graham (27253) *(G-6680)*	
Bray S Recapping Service Inc (PA)	336 786-6182
1120 W Lebanon St Mount Airy (27030) *(G-11486)*	
Bread & Butter Custom Scrn Prt	919 942-3198
1201 Raleigh Rd Ste 100 Chapel Hill (27517) *(G-1995)*	
Bread N Butter Screenprinting, Chapel Hill Also Called: Bread & Butter Custom Scrn Prt *(G-1995)*	
Breathingair Systems, Randleman Also Called: Sub-Aquatics Inc *(G-13492)*	
Breezeplay LLC	980 297-0885
8045 Corporate Center Dr Charlotte (28226) *(G-2350)*	
Breezer Holdings LLC	844 233-5673
4835 Sirona Dr Ste 400 Charlotte (28273) *(G-2351)*	
Breezer Mobile Cooling, Charlotte Also Called: Breezer Holdings LLC *(G-2351)*	
Brembo North America Inc	704 799-0530
7275 Westwinds Blvd Nw Concord (28027) *(G-4214)*	
Bremeo North America, Concord Also Called: Brembo North America Inc *(G-4214)*	
Brenthaven, High Point Also Called: Pioneer Square Brands Inc *(G-8485)*	
Bretagne LLC	336 299-8729
814 Pebble Dr Greensboro (27410) *(G-6850)*	
Brett McHenry Logging LLC	252 243-7285
3204 Nash St N Ste C Wilson (27896) *(G-16478)*	
Brett Salter	828 252-4311
9 Webb Cove Rd Asheville (28804) *(G-572)*	
Brevard Business Ctr	828 883-4363
9 Encompass Plz E Brevard (28712) *(G-1272)*	
Brevard Laser, Pisgah Forest Also Called: Jonathan Stamey *(G-12324)*	

ALPHABETIC SECTION

Brew Candle Company.. 980 275-9355
115b Corby Ct Boone (28607) *(G-1182)*

Brew Masters of Goldsboro.. 919 288-2014
2402 E Ash St Goldsboro (27534) *(G-6596)*

Brew Publik Incorporated... 704 231-2703
312 W Park Ave Charlotte (28203) *(G-2352)*

Brewitt & Dreenkupp Inc.. 704 525-3366
4321 Stuart Andrew Blvd Ste I Charlotte (28217) *(G-2353)*

Brewmasters Inc... 252 991-6035
2117 Forest Hills Rd W Wilson (27893) *(G-16479)*

Brewpub, Charlotte *Also Called: Salud LLC* *(G-3485)*

Brian Allen Artisan Printer.. 919 609-8992
807 E Main St Ste 3141 Durham (27701) *(G-4976)*

Brian McGregor Enterprise.. 919 732-2317
2207 Leah Dr Hillsborough (27278) *(G-8640)*

Brice Manufacturing Co Inc....................................... 818 896-2938
8010 Piedmont Triad Pkwy Greensboro (27409) *(G-6851)*

Brick & Mortar Grill... 919 639-9700
8 N Broad St E Ste 200 Angier (27501) *(G-133)*

Brick City Gaming Inc... 919 297-2081
80 Hamilton Hedge Pl Cary (27519) *(G-1713)*

Brick City Phenomicon, Sanford *Also Called: Hugger Mugger LLC* *(G-14134)*

Brick Mason Masonry.. 704 502-4907
1122 Goodman Rd Charlotte (28214) *(G-2354)*

Brickfields Incorporated... 704 351-1524
6109 Hickory Forest Dr Charlotte (28277) *(G-2355)*

Bricks & Quarters LLC.. 704 321-0124
3014 Shalford Ln Matthews (28104) *(G-10305)*

Brickstone Publishing... 919 522-4052
133 Clay Ridge Way Ste 200 Holly Springs (27540) *(G-8692)*

Bridge, Raleigh *Also Called: Getbridge LLC* *(G-12799)*

Bridgestone Ret Operations LLC............................. 919 471-4468
3809 N Duke St Durham (27704) *(G-4977)*

Bridgestone Ret Operations LLC............................. 910 864-4106
660 Cross Creek Mall Fayetteville (28303) *(G-5775)*

Bridgestone Ret Operations LLC............................. 704 861-8146
142 N New Hope Rd Gastonia (28054) *(G-6360)*

Bridgestone Ret Operations LLC............................. 919 778-0230
507 N Berkeley Blvd Goldsboro (27534) *(G-6597)*

Bridgestone Ret Operations LLC............................. 336 282-6646
3311 Battleground Ave Greensboro (27410) *(G-6852)*

Bridgestone Ret Operations LLC............................. 336 852-8524
3937 W Gate City Blvd Greensboro (27407) *(G-6853)*

Bridgestone Ret Operations LLC............................. 252 522-5126
1901 W Vernon Ave Kinston (28504) *(G-9347)*

Bridgestone Ret Operations LLC............................. 919 872-6402
5058 N New Hope Rd Raleigh (27604) *(G-12573)*

Bridgestone Ret Operations LLC............................. 919 872-6566
4305 Wake Forest Rd Raleigh (27609) *(G-12574)*

Bridgestone Ret Operations LLC............................. 252 243-5189
1401 Ward Blvd Wilson (27893) *(G-16480)*

Bridgestone Ret Operations LLC............................. 336 725-1580
2743 Reynolda Rd Winston Salem (27106) *(G-16636)*

Bridgetower Media LLC (PA)..................................... 612 317-9420
7025 Albert Pick Rd Ste 200 Greensboro (27409) *(G-6854)*

Bridgewater Blinds Interi... 910 408-1900
1132 New Pointe Blvd Ste 5 Leland (28451) *(G-9530)*

Bridgport Restoration Svcs Inc................................. 336 996-1212
742 Park Lawn Ct Kernersville (27284) *(G-9169)*

Brig Homes NC.. 252 459-7026
1001 Eastern Ave Nashville (27856) *(G-11737)*

Briggs Boat Works Incorporated.............................. 252 473-2393
370 Harbor Rd Wanchese (27981) *(G-15643)*

Briggs-Shaffner Acquisition Co (PA)...................... 336 463-4272
1448 Us 601 Hwy Yadkinville (27055) *(G-17034)*

Briggs-Shaffner Company, Yadkinville *Also Called: Briggs-Shaffner Acquisition Co* *(G-17034)*

Bright Angle LLC.. 828 771-6966
207 Coxe Ave Asheville (28801) *(G-573)*

Bright Fabrication LLC... 704 660-3151
133 Waderich Ln Mooresville (28117) *(G-10888)*

Bright Path Laboratories Inc..................................... 858 281-8121
150 N Research Campus Dr Kannapolis (28081) *(G-9112)*

Bright View Technologies Corp................................. 919 228-4370
4022 Stirrup Creek Dr Ste 301 Durham (27703) *(G-4978)*

Brightbell Creative, Greensboro *Also Called: Songs of Water LLC* *(G-7349)*

Brightfish Press.. 919 452-5737
2514 State St Durham (27704) *(G-4979)*

Brightleaf Wldg & Mch Repr LLC............................. 919 934-3300
2850 S Brightleaf Blvd Smithfield (27577) *(G-14451)*

Brightly Software Inc (PA).. 919 816-8237
11000 Regency Pkwy Ste 110 Cary (27518) *(G-1714)*

Brightwill Technologies LLC.................................... 919 757-3176
3613 Cathedral Bell Rd Raleigh (27614) *(G-12575)*

Brigman Electric Motors Inc..................................... 828 492-0568
6110 Old Clyde Rd Canton (28716) *(G-1603)*

Brii Biosciences Inc.. 919 240-5605
110 N Corcoran St Unit 5-130 Durham (27701) *(G-4980)*

Brilliant Pos LLC... 704 315-2352
15210 Pangborn Pl Charlotte (28278) *(G-2356)*

Brilliant Sole Inc... 339 222-8528
1930 Senova Trce Wilmington (28405) *(G-16143)*

Brilliant You LLC... 336 343-5535
1451 S Elm Eugene St Ste 1102 Greensboro (27406) *(G-6855)*

Brisk Transport 910 LLC... 910 527-7398
232 Old Montague Way Cameron (28326) *(G-1560)*

Brispa Investments Inc.. 336 668-3636
4833 W Gate City Blvd Greensboro (27407) *(G-6856)*

Bristol-Myers Squibb, Charlotte *Also Called: Bristol-Myers Squibb Company* *(G-2357)*

Bristol-Myers Squibb Company................................ 800 321-1335
Charlotte (28275) *(G-2357)*

Bristol-Myers Squibb Company................................ 336 855-5500
211 American Ave Greensboro (27409) *(G-6857)*

Brite Sky LLC... 757 589-4676
6461 Sherrill Baggett Rd Godwin (28344) *(G-6576)*

Brittany Smith... 912 313-0588
2508 Glenhaven Dr Greensboro (27406) *(G-6858)*

Brittenhams Rebuilding Service............................... 252 332-3181
2314 Us Hwy13 S Ahoskie (27910) *(G-57)*

Broach Custom Signs, Wendell *Also Called: Broach Custom Signs NC LLC* *(G-15893)*

Broach Custom Signs NC LLC.................................. 919 876-8380
3040 Wendell Blvd Wendell (27591) *(G-15893)*

Broad Branch Distillery, Winston Salem *Also Called: Broad Branch Distillery LLC* *(G-16638)*

Broad Branch Distillery LLC..................................... 336 207-7855
2403 Buena Vista Rd Winston Salem (27104) *(G-16637)*

Broad Branch Distillery LLC..................................... 336 602-2824
756 N Trade St Winston Salem (27101) *(G-16638)*

Broad River Forest Products..................................... 828 287-8003
2250 Us 221 Hwy N Rutherfordton (28139) *(G-13868)*

Broadcom Corporation.. 919 865-2954
1030 Swabia Ct Ste 400 Durham (27703) *(G-4981)*

Broadsight Systems Inc... 336 837-1272
1023 Corporate Park Dr Mebane (27302) *(G-10401)*

Broadway Chipping Co., New Bern *Also Called: Broadway Logging Co Inc* *(G-11778)*

Broadway Logging Co Inc.. 252 633-2693
1525 Saints Delight Church Rd New Bern (28560) *(G-11778)*

Broadwick, Morrisville *Also Called: Icontact LLC* *(G-11356)*

Broadwind Indus Solutions LLC............................... 919 777-2907
1824 Boone Trail Rd Sanford (27330) *(G-14096)*

Brock & Triplett Machine, Moravian Falls *Also Called: Brock and Triplett Machine Sp* *(G-11142)*

Brock and Triplett Machine Sp.................................. 336 667-6951
285 E Meadows Rd Moravian Falls (28654) *(G-11142)*

Brodie-Jones Printing Co Inc.................................... 252 438-7992
253 Ronald Tharrington Rd Louisburg (27549) *(G-9981)*

Bromley Plastics, Fletcher *Also Called: Mdt Bromley LLC* *(G-6021)*

Bromma Inc... 919 620-8039
4400 Ben Franklin Blvd Ste 200 Durham (27704) *(G-4982)*

Bronto Software LLC... 919 595-2500
324 Blackwell St Ste 410 Durham (27701) *(G-4983)*

Brookhurst Associates.. 919 792-0987
2400 Saint Pauls Sq Raleigh (27614) *(G-12576)*

Brookline Inc.. 704 824-1390
112 Cramer Mountain Woods Cramerton (28032) *(G-4600)*

Brookline Furniture, Archdale Also Called: Brookline Furniture Co Inc **(G-270)**
Brookline Furniture Co Inc... 336 841-8503
   4015 Cheyenne Dr Archdale (27263) **(G-270)**
Brooks Boatworks Inc.. 252 974-1005
   403 Handy Ln Bath (27808) **(G-914)**
Brooks Equipment, Charlotte Also Called: Beco Holding Company Inc **(G-2295)**
Brooks Machine & Design Inc.. 919 404-0901
   1424 Old Us Highway 264 Zebulon (27597) **(G-17122)**
Brooks Manufacturing Solutions... 336 438-1280
   1017 Davis Ln Graham (27253) **(G-6681)**
Brooks Mfg Solutions Inc.. 336 438-1280
   418 N Main St Burlington (27217) **(G-1379)**
Brooks of Dallas Inc.. 704 922-5219
   203 E Lay St Dallas (28034) **(G-4635)**
Brooks Tool Inc... 704 283-0112
   524 Marshall St Monroe (28112) **(G-10669)**
Brookshire Buiulders, Asheville Also Called: Brookshire Woodworking Inc **(G-574)**
Brookshire Woodworking Inc (PA)... 828 779-2119
   355 Haywood Rd Asheville (28806) **(G-574)**
Brookshire Woodworking Inc... 828 779-2119
   99 Dodd Rd Barnardsville (28709) **(G-906)**
Brookstone Baptist Church.. 828 658-9443
   90 Griffee Rd Weaverville (28787) **(G-15840)**
Brookwood Farms Inc... 919 663-3612
   1015 Alston Bridge Rd Siler City (27344) **(G-14401)**
Broome Sign Company... 704 782-0422
   348 Spring St Nw Concord (28025) **(G-4215)**
Broomes Poultry Inc.. 704 983-0965
   24816 Austin Rd Albemarle (28001) **(G-75)**
Brothers Metal Fab Inc... 336 270-3761
   330 Holly Hill Ln Burlington (27215) **(G-1380)**
Brown & Church Neck Wear Co.. 336 368-5502
   118 Mary Moore Ln Pilot Mountain (27041) **(G-12196)**
Brown Brothers Construction Co.. 828 297-2131
   10801 Us Highway 421 N Zionville (28698) **(G-17148)**
Brown Brothers Lumber... 828 632-6486
   1388 Little River Church Rd Taylorsville (28681) **(G-15132)**
Brown Building Corporation.. 919 782-1800
   1111 Copeland Oaks Dr Morrisville (27560) **(G-11308)**
Brown Cabinet Co.. 704 933-2731
   1510 N Ridge Ave Kannapolis (28083) **(G-9113)**
Brown Creek Timber Company Inc.. 704 694-3529
   2691 Nc 742 N Wadesboro (28170) **(G-15504)**
Brown Equipment and Capitl Inc... 704 921-4644
   650 Broome St Monroe (28110) **(G-10670)**
Brown Lady Publishing LLC.. 980 833-0398
   9137 Austin Ridge Ln Charlotte (28214) **(G-2358)**
Brown Mitchell Hodges LLC.. 800 477-8982
   4111 Rose Lake Dr Ste E Pmb 678 Charlotte (28217) **(G-2359)**
Brown Printing Inc.. 704 849-9292
   9129 Monroe Rd Ste 160 Charlotte (28270) **(G-2360)**
Browns Woodworking LLC... 704 983-5917
   210 Charter St Albemarle (28001) **(G-76)**
Brp Spruce Pine, Spruce Pine Also Called: Brp US Inc **(G-14631)**
Brp Spruce Pine Distribution, Spruce Pine Also Called: Brp US Inc **(G-14630)**
Brp US Inc... 828 766-1164
   12934 S Highway 226 Spruce Pine (28777) **(G-14630)**
Brp US Inc... 828 766-1100
   1211 Greenwood Rd Spruce Pine (28777) **(G-14631)**
Brs Aerospace, Pinebluff Also Called: Ballistic Recovery Systems Inc **(G-12213)**
Brucato Power Inc... 919 234-1776
   122 N Salem St Ste 201 Apex (27502) **(G-173)**
Bruce Julian Heritage Foods, Charlotte Also Called: Bevs & Bites LLC **(G-2305)**
Bruce Stanley... 828 683-1265
   570 Clarks Branch Rd Leicester (28748) **(G-9508)**
Bruce Trull Sawing Mill... 828 667-1148
   26 Doyce Dr Candler (28715) **(G-1572)**
Bruex Inc... 828 754-1186
   312 Lutz St Sw Lenoir (28645) **(G-9592)**
Brumley-South, Mooresville Also Called: Brumley/South Inc **(G-10889)**
Brumley/South Inc... 704 664-9251
   422 N Broad St Mooresville (28115) **(G-10889)**

Brun Millworks LLC... 704 989-3145
   16300 Blackberry Hills Dr Midland (28107) **(G-10458)**
Bruning and Federle Mfg Co (PA)... 704 873-7237
   2503 Northside Dr Statesville (28625) **(G-14766)**
Brunner & Lay Inc... 828 274-2770
   90 Reeds Way Flat Rock (28731) **(G-5961)**
Brunson Marine Group LLC... 252 291-0271
   4155 Dixie Inn Rd Wilson (27893) **(G-16481)**
Brunswick Beacon Inc.. 910 754-6890
   208 Smith Ave Shallotte (28470) **(G-14270)**
Brunswick Cabinets Countertops, Supply Also Called: Bcac Holdings LLC **(G-15006)**
Brunswick Screen Prtg & EMB... 910 579-1234
   570 Meadow Summit Dr Ocean Isle Beach (28469) **(G-12087)**
Brushy Mountain Bee Farm Inc (PA)... 336 921-3640
   101 S Stratford Rd Ste 210 Winston Salem (27104) **(G-16639)**
Brushy Mountain Dry Kilns LLC... 336 379-8314
   10 Branch Ct Greensboro (27408) **(G-6859)**
Brushy Mountain Publishing... 828 298-6687
   221 Long Branch Rd Swannanoa (28778) **(G-15021)**
Brushy Mtn Cstm Woodworks Inc.. 336 921-3510
   10350 Brushy Mountain Rd Moravian Falls (28654) **(G-11143)**
Bryan Austin.. 336 841-6573
   1589 Skeet Club Rd Ste 102 High Point (27265) **(G-8276)**
Bryan Blake James.. 252 729-8021
   134 Shore Dr Gloucester (28528) **(G-6574)**
Bryant Grant Mutual Burial Asn... 828 524-2411
   105 W Main St Franklin (28734) **(G-6117)**
Bryants Fire Extinguisher Co.. 252 563-4111
   108 W Granville St Tarboro (27886) **(G-15098)**
Bryson Industries Inc... 336 931-0026
   416 Albertson Rd Thomasville (27360) **(G-15191)**
Bsci Inc (PA).. 704 664-3005
   170 Barley Park Ln Mooresville (28115) **(G-10890)**
Bsh Home Appliances Corp.. 252 636-4454
   120 Bosch Blvd New Bern (28562) **(G-11779)**
Bsh Home Appliances Corp.. 252 672-9155
   100 Bosch Blvd New Bern (28562) **(G-11780)**
Bsh Home Appls A Ltd Partnr.. 252 636-4200
   100 Bosch Blvd New Bern (28562) **(G-11781)**
Bsh International Trade, New Bern Also Called: Bsh Home Appliances Corp **(G-11780)**
BSN Medical Inc (DH).. 704 554-9933
   5825 Carnegie Blvd Charlotte (28209) **(G-2361)**
BT America Inc... 704 434-8072
   415 S Main St Boiling Springs (28017) **(G-1158)**
Btc Electronic Components LLC (DH)... 919 229-2162
   2709 Connector Dr Wake Forest (27587) **(G-15536)**
Btc Electronic Components Inc, Wake Forest Also Called: Btc Electronic Components LLC **(G-15536)**
Bthec Inc (PA).. 704 596-5112
   4823 N Graham St Charlotte (28269) **(G-2362)**
Bubble, Charlotte Also Called: Ebhc LLC **(G-2681)**
Buchanan Gem Stone Mines Inc.. 828 765-6130
   13780 S 226 Hwy Spruce Pine (28777) **(G-14632)**
Bucher Municipal N Amer Inc.. 704 658-1333
   105 Motorsports Rd Mooresville (28115) **(G-10891)**
Buchi Kombucha, Marshall Also Called: Asheville Kombucha Mamas LLC **(G-10199)**
Buck Lucas Logging Companies.. 252 410-0160
   812 W Hawkins Rd Roanoke Rapids (27870) **(G-13568)**
Buck Marine Diesel, Winterville Also Called: Buck Supply Company Inc **(G-16995)**
Buck Racing Engines Inc.. 336 983-6562
   205 Old Newsome Rd King (27021) **(G-9265)**
Buck Supply Company Inc... 252 215-1252
   3060 Old Highway 11 Winterville (28590) **(G-16995)**
Buckeye Cleaning Center, Charlotte Also Called: Buckeye International Inc **(G-2363)**
Buckeye Fire Equipment Company (PA)..................................... 704 739-7415
   110 Kings Rd Kings Mountain (28086) **(G-9296)**
Buckeye International Inc... 704 523-9400
   4123 Barringer Dr Ste A Charlotte (28217) **(G-2363)**
Buckeye Technologies Inc.. 704 822-6400
   100 Buckeye Dr Mount Holly (28120) **(G-11623)**
BUCKEYE TECHNOLOGIES INC., Mount Holly Also Called: Buckeye Technologies Inc **(G-11623)**

Buckhorn Lumber and Wood Pdts, Brasstown *Also Called: Peachtree Lumber Company Inc* *(G-1268)*

Bucks Woodworks LLC.. 336 764-3979
145 Saint Johns Ct Clemmons (27012) *(G-4033)*

Bucks Wrecker Service... 704 776-0899
2493 Hickory Hwy Statesville (28677) *(G-14767)*

Bud Baumgarner.. 828 256-6230
3551 28th St Ne Hickory (28601) *(G-7954)*

Budd-Piper Roofing Company...................................... 919 682-2121
506 Ramseur St Durham (27701) *(G-4984)*

Buddy Book Publishing... 704 657-6909
104 Nathaniel Ct Mooresville (28117) *(G-10892)*

Buddy Cut Inc... 888 608-4701
760 Redgate Rd Pittsboro (27312) *(G-12333)*

Budget Blinds, Wilmington *Also Called: Synoptix Companies LLC* *(G-16425)*

Budget Printing, Jamestown *Also Called: Geo-Lin Inc* *(G-9050)*

Budget Printing Co.. 910 642-7306
1424 S Jk Powell Blvd Ste B Whiteville (28472) *(G-15960)*

Buds Logging and Trucking.. 704 465-8016
1561 Stanbackfry Ice Plnt Rd Wadesboro (28170) *(G-15505)*

Budsin Wood Craft.. 252 729-1540
142 Moore Ln Marshallberg (28553) *(G-10209)*

Buechel Stone Corp.. 800 236-4474
7274 Us 221 N Marion (28752) *(G-10145)*

Buehler Motor Inc (HQ)... 919 380-3333
1100 Perimeter Park Dr Ste 118 Morrisville (27560) *(G-11309)*

Buffalo City Distillery LLC... 252 256-1477
8821 Caratoke Hwy Point Harbor (27964) *(G-12380)*

Buffalo Creek Farm, Germanton *Also Called: Buffalo Creek Farm & Crmry LLC* *(G-6552)*

Buffalo Creek Farm & Crmry LLC................................ 336 969-5698
3241 Buffalo Creek Farm Rd Germanton (27019) *(G-6552)*

Buffalo Crushed Stone Inc... 919 688-6881
1503 Camden Ave Durham (27704) *(G-4985)*

Buffalo Inv Group NC LLC.. 252 522-0050
1592 Industrial Dr Kinston (28504) *(G-9348)*

Buffaloe Milling Company Inc...................................... 252 438-8637
196 Buffalo Mill Rd Kittrell (27544) *(G-9394)*

Buffer Zone Ceramics... 828 863-2000
655 John Weaver Rd Columbus (28722) *(G-4172)*

Buffingtons Commercial Trim...................................... 919 244-8848
211 Shotts Ct Cary (27511) *(G-1715)*

Buhler Inc... 800 722-7483
100 Aeroglide Dr Cary (27511) *(G-1716)*

Buhlmann Group, Oakboro *Also Called: Buhlmann North America LP* *(G-12068)*

Buhlmann North America LP.. 704 485-4144
527 S Main St Oakboro (28129) *(G-12068)*

Buie and Company, Laurinburg *Also Called: Buie Manufacturing Company* *(G-9470)*

Buie Manufacturing Company...................................... 910 610-3504
105 Sterling Ln Laurinburg (28352) *(G-9470)*

Builders Firstsource Inc... 336 884-5454
7601 Boeing Dr Greensboro (27409) *(G-6860)*

Builders Firstsource Inc... 919 562-6601
45 Mosswood Blvd Youngsville (27596) *(G-17072)*

Builders Firstsource - SE Grp...................................... 910 313-3056
4151 Emerson St Wilmington (28403) *(G-16144)*

Builders Frstsrce - Rleigh LLC..................................... 919 363-4956
23 Red Cedar Way Apex (27523) *(G-174)*

Builders Frstsrce - Sthast Gro.................................... 910 944-2516
900 Pinehurst Dr Aberdeen (28315) *(G-2)*

Building Automation Svcs LLC.................................... 336 884-4026
1515 Bethel Dr High Point (27260) *(G-8277)*

Building Center Inc (PA).. 704 889-8182
10201 Industrial Dr Pineville (28134) *(G-12257)*

Building Envlope Erction Svcs (PA)............................ 252 747-2015
1441 Nahunta Rd Snow Hill (28580) *(G-14499)*

Building Stars of Charlotte, Charlotte *Also Called: Skyview Commercial Cleaning* *(G-3562)*

Buildings R US.. 828 382-0167
242 S Church St Forest City (28043) *(G-6062)*

Buildings R US.. 704 482-3166
1703 E Dixon Blvd Shelby (28152) *(G-14290)*

Built To Last NC LLC.. 252 232-0055
417h Caratoke Hwy Moyock (27958) *(G-11693)*

Bulk Sak International Inc.. 704 833-1361
1302 Industrial Pike Rd Gastonia (28052) *(G-6361)*

Bulk Transport Service Inc... 910 329-0555
169 Preston Wells Rd Holly Ridge (28445) *(G-8680)*

Bull, Charlotte *Also Called: Bull Engineered Products Inc* *(G-2364)*

Bull City Ciderworks, Lexington *Also Called: Cider Bros LLC* *(G-9694)*

Bull City Designs LLC... 919 908-6252
1111 Neville St Durham (27701) *(G-4986)*

Bull City Press LLC... 919 883-5585
1217 Odyssey Dr Durham (27713) *(G-4987)*

Bull City Sheet Metal LLC... 919 354-0993
4008 Comfort Ln Durham (27705) *(G-4988)*

Bull Cy Arts Collaborative LLC.................................... 919 949-4847
401 Foster St Ste B1 Durham (27701) *(G-4989)*

Bull Durham Beer Co LLC.. 919 744-3568
409 Blackwell St Durham (27701) *(G-4990)*

Bull Engineered Products Inc...................................... 704 504-0300
12001 Steele Creek Rd Charlotte (28273) *(G-2364)*

Bulldog Hose Company LLC.. 919 639-6151
141 Junny Rd Angier (27501) *(G-134)*

Bulldog Machine Inc... 704 200-7838
3330 Smith Farm Rd Matthews (28104) *(G-10306)*

Bulldog Printing, Greensboro *Also Called: American Indian Printing Inc* *(G-6800)*

Bulldurhamfabrications Com....................................... 919 479-1919
5004 Mandel Rd Durham (27712) *(G-4991)*

Bumgarners Welding.. 704 764-7041
8701 Landsford Rd Monroe (28112) *(G-10671)*

Bumpkin Skateboards LLC.. 919 821-2037
4924 Kundinger Ct Raleigh (27606) *(G-12577)*

Bunce Buildings, Salisbury *Also Called: Harvest Homes and Handi Houses* *(G-13975)*

Bundy Logging Company Inc...................................... 252 357-0191
37 Main St Gatesville (27938) *(G-6548)*

Bundy Trucking, Gatesville *Also Called: Bundy Logging Company Inc* *(G-6548)*

Bunge Oils Inc... 910 293-7917
376 W Park Dr Warsaw (28398) *(G-15665)*

Bunting Equipment Company Inc............................... 336 626-7300
3846 Caraway Mountain Rd Sophia (27350) *(G-14513)*

Bunzl Processor Dist LLC.. 910 738-8111
124 Hornets Rd Lumberton (28358) *(G-10028)*

Burch Industries, Laurinburg *Also Called: Charles Craft Inc* *(G-9474)*

Burchette Services Corporation................................. 919 225-2890
202 Long Crescent Dr Durham (27712) *(G-4992)*

Burchette Sign Company Inc...................................... 336 996-6501
8705 Triad Dr Colfax (27235) *(G-4143)*

Burco International Inc.. 828 252-4481
1900 Hendersonville Rd Ste 10 Asheville (28803) *(G-575)*

Burco Promotional Printing Inc................................... 864 546-3443
3106 Sweeten Creek Rd Ste B Asheville (28803) *(G-576)*

Burco Welding & Cutng Pdts Inc................................. 336 887-6100
614 Old Thomasville Rd High Point (27260) *(G-8278)*

Burdetts Custom Woodworks Inc............................... 919 592-9903
317 Hemlock St Cary (27513) *(G-1717)*

Burgess Duke Hward Ktrina Kner............................... 704 732-0547
4659 Asbury Church Rd Lincolnton (28092) *(G-9877)*

Burgess Logging, Lincolnton *Also Called: Burgess Duke Hward Ktrina Kner* *(G-9877)*

Burgiss Farm Bed & Breakfast, Laurel Springs *Also Called: Tom Burgiss* *(G-9468)*

Burke Mill... 336 774-2952
3130 Burke Mill Ct Winston Salem (27103) *(G-16640)*

Burke Mills Inc.. 828 874-6341
191 Sterling St Nw Valdese (28690) *(G-15442)*

Burke Veneers Inc.. 828 437-8510
2170 Fr Coffey Rd Morganton (28655) *(G-11203)*

Burkert Fluid Control Systems, Huntersville *Also Called: Burkert USA Corporation* *(G-8798)*

Burkert USA Corporation.. 800 325-1405
11425 Mount Holly Hntrsvlle Rd Huntersville (28078) *(G-8798)*

Burkett Welding Services Inc..................................... 252 635-2814
1401 B St New Bern (28560) *(G-11782)*

Burlan Manufacturing LLC (PA)................................. 704 349-0000
2740 W Franklin Blvd Gastonia (28052) *(G-6362)*

Burlington Chemical Co LLC....................................... 336 584-0111
8646 W Market St Ste 116 Greensboro (27409) *(G-6861)*

Burlington Coat Factory, Cary *Also Called: Burlington Coat Fctry Whse Cor (G-1718)*
Burlington Coat Fctry Whse Cor... 919 468-9312
  1741 Walnut St Cary (27511) *(G-1718)*
Burlington Distributing Co.. 336 292-1415
  2232 Westbrook St Greensboro (27407) *(G-6862)*
Burlington House LLC.. 336 379-6220
  804 Green Valley Rd Ste 300 Greensboro (27408) *(G-6863)*
Burlington Industries III LLC... 336 379-2000
  3330 W Friendly Ave Greensboro (27410) *(G-6864)*
Burlington Industries LLC (DH)... 336 379-6220
  804 Green Valley Rd Ste 300 Greensboro (27408) *(G-6865)*
Burlington Intl Svcs Co (PA)... 336 379-2000
  804 Green Valley Rd # 300 Greensboro (27408) *(G-6866)*
Burlington Investment II Inc... 336 379-2000
  3330 W Friendly Ave Greensboro (27410) *(G-6867)*
Burlington Machine Service... 336 228-6758
  632 Chapel Hill Rd Burlington (27215) *(G-1381)*
Burlington Msclineous Mtls LLC... 336 376-1264
  3406 William Newlin Dr Graham (27253) *(G-6682)*
Burlington Outlet (PA)... 910 278-3442
  5817 E Oak Island Dr Oak Island (28465) *(G-12048)*
Burlington Rigid Box Plant, Burlington *Also Called: Caraustar Brlngton Rgid Box In (G-1383)*
Burlington Worsteds Inc... 336 379-2000
  3330 W Friendly Ave Greensboro (27410) *(G-6868)*
Burlow Promotions Inc.. 336 856-0500
  4802 Tamaron Dr Greensboro (27410) *(G-6869)*
Burnett Darrill Stephen.. 828 287-8778
  137 Williamsburg Dr Spindale (28160) *(G-14604)*
Burnett Machine Company Inc.. 704 867-7786
  924 Hanover St Gastonia (28054) *(G-6363)*
Burnett Welding... 803 360-7406
  870 Sweet Home Church Rd Elizabethtown (28337) *(G-5586)*
Burney Sweets & More Inc (PA)... 910 862-2099
  106-B Martin Luther King Dr Elizabethtown (28337) *(G-5587)*
Burneys Sweets & More, Elizabethtown *Also Called: Burney Sweets & More Inc (G-5587)*
Burns Welding Services LLC.. 336 908-5716
  2443 Flat Shoals Rd Germanton (27019) *(G-6553)*
Burntshirt Vineyards LLC... 828 685-2402
  3737 Howard Gap Rd Hendersonville (28792) *(G-7830)*
Burris Machine Company Inc (PA).. 828 322-6914
  3155 Highland Ave Ne Hickory (28601) *(G-7955)*
Burris Machine Company Inc.. 828 322-6914
  1631 Main Avenue Dr Nw Hickory (28601) *(G-7956)*
Burris Woodworks... 336 746-5286
  1134 John Young Rd Lexington (27292) *(G-9687)*
Burrough Furniture.. 336 841-3129
  1302 Kersey Valley Rd Archdale (27263) *(G-271)*
Burrow Family Corporation... 336 887-3173
  660 Southwest St High Point (27260) *(G-8279)*
Burton Steel Company (PA)... 910 675-9241
  102b Ritter Dr Castle Hayne (28429) *(G-1944)*
Burts Bees Inc (HQ)... 919 998-5200
  210 W Pettigrew St Durham (27701) *(G-4993)*
Burts Bees Inc.. 919 998-5200
  701 Distribution Dr Durham (27709) *(G-4994)*
Burts Bees Inc.. 919 238-6450
  900 Aviation Pkwy Ste 400 Morrisville (27560) *(G-11310)*
Bus Safety Inc.. 336 671-0838
  133 Avgol Dr Mocksville (27028) *(G-10558)*
Bus Safety Solutions, Mocksville *Also Called: Bus Safety Inc (G-10558)*
Busbin Cabinetry... 704 560-4485
  180 Berkshire Ave Belmont (28012) *(G-976)*
Busch Enterprises Inc.. 704 878-2067
  908 Cochran St Statesville (28677) *(G-14768)*
Busiapp Corporation... 877 558-2518
  400 Innovation Ave Ste 150 Morrisville (27560) *(G-11311)*
Busick Brothers Machine Inc... 336 969-2717
  262 Northstar Dr Rural Hall (27045) *(G-13834)*
Business Brokerage Press Inc.. 800 239-5085
  2726 Warlick Dr Wilmington (28409) *(G-16145)*
Business Card Express Raleigh, Morrisville *Also Called: Endaxi Company Inc (G-11338)*

Business Journals (DH).. 704 371-3248
  120 W Morehead St Ste 420 Charlotte (28202) *(G-2365)*
Business Leader, Raleigh *Also Called: Business To Business Inc (G-12579)*
Business Mogul LLC... 919 605-2165
  2120 Breezeway Dr Unit 112 Raleigh (27614) *(G-12578)*
Business North Carolina, Charlotte *Also Called: Red Hand Media LLC (G-3422)*
Business Systems of America.. 704 766-2755
  3020 Prosperity Church Rd Charlotte (28269) *(G-2366)*
Business To Business Inc (PA)... 919 872-7077
  3801 Wake Forest Rd Ste 102 Raleigh (27609) *(G-12579)*
Business Wise Inc... 704 554-4112
  615 S College St Ste 810 Charlotte (28202) *(G-2367)*
Busy BS Monogramming LLC.. 919 870-6106
  1500 Bedford Hills Ct Raleigh (27613) *(G-12580)*
Butchers Best Inc... 252 533-0961
  944 Raleigh St Roanoke Rapids (27870) *(G-13569)*
Butler Trailer Mfg Co Inc... 336 674-8850
  259 Hockett Dairy Rd Randleman (27317) *(G-13453)*
Butler Trieu Inc.. 910 346-4929
  1183 Kellum Loop Rd Jacksonville (28546) *(G-8992)*
Butner-Creedmoor News, Creedmoor *Also Called: Granville Publishing Co Inc (G-4614)*
Butterball LLC.. 919 658-6743
  938 Millers Chapel Rd Goldsboro (27534) *(G-6598)*
Butterball LLC.. 919 658-6743
  1628 Garner Chapel Rd Mount Olive (28365) *(G-11657)*
Butterball LLC.. 910 875-8711
  1140 E Central Ave Raeford (28376) *(G-12415)*
Butterball LLC (HQ)... 919 255-7900
  1 Butterball Ln Garner (27529) *(G-6258)*
Buttercreme Bakery Inc... 336 722-1022
  895 W Northwest Blvd Winston Salem (27101) *(G-16641)*
Butterfields Candies, Nashville *Also Called: Butterfields Candy LLC (G-11738)*
Butterfields Candy LLC.. 252 459-2577
  2155 S Old Franklin Rd Nashville (27856) *(G-11738)*
Buvic LLC.. 910 302-7950
  6798 Weeping Water Run Fayetteville (28314) *(G-5776)*
Buy Smart Inc.. 252 293-4700
  1109 Brookside Dr Nw Wilson (27896) *(G-16482)*
Buzz Saw Inc... 910 321-7446
  1015 Robeson St Ste 103 Fayetteville (28305) *(G-5777)*
Buzzispace Inc (DH)... 336 821-3150
  2880 Ridgewood Park Dr Winston Salem (27107) *(G-16642)*
Bwh Foam and Fiber Inc.. 336 498-6949
  605 Sunset Dr Randleman (27317) *(G-13454)*
Bwi Etn LLC.. 828 682-2645
  19 Crushing Rd Burnsville (28714) *(G-1525)*
Bwx Technologies Inc.. 980 365-4000
  11525 N Community House Rd Ste 600 Charlotte (28277) *(G-2368)*
Bwxt Investment Company (HQ).. 704 625-4900
  13024 Ballantyne Corporate Pl Ste 700 Charlotte (28277) *(G-2369)*
Bwxt Mpower Inc.. 980 365-4000
  11525 N Community House Rd Ste 600 Charlotte (28277) *(G-2370)*
By Faith Logging Inc.. 252 792-0019
  1046 Cedar Hill Dr Williamston (27892) *(G-16058)*
By-Design Black Oxide & TI LLC.. 828 874-0610
  1260 Margaret St Nw Valdese (28690) *(G-15443)*
Byers Prcision Fabricators Inc... 828 693-4088
  675 Dana Rd Hendersonville (28792) *(G-7831)*
Bymonetcrochet.. 443 613-1736
  8536 Caden Lee Way Apt 2208 Charlotte (28273) *(G-2371)*
Byrd Designs Inc... 828 628-0151
  140 Lee Dotson Rd Fairview (28730) *(G-5709)*
Byrnes Enterprises... 919 876-3223
  3216 Wellington Ct # 107 Raleigh (27615) *(G-12581)*
Byron Dale Spivey.. 910 653-3128
  2009 Reynolds Rd Tabor City (28463) *(G-15078)*
C & B Frame Co Inc.. 336 475-0194
  1506 Lexington Ave Thomasville (27360) *(G-15192)*
C & B Salvage Company Inc.. 336 374-3946
  2882 Ararat Rd Ararat (27007) *(G-263)*
C & B Welding & Fab Inc.. 704 435-6942
  2070 Mauney Rd Bessemer City (28016) *(G-1054)*

ALPHABETIC SECTION

Cabinet Creations Inc

C & C Chemical Company Inc.. 828 255-7639
119 Haywood Rd Asheville (28806) *(G-577)*

C & C Chipping Inc.. 252 249-1617
6003 Neuse Rd Grantsboro (28529) *(G-6764)*

C & C Precision Machine Inc.. 704 739-0505
418 Canterbury Rd Kings Mountain (28086) *(G-9297)*

C & D Fabrications Inc.. 919 639-2489
199 Fabrication Ln Angier (27501) *(G-135)*

C & D Woodworking Inc.. 336 476-8722
7139 Wright Rd Thomasville (27360) *(G-15193)*

C & F Custom Cabinets Inc.. 910 424-7475
140 Sanders St Hope Mills (28348) *(G-8733)*

C & J Crosspieces LLC.. 910 652-4955
126 S Lancer Rd Star (27356) *(G-14714)*

C & J Machine Company Inc.. 704 922-5913
3519 Philadelphia Church Rd Dallas (28034) *(G-4636)*

C & J Welding Inc.. 919 552-0275
136 Acorn Ridge Ln Holly Springs (27540) *(G-8693)*

C & L Manufacturing.. 336 957-8359
1519 Oak Ridge Church Rd Hays (28635) *(G-7773)*

C & M Enterprise Inc.. 704 545-1180
6808 Wilgrove Mint Hill Rd Mint Hill (28227) *(G-10524)*

C & M Industrial Supply Co.. 704 483-4001
748 N Hwy 16 Mill Spring (28756) *(G-10484)*

C & M Sawmill, Cleveland Also Called: Myers Forest Products Inc *(G-4077)*

C & M Tag, Mint Hill Also Called: C & M Enterprise Inc *(G-10524)*

C & M Welding Inspections Inc.. 919 762-7345
7225 Blannie Farms Ln Willow Spring (27592) *(G-16076)*

C & R Building Supply Inc.. 910 567-6293
2300 Ernest Williams Rd Autryville (28318) *(G-840)*

C & R Hard Chrome Service Inc.. 704 861-8831
940 Hanover St Gastonia (28054) *(G-6364)*

C & S Antennas Inc.. 828 324-2454
1123 Industrial Dr Sw Conover (28613) *(G-4427)*

C & S Custom.. 336 242-9730
441 Pine Top Rd Lexington (27295) *(G-9688)*

C & S Woodworking.. 828 437-5024
833 Summers Rd Valdese (28690) *(G-15444)*

C & W Mch & Fabrication Inc.. 252 522-5476
1206 Hugo Rd Kinston (28501) *(G-9349)*

C A Perry & Son Inc.. 252 330-2323
683 Dry Ridge Rd Elizabeth City (27909) *(G-5532)*

C A Perry & Son Inc (DH).. 252 221-4463
4033 Virginia Rd Hobbsville (27946) *(G-8675)*

C A Zimmer Inc.. 704 483-4560
731 Crosspoint Dr Denver (28037) *(G-4766)*

C Alan Publications LLC.. 336 272-3920
6 Oak Branch Dr Ste A Greensboro (27407) *(G-6870)*

C and D Welders LLC.. 910 552-3294
3620 S Nc 41 Hwy Wallace (28466) *(G-15619)*

C and L Cabinets LLC.. 828 550-9820
390 Pressley Rd Canton (28716) *(G-1604)*

C B Bunting & Sons Inc.. 252 813-4237
266 Bunting Ln Pinetops (27864) *(G-12241)*

C B C Printing.. 828 497-5510
149 Childrens Home Rd Cherokee (28719) *(G-3853)*

C C S, Greensboro Also Called: Custom Cnverting Solutions Inc *(G-6949)*

C C W, Wilmington Also Called: Creative Custom Wdwkg LLC *(G-16185)*

C D J & P Inc.. 252 446-3611
1911 N Wesleyan Blvd Rocky Mount (27804) *(G-13686)*

C D Stampley Enterprises Inc.. 704 333-6631
6100 Orr Rd Charlotte (28213) *(G-2372)*

C E C, Weaverville Also Called: Conrad Embroidery Company LLC *(G-15842)*

C E Hicks Enterprises Inc.. 919 772-5131
230 Us 70 Hwy E Garner (27529) *(G-6259)*

C E I, Apex Also Called: Computational Engrg Intl Inc *(G-176)*

C E Smith Co Inc.. 336 273-0166
6396 Burnt Poplar Rd Greensboro (27409) *(G-6871)*

C E Smith Co Inc (PA).. 336 273-0166
1001 Bitting St Greensboro (27403) *(G-6872)*

C G C, Cary Also Called: Container Graphics Corp *(G-1733)*

C G P, Clayton Also Called: Dew Group Enterprises Inc *(G-3974)*

C J Manufacturing Inc.. 252 927-4913
2331 Pocosin Rd Pinetown (27865) *(G-12244)*

C L Rabb Inc.. 704 865-0295
103 Wolfpack Rd Gastonia (28056) *(G-6365)*

C L S, Durham Also Called: Custom Light and Sound Inc *(G-5040)*

C M I, Raleigh Also Called: Consolidated Mfg Intl LLC *(G-12638)*

C Murrells Event Planning LLC.. 910 382-2742
1004 Main St Maysville (28555) *(G-10370)*

C O Jelliff Corporation.. 828 428-3672
4292 Providence Mill Rd Maiden (28650) *(G-10100)*

C P Eakes Company.. 336 574-1800
2012 Fairfax Rd Greensboro (27407) *(G-6873)*

C P T, Zirconia Also Called: Carolina Paper Tubes Inc *(G-17151)*

C R Currin Company, Trinity Also Called: Jalco Inc *(G-15347)*

C R Laine Furniture Co Inc.. 828 328-1831
2829 Us Highway 70 Se Hickory (28602) *(G-7957)*

C R Laine Furniture Co Inc.. 336 841-5337
310 N Hamilton St High Point (27260) *(G-8280)*

C R Onsrud Inc (PA).. 704 508-7000
120 Technology Dr Troutman (28166) *(G-15368)*

C S America Inc (HQ) 1305 Graham St Burlington (27217) *(G-1382)*

C S I, Chapel Hill Also Called: Conservation Station Inc *(G-2005)*

C S I, Hickory Also Called: Carolina Solvents Inc *(G-7966)*

C T I, Indian Trail Also Called: Coatings Technologies Inc *(G-8927)*

C T I Pressure Washing, Raleigh Also Called: CTI Property Services Inc *(G-12659)*

C V Industries, Valdese Also Called: Valdese Weavers LLC *(G-15460)*

C W Lawley Incorporated.. 919 467-7782
201 Towerview Ct Cary (27513) *(G-1719)*

C Y Yard, Charlotte Also Called: Lucky Landports *(G-3107)*

C York Law Pllc.. 910 256-1235
2030 Eastwood Rd Ste 2 Wilmington (28403) *(G-16146)*

C-Tron Incorporated.. 919 494-7811
22 N Main St Franklinton (27525) *(G-6151)*

C.V.products, Thomasville Also Called: Xceldyne Group LLC *(G-15307)*

C&A Hockaday Transport LLC.. 252 676-5956
1660 Hill St Roanoke Rapids (27870) *(G-13570)*

C&J Publishing.. 336 722-8005
948 Sportsmans Dr Winston Salem (27101) *(G-16643)*

C&K Plastics Nc LLC.. 833 232-4848
164 Mckenzie Rd Mooresville (28115) *(G-10893)*

C&K Plastics North Carolina, Mooresville Also Called: C&K Plastics Nc LLC *(G-10893)*

C&M Woodworks.. 919 280-9896
2800 Mattlyn Ct Raleigh (27613) *(G-12582)*

C&V Powder Coating.. 910 228-1173
1068 Ashland Way Leland (28451) *(G-9531)*

C2c Plastics Inc.. 910 338-5260
3024 Hall Watters Dr Ste 101 Wilmington (28405) *(G-16147)*

C3 Sealcoating LLC.. 919 880-5515
101 Jordan Ln Wake Forest (27587) *(G-15537)*

C6 Manufacturing.. 704 896-3934
10515 Caldwell Depot Rd Cornelius (28031) *(G-4532)*

Cabarrus Brewing Company LLC.. 704 490-4487
329 Mcgill Ave Nw Concord (28027) *(G-4216)*

Cabarrus Business Magazine, Concord Also Called: Comfort Publishing Svcs LLC *(G-4236)*

Cabarrus Concrete Co (PA).. 704 788-3000
2807 Armentrout Dr Concord (28025) *(G-4217)*

Cabarrus Cycling Company.. 704 938-8735
109 West Ave Kannapolis (28081) *(G-9114)*

Cabarrus Hosiery Dist Inc.. 704 436-3575
8215 W Franklin St Mount Pleasant (28124) *(G-11672)*

Cabarrus Plastics Inc.. 704 784-2100
2845 Armentrout Dr Concord (28025) *(G-4218)*

Cabin Craft American Homes, Rocky Mount Also Called: Log Cabin Homes Ltd *(G-13708)*

Cabinet Connection of NC Inc.. 919 653-1300
1015 Tribayne Ct Apex (27502) *(G-175)*

Cabinet Creations, Mount Pleasant Also Called: Tommy W Smith Inc *(G-11678)*

Cabinet Creations Inc.. 919 542-3722
585 Carl Foushee Rd Moncure (27559) *(G-10616)*

Cabinet Cures of The Carolinas   ALPHABETIC SECTION

Cabinet Cures of The Carolinas, Raleigh Also Called: Gw Industries LLC (G-12825)
Cabinet Door World LLC 877 929-2750
   1711 11th Ave Sw Hickory (28602) (G-7958)
Cabinet Doors For Less 828 351-3510
   908 Industrial Dr Sw Conover (28613) (G-4428)
Cabinet Guy 919 375-4559
   94 Privette Way Zebulon (27597) (G-17123)
Cabinet King Refinishing 704 241-6405
   8500 Pine Hill Rd Mint Hill (28227) (G-10525)
Cabinet Makers Inc 704 876-2808
   534 Jane Sowers Rd Statesville (28625) (G-14769)
Cabinet Man Cabinetry 336 382-0879
   9252 Nc Highway 49 S Denton (27239) (G-4727)
Cabinet Masters and More LLC 828 396-1881
   239 River Bend Dr Granite Falls (28630) (G-6725)
Cabinet Plus 917 698-7708
   13211 Willow Breeze Ln Huntersville (28078) (G-8799)
Cabinet Sales LLC 919 604-9536
   8705 Cliff Top Ct Raleigh (27613) (G-12583)
Cabinet Shop Inc 252 726-6965
   4915 Arendell St Ste 309 Morehead City (28557) (G-11156)
Cabinet Solutions Usa Inc 828 358-2349
   1711 11th Ave Sw Hickory (28602) (G-7959)
Cabinet Transitions Inc 336 382-7154
   5310 Solar Pl Greensboro (27406) (G-6874)
Cabinetry Squared 919 589-7253
   7309 Trouble Rd Willow Spring (27592) (G-16077)
Cabinets 4 U LLC 919 291-4617
   1108 Crown Ct Hillsborough (27278) (G-8641)
Cabinets and Things 828 652-1734
   141 Bill Deck Rd Union Mills (28167) (G-15439)
Cabinets Plus Inc 718 213-3300
   8431 Old Statesville Rd Charlotte (28269) (G-2373)
Cabinets Trim and More 704 680-7076
   46 Charing Pl Sw Concord (28025) (G-4219)
Cabinetworks Group Mich LLC 803 984-2285
   1200 Westinghouse Blvd Ste O Charlotte (28273) (G-2374)
Cabinetworks Group Mich LLC 919 868-8174
   6221 Westgate Rd Ste 100 Raleigh (27617) (G-12584)
Cable Devices Incorporated 704 588-0859
   10736 Nations Ford Rd Charlotte (28273) (G-2375)
Cable Devices Incorporated (HQ) 714 554-4370
   1100 Commscope Pl Se Hickory (28602) (G-7960)
Cable Devices Incorporated 704 588-0859
   10540 Southern Loop Blvd Pineville (28134) (G-12258)
Cable Exchange, Hickory Also Called: Cable Devices Incorporated (G-7960)
Cablenc LLC 919 307-9065
   8012 Spiderlily Ct Zebulon (27597) (G-17124)
Cabo Winery LLC 704 785-9463
   37 Union St S Concord (28025) (G-4220)
Cabot Wrenn, Hickory Also Called: HM Liquidation Inc (G-8058)
Cabot Wrenn, Taylorsville Also Called: Hancock & Moore LLC (G-15144)
Cabot Wrenn, Taylorsville Also Called: Hancock & Moore LLC (G-15145)
Cadence Design Systems Inc 919 380-3900
   11000 Regency Pkwy Ste 401 Cary (27518) (G-1720)
Caesarstone Tech USA Inc (HQ) 818 779-0999
   1401 W Morehead St Ste 100 Charlotte (28208) (G-2376)
Cagle Frames LLC 910 464-1170
   978 Brewer Rd Seagrove (27341) (G-14233)
Cagle Sawmill Inc 336 857-2274
   7065 Charles Mountain Rd Denton (27239) (G-4728)
Cahoon Brothers Logging LLC 252 943-9901
   6073 Free Union Church Rd Pinetown (27865) (G-12245)
Cahoon Logging, Pinetown Also Called: Cahoon Logging Company Inc (G-12246)
Cahoon Logging Company Inc 252 943-6805
   6848 Free Union Church Rd Pinetown (27865) (G-12246)
Cahoon, Bobby Logging, Grantsboro Also Called: C & C Chipping Inc (G-6764)
Cairn Studio Ltd (PA) 704 892-3581
   121 N Main St Davidson (28036) (G-4667)
Cairn Studio Ltd 704 664-7128
   200 Mckenzie Rd Mooresville (28115) (G-10894)

Caison Yachts Inc 910 270-6394
   585 Lewis Rd Hampstead (28443) (G-7641)
Cajah Corporation 828 728-7300
   1905 International Blvd Hudson (28638) (G-8764)
Cajah Mountain Hosiery Mills, Hudson Also Called: Cajah Corporation (G-8764)
Cakerator Inc 919 270-5899
   5924 Swales Way Raleigh (27603) (G-12585)
Cakes, Charlotte Also Called: Swirl Oakhurst LLC (G-3662)
Caky-Q 215 287-9145
   1207 Janrose Ct Nw Concord (28027) (G-4221)
Cal-Cru, Granite Quarry Also Called: Granite Knitwear Inc (G-6760)
Cal-Van, Greensboro Also Called: Horizon Tool Inc (G-7101)
Calco Enterprises Inc (PA) 910 695-0089
   240 Crestline Ln Aberdeen (28315) (G-3)
Calco Sheet Metal Works, Aberdeen Also Called: Calco Enterprises Inc (G-3)
Caldwell Cabinets NC LLC 828 212-0000
   3441 Hickory Blvd Hudson (28638) (G-8765)
Caldwell Hohl Artworks 336 879-9090
   155 Cabin Trl Seagrove (27341) (G-14234)
Caldwell WD Carving Turning Co 828 758-0186
   459 Abington Rd Lenoir (28645) (G-9593)
Caldwells Mt Process Abattoirs 828 428-8833
   3726 Goodson Rd Maiden (28650) (G-10101)
Caldwells Water Conditioning 828 253-6605
   22 Country Spring Dr Asheville (28804) (G-578)
Calhoun Welding Inc 252 281-1455
   7367 Tory Pl Macclesfield (27852) (G-10064)
Cali Metal Polish 704 788-2466
   2044 Wilshire Ct Sw Concord (28025) (G-4222)
Cali Stitches 336 895-4714
   204 S Westgate Dr Greensboro (27407) (G-6875)
Calico Coatings, Denver Also Called: Calico Technologies Inc (G-4767)
Calico Technologies Inc (PA) 704 483-2202
   5883 Balsom Ridge Rd Denver (28037) (G-4767)
Califrnia Grrett Cmmnctons Inc, Mooresville Also Called: Garrettcom Inc (G-10954)
Call Center, Cary Also Called: Pepsi Bottling Ventures LLC (G-1849)
Call Family Distillers LLC 336 990-0708
   1611 Industrial Dr Wilkesboro (28697) (G-16015)
Call Printing & Copying 704 821-6554
   311 Indian Trail Rd S Indian Trail (28079) (G-8925)
Calsak Plastics Inc 704 597-8555
   3000 Crosspoint Center Ln Ste A Charlotte (28269) (G-2377)
Calvin C Mooney Poultry 336 374-6690
   4167 Nc 268 Ararat (27007) (G-264)
Calvin Laws Jay 336 973-4318
   2036 Kendell Town Rd Ferguson (28624) (G-5956)
Calypso Cottage LLC (PA) 252 728-4299
   324 Orange St Beaufort (28516) (G-948)
Calypso Feed Mill, Mount Olive Also Called: Case Farms LLC (G-11659)
CAM Craft LLC 828 681-5183
   54 Atrium Trl Arden (28704) (G-316)
CAM Enterprises Inc 252 946-4877
   5601 Us Highway 264 W Washington (27889) (G-15684)
Camag Scientific Inc 910 343-1830
   515 Cornelius Harnett Dr Wilmington (28401) (G-16148)
Camargo Phrm Svcs LLC 513 618-0325
   800 Taylor St Ste 101 Durham (27701) (G-4995)
Cambbro Manufacturing Company 919 568-8506
   1268 W Holt St Mebane (27302) (G-10402)
Cambrex, Durham Also Called: Avista Pharma Solutions Inc (G-4939)
Cambrex High Point Inc 336 841-5250
   4180 Mendenhall Oaks Pkwy High Point (27265) (G-8281)
Cambro 919 563-0761
   1268 Holt St Mebane (27302) (G-10403)
Camco Manufacturing Inc 336 348-6609
   2900 Vance Street Ext Reidsville (27320) (G-13511)
Camco Manufacturing LLC (PA) 800 334-2004
   121 Landmark Dr Greensboro (27409) (G-6876)
CAMCO MANUFACTURING, INC., Reidsville Also Called: Camco Manufacturing Inc (G-13511)

Camcraft Performance Cams.. 828 492-0950
  442 Phillipsville Loop Canton (28716) *(G-1605)*
Camel City Posters, King *Also Called: Blue Light Images Company Inc (G-9264)*
Camelot Computers Inc.. 704 554-1670
  10020 Park Cedar Dr Ste 205 Charlotte (28210) *(G-2378)*
Camelot Rturn Intrmdate Hldngs (PA).................................... 866 419-0042
  5020 Weston Pkwy Ste 400 Cary (27513) *(G-1721)*
Camelot Software Consulting, Charlotte *Also Called: Camelot Computers Inc (G-2378)*
Cameo Curtains Div, Charlotte *Also Called: Chf Industries Inc (G-2473)*
Cameo Fibers, Conover *Also Called: Fibrix LLC (G-4454)*
Camera To Candle... 339 224-1073
  16016 Loch Raven Rd Huntersville (28078) *(G-8800)*
Camerins Pixel Flare... 704 502-6922
  4066 Glenlea Commons Dr Charlotte (28216) *(G-2379)*
Camfil Usa Inc.. 828 465-2880
  1008 1st St W Conover (28613) *(G-4429)*
Camfil Usa Inc.. 252 975-1141
  200 Creekside Dr Washington (27889) *(G-15685)*
Camoteck LLC... 910 590-3213
  1318 Lisbon St Clinton (28328) *(G-4089)*
Camp Chemical Corporation (PA)... 336 597-2214
  200 Hester St Roxboro (27573) *(G-13797)*
Camp Lejeune Globe... 910 939-0705
  149 Rea St Jacksonville (28546) *(G-8993)*
Camp Publications LLC... 252 908-3684
  1505 Captains Rd Tarboro (27886) *(G-15099)*
Camp S Well and Pump Co Inc... 828 453-7322
  149 Ola Dr Ellenboro (28040) *(G-5634)*
Campbell & Sons Machining Co.. 704 394-0291
  230 W Congress St Lincolnton (28092) *(G-9878)*
Campus Safety Products LLC... 919 321-1477
  2530 Meridian Pkwy Ste 300 Durham (27713) *(G-4996)*
Camstar Systems Inc... 704 227-6600
  13024 Ballantyne Corporate Pl Charlotte (28277) *(G-2380)*
Can-AM Custom Trucks Inc... 704 334-0322
  1734 University Commercial Pl Charlotte (28213) *(G-2381)*
Can-Do Handyman Services, Whitsett *Also Called: Drew Roberts LLC (G-15988)*
Canalta Enterprises LLC... 919 615-1570
  4809 Auburn Knightdale Rd Raleigh (27610) *(G-12586)*
Cancer Diagnostics Inc (PA).. 877 846-5393
  116 Page Point Cir Durham (27703) *(G-4997)*
Candace Rand... 336 643-7082
  8306 Spotswood Rd Summerfield (27358) *(G-14977)*
Candies Italian ICEE LLC.. 980 475-7429
  3428 Nevin Brook Rd Ste 101 Charlotte (28269) *(G-2382)*
Candle Bar... 704 497-6099
  1800 Camden Rd Charlotte (28203) *(G-2383)*
Candy Cane Coatings... 919 605-6997
  7421 Blannie Farms Ln Willow Spring (27592) *(G-16078)*
Candypearls Hair LLC... 252 558-7202
  2417 Blackwolf Run Ln Raleigh (27604) *(G-12587)*
Cane Creek Cycling Cmpnnts Inc.. 828 684-3551
  355 Cane Creek Rd Fletcher (28732) *(G-5991)*
Cangilosi Spcialty Sausage Inc... 336 665-5775
  115 Landmark Dr Greensboro (27409) *(G-6877)*
Canine Cafe, Charlotte *Also Called: Barbaras Canine Catering Inc (G-2277)*
Canipe & Lynn Elc Mtr Repr Inc... 828 322-9052
  1909 1st Ave Sw Hickory (28602) *(G-7961)*
Canis Lupus Enterprises LLC... 828 450-2074
  220 S Rugby Rd Hendersonville (28791) *(G-7832)*
Cannon & Daughters Inc.. 828 254-9236
  2000 Riverside Dr Ste 9 Asheville (28804) *(G-579)*
Cannon Paint and Abbraisives, Lenoir *Also Called: W G Cannon Paint Co Inc (G-9659)*
Canteen Raleigh/Durham, Garner *Also Called: Compass Group Usa Inc (G-6267)*
Canton Dry Kilns LLC... 828 492-0715
  649 Champion Dr Canton (28716) *(G-1606)*
Canton Hardwood Company... 828 492-0715
  5373 Thickety Rd Canton (28716) *(G-1607)*
Canton Mill, Canton *Also Called: Evergreen Packaging LLC (G-1615)*
Canvas Beauty Bar LLC.. 828 355-9688
  181 Meadowview Dr Boone (28607) *(G-1183)*

Canvas Giclee Printing... 910 458-4229
  1018 Lake Park Blvd N Ste 19 Carolina Beach (28428) *(G-1632)*
Canvas of Flesh... 980 234-5957
  6295 S Main St Salisbury (28147) *(G-13931)*
Canvas Sx LLC (HQ)... 980 474-3700
  6325 Ardrey Kell Rd Ste 400 Charlotte (28277) *(G-2384)*
Canvasmasters LLC.. 828 369-0406
  78 Cabe Cove Rd Franklin (28734) *(G-6118)*
Canyon Stone Inc... 919 880-3273
  409 Northbrook Dr Youngsville (27596) *(G-17073)*
Cape Fear Boat Works Inc.. 910 371-3460
  1690 Royster Rd Ne Navassa (28451) *(G-11757)*
Cape Fear Cabinet Co Inc.. 910 703-8760
  2908 Fort Bragg Rd Fayetteville (28303) *(G-5778)*
Cape Fear Chemicals Inc... 910 862-3139
  4271 Us Highway 701 N Elizabethtown (28337) *(G-5588)*
Cape Fear Cnstr Group LLC... 910 344-1000
  102 Autumn Hall Dr Ste 210 Wilmington (28403) *(G-16149)*
Cape Fear Coffee LLC.. 910 383-2429
  511 Olde Waterford Way Leland (28451) *(G-9532)*
Cape Fear Designs, Wilmington *Also Called: Robert Citrano (G-16385)*
Cape Fear Graphics, Wilmington *Also Called: Aesco Inc (G-16096)*
Cape Fear Music Center LLC.. 910 480-2362
  150 Rowan St Fayetteville (28301) *(G-5779)*
Cape Fear Newspapers Inc.. 910 285-2178
  107 N College St Wallace (28466) *(G-15620)*
Cape Fear Orthtics Prsthtics I.. 910 483-0933
  435 W Russell St Fayetteville (28301) *(G-5780)*
Cape Fear Pblications Dist LLC.. 910 762-3451
  2204 Market St Wilmington (28403) *(G-16150)*
Cape Fear Plant, Wilmington *Also Called: Alpek Polyester Usa LLC (G-16108)*
Cape Fear Press... 910 458-4647
  610 Atlanta Ave Carolina Beach (28428) *(G-1633)*
Cape Fear Vineyard Winery LLC... 844 846-3386
  195 Vineyard Dr Elizabethtown (28337) *(G-5589)*
Cape Fear Vineyards, Rose Hill *Also Called: Duplin Wine Cellars Inc (G-13776)*
Cape Fear Vinyrd & Winery LLC... 910 645-4292
  218 Aviation Pkwy Ste C Elizabethtown (28337) *(G-5590)*
Cape Fear Yacht Works LLC... 910 540-1685
  111 Bryan Rd Wilmington (28412) *(G-16151)*
Cape Lookout Canvas & Customs... 252 726-3751
  4444 Arendell St Ste D Morehead City (28557) *(G-11157)*
Capefear Sportswear... 910 620-7844
  901 Upper Reach Dr Wilmington (28409) *(G-16152)*
Capefear Woodworks... 910 988-3306
  551 Town Creek Rd Ne Leland (28451) *(G-9533)*
Capel Incorporated (PA).. 910 572-7000
  831 N Main St Troy (27371) *(G-15402)*
Capel Rugs, Troy *Also Called: Capel Incorporated (G-15402)*
Capital Bumper, Fayetteville *Also Called: Capitol Bumper (G-5782)*
Capital City Cuisine LLC.. 919 432-2126
  4808 Wallingford Dr Raleigh (27616) *(G-12588)*
Capital City Sealants LLC.. 919 427-4077
  3101 Stony Brook Dr Ste 166 Raleigh (27604) *(G-12589)*
Capital Cy Roofg & Shtmtl LLC.. 919 366-1850
  601 Cook St Wendell (27591) *(G-15894)*
Capital Lghtning Prtection Inc.. 919 832-5574
  743 Pershing Rd Raleigh (27608) *(G-12590)*
Capital Lightng Protection, Raleigh *Also Called: Quality Lghtning Prtection Inc (G-13164)*
Capital Marble Creations Inc.. 910 893-2462
  309 W Duncan St Lillington (27546) *(G-9845)*
Capital of Garner... 919 582-0202
  200 Waterfield Ridge Pl Garner (27529) *(G-6260)*
Capital Rdymx Pittsboro LLC.. 919 217-0222
  270 Moncure Pittsboro Rd Moncure (27559) *(G-10617)*
Capital Ready Mix Concrete LLC... 919 217-0222
  512 Three Sisters Rd Knightdale (27545) *(G-9414)*
Capital Sign Solutions LLC... 919 789-1452
  5800 Mchines Pl Ste 110 Raleigh (27616) *(G-12591)*
Capital Value Center Sls & Svc.. 910 799-4060
  5406 Market St Wilmington (28405) *(G-16153)*

Capital Wood Products Inc   **ALPHABETIC SECTION**

Capital Wood Products Inc 704 982-2417
  38081 Saw Mill Rd New London (28127) *(G-11867)*

Capital Wraps, Raleigh *Also Called: Ki Agency LLC (G-12937)*

Capitol Bumper (PA) 919 772-7330
  126 Drake St Fayetteville (28301) *(G-5781)*

Capitol Bumper 919 772-7330
  126 Drake St Fayetteville (28301) *(G-5782)*

Capitol Funds Inc 910 439-5275
  409 N Main St Mount Gilead (27306) *(G-11599)*

Capitol Funds Inc (PA) 704 487-8547
  720 S Lafayette St Shelby (28150) *(G-14291)*

Capitol Funds Inc 704 482-0645
  649 Washburn Switch Rd Shelby (28150) *(G-14292)*

Capitol Woodworks 919 703-9293
  3911 Peachtree Ave Wilmington (28403) *(G-16154)*

Capnostics LLC 610 442-1363
  9724 Colts Neck Ln Concord (28027) *(G-4223)*

Capper McCall Co 919 270-8813
  9650 Strickland Rd Ste 103420 Raleigh (27615) *(G-12592)*

Capps Noble Logging 828 696-9690
  Bob's Creek Road Zirconia (28790) *(G-17150)*

Capre Omnimedia LLC 917 460-3572
  801 N 4th St Apt 404 Wilmington (28401) *(G-16155)*

Capstar Corporation 704 878-2007
  600 Park Dr Statesville (28677) *(G-14770)*

Capt Charlies Seafood Inc 252 796-7278
  508 N Road St Columbia (27925) *(G-4165)*

Capt Neills Seafood Inc 252 796-0795
  508 N Road St Columbia (27925) *(G-4166)*

Captain Charlie's Seafood, Columbia *Also Called: Capt Charlies Seafood Inc (G-4165)*

Captive-Aire Systems Inc (PA) 919 882-2410
  4641 Paragon Park Rd Ste 104 Raleigh (27616) *(G-12593)*

Captive-Aire Systems Inc 704 843-7215
  516 Wyndham Ln Waxhaw (28173) *(G-15748)*

Captive-Aire Systems Inc 919 887-2721
  360 Northbrook Dr Youngsville (27596) *(G-17074)*

Car RE Finish, Greensboro *Also Called: Akzo Nobel Coatings Inc (G-6787)*

Car-Mel Products, Statesville *Also Called: D & F Consolidated Inc (G-14781)*

Caraustar Brlngton Rgid Box In 336 226-1616
  322 Fonville St Burlington (27217) *(G-1383)*

Caraustar Cstm Packg Group Inc 336 498-2631
  4139 Us Hwy 311 Randleman (27317) *(G-13455)*

Caraustar Indus Cnsmr Pdts Gro 336 564-2163
  1485 Plaza South Dr Kernersville (27284) *(G-9170)*

Caraustar Indus Cnsmr Pdts Gro 336 996-4165
  1045 Industrial Park Dr Kernersville (27284) *(G-9171)*

Caraustar Industries Inc 704 333-5488
  4915 Hovis Rd Charlotte (28208) *(G-2385)*

Caraustar Industries Inc 704 554-5796
  8800 Crump Rd Charlotte (28273) *(G-2386)*

Caraustar Industries Inc 336 992-1053
  1496 Plaza South Dr Kernersville (27284) *(G-9172)*

Caraustar Industries Inc 336 498-2631
  4139 Us Highway 311 Randleman (27317) *(G-13456)*

Caraustar Industries Inc 828 246-7234
  5095 Old River Rd Waynesville (28786) *(G-15796)*

Caraway Logging Inc 252 633-1230
  1939 Olympia Rd New Bern (28560) *(G-11783)*

Carbide Saws Incorporated 336 882-6835
  701 Garrison St High Point (27260) *(G-8282)*

Carbo-Cut Inc 828 685-7890
  3937 Chimney Rock Rd Hendersonville (28792) *(G-7833)*

Carbon Conversion Systems LLC 919 883-4238
  95 Wood Laurel Ln Chapel Hill (27517) *(G-1996)*

Carbon Market Exchange LLC 828 545-0140
  28 Schenck Pkwy Ste 200 Asheville (28803) *(G-580)*

Carbon-Less Industries Inc 704 361-1231
  12059 University Cy Blvd Harrisburg (28075) *(G-7703)*

Carbotech USA Inc 704 481-8500
  4031 Dearborn Pl Nw Concord (28027) *(G-4224)*

Carden Farms Soap Inc 919 570-0745
  204 King Dr Franklinton (27525) *(G-6152)*

Carden Printing Company 336 364-2923
  52 Hunters Ln Timberlake (27583) *(G-15313)*

Cardiac Wllness Spplements LLC 252 757-3939
  2459 Emerald Pl Ste 102 Greenville (27834) *(G-7495)*

Cardinal Alaris Products, Creedmoor *Also Called: Carefusion 303 Inc (G-4608)*

Cardinal America Inc 704 810-1620
  165 Commerce Blvd Statesville (28625) *(G-14771)*

Cardinal Bag & Envelope Co Inc 704 225-9636
  2861 Gray Fox Rd Monroe (28110) *(G-10672)*

Cardinal Buildings LLC 919 422-5670
  1641 Us 70 Hwy E Garner (27529) *(G-6261)*

Cardinal Cabinets Distinction, Stedman *Also Called: Cynthia Saar (G-14934)*

Cardinal Cabinetworks Inc 919 829-3634
  4900 Craftsman Dr Ste A Raleigh (27609) *(G-12594)*

Cardinal Container Svcs Inc 336 249-6816
  138 Walser Rd Lexington (27295) *(G-9689)*

Cardinal Creek Cndles Gfts LLC 336 941-3158
  119 Alexandria Ct Advance (27006) *(G-39)*

Cardinal CT Company 336 719-6857
  630 Derby St Mount Airy (27030) *(G-11487)*

Cardinal Fg, Mooresville *Also Called: Cardinal Glass Industries Inc (G-10895)*

Cardinal Foods LLC 910 259-9407
  201 Progress Dr Burgaw (28425) *(G-1334)*

Cardinal Glass Industries Inc 704 660-0900
  342 Mooresville Blvd Mooresville (28115) *(G-10895)*

Cardinal Graphics Inc 704 545-4144
  4475 Morris Park Dr Ste H Mint Hill (28227) *(G-10526)*

Cardinal Health 414, Charlotte *Also Called: Cardinal Health 414 LLC (G-2387)*

Cardinal Health 414 LLC 704 644-7989
  3845 Shopton Rd Ste 18a Charlotte (28217) *(G-2387)*

Cardinal Metalworks LLC 910 259-9990
  1090 E Wilmington Street Ext Burgaw (28425) *(G-1335)*

Cardinal Millwork & Supply Inc 336 665-9811
  7620 W Market St Greensboro (27409) *(G-6878)*

Cardinal Plastics Inc 704 739-9420
  4910 Barrett Rd Kings Mountain (28086) *(G-9298)*

Cardinal Plastics Sales Inc 336 540-9013
  2416 Old Towne Dr Greensboro (27455) *(G-6879)*

Cardinal Stone Company Inc 336 846-7191
  1608 Us Highway 221 N Jefferson (28640) *(G-9087)*

Cardinal Tissue LLC 815 503-2096
  207 Oakland Rd Spindale (28160) *(G-14605)*

Cardiopharma Inc 910 791-1361
  100-A Eastwood Center Dr Ste 117 Wilmington (28403) *(G-16156)*

Cardioxyl Pharmaceuticals Inc 919 869-8586
  1450 Raleigh Rd Ste 212 Chapel Hill (27517) *(G-1997)*

Cardservice of Carolinas, Greensboro *Also Called: Atlantic Bankcard Center Inc (G-6821)*

Care A Lot Pet Supply 757 457-9425
  102 Lark Dr Moyock (27958) *(G-11694)*

Carefusion 303 Inc 919 528-5253
  1515 Ivac Way Creedmoor (27522) *(G-4608)*

Carer Welding 336 558-3906
  10553 Randleman Rd Bldg 6 Randleman (27317) *(G-13457)*

Cargill, Charlotte *Also Called: Cargill Incorporated (G-2388)*

Cargill, Cleveland *Also Called: Cargill Incorporated (G-4069)*

Cargill, Greenville *Also Called: Cargill Incorporated (G-7496)*

Cargill, High Point *Also Called: Cargill & Pendleton Inc (G-8283)*

Cargill Incorporated 704 523-0414
  5000 South Blvd Charlotte (28217) *(G-2388)*

Cargill Incorporated 704 278-2941
  9150 Statesville Blvd Cleveland (27013) *(G-4069)*

Cargill Incorporated 800 227-4455
  1754 River Rd Fayetteville (28312) *(G-5783)*

Cargill & Pendleton Inc 336 882-5510
  330 N Hamilton St High Point (27260) *(G-8283)*

Cargill Incorporated 252 752-1879
  6 Miles East Farmville Greenville (27834) *(G-7496)*

Cargomovement International 704 688-9720
  2111 Lawry Run Dr Charlotte (28273) *(G-2389)*

Cargotec Port Security LLC (DH) 919 620-1763
  4400 Ben Franklin Blvd Ste 200a Durham (27704) *(G-4998)*

ALPHABETIC SECTION — Carolina Container LLC

Caring For Body LLC.. 706 897-9904
12 Whitleigh Ct Arden (28704) *(G-317)*

Carlina Shotwell LLC.. 252 417-8688
204 E Arlington Blvd Ste C-103 Greenville (27858) *(G-7497)*

Carlisle Corporation (HQ)... 704 501-1100
11605 N Community House Rd Charlotte (28277) *(G-2390)*

Carlisle Finishing LLC.. 864 466-4173
804 Green Valley Rd Ste 300 Greensboro (27408) *(G-6880)*

Carlisle Syntec Systems A Div, Charlotte *Also Called: Carlisle Corporation (G-2390)*

Carlson Environmental Cons PC (PA)......................... 704 283-9765
1127 Curtis St Ste 110 Monroe (28112) *(G-10673)*

Carlson Envmtl Cons Prof Corp, Monroe *Also Called: Carlson Environmental Cons PC (G-10673)*

Carlton Enterprizes LLC... 919 534-5424
195 Rocky Point Trng Sch Rd Rocky Point (28457) *(G-13743)*

Carmel By D3sign LLC... 336 617-6383
3408 Winchester Dr Greensboro (27406) *(G-6881)*

Carnes-Miller Gear Company Inc................................ 704 888-4448
362 Browns Hill Rd Locust (28097) *(G-9955)*

Caro-Polymers Inc (PA).. 704 629-5319
611 Bess Town Rd Bessemer City (28016) *(G-1055)*

Carocon, Laurinburg *Also Called: Carolina Container LLC (G-9471)*

Carocraft Cabinets Inc.. 704 376-0022
1932 Statesville Ave Charlotte (28206) *(G-2391)*

Carol Williams.. 252 883-7968
745 Foxridge Ct Rocky Mount (27804) *(G-13687)*

Carolina... 919 851-0906
8204 Tryon Woods Dr Cary (27518) *(G-1722)*

Carolina Academic Press LLC.................................... 919 489-7486
700 Kent St Durham (27701) *(G-4999)*

Carolina Ad Group... 919 628-0549
116 Springfork Dr Cary (27513) *(G-1723)*

Carolina Apparel Group Inc.. 704 694-6544
425 Us Highway 52 S Wadesboro (28170) *(G-15506)*

Carolina Asphalt, Hickory *Also Called: Carolina Paving Hickory Inc (G-7964)*

Carolina Attachments LLC... 336 474-7309
704 Pineywood Rd Thomasville (27360) *(G-15194)*

Carolina Awning and Tent, Rocky Mount *Also Called: Rocky Mount Awning & Tent Co (G-13730)*

Carolina Bargain Trader Inc....................................... 252 756-1500
72 Howell St Greenville (27834) *(G-7498)*

Carolina Bark Products LLC...................................... 252 589-1324
Hwy 186 E Seaboard (27876) *(G-14227)*

Carolina Base - Pac Corp.. 828 728-7304
3157 Freezer Locker Rd Hudson (28638) *(G-8766)*

Carolina Beer Company, Mooresville *Also Called: Carolina Beverage Group LLC (G-10896)*

Carolina Beverage Corporation (PA).......................... 704 636-2191
1413 Jake Alexander Blvd S Salisbury (28146) *(G-13932)*

Carolina Beverage Group LLC (HQ)..........................704 799-2337
110 Barley Park Ln Mooresville (28115) *(G-10896)*

Carolina Bg... 704 847-8840
624 Matthews Mint Hill Rd Ste B Matthews (28105) *(G-10236)*

Carolina Biological Supply Co.................................... 336 446-7600
6537 Judge Adams Rd Whitsett (27377) *(G-15985)*

Carolina Biological Supply Co, Burlington *Also Called: Carolina Biological Supply Company (G-1384)*

Carolina Biological Supply Company (PA).................336 584-0381
2700 York Rd Burlington (27215) *(G-1384)*

Carolina Blind Outlet Inc (PA)....................................828 697-8525
225 Duncan Hill Rd Hendersonville (28792) *(G-7834)*

Carolina Blue Publishing LLC.................................... 704 628-6290
5105 Candleglow Ct Indian Trail (28079) *(G-8926)*

Carolina Bottle Mfr LLC... 704 635-8759
2630 Nelda Dr Ste B Monroe (28110) *(G-10674)*

Carolina Bottling Company.. 704 637-5869
1413 Jake Alexander Blvd S Salisbury (28146) *(G-13933)*

Carolina Brace Systems, Chapel Hill *Also Called: Orthorx Inc (G-2050)*

Carolina Bronze, Seagrove *Also Called: Carolina Bronze Sculpture Inc (G-14235)*

Carolina Bronze Sculpture Inc................................... 336 873-8291
6108 Maple Springs Rd Seagrove (27341) *(G-14235)*

Carolina Brush Company... 704 867-0286
3093 Northwest Blvd Gastonia (28052) *(G-6366)*

Carolina Brush Mfg Co (PA)...................................... 704 867-0286
3093 Northwest Blvd Gastonia (28052) *(G-6367)*

Carolina Building Services Inc (PA)........................... 704 664-7110
207 Timber Rd Mooresville (28115) *(G-10897)*

Carolina Business and.. 704 826-7099
2436 Logan Field Dr Waxhaw (28173) *(G-15749)*

Carolina Business Furn Inc....................................... 336 431-9400
535 Archdale Blvd Archdale (27263) *(G-272)*

Carolina By-Products, Greensboro *Also Called: Valley Proteins (de) Inc (G-7435)*

Carolina By-Products Co.. 336 333-3030
2410 Randolph Ave Greensboro (27406) *(G-6882)*

Carolina Cab Specialist LLC..................................... 919 818-4375
311 Ashville Ave Ste K Cary (27518) *(G-1724)*

Carolina Cabinets of Cedar Pt.................................. 252 393-6236
136 Vfw Rd Swansboro (28584) *(G-15042)*

Carolina Candle.. 336 835-6020
430 Gentry Rd Elkin (28621) *(G-5612)*

Carolina Canners Inc.. 843 537-5281
750 S Bennett St Southern Pines (28387) *(G-14530)*

Carolina Carports Inc (PA)....................................... 336 367-6400
187 Cardinal Ridge Ln Dobson (27017) *(G-4821)*

Carolina Carton.. 704 554-5796
8800 Crump Rd Pineville (28134) *(G-12259)*

Carolina Carton Plant, Charlotte *Also Called: Caraustar Industries Inc (G-2386)*

Carolina Cartridge, Charlotte *Also Called: Carolina Cartridge Systems Inc (G-2392)*

Carolina Cartridge Systems Inc................................ 704 347-2447
516 E Hebron St Charlotte (28273) *(G-2392)*

Carolina Catch Inc.. 252 946-5796
321 N Pierce St Washington (27889) *(G-15686)*

Carolina Cemetery Park Corp................................... 704 528-5543
344 Field Dr Troutman (28166) *(G-15369)*

Carolina Certif Mus Group LLC................................ 984 234-2073
1128 Vermillion Dr Durham (27713) *(G-5000)*

Carolina Chair Inc.. 828 459-1330
1822 Brian Dr Ne Conover (28613) *(G-4430)*

Carolina Chocolatiers Inc... 828 652-4496
20 N Main St Marion (28752) *(G-10146)*

Carolina Classic Manufacturing Inc.......................... 252 237-9105
510 Jones St S Wilson (27893) *(G-16483)*

Carolina Classifiedscom LLC (PA)........................... 704 246-0900
1609 Airport Rd Monroe (28110) *(G-10675)*

Carolina Cltch Brake Rbldrs In................................. 828 327-9358
430 Us Highway 70 Se Hickory (28602) *(G-7962)*

Carolina Co Packaging LLC, Henderson *Also Called: D C Thomas Group Inc (G-7780)*

Carolina Coast Vineyard.. 910 707-1777
1328 Lake Park Blvd N Carolina Beach (28428) *(G-1634)*

Carolina Coastal Coatings....................................... 910 346-9607
400 White St Jacksonville (28546) *(G-8994)*

Carolina Coastal Coatings Inc.................................. 910 346-9607
375 Padgett Rd Maple Hill (28454) *(G-10131)*

Carolina Coating Solutions, Chapel Hill *Also Called: Abcor Supply Inc (G-1981)*

Carolina Commercial Coatings................................. 910 279-6045
20 Wrights Aly Wilmington (28401) *(G-16157)*

Carolina Components Group, Durham *Also Called: Carolina Components Group Inc (G-5001)*

Carolina Components Group Inc.............................. 919 635-8438
1001 Hill Dr Durham (27703) *(G-5001)*

Carolina Compost.. 252 202-6602
191 Lambs Rd Camden (27921) *(G-1556)*

Carolina Concrete Inc.. 704 596-6511
11509 Reames Rd Charlotte (28269) *(G-2393)*

Carolina Concrete Inc (PA)...................................... 704 821-7645
1316 Waxhaw Rd Matthews (28105) *(G-10237)*

Carolina Concrete Materials.................................... 828 686-3040
650 Old Us 70 Hwy Swannanoa (28778) *(G-15022)*

Carolina Connections Inc... 336 786-7030
805 Merita St Mount Airy (27030) *(G-11488)*

Carolina Container Company (HQ).......................... 336 883-7146
909 Prospect St High Point (27260) *(G-8284)*

Carolina Container LLC... 828 322-3380
61 30th St Nw Hickory (28601) *(G-7963)*

Carolina Container LLC... 910 277-0400
16100 Joy St Laurinburg (28352) *(G-9471)*

Carolina Container LLC   ALPHABETIC SECTION

Carolina Container LLC 336 883-7146
1205 Trinity St Thomasville (27360) *(G-15195)*

Carolina Conveying Inc 828 235-1005
162 Great Oak Dr Canton (28716) *(G-1608)*

Carolina Copacking LLC 252 433-0130
860 Commerce Dr Henderson (27537) *(G-7776)*

Carolina Copy Services Inc (PA) 704 375-9099
21300 Blakely Shores Dr Cornelius (28031) *(G-4533)*

Carolina Core Machine LLC 336 342-1141
638 Tamco Rd Reidsville (27320) *(G-13512)*

Carolina Core Solutions LLC 704 900-4208
1605 Norfolk Pl Sw Conover (28613) *(G-4431)*

Carolina Counters, Midland *Also Called: E T Sales Inc (G-10467)*

Carolina Countertops of Garner 919 832-3335
3800 Tryon Rd Ste F Raleigh (27606) *(G-12595)*

Carolina Crate & Pallet Inc 910 245-4001
3281 Us 1 Hwy Vass (28394) *(G-15491)*

Carolina Crating Inc 910 276-7170
430 Hillside Ave Laurinburg (28352) *(G-9472)*

Carolina Creative Cabinets Inc 919 842-2060
517 N Franklin Dr Sanford (27330) *(G-14097)*

Carolina Cstm Cabinets & Furn, Powells Point *Also Called: Carolina Custom Cabinets Inc (G-12396)*

Carolina Cstm Signs & Graphics 336 681-4337
1023 Huffman St Greensboro (27405) *(G-6883)*

Carolina Csual Otdoor Furn Inc 252 491-5171
7359 Caratoke Hwy Jarvisburg (27947) *(G-9083)*

Carolina Custom Booth, High Point *Also Called: Carolina Custom Booth Co LLC (G-8285)*

Carolina Custom Booth Co LLC 336 886-3127
901 W Market Center Dr High Point (27260) *(G-8285)*

Carolina Custom Cabinetry 704 808-1225
6823 Davis Rd Waxhaw (28173) *(G-15750)*

Carolina Custom Cabinets 910 525-3096
104 Andrews Chapel Rd Roseboro (28382) *(G-13783)*

Carolina Custom Cabinets Inc 252 491-5475
102 Park Dr Powells Point (27966) *(G-12396)*

Carolina Custom Coating 704 224-1503
380 Neazer St Rockwell (28138) *(G-13647)*

Carolina Custom Draperies Inc 336 945-5190
5723 Country Club Rd Ste D Winston Salem (27104) *(G-16644)*

Carolina Custom Exteriors Inc 828 232-0402
211 Amboy Rd Asheville (28806) *(G-581)*

Carolina Custom Leather, Conover *Also Called: NC Custom Leather Inc (G-4474)*

Carolina Custom Millwork, Gastonia *Also Called: Contemporary Design Co LLC (G-6386)*

Carolina Custom Pressing, Greensboro *Also Called: Ultimix Records (G-7426)*

Carolina Custom Rubber Inc 704 636-6989
5415 Statesville Blvd Salisbury (28147) *(G-13934)*

Carolina Custom Surfaces, Greensboro *Also Called: McAd Inc (G-7193)*

Carolina Custom Tank LLC 980 406-3200
924 Dr Martin Luther King Jr Way Gastonia (28054) *(G-6368)*

Carolina Custom Towers LLC 252 671-3779
311 Facility Dr Morehead City (28557) *(G-11158)*

Carolina Custom Windows, Belmont *Also Called: Ramsey Industries Inc (G-1005)*

Carolina Dairy LLC 910 569-7070
116 Industrial Park Biscoe (27209) *(G-1105)*

Carolina Data Recovery LLC 704 536-1717
7512 E Independence Blvd Ste 100 Charlotte (28227) *(G-2394)*

Carolina Design & Mfg Inc 919 554-1823
239 Wiggins Rd Louisburg (27549) *(G-9982)*

Carolina Dry Kiln, Lexington *Also Called: J E Jones Lumber Company (G-9732)*

Carolina Duct Fabrication Inc 252 478-9955
360 Barbee St Spring Hope (27882) *(G-14616)*

Carolina Dyeing and Finshg LLC 336 227-2770
220 Elmira St Burlington (27217) *(G-1385)*

Carolina Ear Hring Aid Assoc L 919 876-4327
5900 Six Forks Rd Ste 200 Raleigh (27609) *(G-12596)*

Carolina East Timber Inc 252 638-1914
2145 Saints Delight Church Rd New Bern (28560) *(G-11784)*

Carolina Eastern Inc 252 795-3128
6940 Us Highway 64 Robersonville (27871) *(G-13615)*

Carolina Egg Companies Inc 252 459-2143
10927 Cooper Rd Nashville (27856) *(G-11739)*

Carolina Elctrnic Assmblers In 919 938-1086
132 Citation Ln Smithfield (27577) *(G-14452)*

Carolina Electric Boats, Benson *Also Called: Twin Troller Boats Inc (G-1044)*

Carolina Electric Mtr Repr LLC 704 289-3732
1812 Skyway Dr Monroe (28110) *(G-10676)*

Carolina Embroidery Kenly Inc 919 279-2356
103 N Gardner Ave Kenly (27542) *(G-9146)*

Carolina Energy Concepts LLC 910 833-4203
203 Cole Dr Hampstead (28443) *(G-7642)*

Carolina Envelope, Lexington *Also Called: Ceprint Solutions Inc (G-9691)*

Carolina Event Labor, Charlotte *Also Called: Fairfield Pro AV Inc (G-2746)*

Carolina Expediters LLC 888 537-5330
1415 Fancy Gap Rd Mount Airy (27030) *(G-11489)*

Carolina Extruded Plastics Inc 336 272-1191
728 Utility St Greensboro (27405) *(G-6884)*

Carolina Fab Inc 704 820-8694
2129 Charles Raper Jonas Hwy Mount Holly (28120) *(G-11624)*

Carolina Fabricators, Raleigh *Also Called: Carolina Fabricators LLC (G-12597)*

Carolina Fabricators, Raleigh *Also Called: Kisner Corporation (G-12941)*

Carolina Fabricators LLC 919 510-8410
6016 Triangle Dr Raleigh (27617) *(G-12597)*

Carolina Fairway Cushions LLC 336 434-4292
15 N Robbins St Thomasville (27360) *(G-15196)*

Carolina Farm Table, Sparta *Also Called: Designs In Wood (G-14593)*

Carolina Farmstead LLC 800 822-6219
1012 Hardy Rd Snow Hill (28580) *(G-14500)*

Carolina Fine Snacks, Greensboro *Also Called: KLb Enterprises Incorporated (G-7153)*

Carolina Finshg & Coating Inc 704 730-8233
441 Countryside Rd Kings Mountain (28086) *(G-9299)*

Carolina Fire Journal, Indian Trail *Also Called: Knight Communications Inc (G-8943)*

Carolina Fire Protection Inc 910 892-1700
4055 Hodges Chapel Rd Dunn (28334) *(G-4854)*

Carolina Flare Sportfishng LLC 252 205-5563
5166 Mamie Rd Sims (27880) *(G-14440)*

Carolina Foods LLC 704 333-9812
1807 S Tryon St Charlotte (28203) *(G-2395)*

Carolina Foundry Inc 704 376-3145
228 W Tremont Ave Charlotte (28203) *(G-2396)*

Carolina Frames, Asheboro *Also Called: Chris Isom Inc (G-415)*

Carolina Fur Dressing Company 919 231-0086
900 Freedom Dr Raleigh (27610) *(G-12598)*

Carolina Furniture Mfrs Inc 336 873-7355
1776 Pleasant Ridge Rd Seagrove (27341) *(G-14236)*

Carolina Giant Tires Inc 919 609-9077
389 Americal Rd Henderson (27537) *(G-7777)*

Carolina Glove Company (PA) 828 464-1132
116 S Mclin Creek Rd Conover (28613) *(G-4432)*

Carolina Gloves & Safety Co, Conover *Also Called: Carolina Glove Company (G-4432)*

Carolina Golfco Inc 704 525-7846
209 E Exmore St Charlotte (28217) *(G-2397)*

Carolina Graphic Services LLC 336 668-0871
4328 Federal Dr Ste 105 Greensboro (27410) *(G-6885)*

Carolina Greenhouse Plants Inc 252 523-9300
1504 Cunningham Rd Kinston (28501) *(G-9350)*

Carolina Ground Svc Eqp Inc (PA) 252 565-0288
430 Executive Pkwy New Bern (28562) *(G-11785)*

Carolina Growler Inc 910 948-2114
121 N Green St Robbins (27325) *(G-13597)*

Carolina GSE, New Bern *Also Called: Carolina Ground Svc Eqp Inc (G-11785)*

Carolina Gym Supply Corp 919 732-6999
575 Dimmocks Mill Rd Hillsborough (27278) *(G-8642)*

Carolina Gyps Reclamation LLC 704 895-4506
19109 W Catawba Ave Cornelius (28031) *(G-4534)*

Carolina Heritage Cabinetry, North Wilkesboro *Also Called: Commercial Property LLC (G-12002)*

Carolina Heritg Vinyrd Winery 336 448-4781
170 Heritage Vines Way Elkin (28621) *(G-5613)*

Carolina Home Exteriors LLC 252 637-6599
252 Kale Rd New Bern (28562) *(G-11786)*

Carolina Home Garden 828 692-3230
105 S Main St Hendersonville (28792) *(G-7835)*

Carolina Homes, Lumberton *Also Called: Carolina Mnufactured Homes LLC (G-10029)*

Carolina Hosiery Mills Inc 336 226-5581
710 Koury Dr Burlington (27215) *(G-1386)*

Carolina Hosiery Mills Inc 336 226-5581
735 Koury Dr Burlington (27215) *(G-1387)*

Carolina Hosiery Mills Inc (PA) 336 570-2129
2316 Tucker St. Extension Burlington (27215) *(G-1388)*

Carolina House Furniture Inc (PA) 828 459-7400
5485 Herman Rd Claremont (28610) *(G-3903)*

Carolina Ice Inc 252 527-3178
2466 Old Poole Rd Kinston (28504) *(G-9351)*

Carolina Innvtive Fd Ingrdnts 804 359-9311
4626 Coleman Dr Nashville (27856) *(G-11740)*

Carolina International Inc (HQ) 336 472-7788
110 W Guilford St Thomasville (27360) *(G-15197)*

Carolina Keller LLC 252 237-8181
2401 Stantonsburg Rd Se Wilson (27893) *(G-16484)*

Carolina Knife Company, Asheville *Also Called: Hamilton Indus Grinding Inc (G-647)*

Carolina Laser Cutting Inc 336 292-1474
4400 S Holden Rd Greensboro (27406) *(G-6886)*

Carolina Lasers 919 872-8001
5508 Old Wake Forest Rd Raleigh (27609) *(G-12599)*

Carolina Lawnscape Inc 803 230-5570
13105 Greencreek Dr Charlotte (28273) *(G-2398)*

Carolina Leatherwork, Fleetwood *Also Called: Cranberry Wood Works Inc (G-5974)*

Carolina Leg Supply LLC 828 446-6838
511 Golfview Ct Lenoir (28645) *(G-9594)*

Carolina Loom Reed Company Inc 336 274-7631
3503 Holts Chapel Rd Greensboro (27401) *(G-6887)*

Carolina Lquid Chmistries Corp (PA) 336 722-8910
313 Gallimore Dairy Rd Greensboro (27409) *(G-6888)*

Carolina Machine Works, Belmont *Also Called: Equipment Parts Inc (G-987)*

Carolina Machining Fabrication 919 554-9700
321 N Nassau St Youngsville (27596) *(G-17075)*

Carolina Marble & Granite 704 523-2112
1924 Dilworth Rd W Charlotte (28203) *(G-2399)*

Carolina Marble Products Inc 252 753-3020
3973 W Wilson St Farmville (27828) *(G-5731)*

Carolina Mat Incorporated 252 793-1111
193 Hwy 149 N Plymouth (27962) *(G-12367)*

Carolina Material Handling Inc 336 294-2346
2209 Patterson Ct Greensboro (27407) *(G-6889)*

Carolina Mattress Guild Inc 336 841-8529
385 North Dr Thomasville (27360) *(G-15198)*

Carolina Mch Fayetteville Inc 910 425-9115
3465 Black And Decker Rd Hope Mills (28348) *(G-8734)*

Carolina Mechanical Services Inc 919 477-7100
5100 International Dr Durham (27712) *(G-5002)*

Carolina Metal Fabricators, Raleigh *Also Called: Directus Holdings LLC (G-12686)*

Carolina Metals Inc 828 667-0876
1398 Brevard Rd Asheville (28806) *(G-582)*

Carolina Meter and Supply, Hampstead *Also Called: Utility Metering Solutions Inc (G-7663)*

Carolina Mfg Group LLC 336 413-8335
7840 N Point Blvd Unit 11031 Winston Salem (27116) *(G-16645)*

Carolina Mills Incorporated (PA) 828 428-9911
618 N Carolina Ave Maiden (28650) *(G-10102)*

Carolina Mills Warehouse 828 428-9911
624 N Carolina Ave Maiden (28650) *(G-10103)*

Carolina Mnufactured Homes LLC 910 374-6889
386 Brookgreen Dr Lumberton (28358) *(G-10029)*

Carolina Moldings Inc 704 523-7471
4601 Macie St Charlotte (28217) *(G-2400)*

Carolina Money Saver, Monroe *Also Called: Carolina Classifiedscom LLC (G-10675)*

Carolina Monogram Company 919 285-3091
208 Church St Fuquay Varina (27526) *(G-6186)*

Carolina Movile Bus Systems 336 475-0983
771 Old Emanuel Church Rd Thomasville (27360) *(G-15199)*

Carolina Narrow Fabric Company 336 631-3000
1100 N Patterson Ave Winston Salem (27101) *(G-16646)*

Carolina Newspapers Inc 336 274-7829
807 Summit Ave Greensboro (27405) *(G-6890)*

Carolina Nonwovens LLC 704 735-5600
1106 Jw Abernathy Plant Rd Maiden (28650) *(G-10104)*

Carolina North Granite Corp 336 719-2600
151 Granite Quarry Trl Mount Airy (27030) *(G-11490)*

Carolina North Mfg Inc 336 992-0082
1161 S Park Dr Kernersville (27284) *(G-9173)*

Carolina Nut Inc 910 293-4209
1180 Stanley Chapel Church Rd Mount Olive (28365) *(G-11658)*

Carolina Packaging & Sup Inc (PA) 919 201-5592
5609 Departure Dr Raleigh (27616) *(G-12600)*

Carolina Packers Inc (PA) 919 934-2181
2999 S Brightleaf Blvd Smithfield (27577) *(G-14453)*

Carolina Packing House Sups 910 653-3438
305 Green Sea Rd Tabor City (28463) *(G-15079)*

Carolina Pallet Recycling Inc 828 652-6818
2855 Nc 226 I 40 Marion (28752) *(G-10147)*

Carolina Paper Guys LLC 704 980-3112
5800 Brookshire Blvd Charlotte (28216) *(G-2401)*

Carolina Paper Tubes Inc 828 692-9686
3932 Old Us Highway 25 Zirconia (28790) *(G-17151)*

Carolina Parenting Inc (PA) 704 344-1980
214 W Tremont Ave Ste 302 Charlotte (28203) *(G-2402)*

Carolina Patch & Leather LLC 704 880-7724
203 Old Airport Rd Statesville (28677) *(G-14772)*

Carolina Paving Hickory Inc 828 328-3909
445 9th St Se Hickory (28602) *(G-7964)*

Carolina Paving Hickory Inc (PA) 828 322-1706
3203 Highland Ave Ne Hickory (28601) *(G-7965)*

Carolina Peacemaker, Greensboro *Also Called: Carolina Newspapers Inc (G-6890)*

Carolina Perfumer Inc (PA) 910 295-5600
102 Berwick Ct Pinehurst (28374) *(G-12217)*

Carolina Piping Services Inc 704 405-0297
307 S Cansler St Kings Mountain (28086) *(G-9300)*

Carolina Powder Coating 336 934-6102
3753 Deer Creek Ln Yadkinville (27055) *(G-17035)*

Carolina Prcsion Cmponents Inc 828 496-1045
4181 Us Highway 321a Granite Falls (28630) *(G-6726)*

Carolina Prcsion Fbers Spv LLC 336 527-4140
145 Factory St Ronda (28670) *(G-13763)*

Carolina Prcsion Machining Inc 336 751-7788
1500 N Main St Mocksville (27028) *(G-10559)*

Carolina Precast Concrete 910 230-0028
452 Webb Rd Dunn (28334) *(G-4855)*

Carolina Precision Fibers Inc 336 527-4140
145 Factory St Ronda (28670) *(G-13764)*

Carolina Precision Machining 336 751-7788
130 Funder Dr Mocksville (27028) *(G-10560)*

Carolina Precision Plas LLC 336 283-4700
111 Cpp Global Dr Mocksville (27028) *(G-10561)*

Carolina Precision Plastics L (HQ) 336 498-2654
405 Commerce Pl Asheboro (27203) *(G-412)*

Carolina Precision Tech LLC 215 675-4590
1055 Gateway Dr Ste A Mooresville (28115) *(G-10898)*

Carolina Prime, Lenoir *Also Called: Carolina Prime Pet Inc (G-9595)*

Carolina Prime Pet Inc 888 370-2360
2040 Morganton Blvd Sw Lenoir (28645) *(G-9595)*

Carolina Print Mill 919 607-9452
527 E Chatham St Cary (27511) *(G-1725)*

Carolina Print Works Inc 704 637-6902
600 N Long St Ste B Salisbury (28144) *(G-13935)*

Carolina Printing & Converting, Wilkesboro *Also Called: Interflex Acquisition Co LLC (G-16027)*

Carolina Printing Associates 704 477-0626
1707 N Post Rd Shelby (28150) *(G-14293)*

Carolina Printing Co 919 834-0433
640 Quarterhorse Rd Princeton (27569) *(G-12399)*

Carolina Products Inc 704 364-9029
1132 Pro Am Dr Charlotte (28211) *(G-2403)*

Carolina Prtg Wilmington Inc 910 762-2453
2790 Sea Vista Dr Sw Supply (28462) *(G-15007)*

Carolina Publishing Company 252 206-1633
1131 Anderson St Nw Wilson (27893) *(G-16485)*

Carolina Pumps Instrumentation, Winston Salem *Also Called: Hoh Corporation (G-16747)*

Carolina Pwr Signalization LLC..910 323-5589
1416 Middle River Loop Fayetteville (28312) *(G-5784)*

Carolina Quarries Inc (PA)...704 633-0201
805 Harris Granite Rd Salisbury (28146) *(G-13936)*

Carolina Ready Mix & Build (PA)....................................828 686-3041
606 Old Us 70 Hwy Swannanoa (28778) *(G-15023)*

Carolina Ready-Mix LLC...704 225-1112
1901 Valley Pkwy Ste 100 Monroe (28110) *(G-10677)*

Carolina Resource Corp...919 562-0200
850 Park Ave Youngsville (27596) *(G-17076)*

Carolina Retread LLC...910 642-4123
30 Bitmore Rd Whiteville (28472) *(G-15961)*

Carolina Road Media LLC..844 222-7069
105 Settlers Mill Ln Durham (27713) *(G-5003)*

Carolina Rubber & Spc Inc..336 744-5111
4301 Idlewild Industrial Dr Winston Salem (27105) *(G-16647)*

Carolina Screw Products...336 760-7400
Winston Salem (27113) *(G-16648)*

Carolina Seafood Company Inc.....................................252 322-5455
161 Muddy Creek Rd Aurora (27806) *(G-833)*

Carolina Sgns Grphic Dsgns Inc...................................919 383-3344
3535 Hillsborough Rd Durham (27705) *(G-5004)*

Carolina Sheds LLC...336 623-7433
131 N Van Buren Rd Eden (27288) *(G-5487)*

Carolina Shirt Company Inc..910 575-4447
262 Koolabrew Dr Nw Calabash (28467) *(G-1552)*

Carolina Shower Door Inc...910 343-0009
1901 Blue Clay Rd Ste G1 Wilmington (28405) *(G-16158)*

Carolina Sign Co Inc...704 399-3995
2925 Beatties Ford Rd Charlotte (28216) *(G-2404)*

Carolina Sign Svc...919 247-0927
174 Kinnis Creek Dr Angier (27501) *(G-136)*

Carolina Signals and Lightings, Fayetteville *Also Called: Carolina Pwr Signalization LLC (G-5784)*

Carolina Signs..704 622-1939
3319 Lincoln Ln Gastonia (28056) *(G-6369)*

Carolina Signs & Lighting Inc.......................................336 399-1400
928 Spainhour Rd King (27021) *(G-9266)*

Carolina Signs and Graphics,, Durham *Also Called: Carolina Sgns Grphic Dsgns Inc (G-5004)*

Carolina Signs and Wonders Inc...................................704 286-1343
1700 University Commercial Pl Charlotte (28213) *(G-2405)*

Carolina Siteworks Inc..704 855-7483
300 Wade Dr China Grove (28023) *(G-3881)*

Carolina Solar Structures Inc.......................................828 684-9900
1007 Tunnel Rd Asheville (28805) *(G-583)*

Carolina Solvents Inc...828 322-1920
2274 1st St Se Hickory (28602) *(G-7966)*

Carolina Specialties Inc...704 525-9599
4230 Barringer Dr Charlotte (28217) *(G-2406)*

Carolina Spral Duct Fbrction L....................................704 395-3289
11524 Wilmar Blvd Charlotte (28273) *(G-2407)*

Carolina Sputter Solutions, Raleigh *Also Called: Kyma Technologies Inc (G-12949)*

Carolina Square Inc..336 793-3222
1164 Cherry Hill Rd Mocksville (27028) *(G-10562)*

Carolina Stairs Inc..704 664-5032
255 Belk Rd Mount Ulla (28125) *(G-11681)*

Carolina Stake and WD Pdts Inc..................................704 545-7774
11223 Blair Rd Ste 4 Mint Hill (28227) *(G-10527)*

Carolina Stalite Co Ltd Partnr.....................................704 279-2166
16815 Old Beatty Ford Rd Gold Hill (28071) *(G-6580)*

Carolina Stalite Co Ltd Partnr.....................................704 279-2166
17700 Old Beatty Ford Rd Gold Hill (28071) *(G-6581)*

Carolina Stalite Co Ltd Partnr.....................................704 474-3165
12423 Old Aquadale Rd Norwood (28128) *(G-12037)*

Carolina Stalite Co Ltd Partnr (PA)..............................704 637-1515
205 Klumac Rd Salisbury (28144) *(G-13937)*

Carolina Stamping Company.......................................704 637-0260
701 Corporate Cir Salisbury (28147) *(G-13938)*

Carolina Stickers & Signs LLC....................................704 649-7318
422 E 22nd St Ste 3 Charlotte (28206) *(G-2408)*

Carolina Stone LLC..252 208-1633
10600 Nc Highway 55 W Dover (28526) *(G-4834)*

Carolina Store Fixtures LLC..252 508-0110
28333 Us Highway 64 Jamesville (27846) *(G-9079)*

Carolina Strapping Buckles Co, Gastonia *Also Called: Burlan Manufacturing LLC (G-6362)*

Carolina Sunrock, Durham *Also Called: Buffalo Crushed Stone Inc (G-4985)*

Carolina Sunrock LLC (HQ)..919 575-4502
1001 W B St Butner (27509) *(G-1543)*

Carolina Sunrock LLC..919 201-4201
3092 Rock Spring Church Rd Creedmoor (27522) *(G-4609)*

Carolina Sunrock LLC..252 433-4617
214 Sunrock Rd Kittrell (27544) *(G-9395)*

Carolina Sunrock LLC..919 861-1860
8620 Barefoot Industrial Rd Raleigh (27617) *(G-12601)*

Carolina Sunrock LLC..919 554-0500
5043 Unicon Dr Wake Forest (27587) *(G-15538)*

Carolina Surfaces LLC...910 874-1335
242 Woodlief Dr Elizabethtown (28337) *(G-5591)*

Carolina Swatching Inc...828 327-9499
725 14th Street Dr Sw Hickory (28602) *(G-7967)*

Carolina Tailors Inc (PA)...252 247-6469
2896 Highway 24 Ste D Newport (28570) *(G-11899)*

Carolina Tape & Supply Corp....................................828 322-3991
502 19th Street Pl Se Hickory (28602) *(G-7968)*

Carolina Tarwheels Whlchair Bs...............................704 791-5803
2404 Lynn Dr Concord (28025) *(G-4225)*

Carolina Tex Sls Gastonia Inc..................................704 739-1646
521 N Sims St Kings Mountain (28086) *(G-9301)*

Carolina Textile Services Inc (PA)............................910 843-3033
Off Hwy 211 Red Springs (28377) *(G-13496)*

Carolina Textile Sls Gastonia, Kings Mountain *Also Called: Carolina Tex Sls Gastonia Inc (G-9301)*

Carolina Timberworks LLC.......................................828 266-9663
210 Industrial Park Way West Jefferson (28694) *(G-15936)*

Carolina Time, Charlotte *Also Called: Carolina Time Equipment Co Inc (G-2409)*

Carolina Time Equipment Co Inc (PA).....................704 536-2700
1801 Norland Rd Charlotte (28205) *(G-2409)*

Carolina Tractor & Eqp Co......................................828 251-2500
40 Interstate Blvd Asheville (28806) *(G-584)*

CAROLINA TRACTOR & EQUIPMENT COMPANY, Asheville *Also Called: Carolina Tractor & Eqp Co (G-584)*

Carolina Trader..910 433-2229
458 Whitfield St Fayetteville (28306) *(G-5785)*

Carolina Traffic Devices Inc....................................704 588-7055
11900 Goodrich Dr Charlotte (28273) *(G-2410)*

Carolina Turkeys, Mount Olive *Also Called: Butterball LLC (G-11657)*

Carolina Underwear, Thomasville *Also Called: Carolina International Inc (G-15197)*

Carolina Underwear Company (PA).......................336 472-7788
110 W Guilford St Thomasville (27360) *(G-15200)*

Carolina Unplugged..336 965-4443
300 Meadowood St Greensboro (27409) *(G-6891)*

Carolina Urban Lumber..704 755-5110
10412 Rodney St Pineville (28134) *(G-12260)*

Carolina Vinyl Printing...910 603-3036
14 Troon Dr Pinehurst (28374) *(G-12218)*

Carolina Vinyl Products, Grifton *Also Called: Englishs All Wood Homes Inc (G-7600)*

Carolina Vinyl Shack LLC.....................................704 788-9493
7300 Flowes Store Rd Concord (28025) *(G-4226)*

Carolina Warp Prints Inc.....................................704 866-4763
221 Meek Rd Gastonia (28056) *(G-6370)*

Carolina Water Consultants LLC.........................828 251-2420
4 Vaughn Cir Fletcher (28732) *(G-5992)*

Carolina Water Jets..704 853-3663
219 Superior Stainless Rd Gastonia (28052) *(G-6371)*

Carolina WD Pdts Mrshville Inc..........................704 624-2119
1112 Doctor Blair Rd Marshville (28103) *(G-10211)*

Carolina Weekly Newspaper Grou......................704 849-2261
10100 Park Cedar Dr Ste 150 Charlotte (28210) *(G-2411)*

Carolina Welding & Cnstr..................................252 814-8740
1806 N Herritage St Kinston (28501) *(G-9352)*

Carolina Whlchair Basktbal Co..........................828 248-2055
629 Hardin Rd Forest City (28043) *(G-6063)*

Carolina Woman Inc 919 869-8200
1506 E Franklin St Ste 103 Chapel Hill (27514) *(G-1998)*

Carolina Wood Residuals LLC 252 633-3374
1815 Asbury Rd Cove City (28523) *(G-4597)*

Carolina Woodcraft LLC 919 585-2563
325 Old York Cir Clayton (27527) *(G-3961)*

Carolina Woodwork & Stair Inc 704 363-5114
309 E Morehead St Apt 918 Charlotte (28202) *(G-2412)*

Carolina Woodworks Trim of NC 252 492-9259
625 Parham Rd Henderson (27536) *(G-7778)*

Carolina Wren Press Inc 919 560-2738
811 9th St Ste 130-127 Durham (27705) *(G-5005)*

Carolina Yachts, Beaufort *Also Called: Harding Enterprise Inc (G-960)*

Carolina Yarn Processors Inc 828 859-5891
250 Screvens Rd Tryon (28782) *(G-15422)*

Carolina Yogurt Inc 828 754-9685
208 Morganton Blvd Sw Lenoir (28645) *(G-9596)*

Carolina York LLC 704 237-0873
1235 East Blvd Ste E Pmb 248 Charlotte (28203) *(G-2413)*

Carolina-Virginia Mfg Co Inc 336 623-1307
2873 Nc Highway 135 Stoneville (27048) *(G-14954)*

Carolinas Cord Blood Bank 919 668-1102
2400 Pratt St Ste 1400 Durham (27705) *(G-5006)*

Carolinas Top Shelf Cust Cabn 704 376-5844
519 Armour Dr Charlotte (28206) *(G-2414)*

Carolinas Top Shelf Custom CA, Charlotte *Also Called: Carolinas Top Shelf Cust Cabn (G-2414)*

Carolinian Pubg Group LLC 919 834-5558
1504 New Bern Ave Raleigh (27610) *(G-12602)*

Carolon Company 336 969-6001
601 Forum Pkwy Rural Hall (27045) *(G-13835)*

Caromed, Raleigh *Also Called: Bar Squared Inc (G-12543)*

Caromed International Inc 919 878-0578
5605 Spring Ct Raleigh (27616) *(G-12603)*

Carotek, Matthews *Also Called: Carotek Inc (G-10238)*

Carotek Inc (HQ) 704 844-1100
700 Sam Newell Rd Matthews (28105) *(G-10238)*

Carpathian Woodworks Inc 919 669-7546
46 Albemarle Dr Clayton (27527) *(G-3962)*

Carpe, Durham *Also Called: Clutch Inc (G-5022)*

Carpenter Co 828 464-9470
2009 Keisler Dairy Rd Conover (28613) *(G-4433)*

Carpenter Co 828 322-6545
30 29th St Nw Hickory (28601) *(G-7969)*

Carpenter Co 336 861-5730
1021 E Springfield Rd Ste 101 High Point (27263) *(G-8286)*

Carpenter Co 828 632-7061
Hwy 90 E Taylorsville (28681) *(G-15133)*

Carpenter Design, Rutherfordton *Also Called: Carpenter Design Inc (G-13869)*

Carpenter Design Inc 828 248-9070
330 Broyhill Rd Rutherfordton (28139) *(G-13869)*

Carpet One, Asheboro *Also Called: Interrs-Exteriors Asheboro Inc (G-446)*

Carpet Rentals Inc 704 872-4461
1002 Winston Ave Statesville (28677) *(G-14773)*

Carpigiani Corporation America, High Point *Also Called: Ali Group North America Corp (G-8240)*

Carport Central, Mount Airy *Also Called: Central Steel Buildings Inc (G-11496)*

Carport Central Inc 980 321-9898
1372 Boggs Dr Mount Airy (27030) *(G-11491)*

Carport Commander LLC 800 688-6151
238 Willow St Ste 102 Mount Airy (27030) *(G-11492)*

Carport Direct Inc 336 715-8217
737 S Main St Mount Airy (27030) *(G-11493)*

Carr Amplifers 919 545-0747
23 Rectory St Ste E Pittsboro (27312) *(G-12334)*

Carr Amplifiers 919 545-0747
433 W Salisbury St Pittsboro (27312) *(G-12335)*

Carr Mill Supplies Inc 336 883-0135
1015 Manley St High Point (27260) *(G-8287)*

Carr Precast Concrete Inc 910 892-1151
7519 Plainview Hwy Dunn (28334) *(G-4856)*

Carraways Sign & WD Crafts LLC 252 292-7141
1303 Gold St N Wilson (27893) *(G-16486)*

Carriage House Furniture Co, Jacksonville *Also Called: World Art Gallery Incorporated (G-9047)*

Carrier Carolinas 336 292-0909
7203 W Friendly Ave Greensboro (27410) *(G-6892)*

Carrier Chiller Op, Charlotte *Also Called: Carrier Corporation (G-2415)*

Carrier Corporation 704 921-3800
9701 Old Statesville Rd Charlotte (28269) *(G-2415)*

Carrier Corporation 704 494-2600
200 Perimeter Park Dr Ste A Morrisville (27560) *(G-11312)*

CARRIER FIRE & SECURITY AMERICAS CORPORATION, Mebane *Also Called: Carrier Fire SEC Americas Corp (G-10404)*

Carrier Fire SEC Americas Corp 919 563-5911
1027 Corporate Park Dr Mebane (27302) *(G-10404)*

Carriff Corporation Inc (PA) 704 888-3330
3500 Fieldstone Trce Midland (28107) *(G-10459)*

Carriff Engineered Fabrics, Midland *Also Called: Carriff Corporation Inc (G-10459)*

Carrington Court Inc 828 396-1049
2 Winchester Ave Granite Falls (28630) *(G-6727)*

Carrol Poultry LLC 347 203-9637
414 Industrial Dr Bladenboro (28320) *(G-1145)*

Carroll Co 919 779-1900
5771 Nc Highway 42 W Garner (27529) *(G-6262)*

Carroll Companies Inc (PA) 828 264-2521
1640 Old 421 S Boone (28607) *(G-1184)*

Carroll Companies Inc 828 466-5489
1226 Fedex Dr Sw Conover (28613) *(G-4434)*

Carroll Leather, Conover *Also Called: Carroll Companies Inc (G-4434)*

Carroll Russell Mfg Inc 919 779-2273
2009 Carr Pur Dr Raleigh (27603) *(G-12604)*

Carroll Signs & Advertising 336 983-3415
151 Jefferson Church Rd Ste B King (27021) *(G-9267)*

Carroll-Baccari Inc (PA) 561 585-2227
110 Commercial Blvd Flat Rock (28731) *(G-5962)*

Carson Dellosa Education, Greensboro *Also Called: Carson-Dellosa Publishing LLC (G-6893)*

Carson Dellosa Education, Greensboro *Also Called: Carson-Dellosa Publishing LLC (G-6894)*

Carson Dellosa Publishing, Greensboro *Also Called: Unique Collating & Bindery Svc (G-7429)*

Carson Dellosa Publishing Co 336 294-8176
3316 Morris Farm Dr Jamestown (27282) *(G-9048)*

Carson-Dellosa Publishing LLC (PA) 336 632-0084
7027 Albert Pick Rd Ste 300 Greensboro (27409) *(G-6893)*

Carson-Dellosa Publishing LLC 336 632-0084
657 Brigham Rd Ste A Greensboro (27409) *(G-6894)*

Carter, Thomasville *Also Called: Tomlinson of Orlando Inc (G-15292)*

Carter Thomas Wayne Sr 336 623-2177
2141 Moir Mill Rd Reidsville (27320) *(G-13513)*

Carter Furniture, Salisbury *Also Called: Contemporary Furnishings Corp (G-13946)*

Carter Millwork Inc 800 861-0734
117 Cedar Lane Dr Lexington (27292) *(G-9690)*

Carter Office Supplies, Kernersville *Also Called: Carter Publishing Company Inc (G-9174)*

Carter Printing 919 373-0531
1105 Great Falls Ct Ste A Knightdale (27545) *(G-9415)*

Carter Printing & Graphics Inc 919 266-5280
1001 Steeple Square Ct Knightdale (27545) *(G-9416)*

Carter Publishing Company Inc 336 993-2161
300 E Mountain St Kernersville (27284) *(G-9174)*

Carter Traveler Division, Gastonia *Also Called: A B Carter Inc (G-6334)*

Carter-Hubbard Publishing Co 336 838-4117
711 Main St North Wilkesboro (28659) *(G-12000)*

Carteret Canvas Company 252 247-9588
122 Old Causeway Rd Atlantic Beach (28512) *(G-828)*

Carteret Publishing Company (PA) 252 726-7081
5039 Executive Dr Ste 300 Morehead City (28557) *(G-11159)*

Carteret Publishing Company 910 326-5066
774 W Corbett Ave Swansboro (28584) *(G-15043)*

Carters Machine Company Inc 704 784-3106
540 Lake Lynn Rd Concord (28025) *(G-4227)*

Carthage Gazette — ALPHABETIC SECTION

Carthage Gazette, West End *Also Called: Seven Lakes News Corporation (G-15932)*

Cartridge World 336 885-0989
2640 Willard Dairy Rd Ste 114 High Point (27265) *(G-8288)*

Carus LLC 704 822-1441
181 Woodlawn St Belmont (28012) *(G-977)*

CARUS LLC, Belmont *Also Called: Carus LLC (G-977)*

Cary Audio Design LLC 919 355-0010
6301 Chapel Hill Rd Raleigh (27607) *(G-12605)*

Cary Keisler Inc 336 586-9333
1372 Tiki Ln Burlington (27215) *(G-1389)*

Cary Manufacturing Corporation 704 527-4402
10815 John Price Rd Ste E Charlotte (28273) *(G-2416)*

Cary Printing 919 266-9005
1528 Crickett Rd Raleigh (27610) *(G-12606)*

Carypress Publishing 919 346-4907
8801 Fast Park Dr Ste 301 Raleigh (27617) *(G-12607)*

Cas Machine Design LLC 919 515-2834
210 Cox Ave Apt A Raleigh (27605) *(G-12608)*

Casa Di Cupcakes 919 255-9994
2120 Woodwyck Way Raleigh (27604) *(G-12609)*

Casablanca 4 LLC 910 702-4399
4805 Wrightsville Ave Wilmington (28403) *(G-16159)*

Cascadas Nye Corporation 919 834-8128
2109 Avent Ferry Rd Ste 103 Raleigh (27606) *(G-12610)*

Cascade Die Casting, High Point *Also Called: Cascade Die Casting Group Inc (G-8289)*

Cascade Die Casting Group Inc 336 882-0186
1800 Albertson Rd High Point (27260) *(G-8289)*

Cascade Die Casting Group Inc 336 882-0186
501 Old Thomasville Rd High Point (27260) *(G-8290)*

Cascades Moulded Pulp Inc 910 997-2775
112 Cascades Way Rockingham (28379) *(G-13621)*

Cascades Tissue Group, Rockingham *Also Called: Cascades Tissue Group - NC Inc (G-13622)*

Cascades Tissue Group - NC Inc 910 895-4033
805 Midway Rd Rockingham (28379) *(G-13622)*

Cascades Tissue Group-Oregon, Wagram *Also Called: Cascades Tssue Group - Ore Inc (G-15521)*

Cascades Tssue Group - Ore Inc 503 397-2900
19320 Airbase Rd Wagram (28396) *(G-15521)*

Casco Signs Inc 704 788-9055
199 Wilshire Ave Sw Concord (28025) *(G-4228)*

Case & Bear Great Homes LLC 704 595-3832
6535 Greenway Bend Dr Charlotte (28226) *(G-2417)*

Case Basket Creations 828 381-4908
4975 J M Craig Rd Granite Falls (28630) *(G-6728)*

Case By Case LLC 910 814-3288
162 Summerwood Ln Lillington (27546) *(G-9846)*

Case Farms, Goldsboro *Also Called: Case Foods Inc (G-6600)*

Case Farms, Troutman *Also Called: Case Farms Processing Inc (G-15371)*

Case Farms LLC 919 735-5010
330 Pecan Rd Dudley (28333) *(G-4841)*

Case Farms LLC 919 658-2252
330 Westbrook Rd Goldsboro (27530) *(G-6599)*

Case Farms LLC 919 635-2390
188 Broadhurst Rd Mount Olive (28365) *(G-11659)*

Case Farms LLC (PA) 704 528-4501
385 Pilch Rd Troutman (28166) *(G-15370)*

Case Farms Processing Inc 704 528-4501
385 Pilch Rd Troutman (28166) *(G-15371)*

Case Foods, Troutman *Also Called: Case Farms LLC (G-15370)*

Case Foods Inc 919 736-4498
259 Sandhill Dr Goldsboro (27530) *(G-6600)*

Case Foods Inc (PA) 704 528-4501
385 Pilch Rd Troutman (28166) *(G-15372)*

Case Green Cabinetry 828 620-9730
104 Lakeshore Dr Asheville (28804) *(G-585)*

Case Smith Inc 336 969-9786
625 Montroyal Rd Rural Hall (27045) *(G-13836)*

Case Specialists 919 818-4476
2033 Longwood Dr Raleigh (27612) *(G-12611)*

Case-Closed Investigations 336 794-2274
5032 Hwy 70 W Morehead City (28557) *(G-11160)*

Caseiro International LLC 919 530-8333
105 Hood St Ste 7 Durham (27701) *(G-5007)*

Cases For A Cause 704 239-3269
1034 Quail Haven Ln Rockwell (28138) *(G-13648)*

Casetec, Mooresville *Also Called: Casetec Precision Machine LLC (G-10899)*

Casetec Precision Machine LLC 704 663-6043
178 Attleboro Pl Mooresville (28117) *(G-10899)*

Casework Etc Inc 910 763-7119
3116 Kitty Hawk Rd Wilmington (28405) *(G-16160)*

Caseworx, Hudson *Also Called: Caldwell Cabinets NC LLC (G-8765)*

Cashiers Crossroads Chronicles, Cashiers *Also Called: Community Newspapers Inc (G-1935)*

Cashiers Printing Inc 828 787-1324
68 Highlands Walk Highlands (28741) *(G-8613)*

Cashiers Printing & Graphics, Highlands *Also Called: Cashiers Printing Inc (G-8613)*

Cashman Inc 252 995-4319
53392 Hwy 12 Frisco (27936) *(G-6176)*

Cast First Stone Ministry 704 437-1053
106 Justin Dr Troutman (28166) *(G-15373)*

Cast Iron Division, Charlotte *Also Called: Charlotte Pipe and Foundry Co (G-2458)*

Cast Iron Elegance Inc 919 662-8777
831 Purser Dr Ste 103 Raleigh (27603) *(G-12612)*

Cast Stone Systems Inc 252 257-1599
532 N Main St Warrenton (27589) *(G-15657)*

Caster House, Greensboro *Also Called: Carolina Material Handling Inc (G-6889)*

Castle Hayne Hardware LLC 910 675-9205
6301 Castle Hayne Rd Castle Hayne (28429) *(G-1945)*

Castle Hayne Yard, Castle Hayne *Also Called: Martin Marietta Materials Inc (G-1954)*

Castle Shirt Company LLC 336 992-7727
621 Indeneer Dr Ste 1 Kernersville (27284) *(G-9175)*

Casual Crates, Seagrove *Also Called: H & H Furniture Mfrs Inc (G-14239)*

Cat Daddy Ventures LLC 252 229-8617
62 Smokemont Dr Arden (28704) *(G-318)*

CAT Logistics Inc 252 447-2490
7970 Hwy 70 E New Bern (28560) *(G-11787)*

Catalent Greenville Inc 732 537-6200
5440 Martin Luther King Jr Hwy Greenville (27834) *(G-7499)*

Catalent Greenville Inc (DH) 252 752-3800
1240 Sugg Pkwy Greenville (27834) *(G-7500)*

Catalent Pharma Solutions LLC 919 481-4855
140 Southcenter Ct Morrisville (27560) *(G-11313)*

Catalent Pharma Solutions LLC 919 481-4855
160 N Pharma Dr Morrisville (27560) *(G-11314)*

Catalent Pharma Solutions Inc 919 465-8206
160 N Pharma Dr Durham (27703) *(G-5008)*

Catalent Pharma Solutions Inc 919 481-2614
120 Southcenter Ct Ste 100 Morrisville (27560) *(G-11315)*

Cataler North America Corp (DH) 828 970-0026
2002 Cataler Dr Lincolnton (28092) *(G-9879)*

Catamount 55, Concord *Also Called: Belle Embroidery LLC (G-4207)*

Catamount Energy Corporation (DH) 802 773-6684
550 S Tryon St Charlotte (28202) *(G-2418)*

Catawampus Press LLC 201 572-3990
1616 S Mineral Springs Rd Durham (27703) *(G-5009)*

Catawba Farms Enterprises LLC 828 464-5780
1670 Southwest Blvd Newton (28658) *(G-11917)*

Catawba Frames Inc 828 459-7717
4827 S Depot St Claremont (28610) *(G-3904)*

Catawba Plant, Claremont *Also Called: Universal Furniture Intl Inc (G-3941)*

Catawba Valley Fabrication Inc 828 459-1191
1823 Brian Dr Ne Conover (28613) *(G-4435)*

Catawba Valley Finishing LLC (PA) 828 464-2252
1609 Northwest Blvd Newton (28658) *(G-11918)*

Catawba Valley Mills, Newton *Also Called: Ashfar Enterprises Inc (G-11913)*

Catawba Valley Quilters Guild 828 322-4517
1880 6th St Nw Hickory (28601) *(G-7970)*

Catawba Vly Youth Soccer Assoc 828 234-7082
3404 6th Street Dr Nw Hickory (28601) *(G-7971)*

Caterpillar, Clayton *Also Called: Caterpillar Inc (G-3963)*

Caterpillar, New Bern *Also Called: CAT Logistics Inc (G-11787)*

ALPHABETIC SECTION

Caterpillar, Sanford *Also Called: Caterpillar Inc (G-14098)*
Caterpillar Authorized Dealer, Charlotte *Also Called: Arrow Equipment LLC (G-2218)*
Caterpillar Inc.. 919 550-1100
  954 Nc Highway 42 E Clayton (27527) *(G-3963)*
Caterpillar Inc.. 919 777-2000
  5000 Womack Rd Sanford (27330) *(G-14098)*
Cates Mechanical Corporation.. 704 458-5163
  3901 Corporation Cir Charlotte (28216) *(G-2419)*
Cathedral Publishing, Charlotte *Also Called: Catholic News and Herald (G-2420)*
Catholic News and Herald.. 704 370-3333
  1123 S Church St Charlotte (28203) *(G-2420)*
Cathtek LLC.. 336 748-0686
  3825 Reidsville Rd Winston Salem (27101) *(G-16649)*
Catlow Inc... 336 894-3367
  7300 W Friendly Ave Greensboro (27410) *(G-6895)*
Caudle Bedding Supplies... 336 498-2600
  216 Russell Walker Ave Randleman (27317) *(G-13458)*
Cauley Construction Company.. 252 522-1078
  2385 Westdowns Ter Kinston (28504) *(G-9353)*
Causa LLC.. 866 695-7022
  9303 Monroe Rd Charlotte (28270) *(G-2421)*
Causekeepers Inc.. 336 824-2518
  5068 Us Highway 64 E Franklinville (27248) *(G-6167)*
Cava Di Pietra Inc.. 910 338-5024
  1502 N 23rd St Wilmington (28405) *(G-16161)*
Cavalier Home Builders LLC.. 252 459-7026
  1001 Eastern Ave Nashville (27856) *(G-11741)*
Cavco Industries Inc... 910 410-5050
  106 Innovative Way Hamlet (28345) *(G-7618)*
Cavco of North Carolina, Hamlet *Also Called: Cavco Industries Inc (G-7618)*
Cavert Red Line Wire Division, Rural Hall *Also Called: Cavert Wire Company Inc (G-13837)*
Cavert Wire Company Inc (HQ).. 800 969-2601
  620 Forum Pkwy Rural Hall (27045) *(G-13837)*
Cavotec USA Inc (DH).. 704 873-3009
  500 S Main St # 1 Mooresville (28115) *(G-10900)*
Cavu Printing Inc... 336 818-9790
  339 Benham Church Rd Elkin (28621) *(G-5614)*
CB Industries... 704 660-1955
  125 Infield Ct Mooresville (28117) *(G-10901)*
CBA Productions Inc.. 703 568-4758
  579 Baywood Rd Fayetteville (28312) *(G-5786)*
CBA Software Inc... 919 289-9820
  512 Grand Oak Dr Hillsborough (27278) *(G-8643)*
Cbd Open Water Diving... 910 232-3692
  262 Battleship Rd Wilmington (28401) *(G-16162)*
Cbdmd, Charlotte *Also Called: Cbdmd Inc (G-2422)*
Cbdmd Inc (PA).. 704 445-3060
  8845 Red Oak Blvd Charlotte (28217) *(G-2422)*
Cbg Draft Services Lc LLC.. 704 727-3300
  1720 Toal St Charlotte (28206) *(G-2423)*
Cbj Transit LLC... 252 417-9972
  1220 Timber Dr E Garner (27529) *(G-6263)*
Cbm, Bessemer City *Also Called: Conner Brothers Machine Co Inc (G-1056)*
Cbr Logging LLC... 252 791-0494
  105 Ange Dr Plymouth (27962) *(G-12368)*
Cbr Signs LLC... 910 794-8243
  5649 Carolina Beach Rd Wilmington (28412) *(G-16163)*
CBS Radio Holdings Inc... 704 319-9369
  1520 South Blvd Ste 300 Charlotte (28203) *(G-2424)*
CBS Windows & Doors, Mooresville *Also Called: Carolina Building Services Inc (G-10897)*
CC, Durham *Also Called: Collegiate Clors Christn Colors (G-5024)*
CC Boats Inc.. 252 482-3699
  140 Midway Dr Edenton (27932) *(G-5509)*
Ccbb Affl With The Duke Univ S, Durham *Also Called: Carolinas Cord Blood Bank (G-5006)*
Ccbcc Inc.. 704 557-4000
  4115 Coca Cola Plz Charlotte (28211) *(G-2425)*
Ccbcc Operations LLC... 704 557-4038
  4115 Coca Cola Plz Charlotte (28211) *(G-2426)*
Ccbcc Operations LLC... 910 582-3543
  1662 E Us 74 Hwy Hamlet (28345) *(G-7619)*
Ccbcc Operations LLC... 704 872-3634
  2111 W Front St Statesville (28677) *(G-14774)*
Ccbcc Operations LLC... 828 687-1300
  36 Clayton Rd Arden (28704) *(G-319)*
Ccbcc Operations LLC... 828 297-2141
  795 Nc Highway 105 Byp Boone (28607) *(G-1185)*
Ccbcc Operations LLC... 828 488-2874
  441 Industrial Park Rd Bryson City (28713) *(G-1321)*
Ccbcc Operations LLC... 704 359-5600
  4690 First Flight Dr Charlotte (28208) *(G-2427)*
Ccbcc Operations LLC (HQ).. 704 364-8728
  4100 Coca Cola Plz Charlotte (28211) *(G-2428)*
Ccbcc Operations LLC... 704 399-6043
  801 Black Satchel Rd Charlotte (28216) *(G-2429)*
Ccbcc Operations LLC... 980 321-3226
  4901a Chesapeake Dr Charlotte (28216) *(G-2430)*
Ccbcc Operations LLC... 919 359-2966
  977 Shotwell Rd Ste 104 Clayton (27520) *(G-3964)*
Ccbcc Operations LLC... 910 483-6158
  800 Tom Starling Rd Fayetteville (28306) *(G-5787)*
Ccbcc Operations LLC... 336 664-1116
  8200 Capital Dr 067 Greensboro (27409) *(G-6896)*
Ccbcc Operations LLC... 828 322-5097
  820 1st Ave Nw Hickory (28601) *(G-7972)*
Ccbcc Operations LLC... 704 225-1973
  4268 Capital Dr Monroe (28110) *(G-10678)*
Ccbcc Operations LLC... 336 789-7111
  2516 W Pine St Mount Airy (27030) *(G-11494)*
Ccbs & Sign Shop Inc... 252 728-4866
  1626 Live Oak St Beaufort (28516) *(G-949)*
CCI Hair Boutique LLC... 407 216-9213
  3059 N Main St Hope Mills (28348) *(G-8735)*
CCL Label... 919 713-0388
  308 S Rogers Ln Raleigh (27610) *(G-12613)*
CCL Label Inc.. 704 714-4800
  4000 Westinghouse Blvd Charlotte (28273) *(G-2431)*
CCL Label Inc.. 919 713-0388
  308 S Rogers Ln Ste 120 Raleigh (27610) *(G-12614)*
CCL Metal Science LLC... 910 299-0911
  520 E Railroad St Clinton (28328) *(G-4090)*
CCM Press LLC... 704 825-9995
  305 Fieldbrook Pl Charlotte (28209) *(G-2432)*
Cco Holdings LLC.. 828 414-4238
  278 Shoppes On The Parkway Rd Blowing Rock (28605) *(G-1155)*
Cco Holdings LLC.. 828 355-4149
  531 W King St Boone (28607) *(G-1186)*
Cco Holdings LLC.. 910 292-4083
  102 W Divine St Dunn (28334) *(G-4857)*
Cco Holdings LLC.. 828 270-7016
  483 Us Highway 70 Sw Hickory (28602) *(G-7973)*
Cco Holdings LLC.. 919 502-4007
  607 W 2nd St Kenly (27542) *(G-9147)*
Cco Holdings LLC.. 828 394-0635
  1048 Harper Ave Nw Lenoir (28645) *(G-9597)*
Cco Holdings LLC.. 704 308-3361
  644 Center Dr Lincolnton (28092) *(G-9880)*
Cco Holdings LLC.. 828 528-4004
  520 Pineola St Newland (28657) *(G-11883)*
Cco Holdings LLC.. 919 200-6260
  466 Vineyard Rdg Siler City (27344) *(G-14402)*
Cco Holdings LLC.. 828 368-4161
  240 Main St W Valdese (28690) *(G-15445)*
CCS International Circuits LLC....................................... 704 907-1208
  1408 Wyndmere Hills Ln Matthews (28105) *(G-10239)*
Ccw, Concord *Also Called: Client Care Web Inc (G-4234)*
CD Dickie & Associates Inc... 704 527-9102
  3400 S Tryon St Ste D Charlotte (28217) *(G-2433)*
CD Snow Hill LLC.. 252 747-5943
  204 Carolina Dr Snow Hill (28580) *(G-14501)*
Cda Inc
  8500 S Tryon St Charlotte (28273) *(G-2434)*

Cdata Software Inc (PA) 919 928-5214
101 Europa Dr Ste 110 Chapel Hill (27517) *(G-1999)*

Cdb Corporation 910 383-6464
2304 Mercantile Dr Ne Leland (28451) *(G-9534)*

CDM Wireless, Louisburg Also Called: Carolina Design & Mfg Inc *(G-9982)*

Cdp, Charlotte Also Called: Consultants In Data Proc Inc *(G-2542)*

Cdp Inc 336 270-6151
4014 Forbes Way Burlington (27215) *(G-1390)*

Cdv LLC (PA) 919 674-3460
2300 Gateway Centre Blvd Ste 200 Morrisville (27560) *(G-11316)*

Ce Kitchen Inc 910 399-2334
306 Old Dairy Rd Wilmington (28405) *(G-16164)*

Ceast USA Inc 704 423-0081
4816 Sirus Ln Charlotte (28208) *(G-2435)*

Cecil Budd Tire Company LLC 919 742-2322
394 Pine Forest Dr Siler City (27344) *(G-14403)*

Cecil-Johnson Mfg Inc 336 431-5233
1445 Jackson Lake Rd High Point (27263) *(G-8291)*

Ceco Friction Products Inc 704 857-1156
2525 N Hwy 29 Landis (28088) *(G-9450)*

Ceco Publishing, Asheville Also Called: Ceco Publishing Inc *(G-586)*

Ceco Publishing Inc (PA) 828 253-2047
208 Elk Park Dr Asheville (28804) *(G-586)*

Ced, Morganton Also Called: Consolidated Elec Distrs Inc *(G-11207)*

Ced Incorporated 336 378-0044
7910 Industrial Village Rd Greensboro (27409) *(G-6897)*

Cedar Creek Pot & Cft Gallery, Creedmoor Also Called: Ceder Creek Gallery & Pottery *(G-4610)*

Cedar Fork Woodworks LLC 910 340-0821
1362 Fountaintown Rd Beulaville (28518) *(G-1092)*

Cedar Hill Studio & Gallery 828 456-6344
196 N Main St Waynesville (28786) *(G-15797)*

Cedar Rock Home Furnishings 828 396-2361
3483 Hickory Blvd Hudson (28638) *(G-8767)*

Cedar Valley Finishing Co Inc 704 289-9546
603 Broome St Monroe (28110) *(G-10679)*

Cedar Valley Hosiery Mill Inc 828 396-1804
3074 Deal Mill Rd Hudson (28638) *(G-8768)*

Cedarlane, Burlington Also Called: Cedarlane Laboratories USA *(G-1391)*

Cedarlane Laboratories USA 336 513-5135
1210 Turrentine St Burlington (27215) *(G-1391)*

Ceder Creek Gallery & Pottery 919 528-1041
1150 Fleming Rd Creedmoor (27522) *(G-4610)*

CEF, Taylorsville Also Called: Custom Educational Furn LLC *(G-15137)*

Cefla Dental Group America 704 731-5293
6125 Harris Technology Blvd Charlotte (28269) *(G-2436)*

Cefla North America Inc 704 598-0020
6125 Harris Technology Blvd Charlotte (28269) *(G-2437)*

Cekal Specialties Inc 704 822-6206
101 Brickyard Rd Mount Holly (28120) *(G-11625)*

Celand Yarn Dyers Inc 336 472-4400
606 Davidson St Thomasville (27360) *(G-15201)*

Celanese 910 343-5000
4600 Us Highway 421 N Wilmington (28401) *(G-16165)*

Celanese, Grover Also Called: Celanese Intl Corp *(G-7606)*

Celanese Advanced Materials, Charlotte Also Called: Pbi Performance Products Inc *(G-3322)*

Celanese Intl Corp 704 480-5798
2523 Blacksburg Rd Grover (28073) *(G-7606)*

Celcore Inc 828 669-4875
3148 Us Highway 70 W Black Mountain (28711) *(G-1122)*

Celebration Candles Inc 610 360-1545
1333 Hydrangea Ct Leland (28451) *(G-9535)*

Celebrity Dairy LLC 919 742-4931
198 Celebrity Dairy Way Siler City (27344) *(G-14404)*

Celeros Flow Technology LLC (PA) 704 752-3100
14045 Ballantyne Corporate Pl Ste 300 Charlotte (28277) *(G-2438)*

Celesta's, Asheville Also Called: Monogram Asheville *(G-704)*

Celestial Cocoa Co (PA) 704 871-2495
165 Bowman Rd Statesville (28625) *(G-14775)*

Celestial Products Inc 540 338-4040
9632 Skybluff Cir Huntersville (28078) *(G-8801)*

Celestial Publishing 704 701-2027
208 Tournament Dr Sw Concord (28025) *(G-4229)*

Celgard LLC 704 588-5310
13800 S Lakes Dr Charlotte (28273) *(G-2439)*

Celgard LLC (HQ) 800 235-4273
11430 N Community House Rd Ste 350 Charlotte (28277) *(G-2440)*

Celgard LLC 704 720-5200
390 Business Blvd Nw Concord (28027) *(G-4230)*

Cell Microsystems Inc 919 608-2035
801 Capitola Dr Ste 10 Durham (27713) *(G-5010)*

Cellar 910 399-2997
12 Nun St Wilmington (28401) *(G-16166)*

Cellar 4201 LLC 336 699-6030
4201 Apperson Rd East Bend (27018) *(G-5464)*

Celplor LLC 919 961-1961
115 Centrewest Ct Ste B Cary (27513) *(G-1726)*

Celtic Ceramics 919 510-6817
4140 Mardella Dr Raleigh (27613) *(G-12615)*

Celtic Ocean International Inc 828 299-9005
4 Celtic Dr Arden (28704) *(G-320)*

Cem Corporation (HQ) 704 821-7015
3100 Smith Farm Rd Matthews (28104) *(G-10307)*

Cem Holdings Corporation (PA) 704 821-7015
3100 Smith Farm Rd Matthews (28104) *(G-10308)*

Cem-102 Pharmaceuticals Inc 919 576-2306
6320 Quadrangle Dr Ste 360 Chapel Hill (27517) *(G-2000)*

Cemco, Lincolnton Also Called: Umi Company Inc *(G-9932)*

Cemco Electric Inc 704 504-0294
10913 Office Park Dr Charlotte (28273) *(G-2441)*

Cemco Partitions LLC 336 643-6316
5340 Us Highway 220 N Summerfield (27358) *(G-14978)*

Cemco Systems, Charlotte Also Called: Cemco Electric Inc *(G-2441)*

Cemex, Harrisburg Also Called: Cemex Materials LLC *(G-7704)*

Cemex Cnstr Mtls ATL LLC 704 873-3263
2067 Salisbury Hwy Statesville (28677) *(G-14776)*

Cemex Materials LLC 704 455-1100
5601 Pharr Mill Rd Harrisburg (28075) *(G-7704)*

Cemex Materials LLC 800 627-2986
208 Randolph St Thomasville (27360) *(G-15202)*

Cemex Materials LLC 252 243-6153
1600 Thorne Ave S Wilson (27893) *(G-16487)*

Cempra Pharmaceuticals Inc 919 803-6882
6320 Quadrangle Dr Ste 360 Chapel Hill (27517) *(G-2001)*

Cenerx Biopharma Inc 919 234-4072
270 Cornerstone Dr Ste 103 Cary (27519) *(G-1727)*

Cengage Learning Inc 919 829-8181
1791 Varsity Dr Ste 200 Raleigh (27606) *(G-12616)*

Centaur Laboratories Inc 919 249-5072
7715 Peck Watts Rd Oxford (27565) *(G-12119)*

Center for Creative Leadership (PA) 336 288-7210
1 Leadership Pl Greensboro (27410) *(G-6898)*

Center For Ecozoic Studies 919 929-4116
2516 Winningham Rd Chapel Hill (27516) *(G-2002)*

Center For Orthotic & Prosthet 919 585-4173
166 Springbrook Ave Ste 203 Clayton (27520) *(G-3965)*

Center For Orthtic Prsthtic CA (HQ) 919 797-1230
4702 Creekstone Dr Durham (27703) *(G-5011)*

Center For Orthtic Prsthtic Ca, Durham Also Called: Center For Orthtic Prsthtic CA *(G-5011)*

Centeredge Software 336 598-5934
5050 Durham Rd Roxboro (27574) *(G-13798)*

Centice Corporation 919 653-0424
7283 Nc Highway 42 Ste 102 Raleigh (27603) *(G-12617)*

Centor Inc 704 896-7535
5900 Harris Technology Blvd Ste G Charlotte (28269) *(G-2442)*

Centos Project, Raleigh Also Called: Red Hat Inc *(G-13196)*

Central ARC Wldg Solutions LLC 704 858-1614
12524 Vantage Point Ln Huntersville (28078) *(G-8802)*

Central Carolina Btlg Co Inc 919 542-3226
1506 Mays Chapel Rd Bear Creek (27207) *(G-937)*

Central Carolina Concrete LLC (HQ) 336 315-0785
296 Edwardia Dr Greensboro (27409) *(G-6899)*

ALPHABETIC SECTION — Chandler Concrete

Central Carolina Forklift LLC 919 545-9749
  156 Carl Foushee Rd Moncure (27559) *(G-10618)*

Central Carolina Hosiery Inc (PA) 910 428-9688
  211 Shady Oak Dr Biscoe (27209) *(G-1106)*

Central Carolina Printing LLC 910 572-3344
  464 Cheshire Pl Asheboro (27205) *(G-413)*

Central Carolina Products Inc 336 226-1449
  2804 Troxler Rd Burlington (27215) *(G-1392)*

Central Carolina Products Inc (PA) 336 226-0005
  250 W Old Glencoe Rd Burlington (27217) *(G-1393)*

Central Carolina Steel, Stanley Also Called: Metal Roofing Systems LLC *(G-14702)*

Central Concrete, Asheboro Also Called: Chandler Concrete Inc *(G-414)*

Central Machine Company 336 855-0022
  2509 Surrett Dr Archdale (27263) *(G-273)*

Central Site Group LLC 336 380-4121
  15 Scotland St Ocean Isle Beach (28469) *(G-12088)*

Central States Mfg Inc 336 719-3280
  751 Piedmont Triad West Dr Mount Airy (27030) *(G-11495)*

Central Steel Buildings Inc 336 789-7896
  181 Woltz St Mount Airy (27030) *(G-11496)*

Central Tool & Mfg Co Inc 828 328-2383
  1021 17th St Sw Hickory (28602) *(G-7974)*

Centric Brands LLC 646 582-6000
  620 S Elm St Ste 395 Greensboro (27406) *(G-6900)*

Centro Inc 319 626-3200
  2725 Kelly Blvd Claremont (28610) *(G-3905)*

Centurion Industries Inc 704 867-2304
  1990 Industrial Pike Rd Gastonia (28052) *(G-6372)*

Century Case Goods Division, Hickory Also Called: Century Furniture LLC *(G-7976)*

Century Furniture LLC 828 326-8410
  535 27th St Nw Hickory (28601) *(G-7975)*

Century Furniture LLC 828 326-8201
  420 12th Street Dr Nw Hickory (28601) *(G-7976)*

Century Furniture LLC 828 326-8535
  25 18th St Nw Hickory (28601) *(G-7977)*

Century Furniture LLC 828 326-8458
  3086 Main Ave Nw Hickory (28601) *(G-7978)*

Century Furniture LLC 828 326-8410
  420 27th St Nw Hickory (28601) *(G-7979)*

Century Furniture LLC 828 326-8650
  820 21st St Nw Hickory (28601) *(G-7980)*

Century Furniture LLC 828 326-8300
  401 11th St Nw Hickory (28601) *(G-7981)*

Century Furniture LLC 828 326-8495
  126 33rd St Nw Hickory (28601) *(G-7982)*

Century Furniture LLC 336 889-8286
  200 Steele St High Point (27260) *(G-8292)*

Century Furniture Industries, Hickory Also Called: Cv Industries Inc *(G-8001)*

Century Furniture LLC (HQ) 828 267-8739
  401 11th St Nw Hickory (28601) *(G-7983)*

Century Furniture Uphl Plant, Hickory Also Called: Century Furniture LLC *(G-7975)*

Century Hosiery Inc (PA) 336 859-3806
  651 Garner Rd Denton (27239) *(G-4729)*

Century Place Apparel, Charlotte Also Called: Century Place II LLC *(G-2443)*

Century Place II LLC 704 790-0970
  10220 Western Ridge Rd Ste A Charlotte (28273) *(G-2443)*

Century Stone LLC 919 774-3334
  624 Fairway Dr Sanford (27330) *(G-14099)*

Century Textile Mfg Inc 704 869-6660
  803 N Oakland St Gastonia (28054) *(G-6373)*

Ceprint Solutions Inc 336 956-6327
  564 Dixon St Lexington (27292) *(G-9691)*

Ceramawire 252 335-7411
  786 Pitts Chapel Rd Elizabeth City (27909) *(G-5533)*

Ceramco Incorporated 704 588-4814
  11009 Carpet St Charlotte (28273) *(G-2444)*

Ceres Turf Inc 910 256-8974
  2312 N 23rd St Wilmington (28401) *(G-16167)*

Certainteed LLC 828 459-0556
  2651 Penny Rd Claremont (28610) *(G-3906)*

Certainteed LLC 336 696-2007
  1149 Abtco Rd North Wilkesboro (28659) *(G-12001)*

Certainteed LLC 919 603-1971
  200 Certainteed Dr Oxford (27565) *(G-12120)*

Certification Services International LLC 828 458-1573
  510 La White Dr Bldg 12 Fletcher (28732) *(G-5993)*

Certified Fiberglass Inc 252 241-9641
  1063 Hwy 58 Cape Carteret (28584) *(G-1630)*

Certified Lawnmower Inc 704 527-2765
  124 Hubbard St Belmont (28012) *(G-978)*

Certified Machining Inc 919 777-9608
  2710 Wilkins Dr Sanford (27330) *(G-14100)*

Certirx Corporation 919 354-1029
  2 Davis Dr Rtp (27709) *(G-13830)*

Ces, Mount Airy Also Called: Advanced Electronic Svcs Inc *(G-11473)*

Cessna Grnsboro Cttion Svc Ctr, Greensboro Also Called: Textron Aviation Inc *(G-7398)*

CF Steel LLC 704 516-1750
  12322 Old Camden Rd Midland (28107) *(G-10460)*

CFI Ready Mix LLC 910 814-4238
  304 E Mcneill St Lillington (27546) *(G-9847)*

CFS Press Slim Ray 828 505-1030
  8 Pelham Rd Asheville (28803) *(G-587)*

Cgc, Pineville Also Called: Container Graphics Corp *(G-12261)*

Cgi Inc 704 932-1820
  712 N Cannon Blvd Kannapolis (28083) *(G-9115)*

Cgmi Acquisition Company LLC 919 533-6123
  1318 Shields Rd Kernersville (27284) *(G-9176)*

CGR Products Inc (PA) 336 621-4568
  4655 Us Highway 29 N Greensboro (27405) *(G-6901)*

Ch Publishing 336 886-1984
  701 Shamrock Rd High Point (27265) *(G-8293)*

Chaddock, Morganton Also Called: LLC Ferguson Copeland *(G-11229)*

Chaddock Home, Morganton Also Called: Guy Chaddock and Company LLC *(G-11217)*

Chadsworth Incorporated 910 763-7600
  420 Raleigh St Ste A Wilmington (28412) *(G-16168)*

Chained Dragon LLC 919 243-0974
  70 Plott Hound Dr Clayton (27520) *(G-3966)*

Chair Man 610 809-0871
  118 Fort Hugar Way Manteo (27954) *(G-10127)*

Challnge Prtg of Crlnas Inc Th 919 777-2820
  5905 Clyde Rhyne Dr Sanford (27330) *(G-14101)*

Chamblee Graphics, Raleigh Also Called: S Chamblee Incorporated *(G-13221)*

Chameleon Wraps & Designs 910 544-9801
  3273 Fire Tower Rd Orrum (28369) *(G-12115)*

Champion, Charlotte Also Called: Champion LLC *(G-2445)*

Champion, Lillington Also Called: Champion Home Builders Inc *(G-9848)*

Champion Burley 919 693-6285
  1168 Us Highway 158 Ste A Oxford (27565) *(G-12121)*

Champion & Company, Oxford Also Called: Champion Burley *(G-12121)*

Champion Home Builders Inc 910 893-5713
  4055 Us 401 S Lillington (27546) *(G-9848)*

Champion Industries, Winston Salem Also Called: Ali Group North America Corp *(G-16596)*

Champion Industries Inc 336 661-1556
  3765 Champion Blvd Winston Salem (27105) *(G-16650)*

Champion LLC 704 392-1038
  8844 Mount Holly Rd Charlotte (28214) *(G-2445)*

Champion Media LLC 910 506-3021
  915 S Main St Ste H Laurinburg (28352) *(G-9473)*

Champion Powdercoating Inc 704 866-8148
  1220 Industrial Ave Gastonia (28054) *(G-6374)*

Champion Products, Laurel Hill Also Called: Hanesbrands Inc *(G-9460)*

Champion Thread Company (PA) 704 867-6611
  165 Bluedevil Dr Gastonia (28056) *(G-6375)*

Champion Win Co of Charlotte 704 398-0085
  9100 Perimeter Woods Dr Ste C Charlotte (28216) *(G-2446)*

Champion Wndows Sding Ptio Rom, Charlotte Also Called: Champion Win Co of Charlotte *(G-2446)*

Championx LLC 704 506-4830
  2000 Oaks Pkwy Belmont (28012) *(G-979)*

Chandler Con Pdts of Chrstnber 336 226-1181
  1006 S Church St Burlington (27215) *(G-1394)*

Chandler Concrete, Biscoe Also Called: Chandler Concrete Co Inc *(G-1107)*

Chandler Concrete, Greensboro *Also Called: Chandler Concrete Inc (G-6902)*
Chandler Concrete & Bldg Sup, Salisbury *Also Called: Chandler Concrete Inc (G-13939)*
Chandler Concrete Co... 919 742-2627
  804 S Chatham Ave Siler City (27344) *(G-14405)*
Chandler Concrete Co Inc... 910 974-4744
  1517 Us Highway 220 Alt S Biscoe (27209) *(G-1107)*
Chandler Concrete Co Inc (PA)... 336 272-6127
  1006 S Church St Burlington (27215) *(G-1395)*
Chandler Concrete Company, Pittsboro *Also Called: Chandler Concrete Inc (G-12336)*
Chandler Concrete High Co... 828 264-8694
  805 State Farm Rd Ste 203 Boone (28607) *(G-1187)*
Chandler Concrete Inc.. 336 625-1070
  205 W Academy St Asheboro (27203) *(G-414)*
Chandler Concrete Inc.. 336 982-8760
  1992 Nc Highway 16 N Crumpler (28617) *(G-4628)*
Chandler Concrete Inc.. 919 598-1424
  2700 E Pettigrew St Durham (27703) *(G-5012)*
Chandler Concrete Inc.. 336 342-5771
  6354 Main St Eden (27288) *(G-5488)*
Chandler Concrete Inc.. 336 222-9716
  301 W River St Graham (27253) *(G-6683)*
Chandler Concrete Inc.. 336 297-1179
  300 S Swing Rd Greensboro (27409) *(G-6902)*
Chandler Concrete Inc.. 919 644-1058
  1501 Old North Carolina Hwy 10 Hillsborough (27278) *(G-8644)*
Chandler Concrete Inc.. 919 542-4242
  246 Chatham Forest Dr Pittsboro (27312) *(G-12336)*
Chandler Concrete Inc.. 336 599-8343
  121 Burch Ave Roxboro (27573) *(G-13799)*
Chandler Concrete Inc.. 704 636-4711
  400 N Long St Salisbury (28144) *(G-13939)*
Chandler Concrete Inc.. 336 372-4348
  23 Birch Ln Sparta (28675) *(G-14591)*
CHANDLER CONCRETE INC, Eden *Also Called: Chandler Concrete Inc (G-5488)*
CHANDLER CONCRETE INC, Hillsborough *Also Called: Chandler Concrete Inc (G-8644)*
CHANDLER CONCRETE INC, Roxboro *Also Called: Chandler Concrete Inc (G-13799)*
CHANDLER CONCRETE INC, Sparta *Also Called: Chandler Concrete Inc (G-14591)*
Chandler Foods Inc... 336 299-1934
  2727 Immanuel Rd Greensboro (27407) *(G-6903)*
Chanmala Gallery Fine Art Prtg.. 704 975-7695
  306 S White St Wake Forest (27587) *(G-15539)*
Channeladvisor, Morrisville *Also Called: Channeladvisor Corporation (G-11317)*
Channeladvisor Corporation (DH).. 919 228-4700
  1010 Sync St Morrisville (27560) *(G-11317)*
Channeltivity LLC.. 704 408-3560
  301 E John St Matthews (28106) *(G-10240)*
Chaos Worldwide LLC... 336 558-5654
  208 Sandbar Cir Apt 2f Greensboro (27406) *(G-6904)*
Chaotic Terrain Press.. 828 575-7300
  62 Wolf Rd Asheville (28805) *(G-588)*
Chapel Hill Magazine, Chapel Hill *Also Called: Shannon Media Inc (G-2071)*
Chapman Brothers Logging LLC.. 828 437-6498
  8849 Gus Peeler Rd Connelly Springs (28612) *(G-4398)*
Chapman Machine... 704 739-1834
  109 Joanne Dr Kings Mountain (28086) *(G-9302)*
Chapman Welding LLC... 919 951-8131
  4501 Gails Trl Efland (27243) *(G-5524)*
Charah LLC... 704 731-2300
  4235 Southstream Blvd Ste 180 Charlotte (28217) *(G-2447)*
Charah LLC... 502 873-6993
  175 Steam Plant Rd Mount Holly (28120) *(G-11626)*
Charge Onsite LLC.. 888 343-2688
  1015 East Blvd Charlotte (28203) *(G-2448)*
Charles & Colvard, Morrisville *Also Called: Charles & Colvard Ltd (G-11318)*
Charles & Colvard Ltd (PA)... 919 468-0399
  170 Southport Dr Morrisville (27560) *(G-11318)*
Charles & Colvard Direct LLC... 919 468-0399
  300 Perimeter Park Dr Ste A Morrisville (27560) *(G-11319)*
Charles Craft Inc (PA)... 910 844-3521
  21381 Charles Craft Ln Laurinburg (28352) *(G-9474)*
Charles Ferguson Logging... 336 921-3126
  245 Jack Russell Rd Moravian Falls (28654) *(G-11144)*
Charles Hill Enterprises... 828 665-2116
  145 Brooks Cove Rd Candler (28715) *(G-1573)*
Charles Stewart Co... 828 322-9464
  931 18th Street Pl Nw Hickory (28601) *(G-7984)*
Charles White Woodworking.. 252 714-9124
  3024 Church Street Ext Winterville (28590) *(G-16996)*
Charlesandcolvardcom LLC... 877 202-5467
  170 Southport Dr Morrisville (27560) *(G-11320)*
Charlies Heating & Cooling LLC... 336 260-1973
  8277 Bethel South Fork Rd Snow Camp (27349) *(G-14495)*
Charlott Custom Woodworks.. 704 634-0863
  20428 Willow Pond Rd Cornelius (28031) *(G-4535)*
Charlotte Aarrow LLC... 704 909-7692
  401 Hawthorne Ln Ste 110-256 Charlotte (28204) *(G-2449)*
Charlotte Block Inc... 704 399-4526
  5125 Rozzelles Ferry Rd Charlotte (28216) *(G-2450)*
Charlotte Branch, Charlotte *Also Called: Form Tech Concrete Forms Inc (G-2787)*
Charlotte Business Journal, Charlotte *Also Called: American City Bus Journals Inc (G-2182)*
Charlotte Cabinetry LLC... 704 966-2500
  156 S South St Ste 201 Gastonia (28052) *(G-6376)*
Charlotte Compressor Llc.. 704 399-9993
  338 S Sharon Amity Rd Ste 201 Charlotte (28211) *(G-2451)*
Charlotte Instyle Inc... 704 665-8880
  801 Pressley Rd Ste 1071 Charlotte (28217) *(G-2452)*
Charlotte Metal Finishing Inc... 704 732-7570
  2708 E Main St Lincolnton (28092) *(G-9881)*
Charlotte Observer.. 704 358-5000
  550 S Caldwell St Ste 1010 Charlotte (28202) *(G-2453)*
Charlotte Observer, Charlotte *Also Called: Charlotte Observer Pubg Co (G-2455)*
Charlotte Observer, Charlotte *Also Called: Charlotte Observer Pubg Co (G-2456)*
Charlotte Observer, Matthews *Also Called: Charlotte Observer Pubg Co (G-10241)*
Charlotte Observer Pubg Co... 704 987-3660
  9140 Research Dr Ste C1 Charlotte (28262) *(G-2454)*
Charlotte Observer Pubg Co... 704 572-0747
  3100 Yorkmont Rd Charlotte (28208) *(G-2455)*
Charlotte Observer Pubg Co (DH)... 704 358-5000
  550 S Caldwell St Ste 1010 Charlotte (28202) *(G-2456)*
Charlotte Observer Pubg Co... 704 358-6020
  10810 Independence Pointe Pkwy Ste H Matthews (28105) *(G-10241)*
Charlotte Parent, Charlotte *Also Called: Carolina Parenting Inc (G-2402)*
Charlotte Pipe and Foundry Co (PA)...................................... 704 372-5030
  2109 Randolph Rd Charlotte (28207) *(G-2457)*
Charlotte Pipe and Foundry Co.. 704 348-5416
  1335 S Clarkson St Charlotte (28208) *(G-2458)*
Charlotte Pipe and Foundry Co.. 704 372-3650
  4210 Old Charlotte Hwy Monroe (28110) *(G-10680)*
Charlotte Pipe and Foundry Co.. 704 887-8015
  10145 Lighthouse Rd Oakboro (28129) *(G-12069)*
Charlotte Pipe and Foundry Com... 704 379-0700
  2109 Randolph Rd Charlotte (28207) *(G-2459)*
Charlotte Pipe Inc... 704 291-3269
  Monroe (28111) *(G-10681)*
Charlotte Plastics, Monroe *Also Called: Charlotte Pipe and Foundry Co (G-10680)*
Charlotte Plating Inc.. 704 552-2100
  8421 Kirchenbaum Dr Charlotte (28210) *(G-2460)*
Charlotte Post, Charlotte *Also Called: Charlotte Post Pubg Co Inc (G-2461)*
Charlotte Post Pubg Co Inc.. 704 376-0496
  5118 Princess St Charlotte (28269) *(G-2461)*
Charlotte Printing Company Inc (PA)..................................... 704 888-5181
  3751 Dakeita Cir Concord (28025) *(G-4231)*
Charlotte Publishing Company.. 704 547-0900
  9140 Research Dr Charlotte (28262) *(G-2462)*
Charlotte Recycling Plant, Charlotte *Also Called: Caraustar Industries Inc (G-2385)*
Charlotte Shutter and Shades.. 336 351-3391
  1825 Pell Rd Westfield (27053) *(G-15951)*
Charlotte Sock Basket.. 704 910-2388
  9200 Harris Corners Pkwy Ste B Charlotte (28269) *(G-2463)*
Charlotte Springfree Trmpoline.. 704 312-1212
  9848 Rea Rd Ste E Charlotte (28277) *(G-2464)*

ALPHABETIC SECTION — Chicopee

Charlotte T Shirt Authority, Charlotte *Also Called: Kna (G-3058)*
Charlotte Tent & Awning Co, Charlotte *Also Called: DLM Sales Inc (G-2647)*
Charlotte Trimming Company Inc (PA) 704 529-8427
 900 Pressley Rd Charlotte (28217) *(G-2465)*
Charlotte Weekly 704 849-2261
 9506 Monroe Rd Ste A Charlotte (28270) *(G-2466)*
Charlotte World, The, Charlotte *Also Called: World Newspaper Publishing (G-3824)*
Charlottes Crown, Matthews *Also Called: Jody Stowe (G-10256)*
Charltte McKlnburg Dream Ctr I 704 421-4440
 129 W Trade St Charlotte (28202) *(G-2467)*
Charmed Wright LLC 704 850-8186
 108 Saye Pl Mooresville (28115) *(G-10902)*
Charming Pot Candle Co LLC 828 768-4827
 427 Luther Rd Candler (28715) *(G-1574)*
Charnel Inc 910 763-8476
 110 Dock St Wilmington (28401) *(G-16169)*
Charter Dura-Bar Inc 704 637-1906
 770 Cedar Springs Rd Salisbury (28147) *(G-13940)*
Charter Furniture, Siler City *Also Called: Lodging By Liberty Inc (G-14423)*
Charter Jet Transport Inc 704 359-8833
 5400 Airport Dr Charlotte (28208) *(G-2468)*
Charter Medical Ltd 336 768-6447
 3948 Westpoint Blvd Ste A Winston Salem (27103) *(G-16651)*
Chartreuse Shepherd 252 532-2708
 200 Mill St Weldon (27890) *(G-15881)*
Chase Corporation 828 396-2121
 3908 Hickory Blvd Granite Falls (28630) *(G-6729)*
Chase Corporation 828 855-9316
 1954 Main Ave Se Hickory (28602) *(G-7985)*
Chase Corporation 828 649-5578
 1527 7th Street Ln Se Hickory (28602) *(G-7986)*
Chase Corporation 828 726-6023
 2012 Hickory Blvd Sw Lenoir (28645) *(G-9598)*
Chase Laminating Inc 828 632-6666
 138 Wittenburg Rd Taylorsville (28681) *(G-15134)*
Chase-Logeman Corporation 336 665-0754
 303 Friendship Dr Greensboro (27409) *(G-6905)*
Chateau DAx USA Ltd 336 885-9777
 1838 Eastchester Dr Ste 106 High Point (27265) *(G-8294)*
Chateau Jourdain LLC 786 273-2869
 2406 Swan Creek Rd Jonesville (28642) *(G-9094)*
Chatham News, Siler City *Also Called: Chatham News Publishing Co (G-14406)*
Chatham News Publishing Co (PA) 919 663-4042
 303 W Raleigh St Siler City (27344) *(G-14406)*
Chatham Steel Corporation 912 233-4182
 2702 Cheek Rd Durham (27704) *(G-5013)*
Chatsworth Products Inc 252 514-2779
 701 Industrial Dr New Bern (28562) *(G-11788)*
Chatter Free Tling Sltions Inc 828 659-7379
 1877 Rutherford Rd Marion (28752) *(G-10148)*
Chaudhry Meat Company 919 742-9292
 380 Stockyard Rd Staley (27355) *(G-14663)*
Chd, Cherryville *Also Called: Custom Hydraulics & Design (G-3865)*
Cheadles Auto Art & Sign 828 254-2600
 6 Business Park Cir Arden (28704) *(G-321)*
Check Printers Inc 336 724-5980
 2709 Boulder Park Ct Winston Salem (27101) *(G-16652)*
Checkfree Mobius, Durham *Also Called: Checkfree Services Corporation (G-5014)*
Checkfree Services Corporation 919 941-2640
 4819 Emperor Blvd Ste 300 Durham (27703) *(G-5014)*
Cheeky Lather LLC 919 672-8071
 4117 High Rock Rd Efland (27243) *(G-5525)*
Cheerwine, Salisbury *Also Called: Carolina Beverage Corporation (G-13932)*
Chef Martini LLC 919 327-3183
 1908 Falls Of Neuse Rd Ste 215 Raleigh (27615) *(G-12618)*
Chelsea Therapeutics International Ltd 704 341-1516
 3530 Toringdon Way Ste 200 Charlotte (28277) *(G-2469)*
Chem-Tech Solutions Inc 704 829-9202
 427 Brook St Belmont (28012) *(G-980)*
Chem-Tex Laboratories Inc 706 602-8600
 180 Gee Rd Concord (28025) *(G-4232)*
Chemist 828 505-8778
 151 Coxe Ave Asheville (28801) *(G-589)*
Chemogenics Biopharma LLC (PA) 919 323-8133
 3325 Durham Chapel Hill Blvd Ste 250 Durham (27707) *(G-5015)*
Chemol Company Inc 336 333-3050
 2300 Randolph Ave Greensboro (27406) *(G-6906)*
Chemours Company 910 483-4681
 22828 Nc Highway 87 W Fayetteville (28306) *(G-5788)*
Chemours Company Fc LLC 910 678-1314
 22828 Nc Highway 87 W Fayetteville (28306) *(G-5789)*
Chemring Detection Systems, Charlotte *Also Called: Chemring Snsors Elctrnic Syste (G-2470)*
Chemring Snsors Elctrnic Syste 980 235-2200
 4205 Westinghouse Commons Dr Charlotte (28273) *(G-2470)*
Chemtech Industrial Inc 919 400-5743
 61 T Kemp Rd Louisburg (27549) *(G-9983)*
Chemtech North Carolina LLC 910 514-9575
 1030 S Main St Lillington (27546) *(G-9849)*
Chemtrade Logistics (us) Inc (HQ) 773 646-2500
 814 Tyvola Rd Ste 126 Charlotte (28217) *(G-2471)*
Chentech Corp 919 749-8765
 524 Texanna Way Holly Springs (27540) *(G-8694)*
Chep Recycled Pallet Solu 704 718-8199
 5808 Long Creek Park Dr Charlotte (28269) *(G-2472)*
Cherokee Instruments Inc (PA) 919 552-0554
 100 Logan Ct Angier (27501) *(G-137)*
Cherokee Publications 828 627-2424
 66 Luftee Lake Rd Cherokee (28719) *(G-3854)*
Cherokee Publications Inc 828 627-2424
 186 Bobcat Trl Clyde (28721) *(G-4121)*
Cherokee Publishing Co Inc 919 674-6020
 301 Cascade Pointe Ln Cary (27513) *(G-1728)*
Cherokee Transfer Station 828 497-4519
 Aloveit Church Rdd Cherokee (28719) *(G-3855)*
Cherry Contracting Inc 336 969-1825
 8640 Broad St Rural Hall (27045) *(G-13838)*
Cherry Precast, Rural Hall *Also Called: Cherry Contracting Inc (G-13838)*
Cherryrich Publishing LLC 336 587-0805
 2303 Phoenix Dr Greensboro (27406) *(G-6907)*
Cherryville Distrg Co Inc 704 435-9692
 322 E Main St Cherryville (28021) *(G-3863)*
Chesapeake Graphics Inc 704 827-7172
 8261 Nc 73 Hwy Ste A Stanley (28164) *(G-14688)*
Chesnick Corporation 919 231-2899
 3236 Lake Woodard Dr Raleigh (27604) *(G-12619)*
Chester Lewis Newsome 919 605-4887
 200 Lancaster Dr Greenville (27834) *(G-7501)*
Chesterfield Wood Products Inc 828 433-0042
 1810 Us 64 Morganton (28655) *(G-11204)*
Chestnut Land Company 828 299-9108
 3 S Tunnel Rd Ste B-8 Asheville (28805) *(G-590)*
Chestnut Trail Vineyard LLC 336 655-4755
 640 Cedar Grove Church Rd Mocksville (27028) *(G-10563)*
Chf Industries Inc 212 951-7800
 9741 Southern Pine Blvd Ste A Charlotte (28273) *(G-2473)*
CHI Resources 828 835-7878
 1115 Horton Rd Murphy (28906) *(G-11707)*
Chic Monogram 910 431-8704
 1222 Columbus Cir Apt C Wilmington (28403) *(G-16170)*
Chicadoo 704 562-8796
 8040 Providence Rd Ste 100 Charlotte (28277) *(G-2474)*
Chicago Pneumatic Tool Co LLC 704 504-6937
 11313 Steele Creek Rd Charlotte (28273) *(G-2475)*
Chicago Tube and Iron, Locust *Also Called: Chicago Tube and Iron Company (G-9956)*
Chicago Tube and Iron Company 704 781-2060
 421 Browns Hill Rd Locust (28097) *(G-9956)*
Chichibone Inc (PA) 919 785-0090
 Kernersville (27284) *(G-9177)*
Chichibone Inc 919 785-0090
 600 Airport Blvd Ste 1400 Morrisville (27560) *(G-11321)*
Chicopee, Charlotte *Also Called: Pgi Polymer Inc (G-3336)*

Chicopee Inc 919 894-4111
 1203 Chicopee Rd Benson (27504) *(G-1032)*

Chicopee Inc (DH) 704 697-5100
 9335 Harris Corners Pkwy Ste 300 Charlotte (28269) *(G-2476)*

Chief Corporation 704 916-4521
 10926 David Taylor Dr Ste 300 Charlotte (28262) *(G-2477)*

Chief Feed Mill, Rose Hill Also Called: Murphy-Brown LLC *(G-13779)*

Childers Concrete Company 336 841-3111
 200 Wise Ave High Point (27260) *(G-8295)*

Childress Vineyards LLC 336 236-9463
 1000 Childress Vinyard Rd Lexington (27295) *(G-9692)*

Childress Winery LLC 336 775-0522
 9160 Hampton Rd Lexington (27295) *(G-9693)*

Chimerix Inc (PA) 919 806-1074
 2505 Meridian Pkwy Ste 100 Durham (27713) *(G-5016)*

Chimneyrock Storage 828 685-2893
 175 Fascination Dr Hendersonville (28792) *(G-7836)*

China Free Press Inc 919 308-9826
 4711 Hope Valley Rd 122 Durham (27707) *(G-5017)*

Chirazyme Labs Inc 252 717-1112
 1520 Whootentown Rd Washington (27889) *(G-15687)*

Chiron America Inc (DH) 704 587-9526
 10950 Withers Cove Park Dr Charlotte (28278) *(G-2478)*

Chiron Publications LLC 828 285-0838
 451 Beaucatcher Rd Asheville (28805) *(G-591)*

Chocolate Fetish LLC 828 258-2353
 36 Haywood St Asheville (28801) *(G-592)*

Chocolate Heaven Company 828 421-2042
 2254 Dillard Rd Highlands (28741) *(G-8614)*

Chocolate Smiles Village LLC 919 469-5282
 312 W Chatham St Ste 101 Cary (27511) *(G-1729)*

Choice Awards & Signs 704 844-0860
 4036 Matthews Indian Trail Rd Matthews (28104) *(G-10309)*

Choice Printing LLC 919 790-0680
 4100 Wingate Dr Raleigh (27609) *(G-12620)*

Choice USA Beverage Inc 704 861-1029
 809 E Franklin Blvd Gastonia (28054) *(G-6377)*

Choice USA Beverage Inc (PA) 704 823-1651
 603 Groves St Lowell (28098) *(G-10007)*

Choice USA Beverage Inc 704 487-6951
 2440 S Lafayette St Shelby (28152) *(G-14294)*

Chopin Vodka 336 707-8305
 4 Asheland Ridge Ct Greensboro (27410) *(G-6908)*

Choppers and Hotrods 336 993-3939
 1527 Union Cross Rd Kernersville (27284) *(G-9178)*

Chowan Herald, Edenton Also Called: Cox Nrth Crlina Pblcations Inc *(G-5510)*

Chris Isom Inc 336 629-0240
 1228 Green Farm Rd Asheboro (27205) *(G-415)*

Chrisco Machine Shop LLC 828 428-9966
 4280 Maiden Hwy Lincolnton (28092) *(G-9882)*

Christian Focus Magazine 252 240-1656
 706 Wagon Cir Morehead City (28557) *(G-11161)*

Christine N Honeywell PT 802 496-6509
 76 Pine Lake Dr Whispering Pines (28327) *(G-15953)*

Christopher Ridley 919 291-9999
 8426 Old Ponderosa Cir Raleigh (27603) *(G-12621)*

Chroma Color Corporation 336 629-9184
 1134 Nc Highway 49 S Asheboro (27205) *(G-416)*

Chroma Color Corporation 704 637-7000
 100 E 17th St Salisbury (28144) *(G-13941)*

Chrome Bubbles By Maurice 704 224-8866
 7233 Point Lake Dr # 108 Charlotte (28227) *(G-2479)*

Chrome Man 704 550-6423
 10090 Bethel Church Rd Midland (28107) *(G-10461)*

Chromed Out Frame Covers Inc 704 813-8811
 7900 Waterford Tide Loop Apt 3121 Charlotte (28226) *(G-2480)*

Chronicle Mill Land LLC 704 527-3227
 3826 S New Hope Rd Ste 4 Gastonia (28056) *(G-6378)*

Chronicle Research Inc 919 259-0970
 409 Walnut Woods Dr Morrisville (27560) *(G-11322)*

Chronicle-Of-Victoriacom 336 258-2022
 110 S Arlington Ave Jonesville (28642) *(G-9095)*

Chronicles 252 617-1774
 121 Mendover Dr Jacksonville (28546) *(G-8995)*

Chrysalis, Morganton Also Called: Material Return LLC *(G-11231)*

Chrysler Freight Liner, Cleveland Also Called: Daimler Truck North Amer LLC *(G-4071)*

Cht R Beitlich Corporation 704 523-4242
 5046 Old Pineville Rd Charlotte (28217) *(G-2481)*

Chudy Group LLC 262 279-5307
 106 Roche Dr Durham (27703) *(G-5018)*

Church & Church Lumber LLC 336 838-1256
 185 Hensley Eller Rd Millers Creek (28651) *(G-10492)*

Church & Church Lumber LLC 336 973-4297
 Brown Ford Rd Wilkesboro (28697) *(G-16016)*

Church & Church Lumber LLC (PA) 336 973-5700
 863 New Browns Ford Rd Wilkesboro (28697) *(G-16017)*

Church Initiative Inc 919 562-2112
 250 S Allen Rd Wake Forest (27587) *(G-15540)*

Church Production Magazine, Raleigh Also Called: Production Media Inc *(G-13149)*

Chushion Division, High Point Also Called: Snyder Paper Corporation *(G-8539)*

CIC, Concord Also Called: Controls Instrumentation Inc *(G-4243)*

Cicero Inc (PA) 919 380-5000
 2500 Regency Pkwy Cary (27518) *(G-1730)*

Cider Bros LLC 919 943-9692
 599 S Railroad St Lexington (27292) *(G-9694)*

Cii Technologies, Fairview Also Called: Te Connectivity Corporation *(G-5719)*

Cincinnati Thermal Spray Inc 910 675-2909
 11766 Nc Hwy 210 Rocky Point (28457) *(G-13744)*

Cincro, Liberty Also Called: Leggett & Platt Incorporated *(G-9819)*

Cindy Blackburn 336 643-3822
 7650 Anthony Rd Kernersville (27284) *(G-9179)*

Cindys Souther Scents 828 492-0562
 191 Miller Cove Rd Canton (28716) *(G-1609)*

Cinema III Theaters, Whiteville Also Called: J L Powell & Co Inc *(G-15967)*

Cintas, Greensboro Also Called: Cintas Corporation No 2 *(G-6909)*

Cintas Corporation No 2 .... 336 632-4412
 4345 Federal Dr Greensboro (27410) *(G-6909)*

Cinters Inc 336 267-3051
 4501 New Bern Ave # 130-308 Raleigh (27610) *(G-12622)*

Cintoms Inc 828 684-1317
 3080 Sweeten Creek Rd Asheville (28803) *(G-593)*

Circa 1801 .... 828 397-7003
 1 Jacquard Dr Connelly Springs (28612) *(G-4399)*

Circle Graphics Inc 919 864-4518
 10700 World Trade Blvd Raleigh (27617) *(G-12623)*

Circor Precision Metering LLC (DH) 704 289-6511
 1710 Airport Rd Monroe (28110) *(G-10682)*

Circor Precision Metering LLC 919 774-7667
 5910 Elwin Buchanan Dr Sanford (27330) *(G-14102)*

Circor Pumping Technologies, Monroe Also Called: Circor Pumps North America LLC *(G-10684)*

Circor Pumps North America LLC (DH) 704 289-6511
 1710 Airport Rd Monroe (28110) *(G-10683)*

Circor Pumps North America LLC 877 853-7867
 1710 Airport Rd Monroe (28110) *(G-10684)*

Circuit Board Assemblers Inc 919 556-7881
 130 Mosswood Blvd Youngsville (27596) *(G-17077)*

Circuits, Indian Trail Also Called: Hitech Circuits Inc *(G-8939)*

Cisco Systems, Carolina Beach Also Called: Cisco Systems Inc *(G-1635)*

Cisco Systems, Charlotte Also Called: Cisco Systems Inc *(G-2482)*

Cisco Systems, Morrisville Also Called: Cisco Systems Inc *(G-11323)*

Cisco Systems, Morrisville Also Called: Cisco Systems Inc *(G-11324)*

Cisco Systems Inc 910 707-1052
 1004 North Carolina Ave Carolina Beach (28428) *(G-1635)*

Cisco Systems Inc 704 338-7350
 1900 South Blvd Ste 200 Charlotte (28203) *(G-2482)*

Cisco Systems Inc 919 392-2000
 7100 Kit Creek Rd Morrisville (27560) *(G-11323)*

Cisco Systems Inc 919 392-2000
 7025 Kit Creek Rd Morrisville (27560) *(G-11324)*

Citgo Quik Lube of Clayton 919 550-0935
 11133 Us 70 Business Hwy W Clayton (27520) *(G-3967)*

ALPHABETIC SECTION

Citi Energy LLC.. 336 379-0800
2309 W Cone Blvd Ste 200 Greensboro (27408) *(G-6910)*

Citilift Company.. 704 241-6477
4732 West Blvd Ste D Charlotte (28208) *(G-2483)*

Citizen Media Inc.. 704 363-6062
403 N Old Statesville Rd Huntersville (28078) *(G-8803)*

Citrix Sharefile, Raleigh *Also Called: Cloud Sftwr Group Holdings Inc (G-12631)*

Citrix System... 919 607-9973
1304 Dexter Ridge Dr Holly Springs (27540) *(G-8695)*

City Biscuit Bus, Charlotte *Also Called: Sistas 4 Life Food Svcs LLC (G-3557)*

City Compressor Rebuilders (PA).......................... 704 947-1811
9750 Twin Lakes Pkwy Charlotte (28269) *(G-2484)*

City Compressor Rebuilders................................ 704 947-1811
9750 Twin Lakes Pkwy Charlotte (28269) *(G-2485)*

City Graphics Inc.. 704 529-6448
3139 Westinghouse Blvd Ste C Charlotte (28273) *(G-2486)*

City Machine Company Inc.................................. 828 754-9661
723 Virginia St Sw Lenoir (28645) *(G-9599)*

City of Charlotte-Atando.................................. 704 336-2722
1031 Atando Ave Charlotte (28206) *(G-2487)*

City of Graham... 336 570-6811
111 E Crescent Square Dr Graham (27253) *(G-6684)*

City of Greensboro... 336 373-5855
1041 Battleground Ave Greensboro (27408) *(G-6911)*

City of Lexington.. 336 248-3945
425 Carolina Ave Lexington (27292) *(G-9695)*

City of Morganton.. 828 584-1460
100 Coulter St Morganton (28655) *(G-11205)*

City of Shelby... 704 484-6840
824 W Grover St Shelby (28150) *(G-14295)*

City Prints LLC.. 404 273-5741
5008 Helena Park Ln Matthews (28105) *(G-10242)*

Cityview Magazine, Fayetteville *Also Called: Cityview Publishing LLC (G-5790)*

Cityview Publishing LLC.................................... 910 423-6500
2533 Raeford Rd Ste A Fayetteville (28305) *(G-5790)*

Civentichem Usa LLC.. 919 672-8865
329 Matilda Pl Cary (27513) *(G-1731)*

Cives Corp... 919 518-2140
1621 Morning Mountain Rd Raleigh (27614) *(G-12624)*

CJ Partners LLC.. 336 838-3080
1702 W Us Highway 421 P Wilkesboro (28697) *(G-16018)*

CJ Stallings Logging Inc................................... 252 297-2272
1307 Acorn Hill Rd Belvidere (27919) *(G-1021)*

Cjc Enterprises.. 919 266-3158
7608 Ligon Mill Rd Wake Forest (27587) *(G-15541)*

Cjk Custom Printing and D.................................. 910 488-1288
2110 Murchison Rd Unit A Fayetteville (28301) *(G-5791)*

Cjm Industries LLC... 704 506-5926
276 Whippoorwill Rd Mooresville (28117) *(G-10903)*

Cjr Products Inc... 336 766-2710
6206 Hacker Bend Ct Winston Salem (27103) *(G-16653)*

CJS Welding.. 252 972-5711
4946 Temperance Hall Rd Elm City (27822) *(G-5648)*

Cjt Machine, Hendersonville *Also Called: Cjt Machine Inc (G-7837)*

Cjt Machine Inc.. 828 376-3693
1172 Terrys Gap Rd Hendersonville (28792) *(G-7837)*

Ckke Publishing.. 704 236-5981
6415 Yateswood Dr Charlotte (28212) *(G-2488)*

Cks Packaging.. 704 663-6510
289 Rolling Hill Rd Mooresville (28117) *(G-10904)*

CKS Packaging Inc.. 336 578-5800
943 Trollingwood Road Graham (27253) *(G-6685)*

CKS Packaging Inc.. 704 663-6510
289 Rolling Hill Rd Mooresville (28117) *(G-10905)*

Cla Properties LLC... 336 476-7828
200 Echo Trl Thomasville (27360) *(G-15203)*

Clapp Fertilizer and Trckg Inc............................. 336 449-6103
2225 Herron Rd Whitsett (27377) *(G-15986)*

Clar-Mar Inc... 704 435-9776
3912 Tryon Courthouse Rd Cherryville (28021) *(G-3864)*

Clarcor, Washington *Also Called: Clarcor Eng MBL Solutions LLC (G-15688)*

Clarcor Eng MBL Solutions LLC.............................. 860 992-3496
230 Clarks Neck Rd Washington (27889) *(G-15688)*

Claremont Products LLC..................................... 704 325-3580
2932 Bethany Church Rd Claremont (28610) *(G-3907)*

Clariant, Charlotte *Also Called: Clariant Corporation (G-2491)*

Clariant Corporation....................................... 704 331-7000
4331 Chesapeake Dr Charlotte (28216) *(G-2489)*

Clariant Corporation....................................... 704 371-3272
11701 Mount Holly Rd Charlotte (28214) *(G-2490)*

Clariant Corporation (HQ).................................. 704 331-7000
500 E Morehead St Ste 400 Charlotte (28202) *(G-2491)*

Clariant Corporation....................................... 704 235-5700
337 Timber Rd Mooresville (28115) *(G-10906)*

Clariant Corporation....................................... 704 822-2100
625 E Catawba Ave Mount Holly (28120) *(G-11627)*

Clarios LLC.. 866 589-8883
9844 Southern Pine Blvd Charlotte (28273) *(G-2492)*

Clarios LLC.. 336 884-5832
211 S Hamilton St High Point (27260) *(G-8296)*

Clarios LLC.. 336 761-1550
2701 Johnson Controls Dr Kernersville (27284) *(G-9180)*

Clarios LLC.. 252 754-0782
4125 Bayswater Rd Winterville (28590) *(G-16997)*

Clarity Vision of Smithfield............................... 919 938-6101
1680 E Booker Dairy Rd Smithfield (27577) *(G-14454)*

Clark Art Shop Inc... 919 832-8319
12705 Scenic Dr Raleigh (27614) *(G-12625)*

Clark Co Cstm Trim & Wdwkg Inc............................. 704 905-7131
3031 Valley Acres Dr Midland (28107) *(G-10462)*

Clark Communications, Asheville *Also Called: Clarks Printing Service Inc (G-594)*

Clark Sign Corporation..................................... 336 431-4944
11530 N Main St Archdale (27263) *(G-274)*

Clark Tire & Auto Service, Boone *Also Called: Mr Tire Inc (G-1225)*

Clarke Harland Corp.. 210 697-8888
4475 Premier Dr High Point (27265) *(G-8297)*

Clarks Printing Service Inc................................ 828 254-1432
2 Westside Dr Asheville (28806) *(G-594)*

Clarolux Inc... 336 378-6800
2501 Greengate Dr Greensboro (27406) *(G-6912)*

Clary Lumber Company....................................... 252 537-2558
204 Mitchell St Gaston (27832) *(G-6330)*

Classic Address Signs...................................... 919 734-4482
697 Sandhill Dr Dudley (28333) *(G-4842)*

Classic Car Metal & Parts LLC.............................. 919 567-0693
3600 Knightcroft Pl Fuquay Varina (27526) *(G-6187)*

Classic Carburetor Rebuilders.............................. 336 613-5715
1909 Stovall St Eden (27288) *(G-5489)*

Classic Cleaning LLC....................................... 800 220-7101
8601 Six Forks Rd Ste 400 Raleigh (27615) *(G-12626)*

Classic Industrial Services................................ 919 209-0909
1305 S Brightleaf Blvd Ste 103 Smithfield (27577) *(G-14455)*

Classic Industrial Services, Smithfield *Also Called: Classic Industrial Services (G-14455)*

Classic Leather Inc (PA)................................... 828 328-2046
309 Simpson St Sw Conover (28613) *(G-4436)*

Classic Molders, Monroe *Also Called: Rs Industries Inc (G-10800)*

Classic Packaging Company.................................. 336 922-4224
5570 Bethania Rd Pfafftown (27040) *(G-12187)*

Classic Scent.. 828 645-5171
72 Hillcrest Dr Weaverville (28787) *(G-15841)*

Classic Seafood Group Inc.................................. 252 746-2818
7178 Nc 11 S Ayden (28513) *(G-849)*

Classic Sign Services LLC.................................. 704 401-1466
2242 W Roosevelt Blvd Ste F Monroe (28110) *(G-10685)*

Classic Steel Buildings Inc................................ 252 465-4184
530 Folly Rd Sunbury (27979) *(G-14995)*

Classic Wood Manufacturing................................. 336 691-1344
1006 N Raleigh St Greensboro (27405) *(G-6913)*

Classical Elements... 828 575-9145
9 Sweeten Creek Xing Asheville (28803) *(G-595)*

Classics, High Point *Also Called: Swaim Inc (G-8559)*

Classy Dolls Massage & Btq LLC............................. 336 209-3933
1901 Ashwood Ct Ste E Greensboro (27455) *(G-6914)*

ALPHABETIC SECTION

Classy Glass Inc 828 452-2242
  12 Cougar Ct Waynesville (28786) *(G-15798)*

Clausen Carolina Lasers, Raleigh *Also Called: Carolina Lasers (G-12599)*

Clausen Craftworks LLC 704 252-5048
  900 Pressley Rd Ste C Charlotte (28217) *(G-2493)*

Clay County Food Pantry Inc 828 389-1657
  2278 Hinton Center Rd Hayesville (28904) *(G-7761)*

Clay County Progress, Hayesville *Also Called: Community Newspapers Inc (G-7763)*

Clay Creek Athletics, Burlington *Also Called: Fuller Specialty Company Inc (G-1417)*

Clay Kinnakeet Inc 252 995-0101
  40462 N End Rd Avon (27915) *(G-844)*

Clay Taylor Products Inc 704 636-2411
  1225 Chuck Taylor Ln Salisbury (28147) *(G-13942)*

Claybourn Walters Log Co Inc 910 628-7075
  16071 Nc Highway 130 E Fairmont (28340) *(G-5701)*

Claybrook Tire Inc 336 573-3135
  101 N Glenn St Stoneville (27048) *(G-14955)*

Claypro LLC 828 301-6309
  343 Warren Plains Norlina Rd Norlina (27563) *(G-11995)*

Clayton & Co, High Point *Also Called: Oakhurst Company Inc (G-8468)*

Clayton Electric Mtr Repr Inc 336 584-3756
  1407 N Nc Highway 87 Elon College (27244) *(G-5664)*

Clayton Homes Inc 828 667-8701
  651 Smoky Park Hwy Candler (28715) *(G-1575)*

Clayton Homes Inc 828 684-1550
  5250 Hendersonville Rd Fletcher (28732) *(G-5994)*

Clayton Welding 252 717-5909
  451 Barwick Dr Washington (27889) *(G-15689)*

Clean and Vac 919 753-7951
  2013 Sterling Hill Dr Fuquay Varina (27526) *(G-6188)*

Clean As A Whistle 919 949-7738
  706 Justice St Durham (27704) *(G-5019)*

Clean Catch Fish Market LLC 704 333-1212
  2820 Selwyn Ave Ste 150 Charlotte (28209) *(G-2494)*

Clean Green Inc 919 596-3500
  928 Harvest Rd Durham (27704) *(G-5020)*

Clean Green Environmental Svcs, Durham *Also Called: Clean Green Inc (G-5020)*

Clean Green Sustainable Lf LLC 855 946-8785
  610 N Elam Ave Greensboro (27408) *(G-6915)*

Clean Press 4 Less 919 942-4141
  11312 Us 15 501 N Chapel Hill (27517) *(G-2003)*

Clean Solutions LLC 919 391-8047
  6525 Providence Farm Ln Apt 5115 Charlotte (28277) *(G-2495)*

Clean-Sweep Solutions Inc 469 450-8317
  1017 Main Campus Dr Raleigh (27606) *(G-12627)*

Cleanaire Inc 252 623-4010
  112 S Respess St Washington (27889) *(G-15690)*

Clear Channel Communications, Waynesville *Also Called: Wmxf AM 1400 (G-15834)*

Clear Defense LLC 336 370-1699
  2000 N Church St Greensboro (27405) *(G-6916)*

Clear Path Recycling LLC 877 387-3738
  3500 Cedar Creek Rd Fayetteville (28312) *(G-5792)*

Clear Stone Coating Inc 424 543-0811
  608 Wahlbrink Dr Wake Forest (27587) *(G-15542)*

Clear-Flo Air Filters, Charlotte *Also Called: United Air Filter Company Corp (G-3750)*

Clearlight Glass and Mirror, Kernersville *Also Called: Cgmi Acquisition Company LLC (G-9176)*

Clearwater Paper Shelby LLC 704 476-3802
  671 Washburn Switch Rd Shelby (28150) *(G-14296)*

Clearwater Services LLC 704 995-9260
  563 Webb Rd Concord (28025) *(G-4233)*

Cleaver Returns Inc 630 508-8062
  608 Bristlecone Pine Dr Fuquay Varina (27526) *(G-6189)*

Clement Pappas Nc LLC 856 455-1000
  125 Industrial Park Rd Hendersonville (28792) *(G-7838)*

Clemmons Courier, Mocksville *Also Called: Davie County Publishing Co (G-10565)*

Clemmons Hardwoods Cabinet Sp 336 773-0551
  790 E 21st St Winston Salem (27105) *(G-16654)*

Clemmons Pallet Skid Works Inc 336 766-5462
  3449 Hwy 158 E Clemmons (27012) *(G-4034)*

Cleos Alpacas LLC 704 663-9785
  585 Isle Of Pines Rd Mooresville (28117) *(G-10907)*

Cleveland Compounding Inc 704 487-1971
  701 E Grover St # 2 Shelby (28150) *(G-14297)*

Cleveland Freightliner Truck 704 645-5000
  11550 Statesville Blvd Cleveland (27013) *(G-4070)*

Cleveland Lumber Company (PA) 704 487-5263
  217 Arrowood Dr Shelby (28150) *(G-14298)*

Cleveland Yutaka Corporation 704 480-9290
  2081 W Dixon Blvd Shelby (28152) *(G-14299)*

Cleveland-Cliffs Piedmont, Newton *Also Called: Cleveland-Cliffs Plate LLC (G-11919)*

Cleveland-Cliffs Plate LLC 828 464-9214
  2027 S Mclin Creek Rd Newton (28658) *(G-11919)*

Click Electronics LLC 704 840-6855
  4030 Wake Forest Rd Ste 349 Raleigh (27609) *(G-12628)*

Client Care Web Inc 704 787-9901
  4078 Morris Burn Dr Sw Concord (28027) *(G-4234)*

Clifford W Estes Co Inc 336 622-6410
  2637 Old 421 Rd Staley (27355) *(G-14664)*

Clift Industries Inc 704 752-0031
  201 Westland Farm Rd Mount Holly (28120) *(G-11628)*

Climate Seal, Charlotte *Also Called: Envirnmental Win Solutions LLC (G-2717)*

Cline Printing Inc 704 394-8144
  3445 Carolina Ave Ste A Charlotte (28208) *(G-2496)*

Clinetic Inc 513 295-1332
  520 Guilford Cir Raleigh (27608) *(G-12629)*

Clinical Workflow Consulting, Cary *Also Called: Siemens Med Solutions USA Inc (G-1887)*

Clinicians Advocacy Group Inc 704 751-9515
  1433 Emerywood Dr Ste A Charlotte (28210) *(G-2497)*

Clinton Grains, Garland *Also Called: Garland Farm Supply Inc (G-6244)*

Clinton Press Inc 336 275-8491
  2100 Tennyson Dr Greensboro (27410) *(G-6917)*

Clondalkin Pharma & Healthcare 336 292-4555
  1072 Boulder Rd Greensboro (27409) *(G-6918)*

Closets By Design 704 361-6424
  1108 Continental Blvd Ste A Charlotte (28273) *(G-2498)*

Closure Medical Corporation 919 876-7800
  5250 Greens Dairy Rd Raleigh (27616) *(G-12630)*

Cloth Barn Inc 919 735-3643
  1701 E Ash St Goldsboro (27530) *(G-6601)*

Clothes Cleaning System LLC 252 243-3752
  4475 Technology Dr Nw Wilson (27896) *(G-16488)*

Cloud Nine Foods Inc 817 909-8988
  160 Live Oak Rd Newport (28570) *(G-11900)*

Cloud Pharmaceuticals Inc 919 558-1254
  6 Davis Dr Durham (27709) *(G-5021)*

Cloud Sftwr Group Holdings Inc 919 839-6139
  120 S West St Raleigh (27603) *(G-12631)*

Cloud Software Group Inc 919 969-6500
  200 W Franklin St Ste 250 Chapel Hill (27516) *(G-2004)*

Cloud Stream Systems LLC 704 916-9664
  415 Williams Rd Harrisburg (28075) *(G-7705)*

Cloud9 Coatings LLc 704 252-0287
  11219 Stony Path Dr Charlotte (28214) *(G-2499)*

Cloudgenera Inc 980 332-4040
  1824 Statesville Ave Ste 103 Charlotte (28206) *(G-2500)*

Clover Garden Soaps 828 970-7289
  506 E Main St Maiden (28650) *(G-10105)*

Cloverdale Co Inc Roanoke Co, Newport *Also Called: Veneer Technologies Inc (G-11910)*

Cloverleaf Mixing Inc 336 765-7900
  121 Cloverleaf Dr Winston Salem (27103) *(G-16655)*

Clt 2016 Inc 704 886-1555
  1836 Equitable Pl Charlotte (28213) *(G-2501)*

Clt Machine LLc 704 778-8305
  14604 Arlandes Dr Charlotte (28278) *(G-2502)*

Club The Nantahala Bicycle Inc 828 524-4900
  1863 Georgia Rd Franklin (28734) *(G-6119)*

Clutch Inc 919 448-8654
  120 W Parrish St Durham (27701) *(G-5022)*

Clutch Climbing Gear LLC 336 262-9719
  1215 Rom Eller Rd Ferguson (28624) *(G-5957)*

Clyde Moore Logging, Whiteville *Also Called: H Clyde Moore Jr (G-15965)*

Clyde Union (us) Inc (HQ) 704 808-3000
  14045 Ballantyne Corporate Pl Ste 300 Charlotte (28277) *(G-2503)*

ALPHABETIC SECTION — Coatings and Adhesives Corp

Clydeunion Pumps, Charlotte Also Called: Clyde Union (us) Inc *(G-2503)*
Clydeunion Pumps Inc.. 704 808-3848
13320 Ballantyne Corporate Pl Charlotte (28277) *(G-2504)*
CM Supply, Robbinsville Also Called: Robbinsville Cstm Molding Inc *(G-13610)*
CM Welding.. 704 791-0572
9851 Reed Mine Rd Midland (28107) *(G-10463)*
CMA Signs LLC.. 919 245-8339
610 Meadowlands Dr Hillsborough (27278) *(G-8645)*
CMC, Waynesville Also Called: Sanders Industries Inc *(G-15820)*
CMC Rebar.. 704 865-8571
2528 N Chester St Gastonia (28052) *(G-6379)*
CMC Rebar, Gastonia Also Called: Commercial Metals Company *(G-6381)*
CMC Sencon Inc (PA).. 919 938-3216
132 Citation Ln Smithfield (27577) *(G-14456)*
Cmd Land Services LLC.. 919 554-2281
532 S Wingate St Wake Forest (27587) *(G-15543)*
CMF, Lincolnton Also Called: Charlotte Metal Finishing Inc *(G-9881)*
Cmfi, Youngsville Also Called: Carolina Machining Fabrication *(G-17075)*
CMH, Rockwell Also Called: CMH Manufacturing Inc *(G-13649)*
CMH Manufacturing Inc.. 704 279-4659
508 Palmer Rd Rockwell (28138) *(G-13649)*
CMI Enterprises.. 305 685-9651
135 Pine St Forest City (28043) *(G-6064)*
CMI Plastics, Ayden Also Called: Consolidated Models Inc *(G-851)*
CMI Plastics Inc.. 252 746-2171
222 Pepsi Way Ayden (28513) *(G-850)*
Cmisolutions Inc.. 704 759-9950
7520 E Independence Blvd Ste 400 Charlotte (28227) *(G-2505)*
Cml Micro Circuit USA.. 336 744-5050
486 N Patterson Ave Ste 301 Winston Salem (27101) *(G-16656)*
Cmm Quarterly Inc.. 704 995-3007
13720 Woody Point Rd Charlotte (28278) *(G-2506)*
Cmp Pharma Inc.. 252 753-7111
8026 East Marlboro Rd Farmville (27828) *(G-5732)*
CMS Associates Inc.. 919 365-0881
7308 Siemens Rd Ste D Wendell (27591) *(G-15895)*
CMS Printing Services, Raeford Also Called: Currie Motorsports Inc *(G-12418)*
CMS Tool and Die Inc.. 910 458-3322
1331 Bridge Barrier Rd Carolina Beach (28428) *(G-1636)*
Cmt Metal Finishes.. 828 400-0626
1570 S Main St Waynesville (28786) *(G-15799)*
Cmw Holding, Salisbury Also Called: Lgc Consulting Inc *(G-14003)*
Cmw Manufacturing LLC.. 704 216-0171
1217 Speedway Blvd Salisbury (28146) *(G-13943)*
Cmw Mfg LLC.. 330 283-5551
9821 Longstone Ln Charlotte (28277) *(G-2507)*
CNA Technology LLC.. 954 312-1200
220 Indl Blvd Greenville (27834) *(G-7502)*
Cnc, Maiden Also Called: Carolina Nonwovens LLC *(G-10104)*
Cnc Creations.. 704 508-2668
120 Corporate Dr Troutman (28166) *(G-15374)*
Cnc Laser Shop, Wilmington Also Called: Hanover Iron Works Shtmtl Inc *(G-16246)*
Cnc Performance Eng LLC.. 704 599-2555
11125 Metromont Pkwy Charlotte (28269) *(G-2508)*
Cnc-Ke Inc.. 704 333-0145
1340 Amble Dr Charlotte (28206) *(G-2509)*
Cnd, Oxford Also Called: Revlon Consumer Products Corp *(G-12150)*
Cni Regional, Franklin Also Called: Community Newspapers Inc *(G-6121)*
Co-Da, Indian Trail Also Called: Audio Vdeo Concepts Design Inc *(G-8921)*
Coalition Targets, Concord Also Called: Atwell Fabrication LLC *(G-4201)*
Coalogix Inc.. 704 827-8933
11707 Steele Creek Rd Charlotte (28273) *(G-2510)*
Coast Lamp Manufacturing Inc.. 828 648-7876
35 Church St Canton (28716) *(G-1610)*
Coast To Coast Carports Inc.. 336 783-3015
170 Holly Springs Rd Mount Airy (27030) *(G-11497)*
COAST TO COAST CARPORTS INC., Mount Airy Also Called: Coast To Coast Carports Inc *(G-11497)*
Coast To Coast Lea & Vinyl Inc.. 336 886-5050
1022 Porter St High Point (27263) *(G-8298)*
Coastal Agrobusiness Inc.. 828 697-2220
814 Mcmurray Rd Flat Rock (28731) *(G-5963)*
Coastal Agrobusiness Inc (PA).. 252 238-7391
112 Staton Rd Greenville (27834) *(G-7503)*
Coastal Agrobusiness Inc.. 252 798-3481
12011 Nc 125 Hamilton (27840) *(G-7613)*
Coastal Awngs Hrrcane Shutters, Morehead City Also Called: Coastal Awnings Inc *(G-11162)*
Coastal Awnings Inc.. 252 222-0707
5300 High St Unit 0 Morehead City (28557) *(G-11162)*
Coastal Cabinetry Inc.. 910 367-8864
5017 Songline St Shallotte (28470) *(G-14271)*
Coastal Cabinets, Wilmington Also Called: Mike Powell Inc *(G-16324)*
Coastal Cabinets & Granite LLC.. 252 717-0611
2845b Edwards Drive Simpson (27879) *(G-14437)*
Coastal Cabinets of New Bern.. 252 514-5030
121 Premier Dr New Bern (28562) *(G-11789)*
Coastal Canvas, Beaufort Also Called: Coastal Canvas Mfg Inc *(G-950)*
Coastal Canvas Mfg Inc.. 252 728-4946
1403 Harkers Island Rd Beaufort (28516) *(G-950)*
Coastal Carolina Clean Pwr LLC.. 910 296-1909
1838 N Nc 11 903 Hwy Kenansville (28349) *(G-9141)*
Coastal Carolina Cutng Boards, Holly Ridge Also Called: Dean Company of North Carolina *(G-8681)*
Coastal Carolina Gin, Pantego Also Called: Coastal Carolina Gin LLC *(G-12162)*
Coastal Carolina Gin LLC.. 252 943-6990
4851 Terra Ceia Rd Pantego (27860) *(G-12162)*
Coastal Carolina Loggin.. 252 474-2165
250 Aurora Rd Ernul (28527) *(G-5686)*
Coastal Carolina Winery.. 843 443-9463
10301 Carriage Ct Cornelius (28031) *(G-4536)*
Coastal Custom Wood Works LLC.. 252 675-8732
111 Premier Dr New Bern (28562) *(G-11790)*
Coastal Fabrica Tion.. 910 399-4460
1409 Audubon Blvd Wilmington (28403) *(G-16171)*
Coastal Fish Prints LLC.. 910 200-7005
1675 Corcus Ferry Rd Hampstead (28443) *(G-7643)*
Coastal Impressions Inc.. 252 480-1717
3022 S Croatan Hwy Nags Head (27959) *(G-11719)*
Coastal Machine & Welding Inc.. 910 754-6476
146 Wall St Shallotte (28470) *(G-14272)*
Coastal Millwork Supply Co.. 910 763-3300
1301 S 13th St Wilmington (28401) *(G-16172)*
Coastal Office Eqp & Computers.. 252 335-9427
501 E Church St Ste A Elizabeth City (27909) *(G-5534)*
Coastal Precast Systems LLC.. 910 444-4682
5125 Us Highway 421 N Wilmington (28401) *(G-16173)*
Coastal Press Inc.. 252 726-1549
502 Arendell St Morehead City (28557) *(G-11163)*
Coastal Protein Products Inc.. 910 567-6102
1600 Martin Rd Godwin (28344) *(G-6577)*
Coastal Proteins, Godwin Also Called: Kansas City Sausage Co LLC *(G-6578)*
Coastal Sales Inc.. 252 717-3542
164 Periwinkle Ln Washington (27889) *(G-15691)*
Coastal Tides Soap Candles LLC.. 910 833-2132
5305 Lord Tennyson Dr Wilmington (28405) *(G-16174)*
Coastal Treated Products LLC.. 252 410-0180
1433 Georgia Ave Roanoke Rapids (27870) *(G-13571)*
Coastal Trimworks Inc.. 910 231-8532
1114 Maplechase Dr Se Leland (28451) *(G-9536)*
Coastal Wood Products Inc.. 252 943-6650
6650 Free Union Church Rd Pinetown (27865) *(G-12247)*
Coastal Woodworking.. 910 477-1330
816 Folly Dr Se Bolivia (28422) *(G-1163)*
Coaster Magazine Carteret Cnty, Morehead City Also Called: Ncoast Communications *(G-11183)*
Coastland Times, Manteo Also Called: Times Printing Company *(G-10130)*
Coates Designers & Crafstmen.. 828 349-9700
57 Mill St Franklin (28734) *(G-6120)*
Coating Concepts Inc.. 704 391-0499
8154 Westbourne Dr Charlotte (28216) *(G-2511)*
Coatings and Adhesives Corp (PA).. 910 371-3184
1901 Popular St Leland (28451) *(G-9537)*

Coatings Technologies Inc — ALPHABETIC SECTION

Coatings Technologies Inc 704 821-8231
214 Plyler Rd Indian Trail (28079) *(G-8927)*

Coats & Clark Inc (HQ) 704 542-5959
13850 Ballantyne Corporate Pl Ste 250 Charlotte (28277) *(G-2512)*

Coats American Inc (HQ) 800 242-8095
14120 Ballantyne Corporate Pl Ste 300 Charlotte (28277) *(G-2513)*

Coats HP Inc (DH) 704 329-5800
14120 Ballantyne Corporate Pl Ste 300 Charlotte (28277) *(G-2514)*

Coats HP Inc 704 824-9904
300 Dickson Rd Mc Adenville (28101) *(G-10377)*

Coats N Amer De Rpblica Dmncan (HQ) 800 242-8095
14120 Ballantyne Corporate Pl Ste 300 Charlotte (28277) *(G-2515)*

Coats N Amer De Rpblica Dmncan, Charlotte Also Called: Coats & Clark Inc *(G-2512)*

Coats North America, Charlotte Also Called: Coats American Inc *(G-2513)*

Coaxle Optical Device and Eqp, Hickory Also Called: Code LLC *(G-7987)*

Cobb Clark Richard II 704 274-5479
12723 Cliffcreek Dr Huntersville (28078) *(G-8804)*

Cobb Sign Company Incorporated 336 227-0181
528 Elmira St Burlington (27217) *(G-1396)*

Cobble Creek Lumber LLC 336 844-2620
225 Hice Ave West Jefferson (28694) *(G-15937)*

Coble Printing Co Inc 919 693-4622
120 Hillsboro St Oxford (27565) *(G-12122)*

Coc USA Inc 888 706-0059
624 Matthews Mint Hill Rd Ste C Matthews (28105) *(G-10243)*

Coca Cola Bottling Co 704 509-1812
5020 W W T Harris Blvd Charlotte (28269) *(G-2516)*

Coca-Cola, Arden Also Called: Ccbcc Operations LLC *(G-319)*
Coca-Cola, Boone Also Called: Ccbcc Operations LLC *(G-1185)*
Coca-Cola, Bryson City Also Called: Ccbcc Operations LLC *(G-1321)*
Coca-Cola, Charlotte Also Called: Ccbcc Operations LLC *(G-2426)*
Coca-Cola, Charlotte Also Called: Ccbcc Operations LLC *(G-2427)*
Coca-Cola, Charlotte Also Called: Ccbcc Operations LLC *(G-2428)*
Coca-Cola, Charlotte Also Called: Ccbcc Operations LLC *(G-2429)*
Coca-Cola, Charlotte Also Called: Ccbcc Operations LLC *(G-2430)*
Coca-Cola, Charlotte Also Called: Coca-Cola Consolidated Inc *(G-2517)*
Coca-Cola, Charlotte Also Called: Coca-Cola Consolidated Inc *(G-2518)*
Coca-Cola, Charlotte Also Called: Coca-Cola Consolidated Inc *(G-2519)*
Coca-Cola, Charlotte Also Called: Piedmont Coca-Cola Btlg Partnr *(G-3339)*
Coca-Cola, Clayton Also Called: Ccbcc Operations LLC *(G-3964)*
Coca-Cola, Clayton Also Called: Coca-Cola Consolidated Inc *(G-3968)*
Coca-Cola, Elizabeth City Also Called: Coca-Cola Consolidated Inc *(G-5535)*
Coca-Cola, Fayetteville Also Called: Ccbcc Operations LLC *(G-5787)*
Coca-Cola, Greensboro Also Called: Ccbcc Operations LLC *(G-6896)*
Coca-Cola, Greenville Also Called: Piedmont Coca-Cola Btlg Partnr *(G-7574)*
Coca-Cola, Halifax Also Called: Piedmont Coca-Cola Btlg Partnr *(G-7611)*
Coca-Cola, Hamlet Also Called: Ccbcc Operations LLC *(G-7619)*
Coca-Cola, Hickory Also Called: Ccbcc Operations LLC *(G-7972)*
Coca-Cola, Kinston Also Called: Coca-Cola Consolidated Inc *(G-9354)*
Coca-Cola, Leland Also Called: Coca-Cola Consolidated Inc *(G-9538)*
Coca-Cola, Monroe Also Called: Ccbcc Operations LLC *(G-10678)*
Coca-Cola, Mount Airy Also Called: Ccbcc Operations LLC *(G-11494)*
Coca-Cola, New Bern Also Called: Piedmont Coca-Cola Btlg Partnr *(G-11836)*
Coca-Cola, Newton Also Called: Coca-Cola Consolidated Inc *(G-11920)*
Coca-Cola, Raleigh Also Called: Durham Coca-Cola Bottling Co *(G-12711)*
Coca-Cola, Sanford Also Called: Sanford Coca-Cola Bottling Co *(G-14180)*
Coca-Cola, Statesville Also Called: Ccbcc Operations LLC *(G-14774)*

Coca-Cola Consolidated Inc 704 398-2252
801 Black Satchel Rd Charlotte (28216) *(G-2517)*

Coca-Cola Consolidated Inc 980 321-3001
5001 Chesapeake Dr Charlotte (28216) *(G-2518)*

Coca-Cola Consolidated Inc (PA) 704 557-4400
4100 Coca Cola Plz Ste 100 Charlotte (28211) *(G-2519)*

Coca-Cola Consolidated Inc 919 550-0611
977 Shotwell Rd Ste 104 Clayton (27520) *(G-3968)*

Coca-Cola Consolidated Inc 252 334-1820
1210 George Wood Dr Elizabeth City (27909) *(G-5535)*

Coca-Cola Consolidated Inc 704 551-4500
4194 W Vernon Ave Kinston (28504) *(G-9354)*

Coca-Cola Consolidated Inc 919 763-3172
2210 Mercantile Dr Leland (28451) *(G-9538)*

Coca-Cola Consolidated Inc 828 322-5096
820 E 1st St Newton (28658) *(G-11920)*

Cochrane Steel, Monroe Also Called: Cochrane Steel Industries Inc *(G-10686)*

Cochrane Steel Industries Inc 704 291-9330
5529 Cannon Dr Monroe (28110) *(G-10686)*

Coco Lumber Company LLC 336 906-3754
2101 Sardis Rd N Ste 201 Charlotte (28227) *(G-2520)*

Coconut Paradise Inc 704 662-3443
803 Performance Rd Mooresville (28115) *(G-10908)*

Code LLC 828 328-6004
2013 1st St Se Hickory (28602) *(G-7987)*

Coder Foundry 704 910-3077
8430 University Exec Park Dr Charlotte (28262) *(G-2521)*

Coding Institute LLC 239 280-2300
2222 Sedwick Rd Ste 1 Durham (27713) *(G-5023)*

Coeur Inc 252 946-1963
209 Creekside Dr Washington (27889) *(G-15692)*

Cog Glbal Media/Consulting LLC 980 239-8042
738 Ablow Dr Matthews (28105) *(G-10244)*

Cog In Games LLP 704 763-4609
10144 Elizabeth Crest Ln Charlotte (28277) *(G-2522)*

Cogent Dynamics Inc 828 628-9025
33 Meadow Brook Dr Fletcher (28732) *(G-5995)*

Cognito Promo, Raleigh Also Called: Tannis Root Productions Inc *(G-13327)*

Cohera Medical Inc (PA) 800 641-7458
227 Fayetteville St Ste 900 Raleigh (27601) *(G-12632)*

Coil Masters LLC 704 500-8341
139 White Dove Way Mocksville (27028) *(G-10564)*

Coker Feed Mill Inc 919 778-3491
1439 Hood Swamp Rd Goldsboro (27534) *(G-6602)*

Col-Eve Metal Products Co 336 472-7039
702 Bryant Rd Lexington (27292) *(G-9696)*

Cold Mountain Capital LLC (PA) 828 210-8129
2 Town Square Blvd Asheville (28803) *(G-596)*

Cold Mtn Cabinetry 828 577-8582
40 Meadow Dr Horse Shoe (28742) *(G-8739)*

Cold Off Press LLC 984 444-9006
416 W South St Ste 100 Raleigh (27601) *(G-12633)*

Cole Machine Inc 336 222-8381
6144 Patterson Rd Snow Camp (27349) *(G-14496)*

Colefields Publishing Inc 704 661-1599
2626 Hampton Ave Charlotte (28207) *(G-2523)*

Coleman Cable LLC 828 389-8013
788 Tusquittee Rd Hayesville (28904) *(G-7762)*

Coleys Printing 704 785-8837
160 Warren C Coleman Blvd N 23 Concord (28027) *(G-4235)*

Colfax Amrcas Engnered Systems 704 289-6511
1710 Airport Rd Monroe (28110) *(G-10687)*

Colfax Pump Group 704 289-6511
1710 Airport Rd Monroe (28110) *(G-10688)*

Colfax Trailer & Repair LLC 336 993-8511
8426a Norcross Rd Colfax (27235) *(G-4144)*

Collegate Clors Christn Colors 919 536-8179
4204 Destrier Dr Durham (27703) *(G-5024)*

College Sun Do 910 521-9189
701 W 3rd St Pembroke (28372) *(G-12181)*

Collier Industries NC 980 263-0510
716 Murphy St Stanley (28164) *(G-14689)*

Colliers Welding LLC 910 818-5728
773 Mary Jordan Ln Fayetteville (28311) *(G-5793)*

Collin Manufacturing Inc 919 917-5969
12271 Capital Blvd Wake Forest (27587) *(G-15544)*

Collin Mfg Inc 919 917-6264
99 Pelican Cir Oriental (28571) *(G-12109)*

Collins Aerospace 704 423-7000
2730 W Tyvola Rd Charlotte (28217) *(G-2524)*

Collins Aerospace, Charlotte Also Called: Goodrich Corporation *(G-2847)*

ALPHABETIC SECTION — Common Scents

Collins Aerospace, Winston Salem *Also Called: B/E Aerospace Inc (G-16612)*
Collins Aerospace, Winston Salem *Also Called: B/E Aerospace Inc (G-16617)*
Collins Aerospace, Winston Salem *Also Called: Rockwell Collins Inc (G-16886)*
Collins Aerospace, Winston Salem *Also Called: Rockwell Collins Inc (G-16888)*
Collins Banks Investments Inc 252 439-1200
  311 Staton Rd Greenville (27834) *(G-7504)*
Collins Fabrication & Wldg LLC 704 861-9326
  1204 N Chester St Gastonia (28052) *(G-6380)*
Colonial LLC 336 434-5600
  536 Townsend Ave High Point (27263) *(G-8299)*
Colonial Braided Rug Co NC 704 538-1824
  3414 W Stage Coach Trl Shelby (28150) *(G-14300)*
Colonial Cabinets LLC 910 579-2954
  259 Koolabrew Dr Nw Calabash (28467) *(G-1553)*
Colonial Tin Works Inc 336 668-4126
  7609 Canoe Rd Greensboro (27409) *(G-6919)*
Colony Gums LLC 704 226-9666
  2626 Executive Point Dr Monroe (28110) *(G-10689)*
Colony Tire Corporation 252 973-0004
  1463 N Wesleyan Blvd Rocky Mount (27804) *(G-13688)*
Color Spot 336 778-3982
  6220 Hacker Bend Ct Ste A Winston Salem (27103) *(G-16657)*
Colored Metal Products Inc 704 482-1407
  103 Cameron St Shelby (28152) *(G-14301)*
Coloring Pen The, Pittsboro *Also Called: Snipes Group LLC (G-12350)*
Colowrap LLC 888 815-3376
  3333 Durham Chapel Hill Blvd Ste A200 Durham (27707) *(G-5025)*
Colquimica Adhesives Inc 704 318-4750
  2205 Beltway Blvd Ste 200 Charlotte (28214) *(G-2525)*
Colsenkeane Leather LLC 704 750-9887
  1707 E 7th St Charlotte (28204) *(G-2526)*
Colt Welding 361 244-2513
  404 Beaverdam Lake Dr Fuquay Varina (27526) *(G-6190)*
Coltec Industries Inc 704 731-1500
  5605 Carnegie Blvd Ste 500 Charlotte (28209) *(G-2527)*
Columbia Carolina Division, Old Fort *Also Called: Columbia Plywood Corporation (G-12100)*
Columbia Flooring 304 239-2633
  2000 Pergo Pkwy Garner (27529) *(G-6264)*
Columbia Forest Products Inc 336 605-0429
  Centruty Drive Ste 200 Greensboro (27401) *(G-6920)*
Columbia Panel Mfg Co Inc 336 861-4100
  100 Giles St High Point (27263) *(G-8300)*
Columbia Plywood Corporation 828 724-4191
  369 Columbia Carolina Rd Old Fort (28762) *(G-12100)*
Columbia Silica Sand LLC 803 755-1036
  1410 Commonwealth Dr Ste 201 Wilmington (28403) *(G-16175)*
Columbia West Virginia Corp (HQ) 336 605-0429
  7820 Thorndike Rd Greensboro (27409) *(G-6921)*
Columbiana Hi Tech LLC (PA) 336 497-3600
  1621 Old Greensboro Rd Kernersville (27284) *(G-9181)*
Columbus Industries LLC (PA) 910 872-1625
  941 Cabbage Rd Bladenboro (28320) *(G-1146)*
Columbus McKinnon, Wadesboro *Also Called: Columbus McKinnon Corporation (G-15507)*
Columbus McKinnon Corporation 704 694-2156
  2020 Country Club Rd Wadesboro (28170) *(G-15507)*
Columbus Pallet Company Inc 910 655-4513
  813 Lennon Rd Delco (28436) *(G-4720)*
Column & Post, Fuquay Varina *Also Called: Column & Post Inc (G-6191)*
Column & Post Inc 919 255-1533
  8013 Purfoy Rd Fuquay Varina (27526) *(G-6191)*
Coman Publishing Co Inc (PA) 919 688-0218
  324 Blackwell St Ste 560 Durham (27701) *(G-5026)*
Combat Medical Systems LLC 704 705-1222
  5555 Harrisburg Ind Pk Dr Harrisburg (28075) *(G-7706)*
Combilift USA LLC 336 378-8884
  303 Concord St Greensboro (27406) *(G-6922)*
Combinations Embroidery, Thomasville *Also Called: Combintons Screen Prtg EMB Inc (G-15204)*
Combintons Screen Prtg EMB Inc 336 472-4420
  4 N Robbins St Thomasville (27360) *(G-15204)*
Combs Welding LLC 336 984-3832
  976 Dellaplane Rd Roaring River (28669) *(G-13592)*
Combs Welding LLC 336 452-1386
  290 Froglevel Rd Ronda (28670) *(G-13765)*
Comedycd 336 273-0077
  400 Nottingham Rd Greensboro (27408) *(G-6923)*
Comer Sanitary Service Inc 336 629-8311
  3039 Greensboro Street Ext Lexington (27295) *(G-9697)*
Comer Trucking, Lexington *Also Called: Comer Sanitary Service Inc (G-9697)*
Comfort Bay Home Fashions Inc 843 442-7477
  2200 Main Ave Se Hickory (28602) *(G-7988)*
Comfort Bilt, Morrisville *Also Called: Smg Hearth and Home LLC (G-11430)*
Comfort Engineers Inc (PA) 919 383-0158
  4008 Comfort Ln Durham (27705) *(G-5027)*
Comfort Publishing Svcs LLC 704 907-7848
  8890 Brandon Cir Concord (28025) *(G-4236)*
Comfort Seals, Biscoe *Also Called: Comfort Tech Inc (G-1108)*
Comfort Sleep LLC 336 267-5853
  1100 National Hwy Ste L Thomasville (27360) *(G-15205)*
Comfort Tech Inc 910 428-1779
  Hgwy 2427 Biscoe (27209) *(G-1108)*
Comfortland International LLC 866 277-3135
  709 A O Smith Rd Mebane (27302) *(G-10405)*
Comm Scope Network, Claremont *Also Called: Commscope Inc North Carolina (G-3910)*
Comm Scope Network Cable Div, Newton *Also Called: Commscope Inc North Carolina (G-11922)*
Comm-Kab Inc 336 873-8787
  1865 Spero Rd Asheboro (27205) *(G-417)*
Commdoor Inc 800 565-1851
  5555 Yorke St Nw Concord (28027) *(G-4237)*
Commercial Cnstr Jantr Svcs, Raleigh *Also Called: Classic Cleaning LLC (G-12626)*
Commercial Enterprises NC Inc 910 592-8163
  103 E Morisey Blvd Clinton (28328) *(G-4091)*
Commercial Fabricators Inc 828 465-1010
  2045 Industrial Dr Newton (28658) *(G-11921)*
Commercial Flter Svc of Triad 336 272-1443
  107 Creek Ridge Rd Ste F Greensboro (27406) *(G-6924)*
Commercial Metals Company 336 584-0333
  Park Road Burlington (27216) *(G-1397)*
Commercial Metals Company 704 375-5937
  419 Atando Ave Charlotte (28206) *(G-2528)*
Commercial Metals Company 704 399-9020
  301 Black Satchel Rd Charlotte (28216) *(G-2529)*
Commercial Metals Company 919 833-9737
  2528 N Chester St Gastonia (28052) *(G-6381)*
Commercial Printing, Lincolnton *Also Called: Commercial Prtg Lincolnton NC (G-9883)*
Commercial Printing Company 919 832-2828
  3731 Centurion Dr Garner (27529) *(G-6265)*
Commercial Property LLC 336 818-1078
  209 Elkin Hwy North Wilkesboro (28659) *(G-12002)*
Commercial Prtg Co of Clinton 910 592-8163
  103 E Morisey Blvd Clinton (28328) *(G-4092)*
Commercial Prtg Lincolnton NC 704 735-6831
  523 N Aspen St Lincolnton (28092) *(G-9883)*
Commercial Prtg Solutuions 828 764-4137
  3640 Nc 18 S Morganton (28655) *(G-11206)*
Commercial Ready Mix Pdts Inc 252 332-3590
  100 Hayes St E Ahoskie (27910) *(G-58)*
Commercial Ready Mix Pdts Inc 252 335-9740
  168 Knobbs Creek Dr Elizabeth City (27909) *(G-5536)*
Commercial Ready Mix Pdts Inc 252 232-1250
  115 Windchaser Way Moyock (27958) *(G-11695)*
Commercial Ready Mix Pdts Inc 252 585-1777
  1231 Vougemills Rd Pendleton (27862) *(G-12185)*
Commercial Seaming Co Inc 252 492-6178
  501 Walnut St Henderson (27536) *(G-7779)*
Commercial Spclty Trck Hldngs 859 234-1100
  1425 Brittney Ln Burlington (27215) *(G-1398)*
Commercial Vehicle Group Inc 704 886-6407
  2845 Armentrout Dr Concord (28025) *(G-4238)*
Common Part Groupings LLC 704 948-0097
  11601 Hambright Rd Huntersville (28078) *(G-8805)*
Common Scents 704 780-2230
  6812 Malagant Ln Charlotte (28213) *(G-2530)*

Common Scents Solutions 812 344-4312
705 Glenarthur Dr Wilmington (28412) *(G-16176)*

Commonwealth Brands Inc 336 634-4200
714 Green Valley Rd Greensboro (27408) *(G-6925)*

Commonwealth Graphics Inc 704 997-8501
191 Knoxview Ln Mooresville (28117) *(G-10909)*

Commonwealth Hosiery, Randleman *Also Called: Commonwealth Hosiery Mills Inc (G-13459)*

Commonwealth Hosiery Mills Inc 336 498-2621
4964 Island Ford Rd Randleman (27317) *(G-13459)*

Commscope, Claremont *Also Called: Commscope Inc North Carolina (G-3909)*

COMMSCOPE, Claremont *Also Called: Commscope Holding Company Inc (G-3913)*

Commscope Inc North Carolina 828 459-5001
3565 Centennial Blvd Claremont (28610) *(G-3908)*

Commscope Inc North Carolina (DH) 828 324-2200
3642 E Us Highway 70 Claremont (28610) *(G-3909)*

Commscope Inc North Carolina 828 459-5000
3642 E Us Highway 70 Claremont (28610) *(G-3910)*

Commscope Inc North Carolina 828 324-2200
2908 2nd Ave Nw Hickory (28601) *(G-7989)*

Commscope Inc North Carolina 828 466-8600
1545 Saint James Church Rd Newton (28658) *(G-11922)*

Commscope LLC (HQ) 828 324-2200
3642 E Us Highway 70 Claremont (28610) *(G-3911)*

Commscope Cnnctvity Sltons LLC 828 324-2200
1100 Commscope Pl Se Hickory (28602) *(G-7990)*

Commscope Connectivity LLC (HQ) 828 324-2200
3642 E Us Highway 70 Claremont (28610) *(G-3912)*

Commscope Dsl Systems LLC 828 324-2200
1100 Commscope Pl Se Hickory (28602) *(G-7991)*

Commscope Holding Company Inc (PA) 828 459-5000
3642 E Us Highway 70 Claremont (28610) *(G-3913)*

Commscope Intl Holdings LLC 828 324-2200
3642 E Us Highway 70 Claremont (28610) *(G-3914)*

Commscope Technologies Fin LLC 828 323-4970
3642 E Us Highway 70 Claremont (28610) *(G-3915)*

Commscope Technologies LLC 828 324-2200
3642 E Us Highway 70 Claremont (28610) *(G-3916)*

Commscope Technologies LLC 919 329-8700
620 N Greenfield Pkwy Garner (27529) *(G-6266)*

Commscope Technologies LLC 336 665-6000
8420 Triad Dr Greensboro (27409) *(G-6926)*

Commscope Technologies LLC 828 324-2200
1100 Commscope Pl Se Hickory (28602) *(G-7992)*

Commscope Technologies LLC 919 934-9711
1315 Industrial Park Dr Smithfield (27577) *(G-14457)*

Commscope, Inc., Claremont *Also Called: Commscope LLC (G-3911)*

Communications & Pwr Inds LLC 828 241-5735
1472 Joe Johnson Rd Catawba (28609) *(G-1963)*

Communications & Pwr Inds LLC 650 846-2900
1700 Cable Dr Ne Conover (28613) *(G-4437)*

Community Brewing Ventures LLC (PA) 800 579-6539
116 W A St Newton (28658) *(G-11923)*

Community First Media Inc 704 482-4142
503 N Lafayette St Shelby (28150) *(G-14302)*

Community Newspapers Inc 828 743-5101
426 Nc 107 S Cashiers (28717) *(G-1935)*

Community Newspapers Inc 828 369-3430
690 Wayah St Franklin (28734) *(G-6121)*

Community Newspapers Inc 828 389-8431
43 Main St Hayesville (28904) *(G-7763)*

Community Newspapers Inc 828 479-3383
720 Tallulah Rd Robbinsville (28771) *(G-13606)*

Community Newspapers Inc 828 765-7169
261 Locust St Spruce Pine (28777) *(G-14633)*

Communitys Kitchen L3c 828 817-2308
835 N Trade St Ste A Tryon (28782) *(G-15423)*

Comp Environmental Inc 919 316-1321
5007 Southpark Dr Ste 200e Durham (27713) *(G-5028)*

Compagnie Parento Inc 828 758-2525
340 Industrial Ct Lenoir (28645) *(G-9600)*

Compass Color & Coating LLC 704 393-6745
3825 Corporation Cir Charlotte (28216) *(G-2531)*

Compass Group Usa Inc 704 398-6515
3112 Horseshoe Ln Charlotte (28208) *(G-2532)*

Compass Group Usa Inc 919 381-9577
3300 Waterfield Dr Garner (27529) *(G-6267)*

Compass Group Usa Inc 252 291-7733
2102 Industrial Park Dr Se Wilson (27893) *(G-16489)*

Compass Precision LLC (PA) 704 790-6764
4600 Westinghouse Blvd Charlotte (28273) *(G-2533)*

Compass Woodworks Co 704 232-0272
440 Waters Rd Salisbury (28146) *(G-13944)*

Competition Cages 919 644-1334
522 East Dr Hillsborough (27278) *(G-8646)*

Competition Tooling Inc 336 887-4414
219 Dublin Ave High Point (27260) *(G-8301)*

Competitive Edge Inc 704 881-4157
535 Davie Ave Statesville (28677) *(G-14777)*

Competitive Solutions Inc (PA) 919 851-0058
8340 Bandford Way Ste 103 Raleigh (27615) *(G-12634)*

Complete Comp St of Ralgh Inc 919 828-5227
3016 Hillsborough St Ste 100 Raleigh (27607) *(G-12635)*

Complete Trnsp & Dist Ctr Inc 336 457-6960
3211 Stonypointe Dr Greensboro (27406) *(G-6927)*

Compmillennia LLC 252 628-8065
706 Hackney Ave Washington (27889) *(G-15693)*

Component Manufacturing & Mch 336 699-4204
Lewisville (27023) *(G-9665)*

Component Sourcing Intl, Charlotte *Also Called: Remedios LLC (G-3429)*

Component Sourcing Intl LLC 704 843-9292
1301 Westinghouse Blvd Ste 1 Charlotte (28273) *(G-2534)*

Component Technology Intl Inc 704 331-0888
1000 Upper Asbury Ave Charlotte (28206) *(G-2535)*

Composite Fabrics America LLC 828 632-5220
105 Pierpoint Ln Taylorsville (28681) *(G-15135)*

Composite Factory LLC 484 264-3306
255 Raceway Dr Mooresville (28117) *(G-10910)*

Composites.com, Beaufort *Also Called: Beaufort Composite Tech Inc (G-946)*

Compressed Gas Solutions, Raleigh *Also Called: American Welding & Gas Inc (G-12501)*

Compton Tape & Label Inc 336 548-4400
3520 Us Highway 220 Madison (27025) *(G-10070)*

Compton Tape and Converting, Madison *Also Called: Compton Tape & Label Inc (G-10070)*

Computational Engrg Intl Inc (HQ) 919 363-0883
2166 N Salem St Ste 101 Apex (27523) *(G-176)*

Computer Task Group Inc 919 677-1313
8801 Fast Park Dr Ste 101 Raleigh (27617) *(G-12636)*

Computerway Food Systems Inc 336 841-7289
2700 Westchester Dr High Point (27262) *(G-8302)*

Comset Management Group 910 574-6007
3926 Gaithersburg Ln Hope Mills (28348) *(G-8736)*

Comtech Group Inc 919 313-4800
4819 Emperor Blvd Ste 400 Durham (27703) *(G-5029)*

Con Met, Canton *Also Called: Consolidated Metco Inc (G-1611)*

Con-Tab Inc 336 476-0104
4001 Ball Park Rd Thomasville (27360) *(G-15206)*

Concept Frames Inc 828 465-2015
2015 Industrial Dr Newton (28658) *(G-11924)*

Concept Fusion, Middlesex *Also Called: Concept Fusion LLC (G-10445)*

Concept Fusion LLC 252 406-7052
8200 Planer Mill Rd Middlesex (27557) *(G-10445)*

Concept Plastics Inc (PA) 336 889-2001
1210 Hickory Chapel Rd High Point (27260) *(G-8303)*

Concept Steel Inc 704 874-0414
1801 Bradbury Ct Gastonia (28052) *(G-6382)*

Concierge Consulting - Itsm, Charlotte *Also Called: Concierge Transit LLC (G-2536)*

Concierge Transit LLC 704 778-0755
1623 Swan Dr Charlotte (28216) *(G-2536)*

Concise Manufacturing Inc 704 796-8419
630 Corporate Cir Salisbury (28147) *(G-13945)*

Concord Custom Cabinets 704 773-0081
4530 Cochran Farm Rd Sw Concord (28027) *(G-4239)*

Concord Printing Company Inc 704 786-3717
660 Abington Dr Ne Concord (28025) *(G-4240)*

ALPHABETIC SECTION

Concord Trading Inc 704 375-3333
225 Wilshire Ave Sw Concord (28025) *(G-4241)*

Concrete Pipe & Precast LLC 910 892-6411
452 Webb Rd Dunn (28334) *(G-4858)*

Concrete Pipe & Precast LLC 704 485-4614
20047 Silver Rd Oakboro (28129) *(G-12070)*

Concrete Pumping By Macleod, Charlotte *Also Called: Macleod Construction Inc (G-3116)*

Concrete Service Co Inc (HQ) 910 483-0396
130 Builders Blvd Fayetteville (28301) *(G-5794)*

Concrete Service Company 910 590-0035
3095 Turkey Hwy Clinton (28328) *(G-4093)*

Concrete Supply Co LLC (HQ) 864 517-4055
3823 Raleigh St Charlotte (28206) *(G-2537)*

Concrete Supply Holdings Inc (PA) 704 372-2930
3823 Raleigh St Charlotte (28206) *(G-2538)*

Condar Company, Columbus *Also Called: Woodlane Envmtl Tech Inc (G-4182)*

Cone Denim LLC (DH) 336 379-6165
804 Green Valley Rd Ste 300 Greensboro (27408) *(G-6928)*

Cone Denim Mills, Greensboro *Also Called: Cone Denim LLC (G-6928)*

Cone Jacquards LLC (DH) 336 379-6220
804 Green Valley Rd Ste 300 Greensboro (27408) *(G-6929)*

Conestoga Wood Spc Corp 919 284-2258
621 Johnston Pkwy Kenly (27542) *(G-9148)*

Conetoe Land & Timber LLC 252 717-4648
3820 Stevens Mill Rd Goldsboro (27530) *(G-6603)*

Confab Manufacturing Co LLC 704 366-7140
6525 Morrison Blvd Ste 300 Charlotte (28211) *(G-2539)*

Conference Inc 704 349-0203
259 W Main Ave Gastonia (28052) *(G-6383)*

Conitex Sonoco Usa Inc 704 864-5406
1302 Industrial Pike Rd Gastonia (28052) *(G-6384)*

Conjet Inc 636 485-4724
3400 International Airport Dr Ste 100 Charlotte (28208) *(G-2540)*

Conmech Industries LLC 919 306-6228
117 Beaver Creek Rd Apex (27502) *(G-177)*

Conmet, Monroe *Also Called: Consolidated Metco Inc (G-10693)*

Conn-Selmer Inc 704 289-6459
2806 Mason St Monroe (28110) *(G-10690)*

Connected 2k LLC 910 321-7446
1015 Robeson St Ste 103 Fayetteville (28305) *(G-5795)*

Connectivity Group LLC 910 799-9023
837 S Kerr Ave Wilmington (28403) *(G-16177)*

Connectmedia Ventures LLC 773 551-7446
425 N Boylan Ave Raleigh (27603) *(G-12637)*

Conner Brothers Machine Co Inc 704 864-6084
3200 Bessemer City Rd Bessemer City (28016) *(G-1056)*

Connexion Technologies 919 674-0036
111 Corning Rd Ste 250 Cary (27518) *(G-1732)*

Conopco Inc 910 875-4121
100 Faberge Blvd Raeford (28376) *(G-12416)*

Conover Lumber Company Inc 828 464-4591
311 Conover Blvd E Conover (28613) *(G-4438)*

Conover Machine and Design Inc 828 328-6737
231 33rd Street Dr Se Hickory (28602) *(G-7993)*

Conover Metal Products Inc 828 464-9414
315 S Mclin Creek Rd Conover (28613) *(G-4439)*

Conover Plastics, Conover *Also Called: Plastics Mlding Dsign Plus LLC (G-4482)*

Conrad Embroidery Company LLC 828 645-3015
22 A B Emblem Dr Weaverville (28787) *(G-15842)*

Conrad Industries Inc (PA) 828 645-3015
22 A B Emblem Dr Weaverville (28787) *(G-15843)*

Conrad Tire & Automotive, Thomasville *Also Called: John Conrad Inc (G-15239)*

Conroll Corporation 910 202-4292
3302 Kitty Hawk Rd Ste 100 Wilmington (28405) *(G-16178)*

Conservation Station Inc 919 932-9201
60 Sun Forest Way Chapel Hill (27517) *(G-2005)*

Consoldted Elctrnic Rsrces Inc 919 321-0004
2933 S Miami Blvd Ste 124 Durham (27703) *(G-5030)*

Consoldted Grphics - PBM Grphi 919 544-6222
3700 S Miami Blvd Durham (27703) *(G-5031)*

Consolidated Diesel Inc 252 437-6611
9377 N Us Highway 301 Whitakers (27891) *(G-15956)*

Consolidated Elec Distrs Inc 828 433-4689
208 W Fleming Dr Ste D Morganton (28655) *(G-11207)*

Consolidated EMC Inc 980 245-2859
2240 Stevens Mill Rd Matthews (28104) *(G-10310)*

Consolidated Inspections Inc 919 658-5800
526 Norwood Ezzell Rd Mount Olive (28365) *(G-11660)*

Consolidated Metco Inc 360 828-2689
90 Christ School Rd Arden (28704) *(G-322)*

Consolidated Metco Inc 828 488-5126
1821 Hwy 19 Bryson City (28713) *(G-1322)*

Consolidated Metco Inc 828 488-5114
171 Great Oak Dr Canton (28716) *(G-1611)*

Consolidated Metco Inc 704 289-6492
780 Patton Ave Monroe (28110) *(G-10691)*

Consolidated Metco Inc 704 289-6491
1700 N Charlotte Ave Monroe (28110) *(G-10692)*

Consolidated Metco Inc 704 226-5246
4220 Propel Way Monroe (28110) *(G-10693)*

Consolidated Mfg Intl LLC (PA) 919 781-3411
5816 Triangle Dr Raleigh (27617) *(G-12638)*

Consolidated Models Inc 252 746-2171
222 Pepsi Way Ayden (28513) *(G-851)*

Consolidated Pipe & Sup Co Inc 336 294-8577
2410 Binford St Greensboro (27407) *(G-6930)*

Consolidated Press 704 283-0776
2106 W Roosevelt Blvd Monroe (28110) *(G-10694)*

Consolidated Press Inc 704 372-6785
3900 Greensboro St Charlotte (28206) *(G-2541)*

Consolidated Press Charlotte, Charlotte *Also Called: Consolidated Press Inc (G-2541)*

Consolidated Sciences Inc 919 870-0344
8390 Six Forks Rd Ste 101 Raleigh (27615) *(G-12639)*

Consolidated Truck Parts Inc 704 279-5543
7665 Hwy 52 North Rockwell (28138) *(G-13650)*

Construction Attachments, Lenoir *Also Called: Construction Attachments Inc (G-9601)*

Construction Attachments Inc 828 758-2674
1160 Cal Ct Lenoir (28645) *(G-9601)*

Construction Metal Pdts Inc 704 871-8704
2204 W Front St Statesville (28677) *(G-14778)*

Consuldated Media Group, Durham *Also Called: Triangle Tribune (G-5411)*

Consultants In Data Proc Inc 704 542-6339
6911 Shannon Willow Rd Ste 100 Charlotte (28226) *(G-2542)*

Consulting & Management Svcs, Raleigh *Also Called: Volta Group Corporation LLC (G-13408)*

Consumer Concepts 252 247-7000
1506 Bridges St Morehead City (28557) *(G-11164)*

Consumer Specialty Inc 828 396-2195
4003 Us Highway 321a Hudson (28638) *(G-8769)*

Contagious Graphics Inc 704 529-5600
5901 Orr Rd Charlotte (28213) *(G-2543)*

Container Graphics Corp (PA) 919 481-4200
114 Edinburgh South Dr Ste 104 Cary (27511) *(G-1733)*

Container Graphics Corp 704 588-7230
10430 Southern Loop Blvd Pineville (28134) *(G-12261)*

Container Products Corporation (PA) 910 392-6100
112 N College Rd Wilmington (28405) *(G-16179)*

Container Systems Incorporated 919 496-6133
6863 N Carolina 56 Hwy E Franklinton (27525) *(G-6153)*

Container Technology, Wilmington *Also Called: Container Technology Inc (G-16180)*

Container Technology Inc 910 350-1303
430 Raleigh St Wilmington (28412) *(G-16180)*

Contaminant Control 704 886-0205
440 Action Dr Nw Concord (28027) *(G-4242)*

Contec LLC 408 389-7206
6800 Steele Creek Rd Charlotte (28217) *(G-2544)*

CONTEC LLC, Charlotte *Also Called: Contec LLC (G-2544)*

Contech Engnered Solutions LLC 704 596-4226
4242 Raleigh St Charlotte (28213) *(G-2545)*

Contech Engnered Solutions LLC 919 858-7820
4917 Waters Edge Dr Ste 271 Raleigh (27606) *(G-12640)*

Contech Engnered Solutions LLC 919 851-2880
6115 Chapel Hill Rd Raleigh (27607) *(G-12641)*

Contego Medical Inc.. 919 606-3917
  3801 Lake Boone Trl Ste 100 Raleigh (27607) *(G-12642)*

Contempora Fabrics Inc.. 910 345-0150
  351 Contempora Dr Lumberton (28358) *(G-10030)*

Contemporary Concepts Inc.. 704 864-9572
  2940 Audrey Dr Gastonia (28054) *(G-6385)*

Contemporary Design Co LLC.. 704 375-6030
  513 N Broad St Gastonia (28054) *(G-6386)*

Contemporary Furnishings Corp... 336 857-2988
  6550 Scarlet Oak Dr Denton (27239) *(G-4730)*

Contemporary Furnishings Corp (PA)... 704 633-8000
  1000 N Long St Salisbury (28144) *(G-13946)*

Contemporary Products Inc... 919 779-4228
  275 Hein Dr Garner (27529) *(G-6268)*

Contemporary Publishing Co... 919 834-4432
  1460 Diggs Dr Ste C Raleigh (27603) *(G-12643)*

Continental Auto Systems Inc... 828 654-2000
  1 Quality Way Fletcher (28732) *(G-5996)*

Continental Auto Systems Inc... 828 584-4500
  1103 Jamestown Rd Morganton (28655) *(G-11208)*

Continental Auto Systems Inc... 828 584-4500
  1103 Johnstown Rd Valdese (28690) *(G-15446)*

Continental Manufacturing Co... 336 697-2591
  814c Knox Rd Ste E Mc Leansville (27301) *(G-10386)*

Continental Stone Company.. 336 951-2945
  159 Harvest Rd Reidsville (27320) *(G-13514)*

Continental Teves, Morganton Also Called: Continental Auto Systems Inc *(G-11208)*

Continental Ticking Corp Amer (PA)... 336 570-0091
  4101 South Nc 62 Alamance (27201) *(G-68)*

Continental Tool Works Inc.. 828 692-2578
  690 Shepherd St Hendersonville (28792) *(G-7839)*

Contour Enterprises LLC... 828 328-1550
  3345 Clarence Towery Cir Hildebran (28637) *(G-8620)*

Contract Furniture Restoration, Davidson Also Called: Davidson House Inc *(G-4670)*

Contract Manufacturing Div, Belmont Also Called: Custom Industries Inc *(G-981)*

Contract Printing & Graphics.. 919 832-7178
  2417 Bertie Dr Raleigh (27610) *(G-12644)*

Contract Seating Inc.. 828 322-6662
  796 20th St Ne 4 Hickory (28601) *(G-7994)*

Control and Barricade LLC.. 704 315-2138
  2025 October Dr Durham (27703) *(G-5032)*

Controlled Products Systems G... 704 392-2859
  1859 Lindbergh St Ste 300 Charlotte (28208) *(G-2546)*

Controlled Release Tech Inc... 704 487-0878
  1016 Industry Dr Shelby (28152) *(G-14303)*

Controlled Rock Drillilng & Bl... 704 876-9004
  1047 Olin Loop Olin (28660) *(G-12107)*

Controls Group, Charlotte Also Called: Clarios LLC *(G-2492)*

Controls Instrumentation Inc.. 704 786-1700
  272 International Dr Nw Concord (28027) *(G-4243)*

Controls Southeast Inc.. 704 644-5000
  12201 Nations Ford Rd Pineville (28134) *(G-12262)*

Convatec Inc... 336 855-5500
  7815 National Service Rd Ste 600 Greensboro (27409) *(G-6931)*

Convatec Inc... 336 297-3021
  7815 National Service Rd Ste 600 Greensboro (27409) *(G-6932)*

Convatec Purchasing Department.. 336 297-3021
  7900 Triad Center Dr Ste 400 Greensboro (27409) *(G-6933)*

Convenient Pallets LLc.. 919 648-3396
  379 Savannah Rd Seven Springs (28578) *(G-14266)*

Convergence Technologies, Burlington Also Called: RG Convergence Tech LLC *(G-1484)*

Convergent Integration Inc.. 704 516-5922
  10205 Foxhall Dr Charlotte (28210) *(G-2547)*

Conversant Products Inc.. 919 465-3456
  120 Preston Executive Dr Ste 200 Cary (27513) *(G-1734)*

Convert-A-Stair LLC... 888 908-5657
  3013 Hall Watters Dr Ste C Wilmington (28405) *(G-16181)*

Converting Division, Raleigh Also Called: Pratt Industries Inc *(G-13131)*

Converting Technology Inc... 336 333-2386
  514 Teague St Greensboro (27406) *(G-6934)*

Conveying Solutions LLC... 704 636-4241
  804 Julian Rd Salisbury (28147) *(G-13947)*

Conveying Solutions LLC NC, Salisbury Also Called: Conveying Solutions LLC *(G-13947)*

Conveyor Tech LLC.. 919 776-7227
  751 S Church St Goldston (27252) *(G-6674)*

Conveyor Technologies, Goldston Also Called: Conveyor Tech LLC *(G-6674)*

Conveyor Technologies Inc... 919 732-8291
  1218 Blacksmith Rd Efland (27243) *(G-5526)*

Conveyor Technologies of Sanford NC Inc................................... 919 776-7227
  5313 Womack Rd Sanford (27330) *(G-14103)*

Conway Development Inc (PA)... 252 756-2168
  2218 Dickinson Ave Greenville (27834) *(G-7505)*

Conway Entps Carteret Cnty LLC.. 252 504-3518
  313 Laurel Rd Beaufort (28516) *(G-951)*

Conxit Technology Group Inc... 877 998-4227
  9101 Southern Pine Blvd # 250 Charlotte (28273) *(G-2548)*

Cook & Boardman Group LLC (HQ).. 336 768-8872
  3064 Salem Industrial Dr Winston Salem (27127) *(G-16658)*

Cook & Boardman Nc LLC.. 336 768-8872
  3916 Westpoint Blvd Winston Salem (27103) *(G-16659)*

Cook Brothers Lumber Co Inc... 828 524-4857
  85 Peaceful Cove Rd Franklin (28734) *(G-6122)*

Cook Endoscopy, Winston Salem Also Called: Wilson-Cook Medical Inc *(G-16977)*

Cook Group Inc... 336 605-5557
  147 Forest Glen Rd Mooresville (28115) *(G-10911)*

Cook Group Inc... 336 744-0157
  5941 Grassy Creek Blvd Winston Salem (27105) *(G-16660)*

Cook Incorporated.. 336 744-0157
  4900 Bethania Station Rd Winston Salem (27105) *(G-16661)*

Cook Medical Endoscopy Div, Winston Salem Also Called: Cook Group Inc *(G-16660)*

Cooke Communications NC LLC.. 252 329-9500
  1150 Sugg Pkwy Greenville (27834) *(G-7506)*

Cooke Companies Intl... 919 968-0848
  105 York Pl Chapel Hill (27517) *(G-2006)*

Cooke Training, Chapel Hill Also Called: Cooke Companies Intl *(G-2006)*

Cool Runnings Jamaican LLC (PA).. 919 818-9220
  2700 Hidden Glen Ln Raleigh (27606) *(G-12645)*

Coolant & Cleaning Tech Inc.. 704 753-1333
  7421 Morgan Mill Rd Monroe (28110) *(G-10695)*

Coomers Welding LLC... 919 708-8087
  473 Peele Ln Sanford (27332) *(G-14104)*

Cooper, Goldsboro Also Called: Cooper-Standard Automotive Inc *(G-6604)*

Cooper B-Line Inc.. 704 522-6272
  3810 Ayscough Rd Charlotte (28211) *(G-2549)*

Cooper Bussmann LLC... 252 566-0278
  4758 Washington St La Grange (28551) *(G-9438)*

Cooper Crouse-Hinds LLC... 252 566-3014
  4758 Washington St La Grange (28551) *(G-9439)*

Cooper Industries LLC... 304 545-1482
  3912 Battleground Ave Greensboro (27410) *(G-6935)*

Cooper Technical Services Inc.. 910 285-2925
  4527 S Us Highway 117 Rose Hill (28458) *(G-13774)*

Cooper Thomas & Benton, Chapel Hill Also Called: Quick Color Solutions Inc *(G-2060)*

Cooper Thomas & Benton Prtg Co.. 336 698-0951
  829 Knox Rd Mc Leansville (27301) *(G-10387)*

Cooper-Standard Automotive Inc... 919 735-5394
  308 Fedelon Trl Goldsboro (27530) *(G-6604)*

Coopercraft Pens.. 910 603-1191
  2816 Fowler Ave Raleigh (27607) *(G-12646)*

Coopers Fayetteville Inc.. 910 483-0606
  1326 Sapona Rd Fayetteville (28312) *(G-5796)*

Copia Labs Inc.. 910 904-1000
  2501 Us Hwy 401 Bus Raeford (28376) *(G-12417)*

Copland, Burlington Also Called: Copland Fabrics Inc *(G-1399)*

Copland Fabrics Inc.. 336 226-0272
  1714 Carolina Mill Rd Burlington (27217) *(G-1399)*

Copland Industries Inc.. 336 226-0272
  1714 Carolina Mill Rd Burlington (27217) *(G-1400)*

Copper Barrel Distillery LLC.. 336 262-6500
  508 Main St North Wilkesboro (28659) *(G-12003)*

Copper Line Custom... 704 956-0734
  213 English Hills Dr Mooresville (28115) *(G-10912)*

Copy Cat Instant Prtg Chrltte.. 704 529-6606
  4612 South Blvd Ste B Charlotte (28209) *(G-2550)*

ALPHABETIC SECTION — Cottage

Copy Express Charlotte Inc 704 527-1750
4004 South Blvd Ste A Charlotte (28209) *(G-2551)*

Copy King Inc (PA) 336 333-9900
611 W Gate City Blvd Greensboro (27403) *(G-6936)*

Copy King Printing, Greensboro Also Called: Copy King Inc *(G-6936)*

Copy That Business Services 980 297-7088
2130 Ayrsley Town Blvd Ste B Charlotte (28273) *(G-2552)*

Copy Works 828 698-7622
348 7th Ave E Hendersonville (28792) *(G-7840)*

Copycat Print Shop Inc 910 799-1500
637 S Kerr Ave Wilmington (28403) *(G-16182)*

Copymasters Printing Svcs Inc 828 324-0532
818 1st Ave Sw Hickory (28602) *(G-7995)*

Copymatic Document Solutions, Raleigh Also Called: Easter Seals Ucp NC & VA Inc *(G-12717)*

Copymatic of Greenville, Greenville Also Called: Copymatic United Cerebral *(G-7507)*

Copymatic United Cerebral 252 695-6155
200 W 4th St Greenville (27858) *(G-7507)*

Copyrite, Shelby Also Called: Westmoreland Printers Inc *(G-14382)*

Coramdeo Lighting Industries 704 906-8864
116 Gasoline Aly Ste 119 Mooresville (28117) *(G-10913)*

Corbett Package Company 910 763-9991
1200 Castle Hayne Rd Wilmington (28401) *(G-16183)*

Corbett Timber Company 910 406-1129
105 Chuckanut Dr Hampstead (28443) *(G-7644)*

Cordex Instruments Inc 877 836-0764
5309 Monroe Rd Charlotte (28205) *(G-2553)*

Cordset Designs Inc 252 568-4001
100 W New St Pink Hill (28572) *(G-12316)*

Core Beginnings 614 551-1963
420 E Wade St Wadesboro (28170) *(G-15508)*

Core Electric Rebuilders, Mount Airy Also Called: Surry Elc Mtr & Cntrls Inc *(G-11581)*

Core Grip LLC 252 341-7783
2120 E Fire Tower Rd Greenville (27858) *(G-7508)*

Core Sound Imaging Inc 919 277-0636
5510 Six Forks Rd Ste 200 Raleigh (27609) *(G-12647)*

Core Technology Molding Corp 336 294-2018
2911 E Gate City Blvd Ste 201 Greensboro (27401) *(G-6937)*

Coregroup Displays, Mooresville Also Called: Coregrp LLC *(G-10914)*

Coregrp LLC 845 876-5109
631 Brawley School Rd Mooresville (28117) *(G-10914)*

Coriander Designs 425 402-8001
2141 Heavner Rd Lincolnton (28092) *(G-9884)*

Corilam Fabricating Co 336 993-2371
5211 Macy Grove Rd Kernersville (27284) *(G-9182)*

Cork Tee 919 536-3200
3436 Rugby Rd Durham (27707) *(G-5033)*

Cormark International LLC 828 658-8455
179 Reems Creek Rd Weaverville (28787) *(G-15844)*

Cormetech, Charlotte Also Called: Steag SCR-Tech Inc *(G-3626)*

Cormetech Inc (HQ) 919 620-3000
11707 Steele Creek Rd Charlotte (28273) *(G-2554)*

Cornell Lab Publishing Gropu, Cary Also Called: Phoenix St Claire Pubg LLC *(G-1851)*

Cornell Zimmer Organ Builders, Denver Also Called: C A Zimmer Inc *(G-4766)*

Corner Station Olive Oil Co 828 246-0218
224 Branner Ave Waynesville (28786) *(G-15800)*

Corner Stone Plastics Inc 336 629-1828
1027 Luck Rd Asheboro (27205) *(G-418)*

Cornerstone Biopharma Inc 919 678-6501
175 Regency Woods Pl Ste 600 Cary (27518) *(G-1735)*

Cornerstone Bldg Brands (HQ) 281 897-7788
5020 Weston Pkwy Cary (27513) *(G-1736)*

Cornerstone Building Brands, Cary Also Called: Cornerstone Bldg Brands Inc *(G-1736)*

Cornerstone Custom Printi 919 524-7420
149 Claire Dr Clayton (27520) *(G-3969)*

Cornerstone Kitchens Inc 919 510-4200
6300 Westgate Rd Ste C Raleigh (27617) *(G-12648)*

Cornerstone Mfg Co LLC 704 624-6145
4104 Philadelphia Church Rd Marshville (28103) *(G-10212)*

Cornerstone Software, Oak Ridge Also Called: Oakbrook Solutions Inc *(G-12062)*

Cornerstone Woodworks LLC 908 343-3708
1782 Forest Side Ln Charlotte (28213) *(G-2555)*

Corney Transportation Inc 800 354-9111
19214 Us Highway 301 N Saint Pauls (28384) *(G-13904)*

Cornhole Stop 704 728-1550
19235 Dutch Iris Ln Cornelius (28031) *(G-4537)*

Corning, Charlotte Also Called: Corning Optcal Cmmncations LLC *(G-2557)*

Corning, Durham Also Called: Corning Incorporated *(G-5034)*

Corning, Hickory Also Called: Corning Optcal Cmmncations LLC *(G-7996)*

Corning, Midland Also Called: Corning Incorporated *(G-10464)*

Corning, Newton Also Called: Corning Incorporated *(G-11925)*

Corning, Tarboro Also Called: Corning Incorporated *(G-15100)*

Corning, Wilmington Also Called: Corning Incorporated *(G-16184)*

Corning, Winston Salem Also Called: Corning Incorporated *(G-16662)*

Corning, Winston Salem Also Called: Corning Optcal Cmmncations LLC *(G-16663)*

Corning Incorporated 919 620-6200
1 Becton Cir Durham (27712) *(G-5034)*

Corning Incorporated 704 569-6000
14556 S Us Hwy 601 Midland (28107) *(G-10464)*

Corning Incorporated 828 465-0016
1500 Prodelin Dr Newton (28658) *(G-11925)*

Corning Incorporated 252 316-4500
7708 Us Highway 64 Alternate W Tarboro (27886) *(G-15100)*

Corning Incorporated 910 784-7200
310 N College Rd Wilmington (28405) *(G-16184)*

Corning Incorporated 336 771-8000
3180 Centre Park Blvd Winston Salem (27107) *(G-16662)*

Corning Optcal Cmmncations LLC (HQ) 828 901-5000
4200 Corning Pl Charlotte (28216) *(G-2556)*

Corning Optcal Cmmncations LLC 828 901-5000
4200 Corning Pl Charlotte (28216) *(G-2557)*

Corning Optcal Cmmncations LLC 828 327-5290
1164 23rd St Se Hickory (28602) *(G-7996)*

Corning Optcal Cmmncations LLC 336 771-8000
3180 Centre Park Blvd Winston Salem (27107) *(G-16663)*

Corob North America Inc 704 588-8408
4901 Gibbon Rd A Charlotte (28269) *(G-2558)*

Corporate Place LLC 704 808-3848
13320 Ballantyne Corporate Pl Charlotte (28277) *(G-2559)*

Corporate Resources, Kinston Also Called: Kinston Office Supply Co Inc *(G-9373)*

Corrtrac Systems Corporation 252 232-3975
126 E Canvasback Dr Currituck (27929) *(G-4633)*

Corsan LLC 704 765-9979
13201 Reese Blvd W Ste 100 Huntersville (28078) *(G-8806)*

Cortical Metrics LLC 919 903-9943
209 Lloyd St Ste 360 Carrboro (27510) *(G-1646)*

Cortina Systems 919 226-1800
523 Davis Dr Ste 300 Morrisville (27560) *(G-11325)*

Corvac Inc 772 692-5514
1654 Myers Chapel Rd Hayesville (28904) *(G-7764)*

Cosaint Arms, East Flat Rock Also Called: Agile Ventures LLC *(G-5472)*

Cosatron 704 785-8145
640 Church St N Concord (28025) *(G-4244)*

Cosette Pharmaceuticals Inc 704 735-5700
1877 Kawai Rd Lincolnton (28092) *(G-9885)*

Cosette Phrmctcals NC Labs LLC 908 753-2000
1877 Kawai Rd Lincolnton (28092) *(G-9886)*

Cosmopros 704 717-7420
1001 E W T Harris Blvd Charlotte (28213) *(G-2560)*

Costin Welding and Fabrication 910 789-7961
310 Long Branch Ln Burgaw (28425) *(G-1336)*

Cosync Inc (PA) 919 523-8336
106d Fountain Brook Cir Ste D Cary (27511) *(G-1737)*

Cote Timeworks LLC 910 246-1767
106 E Connecticut Ave Southern Pines (28387) *(G-14531)*

Cotner Cabinet 336 498-6199
7653 Adams Farm Rd Randleman (27317) *(G-13460)*

Cotner Cabinet 336 672-1560
3004 Old County Farm Rd Sophia (27350) *(G-14514)*

Cottage 919 872-1441
1430 Canterbury Rd Raleigh (27608) *(G-12649)*

Cottage House Wreaths... 336 234-7079
  7213 Nc Highway 62 N Blanch (27212) *(G-1151)*

Cotton Belt Inc.. 252 689-6847
  310 Staton Rd Greenville (27834) *(G-7509)*

Cotton Creek Chip Co, Mount Gilead *Also Called: Jordan Lumber & Supply Inc (G-11602)*

Cotton Creek Chip Company, Star *Also Called: Jordan Lumber & Supply Inc (G-14717)*

Cotton Gin and Warehouse, Newton Grove *Also Called: Sampson Gin Company Inc (G-11992)*

Cottonwood Manufacturing Inc (PA)..........................704 504-0374
  14328 Arbor Ridge Dr Charlotte (28273) *(G-2561)*

Coty, Sanford *Also Called: Coty US LLC (G-14106)*

Coty Inc.. 919 895-5000
  1400 Broadway Rd Sanford (27332) *(G-14105)*

Coty Sanford Factory, Sanford *Also Called: Coty Inc (G-14105)*

Coty US LLC.. 919 895-5374
  1400 Broadway Rd Sanford (27332) *(G-14106)*

Cougar Run Winery... 704 788-2746
  215 Union St S Concord (28025) *(G-4245)*

Council Tool Company Inc (PA).................................910 646-3011
  345 Pecan Ln Lake Waccamaw (28450) *(G-9448)*

Council Trnsp & Logistics LLC................................. 910 322-7588
  6217 Rhemish Dr Fayetteville (28304) *(G-5797)*

Councill Company LLC.. 336 859-2155
  1156 N Main St Denton (27239) *(G-4731)*

Counter Art.. 704 658-0312
  132 Joe Knox Ave Ste 106 Mooresville (28117) *(G-10915)*

Counter Effect... 252 636-0080
  115 Justin Dr New Bern (28562) *(G-11791)*

Country At Home Furniture Inc................................. 828 464-7498
  2010 Log Barn Rd Newton (28658) *(G-11926)*

Country Corner.. 919 444-9663
  2193 Us 64 Business E Pittsboro (27312) *(G-12337)*

Country Heart Braiding... 828 245-0562
  955 Hopper Rd Rutherfordton (28139) *(G-13870)*

Country Lotus Soaps LLC... 786 384-4174
  2313 Ginger Ln Apt H Charlotte (28213) *(G-2562)*

Country Roads Logging LLC.................................... 252 578-8191
  332 Providence Ln Margarettsville (27853) *(G-10136)*

Country Roads Logging LLC.................................... 252 398-4770
  1130b Boones Bridge Rd Como (27818) *(G-4183)*

County Nws-Ntrprs-Maiden Times, Newton *Also Called: Observer News Enterprise Inc (G-11954)*

County of Alexander... 828 632-1101
  255 Liledoun Rd Taylorsville (28681) *(G-15136)*

County of Anson... 704 848-4849
  567 Filtration Rd Lilesville (28091) *(G-9836)*

County of Dare.. 252 475-5990
  600 S Mustian St Kill Devil Hills (27948) *(G-9255)*

County Press Inc.. 919 894-2112
  113 S Market St Benson (27504) *(G-1033)*

Countync News LLC... 919 650-2767
  235 Rosenberry Hills Dr Cary (27513) *(G-1738)*

Courtesy Ford Inc... 252 338-4783
  1310 N Road St Elizabeth City (27909) *(G-5537)*

Courtesy Ford Lincoln-Mercury, Elizabeth City *Also Called: Courtesy Ford Inc (G-5537)*

Courtesy of Kamdyn LLC... 706 831-5395
  5406 Strive St Apt 104 Charlotte (28262) *(G-2563)*

Courtney Martins Kiln.. 828 467-1414
  3224 Snow Creek Rd Bakersville (28705) *(G-881)*

Covenantmade LLC... 336 434-4725
  2509 Surrett Dr Archdale (27263) *(G-275)*

Covia Holdings Corporation..................................... 828 688-2169
  2241 Nc 197 Bakersville (28705) *(G-882)*

Covia Holdings Corporation..................................... 980 495-2092
  9930 Kincey Ave # 200 Huntersville (28078) *(G-8807)*

Covia Holdings Corporation..................................... 828 765-4823
  Rag Branch Rd Spruce Pine (28777) *(G-14634)*

COVIA HOLDINGS CORPORATION, Bakersville *Also Called: Covia Holdings Corporation (G-882)*

COVIA HOLDINGS CORPORATION, Huntersville *Also Called: Covia Holdings Corporation (G-8807)*

COVIA HOLDINGS CORPORATION, Spruce Pine *Also Called: Covia Holdings Corporation (G-14634)*

Covia Holdings LLC... 828 688-2169
  Red Hill Iota Plant Bakersville (28705) *(G-883)*

Covia Holdings LLC... 828 765-1215
  7638 S 226 Hwy Spruce Pine (28777) *(G-14635)*

Covia Holdings LLC... 828 765-4251
  Us Hwy 19 E Spruce Pine (28777) *(G-14636)*

Covia Holdings LLC... 828 765-4283
  Bakersville Rd Spruce Pine (28777) *(G-14637)*

Covia Holdings LLC... 828 765-1114
  136 Crystal Dr Spruce Pine (28777) *(G-14638)*

Covidien Holding Inc.. 919 878-2930
  8800 Durant Rd Raleigh (27616) *(G-12650)*

Coville Inc (PA).. 336 759-0115
  8065 N Point Blvd Ste O Winston Salem (27106) *(G-16664)*

Covington Barcoding Inc.. 336 996-5759
  1800 Watmead Rd Kernersville (27284) *(G-9183)*

Cowee Mountain Ruby Mine..................................... 828 369-5271
  6771 Sylva Rd Franklin (28734) *(G-6123)*

Cox Machine Co Inc.. 704 296-0118
  2336 Concord Hwy Monroe (28110) *(G-10696)*

Cox Manufacturing Company Inc............................. 828 397-4123
  220 10th St Sw Hickory (28602) *(G-7997)*

Cox Nrth Crlina Pblcations Inc................................ 252 482-4418
  421 S Broad St Edenton (27932) *(G-5510)*

Cox Nrth Crlina Pblcations Inc................................ 252 335-0841
  215 S Water St Elizabeth City (27909) *(G-5538)*

Cox Nrth Crlina Pblcations Inc (DH).........................252 329-9643
  1150 Sugg Pkwy Greenville (27834) *(G-7510)*

Cox Nrth Crlina Pblcations Inc................................ 910 296-0239
  102 Front St Kenansville (28349) *(G-9142)*

Cox Nrth Crlina Pblcations Inc................................ 252 792-1181
  106 W Main St Williamston (27892) *(G-16059)*

Cox Precision Springs Inc....................................... 336 629-8500
  3162 Spoons Chapel Rd Asheboro (27205) *(G-419)*

CP Components LLC.. 330 715-1837
  151 Gray Cliff Dr Mooresville (28117) *(G-10916)*

CP Industries Inc.. 704 816-0580
  660 Westinghouse Blvd Ste 107 Charlotte (28273) *(G-2564)*

CP Liquidation Inc.. 704 921-1100
  5104 N Graham St Charlotte (28269) *(G-2565)*

Cpg, Huntersville *Also Called: Common Part Groupings LLC (G-8805)*

CPI, New Bern *Also Called: Chatsworth Products Inc (G-11788)*

CPI Satcom & Antenna Tech Inc............................. 704 462-7330
  1700 Cable Dr Ne Conover (28613) *(G-4440)*

CPI Satcom & Antenna Tech Inc (DH)......................704 462-7330
  1700 Cable Dr Ne Conover (28613) *(G-4441)*

CPM Acquisition Corp... 972 243-8070
  121 Proctor Ln Lexington (27292) *(G-9698)*

CPM of Nc Inc... 704 467-5819
  4222 Barfield St Concord (28027) *(G-4246)*

CPM Wolverine Proctor LLC.................................... 336 479-2983
  121 Proctor Ln Lexington (27292) *(G-9699)*

CPM Wolverine Proctor LLC.................................... 336 248-5181
  121 Proctor Ln Lexington (27292) *(G-9700)*

Cpp Global, Asheboro *Also Called: Carolina Precision Plastics L (G-412)*

Cpp Global, Mocksville *Also Called: Carolina Precision Plas LLC (G-10561)*

CPS Resources Inc... 704 628-7678
  5712 Stockbridge Dr Monroe (28110) *(G-10697)*

Cpscolor, Charlotte *Also Called: Corob North America Inc (G-2558)*

Cr Appraisal Firm LLC.. 704 344-0909
  704 East Blvd Apt 1 Charlotte (28203) *(G-2566)*

Crackle Holdings LP... 704 927-7620
  1800 Continental Blvd Ste 200c Charlotte (28273) *(G-2567)*

Craft Brew Alliance Inc.. 828 263-1111
  163 Boone Creek Dr Boone (28607) *(G-1188)*

Craft Doors Usa LLC... 828 469-7029
  1516 Mount Olive Church Rd Newton (28658) *(G-11927)*

Craft Revolution LLC (PA).. 347 924-7540
  4001 Yancey Rd Ste A Charlotte (28217) *(G-2568)*

ALPHABETIC SECTION

Craft Village, Morganton *Also Called: South Mountain Crafts (G-11255)*
Craft Woodwork Inc..252 237-7581
   4205 Craft Ln Wilson (27893) *(G-16490)*
Craft-Tex, High Point *Also Called: Concept Plastics Inc (G-8303)*
Crafted Hart Hand..704 539-4808
   176 Butch Branch Rd Union Grove (28689) *(G-15435)*
Craftex Rework Inc..252 239-0123
   500 Woodcrest St Lucama (27851) *(G-10016)*
Craftmaster Furniture Inc (DH)...828 632-9786
   221 Craftmaster Rd Hiddenite (28636) *(G-8214)*
Craftmaster Furniture Inc...828 632-8127
   750 Sharpe Ln Hiddenite (28636) *(G-8215)*
Craftsman Foam Fabricators Inc..336 476-5655
   196 Mason Way Thomasville (27360) *(G-15207)*
Craftwood Veneers Inc...336 434-2158
   822 Herman Ct High Point (27263) *(G-8304)*
Craig & Sandra Blackwell Inc...252 473-1803
   932 Harbor Rd Wanchese (27981) *(G-15644)*
Craig Hart..269 365-5568
   2007 Griffin Run Ct Greensboro (27455) *(G-6938)*
Craig S Printing LLC..336 786-2327
   151 Royal Ln Dobson (27017) *(G-4822)*
Craigscabinet..919 219-3970
   107 Holder Cir Clayton (27527) *(G-3970)*
Cranberry Wood Works Inc..336 877-8771
   13830 Us Highway 221 S Fleetwood (28626) *(G-5974)*
Crane Coffee Roasters LLC..443 960-0654
   908 Cotten Farm Dr Fuquay Varina (27526) *(G-6192)*
Crane Creek Garden, Mooresville *Also Called: Earth-Kind Inc (G-10934)*
Crane Resistoflex, Marion *Also Called: McC Holdings Inc (G-10160)*
Cranford Silk Screen Prcess In..336 434-6544
   7066 Mendenhall Rd Archdale (27263) *(G-276)*
Cranial Technologies Inc..336 760-5530
   1590 Westbrook Plaza Dr Winston Salem (27103) *(G-16665)*
Cranky Creative Group..877 775-9727
   5812 Triangle Dr Raleigh (27617) *(G-12651)*
Craters and Freighters Raleigh, Raleigh *Also Called: Lls Investments Inc (G-12976)*
Craven Sign Services Inc...336 883-7306
   508 Old Thomasville Rd High Point (27260) *(G-8305)*
Craven Tire Inc...252 633-0200
   318 1st St New Bern (28560) *(G-11792)*
Crawford Composites LLC...704 483-4175
   3501 Denver Dr Denver (28037) *(G-4768)*
Crawford Industries Inc..336 884-8822
   108 Lane Ave High Point (27260) *(G-8306)*
Crawford Knitting Company Inc..336 824-1065
   7718 Us Highway 64 E Ramseur (27316) *(G-13442)*
Crawfords Forge..828 280-2555
   4160 Sugarloaf Rd Hendersonville (28792) *(G-7841)*
Crawlspace Press LLC..919 645-7075
   2821 Knowles St Raleigh (27603) *(G-12652)*
Craymer McElwee Holdings Inc..828 326-6100
   6429 Hildebran Shelby Rd Hickory (28602) *(G-7998)*
Crazie Tees..704 898-2272
   177 Brookstone Dr Mount Holly (28120) *(G-11629)*
Crazy Ink Stitches...910 964-2889
   2467 Powell St Fayetteville (28306) *(G-5798)*
Crazy Pig Inc..704 997-2320
   402 S Main St Davidson (28036) *(G-4668)*
CRC..704 664-1242
   2425 Statesville Hwy Mooresville (28115) *(G-10917)*
CRC Machine & Fabrication Inc..980 522-1361
   4375 Dallas Cherryville Hwy Bessemer City (28016) *(G-1057)*
CRC Powder Coating, Mooresville *Also Called: CRC (G-10917)*
CRC Printing Co Inc..704 875-1804
   15700 Old Statesville Rd Huntersville (28078) *(G-8808)*
Creasman D C Mfrs Fine Jewe, Asheville *Also Called: D C Crsman Mfr Fine Jwly Inc (G-601)*
Creasmans Welding..828 667-1875
   43 Sand Hill Ln Asheville (28806) *(G-597)*
Creations By Taylor...410 269-6430
   2892 Long Run Farm Rd Mount Pleasant (28124) *(G-11673)*

Creations Cabinetry Design LLC..919 865-5979
   3825 Junction Blvd Raleigh (27603) *(G-12653)*
Creative Brewing Company LLC..919 297-8182
   809 S 2nd St Smithfield (27577) *(G-14458)*
Creative Caps Inc..919 701-1175
   214 E Broad St Dunn (28334) *(G-4859)*
Creative Closets and Cabinetry...570 952-1702
   6576 Annesbrook Pl Sw Ocean Isle Beach (28469) *(G-12089)*
Creative Clout Agency, Morehead City *Also Called: Christian Focus Magazine (G-11161)*
Creative Conquest LLC...720 481-4372
   728 Mcswain Rd Shelby (28150) *(G-14304)*
Creative Custom Wdwkg LLC..910 431-8544
   2150 Wrightsville Ave Wilmington (28403) *(G-16185)*
Creative Custom Woodworks Inc..910 431-8544
   1290 S 15th St B Wilmington (28401) *(G-16186)*
Creative Documents..704 674-5230
   704 S Skyland Dr Bessemer City (28016) *(G-1058)*
Creative Dyeing & Finshg LLC...704 983-5555
   2035 Kingsley Dr Albemarle (28001) *(G-77)*
Creative Fabric Services LLC..704 861-8383
   1675 Garfield Dr Gastonia (28052) *(G-6387)*
Creative Fish Company Inc..203 515-8631
   106 Short St Kernersville (27284) *(G-9184)*
Creative Images Inc..919 467-2188
   226 E Chatham St Cary (27511) *(G-1739)*
Creative Label Solutions..828 315-9500
   1132 Bugle Ln Newton (28658) *(G-11928)*
Creative Label Solutions Inc...828 320-5389
   1025 19th St Sw Hickory (28602) *(G-7999)*
Creative Lights...336 209-8209
   2541 River Rd Stoneville (27048) *(G-14956)*
Creative Liquid Coatings Inc...336 415-6214
   710 Piedmont Triad West Dr Mount Airy (27030) *(G-11498)*
Creative Metal and Wood Inc...336 475-9400
   8512 Blackstone Dr Colfax (27235) *(G-4145)*
Creative Outdoor Advertising, Shelby *Also Called: Headrick Otdoor Mdia of Crlnas (G-14326)*
Creative Printers, Andrews *Also Called: Creative Printers & Brks Inc (G-125)*
Creative Printers Inc...336 246-7746
   4 N 6th Ave West Jefferson (28694) *(G-15938)*
Creative Printers & Brks Inc..828 321-4663
   980 Main St Andrews (28901) *(G-125)*
Creative Printing Inc...828 265-2800
   1738 Nc Highway 105 Byp Boone (28607) *(G-1189)*
Creative Printing Stanley Inc...704 732-6398
   4147 Stoney Creek Dr Lincolnton (28092) *(G-9887)*
Creative Prosthetics and Ortho..828 994-4808
   3305 16th Ave Se Ste 101 Conover (28613) *(G-4442)*
Creative Prtg Intrnet Svcs LLC..828 265-2800
   1738 Nc Highway 105 Byp Boone (28607) *(G-1190)*
Creative Screening..919 467-5081
   303 E Durham Rd Ste C Cary (27513) *(G-1740)*
Creative Services Usa Inc..336 887-1958
   1231 Montlieu Ave High Point (27262) *(G-8307)*
Creative Signs Inc...910 395-0100
   4305 Oleander Dr Wilmington (28403) *(G-16187)*
Creative Stone, Fayetteville *Also Called: Creative Stone Fyetteville Inc (G-5799)*
Creative Stone Fyetteville Inc (PA).......................................910 491-1225
   6253 Raeford Rd Fayetteville (28304) *(G-5799)*
Creative T-Shirts Imaging LLC..919 828-0204
   2526 Hillsborough St Ste 101 Raleigh (27607) *(G-12654)*
Creative Tees..919 828-0204
   2526 Hillsborough St Raleigh (27607) *(G-12655)*
Creative Textiles Inc...919 693-4427
   615 Hillsboro St Oxford (27565) *(G-12123)*
Creative Tooling Solutions Inc..704 504-5415
   10809 Southern Loop Blvd Pineville (28134) *(G-12263)*
Creative Woodcrafters Inc...828 252-9663
   42 West Rd Leicester (28748) *(G-9509)*
Creative Woodworks...910 233-3042
   109 Fox Run Dr Hampstead (28443) *(G-7645)*
Creativemark Canvas LLC..919 267-4660
   78 Old Grove Ln Apex (27502) *(G-178)*

Creativeminds Design — ALPHABETIC SECTION

Creativeminds Design, Monroe *Also Called: Creativeminds Design LLC (G-10698)*
Creativeminds Design LLC 678 457-6148
5051 Waldorf Ave Monroe (28110) *(G-10698)*

Creativewoodworks Wilmington 910 233-3042
6708 Dorrington Dr Wilmington (28412) *(G-16188)*

Credle Woodworks LLC 919 353-4298
3810 Marklyn Pl Hillsborough (27278) *(G-8647)*

Creedmoor Forest Products 919 529-1779
2128 Hoerner Warldorf Rd Creedmoor (27522) *(G-4611)*

Creek Industries Inc 828 319-7490
87 Island In The Sky Trl Weaverville (28787) *(G-15845)*

Creekraft Cultured Marble Inc 252 636-5488
3205 Old Cherry Point Rd New Bern (28560) *(G-11793)*

Creekside Creative Design Inc 252 243-6272
206 Goldsboro St Sw Wilson (27893) *(G-16491)*

Creeled Inc 919 313-5330
4400 Silicon Dr Durham (27703) *(G-5035)*

Creighton Ab Inc 336 349-8275
205 Watlington Industrial Dr Reidsville (27320) *(G-13515)*

Cres Tobacco Company LLC 336 983-7727
3000 Big Oaks Rd King (27021) *(G-9268)*

Crest Capital LLC 336 664-2400
7800 Mccloud Rd Greensboro (27409) *(G-6939)*

Crest Electronics Inc 336 855-6422
3703 Alliance Dr Ste A Greensboro (27407) *(G-6940)*

Crest Publications 704 277-7194
12701 Netherhall Dr Charlotte (28269) *(G-2569)*

Crestline Software LLC 336 217-1005
2733 Horse Pen Creek Rd Ste 101 Greensboro (27410) *(G-6941)*

Crestview Trading Post, Rockingham *Also Called: Allen Brothers Timber Company (G-13619)*
Crete Solutions LLC 910 726-1686
2005 Eastwood Rd Ste 200 Wilmington (28403) *(G-16189)*

Crh Americas Inc 704 282-8443
1139 N Charlotte Ave Monroe (28110) *(G-10699)*

Cricket Forge LLC 919 680-3513
2314 Operations Dr Durham (27705) *(G-5036)*

Cris Bifaro Woodworks Inc 828 776-2453
37 Langwell Ave Asheville (28806) *(G-598)*

Crisp Printers Inc 704 867-6663
2022 E Ozark Ave Gastonia (28054) *(G-6388)*

Cristal Dragon Candle Company 336 997-4210
3271 Moir Farm Rd Sandy Ridge (27046) *(G-14077)*

Criticore Inc (DH) 704 542-6876
9525 Monroe Rd Ste 150 Charlotte (28270) *(G-2570)*

Crizaf Inc 919 251-7661
2, 1534 Cher Dr, Durham (27713) *(G-5037)*

Crizaf Srl, Durham *Also Called: Crizaf Inc (G-5037)*

Crm A LLC 888 600-7567
8000 Weston Pkwy Ste 100 Cary (27513) *(G-1741)*

Crmnext Inc 415 424-4644
702 Oberlin Rd Ofc Ofc Raleigh (27605) *(G-12656)*

Crmp, Ahoskie *Also Called: Commercial Ready Mix Pdts Inc (G-58)*
Crmp Inc 252 358-5461
115 Hwy 158 W Winton (27986) *(G-17021)*

Crochet By Sue 201 723-4906
533 Fairbluff Ave Salisbury (28146) *(G-13948)*

Crockers Inc 336 366-2005
1821 Joe Layne Mill Rd Elkin (28621) *(G-5615)*

Croft Precision Tools Inc 704 399-4124
4424 Taggart Creek Rd Ste 108 Charlotte (28208) *(G-2571)*

Crompton Instruments 919 557-8698
8000 Purfoy Rd Fuquay Varina (27526) *(G-6193)*

Croscill Home LLC 919 735-7111
200 Ne Outer Loop Oxford (27565) *(G-12124)*

CROSS & CROWN, Ayden *Also Called: Free Will Bptst Press Fndtion (G-852)*
Cross Canvas Company Inc 828 252-0440
63 Glendale Ave Asheville (28803) *(G-599)*

Cross Co 336 856-6110
608 Ashe St High Point (27262) *(G-8308)*

Cross Hose and Fitting, Greensboro *Also Called: Cross Technologies Inc (G-6943)*
Cross Manufacturing LLC 336 269-6542
2505 Parrish St Burlington (27215) *(G-1401)*

Cross Manufacturing LLC 336 603-6926
138 Eugene St Gibsonville (27249) *(G-6557)*

Cross Precision Measurement, Greensboro *Also Called: Cross Technologies Inc (G-6942)*
Cross Technologies Inc (HQ) 800 327-7727
4400 Piedmont Pkwy Greensboro (27410) *(G-6942)*

Cross Technologies Inc 336 370-4673
3012 S Elm Eugene St Ste A Greensboro (27406) *(G-6943)*

Cross Technologies Inc 336 292-0511
6541c Franz Warner Pkwy Whitsett (27377) *(G-15987)*

Cross Technology Inc (PA) 336 725-4700
305 Junia Ave East Bend (27018) *(G-5465)*

Cross-Link Inc 828 657-4477
4734 Us 221a Hwy Cliffside (28024) *(G-4084)*

Crossroad Press 252 340-3952
141 Brayden Dr Hertford (27944) *(G-7917)*

Crossroads Coatings, Statesville *Also Called: Crossroads Coatings Inc (G-14779)*
Crossroads Coatings Inc 704 873-2244
208 Bucks Industrial Rd Statesville (28625) *(G-14779)*

Crossroads Fuel Service Inc 252 426-5216
395 Ocean Hwy N Hertford (27944) *(G-7918)*

Crossroads Tire Store Inc 704 888-2064
4430 Albemarle Rd Midland (28107) *(G-10465)*

Crossties Plus LLC 252 943-7437
383 Industrial Park Rd Plymouth (27962) *(G-12369)*

Croswait Custom Composites Inc 252 423-1245
90 Dusty Ln Wanchese (27981) *(G-15645)*

Crowder Trucking LLC 910 797-4163
6776 Saint Julian Way Fayetteville (28314) *(G-5800)*

Crowdguard Inc 919 605-1948
12218 Bradford Green Sq Ste 151 Cary (27519) *(G-1742)*

Crown Case Co 704 453-1542
801 Atando Ave Ste C Charlotte (28206) *(G-2572)*

Crown Defense Ltd 202 800-8848
2320 N Nc 16 Business Hwy Denver (28037) *(G-4769)*

Crown Equipment Corporation 336 291-2500
8220 Tyner Rd Colfax (27235) *(G-4146)*

Crown Equipment Corporation 704 721-4000
8401 Westmoreland Dr Nw Concord (28027) *(G-4247)*

Crown Equipment Corporation 919 773-4160
1000 N Greenfield Pkwy Ste 1090 Garner (27529) *(G-6269)*

Crown Equipment Corporation 252 522-3088
2000 Dobbs Farm Rd Kinston (28504) *(G-9355)*

Crown Foam Products Inc 336 434-4024
921 Baker Rd Ste 3 High Point (27263) *(G-8309)*

Crown Heritage Inc 336 835-1424
296 Gentry Rd Elkin (28621) *(G-5616)*

Crown Lift Trucks, Colfax *Also Called: Crown Equipment Corporation (G-4146)*
Crown Lift Trucks, Garner *Also Called: Crown Equipment Corporation (G-6269)*
Crown Lift Trucks, Kinston *Also Called: Crown Equipment Corporation (G-9355)*

Crown Town Compost LLC 704 654-5689
1801 Merriman Ave Charlotte (28203) *(G-2573)*

Crown Town Industries LLC 704 579-0387
813 Hydrangea Cir Nw Concord (28027) *(G-4248)*

Crown Trophy Inc 336 851-1011
201 Pomona Dr Ste C Greensboro (27407) *(G-6944)*

Crowntown Tinker LLC 843 614-9566
6227 Hermsley Rd Charlotte (28278) *(G-2574)*

Crp Usa LLC 704 660-0258
127 Goodwin Cir Mooresville (28115) *(G-10918)*

CRS Laboratories, Durham *Also Called: Sciepharm LLC (G-5343)*
CRS/Las Inc 910 392-0883
120 Racine Dr Ste 3 Wilmington (28403) *(G-16190)*

Crt Inc 704 905-9748
7515 Valleybrook Rd Charlotte (28270) *(G-2575)*

Crude LLC 919 391-8185
501 E Davie St Raleigh (27601) *(G-12657)*

Cruise Industry News, Charlotte *Also Called: Mathisen Ventures Inc (G-3141)*
Crump Group USA Inc 936 465-5870
4626 Coleman Dr Nashville (27856) *(G-11742)*

Crumpler Plastic Pipe Inc 910 525-4046
852 Autry Hwy 24 Roseboro (28382) *(G-13784)*

ALPHABETIC SECTION — Cunningham Brick Company

Crww Specialty Composites Inc.. 828 548-5002
   2678 Heart Dr Bldg B Claremont (28610) *(G-3917)*

Cryogen LLC.. 919 649-7027
   2626 Glenwood Ave Ste 140 Raleigh (27608) *(G-12658)*

Cryostop International... 910 452-5556
   105 Oxmoor Pl Wilmington (28403) *(G-16191)*

Cryotherapy of Pines LLC... 910 988-0357
   122 Brucewood Rd Southern Pines (28387) *(G-14532)*

Cryovac LLC (HQ).. 980 430-7000
   2415 Cascade Pointe Blvd Charlotte (28208) *(G-2576)*

Cryovac Intl Holdings Inc (HQ)... 980 430-7000
   2415 Cascade Pointe Blvd Charlotte (28208) *(G-2577)*

Cryovac Leasing Corporation... 980 430-7000
   2415 Cascade Pointe Blvd Charlotte (28208) *(G-2578)*

Cryptic Coatings... 828 994-4474
   2684 Tiffany St Conover (28613) *(G-4443)*

Cryptic Coatings Ltd... 704 966-1617
   6515 Denver Industrial Park Rd Denver (28037) *(G-4770)*

Crypton Mills LLC.. 828 202-5875
   3400 Hwy 221a Cliffside (28024) *(G-4085)*

Crystal Clear Images Inc... 704 708-5420
   8203 White Horse Ln Charlotte (28270) *(G-2579)*

Crystal Coast Boatworks.. 252 723-9370
   1145 Sensation Weigh Beaufort (28516) *(G-952)*

Crystal Coast Composites Inc... 252 838-0025
   2630 Highway 101 Beaufort (28516) *(G-953)*

Crystal Coast Composites Inc (PA).................................... 252 838-0025
   1707 River Dr Morehead City (28557) *(G-11165)*

Crystal Impressions Ltd.. 704 821-7678
   14200 E Independence Blvd Indian Trail (28079) *(G-8928)*

Crystal Plant, Spruce Pine *Also Called: Covia Holdings LLC (G-14638)*

Cs Alloys.. 704 675-5810
   2888 Colony Woods Dr Gastonia (28054) *(G-6389)*

Cs Carolina Inc.. 336 578-0110
   1305 Graham St Burlington (27217) *(G-1402)*

Cs Ink, Madison *Also Called: Custom Screens Inc (G-10071)*

Cs Manufacturing Cs Mfg... 704 837-1701
   4525 Reagan Dr # A Charlotte (28206) *(G-2580)*

Cs Systems Company Inc.. 800 525-9878
   1465 Sand Hill Rd Ste 2050 Candler (28715) *(G-1576)*

Csa Wireless, Conover *Also Called: Amphenol Antenna Solutions (G-4515)*

CSC Awnings Inc... 336 744-5006
   3950 N Liberty St Winston Salem (27105) *(G-16666)*

CSC Family Holdings Inc... 336 993-2680
   9035 Us Hwy 421 Colfax (27235) *(G-4147)*

CSC Family Holdings Inc (PA)... 336 275-9711
   101 Centreport Dr Ste 400 Greensboro (27409) *(G-6945)*

CSC Family Holdings Inc... 252 459-7116
   341 Corbett Rd Nashville (27856) *(G-11743)*

CSC Sheet Metal Inc... 919 544-8887
   1310 E Cornwallis Rd Durham (27713) *(G-5038)*

Csi, Charlotte *Also Called: Component Sourcing Intl LLC (G-2534)*

Csi, Madison *Also Called: Deep South Holding Company Inc (G-10072)*

Csi, Newton *Also Called: Custom Socks Ink Inc (G-11929)*

Csi, Pineville *Also Called: Controls Southeast Inc (G-12262)*

Csi Armoring Inc.. 336 313-8561
   425 Industrial Dr Lexington (27295) *(G-9701)*

Csit Group... 828 233-5750
   205 Newstock Rd Asheville (28804) *(G-600)*

CSM, Graham *Also Called: CSM Manufacturing Inc (G-6686)*

CSM Logistics LLC.. 980 800-2621
   4835 Sirona Dr Ste 300 Charlotte (28273) *(G-2581)*

CSM Manufacturing Inc.. 336 570-2282
   913 Washington St Graham (27253) *(G-6686)*

CSS, Gastonia *Also Called: Barnyard Utlity Bldngs-Strg/TI (G-6351)*

CSS, Greensboro *Also Called: Ddp Spclty Elctrnic Mtls US 9 (G-6962)*

Cstruct, Raleigh *Also Called: Starta Development Inc (G-13299)*

CT Commercial Paper LLC... 704 485-3212
   349 S Main St Oakboro (28129) *(G-12071)*

Ct-Nassau Tape LLC... 336 570-0091
   4101 S N Carolina Hwy 62 Alamance (27201) *(G-69)*

Ct-Nassau Ticking LLC... 336 570-0091
   1504 Anthony Rd Burlington (27215) *(G-1403)*

Ctc, Gastonia *Also Called: Champion Thread Company (G-6375)*

Ctc Holdings LLC (PA).. 704 867-6611
   165 Bluedevil Dr Gastonia (28056) *(G-6390)*

Cth-Shrrill Occsional Furn Div, Hickory *Also Called: Sherrill Furniture Company (G-8148)*

CTI, Wilmington *Also Called: Ceres Turf Inc (G-16167)*

CTI Property Services Inc.. 919 787-3789
   5450 Old Wake Forest Rd Raleigh (27609) *(G-12659)*

CTI Systems, Sanford *Also Called: Conveyor Technologies of Sanford NC Inc (G-14103)*

CTS, Rocky Point *Also Called: Cincinnati Thermal Spray Inc (G-13744)*

CTS Cleaning Systems Inc... 910 483-5349
   2185 Angelia M St Fayetteville (28312) *(G-5801)*

CTS Custom Cabinets.. 704 376-5844
   519 Armour Dr Charlotte (28206) *(G-2582)*

CTX Builders Supply... 704 983-6748
   2100 Sterling Dr Albemarle (28001) *(G-78)*

Cub Creek Kitchens & Baths Inc... 336 651-8983
   309 Wilkesboro Ave North Wilkesboro (28659) *(G-12004)*

Culligan Water Conditioning... 252 646-3800
   4911 Bridges St Ext Morehead City (28557) *(G-11166)*

Culp Inc... 662 844-7144
   2742 Tucker St # A Burlington (27215) *(G-1404)*

Culp Inc (PA).. 336 889-5161
   1823 Eastchester Dr High Point (27265) *(G-8310)*

Culp Inc... 336 885-2800
   7209 Us Highway 158 Stokesdale (27357) *(G-14940)*

Culp Inc... 336 643-7751
   7209 Us Highway 158 Stokesdale (27357) *(G-14941)*

Culp of Mississippi, Burlington *Also Called: Culp Inc (G-1404)*

Culp Ticking, Stokesdale *Also Called: Culp Inc (G-14941)*

Culpeper Roanoke Rapids LLC.. 252 678-3804
   2262 W 10th St Roanoke Rapids (27870) *(G-13572)*

Cultivated Cocktails, Asheville *Also Called: H&H Distillery LLC (G-646)*

Culture Cuisine LLC... 347 278-3210
   801 E Morehead St Charlotte (28202) *(G-2583)*

Culture Shock Toys, Huntersville *Also Called: PCS Collectibles LLC (G-8873)*

Cumberland Grav & Sand Min Co (PA)............................... 828 686-3844
   Old Us Highway 70 Swannanoa (28778) *(G-15024)*

Cumberland Gravel, Marion *Also Called: B V Hedrick Gravel & Sand Co (G-10140)*

Cumberland Gravel & Sand Co.. 704 633-4241
   Salisbury (28145) *(G-13949)*

Cumberland Sand and Gravel.. 704 474-3165
   12423 Old Aquadale Rd Norwood (28128) *(G-12038)*

Cumins Machinery Corp.. 336 622-1000
   312 W Luther Ave Liberty (27298) *(G-9809)*

Cummins, Charlotte *Also Called: Cummins Atlantic LLC (G-2584)*

Cummins, Charlotte *Also Called: Cummins Atlantic LLC (G-2585)*

Cummins, Charlotte *Also Called: Pcai Inc (G-3323)*

Cummins, Greensboro *Also Called: Cummins Atlantic LLC (G-6946)*

Cummins, Kenly *Also Called: Cummins Atlantic LLC (G-9149)*

Cummins Atlantic LLC.. 704 596-7690
   3700 Jeff Adams Dr Charlotte (28206) *(G-2584)*

Cummins Atlantic LLC (HQ)... 704 588-1240
   11101 Nations Ford Rd Charlotte (28273) *(G-2585)*

Cummins Atlantic LLC.. 336 275-4531
   512 Teague St Greensboro (27406) *(G-6946)*

Cummins Atlantic LLC.. 919 284-9111
   350 Cummins Dr Kenly (27542) *(G-9149)*

Cummins Inc... 919 284-9111
   350 Cummins Dr Kenly (27542) *(G-9150)*

Cummins Inc... 704 588-1240
   11101 Nations Ford Rd Pineville (28134) *(G-12264)*

Cumulus - Statesville West, Statesville *Also Called: Fibrix LLC (G-14796)*

Cumulus Fibres - Charlotte, Charlotte *Also Called: Fibrix LLC (G-2758)*

Cumulus Fibres - Statesville, Statesville *Also Called: Fibrix LLC (G-14797)*

Cumulus Fibres Inc... 704 394-2111
   1101 Tar Heel Rd Charlotte (28208) *(G-2586)*

Cunningham Brick Company.. 336 248-8541
   701 N Main St Lexington (27292) *(G-9702)*

Cupcake A La Mo LLC   ALPHABETIC SECTION

Cupcake A La Mo LLC 919 322-8824
  8110 Farmlea Cir Raleigh (27616) *(G-12660)*

Cupcake Bar 919 816-2905
  315 Monmouth Ave Durham (27701) *(G-5039)*

Cupcake Stop Shop LLC 919 457-7900
  6902 Cameron Crest Cir Apt 118 Raleigh (27613) *(G-12661)*

Curious Discoveries Inc 336 643-0432
  7911 Windspray Dr Summerfield (27358) *(G-14979)*

Curlee Machinery Company 919 467-9311
  412 Field St Cary (27513) *(G-1743)*

Curleys Plumbing 252 578-8666
  190 Fairlane Dr Roanoke Rapids (27870) *(G-13573)*

Current Enterprises Inc 919 469-1227
  125 International Dr Ste J Morrisville (27560) *(G-11326)*

Currie Motorsports Inc 910 580-1765
  611 College Dr Raeford (28376) *(G-12418)*

Currier Woodworks Inc 252 725-4233
  1622 Live Oak St Beaufort (28516) *(G-954)*

Curti USA Corporation 910 769-1977
  161 Poole Rd Belville (28451) *(G-1023)*

Curtis L Maclean L C 704 940-5531
  227 Manufacturers Blvd Mooresville (28115) *(G-10919)*

Curtis Packing Company (PA) 336 275-7684
  2416 Randolph Ave Greensboro (27406) *(G-6947)*

Curtiss-Wright Controls Inc (HQ) 704 869-4600
  15801 Brixham Hill Ave Ste 200 Charlotte (28277) *(G-2587)*

Curtiss-Wright Controls Inc 704 869-2320
  3120 Northwest Blvd Gastonia (28052) *(G-6391)*

Curtiss-Wright Controls Inc 704 869-2300
  201 Old Boiling Springs Rd Shelby (28152) *(G-14305)*

Curtiss-Wright Controls Inc 704 481-1150
  201 Old Boiling Springs Rd Shelby (28152) *(G-14306)*

Curtiss-Wright Corporation (PA) 704 869-4600
  130 Harbour Place Dr Ste 300 Davidson (28036) *(G-4669)*

Curtiss-Wright Corporation 704 481-1150
  201 Old Boiling Springs Rd Shelby (28152) *(G-14307)*

Curved Plywood Inc 336 249-6901
  111 E 7th Ave Lexington (27292) *(G-9703)*

Curvemakers Inc 919 690-1121
  115 Corporation Dr Oxford (27565) *(G-12125)*

Curvemakers Inc (PA) 919 821-5792
  703 W Johnson St Raleigh (27603) *(G-12662)*

Cushion Manufacturing Inc 828 324-9555
  1343 9th Ave Ne Hickory (28601) *(G-8000)*

Custom Air Trays Inc (PA) 336 889-8729
  2112 S Elm St High Point (27260) *(G-8311)*

Custom Armor Group Inc 336 617-4667
  4270 Piedmont Pkwy Ste 102 Greensboro (27410) *(G-6948)*

Custom Assemblies Inc 919 202-4533
  330 E Main St Pine Level (27568) *(G-12207)*

Custom Automated Machines Inc 704 289-7038
  509 E Windsor St Monroe (28112) *(G-10700)*

Custom Boatworks Inc 252 235-2461
  8957 Pace Rd Bailey (27807) *(G-869)*

Custom Brick and Supplied Co., Raleigh *Also Called: Custom Brick Company Inc (G-12663)*

Custom Brick Company Inc 919 832-2804
  1833 Capital Blvd Raleigh (27604) *(G-12663)*

Custom Cabinet Works 828 396-6348
  180 N Main St Granite Falls (28630) *(G-6730)*

Custom Cabinets & Rmdlg Inc 828 264-1806
  699 Green Briar Rd Boone (28607) *(G-1191)*

Custom Cabinets By Livengood 704 279-3031
  490 Parks Rd Salisbury (28146) *(G-13950)*

Custom Canvas Inc 2 .... 252 633-0754
  225b S Front St New Bern (28560) *(G-11794)*

Custom Canvas Works Inc 919 662-4800
  540 Dynamic Dr Garner (27529) *(G-6270)*

Custom Chrome & Coatings Inc 704 226-6808
  8208 Lawyers Rd Charlotte (28227) *(G-2588)*

Custom Cnc LLC 828 734-8293
  6989 Carolina Blvd Clyde (28721) *(G-4122)*

Custom Cnverting Solutions Inc 336 292-2616
  1207 Boston Rd Greensboro (27407) *(G-6949)*

Custom Contract Furn LLC 336 882-8565
  667 W Ward Ave High Point (27260) *(G-8312)*

Custom Controls Unlimited LLC 919 812-6553
  2600 Garner Station Blvd Raleigh (27603) *(G-12664)*

Custom Corrugated Cntrs Inc 704 588-0371
  5024 Westinghouse Blvd Charlotte (28273) *(G-2589)*

Custom Creations By Ellen 509 480-0263
  3210 Kentyre Dr Fayetteville (28303) *(G-5802)*

Custom Decks and Woodworking 828 699-2349
  2294 Old Us 25 Hwy Zirconia (28790) *(G-17152)*

Custom Design Inc 704 637-7110
  2001 S Main St Salisbury (28144) *(G-13951)*

Custom Designs and Upholstery 336 882-1516
  1372 Unity St # B Thomasville (27360) *(G-15208)*

Custom Doors Incorporated 704 982-2885
  800 Laton Rd Albemarle (28001) *(G-79)*

Custom Educational Furn LLC 800 255-9189
  2696 Nc Highway 16 S Taylorsville (28681) *(G-15137)*

Custom Electric Mfg LLC 248 305-7700
  180 International Dr Nw Concord (28027) *(G-4249)*

Custom Engines Ltd 910 532-4114
  2560 Wildcat Rd Harrells (28444) *(G-7691)*

Custom Enterprises Inc 336 226-8296
  129 E Ruffin St Burlington (27217) *(G-1405)*

Custom Express 704 845-0900
  1400 Industrial Dr Matthews (28105) *(G-10245)*

Custom Extrusion Inc 336 495-7070
  2971 Taylor Dr Asheboro (27203) *(G-420)*

Custom Fabric Samples Inc 336 472-1854
  261 Sunset Dr Thomasville (27360) *(G-15209)*

Custom Fiberglass Products 252 235-2461
  8957 Pace Rd Bailey (27807) *(G-870)*

Custom Finishers Inc (PA) 336 431-7141
  2213 Shore St High Point (27263) *(G-8313)*

Custom Gears Inc 704 735-6883
  3565 Hwy 155 S Lincolnton (28092) *(G-9888)*

Custom Glass Works Inc 704 597-0290
  2000 W Morehead St Ste F Charlotte (28208) *(G-2590)*

Custom Golf Car Supply Inc 704 855-1130
  1735 Heilig Rd Salisbury (28146) *(G-13952)*

Custom Hydraulics & Design (PA) 704 347-0023
  242 Dick Beam Rd Cherryville (28021) *(G-3865)*

Custom Industries Inc 704 825-3346
  111 Hubbard St Belmont (28012) *(G-981)*

Custom Industries Inc (PA) 336 299-2885
  215 Aloe Rd Greensboro (27409) *(G-6950)*

Custom Ink 704 935-5604
  530 Brandywine Rd Ste C Charlotte (28209) *(G-2591)*

Custom Light and Sound Inc 919 286-1122
  2506 Guess Rd Durham (27705) *(G-5040)*

Custom Machine Company Inc 704 629-5326
  221 White Jenkins Rd Bessemer City (28016) *(G-1059)*

Custom Machining Inc 336 996-0855
  121 Majestic Way Ct Ste D Kernersville (27284) *(G-9185)*

Custom Marble Corporation (PA) 910 215-0679
  150 Safford Dr Pinehurst (28374) *(G-12219)*

Custom Marine Canvas 252 482-0675
  121 Montpelier Dr Edenton (27932) *(G-5511)*

Custom Marine Fabrication Inc 252 638-5422
  2401 Us Highway 70 E New Bern (28560) *(G-11795)*

Custom Marking & Printing Inc 704 866-8245
  907 Bessemer City Rd Gastonia (28052) *(G-6392)*

Custom Medical Specialties Inc 919 202-8462
  330 E Main St Pine Level (27568) *(G-12208)*

Custom Metal Creation LLC 828 302-0623
  4395 Macedonia Church Rd Vale (28168) *(G-15464)*

Custom Metal Finishing 704 445-1710
  617 E Main St B Cherryville (28021) *(G-3866)*

Custom Metal Products, Wilmington *Also Called: Metal-Cad Stl Frmng Systems In (G-16321)*

ALPHABETIC SECTION

Custom Nano Inc.. 919 608-3540
1509 Lorimer Rd Raleigh (27606) *(G-12665)*

Custom Neon & Graphics Inc................................ 704 344-1715
1722 Toal St Charlotte (28206) *(G-2592)*

Custom Packaging Inc... 828 684-5060
20 Beale Rd Arden (28704) *(G-323)*

Custom Packaging of Asheville, Arden Also Called: Custom Packaging Inc *(G-323)*

Custom Patch Hats LLC.. 919 424-7723
1505 Capital Blvd Ste 14b Raleigh (27603) *(G-12666)*

Custom Plastic Forming, Salisbury Also Called: Custom Golf Car Supply Inc *(G-13952)*

Custom Polymers, Charlotte Also Called: Custom Polymers Inc *(G-2593)*

Custom Polymers Inc (PA).................................... 704 332-6070
831 E Morehead St Ste 840 Charlotte (28202) *(G-2593)*

Custom Polymers Pet LLC (PA)............................ 866 717-0716
831 E Morehead St Ste 840 Charlotte (28202) *(G-2594)*

Custom Powder Worx... 828 310-1373
4911 Church Rd Taylorsville (28681) *(G-15138)*

Custom Printing Solutions Inc............................ 336 992-1161
1355 S Park Dr Kernersville (27284) *(G-9186)*

Custom Products Inc... 704 663-4159
1618 Landis Hwy Mooresville (28115) *(G-10920)*

Custom Rehabilitation Spc Inc............................ 910 471-2962
7225 Anaca Point Rd Wilmington (28411) *(G-16192)*

Custom Sample Service Inc................................. 336 861-2010
5415 Surrett Dr Archdale (27263) *(G-277)*

Custom Screens Inc... 336 427-0265
2216 Us Highway 311 Madison (27025) *(G-10071)*

Custom Seatings... 828 879-1964
3011 High Peak Rd Valdese (28690) *(G-15447)*

Custom Sgns - Dsign Mnfcture I, Apex Also Called: Mercury Signs Inc *(G-218)*

Custom Sheetmetal Services Inc......................... 919 282-1088
5109 Neal Rd Durham (27705) *(G-5041)*

Custom Signage Company.................................. 909 215-2404
10423 Dickson Ln Charlotte (28262) *(G-2595)*

Custom Signs.. 336 847-7700
2724 Belmont Dr High Point (27263) *(G-8314)*

Custom Smiles Inc.. 919 331-2090
123 Fish Dr Ste 101 Angier (27501) *(G-138)*

Custom Socks Ink Inc... 828 695-9869
2011 N Main Ave Newton (28658) *(G-11929)*

Custom Spt & Imprintables LLC......................... 910 799-9914
207 Antilles Ct Ste B Wilmington (28405) *(G-16193)*

Custom Steel Incorporated.................................. 919 383-9170
3161 Hillsborough Rd Durham (27705) *(G-5042)*

Custom Steel Boats Inc.. 252 745-7447
102 Yacht Dr Merritt (28556) *(G-10439)*

Custom Steel Fabricators Inc.............................. 336 498-5099
362 Providence Church Rd Randleman (27317) *(G-13461)*

Custom Surfaces Corporation............................. 252 638-3800
115 Justin Dr New Bern (28562) *(G-11796)*

Custom Tees Lab.. 704 804-8706
5121 Vanhoy Ln Charlotte (28269) *(G-2596)*

Custom Win Trtments Dctr Items, Boone Also Called: Bettys Drapery Design Workroom *(G-1176)*

Custom Wood Creations...................................... 252 341-7923
901 Trolling Wood Ct Greenville (27858) *(G-7511)*

Custom Wood Creations...................................... 910 367-8747
9485 Night Harbor Dr Se Leland (28451) *(G-9539)*

Custom Wood Products, Monroe Also Called: Robert Hamms LLC *(G-10797)*

Customer Service Center Repair, Monroe Also Called: Goodrich Corporation *(G-10726)*

Customer Service Department, Cary Also Called: Oxford University Press LLC *(G-1840)*

Customer Service Spare, Monroe Also Called: Goodrich Corporation *(G-10725)*

Cut Above Construction...................................... 828 758-8557
3815 Charles White Ln Lenoir (28645) *(G-9602)*

Cutting Edge Industries....................................... 336 937-2129
3502 Cloverdale Dr Greensboro (27408) *(G-6951)*

Cutting Edge Piping Svcs LLC............................ 704 419-3995
115 Ralph Green Rd Shelby (28152) *(G-14308)*

Cutting Edge Stoneworks, Mooresville Also Called: Cutting Edge Stoneworks Inc *(G-10921)*

Cutting Edge Stoneworks Inc............................. 704 799-1227
161 Mckenzie Rd Mooresville (28115) *(G-10921)*

Cutting Systems Inc.. 704 592-2451
774 Zeb Rd Union Grove (28689) *(G-15436)*

Cutting Up Logging LLC..................................... 910 389-3539
1507 White Oak River Rd Maysville (28555) *(G-10371)*

Cutworm Specialties Inc...................................... 828 389-1999
62 Church St Hayesville (28904) *(G-7765)*

Cv Industries... 919 778-7280
105 Pinehaven Ct Goldsboro (27534) *(G-6605)*

Cv Industries Inc (PA).. 828 328-1851
401 11th St Nw Hickory (28601) *(G-8001)*

Cvc & Equipment, Cherryville Also Called: CVC Equipment Company *(G-3867)*

CVC Equipment Company.................................. 704 300-6242
316 Old Stubbs Rd Ste 1 Cherryville (28021) *(G-3867)*

Cvmr (usa) Inc... 828 288-3768
2702 Centennial Rd Union Mills (28167) *(G-15440)*

Cw Landscapes, Efland Also Called: Chapman Welding LLC *(G-5524)*

Cw Media Inc... 910 302-3066
220 Crestwood Ln Raeford (28376) *(G-12419)*

CWC Fabricating... 704 360-8264
2530 Graham Rd Mount Ulla (28125) *(G-11682)*

Cwi Services LLC... 704 560-9755
3382 Willow Cir Se Southport (28461) *(G-14568)*

Cyber Defense Advisors....................................... 336 899-6072
3336 Wall Rd Greensboro (27407) *(G-6952)*

Cyber Imaging Systems Inc................................ 919 872-5179
8300 Falls Of Neuse Rd Raleigh (27615) *(G-12667)*

Cyberbiota Incorporated...................................... 919 308-3839
405 Gresham Ave Durham (27704) *(G-5043)*

Cyberlux Corporation (PA)................................. 984 363-6894
800 Park Offices Dr Ste 3209 Research Triangle Pa (27709) *(G-13549)*

Cybermatrix Inc... 910 292-9370
1323 Carolee Ct Fayetteville (28314) *(G-5803)*

Cycle Pro LLC.. 704 662-6682
261 Rolling Hill Rd Ste 1a Mooresville (28117) *(G-10922)*

Cycra Racing, Thomasville Also Called: Sv Plastics LLC *(G-15287)*

Cycra Racing Systems, Thomasville Also Called: Next World Design Inc *(G-15256)*

Cygany Inc.. 773 293-2999
2712 Denise Dr Greensboro (27407) *(G-6953)*

Cymbal LLC.. 877 365-9622
2500 Regency Pkwy Cary (27518) *(G-1744)*

Cynthia Drew... 828 301-8697
154 Horseshoe Trl Barnardsville (28709) *(G-907)*

Cynthia Saar... 910 480-2523
5139 Front St Stedman (28391) *(G-14934)*

Cyp, Tryon Also Called: Carolina Yarn Processors Inc *(G-15422)*

Cypress Bend Vineyards Inc............................... 910 369-0411
21904 Riverton Rd Wagram (28396) *(G-15522)*

Cypress Creek Harvesting Inc............................ 805 462-9412
6993 Old Fayetteville Rd Garland (28441) *(G-6241)*

Cypress Mountain Company (HQ)..................... 252 758-2179
107 Staton Ct Greenville (27834) *(G-7512)*

Cyrco Inc... 336 668-0977
120 N Chimney Rock Rd Greensboro (27409) *(G-6954)*

Cyril Bath Company (PA).................................... 704 289-8531
1610 Airport Rd Monroe (28110) *(G-10701)*

Cytonet LLC
801 Capitola Dr Ste 8 Durham (27713) *(G-5044)*

Czechmate Enterprises LLC................................ 704 784-6547
6101 Zion Church Rd Concord (28025) *(G-4250)*

D & B Concepts Inc.. 336 885-8292
613 Prospect St High Point (27260) *(G-8315)*

D & B Printing Co... 919 876-3530
3000 Trawick Rd Raleigh (27604) *(G-12668)*

D & D Displays Inc... 336 667-8765
126 Shaver St North Wilkesboro (28659) *(G-12005)*

D & D Entps Greensboro Inc............................... 336 495-3407
1337 Burnetts Chapel Rd Greensboro (27406) *(G-6955)*

D & D Entps Greensboro Inc............................... 336 495-3407
10458 Us Highway 220 Bus N Randleman (27317) *(G-13462)*

D & D Industries.. 252 331-2528
2299 Delia Dr Elizabeth City (27909) *(G-5539)*

ALPHABETIC SECTION

D & D Machine Works Inc 704 878-0117
111 Dealwood Dr Statesville (28625) *(G-14780)*

D & D Precision Tool, Greensboro *Also Called: D & D Entps Greensboro Inc (G-6955)*

D & D Welding & Repair LLC 336 648-1393
350 Slate Mountain Rd Mount Airy (27030) *(G-11499)*

D & F Consolidated Inc 704 664-6660
2205 Mocaro Dr Statesville (28677) *(G-14781)*

D & L Cabinets Inc 336 376-6009
1010 Rolling Oaks Dr Graham (27253) *(G-6687)*

D & M Logging of Wnc LLC 828 648-4366
1936 Beaverdam Rd Canton (28716) *(G-1612)*

D & M Packing Company 704 982-3716
687 Morgan Rd Albemarle (28001) *(G-80)*

D & S Frames Inc 828 241-5962
1309 Shiloh Rd Claremont (28610) *(G-3918)*

D & S International Inc 336 578-3800
700 Trollingwood Hawflds Rd Mebane (27302) *(G-10406)*

D & T Soy Candles 704 320-2804
152 Hawk Rd Polkton (28135) *(G-12386)*

D & W Logging Inc 919 820-0826
1771 Stricklands Crossroads Rd Four Oaks (27524) *(G-6102)*

D A C, Rural Hall *Also Called: Dac Products Inc (G-13839)*

D A Moore, Concord *Also Called: K&H Acquisition Company LLC (G-4297)*

D Block Metals LLC (PA) 704 705-5895
1111 Jenkins Rd Gastonia (28052) *(G-6393)*

D Block Metals LLC 980 238-2600
1808 Indian Creek Rd Lincolnton (28092) *(G-9889)*

D C Crsman Mfr Fine Jwly Inc 828 252-9891
269 Tunnel Rd Asheville (28805) *(G-601)*

D C Custom Freight LLC 843 658-6484
1901 Landsford Rd Marshville (28103) *(G-10213)*

D C Thomas Group Inc (PA) 336 299-6263
6540 W Market St Greensboro (27409) *(G-6956)*

D C Thomas Group Inc 252 433-0132
860 Commerce Dr Henderson (27537) *(G-7780)*

D D Lawncare Service 336 895-3353
5304 N Nc Highway 87 Gibsonville (27249) *(G-6558)*

D J Enviro Solutions 828 495-7448
334 Riverview Rd Taylorsville (28681) *(G-15139)*

D J Logging Inc 919 219-6853
5199 Hillsborough St Raleigh (27606) *(G-12669)*

D M & E Corporation 704 482-8876
833 S Post Rd Shelby (28152) *(G-14309)*

D M F Incorporated 919 553-5191
5335 Us 70 Bus Hwy W Clayton (27520) *(G-3971)*

D P G Entertainment, Fayetteville *Also Called: Dem Party Gurls Entrmt LLC (G-5811)*

D R Burton Healthcare LLC 252 228-7038
3936 South Fields St Farmville (27828) *(G-5733)*

D R Kincaid Chair Co Inc 828 754-0255
3122 Sheely Rd Lenoir (28645) *(G-9603)*

D T Bracy Logging Inc 252 332-8332
520 Kiwanis St Ahoskie (27910) *(G-59)*

D T M, Kings Mountain *Also Called: Diversified Textile Mchy Corp (G-9304)*

D Winchester Designs 704 607-0678
3121 Duck Point Dr Monroe (28110) *(G-10702)*

D&E Freight LLC 704 977-4847
4427 Knollcrest Dr Charlotte (28208) *(G-2597)*

D&J Sand & Gravel 919 584-8267
380 Claridge Nursery Rd Goldsboro (27530) *(G-6606)*

D&M Embroidery LLC 910 467-3586
1324 Sofia Ct Jacksonville (28540) *(G-8996)*

D&P Pallet, Star *Also Called: Lagael Manufacturing LLC (G-14718)*

D&S Asphalt Materials Inc 828 894-2778
265 Hugh Champion Rd Tryon (28782) *(G-15424)*

D2 Government Solutions LLC (PA) 662 655-4554
820 Aviation Dr Ste 1 New Bern (28562) *(G-11797)*

D2h Advanced Composites Inc 336 239-9637
6210 Hacker Bend Ct Ste G Winston Salem (27103) *(G-16667)*

D3 Software Inc 336 870-9138
277 Creekside Dr High Point (27265) *(G-8316)*

D3 Software Inc 336 776-0202
8411 N Nc Highway 109 Winston Salem (27107) *(G-16668)*

Da Welding LLC 336 231-7691
1645 S Martin Luther King Jr Dr Winston Salem (27107) *(G-16669)*

Dac Products Inc 336 969-9786
625 Montroyal Rd Rural Hall (27045) *(G-13839)*

Daddy Mikes LLC 252 327-1840
1211 Fellowes Ct Winterville (28590) *(G-16998)*

Daddy Petes Plant Pleaser 704 585-2355
1210 Smith Farm Rd Stony Point (28678) *(G-14971)*

Dae Systems, Claremont *Also Called: Dynamic Air Engineering Inc (G-3925)*

Daedalus Composites LLC 252 368-9000
109 Anchors Way Dr Edenton (27932) *(G-5512)*

Daedalus Yachts, Edenton *Also Called: Daedalus Composites LLC (G-5512)*

Daetwyler Cstm Fbrction McHnin, Huntersville *Also Called: Max Daetwyler Corp (G-8853)*

Daewoo-Folger Automotive, Charlotte *Also Called: Subaru Folger Automotive (G-3645)*

Dagenhart Pallet Inc 828 241-2374
2088 Mathis Church Rd Catawba (28609) *(G-1964)*

Dah Inc 910 887-3675
3940 Old Bridge Rd Se Southport (28461) *(G-14569)*

Daikin Applied Americas Inc 704 588-0087
13504 S Point Blvd Ste G Charlotte (28273) *(G-2598)*

Dails Pallet & Produce Inc 252 717-1338
2884 Neuse Rd Kinston (28501) *(G-9356)*

Daily Courier 828 245-6431
162 N Main St Rutherfordton (28139) *(G-13871)*

Daily Dispatch, Henderson *Also Called: Henderson Newspapers Inc (G-7786)*

Daily Grind 919 864-8775
10970 Chapel Hill Rd Ste 122 Morrisville (27560) *(G-11327)*

Daily Grind LLC 910 541-0471
114 N Topsail Dr Surf City (28445) *(G-15015)*

Daily Herald, Roanoke Rapids *Also Called: Wick Communications Co (G-13589)*

Daily Living Solutions Inc 704 614-0977
9711 Stewart Spring Ln Charlotte (28216) *(G-2599)*

Daily Manufacturing Inc 704 782-0700
4820 Pless Rd Rockwell (28138) *(G-13651)*

Daily N-Gine LLC 336 285-8042
909 Thorncroft Rd Greensboro (27406) *(G-6957)*

Daily Record The, Dunn *Also Called: Record Publishing Company (G-4881)*

Daily Reflector, The, Greenville *Also Called: Cox Nrth Crlina Pblcations Inc (G-7510)*

Daily Tarheel, Chapel Hill *Also Called: Dth Publishing Inc (G-2010)*

Daily Victories Inc 704 982-1341
1006 Colonial Dr Albemarle (28001) *(G-81)*

Daimler Truck North Amer LLC 704 645-5000
11550 Statesville Blvd Cleveland (27013) *(G-4071)*

Daimler Truck North Amer LLC 704 868-5700
1400 Tulip Dr Gastonia (28052) *(G-6394)*

Dairy Fresh, Winston Salem *Also Called: New Dairy Opco LLC (G-16819)*

Dairy Queen, Charlotte *Also Called: Lmb Corp (G-3098)*

Dairy Services 919 303-2442
100 Cordova Ct Raleigh (27606) *(G-12670)*

Daisy Pink Co 704 907-3526
10335 Worsley Ln Charlotte (28269) *(G-2600)*

Dak Americas, Fayetteville *Also Called: Alpek Polyester Usa LLC (G-5758)*

Dakota Fab & Welding Inc 919 881-0027
1420 W 3rd St Siler City (27344) *(G-14407)*

Dal Leather Inc 828 302-1667
2139 St Johns Church Rd Ne Conover (28613) *(G-4444)*

Dalco GF Technologies LLC 828 459-2577
2050 Evergreen Dr Ne Conover (28613) *(G-4445)*

Dalco Gft Nonwovens LLC 828 459-2577
2050 Evergreen Dr Ne Conover (28613) *(G-4446)*

Dale Advertising Inc 704 484-0971
2523 Taylor Rd Shelby (28152) *(G-14310)*

Dale Ray Fabrics LLC 704 932-6411
1121 N Main St Kannapolis (28081) *(G-9116)*

Dale Reynolds Cabinets Inc 704 890-5962
301 Kimmswick Rd Charlotte (28214) *(G-2601)*

Dales Welding Service 919 872-6969
7352 Berkshire Downs Dr Raleigh (27616) *(G-12671)*

Daliah Plastics Corp 336 629-0551
134 W Wainman Ave Asheboro (27203) *(G-421)*

ALPHABETIC SECTION — Daughtridge Enterprises Inc

Dallas Fabrication 704 629-4000
1346 Ramseur Rd Bessemer City (28016) *(G-1060)*

Dallas L Pridgen Inc 919 732-4422
104 Morningside Dr Carrboro (27510) *(G-1647)*

Dallas L Pridgen Jewelry, Carrboro Also Called: Dallas L Pridgen Inc *(G-1647)*

Dallas Machine and 704 629-5611
1326 Ramseur Rd Bessemer City (28016) *(G-1061)*

Dallas Machine Company, Bessemer City Also Called: Dallas Machine and *(G-1061)*

Daltons Metal Works, Winston Salem Also Called: Daltons Metal Works Inc *(G-16670)*

Daltons Metal Works Inc 336 731-1442
2411 Gumtree Rd Winston Salem (27107) *(G-16670)*

Daly Company Inc 919 751-3625
4043 Mclain St Goldsboro (27534) *(G-6607)*

Dambach Lagersysteme Inc 704 421-6425
121 W Trade St Ste 2850 Charlotte (28202) *(G-2602)*

Damco Inc 252 633-1404
1103 Us Highway 17 N New Bern (28560) *(G-11798)*

Dampp-Chaser, Hendersonville Also Called: Dampp-Chaser Electronics Corp *(G-7842)*

Dampp-Chaser Electronics Corp 828 692-8271
1410 Spartanburg Hwy Hendersonville (28792) *(G-7842)*

Damsel Dedicated To Defense 910 546-5603
4392 Eagle Bluff Ln Southport (28461) *(G-14570)*

Damsel In Defense 919 362-5972
2821 Evans Rd Apex (27502) *(G-179)*

Damsel In Defense 919 744-8776
109 Lake Point Dr Clayton (27527) *(G-3972)*

Damsel In Defense 919 901-9926
1401 Cuyler Best Rd Goldsboro (27534) *(G-6608)*

Dan Forrest Woodworks Wrap Up 919 532-9190
4209 Waterbury Rd Raleigh (27604) *(G-12672)*

Dan Moore Inc 336 475-8350
405 Albertson Rd Thomasville (27360) *(G-15210)*

Dan Morton Logging 919 693-1898
1671 Sunset Rd Oxford (27565) *(G-12126)*

Dana Fancy Foods 828 685-2937
101 Lytle Rd Hendersonville (28792) *(G-7843)*

Dana Industries 919 496-3262
Timberlake Rd Louisburg (27549) *(G-9984)*

Danaher Indus Sensors Contrls 910 862-5426
2100 W Broad St Elizabethtown (28337) *(G-5592)*

Danbartex LLC 704 323-8728
120 Commercial Dr Ste A Mooresville (28115) *(G-10923)*

Danby Barcoding LLC 770 416-9845
1800 Watmead Rd Kernersville (27284) *(G-9187)*

Dancing Moon Print Sltions Inc 828 689-9353
16 N Main St Mars Hill (28754) *(G-10194)*

Dandy Light Traps Inc 980 223-2744
1256 N Barkley Rd Statesville (28677) *(G-14782)*

DAngelico Guitars 908 451-9606
4111 W 5th St Lumberton (28358) *(G-10031)*

Dani Leather USA Inc 973 598-0890
635 Southwest St Ste A High Point (27260) *(G-8317)*

Daniel A Malpass Logging 910 669-2823
21819 Nc Highway 53 E Kelly (28448) *(G-9137)*

Daniel Carpenter Mustang, Concord Also Called: Mustang Reproductions Inc *(G-4321)*

Daniel Winkler Knifemaker LLC 828 262-3691
141 Leigh Ln Boone (28607) *(G-1192)*

Daniel, Johnny Logging, Denton Also Called: Johnny Daniel *(G-4739)*

Daniels Business Services Inc (PA) 828 277-8250
131 Sweeten Creek Rd 25a Asheville (28803) *(G-602)*

Daniels Graphics, Asheville Also Called: Daniels Business Services Inc *(G-602)*

Daniels House Publications 919 328-0709
201 Monticello Ave Durham (27707) *(G-5045)*

Daniels Lumber Sales Inc 336 622-5486
3224 Staley Store Rd Liberty (27298) *(G-9810)*

Daniels Woodcarving Co Inc 828 632-7336
2325 Nc Highway 90 E Taylorsville (28681) *(G-15140)*

Danisson Trading, Kernersville Also Called: Danisson USA Trading Ltd LLC *(G-9188)*

Danisson USA Trading Ltd LLC 704 965-8317
210 Serenity Pointe Dr Kernersville (27284) *(G-9188)*

Dannies Logging Inc 919 528-2370
2155 Tar River Rd Creedmoor (27522) *(G-4612)*

Danny Huffman Logging LLC 336 973-0555
154 Fletcher Creek Ln Purlear (28665) *(G-12410)*

Dannys Sandblasting 910 876-4596
119 Freeman St Bladenboro (28320) *(G-1147)*

Dante Cabinets 919 306-3261
2905 Sparger Rd Durham (27705) *(G-5046)*

Dantherm Filtration Inc 336 889-5599
150 Transit Ave Thomasville (27360) *(G-15211)*

Dap Products Inc 704 799-9640
125 Infield Ct Mooresville (28117) *(G-10924)*

Daphne Lawson Espino 910 290-2762
413 N Railroad Ave Beulaville (28518) *(G-1093)*

Daramic LLC (DH) 704 587-8599
11430 N Community House Rd Ste 350 Charlotte (28277) *(G-2603)*

Darius All Access, Wilmington Also Called: Darius All Access LLC *(G-16194)*

Darius All Access LLC 910 262-8567
1013 Glenlea Dr Wilmington (28405) *(G-16194)*

Dark City Defense 805 729-8800
178 Cragmont Rd Black Mountain (28711) *(G-1123)*

Dark Hydrogen LLC 530 360-8660
2557 Fallbrook Pl Nw Concord (28027) *(G-4251)*

Dark Moon Distileries LLC 704 222-8063
60 Deer Run, Banner Elk Banner Elk (28604) *(G-895)*

Darla Ward 252 340-1895
1096 Commissary Rd Elizabeth City (27909) *(G-5540)*

Darling Ingredients Inc 910 483-0473
1309 Industrial Dr Fayetteville (28301) *(G-5804)*

Darling Ingredients Inc 704 864-9941
5533 York Hwy Gastonia (28052) *(G-6395)*

Darling Ingredients Inc 910 289-2083
469 Yellowcut Rd Rose Hill (28458) *(G-13775)*

Darling Ingredients Inc 704 694-3701
656 Little Duncan Rd Wadesboro (28170) *(G-15509)*

Darnel Inc 704 625-9869
1809 Airport Rd Monroe (28110) *(G-10703)*

Darran Furniture, High Point Also Called: Darran Furniture Inds Inc *(G-8318)*

Darran Furniture Inds Inc 336 861-2400
2402 Shore St High Point (27263) *(G-8318)*

Darrell Scott Carriker 704 201-7465
Midland (28107) *(G-10466)*

Darrell T Bracy 252 358-1432
520 Kiwanis St Ahoskie (27910) *(G-60)*

Darren Lee Depalo 252 259-4515
108 Crocker Rd Havelock (28532) *(G-7741)*

Darren Moretz Backhoe Ser 828 964-1006
225 Tom Jackson Rd Boone (28607) *(G-1193)*

Dart Container Corp Georgia 336 495-1101
3219 Wesleyan Rd Randleman (27317) *(G-13463)*

Daryl Duff Lockyer 704 658-0695
170 Gabriel Dr Mooresville (28115) *(G-10925)*

Das Oil Werks LLC 919 267-5781
198 Hidden Field Ln New Hill (27562) *(G-11860)*

Dash Cabinet Company LLC 704 746-7382
19701 Bethel Church Rd Ste 201 Cornelius (28031) *(G-4538)*

Data443 Risk Mitigation Inc 919 858-6542
4000 Sancar Way Ste 400 Durham (27709) *(G-5047)*

Database Incorporated 202 684-6252
3342 Rose Of Sharon Rd Durham (27712) *(G-5048)*

Dataforce, Charlotte Also Called: Mjt Us Inc *(G-3189)*

Datamark Graphics Inc 336 629-0267
603 W Bailey St Asheboro (27203) *(G-422)*

Datanyze LLC 866 408-1633
2530 Meridian Pkwy Ste 300 Durham (27713) *(G-5049)*

Datascope North America Inc 980 819-5244
4427 Wilgrove Mint Hill Rd Mint Hill (28227) *(G-10528)*

Dataspectrum 919 341-3300
4700 Falls Of Neuse Rd Raleigh (27609) *(G-12673)*

Daughters & Ryan Inc 919 284-0153
207 Johnston Pkwy Kenly (27542) *(G-9151)*

Daughtridge Enterprises Inc 252 977-7775
1200 East St Rocky Mount (27801) *(G-13665)*

Daughtrys Creations LLC   **ALPHABETIC SECTION**

Daughtrys Creations LLC 704 929-8717
   2134 Land Hbr Newland (28657) *(G-11884)*

Dauntless Discovery LLC 610 909-7383
   808 Aviation Pkwy Ste 1200 Morrisville (27560) *(G-11328)*

Dauntless Mfg Solutions LLC 757 870-2173
   247 Sawyersville Rd Asheboro (27205) *(G-423)*

Davcom Enterprises Inc 919 872-9522
   2621 Spring Forest Rd Ste 105 Raleigh (27616) *(G-12674)*

Dave Mulhollem Logging Inc 919 796-8994
   8853 Covered Bridge Rd Wendell (27591) *(G-15896)*

Dave Steel Company Inc 828 252-2771
   76 Roberts Rd Asheville (28803) *(G-603)*

Dave Steel Company Inc (PA) 828 252-2771
   40 Meadow Rd Asheville (28803) *(G-604)*

David Allen Company Inc (PA) 919 821-7100
   150 Rush St Raleigh (27603) *(G-12675)*

David Beasley 910 891-2557
   306 S Clinton Ave Dunn (28334) *(G-4860)*

David Bennett 919 798-3424
   80 H H Mckoy Ln Fuquay Varina (27526) *(G-6194)*

David Conrad 336 253-6966
   212 Staunton Dr Greensboro (27410) *(G-6958)*

David E Meiggs 252 340-1640
   114 Calm Harbor St Hertford (27944) *(G-7919)*

David J Spain 252 902-6900
   8851 Cherry Run Rd Washington (27889) *(G-15694)*

David Miller Logging LLC 336 831-4052
   2541 Spencer Rd Boonville (27011) *(G-1254)*

David Oreck Candle 336 375-8411
   3500 N Ohenry Blvd Greensboro (27405) *(G-6959)*

David Presnell 336 372-5989
   1397 Us Highway 21 S Sparta (28675) *(G-14592)*

David R Webb Company Inc 336 605-3355
   300 Standard Dr Greensboro (27409) *(G-6960)*

David Raynor Logging Inc 910 980-0129
   4718 Long St Linden (28356) *(G-9939)*

David Rothschild Co Inc 336 342-0035
   618 Grooms Rd Reidsville (27320) *(G-13516)*

David Vizard Motortec Features 865 850-0666
   109 Mistywood Dr Mount Holly (28120) *(G-11630)*

David West 910 271-0757
   9090 Us Hwy 117 N Willard (28478) *(G-16054)*

David Yurman Enterprises LLC 704 366-7259
   4400 Sharon Rd Ste 177 Charlotte (28211) *(G-2604)*

Davidson Daily, Kinston *Also Called: Magic Mile Media Inc (G-9375)*

Davidson House Inc 704 791-0171
   643 Portside Dr Davidson (28036) *(G-4670)*

Davidson Machine Fabrication, Clayton *Also Called: D M F Incorporated (G-3971)*

Davidson Printing Inc 336 357-0555
   223 S Main St Ste D Lexington (27292) *(G-9704)*

Davidson Printing & Machinery 202 558-2055
   6173 Nc Highway 58 S Stantonsburg (27883) *(G-14711)*

Davidson Steel Services LLC 336 775-1234
   11075 Old Us Highway 52 # 100 Winston Salem (27107) *(G-16671)*

Davidson Wine Co LLC 614 738-0051
   10930 Zac Hill Rd Davidson (28036) *(G-4671)*

Davidsonspeed Printing, Lexington *Also Called: Davidson Printing Inc (G-9704)*

Davie County Publishing Co (HQ) 336 751-2120
   171 S Main St Mocksville (27028) *(G-10565)*

Davie Paper Co 425 941-1994
   5303 Grandhaven Dr Durham (27713) *(G-5050)*

Davie Property Restoration LLC 336 923-4018
   177 Sourwood Ln Advance (27006) *(G-40)*

Davis Brothers Roofing 828 578-8561
   2404 N Center St Unit B Hickory (28601) *(G-8002)*

Davis Cabinet Co Wilson Inc 252 291-9052
   6116 Green Pond Rd Sims (27880) *(G-14441)*

Davis Conveyor Components 704 557-1742
   1400 Sharon Rd W Charlotte (28210) *(G-2605)*

Davis Custom Cabinets 336 961-2817
   2545 Union Cross Church Rd Yadkinville (27055) *(G-17036)*

Davis Davis Mch & Wldg Co Inc 252 443-2652
   4956 Community Dr Rocky Mount (27804) *(G-13689)*

Davis Equipment Handlers Inc 704 792-9176
   3860 Abiliene Rd Charlotte (28205) *(G-2606)*

Davis Furniture Industries Inc (PA) 336 889-2009
   2401 College Dr High Point (27260) *(G-8319)*

Davis Machine Co Inc 704 865-2863
   158 Superior Stainless Rd Gastonia (28052) *(G-6396)*

Davis Mechanical Inc 704 272-9366
   4368 Nc 218 Peachland (28133) *(G-12173)*

Davis Newell Company Inc 910 762-3500
   2962 N Kerr Ave Wilmington (28405) *(G-16195)*

Davis Publishing Group In 919 894-4170
   611 Chicopee Rd Benson (27504) *(G-1034)*

Davis Rug, Shelby *Also Called: Davis Rug Company (G-14311)*

Davis Rug Company 704 434-7231
   3938 Barclay Rd Shelby (28152) *(G-14311)*

Davis Sign Company Inc 336 765-2990
   208 Regent Dr Winston Salem (27103) *(G-16672)*

Davis Steel and Iron Co Inc 704 821-7676
   1035 Commercial Dr Matthews (28104) *(G-10311)*

Davis Vogler Enterprises LLC 402 257-7188
   5316 Camilla Dr Charlotte (28226) *(G-2607)*

Davospharma 919 662-8432
   4009 Harriat Dr Apex (27539) *(G-180)*

Dawn Processing Company Inc 704 629-5321
   205 E Alabama Ave Bessemer City (28016) *(G-1062)*

Day & Nght Creal Bar Clmbia SC 719 323-8265
   2316 Foster Gwin Ln Fayetteville (28304) *(G-5805)*

Day 3 Lwncare Ldscpg Prfctnist 910 574-8422
   1637 Woodfield Rd Fayetteville (28303) *(G-5806)*

Day International Prtg Pdts, Arden *Also Called: Flint Group US LLC (G-332)*

Dayco Manufacturing Inc 919 989-1820
   6116 Us 70 W Clayton (27520) *(G-3973)*

Dayco Products LLC 910 843-1024
   16824 Nc Highway 211 W Red Springs (28377) *(G-13497)*

Daydream Education LLC 800 591-6150
   21 Listening Cv Clyde (28721) *(G-4123)*

Daystar Machining Tech Inc 828 684-1316
   356 Cane Creek Rd Fletcher (28732) *(G-5997)*

Daystar Materials Inc 919 734-0460
   200 W Dewey St Goldsboro (27530) *(G-6609)*

Daytech Solutions LLC 336 918-4122
   101 N Chestnut St Ste 211 Winston Salem (27101) *(G-16673)*

Dayton Bag & Burlap Co 704 873-7271
   233 Commerce Blvd Statesville (28625) *(G-14783)*

Dayton Metals 937 615-9812
   Fayetteville (28302) *(G-5807)*

Daztech Inc 800 862-6360
   214 Walnut St Wilmington (28401) *(G-16196)*

Daztech Promotions, Wilmington *Also Called: Daztech Inc (G-16196)*

DB CUSTOM CRAFTS LLC 336 791-0940
   267 Kendall Farms Ct Winston Salem (27107) *(G-16674)*

Db North Carolina Holdings Inc (HQ) 910 323-4848
   458 Whitfield St Fayetteville (28306) *(G-5808)*

Db Power Sports 828 324-1500
   2830 Springs Rd Ne Hickory (28601) *(G-8003)*

Dbt Coatings LLC 336 834-9700
   1908 Fairfax Rd Ste A Greensboro (27407) *(G-6961)*

Dbw Print & Promo 704 906-8551
   6012 Bayfield Pkwy Concord (28027) *(G-4252)*

Dce Inc 704 230-4649
   138 Cayuga Dr Ste C Mooresville (28117) *(G-10926)*

DCE Solar Service Inc 704 659-7474
   19410 Jetton Rd Ste 220 Cornelius (28031) *(G-4539)*

Dcli, Charlotte *Also Called: Direct Chassislink Inc (G-2639)*

DCS USA Corporation 919 535-8000
   3000 Bear Cat Way Ste 118 Morrisville (27560) *(G-11329)*

Ddi, Raleigh *Also Called: Ddi Print (G-12676)*

Ddi Print 919 829-8810
   5210 Western Blvd Raleigh (27606) *(G-12676)*

ALPHABETIC SECTION

Ddm Inc 910 686-1481
210 Sea Shell Ln Wilmington (28411) *(G-16197)*

Ddp Spclty Elctrnic Mtls US 9 .... 336 547-7112
2914 Patterson St Greensboro (27407) *(G-6962)*

De Feet, Hildebran *Also Called: De Feet International Inc (G-8621)*

De Feet International Inc 828 397-7025
371 I40 Access Rd Hildebran (28637) *(G-8621)*

De Little Cabinet Inc 704 888-5994
8267 Nc Hwy 200 Stanfield (28163) *(G-14677)*

De Luxe Packaging Corp 800 845-6051
3436 Toringdon Way Ste 100 Charlotte (28277) *(G-2608)*

DEA Sasso Light of Day 828 258-0141
117 Morningside Dr Asheville (28806) *(G-605)*

Deal Machine Shop Inc 704 872-7618
400 Beulah Rd Statesville (28625) *(G-14784)*

Deal-Rite Feeds Inc 704 873-8646
109 Anna Dr Statesville (28625) *(G-14785)*

Dealer Track Inc 919 554-0972
1890 S Main St Ste 106 Wake Forest (27587) *(G-15545)*

Dean Company of North Carolina 910 622-1012
301 Us Highway 17 S Ste 9 Holly Ridge (28445) *(G-8681)*

Dean S Ready Mixed Inc 704 982-5520
517 Old Charlotte Rd Albemarle (28001) *(G-82)*

Dean St Processing LLC 252 235-0401
5645 Deans St Bailey (27807) *(G-871)*

DEB Manufacturing Inc 704 703-6618
4040 Dearborn Pl Nw Concord (28027) *(G-4253)*

Deb SBS Inc 704 263-4240
1100 S Highway 27 Stanley (28164) *(G-14690)*

Debbing Inspirations, Greensboro *Also Called: Tapestries Ltd (G-7389)*

Deberry Land & Timber Inc 910 572-2698
112 Leslie St Troy (27371) *(G-15403)*

Deberry Precision Machine Inc 704 422-3274
40018 Palmerville Rd New London (28127) *(G-11868)*

Debmed Usa LLC 704 263-4240
2815 Coliseum Centre Dr # 6 Charlotte (28217) *(G-2609)*

Debotech Inc 704 664-1361
130 Infield Ct Mooresville (28117) *(G-10927)*

Decal Source Inc 336 574-3141
804 Knox Rd Mc Leansville (27301) *(G-10388)*

Decarlo Woodworks 919 327-3647
4917 Mashpee Ln Apex (27539) *(G-181)*

December Diamonds Inc 828 926-3308
3425 Dellwood Rd Waynesville (28786) *(G-15801)*

Decicco Woodshop LLC 914 213-8553
207 Penchant Ct Cary (27513) *(G-1745)*

Decima Corporation Inc 734 516-1535
529 W Summit Ave Ste 1c Charlotte (28203) *(G-2610)*

Decker Advanced Fabrication, Charlotte *Also Called: Joseph F Decker (G-3035)*

Deckle Paperboard Sales Inc 910 686-9145
256 Osprey Pl Wilmington (28411) *(G-16198)*

Decocrete 910 358-4175
1120 River St Jacksonville (28540) *(G-8997)*

Decolux USA 704 340-3532
6024 Shining Oak Ln Charlotte (28269) *(G-2611)*

Decorative Def Con Coatings, Aberdeen *Also Called: Tfam Solutions LLC (G-31)*

Decorative Plastics LLC 252 638-6684
203 River Bluffs Dr New Bern (28560) *(G-11799)*

Decore-Ative Spc NC LLC 704 291-9669
701 Industrial Dr Monroe (28110) *(G-10704)*

Dedon Inc (DH) 336 790-1070
657 Brigham Rd Ste C Greensboro (27409) *(G-6963)*

Deep Creek Lures Inc 910 892-1791
603 S Wilson Ave Dunn (28334) *(G-4861)*

Deep Creek Motors Inc 336 599-0000
625 N Madison Blvd Roxboro (27573) *(G-13800)*

Deep Creek Timber, Wadesboro *Also Called: James L Johnson (G-15514)*

Deep Creek Winery 828 341-0592
380 Jonathan Walk Bryson City (28713) *(G-1323)*

Deep River Fabricators Inc 336 824-8881
240 E Main St Franklinville (27248) *(G-6168)*

Deep River Press Inc 910 249-9552
412 Virginia Ave Morehead City (28557) *(G-11167)*

Deep River Printing, Greensboro *Also Called: Deep Rver Mlls Ctd Fabrics Inc (G-6964)*

Deep Rver Mlls Ctd Fabrics Inc (PA) 910 464-3135
1904 Lendew St Greensboro (27408) *(G-6964)*

Deep South Holding Company Inc 336 427-0265
2216 Us Highway 311 Madison (27025) *(G-10072)*

Deere & Company 919 567-6400
6501 S Nc 55 Hwy Fuquay Varina (27526) *(G-6195)*

Deere & Company 336 996-8100
1000 John Deere Rd Kernersville (27284) *(G-9189)*

Deere-Hitachi Cnstr McHy, Kernersville *Also Called: Deere & Company (G-9189)*

Deerhunter Tree Stands Inc 704 462-1116
5944 Leil Rd Hickory (28602) *(G-8004)*

Deetag USA Inc (DH) 828 465-2644
1232 Fedex Dr Sw Conover (28613) *(G-4447)*

Defense Logistics Services LLC 703 449-1620
231 Meed Ct Ste 104 Fayetteville (28303) *(G-5809)*

Defense of Implicit 919 554-2735
144 S Creek Dr Louisburg (27549) *(G-9985)*

Definitive Media Corp (PA) 714 730-4958
2000 Centre Green Way Ste 300 Cary (27513) *(G-1746)*

Defy Hickory 828 222-4144
1843 Catawba Valley Blvd Se Hickory (28602) *(G-8005)*

Degesch America Inc 800 548-2778
1810 Firestone Pkwy Ne Wilson (27893) *(G-16492)*

Dehydration LLC 252 747-8200
963 Hwy 258 S Snow Hill (28580) *(G-14502)*

Dej Holdings LLC (PA) 704 799-4800
349 Cayuga Dr Mooresville (28117) *(G-10928)*

Deka Batteries & Cables, Winston Salem *Also Called: East Penn Manufacturing Co (G-16689)*

Del-Mark Inc 828 322-6180
1225 Main Ave Sw Hickory (28602) *(G-8006)*

Delaby Brace and Limb Co 910 484-2509
405 Owen Dr Fayetteville (28304) *(G-5810)*

Delaney Holdings Co 704 808-3848
13320 Ballantyne Corporate Pl Charlotte (28277) *(G-2612)*

Delarrivo Inc 919 460-9500
3000 Rdu Center Dr Morrisville (27560) *(G-11330)*

Delbert White Logging Inc 252 209-4779
452 White Oak Rd Windsor (27983) *(G-16564)*

Delcor Polymers Inc 704 847-0640
2536 Winterbrooke Dr Matthews (28105) *(G-10246)*

Delfortgroup Printing Services 336 272-9344
206 Bruce St Greensboro (27403) *(G-6965)*

Delgado's Fuego, Charlotte *Also Called: Jhonny Delgado (G-3021)*

Delgados Welding Inc 910 588-4762
1275 Willard Tatum Rd Elizabethtown (28337) *(G-5593)*

Delish Cakery Co 704 724-7743
3425 Back Creek Church Rd Charlotte (28213) *(G-2613)*

Deliveright Logistics Inc 862 279-7332
176 L F I Complex Ln Lexington (27295) *(G-9705)*

Delizza LLC 252 442-0270
6610 Corporation Pkwy Battleboro (27809) *(G-919)*

Delkote Machine Finishing Inc 828 253-1023
69 Bingham Rd Asheville (28806) *(G-606)*

Dellinger Enterprises Ltd 704 825-9687
759 Cason St Belmont (28012) *(G-982)*

Dellinger Precast Inc 704 483-2868
4531 N Nc 16 Business Hwy Denver (28037) *(G-4771)*

Dellinger Woodworks LLC 980 245-6086
1806 Crestgate Dr Waxhaw (28173) *(G-15751)*

Dellner Inc 704 527-2121
4016 Shutterfly Rd Ste 100 Charlotte (28217) *(G-2614)*

Dellner Brakes, Charlotte *Also Called: Dellner Inc (G-2614)*

Delta Contractors Inc 817 410-9481
6309 Castlebrooke Ln Linden (28356) *(G-9940)*

Delta Mold Inc 704 588-6600
9415 Stockport Pl Charlotte (28273) *(G-2615)*

Delta Msrment Cmbstn Cntrls LL 919 623-7133
207 Kettlebridge Dr Cary (27511) *(G-1747)*

Delta Phoenix Inc... 336 621-3960
  4820 Us Hwy 29 N Greensboro (27405) *(G-6966)*

Deltec Homes Inc (PA)... 828 253-0483
  69 Bingham Rd Asheville (28806) *(G-607)*

Deluxe Corp... 704 969-5200
  6125 Lakeview Rd Charlotte (28269) *(G-2616)*

Deluxe Corporation.. 336 851-4600
  3703 Farmington Dr Greensboro (27407) *(G-6967)*

Deluxe Printing Co Inc... 828 322-1329
  10 9th St Nw Hickory (28601) *(G-8007)*

Deluxe Printing Group, Hickory *Also Called: Deluxe Printing Co Inc (G-8007)*

Delve Interiors LLC... 336 274-4661
  7820 Thorndike Rd Greensboro (27409) *(G-6968)*

Delzer Construction.. 919 625-0755
  632 Northwoods Dr Cary (27513) *(G-1748)*

Dem Party Gurls Entrmt LLC...................................... 910 964-3599
  7582 Beverly Dr Fayetteville (28314) *(G-5811)*

Demilo Bros NC LLC.. 704 771-0762
  1807 Palazzo Dr Waxhaw (28173) *(G-15752)*

Demilo Bros., Waxhaw *Also Called: Demilo Bros NC LLC (G-15752)*

Demmel Inc... 828 585-6600
  100 Old World Cir East Flat Rock (28726) *(G-5473)*

Democracy Greensboro.. 336 635-7016
  5214 Skylark Dr Greensboro (27405) *(G-6969)*

Denso Manufacturing NC Inc.................................... 252 754-1000
  1125 Sugg Pkwy Greenville (27834) *(G-7513)*

Denso Manufacturing NC Inc (DH)............................ 704 878-6663
  470 Crawford Rd Statesville (28625) *(G-14786)*

Dental Equipment LLC... 704 588-2126
  11727 Fruehauf Dr Charlotte (28273) *(G-2617)*

Denton Orator... 336 859-3131
  26 N Main St Denton (27239) *(G-4732)*

Denton Wreath Company.. 828 479-4992
  692 Slaybacon Rd Robbinsville (28771) *(G-13607)*

Dentonics Inc.. 704 238-0245
  2833 Top Hill Rd Monroe (28110) *(G-10705)*

DENTSPLY SIRONA, Charlotte *Also Called: Dentsply Sirona Inc (G-2618)*

Dentsply Sirona Inc (PA)... 844 848-0137
  13320 Ballantyne Corporate Pl Charlotte (28277) *(G-2618)*

Denver Global Products Inc..................................... 704 665-1800
  6420 Rea Rd Ste A1 Charlotte (28277) *(G-2619)*

Denver Waterjet LLC.. 980 222-7447
  3865 N Nc 16 Business Hwy Denver (28037) *(G-4772)*

Deohges Welding Service LLC................................. 828 396-2770
  2800 Campground Rd Granite Falls (28630) *(G-6731)*

Depalo Foods Inc.. 704 827-0245
  2010 Oaks Pkwy Belmont (28012) *(G-983)*

Department of Solid Waste, Taylorsville *Also Called: County of Alexander (G-15136)*

Derick Cordon Logging Inc...................................... 252 964-2009
  9040 Nc 99 Hwy South Bath (27808) *(G-915)*

Deringer-Ney Inc... 828 649-3232
  155 Deringer Dr Marshall (28753) *(G-10201)*

Derita Precision Mch Co Inc.................................... 704 392-7285
  605 Toddville Rd Charlotte (28214) *(G-2620)*

Dermasweet LLC... 843 834-1413
  817 Town Center Dr Ste 125- Wilmington (28405) *(G-16199)*

Derrow Enterprises Inc... 252 635-3375
  7001 Us Highway 70 E New Bern (28562) *(G-11800)*

Dersheng Usa Inc... 336 434-5055
  2019 Brevard Rd High Point (27263) *(G-8320)*

Dert Sign Co... 336 225-1800
  984 N Nc Highway 150 Lexington (27295) *(G-9706)*

Descher Automation, Raleigh *Also Called: Descher LLC (G-12677)*

Descher LLC.. 919 828-7708
  1613 Old Louisburg Rd Raleigh (27604) *(G-12677)*

Desco Equipment Company Inc............................... 704 873-2844
  1031 S Meeting St Statesville (28677) *(G-14787)*

Desco Industries Inc.. 919 718-0000
  920 J R Industrial Dr Sanford (27332) *(G-14107)*

Desco Industries Inc.. 919 718-0000
  917 J R Industrial Dr Sanford (27332) *(G-14108)*

Desco Industries Inc.. 919 718-0000
  914 J R Industrial Dr Sanford (27332) *(G-14109)*

Desco Industries Inc.. 919 718-0000
  926 J R Industrial Dr Sanford (27332) *(G-14110)*

Desena Commercial Services LLC............................ 336 786-1111
  525 Holly Springs Rd Mount Airy (27030) *(G-11500)*

Desena Commercial Svc.. 336 786-1111
  268 Old Highway 601 Mount Airy (27030) *(G-11501)*

Design Concepts Incorporated................................. 336 887-1932
  341 South Rd High Point (27262) *(G-8321)*

Design Engnred Fbrications Inc................................ 336 768-8260
  2461 Spaugh Industrial Dr Winston Salem (27103) *(G-16675)*

Design Master Displays, High Point *Also Called: Master Displays Inc (G-8448)*

Design Printing Inc.. 336 472-3333
  1107 Trinity St Thomasville (27360) *(G-15212)*

Design Specialties Inc... 919 772-6955
  3640 Banks Rd Raleigh (27603) *(G-12678)*

Design Surfaces Inc... 919 781-0310
  1212 Front St Raleigh (27609) *(G-12679)*

Design Surfaces of Raleigh, Raleigh *Also Called: Design Surfaces Inc (G-12679)*

Design Theory LLC... 336 912-0155
  1020 Surrett Dr High Point (27260) *(G-8322)*

Design Workshop Incorporated................................ 910 293-7329
  1696 Nc 24 And 50 Hwy Warsaw (28398) *(G-15666)*

Design Workshop, The, Wilmington *Also Called: Diane Britt (G-16200)*

Designcraft... 919 903-5711
  106 Berry Patch Ln Chapel Hill (27514) *(G-2007)*

Designelement.. 919 383-5561
  972 Trinity Rd Raleigh (27607) *(G-12680)*

Designer Woodwork... 910 521-1252
  1616 Hiawatha Rd Pembroke (28372) *(G-12182)*

Designline Corporation.. 704 494-7800
  2309 Nevada Blvd Charlotte (28273) *(G-2621)*

Designline Intl Holdings, Charlotte *Also Called: Designline Corporation (G-2621)*

Designline Usa LLC... 704 494-7800
  2309 Nevada Blvd Charlotte (28273) *(G-2622)*

Designmaster Furniture Inc...................................... 828 324-7992
  1283 23rd St Se Hickory (28602) *(G-8008)*

Designs By Rachel.. 828 783-0698
  220 Reservoir Rd Spruce Pine (28777) *(G-14639)*

Designs In Wood... 336 372-8995
  122 E Doughton St Sparta (28675) *(G-14593)*

Designtek Fabrication Inc.. 910 359-0130
  16824 A Hwy 211 Red Springs (28377) *(G-13498)*

Desmond Office Furniture Inc.................................. 828 235-9400
  865 Beaverdam Rd Canton (28716) *(G-1613)*

Detmer Metals LLC.. 704 997-6114
  168 Beracah Rd Mooresville (28115) *(G-10929)*

Deuces Custom... 704 658-1777
  240 Commodore Loop Mooresville (28117) *(G-10930)*

Deurotech America Inc.. 980 272-6827
  4526 Westinghouse Blvd Ste A Charlotte (28273) *(G-2623)*

Devada, Research Triangle Pa *Also Called: Dzone Inc (G-13550)*

Devan Us Inc.. 704 365-7111
  6525 Morrison Blvd Ste 516 Charlotte (28211) *(G-2624)*

Deverger Systems Inc.. 828 253-2255
  87 Downing St Asheville (28806) *(G-608)*

Devil Dog Manufacturing Co Inc............................... 919 269-7485
  400 E Gannon Ave Zebulon (27597) *(G-17125)*

Devils Kindred MC... 336 712-7689
  310 S Chestnut St Swansboro (28584) *(G-15044)*

Deviney Lumber & Salvage, Casar *Also Called: M O Deviney Lumber Co Inc (G-1934)*

Devmir Legwear Inc... 919 545-5500
  136 Fayetteville St Pittsboro (27312) *(G-12338)*

Devora Designs Inc... 336 782-0964
  1315 Creekshire Way Apt 312 Winston Salem (27103) *(G-16676)*

Dew Group Enterprises Inc...................................... 919 585-0100
  501 Atkinson St Clayton (27520) *(G-3974)*

Dewalt Industrial Tool, Greensboro *Also Called: Black & Decker (us) Inc (G-6840)*

Dewey S Bakery Inc (PA)... 336 748-0230
  3840 Kimwell Dr Winston Salem (27103) *(G-16677)*

ALPHABETIC SECTION

Dewill Inc..919 426-9550
951 High House Rd Cary (27513) *(G-1749)*

Dewoolfson Down, Banner Elk Also Called: Dewoolfson Down Intl Inc *(G-896)*

Dewoolfson Down Intl Inc (PA)..828 963-2750
9452 Nc Highway 105 S Banner Elk (28604) *(G-896)*

Dex Media East LLC..919 297-1600
1001 Winstead Dr Ste 1 Cary (27513) *(G-1750)*

Dex n Dox..910 576-4644
225 Basswood Rd Troy (27371) *(G-15404)*

Dex One Corporation..919 297-1600
1001 Winstead Dr Cary (27513) *(G-1751)*

Dexios Services LLC..704 946-5101
10308 Bailey Rd Ste 430 Cornelius (28031) *(G-4540)*

Dexter Inc..828 459-7904
5718 Oxford School Rd Claremont (28610) *(G-3919)*

Dexter Inc (PA)..919 510-5050
8411 Glenwood Ave Ste 101 Raleigh (27612) *(G-12681)*

Dexter Furniture, Raleigh Also Called: Dexter Inc *(G-12681)*

Dexterity LLC..919 524-7732
104 Azalea Dr Greenville (27858) *(G-7514)*

Df Framing LLC..919 368-7903
510 N Garden Ave Siler City (27344) *(G-14408)*

Dfa Dairy Brands Fluid LLC..704 341-2794
3540 Toringdon Way Ste 200 Charlotte (28277) *(G-2625)*

Dfa Dairy Brands Fluid LLC..336 714-9032
1079 W Saint James St Tarboro (27886) *(G-15101)*

Dfp Inc (PA)..336 841-3028
685 Southwest St High Point (27260) *(G-8323)*

Dg Printing Solutions..919 779-0225
5412 Overdale Ln Raleigh (27603) *(G-12682)*

Dg Solutions LLC..864 605-3223
44 Buck Shoals Rd Ste F2 Arden (28704) *(G-324)*

DH Screen Print Plus..704 609-4823
10917 Wyndham Pointe Dr Charlotte (28213) *(G-2626)*

Dhollandia Us Llc (HQ)..909 251-7979
270 Southridge Pkwy Bessemer City (28016) *(G-1063)*

Dia-Be-Tees LLC..330 687-7792
6501 Hollow Oak Dr Mint Hill (28227) *(G-10529)*

Diabetic Sock Club..800 214-0218
6325 Wilkinson Blvd Ste 103 Belmont (28012) *(G-984)*

Diablo Distilleries LLC..910 467-5017
316 Royal Bluff Rd Jacksonville (28540) *(G-8998)*

Diagnostic Devices..704 599-5908
2701 Hutchison Mcdonald Rd Ste A Charlotte (28269) *(G-2627)*

Diagnostic Shop Inc..704 933-3435
723 Fairview St Kannapolis (28083) *(G-9117)*

Diagnostic Shop and Repair, Kannapolis Also Called: Diagnostic Shop Inc *(G-9117)*

Diamond Apparel..866 578-9708
100 Webb Way Advance (27006) *(G-41)*

Diamond Apparel, Mocksville Also Called: Carolina Square Inc *(G-10562)*

Diamond Brand, Fletcher Also Called: Diamond Brand Gear Company *(G-5998)*

Diamond Brand Canvas Products, Fletcher Also Called: WC&r Interests LLC *(G-6050)*

Diamond Brand Gear Company..828 684-9848
145 Cane Creek Industrial Park Rd Ste 100 Fletcher (28732) *(G-5998)*

Diamond Dog Tools Inc..828 687-3686
75 Old Shoals Rd Arden (28704) *(G-325)*

Diamond Enterprises..828 495-4448
5171 Icard Ridge Rd Hickory (28601) *(G-8009)*

Diamond Finish Car Wash, Charlotte Also Called: G & E Investments Inc *(G-2802)*

Diamond Orthopedic LLC..704 585-8258
1669 Federal St Gastonia (28052) *(G-6397)*

Diamond Outdoor Entps Inc..336 857-1450
9035 Nc Highway 49 S Denton (27239) *(G-4733)*

Diamond Power Intl LLC..704 625-4900
13024 Ballantyne Corporate Pl Ste 700 Charlotte (28277) *(G-2628)*

Diamond Pwr Astrlia Hldngs Inc..704 625-4900
13024 Ballantyne Corporate Pl Ste 700 Charlotte (28277) *(G-2629)*

Diamond Pwr Eqity Invstmnts In..704 625-4900
13024 Ballantyne Corporate Pl Ste 700 Charlotte (28277) *(G-2630)*

Diamond Research and Dev, Hickory Also Called: Diamond Enterprises *(G-8009)*

Diamondback Armor..828 288-6680
207 Oakland Rd Spindale (28160) *(G-14606)*

Diamondback Industries LLC..336 956-8871
4683 Old Salisbury Rd Lexington (27295) *(G-9707)*

Diamondback Products Inc..336 236-9800
40 W 12th Ave Lexington (27292) *(G-9708)*

Diane Britt..910 763-9600
3205 Kitty Hawk Rd Ste 1 Wilmington (28405) *(G-16200)*

Diarkis LLC..704 888-5244
142 Cara Ct Locust (28097) *(G-9957)*

Diazit Company Inc..919 556-5188
8120 Diazit Dr Wake Forest (27587) *(G-15546)*

Dicey Fabrics, Shelby Also Called: Dicey Mills Inc *(G-14312)*

Dicey Mills Inc..704 487-6324
430 Neisler St Shelby (28152) *(G-14312)*

Dickerson Group Inc (PA)..704 289-3111
1111 Metropolitan Ave Ste 1090 Charlotte (28204) *(G-2631)*

Dickie Jones..828 733-5084
883 Whitaker Branch Rd Newland (28657) *(G-11885)*

Dicks Store..336 548-9358
547 Mccollum Rd Madison (27025) *(G-10073)*

Dickson Elberton Mill Inc..336 226-3556
1831 N Park Ave Burlington (27217) *(G-1406)*

Die-Tech Inc..336 475-9186
4 Stanley Ave Thomasville (27360) *(G-15213)*

Diebold Nixdorf Incorporated..704 599-3100
5900 Northwoods Business Pkwy Ste K Charlotte (28269) *(G-2632)*

Dienes Apparatus Inc..704 525-3770
9220 Rodney St Pineville (28134) *(G-12265)*

Digger Specialties Inc..919 255-2533
8013 Purfoy Rd Fuquay Varina (27526) *(G-6196)*

Digger Specialties Inc..336 495-1517
4256 Heath Dairy Rd Randleman (27317) *(G-13464)*

Digi Ronin Games LLC..919 845-9960
12308 Glenlivet Way Raleigh (27613) *(G-12683)*

Digital AP Prtg DBA F4mily Mtt..980 939-8066
3623 Latrobe Dr Charlotte (28211) *(G-2633)*

Digital Audio Corporation..919 572-6767
116 Brightwater Heights Dr Hendersonville (28791) *(G-7844)*

Digital Design & Modeling LLC..336 766-2155
6201 Hacker Bend Ct Winston Salem (27103) *(G-16678)*

Digital Designs Inc..704 790-7100
3540 Toringdon Way Ste 200 Charlotte (28277) *(G-2634)*

Digital High Point, Hickory Also Called: Carolina Container LLC *(G-7963)*

Digital High Point, High Point Also Called: Carolina Container Company *(G-8284)*

Digital Highpoint LLC..336 883-7146
401 Model Farm Rd Ste 101 High Point (27263) *(G-8324)*

Digital Ink Technology Inc..603 707-7843
8107 Arrowridge Blvd Charlotte (28273) *(G-2635)*

Digital Log Cabin Press..336 287-7265
2432 Fairway Dr Winston Salem (27103) *(G-16679)*

Digital Print & Imaging Inc..910 341-3005
3001 Wrightsville Ave Ste C Wilmington (28403) *(G-16201)*

Digital Printing..336 430-8011
4142 Brynwood Dr Colfax (27235) *(G-4148)*

Digital Printing Systems Inc (PA)..704 525-0190
606 E Hebron St Charlotte (28273) *(G-2636)*

Digital Progressions Inc..336 676-6570
5101 W Market St Greensboro (27409) *(G-6970)*

Digital Recorders Inc..919 361-2155
598 Airport Blvd Ste 300 Morrisville (27560) *(G-11331)*

Digital Turbine Media Inc (HQ)..866 254-2453
410 Blackwell St Durham (27701) *(G-5051)*

Digitaurus Inc..910 794-9243
4605 Wrightsville Ave Wilmington (28403) *(G-16202)*

Digitaurus EMB Screen Prtg Inc..910 794-3275
6100 Chilcot Ln Wilmington (28409) *(G-16203)*

Digitome Corporation..860 651-5560
210 Delburg St Davidson (28036) *(G-4672)*

Digiton Corp..919 601-4826
4205 Holly Stream Ct Apex (27539) *(G-182)*

Digits..336 721-0209
306 S Stratford Rd Winston Salem (27103) *(G-16680)*

Digitz   ALPHABETIC SECTION

Digitz, Raleigh Also Called: Complete Comp St of Ralgh Inc *(G-12635)*

Dignify Inc.. 336 500-8668
  3907 N Elm St Greensboro (27455) *(G-6971)*

Dignify Therapeutics LLC.. 919 371-8138
  2 Davis Dr Durham (27709) *(G-5052)*

Dilisym Services Inc... 919 558-1323
  6 Davis Dr Durham (27709) *(G-5053)*

Dill Air Controls Products LLC.. 919 692-2300
  1500 Williamsboro St Oxford (27565) *(G-12127)*

Dillon L Colter L C... 828 242-7750
  513 North St Chapel Hill (27514) *(G-2008)*

Dilworth Custom Framing... 704 370-7660
  125 Remount Rd Ste C2 Charlotte (28203) *(G-2637)*

Dilworth Mattress Company Inc (PA).................................. 704 333-6564
  211 W Worthington Ave Charlotte (28203) *(G-2638)*

Dime EMB LLC... 336 765-0910
  3929 Westpoint Blvd Ste A Winston Salem (27103) *(G-16681)*

Dimension Milling Co Inc.. 336 983-2820
  12885 Nc Highway 47 Denton (27239) *(G-4734)*

Dimension Wood Products Inc.. 828 459-9891
  2885 Kelly Blvd Claremont (28610) *(G-3920)*

Dimensional Metals Inc.. 704 279-9691
  819 S Salisbury Ave Salisbury (28146) *(G-13953)*

Dimill Enterprises LLC.. 919 629-2011
  531 Pylon Dr Raleigh (27606) *(G-12684)*

Dine America, Chapel Hill Also Called: Journalistic Inc *(G-2028)*

Dings Etc.. 252 933-0208
  572 Nc Hwy 58 S Kinston (28504) *(G-9357)*

Diomorph Pharmaceuticals LP.. 919 354-6233
  6340 Quadrangle Dr Ste 120 Chapel Hill (27517) *(G-2009)*

Diply LLC... 828 495-4352
  2425 N Center St Ste 247 Hickory (28601) *(G-8010)*

Direct Action K-9 LLC... 910 246-0806
  160 E Massachusetts Ave Southern Pines (28387) *(G-14533)*

Direct Chassislink Inc (PA).. 704 594-3800
  3525 Whitehall Park Dr Ste 400 Charlotte (28273) *(G-2639)*

Direct Digital LLC (PA)... 704 557-0987
  615 S College St Ste 1300 Charlotte (28202) *(G-2640)*

Direct Discount Carports... 888 642-1910
  743 Slate Mountain Rd Mount Airy (27030) *(G-11502)*

Direct Distribution Inds Inc.. 910 217-0000
  24581 Main St Wagram (28396) *(G-15523)*

Direct Legal Mail LLC... 919 353-9158
  8800 Westgate Park Dr Ste 110 Raleigh (27617) *(G-12685)*

Direct Pack East LLC... 910 331-0071
  612 Airport Rd Rockingham (28379) *(G-13623)*

Direct Promotional, Asheboro Also Called: Web 4 Half LLC *(G-509)*

Direct South Logistics, Sanford Also Called: Southern Elc & Automtn Corp *(G-14187)*

Direct Wholesale Signs LLC.. 704 750-2842
  711 York Rd Kings Mountain (28086) *(G-9303)*

Direct Wood Products.. 336 238-2516
  808 Grimes Blvd Lexington (27292) *(G-9709)*

DIRECT WOOD PRODUCTS, Lexington Also Called: Direct Wood Products *(G-9709)*

Directional, Thomasville Also Called: Directional Buying Group Inc *(G-15214)*

Directional Buying Group Inc.. 336 472-6187
  201 E Holly Hill Rd Thomasville (27360) *(G-15214)*

Directus Holdings LLC (PA)... 919 510-8410
  6016 Triangle Dr Raleigh (27617) *(G-12686)*

Dirty Dog Threads LLC... 704 240-3668
  1841 Wisteria Ln Lincolnton (28092) *(G-9890)*

Disco Hi-TEC America Inc... 919 468-6003
  3000 Aerial Center Pkwy Ste 140 Morrisville (27560) *(G-11332)*

Discount Box & Pallet Inc (PA).. 336 272-2220
  3174 Weeden St Staley (27355) *(G-14665)*

Discount Pallet Services LLC... 910 892-3760
  319 Ira B Tart Rd Dunn (28334) *(G-4862)*

Discount Printing Inc... 704 365-3665
  2914 Crosby Rd Charlotte (28211) *(G-2641)*

Discover Night LLC.. 888 825-6282
  4030 Wake Forest Rd Ste 349 Raleigh (27609) *(G-12687)*

Discovery Insurance Company.. 800 876-1492
  604 N Queen St Kinston (28501) *(G-9358)*

Discovery Map... 435 901-1027
  176 S Dogwood Trl Kitty Hawk (27949) *(G-9400)*

Discovery Map... 910 315-1155
  Pinehurst (28370) *(G-12220)*

Discovery Map, New Bern Also Called: Pinecone Publishing LLC *(G-11837)*

Disher Packing Co, Yadkinville Also Called: If Disher Meat Processing *(G-17041)*

Display Options Woodwork Inc... 704 599-6525
  205 Colonial Dr Belmont (28012) *(G-985)*

Display Techs LLC... 704 966-0679
  4251 Stormy Pointe Ct Denver (28037) *(G-4773)*

Display Your Graphics LLC... 828 489-2282
  140 Jaymar Park Dr Hendersonville (28792) *(G-7845)*

Disruptive Enterprises LLC (PA)... 336 567-0104
  1452 Industry Dr Burlington (27215) *(G-1407)*

Dissonant Skateboards.. 607 793-8210
  147 Edgewood Rd Apt 1 Asheville (28804) *(G-609)*

Disston Co Inc.. 336 547-6300
  7345 W Friendly Ave Ste G Greensboro (27410) *(G-6972)*

Distinction Hospitality Inc... 336 875-3043
  4100 Mendenhall Oaks Pkwy Ste 200 High Point (27265) *(G-8325)*

Distinction Leather Company
  210 Lap Rd Ne Conover (28613) *(G-4448)*

Distinctive Bldg & Design Inc.. 828 456-4730
  24 Chloe Ln Waynesville (28786) *(G-15802)*

Distinctive Cabinets Inc.. 704 529-6234
  319 Old Hebron Rd Ste A Charlotte (28273) *(G-2642)*

Distinctive Furniture Inc (PA).. 828 754-3947
  1750 Taylorsville Rd Se Lenoir (28645) *(G-9604)*

Distinctive Millworks LLC.. 919 263-4337
  3650 Rogers Rd Ste 201 Wake Forest (27587) *(G-15547)*

Distinctive Soul Creations LLC... 704 299-3269
  214 Oakton Glen Ct Charlotte (28262) *(G-2643)*

Distributech.. 800 742-0141
  114 Crosswind Dr Cary (27513) *(G-1752)*

Distributor, Youngsville Also Called: Tar River Trading Post LLC *(G-17104)*

Ditex LLC.. 919 215-3773
  5112 Greyfield Blvd Durham (27713) *(G-5054)*

Diverse Corporate Tech Inc... 828 245-3717
  289 Shiloh Rd Forest City (28043) *(G-6065)*

Diverse Flooring Systems.. 910 425-8915
  2112 Birchcreft Dr Fayetteville (28304) *(G-5812)*

Diverse Security Systems Inc... 919 848-9599
  8831 Westgate Park Dr Ste 100 Raleigh (27617) *(G-12688)*

Diversfied Holdings Dallas Inc.. 704 922-5293
  124 W Catawba Ave Mount Holly (28120) *(G-11631)*

Diversfied McHning Cncepts Inc... 828 665-2465
  5 Sagefield Dr Candler (28715) *(G-1577)*

Diversfied Prtg Techniques Inc... 704 583-9433
  13336 S Ridge Dr Charlotte (28273) *(G-2644)*

Diversified Disposables Mfg, Wilmington Also Called: Ddm Inc *(G-16197)*

Diversified Energy LLC.. 828 266-9800
  148 Highway 105 Ext Ste 202 Boone (28607) *(G-1194)*

Diversified Foam Inc (PA).. 336 463-5512
  1813 Us 601 Hwy Yadkinville (27055) *(G-17037)*

Diversified Signs & Graphics.. 704 392-8165
  5245 Old Dowd Rd Charlotte (28208) *(G-2645)*

DIVERSIFIED SIGNS & GRAPHICS INC, Charlotte Also Called: Diversified Signs & Graphics *(G-2645)*

Diversified Specialties Inc.. 704 825-3671
  10 Airline Ave Belmont (28012) *(G-986)*

Diversified Technologies, Jamestown Also Called: SBS Diversified Tech Inc *(G-9071)*

Diversified Textile Mchy Corp.. 704 739-2121
  133 Kings Rd Kings Mountain (28086) *(G-9304)*

Diversified Welding and Steel... 704 504-1111
  10801 Nations Ford Rd Pineville (28134) *(G-12266)*

Diversified Wood Products Inc... 252 793-6600
  111 W Water St Ste 1 Plymouth (27962) *(G-12370)*

Diversified Woodcrafts Inc.. 336 688-3114
  923 Shamrock Rd High Point (27265) *(G-8326)*

Divine Connection.. 252 975-1320
  408 N Market St Washington (27889) *(G-15695)*

ALPHABETIC SECTION — Domimex

Divine Creations 704 364-5844
216 Glenn Abby Dr Morehead City (28557) *(G-11168)*

Divine Lemonades LLC 336 255-0739
1605 Withersea Ln Reidsville (27320) *(G-13517)*

Divine Llama Vineyards LLC 336 699-2525
4179 Divine Llama Ln East Bend (27018) *(G-5466)*

Divine South Baking Co LLC 828 421-2042
2254 Dillard Rd Highlands (28741) *(G-8615)*

Division 10 .... 919 661-1101
10111 Division Dr Raleigh (27603) *(G-12689)*

Division 5 LLC 336 725-0521
1725 Vargrave St Winston Salem (27107) *(G-16682)*

Division Eight Inc 336 852-1275
2206 N Church St Greensboro (27405) *(G-6973)*

Division II, Hickory Also Called: Unifour Finishers Inc *(G-8194)*

Division of Leggett Platt, Statesville Also Called: Iredell Fiber Inc *(G-14822)*

Division One, Hickory Also Called: Unifour Finishers Inc *(G-8193)*

Division Six Incorporated 910 420-3305
115 Justin Dr New Bern (28562) *(G-11801)*

DIVORCECARE, Wake Forest Also Called: Church Initiative Inc *(G-15540)*

Dix Enterprises Inc 336 558-9512
2436 Lake Oak High Point (27265) *(G-8327)*

Dixie Decoys LLC 703 554-9478
119 Tucker Ave Winston Salem (27104) *(G-16683)*

Dixie Electro Mech Svcs Inc 704 332-1116
2115 Freedom Dr Charlotte (28208) *(G-2646)*

Dixie Reel & Box Co, Charlotte Also Called: Lone Star Container Sales Corp *(G-3102)*

Dixon Custom Cabinetry LLC 336 992-3306
129 Furlong Industrial Dr Kernersville (27284) *(G-9190)*

Dixon Quick Coupling, Dallas Also Called: Dixon Valve & Coupling Co LLC *(G-4637)*

Dixon Valve & Coupling Co LLC 704 334-9175
2925 Chief Ct Dallas (28034) *(G-4637)*

Diy Performance, Oakboro Also Called: Dover Power LLC *(G-12072)*

Dize Awning and Tent Company, Winston Salem Also Called: Dize Company *(G-16684)*

Dize Company 336 722-5181
1512 S Main St Winston Salem (27127) *(G-16684)*

Dj Powder Coating, Kernersville Also Called: Dj Powdercoating Ironwork LLC *(G-9191)*

Dj Powdercoating Ironwork LLC 336 310-4725
232 Industrial Way Dr Ste A Kernersville (27284) *(G-9191)*

DJS Pickles LLC 828 647-0357
570 Brevard Rd Ste 16 Asheville (28806) *(G-610)*

Dkd Apparel, Mooresville Also Called: Daryl Duff Lockyer *(G-10925)*

DL Hopper & Associates Inc 252 838-1062
402 Sea Gate Dr Newport (28570) *(G-11901)*

DLM Sales Inc 704 399-2776
5901 N Hill Cir Charlotte (28213) *(G-2647)*

Dlp Publishing LLC 336 803-2188
2530 Willard Rd High Point (27265) *(G-8328)*

Dlss Manufacturing LLC 919 619-7594
697 Hillsboro St Pittsboro (27312) *(G-12339)*

Dlss Mfg 919 619-6184
2458 Hamlets Chapel Rd Pittsboro (27312) *(G-12340)*

Dm2 .... 336 362-3425
King (27021) *(G-9269)*

Dma Inc 704 527-0992
3123 May St Charlotte (28217) *(G-2648)*

Dma Design Print 336 877-0068
102 Grouse Rdg Lansing (28643) *(G-9454)*

Dmarcian (PA) 828 767-7588
43 S Broad St Ste 203 Brevard (28712) *(G-1273)*

DMC LLC 980 352-9806
1319 Lily Green Ct Nw Concord (28027) *(G-4254)*

DMD Logistics LLC 336 480-8149
2124 Craver Meadows Ct Winston Salem (27127) *(G-16685)*

Dmg Manufacturing LLC 828 855-1997
719 Old Lenoir Rd Hickory (28601) *(G-8011)*

Dmnc Greenville Plant, Greenville Also Called: Denso Manufacturing NC Inc *(G-7513)*

DMV Commissioners Office 704 679-3914
201 W Arrowood Rd Charlotte (28217) *(G-2649)*

DN Yager Woodworks 704 236-3481
709 Catawba Cir N Matthews (28104) *(G-10312)*

Dna Group Inc (PA) 919 881-0889
2841 Plaza Pl Ste 200 Raleigh (27612) *(G-12690)*

Dna Services Inc 910 279-2775
770 Settlers Ln Kure Beach (28449) *(G-9437)*

DNB Humidifier Mfg Inc 336 764-2076
175 Dixie Club Rd Winston Salem (27107) *(G-16686)*

Dnj Engine Comp Onents 704 855-5505
1450 N Main St China Grove (28023) *(G-3882)*

Dnl Services LLC 910 689-8759
64 Blue Heron Dr Harrells (28444) *(G-7692)*

Dnp Imagingcomm America Corp (DH) 704 784-8100
4524 Enterprise Dr Nw Concord (28027) *(G-4255)*

Dnp Photo Imaging, Concord Also Called: Dnp Imagingcomm America Corp *(G-4255)*

Do It Best, Garner Also Called: Hudson S Hardware Inc *(G-6276)*

Dobbins Products 919 580-0621
208 Earl Dr Goldsboro (27530) *(G-6610)*

Doble Engineering Company 919 380-7461
2200 Gateway Centre Blvd Ste 207 Morrisville (27560) *(G-11333)*

Docent Pharma Services LLC 229 310-0111
1533 Armscroft Ln Apex (27502) *(G-183)*

Dock Street Printing Co, Wilmington Also Called: Charnel Inc *(G-16169)*

Dockery Logging 828 557-9149
2020 Bell Hill Rd Murphy (28906) *(G-11708)*

Docmagnet Inc 919 788-7999
6220 Angus Dr Ste 100 Raleigh (27617) *(G-12691)*

Docsite LLC (DH) 866 823-3958
280 S Mangum St Ste 540 Durham (27701) *(G-5055)*

Docu Source of NC 919 459-5900
951 Aviation Pkwy Ste 600 Morrisville (27560) *(G-11334)*

Document Directs Inc 919 829-8810
5210 Western Blvd Raleigh (27606) *(G-12692)*

Document Imaging Systems Inc 919 460-9440
8709 Stage Ford Rd Raleigh (27615) *(G-12693)*

Docurep LLC 919 280-4723
8617 Territory Trl Wake Forest (27587) *(G-15548)*

Docusource North Carolina LLC 919 459-5900
2800 Slater Rd Morrisville (27560) *(G-11335)*

Dodson Defense LLC 336 421-9649
4756 Blanchard Rd Burlington (27217) *(G-1408)*

DOE & Ingalls Investors Inc (HQ) 919 598-1986
4813 Emperor Blvd Ste 300 Durham (27703) *(G-5056)*

DOE & Ingalls Management LLC (DH) 919 598-1986
4813 Emperor Blvd Ste 300 Durham (27703) *(G-5057)*

DOE & Inglls Nrth Crlina Oprti 919 282-1792
4063 Stirrup Creek Dr Durham (27703) *(G-5058)*

Dof Office Seating, Canton Also Called: Desmond Office Furniture Inc *(G-1613)*

Dog Black Services LLC 336 266-0778
6261 Whitney Rd Graham (27253) *(G-6688)*

Doggies r US 336 455-1113
2940 E Market St Greensboro (27405) *(G-6974)*

Dogwood Print 919 906-0617
400 Big Branch Ln Wendell (27591) *(G-15897)*

Doin It Rght Cbnetry More LLC 980 297-3116
5248 King Wilkinson Rd Denver (28037) *(G-4774)*

Dokja Inc (PA) 336 852-5190
602 S Edwardia Dr Greensboro (27409) *(G-6975)*

Dolan LLC 919 829-9333
107 Fayetteville St 3rd Fl Raleigh (27601) *(G-12694)*

Dole Food, Charlotte Also Called: Dole Food Company Inc *(G-2650)*

Dole Food Company Inc (DH) 818 874-4000
200 S Tyron St Ste 600 Charlotte (28202) *(G-2650)*

Dollar Eddie Rev 919 596-7564
4420 Holloman Rd Durham (27703) *(G-5059)*

Domco Technology LLC 888 834-8541
1342 Barnardsville Hwy Ste A Barnardsville (28709) *(G-908)*

Domenicks Furniture Mfr LLC 336 442-3348
1107 Tate St High Point (27260) *(G-8329)*

Domestic Fabrics Blankets Corp 252 523-7948
2002 W Vernon Ave Kinston (28504) *(G-9359)*

Domimex 919 602-3921
421 Chapanoke Rd Raleigh (27603) *(G-12695)*

Domtar Paper Company LLC 252 752-1100
1029 Old Creek Rd Greenville (27834) *(G-7515)*

Domtar Paper Company LLC 252 793-8111
1375 Nc Hwy 149 N Plymouth (27962) *(G-12371)*

Don Koons Inc 919 603-0948
4662 Antioch Rd Oxford (27565) *(G-12128)*

Donald Auton 704 872-7528
841 Reynolds Rd Statesville (28677) *(G-14788)*

Donald Haack Diamonds Inc 704 365-4400
3900 Colony Rd Ste E Charlotte (28211) *(G-2651)*

Donald Hack Diamonds Fine Gems, Charlotte Also Called: Donald Haack Diamonds Inc *(G-2651)*

Donald Henley & Sons Sawmill 336 625-5665
2351 Old Cedar Falls Rd Asheboro (27203) *(G-424)*

Donald R Young Logging Inc 910 934-6769
165 Buie Farm Ln Lillington (27546) *(G-9850)*

Donalds Welding Inc 910 298-5234
1806 S Nc 111 Hwy Chinquapin (28521) *(G-3892)*

Done-Gone Adios Inc 336 993-7300
1318 Shields Rd Kernersville (27284) *(G-9192)*

Dons Disposal 919 542-2208
3692 Nc Highway 87 N Pittsboro (27312) *(G-12341)*

Dons Fine Jewelry Inc 336 724-7826
2503 Lewisville Clemmons Rd Clemmons (27012) *(G-4035)*

Dons Stitches 336 554-6697
4705 Benttree Dr Mc Leansville (27301) *(G-10389)*

Donut Shop 910 640-3317
1602 S Madison St Whiteville (28472) *(G-15962)*

Donzi Marine LLC 252 975-2000
1653 Whichards Beach Rd Washington (27889) *(G-15696)*

Doodle Sasser Distilling LLC 704 806-6594
171 Associate Ln Indian Trail (28079) *(G-8929)*

Door Screen 406 531-4516
1177 Duck Rd Kitty Hawk (27949) *(G-9401)*

Door Store of America Inc 919 781-3200
10681 World Trade Blvd Raleigh (27617) *(G-12696)*

Door Works Huntersville LLC 704 947-1900
11701 Mccord Rd Bldg 11 Huntersville (28078) *(G-8809)*

Doosan Bobcat North Amer Inc 704 883-3500
1293 Glenway Dr Statesville (28625) *(G-14789)*

Dorel Ecommerce Inc 828 378-0092
37 Haywood St Ste 300 Asheville (28801) *(G-611)*

Dorian Corporation 910 352-6939
901 Martin St Wilmington (28401) *(G-16204)*

Doris E Inc 919 858-5419
1027 Lake Moraine Pl Raleigh (27607) *(G-12697)*

Dormer Pramet LLC 800 877-3745
1483 Dogwood Way Mebane (27302) *(G-10407)*

Dorsett Printing Company 910 895-3520
1203 Rockingham Rd Rockingham (28379) *(G-13624)*

Dorsett Technologies Inc (PA) 855 387-2232
100 Woodlyn Dr Yadkinville (27055) *(G-17038)*

DOT Blue Readi-Mix LLC 704 391-3000
1022 Exchange St Charlotte (28208) *(G-2652)*

DOT Blue Readi-Mix LLC 704 247-2778
7406 Millbrook Rd Harrisburg (28075) *(G-7707)*

DOT Blue Readi-Mix LLC 704 247-2777
1703 Morgan Mill Rd Monroe (28110) *(G-10706)*

DOT Blue Readi-Mix LLC 704 978-2331
158 Intercraft Dr Statesville (28625) *(G-14790)*

DOT Blue Services Inc 704 342-2970
11819 Reames Rd Charlotte (28269) *(G-2653)*

DOT Master, Lexington Also Called: Draft DOT International LLC *(G-9710)*

Dotson Metal Finishing Inc 828 298-9844
16 Old Charlotte Hwy Asheville (28803) *(G-612)*

Double Hung LLC 888 235-8956
2801 Patterson St Greensboro (27407) *(G-6976)*

Double O Plastics Inc 704 788-8517
981 Biscayne Dr Concord (28027) *(G-4256)*

Double R Welding & Fabrication 704 340-5825
4441 Motorsports Dr Sw Ste 10 Concord (28027) *(G-4257)*

Doug Bowman Galleries 704 662-5620
188 Hwy 64-74 Chimney Rock (28720) *(G-3879)*

Douglas Battery Mfg Co 336 650-7000
500 Battery Dr Winston Salem (27107) *(G-16687)*

Douglas Duane Sniffen 919 924-8337
101 Oak Hollow Ct Garner (27529) *(G-6271)*

Douglas Fabrication & Mch Inc 919 365-7553
430 Industrial Dr Wendell (27591) *(G-15898)*

Douglas Temple & Son Inc 252 771-5676
1273 Lynchs Corner Rd Elizabeth City (27909) *(G-5541)*

Douglas Wolcott 336 475-0052
48 High Tech Blvd Unit C Thomasville (27360) *(G-15215)*

Dova Pharmaceuticals, Durham Also Called: Dova Pharmaceuticals Inc *(G-5060)*

Dova Pharmaceuticals Inc (HQ) 919 748-5975
240 Leigh Farm Rd Ste 245 Durham (27707) *(G-5060)*

Dove Communications Inc 336 855-5491
7 Wendy Ct Ste B Greensboro (27409) *(G-6977)*

Dove Medical Supply LLC 336 643-9367
8164 Mabe Marshall Rd Bldg 2 Summerfield (27358) *(G-14980)*

Dove Vine LLC 336 751-3794
261 Scenic Dr Mocksville (27028) *(G-10566)*

Dover Foods Inc 800 348-7416
353 Banner Farm Rd Mills River (28759) *(G-10502)*

Dover Power LLC 704 485-2020
16400 Buster Rd Oakboro (28129) *(G-12072)*

Dow Silicones Corporation 336 547-7100
2914 Patterson St Greensboro (27407) *(G-6978)*

Down East Molding Company, Ahoskie Also Called: H T Jones Lumber Company *(G-63)*

Down East Offroad Inc 252 246-9440
1425 Thorne Ave S Wilson (27893) *(G-16493)*

Down East Printing, Morehead City Also Called: Coastal Press Inc *(G-11163)*

Down East Screen Printing LLC 252 808-7742
208 Straits Haven Rd Beaufort (28516) *(G-955)*

Down Range Armory Inc 919 749-5820
5240 Nc 96 Hwy W Ste 104 Youngsville (27596) *(G-17078)*

Down South Logging LLC 843 333-1649
121 Lake Tabor Dr Tabor City (28463) *(G-15080)*

Downeast Cabinets William Brya 252 414-7730
2543 Circle Dr Winterville (28590) *(G-16999)*

Downeast Marine Canvas LLC 252 495-2631
387 S Asbury Church Rd Washington (27889) *(G-15697)*

DOWns&moss A1 Trucking LLC 704 981-0880
7319 Mtthews Mint Hl Rd S Mint Hill (28227) *(G-10530)*

Downsouth Wood Working LLC 910 259-4617
12766 Ashton Rd Burgaw (28425) *(G-1337)*

Downtown Graphics Network Inc 704 637-0855
1409 S Fulton St Salisbury (28144) *(G-13954)*

Downtown Raleigh 919 821-7897
402 Glenwood Ave Raleigh (27603) *(G-12698)*

Downtown Raleigh Publishing, Raleigh Also Called: Raleigh Downtowner *(G-13176)*

Doyle Enterprises, High Point Also Called: W V Doyle Enterprises Inc *(G-8600)*

Doyles Vineyard 919 544-6291
8913 Nc Highway 751 Durham (27713) *(G-5061)*

Dozier Industrial Electric Inc 252 451-0020
1151 Atlantic Ave Rocky Mount (27801) *(G-13666)*

Dp Custom Works LLC 704 221-7291
5210 Horne Rd Marshville (28103) *(G-10214)*

Dp Solutions Inc (DH) 336 854-7700
1801 Stanley Rd Ste 301 Greensboro (27407) *(G-6979)*

Dp Woodworks Inc 704 821-7799
5631 Cannon Dr Ste A Monroe (28110) *(G-10707)*

Dpi, Greenville Also Called: DSM Pharmaceuticals Inc *(G-7519)*

Dpi Newco LLC 252 758-3436
5900 Martin Luther King Jr Hwy Greenville (27834) *(G-7516)*

Dps Molding Inc 732 763-4811
276 Bailey Ln Vanceboro (28586) *(G-15476)*

Dpsi, Greensboro Also Called: Dp Solutions Inc *(G-6979)*

Dr Logging LLC 910 417-9643
506 Bauersfeld St Hamlet (28345) *(G-7620)*

Dr Pepper, West Jefferson Also Called: Dr Ppper Btlg W Jffrson NC In *(G-15939)*

Dr Pepper, Wilmington Also Called: Dr Pepper Co of Wilmington *(G-16205)*

Dr Pepper Co of Wilmington 910 792-5400
415 Landmark Dr Wilmington (28412) *(G-16205)*

Dr Pepper/Seven-Up Bottling 828 322-8090
2401 14th Avenue Cir Nw Hickory (28601) *(G-8012)*

Dr Ppper Btlg W Jffrson NC In 336 846-2433
109 W 3rd St West Jefferson (28694) *(G-15939)*

Dracor Water Systems, Durham *Also Called: Drch Inc (G-5063)*

Dradura USA Corp 252 637-9660
197 Bosch Blvd New Bern (28562) *(G-11802)*

Draft DOT International LLC 336 775-0525
5450 N Nc Highway 150 Lexington (27295) *(G-9710)*

Dragonfly Studios 704 706-2910
190 Pitts School Rd Nw Concord (28027) *(G-4258)*

Draka Communication, Claremont *Also Called: Draka Communications Americas Inc (G-3921)*

Draka Communications Americas Inc 828 459-8456
2512 Penny Rd Claremont (28610) *(G-3921)*

Draka Elevator Products Inc (DH) 252 984-5100
2151 N Church St Rocky Mount (27804) *(G-13690)*

Draka Holdings Usa Inc 828 383-0020
2512 Penny Rd Claremont (28610) *(G-3922)*

Draka Transport USA LLC 828 459-8895
2512 Penny Rd Claremont (28610) *(G-3923)*

Draka Usa Inc 828 459-9787
2512 Penny Rd Claremont (28610) *(G-3924)*

Drake Enterprises Ltd 828 524-7045
219 E Palmer St Franklin (28734) *(G-6124)*

Drake S Fresh Pasta Company 336 861-5454
636 Southwest St High Point (27260) *(G-8330)*

Drake Software LLC 828 524-2922
235 E Palmer St Franklin (28734) *(G-6125)*

Dramar Machine Devices Inc 704 866-0904
108 Chickasaw Rd Gastonia (28056) *(G-6398)*

Dramen of Raleigh LLC 919 828-5464
547 Pylon Dr Raleigh (27606) *(G-12699)*

Drapery Hardware, Huntersville *Also Called: Nova Wildcat Drapery Hdwr LLC (G-8862)*

Draxlor Industries Inc 757 274-6771
228 S Riverdale Dr Durham (27712) *(G-5062)*

Drch Inc 919 383-9421
3518 Medford Rd Durham (27705) *(G-5063)*

Dream Doers Publishing LLC 336 413-7101
110 Norwood Forest Ln Tobaccoville (27050) *(G-15317)*

Dream Kreams LLC 919 491-1984
549 Arbor Hill Rd Apt 5a Kernersville (27284) *(G-9193)*

Dreamcatchers Publishing 336 441-2555
4008 Mitchell Mill Rd Raleigh (27616) *(G-12700)*

Dreamflyer Publications 919 596-1906
1013 Gunston Ln Durham (27703) *(G-5064)*

Dreams Tobacco Mart, Greenville *Also Called: Alnamer Inc (G-7479)*

Dreamseedscom Seeds of Light 239 541-0501
41 Foxridge Dr Fletcher (28732) *(G-5999)*

Dreamship Inc 908 601-8152
12212 Kyle Abbey Ln Raleigh (27613) *(G-12701)*

Dreamshipper, Raleigh *Also Called: Dreamship Inc (G-12701)*

Dreamstone Gran MBL & Quartz, Garner *Also Called: USA Dreamstone LLC (G-6323)*

Dreamweavers Brewery LLC 704 507-7773
115 E North Main St Waxhaw (28173) *(G-15753)*

Drew Roberts LLC 336 497-1679
6627 Barton Creek Dr Whitsett (27377) *(G-15988)*

Drews Cabinets and Cases 919 796-3985
8100 Nc Highway 42 E Selma (27576) *(G-14254)*

Drexel Heritage Furnishings 828 391-6400
825 Visionary St Lenoir (28645) *(G-9605)*

Drexel Heritage Home Furnsngs 336 812-4430
741 W Ward Ave High Point (27260) *(G-8331)*

Drill & Fill Mfg LLC 252 937-4555
5484 S Old Carriage Rd Rocky Mount (27803) *(G-13691)*

Drink A Bull LLC 919 818-3621
921 Holloway St Ste 103 Durham (27701) *(G-5065)*

Driveco Inc 704 615-2111
13519 Norlington Ct Charlotte (28273) *(G-2654)*

Driver Distribution Inc (PA) 984 204-2929
624 N Carolina Ave Bldg 4 Maiden (28650) *(G-10106)*

Driver Distribution Inc 984 204-2929
9413 Owls Nest Dr Raleigh (27613) *(G-12702)*

Driver License, Salisbury *Also Called: North Carolina Dept Trnsp (G-14020)*

Drnc, Conover *Also Called: Blue Inc Usa LLC (G-4423)*

Dromma Bed, Hickory *Also Called: Comfort Bay Home Fashions Inc (G-7988)*

Dronescape Pllc 704 953-3798
9716 Rea Rd Ste B Charlotte (28277) *(G-2655)*

Dropping Gemz Nail Studio LLC (PA) 919 440-4744
7400 Six Forks Rd Ste 4 Raleigh (27615) *(G-12703)*

Drs Consulting, Raleigh *Also Called: Drs Transportation Inc (G-12704)*

Drs Transportation Inc 919 215-2770
10820 Oliver Rd Apt 101 Raleigh (27614) *(G-12704)*

Drug Safety Navigator LLC 919 885-0549
2605 Meridian Pkwy Ste 115 Durham (27713) *(G-5066)*

Drum Beat Fishing LLC 252 455-5114
105 Mariners Vw Kitty Hawk (27949) *(G-9402)*

Drum Filter Media Inc 336 434-4195
901 W Fairfield Rd High Point (27263) *(G-8332)*

Drw Renovations & Custom Wdwkg 910 471-9367
11 Robert E Lee Dr Wilmington (28412) *(G-16206)*

Drydog Barriers LLC 704 334-8222
2034 Van Buren Ave Ste C Indian Trail (28079) *(G-8930)*

Ds Smith Packaging, Asheboro *Also Called: Southcorr LLC (G-482)*

Ds Smith Packaging and Paper 336 668-0871
4328 Federal Dr Ste 105 Greensboro (27410) *(G-6980)*

Ds Smith PLC 919 557-3148
301 Thomas Mill Rd Holly Springs (27540) *(G-8696)*

DSA Master Crafted Doors, Raleigh *Also Called: Door Store of America Inc (G-12696)*

Dsd Press 919 606-9923
245 Memorial Dr Cullowhee (28723) *(G-4631)*

Dse, Mooresville *Also Called: Kgt Enterprises Inc (G-10997)*

DSI Blackpages, Asheville *Also Called: Deverger Systems Inc (G-608)*

DSI Innovations LLC 336 893-8385
42 High Tech Blvd Thomasville (27360) *(G-15216)*

Dsk Biopharma Inc (PA) 919 465-9104
112 Nova Dr Morrisville (27560) *(G-11336)*

Dskow Publishing LLC 321 506-0004
301 Fayetteville St Unit 3309 Raleigh (27601) *(G-12705)*

DSM 408 582-2610
202 Crestline Blvd Greenville (27834) *(G-7517)*

Dsm Inc 919 876-2802
266 W Millbrook Rd Raleigh (27609) *(G-12706)*

DSM Desotech 704 862-5000
1101 N Carolina 27 Stanley (28164) *(G-14691)*

DSM Hpf, Greenville *Also Called: Avient Protective Mtls LLC (G-7490)*

DSM Pharmaceuticals Inc 252 758-3436
5900 Martin Luther King Jr Hwy Greenville (27834) *(G-7518)*

DSM Pharmaceuticals Inc 252 758-3436
5900 Martin Luther King Jr Hwy Greenville (27834) *(G-7519)*

Dst Manufacturing LLC 336 676-6096
166 Regal Dr Randleman (27317) *(G-13465)*

Dt Aerospace Inc 919 417-1895
1220 E Hardscrabble Dr Hillsborough (27278) *(G-8648)*

Dtbtla Inc 336 769-0000
4301 Waterleaf Ct Greensboro (27410) *(G-6981)*

Dth Publishing Inc 919 962-1163
151 E Rosemary St Ste 101 Chapel Hill (27514) *(G-2010)*

Dtp Inc 336 272-5122
1 Wendy Ct Ste E Greensboro (27409) *(G-6982)*

Dublin Woodwork Shop 910 862-2289
N S Hwy 87 E Dublin (28332) *(G-4837)*

Dubose National Enrgy Svcs Inc 704 295-1060
103 Waxhaw Professional Park Dr Ste D Waxhaw (28173) *(G-15754)*

Dubose Strapping Inc (PA) 910 590-1020
906 Industrial Dr Clinton (28328) *(G-4094)*

Ducduc LLC 212 226-1868
3200 Wake Forest Rd Ste 204 Raleigh (27609) *(G-12707)*

Ducduc Nyc, Raleigh *Also Called: Ducduc LLC (G-12707)*

Duck Head LLC 855 457-1865
816 S Elm St Greensboro (27406) *(G-6983)*

Duck-Rabbit Craft Brewery Inc 252 753-7745
   4519 West Pine St Farmville (27828) *(G-5734)*

Duco-SCI Inc 704 289-9502
   6004 Stitt St Monroe (28110) *(G-10708)*

Dudley Inc 704 636-8850
   475 Majolica Rd Salisbury (28147) *(G-13955)*

Dudleys Fence Company 252 566-5759
   4126 Fields Station Rd La Grange (28551) *(G-9440)*

Due Process Stable Trdg Co LLC 910 608-0284
   4111 W 5th St Lumberton (28358) *(G-10032)*

Duff-Norton Company Inc (HQ) 704 588-0510
   9415 Pioneer Ave Charlotte (28273) *(G-2656)*

Duke Athletic Products, Yanceyville *Also Called: Royal Textile Mills Inc (G-17065)*

Duke Energy Center 919 464-0960
   2 E South St Raleigh (27601) *(G-12708)*

Duke Student Publishing Co Inc 919 684-3811
   101 Union Dr Durham (27708) *(G-5067)*

Duke University 919 687-3600
   905 W Main St Ste 19 Durham (27701) *(G-5068)*

Duke University Press, Durham *Also Called: Duke University (G-5068)*

Dukester Productions Entrmt Co, Goldsboro *Also Called: Monk Lekeisha (G-6637)*

Dumpster Mate LLC 919 303-7402
   2600 Hilltop Farms Rd Apex (27502) *(G-184)*

Dunavants Welding & Steel Inc 252 338-6533
   207 Us Highway 158 E Camden (27921) *(G-1557)*

Dunbar Foods Corporation 910 892-3175
   1000 S Fayetteville Ave Dunn (28334) *(G-4863)*

Duncan Design Ltd 919 834-7713
   2308 Wake Forest Rd Ste E Raleigh (27608) *(G-12709)*

Duncan Joseph E & Duncan Billy 828 299-8464
   423 Christian Creek Rd Swannanoa (28778) *(G-15025)*

Duncan Junior D 336 871-3599
   1165 Troy Brown Rd Sandy Ridge (27046) *(G-14078)*

Duncan-Parnell Inc 252 977-7832
   2741 N Wesleyan Blvd Rocky Mount (27804) *(G-13692)*

Duncan, JD Logging, Sandy Ridge *Also Called: Duncan Junior D (G-14078)*

Dunkin Donuts 919 217-9603
   7137 Knightdale Blvd Ste A Knightdale (27545) *(G-9417)*

Dunlop Aircraft Tyres Inc 336 283-0979
   205 Enterprise Way Mocksville (27028) *(G-10567)*

Dunn Manufacturing Corp (PA) 704 283-2147
   1400 Goldmine Rd Monroe (28110) *(G-10709)*

Dunstone Company Inc 704 841-1380
   15050 Choate Cir Ste B Charlotte (28273) *(G-2657)*

Duocraft Cabinets & Dist Co (PA) 252 240-1476
   1306 Bridges St Morehead City (28557) *(G-11169)*

Duotech Services Inc 828 369-5411
   245 Industrial Park Rd Franklin (28734) *(G-6126)*

Duplin Forest Products Inc 910 285-5381
   312 Jack Dale Rd Wallace (28466) *(G-15621)*

Duplin Times, Kenansville *Also Called: Cox Nrth Crlina Pblcations Inc (G-9142)*

Duplin Wine Cellars Inc (PA) 910 289-3888
   505 N Sycamore St Rose Hill (28458) *(G-13776)*

Dupont 919 414-0089
   5816 Raddington St Raleigh (27613) *(G-12710)*

Dupont, Durham *Also Called: Dupont Specialty Pdts USA LLC (G-5070)*

Dupont, Fayetteville *Also Called: Eidp Inc (G-5819)*

Dupont, Grifton *Also Called: Eidp Inc (G-7599)*

Dupont, Kinston *Also Called: Eidp Inc (G-9362)*

Dupont, Leland *Also Called: Eidp Inc (G-9540)*

Dupont Electronic Polymers L P (HQ) 919 248-5135
   14 Tw Alexander Dr Durham (27709) *(G-5069)*

Dupont Specialty Pdts USA LLC 919 248-5109
   4020 Stirrup Creek Dr Durham (27703) *(G-5070)*

Dupont Teijin Films 910 433-8200
   3216 Cedar Creek Rd Fayetteville (28312) *(G-5813)*

Dura-Craft Die Inc 828 632-1944
   1442 Liledoun Rd Taylorsville (28681) *(G-15141)*

Durabar Metals Services Div, Salisbury *Also Called: Charter Dura-Bar Inc (G-13940)*

Durable Wood Preservers Inc 704 537-3113
   7901 Pence Rd Charlotte (28215) *(G-2658)*

Durafiber Technologies 704 912-3700
   13620 Reese Blvd E # 400 Huntersville (28078) *(G-8810)*

Durafiber Technologies (dft) Inc 704 912-3700
   13620 Reese Blvd E Ste 400 Huntersville (28078) *(G-8811)*

Durafiber Technologies (dft) Operations LLC 704 912-3770
   13620 Reese Blvd E Ste 400 Huntersville (28078) *(G-8812)*

Durafiber Technologies DFT Inc 704 639-2722
   7401 Statesville Blvd Salisbury (28147) *(G-13956)*

Durafiber Technologies DFT Inc 919 356-3824
   672 Douglas Farm Rd Sanford (27332) *(G-14111)*

Duraline Imaging Inc 828 692-1301
   580 Upward Rd Ste 1 Flat Rock (28731) *(G-5964)*

Duramax Holdings LLC 704 588-9191
   12700 General Dr Charlotte (28273) *(G-2659)*

Durham Bookcases, Durham *Also Called: Bookcase Shop (G-4972)*

Durham Coca-Cola Bottling Co 919 510-0574
   1 Floretta Pl Raleigh (27613) *(G-12711)*

Durham Coca-Cola Bottling Company (PA) 919 383-1531
   3214 Hillsborough Rd Durham (27705) *(G-5071)*

Durham Distillery Llc 919 937-2121
   711 Washington St Durham (27701) *(G-5072)*

Durham Racing Engines Inc 336 471-1830
   205 Old Embler Rd Thomasville (27360) *(G-15217)*

Durkee Embroidery Inc 980 689-2684
   10620 Bailey Rd Ste G Cornelius (28031) *(G-4541)*

Dustcontrol Inc 910 395-1808
   6720 Amsterdam Way Ste 400 Wilmington (28405) *(G-16207)*

Dustin Ellis Logging 704 732-6027
   1186 Confederate Rd Lincolnton (28092) *(G-9891)*

Dustin Lynn Sink 336 442-5602
   5869 Lacey Ct Trinity (27370) *(G-15340)*

Dusty Pallet 828 524-5676
   52 E Main St Franklin (28734) *(G-6127)*

Dusty Rhoads Hvac Inc 252 261-5892
   3822 Elijah Baum Dr Kitty Hawk (27949) *(G-9403)*

Dutch Kettle LLC 336 468-8422
   5016 Hunting Creek Church Rd Hamptonville (27020) *(G-7669)*

Dutch Kettle, The, Hamptonville *Also Called: Dutch Kettle LLC (G-7669)*

Dutch Miller Auto Group, Charlotte *Also Called: Dutch Miller Charlotte Inc (G-2660)*

Dutch Miller Charlotte Inc 704 522-8422
   7725 South Blvd Charlotte (28273) *(G-2660)*

Dutchman Creek Self-Storage 919 363-8878
   8712 Holly Springs Rd Apex (27539) *(G-185)*

Duty Tire and Service Center, Raleigh *Also Called: Village Tire Center Inc (G-13400)*

Duvall Timber LLC 704 236-2211
   1223 Dobson Dr Waxhaw (28173) *(G-15755)*

Dvd Rulers 336 270-9269
   6303 Muirfield Dr Greensboro (27410) *(G-6984)*

DVine Foods 910 862-2576
   1585 Hwy 107 South Elizabethtown (28337) *(G-5594)*

Dw Beam Publishing 336 813-2451
   222 Red Coat Ln King (27021) *(G-9270)*

Dwd Industries LLC 336 498-6327
   151 Southern Dr Randleman (27317) *(G-13466)*

Dwelling NC Inc 252 619-0226
   103 Brickells Glade Edenton (27932) *(G-5513)*

Dwiggins Metal Masters Inc 336 751-2379
   122 Wilkesboro St Mocksville (27028) *(G-10568)*

DWM INTERNATIONAL INC 646 290-7448
   2151 Hawkins St Ste 1225 Charlotte (28203) *(G-2661)*

Dwp, Plymouth *Also Called: Diversified Wood Products Inc (G-12370)*

Dxterity Solutions, Mooresville *Also Called: 27 Software US Inc (G-10844)*

Dyer Publishing LLC 336 452-2275
   872 S Recreation Rd Wilkesboro (28697) *(G-16019)*

Dymetrol Company Inc (PA) 866 964-8632
   1305 W Seaboard St Bladenboro (28320) *(G-1148)*

Dyna-Tech Manufacturing Inc 704 839-0203
   5639 Cannon Dr Monroe (28110) *(G-10710)*

Dynacast, Charlotte *Also Called: Dynacast LLC (G-2662)*

Dynacast, Charlotte *Also Called: Dynacast US Holdings Inc (G-2665)*

Dynacast LLC (DH) 704 927-2790
   11325 N Community House Rd Ste 300 Charlotte (28277) *(G-2662)*

Dynacast International LLC (DH) 704 927-2790
  14045 Ballantyne Corporate Pl Charlotte (28277) *(G-2663)*
Dynacast US Holdings Inc 704 927-2786
  14045 Ballantyne Corporate Pl Ste 300 Charlotte (28277) *(G-2664)*
Dynacast US Holdings Inc (DH) 704 927-2790
  14045 Ballantyne Corporate Pl Ste 400 Charlotte (28277) *(G-2665)*
Dynagraphics Screenprintng 919 212-2898
  125 Quantum St Holly Springs (27540) *(G-8697)*
Dynamac Corporation 919 544-6428
  1910 Sedwick Rd Ste 300a Durham (27713) *(G-5073)*
Dynamic Air Engineering Inc 714 540-1000
  2421 Bga Dr Claremont (28610) *(G-3925)*
Dynamic Defense Tactics II LLC 703 850-1103
  166 Mount Laurel Pl Canton (28716) *(G-1614)*
Dynamic Fabrication & Wldg Inc 828 390-8377
  4620 Amber Ln Morganton (28655) *(G-11209)*
Dynamic Machine Works LLC 336 462-7370
  2655 Knob Hill Dr Clemmons (27012) *(G-4036)*
Dynamic Machining X Mfg LLC 336 362-3425
  157 Industrial Dr King (27021) *(G-9271)*
Dynamic Mounting 704 978-8723
  120b Pitt Rd Mooresville (28115) *(G-10931)*
Dynamic Nutraceuticals LLC (PA) 704 380-2324
  1441 Wilkesboro Hwy Statesville (28625) *(G-14791)*
Dynamic Stampings of NC I 704 864-1572
  1412 Castle Ct Gastonia (28052) *(G-6399)*
Dynamic Systems Inc 828 683-3523
  104 Morrow Branch Rd Leicester (28748) *(G-9510)*
Dynapar Corporation (HQ) 800 873-8731
  2100 W Broad St Elizabethtown (28337) *(G-5595)*
Dynea, Moncure *Also Called: Arclin USA LLC (G-10614)*
Dynisco Bearing, Hickory *Also Called: Dynisco Instruments LLC (G-8013)*
Dynisco Instruments LLC 828 326-9888
  1291 19th Street Ln Nw Hickory (28601) *(G-8013)*
Dyno Nobel Explosive Blasting 919 771-1522
  1201 Aversboro Rd Ste H101 Garner (27529) *(G-6272)*
Dystar Americas Holding Corp (PA) 704 561-3000
  9844 Southern Pine Blvd Ste A Charlotte (28273) *(G-2666)*
Dystar Carolina Chemical Corp 704 391-6322
  8309 Wilkinson Blvd Charlotte (28214) *(G-2667)*
Dystar LP (DH) 704 561-3000
  9844 Southern Pine Blvd Ste A Charlotte (28273) *(G-2668)*
Dystar LP 336 342-6631
  209 Watlington Industrial Dr Reidsville (27320) *(G-13518)*
Dzone Inc 919 678-0300
  600 Park Offices Dr Ste 150 Research Triangle Pa (27709) *(G-13550)*
E & M Concrete Inc 919 235-7221
  7505 Troy Stone Dr Fuquay Varina (27526) *(G-6197)*
E A Duncan Cnstr Co Inc 910 653-3535
  1475 Savannah Rd Tabor City (28463) *(G-15081)*
E and J Publishing LLC 877 882-2138
  3502 Lukes Dr Charlotte (28216) *(G-2669)*
E By Design LLC 980 231-5483
  20823 N Main St, Ste 115 Cornelius (28031) *(G-4542)*
E C L Inc 919 365-7101
  485-1 Old Wilson Rd Wendell (27591) *(G-15899)*
E C P, Middlesex *Also Called: Eastcoast Packaging Inc (G-10447)*
E C U Univ Prtg & Graphics 252 737-1301
  2612 E 10th St Greenville (27858) *(G-7520)*
E Cache & Co LLC 919 590-0779
  6316 Old Sugar Creek Rd Ste E Charlotte (28269) *(G-2670)*
E F P Inc 336 498-4134
  8013 Adams Farm Rd Randleman (27317) *(G-13467)*
E Feibusch Company Inc 336 434-5095
  516 Townsend Ave High Point (27263) *(G-8333)*
E G A Products Inc 704 664-1221
  208 Mckenzie Rd Mooresville (28115) *(G-10932)*
E Gads Screen Printing & EMB, Elizabeth City *Also Called: Marvin Bailey Screen Printing (G-5556)*
E I Du Pont De Nemours 919 518-1332
  509 Grosvenor Dr Raleigh (27615) *(G-12712)*

E J Victor Inc (PA) 828 437-1991
  110 Wamsutta Mill Rd Morganton (28655) *(G-11210)*
E J Victor Furniture, Morganton *Also Called: E J Victor Inc (G-11210)*
E JS Logging Inc 252 927-3539
  420 Long Ridge Rd Pinetown (27865) *(G-12248)*
E P D, Wendell *Also Called: Electronic Products Design Inc (G-15901)*
E R W Printing 704 201-5642
  1801 N Tryon St Ste 607 Charlotte (28206) *(G-2671)*
E T C of Henderson N C Inc (PA) 252 492-4033
  601 Wakefield Ave Henderson (27536) *(G-7781)*
E T Sales Inc 704 888-4010
  13570 Broadway Ave Midland (28107) *(G-10467)*
E W Godwin S Sons Inc (PA) 910 762-7747
  1207 Castle Hayne Rd Wilmington (28401) *(G-16208)*
E Z Frames 910 464-1813
  978 Brewer Rd Seagrove (27341) *(G-14237)*
E Z Stop Number Two 828 627-9081
  8721 Carolina Blvd Clyde (28721) *(G-4124)*
E- Stitch.com, Snow Hill *Also Called: Happy Jack Incorporated (G-14503)*
E-Liquid Brands LLC 828 385-5090
  120 Commercial Dr Mooresville (28115) *(G-10933)*
E-N-G Mobile Systems LLC (HQ) 925 798-4060
  810 Tom Starling Rd Fayetteville (28306) *(G-5814)*
E-Z Dumper Products LLC 717 762-8432
  150 Vardon Ct Southern Pines (28387) *(G-14534)*
E&C Medical Intelligence Inc 609 228-7898
  100 Regency Forest Dr Ste 200 Cary (27518) *(G-1753)*
E&G Industries Inc 347 665-3039
  202 Hillview Dr Durham (27703) *(G-5074)*
E2m Kitchen LLC 704 985-5903
  1907 Gateway Blvd Charlotte (28208) *(G-2672)*
Eagle Assembly Unlimited Inc 252 462-0408
  8928 Main St Castalia (27816) *(G-1939)*
Eagle Carports Inc (PA) 800 579-8589
  210 Airport Rd Mount Airy (27030) *(G-11503)*
Eagle Compressors, Greensboro *Also Called: Eagle Compressors Inc (G-6985)*
Eagle Compressors Inc (PA) 336 370-4159
  3003 Thurston Ave Greensboro (27406) *(G-6985)*
Eagle Eyes Crrclum Edtrial Svc 910 399-7445
  114 Red Fox Rd Wilmington (28409) *(G-16209)*
Eagle Laser, High Point *Also Called: Custom Finishers Inc (G-8313)*
Eagle Machining Usa Inc 717 235-9383
  13728 Statesville Rd Huntersville (28078) *(G-8813)*
Eagle Products Inc 336 886-5688
  1200 Surrett Dr High Point (27260) *(G-8334)*
Eagle River, Apex *Also Called: Wolfe Products Inc (G-260)*
Eagle Rock Concrete LLC 919 596-7077
  500 Pristine Water Dr Apex (27539) *(G-186)*
Eagle Rock Concrete LLC (PA) 919 781-3744
  8310 Bandford Way Raleigh (27615) *(G-12713)*
Eagle Rock Concrete LLC 919 281-0120
  8311 Bandford Way Ste 7 Raleigh (27615) *(G-12714)*
Eagle Rock Industries LLC 919 799-1021
  2271 S Chatham Avenue Ext Siler City (27344) *(G-14409)*
Eagle Sportswear LLC 919 365-9805
  4251 Wendell Blvd Wendell (27591) *(G-15900)*
Eagle Sportswear LLC 252 235-4082
  10447 S Nash St Middlesex (27557) *(G-10446)*
Eagle Superabrasives Inc 828 261-7281
  141 33rd Street Dr Se Hickory (28602) *(G-8014)*
Eagle USA, Wendell *Also Called: Eagle Sportswear LLC (G-15900)*
Eagleair Inc 336 398-8000
  3003 Thurston Ave Greensboro (27406) *(G-6986)*
Eaglestone Technology Inc 336 476-0244
  1401 Kensington Dr High Point (27262) *(G-8335)*
Earls Precision Machining 919 542-1869
  365 Taylors Chapel Rd Sanford (27330) *(G-14112)*
Early Bird Hosiery Mills Inc 828 324-6745
  1011 10th Street Blvd Nw Hickory (28601) *(G-8015)*
Earnhardt Manufacturing 910 738-9426
  606 E 1st St Lumberton (28358) *(G-10033)*

Earnmoore — ALPHABETIC SECTION

Earnmoore, High Point *Also Called: Cartridge World* *(G-8288)*

Earth Dog Enterprises LLC.. 919 876-7768
2231 E Millbrook Rd Ste 111 Raleigh (27604) *(G-12715)*

Earth Edge LLC.. 828 624-0252
940 23rd St Sw Hickory (28602) *(G-8016)*

Earth Guild, Asheville *Also Called: Grateful Union Family Inc* *(G-640)*

Earth Matters Inc... 410 747-4400
4943 Looking Glass Trl Denver (28037) *(G-4775)*

Earth-Kind Inc.. 701 751-4456
346 E Plaza Dr Ste D Mooresville (28115) *(G-10934)*

Earthknit, Liberty *Also Called: Supertex Inc* *(G-9833)*

Eas Incorporated.. 704 734-4945
420 Canterbury Rd Kings Mountain (28086) *(G-9305)*

East Bay Woodworks... 503 313-4079
249 Woodstream Cir Mooresville (28117) *(G-10935)*

East Carolina Brace Limb Inc... 252 726-8068
209 N 35th St Ste 1 Morehead City (28557) *(G-11170)*

East Carolina Trucks, Garner *Also Called: Carroll Co* *(G-6262)*

East Cast Emrgncy Response Svc, Beulaville *Also Called: Daphne Lawson Espino* *(G-1093)*

East Cast Trckg Bckhoe Svcs LL... 919 209-0198
708 Nc Highway 210 Smithfield (27577) *(G-14459)*

East Coast Bat Company Inc.. 704 305-3649
8427 Dawson Ln Locust (28097) *(G-9958)*

East Coast Biologics.. 717 919-9980
311 Wagoner Dr Fayetteville (28303) *(G-5815)*

East Coast Designs LLC... 910 865-1070
781 Tobermory Rd Fayetteville (28306) *(G-5816)*

East Coast Digital Inc.. 919 304-1142
100 E Ruffin St Mebane (27302) *(G-10408)*

East Coast Digital Prtg Inc.. 919 465-3799
800 Bell Arbor Ct Cary (27519) *(G-1754)*

East Coast Door & Hardware Inc... 704 791-4128
464 Action Dr Nw Concord (28027) *(G-4259)*

East Coast Fab LLC.. 336 285-7444
195 Labrador Dr Randleman (27317) *(G-13468)*

East Coast Firewood LLC... 919 542-0792
840 Moncure Pittsboro Rd Moncure (27559) *(G-10619)*

East Coast Hurricane Shutters... 910 352-5717
4133 Highsmith Rd Burgaw (28425) *(G-1338)*

East Coast Log & Timber Inc... 252 568-4344
305 Kator Dunn Rd Albertson (28508) *(G-115)*

East Coast Logging Inc... 252 794-4054
128 Mizelle Ln Windsor (27983) *(G-16565)*

East Coast Mouldings, North Wilkesboro *Also Called: Ecmd Inc* *(G-12006)*

East Coast Oxygen Inc.. 828 252-7770
310 Elk Park Dr Asheville (28804) *(G-613)*

East Coast Roadster... 336 624-5083
5401 Kingsbridge Rd Winston Salem (27103) *(G-16688)*

East Coast Signs.. 910 462-2632
9757 Mccoll Rd Laurinburg (28352) *(G-9475)*

East Coast Stl Fabrication Inc.. 757 351-2601
116 N Granby St Hertford (27944) *(G-7920)*

East Coast Umbrella Inc.. 910 462-2500
6321 Andrew Jackson Hwy Laurel Hill (28351) *(G-9459)*

East Crlina Metal Treating Inc (PA)....................................... 919 834-2100
1117 Capital Blvd Raleigh (27603) *(G-12716)*

East Crlina Olseed Prcssors LL... 252 935-5553
2015 Nc Highway 45 N Pantego (27860) *(G-12163)*

East Crlina Orthtics Prsthtics, Elizabeth City *Also Called: Albemrle Orthotics Prosthetics* *(G-5531)*

East End Mllwk DBA Avvento Inc... 516 313-7739
1772 Rosebay Ct Sw Ocean Isle Beach (28469) *(G-12090)*

East Fork, Asheville *Also Called: East Fork Pottery LLC* *(G-615)*

East Fork Pottery LLC... 828 237-7200
144 Caribou Rd Ste 70 Asheville (28803) *(G-614)*

East Fork Pottery LLC (PA).. 828 237-7200
531 Short Mcdowell St Asheville (28803) *(G-615)*

East Fork Pottery LLC... 828 575-2150
15 W Walnut St # A Asheville (28801) *(G-616)*

East Industries Inc.. 252 442-9662
1114 Instrument Dr Rocky Mount (27804) *(G-13693)*

East Penn Manufacturing Co.. 336 771-1380
3117 Starlight Dr Ste 200 Winston Salem (27107) *(G-16689)*

East West Design Mfg Dist, Mooresville *Also Called: East West Manufacturing LLC* *(G-10936)*

East West Diversified LLC... 919 671-0301
1609 Gracie Girl Way Wake Forest (27587) *(G-15549)*

East West Manufacturing LLC.. 704 663-5975
1133 N Main St Mooresville (28115) *(G-10936)*

Eastcarolinacustomcabinets... 757 450-7385
122 Quail Run Dr Moyock (27958) *(G-11696)*

Eastcoast Carports... 336 755-3409
510 Riverside Dr Mount Airy (27030) *(G-11504)*

Eastcoast Packaging Inc.. 919 562-6060
10235 E Finch Ave Middlesex (27557) *(G-10447)*

Easter Seals Ucp NC & VA Inc... 919 856-0250
2533 Atlantic Ave Raleigh (27604) *(G-12717)*

Eastern Band Cherokee Indians.. 828 497-6824
2000 Old #4 Rd Cherokee (28719) *(G-3856)*

Eastern Bikes, Maiden *Also Called: Driver Distribution Inc* *(G-10106)*

Eastern Bikes, Raleigh *Also Called: Driver Distribution Inc* *(G-12702)*

Eastern Building Components, New Bern *Also Called: General Wholesale Bldg Sup Co* *(G-11806)*

Eastern Cabinet Company Inc.. 252 237-5245
3100 Meteor Dr Wilson (27893) *(G-16494)*

Eastern Cabinet Installers Inc... 336 774-2966
4735 Kester Mill Rd Winston Salem (27103) *(G-16690)*

Eastern Carolina Mfg Co LLC... 252 824-3794
179 Nc Highway 97 E Tarboro (27886) *(G-15102)*

Eastern Carolina Vault Co Inc.. 252 243-5614
1214 Queen St E Wilson (27893) *(G-16495)*

Eastern Compost LLC... 252 446-3636
8487 Bttleboro Leggett Rd Elm City (27822) *(G-5649)*

Eastern Cornerstone Cnstr LLC.. 919 702-3583
105 S Creek Dr Louisburg (27549) *(G-9986)*

Eastern Crlina Agrculture Svcs, Robersonville *Also Called: Carolina Eastern Inc* *(G-13615)*

Eastern Crlina Vctonal Ctr Inc (PA)...................................... 252 758-4188
2100 N Greene St Greenville (27834) *(G-7521)*

Eastern Elevator Inc... 877 840-2638
176 Mine Lake Ct Raleigh (27615) *(G-12718)*

Eastern Fuel Procurement Inc.. 252 523-2799
3419 Buena Vista Ct Kinston (28504) *(G-9360)*

Eastern Hydraulic & Pwr Transm, Rocky Mount *Also Called: Wilson Iron Works Incorporated* *(G-13677)*

Eastern Manufacturing LLC... 919 580-2058
300 Dixie Trl Goldsboro (27530) *(G-6611)*

Eastern Offset Printing Co.. 252 247-6791
410 W Fort Macon Rd Atlantic Beach (28512) *(G-829)*

Eastern Plastics Company.. 704 542-7786
10724 Carmel Commons Blvd Ste 580 Charlotte (28226) *(G-2673)*

Eastern Sun Communications Inc... 704 408-7668
4019 Sheridan Dr Charlotte (28205) *(G-2674)*

Eastern Wholesale Fence LLC.. 631 698-0975
7401 Statesville Blvd Salisbury (28147) *(G-13957)*

Easth20 Holdings Llc... 919 313-2100
4224 Tudor Ln Ste 101 Greensboro (27410) *(G-6987)*

Eastonsweb Multimedia.. 704 607-0941
4111 Nicole Eileen Ln Charlotte (28216) *(G-2675)*

Easy E Enterprises LLC.. 704 763-7906
2232 Page Rd Ste 104 Durham (27703) *(G-5075)*

Easy Fresh Products... 704 216-4111
5403 Dilda Church Rd Fountain (27829) *(G-6093)*

Easy Light LLC.. 972 313-5474
715 N Church St Charlotte (28202) *(G-2676)*

Easy Mask, Cary *Also Called: Loparex LLC* *(G-1814)*

Easy Stones Corp... 980 201-9506
1440 Westinghouse Blvd Ste A Charlotte (28273) *(G-2677)*

Easyglass Inc... 336 786-1800
1 Andrew Pearson Dr Mount Airy (27030) *(G-11505)*

Easykeyscom Inc.. 877 839-5397
11407 Granite St Charlotte (28273) *(G-2678)*

Easynotes LLC... 919 870-5228
412 Kaywoody Ct Raleigh (27615) *(G-12719)*

ALPHABETIC SECTION

Easynotes Pro, Raleigh *Also Called: Easynotes LLC (G-12719)*

Eatclub Inc..609 578-7942
114 Saint Ayers Way Chapel Hill (27517) *(G-2011)*

Eaton Corporation..828 684-2381
221 Heywood Rd Arden (28704) *(G-326)*

Eaton Corporation..910 677-5375
2900 Doc Bennett Rd Fayetteville (28306) *(G-5817)*

Eaton Corporation..828 286-4157
240 Daniel Rd Forest City (28043) *(G-6066)*

Eaton Corporation..704 937-7411
744 S Battleground Ave Kings Mountain (28086) *(G-9306)*

Eaton Corporation..910 695-2900
15 Centennial Blvd Pinehurst (28374) *(G-12221)*

Eaton Corporation..919 870-3000
8609 Six Forks Rd Raleigh (27615) *(G-12720)*

Eaton Corporation..864 433-1603
8380 Capital Blvd Raleigh (27616) *(G-12721)*

Eaton Corporation..919 872-3020
3301 Spring Forest Rd Raleigh (27616) *(G-12722)*

Eaton Corporation..336 322-0696
2564 Durham Rd Roxboro (27573) *(G-13801)*

Eaton Corporation..919 965-2341
1100 E Preston St Selma (27576) *(G-14255)*

Eaton Power Quality Corp................................919 872-3020
8609 Six Forks Rd Raleigh (27615) *(G-12723)*

Eaton Power Quality Group Inc (DH)..............919 872-3020
8609 Six Forks Rd Raleigh (27615) *(G-12724)*

Eaton Scientific Inc..919 855-9886
2105 Osprey Cir Raleigh (27615) *(G-12725)*

Eaton US Raleigh, Raleigh *Also Called: Eaton Corporation (G-12721)*

Eaton-Schultz Inc...704 331-8004
3800 Woodpark Blvd Ste I Charlotte (28206) *(G-2679)*

Eatumup Lure Company Inc............................336 218-0896
116 S Walnut Cir Greensboro (27409) *(G-6988)*

Eb5 Corporation...503 230-8008
201 Rampart St Charlotte (28203) *(G-2680)*

Ebert Sign Company Inc..................................336 768-2867
7815 N Nc Highway 150 Lexington (27295) *(G-9711)*

Ebhc LLC..704 733-9427
210 E Trade St Charlotte (28202) *(G-2681)*

Ebony & Ivorys Unique Btq LLC.......................704 324-4035
214 Glencroft Dr Wingate (28174) *(G-16574)*

Echo Industries Inc..704 921-2293
11421 Reames Rd Charlotte (28269) *(G-2682)*

Ecii, Whitsett *Also Called: Engineered Controls Intl LLC (G-15989)*

Eclipse Composite Engineering......................801 601-8559
138 Cedar Pointe Dr Mooresville (28117) *(G-10937)*

Eclipse Composites Engineering, Mooresville *Also Called: Eclipse Composite Engineering (G-10937)*

Eclipse Health Outcomes Inc..........................706 589-4086
35 Wilhelm Dr Durham (27705) *(G-5076)*

Ecmd Inc..336 835-1182
541 Gentry Rd Elkin (28621) *(G-5617)*

Ecmd Inc (PA)..336 667-5976
2 Grandview St North Wilkesboro (28659) *(G-12006)*

Eco Building Corporation................................910 736-1540
16824 A Nc-211 Red Springs (28377) *(G-13499)*

Eco Modern Homes LLC..................................252 833-4335
509 Bay Lake Dr Chocowinity (27817) *(G-3894)*

Eco-Kids LLC..207 899-2752
6316 J Richard Dr Ste C Raleigh (27617) *(G-12726)*

Ecoatm LLC..858 324-4111
200 Village Dr Boone (28607) *(G-1195)*

Ecodyst, Apex *Also Called: Ecodyst Inc (G-187)*

Ecodyst Inc..919 599-4963
1010 Goodworth Dr Apex (27539) *(G-187)*

Ecolab, Greensboro *Also Called: Kay Chemical Company (G-7144)*

Ecolab Inc..704 527-5912
9335 Harris Corners Pkwy Ste 100 Charlotte (28269) *(G-2683)*

Ecolab Inc..336 931-2289
8300 Capital Dr Greensboro (27409) *(G-6989)*

Ecolab Inc..336 931-2237
90 Piedmont Industrial Dr Ste 400 Winston Salem (27107) *(G-16691)*

Ecolab Kay Chemical Company, Greensboro *Also Called: Ecolab Inc (G-6989)*

Ecomarc LLC..828 226-4780
1207 Posey Blanton Rd Sylva (28779) *(G-15056)*

Economy Clrs Lillington LLC...........................910 893-3927
235 Skeet Range Rd Coats (27521) *(G-4129)*

Economy Grinding, Charlotte *Also Called: Economy Grinding Straightening (G-2684)*

Economy Grinding Straightening....................704 400-2500
432 Springbrook Rd Charlotte (28217) *(G-2684)*

Ecovehicle Enterprises Inc.............................704 544-9907
15022 Bllntyne Cntry Clb Charlotte (28277) *(G-2685)*

ECR Software Corporation (PA).....................828 265-2907
277 Howard St Boone (28607) *(G-1196)*

Ecrs, Boone *Also Called: ECR Software Corporation (G-1196)*

Ecs Enterprises Inc...704 786-1600
7200 Devonshire Dr Kannapolis (28081) *(G-9118)*

Ecs Group-NC LLC...919 830-1171
6424 Zebulon Rd Wake Forest (27587) *(G-15550)*

Ecu Print Shop, Greenville *Also Called: E C U Univ Prtg & Graphics (G-7520)*

ECVC, Greenville *Also Called: Eastern Crlina Vctonal Ctr Inc (G-7521)*

Ed Kemp Associates, High Point *Also Called: Ed Kemp Associates Inc (G-8336)*

Ed Kemp Associates Inc..................................336 869-2155
3001 N Main St High Point (27265) *(G-8336)*

Ed Majka LLC..570 985-9677
459 Wickham Rd Shiloh (27974) *(G-14391)*

Ed S Tire Laurinburg Inc.................................910 277-0565
300 Biggs St Laurinburg (28352) *(G-9476)*

ED&d, Cary *Also Called: Educated Design & Development Incorporated (G-1755)*

Edc Inc (PA)...336 993-0468
950 Old Winston Rd Kernersville (27284) *(G-9194)*

Edco Products Inc...828 264-1490
643 Greenway Rd Ste J5 Boone (28607) *(G-1197)*

Edd Loftis Backhoe Servic..............................919 971-5740
6484 Carrick Bend Trl Sw Ocean Isle Beach (28469) *(G-12091)*

Eddie Hsr S Prcsion McHning In....................704 750-4244
613 Slater St Kings Mountain (28086) *(G-9307)*

Eddie S Mountain Machine Inc......................828 685-0733
2011 Pilot Mountain Rd Hendersonville (28792) *(G-7846)*

Eddie Ta Mendenhall Logging........................919 718-9293
314 Mendenhall Farm Ln Moncure (27559) *(G-10620)*

Eddies Welding Inc...704 585-2024
213 Halyburton Rd Stony Point (28678) *(G-14972)*

Edelbrock LLC...919 718-9737
5715 Clyde Rhyne Dr Sanford (27330) *(G-14113)*

Eden Dry Cleaners, Charlotte *Also Called: M and R Inc (G-3114)*

Edenton Boatworks LLC.................................252 482-7600
140 Midway Dr Edenton (27932) *(G-5514)*

Edge Broadband Solutions LLC.....................828 785-1420
244 Lea Plant Rd Waynesville (28786) *(G-15803)*

Edge of The Carolinas Magazine, Wilmington *Also Called: Quinlan Publishing Company (G-16374)*

Edge Promo Team LLC....................................919 946-4218
7868 Us 70 Bus Hwy W Ste B Clayton (27520) *(G-3975)*

Edge Welding Supply, Mooresville *Also Called: M 5 Scentific Glassblowing Inc (G-11012)*

Edge-Works Manufacturing Co......................910 455-9834
272 W Stag Park Service Rd Burgaw (28425) *(G-1339)*

Edgewell Per Care Brands LLC......................336 672-4500
2331 Carl Dr Asheboro (27203) *(G-425)*

Edgewell Per Care Brands LLC......................336 629-1581
800 Albemarle Rd Asheboro (27203) *(G-426)*

Edgewell Per Care Brands LLC......................336 672-4500
419 Art Bryan Dr Asheboro (27203) *(G-427)*

Edgeworks, Burgaw *Also Called: Edge-Works Manufacturing Co (G-1339)*

Edit Plus..336 775-2764
900 Leonard Courtyard Blvd Clemmons (27012) *(G-4037)*

EDM Technology Inc..336 882-8115
210 Old Thomasville Rd High Point (27260) *(G-8337)*

Edmiston Hydrlic Swmill Eqp In....................336 921-2304
8540 W Nc Highway 268 Boomer (28606) *(G-1169)*

Eds Pallet World Inc 828 453-8986
559 Race Path Church Rd Ellenboro (28040) *(G-5635)*

Edsel G Barnes Jr Inc 252 793-4170
1458 Morrattock Rd Plymouth (27962) *(G-12372)*

Edtech Systems LLC 919 341-0613
6115 Corporate Ridge Rd Raleigh (27607) *(G-12727)*

Educated Design & Development Incorporated 919 469-9434
901 Sheldon Dr Cary (27513) *(G-1755)*

Education Center LLC 336 854-0309
8886 Rymack Dr Oak Ridge (27310) *(G-12059)*

Educatrx Inc 980 328-0013
504 Kintyre Dr Monroe (28112) *(G-10711)*

Edward & Lamar Publishing 919 433-6625
1418 Leon St Durham (27705) *(G-5077)*

Edward Ferrell Lewis Mittman, High Point *Also Called: Dfp Inc (G-8323)*

Edward Heil Screw Products 828 345-6140
1114 1st St W Conover (28613) *(G-4449)*

Edwards Electronic Systems Inc (DH) 919 359-2239
3821 Powhatan Rd Clayton (27520) *(G-3976)*

Edwards Lawnmower & Wldg Repr 919 235-7173
1616 Wake Dr Wake Forest (27587) *(G-15551)*

Edwards Logging Inc 336 783-0833
119 Crabapple Ln Mount Airy (27030) *(G-11506)*

Edwards Mountain Woodworks LLC 919 932-6050
57 Woodside Trl Chapel Hill (27517) *(G-2012)*

Edwards Timber Company Inc (PA) 704 624-5098
2215 Old Lawyers Rd Marshville (28103) *(G-10215)*

Edwards Transportation, Marshville *Also Called: Edwards Wood Products Inc (G-10216)*

Edwards Unlimited Inc 252 226-4583
3355 Raleigh Rd Henderson (27537) *(G-7782)*

Edwards Wood Pdts Inc/Woodlawn 828 756-4758
8482 Us 221 N Marion (28752) *(G-10149)*

Edwards Wood Products Inc 704 624-5098
9979 Old Liberty Rd Liberty (27298) *(G-9811)*

Edwards Wood Products Inc 336 622-7537
3231 Staley Store Rd Liberty (27298) *(G-9812)*

Edwards Wood Products Inc (PA) 704 624-3624
2215 Old Lawyers Rd Marshville (28103) *(G-10216)*

Edwards Wood Products Inc 910 276-6870
19500 Old Lumberton Rd Laurinburg (28352) *(G-9477)*

Edwin Reaves 901 326-6382
1630 Flintshire Rd Fayetteville (28304) *(G-5818)*

Eekkohart Floors & Lbr Co Inc 336 409-2672
1133 N Main St Mocksville (27028) *(G-10569)*

Efa Inc 336 378-2603
3112 Pleasant Garden Rd Greensboro (27406) *(G-6990)*

Efa Inc (DH) 336 275-9401
3112 Pleasant Garden Rd Greensboro (27406) *(G-6991)*

Efco USA Inc 800 332-6872
11600 Goodrich Dr Charlotte (28273) *(G-2686)*

Effikal LLC 252 522-3031
2630 Airport Rd Kinston (28504) *(G-9361)*

Eg-Gilero, Durham *Also Called: Gilero LLC (G-5115)*

Ega Southeast, Mooresville *Also Called: E G A Products Inc (G-10932)*

Egads Printing Co 252 335-1554
1403 N Road St Elizabeth City (27909) *(G-5542)*

Egger, Linwood *Also Called: Egger Wood Products LLC (G-9943)*

Egger Wood Products LLC 336 843-7000
300 Egger Pkwy Linwood (27299) *(G-9943)*

Egi Associates Inc 704 561-3337
417 Minuet Ln Ste A Charlotte (28217) *(G-2687)*

Egret Boats LLC 252 948-0004
715 Page Rd Washington (27889) *(G-15698)*

Ehs Retail LLC 336 629-4367
405 E Dixie Dr Ste A Asheboro (27203) *(G-428)*

Ei LLC 704 857-0707
380 Knollwood St Ste 700 Winston Salem (27103) *(G-16692)*

Ei Solution Works, Winston Salem *Also Called: Ei LLC (G-16692)*

Eidolon Designs, Raleigh *Also Called: Michael Parker Cabinetry (G-13024)*

Eidp Inc 910 483-4681
22828 Nc Highway 87 W Fayetteville (28306) *(G-5819)*

Eidp Inc 252 522-6111
4693 Highway 11 N Grifton (28530) *(G-7599)*

Eidp Inc 252 522-6286
4693 Hwy 11 N Kinston (28502) *(G-9362)*

Eidp Inc 910 371-4000
3500 Daniels Rd Ne Leland (28451) *(G-9540)*

Eighty Orchard Publishing Inc 980 689-5406
15823 Kelly Park Cir Huntersville (28078) *(G-8814)*

Eisai Inc 919 941-6920
4130 Parklake Ave Ste 500 Raleigh (27612) *(G-12728)*

Eizi Group Llc 919 397-3638
9008 Riverview Park Dr Raleigh (27613) *(G-12729)*

Ej, Apex *Also Called: Ej Usa Inc (G-188)*

Ej Usa Inc 919 362-7744
1006 Investment Blvd Apex (27502) *(G-188)*

Ek Air LLC 704 881-1959
143 Southview Dr Statesville (28677) *(G-14792)*

Ekos Brewmaster LLC 704 973-5640
800 W Hill St Ste 101 Charlotte (28208) *(G-2688)*

El Comal Inc 336 788-8110
2390 E Sprague St Winston Salem (27107) *(G-16693)*

El Mexicano Tires, Warsaw *Also Called: Elias Gonzalez (G-15667)*

El Valle of Lake Norman Inc 704 658-0212
835 Williamson Rd Mooresville (28117) *(G-10938)*

Elan Model Management, Charlotte *Also Called: Hkb Enterprises LLC (G-2912)*

Elan Trading Inc 704 342-1696
3826 Raleigh St Charlotte (28206) *(G-2689)*

Elanco US Inc 812 230-2745
3200 Northline Ave Ste 300 Greensboro (27408) *(G-6992)*

Eland Industries Inc 910 304-5353
353 Washington Acres Rd Hampstead (28443) *(G-7646)*

Elastic Fabric of America, Greensboro *Also Called: Efa Inc (G-6991)*

Elastic Fabrics of America, Greensboro *Also Called: Efa Inc (G-6990)*

Elastic Products, Andrews *Also Called: Industrial Opportunities Inc (G-126)*

Elastic Therapy LLC 336 625-0529
718 Industrial Park Ave Asheboro (27205) *(G-429)*

Elberta Crate & Box Co 252 257-4659
619 N Main St Warrenton (27589) *(G-15658)*

Elborn Holdings LLC 919 917-1419
17408 Lynx Den Ct Davidson (28036) *(G-4673)*

Elder Hosiery Mills Inc 336 226-0673
139 Homewood Ave Burlington (27217) *(G-1409)*

Elders MBL Grinding & Recycl, Marshville *Also Called: MR Fabrications LLC (G-10220)*

Electric Glass Fiber Amer LLC 336 357-8151
473 New Jersey Church Rd Lexington (27292) *(G-9712)*

Electric Glass Fiber Amer LLC (DH) 704 434-2261
940 Washburn Switch Rd Shelby (28150) *(G-14313)*

Electric Meter Division, Raleigh *Also Called: Elster Solutions LLC (G-12732)*

Electric Motor Rewinding Inc 252 338-8856
407 N Poindexter St Elizabeth City (27909) *(G-5543)*

Electric Motor Service of Shelby Inc 704 482-9979
1143 Airport Rd Shelby (28150) *(G-14314)*

Electric Motor Shop, Rocky Mount *Also Called: Electric Mtr Sp Wake Frest Inc (G-13694)*

Electric Motor Svc Ahoskie Inc 252 332-4364
2103 Us Highway 13 S Ahoskie (27910) *(G-61)*

Electric Mtr Sls Svc Pitt Cnty 252 752-3170
202 Hooker Rd Greenville (27834) *(G-7522)*

Electric Mtr Sp Wake Frest Inc 252 446-4173
2421 W Raleigh Blvd Rocky Mount (27803) *(G-13694)*

Electric Mtr Sp Wake Frest Inc (PA) 919 556-3229
1225 N White St Wake Forest (27587) *(G-15552)*

Electrical, Raeford *Also Called: Bennett Elec Maint & Cnstr LLC (G-12414)*

Electrical Apparatus & Mch Co 704 333-2987
5619 Gallagher Dr Gastonia (28052) *(G-6400)*

Electrical Equipment Company 910 276-2141
226 N Wilkinson Dr Laurinburg (28352) *(G-9478)*

Electrical Panel & Contrls Inc 336 434-4445
645 Mcway Dr High Point (27263) *(G-8338)*

Electro Magnetic Research Inc 919 365-3723
9576 Covered Bridge Rd Zebulon (27597) *(G-17126)*

ALPHABETIC SECTION

Electro Switch Corp... 919 833-0707
2010 Yonkers Rd Raleigh (27604) *(G-12730)*

Electro-Motion Agency, Charlotte *Also Called: Alan R Williams Inc (G-2151)*

Electrolux Home Products Inc....................................... 252 527-5100
4850 W Vernon Ave Kinston (28504) *(G-9363)*

Electronic Imaging Svcs Inc... 704 587-3323
1500 Continental Blvd Charlotte (28273) *(G-2690)*

Electronic Products Design Inc..................................... 919 365-9199
2554 Lake Wendell Rd Wendell (27591) *(G-15901)*

Electronic Services, Farmville *Also Called: Esco Electronic Services Inc (G-5735)*

Electropin Technologies LLC... 919 288-1203
110 Centura Dr Goldsboro (27530) *(G-6612)*

Electroswitch, Raleigh *Also Called: Electro Switch Corp (G-12730)*

Electrotek, Fayetteville *Also Called: Energetics Inc (G-5821)*

Elektran Inc.. 910 997-6640
220 River Rd Rockingham (28379) *(G-13625)*

Elektrikredd LLC... 704 805-0110
2123 Stevens Mill Rd Matthews (28104) *(G-10313)*

Element Arbor Inc... 828 550-2250
417 Sunny Dr Waynesville (28786) *(G-15804)*

Element Countertops Inc... 704 641-7145
1724 Clontz Long Rd Monroe (28110) *(G-10712)*

Element Designs, Charlotte *Also Called: Element Designs Inc (G-2691)*

Element Designs Inc.. 704 332-3114
235 Crompton St Charlotte (28273) *(G-2691)*

Element Strategy LLC.. 704 997-5627
13346 Robert Walker Dr Davidson (28036) *(G-4674)*

Element Tree Essentials LLC.. 828 707-0407
3873a Sweeten Creek Rd Arden (28704) *(G-327)*

Element West LLC... 336 853-6118
266 Haywood Rd Lexington (27295) *(G-9713)*

Elemental Bee.. 336 471-9085
4115 Aberdare Dr High Point (27265) *(G-8339)*

Elements Brands, Charlotte *Also Called: Elements Brands LLC (G-2692)*

Elements Brands LLC.. 503 230-8008
1515 Mockingbird Ln Charlotte (28209) *(G-2692)*

Elements Imaging LLC.. 504 258-3317
74 Suddreth Ln Candler (28715) *(G-1578)*

Elements In Focus LLC... 561 289-8641
104 Rozelle Valley Ln Cary (27519) *(G-1756)*

Elephants Corner Wines LLC....................................... 336 782-7084
550 Peters Creek Pkwy Unit No1640 Winston Salem (27101) *(G-16694)*

Elevate Cleaning Service.. 347 928-4030
2120 Fort Bragg Rd Fayetteville (28303) *(G-5820)*

Elevate Textiles Inc... 336 379-6220
906 N Anthony St Burlington (27217) *(G-1410)*

Elevate Textiles Inc (HQ).. 336 379-6220
121 W Trade St Ste 1700 Charlotte (28202) *(G-2693)*

Elevate Textiles Inc... 910 997-5001
740 Old Cheraw Hwy Cordova (28330) *(G-4517)*

Elevate Textiles Holding Corp (PA).............................. 336 379-6220
121 W Trade St Ste 1700 Charlotte (28202) *(G-2694)*

Elevated Cnstr Renovations LLC................................. 910 301-4243
1279 Lewis Mcneill Rd Red Springs (28377) *(G-13500)*

Elevator & Amusement DVC Bur, Raleigh *Also Called: North Carolina Dept Labor (G-13068)*

Elevator Controls and Security, Wake Forest *Also Called: Ecs Group-NC LLC (G-15550)*

Elevators & Conveyors, Charlotte *Also Called: Citilift Company (G-2483)*

Elgi Compressors USA Inc (HQ)................................... 704 943-7966
4610 Entrance Dr Ste A Charlotte (28273) *(G-2695)*

Eli Company... 908 242-3497
79 Luzelle Dr Winston Salem (27103) *(G-16695)*

Eli Lilly and Company.. 317 296-1226
59 Moore Dr Durham (27709) *(G-5078)*

Eli Research It Journals, Durham *Also Called: Academy Association Inc (G-4899)*

Elias Gonzalez.. 910 271-9514
516 S Pine St Warsaw (28398) *(G-15667)*

Elio Inc... 919 708-5554
2555 Hawkins Ave Sanford (27330) *(G-14114)*

Elite Access International Inc (PA)............................... 336 327-8096
3718 Alliance Dr Ste A Greensboro (27407) *(G-6993)*

Elite Auto Lights, Inc., Flat Rock *Also Called: Three GS Enterprises Inc (G-5972)*

Elite Business Solutions LLC.. 910 713-9350
420 Darlington Ave Wilmington (28403) *(G-16210)*

Elite Business Technologies, Wilmington *Also Called: Elite Business Solutions LLC (G-16210)*

Elite Comfort Solutions LLC.. 828 328-2201
1115 Farrington St Sw Bldg 1 Conover (28613) *(G-4450)*

Elite Cushion Company, Conover *Also Called: Richard Shew (G-4491)*

Elite Custom Coatings, Raleigh *Also Called: Cast Iron Elegance Inc (G-12612)*

Elite Displays & Design Inc... 336 472-8200
6771 Pikeview Dr Thomasville (27360) *(G-15218)*

Elite Forestry Solutions LLC... 757 777-2729
9805 Statesville Rd Ste 6058 Charlotte (28269) *(G-2696)*

Elite Furniture Mfg Inc... 336 882-0406
928 Millis St High Point (27260) *(G-8340)*

Elite Marine LLC... 919 495-6388
377 King Mill Rd Four Oaks (27524) *(G-6103)*

Elite Metal Performance LLC.. 704 660-0006
132 Conifer Dr Statesville (28625) *(G-14793)*

Elite Mountain Business LLC.. 828 349-0403
21 Sanderstown Rd Franklin (28734) *(G-6128)*

Elite Textiles Fabrication Inc... 888 337-0977
1124 Roberts Ln High Point (27260) *(G-8341)*

Elite Wldg & Fabrications LLC...................................... 919 224-6007
150 Ridgeway Warrenton Rd Warrenton (27589) *(G-15659)*

Elite Wood Classics Inc... 910 454-8745
4392 Long Beach Rd Se Oak Island (28461) *(G-12049)*

Elite Wood Products.. 828 994-4446
1600 N College Ave Newton (28658) *(G-11930)*

Elizabeth Carbide Die Co, Lexington *Also Called: Elizabeth Carbide NC Inc (G-9715)*

Elizabeth Carbide Die Co Inc.. 336 472-5555
5801 E Us Highway 64 Lexington (27292) *(G-9714)*

Elizabeth Carbide NC Inc.. 336 472-5555
5801 E Us Highway 64 Lexington (27292) *(G-9715)*

Elizabeth City Cotton Mills, Elizabeth City *Also Called: Robinson Manufacturing Company (G-5568)*

Elizabeth City Yard, Elizabeth City *Also Called: Legacy Vulcan LLC (G-5554)*

Elizabeth Logistic LLC... 803 920-3931
1000 Loudoun Rd Indian Trail (28079) *(G-8931)*

Elizabeth S Java Express... 919 777-5282
120 S Moore St Sanford (27330) *(G-14115)*

Elizondo LLC... 910 590-6550
106 W Clark St Ste B Saint Pauls (28384) *(G-13905)*

Elk Products Inc... 828 397-4200
3266 Us Highway 70 Connelly Springs (28612) *(G-4400)*

Elkamet Inc.. 828 233-4001
201 Mills St East Flat Rock (28726) *(G-5474)*

Elkay Ohio Plumbing Pdts Co....................................... 910 739-8181
880 Caton Rd Lumberton (28360) *(G-10034)*

Elkin Creek Vineyard LLC.. 336 526-5119
318 Elkin Creek Mill Rd Elkin (28621) *(G-5618)*

Elkin Furniture, Elkin *Also Called: Vaughan-Bassett Furn Co Inc (G-5631)*

Elkins Sawmill Inc.. 919 362-1235
670 King Rd Moncure (27559) *(G-10621)*

Ella B Candles LLC.. 980 339-8898
9517 Monroe Rd Ste C Charlotte (28270) *(G-2697)*

Elledge Family Inc.. 919 876-2300
2900 Spring Forest Rd Ste 101 Raleigh (27616) *(G-12731)*

Ellenburg Sheet Metal.. 704 872-2089
353 Stamey Farm Rd Statesville (28625) *(G-14794)*

Ellerre Tech Inc... 704 524-9096
107 E Robinson St Dallas (28034) *(G-4638)*

Ellie Industries Inc... 828 626-3935
93 Buena Vista Dr Barnardsville (28709) *(G-909)*

Ellis Backhoe Service Inc.. 336 451-6265
151 Burton Farm Rd Greensboro (27455) *(G-6994)*

Ellis Jewelers, Lexington *Also Called: Jewel Masters Inc (G-9734)*

Ellis Lumber Co and Logs, Shelby *Also Called: Ellis Lumber Company Inc (G-14315)*

Ellis Lumber Company Inc.. 704 482-1414
1681 S Lafayette St Shelby (28152) *(G-14315)*

Ellis Publishing Company Inc....................................... 252 444-1999
3200 Wellons Blvd New Bern (28562) *(G-11803)*

Ellismorris LLC..646 538-1870
  1908 Creekside Landing Dr Apex (27502) *(G-189)*
Ellison Company Inc..704 889-7518
  13501 S Ridge Dr Charlotte (28273) *(G-2698)*
Ellison Technologies Inc....................................704 545-7362
  9724 Southern Pine Blvd Charlotte (28273) *(G-2699)*
Elmore Welding Inc..919 584-7460
  318 Nita Ln Durham (27712) *(G-5079)*
Elnik Systems LLC...973 239-6066
  12004 Carolina Logistics Dr Ste A Pineville (28134) *(G-12267)*
Elomi Inc...904 591-0095
  22 Carpenter Ct Nw Concord (28027) *(G-4260)*
Elsag North America LLC (PA)..........................336 379-7135
  4221 Tudor Ln Greensboro (27410) *(G-6995)*
Elsco Inc (PA)..509 885-4525
  199 Crocker St Seaboard (27876) *(G-14228)*
Elster American Meter Company LLC (HQ).......402 873-8200
  855 S Mint St Charlotte (28202) *(G-2700)*
Elster Electricity, Raleigh *Also Called: Elster Solutions LLC (G-12733)*
Elster Solutions LLC (DH).................................919 212-4800
  208 S Rogers Ln Raleigh (27610) *(G-12732)*
Elster Solutions LLC...919 212-4819
  201 S Rogers Ln Raleigh (27610) *(G-12733)*
Elxsi Corporation..407 849-1090
  6325 Ardrey Kell Rd Ste 400 Charlotte (28277) *(G-2701)*
Ely Tortilleria LLC..704 886-8501
  6301 N Tryon St Ste 112 Charlotte (28213) *(G-2702)*
Em2 Machine Corp..336 297-4110
  7939 Highfill Rd Summerfield (27358) *(G-14981)*
Em2 Machine Corporation.................................336 707-8409
  1030 Boulder Rd Greensboro (27409) *(G-6996)*
Emage Medical LLC..704 904-1873
  15720 Brixham Hill Ave Ste 300 Charlotte (28277) *(G-2703)*
Emanuel Hoggard..252 794-3724
  837 Askewville Rd Windsor (27983) *(G-16566)*
Emanuel Hoggard Logging, Windsor *Also Called: Emanuel Hoggard (G-16566)*
Emath360 LLC..919 744-4944
  302 Parish House Rd Cary (27513) *(G-1757)*
Emb Inc...336 945-0759
  4180 Mendenhall Oaks Pkwy Ste 100 High Point (27265) *(G-8342)*
Embrex LLC (HQ)..919 941-5185
  1040 Swabia Ct Durham (27703) *(G-5080)*
Embrex Poultry Health LLC...............................910 844-5566
  22300 Skyway Church Rd Maxton (28364) *(G-10355)*
Embrex, Inc., Durham *Also Called: Embrex LLC (G-5080)*
Embroid It...704 617-0357
  16324 York Rd Charlotte (28278) *(G-2704)*
Embroid ME, Charlotte *Also Called: Kessel Development LLC (G-3051)*
Embroidery 2, Pineville *Also Called: Blp Products and Services Inc (G-12256)*
Embroidery Authority, Burnsville *Also Called: Amy Smith (G-1522)*
Embroidery Corner..910 817-7586
  136 Glendale Dr Rockingham (28379) *(G-13626)*
Embroidery Nurse LLC......................................919 630-5261
  1812 Falls River Ave Raleigh (27614) *(G-12734)*
Embroidery Store, The, Winston Salem *Also Called: Dime EMB LLC (G-16681)*
Embroidme..919 316-1538
  105 W Nc Highway 54 Ste 261 Durham (27713) *(G-5081)*
Embroidme Lake Norman..................................704 987-9630
  19420 Jetton Rd Ste 104 Cornelius (28031) *(G-4543)*
EMC Contractor LLC...910 576-7101
  3154 Love Joy Rd Troy (27371) *(G-15405)*
EMC Corporation..720 341-3274
  10815 David Taylor Dr Ste 200 Charlotte (28262) *(G-2705)*
EMC Corporation..919 767-0641
  4121 Surles Ct Durham (27703) *(G-5082)*
EMC Corporation..919 851-3241
  701 Corporate Center Dr Ste 425 Raleigh (27607) *(G-12735)*
Emerald Carolina Chemical LLC......................704 393-0089
  8309 Wilkinson Blvd Charlotte (28214) *(G-2706)*
Emerald Hollow Gems, Hiddenite *Also Called: Hiddenite Gems Inc (G-8219)*
Emerald Printing Inc...336 325-3522
  2616 Shoals Rd Pinnacle (27043) *(G-12320)*

Emerald Tool and Mold Inc................................336 996-6445
  106 Furlong Industrial Dr Kernersville (27284) *(G-9195)*
Emerald Village Inc..828 765-6463
  387 Mckinney Mine Rd Little Switzerland (28749) *(G-9948)*
Emergency Energy Systems Inc.......................910 285-6400
  116 W Southerland St Wallace (28466) *(G-15622)*
Emergency Responder Systems, Charlotte *Also Called: Rf Das Systems Inc (G-3446)*
Emergent Tech Solutions Inc............................704 777-1909
  17004 Turtle Point Rd Charlotte (28278) *(G-2707)*
Emerging Technology Institute, Red Springs *Also Called: Eco Building Corporation (G-13499)*
Emergo Therapeutics Inc..................................919 649-5544
  6208 Fayetteville Rd Ste 104 Durham (27713) *(G-5083)*
Emerson, Shelby *Also Called: Emerson Electric Co (G-14316)*
Emerson Electric Co...704 480-8519
  Plant 4I-32 4401 East Dix Shelby (28150) *(G-14316)*
Emerson Process Management........................704 357-0294
  6135 Lakeview Rd Charlotte (28269) *(G-2708)*
Emery Corporation..828 433-1536
  1523 N Green St Morganton (28655) *(G-11211)*
Emf Industries, Dallas *Also Called: Erecto Mch & Fabrication Inc (G-4639)*
EMI, Columbus *Also Called: Energy Management Insulation (G-4173)*
Eminess Technologies Inc................................704 283-2600
  1412 Airport Rd Monroe (28110) *(G-10713)*
Emitbio Inc..919 321-1726
  615 Davis Dr Morrisville (27560) *(G-11337)*
Emmco Sport LLC..336 354-7244
  1355 S Park Dr # A Kernersville (27284) *(G-9196)*
Emp Services, Statesville *Also Called: Elite Metal Performance LLC (G-14793)*
Empire Carpet & Blinds Inc...............................704 541-3988
  10500 Mcmullen Creek Pkwy Charlotte (28226) *(G-2709)*
Employus Inc..919 706-4008
  122 E Chatham St Ste 300 Cary (27511) *(G-1758)*
Empowered Defense LLC..................................919 624-1304
  3602 Mill Run Raleigh (27612) *(G-12736)*
EMR Electric, Zebulon *Also Called: Electro Magnetic Research Inc (G-17126)*
Emrise Corporation...408 200-3040
  2530 Meridian Pkwy Durham (27713) *(G-5084)*
Emtelle USA Inc..828 707-9970
  101 Mills Gap Rd Unit A Fletcher (28732) *(G-6000)*
En Fleur Corporation...919 556-1623
  124 Fairview Rd Louisburg (27549) *(G-9987)*
Ena Advanced Rubber Tech..............................919 235-0245
  3032 Barrow Dr Raleigh (27616) *(G-12737)*
Enc Conveyance, Rocky Mount *Also Called: Enc Conveyance LLC (G-13667)*
Enc Conveyance LLC..252 378-9990
  4314 Bulluck School Rd Rocky Mount (27801) *(G-13667)*
Enc Industrial Supply.......................................252 862-8300
  423 Railroad St N Ahoskie (27910) *(G-62)*
Encertec Inc..336 288-7226
  415 Pisgah Church Rd Ste 302 Greensboro (27455) *(G-6997)*
Encore Group Inc..336 768-7859
  111 Cloverleaf Dr Winston Salem (27103) *(G-16696)*
Encore Label & Packaging, Charlotte *Also Called: Grand Encore Charlotte LLC (G-2854)*
Encube Ethicals Inc..984 439-2761
  200 Meredith Dr Ste 202 Durham (27713) *(G-5085)*
End Camp North..980 337-4600
  300 Camp Rd Charlotte (28206) *(G-2710)*
End of Days Distillery.......................................910 399-1133
  1815 Castle St Wilmington (28403) *(G-16211)*
Endaxi Company Inc...919 467-8895
  137 Trans Air Dr Morrisville (27560) *(G-11338)*
Endeavor Fabrication Group, Durham *Also Called: Endeavour Fbrication Group Inc (G-5086)*
Endeavour Fbrication Group Inc.......................919 479-1453
  1534 Cher Dr Durham (27713) *(G-5086)*
Endgrain Woodworks LLC.................................980 237-2612
  301 Queens Rd Apt 302 Charlotte (28204) *(G-2711)*
Endless Plastics LLC..336 346-1839
  3704 Alliance Dr Ste B Greensboro (27407) *(G-6998)*
Endura Products LLC..336 991-8818
  210 E Commerce Ave High Point (27260) *(G-8343)*

ALPHABETIC SECTION — Environmental Inks

Endura Products LLC (HQ)..336 668-2472
 8817 W Market St Colfax (27235) *(G-4149)*

Eneco East Inc..828 322-6008
 Hickory (28603) *(G-8017)*

Enepay Corporation...919 788-1454
 7226 Summit Waters Ln Raleigh (27613) *(G-12738)*

Energetics Inc...910 483-2581
 455 Hillsboro St Fayetteville (28301) *(G-5821)*

Energizer Battery Mfg..336 736-7936
 419 Art Bryan Dr Asheboro (27203) *(G-430)*

Energizer Holdings Inc..336 672-3526
 800 Albemarle Rd Asheboro (27203) *(G-431)*

Energy and Entropy Inc...919 933-1365
 301 Palafox Dr Chapel Hill (27516) *(G-2013)*

Energy Conversion Syste...910 892-8081
 10 Carlie Cs Dr Dunn (28334) *(G-4864)*

Energy Management Insulation...828 894-3635
 Columbus (28722) *(G-4173)*

Energy Svers Windows Doors Inc......................................252 758-8700
 1806 Dickinson Ave Greenville (27834) *(G-7523)*

Enerjali LLC..336 451-6479
 7567 Haw Meadows Dr Kernersville (27284) *(G-9197)*

Enertia Building Systems Inc..919 556-2391
 13312 Garffe Sherron Rd Wake Forest (27587) *(G-15553)*

Enfield Tire Service Inc..252 445-5016
 301 N Mcdaniel St Enfield (27823) *(G-5677)*

Enforge LLC..704 983-4146
 1600 Woodhurst Ln Albemarle (28001) *(G-83)*

Eng Solutions Inc..919 831-1830
 1109 Pinehurst Dr Chapel Hill (27517) *(G-2014)*

Engage2excel Inc (PA)..704 872-5231
 115 Corporate Center Dr Ste E Mooresville (28117) *(G-10939)*

Engaged Media Inc..239 280-4202
 3622 Lyckan Pkwy Ste 3003 Durham (27707) *(G-5087)*

Engaging Signs & Graphics...919 371-0885
 11705 Dellcain Ct Raleigh (27617) *(G-12739)*

Engcon North America..203 691-5920
 2827 Earlham Pl High Point (27263) *(G-8344)*

Engine Systems Inc (HQ)..252 977-2720
 175 Freight Rd Rocky Mount (27804) *(G-13695)*

Engine Wellness Inc..503 231-0495
 1067 Canterbury Ln Chapel Hill (27517) *(G-2015)*

Engineered Attachments LLC..336 703-5266
 200 Kapp St Winston Salem (27105) *(G-16697)*

Engineered Coated Fabrics, Rutherfordton Also Called: Trelleborg Ctd Systems US Inc *(G-13895)*

Engineered Controls Intl LLC..336 226-3244
 3181 Lear Dr Burlington (27215) *(G-1411)*

Engineered Controls Intl LLC..828 466-2153
 911 Industrial Dr Sw Conover (28613) *(G-4451)*

Engineered Controls Intl LLC (HQ).....................................336 449-7707
 100 Rego Dr Elon (27244) *(G-5657)*

Engineered Controls Intl LLC..336 449-7706
 1239 Rock Creek Dairy Rd Whitsett (27377) *(G-15989)*

Engineered Processing Eqp LLC..919 321-6891
 5036 Country Club Dr N Wilson (27896) *(G-16496)*

Engineered Recycling Company LLC.................................704 358-6700
 1011 Woodward Ave 1101 Charlotte (28206) *(G-2712)*

Engineered Software...336 299-4843
 615 Guilford Ave Greensboro (27401) *(G-6999)*

Engineered Steel Products LLC..336 495-5266
 4977 Plainfield Rd Sophia (27350) *(G-14515)*

Engineered Steel Products Inc...336 495-5266
 4977 Plainfield Rd Sophia (27350) *(G-14516)*

Engineering Consulting Svcs, Greensboro Also Called: McLean Sbsrface Utility Engrg L *(G-7194)*

Engineering Mfg Svcs Co...704 821-7325
 5634 Cannon Dr Monroe (28110) *(G-10714)*

Engineering Reprographics, Raleigh Also Called: Document Imaging Systems Inc *(G-12693)*

Enginred Plstic Components Inc..919 663-3141
 920 E Raleigh St Siler City (27344) *(G-14410)*

England Inc..336 861-5266
 222 S Main St High Point (27260) *(G-8345)*

Englishs All Wood Homes Inc...252 524-5000
 608 Queen St Grifton (28530) *(G-7600)*

Ennis-Flint..336 477-8439
 505 County Line Rd Thomasville (27360) *(G-15219)*

Ennis-Flint, Thomasville Also Called: Flint Trading Inc *(G-15224)*

Ennis-Flint, Thomasville Also Called: Road Infrstrcture Inv Hldngs I *(G-15271)*

Ennis-Flint Inc (HQ)...800 331-8118
 4161 Piedmont Pkwy Ste 370 Greensboro (27410) *(G-7000)*

Ennis-Flint Inc...800 331-8118
 115 Todd Ct Thomasville (27360) *(G-15220)*

Eno Mt Cabinets James Ray..919 644-1981
 506 Eno Mountain Rd Hillsborough (27278) *(G-8649)*

Eno Scientific LLC..910 778-2660
 1606 Faucette Mill Rd Hillsborough (27278) *(G-8650)*

Enoco LLC..336 398-5650
 112 Maxfield Rd Greensboro (27405) *(G-7001)*

Enovis Corporation..704 289-6511
 1710 Airport Rd Monroe (28110) *(G-10715)*

Enplas Life Tech Inc...828 633-2250
 230 Sardis Rd Asheville (28806) *(G-617)*

Enpoco, Spindale Also Called: Watts Drainage Products Inc *(G-14609)*

Enpro, Charlotte Also Called: Enpro Industries Inc *(G-2713)*

Enpro Industries Inc (PA)..704 731-1500
 5605 Carnegie Blvd Ste 500 Charlotte (28209) *(G-2713)*

Enrg Brand LLC...980 298-8519
 125 Remount Rd Ste C12168 Charlotte (28203) *(G-2714)*

Enriched Abundance Entp LLC...704 369-6363
 15316 Trickling Water Ct Charlotte (28273) *(G-2715)*

Ensales Electrical Assoc Inc...910 298-3305
 140 E Park Dr Unit B Beulaville (28518) *(G-1094)*

Ensinger Polytech Inc (DH)...704 992-8100
 13728 Statesville Rd Huntersville (28078) *(G-8815)*

Entergy Group LLC..866 988-8884
 500 Westover Dr Ste 10447 Sanford (27330) *(G-14116)*

Enterprint Corp..919 821-7897
 606 Wade Ave Ste 100 Raleigh (27605) *(G-12740)*

Enterprise Loggers Company Inc.......................................252 586-4805
 681 Enterprise Rd Littleton (27850) *(G-9951)*

Enterprise Metal Tag Plant, Raleigh Also Called: North Carolina Dept Pub Safety *(G-13069)*

Enterprise Rendering Company..704 485-3018
 28821 Bethlehem Church Rd Oakboro (28129) *(G-12073)*

Enterprise Twd...704 822-6166
 7482 Nc 73 Hwy Stanley (28164) *(G-14692)*

Enterprise, The, Williamston Also Called: Cox Nrth Crlina Pblcations Inc *(G-16059)*

Entex Technologies Inc..919 933-1380
 1340 Environ Way Chapel Hill (27517) *(G-2016)*

Entropy, Rocky Point Also Called: Sea Mark Boats Inc *(G-13749)*

Entropy Solar Integrators LLC..704 936-5018
 13950 Ballantyne Charlotte (28277) *(G-2716)*

Entrust Services LLC...336 274-5175
 130 S Walnut Cir Greensboro (27409) *(G-7002)*

Enttec Americas LLC..919 200-6468
 3874 S Alston Ave Ste 103 Durham (27713) *(G-5088)*

Envirco Corporation (PA)...919 775-2201
 101 Mcneill Rd Sanford (27330) *(G-14117)*

Envirnmental Svcs of Charlotte, Charlotte Also Called: DOT Blue Services Inc *(G-2653)*

Envirnmental Win Solutions LLC..704 200-2001
 1401 Morningside Dr Charlotte (28205) *(G-2717)*

Envirnmntal Cmfort Sltions Inc..980 272-7327
 1400 S Main St Kannapolis (28081) *(G-9119)*

Envirnmntal Prcess Systems Inc.......................................704 827-0740
 227 Lamplighter Ln Mount Holly (28120) *(G-11632)*

Envirnmntal Systems RES Inst I..704 541-9810
 3325 Springbank Ln Ste 200 Charlotte (28226) *(G-2718)*

Enviro-Companies LLC..919 758-6246
 3305 Durham Dr Ste 119 Raleigh (27603) *(G-12741)*

Enviroclean Solutions, Durham Also Called: Bottom Line Technologies Inc *(G-4974)*

Environmental Inks, Morganton Also Called: Siegwerk Eic LLC *(G-11253)*

Environmental Inks and Coatings Canada Ltd.......... 828 433-1922
1 Quality Products Rd Morganton (28655) ***(G-11212)***

Environmental Science US LLC (HQ).......... 800 331-2867
5000 Centre Green Way Ste 400 Cary (27513) ***(G-1759)***

Environmental Specialties LLC (DH).......... 919 829-9300
4412 Tryon Rd Raleigh (27606) ***(G-12742)***

Environmental Supply Co Inc.......... 919 956-9688
708 E Club Blvd Durham (27704) ***(G-5089)***

Enviroserve Chemicals Inc.......... 910 892-1791
603 S Wilson Ave Dunn (28334) ***(G-4865)***

Envirotek Worldwide LLC.......... 704 285-6400
2701 Hutchison Mcdonald Rd Ste A Charlotte (28269) ***(G-2719)***

Envisia Therapeutics Inc.......... 919 973-1440
4301 Emperor Blvd Ste 200 Durham (27703) ***(G-5090)***

Envision Glass Inc.......... 336 283-9701
3950 N Liberty St Winston Salem (27105) ***(G-16698)***

Envision Inc.......... 919 832-8962
625 Hutton St Ste 102 Raleigh (27606) ***(G-12743)***

Enwood Structures, Raleigh *Also Called: Zenecar LLC* ***(G-13436)***

Enzyme Customs.......... 704 888-8278
515 Redah Ave Locust (28097) ***(G-9959)***

Eon Labs Inc.......... 252 234-2222
4700 Sandoz Dr Wilson (27893) ***(G-16497)***

Eoncoat LLC (PA).......... 941 928-9401
3337 Air Park Rd Ste 6 Fuquay Varina (27526) ***(G-6198)***

Eoncoat LLC.......... 941 928-9401
1333 Virginia St Sw Lenoir (28645) ***(G-9606)***

EP Nisbet Company.......... 704 332-7755
1818 Baxter St Charlotte (28204) ***(G-2720)***

Epi Centre Sundries.......... 704 650-9575
210 E Trade St Charlotte (28202) ***(G-2721)***

Epi Group Llc (PA).......... 843 577-7111
4020 Stirrup Creek Dr Durham (27703) ***(G-5091)***

Epic Apparel.......... 980 335-0463
8118 Statesville Rd Charlotte (28269) ***(G-2722)***

Epic Enterprises Inc (PA).......... 910 692-5750
845 Valley View Rd Southern Pines (28387) ***(G-14535)***

Epic Kites LLC.......... 203 209-6831
508 Schooner Ct Kill Devil Hills (27948) ***(G-9256)***

Epic Restorations LLC.......... 866 597-2733
118 Commerce Dr Roxboro (27573) ***(G-13802)***

Epicypher, Durham *Also Called: Epicypher Inc* ***(G-5092)***

Epicypher Inc.......... 855 374-2461
6 Davis Dr Durham (27709) ***(G-5092)***

Epk LLC.......... 980 643-4787
425 Klumac Rd Salisbury (28144) ***(G-13958)***

Epk Industrial Solutions, Salisbury *Also Called: Epk LLC* ***(G-13958)***

Epl, Wake Forest *Also Called: Epl & Solar Corp* ***(G-15554)***

Epl & Solar Corp.......... 201 577-8966
5517 Sedge Wren Dr Wake Forest (27587) ***(G-15554)***

Epoch Solutions, Roxboro *Also Called: P&A Indstrial Fabrications LLC* ***(G-13815)***

Epoch Times Nc Inc.......... 919 649-6014
115 Joseph Pond Ln Cary (27519) ***(G-1760)***

Eppin Pharma Inc.......... 919 608-2984
3909 Windy Hill Rd Chapel Hill (27514) ***(G-2017)***

Epsilon Holdings LLC (PA).......... 336 763-6147
2103 E Town Blvd Ste 105 Greensboro (27455) ***(G-7003)***

Epsiusa.......... 704 827-0740
1124 W Charlotte Ave Mount Holly (28120) ***(G-11633)***

Epv Corporation.......... 704 494-7800
11435 Granite St Ste M Charlotte (28273) ***(G-2723)***

Epv Corporation (PA).......... 704 494-7800
2309 Nevada Blvd Charlotte (28273) ***(G-2724)***

Equagen Engineers, Raleigh *Also Called: Equagen Engineers Pllc* ***(G-12744)***

Equagen Engineers Pllc.......... 919 444-5442
8045 Arco Corporate Dr Ste 220 Raleigh (27617) ***(G-12744)***

Equilibar LLC.......... 828 650-6590
320 Rutledge Rd Fletcher (28732) ***(G-6001)***

Equinom Enterprises LLC.......... 704 817-8489
16310 Magnolia Woods Ln Charlotte (28277) ***(G-2725)***

Equipment & Supply Inc.......... 704 289-6565
4507 W Highway 74 Monroe (28110) ***(G-10716)***

Equipment Dsign Fbrication Inc.......... 704 372-4513
201 Davis Heights Dr Gastonia (28052) ***(G-6401)***

Equipment Enterprises Division, Charlotte *Also Called: Ward Vessel and Exchanger Corp* ***(G-3795)***

Equipment Parts Inc (PA).......... 704 827-7545
795 Cason St Belmont (28012) ***(G-987)***

Equipment Shop, Newland *Also Called: North Carolina Dept Trnsp* ***(G-11891)***

ERA Polymers Corporation.......... 704 931-3675
1101 S Highway 27 Stanley (28164) ***(G-14693)***

Erader Mills Septic Tank Inc.......... 252 478-5960
8374 Savage Rd Spring Hope (27882) ***(G-14617)***

ERC, Charlotte *Also Called: Engineered Recycling Company LLC* ***(G-2712)***

Erdle Perforating Holdings Inc.......... 704 588-4380
1100 Culp Rd # A Charlotte (28241) ***(G-2726)***

Erecto Mch & Fabrication Inc.......... 704 922-8621
3653 Dallas Cherryville Hwy Dallas (28034) ***(G-4639)***

Eric Arnold Klein.......... 828 464-0001
504a W 25th St Newton (28658) ***(G-11931)***

Eric Leffingwell.......... 910 367-1928
2925 Boundary St Ste 21 Wilmington (28405) ***(G-16212)***

Eric Martin Jermey.......... 704 692-0389
1815 Salem Church Rd Bostic (28018) ***(G-1262)***

Erico.......... 704 846-5743
9305 Whitethorn Dr Charlotte (28277) ***(G-2727)***

Erico International Corp.......... 910 944-3355
188 Carolina Rd Aberdeen (28315) ***(G-4)***

Erics Cheesecakes LLC.......... 336 264-4303
2439 Morningside Drive Burlington (27217) ***(G-1412)***

Ericson Foods Inc.......... 336 317-2199
4143 Wycliff Dr Winston Salem (27106) ***(G-16699)***

Erlanger Auto Care Inc.......... 336 249-9674
905 W Center St Lexington (27292) ***(G-9716)***

Erleclair Inc.......... 919 233-7710
301 Ashville Ave Ste 121 Cary (27518) ***(G-1761)***

Ernies Boat Canvas & Awning C.......... 252 491-8279
101 Meadow Lake Cir 158 Jarvisburg (27947) ***(G-9084)***

Ervin Woodworks LLC.......... 919 451-0652
407 Chadwick Ln Efland (27243) ***(G-5527)***

Erythis Inc.......... 704 644-0963
8820 Singleton Ct Huntersville (28078) ***(G-8816)***

Esc Brands LLC (PA).......... 888 331-8332
664 Old Hargrave Rd Lexington (27295) ***(G-9717)***

Escapist.......... 919 806-4448
2530 Meridian Pkwy Ste 200 Durham (27713) ***(G-5093)***

Escazu Artisan Chocolate LLC.......... 919 832-3433
936 N Blount St Raleigh (27604) ***(G-12745)***

Esco Electronic Services Inc.......... 252 753-4433
268 Hwy 121 And 264 Alternate Farmville (27828) ***(G-5735)***

Esco Group LLC.......... 919 900-8226
3221 Durham Dr Ste 118 Raleigh (27603) ***(G-12746)***

Esco Industries Inc.......... 336 495-3772
4717 Island Ford Rd Randleman (27317) ***(G-13469)***

Esequence Inc.......... 919 831-1995
412 W Jones St Raleigh (27603) ***(G-12747)***

Esher LLC.......... 704 975-1463
9911 Rose Commons Dr Huntersville (28078) ***(G-8817)***

Eskimo 7 Limited.......... 252 726-8181
5317 Hwy 70 W Morehead City (28557) ***(G-11171)***

Esri, Charlotte *Also Called: Envirnmntal Systems RES Inst I* ***(G-2718)***

Essay Operations Inc (PA).......... 252 443-6010
3701 Winchester Rd Rocky Mount (27804) ***(G-13696)***

Essay Polyfab, Rocky Mount *Also Called: Essay Operations Inc* ***(G-13696)***

Essence Candles.......... 980 785-4309
576 Perry Rd Troutman (28166) ***(G-15375)***

Essence Noire LLC.......... 704 351-8322
6840 Carradale Way Charlotte (28278) ***(G-2728)***

Essential Soap Co.......... 704 737-2385
4100 Barmettler Dr Charlotte (28211) ***(G-2729)***

Essex Group Inc.......... 704 921-9605
3300 Woodpark Blvd Charlotte (28206) ***(G-2730)***

Esta Extraction USA LP.......... 704 942-8844
301 Mccullough Dr Ste 400 Charlotte (28262) ***(G-2731)***

ALPHABETIC SECTION — Excel Signs and Lighting

Esterline Defense Technologies, Lillington *Also Called: Esterline Technologies Corp (G-9851)*
Esterline Technologies Corp 910 814-1222
   608 E Mcneill St Lillington (27546) *(G-9851)*
Estes Machine Co 336 786-7680
   256 Snowhill Dr Mount Airy (27030) *(G-11507)*
Esymphony Software Solutions I 919 293-0233
   9220 Clubvalley Way Raleigh (27617) *(G-12748)*
Etc Division, Conover *Also Called: CPI Satcom & Antenna Tech Inc (G-4440)*
Eternal Wraps 704 756-1914
   10603 Caldwell Depot Rd Cornelius (28031) *(G-4544)*
Ethan Allen Maiden Division, Maiden *Also Called: Ethan Allen Retail Inc (G-10107)*
Ethan Allen Retail Inc 828 428-9361
   700 S Main Ave Maiden (28650) *(G-10107)*
Ethereon Software Corp 919 510-5112
   8013 Tylerton Dr Raleigh (27613) *(G-12749)*
Etherngton Cnservation Ctr Inc 336 665-1317
   1010 Arnold St Greensboro (27405) *(G-7004)*
Ethicon Endo - Surgery, Cary *Also Called: Ethicon Inc (G-1762)*
Ethicon Inc 919 234-2124
   125 Edinburgh South Dr Ste 201 Cary (27511) *(G-1762)*
Ethics Archery LLC 980 429-2070
   2664 Sam Houser Rd Vale (28168) *(G-15465)*
Ethics Bullets, Vale *Also Called: Ethics Archery LLC (G-15465)*
Ethnicraft Usa LLC 336 885-2055
   101 Prospect St High Point (27260) *(G-8346)*
Etimex USA Inc 704 583-0002
   9405 D Ducks Ln Ste A Charlotte (28273) *(G-2732)*
Etk International Inc 704 819-1541
   1005 Andrea Pl Indian Trail (28079) *(G-8932)*
Etmo TEC LLC 704 878-9979
   111 Crofton Ct Statesville (28677) *(G-14795)*
Ets 919 556-7899
   928 Nc 96 Hwy E Youngsville (27596) *(G-17079)*
Euclid Chemical Company 704 283-2544
   914 N Johnson St Monroe (28110) *(G-10717)*
Euclid Innovations Inc (PA) 877 382-5431
   101 S Tryon St Ste 2410 Charlotte (28280) *(G-2733)*
Eudy's Cabinet Manufacturing, Stanfield *Also Called: S Eudy Cabinet Shop Inc (G-14682)*
Eudys Cabinet Manufacturing 704 888-4454
   12303 Renee Ford Rd Stanfield (28163) *(G-14678)*
Eugenes Trucking Inc 910 267-0555
   10422 Faison Hwy Faison (28341) *(G-5723)*
Euliss Oil Company Inc 336 622-3055
   122 S Foster St Liberty (27298) *(G-9813)*
Eurisko Beer Company 828 774-5055
   255 Short Coxe Ave Asheville (28801) *(G-618)*
Eurodrawer, Mocksville *Also Called: Olon Industries Inc (us) (G-10596)*
Eurogold Art 336 989-6205
   251 N Main St Kernersville (27284) *(G-9198)*
Eurohansa Inc 336 885-1010
   1213 Dorris Ave High Point (27260) *(G-8347)*
Ev Fleet Inc 704 425-6272
   11701 Mount Holly Rd Bldg 32 Charlotte (28214) *(G-2734)*
Evangelistic Press, Concord *Also Called: Charlotte Printing Company Inc (G-4231)*
Evans and McClain LLC 919 374-5578
   555 Fayetteville St # 201 Raleigh (27601) *(G-12750)*
Evans Hosiery, Connelly Springs *Also Called: R Evans Hosiery LLC (G-4408)*
Evans Logging Inc 252 792-3865
   1047 Fleming Cir Jamesville (27846) *(G-9080)*
Evans Machinery Inc 252 243-4006
   5123 Ivy Ct Wilson (27893) *(G-16498)*
Evans, Bill Co, Laurinburg *Also Called: M C C of Laurinburg Inc (G-9486)*
Evelyn T Burney 336 473-9794
   2551 N Church St Rocky Mount (27804) *(G-13697)*
Event Extravaganza LLC 252 679-7004
   407 S Griffin St Ste E Elizabeth City (27909) *(G-5544)*
Eventide Solutions LLC 828 855-0448
   1126 10th Street Ln Nw Hickory (28601) *(G-8018)*
Ever Glo Sign Co Inc 704 633-3324
   4975 S Main St Salisbury (28147) *(G-13959)*

Eveready Mix Concrete Co Inc 336 961-6688
   421 Old Hwy E Yadkinville (27055) *(G-17039)*
Everest Textile Usa LLC 828 245-2696
   1331 W Main St Forest City (28043) *(G-6067)*
Everettes Company Inc 336 956-2097
   4805 Old Linwood Rd Linwood (27299) *(G-9944)*
Everettes Industrial Repr Svc 252 527-4269
   117 Dobbs Pl Goldsboro (27534) *(G-6613)*
Everglow Na Inc 704 841-2580
   1122 Industrial Dr Ste 112 Matthews (28105) *(G-10247)*
Evergreen Forest Products Inc 910 762-9156
   2605 Blue Clay Rd Wilmington (28405) *(G-16213)*
Evergreen Logging LLC 910 654-1662
   686 Homer Nance Rd Evergreen (28438) *(G-5697)*
Evergreen Packaging, Canton *Also Called: Blue Ridge Paper Products LLC (G-1601)*
Evergreen Packaging, Canton *Also Called: Blue Ridge Paper Products LLC (G-1602)*
Evergreen Packaging, Waynesville *Also Called: Blue Ridge Paper Products LLC (G-15795)*
Evergreen Packaging LLC 828 454-0676
   175 Main St Canton (28716) *(G-1615)*
Evergreen Packaging LLC 919 828-9134
   2215 S Wilmington St Raleigh (27603) *(G-12751)*
Evergreen Pallets LLC 828 313-0050
   3815 N Main St Granite Falls (28630) *(G-6732)*
Evergreen Silks, Matthews *Also Called: Evergreen Silks NC Inc (G-10248)*
Evergreen Silks NC Inc 704 845-5577
   901 Sam Newell Rd Ste I Matthews (28105) *(G-10248)*
Everhart Printinc Co 336 764-3978
   241 Jefferson Ave Winston Salem (27107) *(G-16700)*
Everkem Diversified Pdts Inc 336 661-7801
   120 Regent Dr Winston Salem (27103) *(G-16701)*
Eversharp Saw & Tool Inc 828 345-1200
   1241 13th St Ne Hickory (28601) *(G-8019)*
Everview 800 549-4722
   201 Technology Ln Mount Airy (27030) *(G-11508)*
Every Day Carry LLc 203 231-0256
   4716 Black Pine Ct Winnabow (28479) *(G-16580)*
Everyday Fix Cyclery 828 855-9989
   4426 N Center St Hickory (28601) *(G-8020)*
Everything Attachments 828 464-0161
   1506 Emmanuel Church Rd Conover (28613) *(G-4452)*
Everything Hemp Store, The, Asheboro *Also Called: Ehs Retail LLC (G-428)*
Everything Industrial Supply 743 333-2222
   164 N Hawthorne Rd Winston Salem (27104) *(G-16702)*
Evident Fab LLC 973 294-4507
   101 Poplar Rd Havelock (28532) *(G-7742)*
Evil Swingarms 1 LLC 336 847-2476
   4342 Woodfern Rd Seagrove (27341) *(G-14238)*
Evolution Mobile Welding LLC 336 383-9277
   3020 Stratford Dr Greensboro (27408) *(G-7005)*
Evolution of Style LLC 914 329-3078
   2901 N Davidson St Unit 170 Charlotte (28205) *(G-2735)*
Evolution Technologies Inc 919 544-3777
   1121 Situs Ct Ste 130 Raleigh (27606) *(G-12752)*
Evonik Corporation 336 333-3565
   2401 Doyle St Greensboro (27406) *(G-7006)*
Evonik Superabsorber LLC (DH) 336 333-7540
   2401 Doyle St Greensboro (27406) *(G-7007)*
Evoqua Water Technologies LLC 919 477-2161
   1301 S Briggs Ave Ste 116 Durham (27703) *(G-5094)*
Ew Jackson Transportation LLC 919 586-2514
   113 Gingerlilly Ct Holly Springs (27540) *(G-8698)*
Ew Painting LLC 252 375-1403
   3808 E Vancroft Cir Unit M6 Winterville (28590) *(G-17000)*
Ew2 Environmental Inc (PA) 704 542-2444
   7245 Pineville Matthews Rd Ste 100 Charlotte (28226) *(G-2736)*
Exact Cut Inc 336 207-4022
   824 Winston St Greensboro (27405) *(G-7008)*
Exact Fit, Sophia *Also Called: Bunting Equipment Company Inc (G-14513)*
Excel Inc 704 735-6535
   509 Lee Ave Lincolnton (28092) *(G-9892)*
Excel Signs and Lighting 336 257-9225
   5526 Germanton Rd Winston Salem (27105) *(G-16703)*

Excell Home Fashions, Goldsboro Also Called: Glenoit Universal Ltd (G-6616)

Excelsior Sewing LLC 828 398-8056
125 Brickton Dr Fletcher (28732) (G-6002)

Executive Grooming LLC 919 706-5382
5910 Duraleigh Rd Ste 133 Raleigh (27612) (G-12753)

Executive Promotions Inc 704 663-4000
2987 Charlotte Hwy 21 Mooresville (28117) (G-10940)

Exela Drug Substance LLC 828 758-5474
1245 Blowing Rock Blvd Lenoir (28645) (G-9607)

Exela Pharma Sciences LLC (PA) 828 758-5474
1245 Blowing Rock Blvd Lenoir (28645) (G-9608)

Exhibit World Inc 704 882-2272
13701 E Independence Blvd Indian Trail (28079) (G-8933)

Exide 704 357-9845
3308 Oak Lake Blvd Ste A Charlotte (28208) (G-2737)

Exide Battery, Charlotte Also Called: Exide Technologies LLC (G-2738)

Exide Technologies LLC 704 521-8016
648 Griffith Rd Ste G Charlotte (28217) (G-2738)

Exide Technologies LLC 919 553-3578
104 N Tech Dr Clayton (27520) (G-3977)

Exley Custom Woodwork Inc 910 763-5445
2921 Castle Hayne Rd Castle Hayne (28429) (G-1946)

Exlon Extrusion Inc 336 621-1295
2971 Taylor Dr Asheboro (27203) (G-432)

Exotics Power Coat 336 831-3865
745 Cinema Ct Kernersville (27284) (G-9199)

Exp Pharmaceuticals Inc 336 631-2893
635 Vine St Winston Salem (27101) (G-16704)

Expersis Software Inc 919 874-0608
1060 Kennicott Ave Cary (27513) (G-1763)

Explosives Supply Company (PA) 828 765-2762
167 Roan Rd Spruce Pine (28777) (G-14640)

Expogo Inc 910 452-3976
411 Landmark Dr Wilmington (28412) (G-16214)

Expogo Displays & Graphics, Wilmington Also Called: Expogo Inc (G-16214)

Exposure Software LLC 919 832-4124
1111 Haynes St Ste 107 Raleigh (27604) (G-12754)

Express Carport LLC 888 389-2485
875 New Leicester Hwy Asheville (28806) (G-619)

Express Graphics, Winston Salem Also Called: Graphic Productions Inc (G-16729)

Express Printing, Jacksonville Also Called: Print Express Inc (G-9021)

Express Wire Services Inc 704 393-5156
2947 Interstate St Charlotte (28208) (G-2739)

Express Yourself 919 526-0611
10351 Crestgate Ter Apt 206 Raleigh (27617) (G-12755)

Express, The, Wadesboro Also Called: Anson Express (G-15500)

Expressions Cabinetry LLC 828 278-7999
106 Lytle Rd Fletcher (28732) (G-6003)

Expressive Screen Printing 910 739-3221
504 Peterson Dr Lumberton (28358) (G-10035)

Exprolink Corp 919 215-4675
5025 Departure Dr Ste A Raleigh (27616) (G-12756)

Exquisite Air and Water 919 524-4625
1011 Beach Pointe Ave Raleigh (27604) (G-12757)

Exquisite Granite and MBL Inc 336 851-8890
6207 Tri Port Ct Greensboro (27409) (G-7009)

Extensive Builders LLC 980 621-3793
2604 Old Wilkesboro Rd Salisbury (28144) (G-13960)

Exterior Vinyl Wholesale 336 838-7772
1808 Industrial Dr Wilkesboro (28697) (G-16020)

Exteriors Inc Ltd 919 325-2251
650 W Manchester Rd Spring Lake (28390) (G-14625)

Extra-Dimensional Pubg LLC 704 574-4652
516 Academy St Mc Adenville (28101) (G-10378)

Extreme, Morrisville Also Called: Extreme Networks Inc (G-11339)

Extreme Millwork, High Point Also Called: Extreme Scenes Inc (G-8348)

Extreme Networks Inc (PA) 408 579-2800
2121 Rdu Center Dr Ste 300 Morrisville (27560) (G-11339)

Extreme Scenes Inc 336 687-3369
1525 Blandwood Dr High Point (27260) (G-8348)

Extreme Stud Welding LLC 828 217-2587
2949 Cat Square Rd Vale (28168) (G-15466)

Extreme Tractor Parts LLC 919 605-6040
1518 Miranda Woods Ln Fuquay Varina (27526) (G-6199)

Extron Electronics 919 850-1000
2500 N Raleigh Blvd Raleigh (27604) (G-12758)

Eye Dialogue 704 567-7789
412 N Crigler St Charlotte (28216) (G-2740)

Eye Glass Lady LLC 828 669-2154
411 Tomahawk Ave Black Mountain (28711) (G-1124)

EZ Beverage Company Wilmington, Wilmington Also Called: Zeskp LLC (G-16460)

EZ Custom Screen Printing 704 821-8488
600 Union West Blvd Ste B Matthews (28104) (G-10314)

EZ Custom Scrnprinting EMB Inc 704 821-9641
200 Foxton Rd Matthews (28104) (G-10315)

EZ Fabrication Inc 828 674-0661
5882 Crescent Dr Claremont (28610) (G-3926)

EZ Sign Service 919 604-3508
2513 Burlington Mills Rd Wake Forest (27587) (G-15555)

EZ Sign Service 919 554-4300
941 Us 1 Hwy Youngsville (27596) (G-17080)

Ezbrew Inc 833 233-2739
1006 Sw Maynard Rd Cary (27511) (G-1764)

Eztax, Durham Also Called: Billsoft Inc (G-4957)

F & C Repair and Sales LLC 704 907-2461
4720 Brookshire Blvd Charlotte (28216) (G-2741)

F & H Print Sign Design LLC 252 335-0181
1725 City Center Blvd Ste C Elizabeth City (27909) (G-5545)

F & M Steel Products Inc 910 793-1345
3314 Enterprise Dr Wilmington (28405) (G-16215)

F B Publications, Fayetteville Also Called: Up & Coming Magazine (G-5941)

F B Publications Inc 910 484-6200
909 S Mcpherson Church Rd Fayetteville (28303) (G-5822)

F C C LLC 336 883-7314
4045 Premier Dr Ste 200 High Point (27265) (G-8349)

F L Turlington Lumber Co Inc 910 592-7197
229 E Railroad St Clinton (28328) (G-4095)

F-N-D Machinery Services Inc 336 906-2817
1198 N Main St Denton (27239) (G-4735)

Fab Designs Incorporated 704 636-2349
2231 Old Wilkesboro Rd Salisbury (28144) (G-13961)

Fab-Con, Harrisburg Also Called: Fab-Con Machinery Dev Corp (G-7708)

Fab-Con, Oakboro Also Called: Fab-Con Machinery Dev Corp (G-12074)

Fab-Con Machinery Dev Corp 516 883-3999
12145 University City Blvd Harrisburg (28075) (G-7708)

Fab-Con Machinery Dev Corp (PA) 704 486-7120
201 E 10th St Oakboro (28129) (G-12074)

Fab-Tec Inc 704 864-6872
3626 Dallas Hgh Shls Hwy Dallas (28034) (G-4640)

Fabco Industries 919 481-3010
312 N Dixon Ave Cary (27513) (G-1765)

Fabric Services Hickory Inc 828 397-7331
130 Kline Industrial Park 3rd St Ne Hildebran (28637) (G-8622)

Fabricated Solutions LLC 704 982-7789
1210 Poplar St Albemarle (28001) (G-84)

Fabrication Associates Inc 704 535-8050
7950 Pence Rd Charlotte (28215) (G-2742)

Fabrication Automation LLC 704 785-2120
2772 Concord Pkwy S Concord (28027) (G-4261)

Fabricted Parts Assemblies LLC 704 784-4376
5552 Yorke St Nw Concord (28027) (G-4262)

Fabrineering LLC 704 999-9906
1035 Mecklenburg Hwy Mooresville (28115) (G-10941)

Fabrineering LLC 704 661-4877
8955 W Nc 152 Hwy Mooresville (28115) (G-10942)

Fabrix Inc 704 953-1239
231 Foster Ave Ste A Charlotte (28203) (G-2743)

Fac Ette Manufacturing 910 599-7352
208 Beech St Wilmington (28405) (G-16216)

Faces South Inc 336 883-0647
1330 Lincoln Dr High Point (27260) (G-8350)

Facilitydudecom Inc 919 459-6430
11000 Regency Pkwy Ste 200 Cary (27518) (G-1766)

ALPHABETIC SECTION

Factor Inc.. 919 358-0004
   1901 Sedwick Rd Durham (27713) *(G-5095)*
Factory Systems, Raleigh *Also Called: Symbrium Inc (G-13319)*
Fading D Farm LLC.. 704 633-3888
   295 Fading D Farm Rd Salisbury (28144) *(G-13962)*
Fae Nectar, Asheville *Also Called: Asheville Meadery LLC (G-538)*
Faerie Star Forge... 910 743-2862
   206 Halibut Ct Maysville (28555) *(G-10372)*
Fagus Grecon Inc.. 503 641-7731
   648 Griffith Rd Ste A Charlotte (28217) *(G-2744)*
Fahmar Inc... 704 843-1872
   501 Running Horse Ln Waxhaw (28173) *(G-15756)*
Failure Free Reading, Concord *Also Called: Jfl Enterprises Inc (G-4293)*
Fain Enterprises Inc.. 336 724-0417
   309 Deerglade Rd Winston Salem (27104) *(G-16705)*
Fainting Goat Spirits LLC.. 336 273-6221
   321 W Wendover Ave Greensboro (27408) *(G-7010)*
Fair Products Inc... 919 467-1599
   806 Reedy Creek Rd Cary (27513) *(G-1767)*
Fairbanks Nijhuis.. 262 728-7449
   400 Regency Forest Dr Cary (27518) *(G-1768)*
Fairchild Industrial Pdts Co (DH)... 336 659-3400
   3920 Westpoint Blvd Winston Salem (27103) *(G-16706)*
Faircloth Machine Shop Inc.. 336 777-1529
   2355 Farrington Point Dr Winston Salem (27107) *(G-16707)*
Fairfax Digital LLC... 407 822-2918
   7804 Fairview Rd Charlotte (28226) *(G-2745)*
Fairfield Chair Company... 828 785-5571
   606 Kincaid Cir Lenoir (28645) *(G-9609)*
Fairfield Chair Company (PA)... 828 758-5571
   1331 Harper Ave Sw Lenoir (28645) *(G-9610)*
Fairfield Pro AV Inc.. 214 375-8570
   17540 Westmill Ln Charlotte (28277) *(G-2746)*
Fairgrove Furniture Co Inc.. 828 322-8570
   1350 21st Street Dr Se Hickory (28602) *(G-8021)*
Fairmont Metal Finishing Inc.. 336 434-4188
   1301 Corporation Dr Archdale (27263) *(G-278)*
Fairview Town Crier.. 828 628-4547
   1185 Charlotte Hwy Ste G Fairview (28730) *(G-5710)*
Fairview Woodcarving Inc.. 828 428-9491
   2092 Anaconda Ln Maiden (28650) *(G-10108)*
Fairway Insurance and Risk MGT, Charlotte *Also Called: Pma Industries Inc (G-3350)*
Fairway Outdoor Advg LLC.. 919 755-1900
   508 Capital Blvd Raleigh (27603) *(G-12759)*
Fairway Printing Inc... 919 779-4797
   821 Purser Dr Ste A Raleigh (27603) *(G-12760)*
Faith Computer Repairs.. 910 730-1731
   3404 Nc Highway 211 W Lumberton (28360) *(G-10036)*
Faith Farm Inc.. 704 431-4566
   585 W Ritchie Rd Ste A Salisbury (28147) *(G-13963)*
Faith Logging... 828 446-5671
   1722 White Rock Rd Lenoir (28645) *(G-9611)*
Faith Prsthtc-Rthotic Svcs Inc (DH)... 704 782-0908
   1025 Concord Pkwy N Concord (28027) *(G-4263)*
Faizon Global Inc... 704 774-1141
   2115 W Roosevelt Blvd # 70 Monroe (28110) *(G-10718)*
Falcon Industries LLC... 336 229-1048
   2834 Bedford St Burlington (27215) *(G-1413)*
Falls Automotive & Tire Svc, Winston Salem *Also Called: Falls Automotive Service Inc (G-16708)*
Falls Automotive Service Inc.. 336 723-0521
   1548 S Main St Winston Salem (27127) *(G-16708)*
Falls of Neuse Management LLC.. 919 573-2900
   4900 Falls Of Neuse Rd Ste 150 Raleigh (27609) *(G-12761)*
Family Industries Inc.. 919 875-4499
   631 Macon Pl Raleigh (27609) *(G-12762)*
Family Traditions, Gastonia *Also Called: Fidelity Associates Inc (G-6402)*
Famous Amos Signs... 919 820-2211
   111 Averasboro Rd Dunn (28334) *(G-4866)*
Fantasy Sports Breaks LLC.. 276 233-7504
   302 Hodges Mill Rd Dobson (27017) *(G-4823)*

Fanuc America Corporation.. 704 596-5121
   13245 Reese Blvd W Ste 140 Huntersville (28078) *(G-8818)*
Fanuc Robotics, Huntersville *Also Called: Fanuc America Corporation (G-8818)*
Far From A Maid LLC... 803 610-1727
   9716 Rea Rd Ste B Charlotte (28277) *(G-2747)*
Far Niente LLC... 252 715-0154
   6021 Martins Point Rd Kitty Hawk (27949) *(G-9404)*
Farleys Custom Carving Inc... 828 256-9124
   6653 St Peters Church Rd Conover (28613) *(G-4453)*
Farm Chemicals Inc (PA).. 910 875-4277
   2274 Saint Pauls Dr Raeford (28376) *(G-12420)*
Farm Services Inc... 336 226-7381
   125 E Elm St Graham (27253) *(G-6689)*
Farmer Machine Group LLC... 704 629-5133
   308 White Jenkins Rd Bessemer City (28016) *(G-1064)*
Farmhouse Stitching.. 910 308-7308
   1029 Horne Farm Rd Stedman (28391) *(G-14935)*
Farmville Service, Farmville *Also Called: Goldsboro Milling Company (G-5737)*
Faro10 LLC... 757 285-8069
   105 Hasbrouck Dr Apex (27523) *(G-190)*
Farr Knitting Company Inc... 336 625-5561
   171 Boyd Ave Asheboro (27205) *(G-433)*
Farris Belt & Saw Company.. 704 527-6166
   235 Foster Ave Charlotte (28203) *(G-2748)*
Farris Fab & Machine Inc... 704 629-4879
   1941 Bess Town Rd Bessemer City (28016) *(G-1065)*
Farris Fab & Machine Inc... 704 629-4879
   522 Bess Town Rd Bessemer City (28016) *(G-1066)*
Farris Fab & Machine Inc (PA).. 704 629-4879
   1006 W Academy St Cherryville (28021) *(G-3868)*
Farval Lubrication Systems.. 252 527-6001
   2685 Airport Rd Kinston (28504) *(G-9364)*
Farval Lubrication Systems (DH).. 252 527-6001
   808 Aviation Parkway Kinston (28504) *(G-9365)*
Fascoe Realty... 828 963-7600
   133 Echota Pkwy Boone (28607) *(G-1198)*
Fast Arch of Carolinas Inc.. 336 431-2724
   617 Eden Ter Ste B Archdale (27263) *(G-279)*
Fast Lane Signs.. 336 745-5257
   115 Spry Ln Mocksville (27028) *(G-10570)*
Fast Pro Media LLC.. 704 799-8040
   10308 Bailey Rd Ste 422 Cornelius (28031) *(G-4545)*
Fast Pro Media LLC.. 704 799-8040
   10308 Bailey Rd Ste 422 Cornelius (28031) *(G-4546)*
Fastlife Transport LLC (PA)... 484 350-6754
   7710 Holliswood Ct Charlotte (28217) *(G-2749)*
Fastrack Publishing Co Inc... 828 294-0544
   1602 Corral Dr Hickory (28602) *(G-8022)*
Fastsigns.. 252 364-8745
   2294a County Home Rd Greenville (27858) *(G-7524)*
Fastsigns.. 704 360-3805
   119 Midnight Ln Mooresville (28117) *(G-10943)*
Fastsigns, Asheville *Also Called: Playrace Inc (G-735)*
Fastsigns, Charlotte *Also Called: Beaty Corporation (G-2293)*
Fastsigns, Charlotte *Also Called: CD Dickie & Associates Inc (G-2433)*
Fastsigns, Charlotte *Also Called: Qasioun LLC (G-3398)*
Fastsigns, Concord *Also Called: Jr Signs LLC (G-4296)*
Fastsigns, Durham *Also Called: Meredith Media Co (G-5221)*
Fastsigns, Fayetteville *Also Called: Signify It Inc (G-5916)*
Fastsigns, Monroe *Also Called: Classic Sign Services LLC (G-10685)*
Fastsigns, Mooresville *Also Called: Fastsigns (G-10943)*
Fastsigns, Raleigh *Also Called: Davcom Enterprises Inc (G-12674)*
Fastsigns, Wilmington *Also Called: Creative Signs Inc (G-16187)*
Fastzone Dsl & Internet Servic... 828 963-1350
   157 Seven Devils Rd Banner Elk (28604) *(G-897)*
Fat Man Fabrications Inc.. 704 545-0369
   8621c Fairview Rd Mint Hill (28227) *(G-10531)*
Fathom Holdings Inc (PA).. 888 455-6040
   2000 Regency Pkwy Ste 300 Cary (27518) *(G-1769)*
Fathom Offshore, Wilmington *Also Called: Fathom Offshore Holdings LLC (G-16217)*

Fathom Offshore Holdings LLC 910 399-6882
3018 N Kerr Ave Ste A Wilmington (28405) *(G-16217)*

Fawn Industries Inc 252 462-4700
100 Industry Ct Nashville (27856) *(G-11744)*

Fayblock Materials Inc 910 323-9198
130 Builders Blvd Fayetteville (28301) *(G-5823)*

Fayetteville Observer, The, Fayetteville Also Called: Db North Carolina Holdings Inc *(G-5808)*

Fayetteville Observer, The, Fayetteville Also Called: Fayetteville Publishing Co *(G-5824)*

Fayetteville Publishing Co (DH) 910 323-4848
302 Worth St Fayetteville (28301) *(G-5824)*

Fayetteville Steel, Fayetteville Also Called: McCune Technology Inc *(G-5871)*

FCC, Laurinburg Also Called: FCC (north Carolina) LLC *(G-9479)*

FCC (north Carolina) LLC 910 462-4465
18000 Fieldcrest Rd Laurinburg (28352) *(G-9479)*

FCC Butner 919 575-3900
Butner (27509) *(G-1544)*

Fci-An Agricultural Service Co, Raeford Also Called: Farm Chemicals Inc *(G-12420)*

Fe26 LLC 980 875-0170
3150 Rozzelles Ferry Rd Charlotte (28205) *(G-2750)*

FEC Inc 828 765-4599
284 Roan Rd Spruce Pine (28777) *(G-14641)*

Federal Ridge, Greensboro Also Called: Patheon Softgels Inc *(G-7247)*

Fee Kees Wreaths LLC 704 636-1008
1047 Landsdown Dr Salisbury (28147) *(G-13964)*

Feeder Innovations Corporation 910 276-3511
9781 Mccoll Rd Laurinburg (28352) *(G-9480)*

Feedtrail Incorporated 757 618-7760
811 Handsworth Ln Apt 108 Raleigh (27607) *(G-12763)*

Feeneys (PA) 336 617-5874
1603 New Garden Rd Greensboro (27410) *(G-7011)*

Feinberg Enterprises Inc 704 822-2400
3 Caldwell Dr Belmont (28012) *(G-988)*

Felice Hosiery Co Inc 336 996-2371
118 Burke St Kernersville (27284) *(G-9200)*

Feller LLC (DH) 910 383-6920
9100 Industrial Blvd Ne Leland (28451) *(G-9541)*

Felts Lumber Co Inc 336 368-5667
1377 Perch Rd Pinnacle (27043) *(G-12321)*

Femco Radio Controls, Archdale Also Called: Hubbell Industrial Contrls Inc *(G-283)*

Fenwal Safety Systems, Wilson Also Called: Kidde Technologies Inc *(G-16508)*

Ferebee Asphalt, Charlotte Also Called: Ferebee Corporation *(G-2751)*

Ferebee Corporation (HQ) 704 509-2586
10045 Metromont Industrial Blvd Charlotte (28269) *(G-2751)*

Ferguson & Company LLC 704 332-4396
201 S Tryon St Charlotte (28202) *(G-2752)*

Ferguson Box 704 597-0310
10820 Quality Dr Charlotte (28278) *(G-2753)*

Ferguson Cabinet Works 828 433-8710
4188 Nc 181 Morganton (28655) *(G-11213)*

Ferguson Companies
1638 Clyde Fitzgerald Rd Linwood (27299) *(G-9945)*

Ferguson Design Inc 704 394-0120
236 Hawthorne Park Ave Belmont (28012) *(G-989)*

Ferguson Fibers, Linwood Also Called: Ferguson Companies *(G-9945)*

Ferguson Highway Products Inc 704 320-3087
212 Old Dutch Rd W Indian Trail (28079) *(G-8934)*

Ferguson Lumber Inc 336 871-2591
2634 Amostown Rd Sandy Ridge (27046) *(G-14079)*

Ferguson Manufacturing Company 336 661-1116
6275 Raven Forest Ct Winston Salem (27105) *(G-16709)*

Ferguson Supply and Box Mfg Co (PA) 704 597-0310
10820 Quality Dr Charlotte (28278) *(G-2754)*

Ferguson Waterworks 704 540-7225
10039 Industrial Dr Pineville (28134) *(G-12268)*

Ferncrest Fashions Inc 704 283-6422
4813 Starcrest Dr Monroe (28110) *(G-10719)*

Fernel Therapeutics Inc 919 614-2375
408 Gablefield Ln Apex (27502) *(G-191)*

Ferree Trailer, Liberty Also Called: Vision Metals Inc *(G-9834)*

Ferrofab Inc 910 557-5624
1416 Hylan Ave Hamlet (28345) *(G-7621)*

Fertility Tech Resources Inc 404 626-9786
211 Paradise Rd Murphy (28906) *(G-11709)*

Fervent Pharmaceuticals LLC 252 558-9700
740 Greenville Blvd Ste 400-151 Greenville (27834) *(G-7525)*

Fex Straw Manufacturing Inc 910 671-4141
191 Magna Blvd Lumberton (28360) *(G-10037)*

Ffi Holdings III Corp (PA) 800 690-3650
3915 Shopton Rd Charlotte (28217) *(G-2755)*

Ffnc, High Point Also Called: Future Foam Inc *(G-8361)*

Ffnc Inc 336 885-4121
1300 Prospect St High Point (27260) *(G-8351)*

Fg Group Holdings Inc (PA) 704 994-8279
5960 Fairview Rd Ste 275 Charlotte (28210) *(G-2756)*

Fiber Company 336 725-5277
8863 Belhaven Ct Lewisville (27023) *(G-9666)*

Fiber Composites LLC 704 463-7118
44017 Us 52 Hwy N New London (28127) *(G-11869)*

Fiber Composites LLC (HQ) 704 463-7120
181 Random Dr New London (28127) *(G-11870)*

Fiber Cushioning Inc (PA) 336 629-8442
4454 Us Highway 220 Bus S Asheboro (27205) *(G-434)*

Fiber Cushioning Inc 336 887-4782
113 Motsinger St High Point (27260) *(G-8352)*

Fiber Dynamics, High Point Also Called: Fiber Dynamics Inc *(G-8353)*

Fiber Dynamics Inc 336 886-7111
200 S West Point Ave High Point (27260) *(G-8353)*

Fiber Fuels, Marshville Also Called: D C Custom Freight LLC *(G-10213)*

Fiber N C Div, Marion Also Called: Jeld-Wen Inc *(G-10153)*

Fiber Transport Systems Inc 704 905-3549
13000 S Tryon St Ste F-121 Charlotte (28278) *(G-2757)*

Fiber-Line LLC 828 326-8700
280 Performance Dr Se Hickory (28602) *(G-8023)*

Fiberglass Fabrication Inc 828 685-0940
14 Twin Willow Dr Hendersonville (28792) *(G-7847)*

Fiberlink 901 826-8126
151 Flower House Loop Troutman (28166) *(G-15376)*

Fiberlink Inc 828 274-5629
122 Deerlake Dr Asheville (28803) *(G-620)*

Fiberon 704 463-2955
411 International Dr Nw Concord (28027) *(G-4264)*

Fiberon, New London Also Called: Fiber Composites LLC *(G-11870)*

Fiberon Recycling, New London Also Called: Fiber Composites LLC *(G-11869)*

Fibex LLC (PA) 336 605-9002
5280 National Center Dr Colfax (27235) *(G-4150)*

Fibex LLC 336 358-5014
7109 Cessna Dr Greensboro (27409) *(G-7012)*

Fibrecrete Pprsrvtion Tech Inc 336 789-7259
131 Saint James Way Mount Airy (27030) *(G-11509)*

Fibreworks Composites LLC 704 696-1084
143 Thunder Rd Mooresville (28115) *(G-10944)*

Fibrix LLC 704 394-2111
1101 Tar Heel Rd Charlotte (28208) *(G-2758)*

Fibrix LLC (HQ) 828 459-7064
1820 Evans St Ne Conover (28613) *(G-4454)*

Fibrix LLC 704 872-5223
166 Orbit Rd Statesville (28677) *(G-14796)*

Fibrix LLC 704 878-0027
1004 Bucks Industrial Rd Statesville (28625) *(G-14797)*

Fibrix Filtration, Mooresville Also Called: Branford Filtration LLC *(G-10886)*

Fics America Inc 704 329-7391
2815 Coliseum Centre Dr Ste 300 Charlotte (28217) *(G-2759)*

Fiddlin Fish Brewing Co 336 999-8945
772 N Trade St Winston Salem (27101) *(G-16710)*

Fiddlin' Fish Brewing Company, Winston Salem Also Called: Fiddlin Fish Brewing Co *(G-16710)*

Fidelity Associates Inc 704 864-3766
2936 Rousseau Ct Gastonia (28054) *(G-6402)*

Fidelity Pharmaceuticals LLC 704 274-3192
11957 Ramah Church Rd Huntersville (28078) *(G-8819)*

Field Controls LLC (DH) 252 208-7300
2630 Airport Rd Kinston (28504) *(G-9366)*

ALPHABETIC SECTION — Firstmark Controls

Fieldco Machining Inc.. 828 891-4100
5164 Old Haywood Rd Fletcher (28732) *(G-6004)*

Fieldproof Prints LLC.. 270 313-8439
439 Westwood Shopping Ctr Pmb 471 Fayetteville (28314) *(G-5825)*

Fields Industries LLC.. 704 264-3872
14624 Provence Ln Charlotte (28277) *(G-2760)*

Fieldsway Solutions LLC.. 984 920-7791
177 Ridgemoore Ct Four Oaks (27524) *(G-6104)*

Fieldx Inc.. 919 926-7001
7504 Deer Track Dr Raleigh (27613) *(G-12764)*

Fiestic Inc.. 888 935-3999
555 Fayetteville St Ste 201 Raleigh (27601) *(G-12765)*

Fifty Combs LLC.. 252 406-6242
611 Martin Luther King Jr Dr Tarboro (27886) *(G-15103)*

Fil-Chem Inc.. 919 878-1270
3808 Evander Way Raleigh (27613) *(G-12766)*

Filament Fabrics, Burnsville *Also Called: Glen Raven Custom Fabrics LLC (G-1526)*

Filer Micro Welding.. 828 248-1813
251 Terry Filer Rd Forest City (28043) *(G-6068)*

Filet of Chicken.. 336 751-4752
251 Eaton Rd Mocksville (27028) *(G-10571)*

Fill Pac LLC.. 828 322-1916
1140 Tate Blvd Se Hickory (28602) *(G-8024)*

Fillauer North Carolina Inc.. 828 658-8330
220 Merrimon Ave Ste A Weaverville (28787) *(G-15846)*

Filltech Inc.. 704 279-4300
228 W Main St Rockwell (28138) *(G-13652)*

Filltech USA LLC.. 704 279-4300
380 Palmer Cir Rockwell (28138) *(G-13653)*

Filmon Process Corp.. 828 684-1360
100 Baldwin Rd Arden (28704) *(G-328)*

Filspecusa, Ellerbe *Also Called: Richmond Specialty Yarns LLC (G-5643)*

Filtec Precise Inc.. 910 653-5200
218 N Us Highway 701 Byp Tabor City (28463) *(G-15082)*

Filter Srvcng of Chrltte 135.. 704 619-3768
6608 Woodmont Pl Charlotte (28211) *(G-2761)*

Filtex Inc.. 828 874-2100
160 Fashion Ave Rutherford College (28671) *(G-13859)*

Filtration Technology, Greensboro *Also Called: Filtration Technology Inc (G-7013)*

Filtration Technology Inc.. 336 509-9960
110 Pomona Dr Greensboro (27407) *(G-7013)*

Filtration Technology Inc (PA).. 336 294-5655
110 Pomona Dr Greensboro (27407) *(G-7014)*

Filtrona Filters Inc.. 336 362-1333
303 Gallimore Dairy Rd Greensboro (27409) *(G-7015)*

Fimia Inc.. 828 697-8447
201 Arbutus Ln Hendersonville (28739) *(G-7848)*

Finch Industries Incorporated.. 336 472-4499
104 Williams St Thomasville (27360) *(G-15221)*

Finch's Print Shop, Louisburg *Also Called: Brodie-Jones Printing Co Inc (G-9981)*

Find Your Voice LLC.. 301 922-0978
5101 Stoney Pond Ln Apt W Mint Hill (28227) *(G-10532)*

Fine Art Tapestries, Lynn *Also Called: Pure Country Inc (G-10063)*

Fine Line Hosiery Inc.. 336 498-8022
2012 Sunny Ln Asheboro (27205) *(G-435)*

Fine Sheer Industries Inc.. 704 375-3333
225 Wilshire Ave Sw Concord (28025) *(G-4265)*

Fineline Prototyping Inc.. 919 781-7702
3700 Pleasant Grove Church Rd Morrisville (27560) *(G-11340)*

Finely Finished Wdwkg LLC.. 828 553-9549
662 Holiday Dr Hendersonville (28739) *(G-7849)*

Fines and Carriel Inc.. 919 929-0702
1322 Fordham Blvd Ste 5 Chapel Hill (27514) *(G-2018)*

Finishing Partners Inc.. 704 583-7322
1301 Westinghouse Blvd Ste E Charlotte (28273) *(G-2762)*

Finishworks, Hickory *Also Called: RPM Wood Finishes Group Inc (G-8140)*

Finley Enterprises LLC.. 910 747-6679
2826 Green Lane Dr Durham (27712) *(G-5096)*

Finnord North America Corp.. 704 723-4913
14514 Sunset Walk Ln Huntersville (28078) *(G-8820)*

Fintronx LLC.. 919 324-3960
5995 Chapel Hill Rd Ste 119 Raleigh (27607) *(G-12767)*

Fire & Safety Outfitters, Charlotte *Also Called: Lightning X Products Inc (G-3088)*

Fire Flutes.. 321 230-3878
906 Bear Branch Way # 301 Wake Forest (27587) *(G-15556)*

Fire Fly Balloons 2006 LLC.. 704 878-9501
850 Meacham Rd Statesville (28677) *(G-14798)*

Fire Hose Direct, Mooresville *Also Called: Fireresq Incorporated (G-10945)*

Fire Retardant Chem Tech LLC.. 980 253-8880
3465 Gribble Rd Matthews (28104) *(G-10316)*

Firefly Balloons 2010 Inc.. 704 878-9501
850 Meacham Rd Statesville (28677) *(G-14799)*

Firefly Balloons Inc.. 704 878-9501
810 Salisbury Rd Statesville (28677) *(G-14800)*

Firehouse Cabinets.. 704 689-5243
715 Brook Forest Dr Belmont (28012) *(G-990)*

Firehouse Publications.. 609 298-3742
5924 Lunenburg Dr Raleigh (27603) *(G-12768)*

Fireline Shields Llc.. 704 948-3680
15336 Old Statesville Rd Huntersville (28078) *(G-8821)*

Fireplace Guy, The, Kure Beach *Also Called: Dna Services Inc (G-9437)*

Fireproof Office Files, Asheville *Also Called: Blue-Hen Inc (G-567)*

Fireresq Incorporated.. 888 975-0858
115 Corporate Center Dr Ste J Mooresville (28117) *(G-10945)*

Firestone, Durham *Also Called: Bridgestone Ret Operations LLC (G-4977)*

Firestone, Fayetteville *Also Called: Bridgestone Ret Operations LLC (G-5775)*

Firestone, Gastonia *Also Called: Bridgestone Ret Operations LLC (G-6360)*

Firestone, Goldsboro *Also Called: Bridgestone Ret Operations LLC (G-6597)*

Firestone, Greensboro *Also Called: Bridgestone Ret Operations LLC (G-6852)*

Firestone, Greensboro *Also Called: Bridgestone Ret Operations LLC (G-6853)*

Firestone, Kinston *Also Called: Bridgestone Ret Operations LLC (G-9347)*

Firestone, Raleigh *Also Called: Bridgestone Ret Operations LLC (G-12573)*

Firestone, Raleigh *Also Called: Bridgestone Ret Operations LLC (G-12574)*

Firestone, Wilson *Also Called: Bridgestone Ret Operations LLC (G-16480)*

Firestone, Winston Salem *Also Called: Bridgestone Ret Operations LLC (G-16636)*

Firestone Fibers Textiles LLC.. 704 734-2110
100 Firestone Ln Kings Mountain (28086) *(G-9308)*

Firestopping Products Inc.. 336 661-0102
120 Regent Dr Winston Salem (27103) *(G-16711)*

Firetech, Hendersonville *Also Called: Hiviz Lighting Inc (G-7865)*

Firm Ascend LLC.. 704 464-3024
224 Westinghouse Blvd Ste 602 Charlotte (28273) *(G-2763)*

First Alance Logistics MGT LLC.. 704 522-0233
14120 Ballantyne Corporate Pl Charlotte (28277) *(G-2764)*

First Choice, Wilson *Also Called: Buy Smart Inc (G-16482)*

First Choice Properties, Shelby *Also Called: Joe Robin Darnell (G-14333)*

First Class Ridez LLC.. 919 610-6043
472 Mallie Pearce Rd Zebulon (27597) *(G-17127)*

First Coast Energy LLP.. 828 667-0625
301 Smokey Park Hwy Asheville (28806) *(G-621)*

First Due Prints Inc.. 704 320-1251
1202 Technology Dr Ste B Indian Trail (28079) *(G-8935)*

First Impressions Ltd.. 704 536-3622
8500 Monroe Rd Charlotte (28212) *(G-2765)*

First In Fight Skateboards LLC.. 828 449-9150
220 14th Ave Se Apt B Hickory (28602) *(G-8025)*

First Leads Inc.. 919 672-5329
201 W Main St Ste 305 Durham (27701) *(G-5097)*

First Miracle Vine & Wine LLC.. 910 990-5681
365 Johnson Rd Garland (28441) *(G-6242)*

First Noodle Co Inc.. 704 393-3238
333 Oakdale Rd Charlotte (28216) *(G-2766)*

First Prrity Emrgncy Vhcles In.. 908 645-0788
1208 School St Wilkesboro (28697) *(G-16021)*

First Rate Blinds.. 800 655-1080
19701 Bethel Church Rd # 178 Cornelius (28031) *(G-4547)*

Firstmark Aerospace Corp.. 919 956-4200
1176 Telecom Dr Creedmoor (27522) *(G-4613)*

Firstmark Aerospace Corp.. 919 956-4323
921 Holloway St Durham (27701) *(G-5098)*

Firstmark Controls, Creedmoor *Also Called: Firstmark Aerospace Corp (G-4613)*

ALPHABETIC SECTION

Firstreport Software Inc.................... 828 441-0404
369 London Rd Asheville (28803) *(G-622)*

Firstsource Distributors LLC.................... 704 553-8510
710 Peninsula Ln Ste E Charlotte (28273) *(G-2767)*

Fish Getter Lure Co LLC.................... 704 538-9863
254 Hull Rd Casar (28020) *(G-1933)*

Fish Hippie, Mount Airy Also Called: Old North State Winery Inc *(G-11554)*

Fish Sticks LLC.................... 336 984-1791
622 Moore Rd North Wilkesboro (28659) *(G-12007)*

Fishel Steel Company.................... 336 788-2880
760 Palmer Ln Winston Salem (27107) *(G-16712)*

Fisher Athletic Equipment Inc.................... 704 636-5713
2060 Cauble Rd Salisbury (28144) *(G-13965)*

Fisher Scientific Company LLC.................... 800 252-7100
275 Aiken Rd Asheville (28804) *(G-623)*

Fisher Signs Murals & Frames.................... 919 286-0591
2606 Hillsborough Rd Durham (27705) *(G-5099)*

Fisherman Creations Inc.................... 252 725-0138
1175 Hwy 70 Otway Beaufort (28516) *(G-956)*

Fishkillerdaves LLC.................... 252 441-7703
337 Sir Chandler Dr Kill Devil Hills (27948) *(G-9257)*

Fishsticks.................... 919 900-8998
7145 North Ridge Dr Raleigh (27615) *(G-12769)*

Fisk Tool Company.................... 828 684-5454
24 Fisk Dr Arden (28704) *(G-329)*

Fiskars Brands Inc.................... 336 292-6237
322 Edwardia Dr Ste D Greensboro (27409) *(G-7016)*

Fit1media LLC.................... 919 925-2200
8601 Six Forks Rd Ste 400 Raleigh (27615) *(G-12770)*

Fitch Sign Company Inc.................... 704 482-2916
341 N Post Rd Shelby (28152) *(G-14317)*

Fitt Usa Inc.................... 866 348-8872
136 Corporate Park Dr Ste I Mooresville (28117) *(G-10946)*

Fitzbradshaw Racing, Mooresville Also Called: Highline Performance Group *(G-10974)*

Five Points Baking Company LLC.................... 919 349-2033
2009 Carroll Dr Raleigh (27608) *(G-12771)*

Five Star Bodies.................... 262 325-9126
177 Houston Rd Troutman (28166) *(G-15377)*

Five Star Coffee Roasters LLC.................... 919 671-0645
108 Thomas Mill Rd Ste 101 Holly Springs (27540) *(G-8699)*

Fix-A-Latch, Chapel Hill Also Called: Fix-A-Latch Usa LLC *(G-2019)*

Fix-A-Latch Usa LLC (PA).................... 435 901-4146
133 1/2 E Franklin St Ste 104 Chapel Hill (27514) *(G-2019)*

Fix-A-Latch Usa LLC.................... 435 901-4146
122 Marin Dr Chapel Hill (27516) *(G-2020)*

Fixed-NC LLC.................... 252 751-1911
1830a Old Fire Tower Rd Greenville (27858) *(G-7526)*

Fixtures & More.................... 828 855-9093
2220 Us Highway 70 Se Ste 384 Hickory (28602) *(G-8026)*

Fixxus Indus Holdings Co LLC.................... 336 674-3088
6116 Old Mendenhall Rd Archdale (27263) *(G-280)*

Fla Orthopedics Inc (DH).................... 800 327-4110
5825 Carnegie Blvd Charlotte (28209) *(G-2768)*

Flagstone Foods LLC.................... 252 795-6500
201 E 3rd St Robersonville (27871) *(G-13616)*

Flair Designs, Robbins Also Called: Minhas Furniture House Inc *(G-13601)*

Flakeboard America Limited.................... 910 569-7010
157 Atc Dr Biscoe (27209) *(G-1109)*

Flame Tech Inc.................... 336 661-7801
120 Regent Dr Winston Salem (27103) *(G-16713)*

Flame-Tec LLC.................... 844 352-6383
136 Hillview Blvd Hendersonville (28792) *(G-7850)*

Flameoff Coatings Inc (PA).................... 888 816-7468
3915 Beryl Rd Ste 130 Raleigh (27607) *(G-12772)*

Flamingo Group LLC.................... 910 478-9987
1250 Western Blvd Ste L2 Jacksonville (28546) *(G-8999)*

Flanagan Printing Company Inc.................... 828 693-7380
127 3rd Ave W Hendersonville (28792) *(G-7851)*

Flanders Corporation.................... 919 934-3020
2121 Wal Pat Rd Smithfield (27577) *(G-14460)*

Flanders Corporation (DH).................... 252 946-8081
531 Flanders Filter Rd Washington (27889) *(G-15699)*

Flanders Corporation.................... 252 946-0744
531 Flanders Filter Rd Washington (27889) *(G-15700)*

Flanders Filters Inc.................... 252 217-3978
1418 Wal Pat Rd Smithfield (27577) *(G-14461)*

Flanders Filters Inc (DH).................... 252 946-8081
531 Flanders Filter Rd Washington (27889) *(G-15701)*

Flanders Precisionaire, Smithfield Also Called: Flanders Corporation *(G-14460)*

Flanders/Csc LLC.................... 252 946-8081
531 Flanders Filter Rd Washington (27889) *(G-15702)*

Flane Tech, Winston Salem Also Called: Firestopping Products Inc *(G-16711)*

Flare Dichiaro.................... 336 500-5160
3700 Madison Ave Greensboro (27403) *(G-7017)*

Flash Printing Company Inc.................... 704 375-2474
1003 Louise Ave Ste A Charlotte (28205) *(G-2769)*

Flash Technology LLC.................... 980 474-3700
6325 Ardrey Kell Rd Ste 400 Charlotte (28277) *(G-2770)*

Flat Iron Mill Works LLC.................... 828 768-7770
22 Pear Tree Ln Leicester (28748) *(G-9511)*

Flat Rock Signs & Graphics.................... 828 693-0908
578 Upward Rd Unit 8 Flat Rock (28731) *(G-5965)*

Flat Rock Tool & Mold Inc.................... 828 692-2578
690 Shepherd St Hendersonville (28792) *(G-7852)*

Flat Water Corp.................... 704 584-7764
800 Clanton Rd Ste R Charlotte (28217) *(G-2771)*

Flavor Sciences Inc.................... 828 758-2525
715 Houck Mountain Rd Taylorsville (28681) *(G-15142)*

Flavor Seed LLC.................... 704 401-9319
1419 Cavendish Ct Charlotte (28211) *(G-2772)*

Flavors Ice Cream, Raleigh Also Called: Antkar LLC *(G-12509)*

Fleet Fixers Inc.................... 704 986-0066
927a Concord Rd Albemarle (28001) *(G-85)*

Fleet Readiness Center East, Cherry Point Also Called: United States Dept of Navy *(G-3858)*

Fleetgenius of Nc Inc.................... 828 726-3001
1808 Norwood St Sw Lenoir (28645) *(G-9612)*

Fleetwood, Raleigh Also Called: Udm Systems LLC *(G-13375)*

Fleming Wood & Rod LLC.................... 828 278-9194
5001 Us Highway 421 N Vilas (28692) *(G-15495)*

Fletcher Industries Inc.................... 910 692-7133
1485 Central Dr 22 Southern Pines (28387) *(G-14536)*

Fletcher Limestone Company Inc.................... 828 684-6701
639 Faning Bridge Rd Fletcher (28732) *(G-6005)*

Fletcher Machine Inds Inc.................... 336 249-6101
4305 E Us Highway 64 Lexington (27292) *(G-9718)*

Fletcher Printville.................... 828 348-5126
222 Old Airport Rd Fletcher (28732) *(G-6006)*

Flex Finishing Inc.................... 704 342-3600
4811 Worth Pl Charlotte (28216) *(G-2773)*

Flex Tram, Lexington Also Called: Carter Millwork Inc *(G-9690)*

Flexgen Power Systems Inc.................... 855 327-5674
2175 Presidential Dr Ste 100 Durham (27703) *(G-5100)*

Flexgen Power Systems Inc (PA).................... 855 327-5674
280 S Mangum St Ste 150 Durham (27701) *(G-5101)*

Flexi North America LLC.................... 704 588-0785
2405 Center Park Dr Charlotte (28217) *(G-2774)*

Flexo Factor.................... 704 962-5404
2814 Yorkview Ct Charlotte (28270) *(G-2775)*

Flextrol Corporation.................... 704 888-1120
192 Browns Hill Rd Locust (28097) *(G-9960)*

Flextronics Corporation.................... 704 598-3300
6800 Solectron Dr Charlotte (28262) *(G-2776)*

Flextronics Intl USA Inc.................... 704 509-8700
6800 Solectron Dr Charlotte (28262) *(G-2777)*

Flextronics Intl USA Inc.................... 919 998-4000
1000 Innovation Ave Morrisville (27560) *(G-11341)*

Flexview Systems LLC.................... 704 644-3079
7751 Ballantyne C Ste 101 Charlotte (28277) *(G-2778)*

Flint Acquisition Corp.................... 336 475-6600
115 Todd Ct Thomasville (27360) *(G-15222)*

Flint Ennis Inc.................... 800 331-8118
4189 Eagle Hill Dr High Point (27265) *(G-8354)*

Flint Group Inc (PA).................... 828 687-4363
25 Old Shoals Rd Arden (28704) *(G-330)*

Flint Group Flexographic Pdts, Arden *Also Called: Flint Group Inc (G-330)*
Flint Group Print Media N Amer, Arden *Also Called: Flint Group US LLC (G-331)*
Flint Group US LLC 828 687-4309
  95 Glenn Bridge Rd Arden (28704) *(G-331)*
Flint Group US LLC 828 687-2485
  95 Glenn Bridge Rd Arden (28704) *(G-332)*
Flint Group US LLC 828 687-4291
  25 Old Shoals Rd Arden (28704) *(G-333)*
Flint Group US LLC 704 504-2626
  2915 Whitehall Park Dr Ste 600 Charlotte (28273) *(G-2779)*
Flint Hill Textiles Inc 704 434-9331
  2240 Flint Hill Church Rd Shelby (28152) *(G-14318)*
Flint Spinning LLC 336 665-3000
  7736 Mccloud Rd Ste 300 Greensboro (27409) *(G-7018)*
Flint Trading Inc 336 308-3770
  505 County Line Rd Thomasville (27360) *(G-15223)*
Flint Trading Inc 336 475-6600
  115 Todd Ct Thomasville (27360) *(G-15224)*
Flo-Tite Inc Valves & Contrls 910 738-8904
  4815 W 5th St Lumberton (28358) *(G-10038)*
Float Lifts of Carolinas LLC 919 972-1082
  8012 Yellow Daisy Dr Wilmington (28412) *(G-16218)*
Flologic Inc 919 878-1808
  1015 Aviation Pkwy Ste 900 Morrisville (27560) *(G-11342)*
Floor Azzo, Siler City *Also Called: Floorazzo (G-14411)*
Floorazzo 919 663-1684
  215 W 3rd St Siler City (27344) *(G-14411)*
Floorazzo Tile LLC 919 663-1684
  1217 Harold Andrews Rd Siler City (27344) *(G-14412)*
Flooring Manufacturing, Franklin *Also Called: Beasley Flooring Products Inc (G-6116)*
Floraleads Group 919 303-1420
  5308 Dutchman Dr Raleigh (27606) *(G-12773)*
Flores Crane Services LLC 704 243-4347
  8705 Kentucky Derby Dr Waxhaw (28173) *(G-15757)*
Flores Welding Inc 919 838-1060
  961 Palace Garden Way Raleigh (27603) *(G-12774)*
Florida Fire Supply 336 885-5007
  3645 Reed St Winston Salem (27107) *(G-16714)*
Florida Marine Tanks Inc (HQ) 305 620-9030
  120 Peter Gill Rd Henderson (27537) *(G-7783)*
Florida Progress Corporation (DH) 704 382-3853
  410 S Wilmington St Raleigh (27601) *(G-12775)*
Flow Control Group, Charlotte *Also Called: Ffi Holdings III Corp (G-2755)*
Flow Dental, Battleboro *Also Called: Flow X Ray Corporation (G-920)*
Flow Fabrication 704 376-8555
  4110 Monroe Rd Charlotte (28205) *(G-2780)*
Flow Rhythm Inc 704 737-2178
  1520 Mockingbird Ln Charlotte (28209) *(G-2781)*
Flow Sciences Inc 910 763-1717
  2025 Mercantile Dr Leland (28451) *(G-9542)*
Flow X Ray Corporation 631 242-9729
  133 Wolf Rd Battleboro (27809) *(G-920)*
Flowers Bakery, Goldsboro *Also Called: Franklin Baking Company LLC (G-6614)*
Flowers Bakery, Jamestown *Also Called: Flowers Baking Co Newton LLC (G-9049)*
Flowers Bakery, Sanford *Also Called: Flowers Bkg Co Jamestown LLC (G-14118)*
Flowers Bakery of Winston-Salem LLC 336 785-8700
  315 Cassell St Winston Salem (27107) *(G-16715)*
Flowers Bakery Outlet, Winston Salem *Also Called: Flowers Bkg Co Jamestown LLC (G-16716)*
Flowers Baking Co Newton LLC (HQ) 336 841-8840
  801 W Main St Jamestown (27282) *(G-9049)*
Flowers Baking Co Newton LLC 336 903-1345
  802 N Moravian St Wilkesboro (28697) *(G-16022)*
FLOWERS BAKING CO. OF JAMESTOWN, LLC, Henderson *Also Called: Flowers Bkg Co Jamestown LLC (G-7784)*
FLOWERS BAKING CO. OF JAMESTOWN, LLC, Monroe *Also Called: Flowers Bkg Co Jamestown LLC (G-10720)*
Flowers Bkg Co Jamestown LLC 252 492-1519
  875 S Beckford Dr Henderson (27536) *(G-7784)*
Flowers Bkg Co Jamestown LLC 704 296-1000
  5524 W Highway 74 Monroe (28110) *(G-10720)*
Flowers Bkg Co Jamestown LLC 919 776-8932
  708 E Main St Sanford (27332) *(G-14118)*
Flowers Bkg Co Jamestown LLC 336 744-3525
  5610 Shattalon Dr Winston Salem (27105) *(G-16716)*
Flowers Slaughterhouse LLC 252 235-4106
  5154a Saint Rose Church Rd Sims (27880) *(G-14442)*
Flowserve Corporation 704 494-0497
  2801 Hutchison Mcdonald Rd Ste T Charlotte (28269) *(G-2782)*
Flowserve Corporation 910 371-9011
  2216 Mercantile Dr Leland (28451) *(G-9543)*
Flowserve US Inc 972 443-6500
  1900 S Saunders St Raleigh (27603) *(G-12776)*
Floyd S Braces and Limbs Inc 910 763-0821
  709 Parkway Blvd Wilmington (28412) *(G-16219)*
Fluid Power Technology, Charlotte *Also Called: Parmer International Inc (G-3316)*
Fluid Sealing Supply, Concord *Also Called: Michael Simmons (G-4313)*
Flutterby Embroidery 980 225-6053
  8524 Indian Summer Trl Harrisburg (28075) *(G-7709)*
Flying Smiles Inc 252 255-3054
  302 Sea Oats Trl Kitty Hawk (27949) *(G-9405)*
Flynn Burner Corporation 704 660-1500
  225 Mooresville Blvd Mooresville (28115) *(G-10947)*
Flynt/Amtex Inc (PA) 336 226-0621
  2908 Alamance Rd Burlington (27215) *(G-1414)*
FMC Corporation 704 868-5300
  161 Kings Mtn Hwy Bessemer City (28016) *(G-1067)*
FMC Corporation 704 426-5336
  1115 Bessemer City Kings Mtn Hwy Bessemer City (28016) *(G-1068)*
FMC Lithium Division, Bessemer City *Also Called: FMC Corporation (G-1068)*
Fmp Equipment Corp 336 621-2882
  6204 Technology Dr Browns Summit (27214) *(G-1302)*
Fms Enterprises Usa Inc 704 735-4249
  2001 Kawai Rd Lincolnton (28092) *(G-9893)*
Fmt, Henderson *Also Called: Florida Marine Tanks Inc (G-7783)*
Focal Point Architectural Pdts, Tarboro *Also Called: Focal Point Products Inc (G-15104)*
Focal Point Products Inc 252 824-0015
  3006 Anaconda Rd Tarboro (27886) *(G-15104)*
Focke & Co Inc 336 449-7200
  5730 Millstream Rd Whitsett (27377) *(G-15990)*
Focus Newspaper, Hickory *Also Called: Tucker Production Incorporated (G-8190)*
Focusales Inc 919 614-3076
  6113 Chowning Ct Raleigh (27612) *(G-12777)*
Foell Packing Company of NC 919 776-0592
  2209 Boone Trail Rd Sanford (27330) *(G-14119)*
Fogle Computing Corporation 828 697-9080
  131 Camellia Way Hendersonville (28739) *(G-7853)*
Foiled Agin Choclat Coins LLC 919 342-4601
  1488 Mcneill Rd # A Sanford (27330) *(G-14120)*
Folkwear 828 626-3100
  1679 Barnardsville Hwy Barnardsville (28709) *(G-910)*
Fontaine Modification Company (DH) 704 392-8502
  9827 Mount Holly Rd Charlotte (28214) *(G-2783)*
Fontem Us Inc 888 207-4588
  1100 S Tyron Ste 300 Charlotte (28203) *(G-2784)*
Foo Machine & Tool Precision 919 258-5099
  311 W Harrington Ave Broadway (27505) *(G-1296)*
Food Industry, Wendell *Also Called: Magnificent Concessions LLC (G-15907)*
Foot To Die For 704 577-2822
  2545 Valleyview Dr Charlotte (28212) *(G-2785)*
Foothills Brewing 336 997-9484
  3800 Kimwell Dr Winston Salem (27103) *(G-16717)*
Foothills Distillery LLC 704 462-1055
  300 Thornburg Dr Se Unit A Conover (28613) *(G-4455)*
Foothills Fire Defense LLC 828 381-3988
  63 George Baker Dr Hickory (28601) *(G-8027)*
Foothills Fire Defense LLC 828 612-9575
  25 Heron Cove Loop Hickory (28601) *(G-8028)*
Foothills Sug Cured Cntry Hams 336 835-2411
  522 S Main St Jonesville (28642) *(G-9096)*
Foothold Publications Inc 770 891-3423
  2656 Garden Knoll Ln Raleigh (27614) *(G-12778)*

Forage Soaps LLC 828 737-9088
  20 Randall Ln Newland (28657) *(G-11886)*

Forbes Custom Cabinets LLC 919 362-4277
  2025 Production Dr Apex (27539) *(G-192)*

Forbes Fixtures, Apex *Also Called: Forbes Custom Cabinets LLC (G-192)*

Forbes Printing, Lenoir *Also Called: A Forbes Company (G-9566)*

Forbo Belting 704 948-0800
  12201 Vanstory Dr Huntersville (28078) *(G-8822)*

Forbo Movement Systems 704 334-5353
  10125 S Tryon St Charlotte (28273) *(G-2786)*

Forbo Siegling LLC 704 948-0800
  13245 Reese Blvd W Huntersville (28078) *(G-8823)*

Forbo Siegling LLC 704 948-0800
  12120 Herbert Wayne Ct Huntersville (28078) *(G-8824)*

Forbo Siegling LLC (HQ) 704 948-0800
  12201 Vanstory Dr Huntersville (28078) *(G-8825)*

Force Protection Inc 336 597-2381
  3300 Jim Thorpe Hwy Roxboro (27574) *(G-13803)*

Ford Division 336 838-4155
  1422 2nd St North Wilkesboro (28659) *(G-12008)*

Forest City Pallett Co Inc 828 652-8432
  5159 Harmony Grove Rd Nebo (28761) *(G-11760)*

Forest Millwork Inc 828 251-5264
  93 Thompson St Asheville (28803) *(G-624)*

Forever Outdoors, Marion *Also Called: Joseph Sotanski (G-10155)*

Forged Cstm Met Fbrication LLC 910 274-8300
  6804 Holly Shelter Rd Castle Hayne (28429) *(G-1947)*

Forged Timber Company 704 351-7712
  802e Performance Rd Mooresville (28115) *(G-10948)*

Forklift Network 877 327-7260
  20802 Eastpoint Dr Cornelius (28031) *(G-4548)*

Forklift Pro Inc 704 716-3636
  9801 Industrial Dr Pineville (28134) *(G-12269)*

Form Tech Concrete Forms Inc 704 395-9910
  1000 Thomasboro Dr Charlotte (28208) *(G-2787)*

Form Technologies, Charlotte *Also Called: Form Technologies Inc (G-2788)*

Form Technologies Inc (DH) 704 927-2790
  11325 N Community House Rd Ste 300 Charlotte (28277) *(G-2788)*

Forma-Fab Metals Inc 919 563-5630
  5816 Us 70 W Mebane (27302) *(G-10409)*

Formark Corporation 704 922-9516
  7537 Hawkstand Ln Charlotte (28210) *(G-2789)*

Formcut 3d, Cary *Also Called: Size Stream LLC (G-1893)*

Forming Belt Service LLC 828 465-0001
  3280 20th Ave Se Newton (28658) *(G-11932)*

Forrentcom 336 420-9562
  3708 Lexham Ct High Point (27265) *(G-8355)*

Forsyth Family Magazine Inc 336 782-0331
  6255 Towncenter Dr Clemmons (27012) *(G-4038)*

Forsyth Printing Company Inc 336 969-0383
  627 Forum Pkwy Rural Hall (27045) *(G-13840)*

Forsyth Redi-Mix Inc 336 969-0446
  100 Anderson St Rural Hall (27045) *(G-13841)*

Fort Bragg Surplus 828 351-4195
  13774 Cruso Rd Canton (28716) *(G-1616)*

Fortech Inc 704 333-0621
  2124 Wilkinson Blvd Charlotte (28208) *(G-2790)*

Fortem Genus Inc 910 574-5214
  427 Franklin St Fayetteville (28301) *(G-5826)*

Forterra Brick LLC 704 341-8750
  7400 Carmel Executive Park Dr Ste 200 Charlotte (28226) *(G-2791)*

Forterra Pipe & Precast LLC 910 892-6411
  452 Webb Rd Dunn (28334) *(G-4867)*

Fortiline LLC (DH) 704 788-9800
  7025 Northwinds Dr Nw Concord (28027) *(G-4266)*

Fortiline Waterworks, Concord *Also Called: Fortiline LLC (G-4266)*

Fortis Track, Raleigh *Also Called: Smart Cast Group (G-13272)*

Fortner Lumber Inc 704 585-2383
  991 Liberty Church Rd Hiddenite (28636) *(G-8216)*

Fortovia Therapeutics Inc (PA) 919 872-5578
  8540 Colonnade Center Dr Ste 101 Raleigh (27615) *(G-12779)*

Fortrans Inc 919 365-8004
  7400 Siemens Rd Ste B Wendell (27591) *(G-15902)*

Fortrea Holdings Inc (PA) 877 495-0816
  8 Moore Dr Durham (27709) *(G-5102)*

Fortress Forest International, Conover *Also Called: Fortress International Corp NC (G-4456)*

Fortress International Corp NC 336 645-9365
  1808 Emmanuel Church Rd Conover (28613) *(G-4456)*

Fortress Wood Products Inc 336 854-5121
  3874 Bethel Drive Ext High Point (27260) *(G-8356)*

Fortron Industries LLC 910 343-5000
  4600 Us Highway 421 N Wilmington (28401) *(G-16220)*

Forveson Corp 336 292-6237
  322 Edwardia Dr Ste D Greensboro (27409) *(G-7019)*

Forward Design & Print Co Inc 704 776-9304
  1903 Tom Williams Rd Monroe (28112) *(G-10721)*

Forward Dsptching Lgistics LLC 252 907-9797
  3033 Clubway Dr Apt 124 Greenville (27834) *(G-7527)*

Foss Industrial Recycling LLC 336 342-4812
  7037 Us Highway 70 W La Grange (28551) *(G-9441)*

Foster Jackson & Sons LLC 828 674-7941
  10363 Holbert Cove Rd Saluda (28773) *(G-14070)*

Foster Tire Sales Inc 336 248-6726
  1609 S Main St Lexington (27292) *(G-9719)*

Fosters Consulting, Fayetteville *Also Called: Fosterscape LLP (G-5827)*

Fosterscape LLP 910 401-7638
  5694 Juneberry Ln Fayetteville (28304) *(G-5827)*

Foto Grafix 336 570-1885
  341 S Main St Burlington (27215) *(G-1415)*

Foundation Woodworks LLC 828 713-9665
  17 Foundy St Ste 10 Asheville (28801) *(G-625)*

Founders Hemp LLC 888 334-4367
  1157 S Cox St # B Asheboro (27203) *(G-436)*

Founding Fathers Distillery 336 434-0149
  6116 Hickory Creek Rd High Point (27263) *(G-8357)*

Foundry A Print Cmmnctions LLC 703 329-3300
  2725 Abruzzo Dr Apex (27502) *(G-193)*

Foundry Commercial 704 348-6875
  101 N Tryon St Ste 1000 Charlotte (28246) *(G-2792)*

Foundry Group LLC 412 973-9762
  531 Brentwood Rd # 507 Denver (28037) *(G-4776)*

Foundry, The, Apex *Also Called: Foundry A Print Cmmnctions LLC (G-193)*

Fountain Powerboat Inds Inc (HQ) 252 975-2000
  1653 Whichards Beach Rd Washington (27889) *(G-15703)*

Fountain Powerboats, Washington *Also Called: Fountain Powerboats Inc (G-15704)*

Fountain Powerboats Inc 252 975-2000
  1653 Whichards Beach Rd Washington (27889) *(G-15704)*

Four Corners Frmng Gallery Inc 704 662-7154
  148 N Main St Mooresville (28115) *(G-10949)*

Four Corners Home Inc (PA) 828 398-4187
  1 Page Ave Ste 112l Asheville (28801) *(G-626)*

Four Hounds Distilling LLC 757 717-9393
  1117 Lake Park Blvd N Carolina Beach (28428) *(G-1637)*

Four Jaks 828 484-9545
  25 Salem Acres Rd Weaverville (28787) *(G-15847)*

Four Oks/Benson News In Review, Benson *Also Called: County Press Inc (G-1033)*

Four Points Recycling LLC 910 333-5961
  309 King Rd Jacksonville (28540) *(G-9000)*

Fourshare LLC 336 714-0448
  6645 Holder Rd Clemmons (27012) *(G-4039)*

Fox Apparel Inc 336 629-7641
  100 Industrial Park Ave Asheboro (27205) *(G-437)*

Fox Briar Furniture & Wdwkg 980 254-8433
  3580 Us Highway 158 Mocksville (27028) *(G-10572)*

Fox Factory Inc 828 633-6840
  1240 Brevard Rd Asheville (28806) *(G-627)*

Fox Factory Inc 831 421-1791
  169 Gasoline Aly Mooresville (28117) *(G-10950)*

Foxfire Printing 252 329-8181
  300 W Arlington Blvd E Greenville (27834) *(G-7528)*

Foxster Opco LLC 910 297-6996
  118 Circle Dr Hampstead (28443) *(G-7647)*

ALPHABETIC SECTION — Freud America Inc

Fpt Infrastructure, Mount Airy *Also Called: Fibrecrete Pprsrvtion Tech Inc (G-11509)*

Fragrant Passage Candle Co LP 336 375-8411
3500 N Ohenry Blvd Greensboro (27405) *(G-7020)*

Framers Cottage 910 638-0100
58 Pine Ridge Dr Whispering Pines (28327) *(G-15954)*

Framewright Inc 828 459-2284
1824 Brian Dr Ne Conover (28613) *(G-4457)*

Framingsupplies.com, Tryon *Also Called: William L Day Companies Inc (G-15431)*

Frances Machine Shop 910 653-3477
8421 Joe Brown Hwy S Chadbourn (28431) *(G-1975)*

Franchise Signs International 704 209-1087
9905 Old Beatty Ford Rd Rockwell (28138) *(G-13654)*

Francis Simply Publishing Co 910 399-2508
Wilmington (28403) *(G-16221)*

Frank Door Company, Newport *Also Called: TRf Manufacturing NC Inc (G-11909)*

Frank Ficca Woodworking 336 937-2985
6300 Wescott Dr Summerfield (27358) *(G-14982)*

Frank G Shumate 336 784-0828
145 Bluff School Rd Kernersville (27284) *(G-9201)*

Frank Peterson 910 892-6496
285 Stonehenge Dr Dunn (28334) *(G-4868)*

Frank Uncle Productions LLC 910 769-2729
3719 Carolina Beach Rd Wilmington (28412) *(G-16222)*

Franken Signs 704 339-0059
3100 South Blvd Charlotte (28209) *(G-2793)*

Franken Woodworking 910 488-6931
7683 Wilkins Dr Fayetteville (28311) *(G-5828)*

Frankie York Logging Co 252 633-4825
2250 Us Highway 17 N New Bern (28560) *(G-11804)*

Franklin / Kerr Press LLC 828 216-3021
213 Franklin Ave Nw Concord (28025) *(G-4267)*

Franklin Aerospace Inc 336 474-1960
147 Commercial Park Dr Thomasville (27360) *(G-15225)*

Franklin Baking Company LLC (HQ) 919 735-0344
500 W Grantham St Goldsboro (27530) *(G-6614)*

Franklin Baking Company LLC 252 752-4600
1107 Myrtle St Greenville (27834) *(G-7529)*

Franklin Baking Company LLC 910 425-5090
217 Woodington Rd Hope Mills (28348) *(G-8737)*

Franklin Baking Company LLC 919 832-7942
1404 S Bloodworth St Raleigh (27610) *(G-12780)*

Franklin Baking Company LLC 252 410-0255
610 Julian R Allsbrook Hwy Roanoke Rapids (27870) *(G-13574)*

Franklin Baking Company LLC 252 946-3340
5398 Us Highway 264 E Washington (27889) *(G-15705)*

Franklin County Newspapers Inc 919 496-6503
109 S Bickett Blvd Louisburg (27549) *(G-9988)*

Franklin Forest Products LLC 336 982-5550
1260 Old Highway 16 Jefferson (28640) *(G-9088)*

Franklin Industrial Contrs, Aurora *Also Called: Franklin Industrial Contrs Inc (G-834)*

Franklin Industrial Contrs Inc 252 670-6682
8501 Nc Highway 306 S Aurora (27806) *(G-834)*

Franklin Investments, Charlotte *Also Called: Diversfied Prtg Techniques Inc (G-2644)*

Franklin Logistical Services Inc 919 556-6711
112 Franklin Park Dr Youngsville (27596) *(G-17081)*

Franklin Machine Company LLC 828 524-2313
231 Depot St Franklin (28734) *(G-6129)*

Franklin Partleboard, Moncure *Also Called: Aconcagua Timber Corp (G-10612)*

Franklin Sheet Metal, Franklin *Also Called: Franklin Sheet Metal Shop Inc (G-6130)*

Franklin Sheet Metal Shop Inc 828 524-2821
791 Ulco Dr Ste A Franklin (28734) *(G-6130)*

Franklin Times, Louisburg *Also Called: Franklin County Newspapers Inc (G-9988)*

Franklin Veneers Inc 919 494-2284
5735 Nc Hwy 56 E Franklinton (27525) *(G-6154)*

Franklinton Concrete Plant, Franklinton *Also Called: S T Wooten Corporation (G-6163)*

Franks Millwright Services 336 248-6692
1207 Ashland Dr Lexington (27295) *(G-9720)*

Fraser West Inc 910 655-4106
361 Federal Rd Riegelwood (28456) *(G-13558)*

Frazees Trophies 910 892-6722
312 S Powell Ave Dunn (28334) *(G-4869)*

Frazier Holdings LLC 919 868-8651
2009 Pope Ct Clayton (27520) *(G-3978)*

Frct, Matthews *Also Called: Fire Retardant Chem Tech LLC (G-10316)*

Fred L Brown 336 643-7523
2913 Pleasant Ridge Rd Summerfield (27358) *(G-14983)*

Fred Marvin and Associates Inc 330 784-9211
496 Gallimore Dairy Rd Ste D Greensboro (27409) *(G-7021)*

Fred Marvin Associates, Greensboro *Also Called: Fred Marvin and Associates Inc (G-7021)*

Fred R Harrris Logging Inc 919 853-2266
527 Schloss Rd Louisburg (27549) *(G-9989)*

Fred Smith Company, Raleigh *Also Called: Fsc II LLC (G-12785)*

Fred Winfield Lumber Co Inc 828 648-3414
Dutch Cove Rd Canton (28716) *(G-1617)*

Frederick and Frederick Entp 252 235-4849
8520 Hilliard Rd Middlesex (27557) *(G-10448)*

Free Press, The, Kinston *Also Called: Kinston Free Press Company (G-9371)*

Free Will Bptst Press Fndtion (PA) 252 746-6128
3928 Lee St Ayden (28513) *(G-852)*

Freedom Beverage Company 336 316-1260
4319 Waterleaf Ct Ste 101 Greensboro (27410) *(G-7022)*

Freedom Creative Solutions, Winston Salem *Also Called: Freedom Mailing & Mktg Inc (G-16718)*

Freedom Enterprise LLC 502 510-7296
5028 Pender Rd Shallotte (28470) *(G-14273)*

Freedom Industries Inc 252 984-0007
4000 E Old Spring Hope Rd Rocky Mount (27804) *(G-13698)*

Freedom Mailing & Mktg Inc 336 595-6300
427 W End Blvd Winston Salem (27101) *(G-16718)*

Freedom Metals Inc 704 333-1214
2014 Vanderbilt Rd Charlotte (28206) *(G-2794)*

Freedom Steel Welding LLC 704 884-1277
206 W 4th St Cherryville (28021) *(G-3869)*

Freeman Container Company Inc 704 922-7972
121 Freeman Franklin Rd Dallas (28034) *(G-4641)*

Freeman Corrugated Containers, Dallas *Also Called: Freeman Container Company Inc (G-4641)*

Freeman Custom Welding Inc 919 210-6267
2108 Langdon Rd Raleigh (27604) *(G-12781)*

Freeman Screen Printers Inc 704 521-9148
4442 South Blvd Ste B Charlotte (28209) *(G-2795)*

Freeman Transport and Logging 910 220-5358
1163 Tarry Church Rd Star (27356) *(G-14715)*

Freight Company, Charlotte *Also Called: D&E Freight LLC (G-2597)*

Freightliner Parts Plant, Gastonia *Also Called: Daimler Truck North Amer LLC (G-6394)*

Freightpal Inc 704 971-8183
201 Mccullough Dr Ste 300 Charlotte (28262) *(G-2796)*

Freirich Foods Inc 704 636-2621
815 W Kerr St Salisbury (28144) *(G-13966)*

French Apron Manufacturing Co 704 865-7666
1619 Madison St Gastonia (28052) *(G-6403)*

French Broad Boatworks 828 230-6600
211 Amboy Rd Ste D Asheville (28806) *(G-628)*

French Broad Chocolates LLC 828 252-4181
821 Riverside Dr Asheville (28801) *(G-629)*

French Heritage Inc (PA) 336 882-3565
1638 W English Rd High Point (27262) *(G-8358)*

Frenzelit Inc 336 814-4317
4165 Old Salisbury Rd Lexington (27295) *(G-9721)*

Fresenius Kabi Usa LLC 252 991-2692
5200 Corporate Pkwy Wilson (27893) *(G-16499)*

Fresh Air Technologies LLC 704 622-7877
2246 Stevens Mill Rd Ste B Matthews (28104) *(G-10317)*

Fresh As A Daisy, High Point *Also Called: Fresh As A Daisy Inc (G-8359)*

Fresh As A Daisy Inc 336 869-3002
3601 Huntingridge Dr High Point (27265) *(G-8359)*

Fresh LLC 919 592-7255
4700 Archean Way Apt 107 Raleigh (27616) *(G-12782)*

Fresh-N-Mobile LLC 704 251-4643
8640 University City Blvd Ste 135 Charlotte (28213) *(G-2797)*

Freud, High Point *Also Called: Freud America Inc (G-8360)*

Freud America Inc 800 334-4107
218 Feld Ave High Point (27263) *(G-8360)*

Freudenberg Nonwoven, Durham *Also Called: Freudenberg Prfmce Mtls LP (G-5104)*

Freudenberg Nonwovens Limited Partnership................................. 919 620-3900
  3500 Industrial Dr Durham (27704) *(G-5103)*

Freudenberg Prfmce Mtls LP... 828 665-5000
  1301 Sand Hill Rd Candler (28715) *(G-1579)*

Freudenberg Prfmce Mtls LP (HQ).. 919 479-7443
  3500 Industrial Dr Durham (27704) *(G-5104)*

Freudenberg Prfmce Mtls LP... 919 620-3900
  3440 Industrial Dr Durham (27704) *(G-5105)*

Friddles Custom Sawing.. 336 210-0144
  117 Thrush Rd Stokesdale (27357) *(G-14942)*

Friedrich Metal Pdts Co Inc... 336 375-3067
  6204 Technology Dr Browns Summit (27214) *(G-1303)*

Friendship Upholstery Co Inc.. 828 632-9836
  6035 Church Rd Taylorsville (28681) *(G-15143)*

Frisby Aerospace Inc... 336 712-8004
  4520 Hampton Rd Clemmons (27012) *(G-4040)*

Frisby Technologies Inc (PA).. 336 998-6652
  136 Medical Dr Advance (27006) *(G-42)*

Frit Car Inc... 252 638-2675
  Hwy 17 N Ste 2012 Bridgeton (28519) *(G-1294)*

Frito-Lay, Charlotte *Also Called: Frito-Lay North America Inc (G-2798)*

Frito-Lay North America Inc... 704 588-4150
  2911 Nevada Blvd Charlotte (28273) *(G-2798)*

Frito-Lay North America Inc... 980 224-3730
  3215 Kitty Hawk Rd Wilmington (28405) *(G-16223)*

Froehling & Robertson Inc... 804 264-2701
  310 Hubert St Raleigh (27603) *(G-12783)*

Front Line Express LLC.. 800 260-1357
  4086 Clovelly Dr Greensboro (27406) *(G-7023)*

Front Porch Ice Cream, Mooresville *Also Called: Mooresville Ice Cream Company LLC (G-11024)*

Front Prch Cstm Frmng Wodworks.. 252 717-2868
  1043 Zeke Rhodes Ln Williamston (27892) *(G-16060)*

Front Street Vlg Mstr Assn Inc.. 252 838-1524
  2450 Lennoxville Rd Beaufort (28516) *(G-957)*

Frontier Meat Processing Inc.. 704 843-3921
  8303 Lancaster Hwy Waxhaw (28173) *(G-15758)*

Frontier Yarns Inc (HQ).. 919 776-9940
  1823 Boone Trail Rd Sanford (27330) *(G-14121)*

Frontier Yarns Inc.. 919 776-9940
  1823 Boone Trail Rd Sanford (27330) *(G-14122)*

Frostie Bottom At Doors, Claremont *Also Called: Frostie Bottom Tree Stand LLC (G-3927)*

Frostie Bottom Tree Stand LLC.. 828 466-1708
  3280 Yount Rd Claremont (28610) *(G-3927)*

Frozen Dessert Specialists LLC.. 336 362-8707
  10922 Randleman Rd Randleman (27317) *(G-13470)*

Frsteam By Sun Cleaners, Newton *Also Called: Sun Cleaners & Laundry Inc (G-11974)*

Fryeday Coffee Roasters LLC.. 704 879-9083
  106 E 1st St Unit B Lowell (28098) *(G-10008)*

Fs LLC.. 919 309-9727
  4122 Bennett Memorial Rd Ste 304 Durham (27705) *(G-5106)*

Fsc Holdings Inc... 919 782-1247
  6001 Westgate Rd Raleigh (27617) *(G-12784)*

Fsc II LLC (HQ).. 919 783-5700
  701 Corporate Center Dr Ste 101 Raleigh (27607) *(G-12785)*

Fsc Therapeutics LLC.. 704 941-2500
  6100 Fairview Rd Ste 300 Charlotte (28210) *(G-2799)*

Fsm Liquidation Corp.. 919 776-9940
  1823 Boone Trail Rd Sanford (27330) *(G-14123)*

Ft Media Holdings LLC (HQ).. 336 605-0121
  7025 Albert Pick Rd Ste 200 Greensboro (27409) *(G-7024)*

FTM Enterprises Inc... 910 798-2045
  301 N Green Meadows Dr Wilmington (28405) *(G-16224)*

Ftp Co, Greenville *Also Called: Modern Lightning Protection Co (G-7561)*

Fudgeboat Inc.. 910 617-9793
  920 Riptide Ln Carolina Beach (28428) *(G-1638)*

Fuel Doc 16... 919 284-5400
  214 E 2nd St Kenly (27542) *(G-9152)*

Fueltec Systems LLC.. 828 212-1141
  3821 N Main St Granite Falls (28630) *(G-6733)*

Fuji America Inc... 704 527-3854
  10817 Southern Loop Blvd Charlotte (28273) *(G-2800)*

Fuji Foods Inc.. 336 897-3373
  6205 Corporate Park Dr Browns Summit (27214) *(G-1304)*

Fuji Foods Inc (DH).. 336 375-3111
  6206 Corporate Park Dr Browns Summit (27214) *(G-1305)*

Fuji Foods Inc.. 336 226-8817
  363 W Old Glencoe Rd Burlington (27217) *(G-1416)*

Fuji Silysia Chemical Ltd.. 919 484-4158
  1215 Sugg Pkwy Greenville (27834) *(G-7530)*

Fuji Silysia Chemical USA Ltd... 252 413-0003
  1215 Sugg Pkwy Greenville (27834) *(G-7531)*

Fujifilm Diosynth Biotechnolog.. 919 337-4400
  6051 George Watts Hill Dr Durham (27709) *(G-5107)*

Fujifilm Dsynth Btchnlgies USA (DH).. 919 337-4400
  101 J Morris Commons Ln Ste 300 Morrisville (27560) *(G-11343)*

Fulcher Elc Fayetteville Inc... 910 483-7772
  1744 Middle River Loop Fayetteville (28312) *(G-5829)*

Fulfords Restorations (PA)... 252 243-7727
  320 Barnes St S Wilson (27893) *(G-16500)*

Full Circle Grinding LLC.. 919 879-9529
  209 Clearwater Ct Clayton (27520) *(G-3979)*

Full Throttle Fabrication.. 910 770-1180
  1047 Old Cribbtown Rd Chadbourn (28431) *(G-1976)*

Fuller Dynasty Brand LLC... 336 847-3875
  719 Westwood Dr Eden (27288) *(G-5490)*

Fuller Specialty Company Inc... 336 226-3446
  804 Bradley St Burlington (27215) *(G-1417)*

Fuller Wldg & Fabricators Inc... 336 751-3712
  980 Salisbury Rd Mocksville (27028) *(G-10573)*

Fully Invlved Leatherworks LLC... 704 799-9938
  147 Houston Rd Ste E Troutman (28166) *(G-15378)*

Fully Involved Leatherworks... 704 799-9938
  147 Stonefield Dr Statesville (28677) *(G-14801)*

Fully Involved Printing LLC... 980 521-2670
  4008 Parkmont Rd Concord (28025) *(G-4268)*

Fully Promoted, Durham *Also Called: Fully Promoted Durham (G-5108)*

Fully Promoted, Fuquay Varina *Also Called: Fully Promoted Fuquay-Varina (G-6200)*

Fully Promoted Durham.. 919 316-1538
  105 W Nc Highway 54 Ste 261 Durham (27713) *(G-5108)*

Fully Promoted Fuquay-Varina... 919 346-8955
  504 Broad St Fuquay Varina (27526) *(G-6200)*

Fulp Lumber Company Inc... 336 573-3113
  280 Fulp Sawmill Rd Stoneville (27048) *(G-14957)*

Fulton Technology Corporation.. 828 657-1611
  337 S Pea Ridge Rd Mooresboro (28114) *(G-10838)*

Fun Publications Inc... 919 847-5263
  12513 Birchfalls Dr Raleigh (27614) *(G-12786)*

Fun-Tees Inc... 704 788-3003
  2583 Armentrout Rd Concord (28025) *(G-4269)*

Fun-Tees Inc (HQ)... 704 788-3003
  4735 Corporate Dr Nw Ste 100 Concord (28027) *(G-4270)*

Funball, Greensboro *Also Called: Intertech Corporation (G-7120)*

Fundamental Playgrounds, Raleigh *Also Called: Brookhurst Associates (G-12576)*

Funder America Inc (HQ)... 336 751-3501
  200 Funder Dr Mocksville (27028) *(G-10574)*

Funder America Inc.. 336 751-3501
  200 Funder Dr Mocksville (27028) *(G-10575)*

Funny Bone EMB & Screening... 704 663-4711
  829 Plaza Ln Mooresville (28115) *(G-10951)*

Funny Girl Press... 919 247-8861
  6511 Creedmoor Rd Ste 204 Raleigh (27613) *(G-12787)*

Funston Company... 910 383-1425
  1018 Grandiflora Dr Leland (28451) *(G-9544)*

Fuqua Logging Company Inc.. 336 562-5178
  388 Fuqua Rd Leasburg (27291) *(G-9505)*

Fuquay-Varina Baking Co Inc... 919 557-2237
  127 S Main St Fuquay Varina (27526) *(G-6201)*

Furiex Pharmaceuticals LLC.. 919 456-7800
  3900 Paramount Pkwy Ste 150 Morrisville (27560) *(G-11344)*

Furnace Rebuilders Inc.. 704 483-4025
  915 Dove Ct Denver (28037) *(G-4777)*

ALPHABETIC SECTION

Furniture At Work..336 472-6619
  6089 Kennedy Rd Trinity (27370) *(G-15341)*
Furniture City Color, High Point *Also Called: F C C LLC (G-8349)*
Furniture Company...910 686-1937
  822 Santa Maria Ave Wilmington (28411) *(G-16225)*
Furniture Concepts..828 323-1590
  909 10th St Ne Hickory (28601) *(G-8029)*
Furniture Fair Inc..910 455-4044
  418 White St Jacksonville (28546) *(G-9001)*
Furniture Lab, Carrboro *Also Called: Rapp Productions Inc (G-1654)*
Furniture Mfrs Claring Hse Inc...............................866 477-8468
  107 Sunrise Center Dr Thomasville (27360) *(G-15226)*
Furniture Tday Media Group LLC.............................336 605-0121
  7025 Albert Pick Rd Ste 200 Greensboro (27409) *(G-7025)*
Furnlite, Fallston *Also Called: Furnlite Inc (G-5729)*
Furnlite Inc...704 538-3193
  344 Wilson Rd Fallston (28042) *(G-5729)*
Furr Signs..704 455-5849
  929 Patricia Ave Harrisburg (28075) *(G-7710)*
Fusion Fabrication & Wldg LLC..............................704 240-9416
  4720 Reepsville Rd Vale (28168) *(G-15467)*
Fusion Fiber Optics LLC......................................252 933-5244
  1935 Neuse Rd Kinston (28501) *(G-9367)*
Fusion Incorporated (PA)....................................252 244-4300
  276 Bailey Ln Vanceboro (28586) *(G-15477)*
Fusion Sport Inc...720 987-4403
  122 E Parrish St Durham (27701) *(G-5109)*
Fusion Welding..508 320-3525
  37 Brandon Ln Rocky Point (28457) *(G-13745)*
Futrell Precasting LLC......................................252 568-3481
  3430 Old Pink Hill Rd Deep Run (28525) *(G-4716)*
Future Endeavors Hickory LLC............................828 256-5488
  2608 Springs Rd Ne Hickory (28601) *(G-8030)*
Future Energy Svc Publishing..............................336 298-8036
  5302 Chestnut Ridge Dr Summerfield (27358) *(G-14984)*
Future Foam, High Point *Also Called: Ffnc Inc (G-8351)*
Future Foam Inc..336 861-8095
  3803 Comanche Rd Archdale (27263) *(G-281)*
Future Foam Inc..336 885-4121
  1300 Prospect St High Point (27260) *(G-8361)*
Future Prints Inc...704 241-4164
  12517 Preservation Pointe Dr Charlotte (28216) *(G-2801)*
Fxi Inc...336 431-1171
  2222 Surrett Dr High Point (27263) *(G-8362)*
Fyi Press Inc..336 254-3452
  818 Walker Ave Greensboro (27403) *(G-7026)*
G & E Investments Inc....................................704 395-2155
  601 S Kings Dr Charlotte (28204) *(G-2802)*
G & E Software Inc..910 762-5608
  1410 Commonwealth Dr Ste 102b Wilmington (28403) *(G-16226)*
G & G Enterprises...336 764-2493
  210 Industrial Dr Ste 2 Clemmons (27012) *(G-4041)*
G & G Forest Products....................................704 539-5110
  147 Lumber Dr Union Grove (28689) *(G-15437)*
G & G Logging...336 352-5586
  401 Ramey Orchard Rd Lowgap (27024) *(G-10013)*
G & G Lumber Company Inc............................704 539-5110
  179 Lumber Dr Harmony (28634) *(G-7686)*
G & G Management LLC.................................336 444-6271
  1603 Battleground Ave Ste F Greensboro (27408) *(G-7027)*
G & G Moulding Inc......................................828 438-1112
  801 N Green St Morganton (28655) *(G-11214)*
G & H Broadway Logging Inc..........................252 229-4594
  145 Territorial Rd New Bern (28560) *(G-11805)*
G & J Machine Shop Inc (PA)..........................336 668-0996
  7800 Boeing Dr Greensboro (27409) *(G-7028)*
G & M Milling Co Inc...................................704 873-5758
  4000 Taylorsville Hwy Statesville (28625) *(G-14802)*
G A Lankford Construction............................828 254-2467
  333 Old Nc 20 Hwy Alexander (28701) *(G-118)*
G and G Art and Frame, Morganton *Also Called: G & G Moulding Inc (G-11214)*
G B Technologies..919 954-0721
  3222 Wellington Ct Ste 104 Raleigh (27615) *(G-12788)*
G Denver and Co LLC (HQ)...........................704 896-4000
  800 Beaty St Davidson (28036) *(G-4675)*
G Force South, Asheboro *Also Called: Longs Machine & Tool Inc (G-454)*
G H Group LLC..919 264-0939
  2001 Yorkgate Dr Raleigh (27612) *(G-12789)*
G M I, Pine Level *Also Called: General Metals Inc (G-12209)*
G R T Electronics, Raleigh *Also Called: Grt Electronics LLC (G-12823)*
G S I, Greensboro *Also Called: Graphic Systems Intl Inc (G-7059)*
G S Materials Inc.......................................336 584-1745
  1521 Huffman Mill Rd Burlington (27215) *(G-1418)*
G T Racing Heads Inc..................................336 905-7988
  2735 Banner Whitehead Rd Sophia (27350) *(G-14517)*
G-Loc Brakes LLC......................................704 765-0213
  503 Performance Rd Mooresville (28115) *(G-10952)*
G.T.a, Reidsville *Also Called: Global Textile Alliance Inc (G-13520)*
G&N Logging LLC......................................919 524-1555
  11727 Nc 222 Hwy W Middlesex (27557) *(G-10449)*
G1 Therapeutics, Durham *Also Called: G1 Therapeutics Inc (G-5110)*
G1 Therapeutics Inc...................................919 213-9835
  700 Park Offices Dr Ste 200 Durham (27709) *(G-5110)*
G60 Cnc LLC...704 796-0478
  5817 Rocky Trace Ct Nw Concord (28027) *(G-4271)*
GA Communications Inc..............................704 360-1860
  136 Fairview Rd Ste 220 Mooresville (28117) *(G-10953)*
Gabden Entertainment, Statesville *Also Called: Gabden LLC (G-14803)*
Gabden LLC..704 451-8646
  232 N Center St Statesville (28677) *(G-14803)*
Gaines Motor Lines Inc (PA)........................828 322-2000
  2349 13th Ave Sw Hickory (28602) *(G-8031)*
Gains Fitness Gear LLC..............................800 403-2904
  224 E Holding Ave Unit 1616 Wake Forest (27588) *(G-15557)*
Gainsborough Baths LLC............................336 357-0797
  41 Rogers Rd Lexington (27292) *(G-9722)*
Gainsbrough Specialist Bathing, Lexington *Also Called: Gainsborough Baths LLC (G-9722)*
Gainspan Corporation...............................408 627-6500
  3131 Rdu Center Dr Ste 135 Morrisville (27560) *(G-11345)*
Galaxy Electronics Inc..............................704 343-9881
  4233 Trailer Dr Charlotte (28269) *(G-2803)*
Galaxy Graphics Inc.................................704 724-9057
  1028 Brenham Ln Matthews (28105) *(G-10249)*
Galaxy Pressure Washing Inc......................888 299-3129
  10810 Southern Loop Blvd Ste 12 Pineville (28134) *(G-12270)*
Galde Press Inc......................................612 965-5515
  110 Lloyd Barnwell Rd Hendersonville (28792) *(G-7854)*
Gale Global Research Inc..........................910 795-8595
  7007 Robert Ruark Dr Leland (28451) *(G-9545)*
Gale Pacific, Charlotte *Also Called: Gale Pacific Usa Inc (G-2804)*
Gale Pacific Usa Inc (HQ)........................407 772-7900
  5311 77 Center Dr Ste 150 Charlotte (28217) *(G-2804)*
Gallery G, Charlotte *Also Called: Artistic Images Inc (G-2221)*
Gallimore Body Shop, Asheboro *Also Called: Gallimore Fmly Investments Inc (G-438)*
Gallimore Fmly Investments Inc.................336 625-5138
  1431 E Salisbury St Asheboro (27203) *(G-438)*
Gallishaw Elite Rigging LLC.....................757 240-8963
  1409 Lambs Grove Rd Elizabeth City (27909) *(G-5546)*
Gallo Lea Organics LLC..........................828 337-1037
  9 Inglewood Rd Asheville (28804) *(G-630)*
Gallolea Pizza Kits, Asheville *Also Called: Gallo Lea Organics LLC (G-630)*
Galloreecom..704 644-0978
  6211 Moss Bank Ct Charlotte (28262) *(G-2805)*
Galvan Industries Inc............................704 455-5102
  7315 Galvan Way Harrisburg (28075) *(G-7711)*
Galvanizing Consultants Inc...................336 603-4218
  687 Winners Pt Whitsett (27377) *(G-15991)*
Galvix Inc..925 434-6243
  1036 Canyon Shadows Ct Cary (27519) *(G-1770)*
Gamble Associates Inc.........................704 375-9301
  701 Johnson Rd Charlotte (28206) *(G-2806)*

Gamble Pallet & Whse Eqp Co — ALPHABETIC SECTION

Gamble Pallet & Whse Eqp Co, Charlotte *Also Called: Gamble Associates Inc (G-2806)*

Game Box Builders, Greensboro *Also Called: Game Box LLC (G-7029)*

Game Box LLC (PA) 866 241-1882
 143 Industrial Ave Greensboro (27406) *(G-7029)*

Game Day Crochet 704 635-7557
 1005 Dunard Ct Indian Trail (28079) *(G-8936)*

Game Processing Leonards Wild 980 429-7042
 167 Car Farm Rd Lincolnton (28092) *(G-9894)*

Gametime Imagewear, Lincolnton *Also Called: Jax Brothers Inc (G-9897)*

Gannett Media Corp 828 649-1075
 58 Back St Marshall (28753) *(G-10202)*

Gannett Media Corp 919 467-1402
 107b Quail Fields Ct Morrisville (27560) *(G-11346)*

Garage Guys 704 494-8841
 4820 N Graham St Charlotte (28269) *(G-2807)*

Garb Athletics, Statesville *Also Called: Badger Sportswear LLC (G-14758)*

Garcia Brothers Welding LLC 919 207-8190
 7154 Us Highway 264a Bailey (27807) *(G-872)*

Garden Gate Ornamental Iron In 704 922-1635
 406 Miles Rd Dallas (28034) *(G-4642)*

Garden Metalwork 828 733-1077
 3640 Rd Newland (28657) *(G-11887)*

Gardner Asphalt Co 336 784-8924
 1664 S Martin Luther King Jr Dr Winston Salem (27107) *(G-16719)*

Gardner Denver, Inc., Davidson *Also Called: G Denver and Co LLC (G-4675)*

Gardner Gibson, Winston Salem *Also Called: Gardner Asphalt Co (G-16719)*

Gardner Glass Products, North Wilkesboro *Also Called: Gardner Glass Products Inc (G-12010)*

Gardner Glass Products Inc 336 838-2151
 201 Elkin Hwy North Wilkesboro (28659) *(G-12009)*

Gardner Glass Products Inc (PA) 336 651-9300
 301 Elkin Hwy North Wilkesboro (28659) *(G-12010)*

Gardner Machinery Corporation 704 372-3890
 700 N Summit Ave Charlotte (28216) *(G-2808)*

Garick LLC 704 455-6418
 8829 Rocky River Rd Harrisburg (28075) *(G-7712)*

Garland Apparel Group LLC 646 647-2790
 120 S Church Ave Garland (28441) *(G-6243)*

Garland Farm Supply Inc (PA) 910 529-9731
 250 N Belgrade Ave Garland (28441) *(G-6244)*

Garland Heritage NC, Garland *Also Called: Garland Apparel Group LLC (G-6243)*

Garland Langley Gravel 252 450-9022
 2933 Old Mill Rd Rocky Mount (27803) *(G-13699)*

Garland Langley Sand and Grav 252 235-2812
 5312 Roseheath Rd Bailey (27807) *(G-873)*

Garlock Bearings, Charlotte *Also Called: Coltec Industries Inc (G-2527)*

Garmin International Inc 919 337-0116
 100 Regency Forest Dr Cary (27518) *(G-1771)*

Garner Concrete Plant, Garner *Also Called: S T Wooten Corporation (G-6313)*

Garner Concrete Plant, Garner *Also Called: S T Wooten Corporation (G-6314)*

Garner Woodworks LLC 828 775-1790
 304 Patton Hill Rd Swannanoa (28778) *(G-15026)*

Garners Septic Tank Inc 919 718-5181
 8574 Turnpike Rd Raeford (28376) *(G-12421)*

Garnett Component Sales Inc 919 562-5158
 2824 Penfold Ln Wake Forest (27587) *(G-15558)*

Garrettcom Inc (HQ) 510 438-9071
 1113 N Main St Mooresville (28115) *(G-10954)*

Garris Grading and Paving Inc 252 749-1101
 5950 Gay Rd Farmville (27828) *(G-5736)*

Gary Forte Woodworking Inc 704 780-0095
 1424 Forest Ln Monroe (28112) *(G-10722)*

Gary J Younts Machine Company 336 476-7930
 4786 Turnpike Ct Thomasville (27360) *(G-15227)*

Gary Tucker 919 837-5724
 12988 Nc 902 Hwy Bear Creek (27207) *(G-938)*

Garys Garage 828 513-5055
 36 P E M Dr Hendersonville (28792) *(G-7855)*

Gas Dept, Shelby *Also Called: City of Shelby (G-14295)*

Gas-Fired Products Inc (PA) 704 372-3485
 1700 Parker Dr Charlotte (28208) *(G-2809)*

Gasboy International Inc 336 547-5000
 7300 W Friendly Ave Greensboro (27410) *(G-7030)*

Gasp Inc 828 891-1628
 80 Emma Sharp Rd Ste 5 Fletcher (28732) *(G-6007)*

Gasser and Sons 910 471-6907
 5102 Old Myrtle Grove Rd Wilmington (28409) *(G-16227)*

Gastex LLC 704 824-9861
 3051 Aberdeen Blvd Gastonia (28054) *(G-6404)*

Gaston County Dyeing Machine Company 704 822-5000
 1310 Charles Raper Jonas Hwy Mount Holly (28120) *(G-11634)*

Gaston Fabrication, Mount Holly *Also Called: Gaston County Dyeing Machine Company (G-11634)*

Gaston Gazette LLP 704 869-1700
 1893 Remount Rd Gastonia (28054) *(G-6405)*

Gaston Indus Machining LLC 704 825-3346
 125 Robinsons Park Dr Bessemer City (28016) *(G-1069)*

Gaston Printing and Signs LLC 702 267-5633
 7204 W Wilkinson Blvd Belmont (28012) *(G-991)*

Gaston Screen Printing Inc 704 399-0459
 8620 Wilkinson Blvd Charlotte (28214) *(G-2810)*

Gaston Systems Inc 704 263-6000
 200 S Main St Stanley (28164) *(G-14694)*

Gastonia 704 377-3687
 860 Summit Crossing Pl Gastonia (28054) *(G-6406)*

Gastonia Iron Works, Mount Holly *Also Called: Gastonia Ornamental Wldg Inc (G-11635)*

Gastonia Ornamental Wldg Inc 704 827-1146
 624 Legion Rd Mount Holly (28120) *(G-11635)*

Gate City Kitchens LLC 336 378-0870
 201 Creek Ridge Rd Ste D Greensboro (27406) *(G-7031)*

Gate Precast Company 919 603-1633
 3800 Oxford Loop Oxford (27565) *(G-12129)*

Gatehouse Media LLC 336 626-6103
 500 Sunset Ave Asheboro (27203) *(G-439)*

Gates County Index Shopper, Ahoskie *Also Called: Boone Newspapers Inc (G-56)*

Gates Custom Milling Inc (PA) 252 357-0116
 681 Nc Hwy 37 S Gatesville (27938) *(G-6549)*

Gateway Campus 919 833-0096
 1306 Hillsborough St Raleigh (27605) *(G-12790)*

Gathering Place Pubg Co LLC 919 742-5850
 274 Lambert Chapel Rd Siler City (27344) *(G-14413)*

Gayco 252 753-4777
 893 Gay Rd Walstonburg (27888) *(G-15637)*

Gaylord Inc 704 694-2434
 4600 Lebanon Rd Ste K Mint Hill (28227) *(G-10533)*

Gb Biosciences LLC (DH) 336 632-6000
 410 S Swing Rd Greensboro (27409) *(G-7032)*

Gb Industries 828 692-9163
 3005 Spartanburg Hwy East Flat Rock (28726) *(G-5475)*

Gb Labs LLC 919 606-7253
 794 American Way Lexington (27295) *(G-9723)*

Gbc Construction Gbc Cons 704 500-9232
 3482 Fredell Dr Conover (28613) *(G-4458)*

Gbc Distribution LLC 704 341-8473
 10123 Park Rd Charlotte (28210) *(G-2811)*

Gbf Inc 336 665-0205
 2427 Penny Rd High Point (27265) *(G-8363)*

Gc Valves, Charlotte *Also Called: General Control Equipment Co (G-2816)*

Gdais, Greensboro *Also Called: General Dynmics Mssion Systems (G-7034)*

GE, Charlotte *Also Called: GE Vernova International LLC (G-2812)*

GE, Charlotte *Also Called: General Electric Company (G-2817)*

GE, Durham *Also Called: GE Aircraft Engs Holdings Inc (G-5111)*

GE, Indian Trail *Also Called: General Electric Company (G-8937)*

GE, Mebane *Also Called: General Electric Company (G-10410)*

GE Aircraft Engs Holdings Inc 919 361-4400
 3701 S Miami Blvd Durham (27703) *(G-5111)*

GE Aviation, Asheville *Also Called: GE Aviation Systems LLC (G-631)*

GE Aviation Systems LLC 828 210-5076
 502 Sweeten Creek Industrial Park Asheville (28803) *(G-631)*

GE Energy, Garner *Also Called: Bently Nevada LLC (G-6256)*

GE Vernova International LLC 704 587-1300
 12037 Goodrich Dr Charlotte (28273) *(G-2812)*

ALPHABETIC SECTION

Ge-Hitchi Nclear Enrgy Amrcas (HQ) 910 819-5073
3901 Castle Hayne Rd Castle Hayne (28429) *(G-1948)*

Ge-Hitchi Nclear Enrgy Intl LL (HQ) 518 433-4338
3901 Castle Hayne Rd Wilmington (28402) *(G-16228)*

Gea Intec LLC 919 433-0131
4319 S Alston Ave Ste 105 Durham (27713) *(G-5112)*

Geami Ltd 919 654-7700
3401 Gresham Lake Rd Ste 110 Raleigh (27615) *(G-12791)*

Gear Fx Driveline LLC 704 799-9117
185 Mckenzie Rd Mooresville (28115) *(G-10955)*

Gee Spot Mobile Bar LLC 910 581-1786
12 East Dr Jacksonville (28546) *(G-9002)*

Gee-Lock, Mooresville Also Called: G-Loc Brakes LLC *(G-10952)*

Geecee, Smithfield Also Called: Lampe & Malphrus Lumber Co *(G-14470)*

Geeks On Call, Durham Also Called: Comtech Group Inc *(G-5029)*

Gefran Inc 501 442-1521
4209 Stuart Andrew Blvd Ste C Charlotte (28217) *(G-2813)*

Geiger International Inc 828 324-6500
218 Cline Park Dr Hildebran (28637) *(G-8623)*

Gelarto Inc 646 795-3505
18 S Water St Wilmington (28401) *(G-16229)*

Gelder & Associates Inc 919 772-6895
3901 Gelder Dr Raleigh (27603) *(G-12792)*

Gem Asset Acquisition LLC 919 851-0799
200 Travis Park Cary (27511) *(G-1772)*

Gem Asset Acquisition LLC (PA) 704 225-3321
1855 Lindbergh St Ste 500 Charlotte (28208) *(G-2814)*

Gem Asset Acquisition LLC 704 697-9577
1955 Scott Futrell Dr Charlotte (28208) *(G-2815)*

Gem Asset Acquisition LLC 336 854-8200
139 S Walnut Cir Greensboro (27409) *(G-7033)*

Gem Buoy Incorporated 252 469-3680
3004 Lansdowne Dr Tarboro (27886) *(G-15105)*

Gem Mountain, Spruce Pine Also Called: Buchanan Gem Stone Mines Inc *(G-14632)*

Gem Publishing LLC 828 885-5272
1950 Indian Creek Rd Balsam Grove (28708) *(G-891)*

Gem-Dandy, Madison Also Called: Madison Company Inc *(G-10079)*

Gem-Dandy, Madison Also Called: The Madison Company Inc *(G-10088)*

Gemseal, Charlotte Also Called: Gem Asset Acquisition LLC *(G-2814)*

Gemseal Pvments Pdts - Raleigh, Cary Also Called: Gem Asset Acquisition LLC *(G-1772)*

Gemseal Pvmnts Pdts - Chrlotte, Charlotte Also Called: Gem Asset Acquisition LLC *(G-2815)*

Gen Trak, Liberty Also Called: Sfp Research Inc *(G-9831)*

Genco 919 963-4227
130 Four Oaks Pkwy Four Oaks (27524) *(G-6105)*

Gene Franklin Brisson, Bladenboro Also Called: Columbus Industries LLC *(G-1146)*

Gene Leather Mean 910 325-7098
333 Highway 172 Hubert (28539) *(G-8748)*

Genelect Services Inc 828 255-7999
50 Glendale Ave Asheville (28803) *(G-632)*

Generac Distributors, Asheville Also Called: Genelect Services Inc *(G-632)*

General Contracting, Rocky Point Also Called: Carlton Enterprizes LLC *(G-13743)*

General Contractor, Greensboro Also Called: Kcs Imprv & Cnstr Co Inc *(G-7147)*

General Control Equipment Co 704 588-0484
456 Crompton St Charlotte (28273) *(G-2816)*

General Dynamics Corporation 336 698-8571
5440 Millstream Rd Ste W300 Mc Leansville (27301) *(G-10390)*

General Dynamics Worldwide, Fort Bragg Also Called: General Dynmics Mssion Systems *(G-6089)*

General Dynmics Mssion Systems 910 497-7900
6812 Butner Rd And Letterman St Bldg 8 Fort Bragg (28310) *(G-6089)*

General Dynmics Mssion Systems 336 323-9752
3801 Boren Dr Greensboro (27407) *(G-7034)*

General Dynmics Mssion Systems 336 698-8000
5440 Millstream Rd Ste W300 Mc Leansville (27301) *(G-10391)*

General Elastic Corporation 336 431-8714
6086 Old Mendenhall Rd High Point (27263) *(G-8364)*

General Elastic Sales, High Point Also Called: General Elastic Corporation *(G-8364)*

General Electric Company 704 561-5700
4601 Park Rd Ste 400 Charlotte (28209) *(G-2817)*

General Electric Company 704 821-8260
171 Associate Ln Indian Trail (28079) *(G-8937)*

General Electric Company 919 563-7445
I-85 Buckhorn Rd Mebane (27302) *(G-10410)*

General Electric Company 919 563-5561
6801 Industrial Dr Mebane (27302) *(G-10411)*

General Electric Company 910 675-5000
3901 Castle Hayne Rd Wilmington (28401) *(G-16230)*

General Fertilizer Eqp Inc 336 299-4711
429 Edwardia Dr Greensboro (27409) *(G-7035)*

General Foam Plastics Corp 757 857-0153
501 Daniel St Tarboro (27886) *(G-15106)*

General Foods Distributors 919 279-7236
207 E Sycamore St Zebulon (27597) *(G-17128)*

General Glass International, Rockingham Also Called: Ggi Glass Distributors Corp *(G-13627)*

General Industries Inc 919 751-1791
3048 Thoroughfare Rd Goldsboro (27534) *(G-6615)*

General Machining Inc 336 342-2759
37 W Plymouth Reidsville (27320) *(G-13519)*

General Mch Wldg of Burlington 336 227-5400
3304 Maple Ave Burlington (27215) *(G-1419)*

General McRocircuits - E W LLC 704 663-5975
1133 N Main St Mooresville (28115) *(G-10956)*

General Metals Inc 919 202-0100
328 E Main St Pine Level (27568) *(G-12209)*

General Microcircuits Inc 704 663-5975
1133 N Main St Mooresville (28115) *(G-10957)*

General Motor Repair & Svc Inc 336 292-1715
2206 Westbrook St Greensboro (27407) *(G-7036)*

General Painting & Woodwork 828 318-1252
16 Willow Creek Dr Asheville (28803) *(G-633)*

General Precision Svc 919 553-2604
321 E Main St Clayton (27520) *(G-3980)*

General Refrigeration Company 919 661-4727
96 Shipwash Dr Garner (27529) *(G-6273)*

General Shale Brick, Wilmington Also Called: General Shale Brick Inc *(G-16231)*

General Shale Brick Inc 704 937-7431
1622 Longbranch Rd Grover (28073) *(G-7607)*

General Shale Brick Inc 919 775-2121
300 Brick Plant Rd Moncure (27559) *(G-10622)*

General Shale Brick Inc 919 828-0541
8820 Westgate Park Dr Raleigh (27617) *(G-12793)*

General Shale Brick Inc 919 775-2121
2507 Jefferson Davis Hwy Sanford (27332) *(G-14124)*

General Shale Brick Inc 910 452-3498
3750 Us Highway 421 N Wilmington (28401) *(G-16231)*

General Steel Drum LLC (PA) 704 525-7160
4500 South Blvd Charlotte (28209) *(G-2818)*

General Wholesale Bldg Sup Co (PA) 252 638-5861
3321 Neuse Blvd New Bern (28560) *(G-11806)*

General Wood Preserving Co Inc 910 371-3131
1901 Wood Treatment Rd Ne Leland (28451) *(G-9546)*

Generations L LLC 336 835-3095
220 Winston Rd Jonesville (28642) *(G-9097)*

Generator Supercenter Raleigh 919 925-3434
8601 Glenwood Ave Raleigh (27617) *(G-12794)*

Generics Bidco II LLC 980 389-2501
3700 Woodpark Blvd Ste A Charlotte (28206) *(G-2819)*

Generics Bidco II LLC (DH) 704 612-8830
3241 Woodpark Blvd Charlotte (28206) *(G-2820)*

Genesis Water Technologies Inc 704 360-5165
10130 Perimeter Pkwy Ste 200 Charlotte (28216) *(G-2821)*

Genesis Wldg & Fabrication LLC 336 622-9533
6029 Kirkman Street Ext Liberty (27298) *(G-9814)*

Genesys Cloud Services Inc 317 872-3000
4307 Emperor Blvd Ste 300 Durham (27703) *(G-5113)*

Genesys Technology Inc 336 789-0763
506 Bennett St Mount Airy (27030) *(G-11510)*

Genetic Medicine Building, Chapel Hill Also Called: Viiv Healthcare Company *(G-2093)*

Geneva Software Co Inc 336 275-8887
445 Dolley Madison Rd Ste 402 Greensboro (27410) *(G-7037)*

Genie Products, Brevard Also Called: Grey Holdings Inc *(G-1274)*

Genie Trcking Sltons Lbels LLC 919 201-2600
111 Neuse Ridge Dr Clayton (27527) *(G-3981)*

Genixus, Concord *Also Called: Genixus Corp (G-4272)*
Genixus, Kannapolis *Also Called: Genixus Corp (G-9120)*
Genixus Corp.. 877 436-4987
  4715 Corporate Dr Nw Ste 100 Concord (28027) *(G-4272)*
Genixus Corp (PA).. 877 436-4987
  150 N Research Campus Dr Kannapolis (28081) *(G-9120)*
Genotech Inc... 919 369-4947
  413 Legault Dr Cary (27513) *(G-1773)*
Genpak, Charlotte *Also Called: Genpak LLC (G-2823)*
Genpak, Charlotte *Also Called: Great Pacific Entps US Inc (G-2859)*
Genpak LLC... 704 588-6202
  1001 Westinghouse Blvd Charlotte (28273) *(G-2822)*
Genpak LLC (DH).. 800 626-6695
  10601 Westlake Dr Charlotte (28273) *(G-2823)*
Gent of Scent.. 980 505-9903
  15137 Taylor Ridge Ln Charlotte (28273) *(G-2824)*
Gentle Machine and Tool Inc................................... 336 492-5055
  2716 Us Highway 601 N Mocksville (27028) *(G-10576)*
Gentry Mills Inc.. 704 983-5555
  2035 Kingsley Dr Albemarle (28001) *(G-86)*
Gentry Plastics Inc... 704 864-4300
  1808 Bradbury Ct Gastonia (28052) *(G-6407)*
Gentrys Cabnt Doors... 336 957-8787
  2872 Austin Little Mtn Rd Roaring River (28669) *(G-13593)*
Geo Comp, Shelby *Also Called: Geocomp Inc (G-14319)*
Geo Specialty Chemicals Inc.................................... 252 793-2121
  Main St Extension Plymouth (27962) *(G-12373)*
Geo-Lin Inc... 336 884-0648
  107 Hillstone Dr Jamestown (27282) *(G-9050)*
Geocomp Inc.. 704 480-7688
  1901 W Dixon Blvd Shelby (28152) *(G-14319)*
Geographics Screenprinting Inc.............................. 704 357-3300
  3622 Green Park Cir Charlotte (28217) *(G-2825)*
Geometry Workbook... 252 714-3327
  3722 Providence Plan Ln Charlotte (28270) *(G-2826)*
Geonics.. 704 956-7999
  4994 Aztec Dr Concord (28025) *(G-4273)*
George Clinical Inc... 919 789-2022
  120 Penmarc Dr Raleigh (27603) *(G-12795)*
George F Wlson Wldg Fbrication............................. 828 262-1668
  1777 Nc Highway 194 N Boone (28607) *(G-1199)*
George P Gatling Logging....................................... 252 465-8983
  223 Nc Highway 32 S Sunbury (27979) *(G-14996)*
George R Hardie.. 336 263-7920
  5529 Ferguson Rd Liberty (27298) *(G-9815)*
George W Dahl Company Inc.................................. 336 668-4444
  8439 Triad Dr Greensboro (27409) *(G-7038)*
George's Bbq Sauce, Nashville *Also Called: Georges Sauces LLC (G-11745)*
Georges Sauces LLC... 252 459-3084
  1173 Womble Rd Nashville (27856) *(G-11745)*
Georgia Poultry Equipment Co, Newton Grove *Also Called: Hog Slat Incorporated (G-11988)*
Georgia Pratt Box Inc... 919 872-3007
  5620 Departure Dr Raleigh (27616) *(G-12796)*
Georgia-Carolina Quarries Inc (PA)......................... 336 786-6978
  1700 Fancy Gap Rd Mount Airy (27030) *(G-11511)*
Georgia-Pacific, Asheboro *Also Called: Georgia-Pacific LLC (G-440)*
Georgia-Pacific, Dudley *Also Called: Georgia-Pacific LLC (G-4843)*
Georgia-Pacific, Dudley *Also Called: Georgia-Pacific LLC (G-4844)*
Georgia-Pacific, Middleburg *Also Called: Georgia-Pacific LLC (G-10443)*
Georgia-Pacific LLC... 336 629-2151
  200 Mcdowell Rd Asheboro (27205) *(G-440)*
Georgia-Pacific LLC... 919 580-1078
  139 Brewington Dr Dudley (28333) *(G-4843)*
Georgia-Pacific LLC... 919 736-2722
  2457b Old Mt Olive Hwy Dudley (28333) *(G-4844)*
Georgia-Pacific LLC... 252 438-2238
  Hwy 158 And Interstate 85 Middleburg (27556) *(G-10443)*
Georgia-Pacific LLC... 910 642-5041
  1980 Georgia Pacific Rd Whiteville (28472) *(G-15963)*
Geosonics Inc... 919 790-9500
  5874 Faringdon Pl Ste 100 Raleigh (27609) *(G-12797)*

Geosurfaces Southeast Inc...................................... 704 660-3000
  150 River Park Rd Mooresville (28117) *(G-10958)*
Geotrak Incorporated.. 919 303-1467
  2521 Schieffelin Rd Ste 136 Apex (27502) *(G-194)*
Gerald Fisheries LLC.. 907 518-0004
  104 Coree Way New Bern (28562) *(G-11807)*
Gerald Hartsoe... 336 498-3233
  3109 Tom Brown Rd Randleman (27317) *(G-13471)*
Gerald's Yarns, Lincolnton *Also Called: Marilyn Cook (G-9905)*
Gerbing's Heated Clothing, Greensboro *Also Called: Gerbings LLC (G-7039)*
Gerbings LLC... 800 646-5916
  816 S Elm St Ste D Greensboro (27406) *(G-7039)*
Gerdau Ameristeel US Inc....................................... 704 596-0361
  6601 Lakeview Rd Charlotte (28269) *(G-2827)*
Gerdau Ameristeel US Inc....................................... 919 833-9737
  2126 Garner Rd Raleigh (27610) *(G-12798)*
Gerrard Family LLC.. 704 545-5117
  7218 Ashbourne Ln Mint Hill (28227) *(G-10534)*
Gerresheimer Glass Inc... 828 433-5000
  114 Wamsutta Mill Rd Morganton (28655) *(G-11215)*
Gerringer Enterprises.. 336 227-6535
  180 Spoon Dr Burlington (27217) *(G-1420)*
Gersan Industries Incorporated............................... 336 886-5455
  607 Blake Ave High Point (27260) *(G-8365)*
Gerson & Gerson Inc... 252 235-2441
  10601 E Finch Ave Middlesex (27557) *(G-10450)*
Ges Industries (PA).. 252 430-8851
  78 Walter Grissom Rd Kittrell (27544) *(G-9396)*
Gesipa Fasteners Usa Inc.. 336 751-1555
  126 Quality Dr Mocksville (27028) *(G-10577)*
Gesipa Fasteners Usa Inc (PA)................................. 609 208-1740
  126 Quality Dr Mocksville (27028) *(G-10578)*
Get Custom Print... 336 682-3891
  504 Edgewood St Kernersville (27284) *(G-9202)*
Get Stuck Inc.. 336 698-3277
  2710 N Church St Greensboro (27405) *(G-7040)*
Get Wickd Candles.. 704 437-9062
  366 Weathers Creek Rd Troutman (28166) *(G-15379)*
Getbridge LLC.. 919 645-2800
  434 Fayetteville St Fl 9 Raleigh (27601) *(G-12799)*
GF Machining Solutions.. 704 927-8929
  13245 Reese Blvd W Ste 100 Huntersville (28078) *(G-8826)*
Gfl Environmental Company, Raleigh *Also Called: Waste Industries Usa LLC (G-13412)*
Gfm Industries LLC.. 614 439-5349
  3948 Clapp Mill Rd Burlington (27215) *(G-1421)*
Gfsi Holdings LLC (HQ)... 336 519-8080
  9700 Commerce Pkwy Winston Salem (27105) *(G-16720)*
Ggi Glass Distributors Corp.................................... 910 895-2022
  208 Silver Grove Church Rd Rockingham (28379) *(G-13627)*
Ggr, Leland *Also Called: Gale Global Research Inc (G-9545)*
Ggs Technical Publications..................................... 336 256-9600
  420 Gallimore Dairy Rd Ste A Greensboro (27409) *(G-7041)*
Ggs Woodworking... 704 279-5482
  1725 Lower Palmer Rd Salisbury (28146) *(G-13967)*
Ghost Hawk Intel LLC... 910 235-0323
  1 Troy Ct Pinehurst (28374) *(G-12222)*
Giant Cement Co... 704 583-1568
  10910 Texland Blvd Charlotte (28273) *(G-2828)*
Giant Wake Forest LLC.. 919 556-7433
  11216 Capital Blvd Ste 108 Wake Forest (27587) *(G-15559)*
Gibbs Machine Company Incorporated.................. 336 856-1907
  2012 Fairfax Rd Greensboro (27407) *(G-7042)*
Gibbs Performance Spc Inc.................................... 704 746-2225
  7075 Aviation Blvd Nw Ste B Concord (28027) *(G-4274)*
Gibraltar Packaging Inc... 910 439-6137
  5465 Nc Highway 73 W Mount Gilead (27306) *(G-11600)*
Gibson Accumulator LLC.. 336 449-4753
  2208 Airpark Rd Burlington (27215) *(G-1422)*
Gibson Mill Ciderworks, Concord *Also Called: Cabarrus Brewing Company LLC (G-4216)*
Giddy LLC... 813 767-1344
  326 Azalea Dr Chapel Hill (27517) *(G-2021)*

ALPHABETIC SECTION

Gifted Hands Styling Salon... 828 781-2781
　1316 Us Highway 70 Sw Hickory (28602) *(G-8032)*

Gigabeam Corporation 919 206-4426
　4021 Stirrup Creek Dr Ste 400 Durham (27703) *(G-5114)*

Gik Inc... 919 872-9498
　1801 Saint Albans Dr Ste B Raleigh (27609) *(G-12800)*

Gilbarco Inc (HQ).. 336 547-5000
　7300 W Friendly Ave Greensboro (27410) *(G-7043)*

Gilbarco Veeder-Root, Greensboro *Also Called: Gilbarco Inc (G-7043)*

Gilbert Hardwood Centers, Trinity *Also Called: Gilbert Hardwoods Inc (G-15342)*

Gilbert Hardwoods Inc (PA)... 336 431-2127
　12990 Trinity Rd Trinity (27370) *(G-15342)*

Gildan Activewear (eden) Inc... 336 623-9555
　602 E Meadow Rd Eden (27288) *(G-5491)*

Gildan Yarns LLC... 704 633-5133
　2121 Heilig Rd Salisbury (28146) *(G-13968)*

Gilead Sciences Inc... 650 574-3000
　305 Church At North Hills St Raleigh (27609) *(G-12801)*

Gilero LLC (HQ)... 919 595-8220
　4319 S Alston Ave Durham (27713) *(G-5115)*

Giles Chemical Corporation.. 828 452-4784
　75 Giles Pl Waynesville (28786) *(G-15805)*

Giles Chemical Corporation (HQ).. 828 452-4784
　102 Commerce St Waynesville (28786) *(G-15806)*

Giles Chemical Industries, Waynesville *Also Called: Giles Chemical Corporation (G-15806)*

Gilkey Lumber Co Inc... 828 286-9069
　2250 Us 221 Hwy N Rutherfordton (28139) *(G-13872)*

Gillespies Fabrication Design, Salisbury *Also Called: Gillespies Fbrction Design Inc (G-13969)*

Gillespies Fbrction Design Inc... 704 636-2349
　2231 Old Wilkesboro Rd Salisbury (28144) *(G-13969)*

Gilley Printers Inc... 910 295-6317
　22 Rattlesnake Trl Pinehurst (28374) *(G-12223)*

Gillikin Marine Railways Inc... 252 726-7284
　195 Morgan St Beaufort (28516) *(G-958)*

Gilmore Globl Lgstics Svcs Inc.. 919 277-2700
　101 Southcenter Ct Ste 100-E Morrisville (27560) *(G-11347)*

Ginas Processing & Prtg Ctr.. 910 476-0037
　114 Harris Ln Raeford (28376) *(G-12422)*

Ginger Supreme Inc.. 919 812-8986
　4925 Lett Rd Apex (27539) *(G-195)*

Gingers Revenge LLC... 828 505-2462
　829 Riverside Dr Ste 100 Asheville (28801) *(G-634)*

Gingras Sleep Medicine PA.. 704 944-0562
　6207 Park South Dr Ste 101 Charlotte (28210) *(G-2829)*

Gini's Beverages, Cary *Also Called: Sakun Inc (G-1878)*

Ginkgo Print Studio LLC.. 828 275-6300
　1 Grace Ave Asheville (28804) *(G-635)*

Ginkgo Stone LLC.. 704 451-8678
　5340 Camilla Dr Charlotte (28226) *(G-2830)*

Ginny O s Inc... 919 816-7276
　946 Penny Branch Rd Warsaw (28398) *(G-15668)*

Girlie Jams... 704 575-5815
　21200 Cold Spring Ln Cornelius (28031) *(G-4549)*

Gitsum Precision LLC.. 336 453-3998
　390 Duggins Rd Stoneville (27048) *(G-14958)*

Give You Hope Industries Inc... 336 608-2774
　2840 Kensington Rd Winston Salem (27106) *(G-16721)*

Giving Tree Woodworks LLc.. 704 930-5847
　204 Brookstone Dr Mount Holly (28120) *(G-11636)*

GK Software USA, Raleigh *Also Called: GK Software Usa Inc (G-12802)*

GK Software Usa Inc.. 984 255-7995
　9121 Anson Way Ste 150 Raleigh (27615) *(G-12802)*

GKN Automotive, Newton *Also Called: GKN Driveline Newton LLC (G-11933)*

GKN Automotive, Newton *Also Called: GKN Driveline Newton LLC (G-11934)*

GKN Dna Inc... 919 304-7378
　1067 Trollingwood Hawflds Rd Mebane (27302) *(G-10412)*

GKN Driveline Newton LLC (HQ)... 828 428-3711
　1848 Gkn Way Newton (28658) *(G-11933)*

GKN Driveline Newton LLC.. 828 428-5292
　2900 S Us 321 Hwy Newton (28658) *(G-11934)*

GKN Driveline North Amer Inc... 919 304-7252
　1067 Trollingwood Hawflds Rd Mebane (27302) *(G-10413)*

GKN Driveline North Amer Inc... 336 364-6200
　6400 Durham Rd Timberlake (27583) *(G-15314)*

GKN Driveline Roxboro, Timberlake *Also Called: GKN Driveline North Amer Inc (G-15314)*

GKN Sinter Metals LLC.. 828 464-0642
　407 Thornburg Dr Se Conover (28613) *(G-4459)*

Glacier Forestry Inc.. 704 902-2594
　135 Jocelyn Ln Apt 108 Mooresville (28117) *(G-10959)*

Gladiator Enterprises Inc... 336 944-6932
　5505 Weslo Willow Dr Greensboro (27409) *(G-7044)*

Gladsons Logging LLC.. 252 670-8813
　8902 Nc Highway 306 S Aurora (27806) *(G-835)*

Glam Gal, Castle Hayne *Also Called: AC Valor Reyes LLC (G-1941)*

Glaser Designs Inc... 415 552-3188
　2825 Seclusion Ct Apt A Raleigh (27612) *(G-12803)*

Glass & Window Warehouse, Siler City *Also Called: Orare Inc (G-14429)*

Glass Jug.. 919 818-6907
　5410 Nc Highway 55 Ste V Durham (27713) *(G-5116)*

Glass Jug LLC.. 919 813-0135
　5410 Nc Highway 55 Ste V Durham (27713) *(G-5117)*

Glass Unlimited, High Point *Also Called: Glass Unlimited High Point Inc (G-8366)*

Glass Unlimited High Point Inc... 336 889-4551
　2149 Brevard Rd High Point (27263) *(G-8366)*

Glass Works of Hickory Inc.. 828 322-2122
　1040 Old Lenoir Rd Ste B Hickory (28601) *(G-8033)*

Glatfelter, Charlotte *Also Called: Glatfelter Corporation (G-2831)*

Glatfelter Composite Fibers NA, Pisgah Forest *Also Called: Glatfelter Corporation (G-12323)*

Glatfelter Corporation (PA).. 704 885-2555
　4350 Congress St Ste 600 Charlotte (28209) *(G-2831)*

Glatfelter Corporation.. 828 877-2110
　2795 King Rd Pisgah Forest (28768) *(G-12323)*

Glatfelter Inds Asheville Inc... 828 670-0041
　1265 Sand Hill Rd Candler (28715) *(G-1580)*

Glatfelter Mt Holly LLC... 704 812-2299
　100 Buckeye Dr Mount Holly (28120) *(G-11637)*

Glatflter Sntara Old Hckry Inc (DH)... 615 526-2100
　4350 Congress St Ste 600 Charlotte (28209) *(G-2832)*

Glaxosmithkline, Durham *Also Called: Glaxosmithkline LLC (G-5120)*

Glaxosmithkline, Zebulon *Also Called: Glaxosmithkline LLC (G-17129)*

Glaxosmithkline 69 Pharma.. 612 719-4438
　1 Moore Dr Durham (27709) *(G-5118)*

Glaxosmithkline LLC.. 704 962-5786
　8625 Covedale Crossings Cir Cornelius (28031) *(G-4550)*

Glaxosmithkline LLC.. 919 483-5302
　5 3313 Gsk Co Durham (27713) *(G-5119)*

Glaxosmithkline LLC.. 919 483-2100
　410 Blackwell St Durham (27701) *(G-5120)*

Glaxosmithkline LLC.. 252 315-9774
　406 Blackwell St Durham (27701) *(G-5121)*

Glaxosmithkline LLC.. 919 483-2100
　2512 S Tricenter Blvd Durham (27713) *(G-5122)*

Glaxosmithkline LLC.. 336 392-3058
　3408 Old Barn Rd Greensboro (27410) *(G-7045)*

Glaxosmithkline LLC.. 919 628-3630
　7030 Kit Creek Rd Morrisville (27560) *(G-11348)*

Glaxosmithkline LLC.. 919 483-5006
　52069 Five Moore Dr Research Triangle Pa (27709) *(G-13551)*

Glaxosmithkline LLC.. 919 269-5000
　1011 N Arendell Ave Zebulon (27597) *(G-17129)*

Glaxosmithkline Services Inc.. 919 483-2100
　5 Moore Dr Durham (27709) *(G-5123)*

Glen Raven Inc... 336 227-6211
　3726 Altamahaw Union Ridge Rd Altamahaw (27202) *(G-122)*

Glen Raven Custom Fabrics LLC... 828 682-2142
　73 E Us Highway 19e Burnsville (28714) *(G-1526)*

Glen Raven Inc (PA).. 336 227-6211
　192 Glen Raven Rd Burlington (27217) *(G-1423)*

Glen Rven Tchnical Fabrics LLC (HQ)... 336 227-6211
　1831 N Park Ave Burlington (27217) *(G-1424)*

Glen Rven Tchnical Fabrics LLC... 336 229-5576
　1821 N Park Ave Burlington (27217) *(G-1425)*

Glen Touch Division — ALPHABETIC SECTION

Glen Touch Division, Altamahaw Also Called: Glen Raven Inc *(G-122)*

Glendon Pyrophllite Rock Quar, Sanford Also Called: Glendon Pyrophyllite Inc *(G-14125)*

Glendon Pyrophyllite Inc 919 464-5243
1789 Clarence Mckeithen Rd Sanford (27330) *(G-14125)*

Glenmark Phrmceuticals Inc USA 704 218-2600
4147 Goldmine Rd Monroe (28110) *(G-10723)*

Glenn Lumber Company Inc 704 434-7873
145 Rockford Rd Shelby (28152) *(G-14320)*

Glenn Lumber Company Inc 704 434-9661
145 Rockford Rd Boiling Springs (28017) *(G-1159)*

Glenn Mauser Company Inc 828 464-8996
3240 20th Ave Se Newton (28658) *(G-11935)*

Glenn Torrance Models LLC 919 761-1363
50 Ward Dr Youngsville (27596) *(G-17082)*

Glenn Trexler & Sons Log Inc 704 694-5644
1095 Bethel Rd Wadesboro (28170) *(G-15510)*

Glennstone Field Office 919 680-8700
4028 Lady Slipper Ln Durham (27704) *(G-5124)*

Glenoit Universal Ltd (PA) 919 735-7111
One Excell Linde Dr Goldsboro (27533) *(G-6616)*

Glenraven.com, Burlington Also Called: Glen Raven Inc *(G-1423)*

Glenraven.com, Burlington Also Called: Glen Rven Tchnical Fabrics LLC *(G-1424)*

Glenwood Village Exxon, Raleigh Also Called: Wmb of Wake County Inc *(G-13426)*

GLG Corporation (PA) 336 784-0396
3410 Thomasville Rd Winston Salem (27107) *(G-16722)*

Glh Systems & Controls Inc 980 581-1304
4667 Love Mill Rd Stanfield (28163) *(G-14679)*

Glia Beauty, Raleigh Also Called: Cryogen LLC *(G-12658)*

Glidden Professional Paint Ctr, Fayetteville Also Called: PPG Architectural Finishes Inc *(G-5899)*

Glidden Professional Paint Ctr, Gastonia Also Called: PPG Architectural Finishes Inc *(G-6493)*

Glidden Professional Paint Ctr, Greensboro Also Called: PPG Architectural Finishes Inc *(G-7271)*

Glidden Professional Paint Ctr, Matthews Also Called: PPG Architectural Finishes Inc *(G-10282)*

Glidden Professional Paint Ctr, Mooresville Also Called: PPG Architectural Finishes Inc *(G-11056)*

Glidden Professional Paint Ctr, Morganton Also Called: PPG Architectural Finishes Inc *(G-11242)*

Glidden Professional Paint Ctr, Raleigh Also Called: PPG Architectural Finishes Inc *(G-13127)*

Glidden Professional Paint Ctr, Raleigh Also Called: PPG Architectural Finishes Inc *(G-13128)*

Glidden Professional Paint Ctr, Salisbury Also Called: PPG Architectural Finishes Inc *(G-14028)*

Glitzbybritt, Greensboro Also Called: Brittany Smith *(G-6858)*

Global, West Jefferson Also Called: Global Manufacturing Svcs Inc *(G-15940)*

Global Bioprotect LLC 336 861-0162
2714 Uwharrie Rd High Point (27263) *(G-8367)*

Global Dominion Enterprise, Charlotte Also Called: Reginald DWayne Dillard *(G-3427)*

Global Door Controls, Charlotte Also Called: Imperial Usa Ltd *(G-2954)*

Global Ecosciences Inc 252 631-6266
7723 Benthill Ct Wake Forest (27587) *(G-15560)*

Global Emssons Systems Inc-USA 704 585-8490
158 Houston Rd Troutman (28166) *(G-15380)*

Global Envmtl Ctrl III Inc 704 603-6155
585 Bonanza Dr Salisbury (28144) *(G-13970)*

Global Filter Source LLC 919 571-4945
6212 Westgate Rd Ste A Raleigh (27617) *(G-12804)*

Global Forming Tech Ltd 919 234-1384
801 Cascade Pointe Ln Ste 102 Cary (27513) *(G-1774)*

Global Graphics Solution, Thomasville Also Called: Wright of Thomasville Inc *(G-15305)*

Global Laser Enrichment LLC 910 819-7255
3901 Castle Hayne Rd Castle Hayne (28429) *(G-1949)*

Global Manufacturing Svcs Inc 336 846-1674
140 Industrial Park Way West Jefferson (28694) *(G-15940)*

Global Nuclear Fuel LLC 910 819-6181
3901 Castle Hayne Rd Wilmington (28401) *(G-16232)*

Global Nuclear Fuel-Americas LLC (HQ) 910 819-5950
3901 Castle Hayne Rd Castle Hayne (28429) *(G-1950)*

Global Packaging Inc 610 666-1608
106 Marks Creek Ln Hamlet (28345) *(G-7622)*

Global Plasma Solutions Inc 980 279-5622
3101 Yorkmont Rd Ste 400 Charlotte (28208) *(G-2833)*

Global Products & Mfg Svcs Inc 360 870-9876
6000 Fairview Rd Ste 1200 Charlotte (28210) *(G-2834)*

Global Products LLC 336 227-7327
144 Industrial Ave Greensboro (27406) *(G-7046)*

Global Resource Corporation 919 972-7803
9400 Globe Center Dr # 101 Morrisville (27560) *(G-11349)*

Global Resource NC Inc 910 793-4770
1001 Broomsedge Ter Wilmington (28412) *(G-16233)*

Global Sensors 704 827-4331
123 N Main St Mount Holly (28120) *(G-11638)*

Global Sensors LLC 704 827-4331
63 Mcadenville Rd Belmont (28012) *(G-992)*

Global Skyware, Smithfield Also Called: Raven Antenna Systems Inc *(G-14478)*

Global Software LLC 919 872-7800
3200 Atlantic Ave Ste 200 Raleigh (27604) *(G-12805)*

Global Software Labs LLC 404 550-4390
304 W Franklin St Monroe (28112) *(G-10724)*

GLOBAL SOFTWARE, LLC, Raleigh Also Called: Global Software LLC *(G-12805)*

Global Stone Impex LLC 336 609-1113
5088 Bartholomews Ln Greensboro (27407) *(G-7047)*

Global Synergy Group Inc 704 254-9886
13663 Providence Rd Ste 370 Matthews (28104) *(G-10318)*

Global Textile Alliance Inc (PA) 336 217-1300
2361 Holiday Loop Reidsville (27320) *(G-13520)*

Global Veneer Sales Inc 336 885-5061
112 Hodgin St High Point (27262) *(G-8368)*

Globalectronics Inc 919 599-6680
8608 Harps Mill Rd Raleigh (27615) *(G-12806)*

Glossy Wicks LLC 980 349-5908
7419 Quail Wood Dr Apt D Charlotte (28226) *(G-2835)*

Glover Corporation Inc 919 821-5535
2401 Atlantic Ave Raleigh (27604) *(G-12807)*

Glover Materials Inc (PA) 252 536-2660
4493 Us Highway 301 Pleasant Hill (27866) *(G-12364)*

Glover Printing Company, Raleigh Also Called: Glover Corporation Inc *(G-12807)*

Glovers Welding LLC 252 586-7692
638 Oak Grove Church Rd Littleton (27850) *(G-9952)*

Gloves-Online Inc 919 468-4244
231 E Johnson St Ste K Cary (27513) *(G-1775)*

Glow Gorgeous, Fayetteville Also Called: Bignisha Rgrts Chill Cream LLC *(G-5770)*

GLS Products LLC 704 334-2425
1209 Lilac Rd Charlotte (28209) *(G-2836)*

Glycotech Inc 910 371-2234
2271 Andrew Jackson Hwy Ne Leland (28451) *(G-9547)*

Glycyx Pharmaceuticals Ltd 919 862-1097
8510 Colonnade Center Dr Raleigh (27615) *(G-12808)*

Glyphus LLC 336 973-4793
4159 Summit Rd Purlear (28665) *(G-12411)*

GM Defense LLC 800 462-8782
4540 Fortune Ave Concord (28027) *(G-4275)*

GM Nameplate NC Division, Monroe Also Called: Boyd Gmn Inc *(G-10668)*

Gma Creative Inc 919 435-6984
504 S White St Wake Forest (27587) *(G-15561)*

Gmd Logging Inc 704 985-5460
44100 Dennis Rd Albemarle (28001) *(G-87)*

Gmg Group LLC 252 441-8374
115 W Saint Clair St Kill Devil Hills (27948) *(G-9258)*

GNB Ventures LLC 704 488-4468
1800 Associates Ln Charlotte (28217) *(G-2837)*

GNH Pharmaceuticals USA LLC 919 820-3077
125 Remount Rd Ste C1 Charlotte (28203) *(G-2838)*

GNT Usa LLC 914 524-0600
One Exberry Dr Dallas (28034) *(G-4643)*

Go Ask Erin LLC 336 747-3777
328 Virgilina Rd Roxboro (27573) *(G-13804)*

Go Energies LLC 877 712-5999
1410 Commonwealth Dr Ste 102b Wilmington (28403) *(G-16234)*

Go Energies Holdings Inc (PA) 910 762-5802
1410 Commonwealth Dr Ste 102b Wilmington (28403) *(G-16235)*

ALPHABETIC SECTION — Goodstuff Juices LLC

Go Ev and Go Green Corp..704 327-9040
9711 David Taylor Dr Apt 106 Charlotte (28262) *(G-2839)*

Go For Green Fleet Svcs LLC...803 306-3683
1911 Greymouth Rd Apt 305 Charlotte (28262) *(G-2840)*

Go Gloves, Cary Also Called: Gloves-Online Inc *(G-1775)*

Go Green Miracle Balm...630 209-0226
17810 Half Moon Ln Apt A Cornelius (28031) *(G-4551)*

Go Green Plumbing, Greensboro Also Called: Go Green Services LLC *(G-7048)*

Go Green Racing..916 295-2621
409 Performance Rd Mooresville (28115) *(G-10960)*

Go Green Services LLC...336 252-2999
300 Pomona Dr Greensboro (27407) *(G-7048)*

Go Postal In Boone Inc...828 262-0027
207 New Market Ctr Boone (28607) *(G-1200)*

Goaero LLC..815 713-1190
7680 Airline Rd Ste C Greensboro (27409) *(G-7049)*

Goals In Service LLC...919 440-2656
103 Richard Dupree Ln Seven Springs (28578) *(G-14267)*

Gocaissoncom...336 454-4610
3210 Dillon Rd Jamestown (27282) *(G-9051)*

God's Son Plumbing Repair, Wilson Also Called: Gods Son Plumbing Inc *(G-16501)*

Godfrey Group, Cary Also Called: Portable Displays LLC *(G-1855)*

Godfrey Industrial Welding..919 604-0498
439 Ragan Rd Sanford (27330) *(G-14126)*

Godfrey Lumber Company Inc (PA)...704 872-6366
1715 Amity Hill Rd Statesville (28677) *(G-14804)*

Godglamit LLC..336 558-1097
620 N Church St Apt 2216 Charlotte (28202) *(G-2841)*

Gods Son Plumbing Inc..252 299-0983
1711 Roxbury Dr Wilson (27893) *(G-16501)*

Godwin Door & Hardware Inc..919 580-0543
105 E Holly St Goldsboro (27530) *(G-6617)*

Godwin Manufacturing Co Inc (PA)...910 897-4995
17666 Us 421 S Dunn (28334) *(G-4870)*

Goembel Inc...919 303-0485
7303 Vanclaybon Rd Apex (27523) *(G-196)*

Goffstar Inc..704 895-3878
5015 W W T Harris Blvd Ste F Charlotte (28269) *(G-2842)*

Gogofiber, Waynesville Also Called: Edge Broadband Solutions LLC *(G-15803)*

Gogopanels...702 800-1941
1600 Carson St Raleigh (27608) *(G-12809)*

Goins Signs Inc..336 427-5783
1811 Victory Hill Church Rd Stoneville (27048) *(G-14959)*

Gold Bond Building Pdts LLC (HQ)...704 365-7300
2001 Rexford Rd Charlotte (28211) *(G-2843)*

Gold Boy Music Publicatio..919 500-3023
108 Highland Trl Chapel Hill (27516) *(G-2022)*

Gold Canyon Candles...828 358-5729
2724 Knob Hill Dr Connelly Springs (28612) *(G-4401)*

Gold Creek Inc..336 468-4495
3441 Lone Hickory Rd Hamptonville (27020) *(G-7670)*

Gold Leaf Literary Svcs LLC..864 915-0226
308 Cumberland Ave Asheville (28801) *(G-636)*

Gold Leaf Publishers, Raleigh Also Called: News and Observer Pubg Co *(G-13063)*

Gold Medal North Carolina II...336 665-4997
410 Gallimore Dairy Rd Ste G Greensboro (27409) *(G-7050)*

Gold Medal Products Co...336 665-4997
410 Gallimore Dairy Rd Ste G Greensboro (27409) *(G-7051)*

Gold Medal Products-Carolina, Greensboro Also Called: Gold Medal Products Co *(G-7051)*

Gold Refinery...336 501-2977
2177 Scott Rd Browns Summit (27214) *(G-1306)*

Gold Refinery...336 471-4817
3954 Huttons Lake Ct High Point (27265) *(G-8369)*

Gold Star...704 651-8186
129 Oak Park Dr. Mooresville (28115) *(G-10961)*

Gold Toe Stores Inc (DH)..828 464-0751
514 W 21st St Newton (28658) *(G-11936)*

Golden Grove USA, Mount Olive Also Called: Carolina Nut Inc *(G-11658)*

Golden Pop Shop LLC...704 236-9455
9805 Statesville Rd Ste 6012 Charlotte (28269) *(G-2844)*

Golden Rctangle Enterprises Inc..828 389-3336
2966 Nc 69 Hayesville (28904) *(G-7766)*

Golden Valley Mfg Plant Div, Bostic Also Called: Milliken & Company *(G-1265)*

Golding Farms, Winston Salem Also Called: Golding Farms Foods Inc *(G-16723)*

Golding Farms Foods Inc (PA)..336 766-6161
6061 Gun Club Rd Winston Salem (27103) *(G-16723)*

Goldmine Software..704 944-3579
10130 Mallard Creek Rd Ste 300 Charlotte (28262) *(G-2845)*

Goldsboro Mil & Grn Stor Co, Goldsboro Also Called: Goldsboro Milling Company *(G-6618)*

Goldsboro Milling Company..252 753-5371
3628 South Fields St Farmville (27828) *(G-5737)*

Goldsboro Milling Company (PA)..919 778-3130
938 Millers Chapel Rd Goldsboro (27534) *(G-6618)*

Goldsboro Neon Sign Co Inc..919 735-2035
712 N George St Goldsboro (27530) *(G-6619)*

Goldsboro News-Argus, Goldsboro Also Called: Wayne Printing Company Inc *(G-6669)*

Goldsboro Strter Altrntor Svc..919 735-6745
105 E Oak St Goldsboro (27530) *(G-6620)*

Goldsmith By Rudi Ltd..828 693-1030
434 N Main St Hendersonville (28792) *(G-7856)*

Goldtoemoretz LLC...828 464-0751
514 W 21st St Newton (28658) *(G-11937)*

Golf Associates, Asheville Also Called: Pinkston Properties LLC *(G-732)*

Golf Associates Advertising Co...828 252-6544
91 Westside Dr Asheville (28806) *(G-637)*

Golf Associates Score Card Co, Asheville Also Called: Golf Associates Advertising Co *(G-637)*

Golf Pride, Pinehurst Also Called: Eaton Corporation *(G-12221)*

Golf Shop...704 636-7070
747 Club Dr Salisbury (28144) *(G-13971)*

Golfstar Technology LLC...910 420-3122
75 Lakewood Dr Pinehurst (28374) *(G-12224)*

Golfworks...910 796-3160
102 Old Eastwood Rd Ste C2 Wilmington (28403) *(G-16236)*

Gom Americas Inc...704 912-1600
9319 Robert D Snyder Rd 442 & 445 Charlotte (28223) *(G-2846)*

Gonzalez Cab Installers LLC..336 897-1046
2404 New Orleans St Greensboro (27406) *(G-7052)*

Gonzalez Welding Inc..336 270-8179
817 E Parker St Graham (27253) *(G-6690)*

Good Bros Ginger Brew LLC...828 279-2512
516 Roy Forrester Rd Mars Hill (28754) *(G-10195)*

Good Earth Ministries...828 287-9826
156 River Ridge Pkwy Rutherfordton (28139) *(G-13873)*

Good Grief Marketing LLC...336 989-1984
2609 E Market St Greensboro (27401) *(G-7053)*

Good Measure Graphics, Kill Devil Hills Also Called: Gmg Group LLC *(G-9258)*

Good News Iphc Ministries Inc..919 906-2104
102 E Doris Ave Jacksonville (28540) *(G-9003)*

Good Will Publishers Inc (PA)...704 853-3237
1520 S York Rd Gastonia (28052) *(G-6408)*

Goodberry Creamery Inc (PA)..919 878-8870
305 Capcom Ave Wake Forest (27587) *(G-15562)*

Goodberrys Creamery Rest, Wake Forest Also Called: Goodberry Creamery Inc *(G-15562)*

Gooder Grafix Inc..828 349-4097
1021 E Main St Franklin (28734) *(G-6131)*

Goodman Millwork Inc..704 633-2421
201 Lumber St Salisbury (28144) *(G-13972)*

Goodnight Brothers Prod Co Inc (PA)...828 264-8892
372 Industrial Park Dr Boone (28607) *(G-1201)*

Goodrich Corporation (HQ)..704 423-7000
2730 W Tyvola Rd Charlotte (28217) *(G-2847)*

Goodrich Corporation...704 282-2500
4115 Corporate Center Dr Monroe (28110) *(G-10725)*

Goodrich Corporation...704 282-2500
4115 Corporate Center Dr Monroe (28110) *(G-10726)*

Goodson Enterprises Inc...410 303-5053
99 High Meadows Dr Candler (28715) *(G-1581)*

Goodson S All Terrain Log Inc..910 347-7919
173 Goodson Trl Jacksonville (28546) *(G-9004)*

Goodsons All Terrain Log...910 934-8451
137 Rustic Ln Jacksonville (28546) *(G-9005)*

Goodstuff Juices LLC..252 347-2341
803 Moye Blvd Ste A Greenville (27834) *(G-7532)*

Goodwill Employment & Training... 704 873-5005
124 Fourth Crescent Pl Statesville (28625) *(G-14805)*

Goodyear, Holly Springs *Also Called: Goodyear Tire & Rubber Company (G-8700)*

Goodyear, Oxford *Also Called: Perry Brothers Tire Svc Inc (G-12140)*

Goodyear, Statesville *Also Called: Goodyear Tire & Rubber Company (G-14806)*

Goodyear, Winston Salem *Also Called: Goodyear Tire & Rubber Company (G-16724)*

Goodyear Tire & Rubber Company... 910 488-9295
6650 Ramsey St Fayetteville (28311) *(G-5830)*

Goodyear Tire & Rubber Company... 919 552-9340
932 N Main St Holly Springs (27540) *(G-8700)*

Goodyear Tire & Rubber Company... 704 928-4500
108 Business Park Dr Statesville (28677) *(G-14806)*

Goodyear Tire & Rubber Company... 336 794-0035
130 Country Club Ln Winston Salem (27104) *(G-16724)*

Goose and Monkey Brewhouse LLC... 336 239-0206
401 S Railroad St Lexington (27292) *(G-9724)*

Goose and The Monkey Brewhouse, Lexington *Also Called: Goose and Monkey Brewhouse LLC (G-9724)*

Gordon Enterprises... 919 776-8784
3125 Hawkins Ave Sanford (27330) *(G-14127)*

Gordon Wldg & Fabrication LLC... 336 406-7471
5311 Bailey Rd Greensboro (27406) *(G-7054)*

Gore S Mar Met Fabrication Inc... 910 763-6066
302 N Channel Haven Dr Wilmington (28409) *(G-16237)*

Gore S Trlr Manufacturer S Inc... 910 642-2246
305 Gores Trailer Rd Whiteville (28472) *(G-15964)*

Gorilla Offroad Company... 815 715-6003
414 Virginia Water Dr Rolesville (27571) *(G-13757)*

Gormac Custom Mfg Inc... 828 891-9984
28 Wild Dogwood Trl Arden (28704) *(G-334)*

Goshen Engineering Inc... 919 429-9798
439 Nc Highway 55 E Mount Olive (28365) *(G-11661)*

Goshen House & Trading LLC... 832 407-8153
744 E Chatham St Ste G Cary (27511) *(G-1776)*

Goslen Printing Company... 336 768-5775
3250 Healy Dr Winston Salem (27103) *(G-16725)*

Gouge Logging... 828 675-9216
360 Rock Creek Rd Burnsville (28714) *(G-1527)*

Gough Econ Inc... 704 399-4501
9400 N Lakebrook Rd Charlotte (28214) *(G-2848)*

Gould & Goodrich, Lillington *Also Called: Point Blank Enterprises Inc (G-9858)*

Goulston Technologies Inc (HQ)... 704 289-6464
700 N Johnson St Monroe (28110) *(G-10727)*

Gounmanned LLC... 919 835-2140
533 Pylon Dr Raleigh (27606) *(G-12810)*

Gourmet Foods USA LLC... 704 248-1724
10415 Bailey Rd Cornelius (28031) *(G-4552)*

Government Sales LLC... 252 726-6315
4644 Arendell St Ste A Morehead City (28557) *(G-11172)*

GP Fabrication Inc... 336 361-0410
9968 Us 158 Reidsville (27320) *(G-13521)*

GP Foam Fabricators Inc... 336 434-3600
220 Swathmore Ave High Point (27263) *(G-8370)*

GP Technology LLC... 919 876-3666
4807 Beryl Rd Raleigh (27606) *(G-12811)*

Gpi, Gastonia *Also Called: Gentry Plastics Inc (G-6407)*

Gpms, Charlotte *Also Called: Global Products & Mfg Svcs Inc (G-2834)*

Gpx Intelligence Inc... 888 260-0706
620a S Elm St Greensboro (27406) *(G-7055)*

Grace & Glory Goods LLC... 828 575-2166
402 Elk Park Dr Asheville (28804) *(G-638)*

Grace and Company LLC... 336 893-7511
183 Wayside Dr Winston Salem (27107) *(G-16726)*

Grace Apparel Company Inc... 828 242-8172
2 Business Park Cir Arden (28704) *(G-335)*

Grace Communion International (PA)... 626 650-2300
3120 Whitehall Park Dr Charlotte (28273) *(G-2849)*

Grace Construction & Glass... 919 805-8380
671 Jack Rd Clayton (27520) *(G-3982)*

Grace Press LLC... 704 277-4007
1235 East Blvd Ste E Charlotte (28203) *(G-2850)*

Grace Southern Embroidery... 336 254-5585
4351 High Rock Rd Gibsonville (27249) *(G-6559)*

Grace-Everett Press... 828 768-7366
175 Carolina Bluebird Loop Arden (28704) *(G-336)*

Graceful Stitching... 704 964-2121
1511 S New Hope Rd Gastonia (28054) *(G-6409)*

Gracefully Broken LLC... 980 474-0309
14129 Perugia Way Apt 102 Charlotte (28273) *(G-2851)*

Gracefully Gifted Hands LLC... 845 248-8743
8480 Honeycutt Rd Ste 200 Raleigh (27615) *(G-12812)*

Gracie & Lucas LLC... 704 707-3207
224 Wiredell Ave Mooresville (28115) *(G-10962)*

Gracie Goodness Inc... 910 792-0800
113 Portwatch Way Ste 101 Wilmington (28412) *(G-16238)*

Gracili Therapeutics Inc... 617 331-4110
15 Tw Alexander Dr Rtp (27709) *(G-13831)*

Grady & Son Atkins Logging... 919 934-7785
1401 Devils Racetrack Rd Four Oaks (27524) *(G-6106)*

Grady Distributing Co Inc... 919 556-5630
640 Park Ave Youngsville (27596) *(G-17083)*

Grady F Smith & Co Inc... 866 900-0983
1705 Evans St Greenville (27834) *(G-7533)*

Grady-White Boats Inc... 252 752-2111
5121 Martin Luther King Jr Hwy Greenville (27834) *(G-7534)*

Graedon Enterprises Inc... 919 493-0448
5900 Beech Bluff Ln Durham (27705) *(G-5125)*

Grafix Unlimited LLC... 919 291-9035
497 Barrette Ln Wendell (27591) *(G-15903)*

Graham Cracker LLC... 336 288-4440
514 Pisgah Church Rd Greensboro (27455) *(G-7056)*

Graham Dyeing & Finishing Inc... 336 228-9981
240 Hawkins St Burlington (27217) *(G-1426)*

Grahams Transportation LLC... 910 627-6880
6642 Keeler Dr Fayetteville (28303) *(G-5831)*

Grailgame Inc... 804 517-3102
301 N Scales St Reidsville (27320) *(G-13522)*

Gram Furniture... 828 241-2836
4513 Nc Highway 10 E Claremont (28610) *(G-3928)*

Grancreations Inc... 704 332-7625
3400 N Graham St Charlotte (28206) *(G-2852)*

Grand Coulee Consortium... 704 943-4343
10735 David Taylor Dr # 5 Charlotte (28262) *(G-2853)*

Grand Encore Charlotte LLC... 513 482-7500
3700 Rose Lake Dr Charlotte (28217) *(G-2854)*

Grand Manor Furniture Inc... 828 758-5521
929 Harrisburg Dr Sw Lenoir (28645) *(G-9613)*

Grandeur Manufacturing Inc... 336 526-2468
2200 Nc Highway 67 Jonesville (28642) *(G-9098)*

Grandfather Vinyrd Winery LLC... 828 963-2400
225 Vineyard Ln Banner Elk (28604) *(G-898)*

Grandmas Sugar Shack... 336 760-8822
209 S Gordon Dr Winston Salem (27104) *(G-16727)*

Grandwell Industries Inc... 919 557-1221
6109 S Nc 55 Hwy Fuquay Varina (27526) *(G-6202)*

Granges Americas Inc... 704 633-6020
1709 Jake Alexander Blvd S Salisbury (28146) *(G-13973)*

Granite Falls Furnaces LLC... 828 324-4394
1230 Premier Rd Granite Falls (28630) *(G-6734)*

Granite Falls Plant, Granite Falls *Also Called: Chase Corporation (G-6729)*

Granite Knitwear Inc (PA)... 704 279-5526
805 S Salisbury Ave Granite Quarry (28072) *(G-6760)*

Granite Memorials Inc... 336 786-6596
636 S Main St Mount Airy (27030) *(G-11512)*

Granite Tactical Vehicles Inc... 336 789-5555
915 Newsome St Mount Airy (27030) *(G-11513)*

Granite Tape Co... 828 396-5614
4 Cedar St Granite Falls (28630) *(G-6735)*

Granville Equipment LLC... 919 693-1425
4602a Watkins Rd Oxford (27565) *(G-12130)*

Granville Miller LLC... 919 865-0602
5305 Burning Oak Ct Raleigh (27606) *(G-12813)*

ALPHABETIC SECTION

Granville Pallet Co Inc 919 528-2347
   3566 Us Highway 15 Oxford (27565) *(G-12131)*

Granville Publishing Co Inc 919 528-2393
   418 N Main St Creedmoor (27522) *(G-4614)*

Grapgic Design, Huntersville *Also Called: Tudg Multimedia Firm (G-8904)*

Graphic Attack Inc 252 491-2174
   Harbinger Commercial Park Ste 34 Harbinger (27941) *(G-7683)*

Graphic Components LLC 336 542-2128
   2800 Patterson St Greensboro (27407) *(G-7057)*

Graphic Design, Spruce Pine *Also Called: Designs By Rachel (G-14639)*

Graphic Finshg Solutions LLC 336 255-7857
   1207 Boston Rd Greensboro (27407) *(G-7058)*

Graphic Image, Wilmington *Also Called: Graphic Image of Cape Fear Inc (G-16239)*

Graphic Image of Cape Fear Inc 910 313-6768
   2840 S College Rd Wilmington (28412) *(G-16239)*

Graphic Impressions Inc 704 596-4921
   7910 District Dr Charlotte (28213) *(G-2855)*

Graphic Master, Youngsville *Also Called: Via Prnting Graphic Design Inc (G-17112)*

Graphic Packaging Intl LLC 704 588-1750
   800 Westinghouse Blvd Charlotte (28273) *(G-2856)*

Graphic Packaging Intl LLC 336 744-1222
   320 W Hanes Mill Rd Winston Salem (27105) *(G-16728)*

Graphic Printing, Elkin *Also Called: Kathie S Mc Daniel (G-5622)*

Graphic Productions Inc 336 765-9335
   301 N Main St Ste 2104 Winston Salem (27101) *(G-16729)*

Graphic Products Inc 919 894-3661
   105 S Wall St Benson (27504) *(G-1035)*

Graphic Rewards Inc 336 969-2733
   130 Northstar Dr Ste B Rural Hall (27045) *(G-13842)*

Graphic Systems Intl Inc 336 662-8686
   7 Lockheed Ct Greensboro (27409) *(G-7059)*

Graphical Creations Inc 704 888-8870
   106 Conveyor Beltway Dr Stanfield (28163) *(G-14680)*

Graphik Dimensions Limited 800 332-8884
   2103 Brentwood St High Point (27263) *(G-8371)*

Graphix Solution Inc 919 213-0371
   1094 Classic Rd Apex (27539) *(G-197)*

Graphixx Screen Printing Inc 919 736-3995
   601 N James St Ste B Goldsboro (27530) *(G-6621)*

Graphx Printing Inc 828 475-4970
   1243 Burkemont Ave Ste A Morganton (28655) *(G-11216)*

Grasche, Hickory *Also Called: Grasche USA Inc (G-8034)*

Grasche USA Inc 828 322-1226
   240 Performance Dr Se Hickory (28602) *(G-8034)*

Grass America Inc 336 996-4041
   1202 Nc Highway 66 S Kernersville (27284) *(G-9203)*

Grassy Creek Vineyard & Winery 336 835-2458
   235 Chatham Cottage Ln State Road (28676) *(G-14726)*

Grassy Ridge Logging Co 919 935-5355
   315 Hallison Highfalls Rd Robbins (27325) *(G-13598)*

Grateful Steps Foundation 828 277-0998
   119 Buffalo Trl Asheville (28805) *(G-639)*

Grateful Union Family Inc (PA) 828 622-3258
   33 Haywood St Asheville (28801) *(G-640)*

Gratz Industries 828 467-6380
   6 Vance Place Dr Asheville (28801) *(G-641)*

Gravel Monkey Geodes LLC 224 848-0401
   106 Mar Joy Dr Dunn (28334) *(G-4871)*

Graveoke Inc 704 534-3480
   1814 Bradenton Dr Charlotte (28206) *(G-2857)*

Graves Inc 252 792-1191
   1909 W Main St Williamston (27892) *(G-16061)*

Gray Flex Systems Inc (PA) 910 897-3539
   232 N Ida St Coats (27521) *(G-4130)*

Gray Manufacturing Co 615 841-3066
   8548 Highland Glen Dr Charlotte (28269) *(G-2858)*

Gray Manufacturing Tech LLC 704 489-2206
   3570 Denver Dr Denver (28037) *(G-4778)*

Gray Metal South Inc (PA) 910 892-2119
   600 N Powell Ave Dunn (28334) *(G-4872)*

Gray Ox Inc 704 662-8247
   155 Quiet Cove Rd Mooresville (28117) *(G-10963)*

Gray Wolf Log Homes Inc 828 586-4662
   538 Big Oak Springs Rd Sylva (28779) *(G-15057)*

Graybeard Distillery Inc 919 361-9980
   4625 Industry Ln Durham (27713) *(G-5126)*

Grayson Wireless, Garner *Also Called: Commscope Technologies LLC (G-6266)*

Graystone Manor Lake Lure LLC 828 395-2099
   730 N Washington St Rutherfordton (28139) *(G-13874)*

Great Eastern Sun, Asheville *Also Called: Great Eastern Sun Trdg Co Inc (G-642)*

Great Eastern Sun Trdg Co Inc 828 665-7790
   92 Mcintosh Rd Asheville (28806) *(G-642)*

Great Pacific Entps US Inc (DH) 980 256-7729
   10601 Westlake Dr Charlotte (28273) *(G-2859)*

Great Products Inc 910 944-2020
   Us Hwy 15 501 Aberdeen (28315) *(G-5)*

Great Star Industrial Usa LLC (DH) 704 892-4965
   9836 Northcross Center Ct Ste A Huntersville (28078) *(G-8827)*

Great Wagon Road Distlg Co LLC 704 246-8740
   4150 Yancey Rd Charlotte (28217) *(G-2860)*

Great Wagon Road Distlg Co LLC 704 469-9330
   227 Southside Dr Ste B Charlotte (28217) *(G-2861)*

Great-R Good Publishing Inc 919 812-1555
   410 Highfield Ave Cary (27519) *(G-1777)*

Greater Wilmington Business 910 343-8600
   101 N 3rd St Wilmington (28401) *(G-16240)*

Grecon Dimter Inc 828 397-5139
   8658 Huffman Ave Connelly Springs (28612) *(G-4402)*

Grecon Inc (HQ) 503 641-7731
   648 Griffith Rd Ste A Charlotte (28217) *(G-2862)*

Grede II LLC 910 428-2111
   530 E Main St Biscoe (27209) *(G-1110)*

Green Apple Studio 919 377-2239
   590 E Chatham St Cary (27511) *(G-1778)*

Green Bean Counters LLC 919 545-2324
   587 Old Farrington Rd Chapel Hill (27517) *(G-2023)*

Green Creek Winery LLC 828 863-4136
   413 Gilbert Rd Columbus (28722) *(G-4174)*

Green Gate Olive Oils Inc 910 986-0880
   105 Cherokee Rd Ste 1b Pinehurst (28374) *(G-12225)*

Green Karma Labs LLC 704 746-2363
   3226 Taylorsville Hwy Statesville (28625) *(G-14807)*

Green Line Defense LLC 828 707-5236
   36 Renaissance Pl Leicester (28748) *(G-9512)*

Green Line Media Inc 828 251-1333
   2 Wall St Ste 214 Asheville (28801) *(G-643)*

Green Pastures Lawn Care 828 758-9265
   5920 Hollow Springs Cir Boomer (28606) *(G-1170)*

Green Power Producers 704 844-8990
   10600 Nations Ford Rd # 150 Charlotte (28273) *(G-2863)*

Green Quest Inc 828 464-7336
   1555 N Rankin Ave Newton (28658) *(G-11938)*

Green River Resource MGT 828 697-0357
   195 Blueberry Farm Rd Zirconia (28790) *(G-17153)*

Green State Landscape & Nrsry, Lumberton *Also Called: Taylco Inc (G-10057)*

Green Stream Technologies Inc 844 499-8880
   3331 Heritage Trade Dr Ste 101 Wake Forest (27587) *(G-15563)*

Green Waste Management LLC 704 289-0720
   101 N Tryon St Ste 112 Charlotte (28246) *(G-2864)*

Greenbrook Design Center, Shelby *Also Called: Walker Woodworking Inc (G-14381)*

Greenbrook Tms Neurohealth Ctr 855 910-4867
   149 Plantation Ridge Dr Ste 150 Mooresville (28117) *(G-10964)*

Greene Imaging & Design Inc 919 787-3737
   6320 Angus Dr Ste E Raleigh (27617) *(G-12814)*

Greene Logging 336 667-6960
   9145 Boone Trl Purlear (28665) *(G-12412)*

Greene Mountain Outdoors LLC 336 670-2186
   2321 Yellow Banks Rd North Wilkesboro (28659) *(G-12011)*

Greene Precision Products Inc 828 262-0116
   4016 Nc Highway 194 N Boone (28607) *(G-1202)*

Greene Products Inc 336 670-2186
   2321 Yellow Banks Rd North Wilkesboro (28659) *(G-12012)*

Greenes Logging 910 533-2021
   760 Mill Creek Church Rd Roseboro (28382) *(G-13785)*

Greenfield Energy LLC 910 509-1805
213 Seacrest Dr Wrightsville Beach (28480) *(G-17025)*

Greenfield Printing Co 910 763-0647
1536 S Front St Wilmington (28401) *(G-16241)*

Greengate Skatepark LLC 336 333-5800
2616 Greengate Dr Greensboro (27406) *(G-7060)*

Greenheck Fan Co 336 852-5788
3816 Patterson St Greensboro (27407) *(G-7061)*

Greenheck Fan Corporation 704 476-3700
2000 Partnership Dr Shelby (28150) *(G-14321)*

Greenleaf Corporation 828 693-0461
761 Roper Rd East Flat Rock (28726) *(G-5476)*

Greenlights LLC 919 766-8900
1211 Walnut St Cary (27511) *(G-1779)*

Greenline 704 333-3377
3412 Monroe Rd Charlotte (28205) *(G-2865)*

Greenline Corporation 704 333-3377
200 Forsyth Hall Dr Ste E Charlotte (28273) *(G-2866)*

Greenology Products LLC 877 473-3650
7020 Cynrow Blvd Raleigh (27615) *(G-12815)*

Greens Machine & Tool Inc 828 654-0042
8 Park Ridge Dr Fletcher (28732) *(G-6008)*

Greensboro Distilling LLC 336 273-6221
321 W Wendover Ave Greensboro (27408) *(G-7062)*

Greensboro Drifters Inc 336 375-6743
4311 King Arthur Pl Greensboro (27405) *(G-7063)*

Greensboro Industrial Platers, Greensboro Also Called: Nb Corporation *(G-7214)*

Greensboro Industrial Platers, Greensboro Also Called: Nb Corporation *(G-7215)*

Greensboro Metal Parts, Jamestown Also Called: Hemco Wire Products Inc *(G-9052)*

Greensboro News & Record LLC 336 373-7000
3001 S Elm Eugene St Greensboro (27406) *(G-7064)*

Greensboro Platers 336 274-7654
725 Kenilworth St Greensboro (27403) *(G-7065)*

Greensboro Tire & Auto Service 336 294-9495
4615 W Market St Ste A Greensboro (27407) *(G-7066)*

Greensboro Tire 3, Greensboro Also Called: Greensboro Tire & Auto Service *(G-7066)*

Greensboro Voice 336 255-1006
407 E Washington St Greensboro (27401) *(G-7067)*

Greensboro Wilbert, Greensboro Also Called: Wilbert Funeral Services Inc *(G-7461)*

Greenstory Globl Gvrnment Mlta 828 446-9278
3811 Gordon St Terrell (28682) *(G-15179)*

Greenville Division, Greenville Also Called: Robert Bosch Tool Corporation *(G-7580)*

Greenville Marble & Gran Works, Greenville Also Called: Conway Development Inc *(G-7505)*

Greenville Rdymx Dpd Team Con, Winterville Also Called: Greenville Ready Mix Concrete *(G-17001)*

Greenville Ready Mix Concrete (PA) 252 756-0119
5039 Nc 11 S Winterville (28590) *(G-17001)*

Greenville Seamless Gutters, Greenville Also Called: Team Gsg LLC *(G-7588)*

Greenville Wood Renewal Inc 828 894-5376
836 Hawk Ridge Dr Mill Spring (28756) *(G-10485)*

Greenwich Bay Trading Co Inc 919 781-5008
5809 Triangle Dr Ste C Raleigh (27617) *(G-12816)*

Greenworks North America LLC (PA) 704 658-0539
500 S Main St Ste 450 Mooresville (28115) *(G-10965)*

Greenworks Tools, Mooresville Also Called: Greenworks North America LLC *(G-10965)*

Greer and Associates Inc 919 383-3500
972 Trinity Rd Raleigh (27607) *(G-12817)*

Greer Laboratories Inc 828 758-2388
Hwy 90 Lenoir (28645) *(G-9614)*

Greer Laboratories Inc (DH) 828 754-5327
639 Nuway Cir Lenoir (28645) *(G-9615)*

Greg Goodwin PA 828 657-5371
1269 Us Highway 221a Forest City (28043) *(G-6069)*

Greg Price 847 778-4426
107 Patton Ln Hampstead (28443) *(G-7648)*

Gregory Hill Frame 828 428-0007
108 W Cemetery St Maiden (28650) *(G-10109)*

Gregory Pallet Co 336 349-2212
11177 Cherry Grove Rd Reidsville (27320) *(G-13523)*

Gregory Pallet Co LLC 336 342-3590
745 Underwood Rd Elon (27244) *(G-5658)*

Gregory Poole Equipment Co 252 931-5100
5200 Martin Luther King Jr Hwy Greenville (27834) *(G-7535)*

Gregory Poole Equipment Co 919 872-2691
2620 Discovery Dr Raleigh (27616) *(G-12818)*

Gregory Vineyards 919 427-9409
275 Bowling Spring Dr Angier (27501) *(G-139)*

Greif Inc 704 588-3895
900 Westinghouse Blvd Charlotte (28273) *(G-2867)*

Greiner Bio-One North Amer Inc (DH) 704 261-7800
4238 Capital Dr Monroe (28110) *(G-10728)*

Greiner-Bio-One, Monroe Also Called: Greiner Bio-One North Amer Inc *(G-10728)*

Grenade Mentality Pubg Co 704 865-7786
4217 Sunflower Ct Gastonia (28052) *(G-6410)*

Gresco Manufacturing Inc 336 475-8101
216 E Holly Hill Rd Thomasville (27360) *(G-15228)*

Gresham Lake Concrete Plant, Raleigh Also Called: S T Wooten Corporation *(G-13224)*

Grey Area News 919 637-6973
70 Harrison St Zebulon (27597) *(G-17130)*

Grey Holdings Inc 828 862-4772
283 Old Rosman Hwy Brevard (28712) *(G-1274)*

Grey House Publishing, Concord Also Called: Grey House Publishing Inc *(G-4276)*

Grey House Publishing Inc 704 784-0051
624 Foxwood Dr Se Concord (28025) *(G-4276)*

Grey Star Woodworks 919 903-8471
421 Bruce Burns Rd Moncure (27559) *(G-10623)*

Greybeard Printing Inc 828 252-3082
1304c Patton Ave Ste C Asheville (28806) *(G-644)*

Greyberry Printing 919 649-3187
8301 Hempshire Pl Apt 106 Raleigh (27613) *(G-12819)*

Greystone Concrete Pdts Inc 252 438-5144
2100 Us 1/158 Hwy Henderson (27537) *(G-7785)*

Grice Showcase Display Mfg Inc 704 423-8888
5001 White Oak Rd Charlotte (28210) *(G-2868)*

Grid Research LLC 704 345-9774
13310 Fairington Oaks Dr Mint Hill (28227) *(G-10535)*

Gridlock Enterprises LLC 910 939-4867
3165 Northwoods Dr Jacksonville (28540) *(G-9006)*

Griffin Automotive Marine Inc 252 940-0714
450 Herring Club Rd Washington (27889) *(G-15706)*

Griffin Industries LLC 704 624-9140
5805 Highway 74 E Marshville (28103) *(G-10217)*

Griffin Manufacturing LLC 704 984-2070
210b Charter St Albemarle (28001) *(G-88)*

Griffin Marketing Group 336 558-5802
4608 Knightbridge Rd Greensboro (27455) *(G-7068)*

Griffin Motion LLC 919 577-6333
1040 Classic Rd Apex (27539) *(G-198)*

Griffin Printing Inc 919 832-6931
500 Uwharrie Ct Ste A Raleigh (27606) *(G-12820)*

Griffin Tubing Company Inc 336 449-4822
906 Burlington Ave Gibsonville (27249) *(G-6560)*

Griffiths Corporation 704 552-6793
10134 Industrial Dr Pineville (28134) *(G-12271)*

Griffiths Corporation 704 554-5657
10240 Industrial Dr Pineville (28134) *(G-12272)*

Griffn S Brbcue Wlliamston Inc 252 792-4887
5362 Fire Dept Rd Williamston (27892) *(G-16062)*

Grifols, Clayton Also Called: Grifols Therapeutics LLC *(G-3984)*

Grifols Inc 919 553-5011
8368 Us 70 Bus Hwy W Clayton (27520) *(G-3983)*

Grifols Therapeutics LLC 919 359-7069
9257 Us 70 Bus Hwy W Ste B-302 Clayton (27520) *(G-3984)*

Grifols Therapeutics LLC 919 553-0172
8368 Us 70 Bus Hwy W Clayton (27520) *(G-3985)*

Grifols Therapeutics LLC (DH) 919 316-6300
79 Tw Alexander Dr Durham (27709) *(G-5127)*

Grifols Therapeutics LLC 919 316-6668
79 Tw Alexander Dr Durham (27709) *(G-5128)*

Grifols Therapeutics LLC 919 316-6214
85 Tw Alexander Dr Durham (27709) *(G-5129)*

Grifols Therapeutics LLC 919 316-6612
1017 Main Campus Dr Ste 2580 Raleigh (27606) *(G-12821)*

Griggs Custom Woodwork.. 828 719-1503
114 S Slope Cir Banner Elk (28604) *(G-899)*

Grimes Mill LLC.. 336 470-6864
4 E 1st Ave Lexington (27292) *(G-9725)*

Grimme Services LLC... 828 490-6366
26 Pelzer St Asheville (28804) *(G-645)*

Grind Athletics LLC.. 910 228-0035
8119 Yellow Daisy Dr Wilmington (28412) *(G-16242)*

Grinding & Metals Inc.. 704 588-5999
1200 Westinghouse Blvd Charlotte (28273) *(G-2869)*

Grindtec Enterprises Corp.. 704 636-1825
3402 Mooresville Rd Salisbury (28147) *(G-13974)*

Grins Beverages, Winston Salem Also Called: Grins Enterprises LLC *(G-16730)*

Grins Enterprises LLC.. 336 831-0534
1051 Arbor Rd Winston Salem (27104) *(G-16730)*

Grip Pod Systems Intl LLC.. 239 233-3694
6321 Swallow Cove Ln Raleigh (27614) *(G-12822)*

Grits and Gravel Services LLC... 919 758-8975
251 Meadow Beauty Dr Apex (27539) *(G-199)*

Grizzly Cookware LLC... 704 322-3521
2030 S Tryon St Ste 3g Charlotte (28203) *(G-2870)*

Groninger USA LLC... 704 588-3873
14045 S Lakes Dr Charlotte (28273) *(G-2871)*

Ground Control Landscape MGT... 704 472-3448
506 W Dixon Blvd Shelby (28152) *(G-14322)*

Groundswell Renovation & Repr, Wilmington Also Called: Bowie Machine Works LLC *(G-16142)*

Group 6 Holdings Inc... 888 804-5008
1806 N Nc 16 Business Hwy Denver (28037) *(G-4779)*

Groupe Lacasse LLC... 336 778-2098
2235 Lewisville Clemmons Rd Ste D Clemmons (27012) *(G-4042)*

Grove Cabinet LLC.. 828 575-4463
6 Miller Rd Fairview (28730) *(G-5711)*

Grove Stone & Sand, Swannanoa Also Called: B V Hedrick Gravel & Sand Co *(G-15020)*

Grove Stone & Sand Division, Salisbury Also Called: B V Hedrick Gravel & Sand Co *(G-13928)*

Grove Vineyards & Winery, Gibsonville Also Called: Haw River Valley Entps LLC *(G-6562)*

Grover Gaming Inc (PA).. 252 329-7900
3506 Greenville Blvd Ne Greenville (27834) *(G-7536)*

Grover Industries Inc (PA)... 828 859-9125
219 Laurel Ave Grover (28073) *(G-7608)*

Growler Manufacturing & Engrg, Robbins Also Called: Carolina Growler Inc *(G-13597)*

Grp Inc.. 919 776-9940
1823 Boone Trail Rd Sanford (27330) *(G-14128)*

Grt Electronics LLC... 919 821-1996
3805 Beryl Rd Raleigh (27607) *(G-12823)*

Grubb & Son Sawmill Inc.. 336 241-2252
1498 Summey Town Rd Trinity (27370) *(G-15343)*

Gruma Corporation.. 919 778-5553
401 Gateway Dr Goldsboro (27534) *(G-6622)*

Grund America LLC.. 704 287-1805
220 Reefton Rd Matthews (28104) *(G-10319)*

Gryphon House Inc.. 800 638-0928
1310 Lewisville Clemmons Rd Lewisville (27023) *(G-9667)*

GS Fab Inc.. 704 799-1227
235 Rolling Hill Rd Ste 10 Mooresville (28117) *(G-10966)*

Gsam Residuals LLC.. 704 200-2634
2901 Coltsgate Rd Charlotte (28211) *(G-2872)*

GSE Dispensing.. 704 509-2651
2625 Rustic Ridge Ct Charlotte (28270) *(G-2873)*

Gso Printing.. 336 292-1601
317 S Westgate Dr Ste A Greensboro (27407) *(G-7069)*

Gso Printing Inc.. 336 288-5778
2 Hill Valley Ct Greensboro (27410) *(G-7070)*

Gt Rhyno Construction LLC.. 919 737-3620
7061 Fox Meadow Ln Apt 911 Raleigh (27616) *(G-12824)*

Gtg Engineering, Clarendon Also Called: Gtg Engineering Inc *(G-3947)*

Gtg Engineering Inc.. 877 569-8572
768 Furnie Hammond Rd Clarendon (28432) *(G-3946)*

Gtg Engineering Inc (PA).. 877 569-8572
766 Furnie Hammond Rd Clarendon (28432) *(G-3947)*

Gtg Engineering Inc.. 910 457-0068
4956 Long Beach Rd Se Ste 14 Southport (28461) *(G-14571)*

GTW Woodworks.. 704 640-5402
174 Brawley Rd Cleveland (27013) *(G-4072)*

Guardian Strapping, Clinton Also Called: Dubose Strapping Inc *(G-4094)*

Guerrero Enterprises Inc.. 828 286-4900
1621 Poors Ford Rd Rutherfordton (28139) *(G-13875)*

Guerrilla Rf Inc.. 336 510-7840
2000 Pisgah Church Rd Greensboro (27455) *(G-7071)*

Guest Interiors.. 828 244-5738
904 3rd Ave Nw Hickory (28601) *(G-8035)*

Guilford Business Forms, High Point Also Called: Gbf Inc *(G-8363)*

Guilford Fabricators Inc... 336 434-3163
5261 Glenola Industrial Dr High Point (27263) *(G-8372)*

Guilford Mills LLC.. 910 794-5810
1001 Military Cutoff Rd Ste 300 Wilmington (28405) *(G-16243)*

Guilford Orthtic Prothetic Inc... 336 676-5394
405 Parkway St Ste G Greensboro (27401) *(G-7072)*

Guilford Performance Textiles... 910 296-5362
1754 Nc-903 Kenansville (28349) *(G-9143)*

Guilford Performance Textiles, Wilmington Also Called: Lear Corporation *(G-16294)*

Gulfstream Plans & Design Inc.. 704 641-2544
18725 The Commons Blvd Cornelius (28031) *(G-4553)*

Gulfstream Publications Inc... 252 449-2222
4425 N Croatan Hwy Kitty Hawk (27949) *(G-9406)*

Gullistan Carpet, Aberdeen Also Called: Hampton Capital Partners LLC *(G-6)*

Gum Drop Cases LLC... 206 805-0818
1515 W Green Dr High Point (27260) *(G-8373)*

Gum Ridge Milling Company... 336 877-8894
650b Bear Ridge Trl Fleetwood (28626) *(G-5975)*

Gunboat International Ltd.. 252 305-8700
829 Harbor Rd Wanchese (27981) *(G-15646)*

Gunk, Indian Trail Also Called: Radiator Specialty Company *(G-8959)*

Gunmar Machine Corporation.. 910 738-6295
310 Hines St Lumberton (28358) *(G-10039)*

Gunpowder Creek Distillers LLC... 828 851-0799
1260 25th Street Pl Se Hickory (28602) *(G-8036)*

Guns Welding LLC.. 336 786-1020
496 Belton Rd Mount Airy (27030) *(G-11514)*

Gusto Packing Company, Garner Also Called: Butterball LLC *(G-6258)*

Guy Chaddock and Company LLC..................................... 828 584-0664
100 Reep Dr Morganton (28655) *(G-11217)*

Guy N Langley... 252 972-9875
2026 Leggett Rd Rocky Mount (27801) *(G-13668)*

Guyclee Millwork... 919 202-5738
1251 S Pollock St Selma (27576) *(G-14256)*

Gw Industries LLC... 919 608-1911
2013 New Hope Church Rd Raleigh (27604) *(G-12825)*

Gwg Boatworks LLC.. 252 422-0757
902 Oxford Dr Morehead City (28557) *(G-11173)*

Gxs Wraps, Apex Also Called: Graphix Solution Inc *(G-197)*

Gym 30, Wake Forest Also Called: Trickfit & Suepack Training *(G-15606)*

H & B Tool & Die Supply Co... 704 376-8531
5005 W Wt Harris Blvd Ste A Charlotte (28269) *(G-2874)*

H & C Erectors and Welding LLC.. 704 615-9849
6505 Nevin Glen Dr Charlotte (28269) *(G-2875)*

H & H Farm Machine Co Inc.. 704 753-1555
7916 Unionville Brief Rd Monroe (28110) *(G-10729)*

H & H Furniture Mfrs Inc... 336 873-7245
236 N Broad St Seagrove (27341) *(G-14239)*

H & H Login... 704 272-8763
2355 Tarpin Town Rd Polkton (28135) *(G-12387)*

H & H Polishing Inc... 704 393-8728
4256 Golf Acres Dr Charlotte (28208) *(G-2876)*

H & H Products Incorporated (PA)..................................... 910 891-4276
275 Carlie Cs Dr Dunn (28334) *(G-4873)*

H & H Representatives Inc.. 704 596-6950
University Parkway Charlotte (28229) *(G-2877)*

H & H REPRESENTATIVES, INC, Charlotte Also Called: H & H Representatives Inc *(G-2877)*

H & H Wood Products Inc.. 704 233-4148
3349 Us Hwy 74 E Wingate (28174) *(G-16575)*

H & H Woodworking LLC — ALPHABETIC SECTION

H & H Woodworking LLC 336 676-6524
  4159 Keeley Rd Mc Leansville (27301) *(G-10392)*

H & H Woodworking Inc 336 884-5848
  530 Gatewood Ave High Point (27262) *(G-8374)*

H & L Logging Inc 252 793-2778
  1166 Long Ridge Rd Plymouth (27962) *(G-12374)*

H & P Wood Turnings Inc 910 675-2784
  9375 Us Hwy 117 S Rocky Point (28457) *(G-13746)*

H & R Mullis Machine Inc 704 791-4149
  151 Highway 24 27 E Midland (28107) *(G-10468)*

H & T Chair Co Inc 828 264-7742
  1598 Meat Camp Rd Boone (28607) *(G-1203)*

H & V Processing Inc 336 224-2985
  251 Primrose Drive Ext Lexington (27292) *(G-9726)*

H + M USA Management Co Inc 704 599-9325
  2020 Starita Rd Ste I Charlotte (28206) *(G-2878)*

H and H Woodworks 704 827-4506
  121 Griffin Rd Stanley (28164) *(G-14695)*

H Brothers Fine Wdwkg LLC 931 216-1955
  1512 Earpsboro Rd Zebulon (27597) *(G-17131)*

H C Production Co 910 483-5267
  218 Tolar St Fayetteville (28306) *(G-5832)*

H Clyde Moore Jr 910 642-3507
  790 Honey Field Rd Whiteville (28472) *(G-15965)*

H D Technologies, Morganton *Also Called: Barefoot Cnc Inc (G-11199)*

H F I, Randleman *Also Called: Hughes Furniture Inds Inc (G-13473)*

H Horseshoe 336 853-5913
  194 Sandy Creek Ln Lexington (27295) *(G-9727)*

H M Elliott Inc 704 663-8226
  387 Pitt Rd Mooresville (28115) *(G-10967)*

H Parsons Incorporated 828 757-9191
  100 Parsons Park Dr Lenoir (28645) *(G-9616)*

H S G, Swansboro *Also Called: High Speed Gear Inc (G-15045)*

H T Jones Lumber Company 252 332-4135
  204 Catherine Creek Rd N Ahoskie (27910) *(G-63)*

H T Wade Enterprises Inc 336 375-8900
  5838 Rudd Station Rd Browns Summit (27214) *(G-1307)*

H W Andersen Products Inc 336 376-3000
  3202 Caroline Dr Haw River (27258) *(G-7752)*

H W Culp Lumber Company 704 463-7311
  491 Us Hwy 52 N New London (28127) *(G-11871)*

H W S Company Inc (HQ) 828 322-8624
  856 7th Ave Se Hickory (28602) *(G-8037)*

H-T-L Perma USA Ltd Partnr (PA) 704 377-3100
  10333 Westlake Dr Charlotte (28273) *(G-2879)*

H.E.A.L. Marketplace, Rutherfordton *Also Called: Heal (G-13878)*

H&H Distillery LLC 828 338-9779
  204 Charlotte Hwy Ste D Asheville (28803) *(G-646)*

H&H Metal Fab 828 757-3747
  3050 Mcmillan Pl Lenoir (28645) *(G-9617)*

H&M Woodworks Inc 919 496-5993
  504 S Bickett Blvd Louisburg (27549) *(G-9990)*

H&R Transport LLC 910 588-4410
  1315 Bull St Garland (28441) *(G-6245)*

H&S Autoshot LLC 847 662-8500
  302 Rolling Hill Rd Mooresville (28117) *(G-10968)*

H2h Blinds 704 628-5084
  13137 Bleinheim Ln Matthews (28105) *(G-10250)*

Haand 336 350-7597
  413 Tucker St Burlington (27215) *(G-1427)*

Haand Hospitality, Burlington *Also Called: Haand (G-1427)*

Hackner Home LLC 980 552-9573
  806 W Warren St Shelby (28150) *(G-14323)*

Hackney, Washington *Also Called: Transportation Tech Inc (G-15734)*

Hackney & Sons Midwest Inc 252 946-6521
  911 W 5th St Washington (27889) *(G-15707)*

Hackney A Div VT Spclzed Vhcle, Washington *Also Called: VT Hackney Inc (G-15737)*

Haeco Americas, Greensboro *Also Called: Haeco Americas LLC (G-7073)*

Haeco Americas LLC (DH) 336 668-4410
  623 Radar Rd Greensboro (27410) *(G-7073)*

Haeco Americas Cabin Solutions, Greensboro *Also Called: Brice Manufacturing Co Inc (G-6851)*

Haeco Americas Cabin Solutions, Greensboro *Also Called: Haeco Cabin Solutions LLC (G-7074)*

Haeco Americas Cabin Solutions, Winston Salem *Also Called: Haeco Cabin Solutions LLC (G-16731)*

Haeco Cabin Solutions LLC (DH) 336 862-1418
  8010 Piedmont Triad Pkwy Greensboro (27409) *(G-7074)*

Haeco Cabin Solutions LLC 336 464-0122
  5568 Gumtree Rd Winston Salem (27107) *(G-16731)*

Hager Cabinet Works John E Hag 704 799-8113
  111 Barksdale Ln Mooresville (28117) *(G-10969)*

Haigler Electric & Cnstr, Monroe *Also Called: Trimworks Inc (G-10823)*

Haines Corporation 704 545-4361
  3622 Glen Lyon Dr Matthews (28105) *(G-10251)*

Hair Collection, The, Raleigh *Also Called: Magazine Nakia Lashawn (G-12987)*

Hair Socety Inc 919 588-1453
  117 Station Dr Morrisville (27560) *(G-11350)*

Haircutters of Raleigh Inc 919 781-3465
  4024 Barrett Dr Ste 102 Raleigh (27609) *(G-12826)*

Hairfield Wilbert Burial Vlt 828 437-4319
  3098 Morganton Furniture Rd Morganton (28655) *(G-11218)*

Hais Kookies & More 980 819-8256
  600 Hartford Ave Charlotte (28209) *(G-2880)*

Halcore Group Inc 336 982-9824
  101 Gates Ln Jefferson (28640) *(G-9089)*

Halcore Group Inc 336 846-8010
  101 Gates Ln Jefferson (28640) *(G-9090)*

Haldex Inc 828 652-9308
  5334 Us Hwy 221 N Marion (28752) *(G-10150)*

Hale's Sample Shop, High Point *Also Called: Solid Frames Inc (G-8541)*

Hales Welding and Fabrication 252 907-5508
  900 Carr Farm Rd Macclesfield (27852) *(G-10065)*

Haley Promotions Inc 336 402-7450
  200 Park At North Hills St Apt 1606 Raleigh (27609) *(G-12827)*

Halifax EMC 252 445-5111
  12867 Nc Highway 481 Enfield (27823) *(G-5678)*

Halifax Media Group 704 869-1700
  1893 Remount Rd Gastonia (28054) *(G-6411)*

Halifax Media Holdings LLC 828 692-5763
  1717 Four Seasons Blvd Hendersonville (28792) *(G-7857)*

Hall Tire and Battery Co Inc 336 275-3812
  2222 Martin Luther King Jr Dr Greensboro (27406) *(G-7075)*

Halls Auto Repair 919 879-9946
  200 W Broad St Dunn (28334) *(G-4874)*

Halogen Software US Inc 866 566-7778
  15801 Brixham Hill Ave Ste 430 Charlotte (28277) *(G-2881)*

Ham Brothers Inc 704 827-1303
  205 Shamrock Rd Gastonia (28056) *(G-6412)*

Ham Wayco Company 919 735-3962
  506 N William St Goldsboro (27530) *(G-6623)*

Hamby Brother S Incorporated 336 667-1154
  Us Hwy 421 North Wilkesboro (28659) *(G-12013)*

Hamby Brothers Concrete Inc 828 754-2176
  2051 Morganton Blvd Sw Lenoir (28645) *(G-9618)*

Hamilton 704 896-1427
  400 Avinger Ln Davidson (28036) *(G-4676)*

Hamilton Beach Brands Inc 252 975-0444
  234 Springs Rd Washington (27889) *(G-15708)*

Hamilton Drywall Products, Monroe *Also Called: Mbp Acquisition LLC (G-10768)*

Hamilton Indus Grinding Inc 828 253-6796
  224 Mulvaney St Asheville (28803) *(G-647)*

Hamilton Machine Works LLC 919 779-6892
  908 Withers Rd Raleigh (27603) *(G-12828)*

Hamilton Sundstrand Corp 860 654-6000
  2730 W Tyvola Rd Charlotte (28217) *(G-2882)*

Hamlet Paper Packaging, Hamlet *Also Called: Hood Packaging Corporation (G-7623)*

Hamlin Sheet Metal Company Inc 919 894-2224
  200 N Walton Ave Benson (27504) *(G-1036)*

Hamlin Sheet Metal Company Incorporated (PA) 919 772-8780
  1411 W Garner Rd Garner (27529) *(G-6274)*

Hammer & Shaw Woodworks 336 339-4829
  910 Mccormick St Greensboro (27403) *(G-7076)*

ALPHABETIC SECTION — Harper Corporation of America

Hammer Publications, Greensboro *Also Called: Rhinoceros Times (G-7310)*
Hammill Construction Co Inc.. 704 279-5309
  5051 St Stephens Church Rd Gold Hill (28071) *(G-6582)*
Hammock Consumer, Charlotte *Also Called: Hammock Pharmaceuticals Inc (G-2883)*
Hammock Pharmaceuticals Inc.. 704 727-7926
  11922 General Dr Unit C Charlotte (28273) *(G-2883)*
Hammond Electric Motor Company.. 704 983-3178
  811 Concord Rd Albemarle (28001) *(G-89)*
Hampstead Publishing, Hampstead *Also Called: Topsail Voice LLC (G-7662)*
Hampton Art Inc.. 252 975-7207
  1481 W 2nd St Ste 109 Washington (27889) *(G-15709)*
Hampton Capital Partners LLC
  3140 Nc Highway 5 Aberdeen (28315) *(G-6)*
Hamrick Fence Company.. 704 434-5011
  407 E College Ave Boiling Springs (28017) *(G-1160)*
Hamrick Precast LLC.. 704 434-6551
  415 W College Ave Shelby (28152) *(G-14324)*
Hanak Enterprises.. 704 315-5249
  2133 Rocky Falls Ln Gastonia (28054) *(G-6413)*
Hancock & Grandson Inc.. 252 728-2416
  971 Harkers Island Rd Beaufort (28516) *(G-959)*
Hancock & Moore LLC (HQ).. 828 495-8235
  166 Hancock And Moore Ln Taylorsville (28681) *(G-15144)*
Hancock & Moore LLC.. 828 495-8235
  405 Rink Dam Rd Taylorsville (28681) *(G-15145)*
Hand 2 Hand Signs.. 919 401-2420
  17 Streamview Ct Durham (27713) *(G-5130)*
Hanes, Winston Salem *Also Called: Hanesbrands Inc (G-16734)*
Hanes Companies Inc.. 828 464-4673
  500 N Mclin Creek Rd Conover (28613) *(G-4460)*
Hanes Companies Inc (HQ).. 336 747-1600
  815 Buxton St Winston Salem (27101) *(G-16732)*
Hanes Inds A Div Hnes Cmpanies, Conover *Also Called: Hanes Companies Inc (G-4460)*
Hanes Industries, Winston Salem *Also Called: Hanes Companies Inc (G-16732)*
Hanes Industries-Newton.. 828 469-2000
  2042 Fairgrove Church Rd Newton (28658) *(G-11939)*
Hanesbrands Export Canada LLC.. 336 519-8080
  1000 E Hanes Mill Rd Winston Salem (27105) *(G-16733)*
Hanesbrands Inc.. 910 462-2001
  18400 Fieldcrest Rd Laurel Hill (28351) *(G-9460)*
Hanesbrands Inc.. 336 789-6118
  645 W Pine St Mount Airy (27030) *(G-11515)*
Hanesbrands Inc.. 336 519-8080
  710 Almondridge Dr Rural Hall (27045) *(G-13843)*
Hanesbrands Inc (PA).. 336 519-8080
  1000 E Hanes Mill Rd Winston Salem (27105) *(G-16734)*
Haney's Tire, Laurinburg *Also Called: Haneys Tire Recapping Svc LLC (G-9481)*
Haneys Tire Recapping Svc LLC.. 910 276-2636
  1663 S Main St Laurinburg (28352) *(G-9481)*
Hangcha America, Charlotte *Also Called: Hc Forklift America Corp (G-2895)*
Hanger Clinic, Greensboro *Also Called: Bio-Tech Prsthtics Orthtics In (G-6839)*
Hanging C Farms.. 704 239-6691
  709 China Grove Rd Kannapolis (28083) *(G-9121)*
Hanks Game Calls.. 336 317-3530
  140 Hanks Trl Reidsville (27320) *(G-13524)*
Hanor Co Inc.. 252 977-0035
  6717 Nc 97 W Battleboro (27809) *(G-921)*
Hanover Electric Motor Svc Inc.. 910 762-3702
  602 Wellington Ave Wilmington (28401) *(G-16244)*
Hanover Electric Motors & Sups, Wilmington *Also Called: Hanover Electric Motor Svc Inc (G-16244)*
Hanover Iron Works Inc.. 910 763-7318
  2602 Park Ave Wilmington (28403) *(G-16245)*
Hanover Iron Works Shtmtl Inc.. 910 399-1146
  1861 Dawson St Wilmington (28403) *(G-16246)*
Hans Krug.. 704 370-0809
  4310 Sharon Rd Ste U01 Charlotte (28211) *(G-2884)*
Hanson Brick, Charlotte *Also Called: Forterra Brick LLC (G-2791)*
Hanson Systems Inc.. 828 687-3701
  340 L.A. White Dr Fletcher (28732) *(G-6009)*

Hanson Welding, Fletcher *Also Called: Hanson Systems Inc (G-6009)*
Hanta Rods and Lures LLC.. 919 480-5138
  6612 Viceroy Dr Raleigh (27613) *(G-12829)*
Hanwha Advanced Mtls Amer LLC.. 704 434-2271
  925 Washburn Switch Rd Shelby (28150) *(G-14325)*
Hanwha Shelby, Shelby *Also Called: Hanwha Advanced Mtls Amer LLC (G-14325)*
Hao WEI Lai Inc.. 336 789-9969
  2021 Rockford St Mount Airy (27030) *(G-11516)*
Hap Innovations LLC.. 919 650-6497
  2501 Aerial Center Pkwy Ste 100 Morrisville (27560) *(G-11351)*
Happiteescom.. 704 965-2507
  1060 Tara Ln Charlotte (28213) *(G-2885)*
Happy Jack Incorporated.. 252 747-2911
  2122 Hwy 258 S Snow Hill (28580) *(G-14503)*
Happy Shack Smoke Shop.. 980 833-8053
  4322 Wilkinson Blvd Gastonia (28056) *(G-6414)*
Happy Sign Surprise LLC.. 704 341-3359
  10931 Chamberlain Hall Ct Charlotte (28277) *(G-2886)*
Happy Wax.. 888 400-3053
  120 W Parrish St Durham (27701) *(G-5131)*
Harbisonwalker Intl Inc.. 704 599-6540
  6600 Northpark Blvd Ste E Charlotte (28216) *(G-2887)*
Harbor Lines LLC.. 910 279-3796
  127 Northern Blvd Wilmington (28401) *(G-16247)*
Harbor Welding Inc.. 252 473-3777
  935 Harbor Rd Wanchese (27981) *(G-15647)*
Harborlite, Youngsville *Also Called: Imerys Perlite Usa Inc (G-17085)*
Harco Air LLC.. 252 491-5220
  116 Ballast Rock Rd Unit L Powells Point (27966) *(G-12397)*
Harco Printing Incorporated.. 336 771-0234
  130 Back Forty Dr Winston Salem (27127) *(G-16735)*
Hardie Wood Working, Liberty *Also Called: George R Hardie (G-9815)*
Hardin Company, Hendersonville *Also Called: Hardin Manufacturing Co (G-7858)*
Hardin Manufacturing Co.. 828 685-2008
  1281 Ridge Rd Hendersonville (28792) *(G-7858)*
Harding Enterprise Inc.. 252 725-9785
  1110 Spartina Dr Beaufort (28516) *(G-960)*
Hardison Tire Co Inc.. 252 745-4561
  13504 Nc Highway 55 Bayboro (28515) *(G-935)*
Hardister Logging.. 336 857-2397
  5571 Sandalwood Dr Denton (27239) *(G-4736)*
Hardware Ventures Inc.. 919 818-9039
  213 Ryans Ln Clayton (27520) *(G-3986)*
Hardwood Designs, Hillsborough *Also Called: Athol Arbor Corporation (G-8636)*
HARDWOOD DESIGNS, Hillsborough *Also Called: Kotek Holdings Inc (G-8659)*
Hardwood Publishing Co Inc.. 704 543-4408
  6400 Bannington Rd Charlotte (28226) *(G-2888)*
Hardwood Review Export, Charlotte *Also Called: Hardwood Publishing Co Inc (G-2888)*
Hardwood Store of NC Inc.. 336 449-9627
  106v E Railroad Ave Gibsonville (27249) *(G-6561)*
Hare Asian Trading Company LLC.. 910 524-4667
  49 International Rd Burgaw (28425) *(G-1340)*
Hargenrader Cstm Woodcraft LLC.. 828 896-7182
  2481 23rd St Ne Hickory (28601) *(G-8038)*
Hargrove Countertops & ACC Inc.. 919 981-0163
  5250 Old Wake Forest Rd Ste 100 Raleigh (27609) *(G-12830)*
Hari Krupa Oil and Gas LLC.. 860 805-1704
  6031 Claudias Ln Apt 201 Winston Salem (27103) *(G-16736)*
Harley Owners Group Sttsvlle I.. 704 872-3883
  1226 Morland Dr Statesville (28677) *(G-14808)*
Harley S Woodworks Inc.. 828 776-0120
  917 N Fork Rd Barnardsville (28709) *(G-911)*
Harmony Farm Candles.. 919 698-5200
  404 S First St Mebane (27302) *(G-10414)*
Harmony House Foods Inc.. 800 696-1395
  277 Industrial Park Rd Franklin (28734) *(G-6132)*
Harmony Timberworks, Boone *Also Called: Soha Holdings LLC (G-1236)*
Harper Companies Intl Inc.. 800 438-3111
  11625 Steele Creek Rd Charlotte (28273) *(G-2889)*
Harper Corporation of America (PA).. 704 588-3371
  11625 Steele Creek Rd Charlotte (28273) *(G-2890)*

Harper-Love Adhesives Corp (HQ) 704 588-4395
11101 Westlake Dr Charlotte (28273) *(G-2891)*

Harrah Enterprise Ltd 336 253-3963
10308 Bailey Rd Ste 416 Cornelius (28031) *(G-4554)*

Harrell Proper Transport LLC 336 202-7135
205 Boling Springs Ct Whitsett (27377) *(G-15992)*

Harrins Sand & Gravel Inc 828 254-2744
195 Amboy Rd Asheville (28806) *(G-648)*

Harris Custom Cabinetry LLC 828 289-5620
471 Ivy Dr Rutherfordton (28139) *(G-13876)*

Harris House Furn Inds Inc 336 431-2802
104 Seminole Dr Archdale (27263) *(G-282)*

Harris Industries LLC 410 924-3894
7136 Friar Tuck Ln Mint Hill (28227) *(G-10536)*

Harris Logging LLC 336 859-2786
7508 Brantly Fords Rd Denton (27239) *(G-4737)*

Harris Lumber Company Inc 828 245-2664
1266 Big Island Rd Rutherfordton (28139) *(G-13877)*

Harris Rebar Inc 919 528-8333
803 S Market St Benson (27504) *(G-1037)*

Harris Repair Service, Charlotte Also Called: L3harris Technologies Inc *(G-3066)*

Harris Solar Inc 704 490-8374
356 Belvedere Dr Nw Concord (28027) *(G-4277)*

Harris Teeter LLC 704 846-7117
1811 Matthews Township Pkwy Matthews (28105) *(G-10252)*

Harris Teeter LLC 919 859-0110
5563 Western Blvd Ste 38 Raleigh (27606) *(G-12831)*

Harris Teeter 038, Raleigh Also Called: Harris Teeter LLC *(G-12831)*

Harris Teeter 157, Matthews Also Called: Harris Teeter LLC *(G-10252)*

Harris Welding 336 514-6640
809 Richland St High Point (27260) *(G-8375)*

Harris Wood Products Inc 704 550-5494
40425 Tower Rd New London (28127) *(G-11872)*

Harris-Robinette Inc 252 813-5794
412 Harris Acre Ln Pinetops (27864) *(G-12242)*

Harrison Fence Inc 919 244-6908
1680 E Williams St Apex (27539) *(G-200)*

Harrison Martha Print Studio 949 290-8630
4010 Carlton Dr Claremont (28610) *(G-3992)*

Harrison Woodworks Inc 919 632-3703
2322 Glendale Ave Durham (27704) *(G-5132)*

Harriss & Covington Hosiery, High Point Also Called: Harriss Cvington Hsy Mills Inc *(G-8377)*

Harriss & Covington Hsy Mills 336 882-6811
1232 Hickory Chapel Rd High Point (27260) *(G-8376)*

Harriss Cvington Hsy Mills Inc 336 882-6811
1250 Hickory Chapel Rd High Point (27260) *(G-8377)*

Harsco Metro Rail LLC 980 960-2624
3440 Toringdon Way Ste 100 Charlotte (28277) *(G-2892)*

Harsco Rail LLC (HQ) 980 960-2624
3440 Toringdon Way Ste 100 Charlotte (28277) *(G-2893)*

Hartford Products Inc 919 471-5937
6224 Acorn Ridge Trl Hillsborough (27278) *(G-8651)*

Hartley Brothers Sawmill Inc 336 921-2955
8507 West North Carolina Hwy 268 Boomer (28606) *(G-1171)*

Hartley Loudspeakers Inc 910 392-1200
5732 Oleander Dr Wilmington (28403) *(G-16248)*

Hartley Products Corp 910 392-0500
5732 Oleander Dr Wilmington (28403) *(G-16249)*

Hartley Ready Mix Con Mfg Inc 336 294-5995
1040 Boulder Rd Greensboro (27409) *(G-7077)*

Hartley Ready Mix Con Mfg Inc (PA) 336 788-3928
3510 Rothrock St Winston Salem (27107) *(G-16737)*

Hartman Welding 336 372-2220
23 Rivers Edge Rd Sparta (28675) *(G-14594)*

Harts Striping, Archdale Also Called: Steelcity LLC *(G-299)*

Harvest Homes and Handi Houses (PA) 336 243-2382
2100 S Main St Lexington (27292) *(G-9728)*

Harvest Homes and Handi Houses 704 637-3878
3711 Statesville Blvd Salisbury (28147) *(G-13975)*

Harvest Time Bread Company
501 Piedmont Triad W Dr Mount Airy (27030) *(G-11517)*

Harvey & Sons Net & Twine 252 729-1731
804 Hwy 70 Davis Davis (28524) *(G-4707)*

Harvey Fertilizer and Gas Co 252 753-2063
4419 W Pine St Farmville (27828) *(G-5738)*

Harvey Fertilizer and Gas Co 919 731-2474
2937 N William St Goldsboro (27530) *(G-6624)*

Harvey Fertilizer and Gas Co 252 523-9090
1291 Hwy 258 N Kinston (28504) *(G-9368)*

Harvey Fertilizer and Gas Co (PA) 252 526-4150
303 Bohannon Rd Kinston (28501) *(G-9369)*

Harvey Gin & Cotton, Kinston Also Called: Harvey Fertilizer and Gas Co *(G-9369)*

Harwood Signs 704 857-6203
112 Chippewa Trl China Grove (28023) *(G-3883)*

Hasco America Inc 828 650-2631
270 Rutledge Rd Unit B Fletcher (28732) *(G-6010)*

Hashtag Screen Printing 980 429-5447
5392 W Highway 27 Vale (28168) *(G-15468)*

Hasty Print Works 704 964-6401
821 Heatherly Rd Mooresville (28115) *(G-10970)*

Hat Creek Alpacas 336 552-2284
2141 Moir Mill Rd Reidsville (27320) *(G-13525)*

Hatleys Signs & Service Inc 704 723-4027
4495 Motorsports Dr Sw Ste 110 # 1 Concord (28027) *(G-4278)*

Hatrack River Enterprises Inc 336 282-9848
401 Willoughby Blvd Greensboro (27408) *(G-7078)*

Hatteras Canvas Products, Greenville Also Called: Hatteras Hammocks Inc *(G-7537)*

Hatteras Hammocks Inc 252 758-0641
305 Industrial Blvd Greenville (27834) *(G-7537)*

Hatteras Networks Inc 919 991-5440
637 Davis Dr Morrisville (27560) *(G-11352)*

Hatteras Yachts, New Bern Also Called: White River Marine Group LLC *(G-11856)*

Hatteras Yachts Inc 252 633-3101
110 N Glenburnie Rd New Bern (28560) *(G-11808)*

Haulco LLC 336 781-0468
9057 Hillsville Rd Trinity (27370) *(G-15344)*

Hauser Hvac Installation 336 416-2173
480 S Peace Haven Rd Winston Salem (27103) *(G-16738)*

Have A Shirt Made 910 201-9911
106 Se 58th St Oak Island (28465) *(G-12050)*

Haw River Farmhouse Ales LLC 336 525-9270
1713 Sax-Beth Church Rd Saxapahaw (27340) *(G-14217)*

Haw River Valley Entps LLC 336 584-4060
1183 University Dr Ste 105-1044 Gibsonville (27249) *(G-6562)*

Hawaiian Shaved Ice, Clinton Also Called: Mary Macks Inc *(G-4097)*

Hawe Hydraulics, Huntersville Also Called: Hawe North America Inc *(G-8828)*

Hawe North America Inc (HQ) 704 509-1599
13020 Jamesburg Dr Ste A Huntersville (28078) *(G-8828)*

Hawk Distributors Inc 888 334-1307
2980 Lee Ave Sanford (27332) *(G-14129)*

Hawk Manufacturing Inc 803 802-9777
3004 Arsdale Rd Waxhaw (28173) *(G-15759)*

Haworth Inc 828 328-5600
1610 Deborah Herman Rd Sw Conover (28613) *(G-4461)*

Haworth Inc 336 885-4021
1673 W English Rd High Point (27262) *(G-8378)*

Haworth Conover Manufacturing, Conover Also Called: Haworth Inc *(G-4461)*

Haworth Health Environments LLC 828 328-5600
1610 Deborah Herman Rd Sw Conover (28613) *(G-4462)*

Hawthorne Services 910 436-9013
1 Fort Bragg Fayetteville (28307) *(G-5833)*

Hayes & Lunsford Elec Contrs, Asheville Also Called: Presley Group Ltd *(G-741)*

Hayes Print-Stamp Co Inc 336 667-1116
1150 Foster St Wilkesboro (28697) *(G-16023)*

Hayes Welding 336 989-6171
5033 Walker Mill Rd Sophia (27350) *(G-14518)*

Hayfield Auto Sales, Alexander Also Called: G A Lankford Construction *(G-118)*

Haynes International, Mountain Home Also Called: Haynes Wire Company *(G-11690)*

Haynes International Inc 765 456-6000
158 N Edgerton Rd Mountain Home (28758) *(G-11689)*

Haynes Wire Company 828 692-5791
158 N Edgerton Rd Mountain Home (28758) *(G-11690)*

ALPHABETIC SECTION

Haynes Wire Company, Mountain Home *Also Called: Haynes International Inc (G-11689)*

Hayward Industries Inc (HQ)..908 351-5400
   1415 Vantage Park Dr Pmb 400 Charlotte (28203) *(G-2894)*

Hayward Industries Inc..336 712-9900
   1 Hayward Industrial Dr Clemmons (27012) *(G-4043)*

Hayward Industries Inc..336 712-9900
   1 Hayward Industrial Dr Clemmons (27012) *(G-4044)*

Haywood Pool Products, Charlotte *Also Called: Hayward Industries Inc (G-2894)*

Haze Gray Vineyards, Dobson *Also Called: Haze Gray Vineyards LLC (G-4824)*

Haze Gray Vineyards LLC..610 247-9387
   765 Stony Knoll Rd Dobson (27017) *(G-4824)*

Hazel Keller Cosmetics, Monroe *Also Called: Keller Cosmetics Inc (G-10753)*

HB Fuller Co...415 878-7202
   523 Davis Dr Morrisville (27560) *(G-11353)*

HB Fuller Company..336 294-5939
   2302 W Meadowview Rd Greensboro (27407) *(G-7079)*

Hbb Global LLC..615 306-1270
   8324 Covington Hill Way Apex (27539) *(G-201)*

Hbf Textiles, Hickory *Also Called: Hickory Business Furniture LLC (G-8045)*

Hbi Sourcing LLC (HQ)...336 519-8080
   1000 E Hanes Mill Rd Winston Salem (27105) *(G-16739)*

Hbi Wh Minority Holdings LLC.......................................336 519-8080
   1000 E Hanes Mill Rd Winston Salem (27105) *(G-16740)*

Hc Composites LLC..252 641-8000
   1090 W Saint James St Tarboro (27886) *(G-15107)*

Hc Forklift America Corp..980 888-8335
   1338 Hundred Oaks Dr Ste Dd Charlotte (28217) *(G-2895)*

Hdb Inc..800 403-2247
   3901 Riverdale Dr Greensboro (27406) *(G-7080)*

Hdh Pharma Inc..919 462-1494
   421 Charleville Ct Cary (27519) *(G-1780)*

Hdm Furniture Industries Inc..800 349-4579
   37 9th Street Pl Se Hickory (28602) *(G-8039)*

Hdm Furniture Industries Inc..336 882-8135
   37 9th Street Pl Se Hickory (28602) *(G-8040)*

Hdm Furniture Industries Inc..336 812-4434
   741 W Ward Ave Plant37 High Point (27260) *(G-8379)*

Headbands of Hope LLC..919 323-4140
   7498 Waterside Peak Dr Denver (28037) *(G-4780)*

Headrick Otdoor Mdia of Crlnas.....................................704 487-5971
   600 S Morgan St Shelby (28150) *(G-14326)*

Heal..828 287-8787
   360 Carpenter Rd Rutherfordton (28139) *(G-13878)*

Healey Publishing...919 614-6685
   207 Queensferry Rd Cary (27511) *(G-1781)*

Healing Crafter...336 567-1620
   4435 Garden Club St High Point (27265) *(G-8380)*

Healing Springs Farmacy...336 549-6159
   812 Stoney Hill Cir Greensboro (27406) *(G-7081)*

Health At Home Inc...850 543-4482
   1321 Cavendish Ct Charlotte (28211) *(G-2896)*

Health Choice Pharmacy..281 741-8358
   2690 Hendersonville Rd Arden (28704) *(G-337)*

Health Educator Publications...919 243-1299
   476 Shotwell Rd Ste 102 Clayton (27520) *(G-3987)*

Health Services, Charlotte *Also Called: Unity Hlthcare Lab Billing LLP (G-3754)*

Health Supply Us LLC..888 408-1694
   205 Raceway Dr Ste 3 Mooresville (28117) *(G-10971)*

Health Wyze Media..336 528-4120
   142 Redwood Dr Mocksville (27028) *(G-10579)*

Health Wyze Report, The, Mocksville *Also Called: Health Wyze Media (G-10579)*

Healthline Info Systems Inc..704 655-0447
   705 Northeast Dr Ste 17 Davidson (28036) *(G-4677)*

Healthlink Europe...919 368-2187
   611 Creekside Dr Raleigh (27609) *(G-12832)*

Healthlink Europe...919 783-4142
   3737 Glenwood Ave Ste 100 Raleigh (27612) *(G-12833)*

Healthlink Europe & Intl, Raleigh *Also Called: Healthlink International Inc (G-12834)*

Healthlink International Inc..877 324-2837
   211 E Six Forks Rd Ste 209a Raleigh (27609) *(G-12834)*

Healthspan Dx, Durham *Also Called: Sapere Bio Inc (G-5337)*

Healthy Eaton LLC...980 207-3887
   9016 Griers Pasture Dr Charlotte (28278) *(G-2897)*

Hearsay Guides LLC..336 584-1440
   5005 Windsor Ct Elon (27244) *(G-5659)*

Hearst Corporation...704 348-8000
   3540 Toringdon Way Ste 700 # 7 Charlotte (28277) *(G-2898)*

Hearst Corporation...704 348-8000
   3540 Toringdon Way Ste 700 # 7 Charlotte (28277) *(G-2899)*

Hearst Service Center, Charlotte *Also Called: Hearst Corporation (G-2898)*

Heart Electric, Bessemer City *Also Called: Heart Electric Motor Service (G-1070)*

Heart Electric Motor Service..704 922-4720
   Costner School Rd Rr 1 Bessemer City (28016) *(G-1070)*

Hearth & Home Technologies LLC.................................336 274-1663
   215 Industrial Ave Ste A Greensboro (27406) *(G-7082)*

HEARTH & HOME TECHNOLOGIES, LLC, Greensboro *Also Called: Hearth & Home Technologies LLC (G-7082)*

Heartland Harps...828 329-6477
   172 Highlands Square Dr Hendersonville (28792) *(G-7859)*

Heartland Publications..910 592-8137
   303 W Elizabeth St Clinton (28328) *(G-4096)*

Heartwood Pine Floors Inc..919 542-4394
   2722 Nc 87 S Moncure (27559) *(G-10624)*

Heartwood Refuge..828 513-5016
   389 Courtland Blvd Hendersonville (28791) *(G-7860)*

Heat Press Unlimited LLC..910 273-6831
   6595 Stillwater Dr Fayetteville (28304) *(G-5834)*

Heat Transfer Sales LLC..800 842-3328
   4321 Piedmont Pkwy Greensboro (27410) *(G-7083)*

Heat Transfer Sales LLC (HQ).......................................336 292-8777
   3816 Patterson St Greensboro (27407) *(G-7084)*

Heat Transfer Sales of The Carolinas Inc (PA)..............336 294-3838
   4101 Beechwood Dr Greensboro (27410) *(G-7085)*

Heated Bed Printing LLC...860 230-6142
   808 Advancement Ave Apt 202 Durham (27703) *(G-5133)*

Heath and Sons Management, Rocky Point *Also Called: Heath and Sons MGT Svcs LLC (G-13747)*

Heath and Sons MGT Svcs LLC.....................................910 679-6142
   514 Complex Rd Rocky Point (28457) *(G-13747)*

Heaths R&R Transport LLC..252 558-5215
   875 Spring Frest Rd Apt 1 Greenville (27834) *(G-7538)*

Heatmaster LLC (PA)...919 639-4568
   3625 Benson Rd Angier (27501) *(G-140)*

Heaven & Earth Works..845 797-0902
   102 College Station Dr Brevard (28712) *(G-1275)*

Heavenly Cheesecakes..336 577-9390
   11040 Old Us Highway 52 Winston Salem (27107) *(G-16741)*

Heavy Armor Division LLC...980 328-8883
   7916 Stinson Hartis Rd Indian Trail (28079) *(G-8938)*

Heavy Duty Electric, Goldsboro *Also Called: Prolec-GE Waukesha Inc (G-6646)*

Heavy Metal Fabrication LLC..919 656-2717
   1382 Turkey Hill Rd Winston Salem (27106) *(G-16742)*

Heavy Metal Supply...919 625-3508
   1010 S Saunders St Raleigh (27603) *(G-12835)*

Heavy Metal Supply LLC...919 625-3508
   141 Spring Cove Dr Cary (27511) *(G-1782)*

Heckler Brewing Company..910 748-0085
   5780 Ramsey St Ste 110 Fayetteville (28311) *(G-5835)*

Hedgecock Racing Entps Inc...336 887-4221
   1520 Horneytown Rd High Point (27265) *(G-8381)*

Hedrick B V Gravel & Sand Co......................................704 848-4165
   403 Gravel Plant Rd Lilesville (28091) *(G-9837)*

Hedrick Brothers Lumber Co Inc...................................336 746-5885
   6736 Nc Highway 47 Lexington (27292) *(G-9729)*

Hedrick Construction...336 362-3443
   838 Crosscreek Rd Kernersville (27284) *(G-9204)*

Hedrick Industries, Stanley *Also Called: B V Hedrick Gravel & Sand Co (G-14686)*

Heed Group Inc...877 938-8853
   107 Redding Rd Stanley (28164) *(G-14696)*

Hefner Reels LLC..828 632-5717
   34 Wittenburg Industrial Dr Taylorsville (28681) *(G-15146)*

Hefty Concrete Inc..910 483-1598
   309 Ivan Dr Fayetteville (28306) *(G-5836)*

Heico Fasteners Inc (HQ) 828 261-0184
2377 8th Ave Nw Hickory (28601) *(G-8041)*

Heico Manufacturing Inc 828 304-5499
2377 8th Ave Nw Hickory (28601) *(G-8042)*

Heidelberg Materials Us Inc 252 235-4162
7225 Neverson Rd Sims (27880) *(G-14443)*

Heidelberg Mtls Sthast Agg LLC 252 235-4162
Bailey (27807) *(G-874)*

Heidelberg Mtls Sthast Agg LLC 910 893-8308
3155 Nc 210 S Bunnlevel (28323) *(G-1330)*

Heidelberg Mtls Sthast Agg LLC 910 893-2111
Sr 2016 Lillington (27546) *(G-9852)*

Heidelberg Mtls Sthast Agg LLC 252 222-0812
5101 Business Dr Morehead City (28557) *(G-11174)*

Heidelberg Mtls Sthast Agg LLC 919 936-4221
476 Edwards Rd Princeton (27569) *(G-12400)*

Heidelberg Mtls Sthast Agg LLC 919 787-0613
5001 Duraleigh Rd Raleigh (27612) *(G-12836)*

Heidelberg Mtls Sthast Agg LLC 919 556-4011
10501 Capital Blvd Wake Forest (27587) *(G-15564)*

Heidelberg Mtls US Cem LLC 919 682-5791
1031 Drew St Durham (27701) *(G-5134)*

Heintz Bros Automotives Inc 704 872-8081
1475 Old Mountain Rd Statesville (28677) *(G-14809)*

Heist Brewery, Charlotte Also Called: Heist Brewing Company LLC *(G-2900)*

Heist Brewing Company LLC 603 969-8012
525 Oakland Ave Apt 1 Charlotte (28204) *(G-2900)*

Helena Agri-Enterprises LLC 828 685-1182
3642 Chimney Rock Rd Hendersonville (28792) *(G-7861)*

Helena Agri-Enterprises LLC 910 422-8901
13866 Hwy 301 S Rowland (28383) *(G-13789)*

Helium Agency LLC 919 833-1358
2207 Alexander Rd Raleigh (27608) *(G-12837)*

Helium Brands LLC 561 350-1328
109 Granby Ct Cary (27511) *(G-1783)*

Hell On Horsecreek Brewing, Madison Also Called: Lichtenberg Inc *(G-10078)*

Hello PHD LLC 919 414-3215
1519 Rutoni Dr Hillsborough (27278) *(G-8652)*

Hello Signs LLC 704 572-4853
4724 Old Pineville Rd Ste H Charlotte (28217) *(G-2901)*

Helmet Halo 828 407-3742
2 Williams St Asheville (28803) *(G-649)*

Helms Machine Company 704 289-5571
216 N Bivens Rd Monroe (28110) *(G-10730)*

Help/Systems LLC 844 425-2966
2435 Lynn Rd Ste 100 Raleigh (27612) *(G-12838)*

Helping Hands Concrete Llc 828 817-1288
112 Carson Cove Rd Mill Spring (28756) *(G-10486)*

Helpmehelpu, Raleigh Also Called: Holley Selinda *(G-12851)*

Hemco Wire Products Inc 336 454-7280
301 Scientific St Jamestown (27282) *(G-9052)*

Hemispheres Magazine 336 255-0195
1301 Carolina St Greensboro (27401) *(G-7086)*

Hemo Bioscience Inc 919 313-2888
4022 Stirrup Creek Dr Ste 311 Durham (27703) *(G-5135)*

Hemosonics LLC 800 280-5589
4020 Stirrup Creek Dr Durham (27703) *(G-5136)*

Hemosonics LLC 800 280-5589
4020 Stirrup Creek Dr Ste 105 Durham (27703) *(G-5137)*

Hemp and Tea Company LLC 704 248-8657
15906 Old Statesville Rd Ste 100 Huntersville (28078) *(G-8829)*

Henco North 828 552-3671
1445 Merrimon Ave Asheville (28804) *(G-650)*

Hendersnvlle Affrdbl Hsing Cor 828 692-6175
203 N Justice St Hendersonville (28739) *(G-7862)*

Henderson & Kirkland Inc 252 355-0224
223 Forlines Rd Winterville (28590) *(G-17002)*

Henderson Newspapers Inc 252 436-2700
420 S Garnett St Henderson (27536) *(G-7786)*

Hendersonville Phrm RES 828 696-2483
709 5th Ave W Hendersonville (28739) *(G-7863)*

Hendrens Racg Engs Chassis Inc 828 286-0780
1310 Us 221 Hwy N Rutherfordton (28139) *(G-13879)*

Hendrix Batting Company 336 431-1181
2310 Surrett Dr High Point (27263) *(G-8382)*

Henkel Corporation 704 633-1731
485 Cedar Springs Rd Salisbury (28147) *(G-13976)*

Henkel Corporation, Salisbury Also Called: Henkel Corporation *(G-13976)*

Henkel Electronic Materials, Salisbury Also Called: Henkel US Operations Corp *(G-13977)*

Henkel US Operations Corp 704 799-0385
150 Fairview Rd Ste 225 Mooresville (28117) *(G-10972)*

Henkel US Operations Corp 704 647-3500
825 Cedar Springs Rd Salisbury (28147) *(G-13977)*

Henley Sawmill, Asheboro Also Called: Donald Henley & Sons Sawmill *(G-424)*

Henniges Automotive N Amer Inc (DH) 336 342-9300
226 Watlington Industrial Dr Reidsville (27320) *(G-13526)*

Henry & Rye Incorporated 919 365-7045
485 Old Wilson Rd Ste 1 Wendell (27591) *(G-15904)*

Henry The Great, High Point Also Called: Henry Williams Jr *(G-8383)*

Henry Williams Jr (PA) 336 897-8714
455 S Main St High Point (27260) *(G-8383)*

Hensel Phelps 828 585-4689
171 Wright Brothers Way Fletcher (28732) *(G-6011)*

Hensel Wood Products Corp 336 725-7568
2924 Buena Vista Rd Winston Salem (27106) *(G-16743)*

Hensley Corporation 828 230-9447
9 Madelyn Ln Fairview (28730) *(G-5712)*

Henson Family Investments LLC 910 817-9450
395 Ledbetter Rd Rockingham (28379) *(G-13628)*

Henson's Printing, Smithfield Also Called: Hinsons Typing & Printing *(G-14462)*

Hepsco, Charlotte Also Called: Hydralic Engnered Pdts Svc Inc *(G-2940)*

Heraeus Quartz North Amer LLC 910 799-6230
3016 Boundary St Wilmington (28405) *(G-16250)*

Herald A Pierre LLC 919 730-2965
707 Church St Fairmont (28340) *(G-5702)*

Herald Huntersville 704 766-2100
200 S Old Statesville Rd Huntersville (28078) *(G-8830)*

Herald Printing Co Inc 252 537-2505
916 Roanoke Ave Roanoke Rapids (27870) *(G-13575)*

Herald Printing Inc 252 726-3534
201 N 17th St Morehead City (28557) *(G-11175)*

Herald Sanford Inc 919 708-9000
208 Saint Clair Ct Sanford (27330) *(G-14130)*

Herald-Sun, The, Durham Also Called: News and Observer Pubg Co *(G-5245)*

Herbal Ingenuity, Wilkesboro Also Called: Herbal Innovations LLC *(G-16024)*

Herbal Innovations LLC 336 818-2332
151 Herbal Ingenuity Way Wilkesboro (28697) *(G-16024)*

Herbal Spectacle Inc 540 270-7543
1 Mosers Pl Candler (28715) *(G-1582)*

Herbalife Manufacturing LLC 336 970-6400
3200 Temple School Rd Winston Salem (27107) *(G-16744)*

Herbs Gaia Inc (PA) 828 884-4242
101 Gaia Herbs Rd Brevard (28712) *(G-1276)*

Hercules Steel Company Inc (PA) 910 488-5110
950 Country Club Dr Fayetteville (28301) *(G-5837)*

Herd Woodworking LLC 704 778-0556
36589 Millingport Rd New London (28127) *(G-11873)*

Herff Jones 910 399-2740
105 Portwatch Way Ste C Wilmington (28412) *(G-16251)*

Herff Jones, Charlotte Also Called: Herff Jones LLC *(G-2902)*

Herff Jones LLC 704 962-1483
14931 Santa Lucia Dr Charlotte (28277) *(G-2902)*

Herff Jones LLC 704 845-3355
9525 Monroe Rd Ste 150 Charlotte (28270) *(G-2903)*

Herff Jones LLC 704 873-5563
307 E Front St Statesville (28677) *(G-14810)*

Heritage Building Company LLC 704 431-4494
114 N Center St Ste 300 Statesville (28677) *(G-14811)*

Heritage Cabinet Company Inc 252 648-8151
5030 Business Dr Morehead City (28557) *(G-11176)*

Heritage Classic Wovens LLC 828 247-6010
155 Westerly Hills Dr Forest City (28043) *(G-6070)*

ALPHABETIC SECTION — Hickory Springs Mfg Rubbr

Heritage Clssic Wven Mllstreet, Forest City *Also Called: Liberty Street LLC (G-6075)*

Heritage Concrete, Sanford *Also Called: Heritage Concrete Service Corp (G-14131)*

Heritage Concrete Service Corp.. 910 892-4445
1300 N Mckay Ave Dunn (28334) *(G-4875)*

Heritage Concrete Service Corp (PA).. 919 775-5014
140 Deep River Rd Sanford (27330) *(G-14131)*

Heritage Custom Signs & Disp.. 704 655-1465
2731 Interstate St Charlotte (28208) *(G-2904)*

Heritage Knitting Co LLC.. 704 872-7653
240 Wilson Park Rd Statesville (28625) *(G-14812)*

Heritage Prtg & Graphics Inc.. 704 551-0700
2739 Interstate St Charlotte (28208) *(G-2905)*

Heritage Steel LLC.. 704 431-4097
3870 Statesville Blvd Salisbury (28147) *(G-13978)*

Heritage Woodworks LLC.. 919 774-1554
205 Mciver St Sanford (27330) *(G-14132)*

Herman Reeves Sheet Metal, Gastonia *Also Called: Herman Reeves Tex Shtmtl Inc (G-6415)*

Herman Reeves Tex Shtmtl Inc... 704 865-2231
1617 E Ozark Ave Gastonia (28054) *(G-6415)*

Hermes Marine LLC (PA)... 252 368-9000
109 Anchors Way Dr Edenton (27932) *(G-5515)*

Hermes Medical Solutions Inc... 252 355-4373
710 Cromwell Dr Ste A Greenville (27858) *(G-7539)*

Hermit Feathers Press LLC.. 336 404-8229
3520 Saint Leonards Ct Clemmons (27012) *(G-4045)*

Herrin Bros Coal & Ice Co... 704 332-2193
315 E 36th St Charlotte (28206) *(G-2906)*

Hersey Meters Co LLC... 704 278-2221
10210 Statesville Blvd Cleveland (27013) *(G-4073)*

Hersey Meters Division, Cleveland *Also Called: Mueller Systems LLC (G-4076)*

Hershey, Kenly *Also Called: Hershey Company (G-9153)*

Hershey Company... 919 284-0272
104 Hershey Dr Kenly (27542) *(G-9153)*

Hershey Group LLC... 336 855-3888
2010 New Garden Rd Ste A Greensboro (27410) *(G-7087)*

Hertford ABC Board.. 252 426-5290
803 S Church St Hertford (27944) *(G-7921)*

Hertford Printing Signs... 252 426-5505
2713 Peartree Rd Elizabeth City (27909) *(G-5547)*

Hertz Kompressoren USA Inc.. 704 579-5900
3320 Service St Charlotte (28206) *(G-2907)*

Hess Manufacturing Inc... 704 637-3300
185 Piper Ln Salisbury (28147) *(G-13979)*

Hester Cabinets... 336 376-0186
6662 S Nc Highway 87 Graham (27253) *(G-6691)*

Hester Enterprises Inc.. 704 865-4480
214 Superior Stainless Rd Gastonia (28052) *(G-6416)*

Heubach Colorants USA LLC... 408 686-2935
5500 77 Center Dr Charlotte (28217) *(G-2908)*

Hewlin Brothers Lumber Co.. 252 586-6473
18555 Nc Highway 48 Enfield (27823) *(G-5679)*

Hexatech Inc... 919 481-4412
991 Aviation Pkwy Ste 800 Morrisville (27560) *(G-11354)*

Hexatech Inc... 919 633-0583
8311 Brier Creek Pkwy Raleigh (27617) *(G-12839)*

Hexion Inc.. 910 483-1311
1411 Industrial Dr Fayetteville (28301) *(G-5838)*

Hexion Inc.. 336 884-8918
1717 W Ward Ave High Point (27260) *(G-8384)*

Hexion Inc.. 828 584-3800
114 Industrial Blvd Morganton (28655) *(G-11219)*

Hexpol, Statesville *Also Called: Hexpol Compounding NC Inc (G-14813)*

Hexpol Compounding NC Inc... 704 872-1585
280 Crawford Rd Statesville (28625) *(G-14813)*

Heyel Custom Metal... 919 957-8442
1224 Home Ct Raleigh (27603) *(G-12840)*

Heyel Custom Metal Inc... 919 957-8442
1224 Home Ct Raleigh (27603) *(G-12841)*

Hf Group LLC.. 336 931-0800
1010 Arnold St Greensboro (27405) *(G-7088)*

HFC Prestige Products Inc... 919 895-5300
1400 Broadway Rd Sanford (27332) *(G-14133)*

Hfi Wind Down Inc... 828 438-5767
109 E Fleming Dr 7 Morganton (28655) *(G-11220)*

Hfi Wind Down Inc... 828 430-3355
410 Hogan St Morganton (28655) *(G-11221)*

Hhh Tempering Resources Inc.. 336 201-5396
5901 Gun Club Rd Winston Salem (27103) *(G-16745)*

HI & Dri Boat Lift Systems Inc.. 704 663-5438
1277 River Hwy Mooresville (28117) *(G-10973)*

Hi-TEC Machine Corp.. 828 652-1060
2082 Silvers Welch Rd Old Fort (28762) *(G-12101)*

Hi-TEC Plating Inc... 704 872-8969
1603 Salisbury Rd Statesville (28677) *(G-14814)*

Hi-Tech Fabrication Inc... 919 781-6150
222 Glenwood Ave Apt 503 Raleigh (27603) *(G-12842)*

Hi-Tech Screens Inc.. 828 452-5151
364 Lea Plant Rd Waynesville (28786) *(G-15807)*

Hi-Tech Signs, Charlotte *Also Called: S Tri Inc (G-3477)*

Hiab, Cornelius *Also Called: Hiab USA Inc (G-4555)*

Hiab USA Inc... 704 896-9089
18627 Starcreek Dr Cornelius (28031) *(G-4555)*

Hiatus Inc.. 844 572-6185
1515 Mockingbird Ln Charlotte (28209) *(G-2909)*

Hibco Plastics Inc.. 336 463-2391
1820 Us 601 Hwy Yadkinville (27055) *(G-17040)*

Hickman, Arden *Also Called: Wph Ventures Inc (G-392)*

Hickman Oil & Ice, Troy *Also Called: Hickman Oil & Ice Co Inc (G-15406)*

Hickman Oil & Ice Co Inc.. 910 576-2501
165 Lemonds Drywall Rd Troy (27371) *(G-15406)*

Hickory Adchem Inc.. 828 327-0936
123 23rd St Sw Hickory (28602) *(G-8043)*

Hickory Brands Inc.. 828 322-2600
429 27th St Nw Hickory (28601) *(G-8044)*

Hickory Business Furniture LLC (HQ)....................................... 828 328-2064
900 12th Street Dr Nw Hickory (28601) *(G-8045)*

Hickory Chair, Hickory *Also Called: Hickory Chair Company (G-8046)*

Hickory Chair Company... 800 225-0265
37 9th Street Pl Se Hickory (28602) *(G-8046)*

Hickory Color & Chemical Co, High Point *Also Called: Marlowe-Van Loan Sales Co (G-8441)*

Hickory Daily Record, Hickory *Also Called: Hickory Publishing Co Inc (G-8049)*

Hickory Dyg & Winding Co Inc... 828 322-1550
1025 10th St Ne Hickory (28601) *(G-8047)*

Hickory Heritage of Falling Creek Inc
3211b Falling Creek Rd Hickory (28601) *(G-8048)*

Hickory Leather Company, Vale *Also Called: Meghan Blake Industries Inc (G-15469)*

Hickory Mfg Division, Hickory *Also Called: Sherrill Furniture Company (G-8147)*

Hickory Printing Group Inc H.. 828 465-3431
725 Reese Dr Sw Conover (28613) *(G-4463)*

Hickory Printing Solutions LLC.. 828 465-3431
725 Reese Dr Sw Conover (28613) *(G-4464)*

Hickory Publishing Co Inc.. 828 322-4510
1100 Park Place 11th Ave Se Hickory (28601) *(G-8049)*

Hickory Saw & Tool Inc... 828 324-5585
406 9th St Se Hickory (28602) *(G-8050)*

Hickory Springs California LLC.. 828 328-2201
235 2nd Ave Nw Hickory (28601) *(G-8051)*

Hickory Springs Manufacturing Company (PA)....................... 828 328-2201
235 2nd Ave Nw Hickory (28601) *(G-8052)*

Hickory Springs Mfg Co... 828 322-7994
871 Highland Ave Ne Hickory (28601) *(G-8053)*

Hickory Springs Mfg Co... 828 328-2201
2230 Main Ave Se Hickory (28602) *(G-8054)*

Hickory Springs Mfg Co... 828 632-9733
Sharpe Rd Hiddenite (28636) *(G-8217)*

Hickory Springs Mfg Co... 336 861-4195
1325 Baker Rd High Point (27263) *(G-8385)*

Hickory Springs Mfg Co... 336 491-4131
1905 Alleghany St High Point (27263) *(G-8386)*

Hickory Springs Mfg Co... 828 728-9274
2145 Norwood St Sw Lenoir (28645) *(G-9619)*

Hickory Springs Mfg Rubbr, Lenoir *Also Called: Hickory Springs Mfg Co (G-9619)*

Hickory Throwing Company 828 322-1158
520 20th St Se Hickory (28602) *(G-8055)*

Hickory White Company, Hickory *Also Called: H W S Company Inc (G-8037)*

Hickory Wire Inc 828 322-9473
1711 11th Ave Sw Hickory (28602) *(G-8056)*

Hickory Yarns, Hickory *Also Called: Hickory Dyg & Winding Co Inc (G-8047)*

Hickory Youth Sports Inc 828 327-9550
425 44th Avenue Dr Nw Hickory (28601) *(G-8057)*

Hicks Mechanical, Mount Airy *Also Called: Hicks Wterstoves Solar Systems (G-11518)*

Hicks Wterstoves Solar Systems 336 789-4977
2649 S Main St Mount Airy (27030) *(G-11518)*

Hidden Path Publication Inc 704 878-6986
304 Brierwood Rd Statesville (28677) *(G-14815)*

Hiddenite Conference Ctr LLC 828 352-9200
471 Sulphur Springs Rd Hiddenite (28636) *(G-8218)*

Hiddenite Gems Inc 828 632-3394
484 Emerald Hollow Mine Dr Hiddenite (28636) *(G-8219)*

High and High Inc 252 257-2390
268 Country Club Dr Henderson (27536) *(G-7787)*

High Branch Brewing Co LLC 704 706-3807
325 Mcgill Ave Nw Ste 148 Concord (28027) *(G-4279)*

High Cntry Tmbrframe Gllery WD 828 264-8971
689 George Wilson Rd Boone (28607) *(G-1204)*

High Concepts LLC 704 377-3467
7806 Creek Park Dr Denver (28037) *(G-4781)*

High Cotton Fabrication LLC 910 408-6961
3126 Kitty Hawk Rd Ste 5 Wilmington (28405) *(G-16252)*

High Cotton Screenprinting 704 872-7630
809 Sharon School Rd Statesville (28625) *(G-14816)*

High Country Candles, Blowing Rock *Also Called: Wildflwers Btq of Blowing Rock (G-1157)*

High Country Chair Weaving, Lansing *Also Called: Jerry Blevins (G-9455)*

High Country Electric Mtrs LLC 336 838-4808
1268 Suncrest Orchard Rd North Wilkesboro (28659) *(G-12014)*

High Country Media LLC 828 733-2448
428 Pineola St Newland (28657) *(G-11888)*

High Country News Inc 828 264-2262
1600 Highway 105 Boone (28607) *(G-1205)*

High Creek Woodworks 919 418-1210
2921 Miller Rd Hillsborough (27278) *(G-8653)*

High Definition Tool Corp 828 397-2467
7600 Carolina Tool Dr Connelly Springs (28612) *(G-4403)*

High Falls Publishing 904 234-0015
11 Flycatcher Way # 201 Arden (28704) *(G-338)*

High Five Enterprises Inc 828 279-5962
12 Strawberry Ln Weaverville (28787) *(G-15848)*

High Ground Incorporated 704 372-6620
2209 Park Rd Ste 1 Charlotte (28203) *(G-2910)*

High Mobility Solutions Inc 704 849-8242
648 Matthews Mint Hill Rd Ste D Matthews (28105) *(G-10253)*

High Noon Coffee Roasters LLC 770 851-7004
191 Charlotte St Ste 101 Asheville (28801) *(G-651)*

High Performance Adaptive, Denver *Also Called: Crawford Composites LLC (G-4768)*

High Performance Marketing Inc 919 870-9915
158 Wind Chime Ct Raleigh (27615) *(G-12843)*

High Point Enterprise Inc 336 434-2716
213 Woodbine St High Point (27260) *(G-8387)*

High Point Enterprise Inc 336 883-2839
712 W Lexington Ave High Point (27262) *(G-8388)*

High Point Enterprise Inc (PA) 336 888-3500
213 Woodbine St High Point (27260) *(G-8389)*

High Point Enterprise Inc 336 472-9500
512 Turner St Thomasville (27360) *(G-15229)*

High Point Fibers Inc 336 887-8771
601 Old Thomasville Rd High Point (27260) *(G-8390)*

High Point Furniture 0n64, High Point *Also Called: Leggett & Platt Incorporated (G-8430)*

High Point Furniture Inds Inc (PA) 336 431-7101
1104 Bedford St High Point (27263) *(G-8391)*

High Point Pharmaceuticals Inc 336 841-0300
4170 Mendenhall Oaks Pkwy High Point (27265) *(G-8392)*

High Point Precast Pdts Inc 336 434-1815
4130 W Us Highway 64 Lexington (27295) *(G-9730)*

High Point Quilting Inc 336 861-4180
1601 Blandwood Dr High Point (27260) *(G-8393)*

High Point Showroom, High Point *Also Called: Ofs Brands Inc (G-8470)*

High Point Spring 1506, High Point *Also Called: Leggett & Platt Incorporated (G-8429)*

High Rise Service Company Inc 910 371-2325
1690 Royster Rd Ne Leland (28451) *(G-9548)*

High Speed Gear Inc 910 325-1000
87 Old Hammock Rd Swansboro (28584) *(G-15045)*

High Speed Welding LLC 910 632-4427
1536 Castle Hayne Rd 6 Wilmington (28405) *(G-16253)*

High Street Baptist Church 336 234-0400
11759 Academy St Milton (27305) *(G-10515)*

High Tech Signs Inc 919 859-3206
8601 Battom Ct Raleigh (27613) *(G-12844)*

High Tide Canvas & Uphl Inc 910 409-5903
311 Judges Rd Ste 12a Wilmington (28405) *(G-16254)*

High Velocity Archery LLC 910 620-5215
18879 Nc Highway 53 E Kelly (28448) *(G-9138)*

High Velocity Defense 704 738-3574
195 Lone Star St Salisbury (28146) *(G-13980)*

High-Tech Fabrications Inc 336 871-2990
3045 Nc 704 Hwy E Lawsonville (27022) *(G-9503)*

Highcorp Incorporated 910 642-4104
127 W Columbus St Whiteville (28472) *(G-15966)*

Highiq LLC 704 956-8716
261 Lincoln St Sw Concord (28025) *(G-4280)*

Highland, Asheville *Also Called: Highland Brewing Company Inc (G-652)*

Highland Brewing Company Inc 828 299-3370
12 Old Charlotte Hwy Ste H Asheville (28803) *(G-652)*

Highland Composites 704 924-3090
416 Gallimore Dairy Rd Ste N Greensboro (27409) *(G-7089)*

Highland Containers Inc (DH) 336 887-5400
100 Ragsdale Rd Jamestown (27282) *(G-9053)*

Highland Containers Inc 336 887-5400
3520 Dillon Rd Jamestown (27282) *(G-9054)*

Highland Craftsmen Inc 828 765-9010
534 Oak Ave Spruce Pine (28777) *(G-14642)*

Highland Foam Inc 828 327-0400
1560 Deborah Herman Rd Sw Conover (28613) *(G-4465)*

Highland House, Hickory *Also Called: Century Furniture LLC (G-7981)*

Highland House, Hickory *Also Called: Century Furniture LLC (G-7983)*

Highland Industries Inc 336 855-0625
10 Northline Pl Greensboro (27410) *(G-7090)*

Highland Industries Inc 336 547-1600
629 Green Valley Rd Ste 300 Greensboro (27408) *(G-7091)*

Highland International 828 265-2513
160b Den-Mac Dr Boone (28607) *(G-1206)*

Highland International LLC 828 265-2513
465 Industrial Park Dr Boone (28607) *(G-1207)*

Highland Mills, Concord *Also Called: Fine Sheer Industries Inc (G-4265)*

Highland Paving Co LLC 910 482-0080
1351 Wilmington Hwy Fayetteville (28306) *(G-5839)*

Highland Tank NC Inc 336 218-0801
2700 Patterson St Greensboro (27407) *(G-7092)*

Highland Tool, Mills River *Also Called: Highland Tool and Gauge Inc (G-10503)*

Highland Tool and Gauge Inc 828 891-8557
5500 Old Haywood Rd Mills River (28759) *(G-10503)*

Highlander Unmanned Drone 828 776-6061
35 Kirkpatrick Ln Fairview (28730) *(G-5713)*

Highlight Industries Inc 704 661-1734
537 Geary St Nw Concord (28027) *(G-4281)*

Highline Performance Group 704 799-3500
114 Meadow Hill Cir Mooresville (28117) *(G-10974)*

Highpoint Century Showroom, High Point *Also Called: Century Furniture LLC (G-8292)*

Highs Welding Shop 704 624-5707
1027 Unarco Rd Marshville (28103) *(G-10218)*

Hightower Group LLC 816 286-1051
211 Fraley Rd High Point (27263) *(G-8394)*

Highway Maintenance Ofc 252 534-4031
Hwy 305 Jackson (27845) *(G-8982)*

Highway Patrol, Kinston *Also Called: North Crlina Dept Crime Ctrl P (G-9379)*

ALPHABETIC SECTION — Hog Slat Incorporated

Hildreth Mechanical & Maint, Laurel Hill *Also Called: Tony D Hildreth* *(G-9465)*

Hildreth Ready Mix LLC 704 694-2034
518 W Us Highway 74 Rockingham (28379) *(G-13629)*

Hildreth Wood Products Inc 704 826-8326
825 Mount Vernon Rd Wadesboro (28170) *(G-15511)*

Hill & Ferencz Elc Mtr Co Inc 919 736-7373
301 S George St Goldsboro (27530) *(G-6625)*

Hill Country Woodworks, Chapel Hill *Also Called: Nobscot Construction Co Inc* *(G-2048)*

Hill Hosiery Mill Inc 336 472-7908
602 Davidson St Thomasville (27360) *(G-15230)*

Hill Printing Company 919 833-5934
606 Glenwood Ave Raleigh (27603) *(G-12845)*

Hill Spinning Division, Thomasville *Also Called: Hill Hosiery Mill Inc* *(G-15230)*

Hill-Pak Inc 336 431-3833
5453 Lilly Flower Rd High Point (27263) *(G-8395)*

Hill-Publications LLC 704 399-7002
2018 Mt Holly Huntersville Rd Charlotte (28214) *(G-2911)*

Hill-Rom Inc 919 854-3600
1225 Crescent Green Ste 300 Cary (27518) *(G-1784)*

Hill's Tire & Auto, Goldsboro *Also Called: Super Retread Center Inc* *(G-6663)*

Hilliard Fabricators LLC 336 861-8833
501 Carolina Ave Thomasville (27360) *(G-15231)*

Hills Machinery Company LLC 828 820-5265
5481 Old Haywood Rd Mills River (28759) *(G-10504)*

Hillshire Brands Company 336 519-8080
470 W Hanes Mill Rd Frnt Frnt Winston Salem (27105) *(G-16746)*

Hillsville Welding 336 861-0732
9055 Hillsville Rd Trinity (27370) *(G-15345)*

Hilton Vineyards LLC 704 776-9656
3310 Crow Rd Monroe (28112) *(G-10731)*

Him Inc 336 409-7795
King (27021) *(G-9272)*

Himcen Battery, Apex *Also Called: Himcen Battery Inc* *(G-202)*

Himcen Battery Inc 408 828-8744
2313 Blue Cedar Ct Apex (27523) *(G-202)*

Hinderer & Muehlich, Charlotte *Also Called: H + M USA Management Co Inc* *(G-2878)*

Hinnant Farms Vineyard LLC 919 965-3350
826 Pine Level Micro Road Pine Level (27568) *(G-12210)*

Hinson Industries Inc 252 937-7171
109 Zebulon Ct Rocky Mount (27804) *(G-13700)*

Hinson Metal Fabrication 828 944-0908
30 Tess Ln Maggie Valley (28751) *(G-10094)*

Hinsons Typing & Printing 919 934-9036
1294 W Market St Smithfield (27577) *(G-14462)*

Hipra Scientific USA 919 605-8256
1001 William Moore Dr Raleigh (27607) *(G-12846)*

Hirschfeld Industries, Greensboro *Also Called: CSC Family Holdings Inc* *(G-6945)*

Hirschfeld Industries Brdg LLC 336 271-8252
101 Centreport Dr Ste 400 Greensboro (27409) *(G-7093)*

Hirschfeld Industries-Bridge, Greensboro *Also Called: Hirschfeld Industries Brdg LLC* *(G-7093)*

His Company Inc 800 537-0351
2516 Independence Blvd Ste 201 Wilmington (28412) *(G-16255)*

His Glassworks Inc 828 254-2559
2000 Riverside Dr Ste 19 Asheville (28804) *(G-653)*

His Glory Creations Pubg LLC 919 618-0262
4595 Wendell Blvd Wendell (27591) *(G-15905)*

His Specialty Fab LLC 704 279-1638
3250 Poole Rd Salisbury (28146) *(G-13981)*

Historic Interpretations Inc 919 339-1558
Raleigh (27661) *(G-12847)*

Historical Aviation Tshirts, Greensboro *Also Called: 3d Upfitters LLC* *(G-6766)*

Hitachi ABB Power Grids, Raleigh *Also Called: Hitachi Energy USA Inc* *(G-12848)*

Hitachi Energy USA Inc 919 649-7022
901 Main Campus Dr Raleigh (27606) *(G-12848)*

Hitachi Energy USA Inc 919 324-5403
1345 Express Dr Raleigh (27603) *(G-12849)*

Hitachi Energy USA Inc (HQ) 919 856-2360
901 Main Campus Dr Raleigh (27606) *(G-12850)*

Hitachi Metals NC Ltd 704 855-2800
1 Hitachi Metals Dr China Grove (28023) *(G-3884)*

Hitch Crafters LLC 336 859-3257
853 Cid Rd Lexington (27292) *(G-9731)*

Hitech Circuits Inc 336 838-3420
7711 Idlewild Rd Indian Trail (28079) *(G-8939)*

Hitech Controls Inc 336 498-1534
1348 Plantation Ct Randleman (27317) *(G-13472)*

Hitork USA LLC 803 446-7513
8311 Hampton Fare Ln Waxhaw (28173) *(G-15760)*

Hiviz Led Lighting LLC 703 662-3458
149 Twin Springs Rd Hendersonville (28792) *(G-7864)*

Hiviz Lighting Inc 703 382-5675
149 Twin Springs Rd Hendersonville (28792) *(G-7865)*

HK Publishing Inc 727 459-7724
2 Sunset Dr Asheville (28804) *(G-654)*

Hkb Enterprises LLC 704 831-0402
4936 Osage Cir Charlotte (28269) *(G-2912)*

HL James LLC 516 398-3311
1911 W Club Blvd Durham (27705) *(G-5138)*

Hlm Legacy Group Inc 704 878-8823
129 Honeycutt Rd Troutman (28166) *(G-15381)*

Hlmf Logistics Inc 704 782-0356
11516 Downs Rd Pineville (28134) *(G-12273)*

HM Frame Company Inc 828 428-3354
1903 Gkn Way Newton (28658) *(G-11940)*

HM Liquidation Inc 828 495-8235
166 Hancock & Moore Ln Hickory (28601) *(G-8058)*

Hmf Inc 704 821-6765
3479 Gribble Rd Matthews (28104) *(G-10320)*

Hmi USA, High Point *Also Called: Home Meridian Group LLC* *(G-8399)*

HMS Protec Inc 954 803-2319
5667 Soco Rd Maggie Valley (28751) *(G-10095)*

Hobes Country Hams Inc (PA) 336 670-3401
389 Elledge Mill Rd North Wilkesboro (28659) *(G-12015)*

Hockmeyer Equipment Corp 252 338-4705
6 Kitty Hawk Ln Elizabeth City (27909) *(G-5548)*

HOCKMEYER EQUIPMENT CORP., Elizabeth City *Also Called: Hockmeyer Equipment Corp* *(G-5548)*

Hodge Farms LLC 704 278-2684
11235 Nc Highway 801 Mount Ulla (28125) *(G-11683)*

Hodge Industries Inc 704 491-0104
1804 Dearmon Dr Charlotte (28205) *(G-2913)*

Hodges Precision Machine 336 366-3024
116 Tobe Hudson Rd Dobson (27017) *(G-4825)*

Hoffer Calibration Svcs LLC 252 338-6379
1100 W Ehringhaus St Ste C Elizabeth City (27909) *(G-5549)*

Hoffer Flow Controls Inc 252 331-1997
107 Kitty Hawk Ln Elizabeth City (27909) *(G-5550)*

Hoffman Building Tech Inc 336 292-8777
3816 Patterson St Greensboro (27407) *(G-7094)*

Hoffman Materials LLC 717 243-2011
230 Timberbrook Ln Granite Falls (28630) *(G-6736)*

Hoffman Materials Inc 717 243-2011
230 Timberbrook Ln Granite Falls (28630) *(G-6737)*

Hoffman Materials LLC 828 212-1669
230 Timberbrook Ln Granite Falls (28630) *(G-6738)*

Hoffman Plasti, High Point *Also Called: Hoffman Plasti-Form Company* *(G-8396)*

Hoffman Plasti-Form Company 336 431-2934
5432 Edgar Rd High Point (27263) *(G-8396)*

Hoffman Steinberg 336 292-5501
1806 Fairfax Rd Ste A Greensboro (27407) *(G-7095)*

Hofler H S & Sons Lumber Co 252 465-8603
577 Nc Highway 32 N Sunbury (27979) *(G-14997)*

Hofler Logging Inc 252 465-8921
491 Nc Highway 32 S Sunbury (27979) *(G-14998)*

Hog Slat Incorporated 252 209-0092
440 Nc Highway 561 W Aulander (27805) *(G-830)*

Hog Slat Incorporated 910 862-7081
2229 Us Highway 701 N Elizabethtown (28337) *(G-5596)*

Hog Slat Incorporated (PA) 800 949-4647
206 Fayetteville St Newton Grove (28366) *(G-11988)*

Hog Slat Incorporated 800 949-4647
117 W Weeksdale St Newton Grove (28366) *(G-11989)*

Hog Slat Incorporated 919 663-3321
   17720 Us Highway 64 W Siler City (27344) *(G-14414)*
Hoh Corporation 336 723-9274
   1701 Vargrave St Winston Salem (27107) *(G-16747)*
Hohn Welding Services LLC 336 870-9617
   2132 Crssing Way Crt Apt High Point (27262) *(G-8397)*
Holder Backhoe & Hauling Inc 336 622-7388
   4660 Randolph Church Rd Liberty (27298) *(G-9816)*
Holder Machine & Mfg Co 828 479-8627
   1483 Fontana Rd Robbinsville (28771) *(G-13608)*
Holders Restaurant Furniture 828 754-8383
   2310 Morganton Blvd Sw Lenoir (28645) *(G-9620)*
Holland Industrial, Henderson Also Called: Holland Supply Company *(G-7788)*
Holland Sign Plus Engrv Sltons 252 339-5389
   1123 Macedonia Rd Edenton (27932) *(G-5516)*
Holland Supply Company 252 492-7541
   518 W Montgomery St Henderson (27536) *(G-7788)*
Hollands Floor Covering LLC 602 703-1951
   203 Nydegg Rd New Bern (28562) *(G-11809)*
Holley Selinda 919 351-9466
   700 Peterson St Raleigh (27610) *(G-12851)*
Hollifield Enterprises 828 766-7552
   10 Ellis Road Ext Spruce Pine (28777) *(G-14643)*
Hollingsworth & Vose Company 704 708-5913
   143 Sardis Pointe Rd Matthews (28105) *(G-10254)*
Hollingsworth Custom Shop 910 251-8849
   2915 Castle Hayne Rd Castle Hayne (28429) *(G-1951)*
Hollingsworth Heating Air Cond 252 824-0355
   1893 Mcnair Rd Tarboro (27886) *(G-15108)*
Hollingswrth Cbnets Intrors LL 910 251-1490
   2913 Castle Hayne Rd Castle Hayne (28429) *(G-1952)*
Hollister Incorporated 919 792-2095
   5959 Triangle Town Blvd Ste 1085 Raleigh (27616) *(G-12852)*
Hollywood Fit LLC 704 879-7426
   4491 Posterity Ct Gastonia (28056) *(G-6417)*
Holman & Moody Inc 704 394-4141
   9119 Forsyth Park Dr Charlotte (28273) *(G-2914)*
Holman Automotive Inc 704 583-2888
   9119 Forsyth Park Dr Charlotte (28273) *(G-2915)*
Holmes Logging - Wallace LLC 910 271-1216
   2788 Lightwood Bridge Rd Wallace (28466) *(G-15623)*
Holmes Welding LLC 919 779-8844
   9408 Middleberry Ln Raleigh (27603) *(G-12853)*
Holsters For Life LLC 704 862-0212
   4531 Binwhe Ln Gastonia (28052) *(G-6418)*
Holt Group, High Point Also Called: Holt Group Inc *(G-8398)*
Holt Group Inc (PA) 336 668-2770
   4198 Eagle Hill Dr Ste 105 High Point (27265) *(G-8398)*
Holt Hosiery Mills Inc 336 227-1431
   733 Koury Dr Burlington (27215) *(G-1428)*
Holt Sublimation Prtg Pdts Inc (PA) 336 222-3600
   2208 Airpark Rd Burlington (27215) *(G-1429)*
Holten Industries LLC 919 810-8467
   2009 Lake Trout Ln Raleigh (27610) *(G-12854)*
Holy Cow Publications LLC 704 900-5779
   811 Queens Rd Apt 1 Charlotte (28207) *(G-2916)*
Holy Mountain Printing 801 634-3462
   301 Catalpa Ct Raleigh (27609) *(G-12855)*
Holz-Her Us Inc (DH) 704 587-3400
   124 Crosslake Park Dr Mooresville (28117) *(G-10975)*
Home City Ltd (PA) 910 428-2196
   2086 Hwy 2427 W Biscoe (27209) *(G-1111)*
Home Elevators & Lift, Sunset Beach Also Called: Home Elevators & Lift Pdts LLC *(G-14999)*
Home Elevators & Lift Pdts LLC 910 427-0006
   8311 Ocean Hwy W Sunset Beach (28468) *(G-14999)*
Home Fabrics, Goldsboro Also Called: Cloth Barn Inc *(G-6601)*
Home Impressions Inc 828 328-1142
   420 3rd Ave Nw Hickory (28601) *(G-8059)*
Home Imprv Solutions NC LLC 919 876-3230
   2013 New Hope Church Rd Ste K Raleigh (27604) *(G-12856)*
Home Meridian Group LLC (HQ) 336 819-7200
   2485 Penny Rd High Point (27265) *(G-8399)*

Home Meridian Holdings Inc 336 887-1985
   2485 Penny Rd High Point (27265) *(G-8400)*
Home Security Bars, Greenville Also Called: Energy Svers Windows Doors Inc *(G-7523)*
Home State Apparel, Greensboro Also Called: Mischief Makers Local 816 LLC *(G-7202)*
Home T LLC 646 797-4768
   652 Griffith Rd Ste I Charlotte (28217) *(G-2917)*
Home Team Athletics Inc 910 938-0862
   242 Wilmington Hwy 17 Jacksonville (28540) *(G-9007)*
Homeland Creamery LLC 336 685-6455
   6506 Bowman Dairy Rd Julian (27283) *(G-9105)*
Homes & Land Mag of High S, Boone Also Called: Ty Brown *(G-1244)*
Homeserve NC LLC 740 552-8497
   2225 Castle Rock Farm Rd Pittsboro (27312) *(G-12342)*
Homestead Country Built Furn (PA) 910 799-6489
   4942 Tanbark Dr Wilmington (28412) *(G-16256)*
Hometown Cabinets Inc 919 245-3554
   903 Apple Ln Hillsborough (27278) *(G-8654)*
Hometown Sports Embroidery, Hillsborough Also Called: Hometown Sports Inc *(G-8655)*
Hometown Sports Inc 919 732-7090
   3301 St Marys Rd Hillsborough (27278) *(G-8655)*
Honda Aero Inc (HQ) 336 226-2376
   2989 Tucker Street Ext Burlington (27215) *(G-1430)*
Honda Aircraft Co Service Ctr, Greensboro Also Called: Honda Aircraft Company LLC *(G-7097)*
Honda Aircraft Company LLC 336 662-0849
   6423 Bryan Blvd Ste B Greensboro (27409) *(G-7096)*
Honda Aircraft Company LLC 336 662-0246
   6420 Ballinger Rd Bldg 400 Greensboro (27410) *(G-7097)*
Honda Aircraft Company LLC 336 662-0246
   404 S Chimney Rock Rd Greensboro (27409) *(G-7098)*
Honda Aircraft Company LLC (HQ) 336 662-0246
   6430 Ballinger Rd Greensboro (27410) *(G-7099)*
Hones Enterprises 336 378-9351
   1102 Briarcliff Rd Greensboro (27408) *(G-7100)*
Honeycutt Custom Cabinets Inc 910 567-6766
   1068 Baptist Chapel Rd Autryville (28318) *(G-841)*
Honeygirl Meadery LLC 919 399-3056
   105 Hood St Ste 6 Durham (27701) *(G-5139)*
Honeywell 734 942-5823
   13509 S Point Blvd Ste 150 Charlotte (28273) *(G-2918)*
Honeywell, Charlotte Also Called: Honeywell *(G-2918)*
Honeywell, Charlotte Also Called: Honeywell International Inc *(G-2919)*
Honeywell, Fort Bragg Also Called: Honeywell International Inc *(G-6090)*
Honeywell, Raleigh Also Called: Honeywell International Inc *(G-12857)*
Honeywell Authorized Dealer, Charlotte Also Called: Carolina Products Inc *(G-2403)*
Honeywell Authorized Dealer, Kitty Hawk Also Called: Dusty Rhoads Hvac Inc *(G-9403)*
Honeywell Authorized Dealer, Littleton Also Called: Airboss Heating and Coolg Inc *(G-9950)*
Honeywell Authorized Dealer, Raleigh Also Called: Allen Kelly & Co Inc *(G-12490)*
Honeywell Authorized Dealer, Wilmington Also Called: Kenny Fowler Heating and A Inc *(G-16288)*
Honeywell International Inc (PA) 704 627-6200
   855 S Mint St Charlotte (28202) *(G-2919)*
Honeywell International Inc 910 436-5144
   1 Fort Bragg Fort Bragg (28307) *(G-6090)*
Honeywell International Inc 919 662-7539
   201 S Rogers Ln Raleigh (27610) *(G-12857)*
Honeywell International Inc 252 977-2100
   3475 N Wesleyan Blvd Rocky Mount (27804) *(G-13701)*
Hood Container Corporation 336 887-5400
   3520 Dillon Rd Jamestown (27282) *(G-9055)*
Hood Container Corporation 336 784-0445
   555 Aureole St Winston Salem (27107) *(G-16748)*
Hood Packaging Corporation 910 582-1842
   740 Cheraw Rd Hamlet (28345) *(G-7623)*
Hoodoo Honey LLC 252 548-0697
   3600 N Duke St Ste 1 Durham (27704) *(G-5140)*
Hook Publications 219 808-3989
   11124 S Lowell Rd Bahama (27503) *(G-863)*
Hook-It-Up 980 253-4542
   3837 Bon Rea Dr Charlotte (28226) *(G-2920)*

Hooker Furniture Corporation..336 819-7200
2485 Penny Rd Fl 2 High Point (27265) *(G-8401)*

Hooks Inc Chris..704 516-1529
6500 Tall Oaks Trl Charlotte (28210) *(G-2921)*

Hooks Vineyard...919 917-5658
8145 Caliber Woods Dr Raleigh (27616) *(G-12858)*

Hootenanny Brewing Company LLC..............................704 254-6190
187 Shinnville Rd Mooresville (28115) *(G-10976)*

Hoover Bb Inc..615 872-4510
2129 Kingstree Cir Gastonia (28054) *(G-6419)*

Hoover Custom Tops, Kinston *Also Called: Buffalo Inv Group NC LLC (G-9348)*

Hoover Treated Wood Pdts Inc...866 587-8761
1772 Trueblood Rd Weldon (27890) *(G-15882)*

Hop A Chopper Inc...704 624-6794
6703 Old Pglnd Marshvl Rd Marshville (28103) *(G-10219)*

Hope Counseling Ctr..910 741-0538
971 Chadwick Shores Dr Sneads Ferry (28460) *(G-14491)*

Hope Renovations..919 960-1957
3 Bolin Hts Chapel Hill (27514) *(G-2024)*

Hope Tree Publishing LLC..336 858-5301
916 Big Creek Ct High Point (27265) *(G-8402)*

Hopewriters LLC..317 414-3342
4405 Gwen Hartis Ct Monroe (28110) *(G-10732)*

Hopkins Poultry Company..336 656-3361
7741 Doggett Rd Browns Summit (27214) *(G-1308)*

Hopperncleve Designs LLC..919 721-4406
423 Crutchfield Dr Cameron (28326) *(G-1561)*

Hoptown, Mooresville *Also Called: Hootenanny Brewing Company LLC (G-10976)*

Horballs Inc..919 925-0483
1009 Lila Ln Raleigh (27614) *(G-12859)*

Horiba Instruments Inc..828 676-2801
270 Rutledge Rd Unit D Fletcher (28732) *(G-6012)*

Horizon Forest Products, Raleigh *Also Called: Horizon Frest Pdts Wlmngton LP (G-12860)*

Horizon Forest Products Co LP......................................336 993-9663
9050 W Market St Colfax (27235) *(G-4151)*

Horizon Frest Pdts Wlmngton LP...................................919 424-8265
4115 Commodity Pkwy Raleigh (27610) *(G-12860)*

Horizon Home Imports Inc..704 859-5133
6211 Clementine Dr Clemmons (27012) *(G-4046)*

Horizon Lab Systems LLC...919 896-7737
8601 Six Forks Rd Ste 160 Raleigh (27615) *(G-12861)*

Horizon Publications Inc..828 464-0221
309 N College Ave Newton (28658) *(G-11941)*

Horizon Tool Inc..336 299-4182
7918 Industrial Village Rd Greensboro (27409) *(G-7101)*

Horizon Vision Research Inc..910 796-8600
1717 Shipyard Blvd Ste 140 Wilmington (28403) *(G-16257)*

Hormel, Charlotte *Also Called: Hormel Foods Corp Svcs LLC (G-2922)*

Hormel Foods Corp Svcs LLC..704 527-1535
3420 Toringdon Way Charlotte (28277) *(G-2922)*

Hornet Capital LLC (PA)..252 641-8000
1090 W Saint James St Tarboro (27886) *(G-15109)*

Hornwood Inc (PA)..704 848-4121
766 Haileys Ferry Rd Lilesville (28091) *(G-9838)*

Hornwood Inc...704 694-3009
204 E Wade St Wadesboro (28170) *(G-15512)*

Horseware Triple Crown Blanket....................................252 208-0080
1030 N Rogers Ln Raleigh (27610) *(G-12862)*

Hortonworks Inc..855 846-7866
312 Blackwell St Ste 100 Durham (27701) *(G-5141)*

Hos Woodworking Inc...712 298-1985
2704 Old Course Rd Monroe (28112) *(G-10733)*

Hose Products Division, Greensboro *Also Called: Parker-Hannifin Corporation (G-7245)*

Hoser Inc..704 989-7151
1132 Curtis St Monroe (28112) *(G-10734)*

Hosmer Woodworks..415 730-5401
321 E Renovah Cir Wilmington (28403) *(G-16258)*

Hospira Inc..252 977-5111
6551 N Us Highway 301 Battleboro (27809) *(G-922)*

Hospira Inc..704 335-1300
2815 Coliseum Centre Dr Ste 250 Charlotte (28217) *(G-2923)*

Hospira Inc..919 553-3831
8484 Us 70 Bus Hwy W Clayton (27520) *(G-3988)*

Hospira Inc..252 977-5500
Highway 301 North Rocky Mount (27801) *(G-13669)*

Hospira Inc..252 977-5111
4285 N Wesleyan Blvd Rocky Mount (27804) *(G-13702)*

Hospitality Mints LLC..828 262-0950
996 George Wilson Rd Boone (28607) *(G-1208)*

Hostetler Sawmill..336 468-1800
5400 Saint Paul Church Rd Hamptonville (27020) *(G-7671)*

Hot Box Power Coating Inc...704 398-8224
1033 Berryhill Rd Charlotte (28208) *(G-2924)*

Hot Chillys, Southern Pines *Also Called: Performance Apparel LLC (G-14544)*

Hot Shot Services LLC..336 244-0331
2202 Us 21 State Road (28676) *(G-14727)*

Hotchkis Bryde Incorporated..704 660-3060
118 Infield Ct Ste A Mooresville (28117) *(G-10977)*

Hotchkis Performance Mfg Inc.......................................704 660-3060
118 Infield Ct Ste A Mooresville (28117) *(G-10978)*

Houdiniesq, Durham *Also Called: Logicbit Software LLC (G-5194)*

House of Guns Inc..910 381-0732
377 Bannermans Mill Rd Richlands (28574) *(G-13555)*

House of Hops...919 819-0704
6909 Glenwood Ave Raleigh (27612) *(G-12863)*

House of Raeford Farms Inc..910 289-3191
1000 E Central Ave Raeford (28376) *(G-12423)*

House of Raeford Farms Inc (HQ).................................912 222-4090
3333 S Us Highway 117 Rose Hill (28458) *(G-13777)*

House of Raeford Farms Inc..910 763-0475
118 Cardinal Drive Ext Ste 102 Wilmington (28405) *(G-16259)*

House of Raeford Farms La LLC...................................336 751-4752
251 Eaton Rd Mocksville (27028) *(G-10580)*

House of Stitches...570 768-6930
2983 Simpson Mill Rd Dobson (27017) *(G-4826)*

House Staffer, Durham *Also Called: First Leads Inc (G-5097)*

House-Autry Mills Inc (PA)...919 963-6200
7000 Us Highway 301 S Four Oaks (27524) *(G-6107)*

Hovis Metal Fabricating Inc...704 922-5293
842 Lower Dallas Hwy Dallas (28034) *(G-4644)*

How Great Thou Art Publication....................................704 851-3117
Hwy 52 Sr 1003 Ste 357 Mc Farlan (28102) *(G-10381)*

Howard & Sons, Cary *Also Called: Beach Craft Woodworking LLC (G-1700)*

Howard Brothers Mfg LLC..919 772-4800
1321 Bobbitt Dr Garner (27529) *(G-6275)*

Howard Steel Inc...704 376-9631
3528 N Graham St Charlotte (28206) *(G-2925)*

Howell & Sons Canvas Repairs.....................................704 892-7913
29015 North Main St Cornelius (28031) *(G-4556)*

Howling Moon Distillery Inc...828 208-1469
42 Old Elk Mountain Rd Asheville (28804) *(G-655)*

Howmet Aerospace Inc...704 334-7276
301 N Smith St Charlotte (28202) *(G-2926)*

Howmet Aerospace Inc, Charlotte *Also Called: Howmet Aerospace Inc (G-2926)*

HP, Charlotte *Also Called: HP Inc (G-2927)*

HP Inc..704 523-3548
4035 South Blvd Charlotte (28209) *(G-2927)*

HP Textile, Winston Salem *Also Called: Hpfabrics Inc (G-16749)*

Hpc NC...704 978-0103
280 Crawford Rd Statesville (28625) *(G-14817)*

Hpfabrics Inc...336 231-0278
3821 Kimwell Dr Winston Salem (27103) *(G-16749)*

Hpfi, High Point *Also Called: High Point Furniture Inds Inc (G-8391)*

Hpt Hitoms LLC...336 541-8093
3008 Redford Dr Greensboro (27408) *(G-7102)*

Hrtms Incorporated...919 741-5099
801 Corporate Center Dr Ste 130 Raleigh (27607) *(G-12864)*

Hsm, Matthews *Also Called: High Mobility Solutions Inc (G-10253)*

Hsm Solutions, Hickory *Also Called: Hickory Springs Manufacturing Company (G-8052)*

Htc Logging Inc...828 625-1601
1055 Cooper Gap Rd Mill Spring (28756) *(G-10487)*

Htm Concepts Martin Entps LLC 252 789-0508
   23366 Nc Highway 125 Williamston (27892) *(G-16063)*

Htx Imaging, Carrboro *Also Called: Htx Technologies LLC (G-1648)*

Htx Technologies LLC 919 928-5688
   610 Jones Ferry Rd Ste 207 Carrboro (27510) *(G-1648)*

Hubbard Iron Inc 828 776-7168
   4383 Mintwood Dr Gastonia (28056) *(G-6420)*

Hubbell Incorporated 828 687-8505
   20 Glenn Bridge Rd Arden (28704) *(G-339)*

Hubbell Industrial Contrls Inc (HQ) 336 434-2800
   4301 Cheyenne Dr Archdale (27263) *(G-283)*

Hubbell Premise Wiring, Arden *Also Called: Hubbell Incorporated (G-339)*

Huber + Suhner Inc (DH) 704 790-7300
   8530 Steele Creek Place Dr Ste H Charlotte (28273) *(G-2928)*

Huber + Suhner North Amer Corp (HQ) 704 790-7300
   8530 Steele Creek Place Dr Ste H Charlotte (28273) *(G-2929)*

Huber Engineered Woods LLC (HQ) 800 933-9220
   10925 David Taylor Dr Ste 300 Charlotte (28262) *(G-2930)*

Huber Suhner USA Corporation, Charlotte *Also Called: Huber + Suhner North Amer Corp (G-2929)*

Huber Technology Inc (DH) 704 949-1010
   1009 Airlie Pkwy Denver (28037) *(G-4782)*

Huber Usa Inc 919 674-4266
   1101 Nowell Rd # 110 Raleigh (27607) *(G-12865)*

Hubergroup Usa Inc 336 292-5501
   651 Brigham Rd Ste C Greensboro (27409) *(G-7103)*

Huck Cycles Corporation 704 275-1735
   11020 Bailey Rd Ste D Cornelius (28031) *(G-4557)*

Huddle Furniture Inc (PA) 828 874-8888
   1801 Main St E Valdese (28690) *(G-15448)*

Hudson Industries LLC 704 480-0014
   439 Neisler St Shelby (28152) *(G-14327)*

Hudson Overall Company Inc 336 314-5024
   527 S Elm St Greensboro (27406) *(G-7104)*

Hudson Paving Inc 910 895-5910
   120 Yates Hill Rd Rockingham (28379) *(G-13630)*

Hudson S Hardware Inc (PA) 919 553-3030
   305 Benson Rd Garner (27529) *(G-6276)*

Hudson's Hardware, Castle Hayne *Also Called: Castle Hayne Hardware LLC (G-1945)*

Hudson's Hill, Greensboro *Also Called: Hudson Overall Company Inc (G-7104)*

Huff Mj LLC 910 313-3163
   5617 Carolina Beach Rd Wilmington (28412) *(G-16260)*

Huffman Finishing Company Inc 828 396-1741
   4919 Hickory Blvd Granite Falls (28630) *(G-6739)*

Huffman Sales and Service LLC 828 234-0693
   326 Macarthur Ln Burlington (27217) *(G-1431)*

Hugger Inc 704 735-7422
   1443 E Gaston St Lincolnton (28092) *(G-9895)*

Hugger Mugger LLC 910 585-2749
   229 Wicker St Sanford (27330) *(G-14134)*

Hugh's Sheet Metal, Statesville *Also Called: Hughs Sheet Mtal Sttsvlle LLC (G-14818)*

Hughes Furniture Inds Inc (PA) 336 498-8700
   952 S Stout Rd Randleman (27317) *(G-13473)*

Hughes Metal Works, Greensboro *Also Called: Hughes Metal Works LLC (G-7105)*

Hughes Metal Works LLC 336 297-0808
   1914 Fairfax Rd Greensboro (27407) *(G-7105)*

Hughes Products Co Inc 336 769-3788
   241 Emily Ann Dr Winston Salem (27107) *(G-16750)*

Hughes Products Co Inc 336 475-0091
   4422 Wallburg Rd Winston Salem (27107) *(G-16751)*

Hughes Sup of Thomasville Inc 336 475-8146
   175 Kanoy Rd Thomasville (27360) *(G-15232)*

Hughes Welding & Crane Svc LLC 910 895-9767
   121 Mill Rd Rockingham (28379) *(G-13631)*

Hughs Sheet Mtal Sttsvlle LLC 704 872-4621
   1312 N Barkley Rd Statesville (28677) *(G-14818)*

Huitt Mills Inc (PA) 828 322-8628
   115 10th St Ne Hildebran (28637) *(G-8624)*

Hull Brothers Lumber Co Inc 336 789-5252
   579 Maple Hollow Rd Mount Airy (27030) *(G-11519)*

Hull's Wall Covering, Bessemer City *Also Called: Patricia Hall (G-1077)*

Humber Street Facility Inc 919 775-3628
   105 E Humber St Sanford (27330) *(G-14135)*

Humble Tree Naturals 704 770-1007
   4544 Randolph Rd Apt 70 Charlotte (28211) *(G-2931)*

Humbly Made Brand 740 506-1554
   2411 Still Forest Pl Apt 303 Raleigh (27607) *(G-12866)*

Humboldt Mfg Co Inc 919 832-6509
   2525 Atlantic Ave Raleigh (27604) *(G-12867)*

Humility Bracelets 704 277-5896
   5516 Challis View Ln Charlotte (28226) *(G-2932)*

Hummingbird 3d Solutions LLC 336 792-6637
   256 W Trade St Burlington (27217) *(G-1432)*

Hummingbird Naturals LLC 774 276-0889
   1304 Colton Creek Rd Knightdale (27545) *(G-9418)*

Hunckler Fabrication LLC 336 753-0905
   123 S Park Pl Mocksville (27028) *(G-10581)*

Huneywood Inc 704 385-9785
   7123 Sugar And Wine Rd Monroe (28110) *(G-10735)*

Huneywood Frames, Monroe *Also Called: Huneywood Inc (G-10735)*

Hunsucker Printing Co Inc 336 629-9125
   522 N Fayetteville St Asheboro (27203) *(G-441)*

Hunt Country Component LLC 336 475-7000
   1120 Trinity St Thomasville (27360) *(G-15233)*

Hunt Kendall Publishing 919 510-0160
   11717 Stannary Pl Raleigh (27613) *(G-12868)*

Hunt Logging Co 919 853-2850
   2233 Person Rd Louisburg (27549) *(G-9991)*

Hunter Fan Company 704 896-9250
   20464 Chartwell Center Dr Ste H Cornelius (28031) *(G-4558)*

Hunter Farms 336 822-2300
   1900 N Main St High Point (27262) *(G-8403)*

Hunter Farms, High Point *Also Called: Hunter Farms (G-8403)*

Hunter Innovations Ltd 919 848-8814
   1201 Corporation Pkwy Raleigh (27610) *(G-12869)*

Hunter Liver Mush Inc 828 652-7902
   98 Poteat Rd Marion (28752) *(G-10151)*

Hunter Millwork Inc 704 821-0144
   422 Seaboard Dr Matthews (28104) *(G-10321)*

Huntington House Inc 828 495-4400
   210 Bethlehem Park Ln Taylorsville (28681) *(G-15147)*

Huntington House Inc (PA) 828 495-4400
   661 Rink Dam Rd Hickory (28601) *(G-8060)*

Huntpack Inc 704 986-0684
   320 Anderson Rd Albemarle (28001) *(G-90)*

Huntsman Corporation 706 272-4020
   3400 Westinghouse Blvd Charlotte (28273) *(G-2933)*

Huntsman International LLC 704 588-6082
   3400 Westinghouse Blvd Charlotte (28273) *(G-2934)*

Huntsman Textile Effects 704 587-5000
   3400 Westinghouse Blvd Charlotte (28273) *(G-2935)*

Huo LI Juice & Co LLC 804 299-0806
   11104 Bryton Pkwy # 5113 Huntersville (28078) *(G-8831)*

Hurleys Ornamental Iron 910 576-4731
   2179 Love Joy Rd Troy (27371) *(G-15407)*

Hurricane Aqua Sports Inc 910 293-2941
   170 Water Tank Rd Warsaw (28398) *(G-15669)*

Hurricane Kayaks, Warsaw *Also Called: Hurricane Aqua Sports Inc (G-15669)*

Hurst Jaws of Life Inc (HQ) 704 487-6961
   711 N Post Rd Shelby (28150) *(G-14328)*

Hush Greensboro 336 676-6133
   433 Spring Garden St Greensboro (27401) *(G-7106)*

Husky Rack and Wire, Denver *Also Called: Wireway/Husky Corp (G-4815)*

Husqvarna Forest & Garden, Charlotte *Also Called: Husqvma Cnsmr Otdoor Pdts NA (G-2936)*

Husqvarna Prof Outdoor Pdts, Charlotte *Also Called: Husqvrna Cnsmr Otdoor Pdts NA (G-2937)*

Husqvrna Cnsmr Otdoor Pdts NA (HQ) 704 597-5000
   9335 Harris Corners Pkwy Ste 500 Charlotte (28269) *(G-2936)*

Husqvrna Cnsmr Otdoor Pdts NA 704 597-5000
   7349 Statesville Rd Charlotte (28269) *(G-2937)*

Husqvrna Cnsmr Otdoor Pdts NA 704 494-4810
   8825 Statesville Rd Charlotte (28269) *(G-2938)*

ALPHABETIC SECTION

Hutton Vineyards LLC.. 336 374-2321
103 Buck Fork Rd Dobson (27017) *(G-4827)*

Huvepharma Inc.. 910 506-4649
22300 Skyway Church Rd Maxton (28364) *(G-10356)*

Hvte Inc.. 919 274-8899
90 Mosswood Blvd Ste 100 Youngsville (27596) *(G-17084)*

Hycorr LLC... 216 570-7408
10115 Kincey Ave Huntersville (28078) *(G-8832)*

Hydac Technology Corp... 610 266-0100
1051 Airlie Pkwy Denver (28037) *(G-4783)*

Hyde Park Partners Inc (PA)... 704 587-4819
11529 Wilmar Blvd Charlotte (28273) *(G-2939)*

Hydra Cut LLC... 252 814-1654
4745 Reedy Branch Rd Winterville (28590) *(G-17003)*

Hydralic Engnered Pdts Svc Inc.. 704 374-1306
803 Pressley Rd Ste 101 Charlotte (28217) *(G-2940)*

Hydrant Mechanics.. 919 922-3829
7303 Hickory Crossroads Rd Princeton (27569) *(G-12401)*

Hydraulic Hose Depot Inc.. 252 356-1862
1520c River Rd Cofield (27922) *(G-4135)*

Hydraulic Valve Division, Forest City *Also Called: Parker-Hannifin Corporation (G-6079)*

Hydraulics Express.. 828 251-2500
40 Interstate Blvd Asheville (28806) *(G-656)*

Hydreco Inc.. 704 295-7575
1500 Continental Blvd Ste Z Charlotte (28273) *(G-2941)*

Hydro Extrusion Usa LLC.. 336 227-8826
1512 Industry Dr Burlington (27215) *(G-1433)*

Hydro Service & Supplies Inc (PA).. 919 544-3744
513 United Dr Durham (27713) *(G-5142)*

Hydro Tube Enterprises Inc... 919 258-3070
2645 Mount Pisgah Church Rd Sanford (27332) *(G-14136)*

Hydro Tube South LLC.. 919 258-3070
2645 Mount Pisgah Church Rd Sanford (27332) *(G-14137)*

Hydroeye Marine Group LLC... 828 394-4406
8326 Mount Harmony Rd Connelly Springs (28612) *(G-4404)*

Hydrohoist of North Carolina... 704 799-1910
1258 River Hwy Mooresville (28117) *(G-10979)*

Hydrohoist of The Carolinas, Mooresville *Also Called: Hydrohoist of North Carolina (G-10979)*

Hydromer Inc (PA)... 908 526-2828
4715 Corporate Dr Nw Ste 200 Concord (28027) *(G-4282)*

Hydrotex Usa Inc... 919 876-4170
1065 Bullard Ct Raleigh (27615) *(G-12870)*

Hygeia Corporation.. 704 933-5190
Kannapolis (28082) *(G-9122)*

Hygeia Marketing Corporation... 704 933-5190
729 S Main St Kannapolis (28081) *(G-9123)*

Hygiene Systems Inc... 910 462-2661
10442 Old Wire Rd Laurel Hill (28351) *(G-9461)*

Hylite Led, Charlotte *Also Called: Arva LLC (G-2223)*

Hyman Furniture Warehouse, Winston Salem *Also Called: Hyman Furniture Warehouse LLC (G-16752)*

Hyman Furniture Warehouse LLC.. 336 528-4950
1901 Margaret St Winston Salem (27103) *(G-16752)*

Hyosung Holdings Usa Inc (HQ).. 704 790-6134
15801 Brixham Hill Ave Ste 575 Charlotte (28277) *(G-2942)*

Hyosung Usa Inc (DH)... 704 790-6100
15801 Brixham Hill Ave Ste 575 Charlotte (28277) *(G-2943)*

Hyper Analytical Software LLC.. 919 267-4897
822 Blackmar St Cary (27519) *(G-1785)*

Hyper Networks LLC... 704 837-8411
12249 Nations Ford Rd Pineville (28134) *(G-12274)*

Hyperbranch, Durham *Also Called: Stryker Corporation (G-5378)*

Hyperbranch Medical Tech Inc.. 919 433-3325
800 Capitola Dr Ste 12 Durham (27713) *(G-5143)*

Hypernova Inc.. 704 360-0096
1228 Archdale Dr Apt E Charlotte (28217) *(G-2944)*

Hypernova Solutions, Charlotte *Also Called: Hypernova Inc (G-2944)*

Hyster-Yale Group Inc.. 252 931-5100
1400 Sullivan Dr Greenville (27834) *(G-7540)*

Hyster-Yale Group Inc.. 252 931-5100
5200 Martin Luther King Jr Hwy Greenville (27834) *(G-7541)*

Hyster-Yale Group Inc (HQ)... 252 931-5100
1400 Sullivan Dr Greenville (27834) *(G-7542)*

Hysucat USA LLC.. 919 345-0240
12608 Leatherwood Ct Raleigh (27613) *(G-12871)*

Hzo, Morrisville *Also Called: Hzo Inc (G-11355)*

Hzo Inc (PA).. 919 439-0505
5151 Mccrimmon Pkwy Ste 208 Morrisville (27560) *(G-11355)*

I & I Sling Inc... 336 323-1532
3824 Patterson St Greensboro (27407) *(G-7107)*

I A C, Red Springs *Also Called: Industrial and Agricultural Chemicals Incorporated (G-13501)*

I C E S Gaston County Inc.. 704 263-1418
102 Mariposa Rd Stanley (28164) *(G-14697)*

I G M, Charlotte *Also Called: IGM Resins USA Inc (G-2950)*

I G P... 828 728-5338
1477 Connelly Springs Rd Lenoir (28645) *(G-9621)*

I I G Logging Inc.. 704 984-3175
10342 Highway 145 Morven (28119) *(G-11471)*

I Mix 4 U LLC... 336 307-6297
219 Santa Fe Cir Thomasville (27360) *(G-15234)*

I Must Garden LLC.. 919 929-2299
1500 Garner Rd Ste D Raleigh (27610) *(G-12872)*

I N I, Morrisville *Also Called: Ini Power Systems Inc (G-11359)*

I Print Ttees LLC... 336 202-8148
241 E Market St Greensboro (27401) *(G-7108)*

I R C, Boone *Also Called: Tresco (G-1242)*

I S A, Durham *Also Called: International Society Automtn (G-5162)*

I S G, Raleigh *Also Called: Insurance Systems Group Inc (G-12894)*

I T G, Greensboro *Also Called: Itg Holdings Inc (G-7126)*

I T G Raeford... 910 875-3736
1001 Turnpike Rd Raeford (28376) *(G-12424)*

I W S, High Point *Also Called: Interior Wood Specialties Inc (G-8413)*

I-40 Machine and Tool Inc... 704 881-0242
223 Commerce Blvd Statesville (28625) *(G-14819)*

I-Leadr Inc.. 910 431-5252
2220 Lazy Ln Sherrills Ford (28673) *(G-14385)*

I-Lumenate... 704 966-1910
2830 Hagers Ct Denver (28037) *(G-4784)*

I-Lumenate... 336 448-0356
353 Jonestown Rd Winston Salem (27104) *(G-16753)*

I2e Group LLC... 336 884-2014
2108 S Elm St High Point (27260) *(G-8404)*

I2m LLC... 984 202-0582
801 Corporate Center Dr Ste 128 Raleigh (27607) *(G-12873)*

IAMS, Henderson *Also Called: Mars Petcare Us Inc (G-7798)*

Ibd Outdoor Rooms, Concord *Also Called: Mystic Lifestyle Inc (G-4322)*

Ibeny Embroidering LLC.. 347 286-1299
4800 Express Dr Charlotte (28208) *(G-2945)*

IBM, Durham *Also Called: International Bus Mchs Corp (G-5161)*

Ibolili Natural Fibers... 866 834-9857
104 Leonard Dr Greensboro (27410) *(G-7109)*

Ibolili Natural Home Furn, Greensboro *Also Called: Ibolili Natural Fibers (G-7109)*

Ibx Lumber LLC... 252 935-4050
405 Mainstem Rd Pantego (27860) *(G-12164)*

Ica Mid-Atlantic Inc.. 336 447-4546
6532 Judge Adams Rd Whitsett (27377) *(G-15993)*

Ica(usa)inc... 704 798-3488
1728 Jonestown Rd Winston Salem (27103) *(G-16754)*

Icagen LLC... 919 941-5206
1035 Swabia Ct Ste 110 Durham (27703) *(G-5144)*

Ican Clothes Company.. 910 670-1494
1617 Owen Dr Fayetteville (28304) *(G-5840)*

Icare Tonometer, Raleigh *Also Called: Icare Usa Inc (G-12874)*

Icare Usa Inc.. 919 877-9607
809 Faulkner Pl Raleigh (27609) *(G-12874)*

ICC, High Point *Also Called: Industrial Container Corp (G-8408)*

Ice, Matthews *Also Called: International Cnstr Eqp Inc (G-10322)*

Ice Box Company Inc... 910 579-3273
570 Meadow Summit Dr Ste 19 Ocean Isle Beach (28469) *(G-12092)*

Ice Companies Inc (PA)... 910 791-1970
2820 Carolina Beach Rd Wilmington (28412) *(G-16261)*

ALPHABETIC SECTION

Ice Cube Recording Studios......... 910 260-7616
801 Greenfield St Wilmington (28401) *(G-16262)*

Ice River Springs Usa Inc (HQ)......... 519 925-2929
601 E Union St Morganton (28655) *(G-11222)*

Ice River Springs Water, Morganton *Also Called: Ice River Springs Usa Inc (G-11222)*

ICEE Company......... 704 357-6865
1901 Associates Ln Ste A Charlotte (28217) *(G-2946)*

ICEE Company......... 910 346-3937
13 E Doris Ave Ste H Jacksonville (28540) *(G-9008)*

ICI Copy Forms & Printing, Charlotte *Also Called: Insta Copy Shop Ltd (G-2977)*

Ickler Manufacturing LLC......... 704 658-1195
229 Pitt Rd Mooresville (28115) *(G-10980)*

Icon Boiler Inc......... 844 562-4266
2025 16th St Greensboro (27405) *(G-7110)*

Icon Coolers LLC......... 855 525-4266
7213 Ogden Business Ln Wilmington (28411) *(G-16263)*

Icon Sign Systems Inc......... 828 253-4266
23 Villemagne Dr Asheville (28804) *(G-657)*

Iconic Marine Group LLC (PA)......... 252 975-2000
1653 Whichards Beach Rd Chocowinity (27817) *(G-3895)*

Icons America LLC......... 704 922-0041
1055 Gastonia Technology Pkwy Dallas (28034) *(G-4645)*

Icontact LLC......... 919 957-6150
2450 Perimeter Park Dr Ste 105 Morrisville (27560) *(G-11356)*

ICP, Winston Salem *Also Called: Industrial Control Panels Inc (G-16758)*

Ics North America Corp......... 704 794-6620
323 Corban Ave Sw Ste 504 Concord (28025) *(G-4283)*

Ict/Data On Cd Inc......... 704 841-8404
9123 Monroe Rd Ste 145 Charlotte (28270) *(G-2947)*

ID Images LLC......... 704 494-0444
2311 Distribution Center Dr Ste A Charlotte (28269) *(G-2948)*

ID Pros LLC......... 904 887-6210
2618 Crowders Creek Rd Gastonia (28052) *(G-6421)*

Idael Mfg Co......... 919 480-1329
6300 Creedmoor Rd Raleigh (27612) *(G-12875)*

Idaho Timber NC LLC (HQ)......... 252 430-0030
1431 Nicholas St Henderson (27536) *(G-7789)*

Idaho Wood Inc......... 208 263-9521
114 Southgate Dr Oxford (27565) *(G-12132)*

Idea People Inc......... 704 398-4437
14311 Reese Blvd W Huntersville (28078) *(G-8833)*

Idea Software Inc......... 407 453-3883
10814 Greater Hills St Raleigh (27614) *(G-12876)*

Ideablock LLC......... 919 551-5054
212 W Main St Ste 302 Durham (27701) *(G-5145)*

Ideacode Inc......... 919 341-5170
11010 W Northwood St Greensboro (27408) *(G-7111)*

Ideaitlia Cntmporary Furn Corp......... 828 464-1000
1902 Emmanuel Church Rd Conover (28613) *(G-4466)*

Ideal Accessories, Oxford *Also Called: Ideal Fastener Corporation (G-12133)*

Ideal Fastener Corporation (PA)......... 919 693-3115
603 W Industry Dr Oxford (27565) *(G-12133)*

Ideal Liquidation Inc......... 828 632-3771
171 5th Ave Sw Taylorsville (28681) *(G-15148)*

Ideal Precast Inc......... 919 801-8287
7020 Mount Hermon Church Rd Durham (27705) *(G-5146)*

Ideal Precision Meter Inc......... 919 571-2000
5816 Creedmoor Rd Ste 103 Raleigh (27612) *(G-12877)*

Ideal Printing......... 336 754-4050
4926 Harley Dr Walkertown (27051) *(G-15614)*

Ideal Printing Services Inc......... 336 784-0074
4240 Kernersville Rd Ste D Kernersville (27284) *(G-9205)*

Ideas Aesthetech, Wendell *Also Called: Modern Tool Service (G-15909)*

Identify Yourself LLC......... 252 202-1452
6146 N Croatan Hwy Unit C Kitty Hawk (27949) *(G-9407)*

Identigraph Signs & Awnings......... 704 635-7911
1132 Curtis St Monroe (28112) *(G-10736)*

Identity Custom Signage Inc......... 336 882-7446
324 Burton Ave High Point (27262) *(G-8405)*

Idexx Pharmaceuticals Inc......... 336 834-6500
7009 Albert Pick Rd Greensboro (27409) *(G-7112)*

Idustrial Burkett Services......... 252 244-0143
2050 Nc Highway 43 Vanceboro (28586) *(G-15478)*

Idx Corporation......... 252 948-2048
234 Springs Rd Washington (27889) *(G-15710)*

Idx Impressions LLC (DH)......... 703 550-6902
234 Springs Rd Washington (27889) *(G-15711)*

Idx North Carolina, Washington *Also Called: Idx Corporation (G-15710)*

Ie Furniture Inc (PA)......... 336 475-5050
1121 Corporation Dr Archdale (27263) *(G-284)*

Ientertainment Network Inc (PA)......... 919 238-4090
100 Club Dr Ste 203 Burnsville (28714) *(G-1528)*

If Armor International LLC......... 704 482-1399
2501 W Dixon Blvd Shelby (28152) *(G-14329)*

If Disher Meat Processing......... 336 463-2907
1437 Old Stage Rd Yadkinville (27055) *(G-17041)*

If Tees Could Talk LLC......... 919 938-8031
549 E Main St Clayton (27520) *(G-3989)*

Ifab Corp......... 704 864-3032
2408 Forbes Rd Gastonia (28056) *(G-6422)*

Ifanatic LLC (PA)......... 919 387-6062
105 Shalon Ct Apex (27502) *(G-203)*

Ifb Solutions, Winston Salem *Also Called: Winstn-Slem Inds For Blind Inc (G-16979)*

Ifpo - Ifmo/American Image Inc......... 336 945-9867
5043 Highland Grove Pl Hamptonville (27020) *(G-7672)*

Ifs, Burlington *Also Called: Impact Fulfillment Svcs LLC (G-1434)*

Ifs Industries, Morrisville *Also Called: Ifs Industries Inc (G-11357)*

Ifs Industries Inc......... 919 234-1397
100 Southcenter Ct Ste 300 Morrisville (27560) *(G-11357)*

Ifta Usa Inc......... 919 659-8393
4819 Emperor Blvd Ste 400 Durham (27703) *(G-5147)*

Igh Enterprises Inc......... 704 372-6744
2001 W Morehead St Charlotte (28208) *(G-2949)*

IGM Resins USA Inc (DH)......... 704 588-2500
3300 Westinghouse Blvd Charlotte (28273) *(G-2950)*

Igm Specialties Holding Inc (DH)......... 704 945-8702
3300 Westinghouse Blvd Charlotte (28273) *(G-2951)*

Ignite Dirt Sports LLC......... 704 770-7806
19825 North Cove Rd Ste 171 Cornelius (28031) *(G-4559)*

Igniterate LLC......... 919 473-9560
600 Park Offices Dr Ste 300-137 Durham (27709) *(G-5148)*

Ika, Wilmington *Also Called: Ika-Works Inc (G-16264)*

Ika-Works Inc (HQ)......... 910 452-7059
2635 Northchase Pkwy Se Wilmington (28405) *(G-16264)*

Ilco Unican Holding Corp......... 252 446-3321
400 Jeffreys Rd Rocky Mount (27804) *(G-13703)*

Illinois Tool Works Inc......... 336 996-7046
1210 S Park Dr Kernersville (27284) *(G-9206)*

Ilmor Marine LLC......... 704 360-1901
186 Penske Way Mooresville (28115) *(G-10981)*

Ilsemann Corp......... 610 323-4143
2555 Westinghouse Blvd Charlotte (28273) *(G-2952)*

Iluka Resources Inc......... 904 284-9832
4208 Six Forks Rd Ste 1000 Raleigh (27609) *(G-12878)*

Iluma Alliance, Durham *Also Called: Premex Inc (G-5304)*

Ilumivu Inc......... 410 570-8846
1200 Ridgefield Blvd Ste 170 Asheville (28806) *(G-658)*

Imaflex Usa Inc......... 336 885-8131
7137 Prospect Church Rd Thomasville (27360) *(G-15235)*

Imaflex Usa Inc (HQ)......... 336 474-1190
1201 Unity St Thomasville (27360) *(G-15236)*

Image 360, Raleigh-Rtp, Raleigh *Also Called: Greene Imaging & Design Inc (G-12814)*

Image 420 Screen Printing, Asheville *Also Called: Image 420 Screenprinting Inc (G-659)*

Image 420 Screenprinting Inc......... 828 253-9420
420 Haywood Rd Asheville (28806) *(G-659)*

Image Design......... 910 862-8988
113 W Broad St Elizabethtown (28337) *(G-5597)*

Image Designs Ink LLC......... 252 235-1964
12687 Sanford St Bailey (27807) *(G-875)*

Image Industries NC Inc......... 828 464-8882
1848 Saint Pauls Church Rd Newton (28658) *(G-11942)*

Image Matters Inc......... 336 940-3000
1808 Ramhurst Dr Clemmons (27012) *(G-4047)*

ALPHABETIC SECTION

Image Solutions.. 336 769-8403
  332b Shellybrook Dr Pilot Mountain (27041) *(G-12197)*
Image Works Inc... 336 668-3338
  120 Wade St Ste A Jamestown (27282) *(G-9056)*
Image360 North Raleigh NC....................................... 919 307-4119
  8471 Garvey Dr Ste 101 Raleigh (27616) *(G-12879)*
Imagemark, Gastonia Also Called: Imagemark Business Svcs Inc *(G-6423)*
Imagemark Business Svcs Inc (PA)............................ 704 865-4912
  3145 Northwest Blvd Gastonia (28052) *(G-6423)*
Images of America Inc... 336 475-7106
  829 Blair St Thomasville (27360) *(G-15237)*
Imagesmith, Arden Also Called: Smith & Fox Inc *(G-377)*
Imagination Fabrication... 919 280-4430
  810 Center St Apex (27502) *(G-204)*
Imagine One LLC.. 828 324-6454
  420 3rd Ave Nw Hickory (28601) *(G-8061)*
Imagine One Resources LLC..................................... 828 328-1142
  420 3rd Ave Nw Hickory (28601) *(G-8062)*
Imagine That Creations LLC...................................... 480 528-6775
  104 Eastside Dr Black Mountain (28711) *(G-1125)*
Imagineoptix Corporation... 919 757-4945
  20 Tw Alexander Dr Ste 100 Durham (27709) *(G-5149)*
Imaginesoftware, Charlotte Also Called: Technology Partners LLC *(G-3677)*
Imbrium Therapeutics LP.. 984 439-1075
  400 Park Offices Dr Ste Ll 102 Morrisville (27560) *(G-11358)*
IMC, Shelby Also Called: Imc-Metalsamerica LLC *(G-14330)*
Imc-Metalsamerica LLC (HQ)..................................... 704 482-8200
  135 Old Boiling Springs Rd Shelby (28152) *(G-14330)*
Imerys Clays Inc.. 828 648-2668
  125 N Main St Canton (28716) *(G-1618)*
Imerys Mica Kings Mountain Inc................................. 704 739-3616
  1469 S Battleground Ave Kings Mountain (28086) *(G-9309)*
Imerys Perlite Usa Inc... 919 562-0031
  100 Robert Blunt Dr Youngsville (27596) *(G-17085)*
Immedia Print, Winston Salem Also Called: Baicy Communications Inc *(G-16622)*
Immi Safeguard, High Point Also Called: Indiana Mills & Manufacturing *(G-8407)*
Immixt LLC.. 336 207-8679
  9743 Silk Hope Liberty Rd Siler City (27344) *(G-14415)*
Immunotek Bio Centers LLC..................................... 828 569-6264
  1040 2nd St Ne Hickory (28601) *(G-8063)*
Immunotek Bio Centers LLC..................................... 336 781-4901
  1628 S Main St Ste 105 High Point (27260) *(G-8406)*
IMO Industries Inc (HQ)... 301 323-9000
  420 National Business Pkwy Fl 5 Monroe (28110) *(G-10737)*
IMO Industries Inc.. 704 289-6511
  1710 Airport Rd Monroe (28110) *(G-10738)*
IMO Pump, Monroe Also Called: Colfax Pump Group *(G-10688)*
Impact Digital Printing Inc.. 704 609-7638
  18605 Northline Dr Ste E11 Cornelius (28031) *(G-4560)*
Impact Fulfillment Svcs LLC (PA)................................ 336 227-1130
  1601 Anthony Rd Burlington (27215) *(G-1434)*
Impact Plastics Inc... 910 205-1493
  1057 County Home Rd Hamlet (28345) *(G-7624)*
Impact Printing and Design LLC................................. 919 377-9747
  2908 N Main St Ste 112 Fuquay Varina (27526) *(G-6203)*
Impact Technologies LLC... 704 400-5364
  4171 Deerfield Dr Nw Concord (28027) *(G-4284)*
Impeccable Improvements NC, Salisbury Also Called: Shield & Steel Enterprises LLC *(G-14043)*
Imperial Falcon Group Inc.. 646 717-1128
  3440 Toringdon Way Ste 205 Charlotte (28277) *(G-2953)*
Imperial Machine Co, Bessemer City Also Called: Imperial Machine Company Inc *(G-1071)*
Imperial Machine Company Inc.................................. 704 739-8038
  4429 Kings Mountain Hwy Bessemer City (28016) *(G-1071)*
Imperial Printing Pdts Co Inc.................................... 704 554-1188
  141 Robins St Lowell (28098) *(G-10009)*
Imperial Usa Ltd.. 704 596-2444
  1535 Elizabeth Ave Ste 201 Charlotte (28204) *(G-2954)*
Imperial Vault Company... 336 983-6343
  1 Sun Dr King (27021) *(G-9273)*
Implus Footcare LLC (DH).. 800 446-7587
  2001 Tw Alexander Dr Durham (27709) *(G-5150)*

Implus LLC.. 828 485-3318
  1279 19th Street Ln Nw Hickory (28601) *(G-8064)*
Imprint Publishing LLC... 678 650-1140
  3403 Arsenal Ct Apt 311 Charlotte (28273) *(G-2955)*
Imprinting Systems Spcalty Inc.................................. 704 527-4545
  803 Pressley Rd Ste 104 Charlotte (28217) *(G-2956)*
Improved Nature LLC... 919 588-2299
  101 Vandora Springs Rd Garner (27529) *(G-6277)*
Impulse NC, Mount Olive Also Called: AFL Network Services Inc *(G-11653)*
Impulse NC LLC... 919 658-2311
  100 Impulse Way Mount Olive (28365) *(G-11662)*
IMS, Winston Salem Also Called: International McHy Sls Inc *(G-16763)*
IMS Fabrication Inc... 704 216-0255
  150 Summit Park Dr Salisbury (28146) *(G-13982)*
IMS Intrnational Mfrs Showroom................................ 336 454-0388
  4250 Furniture Ave Jamestown (27282) *(G-9057)*
IMS Usa LLC.. 910 796-2040
  110 Portwatch Way Ste 103 Wilmington (28412) *(G-16265)*
In Acorda Therapeutics.. 914 347-4300
  5300 Balmy Dawn Ct Raleigh (27613) *(G-12880)*
In Blue Handmade Inc.. 828 774-5094
  20 Westside Dr Asheville (28806) *(G-660)*
In Pink... 919 380-1487
  112 Swiss Stone Ct Cary (27513) *(G-1786)*
In Stitches Custom EMB LLC..................................... 336 655-3498
  6011 Rollingreen Dr Winston Salem (27103) *(G-16755)*
In Style Kitchen Cabinetry.. 336 769-9605
  8570 N Nc Highway 109 Winston Salem (27107) *(G-16756)*
In Your Business Inc... 704 443-1330
  4820 Pimlico Ln Waxhaw (28173) *(G-15761)*
Incantare Art By Marilyn LLC..................................... 704 713-8846
  15701 Pedlar Mills Rd Charlotte (28278) *(G-2957)*
Ind Fab Inc... 252 977-0811
  8311 Vickers Rd Elm City (27822) *(G-5650)*
Indapharma LLC... 919 968-4500
  512 Booth Rd Chapel Hill (27516) *(G-2025)*
Indaux Usa Inc.. 336 861-0740
  548 Nc Highway 801 N Advance (27006) *(G-43)*
Independence Holdings Inc....................................... 704 588-6202
  1001 Westinghouse Blvd Charlotte (28273) *(G-2958)*
Independence Lumber.. 336 366-3400
  350 Elkin Wildlife Rd Elkin (28621) *(G-5619)*
Independence Lumber Inc... 276 773-3744
  18900 Riverwind Ln Davidson (28036) *(G-4678)*
Independence Printing... 336 771-0234
  130 Back Forty Dr Winston Salem (27127) *(G-16757)*
Independent Beverage Co LLC (PA)............................ 704 399-2504
  3936 Corporation Cir Charlotte (28216) *(G-2959)*
Indestructible LLC.. 804 601-4097
  525 N Tryon St Ste 1600 Charlotte (28202) *(G-2960)*
Indian Head Industries Inc (PA)................................. 704 547-7411
  6200 Harris Technology Blvd Charlotte (28269) *(G-2961)*
Indian Head Industries Inc....................................... 704 547-7411
  229 Park Ave Murphy (28906) *(G-11710)*
Indian Health Spring Water, Murphy Also Called: CHI Resources *(G-11707)*
Indian Motorcycle Charlotte, Lowell Also Called: Indian Motorcycle Company *(G-10010)*
Indian Motorcycle Company....................................... 704 879-4560
  110 Indian Walk Lowell (28098) *(G-10010)*
Indian Tff-Tank Greensboro Inc................................. 336 625-2629
  2491 Mountain Lake Rd Asheboro (27205) *(G-442)*
Indiana Chair Frame 3200, Liberty Also Called: Indiana Chair Frame Company *(G-9817)*
Indiana Chair Frame Company.................................... 574 825-9355
  330 N Greensboro St Liberty (27298) *(G-9817)*
Indiana Mills & Manufacturing.................................... 336 862-7519
  200 Swathmore Ave High Point (27263) *(G-8407)*
Indie Publishing... 919 435-6215
  2623 Hamlet Green Dr Raleigh (27614) *(G-12881)*
Indie Services... 336 524-6966
  205 E Davis St Burlington (27215) *(G-1435)*
Indivior Manufacturing LLC....................................... 804 594-0974
  8900 Capital Blvd Raleigh (27616) *(G-12882)*

Indorama Ventures USA Inc (DH).. 336 672-0101
801 Pineview Rd Asheboro (27203) *(G-443)*

Indramat Div, Charlotte *Also Called: Bosch Rexroth Corporation* *(G-2336)*

Induction Food Systems Inc.. 919 907-0179
2609 Discovery Dr Ste 115 Raleigh (27616) *(G-12883)*

Indulgent Essential Spices, Franklinton *Also Called: Indulgent Essential Spices LLC* *(G-6155)*

Indulgent Essential Spices LLC... 919 973-3069
7 W Mason St Ste A Franklinton (27525) *(G-6155)*

Indulor America LP.. 336 578-6855
932 E Elm St Graham (27253) *(G-6692)*

Induspac USA... 919 484-9484
3829 S Miami Blvd Durham (27703) *(G-5151)*

Industrial Air Inc... 336 292-1030
428 Edwardia Dr Greensboro (27409) *(G-7113)*

Industrial and Agricultural Chemicals Incorporated.................. 910 843-2121
2042 Buie Philadelphus Rd Red Springs (28377) *(G-13501)*

Industrial Anodizing.. 336 434-2110
112 School Rd Trinity (27370) *(G-15346)*

Industrial Automation Company... 877 727-8757
544 Pylon Dr Raleigh (27606) *(G-12884)*

Industrial Cleaning Eqp Co, Wilmington *Also Called: Ice Companies Inc* *(G-16261)*

Industrial Cnnctons Sltons LLC (DH)..................................... 203 229-3932
305 Gregson Dr Cary (27511) *(G-1787)*

Industrial Coatings, Greensboro *Also Called: PPG Industries Inc* *(G-7273)*

Industrial Construction, Sylva *Also Called: Wnc White Corporation* *(G-15076)*

Industrial Container Corp... 336 886-7031
107 Motsinger St High Point (27260) *(G-8408)*

Industrial Container Inc... 336 882-1310
107 Motsinger St High Point (27260) *(G-8409)*

Industrial Control Panels Inc.. 336 661-3037
152 Capp St Ste A Winston Salem (27105) *(G-16758)*

Industrial Ctd Fabrics Group, Rutherfordton *Also Called: Trelleborg Ctd Systems US Inc* *(G-13897)*

Industrial Cting Solutions Inc... 910 398-7556
9049 Industrial Blvd Ne Leland (28451) *(G-9549)*

Industrial Elcpltg Co Inc... 704 867-4547
1401 Gaston Ave Gastonia (28052) *(G-6424)*

Industrial Elcpltg Co Inc (PA)... 704 867-4547
307 Linwood Rd Gastonia (28052) *(G-6425)*

Industrial Glass Tech LLC... 704 853-2429
112 Superior Stainless Rd Gastonia (28052) *(G-6426)*

Industrial Glass Technologies, Gastonia *Also Called: Industrial Glass Tech LLC* *(G-6426)*

Industrial Hard Carbon LLC.. 704 489-1488
771 Crosspoint Dr Denver (28037) *(G-4785)*

Industrial Heat LLC.. 919 743-5727
1017 Main Campus Dr Raleigh (27606) *(G-12885)*

Industrial Lubricants Inc.. 336 767-0013
1110 Fairchild Rd Winston Salem (27105) *(G-16759)*

Industrial Machine & Wldg Inc... 910 251-1393
1918 Castle Hayne Rd Wilmington (28401) *(G-16266)*

Industrial Machine Company... 704 922-9750
103 Nelda St Dallas (28034) *(G-4646)*

Industrial Mechanical Services.. 828 397-3231
2354 Us Hwy 70 Hildebran (28637) *(G-8625)*

Industrial Mechatronics Inc... 704 900-2407
117 Freeland Ln Charlotte (28217) *(G-2962)*

Industrial Metal Craft Inc... 704 864-3416
901 Tulip Dr Gastonia (28052) *(G-6427)*

Industrial Metal Maint Inc.. 910 285-3240
164 John Deere Rd Teachey (28464) *(G-15177)*

Industrial Metal Products of... 910 944-8110
461 Carolina Rd Aberdeen (28315) *(G-7)*

Industrial Mgmt of Materials.. 704 359-9928
647 Michael Wylie Dr Charlotte (28217) *(G-2963)*

Industrial Motions Inc.. 734 284-8944
1401 Boxwood Ln Apex (27502) *(G-205)*

Industrial Mtal Flame Spryers.. 919 596-9381
419 Salem St Durham (27703) *(G-5152)*

Industrial Opportunities Inc... 828 321-4754
2586 Business 19 Andrews (28901) *(G-126)*

Industrial Panel Company LLC (PA)..................................... 866 736-1290
121 E Market St Burlington (27217) *(G-1436)*

Industrial Panel Company LLC.. 866 736-1290
147 N Main St Burlington (27217) *(G-1437)*

Industrial Piping Inc... 704 588-1100
212 S Tryon St Ste 1050 Charlotte (28281) *(G-2964)*

Industrial Power Inc (PA)... 910 483-4230
703 Whitfield St Fayetteville (28306) *(G-5841)*

Industrial Prcess Slutions Inc.. 336 926-1511
915 Germantown Rd Wilkesboro (28697) *(G-16025)*

Industrial Recycling Services.. 704 462-1882
2815 Woodtech Dr Newton (28658) *(G-11943)*

Industrial Rlblity Spclsts Inc... 513 652-9337
2629 Blue Clay Rd Wilmington (28405) *(G-16267)*

Industrial Services, Raleigh *Also Called: Robert Gregory* *(G-13210)*

Industrial Sheet Metal Works.. 828 654-9655
149 Old Shoals Rd Arden (28704) *(G-340)*

Industrial Sign & Graphics Inc (PA)....................................... 704 371-4985
4227 N Graham St Charlotte (28206) *(G-2965)*

Industrial Sup Solutions Inc (PA)... 704 636-4241
804 Julian Rd Salisbury (28147) *(G-13983)*

Industrial Timber LLC (PA).. 704 919-1215
6441 Hendry Rd Ste A Charlotte (28269) *(G-2966)*

Industrial Timber LLC.. 704 919-1215
330 White Plains Rd Hiddenite (28636) *(G-8220)*

Industrial Tling Svcs Ashvlle.. 828 683-4168
1259 Alexander Rd Leicester (28748) *(G-9513)*

Industrial Welding &.. 910 309-8540
5936 Tabor Church Rd Fayetteville (28312) *(G-5842)*

Industrial Wood Products Inc (PA).. 336 333-5959
9205 Hwy 22 S Climax (27233) *(G-4086)*

Industries of Blind Inc (PA).. 336 274-1591
920 W Gate City Blvd Greensboro (27403) *(G-7114)*

Industry Choice Solutions LLC... 828 628-1991
98 Bishop Cove Rd Fairview (28730) *(G-5714)*

Industry Nine LLC.. 828 210-5113
21 Old County Home Rd Asheville (28806) *(G-661)*

Indy Week.. 919 832-8774
709 W Jones St Raleigh (27603) *(G-12886)*

Ineo Usa Inc... 919 467-2199
120 James Jackson Ave Unit 16 Cary (27513) *(G-1788)*

Ineos Automotive Americas LLC.. 404 513-8577
2020 Progress Ct Ste 100-112 Raleigh (27608) *(G-12887)*

Inferensys Inc.. 910 398-1200
112 Dare Pines Way Durham (27703) *(G-5153)*

Infinite Controls Inc... 919 623-4818
Chapel Hill (27516) *(G-2026)*

Infinite Software Resorces LLC (PA)................................... 704 509-0031
3020 Prosperity Church Rd 1 Charlotte (28269) *(G-2967)*

Infinity Communications LLC (PA)....................................... 919 797-2334
5201 International Dr Durham (27712) *(G-5154)*

Infinity Learning Solutions.. 828 665-8292
1463 Sand Hill Rd Ste 324 Candler (28715) *(G-1583)*

Infinity S End Inc (PA)... 704 900-8355
7804 Fairview Rd Ste C Charlotte (28226) *(G-2968)*

Infinity Signs and Screen Prtg, Charlotte *Also Called: Infinity S End Inc* *(G-2968)*

Infinity Stingray Products, Otto *Also Called: J Culpepper & Co* *(G-12118)*

Infisoft Software... 704 307-2619
7422 Carmel Executive Park Dr Charlotte (28226) *(G-2969)*

Info-Gel LLC (PA)... 704 599-5770
2311 Distribution Center Dr Ste F Charlotte (28269) *(G-2970)*

Infobelt LLC (PA)... 980 223-4000
4100 Beresford Rd Charlotte (28211) *(G-2971)*

Information Age Publishing Inc.. 704 752-9125
11600 N Community House Rd # R Charlotte (28277) *(G-2972)*

Information Tech Works LLC (HQ)....................................... 919 232-5332
4809 Little Falls Dr Raleigh (27609) *(G-12888)*

Informtion Rtrval Cmpanies Inc... 919 460-7447
3500 Regency Pkwy Ste 140 Cary (27518) *(G-1789)*

Ing Source LLC.. 828 855-0481
1340 14th Avenue Ct Sw Hickory (28602) *(G-8065)*

Ingalls Alton... 252 975-2056
115 N Respess St Washington (27889) *(G-15712)*

ALPHABETIC SECTION — Insightsoftware

Ingalls and Associates, Washington Also Called: Ingalls Alton *(G-15712)*

Ingersoll Rand Inc.. 704 774-4290
 6000 General Commerce Dr Charlotte (28213) *(G-2973)*

INGERSOLL RAND INC (PA)..................................... 704 896-4000
 525 Harbour Place Dr Ste 600 Davidson (28036) *(G-4679)*

Ingersoll-Rand, Charlotte Also Called: Ingersoll-Rand Company *(G-2974)*

Ingersoll-Rand, Southern Pines Also Called: Trane Technologies Company LLC *(G-14558)*

Ingersoll-Rand Company.. 704 655-4836
 10000 Twin Lakes Pkwy Charlotte (28269) *(G-2974)*

Ingersoll-Rand Indus US Inc (HQ)............................ 704 896-4000
 525 Harbour Place Dr Ste 600 Davidson (28036) *(G-4680)*

Ingersoll-Rand Intl Holdg.. 704 655-4000
 800 Beaty St Davidson (28036) *(G-4681)*

Ingersoll-Rand US Holdco Inc.................................. 704 655-4000
 800 Beaty St Ste E Davidson (28036) *(G-4682)*

Ingle Protective Systems Inc................................... 704 788-3327
 231 Pounds Ave Sw Concord (28025) *(G-4285)*

Ingles, Boiling Springs Also Called: Ingles Markets Incorporated *(G-1161)*

Ingles Markets Incorporated.................................. 704 434-0096
 214 N Main St Boiling Springs (28017) *(G-1161)*

Ingram Machine & Balancing................................. 828 254-3420
 48 Ben Lippen Rd Asheville (28806) *(G-662)*

Ingram Racing Engines, Asheville Also Called: Ingram Machine & Balancing *(G-662)*

Ingram Woodyards Inc... 910 556-1250
 1925 Jefferson Davis Hwy Sanford (27330) *(G-14138)*

Ingredion Incorporated... 336 785-0100
 4501 Overdale Rd Winston Salem (27107) *(G-16760)*

Inhalon Biopharma Inc.. 650 439-0110
 104 Tw Alexander Dr Rm 2021rtp Durham (27709) *(G-5155)*

Ini Power Systems Inc... 919 677-7112
 137 Trans Air Dr Morrisville (27560) *(G-11359)*

Injection Technology Corporation........................... 828 684-1362
 199 Airport Rd Arden (28704) *(G-341)*

Ink City Screen Printing LLC................................... 347 729-5870
 610 Cavendish Ln Waxhaw (28173) *(G-15762)*

Ink n Stitches LLC.. 336 633-3898
 2739 Us Highway 220 Bus S Asheboro (27205) *(G-444)*

Ink Pallets & Stitches LLC..................................... 239 826-4772
 118 Villa Park Dr Hubert (28539) *(G-8749)*

Ink Tec Inc... 828 465-6411
 1838 Saint Pauls Church Rd Newton (28658) *(G-11944)*

Ink Well.. 336 727-9750
 1650 Hutton St Winston Salem (27127) *(G-16761)*

Ink Well, Durham Also Called: Ink Well Inc *(G-5156)*

Ink Well, Winston Salem Also Called: Ink Well *(G-16761)*

Ink Well Inc... 919 682-8279
 3112 N Roxboro St Durham (27704) *(G-5156)*

Ink Well Tatoo... 919 682-8279
 2416 Lindmont Ave Durham (27704) *(G-5157)*

Inka Outdoor LLC.. 828 539-0842
 1236 Industrial Ave # 107 Gastonia (28054) *(G-6428)*

Inkwell... 919 433-7539
 2823 Bragg Blvd Fayetteville (28303) *(G-5843)*

Inman Septic Tank Service Inc................................ 910 763-1146
 2631 Blue Clay Rd Wilmington (28405) *(G-16268)*

Inmylife Inc... 336 644-8856
 900 Troublesome Creek Dr Greensboro (27455) *(G-7115)*

Inn-Flow Inc... 919 277-9027
 5640 Dillard Dr Ste 300 Cary (27518) *(G-1790)*

Inn-Flow Hotel Software, Cary Also Called: Inn-Flow Inc *(G-1790)*

Innait, Charlotte Also Called: Innait Inc *(G-2975)*

Innait Inc.. 406 241-5245
 5524 Joyce Dr Charlotte (28215) *(G-2975)*

Innavasc Medical Inc.. 813 902-2228
 110 Swift Ave Durham (27705) *(G-5158)*

Innerer Klang Letter Press.................................... 828 253-3711
 5 Balsam Rd Black Mountain (28711) *(G-1126)*

Inneroptic Technology Inc..................................... 919 732-2090
 3421 Carriage Trl Hillsborough (27278) *(G-8656)*

Inniah Production Incorporated............................. 828 765-6800
 152 Summit Ave Spruce Pine (28777) *(G-14644)*

Innisbrook Wraps, Greensboro Also Called: Shamrock Corporation *(G-7334)*

Innobioactives LLC.. 336 235-0838
 7325 W Friendly Ave Ste H Greensboro (27410) *(G-7116)*

Innocrin Pharmaceuticals Inc................................ 919 467-8539
 701 Wagstaff Rd Fuquay Varina (27526) *(G-6204)*

Innofa Usa LLC... 336 635-2900
 716 Commerce Dr Eden (27288) *(G-5492)*

Innospec, High Point Also Called: Innospec Active Chemicals LLC *(G-8410)*

Innospec Active Chemicals LLC (HQ)...................... 336 882-3308
 510 W Grimes Ave High Point (27260) *(G-8410)*

Innospec Active Chemicals LLC.............................. 704 633-8028
 500 Hinkle Ln Salisbury (28144) *(G-13984)*

Innospec Inc... 704 633-8028
 500 Hinkle Ln Salisbury (28144) *(G-13985)*

Innospec Inc... 704 633-8028
 500 Hinkle Ln Salisbury (28144) *(G-13986)*

Innospec Performance Chemicals, Salisbury Also Called: Innospec Active Chemicals LLC *(G-13984)*

Innospec Performance Chemicals, Salisbury Also Called: Innospec Inc *(G-13985)*

Innospec Performance Chemicals, Salisbury Also Called: Innospec Inc *(G-13986)*

Innova-Con Incorporated..................................... 919 303-1467
 2521 Schieffelin Rd Ste 136 Apex (27502) *(G-206)*

Innovaknits LLC.. 828 536-9348
 350 5th Ave Se Conover (28613) *(G-4467)*

Innovasource LLC... 704 584-0072
 11515 Vanstory Dr Ste 110 Huntersville (28078) *(G-8834)*

Innovation Brewing LLC....................................... 828 586-9678
 414 W Main St Sylva (28779) *(G-15058)*

Innovative Awngs & Screens LLC........................... 833 337-4233
 19825 North Cove Rd Ste B Cornelius (28031) *(G-4561)*

Innovative Business Growth LLC............................ 888 334-4367
 1157 S Cox St Asheboro (27203) *(G-445)*

Innovative Cushions LLC...................................... 336 861-2060
 4010 Cheyenne Dr Archdale (27263) *(G-285)*

Innovative Custom Cabinets Inc............................. 813 748-0655
 1018 Robinhood Ln Kannapolis (28081) *(G-9124)*

Innovative Design Tech LLC.................................. 919 331-0204
 475 S Raleigh St Angier (27501) *(G-141)*

Innovative Kitchens Baths Inc............................... 336 279-1188
 2912 Manufacturers Rd Greensboro (27406) *(G-7117)*

Innovative Knitting LLC....................................... 336 350-8122
 3720 S Church St Burlington (27215) *(G-1438)*

Innovative Laminations Company.......................... 252 745-8133
 51a Halls Creek Rd New Bern (28560) *(G-11810)*

Innovative Mfg Solutions Inc................................. 919 219-2424
 675 Wooded Lake Dr Apex (27523) *(G-207)*

Innovative Technology Mfg LLC............................. 980 248-3731
 136 Lugnut Ln Ste C Mooresville (28117) *(G-10982)*

Innovtive Msrment Slutions Inc.............................. 757 560-0820
 1201 Arrowhead Trl Edenton (27932) *(G-5517)*

Innovtors In McRwave Technolgy, Matthews Also Called: Cem Corporation *(G-10307)*

Innowera Ltd Liability Company............................ 214 295-9508
 8529 Six Forks Rd Ste 400 Raleigh (27615) *(G-12889)*

Innspector Software LLC..................................... 828 712-7127
 65 Gray Duster Cir Biltmore Lake (28715) *(G-1100)*

Inotec AMD Inc... 888 354-9772
 1350 4th St Nw Hickory (28601) *(G-8066)*

Inovaetion Inc.. 919 651-1628
 8601 Six Forks Rd Ste 400 Raleigh (27615) *(G-12890)*

Inovative Vapes of Boone..................................... 828 386-1041
 244 Shadowline Dr Boone (28607) *(G-1209)*

Inpernum Pharma Solutions LLC........................... 919 599-5501
 3815 Saint Marks Rd Durham (27707) *(G-5159)*

Inplac North America Inc..................................... 704 587-1151
 10926 S Tryon St Ste F Charlotte (28273) *(G-2976)*

Inprimo Solutions Inc... 919 390-7776
 7925 Vandemere Ct Raleigh (27615) *(G-12891)*

Inquire Journal, The, Monroe Also Called: Paxton Media Group *(G-10784)*

Insect Shield LLC (PA)... 336 272-4157
 814 W Market St Greensboro (27401) *(G-7118)*

Insightsoftware, Raleigh Also Called: Insightsoftware LLC *(G-12892)*

Insightsoftware LLC (PA)...........................919 872-7800
8529 Six Forks Rd Raleigh (27615) *(G-12892)*

Insource Sftwr Solutions Inc...........................704 895-1052
19421 Liverpool Pkwy Ste A Cornelius (28031) *(G-4562)*

Inspectionxpert Corporation...........................919 249-6442
1 Glenwood Ave Ste 500 Raleigh (27603) *(G-12893)*

Inspiration Leather Design Inc...........................336 420-2265
4713 Barrington Place Ct Jamestown (27282) *(G-9058)*

Inspire Creative Studios Inc...........................910 395-0200
720 N 3rd St Ste 101 Wilmington (28401) *(G-16269)*

Insta Copy Shop Ltd...........................704 376-1350
4311 South Blvd Ste D Charlotte (28209) *(G-2977)*

Instant Imprints...........................704 864-1510
2258 Helen Dr Gastonia (28054) *(G-6429)*

Instant Imprints...........................919 468-9808
10970 Chapel Hill Rd Ste 118 Morrisville (27560) *(G-11360)*

Instant Imprints, Raleigh *Also Called: Nine Thirteen LLC (G-13064)*

Instant Imprints Greenville...........................252 364-3254
1011 Charles Blvd Greenville (27858) *(G-7543)*

Insteel, Mount Airy *Also Called: Insteel Industries Inc (G-11520)*

Insteel Industries Inc (PA)...........................336 786-2141
1373 Boggs Dr Mount Airy (27030) *(G-11520)*

Insteel Wire Products Company (HQ)...........................336 719-9000
1373 Boggs Dr Mount Airy (27030) *(G-11521)*

Institute For Resch Biotecnoly...........................252 689-2205
2905 S Memorial Dr Greenville (27834) *(G-7544)*

Instrotek Inc (PA)...........................919 875-8371
1 Triangle Dr Durham (27709) *(G-5160)*

Instrument Trans Eqp Corp...........................704 282-4331
2402 Walkup Ave Monroe (28110) *(G-10739)*

Insty-Prints, Raleigh *Also Called: Pamela A Adams (G-13096)*

Insul Kor, Greensboro *Also Called: Quality Housing Corporation (G-7300)*

Insulsure, Mooresville *Also Called: Attic Tent Inc (G-10864)*

Insurance Systems Group Inc...........................919 834-4907
827 N Bloodworth St Raleigh (27604) *(G-12894)*

Insurrection Industries LLC...........................443 801-7356
4112 Glencove Ct Winston Salem (27106) *(G-16762)*

Intas Pharmaceuticals Limited...........................919 941-7878
8041 Arco Corporate Dr Ste 200 Raleigh (27617) *(G-12895)*

Integra Foods LLC...........................910 984-2007
476 Industrial Dr Bladenboro (28320) *(G-1149)*

Integrated Info Systems Inc...........................919 488-5000
460 Boardwalk Dr Youngsville (27596) *(G-17086)*

Integrated Print Services Inc...........................704 307-4495
8534 Dennington Grove Ln Charlotte (28277) *(G-2978)*

Integrated Roe Security LLC...........................919 297-8036
2308 Basil Dr Raleigh (27612) *(G-12896)*

Integrity Medical Solutions, Shelby *Also Called: Tube Enterprises Incorporated (G-14376)*

Integrity Plastics...........................828 247-8801
291 Shiloh Rd Forest City (28043) *(G-6071)*

Integrity Welding LLC...........................919 556-5144
75 Eastwind Rd Louisburg (27549) *(G-9992)*

Integrted Cble Assmbly Hldings, Whitsett *Also Called: Ica Mid-Atlantic Inc (G-15993)*

Intelligent Apps LLC...........................919 628-6256
12113 Oakwood View Dr Apt 202 Raleigh (27614) *(G-12897)*

Intelligent Endoscopy LLC...........................336 608-4375
4740 Commercial Park Ct Ste 1 Clemmons (27012) *(G-4048)*

Intelligent Tool Corp...........................704 799-0449
1151 Biscayne Dr Concord (28027) *(G-4286)*

Intensa Inc...........................336 884-4096
1810 S Elm St High Point (27260) *(G-8411)*

Intensa Inc...........................336 884-4003
1810 S Elm St High Point (27260) *(G-8412)*

Inteplast Group Corporation...........................704 504-3200
10701 S Commerce Blvd Ste A Charlotte (28273) *(G-2979)*

Inter-Continental Corporation...........................828 464-8250
2575 N Ashe Ave Newton (28658) *(G-11945)*

Inter-Continental Gear & Brake (PA)...........................704 599-3420
6431 Reames Rd Charlotte (28216) *(G-2980)*

Interactive Intelligence, Durham *Also Called: Genesys Cloud Services Inc (G-5113)*

Interactive Safety Pdts Inc...........................704 664-7377
9825 Northcross Center Ct Ste A Huntersville (28078) *(G-8835)*

Interconnect Products and Services Inc (PA)...........................336 667-3356
1206 Industrial Park Rd Wilkesboro (28697) *(G-16026)*

Intercontinental Metals Corp...........................336 786-2141
1373 Boggs Dr Mount Airy (27030) *(G-11522)*

Intereco USA Belt Filter Press...........................919 349-6041
7474 Creedmoor Rd Raleigh (27613) *(G-12898)*

Interface Fabrics Group...........................336 526-0407
304 E Main St Elkin (28621) *(G-5620)*

Interflex Acquisition Co LLC...........................336 921-3505
3200 W Nc Highway 268 Wilkesboro (28697) *(G-16027)*

Interflex Acquisition Co LLC...........................336 921-3505
3200 Hwy 268 W Wilkesboro (28697) *(G-16028)*

Interflex Acquisition Co LLC (HQ)...........................336 921-3505
3200 W Nc Highway 268 Wilkesboro (28697) *(G-16029)*

Interflex Acquisition Co LLC...........................336 921-3505
251 Industrial Dr Ext Wilkesboro (28697) *(G-16030)*

Interflex Acquisition Co LLC...........................336 921-3505
3200 W Nc Highway 268 Wilkesboro (28697) *(G-16031)*

Interflex Group, Wilkesboro *Also Called: Interflex Acquisition Co LLC (G-16029)*

Interior Trim Creations, Matthews *Also Called: Itc Millwork LLC (G-10323)*

Interior Trim Creations Inc...........................704 821-1470
11912 Erwin Ridge Ave Charlotte (28213) *(G-2981)*

Interior Wood Specialties Inc...........................336 431-0068
1130 Bedford St High Point (27263) *(G-8413)*

Interior Wood Works LLC...........................910 754-3987
325 Colonial Landing Rd Se Bolivia (28422) *(G-1164)*

Interlam Corporation...........................336 786-6254
391 Hickory St Mount Airy (27030) *(G-11523)*

Intermarket Technology Inc...........................252 623-2199
932 Page Rd Washington (27889) *(G-15713)*

International, Charlotte *Also Called: Notepad Enterprises LLC (G-3271)*

International Bus Connection...........................251 391-1158
1148 Kildaire Farm Rd Cary (27511) *(G-1791)*

International Bus Mchs Corp...........................919 543-6919
3039 Cornwallis Rd Durham (27709) *(G-5161)*

International Cabinetry Inc...........................828 393-7998
1437 Dana Rd Hendersonville (28792) *(G-7866)*

International Cnstr Eqp Inc (PA)...........................704 821-8200
301 Warehouse Dr Matthews (28104) *(G-10322)*

International Embroidery...........................704 792-0641
2890 Highway 49 N Concord (28025) *(G-4287)*

International Foam Pdts Inc (PA)...........................704 588-0080
10530 Westlake Dr Charlotte (28273) *(G-2982)*

International Furnishings Inc...........................336 472-8422
1506 Lexington Ave Thomasville (27360) *(G-15238)*

International Furniture, Greensboro *Also Called: Schnadig Corporation (G-7327)*

International Instrumentation...........................919 496-4208
382 N Carolina 98 Hwy W Bunn (27508) *(G-1328)*

International McHy Sls Inc...........................336 759-9548
8065 N Point Blvd Ste J Winston Salem (27106) *(G-16763)*

International Minute Press...........................919 762-0054
316 Angier Rd Fuquay Varina (27526) *(G-6205)*

International Minute Press...........................336 854-1589
2417 Spring Garden St Greensboro (27403) *(G-7119)*

International Minute Press...........................704 827-7173
9633 Sunset Grove Dr Huntersville (28078) *(G-8836)*

International Minute Press...........................704 246-3758
11100 Monroe Rd Ste H Matthews (28105) *(G-10255)*

International Minute Press...........................910 725-1148
280 Pinehurst Ave Ste 6 Southern Pines (28387) *(G-14537)*

International Minute Press...........................336 231-3178
3490 Reynolda Rd Winston Salem (27106) *(G-16764)*

International Minute Press, Clinton *Also Called: Commercial Enterprises NC Inc (G-4091)*

International Minute Press, Fayetteville *Also Called: Os Press LLC (G-5890)*

International Minute Press, Gastonia *Also Called: Better Business Printing Inc (G-6353)*

International Minute Press, High Point *Also Called: James G Gouge (G-8415)*

International Minute Press, Pineville *Also Called: Roark Printing Inc (G-12295)*

International Minute Press, Raleigh *Also Called: Js Printing LLC (G-12925)*

International Minute Press, Raleigh *Also Called: Welloyt Enterprises Inc (G-13418)*

International Moulding NC, Morganton *Also Called: T Distribution NC Inc (G-11259)*

ALPHABETIC SECTION — Ipex USA LLC

International Paper, Burgaw *Also Called: International Paper Company* *(G-1341)*
International Paper, Charlotte *Also Called: International Paper Company* *(G-2983)*
International Paper, Charlotte *Also Called: International Paper Company* *(G-2985)*
International Paper, Charlotte *Also Called: International Paper Company* *(G-2986)*
International Paper, Charlotte *Also Called: International Paper Company* *(G-2987)*
International Paper, Lumberton *Also Called: International Paper Company* *(G-10040)*
International Paper, Manson *Also Called: International Paper Company* *(G-10124)*
International Paper, New Bern *Also Called: International Paper Company* *(G-11811)*
International Paper, Raleigh *Also Called: International Paper Company* *(G-12899)*
International Paper, Riegelwood *Also Called: International Paper Company* *(G-13559)*
International Paper, Riegelwood *Also Called: International Paper Company* *(G-13560)*
International Paper, Vanceboro *Also Called: International Paper Company* *(G-15479)*

International Paper Com 828 200-9284
35 Martindale Rd Asheville (28804) *(G-663)*

International Paper Company 910 259-1723
3870 Highsmith Rd Burgaw (28425) *(G-1341)*

International Paper Company 704 393-8210
11020 David Taylor Dr Charlotte (28262) *(G-2983)*

International Paper Company 704 588-8522
10601 Westlake Dr Charlotte (28273) *(G-2984)*

International Paper Company 704 398-8354
5419 Hovis Rd Charlotte (28208) *(G-2985)*

International Paper Company 704 334-5222
201 E 28th St Charlotte (28206) *(G-2986)*

International Paper Company 704 588-8522
3700 Display Dr Charlotte (28273) *(G-2987)*

International Paper Company 910 738-8930
2060 W 5th St Lumberton (28358) *(G-10040)*

International Paper Company 910 738-6214
820 Caton Rd Lumberton (28360) *(G-10041)*

International Paper Company 252 456-3111
967 Us Highway 1 S Manson (27553) *(G-10124)*

International Paper Company 252 633-7407
1785 Weyerhaeuser Rd New Bern (28563) *(G-11811)*

International Paper Company 828 464-3841
1525 Mount Olive Church Rd Newton (28658) *(G-11946)*

International Paper Company 919 831-4764
5 W Hargett St Rm 914 Raleigh (27601) *(G-12899)*

International Paper Company 910 655-2211
1865 John Riegel Rd Riegelwood (28456) *(G-13559)*

International Paper Company 910 362-4900
865 John L Regel Rd Riegelwood (28456) *(G-13560)*

International Paper Company 704 872-6541
930 Meacham Rd Statesville (28677) *(G-14820)*

International Paper Company 252 633-7509
1785 Weyerhaeuser Rd Vanceboro (28586) *(G-15479)*

International Pet ACC LLC 919 964-0738
11842 Canemount St Raleigh (27614) *(G-12900)*

International Precast Inc 919 742-4241
2469 Old Us 421 N Siler City (27344) *(G-14416)*

International Ptnrshp For Vacc 919 367-0379
114 Burgwin Wright Way Cary (27519) *(G-1792)*

International Society Automtn (PA) 919 206-4176
67 T W Alexander Dr Durham (27709) *(G-5162)*

International Tela-Com Inc 828 651-9801
103 Underwood Rd Unit C Fletcher (28732) *(G-6013)*

International Thermodyne Inc 704 579-8218
3120 Latrobe Dr Ste 110 Charlotte (28211) *(G-2988)*

International Vault, Siler City *Also Called: International Vault Inc* *(G-14417)*

International Vault Inc (PA) 919 742-3132
2469 Old Us 421 N Siler City (27344) *(G-14417)*

International Wood Svcs Inc 910 549-8142
330 Shipyard Blvd Ste D Wilmington (28412) *(G-16270)*

Interntnal Agrclture Group LLC 908 323-3246
106 Langtree Village Dr Ste 301 Mooresville (28117) *(G-10983)*

Interntnal Instlltion Group LL 704 231-1868
312 Riverside Dr Sparta (28675) *(G-14595)*

Interntnal Tray Pads Packg Inc 910 944-1800
3299 Nc Highway 5 Aberdeen (28315) *(G-8)*

Interntonal Specialty Pdts Inc 828 326-9053
1720 Tate Blvd Se Hickory (28602) *(G-8067)*

Interordnance Amer Ltd Partnr 321 212-7801
3305 Westwood Indus Dr Monroe (28110) *(G-10740)*

Interpace Pharma Solutions Inc 919 678-7024
133 Southcenter Ct Ste 400 Morrisville (27560) *(G-11361)*

Interroll Corporation 910 799-1100
3000 Corporate Dr Wilmington (28405) *(G-16271)*

Interroll USA Holding LLC 910 799-1100
3000 Corporate Dr Wilmington (28405) *(G-16272)*

Interrs-Exteriors Asheboro Inc 336 629-2148
2013 S Fayetteville St Asheboro (27205) *(G-446)*

Intersport Group Inc 814 968-3085
336 Willowdale Church Rd Vilas (28692) *(G-15496)*

Interstate All Batteries Ctr 704 979-3430
8605 Concord Mills Blvd Concord (28027) *(G-4288)*

Interstate Fabrications LLC 704 209-0263
121 N Salisbury Gq Ave Salisbury (28146) *(G-13987)*

Interstate Foam & Supply Inc 828 459-9700
306 Comfort Dr Ne Conover (28613) *(G-4468)*

Interstate Narrow Fabrics Inc 336 578-1037
1101 Porter Ave Haw River (27258) *(G-7753)*

Interstate Sign Company Inc 336 789-3069
1990 Rockford St Mount Airy (27030) *(G-11524)*

Intertape Polymer Corp 252 792-2083
1622 Twin Bridges Rd Everetts (27825) *(G-5695)*

Intertape Polymer Corp 980 907-4871
13722 Bill Mcgee Rd Midland (28107) *(G-10469)*

Intertape Polymer Corp 704 279-3011
3725 Faith Rd Salisbury (28146) *(G-13988)*

Intertape Polymer Group, Midland *Also Called: Intertape Polymer Corp* *(G-10469)*

Intertech Corporation 336 621-1891
3240 N Ohenry Blvd Greensboro (27405) *(G-7120)*

Intracoastal Woodworks Inc 910 270-5515
390 Knollwood Dr Hampstead (28443) *(G-7649)*

Intrinsic Advanced Mtls LLC 704 874-5000
531 Cotton Blossom Cir Gastonia (28054) *(G-6430)*

Inventive Graphics Inc 704 814-4900
9129 Monroe Rd Ste 160 Charlotte (28270) *(G-2989)*

Investorcookbookscom 919 280-8600
301 Crickentree Dr Cary (27518) *(G-1793)*

Invictus Lighting LLC 828 855-9324
1401 Main Ave Sw Hickory (28602) *(G-8068)*

Invisible Fencing of Mtn Reg 828 667-8847
176 Pete Luther Rd Candler (28715) *(G-1584)*

Invista Capital Management LLC 704 636-6000
Hwy 70 W Salisbury (28145) *(G-13989)*

Invista Capital Management LLC 316 828-1000
4600 Us Highway 421 N Wilmington (28401) *(G-16273)*

Invitation Duck LLC 919 341-3739
111 James Jackson Ave Ste 209 Cary (27513) *(G-1794)*

INX International, Charlotte *Also Called: INX International Ink Co* *(G-2990)*

INX International Ink Co 704 372-2080
10820 Withers Cove Park Dr Charlotte (28278) *(G-2990)*

Ioa Healthcare Furniture, Thomasville *Also Called: Images of America Inc* *(G-15237)*

Iodine Poetry Journal 704 595-9526
1543 Rumstone Ln Charlotte (28262) *(G-2991)*

Ioto Usa LLC 252 413-7343
1997 N Greene St Greenville (27834) *(G-7545)*

Ipas 919 967-7052
4711 Hope Valley Rd Durham (27707) *(G-5163)*

IPC Corporation 704 821-7084
3330 Smith Farm Rd Stallings (28104) *(G-14671)*

Ipd Co 704 999-4484
505 White Water Falls Dr Apt 716 Charlotte (28217) *(G-2992)*

Iperionx Limited 704 578-3217
129 W Trade St Ste 1405 Charlotte (28202) *(G-2993)*

Iperionx Technology LLC 704 578-3217
129 W Trade St Ste 1405 Charlotte (28202) *(G-2994)*

Ipex USA LLC 704 889-2431
7125 Logistics Center Dr Charlotte (28273) *(G-2995)*

Ipex USA LLC (DH) 704 889-2431
10100 Rodney St Pineville (28134) *(G-12275)*

Ipex USA LLC 704 889-2431
10100 Rodney St Pineville (28134) *(G-12276)*

Ipi Acquisition LLC 704 588-1100
13504 S Point Blvd Ste M Charlotte (28273) *(G-2996)*

Ips 704 788-3327
338 Webb Rd Concord (28025) *(G-4289)*

Ips Corporation 919 598-2400
600 Ellis Rd Durham (27703) *(G-5164)*

Ips Perforating Inc 704 881-0050
1821 Weinig St Statesville (28677) *(G-14821)*

Ips Structural Adhesives Inc (DH) 919 598-2400
600 Ellis Rd Durham (27703) *(G-5165)*

Iq Brands Inc (HQ) 336 751-0040
129 Nc Highway 801 S Advance (27006) *(G-44)*

Iqe North Carolina LLC 336 609-6270
494 Gallimore Dairy Rd Greensboro (27409) *(G-7121)*

Iqmetrix USA Inc 704 987-9903
184 Longboat Rd Mooresville (28117) *(G-10984)*

Iqvia Pharma Inc (HQ) 919 998-2000
4820 Emperor Blvd Durham (27703) *(G-5166)*

Irc, Cary *Also Called: Informtion Rtrval Cmpanies Inc (G-1789)*

Iredell Fiber Inc 704 878-0884
124 Fanjoy Rd Statesville (28625) *(G-14822)*

Iredell Holding LLC 828 506-2555
3724 Bunker Hill School Rd Claremont (28610) *(G-3930)*

Iron Box, Raleigh *Also Called: Iron Box LLC (G-12901)*

Iron Box LLC 919 890-0025
1349 Express Dr Raleigh (27603) *(G-12901)*

Iron Forged Woodworks 910 581-6574
400 Mccall Dr Jacksonville (28540) *(G-9009)*

Iron Men Fabrication 336 929-6263
1296 Little Point Rd Randleman (27317) *(G-13474)*

Iron-Crete Designs 919 738-2803
595 Dollard Town Rd Goldsboro (27534) *(G-6626)*

Ironbound Waste Management, Wilmington *Also Called: Secured Traffic Control LLC (G-16398)*

Ironlungs Boxing & Personal 919 332-8966
5608 Spring Ct Raleigh (27616) *(G-12902)*

Ironmex Fabrication Inc 336 937-1045
2001 Carpenter St Greensboro (27403) *(G-7122)*

Ironworks Motorcycles 336 542-7868
313 W Fisher Ave Greensboro (27401) *(G-7123)*

Irsi Automation Inc 336 303-5320
3703 Hines Chapel Rd Mc Leansville (27301) *(G-10393)*

Irvan-Smith Inc 704 788-2554
1027 Central Dr Nw Frnt Concord (28027) *(G-4290)*

Irwin 704 987-4339
8936 N Pointe Executive P Huntersville (28078) *(G-8837)*

Irwin Construction Accessories, Huntersville *Also Called: Irwin Industrial Tool Company (G-8838)*

Irwin Industrial Tool Company (HQ) 704 987-4555
8935 N Pointe Executive Park Dr Huntersville (28078) *(G-8838)*

ISA 919 549-8411
67 Alexander Dr Durham (27709) *(G-5167)*

Isabellas Fine Olive Oils & Vi 704 237-4949
16835 Birkdale Commons Pkwy Huntersville (28078) *(G-8839)*

Isabellas Oils LLC 828 221-4274
5152 Sulphur Springs Rd Ne Hickory (28601) *(G-8069)*

Isana LLC 704 439-6761
611 Cricketwood Ln Charlotte (28215) *(G-2997)*

Isenhour Furniture Company (PA) 828 632-8849
486 S Center St Taylorsville (28681) *(G-15149)*

Island Gazette Newspaper, The, Carolina Beach *Also Called: Seaside Press Co Inc (G-1641)*

Island Machining LLC 704 278-3553
265 Pitt Rd Mooresville (28115) *(G-10985)*

Island Timez 919 351-0346
1206 N Berkeley Blvd Goldsboro (27534) *(G-6627)*

Island Wood Crafts Ltd 252 473-5363
776 Old Wharf Rd Wanchese (27981) *(G-15648)*

Island Xpertees, Nags Head *Also Called: Island Xprtees of Oter Bnks In (G-11720)*

Island Xprtees of Oter Bnks In 252 480-3990
2224 S Lark Ave Nags Head (27959) *(G-11720)*

Ism Inc
149 Old Shoals Rd Arden (28704) *(G-342)*

Isometrics Inc 336 342-4150
7537 Nc Highway 87 Reidsville (27320) *(G-13527)*

Isometrics Inc (PA) 336 349-2329
1266 N Scales St Reidsville (27320) *(G-13528)*

ISS 919 317-8314
3108 Thistlecone Way Durham (27707) *(G-5168)*

Issi, Salisbury *Also Called: Industrial Sup Solutions Inc (G-13983)*

Issuer Direct, Raleigh *Also Called: Issuer Direct Corporation (G-12903)*

Issuer Direct Corporation (PA) 919 481-4000
1 Glenwood Ave Ste 1001 Raleigh (27603) *(G-12903)*

It Is Sew 252 531-7859
926 Thomas St Greenville (27834) *(G-7546)*

Itc Millwork LLC (PA) 704 821-1470
3619 Gribble Rd Matthews (28104) *(G-10323)*

Itec 704 282-4331
2402 Walkup Ave Monroe (28110) *(G-10741)*

Itech, Arden *Also Called: Injection Technology Corporation (G-341)*

Itek Graphics LLC 704 357-6002
7075 Aviation Blvd Nw Ste B Concord (28027) *(G-4291)*

Itg Brands 336 335-6600
420 N English St Greensboro (27405) *(G-7124)*

Itg Brands 919 366-0220
900 E Six Forks Rd Unit 210 Raleigh (27604) *(G-12904)*

Itg Brands LLC (HQ) 336 335-7000
714 Green Valley Rd Greensboro (27408) *(G-7125)*

Itg Holdings Inc 336 379-6220
804 Green Valley Rd Ste 300 Greensboro (27408) *(G-7126)*

Itg Holdings USA Inc 954 772-9000
714 Green Valley Rd Greensboro (27408) *(G-7127)*

Itl Corp 828 659-9663
203 College Dr Marion (28752) *(G-10152)*

Itlaq Technologies 305 549-8561
11420 Delores Ferguson Ln Charlotte (28277) *(G-2998)*

Itm Ltd South 336 883-2400
1903 Brassfield Rd Greensboro (27410) *(G-7128)*

Itron Inc 919 876-2600
8529 Six Forks Rd Ste 100 Raleigh (27615) *(G-12905)*

Its A Snap 828 254-3456
66 Asheland Ave Asheville (28801) *(G-664)*

Its Your Time Business Center 336 754-4456
2735 Old Hollow Rd Walkertown (27051) *(G-15615)*

ITT LLC 704 716-7600
4828 Parkway Plaza Blvd # 200 Charlotte (28217) *(G-2999)*

ITT LLC 336 662-0113
8511 Norcross Rd Colfax (27235) *(G-4152)*

Iv-S Metal Stamping Inc 336 861-2100
2400 Shore St Archdale (27263) *(G-286)*

Ivars Display 909 923-2761
2001 Partnership Dr Shelby (28150) *(G-14331)*

Ivars Sportswear Inc 336 227-9683
408 W Interstate Service Rd Graham (27253) *(G-6693)*

Ivey Fixture & Design Inc 704 283-4398
2814 N Rocky River Rd Monroe (28110) *(G-10742)*

Ivey Icenhour DBA 704 786-0676
5690 Barrier Georgeville Rd Mount Pleasant (28124) *(G-11674)*

Ivey Lane, Greensboro *Also Called: Ivey Ln Inc (G-7129)*

Ivey Ln Inc 336 230-0062
103 Ward Rd Greensboro (27405) *(G-7129)*

Ivm Chemicals Inc 407 506-4913
301 Mccullough Dr Fl 4 Charlotte (28262) *(G-3000)*

Ivp Forest Products LLC 252 241-8126
125 Horton Dr Morehead City (28557) *(G-11177)*

Ivy Brand LLC 980 225-7866
106 Foster Ave Charlotte (28203) *(G-3001)*

Iwanna 828 505-7319
31 College Pl Ste B100 Asheville (28801) *(G-665)*

Ixc Discovery Inc (PA) 919 941-5206
4222 Emperor Blvd Ste 350 Durham (27703) *(G-5169)*

Izitleather, Mount Airy *Also Called: Willow Tex LLC (G-11595)*

ALPHABETIC SECTION

J & B Hardwood Inc 828 226-2326
592 Beaverdam Rd Canton (28716) *(G-1619)*

J & B Logging and Timber Co 919 934-4115
524 Brogden Rd Smithfield (27577) *(G-14463)*

J & B Tool Making Inc 704 827-4805
14522 Lucia Riverbend Hwy Mount Holly (28120) *(G-11639)*

J & D Thorpe Enterprises Inc 919 553-0918
116 Shady Meadow Ln Clayton (27520) *(G-3990)*

J & D Welding & Fabg Corp 704 393-9115
6120 Brookshire Blvd Charlotte (28216) *(G-3002)*

J & D Wood Inc 910 628-9000
4940 Centerville Church Rd Fairmont (28340) *(G-5703)*

J & E Digital Printing Inc 919 803-8913
3524 Pinnacle Peak Dr Raleigh (27604) *(G-12906)*

J & J Logging Inc 252 430-1110
255 J P Taylor Rd Henderson (27537) *(G-7790)*

J & J Machine Works Inc 336 434-4081
1300 Corporation Dr Archdale (27263) *(G-287)*

J & J Metal Fabrication LLC 704 746-5279
170 Rooster Tail Ln Troutman (28166) *(G-15382)*

J & K Logging, Washington *Also Called: David J Spain (G-15694)*

J & K Tools LLC 828 299-0589
490 Upper Grassy Br Rd Asheville (28805) *(G-666)*

J & L Bckh/Nvrnmental Svcs Inc 910 237-7351
3043 Tom Geddie Rd Eastover (28312) *(G-5481)*

J & M Cabinet Installers LLC 336 500-7148
2811 Bears Creek Rd Greensboro (27406) *(G-7130)*

J & M Pavers LLC 704 776-6613
1504 Citrus Dr Monroe (28110) *(G-10743)*

J & M Woodworking Inc 828 728-3253
432 Pine Mountain Rd Hudson (28638) *(G-8770)*

J & P Entrprses of Crlinas Inc 704 861-1867
5640 Gallagher Dr Gastonia (28052) *(G-6431)*

J & P Machine Works Inc 252 758-1719
4291 Us Highway 264 E Greenville (27834) *(G-7547)*

J & R Sales Inc 828 632-7402
380 Old Mountain Rd Hiddenite (28636) *(G-8221)*

J & S Fab Inc 704 528-4251
354 S Eastway Dr Troutman (28166) *(G-15383)*

J & S Parkside LLC 919 434-1293
7169 Okelly Chapel Rd Cary (27519) *(G-1795)*

J & S Tools Inc 252 514-7805
100 Liestal Ln New Bern (28562) *(G-11812)*

J & W Service Incorporated 336 449-4584
7471 Danford Rd Whitsett (27377) *(G-15994)*

J & W Steel Inc 980 579-0452
9601 Parkridge Dr Charlotte (28214) *(G-3003)*

J &D Contractor Service Inc 919 427-0218
246 Scotts Ln Angier (27501) *(G-142)*

J A King 800 327-7727
7239 Acc Blvd Ste 101 Raleigh (27617) *(G-12907)*

J Ali Candles 910 603-2997
172 Tanner Ln West End (27376) *(G-15927)*

J B I Custom Cabinets 910 538-3831
4619 Filmore Dr Apt B Wilmington (28403) *(G-16274)*

J C Custom Sewing Inc 336 449-4586
106 E Railroad Ave Gibsonville (27249) *(G-6563)*

J C Enterprises 336 986-1688
936 Washington Ave Winston Salem (27101) *(G-16765)*

J C I, Selma *Also Called: Johnston County Industries Inc (G-14257)*

J C Lawrence Co 919 553-3044
9526 Connie Cove Rd Oriental (28571) *(G-12110)*

J C Stair Erectors 336 240-0560
7981 Us Highway 220 Bus N Randleman (27317) *(G-13475)*

J Charles Saunders Co Inc 704 866-9156
1004 E Long Ave Gastonia (28054) *(G-6432)*

J Culpepper & Co 828 524-6842
8285 Georgia Rd Otto (28763) *(G-12118)*

J E Carpenter Logging Co Inc 252 633-0037
4911 Hermitage Rd Trent Woods (28562) *(G-15328)*

J E Herndon Company (HQ) 704 739-4711
1020 Je Herndon Access Rd Kings Mountain (28086) *(G-9310)*

J E Ingram LLC 770 354-5599
5401 Amsterdam Pl Raleigh (27606) *(G-12908)*

J E Jones Lumber Company 336 472-3478
7255 E Us Highway 64 Lexington (27292) *(G-9732)*

J E Kerr Timber Co Corp 252 537-0544
1005 Old Halifax Rd Roanoke Rapids (27870) *(G-13576)*

J F Fabricators LLC (PA) 704 454-7224
7315 Millbrook Rd Harrisburg (28075) *(G-7713)*

J F Heat Treating Inc 704 864-0998
409 Airport Rd Gastonia (28056) *(G-6433)*

J J Jenkins Incorporated 704 821-6648
3380 Smith Farm Rd Matthews (28104) *(G-10324)*

J L Anderson Co Inc 704 289-9599
4812 W Highway 74 Monroe (28110) *(G-10744)*

J L Frame Shop Inc 828 256-6290
1310 Houston Mill Rd Conover (28613) *(G-4469)*

J L Powell & Co Inc (PA) 910 642-8989
135 E Main St Whiteville (28472) *(G-15967)*

J L Smith & Co Inc (PA) 704 521-1088
901 Blairhill Rd Ste 400 Charlotte (28217) *(G-3004)*

J M C Tool and Machine, Sanford *Also Called: Bnp Inc (G-14094)*

J M I Barcodes 919 289-4125
9400 Ransdell Rd Ste 9 Raleigh (27603) *(G-12909)*

J Morgan Signs Inc 336 274-6509
4421 S Elm Eugene St Greensboro (27406) *(G-7131)*

J R B and J Knitting Inc 910 439-4242
4543 Nc Highway 109 S Mount Gilead (27306) *(G-11601)*

J R Cole Industries Inc 704 523-6622
10708 Granite St Charlotte (28273) *(G-3005)*

J R Cole Industries Inc (PA) 704 523-6622
435 Minuet Ln Charlotte (28217) *(G-3006)*

J R Craver & Associates Inc 336 769-3330
265 Ashbourne Lake Ct Clemmons (27012) *(G-4049)*

J R Nixon Welding 252 221-4574
212 Center Hill Rd Tyner (27980) *(G-15434)*

J S Myers Co Inc 336 463-5572
2129 Ray T Moore Rd Yadkinville (27055) *(G-17042)*

J Signs and Graphics LLC 910 315-2657
1345 N Sandhills Blvd Ste 1 Aberdeen (28315) *(G-9)*

J Stahl Sales & Sourcing Inc (PA) 828 645-3005
81 Monticello Rd Weaverville (28787) *(G-15849)*

J T Metals LLC 336 737-4189
3032 Nc Highway 42 Goldston (27252) *(G-6675)*

J W Jones Lumber Company Inc (PA) 252 771-2497
1443 Northside Rd Elizabeth City (27909) *(G-5551)*

J Wise Inc 828 202-5563
313a Motz Ave Lincolnton (28092) *(G-9896)*

J-M Manufacturing Company Inc 919 575-6515
2602 W Lyon Station Rd Creedmoor (27522) *(G-4615)*

J&B Welding LLC 910 316-5838
2188 Moores Ln Lumberton (28358) *(G-10042)*

J&C Welding and Fabrication 704 654-8253
3550 Briarthorne Dr Charlotte (28269) *(G-3007)*

J&D Logging Inc 910 271-0750
1644 Veachs Mill Rd Warsaw (28398) *(G-15670)*

J&J Millworks Inc 336 252-2868
3528 Thomasville Rd Winston Salem (27107) *(G-16766)*

J&J Outdoor Accessories 910 742-1969
26955 Andrew Jackson Hwy E Delco (28436) *(G-4721)*

J&J Precision Services LLC 970 412-4683
1817 Brierwood Rd Wilmington (28405) *(G-16275)*

J&J Woodworking LLC 704 941-9537
1004 Raywood Ct Matthews (28104) *(G-10325)*

J&L Machine & Fabrication Inc 704 755-5552
201 S Buckoak St Stanley (28164) *(G-14698)*

J&L Manufacturing Inc 919 801-3219
192 Jarco Dr Fuquay Varina (27526) *(G-6206)*

J&P Metal Arts Inc 704 684-5140
5923 Stockbridge Dr Ste B Monroe (28110) *(G-10745)*

J&R Cohoon Logging & Tidewater 252 943-6300
25912 Us Highway 264 E Pantego (27860) *(G-12165)*

ALPHABETIC SECTION

J&R Precision Heating and Air..910 480-8322
1625 Cumberland Dr Fayetteville (28311) *(G-5844)*

J&R SERvices/J&r Lumber Co..956 778-7005
1319 Military Cutoff Rd Ste Cc Pmb 173 Wilmington (28405) *(G-16276)*

J4 Construction LLC..704 550-7970
2634 W Hwy 74 W Wadesboro (28170) *(G-15513)*

J6 & Company LLC..336 997-4497
5077 Bismark St Winston Salem (27105) *(G-16767)*

JA Smith Inc..704 860-4910
305 Plainsview Church Rd Lawndale (28090) *(G-9500)*

Jab Lures..860 885-9314
105 Taylor Leigh Dr South Mills (27976) *(G-14524)*

Jab-C LLC..704 507-6196
5912 Waxhaw Hwy Mineral Springs (28108) *(G-10517)*

Jabb of Carolinas Inc..919 965-9007
302 E Brown St Pine Level (27568) *(G-12211)*

Jabec Enterprise Inc (PA)..336 655-8441
5224 Mountain View Rd Winston Salem (27104) *(G-16768)*

Jabil Inc..828 684-3141
100 Vista Blvd Arden (28704) *(G-343)*

Jabil Inc..828 209-4202
724 Broadpointe Dr Mills River (28759) *(G-10505)*

Jack Cartwright Incorporated..336 889-9400
2014 Chestnut Street Ext High Point (27262) *(G-8414)*

Jack M Jarrett..336 772-4108
512 N Mendenhall St Greensboro (27401) *(G-7132)*

Jack Pagan & Assoc Inc..919 872-0159
1001 Thoreau Dr Raleigh (27609) *(G-12910)*

Jack Stevens Inc..919 363-8589
833 Us 64 Hwy W Apex (27523) *(G-208)*

Jackie Lewis Photography Aka..910 640-1550
2458 Union Valley Rd Whiteville (28472) *(G-15968)*

Jacks Motor Parts Inc..910 642-4077
Hwy 701 Whiteville (28472) *(G-15969)*

Jackson Arts Market LLC..415 659-0710
533 W Main St Sylva (28779) *(G-15059)*

Jackson Corrugated LLC..828 608-0931
1000 Chain Dr Morganton (28655) *(G-11223)*

Jackson Logging..919 658-2757
2936 Summerlins Crossroad Rd Mount Olive (28365) *(G-11663)*

Jackson Paper Manufacturing Co (PA)..828 586-5534
152 W Main St Sylva (28779) *(G-15060)*

Jackson Products Inc..704 598-4949
1109 Monterey Bay Dr Wake Forest (27587) *(G-15565)*

Jackson Wine..828 508-9292
183 King St Brevard (28712) *(G-1277)*

Jacksonville Metal Mfg Inc..910 938-7635
181 Piney Green Rd Jacksonville (28546) *(G-9010)*

Jackway Software LLC..919 747-1190
552 Wanderview Ln Holly Springs (27540) *(G-8701)*

Jacob Holm Industries Amer Inc..828 490-6017
145 Cane Creek Indus Park Fletcher (28732) *(G-6014)*

Jacob Holtz Company..828 328-1003
747 22nd Street Pl Se Hickory (28602) *(G-8070)*

JACOB HOLTZ COMPANY, Hickory Also Called: *Jacob Holtz Company (G-8070)*

Jacobs Creek Stone Company Inc..336 857-2602
2081 W Slate Mine Rd Denton (27239) *(G-4738)*

Jacody Publishing..336 438-1579
3065 Gwyn Rd Elon (27244) *(G-5660)*

Jacqueline Cole..828 277-3566
676 Fairview Rd Asheville (28803) *(G-667)*

Jadas Hats..919 561-4373
5812 Magellan Way Apt 102 Raleigh (27612) *(G-12911)*

Jaeco Precision Inc..336 633-1025
721 Jaeco Caudill Dr Asheboro (27205) *(G-447)*

Jag Graphics Inc..828 259-9020
231 Biltmore Ave Asheville (28801) *(G-668)*

Jag Industries LLC..704 655-2507
10408 Remembrance Trl Huntersville (28078) *(G-8840)*

Jaggaer, Morrisville Also Called: *Jaggaer LLC (G-11362)*

Jaggaer LLC (HQ)..919 659-2100
3020 Carrington Mill Blvd Ste 100 Morrisville (27560) *(G-11362)*

Jak Moulding & Supply Inc..252 753-5546
1565 Strickland Rd Walstonburg (27888) *(G-15638)*

Jala Woodshop LLC..704 439-6119
10301 Conistan Pl Cornelius (28031) *(G-4563)*

Jalco Inc..336 434-5909
3621 Steeplegate Dr Trinity (27370) *(G-15347)*

Jalilud Embroidery LLC..704 425-3492
9419 Silverdale Ln Charlotte (28269) *(G-3008)*

James Bunn..252 293-4867
4167 Black Creek Rd S Wilson (27893) *(G-16502)*

James Cotter Ironworks..919 644-2664
5102 Eno Cemetery Rd Cedar Grove (27231) *(G-1971)*

James E Latta..919 682-5793
2725 Beck Rd Durham (27704) *(G-5170)*

James Embroidery Company..704 467-1224
3270 Jackson Rd Mooresville (28115) *(G-10986)*

James Fods Frnchise Corp Amer..336 437-0393
611 E Gilbreath St Graham (27253) *(G-6694)*

James Foods Inc..336 437-0393
611 E Gilbreath St Graham (27253) *(G-6695)*

James G Gouge..336 854-1551
1001 Phillips Ave High Point (27262) *(G-8415)*

James Iron & Steel Inc..704 309-8507
3010 W Beach Dr Oak Island (28465) *(G-12051)*

James Iron & Steel Inc..704 283-2299
2819 Top Hill Rd Monroe (28110) *(G-10746)*

James Keith Nations..828 421-5391
69 Thomas Valley Rd Whittier (28789) *(G-16007)*

James King..910 308-8818
9998 Fayetteville Rd Fayetteville (28304) *(G-5845)*

James L Johnson..704 694-0103
2151 Beaver Rd Wadesboro (28170) *(G-15514)*

James Lammers..252 491-2303
7715 Caratoke Hwy Powells Point (27966) *(G-12398)*

James M Pleasants Company Inc (PA)..336 275-3152
603 Diamond Hill Ct Greensboro (27406) *(G-7133)*

James M Pleasants Company Inc..888 902-8324
206 E Seneca Rd Greensboro (27406) *(G-7134)*

James Michael Vineyards LLC..704 539-4749
440 Lake Mullis Rd Harmony (28634) *(G-7687)*

James Moore & Son Logging..336 656-9858
7435 Friendship Church Rd Browns Summit (27214) *(G-1309)*

James O 2, Hickory Also Called: *James Oxygen and Supply Co (G-8071)*

James Oxygen and Supply Co (PA)..704 322-5438
30 Us Highway 321 Nw Hickory (28601) *(G-8071)*

James Ricks, Fayetteville Also Called: *Rk Enterprises LLC (G-5908)*

James River Equipment..704 821-7399
2112 Morgan Mill Rd Monroe (28110) *(G-10747)*

James T White Company..704 865-9811
4415 Little Mountain Rd Gastonia (28056) *(G-6434)*

James Tool Company, Morganton Also Called: *James Tool Machine & Engrg Inc (G-11224)*

James Tool Machine & Engrg Inc (PA)..828 584-8722
130 Reep Dr Morganton (28655) *(G-11224)*

James W McManus Inc..828 688-2560
2419 Beans Creek Rd Bakersville (28705) *(G-884)*

Jamestown News..336 841-4933
206 E Main St Ste 1a Jamestown (27282) *(G-9059)*

Jamie M Dollahan..571 435-2060
112 Hardin Dr Maysville (28555) *(G-10373)*

Jamn Tees..336 444-4327
244 Ararat Longhill Rd Pilot Mountain (27041) *(G-12198)*

Janco LLC..919 847-8816
128 Yorkchester Way Raleigh (27615) *(G-12912)*

Janellco Products Inc..704 896-1415
400 Avinger Ln Apt 415 Davidson (28036) *(G-4683)*

Janesville LLC..828 668-9251
157 Lackey Town Rd Old Fort (28762) *(G-12102)*

Janet W Whitbeck Inc..252 986-2800
57158 Altona Ln Hatteras (27943) *(G-7737)*

Jantec Sign Group LLC..336 429-5010
196 Sexton Rd Mount Airy (27030) *(G-11525)*

ALPHABETIC SECTION

Janus Development Group Inc..252 551-9042
308 W Arlington Blvd Ste 300 Greenville (27834) *(G-7548)*

Jared Munday Electric Inc..828 355-9024
123 Tarheel Ln Boone (28607) *(G-1210)*

Jared Sasnett Logging Co Inc..252 939-6289
1976 Neuse Rd Kinston (28501) *(G-9370)*

Jarrett Bay Offshore..919 803-1990
4209 Lassiter Mill Rd Ste 126 Raleigh (27609) *(G-12913)*

Jarrett Brothers..828 433-8036
200 Carbondale Ln Morganton (28655) *(G-11225)*

Jarrett Press Publications...919 862-0551
2805 Spring Forest Rd Ste 201 Raleigh (27616) *(G-12914)*

Jarrett Shane DBA Jarrett Stuc......................................828 768-8385
19 Broadview Dr Asheville (28803) *(G-669)*

Jasie Blanks LLC...910 485-0016
3725 Ramsey St Ste 103c Fayetteville (28311) *(G-5846)*

Jasmine Wade Co LLC..704 345-8301
15120 Kellington Ct Charlotte (28273) *(G-3009)*

Jason Case Corp..212 786-2288
4809 Hillsborough Rd Durham (27705) *(G-5171)*

Jason Culbertson...910 733-6794
357 Lighthouse Rd Maxton (28364) *(G-10357)*

Jasper Engine Exchange Inc..704 664-2300
200 Penske Way Mooresville (28115) *(G-10987)*

Jasper Library Furniture, Troutman *Also Called: Jasper Seating Company Inc (G-15384)*

Jasper Library Furniture, Troutman *Also Called: Liat LLC (G-15386)*

Jasper Motor Sports, Mooresville *Also Called: Jasper Engine Exchange Inc (G-10987)*

Jasper Penske Engines..704 788-8996
4361 Motorsports Dr Sw Concord (28027) *(G-4292)*

Jasper Seating Company Inc..704 528-4506
694 N Main St Troutman (28166) *(G-15384)*

Jax Brothers Inc..704 732-3351
536 N Generals Blvd Lincolnton (28092) *(G-9897)*

Jax Specialty Welding LLC...704 380-3548
621 Bristol Dr Statesville (28677) *(G-14823)*

Jaxonsigns...910 467-3409
874 E Ocean Hwy Holly Ridge (28445) *(G-8682)*

Jayson Concepts Inc...828 654-8900
115 Vista Blvd Arden (28704) *(G-344)*

JB Cabinets, Hickory *Also Called: Bud Baumgarner (G-7954)*

JB II Printing LLC...336 222-0717
825 S Main St Burlington (27215) *(G-1439)*

Jb-Isecurity LLC...910 824-7601
505 Toxaway Ct Fayetteville (28314) *(G-5847)*

Jbb Packaging LLC..201 470-8501
100 Grace Dr Weldon (27890) *(G-15883)*

Jbm Manufacturing, Morehead City *Also Called: Jones Brothers Marine Mfg Inc (G-11178)*

Jbr Properties of Greenville Inc....................................252 355-9353
133 Forlines Rd Winterville (28590) *(G-17004)*

Jbs Case Ready, Lenoir *Also Called: Jbs USA LLC (G-9622)*

Jbs Ordnance Inc..980 722-3659
9036 Bremerton Ct Charlotte (28227) *(G-3010)*

Jbs USA LLC..828 855-9571
1207 25th Street Pl Se Hickory (28602) *(G-8072)*

Jbs USA LLC..828 725-7000
1450 Homegrown Ct Lenoir (28645) *(G-9622)*

Jbs2 Inc...828 236-1300
875 Warren Wilson Rd Swannanoa (28778) *(G-15027)*

Jbt Aerotech Services..336 740-3737
6035 Old Oak Ridge Rd Greensboro (27410) *(G-7135)*

JC Powder Coating LLC...919 362-9311
9016 Barker Rd New Hill (27562) *(G-11861)*

JC Signs Inc..704 995-0988
2336 Kenmore Ave Unit F Charlotte (28204) *(G-3011)*

JC Signs Charlotte...704 370-2725
9700 Research Dr Charlotte (28262) *(G-3012)*

JC Welding and Machine LLC..336 306-2026
429 Hege Rd Lexington (27295) *(G-9733)*

JC Wicks LLC..828 514-9788
1220 Ballina Way Charlotte (28214) *(G-3013)*

Jci Jones Chemicals Inc...704 392-9767
1500 Tar Heel Rd Charlotte (28208) *(G-3014)*

Jctm, Charlotte *Also Called: Jctm LLC (G-3015)*

Jctm LLC...252 571-8678
16710 Tulloch Rd Charlotte (28278) *(G-3015)*

Jcv Communications, Wilmington *Also Called: Jcv Communications Inc (G-16277)*

Jcv Communications Inc (PA)...844 399-8282
4563 Technology Dr Ste 7 Wilmington (28405) *(G-16277)*

JD Apparel Inc..704 289-5600
1680 Williams Rd Monroe (28110) *(G-10748)*

JD Steel LLC...843 367-7456
12324 Buxton Dr Pineville (28134) *(G-12277)*

Jd2 Company LLC..800 811-6441
3527 Governors Island Dr Denver (28037) *(G-4786)*

JDG Woodworks Inc...910 367-8806
1002 Shakespeare Dr Wilmington (28405) *(G-16278)*

Jdh Capital LLC (PA)...704 357-1220
3735 Beam Rd Unit B Charlotte (28217) *(G-3016)*

Jds Logging LLC..910 713-5980
6020 Ludlum Rd Nw Ash (28420) *(G-395)*

JE Ekornes Usa Inc..828 764-4001
115 Wamsutta Mill Rd Morganton (28655) *(G-11226)*

Je Freeze LLC..980 231-5365
20045 Verlaine Dr Davidson (28036) *(G-4684)*

Jean Dupree..919 821-4020
476 Pepperstone Dr Salisbury (28146) *(G-13990)*

Jeans Printshop LLC..704 564-4348
4221 W Sugar Creek Rd Charlotte (28269) *(G-3017)*

Jebco Inc..919 557-2001
121 Thomas Mill Rd Holly Springs (27540) *(G-8702)*

Jeff Anderson..910 481-8923
3741 Butler Nursery Rd Fayetteville (28306) *(G-5848)*

Jeff Weaver Logging..864 909-1758
617 John Weaver Rd Columbus (28722) *(G-4175)*

Jefferies Socks LLC..336 226-7316
2203 Tucker St Burlington (27215) *(G-1440)*

Jeffers Logging Inc...919 708-2193
279 Garner Rd Sanford (27330) *(G-14139)*

Jefferson Group Inc...252 752-6195
225 Martin St Greenville (27834) *(G-7549)*

Jeffrey Ancheta..919 552-0892
4817 Frankie Rd Fuquay Varina (27526) *(G-6207)*

Jeffrey Sheffer..919 861-9126
3901 Commerce Park Dr Raleigh (27610) *(G-12915)*

Jeffrey's Seafood, Hatteras *Also Called: Janet W Whitbeck Inc (G-7737)*

Jeffreys Division, Colfax *Also Called: Phillips Corporation (G-4157)*

Jeld Wen International Supply, Charlotte *Also Called: Jeld-Wen Inc (G-3018)*

Jeld-Wen, Charlotte *Also Called: Jeld-Wen Holding Inc (G-3019)*

Jeld-Wen Inc (HQ)...800 535-3936
2645 Silver Crescent Dr Charlotte (28273) *(G-3018)*

Jeld-Wen Inc..828 724-9511
100 Henry Mccall Rd Marion (28752) *(G-10153)*

Jeld-Wen Inc..336 838-0292
205 Lanes Dr North Wilkesboro (28659) *(G-12016)*

Jeld-Wen Composite, North Wilkesboro *Also Called: Jeld-Wen Inc (G-12016)*

Jeld-Wen Holding Inc (PA)...704 378-5700
2645 Silver Crescent Dr Charlotte (28273) *(G-3019)*

Jem Acres Inc...252 823-3483
506 Trade St Tarboro (27886) *(G-15110)*

Jenesis Software Inc..828 245-1171
294 S Broadway St Forest City (28043) *(G-6072)*

Jenkins, Charlotte *Also Called: Jenkins Electric Company (G-3020)*

Jenkins Electric Company..800 438-3003
5933 Brookshire Blvd Charlotte (28216) *(G-3020)*

Jenkins Foods Inc...704 434-2347
2119 New House Rd Shelby (28150) *(G-14332)*

Jenkins Interiors, North Wilkesboro *Also Called: Jenkins Properties Inc (G-12017)*

Jenkins Millwork LLC...336 667-3344
1603 Industrial Dr Wilkesboro (28697) *(G-16032)*

Jenkins Properties Inc..336 667-4282
102 Chestnut St Ste 101 North Wilkesboro (28659) *(G-12017)*

Jenkins Services Group LLC...704 881-3210
5577 Little Mountain Rd Catawba (28609) *(G-1965)*

Jenni K Jewelry, Greenville *Also Called: Jkl Inc (G-7550)*

Jennifer E Smith ND.. 704 871-1229
110 Stockton St Ste J Statesville (28677) *(G-14824)*

Jennifer Mowrer.. 336 714-6462
150 Kimel Park Dr Ste 100 Winston Salem (27103) *(G-16769)*

Jennifer Niten Logging.. 336 428-6245
823 Edwards Lakeview Dr Elkin (28621) *(G-5621)*

Jensen Activewear.. 704 982-3005
703 Concord Rd Albemarle (28001) *(G-91)*

Jepp Industries Inc... 910 232-8715
6644 Shire Ln Wilmington (28411) *(G-16279)*

Jeremy Weitzel... 919 878-4474
1228 United Dr Raleigh (27603) *(G-12916)*

Jerky Man Inc... 828 749-3685
4035 Fork Creek Rd Saluda (28773) *(G-14071)*

Jerky Outpost... 828 260-6221
2107 Broadstone Rd Banner Elk (28604) *(G-900)*

Jerry Blevins... 336 384-3726
1162 Deep Ford Rd Lansing (28643) *(G-9455)*

Jerry Cox Logging.. 919 742-6089
7598 Old Siler City Rd Ramseur (27316) *(G-13443)*

Jerry G Williams & Sons Inc... 919 934-4115
524 Brogden Rd Smithfield (27577) *(G-14464)*

Jerry Huffman Sawmill.. 336 973-3606
287 Cactus Ln Wilkesboro (28697) *(G-16033)*

Jerry Huffman Sawmill & Log, Wilkesboro *Also Called: Jerry Huffman Sawmill (G-16033)*

Jerry Williams & Son Inc.. 919 934-4115
524 Brogden Rd Smithfield (27577) *(G-14465)*

Jersey City Sports, Winston Salem *Also Called: Twin City Sports LLC (G-16958)*

Jerseybincom.. 828 545-0445
61 N Merrimon Ave # 407 Asheville (28804) *(G-670)*

Jeskri Associates Inc... 704 291-9991
1821 N Rocky River Rd Monroe (28110) *(G-10749)*

Jessica Charles LLC.. 336 434-2124
535 Townsend Ave High Point (27263) *(G-8416)*

Jester-Crown Inc.. 919 872-1070
4721 Atlantic Ave Ste 119 Raleigh (27604) *(G-12917)*

Jestines Jewels Inc.. 704 904-0191
512 Klumac Rd Ste 4 Salisbury (28144) *(G-13991)*

Jesus Daily Group LLC.. 336 727-4781
726 Morris Rd Winston Salem (27101) *(G-16770)*

Jewel Masters Inc (PA).. 336 243-2711
221 W Us Highway 64 Lexington (27295) *(G-9734)*

Jewelry By Gail Inc.. 252 441-5387
207 E Driftwood St Nags Head (27959) *(G-11721)*

Jewelry Spoken Here... 828 225-8464
86 Lanvale Ave Asheville (28806) *(G-671)*

Jewers Doors Us Inc... 888 510-5331
3714 Alliance Dr Ste 305 Greensboro (27407) *(G-7136)*

JFK Conferences LLC... 980 255-3336
322 Ridgeway Ct Fayetteville (28311) *(G-5849)*

Jfl Enterprises Inc... 704 786-7838
82 Spring St Sw Concord (28025) *(G-4293)*

JG Agnew Holdings Inc... 704 594-0900
2535 Red Maple Ln Harrisburg (28075) *(G-7714)*

Jgi Inc (PA)... 704 522-8860
10108 Industrial Dr Pineville (28134) *(G-12278)*

Jh Logging... 336 599-0278
1300 Virgilina Rd Roxboro (27573) *(G-13805)*

Jhd Enterprise LLC.. 919 612-1787
1102 Lake Ridge Dr Creedmoor (27522) *(G-4616)*

Jhonny Delgado... 704 218-9424
7321 William Reynolds Dr Charlotte (28215) *(G-3021)*

Jhons Wood Work LLC.. 828 231-6240
255 Tipton Hill Rd Leicester (28748) *(G-9514)*

Jhrg LLC... 252 478-4997
303 S Pine St Spring Hope (27882) *(G-14618)*

Jhrg Manufacturing LLC.. 252 478-4977
303 S Pine St Spring Hope (27882) *(G-14619)*

Jif Logging Inc... 252 398-2249
411 E Woodrow School Rd Murfreesboro (27855) *(G-11699)*

Jiffy Division, High Point *Also Called: Sealed Air Corporation (G-8520)*

Jim Fab of North Carolina Inc.. 704 278-1000
10230 Statesville Blvd Cleveland (27013) *(G-4074)*

Jim Hammonds Enterprises LLC....................................... 828 775-8805
349 Miller Branch Rd Mars Hill (28754) *(G-10196)*

Jim John... 336 352-4650
1223 Laurel Springs Church Rd Mount Airy (27030) *(G-11526)*

Jim Myers & Sons Inc.. 704 554-8397
5120 Westinghouse Blvd Charlotte (28273) *(G-3022)*

Jimbuilt, Connelly Springs *Also Called: Jimbuilt Machines Inc (G-4405)*

Jimbuilt Machines Inc.. 828 874-3530
2555 Israel Chapel Rd Connelly Springs (28612) *(G-4405)*

Jimmie A Hogan... 910 428-2535
392 Cedar Creek Rd Biscoe (27209) *(G-1112)*

Jimmie Nelms Trucking, Louisburg *Also Called: Jimmy D Nelms Logging Inc (G-9993)*

Jimmy D Nelms Logging Inc... 919 853-2597
4021 Nc 561 Hwy Louisburg (27549) *(G-9993)*

Jimmy Keith Surfboards Inc.. 910 297-9719
453 Shipyard Blvd Wilmington (28412) *(G-16280)*

Jimmys Coating Unlimited Inc.. 704 915-2420
420 N Morehead St Gastonia (28054) *(G-6435)*

Jj Electronic Solutions Div, Sanford *Also Called: Desco Industries Inc (G-14107)*

Jj Hernandez Logging LLC... 919 742-3381
4272 Piney Grove Church Rd Siler City (27344) *(G-14418)*

Jj Led Solution Inc... 704 261-4279
5413 Stowe Derby Dr Charlotte (28278) *(G-3023)*

Jk Logging LLC.. 910 648-5471
3564 Paul Willoughby Rd Evergreen (28438) *(G-5698)*

Jka Industries... 980 225-5350
353 Grayson Dr Salisbury (28147) *(G-13992)*

Jkl Inc (PA)... 252 355-6714
727 Red Banks Rd Greenville (27858) *(G-7550)*

JKS Motorsports Inc (PA)... 336 722-4129
301 Welcome Center Blvd Lexington (27295) *(G-9735)*

Jl Hosiery LLC.. 910 974-7156
130 S Main St Candor (27229) *(G-1593)*

Jlmade LLC.. 252 515-2195
2226 Jasper Forest Trl Winnabow (28479) *(G-16581)*

Jls Masonry Inc.. 704 307-1219
4509 Parkwood School Rd Monroe (28112) *(G-10750)*

Jly Invstmnts Inc Fka Nwman Mc (HQ)............................ 336 273-8261
2949 Lees Chapel Rd Browns Summit (27214) *(G-1310)*

JM Graphics Inc... 704 375-1147
3400 International Airport Dr Ste 950 Charlotte (28208) *(G-3024)*

JM Innovations LLC... 704 495-4841
7222 Lillian Way Charlotte (28226) *(G-3025)*

JM Williams Timber Company.. 919 362-1333
4525 Green Level West Rd Apex (27523) *(G-209)*

Jmc Tool & Machine Co.. 919 775-7070
5910 Elwin Buchanan Dr Sanford (27330) *(G-14140)*

Jmedic Inc.. 336 744-4444
160 Hanes Mall Cir Winston Salem (27103) *(G-16771)*

Jmk Tool & Die Inc... 910 897-6373
3482 Nc Hwy 27 E Coats (27521) *(G-4131)*

JMP Statistical Discovery Llc... 877 594-6567
100 Matrix Dr 8000 Cary (27513) *(G-1796)*

JMS Southeast Inc.. 704 873-1835
105 Temperature Ln Statesville (28677) *(G-14825)*

Jmw Logging LLC.. 919 934-4115
524 Brogden Rd Smithfield (27577) *(G-14466)*

Jna, Mooresville *Also Called: Bucher Municipal N Amer Inc (G-10891)*

Jo Mangum... 919 271-8822
60 Linden Ave Asheville (28801) *(G-672)*

Jo-Mar Group LLC... 704 825-5000
701 Plum St Belmont (28012) *(G-993)*

Jo-Mar Spinning, Belmont *Also Called: Jo-Mar Group LLC (G-993)*

Jo-Natta Transportation LLC... 888 424-8789
348 Foothill Ln Fayetteville (28311) *(G-5850)*

Joanna Division Ch F Inds.. 704 522-5000
8701 Red Oak Blvd Ste 400 Charlotte (28217) *(G-3026)*

Job Finder USA, Cary *Also Called: Prism Publishing Inc (G-1860)*

ALPHABETIC SECTION — Jolo Winery & Vineyards LLC

Job Shop Fabricators Inc 336 427-7300
3522 Us Highway 220 Madison (27025) *(G-10074)*

Jobs Magazine LLC 919 319-6816
1240 Se Maynard Rd Ste 104 Cary (27511) *(G-1797)*

Jocephus Originals Inc 336 229-9600
1003 W Main St Ste A4 Haw River (27258) *(G-7754)*

Jochum Industries 336 288-7975
710 Freemasons Dr Greensboro (27407) *(G-7137)*

Jody Stowe 704 519-6560
2848 Lakeview Cir Matthews (28105) *(G-10256)*

Joe and Kitty Brown Inc 704 629-4327
1312 Ramseur Rd Bessemer City (28016) *(G-1072)*

Joe and La Inc 336 585-0313
326 Mcarthur Ln Burlington (27217) *(G-1441)*

Joe Armstrong 336 207-6503
3205 Liberty Rd Greensboro (27406) *(G-7138)*

Joe Robin Darnell 704 482-1186
2115 Chatfield Rd Shelby (28150) *(G-14333)*

Joel Moretz 828 355-9936
209 Blairmont Dr Boone (28607) *(G-1211)*

Joerns Healthcare Parent LLC (PA) 800 966-6662
2430 Whitehall Park Dr Ste 100 Charlotte (28273) *(G-3027)*

Joesigns Inc 252 638-1622
2617 Trent Rd New Bern (28562) *(G-11813)*

Joey Manic Inc 919 772-7756
122 Wall St Oxford (27565) *(G-12134)*

Joeys Woodworking Gifts 336 427-5263
1601 Gold Hill Rd Madison (27025) *(G-10075)*

Jofra Graphics Inc 910 259-1717
401 Us Highway 117 S Burgaw (28425) *(G-1342)*

John Conrad Inc 336 475-8144
1028 Johnsontown Rd Thomasville (27360) *(G-15239)*

John Deere, Cary *Also Called: John Deere Consumer Pdts Inc (G-1798)*

John Deere, Fuquay Varina *Also Called: Revels Turf and Tractor LLC (G-6226)*

John Deere Authorized Dealer, Monroe *Also Called: James River Equipment (G-10747)*

John Deere Consumer Pdts Inc (HQ) 919 804-2000
2000 John Deere Run Cary (27513) *(G-1798)*

John Deere Kernersville LLC 336 996-8100
1000 John Deere Rd Kernersville (27284) *(G-9207)*

John Deere Turf Care, Fuquay Varina *Also Called: Deere & Company (G-6195)*

John Glen Alexander Corp 704 309-7258
10015 Andres Duany Dr Huntersville (28078) *(G-8841)*

John H Peterson Jr 910 762-9957
51 Feather Ln Rocky Point (28457) *(G-13748)*

John J Morton Company Inc (PA) 704 332-6633
2211 W Morehead St Charlotte (28208) *(G-3028)*

John Jenkins Company 336 375-3717
5949 Summit Ave Browns Summit (27214) *(G-1311)*

John Jones DBA Grass Choppers 336 413-6613
393 Slater Rd Lewisville (27023) *(G-9668)*

John K Chenausky 336 427-2495
3494 Ayersville Rd Mayodan (27027) *(G-10364)*

John K Chenausky, Owner, Mayodan *Also Called: John K Chenausky (G-10364)*

John Laughter Jewelry Inc 828 456-4772
146 N Main St Waynesville (28786) *(G-15808)*

John Lindenberger 919 337-6741
6429 Grassy Knoll Ln Raleigh (27616) *(G-12918)*

John R Bell 252 297-2499
112 Ridge Rd Belvidere (27919) *(G-1022)*

John W Foster Sales Inc 704 821-3822
3491 Gribble Rd Matthews (28104) *(G-10326)*

John West Auto Service Inc 919 250-0825
3216 Lake Woodard Dr Raleigh (27604) *(G-12919)*

Johnie Gregory Trck Bodies Inc 252 264-2626
337 Old Us Highway 17 Hertford (27944) *(G-7922)*

Johnny Daniel 336 859-2480
230 Bringle Ferry Rd Denton (27239) *(G-4739)*

Johnny Slicks Inc 910 803-2159
624 Us Highway 17 S Unit 1 Holly Ridge (28445) *(G-8683)*

Johnnys Tire Sales and Svc Inc 252 353-8473
2400 S Memorial Dr Ste 3a Greenville (27834) *(G-7551)*

Johnson Cabinet Co 252 714-2051
Simpson (27879) *(G-14438)*

Johnson Cnc LLC 910 428-1245
133 S Main St Star (27356) *(G-14716)*

Johnson Concrete Company 704 786-4204
106 Old Davidson Pl Nw Concord (28027) *(G-4294)*

Johnson Concrete Company 336 248-2918
514 Burgin Dr Lexington (27292) *(G-9736)*

Johnson Concrete Company (PA) 704 636-5231
217 Klumac Rd Salisbury (28144) *(G-13993)*

Johnson Concrete Company 704 636-5231
1401 Nc 42 Hwy Willow Spring (27592) *(G-16079)*

Johnson Concrete Products, Concord *Also Called: Johnson Concrete Company (G-4294)*

Johnson Concrete Products, Salisbury *Also Called: Johnson Concrete Company (G-13993)*

Johnson Controls 704 501-0500
9826 Southern Pine Blvd Charlotte (28273) *(G-3029)*

Johnson Controls, Asheville *Also Called: Johnson Controls Inc (G-673)*

Johnson Controls, Charlotte *Also Called: Johnson Controls Inc (G-3030)*

Johnson Controls, Charlotte *Also Called: Johnson Controls Inc (G-3031)*

Johnson Controls, Durham *Also Called: Johnson Controls Inc (G-5172)*

Johnson Controls, High Point *Also Called: Clarios LLC (G-8296)*

Johnson Controls, Kernersville *Also Called: Clarios LLC (G-9180)*

Johnson Controls, Raleigh *Also Called: Johnson Controls Inc (G-12920)*

Johnson Controls, Wilmington *Also Called: Johnson Controls Inc (G-16281)*

Johnson Controls, Winterville *Also Called: Clarios LLC (G-16997)*

Johnson Controls Inc 828 225-3200
905 Riverside Dr Asheville (28804) *(G-673)*

Johnson Controls Inc 704 521-8889
9844 Southern Pine Blvd Ste B Charlotte (28273) *(G-3030)*

Johnson Controls Inc 919 905-5745
5 Moore Dr Durham (27709) *(G-5172)*

Johnson Controls Inc 866 285-8345
2700 Perimeter Park Dr Morrisville (27560) *(G-11363)*

Johnson Controls Inc 919 743-3500
633 Hutton St Ste 104 Raleigh (27606) *(G-12920)*

Johnson Controls Inc 910 392-2372
395 N Green Meadows Dr Wilmington (28405) *(G-16281)*

Johnson Controls Inc 704 521-8889
9844 Southern Pine Blvd Charlotte (28273) *(G-3031)*

Johnson Custom Boats Inc 910 232-4594
6820a Market St Wilmington (28405) *(G-16282)*

Johnson Global Cmplnce Contrls 704 552-1119
13950 Ballantyne Corporate Pl Charlotte (28277) *(G-3032)*

Johnson Harn Vngar Gee GL Pllc 919 213-6163
434 Fayetteville St Ste 2200 Raleigh (27601) *(G-12921)*

Johnson Industrial Mchy Svcs 252 239-1944
7160 Us Highway 117 Lucama (27851) *(G-10017)*

Johnson Lumber Products Inc 910 532-4201
911 Eddie L Jones Rd Ivanhoe (28447) *(G-8981)*

Johnson Machine Co Inc 252 638-2620
8 Batts Hill Rd New Bern (28562) *(G-11814)*

Johnson Nash & Sons Farms Inc (PA) 910 289-3113
3385 Us Hwy 117 S Rose Hill (28458) *(G-13778)*

Johnson Paving Company Inc 828 652-4911
3101 Us 221 North Marion (28752) *(G-10154)*

Johnson's Industrial Coatings, Clemmons *Also Called: Paint Company of NC (G-4054)*

Johnston Casuals Furniture Inc 336 838-5178
121 Shaver St North Wilkesboro (28659) *(G-12018)*

Johnston County Industries Inc 919 743-8700
1100 E Preston St Selma (27576) *(G-14257)*

Johnston Knife and Tool Inc 704 208-9191
6400 Lake Rd Mint Hill (28227) *(G-10537)*

Joie of Seating Inc 704 795-7474
4537 Orphanage Rd Concord (28027) *(G-4295)*

Joines Custom Woodwork 336 984-7237
485 Pennell Rd Moravian Falls (28654) *(G-11145)*

Joken Publications 704 957-7030
3712 Charterhall Ln Charlotte (28215) *(G-3033)*

Jolo Winery & Vineyards LLC 954 816-5649
219 Jolo Winery Ln Pilot Mountain (27041) *(G-12199)*

ALPHABETIC SECTION

Jon Mitchell Cabinets..336 229-6261
   1413 Mccuiston Dr Burlington (27215) *(G-1442)*

Jonathan Holt LLC...919 391-7062
   1115 Old School Rd Chapel Hill (27516) *(G-2027)*

Jonathan Stamey..828 577-0450
   1 Old Hendersonville Hwy Pisgah Forest (28768) *(G-12324)*

Jones Brothers Marine Mfg Inc...............................252 240-1995
   100 Bateau Blvd Morehead City (28557) *(G-11178)*

Jones Doors & Windows Inc...................................336 998-8624
   533 Joe Rd Mocksville (27028) *(G-10582)*

Jones Fab LLC..336 940-2769
   897 Underpass Rd Advance (27006) *(G-45)*

Jones Fabricare Inc (PA)..336 272-7261
   502 E Cornwallis Dr Greensboro (27405) *(G-7139)*

Jones Frame Inc...336 434-2531
   5456 Uwharrie Rd High Point (27263) *(G-8417)*

Jones Furs, Greensboro *Also Called: Jones Fabricare Inc (G-7139)*

Jones Marine Inc..704 639-0173
   10285 Bringle Ferry Rd Salisbury (28146) *(G-13994)*

Jones Media..828 264-3612
   474 Industrial Park Dr Boone (28607) *(G-1212)*

Jones Ornamental Concrete...................................828 685-3740
   417 Pilot Mountain Rd Hendersonville (28792) *(G-7867)*

Jones Printing Company Inc..................................919 774-9442
   104 Hawkins Ave Sanford (27330) *(G-14141)*

Jones Salsa, Hendersonville *Also Called: Tina M Jones (G-7907)*

Jones Sign..828 478-4780
   9325 Azalea Rd Sherrills Ford (28673) *(G-14386)*

Jones Vndrhle Vineyards Winery, Thurmond *Also Called: Jones Vondrehle Vineyards LLC (G-15310)*

Jones Vondrehle Vineyards LLC............................336 874-2800
   964 Old Railroad Grade Rd Thurmond (28683) *(G-15310)*

Jones Welding..828 508-0080
   512 Country Knoll Dr Sylva (28779) *(G-15061)*

Jonesville Water Plant, Jonesville *Also Called: Town of Jonesville (G-9102)*

Jonnie Chardonn..910 471-0418
   6027 Mount Carmel Parke Wilmington (28412) *(G-16283)*

Jordan Electric Motors Inc.....................................919 708-7010
   3307 Lee Ave Sanford (27332) *(G-14142)*

Jordan Group Corporation.....................................803 309-9988
   7007 Berolina Ln Apt 1613 Charlotte (28226) *(G-3034)*

Jordan Innvtive Fbrication LLC..............................910 428-2368
   275 Sedberry Rd Biscoe (27209) *(G-1113)*

Jordan Lumber & Supply Inc.................................910 439-6121
   1939 Nc Highway 109 S Mount Gilead (27306) *(G-11602)*

Jordan Lumber & Supply Inc (PA).........................910 439-6121
   1939 Nc Highway 109 S Mount Gilead (27306) *(G-11603)*

Jordan Lumber & Supply Inc.................................910 428-9048
   4483 Spies Rd Star (27356) *(G-14717)*

Jordan Piping Inc...336 818-9252
   300 8th St North Wilkesboro (28659) *(G-12019)*

Jordan-Holman Lumber Co Inc...............................828 396-3101
   650 N Main St Granite Falls (28630) *(G-6740)*

Jorlink Usa Inc...336 288-1613
   3714 Alliance Dr Ste 100 Greensboro (27407) *(G-7140)*

Jorlink.com, Greensboro *Also Called: Jorlink Usa Inc (G-7140)*

Joseph and Jerry Curtis...704 663-4811
   342 Kistler Farm Rd Mooresville (28115) *(G-10988)*

Joseph C Woodard Prtg Co Inc.............................919 829-0634
   2815 S Saunders St Raleigh (27603) *(G-12922)*

Joseph Decicco...910 262-9701
   121 Topsail Lake Dr Hampstead (28443) *(G-7650)*

Joseph F Decker..704 335-0021
   341 Dalton Ave Charlotte (28206) *(G-3035)*

Joseph Halker...336 769-4734
   481 Shady Grove Church Rd Winston Salem (27107) *(G-16772)*

Joseph Sotanski...407 324-6187
   632 College Dr Marion (28752) *(G-10155)*

Josey Lumber Company Inc..................................252 826-5614
   476 Lees Meadow Rd Scotland Neck (27874) *(G-14219)*

Josh Allred..336 873-1006
   335 N Broad St Seagrove (27341) *(G-14240)*

Josh Lane Logging LLC...828 289-4052
   2575 Camp Creek Rd Union Mills (28167) *(G-15441)*

Jostens, Winston Salem *Also Called: Jostens Inc (G-16773)*

Jostens Inc...336 765-0070
   2505 Empire Dr Winston Salem (27103) *(G-16773)*

Joulin, Hickory *Also Called: Vacuum Handling North Amer LLC (G-8201)*

Journal Doctors Inc...919 469-1438
   1209 Chalk Maple Dr Cary (27519) *(G-1799)*

Journal Vacuum Science & Tech...........................919 361-2787
   51 Kilmayne Dr Ste 104 Cary (27511) *(G-1800)*

Journalbooks, Charlotte *Also Called: Timeplanner Calendars Inc (G-3695)*

Journalistic Inc..919 945-0700
   101 Europa Dr Ste 150 Chapel Hill (27517) *(G-2028)*

Jowat Adhesives, Archdale *Also Called: Jowat Corporation (G-289)*

Jowat Corporation..336 434-9356
   5637 Evelyn View Dr Archdale (27263) *(G-288)*

Jowat Corporation (HQ)...336 434-9000
   5608 Uwharrie Rd Archdale (27263) *(G-289)*

Jowat International Corp.......................................336 434-9000
   5608 Uwharrie Rd Archdale (27263) *(G-290)*

Jowat Properties Corp..336 434-9000
   5608 Uwharrie Rd Archdale (27263) *(G-291)*

Joy Dental Lab, Angier *Also Called: Custom Smiles Inc (G-138)*

Joyce Heflin President...919 451-0003
   5015 Lazywood Ln Durham (27712) *(G-5173)*

JP Leather Arcona Division, Hudson *Also Called: Arcona Leather Company LLC (G-8761)*

JP Leather Company Inc..828 396-7728
   2615 Mission Rd Hudson (28638) *(G-8771)*

JP Mechanic & Welding Inc...................................919 650-7438
   1924 Stockyard Rd Staley (27355) *(G-14666)*

Jph III Logging Inc...910 610-9338
   11241 Barnes Bridge Rd Laurinburg (28352) *(G-9482)*

Jpi Coastal..704 310-5867
   1114 Old Concord Rd Salisbury (28146) *(G-13995)*

Jpm, Greensboro *Also Called: James M Pleasants Company Inc (G-7133)*

JPS Communications Inc......................................919 534-1168
   5800 Departure Dr Raleigh (27616) *(G-12923)*

JPS Composite Materials Corp.............................704 872-9831
   535 Connor St Statesville (28677) *(G-14826)*

Jps Cupcakery LLC..919 894-5000
   111 S Railroad St Benson (27504) *(G-1038)*

JPS Elstmerics Westfield Plant.............................336 351-0938
   1535 Elastic Plant Rd Westfield (27053) *(G-15952)*

JPS Intrprbility Solutions Inc................................919 332-5009
   5800 Departure Dr Raleigh (27616) *(G-12924)*

Jq Pro Detailing LLC..336 543-0663
   2524 Yow Rd Greensboro (27407) *(G-7141)*

JR Mooresville Inc..973 434-6453
   1515 E Broad St Statesville (28625) *(G-14827)*

Jr S Custom Woodworks..336 643-1524
   7951 Lester Rd Stokesdale (27357) *(G-14943)*

Jr Signs LLC..980 255-3083
   147 Union St S Concord (28025) *(G-4296)*

Jrg Technologies Corp...850 362-4310
   9300 Harris Corners Pkwy Ste 450 Charlotte (28269) *(G-3036)*

Jri Development Group LLC..................................704 660-8346
   136 Knob Hill Rd Mooresville (28117) *(G-10989)*

Jri Shocks LLC...704 660-8346
   116 Infield Ct Mooresville (28117) *(G-10990)*

Jrm Inc...888 576-7007
   8491 N Nc Hwy 150 Clemmons (27012) *(G-4050)*

JRs Custom Framing...704 449-2830
   7604 Waterford Lakes Dr Charlotte (28210) *(G-3037)*

Jrt Logging Inc..704 322-0458
   117 Pine Log Rd Polkton (28135) *(G-12388)*

Js Fiber Co Inc (PA)..704 871-1582
   290 Marble Rd Statesville (28625) *(G-14828)*

Js Linens and Curtain Outlet (PA)........................704 871-1582
   290 Marble Rd Statesville (28625) *(G-14829)*

Js Printing LLC..919 773-1103
   1824 Garner Station Blvd Raleigh (27603) *(G-12925)*

Js Royal Home Usa Inc.. 704 542-2304
13451 S Point Blvd Charlotte (28273) *(G-3038)*

Jsbd Software LLC... 919 841-1218
5409 Wynneford Way Raleigh (27614) *(G-12926)*

Jtc Awards and Printing.. 910 346-9522
1423 N Marine Blvd Jacksonville (28540) *(G-9011)*

Jtec Radiowave... 704 799-1658
129 Loc Doc Pl # B Mooresville (28115) *(G-10991)*

Jts Venom Performance.. 704 214-7849
108 Bost Nursery Rd Maiden (28650) *(G-10110)*

Juan J Hernandez... 919 742-3381
4272 Piney Grove Church Rd Siler City (27344) *(G-14419)*

Juan Pino Signs Inc... 336 764-4422
2041 Gumtree Rd Winston Salem (27107) *(G-16774)*

Jubilee Screen Printing Inc... 910 673-4240
314 Grant St Ste F West End (27376) *(G-15928)*

Jugtown Pottery... 910 464-3266
330 Jugtown Rd Seagrove (27341) *(G-14241)*

Julia Lipscomb... 919 528-1800
10408 Boyce Rd Creedmoor (27522) *(G-4617)*

Julia's Pantry, Raleigh *Also Called: Julias Southern Foods LLC (G-12927)*

Julian Freirich Co, Salisbury *Also Called: Julian Freirich Food Products (G-13997)*

Julian Freirich Company Inc.. 704 636-2621
815 W Kerr St Salisbury (28144) *(G-13996)*

Julian Freirich Food Products..................................... 704 636-2621
815 W Kerr St Salisbury (28144) *(G-13997)*

Julias Southern Foods LLC... 919 609-6745
5608 Primavera Ct Ste G Raleigh (27616) *(G-12927)*

Jumbo Co... 919 637-0313
7301 Indian Rock Rd Wendell (27591) *(G-15906)*

Junaluska Mill Engineering.. 828 321-3693
181 Gipp Creek Rd Andrews (28901) *(G-127)*

Junes Craftmanship Inc... 704 230-0901
185 Oliphant Rd Mooresville (28115) *(G-10992)*

Junior Johnson Country Hams, Wilkesboro *Also Called: Suncrest Farms Cntry Hams Inc (G-16044)*

Juniper Networks Inc.. 888 586-4737
1730 Varsity Dr Ste 10 Raleigh (27606) *(G-12928)*

Junk Food Clothing Inc.. 910 483-2500
1 Soffe Dr Fayetteville (28312) *(G-5851)*

Jupiter Bathware Inc... 800 343-8295
510 Jones St S Wilson (27893) *(G-16503)*

Jus Doors Inc.. 888 510-5331
3714 Alliance Dr Ste 305 Greensboro (27407) *(G-7142)*

Just Black LLC... 252 204-5437
1124 Crowders Woods Dr Gastonia (28052) *(G-6436)*

Just n Tyme Trucking LLC.. 704 804-9519
6015 Lake Forest Rd E Charlotte (28227) *(G-3039)*

Just Sayin Socks LLC... 828 513-1517
225 Winding Meadows Dr Flat Rock (28731) *(G-5966)*

Just Stitchin Quilts LLc.. 828 644-3368
321 Hwy 64 W Hayesville (28904) *(G-7767)*

Just Suspension, Denver *Also Called: Suspensions LLC (G-4804)*

Justenough Software Corp Inc.................................... 800 949-3432
1009 Slater Rd Ste 420 Durham (27703) *(G-5174)*

Justi LLC.. 919 434-5002
109 Oxyard Way Cary (27519) *(G-1801)*

Justice.. 910 392-1581
3500 Oleander Dr Ste 1054 Wilmington (28403) *(G-16284)*

Justice Bearing LLC... 800 355-2500
243 Overhill Dr Ste D Mooresville (28117) *(G-10993)*

Justice Bearings, Mooresville *Also Called: Justice Bearing LLC (G-10993)*

Justin Moretz & Greg Moretz Db................................. 828 263-8668
153 Monte Verde Rd Deep Gap (28618) *(G-4709)*

Justneem LLC.. 919 414-8826
2416 Maxton Crest Dr Apex (27539) *(G-210)*

Justneem Body Care, Apex *Also Called: Justneem LLC (G-210)*

Justrite Manufacturing.. 336 990-0918
2745 Statesville Rd North Wilkesboro (28659) *(G-12020)*

Jvst, Cary *Also Called: Journal Vacuum Science & Tech (G-1800)*

JW Metal Products, Monroe *Also Called: Stainless Supply Inc (G-10814)*

JW Wraps LLC... 614 401-9164
4511 Staffordshire Dr Apt 2 Wilmington (28412) *(G-16285)*

K & C Machine Co Inc... 336 373-0745
601 Industrial Ave Greensboro (27406) *(G-7143)*

K & D Signs LLC... 336 786-1111
1078 S Main St Mount Airy (27030) *(G-11527)*

K & J Ashworth Logging LLC...................................... 336 879-2388
8797 Erect Rd Seagrove (27341) *(G-14242)*

K & K Industries.. 336 689-4293
427 Hannersville Rd Lexington (27292) *(G-9737)*

K & K Stitch & Screen... 336 246-5477
240 Helen Blevins Rd Unit 1 West Jefferson (28694) *(G-15941)*

K & L Resources... 910 494-3736
7809 Gallant Ridge Dr Fayetteville (28314) *(G-5852)*

K & M Products of NC Inc.. 828 524-5905
3248 Patton Rd Franklin (28734) *(G-6133)*

K & S Tool & Manufacturing Co................................... 336 410-7260
1247 Elon Pl High Point (27263) *(G-8418)*

K & S Tool & Manufacturing Co (PA)........................... 336 410-7260
614 Hendrix St High Point (27260) *(G-8419)*

K & W Welding LLC... 910 895-9220
180 Old 74 Hwy Rockingham (28379) *(G-13632)*

K & W Welding LLC... 910 844-2288
12721 Airport Rd Maxton (28364) *(G-10358)*

K B I Biopharma, Durham *Also Called: Kbi Biopharma Inc (G-5177)*

K D S, Etowah *Also Called: Kiln Drying Systems Cmpnnts In (G-5692)*

K Formula Enterprises Inc.. 910 323-3315
829 Gillespie St Ste A Fayetteville (28306) *(G-5853)*

K L Butler Logging Inc.. 910 648-6016
12237 Nc 41 Hwy W Bladenboro (28320) *(G-1150)*

K P Welding Inc... 540 250-7187
3133 Swan Creek Rd Jonesville (28642) *(G-9099)*

K W, Charlotte *Also Called: Kem-Wove Inc (G-3049)*

K-Flex USA LLC... 919 556-3475
100 K Flex Way Youngsville (27596) *(G-17087)*

K-M Machine Company Inc.. 910 428-2368
275 Sedberry Rd Biscoe (27209) *(G-1114)*

K-Tek Crlina Prcsion Spclty Mf, Pineville *Also Called: Griffiths Corporation (G-12272)*

K&B Galleries, Raleigh *Also Called: Kitchen Bath Gllries N Hlls LL (G-12942)*

K&H Acquisition Company LLC................................... 704 788-1128
36 Oak Dr Sw Concord (28027) *(G-4297)*

K&K Holdings Inc.. 704 341-5567
1310 S Church St Charlotte (28203) *(G-3040)*

K&M Sheet Metal LLC... 919 544-8887
1310 E Cornwallis Rd Durham (27713) *(G-5175)*

K&S Custom LLC.. 336 861-1607
2316 Windsong Rd Sophia (27350) *(G-14519)*

K&S Rustic Woodworks.. 336 504-6988
3315 Pine Valley Rd High Point (27265) *(G-8420)*

K12 Computers.. 336 754-6111
1203 Winston Rd Lexington (27295) *(G-9738)*

K2 Scientific LLC.. 800 218-7613
3029 Horseshoe Ln Ste D Charlotte (28208) *(G-3041)*

K2 Solutions Inc.. 910 692-6898
5735 Us Hwy 1 N Southern Pines (28387) *(G-14538)*

K9 Installs Inc.. 743 207-1507
6255 Towncenter Dr Ste 875 Clemmons (27012) *(G-4051)*

Ka-Ex LLC.. 704 343-5143
125 Remount Rd Ste C1 Pmb 2002 Charlotte (28203) *(G-3042)*

Kaba Access Control, Winston Salem *Also Called: Kaba Ilco Corp (G-16775)*

Kaba Ilco Corp (HQ)... 252 446-3321
400 Jeffreys Rd Rocky Mount (27804) *(G-13704)*

Kaba Ilco Corp... 336 725-1331
2941 Indiana Ave Winston Salem (27105) *(G-16775)*

Kabinet Werks LLC.. 704 359-7311
8501 Middleton Cir Harrisburg (28075) *(G-7715)*

Kahne Screen Print LLC.. 704 662-8549
265 Cayuga Dr Mooresville (28117) *(G-10994)*

Kalajdzic Inc... 855 465-4225
1415 River Ridge Dr Clemmons (27012) *(G-4052)*

Kaleida Systems Inc... 704 814-4429
2530 Plantation Center Dr Ste A Matthews (28105) *(G-10257)*

Kaleido Inc

ALPHABETIC SECTION

Kaleido Inc... 984 205-9436
16 W Martin St Fl 7 Raleigh (27601) *(G-12929)*

Kalinka Arms, Southport *Also Called: Aboard Trade LLC (G-14563)*

Kalo Foods, Stokesdale *Also Called: Kalo Foods LLC (G-14944)*

Kalo Foods LLC... 336 949-4802
119 Carlton Park Dr Stokesdale (27357) *(G-14944)*

KAM Tool & Die Inc... 919 269-5099
530 N Industrial Dr Zebulon (27597) *(G-17132)*

Kamlar Corporation (PA)... 252 443-2576
444 Kamlar Rd Rocky Mount (27804) *(G-13705)*

Kamp Usa Inc.. 336 668-1169
2321 E Martin Luther King Jr Dr High Point (27260) *(G-8421)*

Kannapolis Awards and Graphics................................. 704 224-3695
1103 Central Dr Kannapolis (28083) *(G-9125)*

Kansas City Sausage Co LLC...................................... 910 567-5604
1600 Martin Rd Godwin (28344) *(G-6578)*

Kanthal, Concord *Also Called: Custom Electric Mfg LLC (G-4249)*

Kanthal Thermal Process Inc....................................... 704 784-3001
180 International Dr Nw Ste A Concord (28027) *(G-4298)*

KAO Specialties Americas LLC (HQ).......................... 336 884-2214
243 Woodbine St High Point (27260) *(G-8422)*

Kapstone Kraft Paper, Roanoke Rapids *Also Called: Westrock Paper and Packg LLC (G-13587)*

Kapstone Paper Packaging, Morrisville *Also Called: Westrock Paper and Packg LLC (G-11466)*

Karamedica Inc... 919 302-1325
509 W North St Raleigh (27603) *(G-12930)*

Karastan... 336 627-7200
335 Summit Rd Eden (27288) *(G-5493)*

Karess Krafters.. 919 961-5575
Holly Springs (27540) *(G-8703)*

Karl Ogden Enterprises Inc.. 704 845-2785
1320 Industrial Dr Matthews (28105) *(G-10258)*

Karl Rl Manufacturing.. 919 846-3801
11937 Appaloosa Run E Raleigh (27613) *(G-12931)*

Kart Precision Barrel Corp... 910 754-5212
3975 Garner St Sw Shallotte (28470) *(G-14274)*

Karwin Technologies Inc.. 919 612-3974
2012 Briarwood Cir Clayton (27520) *(G-3991)*

Kashif Mazhar... 919 314-2891
68 Tw Alexander Dr Durham (27709) *(G-5176)*

Kask America Inc.. 704 960-4851
301 W Summit Ave Charlotte (28203) *(G-3043)*

Kat Designs Inc... 336 789-7288
280 Hickory St Mount Airy (27030) *(G-11528)*

Katchi Tees Incorporated.. 252 315-4691
1108 Gold St N Wilson (27893) *(G-16504)*

Katesville Pallet Mill Inc.. 919 496-3162
7119 Nc 56 Hwy Franklinton (27525) *(G-6156)*

Kathie S Mc Daniel... 336 835-1544
765 Oakland Dr Elkin (28621) *(G-5622)*

Kathys Signs For Less.. 910 840-1447
1145 Bird Cage Rd Chadbourn (28431) *(G-1977)*

Kattermann Ventures Inc.. 828 651-8737
282 Cane Creek Rd Fletcher (28732) *(G-6015)*

Kauffman & Co.. 716 969-2005
1420 S Mint St Charlotte (28203) *(G-3044)*

Kaufman Trailers Inc... 336 790-6800
702 N Silver St Lexington (27292) *(G-9739)*

Kavo Kerr Group... 704 927-0617
11727 Fruehauf Dr Charlotte (28273) *(G-3045)*

Kay & Sons Woodworks Inc.. 919 556-1060
2040 Forestville Rd Wake Forest (27587) *(G-15566)*

Kay Chemical Company.. 336 668-7290
8300 Capital Dr Greensboro (27409) *(G-7144)*

Kaye Products Inc... 919 732-6444
535 Dimmocks Mill Rd Hillsborough (27278) *(G-8657)*

Kayla Jonise Bernhardt Crutch................................... 252 457-5367
115 Carver St Elizabeth City (27909) *(G-5552)*

Kayne & Son Custom Hdwr Inc................................... 828 665-1988
100 Daniel Ridge Rd Candler (28715) *(G-1585)*

Kayne & Son Hardware, Candler *Also Called: Kayne & Son Custom Hdwr Inc (G-1585)*

Kayser-Roth Corporation (DH).................................... 336 852-2030
102 Corporate Center Blvd Greensboro (27408) *(G-7145)*

Kayser-Roth Hosiery Inc... 336 229-2269
714 W Interstate Service Rd Graham (27253) *(G-6696)*

Kayser-Roth Hosiery Inc... 336 852-2030
102 Corporate Center Blvd Greensboro (27408) *(G-7146)*

KB Sign Solutions LLC.. 217 474-5861
4555 Mtrsprts Dr Sw Ste 1 Concord (28027) *(G-4299)*

KB Socks Inc.. 336 719-8000
661 Linville Rd Mount Airy (27030) *(G-11529)*

Kbb Towers LLC... 828 243-1812
75 Jackson Rd Fletcher (28732) *(G-6016)*

Kbc of Nc LLC.. 704 589-3711
4114 Western Union School Rd Waxhaw (28173) *(G-15763)*

Kberg Consultants, Raleigh *Also Called: Kberg Productions LLC (G-12932)*

Kberg Productions LLC.. 910 232-0342
4234 Massey Preserve Trl Raleigh (27616) *(G-12932)*

Kbi Biopharma Inc (PA)... 919 479-9898
1101 Hamlin Rd Durham (27704) *(G-5177)*

Kbi Biopharma Inc.. 919 479-9898
2 Triangle Dr Durham (27709) *(G-5178)*

KBK Cabinetry Inc.. 704 506-0088
9812 Running Cedar Ln Indian Trail (28079) *(G-8940)*

KBK Cstom Dsgns Essential Oils, Rocky Mount *Also Called: Malinda Rackley (G-13709)*

Kbs Sales Co, Stanfield *Also Called: Eudys Cabinet Manufacturing (G-14678)*

Kc Stone Enterprise Inc.. 704 907-1361
3006 Sardis Dr Indian Trail (28079) *(G-8941)*

Kc Stone Inc... 704 907-1361
3821 Wesley Chapel Rd Matthews (28104) *(G-10327)*

Kc-46a Pegasus, Sjafb *Also Called: Boeing Company (G-14446)*

Kch Engineered Systems, Forest City *Also Called: Kch Services Inc (G-6073)*

Kch Services Inc... 828 245-9836
144 Industrial Dr Forest City (28043) *(G-6073)*

Kci... 910 612-4914
2611 Hidden Pointe Dr Wilmington (28411) *(G-16286)*

Kci, Charlotte *Also Called: Kincol Industries Incorporated (G-3055)*

Kck Holding Company... 336 513-0002
2215 Airpark Rd Burlington (27215) *(G-1443)*

Kcp Inc.. 919 854-7824
6807 Breezewood Rd Raleigh (27607) *(G-12933)*

Kcs Imprv & Cnstr Co Inc... 336 288-3865
510 N Church St Ste C Greensboro (27401) *(G-7147)*

Kd Cabinets Inc.. 828 689-3848
474 Wolf Branch Rd Marshall (28753) *(G-10203)*

Kdh Defense Systems, Eden *Also Called: Kdh Defense Systems Inc (G-5494)*

Kdh Defense Systems Inc... 336 635-4158
750a W Fieldcrest Rd Eden (27288) *(G-5494)*

Kdm Enterprise LLC... 919 689-9720
1594 Us Highway 13 S Goldsboro (27530) *(G-6628)*

Kdr Visuality, Charlotte *Also Called: Kdr Visuality LLC (G-3046)*

Kdr Visuality LLC... 704 451-1290
9922 Nations Ford Rd Charlotte (28273) *(G-3046)*

Kds Fabricating and Mch Sp LLC................................ 828 632-5091
4838 Nc Highway 90 E Hiddenite (28636) *(G-8222)*

Kdy Automation Solutions Inc..................................... 888 219-0049
150 Dominion Dr Ste E Morrisville (27560) *(G-11364)*

Keani Furniture Inc... 336 303-5484
1546 N Fayetteville St Asheboro (27203) *(G-448)*

Kearfott Corporation... 828 350-5300
2858 Us 70 Hwy Black Mountain (28711) *(G-1127)*

Keck Logging & Chipping Inc...................................... 336 538-6903
576 Browns Chapel Rd Gibsonville (27249) *(G-6564)*

Keck Logging Company... 336 538-6903
576 Browns Chapel Rd Gibsonville (27249) *(G-6565)*

Kedplasma.. 704 691-3287
588 N New Hope Rd Gastonia (28054) *(G-6437)*

Kee Auto Top Manufacturing Co................................. 704 332-8213
3018 Stewart Creek Blvd Charlotte (28216) *(G-3047)*

Keebler, Sanford *Also Called: Keebler Company (G-14143)*

Keebler Company 919 774-6431
5801 Mockingbird Ln Sanford (27332) *(G-14143)*

Keel Labs Inc 917 848-9066
1015 Aviation Pkwy Ste 400 Morrisville (27560) *(G-11365)*

Keener Lumber Company Inc (PA) 919 934-1087
1209 W Market St Smithfield (27577) *(G-14467)*

Keener Wood Products Inc 828 428-1562
4274 Providence Mill Rd Maiden (28650) *(G-10111)*

Keep Stanly Beautiful Corp 704 982-2649
505 Muirfield Dr Albemarle (28001) *(G-92)*

Keffer Auto Huntersville LLC 877 260-4062
13651 Statesville Rd Huntersville (28078) *(G-8842)*

Kefi Winery Inc 704 591-5791
3109 Plyler Mill Rd Monroe (28112) *(G-10751)*

Keglers Woodworks LLC 919 608-7220
330 Dupont Cir Raleigh (27603) *(G-12934)*

Keim Mineral Coatings Amer Inc 704 588-4811
3935 Perimeter W Dr Ste 100 Charlotte (28214) *(G-3048)*

Keith Call Logging LLC 336 262-3681
Millers Creek (28651) *(G-10493)*

Keith Laws 336 973-7220
1001 N Marley Ford Rd Wilkesboro (28697) *(G-16034)*

Keith Nations Log Company, Whittier *Also Called: James Keith Nations (G-16007)*

Keiths Cleaning LLC 336 701-0185
54 Hoskins Dr Winston Salem (27105) *(G-16776)*

Keiths Kustomz LLC 704 524-8684
1676 Lowell Bethesda Rd Apt B Gastonia (28056) *(G-6438)*

Kelhorn Corporation 828 837-5833
199 Waldroup Rd Brasstown (28902) *(G-1266)*

Kelishek Workshop, Brasstown *Also Called: Kelhorn Corporation (G-1266)*

Kelken Enterprises LLC 910 890-7211
12 Caco Dr Lillington (27546) *(G-9853)*

Kellanova 704 370-1658
13801 Reese Blvd W Huntersville (28078) *(G-8843)*

Kellanova 704 241-6977
1007 Omaha Dr Monroe (28110) *(G-10752)*

Keller Companies Inc 919 776-4641
1600 Colon Rd Sanford (27330) *(G-14144)*

Keller Cosmetics Inc 704 399-2226
2620 Stitt St Monroe (28110) *(G-10753)*

Keller Cres U To Be Phrmgraphi 336 851-1150
1072 Boulder Rd Greensboro (27409) *(G-7148)*

Keller Technology Corporation 704 875-1605
11905 Vanstory Dr Huntersville (28078) *(G-8844)*

Kellex Corp 828 874-0389
501 Hoyle St Sw Valdese (28690) *(G-15449)*

Kelley G Cupcakes 314 368-5316
2341 Huron St Durham (27707) *(G-5179)*

Kelleys Sports and Awards Inc 828 728-4600
2636 Hickory Blvd Hudson (28638) *(G-8772)*

Kellog, Huntersville *Also Called: Kellanova (G-8843)*

Kellogg, Monroe *Also Called: Kellanova (G-10752)*

Kelly Hosiery Mill Inc 828 324-6456
6450 Applehill Dr Hickory (28602) *(G-8073)*

Kelly Printing LLC 336 760-0505
3490 Reynolda Rd Winston Salem (27106) *(G-16777)*

Kelly Signs 828 778-4146
309 White St Hendersonville (28739) *(G-7868)*

Kellys Embroidery 919 738-5072
843 Norwood Ezzell Rd Mount Olive (28365) *(G-11664)*

Kem-Wove Inc (PA) 704 588-0080
10530 Westlake Dr Charlotte (28273) *(G-3049)*

Kemet Electronics Corporation 864 963-6300
2501 W Dixon Blvd Shelby (28152) *(G-14334)*

Kemmler Products Inc 704 663-5678
250 Canvasback Rd Mooresville (28117) *(G-10995)*

Ken Garner Mfg, Rural Hall *Also Called: Ken Garner Mfg - RHO Inc (G-13844)*

Ken Garner Mfg - RHO Inc 336 969-0416
8610 Chipboard Rd Rural Hall (27045) *(G-13844)*

Ken Horton Logging LLC 336 789-2849
120 W Elm St Mount Airy (27030) *(G-11530)*

Ken Krause Co, Vass *Also Called: Kendall E Krause (G-15492)*

Ken Staley Co Inc 336 685-4294
4675 Us Highway 64 E Bldg 16 Franklinville (27248) *(G-6169)*

Ken Wood Corp 252 792-6481
1660 Arthur Corey Rd Williamston (27892) *(G-16064)*

Kencraft Manufacturing Inc 252 291-0271
4078 Us Highway 117 Wilson (27893) *(G-16505)*

Kendall E Krause 910 690-4119
148 Rice Rd Vass (28394) *(G-15492)*

Kendrion, Shelby *Also Called: Linnig Corporation (G-14338)*

Kenly News, Kenly *Also Called: Richard D Stewart (G-9156)*

Kenmar Inc 336 884-8722
2531 Willard Dairy Rd High Point (27265) *(G-8423)*

Kenn M LLC 678 755-6607
6046 Inona Pl Raleigh (27606) *(G-12935)*

Kennametal Inc 336 672-3313
201 Yzex St Asheboro (27203) *(G-449)*

Kennametal Inc 704 588-4777
8910 Lenox Pointe Dr Ste F Charlotte (28273) *(G-3050)*

Kennametal Inc 252 492-4163
139 Warehouse Rd Henderson (27537) *(G-7791)*

Kennametal Inc 252 536-5209
100 Kennametal Dr Weldon (27890) *(G-15884)*

Kennedy Woodworking LLC 704 278-9444
955 Umberger Rd Mount Ulla (28125) *(G-11684)*

Kennel-Aire LLC (PA) 704 459-0044
17382 Randalls Ferry Rd Norwood (28128) *(G-12039)*

Kennelpro, Concord *Also Called: Sunbelt Enterprises Inc (G-4368)*

Kenneth Moore Signs 910 458-6428
6220 Riverwoods Dr Apt 103 Wilmington (28412) *(G-16287)*

Kenneth Perkins 919 267-9396
225 Marsh Landing Dr Holly Springs (27540) *(G-8704)*

Kenny Fowler Heating and A Inc (PA) 910 508-4553
711 Wellington Ave Wilmington (28401) *(G-16288)*

Kenny Robinson S Wldg Svc Inc 760 213-6454
8975 Moody Rd Liberty (27298) *(G-9818)*

Kennys Fiberglass Restoration 704 252-0979
210 Sparta Dr Mooresville (28117) *(G-10996)*

Kens Candles and Soaps 919 207-2880
1302 Old Fairground Rd Willow Spring (27592) *(G-16080)*

Kens Custom Cabinets Inc 252 637-3378
4685 E Us 70 Hwy New Bern (28562) *(G-11815)*

Kens Trim & Stairs Ken Swarey 336 835-4298
506 W Main St Elkin (28621) *(G-5623)*

Kenson Parenting Solutions 919 637-1499
1404 Wall Rd Ste 200 Wake Forest (27587) *(G-15567)*

Kenzie Layne Company 704 485-2282
506 Running Creek Ch Rd Locust (28097) *(G-9961)*

Keowee Publishing Co Inc 828 877-4742
96 Merle Farm Ln Pisgah Forest (28768) *(G-12325)*

Kepley-Frank Hardwood Co Inc 336 746-5419
975 Conrad Hill Mine Rd Lexington (27292) *(G-9740)*

Keranetics LLC 336 725-0621
200 E 1st St Box 4 Winston Salem (27101) *(G-16778)*

Kerdea Technologies Inc 971 900-1113
1800 N Greene St Greenville (27834) *(G-7552)*

Kern-Liebers USA Textile Inc 704 329-7153
921 Matthews Mint Hill Rd Matthews (28105) *(G-10259)*

Kernersville Adhesives Plant, Kernersville *Also Called: Caraustar Indus Cnsmr Pdts Gro (G-9170)*

Kernsville Tube Plant, Kernersville *Also Called: Caraustar Indus Cnsmr Pdts Gro (G-9171)*

Kerr Lake Cornhole & Printing 252 430-7144
335 N Chestnut St Henderson (27536) *(G-7792)*

Kerr's H R M Concrete, Hickory *Also Called: Kerrs Hickry Ready-Mixed Con (G-8074)*

Kerrs Hickry Ready-Mixed Con (PA) 828 322-3157
1126 1st Ave Sw Hickory (28602) *(G-8074)*

Kerrybeth Home Improvements, Arden *Also Called: Khi LLC (G-345)*

Keryflex Podadvance Inc 888 763-2382
9132 Fawn Hill Ct Raleigh (27617) *(G-12936)*

Keselowski Advanced Mfg LLC 704 799-0206
258 Aviation Dr Statesville (28677) *(G-14830)*

Kessebohmer USA Inc 910 338-5080
  106 Market St # 300 Wilmington (28401) *(G-16289)*

Kessel Development LLC 704 752-4282
  16131 Lancaster Hwy Ste 6 Charlotte (28277) *(G-3051)*

Kessler Inc 248 717-0027
  7171 Stinson Hartis Rd Indian Trail (28079) *(G-8942)*

Kestrel I Acquisition Corporation 919 990-7500
  1035 Swabia Ct Durham (27703) *(G-5180)*

Ketchie Marble Co Inc 704 279-8377
  1920 Saint Luke Church Rd Salisbury (28146) *(G-13998)*

Ketchie-Houston, Concord *Also Called: Ketchie-Houston Inc (G-4300)*

Ketchie-Houston Inc 704 786-5101
  201 Winecoff School Rd Concord (28027) *(G-4300)*

Keter Us Inc 704 263-1967
  2369 Charles Raper Jonas Hwy Stanley (28164) *(G-14699)*

Kettu Woodworks 919 699-4173
  7409 Lakefall Dr Wake Forest (27587) *(G-15568)*

Kevins Backhoe Service 336 591-7751
  1108 Brook Crossing Rd Germanton (27019) *(G-6554)*

Kevins Sheet Metal 910 253-6203
  933 Forest Way Ne Leland (28451) *(G-9550)*

Kevs Woodworking LLC 850 559-3228
  219 Toucan Way Hubert (28539) *(G-8750)*

Kewaunee Scientific Corp (PA) 704 873-7202
  2700 W Front St Statesville (28677) *(G-14831)*

Key City Furniture Company Inc 336 818-1161
  1804 River St Wilkesboro (28697) *(G-16035)*

Key Gas Components Inc (PA) 828 655-1700
  160 Clay St Marion (28752) *(G-10156)*

Key Packing Company Inc 910 464-5054
  596 Maness Rd Robbins (27325) *(G-13599)*

Key Printing Inc 252 459-4783
  1036 E Washington St Nashville (27856) *(G-11746)*

Keya USA, High Point *Also Called: Kamp Usa Inc (G-8421)*

Keymac USA LLC 704 877-5137
  8301 Arrowridge Blvd Ste I Charlotte (28273) *(G-3052)*

Keyper Systems, Harrisburg *Also Called: Marcon International Inc (G-7717)*

Keypoint LLC 704 962-8110
  8002 New Town Rd Waxhaw (28173) *(G-15764)*

Keypoint Fabrication, Waxhaw *Also Called: Keypoint LLC (G-15764)*

Keystone Foods LLC 336 342-6601
  227 Equity Dr Reidsville (27320) *(G-13529)*

Keystone Powdered Metal Co 704 435-4036
  100 Commerce Dr Cherryville (28021) *(G-3870)*

Keystone Powdered Metal Co 704 730-8805
  779 Sunnyside Shady Rest Rd Kings Mountain (28086) *(G-9311)*

Keytune Mus Pubg Wrld Wide LLC 910 286-7868
  505 Cypress Trace Dr Fayetteville (28314) *(G-5854)*

Kfh, Lexington *Also Called: Kepley-Frank Hardwood Co Inc (G-9740)*

Kgi Trading NC, Charlotte *Also Called: Moon N Sea Nc LLC (G-3202)*

Kgt Enterprises Inc 704 662-3272
  185 Mckenzie Rd Mooresville (28115) *(G-10997)*

Khi LLC 828 654-9916
  Arden (28704) *(G-345)*

Ki Agency LLC 919 977-7075
  5812 Triangle Dr Raleigh (27617) *(G-12937)*

Kidde Safety, Mebane *Also Called: Walter Kidde Portable Eqp Inc (G-10435)*

Kidde Technologies Inc 252 237-7004
  4200 Airport Dr Nw Wilson (27896) *(G-16506)*

Kidde Technologies Inc 252 237-7004
  4200 Airport Dr Nw Wilson (27896) *(G-16507)*

Kidde Technologies Inc (DH) 252 237-7004
  4200 Airport Dr Nw Wilson (27896) *(G-16508)*

Kidkusion Inc 252 946-7162
  623 River Rd Washington (27889) *(G-15714)*

Kids Playhouse LLC 704 299-4449
  10823 John Price Rd Charlotte (28273) *(G-3053)*

Kidsvidz Productions 704 663-4487
  694 Big Indian Loop Mooresville (28117) *(G-10998)*

Kieffer Starlite Company 800 659-2493
  609 Junction St Mount Airy (27030) *(G-11531)*

Kildaire Regency Publishing 919 469-5851
  100 Crestview Ct Cary (27518) *(G-1802)*

Kiln Drying Systems Cmpnnts In 828 891-8115
  234 Industrial Dr Etowah (28729) *(G-5692)*

Kiln-Directcom 910 259-9794
  200a Progress Dr Burgaw (28425) *(G-1343)*

Kilop USA Inc 336 297-4999
  3714 Alliance Dr Ste 401 Greensboro (27407) *(G-7149)*

Kimballs Screen Print Inc 704 636-0488
  1315 Union Church Rd Salisbury (28146) *(G-13999)*

Kimbees Inc 336 323-8773
  317 Martin Luthe Greensboro (27406) *(G-7150)*

Kimberly Gordon Studios Inc 980 287-6420
  525 N Tryon St Charlotte (28202) *(G-3054)*

Kimberly-Clark Corporation 828 698-5230
  32 Smyth Ave Hendersonville (28792) *(G-7869)*

Kimmys Customs LLC 904 699-2933
  2339 Whisperwood St Rural Hall (27045) *(G-13845)*

Kincaid Furniture Company Inc (HQ) 828 728-3261
  240 Pleasant Hill Rd Hudson (28638) *(G-8773)*

Kincol Industries Incorporated 704 372-8435
  1721 Toal St Charlotte (28206) *(G-3055)*

Kindermusik, Greensboro *Also Called: Kindermusik International Inc (G-7151)*

Kindermusik International Inc 800 628-5687
  237 Burgess Rd Greensboro (27409) *(G-7151)*

Kindred Rolling Doors LLC 704 905-3806
  3420 Country Club Dr Gastonia (28056) *(G-6439)*

Kinetic Performance Llc 910 248-2121
  393 Gable Dr Raeford (28376) *(G-12425)*

Kinetic Sltons Fabrication LLC 607 749-0946
  405 Salvo Ct Holly Ridge (28445) *(G-8684)*

Kinetic Systems Inc 919 322-7200
  4900 Prospectus Dr Ste 500 Durham (27713) *(G-5181)*

King Aerospace and Tech, New Bern *Also Called: Accuking Inc (G-11765)*

King Bio Inc 828 398-6058
  150 Westside Dr Asheville (28806) *(G-674)*

King Bio Inc (PA) 828 255-0201
  3 Westside Dr Asheville (28806) *(G-675)*

King Business Service Inc 910 610-1030
  1680 S Main St Laurinburg (28352) *(G-9483)*

King Charles Industries LLC 704 848-4121
  766 Haileys Ferry Rd Lilesville (28091) *(G-9839)*

King Charles Industries LLC 910 974-4114
  520 E Main St Candor (27229) *(G-1594)*

King Features Syndicate, Charlotte *Also Called: Hearst Corporation (G-2899)*

King Hickory Furniture Company 828 324-0472
  728 Highland Ave Ne Hickory (28601) *(G-8075)*

King Hickory Furniture Company (PA) 828 322-6025
  1820 Main Ave Se Hickory (28602) *(G-8076)*

King Hickory Furniture Company 336 841-6140
  2016 W Green Dr High Point (27260) *(G-8424)*

King International Corporation 336 983-5171
  275 S Main St King (27021) *(G-9274)*

King Pharmaceutical R & D, Cary *Also Called: King Phrmceuticals RES Dev LLC (G-1803)*

King Phrmceuticals RES Dev LLC 919 653-7001
  4000 Centre Green Way Ste 300 Cary (27513) *(G-1803)*

King Signs, Fayetteville *Also Called: Mass Connection Inc (G-5868)*

King Splash, Kings Mountain *Also Called: Specialty Textiles Inc (G-9333)*

King Stone Innovation LLC 704 352-1134
  7313 Mossborough Ct Charlotte (28227) *(G-3056)*

King Tutt Graphics 919 977-6901
  1100 Corporation Pkwy Ste 122 Raleigh (27610) *(G-12938)*

King Tutt Graphics LLC 877 546-4888
  1113 Transport Dr Raleigh (27603) *(G-12939)*

Kingdom Prints LLC 828 894-8851
  190 Hatley Dr Columbus (28722) *(G-4176)*

Kingdom Woodworks Inc 704 678-8134
  405 Margrace Rd Kings Mountain (28086) *(G-9312)*

Kings Chandelier Company 336 623-6188
  1023 Friendly Rd Eden (27288) *(G-5495)*

Kings Mountain Intl Inc 704 739-4227
  1755 S Battleground Ave Kings Mountain (28086) *(G-9313)*

ALPHABETIC SECTION — Korber Medipak Systems NA Inc

Kings Plush Inc 704 739-9931
515 Marie St Kings Mountain (28086) *(G-9314)*

Kings Prtble Wldg Fbrction LLC 336 789-2372
832 W Lebanon St Mount Airy (27030) *(G-11532)*

Kings Queens Plus Size Fashion 704 223-4377
107 Assembly Dr Unit 110 Mooresville (28117) *(G-10999)*

Kingsdown Incorporated (HQ) 919 563-3531
110 S Fourth St Mebane (27302) *(G-10415)*

Kingtuttgraphics 919 748-0843
8809 Amerjack Ct Raleigh (27603) *(G-12940)*

Kinston Free Press Company 252 527-3191
2103 N Queen St Kinston (28501) *(G-9371)*

Kinston Neuse Corporation 252 522-3088
2000 Dobbs Farm Rd Kinston (28504) *(G-9372)*

Kinston Office Supply Co Inc (PA) 252 523-7654
704 Plaza Blvd Ste B Kinston (28501) *(G-9373)*

Kintor Pharmaceuticals Inc 984 208-1255
1011 S Hamilton Rd Chapel Hill (27517) *(G-2029)*

Kirk & Blum Manufacturing Co 801 728-6533
8735 W Market St Greensboro (27409) *(G-7152)*

Kishwa Leather LLC 828 234-4592
4331 1st Street Dr Nw Hickory (28601) *(G-8077)*

Kisner Corporation 919 510-8410
6016 Triangle Dr Raleigh (27617) *(G-12941)*

Kiss Manufacturing Co Inc 828 524-6293
188 Falling Rock Rd Franklin (28734) *(G-6134)*

Kitchen & Bath Decisions, Winterville Also Called: Henderson & Kirkland Inc *(G-17002)*

Kitchen Art, Greensboro Also Called: Marsh Furniture Company *(G-7182)*

Kitchen Bath Gllries N Hlls LL 919 600-6200
4209 Lassiter Mill Rd Ste 130 Raleigh (27609) *(G-12942)*

Kitchen Cabinet Designers LLC 919 833-6532
2114 Atlantic Ave Ste 106 Raleigh (27604) *(G-12943)*

Kitchen Cabinet Distributors, Raleigh Also Called: Kitchen Cabinet Designers LLC *(G-12943)*

Kitchen Cabinets and Design 828 779-4453
60 N Merrimon Ave Unit 107 Asheville (28804) *(G-676)*

Kitchen Cabinets of Raleigh 919 291-4397
2816 Kimmon Way Wake Forest (27587) *(G-15569)*

Kitchen Distributors of South, Matthews Also Called: Mid Carolina Cabinets Inc *(G-10273)*

Kitchen Man Inc 910 408-1322
6361 Ocean Hwy E Ste 1 Winnabow (28479) *(G-16582)*

Kitchen Masters Charlotte LLC 704 375-3320
504 Sarazen Way Salisbury (28144) *(G-14000)*

Kitchen Vntilation Systems LLC 704 476-3565
212 Commerce Blvd Kings Mountain (28086) *(G-9315)*

Kitchens Unlimited Asheville, Asheville Also Called: Sjr Incorporated *(G-773)*

Kitchens.com, Cornelius Also Called: White Picket Media Inc *(G-4594)*

Kitten Kaboodle Alpacas 252 289-5654
327 Fairlane Rd Plymouth (27962) *(G-12375)*

Kitty Hawk Chairs, Kitty Hawk Also Called: Drum Beat Fishing LLC *(G-9402)*

Kitty Hawk Kites Inc 252 441-4124
3933 S Croatan Hwy Nags Head (27959) *(G-11722)*

Kituwah Industries LLC 828 477-4616
1158 Seven Clans Ln Whittier (28789) *(G-16008)*

Kkb Biltmore Inc 828 274-6711
479 Hendersonville Rd Asheville (28803) *(G-677)*

Klazzy Magazine Inc 704 293-8321
100 N Tryon St Ste B220-127 Charlotte (28202) *(G-3057)*

Klazzy.com The Magazine, Charlotte Also Called: Klazzy Magazine Inc *(G-3057)*

KLb Enterprises Incorporated 336 605-0773
209 Citation Ct Greensboro (27409) *(G-7153)*

Klearoptics Inc 760 224-6770
150 N Rsrch Cmpus Dr Ste Lattimore (28089) *(G-9457)*

Kleiberit Adhesives USA Inc 704 843-3339
109b Howie Mine Rd Waxhaw (28173) *(G-15765)*

Kliersolutions 919 806-1287
4041 Brook Cross Dr Apex (27539) *(G-211)*

Klingspor, Hickory Also Called: Klingspor Abrasives Inc *(G-8078)*

Klingspor Abrasives Inc (HQ) 828 322-3030
2555 Tate Blvd Se Hickory (28602) *(G-8078)*

Kloud Hemp Co 336 740-2528
2701 S Elm Eugene St Ste E Greensboro (27406) *(G-7154)*

Kme Consolidated Inc 704 847-9888
529 Crestdale Rd Matthews (28105) *(G-10260)*

Kn Furniture Inc 336 953-3259
244 Nc Highway 22 N Ramseur (27316) *(G-13444)*

Kna 704 847-4280
9535 Monroe Rd Ste 150 Charlotte (28270) *(G-3058)*

Knapheide Trck Eqp Co Midsouth 910 484-0558
3572 Fieldstone Trce Midland (28107) *(G-10470)*

Knapheide Truck Equipment Ctrs, Midland Also Called: Knapheide Trck Eqp Co Midsouth *(G-10470)*

Knight Communications Inc 704 568-7804
6301 Creft Cir Indian Trail (28079) *(G-8943)*

Knight Safety Coatings Co Inc 910 458-3145
201 Beval Rd Wilmington (28401) *(G-16290)*

Knit Tech Inc 336 584-8999
2448 Pitt Rd # A Elon College (27244) *(G-5665)*

Knit-Rite Inc 910 557-5378
167 Marks Creek Ln Hamlet (28345) *(G-7625)*

Knit-Wear Fabrics Inc (PA) 336 226-4342
145 N Cobb Ave Burlington (27217) *(G-1444)*

Knitwear America Inc 704 396-1193
5740 Rocky Mount Rd Granite Falls (28630) *(G-6741)*

Knooosc Inc 415 640-0080
208 Lord Granville Dr Morehead City (28557) *(G-11179)*

Knorr Brake Truck Systems Co 888 836-6922
115 Summit Park Dr Salisbury (28146) *(G-14001)*

Knowledge Management Assoc LLC 781 250-2001
8529 Six Forks Rd Ste 400 Raleigh (27615) *(G-12944)*

Knowlton Woodworking LLC 336 588-3502
523 Gap Rd Seagrove (27341) *(G-14243)*

Knuckleheadz Kustomz Inc 252 646-3354
5306 High St Morehead City (28557) *(G-11180)*

Kodak 919 559-7232
1100 Perimeter Park Dr Ste 108 Morrisville (27560) *(G-11366)*

Kodak, Morrisville Also Called: Kodak *(G-11366)*

Kohnle Cabinetry 828 640-2498
250 Rocky Acres Rd Hickory (28601) *(G-8079)*

Koi Fish Publishing House LLC 704 540-8805
10705 Sapona Ct Charlotte (28277) *(G-3059)*

Koi Pond Brewing Company LLC 252 231-1660
1107 Falls Rd Rocky Mount (27804) *(G-13706)*

Kol Incorporated 919 872-2340
5700 Buffaloe Rd Raleigh (27616) *(G-12945)*

Kolb Boyette & Assoc Inc 919 544-7839
514 United Dr Ste A Durham (27713) *(G-5182)*

Kolcraft Enterprises Inc 910 944-9345
10832 Nc 211 Hwy Aberdeen (28315) *(G-10)*

Konica Mnlta Hlthcare Amrcas I 919 792-6420
2217 Us 70 Hwy E Garner (27529) *(G-6278)*

Konptec Publishing LLC 704 873-4262
142 Sweet Gum Ln Statesville (28625) *(G-14832)*

Kontane Logistics Inc (PA) 828 397-5501
3876 Martin Fish Pond St Hickory (28602) *(G-8080)*

Kontoor Brands, Greensboro Also Called: Kontoor Brands Inc *(G-7156)*

Kontoor Brands Inc 336 332-3586
400 N Elm St Greensboro (27401) *(G-7155)*

Kontoor Brands Inc (PA) 336 332-3400
400 N Elm St Greensboro (27401) *(G-7156)*

Kontoor Brands Inc 336 332-3577
1421 S Elm Eugene St Greensboro (27406) *(G-7157)*

Kooks Custom Headers 704 838-1110
2333 Salisbury Hwy Statesville (28677) *(G-14833)*

Kooks Custom Headers Inc 704 768-2288
141 Advantage Pl Statesville (28677) *(G-14834)*

Koolabrew LLC 910 579-6711
44 Red Bug Rd Sw Shallotte (28470) *(G-14275)*

Koonts Manufacturing Inc 336 300-8009
1447 Rowe Rd Lexington (27295) *(G-9741)*

Korber Medipak Systems N Amer, Morrisville Also Called: Korber Medipak Systems NA Inc *(G-11367)*

Korber Medipak Systems NA Inc 727 538-4644
8000 Regency Pkwy Ste 403 Cary (27518) *(G-1804)*

Korber Medipak Systems NA Inc 727 538-4644
  1001 Aviation Pkwy Ste 200 Morrisville (27560) *(G-11367)*
Korber Medipak Systems Na Inc., Cary *Also Called: Korber Medipak Systems NA Inc (G-1804)*
Kordsa Inc 910 462-2051
  17780 Armstrong Rd Laurel Hill (28351) *(G-9462)*
Kornegay Logging & Timber Co 919 658-5716
  1404 Red Hill Rd Mount Olive (28365) *(G-11665)*
Koru Naturals LLC 800 253-7011
  218 S Churton St Hillsborough (27278) *(G-8658)*
Kosa, Wilmington *Also Called: Invista Capital Management LLC (G-16273)*
Kotek Holdings Inc 919 643-1100
  511 Valley Forge Rd Hillsborough (27278) *(G-8659)*
Kotohira 336 667-0150
  1206 River St Wilkesboro (28697) *(G-16036)*
Kowa Research Institute Inc 919 433-1600
  430 Davis Dr Ste 200 Morrisville (27560) *(G-11368)*
Kr Publications 910 852-1525
  4100 Nelson Way Lumberton (28360) *(G-10043)*
Kraft Cabin LLc 224 409-4374
  3928 Tyler Bluff Ln Raleigh (27616) *(G-12946)*
Kraft Foods, Charlotte *Also Called: Kraft Heinz Foods Company (G-3060)*
Kraft Heinz Foods Company 704 565-5500
  2815 Coliseum Centre Dr Ste 100 Charlotte (28217) *(G-3060)*
Kraftsman Inc 336 824-1114
  10051 Us Highway 64 E Ramseur (27316) *(G-13445)*
Kraftsman Tactical Inc 336 465-3576
  1650 Woodhurst Ln Albemarle (28001) *(G-93)*
Kraken-Skulls 910 500-9100
  822 Shannon Dr Fayetteville (28303) *(G-5855)*
Kral USA Inc 704 814-6164
  901a Matthews Mint Hill Rd Matthews (28105) *(G-10261)*
Kranken Signs Vehicle Wraps 704 339-0059
  310 N Polk St Pineville (28134) *(G-12279)*
Kratos Antenna Solutions Corp 919 934-9711
  1315 Industrial Park Dr Smithfield (27577) *(G-14468)*
Kraze Custom Prints, Monroe *Also Called: Faizon Global Inc (G-10718)*
Kreber 336 861-2700
  221 Swathmore Ave High Point (27263) *(G-8425)*
Kreber Enterprises, High Point *Also Called: Kreber (G-8425)*
Krebs Corporation 336 548-3250
  703 W Decatur St Madison (27025) *(G-10076)*
Krenitsky Pharmaceuticals Inc 919 493-4631
  2516 Homestead Rd Chapel Hill (27516) *(G-2030)*
Krieg Corp 704 361-1223
  8501 Castleby Dr Charlotte (28277) *(G-3061)*
Krieger Cabinets Dewayne 704 630-0609
  415 Sailboat Dr Salisbury (28146) *(G-14002)*
Krigen Pharmaceuticals LLC 919 523-7530
  800 Edwards Dr Lillington (27546) *(G-9854)*
Krigen Pharmaceuticals LLC 919 961-3751
  800 Edwards Brothers Dr Lillington (27546) *(G-9855)*
Krispy Kreme, Gastonia *Also Called: Krispy Kreme Doughnut Corp (G-6440)*
Krispy Kreme, Greensboro *Also Called: Krispy Kreme Doughnut Corp (G-7158)*
Krispy Kreme, Winston Salem *Also Called: Krispy Kreme Doughnut Corp (G-16779)*
Krispy Kreme, Winston Salem *Also Called: Krispy Kreme Doughnuts Inc (G-16781)*
Krispy Kreme Doughnut Corp (DH) 980 270-7117
  2116 Hawkins St Ste 102 Charlotte (28203) *(G-3062)*
Krispy Kreme Doughnut Corp 919 669-6151
  2990 E Franklin Sq Gastonia (28056) *(G-6440)*
Krispy Kreme Doughnut Corp 336 854-8275
  3704 W Gate City Blvd Greensboro (27407) *(G-7158)*
Krispy Kreme Doughnut Corp 336 733-3780
  259 S Stratford Rd Winston Salem (27103) *(G-16779)*
Krispy Kreme Doughnut Corp 336 726-8908
  3190 Centre Park Blvd Winston Salem (27107) *(G-16780)*
Krispy Kreme Doughnuts Inc (HQ) 336 725-2981
  370 Knollwood St Winston Salem (27103) *(G-16781)*
Kristen Screen Printing & EMB 980 256-4561
  4115 Bloomdale Dr Apt 10 Charlotte (28211) *(G-3063)*
Krodsa USA Inc 910 462-2041
  17780 Armstrong Rd Laurel Hill (28351) *(G-9463)*

Kronos Carolinas, Greensboro *Also Called: Ukg Kronos Systems LLC (G-7425)*
Krs Plastics Inc 910 653-3602
  26 Tabor Industrial Park Rd Tabor City (28463) *(G-15083)*
Krueger International Inc 336 434-5011
  217 Feld Ave High Point (27263) *(G-8426)*
Krw Packaging Machinery Inc 828 658-0912
  81 Monticello Rd Weaverville (28787) *(G-15850)*
KS Custom Woodworks Inc 252 714-3957
  3205 Fire Tower Rd Walstonburg (27888) *(G-15639)*
KS Precious Metals LLC 910 687-0244
  Pinehurst (28374) *(G-12226)*
KSA, High Point *Also Called: KAO Specialties Americas LLC (G-8422)*
Ksep Systems LLC 919 339-1850
  598 Airport Blvd Ste 600 Morrisville (27560) *(G-11369)*
Ksm, Shelby *Also Called: Ksm Castings USA Inc (G-14335)*
Ksm Castings USA Inc (DH) 704 751-0559
  120 Blue Brook Dr Shelby (28150) *(G-14335)*
Ksw Logistics & Transport LLC 919 578-5788
  6048 Beale Loop Raleigh (27616) *(G-12947)*
Kudzu Printing Company Inc 828 330-4887
  111 Black Mountain Ave Black Mountain (28711) *(G-1128)*
Kuebler Inc 704 705-4711
  10430 Harris Oak Blvd Ste J Charlotte (28269) *(G-3064)*
Kuenz America Inc 984 255-1018
  9321 Focal Pt Ste 8 Raleigh (27617) *(G-12948)*
Kuntrys Soul-Food & Bbq LLC 910 797-0766
  418 Minnow Ct Fayetteville (28312) *(G-5856)*
Kurrent Wldg & Fabrication Inc 800 738-6114
  187 Deertract Loop Stoneville (27048) *(G-14960)*
Kurt Widenhouse Violins 704 825-3289
  318 Mellon Rd Belmont (28012) *(G-994)*
Kurz Transfer Products LP (HQ) 704 927-3700
  11836 Patterson Rd Huntersville (28078) *(G-8845)*
Kurz Transfer Products LP 336 764-4128
  4939 N Nc Highway 150 Lexington (27295) *(G-9742)*
Kustom Kraft Wdwrks Mt Airy In 336 786-2831
  3096 Westfield Rd Mount Airy (27030) *(G-11533)*
Kute N Klassy By Jen LLc 828 755-5613
  285 Crowe Dairy Rd Forest City (28043) *(G-6074)*
Kwg Music LLC 773 771-2017
  2211 Pear Tree Ln Durham (27703) *(G-5183)*
Kwiatek Innovations LLC 919 455-8295
  108 La Salle St Wilmington (28411) *(G-16291)*
Kwik Elc Mtr Sls & Svc Inc (PA) 252 335-2524
  511 Witherspoon St Elizabeth City (27909) *(G-5553)*
Kwik Kopy Business 704 987-0111
  16630 Northcross Dr Ste 102 Huntersville (28078) *(G-8846)*
Kwik Kopy Printing, Asheville *Also Called: Pope Printing & Design Inc (G-738)*
Kyma Technologies Inc 919 789-8880
  8829 Midway West Rd Raleigh (27617) *(G-12949)*
Kymera International, Durham *Also Called: SCM Metal Products Inc (G-5345)*
Kymera International LLC (PA) 919 544-8090
  2601 Weck Dr Durham (27709) *(G-5184)*
Kyocera Precision Tools Inc (DH) 800 823-7284
  102 Industrial Park Rd Hendersonville (28792) *(G-7870)*
Kyson Leather Incorporated 919 245-0053
  9333 Tapp Rd Hurdle Mills (27541) *(G-8909)*
L & B Custom Woodworking 252 578-8955
  736 Nc Highway 35 Woodland (27897) *(G-17022)*
L & B Jandrew Enterprises 828 687-8927
  1927 Spartanburg Hwy Hendersonville (28792) *(G-7871)*
L & B Monograms Plus 336 229-0152
  413 Maryland Ave Burlington (27217) *(G-1445)*
L & K Machining Inc 336 222-9444
  1312 Whitsett St Burlington (27215) *(G-1446)*
L & R Installations Inc 336 547-8998
  2303 Adams Farm Pkwy Greensboro (27407) *(G-7159)*
L & R Knitting Inc 828 874-2960
  6350 Claude Brittain Rd Hickory (28602) *(G-8081)*
L & R Specialties Inc 704 853-3296
  2757 W Franklin Blvd Gastonia (28052) *(G-6441)*

ALPHABETIC SECTION

L & S Automotive Inc.. 704 391-7657
1214 Caldwell Williams Rd Charlotte (28216) *(G-3065)*

L & S Custom Trailer Service, Charlotte *Also Called: L & S Automotive Inc (G-3065)*

L & W GL Mirror & WD Works LLC.. 336 562-2155
14480 Nc Highway 86 S Prospect Hill (27314) *(G-12407)*

L and L Machine Co Inc... 704 864-5521
158 Superior Stainless Rd Gastonia (28052) *(G-6442)*

L B Plastics Incorporated... 704 663-1543
482 E Plaza Dr Mooresville (28115) *(G-11000)*

L C B of Mount Airy, Mount Airy *Also Called: Travis L Bunker (G-11589)*

L C Industries Inc (PA)... 919 596-8277
4500 Emperor Blvd Durham (27703) *(G-5185)*

L C Industries Inc.. 919 596-8277
4525 Campground Rd Fayetteville (28314) *(G-5857)*

L D Davis, Monroe *Also Called: LD Davis Industries Inc (G-10756)*

L F Delp Lumber Co Inc... 336 359-8202
2601 Nc Highway 113 Laurel Springs (28644) *(G-9466)*

L F I Services Inc... 215 343-0411
1136 Broadway Rd Sanford (27332) *(G-14145)*

L F T Inc.. 828 253-6830
123 Lyman St Asheville (28801) *(G-678)*

L G M, Maiden *Also Called: C O Jelliff Corporation (G-10100)*

L G Sourcing Inc (HQ)... 704 758-1000
1000 Lowes Blvd Mooresville (28117) *(G-11001)*

L L C Batteries of N C.. 919 331-0241
101 Medical Dr Angier (27501) *(G-143)*

L Michelle LLC.. 980 946-0204
137 Autry Ave Mooresville (28117) *(G-11002)*

L P, North Wilkesboro *Also Called: Louisiana-Pacific Corporation (G-12024)*

L T Welding, Gibsonville *Also Called: Larry D Troxler (G-6566)*

L TS Gas and Snaks.. 910 762-7130
2461 Carolina Beach Rd Wilmington (28401) *(G-16292)*

L'Eggs - Hanes - Bali, Mount Airy *Also Called: Hanesbrands Inc (G-11515)*

L&C Cabinetry, Charlotte *Also Called: Royal Maple LLC (G-3464)*

L&L Wings, Carolina Beach *Also Called: Wings Store 765 (G-1642)*

L&P Dstribution Ctr Furn 8814, Conover *Also Called: Leggett & Platt Incorporated (G-4471)*

L3harris Technologies Inc.. 704 588-7126
8406 Mcalpine Dr Charlotte (28217) *(G-3066)*

L6 Realty LLC.. 704 654-3000
2744 Yorkmont Rd Charlotte (28208) *(G-3067)*

La Barge Inc.. 336 812-2400
1925 Eastchester Dr High Point (27265) *(G-8427)*

La Estrella Inc... 919 639-6559
61 W Williams St Angier (27501) *(G-144)*

La Farm Inc... 919 657-0657
4248 Nw Cary Pkwy Cary (27513) *(G-1805)*

La Farm Bakery, Cary *Also Called: La Farm Inc (G-1805)*

La Oaxaquena... 336 274-0173
2708 S Elm Eugene St Greensboro (27406) *(G-7160)*

La Palmas Tortilleria Y Taquer.. 252 206-1683
900 Goldsboro St Sw Wilson (27893) *(G-16509)*

La Signs Inc.. 919 779-1185
1140 Benson Rd Ste 107 Garner (27529) *(G-6279)*

La Sky Creations LLC.. 516 996-1231
3930 Bardstown Ct Apt 103 Fayetteville (28304) *(G-5858)*

La T Da Btq Monogramming.. 336 457-9831
1 Brackenwood Ct Greensboro (27407) *(G-7161)*

La Tortilleria, Winston Salem *Also Called: La Tortilleria LLC (G-16782)*

La Tortilleria LLC... 336 773-0010
2900 Lowery St Winston Salem (27101) *(G-16782)*

LA West Inc... 704 685-2833
8815 Colebridge Ct Sherrills Ford (28673) *(G-14387)*

Lab Designs LLC (PA).. 336 429-4114
391 Hickory St Mount Airy (27030) *(G-11534)*

Lab Dsgns Archtctural Laminate, Mount Airy *Also Called: Lab Designs LLC (G-11534)*

Label & Printing Solutions Inc.. 919 782-1242
201 Buncombe St Raleigh (27609) *(G-12950)*

Label Line Ltd... 336 857-3115
5356 Nc Highway 49 S Asheboro (27205) *(G-450)*

Label Printing Systems Inc.. 336 760-3271
3937 Westpoint Blvd Winston Salem (27103) *(G-16783)*

Label Southeast LLC... 518 796-6320
227 W 4th St Ste 112 Charlotte (28202) *(G-3068)*

Label Store, The, Charlotte *Also Called: Rapid Response Inc (G-3409)*

Labels Tags & Inserts Inc.. 336 227-8485
2302 Airpark Rd Burlington (27215) *(G-1447)*

Labonte Racing Inc... 336 431-1004
5740 Hopewell Church Rd Trinity (27370) *(G-15348)*

Laborie Sons Cstm Wodworks LLC.. 910 769-2524
315 Van Dyke Dr Wilmington (28405) *(G-16293)*

Laceration Lures LLC.. 919 612-3368
5333 Durham Rd Raleigh (27613) *(G-12951)*

Laceys Tree Service.. 910 330-2868
221 Jenkins Rd Jacksonville (28540) *(G-9012)*

Lacquer Craft Hospitality Inc (DH).. 336 822-8086
2575 Penny Rd High Point (27265) *(G-8428)*

Lacy J Miller Machine.. 336 764-0518
7987 Old Us Highway 52 Lexington (27295) *(G-9743)*

Lad Ways of Printing Inc... 252 814-9559
3820 Nc Highway 222 Fountain (27829) *(G-6094)*

Ladder & Things.. 704 779-7211
7316 Rockwood Forest Ln Charlotte (28212) *(G-3069)*

Ladder Carry LLC... 704 245-2359
401 Harlon Dr Cary (27511) *(G-1806)*

Lady C E Crews LLC.. 703 565-3687
2740 6th Street Ct Ne Hickory (28601) *(G-8082)*

Ladybug Vineyard LLC.. 336 366-4701
607 Crossroad Church Rd Dobson (27017) *(G-4828)*

Ladybugs Medibles LLC.. 704 635-7596
2003 Shady Ln Monroe (28110) *(G-10754)*

Lafauci.. 919 244-5912
5001 Sunset Forest Cir Holly Springs (27540) *(G-8705)*

Lagael Manufacturing LLC... 910 428-9383
205 Frame Shop Rd Star (27356) *(G-14718)*

Laird Plastics Inc... 704 597-8555
6100 Harris Technology Blvd Ste F Charlotte (28269) *(G-3070)*

Laird Plastics, Inc., Charlotte *Also Called: Laird Plastics Inc (G-3070)*

Laird Thermal Systems Inc.. 919 597-7300
629 Davis Dr Ste 200 Morrisville (27560) *(G-11370)*

Lake City Electric Motor Repr.. 336 248-2377
915 S Talbert Blvd Lexington (27292) *(G-9744)*

Lake Country Alpacas... 252 430-0963
1256 Twnsville Landing Rd Henderson (27537) *(G-7793)*

Lake Creek Logging & Trckg Inc... 910 532-2041
3744 Nc Highway 210 E Harrells (28444) *(G-7693)*

Lake Gaston Gazette, Littleton *Also Called: Womack Publishing Co Inc (G-9954)*

Lake House Enterprises Inc... 919 424-3780
4104 Ridgebluffs Ct Raleigh (27603) *(G-12952)*

Lake Lure Marine.. 828 200-5908
5911 Us 64 74a Hwy Lake Lure (28746) *(G-9447)*

Lake Norman EMB & Monogramming.. 704 892-8450
21228 Catawba Ave Cornelius (28031) *(G-4564)*

Lake Norman Industries LLC... 704 987-9048
19116 Statesville Rd Cornelius (28031) *(G-4565)*

Lake Norman Times, Mooresville *Also Called: Womack Publishing Co Inc (G-11131)*

Lake Nrman Screen Prtg Fctry L.. 704 664-8337
915 River Hwy Mooresville (28117) *(G-11003)*

Lake Printing & Design, Charlotte *Also Called: Goffstar Inc (G-2842)*

Lake Shore Radiator Inc.. 336 271-2626
211c Creek Ridge Rd Greensboro (27406) *(G-7162)*

Lakebrook Corporation... 207 947-4051
3506 E Yacht Dr Oak Island (28465) *(G-12052)*

Lakeland Ledger Publishing, Wilmington *Also Called: Wilmington Star-News Inc (G-16452)*

Lakeshore Cabinet.. 847 508-3594
14034 Holly Springs Dr Huntersville (28078) *(G-8847)*

Lakeside Cstm Tees & Embroider... 704 274-3730
9216 Westmoreland Rd Ste B Cornelius (28031) *(G-4566)*

Lakeside Dyeing & Finshg Inc.. 336 229-0064
423 Lakeside Ave Burlington (27217) *(G-1448)*

Lakeside Mills Inc (PA).. 828 286-4866
398 W Main St Spindale (28160) *(G-14607)*

Lakou LLC... 704 780-5129
10104 Bellhaven Blvd Charlotte (28214) *(G-3071)*

ALPHABETIC SECTION

Lam Factory, The, Canton *Also Called: Coast Lamp Manufacturing Inc* **(G-1610)**

Lambda Technologies Inc.. 919 462-1919
   2200 Gateway Centre Blvd Morrisville (27560) *(G-11371)*

Lamberts Industries.. 980 244-0898
   1012 N 6th St Albemarle (28001) *(G-94)*

Lambeth Dimension Inc... 336 629-3838
   443 Mount Shepherd Road Ext Asheboro (27205) *(G-451)*

Lambeth Frames Inc... 336 953-9805
   443 Mount Shepherd Road Ext Asheboro (27205) *(G-452)*

Lamco Machine Tool Inc.. 252 247-4360
   135 Industrial Dr Morehead City (28557) *(G-11181)*

Lamination Services Inc... 336 643-7369
   6919 Us Highway 158 Stokesdale (27357) *(G-14945)*

Lammers Glass & Design, Powells Point *Also Called: James Lammers* **(G-12398)**

Lampe & Malphrus Lumber Co... 919 934-6152
   37 E Peedin Rd Smithfield (27577) *(G-14469)*

Lampe & Malphrus Lumber Co (PA)................................... 919 934-6152
   37 E Peedin Rd Smithfield (27577) *(G-14470)*

Lampe & Malphrus Lumber Co... 919 934-1124
   210 N 10th St Smithfield (27577) *(G-14471)*

Lanart International Inc... 704 875-1972
   10325 Hambright Rd Huntersville (28078) *(G-8848)*

Lancer Incorporated... 910 428-2181
   135 S Lancer Rd Star (27356) *(G-14719)*

Land and Loft LLC... 315 560-7060
   701 Georgetown Rd Raleigh (27608) *(G-12953)*

Land of Sky Mobile Canning LLC....................................... 303 880-1297
   26 Magnolia Ave Asheville (28801) *(G-679)*

Landfill Gas Producers... 704 844-8990
   10600 Nations Ford Rd # 150 Charlotte (28273) *(G-3072)*

Landmark Coatings, Mocksville *Also Called: Landmark Coatings LLC* **(G-10583)**

Landmark Coatings LLC.. 336 492-2492
   933 Danner Rd Mocksville (27028) *(G-10583)*

Landmark Music Group Inc... 919 800-7277
   412 Henry Dr Garner (27529) *(G-6280)*

Landmark Printing Inc... 919 833-5151
   901 W Hodges St Raleigh (27608) *(G-12954)*

Landmark Printing Co Inc.. 919 833-5151
   901 W Hodges St Raleigh (27608) *(G-12955)*

Landscape Design & Lawn Maint, Charlotte *Also Called: Carolina Lawnscape Inc* **(G-2398)**

Landscaping/Construction, Mill Spring *Also Called: Helping Hands Concrete Llc* **(G-10486)**

Landsdown Mining Corporation... 704 753-5400
   7406 Concord Hwy Monroe (28110) *(G-10755)*

Landshire Inc... 919 650-3544
   150 Dominion Dr Ste G Morrisville (27560) *(G-11372)*

Landsman Forest Lawn Guard.. 828 898-3433
   174 Maple Dr Banner Elk (28604) *(G-901)*

Lane Construction Corporation... 919 876-4550
   3010 Gresham Lake Rd Raleigh (27615) *(G-12956)*

Lane Land & Timber Inc.. 252 443-1151
   5631 Hart Farm Rd Battleboro (27809) *(G-923)*

Langenthal Corporation... 336 969-9551
   1300 Langenthal Dr Rural Hall (27045) *(G-13846)*

Langley & Huther Rf Tech.. 919 880-4968
   3304 E Annaley Dr Raleigh (27604) *(G-12957)*

Langley Indus McHning Fbrction, Sharpsburg *Also Called: Scoggins Industrial Inc* **(G-14280)**

Laniers Screen Printing.. 336 857-2699
   6271 Bombay School Rd Denton (27239) *(G-4740)*

Lannings Farming and Logging... 828 246-8938
   108 Lanning Rd Clyde (28721) *(G-4125)*

Lantal Textiles Inc (HQ).. 336 969-9551
   1300 Langenthal Dr Rural Hall (27045) *(G-13847)*

Lantern of Hendersonville LLC... 828 513-5033
   755 N Main St Hendersonville (28792) *(G-7872)*

Lanxess Corporation.. 704 923-0121
   1225 Gastonia Technology Pkwy Dallas (28034) *(G-4647)*

Lanxess Corporation.. 704 868-7200
   214 W Ruby Ave Gastonia (28054) *(G-6443)*

Large & Small Graphics, Wallace *Also Called: Lsg LLC* **(G-15624)**

Larlin Cushion Company.. 828 465-5599
   1950 Fairgrove Church Rd Hickory (28602) *(G-8083)*

Larry Bissette Inc... 919 773-2140
   8012 Dirt Rd Apex (27539) *(G-212)*

Larry D Troxler.. 336 585-1141
   6170 Nc Highway 87 N Gibsonville (27249) *(G-6566)*

Larry S Cabinet Shop Inc... 252 442-4330
   4217 S Church St Rocky Mount (27803) *(G-13707)*

Larry S Sausage Company.. 910 483-5148
   1624 Middle River Loop Fayetteville (28312) *(G-5859)*

Larry Shackelford.. 919 467-8817
   309 Dunhagan Pl Cary (27511) *(G-1807)*

Larrys Beans Inc.. 919 828-1234
   1507 Gavin St Raleigh (27608) *(G-12958)*

Laru Industries Inc.. 704 821-7503
   115 Business Park Dr Indian Trail (28079) *(G-8944)*

Laser Dynamics Inc... 704 658-9769
   104 Performance Rd Mooresville (28115) *(G-11004)*

Laser Image Printing & Mktg, Durham *Also Called: Laser Ink Corporation* **(G-5186)**

Laser Ink Corporation.. 919 361-5822
   4018 Patriot Dr Ste 200 Durham (27703) *(G-5186)*

Laser Precision Cutting Inc... 828 658-0644
   181 Reems Creek Rd Ste 3 Weaverville (28787) *(G-15851)*

Laser Recharge Carolina Inc.. 919 467-5902
   2474 Walnut St Cary (27518) *(G-1808)*

Lash Out Inc.. 919 342-0221
   117 Georgetowne Dr Clayton (27520) *(G-3992)*

Lassiter Distilling Company... 919 295-0111
   319 N 1st Ave Knightdale (27545) *(G-9419)*

Late Model Digest, Murphy *Also Called: McLoud Media* **(G-11712)**

Latham Inc... 336 857-3702
   6509 Scarlet Oak Dr Denton (27239) *(G-4741)*

Latham-Hall Corporation... 336 475-9723
   5003 Ball Park Rd Thomasville (27360) *(G-15240)*

Lathamscu... 336 477-5008
   376 Ben Anderson Rd Mocksville (27028) *(G-10584)*

Lathers Skin Essentials.. 828 449-9244
   1891 Plaza Dr Hickory (28602) *(G-8084)*

Laticrete International Inc.. 910 582-2252
   299 Industry Dr Hamlet (28345) *(G-7626)*

Latino Communications Inc... 704 319-5044
   7508 E Independence Blvd Ste 109 Charlotte (28227) *(G-3073)*

Latino Communications Inc... 919 645-1680
   150 Fayetteville St Ste 110 Raleigh (27601) *(G-12959)*

Latino Communications Inc (PA)..................................... 336 714-2823
   3067 Waughtown St Winston Salem (27107) *(G-16784)*

Laundry Svc Tech Ltd Lblty Co.. 908 327-1997
   2217 Matthews Township Pkwy Ste D Matthews (28105) *(G-10262)*

Laura Cooke Ceramics... 336 580-4308
   1 Brucemont Cir Apt 3 Asheville (28806) *(G-680)*

Laura Gaskin... 828 628-5891
   922 Garren Creek Rd Fairview (28730) *(G-5715)*

Laurel Gray Vineyards Inc... 336 468-9463
   5726 W Old Us 421 Hwy Hamptonville (27020) *(G-7673)*

Laurel Hill Paper Co.. 910 997-4526
   126 1st St Cordova (28330) *(G-4518)*

Laurel of Asheville LLC.. 828 670-7503
   110 Executive Park Asheville (28801) *(G-681)*

Laurel of Asheville, The, Asheville *Also Called: Laurel of Asheville LLC* **(G-681)**

Laurinburg Exchange, Laurinburg *Also Called: Champion Media LLC* **(G-9473)**

Laurinburg Feed Mill, Laurinburg *Also Called: Murphy-Brown LLC* **(G-9490)**

Laurinburg Machine Company... 910 276-0360
   715 Park Cir Laurinburg (28352) *(G-9484)*

Lava Cable, Fayetteville *Also Called: Mark Stoddard* **(G-5866)**

Lavender Inc.. 704 481-8327
   769 Ware Rd Shelby (28152) *(G-14336)*

Lawing Advg Mktg & Pubg LLC... 704 364-8649
   5210 Lincrest Pl Charlotte (28211) *(G-3074)*

Lawing Marble Co Inc.. 704 732-0360
   2523 E Highway 150 Lincolnton (28092) *(G-9898)*

Lawrence Williams.. 910 462-2332
   10200 Andrew Jackson Hwy Laurel Hill (28351) *(G-9464)*

Laws Distillery Inc... 828 726-3663
   1889 Greasy Creek Rd Lenoir (28645) *(G-9623)*

ALPHABETIC SECTION

Laws Logging 336 973-4318
   2036 Kendell Town Rd Ferguson (28624) *(G-5958)*

Laws Sign Group LLC 919 755-3632
   3119 Belvin Dr Raleigh (27609) *(G-12960)*

Layer27 .... 919 909-9088
   205 Blue Heron Dr Youngsville (27596) *(G-17088)*

Laying Dimes Welding & Fab LLC 704 677-5521
   1240 Regan Rd Lexington (27292) *(G-9745)*

Layton Optics, Greensboro *Also Called: Optics Inc (G-7236)*

Laytons Custom Boatworks LLC 252 482-1504
   103 Anchors Way Dr Edenton (27932) *(G-5518)*

Lazar Industries LLC (PA) 919 742-9303
   3025 Hamp Stone Rd Siler City (27344) *(G-14420)*

Lazar Industries East Inc 919 742-9303
   3025 Hamp Stone Rd Siler City (27344) *(G-14421)*

Lazeredge LLC 336 480-7934
   244 Brunswick Ln Mount Airy (27030) *(G-11535)*

Lazeredge LLC (PA) 336 480-7934
   244 Brunswick Ln Mount Airy (27030) *(G-11536)*

Lba Group Inc (PA) 252 329-9243
   3400 Tupper Dr Greenville (27834) *(G-7553)*

Lba Technology Inc 252 757-0279
   3400 Tupper Dr Greenville (27834) *(G-7554)*

Lbm Industries Inc 828 966-4270
   17668 Rosman Hwy Sapphire (28774) *(G-14213)*

Lbm Industries Inc (PA) 828 966-4270
   2000 Whitewater Rd Sapphire (28774) *(G-14214)*

Lbm Industries Inc 828 631-1227
   21 E Hall Hts Sylva (28779) *(G-15062)*

Lc America Inc 336 676-5129
   8221 Tyner Rd Colfax (27235) *(G-4153)*

Lc Foods LLC 919 510-6688
   3809 Frazier Dr Ste 101 Raleigh (27610) *(G-12961)*

Lcf Enterprise (PA) 208 415-4300
   719 6th Ave Nw Hickory (28601) *(G-8085)*

LCI, Charlotte *Also Called: LCI Corporation International (G-3076)*

LCI, Sanford *Also Called: Lee County Industries Inc (G-14148)*

LCI Corporation International 704 399-7441
   4404b Chesapeake Dr Charlotte (28216) *(G-3075)*

LCI Corporation International 704 399-7441
   4433 Chesapeake Dr Charlotte (28216) *(G-3076)*

LD Davis Industries Inc 704 289-4551
   2031 E Roosevelt Blvd Monroe (28112) *(G-10756)*

LDR Designs 252 375-4484
   3113 Cleere Ct Greenville (27858) *(G-7555)*

Le Bleu Corporation 828 254-5105
   212 Baldwin Rd Arden (28704) *(G-346)*

Le Soigneur Canvas LLC 910 670-3620
   10611 Lanier Club Dr Apt 305 Raleigh (27617) *(G-12962)*

Lea Aid, Raleigh *Also Called: Lea Aid Acquisition Company (G-12963)*

Lea Aid Acquisition Company 919 872-6210
   1717 S Saunders St Raleigh (27603) *(G-12963)*

Lea Industries Inc 336 294-5233
   240 Pleasant Hill Rd Hudson (28638) *(G-8774)*

Lea R N, Raleigh *Also Called: Learnplatform Inc (G-12964)*

Lea Street Press LLC 336 514-2351
   37 Clear Springs Cir Blanch (27212) *(G-1152)*

Leading Edge Safety Systems, New Bern *Also Called: Pucuda Inc (G-11838)*

Leanders, Concord *Also Called: Tameka Burros (G-4369)*

Leapfrog Document Services Inc 704 372-1078
   4651 Charlotte Park Dr Ste 230 Charlotte (28217) *(G-3077)*

Lear Corporation 919 552-5667
   200 Dickens Rd Fuquay Varina (27526) *(G-6208)*

Lear Corporation 910 296-8671
   1754 N Nc 11 903 Hwy Kenansville (28349) *(G-9144)*

Lear Corporation 910 794-5810
   1001 Military Cutoff Rd Ste 300 Wilmington (28405) *(G-16294)*

Lear Enterprises Inc 704 321-0027
   8145 Ardrey Kell Rd Charlotte (28277) *(G-3078)*

Lear Metal Carports LLC 877 219-4677
   149 Tanglewood Dr Mount Airy (27030) *(G-11537)*

Learning Craftsmen Inc 813 321-5003
   1000 Chedington Dr Apex (27502) *(G-213)*

Learningstationcom Inc (PA) 704 926-5400
   8022 Providence Rd Ste 500 Charlotte (28277) *(G-3079)*

Learnplatform Inc 919 247-5998
   509 W North St Raleigh (27603) *(G-12964)*

Leather Miracles LLC 828 464-7448
   3350 20th Ave Se Hickory (28602) *(G-8086)*

Leatherbound Book Works 919 448-7847
   608 Starmont Dr Durham (27705) *(G-5187)*

Lebos Shoe Store Inc 704 987-6540
   20605 Torrence Chapel Rd Cornelius (28031) *(G-4567)*

Led Integrations 336 257-9935
   415 Trail One Burlington (27215) *(G-1449)*

Led Lighting Fixtures Inc 919 991-0700
   617 Davis Dr Ste 200 Morrisville (27560) *(G-11373)*

Ledford Logging Co Inc 828 644-5410
   1737 Sunny Point Rd Murphy (28906) *(G-11711)*

Ledford Upholstery 704 732-0233
   202 W Pine St Lincolnton (28092) *(G-9899)*

Ledford Upholstery & Fabrics, Lincolnton *Also Called: Ledford Upholstery (G-9899)*

Ledger Hardware Inc 828 688-4798
   5489 S 226 Hwy Bakersville (28705) *(G-885)*

Ledger Publishing Company 919 693-2646
   200 W Spring St Oxford (27565) *(G-12135)*

Lee, Greensboro *Also Called: Lee Apparel Company Inc (G-7163)*

Lee Apparel Company Inc (DH) 336 332-3400
   400 N Elm St Greensboro (27401) *(G-7163)*

Lee Brick & Tile Company 919 774-4800
   3704 Hawkins Ave Sanford (27330) *(G-14146)*

Lee Builder Mart Inc
   1000 N Horner Blvd Sanford (27330) *(G-14147)*

Lee Controls LLC 732 752-5200
   8250 River Rd Southport (28461) *(G-14572)*

Lee County Industries Inc 919 775-3439
   2711 Tramway Rd Sanford (27332) *(G-14148)*

Lee Industries LLC (PA) 828 464-8318
   210 4th St Sw Conover (28613) *(G-4470)*

Lee Industries LLC 828 464-8318
   402 W 25th St Newton (28658) *(G-11947)*

Lee Industries LLC 828 464-8318
   1620 Fisher Ct Newton (28658) *(G-11948)*

Lee Linear 800 221-0811
   8250 River Rd Southport (28461) *(G-14573)*

Lee Marks (PA) 919 493-2208
   4304 Amesbury Ln Durham (27707) *(G-5188)*

Lee Paving Solutions LLC 828 302-0415
   688 N Nc 16 Business Hwy Denver (28037) *(G-4787)*

Lee Roys Frame Co Inc 828 241-2513
   2221 Buffalo Shoals Rd Catawba (28609) *(G-1966)*

Lee Spring Company 336 275-3631
   3013 S Elm Eugene St Greensboro (27406) *(G-7164)*

Lee Spring Company LLC 336 275-3631
   104 Industrial Ave Greensboro (27406) *(G-7165)*

Leeboy, Lincolnton *Also Called: St Engineering Leeboy Inc (G-9921)*

Leeboy, Lincolnton *Also Called: VT Leeboy Inc (G-9934)*

Lees Logging Company 910 385-7201
   201 Nc Highway 210 E Harrells (28444) *(G-7694)*

Lees Polishing & Powdercoatin 704 827-4309
   922 S Nc 16 Business Hwy Stanley (28164) *(G-14700)*

Lees Screen Enclosures & More 843 283-7227
   403 Bayberry Ln Sunset Beach (28468) *(G-15000)*

Lees Tackle Inc 910 386-5100
   5316 Us Highway 421 N Wilmington (28401) *(G-16295)*

Legacy Aerospace & Defense, Arden *Also Called: Legacy Aerospace and Def LLC (G-347)*

Legacy Aerospace and Def LLC 828 398-0981
   150 Glenn Bridge Rd Arden (28704) *(G-347)*

Legacy Biogas, Goldsboro *Also Called: Legacy Biogas LLC (G-6629)*

Legacy Biogas LLC 713 253-9013
   107 Cassedale Dr Goldsboro (27534) *(G-6629)*

Legacy Commercial Service LLC 757 831-5291
   13921 Allison Forest Trl Charlotte (28278) *(G-3080)*

Legacy Designs & Graphx LLC — ALPHABETIC SECTION

Legacy Designs & Graphx LLC.. 910 237-2916
198 Windsor Dr Angier (27501) *(G-145)*

Legacy Graphics Inc... 919 741-6262
191 Technology Dr Garner (27529) *(G-6281)*

Legacy Knitting LLC.. 844 762-2678
3310 Kitty Hawk Rd Ste 100 Wilmington (28405) *(G-16296)*

Legacy Mechanical.. 704 225-8558
2715 Gray Fox Rd Monroe (28110) *(G-10757)*

Legacy National Installers LLC... 336 804-1990
425 E Steeple Chase Rd Pleasant Garden (27313) *(G-12357)*

Legacy Paddlesports LLC.. 828 684-1933
210 Old Airport Rd Fletcher (28732) *(G-6017)*

Legacy Pre-Finishing Inc... 704 528-7136
450 S Eastway Dr Troutman (28166) *(G-15385)*

Legacy River Company... 704 618-7260
935 Iberville St Charlotte (28270) *(G-3081)*

Legacy Vulcan LLC.. 828 963-7100
3869 Hwy 105 S Boone (28607) *(G-1213)*

Legacy Vulcan LLC.. 704 788-7833
7680 Poplar Tent Rd Concord (28027) *(G-4301)*

Legacy Vulcan LLC.. 252 338-2201
174 Knobbs Creek Dr Elizabeth City (27909) *(G-5554)*

Legacy Vulcan LLC.. 336 835-1439
12362 Nc 268 Elkin (28621) *(G-5624)*

Legacy Vulcan LLC.. 828 255-8561
Hwy 19 & 23 S Enka (28728) *(G-5683)*

Legacy Vulcan LLC.. 704 279-5566
16745 Old Beatty Ford Rd Gold Hill (28071) *(G-6583)*

Legacy Vulcan LLC.. 252 438-3161
696 Greystone Rd Henderson (27537) *(G-7794)*

Legacy Vulcan LLC.. 828 692-0254
2960 Clear Creek Rd Hendersonville (28792) *(G-7873)*

Legacy Vulcan LLC.. 828 754-5348
2008 Wilkesboro Blvd Lenoir (28645) *(G-9624)*

Legacy Vulcan LLC.. 828 437-2616
Causby Quarry Rd Morganton (28655) *(G-11227)*

Legacy Vulcan LLC.. 336 838-8072
776 Quarry Rd # 115 North Wilkesboro (28659) *(G-12021)*

Legacy Vulcan LLC.. 910 895-2415
353 Galestown Rd Rockingham (28379) *(G-13633)*

Legacy Vulcan LLC.. 336 767-0911
4401 N Patterson Ave Winston Salem (27105) *(G-16785)*

Legalis Dms LLC.. 919 741-8260
1315 Oakwood Ave Raleigh (27610) *(G-12965)*

Legalize Pot Belly Pigs Co LLC... 828 505-7053
40 Old Elk Mountain Rd Asheville (28804) *(G-682)*

Legend Compression Wear.. 877 711-5343
1450 Healing Springs Dr Denton (27239) *(G-4742)*

Legend-Tees.. 828 585-2066
37 Loop Rd Arden (28704) *(G-348)*

Legends Countertops LLC.. 980 230-4501
138 Buffalo Ave Nw Unit 3 Concord (28025) *(G-4302)*

Leggett & Platt.. 336 357-3641
161 Proctor Ln Lexington (27292) *(G-9746)*

Leggett & Platt Incorporated... 336 379-7777
911 Northridge St Greensboro (27403) *(G-7166)*

Leggett & Platt Incorporated... 336 884-4306
1629 Blandwood Dr High Point (27260) *(G-8429)*

Leggett & Platt Incorporated... 336 622-0121
330 N Greensboro St Liberty (27298) *(G-9819)*

Leggett & Platt Incorporated... 704 380-6208
178 Orbit Rd Statesville (28677) *(G-14835)*

Leggett & Platt Incorporated... 828 322-6855
1401 Deborah Herman Rd Sw Conover (28613) *(G-4471)*

Leggett & Platt Incorporated... 336 889-2600
1430 Sherman Ct High Point (27260) *(G-8430)*

Leggett & Platt Incorporated... 336 889-2600
1430 Sherman Ct High Point (27260) *(G-8431)*

Legions Stadium.. 910 341-4604
2221 Carolina Beach Rd Wilmington (28401) *(G-16297)*

Lehr LLC... 704 827-9368
12703 Commerce Station Dr Huntersville (28078) *(G-8849)*

Leighdeux LLC.. 704 965-4889
355 Eastover Rd Charlotte (28207) *(G-3082)*

Leist Studios Inc.. 828 262-5912
381 Tarleton Cir Boone (28607) *(G-1214)*

Leistriz Advanced Turbine Components Inc....................................... 336 969-1352
3050 Wstnghuse Rd Ste 190 Rural Hall (27045) *(G-13848)*

Leisure Craft Holdings LLC... 828 693-8241
940 Upward Rd Flat Rock (28731) *(G-5967)*

Leisure Craft Inc.. 828 693-8241
940 Upward Rd Flat Rock (28731) *(G-5968)*

Leitz Tooling Demp's Div., Archdale *Also Called: Leitz Tooling Systems LP (G-292)*

Leitz Tooling Systems LP... 336 861-3367
401 Interstate Dr Archdale (27263) *(G-292)*

Leiva Strings Inc.. 919 538-6269
3653 Campbell Rd Raleigh (27606) *(G-12966)*

Leke LLC... 704 523-1452
10800 Nations Ford Rd Pineville (28134) *(G-12280)*

Leland Machine Shop Inc.. 910 371-0360
767 Village Rd Ne Leland (28451) *(G-9551)*

Lelantos Group Inc... 704 780-4127
132 Joe Knox Ave Ste 100 Mooresville (28117) *(G-11005)*

Lely Manufacturing Inc... 252 291-7050
4608 Lely Rd Wilson (27893) *(G-16510)*

Len Corporation.. 919 876-2964
525 Hinton Oaks Blvd Knightdale (27545) *(G-9420)*

Lennox International Inc... 828 633-4805
1251 Sand Hill Rd Candler (28715) *(G-1586)*

Lennox Store Asheville, Candler *Also Called: Lennox International Inc (G-1586)*

Lennox Stores (partsplus).. 910 660-7070
3826 Us Highway 421 N Ste 160 Wilmington (28401) *(G-16298)*

Lenoir Concrete Cnstr Co... 828 759-0449
562 Abington Rd Lenoir (28645) *(G-9625)*

Lenoir Mirror Company.. 828 728-3271
401 Kincaid St Lenoir (28645) *(G-9626)*

Lenoir Printing Inc.. 828 758-7260
401 Harper Ave Sw Lenoir (28645) *(G-9627)*

Lenovo (united States) Inc... 919 486-9627
5241 Paramount Pkwy Morrisville (27560) *(G-11374)*

Lenovo (united States) Inc... 919 237-8389
7001 Development Dr Bldg 7 Morrisville (27560) *(G-11375)*

Lenovo (united States) Inc (HQ).. 855 253-6686
8001 Development Dr Morrisville (27560) *(G-11376)*

Lenovo Holding Company Inc (HQ).. 855 253-6686
8001 Development Dr Morrisville (27560) *(G-11377)*

Lenovo International, Morrisville *Also Called: Lenovo (united States) Inc (G-11376)*

Lenovo US Fulfillment Ctr LLC.. 855 253-6686
1009 Think Pl Morrisville (27560) *(G-11378)*

Lenox Birkdale LLC... 704 997-8116
16623 Birkdale Commons Pkwy Huntersville (28078) *(G-8850)*

Lenox Land... 704 507-4877
15925 Bayshore Dr Huntersville (28078) *(G-8851)*

Lenscrafters, Fayetteville *Also Called: Luxottica of America Inc (G-5862)*

Lenscrafters, Goldsboro *Also Called: Luxottica of America Inc (G-6632)*

Leo Gaev Metalworks Inc.. 919 883-4666
616 Nc Highway 54 W Chapel Hill (27516) *(G-2031)*

Leoforce LLC... 919 539-5434
500 W Peace St Raleigh (27603) *(G-12967)*

Leonard Alum Utlity Bldngs Inc... 336 226-9410
2602 Alamance Rd Burlington (27215) *(G-1450)*

Leonard Alum Utlity Bldngs Inc (PA).. 336 789-5018
630 W Independence Blvd Ste 3 Mount Airy (27030) *(G-11538)*

Leonard Alum Utlity Bldngs Inc... 919 872-4442
4239 Capital Blvd Raleigh (27604) *(G-12968)*

Leonard Alum Utlity Bldngs Inc... 910 392-4921
5705 Market St Wilmington (28405) *(G-16299)*

Leonard Automatics Inc... 704 483-9316
5894 Balsom Ridge Rd Denver (28037) *(G-4788)*

Leonard Block Company.. 336 764-0607
2390 Midway School Rd Winston Salem (27107) *(G-16786)*

Leonard Building & Trck Cover, Wilmington *Also Called: Leonard Alum Utlity Bldngs Inc (G-16299)*

ALPHABETIC SECTION

Leonard Building & Trck Covers, Mount Airy *Also Called: Leonard Alum Utlity Bldngs Inc* *(G-11538)*

Leonard Building & Truck ACC, Raleigh *Also Called: Leonard Alum Utlity Bldngs Inc* *(G-12968)*

Leonard Building and Truck ACC, Burlington *Also Called: Leonard Alum Utlity Bldngs Inc* *(G-1450)*

Leonard Electric Mtr Repr Inc 336 625-2375
531 N Fayetteville St Asheboro (27203) *(G-453)*

Leonard Frabrication & Design, Denver *Also Called: Leonard Automatics Inc* *(G-4788)*

Leonard Logging Co 336 857-2776
4057 Salem Church Rd Denton (27239) *(G-4743)*

Leonard McSwain Sptic Tank Svc 704 482-1380
3020 Ramseur Church Rd Shelby (28150) *(G-14337)*

Leonard Products, Oak Island *Also Called: Lakebrook Corporation* *(G-12052)*

Leonine Protection Systems LLC 704 296-2675
309 Dutchmans Meadow Dr Mount Holly (28120) *(G-11640)*

Leons Welding & Decking LLC 919 923-7327
104 Crestwood Cir Lot 18 Chapel Hill (27516) *(G-2032)*

Let It Flo LLC 717 421-3754
3522 Harrisburg Dr Fayetteville (28306) *(G-5860)*

Lets Build It Woodworking 704 352-7131
414 Arlee Cir Sw Concord (28025) *(G-4303)*

Lets Talk Some Shit 704 264-6212
7400 Old Mount Holly Rd Paw Creek (28130) *(G-12172)*

Level Ten Facilities Svcs LLC 704 759-6799
1213 W Morehead St # 500 Charlotte (28208) *(G-3083)*

Levi Innovations Inc 828 684-6640
122 Continuum Dr Fletcher (28732) *(G-6018)*

Levi Strauss International 828 665-2417
800 Brevard Rd Asheville (28806) *(G-683)*

Leviosa Motor Shades, Mooresville *Also Called: Penrock LLC* *(G-11049)*

Leviton Manufacturing Co Inc 828 584-1611
113 Industrial Blvd Morganton (28655) *(G-11228)*

Leviton Manufacturing Co Inc 336 846-3246
618 S Jefferson Ave West Jefferson (28694) *(G-15942)*

Leviton Town Plant 336 846-3246
618 S Jefferson Ave West Jefferson (28694) *(G-15943)*

Lewis Brothers Tire & Algnmt 919 359-9050
451 E Main St Clayton (27520) *(G-3993)*

Lewis Frank Specialty Products, Salisbury *Also Called: Carolina Print Works Inc* *(G-13935)*

Lewis Machine Company Inc 828 668-7752
712 Catawba River Rd Old Fort (28762) *(G-12103)*

Lewis Moore Prtg & Graphics, Raleigh *Also Called: Moore Printing & Graphics Inc* *(G-13041)*

Lewtak Pipe Organ Builders Inc 336 554-2251
211 Parsley Ln Mocksville (27028) *(G-10585)*

Lexington Electric Motor Repr, Lexington *Also Called: Lake City Electric Motor Repr* *(G-9744)*

Lexington Furniture Inds Inc (PA) 336 474-5300
1300 National Hwy Thomasville (27360) *(G-15241)*

Lexington Gas Dept, City of, Lexington *Also Called: City of Lexington* *(G-9695)*

Lexington Home Brands, Thomasville *Also Called: Lexington Furniture Inds Inc* *(G-15241)*

Lexington Home Brands Mfg 336 243-5740
1893 Brown St Lexington (27292) *(G-9747)*

Lexington Plant Nippon Elc GL, Lexington *Also Called: Nippon Electric Glass Co Ltd* *(G-9761)*

Lexington Road Properties Inc 336 650-7209
500 Battery Dr Winston Salem (27107) *(G-16787)*

Lexington Tire & Auto LLC 336 249-2105
1200 S Main St Lexington (27292) *(G-9748)*

Lexitas Pharma Services Inc 919 205-0012
5425 Page Rd Ste 410 Durham (27703) *(G-5189)*

Lgc Consulting Inc 704 216-0171
1217 Speedway Blvd Salisbury (28146) *(G-14003)*

Li-Ion Motors Corp 704 662-0827
158 Rolling Hill Rd Mooresville (28117) *(G-11006)*

Liat LLC 704 528-4506
694 N Main St Troutman (28166) *(G-15386)*

Libasci Woodworks Inc 828 524-7073
401 Dobson Mountain Rd R Franklin (28734) *(G-6135)*

Liberty & Plenty Distillery, Durham *Also Called: Blu Distilling Company LLC* *(G-4965)*

Liberty & Plenty Distilling, Raleigh *Also Called: Blu Distilling Company LLC* *(G-12563)*

Liberty Dry Kiln Corp 336 622-5490
3246 Staley Store Rd Liberty (27298) *(G-9820)*

Liberty Embroidery Inc 336 548-1802
301 K Fork Rd Madison (27025) *(G-10077)*

Liberty Hse Utility Buildings 828 209-3390
65 Dalton Rd Horse Shoe (28742) *(G-8740)*

Liberty Investment & MGT Corp 919 544-0344
455 Kitty Hawk Dr Morrisville (27560) *(G-11379)*

Liberty Lumber Company 336 622-4901
9979 Old Liberty Rd Liberty (27298) *(G-9821)*

Liberty Press 336 996-3667
1356 Amylee Trl Kernersville (27284) *(G-9208)*

Liberty Press, Rutherfordton *Also Called: S Ruppe Inc* *(G-13889)*

Liberty Sign and Lighting LLC 336 703-7465
375 Ridge Rd Lexington (27295) *(G-9749)*

Liberty Street LLC 828 247-6010
155 Westerly Hills Dr Forest City (28043) *(G-6075)*

Liberty Street Baggage, Asheville *Also Called: Saundra D Hall* *(G-763)*

Liberty Trailers LLC 219 866-7141
5806 York Martin Rd Liberty (27298) *(G-9822)*

Liberty Welding 336 964-0640
134 E Dameron Ave Liberty (27298) *(G-9823)*

Liberty Wood Products Inc 828 524-7958
874 Iotla Church Rd Franklin (28734) *(G-6136)*

Libra Life Group Llc 910 550-8664
9371 Cassadine Ct Leland (28451) *(G-9552)*

Libra Logistics/Escort, Leland *Also Called: Libra Life Group Llc* *(G-9552)*

Liburdi, Mooresville *Also Called: Liburdi Dimetrics Corporation* *(G-11007)*

Liburdi Dimetrics Corporation 704 230-2510
2599 Charlotte Hwy Mooresville (28117) *(G-11007)*

Liburdi Turbine Services LLC 704 230-2510
2599 Charlotte Hwy Mooresville (28117) *(G-11008)*

License Plate Agency 910 763-7076
2390 Carolina Beach Rd Wilmington (28401) *(G-16300)*

Lichtenberg Inc 336 949-9438
107 E Murphy St Madison (27025) *(G-10078)*

Lick er Lips Lip Balm LLC 702 355-5433
11512 Ridge Oak Dr Charlotte (28273) *(G-3084)*

Lidseen North Carolina Inc 828 389-8082
6382 Old Hwy 64 W Hayesville (28904) *(G-7768)*

Lie Loft, Raleigh *Also Called: Land and Loft LLC* *(G-12953)*

Liebel-Flarsheim Company LLC 919 878-2930
8800 Durant Rd Raleigh (27616) *(G-12969)*

Liechti America 704 948-1277
13245 Reese Blvd W Ste 100 Huntersville (28078) *(G-8852)*

Life, Cary *Also Called: Living Intntionally For Excell* *(G-1813)*

Life Stories and Beyond 704 579-7161
4001 Wilson Dr Charlotte (28270) *(G-3085)*

Life Style Publishing Inc 828 507-2209
Cashiers (28717) *(G-1936)*

Liferay Inc 703 957-8542
7151 Okelly Chapel Rd Cary (27519) *(G-1809)*

Lifespan Incorporated (PA) 704 944-5100
1511 Shopton Rd Ste A Charlotte (28217) *(G-3086)*

Lifespan Incorporated 336 838-2614
2070 River Rd Liberty Grove Rd North Wilkesboro (28659) *(G-12022)*

Lifestory Publishing LLC 601 594-0018
48 Greenwood Rd Asheville (28803) *(G-684)*

Lift Bodies Inc 336 667-2588
1675 Elkin Hwy 268 North Wilkesboro (28659) *(G-12023)*

Lift Equipment Inc 704 799-3355
660 Millswood Dr Mooresville (28115) *(G-11009)*

Liggett Group LLC (DH) 919 304-7700
100 Maple Ln Mebane (27302) *(G-10416)*

Light Place, The, Hickory *Also Called: Fixtures & More* *(G-8026)*

Light Source Usa Inc 704 504-8399
3935 Westinghouse Blvd Charlotte (28273) *(G-3087)*

Light-Beams Publishing 603 659-1300
111 Island Palms Dr Carolina Beach (28428) *(G-1639)*

Lightcreed Labs, Durham *Also Called: Wolfspeed Inc* *(G-5443)*

Lightform Inc 908 281-9098
403 Shelwood Cir Apt H Asheville (28804) *(G-685)*

Lighthouse Led — ALPHABETIC SECTION

Lighthouse Led 252 756-1158
  4776 Reedy Branch Rd Winterville (28590) *(G-17005)*

Lighthouse Led Inc 252 916-0998
  3602 Huntington Rd Greenville (27858) *(G-7556)*

Lighthouse of Wayne County Inc 919 736-1313
  405 E Walnut St Goldsboro (27530) *(G-6630)*

Lighthouse Press Inc 919 371-8640
  102 Eagle Meadow Ct Cary (27519) *(G-1810)*

Lighthouse Press Inc 919 371-8640
  5448 Apex Peakway Apex (27502) *(G-214)*

Lighting 919 828-0351
  1608 N Market Dr Raleigh (27609) *(G-12970)*

Lightjunction 919 607-9717
  400 Innovation Ave # 150 Morrisville (27560) *(G-11380)*

Lightjunction, Morrisville Also Called: Busiapp Corporation *(G-11311)*

Lightning Bolt Ink LLC 828 281-1274
  100 N Lexington Ave Asheville (28801) *(G-686)*

Lightning Protection, Waynesville Also Called: Alp Systems Inc *(G-15792)*

Lightning Prtction Systems LLC 252 213-9900
  5901 Triangle Dr Raleigh (27617) *(G-12971)*

Lightning X Products Inc 704 295-0299
  2365 Tipton Dr Charlotte (28206) *(G-3088)*

Lights-Lights LLC 919 798-2317
  1206 Bill Avery Rd Coats (27521) *(G-4132)*

Lightwave Fabrication Mch LLC 252 927-1591
  333 Windley Canal Rd Pantego (27860) *(G-12166)*

Ligna Machinery Inc 336 584-0030
  315 Macarthur Ln Burlington (27217) *(G-1451)*

Likeable Press LLC 844 882-8340
  227 W 4th St Charlotte (28202) *(G-3089)*

Lilas Trunk 919 548-0784
  145 Cc Routh Rd Bear Creek (27207) *(G-939)*

Lillianonline LLC 919 850-4594
  3641 Top Of The Pines Ct Raleigh (27604) *(G-12972)*

Lillies Intriors Cstm Quilting, Thomasville Also Called: Lillys Interiors Cstm Quilting *(G-15242)*

Lillys Interiors Cstm Quilting 336 475-1421
  1165 Hillside Dr Thomasville (27360) *(G-15242)*

Lily Belles 828 246-0894
  305 Castle Creek Dr Waynesville (28786) *(G-15809)*

Lime-Chem Inc 910 843-2121
  8135 Red Rd Rockwell (28138) *(G-13655)*

Limestone Products Inc (PA) 704 283-9492
  3302 W Highway 74 B Monroe (28110) *(G-10758)*

Limitless Prfmce Fbrication LL 910 799-5441
  4921 Berry Ct Wilmington (28412) *(G-16301)*

Limitless Wldg Fabrication LLC 252 753-0660
  3543 South Fields St Farmville (27828) *(G-5739)*

Lin Wggins Mem Schlarship Fund 919 749-2340
  5653 Soft Wind Dr Fuquay Varina (27526) *(G-6209)*

Lin-Ink Publishing LLC 704 485-5823
  825 Old Farm Rd Oakboro (28129) *(G-12075)*

Linamar Forgings Carolina Inc 252 237-8181
  2401 Old Stantonsburg Rd Wilson (27894) *(G-16511)*

Linamar Light Metal S-Mr LLC 828 348-4010
  490 Ferncliff Park Dr Mills River (28732) *(G-10506)*

Linamar North Carolina Inc 828 348-5343
  2169 Hendersonville Rd Arden (28704) *(G-349)*

Lincoln County Fabricators Inc 704 735-1398
  513 Jason Rd Lincolnton (28092) *(G-9900)*

Lincoln Financial, Greensboro Also Called: Abe Entercom Holdings LLC *(G-6773)*

Lincoln Herald LLC 704 735-3620
  611 N Laurel St Lincolnton (28092) *(G-9901)*

Lincolnton Bearing Plant 704 794-5964
  1000 Timken Pl Iron Station (28080) *(G-8974)*

Lincotek Surface Solutions, Hickory Also Called: Turbocoating Corp *(G-8191)*

Linde Advanced Mtl Tech Inc 828 862-4772
  283 Old Rosman Hwy Brevard (28712) *(G-1278)*

Linde Gas & Equipment Inc 919 380-7411
  1120 W Chatham St Cary (27511) *(G-1811)*

Linde Gas & Equipment Inc 704 587-7096
  3810 Shutterfly Rd Ste 100 Charlotte (28217) *(G-3090)*

Linde Gas & Equipment Inc 919 549-0633
  11 Triangle Dr Durham (27709) *(G-5190)*

Linde Gas & Equipment Inc 866 543-3427
  1304 Roosevelt Ct Whitsett (27377) *(G-15995)*

Linde Gas North America, Cary Also Called: Linde Gas & Equipment Inc *(G-1811)*

Linde Gas North America, Charlotte Also Called: Linde Gas & Equipment Inc *(G-3090)*

Linde Gas North America, Durham Also Called: Linde Gas & Equipment Inc *(G-5190)*

Linde Gas North America, Whitsett Also Called: Linde Gas & Equipment Inc *(G-15995)*

Linde Inc 910 343-0241
  Hwy 421 N Wilmington (28405) *(G-16302)*

Linder Industrial Machinery Co 980 777-8345
  5733 Davidson Hwy Concord (28027) *(G-4304)*

Lindley Laboratories Inc (PA) 336 449-7521
  106 E Railroad Ave Gibsonville (27249) *(G-6567)*

Lindley Mills Inc 336 376-6190
  7763 Lindley Mill Rd Graham (27253) *(G-6697)*

Lindsay Precast Inc 919 494-7600
  2675 Us1 Hwy Franklinton (27525) *(G-6157)*

LINDSAY PRECAST, INC., Franklinton Also Called: Lindsay Precast Inc *(G-6157)*

Line Drive Sports Center Inc 336 824-1692
  161 Crestwick Rd Ramseur (27316) *(G-13446)*

Lines and Lineage LLC 919 783-7517
  809 Munt Vrnon Rd Ste 103 Raleigh (27607) *(G-12973)*

Lines Unlimited Inc 336 996-6603
  1114 Oakwood Dr Walnut Cove (27052) *(G-15632)*

Lingle Electric Repair Inc 704 636-5591
  600 N Main St Salisbury (28144) *(G-14004)*

Linkone Src LLC 252 206-0960
  2018 Beeler Rd S Wilson (27893) *(G-16512)*

Linkous Carpentry & Wdwkg LLC 828 460-5610
  415 Melody Cir Swannanoa (28778) *(G-15028)*

Linnig Corporation 704 482-9582
  1100 Airport Rd Shelby (28150) *(G-14338)*

Linor Technology Inc 336 485-6199
  4741 S Main St Winston Salem (27127) *(G-16788)*

Linprint Company 910 763-5103
  3405 Market St Unit 2 Wilmington (28403) *(G-16303)*

Linrene Furniture Inc 919 742-9391
  2535 Us Hwy 421 N Siler City (27344) *(G-14422)*

Linter North America Corp (DH) 828 645-4261
  48 Patton Ave Asheville (28801) *(G-687)*

Lintons Gas Piping & Service 828 734-6259
  1549 Kims Cove Rd Canton (28716) *(G-1620)*

Linville Falls Winery 828 733-9021
  9557 Linville Falls Hwy Newland (28657) *(G-11889)*

Linwood Inc 336 300-8307
  3979 Old Linwood Rd Lexington (27292) *(G-9750)*

Lionel LLC (PA) 704 454-4200
  6301 Performance Dr Sw Concord (28027) *(G-4305)*

Lions Services Inc 704 921-1527
  4600 N Tryon St Ste A Charlotte (28213) *(G-3091)*

Lionstar Transport LLC 336 448-0166
  2597 Landmark Dr Winston Salem (27103) *(G-16789)*

Liposcience, Morrisville Also Called: Liposcience Inc *(G-11381)*

Liposcience Inc 919 212-1999
  100 Perimeter Park Dr Ste C Morrisville (27560) *(G-11381)*

Lipstick Chatter LLC 919 285-3439
  149 Smith Rock Dr Holly Springs (27540) *(G-8706)*

Lipstick Ministries Inc 910 228-0097
  4809 Elmhurst Ridge Ct Raleigh (27616) *(G-12974)*

Liqui-Box Corporation (HQ) 804 325-1400
  2415 Cascade Pointe Blvd Charlotte (28208) *(G-3092)*

Liquid Ice Corporation 704 882-3505
  500 Union West Blvd Ste C Matthews (28104) *(G-10328)*

Liquid Moly, Salisbury Also Called: Lockrey Company LLC *(G-14005)*

Liquid Process Systems Inc 704 821-1115
  1025 Technology Dr Ste A Indian Trail (28079) *(G-8945)*

Liquidating Reichhold Inc 919 990-7500
  1035 Swabia Ct Durham (27703) *(G-5191)*

Liquidehr Inc 866 618-1531
  1939 High House Rd Ste 107 Cary (27519) *(G-1812)*

Litbywhit LLC...... 704 293-5743
2810 Chalgrove Ln Charlotte (28216) *(G-3093)*

Lite Logging LLC...... 252 560-8131
7091 Nc Highway 903 S La Grange (28551) *(G-9442)*

Litex Industries Inc...... 704 799-3758
120 N Commercial Dr Mooresville (28115) *(G-11010)*

Litho Priting Inc...... 919 755-9542
1501 S Blount St Raleigh (27603) *(G-12975)*

Lithography Design, Raleigh Also Called: Litho Priting Inc *(G-12975)*

Litholyte Corporation LLC...... 252 671-2032
3505 Barons Way Trent Woods (28562) *(G-15329)*

Little Beekeeper LLC...... 704 215-9690
3978 Stoney Creek Dr Lincolnton (28092) *(G-9902)*

Little Blank Canvas LLC...... 336 887-6133
3623 Single Leaf Ct High Point (27265) *(G-8432)*

Little Leaps Press Inc...... 404 664-1842
2 Lynwood Rd Asheville (28804) *(G-688)*

Little Logging Inc...... 704 201-8185
1513 N Main St Oakboro (28129) *(G-12076)*

Little Red Wagon Granola, Durham Also Called: Lrw Holdings Inc *(G-5196)*

Little Reds Engraving LLC...... 910 599-7747
304 Lake Dr Burgaw (28425) *(G-1344)*

Little River Furniture, Ether Also Called: Blackstone Furniture Inds Inc *(G-5690)*

Little River Metalworks LLC...... 919 920-0292
132 Blueberry Rd Goldsboro (27530) *(G-6631)*

Little River Naturals LLC...... 919 760-3708
7408 Riley Hill Rd Zebulon (27597) *(G-17133)*

Little River Yachts LLC...... 828 323-4955
1100 Commscope Pl Se Hickory (28602) *(G-8087)*

Little Stitches EMB & Prtg LLC...... 828 352-7550
196 Westgate Dr Taylorsville (28681) *(G-15150)*

Litton Systems Inc...... 704 588-2340
1201 Continental Blvd Charlotte (28273) *(G-3094)*

Live It Boutique LLC...... 704 492-2402
509 Old Vine Ct Charlotte (28214) *(G-3095)*

Livedo Usa Inc...... 252 237-1373
4925 Livedo Dr Wilson (27893) *(G-16513)*

Livengood Innovations LLC...... 336 925-7604
12068 S Nc Highway 150 Linwood (27299) *(G-9946)*

Livin' Rooms, Claremont Also Called: Dexter Inc *(G-3919)*

Living Intntionally For Excell...... 810 600-3425
200 Commonwealth Ct Ste 200 Cary (27511) *(G-1813)*

Living Water Filter Co Inc...... 252 438-6600
123 Horner St Henderson (27536) *(G-7795)*

Living Wise, High Point Also Called: Wise Living Inc *(G-8606)*

Livingston & Haven, Charlotte Also Called: Hyde Park Partners Inc *(G-2939)*

Livingston & Haven LLC (HQ)...... 704 588-3670
11529 Wilmar Blvd Charlotte (28273) *(G-3096)*

Lizard Lick Brewing & Dist LLC...... 919 887-4369
138 E Vance St Zebulon (27597) *(G-17134)*

Lizard Lick Brewing and Dist, Zebulon Also Called: Lizard Lick Brewing & Dist LLC *(G-17134)*

Lizmere Cavaliers...... 704 418-2543
403 S Washington St Shelby (28150) *(G-14339)*

Lizzys Logos Inc...... 704 321-2588
3118 Savannah Hills Dr Matthews (28105) *(G-10263)*

Lj Cbg Acquisition Company...... 336 768-8872
3916 Westpoint Blvd Winston Salem (27103) *(G-16790)*

Ljm Machine Co Inc...... 336 764-0518
7987 Old Us Highway 52 Lexington (27295) *(G-9751)*

Lkf Inc...... 336 475-7400
111 Todd Ct Thomasville (27360) *(G-15243)*

Lkn Perform LLC...... 704 215-4900
11020 Bailey Rd Ste J Cornelius (28031) *(G-4568)*

LL Cultured Marble Inc...... 336 789-3908
1184 Maple Grove Church Rd Mount Airy (27030) *(G-11539)*

LLC Diamond Bell...... 704 806-4705
6420 Rea Rd Ste A1 # 25 Charlotte (28277) *(G-3097)*

LLC Ferguson Copeland (HQ)...... 828 584-0664
100 Reep Dr Morganton (28655) *(G-11229)*

LLC Stanton Gray...... 704 975-9392
202 N Main Ave Newton (28658) *(G-11949)*

Llewellyn Mtal Fabricators Inc...... 704 283-4816
4816 Persimmon Ct Monroe (28110) *(G-10759)*

Llf, Morrisville Also Called: Led Lighting Fixtures Inc *(G-11373)*

Llflex LLC...... 336 777-5000
220 Polo Rd Winston Salem (27105) *(G-16791)*

Lloyds Chatham Ltd Partnership...... 919 742-4692
511 Dorado Dr High Point (27265) *(G-8433)*

Lloyds Fabricating Solutions...... 336 250-0154
5896 Denton Rd Thomasville (27360) *(G-15244)*

Lloyds Oyster House Inc...... 910 754-6958
1642 Village Point Rd Sw Shallotte (28470) *(G-14276)*

Lls Investments Inc (PA)...... 919 662-7283
3400 Lake Woodard Dr Raleigh (27604) *(G-12976)*

Lm, Granite Falls Also Called: Lubrimetal Corporation *(G-6742)*

Lm Shea LLC...... 919 608-1901
8201 Candelaria Dr Raleigh (27616) *(G-12977)*

Lmb Corp...... 704 547-8886
3020 Prosperity Church Rd Ste D Charlotte (28269) *(G-3098)*

Lmg Holdings Inc...... 919 653-0910
4920 S Alston Ave Durham (27713) *(G-5192)*

Ln Woodworks...... 509 480-0263
3210 Kentyre Dr Fayetteville (28303) *(G-5861)*

Lns Turbo Inc (DH)...... 704 739-7111
203 Turbo Dr Kings Mountain (28086) *(G-9316)*

Lns Turbo North America...... 704 435-6376
242 Dick Beam Rd Cherryville (28021) *(G-3871)*

Lo & Behold LLC...... 336 988-0589
202 E Maynard Ave Durham (27704) *(G-5193)*

Loading Republic Inc...... 704 561-1077
191 Crowell Dr Nw Concord (28025) *(G-4306)*

Loba-Wakol LLC...... 704 527-5919
2732 Us Highway 74 W Wadesboro (28170) *(G-15515)*

Lobbyguard Solutions Inc...... 919 785-3301
4700 Six Forks Rd Ste 300 Raleigh (27609) *(G-12978)*

Local Print...... 919 620-9050
14 Rountree Ln Bahama (27503) *(G-864)*

Lock Drives Inc...... 704 588-1844
11198 Downs Rd Pineville (28134) *(G-12281)*

Locklear Cabinet and Woodworks, Rowland Also Called: Locklear Cabinets Wdwrk Sp Inc *(G-13790)*

Locklear Cabinets Wdwrk Sp Inc...... 910 521-4463
4659 Cabinet Shop Rd Rowland (28383) *(G-13790)*

Lockrey Company LLC (PA)...... 856 665-4794
614 Emerald Bay Dr Salisbury (28146) *(G-14005)*

Locktite Log Systems, Salisbury Also Called: Log Home Builders Inc *(G-14007)*

Lockwood Identity Inc...... 704 597-9801
6225 Old Concord Rd Charlotte (28213) *(G-3099)*

Locust Monument LLC...... 704 888-5600
713 Main St W Locust (28097) *(G-9962)*

Locust Plastics Inc...... 704 636-2742
630 Industrial Ave Salisbury (28144) *(G-14006)*

Lodging By Liberty Inc...... 336 622-2201
50 Industrial Park Dr Siler City (27344) *(G-14423)*

Loflin Concrete Co Inc...... 336 904-2788
2105 Pisgah Church Rd Kernersville (27284) *(G-9209)*

Loflin Fabrication, Denton Also Called: Loflin Fabrication LLC *(G-4744)*

Loflin Fabrication LLC...... 336 859-4333
1382 Cranford Rd Denton (27239) *(G-4744)*

Loflin Handle Co Inc...... 336 463-2422
2625 Courtney Huntsville Rd Yadkinville (27055) *(G-17043)*

Loflin Materials Inc...... 336 993-2432
4880 Old Hollow Rd Kernersville (27284) *(G-9210)*

Loftin & Company Inc...... 704 393-9393
1908 Gateway Blvd Charlotte (28208) *(G-3100)*

Loftin & Company Printers, Charlotte Also Called: Loftin & Company Inc *(G-3100)*

Log Cabin Homes Ltd...... 252 454-1548
7677 N Halifax Rd Battleboro (27809) *(G-924)*

Log Cabin Homes Ltd (PA)...... 252 454-1500
513 Keen St # 515 Rocky Mount (27804) *(G-13708)*

Log Home Builders Inc...... 704 638-0677
470 B Leazer Rd Salisbury (28147) *(G-14007)*

ALPHABETIC SECTION

Logan Text Fabrics, Greensboro Also Called: Oakhurst Textiles Inc *(G-7229)*

Logangate Homes Timber Homes, Asheville Also Called: Rclgh Inc *(G-753)*

Logger Head Logging 919 842-0249
   538 Pea Ridge Rd New Hill (27562) *(G-11862)*

Logic Hydraulic Controls Inc 910 791-9293
   6616 Windmill Way Wilmington (28405) *(G-16304)*

Logic Manufacturing Inc 704 821-0535
   4009 Fawnbrooke Dr Indian Trail (28079) *(G-8946)*

Logicbay Corp 888 301-0751
   2002 Eastwood Rd Ste 306 Wilmington (28403) *(G-16305)*

Logicbit Software LLC 888 366-2280
   2530 Meridian Pkwy Ste 300 Durham (27713) *(G-5194)*

Logicom Computer Systems Inc 910 256-5916
   1121 Military Cutoff Rd Ste C Wilmington (28405) *(G-16306)*

Logiksavvy Solutions LLC 336 392-6149
   2204 Flora Vista Ct Greensboro (27406) *(G-7167)*

Logistimatics, Greensboro Also Called: Gpx Intelligence Inc *(G-7055)*

Logo Dogz 888 827-8666
   4808 Persimmon Ct Monroe (28110) *(G-10760)*

Logo Label Printing Company 919 309-0007
   4416 Bennett Memorial Rd Ste 101 Durham (27705) *(G-5195)*

Logo Shop , The, Mooresville Also Called: Cook Group Inc *(G-10911)*

Logo Wear Graphics LLC 336 382-0455
   300 Norman Farm Rd Summerfield (27358) *(G-14985)*

Logodogz, Monroe Also Called: Reliance Management Group Inc *(G-10796)*

Logonation Inc 704 799-0612
   128 Overhill Dr Ste 102 Mooresville (28117) *(G-11011)*

Logosdirect LLC 866 273-2335
   6303 Oleander Dr Ste 102b Wilmington (28403) *(G-16307)*

Logothreads Inc 704 892-9433
   20480 Chartwell Center Dr Ste H Cornelius (28031) *(G-4569)*

Logowear 336 969-0444
   8003 Mathison Creek Dr Rural Hall (27045) *(G-13849)*

Lollipop Cenral 704 934-0015
   3111 Mocking Bird Ln Kannapolis (28083) *(G-9126)*

Lomar Specialty Advg Inc 704 788-4380
   7148 Weddington Rd Nw Ste 110 Concord (28027) *(G-4307)*

London Garment Mfg LLC 336 573-9300
   1731 Price Grange Rd Stoneville (27048) *(G-14961)*

London Luxury LLC 980 819-1966
   3540 Toringdon Way Ste 200 Charlotte (28277) *(G-3101)*

Lone Star Container Sales Corp 704 588-1737
   10901 Carpet St Charlotte (28273) *(G-3102)*

Long Asp Pav Trckg of Grnsburg 336 643-4121
   4349 Us Highway 220 N Summerfield (27358) *(G-14986)*

Long Branch Partners LLC 828 837-1400
   1960 Brasstown Rd Brasstown (28902) *(G-1267)*

Long J E & Sons Grading Inc (PA) 336 228-9706
   3218 Foy Jane Trl Burlington (27217) *(G-1452)*

Long Life Lighting Inc 919 833-1292
   8810 Westgate Park Dr Ste 100 Raleigh (27617) *(G-12979)*

Long Trailer Co Inc 252 823-8828
   313 Bass Ln Tarboro (27886) *(G-15111)*

Long, J E Sand & Stone, Burlington Also Called: Long J E & Sons Grading Inc *(G-1452)*

Longleaf Services Inc 800 848-6224
   116 S Boundary St Chapel Hill (27514) *(G-2033)*

Longleaf Truss Company 910 673-4711
   4476 Nc Highway 211 West End (27376) *(G-15929)*

Longleaf Vineyard 828 435-3555
   36 Hallaran Dr Marshall (28753) *(G-10204)*

Longs Machine & Tool Inc 336 625-3844
   2224 S Fayetteville St Asheboro (27205) *(G-454)*

Longwood Industries Inc (DH) 336 272-3710
   706 Green Valley Rd Ste 212 Greensboro (27408) *(G-7168)*

Longworth Industries Inc 910 974-3068
   480 E Main St Candor (27229) *(G-1595)*

Longworth Industries Inc (DH) 910 673-5290
   565 Air Tool Dr Ste K Southern Pines (28387) *(G-14539)*

Lonza Rtp 800 748-8979
   523 Davis Dr Ste 400 Morrisville (27560) *(G-11382)*

Looc Studio Inc 336 472-6877
   2066 Industrial Dr Newton (28658) *(G-11950)*

Looking Glass Creamery LLC 828 458-0088
   115 Harmon Dairy Ln Columbus (28722) *(G-4177)*

Looking Glass Technology LLC 910 679-8060
   1901 Edgemont Ln Wilmington (28405) *(G-16308)*

Lookout Boat Window Frames LLC 252 723-2222
   2500 Bridges St Ste W19 Morehead City (28557) *(G-11182)*

Lookwhatqmade LLC 980 330-1995
   101 N Tryon St Ste 112 Charlotte (28246) *(G-3103)*

Loparex LLC (DH) 919 678-7700
   1255 Crescent Green Ste 400 Cary (27518) *(G-1814)*

Loparex LLC 336 635-0192
   816 W Fieldcrest Rd Eden (27288) *(G-5496)*

Lord Corporation 877 275-5673
   200 Lord Dr Cary (27511) *(G-1815)*

Lord Corporation 919 342-3380
   406 Gregson Dr Cary (27511) *(G-1816)*

Lord Corporation (HQ) 919 468-5979
   111 Lord Dr Cary (27511) *(G-1817)*

Lord Corporation 919 469-2500
   110 Lord Dr Cary (27511) *(G-1818)*

Lord Far East Inc 919 468-5979
   111 Lord Dr Cary (27511) *(G-1819)*

Lorillard LLC (DH) 336 741-2000
   401 N Main St Winston Salem (27101) *(G-16792)*

Lorillard Q-Tech Inc 877 703-0386
   714 Green Valley Rd Greensboro (27408) *(G-7169)*

Lorillard Tobacco Company LLC 336 335-6600
   714 Green Valley Rd Greensboro (27408) *(G-7170)*

Los Vientos Windpower Ib LLC 704 594-6200
   526 S Church St Charlotte (28202) *(G-3104)*

Lots of Labels 252 410-1611
   210 E 10th St Roanoke Rapids (27870) *(G-13577)*

Lotus Bakeries Us LLC 415 956-8956
   2010 Park Center Dr Mebane (27302) *(G-10417)*

Loud Lemon Beverage LLC 919 949-7649
   8512 Meadow View Ln Bahama (27503) *(G-865)*

Louise L Nona L C 704 242-0929
   25425 Rowland Rd Locust (28097) *(G-9963)*

Louisiana-Pacific Corporation 336 696-2751
   1068 Abtco Rd North Wilkesboro (28659) *(G-12024)*

Louisiana-Pacific Corporation 336 696-2751
   1151 Abtco Rd Roaring River (28669) *(G-13594)*

Louisiana-Pacific Corporation 336 599-8080
   10475 Boston Rd Roxboro (27574) *(G-13806)*

Louisiana-Pacific Southern Div, Roxboro Also Called: Louisiana-Pacific Corporation *(G-13806)*

Love Knot Candles 336 456-1619
   4603 Barn Owl Ct Greensboro (27406) *(G-7171)*

Love Thy Skin LLC 910 703-2321
   227 Remington Dr Coats (27521) *(G-4133)*

Lovegrass Kitchen Inc 919 234-7541
   5305 Hilltop Needmore Rd Fuquay Varina (27526) *(G-6210)*

Lovekin & Young PC 828 322-5435
   110 N Center St Hickory (28601) *(G-8088)*

Loven Ready Mix LLC 828 265-4671
   1996 Us Highway 421 N Boone (28607) *(G-1215)*

Low Country Steel SC LLC (PA) 336 283-9611
   2529 Viceroy Dr Winston Salem (27103) *(G-16793)*

Low Impact Tech USA Inc 828 428-6310
   269 Cane Creek Rd Fletcher (28732) *(G-6019)*

Lowder Steel Inc 336 431-9000
   2450 Coltrane Mill Rd Archdale (27263) *(G-293)*

Lowes Global Sourcing, Mooresville Also Called: L G Sourcing Inc *(G-11001)*

Lowes Welding and Camper Repr 336 214-9058
   2417 S Nc Highway 87 Graham (27253) *(G-6698)*

Lowland Seafood Inc 252 745-3751
   569 Kelly Watson Rd Lowland (28552) *(G-10014)*

Lowman Publishing 919 929-7829
   104 Chesley Ln Chapel Hill (27514) *(G-2034)*

Loy & Loy Inc 919 942-6356
   205 Travora St Graham (27253) *(G-6699)*

ALPHABETIC SECTION

Lpm Inc 704 922-6137
  2703 Ashbourne Dr Gastonia (28056) *(G-6444)*

Lpmylan Specialty, Greensboro *Also Called: Mylan Pharmaceuticals Inc (G-7211)*

Lps Tag & Label, Winston Salem *Also Called: Label Printing Systems Inc (G-16783)*

Lq3 Pharmaceuticals, Morrisville *Also Called: Lq3 Pharmaceuticals Inc (G-11383)*

Lq3 Pharmaceuticals Inc 919 794-7391
  419 Davis Dr Ste 100 Morrisville (27560) *(G-11383)*

Lr Manufacturing Inc 910 399-1410
  60 Dream Ave Delco (28436) *(G-4722)*

Lrc, Cary *Also Called: Laser Recharge Carolina Inc (G-1808)*

Lrs Technology Inc (PA) 336 669-5982
  1802 Cotton Grove Rd Lexington (27292) *(G-9752)*

Lrw Holdings Inc 919 609-4172
  2310 Sparger Rd Ste B Durham (27705) *(G-5196)*

Ls Cable & System USA Inc 252 824-3553
  2801 Anaconda Rd Tarboro (27886) *(G-15112)*

Ls of Raleigh 919 457-0340
  10208 Cerny St Ste 210 Raleigh (27617) *(G-12980)*

LS Starrett Company 336 789-5141
  1372 Boggs Dr Mount Airy (27030) *(G-11540)*

Ls Woodworks, Wilmington *Also Called: Laborie Sons Cstm Wodworks LLC (G-16293)*

Lsa, Concord *Also Called: Lomar Specialty Advg Inc (G-4307)*

Lsc Communications Inc 704 889-5800
  10519 Industrial Dr Pineville (28134) *(G-12282)*

Lsg LLC 919 878-5500
  268 Hc Powers Rd Wallace (28466) *(G-15624)*

Lsrwm Corp 704 866-8533
  1225 Isley Rd Gastonia (28052) *(G-6445)*

Lsrwm Corp 704 866-8533
  1225 Isley Rd Gastonia (28052) *(G-6446)*

Ltd Industries LLC (PA) 704 897-2182
  5509 David Cox Rd Charlotte (28269) *(G-3105)*

Ltlb Holding Company (PA) 828 624-1460
  1350 4th St Dr Nw Hickory (28601) *(G-8089)*

Ltlb Holding Company 704 585-2908
  1095 Mcclain Rd Hiddenite (28636) *(G-8223)*

Lubrimetal Corporation 828 212-1083
  2889 Countryside Dr Granite Falls (28630) *(G-6742)*

Lubrizol Global Management Inc 704 865-7451
  207 Telegraph Dr Gastonia (28056) *(G-6447)*

Lucas Concrete Products Inc 704 525-9622
  401 Rountree Rd Charlotte (28217) *(G-3106)*

Lucerno Dynamics LLC 317 294-1395
  140 Towerview Ct Cary (27513) *(G-1820)*

Luck Fabrication Incorporated 336 498-0905
  616 New Salem Rd Randleman (27317) *(G-13476)*

Luck Stone - Pittsboro, Moncure *Also Called: Luck Stone Corporation (G-10625)*

Luck Stone Corporation 919 545-0027
  4189 Nc Highway 87 S Moncure (27559) *(G-10625)*

Luck Stone Corporation 336 786-4693
  525 Quarry Rd Mount Airy (27030) *(G-11541)*

Lucky Country USA LLC 828 428-8313
  3333 Finger Mill Rd Lincolnton (28092) *(G-9903)*

Lucky Landports 704 399-9880
  6510 Rozzelles Ferry Rd Charlotte (28214) *(G-3107)*

Lucky Man Inc (HQ) 828 251-0090
  160 Broadway St Asheville (28801) *(G-689)*

Lucky Tusk 704 985-1127
  1465 Us 52 North Albemarle (28001) *(G-95)*

Lucy In Rye LLC 828 586-4601
  612 W Main St Sylva (28779) *(G-15063)*

Lucy V Dierks Ceramics Inc 757 692-5145
  105 Kimberly Knoll Rd Asheville (28804) *(G-690)*

Ludlam Family Foods LLC (PA) 919 805-6061
  9 Saint James Pl Chapel Hill (27514) *(G-2035)*

Ludlam Family Foods LLC 919 805-6061
  1408 Christian Ave Ste 3 Durham (27705) *(G-5197)*

Ludwig Industries, Monroe *Also Called: Conn-Selmer Inc (G-10690)*

Lulaza Aerospace LLC 919 371-4240
  627 Distribution Dr Ste D Morrisville (27560) *(G-11384)*

Lullicoin LLC 336 955-1159
  3540 Toringdon Way Charlotte (28277) *(G-3108)*

Lulu Press Inc 919 447-3290
  700 Park Offices Dr Ste 250 Durham (27709) *(G-5198)*

Lulu Technology Circus Inc 919 459-5858
  860 Aviation Pkwy Ste 300 Morrisville (27560) *(G-11385)*

Lulu.com, Morrisville *Also Called: Lulu Technology Circus Inc (G-11385)*

Lululemon 336 723-3002
  312 S Stratford Rd Winston Salem (27103) *(G-16794)*

Lumedica Inc 919 886-1863
  1312 Dollar Ave Durham (27701) *(G-5199)*

Lumenfocus, Henderson *Also Called: Lumenfocus LLC (G-7796)*

Lumenfocus LLC 252 430-6970
  880 Facet Rd Henderson (27537) *(G-7796)*

Lumeova Inc 908 229-4651
  3801 Lake Boone Trl Ste 260 Raleigh (27607) *(G-12981)*

Lumina Embroidery LLC 910 371-1384
  734 Remount Ct Se Leland (28451) *(G-9553)*

Lumina News 910 256-6569
  7232 Wrightsville Ave Wilmington (28403) *(G-16309)*

Lumsden Steel, Wilmington *Also Called: Lumsden Welding Company (G-16310)*

Lumsden Welding Company 910 791-6336
  6736 Carolina Beach Rd Wilmington (28412) *(G-16310)*

Luna Metal Buildings and Con 336 628-0273
  468 N Fayetteville St Asheboro (27203) *(G-455)*

Lunar International Tech LLC 800 975-7153
  338 S Sharon Amity Rd Charlotte (28211) *(G-3109)*

Luray Textiles Inc 336 670-3725
  300 Luray Rd North Wilkesboro (28659) *(G-12025)*

Luray Textiles & Knitting, North Wilkesboro *Also Called: Luray Textiles Inc (G-12025)*

Lures Galore LLC 336 643-0948
  5243 Larue Ct Summerfield (27358) *(G-14987)*

Lustar Dyeing and Finshg Inc 828 274-2440
  144 Caribou Rd Asheville (28803) *(G-691)*

Lusty Monk LLC 828 645-5056
  29 Canoe Ln Asheville (28804) *(G-692)*

Lutheran Svcs For The Aging 910 457-5604
  4843 Southport Supply Rd Se Southport (28461) *(G-14574)*

Luthiers Workshop LLC 919 241-4578
  2207 Leah Dr Ste 102 Hillsborough (27278) *(G-8660)*

Lutze Inc 704 504-0222
  13330 S Ridge Dr Charlotte (28273) *(G-3110)*

Luxebright Skin Care, Matthews *Also Called: Luxebright Skin Care LLC (G-10264)*

Luxebright Skin Care LLC 877 614-9128
  2704 Cross Point Cir Apt 21 Matthews (28105) *(G-10264)*

Luxemark Company 919 863-0101
  6909 Glenwood Ave Ste 106 Raleigh (27612) *(G-12982)*

Luxfer, Graham *Also Called: Metal Impact East LLC (G-6702)*

Luxor Hydration LLC 919 568-5047
  3600 N Duke St Durham (27704) *(G-5200)*

Luxottica of America Inc 910 867-0200
  302 Cross Creek Mall Fayetteville (28303) *(G-5862)*

Luxottica of America Inc 919 778-5692
  611 N Berkeley Blvd Ste B Goldsboro (27534) *(G-6632)*

Luxuriously Natural Products 919 345-9050
  4158 Winchester Ln Franklinton (27525) *(G-6158)*

Luxury Escapes LLC 706 373-8500
  8480 Honeycutt Rd Ste 200 Raleigh (27615) *(G-12983)*

Luxury Tresses Collection LLC 910 501-4451
  1301 Franklin Ave Laurinburg (28352) *(G-9485)*

Lws Tools Inc 919 247-1913
  1139 Mabry Rd Angier (27501) *(G-146)*

Lxd Research & Display LLC 919 600-6440
  7516 Precision Dr Ste 100 Raleigh (27617) *(G-12984)*

Lydall Inc 336 468-8522
  1241 Buck Shoals Rd Hamptonville (27020) *(G-7674)*

Lydall Inc 336 468-1323
  2029 Anna Dr Yadkinville (27055) *(G-17044)*

Lydall Thermal/Acoustical Inc (DH) 336 468-8522
  1241 Buck Shoals Rd Hamptonville (27020) *(G-7675)*

Lydall Thermal/Acoustical Inc 336 468-8522
  1241 Buck Shoals Rd Hamptonville (27020) *(G-7676)*

Lyerlys Wldg & Fabrication Inc 704 680-2317
  215 Woodson Rd Gold Hill (28071) *(G-6584)*

Lyf-Tym Building Products ALPHABETIC SECTION

Lyf-Tym Building Products, Charlotte *Also Called: Beacon Roofing Supply Inc (G-2291)*

Lynchs Office Supply Co Inc (PA) 252 537-6041
921 Roanoke Ave Roanoke Rapids (27870) *(G-13578)*

Lyndon Steel Company LLC (DH) 336 785-0848
1947 Union Cross Rd Winston Salem (27107) *(G-16795)*

Lynn Electronics Corporation 704 369-0093
5409 Shoreview Dr Concord (28025) *(G-4308)*

Lynn Jones Race Cars 252 522-0705
1168 Woodington Rd Kinston (28504) *(G-9374)*

Lynn Ladder Scaffolding Co Inc 301 336-4700
3801 Corporation Cir Charlotte (28216) *(G-3111)*

Lynx Defense Corporation 919 701-9411
212 Ivey Rd Four Oaks (27524) *(G-6108)*

Lynx Outdoor Gear, Four Oaks *Also Called: Lynx Defense Corporation (G-6108)*

Lyon Logging 336 957-3131
3256 S Center Church Rd Thurmond (28683) *(G-15311)*

Lyon Metal & Supply, Hildebran *Also Called: Lyon Roofing Inc (G-8626)*

Lyon Roofing Inc 828 397-2301
323 S Center St Hildebran (28637) *(G-8626)*

Lyons Hosiery Inc 336 789-2651
719 S South St Mount Airy (27030) *(G-11542)*

M & A Equipment Inc (PA) 704 703-9400
7110 Expo Dr Ste D Charlotte (28269) *(G-3112)*

M & G Polymers Usa LLC 910 509-4414
1979 Eastwood Rd Wilmington (28403) *(G-16311)*

M & G Screen Service, Sanford *Also Called: Ralph B Hall (G-14173)*

M & J Marine LLC 252 249-0522
1218 Lupton Dr Oriental (28571) *(G-12111)*

M & J Stucco LLC 704 634-2249
Monroe (28111) *(G-10761)*

M & K Logging LLC 252 349-8975
310 Parker Rd New Bern (28562) *(G-11816)*

M & M Electric Service Inc 704 867-0221
1680 Garfield Dr Gastonia (28052) *(G-6448)*

M & M Electric Service NC, Gastonia *Also Called: M & M Electric Service Inc (G-6448)*

M & M Entps Banner Elk Inc 828 898-2401
318 Outback Ln Banner Elk (28604) *(G-902)*

M & M Frame Company Inc 336 859-8166
18847 S Nc Highway 109 Denton (27239) *(G-4745)*

M & M Graphics, Charlotte *Also Called: S&A Marketing Inc (G-3478)*

M & M Signs and Awnings Inc 336 352-4300
1465 Ladonia Church Rd Mount Airy (27030) *(G-11543)*

M & M Stone Sculpting & Engrv 336 877-3842
498 Carter Miller Rd Todd (28684) *(G-15323)*

M & M Technology Inc 704 882-9432
7711 Idlewild Rd Indian Trail (28079) *(G-8947)*

M & M Tire and Auto Inc 336 643-7877
5570 Spotswood Cir Summerfield (27358) *(G-14988)*

M & N Equipment Rental, Colfax *Also Called: M&N Construction Supply Inc (G-4154)*

M & P Polymers Inc 910 246-6585
135 Applecross Rd Pinehurst (28374) *(G-12227)*

M & R Forestry Service Inc 980 439-1261
24062 Sam Rd Albemarle (28001) *(G-96)*

M & R Retreading & Oil Co Inc 704 474-4101
337 W Whitley St Norwood (28128) *(G-12040)*

M & S Manufacturing, Lenoir *Also Called: M & S Warehouse Inc (G-9628)*

M & S Systems, Kernersville *Also Called: M & S Systems Inc (G-9211)*

M & S Systems Inc 336 996-7118
951 Nc Highway 66 S Ste 6b Kernersville (27284) *(G-9211)*

M & S Warehouse Inc (PA) 828 728-3733
1712 Hickory Blvd Lenoir (28645) *(G-9628)*

M & W Fab, Smithfield *Also Called: Ace Fabrication Inc (G-14448)*

M & W Industries Inc (PA) 704 837-0331
3426 Toringdon Way Ste 100 Charlotte (28277) *(G-3113)*

M 5 Scentific Glassblowing Inc 704 663-0101
706c Performance Rd Mooresville (28115) *(G-11012)*

M A I N, Asheville *Also Called: Mountain Area Info Netwrk (G-707)*

M and H Masonry 704 858-7230
503 N Bragg St Monroe (28112) *(G-10762)*

M and M Docks LLC 336 537-0092
10235 Nc Highway 8 Lexington (27292) *(G-9753)*

M and R Inc 704 332-5999
820 E 7th St Ste C Charlotte (28202) *(G-3114)*

M C B Displays, Greensboro *Also Called: Quality Prtg Cartridge Fctry (G-7301)*

M C C of Laurinburg Inc 910 276-0519
200 Johns Rd Laurinburg (28352) *(G-9486)*

M C H, Concord *Also Called: Moores Cylinder Heads LLC (G-4318)*

M D C Graphics LLC 336 454-6467
2410 E Martin Luther King Jr Dr High Point (27260) *(G-8434)*

M D I, Shelby *Also Called: Modern Densifying Inc (G-14348)*

M D N Cabinets, Garner *Also Called: MDN Cabinets Inc (G-6285)*

M D Prevatt Inc 919 796-4944
338 Winding Oak Way Clayton (27520) *(G-3994)*

M Davis and Associates LLC (PA) 336 337-7089
1918 Bradford St Greensboro (27405) *(G-7172)*

M F C Inc 252 322-5004
Hwy 33 Aurora (27806) *(G-836)*

M G Newell Corporation (PA) 336 393-0100
301 Citation Ct Greensboro (27409) *(G-7173)*

M H Investments, Fayetteville *Also Called: Muriel Harris Investments Inc (G-5879)*

M I, Durham *Also Called: Measurement Incorporated (G-5213)*

M I Connection 704 662-3255
435 S Broad St Mooresville (28115) *(G-11013)*

M J E J Inc 910 399-3795
3310 Kitty Hawk Rd Ste 100 Wilmington (28405) *(G-16312)*

M J Soffe Co (HQ) 910 435-3138
1 Soffe Dr Fayetteville (28312) *(G-5863)*

M M & D Harvesting Inc 252 793-4074
385 Roxie Reese Rd Plymouth (27962) *(G-12376)*

M M M Inc (PA) 252 527-0229
501 W Railroad St La Grange (28551) *(G-9443)*

M O Deviney Lumber Co Inc (PA) 704 538-9071
838 Moriah School Rd Casar (28020) *(G-1934)*

M P I Lable Systems Carolina, Charlotte *Also Called: Miller Products Inc (G-3182)*

M Press Inc 336 292-5005
3400 W Wendover Ave Greensboro (27407) *(G-7174)*

M S I Precision Machine Inc 704 629-9375
725 E Maine Ave Bessemer City (28016) *(G-1073)*

M T I, Mills River *Also Called: Medical Cable Specialists Inc (G-10507)*

M T Industries Inc 828 697-2864
1584 Airport Rd Hendersonville (28792) *(G-7874)*

M Vision Software Inc 703 530-9900
58 Highland View Dr Southern Pines (28387) *(G-14540)*

M-B Industries Inc 828 862-4201
9205 Rosman Hwy Rosman (28772) *(G-13786)*

M-M Components, Denton *Also Called: M & M Frame Company Inc (G-4745)*

M-Prints Inc 828 265-4929
713 W King St Boone (28607) *(G-1216)*

M.C. Exteriors, Fuquay Varina *Also Called: E & M Concrete Inc (G-6197)*

M.J. SOFFE, LLC, Rowland *Also Called: MJ Soffe LLC (G-13791)*

M&J Oldco Inc 336 854-0309
3515 W Market St Ste 200 Greensboro (27403) *(G-7175)*

M&M Bioplastic LLC 877 366-5227
4021 Highway 108 E Mill Spring (28756) *(G-10488)*

M&N Construction Supply Inc 336 996-7740
8431 Norcross Rd Colfax (27235) *(G-4154)*

M&N Construction Supply Inc 910 791-0908
323 Eastwood Rd Ste A Wilmington (28403) *(G-16313)*

M&S Enterprises Inc 910 259-1763
784 New Rd Burgaw (28425) *(G-1345)*

M2 Optics Inc 919 342-5619
5621 Departure Dr Ste 117 Raleigh (27616) *(G-12985)*

M3 Products Com 631 938-1245
1537 Golden Rain Dr Matthews (28104) *(G-10329)*

Maag Reduction Inc (HQ) 704 716-9000
9401 Southern Pine Blvd Ste Q Charlotte (28273) *(G-3115)*

Mable Mullen 252 599-1181
111 Bayberry Dr Elizabeth City (27909) *(G-5555)*

Mables Headstone & Monu Co LLP (PA) 919 724-8705
206 West Wilton Ave Creedmoor (27522) *(G-4618)*

Mabry Industries Inc 336 584-1311
2903 Gibsonville Ossipee Rd Elon College (27244) *(G-5666)*

ALPHABETIC SECTION

MAC Grading Co..910 531-4642
971 Leroy Autry Rd Autryville (28318) *(G-842)*

Mac Panel, High Point Also Called: Mac Panel Company *(G-8435)*

Mac Panel Company (PA)..336 861-3100
551 W Fairfield Rd High Point (27263) *(G-8435)*

Mac-Vann Inc...919 577-0746
4792 Rawls Church Rd Fuquay Varina (27526) *(G-6211)*

Mac/Fab Company Inc..704 822-1103
913 W Catawba Ave Mount Holly (28120) *(G-11641)*

Machine Builders & Design Inc................................704 482-3456
806 N Post Rd Shelby (28150) *(G-14340)*

Machine Consulting Svcs Inc...................................919 596-3033
1545 Cooper St Durham (27703) *(G-5201)*

Machine Control Company Inc.................................704 708-5782
1030 Industrial Dr Matthews (28105) *(G-10265)*

Machine Nunn Cnc Shop LLC....................................704 873-4931
1235 Old Mountain Rd Statesville (28677) *(G-14836)*

Machine Shop..910 246-0720
203 Country Ridge Ln Carthage (28327) *(G-1663)*

Machine Shop, Mooresville Also Called: Island Machining LLC *(G-10985)*

Machine Shop, Wilmington Also Called: Penco Precision LLC *(G-16350)*

Machine Shop of Charlotte, The, Mount Holly Also Called: Modern Mold & Tool Company *(G-11643)*

Machine Shop, Job Shop, Burlington Also Called: L & K Machining Inc *(G-1446)*

Machine Specialties LLC..336 603-1919
6511 Franz Warner Pkwy Whitsett (27377) *(G-15996)*

Machine Tool Components LLC................................866 466-0120
1507 Turring Dr Ste D Indian Trail (28079) *(G-8948)*

Machinery Sales...704 822-0110
7659 Old Plank Rd Stanley (28164) *(G-14701)*

Machinery Sales and Service, Stanley Also Called: Machinery Sales *(G-14701)*

Machinex..336 665-5030
716 Gallimore Dairy Rd High Point (27265) *(G-8436)*

Machinex Technologies Inc.....................................773 867-8801
716 Gallimore Dairy Rd High Point (27265) *(G-8437)*

Machining, Statesville Also Called: D & D Machine Works Inc *(G-14780)*

Machining Solutions Inc...704 528-5436
102 Corporate Dr Troutman (28166) *(G-15387)*

Machining Technology Services...............................704 282-1071
1817 N Rocky River Rd Monroe (28110) *(G-10763)*

Mack Industries...252 977-3733
4879 Us 301 N Elm City (27822) *(G-5651)*

Mack Molding Company Inc....................................704 878-9641
149 Water Tank Rd Statesville (28677) *(G-14837)*

Mack S Liver Mush Inc...704 434-6188
6126 Mckee Rd Shelby (28150) *(G-14341)*

Mack Trucks Inc..336 291-9064
496 Gallimore Dairy Rd Ste D Greensboro (27409) *(G-7176)*

Mack Trucks Inc (HQ)..336 291-9001
7900 National Service Rd Greensboro (27409) *(G-7177)*

Mack's Livermush & Meats, Shelby Also Called: Mack S Liver Mush Inc *(G-14341)*

Macleod Construction Inc (PA)...............................704 483-3580
4304 Northpointe Industrial Blvd Charlotte (28216) *(G-3116)*

Maco Inc...704 434-6800
521 Plato Lee Rd Shelby (28150) *(G-14342)*

Macom Technology Solutions Inc............................919 807-9100
523 Davis Dr Ste 500 Morrisville (27560) *(G-11386)*

Macon Printing, Franklin Also Called: Drake Enterprises Ltd *(G-6124)*

Macs Farms Sausage Co Inc....................................910 594-0095
209 Raleigh Rd Newton Grove (28366) *(G-11990)*

Mad Rush Media..336 816-3972
208 Oakwood Ct Winston Salem (27103) *(G-16796)*

Madame Gigi's Cottage, Apex Also Called: Renaissance Innovations LLC *(G-239)*

Made By Custom LLC...704 980-9840
3206 N Davidson St Charlotte (28205) *(G-3117)*

Madem-Moorecraft Reels USA Inc...........................252 823-2510
3006 Anaconda Rd Tarboro (27886) *(G-15113)*

Madern Usa Inc...919 363-4248
1010 Burma Dr Apex (27539) *(G-215)*

Madison Ave, Concord Also Called: Minka Lighting Inc *(G-4316)*

Madison Ave Cases..843 214-0476
1005 Deepwood Ct Winston Salem (27104) *(G-16797)*

Madison Company Inc (PA)....................................336 548-9624
200 W Academy St Madison (27025) *(G-10079)*

Madison Manufacturing Company...........................828 622-7500
172 S Andrews Ave Hot Springs (28743) *(G-8745)*

Madison Woodworking..704 634-1143
10015 Metromont Indstrl Charlotte (28269) *(G-3118)*

Madix...804 456-3007
2326 Hales Rd Raleigh (27608) *(G-12986)*

Mae Rodgers Cola..252 797-4253
1703 Davenport Fork Rd Creswell (27928) *(G-4626)*

Maelle Kids Inc..252 799-7312
252 W Pine St Williamston (27892) *(G-16065)*

Mafic USA LLC..704 967-8006
119 Metrolina Plz Shelby (28150) *(G-14343)*

Magazine Nakia Lashawn.......................................919 875-1156
2833 Roundleaf Ct Raleigh (27604) *(G-12987)*

Maggie Valley Sanitary Dst, Maggie Valley Also Called: Town of Maggie Valley Inc *(G-10096)*

Magic Mile Media Inc...252 572-1330
105 W Blount St Kinston (28501) *(G-9375)*

Magna Composites LLC..704 797-8744
6701 Statesville Blvd Salisbury (28147) *(G-14008)*

Magna Machining Inc...704 463-9904
111 3rd Park Dr Richfield (28137) *(G-13552)*

Magna Ready LLC..617 909-4166
7721 Harps Mill Rd Raleigh (27615) *(G-12988)*

Magna Sign Intl..813 727-0205
2200 Prairie Dog Dr Wake Forest (27587) *(G-15570)*

Magnarep Incorporated...919 949-5488
1618 Crystal Creek Dr Durham (27712) *(G-5202)*

Magnet America, King Also Called: Magnet America Inc *(G-9275)*

Magnet America Intl Inc..336 985-0320
512 Newsome Rd King (27021) *(G-9275)*

Magnet Guys...816 259-5201
100 Capitola Dr Ste 101 Durham (27713) *(G-5203)*

Magnevolt Inc..919 553-2202
5335 Us 70 Bus Hwy W Clayton (27520) *(G-3995)*

Magnificent Concessions LLC.................................919 413-1558
106 Northwinds North Dr Wendell (27591) *(G-15907)*

Magnum Enterprize Inc...252 524-5391
525 Country Acres Rd Grifton (28530) *(G-7601)*

Magnum Mobile Welding Wrap Up.........................910 372-3380
171 Reedy Ln Beulaville (28518) *(G-1095)*

Magnum Telemetry, Grifton Also Called: Magnum Enterprize Inc *(G-7601)*

Magnussen, Greensboro Also Called: Magnussen Home Furnishings Inc *(G-7178)*

Magnussen Home Furnishings Inc (HQ).................336 841-4424
4523 Green Point Dr Ste 109 Greensboro (27410) *(G-7178)*

Mahle Motorsports Inc..888 255-1942
270 Rutledge Rd Unit C Fletcher (28732) *(G-6020)*

Maia LLC...828 612-6109
3327 Henderson Mill Rd Morganton (28655) *(G-11230)*

Maia Stave, Morganton Also Called: Maia LLC *(G-11230)*

Maiden Casting Company......................................704 735-6812
3540 Anderson Mountain Rd Maiden (28650) *(G-10112)*

Mail Box Book Company, The, Greensboro Also Called: M&J Oldco Inc *(G-7175)*

Mail Management Services LLC..............................828 236-0076
88 Roberts St Asheville (28801) *(G-693)*

Mailbox, The, Oak Ridge Also Called: Education Center LLC *(G-12059)*

Mailing Solutions Plus, Mooresville Also Called: Executive Promotions Inc *(G-10940)*

Main Filter LLC..704 735-0009
1443 E Gaston St Lincolnton (28092) *(G-9904)*

Main Street Monograms..704 233-5393
411 Maye St Wingate (28174) *(G-16576)*

Main Street Rag Publishing Co...............................704 573-2516
4614 Wilgrove Mint Hill Rd Ste G3 Mint Hill (28227) *(G-10538)*

Main Street Vinyl LLC..336 585-3089
321 S Main St Burlington (27215) *(G-1453)*

Maines Woodworks Cstm Mil LLC...........................336 263-0799
1224 Crowsnest Dr Hurdle Mills (27541) *(G-8910)*

Maiweave, Salisbury Also Called: Intertape Polymer Corp *(G-13988)*

Majestic Xpress Handwash Inc 919 440-7611
103 N John St Ste D Goldsboro (27530) *(G-6633)*

Majic TNT Inc 252 425-0489
419 E Starmount Ave Liberty (27298) *(G-9824)*

Major Display Inc 800 260-1067
131 Franklin Plaza Dr Ste 363 Franklin (28734) *(G-6137)*

Majorpharma US Inc 919 799-2010
4801 Glenwood Ave Raleigh (27612) *(G-12989)*

Majorpower Corporation 919 563-6610
7011 Industrial Dr Mebane (27302) *(G-10418)*

Make An Impression Inc 919 557-7400
202 Premier Dr Holly Springs (27540) *(G-8707)*

Make Solutions Inc 623 444-0098
23 Tacoma St Asheville (28801) *(G-694)*

Makhteshim Agan North Amer Inc (DH) 919 256-9300
8601 Six Forks Rd Ste 300 Raleigh (27615) *(G-12990)*

Malcolms Metal & More 828 286-1419
356 Winnies Rd Bostic (28018) *(G-1263)*

Malinda Rackley 252 886-3315
1384 Northridge Dr Rocky Mount (27804) *(G-13709)*

Mallard Creek Polymers, Charlotte *Also Called: Mallard Creek Polymers LLC (G-3121)*

Mallard Creek Polymers LLC 877 240-0171
2800 Morehead Rd Charlotte (28262) *(G-3119)*

Mallard Creek Polymers LLC 704 547-0622
14800 Mallard Creek Rd Charlotte (28262) *(G-3120)*

Mallard Creek Polymers LLC (PA) 704 547-0622
8901 Research Dr Charlotte (28262) *(G-3121)*

Mallard Creek Polymers LLC 704 547-0622
2388 Speedrail Dr Harrisburg (28075) *(G-7716)*

Mallinckrodt LLC 919 878-2800
8801 Capital Blvd Raleigh (27616) *(G-12991)*

Mallinckrodt LLC 919 878-2900
8800 Durant Rd Raleigh (27616) *(G-12992)*

Mama Neds Subscription Box LLC 954 703-9308
2880 Old Murphy Rd Franklin (28734) *(G-6138)*

Mammoth Industries LLC 919 749-8183
8013 Wesley Farm Dr Raleigh (27616) *(G-12993)*

Mammoth Machine and Design LLC 704 727-3330
197 Pitt Rd Mooresville (28115) *(G-11014)*

Man Around House 919 625-5933
908 Grandview Dr Durham (27703) *(G-5204)*

Man Lift, Shelby *Also Called: If Armor International LLC (G-14329)*

Man Lift Mfg Co 414 486-1760
2501 W Dixon Blvd Shelby (28152) *(G-14344)*

Mana Nutrition, Matthews *Also Called: Mana Nutritive Aid Pdts Inc (G-10266)*

Mana Nutritive Aid Pdts Inc (PA) 855 438-6262
130 Library Ln Ste A Matthews (28105) *(G-10266)*

Manda Pandas LLC 919 452-7917
109 Stinhurst Dr Durham (27713) *(G-5205)*

Mang Systems Inc 704 292-1041
500 Union West Blvd Ste B Matthews (28104) *(G-10330)*

Manhattan Amrcn Terrazzo Strip 336 622-4247
2433 Us Hwy 421 Staley (27355) *(G-14667)*

Manhattan Woodworking Inc 704 528-5733
302 Compton Park Rd Statesville (28677) *(G-14838)*

Mann Custom Boats Inc 252 473-1716
6300 Us Highway 64 # 264 Manns Harbor (27953) *(G-10122)*

Mann Media Inc 336 286-0600
800 Green Valley Rd Ste 106 Greensboro (27408) *(G-7179)*

Mann+hmmel Fltrtion Tech Group (DH) 704 869-3300
1 Wix Way Gastonia (28054) *(G-6449)*

Mann+hmmel Fltrtion Tech Intrm (DH) 704 869-3300
1 Wix Way Gastonia (28054) *(G-6450)*

Mann+hmmel Fltrtion Tech US LL 704 869-3700
1 Wix Way Gastonia (28054) *(G-6451)*

Mann+hmmel Fltrtion Tech US LL (DH) 704 869-3300
1 Wix Way Gastonia (28054) *(G-6452)*

Mann+hmmel Prlator Filters LLC (DH) 910 425-4181
3200 Natal St Ste 64069 Fayetteville (28306) *(G-5864)*

Mann+hmmel Prlator Filters LLC 910 425-4181
3200 Natal St Fayetteville (28306) *(G-5865)*

Mann+hmmel Prlator Filters LLC 704 869-3441
1 Wix Way Gastonia (28054) *(G-6453)*

Mann+hummel Filtration Technol 704 869-3500
2900 Northwest Blvd Gastonia (28052) *(G-6454)*

Mann+hummel Filtration Technol 704 869-3952
1551 Mount Olive Church Rd Gastonia (28052) *(G-6455)*

Mann+hummel Filtration Technol 704 869-3501
2900 Northwest Blvd Gastonia (28052) *(G-6456)*

Mann+hummel Filtration Technology Holdings Inc 704 869-3300
1 Wix Way Gastonia (28054) *(G-6457)*

Manna Corp North Carolina (PA) 828 696-3642
508 N Main St Hendersonville (28792) *(G-7875)*

Manna Designs, Hendersonville *Also Called: Manna Corp North Carolina (G-7875)*

Mannhmmel Fltration Tech Group, Gastonia *Also Called: Mann+hmmel Fltrtion Tech US LL (G-6452)*

Manning and Co., Pinehurst *Also Called: Manning Fabrics Inc (G-12228)*

Manning Building Products LLC 919 662-9894
108 Professional Ct Ste A Garner (27529) *(G-6282)*

Manning Fabrics Inc 910 295-1970
42028 Us 1 Hwy Pinebluff (28373) *(G-12215)*

Manning Fabrics Inc (PA) 910 295-1970
650a Page St Pinehurst (28374) *(G-12228)*

Mannington Mills Inc 336 884-5600
210 N Pendleton St High Point (27260) *(G-8438)*

Mannington Mills Inc 704 824-3551
200 Saxony Dr Mc Adenville (28101) *(G-10379)*

Manroy Defense Systems, Spindale *Also Called: Manroy Usa LLC (G-14608)*

Manroy Usa LLC 828 286-9274
159 Yelton St Spindale (28160) *(G-14608)*

Mantissa Corporation 704 525-1749
616 Pressley Rd Charlotte (28217) *(G-3122)*

Mantissa Material Handling, Charlotte *Also Called: Mantissa Corporation (G-3122)*

Manual Woodworkers Weavers Inc (PA) 828 692-7333
3737 Howard Gap Rd Hendersonville (28792) *(G-7876)*

Manufactur LLC 919 937-2090
201 W Main St Durham (27701) *(G-5206)*

Manufacturer, Hickory *Also Called: Purthermal LLC (G-8129)*

Manufacturing, Fuquay Varina *Also Called: Boehrnger Inglheim Anmal Hlth (G-6185)*

Manufacturing, Raleigh *Also Called: Progress Solar Solutions LLC (G-13150)*

Manufacturing, Rocky Mount *Also Called: Babington Technology LLC (G-13682)*

Manufacturing Analysis Inc 919 434-3005
106 Amber Ct Carrboro (27510) *(G-1649)*

Manufacturing Methods LLC 910 371-1700
9244 Industrial Blvd Ne Leland (28451) *(G-9554)*

Manufacturing Services Inc 704 629-4163
725 E Maine Ave Bessemer City (28016) *(G-1074)*

Manufacturing Strategies LLC 828 758-9092
1301 Mountain Circle Dr Lenoir (28645) *(G-9629)*

Manufacturing Structures LLC 828 264-6198
355 Industrial Park Dr Boone (28607) *(G-1217)*

Manufacturing Systems Eqp Inc 704 283-2086
2812 Chamber Dr Monroe (28110) *(G-10764)*

Maola Milk and Ice Cream Co 252 756-3160
107 Hungate Dr Greenville (27858) *(G-7557)*

Maola Milk and Ice Cream Co 844 287-1970
307 N First Ave New Bern (28560) *(G-11817)*

MAOLA MILK AND ICE CREAM COMPANY, Greenville *Also Called: Maola Milk and Ice Cream Co (G-7557)*

Map Shop LLC 704 332-5557
3421 St Vardell Ln Ste H Charlotte (28217) *(G-3123)*

Map Supply Inc 336 731-3230
132 Poplar Loop Dr Flat Rock (28731) *(G-5969)*

Mapjoy LLC 919 450-8360
4501 Marena Pl Durham (27707) *(G-5207)*

Maple View Ice Cream 919 960-5535
6900 Rocky Ridge Rd Hillsborough (27278) *(G-8661)*

Maplewood Imaging Ctr 336 397-6000
3155 Maplewood Ave Winston Salem (27103) *(G-16798)*

Maplight Therapeutics Inc 603 553-9013
1240 Sugg Pkwy Greenville (27834) *(G-7558)*

Maranz Inc 336 996-7776
2860 Lowery St Winston Salem (27101) *(G-16799)*

ALPHABETIC SECTION — Marsh Furniture Company

Marathon Publications Inc 651 341-4202
  1068 Maplewood Ct Hendersonville (28791) *(G-7877)*
Marbach America Inc 704 644-4900
  100 Forsyth Hall Dr Ste B Charlotte (28273) *(G-3124)*
Marc Machine Works Inc 704 865-3625
  5042 York Hwy Gastonia (28052) *(G-6458)*
Marc Staples Sculpture 919 475-9633
  3801 Shoccoree Dr Durham (27705) *(G-5208)*
Marcal Paper Mills LLC 828 322-1805
  612 3rd Ave Ne Hickory (28601) *(G-8090)*
March Furniture Manufacturing Inc 336 824-4413
  447 Reed Creek Rd Ramseur (27316) *(G-13447)*
Marching Orders Incorporated 336 497-4251
  1014 Grays Land Ct Apt 125 Kernersville (27284) *(G-9212)*
Marco Pproducts, New Bern Also Called: Marco Products Inc *(G-11818)*
Marco Products Inc 215 956-0313
  214 Kale Rd New Bern (28562) *(G-11818)*
Marcon International 704 455-9400
  5679 Harrisburg Ind Pk Dr Harrisburg (28075) *(G-7717)*
Marcott Hosiery LLC 704 485-8702
  349 Rocky River Rd Oakboro (28129) *(G-12077)*
Marian Manufacturing Plant, Marion Also Called: ABB Motors and Mechanical Inc *(G-10137)*
Marie Sharps Usa LLC 336 701-0377
  1976 Runnymede Rd Winston Salem (27104) *(G-16800)*
Marietta Martin Materials Inc 704 525-7740
  8701 Red Oak Blvd Ste 540 Charlotte (28217) *(G-3125)*
Marietta Martin Materials Inc 252 749-2641
  5368 Allen Gay Rd Fountain (27829) *(G-6095)*
Marietta Martin Materials Inc 919 772-3563
  1111 E Garner Rd Garner (27529) *(G-6283)*
Marietta Martin Materials Inc 336 668-3253
  413 S Chimney Rock Rd Greensboro (27409) *(G-7180)*
Marietta Martin Materials Inc 828 322-8386
  1989 11th Ave Se Hickory (28602) *(G-8091)*
Marietta Martin Materials Inc 336 886-5015
  5725 Riverdale Dr Jamestown (27282) *(G-9060)*
Marietta Martin Materials Inc 336 769-3803
  4572 High Point Rd Kernersville (27284) *(G-9213)*
Marietta Martin Materials Inc 704 739-4761
  181 Quarry Rd Kings Mountain (28086) *(G-9317)*
Marietta Martin Materials Inc 910 743-6471
  2998 Belgrade Swansboro Rd Maysville (28555) *(G-10374)*
Marietta Martin Materials Inc 704 283-4915
  2111 N Rocky River Rd Monroe (28110) *(G-10765)*
Marietta Martin Materials Inc 919 788-4392
  6028 Triangle Dr Raleigh (27617) *(G-12994)*
Marietta Martin Materials Inc 336 349-3333
  7639 Nc Highway 87 Reidsville (27320) *(G-13530)*
Marietta Martin Materials Inc 704 636-6372
  3825 Trexler St Salisbury (28147) *(G-14009)*
Marietta Martin Materials Inc 704 873-8191
  220 Quarry Rd Statesville (28677) *(G-14839)*
Marietta Martin Materials Inc 336 475-9134
  691 Upper Lake Rd Thomasville (27360) *(G-15245)*
Marietta Martin Materials Inc 704 278-2218
  720 Quarry Rd Woodleaf (27054) *(G-17023)*
Marilyn Cook 704 735-4414
  2628 Buffalo Forest Rd Lincolnton (28092) *(G-9905)*
Marine & Industrial Plastics 252 224-1000
  Hwy 17 Sermon Lane Pollocksville (28573) *(G-12393)*
Marine Fabrications LLC 252 473-4767
  31 Beverly Dr Wanchese (27981) *(G-15649)*
Marine Systems Inc 828 254-5354
  7 Westside Dr Asheville (28806) *(G-695)*
Marine Tooling Technology Inc 336 887-9577
  2100 E Martin Luther King Jr Dr Ste 106 High Point (27260) *(G-8439)*
Marinemax, Wrightsville Beach Also Called: Marinemax of North Carolina *(G-17026)*
Marinemax of North Carolina 910 256-8100
  130 Short St Wrightsville Beach (28480) *(G-17026)*
Marion Cultured Marble Inc 828 724-4782
  4805 Highway 70 W Marion (28752) *(G-10157)*
Marion Machine Div, Marion Also Called: Superior Machine Co SC Inc *(G-10181)*
Marion Machine LLC 800 627-1639
  169 Machine Shop Rd Marion (28752) *(G-10158)*
Mariscos Nayarit Corp Inc 919 615-4347
  1428 Garner Station Blvd Raleigh (27603) *(G-12995)*
Mark III Logging Inc 910 862-4820
  16324 Nc Highway 87 W Tar Heel (28392) *(G-15089)*
Mark Johnson 919 834-1157
  204 Plainview Ave Raleigh (27604) *(G-12996)*
Mark L Wood 919 977-6507
  1140 Stone Kirk Dr Raleigh (27614) *(G-12997)*
Mark Lindsay Looper 828 234-5453
  6290 Duck Creek Rd Lenoir (28645) *(G-9630)*
Mark Stoddard 910 797-7214
  1935 Brawley Ave Fayetteville (28314) *(G-5866)*
Mark T Galvin 828 627-0823
  324 Upper Crabtree Rd Clyde (28721) *(G-4126)*
Mark Trece, Greensboro Also Called: Mark/Trece Inc *(G-7181)*
Mark W McKenzie 860 529-2476
  182 Isham Dr Bostic (28018) *(G-1264)*
Mark/Trece Inc 973 884-1005
  902 Norwalk St Greensboro (27407) *(G-7181)*
Mark/Trece Inc 336 292-3424
  6799 Leaf Crest Dr Apt 2c Whitsett (27377) *(G-15997)*
Markell Printing and Prom Pdts, Burlington Also Called: Markell Publishing Company Inc *(G-1454)*
Markell Publishing Company Inc 336 226-7148
  718 E Davis St Burlington (27215) *(G-1454)*
Market of Raleigh LLC 919 212-2100
  4111 New Bern Ave Raleigh (27610) *(G-12998)*
Marketing One Sportswear Inc 704 334-9333
  3101 Yorkmont Rd Ste 1100 Charlotte (28208) *(G-3126)*
Markets Global Publishing 828 783-0599
  15 Deer Park Loop Apt A1 Spruce Pine (28777) *(G-14645)*
Markham Woodworks LLC 252 492-5823
  82 Epsom Rocky Ford Rd Henderson (27537) *(G-7797)*
Markraft Cabinets Direct Sales 910 762-1986
  2422 Castle Hayne Rd Wilmington (28401) *(G-16314)*
Marlatex Corporation 704 829-7797
  8425 Winged Bourne Charlotte (28210) *(G-3127)*
Marley Company LLC (DH) 704 752-4400
  13515 Ballantyne Corporate Pl Charlotte (28277) *(G-3128)*
Marley-Wylain Company 336 627-6000
  523 S New St Eden (27288) *(G-5497)*
Marlin Company Inc 828 758-9999
  1211 Underdown Ave Sw Lenoir (28645) *(G-9631)*
Marlin Company Inc (HQ) 828 754-0980
  1333 Virginia St Sw Lenoir (28645) *(G-9632)*
Marlinwoodworks LLC 919 343-2605
  50 Otto Rd Lillington (27546) *(G-9856)*
Marlowe Loans Sales, High Point Also Called: Marlowe-Van Loan Corporation *(G-8440)*
Marlowe-Van Loan Corporation 336 886-7126
  1224 W Ward Ave High Point (27260) *(G-8440)*
Marlowe-Van Loan Sales Co 336 882-3351
  1224 W Ward Ave High Point (27260) *(G-8441)*
Marmon Engine Controls LLC 843 701-5145
  2519 Dana Dr Laurinburg (28352) *(G-9487)*
Marmon Holdings Inc 910 291-2571
  2519 Dana Dr Laurinburg (28352) *(G-9488)*
Marmon Powertrain Controls, Aberdeen Also Called: Rostra Precision Controls Inc *(G-27)*
Marmonpowertrain, Laurinburg Also Called: Marmon Engine Controls LLC *(G-9487)*
Marpac LLC (PA) 910 602-1421
  3870 Us Highway 421 N Wilmington (28401) *(G-16315)*
Marquis Contract Corporation (PA) 336 884-8200
  231 South Rd High Point (27262) *(G-8442)*
Marquis Seating, High Point Also Called: Marquis Contract Corporation *(G-8442)*
Marrone Bio Innovations, Raleigh Also Called: Pro Farm Group Inc *(G-13147)*
Mars Petcare Us Inc 252 438-1600
  845 Commerce Dr Henderson (27537) *(G-7798)*
Marsh Furniture Company 336 229-5122
  605 W Harden St Graham (27253) *(G-6700)*

Marsh Furniture Company...... 336 273-8196
2503 Greengate Dr Greensboro (27406) *(G-7182)*

Marsh Furniture Company...... 336 884-7393
1015 S Centennial St High Point (27260) *(G-8443)*

Marsh Furniture Company (PA)...... 336 884-7363
1001 S Centennial St High Point (27260) *(G-8444)*

Marsh Furniture Company...... 336 765-7832
420 Jonestown Rd Ste D Winston Salem (27104) *(G-16801)*

Marsh Kitchens, High Point Also Called: Marsh Furniture Company *(G-8444)*

Marsh Kitchens, Winston Salem Also Called: Marsh Furniture Company *(G-16801)*

Marsh Kitchens of High Point, High Point Also Called: Marsh Furniture Company *(G-8443)*

Marsh Welding...... 919 335-5332
1608 Sherron Rd Durham (27703) *(G-5209)*

Marsh-Armfield Incorporated...... 336 882-4175
1237 Hickory Chapel Rd High Point (27260) *(G-8445)*

Marshall Air Systems Inc...... 704 525-6230
419 Peachtree Dr S Charlotte (28217) *(G-3129)*

Marshall Group of NC Inc...... 252 638-8585
2400 Trent Rd New Bern (28562) *(G-11819)*

Marshall Middleby Inc...... 919 762-1000
1100 Old Honeycutt Rd Fuquay Varina (27526) *(G-6212)*

Marshall USA LLC...... 301 481-1241
111 W Lewis St Greensboro (27406) *(G-7183)*

Marties Miniatures...... 336 869-5952
392 Northbridge Dr High Point (27265) *(G-8446)*

Martin Industries, Albemarle Also Called: Ram Industries Inc *(G-102)*

Martin Innovations, Rocky Mount Also Called: Martin Manufacturing Co LLC *(G-13710)*

Martin Logging, Bostic Also Called: Eric Martin Jermey *(G-1262)*

Martin Lumber & Mulch LLC...... 252 935-5294
301 Mainstem Rd Pantego (27860) *(G-12167)*

Martin Manufacturing Co LLC...... 919 741-5439
2585 Eastern Ave Rocky Mount (27804) *(G-13710)*

Martin Marietta, Garner Also Called: Marietta Martin Materials Inc *(G-6283)*

Martin Marietta, Raleigh Also Called: Martin Marietta Materials Inc *(G-13001)*

Martin Marietta, Randleman Also Called: Martin Marietta Materials Inc *(G-13478)*

Martin Marietta Aggregates, Benson Also Called: Martin Marietta Materials Inc *(G-1039)*

Martin Marietta Aggregates, Burlington Also Called: Martin Marietta Materials Inc *(G-1455)*

Martin Marietta Aggregates, Castle Hayne Also Called: Martin Marietta Materials Inc *(G-1953)*

Martin Marietta Aggregates, Charlotte Also Called: Marietta Martin Materials Inc *(G-3125)*

Martin Marietta Aggregates, Charlotte Also Called: Martin Marietta Materials Inc *(G-3130)*

Martin Marietta Aggregates, Charlotte Also Called: Martin Marietta Materials Inc *(G-3131)*

Martin Marietta Aggregates, Charlotte Also Called: Martin Marietta Materials Inc *(G-3132)*

Martin Marietta Aggregates, China Grove Also Called: Martin Marietta Materials Inc *(G-3885)*

Martin Marietta Aggregates, Concord Also Called: Martin Marietta Materials Inc *(G-4309)*

Martin Marietta Aggregates, Fountain Also Called: Martin Marietta Materials Inc *(G-6095)*

Martin Marietta Aggregates, Fuquay Varina Also Called: Martin Marietta Materials Inc *(G-6213)*

Martin Marietta Aggregates, Greensboro Also Called: Marietta Martin Materials Inc *(G-7180)*

Martin Marietta Aggregates, Greensboro Also Called: Martin Marietta Materials Inc *(G-7184)*

Martin Marietta Aggregates, Greensboro Also Called: Martin Marietta Materials Inc *(G-7185)*

Martin Marietta Aggregates, Hickory Also Called: Marietta Martin Materials Inc *(G-8091)*

Martin Marietta Aggregates, Kings Mountain Also Called: Marietta Martin Materials Inc *(G-9317)*

Martin Marietta Aggregates, Landis Also Called: Martin Marietta Materials Inc *(G-9451)*

Martin Marietta Aggregates, Leland Also Called: Martin Marietta Materials Inc *(G-9555)*

Martin Marietta Aggregates, Lenoir Also Called: Martin Marietta Materials Inc *(G-9633)*

Martin Marietta Aggregates, Matthews Also Called: Martin Marietta Materials Inc *(G-10267)*

Martin Marietta Aggregates, Maysville Also Called: Marietta Martin Materials Inc *(G-10374)*

Martin Marietta Aggregates, Monroe Also Called: Martin Marietta Materials Inc *(G-10765)*

Martin Marietta Aggregates, New Bern Also Called: Martin Marietta Materials Inc *(G-11820)*

Martin Marietta Aggregates, Raleigh Also Called: Marietta Martin Materials Inc *(G-12994)*

Martin Marietta Aggregates, Raleigh Also Called: Marietta Martin Materials Inc *(G-13000)*

Martin Marietta Aggregates, Randleman Also Called: Martin Marietta Materials Inc *(G-13477)*

Martin Marietta Aggregates, Reidsville Also Called: Martin Marietta Materials Inc *(G-13530)*

Martin Marietta Aggregates, Richlands Also Called: Martin Marietta Materials Inc *(G-13556)*

Martin Marietta Aggregates, Salisbury Also Called: Marietta Martin Materials Inc *(G-14009)*

Martin Marietta Aggregates, Sanford Also Called: Martin Marietta Materials Inc *(G-14149)*

Martin Marietta Aggregates, Statesville Also Called: Marietta Martin Materials Inc *(G-14839)*

Martin Marietta Aggregates, Thomasville Also Called: Marietta Martin Materials Inc *(G-15245)*

Martin Marietta Aggregates, Woodleaf Also Called: Marietta Martin Materials Inc *(G-17023)*

Martin Marietta Materia...... 336 372-6311
140 S Sparta Pkwy Sparta (28675) *(G-14596)*

Martin Marietta Materials Inc...... 919 894-2003
13661 Raleigh Rd Benson (27504) *(G-1039)*

Martin Marietta Materials Inc...... 336 584-8875
1671 Huffman Mill Rd Burlington (27215) *(G-1455)*

Martin Marietta Materials Inc...... 910 675-2283
5408 Holly Shelter Rd Castle Hayne (28429) *(G-1953)*

Martin Marietta Materials Inc...... 910 602-6058
5635 Holly Shelter Rd Castle Hayne (28429) *(G-1954)*

Martin Marietta Materials Inc...... 919 929-7131
1807 Hwy 54 W Chapel Hill (27516) *(G-2036)*

Martin Marietta Materials Inc...... 704 392-1333
4551 Beatties Ford Rd Charlotte (28216) *(G-3130)*

Martin Marietta Materials Inc...... 704 547-9775
575 E Mallard Creek Church Rd Charlotte (28262) *(G-3131)*

Martin Marietta Materials Inc...... 704 588-1471
11325 Texland Blvd Charlotte (28273) *(G-3132)*

Martin Marietta Materials Inc...... 704 932-4377
2270 China Grove Rd China Grove (28023) *(G-3885)*

Martin Marietta Materials Inc...... 704 786-8415
7219 Weddington Rd Nw Concord (28027) *(G-4309)*

Martin Marietta Materials Inc...... 919 557-7412
7400 Buckhorn Duncan Road Fuquay Varina (27526) *(G-6213)*

Martin Marietta Materials Inc...... 336 375-7584
5800 Eckerson Rd Greensboro (27405) *(G-7184)*

Martin Marietta Materials Inc...... 336 674-0836
3957 Liberty Rd Greensboro (27406) *(G-7185)*

Martin Marietta Materials Inc...... 704 932-4379
Landis (28088) *(G-9451)*

Martin Marietta Materials Inc...... 910 371-3848
1635 Malmo Loop Rd Ne Leland (28451) *(G-9555)*

Martin Marietta Materials Inc...... 828 754-3077
1325 Bradford Mountain Rd Lenoir (28645) *(G-9633)*

Martin Marietta Materials Inc...... 704 847-3087
1601 Sam Newell Rd Matthews (28105) *(G-10267)*

Martin Marietta Materials Inc...... 252 633-5308
1315 Old Us 70 W New Bern (28560) *(G-11820)*

Martin Marietta Materials Inc...... 360 424-3441
4123 Parklake Ave Raleigh (27612) *(G-12999)*

Martin Marietta Materials Inc...... 919 863-4305
2501 Blue Ridge Rd Raleigh (27607) *(G-13000)*

Martin Marietta Materials Inc (PA)...... 919 781-4550
4123 Parklake Ave Raleigh (27612) *(G-13001)*

Martin Marietta Materials Inc...... 919 664-1700
2235 Gateway Access Pt Ste 400 Raleigh (27607) *(G-13002)*

Martin Marietta Materials Inc...... 336 672-1501
2757 Hopewood Rd Randleman (27317) *(G-13477)*

Martin Marietta Materials Inc...... 336 672-1501
2757 Hopewood Rd Randleman (27317) *(G-13478)*

Martin Marietta Materials Inc...... 910 324-7430
131 Duffy Field Rd Richlands (28574) *(G-13556)*

Martin Marietta Materials Inc...... 919 788-4391
1227 Willett Rd Sanford (27332) *(G-14149)*

Martin Materials Inc...... 336 697-1800
4801 Burlington Rd Greensboro (27405) *(G-7186)*

Martin Meats, Godwin Also Called: Coastal Protein Products Inc *(G-6577)*

Martin Obrien Cabinetmaker...... 336 773-1334
1940 Brantley St Winston Salem (27103) *(G-16802)*

Martin Sprocket & Gear Inc...... 817 258-3000
306 Bethany Rd Albemarle (28001) *(G-97)*

Martin Sprocket & Gear Inc...... 704 394-9111
3901 Scott Futrell Dr Charlotte (28208) *(G-3133)*

Martin Welding Inc...... 919 436-8805
816 Old Crowder Dr Garner (27529) *(G-6284)*

Martin Wood Products Inc...... 336 548-3470
680 Bald Hill Loop Madison (27025) *(G-10080)*

Martinez Wldg Fabrication Corp...... 919 957-8904
2901 Carpenter Pond Rd Raleigh (27613) *(G-13003)*

ALPHABETIC SECTION — Matthew Warren Inc

Martins Fmous Pstry Shoppe Inc 800 548-1200
1933 Scott Futrell Dr Charlotte (28208) *(G-3134)*

Martins Fmous Pstry Shoppe Inc 800 548-1200
2320 Southern Ave Fayetteville (28306) *(G-5867)*

Martins Fmous Pstry Shoppe Inc 800 548-1200
1031 E Mountain St Bldg 314 Kernersville (27284) *(G-9214)*

Martins Woodworking, Lattimore *Also Called: Martins Woodworking LLC (G-9458)*

Martins Woodworking LLC 704 473-7617
100 Martin St Lattimore (28089) *(G-9458)*

Marus Dental, Charlotte *Also Called: Dental Equipment LLC (G-2617)*

Marvel-Schbler Arcft Crbrtors 336 446-0002
2208 Airpark Rd Burlington (27215) *(G-1456)*

Marvell Semiconductor Inc 408 222-2500
3015 Carrington Mill Blvd Morrisville (27560) *(G-11387)*

Marves Industries Inc 828 397-4400
205 Cline Park Dr Hildebran (28637) *(G-8627)*

Marvica McLendon LLC 704 965-9408
5906 Old Coach Rd Charlotte (28215) *(G-3135)*

Marvida Acres LLC 336 392-0414
2011 Vanstory St Greensboro (27403) *(G-7187)*

Marvin Bailey Screen Printing 252 335-1554
1403 N Road St Elizabeth City (27909) *(G-5556)*

Marvin Saltzman 919 942-7091
717 Emory Dr Chapel Hill (27517) *(G-2037)*

Marx LLC 828 396-6700
4276 Helena St Granite Falls (28630) *(G-6743)*

Marx Industries, Hudson *Also Called: Marx Industries Incorporated (G-8775)*

Marx Industries Incorporated 828 396-6700
4276 Helena St Hudson (28638) *(G-8775)*

Mary Bogest Impressions 336 848-0910
2913 Mossy Meadow Dr High Point (27265) *(G-8447)*

Mary Kay Inc 336 998-1663
685 Redland Rd Advance (27006) *(G-46)*

Mary Macks Inc 770 234-6333
214 Armory Dr Clinton (28328) *(G-4097)*

Mas Acme USA 336 625-2161
159 North St Asheboro (27203) *(G-456)*

Mas Defense LLC 980 265-1005
8334 Pineville Matthews Rd Ste 103 Charlotte (28226) *(G-3136)*

Masco, Mooresville *Also Called: Masco Corporation (G-11015)*

Masco Corporation 704 658-9646
344 E Plaza Dr Mooresville (28115) *(G-11015)*

Mason Inlet Distillery LLC 910 200-4584
611 Everbreeze Ln Wilmington (28411) *(G-16316)*

Mason International 704 921-3407
1525 E Worthington Ave Charlotte (28203) *(G-3137)*

Masonite Corporation 704 599-0235
7300 Reames Rd Charlotte (28216) *(G-3138)*

Masonite International Corp 919 575-3700
1712 E D St Butner (27509) *(G-1545)*

Masonry Reinforcing Corp Amer (PA) 704 525-5554
400 Rountree Rd Charlotte (28217) *(G-3139)*

Mass Connection Inc 910 424-0940
2828 Enterprise Ave Fayetteville (28306) *(G-5868)*

Mass Enterprises LLC 443 585-0732
4310 Us Highway 70 E New Bern (28560) *(G-11821)*

Massey Ready-Mix Concrete Inc 336 221-8100
1421 Railroad St Burlington (27217) *(G-1457)*

Mast General Store Inc 423 895-1632
996 George Wilson Rd Boone (28607) *(G-1218)*

Mast General Store CPC, Boone *Also Called: Mast General Store Inc (G-1218)*

Mast Woodworks 336 468-1194
5328 Saint Paul Church Rd Hamptonville (27020) *(G-7677)*

Master Displays Inc 336 884-5575
5657 Prospect St High Point (27263) *(G-8448)*

Master Form Inc 704 292-1041
500 Union West Blvd Ste B Matthews (28104) *(G-10331)*

Master Hatchery, Siler City *Also Called: Mountaire Farms LLC (G-14424)*

Master Kraft Inc 704 234-2673
3350 Smith Farm Rd Matthews (28104) *(G-10332)*

Master Machining Inc 910 675-3660
410 Hermitage Rd Castle Hayne (28429) *(G-1955)*

Master Marketing Group LLC (PA) 870 932-4491
4801 Glenwood Ave Ste 310 Raleigh (27612) *(G-13004)*

Master Screens South LLC 704 226-9600
600 Broome St Monroe (28110) *(G-10766)*

Master Tow Inc 910 630-2000
783 Slocomb Rd Fayetteville (28311) *(G-5869)*

Masterbrand Cabinets Inc 252 523-4131
651 Collier Loftin Rd Kinston (28504) *(G-9376)*

Masterbrand Cabinets Inc 765 491-2385
632 Dixon St Lexington (27292) *(G-9754)*

MASTERBRAND CABINETS, INC., Kinston *Also Called: Masterbrand Cabinets Inc (G-9376)*

Mastercraft, Raleigh *Also Called: National Mastercraft Inds Inc (G-13055)*

Mastercraft Lamp Intl Furn 336 882-1535
156 S Main St High Point (27260) *(G-8449)*

Masterfield Furniture Co Inc 828 632-8535
6463 Church Rd Taylorsville (28681) *(G-15151)*

Masterpiece Staircase LLC 704 806-2894
3368 Smith Farm Rd Matthews (28104) *(G-10333)*

Masters Craftsman 919 800-0096
832 Purser Dr Ste 202 Raleigh (27603) *(G-13005)*

Masters Hand Print Works Inc 828 652-5833
5 Old Greenlee Rd W Marion (28752) *(G-10159)*

Masters Imaging Screen PR 704 500-1039
220 W Wilson Ave Mooresville (28115) *(G-11016)*

Masters Moving Services Inc 919 523-9836
4220 Gallatree Ln Raleigh (27616) *(G-13006)*

Mastertent, Charlotte *Also Called: Zingerle Group Usa Inc (G-3851)*

Masterwork USA Inc 704 288-9506
3700 Rose Lake Dr Charlotte (28217) *(G-3140)*

Masterwrap Inc 336 243-4515
969 American Way Lexington (27295) *(G-9755)*

Matchem Inc 336 886-5000
1115 Clinton Ave High Point (27260) *(G-8450)*

Matcor Mtal Fbrction Wlcome In 336 731-5700
835 Salem Rd Lexington (27295) *(G-9756)*

Mateenbar USA Inc 704 662-2005
2011 Highway 49 S Concord (28027) *(G-4310)*

Material Handling, Mount Airy *Also Called: T P Supply Co Inc (G-11585)*

Material Handling Tech - NC, Morrisville *Also Called: Material Handling Technologies Inc (G-11388)*

Material Handling Technologies Inc (PA) 919 388-0050
113 International Dr Morrisville (27560) *(G-11388)*

Material Return LLC 828 234-5368
647 Hopewell Rd Morganton (28655) *(G-11231)*

Materials Division, Cary *Also Called: Lord Corporation (G-1816)*

Matheson Tri-Gas Inc 919 556-6461
326 Forestville Rd Wake Forest (27587) *(G-15571)*

Mathis Elec Sls & Svc Inc 828 274-5925
102a Caribou Rd Asheville (28803) *(G-696)*

Mathis Electronics, Asheville *Also Called: Mathis Elec Sls & Svc Inc (G-696)*

Mathis Quarries Inc 336 984-4010
873 Cove Creek Dr North Wilkesboro (28659) *(G-12026)*

Mathisen Ventures Inc 212 986-1025
17343 Meadow Bottom Rd Charlotte (28277) *(G-3141)*

Matlab Inc (PA) 336 629-4161
1112 Nc Highway 49 S Asheboro (27205) *(G-457)*

Matrix Technologies Inc 414 291-1000
3109 Poplarwood Ct Ste 217 Raleigh (27604) *(G-13007)*

Matsusada Precision Inc 704 496-2644
5960 Fairview Rd Ste 400 Charlotte (28210) *(G-3142)*

Matt Bieneman Enterprises LLC 704 856-0200
1375 Deal Rd Mooresville (28115) *(G-11017)*

Matt's Auto Shop, Raleigh *Also Called: Scattered Wrenches Inc (G-13236)*

Mattamuskeet Seafood Inc 252 926-2431
24694 Us Highway 264 Swanquarter (27885) *(G-15039)*

Matthew Johnson Logging 919 291-0197
536 Farrell Rd Sanford (27330) *(G-14150)*

Matthew Laws 828 313-2204
12 Falls Ave Ste 3 Granite Falls (28630) *(G-6744)*

Matthew Warren Inc (DH) 704 837-0331
3426 Toringdon Way Ste 100 Charlotte (28277) *(G-3143)*

Matthews Building Supply Co... 704 847-2106
325 W Matthews St Matthews (28105) *(G-10268)*

Matthews Industrial... 704 239-5925
216 N Yadkin Ave Spencer (28159) *(G-14601)*

Matthews Millwork Inc.. 704 821-4499
1105 Jim Cir Monroe (28110) *(G-10767)*

Matthews Mobile Media LLC... 336 303-4982
6343 Burnt Poplar Rd Greensboro (27409) *(G-7188)*

Matthews Spcialty Vehicles Inc... 336 297-9600
211 American Ave Greensboro (27409) *(G-7189)*

Matthews Welding Service.. 828 862-4510
169 Cherryfield Loop Brevard (28712) *(G-1279)*

Mattress Firm... 910 868-0950
1920 Skibo Rd Fayetteville (28314) *(G-5870)*

Mattress Firm... 252 443-1259
794 Sutters Creek Blvd Rocky Mount (27804) *(G-13711)*

Mattress Warehouse.. 919 463-0329
5028 Arco St Cary (27519) *(G-1821)*

Mauser Usa LLC... 704 398-2325
1209 Tar Heel Rd Charlotte (28208) *(G-3144)*

Mauser Usa LLC... 704 625-0737
701 Lawton Rd Charlotte (28216) *(G-3145)*

Mauser Usa LLC... 704 455-2111
12180 University Cy Blvd Harrisburg (28075) *(G-7718)*

Maverick Biofeuls... 919 749-8717
104 Tw Alexander Dr Bldg 4a Durham (27709) *(G-5210)*

Maverick Biofuels.. 919 931-1434
104 Tw Alexander Dr Durham (27709) *(G-5211)*

Maverick Metalworks LLC... 919 609-1274
1108 Vannstone Dr Raleigh (27603) *(G-13008)*

Mavidon, Flat Rock *Also Called: Carroll-Baccari Inc (G-5962)*

Max B Smith Jr.. 828 434-0238
1055 Blowing Rock Rd Boone (28607) *(G-1219)*

Max Daetwyler Corp (DH).. 704 875-1200
13420 Reese Blvd W Huntersville (28078) *(G-8853)*

Max Patterson... 910 947-2524
1910 Autumn Ct Sanford (27330) *(G-14151)*

Max Solutions Inc (PA)... 203 683-8094
700 Derita Rd Bldg B Concord (28027) *(G-4311)*

Max Solutions USA, Concord *Also Called: Max Solutions Inc (G-4311)*

Max Woodworks Inc... 786 286-2668
151 Nc 9 Hwy Black Mountain (28711) *(G-1129)*

Maxam North America Inc (PA)... 214 736-8100
133 River Park Rd Ste 106 Mooresville (28117) *(G-11018)*

Maxim Label Packg High Pt Inc (PA)... 336 861-1666
506 Townsend Ave High Point (27263) *(G-8451)*

Maxime Knitting International.. 803 627-2768
4925 Sirona Dr Ste 200 Charlotte (28273) *(G-3146)*

Maximizer Systems Inc.. 828 345-6036
1010 21st Street Dr Se Hickory (28602) *(G-8092)*

Maximum Asp... 919 544-7900
9221 Globe Center Dr # 120 Morrisville (27560) *(G-11389)*

Maxpro Manufacturing LLC... 910 640-5505
31 Industrial Blvd Whiteville (28472) *(G-15970)*

Maxson & Associates... 336 632-0524
2618 Battleground Ave Greensboro (27408) *(G-7190)*

Maxson and Assoc Greensboro, Greensboro *Also Called: Maxson & Associates (G-7190)*

Maxtronic Technologies LLC... 704 756-5354
9545 Greyson Ridge Dr Charlotte (28277) *(G-3147)*

Maxxdrive LLC.. 704 600-8684
1847 E Dixon Blvd Shelby (28152) *(G-14345)*

May-Craft Fiberglass Pdts Inc... 919 934-3000
96 Hillsboro Rd Four Oaks (27524) *(G-6109)*

Mayberry Distillery... 336 719-6860
461 N South St Mount Airy (27030) *(G-11544)*

Maybin Emergency Power Inc... 828 697-1195
197 Mountain Valley Cemetery Rd Zirconia (28790) *(G-17154)*

Mayflower Vehicle Systems LLC (HQ)... 704 937-4400
629 S Battleground Ave Kings Mountain (28086) *(G-9318)*

Maymead Materials.. 828 758-9299
2008 Wilkesboro Blvd Lenoir (28645) *(G-9634)*

Maynard Frame Shop Inc... 910 428-2033
306 Mcbride Lumber Rd Star (27356) *(G-14720)*

Maynard S Fabricators Inc.. 336 230-1048
2227 W Lee St Ste A Greensboro (27403) *(G-7191)*

Mayne Pharma Commercial LLC... 984 242-1400
3301 Benson Dr Ste 401 Raleigh (27609) *(G-13009)*

Mayne Pharma Ventures LLC.. 252 752-3800
3301 Benson Dr Ste 401 Raleigh (27609) *(G-13010)*

Mayo, Tarboro *Also Called: Mayo Knitting Mill Inc (G-15114)*

Mayo Knitting Mill Inc (PA).. 252 823-3101
2204 W Austin St Tarboro (27886) *(G-15114)*

Mayo Resources Inc.. 336 996-7776
2860 Lowery St Winston Salem (27101) *(G-16803)*

Mayse Manufacturing Co Inc (PA).. 828 245-1891
2201 Us Highway 221 S Forest City (28043) *(G-6076)*

Maysteel Porters LLC.. 704 864-1313
469 Hospital Dr Ste A Gastonia (28054) *(G-6459)*

MB Marketing & Mfg Inc.. 828 285-0882
27 Mulvaney St Asheville (28803) *(G-697)*

Mb-F Inc (PA)... 336 379-9352
620 Industrial Ave Greensboro (27406) *(G-7192)*

Mbm, Asheville *Also Called: MB Marketing & Mfg Inc (G-697)*

Mbp Acquisition LLC.. 704 349-5055
6090 Willis Way Monroe (28110) *(G-10768)*

Mc Clatchy Interactive USA... 919 861-1200
1101 Haynes St Raleigh (27604) *(G-13011)*

Mc Controls LLC... 336 518-1303
100 Woodlyn Dr Yadkinville (27055) *(G-17045)*

Mc Cullough Auto Elc & Assoc... 704 376-5388
3219 N Davidson St Charlotte (28205) *(G-3148)*

Mc Farland & Company Inc... 336 246-4460
960 Nc Highway 88 W Jefferson (28640) *(G-9091)*

Mc Gees Crating Inc.. 828 758-4660
1640 Wilkesboro Blvd Lenoir (28645) *(G-9635)*

Mc Kenzie Taxidermy Supply, Salisbury *Also Called: McKenzie Sports Products LLC (G-14011)*

Mc Neely's Store Rental & Eqpt, Sylva *Also Called: Lbm Industries Inc (G-15062)*

MC Precast Concrete Inc... 919 367-3636
520 Pristine Water Dr Apex (27539) *(G-216)*

Mc Stitch & Print... 336 263-3677
864 Rivers Edge Dr Graham (27253) *(G-6701)*

McAd Inc.. 336 299-3030
100 Landmark Dr Greensboro (27409) *(G-7193)*

McBride Lumber Co Partnr LLC... 910 428-2747
668 Mcbride Lumber Rd Star (27356) *(G-14721)*

McBryde Publishing LLC.. 252 638-8094
905 Hampton Way Trent Woods (28562) *(G-15330)*

McC Holdings Inc.. 828 724-4000
1 Quality Way Marion (28752) *(G-10160)*

McCabes Costumes LLC.. 252 295-7691
4054 S Memorial Dr Ste O Winterville (28590) *(G-17006)*

McCabes Indus Mllwrght Mfg Inc.. 910 843-8699
9502 Nc Highway 71 N Red Springs (28377) *(G-13502)*

McCarthy Tire Service Company... 910 791-0132
118 Portwatch Way Wilmington (28412) *(G-16317)*

McClellan Patric Michael... 336 385-1878
219 Moose Creek Dr Creston (28615) *(G-4623)*

McClure Metal Specialties Inc... 252 792-8624
308 E Franklin St Williamston (27892) *(G-16066)*

McComb Industries Lllp... 336 229-9139
1311 Industry Dr Burlington (27215) *(G-1458)*

McCombs Steel.. 828 572-7600
3620 Cameo Ln Lenoir (28645) *(G-9636)*

McCombs Steel Company Inc (PA)... 704 873-7563
117 Slingshot Rd Statesville (28677) *(G-14840)*

McCorkle Sign Company Inc... 919 687-7080
1107 E Geer St Durham (27704) *(G-5212)*

McCoy Motorsports.. 704 929-8802
999 Triplett Rd Cleveland (27013) *(G-4075)*

McCreary Modern Inc (PA)... 828 464-6465
2564 S Us 321 Hwy Newton (28658) *(G-11951)*

ALPHABETIC SECTION

McCrorie Group LLC (PA)..828 328-4538
  330 19th St Se Hickory (28602) *(G-8093)*
McCrorie Wood Products, Hickory *Also Called: McCrorie Group LLC (G-8093)*
McCune Technology Inc..910 424-2978
  4801 Research Dr Fayetteville (28306) *(G-5871)*
McDaniel Delmar (PA)..336 284-6377
  144 Whetstone Dr Mocksville (27028) *(G-10586)*
McDaniel Awning Co..704 636-8503
  225 White Farm Rd Salisbury (28147) *(G-14010)*
McDaniel Awning Manufacturing, Salisbury *Also Called: McDaniel Awning Co (G-14010)*
McDonald Services Inc..704 597-0590
  1734 University Commercial Pl Charlotte (28213) *(G-3149)*
McDonald Services Inc (PA)..704 753-9669
  7427 Price Tucker Rd Monroe (28110) *(G-10769)*
McDonald's, Pinehurst *Also Called: McDonalds (G-12229)*
McDonalds..910 295-1112
  260 Ivey Ln Pinehurst (28374) *(G-12229)*
McDowell Cement Products Co (HQ)..828 652-5721
  S Garden St Marion (28752) *(G-10161)*
McDowell Cement Products Co..828 765-2762
  167 Roan Rd Spruce Pine (28777) *(G-14646)*
McDowell County Millwork LLC..828 682-6215
  4 Old West Henderson St Marion (28752) *(G-10162)*
McDowell Pressure Washing..828 620-2141
  129 Hill Rd Marion (28752) *(G-10163)*
McDowells Mch Fabrication Inc..336 720-9944
  2312a Cragmore Rd Winston Salem (27107) *(G-16804)*
McF Operating LLC..828 685-8821
  352 Jet St Hendersonville (28792) *(G-7878)*
McFarlin Cabinets..828 310-9906
  108 W Cemetery St Maiden (28650) *(G-10113)*
McGee Brothers Machine & Wldg..828 766-9122
  2585 Halltown Rd Spruce Pine (28777) *(G-14647)*
McGee Brothers Mch & Wldg Co, Spruce Pine *Also Called: McGee Brothers Machine & Wldg (G-14647)*
McGee Corporation..980 721-1911
  12100 Stallings Commerce Dr Matthews (28105) *(G-10269)*
McGee Corporation..704 882-1500
  12701 E Independence Blvd Matthews (28105) *(G-10270)*
McGill Advsory Pblications Inc..866 727-6100
  8816 Red Oak Blvd Ste 240 Charlotte (28217) *(G-3150)*
McGill Corporation..919 467-1993
  1220 Se Maynard Rd Cary (27511) *(G-1822)*
McGrann Digital Imaging, Charlotte *Also Called: McGrann Paper Corporation (G-3151)*
McGrann Paper Corporation (PA)..800 240-9455
  13400 Sage Thrasher Ln Charlotte (28278) *(G-3151)*
MCI Packing Company LLC..910 464-3507
  596 Maness Rd Robbins (27325) *(G-13600)*
McIntyre Manufacturing Group Inc..336 476-3646
  310 Kendall Mill Rd Thomasville (27360) *(G-15246)*
McJast Inc..828 884-4809
  6497 Old Hendersonville Hwy Pisgah Forest (28768) *(G-12326)*
McKay Logging Inc..910 334-3448
  151 Glendale Dr Rockingham (28379) *(G-13634)*
McKeel & Sons Logging Inc..252 244-3903
  170 Spruill Town Rd Vanceboro (28586) *(G-15480)*
McKelvey Fulks..704 357-1550
  1432 Center Park Dr Charlotte (28217) *(G-3152)*
McKenzie Industries Inc..336 870-9229
  216 Lady Slipper Ln Jamestown (27282) *(G-9061)*
McKenzie Sports Products LLC (PA)..704 279-7985
  1910 Saint Luke Church Rd Salisbury (28146) *(G-14011)*
McKenzie Supply Company..910 276-1691
  1600 Us Highway 401 Byp S Laurinburg (28352) *(G-9489)*
McKenzies Tree Service & Log..910 995-1576
  670 Boyd Lake Rd Hamlet (28345) *(G-7627)*
McKinley Leather Hickory Inc..828 459-2884
  3131 W Main St Claremont (28610) *(G-3931)*
McKinney Electric & Mch Co Inc..828 765-7910
  12923 S 226 Hwy Spruce Pine (28777) *(G-14648)*
McKinney Garbage Service, Spruce Pine *Also Called: McKinney Lwncare Grbage Svc LL (G-14649)*
McKinney Lwncare Grbage Svc LL..828 766-9490
  1113 Dale Rd Spruce Pine (28777) *(G-14649)*
McKoys Logging Company Inc..910 862-2706
  3006 W Broad St Elizabethtown (28337) *(G-5598)*
McLamb Group Inc..704 333-1171
  1003-B Louise Ave Charlotte (28205) *(G-3153)*
McLaughlin Farmhouse..704 660-0971
  15725 Mooresville Rd Mooresville (28115) *(G-11019)*
McLean Lighting Works, Greensboro *Also Called: A M Moore and Company Inc (G-6767)*
McLean Precision Cabinetry Inc..910 327-9217
  2507 Nc Highway 172 Sneads Ferry (28460) *(G-14492)*
McLean Sbsrface Utlity Engrg L..336 340-0024
  3015 E Bessemer Ave Greensboro (27405) *(G-7194)*
McLendon Logging Incorporated..910 439-6223
  671 Nc Highway 731 W Mount Gilead (27306) *(G-11604)*
McLoud Media..828 837-9539
  1192 Andrews Rd Ste H Murphy (28906) *(G-11712)*
McLoud Trucking & Rigging, Yadkinville *Also Called: Advantage Machinery Svcs Inc (G-17030)*
McManus Microwave, Bakersville *Also Called: James W McManus Inc (G-884)*
McMichael Mills Inc..336 584-0134
  2050 Willow Spring Ln Burlington (27215) *(G-1459)*
McMichael Mills Inc (PA)..336 548-4242
  130 Shakey Rd Mayodan (27027) *(G-10365)*
McMurray Fabrics Inc (PA)..910 944-2128
  105 Vann Pl (Sandhills Industrial Park) Aberdeen (28315) *(G-11)*
McMurray Fabrics Inc..704 732-9613
  1140 N Flint St Lincolnton (28092) *(G-9906)*
McNamara & Company, Kernersville *Also Called: Chichibone Inc (G-9177)*
McNaughton-Mckay Southeast Inc..910 392-0940
  6719 Amsterdam Way Wilmington (28405) *(G-16318)*
McNeely Accounting & Tax Svc..828 652-7405
  3562 Us 221 S Marion (28752) *(G-10164)*
McNeely Motorsports Inc..704 426-7430
  340 Seaboard Dr Matthews (28104) *(G-10334)*
McNeely Trucking Co..828 966-4270
  17692 Rosman Hwy Sapphire (28774) *(G-14215)*
McNeelys Store Rental & Eqp, Sapphire *Also Called: Lbm Industries Inc (G-14214)*
McNeill Frame Inc..336 873-7934
  3631 Alternate Rd Seagrove (27341) *(G-14244)*
McNeilly Champion Furniture, Lawndale *Also Called: McNeillys Inc (G-9501)*
McNeillys Inc..704 300-1712
  229 Carpenters Grove Church Rd Lawndale (28090) *(G-9501)*
McPherson Beverages Inc..252 537-3571
  1330 Stancell St Roanoke Rapids (27870) *(G-13579)*
McRae Industries Inc..910 439-6149
  125 Wadeville Fire Station Rd Mount Gilead (27306) *(G-11605)*
McRae Industries Inc (PA)..910 439-6147
  400 N Main St Mount Gilead (27306) *(G-11606)*
McRitchie Wine Company LLC..336 874-3003
  315 Thurmond Rd Thurmond (28683) *(G-15312)*
MCS, Durham *Also Called: Machine Consulting Svcs Inc (G-5201)*
MCS of Fayetteville..252 234-6001
  2810 Contentnea Rd S Wilson (27893) *(G-16514)*
McShan Inc..980 355-9790
  16607 Riverstone Way # 200 Charlotte (28277) *(G-3154)*
McW Custom Doors, Madison *Also Called: Martin Wood Products Inc (G-10080)*
Mdb Investors LLC..704 507-6850
  4000 Sam Wilson Rd Charlotte (28214) *(G-3155)*
Mdcsat, Havelock *Also Called: Darren Lee Depalo (G-7741)*
Mdi Solutions LLC..845 721-6758
  760 Choate Rd Salisbury (28146) *(G-14012)*
Mdkscrubs LLC..980 250-4708
  8401 Parkland Cir Apt 102 Charlotte (28227) *(G-3156)*
Mdm Mfg LLC..919 908-6574
  206 Stockbridge Pl Hillsborough (27278) *(G-8662)*
MDN Cabinets Inc..919 662-1090
  3411 Integrity Dr Ste 100 Garner (27529) *(G-6285)*
Mdsi Inc..919 783-8730
  3505 Lake Herman Dr Bldg A Browns Summit (27214) *(G-1312)*
Mdt Bromley LLC..828 651-8737
  282 Cane Creek Rd Fletcher (28732) *(G-6021)*

Meacham Logging Inc   ALPHABETIC SECTION

Meacham Logging Inc 910 652-2794
    1530 Grassy Island Rd Ellerbe (28338) *(G-5642)*
Meadow Burke Products, Charlotte *Also Called: Merchants Metals Inc (G-3165)*
Meadows Frozen Custar 336 298-7246
    2205 Oak Ridge Rd Ste F Oak Ridge (27310) *(G-12060)*
Meadows Mills Inc 336 838-2282
    1352 W D St North Wilkesboro (28659) *(G-12027)*
Meadwestvaco Research Center, Raleigh *Also Called: Westrock Mwv LLC (G-13419)*
Measurement Controls Inc 704 921-1101
    6131 Old Concord Rd Charlotte (28213) *(G-3157)*
Measurement Incorporated (PA) 919 683-2413
    423 Morris St Durham (27701) *(G-5213)*
Meat Farm, Pinetown *Also Called: Acre Station Meat Farm Inc (G-12243)*
Meatinternational LLC 910 628-8267
    266 Bethesda Church Rd Fairmont (28340) *(G-5704)*
Mebane Enterprise, Mebane *Also Called: Womack Publishing Co Inc (G-10437)*
Mebane Machine & Tool LLC 919 597-1169
    317 Canterwood Dr Mebane (27302) *(G-10419)*
Mecha 919 858-0372
    6204 Daimler Way Ste 107 Raleigh (27607) *(G-13012)*
Mechanical Maintenance Inc 336 676-7133
    6028 Liberty Rd Climax (27233) *(G-4087)*
Mechanical Specialty Inc 336 272-5606
    1901 E Wendover Ave Greensboro (27405) *(G-7195)*
Mechlanburg Newspaper Group, Huntersville *Also Called: Herald Huntersville (G-8830)*
Meco Inc 919 557-7330
    501 Community Dr Fuquay Varina (27526) *(G-6214)*
Med Express/Medical Spc Inc 919 572-2568
    4620 Industry Ln Ste A Durham (27713) *(G-5214)*
Medaccess Inc 828 264-4085
    1236 Gladdens Creek Rd Robbinsville (28771) *(G-13609)*
Medallion Athletic Products, Mooresville *Also Called: Geosurfaces Southeast Inc (G-10958)*
Medallion Company Inc (HQ) 919 990-3500
    250 Crown Blvd Timberlake (27583) *(G-15315)*
Medaloni Cellars LLC 336 398-7818
    811 Eula St Ste A Greensboro (27403) *(G-7196)*
Medaloni Cellars LLC 305 509-2004
    470 Yadkin Valley Trl Lewisville (27023) *(G-9669)*
Medals To Honor Inc 910 326-4275
    176 Oyster Ln Hubert (28539) *(G-8751)*
Medaptus Inc 617 896-4000
    4917 Waters Edge Dr Ste 135 Raleigh (27606) *(G-13013)*
Medcor Inc 888 579-1050
    550 Scout Rd Lexington (27292) *(G-9757)*
Medi Mall Inc 877 501-6334
    189 Continuum Dr Fletcher (28732) *(G-6022)*
Media Publishing LLC 919 273-0488
    122 S Berkeley Blvd Goldsboro (27534) *(G-6634)*
Media Wilimington Co 910 791-0688
    6700 Netherlands Dr Unit A Wilmington (28405) *(G-16319)*
Medical Action, Arden *Also Called: Medical Action Industries Inc (G-350)*
Medical Action Industries Inc (HQ)   25 Heywood Rd Arden (28704) *(G-350)*
Medical Cable Specialists Inc 828 890-2888
    2133 Old Fanning Bridge Rd Mills River (28759) *(G-10507)*
Medical Device Bus Svcs Inc 704 423-0033
    900 Center Park Dr Ste Bc Charlotte (28217) *(G-3158)*
Medical Engineering Labs 704 487-0166
    3039 Longwood Dr Shelby (28152) *(G-14346)*
Medical Missionary Press 828 649-3976
    491 Blue Hill Rd Marshall (28753) *(G-10205)*
Medical Murray, Charlotte *Also Called: Murray Inc (G-3222)*
Medical Spclties of Crlnas Inc 704 575-4542
    565 Meadow Ridge Sunset Beach (28468) *(G-15001)*
Medical Spec Mfg, Mint Hill *Also Called: Gaylord Inc (G-10533)*
Medical Specialties Inc 704 694-2434
    308 Parson St Wadesboro (28170) *(G-15516)*
Medicor Imaging Inc 704 332-5532
    1927 S Tryon St Ste 200 Charlotte (28203) *(G-3159)*
Medimassager.com, Fletcher *Also Called: Medi Mall Inc (G-6022)*
Medkoo Inc 919 636-5577
    2224 Sedwick Rd Ste 102 Durham (27713) *(G-5215)*
Medkoo Biosciences, Durham *Also Called: Medkoo Inc (G-5215)*
Medley S Garage Welding 336 674-0422
    5879 Cherokee Trl Pleasant Garden (27313) *(G-12358)*
Medlin Office Supply, Oriental *Also Called: J C Lawrence Co (G-12110)*
Medlio, Durham *Also Called: Medlio Inc (G-5216)*
Medlio Inc 919 599-4870
    3313 Old Chapel Hill Rd Durham (27707) *(G-5216)*
Medlit Solutions 919 878-6789
    191 Technology Dr Garner (27529) *(G-6286)*
Medlit Solutions LLC (HQ) 919 878-6789
    191 Technology Dr Garner (27529) *(G-6287)*
Medtrnic Sofamor Danek USA Inc 919 457-9982
    2000 Regency Pkwy Ste 270 Cary (27518) *(G-1823)*
Medtronic, Cary *Also Called: Medtrnic Sofamor Danek USA Inc (G-1823)*
Medvertical LLC 919 867-4268
    3725 National Dr Ste 160 Raleigh (27612) *(G-13014)*
Meera Industries Usa LLC 336 906-7570
    2020 W Green Dr High Point (27260) *(G-8452)*
Meerkat Press LLC 678 984-5489
    216 Patton Mountain Rd Asheville (28804) *(G-698)*
Mega Machine Shop Inc 336 492-2728
    130 Macy Langston Ln Mocksville (27028) *(G-10587)*
Megawood Inc 910 572-3796
    670 Allenton St Mount Gilead (27306) *(G-11607)*
Megawood Holdings Inc 910 439-2124
    610 W Allenton St Mount Gilead (27306) *(G-11608)*
Meghan Blake Industries Inc 704 462-2988
    7514 W Nc 10 Hwy Vale (28168) *(G-15469)*
Megtec India Holdings LLC 704 625-4900
    13024 Ballantyne Corporate Pl Ste 700 Charlotte (28277) *(G-3160)*
Megtec Turbosonic Tech Inc 704 625-4900
    13024 Ballantyne Corporate Pl Ste 700 Charlotte (28277) *(G-3161)*
Meherrin River Forest Pdts Inc 252 558-4238
    1478 Trueblood Rd Weldon (27890) *(G-15885)*
MEI Tai Baby LLC 919 260-4022
    103 Wrenn Pl Chapel Hill (27516) *(G-2038)*
Mel, Shelby *Also Called: Medical Engineering Labs (G-14346)*
Mel Schlesinger 336 525-6357
    1001 S Marshall St # 290 Winston Salem (27101) *(G-16805)*
Melatex Incorporated 704 332-5046
    3818 Northmore St Charlotte (28205) *(G-3162)*
Melendez Signs LLC 980 298-4057
    271 Crowell Dr Nw Concord (28025) *(G-4312)*
Melinta Therapeutics Inc 919 313-6601
    6340 Quadrangle Dr Ste 100 Chapel Hill (27517) *(G-2039)*
Melinta Therapeutics, Inc., Chapel Hill *Also Called: Melinta Therapeutics Inc (G-2039)*
Melissae Meadery & Winery LLC 336 207-7097
    272 Plantation Dr Marion (28752) *(G-10165)*
Mellineum Printing 919 267-5752
    2015 Production Dr Apex (27539) *(G-217)*
Melltronics Industrial Inc (PA) 704 821-6651
    3479 Gribble Rd Matthews (28104) *(G-10335)*
Melodia Goods and Embroidery 910 674-3934
    1306 Redwood Ct Lumberton (28358) *(G-10044)*
Melt Your Heart, Leicester *Also Called: Melt Your Heart LLC (G-9515)*
Melt Your Heart LLC 828 989-6749
    162 Brookshire Rd Leicester (28748) *(G-9515)*
Melton Backhoe Service Inc 828 779-6728
    103 Chestnut Hill Rd Black Mountain (28711) *(G-1130)*
Memere Publishing 704 597-9160
    6247 Half Dome Dr Charlotte (28269) *(G-3163)*
Memios LLC 336 664-5256
    7609 Business Park Dr # B Greensboro (27409) *(G-7197)*
Memories, Mooresville *Also Called: Memories of Orangeburg Inc (G-11020)*
Memories In Stitches 910 725-0512
    1150 Old Us 1 Hwy Ste 10 Southern Pines (28387) *(G-14541)*
Memories of Orangeburg Inc 803 533-0035
    126 Foxfield Park Dr Mooresville (28115) *(G-11020)*
Memoryc, Charlotte *Also Called: Memoryc Inc (G-3164)*
Memoryc Inc 980 224-2875
    8008 Corp Ctr Dr Ste 200 Charlotte (28226) *(G-3164)*

ALPHABETIC SECTION — Metal Inc Triad

Memscap Inc (HQ) 919 248-4102
  3021 E Cornwallis Rd Research Triangle Pk Durham (27709) *(G-5217)*

Memscap Inc 919 248-1441
  3026 Cornwallis Rd Durham (27709) *(G-5218)*

Men With Wings Press 828 989-6124
  17 Shelby Dr Asheville (28803) *(G-699)*

Mendez Welding LLC 336 618-9337
  133 Hillcrest St Mocksville (27028) *(G-10588)*

Mendoza Logging Inc 252 935-5560
  115 Loop Road Number 1 Pantego (27860) *(G-12168)*

Mendozas Powder Coating LLC 336 877-0783
  189 Von Turner Rd West Jefferson (28694) *(G-15944)*

Mennel Mil & Bky Mix NC LLC 828 468-6015
  11 N Brady Ave Newton (28658) *(G-11952)*

Mepla-Alfit Incorporated 336 289-2300
  1202 Nc Highway 66 S Kernersville (27284) *(G-9215)*

Merch Inc 919 933-6037
  101 Lloyd St Carrboro (27510) *(G-1650)*

Merch Connect Studios Inc 336 501-6722
  1724 Holbrook St Greensboro (27403) *(G-7198)*

Merchant 1 Manufacturing LLC 336 617-3008
  200 Starview Ln Summerfield (27358) *(G-14989)*

Merchant 1 Marketing LLC 888 853-9992
  2900 Pacific Ave Greensboro (27406) *(G-7199)*

Merchants, Havelock *Also Called: Merchants Inc (G-7743)*

Merchants Inc 252 447-2121
  174 Us Highway 70 W Havelock (28532) *(G-7743)*

Merchants Metals, Raleigh *Also Called: Merchants Metals LLC (G-13015)*

Merchants Metals, Statesville *Also Called: Merchants Metals LLC (G-14841)*

Merchants Metals Inc 704 921-9192
  3401 Woodpark Blvd Ste A Charlotte (28206) *(G-3165)*

Merchants Metals LLC 919 598-8471
  6512 Mount Herman Rd Raleigh (27617) *(G-13015)*

Merchants Metals LLC 704 878-8706
  165 Fanjoy Rd Statesville (28625) *(G-14841)*

Merck 919 423-4328
  214 Towne Ridge Ln Chapel Hill (27516) *(G-2040)*

Merck, Charlotte *Also Called: Merck & Co Inc (G-3166)*

Merck, Durham *Also Called: Merck Sharp & Dohme LLC (G-5219)*

Merck & Co Inc 908 423-3000
  10301 David Taylor Dr Charlotte (28262) *(G-3166)*

Merck Sharp & Dohme LLC 919 425-4000
  5325 Old Oxford Rd Durham (27712) *(G-5219)*

Merck Sharp & Dohme LLC 252 243-2011
  4633 Merck Rd W Wilson (27893) *(G-16515)*

Merck Teknika LLC 919 620-7200
  100 Rodolphe St Bldg 1300 Durham (27712) *(G-5220)*

Mercury Signs Inc 919 808-1205
  7306 Vanclaybon Rd Apex (27523) *(G-218)*

Meredith - Webb Prtg Co Inc 336 228-8378
  334 N Main St Burlington (27217) *(G-1460)*

Meredith Media Co 919 748-4808
  4015 University Dr Ste 2d Durham (27707) *(G-5221)*

Merfin Systems LLC 800 874-6373
  105 Industrial Dr King (27021) *(G-9276)*

Merge LLC 919 832-3924
  1410 Hillsborough St Raleigh (27605) *(G-13016)*

Merge Media Ltd 919 688-9969
  104 S Christopher Rd Chapel Hill (27514) *(G-2041)*

Merge Records, Chapel Hill *Also Called: Merge Media Ltd (G-2041)*

Merge Scientific Solutions LLC 919 346-0999
  208 Technology Park Ln Ste 108 Fuquay Varina (27526) *(G-6215)*

Merhi Glass Inc 919 961-5930
  6925 Old Wake Forest Rd Raleigh (27616) *(G-13017)*

merica Labz LLC (PA) 844 445-5735
  1415 Wilkesboro Hwy Statesville (28625) *(G-14842)*

Meridian Brick LLC 704 636-0131
  700 S Long St Salisbury (28144) *(G-14013)*

Meridian Dyed Yarn Group, Gastonia *Also Called: Meridian Industries Inc (G-6460)*

Meridian Granite Company 919 781-4550
  2710 Wycliff Rd Raleigh (27607) *(G-13018)*

Meridian Industries Inc 704 824-7880
  40 Rex Ave Gastonia (28054) *(G-6460)*

Meridian Kiosks, Aberdeen *Also Called: Meridian Zero Degrees LLC (G-12)*

Meridian Point of Sale Inc 336 315-9800
  7343 W Friendly Ave Ste L Greensboro (27410) *(G-7200)*

Meridian Spcalty Yrn Group Inc (HQ) 828 874-2151
  312 Colombo St Sw Valdese (28690) *(G-15450)*

Meridian Zero Degrees LLC (PA) 866 454-6757
  312 S Pine St Aberdeen (28315) *(G-12)*

Meritor Inc 910 425-4181
  3200 Natal St Fayetteville (28306) *(G-5872)*

Meritor Inc 828 687-2000
  1000 Rockwell Dr Fletcher (28732) *(G-6023)*

Meritor Inc 828 687-2000
  1000 Rockwell Dr Fletcher (28732) *(G-6024)*

Meritor Inc 828 247-0440
  160 Ash Dr Forest City (28043) *(G-6077)*

Meritor Inc 910 844-9401
  22021 Skyway Church Rd Ste B Maxton (28364) *(G-10359)*

Meritor Inc 910 844-9401
  22021 Skyway Church Rd Ste A Maxton (28364) *(G-10360)*

Meritor Inc 828 433-4600
  105 Wamsutta Mill Rd Morganton (28655) *(G-11232)*

Merlins Machine Shop 910 399-3677
  4301 Deer Creek Ln Wilmington (28405) *(G-16320)*

Merrill Resources Inc 828 877-4450
  99 Cascade Lake Rd Penrose (28766) *(G-12186)*

Merritt Logging & Chipping Co 910 862-4905
  1109 W Swanzy St Elizabethtown (28337) *(G-5599)*

Merritts Pottery Inc 910 862-3774
  3943 Us Highway 701 N Elizabethtown (28337) *(G-5600)*

Mertek Solutions Inc 919 774-7827
  3913 Hawkins Ave Sanford (27330) *(G-14152)*

Merz, Raleigh *Also Called: Merz Incorporated (G-13019)*

Merz Incorporated 919 582-8196
  6501 Six Forks Rd Raleigh (27615) *(G-13019)*

Merz North America Inc (DH) 919 582-8000
  6501 Six Forks Rd Raleigh (27615) *(G-13020)*

Merz Pharmaceuticals LLC 919 582-8000
  6601 Six Forks Rd Ste 430 Raleigh (27615) *(G-13021)*

Mesa International 207 774-5946
  1408 Unity St Thomasville (27360) *(G-15247)*

Mesa Quality, Hendersonville *Also Called: Mesa Quality Fenestration Inc (G-7879)*

Mesa Quality Fenestration Inc 828 393-0132
  968 Crab Creek Rd Hendersonville (28739) *(G-7879)*

Messer LLC 704 583-0313
  2820 Nevada Blvd Charlotte (28273) *(G-3167)*

Mesurio Inc 919 633-8773
  1210 Holly Creek Ln Chapel Hill (27516) *(G-2042)*

Metal & Materials Proc LLC 260 438-8901
  3250 Nc Highway 5 Aberdeen (28315) *(G-13)*

Metal ARC 910 770-1180
  5547 James B White Hwy S Whiteville (28472) *(G-15971)*

Metal Buildings Charlotte 980 365-6583
  420 Highway 24 27 W Midland (28107) *(G-10471)*

Metal Crafters of Goldsboro NC 919 778-7200
  855 Nc 111 Hwy S Goldsboro (27534) *(G-6635)*

Metal Creations, Fletcher *Also Called: Welding Solutions LLC (G-6051)*

Metal Depots, Raleigh *Also Called: Nci Group Inc (G-13059)*

Metal Fabrication, Henderson *Also Called: Edwards Unlimited Inc (G-7782)*

Metal Graphic, Raleigh *Also Called: Knowledge Management Assoc LLC (G-12944)*

Metal Impact East LLC 336 578-4515
  235 Riverbend Rd Graham (27253) *(G-6702)*

Metal Impact East LLC 743 205-1900
  1200 Jay Ln Graham (27253) *(G-6703)*

Metal Improvement Company LLC 704 525-3818
  500 Springbrook Rd Charlotte (28217) *(G-3168)*

Metal Improvement Company LLC 414 536-1573
  1931 Jordache Ct Gastonia (28052) *(G-6461)*

Metal Inc Triad 980 429-2278
  108 Industrial Park Rd Lincolnton (28092) *(G-9907)*

(PA)=Parent Co (HQ)=Headquarters (DH)=Div Headquarters

Metal Processors Inc 336 993-2181
1010 W Mountain St Kernersville (27284) *(G-9216)*

Metal Roofing Systems LLC 704 820-3110
7687 Mikron Dr Stanley (28164) *(G-14702)*

Metal Sales Manufacturing Corp 704 859-0550
188 Quality Dr Mocksville (27028) *(G-10589)*

Metal Solutions LLC 252 702-7523
4865 Hwy 258 S Snow Hill (28580) *(G-14504)*

Metal Stamping Solutions, Sanford *Also Called: Wolverine Mtal Stmping Sltons (G-14208)*

Metal Structures Plus LLC 704 896-7155
561 Oak Tree Rd Mooresville (28117) *(G-11021)*

Metal Tech Murfreesboro Inc (PA) 252 398-4041
314 W Broad St Murfreesboro (27855) *(G-11700)*

Metal Tech of Murfreesboro, Murfreesboro *Also Called: Metal Tech Murfreesboro Inc (G-11700)*

Metal Treating Div, Gastonia *Also Called: Mik All Machine Co Inc (G-6465)*

Metal Works 828 898-8582
116 Duke St Granite Falls (28630) *(G-6745)*

Metal Works High Point Inc 336 886-4612
918 W Kivett Dr High Point (27262) *(G-8453)*

Metal Works Mfg Co 704 482-1399
2501 W Dixon Blvd Shelby (28152) *(G-14347)*

Metal-Cad Stl Frmng Systems In 910 343-3338
150 Division Dr Wilmington (28401) *(G-16321)*

Metalcraft & Mech Svc Inc 919 736-1029
147 Aycock Dr Goldsboro (27530) *(G-6636)*

Metalcraft Air Filtration, Washington *Also Called: Camfil Usa Inc (G-15685)*

Metalcraft Fabricating Company 919 477-2117
1316 Old Oxford Rd Durham (27704) *(G-5222)*

Metalcraft Specialties Inc 828 779-2523
64 Old Josh Creek Dr Candler (28715) *(G-1587)*

Metalfab of North Carolina LLC 704 841-1090
11145 Monroe Rd Matthews (28105) *(G-10271)*

Metallix Refining Inc 252 413-0346
251 Industrial Blvd Greenville (27834) *(G-7559)*

Metallum Structures Inc 877 517-4422
1618 S Main St Mount Airy (27030) *(G-11545)*

Metallus Inc 330 471-6293
205 Industrial Park Dr Columbus (28722) *(G-4178)*

Metaltek, Morrisville *Also Called: Liberty Investment & MGT Corp (G-11379)*

Metchem Inc 910 944-1405
106 Jordan Pl Aberdeen (28315) *(G-14)*

Metro Fire Lifesafety LLC 704 529-7348
2714 Forbes Rd Gastonia (28056) *(G-6462)*

Metro Print Inc 704 827-3796
800 W Central Ave Mount Holly (28120) *(G-11642)*

Metro Productions Inc 919 851-6420
6005 Chapel Hill Rd Raleigh (27607) *(G-13022)*

Metro Woodcrafter, Charlotte *Also Called: Metro Woodcrafter of Nc Inc (G-3169)*

Metro Woodcrafter of Nc Inc 704 394-9622
3710 Performance Rd Charlotte (28214) *(G-3169)*

Metrographics Printing, Charlotte *Also Called: Flash Printing Company Inc (G-2769)*

Metrohose Incorporated 252 329-9891
2009 N Greene St Greenville (27834) *(G-7560)*

Metrolina Sign Co 704 343-0885
801 Atando Ave Ste D Charlotte (28206) *(G-3170)*

Metrolina Sign Supply LLC 704 343-0885
801 Atando Ave Ste D Charlotte (28206) *(G-3171)*

Metrolina Woodworks Inc 704 821-9095
3475 Gribble Rd Stallings (28104) *(G-14672)*

Metromont Materials Corp 828 253-9383
190 Meadow Rd Asheville (28803) *(G-700)*

Metropolitan Woodworks Inc 704 215-5018
2005 W Poplar St Gastonia (28052) *(G-6463)*

Metso Outotec USA Inc 877 677-2005
3200 Bessemer City Rd Bessemer City (28016) *(G-1075)*

METSO OUTOTEC USA INC., Bessemer City *Also Called: Metso Outotec USA Inc (G-1075)*

Metso Power USA, Charlotte *Also Called: Valmet Inc (G-3763)*

Mettech (PA) 919 833-9460
105 S Wilmington St Raleigh (27601) *(G-13023)*

Metyx USA Inc 704 824-1030
2504 Lowell Rd Gastonia (28054) *(G-6464)*

Metzgers Burl Wood Gallery 828 452-2550
101 N Main St Waynesville (28786) *(G-15810)*

Meusburger Us Inc 704 526-0330
4600 Lebanon Rd Ste A-1 Mint Hill (28227) *(G-10539)*

Mexichem Spcalty Compounds Inc 704 889-7821
9635 Industrial Dr Pineville (28134) *(G-12283)*

Mey Corporation (PA) 919 932-5800
121 S Estes Dr Ste 101 Chapel Hill (27514) *(G-2043)*

Meyer Decorative Surfaces 910 794-7225
3002 Corporate Dr Wilmington (28405) *(G-16322)*

Mfi Products Inc (HQ) 910 944-2128
105 Vann Pl Aberdeen (28315) *(G-15)*

Mg Foods Inc 336 724-6327
3195 Centre Park Blvd Winston Salem (27107) *(G-16806)*

Mg12 LP 828 440-1144
874 S Trade St Tryon (28782) *(G-15425)*

MGe Products LLC 828 443-3214
4830 Crawley Dale St Morganton (28655) *(G-11233)*

MGM Brakes, Charlotte *Also Called: Indian Head Industries Inc (G-2961)*

MGM Brakes, Murphy *Also Called: Indian Head Industries Inc (G-11710)*

Mh Libman Woodturning 828 360-5530
191 Lyman St Asheville (28801) *(G-701)*

MHS Ltd 336 767-2641
4961 Home Rd Ste A Winston Salem (27106) *(G-16807)*

MHS Ltd (PA) 336 767-2641
4959 Home Rd Winston Salem (27106) *(G-16808)*

MI Screen Printing Inc 704 500-1039
114 Vincent Pl Apt 106 Mooresville (28115) *(G-11022)*

Mi-, Durham *Also Called: Advanced Digital Systems Inc (G-4904)*

Miahna Moon LLC 704 449-9495
5409 Prosperity Ridge Rd Apt 102 Charlotte (28269) *(G-3172)*

Mias Inc 704 665-1098
14240 S Lakes Dr Charlotte (28273) *(G-3173)*

Mias Group, Charlotte *Also Called: Mias Inc (G-3173)*

Mic Equip Rebuild, Gastonia *Also Called: Metal Improvement Company LLC (G-6461)*

Micell Technologies Inc 919 313-2102
801 Capitola Dr Ste 1 Durham (27713) *(G-5223)*

Michael D Pressley 828 652-8292
198 Emerson Ln Nebo (28761) *(G-11761)*

Michael Edits 704 737-5220
401 Michelle Linnea Dr Apt 11 Charlotte (28262) *(G-3174)*

Michael H Branch Inc 252 532-0930
1621 Old Emporia Rd Gaston (27832) *(G-6331)*

Michael L Goodson Logging Inc 910 346-8399
171 Goodson Trl Jacksonville (28546) *(G-9013)*

Michael Parker Cabinetry 919 833-5117
414 Dupont Cir Ste 4 Raleigh (27603) *(G-13024)*

Michael Ray McKinney 828 765-7001
1202 Mckinney Mine Rd Spruce Pine (28777) *(G-14650)*

Michael S North Wilkesboro Inc 336 838-5964
900 Main St North Wilkesboro (28659) *(G-12028)*

Michael Simmons 704 298-1103
6012 Bayfield Pkwy Ste 302 Concord (28027) *(G-4313)*

Michael Tate 336 374-4695
1455 Simpson Mill Rd Mount Airy (27030) *(G-11546)*

Michaelian & Kohlberg Inc (PA) 828 891-8511
5216 Brevard Rd Horse Shoe (28742) *(G-8741)*

Michaels Creamery Inc 910 292-4172
439 Westwood Shopping Ctr Ste 148 Fayetteville (28314) *(G-5873)*

Michaels Jewelry, North Wilkesboro *Also Called: Michael S North Wilkesboro Inc (G-12028)*

Micheal Langdon Logging Inc 910 890-5295
7249 Ross Rd Erwin (28339) *(G-5687)*

Michelles Scrubs and More 980 215-9461
829 Joseph Antoon Cir Stanley (28164) *(G-14703)*

Michelson Enterprises Inc 828 693-5500
701 Oriole Dr Hendersonville (28792) *(G-7880)*

Michigan Packaging Company 704 455-4206
2215 Mulberry Rd Concord (28025) *(G-4314)*

Mickey Blanton Logging 828 289-9344
277 Henry Jenkins Rd Mooresboro (28114) *(G-10839)*

Mickey Truck Bodies Inc 336 882-6806
1425 Bethel Dr High Point (27260) *(G-8454)*

ALPHABETIC SECTION

Mickey Truck Bodies Inc (PA) 336 882-6806
1305 Trinity Ave High Point (27260) *(G-8455)*

Mickey Truck Bodies Inc 336 882-6806
Hwy 29-70 Thomasville (27360) *(G-15248)*

Micro Epsilon Amer Ltd Partnr (PA) 919 787-9707
8120 Brownleigh Dr Raleigh (27617) *(G-13025)*

Micro Epsilon America, Raleigh *Also Called: Micro Epsilon Amer Ltd Partnr (G-13025)*

Micro Lens Technology Inc 704 893-2109
2001 Van Buren Ave Indian Trail (28079) *(G-8949)*

Micro Lens Technology Inc (PA) 704 847-9234
3308 Mikelynn Dr Matthews (28105) *(G-10272)*

Micro Measurements, Wendell *Also Called: Vishay Measurements Group Inc (G-15923)*

Micro Technology Unlimited, Raleigh *Also Called: Consolidated Sciences Inc (G-12639)*

Micro-OHM Corporation 800 845-5167
14460 Falls Of Neuse Rd Ste 149-273 Raleigh (27614) *(G-13026)*

Microban, Huntersville *Also Called: Microban Products Company (G-8854)*

Microban Products Company 704 766-4267
11400 Vanstory Dr Huntersville (28078) *(G-8854)*

Microbrush International, Monroe *Also Called: Dentonics Inc (G-10705)*

Microchip Technology Inc 919 844-7510
7901 Strickland Rd Ste 101 Raleigh (27615) *(G-13027)*

Microfine Inc 336 768-1480
100 Cloverleaf Dr Winston Salem (27103) *(G-16809)*

Micronics Tig-Welding 828 691-0755
42 Willie Mae Way Fletcher (28732) *(G-6025)*

Micronova Systems Inc 910 202-0564
2038 Oleander Dr Wilmington (28403) *(G-16323)*

Micropore Technologies Inc 984 344-7499
2121 Tw Alexander Dr Ste 124-8 Morrisville (27560) *(G-11390)*

Microsoft, Charlotte *Also Called: Microsoft Corporation (G-3175)*

Microsoft Corporation 704 527-2987
8055 Microsoft Way Charlotte (28273) *(G-3175)*

Microsolv Technology Corp 720 949-1302
9158 Industrial Blvd Ne Leland (28451) *(G-9556)*

Micross Advnced Intrcnnect TEC 919 248-1872
3021 Cornwallis Rd Durham (27709) *(G-5224)*

Micross Components, Durham *Also Called: Micross Advnced Intrcnnect TEC (G-5224)*

Microtech, Mills River *Also Called: Microtech Knives Inc (G-10508)*

Microtech Defense Inds Inc 828 684-4355
15a National Ave Fletcher (28732) *(G-6026)*

Microtech Knives Inc (PA) 828 684-4355
321 Fanning Fields Rd Mills River (28759) *(G-10508)*

Microthermics Inc 919 878-8045
3216 Wellington Ct Ste 102 Raleigh (27615) *(G-13028)*

Microtronic Us LLC 336 869-0429
401 Dorado Dr High Point (27265) *(G-8456)*

Mid Atlantic Book Bindery, Greensboro *Also Called: Hf Group LLC (G-7088)*

Mid Atlantic Hydraulics & Mch, Washington *Also Called: Mid-Atlantic Tool and Die Inc (G-15715)*

Mid Carolina Cabinets Inc 704 358-9950
1418 Industrial Dr Matthews (28105) *(G-10273)*

Mid Pines Hosiery Company, Sanford *Also Called: Midpines Hosiery Inc (G-14153)*

Mid South Management NC Inc 336 835-1513
214 E Main St Elkin (28621) *(G-5625)*

Mid Town Dixie Express Fuel 336 318-1200
455 W Salisbury St Asheboro (27203) *(G-458)*

Mid-Atlantic Concrete Pdts Inc 336 774-6544
2460 Armstrong Dr Winston Salem (27103) *(G-16810)*

Mid-Atlantic Crane and Eqp Co 919 790-3535
3224 Northside Dr Raleigh (27615) *(G-13029)*

Mid-Atlantic Drainage Inc (PA) 828 324-0808
105 Ge Plant Rd Sw Conover (28613) *(G-4472)*

Mid-Atlantic Specialties Inc 919 212-1939
5200 Trademark Dr Ste 102 Raleigh (27610) *(G-13030)*

Mid-Atlantic Tool and Die Inc 252 946-2598
5324 Us Highway 264 W Washington (27889) *(G-15715)*

Midas Spring Water Btlg Co LLC 704 392-2150
416 Armour St Davidson (28036) *(G-4685)*

Midcoastal Development Corp 336 622-3091
2435 Old 421 Rd Staley (27355) *(G-14668)*

Middle of Nowhere Music LLC 301 237-7290
112 Nc 54 Apt B8 Carrboro (27510) *(G-1651)*

Middleby Marshall Inc (HQ) 919 762-1000
1100 Old Honeycutt Rd Fuquay Varina (27526) *(G-6216)*

Middlesex Plant 252 235-2121
8171 Planer Mill Rd Middlesex (27557) *(G-10451)*

Mideast Division, Concord *Also Called: Legacy Vulcan LLC (G-4301)*

Midland Bottling LLC 919 865-2300
4141 Parklake Ave Ste 600 Raleigh (27612) *(G-13031)*

Midnight Machining, Marion *Also Called: New World Technologies Inc (G-10169)*

Midnight Mndance Vineyards LLC 336 835-6681
5040 Howell School Rd Jonesville (28642) *(G-9100)*

Midnight Publishing Group Inc 919 809-4277
107 Hawks Nest Ct Cary (27513) *(G-1824)*

Midpines Hosiery Inc 919 774-3888
840 White Hill Rd Sanford (27332) *(G-14153)*

Midsouth Power Eqp Co Inc 336 389-0515
518 Corliss St Greensboro (27406) *(G-7201)*

Midstate Mills Inc 828 464-1611
11 N Brady Ave Newton (28658) *(G-11953)*

Midway Blind & Awning Co Inc 336 226-4532
1836 E Webb Ave Burlington (27217) *(G-1461)*

Midwood Barkery LLC 980 395-0498
3100 Monroe Rd Charlotte (28205) *(G-3176)*

Mign Inc 609 304-1617
301 Camp Rd Ste 105 Charlotte (28206) *(G-3177)*

Mijo Enterprises Inc 252 442-6806
2220 N Wesleyan Blvd Rocky Mount (27804) *(G-13712)*

Mik All Machine Co Inc (PA) 704 866-4302
905 Hanover St Gastonia (28054) *(G-6465)*

Mike Atkins & Son Logging Inc 919 965-8002
4336 Browns Pond Rd Selma (27576) *(G-14258)*

Mike Beasley Services Inc 910 892-6216
663 Ammons Rd 244 Dunn (28334) *(G-4876)*

Mike DS Bbq LLC 866 960-8652
455 S Driver St Durham (27703) *(G-5225)*

Mike Goodwin Logging 704 848-8222
338 Horseback Ln Lilesville (28091) *(G-9840)*

Mike Luszcz 252 717-6282
3424 Sagewood Ct Winterville (28590) *(G-17007)*

Mike Powell Inc 910 792-6152
3407a Enterprise Dr Wilmington (28405) *(G-16324)*

Mike S Custom Cabinets Inc 252 224-5351
587 Island Creek Rd Pollocksville (28573) *(G-12394)*

Mike's Hosiery, Mount Airy *Also Called: Michael Tate (G-11546)*

Mikes Core & Battery Inc 910 920-4490
119 Drake St Fayetteville (28301) *(G-5874)*

Mikes Welding & Fabricating 336 472-5804
2871 Old Highway 29 Thomasville (27360) *(G-15249)*

Mikes Welding & Fabrication 336 472-5804
2871 Old Highway 29 Thomasville (27360) *(G-15250)*

Mikes Welding Service of Conc 704 786-9795
643 Firecrest St Se Concord (28025) *(G-4315)*

Mikron Industries 253 398-1382
2505 Meridian Pkwy # 250 Durham (27713) *(G-5226)*

Mikron Industries Inc (HQ) 713 961-4600
2505 Meridian Pkwy Ste 250 Durham (27713) *(G-5227)*

Mikropor America Inc
10512 Kilmory Ter Charlotte (28210) *(G-3178)*

Mikropul LLC 704 998-2600
4500 Chesapeake Dr Charlotte (28216) *(G-3179)*

Mil-Comm Products Inc 704 450-6415
1010 Salisbury Rd Statesville (28677) *(G-14843)*

Mil3 Inc 919 362-1217
500 Upchurch St Apex (27502) *(G-219)*

Milesi Wood Coatings, Charlotte *Also Called: Ivm Chemicals Inc (G-3000)*

Military Products Inc 910 637-0315
5425 Nc Highway 211 West End (27376) *(G-15930)*

Military Wraps Inc 910 671-0008
3400a David St Lumberton (28358) *(G-10045)*

Milkco, Asheville *Also Called: Milkco Inc (G-702)*

Milkco Inc 828 254-8428
220 Deaverview Rd Asheville (28806) *(G-702)*

Mill Art Wood 919 828-7376
1500 Capital Blvd Raleigh (27603) *(G-13032)*

Mill Camp, Boone *Also Called: Mill Camp Wines & Ciders LLC (G-1220)*

Mill Camp Wines & Ciders LLC (PA) 810 923-7339
1624 Tom Jackson Rd Boone (28607) *(G-1220)*

Mill Camp Wines & Ciders LLC 810 923-7339
187 Rivers Crest Rd Boone (28607) *(G-1221)*

Mill Creek Post & Beam Co 828 749-8000
1970 Holbert Cove Rd Saluda (28773) *(G-14072)*

Mill-Chem Manufacturing Inc 336 889-8038
650 Bassett Dr Thomasville (27360) *(G-15251)*

Millar Industries Inc 828 687-0639
20 Loop Rd Arden (28704) *(G-351)*

Millenia Usa LLC
3211c Falling Creek Rd Hickory (28601) *(G-8094)*

Millenium Print Group, Morrisville *Also Called: Park Communications LLC (G-11405)*

Millennium Buildings Inc 866 216-8499
317 W Atkins St Dobson (27017) *(G-4829)*

Millennium Landscaping, High Point *Also Called: True Portion Inc (G-8579)*

Millennium Mfg or US Chem, Boone *Also Called: US Buildings LLC (G-1245)*

Millennium Mfg Structures LLC 828 265-3737
353 Industrial Park Dr Boone (28607) *(G-1222)*

Millennium Pharmaceuticals Inc 866 466-7779
10430 Harris Oak Blvd Ste 1 Charlotte (28269) *(G-3180)*

Millennium Print Group, Morrisville *Also Called: Unlimted Potential Sanford Inc (G-11460)*

Miller Bee Supply Inc 336 670-2249
496 Yellow Banks Rd North Wilkesboro (28659) *(G-12029)*

Miller Brothers Lumber Co, Elkin *Also Called: Miller Brothers Lumber Co Inc (G-5626)*

Miller Brothers Lumber Co Inc 336 366-3400
350 Elkin Wildlife Rd Elkin (28621) *(G-5626)*

Miller Ctrl Mfg Inc Clinton NC 910 592-5112
1008 Southwest Blvd Clinton (28328) *(G-4098)*

Miller Dumpster Service LLC 704 504-9300
16450 Shallow Pond Rd Charlotte (28278) *(G-3181)*

Miller Glass 828 681-8083
72 Bradley Branch Rd Arden (28704) *(G-352)*

Miller Logging Co Inc 252 229-9860
7901 Main St Vanceboro (28586) *(G-15481)*

Miller Meat Processing LLC 252 589-0004
2365 Big Johns Store Rd Seaboard (27876) *(G-14229)*

Miller Products Inc 704 587-1870
4100 Turtle Creek Ln Charlotte (28273) *(G-3182)*

Miller Products Co, Greensboro *Also Called: Easth20 Holdings Llc (G-6987)*

Miller S Utility MGT Inc 910 298-3847
163 Jackson Store Rd Beulaville (28518) *(G-1096)*

Miller Saws & Supplies Inc 252 636-3347
115 Ridgewood Trl New Bern (28560) *(G-11822)*

Miller Sheet Metal Co Inc 336 751-2304
2038 Us Highway 601 S Mocksville (27028) *(G-10590)*

Millers Sports and Trophies 252 792-2050
101 Washington St Williamston (27892) *(G-16067)*

Milligan House Movers Inc (PA) 910 653-2272
2115 Swamp Fox Hwy E Tabor City (28463) *(G-15084)*

Milliken & Company 828 247-4300
2080 Nc Highway 226 Bostic (28018) *(G-1265)*

Milliken & Company 336 548-5680
109 Turner Rd Mayodan (27027) *(G-10366)*

Milliken Calabash Seafood, Shallotte *Also Called: Lloyds Oyster House Inc (G-14276)*

Mills Manufacturing Corp (PA) 828 645-3061
22 Mills Pl Asheville (28804) *(G-703)*

Millstreet Design, Forest City *Also Called: Heritage Classic Wovens LLC (G-6070)*

Millwood, Charlotte *Also Called: Millwood Inc (G-3183)*

Millwood Inc 704 817-7541
5950 Fairview Rd Ste 250 Charlotte (28210) *(G-3183)*

Millys Jamaican Jerk Seasoning, Raleigh *Also Called: Cool Runnings Jamaican LLC (G-12645)*

Milspec Plastics, Candler *Also Called: Cs Systems Company Inc (G-1576)*

Milton Gorham 919 816-8348
120 Wee Loch Dr Ste 101 Cary (27511) *(G-1825)*

Milwaukee Instruments Inc 252 443-3630
2950 Business Park Dr Rocky Mount (27804) *(G-13713)*

Minas Equity Partners LLC 336 724-5152
2710 Boulder Park Ct Winston Salem (27101) *(G-16811)*

Mincar Group Inc 919 772-7170
215 Tryon Rd Raleigh (27603) *(G-13033)*

Mind Flow Pubg & Prod LLC 910 339-0005
1784 Inverness Dr Fayetteville (28304) *(G-5875)*

Minda North America LLC 828 313-0092
10 N Summit Ave Granite Falls (28630) *(G-6746)*

Minelli Usa LLC 828 578-6734
1245 26th St Se Hickory (28602) *(G-8095)*

Mineral Research & Development, Harrisburg *Also Called: Venator Chemicals LLC (G-7733)*

Mineral Springs Fertilizer Inc 704 843-2683
5901 Eubanks Mineral Springs (28108) *(G-10518)*

Minges Bottling Group 252 636-5898
256 Middle St New Bern (28560) *(G-11823)*

Minges Printing & Advg Co 704 867-6791
323 S Chestnut St Gastonia (28054) *(G-6466)*

Minges Printing Company, Gastonia *Also Called: Minges Printing & Advg Co (G-6466)*

Minhas Furniture House Inc 910 898-0808
6844 Nc 705 Hwy Robbins (27325) *(G-13601)*

Mini Semi Logging 828 284-1360
346 Hunter St Burnsville (28714) *(G-1529)*

Mini Storage of North Carolina, Statesville *Also Called: Betco Inc (G-14762)*

Miningstore, Cary *Also Called: Aurum Capital Ventures Inc (G-1695)*

Minipro LLC 844 517-4776
1289 Fordham Blvd Ste 263 Chapel Hill (27514) *(G-2044)*

Minka Lighting Inc 704 785-9200
435 Business Blvd Nw Concord (28027) *(G-4316)*

Minnewawa Inc 865 522-8103
130 Sunrise Center Dr Thomasville (27360) *(G-15252)*

Minnewawa Inc 865 522-8103
10612 Providence Rd Ste D Charlotte (28277) *(G-3184)*

Minnie ME Monograms Inc 919 243-8367
104 Hibiscus Dr Clayton (27527) *(G-3996)*

Minor Press 919 628-3044
2715 W Sugar Creek Rd Charlotte (28262) *(G-3185)*

Mint Hill Cabinet Shop, Monroe *Also Called: Mint Hill Cabinet Shop Inc (G-10770)*

Mint Hill Cabinet Shop Inc 704 821-9373
5519 Cannon Dr Monroe (28110) *(G-10770)*

Mint Hill Industries 704 545-8852
7313 Old Oak Ln Mint Hill (28227) *(G-10540)*

Mint Machining A North Car 440 479-9074
4321 Sawmill Trace Dr Charlotte (28213) *(G-3186)*

Minute Man Anchors, East Flat Rock *Also Called: Mma Manufacturing Inc (G-5478)*

Minute-Man Products Inc 828 692-0256
305 W King St East Flat Rock (28726) *(G-5477)*

Minuteman Press 336 270-4426
236 Riverbend Rd Graham (27253) *(G-6704)*

Minuteman Press, Charlotte *Also Called: Babusci Crtive Prtg Imging LLC (G-2260)*

Minuteman Press, Clinton *Also Called: Commercial Prtg Co of Clinton (G-4092)*

Minuteman Press, Gastonia *Also Called: Minuteman Press of Gastonia (G-6467)*

Minuteman Press, Graham *Also Called: Minuteman Press (G-6704)*

Minuteman Press, Pineville *Also Called: Rocco Marie Ventures LLC (G-12296)*

Minuteman Press, Sneads Ferry *Also Called: Zeri Consulting Inc (G-14494)*

Minuteman Press of Gastonia 704 867-3366
495 E Long Ave Gastonia (28054) *(G-6467)*

Minuteman Provision Co LLC 252 996-0856
8740 Us 158 Reidsville (27320) *(G-13531)*

Minuteman Quick Copy Svc Inc 910 455-5353
207 W Bayshore Blvd Jacksonville (28540) *(G-9014)*

Miracle Recreation Eqp Co 704 875-6550
11515 Vanstory Dr Ste 100 Huntersville (28078) *(G-8855)*

Mirchandani Inc 919 872-8871
3904 Peppertree Pl Raleigh (27604) *(G-13034)*

Mirror Image Publishing LLC 336 643-7638
9091 Us Highway 158 Stokesdale (27357) *(G-14946)*

Mirror Tech Inc 336 342-6041
1011 Freeway Dr Reidsville (27320) *(G-13532)*

ALPHABETIC SECTION — Moduslink Corporation

Mirrormate LLC..704 390-7377
  9317 Monroe Rd Ste A Charlotte (28270) *(G-3187)*

Mischief Makers Local 816 LLC......................................336 763-2003
  1504 Rainbow Dr Greensboro (27403) *(G-7202)*

Miss Kelly's Cookin', Southern Pines *Also Called: Miss Kllys Jllies Jams Such LL (G-14542)*

Miss Kllys Jllies Jams Such LL....................................910 988-8042
  540 Highland Rd Southern Pines (28387) *(G-14542)*

Miss Tortillas Inc...919 598-8646
  3801 Wake Forest Rd Ste 106 Durham (27703) *(G-5228)*

Mission Foods, Goldsboro *Also Called: Gruma Corporation (G-6622)*

Mission Srgcal Innovations LLC....................................810 965-7455
  9004 Shellwood Ct Raleigh (27617) *(G-13035)*

Mistretta Laser Engraving...704 418-5786
  272 Nursery Rd Forest City (28043) *(G-6078)*

Mitchell Concrete Products Inc.....................................919 934-4333
  490 W Market St Smithfield (27577) *(G-14472)*

Mitchell Gold Bob Williams, Taylorsville *Also Called: Mitchell Gold Co LLC (G-15153)*

Mitchell Gold Co LLC..828 632-7916
  804 Old Landfill Rd Taylorsville (28681) *(G-15152)*

Mitchell Gold Co LLC (PA) 135 One Comfortable Pl Taylorsville (28681) *(G-15153)*

Mitchell Meat Processing, Walnut Cove *Also Called: Mitchells Meat Processing (G-15633)*

Mitchell Medlin Machine Shop......................................704 289-2840
  1394 Walkup Ave Ste C Monroe (28110) *(G-10771)*

Mitchell Water/Filtering Plant, Greensboro *Also Called: City of Greensboro (G-6911)*

Mitchell Welding Inc..828 765-2620
  7080 Us 19e Spruce Pine (28777) *(G-14651)*

Mitchells Meat Processing..336 591-7420
  401 Mitchell St Walnut Cove (27052) *(G-15633)*

Mitchum Quality Snack, Charlotte *Also Called: Igh Enterprises Inc (G-2949)*

Miter Point LLC...910 864-3645
  6423 Greyfield Rd Fayetteville (28303) *(G-5876)*

Miters Touch, Banner Elk *Also Called: Miters Touch Inc (G-903)*

Miters Touch Inc...828 963-4445
  591 Old Hartley Rd Banner Elk (28604) *(G-903)*

Mitsubishi Chem Methacrylates, Charlotte *Also Called: Mitsubishi Chemical Amer Inc (G-3188)*

Mitsubishi Chemical Amer Inc (DH)..............................980 580-2839
  9115 Harris Corners Pkwy Ste 300 Charlotte (28269) *(G-3188)*

Mitsubishi Materials USA Corp.....................................980 312-3100
  105 Corporate Center Dr Ste A Mooresville (28117) *(G-11023)*

Mitt S Nitts Inc..919 596-6793
  1014 S Hoover Rd Durham (27703) *(G-5229)*

Mixon Mills Inc..828 297-5431
  4965 Us Highway 421 N Vilas (28692) *(G-15497)*

Mixx Pt 5, Swannanoa *Also Called: Mixx-Point 5 Project LLC (G-15029)*

Mixx-Point 5 Project LLC..858 298-4625
  107 W Buckeye Rd Swannanoa (28778) *(G-15029)*

Mizelle Industries LLC...252 940-5506
  2032 Nc Highway 171 N Washington (27889) *(G-15716)*

Mj Printing..336 992-3828
  1490 Plaza South Dr Ste 9 Kernersville (27284) *(G-9217)*

Mj Soffe, Fayetteville *Also Called: M J Soffe Co (G-5863)*

MJ Soffe LLC...910 422-9002
  13750 Us Highway 301 S Rowland (28383) *(G-13791)*

Mjpc Transport LLC (PA)..877 590-9512
  3201 Edwards Mill Rd Ste 141 Raleigh (27612) *(G-13036)*

Mjt Us Inc...704 826-7828
  6801 Northpark Blvd Ste A Charlotte (28216) *(G-3189)*

Mk Global Holdings LLC (DH)......................................704 334-1904
  5101 Terminal St Charlotte (28208) *(G-3190)*

Mkc85 Inc (PA)...910 762-1986
  2705 Castle Creek Ln Wilmington (28401) *(G-16325)*

Mlb Screen Printing..704 363-6124
  12008 Regal Lily Ln Huntersville (28078) *(G-8856)*

Mlf Company LLC...919 231-9401
  3248 Lake Woodard Dr Raleigh (27604) *(G-13037)*

Mlg Trnscndent Trckg Trnsp Svc.................................336 905-1192
  3495 Hickswood Forest Dr High Point (27265) *(G-8457)*

Mm Clayton LLC...919 553-4113
  1000 Ccc Dr Clayton (27520) *(G-3997)*

Mma Manufacturing Inc..828 692-0256
  305 W King St East Flat Rock (28726) *(G-5478)*

Mmb One Inc (PA)..704 523-8163
  4629 Dwight Evans Rd Charlotte (28217) *(G-3191)*

Mmdi Inc...704 882-4550
  200 Beltway Blvd Matthews (28104) *(G-10336)*

Mmj Machining and Fabg Inc.......................................336 495-1029
  1332 Gene Allred Dr Randleman (27317) *(G-13479)*

MMS Logistics Incorporated..336 214-3552
  1509 Guinness Dr Mc Leansville (27301) *(G-10394)*

MN Logging LLC...828 286-9262
  449 Mountain Creek Rd Rutherfordton (28139) *(G-13880)*

Mobay Sportswear Embroidery....................................704 262-7783
  550 Cabarrus Ave W Concord (28027) *(G-4317)*

Mobile Mini - Stor Tanks Pumps..................................919 365-0377
  618 Nc-2655 Knightdale (27545) *(G-9421)*

Mobile Mini Inc...480 894-6311
  618 Three Sisters Rd Knightdale (27545) *(G-9422)*

Mobile Mini Inc...919 365-3057
  2231 Lake Wendell Rd #c Wendell (27591) *(G-15908)*

Mobius Imaging, Charlotte *Also Called: Mobius Imaging LLC (G-3192)*

Mobius Imaging LLC..704 773-7652
  1723 Beverly Dr Charlotte (28207) *(G-3192)*

Mocaro Dyeing & Finishing, Monroe *Also Called: Sdfc LLC (G-10804)*

Mocaro Dyeing & Finishing Inc....................................704 878-6645
  2201 Mocaro Dr Statesville (28677) *(G-14844)*

Mocaro Industries Inc..704 878-6645
  2201 Mocaro Dr Statesville (28677) *(G-14845)*

Mocha Memoir Press..336 404-7445
  931 S Main St Kernersville (27284) *(G-9218)*

Mock Tire & Automotive Inc..336 753-8473
  132 Interstate Dr Mocksville (27028) *(G-10591)*

Mock Tire & Automotive Inc..336 774-0081
  834 S Stratford Rd Winston Salem (27103) *(G-16812)*

Mock Tire & Automotive Inc (PA)................................336 768-1010
  4752 Country Club Rd Winston Salem (27104) *(G-16813)*

Modacam Incorporated..704 489-8500
  3762 Deer Run Denver (28037) *(G-4789)*

Modena Southern Dyeing Corp...................................704 866-9156
  1010 E Ozark Ave Gastonia (28054) *(G-6468)*

Modern Densifying Inc...704 434-8335
  662 Plato Lee Rd Shelby (28150) *(G-14348)*

Modern Information Svcs Inc......................................704 872-1020
  436 S Center St Statesville (28677) *(G-14846)*

Modern Lightning Protection Co.................................252 756-3006
  302 Queen Annes Rd Greenville (27858) *(G-7561)*

Modern Machine and Metal Fabricators Inc...............336 993-4808
  3201 Centre Park Blvd Winston Salem (27107) *(G-16814)*

Modern Machining Inc...919 775-7332
  115 Brady Rd Sanford (27330) *(G-14154)*

Modern Marble & Glass Inc...336 668-4197
  107 Arrow Rd Greensboro (27409) *(G-7203)*

Modern Mold & Tool Company....................................704 377-2300
  1050 Ironwood Dr Mount Holly (28120) *(G-11643)*

Modern Polymers Inc...704 435-5825
  875 W Academy St Cherryville (28021) *(G-3872)*

Modern Polymers Inc...704 435-5825
  901 W Academy St Cherryville (28021) *(G-3873)*

Modern Recreational Tech...847 272-2278
  2220 Us Highway 70 Se Ste 100 Hickory (28602) *(G-8096)*

Modern Structure Solutions LLC.................................984 286-2447
  2601 Withers Dr Hudson (28638) *(G-8776)*

Modern Tool Service..919 365-7470
  100 Walnut St Wendell (27591) *(G-15909)*

Modern Workbench LLC..828 845-4466
  31 Amber Dr Horse Shoe (28742) *(G-8742)*

Modlins Anonized Aluminum Wldg..............................252 753-7274
  4551 Nc Highway 121 Farmville (27828) *(G-5740)*

Modoral Brands Inc..336 741-7230
  401 N Main St Winston Salem (27101) *(G-16815)*

Moduslink Corporation..781 663-5000
  990 N Greenfield Pkwy Garner (27529) *(G-6288)*

Moe Jt Enterprises Inc.. 423 512-1427
130 Back Forty Dr Winston Salem (27127) *(G-16816)*

Moehring-Group, Beaufort *Also Called: Atlantic Veneer Company LLC (G-943)*

Moen, New Bern *Also Called: Moen Incorporated (G-11824)*

Moen Incorporated.. 252 638-3300
101 Industrial Dr New Bern (28562) *(G-11824)*

Moes Hndy Svcs Fnce Instl Mno.. 910 712-1402
185 Desert Orchid Cir Raeford (28376) *(G-12426)*

Moffitt Machine Company Inc... 910 485-2159
232 Winslow St Fayetteville (28301) *(G-5877)*

Mohawk Industries, Garner *Also Called: Mohawk Industries Inc (G-6290)*

Mohawk Industries Inc... 919 609-4759
800 N Greenfield Pkwy Garner (27529) *(G-6289)*

Mohawk Industries Inc... 919 661-5590
2000 Pergo Pkwy Garner (27529) *(G-6290)*

Mohawk Industries Inc... 910 439-6959
149 Homanit Usa Rd Mount Gilead (27306) *(G-11609)*

Mohawk Industries Inc... 336 313-4156
550 Cloniger Dr Thomasville (27360) *(G-15253)*

Mohawk Laminate & Hardwood, Thomasville *Also Called: Mohawk Industries Inc (G-15253)*

Mohican Mills Inc... 704 735-3343
1419 E Gaston St Lincolnton (28092) *(G-9908)*

Moire Creations America LLC (PA)................................... 704 482-9860
1808 Country Garden Dr Shelby (28150) *(G-14349)*

Moissanite.com, LLC, Morrisville *Also Called: Charlesandcolvardcom LLC (G-11320)*

Mojo Sportswear Inc.. 252 758-4176
1016 Myrtle St Greenville (27834) *(G-7562)*

Mojo Sportswear, Greenville *Also Called: Mojo Sportswear Inc (G-7562)*

Mold Trans LLC... 828 356-5181
279 Hutch Mountain Rd Fletcher (28732) *(G-6027)*

Molded Fiber Glass, Morganton *Also Called: Molded Fibr GL Cmpny/Nrth Crli (G-11234)*

Molded Fibr GL Cmpny/Nrth Crli..................................... 828 584-4974
213 Reep Dr Morganton (28655) *(G-11234)*

Molds of Bethlehem, Hickory *Also Called: Bethlehem Manufacturing Co (G-7949)*

Molecular Toxicology Inc... 828 264-9099
157 Industrial Park Dr Boone (28607) *(G-1223)*

Moltox, Boone *Also Called: Molecular Toxicology Inc (G-1223)*

Momentive Performance Mtls Inc..................................... 704 805-6252
9129 Southern Pine Blvd Charlotte (28273) *(G-3193)*

Momentive Performance Mtls Inc..................................... 704 805-6200
13620 Reese Blvd E Ste 310 Huntersville (28078) *(G-8857)*

Momentive Performance Mtls USA, Huntersville *Also Called: Momentive Performance Mtls Inc (G-8857)*

Mommamade Scents LLC.. 704 458-5901
13626 Riding Hill Ave Charlotte (28213) *(G-3194)*

Mommi & ME Kozmeticz LLC.. 704 620-0082
1822 Mcdonald St Charlotte (28216) *(G-3195)*

Mommy's Numbers, Raeford *Also Called: Cw Media Inc (G-12419)*

Mon Macaron LLC.. 984 200-1387
111 Seaboard Ave Ste 118 Raleigh (27604) *(G-13038)*

Mona Lisa Foods, Hendersonville *Also Called: Barry Callebaut USA LLC (G-7823)*

Monarch Color Corporation (PA)...................................... 704 394-4626
5327 Brookshire Blvd Charlotte (28216) *(G-3196)*

Monarch Educational Svcs LLC... 910 785-4087
309 Collinsworth Dr Clayton (27527) *(G-3998)*

Monarch Knitting McHy Corp.. 704 283-8171
601 Mcarthur Cir Monroe (28110) *(G-10772)*

Monarch Knitting McHy Corp (PA)................................... 704 291-3300
115 N Secrest Ave Monroe (28110) *(G-10773)*

Monarch Manufacturing, Monroe *Also Called: Monarch Knitting McHy Corp (G-10773)*

Monarch Manufacturing Corp.. 704 283-8171
115 N Secrest Ave Monroe (28110) *(G-10774)*

Monarch Medical Tech LLC... 704 335-1300
112 S Tryon St Ste 800 Charlotte (28284) *(G-3197)*

Monarch Printers.. 704 376-1533
3900 Greensboro St Charlotte (28206) *(G-3198)*

Money 4 Lyfe.. 704 606-8671
6426 Covecreek Dr Charlotte (28215) *(G-3199)*

Mongoose LLC... 919 400-0772
423 Lakeside Ave Burlington (27217) *(G-1462)*

Monical Enterprises Inc.. 757 692-1345
499 Lea Dr Hampstead (28443) *(G-7651)*

Monitor Roller Mill Inc... 336 591-4126
109 E 4th St Walnut Cove (27052) *(G-15634)*

Monk Lekeisha... 910 385-0361
Goldsboro (27533) *(G-6637)*

Monkey Jct Mulch & Stone Inc.. 910 793-9111
6512 Carolina Beach Rd Wilmington (28412) *(G-16326)*

Mono Plate Inc... 631 643-3100
2404 Pilsley Rd Apex (27539) *(G-220)*

Mono Systems Inc.. 914 934-2075
1506 Niall Ln Waxhaw (28173) *(G-15766)*

Monogram Asheville.. 828 707-8110
800 Brevard Rd Ste 812 Asheville (28806) *(G-704)*

Monogram Asheville LLC... 828 545-5367
19 E Owl Creek Ln Fairview (28730) *(G-5716)*

Monogram Food Solutions LLC (PA)................................ 901 685-7167
2330 E 5th St Charlotte (28204) *(G-3200)*

Monogram This.. 336 528-9980
784 Sheffield Rd Mocksville (27028) *(G-10592)*

Monogram Whimsy.. 704 904-1476
1901 Crestgate Dr Waxhaw (28173) *(G-15767)*

Monograms Etc.. 336 769-8358
1056 N Peace Haven Rd Winston Salem (27104) *(G-16817)*

Monolith Corporation (HQ)... 919 878-1900
12339 Wake Union Church Rd Ste 107 Wake Forest (27587) *(G-15572)*

Monroe Metal Manufacturing, Monroe *Also Called: Monroe Metal Manufacturing Inc (G-10775)*

Monroe Metal Manufacturing Inc.................................... 800 366-1391
6025 Stitt St Monroe (28110) *(G-10775)*

Monsanto Company... 252 212-5421
5746 Pearsall St Battleboro (27809) *(G-925)*

MONSANTO COMPANY, Battleboro *Also Called: Monsanto Company (G-925)*

Monsted Mix Inc... 704 979-6911
3323 Holt St Charlotte (28205) *(G-3201)*

Monster Brewing Company LLC....................................... 828 883-2337
342 Mountain Industrial Dr Brevard (28712) *(G-1280)*

Monte Enterprises Inc.. 252 637-5803
3204 Neuse Blvd New Bern (28560) *(G-11825)*

Monte Printing Co, New Bern *Also Called: Monte Enterprises Inc (G-11825)*

Montgomery Herald... 910 576-6051
341 N Main St # B Troy (27371) *(G-15408)*

Montgomery Logging Inc.. 910 572-2806
207 Atkins Dairy Rd Troy (27371) *(G-15409)*

Month9 Books LLC (PA)... 919 645-5786
4208 Six Forks Rd Ste 1000 Raleigh (27609) *(G-13039)*

Monticello Labs Inc... 919 623-6390
4604 Brodog Ter Hurdle Mills (27541) *(G-8911)*

Montrose Hanger Co, Wilson *Also Called: Swofford Inc (G-16545)*

Montys Welding & Fabrication.. 919 337-7859
157 Creek Commons Ave Garner (27529) *(G-6291)*

Moog Components Group, Murphy *Also Called: Moog Inc (G-11713)*

Moog Inc.. 828 837-5115
1995 Nc Highway 141 Murphy (28906) *(G-11713)*

Mool Law Firm LLC.. 217 496-3355
163 Farm Valley Ln Boone (28607) *(G-1224)*

Moon and Lola Inc (PA)... 919 306-2257
2024 Saint Marys St Raleigh (27608) *(G-13040)*

Moon Audio... 919 649-5018
1157 Executive Cir Ste 101 Cary (27511) *(G-1826)*

Moon N Sea Nc LLC... 704 588-1963
12810 Virkler Dr Charlotte (28273) *(G-3202)*

Moondance Soaps & More, Raleigh *Also Called: Rachel Dubois (G-13169)*

Moonshine Press.. 828 371-8519
162 Riverwood Dr Franklin (28734) *(G-6139)*

Moore Dumpster Service LLC... 704 560-4410
1617 Salmon Ln Sw Ocean Isle Beach (28469) *(G-12093)*

Moore Machine Products Inc... 910 592-2718
919 Rowan Rd Clinton (28328) *(G-4099)*

Moore Printing & Graphics Inc.. 919 821-3293
5320 Departure Dr Raleigh (27616) *(G-13041)*

Moore S Welding Service Inc... 919 837-5769
142 Elmer Moore Rd Bear Creek (27207) *(G-940)*

ALPHABETIC SECTION — Motor Sports Designs Holding

Moore Signs, Wilmington Also Called: Kenneth Moore Signs (G-16287)
Moore, James R, Greensboro Also Called: Moores Printing (G-7204)
Moorecraft Reels Inc 252 823-2510
   101 Royster St Tarboro (27886) (G-15115)
Moorecraft Wood Proucts Inc 252 823-2510
   101 Royster St Tarboro (27886) (G-15116)
Moores Cylinder Heads LLC (PA) 704 786-8412
   323 Corban Ave Sw Ste 515 Concord (28025) (G-4318)
Moores Fiberglass Inc 252 753-2583
   926 Howell Swamp Church Rd Walstonburg (27888) (G-15640)
Moores Marine Yacht Center Inc 252 504-7060
   182 Lewistown Rd Beaufort (28516) (G-961)
Moores Mch Co Fayetteville Inc (PA) 919 837-5354
   13120 Nc 902 Hwy Bear Creek (27207) (G-941)
Moores Printing 336 856-0540
   4209 Princeton Ave Greensboro (27407) (G-7204)
Moores Upholstering Interiors 704 240-8393
   308 S Poplar St Lincolnton (28092) (G-9909)
Mooresville Ice Cream Company LLC 704 664-5456
   172 N Brd St Mooresville (28115) (G-11024)
Mooresville NC 704 909-6459
   174 Mandarin Dr Mooresville (28117) (G-11025)
Mooresville Parlor LLC 704 450-1836
   168 N Broad St Mooresville (28115) (G-11026)
Mooresville Tax Service Inc 704 360-1040
   907 Brawley School Rd Mooresville (28117) (G-11027)
Mooresville Tribune 704 872-0148
   1100 11th Avenue Blvd Se Hickory (28602) (G-8097)
Mooresvlle Blue Dvil Band Bste 704 787-2994
   659 E Center Ave Mooresville (28115) (G-11028)
Mooresvlle Pub Wrks Snttion De 704 664-4278
   2523 Charlotte Hwy Mooresville (28117) (G-11029)
Moose Candle Company 828 244-1384
   2548 Belshire Dr Conover (28613) (G-4473)
Moose-Tek Industries Inc 336 416-7034
   595 Lake Forest Dr New London (28127) (G-11874)
Morbern LLC 336 883-4332
   401 Fraley Rd High Point (27263) (G-8458)
Morbern USA Inc (HQ) 336 883-4332
   401 Fraley Rd High Point (27263) (G-8459)
Mordecai Beverage Co 919 831-9125
   2425 Crabtree Blvd Raleigh (27604) (G-13042)
More Than Billboards Inc 336 723-1018
   2737 W Mountain St Kernersville (27284) (G-9219)
Moretz & Sipe Inc 828 327-8661
   3261 Highland Ave Ne Hickory (28601) (G-8098)
Moretz Bldg & Woodworks LLC 828 406-4672
   13830 Us Highway 221 S Unit A Fleetwood (28626) (G-5976)
Moretz Signs Inc 828 387-4600
   125 Staghorn Hollow Rd Beech Mountain (28604) (G-972)
Morgan & Son Logging 828 389-9618
   111 Sally Gap Trl Hayesville (28904) (G-7769)
Morgan Advanced Mtls Tech Inc 910 892-9677
   504 N Ashe Ave Dunn (28334) (G-4877)
Morgan Creek Seafood, Beaufort Also Called: Gillikin Marine Railways Inc (G-958)
Morgan Fertilizer, Farmville Also Called: Harvey Fertilizer and Gas Co (G-5738)
Morgan Manufacturing 336 497-5763
   211 Berry Garden Rd Kernersville (27284) (G-9220)
Morgan Printers Inc 252 355-5588
   4120 Bayswater Rd Winterville (28590) (G-17008)
Morgan Tool & Die LLC 910 281-0201
   911 Rose Ridge Rd Aberdeen (28315) (G-16)
Morgans Cabinets Inc 704 485-8693
   8056 Rocky River Rd Oakboro (28129) (G-12078)
Morganton Pressure Vessels LLC, Marion Also Called: Mpv Mrgnton Prssure Vssels NC (G-10168)
Morganton Service League, Morganton Also Called: Morganton Service League Inc (G-11235)
Morganton Service League Inc 828 439-9525
   112 Terrace Pl Morganton (28655) (G-11235)
Morinaga America, Mebane Also Called: Morinaga America Foods Inc (G-10420)

Morinaga America Foods Inc 919 643-2439
   4391 Wilson Rd Mebane (27302) (G-10420)
Morningstar Signs and Banners 704 861-0020
   307 E Franklin Blvd Gastonia (28054) (G-6469)
Moroil Corp 704 795-9595
   6867 Belt Rd Concord (28027) (G-4319)
Moroil Technologies, Concord Also Called: Moroil Corp (G-4319)
Morris & Associates Inc 919 582-9200
   803 Morris Dr Garner (27529) (G-6292)
Morris East, Charlotte Also Called: Morris Family Theatrical Inc (G-3203)
Morris Family Theatrical Inc (PA) 704 332-3304
   6900 Morris Estate Dr Charlotte (28262) (G-3203)
Morris Group 973 713-2211
   1707 Pennyroyal Rd New Bern (28562) (G-11826)
Morris Machine Company Inc 704 824-4242
   122 Stroupe Rd Gastonia (28056) (G-6470)
Morris Machine Sales, Gastonia Also Called: Morris Machine Company Inc (G-6470)
Morris South LLC 704 523-6008
   12428 Sam Neely Rd Ste A Charlotte (28278) (G-3204)
Morris South M T S, Charlotte Also Called: Morris South LLC (G-3204)
Morrisette Paper Company Inc 336 342-5570
   105 E Harrison St Reidsville (27320) (G-13533)
Morrison Mill Work 828 774-5415
   51 Thompson St Asheville (28803) (G-705)
Morton Buildings Inc 252 291-1300
   3042 Forest Hills Rd Sw Ste C Wilson (27893) (G-16516)
Morton Metalcraft Company N 336 731-5700
   Welcome (27374) (G-15873)
Morven Partners LP 252 482-2193
   185 Peanut Dr Edenton (27932) (G-5519)
Morven Partners LP 252 794-3435
   406 Spring St Windsor (27983) (G-16567)
Mosack Group LLC 888 229-2874
   11210 Allen Station Dr Mint Hill (28227) (G-10541)
Moses, David, Monroe Also Called: Interordnance Amer Ltd Partnr (G-10740)
Mosley 910 409-5814
   4917 Gate Post Ln Wilmington (28412) (G-16327)
Moss Brothers Tires & Svc Inc 910 895-4572
   190 W Us Highway 74 Rockingham (28379) (G-13635)
Moss Sign Company Inc 828 299-7766
   526 Swannanoa River Rd Asheville (28805) (G-706)
Moss Supply Company (PA) 704 596-8717
   5001 N Graham St Charlotte (28269) (G-3205)
Mosse Quick Farm, Creston Also Called: McClellan Patric Michael (G-4623)
Mother Earth Brewing LLC 252 208-2437
   311 N Herritage St Kinston (28501) (G-9377)
Mother Murphys Labs Inc 336 273-1737
   300 Dougherty St Greensboro (27406) (G-7205)
Mother Murphys Labs Inc (PA) 336 273-1737
   2826 S Elm Eugene St Greensboro (27406) (G-7206)
Mother of Pearl Co Inc 828 524-6842
   86 Belden Terrace Ln Franklin (28734) (G-6140)
Mother Sand Fathers Black Sons 919 301-8161
   1413 Beichler Rd Garner (27529) (G-6293)
Motion Control Integration 704 608-1279
   9611 Brookdale Dr Ste 100 Charlotte (28215) (G-3206)
Motion Sensors Inc 252 335-7294
   786 Pitts Chapel Rd Elizabeth City (27909) (G-5557)
Motion-Eaze, Randleman Also Called: North Carolina Lumber Company (G-13481)
Motioncraft By Sherrill Div, Morganton Also Called: Sherrill Furniture Company (G-11252)
Motivo Furniture, High Point Also Called: Ariston Hospitality Inc (G-8254)
Moto Group LLC 828 350-7653
   40 Cane Creek Industrial Park Rd Fletcher (28732) (G-6028)
Motor Raceways Inc 252 715-3990
   4025 W Soundside Rd Nags Head (27959) (G-11723)
Motor Rite Inc 919 625-3653
   1001 Corporation Pkwy Ste 100 Raleigh (27610) (G-13043)
Motor Shop Inc 704 867-8488
   5001 York Hwy Gastonia (28052) (G-6471)
Motor Sports Designs Holding, High Point Also Called: M D C Graphics LLC (G-8434)

Motor Vhcles Lcense Plate Agcy...................................... 252 338-6965
  1545 N Road St Ste E Elizabeth City (27909) *(G-5558)*

Motoring Inc... 704 809-1265
  139 Golden Pond Ln Mooresville (28117) *(G-11030)*

Motorola Mobility LLC... 919 294-1289
  7001 Development Dr Morrisville (27560) *(G-11391)*

Motorsport Innovations Inc.. 704 728-7837
  19220 Callaway Hills Ln Davidson (28036) *(G-4686)*

Motorsports Designs Inc.. 336 454-1181
  300 Old Thomasville Rd High Point (27260) *(G-8460)*

Motorsports Machining Tech LLC............................ 336 475-3742
  37 High Tech Blvd Thomasville (27360) *(G-15254)*

Motsinger Block Plant Inc.. 336 764-0350
  199 Disher Rd Winston Salem (27107) *(G-16818)*

Moulding Millwork LLC.. 704 504-9880
  11445 Granite St Unit C Charlotte (28273) *(G-3207)*

Moulding Source Incorporated................................. 704 658-1111
  184 Azalea Rd Mooresville (28115) *(G-11031)*

Mount Airy Signs & Letters Inc................................. 336 786-5777
  1543 Fancy Gap Rd Mount Airy (27030) *(G-11547)*

Mount Holly West Plant, Mount Holly Also Called: Clariant Corporation *(G-11627)*

Mount Hope Machinery Co
  2000 Donald Ross Rd Charlotte (28208) *(G-3208)*

Mount Olive Pickle Company..................................... 704 867-5585
  1534 Union Rd Ste A Gastonia (28054) *(G-6472)*

Mount Olive Pickle Company Inc.............................. 704 867-5585
  1534 Union Rd Ste A Gastonia (28054) *(G-6473)*

Mount Olive Pickle Company Inc (PA)...................... 919 658-2535
  1 Cucumber Blvd Mount Olive (28365) *(G-11666)*

Mount Olive Tribune, Mount Olive Also Called: Benmot Publishing Company Inc *(G-11655)*

Mount Vernon Chemicals LLC................................... 336 226-1161
  2001 Willow Spring Ln Burlington (27215) *(G-1463)*

Mount Vernon Mills Inc.. 336 226-1161
  2001 Willow Spring Ln Burlington (27215) *(G-1464)*

Mountain Area Info Netwrk.. 828 255-0182
  34 Wall St Ste 407 Asheville (28801) *(G-707)*

Mountain Bear & Co Inc.. 828 631-0156
  28 Church St Dillsboro (28725) *(G-4817)*

Mountain Cabinetry Closets LLC.............................. 828 966-9000
  309 S Country Club Rd Brevard (28712) *(G-1281)*

Mountain Graphics, Asheville Also Called: Art Enterprises Inc *(G-528)*

Mountain Homes of Wnc LLC.................................... 828 216-2546
  12 White Walnut Dr Weaverville (28787) *(G-15852)*

Mountain Intaglio LLC.. 713 725-7926
  180 Skycliff Dr Asheville (28804) *(G-708)*

Mountain International LLC....................................... 828 606-0194
  1345 Old Hendersonville Hwy Brevard (28712) *(G-1282)*

Mountain Khakis, Charlotte Also Called: Mk Global Holdings LLC *(G-3190)*

Mountain Leisure Hot Tubs LLC............................... 828 649-7727
  40 Business Park Cir Ste 60 Arden (28704) *(G-353)*

Mountain Machine, Hendersonville Also Called: Eddie S Mountain Machine Inc *(G-7846)*

Mountain Manner Exotic Jellies, Marble Also Called: Pamela Stoeppelwerth *(G-10133)*

Mountain Rcrtion Log Cbins LLC.............................. 828 387-6688
  8007 Linville Falls Hwy Newland (28657) *(G-11890)*

Mountain Showcase, Hendersonville Also Called: Mountain Showcase Group Inc *(G-7881)*

Mountain Showcase Group Inc................................. 828 692-9494
  211 Sugarloaf Rd Hendersonville (28792) *(G-7881)*

Mountain Snow LLC... 828 403-7535
  172 Mountain View Rd Marion (28752) *(G-10166)*

Mountain Times, Boone Also Called: Sundown Times Inc *(G-1240)*

Mountain Times Inc.. 336 246-6397
  7 W Main St West Jefferson (28694) *(G-15945)*

Mountain Top Woodworking..................................... 336 982-4059
  816 Old Obids Rd West Jefferson (28694) *(G-15946)*

Mountain Valley Logging LLC.................................. 828 551-0861
  297 Fate Maybin Ln Zirconia (28790) *(G-17155)*

Mountain Vista Extracts LLC..................................... 910 489-3948
  824 Inlet View Dr Wilmington (28409) *(G-16328)*

Mountain Xpress, Asheville Also Called: Green Line Media Inc *(G-643)*

Mountaineer Enterprise... 828 670-5425
  83 Lake Dr Biltmore Lake (28715) *(G-1101)*

Mountaineer Inc.. 828 452-0661
  220 N Main St Waynesville (28786) *(G-15811)*

Mountaintop Cheesecakes LLC................................ 336 391-9127
  209 Sunburst Ln Mocksville (27028) *(G-10593)*

Mountaire Farms LLC... 910 974-3232
  203 Morris Farm Rd Candor (27229) *(G-1596)*

Mountaire Farms LLC... 910 843-5942
  17269 N Carolina Hwy 71 Lumber Bridge (28357) *(G-10020)*

Mountaire Farms LLC... 910 843-3332
  17269 Nc 71 Hwy N Lumber Bridge (28357) *(G-10021)*

Mountaire Farms LLC... 919 663-1768
  4555 Old Us Hwy 421 N Siler City (27344) *(G-14424)*

Mountaire Farms LLC... 704 978-3055
  2206 W Front St Statesville (28677) *(G-14847)*

Mountaire Farms Inc... 910 843-5942
  17269 Hwy 71 Lumber Bridge (28357) *(G-10022)*

Mountaire Farms Inc... 910 844-3126
  10800 Pell Dr Maxton (28364) *(G-10361)*

Mountaire Farms Inc... 919 663-0848
  1101 E 3rd St Siler City (27344) *(G-14425)*

Mountaire Farms Inc... 704 978-3055
  2206 W Front St Statesville (28677) *(G-14848)*

Mountaire Farms North Carolina, Candor Also Called: Mountaire Farms LLC *(G-1596)*

Mountaire Farms, L.L.C., Lumber Bridge Also Called: Mountaire Farms LLC *(G-10020)*

Movers and Shakers LLC... 980 771-0505
  1016 W Craighead Rd Charlotte (28206) *(G-3209)*

Movex Usa Inc.. 434 616-2590
  1311 Rio Falls Dr Raleigh (27614) *(G-13044)*

Moving Screens Incorporated................................... 336 364-9259
  7807 Helena Moriah Rd Rougemont (27572) *(G-13787)*

Moxie... 646 481-7807
  2030 Eastwood Rd Ste 1 Wilmington (28403) *(G-16329)*

Moya Custom Designs LLC....................................... 984 208-3118
  789 Ss Edwards Rd Siler City (27344) *(G-14426)*

Mp Digital Print & Signs Inc...................................... 571 315-1562
  20325 Sterling Bay Ln W Cornelius (28031) *(G-4570)*

Mpe Usa Inc.. 704 340-4910
  10424 Rodney St Pineville (28134) *(G-12284)*

Mpressive Shirt Works LLC...................................... 919 395-8295
  3402 Tuckland Dr Raleigh (27610) *(G-13045)*

MPS Greensboro, Greensboro Also Called: Multi Packaging Solutions *(G-7207)*

Mpv Morganton Pressu.. 828 652-3704
  1 Alfredo Baglioni Dr Marion (28752) *(G-10167)*

Mpv Mrgnton Prssure Vssels NC............................. 828 652-3704
  1 Alfredo Baglioni Dr Marion (28752) *(G-10168)*

Mpx Manufacturing Inc.. 704 762-9207
  1531 S Main St Salisbury (28144) *(G-14014)*

Mqh LLC... 570 417-3165
  1625 Grooms Rd Reidsville (27320) *(G-13534)*

Mr Bs Fun Foods Inc (PA).. 828 879-1901
  2616 Israel Chapel Rd Connelly Springs (28612) *(G-4406)*

MR Fabrications LLC.. 980 785-3943
  9403 Highway 742 Marshville (28103) *(G-10220)*

Mr Handyman Western Wake Cnty, Raleigh Also Called: Lake House Enterprises Inc *(G-12952)*

Mr Hardwood Floors Inc.. 919 369-8027
  9650 Neils Branch Rd Raleigh (27603) *(G-13046)*

Mr Home Genius LLC... 252 902-4663
  2072 Sinmar Ln Winterville (28590) *(G-17009)*

Mr Tire Inc... 828 262-3555
  1563 Blowing Rock Rd Boone (28607) *(G-1225)*

Mr Tire Inc... 704 483-1500
  357 N Nc 16 Business Hwy Denver (28037) *(G-4790)*

Mr Tire Inc... 828 322-8130
  2105 N Center St Hickory (28601) *(G-8099)*

Mr Tire Inc... 704 739-6456
  407 S Battleground Ave Kings Mountain (28086) *(G-9319)*

Mr Tire Inc... 828 758-0047
  1306 Morganton Blvd Sw Lenoir (28645) *(G-9637)*

Mr Tire Inc... 704 735-8024
  609 E Main St Lincolnton (28092) *(G-9910)*

ALPHABETIC SECTION — Murphy-Brown LLC

Mr Tire Inc 704 484-0816
315 S Dekalb St Shelby (28150) *(G-14350)*

Mr Tire Inc 704 872-4127
149 E Front St Statesville (28677) *(G-14849)*

Mr Tobacco 919 747-9052
4011 Capital Blvd Ste 125 Raleigh (27604) *(G-13047)*

Mra Services Inc 704 933-4300
2500 S Cannon Blvd Kannapolis (28083) *(G-9127)*

Mre-Star 407 403-3889
2099 Brevard Rd Arden (28704) *(G-354)*

Mrf Technologies LLC 919 714-2852
622 Devereux St Raleigh (27605) *(G-13048)*

Mro Stop LLC (HQ) 704 587-5429
11616 Wilmar Blvd Charlotte (28273) *(G-3210)*

Mrr Southern LLC 919 436-3571
5842 Faringdon Pl Ste 1 Raleigh (27609) *(G-13049)*

Mrs GS Tees 704 372-0610
2108 Double Oaks Rd Charlotte (28206) *(G-3211)*

Mrschis Sticker N Tees 919 606-1940
2690 Polenta Rd Clayton (27520) *(G-3999)*

Ms Whlchair N CA AM State Coor 828 230-1129
61 Cheek Rd Weaverville (28787) *(G-15853)*

MSA Safety Sales LLC 910 353-1540
352 White St Jacksonville (28546) *(G-9015)*

MSE Beautyshapewear LLC 910 500-0179
511 N Reilly Rd Ste A-90 Fayetteville (28303) *(G-5878)*

MSI, Bessemer City *Also Called: Manufacturing Services Inc (G-1074)*

MSI, Mooresville *Also Called: MSI Defense Solutions LLC (G-11032)*

MSI, Wilmington *Also Called: Industrial Rlblity Spclsts Inc (G-16267)*

MSI Defense Solutions LLC 704 660-8348
136 Knob Hill Rd Mooresville (28117) *(G-11032)*

Mt Airy Meat Center Inc 336 786-2023
133 Old Buck Shoals Rd Mount Airy (27030) *(G-11548)*

Mt Gilead Cut & Sew Inc 910 439-9909
112 N Main St Mount Gilead (27306) *(G-11610)*

Mt Holly Plant, Charlotte *Also Called: Clariant Corporation (G-2490)*

Mt Press Services Inc 647 979-8675
7928 Goodall Ct Mint Hill (28227) *(G-10542)*

MTI Medical Cables LLC 828 890-2888
2133 Old Fanning Bridge Rd Fletcher (28732) *(G-6029)*

MTS Communication Products, Clayton *Also Called: Multi Technical Services Inc (G-4000)*

MTS Holdings Corp Inc 336 227-0151
2900 Tucker St Burlington (27215) *(G-1465)*

MTS Sensors Division, Cary *Also Called: MTS Systems Corporation (G-1827)*

MTS Systems Corporation 919 677-2352
3001 Sheldon Dr Cary (27513) *(G-1827)*

MTS Systems Roehrig, Greensboro *Also Called: Roehrig Engineering Inc (G-7316)*

Mtz Welding Inc 919 708-8288
1108 Lemmond Dr Sanford (27330) *(G-14155)*

Mud Duck Construction, Bolivia *Also Called: Mud Duck Operations (G-1165)*

Mud Duck Operations 910 253-7669
1470 Old Lennon Rd Se Bolivia (28422) *(G-1165)*

Muddy Creek Mill Works Inc 828 659-5558
2854 Muddy Creek Rd Nebo (28761) *(G-11762)*

Muddy Dog LLC 919 371-2818
511 Edgemore Ave Cary (27519) *(G-1828)*

Muddy Dog Roasting Co, Cary *Also Called: Muddy Dog LLC (G-1828)*

Muddy River Distillery LLC 336 516-4190
1500 River Dr Ste 100 Belmont (28012) *(G-995)*

Mudgear LLC 347 674-9102
2522 Handley Pl Charlotte (28226) *(G-3212)*

Mueller Die Cut Solutions Inc (HQ) 704 588-3900
10415 Westlake Dr Charlotte (28273) *(G-3213)*

Mueller Steam Specialty (DH) 910 865-8241
1491 Nc Highway 20 W Saint Pauls (28384) *(G-13906)*

Mueller Steam Specialty, Saint Pauls *Also Called: Mueller Steam Specialty (G-13906)*

Mueller Systems LLC 704 278-2221
10210 Statesville Blvd Cleveland (27013) *(G-4076)*

Mugo Gravel & Grading Inc (PA) 704 782-3478
2600 Concord Pkwy S Concord (28027) *(G-4320)*

Mulberry Street Inc 252 638-3195
101 Timberwolf Ct New Bern (28560) *(G-11827)*

Mulch Magicians, Waxhaw *Also Called: Pressure Washing Near Me LLC (G-15770)*

Mulch Masters, Raleigh *Also Called: Mulch Masters of NC Inc (G-13050)*

Mulch Masters of NC Inc 919 676-0031
10200 Durant Rd Raleigh (27614) *(G-13050)*

Mulch Solutions LLC 704 893-5302
1011 Thessallian Ln Indian Trail (28079) *(G-8950)*

Mull's Concrete & Septic Tanks, Morganton *Also Called: Mulls Con & Septic Tanks Inc (G-11236)*

Mullen Publications Inc 704 527-5111
9301 Forsyth Park Dr Ste A Charlotte (28273) *(G-3214)*

Mullis Mechanical Inc 704 254-5229
609 Belmont Church Rd Monroe (28112) *(G-10776)*

Mullis Millwork Inc 919 496-5993
904 Jewell Ct New Bern (28560) *(G-11828)*

Mulls Con & Septic Tanks Inc 828 437-0959
2416 Mount Home Church Rd Morganton (28655) *(G-11236)*

Multi Form, Wilmington *Also Called: Micronova Systems Inc (G-16323)*

Multi Packaging Solutions 336 855-7142
7915 Industrial Village Rd Greensboro (27409) *(G-7207)*

Multi Technical Services Inc 919 553-2995
950 Nc Highway 42 W Clayton (27520) *(G-4000)*

Multi-Color Corporation 828 658-6800
15 Conrad Industrial Dr Weaverville (28787) *(G-15854)*

Multi-Shifter Inc 704 588-9611
11110 Park Charlotte Blvd Charlotte (28273) *(G-3215)*

Multidrain Systems, Inc., Statesville *Also Called: ABT Foam Inc (G-14734)*

Multigen Diagnostics LLC 336 510-1120
1100 Revolution Mill Dr Ste 1 Greensboro (27405) *(G-7208)*

Multisite Led LLC 650 823-7247
6715 Fairview Rd Charlotte (28210) *(G-3216)*

Multitrode Inc 561 994-8090
14125 S Bridge Cir Charlotte (28273) *(G-3217)*

Muncy Winds, Vilas *Also Called: MW Enterprises Inc (G-15498)*

Mundo Uniformes LLC 704 287-1527
10806 Reames Rd Ste W Charlotte (28269) *(G-3218)*

Mundy Machine & Fabricating Co, Dallas *Also Called: Mundy Machine Co Inc (G-4648)*

Mundy Machine Co Inc 704 922-8663
3934 Puetts Chapel Rd Dallas (28034) *(G-4648)*

Munibilling 800 259-7020
3300 Battleground Ave Ste 402 Greensboro (27410) *(G-7209)*

Murano Corporation 919 294-8233
68 Tw Alexander Dr Ste 207 Durham (27709) *(G-5230)*

Murata Machinery Usa Inc (DH) 704 875-9280
2120 Queen City Dr Charlotte (28208) *(G-3219)*

Murata McHy USA Holdings Inc (HQ) 704 394-8331
2120 Queen City Dr Charlotte (28208) *(G-3220)*

Muratatec, Charlotte *Also Called: Murata McHy USA Holdings Inc (G-3220)*

Muratec, Charlotte *Also Called: Murata Machinery Usa Inc (G-3219)*

Murdock Bldg Portable Sawmill, Rolesville *Also Called: Murdock Building Company (G-13758)*

Murdock Building Company 919 669-1859
109 Watkins Farm Rd Rolesville (27571) *(G-13758)*

Murdock Webbing Company Inc 252 823-1131
1052 W Saint James St Tarboro (27886) *(G-15117)*

Muriel Harris Investments Inc 800 932-3191
3900 Murchison Rd Fayetteville (28311) *(G-5879)*

Murphy Printing & Vinyl LLC 828 835-4848
180 Beulah Ln Murphy (28906) *(G-11714)*

Murphy S Custom Cabinetry Inc 828 891-3050
351 Hidden Woods Ln Hendersonville (28791) *(G-7882)*

Murphy USA, Lenoir *Also Called: Murphy USA Inc (G-9638)*

Murphy USA Inc 828 758-7055
915 Blowing Rock Blvd Lenoir (28645) *(G-9638)*

Murphy-Brown LLC 910 277-8999
19600 Andrew Jackson Hwy Laurinburg (28352) *(G-9490)*

Murphy-Brown LLC 910 293-3434
210 Chief Ln Rose Hill (28458) *(G-13779)*

Murphy-Brown LLC 910 282-4264
152 Farrow To Finish Ln Rose Hill (28458) *(G-13780)*

Murphy-Brown LLC (DH) 910 293-3434
2822 Highway 24 W Warsaw (28398) *(G-15671)*

Murrah Woodcraft 919 302-3661
2112 Vintage Hill Dr Durham (27712) *(G-5231)*

Murrah Woodcraft LLC 919 302-3661
5 Pearse Wynd Rd Bahama (27503) *(G-866)*

Murray Inc 704 329-0400
4508 Westinghouse Blvd Ste B Charlotte (28273) *(G-3221)*

Murray Inc 847 620-7990
8531 Steele Creek Place Dr Unit D Charlotte (28273) *(G-3222)*

Musa Gold LLC 704 579-7894
8425 Cleve Brown Rd Charlotte (28269) *(G-3223)*

Muscadine Naturals Inc 888 628-5898
6332 Cephis Dr Clemmons (27012) *(G-4053)*

Music & Arts 919 329-6069
2566 Timber Dr Garner (27529) *(G-6294)*

Music Garden, Greensboro *Also Called: Music Matters Inc (G-7210)*

Music Matters Inc 336 272-5303
507 Arlington St Greensboro (27406) *(G-7210)*

Musicland Express 828 627-9431
500 Jones Cove Rd Clyde (28721) *(G-4127)*

Musicmedic.com, Wilmington *Also Called: Dorian Corporation (G-16204)*

Mustang Reproductions Inc 704 786-0990
4310 Concord Pkwy S Concord (28027) *(G-4321)*

Mutual Dropcloth, Monroe *Also Called: Dunn Manufacturing Corp (G-10709)*

Mva Leatherwood LLC 704 519-4200
4530 Park Rd Charlotte (28209) *(G-3224)*

Mvi Productions, Charlotte *Also Called: Palmer Senn (G-3309)*

Mvp Group International Inc (HQ) 843 216-8380
430 Gentry Rd Elkin (28621) *(G-5627)*

Mvp Group International Inc 336 527-2238
830 Fowler Rd Mount Airy (27030) *(G-11549)*

Mw Components, Charlotte *Also Called: M & W Industries Inc (G-3113)*

Mw Defense Systems, Lumberton *Also Called: Military Wraps Inc (G-10045)*

MW Enterprises Inc 828 963-7083
5014 Nc Highway 105 S Vilas (28692) *(G-15498)*

Mww On Demand, Hendersonville *Also Called: Manual Woodworkers Weavers Inc (G-7876)*

My Alabaster Box LLC 919 873-1442
5412 Cahaba Way Raleigh (27616) *(G-13051)*

My County Metal Operations LLC 828 765-5265
163 Tempie Mountain Rd Spruce Pine (28777) *(G-14652)*

My Favorite Cheesecake 919 824-0782
4801 Danube Ln Durham (27704) *(G-5232)*

My Kolors, Clemmons *Also Called: Kalajdzic Inc (G-4052)*

My Threesons Gourmet 336 324-5638
2138 Wentworth St Reidsville (27320) *(G-13535)*

My Wine Saver LLC 828 595-2632
162 N Anvil Ave Hendersonville (28792) *(G-7883)*

Mycoatingsolutions 704 619-0308
1410 Crown Forest Ln Monroe (28112) *(G-10777)*

Myers Brothers Logging LLC 828 432-9738
1222 Myers Ridge Ln S Morganton (28655) *(G-11237)*

Myers Forest Products Inc 704 278-4532
355 Barber Junction Rd Cleveland (27013) *(G-4077)*

Myers Logging LLC 919 496-0379
602 T Model Jones Rd Castalia (27816) *(G-1940)*

Myers Quality Machine Co Inc 336 498-4187
1120 N Main St Randleman (27317) *(G-13480)*

Myers Tool and Machine Co Inc 336 956-1324
156 Dixon St Lexington (27292) *(G-9758)*

Myfuturenc Inc 919 649-7834
311 New Bern Ave Unit 26246 Raleigh (27611) *(G-13052)*

Mylan Pharmaceuticals Inc 336 271-6571
2898 Manufacturers Rd Greensboro (27406) *(G-7211)*

Myricks Cabinet Shop Inc 919 266-3720
2329 Hodge Rd Knightdale (27545) *(G-9423)*

Myricks Custom Fab Inc 828 645-5800
181 Reems Creek Rd Ste 2 Weaverville (28787) *(G-15855)*

Mystery Circuits LLC 919 942-4992
3804 Moonlight Dr Chapel Hill (27516) *(G-2045)*

Mystic Farm & Distillery 336 409-0131
1212 N Mineral Springs Rd Durham (27703) *(G-5233)*

Mystic Lifestyle Inc 704 960-4530
184 Academy Ave Nw Concord (28025) *(G-4322)*

N & N Industries Inc 919 770-1311
5319 Womack Rd Sanford (27330) *(G-14156)*

N C Coil Inc 336 983-4440
529b S Main St King (27021) *(G-9277)*

N C Mtor Vhcl Lcnse Plate Agcy, Burlington *Also Called: NC Motor Vhcl Lcnse Plate Agcy (G-1468)*

N C Sock, Hickory *Also Called: North Carolina Sock Inc (G-8104)*

N Style Living Inc 336 938-4014
265 Eastchester Dr High Point (27262) *(G-8461)*

N W L Capacitors, Snow Hill *Also Called: Nwl Inc (G-14505)*

N-Zyme Specialist LLC 919 349-2429
8121 Hawkshead Rd Wake Forest (27587) *(G-15573)*

N2 Company (PA) 910 202-0917
5051 New Centre Dr Wilmington (28403) *(G-16330)*

N2 Everything LLC 704 232-1407
1070 Cannon St Rockwell (28138) *(G-13656)*

N2 Publishing 336 293-3845
161 Shallowbrook Dr Advance (27006) *(G-47)*

N2 Publishing 828 337-9380
139 Dove Cottage Ln Cary (27519) *(G-1829)*

N2 Publishing 910 363-6919
3721 Stormy Gale Pl Castle Hayne (28429) *(G-1956)*

N2 Publishing 704 492-7206
2555 Stockbridge Dr Apt B Charlotte (28210) *(G-3225)*

N2 Publishing 704 497-7087
6322 Adobe Rd Charlotte (28277) *(G-3226)*

N2 Publishing 919 795-6347
5116 Greyfield Blvd Durham (27713) *(G-5234)*

N2 Publishing 919 280-9566
1010 Beyer Pl Durham (27703) *(G-5235)*

N2 Publishing 410 370-5530
516 Ernst Pt Mount Holly (28120) *(G-11644)*

N2 Publishing, Wilmington *Also Called: N2 Company (G-16330)*

N2god Print Center LLC 910 318-4259
202 S Caledonia Rd Laurinburg (28352) *(G-9491)*

N3xt Inc 704 905-2209
2708 Oakmeade Dr Charlotte (28270) *(G-3227)*

Naarva 704 333-3070
614 Chipley Ave Charlotte (28205) *(G-3228)*

Nabell USA Corporation 704 986-2455
208 Charter St Albemarle (28001) *(G-98)*

Nacho Industries Inc 919 937-9471
8 Heath Pl Durham (27705) *(G-5236)*

Nachos & Beer LLC 828 298-2280
230 Charlotte Hwy Asheville (28803) *(G-709)*

Naes-Oms 252 536-4525
1200 Julian R Allsbrook Hwy Weldon (27890) *(G-15886)*

Nafshi Enterprises LLC 910 986-9888
14796 Us Highway 15 501 Aberdeen (28315) *(G-17)*

Nags Head Hammock Co, Nags Head *Also Called: Nags Head Hammocks LLC (G-11724)*

Nags Head Hammocks LLC (PA) 252 441-6115
1801 Croatan Hwy Nags Head (27959) *(G-11724)*

Nails Sparty LLC 910 794-5406
3224 N College Rd Ste D Wilmington (28405) *(G-16331)*

Nakos Paper Products Inc 704 238-0717
2020 Starita Rd Ste G Charlotte (28206) *(G-3229)*

Nala Membranes Inc 540 230-5606
2 Davis Dr # 113 Durham (27709) *(G-5237)*

Nane Publishing LLC 704 477-3462
106 Southern Pines Dr Shelby (28152) *(G-14351)*

Nano-Purification Solutions, Charlotte *Also Called: Air & Gas Solutions LLC (G-2146)*

Nantahala Bicycle Shop, Franklin *Also Called: Club The Nantahala Bicycle Inc (G-6119)*

Nantahala Talc & Limestone Co 828 321-4239
720 Hewitts Rd Topton (28781) *(G-15326)*

NANTAHALA TALC & LIMESTONE CO, Topton *Also Called: Nantahala Talc & Limestone Co (G-15326)*

NAPA Auto Parts, Four Oaks *Also Called: Roy Dunn (G-6111)*

NAPA Filters 704 864-6748
1 Wix Way Gastonia (28054) *(G-6474)*

ALPHABETIC SECTION

Napco, Sparta *Also Called: Napco Inc (G-14597)*
Napco Inc (DH) 336 372-5214
   120 Trojan Ave Sparta (28675) *(G-14597)*
Napoleon James 413 331-9560
   7125 Spring Morning Ln Charlotte (28227) *(G-3230)*
Narricot Industries LLC 215 322-3908
   804 Green Valley Rd Ste 300 Greensboro (27408) *(G-7212)*
Narron Woodworks 252 258-2151
   1209 Sutton Dr Kinston (28501) *(G-9378)*
Nasaspaceflight LLC 980 430-9535
   10926 Quality Dr Unit 39442 Charlotte (28278) *(G-3231)*
Nascent, Charlotte *Also Called: Nascent Technology LLC (G-3232)*
Nascent Technology LLC 704 654-3035
   2744 Yorkmont Rd Charlotte (28208) *(G-3232)*
Nash Brick Company 252 443-4965
   532 Nash Brick Rd Enfield (27823) *(G-5680)*
Nash Building Systems Inc 252 823-1905
   1803 Anaconda Rd Tarboro (27886) *(G-15118)*
Nash County Newspapers Inc 252 459-7101
   203 W Washington St Nashville (27856) *(G-11747)*
Nashville Graphic, Nashville *Also Called: Nash County Newspapers Inc (G-11747)*
Nashville Wldg & Mch Works Inc 252 243-0113
   2356 Firestone Pkwy Ne Wilson (27893) *(G-16517)*
Nassau Tape, Alamance *Also Called: Ct-Nassau Tape LLC (G-69)*
Nat, Fletcher *Also Called: North American Trade LLC (G-6030)*
Nat Black Logging Inc 704 826-8834
   Mcbride Rd Ansonville (28007) *(G-153)*
Natel Inc 336 227-1227
   1257 S Church St Burlington (27215) *(G-1466)*
Nathan Beiler 252 935-5141
   2685 Nc Highway 45 N Pantego (27860) *(G-12169)*
National Air Filters Inc 919 231-8596
   1109 N New Hope Rd Raleigh (27610) *(G-13053)*
National Carton and Coating Co 704 647-0705
   215 Newport Dr Salisbury (28144) *(G-14015)*
National Coatings & Supplies, Raleigh *Also Called: Falls of Neuse Management LLC (G-12761)*
National Color Graphics Inc 704 263-3187
   98 Rutledge Rd Mount Holly (28120) *(G-11645)*
National Container Group LLC 704 393-9050
   1209c Tar Heel Rd Charlotte (28208) *(G-3233)*
National Conveyors Company Inc 860 325-4011
   4404a Chesapeake Dr Charlotte (28216) *(G-3234)*
National Ctr For Social Impact 984 212-2285
   1053 E Whitaker Mill Rd Ste 115 Raleigh (27604) *(G-13054)*
National Foam Inc (PA) 919 639-6100
   141 Junny Rd Angier (27501) *(G-147)*
National Foam Inc 919 639-6151
   141 Junny Rd Angier (27501) *(G-148)*
National Gyps Receivables LLC 704 365-7300
   2001 Rexford Rd Charlotte (28211) *(G-3235)*
National Gypsum, Charlotte *Also Called: Gold Bond Building Pdts LLC (G-2843)*
National Gypsum Comp, Wilmington *Also Called: Proform Finishing Products LLC (G-16371)*
National Gypsum Company, Charlotte *Also Called: Proform Finishing Products LLC (G-3392)*
National Gypsum Services Co 704 365-7300
   2001 Rexford Rd Charlotte (28211) *(G-3236)*
National Marble Products Inc 910 326-3005
   404 Channel Dr Emerald Isle (28594) *(G-5670)*
National Mastercraft Inds Inc 919 896-8858
   14 Glenwood Ave Ste 22 Raleigh (27603) *(G-13055)*
National Peening Inc (DH) 704 872-0113
   1902 Weinig St Statesville (28677) *(G-14850)*
National Pipe & Plastics Inc 336 996-2711
   9609 W Market St Colfax (27235) *(G-4155)*
National Print Services Inc 704 892-9209
   678 Big Indian Loop Mooresville (28117) *(G-11033)*
National Reconition, Greensboro *Also Called: Crown Trophy Inc (G-6944)*
National Roller Supply Inc 704 853-1174
   811 Grover St Gastonia (28054) *(G-6475)*
National Salvage & Svc Corp 919 739-5633
   430 Old Mt Olive Hwy Dudley (28333) *(G-4845)*

National Sign & Decal Inc 828 478-2123
   2199 Lynmore Dr Sherrills Ford (28673) *(G-14388)*
National Spinning Co Inc 910 298-3131
   326 Lyman Rd Beulaville (28518) *(G-1097)*
National Spinning Co Inc 336 226-0141
   226 Glen Raven Rd Burlington (27217) *(G-1467)*
National Spinning Co Inc (PA) 252 975-7111
   1481 W 2nd St Ste 103 Washington (27889) *(G-15717)*
National Spinning Co Inc 910 642-4181
   Hwy 130 240 Spinning Rd Whiteville (28472) *(G-15972)*
National Spnning Oprations LLC 252 975-7111
   1481 W 2nd St Ste 103 Washington (27889) *(G-15718)*
National Tank Monitor Inc 704 335-8265
   9801 Ferguson Rd Charlotte (28227) *(G-3237)*
National Textile Engravers, Charlotte *Also Called: Graveoke Inc (G-2857)*
National Textile Supply, Charlotte *Also Called: W M Plastics Inc (G-3789)*
National Voctnl Tech Honor Soc 828 698-8011
   1011 Airport Rd Flat Rock (28731) *(G-5970)*
National Wden Pllet Cont Assoc 919 837-2105
   2340 Ike Brooks Rd Siler City (27344) *(G-14427)*
National Wiper Alliance, Swannanoa *Also Called: Jbs2 Inc (G-15027)*
National Wood Products, Mills River *Also Called: Alan Kimzey (G-10498)*
Nationwide Analgesics LLC 704 651-5551
   3116 Weddington Rd # 900 Matthews (28105) *(G-10274)*
Native Amercn Collections Xii, Cherokee *Also Called: Cherokee Publications (G-3854)*
Native Naturalz Inc 336 334-2984
   805 Stoney Hill Cir Greensboro (27406) *(G-7213)*
Natives Rest Candles 828 774-9838
   2132 Gerton Hwy Hendersonville (28792) *(G-7884)*
Natsol LLC 704 302-1246
   11100 Muses Ct Matthews (28105) *(G-10275)*
Natural Adhesive LLC 616 217-8392
   9106 Booth Bay Ct Wilmington (28411) *(G-16332)*
Natural Elements Bath and Body 828 226-0853
   60 W Main St Brevard (28712) *(G-1283)*
Natural Granite & Marble Inc 919 872-1508
   3100 Stony Brook Dr Ste N1 Raleigh (27604) *(G-13056)*
Naturally ME Boutique Inc 919 519-0783
   3231 Shannon Rd Apt 31c Durham (27707) *(G-5238)*
Natures Cup LLC 910 795-2700
   1930 Club Pond Rd Raeford (28376) *(G-12427)*
Natures Own Gallery, Rocky Mount *Also Called: Mijo Enterprises Inc (G-13712)*
Natures Pharmacy Inc 828 251-0094
   752 Biltmore Ave Asheville (28803) *(G-710)*
Naturesrules Inc 336 427-2526
   2094 Ellisboro Rd Madison (27025) *(G-10081)*
Natvar, Clayton *Also Called: Tekni-Plex Inc (G-4017)*
Nautilus Holdco Inc 919 859-1302
   4505 Emperor Blvd Ste 200 Durham (27703) *(G-5239)*
Naval Air Warfare, Cherry Point *Also Called: United States Dept of Navy (G-3859)*
Navelite LLC 336 509-9924
   3220 Peninsula Dr Jamestown (27282) *(G-9062)*
Navex Global Inc 866 297-0224
   13950 Ballantyne Corporate Pl Ste 300 Charlotte (28277) *(G-3238)*
Navia Inc 626 372-9791
   4313 Quail Hollow Dr Raleigh (27609) *(G-13057)*
Navistar Inc 704 596-3860
   3325 Rotary Dr Charlotte (28269) *(G-3239)*
Nb Corporation 336 852-8786
   123 S Edwardia Dr Greensboro (27409) *(G-7214)*
Nb Corporation (PA) 336 274-7654
   725 Kenilworth St Greensboro (27403) *(G-7215)*
NBC, Fayetteville *Also Called: NBC Enterprises Inc (G-5880)*
NBC Enterprises Inc 910 705-5781
   2905 Bakers Mill Rd Fayetteville (28306) *(G-5880)*
Nbn Sports Inc 919 824-5143
   616 Clarion Dr Durham (27705) *(G-5240)*
NC Agriculture Teachers Assoc 704 290-1513
   722 Brewer Dr Monroe (28112) *(G-10778)*
NC Backyard Coops 336 250-0838
   154 Morgan Acres Gold Hill (28071) *(G-6585)*

ALPHABETIC SECTION

NC Carolina Venom..704 635-8696
  6100 Flagstone Ln Apt 204 Indian Trail (28079) *(G-8951)*

NC Custom Leather Inc..828 404-2973
  1118 1st St W Conover (28613) *(G-4474)*

NC Diesel Performance LLC..704 431-3257
  5213 Mooresville Rd Salisbury (28147) *(G-14016)*

NC Filtration of Florida LLC..704 822-4444
  1 Miller St Belmont (28012) *(G-996)*

NC Graphic Pros LLC..252 492-7326
  2232 Rocky Ford Rd Kittrell (27544) *(G-9397)*

NC Imprints Inc..336 790-4546
  3199 E Holly Grove Rd Lexington (27292) *(G-9759)*

NC License Plate..336 889-8247
  1701 Westchester Dr # 220 High Point (27262) *(G-8462)*

NC License Plate Agency..910 347-1000
  521 Yopp Rd Jacksonville (28540) *(G-9016)*

NC Logging & Clearing LLC..919 524-4878
  207 Wilson Rd Sanford (27332) *(G-14157)*

NC Metal Crafters Inc..336 425-9727
  1505 Penny Rd High Point (27265) *(G-8463)*

NC Motor Vhcl Lcnse Plate Agcy..336 228-7152
  2668 Ramada Rd Burlington (27215) *(G-1468)*

NC Moulding Acquisition LLC..336 249-7309
  808 Martin Luther King Jr Blvd Lexington (27292) *(G-9760)*

NC Pallet Manufacturer LLC..910 576-4902
  105 Poole Rd Troy (27371) *(G-15410)*

NC Patches..703 314-3428
  1225 W Market Center Dr High Point (27260) *(G-8464)*

NC Printing LLC...828 393-4615
  1524 Haywood Rd Hendersonville (28791) *(G-7885)*

NC Products, Raleigh Also Called: Oldcastle Infrastructure Inc *(G-13082)*

NC Quality Sales LLC..336 786-7211
  136 Greyhound Rd Mount Airy (27030) *(G-11550)*

NC River Riders LLC..336 244-6220
  201 Big Bend Rd Ronda (28670) *(G-13766)*

NC Sand and Rock Inc...919 538-9001
  9520 Kennebec Rd Willow Spring (27592) *(G-16081)*

NC Saturn Parts LLC...704 802-5277
  6603 Reafield Dr Apt 1 Charlotte (28226) *(G-3240)*

NC Sign and Lighting Svc LLC...586 764-0563
  213 Hillstone Pl Jamestown (27282) *(G-9063)*

NC Softball Sales...704 663-2134
  117 E Statesville Ave Mooresville (28115) *(G-11034)*

NC Solar, Raleigh Also Called: NC Solar Now Inc *(G-13058)*

NC Solar Now Inc...919 833-9096
  2517 Atlantic Ave Raleigh (27604) *(G-13058)*

NC Stairs and Rails Inc..336 460-5687
  5504 Foushee Rd Ramseur (27316) *(G-13448)*

NC Steel Services Inc..252 393-7888
  141 Seth Thomas Ln Swansboro (28584) *(G-15046)*

Ncfi, Mount Airy Also Called: Ncfi Polyurethanes *(G-11551)*

Ncfi Polyurethanes..336 789-9161
  1515 Carter St Mount Airy (27030) *(G-11551)*

Ncfi Polyurethanes, Mount Airy Also Called: Barnhardt Manufacturing Co *(G-11481)*

Nci Group Inc..919 926-4800
  5115 New Bern Ave Raleigh (27610) *(G-13059)*

Ncino, Wilmington Also Called: Ncino Inc *(G-16333)*

Ncino Inc (PA)...888 676-2466
  6770 Parker Farm Dr Ste 100 Wilmington (28405) *(G-16333)*

Ncino Opco Inc (HQ)...888 676-2466
  6770 Parker Farm Dr Ste 200 Wilmington (28405) *(G-16334)*

Nclogowearcom...919 821-4646
  414 Dupont Cir Raleigh (27603) *(G-13060)*

NCM, Goldsboro Also Called: North Carolina Mfg Inc *(G-6638)*

Ncoast Communications (PA)..252 247-7442
  201 N 17th St Morehead City (28557) *(G-11183)*

Ncontact Surgical LLC..
  1001 Aviation Pkwy Ste 400 Morrisville (27560) *(G-11392)*

NCR, Cary Also Called: NCR Voyix Corporation *(G-1830)*

NCR Lcal - Ohio Dtroit Aloha P.......................................440 202-3068
  306 Rl Honeycutt Dr Wilmington (28412) *(G-16335)*

NCR Voyix Corporation..937 445-5000
  115 Centrewest Ct Cary (27513) *(G-1830)*

NCSMJ Inc...704 544-1118
  9433 Pineville Matthews Rd Pineville (28134) *(G-12285)*

ND Southeastern Fastener...704 329-0033
  2220 Center Park Dr Ste C Charlotte (28217) *(G-3241)*

Ndsl Inc...919 790-7877
  1000 Parliament Ct Durham (27703) *(G-5241)*

Neal S Pallet Company Inc..704 393-8568
  8808 Wilkinson Blvd Charlotte (28214) *(G-3242)*

Neals Carpentry & Cnstr...910 346-6154
  153 White Oak Blvd Jacksonville (28546) *(G-9017)*

Neals Pallet Co Inc No 2...704 393-0308
  5100 Terminal St Charlotte (28208) *(G-3243)*

Near Urban LLC...828 631-6213
  714 W Main St Sylva (28779) *(G-15064)*

Neat Feet Hosiery Inc..336 573-2177
  304 Main St Stoneville (27048) *(G-14962)*

Neco Division, Salisbury Also Called: Pyrotek Incorporated *(G-14033)*

Nederman Inc..336 821-0827
  150 Transit Ave Thomasville (27360) *(G-15255)*

Nederman Corporation (HQ)..704 399-7441
  4404a Chesapeake Dr Charlotte (28216) *(G-3244)*

Nederman Manufacturing..704 898-7945
  4500 Chesapeake Dr Charlotte (28216) *(G-3245)*

Nederman Mikropul LLC (DH)...704 998-2600
  4404a Chesapeake Dr Charlotte (28216) *(G-3246)*

Nederman Mikropul Canada Inc (DH).............................704 998-2606
  4404a Chesapeake Dr Charlotte (28216) *(G-3247)*

Need T-Shirts Now..910 644-0455
  1830 Owen Dr Fayetteville (28304) *(G-5881)*

Neet Scrubs...704 431-5019
  618 E Franklin St Salisbury (28144) *(G-14017)*

Neff Tool and Machine LLC...507 226-1708
  104 Dixie Dr Chapel Hill (27514) *(G-2046)*

Neighborhood Smoothie LLC..919 845-5513
  10115 Second Star Ct Raleigh (27613) *(G-13061)*

Neighborhood Union Burial Soc......................................252 448-0581
  387 1st Ave Trenton (28585) *(G-15333)*

Neil Allen Industries Inc...336 887-6500
  2101 E Martin Luther King Jr Dr High Point (27260) *(G-8465)*

Nelson Holdings Nc Inc...828 322-9226
  5 20th St Sw Hickory (28602) *(G-8100)*

Nelson Logging Company Inc..919 849-2547
  9557 Nc Highway 96 Oxford (27565) *(G-12136)*

Nelson Oil Company, Hickory Also Called: Nelson Holdings Nc Inc *(G-8100)*

Nelson Rodriguez...828 433-1223
  341 E Parker Rd Morganton (28655) *(G-11238)*

Neocase, Clemmons Also Called: Groupe Lacasse LLC *(G-4042)*

Neocutis, Raleigh Also Called: Merz North America Inc *(G-13020)*

Neomonde Bakery, Morrisville Also Called: Neomonde Baking Company *(G-11393)*

Neomonde Baking Company (PA)...................................919 469-8009
  220 Dominion Dr Ste A Morrisville (27560) *(G-11393)*

Neon Rooster LLC...330 806-7291
  114 Knight St Aberdeen (28315) *(G-18)*

Neopac Us Inc..908 342-0990
  4940 Lamm Rd Wilson (27893) *(G-16518)*

Neptco, Lenoir Also Called: Neptco Incorporated *(G-9639)*

Neptco Incorporated..828 313-0149
  3908 Hickory Blvd Granite Falls (28630) *(G-6747)*

Neptco Incorporated..828 728-5951
  2012 Hickory Blvd Sw Lenoir (28645) *(G-9639)*

Neptune Hlth Wllness Innvtion......................................888 664-9166
  408 S Mclin Creek Rd Conover (28613) *(G-4475)*

Nerdpopprints..910 514-2279
  390 Kramer Rd Lillington (27546) *(G-9857)*

Nerdy Llama LLC..571 431-8933
  904 Plantation Dr Lenoir (28645) *(G-9640)*

Nester Hosiery, Mount Airy Also Called: Nester Hosiery LLC *(G-11553)*

Nester Hosiery Inc...336 789-0026
  1400 Carter St Mount Airy (27030) *(G-11552)*

ALPHABETIC SECTION

Nester Hosiery LLC (PA)..336 789-0026
　1546 Carter St Mount Airy (27030) *(G-11553)*
NESTER HOSIERY, INC., Mount Airy *Also Called: Nester Hosiery Inc (G-11552)*
Nestle Purina Petcare Company..314 982-1000
　863 E Meadow Rd Eden (27288) *(G-5498)*
Netapp Inc..919 476-4571
　7301 Kit Creek Rd Durham (27709) *(G-5242)*
Netceed, Lexington *Also Called: Walker and Associates Inc (G-9800)*
Netqem LLC...919 544-4122
　1012 Park Glen Pl Durham (27713) *(G-5243)*
Network Integrity Systems, Hickory *Also Called: Network Integrity Systems Inc (G-8101)*
Network Integrity Systems Inc...828 322-2181
　1937 Tate Blvd Se Hickory (28602) *(G-8101)*
Neu Spice and Seasonings Llc..252 378-7912
　4571 Us Highway 264 W Washington (27889) *(G-15719)*
Neurametrix Inc...408 507-2366
　18 Lookout Rd Asheville (28804) *(G-711)*
Neuronex Inc...919 460-9500
　9001 Aerial Center Pkwy Ste 110 Morrisville (27560) *(G-11394)*
Neurotronik Inc...919 883-4155
　4021 Stirrup Creek Dr Ste 210 Durham (27703) *(G-5244)*
Neverson Quarry, Sims *Also Called: Heidelberg Materials Us Inc (G-14443)*
New Beginnings Trnsp LLC..704 293-0493
　5904 Johnnette Dr Charlotte (28212) *(G-3248)*
New Bern Asphalt Plant, New Bern *Also Called: S T Wooten Corporation (G-11842)*
New Bern Craven Co Bd of Educ..252 635-1822
　2922 Trent Rd New Bern (28562) *(G-11829)*
New Bern Magazine...252 626-5812
　219 Pecan Grove Ct New Bern (28562) *(G-11830)*
New Boston Fruit Slice & Confe..919 775-2471
　2627 Watson Ave Sanford (27332) *(G-14158)*
New Can Company Inc..704 853-3711
　121 Crowders Creek Rd Gastonia (28052) *(G-6476)*
New Dairy Opco LLC...336 725-8141
　800 E 21st St Winston Salem (27105) *(G-16819)*
New Directions Enterprises Inc...980 428-1866
　2809 Mayfair Ave Charlotte (28208) *(G-3249)*
New Drections Screen Prtrs Inc..704 393-1769
　241 I K Beatty St Charlotte (28214) *(G-3250)*
New East Cartridge Inc...252 329-0837
　1809 Dickinson Ave Greenville (27834) *(G-7563)*
New Element..704 890-7292
　1021 Polk St Charlotte (28206) *(G-3251)*
New England Wood Works...706 491-5885
　152 Four Wheel Dr Whittier (28789) *(G-16009)*
New Finish Inc...704 474-4116
　8353 Us 52 Hwy S Norwood (28128) *(G-12041)*
New Generation Yarn Corp..336 449-5607
　1248 Springwood Church Rd Gibsonville (27249) *(G-6568)*
New Hanover Printing, Wilmington *Also Called: New Hanover Printing and Pubg (G-16336)*
New Hanover Printing & Pubg, Wilmington *Also Called: Aztech Products Inc (G-16129)*
New Hanover Printing and Pubg..910 520-7173
　2145 Wrightsville Ave Wilmington (28403) *(G-16336)*
New Innovative Products Inc..919 631-6759
　2180 Hyw 70 E Pine Level (27568) *(G-12212)*
New Journey Now..336 234-1534
　4413 W Market St Greensboro (27407) *(G-7216)*
New Life Cbd..828 545-7203
　339 Lytle Cove Rd Swannanoa (28778) *(G-15030)*
New Life Medicals Inc...610 615-1483
　146 Donmoor Ct Garner (27529) *(G-6295)*
New Market, Greenville *Also Called: Grover Gaming Inc (G-7536)*
New Media Golf Inc...828 533-9954
　381 Main St Highlands (28741) *(G-8616)*
New Paradigm Therapeutics Inc...919 259-0026
　8024 Burnette Womack 100 Chapel Hill (27599) *(G-2047)*
New Peco Inc...828 684-1234
　10 Walden Dr Arden (28704) *(G-355)*
New Phoenix Aerospace Inc..919 380-8500
　6008 Triangle Dr Ste 101 Raleigh (27617) *(G-13062)*
New River Distilling Co LLC..732 673-4852
　180 W Yuma Ln Deep Gap (28618) *(G-4710)*

New River Fabrics Inc...704 462-1401
　106 Oak St Lawndale (28090) *(G-9502)*
New River Mills..336 385-1446
　2533 Ed Little Rd Creston (28615) *(G-4624)*
New Sarum Brewing Co LLC...704 310-5048
　109 N Lee St Salisbury (28144) *(G-14018)*
New South Fabricator LLC..704 922-2072
　930 Ashebrook Park Rd Dallas (28034) *(G-4649)*
New South Lumber Company Inc..336 376-3130
　4408 Mount Hermon Rock Crk Rd Graham (27253) *(G-6705)*
New Standard Corporation..252 446-5481
　3883 S Church St Rocky Mount (27803) *(G-13714)*
New Vision Investments Inc...336 757-1120
　4310 Enterprise Dr Ste I Winston Salem (27106) *(G-16820)*
New Vision Logging LLC...910 594-0571
　180 Kenan Weeks Rd Newton Grove (28366) *(G-11991)*
New Vision Momentum Entp LLC.......................................800 575-1244
　4456 The Plaza Ste E Charlotte (28215) *(G-3252)*
New Wave Acrylics, Charlotte *Also Called: TFS Management Group LLC (G-3685)*
New World Technologies Inc..828 652-8662
　78 W Marion Business Park Marion (28752) *(G-10169)*
New York Air Brake LLC...315 786-5200
　985 Whitney Dr Salisbury (28147) *(G-14019)*
Newco, Greenville *Also Called: Dpi Newco LLC (G-7516)*
Newcomb Spring Corp...704 588-2043
　2633 Plastics Dr Gastonia (28054) *(G-6477)*
Newcomb Spring of Carolina, Gastonia *Also Called: Newcomb Spring Corp (G-6477)*
Newell, Roxboro *Also Called: Newell & Sons Inc (G-13807)*
Newell & Sons Inc..336 597-2248
　211 Clayton Ave Roxboro (27573) *(G-13807)*
Newell Brands Distribution LLC...770 418-7000
　3211 Aberdeen Blvd Gastonia (28054) *(G-6478)*
Newell Brands Inc...336 812-8181
　4110 Premier Dr High Point (27265) *(G-8466)*
Newell Brands Inc...704 987-4760
　9815 Northcross Center Ct Ste 8 Huntersville (28078) *(G-8858)*
Newell Brands Inc...704 895-8082
　8935 N Pointe Executive Park Dr Huntersville (28078) *(G-8859)*
Newell Novelty Co Inc...336 597-2246
　25 Weeks Dr Roxboro (27573) *(G-13808)*
Newfound Tire & Quick Lube Inc..828 683-3232
　642 Newfound Rd Leicester (28748) *(G-9516)*
Newgard Industries Inc...704 283-6011
　3132 Drake Ln Monroe (28110) *(G-10779)*
Newgrass Brewing Company LLC.......................................704 477-2795
　101 Columns Cir Shelby (28150) *(G-14352)*
Newman-Whitney, Browns Summit *Also Called: Jly Invstmnts Inc Fka Nwman Mc (G-1310)*
Newport/Morehead Cy Con Plant, Garner *Also Called: S T Wooten Corporation (G-6312)*
Newriverwelding...336 413-3040
　271 Merrells Lake Rd Mocksville (27028) *(G-10594)*
News & Observer Recycling Ctr, Garner *Also Called: News and Observer Pubg Co (G-6296)*
News & Record..336 627-1781
　1921 Vance St Reidsville (27320) *(G-13536)*
News & Record Commercial Prtg.......................................336 373-7300
　200 E Market St Greensboro (27401) *(G-7217)*
News 14 Carolina...704 973-5700
　316 E Morehead St Ste 316 Charlotte (28202) *(G-3253)*
News and Observer Pubg Co..919 894-4170
　611 Chicopee Rd Benson (27504) *(G-1040)*
News and Observer Pubg Co..919 419-6500
　2530 Meridian Pkwy Ste 300 Durham (27713) *(G-5245)*
News and Observer Pubg Co..919 829-8903
　1402 Mechanical Blvd Garner (27529) *(G-6296)*
News and Observer Pubg Co (DH)......................................919 829-4500
　421 Fayetteville St Ste 104 Raleigh (27601) *(G-13063)*
News From An Angel..336 456-5429
　3010 Lacy Ave Greensboro (27405) *(G-7218)*
News of Orange County, Hillsborough *Also Called: Womack Publishing Co Inc (G-8673)*
News Reporter, Whiteville *Also Called: Highcorp Incorporated (G-15966)*
Newsome Home Improvement, Greenville *Also Called: Chester Lewis Newsome (G-7501)*

Newton Instrument Company (PA).. 919 575-6426
111 E A St Butner (27509) *(G-1546)*

Newton Machine Co Inc.. 704 394-2099
1120 N Hoskins Rd Charlotte (28216) *(G-3254)*

Newton Sign Co Inc... 910 347-1661
310 Preston Rd Jacksonville (28540) *(G-9018)*

Nexans USA Inc (DH)... 828 323-2660
39 2nd St Nw Hickory (28601) *(G-8102)*

Nexjen Systems LLC.. 704 969-7070
5933 Brookshire Blvd Charlotte (28216) *(G-3255)*

Nexperia USA Inc (DH)... 919 740-6235
630 Davis Dr Ste 200 Durham (27713) *(G-5246)*

Next Generation Beer Co... 828 989-7662
21 Westside Dr Asheville (28806) *(G-712)*

Next Generation Plastics Inc.. 828 453-0221
161 Bugger Hollow Rd Ellenboro (28040) *(G-5636)*

Next Generation Snacks Inc.. 919 797-9623
615 Davis Dr Ste 900 Morrisville (27560) *(G-11395)*

Next Magazine... 910 609-0638
458 Whitfield St Fayetteville (28306) *(G-5882)*

Next Safety Inc... 336 246-7700
676 S Main St Jefferson (28640) *(G-9092)*

Next World Design Inc... 800 448-1223
42 High Tech Blvd Thomasville (27360) *(G-15256)*

Nexxt Level Trucking LLC.. 980 205-4425
627 Minuet Ln Charlotte (28217) *(G-3256)*

Nexxus Lighting Inc... 407 857-9900
124 Floyd Smith Office Park Dr Ste 300 Charlotte (28262) *(G-3257)*

Nexxussoft Corporation.. 561 352-5232
6511 Bells Mill Dr Charlotte (28269) *(G-3258)*

Ng Corporate LLC.. 704 365-7300
2001 Rexford Rd Charlotte (28211) *(G-3259)*

Ng Operations LLC (PA).. 704 365-7300
2001 Rexford Rd Charlotte (28211) *(G-3260)*

Ng Operations LLC... 704 916-2082
5901 Carnegie Blvd Charlotte (28209) *(G-3261)*

NG OPERATIONS, LLC, Charlotte *Also Called: Ng Operations LLC (G-3261)*

Ngc Receivables, Charlotte *Also Called: National Gyps Receivables LLC (G-3235)*

NGK Ceramics Usa Inc (HQ)... 704 664-7000
119 Mazeppa Rd Mooresville (28115) *(G-11035)*

Ngx... 866 782-7749
3002 Anaconda Rd Tarboro (27886) *(G-15119)*

Nhanced Semiconductors Inc.. 630 561-6813
800 Perimeter Park Dr Ste B Morrisville (27560) *(G-11396)*

Ni4I Antennas and Elec LLC.. 828 738-6445
3861 Mount Olive Church Rd Moravian Falls (28654) *(G-11146)*

Niagara Bottling LLC.. 909 815-6310
178 Mooresville Blvd Mooresville (28115) *(G-11036)*

Nic Nac Welding Co.. 704 502-5178
550 W 32nd St Charlotte (28206) *(G-3262)*

Nice Blends Corp.. 910 640-1000
222 Industrial Blvd Whiteville (28472) *(G-15973)*

Nichols Spdmtr & Instr Co Inc... 336 273-2881
1336 Oakland Ave Greensboro (27403) *(G-7219)*

Nichols Speedometer & Instr Co, Greensboro *Also Called: Nichols Spdmtr & Instr Co Inc (G-7219)*

Nicholsons Pallet Services Inc.. 704 826-8405
122 Ansonville Polkton Rd Ansonville (28007) *(G-154)*

Nico Solid Maple Cabinets LLC... 602 319-2758
2925 Battleground Ave Greensboro (27408) *(G-7220)*

Niels Jorgensen Company Inc... 910 259-1624
200 Progress Dr Burgaw (28425) *(G-1346)*

Night, Raleigh *Also Called: Discover Night LLC (G-12687)*

Nigoche Welding Services LLC.. 252 373-8306
5608 Raccoon Ct Nw Wilson (27896) *(G-16519)*

Nine Thirteen LLC... 919 876-8070
5300 Atlantic Ave Ste 105 Raleigh (27609) *(G-13064)*

Nine-Ai Inc... 781 825-3267
359 Armour St Davidson (28036) *(G-4687)*

Ninos Wldg & Cnstr Svcs LLC... 980 214-5804
11901 Everett Keith Rd Huntersville (28078) *(G-8860)*

Nippon Electric Glass, Shelby *Also Called: Electric Glass Fiber Amer LLC (G-14313)*

Nippon Electric Glass Co Ltd.. 336 357-8151
473 New Jersey Church Rd Lexington (27292) *(G-9761)*

Niras Inc... 919 439-4562
1000 Centre Green Way Ste 200 Cary (27513) *(G-1831)*

Nissens Cooling Solutions Inc... 704 696-8575
110 Oakpark Dr Ste 105 Mooresville (28115) *(G-11037)*

Nite Crawlers LLC... 910 309-0543
3626 Latrobe Dr Charlotte (28211) *(G-3263)*

Nitro Manufacturing Inc... 704 663-3155
510 Performance Rd Mooresville (28115) *(G-11038)*

Nitronex LLC.. 919 807-9100
523 Davis Dr Ste 500 Morrisville (27560) *(G-11397)*

Nitta Gelatin Usa Inc... 910 484-0457
4341 Production Dr Fayetteville (28306) *(G-5883)*

Nivedtech... 336 823-9501
1101 Mendenhall St Thomasville (27360) *(G-15257)*

Nkt Cables, Cary *Also Called: Nkt Inc (G-1832)*

Nkt Inc... 919 601-1970
1255 Crescent Green Cary (27518) *(G-1832)*

Nls, Lexington *Also Called: Nutraceutical Lf Sciences Inc (G-9765)*

Nmhg.. 252 229-0071
3953 Dunhagan Rd Greenville (27858) *(G-7564)*

Nn Inc (PA)... 980 264-4300
6210 Ardrey Kell Rd Ste 600 Charlotte (28277) *(G-3264)*

No Evil Foods LLC... 828 367-1536
108 Monticello Rd Ste 2000 Weaverville (28787) *(G-15856)*

No Nonsense, Greensboro *Also Called: Kayser-Roth Corporation (G-7145)*

No Sweat Specialties, Pilot Mountain *Also Called: Sports Solutions Inc (G-12202)*

No1 Can Do It Betta Trckg LLC... 336 858-7693
1418 Bragg Ave High Point (27265) *(G-8467)*

Noa, Swannanoa *Also Called: Nonwovens of America Inc (G-15031)*

Noa Living, Burlington *Also Called: Mongoose LLC (G-1462)*

Noble Bros Cabinets Mllwk LLC (PA).. 252 482-9100
107 Marine Dr Edenton (27932) *(G-5520)*

Noble Bros Cabinets Mllwk LLC... 252 335-1213
505 E Church St Apt 2 Elizabeth City (27909) *(G-5559)*

Noble Brothers Logging Company.. 252 355-2587
237 W Meath Dr Winterville (28590) *(G-17010)*

Noble Custom Coatings LLC... 910 228-6216
2725 Old Wrightsboro Rd Ste 15-3 Wilmington (28405) *(G-16337)*

Noble Oil Services Inc.. 919 774-8180
5617 Clyde Rhyne Dr Sanford (27330) *(G-14159)*

Noble Printers.. 877 786-6253
5812 Triangle Dr Raleigh (27617) *(G-13065)*

Noble Wholesalers Inc... 409 739-3803
356 Trenburg Pl Clayton (27520) *(G-4001)*

Nobscot Construction Co Inc... 919 929-2075
2113 Old Greensboro Rd Chapel Hill (27516) *(G-2048)*

Nocturnal Product Dev LLC... 919 321-1331
8128 Renaissance Pkwy Ste 210 Durham (27713) *(G-5247)*

Noel Group LLC (PA)... 919 269-6500
501 Innovative Way Zebulon (27597) *(G-17135)*

Nokia of America Corporation.. 919 850-6000
2301 Sugar Bush Rd Ste 300 Raleigh (27601) *(G-13066)*

Nolan Manufacturing LLC... 336 490-0086
18868 S Nc Highway 109 Denton (27239) *(G-4746)*

Nolarec, Carthage *Also Called: Stevens Lighting Inc (G-1668)*

Nolen Machine Co Inc.. 704 867-7851
119 Bob Nolen Rd Gastonia (28056) *(G-6479)*

Noles Cabinets Inc.. 919 552-4257
2290 N Grassland Dr Fuquay Varina (27526) *(G-6217)*

Nomaco Inc (HQ)... 919 269-6500
501 Innovative Way Zebulon (27597) *(G-17136)*

Nomacorc Holdings LLC... 919 460-2200
400 Vintage Park Dr Zebulon (27597) *(G-17137)*

Nomad Houseboats Inc.. 252 288-5670
208 Outrigger Rd New Bern (28562) *(G-11831)*

Nomadic Display, Greensboro *Also Called: Nomadic North America LLC (G-7222)*

Nomadic Display LLC... 800 336-5019
7602 Business Park Dr Greensboro (27409) *(G-7221)*

ALPHABETIC SECTION — North State Millwork

Nomadic North America LLC (HQ) 703 866-9200
7602 Business Park Dr Greensboro (27409) *(G-7222)*

Nomadic State of Mind, Fayetteville *Also Called: CBA Productions Inc (G-5786)*

None 336 408-6008
1411 Plaza West Rd Winston Salem (27103) *(G-16821)*

Noni Bacca Winery 910 397-7617
420 Eastwood Rd Wilmington (28403) *(G-16338)*

Nontoxic Pthgen Erdction Cons 800 308-1094
1258 Mann Dr Ste 200 Matthews (28105) *(G-10276)*

Nonwoven Medical Tech LLC 888 978-6199
635 Atando Ave Ste I Charlotte (28206) *(G-3265)*

Nonwovens of America Inc 828 236-1300
875 Warren Wilson Rd Swannanoa (28778) *(G-15031)*

Norag Technology LLC (PA) 336 316-0417
1214 Nc Highway 700 Pelham (27311) *(G-12177)*

Noralex Inc (PA) 252 974-1253
215 Wilmar Rd Vanceboro (28586) *(G-15482)*

Noralex Timber, Vanceboro *Also Called: Noralex Inc (G-15482)*

Norca Engineered Products LLC 919 846-2010
7201 Creedmoor Rd Ste 150 Raleigh (27613) *(G-13067)*

Norcep Industries 910 762-5933
2921 Blue Clay Rd Castle Hayne (28429) *(G-1957)*

Norcraft Companies LP 336 622-4281
6163 Old 421 Rd Liberty (27298) *(G-9825)*

Nord Gear Corporation 888 314-6673
300 Forsyth Hall Dr Charlotte (28273) *(G-3266)*

Nordfab, Thomasville *Also Called: Dantherm Filtration Inc (G-15211)*

Nordfab Ducting 336 821-0840
4404 Chesapeake Dr Charlotte (28216) *(G-3267)*

Nordfab LLC 336 821-0829
150 Transit Ave Thomasville (27360) *(G-15258)*

Nordic Custom Woodworks 203 209-5854
616 Windchime Dr Wilmington (28412) *(G-16339)*

Nordson Corporation 724 656-5600
1291 19th Street Ln Nw Hickory (28601) *(G-8103)*

Nordson Xaloy, Hickory *Also Called: Nordson Corporation (G-8103)*

Nordson Xaloy, Hickory *Also Called: Xaloy Extrusion LLC (G-8212)*

Noregon Systems Inc 336 615-8555
7823 National Service Rd Ste 100 Greensboro (27409) *(G-7223)*

Norell Inc 828 584-2600
1377 Old Dry Creek Rd Morganton (28655) *(G-11239)*

Norfield LLC 530 879-3121
264 Hein Dr Garner (27529) *(G-6297)*

Normac, Hendersonville *Also Called: Normac Incorporated (G-7886)*

Normac Incorporated (PA) 828 209-9000
93 Industrial Dr Hendersonville (28739) *(G-7886)*

Normac Kitchens Inc 704 485-1911
607 N Central Ave Locust (28097) *(G-9964)*

Normac Kitchens Inc (HQ) 704 485-1911
226 S Main St Oakboro (28129) *(G-12079)*

Norman E Clark 336 573-9629
251 Duck Rd Stoneville (27048) *(G-14963)*

Norman Lake Cabinet Company 704 498-6647
3342 Streamside Dr Davidson (28036) *(G-4688)*

Norman Lake Graphics Inc 704 896-8444
16630 Northcross Dr Ste 102 Huntersville (28078) *(G-8861)*

Norman Lake High 336 971-7348
135 Northbridge Dr Mooresville (28115) *(G-11039)*

Normandie Bakery Inc 910 686-1372
7316 Market St Wilmington (28411) *(G-16340)*

Normtex Incorporated 828 428-3363
1700 Verrazzano Pl Wilmington (28405) *(G-16341)*

Norsan Media LLC 704 494-7181
4801 E Independence Blvd Ste 800 Charlotte (28212) *(G-3268)*

North Amercn Aerodynamics Inc (PA) 336 599-9266
1803 N Main St Roxboro (27573) *(G-13809)*

North Amercn Bio-Energies Inc 828 759-7101
815d Virginia St Sw Lenoir (28645) *(G-9641)*

North American Attachments, Winston Salem *Also Called: Engineered Attachments LLC (G-16697)*

North American Implements 336 476-2904
12608 E Old Us Highway 64 Lexington (27292) *(G-9762)*

North American Implements Inc 336 476-2904
215 Washboard Rd Thomasville (27360) *(G-15259)*

North American Trade LLC 828 712-3004
388 Cane Creek Rd Ste 22 Fletcher (28732) *(G-6030)*

North Beach Sun, Kitty Hawk *Also Called: Gulfstream Publications Inc (G-9406)*

North Buncombe Quarry, Weaverville *Also Called: B V Hedrick Gravel & Sand Co (G-15837)*

North Buncombe Small Engines 828 707-4874
187 Dula Springs Rd Weaverville (28787) *(G-15857)*

North Cape Fear Logging LLC 910 876-3197
125 Charlie Smith Dr Harrells (28444) *(G-7695)*

North Carolina Converting LLC 704 871-2912
1001 Bucks Industrial Rd Statesville (28625) *(G-14851)*

North Carolina Department of A 828 684-8188
785 Airport Rd Arden (28704) *(G-356)*

North Carolina Dept Labor 919 807-2770
1101 Mail Service Ctr Raleigh (27699) *(G-13068)*

North Carolina Dept Pub Safety 919 733-0867
1150 Martin Luther King Jr Blvd Raleigh (27601) *(G-13069)*

North Carolina Dept Trnsp 828 733-9002
North Carolina Hwy 181 Newland (28657) *(G-11891)*

North Carolina Dept Trnsp 704 633-5873
5780 S Main St Salisbury (28147) *(G-14020)*

North Carolina Industrial Sand 910 205-8535
943 Airport Rd Rockingham (28379) *(G-13636)*

North Carolina Lawyers Weekly, Raleigh *Also Called: Dolan LLC (G-12694)*

North Carolina Lumber Company 336 498-6600
1 Parrish Dr Randleman (27317) *(G-13481)*

North Carolina McGee, Matthews *Also Called: McGee Corporation (G-10270)*

North Carolina Mfg Inc 919 734-1115
100 Industry Ct Goldsboro (27530) *(G-6638)*

North Carolina Moulding Co, Lexington *Also Called: NC Moulding Acquisition LLC (G-9760)*

North Carolina Mulch Inc 252 478-4609
3277 Prong Creek Rd Middlesex (27557) *(G-10452)*

North Carolina Plywood LLC 850 948-2211
512 E Main St Whiteville (28472) *(G-15974)*

North Carolina Sock Inc 828 327-4664
5521 Suttlemyre Ln Hickory (28601) *(G-8104)*

North Carolina Sportsman Mag, Wilson *Also Called: Carolina Publishing Company (G-16485)*

North Carolina State Dar Plant, Raleigh *Also Called: North Carolina State Univ (G-13070)*

North Carolina State Univ 919 515-2760
Food Science Bldg Rm 12 Raleigh (27695) *(G-13070)*

North Carolina Tobacco Mfg LLC 252 238-6514
7427 N. Carolina Way Stantonsburg (27883) *(G-14712)*

North Crlina Dept Crime Ctrl P 252 522-1511
2214 W Vernon Ave Kinston (28504) *(G-9379)*

North Crlina Dept Crime Ctrl P 336 599-9233
3434 Burlington Rd Roxboro (27574) *(G-13810)*

North Crlina Lcense Plate Agcy 910 485-1590
815 Elm St Fayetteville (28303) *(G-5884)*

North Crlina Orthtics Prsthtic 919 210-0906
2717 Leighton Ridge Dr Wake Forest (27587) *(G-15574)*

North Crlina Rnwable Prpts LLC 407 536-5346
176 Mine Lake Ct Ste 100 Raleigh (27615) *(G-13071)*

North Crlina Soc For Rsprtory 919 619-4206
732 Phelps Rd Hillsborough (27278) *(G-8663)*

North Crlina Spnning Mills Inc 704 732-1171
104 Industrial Park Rd Lincolnton (28092) *(G-9911)*

North Drham Wtr Rclmtion Fclty 919 560-4384
1900 E Club Blvd Durham (27704) *(G-5248)*

North Fork Electric Inc 336 982-4020
1309 Willie Brown Rd Crumpler (28617) *(G-4629)*

North Iredell Grinding Inc 704 902-4771
542 Fairmount Rd Statesville (28625) *(G-14852)*

North Sports Inc 252 995-4970
Waterside Shops Hwy 45 Avon (27915) *(G-845)*

North Star Fbrication Repr Inc 704 393-5243
124 Carothers St Charlotte (28216) *(G-3269)*

North State Flexibles, Greensboro *Also Called: St Johns Packaging Usa LLC (G-7362)*

North State Machine Inc 336 956-1441
1775 Tyro Rd Lexington (27295) *(G-9763)*

North State Millwork 252 442-9090
2950 Raleigh Rd Rocky Mount (27803) *(G-13715)*

North State Packaging   **ALPHABETIC SECTION**

North State Packaging, Greensboro *Also Called: NS Packaging LLC* **(G-7226)**

North State Signs Inc 919 977-7053
   553 Pylon Dr Ste D Raleigh (27606) **(G-13072)**

North State Steel Inc 919 496-2506
   1801 Nc 98 Hwy W Louisburg (27549) **(G-9994)**

North State Steel At Louisburg, Louisburg *Also Called: North State Steel Inc* **(G-9994)**

North State Steel Inc (PA) 252 830-8884
   1010 W Gum Rd Greenville (27834) **(G-7565)**

Northampton Peanut Company 252 585-0916
   413 Main St Severn (27877) **(G-14268)**

Northeast Foods Inc 919 585-5178
   68 Harvest Mill Ln Clayton (27520) **(G-4002)**

Northeast Textiles 704 799-2235
   105 Oakpark Dr Ste A Mooresville (28115) **(G-11040)**

Northeast Tool and Mfg Company 704 882-1187
   15200 Idlewild Rd Matthews (28104) **(G-10337)**

Northeastern Ready Mix 252 335-1931
   183 Knobbs Creek Dr Elizabeth City (27909) **(G-5560)**

Northern Cres Ir / Matt Wldrop 828 848-8884
   16 Kay Rd Zirconia (28790) **(G-17156)**

Northern Star Technologies Inc 516 353-3333
   1712 Price Rd Indian Trail (28079) **(G-8952)**

Northline Nc LLC 336 283-4811
   262 Northstar Dr Ste 122 Rural Hall (27045) **(G-13850)**

Northrop Grmman Gdnce Elec Inc 704 588-2340
   1201 Continental Blvd Charlotte (28273) **(G-3270)**

Northrop Grmman Tchncal Svcs I 252 447-7575
   4280 6th Ave Cherry Point Air Station Havelock (28532) **(G-7744)**

Northrop Grmman Technical Svcs, Atlantic *Also Called: Northrop Grumman Systems Corp* **(G-827)**

Northrop Grumman Info Systems, Morrisville *Also Called: Northrop Grumman Systems Corp* **(G-11398)**

Northrop Grumman Systems Corp 252 225-0911
   Bldg 7029 Atlantic (28511) **(G-827)**

Northrop Grumman Systems Corp 252 447-7557
   Bldg 4280 Cherry Point (28533) **(G-3857)**

Northrop Grumman Systems Corp 919 465-5020
   3005 Carrington Mill Blvd Morrisville (27560) **(G-11398)**

Northside Millwork Inc 919 732-6100
   301 Millstone Dr Hillsborough (27278) **(G-8664)**

Northsouth Biomagnetics Inc 828 478-2277
   3682 Burton St Sherrills Ford (28673) **(G-14389)**

Northstar Computer Tech Inc 980 272-1969
   5014 Hampton Meadows Rd Monroe (28110) **(G-10780)**

Northstar Travel Media 336 714-3328
   331 High St Winston Salem (27101) **(G-16822)**

Northwest AG Product 509 547-8234
   1001 Winstead Dr Ste 480 Cary (27513) **(G-1833)**

Northwest Coatings Systems Inc 336 924-1459
   5640 Clinedale Ct Pfafftown (27040) **(G-12188)**

Norton Door Controls 704 233-4011
   3000 E Highway 74 Monroe (28112) **(G-10781)**

Norton Door Controls Yale SEC, Monroe *Also Called: Assa Abloy Accessories and* **(G-10654)**

Nortria Inc 919 440-3253
   8801 Fast Park Dr Ste 301 Raleigh (27617) **(G-13073)**

Norwood Manufacturing Inc 704 474-0505
   680 Lanier Rd Norwood (28128) **(G-12042)**

Not Just Archery 828 294-7727
   2201 Moss Farm Rd Hickory (28602) **(G-8105)**

Notemeal Inc 312 550-2049
   122 E Parrish St Durham (27701) **(G-5249)**

Notepad Enterprises LLC 704 377-3467
   901 N Tryon St Ste G Charlotte (28206) **(G-3271)**

Noteworthy Software Inc 828 604-1123
   5291 Mineral Springs Mountain Ave Valdese (28690) **(G-15451)**

Nouveau Verre Holdings Inc (DH) 336 545-0011
   3802 Robert Porcher Way Greensboro (27410) **(G-7224)**

Nova Enterprises Inc (PA) 828 687-8770
   305 Airport Rd Arden (28704) **(G-357)**

Nova Kitchen & Bath, Arden *Also Called: Nova Enterprises Inc* **(G-357)**

Nova Mobility Systems Inc 800 797-9861
   8604 Cliff Cameron Dr Ste 152 Charlotte (28269) **(G-3272)**

Nova Wildcat Drapery Hdwr LLC 704 696-5110
   10115 Kincey Ave Ste 210 Huntersville (28078) **(G-8862)**

Novabus, Greensboro *Also Called: Prevost Car (us) Inc* **(G-7281)**

Novaerus US Inc (PA) 813 304-2468
   3540 Toringdon Way,Ste 200 Charlotte (28277) **(G-3273)**

Novaflex Hose Inc 336 578-2161
   449 Trollingwood Rd Haw River (27258) **(G-7755)**

Novak Industries LLC 704 662-2982
   3898 Joe Crouse Rd Maiden (28650) **(G-10114)**

Novakon 336 813-2309
   2169 Griffith Rd Winston Salem (27103) **(G-16823)**

Novalent Ltd 336 375-7555
   2319 Joe Brown Dr Greensboro (27405) **(G-7225)**

Novant Health Appel 704 316-5025
   1901 Brunswick Ave Ste 200 Charlotte (28207) **(G-3274)**

Novartis Vccnes Dagnostics Inc (HQ) 617 871-7000
   475 Green Oaks Pkwy Holly Springs (27540) **(G-8708)**

Novas Bakery Inc (PA) 704 333-5566
   1800 Odessa Ln Charlotte (28216) **(G-3275)**

Novasearch Cons & Pubg LLC 828 788-2332
   336 Berry Ln Bryson City (28713) **(G-1324)**

Novem Industries Inc 704 660-6460
   1801 Cottonwood St Charlotte (28206) **(G-3276)**

Novex Innovations LLC 336 231-6693
   101 N Chestnut St Ste 303 Winston Salem (27101) **(G-16824)**

Novisystems Inc 919 205-5005
   1315 Ileagnes Rd Raleigh (27603) **(G-13074)**

Novo Nordisk Phrm Inds LP 919 820-9985
   3611 Powhatan Rd Clayton (27527) **(G-4003)**

Novo Nordisk Phrm Inds LP 919 820-9985
   646 Glp Oneway Clayton (27527) **(G-4004)**

Novo Nordisk Phrm Inds LP 919 550-2200
   5235 International Dr Durham (27712) **(G-5250)**

Novoclem, Morrisville *Also Called: Vast Therapeutics Inc* **(G-11462)**

Novolex Holdings LLC 980 498-4082
   3436 Toringdon Way Ste 100 Charlotte (28277) **(G-3277)**

Novozymes, Franklinton *Also Called: Novozymes North America Inc* **(G-6160)**

Novozymes Inc 919 494-3950
   77 Perrys Chapel Church Rd Franklinton (27525) **(G-6159)**

Novozymes North America Inc (HQ) 919 494-2014
   77 Perrys Chapel Church Rd Franklinton (27525) **(G-6160)**

Novozymes North America Inc 919 494-3220
   9000 Development Dr Morrisville (27560) **(G-11399)**

Noxon Automation USA LLC 919 390-1560
   150 Dominion Dr Ste B Morrisville (27560) **(G-11400)**

NPC Corporation 336 998-2386
   140 Theodore Dr Mocksville (27028) **(G-10595)**

NPS Holdings LLC 828 757-7501
   1427 Yadkin River Rd Lenoir (28645) **(G-9642)**

Npx One LLC 910 997-2217
   112 Sonoco Paper Mill Rd Rockingham (28379) **(G-13637)**

Nrfp Logging LLC 919 738-0989
   206 Connie Cir Goldsboro (27530) **(G-6639)**

Nrs Printing & Displays LLC 704 907-2887
   1516 Wandering Way Dr Charlotte (28226) **(G-3278)**

NS Packaging LLC 800 688-7391
   2600 Phoenix Dr Greensboro (27406) **(G-7226)**

Nsi Holdings Inc 704 439-2420
   9730 Northcross Center Ct Huntersville (28078) **(G-8863)**

NSi Holdings Inc (PA) 914 664-3542
   13235 Reese Blvd W Huntersville (28078) **(G-8864)**

Nsi Industries 800 321-5847
   9730 Northcross Center Ct Huntersville (28078) **(G-8865)**

Nsi Industries LLC (PA) 800 321-5847
   13235 Reese Blvd W Huntersville (28078) **(G-8866)**

Nsi Lab Solutions Inc 919 789-3000
   7212 Acc Blvd Raleigh (27617) **(G-13075)**

Nsi Tork, Huntersville *Also Called: Nsi Industries LLC* **(G-8866)**

Ntb, Greensboro *Also Called: Tbc Retail Group Inc* **(G-7392)**

Nterline, Morrisville *Also Called: Xschem Inc* **(G-11467)**

NTI Systems, High Point *Also Called: I2e Group LLC* **(G-8404)**

ALPHABETIC SECTION

Nu Expression, Clemmons Also Called: Print Express Enterprises Inc *(G-4055)*
Nu-Tech, East Bend Also Called: Cross Technology Inc *(G-5465)*
Nu-Tech Enterprises Inc 336 725-1691
   305 Junia Ave Winston Salem (27127) *(G-16825)*
Nuclamp, Oak Ridge Also Called: Nuclamp System LLC *(G-12061)*
Nuclamp System LLC 336 643-1766
   8585 Benbow Merrill Rd Oak Ridge (27310) *(G-12061)*
Nuclear Energy Ne US, Wilmington Also Called: Ge-Hitchi Nclear Enrgy Intl LL *(G-16228)*
Nucon Welding Inc 980 253-9369
   3706 Kilmarsh Ct Charlotte (28262) *(G-3279)*
Nucor, Charlotte Also Called: Nucor Corporation *(G-3281)*
Nucor Castrip Arkansas LLC 704 366-7000
   1915 Rexford Rd Charlotte (28211) *(G-3280)*
Nucor Corporation (PA) 704 366-7000
   1915 Rexford Rd Ste 400 Charlotte (28211) *(G-3281)*
Nucor Corporation 252 356-3700
   1505 River Rd Cofield (27922) *(G-4136)*
Nucor Energy Holdings Inc 704 366-7000
   1915 Rexford Rd Charlotte (28211) *(G-3282)*
Nucor Harris Rebar NC Inc 910 739-9747
   2790 Kenny Biggs Rd Lumberton (28358) *(G-10046)*
NUCOR HARRIS REBAR NORTH CAROLINA INC., Lumberton Also Called: Nucor Harris Rebar NC Inc *(G-10046)*
Nucor Steel Sales Corporation 302 622-4066
   1915 Rexford Rd Charlotte (28211) *(G-3283)*
Nufabrx LLC 888 683-2279
   1515 Mockingbird Ln Ste 400 Charlotte (28209) *(G-3284)*
Nufced Custom T-Shirts & More, Mooresville Also Called: Walk In Faith LLC *(G-11122)*
Nunn Probst Installations Inc 704 822-9443
   6428 W Wilkinson Blvd Belmont (28012) *(G-997)*
Nunnery-Freeman Inc 252 438-3149
   2117 Coleman Pl Henderson (27536) *(G-7799)*
Nunnery-Freeman Mfg Co, Henderson Also Called: Nunnery-Freeman Inc *(G-7799)*
Nussbaum Auto Solutions LP 704 864-2470
   1932 Jorache Ct Gastonia (28052) *(G-6480)*
Nutec Inc 877 318-2430
   11830 Mount Holly Hntrsvlle Rd Huntersville (28078) *(G-8867)*
Nutex Concepts NC Corp 828 726-8801
   2424 Norwood St Sw Lenoir (28645) *(G-9643)*
Nutkao USA Inc 252 595-1000
   7044 Nc 48 Battleboro (27809) *(G-926)*
Nutra-Pharma Mfg Corp NC 631 846-2500
   130 Lexington Pkwy Lexington (27295) *(G-9764)*
Nutraceutical Lf Sciences Inc 336 956-0800
   130 Lexington Pkwy Lexington (27295) *(G-9765)*
Nutraheal, Chapel Hill Also Called: Sapphire Innvtive Thrapies LLC *(G-2067)*
Nutrien AG Solutions Inc 252 322-4111
   1530 Nc Highway 306 S Aurora (27806) *(G-837)*
Nutrien AG Solutions Inc 252 235-4161
   9702 Global Rd Bailey (27807) *(G-876)*
Nutrien AG Solutions Inc 252 585-0282
   Ampac Rd Conway (27820) *(G-4516)*
Nutrien AG Solutions Inc 252 977-2025
   1160 Brake Rd Rocky Mount (27801) *(G-13670)*
Nutrien Phosphate, Aurora Also Called: Nutrien AG Solutions Inc *(G-837)*
Nutrotonic LLC 855 948-0008
   5031 W W T Harris Blvd Ste H Charlotte (28269) *(G-3285)*
Nuvasive Inc 336 430-3169
   1250 Revolution Mill Dr Greensboro (27405) *(G-7227)*
Nuvotronics Inc (DH) 984 666-3543
   2305 Presidential Dr Durham (27703) *(G-5251)*
Nuworks 919 223-2587
   1208 N Berkeley Blvd Goldsboro (27534) *(G-6640)*
Nv-Ths, Flat Rock Also Called: National Voctnl Tech Honor Soc *(G-5970)*
Nvent Thermal LLC 919 552-3811
   8000 Purfoy Rd Fuquay Varina (27526) *(G-6218)*
Nvh Inc (DH) 336 545-0011
   3802 Robert Porcher Way Greensboro (27410) *(G-7228)*
Nvidia Corporation 408 486-2000
   2600 Meridian Pkwy Durham (27713) *(G-5252)*

Nvizion Inc 336 985-3862
   129 Charles Rd King (27021) *(G-9278)*
Nvn Liquidation Inc (PA) 919 485-8080
   Pittsboro (27312) *(G-12343)*
Nvr Inc 704 484-7170
   132 Riverside Ct Kings Mountain (28086) *(G-9320)*
NVR Building Products, Kings Mountain Also Called: Nvr Inc *(G-9320)*
Nwl Inc 252 747-5943
   204 Carolina Dr Snow Hill (28580) *(G-14505)*
Nwl Capacitors, Snow Hill Also Called: CD Snow Hill LLC *(G-14501)*
Nxp Usa Inc 919 468-3251
   113 Fieldbrook Ct Cary (27519) *(G-1834)*
Nyp Corp Frmrly New Yrkr-Pters 910 739-4403
   299 Osterneck Robetex Dr Lumberton (28358) *(G-10047)*
Nypro, Arden Also Called: Nypro Asheville Inc *(G-358)*
Nypro Asheville Inc 828 684-3141
   100 Vista Blvd Arden (28704) *(G-358)*
Nypro Inc 919 304-1400
   1018 Corporate Park Dr Mebane (27302) *(G-10421)*
Nypro Mebane, Mebane Also Called: Nypro Inc *(G-10421)*
Nypro Oregon Inc 541 753-4700
   100 Vista Blvd Arden (28704) *(G-359)*
Nzuri Accessories & Co LLC 980 333-9530
   6201 Fairview Rd Ste 200 Charlotte (28210) *(G-3286)*
O D Eyecarecenter P A 252 443-7011
   3044 Sunset Ave Rocky Mount (27804) *(G-13716)*
O Grayson Company 704 932-6195
   6509 Grayson Ln Kannapolis (28081) *(G-9128)*
O Henry House Ltd 336 431-5350
   308 Greenoak Dr Archdale (27263) *(G-294)*
O P S Holding Company LLC 361 446-8376
   12243 Nations Ford Rd Pineville (28134) *(G-12286)*
O R Prdgen Sons Sptic Tank I 252 442-3338
   4824 S Halifax Rd Rocky Mount (27803) *(G-13717)*
Oak & Axe Custom Woodworking 919 434-1939
   1105 Highland Trl Cary (27511) *(G-1835)*
Oak & Bull Distilling LLC 978 732-4531
   916 Palace Garden Way Raleigh (27603) *(G-13076)*
Oak & Grist Distilling Co LLC 914 450-0589
   40 West St Asheville (28801) *(G-713)*
Oak & Grist Distilling Co LLC 828 357-5750
   1556 Grovestone Rd Black Mountain (28711) *(G-1131)*
Oak City Artisans LLC 347 738-1228
   2325 Woodrow Dr Raleigh (27609) *(G-13077)*
Oak City Columns LLC 919 848-8814
   1201 Corporation Pkwy Raleigh (27610) *(G-13078)*
Oak City Distilling Inc 919 520-4102
   514 Daniels St Raleigh (27605) *(G-13079)*
Oak City Metal LLC 919 375-4535
   700 Pony Rd Ste C Zebulon (27597) *(G-17138)*
Oak City Sign Solutions Inc 919 792-8077
   4904 Alpinis Dr Ste 108 Raleigh (27616) *(G-13080)*
Oak City Woodshop LLC 937 830-0808
   103 Fox Ct Cary (27513) *(G-1836)*
Oak City Woodworks 919 247-5984
   904 Willow Ridge Dr Knightdale (27545) *(G-9424)*
Oak Ridge Industries LLC 252 833-4061
   1228 Page Rd Washington (27889) *(G-15720)*
Oak Street Mfg 877 465-4344
   1903 Clayton St Statesville (28677) *(G-14853)*
Oak-Bark Corporation 910 655-2263
   1507 Cronly Dr Riegelwood (28456) *(G-13561)*
Oak-Bark Corporation (PA)   514 Wayne Dr Wilmington (28403) *(G-16342)*
Oakbrook Solutions Inc 336 714-0321
   5930 Tarleton Dr Oak Ridge (27310) *(G-12062)*
Oakdale Cotton Mills 336 454-1144
   409 E Main St Jamestown (27282) *(G-9064)*
Oakdale Cotton Mills 336 454-1144
   710 Oakdale Rd Jamestown (27282) *(G-9065)*
Oakhurst Company Inc (PA) 336 474-4600
   2016 Van Buren St # 101 High Point (27260) *(G-8468)*

(PA)=Parent Co (HQ)=Headquarters (DH)=Div Headquarters

Oakhurst Textiles Inc 336 668-0733
203 Citation Ct Greensboro (27409) *(G-7229)*

Oakie S Tire & Recapping Inc 704 482-5629
800 W Warren St Shelby (28150) *(G-14353)*

Oaks Unlimited Inc (PA) 828 926-1621
3530 Jonathan Creek Rd Waynesville (28785) *(G-15812)*

Oakstone Associates LLC 704 946-5101
10308 Bailey Rd Ste 430 Cornelius (28031) *(G-4571)*

Oakwood Homes, Fletcher Also Called: Clayton Homes Inc *(G-5994)*

Oasis Akhal-Tekes 704 843-3139
6528 Rehobeth Rd Waxhaw (28173) *(G-15768)*

Oasis Denistry 704 332-8188
2711 Randolph Rd Charlotte (28207) *(G-3287)*

Oasis Magazine LLC 888 559-7549
10225 Hickorywood Hill Ave Huntersville (28078) *(G-8868)*

Oasys Mobile Inc 919 807-5600
8000 Regency Pkwy Ste 285 Cary (27518) *(G-1837)*

Oberle Group 336 399-6833
4721 Sherborne Dr Pfafftown (27040) *(G-12189)*

Obi Machine & Tool Inc 252 946-1580
411 Patrick Ln Chocowinity (27817) *(G-3896)*

Objective Security Corporation 415 997-9967
555 Fayetteville St Ste 201 Raleigh (27601) *(G-13081)*

OBrian Tarping Systems Inc 252 291-6710
110 Beacon St W Wilson (27893) *(G-16520)*

OBrian Tarping Systems Inc (PA) 252 291-2141
2330 Womble Brooks Rd E Wilson (27893) *(G-16521)*

OBrien Logging Co 910 655-3830
988 Livingston Chapel Rd Delco (28436) *(G-4723)*

Obscura Mfg LLC 336 419-5648
3031 Sheely Rd Lenoir (28645) *(G-9644)*

Observer News Enterprise, Newton Also Called: Horizon Publications Inc *(G-11941)*

Observer News Enterprise Inc 828 464-0221
309 N College Ave Newton (28658) *(G-11954)*

Obx Boatworks LLC 336 878-9490
2100 E Martin Luther King Jr Dr Ste 121 High Point (27260) *(G-8469)*

Obx Granola, Chapel Hill Also Called: Ludlam Family Foods LLC *(G-2035)*

Obx Metalworks LLC 757 434-0211
281 Woodleigh Rd Knotts Island (27950) *(G-9435)*

Occasions Group Inc 919 751-2400
305 N Spence Ave Goldsboro (27534) *(G-6641)*

Occasions Group Inc 252 321-5805
1055 Greenville Blvd Sw Greenville (27834) *(G-7566)*

Occidental Chemical Corp 910 675-7200
5408 Holly Shelter Rd Castle Hayne (28429) *(G-1958)*

Ocean 10 Security LLC 828 484-1481
329 Gashes Creek Rd Asheville (28803) *(G-714)*

Ocean Road Graphics Signs 919 404-1444
914 Parkertown Rd Four Oaks (27524) *(G-6110)*

Ocean Woodworking Inc 910 579-2233
6863 Beach Dr Sw Ocean Isle Beach (28469) *(G-12094)*

Oceania Hardwoods LLC 910 862-4447
474 Sweet Home Church Rd Elizabethtown (28337) *(G-5601)*

Oceans Flavor 828 277-7564
123 Cloverleaf Ln Asheville (28803) *(G-715)*

Ocracoke Sauce Company LLC 443 904-7972
58 Water Plant Rd Ocracoke (27960) *(G-12096)*

Ocufii Inc 804 874-4036
11211 James Coy Rd Huntersville (28078) *(G-8869)*

Ocutech Inc 919 967-6460
105 Conner Dr Ste 2105 Chapel Hill (27514) *(G-2049)*

Odd Sock Inc 704 451-4298
610 Jetton St Ste 120-121 Davidson (28036) *(G-4689)*

Odell Custom Cabinets 704 201-6975
5424 Concord Hwy Monroe (28110) *(G-10782)*

Odens Fish & Oil Co Inc 252 588-0036
Ocracoke (27960) *(G-12097)*

Odigia Inc 336 462-8056
300 S Liberty St Ste 210 Winston Salem (27101) *(G-16826)*

Odin Technologies LLC 408 309-1925
4810 Ashley Park Ln Unit C1-1307 Charlotte (28210) *(G-3288)*

Oe Filters, Fayetteville Also Called: Mann+hmmel Prlator Filters LLC *(G-5864)*

Oerlikon AM US Inc 980 260-2827
12012 Vanstory Dr Huntersville (28078) *(G-8870)*

Oerlikon Metco (us) Inc 713 715-6300
12012 Vanstory Dr Huntersville (28078) *(G-8871)*

Ofc Fabricators, Statesville Also Called: Ohio Foam Corporation *(G-14854)*

Off Road Addiction 910 620-4675
2090 Angelia M St Fayetteville (28312) *(G-5885)*

Offerisor LLC 704 970-9700
1014 Brightmoor Dr Matthews (28105) *(G-10277)*

Office Furniture Marketing, Holly Springs Also Called: Ofm LLC *(G-8709)*

Office of Printing, Boone Also Called: Appalachian State University *(G-1174)*

Office Sup Svcs Inc Charlotte (PA) 704 786-4677
4490 Artdale Rd Sw Concord (28027) *(G-4323)*

Office Supply Services, Concord Also Called: Office Sup Svcs Inc Charlotte *(G-4323)*

Offshore Marine Elec LLC 252 504-2624
1381 Old Winberry Rd Newport (28570) *(G-11902)*

Ofm LLC 919 303-6389
161 Tradition Trl Holly Springs (27540) *(G-8709)*

Ofm Inc 919 303-6389
1003 Investment Blvd Ste A Apex (27502) *(G-221)*

Ofs Brands Inc 800 763-0212
1264 Jackson Lake Rd High Point (27263) *(G-8470)*

Ogburn Village Solutions, Winston Salem Also Called: Village Produce & Cntry Str In *(G-16962)*

Ogden Enterprises, Matthews Also Called: Karl Ogden Enterprises Inc *(G-10258)*

OH So Nice 704 263-2668
112 Rollins St Stanley (28164) *(G-14704)*

OHerns Welding Inc 910 484-2087
5379 Butler Nursery Rd Fayetteville (28306) *(G-5886)*

Ohilda Bombardier 704 658-7134
221 Woodwinds St Locust (28097) *(G-9965)*

Ohio Electric Motors Inc 828 626-2901
30 Paint Fork Rd Barnardsville (28709) *(G-912)*

Ohio Foam Corporation 704 883-8402
2185 Salisbury Hwy Statesville (28677) *(G-14854)*

Ohio Mat Lcnsing Cmpnnts Group (DH) 336 861-3500
1 Office Parkway Rd Trinity (27370) *(G-15349)*

Ohio-Sealy Mattress Mfg Co 336 861-3500
1 Office Parkway Rd Trinity (27370) *(G-15350)*

Ohlins Usa Inc 828 692-4525
703 S Grove St Hendersonville (28792) *(G-7887)*

Oil and Vinegar Market Inc 919 491-9225
264 Crimson Oak Dr Durham (27713) *(G-5253)*

Oil Mill Salvage Recyclers Inc 910 268-2111
13840 Oil Mill Rd Gibson (28343) *(G-6555)*

Oiles America Corporation (HQ) 704 784-4500
4510 Enterprise Dr Nw Concord (28027) *(G-4324)*

Oilkleen Inc 480 650-8711
123 Poplar Pointe Dr Ste G Mooresville (28117) *(G-11041)*

Oilkleen LLC (PA) 480 650-8711
123 Poplar Pointe Dr Unit G Mooresville (28117) *(G-11042)*

Okaya Shinnichi Corp America 704 588-3131
300 Crompton St Charlotte (28273) *(G-3289)*

Oklawaha Brewing Company LLC 828 595-9956
147 1st Ave E Hendersonville (28792) *(G-7888)*

Okuma America Corporation (HQ) 704 588-7000
11900 Westhall Dr Charlotte (28278) *(G-3290)*

Ola Marimba Inc 919 479-9995
3600 N Duke St Ste 29 Durham (27704) *(G-5254)*

Old Belt Extracts LLC 336 530-5784
317 Lucy Garrett Rd Roxboro (27574) *(G-13811)*

Old Castle Apg South Inc 919 383-2521
106 S Lasalle St Durham (27705) *(G-5255)*

Old Castle Service Inc 336 992-1601
920 Old Winston Rd Kernersville (27284) *(G-9221)*

Old Dell Designs 910 532-6066
199 E Magnolia Lisbon Rd Magnolia (28453) *(G-10098)*

Old Dominion Win Door Hanover, Charlotte Also Called: Moss Supply Company *(G-3205)*

Old Growth Riverwood Inc 910 762-4077
1407b Castle Hayne Rd Wilmington (28401) *(G-16343)*

Old Hickory Log Homes Inc..704 489-8989
  4279 Burnwood Trl Denver (28037) *(G-4791)*
Old Hickory Stainless Stl Inc..910 567-6751
  8759 Fayetteville Hwy Godwin (28344) *(G-6579)*
Old Hickory Tannery Inc (PA)...828 465-6599
  970 Locust St Newton (28658) *(G-11955)*
Old Homeplace Vineyard LLC...336 399-7293
  623 Mcgee Rd Winston Salem (27107) *(G-16827)*
Old Made Quilts...919 692-1060
  1156 Grassy Crk Virgilina Oxford (27565) *(G-12137)*
Old Master Cabinets, Greensboro Also Called: Burlington Distributing Co *(G-6862)*
Old Mill Precision Gun Works &..704 284-2832
  323 Old Mill Rd Bessemer City (28016) *(G-1076)*
Old North State Winery Inc...336 789-9463
  308 N Main St Mount Airy (27030) *(G-11554)*
Old Salem Incorporated..336 721-7305
  730 S Poplar St Winston Salem (27101) *(G-16828)*
Old Salem Town Merchant, Winston Salem Also Called: Old Salem Incorporated *(G-16828)*
Old Saratoga Inc...252 238-2175
  6351 Nc Hwy 222 Saratoga (27873) *(G-14216)*
Old School Crushing Co Inc...919 661-0011
  250 Old Mechanical Ct Garner (27529) *(G-6298)*
Old School Mill Inc (PA)..704 781-5451
  139 Concord St Unit 4 Stanfield (28163) *(G-14681)*
Old South Monograms & EMB LLC.....................................704 921-8115
  2423 Christenbury Hall Dr Nw Concord (28027) *(G-4325)*
Old Style Printing..828 452-1122
  1046 Sulphur Springs Rd Waynesville (28786) *(G-15813)*
Old Town Soap Co..704 796-8775
  104 S Main St China Grove (28023) *(G-3886)*
OLD-TIME HERALD, Durham Also Called: Old-Time Music Group Inc *(G-5256)*
Old-Time Music Group Inc..919 286-2041
  1109 Clarendon St Durham (27705) *(G-5256)*
Oldcastle Adams..336 310-0542
  3415 Sandy Ridge Rd Colfax (27235) *(G-4156)*
Oldcastle Apg, Cornelius Also Called: Oldcastle Retail Inc *(G-4572)*
Oldcastle Buildingenvelope Inc...704 504-0345
  10405 Granite St Ste M Charlotte (28273) *(G-3291)*
Oldcastle Infrastructure Inc...704 788-4050
  4905 Stough Rd Sw Concord (28027) *(G-4326)*
Oldcastle Infrastructure Inc...910 433-2931
  3960 Cedar Creek Rd Fayetteville (28312) *(G-5887)*
Oldcastle Infrastructure Inc...919 552-2252
  1431 Products Rd Fuquay Varina (27526) *(G-6219)*
Oldcastle Infrastructure Inc...919 552-5715
  1424 Products Rd Fuquay Varina (27526) *(G-6220)*
Oldcastle Infrastructure Inc...919 772-6269
  920 Withers Rd Raleigh (27603) *(G-13082)*
Oldcastle Retail Inc (DH)..704 525-1621
  625 Griffith Rd Ste 100 Charlotte (28217) *(G-3292)*
Oldcastle Retail Inc..704 799-8083
  18637 Northline Dr Ste S Cornelius (28031) *(G-4572)*
Olde Lexington Products Inc...336 956-2355
  480 Cedarwood Dr Linwood (27299) *(G-9947)*
Ole Mexican Foods Inc...704 587-1763
  11001a S Commerce Blvd Charlotte (28273) *(G-3293)*
Ole Pelicans Custom Wdwkg...252 808-7633
  337 E Southwinds Dr Newport (28570) *(G-11903)*
Ole-Charlotte Distribution Ctr, Charlotte Also Called: Ole Mexican Foods Inc *(G-3293)*
Oleksynprannyk LLC..704 450-0182
  149 Cayuga Dr Ste A3 Mooresville (28117) *(G-11043)*
Olens B Enterprises, Greensboro Also Called: Spring Repair Service Inc *(G-7360)*
Olin Black Enterprise LLC...704 363-5675
  11695 Troutman Rd Midland (28107) *(G-10472)*
Olive Beaufort Oil Company..252 504-2474
  300 Front St Ste 4 Beaufort (28516) *(G-962)*
Olive Beaufort Oil Company..910 325-1556
  105 W Church St Swansboro (28584) *(G-15047)*
Olive Euro Oil LLC..336 310-4624
  1369 S Park Dr Kernersville (27284) *(G-9222)*
Olive Hill Wldg & Fabrication, Roxboro Also Called: Olive Hl Wldg Fabrication Inc *(G-13812)*
Olive Hl Wldg Fabrication Inc...336 597-0737
  1940 Semora Rd Roxboro (27574) *(G-13812)*
Olive Pinehurst Oil Co..910 315-9923
  124 Newington Way Aberdeen (28315) *(G-19)*
Olive Press LLC...910 622-6718
  7645 High Market St Unit 4 Sunset Beach (28468) *(G-15002)*
Olive Wagon LLC...919 559-0845
  8490 Honeycutt Rd Ste 106 Raleigh (27615) *(G-13083)*
Oliventures Inc (PA)...800 231-2619
  6325 Falls Of Neuse Rd Ste 35-122 Raleigh (27615) *(G-13084)*
Oliver Rubber Company LLC..336 629-1436
  408 Telephone Ave Asheboro (27205) *(G-459)*
Olivers Drive Shaft Repair...719 539-1823
  707 E 12 1/2 St Winston Salem (27101) *(G-16829)*
Olivia Machine & Tool Inc...919 499-6021
  815 Seawell Rosser Rd Sanford (27332) *(G-14160)*
Ollis Enterprises Inc..828 265-0004
  1613 Industrial Dr Wilkesboro (28697) *(G-16037)*
Olon Industries Inc (us)...630 232-4705
  279 Bethel Church Rd Mocksville (27028) *(G-10596)*
Olpr.leather Goods Co., Mooresville Also Called: Oleksynprannyk LLC *(G-11043)*
OLT Logging Inc...919 894-4506
  451 Marshall Ln Smithfield (27577) *(G-14473)*
Olympian Welding..919 608-3829
  3660 Windsor Dr Franklinton (27525) *(G-6161)*
Olympic Products LLC (PA)..336 378-9620
  4100 Pleasant Garden Rd Greensboro (27406) *(G-7230)*
Olympic Products LLC..336 378-9620
  4100 Pleasant Garden Rd Greensboro (27406) *(G-7231)*
Omega Manufacturing Corp..704 597-0418
  1800 Industrial Center Cir Charlotte (28213) *(G-3294)*
Omega Precious Metals..269 903-9330
  40 Shorrey Pl Youngsville (27596) *(G-17089)*
Omega Products...704 684-1920
  600 Radiator Rd Indian Trail (28079) *(G-8953)*
Omega Studios Inc..704 889-5800
  10519 Industrial Dr Pineville (28134) *(G-12287)*
Omega Tees + Screen Prtg LLC...828 268-0600
  115 Apple Rd Boone (28607) *(G-1226)*
Omni Group LLC...828 404-3104
  1140 Tate Blvd Se Hickory (28602) *(G-8106)*
Omni Mold & Die LLC..336 724-5152
  2710 Boulder Park Ct Winston Salem (27101) *(G-16830)*
Omni Systems, Laurel Hill Also Called: Hygiene Systems Inc *(G-9461)*
Omnia Industries LLC..704 707-6062
  1430 Industrial Dr Ste A Matthews (28105) *(G-10278)*
Omnia LLC..919 696-2193
  115 Certainteed Dr Oxford (27565) *(G-12138)*
Omnia Products, Oxford Also Called: Omnia LLC *(G-12138)*
Omnia Products LLC...919 514-3977
  115 Certainteed Dr Oxford (27565) *(G-12139)*
Omnicell...910 538-2141
  1705 Kings Landing Rd Hampstead (28443) *(G-7652)*
Omninvest LLC (PA)...336 623-1717
  4213 Abernathy Pl Harrisburg (28075) *(G-7719)*
Omtex, Rutherford College Also Called: Aquafil OMara Inc *(G-13858)*
On Demand Hemp Company LLC...336 757-0320
  6880 Rolling View Dr Tobaccoville (27050) *(G-15318)*
On Demand Screen Printing LLC...704 661-0788
  2242 Roberta Rd Concord (28027) *(G-4327)*
On Foot Innovations LLC..336 301-3732
  1820 Harris Houston Rd Unit 620242 Charlotte (28262) *(G-3295)*
On Point Mobile Detailing LLC..404 593-8882
  10906 Featherbrook Rd Charlotte (28262) *(G-3296)*
On The Inside LLC..828 606-8483
  244 Bear Creek Rd Asheville (28806) *(G-716)*
On The Spot Grilling LLC...704 963-4105
  2814 Royal Fern Ln Charlotte (28215) *(G-3297)*
On Time Metal LLC...828 635-1001
  31 Wayfound Church Rd Hiddenite (28636) *(G-8224)*
On-Site Hose Inc...919 303-3840
  1001 Goodworth Dr Apex (27539) *(G-222)*

Onc Tees 252 671-7576
204 Freemason St Oriental (28571) *(G-12112)*

Oncoceutics Inc 678 897-0563
2505 Meridian Pkwy Ste 100 Durham (27713) *(G-5257)*

One Black Sock LLC 919 967-6855
203 Oak Ave Carrboro (27510) *(G-1652)*

One Furniture Group Corp 336 235-0221
6520 Arprt Ctr Dr Ste 204 Greensboro (27409) *(G-7232)*

One Hundred Ten Percent Screen 252 728-3848
150 Lake Rd Beaufort (28516) *(G-963)*

One Library At A Time Inc 704 578-1812
4107 Crossgate Rd Charlotte (28226) *(G-3298)*

One More Cast 252 995-6026
40075 N End Rd Avon (27915) *(G-846)*

One On One Press LLC 910 228-8821
616 Princess St Wilmington (28401) *(G-16344)*

One Packaging Excel Inc 919 268-9330
6446 Stag Trl Wendell (27591) *(G-15910)*

One Source Document Solutions 336 482-2360
311 Pomona Dr Ste D Greensboro (27407) *(G-7233)*

One Source SEC & Sound Inc 281 850-9487
122 Summerville Dr Ste 101 Mooresville (28115) *(G-11044)*

One Srce Dcument Solutions Inc 800 401-9544
4355 Federal Dr Ste 140 Greensboro (27410) *(G-7234)*

One Stop Shipg & Prtg Etc LLC 910 745-9733
3308 Bragg Blvd Ste 108 Fayetteville (28303) *(G-5888)*

One Valley Studios LLC 980 938-0465
1933 Pegram St Charlotte (28205) *(G-3299)*

Oneaka Dance Company 704 299-7432
4430 The Plaza # 13 Charlotte (28215) *(G-3300)*

Oneh2 Inc 844 996-6342
620 23rd St Nw Hickory (28601) *(G-8107)*

Oneida Molded Plastics LLC 919 663-3141
920 E Raleigh St Siler City (27344) *(G-14428)*

Onion Peel Software Inc 919 460-1789
1 Copley Pkwy Ste 480 Morrisville (27560) *(G-11401)*

Onixx Manufacturing LLC 828 298-4625
107 W Buckeye Rd Swannanoa (28778) *(G-15032)*

Online Memorial Services LLC 914 471-6852
810 9th St Apt 340 Durham (27705) *(G-5258)*

Only Bitters 617 413-6571
517 W Cabarrus St Ste A Raleigh (27603) *(G-13085)*

Onsat Magazine, Shelby *Also Called: Triple D Publishing Inc (G-14375)*

Onsight Inc 704 747-4168
2725 Westinghouse Blvd Ste 200 Charlotte (28273) *(G-3301)*

Onsite Woodwork Corporation 704 523-1380
645 Pressley Rd Ste E Charlotte (28217) *(G-3302)*

Onslow Bay Boatworks & Marine 910 270-3703
175 Sloop Point Loop Rd Hampstead (28443) *(G-7653)*

OnTarget Labs Inc (PA) 919 846-3877
8605 Bell Grove Way Raleigh (27615) *(G-13086)*

Ontario Spcialty Coatings Corp 980 207-3944
2905 Westinghouse Blvd Charlotte (28273) *(G-3303)*

Ontex North America, Stokesdale *Also Called: Ontex Operations Usa LLC (G-14947)*

Ontex Operations Usa LLC (HQ) 770 346-9250
9300 Nc Highway 65 Stokesdale (27357) *(G-14947)*

Ontic Engineering and Mfg Inc 919 395-3908
1176 Telecom Dr Creedmoor (27522) *(G-4619)*

Onward Energy Holdings LLC 980 294-0204
7621 Little Ave Ste 350 Charlotte (28226) *(G-3304)*

Onyx, Stanley *Also Called: Onyx Environmental Solutions Inc (G-14705)*

Onyx Environmental Solutions Inc 800 858-3533
7781 S Little Egypt Rd Stanley (28164) *(G-14705)*

Open Book Extracts, Roxboro *Also Called: Old Belt Extracts LLC (G-13811)*

Open South Imports, Hillsborough *Also Called: Sommerville Enterprises LLC (G-8668)*

Openfire Systems 336 251-3991
5450 Boone Trl Millers Creek (28651) *(G-10494)*

Operable Inc 757 617-0935
1209 Winkworth Way Wake Forest (27587) *(G-15575)*

Operating Shelby LLC Tag 704 482-1399
2501 W Dixon Blvd Shelby (28152) *(G-14354)*

Operation Wheelchair 910 391-1945
538 Mayview St Fayetteville (28306) *(G-5889)*

Opportunity Knocks Twice Inc 919 672-5374
1011 Glenrose Dr Durham (27703) *(G-5259)*

Optical Place Inc (PA) 336 274-1300
2633 Randleman Rd Greensboro (27406) *(G-7235)*

Optical Wholesale, Greensboro *Also Called: Optical Place Inc (G-7235)*

Opticare, Rocky Mount *Also Called: O D Eyecarecenter P A (G-13716)*

Opticoncepts Inc 828 320-0138
925b Old Lenoir Rd Hickory (28601) *(G-8108)*

Opticoncepts Inc 828 874-0667
911 W Union St Morganton (28655) *(G-11240)*

Optics Inc 336 288-9504
1607 Westover Ter Ste B Greensboro (27408) *(G-7236)*

Optics Inc (PA) 336 884-5677
1105 N Lindsay St Side Side High Point (27262) *(G-8471)*

Optimal Industries LLC 601 530-5222
285 Cauble Stout Cir Salisbury (28146) *(G-14021)*

Optimum Lighting, Henderson *Also Called: Optimum Lighting LLC (G-7800)*

Optimum Lighting LLC 508 646-3324
880 Facet Rd Henderson (27537) *(G-7800)*

Optimum Sign Age 919 372-8018
106 Okehampton Ct Cary (27518) *(G-1838)*

Option 1 Distribution LLC 704 325-3001
103 N Mclin Creek Rd Conover (28613) *(G-4476)*

Opto Alignment Technology Inc 704 893-0399
1034 Van Buren Ave Ste A Indian Trail (28079) *(G-8954)*

Optometric Eyecare Center Inc 910 326-3050
775 W Corbett Ave Swansboro (28584) *(G-15048)*

Optomill Solutions LLC 704 560-4037
1223 Clover Ln Matthews (28104) *(G-10338)*

Optopol Usa Inc 833 678-6765
3915 Beryl Rd Ste 130 Raleigh (27607) *(G-13087)*

Opulence of Southern Pine 919 467-1781
400 Daniels St Raleigh (27605) *(G-13088)*

Opw Feling Containment Systems, Smithfield *Also Called: Opw Fueling Components Inc (G-14475)*

Opw Fling Cntnment Systems Inc (DH) 919 209-2280
3250 Us Highway 70 Bus W Smithfield (27577) *(G-14474)*

Opw Fueling Components Inc 919 464-4569
3250 Us Highway 70 Bus W Smithfield (27577) *(G-14475)*

Ora Inc 540 903-7177
315 Baldwin Ave Marion (28752) *(G-10170)*

Oracle, Matthews *Also Called: Oracle Systems Corporation (G-10279)*

Oracle, Morrisville *Also Called: Oracle Corporation (G-11402)*

Oracle, Morrisville *Also Called: Oracle Corporation (G-11403)*

Oracle, Raleigh *Also Called: Oracle of God Ministries Nc (G-13089)*

Oracle, Raleigh *Also Called: Oracle Systems Corporation (G-13090)*

Oracle Corporation 919 595-2500
5200 Paramount Pkwy Ste 100 Morrisville (27560) *(G-11402)*

Oracle Corporation 919 205-6000
5200 Paramount Pkwy Ste 100 Morrisville (27560) *(G-11403)*

Oracle Flexible Packaging Inc 336 777-5000
220 Polo Rd Winston Salem (27105) *(G-16831)*

Oracle Hearing Group 732 349-6804
1016 Striking Island Dr Wilmington (28403) *(G-16345)*

Oracle of God Ministries Nc 919 522-2113
5731 New Bern Ave Raleigh (27610) *(G-13089)*

Oracle Packaging, Winston Salem *Also Called: Llflex LLC (G-16791)*

Oracle Systems Corporation 704 423-1426
1608 Nightshade Pl Matthews (28105) *(G-10279)*

Oracle Systems Corporation 919 257-2300
8081 Arco Corporate Dr Ste 270 Raleigh (27617) *(G-13090)*

Oramental Post 704 376-8111
10108 Industrial Dr Pineville (28134) *(G-12288)*

Orange Bakery Inc 704 875-3003
13400 Reese Blvd W Huntersville (28078) *(G-8872)*

Orange Steel Roofing Products, Fayetteville *Also Called: Union Corrugating Company (G-5937)*

Orare Inc 919 742-1003
812 E 3rd St Siler City (27344) *(G-14429)*

ALPHABETIC SECTION — Oxford Public Ledger

Orbita Corporation 910 256-5300
  6740 Netherlands Dr Ste D Wilmington (28405) *(G-16346)*
Orca Tactical, Norlina *Also Called: Claypro LLC (G-11995)*
Organized Cabinet LLC 517 402-8639
  100 Dominion Dr Ste 102 Morrisville (27560) *(G-11404)*
Organizer Llc 336 391-7591
  274 Glen Eagles Dr Winston Salem (27104) *(G-16832)*
Orgbook Inc 615 483-5410
  4307 Emperor Blvd Ste 300 Durham (27703) *(G-5260)*
Orgspan Inc 855 674-7726
  4307 Emperor Blvd Ste 300 Durham (27703) *(G-5261)*
Ori Diagnostic Instruments LLC 919 864-8140
  3407 Middlebrook Dr Durham (27705) *(G-5262)*
Orianna Naturals LLC 336 877-1560
  241 Great Sky Vly Todd (28684) *(G-15324)*
Oriel Therapeutics Inc 919 313-1290
  630 Davis Dr Ste 120 Durham (27713) *(G-5263)*
Origin Food Group LLC 704 768-9000
  306 Stamey Farm Rd Statesville (28677) *(G-14855)*
Original Image 919 781-0064
  229 Rosehaven Dr Raleigh (27609) *(G-13091)*
Original New York Seltzer LLC (HQ) 323 500-0757
  19109 W Catawba Ave Ste 200 Cornelius (28031) *(G-4573)*
Original Nuthouse Brand, Edenton *Also Called: Morven Partners LP (G-5519)*
Oriole Mill, The, Hendersonville *Also Called: Michelson Enterprises Inc (G-7880)*
Orion Manufacturing LLC 714 633-5850
  20016 Bear Creek Ch Rd Richfield (28137) *(G-13553)*
Orlandos Cstm Design T-Shirts 919 220-5515
  2824 N Roxboro St Durham (27704) *(G-5264)*
Ornamental, Archdale *Also Called: Ornamental Mouldings LLC (G-295)*
Ornamental Mouldings LLC (DH) 336 431-9120
  3804 Comanche Rd Archdale (27263) *(G-295)*
Ornamental Specialties Inc 704 821-9154
  3488 Gribble Rd Matthews (28104) *(G-10339)*
Oro Manufacturing Company 704 283-2186
  5000 Stitt St Monroe (28110) *(G-10783)*
Orpak Usa Inc 201 441-9820
  7300 W Friendly Ave Greensboro (27410) *(G-7237)*
Orthopedic Appliance Company 828 254-6305
  75 Victoria Rd Asheville (28801) *(G-717)*
Orthopedic Appliance Company 828 348-1960
  910 Tate Blvd Se Hickory (28602) *(G-8109)*
Orthopedic Services 336 716-3349
  3303 Healy Dr Winston Salem (27103) *(G-16833)*
Orthorx Inc 919 929-5550
  400 Meadowmont Village Cir # 425 Chapel Hill (27517) *(G-2050)*
Oryx Systems Inc 704 519-8803
  1064 Van Buren Ave Ste 6 Indian Trail (28079) *(G-8955)*
Os Press LLC 910 485-7955
  1005 Arsenal Ave Fayetteville (28305) *(G-5890)*
Osa, Charlotte *Also Called: Okaya Shinnichi Corp America (G-3289)*
Oscc, Charlotte *Also Called: Ontario Spcialty Coatings Corp (G-3303)*
Osceola Custom Woodworks 336 514-3720
  1551 Brooks Rd Reidsville (27320) *(G-13537)*
Oslo Press Inc 919 606-2028
  2316 Foxtrot Rd Raleigh (27610) *(G-13092)*
Osprea Logistics USA, Charlotte *Also Called: Osprea Logistics Usa LLC (G-3305)*
Osprea Logistics Usa LLC 704 504-1677
  11108 Quality Dr Charlotte (28273) *(G-3305)*
Ossid LLC (DH) 252 446-6177
  4000 College Rd Battleboro (27809) *(G-927)*
Ossiriand Inc 336 385-1100
  106 Hidden Valley Rd Creston (28615) *(G-4625)*
Ostec Industries Corp 704 488-3841
  4103 Sinclair St Denver (28037) *(G-4792)*
OSteel Buildings Inc (PA) 704 824-6061
  1180 Old Redbud Dr Gastonia (28056) *(G-6481)*
Ostwalt Leasing Co Inc 704 528-4528
  867 S Main Troutman (28166) *(G-15388)*
Ostwalt Machine Company Inc 704 528-5730
  140 Apple Hill Rd Troutman (28166) *(G-15389)*
Ostwalt-Vault Co, Troutman *Also Called: Carolina Cemetery Park Corp (G-15369)*
Otb Machinery Inc 336 323-1035
  51 Proctor Rd Thomasville (27360) *(G-15260)*
Otis Elevator Company 828 251-1248
  203 Elk Park Dr Asheville (28804) *(G-718)*
Otis Elevator Company 704 519-0100
  9625 Southern Pine Blvd Ste G Charlotte (28273) *(G-3306)*
Ottaway Associates LLC 919 467-9988
  1300 Wimberly Rd Apex (27523) *(G-223)*
Ottenweller Co Inc 336 783-6959
  401 Technology Ln Mount Airy (27030) *(G-11555)*
Otter Publications 336 643-5387
  8011 Pate Dr Oak Ridge (27310) *(G-12063)*
Otto & Moore Furn Designers, High Point *Also Called: Otto and Moore Inc (G-8472)*
Otto and Moore Inc 336 887-0017
  701 Eastchester Dr High Point (27262) *(G-8472)*
Otto Environmental Systems, Charlotte *Also Called: Duramax Holdings LLC (G-2659)*
Our Daily Living 919 220-8160
  102 E Murray Ave Durham (27704) *(G-5265)*
Our Pride Foods, Roxboro *Also Called: Our Pride Foods Roxboro Inc (G-13813)*
Our Pride Foods Roxboro Inc 336 597-4978
  1128 N Main St Roxboro (27573) *(G-13813)*
Our State Magazine, Greensboro *Also Called: Mann Media Inc (G-7179)*
Outdoor Paths LLC 828 669-1526
  7 Amys Way Black Mountain (28711) *(G-1132)*
Outdura, Hudson *Also Called: Sattler Corp (G-8778)*
Outer Banks Centinel, Nags Head *Also Called: Slam Publications LLC (G-11726)*
Outer Banks Craft Distlg LLC 252 423-3011
  510 Budleigh St Manteo (27954) *(G-10128)*
Outer Banks Distilling, Manteo *Also Called: Outer Banks Craft Distlg LLC (G-10128)*
Outer Banks Hammocks Inc 910 256-4001
  7228 Wrightsville Ave Wilmington (28403) *(G-16347)*
Outer Banks Internet Inc 252 441-6698
  3116 N Croatan Hwy Ste 104 Kill Devil Hills (27948) *(G-9259)*
Outer Banks Olive Oil Company 252 449-8229
  2200 N Croatan Hwy Kill Devil Hills (27948) *(G-9260)*
Outkast Timber Harvesting LLC 336 906-0962
  7209 Cedar Square Rd Randleman (27317) *(G-13482)*
Outlaw Step Co 252 568-4384
  2491 Burncoat Rd Deep Run (28525) *(G-4717)*
Outlet Marine Engines Inc 919 279-3338
  120 Centrewest Ct Ste 695 Cary (27513) *(G-1839)*
Outside Lines 919 327-3041
  1408 Kenbrook Dr Garner (27529) *(G-6299)*
Over Rainbow Inc 704 332-5521
  1431 Bryant St Charlotte (28208) *(G-3307)*
Over Rainbow Publishing 704 360-4075
  262 Stonemarker Rd Mooresville (28117) *(G-11045)*
Overkill Fabrication 336 480-1787
  1700 Nebo Rd Boonville (27011) *(G-1255)*
Overman Building Supply, Burlington *Also Called: Overman Cabinet & Supply LLC (G-1469)*
Overman Cabinet & Supply LLC 336 584-1349
  1168 Saint Marks Church Rd Burlington (27215) *(G-1469)*
Overstreet Sign Contrs Inc 919 596-7300
  2210 Page Rd Ste 101 Durham (27703) *(G-5266)*
Owen G Dunn Co Inc (PA) 252 633-3197
  3731 Trent Rd New Bern (28562) *(G-11832)*
Owens Corning Gastonia Plant, Dallas *Also Called: Owens Crning Nn-Woven Tech LLC (G-4650)*
Owens Corning Glass Metal Svcs 704 721-2000
  4535 Enterprise Dr Nw Concord (28027) *(G-4328)*
Owens Corning Sales LLC 419 248-8000
  3321 Durham Rd Roxboro (27573) *(G-13814)*
Owens Crning Nn-Woven Tech LLC 740 321-6131
  1230 Gastonia Technology Pkwy Dallas (28034) *(G-4650)*
Owens Quilting Inc 828 695-1495
  101 E 11th St Ste 13 Newton (28658) *(G-11956)*
Owner Tryon Backdoor Dist 864 237-1667
  11 Depot St Tryon (28782) *(G-15426)*
Oxford Public Ledger, Oxford *Also Called: Ledger Publishing Company (G-12135)*

Oxford University Press LLC... 919 677-0977
    4000 Centre Green Way Cary (27513) *(G-1840)*

Oxlife of NC LLC.. 828 684-7353
    110 Big Willow Rd Hendersonville (28739) *(G-7889)*

Oyama Cabinet Inc... 828 327-2668
    115 Ge Plant Rd Sw Conover (28613) *(G-4477)*

P & C Logging LLC... 919 552-3420
    305 Spence Mill Rd Fuquay Varina (27526) *(G-6221)*

P & D Archtectural Precast Inc....................................... 252 566-9811
    323 E Railroad St La Grange (28551) *(G-9444)*

P & G Manufacturing Wash Inc....................................... 252 946-9110
    339 Old Bath Hwy Washington (27889) *(G-15721)*

P & P Distributing Company... 910 582-1968
    307 Industry Dr Hamlet (28345) *(G-7628)*

P & S Welding Inc... 910 285-3126
    8414 Us Hwy 117 N Willard (28478) *(G-16055)*

P A Indl Fabrications... 252 329-8881
    1413 Evans St Ste E Greenville (27834) *(G-7567)*

P C S, Winston Salem *Also Called: Personal Communication Systems Inc (G-16846)*

P P Kiln Erectors.. 980 825-2263
    5351 Faith Rd Salisbury (28146) *(G-14022)*

P P M Cycle and Custom... 336 434-5243
    112 School Rd Trinity (27370) *(G-15351)*

P R Sparks Enterprises Inc.. 336 272-7200
    1333 Headquarters Dr Greensboro (27405) *(G-7238)*

P S G, Greensboro *Also Called: Printing Svcs Greensboro Inc (G-7285)*

P S I, High Point *Also Called: Powder Systems Inc (G-8490)*

P T I, Conover *Also Called: Plastic Technology Inc (G-4481)*

P W I Computer Accessories, Winston Salem *Also Called: Panel Wholesalers Incorporated (G-16835)*

P&A Indstrial Fabrications LLC (PA)............................... 336 322-1766
    1841 N Main St Roxboro (27573) *(G-13815)*

P&S Machining Fabrication LLC..................................... 336 227-0151
    2900 Tucker St Burlington (27215) *(G-1470)*

P1 Catawba Development Co LLC.................................. 704 462-1882
    2815 Woodtech Dr Newton (28658) *(G-11957)*

Pace Incorporated (PA).. 910 695-7223
    346 Grant Rd Vass (28394) *(G-15493)*

Pace Communications Inc (PA)...................................... 336 378-6065
    1301 Carolina St Ste 200 Greensboro (27401) *(G-7239)*

Pace Scientific Inc.. 704 799-0688
    112 Paul Critcher Dr Boone (28607) *(G-1227)*

Pace Worldwide, Vass *Also Called: Pace Incorporated (G-15493)*

Paceline, Monroe *Also Called: Spt Technology Inc (G-10812)*

Paceline Inc (PA).. 704 290-5007
    10737 Independence Pointe Pkwy Ste 103 Matthews (28105) *(G-10280)*

Pacific Cabinets... 919 695-3640
    312 S Miami Blvd Durham (27703) *(G-5267)*

Pacific Coast Feather LLC... 252 492-0051
    100 Comfort Dr Henderson (27537) *(G-7801)*

Pacific Seacraft LLC... 252 948-1421
    1481 W 2nd St Washington (27889) *(G-15722)*

Pack Brothers Log & Grading, Mill Spring *Also Called: Pack Brothers Logging (G-10489)*

Pack Brothers Logging... 828 894-2191
    1559 Highway 9 S Mill Spring (28756) *(G-10489)*

Pack Your Wings, Black Mountain *Also Called: Eye Glass Lady LLC (G-1124)*

Package Craft LLC (DH).. 252 825-0111
    146 Package Craft Rd Bethel (27812) *(G-1090)*

Package Crafters Incorporated...................................... 336 431-9700
    1040 E Springfield Rd High Point (27263) *(G-8473)*

Packaging and Supply Solutions, Wilmington *Also Called: Atlantic Corporation (G-16122)*

Packaging Corporation America..................................... 252 753-8450
    9156 West Marlboro Rd Farmville (27828) *(G-5741)*

Packaging Corporation America..................................... 336 434-0600
    801 N William St Goldsboro (27530) *(G-6642)*

Packaging Corporation America..................................... 704 664-5010
    307 Oates Rd Ste B Mooresville (28117) *(G-11046)*

Packaging Corporation America..................................... 828 584-1511
    114 Dixie Blvd Morganton (28655) *(G-11241)*

Packaging Corporation America..................................... 828 286-9156
    321 Industrial Park Rd Rutherfordton (28139) *(G-13881)*

Packaging Corporation America..................................... 704 633-3611
    1302 N Salisbury Ave Salisbury (28144) *(G-14023)*

Packaging Corporation America..................................... 336 434-0600
    212 Roelee St Trinity (27370) *(G-15352)*

Packaging Plus North Carolina....................................... 336 643-4097
    8301 Sangor Dr Summerfield (27358) *(G-14990)*

Packaging Services... 919 630-4145
    4112 Willow Oak Rd Raleigh (27604) *(G-13093)*

Packaging Unlimited NC Inc (DH)................................... 704 732-7100
    1880 Riverview Rd Lincolnton (28092) *(G-9912)*

Packet Pushers Interactive LLC..................................... 928 793-2450
    500 Westover Dr Ste 16993 Sanford (27330) *(G-14161)*

Packiq, Fayetteville *Also Called: Packiq LLC (G-5891)*

Packiq LLC... 910 964-4331
    800 Technology Dr Ste 110 Fayetteville (28306) *(G-5891)*

Packo Bottling Inc.. 919 496-4286
    42 Golden Leaf Dr Louisburg (27549) *(G-9995)*

Pacon Manufacturing Corp LLC...................................... 732 764-9070
    100 Quality Dr Ne Navassa (28451) *(G-11758)*

Pacrim Inc... 919 363-7711
    1041 Classic Rd Apex (27539) *(G-224)*

Pactiv LLC... 910 944-1800
    3299 Nc Hwy 5 Aberdeen (28315) *(G-20)*

Pactiv LLC... 828 396-2373
    3825 N Main St Granite Falls (28630) *(G-6748)*

Pactiv LLC... 336 292-2796
    520 Radar Rd Greensboro (27410) *(G-7240)*

Pactiv LLC... 252 527-6300
    1447 Enterprise Blvd Kinston (28504) *(G-9380)*

Pactiv LLC... 828 758-7580
    303 Advantage Ct Lenoir (28645) *(G-9645)*

Pag Asb LLC.. 336 883-4187
    2410 Schirra Pl High Point (27263) *(G-8474)*

Page Plantation Shuttering Co, Hamlet *Also Called: P & P Distributing Company (G-7628)*

Pages Hydro Dipping Coatings...................................... 910 322-2077
    7455 Lane Rd Linden (28356) *(G-9941)*

Pages Screen Printing LLC.. 336 759-7979
    4110 Cherry St Winston Salem (27105) *(G-16834)*

Pai Services LLC.. 856 231-4667
    11215 N Community House Rd Ste 800 Charlotte (28277) *(G-3308)*

Painpathways Magazine, Winston Salem *Also Called: Jennifer Mowrer (G-16769)*

Paint Company of NC... 336 764-1648
    10436 N Nc Hwy 150 Clemmons (27012) *(G-4054)*

Paintbox Press LLC... 919 969-7512
    208 Glandon Dr Chapel Hill (27514) *(G-2051)*

Painted Canvas.. 770 331-2462
    3809 Heartpine Dr Fayetteville (28306) *(G-5892)*

Painting By Bill, Fayetteville *Also Called: Peaches Enterprises Inc (G-5895)*

Painting By Colors LLC... 919 963-2300
    562 Rock Pillar Rd Clayton (27520) *(G-4005)*

Pair Cutoms Boats, Washington *Also Called: Pair Marine Inc (G-15723)*

Pair Marine Inc.. 252 717-7009
    106 Tarheel Dr Washington (27889) *(G-15723)*

Pak-Lite Inc... 919 563-1097
    6508 E Washington Street Ext Mebane (27302) *(G-10422)*

Pakaraima Fiber Optics Inc... 704 671-2229
    1602 Backcreek Ln Gastonia (28054) *(G-6482)*

Palace Green, Raleigh *Also Called: Palace Green LLC (G-13094)*

Palace Green LLC... 919 827-7950
    4701 Violet Fields Way Raleigh (27612) *(G-13094)*

Paladin Custom Works.. 336 996-2796
    230 Perry Rd Kernersville (27284) *(G-9223)*

Paladin Furniture, Hiddenite *Also Called: Paladin Industries Inc (G-8225)*

Paladin Industries Inc... 828 635-0448
    5270 Nc Highway 90 E Hiddenite (28636) *(G-8225)*

Paletria La Mnrca McHacana LLC.................................. 919 803-0636
    3901 Capital Blvd Ste 155 Raleigh (27604) *(G-13095)*

Pallet Alliance Inc.. 919 442-1400
    318 Blackwell St Ste 260 Durham (27701) *(G-5268)*

Pallet Express Inc.. 336 621-2266
    6306 Old 421 Rd Liberty (27298) *(G-9826)*

ALPHABETIC SECTION

Pallet Plus Inc..336 887-1810
12990 Trinity Rd Trinity (27370) *(G-15353)*

Pallet Rack World..336 253-8766
6404 Birkdale Dr Greensboro (27410) *(G-7241)*

Pallet Resource of NC Inc...................................336 731-8338
4572 N Nc Highway 150 Lexington (27295) *(G-9766)*

Pallet World...919 800-1113
670 John Lee Rd Dunn (28334) *(G-4878)*

Pallet World USA Inc..828 298-7270
124 Sondley Pkwy Asheville (28805) *(G-719)*

Palletone, Siler City Also Called: Palletone North Carolina Inc *(G-14430)*

Palletone North Carolina Inc.............................919 575-6491
10 26th St Butner (27509) *(G-1547)*

Palletone North Carolina Inc.............................336 492-5565
165 Turkey Foot Rd Mocksville (27028) *(G-10597)*

Palletone North Carolina Inc (HQ).....................704 462-1882
2340 Ike Brooks Rd Siler City (27344) *(G-14430)*

Pallets & Such, Bessemer City Also Called: Ross Woodworking Inc *(G-1081)*

Pallets & Such, Bessemer City Also Called: Ross Woodworking Inc *(G-1082)*

Pallets and More..919 815-6134
119 N Cheatham St Franklinton (27525) *(G-6162)*

Palmer Instruments Inc.....................................828 658-3131
234 Old Weaverville Rd Asheville (28804) *(G-720)*

Palmer Senn...704 451-3971
3113 Airlie St Charlotte (28205) *(G-3309)*

Palmer Wahl Instrmnttion Group, Asheville Also Called: Palmer Instruments Inc *(G-720)*

Palmer Wahl Instrmnttion Group, Asheville Also Called: Palmer Wahl Instruments Inc *(G-721)*

Palmer Wahl Instruments Inc............................828 658-3131
234 Old Weaverville Rd Asheville (28804) *(G-721)*

Palmetto and Associate LLC..............................336 382-7432
223 S Elm St Greensboro (27401) *(G-7242)*

Palmetto Brick-Florence, Monroe Also Called: J L Anderson Co Inc *(G-10744)*

Palziv North America, Louisburg Also Called: Palziv North America Inc *(G-9996)*

Palziv North America Inc...................................919 497-0010
7966 Nc 56 Hwy Louisburg (27549) *(G-9996)*

Pam Trading Corporation..................................336 668-0901
1135 Snow Bridge Ln Kernersville (27284) *(G-9224)*

Pamela A Adams..919 876-5949
3812 Tarheel Dr Ste D Raleigh (27609) *(G-13096)*

Pamela Stoeppelwerth......................................828 837-7293
929 Coalville Rd Marble (28905) *(G-10133)*

Pamlico Air, Washington Also Called: Cleanaire Inc *(G-15690)*

Pamlico Air Inc (DH)..252 995-6267
112 S Respess St Washington (27889) *(G-15724)*

Pamlico Packing Co Inc (PA).............................252 745-3688
66 Cross Rd S Grantsboro (28529) *(G-6765)*

Pamlico Packing Co Inc....................................252 745-3688
28 N First St Vandemere (28587) *(G-15489)*

Pamlico Screen Printing Inc.............................252 944-6001
7669 Broad Creek Rd Washington (27889) *(G-15725)*

Pamlico Shores Inc...252 926-0011
14166 Us Highway 264 Swanquarter (27885) *(G-15040)*

Pammyts Monogram Gifts................................252 363-6331
4942 Strickland Rd Bailey (27807) *(G-877)*

Pamor Fine Print..919 559-2846
5924 Crepe Myrtle Ct Raleigh (27609) *(G-13097)*

Pampering Moms Ntral Skin Care.....................706 490-3083
6401 Ashire Xing Apt G Raleigh (27616) *(G-13098)*

Pan American Screw LLC..................................828 466-0060
630 Reese Dr Sw Conover (28613) *(G-4478)*

Pan Glo, Charlotte, Charlotte Also Called: Russell T Bundy Associates Inc *(G-3473)*

Panaceutics Nutrition Inc..................................919 797-9623
6 Davis Dr Durham (27709) *(G-5269)*

Panel Wholesalers Incorporated......................336 765-4040
3841 Kimwell Dr Winston Salem (27103) *(G-16835)*

Panels By Paith Inc...336 599-3437
2728 Allensville Rd Roxboro (27574) *(G-13816)*

Panenergy Corp (DH)..704 594-6200
526 S Church St Charlotte (28202) *(G-3310)*

Papa Lonnies Inc...336 573-9313
154 Dogwood Rd Stoneville (27048) *(G-14964)*

Papa Parusos Foods Inc....................................910 484-8801
716 Whitfield St Fayetteville (28306) *(G-5893)*

Paper Development, Reidsville Also Called: Morrisette Paper Company Inc *(G-13533)*

Paper Perfector LLC...910 695-1092
125 Brookfield Dr Pinehurst (28374) *(G-12230)*

Paper Route Transportation LLC.......................919 478-6615
347 Longstreet Rd Sanford (27330) *(G-14162)*

Paper Specialties Inc..919 431-0028
2708 Discovery Dr Ste J Raleigh (27616) *(G-13099)*

Papersassy Boutique, Winston Salem Also Called: Devora Designs Inc *(G-16676)*

Paperwhites Press...855 348-9848
3134 Mantle Ridge Dr Apex (27502) *(G-225)*

Paperworks...704 548-9057
3040 Parker Green Trl Charlotte (28269) *(G-3311)*

Paperworks Industries Inc................................910 439-6137
5465 Nc Highway 73 W Mount Gilead (27306) *(G-11611)*

Paperworks Industries Inc................................336 447-7278
6530 Franz Warner Pkwy Whitsett (27377) *(G-15998)*

Paps Performance & Machine LLC....................336 225-1877
587 Lanier Rd Lexington (27295) *(G-9767)*

Paraclete Xp Sky Venture LLC...........................910 848-2600
190 Paraclete Dr Raeford (28376) *(G-12428)*

Paraclete Xp Skyventure LLC............................910 904-0027
925 Doc Brown Rd Raeford (28376) *(G-12429)*

Paradigm Solutions Inc.....................................910 392-2611
1213 Culbreth Dr Wilmington (28405) *(G-16348)*

Paradise Printers...336 570-2922
3651 Alamance Rd Burlington (27215) *(G-1471)*

Paragon Films Inc...828 632-5552
255 We Baab Industrial Dr Taylorsville (28681) *(G-15154)*

Paragon Medical - Southington, Charlotte Also Called: Matthew Warren Inc *(G-3143)*

Paragon Navigator Inc......................................336 316-1206
2801 Lawndale Dr Greensboro (27408) *(G-7243)*

Paramason, Louisburg Also Called: En Fleur Corporation *(G-9987)*

Parameter Generation Ctrl Inc..........................828 669-8717
1054 Old Us Hwy 70 W Black Mountain (28711) *(G-1133)*

Parata Systems LLC..919 363-2454
205 Serence Ct Cary (27518) *(G-1841)*

Parata Systems LLC (HQ)..................................888 727-2821
106 Roche Dr Durham (27703) *(G-5270)*

Parchment Press..931 347-2393
140 Old Mountain Rd Hiddenite (28636) *(G-8226)*

Parchment Press, Hiddenite Also Called: Hiddenite Conference Ctr LLC *(G-8218)*

Parhelion Incorporated.....................................866 409-1839
126 N Salem St Ste 200 Apex (27502) *(G-226)*

Parish Sign & Service Inc.................................910 875-6121
627 Laurinburg Rd Raeford (28376) *(G-12430)*

Park Ave Division, Burlington Also Called: Glen Rven Tchnical Fabrics LLC *(G-1425)*

Park Avenue Metalcraft Inc...............................919 554-2233
850 Park Ave Youngsville (27596) *(G-17090)*

Park Communications LLC (HQ).......................919 852-1117
9301 Globe Center Dr Ste 120 Morrisville (27560) *(G-11405)*

Park Court Properties RE Inc............................919 304-3110
1404 Dogwood Way Unit C Mebane (27302) *(G-10423)*

Park Elevator Co, Gastonia Also Called: Park Manufacturing Company *(G-6483)*

Park Manufacturing Company (PA)..................704 869-6128
3112 Northwest Blvd Gastonia (28052) *(G-6483)*

Park Shirt Company...931 879-5894
321 E Russell St Fayetteville (28301) *(G-5894)*

Parkdale Incorporated (PA)..............................704 874-5000
531 Cotton Blossom Cir Gastonia (28054) *(G-6484)*

Parkdale America LLC (HQ)..............................704 874-5000
531 Cotton Blossom Cir Gastonia (28054) *(G-6485)*

Parkdale America LLC.......................................704 739-7411
500 S Railroad Ave Kings Mountain (28086) *(G-9321)*

Parkdale Mills Incorporated..............................704 825-5324
103 E Woodrow Ave Belmont (28012) *(G-998)*

Parkdale Mills Incorporated..............................704 913-3917
1000 Parkdale Dr Belmont (28012) *(G-999)*

Parkdale Mills Incorporated..............................704 825-2529
501 10th St Belmont (28012) *(G-1000)*

Parkdale Mills Incorporated (HQ)... 704 874-5000
531 Cotton Blossom Cir Gastonia (28054) *(G-6486)*

Parkdale Mills Incorporated... 704 739-7411
500 S Railroad Ave Kings Mountain (28086) *(G-9322)*

Parkdale Mills Incorporated... 704 855-3164
100 S Main St Landis (28088) *(G-9452)*

Parkdale Mills Incorporated... 336 243-2141
100 Mill St Lexington (27295) *(G-9768)*

Parkdale Mills Incorporated... 704 292-1255
Hwy 75 Mineral Springs (28108) *(G-10519)*

Parkdale Mills Incorporated... 704 822-0778
101 Mill St Mount Holly (28120) *(G-11646)*

Parkdale Mills Incorporated... 919 774-7401
1921 Boone Trail Rd Sanford (27330) *(G-14163)*

Parkdale Mills Incorporated... 336 476-3181
400 Carmalt St Thomasville (27360) *(G-15261)*

Parkdale Mills Incorporated... 336 591-4644
1660 Us 311 Hwy N Walnut Cove (27052) *(G-15635)*

Parkdale Mills Inc... 704 857-3456
414 N Meriah St Landis (28088) *(G-9453)*

Parkdale Plant 23, Landis Also Called: Parkdale Mills Incorporated *(G-9452)*

Parkdale Plant 24, Landis Also Called: Parkdale Mills Inc *(G-9453)*

Parkdale Plant 26, Walnut Cove Also Called: Parkdale Mills Incorporated *(G-15635)*

Parkdale Plant 29, Sanford Also Called: Parkdale Mills Incorporated *(G-14163)*

Parkdale Plant 5, Kings Mountain Also Called: Parkdale Mills Incorporated *(G-9322)*

Parkdale Plant 68, Mount Holly Also Called: Parkdale Mills Incorporated *(G-11646)*

Parkdale Plants 3 & 4, Lexington Also Called: Parkdale Mills Incorporated *(G-9768)*

Parkdale1, Gastonia Also Called: Parkdale America LLC *(G-6485)*

Parker Athletic Products LLC... 704 370-0400
2401 Distribution St Charlotte (28203) *(G-3312)*

Parker Brothers Incorporated... 910 564-4132
825 Kitty Fork Rd Clinton (28328) *(G-4100)*

Parker Editing LLC... 919 544-8557
108 Maybank Ct Durham (27713) *(G-5271)*

Parker Gas Company Inc (PA)... 800 354-7250
1504 Sunset Ave Clinton (28328) *(G-4101)*

Parker Hosiery Company Inc... 828 668-7628
78 Catawba Ave Old Fort (28762) *(G-12104)*

Parker Hydraulics, Kings Mountain Also Called: Parker-Hannifin Corporation *(G-9323)*

Parker Industries Inc... 828 437-7779
4867 Rhoney Rd Connelly Springs (28612) *(G-4407)*

Parker Legwear, Old Fort Also Called: Parker Hosiery Company Inc *(G-12104)*

Parker Marine Enterprises Inc... 252 728-5621
2570 Nc Highway 101 Beaufort (28516) *(G-964)*

Parker Medical Associates LLC... 704 344-9998
2400 Distribution St Charlotte (28203) *(G-3313)*

Parker Medical Associates LLC (PA)... 704 344-9998
2400 Distribution St Charlotte (28203) *(G-3314)*

Parker Metal Finishing Company... 336 275-9657
719 W Gate City Blvd Ste D Greensboro (27403) *(G-7244)*

Parker Oil Inc... 828 253-7265
290 Depot St Asheville (28801) *(G-722)*

Parker Service Center, Mooresville Also Called: Parker-Hannifin Corporation *(G-11047)*

Parker Southern Inc... 828 428-3506
15 W Holly St Maiden (28650) *(G-10115)*

Parker-Binns Vineyard LLC... 828 894-0154
7382 Highway 108 E Mill Spring (28756) *(G-10490)*

Parker-Hannifin Corporation... 704 588-3246
9225 Forsyth Park Dr Charlotte (28273) *(G-3315)*

Parker-Hannifin Corporation... 828 245-3233
203 Pine St Forest City (28043) *(G-6079)*

Parker-Hannifin Corporation... 336 373-1761
125 E Meadowview Rd Greensboro (27406) *(G-7245)*

Parker-Hannifin Corporation... 704 739-9781
101 Canterbury Rd Kings Mountain (28086) *(G-9323)*

Parker-Hannifin Corporation... 704 664-1922
2559 Charlotte Hwy Mooresville (28117) *(G-11047)*

Parker-Hannifin Corporation... 704 662-3500
149 Crawford Rd Statesville (28625) *(G-14856)*

Parker-Lord, Cary Also Called: Lord Corporation *(G-1817)*

Parkers Equipment Company... 252 560-0088
3204 Hwy 258 S Snow Hill (28580) *(G-14506)*

Parks Family Meats LLC... 217 446-4600
1618 Nc 24 And 50 Hwy Warsaw (28398) *(G-15672)*

Parkway Asheville, Arden Also Called: Parkway Products LLC *(G-360)*

Parkway Products LLC... 828 684-1362
199 Airport Rd Arden (28704) *(G-360)*

Parkway Vineyard & Winery LLC... 828 765-1400
9557 Linville Falls Hwy Newland (28657) *(G-11892)*

Parkwood Corporation... 910 815-4300
3506 E Yacht Dr Oak Island (28465) *(G-12053)*

Parmer International Inc... 704 374-0066
1225 Graphic Ct Ste D Charlotte (28206) *(G-3316)*

Parrish Contracting LLC... 828 524-9100
3370 Bryson City Rd Franklin (28734) *(G-6141)*

Parrish Tire Company... 704 372-2013
300 E 36th St Charlotte (28206) *(G-3317)*

Parrish Tire Company... 336 334-9979
2809 Thurston Ave Greensboro (27406) *(G-7246)*

Parrish Tire Company... 704 872-6565
547 Winston Rd Jonesville (28642) *(G-9101)*

Parrish Tire Company (PA)... 800 849-8473
5130 Indiana Ave Winston Salem (27106) *(G-16836)*

Parrish Welding... 336 707-3878
6711 Sandylea Rd Oak Ridge (27310) *(G-12064)*

Parsons Metal Fabricators Inc... 828 758-7521
265 Wildwood Rd Lenoir (28645) *(G-9646)*

Parton Export, Rutherfordton Also Called: Parton Lumber Company Inc *(G-13883)*

Parton Forest Products Inc... 828 287-4257
251 Parton Rd Rutherfordton (28139) *(G-13882)*

Parton Lumber Company Inc (PA)... 828 287-4257
251 Parton Rd Rutherfordton (28139) *(G-13883)*

Parts and Systems Company Inc... 828 684-7070
44 Buck Shoals Rd Ste D2 Arden (28704) *(G-361)*

Party Tables Land Co LLC... 919 596-3521
2455 S Alston Ave Durham (27713) *(G-5272)*

Party Time Inc... 910 454-4577
1658 N Howe St Ste 1 Southport (28461) *(G-14575)*

Pas USA Inc... 252 974-5500
2010 W 15th St Washington (27889) *(G-15726)*

Pasb Inc... 704 490-2556
303 N Cannon Blvd Kannapolis (28083) *(G-9129)*

Paschal Associates Ltd... 336 625-2535
324 S Wilmington St Raleigh (27601) *(G-13100)*

Pasco, Arden Also Called: Parts and Systems Company Inc *(G-361)*

Pashes LLC... 704 682-6535
328 E Broad St Statesville (28677) *(G-14857)*

Pass & Seymour Inc... 315 468-6211
4515 Enterprise Dr Nw Concord (28027) *(G-4329)*

Pass & Seymour Legrand, Concord Also Called: Pass & Seymour Inc *(G-4329)*

Passport Health Triangle... 919 781-0053
8450 Chapel Hill Rd Ste 205 Cary (27513) *(G-1842)*

Pasture Management Systems Inc... 704 436-6401
10325 Nc Highway 49 N Mount Pleasant (28124) *(G-11675)*

Patch Rubber Company... 252 536-2574
100 Patch Rubber Rd Weldon (27890) *(G-15887)*

Pate Industries... 704 889-2376
9920 Pineville Matthews Rd Pineville (28134) *(G-12289)*

Patel Deepal... 704 634-5141
4898 Aldridge Pl Nw Concord (28027) *(G-4330)*

Patheon, Morrisville Also Called: Patheon Pharmaceuticals Inc *(G-11407)*

Patheon, Morrisville Also Called: Patheon Phrmceuticals Svcs Inc *(G-11408)*

Patheon Calculus Merger LLC... 919 226-3200
3900 Paramount Pkwy Morrisville (27560) *(G-11406)*

Patheon Inc... 919 226-3200
4815 Emperor Blvd Ste 100 Durham (27703) *(G-5273)*

Patheon Inc... 919 226-3200
4815 Emperor Blvd Ste 100 Durham (27703) *(G-5274)*

Patheon Manufacturing Svcs LLC... 252 758-3436
5900 Martin Luther King Jr Hwy Greenville (27834) *(G-7568)*

Patheon Pharmaceuticals Inc... 866 728-4366
4125 Premier Dr High Point (27265) *(G-8475)*

ALPHABETIC SECTION — Peaberry Press LLC

Patheon Pharmaceuticals Inc (DH) 919 226-3200
3900 Paramount Pkwy Morrisville (27560) *(G-11407)*

Patheon Phrmceuticals Svcs Inc (DH) 919 226-3200
3900 Paramount Pkwy Morrisville (27560) *(G-11408)*

Patheon Softgels Inc 336 812-8700
7902 Indlea Point Ste 112 Greensboro (27409) *(G-7247)*

Patheon Softgels Inc (DH) 336 812-8700
4125 Premier Dr High Point (27265) *(G-8476)*

Patholdco Inc (HQ) 919 212-1300
108 Nova Dr Morrisville (27560) *(G-11409)*

Pathway Technologies Inc (PA) 919 847-2680
8400 Six Forks Rd Ste 202 Raleigh (27615) *(G-13101)*

Patria Vineyard, Winston Salem *Also Called: Patria Vineyard LLC (G-16837)*

Patria Vineyard LLC 336 407-8254
550 Peters Creek Pkwy Unit 1409 Winston Salem (27101) *(G-16837)*

Patricia Hall 704 729-6133
128 Terrace Dr Bessemer City (28016) *(G-1077)*

Patricia Schaefer 919 302-2726
5448 Apex Peakway Apex (27502) *(G-227)*

Patrick 336 846-4759
348 Old Buffalo Rd West Jefferson (28694) *(G-15947)*

Patrick Yarn Mill Inc 704 739-4119
501 York Rd Kings Mountain (28086) *(G-9324)*

Patrick Yarns, Kings Mountain *Also Called: Patrick Yarn Mill Inc (G-9324)*

Patricks Small Engines 910 653-2061
16624 Seven Creeks Hwy Tabor City (28463) *(G-15085)*

Patriot Jerky LLC 828 850-9160
1297 Keri Pl Conover (28613) *(G-4479)*

Pats Mobile Welding 910 891-9581
2503 Erwin Rd Dunn (28334) *(G-4879)*

Pattern Box 704 535-8743
8325 Nathanael Greene Ln Charlotte (28227) *(G-3318)*

Patterson Custom Drapery 910 791-4332
4315 Deer Creek Ln Wilmington (28405) *(G-16349)*

Patterson Marque 336 661-7520
3919 Waddill St Winston Salem (27105) *(G-16838)*

Patti Boo Inc 828 648-6495
1659 N Canton Rd Canton (28716) *(G-1621)*

Patti Boo Designs Inc 828 648-6495
1659 N Canton Rd Canton (28716) *(G-1622)*

Pattons Medical, Charlotte *Also Called: Pattons Medical LLC (G-3319)*

Pattons Medical LLC 704 529-5442
4610 Entrance Dr Ste H Charlotte (28273) *(G-3319)*

Patty Cakes 828 696-8240
5 Star Ln Hendersonville (28791) *(G-7890)*

Patty Knio 919 995-2670
3008 Campbell Rd Raleigh (27606) *(G-13102)*

Paul Brayton Designs, Archdale *Also Called: Baypointe Partners LLC (G-269)*

Paul Casper Inc 919 269-5362
3533 Rosinburg Rd Zebulon (27597) *(G-17139)*

Paul Charles Englert 704 824-2102
1820 Spencer Mountain Rd Gastonia (28054) *(G-6487)*

Paul Davis Restoration, Winston Salem *Also Called: Moe Jt Enterprises Inc (G-16816)*

Paul Hoge Creations Inc 704 624-6860
7105 E Marshville Blvd Marshville (28103) *(G-10221)*

Paul James O'Brian, Delco *Also Called: Preferred Logging (G-4724)*

Paul Norman Company Inc 704 399-4221
8700 Wilkinson Blvd Charlotte (28214) *(G-3320)*

Paul P Poovey Jr 828 465-2975
2538 Newton St (28658) *(G-11958)*

Paul Robert, Taylorsville *Also Called: Paul Robert Chair Inc (G-15155)*

Paul Robert Chair Inc (PA) 828 632-7021
266 Martin Luther King Dr Taylorsville (28681) *(G-15155)*

Paulas Pretty Things Inc 919 656-1163
770 Vail Rd Pikeville (27863) *(G-12193)*

Pauls Cstm Fbrication Mch LLC 757 746-2743
166 Us Highway 158 W Camden (27921) *(G-1558)*

Pauls Custom Woodworking Inc 828 712-6234
190 Eastside Dr Black Mountain (28711) *(G-1134)*

Pauls Water Treatment LLC 336 886-5600
1224 W Ward Ave High Point (27260) *(G-8477)*

Pavco Inc 704 496-6800
9401 Nations Ford Rd Charlotte (28273) *(G-3321)*

Pave Wellness LLC 919 335-3575
420 Glenview Ln Durham (27703) *(G-5275)*

Paw Pharma Services LLC 919 367-0413
304 Kettlebridge Dr Cary (27511) *(G-1843)*

Paws and Claws Publishing LLC 336 541-3997
1589 Skeet Club Rd Ste 102-175 High Point (27265) *(G-8478)*

Paxton Media Group 704 289-1541
1508 Skyway Dr Monroe (28110) *(G-10784)*

Payload Media Inc 919 367-2969
129 Parkcrest Dr Cary (27519) *(G-1844)*

Payload Trailers Inc 833 239-6565
4001 Ball Park Rd Thomasville (27360) *(G-15262)*

Payment Collect LLC 828 214-5550
70 Charlotte St Asheville (28801) *(G-723)*

Payne Leather and Tool LLC 336 391-8964
179 Monticello Rd Weaverville (28787) *(G-15858)*

Pb & J Industries Inc 919 661-2738
8805 Running Oak Dr Raleigh (27617) *(G-13103)*

Pbc of Aberdeen, Aberdeen *Also Called: Builders Frstsrce - Sthast Gro (G-2)*

Pbf LLC 828 252-1742
19 Fieldcrest Cir Asheville (28806) *(G-724)*

Pbi Performance Products Inc (PA) 704 554-3378
9800 Southern Pine Blvd Ste D Charlotte (28273) *(G-3322)*

PBM Graphics Inc 919 544-6222
4102 S Miami Blvd Durham (27703) *(G-5276)*

PBM Graphics Inc (DH) 919 544-6222
3700 S Miami Blvd Durham (27703) *(G-5277)*

PBM Graphics Inc 336 664-5800
415 Westcliff Rd Greensboro (27409) *(G-7248)*

Pbrandecom 336 294-9771
4842 Tower Rd Unit C Greensboro (27410) *(G-7249)*

Pbs Ventures Inc 252 235-2001
5469 Us Highway 264a Bailey (27807) *(G-878)*

PC Satellite Solutions 252 217-7237
325 Jones White Rd Roper (27970) *(G-13770)*

PC Signs & Graphics LLC 919 661-5801
180 Hein Dr Garner (27529) *(G-6300)*

PCA, Farmville *Also Called: Packaging Corporation America (G-5741)*
PCA, Goldsboro *Also Called: Packaging Corporation America (G-6642)*
PCA, Lenoir *Also Called: Polychem Alloy Inc (G-9648)*
PCA/High Point 334, Trinity *Also Called: Packaging Corporation America (G-15352)*
Pca/Morganton 354, Morganton *Also Called: Packaging Corporation America (G-11241)*
Pca/Regional Design Center, Mooresville *Also Called: Packaging Corporation America (G-11046)*
Pca/Salisbury 375, Salisbury *Also Called: Packaging Corporation America (G-14023)*

Pcai Inc 704 588-1240
11101 Nations Ford Rd Charlotte (28206) *(G-3323)*

PCC Airfoils LLC 919 774-4300
5105 Rex Mcleod Dr Sanford (27330) *(G-14164)*

PCI of North Carolina LLC 919 467-5151
100 Falcone Pkwy Cary (27511) *(G-1845)*

Pcore 919 734-0460
200 W Dewey St Goldsboro (27530) *(G-6643)*

PCS Collectibles LLC (PA) 805 306-1140
9825 Northcross Center Ct Huntersville (28078) *(G-8873)*

Pcs Phosphate 252 402-5779
535 Prescott Rd New Bern (28560) *(G-11833)*

Pcs Phosphate Company Inc 252 322-4111
Aurora (27806) *(G-838)*

Pcsi, Gastonia *Also Called: Powder Coating Services Inc (G-6491)*

Pcx Holding LLC 919 550-2800
370 Spectrum Dr Knightdale (27545) *(G-9425)*

Pdf and Associates 252 332-7749
116 Luther Brown Rd Colerain (27924) *(G-4139)*

PDM Lighting LLC 919 771-3230
3737 Glenwood Ave Ste 100 Raleigh (27612) *(G-13104)*

Peaberry, Asheville *Also Called: Peaberry Press LLC (G-725)*

Peaberry Press LLC 828 773-1489
802 Fairview Rd Ste 800 Asheville (28803) *(G-725)*

Peace of Mind Publications — ALPHABETIC SECTION

Peace of Mind Publications 919 308-5137
1321 Shiley Dr Durham (27704) *(G-5278)*

Peaches 'n Cream, Burlington *Also Called: Bonaventure Co LLC (G-1378)*

Peaches Enterprises Inc 910 868-5800
1014 Cain Rd Fayetteville (28303) *(G-5895)*

Peachland Dsign Fbrication LLC 704 272-9296
3129 Deep Springs Church Rd Peachland (28133) *(G-12174)*

Peachtree Audio, Matthews *Also Called: Signal Path International LLC (G-10290)*

Peachtree Lumber Company Inc 828 837-0118
6926 Highway 64 W Brasstown (28902) *(G-1268)*

Peak City Candles Inc 919 601-8223
916 Branch Line Ln Apex (27502) *(G-228)*

Peak Demand Inc 252 360-2777
605 Tarboro Street Anx Sw Wilson (27893) *(G-16522)*

Peak Level Media Solutions LLC 919 917-8002
17104 Musselburgh Dr Cary (27518) *(G-1846)*

Peak Steel LLC 919 362-5955
1610 N Salem St Apex (27523) *(G-229)*

Peak Truss Builders LLC 919 552-5933
1220 N Main St Holly Springs (27540) *(G-8710)*

Peanut, Dublin *Also Called: Peanut Processors Inc (G-4838)*

Peanut Butter Fingers LLC 704 997-5787
17131 Green Dolphin Ln Cornelius (28031) *(G-4574)*

Peanut Butter Project 704 654-0212
14720 Asheton Creek Dr Charlotte (28273) *(G-3324)*

Peanut Processors Inc (PA) 910 862-2136
7329 Albert St Dublin (28332) *(G-4838)*

Peanut Processors Sherman Inc 910 862-2136
7329 Albert St Dublin (28332) *(G-4839)*

Pearl Black Fashion Inc 252 689-6799
652 E Arlington Blvd Greenville (27858) *(G-7569)*

Pearl River Group LLC 704 283-4667
6027 Stitt St Monroe (28110) *(G-10785)*

Pearson Company, Hickory *Also Called: Hdm Furniture Industries Inc (G-8040)*

Pearson Textiles Inc 919 776-8730
7975 Villanow Dr Sanford (27332) *(G-14165)*

Peco, Arden *Also Called: Peco Inc (G-362)*

Peco Inc 828 684-1234
100 Airport Rd Arden (28704) *(G-362)*

Peculiar Roots LLC 845 379-4039
3709 Alliance Dr Ste A Greensboro (27407) *(G-7250)*

Pedal 2 Metal LLP 910 723-2289
2069 Osceola Dr Fayetteville (28301) *(G-5896)*

Peelle Company 631 231-6000
115 N Secrest Ave Monroe (28110) *(G-10786)*

Peerless Blowers, Hot Springs *Also Called: Madison Manufacturing Company (G-8745)*

Peformance Chassis 919 319-3484
214 Hillsboro St Cary (27513) *(G-1847)*

Pegasus Art and Signs LLC 704 588-4948
11908 Tanton Ln Charlotte (28273) *(G-3325)*

Pegasus Builders Supply LLC 919 244-1586
2228 Page Rd Ste 108 Durham (27703) *(G-5279)*

Peggs Recreation Inc 704 660-0007
408 N Main St Mooresville (28115) *(G-11048)*

Pelican Ventures LLC 919 518-8203
5924 Wild Orchid Trl Raleigh (27613) *(G-13105)*

Pelton & Crane Company 704 588-2126
11727 Fruehauf Dr Charlotte (28273) *(G-3326)*

Pemmco Manufacturing Inc 336 625-1122
631 Veterans Loop Rd Asheboro (27205) *(G-460)*

Pen-Cell Plastics Inc 252 467-2210
546 English Rd Rocky Mount (27804) *(G-13718)*

Pencco Inc 252 235-5300
10143 Us 264a Middlesex (27557) *(G-10453)*

Penco Precision LLC 910 292-6542
1901 Blue Clay Rd Ste I Wilmington (28405) *(G-16350)*

Penco Products Inc (DH) 252 917-5287
1820 Stonehenge Dr Greenville (27858) *(G-7570)*

Penco Products Inc 252 798-4000
1301 Penco Dr Hwy 125 Hamilton (27840) *(G-7614)*

Pendel, Raleigh *Also Called: Pendulum Electromagnetics Inc (G-13106)*

Pendergast Industries LLC 919 636-1621
203 Glenview Pl Chapel Hill (27514) *(G-2052)*

Pendulum Electromagnetics Inc 919 571-9970
6304 Westgate Rd Ste D Raleigh (27617) *(G-13106)*

Pendulum Inc 704 491-6320
6128 Brookshire Blvd Ste A Charlotte (28216) *(G-3327)*

Peninsula Polymers 336 885-8185
1709 Blandwood Dr High Point (27260) *(G-8479)*

Penn, Smithfield *Also Called: Penn Compression Moulding Inc (G-14476)*

Penn Compression Moulding Inc (PA) 919 934-5144
309 Components Dr Smithfield (27577) *(G-14476)*

Penn Engineering & Mfg Corp 336 631-8741
2400 Lowery St Winston Salem (27101) *(G-16839)*

Pennsylvania Press Metals, Conover *Also Called: GKN Sinter Metals LLC (G-4459)*

Pennsylvania Trans Tech Inc 910 875-7600
201 Carolina Dr Raeford (28376) *(G-12431)*

Pennsylvania Transformer Co, Raeford *Also Called: Pennsylvania Trans Tech Inc (G-12431)*

Penny Connected Cafe LLC 984 214-2131
66 Easy St Pittsboro (27312) *(G-12344)*

Penrock LLC 704 800-6722
251 Knoxview Ln Mooresville (28117) *(G-11049)*

Penske Racing South Inc (DH) 704 664-2300
200 Penske Way Mooresville (28115) *(G-11050)*

Pentair Pool Products, Sanford *Also Called: Pentair Water Pool and Spa Inc (G-14166)*

Pentair Water Pool and Spa Inc 919 463-4640
400 Regency Forest Dr Ste 300 Cary (27518) *(G-1848)*

Pentair Water Pool and Spa Inc (DH) 919 566-8000
1620 Hawkins Ave Sanford (27330) *(G-14166)*

People's Pharmacy, The, Durham *Also Called: Graedon Enterprises Inc (G-5125)*

Pep Filters, Mooresville *Also Called: Pep Filters Inc (G-11051)*

Pep Filters Inc 704 662-3133
120 Talbert Rd Ste J Mooresville (28117) *(G-11051)*

Pepsi Bottling Group 828 286-4406
1621 Poors Ford Rd Rutherfordton (28139) *(G-13884)*

Pepsi Bottling Group Inc 704 507-4031
5047 Highway 24 27 E Midland (28107) *(G-10473)*

Pepsi Bottling Ventures LLC 800 879-8884
500 Gregson Dr Cary (27511) *(G-1849)*

Pepsi Bottling Ventures LLC 828 264-7702
7467 Old 421 S Deep Gap (28618) *(G-4711)*

Pepsi Bottling Ventures LLC 252 335-4355
109 Corporate Dr Elizabeth City (27909) *(G-5561)*

Pepsi Bottling Ventures LLC 919 863-4000
1900 Pepsi Way Fl 1 Garner (27529) *(G-6301)*

Pepsi Bottling Ventures LLC 919 865-2388
1900 Treygan Rd Garner (27529) *(G-6302)*

Pepsi Bottling Ventures LLC 919 778-8300
2707 N Park Dr Goldsboro (27534) *(G-6644)*

Pepsi Bottling Ventures LLC 704 455-0800
22 Pepsi Way Harrisburg (28075) *(G-7720)*

Pepsi Bottling Ventures LLC (DH) 919 865-2300
4141 Parklake Ave Ste 600 Raleigh (27612) *(G-13107)*

Pepsi Bottling Ventures LLC 252 451-1811
620 Health Dr Rocky Mount (27804) *(G-13719)*

Pepsi Bottling Ventures LLC 910 865-1600
137 Pepsi Way Saint Pauls (28384) *(G-13907)*

Pepsi Bottling Ventures LLC 704 873-0249
1703 Gregory Rd Statesville (28677) *(G-14858)*

Pepsi Bottling Ventures LLC 910 792-5400
415 Landmark Dr Wilmington (28412) *(G-16351)*

Pepsi Bottling Ventures LLC 336 464-9227
295 Business Park Dr Winston Salem (27107) *(G-16840)*

Pepsi Bottling Ventures LLC 336 464-9227
390 Business Park Dr Winston Salem (27107) *(G-16841)*

Pepsi Bottling Ventures LLC 336 724-4800
3425 Myer Lee Dr Winston Salem (27101) *(G-16842)*

Pepsi Cola Bottling Co 828 650-7800
200 Fanning Field Fletcher (28732) *(G-6031)*

Pepsi Cola Co 704 357-9166
3530 Toringdon Way Ste 400 Charlotte (28277) *(G-3328)*

Pepsi-Cola, Cherryville *Also Called: Pepsi-Cola Metro Btlg Co Inc (G-3874)*

ALPHABETIC SECTION — Performnce Strl Con Sltons LLC

Pepsi-Cola, Deep Gap *Also Called: Pepsi Bottling Ventures LLC (G-4711)*
Pepsi-Cola, Garner *Also Called: Pepsi Bottling Ventures LLC (G-6301)*
Pepsi-Cola, Goldsboro *Also Called: Pepsi Bottling Ventures LLC (G-6644)*
Pepsi-Cola, Granite Falls *Also Called: Pepsi-Cola Btlg Hickry NC Inc (G-6749)*
Pepsi-Cola, Harrisburg *Also Called: Pepsi Bottling Ventures LLC (G-7720)*
Pepsi-Cola, Hickory *Also Called: Pepsi-Cola Btlg Hickry NC Inc (G-8110)*
Pepsi-Cola, Hickory *Also Called: Pepsi-Cola Btlg Hickry NC Inc (G-8111)*
Pepsi-Cola, New Bern *Also Called: Pepsi-Cola Btlg New Bern Inc (G-11834)*
Pepsi-Cola, Raleigh *Also Called: Pepsi Bottling Ventures LLC (G-13107)*
Pepsi-Cola, Rocky Mount *Also Called: Pepsi Bottling Ventures LLC (G-13719)*
Pepsi-Cola, Rocky Mount *Also Called: Pepsi-Cola Metro Btlg Co Inc (G-13720)*
Pepsi-Cola, Statesville *Also Called: Pepsi Bottling Ventures LLC (G-14858)*
Pepsi-Cola, Whittier *Also Called: Pepsi-Cola Btlg Hickry NC Inc (G-16010)*
Pepsi-Cola, Wilmington *Also Called: Pepsi Bottling Ventures LLC (G-16351)*
Pepsi-Cola, Winston Salem *Also Called: Pepsi Bottling Ventures LLC (G-16840)*
Pepsi-Cola, Winston Salem *Also Called: Pepsi Bottling Ventures LLC (G-16842)*
Pepsi-Cola, Winston Salem *Also Called: Pepsi-Cola Metro Btlg Co Inc (G-16843)*
Pepsi-Cola Bottler, Winston Salem *Also Called: Pepsi Bottling Ventures LLC (G-16841)*
Pepsi-Cola Btlg Hickry NC Inc 828 322-8090
47 Duke St Granite Falls (28630) *(G-6749)*
Pepsi-Cola Btlg Hickry NC Inc 828 322-8090
2640 Main Ave Nw Hickory (28601) *(G-8110)*
Pepsi-Cola Btlg Hickry NC Inc (PA) 828 322-8090
2401 14th Avenue Cir Nw Hickory (28601) *(G-8111)*
Pepsi-Cola Btlg Hickry NC Inc 828 497-1235
1060 Gateway Rd Whittier (28789) *(G-16010)*
Pepsi-Cola Btlg New Bern Inc (PA) 252 522-0232
3610 Dr M L King Jr Blvd New Bern (28562) *(G-11834)*
Pepsi-Cola Metro Btlg Co Inc 980 581-1099
2820 South Blvd Charlotte (28209) *(G-3329)*
Pepsi-Cola Metro Btlg Co Inc 704 736-2640
152 Commerce Dr Cherryville (28021) *(G-3874)*
Pepsi-Cola Metro Btlg Co Inc 252 446-7181
620 Health Dr Rocky Mount (27804) *(G-13720)*
Pepsi-Cola Metro Btlg Co Inc 336 896-4000
1100 Reynolds Blvd Winston Salem (27105) *(G-16843)*
Pepsico, Charlotte *Also Called: Pepsi Cola Co (G-3328)*
Pepsico, Charlotte *Also Called: Pepsi-Cola Metro Btlg Co Inc (G-3329)*
Pepsico, Marion *Also Called: Pepsico Inc (G-10171)*
Pepsico, Midland *Also Called: Pepsi Bottling Group Inc (G-10473)*
Pepsico, Roanoke Rapids *Also Called: McPherson Beverages Inc (G-13579)*
Pepsico, Rutherfordton *Also Called: Pepsi Bottling Group (G-13884)*
Pepsico, Saint Pauls *Also Called: Pepsi Bottling Ventures LLC (G-13907)*
Pepsico, Winston Salem *Also Called: Pepsico Inc (G-16844)*
Pepsico Inc 828 756-4662
8337 Us 221 N Marion (28752) *(G-10171)*
Pepsico Inc 914 253-2000
Winston Salem (27105) *(G-16844)*
Perdue Agribusiness, Cofield *Also Called: Perdue Farms Inc (G-4137)*
Perdue Ecop Crushing, Pantego *Also Called: East Crlina Olseed Prcssors LL (G-12163)*
Perdue Farms, Candor *Also Called: Perdue Farms Inc (G-1597)*
Perdue Farms, Elkin *Also Called: Perdue Farms Inc (G-5628)*
Perdue Farms, Halifax *Also Called: Perdue Farms Inc (G-7610)*
Perdue Farms, Kenly *Also Called: Perdue Farms Inc (G-9154)*
Perdue Farms, Murfreesboro *Also Called: Perdue Farms Inc (G-11701)*
Perdue Farms, Nashville *Also Called: Perdue Farms Inc (G-11748)*
Perdue Farms, Winston Salem *Also Called: Perdue Farms Inc (G-16845)*
Perdue Farms, Yadkinville *Also Called: Perdue Farms Inc (G-17046)*
Perdue Farms Inc 252 348-4287
2108 Us Highway 13 S Ahoskie (27910) *(G-64)*
Perdue Farms Inc 910 673-4148
Hwy 211 S Candor (27229) *(G-1597)*
Perdue Farms Inc 704 278-2228
9150 Statesville Blvd Cleveland (27013) *(G-4078)*
Perdue Farms Inc 252 358-8245
242 Perdue Rd Cofield (27922) *(G-4137)*
Perdue Farms Inc 704 789-2400
862 Harris St Nw Concord (28025) *(G-4331)*
Perdue Farms Inc 252 338-1543
1268 Us Highway 17 S Elizabeth City (27909) *(G-5562)*
Perdue Farms Inc 336 366-2591
105 Greenwood Cir Elkin (28621) *(G-5628)*
Perdue Farms Inc 252 758-2141
1623 N Greene St Greenville (27834) *(G-7571)*
Perdue Farms Inc 252 583-5731
1201 State Rd Halifax (27839) *(G-7610)*
Perdue Farms Inc 919 284-2033
9266 Revell Rd Kenly (27542) *(G-9154)*
Perdue Farms Inc 252 348-4200
3539 Governors Rd Lewiston Woodville (27849) *(G-9662)*
Perdue Farms Inc 910 738-8581
1801 Godwin Ave Lumberton (28358) *(G-10048)*
Perdue Farms Inc 252 398-5112
Hwy 158 W Murfreesboro (27855) *(G-11701)*
Perdue Farms Inc 252 459-9763
1835 Us Highway 64a Nashville (27856) *(G-11748)*
Perdue Farms Inc 336 896-9121
7996 N Point Blvd Winston Salem (27106) *(G-16845)*
Perdue Farms Inc 336 679-7733
806 W Main St Yadkinville (27055) *(G-17046)*
PERDUE FARMS INC., Ahoskie *Also Called: Perdue Farms Inc (G-64)*
PERDUE FARMS INC., Elizabeth City *Also Called: Perdue Farms Inc (G-5562)*
PERDUE FARMS INC., Lewiston Woodville *Also Called: Perdue Farms Inc (G-9662)*
PERDUE FARMS INC., Lumberton *Also Called: Perdue Farms Inc (G-10048)*
Perdue Farms Incorporated 910 997-8600
416 S Long Dr Rockingham (28379) *(G-13638)*
Perdue Farms Warehouse, Greenville *Also Called: Perdue Farms Inc (G-7571)*
Perdue Grain Market, Cleveland *Also Called: Perdue Farms Inc (G-4078)*
Perfect 10 Brands LLC 702 738-0183
129 Glenmore Rd Cary (27519) *(G-1850)*
Perfect Cube LLC 970 481-5785
2405 Paula St Raleigh (27608) *(G-13108)*
Perfect Fit Industries LLC 800 864-7618
8501 Tower Point Dr Ste C Charlotte (28227) *(G-3330)*
Perfect Match Candles LLC 919 482-6649
609 Culvert St Apex (27502) *(G-230)*
Perfect Square Music Inc 478 718-5702
28 Fox Hollow Ct Arden (28704) *(G-363)*
Perfection Fabrics Inc 828 328-3322
841a F Avenue Dr Se Hickory (28602) *(G-8112)*
Perfection Gear Inc (DH) 828 253-0000
9 N Bear Creek Rd Asheville (28806) *(G-726)*
Perfection Products Co, Greensboro *Also Called: P R Sparks Enterprises Inc (G-7238)*
Perfectly Threaded LLC 336 229-0152
6578 Bethel Church Rd Gibsonville (27249) *(G-6569)*
Performance Additives LLC 215 321-4388
160 W New York Ave Unit 2b Southern Pines (28387) *(G-14543)*
Performance Apparel LLC 805 541-0989
565 Air Tool Dr Ste K Southern Pines (28387) *(G-14544)*
Performance Center, Mooresville *Also Called: Performance Racing Whse Inc (G-11053)*
Performance Entps & Parts Inc 336 621-6572
4104 Burlington Rd Greensboro (27405) *(G-7251)*
Performance Fibers 704 947-7193
12721 Longstock Ct Huntersville (28078) *(G-8874)*
Performance Goods LLC 704 361-8600
4365 School House Cmns Ste 500 # 143 Harrisburg (28075) *(G-7721)*
Performance Machine & Fab Inc 336 983-0414
1050 Denny Rd King (27021) *(G-9279)*
Performance Orthotics 704 945-7790
2024 Randolph Rd # B Charlotte (28207) *(G-3331)*
Performance Parts Intl LLC 704 660-1084
104 Blue Ridge Trl Mooresville (28117) *(G-11052)*
Performance Plastics Pdts Inc 336 454-0350
126 Wade St Ste D Jamestown (27282) *(G-9066)*
Performance Print Services LLC 919 957-9995
1 Tw Alexander Dr Ste 130 Durham (27709) *(G-5280)*
Performance Racing Whse Inc 704 838-1400
145 Blossom Ridge Dr Mooresville (28117) *(G-11053)*
Performnce Strl Con Sltons LLC 980 333-6414
Davidson (28036) *(G-4690)*

Perfusio Corp... 252 656-0404
   102a Hungate Dr Greenville (27858) *(G-7572)*
Perigen, Cary *Also Called: E&C Medical Intelligence Inc (G-1753)*
Perkem Technology, Stanley *Also Called: DSM Desotech Inc (G-14691)*
Perkins Fabrications Inc................................... 828 688-3157
   5632 Nc 261 Bakersville (28705) *(G-886)*
Perlman Inc... 704 332-1164
   5312 Wingedfoot Rd Charlotte (28226) *(G-3332)*
Perma Flex Rller Tchnlgy-Rgnge, Salisbury *Also Called: Perma-Flex Rollers Inc (G-14025)*
Perma Flex Roller Technology (PA)....................... 704 633-1201
   1415 Jake Alexander Blvd S Salisbury (28146) *(G-14024)*
Perma-Flex Rollers Inc..................................... 704 633-1201
   1415 Jake Alexander Blvd S Salisbury (28146) *(G-14025)*
Permatech, LLC, Graham *Also Called: Vesuvius Nc LLC (G-6715)*
Perry Brothers Tire Svc Inc................................ 919 693-2128
   606 Lewis St Oxford (27565) *(G-12140)*
Perry Brothers Tire Svc Inc (PA).......................... 919 775-7225
   610 Wicker St Sanford (27330) *(G-14167)*
Perry Glass Co, Henderson *Also Called: A R Perry Corporation (G-7774)*
Perrycraft Inc.. 336 372-2545
   1549 Us Highway 21 S Sparta (28675) *(G-14598)*
Perrys Frame Inc.. 828 327-4681
   3785 Thompson St Newton (28658) *(G-11959)*
Perseus Intermediate Inc................................... 919 474-6700
   4721 Emperor Blvd Ste 100 Durham (27703) *(G-5281)*
Person County Recycle Center............................ 336 597-4437
   Madison Blvd Roxboro (27573) *(G-13817)*
Person Printing Company Inc............................. 336 599-2146
   115 Clayton Ave Roxboro (27573) *(G-13818)*
Personal Communication Systems Inc.................... 336 722-4917
   301 N Main St Winston Salem (27101) *(G-16846)*
Personal Defense Trainin.................................. 910 455-4473
   213 Maplehurst Dr Jacksonville (28540) *(G-9019)*
Personal Xpressionz LLC.................................. 919 587-7462
   600 Park Offices Dr Ste 300 Pmb 103 Durham (27709) *(G-5282)*
Personalized Learning, Mint Hill *Also Called: Dia-Be-Tees LLC (G-10529)*
Perusi Woodcarving.. 828 734-6121
   103 Waldonpond Pl Waynesville (28786) *(G-15814)*
Pet Love Publishing LLC................................... 252 489-3832
   1229 S Virginia Dare Trl Kill Devil Hills (27948) *(G-9261)*
Petco, Kenly *Also Called: Petroleum Tank Corporation (G-9155)*
Peter J Hamann.. 910 484-7877
   337 Mcmillan St Fayetteville (28301) *(G-5897)*
Peterson Welding Inc....................................... 336 480-4152
   107 Hillside Manor Dr Lewisville (27023) *(G-9670)*
Petnet Solutions Inc... 919 572-5544
   2310 Presidential Dr Ste 108 Durham (27703) *(G-5283)*
Petnet Solutions Inc... 865 218-2000
   3908 Westpoint Blvd Ste E Winston Salem (27103) *(G-16847)*
Petra Precision Machining.................................. 919 751-3461
   3413 Central Heights Rd Goldsboro (27534) *(G-6645)*
Petra Technologies Inc..................................... 704 577-0687
   3902 Alden St Indian Trail (28079) *(G-8956)*
Petro Equipment Sls & Svc LLC.......................... 828 492-0700
   151 Flower House Loop Troutman (28166) *(G-15390)*
Petroleum Tank Corporation............................... 919 284-2418
   600 N Gardner Ave Kenly (27542) *(G-9155)*
Petroliance LLC.. 336 472-3000
   814 Lexington Ave Thomasville (27360) *(G-15263)*
Petteway Body Shop Inc................................... 910 455-3272
   1362 Old Maplehurst Rd Jacksonville (28540) *(G-9020)*
Petteway Rentals, Jacksonville *Also Called: Petteway Body Shop Inc (G-9020)*
Petty Machine Company Inc.............................. 704 864-3254
   2403 E Forbes Rd Gastonia (28056) *(G-6488)*
Pexco LLC.. 336 493-7500
   2971 Taylor Dr Asheboro (27203) *(G-461)*
Pf2 Eis LLC.. 704 549-6931
   10735 David Taylor Dr Ste 100 Charlotte (28262) *(G-3333)*
Pfaff Molds Ltd Partnership................................ 704 423-9484
   11825 Westhall Dr Charlotte (28278) *(G-3334)*
PFC Group LLC... 704 393-4040
   5900 Old Mount Holly Rd Charlotte (28208) *(G-3335)*

Pfi, Graham *Also Called: Pure Flow Inc (G-6709)*
Pfizer, Durham *Also Called: Pfizer Inc (G-5284)*
Pfizer Inc... 252 382-3309
   6563 N Us Highway 301 Battleboro (27809) *(G-928)*
Pfizer Inc... 919 941-5185
   1040 Swabia Ct Durham (27703) *(G-5284)*
Pfizer Inc... 252 977-5111
   4285 N Wesleyan Blvd Rocky Mount (27804) *(G-13721)*
Pfizer Inc... 919 775-7100
   4300 Oak Park Rd Sanford (27330) *(G-14168)*
Pflag Hickory... 828 244-5578
   3065 44th Avenue Dr Ne Hickory (28601) *(G-8113)*
Pg Technichians... 910 742-1017
   4106 Kettering Pl Wilmington (28412) *(G-16352)*
Pgi Nonwovens, Charlotte *Also Called: Chicopee Inc (G-2476)*
Pgi Polymer Inc.. 704 697-5100
   9335 Harris Corners Pkwy Ste 300 Charlotte (28269) *(G-3336)*
Pharmaceutic Litho Label Inc............................. 336 785-4000
   3360 Old Lexington Rd Winston Salem (27107) *(G-16848)*
Pharmaceutical Dimensions............................... 336 297-4851
   7353 W Friendly Ave # A Greensboro (27410) *(G-7252)*
Pharmaceutical Equipment Svcs......................... 239 699-9120
   15 Magnolia Hill Ct Asheville (28806) *(G-727)*
Pharmacutical Dimension................................. 336 664-5287
   7353 W Friendly Ave # A Greensboro (27410) *(G-7253)*
Pharmagra Holding Company LLC....................... 828 884-8656
   158 Mclean Rd Brevard (28712) *(G-1284)*
Pharmasone LLC.. 910 679-8364
   1800 Sir Tyler Dr Wilmington (28405) *(G-16353)*
Pharmdawg Vineyards LLC................................ 770 596-0960
   501 Mining School Rd State Road (28676) *(G-14728)*
Pharmgate Animal Health LLC............................ 910 679-8364
   1800 Sir Tyler Dr Wilmington (28405) *(G-16354)*
Pharmgate Inc (HQ)... 910 679-8364
   1800 Sir Tyler Dr Wilmington (28405) *(G-16355)*
Pharr Fibers and Yarns, Mc Adenville *Also Called: Mannington Mills Inc (G-10379)*
Pharr McAdenville Corporation (PA).................... 704 824-3551
   100 Main St Mc Adenville (28101) *(G-10380)*
Pharr Ph/Crescent Plant, Mc Adenville *Also Called: Coats HP Inc (G-10377)*
Phase II Creations Inc..................................... 336 249-0673
   109 E 7th Ave Lexington (27292) *(G-9769)*
Phelps Wood Products LLC............................... 336 284-2149
   12010 Statesville Blvd Cleveland (27013) *(G-4079)*
Phil Barker's Refinishing, Greensboro *Also Called: Barker and Martin Inc (G-6831)*
Phil Parkey & Associates, Candler *Also Called: Southern Organ Services Ltd (G-1589)*
Phil S Tire Service Inc..................................... 828 682-2421
   617 W Main St Burnsville (28714) *(G-1530)*
Philantrophy Journal.. 919 890-6240
   220 Fayetteville St Raleigh (27601) *(G-13109)*
Philip Brady.. 336 581-3999
   185 Charlie Garner Rd Bennett (27208) *(G-1027)*
Philip Morris, Winston Salem *Also Called: Philip Morris USA Inc (G-16849)*
Philip Morris USA Inc...................................... 336 744-4401
   4338 Grove Ave Winston Salem (27105) *(G-16849)*
Philip Products, Asheville *Also Called: Tompkins Industries Inc (G-802)*
Philips Semiconductors, Cary *Also Called: Nxp Usa Inc (G-1834)*
Phillip Dunn Logging Co Inc.............................. 252 633-4577
   508 Madam Moores Ln New Bern (28562) *(G-11835)*
Phillip Rice Woodworking LLC........................... 919 339-4543
   113 Rayland St Oxford (27565) *(G-12141)*
Phillips Corporation... 336 665-1080
   8500 Triad Dr Colfax (27235) *(G-4157)*
Phillips Iron Works, Raleigh *Also Called: Canalta Enterprises LLC (G-12586)*
Phillips Mobile Home Vlg LLC............................ 704 298-4648
   7740 Freeze Rd Kannapolis (28081) *(G-9130)*
Phillips Plating Co Inc..................................... 252 637-2695
   1617 Hwy 17 N Ste 1617 Bridgeton (28519) *(G-1295)*
Philosophy Inc (HQ).. 602 794-8701
   1400 Broadway Rd Sanford (27332) *(G-14169)*
Philpott Motors Ltd... 704 566-2400
   5401 E Independence Blvd Charlotte (28212) *(G-3337)*

ALPHABETIC SECTION — Piedmont Precision Products

Phitech Laboratories Inc 910 420-1020
12 Forest Lake Dr Jackson Springs (27281) *(G-8983)*

Phitonex Inc 855 874-4866
701 W Main St Ste 200 Durham (27701) *(G-5285)*

Phoenix Aluminum, Winston Salem Also Called: Alpha Aluminum LLC *(G-16600)*

Phoenix Assembly NC LLC 252 801-4250
7101 N Us Highway 301 Battleboro (27809) *(G-929)*

Phoenix Epoxy Systems LLC 252 747-3735
123 Main St Hookerton (28538) *(G-8729)*

Phoenix Home Furnishings Inc
2485 Penny Rd High Point (27265) *(G-8480)*

Phoenix Packaging Inc 336 724-1978
111 E 10th St Winston Salem (27101) *(G-16850)*

Phoenix Rising Press LLC 480 284-1250
157 Starling Pass Asheville (28804) *(G-728)*

Phoenix Sign Pros Inc 252 756-5685
4409 Corey Rd Winterville (28590) *(G-17011)*

Phoenix Software Systems Inc 252 756-6451
111 Asbury Rd Greenville (27858) *(G-7573)*

Phoenix St Claire Pubg LLC 919 303-3223
321 Glen Echo Ln Apt C Cary (27518) *(G-1851)*

Phoenix Tapes Usa LLC 704 588-3090
10900 S Commerce Blvd Charlotte (28273) *(G-3338)*

Phoenix Trimming, Tarboro Also Called: Murdock Webbing Company Inc *(G-15117)*

Phononic Inc 919 908-6300
800 Capitola Dr Ste 7 Durham (27713) *(G-5286)*

Photo Emblem Incorporated 336 784-4000
5010 S Main St Winston Salem (27107) *(G-16851)*

Photon Energy Corp 888 336-8128
1095 Hendersonville Rd Asheville (28803) *(G-729)*

Photonicare Inc 866 411-3277
2800 Meridian Pkwy Ste 175 Durham (27713) *(G-5287)*

Phyllis Pulling 336 643-8201
5935 Tarleton Dr Oak Ridge (27310) *(G-12065)*

Phynix Pc Inc 503 890-1444
51 Abba Cir Middlesex (27557) *(G-10454)*

Picassomoesllc 216 703-4547
513 Patriots Pointe Dr Hillsborough (27278) *(G-8665)*

Piccione Vinyards 312 342-0181
2364 Cedar Forest Rd Ronda (28670) *(G-13767)*

Pickett Hosiery Mills Inc 336 227-2716
733 Koury Dr Burlington (27215) *(G-1472)*

Pickles Manufacturing LLC 910 267-4711
354 N Faison Ave Faison (28341) *(G-5724)*

Pics and Prints LLC 917 753-3542
8473 Mossy Cup Trl Harrisburg (28075) *(G-7722)*

Pictureframes.com, High Point Also Called: Graphik Dimensions Limited *(G-8371)*

Pie Pushers 919 901-0743
625 Hugo St Durham (27704) *(G-5288)*

Piece of Pie LLC 919 286-7421
904 9th St Durham (27705) *(G-5289)*

Piedmont Animal Health Inc 336 544-0320
204 Muirs Chapel Rd Ste 200 Greensboro (27410) *(G-7254)*

Piedmont AVI Cmponent Svcs LLC 336 423-5100
7102 Cessna Dr Greensboro (27409) *(G-7255)*

Piedmont Block, Lexington Also Called: Johnson Concrete Company *(G-9736)*

Piedmont Business Forms Inc 828 464-0010
703 W C St Newton (28658) *(G-11960)*

Piedmont Candy Company (PA) 336 248-2477
404 Market St Lexington (27292) *(G-9770)*

Piedmont Cheerwine Bottling, Colfax Also Called: Piedmont Cheerwine Bottling Co *(G-4158)*

Piedmont Cheerwine Bottling Co 336 993-7733
2913 Sandy Ridge Rd Colfax (27235) *(G-4158)*

Piedmont Chemical Inds I LLC 336 885-5131
331 Burton Ave High Point (27262) *(G-8481)*

Piedmont Cmposites Tooling LLC 828 632-8883
33 Lewittes Rd Taylorsville (28681) *(G-15156)*

Piedmont Coca-Cola Btlg Partnr (HQ) 704 551-4400
4115 Coca Cola Plz Charlotte (28211) *(G-3339)*

Piedmont Coca-Cola Btlg Partnr 252 752-2446
1051 Staton Rd Greenville (27834) *(G-7574)*

Piedmont Coca-Cola Btlg Partnr 252 536-3611
80 Industrial Dr Halifax (27839) *(G-7611)*

Piedmont Coca-Cola Btlg Partnr 252 637-3157
3710 Dr M L King Jr Blvd New Bern (28562) *(G-11836)*

Piedmont Components, Mount Gilead Also Called: Capitol Funds Inc *(G-11599)*

Piedmont Components Division, Shelby Also Called: Capitol Funds Inc *(G-14291)*

Piedmont Components Division, Shelby Also Called: Capitol Funds Inc *(G-14292)*

Piedmont Corrugated, Valdese Also Called: Piedmont Corrugated Specialty *(G-15452)*

Piedmont Corrugated Specialty 828 874-1153
340 Morgan St Se Valdese (28690) *(G-15452)*

Piedmont Custom Meats Inc 336 628-4949
430 Nc Highway 49 S Asheboro (27205) *(G-462)*

Piedmont Directional Signs Inc 704 607-6809
4004 Beechwood Spring Ln Belmont (28012) *(G-1001)*

Piedmont Distillers Inc 336 445-0055
3960 Us Highway 220 Madison (27025) *(G-10082)*

Piedmont Elc Mtr Repr Inc Ashb 336 495-0500
4635 Us Highway 220 Bus N Asheboro (27203) *(G-463)*

Piedmont Fabrication 336 634-0096
116 Industrial Ave Greensboro (27406) *(G-7256)*

Piedmont Fiberglass Inc 828 632-8883
1166 Bunch Dr Statesville (28677) *(G-14859)*

Piedmont First Aid, Statesville Also Called: Carpet Rentals Inc *(G-14773)*

Piedmont Flight Inc 336 776-6070
3789 N Liberty St Winston Salem (27105) *(G-16852)*

Piedmont Flight Training, Winston Salem Also Called: Piedmont Flight Inc *(G-16852)*

Piedmont Graphics Inc 336 230-0040
6903 International Dr Greensboro (27409) *(G-7257)*

Piedmont Hardware Brands, Huntersville Also Called: Amerock LLC *(G-8791)*

Piedmont Hardwood Lbr Co Inc 704 436-9311
9000 Nc Highway 49 N Mount Pleasant (28124) *(G-11676)*

Piedmont Hoist and Crane Inc (PA) 336 992-1355
3350 Temple School Rd Winston Salem (27107) *(G-16853)*

Piedmont Indus Coatings Inc 336 377-3399
160 University Center Dr Winston Salem (27105) *(G-16854)*

Piedmont Lithium Carolinas Inc (HQ) 434 664-7643
42 E Catawba St Belmont (28012) *(G-1002)*

Piedmont Lithium Inc (PA) 704 461-8000
42 E Catawba St Belmont (28012) *(G-1003)*

Piedmont Lminating Coating Inc 336 272-1600
1812 Sullivan St Greensboro (27405) *(G-7258)*

Piedmont Logging LLC 919 562-1861
870 Park Ave Youngsville (27596) *(G-17091)*

Piedmont Machine & Mfg, Concord Also Called: Elomi Inc *(G-4260)*

Piedmont Marble Inc 336 274-1800
5014 Robdot Dr Oak Ridge (27310) *(G-12066)*

Piedmont Mediaworks Inc 828 575-2250
5a Hedgerose Ct Asheville (28805) *(G-730)*

Piedmont Metals Burlington Inc 336 584-7742
215 Macarthur Ln Burlington (27217) *(G-1473)*

Piedmont Metalworks LLC 919 598-6500
5902 Us 70 W Mebane (27302) *(G-10424)*

Piedmont Office Products, Newton Also Called: Piedmont Business Forms Inc *(G-11960)*

Piedmont Packaging Inc (PA) 336 886-5043
1141 Foust Ave High Point (27260) *(G-8482)*

Piedmont Pallet & Cont Inc 336 284-6302
667 Hendrix Farm Circle Ln Woodleaf (27054) *(G-17024)*

Piedmont Paper Stock LLC 336 285-8592
3909 Riverdale Dr Greensboro (27406) *(G-7259)*

Piedmont Parachute Inc 336 597-2225
2712 Durham Rd Roxboro (27573) *(G-13819)*

Piedmont Pipe Mfg LLC 704 489-0911
7871 Commerce Dr Denver (28037) *(G-4793)*

Piedmont Plastics Inc (PA) 704 597-8200
5010 W W T Harris Blvd Charlotte (28269) *(G-3340)*

Piedmont Plating Corporation 336 272-2311
3005 Holts Chapel Rd Greensboro (27401) *(G-7260)*

Piedmont Poultry, Lumber Bridge Also Called: Mountaire Farms LLC *(G-10021)*

Piedmont Precision Products 828 304-0791
347 Highland Ave Se Hickory (28602) *(G-8114)*

Piedmont Printing
ALPHABETIC SECTION

Piedmont Printing, Asheboro Also Called: Asheboro Piedmont Printing Inc *(G-406)*

Piedmont Publishing 336 727-4099
418 N Marshall St Winston Salem (27101) *(G-16855)*

Piedmont Sales, Sanford Also Called: Piedmont Sales & Rentals LLC *(G-14170)*

Piedmont Sales & Rentals LLC 919 499-9888
5074 Nc 87 N Sanford (27332) *(G-14170)*

Piedmont Sand, Swannanoa Also Called: Cumberland Grav & Sand Min Co *(G-15024)*

Piedmont Signs 704 291-2345
2330 Concord Hwy Monroe (28110) *(G-10787)*

Piedmont Springs Company Inc 828 322-5347
118 11th Street Pl Sw Hickory (28602) *(G-8115)*

Piedmont Stairworks LLC (PA) 704 697-0259
2246 Old Steele Creek Rd Charlotte (28208) *(G-3341)*

Piedmont Stairworks LLC 704 483-3721
8135 Mallard Rd Denver (28037) *(G-4794)*

Piedmont Steel Company LLC 336 875-5133
1838 Eastchester Dr Ste 108 High Point (27265) *(G-8483)*

Piedmont Surfaces of Triad LLC 336 627-7790
615 Monroe St Eden (27288) *(G-5499)*

Piedmont Technical Services 770 530-8313
9127 Arbor Glen Ln Charlotte (28210) *(G-3342)*

Piedmont Triad Printing Inc 336 235-3080
6520 Airport Center Dr Greensboro (27409) *(G-7261)*

Piedmont Truck Tires Inc 828 277-1549
125 Sweeten Creek Rd Asheville (28803) *(G-731)*

Piedmont Truck Tires Inc 828 202-5337
1317 Emmanuel Church Rd Conover (28613) *(G-4480)*

Piedmont Truck Tires Inc 336 223-9412
704 Myrtle Dr Graham (27253) *(G-6706)*

Piedmont Truck Tires Inc (HQ) 336 668-0091
312 S Regional Rd Greensboro (27409) *(G-7262)*

Piedmont Turning & Wdwkg Co 336 475-7161
328 Jarrett Rd Thomasville (27360) *(G-15264)*

Piedmont Weld & Pipe Inc 704 782-7774
172 Buffalo Ave Nw Concord (28025) *(G-4332)*

Piedmont Well Covers Inc 704 664-8488
1135 Mazeppa Rd Mount Ulla (28125) *(G-11685)*

Piedmont Wood Products Inc 828 632-4077
1924 Black Oak Ridge Rd Taylorsville (28681) *(G-15157)*

Pierce Farrier Supply Inc 704 753-4358
9705 Pierce Rd Indian Trail (28079) *(G-8957)*

Pierre Foods, Claremont Also Called: Advancepierre Foods Inc *(G-3900)*

Pigeon Rver Cstm Mtalworks LLC 828 619-0559
177 Academy St Canton (28716) *(G-1623)*

Pike Electric, Greensboro Also Called: Pike Electric LLC *(G-7263)*

Pike Electric LLC 336 316-7068
3511 W Market St Greensboro (27403) *(G-7263)*

Pilgrim LLC 980 224-9567
6428 Long Meadow Rd Charlotte (28210) *(G-3343)*

Pilgrim Tract Society Inc 336 495-1241
105 Depot St Randleman (27317) *(G-13483)*

Pilgrims Pride Chkn Oprtons Di, Concord Also Called: Pilgrims Pride Corporation *(G-4333)*

Pilgrims Pride Corporation 704 721-3585
2925 Armentrout Dr Concord (28025) *(G-4333)*

Pilgrims Pride Corporation 704 624-2171
5901 Hwy 74 E Marshville (28103) *(G-10222)*

Pilgrims Pride Corporation 919 774-7333
484 Zimmerman Rd Sanford (27330) *(G-14171)*

Pilgrims Pride Corporation 336 622-4251
2607 Old 421 Rd Staley (27355) *(G-14669)*

Pilgrims Pride Corporation 704 233-4047
205 Edgewood Dr Wingate (28174) *(G-16577)*

Pilkington 828 357-8043
207 Ruby Ave Black Mountain (28711) *(G-1135)*

Pilkington Group Inc 336 545-0425
3307 Timberview Cir Greensboro (27410) *(G-7264)*

Pilkington North America Inc 910 276-5630
13121 S Rocky Ford Rd Laurinburg (28352) *(G-9492)*

Pilot LLC 864 430-6337
375 E Connecticut Ave Southern Pines (28387) *(G-14545)*

Pilot LLC (PA) 910 692-7271
145 W Pennsylvania Ave Southern Pines (28387) *(G-14546)*

Pilot Mountain Vineyards LLC 828 400-9533
1162 Bradley Rd Pinnacle (27043) *(G-12322)*

Pilot Press LLC 910 692-8366
175 Davis St Southern Pines (28387) *(G-14547)*

Pilot Rack Company 336 351-5851
2220 Riverside Dr Mount Airy (27030) *(G-11556)*

Pilot View Wood Works, High Point Also Called: Pilot View Wood Works Inc *(G-8484)*

Pilot View Wood Works Inc 336 883-2511
412 Berkley St High Point (27260) *(G-8484)*

Pilothouse Marine Services LLC 252 732-6427
277 Tosto Rd Beaufort (28516) *(G-965)*

Pinball Literary 919 240-4012
15 S Circle Dr Chapel Hill (27516) *(G-2053)*

Pinco Usa Inc 704 895-5766
10620 Bailey Rd Ste A Cornelius (28031) *(G-4575)*

Pine Creek Products LLC 336 399-8806
2856 Country Club Rd Winston Salem (27104) *(G-16856)*

Pine Glo Products Inc 919 556-7787
115 Legacy Crest Ct Zebulon (27597) *(G-17140)*

Pine Hall Brick Co Inc 336 721-7500
634 Lindsey Bridge Rd Madison (27025) *(G-10083)*

Pine Hall Brick Co Inc (PA) 336 721-7500
2701 Shorefair Dr Winston Salem (27105) *(G-16857)*

Pine Island Sportswear, Monroe Also Called: JD Apparel Inc *(G-10748)*

Pine Log 118 Trdtnal Living Rd, State Road Also Called: Pine Log Co Inc *(G-14729)*

Pine Log Co Inc 336 366-2770
118 Traditonal Living Rd State Road (28676) *(G-14729)*

Pine RES Instrumentation Inc 919 782-8320
2741 Campus Walk Ave Bldg 100 Durham (27705) *(G-5290)*

Pine State Corporate AP LLC 336 789-9437
219 Frederick St Mount Airy (27030) *(G-11557)*

Pine State Corporative Apparel, Mount Airy Also Called: Pine State Corporate AP LLC *(G-11557)*

Pine State Welding 910 639-3631
3 New Day Way Whispering Pines (28327) *(G-15955)*

Pine Top Distillery LLC 888 261-5287
3036 Farrior Rd Raleigh (27607) *(G-13110)*

Pine Tree Poetry 336 584-0631
3529 Elk St Burlington (27215) *(G-1474)*

Pine View Buildings LLC 704 876-1501
933 Tomlin Mill Rd Statesville (28625) *(G-14860)*

Pinecone Publishing LLC 252 649-0973
4910 Spring Green Pass New Bern (28562) *(G-11837)*

Pineland Cutlery Inc 910 757-0035
625 Se Service Rd Southern Pines (28387) *(G-14548)*

Ping Gps Inc 704 806-7945
19825 North Cove Rd Cornelius (28031) *(G-4576)*

Pink Zebra Moving Charlotte NC, Charlotte Also Called: Movers and Shakers LLC *(G-3209)*

Pinkston Properties LLC 828 252-9867
91 Westside Dr Asheville (28806) *(G-732)*

Pinnacle Converting Eqp & Svcs 704 376-3855
11325 Nations Ford Rd Ste A Pineville (28134) *(G-12290)*

Pinnacle Converting Eqp Inc (PA) 704 376-3855
11325 Nations Ford Rd Ste A Pineville (28134) *(G-12291)*

Pinnacle Furnishings Inc 910 944-0908
10570 Nc Highway 211 E Ste G Aberdeen (28315) *(G-21)*

Pinnix Distillery Inc 828 412-5441
101 Fairview Rd Asheville (28803) *(G-733)*

Pins and Needles 910 639-9662
110 N Ridgecrest St Pinebluff (28373) *(G-12216)*

Pioneer, Sparta Also Called: Amano Pioneer Eclipse Corp *(G-14588)*

Pioneer Cabinets Inc 828 688-2642
102 Alfred Woody Dr Bakersville (28705) *(G-887)*

Pioneer Diversities, Newton Also Called: Eric Arnold Klein *(G-11931)*

Pioneer Machine Works Inc 704 864-5528
1221 W 2nd Ave Gastonia (28052) *(G-6489)*

Pioneer Motor Bearing Company 704 937-7000
129 Battleground Rd Kings Mountain (28086) *(G-9325)*

Pioneer Printing Company Inc 336 789-4011
203 N South St Mount Airy (27030) *(G-11558)*

Pioneer Square Brands Inc (PA) 360 733-5608
1515 W Green Dr High Point (27260) *(G-8485)*

ALPHABETIC SECTION — Plexus Corp

Pioneer Srgcal Orthblogics Inc (DH)..................252 355-4405
  1800 N Greene St Ste A Greenville (27834) *(G-7575)*
Pioneer Srgical Orthobiologics, Greenville Also Called: Angstrom Medica Inc *(G-7483)*
PIP Printing, Burlington Also Called: JB II Printing LLC *(G-1439)*
PIP Printing, Burlington Also Called: PIP Printing & Document Servic *(G-1475)*
PIP Printing, Burlington Also Called: Postal Instant Press *(G-1477)*
PIP Printing, Cary Also Called: Triangle Solutions Inc *(G-1912)*
PIP Printing, Rocky Mount Also Called: C D J & P Inc *(G-13686)*
PIP Printing, Sanford Also Called: Sillaman & Sons Inc *(G-14184)*
PIP Printing, Winston Salem Also Called: Rite Instant Printing Inc *(G-16885)*
PIP Printing & Document Servic..................336 222-0717
  717 Chapel Hill Rd Burlington (27215) *(G-1475)*
Pipe Bridge Products Inc..................919 786-4499
  5208 Rembert Dr Raleigh (27612) *(G-13111)*
Pipeline Plastics LLC..................817 693-4100
  15159 Andrew Jackson Hwy Sw Fair Bluff (28439) *(G-5699)*
Piranha, Greensboro Also Called: Piranha Nail and Staple Inc *(G-7265)*
Piranha Industries Inc..................704 248-7843
  2515 Allen Rd S Charlotte (28269) *(G-3344)*
Piranha Nail and Staple Inc..................336 852-8358
  901 Norwalk St Ste E Greensboro (27407) *(G-7265)*
Pirate Press LLC..................919 720-2736
  104 Trackimire Ln Apex (27539) *(G-231)*
Pirtek Wilmington, Wilmington Also Called: Under Pressure Wilmington LLC *(G-16438)*
Pisgah It Company LLC..................828 884-5290
  577 Island Ford Rd Brevard (28712) *(G-1285)*
Pisgah Laboratories Inc..................828 884-2789
  3222 Old Hendersonville Hwy Pisgah Forest (28768) *(G-12327)*
Pitch & Burl LLC..................512 653-9413
  4215 Hiddenbrook Dr Charlotte (28205) *(G-3345)*
Pitman Knits Inc..................704 276-3262
  7625 Palm Tree Church Rd Vale (28168) *(G-15470)*
Pitney Bowes, Greensboro Also Called: Pitney Bowes Inc *(G-7266)*
Pitney Bowes, Raleigh Also Called: Pitney Bowes Inc *(G-13112)*
Pitney Bowes Inc..................336 805-3320
  4161 Piedmont Pkwy Greensboro (27410) *(G-7266)*
Pitney Bowes Inc..................919 785-3480
  3150 Spring Forest Rd Ste 122 Raleigh (27616) *(G-13112)*
Pitt Road Ex Lube & Car Wash, Elizabeth City Also Called: Pitt Road LLC *(G-5563)*
Pitt Road LLC..................252 331-5818
  711 N Hughes Blvd Elizabeth City (27909) *(G-5563)*
Pittmanbac..................252 430-4745
  1079 Eaves Rd Henderson (27537) *(G-7802)*
Pk Woodworks..................828 284-4570
  480 Fruit Tree Ln Burnsville (28714) *(G-1531)*
PL&e Sales Inc..................704 561-9650
  11925 Sam Roper Dr Ste B Charlotte (28269) *(G-3346)*
Plan B Chipping and Logging..................336 942-2692
  2539 Beckerdite Rd Sophia (27350) *(G-14520)*
Plan B Enterprises LLC..................919 387-4856
  3217 Hinsley Rd New Hill (27562) *(G-11863)*
Plan Nine Publishing Inc..................336 454-7766
  1237 Elon Pl High Point (27263) *(G-8486)*
Plane Defense Ltd..................828 254-6061
  175 N Mason Way Hendersonville (28792) *(G-7891)*
Planet Logo Inc..................910 763-2554
  23 N Front St # 3 Wilmington (28401) *(G-16356)*
Planet Smoothie, Mooresville Also Called: Yummy Tummy Ga LLC *(G-11138)*
Plant 15, Belmont Also Called: Parkdale Mills Incorporated *(G-998)*
Plant 17, Belmont Also Called: Parkdale Mills Incorporated *(G-999)*
Plant 21, Mineral Springs Also Called: Parkdale Mills Incorporated *(G-10519)*
Plant 6, Lenoir Also Called: Bernhardt Furniture Company *(G-9585)*
Plant 6 & 7, Thomasville Also Called: Parkdale Mills Incorporated *(G-15261)*
Plantation House Foods Inc..................919 381-5495
  3316 Stoneybrook Dr Durham (27705) *(G-5291)*
Plantation Shutter Pros Inc..................843 591-6634
  5811 Kristi Ln Midland (28107) *(G-10474)*
Plantd Inc..................434 906-3445
  3220 Knotts Grove Rd Oxford (27565) *(G-12142)*

Plasgad Usa LLC..................704 775-6461
  933 Meacham Rd Ste C Statesville (28677) *(G-14861)*
Plaskolite LLC..................704 588-3800
  1100 Bond St Charlotte (28208) *(G-3347)*
Plasma Games..................252 721-3294
  208 Bracken Ct Raleigh (27615) *(G-13113)*
Plasma Games Inc..................919 627-1252
  112 Wind Chime Ct Raleigh (27615) *(G-13114)*
Plasma Surgical..................704 608-6756
  9924 Bayart Way Huntersville (28078) *(G-8875)*
Plasma Web Services Inc..................561 703-0485
  14129 Perugia Way Apt 102 Charlotte (28273) *(G-3348)*
Plastek Group..................910 895-2089
  206 Enterprise Dr Rockingham (28379) *(G-13639)*
Plastek Group, Hamlet Also Called: Plastek Industries Inc *(G-7629)*
Plastek Industries Inc..................814 878-4457
  1015 County Home Rd Hamlet (28345) *(G-7629)*
Plastering..................336 402-0445
  5405 Woodlane Dr Julian (27283) *(G-9106)*
Plastex Fabricators, Charlotte Also Called: PFC Group LLC *(G-3335)*
Plasti-Form, Asheville Also Called: Braiform Enterprises Inc *(G-571)*
Plastic Art Design Inc..................919 878-1672
  5811 Mchines Pl Raleigh (27616) *(G-13115)*
Plastic Ingenuity Inc..................919 693-2009
  113 Certainteed Dr Oxford (27565) *(G-12143)*
Plastic Molding Connection..................910 512-0834
  4164 Breezewood Dr # 102 Wilmington (28412) *(G-16357)*
Plastic Oddities, Forest City Also Called: Diverse Corporate Tech Inc *(G-6065)*
Plastic Oddities Inc..................704 484-1830
  1701 Burke Rd Shelby (28152) *(G-14355)*
Plastic Products Inc (PA)..................704 739-7463
  1413 Bessemer City Kings Mtn Hwy Bessemer City (28016) *(G-1078)*
Plastic Products Inc..................704 739-7463
  1051 York Rd Kings Mountain (28086) *(G-9326)*
Plastic Solutions Inc..................678 353-2100
  324 Tiney Rd Ellenboro (28040) *(G-5637)*
Plastic Technology Inc..................828 328-8570
  1101 Farrington St Sw # 3 Conover (28613) *(G-4481)*
Plastic Technology Inc (HQ)..................828 328-2201
  235 2nd Ave Nw Hickory (28601) *(G-8116)*
Plasticard Products Inc..................828 665-7774
  99 Pond Rd Asheville (28806) *(G-734)*
Plastics Color, Asheboro Also Called: Chroma Color Corporation *(G-416)*
Plastics Mlding Dsign Plus LLC..................828 459-7853
  1803 Conover Blvd E Conover (28613) *(G-4482)*
Plastiflex North Carolina LLC..................704 871-8448
  2101 Sherrill Dr Statesville (28625) *(G-14862)*
Plat LLC..................828 358-4564
  5740 Rocky Mount Rd Granite Falls (28630) *(G-6750)*
Platesetterscom..................888 380-7483
  114 Industrial Ave Greensboro (27406) *(G-7267)*
Platipus Anchors Ltd..................919 662-0900
  1427 Mechanical Blvd Garner (27529) *(G-6303)*
Player Made LLC..................704 303-6626
  1413 Russell Ave Charlotte (28216) *(G-3349)*
Playerz Haul, Charlotte Also Called: Brown Mitchell Hodges LLC *(G-2359)*
Playpower Inc (DH)..................704 949-1600
  11515 Vanstory Dr Ste 100 Huntersville (28078) *(G-8876)*
Playrace Inc..................828 251-2211
  1202 Patton Ave Asheville (28806) *(G-735)*
Playtex Dorado LLC..................336 519-8080
  1000 E Hanes Mill Rd Winston Salem (27105) *(G-16858)*
Plazit-Polygal, Charlotte Also Called: Plaskolite LLC *(G-3347)*
Pleasant Garden Dry Kiln..................336 674-2863
  1221 Briarcrest Dr Pleasant Garden (27313) *(G-12359)*
Pleasant Gardens Machine Inc..................828 724-4173
  2708 Us 70 W Marion (28752) *(G-10172)*
Pleb Urban Winery..................828 767-6445
  289 Lyman St Asheville (28801) *(G-736)*
Plexus Corp..................919 807-8000
  5511 Capital Center Dr Ste 600 Raleigh (27606) *(G-13116)*

Plm Inc 336 788-7529
2371 Farrington Point Dr Winston Salem (27107) *(G-16859)*

Plott Bakery Products, Rocky Mount Also Called: Evelyn T Burney *(G-13697)*

Plum Print Inc 828 633-5535
45 S French Broad Ave Ste 100 Asheville (28801) *(G-737)*

Plush Comforts 336 882-9185
508 Ashe St High Point (27262) *(G-8487)*

Plushh LLC 919 647-7911
3633 Top Of The Pines Ct Raleigh (27604) *(G-13117)*

Pluto Labs LLC 919 691-3550
1217 Lewis St Oxford (27565) *(G-12144)*

Ply Gem, Cary Also Called: Ply Gem Holdings Inc *(G-1852)*

Ply Gem Holdings Inc (DH) 919 677-3900
5020 Weston Pkwy Ste 400 Cary (27513) *(G-1852)*

Ply Gem Industries, Cary Also Called: Ply Gem Industries Inc *(G-1853)*

Ply Gem Industries Inc (DH) 919 677-3900
5020 Weston Pkwy Ste 400 Cary (27513) *(G-1853)*

Plycem Usa LLC 336 696-2007
1149 Abtco Rd North Wilkesboro (28659) *(G-12030)*

Plymouth Mill, Plymouth Also Called: Domtar Paper Company LLC *(G-12371)*

Plywood Plant, Whiteville Also Called: Georgia-Pacific LLC *(G-15963)*

Pma Industries Inc 704 575-6200
3834 Stokes Ave Charlotte (28210) *(G-3350)*

Pmb Industries Inc 336 453-3121
632 Dixon St Lexington (27292) *(G-9771)*

PME, Mooresville Also Called: Pro-Motor Engines Inc *(G-11063)*

PMG Acquisition Corp 828 758-7381
123 Pennton Ave Lenoir (28645) *(G-9647)*

PMG Acquisitions Group Div, Lenoir Also Called: PMG Acquisition Corp *(G-9647)*

PMG SM Holdings LLC 336 548-3250
703 W Decatur St Madison (27025) *(G-10084)*

PMG-DH Company 919 419-6500
1530 N Gregson St Ste 2a Durham (27701) *(G-5292)*

Pnb Manufacturing 336 883-0021
2315 E Martin Luther King Jr Dr Ste A High Point (27260) *(G-8488)*

Pneumax Automation LLC 704 215-6991
128 Durkee Ln Dallas (28034) *(G-4651)*

Poblocki Sign Company LLC 919 354-3800
210 Kitty Hawk Dr Ste 100 Morrisville (27560) *(G-11410)*

Pocket Yacht Company, New Bern Also Called: Mass Enterprises, LLC *(G-11821)*

Pocono Coated Products LLC 704 445-7891
100 Sweetree St Cherryville (28021) *(G-3875)*

Poehler Enterprises Inc 704 239-1166
10515 Jim Sossoman Rd Midland (28107) *(G-10475)*

Pogo, Raleigh Also Called: Pogo Software Inc *(G-13118)*

Pogo Software Inc 407 267-4864
8212 Oak Leaf Ct Raleigh (27615) *(G-13118)*

Pogomaxy Inc 919 623-0118
3737 Benson Dr Raleigh (27609) *(G-13119)*

Point Blank Enterprises Inc 910 893-2071
709 E Mcneill St Lillington (27546) *(G-9858)*

Point Harbor Art 804 852-3633
103 Sumac Ln Point Harbor (27964) *(G-12381)*

Polarean Inc 919 206-7900
2500 Meridian Pkwy Ste 175 Durham (27713) *(G-5293)*

Polarmax/Xgo, Southern Pines Also Called: Longworth Industries Inc *(G-14539)*

Polished Pen 704 451-4077
128 Shagbark Ln Mooresville (28115) *(G-11054)*

Polk Sawmill LLC 828 863-0436
206 Will Green Rd Tryon (28782) *(G-15427)*

Polli Garment, Raleigh Also Called: Caromed International Inc *(G-12603)*

Polly & Crackers LLC 716 680-2456
520 Dock St Wilmington (28401) *(G-16358)*

Polly and Associates LLC 910 319-7564
7426 Janice Ln Wilmington (28411) *(G-16359)*

Poly One Distribution 704 872-8168
114 Morehead Rd Statesville (28677) *(G-14863)*

Poly Packaging Systems Inc 336 889-8334
2150 Brevard Rd High Point (27263) *(G-8489)*

Poly Plastic Products NC Inc 704 624-2555
1206 Traywick Rd Marshville (28103) *(G-10223)*

Poly-Tech Industrial Inc 704 992-8100
11330 Vanstory Dr Huntersville (28078) *(G-8877)*

Poly-Tech Industrial Inc 704 948-8055
13728 Statesville Rd Huntersville (28078) *(G-8878)*

Polychem Alloy Inc 828 754-7570
240 Polychem Ct Lenoir (28645) *(G-9648)*

Polycor Holdings Inc (PA) 828 459-7064
1820 Evans St Ne Conover (28613) *(G-4483)*

Polygal Inc (HQ) 704 588-3800
1100 Bond St Charlotte (28208) *(G-3351)*

Polyhose Incorporated 732 512-9141
353 Acme Way Wilmington (28401) *(G-16360)*

Polymask Corporation 828 465-3053
500 Thornburg Dr Se Conover (28613) *(G-4484)*

Polymer Concepts Inc 336 495-7713
124 Regal Dr Randleman (27317) *(G-13484)*

Polymer Group, Benson Also Called: Chicopee Inc *(G-1032)*

Polyone Corporation 704 838-0457
114 Morehead Rd Statesville (28677) *(G-14864)*

Polyone Distribution 919 413-4547
118 Brandi Dr Rolesville (27571) *(G-13759)*

Polypore Inc 704 587-8409
11430 N Community House Rd Ste 350 Charlotte (28277) *(G-3352)*

Polypore International LP (HQ) 704 587-8409
11430 N Community House Rd Ste 350 Charlotte (28277) *(G-3353)*

Polyprint Usa Inc 888 389-8618
1704 East Blvd Charlotte (28203) *(G-3354)*

Polyquest Incorporated (PA) 910 342-9554
1979 Eastwood Rd Ste 201 Wilmington (28403) *(G-16361)*

Polyspintex Inc 704 523-4382
1301 Townes Rd Charlotte (28209) *(G-3355)*

Polystone Columns, Wilmington Also Called: Chadsworth Incorporated *(G-16168)*

Polytec Inc (PA) 704 277-3960
191 Barley Park Ln Mooresville (28115) *(G-11055)*

Polyvlies Usa Inc 336 769-0206
260 Business Park Dr Winston Salem (27107) *(G-16860)*

Polyvnyl Fnce By Digger Spc In, Randleman Also Called: Digger Specialties Inc *(G-13464)*

Polyzen LLC 919 319-9599
1041 Classic Rd Apex (27539) *(G-232)*

Polyzen Inc 919 319-9599
115 Woodwinds Industrial Ct Cary (27511) *(G-1854)*

Polyzen, Inc., Apex Also Called: Polyzen LLC *(G-232)*

Pomdevices LLC 919 200-6538
178 Colvard Park Dr Durham (27713) *(G-5294)*

Ponderosa News LLC 910 867-6571
5338 Plateau Ct Fayetteville (28303) *(G-5898)*

Ponysaurus Brewing LLC 919 455-3737
219 Hood St Durham (27701) *(G-5295)*

Poochpad Products, Winston Salem Also Called: Microfine Inc *(G-16809)*

Pool Tables Plus (PA) 704 535-8002
4445 E Independence Blvd Charlotte (28205) *(G-3356)*

Poole Company LLC 828 275-0460
5 E Owl Creek Ln Fairview (28730) *(G-5717)*

Poole Printing Company, Raleigh Also Called: Readable Communications Inc *(G-13193)*

Poole Printing Company Inc 919 876-5260
1400 Mapleside Ct Raleigh (27609) *(G-13120)*

Poovey Frame, Newton Also Called: Paul P Poovey Jr *(G-11958)*

Pop Designs Mktg Solutions LLC 336 444-4033
1153 Holly Springs Rd Mount Airy (27030) *(G-11559)*

Pop Products LLC 336 263-1884
532 Circle Dr Burlington (27215) *(G-1476)*

Pope Printing & Design Inc 828 274-5945
485 Hendersonville Rd Ste 7 Asheville (28803) *(G-738)*

Popembroiderydesigns 828 575-4252
37 Bakers Acres Ln Leicester (28748) *(G-9517)*

Poplin & Sons Machine Co Inc 704 289-2079
2118 Stafford Street Ext Monroe (28110) *(G-10788)*

Poppe Inc 828 345-6036
313 Main Ave Ne Hickory (28601) *(G-8117)*

Poppelmann Plastics USA 828 466-9500
4436 Old Catawba Rd Claremont (28610) *(G-3932)*

ALPHABETIC SECTION — Powers Boatworks

Poppelmann Plastics USA LLC.. 828 466-9500
2180 Heart Dr Claremont (28610) *(G-3933)*

Poppelmann Properties USA LLC... 828 466-9500
2180 Heart Dr Claremont (28610) *(G-3934)*

Poppies LLC... 704 896-3433
16815 Cranlyn Rd Ste A Huntersville (28078) *(G-8879)*

Poppies International I Inc... 252 442-4016
6610 Corporation Pkwy Battleboro (27809) *(G-930)*

Poppy Handcrafted Popcorn Inc (PA)...................................... 828 552-3149
127 Old Us Hwy 70 E Black Mountain (28711) *(G-1136)*

Poppy Handcrafted Popcorn LLC... 828 552-3149
78 Catawba Ave Ste A Old Fort (28762) *(G-12105)*

Poppy Handcrafted Popcorn LLC, Old Fort Also Called: Poppy Handcrafted Popcorn LLC *(G-12105)*

Pork Company... 910 293-2157
139 Carter Best Rd Warsaw (28398) *(G-15673)*

Port City Cabinets LLC... 910 622-0375
109 S Palm Dr Winnabow (28479) *(G-16583)*

Port City Elevator Inc (PA).. 910 790-9300
5704 Nixon Ln Castle Hayne (28429) *(G-1959)*

Port City Films, Wilmington Also Called: Inspire Creative Studios Inc *(G-16269)*

Port City Signs & Graphics Inc... 910 350-8242
4011 Oleander Dr Wilmington (28403) *(G-16362)*

Port City Wood Works Inc.. 910 398-8274
122 Country Place Rd Wilmington (28409) *(G-16363)*

Portable Displays LLC.. 919 544-6504
5640 Dillard Dr Ste 301 Cary (27518) *(G-1855)*

Portable Outdoor Equipment, Durham Also Called: Bolton Investors Inc *(G-4971)*

Porter Paints, Raleigh Also Called: PPG Architectural Finishes Inc *(G-13126)*

Porter's Fabrications, Gastonia Also Called: Porters Group LLC *(G-6490)*

Porters Group LLC.. 704 864-1313
469 Hospital Dr Ste A Gastonia (28054) *(G-6490)*

Porters Tavern Wood Works... 910 639-4519
731 Jesse Phillips Rd Robbins (27325) *(G-13602)*

Posh Industries LLC... 919 596-8434
604 Lindley Dr Durham (27703) *(G-5296)*

Posh Pad.. 910 988-4800
700 Mill Bay Dr Stedman (28391) *(G-14936)*

Posh Pickle Company LLC... 336 870-6712
4901 Hackamore Rd Greensboro (27410) *(G-7268)*

Positive Prints Prof Svcs LLC... 336 701-2330
1821 Hillandale Rd Ste 1b Pmb 256 Durham (27705) *(G-5297)*

Positively Haywood, Waynesville Also Called: Vicinitus LLC *(G-15831)*

Post & Courier, The, Durham Also Called: Epi Group Llc *(G-5091)*

Post Consumer Brands LLC.. 336 672-0124
2525 Bank St Asheboro (27203) *(G-464)*

Post EC Holdings Inc.. 919 989-0175
207a Computer Dr Smithfield (27577) *(G-14477)*

Post Publishing Company... 704 633-8950
131 W Innes St Salisbury (28144) *(G-14026)*

Post Voice LLC.. 910 259-9111
201 E Fremont St Burgaw (28425) *(G-1347)*

Postal Express Plus... 336 626-0162
2029 Woods Stream Ln Asheboro (27205) *(G-465)*

Postal Instant Press... 336 222-0717
825 S Main St Burlington (27215) *(G-1477)*

Postal Liquidation Inc
3791 S Alston Ave Durham (27713) *(G-5298)*

Postmark, Kernersville Also Called: Salem One Inc *(G-9231)*

Potash Corp Saskatchewan Inc.. 252 322-4111
1530 Hwy 306 S Aurora (27806) *(G-839)*

Poteet Printing Systems LLC... 704 588-0005
9103 Forsyth Park Dr Charlotte (28273) *(G-3357)*

Potter Logging... 704 483-2738
2037 Cameron Heights Cir Denver (28037) *(G-4795)*

Potter's Lumber, Creston Also Called: Ossiriand Inc *(G-4625)*

Potterwyx Scnted Candles Soaps... 336 245-8560
1351 Lwsville Clemmons Rd Lewisville (27023) *(G-9671)*

Potts Logging Inc... 704 463-7549
39342 Holly Ridge Rd New London (28127) *(G-11875)*

Powder Coat USA.. 919 954-7170
4200 Atlantic Ave Ste 130 Raleigh (27604) *(G-13121)*

Powder Coating By 3 S X... 704 784-3724
4317 Triple Crown Dr Sw Concord (28027) *(G-4334)*

Powder Coating Services Inc.. 704 349-4100
1260 Shannon Bradley Rd Gastonia (28052) *(G-6491)*

Powder River Technologies Inc.. 828 465-2894
1987 Industrial Dr Newton (28658) *(G-11961)*

Powder Systems Inc.. 336 885-1352
1018 Roberts Ln Ste C High Point (27260) *(G-8490)*

Powder Works Inc.. 336 475-7715
6698 Pikeview Dr Thomasville (27360) *(G-15265)*

Powdertek... 828 225-3250
6 Bagwell Mill Rd Arden (28704) *(G-364)*

Powell & Stokes Inc... 252 794-2138
217 Us Highway 13 N Windsor (27983) *(G-16568)*

Powell Industries Inc (PA)... 828 926-9114
4595 Jonathan Creek Rd Waynesville (28785) *(G-15815)*

Powell Ink Inc... 828 253-6886
191 Charlotte St Asheville (28801) *(G-739)*

Powell Welding Inc... 828 433-0831
3156 Hwy 70 Drexel (28619) *(G-4836)*

Powell Wholesale Lumber, Waynesville Also Called: Powell Industries Inc *(G-15815)*

Powell's Ready-Mix, Roanoke Rapids Also Called: Allie M Powell III *(G-13565)*

Power Adhesives, Charlotte Also Called: GLS Products LLC *(G-2836)*

Power Adhesives Ltd... 704 578-9984
1209 Lilac Rd Charlotte (28209) *(G-3358)*

Power and Ctrl Solutions LLC.. 704 609-9623
6205 Boykin Spaniel Rd Charlotte (28277) *(G-3359)*

Power Business Products LLC... 704 604-2844
1001 Somersby Ln Matthews (28105) *(G-10281)*

Power Chem Inc... 919 365-3400
7316b Siemens Rd Wendell (27591) *(G-15911)*

Power Clean Chem, Concord Also Called: Patel Deepal *(G-4330)*

Power Components Inc... 704 321-9481
10837 Coachman Cir Charlotte (28277) *(G-3360)*

Power Coolant & Chemical LLC... 704 759-3435
109 Tanglewood Ct Southern Pines (28387) *(G-14549)*

Power Curbers Inc (PA).. 704 636-5871
727 Bendix Dr Salisbury (28146) *(G-14027)*

Power Generation Mfg Oper Div, Rural Hall Also Called: Siemens Energy Inc *(G-13853)*

Power Integrity Corp... 336 379-9773
2109 Patterson St Greensboro (27407) *(G-7269)*

Power Logistixs LLC... 919 799-0303
108 Shady Grove Ct Selma (27576) *(G-14259)*

Power Pros, Zebulon Also Called: Asp Holdings Inc *(G-17121)*

Power Tech Engines, Concord Also Called: Jasper Penske Engines *(G-4292)*

Power Technologies, Raleigh Also Called: ABB Enterprise Software Inc *(G-12455)*

Power Washer Pros... 252 446-4643
8740 Bend Of The River Rd Rocky Mount (27803) *(G-13722)*

Power-Utility Products Company (PA).................................. 704 375-0776
8710 Air Park West Dr Ste 100 Charlotte (28214) *(G-3361)*

Poweramerica Institute... 919 515-6013
930 Main Campus Dr Ste 20 Raleigh (27606) *(G-13122)*

Powerbrake Corporation.. 704 804-2438
14514 Sunset Walk Ln Huntersville (28078) *(G-8880)*

Powercat Group, Tarboro Also Called: Hc Composites LLC *(G-15107)*

Powerfab... 336 674-0624
1410 Coltrane Mill Rd Randleman (27317) *(G-13485)*

Powergpu LLC... 919 702-6757
762 Park Ave Youngsville (27596) *(G-17092)*

Powerhouse Dugout... 704 215-6604
246 N New Hope Rd 127 Gastonia (28054) *(G-6492)*

Powerhouse Resources Intl LLC... 919 291-1783
2710 Wycliff Rd Ste 105 Raleigh (27607) *(G-13123)*

Powerlab Inc.. 336 650-0706
3352 Old Lexington Rd Bldg 43 Winston Salem (27107) *(G-16861)*

Powerlyte Paintball Game Pdts.. 919 713-4317
5811 Mchines Pl Ste 105 Raleigh (27616) *(G-13124)*

Powermolekul Inc (PA)... 919 264-8487
205 Coltsgate Dr Ste 100 Cary (27518) *(G-1856)*

Powers Boatworks.. 910 762-3636
2725 Old Wrightsboro Rd Unit 8a Wilmington (28405) *(G-16364)*

Powersecure   ALPHABETIC SECTION

Powersecure, Wake Forest *Also Called: Powersecure International Inc (G-15576)*

Powersecure Inc... 919 818-8700
  6137 Princeton Kenly Rd Princeton (27569) *(G-12402)*

Powersecure International Inc........................... 919 556-3056
  1609 Heritage Commerce Ct Wake Forest (27587) *(G-15576)*

Powersecure Solar, Durham *Also Called: Powersecure Solar LLC (G-5299)*

Powersecure Solar LLC...................................... 919 213-0798
  4068 Stirrup Creek Dr Durham (27703) *(G-5299)*

Powerserv International, Cary *Also Called: Powermolekul Inc (G-1856)*

Powersigns Inc.. 910 343-1789
  3617 1/2 Market St Wilmington (28403) *(G-16365)*

Powersnds Ppeline Partners LLC....................... 980 237-8900
  129 W Trade St Ste 1405 Charlotte (28202) *(G-3362)*

Powersolve Corporation LLC............................. 919 662-8515
  117b Pierce Rd Garner (27529) *(G-6304)*

Powertac Usa Inc... 919 239-4470
  3702 Alliance Dr Ste C Greensboro (27407) *(G-7270)*

Powertec Industrial Motors Inc.......................... 704 227-1580
  13509 S Point Blvd Ste 190 Charlotte (28273) *(G-3363)*

Pozen Inc.. 919 913-1030
  8310 Bandford Way Raleigh (27615) *(G-13125)*

Ppa Industries Inc (PA)...................................... 828 328-1142
  420 3rd Ave Nw Hickory (28601) *(G-8118)*

Ppd, Wilmington *Also Called: Ppd Inc (G-16366)*

Ppd Inc (HQ).. 910 251-0081
  929 N Front St Wilmington (28401) *(G-16366)*

Ppd International Holdings LLC (DH)................ 910 251-0081
  929 N Front St Wilmington (28401) *(G-16367)*

PPG 4434, Wilmington *Also Called: PPG Industries Inc (G-16368)*
PPG 4650, Cary *Also Called: PPG Industries Inc (G-1857)*
PPG 4655, Kill Devil Hills *Also Called: PPG Industries Inc (G-9262)*
PPG 4668, Charlotte *Also Called: PPG Industries Inc (G-3365)*
PPG 4669, Raleigh *Also Called: PPG Industries Inc (G-13129)*
PPG 4670, Charlotte *Also Called: PPG Industries Inc (G-3364)*
PPG 4685, Durham *Also Called: PPG Industries Inc (G-5300)*
PPG 9490, Winston Salem *Also Called: PPG Industries Inc (G-16862)*

PPG Architectural Finishes Inc.......................... 910 484-5161
  894 Elm St Ste A Fayetteville (28303) *(G-5899)*

PPG Architectural Finishes Inc.......................... 704 864-6783
  729 E Franklin Blvd Gastonia (28054) *(G-6493)*

PPG Architectural Finishes Inc.......................... 336 273-9761
  5103 W Market St Greensboro (27409) *(G-7271)*

PPG Architectural Finishes Inc.......................... 704 847-7251
  1600 Matthews Mint Hill Rd Ste B Matthews (28105) *(G-10282)*

PPG Architectural Finishes Inc.......................... 704 658-9250
  142 S Cardigan Way Mooresville (28117) *(G-11056)*

PPG Architectural Finishes Inc.......................... 828 438-9210
  511 Burkemont Ave Morganton (28655) *(G-11242)*

PPG Architectural Finishes Inc.......................... 919 981-0600
  5500 Atlantic Springs Rd Ste 110-112 Raleigh (27616) *(G-13126)*

PPG Architectural Finishes Inc.......................... 919 872-6500
  2205 Westinghouse Blvd 11 Raleigh (27604) *(G-13127)*

PPG Architectural Finishes Inc.......................... 919 779-5400
  1458 Garner Station Blvd Raleigh (27603) *(G-13128)*

PPG Architectural Finishes Inc.......................... 704 633-0673
  1333 Klumac Rd Salisbury (28147) *(G-14028)*

PPG Industries Inc... 919 319-0113
  210 Nottingham Dr Cary (27511) *(G-1857)*

PPG Industries Inc... 704 542-8880
  10701 Park Rd Charlotte (28210) *(G-3364)*

PPG Industries Inc... 704 523-0888
  3022 Griffith St Charlotte (28203) *(G-3365)*

PPG Industries Inc... 919 382-3100
  3161 Hillsborough Rd Durham (27705) *(G-5300)*

PPG Industries Inc... 919 772-3093
  4347 Baylor St Greensboro (27455) *(G-7272)*

PPG Industries Inc... 336 856-9280
  109 P P G Rd Greensboro (27409) *(G-7273)*

PPG Industries Inc... 252 480-1970
  2800 N Croatan Hwy Kill Devil Hills (27948) *(G-9262)*

PPG Industries Inc... 704 658-9250
  128 Overhill Dr Ste 104 Mooresville (28117) *(G-11057)*

PPG Industries Inc... 919 981-0600
  5500 Atlantic Springs Rd Raleigh (27616) *(G-13129)*

PPG Industries Inc... 910 452-3289
  4125 Oleander Dr Wilmington (28403) *(G-16368)*

PPG Industries Inc... 336 771-8878
  1455 Trademart Blvd Winston Salem (27127) *(G-16862)*

PPG-Devold LLC... 704 434-2261
  940 Washburn Switch Rd Shelby (28150) *(G-14356)*

Ppi, Mooresville *Also Called: Performance Parts Intl LLC (G-11052)*

PQ Recycling LLC (HQ).................................... 910 342-9554
  1979 Eastwood Rd Ste 201 Wilmington (28403) *(G-16369)*

Practice Fusion Inc (DH).................................... 415 346-7700
  305 Church At North Hills St Ste 100 Raleigh (27609) *(G-13130)*

Practicepro Sftwr Systems Inc.......................... 212 244-2100
  14225 Plantation Pk Blvd Charlotte (28277) *(G-3366)*

Practichem, Morrisville *Also Called: Practichem LLC (G-11411)*

Practichem LLC... 919 714-8430
  10404 Chapel Hill Rd Ste 112 Morrisville (27560) *(G-11411)*

Praetego Inc... 919 237-7969
  68 Tw Alexander Dr Durham (27709) *(G-5301)*

Pramana LLC... 910 233-5118
  709 Dennison Ln Cary (27519) *(G-1858)*

Pratt (jet Corr) Inc.. 704 878-6615
  185 Deer Ridge Dr Statesville (28625) *(G-14865)*

Pratt & Whitney Eng Svcs Inc........................... 860 565-4321
  330 Pratt And Whitney Blvd Asheville (28806) *(G-740)*

Pratt Industries.. 704 864-4022
  975 Tulip Dr Gastonia (28052) *(G-6494)*

Pratt Industries Inc.. 919 334-7400
  5620 Departure Dr Raleigh (27616) *(G-13131)*

Pratt Industries Inc.. 704 878-6615
  185 Deer Ridge Dr Statesville (28625) *(G-14866)*

Pratt Industries USA, Statesville *Also Called: Pratt (jet Corr) Inc (G-14865)*

Pratt Mller Engrg Fbrction LLC......................... 704 977-0642
  9801 Kincey Ave Ste 175 Huntersville (28078) *(G-8881)*

Prattgears.. 414 704-3912
  113 Churchill Dr Salisbury (28144) *(G-14029)*

Praxair, Wilmington *Also Called: Linde Inc (G-16302)*

Pre - War Guitars Co., Hillsborough *Also Called: Luthiers Workshop LLC (G-8660)*

Pre Flight Inc.. 828 758-1138
  1035 Harper Ave Sw Lenoir (28645) *(G-9649)*

Precast Solutions Inc.. 336 656-7991
  7121 Choctaw Ct Browns Summit (27214) *(G-1313)*

Precast Supply Company Inc............................ 704 784-2000
  1201 Biscayne Dr Concord (28027) *(G-4335)*

Precast Terrazzo Entps Inc............................... 919 231-6200
  1107 N New Hope Rd Raleigh (27610) *(G-13132)*

Precedent Furniture, High Point *Also Called: Sherrill Furniture Company (G-8523)*

Precedent Furniture, Newton *Also Called: Sherrill Furniture Company (G-11967)*

Precept, Arden *Also Called: Precept Medical Products Inc (G-365)*

Precept Medical Products Inc (DH)................... 828 681-0209
  370 Airport Rd Arden (28704) *(G-365)*

Precious Oils Up On The Hill, Troutman *Also Called: Up On Hill (G-15397)*

Precise Mobile Welding..................................... 980 785-7085
  7713 Harrington Woods Rd Charlotte (28269) *(G-3367)*

Precise Sheet Metal Mech LLC......................... 336 693-3246
  124 Winterfield Dr Raeford (28376) *(G-12432)*

Precise Technology Inc..................................... 704 576-9527
  4201 Congress St Ste 340 Charlotte (28209) *(G-3368)*

Precision Alloys Inc... 919 231-6329
  1040 Corp Pkwy Ste T Raleigh (27610) *(G-13133)*

Precision Arbatics USA Pty Ltd......................... 770 292-9122
  310 Dragonfly Trl Chapel Hill (27517) *(G-2054)*

Precision Boat Mfg.. 336 395-8795
  808 Carraway Dr Graham (27253) *(G-6707)*

Precision Cabinetry Inc (PA).............................. 828 465-3341
  200 W 4th St Newton (28658) *(G-11962)*

Precision Cabinets Inc...................................... 828 262-5080
  1324 Old 421 S Boone (28607) *(G-1228)*

ALPHABETIC SECTION

Precision Comb Works Inc 704 864-2761
2524 N Chester St Gastonia (28052) *(G-6495)*

Precision Concepts Group LLC 336 761-8572
2701 Boulder Park Ct Winston Salem (27101) *(G-16863)*

Precision Concepts Intl LLC (PA) 704 360-8923
136 Fairview Rd Ste 320 Mooresville (28117) *(G-11058)*

Precision Concepts Mebane LLC (DH) 919 563-9292
1405 Dogwood Way Mebane (27302) *(G-10425)*

Precision Design Machinery 336 889-8157
1509 Bethel Dr High Point (27260) *(G-8491)*

Precision Drive Systems LLC (PA) 704 922-1206
4367 Dallas Cherryville Hwy Bessemer City (28016) *(G-1079)*

Precision Enterprises, Randleman *Also Called: Gerald Hartsoe (G-13471)*

Precision Fabrication Inc 336 885-6091
2000 Nuggett Rd High Point (27263) *(G-8492)*

Precision Fabricators Inc (PA) 336 835-4763
Hwy 268 Ronda (28670) *(G-13768)*

Precision Fabrics Group Inc (PA) 336 281-3049
333 N Greene St Greensboro (27401) *(G-7274)*

Precision Fermentations Inc 919 717-3983
2810 Meridian Pkwy Durham (27713) *(G-5302)*

Precision Genomics Inc 843 737-1911
812 Lumina Ave S Wrightsville Beach (28480) *(G-17027)*

Precision Graphics Inc 252 917-3174
429 Kingold Blvd Snow Hill (28580) *(G-14507)*

Precision Industries Inc 828 465-3418
305 N Mclin Creek Rd Conover (28613) *(G-4485)*

Precision Log & Chipping LLC 828 446-1592
330 Dee Loudermelk Ln Taylorsville (28681) *(G-15158)*

Precision Machine Products Inc 704 865-7490
2347 N Chester St Gastonia (28052) *(G-6496)*

Precision Machine Tools Corp 704 882-3700
500 Union West Blvd Ste A Matthews (28104) *(G-10340)*

Precision Materials LLC (PA) 828 632-8851
6246 Nc Highway 16 S Taylorsville (28681) *(G-15159)*

Precision Mch Components Inc 704 201-8482
8075 Pine Lake Rd Denver (28037) *(G-4796)*

Precision Mch Fabrication Inc 919 231-8648
1100 N New Hope Rd Raleigh (27610) *(G-13134)*

Precision McHning Eddie Husers, Kings Mountain *Also Called: Eddie Hsr S Prcsion McHning In (G-9307)*

Precision Metal Finishing Inc 704 799-0250
962 N Main St Mooresville (28115) *(G-11059)*

Precision Metals LLC 919 762-7481
589 Old Roberts Rd Benson (27504) *(G-1041)*

Precision Mindset Pllc 704 508-1314
130 April Showers Ln Statesville (28677) *(G-14867)*

Precision Mtls - Blue Rdge LLC 828 322-7990
3050 Main Ave Nw Hickory (28601) *(G-8119)*

Precision Optics LLC 919 619-4468
1015 Wave Rd Chapel Hill (27517) *(G-2055)*

Precision Packaging Services I 919 806-8152
2910 Weck Dr Durham (27709) *(G-5303)*

Precision Pallet LLC 252 935-5355
405 Mainstem Rd Pantego (27860) *(G-12170)*

Precision Part Systems, Winston Salem *Also Called: Precision Part Systems Wnstn-S (G-16864)*

Precision Part Systems Wnstn-S 336 723-5210
1035 W Northwest Blvd Winston Salem (27101) *(G-16864)*

Precision Partners LLC 704 560-6442
1830 Statesville Ave Charlotte (28206) *(G-3369)*

Precision Partners LLC 800 545-3121
1830 Statesville Ave Ste C Charlotte (28206) *(G-3370)*

Precision Pdts Asheville Inc (PA) 828 684-4207
118 Glenn Bridge Rd Arden (28704) *(G-366)*

Precision Pdts Prfmce Ctr Inc 828 684-8569
191 Airport Rd Arden (28704) *(G-367)*

Precision Printing 252 338-2450
307 S Road St Elizabeth City (27909) *(G-5564)*

Precision Printing 336 273-5794
2832 Randleman Rd Ste D Greensboro (27406) *(G-7275)*

Precision Printing, Wilkesboro *Also Called: Ollis Enterprises Inc (G-16037)*

Precision Processing System, Statesville *Also Called: Southern Prestige Industries Inc (G-14893)*

Precision Products Inc 336 688-0298
1219 Dorris Ave Apt A High Point (27260) *(G-8493)*

Precision Prtcle Msrements Inc 919 667-6960
1514 Saddle Club Rd Mebane (27302) *(G-10426)*

Precision Saw Works Inc 704 272-8326
10424 Highway 742 N # 742n Polkton (28135) *(G-12389)*

Precision Signs Inc 919 615-0979
5455 Raynor Rd Garner (27529) *(G-6305)*

Precision Sports Paintball 828 212-0415
4994 Hickory Blvd Hickory (28601) *(G-8120)*

Precision Stampers Inc 919 366-3333
480 Old Wilson Rd Wendell (27591) *(G-15912)*

Precision Steel Works LLC 252 467-0338
1100 Atlantic Ave Rocky Mount (27801) *(G-13671)*

Precision Textiles, High Point *Also Called: Precision Textiles LLC (G-8494)*

Precision Textiles LLC 336 861-0168
5522 Uwharrie Rd High Point (27263) *(G-8494)*

Precision Time Systems Inc 910 253-9850
959 Little Macedonia Rd Nw Supply (28462) *(G-15008)*

Precision Tool & Stamping Inc 910 592-0174
800 Warsaw Rd Clinton (28328) *(G-4102)*

Precision Tool Dye and Mold 828 687-2990
69 Bagwell Mill Rd Arden (28704) *(G-368)*

Precision Walls Inc 336 852-7710
7215 Cessna Dr Greensboro (27409) *(G-7276)*

Precision Welding Mntnc 336 504-5894
5612 Hebron Rd Oxford (27565) *(G-12145)*

Precision Wldg Fbrication Svcs 704 243-1929
7105 Tirzah Church Rd Waxhaw (28173) *(G-15769)*

Precision Wldg Mch Charlotte 704 357-1288
4701 Beam Rd Charlotte (28217) *(G-3371)*

Precisionaire Inc (DH) 252 946-8081
531 Flanders Filter Rd Washington (27889) *(G-15727)*

Precisionaire of Smithfield, Washington *Also Called: Precisionaire Inc (G-15727)*

Precocious Pen LLC 706 338-0010
12427 Toscana Way Charlotte (28273) *(G-3372)*

Precor Incorporated 336 603-1000
1818 Youngs Mill Rd Greensboro (27406) *(G-7277)*

Predatar Inc 919 827-4516
4208 Six Forks Rd Ste 1000 Raleigh (27609) *(G-13135)*

Preferred Communication Inc 919 575-4600
410 Central Ave Butner (27509) *(G-1548)*

Preferred Data Corporation 336 886-3282
3910 Tinsley Dr Ste 105 High Point (27265) *(G-8495)*

Preferred Logging 910 471-4011
969 Livingston Chapel Rd Delco (28436) *(G-4724)*

Preformed Line Products Co 704 983-6161
1700 Woodhurst Ln Albemarle (28001) *(G-99)*

Preformed Line Products Co 336 461-3513
446 Glenbrook Spg New London (28127) *(G-11876)*

Preformed Line Products Co, New London *Also Called: Preformed Line Products Co (G-11876)*

Pregel America, Concord *Also Called: Pregel America Inc (G-4336)*

Pregel America Inc (DH) 704 707-0300
4450 Fortune Ave Nw Concord (28027) *(G-4336)*

Pregis Innovative Packg LLC (DH) 847 597-2200
3825 N Main St Granite Falls (28630) *(G-6751)*

Pregis LLC 828 465-9197
500 Thornburg Dr Se Conover (28613) *(G-4486)*

Pregis LLC 828 396-2373
3825 N Main St Granite Falls (28630) *(G-6752)*

Pregnancy Support Services 919 490-0203
1777 Fordham Blvd Ste 203 Chapel Hill (27514) *(G-2056)*

Preiss Paper & Printing 919 325-3790
1618 Weatherford Cir Raleigh (27604) *(G-13136)*

Prem Corp 704 921-1799
2901 Stewart Creek Blvd Charlotte (28216) *(G-3373)*

Premedia Group LLC 336 274-2421
7605 Business Park Dr Ste F Greensboro (27409) *(G-7278)*

Premex Inc   **ALPHABETIC SECTION**

Premex Inc.. 561 962-4128
   1307 Person St Durham (27703) *(G-5304)*

Premier Body Armor LLC... 704 750-3118
   1552 Union Rd Ste E Gastonia (28054) *(G-6497)*

Premier Cakes, Raleigh *Also Called: Premier Cakes LLC (G-13137)*

Premier Cakes LLC... 919 274-8511
   6617 Falls Of Neuse Rd Ste 105 Raleigh (27615) *(G-13137)*

Premier Kit & Cabinetry Design................................. 910 224-5018
   1705 Crest Dr Aberdeen (28315) *(G-22)*

Premier Magnesia LLC (PA)....................................... 828 452-4784
   75 Giles Pl Waynesville (28786) *(G-15816)*

Premier Mfg Co.. 704 781-4001
   3520 Fieldstone Trce Midland (28107) *(G-10476)*

Premier Powder Coating Inc....................................... 336 672-3828
   1948 N Fayetteville St Asheboro (27203) *(G-466)*

Premier Printing & Apparel... 910 805-0545
   1939 Kent St Wilmington (28403) *(G-16370)*

Premier Quilting Corporation..................................... 919 693-1151
   720 W Industry Dr Oxford (27565) *(G-12146)*

Premier Stucco LLC.. 919 676-2306
   10009 Friedel Pl Raleigh (27613) *(G-13138)*

Premier Tool LLC.. 704 895-8223
   20409 Zion Ave Cornelius (28031) *(G-4577)*

Premiere Fibers LLC... 704 826-8321
   10056 Hwy 52 N Ansonville (28007) *(G-155)*

Premium Cushion Inc... 828 464-4783
   1009 1st St W Conover (28613) *(G-4487)*

Premium Fabricators LLC.. 828 464-3818
   419 4th St Sw Conover (28613) *(G-4488)*

Premix North Carolina LLC.. 704 412-7922
   52a Ervin St Belmont (28012) *(G-1004)*

Prepac Manufacturing US LLC.................................. 800 665-1266
   3031 Hendren Rd Whitsett (27377) *(G-15999)*

Presicion Wall, Raleigh *Also Called: Design Specialties Inc (G-12678)*

Presley Group Ltd (DH)... 828 254-9971
   739 Dogwood Rd Asheville (28806) *(G-741)*

Presnells Prtg & Photography, Sparta *Also Called: David Presnell (G-14592)*

Press.. 336 516-6074
   215 Benjamin Ct Burlington (27215) *(G-1478)*

Press 53 LLC... 336 414-5599
   560 N Trade St Ste 103 Winston Salem (27101) *(G-16865)*

Press Air LLC.. 240 313-6832
   1303 Westpointe Dr Apt 7 Greenville (27834) *(G-7576)*

Press Coffee+crepes.. 336 263-1180
   133 N Main St Graham (27253) *(G-6708)*

Press Flex LLC.. 919 636-4551
   101 Lloyd St Carrboro (27510) *(G-1653)*

Press Ganey Associates Inc...................................... 800 232-8032
   700 E Morehead St Ste 100 Charlotte (28202) *(G-3374)*

Press Glass Inc (HQ)... 336 573-2393
   8901 Us Highway 220 Stoneville (27048) *(G-14965)*

Press Play Counseling Pllc.. 336 223-4234
   5605 Clustermill Dr Greensboro (27407) *(G-7279)*

Pressed Design & Printing Llc.................................. 252 314-6036
   8884 Taylor Woods Cir Rocky Mount (27803) *(G-13723)*

Pressure Power Systems, Kernersville *Also Called: Spartan Manufacturing Corp (G-9237)*

Pressure Washing Near Me LLC................................ 704 280-0351
   10002 King George Ln Waxhaw (28173) *(G-15770)*

Prestage Foods Inc.. 910 865-6611
   4470 Nc Hwy 20 E Saint Pauls (28384) *(G-13908)*

Prestige Cleaning Incorporated................................. 704 752-7747
   13903 Ballantyne Meadows Dr Charlotte (28277) *(G-3375)*

Prestige Fabricators Inc... 336 626-4595
   905 Nc Highway 49 S Asheboro (27205) *(G-467)*

Prestige Farms Inc... 919 861-8867
   2414 Crabtree Blvd Raleigh (27604) *(G-13139)*

Prestige Label, Burgaw *Also Called: Atlantic Corp Wilmington Inc (G-1333)*

Prestige Millwork Inc.. 910 428-2360
   671 Spies Rd Star (27356) *(G-14722)*

Prestress of Carolinas LLC.. 704 587-4273
   11630 Texland Blvd Charlotte (28273) *(G-3376)*

Pretinned Carbide Co Inc.. 704 871-9644
   251 Commerce Blvd Unit G Statesville (28625) *(G-14868)*

Pretium Packaging, Greensboro *Also Called: Pretium Packaging LLC (G-7280)*

Pretium Packaging LLC.. 336 621-1891
   3240 N Ohenry Blvd Greensboro (27405) *(G-7280)*

Pretoria Transit Interiors Inc..................................... 615 867-8515
   13501 S Ridge Dr Charlotte (28273) *(G-3377)*

Pretty Baby Herbal Soaps... 704 209-0669
   1050 Winding Brook Ln Salisbury (28146) *(G-14030)*

Pretty Honest LLC.. 804 837-1038
   8232 Meadowdale Ln Charlotte (28227) *(G-3378)*

Preventech, Indian Trail *Also Called: Preventive Technologies Inc (G-8958)*

Preventive Technologies Inc..................................... 704 684-1211
   4330 Matthews Indian Trail Rd Indian Trail (28079) *(G-8958)*

Prevette & Sons Hauling LLC.................................... 336 909-2717
   566 Duke Whittaker Rd Mocksville (27028) *(G-10598)*

Prevost Car (us) Inc (DH)... 908 222-7211
   7817 National Service Rd Greensboro (27409) *(G-7281)*

Prevost Car (us) Inc... 336 812-3504
   1951 Eastchester Dr Unit E High Point (27265) *(G-8496)*

Preyer Brewing Company LLC................................... 336 420-0902
   600 Battleground Ave Greensboro (27401) *(G-7282)*

Prezioso Ventures LLC... 704 793-1602
   5410 Powerhouse Ct Concord (28027) *(G-4337)*

Price Logging Inc... 252 792-5687
   1901 Mill Rd Jamesville (27846) *(G-9081)*

Price Metal Spinning Inc... 704 922-3195
   3202 Puetts Chapel Rd Dallas (28034) *(G-4652)*

Pricely Inc... 336 431-2055
   7210 Suits Rd High Point (27263) *(G-8497)*

Pride Communications Inc.. 704 375-9553
   8401 University Exec Park Dr Ste 122 Charlotte (28262) *(G-3379)*

Pride Magazine, Charlotte *Also Called: Pride Communications Inc (G-3379)*

Pride Publishing & Typsg Inc.................................... 704 531-9988
   920 Central Ave Charlotte (28204) *(G-3380)*

Pridgen Woodwork Inc... 910 642-7175
   910 Jefferson St Whiteville (28472) *(G-15975)*

Pridgen-Lucas Latisha... 252 360-7866
   3712 Stonehenge Ln W Wilson (27893) *(G-16523)*

Prima Elements LLC.. 910 483-8406
   124 Anderson St Fayetteville (28301) *(G-5900)*

Primaforce, Burlington *Also Called: Disruptive Enterprises LLC (G-1407)*

Primax Pumps, Charlotte *Also Called: Primax Usa Inc (G-3381)*

Primax Usa Inc... 704 587-3377
   11000 S Commerce Blvd Ste A Charlotte (28273) *(G-3381)*

Prime Beverage Group LLC (PA)................................ 704 385-5450
   1858 Kannapolis Pkwy Concord (28027) *(G-4338)*

Prime Beverage Group LLC....................................... 704 385-5451
   215 International Dr Nw Ste B Concord (28027) *(G-4339)*

Prime Coatings... 828 217-8287
   609 2nd St Ne Hickory (28601) *(G-8121)*

Prime Coatings LLC... 828 855-1136
   442 Highland Ave Se Hickory (28602) *(G-8122)*

Prime Credit LLC.. 704 729-7000
   118 Morlake Dr Ste 204 Mooresville (28117) *(G-11060)*

Prime Mill LLC.. 336 819-4300
   1946 W Green Dr High Point (27260) *(G-8498)*

Prime Source Opc LLC.. 336 661-3300
   320 Perimeter Point Blvd Winston Salem (27105) *(G-16866)*

Prime Syntex LLC... 828 324-5496
   6980 Pikeview Dr Thomasville (27360) *(G-15266)*

Prime Water Services Inc.. 919 504-1020
   9400 Ransdell Rd Ste 9 Raleigh (27603) *(G-13140)*

Prime Wire and Cable.. 704 799-6000
   179 Gasoline Aly Ste 103 Mooresville (28117) *(G-11061)*

Primesource Corporation... 336 661-3300
   320a Perimeter Point Blvd Winston Salem (27105) *(G-16867)*

Primevigilance Inc.. 781 703-5540
   5430 Wade Park Blvd Ste 208 Raleigh (27607) *(G-13141)*

Primo Inc... 888 822-5815
   19009 Peninsula Point Dr Cornelius (28031) *(G-4578)*

ALPHABETIC SECTION

Primo Print, Cornelius *Also Called: Primo Inc (G-4578)*

Prince Group LLC 828 681-8860
209 Broadpointe Dr Mills River (28759) *(G-10509)*

Prince Manufacturing Corp 828 681-8860
209 Broadpointe Dr Mills River (28759) *(G-10510)*

Prince Mfg - Asheville, Mills River *Also Called: Prince Manufacturing Corp (G-10510)*

Prince Mfg - Greenville, Mills River *Also Called: Prince Group LLC (G-10509)*

Princeton Asphalt Plant, Princeton *Also Called: S T Wooten Corporation (G-12403)*

Princeton Information 980 224-7114
201 S College St Charlotte (28244) *(G-3382)*

Prinston Laboratories, Charlotte *Also Called: Generics Bidco II LLC (G-2819)*

Prinston Laboratories, Charlotte *Also Called: Generics Bidco II LLC (G-2820)*

Print & Pack Sense LLC 336 394-6930
708 Meadowgreen Village Dr Apt 2a Eden (27288) *(G-5500)*

Print 4 ME Inc 336 854-1589
104 Meadowood St Ste G Greensboro (27409) *(G-7283)*

Print Advisors LLC 704 385-4315
15905 Brookway Dr Ste 4105 Huntersville (28078) *(G-8882)*

Print Charlotte Inc 704 488-5896
5727 N Sharon Amity Rd Ste C Charlotte (28215) *(G-3383)*

Print Doc Pack and 910 454-9104
114 E Nash St Southport (28461) *(G-14576)*

Print Express Enterprises Inc 336 765-5505
6255 Towncenter Dr Clemmons (27012) *(G-4055)*

Print Express Inc 910 455-4554
117 N Marine Blvd Jacksonville (28540) *(G-9021)*

Print Express Plus 252 541-4444
310 Roanoke Ave Roanoke Rapids (27870) *(G-13580)*

Print Haus Inc 828 456-8622
641 N Main St Waynesville (28786) *(G-15817)*

Print Magic Transfers Llc 848 250-9906
6040 Sycamore Gardens Ln Apt 1404 Charlotte (28273) *(G-3384)*

Print Management Group LLC 704 821-0114
425 E Arrowhead Dr Charlotte (28213) *(G-3385)*

Print Marks Screen Prtg & EMB, Durham *Also Called: Lee Marks (G-5188)*

Print Media Associates Inc 704 529-0555
834 Tyvola Rd Ste 110 Charlotte (28217) *(G-3386)*

Print Mine Tees 336 972-1245
4604 Oak Ridge Dr Winston Salem (27105) *(G-16868)*

Print Path 843 615-7882
926 Lenoir Rhyne Blvd Se Hickory (28602) *(G-8123)*

Print Path LLC 828 855-9966
1215 15th Street Dr Ne Hickory (28601) *(G-8124)*

Print Professionals 607 279-3335
280 Oakmont Cir Pinehurst (28374) *(G-12231)*

Print Shoppe of Rocky Mt Inc 252 442-9912
140 S Business Ct Rocky Mount (27804) *(G-13724)*

Print Social 980 430-4483
403 Gilead Rd Ste A Huntersville (28078) *(G-8883)*

Print Usa Inc 910 485-2254
505 S Eastern Blvd Fayetteville (28301) *(G-5901)*

Print Works Fayetteville Inc 910 864-8100
3724 Sycamore Dairy Rd Ste 100 Fayetteville (28303) *(G-5902)*

Print Zilla LLC 800 340-6120
624 Tyvola Rd Ste 103 Charlotte (28217) *(G-3387)*

Printcraft Company Inc 336 248-2544
259 City Lake Rd Lexington (27295) *(G-9772)*

Printcraft Company Inc 336 248-2544
259 City Lake Rd Lexington (27295) *(G-9773)*

Printcrafters Incorporated 704 873-7387
115 W Water St Statesville (28677) *(G-14869)*

Printech, Charlotte *Also Called: Ceramco Incorporated (G-2444)*

Printer Solutions Inc 919 592-1077
5100 Pointe Water Ct Raleigh (27603) *(G-13142)*

Printery 336 852-9774
2100 Fairfax Rd Ste 101a Greensboro (27407) *(G-7284)*

Printful Inc (PA) 818 351-7181
11025 Westlake Dr Charlotte (28273) *(G-3388)*

Printing 770 815-3567
1328 Patton Ave Ste B Asheville (28806) *(G-742)*

Printing & Packaging Inc 704 482-3866
1015 Buffalo St Shelby (28150) *(G-14357)*

Printing Partners Inc 336 996-2268
365 W Bodenhamer St Kernersville (27284) *(G-9225)*

Printing Press 828 299-1234
16 Pleasant Ridge Dr Asheville (28805) *(G-743)*

Printing Pro 704 748-9396
1310 L R Schronce Ln Iron Station (28080) *(G-8975)*

Printing Svcs Greensboro Inc 336 274-7663
2206 N Church St Greensboro (27405) *(G-7285)*

Printlogic Inc 336 626-6680
2753 Us Highway 220 Bus S Asheboro (27205) *(G-468)*

Printmarketing LLC 828 261-0063
320 19th St Se Hickory (28602) *(G-8125)*

Printology Signs Graphics LLC 843 473-4984
10931 Zac Hill Rd Davidson (28036) *(G-4691)*

Printpack Inc 828 693-1723
3510 Asheville Hwy Hendersonville (28791) *(G-7892)*

Printpack Inc 828 649-3800
100 Kenpak Ln Marshall (28753) *(G-10206)*

Printpack Medical Store, Marshall *Also Called: Printpack Inc (G-10206)*

Prints On Parade LLC 713 387-9061
6148 Liberty Rd Julian (27283) *(G-9107)*

Prints Plus 828 389-7190
1124 Nc 69 Ste 105 Hayesville (28904) *(G-7770)*

Printsurge Incorporated 919 854-4376
2308 Beaver Oaks Ct Raleigh (27606) *(G-13143)*

Printville 828 225-3777
1 Page Ave Ste 107 Asheville (28801) *(G-744)*

Printworks Inc 919 649-1547
7649 Summerglen Dr Raleigh (27615) *(G-13144)*

Printworld, Monroe *Also Called: Synthomer Inc (G-10819)*

Priority Backgrounds LLC 919 557-3247
118 N Johnson St Fuquay Varina (27526) *(G-6222)*

Priority Prtg Charlotte Inc 802 374-8360
3126 Milton Rd Ste E Charlotte (28215) *(G-3389)*

Priscllas Crystal Cast Wnes In 252 422-8336
187 Hibbs Road Ext Newport (28570) *(G-11904)*

Prism Printing & Design Inc 919 706-5977
109 Loch Haven Ln Cary (27518) *(G-1859)*

Prism Publishing Inc (PA) 919 319-6816
1240 Se Maynard Rd Ste 104 Cary (27511) *(G-1860)*

Prism Research Glass Inc 919 571-0078
6004 Triangle Dr Ste B Raleigh (27617) *(G-13145)*

Prism Specialties NC, Raleigh *Also Called: Dimill Enterprises LLC (G-12684)*

Prismaflex Usa Inc 910 862-3550
113 E Broad St Elizabethtown (28337) *(G-5602)*

Pritchard Logging LLC 828 447-4354
1651 Piney Knob Rd Rutherfordton (28139) *(G-13885)*

Private Label Digital Prtg LLC 919 929-6053
630 Arlington St Chapel Hill (27514) *(G-2057)*

Private Label Manufacturing, Winston Salem *Also Called: Plm Inc (G-16859)*

Privette Enterprises Inc 704 634-3291
2751 Old Charlotte Hwy Monroe (28110) *(G-10789)*

Prize Management LLC 252 532-1939
8287 Nc Hwy 46 Garysburg (27831) *(G-6329)*

Prn Uniforms, Charlotte *Also Called: Formark Corporation (G-2789)*

Pro Cal Prof Decals Inc (PA) 704 795-6090
4366 Triple Crown Dr Sw Concord (28027) *(G-4340)*

Pro Choice Contractors Corp 919 696-7383
2405 Churchill Rd Raleigh (27608) *(G-13146)*

Pro Custom Cabinets LLC 704 239-6054
1440 Upper Palmer Rd Salisbury (28146) *(G-14031)*

Pro Farm Group Inc (PA) 530 750-2800
7780 Brier Creek Pkwy Ste 420 Raleigh (27617) *(G-13147)*

Pro Feet, Burlington *Also Called: Wilson Brown Inc (G-1518)*

Pro Laundry Equipment, Matthews *Also Called: Laundry Svc Tech Ltd Lblty Co (G-10262)*

Pro Pallet South Inc 910 576-4902
105 Poole Rd Troy (27371) *(G-15411)*

Pro Refrigeration Inc 336 283-7281
319 Farmington Rd Mocksville (27028) *(G-10599)*

Pro Storage Plus, Richfield *Also Called: Richfeld Prtable Buildings Inc (G-13554)*

Pro Tool Company Inc 336 998-9212
1765 Peoples Creek Rd Advance (27006) *(G-48)*

Pro Tronics — ALPHABETIC SECTION

Pro Tronics, Knightdale *Also Called: Protronics Inc (G-9427)*
Pro-Blend Chemical Co, Winston Salem *Also Called: Industrial Lubricants Inc (G-16759)*
Pro-Face America LLC (HQ) 734 477-0600
  235 Burgess Rd Ste D Greensboro (27409) *(G-7286)*
Pro-Fit Boat Canvas LLC 704 340-7733
  134 Palmer Marsh Pl Mooresville (28117) *(G-11062)*
Pro-Kay Supply Inc 910 628-0882
  5032 Atkinson Rd Orrum (28369) *(G-12116)*
Pro-Motor Engines Inc 704 664-6800
  102 S Iredell Industrial Park Rd Mooresville (28115) *(G-11063)*
Pro-System Inc 704 799-8100
  121 Oakpark Dr Mooresville (28115) *(G-11064)*
Pro-Tech Inc 704 872-6227
  1256 N Barkley Rd Statesville (28677) *(G-14870)*
Proash LLC (HQ) 336 597-8734
  1514 Dunnaway Rd Semora (27343) *(G-14264)*
Problem Solver Inc 919 596-5555
  3200 Glen Royal Rd Ste 112 Raleigh (27617) *(G-13148)*
Process Automation Tech Inc 828 298-1055
  3113 Sweeten Creek Rd Asheville (28803) *(G-745)*
Process Electronics Corp 704 827-9019
  100 Brickyard Rd Mount Holly (28120) *(G-11647)*
Procoaters Inc 336 992-0012
  216 Industrial Way Dr Kernersville (27284) *(G-9226)*
Procter & Gamble, Browns Summit *Also Called: Procter & Gamble Mfg Co (G-1314)*
Procter & Gamble, Greensboro *Also Called: Procter & Gamble Mfg Co (G-7287)*
Procter & Gamble Mfg Co 336 954-0000
  6200 Bryan Park Rd Browns Summit (27214) *(G-1314)*
Procter & Gamble Mfg Co 336 954-0000
  100 S Swing Rd Greensboro (27409) *(G-7287)*
Proctorfree Inc 704 759-6569
  210 Delburg St Davidson (28036) *(G-4692)*
Producers Gin Murfreesboro LLC 252 398-3762
  336 Benthall Bridge Rd Murfreesboro (27855) *(G-11702)*
Product Finishing Solutions Co 704 785-8941
  157 Softwind Ln Concord (28025) *(G-4341)*
Product Identification Inc 919 544-4136
  1725 Carpenter Fletcher Rd Ste 201 Durham (27713) *(G-5305)*
Product Quest Manufacturing Inc 386 239-8787
  380 Knollwood St Ste 700 Winston Salem (27103) *(G-16869)*
Product Quest Manufacturing LLC 386 239-8787
  380 Knollwood St Ste 700 Winston Salem (27103) *(G-16870)*
Product Quest Mfg LLC 321 255-3250
  380 Knollwood St Ste 700 Winston Salem (27103) *(G-16871)*
Production Division, Kinston *Also Called: Sanderson Farms Inc (G-9383)*
Production Media Inc 919 325-0120
  2501 Blue Ridge Rd Ste 250 Raleigh (27607) *(G-13149)*
Production Systems Inc 336 886-7161
  1500 Trinity Ave High Point (27260) *(G-8499)*
Production Tool and Die Co Inc 704 525-0498
  537 Scholtz Rd Charlotte (28217) *(G-3390)*
Production Wldg Fbrication Inc 828 687-7466
  1791 Brevard Rd Arden (28704) *(G-369)*
Productive Tool, Dallas *Also Called: Brooks of Dallas Inc (G-4635)*
Proedge Precision LLC 704 872-3393
  113 Hatfield Rd Statesville (28625) *(G-14871)*
Proface America, Greensboro *Also Called: Pro-Face America LLC (G-7286)*
Profection Embroidery, Concord *Also Called: Tef Inc (G-4375)*
Professinal Sales Associates 336 210-2756
  2783 Nc Highway 68 S # 116 High Point (27265) *(G-8500)*
Professional Bus Systems Inc 704 333-2444
  201 E Cama St Charlotte (28217) *(G-3391)*
Professional Image 336 294-6200
  4602 W Market St Greensboro (27407) *(G-7288)*
Professional Laminating, Cary *Also Called: Professional Laminating LLC (G-1862)*
Professional Laminating LLC 919 465-0400
  107 Turnberry Ln Cary (27518) *(G-1861)*
Professional Laminating LLC 919 465-0400
  233 E Johnson St Ste M Cary (27513) *(G-1862)*
Professional Sheet Metal LLC 336 755-3794
  2957 Park Dr Mount Airy (27030) *(G-11560)*
Professnal Alterations EMB Inc 910 577-8484
  2113 Lejeune Blvd Jacksonville (28546) *(G-9022)*
Professnal Prprty Prservations, Raeford *Also Called: William Brantley (G-12445)*
Profile Products LLC 828 327-4165
  219 Simpson St Sw Conover (28613) *(G-4489)*
Profilform Us Inc 252 430-0392
  101 Eastern Minerals Rd Henderson (27537) *(G-7803)*
Proform Finishing Products LLC (DH) 704 365-7300
  2001 Rexford Rd Charlotte (28211) *(G-3392)*
Proform Finishing Products LLC 704 398-3900
  1725 Wester Rd Mount Holly (28120) *(G-11648)*
Proform Finishing Products LLC 910 799-3954
  838 Sunnyvale Dr Wilmington (28412) *(G-16371)*
Proforma Hanson Branding 210 437-3061
  4257 Wallburg High Point Rd High Point (27265) *(G-8501)*
Proforma Print Source 919 383-2070
  3600 N Duke St Durham (27704) *(G-5306)*
Proforma Promographix, Carolina Beach *Also Called: Promographix Inc (G-1640)*
Proforma Tierney Printing 910 392-2611
  1213 Culbreth Dr Wilmington (28405) *(G-16372)*
Progress Energy Florida, Raleigh *Also Called: Florida Progress Corporation (G-12775)*
Progress Software Corp 919 461-4200
  3005 Carrington Mill Blvd Morrisville (27560) *(G-11412)*
Progress Solar Solutions LLC 919 363-3738
  1108 N New Hope Rd Raleigh (27610) *(G-13150)*
Progressive Business Media, Greensboro *Also Called: Ft Media Holdings LLC (G-7024)*
Progressive Elc Greenville LLC 252 413-6957
  8606 Canal Dr Emerald Isle (28594) *(G-5671)*
Progressive Furniture Inc 828 459-2151
  2555 Penny Rd Claremont (28610) *(G-3935)*
Progressive Industries Inc 919 267-6948
  1020 Goodworth Dr Apex (27539) *(G-233)*
Progressive Intl Elec Inc 919 266-4442
  1106 Great Falls Ct Knightdale (27545) *(G-9426)*
Progressive Service Die Co 910 353-4836
  226 White St Jacksonville (28546) *(G-9023)*
Progressive Tool & Mfg Inc 336 664-1130
  245 Standard Dr Greensboro (27409) *(G-7289)*
Project Bean LLC 201 438-1598
  5555 Harrisburg Ind Pk Dr Harrisburg (28075) *(G-7723)*
Prokidney LLC 336 448-2857
  3929 Westpoint Blvd Ste G Winston Salem (27103) *(G-16872)*
Prokidney Corp 336 999-7028
  2000 Frontis Plaza Blvd Ste 250 Winston Salem (27103) *(G-16873)*
Prolec-GE Waukesha Inc 919 734-8900
  2701 Us Highway 117 S Goldsboro (27530) *(G-6646)*
Promatic Automation Inc 828 684-1700
  9a National Ave Fletcher (28732) *(G-6032)*
Prometals Inc 919 693-8884
  510 1/2 Hillsboro St Oxford (27565) *(G-12147)*
Promethera Biosciences LLC 919 354-1930
  6 Davis Dr Durham (27709) *(G-5307)*
Promethera Biosciences LLC (PA) 919 354-1933
  4700 Falls Of Neuse Rd Ste 400 Raleigh (27609) *(G-13151)*
Prometheus Group Holdings LLC 919 835-0810
  4601 Six Forks Rd Ste 220 Raleigh (27609) *(G-13152)*
Prominence Furniture Inc 336 475-6505
  415 Commercial Park Dr Thomasville (27360) *(G-15267)*
Promographix Inc 919 846-1379
  406 Fayetteville Ave Carolina Beach (28428) *(G-1640)*
Promos Inc 336 251-1134
  1316 Westgate Center Dr Winston Salem (27103) *(G-16874)*
Promothreads Inc 704 248-0942
  19824 W Catawba Ave Ste C Cornelius (28031) *(G-4579)*
Promotional Products Plus, Newport *Also Called: Carolina Tailors Inc (G-11899)*
Propak Logistics 704 471-1070
  200 Wal Mart Dr Shelby (28150) *(G-14358)*
Propane Trucks & Tanks Inc (PA) 919 362-5000
  1600 E Williams St Apex (27539) *(G-234)*
Propella Therapeutics Inc 703 631-7523
  120 Mosaic Blvd Ste 120-3 Pittsboro (27312) *(G-12345)*

ALPHABETIC SECTION

Propharma Group LLC (HQ) 888 242-0559
107 W Hargett St Raleigh (27601) *(G-13153)*

Prophysics Innovations Inc 919 245-0406
1911 Evans Rd Cary (27513) *(G-1863)*

Prosapient, Raleigh Also Called: Prosapient Inc *(G-13154)*

Prosapient Inc 984 282-2823
555 Fayetteville St Ste 700 Raleigh (27601) *(G-13154)*

Prosign 919 222-6907
504 Rosewood Rd Goldsboro (27530) *(G-6647)*

Prospective Communications LLC 336 287-5535
1959 N Peace Haven Rd Winston Salem (27106) *(G-16875)*

Prostar Printing Prom Pro 704 839-0253
6010 Bluebird Hill Ln Matthews (28104) *(G-10341)*

Protech Fabrication Inc 704 663-1721
575 Edmiston Rd Mount Ulla (28125) *(G-11686)*

Protech Metals LLC 910 295-6905
3619 Murdocksville Rd Pinehurst (28374) *(G-12232)*

Protechnologies Inc 336 368-1375
331 Shellybrook Dr Pilot Mountain (27041) *(G-12200)*

Protect Adoptable Labs 253 383-2733
23 Timber Ln Asheville (28806) *(G-746)*

Protect Plus Pro LLC 828 328-1142
420 3rd Ave Nw Ste A Hickory (28601) *(G-8126)*

Protection Products Inc 828 324-2173
1010 3rd Ave Nw Hickory (28601) *(G-8127)*

Protein For Pets Opco LLC 252 206-0960
2018 Beeler Rd S Wilson (27893) *(G-16524)*

Protek Services LLC 910 556-4121
905 Cranes Creek Rd Cameron (28326) *(G-1562)*

Protex Sport Products Inc 336 956-2419
1029 S Main St Salisbury (28144) *(G-14032)*

Proto Labs Inc 833 245-8827
3700 Pleasant Grove Church Rd Morrisville (27560) *(G-11413)*

Prototech Manufacturing Inc 508 646-8849
514 Telfair St Washington (27889) *(G-15728)*

Prototype Tooling Co 704 864-7777
1811 W Franklin Blvd Gastonia (28052) *(G-6498)*

Protronics Inc 919 217-0007
861 Old Knight Rd Ste 102 Knightdale (27545) *(G-9427)*

Proveer 800 542-9941
331 Sherwee Dr Raleigh (27603) *(G-13155)*

Providencia Usa Inc 704 881-2837
200 Deer Ridge Dr Statesville (28625) *(G-14872)*

Provision Cabinetry 336 442-3537
107 Sprucewood Ct Archdale (27263) *(G-296)*

Provizion Led, Charlotte Also Called: Carolina Signs and Wonders Inc *(G-2405)*

Prowl Precision and Power LLC 336 580-1558
3022 Forestdale Dr Burlington (27215) *(G-1479)*

Proximal Design Labs LLC 919 599-5742
1421 Carolina Pines Ave Raleigh (27603) *(G-13156)*

Proximity Bakery, Greensboro Also Called: Proximity Foods Corporation *(G-7290)*

Proximity Foods Corporation 336 691-1700
1117 W Cornwallis Dr Greensboro (27408) *(G-7290)*

Prp Ventures Inc 919 554-8734
2811 Superior Dr Ste 101 Wake Forest (27587) *(G-15577)*

Prs Dunn LLC 828 736-4907
56 Rex Dr Asheville (28806) *(G-747)*

Prs Group LLC 910 550-0088
500 Westover Dr Sanford (27330) *(G-14172)*

Prysmian Cables & Systems USA, Claremont Also Called: Draka Holdings Usa Inc *(G-3922)*

Prysmian Cbles Systems USA LLC 828 322-9473
1711 11th Ave Sw Hickory (28602) *(G-8128)*

PS Cisco, Statesville Also Called: Tube Specialties Co Inc *(G-14920)*

Psa Incorporated 910 371-1115
150 Backhoe Rd Ne Belville (28451) *(G-1024)*

Psalm 32 Publishing LLC 704 799-7637
200 Collingswood Rd Mooresville (28117) *(G-11065)*

PSI Control Solutions LLC (PA) 704 596-5617
9900 Twin Lakes Pkwy Charlotte (28269) *(G-3393)*

PSI Global USA 704 544-1893
2725 Westinghouse Blvd Ste 100 Charlotte (28273) *(G-3394)*

PSI Liquidating Inc 704 888-9930
605 N Central Ave Ste A Locust (28097) *(G-9966)*

PSI Pharma Support America Inc 919 249-2660
10 Laboratory Dr Durham (27709) *(G-5308)*

PSI Power & Controls, Charlotte Also Called: PSI Control Solutions LLC *(G-3393)*

Psi-Polymer Systems Inc 828 468-2600
1703 Pineview St Se Conover (28613) *(G-4490)*

PSM Enterprises Inc 336 789-8888
219 Frederick St Mount Airy (27030) *(G-11561)*

Psnc Energy 919 367-2735
2451 Schieffelin Rd Apex (27502) *(G-235)*

Pt Marketing Incorporated 412 471-8995
8360 Six Forks Rd Ste 204 Raleigh (27615) *(G-13157)*

PT&D, Charlotte Also Called: Production Tool and Die Co Inc *(G-3390)*

Ptc, Winston Salem Also Called: Parrish Tire Company *(G-16836)*

Pteris Global (usa) Inc 980 253-3267
2401 Whitehall Park Dr Ste 1000 Charlotte (28273) *(G-3395)*

Pti, Hickory Also Called: Plastic Technology Inc *(G-8116)*

Pti, Pilot Mountain Also Called: Protechnologies Inc *(G-12200)*

Public Health Corps Inc 336 545-2999
3300 Battleground Ave Ste 270 Greensboro (27410) *(G-7291)*

Public Safety UAS LLC 336 601-7578
50 Falcon Ct Gibsonville (27249) *(G-6570)*

Publishing Group Inc 704 847-7150
211 W Matthews St Ste 105 Matthews (28105) *(G-10283)*

Publishing Group, The, Matthews Also Called: Publishing Group Inc *(G-10283)*

Publishing Your Story LLC 704 543-6555
2317 Kingsmill Ter Charlotte (28270) *(G-3396)*

Publishing/Education, Shelby Also Called: Silver Ink Publishing Inc *(G-14367)*

Pucuda Inc 860 526-8004
3100 Oaks Rd New Bern (28560) *(G-11838)*

Puett Trucking & Logging 919 853-2071
1796 Person Rd Louisburg (27549) *(G-9997)*

Puffing Monkey 919 556-7779
2115 S Main St Wake Forest (27587) *(G-15578)*

Pulaski Furniture, High Point Also Called: Home Meridian Holdings Inc *(G-8400)*

Pullover Pal 910 340-1801
305 Thomas Dr Jacksonville (28546) *(G-9024)*

Pulp Mill, Vanceboro Also Called: Weyerhaeuser Company *(G-15485)*

Pumpkin Pacific LLC 704 226-4176
10206 Pineshadow Dr Apt 107 Charlotte (28262) *(G-3397)*

Pumps Blowers & Elc Mtrs LLC 919 286-4975
2712 Edmund St Durham (27705) *(G-5309)*

Pungo River Timber Company, Pantego Also Called: Nathan Beiler *(G-12169)*

Punker LLC 828 322-1951
1112 Lincoln County Pkwy Lincolnton (28092) *(G-9913)*

Puny Human LLC 919 420-4538
6278 Glenwood Ave Raleigh (27612) *(G-13158)*

Pupco, Charlotte Also Called: Power-Utility Products Company *(G-3361)*

Purdue Pharmaceuticals LP 252 265-1900
4701 International Blvd Wilson (27893) *(G-16525)*

Pure Country Inc 828 859-9916
81 Skylar Dr Lynn (28750) *(G-10063)*

Pure Flow Inc (PA) 336 532-0300
1241 Jay Ln Graham (27253) *(G-6709)*

Pure Soy Scents 980 722-1483
1245 Blake Dr Mount Holly (28120) *(G-11649)*

Pure Water Innovations Inc 919 301-8189
272 Williams Rd Spring Hope (27882) *(G-14620)*

Purely Pallets 336 676-7107
4701 Olde Forest Dr Greensboro (27406) *(G-7292)*

Pureon Inc 480 505-3409
1412 Airport Rd Monroe (28110) *(G-10790)*

Purilum LLC 252 931-8020
967 Woodridge Park Rd Greenville (27834) *(G-7577)*

Purina Mills, Statesville Also Called: Purina Mills LLC *(G-14873)*

Purina Mills LLC 704 872-0456
173 Mcness Rd Statesville (28677) *(G-14873)*

Purolator Advanced Filtration, Greensboro Also Called: Purolator Facet Inc *(G-7293)*

Purolator Facet Inc (HQ) 336 668-4444
8439 Triad Dr Greensboro (27409) *(G-7293)*

Purple Star Graphics Inc   **ALPHABETIC SECTION**

Purple Star Graphics Inc 704 723-4020
    32 Union St S Concord (28025) *(G-4342)*
Purser Centl Rewinding Co Inc (PA) 704 786-3131
    865 Concord Pkwy N Concord (28027) *(G-4343)*
Purthermal LLC 828 855-0108
    1720 Tate Blvd Se Hickory (28602) *(G-8129)*
Putsch, Fletcher *Also Called: Putsch & Company Inc (G-6033)*
Putsch & Company Inc (HQ) 828 684-0671
    352 Cane Creek Rd Fletcher (28732) *(G-6033)*
Puzzle Piece LLC 910 688-7119
    2287 Underwood Rd Carthage (28327) *(G-1664)*
Puzzles From Past LLC 704 231-5878
    17424 Invermere Ave Huntersville (28078) *(G-8884)*
Pyramid Cement Products Inc 704 373-2529
    9724 Industrial Dr Pineville (28134) *(G-12292)*
Pyramid Software Inc 336 209-2684
    7410 Denlee Rd Raleigh (27603) *(G-13159)*
Pyrotek Incorporated 704 642-1993
    970 Grace Church Rd Salisbury (28147) *(G-14033)*
Pyxus International Inc 252 753-8000
    8958 West Marlboro Rd Farmville (27828) *(G-5742)*
Q C Apparel Inc 828 586-5663
    330 Scotts Creek Rd Sylva (28779) *(G-15065)*
Q T Corporation 252 399-7600
    2700 Forest Hills Rd Sw Wilson (27893) *(G-16526)*
Q-Edge Corporation 919 935-8167
    4018 Patriot Dr Ste 175 Durham (27703) *(G-5310)*
Qasioun LLC 704 531-8000
    4845 E Independence Blvd Unit B Charlotte (28212) *(G-3398)*
Qatch Technologies LLC 678 908-3112
    551 Dairy Glen Rd Chapel Hill (27516) *(G-2058)*
Qatch Techologies, Chapel Hill *Also Called: Qatch Technologies LLC (G-2058)*
Qc LLC (DH) 800 883-0010
    1001 Winstead Dr Ste 480 Cary (27513) *(G-1864)*
Qcs Acquisition Corporation 252 446-5000
    130 N Business Ct Rocky Mount (27804) *(G-13725)*
Qde Press 256 390-4668
    104 W Raintree Ln Goldsboro (27534) *(G-6648)*
Qi Signs LLC 336 625-0938
    370 W Salisbury St Asheboro (27203) *(G-469)*
QMAX Industries, Pineville *Also Called: QMAX Industries LLC (G-12293)*
QMAX Industries LLC 704 643-7299
    520 Eagleton Downs Dr Ste A Pineville (28134) *(G-12293)*
QMF Mtal Elctrnic Slutions Inc 336 992-8002
    324 Berry Garden Rd Kernersville (27284) *(G-9227)*
Qni, Raleigh *Also Called: Qualia Networks Inc (G-13162)*
Qorvo, Greensboro *Also Called: Qorvo Inc (G-7295)*
Qorvo Inc 336 664-1233
    7908 Piedmont Triad Pkwy Bldg D Greensboro (27409) *(G-7294)*
Qorvo Inc (PA) 336 664-1233
    7628 Thorndike Rd Greensboro (27409) *(G-7295)*
Qorvo International Holdg Inc (DH) 336 664-1233
    7628 Thorndike Rd Greensboro (27409) *(G-7296)*
Qorvo International Svcs Inc 336 664-1233
    7628 Thorndike Rd Greensboro (27409) *(G-7297)*
Qorvo Us Inc 336 662-1150
    7907 Piedmont Triad Pkwy Greensboro (27409) *(G-7298)*
Qorvo Us Inc 336 931-8298
    7914 Piedmont Triad Pkwy Greensboro (27409) *(G-7299)*
Qorvo Us Inc 503 615-9000
    4113 Devondale Ct Jamestown (27282) *(G-9067)*
Qplot Corporation 949 302-7928
    3245 Lewis Farm Rd Raleigh (27607) *(G-13160)*
Qrmc Ltd 828 696-2000
    11 S Egerton Rd Hendersonville (28792) *(G-7893)*
Qspac Industries Inc 704 635-7815
    506 Miller St Monroe (28110) *(G-10791)*
Qst Industries Inc 336 751-1000
    140 Lionheart Dr Mocksville (27028) *(G-10600)*
Quad City High Prfmce Coatings 937 623-2282
    1427 Green Hill Rd Ne Leland (28451) *(G-9557)*

Quad/Graphics Inc 706 648-5456
    10911 Granite St Charlotte (28273) *(G-3399)*
QUAD/GRAPHICS INC., Charlotte *Also Called: Quad/Graphics Inc (G-3399)*
Quadalupe Industries Inc 786 241-0315
    74 Saint Dunstans Cir Asheville (28803) *(G-748)*
Quadsaw Usa LLC 980 339-8554
    6739 Fairway Row Ln Charlotte (28277) *(G-3400)*
Quail Dry Cleaning 704 947-7335
    5818 Prosperity Church Rd Charlotte (28269) *(G-3401)*
Quailwood Screen Prtg & EMB 704 910-2385
    4804 Quail Ridge Dr Mint Hill (28227) *(G-10543)*
Qualcomm, Clemmons *Also Called: Qualcomm Incorporated (G-4056)*
Qualcomm Datacenter Tech Inc 858 567-1121
    8045 Arco Corporate Dr Raleigh (27617) *(G-13161)*
Qualcomm Incorporated 336 323-3300
    6209 Ramada Dr Ste A Clemmons (27012) *(G-4056)*
Qualia Networks Inc 805 637-2083
    3732 Westbury Lake Dr Raleigh (27603) *(G-13162)*
Qualicaps Inc (DH) 336 449-3900
    6505 Franz Warner Pkwy Whitsett (27377) *(G-16000)*
Qualice, Hamlet *Also Called: Qualice LLC (G-7630)*
Qualice LLC 910 419-6589
    11 Ev Hogan Dr Hamlet (28345) *(G-7630)*
Qualiseal Technology LLC 704 731-1522
    5605 Carnegie Blvd Ste 500 Charlotte (28209) *(G-3402)*
Qualitrol Company LLC 704 587-9267
    3030 Whitehall Park Dr Charlotte (28273) *(G-3403)*
Quality Beverage LLC 910 371-3596
    157 Poole Rd Belville (28451) *(G-1025)*
Quality Beverage LLC (PA) 704 637-5881
    1413 Jake Alexander Blvd S Salisbury (28146) *(G-14034)*
Quality Beverage Brands, Salisbury *Also Called: Quality Beverage LLC (G-14034)*
Quality Cabinets Woodworks 252 536-0568
    906 Poplar Ln Halifax (27839) *(G-7612)*
Quality Cleaning Services LLC 919 638-4969
    3639 Guess Rd Durham (27705) *(G-5311)*
Quality Concrete Co Inc 910 483-7155
    1587 Wilmington Hwy Fayetteville (28306) *(G-5903)*
Quality Contemporary Furniture 919 758-7277
    2517 Floyd Dr B Raleigh (27610) *(G-13163)*
Quality Conveyor Solutions, Rocky Mount *Also Called: Qcs Acquisition Corporation (G-13725)*
Quality Custom Woodworks Inc 704 843-1584
    5019 Pleasant Springs Rd Waxhaw (28173) *(G-15771)*
Quality Equipment LLC 919 493-3545
    3821 Durham Chapel Hill Blvd Durham (27707) *(G-5312)*
Quality Fabricators 336 622-3402
    1151 Langley Rd Staley (27355) *(G-14670)*
Quality Foods From Sea Inc 252 338-5455
    173 Knobbs Creek Dr Elizabeth City (27909) *(G-5565)*
Quality Home Fashions Inc 704 983-5906
    28569 Flint Ridge Rd Albemarle (28001) *(G-100)*
Quality Housing Corporation 336 274-2622
    1400 Battleground Ave Ste 205 Greensboro (27408) *(G-7300)*
Quality Information Publs Inc 919 593-4715
    84 Solomon Rd Leicester (28748) *(G-9518)*
Quality Instant Printing Inc 919 544-1777
    1920 E Nc Highway 54 Ste 30 Durham (27713) *(G-5313)*
Quality Insulation Company 252 438-3711
    132 Carey Chapel Rd Henderson (27537) *(G-7804)*
Quality Investments Inc 252 492-8777
    1902 N Garnett St Henderson (27536) *(G-7805)*
Quality Lghtning Prtection Inc (PA) 919 832-9399
    743 Pershing Rd Raleigh (27608) *(G-13164)*
Quality Lightning Protection, Raleigh *Also Called: Capital Lghtning Prtection Inc (G-12590)*
Quality Machine & Tool 336 769-9131
    1793 Union Cross Rd Kernersville (27284) *(G-9228)*
Quality Marble 336 472-1000
    416 Julian Ave Thomasville (27360) *(G-15268)*
Quality Mch & Fabrication Inc 252 435-6041
    444 Guinea Mill Rd Moyock (27958) *(G-11697)*

ALPHABETIC SECTION

Quality Mechanical Contrs LLC..336 228-0638
3032a Rock Hill Rd Burlington (27215) *(G-1480)*

Quality Packaging Corp (PA)..336 881-5300
255 Swathmore Ave High Point (27263) *(G-8502)*

Quality Precast Inc..919 497-0660
100 Gayline Dr Louisburg (27549) *(G-9998)*

Quality Printing Solutions Inc...919 261-9527
4800 Frenchill Cir Raleigh (27610) *(G-13165)*

Quality Prtg Cartridge Fctry..336 852-2505
6700 W Market St Greensboro (27409) *(G-7301)*

Quality Salvage Industries..336 884-4433
1433 National Hwy Thomasville (27360) *(G-15269)*

Quality Saw Shop Inc..336 882-1722
1208 Elon Pl High Point (27263) *(G-8503)*

Quality Seafood Co Inc...252 338-2800
177 Knobbs Creek Dr Elizabeth City (27909) *(G-5566)*

Quality Steel Fabrication Inc..336 961-2670
1301 Union Cross Church Rd Yadkinville (27055) *(G-17047)*

Quality Steel Structure LLC..910 975-3409
375 Highway 105 Ext Apt 203 Boone (28607) *(G-1229)*

Quality Trck Bodies & Repr Inc..252 245-5100
5316 Rock Quarry Rd Elm City (27822) *(G-5652)*

Quality Turf Hauling LLC..336 516-1156
325 Chris St Haw River (27258) *(G-7756)*

Quality Veneer Company...336 622-2211
237 Teague Ave Liberty (27298) *(G-9827)*

Quality Welding..910 754-3232
4916 Arnold St Shallotte (28470) *(G-14277)*

Qualpak LLC...910 610-1213
16000 Joy St Laurinburg (28352) *(G-9493)*

Qualtech Industries Inc..704 734-0345
311 Industrial Dr Kings Mountain (28086) *(G-9327)*

Quantico Tactical Incorporated..910 944-5800
9796 Aberdeen Rd Aberdeen (28315) *(G-23)*

Quantico Water & Sewer LLC...336 528-9299
260 Fern Cliff Ln Clemmons (27012) *(G-4057)*

Quantum Insulation Inc..252 752-7828
2554 Black Jack Grimesland Rd Greenville (27858) *(G-7578)*

Quantum Machinery Group, Charlotte Also Called: M & A Equipment Inc *(G-3112)*

Quantum Materials LLC (HQ)..336 605-9002
5280 National Center Dr Colfax (27235) *(G-4159)*

Quantum Newswire...919 439-8800
150 Fayetteville St 2800d108 Raleigh (27601) *(G-13166)*

Quantum Plastics Raleigh, Kenly Also Called: Rpp Acquisition LLC *(G-9157)*

Quantum Solutions..828 615-7500
365 Main Ave Sw Hickory (28602) *(G-8130)*

Quantum Usa LLP...919 704-8266
15 Grey Squirrel Ct Chapel Hill (27517) *(G-2059)*

Quarries Petroleum...919 387-0986
2540 Schieffelin Rd Apex (27502) *(G-236)*

Quarry & Kiln LLC..704 888-0775
1334 Nc-24 W Midland (28107) *(G-10477)*

Quarter Turn LLC..336 712-0811
8340 Holler Farm Rd Clemmons (27012) *(G-4058)*

Quartz, Spruce Pine Also Called: Quartz Corp USA *(G-14654)*

Quartz Corp USA...828 765-8950
797 Altapass Hwy Spruce Pine (28777) *(G-14653)*

Quartz Corp USA (DH)...828 766-2104
8342 S 226 Bypass Spruce Pine (28777) *(G-14654)*

Quartz Matrix LLC...828 631-3207
283 Winding Ridge Dr Sylva (28779) *(G-15066)*

Quatrobio LLC..919 460-9500
3000 Rdu Center Dr Morrisville (27560) *(G-11414)*

Que Pasa, Winston Salem Also Called: Latino Communications Inc *(G-16784)*

Que Pasa Charlotte, Charlotte Also Called: Latino Communications Inc *(G-3073)*

Queen City Engrg & Design...704 918-5651
369 Corban Ave Sw Concord (28025) *(G-4344)*

Queen City Event Mgmt Cnsltng..704 780-7611
1700 Lumarka Dr Charlotte (28212) *(G-3404)*

Queen City Pastry Llc...704 660-5706
137 Speedway Ln Mooresville (28117) *(G-11066)*

Queen of Wines LLC..919 348-6630
122 Wright Hill Dr Durham (27712) *(G-5314)*

Queen Wrist Bling Inc..980 635-0287
3066 Clover Rd Nw Concord (28027) *(G-4345)*

Queens Creek Seafood..910 326-4801
105 Huffman Ln Hubert (28539) *(G-8752)*

Queensboro Industries Inc..910 251-1251
1400 Marstellar St Wilmington (28401) *(G-16373)*

Queensboro Shirt Company, Wilmington Also Called: Queensboro Industries Inc *(G-16373)*

Queercos.com, Durham Also Called: Finley Enterprises LLC *(G-5096)*

Quest Software Inc...919 337-4719
133 Southcenter Ct Morrisville (27560) *(G-11415)*

QUEST SOFTWARE, INC., Morrisville Also Called: Quest Software Inc *(G-11415)*

Quick Color Solutions..336 698-0951
829 Knox Rd Mc Leansville (27301) *(G-10395)*

Quick Color Solutions Inc...336 282-3900
1801 E Franklin St Ste 208b Chapel Hill (27514) *(G-2060)*

Quick Copy Print Shop, Salisbury Also Called: Baileys Quick Copy Shop Inc *(G-13929)*

Quick N Easy 12 Nc739..336 824-3832
8112 Us Highway 64 E Ramseur (27316) *(G-13449)*

Quick Practice, Charlotte Also Called: Practicepro Sftwr Systems Inc *(G-3366)*

Quick Print, Brevard Also Called: Blue Ridge Quick Print Inc *(G-1270)*

Quick Print, Fletcher Also Called: Asheville Quickprint *(G-5984)*

Quick Print, Salisbury Also Called: Quick Print of Concord *(G-14035)*

Quick Print of Concord..704 782-6634
700 N Long St Ste C Salisbury (28144) *(G-14035)*

Quickie Manufacturing Corp...910 737-6500
2880 Kenny Biggs Rd Lumberton (28358) *(G-10049)*

Quickshipkeys.com, Charlotte Also Called: Easykeyscom Inc *(G-2678)*

Quik Print Inc...910 738-6775
232 E 4th St Lumberton (28358) *(G-10050)*

Quiknit Crafting Inc..704 861-1030
1916 S York Rd Gastonia (28052) *(G-6499)*

Quikrete Companies LLC..704 272-7677
13471 Us Highway 74 W Peachland (28133) *(G-12175)*

Quikrete Peachland, Peachland Also Called: Quikrete Companies LLC *(G-12175)*

Quiktron Inc..828 327-6009
925 Old Lenoir Rd Hickory (28601) *(G-8131)*

Quillen Welding Services LLC..252 269-4908
110 Bonner Ave Morehead City (28557) *(G-11184)*

Quillsedge Press Inc..410 207-0841
365 Anterbury Dr Apex (27502) *(G-237)*

Quilt Lizzy..252 257-3800
4260 Lee St Ayden (28513) *(G-853)*

Quilt Shop...828 263-8691
251 Katie Way Boone (28607) *(G-1230)*

Quinlan Publishing Company...229 886-7995
2102 Pender Ave Wilmington (28403) *(G-16374)*

Quinn Powder Coating...252 235-0200
8246 Planer Mill Rd Middlesex (27557) *(G-10455)*

Quinn Publishing Company..828 668-4622
Asheville (28815) *(G-749)*

Quinnessential Tools Company...540 623-7965
117 Kirkland Pl Raeford (28376) *(G-12433)*

Quinsite LLC Fka Mile 5 Anlyti..317 313-5152
1818 Martin Luther King Jr Blvd Pmb 185 Chapel Hill (27514) *(G-2061)*

Quintiles Pharma, Inc., Durham Also Called: Iqvia Pharma Inc *(G-5166)*

Quo Vademus LLC...910 296-1632
277 Faison W Mcgowan Rd Kenansville (28349) *(G-9145)*

Qws LLC...252 723-2106
110 Bonner Ave Morehead City (28557) *(G-11185)*

R & A Masonry LLC..919 672-6253
1509 N Miami Blvd Durham (27701) *(G-5315)*

R & B Partnership...828 298-7988
940 Tunnel Rd Asheville (28805) *(G-750)*

R & D Label LLC..336 889-2900
117 Wade St Jamestown (27282) *(G-9068)*

R & D Weaving Inc..828 248-1910
376 Pinehurst Rd Ellenboro (28040) *(G-5638)*

R & H Welding LLC...919 763-7955
3020 Cornwallis Rd Garner (27529) *(G-6306)*

R & J Mechanical & Welding LLC.. 919 362-6630
554 E Williams St Apex (27502) *(G-238)*

R & J Road Service Inc.. 252 239-1404
5014 Saint Marys Church Rd Lucama (27851) *(G-10018)*

R & L, Kings Mountain *Also Called: R and L Collision Center Inc (G-9328)*

R & R Ironworks Inc... 828 448-0524
501 Salem Rd Morganton (28655) *(G-11243)*

R & R Logging Inc.. 704 483-5733
1040 N Ingleside Farm Rd Iron Station (28080) *(G-8976)*

R & R Powder Coating Inc.. 704 853-0727
190 Gibson Ct Dallas (28034) *(G-4653)*

R & S Logging Inc.. 252 426-5880
771 Lake Rd Hertford (27944) *(G-7923)*

R & S Precision Customs LLC... 704 984-3480
338 E Main St Albemarle (28001) *(G-101)*

R & S Sporting Goods Ctr Inc... 336 599-0248
515 S Morgan St Roxboro (27573) *(G-13820)*

R A G S, Wilmington *Also Called: Ruth Arnold Graphics & Signs (G-16390)*

R A Serafini Inc.. 704 864-6763
111 Lagrande St Gastonia (28056) *(G-6500)*

R and L Collision Center Inc.. 704 739-2500
1207 S Battleground Ave Kings Mountain (28086) *(G-9328)*

R D Jones Packing Co Inc.. 910 267-2846
192 N Nc Hwy 50 Faison (28341) *(G-5725)*

R D Tillson & Associates Inc.. 336 454-1410
105 Cottonwood Dr Jamestown (27282) *(G-9069)*

R E B B Industries, Yadkinville *Also Called: Viewriver Machine Corporation (G-17061)*

R E Bengel Sheet Metal Co... 252 637-3404
1311 N Craven St New Bern (28560) *(G-11839)*

R E Mason Enterprises Inc (PA)... 910 483-5016
515 Person St Fayetteville (28301) *(G-5904)*

R Evans Hosiery LLC... 828 397-3715
8177 Grover Evans Sr Rd Connelly Springs (28612) *(G-4408)*

R Gregory Jewelers Inc (PA).. 704 872-6669
122 W Broad St Statesville (28677) *(G-14874)*

R H Bolick & Company Inc.. 828 322-7847
1210 9th Ave Ne Hickory (28601) *(G-8132)*

R J Reynolds Tobacco Company.. 336 741-0400
100 Moore-Rjr Dr Tobaccoville (27050) *(G-15319)*

R J Reynolds Tobacco Company.. 919 366-0220
7408 Siemens Rd Ste D Wendell (27591) *(G-15913)*

R J Reynolds Tobacco Company.. 252 291-4700
1500 Charleston St Se Wilson (27893) *(G-16527)*

R J Reynolds Tobacco Company.. 336 741-2132
950 Reynolds Blvd Bldg 605-12 Winston Salem (27105) *(G-16876)*

R J Reynolds Tobacco Company (DH).. 336 741-5000
401 N Main St Winston Salem (27101) *(G-16877)*

R J Rynolds Tob Holdings Inc (DH).. 336 741-5000
401 N Main St Winston Salem (27101) *(G-16878)*

R J Yeller Distribution Inc.. 800 944-2589
1835 Lindbergh St Charlotte (28208) *(G-3405)*

R Jacobs Fine Plbg & Hdwr Inc.. 919 720-4202
8613 Glenwood Ave Ste 103 Raleigh (27617) *(G-13167)*

R Jones Fabrication LLC.. 937 779-0826
270 Deerfield Dr Mooresville (28115) *(G-11067)*

R L Lasater Printing.. 919 639-6662
32 E Depot St Angier (27501) *(G-149)*

R L Roten Woodworking LLC... 336 982-3830
1312 Howard Colvard Rd Crumpler (28617) *(G-4630)*

R M Gear Harness... 336 498-1169
420 High Point St Randleman (27317) *(G-13486)*

R O Givens Signs Inc... 252 338-6578
1145 Parsonage St Elizabeth City (27909) *(G-5567)*

R R Donnelley, Gastonia *Also Called: R R Donnelley & Sons Company (G-6501)*

R R Donnelley, Wilson *Also Called: R R Donnelley & Sons Company (G-16528)*

R R Donnelley & Sons Company.. 919 596-8942
1 Litho Way Durham (27703) *(G-5316)*

R R Donnelley & Sons Company.. 704 864-5717
1205 Isley Rd Gastonia (28052) *(G-6501)*

R R Donnelley & Sons Company.. 252 243-0337
1900 Charleston St Se Wilson (27893) *(G-16528)*

R R Mickey Logging Inc.. 910 205-0525
1014 Boyd Lake Rd Hamlet (28345) *(G-7631)*

R Rabbit Inc... 910 297-6764
604 Woodland Forest Ct Wilmington (28403) *(G-16375)*

R Riveter LLC.. 406 321-2315
154 Nw Broad St Southern Pines (28387) *(G-14550)*

R S Integrators Inc... 704 588-8288
11172 Downs Rd Pineville (28134) *(G-12294)*

R S Skillen... 828 433-5353
2080 Us 70 E Morganton (28655) *(G-11244)*

R S Welding LLC.. 828 437-0768
5697 Morris Loop Morganton (28655) *(G-11245)*

R T Barbee Company Inc... 704 375-4421
724 Montana Dr Ste F Charlotte (28216) *(G-3406)*

R W Britt Logging Inc.. 252 799-7682
7281 Long Ridge Rd Pinetown (27865) *(G-12249)*

R W Garcia Co Inc... 828 428-0115
3181 Progress Dr Lincolnton (28092) *(G-9914)*

R-Anell Custom Homes Inc... 704 483-5511
3549 N Nc 16 Business Hwy Denver (28037) *(G-4797)*

R-Anell Housing Group LLC... 704 445-9610
235 Anthony Grove Rd Crouse (28033) *(G-4627)*

R. R. Donnelley & Sons, Durham *Also Called: PBM Graphics Inc (G-5277)*

R/W Connection Inc... 252 446-0114
136 S Business Ct Rocky Mount (27804) *(G-13726)*

R&D Plastics of Hickory Ltd.. 828 431-4660
345 26th Street Dr Se Hickory (28602) *(G-8133)*

R&H Machining Fabrication Inc.. 828 253-8930
329 Emma Rd Asheville (28806) *(G-751)*

R&J Custom Exhaust, Apex *Also Called: R & J Mechanical & Welding LLC (G-238)*

R&R Custom Embroidery LLC.. 336 693-5029
26 Bridger Farm Rd Hurdle Mills (27541) *(G-8912)*

R&R Iron Works, Morganton *Also Called: R & R Ironworks Inc (G-11243)*

R3cycle Industries LLC.. 404 754-4499
4417 Helms Rd Waxhaw (28173) *(G-15772)*

R65 Labs Inc.. 919 219-1983
108.5 E Parrish St Durham (27701) *(G-5317)*

R82 Inc... 704 882-0668
13137 Bleinheim Ln Matthews (28105) *(G-10284)*

RA Fountain LLC... 252 749-3228
6754 E Wilson St Fountain (27829) *(G-6096)*

Ra Printing & Sign LLC... 704 393-0264
8524 Walden Ridge Dr Charlotte (28216) *(G-3407)*

Rabbit Bottom Logging Co, Warrenton *Also Called: Rabbit Bottom Logging Co Inc (G-15660)*

Rabbit Bottom Logging Co Inc... 252 257-3585
Hc 151 Warrenton (27589) *(G-15660)*

Rabbit Press LLC... 919 703-8206
2029 Rabbit Run Raleigh (27603) *(G-13168)*

Rabbit Town Molding & Trim LLC.. 336 688-2162
3429 Miller Farm Dr Trinity (27370) *(G-15354)*

Rabid Games LLC... 704 754-6382
404 S Carolina Ave Spencer (28159) *(G-14602)*

Race Tech Race Cars Cmpnnts In... 336 538-4941
403 Macarthur Ln Burlington (27217) *(G-1481)*

Race Technologies Concord NC... 704 799-0530
7275 Westwinds Blvd Nw Concord (28027) *(G-4346)*

Rachel Dubois.. 919 870-8063
6013 Old Horseman Trl Raleigh (27613) *(G-13169)*

Rack Works Inc.. 336 368-1302
207 Premier Ln Pilot Mountain (27041) *(G-12201)*

Rackwise, Raleigh *Also Called: Rackwise Inc (G-13170)*

Rackwise Inc.. 919 533-5533
4020 Westchase Blvd Ste 470 Raleigh (27607) *(G-13170)*

Radcon Inc... 919 806-5233
1717 Southpoint Crossing Dr Durham (27713) *(G-5318)*

Radford Quarries Inc (PA).. 828 264-7008
5605 Bamboo Rd Boone (28607) *(G-1231)*

Radiator Specialty Company (PA).. 704 688-2302
600 Radiator Rd Indian Trail (28079) *(G-8959)*

Radon Control Inc.. 828 265-9534
Boone (28607) *(G-1232)*

ALPHABETIC SECTION

Raffaldini Vneyards Winery LLC... 336 835-9463
  450 Groce Rd Ronda (28670) *(G-13769)*
Rafters and Walls LLC.. 980 404-0209
  2312 W Randolph Rd Shelby (28150) *(G-14359)*
Ragg Co Inc... 336 838-4895
  627 Elkin Hwy North Wilkesboro (28659) *(G-12031)*
Rags Signs + Graphics LLC.. 910 793-9087
  102 Portwatch Way Ste C Wilmington (28412) *(G-16376)*
Rai Services Company... 336 741-6774
  401 N Main St Winston Salem (27101) *(G-16879)*
Rail-Scale-Models... 248 421-6276
  140 Tallowwood Dr Garner (27529) *(G-6307)*
Railroad Friction Pdts Corp.. 910 844-9709
  13601 Airport Rd Maxton (28364) *(G-10362)*
Rainbow Upholstery & Furniture, Wake Forest Also Called: Rufco Inc *(G-15585)*
Rainey and Wilson Logistics.. 910 736-8540
  1308 Checker Dr Raeford (28376) *(G-12434)*
Rainforest Nutritionals Inc... 919 847-2221
  9201 Leesville Rd Ste 120c Raleigh (27613) *(G-13171)*
Raleigh... 919 306-3208
  1216 Nikole Ct Raleigh (27612) *(G-13172)*
Raleigh Area Masters.. 919 233-6713
  13200 Falls Of Neuse Rd Raleigh (27614) *(G-13173)*
Raleigh Cabinet Works.. 919 412-7750
  4713 Grand Cypress Ct Raleigh (27604) *(G-13174)*
Raleigh Custom Woodwork Inc... 919 522-6621
  4712 Radcliff Rd Raleigh (27609) *(G-13175)*
Raleigh Denim, Raleigh Also Called: Raleigh Workshop Inc *(G-13188)*
Raleigh Downtowner... 919 821-9000
  12 E Hargett St Raleigh (27601) *(G-13176)*
Raleigh Engraving Co.. 919 832-5557
  806 N West St Raleigh (27603) *(G-13177)*
Raleigh Engraving Press, Raleigh Also Called: Raleigh Engraving Co *(G-13177)*
Raleigh Facility, Raleigh Also Called: Evergreen Packaging LLC *(G-12751)*
Raleigh Magazine.. 919 307-3047
  6511 Creedmoor Rd Ste 207 Raleigh (27613) *(G-13178)*
Raleigh Mechanical & Mtls Inc.. 919 598-4601
  7405 Acc Blvd Raleigh (27617) *(G-13179)*
Raleigh Plant, Raleigh Also Called: Eagle Rock Concrete LLC *(G-12714)*
Raleigh Powder Coating Co.. 919 301-8065
  2100 Garner Rd Raleigh (27610) *(G-13180)*
Raleigh Printing, Raleigh Also Called: Raleigh Printing & Typing Inc *(G-13181)*
Raleigh Printing & Typing Inc.. 919 662-8001
  5415 Fayetteville Rd Raleigh (27603) *(G-13181)*
Raleigh Ringers Inc... 919 847-7574
  2200 E Millbrook Rd Ste 113 Raleigh (27604) *(G-13182)*
Raleigh Road Box Corporation.. 252 438-7401
  Rr 9 Box 403 Henderson (27536) *(G-7806)*
Raleigh Rolls.. 919 559-0451
  411 W Morgan St Raleigh (27603) *(G-13183)*
Raleigh Saw Co Inc... 919 832-2248
  5805 Departure Dr Ste C Raleigh (27616) *(G-13184)*
Raleigh Screen Print Inc.. 919 662-0358
  307 Fields Dr Aberdeen (28315) *(G-24)*
Raleigh Shirt Printer.. 919 261-6628
  3125 Gresham Lake Rd Ste 104 Raleigh (27615) *(G-13185)*
Raleigh Sign Design... 919 244-1802
  5316 Shadow Valley Rd Holly Springs (27540) *(G-8711)*
Raleigh Sign Solutions LLC... 919 578-7255
  6548 English Oaks Dr Raleigh (27615) *(G-13186)*
Raleigh Tees.. 919 850-3378
  4909 Alpinis Dr Ste 113 Raleigh (27616) *(G-13187)*
Raleigh Ventures Inc... 910 350-0036
  6725 Amsterdam Way Wilmington (28405) *(G-16377)*
Raleigh Workshop Inc... 919 917-8969
  319 W Martin St Raleigh (27601) *(G-13188)*
Ralph B Hall... 919 258-3634
  804 Cox Maddox Rd Sanford (27332) *(G-14173)*
Ralph Harris Leather Inc... 336 874-2100
  219 Pat Nixon Rd State Road (28676) *(G-14730)*
Ralph Lauren Corporation... 336 632-5000
  4100 Beechwood Dr Greensboro (27410) *(G-7302)*
Ralph Lauren Corporation... 336 632-5000
  4190 Eagle Hill Dr High Point (27265) *(G-8504)*
Ralph S Frame Works Inc... 336 431-2168
  2231 Shore St High Point (27263) *(G-8505)*
Ram Industries Inc.. 704 982-4015
  1135 Montgomery Ave Albemarle (28001) *(G-102)*
Ram Jack Foundation Repair, Durham Also Called: Fs LLC *(G-5106)*
Ram Welding & Fabrication Inc... 704 985-8486
  1903 Lorelei Ct Mount Pleasant (28124) *(G-11677)*
Rama Sadri.. 919 875-8088
  4420 Jacqueline Ln Raleigh (27616) *(G-13189)*
Ramco.. 704 794-6620
  323 Corban Ave Sw Concord (28025) *(G-4347)*
Ramco Machine & Pump Svc Inc... 910 371-3388
  1054 Thistle Downs St Se Leland (28451) *(G-9558)*
Ramirezstucco Company... 828 458-8495
  62 Alverson Ln Hendersonville (28791) *(G-7894)*
Ramons Custom Framing LLC.. 252 208-8093
  3720 Buck Moore Rd Macclesfield (27852) *(G-10066)*
Ramseur Inter-Lock Knitting Co.. 336 824-2427
  2409 Old Lexington Rd Asheboro (27205) *(G-470)*
Ramsey Industries Inc... 704 827-3560
  816 Woodlawn St Belmont (28012) *(G-1005)*
Ramsey Products Corporation... 704 394-0322
  135 Performance Dr Belmont (28012) *(G-1006)*
Rancho Park Publishing Inc... 919 942-9493
  8 Matchwood Pittsboro (27312) *(G-12346)*
Rand Ange Enterprises Inc... 336 472-7313
  800 Bryan Rd Thomasville (27360) *(G-15270)*
Randall Printing Inc... 336 272-3333
  1029 Huffman St Greensboro (27405) *(G-7303)*
Randall Supply Inc (PA).. 704 289-6479
  2409 Walkup Ave Monroe (28110) *(G-10792)*
Randall-Reilly LLC... 704 814-1390
  1509 Orchard Lake Dr Ste E Charlotte (28270) *(G-3408)*
Randleman Carton Plant, Randleman Also Called: Caraustar Cstm Packg Group Inc *(G-13455)*
Randolph Goodson Logging Inc... 910 347-5117
  170 Jenkins Rd Jacksonville (28540) *(G-9025)*
Randolph Machine Inc (PA).. 336 625-0411
  1206 Uwharrie St Asheboro (27203) *(G-471)*
Randolph Machine Inc... 336 799-1039
  498 Pointe South Dr Randleman (27317) *(G-13487)*
Randolph Packing Company.. 336 672-1470
  403 W Balfour Ave Asheboro (27203) *(G-472)*
Random & Kind LLC.. 919 249-8809
  1348 Scholar Dr Durham (27703) *(G-5319)*
Random Rues Botanical LLC.. 252 214-2759
  1290 E Arlington Blvd Greenville (27858) *(G-7579)*
Randy Chappell Logging LLC.. 910 439-6690
  142 Hamilton Dr Mount Gilead (27306) *(G-11612)*
Randy D Miller Lumber Co Inc.. 336 973-7515
  538 Hwy 16 N Wilkesboro (28697) *(G-16038)*
Randy Smith and Sons Logging.. 828 263-0574
  826 Lawrence Greene Rd Deep Gap (28618) *(G-4712)*
Ranpak Corp.. 919 790-8225
  3401 Gresham Lake Rd Raleigh (27615) *(G-13190)*
Rapid Connector.. 843 315-4700
  136 Carolina Ct W Manteo (27954) *(G-10129)*
Rapid Cut, Wilmington Also Called: US Prototype Inc *(G-16439)*
Rapid Exchange, Clinton Also Called: Parker Gas Company Inc *(G-4101)*
Rapid Response Inc.. 704 588-8890
  218 Westinghouse Blvd Charlotte (28273) *(G-3409)*
Rapid Response Technology LLC.. 910 763-3856
  1900 Eastwood Rd Ste 27 Wilmington (28403) *(G-16378)*
Rapid River Magazine... 828 646-0071
  85 N Main St Canton (28716) *(G-1624)*
Rapid Run Transport LLC... 704 615-3458
  12430 Clackwyck Ln Charlotte (28262) *(G-3410)*
Rapidform Inc.. 408 856-6200
  1001 Winstead Dr Ste 400 Cary (27513) *(G-1865)*

Rapp Productions Inc... 919 913-0270
   103 W Weaver St Carrboro (27510) *(G-1654)*

Rapport Magazine Inc... 919 435-7690
   4262 Cherry Laurel Dr Se Southport (28461) *(G-14577)*

Raptor Attachments, Archdale Also Called: US Metal Crafters LLC *(G-301)*

Rasa Malaysia... 919 601-1765
   410 Market St Chapel Hill (27516) *(G-2062)*

Rated Best of Charlotte... 704 309-3810
   16151 Lancaster Hwy Ste A Charlotte (28277) *(G-3411)*

Ratoon Agroprocessing LLC.. 828 273-9114
   5290 Nc 226 S Marion (28752) *(G-10173)*

Rave Networx Inc... 910 808-9346
   1421 E Broad St Ste 408 Fuquay Varina (27526) *(G-6223)*

Raven Antenna Systems Inc....................................... 919 934-9711
   1315 Outlet Center Dr Smithfield (27577) *(G-14478)*

Raven Rock Manufacturing Inc................................... 910 308-8430
   803 E Broad St Dunn (28334) *(G-4880)*

Raven Sinclaire LLC... 828 423-3819
   177 Woodland Rd Asheville (28804) *(G-752)*

Ravenox, Burlington Also Called: Sgb13 LLC *(G-1492)*

Ravenox Rope... 336 226-5260
   2824 Anthony Rd Burlington (27215) *(G-1482)*

Raw Design Woodworks LLC..................................... 516 477-1963
   3825 Monticello St Indian Trail (28079) *(G-8960)*

Raw Earth Energy Corporation................................... 704 492-0793
   5004 Wilkinson Blvd Charlotte (28208) *(G-3412)*

Raw Elements... 704 307-8025
   8538 Carolina Lily Ln Charlotte (28262) *(G-3413)*

Rawco LLC... 908 832-7700
   18435 Train Station Dr Cornelius (28031) *(G-4580)*

Rawco Precision Manufacturing, Cornelius Also Called: Rawco LLC *(G-4580)*

Raxter Custom Bags... 864 421-5181
   1129 Brason Ln Wake Forest (27587) *(G-15579)*

Ray Houses Machine Shop... 919 553-1249
   110 N Tech Dr Clayton (27520) *(G-4006)*

Ray Publishing... 336 407-4843
   2360 Darwick Rd Winston Salem (27127) *(G-16880)*

Ray Roofing Company Inc... 704 372-0100
   2921 N Tryon St Charlotte (28206) *(G-3414)*

Raybow Usa Inc... 828 884-8656
   158 Mclean Rd Brevard (28712) *(G-1286)*

Raylen Vineyards Inc.. 336 998-3100
   3055 Heather Meadow Dr Winston Salem (27106) *(G-16881)*

Raymond Brown Well Company Inc........................... 336 374-4999
   1109 N Main St Danbury (27016) *(G-4663)*

Rays Classic Vinyl Repair Inc..................................... 910 520-1626
   440 Crooked Creek Rd Hampstead (28443) *(G-7654)*

Raysweathercom.. 828 264-2030
   240 Shadowline Dr Ste L Boone (28607) *(G-1233)*

Razor Motorsports... 704 517-0649
   3410 Country Club Dr Charlotte (28205) *(G-3415)*

Rb3 Digital Graphics, Wake Forest Also Called: Rb3 Enterprises Inc *(G-15580)*

Rb3 Enterprises Inc... 919 795-5822
   4701 Rogers Rd Wake Forest (27587) *(G-15580)*

Rbc Inc... 336 889-7573
   310 S Elm St High Point (27260) *(G-8506)*

Rbc Inc (PA).. 336 889-7333
   7310 Us Highway 311 Sophia (27350) *(G-14521)*

Rbi.. 336 605-0121
   7025 Albert Pick Rd Ste 200 Greensboro (27409) *(G-7304)*

Rbi Manufacturing Inc... 252 977-6764
   4642 S Us Highway 301 Rocky Mount (27803) *(G-13727)*

Rbi Precision, Rocky Mount Also Called: Rbi Manufacturing Inc *(G-13727)*

Rbw LLC... 919 319-1289
   105 Graywick Way Cary (27513) *(G-1866)*

RC Boldt Publishing LLC (PA)..................................... 904 624-0033
   804 Ocean Dr Oak Island (28465) *(G-12054)*

RC Boldt Publishing LLC.. 904 624-0033
   701 N Howe St Ste 6 Southport (28461) *(G-14578)*

RC Industries.. 828 693-1953
   931 Mid Allen Rd Hendersonville (28792) *(G-7895)*

RC Investment Company.. 336 226-5511
   2727 Tucker St Extension Burlington (27215) *(G-1483)*

Rclgh Inc.. 828 707-4383
   69 Bingham Rd Asheville (28806) *(G-753)*

RCM Industries Inc.. 828 286-4003
   401 Aallied Dr Rutherfordton (28139) *(G-13886)*

Rcnc Inc... 919 728-6691
   8817 Timberland Dr Wake Forest (27587) *(G-15581)*

Rcr Welding LLC.. 704 200-8527
   6011 Delta Crossing Ln Apt A Charlotte (28212) *(G-3416)*

Rcws Inc (PA).. 919 680-2655
   421 W Corporation St Durham (27701) *(G-5320)*

RDc Debris Removal Cnstr LLC.................................. 323 614-2353
   149 Rainbow Ln Smithfield (27577) *(G-14479)*

Rdd Pharma Inc.. 302 319-9970
   8480 Honeycutt Rd Ste 120 Raleigh (27615) *(G-13191)*

RDM Industrial Electronics Inc (PA)........................... 828 652-8346
   850 Harmony Grove Rd Nebo (28761) *(G-11763)*

Rdu Print Studio LLC.. 919 260-0173
   1509 Ward St Durham (27707) *(G-5321)*

RE Shads Group LLC... 704 299-8972
   5819 Creola Rd Charlotte (28270) *(G-3417)*

Re-Crtion Sstainable Wdwkg LLC.............................. 919 612-4791
   315 Yadkin Dr Raleigh (27609) *(G-13192)*

React Innovations LLC... 704 773-1276
   1809 Browning Ave Charlotte (28205) *(G-3418)*

Readable Communications Inc................................... 919 876-5260
   2609 Spring Forest Rd Raleigh (27616) *(G-13193)*

Readers Publishing LLC.. 910 728-2911
   307 N Green St Parkton (28371) *(G-12171)*

Readilite & Barricade Inc (PA).................................... 919 231-8309
   708 Freedom Dr Raleigh (27610) *(G-13194)*

Ready Mix, Charlotte Also Called: Redi-Mix LP *(G-3423)*

Ready Mix Concrete, Durham Also Called: Chandler Concrete Inc *(G-5012)*

Ready Mix Concrete, Washington Also Called: Argos USA LLC *(G-15682)*

Ready Mix Concrete Co, Sims Also Called: Argos USA LLC *(G-14439)*

Ready Mix Concrete of Sanford, Raleigh Also Called: Argos USA LLC *(G-12521)*

Ready Mix of Carolinas Inc.. 704 888-3027
   364 Browns Hill Rd Locust (28097) *(G-9967)*

Ready Mixed Concrete.. 252 758-1181
   3928 Jolly Rd Ayden (28513) *(G-854)*

Ready Mixed Concrete, Clinton Also Called: Argos USA LLC *(G-4088)*

Ready Mixed Concrete, New Bern Also Called: Smyrna Ready Mix Concrete LLC *(G-11847)*

Ready Mixed Concrete, Williamston Also Called: Argos USA LLC *(G-16057)*

Ready Mixed Concrete Co, Dunn Also Called: Argos USA LLC *(G-4852)*

Ready Mixed Concrete Co, Raleigh Also Called: Argos USA LLC *(G-12520)*

Ready Mixed Concrete Co, Roanoke Rapids Also Called: Argos USA LLC *(G-13566)*

Ready Mixed Concrete Co Fuquay, Fuquay Varina Also Called: Argos USA LLC *(G-6180)*

Ready Mixed Concrete Company, Raleigh Also Called: Argos Ready Mix (carolinas) Corp *(G-12519)*

Ready Solutions Inc.. 704 534-9221
   112 Eden St Davidson (28036) *(G-4693)*

Ready When You Are... 828 243-7514
   7 Sabrina Dr Arden (28704) *(G-370)*

Readymixed, Newport Also Called: Argos USA LLC *(G-11897)*

Reagan Enterprises LLC.. 704 564-7588
   183 Natures Trl Statesville (28625) *(G-14875)*

Real Estate Book, The, Charlotte Also Called: Colefields Publishing Inc *(G-2523)*

Real Producers, Mooresville Also Called: Roosterfish Media LLC *(G-11072)*

Real Prprty Mngment Trstworthy, Durham Also Called: Burchette Services Corporation *(G-4992)*

Real Time Content, Charlotte Also Called: Randall-Reilly LLC *(G-3408)*

Reality Check Sports, Concord Also Called: Ics North America Corp *(G-4283)*

Realxperience LLC.. 512 775-4386
   5109 Sweet Clover Ct Durham (27703) *(G-5322)*

Reaper Custom Fabrication LLC................................ 336 972-4065
   7245 Donnaha Rd Tobaccoville (27050) *(G-15320)*

Reapers Relgous Secret Soc, Concord Also Called: Dark Hydrogen LLC *(G-4251)*

Rebb Industries Inc... 336 463-2311
   1617 Fern Valley Rd Yadkinville (27055) *(G-17048)*

ALPHABETIC SECTION

Rebecca Kaye International, Raeford Also Called: Rebecca Trickey (G-12435)
Rebecca Trickey..910 584-5549
  389 Gibson Dr Raeford (28376) (G-12435)
Rec Plus Inc..704 375-9098
  1101 Central Ave Charlotte (28204) (G-3419)
Recap Inc..336 299-8794
  5201 Woodberry Forest Rd Greensboro (27406) (G-7305)
Recipharm Laboratories Inc.......................................919 884-2064
  511 Davis Dr Ste 100 Morrisville (27560) (G-11416)
Reclaim, Wake Forest Also Called: Reclaim Filters and Systems (G-15582)
Reclaim Filters and Systems (PA).............................919 528-1787
  1129 Hidden Hills Dr Wake Forest (27587) (G-15582)
Recon Usa LLC...252 206-1391
  4744 Potato House Ct Wilson (27893) (G-16529)
Reconditioning Dept, Thomasville Also Called: Mickey Truck Bodies Inc (G-15248)
Record Publishing Company......................................910 230-1948
  99 W Broad St Dunn (28334) (G-4881)
Record Stor Depot-Shred Depo, Greensboro Also Called: Piedmont Paper Stock LLC (G-7259)
Record Usa Inc (PA)...704 289-9212
  4324 Phil Hargett Ct Monroe (28110) (G-10793)
Recoupl Inc..704 544-0202
  16430 Redstone Mtn Ln Charlotte (28277) (G-3420)
Red 5 Printing LLC..704 996-3848
  18631 Northline Dr Cornelius (28031) (G-4581)
Red Aamerosa Leatherworks LLC.............................717 991-0308
  26381 Red Barn Trl Locust (28097) (G-9968)
Red Adept Publishing LLC...919 798-7410
  104 Bugenfield Ct Garner (27529) (G-6308)
Red Bull Distribution Co Inc......................................910 500-1566
  95 Outer Banks Dr Havelock (28532) (G-7745)
Red Clay Ciderworks..980 498-0676
  245 Clanton Rd Charlotte (28217) (G-3421)
Red Dog Publications Inc..919 782-4422
  3804 City Of Oaks Wynd Raleigh (27612) (G-13195)
Red Gremlin Design Studio, Boone Also Called: Max B Smith Jr (G-1219)
Red Hand Media LLC (PA)...704 523-6987
  1230 W Morehead St Ste 308 Charlotte (28208) (G-3422)
Red Hat Inc (HQ)..919 754-3700
  100 E Davie St Raleigh (27601) (G-13196)
Red Hat SA I LLC (DH)...919 754-3700
  100 E Davie St Raleigh (27601) (G-13197)
Red House Cabinets LLC..919 201-2101
  9660 Falls Of Neuse Rd Raleigh (27615) (G-13198)
Red Maple Logging Company Inc............................704 279-6379
  10007 Meismer Ln Rockwell (28138) (G-13657)
Red Oak Sales Company (PA)...................................704 483-8464
  7912 Commerce Dr Denver (28037) (G-4798)
Red Pepper Salsa...503 799-9170
  336 Cheltenham Dr Winston Salem (27103) (G-16882)
Red Shed Woodworks Inc...828 768-3854
  200 Carl Bowman Rd Marshall (28753) (G-10207)
Red Sky Shelters LLC..828 258-8417
  2002 Riverside Dr Ste 42h Asheville (28804) (G-754)
Red Springs Distribution Ctr, Red Springs Also Called: Dayco Products LLC (G-13497)
Red Wolfe Industries LLC..336 570-2282
  1118 Crowsnest Dr Hurdle Mills (27541) (G-8913)
Redbird Screen Printing LLC....................................919 946-0005
  8711 Owl Roost Pl Raleigh (27617) (G-13199)
Reddick & Reddick LLC..919 845-7333
  5500 Somerford Ln Raleigh (27614) (G-13200)
Reddick Equipment Co NC LLC................................252 792-1191
  1909 W Main St Williamston (27892) (G-16068)
Reddy Ice Group Inc..704 824-4611
  2306 Lowell Rd Gastonia (28054) (G-6502)
Redhawk Publishing...919 274-6477
  2312 Quartz Ct Raleigh (27610) (G-13201)
Redhill Biopharma Inc...984 444-7010
  8045 Arco Corporate Dr Raleigh (27617) (G-13202)
Redi-Frame Inc...828 322-4227
  207 20th St Se Hickory (28602) (G-8134)

Redi-Mix Concrete, Castle Hayne Also Called: Argos USA LLC (G-1943)
Redi-Mix Concrete, Denver Also Called: Argos USA LLC (G-4763)
Redi-Mix Concrete, Garner Also Called: Argos USA LLC (G-6255)
Redi-Mix Concrete, Hickory Also Called: Argos USA LLC (G-7941)
Redi-Mix Concrete, Mooresville Also Called: Argos USA LLC (G-10862)
Redi-Mix Concrete, Winston Salem Also Called: Argos USA LLC (G-16609)
Redi-Mix LP...704 596-6511
  11509 Reames Rd Charlotte (28269) (G-3423)
Redrum Press..910 399-1334
  3128 Kitty Hawk Rd Wilmington (28405) (G-16379)
Redrum Press..866 374-7881
  414 S 5th Ave Wilmington (28401) (G-16380)
Redtail Group LLC..828 539-4700
  2131 Us 70 Hwy Unit C Swannanoa (28778) (G-15033)
Redux Beverages LLC..951 304-1144
  2318 Oakhurst Trl Hillsborough (27278) (G-8666)
Redy Mix of Carolinas Inc...704 888-2224
  364 Browns Hill Rd Locust (28097) (G-9969)
Reeb Millwork Corporation.......................................336 751-4650
  346 Bethel Church Rd Mocksville (27028) (G-10601)
Reecewreathandcraftsetsycom................................828 252-6228
  121 Old Nc 20 Hwy Alexander (28701) (G-119)
Reeder Pallet Company Inc......................................336 879-3095
  435 Reeder Rd Seagrove (27341) (G-14245)
Reedy Chem Foam Spclty Addtves, Charlotte Also Called: Reedy International Corp (G-3424)
Reedy International Corp (PA)..................................980 819-6930
  9301 Forsyth Park Dr Ste A Charlotte (28273) (G-3424)
Reel Solutions Inc..910 947-3117
  1341 Red Branch Rd Carthage (28327) (G-1665)
Reel-Scout Inc..704 348-1484
  1900 Abbott St Ste 100 Charlotte (28203) (G-3425)
Reel-Tex Inc..704 868-4419
  4905 Sparrow Dairy Rd Gastonia (28056) (G-6503)
Reese Sign Service, Goldsboro Also Called: Reese Sign Service Inc (G-6649)
Reese Sign Service Inc...919 580-0705
  3271 Us Highway 117 N Goldsboro (27530) (G-6649)
Reeses Balloon Art..919 303-2147
  114 Seymour Creek Dr Cary (27519) (G-1867)
Reeves Indus Wldg Fabrication...............................910 399-7127
  5479 Goose Neck Rd Ne Riegelwood (28456) (G-13562)
Refab Wood LLC..919 272-2589
  1501 S Blount St Raleigh (27603) (G-13203)
Refined Outdoors LLC...704 634-4027
  2004 Ridge Rd Monroe (28110) (G-10794)
Refinery 56 LLC..910 215-0596
  8 Apawamis Rd Pinehurst (28374) (G-12233)
Refractory Construction, Salisbury Also Called: Virginia Carolina Refr Inc (G-14062)
Refresco Beverages US Inc......................................252 234-0493
  4843 International Blvd Wilson (27893) (G-16530)
Refresco Beverages US Inc......................................252 234-0493
  1805 Purina Cir S Wilson (27893) (G-16531)
Refresco Wilson, Wilson Also Called: Refresco Beverages US Inc (G-16530)
Regal Rexnord Corporation......................................800 825-6544
  701 Carrier Dr Charlotte (28216) (G-3426)
Regency Fibers LLC...828 459-7645
  2788 S Oxford St Claremont (28610) (G-3936)
Regimental Flag & T Shirts.......................................919 496-2888
  29 Secession Ln Louisburg (27549) (G-9999)
Reginald DWayne Dillard..980 254-5505
  13026 Planters Row Dr Charlotte (28278) (G-3427)
Region 3 Tasc Services, High Point Also Called: High Point Enterprise Inc (G-8388)
Regional Truckng Company LLC..............................910 228-0245
  389 Darlington Ave # 102 Wilmington (28403) (G-16381)
Rego, Burlington Also Called: Engineered Controls Intl LLC (G-1411)
Regulator Marine Inc...252 482-3837
  187 Peanut Dr Edenton (27932) (G-5521)
Rehab Solutions Inc..800 273-3418
  3029 Senna Dr Matthews (28105) (G-10285)
Reich LLC..828 651-9019
  140 Vista Blvd Arden (28704) (G-371)

Reichhold Holdings Us Inc

Reichhold Holdings Us Inc... 919 990-7500
   1035 Swabia Ct Durham (27703) *(G-5323)*

Reichhold Liquidation, Inc., Durham Also Called: Liquidating Reichhold Inc *(G-5191)*

Reid For Read Publishing LLC.. 910 263-8090
   6402 Redcliff Dr Fayetteville (28311) *(G-5905)*

Reissmann Entertainment Inc... 734 641-4434
   126 Upper Lake Dr Statesville (28677) *(G-14876)*

Relentless Wldg & Fabrication.. 336 402-3749
   903 Londonderry Dr High Point (27265) *(G-8507)*

Reliable Bedding Company.. 336 883-0648
   7147 Mendenhall Rd Archdale (27263) *(G-297)*

Reliable Bedding Company.. 336 886-7036
   414 South Rd High Point (27262) *(G-8508)*

Reliable Construction Co Inc... 704 289-1501
   100 N Sutherland Ave Ste A Monroe (28110) *(G-10795)*

Reliable Hauling and Grading, Concord Also Called: Reliable Woodworks Inc *(G-4349)*

Reliable Quilting, High Point Also Called: Reliable Bedding Company *(G-8508)*

Reliable Quilting Company.. 336 886-7036
   414 South Rd High Point (27262) *(G-8509)*

Reliable Wallcovering LLC.. 980 565-5224
   7156 Weddington Rd Nw Concord (28027) *(G-4348)*

Reliable Woodworks Inc.. 704 785-9663
   2989 Old Salisbury Concord Rd Concord (28025) *(G-4349)*

Reliance Management Group Inc... 704 282-2255
   4910 Starcrest Dr Monroe (28110) *(G-10796)*

Reliant Rubber Co, Wake Forest Also Called: Tim P Krahulec *(G-15603)*

Relic Wood LLC... 828 855-8924
   1050 Sipe Rd Taylorsville (28681) *(G-15160)*

Relyus, Hope Mills Also Called: William George Printing LLC *(G-8738)*

Reman Technologies Inc... 704 921-2293
   11421 Reames Rd Charlotte (28269) *(G-3428)*

Remedios LLC... 203 453-6000
   1301 Westinghouse Blvd Ste I Charlotte (28273) *(G-3429)*

Remington 1816 Foundation... 866 686-7778
   1435 W Morehead St Ste 120 Charlotte (28208) *(G-3430)*

Remington Arms Company LLC... 800 544-8892
   870 Remington Dr Madison (27025) *(G-10085)*

Remington Arms Company LLC... 800 544-8892
   870 Remington Dr Madison (27025) *(G-10086)*

Remodeez LLC.. 704 428-9050
   1920 Abbott St Ste 303 Charlotte (28203) *(G-3431)*

Rempac LLC.. 910 737-6557
   2005 Starlite Dr Lumberton (28358) *(G-10051)*

Rena Sales... 704 364-3006
   3120 Latrobe Dr Ste 230 Charlotte (28211) *(G-3432)*

Renaissance Fiber LLC.. 860 857-5987
   500 W 5th St Ste 400 Winston Salem (27101) *(G-16883)*

Renaissance Innovations LLC (PA).. 844 473-7246
   1322 Gloriosa St Apex (27523) *(G-239)*

Renaissance Innovations LLC... 774 901-4642
   2534 Whilden Dr Durham (27713) *(G-5324)*

Renew Life Cleansing Co, Durham Also Called: Renew Life Formulas LLC *(G-5325)*

Renew Life Formulas LLC (HQ).. 727 450-1061
   210 W Pettigrew St Durham (27701) *(G-5325)*

Renew Protect LLC... 828 318-5654
   127 Windago Rd Weaverville (28787) *(G-15859)*

Renew Recycling LLC... 919 550-8012
   440 S Tech Park Ln Clayton (27520) *(G-4007)*

Renewable Power Producers LLC.. 704 844-8990
   10600 Nations Ford Rd # 150 Charlotte (28273) *(G-3433)*

Renewble Enrgy Intgrtion Group... 704 596-6186
   9115 Old Statesville Rd Ste A Charlotte (28269) *(G-3434)*

Renewco-Meadow Branch LLC.. 404 584-3552
   1609 Heritage Commerce Ct Wake Forest (27587) *(G-15583)*

Renfro Brands, Mount Airy Also Called: Renfro LLC *(G-11563)*

Renfro LLC.. 336 719-8290
   801 W Lebanon St Mount Airy (27030) *(G-11562)*

Renfro LLC (HQ).. 336 719-8000
   661 Linville Rd Mount Airy (27030) *(G-11563)*

Renfro LLC.. 336 786-3000
   304 Willow St Mount Airy (27030) *(G-11564)*

Renfro Mexico Holdings LLC.. 336 786-3501
   661 Linville Rd Mount Airy (27030) *(G-11565)*

Rennasentient Inc.. 919 233-7710
   301 Ashville Ave Cary (27518) *(G-1868)*

Renner Usa Corp.. 704 527-9261
   651 Michael Wylie Dr Charlotte (28217) *(G-3435)*

Renner Wood Companies.. 704 527-9261
   651 Michael Wylie Dr Charlotte (28217) *(G-3436)*

Rent A Guy Now LLC... 919 637-1104
   404 Butler Dr Garner (27529) *(G-6309)*

Rent Path Inc.. 919 567-8166
   913 Old Baron Dr Fuquay Varina (27526) *(G-6224)*

Renwood Mills, Newton Also Called: Renwood Mills LLC *(G-11963)*

Renwood Mills LLC.. 828 465-0302
   11 N Brady Ave Newton (28658) *(G-11963)*

Repair Services, Mills River Also Called: Western Crlina TI Mold Corp In *(G-10514)*

Replar Mfg Inc... 919 622-5942
   5 Beaufort Ct Durham (27713) *(G-5326)*

Resco Products Inc... 336 299-1441
   3600 W Wendover Ave Greensboro (27407) *(G-7306)*

Resco Products Inc... 336 299-1441
   3600 W Wendover Ave Greensboro (27407) *(G-7307)*

Rescued Wood Rehab LLC... 984 500-7904
   718 N Main St Fuquay Varina (27526) *(G-6225)*

Research Instruments Inc... 919 383-2775
   2618 Pleasant Green Rd Durham (27705) *(G-5327)*

Research Triangle Software Inc.. 919 233-8796
   109 Lochview Dr Cary (27518) *(G-1869)*

Research Trngle Edtrial Sltons... 919 808-2719
   9 Amador Pl Durham (27712) *(G-5328)*

Reservoir Group LLC.. 610 764-0269
   9219 Heritage Woods Pl Charlotte (28269) *(G-3437)*

Resident Culture Brewing LLC.. 704 333-1862
   2101 Central Ave Charlotte (28205) *(G-3438)*

Residential/Commercial Cnstr, Harrisburg Also Called: AMP Agency *(G-7701)*

Resinall Corp.. 252 585-1445
   302 Water St Severn (27877) *(G-14269)*

RESINALL CORP., Severn Also Called: Resinall Corp *(G-14269)*

Resinart East Inc... 828 687-0215
   201 Old Airport Rd Fletcher (28732) *(G-6034)*

Resolute Fabricators LLC.. 704 728-1249
   18708 W Catawba Ave Cornelius (28031) *(G-4582)*

Resource Management Associates.. 919 841-9642
   5720 Six Forks Rd Ste 201 Raleigh (27609) *(G-13204)*

Resource Recovery Company, Hickory Also Called: Poppe Inc *(G-8117)*

Restaurant Furniture Inc... 828 459-9992
   2688 E Us Highway 70 Claremont (28610) *(G-3937)*

Restoration Hardware Inc... 919 544-4196
   8030 Renaissance Pkwy Ste 805 Durham (27713) *(G-5329)*

Retail, Charlotte Also Called: Live It Boutique LLC *(G-3095)*

Retail Installation Svcs LLC... 336 818-1333
   142 Lexi Dr Millers Creek (28651) *(G-10495)*

Retail Market Place.. 984 201-1948
   950 W Market St Smithfield (27577) *(G-14480)*

Rethink Respironics, Davidson Also Called: Rethink Technologies Inc *(G-4694)*

Rethink Technologies Inc.. 980 250-4683
   605 Jetton St Davidson (28036) *(G-4694)*

Retro Meadery LLC.. 910 622-7098
   580 Meadow Ln Burgaw (28425) *(G-1348)*

Retrofix Screws LLC.. 980 432-8412
   821 Mitchell Ave Salisbury (28144) *(G-14036)*

Retroject Inc... 919 619-3042
   1125 Pinehurst Dr Chapel Hill (27517) *(G-2063)*

Reuben James Auto Electric... 910 980-1056
   7386 N West St Falcon (28342) *(G-5727)*

Reuel, Goldsboro Also Called: Pcore *(G-6643)*

Reuel Inc... 919 734-0460
   200 W Dewey St Goldsboro (27530) *(G-6650)*

Revels Turf and Tractor LLC (PA)... 919 552-5697
   2217 N Main St Fuquay Varina (27526) *(G-6226)*

Revi Technical Wear, Greensboro Also Called: Eatumup Lure Company Inc *(G-6988)*

ALPHABETIC SECTION — Richmond Investment

Revloc Reclamation Service Inc 704 625-4900
13024 Ballantyne Corporate Pl Ste 700 Charlotte (28277) *(G-3439)*

Revlon Inc 919 603-2782
1501 Williamsboro St Oxford (27565) *(G-12148)*

Revlon Inc 919 603-2000
1501 Williamsboro St Oxford (27565) *(G-12149)*

Revlon Accounts Payable, Oxford Also Called: Revlon Inc *(G-12148)*

Revlon Consumer Products Corp 919 603-2000
1501 Williamsboro St Oxford (27565) *(G-12150)*

Revmax Performance LLC 877 780-4334
4400 Westinghouse Blvd 2 Charlotte (28273) *(G-3440)*

Revolution Pd LLC 919 949-0241
379 White Smith Rd Pittsboro (27312) *(G-12347)*

Revolution Screen Printing LLC 704 340-4406
337 Dalton Ave Charlotte (28206) *(G-3441)*

Revoultion Oil Inc 704 577-2546
291 Cayuga Dr Mooresville (28117) *(G-11068)*

Revware Inc 919 790-0000
1645 Old Louisburg Rd Raleigh (27604) *(G-13205)*

Rex Oil Company, Thomasville Also Called: Petroliance LLC *(G-15263)*

Rexam Beauty and Closures Inc 704 551-1500
4201 Congress St Ste 340 Charlotte (28209) *(G-3442)*

Rexam Cosmetic Packaging, Charlotte Also Called: Rexam Beauty and Closures Inc *(G-3442)*

Reynaers Inc 480 272-9688
9347 D Ducks Ln Charlotte (28273) *(G-3443)*

Reynolda Mfg Solutions Inc 336 699-4204
1200 Flint Hill Rd East Bend (27018) *(G-5467)*

Reynolda Mfg Solutions Inc 336 699-4204
1200 Flint Hill Rd East Bend (27018) *(G-5468)*

Reynolds & Reynolds, Charlotte Also Called: Reynolds and Reynolds Company *(G-3445)*

Reynolds Advanced Mtls Inc 704 357-0600
10725a John Price Rd Charlotte (28273) *(G-3444)*

Reynolds American Inc (HQ) 336 741-2000
401 N Main St Winston Salem (27101) *(G-16884)*

Reynolds and Reynolds Company 321 287-3939
6000 Monroe Rd Ste 340 Charlotte (28212) *(G-3445)*

Reynolds Consumer Products, Huntersville Also Called: Reynolds Consumer Products Inc *(G-8885)*

Reynolds Consumer Products Inc 704 371-5550
14201 Meacham Farm Dr Huntersville (28078) *(G-8885)*

Rf Das Systems Inc 980 279-2388
8230 Trail View Dr Charlotte (28226) *(G-3446)*

Rf Micro Devices Inc 336 664-1233
7628 Thorndike Rd Greensboro (27409) *(G-7308)*

RFH Tactical Mobility Inc 910 916-0284
748 Dotmond Rd Milton (27305) *(G-10516)*

Rfhic US Corporation 919 677-8780
920 Morrisville Pkwy Morrisville (27560) *(G-11417)*

Rfmd, Greensboro Also Called: Rf Micro Devices Inc *(G-7308)*

Rfmd LLC 336 664-1233
7628 Thorndike Rd Greensboro (27409) *(G-7309)*

Rfmd Infrstrcture PDT Group In 704 996-2997
327 Hillsborough St Raleigh (27603) *(G-13206)*

Rfr, Oxford Also Called: Rfr Metal Fabrication Inc *(G-12151)*

Rfr Metal Fabrication Inc 919 693-1354
3204 Knotts Grove Rd Oxford (27565) *(G-12151)*

Rfsprotech LLC 704 845-2785
1320 Industrial Dr Matthews (28105) *(G-10286)*

RG Convergence Tech LLC 336 953-2796
1325 N Church St B Burlington (27217) *(G-1484)*

Rga Enterprises Inc (PA) 704 398-0487
4001 Performance Rd Charlotte (28214) *(G-3447)*

Rgees LLC 828 708-7178
170 Bradley Branch Rd Ste 6&7 Arden (28704) *(G-372)*

Rgf Printing 201 832-5233
6965 Snow Camp Rd Snow Camp (27349) *(G-14497)*

Rgpack Concrete LLC 919 561-0855
1255 Lyman Rd Chinquapin (28521) *(G-3893)*

Rhd Service LLC 919 297-1600
1001 Winstead Dr Ste 1 Cary (27513) *(G-1870)*

Rheem Manufacturing Company 336 495-6800
4744 Island Ford Rd Randleman (27317) *(G-13488)*

Rheem Sales Company, Randleman Also Called: Rheem Manufacturing Company *(G-13488)*

Rhf Investments Inc (PA) 828 326-8350
401 11th St Nw Hickory (28601) *(G-8135)*

Rhf Investments Inc 828 632-7070
165 Matheson Park Ave Taylorsville (28681) *(G-15161)*

Rhino Networks LLC 855 462-9434
1025 Brevard Rd Ste 8 Asheville (28806) *(G-755)*

Rhino Times, Greensboro Also Called: Snap Publications LLC *(G-7346)*

Rhinoceros Times 336 763-4170
216 W Market St Greensboro (27401) *(G-7310)*

Rhinoshelf.com, Angier Also Called: Innovative Design Tech LLC *(G-141)*

Rhoddie Bicycle Outfitters Inc 828 414-9800
257 Sunset Dr Blowing Rock (28605) *(G-1156)*

Rhyno Enterprises 252 291-6700
709 Tarboro St Sw Wilson (27893) *(G-16532)*

Rhythms Welding LLC 910 477-7150
596 Makatoka Rd Nw Supply (28462) *(G-15009)*

Riba Fairfield 919 294-4819
4116 Colville Rd Durham (27707) *(G-5330)*

Ribbon Enterprises Inc 828 264-6444
1640 Old 421 S Boone (28607) *(G-1234)*

Ribometrix 919 744-9634
701 W Main St Ste 200 Durham (27701) *(G-5331)*

Rice S Glass Company Inc 919 967-9214
107 Lloyd St Carrboro (27510) *(G-1655)*

Ricewrap Foods Corporation 919 614-1179
300 Business Park Dr Butner (27509) *(G-1549)*

Richa Inc 704 944-0230
231 E Tremont Ave Charlotte (28203) *(G-3448)*

Richa Inc (PA) 704 331-9744
800 N College St Charlotte (28206) *(G-3449)*

RICHA GRAPHICS, Charlotte Also Called: Richa Inc *(G-3449)*

Richard C Jones 919 853-2096
7823 Nc 561 Hwy Louisburg (27549) *(G-10000)*

Richard Chldress Racg Entps In 336 731-3334
236 Industrial Dr Welcome (27374) *(G-15874)*

Richard Chldress Racg Entps In (PA) 336 731-3334
425 Industrial Dr Welcome (27374) *(G-15875)*

Richard D Stewart 919 284-2295
201 W 2nd St Kenly (27542) *(G-9156)*

Richard E Page 704 988-7090
8500 Andrew Carnegie Blvd Charlotte (28262) *(G-3450)*

Richard Lewis Von 910 628-9292
1928 Indian Swamp Rd Orrum (28369) *(G-12117)*

Richard Petty Motorsports, Statesville Also Called: Rpac Racing LLC *(G-14879)*

Richard Scarborough Boat Works 252 473-3646
Ficket Lump Rd Wanchese (27981) *(G-15650)*

Richard Schwartz 914 358-4518
322 S College Rd Wilmington (28403) *(G-16382)*

Richard Shew 828 781-3294
6202 N Nc 16 Hwy Conover (28613) *(G-4491)*

Richard West Co Inc 252 793-4440
1174 Us Highway 64 W Plymouth (27962) *(G-12377)*

Richard Wilcox 919 218-5907
1400 Struble Cir Willow Spring (27592) *(G-16082)*

Richards Southern Soul Fd LLC 919 210-8275
6500 Paces Arbor Cir Apt 113 Raleigh (27609) *(G-13207)*

Richards Welding and Repr Inc 828 396-8705
3080 Dry Ponds Rd Granite Falls (28630) *(G-6753)*

Richards Wldg Met Fbrction LLC 919 626-0134
7324 Siemens Rd Wendell (27591) *(G-15914)*

Richardson Enterprises NC Inc 704 675-8666
3201 Puetts Chapel Rd Dallas (28034) *(G-4654)*

Richardson Racing Products Inc 704 784-2602
1028 Central Dr Nw Unit C Concord (28027) *(G-4350)*

Richfeld Prtable Buildings Inc 704 463-1802
321 W Church St Richfield (28137) *(G-13554)*

Richmond Dental and Medical, Charlotte Also Called: Barnhardt Manufacturing Company *(G-2283)*

Richmond Investment (PA) 910 410-8200
611 Airport Rd Rockingham (28379) *(G-13640)*

Richmond Millwork LLC... 910 331-1009
707 Haywood St Rockingham (28379) *(G-13641)*

Richmond Observer LLP... 910 817-3169
505 Rockingham Rd Rockingham (28379) *(G-13642)*

Richmond Specialty Yarns LLC................................ 910 652-5554
1748 N Us Highway 220 Ellerbe (28338) *(G-5643)*

Richmond Steel Welding.. 910 582-4026
895 Airport Rd Rockingham (28379) *(G-13643)*

Rickety Bridge Winery Inc USA................................ 336 781-0645
518 N Hamilton St High Point (27262) *(G-8510)*

Ricks Custom Marine Canvas.................................. 937 623-1672
20213 Middletown Rd Cornelius (28031) *(G-4583)*

Ricky Don Thornton... 910 271-2989
131 Whitted Ln Teachey (28464) *(G-15178)*

Ricky Locklair & Randy Locklai............................... 910 470-3222
619 Kelly Rd Wilmington (28409) *(G-16383)*

Ricky Wyatt Logging... 336 984-3145
5209 Speedway Rd North Wilkesboro (28659) *(G-12032)*

Rickys Welding Inc.. 252 336-4437
899 S Sandy Hook Rd Shiloh (27974) *(G-14392)*

Ricura Corporation... 704 875-0366
11515 Vanstory Dr Ste 110 Huntersville (28078) *(G-8886)*

Riddle & Company LLC.. 336 229-1856
1214 Turrentine St Burlington (27215) *(G-1485)*

Riddle Home & Gift, Burlington Also Called: Riddle & Company LLC *(G-1485)*

Riddle Inc... 919 724-3272
9117 Colony Village Ln Raleigh (27617) *(G-13208)*

Riddley Metals Inc... 704 435-8829
639 Washburn Switch Rd Shelby (28150) *(G-14360)*

Riddley Retail Fixtures Inc....................................... 704 435-8829
119 Bess Rd Kings Mountain (28086) *(G-9329)*

Ride Best LLC.. 252 489-2959
24267 Hwy 12 Rodanthe (27968) *(G-13756)*

Ridge Line Homes, Franklin Also Called: Elite Mountain Business LLC *(G-6128)*

Rifled Air Conditioning Inc....................................... 800 627-1707
2810 Earlham Pl High Point (27263) *(G-8511)*

Rigem Right.. 252 726-9508
173 Hankison Dr Newport (28570) *(G-11905)*

Rikki Tikki Tees.. 828 454-0515
764 S Haywood St Waynesville (28786) *(G-15818)*

Riley Defense Inc... 704 507-9224
25 18th St Nw Hickory (28601) *(G-8136)*

Riley Jaron.. 929 462-8300
509 Houston St Greensboro (27401) *(G-7311)*

Riley Power Group, Pinehurst Also Called: Riley Power Group LLC *(G-12234)*

Riley Power Group LLC.. 910 420-6999
100 Magnolia Rd Ste 2207 Pinehurst (28374) *(G-12234)*

Riley Technologies LLC... 704 663-6319
170 Overhill Dr Mooresville (28117) *(G-11069)*

Rim-TEC Castings Eastern LLC............................. 336 302-0912
421 Inwood Rd Asheboro (27205) *(G-473)*

Rim-TEC Castings Eastern LLC (PA).................... 336 302-0912
16109 Halle Marie Cir Ste 33 Davidson (28036) *(G-4695)*

Rinehart Racing Inc.. 828 350-7653
40 Cane Creek Industrial Park Rd Fletcher (28732) *(G-6035)*

Ringadoc, Raleigh Also Called: Practice Fusion Inc *(G-13130)*

Ringneck and Lure LLC.. 704 377-8581
661 Hempstead Pl Charlotte (28207) *(G-3451)*

Rings True LLC... 919 265-7600
200 N Greensboro St Ste B9 Carrboro (27510) *(G-1656)*

Rinker Materials.. 704 455-1100
2268 Speedrail Dr Harrisburg (28075) *(G-7724)*

Rinker Materials.. 704 827-8175
1725 Drywall Dr Mount Holly (28120) *(G-11650)*

Ripari Automotive LLC... 585 267-0228
2910 Patishall Ln Charlotte (28214) *(G-3452)*

Ripe Revival Produce LLC..................................... 252 567-8305
161 English Rd Rocky Mount (27804) *(G-13728)*

Ripoff Holsters, Wilmington Also Called: Arma Co LLC *(G-16117)*

Ripstop By Roll LLC... 877 525-7210
2101 Tobacco Rd Durham (27704) *(G-5332)*

Riptide Publishing LLC... 908 295-4517
128 Academy St Burnsville (28714) *(G-1532)*

Rise Over Run Inc (PA).. 303 819-1566
2131 Us 70 Hwy Unit C Swannanoa (28778) *(G-15034)*

Ritas One Inc... 919 650-2415
208 Dowington Ln Cary (27519) *(G-1871)*

Ritch Face Veneer Company................................. 336 883-4184
1330 Lincoln Dr High Point (27260) *(G-8512)*

Ritchie Foam Company Inc.................................... 704 663-2533
214 E Waterlynn Rd Mooresville (28117) *(G-11070)*

Ritchie Woodworks.. 980 322-7779
114 S Main St China Grove (28023) *(G-3887)*

Rite Instant Printing Inc... 336 768-5061
1011 Burke St Winston Salem (27101) *(G-16885)*

Ritenis Woodworks... 336 643-6426
3205 Oak Ridge Rd Summerfield (27358) *(G-14991)*

Riteway Express Inc of NC.................................... 828 966-4822
1106 Rosman Hwy Brevard (28712) *(G-1287)*

Ritter Fab LLC... 336 879-2428
5829 Riverside Rd Seagrove (27341) *(G-14246)*

Riverbank Screen Printing Co................................ 910 248-4647
470 Sherwood Rd Lumberton (28358) *(G-10052)*

Riverbed Technology LLC...................................... 415 247-8800
5425 Page Rd Ste 200 Durham (27703) *(G-5333)*

Riverbend Frameworks, Claremont Also Called: Carolina House Furniture Inc *(G-3903)*

Rivers Edge Woodworkers LLC............................. 252 443-5099
2728 Buff Rd Rocky Mount (27803) *(G-13729)*

Riverside, Wilmington Also Called: Riverside Adventure Company *(G-16384)*

Riverside Adventure Company............................... 910 457-4944
5 S Water St Wilmington (28401) *(G-16384)*

Riverside Brick & Supply, Winston Salem Also Called: Pine Hall Brick Co Inc *(G-16857)*

Riverside Cement Co.. 760 245-5321
2710 Wycliff Rd Raleigh (27607) *(G-13209)*

Riverside Knitting Dept.. 336 719-8252
661 Linville Rd Mount Airy (27030) *(G-11566)*

Riverside Mattress Co Inc..................................... 910 483-0461
225 Dunn Rd Fayetteville (28312) *(G-5906)*

Riverview Cabinet & Supply Inc............................ 336 228-1486
1111 N Riverview Dr Burlington (27217) *(G-1486)*

Riverwood Casual, Lexington Also Called: Riverwood Inc *(G-9774)*

Riverwood Inc.. 336 956-3034
632 Dixon St Lexington (27292) *(G-9774)*

Rize LLC... 910 487-9759
1882 Spiralwood Dr Fayetteville (28304) *(G-5907)*

Rk Enterprises LLC.. 910 481-0777
121 N Racepath St Fayetteville (28301) *(G-5908)*

RLM/Universal Packaging Inc................................ 336 644-6161
8607 Cedar Hollow Rd Greensboro (27455) *(G-7312)*

Rls Commercial Interiors Inc.................................. 919 365-4086
7212 Siemens Rd Wendell (27591) *(G-15915)*

Rm Liquidation Inc (PA)... 828 274-7996
81 Thompson St Asheville (28803) *(G-756)*

Rmb Custom Leather LLC..................................... 704 762-1614
966 Bay Dr Oakboro (28129) *(G-12080)*

RMC Advanced Technologies Inc......................... 704 325-7100
1400 Burris Rd Newton (28658) *(G-11964)*

Rmg Leather Usa LLC... 828 466-5489
1226 Fedex Dr Sw Conover (28613) *(G-4492)*

Rmi Plastic... 704 995-9489
184 Ringneck Trl Mooresville (28117) *(G-11071)*

RNS International Inc... 704 329-0444
5001 Sirus Ln Charlotte (28208) *(G-3453)*

Road Infrstrcture Inv Hldngs I (HQ)...................... 336 475-6600
115 Todd Ct Thomasville (27360) *(G-15271)*

Road King Trailers Inc... 828 670-8012
2240 Smoky Park Hwy Candler (28715) *(G-1588)*

Roadactive Suspension Inc................................... 704 523-2646
330 E Hebron St Ste D Charlotte (28273) *(G-3454)*

Roadmaster Truck Company, Grifton Also Called: Roadmster Trck Conversions Inc *(G-7602)*

Roadmasters Traffic Ctrl LLC................................ 704 585-9635
120 Tweety Bird Ln Statesville (28625) *(G-14877)*

ALPHABETIC SECTION — Rockwell Collins Inc

Roadmster Trck Conversions Inc.. 252 412-3980
   6482 N Highland Blvd Grifton (28530) *(G-7602)*

Roadrnner Mtrcycle Turing Trvl.. 336 765-7780
   2245 Lewisville Clemmons Rd Ste D Clemmons (27012) *(G-4059)*

Roadrunner Powder Coating... 919 749-5290
   12900 Raleigh Rd Benson (27504) *(G-1042)*

Roadsafe Traffic Systems Inc.. 919 772-9401
   913 Finch Ave High Point (27263) *(G-8513)*

Roanke Beacon, The, Plymouth Also Called: Washington Cnty Newspapers Inc *(G-12378)*

Roanoke Chowan Ready Mix Inc.. 252 332-7995
   108 Williford Rd Ahoskie (27910) *(G-65)*

Roanoke Truss Inc.. 252 537-0012
   711 E 15th St Roanoke Rapids (27870) *(G-13581)*

Roanoke Valley Steel Corp.. 252 538-4137
   101 Kennametal Dr Weldon (27890) *(G-15888)*

Roaring Lion Publishing... 828 350-1454
   47 Stone River Dr Asheville (28804) *(G-757)*

Roark Printing Inc.. 704 889-5544
   209 Main St Pineville (28134) *(G-12295)*

Robar Rpp LLC.. 860 480-6498
   700 Durant St Apt 102 Chapel Hill (27517) *(G-2064)*

Robbins Beane Inc... 336 953-5919
   621 Hazelwood St Asheboro (27205) *(G-474)*

Robbins Sign Supply Inc.. 828 758-1954
   2435 Hunt Ln Lenoir (28645) *(G-9650)*

Robbinsville Cstm Molding Inc.. 828 479-2317
   1450 Old Hwy 129 Robbinsville (28771) *(G-13610)*

Robbinsville Plant, Charlotte Also Called: CCL Label Inc *(G-2431)*

Robco Manufacturing Inc.. 252 438-7399
   651 Bearpond Rd Henderson (27537) *(G-7807)*

Roberson Logging LLC... 252 799-7076
   1834 Holly Springs Church Rd Williamston (27892) *(G-16069)*

Robert Abbey Inc (PA)... 828 322-3480
   3166 Main Ave Se Hickory (28602) *(G-8137)*

Robert Bergelin Company (PA)... 828 437-6409
   120 S Sterling St Morganton (28655) *(G-11246)*

Robert Blake.. 704 720-9341
   1522 La Forest Ln Concord (28027) *(G-4351)*

Robert Bosch Tool Corporation... 252 551-7512
   310 Staton Rd Greenville (27834) *(G-7580)*

Robert Bosch Tool Corporation... 704 735-7464
   1980 Indian Creek Rd Lincolnton (28092) *(G-9915)*

Robert Citrano... 910 264-7746
   1710 Dawson St Ste C Wilmington (28403) *(G-16385)*

Robert D Starr... 336 697-0286
   1211 Youngs Mill Rd Greensboro (27405) *(G-7313)*

Robert Gregory.. 919 821-9188
   309 Burkwood Ln Raleigh (27609) *(G-13210)*

Robert H Wager Company Inc.. 336 969-6909
   570 Montroyal Rd Rural Hall (27045) *(G-13851)*

Robert Hamms LLC... 704 605-8057
   3028 Proverbs Ct Monroe (28110) *(G-10797)*

Robert L Rich Tmber Hrvstg Inc.. 910 529-7321
   360 Rich Rd Garland (28441) *(G-6246)*

Robert Laskowski.. 203 732-0846
   232 Stony Branch Rd New Bern (28562) *(G-11840)*

Robert Raper Welding Inc... 252 399-0598
   5326 Evansdale Rd Wilson (27893) *(G-16533)*

Robert S Concrete Service Inc.. 910 391-3973
   508 Lamon St Fayetteville (28301) *(G-5909)*

Robert St Clair Co Inc... 919 847-8611
   7701 Leesville Rd Raleigh (27613) *(G-13211)*

Robert Wiggins Wood Work LLC.. 828 254-5644
   2 Lornelle Pl Asheville (28804) *(G-758)*

Robert Wrren MBL TV Prductions.. 910 483-4777
   2121 Middle Rd Eastover (28312) *(G-5482)*

Roberts Company, The, Winterville Also Called: Jbr Properties of Greenville Inc *(G-17004)*

Roberts Family Enterprises LLP... 919 785-3111
   7101 Ebenezer Church Rd Raleigh (27612) *(G-13212)*

Roberts Polypro Inc... 704 588-1794
   5416 Wyoming Ave Charlotte (28273) *(G-3455)*

Robertsons Woodworking... 336 841-7221
   6967 Weant Rd High Point (27263) *(G-8514)*

Robetex Inc (PA)... 910 671-8787
   2504 Fayetteville Rd Lumberton (28358) *(G-10053)*

Robins Lane Press, Lewisville Also Called: Gryphon House Inc *(G-9667)*

Robinson & Son Machine Inc.. 910 592-4779
   446 Faison Hwy Clinton (28328) *(G-4103)*

Robinson Hosiery Mill Inc.. 828 874-2228
   113 Robinson St Se Valdese (28690) *(G-15453)*

Robinson Manufacturing Company... 252 335-2985
   451 N Hughes Blvd Elizabeth City (27909) *(G-5568)*

Robinson Mch & Cutter Grinding... 704 629-5591
   1346 Ramseur Rd Bessemer City (28016) *(G-1080)*

Robinsons Welding Service.. 336 622-3150
   3465 Staley Store Rd Liberty (27298) *(G-9828)*

Robinwood Enterprises... 910 571-0145
   725 Railroad Ave Troy (27371) *(G-15412)*

Robix America Inc... 336 668-9555
   7104 Cessna Dr Greensboro (27409) *(G-7314)*

Robling Medical, Youngsville Also Called: Robling Medical LLC *(G-17093)*

Robling Medical LLC... 919 570-9605
   90 Weathers Ct Youngsville (27596) *(G-17093)*

Roblon US Inc.. 828 396-2121
   3908 Hickory Blvd Granite Falls (28630) *(G-6754)*

Robs Backhoe Service.. 910 295-3317
   1215 Foxfire Rd Aberdeen (28315) *(G-25)*

ROC-N-Soc Inc.. 828 452-1736
   151 Kelly Park Ln Waynesville (28786) *(G-15819)*

Rocas Welding LLC... 252 290-2233
   923 E Trinity Ave Ste F Durham (27704) *(G-5334)*

Rocco Inc... 252 634-1642
   1415 E Main St Havelock (28532) *(G-7746)*

Rocco Marie Ventures LLC... 704 341-8800
   209 Main St Pineville (28134) *(G-12296)*

Rochling Engineering, Dallas Also Called: Roechling Indus Gastonia LP *(G-4655)*

Rock Ages Winery & Vineyard.. 336 364-7625
   2150 Charlie Long Rd Hendersonville (28739) *(G-7896)*

Rock Ages Winery & Vinyrd Inc.. 336 364-7625
   1890 Charlie Long Rd Hurdle Mills (27541) *(G-8914)*

Rock Creek Welding Inc.. 828 385-1554
   58 Wildscreek Rd Bakersville (28705) *(G-888)*

Rock Industrial Services Inc.. 910 652-6267
   157 S Railroad St Ellerbe (28338) *(G-5644)*

Rock of Ages, Salisbury Also Called: Carolina Quarries Inc *(G-13936)*

Rock-Tenn Converting, Winston Salem Also Called: Westrock Converting LLC *(G-16972)*

Rock-Weld Industries Inc.. 336 375-6862
   3515 Associate Dr Greensboro (27405) *(G-7315)*

Rocket Installation LLC... 704 657-9492
   329 Talley St Troutman (28166) *(G-15391)*

Rockfish Creek Winery LLC.. 910 729-0648
   1709 Arabia Rd Raeford (28376) *(G-12436)*

Rockingham Now.. 336 349-4331
   1921 Vance St Reidsville (27320) *(G-13538)*

Rockingham Plant, Rockingham Also Called: Perdue Farms Incorporated *(G-13638)*

Rocks Remodeling Dirt & Gravel, Maxton Also Called: Jason Culbertson *(G-10357)*

Rocktenn In-Store Solutions Inc.. 828 245-9871
   376 Pine St Forest City (28043) *(G-6080)*

Rockwell Automation Inc... 919 804-0200
   113 Edinburgh South Dr Ste 200 Cary (27511) *(G-1872)*

Rockwell Automation Inc... 704 665-6000
   9401 Southern Pine Blvd Ste E Charlotte (28273) *(G-3456)*

Rockwell Automation Inc... 828 652-0074
   510 Rockwell Dr Marion (28752) *(G-10174)*

Rockwell Automation Inc... 828 645-4235
   70 Reems Creek Rd Weaverville (28787) *(G-15860)*

Rockwell Collins, Winston Salem Also Called: B/E Aerospace Inc *(G-16613)*

Rockwell Collins Inc... 336 744-3288
   190 Oak Plaza Blvd Winston Salem (27105) *(G-16886)*

Rockwell Collins Inc... 336 776-3444
   2599 Empire Dr Winston Salem (27103) *(G-16887)*

Rockwell Collins Inc... 336 744-1097
   1455 Fairchild Rd Winston Salem (27105) *(G-16888)*

Rockwood Lithium — ALPHABETIC SECTION

Rockwood Lithium.. 704 739-2501
  348 Holiday Inn Dr Kings Mountain (28086) *(G-9330)*
Rocky Mount Awning & Tent Co............................... 252 442-0184
  602 N Church St Rocky Mount (27804) *(G-13730)*
Rocky Mount Cord Company.................................... 252 977-9130
  381 N Grace St Rocky Mount (27804) *(G-13731)*
Rocky Mount Electric Motor LLC............................. 252 446-1510
  3870 S Church St Rocky Mount (27803) *(G-13732)*
Rocky Mount Mill LLC.. 919 890-6000
  2619 Western Blvd Raleigh (27606) *(G-13213)*
Rocky River Vineyards LLC..................................... 704 781-5035
  11685 Reed Mine Rd Midland (28107) *(G-10478)*
Rocky Springs Applicator....................................... 704 546-7560
  698 Rock Springs Rd Harmony (28634) *(G-7688)*
Roctool Inc... 888 364-6321
  5900 Westover Dr #15609 Sanford (27330) *(G-14174)*
Rod Jahner... 919 435-7580
  157 Crooked Gulley Cir Sunset Beach (28468) *(G-15003)*
Rod Rand Inc.. 336 565-4874
  5524 Eulis Rd Liberty (27298) *(G-9829)*
Rodeco Company.. 919 775-7149
  5811 Elwin Buchanan Dr Sanford (27330) *(G-14175)*
Roderick Mch Erectors Wldg Inc............................. 910 343-0381
  2701 Blue Clay Rd Wilmington (28405) *(G-16386)*
Rodney S Cstm Cut Sign Co Inc.............................. 919 362-9669
  600 Irving Pkwy Holly Springs (27540) *(G-8712)*
Rodney Tyler... 336 629-0951
  530 Albemarle Rd Asheboro (27203) *(G-475)*
Rodney's Sign Company, Holly Springs Also Called: Rodney S Cstm Cut Sign Co Inc *(G-8712)*
Rodriguez Welding LLC.. 980 299-9449
  4051 Walkers Cove Trl Charlotte (28214) *(G-3457)*
Roechling Indus Gastonia LP (DH).......................... 704 922-7814
  903 Gastonia Technology Pkwy Dallas (28034) *(G-4655)*
Roehrig Engineering Inc.. 336 956-3800
  603 Woodland Dr Greensboro (27408) *(G-7316)*
Roger D Thomas... 919 258-3148
  8313 Hillcrest Farm Rd Sanford (27330) *(G-14176)*
Rogers Express Lube LLC....................................... 828 648-7772
  167 Pisgah Dr Canton (28716) *(G-1625)*
Rogers Group Inc... 828 657-9331
  1385 Ferry Rd Mooresboro (28114) *(G-10840)*
Rogers Knitting Inc.. 336 789-4155
  181 Beasley Rd Mount Airy (27030) *(G-11567)*
Rogers Manufacturing Company (PA)..................... 910 259-9898
  505 W Wilmington St Burgaw (28425) *(G-1349)*
Rogers Portable Buildings, Burgaw Also Called: Rogers Manufacturing Company *(G-1349)*
Rogers Screenprinting EMB Inc (PA)....................... 910 628-1983
  10306 Nc Highway 41 S Fairmont (28340) *(G-5705)*
Rogers Screenprinting EMB Inc.............................. 910 738-6208
  1988 N Roberts Ave Lumberton (28358) *(G-10054)*
Rogue Custom Kote LLC.. 919 498-5000
  347 Altons Ln Sanford (27332) *(G-14177)*
Roi Sales Solutions Inc... 704 564-9748
  3313 Thaxton Pl Charlotte (28226) *(G-3458)*
Rol-Mol Inc.. 828 328-1210
  2205 Us Highway 70 Sw Hickory (28602) *(G-8138)*
Roland Brothers LLC.. 336 385-9013
  649 Carl Eastridge Rd Warrensville (28693) *(G-15653)*
Rolf Koerner, Charlotte Also Called: Rolf Koerner LLC *(G-3459)*
Rolf Koerner LLC.. 704 714-8866
  514 Springbrook Rd Ste B Charlotte (28217) *(G-3459)*
Roll-Tech, Hickory Also Called: Roll-Tech Molding Products LLC *(G-8139)*
Roll-Tech Molding Products LLC............................. 828 431-4515
  243 Performance Dr Se Hickory (28602) *(G-8139)*
Rollease Acmeda Inc.. 800 552-5100
  375 Workman St Sw Conover (28613) *(G-4493)*
Rollease Acmeda Dist Ctr, Conover Also Called: Rollease Acmeda Inc *(G-4493)*
Rolls Enterprises Inc.. 919 545-9401
  2277 Otis Johnson Rd Pittsboro (27312) *(G-12348)*
Romac Industries Inc.. 704 915-3317
  400 E Fields St Dallas (28034) *(G-4656)*
Romanos Pizza... 704 782-5020
  349 Copperfield Blvd Ne Ste A Concord (28025) *(G-4352)*
Romanos Pizza Italian Rest, Concord Also Called: Romanos Pizza *(G-4352)*
Romeo Six LLC... 919 589-7150
  260 Premier Dr Holly Springs (27540) *(G-8713)*
Romoco, Rocky Mount Also Called: Rocky Mount Cord Company *(G-13731)*
Ron Clearfield.. 828 683-4425
  21 Clear Water Creek Rd Leicester (28748) *(G-9519)*
Ronak LLC... 781 589-1973
  2302 Skye Ln Cary (27518) *(G-1873)*
Ronald... 828 433-1377
  205 N Sterling St Morganton (28655) *(G-11247)*
Ronald Lee Fulbright Lbr Inc................................. 704 462-1421
  6092 Smith Rd Vale (28168) *(G-15471)*
Rondol Cordon Logging Inc.................................... 252 944-9220
  101 Raccoon Run Washington (27889) *(G-15729)*
Ronnie A Mabe... 336 994-2257
  1122 Covington Rd King (27021) *(G-9280)*
Ronnie Boyds Logging LLC.................................... 336 613-0229
  153 Nance St Eden (27288) *(G-5501)*
Ronnie Garrett Logging... 828 894-8413
  4625 Landrum Rd Columbus (28722) *(G-4179)*
Ronnie L Poole... 336 657-3956
  14596 Nc Highway 18 N Ennice (28623) *(G-5685)*
Ronny D Phelps.. 828 206-6339
  12 E Lawson Rd Hot Springs (28743) *(G-8746)*
Roobrik Inc.. 919 667-7750
  301 S Elm St Ste 421 Greensboro (27401) *(G-7317)*
Roofing Supply... 919 779-6223
  3609 Jones Sausage Rd Garner (27529) *(G-6310)*
Roofing Tools and Eqp Inc (PA)............................. 252 291-1800
  3710 Weaver Rd Wilson (27893) *(G-16534)*
Roosevelt Tire Service Inc..................................... 704 864-5464
  191 E Franklin Blvd Gastonia (28052) *(G-6504)*
Roostem Hunting Products LLC.............................. 919 693-3359
  3000 Roostem Way Oxford (27565) *(G-12152)*
Roosterfish Media LLC.. 980 722-7454
  129 Ashford Hollow Ln Mooresville (28117) *(G-11072)*
Root Spring Scraper Co.. 269 382-2025
  1 York Pl Pinehurst (28374) *(G-12235)*
Roots Originals LLC... 573 673-1669
  4451 Cheyenne Ct Winston Salem (27106) *(G-16889)*
Roots Run Deep LLC... 919 909-9117
  90 Oak Leaf Trl Youngsville (27596) *(G-17094)*
Rose Ice & Coal Company..................................... 910 762-2464
  1202 Market St Wilmington (28401) *(G-16387)*
Rose Media Inc.. 919 736-1154
  200 N Cottonwood Dr Goldsboro (27530) *(G-6651)*
Rose of City Prints... 980 201-9133
  15120 Arbor Trail Ct Apt 1015 Charlotte (28277) *(G-3460)*
Rose Publishing... 828 669-1629
  12 W Cotton Ave Black Mountain (28711) *(G-1137)*
Rose Reprographics.. 336 222-0727
  2030 S Church St Burlington (27215) *(G-1487)*
Rose Welding & Crane Service I............................ 252 796-9171
  1060 S Gum Neck Rd Columbia (27925) *(G-4167)*
Rosendahl Nextrom USA Inc.................................. 828 464-2543
  4260 Nc Highway 10 E Claremont (28610) *(G-3938)*
Rositas Tortillas Inc... 910 944-0577
  1317 N Sandhills Blvd Aberdeen (28315) *(G-26)*
Ross Phelps Logging Co Inc.................................. 252 356-2560
  1548 Wakelon Rd Colerain (27924) *(G-4140)*
Ross Skid Products Inc... 828 652-7450
  7 Landis Rd Marion (28752) *(G-10175)*
Ross Woodworking Inc.. 704 629-4551
  125 L E Perry Rd Bessemer City (28016) *(G-1081)*
Ross Woodworking Inc (PA)................................... 704 629-4551
  1004 Dameron Rd Bessemer City (28016) *(G-1082)*
Rostra Powertrain Controls, Laurinburg Also Called: Marmon Holdings Inc *(G-9488)*
Rostra Precision Controls Inc................................ 910 291-2502
  3056 Nc Hwy 5 Aberdeen (28315) *(G-27)*

Rotary Club Statesville.. 704 872-6851
318 N Center St Statesville (28677) *(G-14878)*

Rotating Machinery Analys.. 512 743-1248
66 Quanv Ct Brevard (28712) *(G-1288)*

Rotec North American... 828 681-0151
95 Glenn Bridge Rd Arden (28704) *(G-373)*

Rotens Logging LLC.. 336 981-7019
466 Dowell Ridge Ln North Wilkesboro (28659) *(G-12033)*

Rothrock Industries.. 336 454-4549
103 Newberry St Jamestown (27282) *(G-9070)*

Roto-Plate Inc... 336 226-4965
2025 Cesnna Dr Burlington (27215) *(G-1488)*

Rotork-Fairchild Indus Pdts Co... 336 659-3400
3920 Westpoint Blvd Winston Salem (27103) *(G-16890)*

Rotron Incorporated... 336 449-3400
1210 Nc Highway 61 Whitsett (27377) *(G-16001)*

Round Peak Vineyards LLC... 336 352-5595
765 Round Peak Church Rd Mount Airy (27030) *(G-11568)*

Roundwood Logging Inc.. 252 230-9980
8421 Amber Rd Sims (27880) *(G-14444)*

Rouse Custom Stone... 336 655-1613
6680 Shallowford Rd Lewisville (27023) *(G-9672)*

Roush & Yates Racing Engs LLC.. 704 799-6216
112 Byers Creek Rd Mooresville (28117) *(G-11073)*

Roush & Yates Racing Engs LLC (PA)... 704 799-6216
297 Rolling Hill Rd Mooresville (28117) *(G-11074)*

Roush Yates Mfg Solutions, Mooresville *Also Called: Roush & Yates Racing Engs LLC* *(G-11073)*

Roush's Racing, Concord *Also Called: Rp Motor Sports Inc* *(G-4353)*

Router Bit Service Company Inc... 336 431-5535
7018 Tomball Rd High Point (27263) *(G-8515)*

Routh Sign Service.. 336 272-0895
318 Creek Ridge Rd Ste B Greensboro (27406) *(G-7318)*

Rovertym.. 704 635-7305
3308 Westwood Industrial Dr Ste E Monroe (28110) *(G-10798)*

Rowan Custom Cabinets Inc... 704 855-4778
2515 S Us 29 Hwy China Grove (28023) *(G-3888)*

Rowan Monuments LLC... 704 905-6651
116 Statesville Blvd Ste B Salisbury (28144) *(G-14037)*

Rowan Precision Machining Inc.. 704 279-6092
707 N Salisbury Ave Granite Quarry (28072) *(G-6761)*

Rowdy Manufacturing, Mooresville *Also Called: Rowdy Manufacturing LLC* *(G-11075)*

Rowdy Manufacturing LLC.. 704 662-0000
161 Byers Creek Rd Mooresville (28117) *(G-11075)*

Rowes... 828 241-2609
7546 Long Island Rd Catawba (28609) *(G-1967)*

Rowland Woodworking Inc.. 336 887-0700
111 E Market Center Dr High Point (27260) *(G-8516)*

Rowlett Publishing LLC... 828 285-2351
225 Lovely Ln Asheville (28803) *(G-759)*

Rowmark LLC.. 252 448-9900
182 Industrial Park Dr Trenton (28585) *(G-15334)*

Roxboro Broom Works, Roxboro *Also Called: Newell Novelty Co Inc* *(G-13808)*

Roxboro Ewp Mill, Roxboro *Also Called: Boise Cascade Wood Pdts LLC* *(G-13795)*

Roxboro Welding.. 336 364-2307
3735 Cates Mill Rd Roxboro (27574) *(G-13821)*

Roy Bridgmohan... 804 426-9652
596 Industry Dr Henderson (27537) *(G-7808)*

Roy Dunn.. 919 963-3700
101 Dunn St Four Oaks (27524) *(G-6111)*

Royal Appliance Manufacturing, Charlotte *Also Called: TTI Floor Care North Amer Inc* *(G-3736)*

Royal Baths Manufacturing Co.. 704 837-1701
4525 Reagan Dr # A Charlotte (28206) *(G-3461)*

Royal Blunts Connections Inc... 919 961-4910
4900 Thornton Rd Ste 109 Raleigh (27616) *(G-13214)*

Royal Brass & Hose... 704 847-2156
3731 Woodpark Blvd Ste A Charlotte (28206) *(G-3462)*

Royal Cheesecake Varieties LLC.. 919 670-8766
8458 Reedy Ridge Ln Raleigh (27613) *(G-13215)*

Royal Colony Furniture Inc... 336 472-8833
20 Carolina Ave Thomasville (27360) *(G-15272)*

Royal Cup Inc... 704 597-5756
3010 Hutchison Mcdonald Rd Ste F Charlotte (28269) *(G-3463)*

Royal Faires Inc (PA).. 704 896-5555
16445 Poplar Tent Rd Huntersville (28078) *(G-8887)*

Royal Hosiery Company Inc (PA).. 828 496-2200
10 N Summit Ave Granite Falls (28630) *(G-6755)*

Royal Impressions LLC.. 910 340-5955
2603 W Woodlyn Way Greensboro (27407) *(G-7319)*

Royal Manufacturing, Charlotte *Also Called: Royal Baths Manufacturing Co* *(G-3461)*

Royal Maple LLC (PA)... 704 900-5086
2908 Stewart Creek Blvd Charlotte (28216) *(G-3464)*

Royal Oak Stairs Inc... 919 855-8988
3201 Wellington Ct Ste 104 Raleigh (27615) *(G-13216)*

Royal Park Uniforms Inc... 336 562-3345
14139 Nc Highway 86 S Prospect Hill (27314) *(G-12408)*

Royal Textile Mills Inc... 336 694-4121
929 Firetower Rd Yanceyville (27379) *(G-17065)*

Royal Textile Products Sw LLC... 602 276-4598
2918 Caldwell Ridge Pkwy Charlotte (28213) *(G-3465)*

Royal Welding Inc.. 704 750-9353
413 N Polk St Pineville (28134) *(G-12297)*

Royal Welding LLC... 704 750-9353
413 N Polk St Unit H Pineville (28134) *(G-12298)*

Royal Wire Products Inc... 704 596-2110
7500 Grier Rd Charlotte (28213) *(G-3466)*

Royale Comfort Seating Inc.. 828 352-9021
140 Alspaugh Dam Rd Taylorsville (28681) *(G-15162)*

Royale Komfort Bedding Inc... 828 632-5631
2320 All Healing Springs Rd Taylorsville (28681) *(G-15163)*

Royalkind LLC... 252 355-7484
2131 Jubilee Ln Winterville (28590) *(G-17012)*

Royall Development Co Inc... 336 889-2569
325 Kettering Rd High Point (27263) *(G-8517)*

Royce Apparel Inc... 704 933-6000
408 Long Meadow Dr Salisbury (28147) *(G-14038)*

Royce Company, Knightdale *Also Called: Len Corporation* *(G-9420)*

Royce Company LLC... 910 395-0046
6500 Windmill Way Wilmington (28405) *(G-16388)*

Royce Too LLC (HQ)... 212 356-1627
3330 Healy Dr Ste 200 Winston Salem (27103) *(G-16891)*

Roz Inc.. 704 737-7940
206 N Hayne St Ste C Monroe (28112) *(G-10799)*

Rp Fletcher Machine Co Inc... 336 249-6101
4305 E Us Highway 64 Lexington (27292) *(G-9775)*

Rp Motor Sports Inc.. 704 720-4200
4202 Roush Pl Nw Concord (28027) *(G-4353)*

Rpac Racing LLC.. 704 696-8650
310 Aviation Dr Statesville (28677) *(G-14879)*

Rpj Honeycutt MBL Detail Press... 704 640-5987
895 Corriher Springs Rd China Grove (28023) *(G-3889)*

RPM Installions Inc... 704 907-0868
19843 Henderson Rd Cornelius (28031) *(G-4584)*

RPM Plastics, Statesville *Also Called: RPM Plastics Inc* *(G-14880)*

RPM Plastics Inc.. 704 871-0518
2301 Speedball Rd Statesville (28677) *(G-14880)*

RPM Plastics LLC... 704 871-0518
933 Meacham Rd Statesville (28677) *(G-14881)*

RPM Products Inc.. 704 871-0518
2301 Speedball Rd Statesville (28677) *(G-14882)*

RPM Wood Finishes Group Inc (HQ).. 828 261-0325
2220 Us Highway 70 Se Ste 100 Hickory (28602) *(G-8140)*

RPM Wood Finishes Group Inc... 828 261-0325
22 S Center St Hickory (28602) *(G-8141)*

RPM Wood Finishes Group Inc... 828 261-0325
22 S Center St Hickory (28602) *(G-8142)*

RPM Wood Finishes Group Inc... 828 728-8266
3190 Hickory Blvd Hudson (28638) *(G-8777)*

Rpp Acquisition LLC.. 919 248-9001
131 Johnston Pkwy Kenly (27542) *(G-9157)*

Rq Industries Inc... 704 701-1071
19 Franklin Ave Nw Concord (28025) *(G-4354)*

RR Donnelley, Durham *Also Called: R R Donnelley & Sons Company (G-5316)*
RR Powder Coatings..704 240-3266
569 S Grove Street Ext Lincolnton (28092) *(G-9916)*
Rrd Packaging Solutions, Greensboro *Also Called: PBM Graphics Inc (G-7248)*
Rs Bostic Service Inc..252 527-4781
2280 Hwy 258 S Kinston (28504) *(G-9381)*
Rs Industries Inc..704 289-2734
524 Marshall St Monroe (28112) *(G-10800)*
Rsa Security LLC..704 847-4725
250 N Trade St Matthews (28105) *(G-10287)*
RSC Bio Solutions LLC (HQ)..800 661-3558
2318 Arty Ave Charlotte (28208) *(G-3467)*
RSC Chemical Solutions LLC...704 821-7643
600 Radiator Rd Indian Trail (28079) *(G-8961)*
Rsf Solid State Lighting Inc..252 478-9915
3469 Peachtree Hills Rd Spring Hope (27882) *(G-14621)*
RSI Home Products Inc..828 428-6300
838 Lincoln County Pkwy Lincolnton (28092) *(G-9917)*
RSI Leasing Inc NS Tbt..704 587-9300
2820 Nevada Blvd Charlotte (28273) *(G-3468)*
Rsk Industries LLC..216 905-4014
841 Traditions Ridge Dr Wake Forest (27587) *(G-15584)*
RSR Fitness Inc..919 255-1233
1207 N New Hope Rd Raleigh (27610) *(G-13217)*
Rssbus Inc..919 969-7675
490 Sun Forest Way Chapel Hill (27517) *(G-2065)*
Rstack Solutions LLC..980 337-1295
3540 Toringdon Way Ste 200 Charlotte (28277) *(G-3469)*
Rt Cardiac Systems Inc..954 908-1074
5420 Deer Forest Trl Raleigh (27614) *(G-13218)*
RTC Ventures LLC..704 247-9781
4520 Westinghouse Blvd Ste B Charlotte (28273) *(G-3470)*
RTD Precision LLC..910 624-2624
7653 Spurge Dr Fayetteville (28311) *(G-5910)*
RTO Services LLC..919 596-5406
2805 E Us 70 Hwy Durham (27703) *(G-5335)*
Rtp Machine Inc..919 279-3338
120 Centrewest Ct Ste 111 Cary (27513) *(G-1874)*
RTS Screen Printing..252 972-3599
2259 Sandy Cross Rd Nashville (27856) *(G-11749)*
Rtst LLC..704 999-9906
243 Collingswood Rd Mooresville (28117) *(G-11076)*
Rtt Machine & Welding Svc Inc......................................919 269-6863
12671 W Nc 97 Zebulon (27597) *(G-17141)*
Rubber Mill, Liberty *Also Called: Rubber Mill Inc (G-9830)*
Rubber Mill Inc..336 622-1680
3109 15th Avenue Blvd Se Conover (28613) *(G-4494)*
Rubber Mill Inc..336 622-1680
9897 Old Liberty Rd Liberty (27298) *(G-9830)*
Rubbermaid, Huntersville *Also Called: Rubbermaid Commercial Pdts LLC (G-8888)*
Rubbermaid, Huntersville *Also Called: Rubbermaid Incorporated (G-8889)*
Rubbermaid, Huntersville *Also Called: Rubbermaid Incorporated (G-8890)*
Rubbermaid Commercial Pdts LLC (DH)........................540 667-8700
8900 N Pointe Executive Park Dr Huntersville (28078) *(G-8888)*
Rubbermaid Incorporated..888 859-8294
16905 Northcross Dr Ste 120 Huntersville (28078) *(G-8889)*
Rubbermaid Incorporated..704 987-4339
8936 N Pointe Executive Park Dr Huntersville (28078) *(G-8890)*
Rucker Intrgrted Logistics LLC......................................704 352-2018
15519 Rathangan Dr Charlotte (28273) *(G-3471)*
Ruckus Wireless Inc..919 677-0571
101 Stamford Dr Cary (27513) *(G-1875)*
Ruddick Operating Company LLC................................704 372-5404
301 S Tryon St Ste 1800 Charlotte (28282) *(G-3472)*
Rudisill Frame Shop Inc..828 464-7020
780 Buchanan Pl Newton (28658) *(G-11965)*
Rudys Logging Inc..910 918-2993
4006 Long Bow Ct Leland (28451) *(G-9559)*
Rufco Inc (PA)..919 829-1332
5101 Unicon Dr Wake Forest (27587) *(G-15585)*
Rufton Brewhouse..828 289-8060
177 N Main St Rutherfordton (28139) *(G-13887)*

Rufus N Ivie III..704 482-2559
4007 Hillview Dr Shelby (28152) *(G-14361)*
Rug & Home, Asheville *Also Called: Rug & Home Inc (G-760)*
Rug & Home Inc..828 785-4480
5 Rocky Ridge Rd Asheville (28806) *(G-760)*
Rugby Acquisition LLC..336 993-8686
637 Graves St Kernersville (27284) *(G-9229)*
Rugers Welding..919 471-8795
3617 Red Mountain Rd Rougemont (27572) *(G-13788)*
Rugged Metal Designs Inc..336 352-5150
1004 Red Hill Creek Rd Dobson (27017) *(G-4830)*
Ruhl Inc..910 497-3172
26 Mockingbird Ln Spring Lake (28390) *(G-14626)*
Ruhl Tech Engineering, Spring Lake *Also Called: Ruhl Inc (G-14626)*
Ruppards Welding Service LLC......................................828 386-8191
816 Millers Pond Ln Boone (28607) *(G-1235)*
Rusco Fixture, Norwood *Also Called: Rusco Fixture Company Inc (G-12043)*
Rusco Fixture Company Inc..704 474-3184
11635 Nc 138 Hwy Norwood (28128) *(G-12043)*
Rush Masonry Management LLC..................................910 787-9100
234 Clayton James Rd Jacksonville (28540) *(G-9026)*
Rushfurnitiure.com, High Point *Also Called: Vrush Industries Inc (G-8597)*
Ruskin Inc..828 324-6500
1189 27th Street Dr Se Hickory (28602) *(G-8143)*
Ruskin LLC..919 583-5444
166 Nc 581 Hwy S Goldsboro (27530) *(G-6652)*
Russ Knits Inc..910 974-4114
520 E Main St Candor (27229) *(G-1598)*
Russ Simmons..910 686-1656
414 Biscayne Dr Wilmington (28411) *(G-16389)*
Russell Custom Stone LLC..336 859-5755
2741 Highway 49 New London (28127) *(G-11877)*
Russell Finex Inc..704 588-9808
625 Eagleton Downs Dr Pineville (28134) *(G-12299)*
Russell Loudermilk Logging..828 632-4968
330 Dee Loudermelk Ln Taylorsville (28681) *(G-15164)*
Russell Printing Inc..404 366-0552
2589 Deep Creek Church Rd Burlington (27217) *(G-1489)*
Russell Standard, Greensboro *Also Called: Russell Standard Nc LLC (G-7321)*
Russell Standard Corporation......................................336 292-6875
1124 S Holden Rd Greensboro (27407) *(G-7320)*
Russell Standard Nc LLC..336 292-6875
1124 S Holden Rd Greensboro (27407) *(G-7321)*
Russell T Bundy Associates Inc....................................704 523-6132
3400 Pelton St Charlotte (28217) *(G-3473)*
Russell-Fshion Foot Hsy Mlls I......................................336 299-0741
875 N Main St Troy (27371) *(G-15413)*
Russian Chapel Hills Winery..828 863-0541
2662 Green Creek Dr Columbus (28722) *(G-4180)*
Rust-Oleum, Mooresville *Also Called: Rust-Oleum Corporation (G-11077)*
Rust-Oleum Corporation..704 662-7730
157 Cedar Pointe Dr Ste A Mooresville (28117) *(G-11077)*
Rust911 Inc..607 425-2882
925 3rd Ave Se Ste 102 Hickory (28602) *(G-8144)*
Rustic Grape LLC..828 319-7939
28 Greenwood Fields Dr Asheville (28804) *(G-761)*
Rustic Innovations LLC..804 822-2492
3138 Groveshire Dr Raleigh (27616) *(G-13219)*
Rustic Oak Sign Co..919 619-4452
4717 Longhill Ln Raleigh (27612) *(G-13220)*
Rut Manufacturing Inc..336 859-0328
211 Bingham Industrial Dr Denton (27239) *(G-4747)*
Ruth Arnold Graphics & Signs......................................910 793-9087
102 Portwatch Way Ste C Wilmington (28412) *(G-16390)*
Ruth Hicks Enterprise Inc..704 469-4741
9417 Marvin School Rd Waxhaw (28173) *(G-15773)*
Rutland Fire Clay Company..802 775-5519
1430 Environ Way Chapel Hill (27517) *(G-2066)*
Rutland Group Inc..704 553-0046
13827 Carowinds Blvd Ste A Charlotte (28273) *(G-3474)*
Rutland Group Inc (HQ)..704 553-0046
10021 Rodney St Pineville (28134) *(G-12300)*

ALPHABETIC SECTION

Rutland Holdings LLC (PA)..704 553-0046
10021 Rodney St Pineville (28134) *(G-12301)*

Rutland Plastic Technologies, Pineville *Also Called: Rutland Holdings LLC (G-12301)*

Rv One Superstores Charlotte, Concord *Also Called: Axle Holdings LLC (G-4203)*

Rvb Systems Group Inc...919 362-5211
5504 Quails Call Ct Garner (27529) *(G-6311)*

Rwm Casters, Gastonia *Also Called: Lsrwm Corp (G-6445)*

Rwm Casters, Gastonia *Also Called: Lsrwm Corp (G-6446)*

Rwm Casters, Greensboro *Also Called: Staunton Capital Inc (G-7368)*

Rx Textiles, Matthews *Also Called: Paceline Inc (G-10280)*

Ryjak Enterprises LLC..910 638-0716
1050 N May St Southern Pines (28387) *(G-14551)*

Rymon Company Inc..704 519-5310
2015 Ayrsley Town Blvd Ste 202 Charlotte (28273) *(G-3475)*

S & A Cherokee LLC...919 674-6020
301 Cascade Pointe Ln Ste 101 Cary (27513) *(G-1876)*

S & A Cherokee Publishing, Cary *Also Called: S & A Cherokee LLC (G-1876)*

S & B Scents Inc..828 287-9410
555 Mcentire Rd Rutherfordton (28139) *(G-13888)*

S & D Coffee Inc (HQ)..704 782-3121
300 Concord Pkwy S Concord (28027) *(G-4355)*

S & D Coffee and Tea, Concord *Also Called: S & D Coffee Inc (G-4355)*

S & D Machine & Tool Inc...919 479-8433
1404 Old Oxford Rd Durham (27704) *(G-5336)*

S & K Logging Inc..252 794-2045
1408 S King St Windsor (27983) *(G-16569)*

S & K Sand LLC...252 964-3144
380 Mill Creek Ln Bath (27808) *(G-916)*

S & L Creations Inc..704 824-1930
120 E 1st St Lowell (28098) *(G-10011)*

S & L Sawmill Inc...704 483-3264
3044 N Nc 16 Business Hwy Denver (28037) *(G-4799)*

S & S Deer Processing...704 827-6884
216 Helms Dr Mount Holly (28120) *(G-11651)*

S & S Repair Service Inc..252 756-5989
1196 Pocosin Rd Winterville (28590) *(G-17013)*

S & S Samples Inc...336 472-0402
880 Whitehart School Rd Thomasville (27360) *(G-15273)*

S & S Screenprinters LLC...704 707-5497
4135 Beauvista Dr Charlotte (28269) *(G-3476)*

S & S Trawl Shop Inc...910 842-9197
896 Stanbury Rd Sw Supply (28462) *(G-15010)*

S & S Trucking Company..910 843-6264
604 E 4th Ave Red Springs (28377) *(G-13503)*

S & W Metal Works Inc..252 641-0912
1813 Anaconda Rd Tarboro (27886) *(G-15120)*

S & W Ready Mix Con Co LLC (DH)....................................910 592-1733
217 Lisbon St Clinton (28328) *(G-4104)*

S & W Ready Mix Con Co LLC..910 592-2191
1395 Turkey Hwy Clinton (28328) *(G-4105)*

S & W Ready Mix Con Co LLC..910 645-6868
1460 Mercer Mill Rd Elizabethtown (28337) *(G-5603)*

S & W Ready Mix Con Co LLC..910 864-0939
1309 S Reilly Rd Fayetteville (28314) *(G-5911)*

S & W Ready Mix Con Co LLC..919 751-1796
624 Powell Rd Goldsboro (27534) *(G-6653)*

S & W Ready Mix Con Co LLC..910 329-1201
307 W Ocean Rd Holly Ridge (28445) *(G-8685)*

S & W Ready Mix Con Co LLC..252 527-1881
604 E New Bern Rd Kinston (28504) *(G-9382)*

S & W Ready Mix Con Co LLC..252 726-2566
5161 Business Dr Morehead City (28557) *(G-11186)*

S & W Ready Mix Con Co LLC..252 633-2115
1300 Us Highway 17 N New Bern (28560) *(G-11841)*

S & W Ready Mix Con Co LLC..910 496-3232
545 W Manchester Rd Spring Lake (28390) *(G-14627)*

S & W Ready Mix Con Co LLC..910 285-2191
768 Sw Railroad St Wallace (28466) *(G-15625)*

S & W Ready Mix Concrete, Elizabethtown *Also Called: S & W Ready Mix Con Co LLC (G-5603)*

S & W Ready Mix Concrete, Holly Ridge *Also Called: S & W Ready Mix Con Co LLC (G-8685)*

S A L T Soak Away Lfes Trubles..910 238-2695
108 Skipping Stone Ln Jacksonville (28546) *(G-9027)*

S and D Publishing Corporation..301 642-6425
2409 Blanche Dr Burlington (27215) *(G-1490)*

S and R Sheet Metal Inc..336 476-1069
521 Broad St Thomasville (27360) *(G-15274)*

S Banner Cabinets Incorporated..828 733-2031
299 Watauga St Newland (28657) *(G-11893)*

S Boyd Welding...336 349-8349
10044 Nc Highway 87 Reidsville (27320) *(G-13539)*

S C C, Reidsville *Also Called: Smith-Carolina Corporation (G-13540)*

S C I A Inc...919 387-7000
204 Dundalk Way Cary (27511) *(G-1877)*

S Chamblee Incorporated...919 833-7561
1300 Hodges St Raleigh (27604) *(G-13221)*

S Choice Baker Inc..919 556-1188
343 S White St Ste B Wake Forest (27587) *(G-15586)*

S Dorsett Upholstery Inc..336 472-7076
406 Aycock St Thomasville (27360) *(G-15275)*

S Duff Fabricating Inc..910 298-3060
228 N Nc 41 Hwy Beulaville (28518) *(G-1098)*

S E Board Inc..336 885-7230
1102 Dorris Ave High Point (27260) *(G-8518)*

S Ernie Machine Co Inc...336 852-6355
4722 Old Julian Rd Julian (27283) *(G-9108)*

S Eudy Cabinet Shop Inc...704 888-4454
12303 Renee Ford Rd Stanfield (28163) *(G-14682)*

S F M, Lexington *Also Called: Special Fab & Machine Inc (G-9784)*

S Foil Incorporated..704 455-5134
2283 Nc Highway 49 S Harrisburg (28075) *(G-7725)*

S G L Carbon, Morganton *Also Called: Sgl Carbon LLC (G-11251)*

S H Woodworking...336 463-2885
1316 Travis Rd Yadkinville (27055) *(G-17049)*

S K Bowling Inc...252 243-1803
4475 Technology Dr Nw Wilson (27896) *(G-16535)*

S Kivett Inc...910 592-0161
711 Southwest Blvd Clinton (28328) *(G-4106)*

S Loflin Enterprises Inc..704 633-1159
133 S Main St Salisbury (28144) *(G-14039)*

S M Company Inc..828 274-0827
170 Broadway St Asheville (28801) *(G-762)*

S Oakley Machine Shop Inc..336 599-6105
126 W Gordon St Roxboro (27573) *(G-13822)*

S P Co Inc..919 848-3599
200 W Millbrook Rd Raleigh (27609) *(G-13222)*

S P X, Charlotte *Also Called: Marley Company LLC (G-3128)*

S Ruppe Inc..828 287-4936
137 Taylor St Rutherfordton (28139) *(G-13889)*

S S C 7516-7, Asheboro *Also Called: Southern States Coop Inc (G-484)*

S S C 7579 7, Creedmoor *Also Called: Southern States Coop Inc (G-4621)*

S S C 7793-7, Mount Airy *Also Called: Southern States Coop Inc (G-11575)*

S S C 7795-7, Mount Olive *Also Called: Southern States Coop Inc (G-11669)*

S S C 7883-7, Roxboro *Also Called: Southern States Coop Inc (G-13824)*

S S C 7912-7, Statesville *Also Called: Southern States Coop Inc (G-14896)*

S S C Oxford Svc, Oxford *Also Called: Southern States Coop Inc (G-12157)*

S S I, Brevard *Also Called: Smith Systems Inc (G-1289)*

S S I, Charlotte *Also Called: Schaefer Systems International Inc (G-3499)*

S Shelton Inc..336 643-5916
9037 Ellisboro Rd Stokesdale (27357) *(G-14948)*

S Strickland Diesel Svc Inc...252 291-6999
5451 Old Raleigh Rd Wilson (27893) *(G-16536)*

S T I, Winston Salem *Also Called: Salem Technologies Inc (G-16895)*

S T Wooten Corporation...919 363-3141
51 Red Cedar Way Apex (27523) *(G-240)*

S T Wooten Corporation...919 562-1851
255 Material Rd Franklinton (27525) *(G-6163)*

S T Wooten Corporation...919 772-7991
3625 Banks Rd Fuquay Varina (27526) *(G-6227)*

S T Wooten Corporation...252 393-2206
12200 Cleveland Rd Garner (27529) *(G-6312)*

S T Wooten Corporation... 919 779-6089
  925 E Garner Rd Garner (27529) *(G-6313)*
S T Wooten Corporation... 919 779-7589
  12204 Cleveland Rd Garner (27529) *(G-6314)*
S T Wooten Corporation... 252 636-2568
  245 Parker Rd New Bern (28562) *(G-11842)*
S T Wooten Corporation... 919 965-7176
  6401 Us Highway 70 E Princeton (27569) *(G-12403)*
S T Wooten Corporation... 919 965-9880
  6401 Us Highway 70 E Princeton (27569) *(G-12404)*
S T Wooten Corporation... 919 783-5507
  9001 Fortune Way Raleigh (27613) *(G-13223)*
S T Wooten Corporation... 252 291-5165
  6937 Capital Blvd Raleigh (27616) *(G-13224)*
S T Wooten Corporation... 919 776-2736
  966 Rocky Fork Church Rd Sanford (27332) *(G-14178)*
S T Wooten Corporation... 910 762-1940
  220 Sutton Lake Rd Wilmington (28401) *(G-16391)*
S T Wooten Corporation... 252 291-5165
  2710 Commerce Rd S Wilson (27893) *(G-16537)*
S T Wooten Corporation (PA)....................................... 252 291-5165
  3801 Black Creek Rd Se Wilson (27893) *(G-16538)*
S Tri Inc... 704 542-8186
  10110 Johnston Rd Ste 12 Charlotte (28210) *(G-3477)*
S W G, Durham *Also Called: Smart Wires Inc (G-5359)*
S Y Shop Inc.. 704 545-7710
  4475 Morris Park Dr Ste G Mint Hill (28227) *(G-10544)*
S Zaytoun Custom Cabinets Inc................................... 252 638-8390
  1206 Pollock St New Bern (28560) *(G-11843)*
S-L Snacks National LLC (DH)..................................... 704 554-1421
  13024 Balntyn Corp Pl Charlotte (28277) *(G-3480)*
S-L Snacks Pa LLC.. 704 554-1421
  13024 Balntyn Corp Pl Charlotte (28277) *(G-3481)*
S. T. Wooten, Wilson *Also Called: S T Wooten Corporation (G-16538)*
S&A Marketing Inc... 704 376-0938
  2526 S Tyron St Charlotte (28203) *(G-3478)*
S&F Products... 714 412-1298
  6112 N Deer Ridge Dr Holly Springs (27540) *(G-8714)*
S&R Investments LLC... 408 597-7007
  13001 General Dr Charlotte (28273) *(G-3479)*
S&S Metal Structures LLC... 336 466-7929
  102 Solo Ln Mount Airy (27030) *(G-11569)*
S&S Welding.. 828 408-2794
  105 Old Hickory Dr Morganton (28655) *(G-11248)*
Saab Barracuda LLC.. 910 814-3088
  608 E Mcneill St Lillington (27546) *(G-9859)*
Sac, Charlotte *Also Called: Southeast Air Control Inc (G-3587)*
Sachs Peanuts LLC... 910 647-4711
  9323 Hwy 70 Clarkton (28433) *(G-3948)*
Sack-UPS Corporation... 828 584-4579
  1611 Jamestown Rd Morganton (28655) *(G-11249)*
Sackner Products Inc... 704 873-1086
  178 Orbit Rd Statesville (28677) *(G-14883)*
Saertex Multicom LP (DH)... 704 946-9229
  12200 Mount Holly Hntrsvlle Rd Huntersville (28078) *(G-8891)*
Saertex Multicom LP.. 704 946-9229
  12200 Mount Holly Hntrsvlle Rd Ste A Huntersville (28078) *(G-8892)*
Saertex Usa LLC (DH).. 704 464-5998
  12200 Mount Holly Hntrsvlle Rd Huntersville (28078) *(G-8893)*
Saf-Holland Inc... 336 310-4595
  952 Kensal Green Dr Kernersville (27284) *(G-9230)*
Safariland Group... 919 779-6141
  3319 Anvil Pl Raleigh (27603) *(G-13225)*
Safe Air Systems Inc.. 336 674-0749
  210 Labrador Dr Randleman (27317) *(G-13489)*
Safe Care Rx, Asheville *Also Called: King Bio Inc (G-675)*
Safe Fire Detection Inc... 704 821-7920
  5915 Stockbridge Dr Monroe (28110) *(G-10801)*
Safe Home Pro Inc... 704 662-2299
  18635 Starcreek Dr Ste B Cornelius (28031) *(G-4585)*
Safe Ride Wheelchair Tran.. 336 995-7529
  Winston Salem (27116) *(G-16892)*

Safe Tire & Auto Services, Clinton *Also Called: Safe Tire & Autos LLC (G-4107)*
Safe Tire & Autos LLC.. 910 590-3101
  1308 Hobbton Hwy Clinton (28328) *(G-4107)*
Safe Waze, Concord *Also Called: VH Industries Inc (G-4385)*
Safeguard America, Harrisburg *Also Called: Combat Medical Systems LLC (G-7706)*
Safeguard Medical... 855 428-6074
  5555 Harrisburg Ind Pk Dr Harrisburg (28075) *(G-7726)*
Safeguard Medical Alarms Inc (PA)............................... 312 506-2900
  5555 Harrisburg Ind Pk Dr Harrisburg (28075) *(G-7727)*
Safetek Medical, Charlotte *Also Called: Nonwoven Medical Tech LLC (G-3265)*
Safety & Security Intl Inc.. 336 285-8673
  4270 Piedmont Pkwy Ste 102 Greensboro (27410) *(G-7322)*
Safety Wheelchair Company...................................... 919 819-3775
  108 Seastone St Raleigh (27603) *(G-13226)*
Safewaze LLC... 704 262-7893
  225 Wilshire Ave Sw Concord (28025) *(G-4356)*
Saft America Inc.. 828 874-4111
  313 Crescent St Ne Valdese (28690) *(G-15454)*
Sag Harbor Industries Inc... 252 753-7175
  3595 Mandarin Dr Farmville (27828) *(G-5743)*
Sage Mule... 336 209-9183
  608 Battleground Ave Greensboro (27401) *(G-7323)*
Sage Payroll Services, Charlotte *Also Called: Pai Services LLC (G-3308)*
Sagent Pharmaceuticals Inc....................................... 919 327-5500
  8900 Capital Blvd Raleigh (27616) *(G-13227)*
Sailcraft Service, Oriental *Also Called: M & J Marine LLC (G-12111)*
Sain Grading & Backhoe... 704 481-9179
  121 Melton Dr Shelby (28152) *(G-14362)*
Saint Benedict Press LLC... 704 731-0651
  13315 Carowinds Blvd Ste 2 Charlotte (28273) *(G-3482)*
Saint Paul Mountain Vineyards................................... 828 685-4002
  588 Chestnut Gap Rd Hendersonville (28792) *(G-7897)*
Saint-Gobain Vetrotex Amer Inc.................................. 704 895-5906
  8936 N Pointe Executive Park Dr Ste 165 Huntersville (28078) *(G-8894)*
Sakun Inc... 919 255-2994
  114 Doric Ct Cary (27519) *(G-1878)*
Sal and Sons Woodworking LLC................................... 910 489-5373
  1402 Saint Johns Loop Raeford (28376) *(G-12437)*
Salazar Custom Framing LLC...................................... 919 349-0830
  111 Raynor Sands Dr Dunn (28334) *(G-4882)*
Salem Baking Company, Winston Salem *Also Called: Dewey S Bakery Inc (G-16677)*
Salem Carpet Mills, Charlotte *Also Called: Shaw Industries Group Inc (G-3537)*
Salem Collection, The, Clemmons *Also Called: J R Craver & Associates Inc (G-4049)*
Salem Neckwear Corporation..................................... 336 498-2022
  116 W Academy St Randleman (27317) *(G-13490)*
Salem One Inc... 336 722-2886
  1155 Distribution Ct Kernersville (27284) *(G-9231)*
Salem One Inc (PA).. 336 744-9990
  5670 Shattalon Dr Winston Salem (27105) *(G-16893)*
Salem Printing, Winston Salem *Also Called: Salem One Inc (G-16893)*
Salem Professional Anesthesia.................................... 336 998-3396
  128 Peachtree Ln Ste B Advance (27006) *(G-49)*
Salem Sports Inc (PA).. 336 722-2444
  1519 S Martin Luther King Jr Dr Winston Salem (27107) *(G-16894)*
Salem Stitches, Winston Salem *Also Called: Three Fifty Six Inc (G-16942)*
Salem Stone Quarry, Kernersville *Also Called: Marietta Martin Materials Inc (G-9213)*
Salem Technologies Inc... 336 777-3652
  2580 Salem Point Ct Winston Salem (27103) *(G-16895)*
Salem Woodworking Company................................... 336 768-7443
  4849 Kester Mill Rd Winston Salem (27103) *(G-16896)*
Salice, Charlotte *Also Called: Salice America Inc (G-3483)*
Salice America Inc (DH)... 704 841-7810
  2123 Crown Centre Dr Charlotte (28227) *(G-3483)*
Salient Sciences, Hendersonville *Also Called: Digital Audio Corporation (G-7844)*
Salisbury Millwork Inc... 704 603-4501
  1910 S Martin Luther King Jr. Ave Salisbury (28144) *(G-14040)*
Salisbury Mtal Fabrication LLC.................................... 704 278-0785
  565 Trexler Loop Salisbury (28144) *(G-14041)*
Salisbury Operations, Salisbury *Also Called: Teijin Automotive Tech Inc (G-14049)*
Salisbury Post, Salisbury *Also Called: Post Publishing Company (G-14026)*

ALPHABETIC SECTION

Salon & Spa Design Services.. 919 556-6380
7208 Ledford Grove Ln Wake Forest (27587) *(G-15587)*

Salon Couture.. 910 693-1611
180 Council Way Southern Pines (28387) *(G-14552)*

Salonexclusive Beauty LLC... 704 488-3909
3015 Kraus Glen Dr Charlotte (28214) *(G-3484)*

Salsa Greensboro... 781 648-4140
512 S Elm St Greensboro (27406) *(G-7324)*

Salt Boatworks Inc... 919 394-3795
117 Adams Ct Newport (28570) *(G-11906)*

Salt Life Canvas LLC... 252 722-2314
128 Tabernacle Ln Aydlett (27916) *(G-861)*

Salt Marsh Home, Jarvisburg *Also Called: Carolina Csual Otdoor Furn Inc (G-9083)*

Salt Water Lite, Jonesville *Also Called: Grandeur Manufacturing Inc (G-9098)*

Salt Wood Products Inc (PA).. 252 830-8875
3016 Jones Park Rd Greenville (27834) *(G-7581)*

Salt Wood Products 2, Greenville *Also Called: Salt Wood Products Inc (G-7581)*

Salty Dog Snacks Inc.. 252 532-2109
507 W Washington St La Grange (28551) *(G-9445)*

Salty Landing... 404 245-5699
6577 Brevard Rd Etowah (28729) *(G-5693)*

Salty Turtle Beer Company.. 910 803-2019
103 Triton Ln Surf City (28445) *(G-15016)*

Salubrent Phrma Solutions Corp.. 301 980-7224
150 N Research Campus Dr Ste 3700 Kannapolis (28081) *(G-9131)*

Salud LLC.. 980 495-6612
3306 N Davidson St Charlotte (28205) *(G-3485)*

Saluda Mountain Products Inc.. 828 696-2296
561 S Allen Rd Flat Rock (28731) *(G-5971)*

Saluda Yarn Co Inc... 828 749-2861
Greenville & Walnut Streets Saluda (28773) *(G-14073)*

Salute Industries Inc... 844 937-2588
105 Apache Dr Archdale (27263) *(G-298)*

Salvin Dental Specialties LLC... 704 442-5400
3450 Latrobe Dr Charlotte (28211) *(G-3486)*

Sam M Butler Inc.. 704 364-8647
447 S Sharon Amity Rd Ste 125 Charlotte (28211) *(G-3487)*

Sam M Butler Inc.. 910 276-2360
504 King St Laurinburg (28352) *(G-9494)*

Sam M Butler Inc (PA)... 910 277-7456
17900 Dana Dr Laurinburg (28352) *(G-9495)*

Sam Software Corp... 910 233-9924
103 Oxmoor Pl Wilmington (28403) *(G-16392)*

Samoa Corporation... 828 645-2290
90 Monticello Rd Weaverville (28787) *(G-15861)*

Samos Polymers Corporation... 704 241-2065
1101 S Highway 27 Stanley (28164) *(G-14706)*

Sample Group Inc (PA).. 828 658-9040
179 Merrimon Ave Ste 100 Weaverville (28787) *(G-15862)*

Sample House Inc... 828 327-4786
721 17th St Sw Hickory (28602) *(G-8145)*

Sampletech Inc.. 336 882-1717
2101 W Green Dr High Point (27260) *(G-8519)*

Sampson Gin Company Inc... 910 567-5111
5625 Newton Grove Hwy Newton Grove (28366) *(G-11992)*

Sampson Weekly Inc... 910 590-2102
414b Northeast Blvd Clinton (28328) *(G-4108)*

Sams Motor Rewinding, Jacksonville *Also Called: Stone Cllins Mtr Rewinding Inc (G-9041)*

Samson Marketing, High Point *Also Called: Lacquer Craft Hospitality Inc (G-8428)*

Samsung Semiconductor Inc... 919 380-8483
8000 Regency Pkwy Ste 585 Cary (27518) *(G-1879)*

Samswoodworks... 336 893-5499
2648 Fairlawn Dr Winston Salem (27106) *(G-16897)*

San Kawa LLC... 704 982-4527
403 W Main St Albemarle (28001) *(G-103)*

Sanctuary Systems LLC... 305 989-0953
701 S Wilson St Fremont (27830) *(G-6173)*

Sanctuary Vineyards... 252 491-2387
7005 Caratoke Hwy Jarvisburg (27947) *(G-9085)*

Sand Hammer Forging Inc.. 919 554-9554
594 Bert Winston Rd Youngsville (27596) *(G-17095)*

Sandalwood Healing Center Inc... 828 228-4517
935 E Mountain St Ste L Kernersville (27284) *(G-9232)*

Sanders Company Inc... 252 338-3995
410 N Poindexter St Elizabeth City (27909) *(G-5569)*

Sanders Electric Motor Svc, Lenoir *Also Called: Sanders Electric Motor Svc Inc (G-9651)*

Sanders Electric Motor Svc Inc... 828 754-0513
285 Wildwood Rd Lenoir (28645) *(G-9651)*

Sanders Industries Inc... 410 277-8565
559 Bow And Arrow Cv Waynesville (28785) *(G-15820)*

Sanders Ridge Inc (PA).. 336 677-1700
3200 Round Hill Rd Boonville (27011) *(G-1256)*

Sanders Ridge Vinyrd & Winery, Boonville *Also Called: Sanders Ridge Inc (G-1256)*

Sanderson Farms Inc... 252 208-0036
1536 Smithfield Way Kinston (28504) *(G-9383)*

Sanderson Farms LLC Proc Div... 910 274-0220
2076 Nc Highway 20 W Saint Pauls (28384) *(G-13909)*

Sandhills Cnsld Svcs Inc... 919 718-7909
200 E Williams St Sanford (27332) *(G-14179)*

Sandhills Sentinel Inc.. 910 944-0992
624 Longleaf Rd Aberdeen (28315) *(G-28)*

Sandhlls Fbrctors Crane Svcs I... 910 673-4573
6536 7 Lakes Vlg West End (27376) *(G-15931)*

Sandoz Inc.. 252 234-2222
4700 Sandoz Dr Wilson (27893) *(G-16539)*

Sandvik Inc (HQ).. 919 563-5008
1483 Dogwood Way Mebane (27302) *(G-10427)*

Sandvik Coromant, Mebane *Also Called: Sandvik Inc (G-10427)*

Sandvik McHning Sltons USA LLC... 919 563-5008
295 Maple Ln Mebane (27302) *(G-10428)*

Sandvik Tooling... 919 563-5008
1483 Dogwood Way Mebane (27302) *(G-10429)*

Sandviper, Morganton *Also Called: Sack-UPS Corporation (G-11249)*

Sandy Creek Woodworks... 919 853-3415
115 Leonard Rd Louisburg (27549) *(G-10001)*

Sandy Land Peanut Company Inc.. 252 356-2679
229 Swains Mill Rd Harrellsville (27942) *(G-7698)*

Sandy Ridge Pork... 919 989-8878
2080 Wilsons Mills Rd Smithfield (27577) *(G-14481)*

Sanford Asphalt Plant, Sanford *Also Called: S T Wooten Corporation (G-14178)*

Sanford Coca-Cola Bottling Co... 919 774-4111
1605 Hawkins Ave Sanford (27330) *(G-14180)*

Sanford Kitchen & Bath Inc.. 919 708-9080
1062 Hickory House Rd Sanford (27332) *(G-14181)*

Sanford S Atv Repair LLC... 252 438-2730
887 Weldon Rd Henderson (27537) *(G-7809)*

Sanford Steel Corporation... 919 898-4799
375 Claude Hash Rd Goldston (27252) *(G-6676)*

Sanford Transition Company Inc.. 919 775-4989
5108 Rex Mcleod Dr Sanford (27330) *(G-14182)*

Sanher Stucco & Lather Inc... 704 241-8517
1101 Tyvola Rd Ste 110 Charlotte (28217) *(G-3488)*

Sanicap, Greensboro *Also Called: Public Health Corps Inc (G-7291)*

Sans, Gastonia *Also Called: Sans Technical Fibers LLC (G-6505)*

Sans Technical Fibers LLC.. 704 869-8311
2020 Remount Rd Gastonia (28054) *(G-6505)*

Santa Fe Natural Tob Co Inc... 919 690-1905
104 Enterprise Ct Oxford (27565) *(G-12153)*

Santa Fe Natural Tobacco, Winston Salem *Also Called: Santa Fe Natural Tobacco Company Foundation (G-16898)*

Santa Fe Natural Tobacco Company Foundation (DH)..................... 800 332-5595
401 N Main St Winston Salem (27101) *(G-16898)*

Santa Fe Ntural Tob Foundation... 919 690-0880
3220 Knotts Grove Rd Oxford (27565) *(G-12154)*

Santarus Inc... 919 862-1000
8510 Colonnade Center Dr Raleigh (27615) *(G-13228)*

Sapere Bio Inc... 919 260-2565
400 Park Offices Dr Ste 113 Durham (27709) *(G-5337)*

Sapiens Americas Corporation (DH)... 919 405-1500
801 Corporate Center Dr Ste 310 # 320 Raleigh (27607) *(G-13229)*

Sapona Manufacturing Co Inc... 336 873-8700
7039 Us Highway 220 S Asheboro (27205) *(G-476)*

Sapona Manufacturing Co Inc.. 336 625-2161
   159 North St Asheboro (27203) *(G-477)*
Sapona Manufacturing Co Inc (PA)...................................... 336 625-2727
   2478 Cedar Falls Rd Cedar Falls (27230) *(G-1969)*
Sapona Plastic LLC... 336 873-7201
   798 Nc Highway 705 Seagrove (27341) *(G-14247)*
Sapona Plastics, Asheboro Also Called: Sapona Manufacturing Co Inc *(G-476)*
Sapona Plastics LLC.. 336 873-8700
   7039 Us Highway 220 S Asheboro (27205) *(G-478)*
Sapphire Innvtive Thrapies LLC... 877 402-4325
   510 Meadowmont Village Cir Chapel Hill (27517) *(G-2067)*
Sapphire Tchncal Solutions LLC.. 704 561-3100
   10230 Rodney St Pineville (28134) *(G-12302)*
Sapps Ventures... 910 824-0762
   994 Wayside Rd Raeford (28376) *(G-12438)*
Saputo Cheese USA Inc... 910 569-7070
   116 Industrial Park Biscoe (27209) *(G-1115)*
Saputo Cheese USA Inc... 847 267-1100
   131 Wright Way Troy (27371) *(G-15414)*
Sara Lee, Winston Salem Also Called: Hillshire Brands Company *(G-16746)*
Sara Lee Bakery Outlet, Tarboro Also Called: Bimbo Bakeries Usa Inc *(G-15096)*
Sara Lee Socks.. 336 789-6118
   100 Woltz St Mount Airy (27030) *(G-11570)*
Sarahs Salsa Inc... 336 508-3033
   622 Myers Ln Greensboro (27408) *(G-7325)*
Saraz Musical Instruments.. 828 782-8896
   90 Sean Dr Swannanoa (28778) *(G-15035)*
Sarda Technologies Inc... 919 757-6825
   100 Capitola Dr Ste 308 Durham (27713) *(G-5338)*
Sare Granite & Tile... 828 676-2666
   128 Greene Rd Arden (28704) *(G-374)*
Sare Kitchen and Bed, Arden Also Called: Sare Granite & Tile *(G-374)*
Sarstedt Inc (PA).. 828 465-4000
   1025 Saint James Church Rd Newton (28658) *(G-11966)*
Sas Federal LLC.. 919 531-7505
   100 Sas Campus Dr Cary (27513) *(G-1880)*
SAS Industries Inc.. 631 727-1441
   100 Corporate Dr Elizabeth City (27909) *(G-5570)*
Sas Industries Company LLC.. 704 323-9098
   12208 Winghurst Dr Pineville (28134) *(G-12303)*
Sas Institute Inc.. 954 494-8189
   940 Nw Cary Pkwy Cary (27513) *(G-1881)*
Sas Institute Inc.. 919 677-8000
   Cary (27512) *(G-1882)*
Sas Institute Inc.. 919 531-4153
   820 Sas Campus Dr # C Cary (27513) *(G-1883)*
Sas Institute Inc (PA)... 919 677-8000
   100 Sas Campus Dr Cary (27513) *(G-1884)*
Sas Institute Inc.. 704 831-5595
   2200 Interstate North Dr Charlotte (28280) *(G-3489)*
Sas Institute Inc.. 704 331-3956
   525 N Tryon St Ste 1600 Charlotte (28202) *(G-3490)*
Sas of Carolinas LLC.. 704 332-7165
   5426 Old Pineville Rd Charlotte (28217) *(G-3491)*
Sas R & D Services Inc.. 954 432-2345
   13929 Ballantyne Meadows Dr Charlotte (28277) *(G-3492)*
Sas Solutions Inc.. 919 369-4424
   1449 Luther Rd Apex (27523) *(G-241)*
Sash and Saber Castings.. 919 870-5513
   119 Dublin Rd Raleigh (27609) *(G-13230)*
Sassy Queen Collection LLC.. 919 949-0085
   215 Cheryl Ave Durham (27712) *(G-5339)*
Sassy Stitches-N-Such Inc.. 919 658-6105
   608 N Breazeale Ave Mount Olive (28365) *(G-11667)*
Satco Truck Equipment Inc... 919 383-5547
   2007 Cheek Rd Durham (27704) *(G-5340)*
Satellite & Cellular, Waynesville Also Called: Sbg Digital Inc *(G-15821)*
Sato America, Charlotte Also Called: Sato America LLC *(G-3493)*
Sato America LLC (HQ).. 704 644-1650
   14125 S Bridge Cir Charlotte (28273) *(G-3493)*
Sato Global Solutions Inc... 954 261-3279
   10350 Nations Ford Rd Ste A Charlotte (28273) *(G-3494)*

Sato Inc.. 980 613-2022
   136 Acorn Ln Mooresville (28117) *(G-11078)*
Satsuma Pharmaceuticals Inc... 650 410-3200
   4819 Emperor Blvd Ste 340 Durham (27703) *(G-5341)*
Sattler Corp... 828 759-2100
   447 Main St Hudson (28638) *(G-8778)*
Sauder Woodworking Co... 704 799-6782
   119 Magnolia Park Dr Mooresville (28117) *(G-11079)*
Saueressig North America Inc.. 336 395-6200
   2056 Willow Spring Ln Burlington (27215) *(G-1491)*
Sauers & Co Processed Veneers, Lexington Also Called: Sauers & Company Inc *(G-9776)*
Sauers & Company Inc... 336 956-1200
   363 Dixon St Lexington (27292) *(G-9776)*
Saunders Phrad, Gastonia Also Called: Modena Southern Dyeing Corp *(G-6468)*
Saunders Thread Company, Gastonia Also Called: J Charles Saunders Co Inc *(G-6432)*
Saundra D Hall.. 828 251-9859
   237 S Liberty St Asheville (28801) *(G-763)*
Savage Pros LLC... 919 971-3153
   1213 Brown Straw Dr Raleigh (27610) *(G-13231)*
Savannah Boats, Four Oaks Also Called: Elite Marine LLC *(G-6103)*
Savatech Corp... 386 760-0706
   715 Railroad Ave Rutherfordton (28139) *(G-13890)*
Save-A-Load Inc.. 704 650-4947
   327 W Tremont Ave Ste A Charlotte (28203) *(G-3495)*
Savoye Solutions Inc... 919 466-9784
   5408 Von Hoyt Dr Raleigh (27613) *(G-13232)*
Savvy - Discountscom News Ltr... 252 729-8691
   195 Old Nassau Road Williston Smyrna (28579) *(G-14490)*
Savvy Millwork LLC.. 919 625-5387
   4504 Fox Rd Raleigh (27616) *(G-13233)*
Savvy Parrot Partners.. 919 417-8865
   3914 Center Creek Cir Raleigh (27612) *(G-13234)*
Sawgrass Industries.. 912 884-4008
   1298 Ozone Dr Saluda (28773) *(G-14074)*
Sawmill Catering LLC... 910 769-7455
   2528 Castle Hayne Rd Wilmington (28401) *(G-16393)*
Sawmill Opration Solutions LLC.. 828 442-5907
   99 Glasgow Trl Black Mountain (28711) *(G-1138)*
Sawyer Creek Soaps LLC... 910 231-5013
   181 Sawyer Ln Wallace (28466) *(G-15626)*
Sawyers Sign Service Inc...
   608 Allred Mill Rd Mount Airy (27030) *(G-11571)*
Saybolt LP.. 910 763-8444
   2321 Burnett Blvd Wilmington (28401) *(G-16394)*
Sbfi-North America Inc (DH).. 828 236-3993
   123 Lyman St Asheville (28801) *(G-764)*
Sbg Digital Inc... 828 476-0030
   1562 S Main St Waynesville (28786) *(G-15821)*
Sbm Industries LLC.. 919 625-3672
   3948 Browning Pl Ste 208 Raleigh (27609) *(G-13235)*
Sbrc Hobbies & Raceway LLC.. 336 782-8420
   341 W Wall St Rural Hall (27045) *(G-13852)*
SBS Diversified Tech Inc.. 336 884-5564
   125 Wade St Jamestown (27282) *(G-9071)*
SC Johnson Prof USA Inc (DH)... 443 521-1606
   2815 Coliseum Centre Dr Ste 600 Charlotte (28217) *(G-3496)*
SC Johnson Prof USA Inc... 704 263-4240
   2408 Doyle St Greensboro (27406) *(G-7326)*
SC Johnson Prof USA Inc... 704 263-4240
   1100 S Highway 27 Stanley (28164) *(G-14707)*
SC Johnson Professional.. 704 263-4240
   1100 S Hwy Stanley (28164) *(G-14708)*
Scaffold Mart, Greenville Also Called: Grady F Smith & Co Inc *(G-7533)*
Scalable Software Inc... 713 316-4900
   9320 Old Barnette Pl Huntersville (28078) *(G-8895)*
Scalawag.. 917 671-7240
   318 Blackwell St Durham (27701) *(G-5342)*
Scaltrol Inc.. 678 990-0858
   2010 Sterling Rd Charlotte (28209) *(G-3497)*
Scattered Wrenches Inc.. 919 480-1605
   130 Annaron Ct Raleigh (27603) *(G-13236)*

ALPHABETIC SECTION — Screen Master

Scenery Solutions, Erwin Also Called: Vegherb LLC *(G-5689)*
Scenic Scape, Lexington Also Called: Cunningham Brick Company *(G-9702)*
Scentair Technologies LLC (PA) 704 504-2320
3810 Shutterfly Rd Ste 900 Charlotte (28217) *(G-3498)*
Scentual Candles 252 281-4919
1011 Tarboro St Sw Wilson (27893) *(G-16540)*
Schaefer Shelving, Charlotte Also Called: Schaefer Systems Intl Inc *(G-3500)*
Schaefer Systems International Inc (HQ) 704 944-4500
10021 Westlake Dr Charlotte (28273) *(G-3499)*
Schaefer Systems Intl Inc 704 944-4500
10125 Westlake Dr Bldg 3 Charlotte (28273) *(G-3500)*
Schaefer Systems Intl Inc 704 944-4550
10124 Westlake Dr Charlotte (28273) *(G-3501)*
Schafer Manufacturing Co LLC 704 528-5321
551 N Main St Troutman (28166) *(G-15392)*
Schelling America Inc 919 544-0430
301 Kitty Hawk Dr Morrisville (27560) *(G-11418)*
Schenck USA Corp 704 529-5300
1232 Commerce St Sw Conover (28613) *(G-4495)*
Schindler 9749, Clinton Also Called: Schindler Elevator Corporation *(G-4109)*
Schindler Elevator Corporation 910 590-5590
821 Industrial Dr Clinton (28328) *(G-4109)*
Schlaadt Plastics Limited 252 634-9494
198 Bosch Blvd New Bern (28562) *(G-11844)*
Schleich USA Inc 704 659-7997
10000 Twin Lakes Pkwy Ste A Charlotte (28269) *(G-3502)*
Schletter NA Inc 704 595-4200
11529 Wilmar Blvd Charlotte (28273) *(G-3503)*
Schmalz Inc 919 713-0880
5850 Oak Forest Dr Raleigh (27616) *(G-13237)*
Schnadig Corporation (HQ) 336 389-5200
1150 Pleasant Ridge Rd Ste A Greensboro (27409) *(G-7327)*
Schneider Automation Inc 919 855-1262
2641 Sumner Blvd Raleigh (27616) *(G-13238)*
Schneider Electric, Knightdale Also Called: Schneider Electric Usa Inc *(G-9428)*
Schneider Electric, Morrisville Also Called: Schneider Electric Usa Inc *(G-11419)*
Schneider Electric Usa Inc 919 266-3671
Hwy 64 East Knightdale (27545) *(G-9428)*
Schneider Electric Usa Inc 888 778-2733
1101 Shiloh Glenn Dr # 100 Morrisville (27560) *(G-11419)*
Schneider Mills Inc (PA) 828 632-8181
1170 Nc Highway 16 N Taylorsville (28681) *(G-15165)*
Schnitzer Group Usa Inc 347 982-6880
121 W Trade St Ste 2900 Charlotte (28202) *(G-3504)*
Schoenberg Salt Co 336 766-0600
4927 Home Rd Winston Salem (27106) *(G-16899)*
School Directorease LLC 240 206-6273
1213 W Morehead St Charlotte (28208) *(G-3505)*
School of Rock Charlotte 704 842-3172
1105 Greenwood Clfs Charlotte (28204) *(G-3506)*
School Team Socks 704 500-1738
4413 Mickleton Rd Charlotte (28226) *(G-3507)*
Schooldude.com, Cary Also Called: Brightly Software Inc *(G-1714)*
Schott Sauce, Charlotte Also Called: Schott Ventures LLC *(G-3508)*
Schott Ventures LLC 252 813-9660
4416 Monroe Rd Ste D1 Charlotte (28205) *(G-3508)*
Schubert Packaging Systems LLC 941 757-8380
8848 Red Oak Blvd Ste H Charlotte (28217) *(G-3509)*
Schueler Industries Inc 847 613-0673
121 Pleasant Point Dr Hickory (28601) *(G-8146)*
Schunk, Morrisville Also Called: Schunk Intec Inc *(G-11420)*
Schunk Intec Inc 919 572-2705
211 Kitty Hawk Dr Morrisville (27560) *(G-11420)*
Schwartz Steel Service Inc 704 865-9576
525 N Broad St Gastonia (28054) *(G-6506)*
Schweitzer-Mauduit Intl Inc 252 360-4666
2711 Commerce Rd S Wilson (27893) *(G-16541)*
SCI Sharp Controls Inc 704 394-1395
11331 Downs Rd Pineville (28134) *(G-12304)*
Science Applications Intl Corp 910 822-2100
4317 Ramsey St Ste 303 Fayetteville (28311) *(G-5912)*
Scienscope Products, Matthews Also Called: M3 Products Com *(G-10329)*
Scientigo Inc (PA) 704 837-0500
6701 Carmel Rd Ste 205 Charlotte (28226) *(G-3510)*
Sciepharm LLC 307 352-9559
5441 Lumley Rd Ste 103 Durham (27703) *(G-5343)*
Scinovia Corp 703 957-0396
8801 Fast Park Dr Ste 301 Raleigh (27617) *(G-13239)*
Scion International US 919 570-9303
2520 Laurelford Ln Wake Forest (27587) *(G-15588)*
Scipher Medicine Corporation 781 755-2063
4134 S Alston Ave Ste 104 Durham (27713) *(G-5344)*
Sciquest, Morrisville Also Called: Biosupplynet Inc *(G-11304)*
Sciquest Holdings Inc 919 659-2100
5151 Mccrimmon Pkwy Ste 216 Morrisville (27560) *(G-11421)*
Sciquest Parent LLC (PA) 919 659-2100
3020 Carrington Mill Blvd Ste 100 Morrisville (27560) *(G-11422)*
Sciteck Diagnostics Inc 828 650-0409
317 Rutledge Rd Fletcher (28732) *(G-6036)*
Scivolutions Inc 704 853-0100
811 Floyd St Kings Mountain (28086) *(G-9331)*
SCM Metal Products Inc (HQ) 919 544-8090
2601 Weck Dr Durham (27709) *(G-5345)*
SCM Publishing LLC 252 456-2132
489 Liberation Rd Manson (27553) *(G-10125)*
Scoggins Industrial Inc 252 977-9222
4842 Us-301 Sharpsburg (27878) *(G-14280)*
Scootatrailertm 336 671-0444
1370 Payne Rd Lexington (27295) *(G-9777)*
Scorpio Acquisition Corp 704 697-5100
9335 Harris Corners Pkwy Ste 300 Charlotte (28269) *(G-3511)*
Scorpion Products Inc 336 813-3241
741 Spainhour Rd King (27021) *(G-9281)*
Scorpius Holdings Inc (PA) 919 240-7133
627 Davis Dr Ste 400 Morrisville (27560) *(G-11423)*
Scotland Neck Heart Pine Inc 252 826-2755
25574 Hwy 125 Scotland Neck (27874) *(G-14220)*
Scott Automation, Charlotte Also Called: Scott Systems Intl Inc *(G-3512)*
Scott Bader Inc 330 920-4410
212 Quality Dr Mocksville (27028) *(G-10602)*
Scott Foresman Publishers 252 946-7488
108 Connecticut Dr Chocowinity (27817) *(G-3897)*
Scott Meek Woodworks 828 283-0796
261 Bear Creek Rd Asheville (28806) *(G-765)*
Scott Safety, Monroe Also Called: Scott Technologies Inc *(G-10802)*
Scott Systems Intl Inc (DH) 704 362-1115
2205 Beltway Blvd Ste 100 Charlotte (28214) *(G-3512)*
Scott Technologies Inc (HQ) 704 291-8300
4320 Goldmine Rd Monroe (28110) *(G-10802)*
Scott Technologies Inc 704 291-8300
4320 Goldmine Rd Monroe (28110) *(G-10803)*
Scott Woodworking 828 550-4742
55 Memory Ln Asheville (28805) *(G-766)*
Scotts & Associates Inc 336 581-3141
1699 Hoyt Scott Rd Bear Creek (27207) *(G-942)*
Scotts Cabinet Store LLC 919 725-2530
605 Rookwood Ct Wake Forest (27587) *(G-15589)*
Scotts Company LLC 704 663-6088
319 Oates Rd Ste A Mooresville (28117) *(G-11080)*
SCR Controls Inc 704 821-6651
3479 Gribble Rd Matthews (28104) *(G-10342)*
SCR-Tech LLC 704 504-0191
11707 Steele Creek Rd Charlotte (28273) *(G-3513)*
SCR/ Melltronics, Matthews Also Called: SCR Controls Inc *(G-10342)*
Scrappy's Metal Recycling, Gastonia Also Called: Paul Charles Englert *(G-6487)*
Scrappys Metal LLC 828 557-5861
701 Regal St Murphy (28906) *(G-11715)*
Screen and Embroidery 919 557-3151
704 Broad St Fuquay Varina (27526) *(G-6228)*
Screen It 919 581-9981
1907 E Ash St Goldsboro (27530) *(G-6654)*
Screen Master 252 492-8407
904 Buckhorn St Henderson (27536) *(G-7810)*

Screen Printers Unlimited LLC 336 667-8737
331 E Main St Ste 1 Wilkesboro (28697) *(G-16039)*

Screen Specialty Shop Inc 336 982-4135
8406 Nc Highway 163 West Jefferson (28694) *(G-15948)*

Screens Stitches & Stones LLC 704 622-1660
208 Waterlynn Ridge Rd Unit E Mooresville (28117) *(G-11081)*

Scribbles Software LLC 704 390-5690
10617 Southern Loop Blvd Pineville (28134) *(G-12305)*

Scriptorium Pubg Svcs Inc 919 481-2701
4220 Apex Hwy Ste 340 Durham (27713) *(G-5346)*

Scs Wood Products, Sanford *Also Called: Sandhills Cnsld Svcs Inc (G-14179)*

Sculptural Arts Coating Inc 336 379-7651
2912 Baltic Ave Greensboro (27406) *(G-7328)*

Sdfc LLC 704 878-6645
3511 Essex Pointe Dr Monroe (28110) *(G-10804)*

Sdp Impress ME 919 947-1197
315 N Spence Ave Goldsboro (27534) *(G-6655)*

SDV MEDICAL SERVICES, Asheville *Also Called: Sdv Office Systems LLC (G-767)*

Sdv Office Systems LLC (PA) 844 968-9500
26 Macallan Ln Asheville (28805) *(G-767)*

Sdv Office Systems LLC 844 968-9500
34 Redmond Dr Apt C Fletcher (28732) *(G-6037)*

SE Co-Brand Ventures LLC 704 598-9322
6801 Northlake Mall Dr Ste 188 Charlotte (28216) *(G-3514)*

SE Logo Wear 336 748-1735
303 S Broad St Winston Salem (27101) *(G-16900)*

Sea & Tee Rsort Rsdntial Prpts 910 231-8212
922 Shelton Ct Wilmington (28412) *(G-16395)*

Sea Food Express, Elizabeth City *Also Called: Quality Foods From Sea Inc (G-5565)*

Sea Mark Boats Inc 910 675-1877
13991 Nc Hwy 210 Rocky Point (28457) *(G-13749)*

Sea Striker Inc 252 247-4113
158 Little Nine Rd Morehead City (28557) *(G-11187)*

Sea Supreme Inc 919 556-1188
343 S White St Ste B Wake Forest (27587) *(G-15590)*

Seabrook Ingredients, Edenton *Also Called: Universal Blanchers LLC (G-5522)*

Seac Banche Usa Inc 919 360-6442
1202 Raleigh Rd Chapel Hill (27517) *(G-2068)*

Seacon Corp 704 331-3920
525 N Tryon St Ste 1600 Charlotte (28202) *(G-3515)*

Seacon Corporation (PA) 704 333-6000
1917 John Crosland Jr Dr Charlotte (28208) *(G-3516)*

Seafarer LLC (PA) 704 624-3200
220 E Main St Marshville (28103) *(G-10224)*

Seagate Technology LLC 910 821-8310
7211 Ogden Business Ln Ste 201 Wilmington (28411) *(G-16396)*

Seagoing Uniform, Marshville *Also Called: Seafarer LLC (G-10224)*

Seagrove Lumber LLC 910 428-9663
558 Little River Golf Dr Seagrove (27341) *(G-14248)*

Seal Innovation Inc 919 302-7870
2520 Kenmore Dr Raleigh (27608) *(G-13240)*

Seal It Services Inc 919 777-0374
3301 Industrial Dr Sanford (27332) *(G-14183)*

Seal Master, Madison *Also Called: Krebs Corporation (G-10076)*

Seal Master, Madison *Also Called: PMG SM Holdings LLC (G-10084)*

Seal Seasons Inc 919 245-3535
4426 S Miami Blvd # 105 Durham (27703) *(G-5347)*

Sealco Manufacturing LLC 704 662-2850
105 Keel Ct Mooresville (28117) *(G-11082)*

Sealed Air, Charlotte *Also Called: Sealed Air Corporation (G-3517)*

Sealed Air Corporation (PA) 980 221-3235
2415 Cascade Pointe Blvd Charlotte (28208) *(G-3517)*

Sealed Air Corporation 336 883-9184
2150 Brevard Rd High Point (27263) *(G-8520)*

Sealed Air Corporation 828 728-6610
2001 International Blvd Hudson (28638) *(G-8779)*

Sealed Air Corporation 828 726-2100
2075 Valway Rd Lenoir (28645) *(G-9652)*

Sealed Air Corporation (us) 201 791-7600
2415 Cascade Pointe Blvd Charlotte (28208) *(G-3518)*

Sealed Air Intl Holdings LLC 980 221-3235
2415 Cascade Pointe Blvd Charlotte (28208) *(G-3519)*

Sealed Air LLC 980 430-7000
2415 Cascade Pointe Blvd Charlotte (28208) *(G-3520)*

Sealed Edge Cutting 828 859-2840
2400 Us 176 Hwy Tryon (28782) *(G-15428)*

Sealmaster, Raleigh *Also Called: Thorworks Industries Inc (G-13348)*

Sealy & Company, Trinity *Also Called: Sealy Corporation (G-15355)*

Sealy Corporation (HQ) 336 861-3500
1 Office Parkway Rd Trinity (27370) *(G-15355)*

Sealy Mattress, Trinity *Also Called: Sealy Mattress Mfg Co LLC (G-15358)*

Sealy Mattress Co SW Virginia 336 861-3500
1 Office Parkway Rd Trinity (27370) *(G-15356)*

Sealy Mattress Company (DH) 336 861-3500
1 Office Parkway Rd Trinity (27370) *(G-15357)*

Sealy Mattress Mfg Co LLC 336 861-2900
239 Sealy Dr Trinity (27370) *(G-15358)*

Seam-Craft Inc 336 861-4156
702 Prospect St High Point (27260) *(G-8521)*

Seamare Press LLC 919 846-3540
2004 Falls Farm Xing Raleigh (27614) *(G-13241)*

Seamless Satellite Solutions 828 421-8988
591 Town Mountain Dr Franklin (28734) *(G-6142)*

Seans Transportation LLC 646 603-8128
6826 Centerline Dr Charlotte (28278) *(G-3521)*

Seaport Crane, Wilmington *Also Called: Roderick Mch Erectors Wldg Inc (G-16386)*

Seas Publications 919 266-0035
3608 Ladywood Ct Raleigh (27616) *(G-13242)*

Seashore Builders Inc 910 259-3404
266 Nelson Park Rd Maple Hill (28454) *(G-10132)*

Seaside Press Co Inc 910 458-8156
1003 Bennet Ln Ste F Carolina Beach (28428) *(G-1641)*

Seaside Woodworks 910 523-1377
1620 Goley Hewett Rd Se Unit 307 Bolivia (28422) *(G-1166)*

Seasons Inspirations 336 990-0072
113 W Main St Wilkesboro (28697) *(G-16040)*

Seaward Action Inc 252 671-1684
219 Oakcrest Dr Wilmington (28403) *(G-16397)*

Seaway Printing & Mailing, Southport *Also Called: Seaway Printing Company (G-14579)*

Seaway Printing Company 910 457-6158
4130 Long Beach Rd Se Southport (28461) *(G-14579)*

Second Earth Inc 336 740-9333
3716 Alliance Dr Ste C Greensboro (27407) *(G-7329)*

Second Green Holdings Inc 336 996-6073
9501 W Market St Colfax (27235) *(G-4160)*

Second Main Phase Slutions LLC 704 303-0090
407 Clairview Ln Matthews (28105) *(G-10288)*

Second Nature, New Bern *Also Called: Test ME Out Inc (G-11849)*

Secret Spot Inc 252 441-4030
2815 S Croatan Hwy Nags Head (27959) *(G-11725)*

Secret Spot Surf Shop, Nags Head *Also Called: Secret Spot Inc (G-11725)*

Secure Bag Custom Prints 856 834-9037
5225 Noble Dr Apt 201 Concord (28027) *(G-4357)*

Secure Canopy LLC 980 322-0590
1215 Pineview St Albemarle (28001) *(G-104)*

Secured Shred 443 288-6375
3901 Barrett Dr Ste 306 Raleigh (27609) *(G-13243)*

Secured Traffic Control LLC 910 233-8148
2801 Bloomfield Ln Wilmington (28412) *(G-16398)*

Security 101 Raleigh, Durham *Also Called: A&B Integrators LLC (G-4897)*

Security Consult Inc 704 531-8399
1318 Beechdale Dr Charlotte (28212) *(G-3522)*

Security Self Storage 919 544-3969
1945 E Cornwallis Rd Durham (27713) *(G-5348)*

Security Ultraviolet, Cary *Also Called: S C I A Inc (G-1877)*

Sedgefield By Adams, High Point *Also Called: Adams Wood Turning Inc (G-8232)*

Sedgewick Industries, High Point *Also Called: Whitewood Contracts LLC (G-8603)*

Sedia Systems Inc 336 887-3818
335 Commerce Pl Asheboro (27203) *(G-479)*

See Clearly Inc 929 464-6887
207 S Westgate Dr Ste B Greensboro (27407) *(G-7330)*

Seeco, Indian Trail *Also Called: Southern Electrical Eqp Co Inc (G-8964)*

ALPHABETIC SECTION — Sgl Carbon LLC

Seema Intl Custom Cabinetry 917 703-0820
1012 Lightfoot Ct Wake Forest (27587) *(G-15591)*

Seemingly Overzealous LLC 770 634-7653
2205 Remount Rd Charlotte (28208) *(G-3523)*

Seg Systems LLC 704 579-5800
10701 Hambright Rd Huntersville (28078) *(G-8896)*

SEI Technologies, Hickory Also Called: Solomon Engineering Inc *(G-8162)*

Seiren North America LLC (HQ) 828 430-3456
1500 E Union St Morganton (28655) *(G-11250)*

Seldon Cele 910 274-8070
126 Ne 25th St Oak Island (28465) *(G-12055)*

Select Air Systems, Monroe Also Called: Select Air Systems Usa Inc *(G-10805)*

Select Air Systems Usa Inc 704 289-1122
2716 Chamber Dr Monroe (28110) *(G-10805)*

Select Frame Shop Inc 910 428-1225
138 Coggins Rd Biscoe (27209) *(G-1116)*

Select Furniture Company Inc 336 886-3572
408 South Rd High Point (27262) *(G-8522)*

Select Hardwoods Div, Millers Creek Also Called: Church & Church Lumber LLC *(G-10492)*

Select Mold Service Inc 910 323-1287
419 Glidden St Fayetteville (28301) *(G-5913)*

Select Stainless, Matthews Also Called: Metalfab of North Carolina LLC *(G-10271)*

Select Stainless Products LLC 888 843-2345
7621 Little Ave Ste 212 Charlotte (28226) *(G-3524)*

Selectbuild Construction Inc 208 331-4300
4800 Falls Of Neuse Rd Ste 400 Raleigh (27609) *(G-13244)*

Selective Enterprises Inc (PA) 704 588-3310
10701 Texland Blvd Charlotte (28273) *(G-3525)*

Selee Corporation (DH) 828 693-0256
700 Shepherd St Hendersonville (28792) *(G-7898)*

Selenis North America LLC 210 380-2723
3218 Cedar Creek Rd Fayetteville (28312) *(G-5914)*

Selex Es LLC 336 379-7135
4221 Tudor Ln Greensboro (27410) *(G-7331)*

Self Helpers, Raleigh Also Called: Therapeutics *(G-13343)*

Selina Naturally, Arden Also Called: Celtic Ocean International Inc *(G-320)*

Selpro LLC 336 513-0550
408 Gallimore Dairy Rd Ste C Greensboro (27409) *(G-7332)*

Sels Smart ERA Ltg Systems 336 661-8031
2995 Starlight Dr Winston Salem (27107) *(G-16901)*

Semper FI Water LLC 910 381-3569
508 Cozy Crow Trl Jacksonville (28540) *(G-9028)*

Seneca Devices Inc 301 412-3576
2 Davis Dr Durham (27709) *(G-5349)*

Sennett Security Products LLC 336 375-1134
6109 Corporate Park Dr Browns Summit (27214) *(G-1315)*

Senox Corporation 704 371-5043
3500 Woodpark Blvd Charlotte (28206) *(G-3526)*

Sensational Signs 704 358-1099
2100 N Davidson St Charlotte (28205) *(G-3527)*

Sense and Defenseability LLC 704 880-0165
149 Walk On Rd Stony Point (28678) *(G-14973)*

Sensory Analytics LLC 336 315-6090
405b Pomona Dr Greensboro (27407) *(G-7333)*

Sensus 919 376-2617
113 Gorecki Pl Cary (27513) *(G-1885)*

Sensus, Morrisville Also Called: Sensus USA Inc *(G-11425)*

Sensus Metering Systems, Morrisville Also Called: Sensus USA Inc *(G-11426)*

Sensus USA Inc 919 879-3200
639 Davis Dr Morrisville (27560) *(G-11424)*

Sensus USA Inc (HQ) 919 845-4000
637 Davis Dr Morrisville (27560) *(G-11425)*

Sensus USA Inc 919 576-6185
400 Perimeter Park Dr Ste K Morrisville (27560) *(G-11426)*

Sentek Dynamics Inc 980 556-7081
1548 Roger Dale Carter Dr Ste A Kannapolis (28081) *(G-9132)*

Sentinel Door Controls LLC 704 921-4627
3020 Hutchison Mcdonald Rd Ste D Charlotte (28269) *(G-3528)*

Sentinel Newspapers (PA) 828 389-8338
23 Riverwalk Cir Hayesville (28904) *(G-7771)*

Sentry Vault Service Inc 252 243-2241
6905 Shallingtons Mill Rd Elm City (27822) *(G-5653)*

Separation Technologies LLC 336 597-9814
1514 Dunnaway Rd Semora (27343) *(G-14265)*

Sephora Inside Jcpenney 919 778-4800
607 N Berkeley Blvd Goldsboro (27534) *(G-6656)*

September Signs & Graphics LLC 910 791-9084
6731 Amsterdam Way Ste 4 Wilmington (28405) *(G-16399)*

Seqirus Inc (DH) 919 577-5000
475 Green Oaks Pkwy Holly Springs (27540) *(G-8715)*

Serenity Home Services LLC 910 233-8733
767 Morrison Farm Rd Troutman (28166) *(G-15393)*

Serigraph Techniques Inc 336 454-5066
101 Oakdale Rd # 1254 Jamestown (27282) *(G-9072)*

Serio Self Defense School of 225 245-0693
38 Church St Waynesville (28786) *(G-15822)*

Serra Wireless Inc 980 318-0873
2431 Tallet Trce Charlotte (28216) *(G-3529)*

Serum Source International Inc 704 588-6607
406 Belvedere Ln Waxhaw (28173) *(G-15774)*

Service and Equipment Company 910 545-5886
521 Yopp Rd Ste 214 Jacksonville (28540) *(G-9029)*

Service Electric and Control 704 888-5100
703 Redah Ave Locust (28097) *(G-9970)*

Service Rofg Shtmtl Wlmngton I 910 343-9860
4838 Us Highway 421 N Wilmington (28401) *(G-16400)*

Service Roofing and Shtmtl Co 252 758-2179
107 Staton Ct Greenville (27834) *(G-7582)*

Service Team Prfssnals Stop Ch, Huntersville Also Called: John Glen Alexander Corp *(G-8841)*

Service Thread Co, Charlotte Also Called: Sam M Butler Inc *(G-3487)*

Service Thread Manufacturing, Laurinburg Also Called: Sam M Butler Inc *(G-9494)*

Service Thread Manufacturing, Laurinburg Also Called: Sam M Butler Inc *(G-9495)*

Serving Our Cmnty Kids Scks SC 704 814-4704
11203 Sir Francis Drake Dr Charlotte (28277) *(G-3530)*

Sesame Technologies Inc 252 964-2205
3718 River Rd Washington (27889) *(G-15730)*

Sesmfg LLC 803 917-3248
8404 Woodford Bridge Dr Charlotte (28216) *(G-3531)*

Seven Cast 704 335-0692
901 N Church St Charlotte (28206) *(G-3532)*

Seven Lakes News Corporation 910 685-0320
2033 7 Lks S West End (27376) *(G-15932)*

Seven Pines Vineyard Inc 252 717-2283
544 Seven Pines Rd Fountain (27829) *(G-6097)*

Seven Thunders Publishing Inc 828 236-0221
6 Sunrise Vly Leicester (28748) *(G-9520)*

Seventy Eight C Inc 919 602-0677
2660 Discovery Dr Ste 136 Raleigh (27616) *(G-13245)*

Sew Blessed Embroidery 704 840-7571
1775 E Brief Rd Monroe (28110) *(G-10806)*

Sew Trendy 252 240-9796
3906b Arendell St Morehead City (28557) *(G-11188)*

Sewerkote 919 598-1974
150 Providence Rd Chapel Hill (27514) *(G-2069)*

Sewerkote LLC 919 602-8002
3612 Courtland Dr Durham (27704) *(G-5350)*

Sewing Plus LLC 704 616-1750
120 Pilots Ridge Dr Bessemer City (28016) *(G-1083)*

Seymour Advanced Tech LLC 704 709-9070
3593 Denver Dr Unit 964 Denver (28037) *(G-4800)*

Sfd Industries Inc 336 829-5796
2358 Motsinger Rd Winston Salem (27107) *(G-16902)*

Sfp Research Inc 336 622-5266
121 W Swannanoa Ave Liberty (27298) *(G-9831)*

Sg-Clw Inc 336 865-4980
1700 N Liberty St Winston Salem (27105) *(G-16903)*

Sgb13 LLC 844 627-5381
2824 Anthony Rd Burlington (27215) *(G-1492)*

Sgl Inc 910 790-3631
8215 Mainsail Ln Wilmington (28412) *(G-16401)*

Sgl Carbon LLC 828 437-3221
307 Jamestown Rd Morganton (28655) *(G-11251)*

Sgl Carbon LLC (DH)... 704 593-5100
10715 David Taylor Dr Ste 460 Charlotte (28262) *(G-3533)*

Sgl Composites Inc.. 704 593-5100
10715 David Taylor Dr Ste 460 Charlotte (28262) *(G-3534)*

Sgl Technologies LLC.. 704 593-5100
10715 David Taylor Dr Ste 460 Charlotte (28262) *(G-3535)*

Sgr Welding & Fabrication LLC... 252 299-3629
4364 Massey Rd Zebulon (27597) *(G-17142)*

Sgrtex LLC.. 336 635-9420
335 Summit Rd Eden (27288) *(G-5502)*

Shades and Shelves LLC.. 910 603-4906
105 Spring Lake Dr Pinehurst (28374) *(G-12236)*

Shadow Creek Consulting Inc... 716 860-7397
124 Commerce Blvd Statesville (28625) *(G-14884)*

Shadow Line Vineyard LLC... 828 234-5773
2550 Shadow Line Ln Granite Falls (28630) *(G-6756)*

Shadow Springs Vineyard Inc... 336 998-6598
264 James Way Advance (27006) *(G-50)*

Shadowtrack 24/7, Fletcher *Also Called: Shadowtrack 247 LLC (G-6038)*

Shadowtrack 247 LLC.. 828 398-0980
45 Park Ridge Dr Fletcher (28732) *(G-6038)*

Shalag Nonwovents, Oxford *Also Called: Shalag US Inc (G-12155)*

Shalag US Inc... 919 690-0250
917 Se Industry Dr Oxford (27565) *(G-12155)*

Shallco Inc.. 919 934-3135
308 Components Dr Smithfield (27577) *(G-14482)*

Shallowford Farms Popcorn, Yadkinville *Also Called: Shallowford Farms Popcorn Inc (G-17050)*

Shallowford Farms Popcorn Inc... 336 463-5938
3732 Hartman Rd Yadkinville (27055) *(G-17050)*

Shamrock Corporation (PA)... 336 574-4200
422 N Chimney Rock Rd Greensboro (27410) *(G-7334)*

Shanes Carolina Jerky LLC... 336 653-3673
220 Cedar Lodge Rd Thomasville (27360) *(G-15276)*

Shannon Media Inc.. 919 933-1551
212 Village Gate Dr Chapel Hill (27514) *(G-2070)*

Shannon Media Inc.. 919 933-1551
1777 Fordham Blvd Ste 105 Chapel Hill (27514) *(G-2071)*

Share Adventures Pubg Inc... 919 973-1299
10110 Knotty Pine Ln Raleigh (27617) *(G-13246)*

Sharewell Coffee Company LLC... 828 290-8188
416 N Main St Hendersonville (28792) *(G-7899)*

Sharkflight Publishing LLC.. 919 744-5997
2233 Tanners Mill Dr Durham (27703) *(G-5351)*

Sharp Fiberglass LLC.. 610 760-0638
6032 Us 1 Byp S Kittrell (27544) *(G-9398)*

Sharp Stone Supply Inc... 336 659-7777
126 Griffith Plaza Dr Winston Salem (27103) *(G-16904)*

Sharpe Co (PA).. 336 724-2871
230 Charlois Blvd Winston Salem (27103) *(G-16905)*

Sharpe Images, Winston Salem *Also Called: Sharpe Images Properties Inc (G-16906)*

Sharpe Images Properties Inc (PA).. 336 724-2871
230 Charlois Blvd Winston Salem (27103) *(G-16906)*

Shat-R-Shield Lighting Inc... 800 223-0853
116 Ryan Patrick Dr Salisbury (28147) *(G-14042)*

Shaver Wood Products Inc.. 704 278-1482
14440 Statesville Blvd Cleveland (27013) *(G-4080)*

Shaw Fine Woodworking... 336 529-4080
241 Rifle Range Rd Sparta (28675) *(G-14599)*

Shaw Industries Inc.. 828 369-1701
301 Depot St Franklin (28734) *(G-6143)*

Shaw Industries Group Inc.. 877 996-5942
10901 Texland Blvd Charlotte (28273) *(G-3536)*

Shaw Industries Group Inc.. 877 996-5942
10901 Texland Blvd Charlotte (28273) *(G-3537)*

Shawmut Corporation... 336 229-5576
1821 N Park Ave Burlington (27217) *(G-1493)*

Shawmut Corporation, Burlington *Also Called: Shawmut Corporation (G-1493)*

Shawn Trucking and Towing, Charlotte *Also Called: Seans Transportation LLC (G-3521)*

Shealy Designed Wood Pdts LLC... 704 308-9435
101 Cricket Creek Dr Cherryville (28021) *(G-3876)*

Shearline Boatworks LLC.. 252 726-6916
127 Hestron Dr Morehead City (28557) *(G-11189)*

Shed Brand Inc (PA).. 704 523-0096
216 Iverson Way Ste A Charlotte (28203) *(G-3538)*

Shed Brand Studios LLC... 704 523-0096
216 Iverson Way Ste A Charlotte (28203) *(G-3539)*

Sheet Metal Duct Suppliers LLC.. 919 732-4362
214 Millstone Dr Hillsborough (27278) *(G-8667)*

Sheet Metal Products Inc.. 919 954-9950
3728 Overlook Rd Raleigh (27616) *(G-13247)*

Sheets Laundry Club Inc.. 704 662-8696
211 Mckenzie Rd Mooresville (28115) *(G-11083)*

Sheets Smith Wealth MGT Inc.. 336 765-2020
120 Club Oaks Ct Ste 200 Winston Salem (27104) *(G-16907)*

Sheffibilt Inc.. 336 963-0086
1429 Cable Creek Rd Asheboro (27205) *(G-480)*

Shelby Business Cards.. 704 481-8341
2020 E Dixon Blvd Shelby (28152) *(G-14363)*

Shelby Candles... 336 804-4182
900 Alice Dr Thomasville (27360) *(G-15277)*

Shelby Elastics, Shelby *Also Called: Shelby Elastics of North Carolina LLC (G-14364)*

Shelby Elastics of North Carolina LLC.................................... 704 487-4301
639 N Post Rd Shelby (28150) *(G-14364)*

Shelby Freedom Star Inc... 704 484-7000
315 E Graham St Shelby (28150) *(G-14365)*

Shelby Kendrion Inc... 704 482-9582
1100 Airport Rd Shelby (28150) *(G-14366)*

Shelby Star The, Shelby *Also Called: Shelby Freedom Star Inc (G-14365)*

Shelf Genie, Raleigh *Also Called: Home Imprv Solutions NC LLC (G-12856)*

Shelf Genie, Wilmington *Also Called: Shelfgenie Coastal Carolinas (G-16402)*

Shelfgenie.. 704 705-0005
4111 Kronos Pl Charlotte (28210) *(G-3540)*

Shelfgenie Coastal Carolinas.. 910 547-9595
4144 Pine Hollow Dr Wilmington (28412) *(G-16402)*

Shelton Logging & Chipping Inc.. 336 548-3860
2861 Anglin Mill Rd Stoneville (27048) *(G-14966)*

Shelton Vineyards Inc.. 336 366-4818
286 Cabernet Ln Dobson (27017) *(G-4831)*

Shenandoah Wood Preservers Inc... 252 826-4151
301 E 16th St Scotland Neck (27874) *(G-14221)*

Shenk Industries Inc.. 828 808-3327
18 Cedar Hill Dr Asheville (28803) *(G-768)*

Shep Berryhill Woodworking.. 828 242-3227
197 Deaverview Rd Asheville (28806) *(G-769)*

Shepherd Family Logging LLC.. 910 572-4098
138 Ivey St Troy (27371) *(G-15415)*

Sherri Gossett.. 910 367-0099
801 Bragg Dr Wilmington (28409) *(G-16403)*

Sherrill Contract Mfg Inc (PA)... 704 922-7871
110 Durkee Ln Dallas (28034) *(G-4657)*

Sherrill Furniture, Hickory *Also Called: Sherrill Furniture Company (G-8149)*

Sherrill Furniture Company.. 828 322-8624
856 7th Ave Se Hickory (28602) *(G-8147)*

Sherrill Furniture Company.. 828 328-5241
2425 Highland Ave Ne Hickory (28601) *(G-8148)*

Sherrill Furniture Company (PA)... 828 322-2640
2405 Highland Ave Ne Hickory (28601) *(G-8149)*

Sherrill Furniture Company.. 336 884-0974
301 Steele St Ste 4 High Point (27260) *(G-8523)*

Sherrill Furniture Company.. 828 437-2256
516 Drexel Rd Morganton (28655) *(G-11252)*

Sherrill Furniture Company.. 828 465-0844
1425 Smyre Farm Rd Newton (28658) *(G-11967)*

Sherwin-Williams, Charlotte *Also Called: Sherwin-Williams Company (G-3541)*

Sherwin-Williams, Greensboro *Also Called: Sherwin-Williams Company (G-7335)*

Sherwin-Williams, Raleigh *Also Called: Sherwin-Williams Company (G-13248)*

Sherwin-Williams, Statesville *Also Called: Sherwin-Williams Company (G-14885)*

Sherwin-Williams Company... 704 548-2820
10300 Claude Freeman Dr Charlotte (28262) *(G-3541)*

Sherwin-Williams Company... 336 292-3000
113 Stage Coach Trl Greensboro (27409) *(G-7335)*

Sherwin-Williams Company 919 436-2460
5301 Capital Blvd Raleigh (27616) *(G-13248)*

Sherwin-Williams Company 704 881-0245
188 Side Track Dr Statesville (28625) *(G-14885)*

Sherwood Refractores, Sanford *Also Called: PCC Airfoils LLC (G-14164)*

Shield & Steel Enterprises LLC 704 607-0869
417b Peach Orchard Rd Salisbury (28147) *(G-14043)*

Shiftwizard Inc 866 828-3318
909 Aviation Pkwy Ste 700 Morrisville (27560) *(G-11427)*

Shiloh Products Inc 336 548-6035
203 N 1st Ave Mayodan (27027) *(G-10367)*

Shimadzu Scientific Instrs Inc 919 425-1010
4022 Stirrup Creek Dr Ste 312 Durham (27703) *(G-5352)*

Shiners Stash Jerky 828 302-6359
272 Moore Ln Taylorsville (28681) *(G-15166)*

Shipman Technologies Inc 919 294-8405
2933-122 South Miami Blvd Durham (27703) *(G-5353)*

Shipwreck Rum Inc 215 896-6172
2308 High Chaparral Dr Clayton (27527) *(G-4008)*

Shira Forge 828 226-5687
502 Utica Trl Sylva (28779) *(G-15067)*

Shirleys Prof Alterations EMB, Jacksonville *Also Called: Professnal Alterations EMB Inc (G-9022)*

Shirtails 910 277-0960
115 E Bizzell St Laurinburg (28352) *(G-9496)*

Shm Jarrett Bay Trs LLC 972 488-1314
530 Sensation Weigh Beaufort (28516) *(G-966)*

Shoaf Precast Septic Tank Inc 336 787-5826
4130 W Us Highway 64 Lexington (27295) *(G-9778)*

Shoaf Precasting, Lexington *Also Called: Shoaf Precast Septic Tank Inc (G-9778)*

Shock Absorber Division, Mooresville *Also Called: Thyssenkrupp Bilstein Amer Inc (G-11112)*

Shocktec Inc 704 663-5678
250 Canvasback Rd Mooresville (28117) *(G-11084)*

Shodja Textiles Inc 910 914-0456
68 Industrial Dr Whiteville (28472) *(G-15976)*

Shoe Venom 919 763-4512
5433 Neuse View Dr Raleigh (27610) *(G-13249)*

Shoffner Industries Inc 336 226-9356
5631 S Nc Highway 62 Burlington (27215) *(G-1494)*

Shop Dawg Signs LLC 919 556-2672
4154 Shearon Farms Ave Ste 109 Wake Forest (27587) *(G-15592)*

Shopbot Tools Inc 919 680-4600
3333b Industrial Dr Durham (27704) *(G-5354)*

Shopper 252 633-1153
3200 Wellons Blvd New Bern (28562) *(G-11845)*

Shopper The, New Bern *Also Called: Shopper (G-11845)*

Shoreline Industries Inc 910 571-0111
798 Nc Highway 109 N Troy (27371) *(G-15416)*

Short Circuit Audio LLC 908 868-7077
3501 Yanceyville St Greensboro (27405) *(G-7336)*

Short Run Pro LLC 704 825-1599
710 E Catawba St Ste A Belmont (28012) *(G-1007)*

Shortway Brewing Company LLC (PA) 252 777-3065
228 Chatham St Newport (28570) *(G-11907)*

Shower Glass LLC 980 785-4030
1013 Tiger Eye Ave Indian Trail (28079) *(G-8962)*

Shower ME With Love LLC 704 302-1555
4845 Ashley Park Ln Ste H Charlotte (28210) *(G-3542)*

Showline Inc (PA) 919 255-9160
2114 Atlantic Ave Ste 160 Raleigh (27604) *(G-13250)*

Showline Automotive Pdts Inc (PA) 919 255-9160
1108 N New Hope Rd Raleigh (27610) *(G-13251)*

Showroom, High Point *Also Called: King Hickory Furniture Company (G-8424)*

Shred Instead, Raleigh *Also Called: Secured Shred (G-13243)*

Shred-Tech Usa LLC 919 387-8220
4701 Trademark Dr Raleigh (27610) *(G-13252)*

Shuford Mills LLC (HQ) 828 324-4265
1985 Tate Blvd Se Ste 54 Hickory (28602) *(G-8150)*

Shuford Yarns, Hickory *Also Called: Shuford Mills LLC (G-8150)*

Shuford Yarns LLC 828 396-2342
5100 Burns Rd Granite Falls (28630) *(G-6757)*

Shuford Yarns LLC (PA) 828 324-4265
1985 Tate Blvd Se Ste 54 Hickory (28602) *(G-8151)*

Shuford Yarns Management Inc 828 324-4265
1985 Tate Blvd Se Ste 54 Hickory (28602) *(G-8152)*

Shur Line Inc 317 442-8850
116 Exmore Rd Mooresville (28117) *(G-11085)*

Shurtape Technologies LLC 704 553-9441
4725 Piedmont Row Dr Ste 210 Charlotte (28210) *(G-3543)*

Shurtape Technologies LLC 828 304-8302
1985 Tate Blvd Se Hickory (28603) *(G-8153)*

Shurtape Technologies LLC 828 322-2700
1620 Highland Ave Ne Hickory (28601) *(G-8154)*

Shurtech Brands, Hickory *Also Called: Stm Industries Inc (G-8170)*

Shurtech Brands LLC 704 799-0779
150 Fairview Rd Mooresville (28117) *(G-11086)*

Shutter Factory Inc 252 974-2795
6139w Us Highway 264 W Washington (27889) *(G-15731)*

Shutter Production Inc 910 289-2620
227 1st St Rose Hill (28458) *(G-13781)*

Shutter Works, The, Middlesex *Also Called: Frederick and Frederick Entp (G-10448)*

Shutterbug Grafix & Signs 910 315-1556
300 Kelly Rd Ste B3 Pinehurst (28374) *(G-12237)*

Shutterhutch 704 918-7852
5416 Midvale Ter Charlotte (28215) *(G-3544)*

Shytle Sign and Ltg Svcs LLC 828 429-4120
567 Terry Rd Ellenboro (28040) *(G-5639)*

Sia Abrasives Inc USA 704 587-7355
1980 Indian Creek Rd Lincolnton (28092) *(G-9918)*

Sibelco 828 765-1114
107 Harris Mining Company Rd Spruce Pine (28777) *(G-14655)*

Sibelco North America Inc 828 766-6050
74 Harris Mining Company Rd Spruce Pine (28777) *(G-14656)*

Sibelco North America Inc 828 766-6050
136 Crystal Dr Spruce Pine (28777) *(G-14657)*

Sicel Technologies Inc 919 465-2236
3800 Gateway Centre Blvd Morrisville (27560) *(G-11428)*

Sid Jenkins Inc 336 632-0707
3004 Harnett Dr Greensboro (27407) *(G-7337)*

Side Hustle Ventures LLC 919 816-2324
8471 Garvey Dr Ste 115 Raleigh (27616) *(G-13253)*

Sideboard 910 612-4398
4107 Oleander Dr Ste C Wilmington (28403) *(G-16404)*

Sides Custom Furniture, High Point *Also Called: Sides Furniture Inc (G-8524)*

Sides Furniture Inc 336 869-5509
1812 Horneytown Rd High Point (27265) *(G-8524)*

Sides Spreader and Eqp Co Inc 336 978-6732
1010 American Way Lexington (27295) *(G-9779)*

Sidney Perry Cooper III 252 257-3886
445 Nc Highway 58 Warrenton (27589) *(G-15661)*

Siebenwurst US Inc 704 333-7790
112 S Tryon St Ste 1130 Charlotte (28284) *(G-3545)*

Sieber Industrial Inc 252 746-2003
221 Pepsi Way Ayden (28513) *(G-855)*

Siegwerk Eic LLC (DH) 800 368-4657
1 Quality Products Rd Morganton (28655) *(G-11253)*

Siemens Airport 704 359-5551
5601 Wilkinson Blvd Charlotte (28208) *(G-3546)*

Siemens Corporation 919 465-1287
3333 Regency Pkwy Cary (27518) *(G-1886)*

Siemens Energy Inc 704 551-5100
5101 Westinghouse Blvd Charlotte (28273) *(G-3547)*

Siemens Energy Inc 336 969-1351
3050 Westinghouse Rd Rural Hall (27045) *(G-13853)*

Siemens Energy Inc 919 365-2200
7000 Siemens Rd Wendell (27591) *(G-15916)*

Siemens Industry Inc 919 365-2200
7000 Siemens Rd Wendell (27591) *(G-15917)*

Siemens Industry Software Inc 704 227-6600
13024 Ballantyne Corporate Pl Charlotte (28277) *(G-3548)*

Siemens Med Solutions USA Inc 919 468-7400
221 Gregson Dr Cary (27511) *(G-1887)*

Siemens PLM Software

ALPHABETIC SECTION

Siemens PLM Software, Charlotte *Also Called: Siemens Industry Software Inc (G-3548)*

Siemens Power Transmission & Distribution Inc.. 919 463-8702
110 Macalyson Ct Cary (27511) *(G-1888)*

Sierra Nevada Corporation.. 919 595-8551
1030 Swabia Ct Ste 100 Durham (27703) *(G-5355)*

Sierra Nevada Corporation.. 910 307-0362
3139 Doc Bennett Rd Fayetteville (28306) *(G-5915)*

Sierra Nevada Corporation.. 775 331-0222
795 Sw Broad St Southern Pines (28387) *(G-14553)*

Sierra Software LLC.. 877 285-2867
143 Industrial Ave Greensboro (27406) *(G-7338)*

Siggbey Industries LLC.. 336 483-6035
717 Shelby Dr Greensboro (27409) *(G-7339)*

Sighttech LLC.. 855 997-4448
9421 Perimeter Station Dr Apt 101 Charlotte (28216) *(G-3549)*

Sigma Engineered Solutions PC (PA).. 919 773-0011
120 Sigma Dr Garner (27529) *(G-6315)*

Sigma Plastics Group.. 336 885-8091
2319 W English Rd High Point (27262) *(G-8525)*

Sigma PM.. 269 903-9330
30 Monarch Ct Youngsville (27596) *(G-17096)*

Sigma Xi Scntfic RES Hnor Soc.. 919 549-4691
3200 Chapel Hill Nelson Hwy Ste 300 Durham (27709) *(G-5356)*

Sign & Awning Systems Inc.. 919 892-5900
2785 Us 301 N Dunn (28334) *(G-4883)*

Sign A Rama, Raleigh *Also Called: Sign-A-Rama (G-13255)*

Sign A Rama Inc.. 336 893-8042
5054 Styers Ferry Rd Lewisville (27023) *(G-9673)*

Sign and Doodle.. 704 763-7501
88 Church St Ne Concord (28025) *(G-4358)*

Sign and Graphics, Roxboro *Also Called: R & S Sporting Goods Ctr Inc (G-13820)*

Sign and Print Shop.. 919 542-0727
295 Hillsboro St Pittsboro (27312) *(G-12349)*

Sign Art, Charlotte *Also Called: Lockwood Identity Inc (G-3099)*

Sign Company of Wilmington Inc.. 910 392-1414
428 Landmark Dr Wilmington (28412) *(G-16405)*

Sign Connection Inc.. 704 868-4500
1660 Pacolet Dr Gastonia (28052) *(G-6507)*

Sign Gypsies Hickory.. 828 244-3085
2017 Conover Blvd E Conover (28613) *(G-4496)*

Sign Here, Denver *Also Called: Sign Here of Lake Norman Inc (G-4801)*

Sign Here of Lake Norman Inc.. 704 483-6454
422 N Nc 16 Business Hwy Denver (28037) *(G-4801)*

Sign Manufacturing, Fayetteville *Also Called: Connected 2k LLC (G-5795)*

Sign Medic Inc.. 336 789-5972
1410 Boggs Dr Mount Airy (27030) *(G-11572)*

Sign Mine Inc.. 336 884-5780
2211 Eastchester Dr High Point (27265) *(G-8526)*

Sign O Rama.. 704 443-0092
3601 Matthews Mint Hill Rd Matthews (28105) *(G-10289)*

Sign On Time.. 704 507-2486
124 Avalon Reserve Dr Mooresville (28115) *(G-11087)*

Sign Resources of NC.. 336 310-4611
673 Gralin St Ste B Kernersville (27284) *(G-9233)*

Sign Scientist LLC.. 919 685-7641
335 Sherwee Dr Ste 103 Raleigh (27603) *(G-13254)*

Sign Shop of The Triangle Inc.. 919 363-3930
4001 Midstream Ct Apex (27539) *(G-242)*

Sign Shoppe Inc.. 910 754-5144
782 Ocean Hwy W Supply (28462) *(G-15011)*

Sign Solutions LLC.. 828 687-9789
90 Old Shoals Rd Ste 105 Arden (28704) *(G-375)*

Sign Systems Inc.. 828 322-5622
315 9th St Se Hickory (28602) *(G-8155)*

Sign Systems Inc.. 828 785-1722
301 College St Asheville (28801) *(G-770)*

Sign Technology Inc.. 336 887-3211
311 Berkley St High Point (27260) *(G-8527)*

Sign With Anderson LLC.. 704 599-6977
1820 Spencer Mountain Rd Ste 110-A Gastonia (28054) *(G-6508)*

Sign With Ease Inc.. 919 285-3224
132 Trevor Ridge Dr Holly Springs (27540) *(G-8716)*

Sign World Inc.. 704 529-4440
200 Foster Ave Charlotte (28203) *(G-3550)*

Sign Worxpress.. 336 437-9889
2529 S Church St Burlington (27215) *(G-1495)*

Sign-A-Rama.. 919 383-5561
972 Trinity Rd Raleigh (27607) *(G-13255)*

Sign-A-Rama, Asheville *Also Called: Piedmont Mediaworks Inc (G-730)*

Sign-A-Rama, Charlotte *Also Called: Baac Business Solutions Inc (G-2257)*

Sign-A-Rama, Clayton *Also Called: J & D Thorpe Enterprises Inc (G-3990)*

Sign-A-Rama, Fayetteville *Also Called: Buzz Saw Inc (G-5777)*

Sign-A-Rama, Greensboro *Also Called: Vic Inc (G-7443)*

Sign-A-Rama, Lewisville *Also Called: Sign A Rama Inc (G-9673)*

Sign-A-Rama, Raleigh *Also Called: Greer and Associates Inc (G-12817)*

Sign-A-Rama, Raleigh *Also Called: Jester-Crown Inc (G-12917)*

Sign-A-Rama, Roxboro *Also Called: Signarama of Roxboro (G-13823)*

Sign-A-Rama, Wilmington *Also Called: Global Resource NC Inc (G-16233)*

Signage Innovations Group LLC.. 704 392-8165
5245 Old Dowd Rd Unit 4 Charlotte (28208) *(G-3551)*

Signal Path International LLC.. 704 391-9337
13087 Bleinheim Ln Ste C Matthews (28105) *(G-10290)*

Signal Signs of Ga Inc.. 828 494-4913
15 Running Bear Rd Murphy (28906) *(G-11716)*

Signal Technologies, Granite Falls *Also Called: Matthew Laws (G-6744)*

Signalscape Inc.. 919 859-4565
200 Regency Forest Dr Ste 310 Cary (27518) *(G-1889)*

Signarama of Roxboro.. 336 322-1663
1680 Gentry Dunkley Rd Roxboro (27574) *(G-13823)*

Signarc of Matthews LLC.. 704 209-4444
14101 E Independence Blvd Matthews (28104) *(G-10343)*

Signature Custom Cabinets LLC.. 704 753-4874
2106 E Highway 218 Monroe (28110) *(G-10807)*

Signature Custom Wdwkg Inc.. 336 983-9905
1050 Denny Rd King (27021) *(G-9282)*

Signature Flight Air Inc.. 919 840-4400
1725 E International Dr Morrisville (27560) *(G-11429)*

Signature Mailings.. 919 981-5736
3194 Retama Run New Hill (27562) *(G-11864)*

Signature Seasonings LLC.. 252 746-1001
3254 Nc 102 E Ayden (28513) *(G-856)*

Signature Seating Inc.. 828 325-0174
1718 9th Ave Nw Hickory (28601) *(G-8156)*

Signature Signs Inc.. 336 431-2072
211 Berkley St High Point (27260) *(G-8528)*

Signcaster Corporation.. 336 712-2525
6210 Hacker Bend Ct Ste B Winston Salem (27103) *(G-16908)*

Signcraft Solutions, Wake Forest *Also Called: Shop Dawg Signs LLC (G-15592)*

Signergy LLC.. 919 876-1370
12208 Warwickshire Way Raleigh (27613) *(G-13256)*

Signfactory Direct Inc.. 336 903-0300
1202 Industrial Park Rd Wilkesboro (28697) *(G-16041)*

Significant Others.. 919 539-7551
2201 Digby Ct Raleigh (27613) *(G-13257)*

Signify It Inc.. 910 678-8111
700 Ramsey St Fayetteville (28301) *(G-5916)*

Signlite Services Inc.. 336 751-9543
151 Industrial Blvd Mocksville (27028) *(G-10603)*

Signlogic Inc.. 910 862-8965
174 S Poplar St Elizabethtown (28337) *(G-5604)*

Signs By Design.. 919 217-8000
10350 Sugarberry Ct # 204 Raleigh (27614) *(G-13258)*

Signs By Design.. 919 217-8000
4112 Pleasant Valley Rd Ste 120 Raleigh (27612) *(G-13259)*

Signs By Tomorrow.. 704 527-6100
2440 Whitehall Park Dr Ste 100 Charlotte (28273) *(G-3552)*

Signs By Tomorrow, Beech Mountain *Also Called: Moretz Signs Inc (G-972)*

Signs Designed LLC.. 704 332-4800
268 Unionville Indian Trail Rd W Indian Trail (28079) *(G-8963)*

Signs Done Right.. 910 384-2007
12008 Purcell Rd Laurinburg (28352) *(G-9497)*

Signs Etc.. 336 722-9341
2432 Cherokee Ln Winston Salem (27103) *(G-16909)*

ALPHABETIC SECTION

Signs Etc, Charlotte *Also Called: Signs Etc of Charlotte* **(G-3554)**
Signs Etc, Pineville *Also Called: Jgi Inc* **(G-12278)**
Signs Etc of Charlotte (PA).. 704 522-8860
   4941 Chastain Ave Charlotte (28217) **(G-3553)**
Signs Etc of Charlotte.. 704 522-8860
   4044 South Blvd Charlotte (28209) **(G-3554)**
Signs Now... 410 923-3534
   3724 Sycamore Dairy Rd Ste 100 Fayetteville (28303) **(G-5917)**
Signs Now... 919 546-0006
   2424 Atlantic Ave Raleigh (27604) **(G-13260)**
Signs Now, Chapel Hill *Also Called: Fines and Carriel Inc* **(G-2018)**
Signs Now, Charlotte *Also Called: K&K Holdings Inc* **(G-3040)**
Signs Now, Fayetteville *Also Called: Signs Now* **(G-5917)**
Signs Now, Gastonia *Also Called: Signz Inc* **(G-6509)**
Signs Now, Greenville *Also Called: Signs Now 103 LLC* **(G-7583)**
Signs Now, Morrisville *Also Called: AAA Mobile Signs LLC* **(G-11274)**
Signs Now, Nashville *Also Called: Signs Now of Greenville* **(G-11750)**
Signs Now, Pineville *Also Called: Signs Now Charlotte* **(G-12306)**
Signs Now, Rocky Mount *Also Called: AAA Mobile Signs LLC* **(G-13678)**
Signs Now 103 LLC... 252 355-0768
   118b Greenville Blvd Se Greenville (27858) **(G-7583)**
Signs Now Charlotte... 704 844-0552
   600 Towne Centre Blvd Ste 404 Pineville (28134) **(G-12306)**
Signs Now of Greenville... 252 382-0020
   6703 N Nc Highway 58 Nashville (27856) **(G-11750)**
Signs Plus.. 704 219-0290
   6106 Olive Branch Rd Wingate (28174) **(G-16578)**
Signs Sealed Delivered.. 919 213-1280
   6409 Fayetteville Rd Durham (27713) **(G-5357)**
Signs Unlimited Inc... 919 596-7612
   6801 Mount Hermon Church Rd Unit C Durham (27705) **(G-5358)**
Signsations Ltd... 571 340-3330
   104 Concord Dr Chapel Hill (27516) **(G-2072)**
Signsmith Custom Signs & Awnin..................................... 252 752-4321
   1709 Evans St Greenville (27834) **(G-7584)**
Signz Inc... 704 824-7446
   3608 S New Hope Rd Gastonia (28056) **(G-6509)**
Sii Dry Kilns, Lexington *Also Called: Southeastern Installation Inc* **(G-9783)**
Sika Corporation (DH)... 704 810-0500
   1909 Kyle Ct Gastonia (28052) **(G-6510)**
Sikora Aerospace Tech Inc.. 336 870-6351
   219 Lucerne Ln Winston Salem (27104) **(G-16910)**
Sikorsky Aircraft Corporation.. 252 447-5050
   Us Highway 70 East New Bern (28560) **(G-11846)**
Silanna Semicdtr N Amer Inc... 984 444-6500
   1130 Situs Ct Ste 100 Raleigh (27606) **(G-13261)**
Silar LLC (DH)... 910 655-4212
   333 Neils Eddy Rd Riegelwood (28456) **(G-13563)**
Silar Laboratories, Riegelwood *Also Called: Silar LLC* **(G-13563)**
Silicones Inc.. 336 886-5018
   211 Woodbine St High Point (27260) **(G-8529)**
Silicones Inc.. 336 886-5018
   1828 Blandwood Dr High Point (27260) **(G-8530)**
Silkscreen Specialists.. 910 353-8859
   2239 Lejeune Blvd Jacksonville (28546) **(G-9030)**
Sillaman & Sons Inc... 919 774-6324
   356 Wilson Rd Sanford (27332) **(G-14184)**
Silver City, Siler City *Also Called: Enginred Plstic Components Inc* **(G-14410)**
Silver Ink Publishing Inc.. 704 473-0192
   917 Beau Rd Shelby (28152) **(G-14367)**
Silver Miller Holdings Llc.. 828 652-6677
   70 Anderson Dr Marion (28752) **(G-10176)**
Silver Moon Nutraceuticals LLC.. 828 698-5795
   111 Fletcher Commercial Dr Ste B Fletcher (28732) **(G-6039)**
Silver-Line Plastics LLC (DH).. 828 252-8755
   900 Riverside Dr Asheville (28804) **(G-771)**
Silverlining Screen Prtrs Inc.. 919 554-0340
   90 Mosswood Blvd Ste 600 Youngsville (27596) **(G-17097)**
Simmie Bullard... 910 600-3191
   787 Goins Rd Pembroke (28372) **(G-12183)**

Simmie Bullard Construction, Pembroke *Also Called: Simmie Bullard* **(G-12183)**
Simmon, W P, Mount Airy *Also Called: WP Simmons Inc* **(G-11597)**
Simmons, Charlotte *Also Called: Ssb Manufacturing Company* **(G-3615)**
Simmons Cstm Cbnetry Mllwk Inc.................................... 252 240-1020
   5312 High St Morehead City (28557) **(G-11190)**
Simmons Hosiery Mill Inc (PA).. 828 327-4890
   3715 9th Street Cir Ne Hickory (28601) **(G-8157)**
Simmons Logging & Trucking Inc.................................... 910 287-6344
   5923 Simmons Rd Nw Ash (28420) **(G-396)**
Simmons Scientific Products, Wilmington *Also Called: Russ Simmons* **(G-16389)**
Simon Industries Inc.. 919 469-2004
   2910 Industrial Dr Raleigh (27609) **(G-13262)**
Simontic Composite Inc.. 336 897-9885
   2901 E Gate City Blvd Ste 2500 Greensboro (27401) **(G-7340)**
Simonton Windows & Doors Inc....................................... 919 677-3938
   5020 Weston Pkwy Ste 300 Cary (27513) **(G-1890)**
Simple & Sentimental LLC.. 252 320-9458
   6248 Nc 11 S Ayden (28513) **(G-857)**
Simple Baking.. 704 523-4962
   617 W Arrowood Rd Charlotte (28217) **(G-3555)**
Simple Graphx LLC... 828 428-1567
   3554 Walker Rd Maiden (28650) **(G-10116)**
Simple Supplies LLC... 336 358-7704
   2945 Cottage Pl Apt G Greensboro (27455) **(G-7341)**
Simplecertifiedmailcom LLC... 888 462-1750
   111 Commonwealth Ct Ste 103 Cary (27511) **(G-1891)**
Simpleshot Inc... 888 202-7475
   2000 Riverside Dr Ste 5a Asheville (28804) **(G-772)**
Simplicity Sofas Inc... 800 813-2889
   414 Grayson St High Point (27260) **(G-8531)**
Simplicti, Cary *Also Called: Simplicti Sftwr Solutions Inc* **(G-1892)**
Simplicti Sftwr Solutions Inc.. 919 858-8898
   1255 Crescent Green Ste 145 Cary (27518) **(G-1892)**
Simplifyber Inc... 919 396-8355
   625 Hutton St Ste 106 Raleigh (27606) **(G-13263)**
Simply Btiful Events Decor LLC....................................... 252 375-3839
   1263 Windsong Dr Greenville (27858) **(G-7585)**
Simply Natural Creamery LLC.. 252 746-3334
   1265 Carson Edwards Rd Ayden (28513) **(G-858)**
Simply Stitching, Advance *Also Called: Twg Inc* **(G-52)**
Simply TS Inc... 828 586-1113
   50 W Sylva Shopping Area Sylva (28779) **(G-15068)**
Simplyhome Inc... 828 684-8441
   48 Fisk Dr Arden (28704) **(G-376)**
Simpson Sawmill LLC... 704 485-8814
   12733 Hazard Rd Oakboro (28129) **(G-12081)**
Simpson Strong-Tie Company Inc.................................... 336 841-1338
   4485 Premier Dr Ste 101 High Point (27265) **(G-8532)**
Simrek Corporation... 336 497-5331
   764 Eagle Point Dr Kernersville (27284) **(G-9234)**
Sincere Scents Co LLC... 910 616-4697
   7300 River Rd Se Trlr 84 Southport (28461) **(G-14580)**
Sine Wave Technologies Inc... 704 765-9636
   19232 Wildcat Trl Davidson (28036) **(G-4696)**
Singer Equipment Company Inc...................................... 910 484-1128
   933 Robeson St Fayetteville (28305) **(G-5918)**
Singer T&L, Fayetteville *Also Called: Singer Equipment Company Inc* **(G-5918)**
Single Temperature Contrls Inc....................................... 704 504-4800
   14201 S Lakes Dr Ste B Charlotte (28273) **(G-3556)**
Singley Specialty Co Inc... 336 852-8581
   1025 Willowbrook Dr Greensboro (27403) **(G-7342)**
Singsa... 336 882-9160
   2401 Penny Rd High Point (27265) **(G-8533)**
Sinnovatek Inc... 919 694-0974
   2609 Discovery Dr Ste 115 Raleigh (27616) **(G-13264)**
Sinnovita Inc.. 919 694-0974
   2609 Discovery Dr Ste 115 Raleigh (27616) **(G-13265)**
Sinowest Mfg LLC.. 919 289-9337
   5915 Oak Frest Dr Ste 103 Raleigh (27616) **(G-13266)**
Sipe Lumber Company Inc.. 828 632-4679
   2750 Us Highway 64 90 W Taylorsville (28681) **(G-15167)**

ALPHABETIC SECTION

Sipes Carving Shop Inc.. 828 327-3077
   1450 10th Ave Sw Hickory (28602) *(G-8158)*

Sippin Snax Cft Beer Wine Snck, Greensboro *Also Called: See Clearly Inc (G-7330)*

Siqnarama Pinevillw... 704 835-1123
   10615 Industrial Dr Ste 200 Pineville (28134) *(G-12307)*

Sir Plasma.. 919 232-1961
   9005 Brook Garden Ct Raleigh (27615) *(G-13267)*

Sir Speedy, Asheville *Also Called: Jag Graphics Inc (G-668)*

Sir Speedy, Burlington *Also Called: Natel Inc (G-1466)*

Sir Speedy, Durham *Also Called: Bennett & Associates Inc (G-4955)*

Sir Speedy, Greensboro *Also Called: Dokja Inc (G-6975)*

Sir Speedy, High Point *Also Called: Weber & Weber Inc (G-8602)*

Sir Speedy, Mooresville *Also Called: Sir Speedy Printing (G-11088)*

Sir Speedy, Raleigh *Also Called: Cascadas Nye Corporation (G-12610)*

Sir Speedy, Raleigh *Also Called: Gik Inc (G-12800)*

Sir Speedy, Statesville *Also Called: Modern Information Svcs Inc (G-14846)*

Sir Speedy, Winston Salem *Also Called: Weber and Weber Inc (G-16968)*

Sir Speedy Printing... 704 664-1911
   124 E Plaza Dr Ste C Mooresville (28115) *(G-11088)*

Sirchie Acquisition Co LLC (PA)................................. 800 356-7311
   100 Hunter Pl Youngsville (27596) *(G-17098)*

Sirchie Finger Print Labs, Youngsville *Also Called: Sirchie Acquisition Co LLC (G-17098)*

Sire Tees... 919 787-6843
   6104 Westgate Rd Ste 115 Raleigh (27617) *(G-13268)*

Sirius Energies Corporation (PA)................................. 704 425-6272
   545 Hamberton Ct Nw Concord (28027) *(G-4359)*

Sirius Tactical Entps LLC... 704 256-3660
   679 Brandy Ct Waxhaw (28173) *(G-15775)*

Sisco Safety, Charlotte *Also Called: GNB Ventures LLC (G-2837)*

Sistas 4 Life Food Svcs LLC.. 704 957-6437
   5115 Speyside Ct Charlotte (28215) *(G-3557)*

Sitech Precision, Raleigh *Also Called: GP Technology LLC (G-12811)*

Sitelink Software LLC... 919 865-0789
   3301 Atlantic Ave Raleigh (27604) *(G-13269)*

Sitework Solutions, Apex *Also Called: Sas Solutions Inc (G-241)*

Sitzer & Spuria Inc... 919 929-0299
   601 W Rosemary St Unit 111 Chapel Hill (27516) *(G-2073)*

Sitzer Spuria Studios, Chapel Hill *Also Called: Sitzer & Spuria Inc (G-2073)*

Six Waterpots Vinyrd & Winery................................... 828 728-5099
   4040 James Dr Hudson (28638) *(G-8780)*

Size Stream LLC... 919 355-5708
   223 Commonwealth Ct Cary (27511) *(G-1893)*

Sizemore Custom Jewelry Repair................................ 336 633-8979
   6212 Russwood Dr Pleasant Garden (27313) *(G-12360)*

Sizemore Printing... 910 228-8749
   1547 Cameron Ct Wilmington (28401) *(G-16406)*

Sizzlewich LLC.. 980 299-1389
   3607 Whitehall Park Dr Ste 1200 Charlotte (28273) *(G-3558)*

Sjr Incorporated.. 828 254-8966
   120 New Leicester Hwy Asheville (28806) *(G-773)*

Sk Enterprises Mfg LLC... 919 721-1458
   129 Flowers Ln Sanford (27332) *(G-14185)*

Sk Publishing LLC.. 336 885-3637
   4112 Saint Johns St High Point (27265) *(G-8534)*

Skamol Americas Inc... 704 544-1015
   Charlotte (28226) *(G-3559)*

Skan US Inc.. 919 354-6380
   7409 Acc Blvd Ste 200 Raleigh (27617) *(G-13270)*

Skatells Mfg Jewelers, Pineville *Also Called: NCSMJ Inc (G-12285)*

Skc1 LLC... 937 620-5187
   18802 Peninsula Club Dr Cornelius (28031) *(G-4586)*

Skeen Decorative Fabrics Inc...................................... 336 884-4044
   1220 W Market Center Dr High Point (27260) *(G-8535)*

Skeen Textiles Inc.. 336 884-4044
   1900 S Elm St High Point (27260) *(G-8536)*

Skeen Txtiles Auto Fabrics Inc.................................... 336 884-4044
   1900 S Elm St High Point (27260) *(G-8537)*

Skeeter Beaters.. 919 285-6054
   3021 Jackson King Rd Willow Spring (27592) *(G-16083)*

Skelly Inc... 828 433-7070
   628 E Meeting St Morganton (28655) *(G-11254)*

Skettis Woodworks... 336 671-9866
   2225 Sedgemont Dr Winston Salem (27103) *(G-16911)*

Ski Time Industries Inc... 704 455-3870
   6650 Kee Ln Harrisburg (28075) *(G-7728)*

Skidril Industries LLC... 800 843-3745
   235 Labrador Dr Randleman (27317) *(G-13491)*

Skin Boys LLC.. 910 259-2232
   140 Industrial Dr Burgaw (28425) *(G-1350)*

Skin So Soft Spa Inc.. 800 674-7554
   4456 The Plaza Ste 5e Charlotte (28215) *(G-3560)*

Skin Wellness By Patricia Inc...................................... 704 634-6635
   158 Saye Pl Mooresville (28115) *(G-11089)*

Skinner Company... 336 580-4716
   414 E Montcastle Dr Greensboro (27406) *(G-7343)*

Skipper Graphics.. 910 754-8729
   209 Village Rd Sw Shallotte (28470) *(G-14278)*

Skj Moore Logging LLC... 910 642-5724
   351 Sp Long Rd Nakina (28455) *(G-11731)*

Sklar Bov Solutions Inc.. 704 872-7277
   1105 E Garner Bagnal Blvd Statesville (28677) *(G-14886)*

Skyland Prsthtics Orthtics Inc...................................... 828 684-1644
   3845 Hendersonville Rd Fletcher (28732) *(G-6040)*

Skyline Plastic Systems Inc... 828 891-2515
   2220 Jeffress Rd Mills River (28759) *(G-10511)*

Skyline Welding LLC.. 336 479-0166
   2597 Michael Rd Lexington (27295) *(G-9780)*

Skyspy LLC... 703 472-4639
   3208 Eastover Ridge Dr Unit 633 Charlotte (28211) *(G-3561)*

Skyview Commercial Cleaning.................................... 704 858-0134
   5725 Carnegie Blvd Charlotte (28209) *(G-3562)*

Skyworks Solutions Inc.. 336 291-4200
   406 Gallimore Dairy Rd Greensboro (27409) *(G-7344)*

SL - Laser Systems LLC... 704 561-9990
   2406 Dunavant St Charlotte (28203) *(G-3563)*

SL Liquidation LLC... 910 353-3666
   408 White St Jacksonville (28546) *(G-9031)*

SL Liquidation LLC (DH).. 860 525-0821
   405 White St Jacksonville (28546) *(G-9032)*

SL Liquidation LLC... 910 353-3666
   405 White St Jacksonville (28546) *(G-9033)*

Slack & Parr International (HQ)................................... 704 527-2975
   Hwy 321 Dallas (28034) *(G-4658)*

Slade, Statesville *Also Called: Slade Operating Company LLC (G-14887)*

Slade Operating Company LLC................................... 704 873-1366
   181 Crawford Rd Statesville (28625) *(G-14887)*

Slam Publications LLC... 252 480-2234
   2910 S Croatan Hwy Unit 19 Nags Head (27959) *(G-11726)*

Slane Hosiery Mills Inc... 336 883-4136
   313 S Centennial St High Point (27260) *(G-8538)*

Slane O W Glass Co Inc... 704 872-4291
   606 Meacham Rd Statesville (28677) *(G-14888)*

Sleepworthy, Greenville *Also Called: Cotton Belt Inc (G-7509)*

Sleepy Bee Worx LLC.. 336 824-6998
   3709 Arthurs Ct Franklinville (27248) *(G-6170)*

Sleepy Creek Turkeys LLC.. 919 778-3130
   938 Millers Chapel Rd Goldsboro (27534) *(G-6657)*

Sleepy Creek Turkeys, Inc., Goldsboro *Also Called: Sleepy Creek Turkeys LLC (G-6657)*

Slickedit Inc... 919 473-0070
   408 Bathgate Ln Cary (27513) *(G-1894)*

Sloans Machine Shop.. 919 499-5655
   1186 Walker Rd Sanford (27332) *(G-14186)*

Sloop Pt Vlntr Fire Dept Inc... 910 270-3267
   19470 Us Highway 17 Hampstead (28443) *(G-7655)*

Sls Baking Company.. 704 421-2763
   15720 Brixham Hill Ave Charlotte (28277) *(G-3564)*

Slum Dog Head Gear LLC.. 704 713-8125
   9912 Jeanette Cir Charlotte (28213) *(G-3565)*

SMA Enterprise LLC... 980 616-0140
   4572 Kellybrook Dr Concord (28025) *(G-4360)*

ALPHABETIC SECTION — Snap One

Small Brothers Tire Co Inc.. 704 289-3531
1725 Concord Ave Monroe (28110) *(G-10808)*

Small Business Software LLC... 919 400-8298
5117 Wickham Rd Raleigh (27606) *(G-13271)*

Small Tire Company, Monroe Also Called: Small Brothers Tire Co Inc *(G-10808)*

Smallhd LLC (DH)... 919 439-2166
301 Gregson Dr Cary (27511) *(G-1895)*

Smart Cast Group.. 855 971-2287
5540 Centerview Dr Ste 204 Raleigh (27606) *(G-13272)*

Smart Electric North Amer LLC... 828 323-1200
1550 Deborah Herman Rd Sw Conover (28613) *(G-4497)*

Smart Play USA... 252 747-2587
417 Kingold Blvd Snow Hill (28580) *(G-14508)*

Smart Start Inc... 828 328-2822
216 10th St Nw Ste 1 Hickory (28601) *(G-8159)*

Smart Way, Charlotte Also Called: Smartway of Carolinas LLC *(G-3566)*

Smart Wires Inc (PA)... 919 294-3999
1035 Swabia Ct Ste 130 Durham (27703) *(G-5359)*

Smartlink Mobile Systems LLC... 919 674-8400
1000 Centre Green Way Ste 250 Cary (27513) *(G-1896)*

Smartrac Tech Fletcher Inc... 828 651-6051
267 Cane Creek Rd Fletcher (28732) *(G-6041)*

Smartrac Technology, Fletcher Also Called: Upm Raflatac Inc *(G-6048)*

Smartware Group Inc.. 866 858-7800
11000 Regency Pkwy Ste 110 Cary (27518) *(G-1897)*

Smartway of Carolinas Inc.. 704 900-7877
3304 Eastway Dr Charlotte (28205) *(G-3566)*

SMC Corporation of America.. 704 947-7556
9801 Kincey Ave Ste 150 Huntersville (28078) *(G-8897)*

SMC Holdco Inc.. 910 844-3956
22261 Skyway Church Rd Laurinburg (28353) *(G-9498)*

Smg Hearth and Home LLC... 919 973-4079
9241 Globe Center Dr Ste 120 Morrisville (27560) *(G-11430)*

SMI, Charlotte Also Called: Specialty Manufacturing Inc *(G-3598)*

Smiling Hara LLC.. 828 545-4150
735 N Fork Rd Barnardsville (28709) *(G-913)*

Smiling Hara Tempeh, Barnardsville Also Called: Smiling Hara LLC *(G-913)*

Smissons Inc.. 660 537-3219
425 Swann Trl Clayton (27527) *(G-4009)*

Smith & Associates, Cary Also Called: Cherokee Publishing Co Inc *(G-1728)*

Smith & Fox Inc.. 828 684-4512
19 Walden Dr Arden (28704) *(G-377)*

Smith Architectural Metals LLC.. 336 273-1970
4536 S Holden Rd Greensboro (27406) *(G-7345)*

Smith Brothers Logging.. 828 265-1506
136 Clyde Ln Deep Gap (28618) *(G-4713)*

Smith Companies Lexington Inc (PA)................................. 336 249-4941
720 W Center St Lexington (27292) *(G-9781)*

Smith Creations LLC.. 704 771-6749
56 Harrison Hill Rd Swannanoa (28778) *(G-15036)*

Smith Draperies Inc.. 336 226-2183
2347 W Hanford Rd Burlington (27215) *(G-1496)*

Smith Electric Co, Lawndale Also Called: JA Smith Inc *(G-9500)*

Smith Fabrication Inc.. 704 660-5170
2136 Coddle Creek Hwy Mooresville (28115) *(G-11090)*

Smith Family Screen Printing... 336 317-4849
5311 Appomattox Rd Pleasant Garden (27313) *(G-12361)*

Smith Holdings... 704 472-4937
411 Beaumonde Ave Shelby (28150) *(G-14368)*

Smith Milling Company... 336 957-8108
1265 Wagon Ridge Rd Roaring River (28669) *(G-13595)*

Smith Millwork Inc.. 800 222-8498
920 Robbins Cir Lexington (27292) *(G-9782)*

Smith Novelty Company Inc.. 704 982-7413
2120 W Main St Albemarle (28001) *(G-105)*

Smith Printing Company LLC.. 704 575-9235
3812 Coopersdale Rd Charlotte (28273) *(G-3567)*

Smith Setzer and Sons Inc.. 828 241-3161
4708 E Nc 10 Hwy Catawba (28609) *(G-1968)*

Smith Systems Inc... 828 884-3490
6 Mill Creek Ctr Brevard (28712) *(G-1289)*

Smith Utility Buildings.. 336 957-8211
13721 Longbottom Rd Traphill (28685) *(G-15327)*

Smith Woodturning Inc... 828 464-2230
2427 Claremont Rd Newton (28658) *(G-11968)*

Smith Woodworks Inc... 910 890-2923
1607 Clayhole Rd Dunn (28334) *(G-4884)*

Smith-Carolina Corporation.. 336 349-2905
654 Freeway Dr Reidsville (27320) *(G-13540)*

Smithfeld Fresh Meats Sls Corp... 910 862-7675
15855 Hwy 87 W Tar Heel (28392) *(G-15090)*

Smithfield Ced... 919 934-5041
412 S 7th St Smithfield (27577) *(G-14483)*

Smithfield Foods Inc... 910 299-3009
424 E Railroad St Clinton (28328) *(G-4110)*

Smithfield Foods Inc... 704 298-0936
2975 Dale Earnhardt Blvd Kannapolis (28083) *(G-9133)*

Smithfield Foods Inc... 252 208-4700
1780 Smithfield Way Kinston (28504) *(G-9384)*

Smithfield Foods Inc... 910 241-1022
16261 Nc Highway 87 W Tar Heel (28392) *(G-15091)*

Smithfield Foods Inc... 910 862-7675
15855 Nc Highway 87 W Tar Heel (28392) *(G-15092)*

Smithfield Hog Production, Warsaw Also Called: Murphy-Brown LLC *(G-15671)*

Smithfield Packing Company Inc.. 910 592-2104
424 E Railroad St Clinton (28328) *(G-4111)*

Smithgroup, Winston Salem Also Called: Sg-Clw Inc *(G-16903)*

Smiths Aerospace Components.. 828 274-4540
401 Sweeten Way Asheville (28803) *(G-774)*

Smiths Custom Kitchen Inc... 828 652-9033
58 Butterfly Dr Marion (28752) *(G-10177)*

Smiths Garage and Machine Shop..................................... 828 452-1664
710 Hyatt Creek Rd Waynesville (28786) *(G-15823)*

Smiths Logging.. 910 653-4422
13169 Swamp Fox Hwy E Tabor City (28463) *(G-15086)*

Smiths Mower Marine & Wldg LLC..................................... 919 729-0070
1149 Ronald Tharrington Rd Louisburg (27549) *(G-10002)*

Smithway Inc... 828 628-1756
20 Smith Farm Rd Fairview (28730) *(G-5718)*

Sml Raleigh LLC.. 919 585-0100
501 Atkinson St Clayton (27520) *(G-4010)*

Sml Transportation LLC.. 704 402-6744
354 Mount Bethel Rd Harmony (28634) *(G-7689)*

Smoke House Lumber Company.. 252 257-3303
2711 Nc Highway 58 Warrenton (27589) *(G-15662)*

Smokey Mountain Amusements... 828 479-2814
5660 Tallulah Rd Robbinsville (28771) *(G-13611)*

Smokey Mountain Logging, Leicester Also Called: Bruce Stanley *(G-9508)*

Smokey Mountain Lumber Inc (PA).................................... 828 298-3958
19 Lower Grassy Branch Rd Asheville (28805) *(G-775)*

Smoky Mountain Jet Boats LLC.. 828 488-0522
414 Black Hill Rd Bryson City (28713) *(G-1325)*

Smoky Mountain Machining Inc... 828 665-1193
80 Mcintosh Rd Asheville (28806) *(G-776)*

Smoky Mountain News Inc (PA)... 828 452-4251
144 Montgomery St Waynesville (28786) *(G-15824)*

Smoky Mountain Timberwrights.. 828 252-4205
904 Old Fairview Rd Asheville (28803) *(G-777)*

Smoky Mtn Nativ Plant Assn.. 828 479-8788
546 Upper Tuskeegee Rd Robbinsville (28771) *(G-13612)*

Smoothie Fabrication LLC.. 704 291-7728
1809 Timber Lane Dr Monroe (28110) *(G-10809)*

Smoothiesorg Inc.. 704 906-4121
416 Queens Rd Apt 14 Charlotte (28207) *(G-3568)*

Smt Inc... 919 782-4804
7300 Acc Blvd Raleigh (27617) *(G-13273)*

Smw, Gastonia Also Called: Speedwell Machine Works Inc *(G-6512)*

Smyrna Ready Mix Concrete LLC....................................... 252 447-5356
417 Miller Blvd Havelock (28532) *(G-7747)*

Smyrna Ready Mix Concrete LLC....................................... 252 637-4155
1715 Race Track Rd New Bern (28562) *(G-11847)*

Snap One, Charlotte Also Called: Snap One Holdings Corp *(G-3570)*

Snap One LLC (HQ) 704 927-7620
1800 Continental Blvd Ste 200 Charlotte (28273) *(G-3569)*

Snap One Holdings Corp (PA) 704 927-7620
1800 Continental Blvd Ste 200 Charlotte (28273) *(G-3570)*

Snap Publications LLC 336 274-8531
216 W Market St Ste A Greensboro (27401) *(G-7346)*

Snap Rite Manufacturing Inc (PA) 910 897-4080
232 N Ida St Coats (27521) *(G-4134)*

Snap-On Power Tools Inc 828 835-4400
250 Snap On Dr Murphy (28906) *(G-11717)*

Snap-On Tools, Murphy *Also Called: Snap-On Power Tools Inc (G-11717)*

Snapav, Charlotte *Also Called: Snap One LLC (G-3569)*

Snapz Software Inc 302 234-0402
52 Quince Ct Smithfield (27577) *(G-14484)*

Snider Tire Inc 704 373-2910
900 Atando Ave Charlotte (28206) *(G-3571)*

Snider Tire Inc 336 691-5480
330 E Lindsay St Greensboro (27401) *(G-7347)*

Snider Tire Inc 828 324-9955
1226 21st Street Dr Se Hickory (28602) *(G-8160)*

Sniders Machine Shop Inc 704 279-6129
8025 Highway 52 Rockwell (28138) *(G-13658)*

Sniff N Rescue Candles LLC 704 909-9853
159 Pampas Ln Mooresville (28117) *(G-11091)*

Sniff To Remember LLC 210 373-2115
1400 Cedarwood Ln Charlotte (28212) *(G-3572)*

Snipes Group LLC 757 266-0488
90 Lucy Mae Page Rd Pittsboro (27312) *(G-12350)*

Snow Electric Co Inc 336 723-2092
428 Brookstown Ave Winston Salem (27101) *(G-16912)*

Snow On Go Trucking LLC 980 892-1791
201 S Institute St Salisbury (28144) *(G-14044)*

Snowbird Logging LLC 828 479-6635
270 Dick Branch Rd Robbinsville (28771) *(G-13613)*

Snowman Software 888 918-4384
3608 Shannon Rd Ste 200 Durham (27707) *(G-5360)*

Snp Inc 919 598-0400
1301 S Briggs Ave Ste 110 Durham (27703) *(G-5361)*

Snyder Custom Creations LLC 704 743-3386
163 Sundown Rd Mooresville (28117) *(G-11092)*

Snyder Packaging, Concord *Also Called: Snyder Packaging Inc (G-4361)*

Snyder Packaging Inc 704 786-3111
788 Harris St Nw Concord (28025) *(G-4361)*

Snyder Paper, Newton *Also Called: Snyder Paper Corporation (G-11969)*

Snyder Paper Corporation 800 222-8562
85 Thompson St Asheville (28803) *(G-778)*

Snyder Paper Corporation 336 884-1172
1104 W Ward Ave High Point (27260) *(G-8539)*

Snyder Paper Corporation 828 464-1189
1813 Mount Olive Church Rd Newton (28658) *(G-11969)*

Snyder's-Lance, Charlotte *Also Called: Snyders-Lance Inc (G-3574)*

Snyders-Lance Inc 704 557-8013
1900 Continental Blvd Charlotte (28273) *(G-3573)*

Snyders-Lance Inc (HQ) 704 554-1421
13515 Ballantyne Corporate Pl Charlotte (28277) *(G-3574)*

So & So Socks 919 437-6458
6325 Falls Of Neuse Rd Raleigh (27615) *(G-13274)*

Sobi Inc 844 506-3682
240 Leigh Farm Rd Ste 245 Durham (27707) *(G-5362)*

Social Grind Gourmet Cof LLC 919 937-9503
4527 American Dr Durham (27705) *(G-5363)*

Socialtopias LLC 704 910-1713
1415 S Church St Ste C Charlotte (28203) *(G-3575)*

Society Awards, Charlotte *Also Called: DWM INTERNATIONAL INC (G-2661)*

Sock Basket LLC 828 251-7072
99 Edgewood Rd Apt A Asheville (28804) *(G-779)*

Sock Factory Inc 828 328-5207
1371 13th St Sw Hickory (28602) *(G-8161)*

Sock Inc 561 254-2223
1908 Belvedere Ave Charlotte (28205) *(G-3576)*

Socks and Other Things LLC 704 904-2472
4413 Mickleton Rd Charlotte (28226) *(G-3577)*

Socks Vterinary Hse Calls Pllc 919 244-2826
116 Benedum Pl Cary (27518) *(G-1898)*

Software Goldsmith Inc 919 346-0403
5305 Lake Edge Dr Holly Springs (27540) *(G-8717)*

Software Professionals Inc 503 860-4507
8529 Six Forks Rd Ste 400 Raleigh (27615) *(G-13275)*

Software Publishers, Gastonia *Also Called: ID Pros LLC (G-6421)*

Sofware, Hendersonville *Also Called: Sofware LLC (G-7900)*

Sofware LLC 757 287-7409
217 Covington Cove Ln Hendersonville (28739) *(G-7900)*

Soha Holdings LLC 828 264-2314
645 Roby Greene Rd Boone (28607) *(G-1236)*

Soisa Inc 336 940-4006
111 Dalton Business Ct Ste 101 Mocksville (27028) *(G-10604)*

Sol-Rex Miniature Lamp Works 845 292-1510
802 Mulberry St Beaufort (28516) *(G-967)*

Sola Publishing 336 226-8240
1074 W Main St Graham (27253) *(G-6710)*

Solace Healthcare Furn LLC 336 884-0046
314 Mandustry St Ste 5 High Point (27262) *(G-8540)*

Solacure LLC 336 601-2868
6208 Technology Dr Browns Summit (27214) *(G-1316)*

Solar Connection LLC 828 484-9163
632 College Dr Marion (28752) *(G-10178)*

Solar Hot Limited 919 439-2387
1105 Transport Dr Raleigh (27603) *(G-13276)*

Solar Hot USA, Raleigh *Also Called: Solar Hot Limited (G-13276)*

Solar Pack 919 515-2194
1791 Varsity Dr Raleigh (27606) *(G-13277)*

Solara Automation, Morrisville *Also Called: Solara Solutions LLC (G-11431)*

Solara of Carolinas 910 723-1270
10255 Ramsey St Linden (28356) *(G-9942)*

Solara Solutions LLC 919 534-1500
155 Kitty Hawk Dr Morrisville (27560) *(G-11431)*

Solarbrook Water and Pwr Corp (PA) 919 231-3205
1220 Corporation Pkwy Ste 103 Raleigh (27610) *(G-13278)*

Solarh2ot Ltd 919 439-2387
1105 Transport Dr Raleigh (27603) *(G-13279)*

Solarhot, Raleigh *Also Called: Solarh2ot Ltd (G-13279)*

Solarpack, Raleigh *Also Called: Solar Pack (G-13277)*

Solid Frames Inc 336 882-5082
501 Garrison St High Point (27260) *(G-8541)*

Solid Holdings LLC 704 423-0260
3820 Rose Lake Dr Charlotte (28217) *(G-3578)*

Solid Woodworker 336 786-7385
305 Tanglewood Dr Mount Airy (27030) *(G-11573)*

Solo Foods LLC 910 259-9407
201w Progress Dr Burgaw (28425) *(G-1351)*

Solo Solutions Corporation 336 992-2585
102b Furlong Industrial Dr Kernersville (27284) *(G-9235)*

Solo Wheels and Accessories 919 333-2945
100 N Moon Cir Dunn (28334) *(G-4885)*

Solomon Engineering Inc 828 855-1652
340 9th St Se Hickory (28602) *(G-8162)*

Solutions In Wood 828 696-2996
65 Lake Pointe Cir Hendersonville (28792) *(G-7901)*

Solvay USA Inc 919 786-4555
9650 Strickland Rd Ste 103 Raleigh (27615) *(G-13280)*

SOLVAY USA INC., Raleigh *Also Called: Solvay USA Inc (G-13280)*

Solvekta LLC 336 944-4677
2110 Rockglen Ln Greensboro (27410) *(G-7348)*

Solvere LLC 704 829-1015
69 Mcadenville Rd Belmont (28012) *(G-1008)*

Soma, Charlotte *Also Called: Soma Intimates LLC (G-3579)*

Soma Intimates LLC 704 365-1153
4400 Sharon Rd Ste G07 Charlotte (28211) *(G-3579)*

Somers Lumber and Mfg Inc
126 Oakleaf Rd Harmony (28634) *(G-7690)*

Something For Youth 252 799-8837
503 E Main St Williamston (27892) *(G-16070)*

Sommerville Enterprises LLC 919 924-1594
202 Holiday Park Rd Hillsborough (27278) *(G-8668)*

ALPHABETIC SECTION — Southeastern Installation Inc

Sona Autocomp USA LLC 919 965-5555
500 Oak Tree Dr Selma (27576) *(G-14260)*

Sona Blw Precision Forge Inc 919 828-3375
500 Oak Tree Dr Selma (27576) *(G-14261)*

Sonablate Corp (PA) 888 874-4384
10130 Perimeter Pkwy Ste 410 Charlotte (28216) *(G-3580)*

Sonaron LLC 808 232-6168
7790 Cottonwood Ave Fayetteville (28314) *(G-5919)*

Sonaspection International 704 262-3384
6851 Belt Rd Concord (28027) *(G-4362)*

Song of Wood Ltd 828 669-7675
203 W State St Black Mountain (28711) *(G-1139)*

Songs of Water LLC 336 337-4674
3204 Wingrave Ter Greensboro (27410) *(G-7349)*

Sonoco, Elon College *Also Called: Sonoco Products Company (G-5667)*

Sonoco, Forest City *Also Called: Sonoco Products Company (G-6082)*

Sonoco Hickory Inc 828 286-1356
681 Piney Ridge Rd Forest City (28043) *(G-6081)*

Sonoco Hickory Inc (HQ) 828 328-2466
1246 Main Ave Se Hickory (28602) *(G-8163)*

Sonoco Products Company 828 648-1987
6175 Pigeon Rd Canton (28716) *(G-1626)*

Sonoco Products Company 704 875-2685
12000 Vance Davis Dr Charlotte (28269) *(G-3581)*

Sonoco Products Company 336 449-7731
212 Cook Rd Elon College (27244) *(G-5667)*

Sonoco Products Company 828 245-0118
323 Pine St Forest City (28043) *(G-6082)*

Sonoco Products Company 828 322-8844
1214 Highland Ave Ne Hickory (28601) *(G-8164)*

Sonoco Products Company 910 455-6903
417 Meadowview Rd Jacksonville (28540) *(G-9034)*

Sonoco Products Company 919 556-1504
243 Tillamook Dr Wake Forest (27587) *(G-15593)*

Sonoco Recycling, Jacksonville *Also Called: Sonoco Products Company (G-9034)*

Sonshine Promises, Waynesville *Also Called: Cedar Hill Studio & Gallery (G-15797)*

Sony Music Holdings Inc 336 886-1807
921 Eastchester Dr High Point (27262) *(G-8542)*

Sorbe Ltd 704 562-2991
111 Cupped Oak Dr Ste A Matthews (28104) *(G-10344)*

Sornig Cstm Wdwrks Thmas Srnig 734 925-3905
349 Covington Dr Advance (27006) *(G-51)*

Sorrells Cabinet Co Inc 919 639-4320
490 Chesterfield Lake Rd Lillington (27546) *(G-9860)*

Sorrells Sheree White (PA) 828 452-4864
1834 Cove Creek Rd Waynesville (28785) *(G-15825)*

SOS Printing Inc 828 264-4262
869 Highway 105 Ext Ste 3 Boone (28607) *(G-1237)*

Sostram Corporation 919 226-1195
2525 Meridian Pkwy Ste 350 Durham (27713) *(G-5364)*

Sota Vision Inc 800 807-7187
1325 Aj Tucker Loop Midland (28107) *(G-10479)*

Soto Industries LLC 706 643-5011
6201 Fairview Rd Ste 200 Charlotte (28210) *(G-3582)*

Soul Defense LLC 704 726-7898
1839 S Wendover Rd Charlotte (28211) *(G-3583)*

Soulku LLC (PA) 828 273-4278
45 S French Broad Ave Ste 180 Asheville (28801) *(G-780)*

Soulshine Publishing Co LLC 336 688-4612
344 Countryside Acres Dr Asheboro (27205) *(G-481)*

Sound Heavy Machinery Inc (PA) 910 782-2477
1809 Blue Clay Rd Wilmington (28405) *(G-16407)*

Sound Parts & Service, Wilmington *Also Called: Sound Heavy Machinery Inc (G-16407)*

Sound Trees, Davis *Also Called: Harvey & Sons Net & Twine (G-4707)*

Soundside Orthtics Prsthtics L 910 238-2026
1715 Country Club Rd Ste B Jacksonville (28546) *(G-9035)*

Soundside Recycling & Mtls Inc 252 491-8666
7565 Caratoke Hwy Jarvisburg (27947) *(G-9086)*

Soup Maven LLC 727 919-5242
117 Longspur Lane Ext Asheville (28804) *(G-781)*

Source Technolgies Holdings, Charlotte *Also Called: St Investors Inc (G-3618)*

South / Win LLC (DH) 336 398-5650
112 Maxfield Rd Greensboro (27405) *(G-7350)*

South Atlantic LLC 336 376-0410
3025 Steelway Dr Graham (27253) *(G-6711)*

South Atlantic LLC (DH) 910 332-1900
1907 S 17th St Ste 2 Wilmington (28401) *(G-16408)*

South Atlantic Galvanizing, Graham *Also Called: South Atlantic LLC (G-6711)*

South Atlantic Galvanizing, Wilmington *Also Called: South Atlantic LLC (G-16408)*

South Boulevard Associates Inc 704 525-7160
186 Cherokee Rd Charlotte (28207) *(G-3584)*

South Central Oil and Prpn Inc 704 982-2173
2121 W Main St Albemarle (28001) *(G-106)*

South City Print, Charlotte *Also Called: Print Media Associates Inc (G-3386)*

South East Manufacturing Co 252 291-0925
113 Walnut St W Wilson (27893) *(G-16542)*

South East Welding 980 428-0742
10935 Winds Crossing Dr Ste 10 Charlotte (28273) *(G-3585)*

South Eastern Electric Whl 252 826-0123
34747 Nc 903 Scotland Neck (27874) *(G-14222)*

South Florida Business Journal, Charlotte *Also Called: American City Bus Journals Inc (G-2181)*

South Fork Industries Inc 828 428-9921
100 W Pine St Maiden (28650) *(G-10117)*

South Mountain Crafts 828 433-2607
300 Enola Rd Morganton (28655) *(G-11255)*

South Point Hospitality Inc 704 542-2304
13451 S Point Blvd Charlotte (28273) *(G-3586)*

South Side Bargain Center, Winston Salem *Also Called: GLG Corporation (G-16722)*

South-East Lumber Company 336 996-5322
1896 W Mountain St Kernersville (27284) *(G-9236)*

South-Tek Systems LLC 910 332-4173
3700 Us Highway 421 N Wilmington (28401) *(G-16409)*

Southag Mfg Inc 919 365-5111
2023 Wendell Blvd Wendell (27591) *(G-15918)*

Southandenglish LLC 336 888-8333
1314 Starr Dr High Point (27260) *(G-8543)*

Southbend, Fuquay Varina *Also Called: Middleby Marshall Inc (G-6216)*

Southbridge Inc 828 350-9112
2000 Riverside Dr Ste 5 Asheville (28804) *(G-782)*

Southco Industries Inc 704 482-1477
1840 E Dixon Blvd Shelby (28152) *(G-14369)*

Southcorr LLC 336 498-1700
3021 Taylor Dr Asheboro (27203) *(G-482)*

Southeast Air Control Inc (PA) 704 392-0149
7700 Frosch Rd Charlotte (28278) *(G-3587)*

Southeast Blastg & Coating LLC 252 725-0010
1705 Olde Farm Rd Morehead City (28557) *(G-11191)*

Southeast Leather, High Point *Also Called: Coast To Coast Lea & Vinyl Inc (G-8298)*

Southeast Tubular Products Inc 704 883-8883
1308 Industrial Dr Statesville (28625) *(G-14889)*

Southeast Wldg Fabrication LLC 828 385-1380
24 Reidy Rd Bakersville (28705) *(G-889)*

Southeast Wood Products Inc 910 285-4359
444 Jack Dale Rd Wallace (28466) *(G-15627)*

Southeaster Plastic Inc 336 275-6616
605 Diamond Hill Ct Greensboro (27406) *(G-7351)*

Southeastern Concrete Pdts Co 704 873-2226
2325 Salisbury Hwy Statesville (28677) *(G-14890)*

Southeastern Container Inc (PA) 828 350-7200
1250 Sand Hill Rd Enka (28728) *(G-5684)*

Southeastern Corrugated LLC (PA) 980 224-9551
10901 Carpet St Charlotte (28273) *(G-3588)*

Southeastern Die of NC 336 275-5212
510 Corliss St Greensboro (27406) *(G-7352)*

Southeastern Elevator Inc 252 726-9983
143 Industrial Dr Morehead City (28557) *(G-11192)*

Southeastern Enterprises (HQ) 704 373-1750
3545 Asbury Ave Charlotte (28206) *(G-3589)*

Southeastern Hardwoods Inc 828 581-0197
734 Bee Tree Rd Swannanoa (28778) *(G-15037)*

Southeastern Installation Inc (PA) 704 352-7146
207 Cedar Lane Dr Lexington (27292) *(G-9783)*

Southeastern MBL Wldg Repr LLC 919 521-7039
1321 Greenbranch Ln Raleigh (27603) *(G-13281)*

Southeastern Mch & Wldg Co Inc 910 791-6661
142 Shipyard Blvd Wilmington (28412) *(G-16410)*

Southeastern Minerals Inc 252 492-0831
170 Eastern Minerals Rd Henderson (27537) *(G-7811)*

SOUTHEASTERN MINERALS, INC., Henderson Also Called: Southeastern Minerals Inc *(G-7811)*

Southeastern Outdoor Pdts Inc 910 608-0015
1825 N Roberts Ave Lumberton (28358) *(G-10055)*

Southeastern Packg Plant 2, Concord Also Called: Michigan Packaging Company *(G-4314)*

Southeastern Plastics, Greensboro Also Called: Southeaster Plastic Inc *(G-7351)*

Southeastern Sign Works Inc 336 789-5516
609 Junction St Mount Airy (27030) *(G-11574)*

Southeastern Steel Cnstr Inc 910 346-4462
225 Ellis Blvd Jacksonville (28540) *(G-9036)*

Southeastern Tool & Die Inc 910 944-7677
105 Taylor St Aberdeen (28315) *(G-29)*

Southeastern Transformer Co, Dunn Also Called: Trans East Inc *(G-4887)*

Souther Signs Company, Wilmington Also Called: Cbr Signs LLC *(G-16163)*

Souther Williams Vineyard LLC 828 651-8011
655 Hoopers Creek Rd Fletcher (28732) *(G-6042)*

Southern Aero LLC 336 476-9094
142 Commercial Park Dr Thomasville (27360) *(G-15278)*

Southern AG Insecticides, Boone Also Called: Southern AG Insecticides Inc *(G-1238)*

Southern AG Insecticides Inc 828 264-8843
395 Brook Hollow Rd Boone (28607) *(G-1238)*

Southern AG Insecticides Inc 828 692-2233
511 Maple St Hendersonville (28792) *(G-7902)*

Southern Aggregates, Staley Also Called: Midcoastal Development Corp *(G-14668)*

Southern ATL Spring Mfg Sls LL 704 279-1331
127 Rowan St Granite Quarry (28072) *(G-6762)*

Southern Bag Corporation Ltd 910 582-1842
740 Cheraw Rd Hamlet (28345) *(G-7632)*

Southern Baptist Church, Weaverville Also Called: Brookstone Baptist Church *(G-15840)*

Southern Block Company 910 293-7844
510 W Hill St Warsaw (28398) *(G-15674)*

Southern Cabinet Co Inc 704 373-2299
1418 Industrial Dr Matthews (28105) *(G-10291)*

Southern Cast Inc 704 335-0692
901 N Church St Charlotte (28206) *(G-3590)*

Southern Classic Seating LLC 336 498-3130
7064 Us Highway 311 Sophia (27350) *(G-14522)*

Southern Classic Stairs Inc 828 285-9828
24 Carl Roberts Rd Alexander (28701) *(G-120)*

Southern Comfort A Systems LLC (PA) 919 324-6336
141 Kitty Hawk Dr Morrisville (27560) *(G-11432)*

Southern Concrete Incorporated 919 906-4069
3560 Mcarthur Rd Broadway (27505) *(G-1297)*

Southern Concrete Materials 704 641-9604
2807 Armentrout Dr Concord (28025) *(G-4363)*

Southern Concrete Materials, Charlotte Also Called: Charlotte Block Inc *(G-2450)*

Southern Concrete Materials Inc (HQ) 828 253-6421
35 Meadow Rd Asheville (28803) *(G-783)*

Southern Concrete Mtls Inc 828 684-3636
Hendersonville Rd Arden (28704) *(G-378)*

Southern Concrete Mtls Inc 828 670-6450
80 Pond Rd Asheville (28806) *(G-784)*

Southern Concrete Mtls Inc 828 682-2298
129 Depot St Burnsville (28714) *(G-1533)*

Southern Concrete Mtls Inc 704 394-2346
11609 Texland Blvd Charlotte (28273) *(G-3591)*

Southern Concrete Mtls Inc 704 394-2344
715 State St Charlotte (28208) *(G-3592)*

Southern Concrete Mtls Inc 828 681-5178
250 Old Hendersonville Rd Fletcher (28732) *(G-6043)*

Southern Concrete Mtls Inc 828 524-3555
493 Wells Grove Rd Franklin (28734) *(G-6144)*

Southern Concrete Mtls Inc 828 692-6517
715 Shepherd St Hendersonville (28792) *(G-7903)*

Southern Concrete Mtls Inc 877 788-3001
1155 Chuck Taylor Ln Salisbury (28147) *(G-14045)*

Southern Concrete Mtls Inc 828 586-5280
1362 W Main St Sylva (28779) *(G-15069)*

Southern Concrete Mtls Inc 828 456-9048
201 Boundary St Waynesville (28786) *(G-15826)*

Southern Custom Doors James NA 919 986-6943
2025 Travianna Ct Raleigh (27609) *(G-13282)*

Southern Custom Doors LLC 919 889-5404
8308 Grey Abbey Pl Raleigh (27615) *(G-13283)*

Southern Data Systems Inc 919 781-7603
7758 Nc Highway 96 Oxford (27565) *(G-12156)*

Southern Design Cabinetry LLC 919 340-1858
740 Merritt Capital Dr Ste 120 Wake Forest (27587) *(G-15594)*

Southern Devices Inc 828 584-1611
113 Industrial Blvd Morganton (28655) *(G-11256)*

Southern Digital Watch Repair 336 299-6718
4009 Groometown Rd Greensboro (27407) *(G-7353)*

Southern Distilling Co LLC 704 677-4069
211 Jennings Rd Statesville (28625) *(G-14891)*

Southern Distilling Company, Statesville Also Called: Southern Distilling Co LLC *(G-14891)*

Southern Elc & Automtn Corp 919 718-0122
800 Hawkins Ave Sanford (27330) *(G-14187)*

Southern Electric Motor Co 919 688-7879
2121 Front St # 25 Durham (27705) *(G-5365)*

Southern Electrical Eqp Co Inc (PA) 704 392-1396
4045 Hargrove Ave Charlotte (28208) *(G-3593)*

Southern Electrical Eqp Co Inc 704 392-1396
1015 Van Buren Ave Indian Trail (28079) *(G-8964)*

Southern Elegance Candle LLC 706 825-7658
174 Stream Fall Ct Raeford (28376) *(G-12439)*

Southern Elements Hardscapes 240 626-1586
301 Bruce Coggins Rd Sanford (27332) *(G-14188)*

Southern Engraving Company 336 656-0084
3008 Windchase Ct High Point (27265) *(G-8544)*

Southern Environmental Cons, Raleigh Also Called: Tower Engrg Professionals Inc *(G-13355)*

Southern Equipment Company, Ayden Also Called: Ready Mixed Concrete *(G-854)*

Southern Estates Metal Roofing 704 245-2023
614 Maple St Locust (28097) *(G-9971)*

Southern Fabricators Inc 704 272-7615
8188 Us Highway 74 W Polkton (28135) *(G-12390)*

Southern Fiber Inc (PA) 704 736-0011
1041 S Grove Extension Lincolnton (28093) *(G-9919)*

Southern Film Extruders, High Point Also Called: Sigma Plastics Group *(G-8525)*

Southern Film Extruders Inc 336 885-8091
2319 W English Rd High Point (27262) *(G-8545)*

Southern Finishing Company Inc (PA) 336 573-3741
100 W Main St Stoneville (27048) *(G-14967)*

Southern Flow Companies, Princeton Also Called: Powersecure Inc *(G-12402)*

Southern Glove Inc 828 464-4884
749 Ac Little Dr Newton (28658) *(G-11970)*

Southern Hardscape Pdts Inc 704 528-6726
126 Orbit Rd Statesville (28677) *(G-14892)*

Southern Hldings Goldsboro Inc 919 920-6998
501 Patetown Rd Ste 4 Goldsboro (27530) *(G-6658)*

Southern Home Spa & Water Pdts, Greensboro Also Called: Southern Home Spa and Wtr Pdts *(G-7354)*

Southern Home Spa and Wtr Pdts 336 286-3564
105 Edwardia Dr Greensboro (27409) *(G-7354)*

Southern Leisure Builders Inc 910 381-0426
2444 Commerce Rd Jacksonville (28546) *(G-9037)*

Southern Lithoplate Inc (PA) 919 556-9400
105 Jeffrey Way Youngsville (27596) *(G-17099)*

Southern Logging Inc 336 859-5057
250 Piedmont School Rd Denton (27239) *(G-4748)*

Southern Machine Services 919 658-9300
300 Waller Rd Mount Olive (28365) *(G-11668)*

Southern Machining, Shelby Also Called: Rufus N Ivie III *(G-14361)*

Southern Made Candles LLC 704 740-7748
39 Salem Rd Weaverville (28787) *(G-15863)*

Southern Marble Co LLC 704 982-4142
2033 W Main St Albemarle (28001) *(G-107)*

Southern Metals Company 704 394-3161
2200 Donald Ross Rd Charlotte (28208) *(G-3594)*

ALPHABETIC SECTION — Southwire

Southern Mllwk By Design Inc 704 309-8854
2105 Blue Iris Dr Matthews (28104) *(G-10345)*

Southern Organ Services Ltd 828 667-8230
3 English Pl Candler (28715) *(G-1589)*

Southern Pdmont Pping Fbrction 704 272-7936
2798 Lower White Store Rd Peachland (28133) *(G-12176)*

Southern Pine Woodworking LLC 910 690-9800
230 S Bennett St Southern Pines (28387) *(G-14554)*

Southern Pipe Inc 704 550-5935
445 N 4th St Albemarle (28001) *(G-108)*

Southern Pipe Inc (PA) 704 463-5202
135 Random Dr New London (28127) *(G-11878)*

Southern Pnt Powdr Coating Co 704 843-5505
7110 Davis Rd Waxhaw (28173) *(G-15776)*

Southern Precision Spring Inc 704 392-4393
2200 Old Steele Creek Rd Charlotte (28208) *(G-3595)*

Southern Prestige Industries Inc 704 872-9524
113 Hatfield Rd Statesville (28625) *(G-14893)*

Southern Prestige Intl LLC 704 872-9524
113 Hatfield Rd Statesville (28625) *(G-14894)*

Southern Printing Company Inc 910 259-4807
203 S Dudley St Burgaw (28425) *(G-1352)*

Southern Products Company Inc 910 281-3189
4303 Us Hwy 1 N Hoffman (28347) *(G-8676)*

Southern Quilters, Henderson *Also Called: Pacific Coast Feather LLC (G-7801)*

Southern Range Brewing LLC 704 289-4049
151 S Stewart St Monroe (28112) *(G-10810)*

Southern Ready Mix LLC 919 988-8448
501 Patetown Rd Ste 4 Goldsboro (27530) *(G-6659)*

Southern Resin Inc 336 475-1348
3440 Denton Rd Thomasville (27360) *(G-15279)*

Southern Resources, Charlotte *Also Called: Elan Trading Inc (G-2689)*

Southern Roots Millwork 336 736-8812
466 Skycrest Country Rd Asheboro (27205) *(G-483)*

Southern Roots Monogramming 706 599-5383
148 Cotton Wood Rd Cleveland (27013) *(G-4081)*

Southern Rubber Company Inc 336 299-2456
2209 Patterson St Greensboro (27407) *(G-7355)*

Southern Scents 910 431-6492
274 Crystal Ct Hampstead (28443) *(G-7656)*

Southern Screen Printers, Wilmington *Also Called: B&Lk Enterprises (G-16130)*

Southern Signworks 828 683-8726
45 Single Tree Gap Rd Leicester (28748) *(G-9521)*

Southern Software Inc 336 879-3350
150 Perry Dr Southern Pines (28387) *(G-14555)*

Southern Software Inc 910 638-8700
7231 Cayman Dr Fayetteville (28306) *(G-5920)*

Southern Spring & Stamping 336 548-3520
2089 Us Highway 220 Stokesdale (27357) *(G-14949)*

Southern Staircase, Charlotte *Also Called: Artistic Southern Inc (G-2222)*

Southern Staircase, Charlotte *Also Called: Southern Staircase Inc (G-3597)*

Southern Staircase Inc 704 363-2123
1108 Continental Blvd Ste O Charlotte (28273) *(G-3596)*

Southern Staircase Inc 704 357-1221
1108 Continental Blvd Ste O Charlotte (28273) *(G-3597)*

Southern Star Cstm Fbrction LL 704 880-8948
1033 Buffalo Shoals Rd Statesville (28677) *(G-14895)*

Southern States Chemical Inc 910 762-5054
4600 Us Highway 421 N Wilmington (28401) *(G-16411)*

Southern States Coop Inc 336 629-3977
504 E Dixie Dr Asheboro (27203) *(G-484)*

Southern States Coop Inc 336 246-3201
2089 Sam Moss Hayes Rd Creedmoor (27522) *(G-4620)*

Southern States Coop Inc 919 528-1516
301 N Main St Creedmoor (27522) *(G-4621)*

Southern States Coop Inc 336 786-7545
202 Snowhill Dr Mount Airy (27030) *(G-11575)*

Southern States Coop Inc 919 658-5061
301 N Chestnut St Mount Olive (28365) *(G-11669)*

Southern States Coop Inc 919 693-6136
607 Hillsboro St Oxford (27565) *(G-12157)*

Southern States Coop Inc 252 823-2520
142 Commercial Rd Princeville (27886) *(G-12406)*

Southern States Coop Inc 336 599-2185
1112 N Main St Roxboro (27573) *(G-13824)*

Southern States Coop Inc 704 872-6364
2504 Davie Ave Statesville (28625) *(G-14896)*

Southern States Coop Inc 910 285-8213
939 Nw Railroad St Wallace (28466) *(G-15628)*

Southern Steel and Wire Inc 336 548-9611
100 Minich Rd Madison (27025) *(G-10087)*

Southern Steelworks LLC 828 548-3660
2251 N 4th St Highlands (28741) *(G-8617)*

Southern Stone Cutting 252 566-3116
108 N Caswell St La Grange (28551) *(G-9446)*

Southern Style Logging LLC 910 259-9897
3595 Little Kelly Rd Rocky Point (28457) *(G-13750)*

Southern Supreme Fruit Cakes, Bear Creek *Also Called: Scotts & Associates Inc (G-942)*

Southern Trade Publications Co (PA) 336 454-3516
6520 Airport Center Dr Ste 204 Greensboro (27409) *(G-7356)*

Southern Traditions Two Inc 919 742-4692
55 Industrial Park Dr Siler City (27344) *(G-14431)*

Southern Trucking & Backhoe 919 548-9723
165 Riverside Rd Siler City (27344) *(G-14432)*

Southern Vinyl Mfg Inc 252 523-2520
2010 Smithfield Way Kinston (28504) *(G-9385)*

Southern Vneer Spclty Pdts LLC 919 642-7004
306 Corinth Rd Moncure (27559) *(G-10626)*

Southern Wicked Distillery Inc 919 539-1620
3211 Imperial Oaks Dr Raleigh (27614) *(G-13284)*

Southern Woodcraft Design LLC 919 693-8995
114 Southgate Dr Oxford (27565) *(G-12158)*

Southern Woods Lumber Inc 919 963-2233
3872 Old School Rd Four Oaks (27524) *(G-6112)*

Southern Woodworking Inc 336 693-5892
418 Hawthorne Ln Burlington (27215) *(G-1497)*

Southfield Ltd 336 434-6220
2224 Shore St High Point (27263) *(G-8546)*

Southfield Upholstered Furn, High Point *Also Called: Southfield Ltd (G-8546)*

Southill Industrial Carving 336 472-5311
1861 N Nc Highway 109 Thomasville (27360) *(G-15280)*

Southland Amusements Vend Inc (PA) 910 343-1809
1611 Castle Hayne Rd Ste D3 Wilmington (28401) *(G-16412)*

Southland Coatings Tech LLC 336 644-8919
1683 Deer Run Ct Oak Ridge (27310) *(G-12067)*

Southland Electrical Sup LLC 336 227-1486
147 N Main St Burlington (27217) *(G-1498)*

Southland Industries 336 989-0944
129 Hartley Dr Apt D High Point (27265) *(G-8547)*

Southland Log Homes Inc 336 449-5388
5692 Millstream Rd Whitsett (27377) *(G-16002)*

Southline Converting LLC 828 781-6414
639 4th Street Pl Sw Conover (28613) *(G-4498)*

Southmark Forest Products 919 300-1596
1209 W Market St Smithfield (27577) *(G-14485)*

Southport Graphics LLC 919 650-3822
9400 Globe Center Dr Ste 101 Morrisville (27560) *(G-11433)*

Southport NC 910 524-7425
5105 Bent Oak Ln Southport (28461) *(G-14581)*

Southport Smoothies LLC 910 363-4526
3703 Cinnamon Fern Dr Southport (28461) *(G-14582)*

Southside Materials LLC 336 388-5613
1524 Rock Quarry Rd Pelham (27311) *(G-12178)*

Southside Protective Coatings 757 938-9188
67 Green Acres Gates (27937) *(G-6545)*

Southstern Archtctural Systems, Charlotte *Also Called: Tom Rochester & Associates Inc (G-3706)*

Southstern Edctl Toy Bk Dstrs 919 954-0140
3071 Business Park Dr # 116 Raleigh (27610) *(G-13285)*

Southstern Prcess Eqp Cntrls I 704 483-1141
7558 Townsend Dr Denver (28037) *(G-4802)*

Southwire, Huntersville *Also Called: Southwire Company LLC (G-8898)*

Southwire Company LLC..704 379-9600
  12331 Commerce Station Dr Huntersville (28078) *(G-8898)*
Southwood Doors LLC..704 625-2578
  1222 Emmanuel Church Rd Ste 6 Conover (28613) *(G-4499)*
Southwood Furniture Corp (PA)..................................828 465-1776
  2860 Nathan St Hickory (28601) *(G-8165)*
Sovereign Technologies LLC......................................828 358-5355
  1108 9th Ave Ne Hickory (28601) *(G-8166)*
Sowers Welding Service..704 929-5617
  111 Red Arrow Pl Mooresville (28117) *(G-11093)*
Soy Clever Candle Co LLC..919 869-5360
  62 Standing Oaks Ln Clayton (27527) *(G-4011)*
Spa and Salon, Fayetteville Also Called: Brandy Thompson *(G-5774)*
Space-Ray, Charlotte Also Called: Gas-Fired Products Inc *(G-2809)*
Spanglercv Inc..910 794-5547
  3111 Kitty Hawk Rd Ste 2 Wilmington (28405) *(G-16413)*
Spanset Inc (HQ)..919 774-6316
  3125 Industrial Dr Sanford (27332) *(G-14189)*
Spantek Expanded Metal Inc......................................704 479-6210
  352 N Generals Blvd Lincolnton (28092) *(G-9920)*
Spark716 LLC...704 439-6864
  6779 Gordon Rd Wilmington (28411) *(G-16414)*
Sparks Mill Works LLC..512 779-5837
  6 Von Ruck Ct Asheville (28801) *(G-785)*
Sparksmith LLC..828 266-0152
  60 Communications Dr Waynesville (28786) *(G-15827)*
Sparta Plastics, High Point Also Called: Prime Mill LLC *(G-8498)*
Spartacraft Inc...828 397-4630
  7690 Sparta Craft Dr Connelly Springs (28612) *(G-4409)*
Spartan Blades LLC...910 757-0035
  625 Se Service Rd Southern Pines (28387) *(G-14556)*
Spartan Dyers Inc..704 829-0467
  217 Sterling St Belmont (28012) *(G-1009)*
Spartan Manufacturing Corp (PA)..............................336 996-5585
  1536 Brookford Industrial Dr Kernersville (27284) *(G-9237)*
Spatial Light LLC..617 213-0314
  1017 Pueblo Ridge Pl Cary (27519) *(G-1899)*
Spc Heating & Cooling, Wendell Also Called: Spc Mechanical Corporation *(G-15919)*
Spc Mechanical Corporation (PA)..............................252 237-9035
  1500 Wendell Rd Wendell (27591) *(G-15919)*
Spc-Usa Inc...910 875-9002
  404 W Edinborough Ave Raeford (28376) *(G-12440)*
Spco., Raleigh Also Called: S P Co Inc *(G-13222)*
Spec, Denver Also Called: Southstern Prcess Eqp Cntrls I *(G-4802)*
Specgx LLC..919 878-4706
  8801 Capital Blvd Raleigh (27616) *(G-13286)*
Special Fab & Machine Inc..336 956-2121
  4133 Old Salisbury Rd Lexington (27295) *(G-9784)*
Special Service Plastic, Charlotte Also Called: Baily Enterprises LLC *(G-2266)*
Special T Hosiery Mills Inc...336 227-2858
  1102 N Anthony St Burlington (27217) *(G-1499)*
Speciality Cox Mfg LLC..828 684-5762
  25 Commerce Way Arden (28704) *(G-379)*
Specialized Packaging Flexo, Greensboro Also Called: Specialized Packaging Radisson LLC *(G-7357)*
Specialized Packaging Radisson LLC........................336 574-1513
  600 Industrial Ave Greensboro (27406) *(G-7357)*
Specialty Boatworks Inc...910 251-5219
  262 Battleship Rd Wilmington (28401) *(G-16415)*
Specialty Fabricators Inc...336 838-7704
  1806 Industrial Dr Wilkesboro (28697) *(G-16042)*
Specialty Lighting LLC...704 538-6522
  4203 Fallston Rd Fallston (28042) *(G-5730)*
Specialty Machine Co Inc..704 853-2102
  1669 Federal St Gastonia (28052) *(G-6511)*
Specialty Manufacturing, Charlotte Also Called: Pretoria Transit Interiors Inc *(G-3377)*
Specialty Manufacturing Inc (HQ)..............................704 247-9300
  13501 S Ridge Dr Charlotte (28273) *(G-3598)*
Specialty Nails Company...336 883-0135
  5050 Prospect St High Point (27263) *(G-8548)*
Specialty National Inc..336 996-8783
  119 Furlong Industrial Dr Ste E Kernersville (27284) *(G-9238)*

Specialty Perf LLC...704 872-9980
  228 Crawford Rd Statesville (28625) *(G-14897)*
Specialty Products Intl Ltd...910 897-4706
  820 N 14th St Erwin (28339) *(G-5688)*
Specialty Textiles Inc...704 710-8657
  822 Floyd St Kings Mountain (28086) *(G-9332)*
Specialty Textiles Inc (PA)...704 739-4503
  515 Marie St Kings Mountain (28086) *(G-9333)*
Specialty Transportation, Newton Also Called: Specialty Trnsp Systems Inc *(G-11971)*
Specialty Trnsp Systems Inc.....................................828 464-9738
  2720 N Main Ave Newton (28658) *(G-11971)*
Specialty Welding...828 248-6229
  737 Hardin Rd Forest City (28043) *(G-6083)*
Specialty Welding & Mch Inc.....................................828 464-1104
  505 E 16th St Newton (28658) *(G-11972)*
Specified Metals Inc..336 786-6254
  391 Hickory St Mount Airy (27030) *(G-11576)*
Spectacle Envy..336 231-3135
  143 Summit Dr Mocksville (27028) *(G-10605)*
Spectacular Publishing Inc..919 672-0289
  3333 Durham Chapel Hill Blvd Ste A101 Durham (27707) *(G-5366)*
Spectra Integrated Systems Inc................................919 876-3666
  4805 Green Rd Ste 110 Raleigh (27616) *(G-13287)*
Spectrasite Communications LLC (HQ).....................919 468-0112
  400 Regency Forest Dr Ste 300 Cary (27518) *(G-1900)*
Spectre Custom Solutions LLC..................................704 450-4428
  142 Hampshire Dr Mooresville (28115) *(G-11094)*
Spectrum Adhesives Inc..828 396-4200
  3815 N Main St Granite Falls (28630) *(G-6758)*
Spectrum Brands Inc...800 854-3151
  15040 Choate Cir Charlotte (28273) *(G-3599)*
Spectrum Brands Inc...704 658-2060
  307 Oates Rd Ste F Mooresville (28117) *(G-11095)*
Spectrum Integrity Inc..805 426-4267
  2973 Autumn Acres Ln Trinity (27370) *(G-15359)*
Spectrum News..919 882-4009
  2505 Atlantic Ave Ste 102 Raleigh (27604) *(G-13288)*
Spectrum Products Inc..919 556-7797
  153 Mosswood Blvd Youngsville (27596) *(G-17100)*
Spectrum Screen Prtg Svc Inc..................................919 481-9905
  214 Hillsboro St Ste 101 Cary (27513) *(G-1901)*
Spee Dee Que Instant Prtg Inc.................................919 683-1307
  301 E Chapel Hill St Durham (27701) *(G-5367)*
Speed Brite Inc..704 639-9771
  1810 W Innes St Salisbury (28144) *(G-14046)*
Speed Energy Drink LLC...704 949-1255
  7100 Weddington Rd Nw Concord (28027) *(G-4364)*
Speed King Manufacturing Inc..................................910 457-1995
  8128 River Rd Southport (28461) *(G-14583)*
Speed Pro Imaging N Charlotte, Cornelius Also Called: Fast Pro Media LLC *(G-4545)*
Speed Pro Imaging N Charlotte, Cornelius Also Called: Fast Pro Media LLC *(G-4546)*
Speed Utv LLC...704 949-1255
  7100 Weddington Rd Nw Concord (28027) *(G-4365)*
Speedball Art Products, Statesville Also Called: Speedball Art Products Co LLC *(G-14898)*
Speedball Art Products Co LLC.................................800 898-7224
  2301 Speedball Rd Statesville (28677) *(G-14898)*
Speedcal Graphics Inc...704 412-3321
  4327 Carlotta St Charlotte (28208) *(G-3600)*
SpeeDee Prints LLC..704 366-1405
  4610 Sharon View Rd Charlotte (28226) *(G-3601)*
Speedgraphics Sign Design Inc................................828 771-0322
  35 Walden Dr Arden (28704) *(G-380)*
Speediprint Inc...910 483-2553
  164 Westwood Shopping Ctr Fayetteville (28314) *(G-5921)*
Speedpro Imaging..704 321-1200
  2301 Crownpoint Executive Dr Charlotte (28227) *(G-3602)*
Speedpro Imaging..704 799-8040
  10308 Bailey Rd Cornelius (28031) *(G-4587)*
Speedpro Imaging..704 495-6749
  103 Masthead Ct Mooresville (28117) *(G-11096)*
Speedpro Imaging..919 578-4338
  2400 Sumner Blvd Ste 110 Raleigh (27616) *(G-13289)*

ALPHABETIC SECTION

Speedpro Imaging Durham.. 919 278-7964
1055 Stillwell Dr Unit 1141 Durham (27707) *(G-5368)*

Speedpro of Northwest Raleigh, Morrisville *Also Called: Triangle Inner Vision Company* *(G-11452)*

Speedway Link Inc.. 704 338-2028
3727 Weddington Ridge Ln Matthews (28105) *(G-10292)*

Speedwell Machine Works Inc.. 704 866-7418
1301 Crowders Creek Rd Gastonia (28052) *(G-6512)*

Speedy Spread, Greensboro *Also Called: General Fertilizer Eqp Inc (G-7035)*

Speer Concrete Inc.. 910 947-3144
4221 Highway 15 501 Carthage (28327) *(G-1666)*

Speer Oil Company LLC.. 910 947-5494
3790 Us 15-501 Hwy Carthage (28327) *(G-1667)*

Speer Operational Tech LLC.. 864 631-2512
315 Baldwin Ave Marion (28752) *(G-10179)*

Spencer Bowman Customs, Oak Ridge *Also Called: B & B Welding Inc (G-12057)*

Spencer Logging.. 910 638-4899
Southern Pines (28388) *(G-14557)*

Spencer Machine Company, Gastonia *Also Called: Wallace Spencer (G-6538)*

Spencer Yachts Inc.. 252 473-2660
5698 Us Highway 64 # 264 Manns Harbor (27953) *(G-10123)*

Spencer-Pettus Machine Co, Bessemer City *Also Called: Tim Conner Enterprises Inc* *(G-1085)*

Spencers Inc Mount Airy N C (PA).. 336 789-9111
290 Quarry Rd Mount Airy (27030) *(G-11577)*

Spenco Medical Corporation.. 919 544-7900
2001 Tw Alexander Dr Durham (27709) *(G-5369)*

Spevco Inc.. 336 924-8100
8118 Reynolda Rd Pfafftown (27040) *(G-12190)*

Spg Prints, Charlotte *Also Called: Spgprints America Inc (G-3603)*

Spgprints America Inc (DH).. 704 598-7171
2121 Distribution Center Dr Ste E Charlotte (28269) *(G-3603)*

Sphenodon Tool Co Inc.. 252 757-3460
3530 Tupper Dr Greenville (27834) *(G-7586)*

SPI Express, Monroe *Also Called: Stegall Petroleum Inc (G-10815)*

Spider Press Inc.. 919 302-2726
303 Hinton St Apex (27502) *(G-243)*

Spinrite Yarns LP.. 252 833-4970
190 Plymouth St Washington (27889) *(G-15732)*

Spintech LLC.. 704 885-4758
159 Walker Rd Statesville (28625) *(G-14899)*

Spiral Graphics Inc.. 919 571-3371
8821 Gulf Ct Ste A Raleigh (27617) *(G-13290)*

Spire Industries Inc.. 435 994-4756
2524 S Wilmington St Raleigh (27603) *(G-13291)*

Spirit Aerosystems Inc.. 252 208-4645
2600 Aerosystems Blvd Kinston (28504) *(G-9386)*

Spirit Aerosystems NC Inc.. 252 208-4645
2626 Glenwood Ave Ste 550 Raleigh (27608) *(G-13292)*

Spiritus Systems, Aberdeen *Also Called: Spiritus Systems Company (G-30)*

Spiritus Systems Company.. 910 637-0196
112 Bud Pl Aberdeen (28315) *(G-30)*

Splendidcrm Software Inc.. 919 604-1258
705 Laurel Bay Ln Holly Springs (27540) *(G-8718)*

Spm Machine Works Inc.. 252 321-2134
4721 Old Nc 11 Ayden (28513) *(G-859)*

Spnc Associates Inc.. 919 467-5151
100 Falcone Pkwy Cary (27511) *(G-1902)*

Spod Inc.. 910 477-6297
316 Cedar Rd Southport (28461) *(G-14584)*

Spoonflower, Durham *Also Called: Spoonflower Inc (G-5370)*

Spoonflower Inc (DH).. 919 886-7885
3871 S Alston Ave Durham (27713) *(G-5370)*

Spoons Bowls N Baking Pans LLC.. 919 662-0494
101 Saint Mellion St Raleigh (27603) *(G-13293)*

Sporting Goods, Winnabow *Also Called: Every Day Carry LLc (G-16580)*

Sports Products LLC.. 919 562-4074
1608 Heritage Commerce Ct Ste 100 Wake Forest (27587) *(G-15595)*

Sports Solutions Inc.. 336 368-1100
614 E Main St Pilot Mountain (27041) *(G-12202)*

Sportsedge Inc.. 704 528-0188
3425 Derby Pl Greensboro (27405) *(G-7358)*

Sportsfield Specialties, Mocksville *Also Called: Sportsfield Specialties Inc (G-10606)*

Sportsfield Specialties Inc.. 704 637-2140
155 Boyce Dr Mocksville (27028) *(G-10606)*

Sportsmans Supply Company Inc.. 336 725-8791
2287 Cloverdale Ave Winston Salem (27103) *(G-16913)*

Spota LLC.. 919 569-6765
1505 Basley St Wake Forest (27587) *(G-15596)*

Spotless Industries LLC.. 980 430-1560
9739 Kings Parade Blvd Unit 318 Charlotte (28273) *(G-3604)*

Spranto America Inc.. 919 741-5095
1870 Lazio Ln Apex (27502) *(G-244)*

Spraying Systems Co.. 704 357-6499
5727 Westpark Dr Ste 204 Charlotte (28217) *(G-3605)*

Spring Air Mattress Corp.. 336 272-1141
401 N Raleigh St Greensboro (27401) *(G-7359)*

Spring Creek Press.. 828 337-8296
159 Atwood Dr Hendersonville (28792) *(G-7904)*

Spring Hope Enterprise Inc.. 252 478-3651
113 N Ash St Spring Hope (27882) *(G-14622)*

Spring Repair Service Inc.. 336 299-5660
5800 W Gate City Blvd Greensboro (27407) *(G-7360)*

Spring Rock Farms Inc.. 336 973-1447
4701 Parsonsville Rd Purlear (28665) *(G-12413)*

Spring Valley Carving Svcs LLC.. 919 553-7906
2024 Spring Valley Dr Clayton (27520) *(G-4012)*

Springlight Creative LLC.. 336 383-8076
1807 Swannanoa Dr Greensboro (27410) *(G-7361)*

Springmill Products Inc.. 336 406-9050
1147 Walter Mabe Rd Lawsonville (27022) *(G-9504)*

Sprinkle of Sugar LLC.. 336 474-8620
11 E Main St Thomasville (27360) *(G-15281)*

Sprout Pharmaceuticals Inc.. 919 882-0850
4350 Lassiter At North Hills Ave Ste 260 Raleigh (27609) *(G-13294)*

Spruce Pine Batch Inc.. 828 765-9876
2490 Us 19e Spruce Pine (28777) *(G-14658)*

Spruce Pine Mica Company.. 828 765-4241
132 Mountain Laurel Dr Spruce Pine (28777) *(G-14659)*

Spt Technology Inc.. 612 332-1880
3107 Chamber Dr Monroe (28110) *(G-10811)*

Spt Technology Inc.. 704 290-5007
4808 Persimmon Ct Monroe (28110) *(G-10812)*

Spunky Sports LLC.. 919 435-0198
7305 Mithrasdowne Ct Wake Forest (27587) *(G-15597)*

Spuntech Industries Inc.. 336 330-9000
555 N Park Dr Roxboro (27573) *(G-13825)*

SPX, Charlotte *Also Called: Clydeunion Pumps Inc (G-2504)*

SPX Cooling Tech LLC.. 630 881-9777
13515 Ballantyne Corporate Pl Charlotte (28277) *(G-3606)*

SPX Cooling Tech, LLC, Charlotte *Also Called: SPX Cooling Tech LLC (G-3606)*

SPX Corporation.. 336 627-6020
523 S New St Eden (27288) *(G-5503)*

SPX CORPORATION, Eden *Also Called: SPX Corporation (G-5503)*

SPX Flow, Charlotte *Also Called: SPX Flow Inc (G-3607)*

SPX Flow Inc (HQ).. 704 752-4400
13320 Ballantyne Corporate Pl Charlotte (28277) *(G-3607)*

SPX Flow Holdings Inc.. 704 808-3848
13320 Ballantyne Corporate Pl Charlotte (28277) *(G-3608)*

SPX Flow Tech Systems Inc.. 704 752-4400
13320 Ballantyne Corporate Pl Charlotte (28277) *(G-3609)*

SPX Flow Technology Usa Inc (DH).. 704 808-3848
13320 Ballantyne Corporate Pl Charlotte (28277) *(G-3610)*

SPX Flow Us LLC.. 919 735-4570
2719 Graves Dr Ste 10 Goldsboro (27534) *(G-6660)*

SPX Latin America Corporation (DH).. 704 808-3848
13320 Ballantyne Corporate Pl Charlotte (28277) *(G-3611)*

Square One Machine LLC.. 704 600-6296
658 Washburn Switch Rd Shelby (28150) *(G-14370)*

Square One Woodworking.. 828 277-5164
33 Dorchester Ave Asheville (28806) *(G-786)*

Square Peg Construction Inc.. 828 277-5164
28 London Rd Asheville (28803) *(G-787)*

(PA)=Parent Co (HQ)=Headquarters (DH)=Div Headquarters

Squarehead Technology LLC 571 299-4849
  200 1st Ave Nw Hickory (28601) *(G-8167)*
Squeaks Logging Inc 252 794-1531
  139 Republican Rd Windsor (27983) *(G-16570)*
Squeegee Tees & More Inc 704 888-0336
  12410 Grey Commercial Rd Midland (28107) *(G-10480)*
Srb Technologies Inc (PA) 336 659-2610
  2580 Landmark Dr Winston Salem (27103) *(G-16914)*
SRI Gear LLC 704 910-2751
  2125 S Tryon St Charlotte (28203) *(G-3612)*
SRI Performance LLC 704 662-6982
  122 Knob Hill Rd Mooresville (28117) *(G-11097)*
SRI Ventures Inc 919 427-1681
  3415 Hawkins Ave Sanford (27330) *(G-14190)*
Srng-Liberty LLC 248 212-7209
  1447 S Tyron St Ste 301 Charlotte (28203) *(G-3613)*
SRNg-T&w LLC 704 271-9889
  1447 S Tyron St Ste 301 Charlotte (28203) *(G-3614)*
SRS Partners, Matthews *Also Called: Surface Renewal Systems LLC (G-10348)*
Ss Handcrafted Art LLC 704 664-2544
  107 Glade Valley Ave Mooresville (28117) *(G-11098)*
Ss Manufacturing Inc 770 317-8121
  703 Mooresville Rd Ste B Kannapolis (28081) *(G-9134)*
Ssb Manufacturing Company 704 596-4935
  5100r Wt Harris Blvd Charlotte (28269) *(G-3615)*
Ssd Designs LLC (PA) 980 245-2988
  9935d Rea Rd # 433 Charlotte (28277) *(G-3616)*
Ssi, Belmont *Also Called: Steel Specialty Co Belmont Inc (G-1010)*
Ssi Services Inc 919 867-1450
  7231 Acc Blvd Ste 107 Raleigh (27617) *(G-13295)*
Ssnc LLC Pba NC Filtration, Belmont *Also Called: NC Filtration of Florida LLC (G-996)*
Sspc Inc
  12016 Steele Creek Rd Charlotte (28273) *(G-3617)*
SSS Logging Inc 828 467-1155
  29 Liberty Drive Marion Marion (28752) *(G-10180)*
St Engineering Leeboy Inc 704 966-3300
  500 Lincoln County Parkway Ext Lincolnton (28092) *(G-9921)*
St Investors Inc 704 969-7500
  4064 Colony Rd Ste 150 Charlotte (28211) *(G-3618)*
St Johns Museum of Art 910 763-0281
  114 Orange St Wilmington (28401) *(G-16416)*
St Johns Packaging Usa LLC 336 292-9911
  2619 Phoenix Dr Greensboro (27406) *(G-7362)*
St Lucie Woodworks Inc 772 626-4778
  366 Bostic Rd Raeford (28376) *(G-12441)*
St of Greensboro LLC 336 851-1600
  6383 Burnt Poplar Rd Greensboro (27409) *(G-7363)*
St Pauls, NC Processing Plant, Saint Pauls *Also Called: Sanderson Farms LLC Proc Div (G-13909)*
St Timothy Chair Co Division, Conover *Also Called: Classic Leather Inc (G-4436)*
St.clair Coatings, Monroe *Also Called: As Inc (G-10651)*
Stabilus, Gastonia *Also Called: Stabilus Inc (G-6513)*
Stabilus Inc (DH) 704 865-7444
  1201 Tulip Dr Gastonia (28052) *(G-6513)*
Stable Holdco Inc 704 866-7140
  1201 Tulip Dr Gastonia (28052) *(G-6514)*
Stackhouse Publishing Inc 203 699-6571
  299 Blackberry Rd Boone (28607) *(G-1239)*
Stacks Kitchen Matthews 704 243-2024
  1315 N Broome St Waxhaw (28173) *(G-15777)*
Stackz Welding 336 564-5481
  8301 Zebedee Ln Stokesdale (27357) *(G-14950)*
Staclean Diffuser, Salisbury *Also Called: Staclean Diffuser Company LLC (G-14047)*
Staclean Diffuser Company LLC (PA) 704 636-8697
  2205 Executive Dr Salisbury (28147) *(G-14047)*
Staclear Inc 919 838-2844
  7250 Acc Blvd Raleigh (27617) *(G-13296)*
Stafford Cutting Dies Inc 704 821-6330
  131 Business Park Dr Indian Trail (28079) *(G-8965)*
Stafford Logging LLC 828 635-8584
  905 Cove Gap Rd Moravian Falls (28654) *(G-11147)*

Stafford Welding 704 774-1837
  1806 Starnes Cemetary Rd Monroe (28112) *(G-10813)*
Stage Dec, Greensboro *Also Called: Stage Decoration and Sups Inc (G-7364)*
Stage Decoration and Sups Inc 336 621-5454
  3519 Associate Dr Greensboro (27405) *(G-7364)*
Stainless & Nickel Alloys LLC 704 201-2898
  1700 W Pointe Dr Ste E Charlotte (28214) *(G-3619)*
Stainless Steel Countertops NC 919 935-0835
  79 Bishops Ct Cameron (28326) *(G-1563)*
Stainless Steel Spc Inc 919 779-4290
  2025 Carr Pur Dr Raleigh (27603) *(G-13297)*
Stainless Stl Fabricators Inc 919 833-3520
  5325 Departure Dr Raleigh (27616) *(G-13298)*
Stainless Supply Inc 704 635-2064
  307 N Secrest Ave Monroe (28110) *(G-10814)*
Stainless Valve Co, Monroe *Also Called: B+e Manufacturing Co Inc (G-10659)*
Stair Tamer Cargo Lifts, Shiloh *Also Called: Stair Tamer LLC (G-14393)*
Stair Tamer LLC 252 336-4437
  899 S Sandy Hook Rd Shiloh (27974) *(G-14393)*
Stairways From Heaven Inc 828 627-3860
  262 Maple Leaf Ln Clyde (28721) *(G-4128)*
Staley Feed Mill, Staley *Also Called: Pilgrims Pride Corporation (G-14669)*
Staley Logging & Grading, Millers Creek *Also Called: William Shawn Staley (G-10496)*
Stallergenes Greer, Lenoir *Also Called: Albion Medical Holdings Inc (G-9571)*
Stallergenes Greer, Lenoir *Also Called: Greer Laboratories Inc (G-9615)*
Stallings Cabinets Inc 252 338-6747
  508 N Hughes Blvd Elizabeth City (27909) *(G-5571)*
Stamp Approval - Anita White 910 433-2279
  2949 Delaware Dr Fayetteville (28304) *(G-5922)*
Stamp-Tech, Wendell *Also Called: Precision Stampers Inc (G-15912)*
Stampco Metal Products Inc 828 645-4271
  108 Herron Cove Rd Weaverville (28787) *(G-15864)*
Stamper Sheet Metal Inc 336 476-5145
  357 Bud Kanoy Rd Thomasville (27360) *(G-15282)*
Stamping & Scrapbooking Rm Inc 336 389-9538
  2806 Randleman Rd Greensboro (27406) *(G-7365)*
Stamping School LLC 407 435-3135
  32 Loggers Run Hendersonville (28739) *(G-7905)*
Stampsource, Charlotte *Also Called: Precision Partners LLC (G-3369)*
Stampsource, Charlotte *Also Called: Precision Partners LLC (G-3370)*
Stan Bunn 1856 Pubg Co LLC 980 613-0633
  2540 Radrick Ln Charlotte (28262) *(G-3620)*
Stanadyne Diesel Systems, Jacksonville *Also Called: SL Liquidation LLC (G-9033)*
Stanadyne Intrmdate Hldngs LLC (HQ) 860 525-0821
  405 White St Jacksonville (28546) *(G-9038)*
Stanadyne Jacksonville LLC 860 683-4553
  405 White St Jacksonville (28546) *(G-9039)*
Stanadyne LLC, Jacksonville *Also Called: SL Liquidation LLC (G-9032)*
Stanadyne Operating Co LLC (PA) 910 353-3666
  405 White St Jacksonville (28546) *(G-9040)*
Standard Mineral Division, Robbins *Also Called: Vanderbilt Minerals LLC (G-13603)*
Standard Tools and Eqp Co 336 697-7177
  4810 Clover Rd Greensboro (27405) *(G-7366)*
Standard Tytape Company Inc 828 693-6594
  1495 N Main St Hendersonville (28792) *(G-7906)*
Stanfast 336 841-7700
  4191 Mendenhall Oaks Pkwy Ste 101 High Point (27265) *(G-8549)*
Stanford Manufacturing LLC 336 999-8799
  3720 Stanford Way Clemmons (27012) *(G-4060)*
Stanley Black & Decker 704 987-2271
  9829 Northcross Center Ct Huntersville (28078) *(G-8899)*
Stanley Black & Decker Inc 704 509-0844
  9115 Old Statesville Rd Ste E Charlotte (28269) *(G-3621)*
Stanley Black & Decker Inc 704 293-9392
  9930 Kincey Ave Huntersville (28078) *(G-8900)*
Stanley Customer Support Divis 704 789-7000
  1000 Stanley Dr Concord (28027) *(G-4366)*
Stanley E Dixon Jr Inc 252 332-5004
  113 Rail Road St Ahoskie (27910) *(G-66)*
Stanley Engineered Fastening, Stanfield *Also Called: Avdel USA LLC (G-14675)*

ALPHABETIC SECTION

Stanley Furniture Company LLC.................................. 336 884-7700
200 N Hamilton St No 200 High Point (27260) *(G-8550)*

Stanleys Woodworking.................................. 828 612-4286
3006 Jack Whitener Rd Newton (28658) *(G-11973)*

Stanly Fixs Acquisition LLC.................................. 704 474-3184
11635 Nc 138 Hwy Norwood (28128) *(G-12044)*

Stanly Fixtures, Norwood *Also Called: Stanly Fixs Acquisition LLC (G-12044)*

Stanly Fixtures Company Inc.................................. 704 474-3184
11635 Nc 138 Hwy Norwood (28128) *(G-12045)*

Stanly Tractor Company.................................. 704 983-1106
37931 Us 52 Hwy N New London (28127) *(G-11879)*

Stans Quality Foods Inc.................................. 336 570-2572
1503 N Graham Hopedale Rd Burlington (27217) *(G-1500)*

Stansell Industries LLC.................................. 864 371-2425
118 Bradley St Asheville (28806) *(G-788)*

Stanza Machinery Inc.................................. 704 599-0623
6801 Northpark Blvd Ste B Charlotte (28216) *(G-3622)*

Star America Inc (PA).................................. 704 788-4700
190 Cabarrus Ave W Concord (28025) *(G-4367)*

Star Food Products Inc (PA).................................. 336 227-4079
727 S Spring St Burlington (27215) *(G-1501)*

Star Milling Company.................................. 704 873-9561
247 Commerce Blvd Unit F Statesville (28625) *(G-14900)*

Star Ready-Mix Inc.................................. 336 725-9401
2865 Lowery St Winston Salem (27101) *(G-16915)*

Star Snax LLC.................................. 828 261-0255
103b Somerset Dr Nw Conover (28613) *(G-4500)*

Star Tickets Plus, Morrisville *Also Called: Tickets Plus Inc (G-11448)*

Star Wipers Inc.................................. 888 511-2656
2260 Raeford Ct Gastonia (28052) *(G-6515)*

Starcke Abrasives Usa Inc.................................. 704 583-3338
9109 Forsyth Park Dr Charlotte (28273) *(G-3623)*

Starcraft Diamonds Inc.................................. 252 717-2548
444 Stewart Pkwy Washington (27889) *(G-15733)*

Stardust Cellars, Winston Salem *Also Called: Stardust Cellars LLC (G-16916)*

Stardust Cellars LLC (PA).................................. 336 466-4454
1764 Camden Rd Winston Salem (27103) *(G-16916)*

Starfangled Press.................................. 804 338-9972
30 Stratford Ave Brevard (28712) *(G-1290)*

Starflite Companies Inc (PA).................................. 252 728-2690
530 Sensation Weigh Beaufort (28516) *(G-968)*

Starhgen Arospc Components LLC.................................. 704 660-1001
333 Oates Rd Mooresville (28117) *(G-11099)*

Starlight Cases, Pine Level *Also Called: New Innovative Products Inc (G-12212)*

Starlight Manufacturing Inc.................................. 252 426-7867
113 Starlight Dr Hertford (27944) *(G-7924)*

Starnes Pallet Service Inc (PA).................................. 704 596-9006
4000 Jeff Adams Dr Charlotte (28206) *(G-3624)*

Starpet, Asheboro *Also Called: Indorama Ventures USA Inc (G-443)*

Starpet Inc.................................. 336 672-0101
801 Pineview Rd Asheboro (27203) *(G-485)*

Starr Training.................................. 336 644-0252
7715 Tall Meadows Dr Kernersville (27284) *(G-9239)*

Starr's Party Ice, Greensboro *Also Called: Robert D Starr (G-7313)*

Starrlight Mead.................................. 919 533-6314
130 Lorax Ln Pittsboro (27312) *(G-12351)*

Starrlight Mead LLC.................................. 919 672-1469
4606 Stillview Dr Durham (27712) *(G-5371)*

Starta Development Inc.................................. 919 865-7700
2610 Wycliff Rd Ste 19 Raleigh (27607) *(G-13299)*

State Electric Supply Company.................................. 336 855-8200
2709 Patterson St Greensboro (27407) *(G-7367)*

State Hwy Patrol-Troop D, Roxboro *Also Called: North Crlina Dept Crime Ctrl P (G-13810)*

State Industries Inc.................................. 704 597-8910
4302 Raleigh St Charlotte (28213) *(G-3625)*

State of ARC Welding.................................. 336 341-9780
4632 Stanley Ct Winston Salem (27101) *(G-16917)*

State of Art Custom Framing.................................. 336 629-7377
150 Sunset Ave Asheboro (27203) *(G-486)*

Statesman Furniture.................................. 828 431-2146
1014 1st St W Conover (28613) *(G-4501)*

Statesville Breeder Feedmill, Statesville *Also Called: Mountaire Farms LLC (G-14847)*

Statesville Brick Company.................................. 704 872-4123
391 Brick Yard Rd Statesville (28677) *(G-14901)*

Statesville High.................................. 704 873-3491
474 N Center St Statesville (28677) *(G-14902)*

Statesville LLC.................................. 704 872-3303
151 Walker Rd Statesville (28625) *(G-14903)*

Statesville Med MGT Svcs LLC.................................. 704 996-6748
1503 E Broad St Statesville (28625) *(G-14904)*

Statesville Pallet Company Inc.................................. 828 632-0268
351 Old Mountain Rd Hiddenite (28636) *(G-8227)*

Statesville Sandlot Basbal Inc.................................. 704 880-1334
165 Eastwood Dr Statesville (28625) *(G-14905)*

Static Control, Sanford *Also Called: Static Control Components Inc (G-14191)*

Static Control Components Inc (DH).................................. 919 774-3808
3010 Lee Ave Sanford (27332) *(G-14191)*

Static Control Ic-Disc Inc.................................. 919 774-3808
3010 Lee Ave Sanford (27332) *(G-14192)*

Staunton Capital Inc (PA).................................. 704 866-8533
3406 W Wendover Ave Ste E Greensboro (27407) *(G-7368)*

Staunton Saw Service.................................. 919 471-3883
1611 Milton Rd Durham (27712) *(G-5372)*

Stay Alert Safety Services Inc.................................. 919 828-5399
1240 Kirkland Rd Raleigh (27603) *(G-13300)*

STAY ALERT SAFETY SERVICES, INC., Raleigh *Also Called: Stay Alert Safety Services Inc (G-13300)*

Stay Online LLC (PA).................................. 888 346-4688
1506 Ivac Way Creedmoor (27522) *(G-4622)*

Stay-Right Pre-Cast Concrete Inc.................................. 919 494-7600
2675 Us1 Hwy Franklinton (27525) *(G-6164)*

STC Precision Cutting Tools, Greenville *Also Called: Sphenodon Tool Co Inc (G-7586)*

Steag SCR-Tech Inc (PA).................................. 704 827-8933
11707 Steele Creek Rd Charlotte (28273) *(G-3626)*

Steeds Service Co.................................. 336 748-1587
109 Pineywood St Thomasville (27360) *(G-15283)*

Steel and Pipe Corporation.................................. 919 776-0751
3709 Hawkins Ave Sanford (27330) *(G-14193)*

Steel City Services LLC.................................. 919 698-2407
1129 E Geer St Durham (27704) *(G-5373)*

Steel Construct Systems LLC.................................. 704 781-5575
118 Pine Forest Rd Locust (28097) *(G-9972)*

Steel Fab.................................. 980 721-8969
161 Gray Cliff Dr Mooresville (28117) *(G-11100)*

Steel Smart Incorporated.................................. 919 736-0681
1042 Airport Rd Ne Pikeville (27863) *(G-12194)*

Steel Specialty Co Belmont Inc (PA).................................. 704 825-4745
5907 W Wilkinson Blvd Belmont (28012) *(G-1010)*

Steel Supply and Erection Co.................................. 336 625-4830
1237 N Fayetteville St Asheboro (27203) *(G-487)*

Steel Tech, Charlotte *Also Called: Waldenwood Group Inc (G-3790)*

Steel Tech, Charlotte *Also Called: Waldenwood Group LLC (G-3791)*

Steel Technologies Carolinas, Clinton *Also Called: Steel Technologies LLC (G-4112)*

Steel Technologies LLC.................................. 910 592-1266
112 Sycamore St Clinton (28328) *(G-4112)*

Steel Technology Inc (PA).................................. 252 937-7122
2620 Business Park Dr Rocky Mount (27804) *(G-13733)*

Steelcity LLC (PA).................................. 336 434-7000
505 Aztec Dr Archdale (27263) *(G-299)*

Steelco Inc.................................. 704 896-1207
1020 Commercial Dr Matthews (28104) *(G-10346)*

Steelcraft Structures LLC.................................. 980 434-5400
1841 Amity Hill Rd Statesville (28677) *(G-14906)*

Steele Rubber Products Inc.................................. 704 483-9343
6180 Highway 150 E Denver (28037) *(G-4803)*

Steelfab Inc (PA).................................. 704 394-5376
3025 Westport Rd Charlotte (28208) *(G-3627)*

Steelfab of Virginia Inc (HQ).................................. 919 828-9545
5105 Bur Oak Cir Ste 100 Raleigh (27612) *(G-13301)*

Steelman Lumber & Pallet LLC.................................. 336 468-2757
4744 Us 21 Hwy Hamptonville (27020) *(G-7678)*

Steelman Milling Company Inc.................................. 336 463-5586
1517 Us 601 Hwy Yadkinville (27055) *(G-17051)*

(PA)=Parent Co (HQ)=Headquarters (DH)=Div Headquarters

Steelpoint — ALPHABETIC SECTION

Steelpoint, Matthews *Also Called: Mmdi Inc (G-10336)*

Steen Inc.. 336 545-3328
5306 Century Oaks Dr Greensboro (27455) *(G-7369)*

Stefano Foods Inc... 704 399-3935
4825 Hovis Rd Charlotte (28208) *(G-3628)*

Stegall Petroleum Inc.. 704 283-5058
1907 Old Charlotte Hwy Monroe (28110) *(G-10815)*

Stein Fibers Ltd... 704 599-2804
10130 Mallard Creek Rd Charlotte (28262) *(G-3629)*

Stein Fibers, Ltd., Charlotte *Also Called: Stein Fibers Ltd (G-3629)*

Stein-Palmer Printing Co.. 740 633-3894
124 Tulip Dr Mooresville (28117) *(G-11101)*

Stella Cabinet Works... 910 358-4248
218 Starlight Ln Maysville (28555) *(G-10375)*

Stellar Innovations Inc... 704 746-2886
21000 Torrence Chapel Rd Ste 104 Cornelius (28031) *(G-4588)*

Stellar Technology... 716 250-1900
111 Lord Dr Cary (27511) *(G-1903)*

Step In Sock.. 704 508-9966
208 Glenway St Belmont (28012) *(G-1011)*

Stephanie Baxter... 803 203-8467
1089 Peach Tree St Lincolnton (28092) *(G-9922)*

Stephanies Mattress LLC.. 704 763-0705
5920 N Tryon St Charlotte (28213) *(G-3630)*

Stephen J McCusker... 336 884-1916
1705 Heathgate Pt High Point (27262) *(G-8551)*

Stephen P Wolfe... 252 792-3001
28228 Us Highway 64 Jamesville (27846) *(G-9082)*

Stephenson Millwork Co Inc..................................... 252 237-1141
210 Harper St Ne Wilson (27893) *(G-16543)*

Steri-Air LLC... 336 434-1166
2109 Brevard Rd High Point (27263) *(G-8552)*

Sterimed, Charlotte *Also Called: Envirotek Worldwide LLC (G-2719)*

Sterling Cleora Corporation...................................... 919 563-5800
3115 Buckingham Rd Durham (27707) *(G-5374)*

Sterling Pharma USA, Cary *Also Called: Sterling Pharma Usa LLC (G-1904)*

Sterling Pharma Usa LLC.. 919 678-0702
1001 Sheldon Dr Ste 101 Cary (27513) *(G-1904)*

Sterling Products Corporation.................................. 646 423-3175
3924 S Holden Rd Greensboro (27406) *(G-7370)*

Sterling Publications LLC.. 919 656-5042
3809 Sparrow Pond Ln Raleigh (27606) *(G-13302)*

Sterling Rack Inc... 704 866-9131
176 Tarheel Dr Gastonia (28056) *(G-6516)*

Sterling Sign, Greensboro *Also Called: Sterling Products Corporation (G-7370)*

Steve & Ray Banks Logging Inc................................ 910 743-3051
7625 New Bern Hwy Maysville (28555) *(G-10376)*

Steve Brooks... 919 248-1458
4725 Regalwood Dr Raleigh (27613) *(G-13303)*

Steve Evans Logging Inc... 252 792-1836
7096 Us Highway 17 Williamston (27892) *(G-16071)*

Steve Noggle Turned Wood..................................... 828 437-8017
638 Enola Rd Morganton (28655) *(G-11257)*

Steve S Seafood Inc.. 910 279-5711
6545 Angels Gift Trl Ne Leland (28451) *(G-9560)*

Steve Whiteside Logging LLC.................................. 828 287-5862
136 Matthew Church Rd Rutherfordton (28139) *(G-13891)*

Steven C Haddock DBA Haddock............................. 252 714-2431
4122 Leary Mills Rd Vanceboro (28586) *(G-15483)*

Steven Meseroll.. 850 264-6079
202 Demaree Ln Matthews (28105) *(G-10293)*

Steven Smoakes... 910 352-4287
595 Sharease Cir Wilmington (28405) *(G-16417)*

Steven-Robert Original Dessert, Pembroke *Also Called: Steven-Robert Originals LLC (G-12184)*

Steven-Robert Originals LLC................................... 910 521-0199
701 S Jones St Pembroke (28372) *(G-12184)*

Stevens Foodservice... 919 322-5470
8392 Six Forks Rd Ste 202 Raleigh (27615) *(G-13304)*

Stevens Lighting Inc (PA).. 910 944-7185
488 Bibey Rd Carthage (28327) *(G-1668)*

Stevens Mill Woodworks LLC.................................. 919 440-8834
3048 Stevens Mill Rd Goldsboro (27530) *(G-6661)*

Stevens Packing Inc.. 336 274-6033
3023 Randleman Rd Greensboro (27406) *(G-7371)*

Stevenso Vestal, Burlington *Also Called: Smith Draperies Inc (G-1496)*

Stevenson Woodworking... 919 362-9121
300 Hickory View Ln Apex (27502) *(G-245)*

Steves Cabinets Plus Inc... 919 351-0454
121 Christopher Ave Princeton (27569) *(G-12405)*

Steves TS & Uniforms Inc....................................... 919 554-4221
3129 Heritage Trade Dr Ste 108 Wake Forest (27587) *(G-15598)*

Stewart Gear Manufacturing, Gastonia *Also Called: Textile Parts and Mch Co Inc (G-6524)*

Stewart Screen Printing Inc..................................... 336 451-9636
1318 Starr Dr High Point (27260) *(G-8553)*

Stewart Sreen Printing.. 336 434-4444
3757 Lynn Oaks Dr Trinity (27370) *(G-15360)*

Stewart Superabsorbents LLC................................. 828 855-9316
1954 Main Ave Se Hickory (28602) *(G-8168)*

Stewarts Garage and Welding Co............................. 336 983-5563
6544 Doral Dr Tobaccoville (27050) *(G-15321)*

Stf Precision, Arden *Also Called: Diamond Dog Tools Inc (G-325)*

STI, Kings Mountain *Also Called: Kings Plush Inc (G-9314)*

STI, Kings Mountain *Also Called: Specialty Textiles Inc (G-9332)*

STI Polymer Inc.. 800 874-5878
5618 Clyde Rhyne Dr Sanford (27330) *(G-14194)*

STI Turf Equipment LLC.. 704 393-8873
4355 Golf Acres Dr Charlotte (28208) *(G-3631)*

Stick Candles.. 315 369-0011
372 Valley Rd Cashiers (28717) *(G-1937)*

Sticker Farm LLC.. 919 332-1342
3516 Keithcastle Ct Charlotte (28210) *(G-3632)*

Stickler Woodworking Inc.. 336 302-0683
458 Burney Rd Asheboro (27205) *(G-488)*

Sticky Fingers Vinyl... 336 859-0262
705 Loflin Rd Denton (27239) *(G-4749)*

Sticky Life... 910 817-4531
321 Goldsboro St Newton Grove (28366) *(G-11993)*

Stiefel Laboratories Inc (DH).................................... 888 784-3335
5 Moore Dr Durham (27709) *(G-5375)*

Stiefel Laboratories Inc... 888 784-3335
410 Blackwell St Durham (27701) *(G-5376)*

Stikeleather Inc... 828 352-9095
146 Windsor Dr Taylorsville (28681) *(G-15168)*

Stiles Mfg Co Inc... 910 592-6344
102 Coharie Dr Clinton (28328) *(G-4113)*

Stiletto Manufacturing Inc.. 252 564-4877
107 S Water St Columbia (27925) *(G-4168)*

Still There... 704 728-1888
12115 Creek Turn Dr Charlotte (28278) *(G-3633)*

Stillwood, Burlington *Also Called: Stillwood Ammun Systems LLC (G-1502)*

Stillwood Ammun Systems LLC................................ 919 721-9096
642 E Webb Ave Burlington (27217) *(G-1502)*

Stine Gear & Machine Company............................... 704 445-1245
2015 Hephzibah Church Rd Bessemer City (28016) *(G-1084)*

Stitch 2 Fit.. 704 677-4842
295 Alcove Rd Mooresville (28117) *(G-11102)*

Stitch 98 Inc... 704 235-5783
154 Talbert Pointe Dr Ste 101 Mooresville (28117) *(G-11103)*

Stitch Barn.. 252 717-1262
1709 Eckerts Ln Greenville (27834) *(G-7587)*

Stitch Count, Ahoskie *Also Called: Stanley E Dixon Jr Inc (G-66)*

Stitch In Time Inc.. 910 497-4171
412 S Main St Spring Lake (28390) *(G-14628)*

Stitch More Big... 910 799-8992
6626 Gordon Rd Ste E Wilmington (28411) *(G-16418)*

Stitch of Royalty... 336 457-1888
721 Pine St Greensboro (27401) *(G-7372)*

Stitch X Stitch LLC.. 704 970-0667
9805 Statesville Rd Charlotte (28269) *(G-3634)*

Stitch-A-Doozy.. 336 573-2339
140 Salems Ln Stoneville (27048) *(G-14968)*

ALPHABETIC SECTION

Stitch-N-Sassy 704 491-8274
10303 Remembrance Trl Huntersville (28078) *(G-8901)*

Stitchcrafters Incorporated 828 397-7656
7923 Houston Ave Hickory (28602) *(G-8169)*

Stitchery Inc 336 248-5604
134 Elk St Lexington (27292) *(G-9785)*

Stitches In Grove 704 791-2402
304 Keller St China Grove (28023) *(G-3890)*

Stitches of Thread 704 840-7215
7300 Sheffingdell Dr Charlotte (28226) *(G-3635)*

Stitches On Critter Pond 919 624-5886
7333 Critter Pond Rd Wake Forest (27587) *(G-15599)*

Stitchinwright 704 219-0697
12235 Winget Rd Charlotte (28278) *(G-3636)*

Stitchmaster, Greensboro Also Called: Stitchmaster LLC *(G-7373)*

Stitchmaster LLC 336 852-6448
309 S Regional Rd Greensboro (27409) *(G-7373)*

Stitchworks Embroidery, Washington Also Called: Uniforms Galore *(G-15735)*

Stm Industries Inc (PA) 828 322-2700
1712 8th Street Dr Se Hickory (28602) *(G-8170)*

Stn Cushion Company 336 476-9100
3 Regency Industrial Blvd Thomasville (27360) *(G-15284)*

Stock Building Supply Holdings LLC 919 431-1000
8020 Arco Corp Dr Ste 400 Raleigh (27617) *(G-13305)*

Stockholm Corporation 704 552-9314
4729 Stockholm Ct Charlotte (28273) *(G-3637)*

Stokes Mfg LLC 336 270-8746
140 Somerset Church Rd Roxboro (27573) *(G-13826)*

Stoltz Automotive Inc 336 595-4218
4861 New Walkertown Rd Walkertown (27051) *(G-15616)*

Stone & Leigh Furniture, Morganton Also Called: Vlr LLC *(G-11265)*

Stone Cllins Mtr Rewinding Inc 910 347-2775
111 Ramsey Rd Jacksonville (28546) *(G-9041)*

Stone Equipment Company Inc 980 202-4448
322 Old Hargrave Rd Lexington (27295) *(G-9786)*

Stone House Creek Logging 252 586-4477
615 Fleming Dairy Rd Littleton (27850) *(G-9953)*

Stone International USA, Thomasville Also Called: Stone Marble Co Inc *(G-15285)*

Stone Marble Co Inc 773 227-1161
7004 Pikeview Dr Thomasville (27360) *(G-15285)*

Stone Mountain Cabinetary 828 676-3600
206 Vista Blvd Arden (28704) *(G-381)*

Stone Resource Inc 336 889-7800
2101 E Martin Luther King Jr Dr High Point (27260) *(G-8554)*

Stone Supply Inc 828 678-9966
159 Depot St Burnsville (28714) *(G-1534)*

Stonefield Cellars LLC 336 632-2391
8220 Nc Highway 68 N Stokesdale (27357) *(G-14951)*

Stonehaven Jewelry Gallery Ltd 919 462-8888
111 Adams St Cary (27513) *(G-1905)*

Stonemaster Inc 704 333-0353
15105 John J Delaney Dr Ste D Charlotte (28277) *(G-3638)*

Stonery LLC 704 662-8702
1077 Mecklenburg Hwy Mooresville (28115) *(G-11104)*

Stonetree Signs 336 625-0938
5321 New Hope Rd Denton (27239) *(G-4750)*

Stoneville Lumber Company Inc 336 623-4311
3442 Nc Highway 135 Stoneville (27048) *(G-14969)*

Stoneworx Inc 252 937-8080
7015 Stanley Park Dr Rocky Mount (27804) *(G-13734)*

Stony Gap Wholesale Co Inc 704 982-5360
40616c Stony Gap Rd Ste C Albemarle (28001) *(G-109)*

Stony Knoll Forge 704 507-0179
1309 Hamiltons Cross Rd Marshville (28103) *(G-10225)*

Stop N Go LLC 919 523-7355
2916 Homebrook Ln Morrisville (27560) *(G-11434)*

Stop-Painting.com, Wake Forest Also Called: Spota LLC *(G-15596)*

Storage System Solutions Inc 336 710-5600
590 Crossingham Rd Mount Airy (27030) *(G-11578)*

Storagemotion Inc 704 746-3700
216 Overhill Dr Ste 104 Mooresville (28117) *(G-11105)*

Store 72, Greensboro Also Called: Consolidated Pipe & Sup Co Inc *(G-6930)*

Stork News, Fayetteville Also Called: Stork News Tm of America *(G-5923)*

Stork News Tm of America (PA) 910 868-3065
5075 Morganton Rd 12a Fayetteville (28314) *(G-5923)*

Stork United Corporation 704 598-7171
3201 Rotary Dr Charlotte (28269) *(G-3639)*

Stormberg Foods LLC 919 947-6011
1002b Sunburst Dr Goldsboro (27534) *(G-6662)*

Storopack Inc 800 827-7225
2598 Empire Dr Ste G Winston Salem (27103) *(G-16918)*

Storybook Farm Metal Shop Inc 919 967-9491
231 Storybook Farm Ln Chapel Hill (27516) *(G-2074)*

Storybook Metal Shop, Chapel Hill Also Called: Storybook Farm Metal Shop Inc *(G-2074)*

Stout Beverages LLC (PA) 704 293-7640
518 N Sims St Kings Mountain (28086) *(G-9334)*

Stout Brands LLC 704 293-7640
518 N Sims St Kings Mountain (28086) *(G-9335)*

Stout Brewing Company LLC 704 288-4042
518 N Sims St Kings Mountain (28086) *(G-9336)*

Stove-Woodward Co, Youngsville Also Called: Stowe Woodward LLC *(G-17101)*

Stovers Precision Tooling Inc 704 876-3673
239 Treebark Rd Statesville (28625) *(G-14907)*

Stowe Woodward Licensco LLC 919 526-1400
8537 Six Forks Rd Ste 300 Raleigh (27615) *(G-13306)*

Stowe Woodward LLC 360 636-0330
14101 Capital Blvd Ste 101 Youngsville (27596) *(G-17101)*

Stowe Woodward LLC 919 556-7235
51 Flex Way Youngsville (27596) *(G-17102)*

Stowed LLC 203 346-5687
1100 W Ward Ave High Point (27260) *(G-8555)*

Stowed Home, High Point Also Called: Stowed LLC *(G-8555)*

Stpi, Statesville Also Called: Southeast Tubular Products Inc *(G-14889)*

Straight Edge Woodworks LLC 704 456-7046
4800 Annelise Dr Harrisburg (28075) *(G-7729)*

Straightline Woodworks 336 469-7029
2845 Mize Rd Yadkinville (27055) *(G-17052)*

Strandberg Engrg Labs Inc 336 274-3775
1302 N Ohenry Blvd Greensboro (27405) *(G-7374)*

Strandh Woodworks LLC 919 703-8056
3501 Johnson Grant Dr New Hill (27562) *(G-11865)*

Strassberg Ceramics 704 315-2034
156 Anniston Way Davidson (28036) *(G-4697)*

Strategic 3d Solutions Inc 919 451-5963
4805 Green Rd Ste 114 Raleigh (27616) *(G-13307)*

Strategic3dsolutions, Raleigh Also Called: Strategic 3d Solutions Inc *(G-13307)*

Stratford Die Casting Inc 336 784-0100
1665 S Martin Luther King Jr Dr Ste A Winston Salem (27107) *(G-16919)*

Stratford Metalfinishing Inc 336 723-7946
1681 S Martin Luther King Jr Dr Winston Salem (27107) *(G-16920)*

Stratford Tool & Die Co Inc 336 765-2030
3841 Kimwell Dr Winston Salem (27103) *(G-16921)*

Stratton Publishing & Mktg Inc 703 914-9200
1457 Quadrant Cir Wilmington (28405) *(G-16419)*

Strawbridge Studios Inc (PA) 919 286-9512
3616 Hillsborough Rd Ste D Durham (27705) *(G-5377)*

Streets Auto Sales & Four WD 704 888-8686
814 Main St W Locust (28097) *(G-9973)*

Stress-Tek, Wendell Also Called: Vishay Transducers Ltd *(G-15924)*

Strickland Backhoe 910 893-5274
3216 Nc 210 S Bunnlevel (28323) *(G-1331)*

Strickland Bros Entps Inc 252 478-3058
3622 Wiggins Rd Spring Hope (27882) *(G-14623)*

Strike & Flame Candles 336 207-4487
3213 Pleasant Garden Rd Apt 2e Greensboro (27406) *(G-7375)*

Stripelight, Apex Also Called: Parhelion Incorporated *(G-226)*

Strong Global Entrmt Inc 704 471-6784
5960 Fairview Rd Ste 275 Charlotte (28210) *(G-3640)*

Strong Manufacturers, Pineville Also Called: Strong Medical Partners LLC *(G-12308)*

Strong Manufacturers, Pineville Also Called: Strong Medical Partners LLC *(G-12309)*

Strong Medical Partners LLC (PA) 716 626-9400
11519 Nations Ford Rd Ste 200 Pineville (28134) *(G-12308)*

Strong Medical Partners LLC   **ALPHABETIC SECTION**

Strong Medical Partners LLC.. 716 507-4476
   11515 Nations Ford Rd Pineville (28134) *(G-12309)*

Stronger By Science Tech LLC.. 336 391-9377
   514 Daniels St 101 Raleigh (27605) *(G-13308)*

Stronghaven Incorporated.. 770 739-6080
   11135 Monroe Rd Matthews (28105) *(G-10294)*

Stroud Logging... 828 541-2721
   480 Coalville Rd Marble (28905) *(G-10134)*

Stroudcraft Marine LLC... 910 623-4055
   13991 Nc Hwy 210 Rocky Point (28457) *(G-13751)*

Stroup Machine & Mfg Inc... 704 394-0023
   2019 W Laporte Dr Charlotte (28216) *(G-3641)*

Stroupe Mirror Co.. 336 475-2181
   2661 Reynolds Dr Winston Salem (27104) *(G-16922)*

Structral Catings Hertford LLC.. 919 553-3034
   930 River Rd Cofield (27922) *(G-4138)*

Structural Materials Inc.. 828 754-6413
   802 Old North Rd Nw Lenoir (28645) *(G-9653)*

Structural Planners Inc... 919 848-8964
   312 Dalton Dr Raleigh (27615) *(G-13309)*

Structural Steel of Carolina, Winston Salem Also Called: Division 5 LLC *(G-16682)*

Structural Steel Products Corp.. 919 359-2811
   8029 Us 70 Bus Hwy W Clayton (27520) *(G-4013)*

Structure Medical LLC... 704 799-3450
   123 Cayuga Dr Mooresville (28117) *(G-11106)*

Strutmasters, Roxboro Also Called: Suspension Experts LLC *(G-13827)*

Stryker Corp... 919 455-6755
   525 Pylon Dr Raleigh (27606) *(G-13310)*

Stryker Corporation.. 919 433-3325
   800 Capitola Dr Ste 12 Durham (27713) *(G-5378)*

STS Packaging Charlotte LLC.. 980 259-2290
   1201 Westinghouse Blvd Charlotte (28273) *(G-3642)*

STS Screen Printing Inc... 704 821-8488
   107 Industrial Dr Matthews (28104) *(G-10347)*

Stuart Dischell.. 336 334-4695
   611 Howard St Greensboro (27403) *(G-7376)*

Stuart Nye Hand Wrought Jwly, Asheville Also Called: R & B Partnership *(G-750)*

Stuart Ryan Kent & Co.. 252 916-8226
   223 Forlines Rd Winterville (28590) *(G-17014)*

Studio 180... 570 998-8746
   606 Hamecon Pl Cedar Grove (27231) *(G-1972)*

Studio Displays Inc.. 704 588-6590
   11150 Rivers Edge Rd Pineville (28134) *(G-12310)*

Studio Griffin LLC.. 919 661-9634
   105 Marianna Pl Garner (27529) *(G-6316)*

Studio Stitch LLC... 336 288-9200
   1616 Battleground Ave Ste D3 Greensboro (27408) *(G-7377)*

Studio Tk LLC.. 919 464-2920
   3940 Us 70 Hwy Business Clayton (27520) *(G-4014)*

Studio Touya.. 910 464-3116
   4911 Busbee Rd Seagrove (27341) *(G-14249)*

Studleys Independent Rods... 704 296-9036
   3229 Waxhaw Hwy Monroe (28112) *(G-10816)*

Stump and Grind LLC.. 704 488-2271
   7420 Ponders End Ln Charlotte (28213) *(G-3643)*

Stump Logging... 910 620-7000
   61 Supply St Se Supply (28462) *(G-15012)*

Stump Printing Co Inc.. 260 723-5171
   525 Lumina Ave S Wrightsville Beach (28480) *(G-17028)*

Stump's, Wrightsville Beach Also Called: Stump Printing Co Inc *(G-17028)*

Sturdy Control Div, Wilmington Also Called: Sturdy Corporation *(G-16420)*

Sturdy Corporation... 910 763-2500
   1822 Carolina Beach Rd Wilmington (28401) *(G-16420)*

Sturdy Power Corporation LLC.. 910 763-2500
   1822 Carolina Beach Rd Wilmington (28401) *(G-16421)*

Sturgeon Creek Home LLC.. 336 843-1403
   90 East 13th Ave Lexington (27292) *(G-9787)*

Sturm Ruger & Company Inc... 336 427-0286
   271 Cardwell Rd Mayodan (27027) *(G-10368)*

Style Upholstering Inc.. 828 322-4882
   33 23rd Ave Ne Hickory (28601) *(G-8171)*

Suarez Bakery Inc.. 704 525-0145
   4245 Park Rd Charlotte (28209) *(G-3644)*

Sub-Aquatics Inc.. 336 674-0749
   210 Labrador Dr Randleman (27317) *(G-13492)*

Subaru Folger Automotive... 704 531-8888
   5701 E Independence Blvd Charlotte (28212) *(G-3645)*

Subsea Video Systems Inc.. 252 338-1001
   611 Hull Dr Elizabeth City (27909) *(G-5572)*

Substance Incorporated... 800 985-9485
   3000 Frazier Dr Claremont (28610) *(G-3939)*

Success In Marketplace LLC.. 919 608-1259
   5300 Six Forks Rd Ste 213 Raleigh (27609) *(G-13311)*

Success Magazine, Raleigh Also Called: Success Publishing Inc *(G-13312)*

Success Publishing Inc.. 919 807-1100
   150 Fayetteville St M Raleigh (27601) *(G-13312)*

Succession Solutions Inc... 704 631-9004
   11108 Downs Rd Pineville (28134) *(G-12311)*

Sudanese Cmnty Schl Greensboro.. 336 763-7761
   604 Orourke Dr Greensboro (27409) *(G-7378)*

Suds ME Up Buttercup.. 704 419-2075
   226 Marys Grove Church Rd Kings Mountain (28086) *(G-9337)*

Sue-Lynn Textiles Inc (PA).. 336 578-0871
   302 Roxboro St Haw River (27258) *(G-7757)*

Sugar Creek Brewing Co LLC.. 704 521-3333
   215 Southside Dr Charlotte (28217) *(G-3646)*

Sugar Mountain Woodworks Inc.. 423 292-6245
   3030 Sugar Mountain 2 Rd Newland (28657) *(G-11894)*

Sugar Pops.. 704 799-0959
   248 N Main St Mooresville (28115) *(G-11107)*

Sugarcane Studios LLC... 828 785-3167
   1550 Hendersonville Rd Asheville (28803) *(G-789)*

Sugarshack Bakery and EMB.. 803 920-3311
   275 Sugar Loaf Rd Troy (27371) *(G-15417)*

Sugg Logging LLC... 910 995-5728
   207 Crawford Rd Ellerbe (28338) *(G-5645)*

Suits US, Mount Airy Also Called: Suits Usa Inc *(G-11579)*

Suits Usa Inc.. 336 786-8808
   1219a W Lebanon St Mount Airy (27030) *(G-11579)*

Sullivan Motorsports Inc.. 252 923-2257
   471 Creek Rd Bath (27808) *(G-917)*

Sullivan Workshop LLC.. 704 560-9900
   1150 Laurel Park Ln Charlotte (28270) *(G-3647)*

Sumitomo Elc Lightwave Corp... 919 541-8100
   201 S Rogers Ln Ste 100 Raleigh (27610) *(G-13313)*

Summer Industries, Welcome Also Called: Summer Industries LLC *(G-15876)*

Summer Industries LLC... 336 731-9217
   262 Welcome Center Court Welcome (27374) *(G-15876)*

Summit Agro Usa LLC... 984 260-0407
   240 Leigh Farm Rd Ste 415 Durham (27707) *(G-5379)*

Summit Aviation Inc... 302 834-5400
   243 Burgess Rd Ste A Greensboro (27409) *(G-7379)*

Summit Logging LLC... 910 734-8787
   1485 Beulah Church Rd Lumberton (28358) *(G-10056)*

Summit Materials, Wilmington Also Called: American Materials Company LLC *(G-16109)*

Summit Peak Pens and WD Works.. 336 404-8312
   412 E Starmount Ave Liberty (27290) *(G-9832)*

Summit Seltzer, Charlotte Also Called: Summit Seltzer Company LLC *(G-3648)*

Summit Seltzer Company LLC... 980 819-6416
   2215 Thrift Rd Charlotte (28208) *(G-3648)*

Summit Yarn LLC... 704 874-5000
   531 Cotton Blossom Cir Gastonia (28054) *(G-6517)*

Summus, Cary Also Called: Oasys Mobile Inc *(G-1837)*

Sumpters Jwly & Collectibles... 704 399-5348
   3501 Wilkinson Blvd Charlotte (28208) *(G-3649)*

Sumter Packaging Corporation.. 704 873-0583
   844 Meacham Rd Statesville (28677) *(G-14908)*

Sun & Surf Containers Inc... 910 754-9600
   2589 Sun And Surf Ln Nw Shallotte (28470) *(G-14279)*

Sun Chemical Corporation... 704 587-4531
   1701 Westinghouse Blvd Charlotte (28273) *(G-3650)*

Sun Cleaners & Laundry Inc.. 704 325-3722
   2306 N Main Ave Newton (28658) *(G-11974)*

ALPHABETIC SECTION

Sun Drop Bottling, Rocky Mount *Also Called: Sun-Drop Btlg Rocky Mt NC Inc (G-13735)*
Sun Drop Bottling Co, Shelby *Also Called: Choice USA Beverage Inc (G-14294)*
Sun Fabricators Inc 336 885-0095
  701 W Ward Ave High Point (27260) *(G-8556)*
Sun Oven, Wilkesboro *Also Called: Sun Ovens International Inc (G-16043)*
Sun Ovens International Inc 630 208-7273
  418 Wilkesboro Blvd Unit 1 Wilkesboro (28697) *(G-16043)*
Sun Path Contracting, Raeford *Also Called: Spc-Usa Inc (G-12440)*
Sun Path Products Inc 910 875-9002
  404 W Edinborough Ave Raeford (28376) *(G-12442)*
Sun Printing Company Inc 336 773-1346
  956 Kenleigh Cir Winston Salem (27106) *(G-16923)*
Sun Publishing Company 919 942-5282
  107 N Roberson St Chapel Hill (27516) *(G-2075)*
Sun River Service Company, Wilson *Also Called: Protein For Pets Opco LLC (G-16524)*
Sun Valley Stl Fabrication Inc 704 289-5830
  1810 Tower Industrial Dr Monroe (28110) *(G-10817)*
Sun-Drop Bottling Co, Lowell *Also Called: Choice USA Beverage Inc (G-10007)*
Sun-Drop Btlg Rocky Mt NC Inc 252 977-4586
  2406 W Raleigh Blvd Rocky Mount (27803) *(G-13735)*
Sun-Journal Incorporated 252 638-8101
  4901 Us Highway 17 S New Bern (28562) *(G-11848)*
Sunbelt Abrasives Inc 336 882-6837
  1507 Bethel Dr High Point (27260) *(G-8557)*
Sunbelt Enterprises Inc 704 788-4749
  263 Litaker Ln Concord (28025) *(G-4368)*
Sunbelt Spring & Stamping, Rosman *Also Called: M-B Industries Inc (G-13786)*
Suncast Corporation 704 274-5394
  9801 Kincey Ave Huntersville (28078) *(G-8902)*
Sunco Powder Systems Inc 704 545-3922
  3230 Valentine Ln Charlotte (28270) *(G-3651)*
Suncrest Farms Cntry Hams Inc 336 667-4441
  1148 Foster St Wilkesboro (28697) *(G-16044)*
Sundance Cstm Painted Cabinets 704 500-3732
  20209 Church St Cornelius (28031) *(G-4589)*
Sunday Drive Holdings Inc 919 825-5613
  421 Fayetteville St # 1100 Raleigh (27601) *(G-13314)*
Sundown Times, West Jefferson *Also Called: Mountain Times Inc (G-15945)*
Sundown Times Inc 828 264-1881
  474 Industrial Park Dr Boone (28607) *(G-1240)*
Sundrop Printing 704 960-1592
  700 N Cannon Blvd Kannapolis (28083) *(G-9135)*
Sundyne Corp 303 249-5350
  5509 Crosshill Ct Charlotte (28277) *(G-3652)*
Sung Industries Inc 919 387-8550
  204 Kellyridge Dr Apex (27502) *(G-246)*
Sunhs Warehouse LLC 919 908-1523
  607 Ellis Rd Bldg 42a Durham (27703) *(G-5380)*
Sunjune Ltrary Cllborative LLC 502 767-2867
  19 Northview St Asheville (28801) *(G-790)*
Sunnex, Charlotte *Also Called: Sunnex Inc (G-3653)*
Sunnex Inc 800 445-7869
  8001 Tower Point Dr Charlotte (28227) *(G-3653)*
Sunninghill Jill Baking Co LLC 704 894-9901
  16618 Flying Jib Rd Cornelius (28031) *(G-4590)*
Sunny View Pallet Company 828 625-9907
  3057 Big Level Rd Mill Spring (28756) *(G-10491)*
Sunqest Inc (PA) 828 325-4910
  1555 N Rankin Ave Newton (28658) *(G-11975)*
Sunray Inc 828 287-7030
  4761 Us 64 74a Hwy Rutherfordton (28139) *(G-13892)*
Sunrise Development LLC 828 453-0590
  650 Nc 120 Hwy Mooresboro (28114) *(G-10841)*
Sunrise Development USA, Mooresboro *Also Called: Sunrise Development LLC (G-10841)*
Sunrise Sawmill Inc 828 277-0120
  68 W Chapel Rd Asheville (28803) *(G-791)*
Sunrock Group Holdings Corp (PA) 919 747-6400
  200 Horizon Dr Ste 100 Raleigh (27615) *(G-13315)*
Sunseeker US Inc 443 253-1546
  311 Post Office Dr Ste 315 Indian Trail (28079) *(G-8966)*

Sunshine Mnfctred Strctres Inc 704 279-6600
  850 Gold Hill Ave Rockwell (28138) *(G-13659)*
Sunstar Heating Products Inc 704 372-3486
  305 Doggett St Charlotte (28203) *(G-3654)*
Sunstar Network LLC 828 684-3571
  100 Thunderland Cir Arden (28704) *(G-382)*
Sunstead Brewing LLC 980 949-6200
  1200 S Graham St Charlotte (28203) *(G-3655)*
Suntech Medical Inc 919 654-2300
  5827 S Miami Blvd Ste 100 Morrisville (27560) *(G-11435)*
Suntex Industries 336 784-1000
  5000 S Main St Winston Salem (27107) *(G-16924)*
Suntory International (DH) 917 756-2747
  4141 Parklake Ave Ste 600 Raleigh (27612) *(G-13316)*
Super G Print Lab LLC 919 864-9351
  813 Onslow St Durham (27705) *(G-5381)*
Super Retread Center Inc (PA) 919 734-0073
  1213 S George St Goldsboro (27530) *(G-6663)*
Super Sagless, Statesville *Also Called: Leggett & Platt Incorporated (G-14835)*
Super Shred, Greenville *Also Called: Collins Banks Investments Inc (G-7504)*
Super Stitchy LLC 919 762-0626
  216 Abbeville Ln Holly Springs (27540) *(G-8719)*
Super-Net, Fuquay Varina *Also Called: American Netting Corp (G-6178)*
Superfast Performance Pdts Inc 828 980-8072
  3379 Harvard Pl Hudson (28638) *(G-8781)*
Superior Cabling Solutions LLC 704 736-9017
  824 Madison St Lincolnton (28092) *(G-9923)*
Superior Custom Cabinets LLC 919 778-1845
  170 Scott St Goldsboro (27534) *(G-6664)*
Superior Dry Kilns Inc 828 754-7001
  2601 Withers Dr Hudson (28638) *(G-8782)*
Superior Envmtl Svcs LLC 919 717-1199
  4033 Village Park Dr Unit 220 Knightdale (27545) *(G-9429)*
Superior Essex Inc 252 823-5111
  2801 Anaconda Rd Tarboro (27886) *(G-15121)*
SUPERIOR ESSEX INTERNATIONAL LP, Tarboro *Also Called: Superior Essex Intl LP (G-15122)*
Superior Essex Intl LP 252 823-5111
  2801 Anaconda Rd Tarboro (27886) *(G-15122)*
Superior Finishing Systems LLC 336 956-2000
  2132 Beckner Rd Lexington (27292) *(G-9788)*
Superior Fire Hose Corp 704 643-5888
  10000 Industrial Dr Ste B Pineville (28134) *(G-12312)*
Superior Machine Co SC Inc 828 652-6141
  169 Machine Shop Rd Marion (28752) *(G-10181)*
Superior Machine Shop Inc 910 675-1336
  354 Sawdust Rd Rocky Point (28457) *(G-13752)*
Superior Manufacturing Company 336 661-1200
  4102 Indiana Ave Winston Salem (27105) *(G-16925)*
Superior Plastics Inc 704 864-5472
  533 N Broad St Gastonia (28054) *(G-6518)*
Superior Powder Coating LLC 704 869-0004
  123 Shannon Bradley Rd Gastonia (28052) *(G-6519)*
Superior Sign Company Inc 336 454-2226
  506 Overbrook Dr High Point (27262) *(G-8558)*
Superior Tooling Inc 919 570-9762
  2800 Superior Dr Wake Forest (27587) *(G-15600)*
Superior Veneers Inc 828 433-6986
  1405 Mountain Shadows Dr Morganton (28655) *(G-11258)*
Superior Wood Products Inc 336 472-2237
  10190 E Us Highway 64 Thomasville (27360) *(G-15286)*
Superskinsystems Inc 336 601-6005
  3329 N Rockingham Rd Greensboro (27407) *(G-7380)*
Supertex Inc 336 622-1000
  312 W Luther Ave Liberty (27298) *(G-9833)*
Suppliers To Wholesalers Inc 704 375-7406
  1816 W Pointe Dr Ste A Charlotte (28214) *(G-3656)*
Supplyone Rockwell Inc 704 279-5650
  729 Palmer Rd Rockwell (28138) *(G-13660)*
Supreme Elastic Corporation 828 302-3836
  325 Spencer Rd Ne Conover (28613) *(G-4502)*

Supreme Murphy Trck Bodies Inc   **ALPHABETIC SECTION**

Supreme Murphy Trck Bodies Inc 252 291-2191
    4000 Airport Dr Nw Wilson (27896) *(G-16544)*

Supreme Sweepers LLC 888 698-9996
    6135 Park South Dr Ste 510 Charlotte (28210) *(G-3657)*

Supreme T-Shirts & Apparel 919 772-9040
    2813 Banks Rd Raleigh (27603) *(G-13317)*

Sure Trip Inc (PA) 704 983-4651
    703a Concord Rd Albemarle (28001) *(G-110)*

Sure Wood Products Inc 828 261-0004
    980 3rd Ave Se Hickory (28602) *(G-8172)*

Surelift Inc 828 963-6899
    151 H O Aldridge Rd Unit B Boone (28607) *(G-1241)*

Suretech Assembly Inc 919 569-0346
    150a Jeffrey Way Youngsville (27596) *(G-17103)*

Surface Buff LLC 919 341-2873
    1140 Kildaire Farm Rd # 303-3 Cary (27511) *(G-1906)*

Surface Renewal Systems LLC 704 207-3596
    5024 Saddle Horn Trl Matthews (28104) *(G-10348)*

Surfline Inc 252 715-1630
    3335 S Virginia Dare Trl Nags Head (27959) *(G-11727)*

Surgical Center of Morehea 252 247-0314
    3714 Guardian Ave Ste W Morehead City (28557) *(G-11193)*

Surgical Guide Systems LLC 919 244-4463
    658 The Preserve Trl Chapel Hill (27517) *(G-2076)*

Surgilum LLC 910 202-2202
    2 N Front St Ste 5 Wilmington (28401) *(G-16422)*

Surratt Hosiery Mill Inc 336 859-4583
    22872 Nc Highway 8 Denton (27239) *(G-4751)*

Surry Chemicals Incorporated 336 786-4607
    241 Hickory St Mount Airy (27030) *(G-11580)*

Surry Collection, Mount Airy *Also Called: Kustom Kraft Wdwrks Mt Airy In (G-11533)*

Surry Elc Mtr & Contrls Inc 336 786-1717
    425 Hadley St Mount Airy (27030) *(G-11581)*

Surry Logistix LLC 336 710-3446
    535 E Pine St Mount Airy (27030) *(G-11582)*

Surry Scene 336 786-4141
    319 N Renfro St Mount Airy (27030) *(G-11583)*

Surteco SE, Greensboro *Also Called: Surteco USA Inc (G-7381)*

Surteco USA Inc 336 668-9555
    7104 Cessna Dr Greensboro (27409) *(G-7381)*

Surtronics Inc 919 834-8027
    4001 Beryl Rd Raleigh (27606) *(G-13318)*

Susan Link Woodworks LLC 828 492-8026
    29 Star Ridge Rd Canton (28716) *(G-1627)*

Susan Strazzella 828 676-1162
    8 Town Square Blvd # 407 Asheville (28803) *(G-792)*

Suspension Experts LLC 855 419-3072
    118 Commerce Dr Roxboro (27573) *(G-13827)*

Suspensions LLC 704 809-1269
    4723 Mountain Creek Ave Denver (28037) *(G-4804)*

Sustain Rng, Charlotte *Also Called: SRNg-T&w LLC (G-3614)*

Sutlers Spirit Company 336 565-6006
    840 Mill Works St Winston Salem (27101) *(G-16926)*

Sutter Street, Claremont *Also Called: Sutter Street Manufacturing (G-3940)*

Sutter Street Manufacturing 828 459-5598
    2973 Kelly Blvd Claremont (28610) *(G-3940)*

Sutton Scientifics Inc 910 428-1600
    246 W College St Star (27356) *(G-14723)*

Sv Plastics LLC 336 472-2242
    42 High Tech Blvd Thomasville (27360) *(G-15287)*

Svcm 305 767-3595
    536 N Generals Blvd Lincolnton (28092) *(G-9924)*

Svcm International, Lincolnton *Also Called: Svcm (G-9924)*

Swaim Inc (PA) 336 885-6131
    1801 S University Pkwy High Point (27260) *(G-8559)*

Swaim Ornamental Iron Works 336 765-5271
    2570 Landmark Dr Winston Salem (27103) *(G-16927)*

Swain & Temple Inc 252 771-8147
    149 Lilly Rd South Mills (27976) *(G-14525)*

Swanson Custom Wood Workin 910 465-3199
    611 Ann St Wilmington (28401) *(G-16423)*

Swanson Custom Woodworking Inc 910 465-3199
    98 N Fayetteville Rd Southport (28461) *(G-14585)*

Swanson Sheetmetal Inc 704 283-3955
    320 Broome St Monroe (28110) *(G-10818)*

Swatch Works Inc 336 626-9971
    453 Oakhurst Rd Asheboro (27205) *(G-489)*

Swatchcraft 336 841-7113
    203 Woodmont Rd Jamestown (27282) *(G-9073)*

Swatchcraft, High Point *Also Called: E Feibusch Company Inc (G-8333)*

Swatchworks Inc 336 626-9971
    730 Industrial Park Ave Asheboro (27205) *(G-490)*

SWB Logging LLC 704 485-3411
    213 Glenwood Dr Oakboro (28129) *(G-12082)*

Sweatnet LLC 847 331-7287
    310 Arlington Ave Unit 229 Charlotte (28203) *(G-3658)*

Sweet Hme Carolna Vinyrd & Win 336 469-9905
    3429 Old Us 421 Hwy E Yadkinville (27055) *(G-17053)*

Sweet Home Yadkin Inc 336 414-9822
    1024 Brookhaven Ln Yadkinville (27055) *(G-17054)*

Sweet Room LLC 336 567-1620
    4435 Garden Club St High Point (27265) *(G-8560)*

Sweet Sanctions LLC 717 222-1859
    48 Petrel Trce Hampstead (28443) *(G-7657)*

Sweet Sssfras Publications Inc 704 340-3862
    5828 Swanston Dr Charlotte (28269) *(G-3659)*

Sweet Taters LLC 252 969-0229
    1121 Falls Rd Rocky Mount (27804) *(G-13736)*

Sweet Tea Girls Patterns 843 907-2727
    137 Watsons Mill Ln Clayton (27527) *(G-4015)*

Sweet Tees Screen Printing LLC 919 497-0500
    651 Woodland Trl Louisburg (27549) *(G-10003)*

Sweet Treats By Treat Lady LLC 336 831-3282
    650 Rugby Row Apt H Winston Salem (27106) *(G-16928)*

Sweet Wick Candle Company LLC 770 687-1519
    120 Serenity Pointe Dr Kernersville (27284) *(G-9240)*

Sweeteasy LLC 252 698-0109
    507 E Main St Ste C Elizabeth City (27909) *(G-5573)*

Sweetgran Prints 919 387-0711
    2410 Vetrina Way Apex (27502) *(G-247)*

Sweets Syrup LLC (PA) 704 989-2156
    6100 Creola Rd Charlotte (28270) *(G-3660)*

Sweettader Custom Composites 910 262-6650
    8118 Market St Wilmington (28411) *(G-16424)*

Swell Home Solutions Inc 919 440-4692
    109 Barfield St Mount Olive (28365) *(G-11670)*

Swimways 252 563-1101
    3002 Anaconda Rd Tarboro (27886) *(G-15123)*

Swiner Publishing Company Inc 919 599-3441
    2 Crawford Ct Durham (27703) *(G-5382)*

Swing Kurve Logistic Trckg LLC 704 506-7371
    2428 Freedom Dr Charlotte (28208) *(G-3661)*

Swir Vision Systems Inc 919 248-0032
    3021 Cornwallis Rd Durham (27709) *(G-5383)*

Swirl Oakhurst LLC 704 258-1209
    1640 Oakhurst Commons Dr Ste 103 Charlotte (28205) *(G-3662)*

Swiss Diamond, Charlotte *Also Called: Swiss Made Brands USA Inc (G-3663)*

Swiss Made Brands USA Inc 704 900-6622
    200 Forsyth Hall Dr Ste H Charlotte (28273) *(G-3663)*

Swk Technologies Inc 336 230-0200
    2309 W Cone Blvd Ste 220 Greensboro (27408) *(G-7382)*

Swm Intl, Wilson *Also Called: Schweitzer-Mauduit Intl Inc (G-16541)*

Swofford Inc 252 478-5969
    301 Railroad St S Wilson (27893) *(G-16545)*

Sword Conservatory Inc 919 557-4465
    112 Tonks Trl Holly Springs (27540) *(G-8720)*

Sycamore Brewing LLC 704 910-3821
    401 W 24th St Charlotte (28206) *(G-3664)*

Sycamore Cabinetry Inc 704 375-1617
    644 Dallas Bessemer City Hwy Dallas (28034) *(G-4659)*

Syd Inc 336 294-8807
    5223c W Market St Ste C Greensboro (27409) *(G-7383)*

ALPHABETIC SECTION

Sylva Herald and Ruralite..828 586-2611
  539 W Main St Sylva (28779) *(G-15070)*

Sylva Herald Pubg Co Incthe..828 586-2611
  539 W Main St Sylva (28779) *(G-15071)*

Sylva Herald, The, Sylva *Also Called: Sylva Herald and Ruralite (G-15070)*

Sylvester Artsan Woodworks LLC.......................................989 529-3573
  751 7 Lks N West End (27376) *(G-15933)*

Symbrium Inc (PA)..919 879-2470
  6021 Triangle Dr Raleigh (27617) *(G-13319)*

Synchrono Group Inc..888 389-0439
  8601 Six Forks Rd Ste 400 Raleigh (27615) *(G-13320)*

Syncot Plastics Inc...704 967-0010
  350 Eastwood Dr Belmont (28012) *(G-1012)*

Syneos Health Consulting Inc..866 462-7373
  1030 Sync St Morrisville (27560) *(G-11436)*

Synereca, Chapel Hill *Also Called: Synereca Pharmaceuticals Inc (G-2077)*

Synereca Pharmaceuticals Inc...919 966-3929
  39519 Glenn Glade Chapel Hill (27517) *(G-2077)*

Synergem Technologies Inc...866 859-0911
  371 Windrush Ln Mount Airy (27030) *(G-11584)*

Synnovator Inc...919 360-0518
  104 Tw Alexander Dr # 1 Durham (27709) *(G-5384)*

Synopsys Inc..919 941-6600
  710 Slater Rd Morrisville (27560) *(G-11437)*

Synoptix Companies LLC...910 790-3630
  130 Cinema Dr Wilmington (28403) *(G-16425)*

Synq Marketing Group LLC..800 380-6360
  338 S Sharon Amity Rd Charlotte (28211) *(G-3665)*

Syntec Inc..336 861-9023
  200 Swathmore Ave High Point (27263) *(G-8561)*

Syntech Abrasives Inc..704 525-8030
  8325 Arrowridge Blvd Ste H Charlotte (28273) *(G-3666)*

Syntech of Burlington Inc...336 570-2035
  1825 Frank Holt Dr Burlington (27215) *(G-1503)*

Syntegon Technology Svcs LLC (PA).................................919 877-0886
  2440 Sumner Blvd Raleigh (27616) *(G-13321)*

Syntha Group Inc (PA)..336 885-5131
  331 Burton Ave High Point (27262) *(G-8562)*

Synthetic Finishing, Hickory *Also Called: Tsg Finishing LLC (G-8188)*

Synthetic Finishing Co, Hickory *Also Called: Tsg Finishing LLC (G-8189)*

Synthetics Finishing, Hickory *Also Called: Tsg Finishing LLC (G-8186)*

Synthomer Inc..704 225-1872
  2011 N Rocky River Rd Monroe (28110) *(G-10819)*

Synthon, Durham *Also Called: Synthon Pharmaceuticals Inc (G-5385)*

Synthon Pharmaceuticals Inc...919 493-6006
  1007 Slater Rd Ste 150 Durham (27703) *(G-5385)*

Synthonix Inc...919 875-9277
  2713 Connector Dr Wake Forest (27587) *(G-15601)*

Syracuse Plastics, Cary *Also Called: PCI of North Carolina LLC (G-1845)*

Syrup and More LLC..781 548-1346
  3702 Kirby Dr Greensboro (27403) *(G-7384)*

Sysmetric USA...704 522-8778
  107 Infield Ct Mooresville (28117) *(G-11108)*

Systel Business Eqp Co Inc...336 808-8000
  3517 W Wendover Ave Greensboro (27407) *(G-7385)*

Systel Office Automation, Greensboro *Also Called: Systel Business Eqp Co Inc (G-7385)*

T - Square Enterprises Inc..704 846-8233
  8318 Pineville Matthews Rd Charlotte (28226) *(G-3667)*

T & J Panel Systems Inc..704 924-8600
  269 Marble Rd Statesville (28625) *(G-14909)*

T & N Manufacturing Inc..704 788-1418
  4345 Shiloh Church Rd Davidson (28036) *(G-4698)*

T & R Signs...919 779-1185
  110 E Main St Garner (27529) *(G-6317)*

T & R Signs & Screen Printing, Garner *Also Called: T & R Signs (G-6317)*

T & S Hardwoods Inc...828 586-4044
  3635 Skyland Dr Sylva (28779) *(G-15072)*

T 2 E, Rocky Mount *Also Called: Trans-Tech Energy Inc (G-13674)*

T Air Inc (PA)...980 595-2840
  11020 David Taylor Dr Ste 350 Charlotte (28262) *(G-3668)*

T and T Timber...252 799-6077
  910 Breezy Banks Rd Roper (27970) *(G-13771)*

T C I, Charlotte *Also Called: Triple Crown International LLC (G-3730)*

T C Logging, Reidsville *Also Called: Carter Thomas Wayne Sr (G-13513)*

T Cs Services Inc...910 655-2796
  286 Jacobs Rd Bolton (28423) *(G-1168)*

T D M Corporation
  333 White Pine Dr Fletcher (28732) *(G-6044)*

T Distribution NC Inc..828 438-1112
  801 N Green St Morganton (28655) *(G-11259)*

T E Garner Logging..252 678-3836
  985 Nc Highway 48 Gaston (27832) *(G-6332)*

T E Johnson Building and Rentl, Four Oaks *Also Called: T E Johnson Lumber Co Inc (G-6113)*

T E Johnson Lumber Co Inc...919 963-2233
  3872 Old School Rd Four Oaks (27524) *(G-6113)*

T E M A, Raleigh *Also Called: The Tarheel Electric Membership Association Incorporated (G-13342)*

T H Blue Inc...910 673-3033
  226 Flowers Rd Eagle Springs (27242) *(G-5461)*

T Hoff Manufacturing Corp (PA)...919 833-8671
  4500 Preslyn Dr D Raleigh (27603) *(G-13322)*

T J S Woodworks...336 299-5913
  707 Shelby Dr Greensboro (27409) *(G-7386)*

T L V, Charlotte *Also Called: Tlv Corporation (G-3698)*

T M S, Raleigh *Also Called: Triangle Microsystems Inc (G-13359)*

T P Supply Co Inc..336 789-2337
  483 Belvue Dr Mount Airy (27030) *(G-11585)*

T Precision Machining Inc..828 250-0993
  123 Lyman St Asheville (28801) *(G-793)*

T R P, Wilson *Also Called: Tobacco Rag Processors Inc (G-16547)*

T Renee Severt LLC...248 540-3741
  101 Conner Dr Ste 401 Chapel Hill (27514) *(G-2078)*

T S Designs Incorporated..336 226-5694
  2053 Willow Spring Ln Burlington (27215) *(G-1504)*

T S E, Fayetteville *Also Called: Tactical Support Equipment Inc (G-5924)*

T Shirt More...828 389-3200
  96 Sanderson St Hayesville (28904) *(G-7772)*

T Simmons Backhoe..336 295-3100
  7507 Doggett Rd Browns Summit (27214) *(G-1317)*

T T Beckham Backhoe Service..252 438-7620
  1870 N Lynnbank Rd Henderson (27537) *(G-7812)*

T T S D Productions LLC...704 829-6666
  27 E Woodrow Ave Belmont (28012) *(G-1013)*

T Toppers, Belmont *Also Called: T T S D Productions LLC (G-1013)*

T V S, Brevard *Also Called: Transylvnia Vcational Svcs Inc (G-1291)*

T W Garner Food Company...336 661-1550
  600 Northgate Park Dr Winston Salem (27106) *(G-16929)*

T W Garner Food Company (PA)..336 661-1550
  614 W 4th St Winston Salem (27101) *(G-16930)*

T W Garner Food Company...336 661-1550
  4045 Indiana Ave Winston Salem (27105) *(G-16931)*

T W Hathcock Logging Inc...704 485-9457
  25341 Millingport Rd Locust (28097) *(G-9974)*

T W Signs & Graphics, Mount Airy *Also Called: Kat Designs Inc (G-11528)*

T-Fab Precision Machining, Asheville *Also Called: T Precision Machining Inc (G-793)*

T-Metrics Inc..704 523-9583
  4430 Stuart Andrew Blvd Charlotte (28217) *(G-3669)*

T-N-T Carports Inc...336 789-3818
  1050 Worth St Mount Airy (27030) *(G-11586)*

T-N-T Carports Inc (PA)...336 789-3818
  170 Holly Springs Rd Mount Airy (27030) *(G-11587)*

T. H. Blue Mulch, Eagle Springs *Also Called: T H Blue Inc (G-5461)*

T&J Sales, Lincolnton *Also Called: Walter Reynolds (G-9935)*

T&L Nursery and Logging LLC..828 387-0448
  325 Clarktown Rd Newland (28657) *(G-11895)*

TA Logging LLC...704 485-8337
  16537 Big Lick Rd Oakboro (28129) *(G-12083)*

Ta Lost Pines Woodwork...828 367-7517
  24 Rose Hill Rd Asheville (28803) *(G-794)*

Tab Steel & Fabricating Inc 828 323-8300
3345 Clarence Towery Cir Hildebran (28637) *(G-8628)*

Table Rock Printers LLC 828 433-1377
205 N Sterling St Morganton (28655) *(G-11260)*

Tabor City Lumber Company (PA) 910 653-3162
510 N Main St Tabor City (28463) *(G-15087)*

Tabur Services 704 483-1650
7845 Commerce Dr Denver (28037) *(G-4805)*

TAC Air, Morrisville *Also Called: Signature Flight Air Inc (G-11429)*

TAC Shield, West End *Also Called: Military Products Inc (G-15930)*

Tactical Coatings Inc 704 692-4511
1028 Railroad Ave Shelby (28152) *(G-14371)*

Tactical Mobility Training, Fayetteville *Also Called: James King (G-5845)*

Tactical Support Equipment Inc 910 425-3360
4039 Barefoot Rd Fayetteville (28306) *(G-5924)*

Tactile Workshop LLC 919 738-9924
1001 S Saunders St Raleigh (27603) *(G-13323)*

Tafford, Charlotte *Also Called: Tafford Uniforms LLC (G-3670)*

Tafford Uniforms LLC 888 823-3673
2121 Distribution Center Dr Ste E Charlotte (28269) *(G-3670)*

Tag Stringing Service Inc 336 294-9394
7 Wendy Ct Ste E Greensboro (27409) *(G-7387)*

Tag-M Prints 919 615-4222
8318 Tierra Del Sol Way Raleigh (27616) *(G-13324)*

Tagtraum Industries Inc 919 809-7797
724 Nash Dr Raleigh (27608) *(G-13325)*

Tailor Cut Wood Products Inc 828 632-2808
35 Wittenburg Industrial Dr Taylorsville (28681) *(G-15169)*

Tailored Chemical, Hickory *Also Called: Tailored Chemical Products Inc (G-8173)*

Tailored Chemical Products Inc (PA) 828 322-6512
700 12th Street Dr Nw Ste B Hickory (28601) *(G-8173)*

Tailored Designs LLC 919 605-6349
11700 Worstel Ln Charlotte (28277) *(G-3671)*

Tailored Visionz & Dreamz LLC 919 340-3613
1406 Lynch Rd Ste B Hollister (27844) *(G-8677)*

Tak Cnc LLC 336 506-7775
1238 Jamestowne Dr Ste C Elon (27244) *(G-5661)*

Tak Manufacturing LLC 704 473-6391
2322 Kings Rd Shelby (28152) *(G-14372)*

Talking Devices Company 828 658-0660
21 Prairie Path Asheville (28805) *(G-795)*

Talladega Mchy & Sup Co NC (PA) 256 362-4124
3510 Gillespie St Fayetteville (28306) *(G-5925)*

Tallahassee Democrat 919 832-9430
4600 Trinity Rd Raleigh (27607) *(G-13326)*

Talledega Machinery & Supply, Fayetteville *Also Called: Talladega Mchy & Sup Co NC (G-5925)*

Tallent Wood Works 704 592-2013
113 Kammerer Dr Statesville (28625) *(G-14910)*

Talley Machinery Corporation (HQ) 336 664-0012
7009 Cessna Dr Greensboro (27409) *(G-7388)*

Taltic Properties LLC 731 656-2735
206 Joe Knox Ave Ste C Mooresville (28117) *(G-11109)*

Tameka Burros 330 338-8941
979 Ramsgate Dr Sw Concord (28025) *(G-4369)*

Tampco Inc 336 835-1895
316 Stainless Way Elkin (28621) *(G-5629)*

Tan Books and Publishers Inc (PA) 704 731-0651
13315 Carowinds Blvd Ste Q Charlotte (28273) *(G-3672)*

Tandemloc Inc 252 447-7155
824 Nc Highway 101 Fontana Blvd Havelock (28532) *(G-7748)*

Tangles Knitting On Main LLC 704 243-7150
200 W North Main St Waxhaw (28173) *(G-15778)*

Tank Fab Inc 910 675-8999
8787 Us Hwy 117 S Rocky Point (28457) *(G-13753)*

Tannis Root Productions Inc 919 832-8552
1720 Capital Blvd Raleigh (27604) *(G-13327)*

Tapestries Ltd 336 883-9864
6 Westmount Ct Greensboro (27410) *(G-7389)*

Tapped Tees LLC 919 943-9692
600 W Main St Apt 613 Durham (27701) *(G-5386)*

Tar Heel Bark, Harrisburg *Also Called: Garick LLC (G-7712)*

Tar Heel Credit Counciling 336 254-0348
2223 N Church St Greensboro (27405) *(G-7390)*

Tar Heel Cuisine Inc 704 435-6979
1009 N Mountain St Cherryville (28021) *(G-3877)*

Tar Heel Enddntic Edctl Fndtio 207 843-6703
2920 Ballybunion Way Raleigh (27613) *(G-13328)*

Tar Heel Fence & Vinyl 336 465-1297
5279 Branson Davis Rd Sophia (27350) *(G-14523)*

Tar Heel Grnd Cmmndery Order K 910 867-6764
1940 Caviness St Fayetteville (28314) *(G-5926)*

Tar Heel Landworks LLC 336 941-3009
6858 Nc Highway 801 S Mocksville (27028) *(G-10607)*

Tar Heel Materials & Hdlg LLC 704 659-5143
725 Kesler Rd Cleveland (27013) *(G-4082)*

Tar Heel Metal Structures 252 208-7171
2200 W Vernon Ave Kinston (28504) *(G-9387)*

Tar Heel Mini Motoring Club 336 391-8084
380 Knollwood St Ste H129 Winston Salem (27103) *(G-16932)*

Tar Heel State Title LLC 704 256-4965
1737 Ridge Haven Rd Waxhaw (28173) *(G-15779)*

Tar Heel Tling Prcsion McHning 919 965-6160
3290 Us Highway 70 E Smithfield (27577) *(G-14486)*

Tar River Mining Inc 252 753-3447
1769 Seven Pines Rd Fountain (27829) *(G-6098)*

Tar River Thinning Inc 919 497-1647
176 Paul Sledge Rd Louisburg (27549) *(G-10004)*

Tar River Trading Post LLC 919 589-3618
385 Fleming Rd Youngsville (27596) *(G-17104)*

Tarason Label Inc 828 464-4743
1640 5th St Nw Hickory (28601) *(G-8174)*

Tarboro Serv, Princeville *Also Called: Southern States Coop Inc (G-12406)*

Tarheel Air & Lube Inc 704 469-1075
195 Davidson Hwy Concord (28027) *(G-4370)*

Tarheel Custom Woodworking Inc 336 237-9344
2550 Jerusalem Rd Lexington (27292) *(G-9789)*

Tarheel Enviromental LLC 910 425-4939
633 Fred Hall Rd Stedman (28391) *(G-14937)*

Tarheel Marble Company Inc 704 888-6003
123 Jefferson Dr Locust (28097) *(G-9975)*

Tarheel Mats Inc 252 325-1903
654 Nc Highway 343 N Camden (27921) *(G-1559)*

Tarheel Monitoring LLC 910 763-1490
709 Princess St Wilmington (28401) *(G-16426)*

Tarheel Oil, Boone *Also Called: BP Oil Corp Distributors (G-1181)*

Tarheel Old English Sheepdog 336 499-6788
8088 Deverow Ct Lewisville (27023) *(G-9674)*

Tarheel Pavement Clg Svcs Inc 704 895-8015
18636 Starcreek Dr Ste G Cornelius (28031) *(G-4591)*

Tarheel Plastics LLC
2018 E Us Highway 64 Lexington (27292) *(G-9790)*

Tarheel Publishing Co 919 553-9042
120 N Tech Dr Ste 102 Clayton (27520) *(G-4016)*

Tarheel Sand & Stone Inc 336 468-4003
1108 Tuckda Way Hamptonville (27020) *(G-7679)*

Tarheel Solid Surfaces, Wilmington *Also Called: Tarheel Wood Designs Inc (G-16427)*

Tarheel Solutions LLC 336 420-9265
6463 Walter Wright Rd Pleasant Garden (27313) *(G-12362)*

Tarheel State Restorations 980 621-3196
2140 Odell School Rd Concord (28027) *(G-4371)*

Tarheel Tool & Gauge LLC 704 213-6924
4665 Miller Rd Salisbury (28147) *(G-14048)*

Tarheel Waves LLC 855 897-2327
3912 Battleground Ave Ste 112 Greensboro (27410) *(G-7391)*

Tarheel Wood Designs Inc 910 395-2226
6609b Windmill Way Wilmington (28405) *(G-16427)*

Tarheel Wood Treating Company 919 467-9176
10309 Chapel Hill Rd Morrisville (27560) *(G-11438)*

Tarheel Woodcrafters Inc 252 432-3035
1570 Hicksboro Rd Henderson (27537) *(G-7813)*

Tarlton Cabinet Shop 704 573-7064
5532 Gristmill Ln Mint Hill (28227) *(G-10545)*

ALPHABETIC SECTION

Tasman Industries Inc 502 587-0701
   1011 Porter St Ste 103 High Point (27263) *(G-8563)*

Tastebuds LLC 704 461-8755
   208 N Main St Belmont (28012) *(G-1014)*

Tastebuds Popcorn, Belmont *Also Called: Tastebuds LLC (G-1014)*

Tat Piedmont, Greensboro *Also Called: Piedmont AVI Cmponent Svcs LLC (G-7255)*

Tate & Lyle Solutions USA LLC 252 482-0402
   841 Avoca Farm Rd Ste 2 Merry Hill (27957) *(G-10441)*

Tatum Galleries Inc 828 963-6466
   5320 Nc Highway 105 S Banner Elk (28604) *(G-904)*

Tatums Trucking & Welding LLC 919 697-6913
   1804 Mill Creek Rd Mebane (27302) *(G-10430)*

Taurus Textiles, Statesville *Also Called: Badger Sportswear LLC (G-14757)*

Tavros Therapeutics Inc 919 602-2631
   8 Davis Dr Ste 100 Durham (27709) *(G-5387)*

Tawnico LLC 704 606-2345
   11612 James Jack Ln Charlotte (28277) *(G-3673)*

Taylco Inc 910 739-0405
   2643 W Carthage Rd Lumberton (28360) *(G-10057)*

Taylor Boat Works 252 726-6374
   200 Pensacola Ave Morehead City (28557) *(G-11194)*

Taylor Business Forms Inc 336 667-0300
   177 Business Center Dr North Wilkesboro (28659) *(G-12034)*

Taylor Business Products, North Wilkesboro *Also Called: Taylor Business Forms Inc (G-12034)*

Taylor Communications Inc 336 841-7700
   4189 Eagle Hill Dr Ste 101 High Point (27265) *(G-8564)*

Taylor Communications Inc 704 282-0989
   1803 N Rocky River Rd Monroe (28110) *(G-10820)*

Taylor Interiors LLC 980 207-3160
   2818 Queen City Dr Charlotte (28208) *(G-3674)*

Taylor King Furniture Inc 828 632-7731
   286 County Home Rd Taylorsville (28681) *(G-15170)*

Taylor Made Cases Inc 919 209-0555
   107 Last Cast Dr Benson (27504) *(G-1043)*

Taylor Manufacturing Inc 910 862-2576
   1585 Us Hwy 701 S Elizabethtown (28337) *(G-5605)*

Taylor Prime Labels & Packg, Goldsboro *Also Called: Occasions Group Inc (G-6641)*

Taylor Prime Labels & Packg, Greenville *Also Called: Occasions Group Inc (G-7566)*

Taylor Printing & Office Sup, Roxboro *Also Called: Person Printing Company Inc (G-13818)*

Taylor Products Inc 910 862-2576
   1585 Us Hwy 701 S Elizabethtown (28337) *(G-5606)*

Taylor Stave LLC 828 659-8880
   2854 Muddy Creek Rd Nebo (28761) *(G-11764)*

Taylor Timber Co LLC 910 588-6214
   113 Mote Fields Rd Harrells (28444) *(G-7696)*

Taylor Timber Transport Inc 252 943-1550
   1977 Old New Bern Rd Chocowinity (27817) *(G-3898)*

Taylorsville Precast Molds Inc 828 632-4608
   128 Taylorsville Mfg Rd Taylorsville (28681) *(G-15171)*

Taylorsville Times 828 632-2532
   24 E Main Ave Taylorsville (28681) *(G-15172)*

Tb Arhaus LLC 828 465-6953
   1211 Keisler Rd Se Conover (28613) *(G-4503)*

Tb Woods Incorporated 704 588-5610
   701 Carrier Dr Charlotte (28216) *(G-3675)*

Tbc Retail Group Inc 336 540-8066
   2514 Battleground Ave Ste B Greensboro (27408) *(G-7392)*

Tc Machine &REpair 336 468-4792
   2517 Campbell Rd Boonville (27011) *(G-1257)*

Tc2 Labs LLC 919 380-2171
   3948 Browning Pl Ste 334 Raleigh (27609) *(G-13329)*

Tc2000.com, Wilmington *Also Called: Worden Brothers Inc (G-16456)*

TCBY, Lenoir *Also Called: Carolina Yogurt Inc (G-9596)*

Tcc Manufacturing 828 970-7620
   4418 Providence Mill Rd Maiden (28650) *(G-10118)*

Tce Coffee LLC 910 336-3439
   408 Trespar Ln Apt 307 Fayetteville (28311) *(G-5927)*

Tce Manufacturing LLC 252 330-9919
   1287 Salem Church Rd Elizabeth City (27909) *(G-5574)*

Tcgrx, Durham *Also Called: Chudy Group LLC (G-5018)*

Tcgrx, Durham *Also Called: Parata Systems LLC (G-5270)*

TCI, Ramseur *Also Called: Tower Components Inc (G-13450)*

TCI Mobility Inc 704 867-8331
   1720 Industrial Pike Rd Gastonia (28052) *(G-6520)*

Tcom, Elizabeth City *Also Called: Tcom Ground Systems LP (G-5576)*

Tcom Limited Partnership 252 330-5555
   190 T Com Dr Elizabeth City (27909) *(G-5575)*

Tcom Ground Systems LP 252 338-3200
   190 T Com Dr Elizabeth City (27909) *(G-5576)*

TCOM, LIMITED PARTNERSHIP, Elizabeth City *Also Called: Tcom Limited Partnership (G-5575)*

Tcp, Hickory *Also Called: Tender Care Products Inc (G-8177)*

TCS Designs Inc 828 324-9944
   1851 9th Ave Ne Hickory (28601) *(G-8175)*

Tcsc, Winston Salem *Also Called: The Computer Solution Company (G-16940)*

Tcu Industries Inc 602 369-7270
   5540 Morehead Rd Ste 2 Harrisburg (28075) *(G-7730)*

Td Cloud, Raleigh *Also Called: Td Cloud Services (G-13330)*

Td Cloud Services 518 258-6788
   3129 Oaklyn Springs Dr Raleigh (27606) *(G-13330)*

Td Fiber, High Point *Also Called: Thomasville-Dexel Incorporated (G-8571)*

Tdc International LLC 704 875-1198
   980 Derita Rd # B Concord (28027) *(G-4372)*

Te Connectivity 336 727-5295
   3700 Reidsville Rd Winston Salem (27101) *(G-16933)*

Te Connectivity, Greensboro *Also Called: Commscope Technologies LLC (G-6926)*

Te Connectivity, Greensboro *Also Called: Tyco Electronics Corporation (G-7424)*

Te Connectivity Corporation 828 338-1000
   1396 Charlotte Hwy Fairview (28730) *(G-5719)*

Te Connectivity Corporation 828 338-1000
   1396 Charlotte Hwy Fairview (28730) *(G-5720)*

Te Connectivity Corporation 919 552-3811
   8000 Purfoy Rd Fuquay Varina (27526) *(G-6229)*

Te Connectivity Corporation 919 557-8425
   8009 Purfoy Rd Fuquay Varina (27526) *(G-6230)*

Te Connectivity Corporation 919 552-3811
   8000 Purfoy Rd Fuquay Varina (27526) *(G-6231)*

Te Connectivity Corporation 336 664-7000
   8000 Piedmont Triad Pkwy Greensboro (27409) *(G-7393)*

Te Connectivity Corporation 336 665-4400
   719 Pegg Rd Bldg 253 Greensboro (27409) *(G-7394)*

Te Connectivity Corporation 336 664-7000
   3900 Reidsville Rd Winston Salem (27101) *(G-16934)*

Te Connectivity Corporation 336 727-5122
   3800 Reidsville Rd Winston Salem (27101) *(G-16935)*

Te Wheel Inc 336 376-1364
   207 Dakota Dr Graham (27253) *(G-6712)*

Tea and Honey Blends LLC 919 673-4273
   444 S Blount St Ste 115b Raleigh (27601) *(G-13331)*

Tea Dogu 818 404-6523
   102 Village Dr Apt 426 Mebane (27302) *(G-10431)*

Tea Rex Teahouse, Charlotte *Also Called: Brewitt & Dreenkupp Inc (G-2353)*

Teabar Publishing Inc 252 764-2453
   201n James Dr Emerald Isle (28594) *(G-5672)*

Team 21st 910 826-3676
   6316 Yadkin Rd Fayetteville (28303) *(G-5928)*

Team Connection 336 287-3892
   2508 Griffith Meadows Dr Winston Salem (27103) *(G-16936)*

Team Gsg LLC 252 830-1032
   851 Black Jack Simpson Rd Greenville (27858) *(G-7588)*

Team Industries Inc 828 837-5377
   3750 Airport Rd Andrews (28901) *(G-128)*

Team Manufacturing - E W LLC 919 554-2442
   35 Weathers Ct Youngsville (27596) *(G-17105)*

Team Penske, Mooresville *Also Called: Penske Racing South Inc (G-11050)*

Team Triangle Cabinets 919 609-1332
   3209 Gresham Lake Rd Ste 105 Raleigh (27615) *(G-13332)*

Team X-Treme LLC 919 562-8100
   600 S Main St Ste C Rolesville (27571) *(G-13760)*

Teamwork Inc 336 578-3456
   1000 Georgetowne Dr Elon (27244) *(G-5662)*

Tearscience Inc 919 459-4880
5151 Mccrimmon Pkwy Ste 250 Morrisville (27560) *(G-11439)*

Tebo Displays LLC 919 832-8525
2609 Discovery Dr Ste 105 Raleigh (27616) *(G-13333)*

TEC Coat 412 215-0152
14030 S Lakes Dr Charlotte (28273) *(G-3676)*

TEC Graphics Inc 919 567-2077
101 Technology Park Ln Fuquay Varina (27526) *(G-6232)*

TEC Tran Brake, Burlington Also Called: Kck Holding Corp *(G-1443)*

TEC-Ops, Hickory Also Called: Blue Lagoon Inc *(G-7951)*

Tecgrachem Inc 336 993-6785
1957 Nc Highway 66 S Kernersville (27284) *(G-9241)*

Tech Marketing, Raleigh Also Called: Pt Marketing Incorporated *(G-13157)*

Tech Medical Plastics Inc 919 563-9272
1403 Dogwood Way Mebane (27302) *(G-10432)*

Tech-Tool Inc 919 906-6229
2561 Country Club Dr Hampstead (28443) *(G-7658)*

Techjournal South 919 832-1858
211 N Boylan Ave Raleigh (27603) *(G-13334)*

Techmet, Hickory Also Called: Techmet Carbides Inc *(G-8176)*

Techmet Carbides Inc 828 624-0222
730 21st Street Dr Se Hickory (28602) *(G-8176)*

Technibilt Ltd (DH) 828 464-7388
700 Technibilt Dr Newton (28658) *(G-11976)*

Technica Editorial Services 919 918-3991
205 W Main St Ste 206 Carrboro (27510) *(G-1657)*

Technical Center, Hickory Also Called: Century Furniture LLC *(G-7977)*

Technical Coating Intl Inc 910 371-0860
150 Backhoe Rd Ne Belville (28451) *(G-1026)*

Technical Development, Concord Also Called: Tdc International LLC *(G-4372)*

Technicon Acoustics, Concord Also Called: Technicon Industries Inc *(G-4373)*

Technicon Industries Inc 704 788-1131
4412 Republic Ct Nw Concord (28027) *(G-4373)*

Technimark 336 736-9366
208 Nc Highway 62 W Randleman (27317) *(G-13493)*

Technimark LLC 336 498-4171
2536 Bank St Asheboro (27203) *(G-491)*

Technimark LLC 336 498-4171
4509 Us Highway 220 Bus N Asheboro (27203) *(G-492)*

Technimark LLC (PA) 336 498-4171
180 Commerce Pl Asheboro (27203) *(G-493)*

Technimark Reynosa LLC 336 498-4171
2510 Bank St Asheboro (27203) *(G-494)*

Technimark Reynosa LLC (HQ) 336 498-4171
180 Commerce Pl Asheboro (27203) *(G-495)*

Technique Chassis LLC 517 819-3579
4101 Roush Pl Nw Concord (28027) *(G-4374)*

Technolio Inc 919 481-4454
114 Bristolwood Cir Morrisville (27560) *(G-11440)*

Technology Partners LLC (PA) 704 553-1004
8757 Red Oak Blvd 2f Charlotte (28217) *(G-3677)*

Technosoft Innovations Inc 919 388-3360
900 Perimeter Park Dr Ste C Morrisville (27560) *(G-11441)*

Techo-Bloc 336 431-4133
5135 Surrett Dr Archdale (27263) *(G-300)*

Techscan Industries LLC (PA) 704 843-4518
4008 Hermes Ln Waxhaw (28173) *(G-15780)*

Techsouth Inc 704 334-1100
601 Union West Blvd Matthews (28104) *(G-10349)*

Techtronic Industries, Charlotte Also Called: TTI Floor Care North Amer Inc *(G-3735)*

Tecworks Inc 704 829-9700
4041 S Cove Ln Belmont (28012) *(G-1015)*

Ted M Hart Logging Inc 919 776-7237
3760 S Plank Rd Sanford (27330) *(G-14195)*

Ted Wheeler 252 438-0820
2651 Hwy 158 Oxford (27565) *(G-12159)*

Ted's Service Company, Oxford Also Called: Ted Wheeler *(G-12159)*

Teddy Soft Paper Products Inc 336 784-5887
535 E Clemmonsville Rd Ste A Winston Salem (27107) *(G-16937)*

Tees Footwear Inc 704 628-0376
2002 Filly Dr Indian Trail (28079) *(G-8967)*

Tees Pretty Things 704 674-0982
2833 Crawford Ave Gastonia (28052) *(G-6521)*

Teeshizzle Printing 336 715-1113
106 Windsong Dr Clemmons (27012) *(G-4061)*

Tef Inc 704 786-9577
3650 Zion Church Rd Concord (28025) *(G-4375)*

Tegna, Asheville Also Called: Asheville Citizen-Times *(G-532)*

Teguar Computers, Charlotte Also Called: Teguar Corporation *(G-3678)*

Teguar Corporation 704 960-1761
2920 Whitehall Park Dr Charlotte (28273) *(G-3678)*

Tehan Company Inc 800 283-7290
2620 Stag Park Rd Burgaw (28425) *(G-1353)*

Tehan Distributing, Burgaw Also Called: Tehan Company Inc *(G-1353)*

Teijin Automotive Tech Inc 828 757-8313
2424 Norwood St Sw Unit 300 Lenoir (28645) *(G-9654)*

Teijin Automotive Tech Inc 828 754-8441
601 Hibriten Dr Sw Lenoir (28645) *(G-9655)*

Teijin Automotive Tech Inc 828 466-7000
1400 Burris Rd Newton (28658) *(G-11977)*

Teijin Automotive Tech Inc 704 797-8744
6701 Statesville Blvd Salisbury (28147) *(G-14049)*

Tekelec, Morrisville Also Called: Tekelec Global Inc *(G-11443)*

Tekelec Inc
5200 Paramount Pkwy Morrisville (27560) *(G-11442)*

Tekelec Global Inc 919 460-5500
5200 Paramount Pkwy Morrisville (27560) *(G-11443)*

Tekni-Plex Inc 919 553-4151
8720 Us 70 Bus Hwy W Clayton (27520) *(G-4017)*

Teknor Apex Company 401 642-3598
3518 Dillon Rd Jamestown (27282) *(G-9074)*

Tektone Sound & Signal Mfg Inc 828 524-9967
324 Industrial Park Rd Franklin (28734) *(G-6145)*

Tektronix, Charlotte Also Called: Tektronix Inc *(G-3679)*

Tektronix, Raleigh Also Called: Tektronix Inc *(G-13335)*

Tektronix Inc 704 527-5000
4400 Stuart Andrew Blvd Ste O Charlotte (28217) *(G-3679)*

Tektronix Inc 919 233-9490
5608 Pine Dr Raleigh (27606) *(G-13335)*

Telair US Cargo Systems, Goldsboro Also Called: Telair US LLC *(G-6665)*

Telair US LLC 919 705-2400
500a Gateway Dr Goldsboro (27534) *(G-6665)*

Telecmmnctons Resource MGT Inc 919 779-0776
156 Annaron Ct Raleigh (27603) *(G-13336)*

Telecommunications Tech Inc 919 556-7100
14101 Capital Blvd Ste 201 Youngsville (27596) *(G-17106)*

Teleflex, Durham Also Called: Teleflex Incorporated *(G-5388)*

Teleflex, Durham Also Called: Teleflex Incorporated *(G-5389)*

Teleflex, Morrisville Also Called: Teleflex Incorporated *(G-11444)*

Teleflex Incorporated 919 433-2575
2917 Weck Dr Research Triangle Park Durham (27709) *(G-5388)*

Teleflex Incorporated 919 433-2575
1805a Tw Alexander Dr Durham (27703) *(G-5389)*

Teleflex Incorporated 919 544-8000
3015 Carrington Mill Blvd Morrisville (27560) *(G-11444)*

Teleflex Medical Incorporated 336 498-4153
312 Commerce Pl Asheboro (27203) *(G-496)*

Teleflex Medical Incorporated 919 544-8000
4024 Stirrup Creek Dr Ste 270 Durham (27703) *(G-5390)*

Teleflex Medical Incorporated (HQ) 919 544-8000
3015 Carrington Mill Blvd Morrisville (27560) *(G-11445)*

Telepathic Graphics Inc (PA) 919 342-4603
6001 Chapel Hill Rd Ste 106 Raleigh (27607) *(G-13337)*

Telepathic Graphics Inc 919 342-4603
1131 Atlantic Ave Rocky Mount (27801) *(G-13672)*

Telephonics Corporation 631 755-7446
1014 Consolidated Rd Elizabeth City (27909) *(G-5577)*

Telephys Inc 312 625-9128
610 Jetton St Ste 120 Davidson (28036) *(G-4699)*

Teletec Corporation 919 954-7300
5617 Departure Dr Ste 107 Raleigh (27616) *(G-13338)*

ALPHABETIC SECTION

Telewire Supply, Cary *Also Called: Ruckus Wireless Inc (G-1875)*

Telit Wireless Solutions Inc (PA) 919 439-7977
5425 Page Rd Ste 120 Durham (27703) *(G-5391)*

Tellad Supply Company 919 572-6700
2320 Presidential Dr # 105 Durham (27703) *(G-5392)*

Telos Group LLC 704 904-0599
11518 Wheat Ridge Rd Charlotte (28277) *(G-3680)*

Tempest Aero Group 336 449-5054
2208 Airpark Rd Burlington (27215) *(G-1505)*

Tempest Aero Group 336 449-5054
1240 Springwood Church Rd Gibsonville (27249) *(G-6571)*

Tempest Environmental, Durham *Also Called: Tempest Envmtl Systems Inc (G-5394)*

Tempest Environmental Corp 919 973-1609
7 Al Acqua Dr Durham (27707) *(G-5393)*

Tempest Envmtl Systems Inc 919 973-1609
7 Al Acqua Dr Durham (27707) *(G-5394)*

Tempest Plus Marketing Group, Gibsonville *Also Called: Tempest Aero Group (G-6571)*

Temple Inc (PA) 828 428-8031
102 S 7th Avenue Ext Maiden (28650) *(G-10119)*

Temple Furniture, Maiden *Also Called: Temple Inc (G-10119)*

Tempo Products LLC 336 434-8649
2130 Brevard Rd High Point (27263) *(G-8565)*

Temposonics LLC 470 380-5103
3001 Sheldon Dr Cary (27513) *(G-1907)*

Temprano Techvestors Inc 877 545-1509
2105 Northwest Blvd Newton (28658) *(G-11978)*

Tempur Sealy International Inc 336 861-2900
1 Office Parkway Rd Trinity (27370) *(G-15361)*

Ten Nails Construction Inc 910 232-4883
449 Landsdowne Cir Hampstead (28443) *(G-7659)*

Tencarva Machinery Company LLC 336 665-1435
1800 Sullivan St Greensboro (27405) *(G-7395)*

Tenda Bake, Newton *Also Called: Midstate Mills Inc (G-11953)*

Tender Care Products Inc 828 726-8241
4151 1st Street Pl Nw Hickory (28601) *(G-8177)*

Tengion, Winston Salem *Also Called: Tengion Inc (G-16938)*

Tengion Inc 336 722-5855
3929 Westpoint Blvd Ste G Winston Salem (27103) *(G-16938)*

Tenn-Tex Plastics Inc 336 931-1100
8011 National Service Rd Colfax (27235) *(G-4161)*

Tennessee Nedgraphics Inc 704 414-4224
1809 Cross Beam Dr Ste E Charlotte (28217) *(G-3681)*

Tenowo Inc (DH) 704 732-3525
1968 Kawai Rd Lincolnton (28092) *(G-9925)*

Tenowo Inc 704 732-3525
1582 Startown Rd Lincolnton (28092) *(G-9926)*

Tenpenny Press 828 423-0799
3 Mulvaney St Asheville (28803) *(G-796)*

Tensor Fiber Optics Tech 828 322-8224
1075 13th St Se Hickory (28602) *(G-8178)*

Teradata Corporation 919 816-1900
5565 Centerview Dr Ste 300 Raleigh (27606) *(G-13339)*

Terarecon Inc (PA) 650 372-1100
4309 Emperor Blvd Ste 310 Durham (27703) *(G-5395)*

Tergus Pharma LLC (PA) 919 549-9700
4018 Stirrup Creek Dr Durham (27703) *(G-5396)*

Terida LLC 910 693-1633
40 Augusta National Dr Pinehurst (28374) *(G-12238)*

Terresolve, Charlotte *Also Called: RSC Bio Solutions LLC (G-3467)*

Terry Leggett Logging Co Inc 252 927-4671
4403 Long Ridge Rd Pinetown (27865) *(G-12250)*

Terry Logging Company 919 477-9170
7917 S Lowell Rd Bahama (27503) *(G-867)*

Terrys Tires & Services LLC 336 251-7366
7849 Nc 67 Hwy East Bend (27018) *(G-5469)*

Tesa Tape Inc (DH) 704 554-0707
5825 Carnegie Blvd Charlotte (28209) *(G-3682)*

Test ME Out Inc 252 635-6770
3262 Wellons Blvd New Bern (28562) *(G-11849)*

Testing Facility, Huntersville *Also Called: Newell Brands Inc (G-8858)*

Tetac 919 369-9106
135 Cedarhurst Ln Franklinton (27525) *(G-6165)*

Tethis Inc 919 808-2866
3401 Spring Forest Rd Raleigh (27616) *(G-13340)*

Tethis Manufacturing LLC 919 808-2866
3401 Spring Forest Rd Raleigh (27616) *(G-13341)*

Tex Care Medical, Burlington *Also Called: Flynt/Amtex Inc (G-1414)*

Tex Tech Industries, Kernersville *Also Called: Tex-Tech Industries Inc (G-9245)*

Tex-Tech Coatings LLC 336 992-7500
215 Drummond St Kernersville (27284) *(G-9242)*

Tex-Tech Coatings LLC (HQ) 336 992-7500
1350 Bridgeport Dr Ste 1 Kernersville (27284) *(G-9243)*

Tex-Tech Engnred Cmposites LLC 207 756-8606
1350 Bridgeport Dr Ste 1 Kernersville (27284) *(G-9244)*

Tex-Tech Industries Inc (PA) 207 756-8606
1350 Bridgeport Dr Ste 1 Kernersville (27284) *(G-9245)*

Texas Refinery 704 213-4990
175 Frances St Salisbury (28147) *(G-14050)*

Texdel, Conover *Also Called: Textile-Based Delivery Inc (G-4504)*

Texinnovate Inc 336 279-7800
7109 Cessna Dr Greensboro (27409) *(G-7396)*

Texlon Industries LLC 252 292-6590
4910 Pompano Ct Wilmington (28403) *(G-16428)*

Texlon Plastics Corp 704 866-8785
135 Wolfpack Rd Gastonia (28053) *(G-6522)*

Texpack USA Inc 704 864-5406
1302 Industrial Pike Rd Gastonia (28052) *(G-6523)*

Textile Designed Machine Co 704 664-1374
1320 Shearers Rd Mooresville (28115) *(G-11110)*

Textile Intl Entps LLC 336 545-0146
4008 Hazel Ln Greensboro (27408) *(G-7397)*

Textile Manufacturing Tech LLC 828 632-3012
3215 Rink Dam Rd Taylorsville (28681) *(G-15173)*

Textile Parts and Mch Co Inc 704 865-5003
1502 W May Ave Gastonia (28052) *(G-6524)*

Textile Piece Dyeing Co Inc 704 732-4200
319 N Generals Blvd Lincolnton (28092) *(G-9927)*

Textile Printing Inc 704 521-8099
2431 Thornridge Rd Charlotte (28226) *(G-3683)*

Textile Products Inc 704 636-6221
119 121 N Main St Salisbury (28144) *(G-14051)*

Textile Rubber and Chem Co Inc 704 376-3582
1020 Forsyth Ave Ste 100 Indian Trail (28079) *(G-8968)*

Textile Sales Intl Inc 704 483-7966
8172 Malibu Pointe Ln Denver (28037) *(G-4806)*

Textile Trends, Siler City *Also Called: Lazar Industries East Inc (G-14421)*

Textile-Based Delivery Inc 866 256-8420
350 5th Ave Se Conover (28613) *(G-4504)*

Textram Inc 704 527-7557
801 Clanton Rd Ste 103 Charlotte (28217) *(G-3684)*

Textrol Laboratories Inc 704 764-3400
111 W Sandy Ridge Rd Monroe (28112) *(G-10821)*

Textron Aviation Inc 336 605-7000
615 Service Center Rd Greensboro (27410) *(G-7398)*

Textum Opco LLC 704 822-2400
3 Caldwell Dr Belmont (28012) *(G-1016)*

Texture Plus Inc 631 218-9200
1477 Roseland Dr Lincolnton (28092) *(G-9928)*

Tfam Solutions LLC 910 637-0266
134 Aqua Shed Ct Aberdeen (28315) *(G-31)*

Tfs Inc 919 556-9161
Wake Forest (27588) *(G-15602)*

TFS Management Group LLC 704 399-3999
4331 Chesapeake Dr Charlotte (28216) *(G-3685)*

TG THERAPEUTICS, Morrisville *Also Called: Tg Therapeutics Inc (G-11446)*

Tg Therapeutics Inc (PA) 212 554-4484
3020 Carrington Mill Blvd Ste 475 Morrisville (27560) *(G-11446)*

Tgi Incorporated 336 768-0139
3570 Vest Mill Rd Ste F Winston Salem (27103) *(G-16939)*

Tgr Enterprises Incorporated 828 665-4427
26 Charity Ln Candler (28715) *(G-1590)*

Th Mills, Statesville *Also Called: Thorneburg Hosiery Mills Inc (G-14912)*

Thanet Inc 704 483-4175
3501 Denver Dr Denver (28037) *(G-4807)*

Tharrington Parts

ALPHABETIC SECTION

Tharrington Parts, Rocky Mount *Also Called: Daughtridge Enterprises Inc (G-13665)*

That Make Scents LLC..919 283-0237
121 Rowan Dr Clayton (27520) *(G-4018)*

That Welder Guy...252 342-0391
468 Bogue Loop Rd Newport (28570) *(G-11908)*

That's Picklicious, Mount Olive *Also Called: Mount Olive Pickle Company Inc (G-11666)*

Thatcher Forest Publishing......................................919 402-9245
3524 Manford Dr Durham (27707) *(G-5397)*

Thayer Coggin, High Point *Also Called: Thayer Coggin Inc (G-8566)*

Thayer Coggin Inc..336 841-6000
230 South Rd High Point (27262) *(G-8566)*

Thayer Coggin Furniture..336 841-6000
230 South Rd High Point (27262) *(G-8567)*

Thb Leisure LLC..828 926-8484
1478 Dellwood Rd Waynesville (28786) *(G-15828)*

The Audio Lab, Wilmington *Also Called: Hartley Loudspeakers Inc (G-16248)*

THE CHRONICLE, Durham *Also Called: Duke Student Publishing Co Inc (G-5067)*

The Computer Solution Company................................336 409-0782
102 W 3rd St Ste 750 Winston Salem (27101) *(G-16940)*

The Design Center, Apex *Also Called: Goembel Inc (G-196)*

The Graham Star, Robbinsville *Also Called: Community Newspapers Inc (G-13606)*

The Havelock News, New Bern *Also Called: Ellis Publishing Company Inc (G-11803)*

The Interflex Group Inc..336 921-3505
3200 W Nc Highway 268 Wilkesboro (28697) *(G-16045)*

The Madison Company Inc..336 548-9624
200 W Academy St Madison (27025) *(G-10088)*

The McQuackins Company LLC..................................980 254-2309
2335 Jenkins Dairy Rd Gastonia (28052) *(G-6525)*

The Physics Teacher Magazine, Boone *Also Called: Appalachian State University (G-1175)*

The Rolling Door Company, Gastonia *Also Called: Kindred Rolling Doors LLC (G-6439)*

The Summer House, Highlands *Also Called: Tiger Mountain Woodworks Inc (G-8618)*

The Tarheel Electric Membership Association Incorporated..........919 876-4603
8730 Wadford Dr Raleigh (27616) *(G-13342)*

The Wheelchair Place LLC......................................828 855-9099
920 Tate Blvd Se Ste 104 Hickory (28602) *(G-8179)*

The Wynsum Gardener, Salisbury *Also Called: Bosmere Inc (G-13930)*

THEM International Inc..336 855-7880
1005 N Eugene St Greensboro (27401) *(G-7399)*

Theo Davis Printing, Zebulon *Also Called: Theo Davis Sons Incorporated (G-17143)*

Theo Davis Sons Incorporated..................................919 269-7401
1415 W Gannon Ave Zebulon (27597) *(G-17143)*

Theodore Alexander..336 689-4178
3407 W Gate City Blvd Ste B Greensboro (27407) *(G-7400)*

Theodore Alexander Uphl LLC..................................336 472-7540
1 Regency Industrial Blvd Thomasville (27360) *(G-15288)*

Therapeutics...919 695-7291
309 Seawell Ave Raleigh (27601) *(G-13343)*

Thermaco Incorporated..336 629-4651
646 Greensboro St Asheboro (27203) *(G-497)*

Thermal Acoustical Group, Hamptonville *Also Called: Lydall Thermal/Acoustical Inc (G-7675)*

Thermal Control Products Inc..................................704 454-7605
6324 Performance Dr Sw Concord (28027) *(G-4376)*

Thermal Metal Treating Inc....................................910 944-3636
9546 Hwy 211 East Aberdeen (28315) *(G-32)*

Thermal Pane Inc..336 722-9977
200 S Main St Lexington (27292) *(G-9791)*

Thermatec, Greensboro *Also Called: Hoffman Building Tech Inc (G-7094)*

Thermcraft Holding Co LLC....................................336 784-4800
3950 Overdale Rd Winston Salem (27107) *(G-16941)*

Thermik Corporation..252 636-5720
3498a Martin Dr New Bern (28562) *(G-11850)*

Thermo Elctron Scntfic Instrs..................................828 281-2651
501 Elk Park Dr Asheville (28804) *(G-797)*

Thermo Electron, Asheville *Also Called: Thermo Elctron Scntfic Instrs (G-797)*

Thermo Fisher Scientific, Asheville *Also Called: Thermo Fsher Scntfic Ashvlle L (G-798)*

Thermo Fisher Scientific Inc....................................800 955-6288
4063 Stirrup Creek Dr Durham (27703) *(G-5398)*

Thermo Fisher Scientific Inc....................................252 707-7093
5900 Martin Luther King Jr Hwy Greenville (27834) *(G-7589)*

Thermo Fisher Scientific Inc....................................800 955-6288
4125 Premier Dr High Point (27265) *(G-8568)*

Thermo Fisher Scientific Inc....................................919 876-2352
3315 Atlantic Ave Raleigh (27604) *(G-13344)*

Thermo Fsher Scntfic Ashvlle L (HQ).........................828 658-2711
275 Aiken Rd Asheville (28804) *(G-798)*

Thermo Fsher Scntfic Ashvlle L................................828 658-2711
220 Merrimon Ave Ste A Weaverville (28787) *(G-15865)*

Thermo King Corporation..732 652-6774
800 Beaty St Davidson (28036) *(G-4700)*

Thermo King Svc, Davidson *Also Called: Thermo King Corporation (G-4700)*

Thermo Products LLC (HQ)....................................800 348-5130
92 W Fourth St Denton (27239) *(G-4752)*

Thermochem Recovery Intl......................................919 606-3282
5201 International Dr Durham (27712) *(G-5399)*

Thermodynamx, Waxhaw *Also Called: Thermodynamx LLC (G-15781)*

Thermodynamx LLC..704 622-1086
514 King St Waxhaw (28173) *(G-15781)*

Thieman Manufacturing Tech LLC.............................828 453-1866
531 Webb Rd Ellenboro (28040) *(G-5640)*

Thieman Technology, Ellenboro *Also Called: Thieman Manufacturing Tech LLC (G-5640)*

Thin Line Saddle Pads Inc......................................919 680-6803
2945 S Miami Blvd Ste 120-120 Durham (27703) *(G-5400)*

Think Welding...980 230-2842
3541 Durham Ln Charlotte (28269) *(G-3686)*

Thinking Maps Inc (PA)..919 678-8778
401 Cascade Pointe Ln Cary (27513) *(G-1908)*

Third Street Screen Print Inc..................................919 365-2725
115 E Third St Wendell (27591) *(G-15920)*

Thirdparty Labs..919 741-5118
220 Fayetteville St Ste 200 Raleigh (27601) *(G-13345)*

This Week Magazine, Morehead City *Also Called: Carteret Publishing Company (G-11159)*

Thistle Meadow Winery Inc....................................800 233-1505
102 Thistle Mdw Laurel Springs (28644) *(G-9467)*

Thomas & Gendics Inc..919 842-7860
2428 Hickory House Rd Sanford (27332) *(G-14196)*

Thomas & Gray, Denton *Also Called: Councill Company LLC (G-4731)*

Thomas B Brugh Mfg Rep......................................858 385-8987
6020 Aynrand Ct Charlotte (28269) *(G-3687)*

Thomas Brothers Foods LLC..................................336 672-0337
1852 Gold Hill Rd Asheboro (27203) *(G-498)*

Thomas Brothers Ham Company, Asheboro *Also Called: Thomas Brothers Foods LLC (G-498)*

Thomas Brothers Meat Proc, North Wilkesboro *Also Called: Thomas Brothers Slaughter Hse (G-12035)*

Thomas Brothers Slaughter Hse..............................336 667-1346
347 Thomas St North Wilkesboro (28659) *(G-12035)*

Thomas Built Buses Inc (DH)..................................336 889-4871
1408 Courtesy Rd High Point (27260) *(G-8569)*

Thomas Buses, High Point *Also Called: Thomas Built Buses Inc (G-8569)*

Thomas Concrete Carolina......................................919 828-6923
609 Tucker St Raleigh (27603) *(G-13346)*

Thomas Concrete Carolina Inc................................704 333-0390
3701 N Graham St Charlotte (28206) *(G-3688)*

Thomas Concrete Carolina Inc................................919 557-3144
140 Pamela Ct Fuquay Varina (27526) *(G-6233)*

Thomas Concrete Carolina Inc................................919 460-5317
220 International Dr Morrisville (27560) *(G-11447)*

Thomas Concrete Carolina Inc (DH).........................919 832-0451
1131 Nw Street Raleigh (27603) *(G-13347)*

Thomas Concrete SC Inc..704 868-4545
5614 Union Rd Gastonia (28056) *(G-6526)*

Thomas Concrete South Carolina, Gastonia *Also Called: Thomas Concrete SC Inc (G-6526)*

Thomas Enterprises, Waynesville *Also Called: Rikki Tikki Tees (G-15818)*

Thomas Fergus...336 447-4289
600 Walnut Crossing Dr Whitsett (27377) *(G-16003)*

Thomas Foods, Greensboro *Also Called: D C Thomas Group Inc (G-6956)*

Thomas Gary Helton..828 726-3694
1523 Gilbert Ln Lenoir (28645) *(G-9656)*

Thomas Golf Inc..704 461-1342
9716 Rea Rd Ste B # 170 Charlotte (28277) *(G-3689)*

ALPHABETIC SECTION — Tileware Global LLC

Thomas Jewelers.. 252 756-1641
714 Greenville Blvd Se Greenville (27858) *(G-7590)*

Thomas Lcklars Cbnets Lrnburg......................... 910 369-2094
21720 Wagram Rd Laurinburg (28352) *(G-9499)*

Thomas Lee Fortner Sawmill................................ 828 632-9525
70 Mount Olive Church Rd Taylorsville (28681) *(G-15174)*

Thomas M Brown Inc... 704 597-0246
1311 Amble Dr Charlotte (28206) *(G-3690)*

Thomas Mendolia MD.. 336 835-5688
116 Quincy Ct Mooresville (28117) *(G-11111)*

Thomas Mfg Co Inc Thomasville........................... 336 474-6030
1024 Randolph St Thomasville (27360) *(G-15289)*

Thomas of High Point.. 336 889-4871
1408 Courtesy Rd High Point (27260) *(G-8570)*

Thomas Timber Inc... 910 532-4542
3344 Nc Highway 210 E Harrells (28444) *(G-7697)*

Thomasville Times, High Point *Also Called: High Point Enterprise Inc (G-8389)*

Thomasville Upholstery Inc................................... 828 345-6225
890 F Avenue Dr Se Hickory (28602) *(G-8180)*

Thomasville-Dexel Incorporated........................... 336 819-5550
2041 Brevard Rd High Point (27263) *(G-8571)*

Thomasvlle Mtal Fbricators Inc (PA)..................... 336 248-4992
200 Prospect Dr Lexington (27292) *(G-9792)*

Thomco Inc... 336 292-3300
2005 Boulevard St Ste F Greensboro (27407) *(G-7401)*

Thompson & Little Inc... 910 484-1128
933 Robeson St Fayetteville (28305) *(G-5929)*

Thompson Apparel Inc... 910 673-4560
3061 7 Lks W West End (27376) *(G-15934)*

Thompson Joinery LLC.. 919 672-2770
912 Burch Ave Durham (27701) *(G-5401)*

Thompson Millwork LLC....................................... 919 596-8236
200 Redman Xing Mebane (27302) *(G-10433)*

Thompson Printing & Packg Inc............................ 704 313-7323
2457 Mccraw Rd Mooresboro (28114) *(G-10842)*

Thompson Sunny Acres Inc................................... 910 206-1801
150 Thompson Farm Rd Rockingham (28379) *(G-13644)*

Thompson Timber Harvest LLC............................. 919 632-4326
350 W Green St Franklinton (27525) *(G-6166)*

Thompson Traders Inc... 336 272-3003
2024 E Market St Greensboro (27401) *(G-7402)*

Thompson Welding & Mechcl Svc........................ 252 536-9431
115 W 13th St Roanoke Rapids (27870) *(G-13582)*

Thompson Wldg & Mech Svc LLC........................ 252 535-4269
Roanoke Rapids (27870) *(G-13583)*

Thomson Plastics Inc.. 336 843-4255
2018 E Us Highway 64 Lexington (27292) *(G-9793)*

Thor.lo, Rockwell *Also Called: Thorneburg Hosiery Mills Inc (G-13661)*

Thorco LLC... 919 363-6234
301 Birdwood Ct Cary (27519) *(G-1909)*

Thornburg Machine & Sup Co Inc......................... 704 735-5421
1699 Smith Farm Rd Lincolnton (28092) *(G-9929)*

Thorneburg Hosiery Mills Inc................................ 704 279-7247
319 Link St Rockwell (28138) *(G-13661)*

Thorneburg Hosiery Mills Inc................................ 704 872-6522
1515 W Front St Statesville (28677) *(G-14911)*

Thorneburg Hosiery Mills Inc (PA)........................ 704 872-6522
2210 Newton Dr Statesville (28677) *(G-14912)*

Thorneburg Hosiery Mills Inc................................ 704 838-6329
1519 W Front St Statesville (28677) *(G-14913)*

Thornton Trucking & Logging, Teachey *Also Called: Ricky Don Thornton (G-15178)*

Thorworks Industries Inc...................................... 919 852-3714
550 Corporate Center Dr Raleigh (27607) *(G-13348)*

Thread, Cary *Also Called: Definitive Media Corp (G-1746)*

Thread Shed Clothing Company, Salisbury *Also Called: S Loflin Enterprises Inc (G-14039)*

Three Fifty Six Inc... 336 631-5356
832 S Main St Winston Salem (27101) *(G-16942)*

Three GS Enterprises Inc...................................... 828 696-2060
100 Tabor Road Ext Flat Rock (28731) *(G-5972)*

Three Gypsies LLC.. 843 337-7799
3918 Belk Mill Rd Wingate (28174) *(G-16579)*

Three Ladies and A Male LLC............................... 704 287-1584
3515 Arsenal Ct Apt 103 Charlotte (28273) *(G-3691)*

Three Sisters Ready Mix LLC................................ 919 217-0222
512 Three Sisters Rd Knightdale (27545) *(G-9430)*

Three Stacks Distilling Co LLC............................. 252 468-0779
906 Atlantic Ave Kinston (28501) *(G-9388)*

Three Stacks Distilling Co., Kinston *Also Called: Three Stacks Distilling Co LLC (G-9388)*

Three Trees Bindery.. 704 724-9409
1600 Burtonwood Cir Charlotte (28212) *(G-3692)*

Three Wishes Monogramming............................... 980 298-2981
8200 Blackjack Oak Ct Harrisburg (28075) *(G-7731)*

Threesixty Graphix Inc.. 704 960-4467
465 Airport Rd Salisbury (28147) *(G-14052)*

Thrift-Tents, Walnut Cove *Also Called: Agricltral-Industrial Fabr Inc (G-15630)*

Thrifty Nickel of Greensboro, Greensboro *Also Called: Want of ADS of Greensboro (G-7454)*

Thrifty Tire.. 919 220-7800
2903 N Roxboro St Durham (27704) *(G-5402)*

Thrills Hauling LLC.. 407 383-3483
173 New Rockwood Rd Arden (28704) *(G-383)*

Throwin Stones LLC.. 828 280-7870
825c Merrimon Ave Ste 123 Asheville (28804) *(G-799)*

Thunder Alley Enterprises..................................... 910 371-0119
1224 Magnolia Village Way Leland (28451) *(G-9561)*

Thunderbird Metals East, Graham *Also Called: Metal Impact East LLC (G-6703)*

Thunderbird Technologies Inc................................ 919 481-3239
5540 Centerview Dr Ste 200 Raleigh (27606) *(G-13349)*

Thunderbolt Tees... 828 855-1124
1010 21st Street Dr Se Hickory (28602) *(G-8181)*

Thundrbird Mlding Grnsboro LLC.......................... 336 668-3636
4833 W Gate City Blvd Greensboro (27407) *(G-7403)*

Thurman Toler... 252 758-4082
1229 Sheppard Mill Rd Greenville (27834) *(G-7591)*

Thurston Genomics LLC....................................... 980 237-7547
7806 Springs Village Ln Charlotte (28226) *(G-3693)*

Thw of Wilson Inc... 252 237-7100
2515 Airport Blvd Nw Ste F Wilson (27896) *(G-16546)*

Thyssenkrupp Bilstein Amer Inc............................ 704 663-7563
293 Timber Rd Mooresville (28115) *(G-11112)*

Tiara Inc... 828 484-8236
2002 Riverside Dr Ste 42k Asheville (28804) *(G-800)*

Tice Kitchens & Interiors LLC............................... 919 366-4117
1504 Capital Blvd Raleigh (27603) *(G-13350)*

Tickets Plus Inc (PA).. 616 222-4000
909 Aviation Pkwy Ste 900 Morrisville (27560) *(G-11448)*

Tico Polishing... 704 788-2466
2044 Wilshire Ct Sw Concord (28025) *(G-4377)*

Tideland News, Swansboro *Also Called: Carteret Publishing Company (G-15043)*

Tiedmont Printing, Asheboro *Also Called: Printlogic Inc (G-468)*

Tier 1 Graphics LLC.. 704 625-6880
18525 Statesville Rd Ste D10 Cornelius (28031) *(G-4592)*

Tier 1 Heating and Air LLC.................................... 910 556-1444
3459 Us Hwy 1 Vass (28394) *(G-15494)*

Tiffany Marble Company, Greensboro *Also Called: Sid Jenkins Inc (G-7337)*

Tiger Mountain Woodworks Inc............................. 828 526-5577
2089 Dillard Rd Highlands (28741) *(G-8618)*

Tiger Precision Products LLC............................... 714 360-4134
138 Cedar Pointe Dr Mooresville (28117) *(G-11113)*

Tiger Products, Elizabethtown *Also Called: Cape Fear Chemicals Inc (G-5588)*

Tiger Steel Inc (PA)... 336 624-4481
1425 Mckinney Rd Mount Airy (27030) *(G-11588)*

Tigerswan LLC.. 919 439-7110
3453 Apex Peakway Apex (27502) *(G-248)*

Tigertek Industrial Services, Stoneville *Also Called: Tigertek Industrial Svcs LLC (G-14970)*

Tigertek Industrial Svcs LLC................................. 336 623-1717
2741 Nc Highway 135 Stoneville (27048) *(G-14970)*

Tigra Usa Inc... 828 324-8227
1106 8th Street Ct Se Hickory (28602) *(G-8182)*

Tileware, Hickory *Also Called: Tileware Global LLC (G-8183)*

Tileware Global LLC.. 828 322-9273
1021 16th St Ne Hickory (28601) *(G-8183)*

Tillery Accessories Inc 704 474-3013
7041 Riverview Rd Norwood (28128) *(G-12046)*

Tillson Engineering Laboratory, Jamestown *Also Called: R D Tillson & Associates Inc*
(G-9069)

Tilson Machine Inc (PA) 828 668-4416
632 College Dr Marion (28752) *(G-10182)*

Tim Con Wood Products Inc 252 793-4819
1438 Cross Rd Roper (27970) *(G-13772)*

Tim Conner Enterprises Inc 704 629-4327
1312 Ramseur Rd Bessemer City (28016) *(G-1085)*

Tim Hlley Excvtg Drctnal Drlg 336 595-3320
5350 Main St Walkertown (27051) *(G-15617)*

Tim Nicholson Race Cars LLC 336 253-6767
205 Se Market St B Reidsville (27320) *(G-13541)*

Tim P Krahulec 919 554-1331
5107 Unicon Dr Ste H Wake Forest (27587) *(G-15603)*

Timber Harvester Inc (PA) 910 346-9754
3862 Richlands Hwy Jacksonville (28540) *(G-9042)*

Timber Ninja Outdoors LLC 828 380-1664
1415 Patton Ave Asheville (28806) *(G-801)*

Timber Specialists Inc 704 902-5146
2123 Shelton Ave Statesville (28677) *(G-14914)*

Timber Specialists LLC 704 873-5756
2511 Heritage Cir Statesville (28625) *(G-14915)*

Timber Stand Improvements Inc 910 439-6121
1939 Nc Highway 109 S Mount Gilead (27306) *(G-11613)*

Timber Wolf Forest Products 828 728-7500
3189 Freezer Locker Rd Hudson (28638) *(G-8783)*

Timber Wolf Wood Creations Inc 704 309-5118
2008 Starbrook Dr Charlotte (28210) *(G-3694)*

Timberlake Cabinet Company, Huntersville *Also Called: American Woodmark Corporation*
(G-8790)

Timberlake Ventures Inc 704 896-7499
1908 Eastwood Rd Ste 327 Wilmington (28403) *(G-16429)*

Timberline, Henderson *Also Called: Timberline Acquisition LLC (G-7814)*

Timberline Acquisition LLC 252 492-6144
235 Warehouse Rd Henderson (27537) *(G-7814)*

Time Warner Cable Inc 704 751-5207
2020 E Dixon Blvd Shelby (28152) *(G-14373)*

Timeless Bedding Inc 336 472-6603
306 Beech Retreat Dr Lexington (27292) *(G-9794)*

Timeplanner Calendars Inc 704 377-0024
1010 Timeplanner Dr Charlotte (28206) *(G-3695)*

Times Journal Inc 828 682-4067
22 N Main St Burnsville (28714) *(G-1535)*

Times News Publishing Company 336 226-4414
707 S Main St Burlington (27215) *(G-1506)*

Times Printing Company (PA) 252 473-2105
501 Budleigh St Manteo (27954) *(G-10130)*

Times Printing Company Inc 252 441-2223
1500 S Croatan Hwy Kill Devil Hills (27948) *(G-9263)*

Times-News, Burlington *Also Called: Times News Publishing Company (G-1506)*

Timken Company 704 736-2700
1000 Timken Pl Iron Station (28080) *(G-8977)*

Timmerman Manufacturing Inc 828 464-1778
102 S Mclin Creek Rd Conover (28613) *(G-4505)*

Timmons Fabrications Inc 919 688-8998
2818 Pervis Rd Durham (27704) *(G-5403)*

Timothy Kornegay 919 222-3184
550 Woodland Church Rd Albertson (28508) *(G-116)*

Timothy Lee Blacjmon 336 481-9038
2658 Johnsontown Rd Thomasville (27360) *(G-15290)*

Timothy W Gillespie 919 567-2687
5028 Salem Ridge Rd Holly Springs (27540) *(G-8721)*

Tin Can Ventures LLC 919 732-9078
2207 Carr Store Rd Cedar Grove (27231) *(G-1973)*

Tin Cans LLC 910 322-2626
510 E Washington St Lillington (27546) *(G-9861)*

Tin Man Customs North Carolina 828 391-8080
1424 Drexel Rd Valdese (28690) *(G-15455)*

Tin Shed LLc 919 928-0600
30062 Benbury Chapel Hill (27517) *(G-2079)*

Tina M Jones 828 685-2937
101 Lytle Rd Hendersonville (28792) *(G-7907)*

Tinas Fabulous Fudge LLC 919 606-2616
4720 Schley Rd Hillsborough (27278) *(G-8669)*

Tinman Candles 828 329-1140
205 Mckinney Rd 1 Etowah (28729) *(G-5694)*

Tint Plus 910 229-5303
2850 Owen Dr Fayetteville (28306) *(G-5930)*

Tipper Tie Inc (HQ) 919 362-8811
2000 Lufkin Rd Apex (27539) *(G-249)*

Tippett Logging LLC 252 301-3170
208 Marks St Whitakers (27891) *(G-15957)*

Tire Kountry LLC 336 637-8320
2300 Freeway Dr Reidsville (27320) *(G-13542)*

Tire Sls Svc Inc Fytteville NC (PA) 910 485-1121
400 Person St Fayetteville (28301) *(G-5931)*

Tires Incorporated of Clinton 910 592-4741
317 Southeast Blvd Clinton (28328) *(G-4114)*

Titan America LLC 336 754-0143
3193 Pine Hall Rd Belews Creek (27009) *(G-973)*

Titan Flow Control Inc (PA) 910 735-0000
290 Corporate Dr Lumberton (28358) *(G-10058)*

Titan Land Group LLC 704 400-1842
8405 Dianthus Ct Unit 104 Charlotte (28277) *(G-3696)*

Titeflex Corporation 647 638-7160
Charlotte (28265) *(G-3697)*

Titus, Tarboro *Also Called: Air System Components Inc (G-15094)*

Tivoli Woodworks LLC 336 602-3512
4850 Bringle Ferry Rd Salisbury (28146) *(G-14053)*

Tk Elevator Corporation 336 272-4563
22 Oak Branch Dr Ste C Greensboro (27407) *(G-7404)*

TLC, Elkin *Also Called: Mvp Group International Inc (G-5627)*

TLC Enterprises 336 454-4981
704 Ragsdale Rd Jamestown (27282) *(G-9075)*

Tlv Corporation 704 597-9070
13901 S Lakes Dr Charlotte (28273) *(G-3698)*

Tm15 Printing Services 704 606-0112
1906 Delaware Dr Apt F Charlotte (28215) *(G-3699)*

Tmb Cranes, Charlotte *Also Called: Thomas M Brown Inc (G-3690)*

Tmcm Services LLC 336 609-4378
3 Long Cove Ct Greensboro (27407) *(G-7405)*

Tmp of Nc Inc 336 463-3225
1201 Old Stage Rd Yadkinville (27055) *(G-17055)*

Tms International LLC 704 604-0287
6601 Lakeview Rd Charlotte (28269) *(G-3700)*

Tms Neurohealth Centers, Mooresville *Also Called: Greenbrook Tms Neurohealth Ctr*
(G-10964)

TNT Services Inc 252 261-3073
3908 Poor Ridge Rd Kitty Hawk (27949) *(G-9408)*

TNT Signs & Graphics 704 460-5050
3131 Suffolk Dr Shelby (28152) *(G-14374)*

TNT Web & Grafix LLC 252 289-8846
619 Western Ave Nashville (27856) *(G-11751)*

Tnw Ventures Inc 828 216-4089
60 Bishop Ln Pisgah Forest (28768) *(G-12328)*

To Knit and Stitch 704 493-2523
7309 Kinsmore Ln Charlotte (28269) *(G-3701)*

To The Point Inc 336 725-5303
130 Stratford Ct Ste E Winston Salem (27103) *(G-16943)*

To The Top Tires and Svc LLC 252 886-3286
327 E Raleigh Blvd Ste 943 Rocky Mount (27801) *(G-13673)*

Tobacco Merchants Association of The United States Inc., Raleigh *Also Called: Tobacco Mrchnts Assn of US Inc (G-13351)*

Tobacco Mrchnts Assn of US Inc 919 872-5040
901 Jones Franklin Rd Ste 102 Raleigh (27606) *(G-13351)*

Tobacco Outlet Products, Charlotte *Also Called: Tobacco Outlet Products LLC (G-3702)*

Tobacco Outlet Products LLC 704 341-9388
6401 Carmel Rd Ste 204 Charlotte (28226) *(G-3702)*

Tobacco Rag Processors Inc (PA) 252 265-0081
4737 Yank Rd Wilson (27893) *(G-16547)*

Tobacco Rag Processors Inc 252 265-0081
4744 Potato House Ct Wilson (27893) *(G-16548)*

ALPHABETIC SECTION

Tobacco Rag Processors Inc.. 252 237-8180
2105 Black Creek Rd Se Bldg 6 Wilson (27893) *(G-16549)*

Tobaccoville Welding LLC.. 336 287-7323
4040 Elizabeth Park Dr Tobaccoville (27050) *(G-15322)*

Tobe Manufacturing Inc... 910 439-6203
603 W Allenton St Mount Gilead (27306) *(G-11614)*

Today's Photographer Magazine, Hamptonville Also Called: Ifpo - Ifmo/American Image Inc *(G-7672)*

Todays Charlotte Woman.. 704 521-6872
5200 Park Rd Ste 126 Charlotte (28209) *(G-3703)*

Todaytec LLC... 704 790-2440
6701 Northpark Blvd Ste K Charlotte (28216) *(G-3704)*

Todco Inc.. 336 248-2001
1123 Roy Lopp Rd Lexington (27292) *(G-9795)*

Toddler Tables... 919 772-4765
3779 Lee St Ayden (28513) *(G-860)*

Toddler Tables, Raleigh Also Called: Vaughan Enterprises Inc *(G-13394)*

Todds Rv & Marine Inc.. 828 651-0007
130 Lyndale Rd Hendersonville (28739) *(G-7908)*

Todrin Fine Woodwork Llc... 413 478-2818
2900 Carl Durham Rd Chapel Hill (27516) *(G-2080)*

Toe River Service Station LLC.. 828 688-6385
4928 S 226 Hwy Bakersville (28705) *(G-890)*

Tokai Carbon GE LLC (DH)... 980 260-1130
6210 Ardrey Kell Rd Ste 270 Charlotte (28277) *(G-3705)*

Tokyos Express... 910 735-0412
2716 N Roberts Ave Lumberton (28358) *(G-10059)*

Toler Welding & Repair, Greenville Also Called: Thurman Toler *(G-7591)*

Tom Burgiss.. 336 359-2995
294 Elk Knob Rd Laurel Springs (28644) *(G-9468)*

Tom Hedrick Express.. 336 798-1293
8034 Nc Highway 8 Lexington (27292) *(G-9796)*

Tom Kleeberg... 336 516-2363
1148 Nc Highway 62 W High Point (27263) *(G-8572)*

Tom Marsh Jr DBA Tm Woodworks.. 910 376-2760
101 Sandtrail Ct Hampstead (28443) *(G-7660)*

Tom Robinsons Carolina Seafood, Carrboro Also Called: Toms Robinson Seafood Inc *(G-1658)*

Tom Rochester & Associates Inc (PA).. 704 896-5805
9325 Forsyth Park Dr Charlotte (28273) *(G-3706)*

Tom's Coin Laundry, Kings Mountain Also Called: B & D Enterprises Inc *(G-9293)*

Tomarjo Corp... 336 762-0065
105 Julian Ave Ste A Thomasville (27360) *(G-15291)*

Tombogancraftsman Com.. 919 932-9878
9622 Greenfield Rd Chapel Hill (27516) *(G-2081)*

Tomlinson of Orlando Inc... 336 475-8000
201 E Holly Hill Rd Thomasville (27360) *(G-15292)*

Tomlinson/Erwin-Lambeth Inc.. 336 472-5005
201 E Holly Hill Rd Thomasville (27360) *(G-15293)*

Tommar Publishing Inc.. 336 463-2690
2937 Lone Hickory Rd Yadkinville (27055) *(G-17056)*

Tommy Signs.. 704 877-1234
8716 Maggie Robinson Rd Waxhaw (28173) *(G-15782)*

Tommy W Smith Inc.. 704 436-6616
9825 Bowman Barrier Rd Mount Pleasant (28124) *(G-11678)*

Tommys Tubing & Stockenettes... 336 449-6461
628 Wood St Gibsonville (27249) *(G-6572)*

Tomorrow Cell LLC.. 704 378-8555
5401 South Blvd Charlotte (28217) *(G-3707)*

Tompkins Industries Inc.. 828 254-2351
150 Westside Dr Asheville (28806) *(G-802)*

Toms Knit Fabrics.. 704 867-4236
699 Carlton Dr Apt A Gastonia (28054) *(G-6527)*

Toms Robinson Seafood Inc.. 919 942-1221
207 Roberson St Carrboro (27510) *(G-1658)*

Toner Machining Tech Inc... 828 432-8007
1523 N Green St Morganton (28655) *(G-11261)*

Toner Machining Technologies... 828 432-8007
212 E Fleming Dr Morganton (28655) *(G-11262)*

Toney Lumber Company Inc... 919 496-5711
309 Bunn Rd Louisburg (27549) *(G-10005)*

Tony D Hildreth.. 910 276-1803
22945 Broadwell Rd Laurel Hill (28351) *(G-9465)*

Tony S Ice Cream Company Inc (PA).. 704 867-7085
604 E Franklin Blvd Gastonia (28054) *(G-6528)*

Tony's Custom Cabinets, Clinton Also Called: Tonys Cabinets *(G-4115)*

TONY'S ICE CREAM CO INC, Gastonia Also Called: Tonys Ice Cream Co Inc *(G-6529)*

Tonyas Crocheted Creations... 704 421-2143
7535 Marlbrook Dr Charlotte (28212) *(G-3708)*

Tonys Cabinets... 910 592-2028
671 Cartertown Rd Clinton (28328) *(G-4115)*

Tonys Ice Cream Co Inc... 704 853-0018
520 E Franklin Blvd Gastonia (28054) *(G-6529)*

Too Hott Customs LLC... 336 722-4919
1249 W Academy St Winston Salem (27103) *(G-16944)*

Tool Rental Depot LLC.. 704 636-6400
2001 S Main St Salisbury (28144) *(G-14054)*

Tool-Weld LLC.. 843 986-4931
180 Cross Ridge Dr Rutherfordton (28139) *(G-13893)*

Toolcraft Inc North Carolina (PA).. 828 659-7379
1877 Rutherford Rd Marion (28752) *(G-10183)*

Tooling Division, Mocksville Also Called: Gesipa Fasteners Usa Inc *(G-10577)*

Toolmarx LLC... 919 725-0122
408 Ricks Dr Winston Salem (27103) *(G-16945)*

Tools USA, Greensboro Also Called: Standard Tools and Eqp Co *(G-7366)*

Top Dawg Landscape Inc... 336 877-7519
605 S Jefferson Ave # 1 West Jefferson (28694) *(G-15949)*

Top Hat Bbcat Backhoe Svcs Inc... 336 382-0068
530 Gold Hill Rd Madison (27025) *(G-10089)*

Top Notch Log Homes Inc.. 828 926-4300
3517 Jonathan Creek Rd Waynesville (28785) *(G-15829)*

Top Tier Paper Products Inc (PA)... 828 994-2222
409 Thornburg Dr Se Conover (28613) *(G-4506)*

Top Tobacco LP... 910 646-3014
204 Top Tobacco Rd Lake Waccamaw (28450) *(G-9449)*

Topgolf.. 704 612-4745
8024 Savoy Corporate Dr Charlotte (28273) *(G-3709)*

Topline Cabinet Co Inc... 919 762-0045
608 Hollymont Dr Holly Springs (27540) *(G-8722)*

Toplink Publishing... 888 375-9818
2227 Natmore Rd Kelly (28448) *(G-9139)*

Topquadrant Inc.. 919 300-7945
930 Main Campus Dr Ste 300 Raleigh (27606) *(G-13352)*

Topsail Sportswear Inc... 910 270-4903
15530 Us Highway 17 Hampstead (28443) *(G-7661)*

Topsail Voice LLC.. 910 270-2944
14886 Us Highway 17 Hampstead (28443) *(G-7662)*

Topsider Building Systems Inc.. 336 766-9300
3710 Dillon Industrial Dr Clemmons (27012) *(G-4062)*

Toque Industries LLC... 704 640-6232
5326 Twin Ln Charlotte (28269) *(G-3710)*

Torches Design Studio Inc.. 704 966-4000
688 N Nc 16 Business Hwy Ste A Denver (28037) *(G-4808)*

Torpedo Specialty Wire Inc... 252 977-3900
1115 Instrument Dr Rocky Mount (27804) *(G-13737)*

Tortillas Carolina, Saint Pauls Also Called: Elizondo LLC *(G-13905)*

Tortillas San Antonio Inc.. 252 459-5459
4981 Old Bailey Hwy Nashville (27856) *(G-11752)*

Tortilleria Duvy LLC... 336 497-1510
1261 Nc Highway 66 S Kernersville (27284) *(G-9246)*

Tortilleria La Favorita.. 910 892-0302
1113 W Broad St Dunn (28334) *(G-4886)*

Tortilleria Los Paisanos... 704 283-8508
1404 Skyway Dr Monroe (28110) *(G-10822)*

Tortilleria Los Remnedios II... 919 658-1714
902 N Breazeale Ave Mount Olive (28365) *(G-11671)*

Tosaf Inc.. 704 396-7097
132 W Virginia Ave Bessemer City (28016) *(G-1086)*

Tosaf Inc (DH)... 980 533-3000
330 Southridge Pkwy Bessemer City (28016) *(G-1087)*

Tosaf Aw Inc... 980 533-3000
330 Southridge Pkwy Bessemer City (28016) *(G-1088)*

Toshiba, Durham *Also Called: Toshiba Globl Cmmrce Sltons In (G-5404)*

Toshiba Globl Cmmrce Sltons In (DH) 984 444-2767
  3901 S Miami Blvd Durham (27703) *(G-5404)*

Total Controls Inc 704 821-6341
  4420 Friendship Dr Ste A Matthews (28105) *(G-10295)*

Total Fire Systems Inc 919 556-9161
  30 Weathers Ct Youngsville (27596) *(G-17107)*

Total Limit Lures 910 330-5786
  3950 Loblolly Ct Sw Concord (28027) *(G-4378)*

Total Print Solutions 336 841-5292
  320 Habersham Rd Ste 105 High Point (27260) *(G-8573)*

Total Solution Industries Inc 919 900-8801
  7613 Pats Branch Dr Raleigh (27612) *(G-13353)*

Total Sono LLC 908 349-8610
  100 Conway Ct Cary (27513) *(G-1910)*

Total Sports Enterprises 704 237-3930
  9624 Belloak Ln Waxhaw (28173) *(G-15783)*

Total Technologies LLC 336 259-5541
  4702 King Crowder Dr Gastonia (28052) *(G-6530)*

Tote Glass Inc 910 515-4187
  621 N 4th St Wilmington (28401) *(G-16430)*

Toter LLC 704 936-5610
  6525 Morrison Blvd Ste 300 Charlotte (28211) *(G-3711)*

Toter LLC (DH) 800 424-0422
  841 Meacham Rd Statesville (28677) *(G-14916)*

Toucan Louie's Gold District, Charlotte *Also Called: Sunstead Brewing LLC (G-3655)*

Touch Tone Tees LLC 919 358-5536
  3316c Capital Blvd Ste 8 Raleigh (27604) *(G-13354)*

Touch Up Solutions Inc 828 428-9094
  4372 Providence Mill Rd Maiden (28650) *(G-10120)*

Touchamerica Inc 919 732-6968
  437 Dimmocks Mill Rd Hillsborough (27278) *(G-8670)*

Touchstone Fine Cabinetry, Rutherfordton *Also Called: US Precision Cabinetry LLC (G-13900)*

Tourist Baseball Inc 828 258-0428
  30 Buchanan Pl Asheville (28801) *(G-803)*

Towel City Tire & Wheel LLC 704 933-2143
  1601 N Ridge Ave Kannapolis (28083) *(G-9136)*

Tower Components Inc 336 824-2102
  5960 Us Highway 64 E Ramseur (27316) *(G-13450)*

Tower Engrg Professionals Inc (PA) 919 661-6351
  326 Tryon Rd Raleigh (27603) *(G-13355)*

Tower House Publishing LLC 917 284-0619
  500 Westover Dr Ste 11228 Sanford (27330) *(G-14197)*

Towerco LLC 919 653-5700
  5000 Valleystone Dr Ste 200 Cary (27519) *(G-1911)*

Town of Jonesville 336 835-2250
  399 Shaw St Jonesville (28642) *(G-9102)*

Town of Maggie Valley Inc 828 926-0145
  45 Water Plant Rd Maggie Valley (28751) *(G-10096)*

Town of Tarboro 252 641-4284
  600 Albemarle Ave Tarboro (27886) *(G-15124)*

Town of Waynesville 828 456-8497
  341 Rocky Branch Rd Waynesville (28786) *(G-15830)*

Toxaway Concrete, Sapphire *Also Called: Lbm Industries Inc (G-14213)*

Toxaway Concrete Inc 828 966-4270
  Hwy 64 E Cashiers (28717) *(G-1938)*

Toxplanet, Wilmington *Also Called: Timberlake Ventures Inc (G-16429)*

Toymakerz LLC 843 267-3477
  2358 Holiday Loop Reidsville (27320) *(G-13543)*

Toza Truss LLC 336 301-6338
  6633 Carl Cox Rd Bennett (27208) *(G-1028)*

Trac Plastics Inc 704 864-9140
  140 Superior Stainless Rd Gastonia (28052) *(G-6531)*

Traceymack Products 919 499-8459
  179 Highmeadow Dr Cameron (28326) *(G-1564)*

Trackx Technology LLC 888 787-2259
  437 Dimmocks Mill Rd Ste 28 Hillsborough (27278) *(G-8671)*

Tractor Country Inc 252 523-3007
  5763 Hwy 70 Dover (28526) *(G-4835)*

Tracy's Gourmet, Asheville *Also Called: Tracys Gourmet LLC (G-804)*

Tracys Gourmet LLC 919 672-1731
  315 Old Haw Creek Rd Asheville (28805) *(G-804)*

Trade Venture Stones LLC 919 803-3923
  365 Spectrum Dr Ste 100 Knightdale (27545) *(G-9431)*

Trademark Landscape Group Inc 910 253-0560
  360 Ocean Hwy E Supply (28462) *(G-15013)*

Trademark Ldscp Cntg Trdmark O, Supply *Also Called: Trademark Landscape Group Inc (G-15013)*

Tradewinds Coffee Co Inc 919 556-1835
  6308 Mitchell Mill Rd Zebulon (27597) *(G-17144)*

Tradition Surfboards LLC 404 229-4223
  568 Boundary Loop Rd Nw Calabash (28467) *(G-1554)*

Traditions Wood Carving & Frms 828 322-5625
  120 11th St Nw Hickory (28601) *(G-8184)*

Trafag Inc 704 343-6339
  8848 Red Oak Blvd Ste I Charlotte (28217) *(G-3712)*

Trailer Plus, New Bern *Also Called: Derrow Enterprises Inc (G-11800)*

Training Grund Pblications LLC 252 568-3922
  4028 Duplin County Rd Pink Hill (28572) *(G-12317)*

Training Industry Inc 919 653-4990
  110 Horizon Dr Ste 110 Raleigh (27615) *(G-13356)*

TRAININGINDUSTRY.COM, Raleigh *Also Called: Training Industry Inc (G-13356)*

Trajan Inc 919 435-1105
  2942 Imperial Oaks Dr Raleigh (27614) *(G-13357)*

Tramway Veneers Inc 919 776-7606
  2603 Tramway Rd Sanford (27332) *(G-14198)*

Trane, Asheville *Also Called: Trane US Inc (G-805)*
Trane, Charlotte *Also Called: Trane US Inc (G-3714)*
Trane, Charlotte *Also Called: Trane US Inc (G-3715)*
Trane, Davidson *Also Called: Trane US Inc (G-4704)*
Trane, Greensboro *Also Called: Trane US Inc (G-7406)*
Trane, Greensboro *Also Called: Trane US Inc (G-7407)*
Trane, Greensboro *Also Called: Trane US Inc (G-7408)*
Trane, Morrisville *Also Called: Trane US Inc (G-11449)*

Trane Company (DH) 704 398-4600
  4500 Morris Field Dr Charlotte (28208) *(G-3713)*

Trane Export LLC 608 788-0569
  800 Beaty St Davidson (28036) *(G-4701)*

Trane Technologies Company LLC (HQ) 704 655-4000
  800 Beaty St Ste E Davidson (28036) *(G-4702)*

Trane Technologies Company LLC 336 751-3561
  501 Sanford Ave Mocksville (27028) *(G-10608)*

Trane Technologies Company LLC 910 692-8700
  1725 Us 1 Hwy N Southern Pines (28387) *(G-14558)*

Trane Technologies Mfg LLC 704 655-4000
  800 Beaty St Davidson (28036) *(G-4703)*

Trane US Inc 828 277-8664
  168 Sweeten Creek Rd Asheville (28803) *(G-805)*

Trane US Inc 704 525-9600
  4501 S Tryon St Charlotte (28217) *(G-3714)*

Trane US Inc 704 697-9006
  8610 Air Park West Dr Ste C Charlotte (28214) *(G-3715)*

Trane US Inc (DH) 704 655-4000
  800 Beaty St Ste E Davidson (28036) *(G-4704)*

Trane US Inc 336 273-6353
  3101 S Elm Eugene St # 100 Greensboro (27406) *(G-7406)*

Trane US Inc 336 378-0670
  1915 N Church St Greensboro (27405) *(G-7407)*

Trane US Inc 336 387-1735
  8408 Triad Dr Greensboro (27409) *(G-7408)*

Trane US Inc 919 781-0458
  401 Kitty Hawk Dr Morrisville (27560) *(G-11449)*

Trans East Inc 910 892-1081
  405 E Edgerton St Dunn (28334) *(G-4887)*

Trans-Tech Energy Inc (PA) 252 446-4357
  14527 Us Highway 64 Alt W Rocky Mount (27801) *(G-13674)*

Trans-Tech Energy LLC 254 840-3355
  14527 Us Highway 64 Alt W Rocky Mount (27801) *(G-13675)*

Transarctic, High Point *Also Called: Transarctic North Carolina Inc (G-8574)*

Transarctic North Carolina Inc 336 861-6116
  5270 Glenola Industrial Dr High Point (27263) *(G-8574)*

ALPHABETIC SECTION

Transbotics Corporation.. 704 362-1115
3400 Latrobe Dr Charlotte (28211) *(G-3716)*

Transcendent Technologies LLC.................................... 704 334-1258
2330 E 5th St Charlotte (28204) *(G-3717)*

Transcontinental AC US LLC (HQ)................................. 704 847-9171
700 Crestdale Rd Matthews (28105) *(G-10296)*

Transcontinental Tvl LLC.. 336 476-3131
1308 Blair St Thomasville (27360) *(G-15294)*

Transdata Solutions Inc.. 919 770-9329
221 N Horner Blvd Sanford (27330) *(G-14199)*

Transeco Energy Corporation.. 828 684-6400
101 Fair Oaks Rd Arden (28704) *(G-384)*

Transenterix Surgical Inc... 919 765-8400
635 Davis Dr Ste 300 Morrisville (27560) *(G-11450)*

Transformational Bible Inst... 702 218-3528
714 Richardson St Elizabeth City (27909) *(G-5578)*

Transformer Sales & Service.. 910 594-1495
1392 Massey Rd Newton Grove (28366) *(G-11994)*

Transit & Level Clinic, Cary Also Called: C W Lawley Incorporated *(G-1719)*

Transmission Div, Maxton Also Called: Meritor Inc *(G-10360)*

Transmission Unlimited, Mooresville Also Called: Gracie & Lucas LLC *(G-10962)*

TransMontaigne, Selma Also Called: TransMontaigne Terminaling Inc *(G-14262)*

TransMontaigne Terminaling Inc..................................... 303 626-8200
2600 W Oak St Selma (27576) *(G-14262)*

Transportation Tech Inc (DH).. 252 946-6521
911 W 5th St Washington (27889) *(G-15734)*

Transtech Pharma LLC (PA)... 336 841-0300
3980 Premier Dr Ste 310 High Point (27265) *(G-8575)*

Transtex Belting.. 704 334-5353
10125 S Tryon St Charlotte (28273) *(G-3718)*

Transtex Belting, Charlotte Also Called: Forbo Movement Systems *(G-2786)*

Transylvnia Vcational Svcs Inc (PA)............................... 828 884-3195
11 Mountain Industrial Dr Brevard (28712) *(G-1291)*

Transylvnia Vcational Svcs Inc....................................... 828 884-1548
1 Quality Way Fletcher (28732) *(G-6045)*

Trash Masher LLC... 786 357-2697
1045 Burke St Winston Salem (27101) *(G-16946)*

Traumtic Drect Trnsfsion Dvcs....................................... 423 364-5828
1007 Woodbriar St Apex (27502) *(G-250)*

Travis Alfrey Woodworking Inc....................................... 910 639-3553
9988 Aberdeen Rd Aberdeen (28315) *(G-33)*

Travis Harrell... 828 279-2937
2936 Orville Wright Way Unit 1 Wilmington (28405) *(G-16431)*

Travis L Bunker... 336 352-3289
6198 W Pine St Mount Airy (27030) *(G-11589)*

Travistees.. 910 506-8827
609 Piner Rd Ste A602 Wilmington (28409) *(G-16432)*

Trawler Incorporated.. 252 745-3751
569 Kelly Watson Rd Lowland (28552) *(G-10015)*

Traxon Technologies LLC.. 201 508-1570
2915 Whitehall Park Dr Charlotte (28273) *(G-3719)*

TRC Acquisition LLC... 252 355-9353
133 Forlines Rd Winterville (28590) *(G-17015)*

Treadz LLC... 704 664-0995
2118 Charlotte Hwy Mooresville (28117) *(G-11114)*

Tree Brand Packaging Inc (PA)...................................... 704 483-0719
7971 Graham Rd Denver (28037) *(G-4809)*

Tree Craft Log Homes Inc... 828 689-2240
43 Back Hollow Rd Mars Hill (28754) *(G-10197)*

Tree Frog Industries LLC... 919 986-2229
246 Dogwood Trl Wendell (27591) *(G-15921)*

Tree Masters Inc.. 828 464-9443
101 E 11th St Ste 1 Newton (28658) *(G-11979)*

Treeforms Inc... 336 292-8998
4242 Regency Dr Greensboro (27410) *(G-7409)*

Treeforms Lockers, Greensboro Also Called: Treeforms Inc *(G-7409)*

Trefena Welds.. 203 551-1370
8408 Exmoor Trce Browns Summit (27214) *(G-1318)*

Treg Tool Inc.. 828 676-0035
10 Summer Meadow Rd Arden (28704) *(G-385)*

Trego Innovations LLC.. 919 374-0089
2301 Wilco Blvd S Wilson (27893) *(G-16550)*

Treklite Inc... 919 610-1788
904 Dorothea Dr Raleigh (27603) *(G-13358)*

Trelleborg Ctd Systems US Inc....................................... 864 576-1210
715 Railroad Ave Rutherfordton (28139) *(G-13894)*

Trelleborg Ctd Systems US Inc....................................... 828 286-9126
631 Rock Rd Rutherfordton (28139) *(G-13895)*

Trelleborg Ctd Systems US Inc (PA).............................. 828 286-9126
715 Railroad Ave Rutherfordton (28139) *(G-13896)*

Trelleborg Ctd Systems US Inc....................................... 828 286-9126
715 Railroad Ave Rutherfordton (28139) *(G-13897)*

Trelleborg Salisbury Inc.. 704 797-8030
510 Long Meadow Dr Salisbury (28147) *(G-14055)*

Trend Performance Products... 828 862-8290
114 Lime Kiln Ln Pisgah Forest (28768) *(G-12329)*

Trendy Nails, Creedmoor Also Called: Jhd Enterprise LLC *(G-4616)*

Trenton Emergency Med Svcs Inc................................... 252 448-2646
105 Cherry St Trenton (28585) *(G-15335)*

Trenton Ems, Trenton Also Called: Trenton Emergency Med Svcs Inc *(G-15335)*

Tresata Inc (PA)... 980 224-2097
1616 Candem Rd Ste 300 Charlotte (28203) *(G-3720)*

Tresco... 361 985-3154
736 Greenway Rd Boone (28607) *(G-1242)*

Tresmc LLC.. 919 900-0868
2509 Ferdinand Dr Knightdale (27545) *(G-9432)*

Treva Mason LLC.. 704 566-7973
8500 Monroe Rd Charlotte (28212) *(G-3721)*

Trevira North America LLC.. 704 910-0970
5206 Leonardslee Ct Charlotte (28226) *(G-3722)*

Trexler Logging Inc... 704 694-5272
2292 Bethel Rd Wadesboro (28170) *(G-15517)*

TRf Manufacturing NC Inc.. 252 223-1112
413 Howard Blvd Newport (28570) *(G-11909)*

Tri City Concrete Co LLC... 828 245-2011
158 Withrow Rd Forest City (28043) *(G-6084)*

Tri County Gastroenterology, Mooresville Also Called: Thomas Mendolia MD *(G-11111)*

Tri Mech Services, Cary Also Called: Trimech Solutions LLC *(G-1914)*

Tri State Componenets, Sparta Also Called: Truss Shop Inc *(G-14600)*

Tri State Plastics Inc... 704 865-7431
507 E Davidson Ave Gastonia (28054) *(G-6532)*

Tri Tech Forensics National La, Leland Also Called: Tri-Tech Forensics Inc *(G-9562)*

Tri-City Concrete LLC... 704 372-2930
3823 Raleigh St Charlotte (28206) *(G-3723)*

Tri-City Mechanical Contrs Inc....................................... 336 272-9495
706 Utility St Greensboro (27405) *(G-7410)*

Tri-City Tire Service, Spindale Also Called: Burnett Darrill Stephen *(G-14604)*

Tri-County Industries Inc... 252 977-3800
1250 Atlantic Ave Rocky Mount (27801) *(G-13676)*

Tri-H Molding Co... 252 491-8530
135 W Side Ln Harbinger (27941) *(G-7684)*

Tri-Star Plastics Corp.. 704 598-2800
1387 N Nc 16 Business Hwy Denver (28037) *(G-4810)*

Tri-State Carports Inc (PA).. 276 755-2081
304 Franklin St Mount Airy (27030) *(G-11590)*

Tri-Steel Fabricators Inc... 252 291-7900
6864 Wagon Wheel Rd Sims (27880) *(G-14445)*

Tri-TEC Ind Inc.. 704 424-5995
200 Peachtree Dr S Charlotte (28217) *(G-3724)*

Tri-Tech Forensics Inc (PA).. 910 457-6600
3811 International Blvd Ne Ste 100 Leland (28451) *(G-9562)*

Tri-W Farms Inc... 910 533-3596
4671 Faison Hwy Clinton (28328) *(G-4116)*

Triac Corporation.. 336 297-1130
611 Norwalk St Greensboro (27407) *(G-7411)*

Triad Anodizing & Plating Inc.. 336 292-7028
3502 Spring Garden St Greensboro (27407) *(G-7412)*

Triad Automation Group, Winston Salem Also Called: Triad Automation Group Inc *(G-16947)*

Triad Automation Group Inc... 336 767-1379
4994 Indiana Ave Ste F Winston Salem (27106) *(G-16947)*

Triad Business Card Assoc... 336 706-2729
3201 Summit Ave Greensboro (27405) *(G-7413)*

Triad Business Journal, Greensboro Also Called: American City Bus Journals Inc *(G-6797)*

Triad Corrugated Metal   **ALPHABETIC SECTION**

Triad Corrugated Metal, Sanford *Also Called: Triad Corrugated Metal Inc* **(G-14200)**
Triad Corrugated Metal Inc (PA) 336 625-9727
   208 Luck Rd Asheboro (27205) **(G-499)**
Triad Corrugated Metal Inc 919 775-1663
   109 Mcneill Rd Sanford (27330) **(G-14200)**
Triad Cutting Tools Inc 336 873-8708
   5527 Us Highway 220 S Asheboro (27205) **(G-500)**
Triad Engines Parts & Svcs Inc 800 334-6437
   3439 S Aviation Dr Burlington (27215) **(G-1507)**
Triad Fabrication and Mch Inc 336 993-6042
   1080 Industrial Park Dr Kernersville (27284) **(G-9247)**
Triad Hosting Inc 336 497-1932
   4602 Joseph Hoskins Rd Summerfield (27358) **(G-14992)**
Triad Marine Center Inc 252 634-1880
   4316 Us Highway 70 E New Bern (28560) **(G-11851)**
Triad Meats, Greensboro *Also Called: Stevens Packing Inc* **(G-7371)**
Triad Power & Controls Inc 336 375-9780
   215 Industrial Ave Ste G Greensboro (27406) **(G-7414)**
Triad Precision Products Inc 336 474-0980
   128 Sunrise Center Dr Thomasville (27360) **(G-15295)**
Triad Prefinish & Lbr Sls Inc 336 375-4849
   3514 Associate Dr Greensboro (27405) **(G-7415)**
Triad Print Promo LLC 336 416-3488
   5336 Courtney Huntsville Rd Yadkinville (27055) **(G-17057)**
Triad Printing NC, Greensboro *Also Called: Triad Printing NC Inc* **(G-7416)**
Triad Printing NC Inc 336 422-8752
   1306 E Wendover Ave Greensboro (27405) **(G-7416)**
Triad Semiconductor Inc 336 774-2150
   1760 Jonestown Rd Ste 100 Winston Salem (27103) **(G-16948)**
Triad Sheet Metal & Mech Inc 336 379-9891
   300 Lowdermilk St Greensboro (27401) **(G-7417)**
Triad Smoothies LLC 336 972-1130
   2541 Bitting Rd Winston Salem (27104) **(G-16949)**
Triad Specialty Products, Greensboro *Also Called: Piedmont Animal Health Inc* **(G-7254)**
Triad Stainless Inc 336 315-5515
   4927 W Market St Greensboro (27407) **(G-7418)**
Triad Welding Contractors Inc 336 882-3902
   146 Silkwind Ct Clemmons (27012) **(G-4063)**
Triad-Fit 336 409-3818
   5677 Harrington Village Dr Winston Salem (27105) **(G-16950)**
Triaga Inc 919 412-6019
   1900 Stantonsburg Rd Se Wilson (27893) **(G-16551)**
Triangel Quarry, Cary *Also Called: Wake Stone Corporation* **(G-1923)**
Triangle Auto Components LLC 704 848-4121
   766 Haileys Ferry Rd Lilesville (28091) **(G-9841)**
Triangle Biosystems Inc 919 361-2663
   2224 Page Rd Ste 108 Durham (27703) **(G-5405)**
Triangle Biosystems Intl, Durham *Also Called: Triangle Biosystems Inc* **(G-5405)**
Triangle Body Works Inc 336 788-0631
   2014 Waughtown St Winston Salem (27107) **(G-16951)**
Triangle Brick Company (PA) 919 544-1796
   6523 Nc Highway 55 Durham (27713) **(G-5406)**
Triangle Brick Company 919 387-9257
   294 King Rd Moncure (27559) **(G-10627)**
Triangle Brick Company 704 695-1420
   2960 Us Highway 52 N Wadesboro (28170) **(G-15518)**
Triangle Brick Merryoaks Plant, Moncure *Also Called: Triangle Brick Company* **(G-10627)**
Triangle Cabinet Company 336 869-6401
   809 Aberdeen Rd High Point (27265) **(G-8576)**
Triangle Chemical Company 919 942-3237
   7100 Old Greensboro Rd Chapel Hill (27516) **(G-2082)**
Triangle Coatings Inc 919 781-6108
   6721 Mount Herman Rd Morrisville (27560) **(G-11451)**
Triangle Converting Corp 919 596-6656
   2021 S Briggs Ave Durham (27703) **(G-5407)**
Triangle Custom Cabinets Inc 919 387-1133
   807 Center St Apex (27502) **(G-251)**
Triangle Custom Woodworks LLC (PA) 919 637-8857
   526 Victoria Hills Dr S Fuquay Varina (27526) **(G-6234)**
Triangle Glass Service Inc 919 477-9508
   1320 Old Oxford Rd Ste 12 Durham (27704) **(G-5408)**

Triangle Hrse Blanket Svcs LLC 919 945-9560
   3528 Fletchers Way Stem (27581) **(G-14939)**
Triangle Indus Sup Hldings LLC (PA) 704 395-0600
   228 Westinghouse Blvd Ste 104 Charlotte (28273) **(G-3725)**
Triangle Inner Vision Company 919 460-6013
   100 Dominion Dr Ste 110 Morrisville (27560) **(G-11452)**
Triangle Installation Svc Inc 919 363-7637
   2445 Reliance Ave Apex (27539) **(G-252)**
Triangle Kitchen Supply 919 562-3888
   336 Bert Winston Rd Youngsville (27596) **(G-17108)**
Triangle Metalworks Inc 919 556-7786
   100 Moores Pond Rd Youngsville (27596) **(G-17109)**
Triangle Microsystems Inc 919 878-1880
   1807 Garner Station Blvd Raleigh (27603) **(G-13359)**
Triangle Microworks Inc 919 870-5101
   2840 Plaza Pl Ste 205 Raleigh (27612) **(G-13360)**
Triangle Pipe Ftting Sltons In 919 696-8635
   102 Stardale Rd Morrisville (27560) **(G-11453)**
Triangle Plastics Inc 919 598-8839
   6435 Mount Herman Rd Raleigh (27617) **(G-13361)**
Triangle Pointer Inc 919 968-4801
   88 Vilcom Center Dr Chapel Hill (27514) **(G-2083)**
Triangle Pointer Magazine, Chapel Hill *Also Called: Triangle Pointer Inc* **(G-2083)**
Triangle Prcsion Dgnostics Inc 919 345-0110
   2 Davis Dr Rm 203 Durham (27709) **(G-5409)**
Triangle Ready Mix LLC 919 859-4190
   241 International Dr Morrisville (27560) **(G-11454)**
Triangle Regulatory Pubg LLC 919 886-4587
   7780 Brier Creek Pkwy Raleigh (27617) **(G-13362)**
Triangle Service Solutions, Morrisville *Also Called: Triangle Pipe Ftting Sltons In* **(G-11453)**
Triangle Sign Solutions 919 302-2482
   5101 Unicon Dr Ste B Wake Forest (27587) **(G-15604)**
Triangle Solutions Inc 919 481-1235
   1074 W Chatham St Cary (27511) **(G-1912)**
Triangle Stainless Inc 919 596-1335
   200 20th St Butner (27509) **(G-1550)**
Triangle Steel Systems LLC 919 615-0282
   133 Us 70 Hwy W Garner (27529) **(G-6318)**
Triangle Systems Inc (PA) 919 544-0090
   882 Pinehurst Dr Chapel Hill (27517) **(G-2084)**
Triangle Systems Inc 919 544-0090
   4364 S Alston Ave Durham (27713) **(G-5410)**
Triangle Trggr-Pint Thrapy Inc 919 845-1818
   184 Wind Chime Ct Ste 202 Raleigh (27615) **(G-13363)**
Triangle Tribune 704 376-0496
   115 Market St Ste 211 Durham (27701) **(G-5411)**
Triangle Web Printing, Durham *Also Called: Kolb Boyette & Assoc Inc* **(G-5182)**
Triangle Woodworks Inc 919 570-0337
   7608 Fullard Dr Wake Forest (27587) **(G-15605)**
Triaxis Games LLC 919 720-7804
   808 Chambord Way Holly Springs (27540) **(G-8723)**
Tribodyn Technologies Inc 859 750-6299
   109 Summerville Dr Mooresville (28115) **(G-11115)**
Tribofilm Research Inc 919 838-2844
   7250 Acc Blvd Raleigh (27617) **(G-13364)**
Tribune Papers Inc 828 606-5050
   Asheville (28813) **(G-806)**
Tribune, The, Elkin *Also Called: Mid South Management NC Inc* **(G-5625)**
Trick Karts Inc 704 883-0089
   935 Shelton Ave Statesville (28677) **(G-14917)**
Trick Tank Inc 980 406-3200
   2250 Toomey Ave Charlotte (28203) **(G-3726)**
Trickfit & Suepack Training 919 737-2231
   918 Gateway Commons Cir Wake Forest (27587) **(G-15606)**
Tricorn Usa Inc 828 369-6682
   66 Van Raalte St Franklin (28734) **(G-6146)**
Trident Fibers Inc 336 605-9002
   7109 Cessna Dr Greensboro (27409) **(G-7419)**
Trident Lure 910 520-4659
   2153 Harrison St Wilmington (28401) **(G-16433)**
Triggermesh Inc 919 228-8049
   109 Harmony Hill Ln Cary (27513) **(G-1913)**

ALPHABETIC SECTION — True World Marine LLC

Trim Inc 336 751-3591
351 Bethel Church Rd Mocksville (27028) *(G-10609)*

Trimaco, Morrisville Also Called: Cdv LLC *(G-11316)*

Trimaco Inc (PA) 919 674-3460
2300 Gateway Centre Blvd Ste 200 Morrisville (27560) *(G-11455)*

Trimantec 336 767-1379
4994 Indiana Ave Winston Salem (27106) *(G-16952)*

Trimech Solutions LLC 919 535-5662
206 High House Rd Ste 104 Cary (27513) *(G-1914)*

Trimech Solutions LLC 704 503-6644
201 Mccullough Dr Ste 300 Charlotte (28262) *(G-3727)*

Trimed LLC 919 615-2784
7429 Acc Blvd Ste 105 Raleigh (27617) *(G-13365)*

Trimfit Inc 336 476-6154
605 Pineywood Rd Thomasville (27360) *(G-15296)*

Trimm, Youngsville Also Called: Trimm International Inc *(G-17110)*

Trimm International Inc 847 362-3700
112 Franklin Park Dr Youngsville (27596) *(G-17110)*

Trimsters Inc 919 639-3126
150 West Rd Angier (27501) *(G-150)*

Trimworks Inc 704 753-4149
4705 Carriker Rd Monroe (28110) *(G-10823)*

Trin-I-Tee Designz LLC 910 520-2032
300 Preswick Dr Rocky Point (28457) *(G-13754)*

Trinicor Technology Incorporat 866 848-1232
1300 S Tryon St Ste F227 Charlotte (28203) *(G-3728)*

Trinity Manufacturing Inc 910 582-5650
11 Ev Hogan Dr Hamlet (28345) *(G-7633)*

Trinity Sock Group LLC 336 226-0237
240 Hawkins St Burlington (27217) *(G-1508)*

Trinity Woodworks LLC 980 938-4765
764 St Stephens Church Rd Gold Hill (28071) *(G-6586)*

Trinket Trunk 910 483-2292
599 Winding Creek Rd Fayetteville (28305) *(G-5932)*

Trinkets and Whimsey 919 368-6044
165 Haynes Blvd Hendersonville (28792) *(G-7909)*

Trinweld Welding Services LLC 704 721-5944
6895 Mission Rd Mount Pleasant (28124) *(G-11679)*

Trio Labs Inc 919 818-9646
133 Southcenter Ct Ste 900 Morrisville (27560) *(G-11456)*

Trion Iaq, Sanford Also Called: Air System Components Inc *(G-14084)*

Tripath Imaging Inc (HQ) 336 222-9707
780 Plantation Dr Burlington (27215) *(G-1509)*

Tripharm Services Inc 984 243-0800
627 Davis Dr Ste 100 Morrisville (27560) *(G-11457)*

Triple B Stone LLC 704 663-5860
319 Doolie Road Terrell (28682) *(G-15180)*

Triple C Brewing Co, Charlotte Also Called: Triple C Brewing Company LLC *(G-3729)*

Triple C Brewing Company LLC 704 372-3212
2900 Griffith St Charlotte (28203) *(G-3729)*

Triple C Companies LLC 704 966-1999
7911 Commerce Dr Denver (28037) *(G-4811)*

Triple Crown International LLC 704 846-4983
12205 Parks Farm Ln Charlotte (28277) *(G-3730)*

Triple D Publishing Inc 704 482-9673
1300 S Dekalb St Shelby (28152) *(G-14375)*

Triple E Equipment LLC 252 448-1002
3899 Nc Highway 58 N Trenton (28585) *(G-15336)*

Triple H Hauling LLC 984 220-4676
390 Shadneck Rd Elizabeth City (27909) *(G-5579)*

Triple M Consolidated Inc 910 484-1303
716 Three Wood Dr Fayetteville (28312) *(G-5933)*

Triple R MBL Cigr Lounge LLC 252 281-7738
163 S Winstead Ave Ste A Rocky Mount (27804) *(G-13738)*

Triplett & Coffey Inc 828 263-0561
204 Jefferson Rd Boone (28607) *(G-1243)*

Triplette Competition Arms, Elkin Also Called: Triplette Fencing Supply Inc *(G-5630)*

Triplette Fencing Supply Inc 336 835-1205
331 Standard St Elkin (28621) *(G-5630)*

Tristate Welding & Fabrication 336 899-5206
704 Ferndale Blvd High Point (27262) *(G-8577)*

Tritech Ventures Inc 919 846-3415
9801 Saint Stephan Ct Raleigh (27615) *(G-13366)*

Triton Glass LLC 704 982-4333
232 S 1st St Albemarle (28001) *(G-111)*

Triton Industries LLC 336 816-3794
830 Fowler Rd Mount Airy (27030) *(G-11591)*

Triton Marine Services Inc 252 728-9958
1050 Sensation Weigh Beaufort (28516) *(G-969)*

Triton Water, Burlington Also Called: Alamance Foods Inc *(G-1362)*

Triumph Acttion Systms-Clmmons, Clemmons Also Called: Triumph Actuation Systems LLC *(G-4064)*

Triumph Actuation Systems LLC (HQ) 336 766-9036
4520 Hampton Rd Clemmons (27012) *(G-4064)*

Triumph Tool Nc Inc 828 676-3677
44 Buck Shoals Rd Ste B3 Arden (28704) *(G-386)*

Triune Business Furniture Inc 336 884-8341
1101 Roberts Ln High Point (27260) *(G-8578)*

Trivantage 800 438-1061
1803 Salisbury Rd Statesville (28677) *(G-14918)*

Trivantage LLC (HQ) 800 786-1876
1831 N Park Ave Burlington (27217) *(G-1510)*

Trivium Packaging USA Inc 336 785-8500
4000 Old Milwaukee Ln Winston Salem (27107) *(G-16953)*

TRM, Raleigh Also Called: Telecmmnctons Resource MGT Inc *(G-13336)*

Trojan Defense, Fletcher Also Called: Moto Group LLC *(G-6028)*

Trophy House Inc (PA) 910 323-1791
3006 Bragg Blvd Fayetteville (28303) *(G-5934)*

Trophy On Maywood LLC 919 803-1333
656 Maywood Ave Raleigh (27603) *(G-13367)*

Tropical Fruit Juice Bar 910 426-5842
419 Cross Creek Mall Fayetteville (28303) *(G-5935)*

Tropical Nut & Fruit Co (PA) 800 438-4470
1100 Continental Blvd Charlotte (28273) *(G-3731)*

Trotters Sewing Company Inc 336 629-4550
321 Industrial Park Ave Asheboro (27205) *(G-501)*

Troutman Careconnect Corp 704 838-9389
191 Timber Lake Dr Troutman (28166) *(G-15394)*

Troutman Chair Company LLC 704 872-7625
134 Rocker Ln Troutman (28166) *(G-15395)*

Troxler Electronic Labs Inc (PA) 919 549-8661
3008 Cornwallis Rd Durham (27709) *(G-5412)*

Troy Ready - Mix Inc 910 572-1011
1739 Nc Highway 24 27 109 W Troy (27371) *(G-15418)*

Trs, Thomasville Also Called: Theodore Alexander Uphl LLC *(G-15288)*

Trs-Sesco LLC 336 996-2220
721 Park Centre Dr Ste A Kernersville (27284) *(G-9248)*

Trtl Inc 844 811-5816
120 Penmarc Dr Ste 118 Raleigh (27603) *(G-13368)*

Tru Colors Brewing, Wilmington Also Called: Spark716 LLC *(G-16414)*

Tru Luck Woodworks 910 642-2753
2122 Pine Level Church Rd Nakina (28455) *(G-11732)*

Tru-Cast Inc 336 294-2370
1208 Rail St Greensboro (27407) *(G-7420)*

Tru-Contour Inc 704 455-8700
165 Brumley Ave Ne Concord (28025) *(G-4379)*

Tru-Contour Precast Division, Concord Also Called: Tru-Contour Inc *(G-4379)*

Truck Parts Inc 704 332-7909
707 Kennedy St Charlotte (28206) *(G-3732)*

Truck Shop, Graham Also Called: Chandler Concrete Inc *(G-6683)*

Trucking, Fayetteville Also Called: Grahams Transportation LLC *(G-5831)*

True Blue Wdcrfting Lser Etchi 609 784-2431
408 Fontana Dr Clayton (27527) *(G-4019)*

True Cabinet LLC 828 855-9200
2401 Us Highway 70 Sw Hickory (28602) *(G-8185)*

True Machine LLC 919 270-2552
6575 Huntsboro Rd Oxford (27565) *(G-12160)*

True Portion Inc 336 362-6326
5220 High Point Rd High Point (27265) *(G-8579)*

True Southern Tees 919 604-6068
166 Cooley Rd Youngsville (27596) *(G-17111)*

True World Marine LLC 252 728-2541
1145 Sensation Weigh Beaufort (28516) *(G-970)*

Truefab LLC... 919 620-8158
  3401 Industrial Dr Durham (27704) *(G-5413)*

Trueflies LLC... 828 337-9716
  815 Quill Gordon Ct Biltmore Lake (28715) *(G-1102)*

Truelook Inc... 833 878-3566
  575 E 4th St Winston Salem (27101) *(G-16954)*

Truelove Fabrications Inc.. 910 343-0195
  1319 S 4th St Wilmington (28401) *(G-16434)*

Trugreen Chemlawn, Candler *Also Called: Charles Hill Enterprises (G-1573)*

Trunk Pump... 910 463-1282
  6620 Gordon Rd Ste J Wilmington (28411) *(G-16435)*

Trunorth Wrrnty Plans N Amer L.. 800 903-7489
  16740 Birkdale Commons Pkwy Huntersville (28078) *(G-8903)*

Trupoint Backyards, Hamptonville *Also Called: Vinyl Structures LLC (G-7680)*

Truss Buildings LLC... 919 377-0217
  1512 Wackena Rd Cary (27519) *(G-1915)*

Truss Shop Inc.. 336 372-6260
  84 Buffalo Rd Sparta (28675) *(G-14600)*

Trusses R US Inc.. 704 361-7004
  200 S High St Waxhaw (28173) *(G-15784)*

Trussway, Whitsett *Also Called: Trussway Manufacturing Inc (G-16004)*

Trussway Manufacturing Inc.. 336 883-6966
  940 Golf House Rd W Ste 201 Whitsett (27377) *(G-16004)*

Truswood Inc (PA)... 800 473-8787
  8816 Running Oak Dr Raleigh (27617) *(G-13369)*

Truventure Logistics, Charlotte *Also Called: Firm Ascend LLC (G-2763)*

Tryhard Infinity LLC... 252 269-0985
  3019 Brunswick Ave New Bern (28562) *(G-11852)*

Tryon Equine Compost LLC.. 914 774-7486
  3661 Nc 108 Hwy E Columbus (28722) *(G-4181)*

Tryon Finishing Corporation... 828 859-5891
  250 Screvens Rd Tryon (28782) *(G-15429)*

Tryon Newsmedia LLC.. 828 859-9151
  16 N Trade St Tryon (28782) *(G-15430)*

Tryton Medical Inc.. 919 226-1490
  1 Floretta Pl Rm 208 Raleigh (27676) *(G-13370)*

TS Krupa LLC... 336 782-1515
  194 Briarcreek Dr Winston Salem (27107) *(G-16955)*

TS Woodworks & RAD Design Inc.. 704 238-1015
  3213 Westwood Industrial Dr Monroe (28110) *(G-10824)*

TSA Griddle System, Lexington *Also Called: CPM Acquisition Corp (G-9698)*

Tsai Winddown Inc... 704 873-3106
  607 Meacham Rd Statesville (28677) *(G-14919)*

Tseng Information Systems Inc.. 919 682-9197
  813 Watts St Durham (27701) *(G-5414)*

Tserings LLC.. 704 283-8811
  1414 Ellen St Monroe (28112) *(G-10825)*

Tsg Finishing LLC.. 828 328-5522
  2246 Us Hwy 70 Hickory (28602) *(G-8186)*

Tsg Finishing LLC.. 828 328-5541
  515 23rd St Sw Hickory (28602) *(G-8187)*

Tsg Finishing LLC.. 828 328-5522
  515 23rd St Sw Hickory (28602) *(G-8188)*

Tsg Finishing LLC.. 828 328-5535
  1006 19th St Ne Hickory (28601) *(G-8189)*

Tsg2 Inc... 704 347-4484
  1235 East Blvd Ste E Charlotte (28203) *(G-3733)*

Tshirts Made By U.. 980 309-9749
  7925 N Tryon St Ste 201 Charlotte (28262) *(G-3734)*

Tshirtskings, Charlotte *Also Called: Napoleon James (G-3230)*

Tsi, Denver *Also Called: Textile Sales Intl Inc (G-4806)*

Tsquared Cabinets.. 336 655-0208
  118 Griffith Plaza Dr Winston Salem (27103) *(G-16956)*

TTI Floor Care North Amer Inc.. 440 996-2000
  8405 Ibm Dr Charlotte (28262) *(G-3735)*

TTI Floor Care North Amer Inc (DH)....................................... 440 996-2000
  8405 Ibm Dr Charlotte (28262) *(G-3736)*

TTI Wireless, Youngsville *Also Called: Telecommunications Tech Inc (G-17106)*

Tube Enterprises Incorporated.. 941 629-9267
  1028 Railroad Ave Shelby (28152) *(G-14376)*

Tube Specialties Co Inc.. 704 818-8933
  1401 Industrial Dr Statesville (28625) *(G-14920)*

Tube-Tech Solar, Raleigh *Also Called: Patty Knio (G-13102)*

Tubs-Usa LLC... 336 884-5737
  322 Fraley Rd High Point (27263) *(G-8580)*

Tubular Resources, Statesville *Also Called: Trick Karts Inc (G-14917)*

Tubular Textile LLC... 336 731-2860
  4157 Old Highway 52 Welcome (27374) *(G-15877)*

Tubular Textile Machinery.. 336 956-6444
  85 Hargrave Rd Lexington (27293) *(G-9797)*

Tucker Logging.. 336 857-2674
  6957 Gravel Hill Rd Denton (27239) *(G-4753)*

Tucker Production Incorporated.. 828 322-1036
  264 1st Ave Nw Hickory (28601) *(G-8190)*

Tucker Welding, Bear Creek *Also Called: Gary Tucker (G-938)*

Tuckers Farm Inc... 704 375-8199
  201 W 31st St Charlotte (28206) *(G-3737)*

Tudg Multimedia Firm... 704 916-9819
  12523 Surreykirt Ln Huntersville (28078) *(G-8904)*

Tuff Shed Inc.. 919 413-2494
  409 Airport Blvd Morrisville (27560) *(G-11458)*

Tuff Temp Corp... 252 398-3400
  310 W Broad St Murfreesboro (27855) *(G-11703)*

Tumi Store - Chrltte Dglas Int... 704 359-8771
  5501 Josh Birmingham Pkwy Unit 21a Charlotte (28208) *(G-3738)*

Tumi Store - Streets South Pt... 919 224-1028
  6910 Fayetteville Rd Ste 168 Durham (27713) *(G-5415)*

Tunnel Creek Venues LLC.. 336 322-3600
  1576 Berryhill Rd Roxboro (27574) *(G-13828)*

Turbocoating Corp... 828 328-8726
  1928 Main Ave Se Hickory (28602) *(G-8191)*

Turbomed LLC.. 973 527-5299
  1830 Owen Dr Ste 9 Fayetteville (28304) *(G-5936)*

Turkington, Clayton *Also Called: Baker Thermal Solutions LLC (G-3957)*

Turmar, Charlotte *Also Called: Turmar Marble Inc (G-3739)*

Turmar Marble Inc... 704 391-1800
  914 Richland Dr Charlotte (28211) *(G-3739)*

Turn Bull Lumber Company.. 910 862-4447
  474 Sweet Home Church Rd Elizabethtown (28337) *(G-5607)*

Turn Key Tire Service Inc... 919 836-8473
  1340 Bobbitt Dr Garner (27529) *(G-6319)*

Turnage Blind Co... 919 736-1809
  415 Sandhill Dr Goldsboro (27530) *(G-6666)*

Turnamics Inc... 828 254-1059
  25 Old County Home Rd Asheville (28806) *(G-807)*

Turnberry Press... 860 670-4892
  150 Crest Rd Southern Pines (28387) *(G-14559)*

Turner & Reeves Fence Co LLC... 910 671-8851
  2016 Pope Ct Clayton (27520) *(G-4020)*

Turner Boys Carrier Svc LLC... 919 946-7553
  1012 Southern Living Dr Raleigh (27610) *(G-13371)*

Turner Equipment Company Inc... 919 734-8328
  1502 Us Highway 117 S Goldsboro (27530) *(G-6667)*

Turner Greenhouses, Goldsboro *Also Called: Turner Equipment Company Inc (G-6667)*

Turner Tire Service, Garner *Also Called: Turn Key Tire Service Inc (G-6319)*

Turning Pges Pctrial Heirlooms.. 704 634-2911
  1113 Northwood Dr Charlotte (28216) *(G-3740)*

Turnkey Technologies Inc... 704 245-6437
  402 Bringle Ferry Rd Salisbury (28144) *(G-14056)*

Turnsmith LLC.. 919 667-9804
  710 Market St Chapel Hill (27516) *(G-2085)*

Turtle Dove Publications.. 828 337-4057
  1106 Montreat Rd Black Mountain (28711) *(G-1140)*

Tuscarora Yarns Inc.. 704 436-6527
  8760 Franklin St E Mount Pleasant (28124) *(G-11680)*

Tutco Inc.. 828 654-1665
  30 Legend Dr Arden (28704) *(G-387)*

Tutcu-Farnam Custom Products.. 828 684-3766
  30 Legend Dr Arden (28704) *(G-388)*

Tvl International LLC.. 704 814-0930
  165 S Trade St Matthews (28105) *(G-10297)*

Tvs, Knightdale *Also Called: Trade Venture Stones LLC (G-9431)*

Twe Nonwovens Us Inc (HQ)... 336 431-7187
  2215 Shore St High Point (27263) *(G-8581)*

ALPHABETIC SECTION

Twg Inc 336 998-9731
652 Nc Highway 801 S Advance (27006) *(G-52)*

Twigs Screen Printing 910 770-1605
5474 Sidney Cherry Grove Rd Tabor City (28463) *(G-15088)*

Twin Attic Publishing Hse Inc 919 426-0322
1415 Cedar Branch Ct Wake Forest (27587) *(G-15607)*

Twin Carports LLC 336 790-8284
1014 Melrose Ct East Bend (27018) *(G-5470)*

Twin Carports LLC (PA) 866 486-3924
202 Hamlin Dr Pilot Mountain (27041) *(G-12203)*

Twin City Custom Cabinets 336 773-7200
1310 N Liberty St Winston Salem (27105) *(G-16957)*

Twin City Sports LLC 336 765-5070
4836 Country Club Rd Winston Salem (27104) *(G-16958)*

Twin Cy Kwnis Fndtion Wnstn-SL 336 784-1649
1 W 4th St Winston Salem (27101) *(G-16959)*

Twin Oaks Gallery & Frmng LLC 704 466-3889
2017 Fairview Rd Shelby (28150) *(G-14377)*

Twin Oaks Service South Inc 704 914-7142
1320 Stony Point Rd Shelby (28150) *(G-14378)*

Twin Troller Boats Inc 919 207-2622
501 S Wall St Ste A Benson (27504) *(G-1044)*

Twinvision North America Inc 919 361-2155
4018 Patriot Dr Ste 100 Durham (27703) *(G-5416)*

Twisted Fire Industires LLC 704 652-8559
9150 Bethel Church Rd Concord (28025) *(G-4380)*

Twisted Infusionz LLC 252 432-4215
14460 Falls Of Neuse Rd Ste 149339 Raleigh (27614) *(G-13372)*

Twisted Metal Fabrication 704 915-1023
3309 Linwood Rd Gastonia (28052) *(G-6533)*

Twisted Paper Products Inc 336 393-0273
7100 Cessna Dr Greensboro (27409) *(G-7421)*

Two Brothers NC LLC 336 516-5181
1601 Anthony Rd Burlington (27215) *(G-1511)*

Two Brothers Wldg Miscellane 704 488-9845
2660 Barringer Dr Charlotte (28208) *(G-3741)*

Two Engravers LLC 919 526-0102
5100 Western Blvd Raleigh (27606) *(G-13373)*

Two Fifty Cleaners 910 397-0071
5601 Carolina Beach Rd Ste C Wilmington (28412) *(G-16436)*

Two Green Thumbs and More Inc 704 614-8703
1109 7th St Ne Hickory (28601) *(G-8192)*

Two Little Birds Screen Ptg 336 988-7488
4810 Carolwood Dr Greensboro (27407) *(G-7422)*

Two of A Kind Publishing LLC 704 497-2879
8239 Romana Red Ln Charlotte (28213) *(G-3742)*

Two Percent LLC 301 401-2750
204 N Laurel St Lincolnton (28092) *(G-9930)*

Two Rivers Plant, Mayodan Also Called: Milliken & Company *(G-10366)*

Two Trees Distilling Co LLC 803 767-1322
17 Continuum Dr Fletcher (28732) *(G-6046)*

Two24 Digital LLC 910 475-7555
1325 Middle Sound Loop Rd Wilmington (28411) *(G-16437)*

Two24 Digital Marketing, Wilmington Also Called: Two24 Digital LLC *(G-16437)*

Twork Technology Inc 704 218-9675
3536 N Davidson St Charlotte (28205) *(G-3743)*

Tws Specialty Woodworking 315 492-1697
609 Killian Rd Stanley (28164) *(G-14709)*

Twyford Printing Company Inc 910 892-3271
200 E Canary St Dunn (28334) *(G-4888)*

Ty Brown 828 264-6865
126 Iris Ln Apt 4 Boone (28607) *(G-1244)*

Tyco Electronics, Greensboro Also Called: Te Connectivity Corporation *(G-7393)*

Tyco Electronics Corporation 717 986-5311
8300 Triad Dr Greensboro (27409) *(G-7423)*

Tyco Electronics Corporation 336 665-4562
719 Pegg Rd Greensboro (27409) *(G-7424)*

Tyler Walston 919 269-9300
3904 Airport Dr Nw Ste A Wilson (27896) *(G-16552)*

Tyndall Machine Technologies, Pittsboro Also Called: Tyndall Machine Tool Inc *(G-12352)*

Tyndall Machine Tool Inc 919 542-4014
154 Dogwood Ln Pittsboro (27312) *(G-12352)*

Tyrata Inc 919 210-8992
101 W Chapel Hill St Ste 200 Durham (27701) *(G-5417)*

Tyratech Inc 919 415-4275
5151 Mccrimmon Pkwy Ste 275 Morrisville (27560) *(G-11459)*

Tyrrell Ready Mix Inc 252 796-0265
1280 Hwy 94 North Columbia (27925) *(G-4169)*

Tysinger Hosiery Mill Inc 336 472-2148
1294 Old Nc Highway 109 Lexington (27292) *(G-9798)*

Tysinger Logging Inc 910 220-5053
499 Brewer St Star (27356) *(G-14724)*

Tyson, Eastover Also Called: Tyson Foods Inc *(G-5483)*
Tyson, Monroe Also Called: Tyson Foods Inc *(G-10826)*
Tyson, Wilkesboro Also Called: Tyson Foods Inc *(G-16046)*
Tyson, Wilkesboro Also Called: Tyson Foods Inc *(G-16047)*
Tyson, Wilkesboro Also Called: Tyson Foods Inc *(G-16048)*

Tyson Foods Inc 910 483-3282
3281 Baywood Rd Eastover (28312) *(G-5483)*

Tyson Foods Inc 704 283-7571
2023 Hasty St Monroe (28112) *(G-10826)*

Tyson Foods Inc 336 838-0083
1600 River St Wilkesboro (28697) *(G-16046)*

Tyson Foods Inc 336 838-2171
115 Factory St Wilkesboro (28697) *(G-16047)*

Tyson Foods Inc 336 838-2171
901 Wilkes St Wilkesboro (28697) *(G-16048)*

Tyson Foods Inc 336 838-2171
706 Factory St Wilkesboro (28697) *(G-16049)*

Tyson Mexican Original Inc 919 777-9428
800 E Main St Sanford (27332) *(G-14201)*

Tyton NC Biofuels LLC 910 878-7820
800 Pate Rd Raeford (28376) *(G-12443)*

U C S, Lincolnton Also Called: Ucs Inc *(G-9931)*
U C S, Lincolnton Also Called: United Canvas & Sling Inc *(G-9933)*
U F P, New London Also Called: Ufp New London LLC *(G-11880)*
U F P, Salisbury Also Called: Ufp Salisbury LLC *(G-14058)*
U K I Supreme, Conover Also Called: Supreme Elastic Corporation *(G-4502)*
U S A T, Chapel Hill Also Called: Usat LLC *(G-2091)*

U S Alloy Co 888 522-8296
825 Groves St Lowell (28098) *(G-10012)*

U S Bottlers McHy Co Inc 704 588-4750
11911 Steele Creek Rd Charlotte (28273) *(G-3744)*

U S Cabinets Express LLC 336 875-4011
2505 N Main St High Point (27262) *(G-8582)*

U S Propeller Service Inc 704 528-9515
844 S Main St Troutman (28166) *(G-15396)*

U Tech Cnc Se LLC 980 500-8263
10234 Rougemont Ln Charlotte (28277) *(G-3745)*

U V Reptile Labs Inc 252 241-4584
107 Craig Dr Hubert (28539) *(G-8753)*

U-Hear of Hickory 704 434-2062
1227 Mount Pleasant Church Rd Mooresboro (28114) *(G-10843)*

U-Teck, Fayetteville Also Called: R E Mason Enterprises Inc *(G-5904)*

Uai Technology Inc 919 541-9339
68 Tw Alexander Dr Durham (27709) *(G-5418)*

Ubora Dens LLC 704 425-3560
1114 Hanford Pl Nw Concord (28027) *(G-4381)*

Uchiyama Mfg Amer LLC 919 731-2364
494 Arrington Bridge Rd Goldsboro (27530) *(G-6668)*

Ucs Inc 704 732-9922
511 Hoffman Rd Lincolnton (28092) *(G-9931)*

Udio Commercial, Hubert Also Called: Udio Commercial LLC *(G-8754)*

Udio Commercial LLC 609 977-2700
101 Gillcrest Ln Hubert (28539) *(G-8754)*

Udm Systems LLC 919 789-0777
6621 Fleetwood Dr Raleigh (27612) *(G-13374)*

Udm Systems LLC (PA) 919 789-0777
8311 Brier Creek Pkwy Ste 105-159 Raleigh (27617) *(G-13375)*

Udp, Trent Woods Also Called: United Decorative Plas NC Inc *(G-15331)*

Ufp Biscoe LLC 910 294-8179
402 Capel St Biscoe (27209) *(G-1117)*

Ufp Mid-Atlantic — ALPHABETIC SECTION

Ufp Mid-Atlantic, Clinton Also Called: Ufp Site Built LLC *(G-4117)*
Ufp Mid-Atlantic, Locust Also Called: Ufp Site Built LLC *(G-9976)*
Ufp New London LLC.. 704 463-1400
  174 Random Dr New London (28127) *(G-11880)*
Ufp Rockwell, Rockwell Also Called: Ufp Rockwell LLC *(G-13662)*
Ufp Rockwell LLC.. 704 279-0744
  175 Old Mail Rd Rockwell (28138) *(G-13662)*
Ufp Salisbury LLC... 704 855-1600
  520 Grace Church Rd Salisbury (28147) *(G-14057)*
Ufp Salisbury LLC (DH).. 704 855-1600
  358 Woodmill Rd Salisbury (28147) *(G-14058)*
UFP SALISBURY, LLC, Salisbury Also Called: Ufp Salisbury LLC *(G-14057)*
Ufp Site Built LLC... 910 590-3220
  254 Superior Dr Clinton (28328) *(G-4117)*
Ufp Site Built LLC... 704 781-2520
  147 Locust Level Dr Locust (28097) *(G-9976)*
UGLy Essentials LLC... 910 319-9945
  8601 Six Forks Rd Ste 400 Raleigh (27615) *(G-13376)*
Ukg Kronos Systems LLC... 800 225-1561
  8801 J M Keynes Dr Ste 240 Charlotte (28262) *(G-3746)*
Ukg Kronos Systems LLC... 800 225-1561
  101 Centreport Dr Ste 340 Greensboro (27409) *(G-7425)*
Ullman Group LLC... 704 246-7333
  10925 Westlake Dr Charlotte (28273) *(G-3747)*
Ullmanique Inc.. 336 885-5111
  323 Old Thomasville Rd High Point (27260) *(G-8583)*
Ultimate Cleaning Servces Dean................................ 865 382-2433
  225 Chinqunpin Trl Old Fort (28762) *(G-12106)*
Ultimate Floor Cleaning.. 704 912-8978
  9625 Commons East Dr Apt L Charlotte (28277) *(G-3748)*
Ultimate Products Inc (PA)... 919 836-1627
  3201 Wellington Ct Ste 115 Raleigh (27615) *(G-13377)*
Ultimate Qm Inc... 704 500-9035
  7149 Brandywine Ln Stanley (28164) *(G-14710)*
Ultimate Textile Inc.. 828 286-8880
  1437 Us 221 Hwy S Rutherfordton (28139) *(G-13898)*
Ultimix Records.. 336 288-7566
  3404 W Wendover Ave Ste E Greensboro (27407) *(G-7426)*
Ultra, Shelby Also Called: Ultra Machine & Fabrication Inc *(G-14379)*
Ultra Coatings Incorporated....................................... 336 883-8853
  3509 Jamac Rd High Point (27260) *(G-8584)*
Ultra Craft Companies, Liberty Also Called: Norcraft Companies LP *(G-9825)*
Ultra Elec Ocean Systems Inc.................................... 781 848-3400
  204 Capcom Ave Wake Forest (27587) *(G-15608)*
Ultra Flex, High Point Also Called: Hickory Springs Mfg Co *(G-8386)*
Ultra Machine & Fabrication Inc................................. 704 482-1399
  2501 W Dixon Blvd Shelby (28152) *(G-14379)*
Ultra Precision Machining, New Bern Also Called: Bannister Inc *(G-11776)*
Ultra Violet Systems Division, Charlotte Also Called: Xylem Lnc *(G-3839)*
Ultra-Mek Inc... 336 859-4552
  487 Bombay Rd Denton (27239) *(G-4754)*
Ultraloop Technologies Inc... 919 636-2842
  1289 Fordham Blvd Chapel Hill (27514) *(G-2086)*
Ultrascope, Charlotte Also Called: Parker Medical Associates LLC *(G-3314)*
Ultratech Industries Inc.. 919 779-2004
  200 Hamlin Rd Benson (27504) *(G-1045)*
Umethod Health Inc... 984 232-6699
  9660 Falls Of Neuse Rd Ste 138-146 Raleigh (27615) *(G-13378)*
Umi Company Inc... 704 479-6210
  352 N Generals Blvd Lincolnton (28092) *(G-9932)*
Umicore USA Inc (HQ).. 919 874-7171
  3600 Glenwood Ave Ste 250 Raleigh (27612) *(G-13379)*
Unadilla Antenna Mfg Co, Moravian Falls Also Called: Ni4l Antennas and Elec LLC *(G-11146)*
UNC Campus Health Services..................................... 919 966-2281
  320 Emergency Room Dr Chapel Hill (27599) *(G-2087)*
Uncle Browns Scented Candles.................................. 704 993-0409
  2311 Honeycutt Simpson Rd Monroe (28110) *(G-10827)*
Under Covers Publishing.. 704 965-8744
  703 Glendale Dr W Wilson (27893) *(G-16553)*
Under Gods Authority... 910 891-1789
  108 High Standard Ln Angier (27501) *(G-151)*

Under One Crown Publishing LLC............................... 919 812-4930
  4826 Rembert Dr Raleigh (27612) *(G-13380)*
Under Pressure Wilmington LLC................................ 910 409-0194
  119e Harley Rd Wilmington (28405) *(G-16438)*
Underbrinks LLC.. 866 495-4465
  705 Hedrick St Salisbury (28144) *(G-14059)*
Underground Baking Co LLC...................................... 828 674-7494
  304 Yon Hill Rd Hendersonville (28792) *(G-7910)*
Underground Printing... 919 525-2029
  133 E Franklin St Chapel Hill (27514) *(G-2088)*
Underground Renovations LLC................................... 202 316-9286
  2834 Friar Tuck Rd Raleigh (27610) *(G-13381)*
Unecol Adhesives N Amer LLC................................... 888 963-8879
  1408 Christian Ave Durham (27705) *(G-5419)*
Uniboard USA LLC... 919 542-2128
  985 Corinth Rd Moncure (27559) *(G-10628)*
Unichem IV Ltd (PA).. 336 578-5476
  916 W Main St Haw River (27258) *(G-7758)*
Unicon Concrete, Statesville Also Called: Argos USA LLC *(G-14752)*
Unicon Concrete, Wake Forest Also Called: Argos USA LLC *(G-15528)*
Unifi, Greensboro Also Called: Unifi Inc *(G-7427)*
Unifi Inc (PA)... 336 294-4410
  7201 W Friendly Ave Greensboro (27410) *(G-7427)*
Unifi Inc... 336 427-1890
  805 Island Dr Madison (27025) *(G-10090)*
Unifi Inc... 336 348-6539
  2920 Vance Street Ext Reidsville (27320) *(G-13544)*
Unifi Inc... 919 774-7401
  1921 Boone Trail Rd Sanford (27330) *(G-14202)*
Unifi Inc... 336 679-3830
  1032 Unifi Industrial Rd Yadkinville (27055) *(G-17058)*
Unifi Kinston LLC... 252 522-6518
  4693 Hwy 11 Kinston (28504) *(G-9389)*
Unifi Manufacturing Inc (HQ)..................................... 336 294-4410
  7201 W Friendly Ave Greensboro (27410) *(G-7428)*
Unifi Manufacturing Inc... 336 427-1515
  601 E Main St Yadkinville (27055) *(G-17059)*
Unifi Manufacturing Inc... 336 679-8891
  1032 Unifi Industrial Rd Yadkinville (27055) *(G-17060)*
Unifi Plant 2, Reidsville Also Called: Unifi Inc *(G-13544)*
Unifi Plant 3, Madison Also Called: Unifi Inc *(G-10090)*
Unified Logistics NC, Moyock Also Called: Andrea L Grizzle *(G-11691)*
Unified Pallets Inc.. 910 891-2571
  2 Dinan Rd Dunn (28334) *(G-4889)*
Unified Scrning Crshing - NC I (PA)............................ 336 824-2151
  136 Crestwick Rd Ramseur (27316) *(G-13451)*
Unified2 Globl Packg Group LLC................................. 774 696-3643
  3829 S Miami Blvd Ste 300 Durham (27703) *(G-5420)*
Uniform Express, Mocksville Also Called: McDaniel Delmar *(G-10586)*
Uniforms Galore... 252 975-5878
  628 River Rd Washington (27889) *(G-15735)*
Unifour Finishers Inc (PA).. 828 322-9435
  120 21st St Nw Hickory (28601) *(G-8193)*
Unifour Finishers Inc... 828 322-9435
  54 29th St Nw Hickory (28601) *(G-8194)*
Unifour Tech Inc.. 828 256-4962
  2845 Robinson Rd Newton (28658) *(G-11980)*
Unigel Inc... 828 228-2095
  1027 19th St Sw Hickory (28602) *(G-8195)*
Unilever.. 910 988-1054
  4152 Turnpike Rd Raeford (28376) *(G-12444)*
Unilever, Raeford Also Called: Conopco Inc *(G-12416)*
Unilin Flooring Nc LLC (HQ)....................................... 336 313-4000
  550 Cloniger Dr Thomasville (27360) *(G-15297)*
Unilin North America LLC.. 919 773-6000
  1001 Pergo Pkwy Garner (27529) *(G-6320)*
Unilin North America LLC.. 919 773-5900
  2000 Pergo Pkwy Garner (27529) *(G-6321)*
Union Concrete, Hillsborough Also Called: Argos USA LLC *(G-8634)*
Union Corrugating Company (DH)............................. 910 483-0479
  701 S King St Fayetteville (28301) *(G-5937)*

Union Grove Saw & Knife Inc.. 704 539-4442
157 Sawtooth Lane Union Grove (28689) *(G-15438)*

Union Masonry Inc.. 919 217-7806
4708 Forestville Rd Raleigh (27616) *(G-13382)*

Union Plastics Company.. 704 624-2112
132 E Union St Marshville (28103) *(G-10226)*

Union Sentinal, Hayesville *Also Called: Sentinel Newspapers (G-7771)*

Unique 3d Printing LLC... 704 843-7367
4423 Bigham Rd Waxhaw (28173) *(G-15785)*

Unique Background Solutions, Mount Airy *Also Called: Carolina Connections Inc (G-11488)*

Unique Body Blends Inc.. 910 302-5484
1108 Strathdon Ave Fayetteville (28304) *(G-5938)*

Unique Carving Inc... 336 472-6215
2285 Todd Dr Trinity (27370) *(G-15362)*

Unique Collating & Bindery Svc.. 336 664-0960
237 Burgess Rd Ste A Greensboro (27409) *(G-7429)*

Unique Concepts.. 919 366-2001
310 Shipwash Dr Ste 101 Garner (27529) *(G-6322)*

Unique Concepts, Wendell *Also Called: Yukon Inc (G-15926)*

Unique Home Theater Inc... 704 787-3239
135 Scalybark Trl Concord (28027) *(G-4382)*

Unique Impressions... 704 873-3241
1906 E Broad St Statesville (28625) *(G-14921)*

Unique Office Solutions Inc.. 336 854-0900
408 Gallimore Dairy Rd Ste E Greensboro (27409) *(G-7430)*

Unique Printer Solutions LLC.. 704 544-4822
9636 Cotton Stand Rd Charlotte (28277) *(G-3749)*

Unique Stone, Rockingham *Also Called: Henson Family Investments LLC (G-13628)*

Unique Stone Incorporated... 910 817-9450
222 Lakeshore Dr Rockingham (28379) *(G-13645)*

Unique Tool and Mfg Co.. 336 498-2614
2054 Bruce Pugh Rd Franklinville (27248) *(G-6171)*

Unique-Skill Precision Inc.. 910 393-0090
90 Fairmont St Ocean Isle Beach (28469) *(G-12095)*

Uniquetex LLC.. 704 457-3003
700 S Battleground Ave Grover (28073) *(G-7609)*

Unison Engine Components Inc... 828 274-4540
401 Sweeten Creek Industrial Park Asheville (28803) *(G-808)*

Unitape (usa) Inc.. 828 464-5695
620 Reese Dr Sw Conover (28613) *(G-4507)*

United Air Filter Company Corp.. 704 334-5311
1000 W Palmer St Charlotte (28208) *(G-3750)*

United Brass Works, Randleman *Also Called: United Brass Works Inc (G-13494)*

United Brass Works Inc (HQ)... 336 498-2661
714 S Main St Randleman (27317) *(G-13494)*

United Canvas & Sling Inc... 704 732-9922
511 Hoffman Rd Lincolnton (28092) *(G-9933)*

United Chemi-Con Inc... 336 384-6903
185 Mcneil Rd Lansing (28643) *(G-9456)*

United Decorative Plas NC Inc.. 252 637-1803
812 Llewellyn Dr Trent Woods (28562) *(G-15331)*

United Finishers Intl Inc.. 336 883-3901
1950 W Green Dr High Point (27260) *(G-8585)*

United Glove Inc.. 828 464-2510
2017 N Stewart Ave Newton (28658) *(G-11981)*

United Group Graphics Inc... 919 596-3932
2608 Carver St Durham (27705) *(G-5421)*

United House Publishing.. 248 605-3787
4671 Garrison Inn Ct Nw Concord (28027) *(G-4383)*

United Lumber Inc... 919 575-6491
10 26th St Butner (27509) *(G-1551)*

United Machine & Metal Fab Inc... 828 464-5167
1220 Fedex Dr Sw Conover (28613) *(G-4508)*

United Machine Works Inc.. 252 752-7434
1716 Nc Highway 903 N Greenville (27834) *(G-7592)*

United Metal Finishing, Greensboro *Also Called: United Mtal Fnshg Inc Grnsboro (G-7431)*

United Mobile Imaging Inc.. 800 983-9840
2554 Lewisville Clemmons Rd Ste 201 Clemmons (27012) *(G-4065)*

United Mtal Fnshg Inc Grnsboro... 336 272-8107
133 Blue Bell Rd Greensboro (27406) *(G-7431)*

United Packaging, Charlotte *Also Called: Apex Packaging Corporation LLC (G-2200)*

United Pallets & Truckin.. 704 493-1636
3435 Northerly Rd Charlotte (28206) *(G-3751)*

United Plastics Corporation.. 336 786-2127
511 Hay St Mount Airy (27030) *(G-11592)*

United Printing Company, Charlotte *Also Called: AEL Services LLC (G-2140)*

United Protective Tech LLC... 704 888-2470
142 Cara Ct Locust (28097) *(G-9977)*

United Services Group LLC (PA)... 980 237-1335
2505 Hutchison Mcdonald Rd Charlotte (28269) *(G-3752)*

United Southern Industries Inc (DH).................................... 866 273-1810
486 Vance St Forest City (28043) *(G-6085)*

United States Dept of Navy... 252 466-4415
Cunningham Bldg 159 Cherry Point (28533) *(G-3858)*

United States Dept of Navy... 252 466-4514
Av 8b Psc Box 8019 Cherry Point (28533) *(G-3859)*

United States Dept of Navy... 252 464-7228
Bldg 137 A St Cherry Point (28533) *(G-3860)*

United States Gypsum Company.. 828 765-9481
510 Altapass Hwy Spruce Pine (28777) *(G-14660)*

United Supply Company, Charlotte *Also Called: Selective Enterprises Inc (G-3525)*

United Technical Services LLC.. 980 237-1335
2505 Hutchison Mcdonald Rd Charlotte (28269) *(G-3753)*

United Therapeutics, Durham *Also Called: United Therapeutics Corp (G-5423)*

United Therapeutics Corp... 919 246-9389
2 Maughan Dr Durham (27709) *(G-5422)*

United Therapeutics Corp... 919 361-6141
55 Tw Alexander Dr Durham (27709) *(G-5423)*

United TI & Stamping Co NC Inc... 910 323-8588
2817 Enterprise Ave Fayetteville (28306) *(G-5939)*

United Visions Corp... 704 953-4555
428 S Main St Ste B Pmb 135 Davidson (28036) *(G-4705)*

United Welding and Iron Work.. 704 281-3706
115 Denver Business Park Dr Ste D Mooresville (28115) *(G-11116)*

United Wood Products Inc.. 336 626-2281
451 Railroad St Asheboro (27203) *(G-502)*

United Writers Press... 828 505-1037
17 Willow Tree Run Asheville (28803) *(G-809)*

Unitex Chemical Corp.. 336 378-0965
520 Broome Rd Greensboro (27406) *(G-7432)*

Unity Hlthcare Lab Billing LLP... 980 209-0402
7508 E Independence Blvd Ste 109 Charlotte (28227) *(G-3754)*

Universal Air Products Corp.. 704 374-0600
4715 Stockholm Ct Charlotte (28273) *(G-3755)*

Universal Bedroom Furniture, High Point *Also Called: Universal Furniture Limited (G-8586)*

Universal Black Oxide Inc.. 704 867-1772
205 Oxford St Gastonia (28054) *(G-6534)*

Universal Blanchers LLC.. 252 482-2112
115 Peanut Dr Edenton (27932) *(G-5522)*

Universal Fibers Inc... 336 672-2600
749 Pineview Rd Asheboro (27203) *(G-503)*

Universal Forest Products, Elizabeth City *Also Called: Universal Forest Products Inc (G-5580)*

Universal Forest Products Inc... 252 338-0319
141 Knobbs Creek Dr Elizabeth City (27909) *(G-5580)*

Universal Furniture Intl Inc... 828 241-3191
4436 Old Catawba Rd Claremont (28610) *(G-3941)*

Universal Furniture Intl Inc... 828 464-0311
1099 2nd Avenue Pl Se Conover (28613) *(G-4509)*

Universal Furniture Limited (PA).. 336 822-8888
2575 Penny Rd High Point (27265) *(G-8586)*

Universal Machine and Tool Inc.. 828 659-2002
1114 W Marion Business Park Marion (28752) *(G-10184)*

Universal Mania Inc... 866 903-0852
1031 Robeson St Ste A Fayetteville (28305) *(G-5940)*

Universal Packaging, Greensboro *Also Called: RLM/Universal Packaging Inc (G-7312)*

Universal Plastic Products Inc... 336 856-0882
3220 Peninsula Dr Jamestown (27282) *(G-9076)*

Universal Preservachem Inc.. 732 568-1266
2390 Park Center Dr Mebane (27302) *(G-10434)*

Universal Printing & Pubg, Durham *Also Called: Atlantis Graphics Inc (G-4933)*

Universal Rubber Products Inc.. 704 483-1249
7780 Forest Oak Dr Denver (28037) *(G-4812)*

Universal Steel NC LLC

ALPHABETIC SECTION

Universal Steel NC LLC 336 476-3105
  630 Bassett Dr Thomasville (27360) *(G-15298)*
Universal Tire Service Inc 919 779-8798
  4608 Fayetteville Rd Raleigh (27603) *(G-13383)*
University Directories LLC 800 743-5556
  2520 Meridian Pkwy Ste 470 Durham (27713) *(G-5424)*
University NC At Chapel Hl 919 962-0369
  116 S Boundary St Chapel Hill (27514) *(G-2089)*
University NC Press, Chapel Hill *Also Called: University NC At Chapel Hl (G-2089)*
University NC Press Inc 919 966-3561
  116 S Boundary St Chapel Hill (27514) *(G-2090)*
UNIVERSITY OF NORTH CAROLINA P, Chapel Hill *Also Called: University NC Press Inc (G-2090)*
Unix Packaging LLC 310 877-7979
  100 Ceramic Tile Dr Morganton (28655) *(G-11263)*
Unlimted Potential Sanford Inc 919 852-1117
  9301 Globe Center Dr Ste 120 Morrisville (27560) *(G-11460)*
Unmdeni Press LLC 209 598-1581
  2105 Glenhaven Dr Waxhaw (28173) *(G-15786)*
Unplugged Incorporated 704 726-0614
  402 W Trade St Ste 104 Charlotte (28202) *(G-3756)*
Unrivaled Metal Buildings LLC 844 848-8676
  814 E Boyd St Maiden (28650) *(G-10121)*
Unruly Mutt Publishing LLC 828 478-9097
  2612 Penngate Dr Sherrills Ford (28673) *(G-14390)*
Unspecified Inc 919 907-2726
  65 Tw Alexander Dr Unit 110324 Durham (27709) *(G-5425)*
Unx Industries Inc 252 355-8433
  1704 E Arlington Blvd Ste A Greenville (27858) *(G-7593)*
Unx Industries Inc 252 756-8616
  201 W 9th St Greenville (27834) *(G-7594)*
Unx Industries, Inc., Greenville *Also Called: Unx Industries Inc (G-7593)*
Unx Industries, Inc., Greenville *Also Called: Unx Industries Inc (G-7594)*
Unx-Christeyns LLC (PA) 252 756-8616
  707 E Arlington Blvd Greenville (27858) *(G-7595)*
Up & Coming Magazine 910 391-3859
  208 Rowan St Fayetteville (28301) *(G-5941)*
Up and Coming Weekly 910 484-6200
  208 Rowan St Fayetteville (28301) *(G-5942)*
Up On Hill 704 664-7971
  129 Fesperman Cir Troutman (28166) *(G-15397)*
Upchurch Machine Co Inc 704 588-2895
  11633 Fruehauf Dr Charlotte (28273) *(G-3757)*
Upel Inc 336 519-8080
  1000 E Hanes Mill Rd Winston Salem (27105) *(G-16960)*
Upfront Well of The Carolinas 919 415-6000
  8800 Westgate Park Dr Ste 108 Raleigh (27617) *(G-13384)*
Upholstery Design, Hickory *Also Called: Upholstery Designs Hickory Inc (G-8196)*
Upholstery Designs Hickory Inc 828 324-2002
  1251 19th St Ne Hickory (28601) *(G-8196)*
Upi, Durham *Also Called: Upl NA Inc (G-5426)*
Upi Chem Distribution Center, Mebane *Also Called: Universal Preservachem Inc (G-10434)*
Upl NA Inc (HQ) 610 491-2800
  5 Laboratory Dr Bldg 1 Ste 1100 Durham (27709) *(G-5426)*
Upm Raflatac Inc 828 335-3289
  535 Cane Creek Rd Fletcher (28732) *(G-6047)*
Upm Raflatac Inc 828 651-4800
  267 Cane Creek Rd Fletcher (28732) *(G-6048)*
Upm Raflatac Inc (HQ) 828 651-4800
  400 Broadpointe Dr Mills River (28759) *(G-10512)*
Upm Raflatac At Fletcher Bus, Fletcher *Also Called: Upm Raflatac Inc (G-6047)*
Upper Coastl Plain Bus Dev Ctr 252 234-5900
  121 Nash St W Wilson (27893) *(G-16554)*
Upper Deck Company 760 496-9149
  1750 Tw Alexander Dr Durham (27703) *(G-5427)*
Upper Rm Outreach Ministry Inc 252 364-8756
  169 Boyd St Winterville (28590) *(G-17016)*
Upper Room 910 540-7719
  1166 Anderson Rd Watha (28478) *(G-15742)*
Upper South Studio Inc 336 724-5480
  330 S Main St Winston Salem (27101) *(G-16961)*

UPS, High Point *Also Called: Bryan Austin (G-8276)*
UPS Stores 2922, The, Laurinburg *Also Called: King Business Service Inc (G-9483)*
Upshinemedical, Charlotte *Also Called: Aj & Raine Scrubs & More LLC (G-2149)*
Uptown Catering Company, The, Charlotte *Also Called: Over Rainbow Inc (G-3307)*
Uptown Publishing Inc 704 543-0690
  8037 Corporate Center Dr Charlotte (28226) *(G-3758)*
Upull LLC 609 977-2700
  101 Gillcrest Ln Hubert (28539) *(G-8755)*
Urban Industries Corp 980 209-9471
  12245 Nations Ford Rd Ste 505 Pineville (28134) *(G-12313)*
Urban News 828 253-5585
  959 Merrimon Ave Ste C Asheville (28804) *(G-810)*
Urban Orchard Cider Company 252 904-5135
  24 Buxton Ave Asheville (28801) *(G-811)*
Urban Orchard Cider Company 828 779-6372
  207 Monticello Rd Weaverville (28787) *(G-15866)*
Urban Spiced LLC 704 741-1174
  15720 Brixham Hill Ave Ste 300 Charlotte (28277) *(G-3759)*
Urban Tactical and Cstm Armory 252 686-0122
  643 Tyree Rd Kinston (28504) *(G-9390)*
Uretek LLC 203 468-0342
  715 Railroad Ave Rutherfordton (28139) *(G-13899)*
Urethane Innovators Inc 252 637-7110
  403 Industrial Dr New Bern (28562) *(G-11853)*
Urovant Sciences Inc 919 323-8528
  324 Blackwell St Bay 11 Durham (27701) *(G-5428)*
US Arms & Ammunition LLC 252 652-7400
  119 Mellen Rd New Bern (28562) *(G-11854)*
US Buildings LLC (PA) 828 264-6198
  355 Industrial Park Dr Boone (28607) *(G-1245)*
US Chemical Storage LLC 828 264-6032
  1806 River St Wilkesboro (28697) *(G-16050)*
US Conec Ltd 828 323-8883
  830 21st Street Dr Se Hickory (28602) *(G-8197)*
US Conec Ltd (PA) 828 323-8883
  1138 25th St Se Hickory (28602) *(G-8198)*
US Cotton LLC (DH) 216 676-6400
  531 Cotton Blossom Cir Gastonia (28054) *(G-6535)*
US Custom Socks Co LLC 336 549-1088
  2522 Brandt Forest Ct Greensboro (27455) *(G-7433)*
US Drainage Systems LLC 828 855-1906
  26 5th St Se Hickory (28602) *(G-8199)*
US Filter 828 274-8282
  1129 Sweeten Creek Rd Asheville (28803) *(G-812)*
US Industrial Piping Inc 336 993-9505
  105 Woodland Trl Kernersville (27284) *(G-9249)*
US Label Corporation 336 332-7000
  2118 Enterprise Rd Greensboro (27408) *(G-7434)*
US Lbm Operating Co 2009 LLC 910 864-8787
  1001 S Reilly Rd Ste 639 Fayetteville (28314) *(G-5943)*
US Legend Cars Intl Inc 704 455-3896
  5245 Nc Highway 49 S Harrisburg (28075) *(G-7732)*
US Logoworks, Fayetteville *Also Called: US Logoworks LLC (G-5944)*
US Logoworks LLC 910 307-0312
  4200 Morganton Rd Ste 105 Fayetteville (28314) *(G-5944)*
US Metal Crafters LLC 336 861-2100
  2400 Shore St Archdale (27263) *(G-301)*
US Microwave Inc 520 891-2444
  164 Fearrington Post Pittsboro (27312) *(G-12353)*
US Mirrors 919 561-6800
  5995 Chapel Hill Rd # 119 Raleigh (27607) *(G-13385)*
US One DOT Com Inc 704 587-0678
  13508 Norlington Ct Charlotte (28273) *(G-3760)*
US Optics 828 874-2242
  100 Beiersdorf Dr Connelly Springs (28612) *(G-4410)*
US Patriot LLC 803 787-9398
  Bldg Z 3252 - 1017 Canopy Lane Fort Bragg (28307) *(G-6091)*
US PATRIOT LLC, Fort Bragg *Also Called: US Patriot LLC (G-6091)*
US Plastic Moldings 800 262-2111
  1711 Gregory Rd Statesville (28677) *(G-14922)*
US Precision Cabinetry LLC 828 351-2020
  160 Executive Dr Rutherfordton (28139) *(G-13900)*

ALPHABETIC SECTION — Vanderbilt Minerals LLC

US Prototype Inc 866 239-2848
341 S College Rd Ste 11 Pmb 3004 Wilmington (28403) *(G-16439)*

US Soaps Manufacturing Co, Raleigh *Also Called: Showline Inc (G-13250)*

US Tobacco Cooperative Inc (PA) 919 821-4560
1304 Annapolis Dr Raleigh (27608) *(G-13386)*

USA Attachments Inc 336 983-0763
105 Industrial Dr King (27021) *(G-9283)*

USA Blind Inc 704 309-5171
6039 Charing Pl Charlotte (28211) *(G-3761)*

USA Display, Flat Rock *Also Called: Leisure Craft Inc (G-5968)*

USA Dreamstone LLC 919 615-4329
128 Yeargan Rd Ste C Garner (27529) *(G-6323)*

USA Drones 937 830-1856
240 Long Leaf Dr Unit 2b Belmont (28012) *(G-1017)*

USA Dutch Inc (PA) 919 732-6956
3604 Southern Dr Efland (27243) *(G-5528)*

USA Dutch Inc 336 227-8600
778 Woody Dr Graham (27253) *(G-6713)*

USA Fuel Service, Kill Devil Hills *Also Called: Fishkillerdaves LLC (G-9257)*

USA Insulation, Harrisburg *Also Called: JG Agnew Holdings Inc (G-7714)*

USA Made Blade 704 798-6478
134 N Lee St Salisbury (28144) *(G-14060)*

USA Metal Structure LLP 336 717-2884
507 W Kapp St Dobson (27017) *(G-4832)*

USa Wholesale and Distrg Inc 888 484-6872
203 Blount St Fayetteville (28301) *(G-5945)*

Usat LLC 919 942-4214
605 Eastowne Dr Chapel Hill (27514) *(G-2091)*

Useable Products 919 870-6693
Raleigh (27624) *(G-13387)*

Usw-Menard Inc 910 371-1899
3600 Andrew Jackson Hwy Ne Leland (28451) *(G-9563)*

UTC Aerospace Systems, Charlotte *Also Called: Hamilton Sundstrand Corp (G-2882)*

Utd Technology Corp 704 612-0121
4455 Morris Park Dr Ste J Mint Hill (28227) *(G-10546)*

Uteck 910 483-5016
159 Rock Hill Rd Fayetteville (28312) *(G-5946)*

Utility Metering Solutions Inc 910 270-2885
231 Sloop Point Loop Rd Hampstead (28443) *(G-7663)*

Utility Precast Inc 704 721-0106
1420 Ivey Cline Rd Concord (28027) *(G-4384)*

Utility Solutions Inc 828 323-8914
101 33rd S Dr Se Hickory (28602) *(G-8200)*

Utsey Duskie & Associates 704 663-0036
243 Overhill Dr Ste B Mooresville (28117) *(G-11117)*

Uwharrie Chair Company LLC 336 431-2055
5873 Parker St High Point (27263) *(G-8587)*

Uwharrie Frames Mfg LLC 336 626-6649
247 Leo Cranford Rd Asheboro (27205) *(G-504)*

Uwharrie Knits Inc 704 474-4123
957 N Main St Norwood (28128) *(G-12047)*

Uwharrie Lumber Co 910 572-3731
335 Page St Troy (27371) *(G-15419)*

V & B Construction Svcs Inc 704 641-9936
8413 Walkup Rd Waxhaw (28173) *(G-15787)*

V and E Components Inc (PA) 336 884-0088
720 W Fairfield Rd High Point (27263) *(G-8588)*

V I P, Henderson *Also Called: Quality Investments Inc (G-7805)*

V M Trucking Inc 984 239-4853
4915 Arendell St Morehead City (28557) *(G-11195)*

V/N Woodwork 704 277-6336
4106 Less Traveled Trl Indian Trail (28079) *(G-8969)*

V1 Pharma, Raleigh *Also Called: V1 Pharma LLC (G-13388)*

V1 Pharma LLC (PA) 919 338-5744
353 E Six Forks Rd # 220 Raleigh (27609) *(G-13388)*

VA Claims LLC 305 984-0936
300 E 1st St Greenville (27858) *(G-7596)*

VA Composites Inc 844 474-2387
707 S Pinehurst St Ste D Aberdeen (28315) *(G-34)*

Vacs America Inc 910 259-9654
3490 Stag Park Rd Burgaw (28425) *(G-1354)*

Vacuum Handling North Amer LLC 828 327-2290
2551 Us Highway 70 Sw Hickory (28602) *(G-8201)*

Vaibas Industries LLC 919 749-4422
6108 Big Sandy Dr Raleigh (27616) *(G-13389)*

Val-U-King Group Inc 980 306-5342
2312 Rufus Ratchford Rd Gastonia (28056) *(G-6536)*

Valassis Communications Inc 919 544-4511
4918 Prospectus Dr Durham (27713) *(G-5429)*

Valassis Communications Inc 919 361-7900
4918 Prospectus Dr Durham (27713) *(G-5430)*

Valassis Durham Printing Div, Durham *Also Called: Valassis Communications Inc (G-5429)*

Valassis Wichita Printing, Durham *Also Called: Valassis Communications Inc (G-5430)*

Vald Group Inc 704 345-5145
2108 South Blvd Ste 115 Charlotte (28203) *(G-3762)*

Valdese Packaging & Label Inc (PA) 828 879-9772
302 Saint Germain Ave Se Valdese (28690) *(G-15456)*

Valdese Packaging & Label Inc 828 879-9772
302 Saint Germain Ave Sw Valdese (28690) *(G-15457)*

Valdese Textiles Inc 828 874-4216
1901 Main St E Valdese (28690) *(G-15458)*

Valdese Weavers, Valdese *Also Called: Valdese Weavers LLC (G-15461)*

Valdese Weavers LLC 828 874-2181
705 Lovelady Rd Ne Valdese (28690) *(G-15459)*

Valdese Weavers LLC 828 874-2181
280 Crescent St Ne Valdese (28690) *(G-15460)*

Valdese Weavers LLC (PA) 828 874-2181
1000 Perkins Rd Se Valdese (28690) *(G-15461)*

Valencell Inc 919 747-3668
4601 Six Forks Rd Ste 103 Raleigh (27609) *(G-13390)*

Valendrawers, Lexington *Also Called: Valendrawers Inc (G-9799)*

Valendrawers Inc 336 956-2118
555 Dixon St Sapona Business Park Lexington (27293) *(G-9799)*

Vallee Industries Inc 910 477-0092
5400 E Yacht Dr Apt C1 Oak Island (28465) *(G-12056)*

Valley Proteins 252 348-4200
3539 Governors Rd Lewiston Woodville (27849) *(G-9663)*

Valley Proteins (de) Inc 336 333-3030
2410 Randolph Ave Greensboro (27406) *(G-7435)*

Valley Proteins (de) Inc 540 877-2533
28844 Bethlehem Church Rd Oakboro (28129) *(G-12084)*

Valley Proteins (de), Inc., Oakboro *Also Called: Valley Proteins (de) Inc (G-12084)*

Valley Run Candles LLC 828 729-8652
2 Spreading Oak Ct Durham (27713) *(G-5431)*

Valmet Inc 704 541-1453
3430 Toringdon Way Charlotte (28277) *(G-3763)*

Valmet Inc 803 289-4900
3440 Toringdon Way Ste 300 Charlotte (28277) *(G-3764)*

Valspar Corporation 704 897-5700
721 Jetton St Davidson (28036) *(G-4706)*

Value Clothing, Salisbury *Also Called: Value Clothing Inc (G-14061)*

Value Clothing Inc (PA) 704 638-6111
1310 Richard St Salisbury (28144) *(G-14061)*

Value Printing Inc 919 380-9883
604 E Chatham St Ste D Cary (27511) *(G-1916)*

Valwood Corporation 828 321-4717
35 Coalville Rd Marble (28905) *(G-10135)*

Van Blake Dixon 336 282-1861
378 Air Harbor Rd Greensboro (27455) *(G-7436)*

Van Duyn Woodwork 919 760-0327
9533 Bells Valley Dr Raleigh (27617) *(G-13391)*

Van Products Inc (PA) 919 878-7110
2521 Noblin Rd Raleigh (27604) *(G-13392)*

Van Welder LLC 919 495-2902
219 Ward St Graham (27253) *(G-6714)*

Van Wingerden Grnhse Co Inc 828 891-7389
4078 Haywood Rd Mills River (28759) *(G-10513)*

Vance Industrial Elec Inc 336 570-1992
1208 Belmont St Burlington (27215) *(G-1512)*

Vanceboro Apparel Inc 252 244-2780
7906 Main St Vanceboro (28586) *(G-15484)*

Vanderbilt Minerals LLC 910 948-2266
400 Spies Rd Robbins (27325) *(G-13603)*

ALPHABETIC SECTION

Vandilay Industries LLC.. 704 962-5140
  11758 James Richard Dr Charlotte (28277) *(G-3765)*
Vanguard Culinary Group Ltd.. 910 484-8999
  716 Whitfield St Fayetteville (28306) *(G-5947)*
Vanguard Furniture, Conover Also Called: Vanguard Furniture Co Inc *(G-4510)*
Vanguard Furniture Co Inc (PA).................................... 828 328-5601
  109 Simpson St Sw Conover (28613) *(G-4510)*
Vanguard Pai Lung LLC... 704 283-8171
  601 Mcarthur Cir Monroe (28110) *(G-10828)*
Vanguard Pailung, Monroe Also Called: Vanguard Pai Lung LLC *(G-10828)*
Vanguard Supreme, Monroe Also Called: Monarch Manufacturing Corp *(G-10774)*
Vanguard Supreme Div, Monroe Also Called: Monarch Knitting McHy Corp *(G-10772)*
Vanilla Print Inc... 919 637-0745
  2301 Cameron Pond Dr Cary (27519) *(G-1917)*
Vann S Wldg & Orna Works Inc.................................... 704 289-6056
  709 Sikes Mill Rd Monroe (28110) *(G-10829)*
Vannoy Construction Arcft LLC.................................... 336 846-7191
  1608 Us Highway 221 N Jefferson (28640) *(G-9093)*
Vans Inc.. 704 364-3811
  4400 Sharon Rd Ste 159 Charlotte (28211) *(G-3766)*
Vans Inc.. 919 792-2555
  5959 Triangle Town Blvd Ste 1152 Raleigh (27616) *(G-13393)*
Vapor Honing Technologies, Lincolnton Also Called: J Wise Inc *(G-9896)*
Varco Pruden Buildings, Greensboro Also Called: Bluescope Buildings N Amer Inc *(G-6843)*
Variety Consult LLC.. 704 275-2284
  3735 Robert Riding Rd Shelby (28150) *(G-14380)*
Variform Inc... 828 277-6420
  12 Gerber Rd Ste A Asheville (28803) *(G-813)*
Vascular Pharmaceuticals Inc...................................... 919 345-7933
  116 Manning Dr Chapel Hill (27599) *(G-2092)*
Vasiliy Yavdoshnyak.. 919 995-9469
  3517 Trawden Dr Wake Forest (27587) *(G-15609)*
Vasonova Inc.. 650 327-1412
  3015 Carrington Mill Blvd Morrisville (27560) *(G-11461)*
Vast Therapeutics Inc... 919 321-1403
  615 Davis Dr Ste 800 Morrisville (27560) *(G-11462)*
Vaughan Enterprises Inc.. 919 772-4765
  834 Purser Dr Ste 102 Raleigh (27603) *(G-13394)*
Vaughan Logging, Wake Forest Also Called: Cjc Enterprises *(G-15541)*
Vaughan-Bassett Furn Co Inc....................................... 336 835-2670
  4109 Poplar Springs Rd Elkin (28621) *(G-5631)*
Vaughan-Bassett Furn Co Inc....................................... 336 889-9111
  210 E Commerce Ave High Point (27260) *(G-8589)*
Vaughn Metals Inc.. 910 791-6576
  1314 S 12th St Wilmington (28401) *(G-16440)*
Vaughn Woodworking Inc.. 828 963-6858
  442 Aldridge Rd Banner Elk (28604) *(G-905)*
Vault Enclosures, High Point Also Called: Vault LLC *(G-8590)*
Vault LLC.. 336 698-3796
  1515 W Green Dr High Point (27260) *(G-8590)*
Vault of Forsyth Inc.. 336 996-2044
  578 Arbor Hill Rd Kernersville (27284) *(G-9250)*
Vav Plastics Nc LLC... 704 325-9332
  8710 Air Park West Dr Ste 200 Charlotte (28214) *(G-3767)*
Vecoplan, Archdale Also Called: Vecoplan LLC *(G-302)*
Vecoplan LLC... 336 861-6070
  5708 Uwharrie Rd Archdale (27263) *(G-302)*
Vector Tobacco Inc.. 919 990-3500
  3800 Paramount Pkwy Ste 250 Morrisville (27560) *(G-11463)*
Vega Construction Company Inc.................................. 336 756-3477
  137 W Main St Unit 8 Pilot Mountain (27041) *(G-12204)*
Vegherb LLC... 800 914-9835
  200 N 13th St Ste 3b Erwin (28339) *(G-5689)*
Veka East Inc... 800 654-5589
  90 Ceramic Tile Dr Morganton (28655) *(G-11264)*
Velco Inc... 828 324-5440
  130 11th St Nw Hickory (28601) *(G-8202)*
Velocita Inc... 336 764-8513
  383 Grant Rd Clemmons (27012) *(G-4066)*
Velocitor Solutions... 704 635-4293
  202 E Woodlawn Rd Ste 146 Charlotte (28217) *(G-3768)*

Ven-Ply Incorporated.. 336 841-4858
  5250 High Point Rd Ste K1 High Point (27265) *(G-8591)*
Venable... 252 430-6208
  563 Thomas Rd Henderson (27537) *(G-7815)*
Venator Chemicals LLC... 704 454-4811
  5910 Pharr Mill Rd Harrisburg (28075) *(G-7733)*
Vencedor, Cary Also Called: Vencedor Software Group Inc *(G-1918)*
Vencedor Software Group Inc..................................... 978 390-1187
  5000 Centre Green Way Ste 500 Cary (27513) *(G-1918)*
Vendelay Industries LLC.. 440 879-8363
  1941 Stagecoach Trl Wendell (27591) *(G-15922)*
Veneer Technologies Inc (PA)..................................... 252 223-5600
  611 Verdun St Newport (28570) *(G-11910)*
Venom Stars Inc... 828 256-8621
  6397 Hayden Dr Hickory (28601) *(G-8203)*
Ventilation Direct... 919 573-1522
  14460 Falls Of Neuse Rd # 14 Raleigh (27614) *(G-13395)*
Ventura Inc... 252 291-7125
  7061 Pennwright Rd Fremont (27830) *(G-6174)*
Ventura Systems Inc.. 704 712-8630
  160 Gibson Ct Dallas (28034) *(G-4660)*
Venture Cabinets... 252 299-0051
  7061 Pennwright Rd Fremont (27830) *(G-6175)*
Venture Products, Asheville Also Called: Venture Products Intl Inc *(G-814)*
Venture Products Intl Inc... 828 285-0495
  27 Mulvaney St Asheville (28803) *(G-814)*
Venture Publishing... 910 670-0552
  2729 Millmann Rd Fayetteville (28304) *(G-5948)*
Venture Shades LLC.. 804 240-2854
  900 E Six Forks Rd Unit 211 Raleigh (27604) *(G-13396)*
Veon Inc... 252 623-2102
  601 W 5th St Washington (27889) *(G-15736)*
Veradigm, Raleigh Also Called: Veradigm LLC *(G-13397)*
Veradigm LLC (HQ).. 919 847-8102
  305 Church At North Hills St Ste 100 Raleigh (27609) *(G-13397)*
Verbatim Americas LLC... 704 547-6551
  7300 Reames Rd Charlotte (28216) *(G-3769)*
Verbatim Americas LLC (PA)....................................... 704 547-6500
  8210 University Exec Park Dr Ste 300 Charlotte (28262) *(G-3770)*
Verbatim Corporation... 704 547-6500
  8210 University Exec Park Dr Ste 300 Charlotte (28262) *(G-3771)*
Verdante, Lenoir Also Called: Verdante Bioenergy Svcs LLC *(G-9657)*
Verdante Bioenergy Svcs LLC..................................... 828 394-1246
  628 Harper Ave Nw # D Lenoir (28645) *(G-9657)*
Verdesian Life Science US LLC (DH).......................... 919 825-1901
  1001 Winstead Dr Ste 480 Cary (27513) *(G-1919)*
Verdesian Life Sciences, Cary Also Called: Verdesian Life Science US LLC *(G-1919)*
Verellen Inc.. 336 889-7379
  5297 Prospect St High Point (27263) *(G-8592)*
Verena Designs Inc (PA)... 336 869-8235
  812 W Green Dr High Point (27260) *(G-8593)*
Veritable Aerospace... 919 258-2230
  410 Lord Berkley Rd Raleigh (27610) *(G-13398)*
Veritiv Operating Company.. 336 834-3488
  3 Centerview Dr Ste 100 Greensboro (27407) *(G-7437)*
Verity Yacht Publications... 760 803-2550
  281 Kinsman Ct Fuquay Varina (27526) *(G-6235)*
Vermeer Manufacturing Company................................ 410 285-0200
  10900 Carpet St Charlotte (28273) *(G-3772)*
Vermont Designs Unlimited LLC.................................. 910 846-4477
  2900 E Lakeview Dr Sw Supply (28462) *(G-15014)*
Vernons Mobile Welding LLC....................................... 336 388-0415
  5566 Park Springs Rd Pelham (27311) *(G-12179)*
Verona Cabinets & Surfaces LLC................................. 704 755-5259
  6700 South Blvd Charlotte (28217) *(G-3773)*
Versatile Machine Fab.. 336 699-8271
  2107 Iron Ridge Dr East Bend (27018) *(G-5471)*
Vertical Access LLC... 800 325-1116
  900 Hwy 258 S Snow Hill (28580) *(G-14509)*
Vertical Solutions of NC Inc... 919 285-2251
  5040 Kinderston Dr Holly Springs (27540) *(G-8724)*

ALPHABETIC SECTION

Verve, Hendersonville *Also Called: Carolina Home Garden (G-7835)*

Verylak Inc 812 442-7281
116 Lowes Foods Dr Lewisville (27023) *(G-9675)*

Vescom America Inc 252 431-6200
2289 Ross Mill Rd Henderson (27537) *(G-7816)*

Vestal Buick Gmc Inc 336 310-0261
900 Hwy 66 South Kernersville (27284) *(G-9251)*

Vestal Pontiac Buick GMC Truck, Kernersville *Also Called: Vestal Buick Gmc Inc (G-9251)*

Vestaron Corporation 919 694-1022
4025 Stirrup Creek Dr Ste 400 Durham (27703) *(G-5432)*

Vestcom Retail Solutions, Charlotte *Also Called: Electronic Imaging Svcs Inc (G-2690)*

Vesuvius Nc LLC 336 578-7728
911 E Elm St Graham (27253) *(G-6715)*

Vesuvius Penn Corporation (HQ) 724 535-4374
5510 77 Center Dr Ste 100 Charlotte (28217) *(G-3774)*

Vesuvius USA Corporation 412 429-1800
5510 77 Center Dr # 100 Charlotte (28217) *(G-3775)*

Veteran Safety Solutions LLC 980 339-2721
10584 Nc Highway 8 S Unit 286 Southmont (27351) *(G-14562)*

Vexea Mx LLC 910 787-9391
205 America Ct Jacksonville (28540) *(G-9043)*

Vextra Technologies LLC 828 464-4419
3642 E Us Highway 70 Claremont (28610) *(G-3942)*

Vf, Greensboro *Also Called: Kontoor Brands Inc (G-7155)*

Vf, Greensboro *Also Called: Workwear Outfitters LLC (G-7467)*

VF Corporation 336 424-6000
105 Corporate Center Blvd Greensboro (27408) *(G-7438)*

VF Corporation 336 424-6000
105 Corp Ctr Blvd Greensboro (27408) *(G-7439)*

VF Corporation 336 332-3400
400 N Elm St Greensboro (27401) *(G-7440)*

Vf Jeanswear Inc (PA) 336 332-3400
105 Corporate Center Blvd Greensboro (27408) *(G-7441)*

Vf Receivables LP 336 424-6000
105 Corporate Center Blvd Greensboro (27408) *(G-7442)*

VFC Lightning Protection, Raleigh *Also Called: Lightning Prtction Systems LLC (G-12971)*

VH Industries Inc 704 743-2400
4451 Raceway Dr Sw Concord (28027) *(G-4385)*

Via Prnting Graphic Design Inc 919 872-8688
5841 Gentle Wind Dr Youngsville (27596) *(G-17112)*

Viasic Inc 336 774-2150
5015 Southpark Dr Ste 240 Durham (27713) *(G-5433)*

Viaticus Inc 252 258-4679
4104 Sterling Trace Dr Winterville (28590) *(G-17017)*

Viavi Solutions Inc 919 388-5100
1100 Perimeter Park Dr Ste 101 Morrisville (27560) *(G-11464)*

Vibration Solutions 704 754-3118
130 Ostwalt Amity Rd Troutman (28166) *(G-15398)*

Vibration Solutions, Charlotte *Also Called: Centor Inc (G-2442)*

Vibration Solutions LLC 704 896-7535
5900 Harris Technology Blvd Ste G Charlotte (28269) *(G-3776)*

Vic Inc 336 545-1124
3410 W Wendover Ave Ste C Greensboro (27407) *(G-7443)*

Vic Panel Sales Division 336 861-2899
5708 Uwharrie Rd Archdale (27263) *(G-303)*

Vicinitus LLC 828 476-6055
788 Springbrook Farm Rd Waynesville (28786) *(G-15831)*

Vicki Vermont Aircraft Sale 828 225-6517
23 Rolling View Dr Asheville (28805) *(G-815)*

Victaulic Company 910 371-5588
2010 Enterprise Dr Ne Leland (28451) *(G-9564)*

Victaulic Leland Facility, Leland *Also Called: Victaulic Company (G-9564)*

Victoria Sweet LLC 336 474-8008
1122 Randolph St Unit 1 Thomasville (27360) *(G-15299)*

Victory 1 Performance Inc 704 799-1955
159 Lugnut Ln Mooresville (28117) *(G-11118)*

Victory Infrstrcture Cnstr LLC 704 572-8247
1511 Doctor Blair Rd Marshville (28103) *(G-10227)*

Victory Press LLC 704 660-0348
114 Eastbend Ct Ste 4 Mooresville (28117) *(G-11119)*

Victory Signs LLC 919 642-3091
2908 N Main St Fuquay Varina (27526) *(G-6236)*

Vida Wood Us Inc 919 934-9904
219 Peedin Rd Ste 102 Smithfield (27577) *(G-14487)*

Videndum Prod Solutions Inc 919 244-0760
215 Trimble Ave Cary (27511) *(G-1920)*

Video Fuel 919 676-9940
6417 Lakeland Dr Raleigh (27612) *(G-13399)*

Video Optimize LLC 818 421-1489
3135 Rustic Ln Castle Hayne (28429) *(G-1960)*

Viewriver Machine Corporation (PA) 336 463-2311
1617 Fern Valley Rd Yadkinville (27055) *(G-17061)*

Vigor LLC 704 661-0891
9905 Devereaux Dr Matthews (28105) *(G-10298)*

Vigor LLC 980 474-1124
1209 S College St Apt 1130 Charlotte (28203) *(G-3777)*

Viiv Healthcare Company 919 445-2770
120 Mason Farm Rd Chapel Hill (27514) *(G-2093)*

Viiv Healthcare Company 919 483-2100
410 Blackwell St Durham (27701) *(G-5434)*

Viiv Healthcare US, Durham *Also Called: Viiv Healthcare Company (G-5434)*

Viking Fire Protection, Winston Salem *Also Called: Florida Fire Supply (G-16714)*

Viking Steel Structures LLC 877 623-7549
113 W Main St , Nc Boonville (27011) *(G-1258)*

Viktors Gran MBL Kit Cnter Top 828 681-0713
28 Beale Rd Arden (28704) *(G-389)*

Villabona Iron Works Inc 252 522-4005
1415 W New Bern Rd Kinston (28504) *(G-9391)*

Village At Duplin Winery LLC 910 285-6814
109 Candlewood Dr Wallace (28466) *(G-15629)*

Village Ceramics Inc 828 685-9491
320 Q P Ln Hendersonville (28792) *(G-7911)*

Village Creamery & Caf Inc 336 447-4726
7111 Summerdale Rd Elon (27244) *(G-5663)*

Village Graphics 252 745-4600
204 Freemason St Oriental (28571) *(G-12113)*

Village Instant Printing Inc 919 968-0000
2204 Damascus Church Rd Chapel Hill (27516) *(G-2094)*

Village Printers, Pinehurst *Also Called: Gilley Printers Inc (G-12223)*

Village Printing Co 336 629-0951
530 Albemarle Rd Asheboro (27203) *(G-505)*

Village Produce & Cntry Str In 336 661-8685
4219 N Liberty St Winston Salem (27105) *(G-16962)*

Village Tire Center Inc 919 862-8500
5220 Atlantic Ave Raleigh (27616) *(G-13400)*

Villari Bros Foods LLC 910 293-2157
135 Carter Best Rd Warsaw (28398) *(G-15675)*

Villari Food Group LLC (PA) 910 293-2157
1015 Ashes Dr Ste 102 Wilmington (28405) *(G-16441)*

Vim Products Inc 919 277-0267
5060 Trademark Dr Raleigh (27610) *(G-13401)*

Vinatoru Enterprises Inc 336 227-4300
209 W Hanover Rd Graham (27253) *(G-6716)*

Vincent L Taylor 252 792-2987
3930 Bear Grass Rd Williamston (27892) *(G-16072)*

Vine & Branch Woodworks LLC 704 663-0077
388 E Plaza Dr Mooresville (28115) *(G-11120)*

Vineyard Bluffton LLC 704 307-2737
1001 Morehead Square Dr Ste 320 Charlotte (28203) *(G-3778)*

Vineyard Hill Distributing LLC 828 684-5113
215 Vineyard Hill Dr Fletcher (28732) *(G-6049)*

Vineyards On Scuppernong LLC 252 796-4727
1894 Nc Highway 94 N Columbia (27925) *(G-4170)*

Vintage Editions Inc 828 632-4185
88 Buff Ln Taylorsville (28681) *(G-15175)*

Vintage South Inc 919 362-4079
1100 Chimney Hill Dr Apex (27502) *(G-253)*

Vintage Vacuum Tubes LLC 336 688-7443
404 Shadowbrook Dr Burlington (27215) *(G-1513)*

Vintners Hill 704 737-8023
3453 Mayhew Forrest Ln Mint Hill (28227) *(G-10547)*

Vinventions Usa LLC 919 460-2200
505 Innovative Way Zebulon (27597) *(G-17145)*

ALPHABETIC SECTION

Vinyl Structures LLC.. 336 468-4311
 4708 Hunting Creek Church Rd Hamptonville (27020) *(G-7680)*

Vinyl Windows & Doors Corp...................................... 910 944-2100
 165 Taylor St Aberdeen (28315) *(G-35)*

Violet Sanford Holdings LLC...................................... 919 775-5931
 2209 Boone Trail Rd Sanford (27330) *(G-14203)*

Violet Studio Games LLC... 919 785-1989
 5417 Parkwood Dr Raleigh (27612) *(G-13402)*

Violino USA Ltd.. 336 889-6623
 123 S Hamilton St High Point (27260) *(G-8594)*

Viovio Inc.. 919 827-1932
 310 W Whitaker Mill Rd Raleigh (27608) *(G-13403)*

VIP Print and Signs... 919 968-0000
 2208 Damascus Church Rd Chapel Hill (27516) *(G-2095)*

VIP Printing and Signs Express, Chapel Hill *Also Called: Village Instant Printing Inc (G-2094)*

Virgilios Premium Vinegars... 919 717-3373
 113 S White St Wake Forest (27587) *(G-15610)*

Virginia Carolina Belting, Rocky Mount *Also Called: R/W Connection Inc (G-13726)*

Virginia Carolina Refr Inc (PA)................................... 704 216-0223
 1123 Speedway Blvd Salisbury (28146) *(G-14062)*

Virginia Mtal Trting Lynchburg, Raleigh *Also Called: East Crlina Metal Treating Inc (G-12716)*

Virginn-Plot Mdia Cmpanies LLC................................ 252 441-3628
 2224 S Croatan Hwy Nags Head (27959) *(G-11728)*

Virscidian Inc... 919 809-7651
 104 Ludlow Ct Cary (27513) *(G-1921)*

Virtue Labs LLC (PA).. 844 782-4247
 426 S Dawson St Raleigh (27601) *(G-13404)*

Virtue Labs LLC... 781 316-5437
 95 W 32nd St Winston Salem (27105) *(G-16963)*

Virtus Entertainment Inc.. 919 467-9700
 114 Mackenan Dr Ste 100 Cary (27511) *(G-1922)*

Vise & Co LLC... 336 354-3702
 5063 Ramillie Run Winston Salem (27106) *(G-16964)*

Vishay Measurements Group Inc (HQ)...................... 336 365-3800
 951 Wendell Blvd Wendell (27591) *(G-15923)*

Vishay Precision Group Inc.. 919 374-5555
 Micro-Measurements Raleigh (27611) *(G-13405)*

Vishay Transducers Ltd (HQ)..................................... 919 365-3800
 951 Wendell Blvd Wendell (27591) *(G-15924)*

Visigraphix Inc.. 336 882-1935
 8911 Cedar Spring Dr Colfax (27235) *(G-4162)*

Vision Contract Mfg LLC... 336 405-8784
 1327 Lincoln Dr High Point (27260) *(G-8595)*

Vision Directional Drilling... 336 570-4621
 3462 Nc Highway 62 E Burlington (27215) *(G-1514)*

Vision Envelope Inc.. 704 392-9090
 2451 Executive St Charlotte (28208) *(G-3779)*

Vision Metals Inc... 336 622-7300
 5806 York Martin Rd Liberty (27298) *(G-9834)*

Vision Motor Cars Inc (PA)... 704 425-6271
 545 Hamberton Ct Nw Concord (28027) *(G-4386)*

Vision Print Solutions, Charlotte *Also Called: Vision Envelope Inc (G-3779)*

Vision Technologies Inc.. 919 387-7878
 8509 Smith Rd Apex (27539) *(G-254)*

Vision Woodworks LLC.. 704 779-0734
 9306 Stawell Dr Huntersville (28078) *(G-8905)*

Visionair Inc... 910 675-9117
 5601 Barbados Blvd Castle Hayne (28429) *(G-1961)*

Visions Interior Designs, Davidson *Also Called: United Visions Corp (G-4705)*

Visions Stairways and Millwork................................... 919 878-5622
 2200 Westinghouse Blvd Ste 108 Raleigh (27604) *(G-13406)*

VISIONS STAIRWAYS AND MILLWORK, Raleigh *Also Called: Visions Stairways and Millwork (G-13406)*

Visitech Systems Inc... 919 387-0524
 1012 Napa Pl Apex (27502) *(G-255)*

Vista Horticultural Group Inc...................................... 828 633-6338
 2099 Brevard Rd Arden (28704) *(G-390)*

Vista Print... 919 400-2736
 5007 N New Hope Rd Apt A2 Raleigh (27604) *(G-13407)*

Vista Products Inc... 910 582-0130
 10 Ev Hogan Dr Hamlet (28345) *(G-7634)*

Vista Tranquila Publishers LLC.................................. 828 586-8401
 53 Lands End Dr Sylva (28779) *(G-15073)*

Visual Impact Prfmce Systems L............................... 704 278-3552
 2720 Amity Hill Rd Cleveland (27013) *(G-4083)*

Visual Impressions, Charlotte *Also Called: Digital Printing Systems Inc (G-2636)*

Visual Products, Charlotte *Also Called: Binders of Jhc LLC (G-2313)*

Visual Products Inc... 336 883-0156
 1019 Porter St High Point (27263) *(G-8596)*

Vita Foam, Greensboro *Also Called: Olympic Products LLC (G-7231)*

Vita Nonwovens, High Point *Also Called: Twe Nonwovens Us Inc (G-8581)*

Vitaflex LLC.. 888 616-8848
 1305 Graham St Burlington (27217) *(G-1515)*

Vitaflex USA, Burlington *Also Called: Vitaflex LLC (G-1515)*

Vital Being.. 828 964-5853
 194 Clay Wilson Dr Zionville (28698) *(G-17149)*

Vittro Sign Studio.. 917 698-1594
 1106 Cameron Woods Dr Apex (27523) *(G-256)*

Vivas Custom Cabinets LLC....................................... 252 650-1103
 515 Gray St Elm City (27822) *(G-5654)*

Vivet Inc... 909 390-1039
 1150 Pleasant Ridge Rd Ste A Greensboro (27409) *(G-7444)*

Vivid Pro Signs.. 919 352-8485
 1671 S Plank Rd Sanford (27330) *(G-14204)*

Viztek LLC.. 919 792-6420
 2217 Us 70 Hwy E Garner (27529) *(G-6324)*

Vlr LLC... 252 355-4610
 1020 N Green St Morganton (28655) *(G-11265)*

Vm Publishing.. 704 547-4322
 106 Colonial Ridge Cir # 22 Mooresville (28117) *(G-11121)*

Vmod Fiber LLC.. 704 525-6851
 811 Pressley Rd Charlotte (28217) *(G-3780)*

Vna Holding Inc (HQ).. 336 393-4890
 7825 National Service Rd Greensboro (27409) *(G-7445)*

VOCATIONAL SOLUTONS, East Flat Rock *Also Called: Vocatnal Sltons Hndrson Cnty I (G-5479)*

Vocatnal Sltons Hndrson Cnty I.................................. 828 692-9626
 2110 Spartanburg Hwy East Flat Rock (28726) *(G-5479)*

Voco America Inc.. 917 923-7698
 1104 Real Quiet Ln Waxhaw (28173) *(G-15788)*

Vocollect Inc.. 980 279-4119
 855 S Mint St Charlotte (28202) *(G-3781)*

Vogenx Inc... 919 659-5677
 3920 S Alston Ave Durham (27713) *(G-5435)*

Voith Fabrics Inc.. 252 291-3800
 3040 Black Creek Rd S Wilson (27893) *(G-16555)*

Volex Inc.. 828 485-4500
 915 Tate Blvd Se Ste 144 Hickory (28602) *(G-8204)*

Volex Inc.. 828 485-4500
 915 Tate Blvd Se Hickory (28602) *(G-8205)*

Volta Group Corporation LLC..................................... 919 637-0273
 300 Fayetteville St Unit 1344 Raleigh (27602) *(G-13408)*

Voltage LLC... 919 391-9405
 1450 Raleigh Rd Ste 208 Chapel Hill (27517) *(G-2096)*

Volumetrics Med Systems LLC................................... 800 472-0900
 4711 Hope Valley Rd Ste 4f Durham (27707) *(G-5436)*

Volvo Group North America LLC (DH)...................... 336 393-2000
 7900 National Service Rd Greensboro (27409) *(G-7446)*

Volvo Group North America LLC................................ 336 393-2000
 8203 Piedmont Triad Pkwy Greensboro (27409) *(G-7447)*

Volvo Group North America LLC................................ 731 968-0151
 7821 National Service Rd 1 Greensboro (27409) *(G-7448)*

Volvo Logistics North America Inc.............................. 336 393-4746
 7900 National Service Rd Greensboro (27409) *(G-7449)*

Volvo Motor Graders Inc... 704 609-3604
 8844 Mount Holly Rd Charlotte (28214) *(G-3782)*

Volvo Trucks North America, Greensboro *Also Called: Volvo Group North America LLC (G-7446)*

Volvo Trucks North America Inc (DH)........................ 336 393-2000
 7900 National Service Rd Greensboro (27409) *(G-7450)*

Vontier Corporation (PA).. 984 275-6000
 5438 Wade Park Blvd Ste 601 Raleigh (27607) *(G-13409)*

Vooner Flogard LLC 980 225-3277
4729 Stockholm Ct Charlotte (28273) *(G-3783)*

Vortant Technologies LLC 828 645-1026
88 High Country Rd Weaverville (28787) *(G-15867)*

Vortex, Raleigh *Also Called: Vortex-Cyclone Technologies (G-13410)*

Vortex Aquatic Structures USA, Cornelius *Also Called: Vortex USA Inc (G-4593)*

Vortex Bottle Shop LLC 980 258-0827
4469 School House Commons Harrisburg (28075) *(G-7734)*

Vortex USA Inc 972 410-3619
11024 Bailey Rd Ste C Cornelius (28031) *(G-4593)*

Vortex-Cyclone Technologies 919 225-1724
4400 Blossom Hill Ct Raleigh (27613) *(G-13410)*

Voyant Solutions, Carolinas, Durham *Also Called: Ditex LLC (G-5054)*

Vpc Foam USA Inc 704 622-0552
1820 Evans St Ne Conover (28613) *(G-4511)*

Vpm Liquidating Inc 336 292-1781
2110 W Gate City Blvd Greensboro (27403) *(G-7451)*

Vrg Components Inc 980 244-3862
3056 Eaton Ave Indian Trail (28079) *(G-8970)*

Vrush Industries Inc 336 886-7700
118 N Wrenn St High Point (27260) *(G-8597)*

VT Hackney Inc 252 946-6521
400 Hackney Ave Washington (27889) *(G-15737)*

VT Leeboy Inc 704 966-3300
500 Lincoln County Parkway Ext Lincolnton (28092) *(G-9934)*

Vtv Therapeutics, High Point *Also Called: Transtech Pharma LLC (G-8575)*

Vtv Therapeutics Inc (PA) 336 841-0300
3980 Premier Dr Ste 310 High Point (27265) *(G-8598)*

Vtv Therapeutics LLC 336 841-0300
3980 Premier Dr Ste 310 High Point (27265) *(G-8599)*

Vulcan Construction Mtls LLC 828 754-3200
609 Wilkesboro Blvd Ne Lenoir (28645) *(G-9658)*

Vulcan Construction Mtls LLC 336 767-1201
3651 Penn Ave Winston Salem (27105) *(G-16965)*

Vulcan Construction Mtls LLC 336 767-0911
4401 N Patterson Ave Winston Salem (27105) *(G-16966)*

Vulcan Materials Company 828 963-7100
3869 Nc Highway 105 S Boone (28607) *(G-1246)*

Vulcan Materials Company 704 545-5687
11435 Brooks Mill Rd Charlotte (28227) *(G-3784)*

Vulcan Materials Company 704 549-1540
11020 David Taylor Dr Ste 105 Charlotte (28262) *(G-3785)*

Vulcan Materials Company 828 692-0039
2284 Clear Creek Rd Hendersonville (28792) *(G-7912)*

Vulcan Materials Company 336 869-2148
2874 Nc Highway 66 S Kernersville (27284) *(G-9252)*

Vulcraft Carrier Corp 704 367-8674
2100 Rexford Rd Charlotte (28211) *(G-3786)*

Vulture Logging LLC 252 578-0377
81 Johnson St Roanoke Rapids (27870) *(G-13584)*

Vwgc, Mills River *Also Called: Van Wingerden Grnhse Co Inc (G-10513)*

Vx Aerospace Corporation 828 433-5353
2080 Us 70 E Morganton (28655) *(G-11266)*

Vx Aerospace Holdings Inc 828 433-5353
2080 Us 70 E Morganton (28655) *(G-11267)*

W & F Manufacturing LLC 336 665-4023
8817 W Market St Colfax (27235) *(G-4163)*

W & S Frame Company Inc 828 728-6078
4833 J M Craig Rd Granite Falls (28630) *(G-6759)*

W & T Logging LLC 252 209-4351
118 Conner Ln Windsor (27983) *(G-16571)*

W A Brown & Son Incorporated (PA) 704 636-5131
209 Long Meadow Dr Salisbury (28147) *(G-14063)*

W and W Truss Builders Inc 252 792-1051
424 Railroad St Williamston (27892) *(G-16073)*

W B Mason Co Inc 888 926-2766
10800 Withers Cove Park Dr Charlotte (28278) *(G-3787)*

W D Lee & Company 704 864-0346
212 Trakas Blvd Gastonia (28052) *(G-6537)*

W E Nixons Wldg & Hdwr Inc 252 221-4348
3036 Rocky Hock Rd Edenton (27932) *(G-5523)*

W F Harris Lighting Inc 704 283-7477
4015 Airport Extension Rd Monroe (28110) *(G-10830)*

W F N Z Radio Station, Charlotte *Also Called: CBS Radio Holdings Inc (G-2424)*

W G Cannon Paint Co Inc (PA) 828 754-5376
1015 Zacks Fork Rd Lenoir (28645) *(G-9659)*

W G of Southwest Raleigh Inc 919 629-7327
413 Redhill Rd Holly Springs (27540) *(G-8725)*

W Gamby C O Hanes Dye & Finish 336 724-9020
600 W Northwest Blvd Winston Salem (27101) *(G-16967)*

W H Bunting Thinning 252 826-4025
2305 Bynums Bridge Rd Scotland Neck (27874) *(G-14223)*

W H Rgers Shtmtl Ir Wrks Inc 704 394-2191
837 Toddville Rd Charlotte (28214) *(G-3788)*

W M Cramer Lumber Co (PA) 828 397-7481
3486 Texs Fish Camp Rd Connelly Springs (28612) *(G-4411)*

W M Plastics Inc 704 599-0511
5301 Terminal St Charlotte (28208) *(G-3789)*

W N C Pallet Forest Pdts Inc 828 667-5426
1414 Smoky Park Hwy Candler (28715) *(G-1591)*

W R Long Inc 252 823-4570
1607 Cedar St Tarboro (27886) *(G-15125)*

W R Rayson Export Ltd 910 686-5802
720 S Dickerson St Burgaw (28425) *(G-1355)*

W R White Inc 252 794-6577
152 W Askewville St Windsor (27983) *(G-16572)*

W T Humphrey Inc (PA) 910 455-3555
2423 N Marine Blvd Jacksonville (28546) *(G-9044)*

W T Mander & Son Inc 336 562-5755
1587 Egypt Rd Prospect Hill (27314) *(G-12409)*

W V Doyle Enterprises Inc 336 885-2035
1816 Belmar St High Point (27260) *(G-8600)*

W W Industries 336 312-1806
2907 Saint Regis Rd Greensboro (27408) *(G-7452)*

W&W-Afco Steel LLC 336 993-2680
9035 W Market St Colfax (27235) *(G-4164)*

W&W-Afco Steel LLC 336 275-9711
101 Centreport Dr Ste 400 Greensboro (27409) *(G-7453)*

W&W-Afco Steel LLC 252 459-7116
341 Corbett Rd Nashville (27856) *(G-11753)*

Wade Biggs Logging Inc 252 927-4470
2173 Biggs Rd Pinetown (27865) *(G-12251)*

Wade Manufacturing Company 910 895-0276
235 River Rd Rockingham (28379) *(G-13646)*

Wade Manufacturing Company (PA) 704 694-2131
76 Mill St Wadesboro (28170) *(G-15519)*

Wag Pet Boutique, Raleigh *Also Called: G H Group LLC (G-12789)*

Wagco Oil and Vinegar Taproom 919 295-6134
861 Old Knight Rd Ste 113 Knightdale (27545) *(G-9433)*

Wager, Rural Hall *Also Called: Robert H Wager Company Inc (G-13851)*

Waggoner Manufacturing Co 704 278-2000
1065 Hall Rd Mount Ulla (28125) *(G-11687)*

Wagon Wheel 828 689-4755
89 Carl Eller Road Mars Hill (28754) *(G-10198)*

Wahah Electric Supply 717 208-2260
3698 Wingfoot Dr Southport (28461) *(G-14586)*

Wainwright Warehouse 252 237-5121
2427 Us Highway 301 S Wilson (27893) *(G-16556)*

Wake Cross Roads Express LLC 919 266-7966
3501 Forestville Rd Raleigh (27616) *(G-13411)*

Wake Forest Gazette 919 556-3409
1255 S Main St Wake Forest (27587) *(G-15611)*

Wake Monument Company Inc (PA) 919 556-3422
213 N Main St Rolesville (27571) *(G-13761)*

Wake Stone Corp 252 985-4411
7379 N Halifax Rd Battleboro (27809) *(G-931)*

Wake Stone Corporation 919 677-0050
222 Star Ln Cary (27513) *(G-1923)*

Wake Stone Corporation (PA) 919 266-1100
6821 Knightdale Blvd Knightdale (27545) *(G-9434)*

Wake Stone Corporation 919 775-7349
9725 Stone Quarry Rd Moncure (27559) *(G-10629)*

Wake Supply Company 252 234-6012
3200 Turnage Rd Wilson (27893) *(G-16557)*

Wakefield Solutions, Raleigh *Also Called: Simon Industries Inc (G-13262)*

Walco International 704 624-2473
531 E Main St Ste B Marshville (28103) *(G-10228)*

Waldensian Style Wines, Durham *Also Called: Drink A Bull LLC (G-5065)*

Waldenwood Group Inc 704 313-8004
3800 Woodpark Blvd Ste I Charlotte (28206) *(G-3790)*

Waldenwood Group LLC 704 331-8004
3800 Woodpark Blvd Ste I Charlotte (28206) *(G-3791)*

Waldos Wldg Met Fbrication LLC 704 638-0462
3185 Bringle Ferry Rd Salisbury (28146) *(G-14064)*

Walex Products Company Inc (PA) 910 371-2242
1949 Popular St Leland (28451) *(G-9565)*

Walflor Industries Inc 360 899-8060
1301 Sand Hill Rd Candler (28715) *(G-1592)*

Walgreen Co 704 525-2628
2215 W Arrowood Rd Charlotte (28217) *(G-3792)*

Walgreens, Charlotte *Also Called: Walgreen Co (G-3792)*

Walk In Faith LLC 704 660-8337
2785 Charlotte Hwy Mooresville (28117) *(G-11122)*

Walker and Associates Inc (DH) 336 731-6391
7129 Old Us Hwy 52 Lexington (27295) *(G-9800)*

Walker Draperies Inc 919 220-1424
2503 Broad St Durham (27704) *(G-5437)*

Walker Logging 336 964-1380
1157 Yates Rd Denton (27239) *(G-4755)*

Walker Pallet Company Inc 910 259-2235
3802 New Savannah Rd Burgaw (28425) *(G-1356)*

Walker Street LLC 919 880-3959
104 Birchland Dr Fuquay Varina (27526) *(G-6237)*

Walker Woodworking Inc (PA) 704 434-0823
112 N Lafayette St Shelby (28150) *(G-14381)*

Walker's, Durham *Also Called: Walker Draperies Inc (G-5437)*

Wallace Printing Inc 828 466-3300
2032 Fairgrove Church Rd Newton (28658) *(G-11982)*

Wallace Spencer 704 865-1147
4306 Derrydowne Ln Gastonia (28056) *(G-6538)*

Wallace Welding Inc 919 934-2488
403 W Market St Smithfield (27577) *(G-14488)*

Wallets For Water 704 564-0763
4228 Wanamassa Dr Charlotte (28269) *(G-3793)*

Wallingford Coffee Mills Inc (PA) 513 771-3131
300 Concord Pkwy S Concord (28027) *(G-4387)*

Wallworx 919 422-8604
200 N Bell Haven St Apex (27539) *(G-257)*

Walnut Cove Furniture Inc 336 591-8008
4730 Nc 89 Hwy E Walnut Cove (27052) *(G-15636)*

Walnut Woodworks 828 290-6438
83 Riley Ln Flat Rock (28731) *(G-5973)*

Walrath Welding 704 771-6640
1360 Chadwick Shores Dr Sneads Ferry (28460) *(G-14493)*

Walter Kidde Portable Eqp Inc (HQ) 919 563-5911
1016 Corporate Park Dr Mebane (27302) *(G-10435)*

Walter Printing Company Inc 704 982-8899
130 Anderson Rd Albemarle (28001) *(G-112)*

Walter Reynolds (PA) 704 735-6050
216 Old Lincolnton Crouse Rd Lincolnton (28092) *(G-9935)*

Walter Tape & Label Co, Albemarle *Also Called: Walter Printing Company Inc (G-112)*

Walton Lumber Co 919 563-6565
302 Circle Dr Mebane (27302) *(G-10436)*

Waltons Distillery Inc 910 347-7770
261 Ben Williams Rd Jacksonville (28540) *(G-9045)*

Wambam Fence Inc 877 778-5733
6935 Reames Rd Ste K Charlotte (28216) *(G-3794)*

Wanchese Dock and Haul LLC 252 473-6424
593 Baumtown Rd Wanchese (27981) *(G-15651)*

Wanda Nickel 828 265-3246
6764 Old 421 S Deep Gap (28618) *(G-4714)*

Wangs and Thangs LLC 980 925-7010
2309 Penny Park Dr Gastonia (28052) *(G-6539)*

Want of ADS of Greensboro 336 297-4300
7715 Kenmont Rd Greensboro (27409) *(G-7454)*

Wanzl North America, Newton *Also Called: Technibilt Ltd (G-11976)*

War Sport LLC 910 948-2237
13117 Nc Highway 24 27 Eagle Springs (27242) *(G-5462)*

War Sport Manufacturing LLC 252 220-6505
111 W Church St Nashville (27856) *(G-11754)*

Ward & Son Inc 252 338-6589
920 Riverside Ave Elizabeth City (27909) *(G-5581)*

Ward Backhoe Bulldozer Svc LLC 252 446-5878
8029 Nc 4 Battleboro (27809) *(G-932)*

Ward Hosiery Company Inc 828 381-2346
1410 13th St Sw Hickory (28602) *(G-8206)*

Ward Specialty Pharmacy LLC 252 459-5544
3646 Sunset Ave Ste 110 Rocky Mount (27804) *(G-13739)*

Ward Vessel and Exchanger Corp (PA) 704 568-3001
6835 E W T Harris Blvd Charlotte (28215) *(G-3795)*

Ward's Grocery, Raleigh *Also Called: Kol Incorporated (G-12945)*

Warden Signs & Service LLC 336 416-4029
2249 Neelie Rd Yadkinville (27055) *(G-17062)*

Warehouse Distillery LLC 828 464-5183
2628 Northwest Blvd Newton (28658) *(G-11983)*

Warehouse Facility, Gastonia *Also Called: Industrial Elcpltg Co Inc (G-6424)*

Warm Industrial Nonwovens, Hendersonville *Also Called: Warm Products Inc (G-7913)*

Warm Products Inc 425 248-2424
581 Old Sunset Hill Rd Hendersonville (28792) *(G-7913)*

Warmack Lumber Co Inc 252 638-1435
321 E Sunset Blvd Cove City (28523) *(G-4598)*

Warming Sun Music Publishing 714 390-8010
107 Deep Crk Pittsboro (27312) *(G-12354)*

Warp Technologies Inc 919 552-2311
601 Irving Pkwy Holly Springs (27540) *(G-8726)*

Warren Oil Co Inc Louisburg 252 764-2171
307 Duck Hvn Swansboro (28584) *(G-15049)*

Warren Oil Company LLC (PA) 910 892-6456
2340 Us 301 N Dunn (28334) *(G-4890)*

Warren Plastics Inc 704 827-9887
511 Rankin Ave Mount Holly (28120) *(G-11652)*

Warren Record, The, Warrenton *Also Called: Womack Publishing Co Inc (G-15663)*

Warrior Boats 336 885-2628
2100 E Martin Luther King Jr Dr High Point (27260) *(G-8601)*

Warsaw Welding Service Inc 910 293-4261
824 N Pine St Warsaw (28398) *(G-15676)*

Washington Alloy, Lowell *Also Called: U S Alloy Co (G-10012)*

Washington Cabinet Company 252 946-3457
4799 Voa Rd Washington (27889) *(G-15738)*

Washington Cnty Newspapers Inc 252 793-2123
212 W Water St Plymouth (27962) *(G-12378)*

Washington Crab, Washington *Also Called: Carolina Catch Inc (G-15686)*

Washington Daily News, Washington *Also Called: Washington News Publishing Co (G-15739)*

Washington News Publishing Co 252 946-2144
217 N Market St Washington (27889) *(G-15739)*

Waste Container Repair Svcs 910 257-4474
2405 Wilmington Hwy Fayetteville (28306) *(G-5949)*

Waste Container Services LLC 910 257-4474
705 W Mountain Dr Fayetteville (28306) *(G-5950)*

Waste Industries Usa LLC (DH) 919 325-3000
3301 Benson Dr Ste 601 Raleigh (27609) *(G-13412)*

Waste Smasher, Winston Salem *Also Called: Trash Masher LLC (G-16946)*

Waste Water Treatment Plant, Cherokee *Also Called: Eastern Band Cherokee Indians (G-3856)*

Wastequip 800 255-4126
841 Meacham Rd Statesville (28677) *(G-14923)*

Wastequip, Charlotte *Also Called: Wastequip LLC (G-3796)*

Wastequip LLC (DH) 704 366-7140
6525 Carnegie Blvd Ste 300 Charlotte (28211) *(G-3796)*

Wastequip Manufacturing Co LLC (DH) 704 504-7597
6525 Morrison Blvd Ste 300 Charlotte (28211) *(G-3797)*

Wastezero Inc (PA) 919 322-1208
4208 Six Forks Rd Ste 1000 Raleigh (27609) *(G-13413)*

ALPHABETIC SECTION

Watauga County Country Hams, Boone *Also Called: Goodnight Brothers Prod Co Inc* *(G-1201)*

Watauga Creek LLC.. 828 369-7881
25 Setser Branch Rd Franklin (28734) *(G-6147)*

Watauga Opportunities Inc (PA).......................... 828 264-5009
642 Greenway Rd Boone (28607) *(G-1247)*

Watauga Ready Mix, Crumpler *Also Called: Chandler Concrete Inc (G-4628)*

Watauga Ready Mixed.. 336 246-6441
525 George Wilson Rd Boone (28607) *(G-1248)*

Water Tech Solutions Inc....................................... 704 408-8391
178 Cayuga Dr Mooresville (28117) *(G-11123)*

Water Treatment Department, Waynesville *Also Called: Town of Waynesville (G-15830)*

Water Treatment Facility...................................... 919 742-2939
955 Water Plant Rd Siler City (27344) *(G-14433)*

Water-Jel Technologies, Harrisburg *Also Called: Project Bean LLC (G-7723)*

Water-Revolution LLC... 336 525-1015
2246 Nc Highway 62 N Blanch (27212) *(G-1153)*

Waterboxer Inc.. 919 279-3338
120 Centrewest Ct Unit 695 Cary (27513) *(G-1924)*

Watercolors By Mista... 828 775-7751
75 Church St Weaverville (28787) *(G-15868)*

Waterdog Wood Works LLC................................. 252 808-7978
195 Port Dr Oriental (28571) *(G-12114)*

Waterline Systems Inc... 910 708-1000
270 Hogans Rd Hubert (28539) *(G-8756)*

Waterplant, Tarboro *Also Called: Town of Tarboro (G-15124)*

Waters Brothers Contrs Inc.................................. 252 446-7141
511 Instrument Dr Rocky Mount (27804) *(G-13740)*

Waters Corporation... 910 270-3137
15430 Us Highway 17 Hampstead (28443) *(G-7664)*

Waterwheel Factory... 828 369-5928
320 Arbor Ln Franklin (28734) *(G-6148)*

Watkins Cabinets LLC... 704 634-1724
1418 Industrial Dr Matthews (28105) *(G-10299)*

Watkins Custom Sewing Inc................................. 252 996-0642
911 Harbor Rd Wanchese (27981) *(G-15652)*

Watkins Wldg Fabrications LLC........................... 828 429-2369
1583 Big Island Rd Rutherfordton (28139) *(G-13901)*

Watson Concrete Pipe Company......................... 828 754-6476
2532 Morganton Blvd Sw Lenoir (28645) *(G-9660)*

Watson Electrical Cnstr Co LLC........................... 252 756-4550
3121 Bismarck St Greenville (27834) *(G-7597)*

Watson Metals Co.. 336 366-4500
2693 Poplar Springs Rd State Road (28676) *(G-14731)*

Watson Party Tables Inc (PA)............................... 919 294-9153
2455 S Alston Ave Durham (27713) *(G-5438)*

Watson Steel & Iron Works LLC........................... 704 821-7140
3624 Gribble Rd Matthews (28104) *(G-10350)*

Watson-Hegner Corporation................................. 704 922-9660
1006 Union Rd Ste C Gastonia (28054) *(G-6540)*

Watts Bumgarner & Brown Inc............................. 828 632-4797
9541 Us Highway 64 90 W Taylorsville (28681) *(G-15176)*

Watts Drainage Products Inc................................ 828 288-2179
100 Watts Rd Spindale (28160) *(G-14609)*

Watts Regulator... 978 689-6066
1491 Nc Highway 20 W Saint Pauls (28384) *(G-13910)*

Watts Regulator Co... 828 286-4151
100 Watts Rd Spindale (28160) *(G-14610)*

Wave Front Computers LLC................................. 919 896-6121
8015 Creedmoor Rd Ste 201 Raleigh (27613) *(G-13414)*

Wave Front Studios, Raleigh *Also Called: Wave Front Computers LLC (G-13414)*

WaveTherm Corporation....................................... 919 307-8071
5995 Chapel Hill Rd Ste 119 Raleigh (27607) *(G-13415)*

Waxhaw Cabinet Company, Waxhaw *Also Called: Brandon Hilbert (G-15747)*

Waxhaw Candle Company LLC............................ 980 245-2827
9830 Rea Rd Ste G Charlotte (28277) *(G-3798)*

Waxhaw Creamery LLC... 704 843-7927
109 E North Main St Waxhaw (28173) *(G-15789)*

Waycaster Nick Stone Co..................................... 828 756-4011
5455 Us 221 N Marion (28752) *(G-10185)*

Waycaster Stone Co, Marion *Also Called: Waycaster Nick Stone Co (G-10185)*

Wayne Dunn Logging LLC................................... 910 439-5478
656 Bowles Rd Mount Gilead (27306) *(G-11615)*

Wayne Farms, Dobson *Also Called: Wayne Farms LLC (G-4833)*

Wayne Farms, Elkin *Also Called: Wayne Farms LLC (G-5632)*

Wayne Farms LLC.. 336 386-8151
802 E Atkins St Dobson (27017) *(G-4833)*

Wayne Farms LLC.. 336 366-4413
10949 Nc 268 Elkin (28621) *(G-5632)*

Wayne Farms LLC.. 770 538-2120
332 E A St Newton (28658) *(G-11984)*

Wayne Industries Inc... 336 434-5017
4107 Cheyenne Dr Archdale (27263) *(G-304)*

Wayne Lamb Logging Co...................................... 910 529-1115
1050 Lisbon Bridge Rd Garland (28441) *(G-6247)*

Wayne Printing Company Inc............................... 919 778-2211
310 N Berkeley Blvd Goldsboro (27534) *(G-6669)*

Wayne Trademark.. 336 887-3173
5356 Nc Highway 49 S Asheboro (27205) *(G-506)*

Wayne Trademark, High Point *Also Called: Burrow Family Corporation (G-8279)*

Wayne Trademark International, Asheboro *Also Called: Wayne Trademark Prtg Packg LLC (G-507)*

Wayne Trademark Prtg Packg LLC...................... 336 887-3173
5346 Nc Highway 49 S Asheboro (27205) *(G-507)*

Wayne Woodworks.. 910 298-5669
880 Sumner Rd Pink Hill (28572) *(G-12318)*

Waynesville Soda Jerks, Waynesville *Also Called: Waynesville Soda Jerks LLC (G-15832)*

Waynesville Soda Jerks LLC................................ 828 278-8589
35 Bridges St Waynesville (28786) *(G-15832)*

WB Embroidery Inc.. 828 432-0076
3076 Nc 18 S Morganton (28655) *(G-11268)*

WB Frames Inc... 828 459-2147
3771 Sandy Ford Rd Hickory (28602) *(G-8207)*

WC&r Interests LLC... 828 684-9848
145 Cane Creek Industrial Park Rd Ste 100 Fletcher (28732) *(G-6050)*

Wcc Television, Charlotte *Also Called: Bahakel Communications Ltd LLC (G-2264)*

Wdm Inc.. 704 283-7508
608 Broome St Monroe (28110) *(G-10831)*

We Cbd LLC.. 336 969-0400
8701 Jefferson Church Rd Rural Hall (27045) *(G-13854)*

We Glowed Up LLC.. 856 266-5000
6805 Walnut Branch Ln Charlotte (28277) *(G-3799)*

We Organize You LLC... 919 773-8990
2031 Production Dr Apex (27539) *(G-258)*

We Partners LLC... 360 750-3500
324 Buncombe St Raleigh (27609) *(G-13416)*

We Print T-Shirts Inc... 910 822-8337
2598 Raeford Rd Fayetteville (28305) *(G-5951)*

Weapon Works LLC... 800 556-9498
1833 Anthony Rd Ste A Burlington (27215) *(G-1516)*

Wear-Flex Slings, Winston Salem *Also Called: MHS Ltd (G-16807)*

Wear-Flex Slings, Winston Salem *Also Called: MHS Ltd (G-16808)*

Wears Industries Inc... 828 575-9466
113 Spivey Mountain Rd Asheville (28806) *(G-816)*

Weather Marine Canvas LLC................................ 336 764-4015
245 Creek Meadow Dr Lexington (27295) *(G-9801)*

Weathercraft Outdoor Furn Inc............................ 336 629-3939
3524 Us Highway 220 Bus S Asheboro (27205) *(G-508)*

Weathers Machine Mfg Inc................................... 919 552-5945
9535 Us 401 N Fuquay Varina (27526) *(G-6238)*

Weathersby Guild Louisville, Shallotte *Also Called: Freedom Enterprise LLC (G-14273)*

Weathervane Creative Inc..................................... 828 542-0136
2359 Us Highway 70 Se Ste 270 Hickory (28602) *(G-8208)*

Weathervane Winery Inc....................................... 336 793-3366
1452 Welcome Arcadia Rd Lexington (27295) *(G-9802)*

Weaver Fabrication.. 336 877-3427
1478 Trojan Horse Cir Fleetwood (28626) *(G-5977)*

Weaveup Inc... 443 540-4201
4810 Hope Valley Rd Ste 210 Durham (27707) *(G-5439)*

Weavexx LLC.. 919 556-7235
14101 Capital Blvd Youngsville (27596) *(G-17113)*

Web 4 Half LLC.. 855 762-4638
720 Industrial Park Ave Asheboro (27205) *(G-509)*

Web-Don   ALPHABETIC SECTION

Web-Don, Charlotte *Also Called: Web-Don Incorporated* **(G-3800)**
Web-Don Incorporated (PA) 800 532-0434
   1400 Ameron Dr Charlotte (28206) *(G-3800)*

Webassign, Raleigh *Also Called: Cengage Learning Inc* **(G-12616)**

Webb of Wnc LLC 828 648-2670
   5717 Dutch Cove Rd Canton (28716) *(G-1628)*

Webb S Maint & Piping Inc 252 972-2616
   217 Daniels Ave Battleboro (27809) *(G-933)*

Webbs Logistics LLC 919 591-4308
   111 Saint Marys St Garner (27529) *(G-6325)*

Weber & Weber Inc 336 889-6322
   117 W Lexington Ave High Point (27262) *(G-8602)*

Weber and Weber Inc (PA) 336 722-4109
   1011 Burke St Winston Salem (27101) *(G-16968)*

Weber Screwdriving Systems Inc 704 360-5820
   149 Knob Hill Rd Mooresville (28117) *(G-11124)*

Weber Stephen Products LLC 704 662-0335
   200 Overhill Dr Mooresville (28117) *(G-11125)*

Webster Entps Jackson Cnty Inc 828 586-8981
   140 Little Savannah Rd Sylva (28779) *(G-15074)*

Webster Fine Art Limited (PA) 919 349-8455
   2800 Perimeter Park Dr Ste A Morrisville (27560) *(G-11465)*

Weddings To Remember 704 608-1181
   9319 Carrot Patch Dr Charlotte (28216) *(G-3801)*

Weddles Signs 276 779-9218
   144 Ridgeview Dr Mount Airy (27030) *(G-11593)*

Wede Corporation 704 864-1313
   133 Industrial Dr Kings Mountain (28086) *(G-9338)*

Wedeco, Charlotte *Also Called: Xylem Water Solutions USA Inc* **(G-3841)**

Wedeco Uv Technologies Inc 704 716-7600
   4828 Parkway Plaza Blvd Ste 200 Charlotte (28217) *(G-3802)*

Wedge Brewing Co 828 505-2792
   125b Roberts St Asheville (28801) *(G-817)*

Wedpics 919 699-5676
   6413 Rushingbrook Dr Raleigh (27612) *(G-13417)*

Weener Plastics Inc 252 206-1400
   2201 Stantonsburg Rd Se Wilson (27893) *(G-16558)*

Weeping Radish Farm Brewry LLC 252 491-5205
   6810 Caratoke Hwy Grandy (27939) *(G-6719)*

Weiss USA LLC 704 282-4496
   2213 Stafford Street Ext Monroe (28110) *(G-10832)*

Weissmann Travel Reports, Winston Salem *Also Called: Northstar Travel Media* **(G-16822)**

Welbuilt Homes Inc 910 323-0098
   2311 Clinton Rd Fayetteville (28312) *(G-5952)*

Welchs Recycling Inc 336 638-9601
   5103 Blakeshire Rd Greensboro (27406) *(G-7455)*

Welcome Industrial Corp 336 329-9640
   717 N Park Ave Burlington (27217) *(G-1517)*

Welders Log 919 473-3045
   108 Craven Hill Ct Cary (27518) *(G-1925)*

Welding - Fbrcation - Repr Inc 828 963-9372
   178 Riley Rd Boone (28607) *(G-1249)*

Welding Company 336 667-0265
   646 Old Us 421 Rd Wilkesboro (28697) *(G-16051)*

Welding Needs 252 902-4082
   3151 Penny Hill Rd Greenville (27834) *(G-7598)*

Welding On Wheels 704 239-7831
   3215 Old Union Church Rd Salisbury (28146) *(G-14065)*

Welding Solutions LLC 828 665-4363
   3632 Butler Bridge Rd Fletcher (28732) *(G-6051)*

Weldingart4u LLC 252 220-0294
   624 Wollett Mill Rd Nashville (27856) *(G-11755)*

Weldon Mills Distillery, Weldon *Also Called: Weldon Mills Distillery LLC* **(G-15889)**

Weldon Mills Distillery LLC (PA) 252 220-4235
   200 Rock Fish Dr Weldon (27890) *(G-15889)*

Weldon Steel Corporation 252 536-2113
   101 Kennametal Dr Weldon (27890) *(G-15890)*

Well Doctor LLC 704 909-9258
   9607 Autumn Applause Dr Charlotte (28277) *(G-3803)*

Well-Bean Coffee & Crumbs LLC 833 777-2326
   4154 Shearon Farms Ave Ste 106 Wake Forest (27587) *(G-15612)*

Well-Bean Coffee Company, Wake Forest *Also Called: Well-Bean Coffee & Crumbs LLC* **(G-15612)**

Wellco Two Inc 828 667-4662
   1835 Old Haywood Rd Asheville (28806) *(G-818)*

Wellington Leisure Products 336 342-4701
   309 Nelson St Pilot Mountain (27041) *(G-12205)*

Wellness Robotronic Industries, Nebo *Also Called: RDM Industrial Electronics Inc* **(G-11763)**

Welloyt Enterprises Inc 919 821-7897
   221 W Martin St Raleigh (27601) *(G-13418)*

Wells Hosiery Mills Inc (PA) 336 633-4881
   1758 S Fayetteville St Asheboro (27205) *(G-510)*

Wells Jnkins Wells Mt Proc Inc 828 245-5544
   145 Rollins Rd Forest City (28043) *(G-6086)*

Wells Mechanical Services LLC 252 532-2632
   628 Raleigh Dr Roanoke Rapids (27870) *(G-13585)*

Wells Pork and Beef Pdts Inc 910 259-2523
   750 Croomsbridge Rd Burgaw (28425) *(G-1357)*

Wells Welding Svc 252 519-2808
   24488 Nc Highway 561 Enfield (27823) *(G-5681)*

Wells Woodworks Gary Wells 828 553-0177
   2121 Big Branch Rd Brevard (28712) *(G-1292)*

Welsh Cstm Sltting Rwnding LLC 336 665-6481
   200 Citation Ct Greensboro (27409) *(G-7456)*

Welsh Paper Company, Youngsville *Also Called: Franklin Logistical Services Inc* **(G-17081)**

Wen Biz Journal 509 663-6730
   5150 Us 25/70 Hwy Marshall (28753) *(G-10208)*

Wen Bray Heating & AC 828 267-0635
   6034 Norcross Ln Hickory (28601) *(G-8209)*

Wendy Bs Cstm EMB Screen Prtg, Morganton *Also Called: WB Embroidery Inc* **(G-11268)**

Wendys Embrdred Spc Screen Prt 704 982-5978
   308 Concord Rd Albemarle (28001) *(G-113)*

Wenker Inc (PA) 704 333-7790
   112 S Tryon St Ste 1130 Charlotte (28284) *(G-3804)*

Wentworth Corporation 336 548-1802
   301 K Fork Rd Madison (27025) *(G-10091)*

Werner Co 704 235-5660
   307 Oask Rd Ste D Mooresville (28115) *(G-11126)*

Wersunsllc 857 209-8701
   615 Saint George Sq Ct Winston Salem (27103) *(G-16969)*

Werywin Corporation 410 322-4917
   70 Mosswood Blvd Ste 300 Youngsville (27596) *(G-17114)*

Weslacova Corp 704 607-1449
   719 Pinewood Cir Mooresville (28115) *(G-11127)*

Wesley Leblanc Racing LLC 336 560-7630
   6815 Mendenhall Rd Archdale (27263) *(G-305)*

West Dynamics Us Inc 704 735-0009
   1443 E Gaston St Lincolnton (28092) *(G-9936)*

West Express 704 276-9001
   4472 W Highway 27 Vale (28168) *(G-15472)*

West Fraser Inc 252 589-2011
   4400 Nc Hwy 186 Seaboard (27876) *(G-14230)*

West Jefferson Service, Creedmoor *Also Called: Southern States Coop Inc* **(G-4620)**

West Pharmaceutical Svcs Inc 252 522-8956
   1028 Innovation Way Kinston (28504) *(G-9392)*

West Pointe Printing 704 806-3670
   3924 Bearwood Ave Charlotte (28205) *(G-3805)*

West Side Industries LLC 980 223-8665
   124 Hatfield Rd Statesville (28625) *(G-14924)*

West Side Prcsion Mch Pdts Inc 908 647-4903
   124 Hatfield Rd Statesville (28625) *(G-14925)*

West Stanly Fabrication Inc 704 254-2967
   16431 Sr 24 27 Oakboro (28129) *(G-12085)*

West Stkes Wldcat Grdron CLB I 336 985-6152
   321 Logan Ct King (27021) *(G-9284)*

Westbend Vineyards Inc 336 768-7520
   599 S Stratford Rd Winston Salem (27103) *(G-16970)*

Westek, Monroe *Also Called: Safe Fire Detection Inc* **(G-10801)**

Western Anmal Dsase Dgnstc Lab, Arden *Also Called: North Carolina Department of A* **(G-356)**

Western Crlina Cstm Cswork Inc 828 669-0459
   2952 Us 70 Hwy Black Mountain (28711) *(G-1141)*

ALPHABETIC SECTION

Western Crlina Mutl Brial Assn..828 837-2577
138 Peachtree St Murphy (28906) *(G-11718)*

Western Crlina TI Mold Corp In..828 890-4448
3 Brandy Branch Rd Mills River (28759) *(G-10514)*

Western Roto Engravers Incorporated (PA)................................336 275-9821
533 Banner Ave Greensboro (27401) *(G-7457)*

Western Technology Inc...336 361-0402
711 County Line Rd Reidsville (27320) *(G-13545)*

Westlift, Goldsboro Also Called: Westlift LLC *(G-6670)*

Westlift LLC..919 242-4379
186 Belfast Rd Goldsboro (27530) *(G-6670)*

Westmoreland Printers Inc..704 482-9100
2020 E Dixon Blvd Shelby (28152) *(G-14382)*

Westpoint Home Inc..910 369-2231
19320 Airbase Rd Wagram (28396) *(G-15524)*

Westrock - Graphics Inc (DH)..610 392-0416
9731 Southern Pine Blvd Ste E Charlotte (28273) *(G-3806)*

Westrock - Southern Cont LLC...704 662-8496
279 Mooresville Blvd Mooresville (28115) *(G-11128)*

Westrock Company..470 484-1183
2690 Kelly Blvd Claremont (28610) *(G-3943)*

Westrock Company..828 248-4815
376 Pine Street Ext Forest City (28043) *(G-6087)*

Westrock Company..770 448-2193
8080 N Point Blvd Winston Salem (27106) *(G-16971)*

Westrock Converting LLC..828 245-9871
376 Pine St Forest City (28043) *(G-6088)*

Westrock Converting LLC..336 661-1700
5900 Grassy Creek Blvd Winston Salem (27105) *(G-16972)*

Westrock Kraft Paper LLC...252 533-6000
100 Gaston Rd Roanoke Rapids (27870) *(G-13586)*

Westrock Merchandising Disp, Winston Salem Also Called: Westrock Rkt LLC *(G-16973)*

Westrock Merchandising Display, Rural Hall Also Called: Westrock Shared Services LLC *(G-13855)*

Westrock Mwv LLC..919 334-3200
1021 Main Campus Dr Raleigh (27606) *(G-13419)*

Westrock Paper and Packg LLC..919 463-3100
5150 Mccrimmon Pkwy Morrisville (27560) *(G-11466)*

Westrock Paper and Packg LLC..252 533-6000
100 Gaston Rd Roanoke Rapids (27870) *(G-13587)*

Westrock Rkt LLC..828 459-8006
2690 Kelly Blvd Claremont (28610) *(G-3944)*

Westrock Rkt LLC..828 464-5560
214 Conover Blvd E Conover (28613) *(G-4512)*

Westrock Rkt LLC..828 655-1303
468 Carolina Ave Marion (28752) *(G-10186)*

Westrock Rkt LLC..770 448-2193
1659 E Court St Marion (28752) *(G-10187)*

Westrock Rkt LLC..704 662-8494
279 Mooresville Blvd Mooresville (28115) *(G-11129)*

Westrock Rkt LLC..336 661-1700
5930 Grassy Creek Blvd Winston Salem (27105) *(G-16973)*

Westrock Rkt LLC..336 661-7180
5900a Grassy Creek Blvd Winston Salem (27105) *(G-16974)*

Westrock Shared Services LLC..336 642-4165
520 Northridge Park Dr Rural Hall (27045) *(G-13855)*

Weststar, Cary Also Called: Weststar Precision Inc *(G-1926)*

Weststar Precision Inc...919 557-2820
101 Fern Bluff Way Cary (27518) *(G-1926)*

Wet Dog Glass LLC..910 428-4111
938 Reynolds Pl Greensboro (27403) *(G-7458)*

Wet Dog Glass LLC..910 428-4111
100 Russell Dr Star (27356) *(G-14725)*

Wetherington Logging Inc..252 393-8435
245 Walters Ln Stella (28582) *(G-14938)*

Wetherington S Mobile Home..910 347-3664
106 Marlo Cir Jacksonville (28540) *(G-9046)*

Wewoka Gas Producers LLC..704 844-8990
10600 Nations Ford Rd Charlotte (28273) *(G-3807)*

Weyerhaeuser, Vanceboro Also Called: Weyerhaeuser New Bern *(G-15486)*

Weyerhaeuser Co..828 464-3841
1525 Mount Olive Church Rd Newton (28658) *(G-11985)*

Weyerhaeuser Company..253 924-2345
10601 Westlake Dr Charlotte (28273) *(G-3808)*

Weyerhaeuser Company..336 835-5100
184 Gentry Rd Elkin (28621) *(G-5633)*

Weyerhaeuser Company..252 746-7200
371 E Hanrahan Rd Grifton (28530) *(G-7603)*

Weyerhaeuser Company..252 791-3200
1000 Nc Hwy 149 N Plymouth (27962) *(G-12379)*

Weyerhaeuser Company..252 633-7100
1785 Weyerhaeuser Rd Vanceboro (28586) *(G-15485)*

Weyerhaeuser New Bern...252 633-7100
1785 Weyerhaeuser Rd Vanceboro (28586) *(G-15486)*

Weyerhaeuser Nr Company..252 633-7100
1482 Weyerhaeuser Rd Vanceboro (28586) *(G-15487)*

Weyerhaueser Nr Co..252 633-7252
1785 Weyerhaeuser Rd Vanceboro (28586) *(G-15488)*

Whaley Foodservice LLC...704 529-6242
8334 Arrowridge Blvd Ste K Charlotte (28273) *(G-3809)*

Wham Aviation LLC...336 605-4663
2611 Oxmoor Rd Summerfield (27358) *(G-14993)*

Wham Bam Monogram..336 712-5109
4050 Dresden Dr Winston Salem (27104) *(G-16975)*

Whatever You Need Screen Print...704 287-8603
531 Brightleaf Pl Nw Concord (28027) *(G-4388)*

Whats Your Sign LLC...919 274-5703
720 Sawmill Rd Raleigh (27615) *(G-13420)*

Whatz Cookin LLC...336 353-0227
123 Old Brintle St Mount Airy (27030) *(G-11594)*

Wheaton Plastic Operations, Youngsville Also Called: Amcor Phrm Packg USA LLC *(G-17066)*

Wheatstone Corporation (PA)...252 638-7000
600 Indl Dr New Bern (28562) *(G-11855)*

Wheel City Wholesale Inc..828 665-2442
200 Smokey Park Hwy Asheville (28806) *(G-819)*

Wheel Pros LLC...336 851-6705
2606 Phoenix Dr Ste 804 Greensboro (27406) *(G-7459)*

Wheeler Industries, Pikeville Also Called: Wheeler Industries Inc *(G-12195)*

Wheeler Industries Inc..919 736-4256
4573 Us Highway 117 N Pikeville (27863) *(G-12195)*

Wheelhouse Builders LLC...828 553-7519
71 Trailcreek Ln Brevard (28712) *(G-1293)*

Whelan Industries LLC...704 506-9515
8621 Fairview Rd Ste I Mint Hill (28227) *(G-10548)*

Whi Sand & Gravel, Fayetteville Also Called: Welbuilt Homes Inc *(G-5952)*

Whimsical Prints Paper & Gifts..919 544-8491
5826 Fayetteville Rd Ste 105 Durham (27713) *(G-5440)*

Whippoorwill Hills Inc...252 537-2765
1509 E 10th St Roanoke Rapids (27870) *(G-13588)*

Whisper Soft Mills, Hampstead Also Called: Babine Lake Corporation *(G-7639)*

Whispering Willow, Denver Also Called: Whispering Willow Soap Co LLC *(G-4813)*

Whispering Willow Soap Co LLC..828 455-0322
5851 Balsom Ridge Rd Ste B Denver (28037) *(G-4813)*

Whistle Stop Press Inc..910 695-1403
175 Davis St Southern Pines (28387) *(G-14560)*

Whitaker Mill Works LLC...919 772-3030
3801 Beryl Rd Raleigh (27607) *(G-13421)*

Whitaker S Tire Service Inc..704 786-6174
530 Concord Pkwy N Concord (28027) *(G-4389)*

Whitakers Tire & Wheel Service, Concord Also Called: Whitaker S Tire Service Inc *(G-4389)*

White Bros Packing Co LLC...252 331-9253
2551 Peartree Rd Elizabeth City (27909) *(G-5582)*

White Cap LP...704 921-4420
5900 W Wt Harris Blvd Charlotte (28269) *(G-3810)*

White Knght Engneered Pdts Inc..828 687-0940
9 Sw Pack Sq Ste 201 Asheville (28801) *(G-820)*

White Knight Engineered Products, Inc., Asheville Also Called: White Knght Engneered Pdts Inc *(G-820)*

White Oak, Spindale Also Called: White Oak Carpet Mills Inc *(G-14611)*

White Oak Carpet Mills Inc..828 287-8892
1553 Old Ballpark Rd Spindale (28160) *(G-14611)*

White Packing Co Inc -Va...540 373-9883
5404 Hillsborough St Ste A Raleigh (27606) *(G-13422)*

White Picket Media Inc — ALPHABETIC SECTION

White Picket Media Inc.. 773 769-8400
21313 Island Forest Dr Cornelius (28031) *(G-4594)*

White River Marine Group LLC.. 252 633-3101
110 N Glenburnie Rd New Bern (28560) *(G-11856)*

White Robert Custom Wdwkg.. 704 489-2005
7606 Townsend Dr Denver (28037) *(G-4814)*

White S Tire Svc Wilson Inc... 252 237-0770
501 Goldsboro St S Wilson (27893) *(G-16559)*

White S Tire Svc Wilson Inc (PA)..................................... 252 237-5426
701 Hines St S Wilson (27893) *(G-16560)*

White Stone Labs Inc... 704 775-5274
178 Cayuga Dr Mooresville (28117) *(G-11130)*

White Street Brewing Co Inc.. 919 647-9439
400 Park Ave Youngsville (27596) *(G-17115)*

White Tiger Btq & Candle Co.. 919 610-7244
3206 Smokey Path Sanford (27330) *(G-14205)*

White Tire and Service LLC... 704 636-0323
200 E Liberty St Salisbury (28144) *(G-14066)*

White Wolf Press LLC... 828 288-2077
961 Painters Gap Rd Rutherfordton (28139) *(G-13902)*

Whitecaps, Monroe Also Called: A C S Enterprises NC Inc *(G-10631)*

Whitefin Vineyards LLC... 219 902-6647
3400 Winding Way Apex (27502) *(G-259)*

Whitehat Seed Farms Inc.. 252 264-2427
102 Whitehat Rd Hertford (27944) *(G-7925)*

Whitener Sales Company... 828 253-0518
91 Carter Cove Rd Asheville (28804) *(G-821)*

Whites Tire Svc New Bern Inc... 252 633-1170
2813 Neuse Blvd New Bern (28562) *(G-11857)*

Whiteside Machine Co, Claremont Also Called: Whiteside Mch & Repr Co Inc *(G-3945)*

Whiteside Mch & Repr Co Inc.. 828 459-2141
4506 Shook Rd Claremont (28610) *(G-3945)*

Whiteville AG... 910 914-0007
3654 James B White Hwy S Whiteville (28472) *(G-15977)*

Whiteville Fabrick, Whiteville Also Called: Shodja Textiles Inc *(G-15976)*

Whiteville Fabrics LLC (PA)... 910 914-0456
68 Industrial Dr Whiteville (28472) *(G-15978)*

Whiteville Fabrics LLC... 910 639-4444
68 Industrial Blvd Whiteville (28472) *(G-15979)*

Whiteville Forklift & Eqp.. 910 642-6642
344 Vinson Blvd Whiteville (28472) *(G-15980)*

Whiteville Plywood Inc.. 910 642-7114
500 E Main St Whiteville (28472) *(G-15981)*

Whiteville Rentals, Whiteville Also Called: Whiteville Forklift & Eqp *(G-15980)*

Whitewood, Thomasville Also Called: Whitewood Industries Inc *(G-15300)*

Whitewood Contracts LLC... 336 885-9300
667 W Ward Ave High Point (27260) *(G-8603)*

Whitewood Industries Inc (PA).. 336 472-0303
100 Liberty Dr Thomasville (27360) *(G-15300)*

Whitewoven Handweaving Studio, Waynesville Also Called: Sorrells Sheree White *(G-15825)*

Whitley Holding Company (PA)....................................... 704 888-2625
3827 Whitley Rd Midland (28107) *(G-10481)*

Whitley Manufacturing, Midland Also Called: Whitley Holding Company *(G-10481)*

Whitley Metals Inc... 919 894-3326
769 Mount Pleasant Rd Willow Spring (27592) *(G-16084)*

Whitley/Monahan Handle LLC... 704 888-2625
3827 Whitley Rd Midland (28107) *(G-10482)*

Whitney Screen Printing.. 910 673-0309
2244 Nc Highway 211 Eagle Springs (27242) *(G-5463)*

Whits Frozen Custard, Davidson Also Called: Je Freeze LLC *(G-4684)*

Whole Harvest, Warsaw Also Called: Whole Harvest Foods LLC *(G-15677)*

Whole Harvest Foods LLC.. 910 293-7917
376 W Park Dr Warsaw (28398) *(G-15677)*

Whole Log Lumber, Zirconia Also Called: Green River Resource MGT *(G-17153)*

Whole Sale Printing Inks, Morganton Also Called: Arpro M-Tec LLC *(G-11198)*

Wholesale, Fayetteville Also Called: Jasie Blanks LLC *(G-5846)*

Wholesale Direct Carports.. 336 399-3221
731 E King St King (27021) *(G-9285)*

Wholesale Distributor, Greensboro Also Called: M Davis and Associates LLC *(G-7172)*

Wholesale Glass Fabricators, Wilmington Also Called: Heraeus Quartz North Amer LLC *(G-16250)*

Wholesale Kennel Supply Co.. 919 742-2515
163 Stockyard Rd Siler City (27344) *(G-14434)*

Wholeseal International... 919 346-0788
192c Lorax Ln Pittsboro (27312) *(G-12355)*

Wichard Inc.. 704 597-1502
3901 Pine Grove Cir Charlotte (28206) *(G-3811)*

Wick Communications Co.. 252 537-2505
1025 Roanoke Ave Roanoke Rapids (27870) *(G-13589)*

Wicked Calm Candles LLc.. 856 343-2499
595 Lockwood Dr Clayton (27527) *(G-4021)*

Wicked Fab-Worx LLC.. 828 492-0112
2962 Asheville Hwy Canton (28716) *(G-1629)*

Wicked Oceans... 252 269-0488
3431 S Buccaneer Dr Nags Head (27959) *(G-11729)*

Wicked Rooster Signs Inc.. 828 844-0404
204 Woods End Dr Hendersonville (28739) *(G-7914)*

Wicked Welds LLC... 704 907-5531
4017 Hartley St Charlotte (28206) *(G-3812)*

Wieland, Wilmington Also Called: Wieland Electric Inc *(G-16442)*

Wieland Copper Products LLC.. 336 445-4500
3990 Us 311 Hwy N Pine Hall (27042) *(G-12206)*

Wieland Electric Inc (DH)... 910 259-5050
8207 Market St Ste P10680 Wilmington (28404) *(G-16442)*

Wigal Wood Works... 580 890-9723
508 Anson Dr Fayetteville (28311) *(G-5953)*

Wiggins Design Fabrication Inc....................................... 252 826-5239
140 Edwards Fork Rd Scotland Neck (27874) *(G-14224)*

Wiggins North State Co Inc (PA)..................................... 919 556-3231
204 S Main St Rolesville (27571) *(G-13762)*

Wikoff Color, Charlotte Also Called: Wikoff Color Corporation *(G-3813)*

Wikoff Color Corporation.. 704 392-4657
2828 Interstate St Charlotte (28208) *(G-3813)*

Wikoff Color Corporation.. 336 668-3423
7212 Cessna Dr Greensboro (27409) *(G-7460)*

Wilbert Inc (HQ)... 704 247-3850
100 N Main St Ste 200 Belmont (28012) *(G-1018)*

Wilbert Burial Vault Company... 910 739-7276
1015 Roberts Ave Lumberton (28358) *(G-10060)*

Wilbert Funeral Services Inc.. 800 828-5879
108 Buchanan Church Rd Greensboro (27405) *(G-7461)*

Wilbert Plastic Services, Belmont Also Called: Wilbert Inc *(G-1018)*

Wilbert Plastic Services, Belmont Also Called: Wilbert Plstic Svcs Acqstion L *(G-1020)*

Wilbert Plastic Services Inc.. 866 273-1810
100 N Main St Ste 200 Belmont (28012) *(G-1019)*

Wilbert Plstic Svcs Acqstion L (DH)................................ 704 822-1423
1000 Oaks Pkwy Belmont (28012) *(G-1020)*

Wilbert Plstic Svcs Acqstion L... 704 455-5191
7301 Caldwell Rd Harrisburg (28075) *(G-7735)*

Wilbert Yates Vault Co Inc... 704 399-8453
2839 Rosemont St Charlotte (28208) *(G-3814)*

Wild Child Custom Graphics LLC.................................... 910 762-5335
3126 Kitty Hawk Rd Ste 1 Wilmington (28405) *(G-16443)*

Wildcat Petroleum Service Inc... 704 379-0132
326 Hawksnest Ct Matthews (28104) *(G-10351)*

Wildcat Territory Inc... 718 361-6726
110 W Guilford St Thomasville (27360) *(G-15301)*

Wildcraft Extracts LLC... 828 273-8173
64 Landmark Dr Sylva (28779) *(G-15075)*

Wilder Tactical LLC... 704 750-7141
120 Wolfpack Rd Gastonia (28056) *(G-6541)*

Wildflour Bakery Inc... 828 749-9224
173 Main St Saluda (28773) *(G-14075)*

Wildflour Bakery & Cafe, Saluda Also Called: Wildflour Bakery Inc *(G-14075)*

Wildflwers Btq of Blowing Rock...................................... 828 295-9655
Old Martin House On Main Street Blowing Rock (28605) *(G-1157)*

Wildwood Lamps & Accents Inc (PA)............................. 252 446-3266
516 Paul St Rocky Mount (27803) *(G-13741)*

Wildwood Studios Inc.. 828 299-8696
2163 Riceville Rd Asheville (28805) *(G-822)*

Wilkes Welding and Mch Co Inc...................................... 336 670-2742
1018 Mulberry Rd Mc Grady (28649) *(G-10382)*

ALPHABETIC SECTION

Willard Rodney White.. 252 794-3245
142 E Askewville St Windsor (27983) *(G-16573)*

William Barnet & Son LLC.. 252 522-2418
1411 Hwy 258 S Kinston (28504) *(G-9393)*

William Bostic.. 336 629-5243
3854 Us Highway 64 E Asheboro (27203) *(G-511)*

William Brantley.. 910 627-7286
637 Dunrobin Dr Raeford (28376) *(G-12445)*

William George Printing LLC...................................... 910 221-2700
3469 Black And Decker Rd Hope Mills (28348) *(G-8738)*

William Goodyear Co (PA)... 704 283-7824
2802 Gray Fox Rd Monroe (28110) *(G-10833)*

William L Day Companies Inc..................................... 828 693-1333
3325 Nc 9 Hwy Tryon (28782) *(G-15431)*

William Shawn Staley... 336 838-9193
838 Green Acres Mill Rd Millers Creek (28651) *(G-10496)*

William Stone & Tile Inc.. 910 353-0914
1525 Freedom Way Hubert (28539) *(G-8757)*

William Travis Jewelry Ltd... 919 968-0011
201 S Estes Dr Ste 400d Chapel Hill (27514) *(G-2097)*

Williams & Son Logging LLC....................................... 252 533-9201
112 Steeplechase Run Roanoke Rapids (27870) *(G-13590)*

Williams Easy Hitch Inc... 919 302-0062
2310 Old Oxford Rd Durham (27704) *(G-5441)*

Williams Electric Mtr Repr Inc..................................... 919 859-9790
2515 Cox Mill Rd Ste A Sanford (27332) *(G-14206)*

Williams Industries Inc (PA).. 919 604-1746
1128 Tyler Farms Dr Raleigh (27603) *(G-13423)*

Williams Logging Inc... 919 542-2740
2371 Charlie Brooks Rd Moncure (27559) *(G-10630)*

Williams Machine & Tool, Laurel Hill *Also Called: Lawrence Williams (G-9464)*

Williams Mech & Wldg Svcs LLC................................ 919 820-5287
674 O W Ln Dunn (28334) *(G-4891)*

Williams Performance Inc... 704 603-4431
3140 Corriher Grange Rd Mount Ulla (28125) *(G-11688)*

Williams Plating Company Inc.................................... 828 681-0301
6 Industrial Dr Arden (28704) *(G-391)*

Williams Printing Inc.. 336 969-2733
286 Northstar Dr Ste 118 Rural Hall (27045) *(G-13856)*

Williams Printing Inc.. 336 969-2733
268 Northstar Dr Ste 118 Rural Hall (27045) *(G-13857)*

Williams Ready Mix Pdts Inc....................................... 704 283-1137
2465 Old Charlotte Hwy Monroe (28110) *(G-10834)*

Williams Seafood Arapahoe Inc.................................. 252 249-0594
2383 Don Lee Rd Arapahoe (28510) *(G-262)*

Williams Signs... 828 321-2338
1025 Main St Andrews (28901) *(G-129)*

Williams Skin Co.. 910 323-2628
1812 Sapona Rd Fayetteville (28312) *(G-5954)*

Williams United LLC.. 336 251-7355
843 Burke Hollow Rd Kernersville (27284) *(G-9253)*

Williamsburg Woodcraft Inc.. 919 965-3363
4901 Nc Highway 96 N Selma (27576) *(G-14263)*

Williamson Greenhouses Inc...................................... 910 592-7072
1469 Beulah Rd Clinton (28328) *(G-4118)*

Williamson Mead & Brewing LLC............................... 661 827-7290
3047 Shawtown Rd Glade Valley (28627) *(G-6573)*

Williamson Mead and Brewing, Glade Valley *Also Called: Williamson Mead & Brewing LLC (G-6573)*

Willis Consulting, Charlotte *Also Called: Goldmine Software (G-2845)*

Willis Defense LLC... 704 609-9953
802 Amity Church Rd Iron Station (28080) *(G-8978)*

Willis Manufacturing, Conover *Also Called: Willis Manufacturing Inc (G-4513)*

Willis Manufacturing Inc... 828 244-0435
1924 Emmanuel Church Rd Conover (28613) *(G-4513)*

Willow Creek Furniture Inc.. 336 889-0076
1949 W Green Dr High Point (27260) *(G-8604)*

Willow Oak Woodworks... 919 906-1232
430 Charlie Monk Rd Hurdle Mills (27541) *(G-8915)*

Willow Street Plant, Mount Airy *Also Called: Renfro LLC (G-11564)*

Willow Tex LLC... 336 789-1009
501 Piedmont Triad West Dr Mount Airy (27030) *(G-11595)*

Willowcroft... 704 540-0367
15301 Marvin Rd Charlotte (28277) *(G-3815)*

Wilmington Box Company... 910 259-0402
101 Industrial Dr Burgaw (28425) *(G-1358)*

Wilmington Camera Service LLC............................... 910 343-1089
905 N 23rd St Wilmington (28405) *(G-16444)*

Wilmington Compost Company LLC.......................... 910 839-3011
1800 Eastwood Rd Apt 232 Wilmington (28403) *(G-16445)*

Wilmington Concrete Plant, Wilmington *Also Called: S T Wooten Corporation (G-16391)*

Wilmington Funeral & Cremation, Wilmington *Also Called: Wilmington Mortuary Svc Inc (G-16449)*

Wilmington Journal Company..................................... 910 762-5502
412 S 7th St Wilmington (28401) *(G-16446)*

Wilmington Journal, The, Wilmington *Also Called: Wilmington Journal Company (G-16446)*

Wilmington Machine Works Inc................................... 910 343-8111
3416 Enterprise Dr Wilmington (28405) *(G-16447)*

Wilmington Machinery Inc... 910 452-5090
4628 Northchase Pkwy Ne Wilmington (28405) *(G-16448)*

Wilmington Mortuary Svc Inc...................................... 910 791-9099
1535 41st St Wilmington (28403) *(G-16449)*

Wilmington National Peening, Statesville *Also Called: National Peening Inc (G-14850)*

Wilmington Rbr & Gasket Co Inc................................ 910 762-4262
321 Raleigh St Wilmington (28412) *(G-16450)*

Wilmington Record Center, Wilmington *Also Called: Raleigh Ventures Inc (G-16377)*

Wilmington Scentific Publr LLC.................................. 910 228-1974
890 S Kerr Ave Ste 1 Wilmington (28403) *(G-16451)*

Wilmington Star-News Inc (HQ)................................. 910 343-2000
1003 S 17th St Ste 112 Wilmington (28401) *(G-16452)*

Wilmington Today LLC.. 910 509-7195
1213 Culbreth Dr Wilmington (28405) *(G-16453)*

Wilmington Wine LLC.. 910 202-4749
605 Castle St Wilmington (28401) *(G-16454)*

Wilmongton Trffic Neighborhood............................... 910 341-7888
206 Operation Center Dr Wilmington (28412) *(G-16455)*

Wilmore Electronics, Hillsborough *Also Called: Wilmore Electronics Company Inc (G-8672)*

Wilmore Electronics Company Inc (PA)..................... 919 732-9351
607 Us Highway 70a E Hillsborough (27278) *(G-8672)*

Wilo Incorporated (DH).. 336 679-4440
350 W Maple St Yadkinville (27055) *(G-17063)*

Wilson Billboard Advg Inc.. 919 934-2421
212 Bridge St Smithfield (27577) *(G-14489)*

Wilson Bros Logging Inc... 252 445-5317
72 Gennie Rd Enfield (27823) *(G-5682)*

Wilson Brown Inc... 336 226-0237
2220 Anthony Rd Burlington (27215) *(G-1518)*

Wilson Concrete Plant, Wilson *Also Called: S T Wooten Corporation (G-16537)*

Wilson Daily Times Inc.. 252 243-5151
126 Nash St. W Wilson (27893) *(G-16561)*

Wilson Grading LLC.. 919 778-1580
132 Blue Bird Ln Goldsboro (27534) *(G-6671)*

Wilson Iron Works Incorporated (PA)........................ 252 291-4465
600 S Washington St Rocky Mount (27801) *(G-13677)*

Wilson Logging Nc LLC.. 336 280-8648
6308 Autumn Crest Ct Summerfield (27358) *(G-14994)*

Wilson Machine & Tool Inc... 919 776-0043
4956 Womack Rd Sanford (27330) *(G-14207)*

Wilson Machine Sho.. 910 673-3505
333 Hoffman Rd West End (27376) *(G-15935)*

Wilson Marble, Marion *Also Called: Marion Cultured Marble Inc (G-10157)*

Wilson Mold & Machine Corp..................................... 252 243-1831
2131 Nc Highway 42 E Wilson (27893) *(G-16562)*

Wilson Outpatient Imaging.. 252 399-7430
1711 Medical Park Dr W Wilson (27893) *(G-16563)*

Wilson Signs, Smithfield *Also Called: Wilson Billboard Advg Inc (G-14489)*

Wilson Tire and Automotive Inc.................................. 336 584-9638
1807 N Nc Highway 87 Elon College (27244) *(G-5668)*

Wilson Trophy & Hayes EMB, Wilson *Also Called: Rhyno Enterprises (G-16532)*

Wilson Wldg & Line Boring LLC................................. 828 406-2078
1263 Charlie Thompson Rd Vilas (28692) *(G-15499)*

Wilson-Cook Medical Inc... 336 744-0157
5941 Grassy Creek Blvd Winston Salem (27105) *(G-16976)*

Wilson-Cook Medical Inc..336 744-0157
4900 Bethania Station Rd Winston Salem (27105) *(G-16977)*

Wilson-Cook Medical Inc., Winston Salem Also Called: Cook Incorporated *(G-16661)*

Wilsonart LLC...866 267-7360
145 Cane Creek Industrial Park Rd Fletcher (28732) *(G-6052)*

Wilsonepes Printing...252 224-0248
1714 Neuse Blvd New Bern (28560) *(G-11858)*

Wilsons Planning & Consulting...919 592-0935
1402 Harth Dr Garner (27529) *(G-6326)*

Winchester Woodworks..828 421-2693
168 Foothill Ln Waynesville (28786) *(G-15833)*

Wind Chime Plaza...919 848-9715
185 Wind Chime Ct Ste 104 Raleigh (27615) *(G-13424)*

Wind Defender LLC...410 913-4660
2690 Salisbury Hwy Statesville (28677) *(G-14926)*

Wind Shear Inc (PA)...704 788-9463
1050 Ivey Cline Rd Concord (28027) *(G-4390)*

Windak Inc...828 322-2292
1661 4th St Sw Conover (28613) *(G-4514)*

Windco LLC...704 846-6029
1505 Turring Dr Ste B Indian Trail (28079) *(G-8971)*

Windlift, Durham Also Called: Windlift Inc *(G-5442)*

Windlift Inc...919 490-8575
2445 S Alston Ave Durham (27713) *(G-5442)*

Window Motor World Inc..800 252-2649
779 Ball Branch Rd Boone (28607) *(G-1250)*

Windows & More, Morehead City Also Called: Eskimo 7 Limited *(G-11171)*

Windridge Sensors LLC..919 272-8714
209 Sunset Grove Dr Holly Springs (27540) *(G-8727)*

Windsor Fiberglass Inc..910 259-0057
301 Progress Dr Burgaw (28425) *(G-1359)*

Windsor Gallery, Salisbury Also Called: Speed Brite Inc *(G-14046)*

Windsor Run Cellars Inc...336 998-6598
264 James Way Advance (27006) *(G-53)*

Windsor Window Company..704 283-7459
2210 Stafford Street Ext Monroe (28110) *(G-10835)*

Windsor Window Company..704 283-7459
2210 Stafford Street Ext Monroe (28110) *(G-10836)*

Windsors Cbnetry For Kit Baths.......................................336 275-0190
1816 Pembroke Rd Ste 2 Greensboro (27408) *(G-7462)*

Windsurfing Hatteras, Avon Also Called: North Sports Inc *(G-845)*

Wine and Canvas Studio..251 591-7219
8320 Pineville Matthews Rd Ste 602 Charlotte (28226) *(G-3816)*

Winecoff Memorials, Statesville Also Called: Winecoff Mmrals Sttesville Inc *(G-14927)*

Winecoff Mmrals Sttesville Inc..704 873-9661
2120 Newton Dr Statesville (28677) *(G-14927)*

Winery Assoc Southeast Inc..919 219-1929
120 Trinity Grove Dr Cary (27513) *(G-1927)*

Winery At The Blueberry Farm, Banner Elk Also Called: Banner Elk Winery Inc *(G-892)*

Winfield Woodworks..828 808-9727
20 American Way Fletcher (28732) *(G-6053)*

Wingfield House of Peace..719 251-0618
2024 Trinity Dr Nashville (27856) *(G-11756)*

Wings Store 765..910 458-0278
1014 Lake Park Blvd N Carolina Beach (28428) *(G-1642)*

Winkler Knives, Boone Also Called: Daniel Winkler Knifemaker LLC *(G-1192)*

Wins Smokehouse Services Ltd..828 884-7476
45 S Ridge Rd Pisgah Forest (28768) *(G-12330)*

Winso Dsgns Screenprinting LLC.....................................704 967-5776
7027 Orr Rd Ste F Charlotte (28213) *(G-3817)*

Winstn-Slem Chronicle Pubg Inc......................................336 722-8624
1300 E 5th St Winston Salem (27101) *(G-16978)*

Winstn-Slem Inds For Blind Inc (PA)...............................336 759-0551
7730 N Point Blvd Winston Salem (27106) *(G-16979)*

Winston Concept Furniture...336 472-7839
1110 Lexington Ave Thomasville (27360) *(G-15302)*

Winston Packaging Division, Winston Salem Also Called: Winston Printing Company *(G-16980)*

Winston Printing Company (PA).......................................336 896-7631
8095 N Point Blvd Winston Salem (27106) *(G-16980)*

Winston Salem Engraving Co...336 725-4268
446 Brookstown Ave Winston Salem (27101) *(G-16981)*

Winston Salem Journal...336 727-7211
418 N Marshall St Winston Salem (27101) *(G-16982)*

Winston Steel Stair Co...336 721-0020
216 Junia Ave Winston Salem (27127) *(G-16983)*

Winston Tool Company Inc..336 983-3722
1025 Gause Dr King (27021) *(G-9286)*

Winston-Salem Casket Company.....................................336 661-1695
4340 Indiana Ave Winston Salem (27105) *(G-16984)*

Winstons Woodworks..919 693-4120
600 Sunset Ave Oxford (27565) *(G-12161)*

Winter Bell Company (PA)...336 887-2651
2018 Brevard Rd High Point (27263) *(G-8605)*

Winter Custom Yachts Inc...910 325-7583
270 Hogans Rd Hubert (28539) *(G-8758)*

Winterville Machine Works Inc...252 756-2130
2672 Mill St Winterville (28590) *(G-17018)*

Winton Products Company..704 399-5151
2500 West Blvd Ste B Charlotte (28208) *(G-3818)*

Wiper Technologies, Greensboro Also Called: Global Products LLC *(G-7046)*

Wire Form, Aberdeen Also Called: Industrial Metal Products of *(G-7)*

Wire-Bond, Charlotte Also Called: Masonry Reinforcing Corp Amer *(G-3139)*

Wireless Communications NC, Charlotte Also Called: McShan Inc *(G-3154)*

Wirenet Inc..513 774-7759
16740 Birkdale Commons Pkwy Ste 306 Huntersville (28078) *(G-8906)*

Wireway/Husky Corp (PA)...704 483-1135
6146 Denver Industrial Park Rd Denver (28037) *(G-4815)*

Wirthwein New Bern Corp..252 634-2871
901 Industrial Dr New Bern (28562) *(G-11859)*

Wirtz Wire Edm LLC..828 696-0830
65a Commercial Hill Dr Hendersonville (28792) *(G-7915)*

Wisdom For Heart...866 482-4253
2703 Jones Franklin Rd Ste 105 Cary (27518) *(G-1928)*

Wisdom House Books Inc...919 883-4669
209 Kousa Trl Chapel Hill (27516) *(G-2098)*

Wise Living Inc...336 991-5346
216 Woodbine St High Point (27260) *(G-8606)*

Wise Storage Solutions LLC..336 789-5141
1372 Boggs Dr Mount Airy (27030) *(G-11596)*

Wishes Fulfilled..704 905-8228
5504 Birchfield Cir Waxhaw (28173) *(G-15790)*

Wispry Inc..919 854-7500
4001 Weston Pkwy St 200 Cary (27513) *(G-1929)*

Wit & Whistle...919 609-5309
929 Manchester Dr Cary (27511) *(G-1930)*

With Purpose Pressure Wshg LLC...................................336 965-9473
2702 Renee Dr Greensboro (27407) *(G-7463)*

Witherspoon Woodworks LLC...919 669-9103
812 Bryan St Raleigh (27605) *(G-13425)*

Witten Vent Company, Gastonia Also Called: WV Holdings Inc *(G-6544)*

Wix By Mel...973 479-0795
110 Sugarloaf Ct Carolina Beach (28428) *(G-1643)*

Wix Filters, Gastonia Also Called: Mann+hummel Filtration Technol *(G-6456)*

Wix Filtration Products, Gastonia Also Called: Mann+hummel Filtration Technol *(G-6455)*

Wizards Wood Werks..252 813-3929
7114 Shallingtons Mill Rd Macclesfield (27852) *(G-10067)*

Wlc Forklift Services LLC...336 345-2571
640 Tamco Rd Reidsville (27320) *(G-13546)*

Wlc LLC..336 852-6422
5509b W Friendly Ave Ste 201 Greensboro (27410) *(G-7464)*

Wldg Honeycutt & Fabrication..252 413-8754
1991 Sound Side Rd Columbia (27925) *(G-4171)*

Wmb of Wake County Inc...919 782-0419
2601 Glenwood Ave Raleigh (27608) *(G-13426)*

Wmc, Thomasville Also Called: Woempner Machine Company Inc *(G-15303)*

Wmf Americas Inc...704 882-3898
3521 Faith Church Rd Indian Trail (28079) *(G-8972)*

Wmf USA, Indian Trail Also Called: Wmf Americas Inc *(G-8972)*

Wmw Marine, Winterville Also Called: Winterville Machine Works Inc *(G-17018)*

Wmxf AM 1400...828 456-8661
54 N Main St Waynesville (28786) *(G-15834)*

ALPHABETIC SECTION — Woodward Compressor Sales

Wnc Cabinetry LLC 828 400-6492
730 N Main St Waynesville (28786) *(G-15835)*

Wnc Craft Beer Export LLC 828 407-9444
159 Burton St Asheville (28806) *(G-823)*

Wnc Dry Kiln Inc (PA) 828 652-0050
65 Jacktown Rd Marion (28752) *(G-10188)*

Wnc Homes & Realstate, Weaverville *Also Called: High Five Enterprises Inc (G-15848)*

Wnc Material Sales 828 658-8368
351 Flat Creek Church Rd Weaverville (28787) *(G-15869)*

Wnc Refab Inc 828 658-8368
125 Old Homestead Trl Weaverville (28787) *(G-15870)*

Wnc Starter, Asheville *Also Called: Blue Ridge Elc Mtr Repr Inc (G-564)*

Wnc White Corporation 828 477-4895
3563 Skyland Dr Sylva (28779) *(G-15076)*

Wnyh LLC 716 853-1800
155 Boyce Dr Mocksville (27028) *(G-10610)*

Wobo Wallet LLC 704 604-6041
5445 Somerset Ln Harrisburg (28075) *(G-7736)*

Woempner Machine Company Inc 336 475-2268
385 Lloyd Murphy Rd Thomasville (27360) *(G-15303)*

Wolf Timber LLC 252 799-0495
1040 David Rogerson Rd Williamston (27892) *(G-16074)*

Wolf X-Ray Corporation 631 242-9729
133 Wolf Rd Battleboro (27809) *(G-934)*

Wolfe Industries, Jamesville *Also Called: Stephen P Wolfe (G-9082)*

Wolfe Products Inc 919 645-7573
2617 Iveysprings Ct Apex (27539) *(G-260)*

Wolfpit Tactical 828 234-1279
1528 N Green St Morganton (28655) *(G-11269)*

Wolfspeed, Durham *Also Called: Wolfspeed Inc (G-5444)*

Wolfspeed Inc 919 407-5300
4601 Silicon Dr 3rd Fl Durham (27703) *(G-5443)*

Wolfspeed Inc (PA) 919 407-5300
4600 Silicon Dr Durham (27703) *(G-5444)*

Wolfspeed Employee Services Co 919 313-5300
4600 Silicon Dr Durham (27703) *(G-5445)*

Wolphs Wood Works Ltd 719 629-6350
374 Andrews Rd Trenton (28585) *(G-15337)*

Wolverine Mtal Stmping Sltons 919 774-4729
5720 Clyde Rhyne Dr Sanford (27330) *(G-14208)*

Wolverine Proctor, Lexington *Also Called: CPM Wolverine Proctor LLC (G-9700)*

Womack Newspaper Inc 336 316-1231
5500 Adams Farm Ln Ste 204 Greensboro (27407) *(G-7465)*

Womack Newspapers, Jamestown *Also Called: Jamestown News (G-9059)*

Womack Publishing Co Inc 919 732-2171
109 E King St Hillsborough (27278) *(G-8673)*

Womack Publishing Co Inc 252 586-2700
378 Lizard Creek Rd Littleton (27850) *(G-9954)*

Womack Publishing Co Inc 919 563-3555
106 N Fourth St Mebane (27302) *(G-10437)*

Womack Publishing Co Inc 704 660-5520
548 Williamson Rd Ste 3 Mooresville (28117) *(G-11131)*

Womack Publishing Co Inc 252 480-2234
2910 S Croatan Hwy Ste 19 Nags Head (27959) *(G-11730)*

Womack Publishing Co Inc 252 257-3341
112 N Main St Warrenton (27589) *(G-15663)*

Wood and Anvil, Hampstead *Also Called: Greg Price (G-7648)*

Wood Barn Inc (PA) 919 496-6714
206 Clifton Ridge Ct Louisburg (27549) *(G-10006)*

Wood Barn Inc 252 826-5538
476 Lees Meadow Rd Scotland Neck (27874) *(G-14225)*

Wood Country Creations LLC 704 545-5966
7901 Allen Black Rd Mint Hill (28227) *(G-10549)*

Wood Creations NC Inc 704 865-1822
2223 Plastics Dr Gastonia (28054) *(G-6542)*

Wood Designs, Monroe *Also Called: Wdm Inc (G-10831)*

Wood Done Right Inc 919 623-4557
525 Colony Woods Dr Chapel Hill (27517) *(G-2099)*

Wood Logging 910 866-4018
361 Gum Spring Rd White Oak (28399) *(G-15958)*

Wood Machine Service Inc 252 446-2142
2 Great State Ln Rocky Mount (27803) *(G-13742)*

Wood N Things 910 990-4448
139 Buckhorn Creek Ln Clinton (28328) *(G-4119)*

Wood Products Packg Intl Inc 704 279-3011
3725 Faith Rd Faith (28041) *(G-5726)*

Wood Right Lumber Company 910 576-4642
225 Basswood Rd Troy (27371) *(G-15420)*

Wood Surgeon 252 728-5767
1403 Lennoxville Rd Beaufort (28516) *(G-971)*

Wood Technology Inc (PA) 828 464-8049
1317 Emmanuel Church Rd Conover (28613) *(G-4515)*

Wood Tone Music Publishing 704 659-1064
287 Massey Deal Rd Statesville (28625) *(G-14928)*

Wood Tooling Shop, Wilmington *Also Called: IMS Usa LLC (G-16265)*

Wood Works 336 580-4134
722 Cannon Rd Greensboro (27410) *(G-7466)*

Wood Works 910 579-1487
9040 Forest Dr Sw Sunset Beach (28468) *(G-15004)*

Wood Works of Ahoskie LLC 252 287-7396
117 Williford Rd Ahoskie (27910) *(G-67)*

Wood-N-Boats Etc Inc 828 682-7470
500 Hawk Branch Rd Burnsville (28714) *(G-1536)*

Woodies Sun Express 704 332-7262
923 S Kings Dr Charlotte (28204) *(G-3819)*

Woodlake Wood Works 919 972-1000
2 Ontario Ct Durham (27713) *(G-5446)*

Woodland Hosiery Inc 910 439-4843
118 Hudson Ln Mount Gilead (27306) *(G-11616)*

Woodland Logging Inc 910 298-3350
596 Hallsville Rd Beulaville (28518) *(G-1099)*

Woodlane Envmtl Tech Inc 828 894-8383
111 Kangaroo Dr Columbus (28722) *(G-4182)*

Woodlawn Quality Plus 828 659-7721
3086 Us 221 N Marion (28752) *(G-10189)*

Woodlawn Tire & Alignment, Marion *Also Called: Woodlawn Tire and Algnmt Inc (G-10190)*

Woodlawn Tire and Algnmt Inc 828 756-4212
8021 Us 221 N Marion (28752) *(G-10190)*

Woodley Enterprises LLC 828 944-0653
22 Turtle Dr Maggie Valley (28751) *(G-10097)*

Woodline Inc 336 476-7100
4695 Turnpike Ct Thomasville (27360) *(G-15304)*

Woodmark Originals Inc 336 841-6409
1920 Jarrell St High Point (27260) *(G-8607)*

Woodmaster Custom Cabinets Inc 919 554-3707
436 Park Ave Youngsville (27596) *(G-17116)*

Woodmaster Woodworking, King *Also Called: Woodmasters Woodworking Inc (G-9287)*

Woodmasters Woodworking Inc 336 985-4000
402 Newsome Rd King (27021) *(G-9287)*

Woodmill Winery Inc 704 276-9911
1350 Woodmill Winery Ln Vale (28168) *(G-15473)*

Woodplay, Raleigh *Also Called: Family Industries Inc (G-12762)*

Woods At Grove Park 336 226-6171
2702 Monticello Ct Burlington (27215) *(G-1519)*

Woods At Lower River LLC 919 544-8044
125 Royal Sunset Dr Durham (27713) *(G-5447)*

Woods Cabinet Company Inc 919 207-1663
1302 N Johnson St Benson (27504) *(G-1046)*

Woods End LLC 910 470-0389
4917 Indian Corn Trl Castle Hayne (28429) *(G-1962)*

Woodshed Software 941 240-1780
925 Mainsail Rd Salisbury (28146) *(G-14067)*

Woodsmiths, Lenoir *Also Called: Woodsmiths Company (G-9661)*

Woodsmiths Company 406 626-3102
418 Prospect St Nw Lenoir (28645) *(G-9661)*

Woodtech/Interiors Inc 704 332-7215
2228 N Brevard St Charlotte (28206) *(G-3820)*

Woodteks LLC 336 244-1718
5243 Captains Trl Jonesville (28642) *(G-9103)*

Woodtreaters Inc 910 675-0038
224 Sawdust Rd Rocky Point (28457) *(G-13755)*

Woodward Compressor Sales, Charlotte *Also Called: Atlas Copco Compressors LLC (G-2236)*

Woodwizards Inc — ALPHABETIC SECTION

Woodwizards Inc 336 427-7698
 4214 Ellisboro Rd Stokesdale (27357) *(G-14952)*

Woodworking At Dinahs Landing 252 402-2248
 90 Dinahs Landing Rd Washington (27889) *(G-15740)*

Woodworking By Robt Wadde 704 236-0883
 218 K Line Dr Ste A Matthews (28104) *(G-10352)*

Woodworking Unlimited 252 235-5285
 6378 Vance St Bailey (27807) *(G-879)*

Woodworking Unlimited Inc 704 903-8080
 675 Bussell Rd Olin (28660) *(G-12108)*

Woodwright Co, Elm City *Also Called: Woodwright of Wilson Co Inc (G-5655)*

Woodwright of Wilson Co Inc 252 243-9663
 5753 Nc 58 Elm City (27822) *(G-5655)*

Woodys Chair Shop 828 765-9277
 784 Dale Rd Spruce Pine (28777) *(G-14661)*

Woodys Welding LLC 828 391-1484
 4576 Saint Pauls Church Rd Morganton (28655) *(G-11270)*

Wool Novelty, High Point *Also Called: Woolfoam Corporation (G-8608)*

Woolfoam Corporation 336 886-4964
 107 Whittier Ave High Point (27262) *(G-8608)*

Wooten Graphics Inc 336 731-4650
 172 Hinkle Ln Welcome (27374) *(G-15878)*

Wooten John 828 322-4031
 3763 1st Ave Sw Hickory (28602) *(G-8210)*

Worden Brothers Inc 919 202-8555
 6315 Boathouse Rd Wilmington (28403) *(G-16456)*

Work Custom LLC 704 488-3113
 5700 Copper Creek Ct Apt 11 Charlotte (28227) *(G-3821)*

Work Well Hydrtion Systems LLC 704 853-7788
 1680 Garfield Dr Gastonia (28052) *(G-6543)*

Workcom Inc 310 586-4000
 1001 Winstead Dr Cary (27513) *(G-1931)*

Workday Inc 919 703-2559
 4801 Glenwood Ave Ste 300 Raleigh (27612) *(G-13427)*

Workflowone 252 215-8880
 3914 Sterling Pointe Dr Unit 1 Winterville (28590) *(G-17019)*

Working Widget Technology LLC 704 684-6277
 7920 Alexander Rd Charlotte (28270) *(G-3822)*

Workman Publishing Co Inc 919 967-0108
 400 Silver Cedar Ct Ste 300 Chapel Hill (27514) *(G-2100)*

Workwear Outfitters LLC 877 824-0613
 No Physical Location Greensboro (27420) *(G-7467)*

World Art Gallery Incorporated 910 989-0203
 1116 Gum Branch Rd Jacksonville (28540) *(G-9047)*

World CAM LLC 704 655-1018
 8000 Tower Point Dr Charlotte (28227) *(G-3823)*

World Elastic Corporation (PA) 704 786-9508
 338 Webb Rd Concord (28025) *(G-4391)*

World Fibers Inc 704 788-3017
 231 Pounds Ave Sw Concord (28025) *(G-4392)*

World Fibers Inc 704 788-3017
 340 Industrial Ct Concord (28025) *(G-4393)*

World Fibers Inc (PA) 704 786-9508
 338 Webb Rd Concord (28025) *(G-4394)*

World Newspaper Publishing 704 548-1737
 8701 Mallard Creek Rd Charlotte (28262) *(G-3824)*

World of RC Parts 252 291-4088
 5320 Us Highway 301 Lucama (27851) *(G-10019)*

World Stone Fabricators Inc 704 372-9668
 4908 Hovis Rd Charlotte (28208) *(G-3825)*

World Stone of Sanford LLC 919 468-8450
 3201 Industrial Dr Sanford (27332) *(G-14209)*

World Wicks Candles 919 791-6123
 357 Gourd St Zebulon (27597) *(G-17146)*

World Wood Company 252 523-0021
 12045 Old Us Highway 70 Cove City (28523) *(G-4599)*

Worldgranite & Stoneart Inc 919 871-0678
 4600 Twisted Oaks Dr Apt 1505 Raleigh (27612) *(G-13428)*

Worldwide Entrmt Mltimedia LLC 704 208-6113
 11511 Sidney Crest Ave Charlotte (28213) *(G-3826)*

Worldwide Protective Pdts LLC (DH) 877 678-4568
 1409 World Wide Ln Wilkesboro (28697) *(G-16052)*

Worldwide Protective Pdts LLC 336 933-8035
 1404 River St Wilkesboro (28697) *(G-16053)*

Worldwide Protective Products, Wilkesboro *Also Called: Worldwide Protective Pdts LLC (G-16052)*

Wormfarmer 252 944-1012
 859 Betsy Elbow Rd Washington (27889) *(G-15741)*

Worsham Sprinkler Co Inc 704 805-9700
 3109 Westinghouse Blvd Charlotte (28273) *(G-3827)*

Worth Products LLC 252 747-9994
 856 Hwy 258 S Snow Hill (28580) *(G-14510)*

Worthington Cylinder Corp 336 777-8600
 1690 Lowery St Winston Salem (27101) *(G-16985)*

Worthyware Dsgns By D McHlle L 803 565-0615
 891 Seigle Point Dr # 101 Charlotte (28204) *(G-3828)*

Wovenart Inc 828 859-6349
 687 N Trade St Tryon (28782) *(G-15432)*

Wovern Art, Tryon *Also Called: Wovenart Inc (G-15432)*

Wp Reidsville LLC 336 342-1200
 109 Sands Rd Reidsville (27320) *(G-13547)*

WP Simmons Inc 336 789-3114
 205 N South St Mount Airy (27030) *(G-11597)*

Wph Ventures Inc 828 676-1700
 4 Commerce Way Arden (28704) *(G-392)*

Wpt LLC 704 770-1311
 1416 E Highway 218 Monroe (28110) *(G-10837)*

Wr Allen LLC 704 390-4032
 4100 Carmel Rd Charlotte (28226) *(G-3829)*

Wrangler, Greensboro *Also Called: Wrangler Apparel Corp (G-7468)*

Wrangler Apparel Corp 336 332-3400
 400 N Elm St Greensboro (27401) *(G-7468)*

Wrangler V K Jeans Wear, Greensboro *Also Called: VF Corporation (G-7440)*

Wrap Attack, Huntersville *Also Called: Cobb Clark Richard II (G-8804)*

Wre/Colortech, Greensboro *Also Called: Western Roto Engravers Incorporated (G-7457)*

Wreathsplusbylyn 252 281-3674
 7050 Gardners School Rd Stantonsburg (27883) *(G-14713)*

Wrenn Brothers Inc 919 742-3329
 902 S Chatham Ave Siler City (27344) *(G-14435)*

Wrenn Brothers Inc 919 742-3717
 1311 N 2nd Ave Siler City (27344) *(G-14436)*

Wright, Riegelwood *Also Called: Oak-Bark Corporation (G-13561)*

Wright & Hobbs Inc 252 537-5817
 105 W Becker Dr Roanoke Rapids (27870) *(G-13591)*

Wright Business Concepts Inc 828 466-1044
 1320 Fairgrove Church Rd Hickory (28603) *(G-8211)*

Wright Chemicals LLC 919 296-1771
 4804 Page Creek Ln Durham (27703) *(G-5448)*

Wright Electric Inc 704 435-6988
 3114 Tryon Courthouse Rd Cherryville (28021) *(G-3878)*

Wright Industries LLC 919 824-2936
 10841 Dry Stone Dr Huntersville (28078) *(G-8907)*

Wright Machine & Tool Co Inc 828 298-8440
 101 Jims Branch Rd Swannanoa (28778) *(G-15038)*

Wright of Thomasville Inc (PA) 336 472-4200
 5115 Prospect St Thomasville (27360) *(G-15305)*

Wright Printing Service Inc 336 427-4768
 1510 W Academy St Madison (27025) *(G-10092)*

Wright Roller Company 336 852-8393
 1800 Fairfax Rd Ste K Greensboro (27407) *(G-7469)*

Writ Press Inc 815 988-7074
 1308 N Duke St Durham (27701) *(G-5449)*

Write Good Stuff LLC 704 522-8242
 7237 Cornwell Ln Charlotte (28217) *(G-3830)*

Write Way Publishing Co LLC 919 606-2681
 322 Fox Hollow Dr Clayton (27527) *(G-4022)*

Writing Penn LLC 301 529-5324
 4400 Turnberry Cir Durham (27712) *(G-5450)*

Wrkco Inc 828 692-6254
 200 Tabor Rd East Flat Rock (28726) *(G-5480)*

Wrkco Inc 919 304-0300
 7411 Oakwood Street Ext Mebane (27302) *(G-10438)*

Wrkco Inc 828 287-9430
 300 Broyhill Rd Rutherfordton (28139) *(G-13903)*

ALPHABETIC SECTION — Yadkin Lumber Company Inc

Wrkco Inc 336 759-7501
8080 N Point Blvd Winston Salem (27106) *(G-16986)*

Wrkco Inc 770 448-2193
5900 Grassy Creek Blvd Winston Salem (27105) *(G-16987)*

Wrkco Inc 336 765-7004
3946 Westpoint Blvd Winston Salem (27103) *(G-16988)*

Wst Logging LLC 336 857-0147
7324 Checkmark Rd Denton (27239) *(G-4756)*

Wto Inc 704 714-7765
13900 S Lakes Dr Ste F Charlotte (28273) *(G-3831)*

Wtvd Television LLC 919 683-1111
411 Liberty St Durham (27701) *(G-5451)*

Wuko Inc 980 938-0512
3505 Associate Dr Greensboro (27405) *(G-7470)*

Wunderkind Press LLC 919 381-0713
601 Watts St Durham (27701) *(G-5452)*

Wurth Revcar Fasteners Inc 919 772-9930
800 N Greenfield Pkwy Ste 810 Garner (27529) *(G-6327)*

Wurtz Woodworks Llc 704 657-6584
117 Misty Spring Rd Troutman (28166) *(G-15399)*

WV Holdings Inc 704 853-8338
404 E Long Ave Gastonia (28054) *(G-6544)*

WW&s Construction Inc 217 620-4042
817 Dallas Spencer Mtn Rd Dallas (28034) *(G-4661)*

Wwj LLC (PA) 704 871-8500
1002 Bucks Industrial Rd Statesville (28625) *(G-14929)*

Www 123 Precious Metal Com, Wilmington *Also Called: 123 Precious Metal Ref LLC* *(G-16087)*

Www.candlevision.com, Marshville *Also Called: Paul Hoge Creations Inc (G-10221)*

Wyatt Woodworks 919 619-8593
1317 Spence Mill Rd Fuquay Varina (27526) *(G-6239)*

Wyeth Holdings LLC 919 775-7100
4300 Oak Park Rd Sanford (27330) *(G-14210)*

Wyeth Pharmaceutical Division, Sanford *Also Called: Wyeth Holdings LLC (G-14210)*

Wyoming Whiskey Inc 561 573-5605
170 Mooresville Commons Way Unit 218 Mooresville (28117) *(G-11132)*

Wyrick Machine and Tool Co 336 841-8261
1215 Kearns Hackett Rd Pleasant Garden (27313) *(G-12363)*

Wysong and Miles Company 336 621-3960
4820 Us 29 N Greensboro (27405) *(G-7471)*

Wysong Parts & Service, Greensboro *Also Called: Wysong and Miles Company (G-7471)*

Wysong Parts and Service, Greensboro *Also Called: Delta Phoenix Inc (G-6966)*

X-Celeprint Inc 919 248-0020
3021 Cornwallis Rd Bldg 1 Durham (27709) *(G-5453)*

X-Jet Technologies Inc 800 983-7467
142 Annaron Ct Raleigh (27603) *(G-13429)*

Xaloy Extrusion LLC 828 326-9888
1291 19th Street Ln Nw Hickory (28601) *(G-8212)*

Xarm Publishing Inc 888 717-3591
324 Ramona St Charlotte (28208) *(G-3832)*

Xavier Power Systems 910 734-7813
885 Shawn Rd Lumberton (28358) *(G-10061)*

XCEL Hrmetic Mtr Rewinding Inc 704 694-6001
2356 Bethel Rd Wadesboro (28170) *(G-15520)*

Xceldyne LLC 336 472-2242
37 High Tech Blvd Thomasville (27360) *(G-15306)*

Xceldyne Group LLC (PA) 336 472-2242
37 High Tech Blvd Thomasville (27360) *(G-15307)*

Xceldyne Technologies LLC 336 475-0201
37 High Tech Blvd Thomasville (27360) *(G-15308)*

Xcelerator Boatworks Inc (PA) 704 622-8978
154 Commerce Blvd Statesville (28625) *(G-14930)*

Xdri Inc 919 361-2155
4018 Patriot Dr Ste 100 Durham (27703) *(G-5454)*

Xelaqua Inc 919 964-4181
404b Glenwood Ave Raleigh (27603) *(G-13430)*

Xelera Inc 855 493-5372
10806 Reames Rd Ste Y Charlotte (28269) *(G-3833)*

Xelera Inc 540 915-6181
137 Cross Center Rd Denver (28037) *(G-4816)*

Xenial, Charlotte *Also Called: Xenial Inc (G-3834)*

Xenial Inc (DH) 800 253-8664
3420 Toringdon Way Ste 400 Charlotte (28277) *(G-3834)*

Xerium, Raleigh *Also Called: Andritz Fabrics and Rolls Inc (G-12506)*

Xerox Corporation 919 428-9718
11000 Weston Pkwy Cary (27513) *(G-1932)*

Xeroxdata Center 704 329-7245
1400 Cross Beam Dr Charlotte (28217) *(G-3835)*

Xilinx Inc 919 846-3922
220 Horizon Dr Ste 114 Raleigh (27615) *(G-13431)*

Xinray Systems Inc 919 701-4100
312 Silver Creek Trl Chapel Hill (27514) *(G-2101)*

Xintek Inc 919 449-5799
312 Silver Creek Trl Chapel Hill (27514) *(G-2102)*

Xl Paws Woodworking LLC 336 309-1173
221 Arlington Dr Cameron (28326) *(G-1565)*

Xo Signs 919 328-9110
414 Currin Rd Durham (27703) *(G-5455)*

Xona Microfluidics Inc 951 553-6400
76 Tw Alexander Dr Durham (27709) *(G-5456)*

Xp Climate Control LLC 828 266-2006
643 Greenway Rd Ste P Boone (28607) *(G-1251)*

Xpc Corporation 919 210-1756
3070 Business Park Dr Ste 108 Raleigh (27610) *(G-13432)*

Xpc Corporation 800 582-4524
7239 Acc Blvd Raleigh (27617) *(G-13433)*

Xpertees Prfmce Screen Prtg 910 763-7703
1406 Castle Hayne Rd Ste 2 Wilmington (28401) *(G-16457)*

Xpres LLC 336 245-1596
111 Cloverleaf Dr Winston Salem (27103) *(G-16989)*

Xpress Line, Winston Salem *Also Called: Encore Group Inc (G-16696)*

Xpress Powder Coat, Gastonia *Also Called: Champion Powdercoating Inc (G-6374)*

Xre Performance Engines LLC 704 663-3505
138 Quiet View Dr Mooresville (28115) *(G-11133)*

Xschem Inc (PA) 919 379-3500
1500 Perimeter Park Dr Ste 300 Morrisville (27560) *(G-11467)*

Xsport Global Inc 212 541-6222
1800 Camden Rd # 107-196 Charlotte (28203) *(G-3836)*

Xsys Global, Arden *Also Called: Xsys North America Corporation (G-393)*

Xsys North America Corporation 828 654-6805
95 Glenn Bridge Rd Arden (28704) *(G-393)*

Xsys North America Corporation 828 687-2485
25 Old Shoals Rd Arden (28704) *(G-394)*

Xsys North America Corporation (DH) 704 504-2626
2915 Whitehall Park Dr Ste 600 Charlotte (28273) *(G-3837)*

Xterior Sales & Service, Raleigh *Also Called: B&C Xterior Cleaning Svc Inc (G-12540)*

Xtinguish LLC 704 868-9500
3021 N Myers St Charlotte (28205) *(G-3838)*

Xtra Light Manufacturing 919 422-7281
1301 Davis Dr Apex (27523) *(G-261)*

Xtreme Fabrication Ltd 336 472-4562
25b High Tech Blvd Thomasville (27360) *(G-15309)*

Xtreme Graphix 704 746-5744
10060 Unity Church Rd Mooresville (28115) *(G-11134)*

Xtreme Postcard Profits System 919 894-8886
22 Boardwalk Ave Benson (27504) *(G-1047)*

Xtreme Power Conversion, Raleigh *Also Called: Xpc Corporation (G-13433)*

Xxxtreme Motorsport 704 663-1500
292 Rolling Hill Rd Mooresville (28117) *(G-11135)*

Xylem, Charlotte *Also Called: Wedeco Uv Technologies Inc (G-3802)*

Xylem Inc 919 772-4126
1328 Bobbitt Dr Garner (27529) *(G-6328)*

Xylem Lnc (DH) 704 409-9700
4828 Parkway Plaza Blvd # 200 Charlotte (28217) *(G-3839)*

Xylem Water Solutions USA Inc (HQ) 704 409-9700
4828 Parkway Plaza Blvd Ste 200 Charlotte (28217) *(G-3840)*

Xylem Water Solutions USA Inc 704 409-9700
14125 S Bridge Cir Charlotte (28273) *(G-3841)*

Yackety Yack Publishing Inc 919 843-5092
Chapel Hill (27514) *(G-2103)*

Yadkin Lumber Company Inc 336 679-2432
800 N State St Yadkinville (27055) *(G-17064)*

ALPHABETIC SECTION

Yadkin Valley Cabinet Co Inc.. 336 786-9860
    135 Red Laurel Ln Mount Airy (27030) *(G-11598)*
Yadkin Valley Herbs Inc... 336 468-4062
    6324 Laurel Gray Ln Hamptonville (27020) *(G-7681)*
Yadkin Valley Paving, Winston Salem *Also Called: Cloverleaf Mixing Inc (G-16655)*
Yadkin Valley Wine Company... 336 467-0257
    6324 Laurel Gray Ln Hamptonville (27020) *(G-7682)*
Yale Industrial Products, Inc., Charlotte *Also Called: Duff-Norton Company Inc (G-2656)*
Yale Material Handling, Greenville *Also Called: Gregory Poole Equipment Co (G-7535)*
Yale Materials Handling, Greenville *Also Called: Hyster-Yale Group Inc (G-7542)*
Yale Rope Technologies Inc... 704 630-0331
    634 Industrial Ave Salisbury (28144) *(G-14068)*
Yamco LLC... 252 747-9267
    310 Kingold Blvd Snow Hill (28580) *(G-14511)*
Yancey Common Times Journal, Burnsville *Also Called: Times Journal Inc (G-1535)*
Yancey Stone Inc.. 828 682-2645
    19 Crushing Rd Burnsville (28714) *(G-1537)*
Yancey Stone Inc.. 828 684-5522
    5 Williams Rd Fletcher (28732) *(G-6054)*
Yancy Common Times Journal... 828 682-2120
    22 N Main St Burnsville (28714) *(G-1538)*
Yancy County Common Times, Burnsville *Also Called: Yancy Common Times Journal (G-1538)*
Yanek LLC.. 252 558-3757
    303 Elm St Snow Hill (28580) *(G-14512)*
Yang Mine Lines, Charlotte *Also Called: Yang Ming America Corporation (G-3842)*
Yang Ming America Corporation... 704 357-3817
    11124 Ascoli Pl Charlotte (28277) *(G-3842)*
Yanjan USA LLC... 704 380-6230
    159 Walker Rd Statesville (28625) *(G-14931)*
Yat Usa Inc.. 480 584-4096
    10506 Bryton Corporate Center Dr Huntersville (28078) *(G-8908)*
Yates American Machine Company.. 336 685-5118
    5309 Burrow Rd Julian (27283) *(G-9109)*
Yates Precision Machining LLC... 704 662-7165
    133 Byers Creek Rd Unit D Mooresville (28117) *(G-11136)*
Yates Wilbert Vault LLC... 704 399-8453
    2839 Rosemont St Charlotte (28208) *(G-3843)*
Yats Stone Masonry Llc... 919 841-2297
    7425 Buck Rd Wendell (27591) *(G-15925)*
Yeeka LLC.. 919 308-9826
    11 Yarmouth Pl Durham (27707) *(G-5457)*
Yellow Dog Design Inc.. 336 553-2172
    112 Oconnor St Greensboro (27406) *(G-7472)*
Yellow Rubber Ball LLC.. 919 357-6307
    4100 Five Oaks Dr Unit 41 Durham (27707) *(G-5458)*
Yelton Milling Co, Spindale *Also Called: Lakeside Mills Inc (G-14607)*
Yentiyahs Naturals LLC... 919 295-4279
    3601 Deering Dr Raleigh (27616) *(G-13434)*
Yepzy Inc... 855 461-2678
    57 Union St S Pmb 1234 Concord (28025) *(G-4395)*
Yes Weekly, Greensboro *Also Called: Womack Newspaper Inc (G-7465)*
Yesco, Greensboro *Also Called: Yesco Sign Lighting Service (G-7473)*
Yesco Sign Lighting Service... 336 285-0795
    5710 W Gate City Blvd Ste K-190 Greensboro (27407) *(G-7473)*
Yg-1 America Inc... 980 318-5348
    11001 Park Charlotte Blvd Charlotte (28273) *(G-3844)*
Yildiz Entegre Usa Inc... 910 763-4733
    1715 Woodbine St Wilmington (28401) *(G-16458)*
YKK AP America Inc... 336 665-1963
    4524 Green Point Dr Ste 106 Greensboro (27410) *(G-7474)*
Yo Zone... 336 270-5262
    309 Huffman Mill Rd Burlington (27215) *(G-1520)*
Yogasleep, Wilmington *Also Called: Marpac LLC (G-16315)*
Yontz & Sons Painting Inc... 336 784-7099
    3803 S Main St Winston Salem (27127) *(G-16990)*
Yorkshire House Inc.. 336 869-9714
    1904 Alleghany St High Point (27263) *(G-8609)*
Young & McQueen Grading Co Inc... 828 682-7714
    25 Crest View Rd Burnsville (28714) *(G-1539)*
Young & Son Mfg LLC.. 704 799-1658
    129 Loc Doc Pl Unit B Mooresville (28115) *(G-11137)*
Young Bat Enterprises Inc... 828 376-3706
    360 Jackson Rd Fletcher (28732) *(G-6055)*
Young Fabrication... 828 776-3203
    265 Morgan Branch Rd Leicester (28748) *(G-9522)*
Young Graphics Inc.. 336 249-3148
    10 Echoview Cir Lexington (27292) *(G-9803)*
Young Logging Company Inc... 919 552-9753
    1517 Clayton Rd Willow Spring (27592) *(G-16085)*
Young Wood Works LLC.. 704 654-1722
    6109 King George Dr Charlotte (28213) *(G-3845)*
Youngs Welding & Machine Svcs... 910 488-1190
    787 Mcarthur Rd Fayetteville (28311) *(G-5955)*
Your Cabinet Connection Inc.. 919 641-2877
    10315 Chapel Hill Rd Morrisville (27560) *(G-11468)*
Your Choice Pregnancy Clinic... 919 577-9050
    607 N Ennis St Fuquay Varina (27526) *(G-6240)*
Your Fire Source Inc.. 828 669-9000
    201 Black Mountain Ave Black Mountain (28711) *(G-1142)*
Your Source For Printing... 704 957-5922
    8116 S Tryon St Charlotte (28273) *(G-3846)*
Yourlogowear.. 704 664-1290
    18700 Statesville Rd Cornelius (28031) *(G-4595)*
Youshirt, Clayton *Also Called: Noble Wholesalers Inc (G-4001)*
Yp Advrtising Pubg LLC Not LLC.. 704 522-5500
    9144 Arrowpoint Blvd Ste 150 Charlotte (28273) *(G-3847)*
Yp Advrtising Pubg LLC Not LLC.. 910 794-5151
    2250 Shipyard Blvd Wilmington (28403) *(G-16459)*
Yukon Inc... 919 366-2001
    485 Old Wilson Rd Ste 8 Wendell (27591) *(G-15926)*
Yukon Medical LLC.. 919 595-8250
    4021 Stirrup Creek Dr Ste 200 Durham (27703) *(G-5459)*
Yummy Tummy Ga LLC.. 704 658-0445
    2105 Brawley School Rd Mooresville (28117) *(G-11138)*
Z Collection LLC.. 919 247-1513
    77 Gennessee Dr Zebulon (27597) *(G-17147)*
Z-Bake Custom Picture Framing.. 919 848-4931
    8412 Aptos Ct Raleigh (27613) *(G-13435)*
Zack Noble Metalworks LLC... 828 688-3468
    4 Blackberry Ln Asheville (28804) *(G-824)*
Zagros Sadjadi Software.. 336 848-8171
    2968 Shady View Dr High Point (27265) *(G-8610)*
Zarges Inc... 704 357-6285
    1440 Center Park Dr Charlotte (28217) *(G-3848)*
Zeal Industries LLC... 828 575-9894
    101 Bee Ridge Rd Asheville (28803) *(G-825)*
Zealousweb... 619 354-3216
    7404 Bosson St Sw Concord (28025) *(G-4396)*
Zebra Communications Inc (PA)... 919 314-3700
    9401 Globe Center Dr Ste 130 Morrisville (27560) *(G-11469)*
Zebra Print Solutions, Morrisville *Also Called: Zebra Communications Inc (G-11469)*
Zebra Technologies, Charlotte *Also Called: Zebra Technologies Corporation (G-3849)*
Zebra Technologies Corporation... 704 517-5271
    9075 Meadowmont View Dr Charlotte (28269) *(G-3849)*
Zekelman Industries Inc.. 704 560-6768
    111 Pin Oak Ln Mooresville (28117) *(G-11139)*
Zelaya Bros LLC... 980 833-0099
    3525 Ritch Ave Charlotte (28206) *(G-3850)*
Zemex Industrial Minerals Inc.. 828 765-5500
    797 Altapass Hwy Spruce Pine (28777) *(G-14662)*
Zenecar LLC.. 919 518-0464
    10224 Durant Rd Ste 201 Raleigh (27614) *(G-13436)*
Zengerle Industries Inc... 919 240-5415
    705 Wellington Dr Chapel Hill (27514) *(G-2104)*
Zenith Pumps, Monroe *Also Called: IMO Industries Inc (G-10737)*
Zeon Technologies Inc... 704 680-9160
    425 Lash Dr Salisbury (28147) *(G-14069)*
Zeri Consulting Inc.. 412 512-2027
    114 Salt Marsh Cv Sneads Ferry (28460) *(G-14494)*
Zeskp LLC.. 910 762-8300
    2027 Capital Dr Wilmington (28405) *(G-16460)*

ALPHABETIC SECTION

Zeta Performance Vhcl Tech LLC..804 690-8979
  11148 Treynorth Dr Ste C Cornelius (28031) *(G-4596)*

ZF Chassis Components LLC..828 468-3711
  1570 E P Street Ext Newton (28658) *(G-11986)*

ZF Lemforder, Newton *Also Called: ZF Chassis Components LLC (G-11986)*

Zibra LLC (PA)..704 271-4503
  172 Broad Sound Pl Mooresville (28117) *(G-11140)*

Zickgraf Enterprises Inc...828 524-2313
  231 Depot St Franklin (28734) *(G-6149)*

Zickgraf Enterprises Inc...704 369-1200
  301 Depot St Franklin (28734) *(G-6150)*

Ziehl-Abegg Inc (DH)..336 834-9339
  719 N Regional Rd Greensboro (27409) *(G-7475)*

Zimmermann - Dynayarn Usa LLC..336 222-8129
  327 E Elm St Graham (27253) *(G-6717)*

Zingerle Group Usa Inc..704 312-1600
  6965 Northpark Blvd Charlotte (28216) *(G-3851)*

Zink, Whitsett *Also Called: Zink Imaging Inc (G-16006)*

Zink Holdings LLC..336 449-8000
  6900 Konica Dr Whitsett (27377) *(G-16005)*

Zink Imaging Inc..336 449-8000
  6900 Konica Dr Whitsett (27377) *(G-16006)*

Zion Industries Inc...828 397-2701
  9480 Neuville Ave Hildebran (28637) *(G-8629)*

Zippy Ice Inc (PA)..980 355-9851
  5701 N Graham St Charlotte (28269) *(G-3852)*

Ziptronix Inc..919 459-2400
  800 Perimeter Park Dr Ste B Morrisville (27560) *(G-11470)*

Zndus Inc (DH)...704 981-8660
  214 James Farm Rd Statesville (28625) *(G-14932)*

Zoallc...910 215-0235
  131 Ampersand Rd Aberdeen (28315) *(G-36)*

Zoes Kitchen Inc..336 748-0587
  205 S Stratford Rd Winston Salem (27103) *(G-16991)*

Zoetic Digital Development..919 720-5945
  401 Scripps Lane Unit 104 Raleigh (27610) *(G-13437)*

Zoetis Inc...919 941-5185
  1040 Swabia Ct Durham (27703) *(G-5460)*

Zoetis Products LLC...336 333-9356
  620 S Elm St Ste 363 Greensboro (27406) *(G-7476)*

Zoeys Btq Style Spclty Trats..910 808-1778
  896 Shawtown Rd Lillington (27546) *(G-9862)*

Zonkd LLC...919 977-6463
  2419 Atlantic Ave Raleigh (27604) *(G-13438)*

Zonnic, Winston Salem *Also Called: Modoral Brands Inc (G-16815)*

Zoom Apparel Inc (PA)..336 993-9666
  303 S Broad St Winston Salem (27101) *(G-16992)*

Zumco Inc..828 891-3300
  199 Forest Knolls Pl Horse Shoe (28742) *(G-8743)*

Zurn Elkay Wtr Solutions Corp...910 501-1853
  102 Elkay Way Lumberton (28358) *(G-10062)*

Zurn Elkay Wtr Solutions Corp...855 663-9876
  5900 Elwin Buchanan Dr Sanford (27330) *(G-14211)*

Zurn Industries LLC...919 775-2255
  5900 Elwin Buchanan Dr Sanford (27330) *(G-14212)*

Zwz Bearing USA, Lincolnton *Also Called: Zwz Bearing USA Inc (G-9937)*

Zwz Bearing USA Inc..734 456-6206
  1574 Startown Rd Lincolnton (28092) *(G-9937)*

Zysense LLC...215 485-1955
  6701 Glen Forrest Dr Chapel Hill (27517) *(G-2105)*

PRODUCT INDEX

- Product categories are listed in alphabetical order.

A

ABRASIVE STONES, EXC GRINDING STONES: Ground Or Whole
ABRASIVES
ABRASIVES: Coated
ACCELERATION INDICATORS & SYSTEM COMPONENTS: Aerospace
ACCELEROMETERS
ACID RESIST: Etching
ACIDS: Sulfuric, Oleum
ACOUSTICAL BOARD & TILE
ACRYLIC RESINS
ACTUATORS: Indl, NEC
ADDITIVE BASED PLASTIC MATERIALS: Plasticizers
ADHESIVES
ADHESIVES & SEALANTS
ADHESIVES: Adhesives, plastic
ADHESIVES: Epoxy
ADRENAL DERIVATIVES
ADVERTISING AGENCIES
ADVERTISING AGENCIES: Consultants
ADVERTISING CURTAINS
ADVERTISING DISPLAY PRDTS
ADVERTISING REPRESENTATIVES: Newspaper
ADVERTISING SPECIALTIES, WHOLESALE
ADVERTISING SVCS: Direct Mail
ADVERTISING SVCS: Display
ADVERTISING SVCS: Outdoor
AERIAL WORK PLATFORMS
AEROSOLS
AGENTS, BROKERS & BUREAUS: Personal Service
AGRICULTURAL DISINFECTANTS
AGRICULTURAL EQPT: BARN, SILO, POULTRY, DAIRY/LIVESTOCK MACH
AGRICULTURAL EQPT: Fertilizing Machinery
AGRICULTURAL EQPT: Fertilizng, Sprayng, Dustng/Irrigatn Mach
AGRICULTURAL EQPT: Grounds Mowing Eqpt
AGRICULTURAL EQPT: Spreaders, Fertilizer
AGRICULTURAL EQPT: Turf & Grounds Eqpt
AGRICULTURAL MACHINERY & EQPT: Wholesalers
AIR CLEANING SYSTEMS
AIR CONDITIONERS: Motor Vehicle
AIR CONDITIONING & VENTILATION EQPT & SPLYS: Wholesales
AIR CONDITIONING EQPT
AIR CONDITIONING EQPT, WHOLE HOUSE: Wholesalers
AIR CONDITIONING REPAIR SVCS
AIR CONDITIONING UNITS: Complete, Domestic Or Indl
AIR MATTRESSES: Plastic
AIR POLLUTION MEASURING SVCS
AIR PURIFICATION EQPT
AIRCRAFT & AEROSPACE FLIGHT INSTRUMENTS & GUIDANCE SYSTEMS
AIRCRAFT & HEAVY EQPT REPAIR SVCS
AIRCRAFT ASSEMBLY PLANTS
AIRCRAFT ENGINES & ENGINE PARTS: Air Scoops
AIRCRAFT ENGINES & ENGINE PARTS: Airfoils
AIRCRAFT ENGINES & ENGINE PARTS: Mount Parts
AIRCRAFT ENGINES & ENGINE PARTS: Research & Development, Mfr
AIRCRAFT ENGINES & PARTS
AIRCRAFT EQPT & SPLYS WHOLESALERS
AIRCRAFT FLIGHT INSTRUMENT REPAIR SVCS
AIRCRAFT LIGHTING
AIRCRAFT MAINTENANCE & REPAIR SVCS
AIRCRAFT PARTS & AUXILIARY EQPT: Assemblies, Fuselage
AIRCRAFT PARTS & AUXILIARY EQPT: Assys, Subassemblies/Parts
AIRCRAFT PARTS & AUXILIARY EQPT: Bodies
AIRCRAFT PARTS & AUXILIARY EQPT: Body Assemblies & Parts
AIRCRAFT PARTS & AUXILIARY EQPT: Military Eqpt & Armament
AIRCRAFT PARTS & AUXILIARY EQPT: Research & Development, Mfr
AIRCRAFT PARTS & AUXILIARY EQPT: Tanks, Fuel
AIRCRAFT PARTS & EQPT, NEC
AIRCRAFT PARTS WHOLESALERS
AIRCRAFT SEATS
AIRCRAFT SERVICING & REPAIRING
AIRCRAFT: Airplanes, Fixed Or Rotary Wing
AIRCRAFT: Motorized
AIRCRAFT: Research & Development, Manufacturer
AIRPORTS, FLYING FIELDS & SVCS
ALARMS: Burglar
ALARMS: Fire
ALCOHOL: Ethyl & Ethanol
ALKALIES & CHLORINE
ALTERNATORS: Automotive
ALUMINUM
ALUMINUM PRDTS
ALUMINUM: Ingots & Slabs
ALUMINUM: Ingots, Primary
ALUMINUM: Rolling & Drawing
AMMUNITION: Cartridges Case, 30 mm & Below
AMMUNITION: Components
AMMUNITION: Small Arms
AMPLIFIERS
AMPLIFIERS: RF & IF Power
AMUSEMENT & RECREATION SVCS: Art Gallery, Commercial
AMUSEMENT ARCADES
AMUSEMENT MACHINES: Coin Operated
AMUSEMENT PARK DEVICES & RIDES
ANALGESICS
ANALYZERS: Blood & Body Fluid
ANALYZERS: Moisture
ANALYZERS: Network
ANALYZERS: Respiratory
ANESTHESIA EQPT
ANIMAL FEED & SUPPLEMENTS: Livestock & Poultry
ANIMAL FEED: Wholesalers
ANIMAL FOOD & SUPPLEMENTS: Chicken Feeds, Prepared
ANIMAL FOOD & SUPPLEMENTS: Dog
ANIMAL FOOD & SUPPLEMENTS: Dog & Cat
ANIMAL FOOD & SUPPLEMENTS: Feed Supplements
ANIMAL FOOD & SUPPLEMENTS: Livestock
ANIMAL FOOD & SUPPLEMENTS: Meat Meal & Tankage
ANIMAL FOOD & SUPPLEMENTS: Pet, Exc Dog & Cat, Canned
ANIMAL FOOD & SUPPLEMENTS: Pet, Exc Dog & Cat, Dry
ANIMAL FOOD & SUPPLEMENTS: Poultry
ANNEALING: Metal
ANODIZING EQPT
ANODIZING SVC
ANTENNAS: Receiving
ANTI-GLARE MATERIAL
ANTIFREEZE
ANTIQUE REPAIR & RESTORATION SVCS, EXC FURNITURE & AUTOS
ANTISEPTICS, MEDICINAL
APPAREL ACCESS STORES
APPAREL DESIGNERS: Commercial
APPAREL FILLING MATERIALS: Cotton Waste, Kapok/Related Matl
APPLIANCE PARTS: Porcelain Enameled
APPLIANCES, HOUSEHOLD: Kitchen, Major, Exc Refrigs & Stoves
APPLIANCES: Household, Refrigerators & Freezers
APPLIANCES: Major, Cooking
APPLIANCES: Small, Electric
APPLICATIONS SOFTWARE PROGRAMMING
AQUARIUM ACCESS, METAL
AQUARIUMS & ACCESS: Glass
ARCHITECTURAL SVCS
ARMATURE REPAIRING & REWINDING SVC
ARMATURES: Ind
ARMOR PLATES
AROMATIC CHEMICAL PRDTS
ART DEALERS & GALLERIES
ART GOODS, WHOLESALE
ART MARBLE: Concrete
ARTIFICIAL FLOWERS & TREES
ARTISTS' MATERIALS, WHOLESALE
ARTS & CRAFTS SCHOOL
ARTWORK: Framed
ASPHALT & ASPHALT PRDTS
ASPHALT COATINGS & SEALERS
ASPHALT MINING & BITUMINOUS STONE QUARRYING SVCS
ASPHALT MIXTURES WHOLESALERS
ASPHALT PLANTS INCLUDING GRAVEL MIX TYPE
ASSEMBLING SVC: Plumbing Fixture Fittings, Plastic
ASSOCIATIONS: Business
ASSOCIATIONS: Real Estate Management
ASSOCIATIONS: Scientists'
ATOMIZERS
ATTENUATORS
AUDIO & VIDEO EQPT, EXC COMMERCIAL
AUDIO COMPONENTS
AUDIO ELECTRONIC SYSTEMS
AUDIO-VISUAL PROGRAM PRODUCTION SVCS
AUTO & HOME SUPPLY STORES: Auto & Truck Eqpt & Parts
AUTO & HOME SUPPLY STORES: Automotive Access
AUTO & HOME SUPPLY STORES: Automotive parts
AUTO & HOME SUPPLY STORES: Batteries, Automotive & Truck
AUTO & HOME SUPPLY STORES: Trailer Hitches, Automotive
AUTO & HOME SUPPLY STORES: Truck Eqpt & Parts
AUTO SPLYS & PARTS, NEW, WHSLE: Exhaust Sys, Mufflers, Etc
AUTOMATIC REGULATING CONTROL: Building Svcs Monitoring, Auto
AUTOMATIC REGULATING CONTROLS: AC & Refrigeration
AUTOMATIC REGULATING CONTROLS: Appliance Regulators
AUTOMATIC REGULATING CONTROLS: Appliance, Exc AirCond/Refr
AUTOMATIC REGULATING CONTROLS: Hardware, Environmental Reg
AUTOMATIC REGULATING CONTROLS: Hydronic Pressure Or Temp
AUTOMATIC REGULATING CONTROLS: Pneumatic Relays, Air-Cond
AUTOMATIC REGULATING CONTROLS: Refrig/Air-Cond Defrost
AUTOMATIC REGULATING CTRLS: Damper, Pneumatic Or Electric
AUTOMATIC TELLER MACHINES
AUTOMOBILES & OTHER MOTOR VEHICLES WHOLESALERS
AUTOMOBILES: Off-Road, Exc Recreational Vehicles
AUTOMOTIVE & TRUCK GENERAL REPAIR SVC
AUTOMOTIVE CUSTOMIZING SVCS, NONFACTORY BASIS
AUTOMOTIVE GLASS REPLACEMENT SHOPS
AUTOMOTIVE PARTS, ACCESS & SPLYS
AUTOMOTIVE PARTS: Plastic
AUTOMOTIVE PRDTS: Rubber
AUTOMOTIVE REPAIR SHOPS: Diesel Engine Repair
AUTOMOTIVE REPAIR SHOPS: Electrical Svcs
AUTOMOTIVE REPAIR SHOPS: Engine Rebuilding
AUTOMOTIVE REPAIR SHOPS: Machine Shop
AUTOMOTIVE REPAIR SHOPS: Rebuilding & Retreading Tires
AUTOMOTIVE REPAIR SHOPS: Sound System Svc & Installation
AUTOMOTIVE REPAIR SHOPS: Tire Recapping
AUTOMOTIVE REPAIR SHOPS: Tire Repair Shop
AUTOMOTIVE REPAIR SHOPS: Trailer Repair
AUTOMOTIVE REPAIR SHOPS: Wheel Alignment
AUTOMOTIVE REPAIR SVC
AUTOMOTIVE SPLYS & PARTS, NEW, WHOLESALE: Hardware
AUTOMOTIVE SPLYS & PARTS, NEW, WHOLESALE: Testing Eqpt, Eng
AUTOMOTIVE SPLYS & PARTS, NEW, WHOLESALE: Trailer Parts

PRODUCT INDEX

AUTOMOTIVE SPLYS & PARTS, NEW, WHOLESALE: Wheels
AUTOMOTIVE SPLYS & PARTS, WHOLESALE, NEC
AUTOMOTIVE SVCS, EXC REPAIR & CARWASHES: Lubrication
AUTOMOTIVE SVCS, EXC RPR/CARWASHES: High Perf Auto Rpr/Svc
AUTOMOTIVE TOWING SVCS
AUTOMOTIVE TRANSMISSION REPAIR SVC
AUTOMOTIVE WELDING SVCS
AUTOMOTIVE: Bodies
AUTOMOTIVE: Seat Frames, Metal
AUTOMOTIVE: Seating
AWNINGS & CANOPIES
AWNINGS & CANOPIES: Awnings, Fabric, From Purchased Matls
AWNINGS & CANOPIES: Canopies, Fabric, From Purchased Matls
AWNINGS: Fiberglass
AWNINGS: Metal
AXLES
AXLES: Rolled Or Forged, Made In Steel Mills

B

BACKHOES
BAGS & BAGGING: Knit
BAGS & CONTAINERS: Textile, Exc Sleeping
BAGS & SACKS: Shipping & Shopping
BAGS: Canvas
BAGS: Duffle, Canvas, Made From Purchased Materials
BAGS: Food Storage & Frozen Food, Plastic
BAGS: Food Storage & Trash, Plastic
BAGS: Paper
BAGS: Paper, Made From Purchased Materials
BAGS: Plastic
BAGS: Plastic & Pliofilm
BAGS: Plastic, Made From Purchased Materials
BAGS: Shipping
BAGS: Shopping, Made From Purchased Materials
BAKERIES, COMMERCIAL: On Premises Baking Only
BAKERIES: On Premises Baking & Consumption
BAKERY MACHINERY
BAKERY PRDTS, FROZEN: Wholesalers
BAKERY PRDTS: Bagels, Fresh Or Frozen
BAKERY PRDTS: Biscuits, Dry
BAKERY PRDTS: Bread, All Types, Fresh Or Frozen
BAKERY PRDTS: Cakes, Bakery, Exc Frozen
BAKERY PRDTS: Cakes, Bakery, Frozen
BAKERY PRDTS: Cookies
BAKERY PRDTS: Cookies & crackers
BAKERY PRDTS: Doughnuts, Exc Frozen
BAKERY PRDTS: Dry
BAKERY PRDTS: Frozen
BAKERY PRDTS: Pastries, Exc Frozen
BAKERY PRDTS: Pretzels
BAKERY PRDTS: Rolls, Bread Type, Fresh Or Frozen
BAKERY PRDTS: Wholesalers
BAKERY: Wholesale Or Wholesale & Retail Combined
BALERS
BALLOONS: Hot Air
BALLOONS: Novelty & Toy
BANKS: Mortgage & Loan
BANNERS: Fabric
BANQUET HALL FACILITIES
BAR
BAR FIXTURES: Wood
BAR JOISTS & CONCRETE REINFORCING BARS: Fabricated
BARBECUE EQPT
BARGES BUILDING & REPAIR
BARRICADES: Metal
BARS & BAR SHAPES: Steel, Cold-Finished, Own Hot-Rolled
BARS: Concrete Reinforcing, Fabricated Steel
BASALT: Crushed & Broken
BASEBOARDS: Metal
BASEMENT WINDOW AREAWAYS: Concrete
BASES, BEVERAGE
BASKETS: Steel Wire
BATH SALTS
BATHROOM ACCESS & FITTINGS: Vitreous China & Earthenware
BATTERIES, EXC AUTOMOTIVE: Wholesalers
BATTERIES: Alkaline, Cell Storage

BATTERIES: Lead Acid, Storage
BATTERIES: Rechargeable
BATTERIES: Storage
BATTERIES: Wet
BATTERY CASES: Plastic Or Plastics Combination
BATTERY CHARGERS
BATTERY CHARGERS: Storage, Motor & Engine Generator Type
BATTS & BATTING: Cotton
BEARINGS & PARTS Ball
BEARINGS: Ball & Roller
BEARINGS: Plastic
BEARINGS: Roller & Parts
BEAUTY & BARBER SHOP EQPT
BEAUTY & BARBER SHOP EQPT & SPLYS WHOLESALERS
BEAUTY SALONS
BEDDING, BEDSPREADS, BLANKETS & SHEETS
BEDDING, FROM SILK OR MANMADE FIBER
BEDS & ACCESS STORES
BEDS: Institutional
BEDSPREADS & BED SETS, FROM PURCHASED MATERIALS
BEDSPREADS, COTTON
BEER & ALE WHOLESALERS
BEER, WINE & LIQUOR STORES: Beer, Packaged
BELLOWS
BELTING: Rubber
BELTS & BELT PRDTS
BELTS: Conveyor, Made From Purchased Wire
BELTS: Seat, Automotive & Aircraft
BEVERAGE BASES & SYRUPS
BEVERAGE PRDTS: Malt, Barley
BEVERAGES, ALCOHOLIC: Ale
BEVERAGES, ALCOHOLIC: Applejack
BEVERAGES, ALCOHOLIC: Beer
BEVERAGES, ALCOHOLIC: Beer & Ale
BEVERAGES, ALCOHOLIC: Bourbon Whiskey
BEVERAGES, ALCOHOLIC: Distilled Liquors
BEVERAGES, ALCOHOLIC: Rum
BEVERAGES, ALCOHOLIC: Wines
BEVERAGES, MALT
BEVERAGES, NONALCOHOLIC: Bottled & canned soft drinks
BEVERAGES, NONALCOHOLIC: Carbonated
BEVERAGES, NONALCOHOLIC: Carbonated, Canned & Bottled, Etc
BEVERAGES, NONALCOHOLIC: Cider
BEVERAGES, NONALCOHOLIC: Flavoring extracts & syrups, nec
BEVERAGES, NONALCOHOLIC: Fruit Drnks, Under 100% Juice, Can
BEVERAGES, NONALCOHOLIC: Soft Drinks, Canned & Bottled, Etc
BEVERAGES, NONALCOHOLIC: Tea, Iced, Bottled & Canned, Etc
BEVERAGES, WINE & DISTILLED ALCOHOLIC, WHOLESALE: Wine
BEVERAGES, WINE/DISTILLED ALCOHOLIC, WHOL: Bttlg Wine/Liquor
BICYCLES, PARTS & ACCESS
BILLIARD & POOL TABLES & SPLYS
BINDING SVC: Books & Manuals
BINDINGS: Bias, Made From Purchased Materials
BIOLOGICAL PRDTS: Agar Culture Media
BIOLOGICAL PRDTS: Blood Derivatives
BIOLOGICAL PRDTS: Exc Diagnostic
BIOLOGICAL PRDTS: Vaccines
BIOLOGICAL PRDTS: Vaccines & Immunizing
BIOLOGICAL PRDTS: Veterinary
BIRTH CONTROL DEVICES: Rubber
BLADES: Knife
BLADES: Saw, Hand Or Power
BLANKBOOKS & LOOSELEAF BINDERS
BLANKBOOKS: Checkbooks & Passbooks, Bank
BLANKETS & BLANKETING, COTTON
BLEACHING YARN & FABRICS: Wool Or Similar Fibers
BLINDS & SHADES: Vertical
BLINDS : Window
BLOCKS & BRICKS: Concrete
BLOCKS: Landscape Or Retaining Wall, Concrete
BLOCKS: Paving
BLOCKS: Standard, Concrete Or Cinder
BLOWERS & FANS
BLOWERS & FANS

BLUEPRINTING SVCS
BOAT & BARGE COMPONENTS: Metal, Prefabricated
BOAT BUILDING & REPAIR
BOAT BUILDING & REPAIRING: Fiberglass
BOAT BUILDING & REPAIRING: Kayaks
BOAT BUILDING & REPAIRING: Motorboats, Inboard Or Outboard
BOAT BUILDING & REPAIRING: Motorized
BOAT BUILDING & REPAIRING: Non-Motorized
BOAT BUILDING & REPAIRING: Yachts
BOAT BUILDING & RPRG: Fishing, Small, Lobster, Crab, Oyster
BOAT DEALERS
BOAT DEALERS: Motor
BOAT LIFTS
BOAT REPAIR SVCS
BOATS & OTHER MARINE EQPT: Plastic
BODIES: Truck & Bus
BODY PARTS: Automobile, Stamped Metal
BOILER REPAIR SHOP
BOILERS & BOILER SHOP WORK
BOILERS: Low-Pressure Heating, Steam Or Hot Water
BOLTS: Metal
BOOK STORES
BOOK STORES: Children's
BOOKS, WHOLESALE
BOOTHS: Spray, Sheet Metal, Prefabricated
BOOTS: Men's
BOTTLED GAS DEALERS: Liquefied Petro, Dlvrd To Customers
BOTTLED GAS DEALERS: Propane
BOTTLES: Plastic
BOX & CARTON MANUFACTURING EQPT
BOXES & CRATES: Rectangular, Wood
BOXES & SHOOK: Nailed Wood
BOXES: Cash & Stamp, Stamped Metal
BOXES: Corrugated
BOXES: Junction, Electric
BOXES: Paperboard, Folding
BOXES: Paperboard, Set-Up
BOXES: Plastic
BOXES: Wooden
BRAKES & BRAKE PARTS
BRAKES: Metal Forming
BRASS & BRONZE PRDTS: Die-casted
BRAZING: Metal
BRICK, STONE & RELATED PRDTS WHOLESALERS
BRICKS & BLOCKS: Structural
BRICKS : Paving, Clay
BRICKS: Clay
BROADCASTING & COMMS EQPT: Antennas, Transmitting/ Comms
BROADCASTING & COMMS EQPT: Trnsmttng TV Antennas/ Grndng Eqpt
BROADCASTING & COMMUNICATIONS EQPT: Cellular Radio Telephone
BROADCASTING & COMMUNICATIONS EQPT: Studio Eqpt, Radio & TV
BROADCASTING STATIONS, RADIO: News
BROKERS' SVCS
BROKERS: Food
BROKERS: Printing
BRONZE FOUNDRY, NEC
BROOMS
BROOMS & BRUSHES
BROOMS & BRUSHES: Household Or Indl
BROOMS & BRUSHES: Paint & Varnish
BROOMS & BRUSHES: Paint Rollers
BROOMS & BRUSHES: Street Sweeping, Hand Or Machine
BUCKETS: Plastic
BUCKLES & PARTS
BUILDING & STRUCTURAL WOOD MEMBERS
BUILDING CLEANING & MAINTENANCE SVCS
BUILDING COMPONENTS: Structural Steel
BUILDING ITEM REPAIR SVCS, MISCELLANEOUS
BUILDING MAINTENANCE SVCS, EXC REPAIRS
BUILDING PRDTS & MATERIALS DEALERS
BUILDING PRDTS: Concrete
BUILDING PRDTS: Stone
BUILDINGS & COMPONENTS: Prefabricated Metal
BUILDINGS: Mobile, For Commercial Use
BUILDINGS: Portable
BUILDINGS: Prefabricated, Metal

PRODUCT INDEX

BUILDINGS: Prefabricated, Wood
BULLETPROOF VESTS
BURIAL VAULTS: Concrete Or Precast Terrazzo
BURNERS: Gas, Indl
BUS BARS: Electrical
BUSHINGS & BEARINGS
BUSINESS ACTIVITIES: Non-Commercial Site
BUSINESS FORMS WHOLESALERS
BUSINESS FORMS: Printed, Manifold
BUSINESS TRAINING SVCS

C

CABINETS & CASES: Show, Display & Storage, Exc Wood
CABINETS: Bathroom Vanities, Wood
CABINETS: Entertainment
CABINETS: Entertainment Units, Household, Wood
CABINETS: Factory
CABINETS: Kitchen, Metal
CABINETS: Kitchen, Wood
CABINETS: Office, Wood
CABINETS: Show, Display, Etc, Wood, Exc Refrigerated
CABLE & OTHER PAY TELEVISION DISTRIBUTION
CABLE TELEVISION
CABLE TELEVISION PRDTS
CABLE: Coaxial
CABLE: Fiber
CABLE: Fiber Optic
CABLE: Noninsulated
CABLE: Ropes & Fiber
CABLE: Steel, Insulated Or Armored
CAFES
CAFETERIAS
CALCULATING & ACCOUNTING EQPT
CALIBRATING SVCS, NEC
CAMPERS: Truck Mounted
CAMSHAFTS
CANDLE SHOPS
CANDLES
CANDLES: Wholesalers
CANDY & CONFECTIONS: Candy Bars, Including Chocolate Covered
CANDY & CONFECTIONS: Chocolate Candy, Exc Solid Chocolate
CANDY & CONFECTIONS: Licorice
CANDY & CONFECTIONS: Nuts, Candy Covered
CANDY & CONFECTIONS: Popcorn Balls/Other Trtd Popcorn Prdts
CANDY, NUT & CONFECTIONERY STORES: Candy
CANDY: Chocolate From Cacao Beans
CANDY: Soft
CANNED SPECIALTIES
CANS & TUBES: Ammunition, Board Laminated With Metal Foil
CANS: Aluminum
CANS: Metal
CANS: Tin
CANVAS PRDTS
CAPACITORS & CONDENSERS
CAPACITORS: NEC
CAR WASH EQPT
CARBIDES
CARBON & GRAPHITE PRDTS, NEC
CARBON BLACK
CARBURETORS
CARDS: Color
CARDS: Greeting
CARDS: Identification
CARDS: Jacquard, Made From Purchased Materials
CARPET & UPHOLSTERY CLEANING SVCS
CARPETS & RUGS: Tufted
CARPETS, RUGS & FLOOR COVERING
CARS: Electric
CARTS: Grocery
CASES: Carrying
CASES: Carrying, Clothing & Apparel
CASES: Plastic
CASES: Shipping, Nailed Or Lock Corner, Wood
CASINGS: Sheet Metal
CAST STONE: Concrete
CASTINGS GRINDING: For The Trade
CASTINGS: Aerospace Investment, Ferrous
CASTINGS: Aerospace, Aluminum
CASTINGS: Aluminum

CASTINGS: Brass, NEC, Exc Die
CASTINGS: Bronze, NEC, Exc Die
CASTINGS: Die, Aluminum
CASTINGS: Die, Nonferrous
CASTINGS: Gray Iron
CASTINGS: Machinery, Aluminum
CASTINGS: Precision
CASTINGS: Steel
CATALOG & MAIL-ORDER HOUSES
CATALOG SALES
CATALYSTS: Chemical
CATERERS
CAULKING COMPOUNDS
CEMENT & CONCRETE RELATED PRDTS & EQPT: Bituminous
CEMENT ROCK: Crushed & Broken
CEMENT: Asbestos, Siding
CEMENT: Heat Resistant
CEMENT: Hydraulic
CEMENT: Masonry
CEMENT: Natural
CHASSIS: Motor Vehicle
CHASSIS: Travel Trailer
CHEMICAL ELEMENTS
CHEMICAL PROCESSING MACHINERY & EQPT
CHEMICALS & ALLIED PRDTS WHOLESALERS, NEC
CHEMICALS & ALLIED PRDTS, WHOLESALE: Adhesives
CHEMICALS & ALLIED PRDTS, WHOLESALE: Chemical Additives
CHEMICALS & ALLIED PRDTS, WHOLESALE: Chemicals, Indl
CHEMICALS & ALLIED PRDTS, WHOLESALE: Chemicals, Indl & Heavy
CHEMICALS & ALLIED PRDTS, WHOLESALE: Detergent/Soap
CHEMICALS & ALLIED PRDTS, WHOLESALE: Detergents
CHEMICALS & ALLIED PRDTS, WHOLESALE: Indl Gases
CHEMICALS & ALLIED PRDTS, WHOLESALE: Oil Additives
CHEMICALS & ALLIED PRDTS, WHOLESALE: Oxygen
CHEMICALS & ALLIED PRDTS, WHOLESALE: Plastics Materials, NEC
CHEMICALS & ALLIED PRDTS, WHOLESALE: Plastics Prdts, NEC
CHEMICALS & ALLIED PRDTS, WHOLESALE: Plastics Sheets & Rods
CHEMICALS & ALLIED PRDTS, WHOLESALE: Resins
CHEMICALS & ALLIED PRDTS, WHOLESALE: Spec Clean/Sanitation
CHEMICALS & ALLIED PRDTS, WHOLESALE: Syn Resin, Rub/Plastic
CHEMICALS & OTHER PRDTS DERIVED FROM COKING
CHEMICALS, AGRICULTURE: Wholesalers
CHEMICALS: Agricultural
CHEMICALS: Alcohols
CHEMICALS: Bromine, Elemental
CHEMICALS: Fire Retardant
CHEMICALS: High Purity Grade, Organic
CHEMICALS: Inorganic, NEC
CHEMICALS: Lithium Compounds, Inorganic
CHEMICALS: Magnesium Compounds Or Salts, Inorganic
CHEMICALS: NEC
CHEMICALS: Phosphates, Defluorinated/Ammoniated, Exc Fertlr
CHEMICALS: Reagent Grade, Refined From Technical Grade
CHEMICALS: Silica Compounds
CHEMICALS: Water Treatment
CHICKEN SLAUGHTERING & PROCESSING
CHILDREN'S & INFANTS' CLOTHING STORES
CHILDREN'S WEAR STORES
CHOCOLATE, EXC CANDY FROM BEANS: Chips, Powder, Block, Syrup
CHOCOLATE, EXC CANDY FROM PURCH CHOC: Chips, Powder, Block
CHRISTMAS TREE LIGHTING SETS: Electric
CHRISTMAS TREES: Artificial
CHROMATOGRAPHY EQPT
CHUCKS
CIGARETTE & CIGAR PRDTS & ACCESS
CIGARETTE FILTERS
CIRCUIT BOARD REPAIR SVCS
CIRCUIT BOARDS: Wiring
CIRCUITS, INTEGRATED: Hybrid
CIRCUITS: Electronic

CIRCULAR KNIT FABRICS DYEING & FINISHING
CLAMPS & COUPLINGS: Hose
CLAMPS: Metal
CLAY, PETROLEUM REFINING: Chemically Processed
CLAY: Filtering, Treated
CLEANING EQPT: Commercial
CLEANING EQPT: Floor Washing & Polishing, Commercial
CLEANING EQPT: High Pressure
CLEANING OR POLISHING PREPARATIONS, NEC
CLEANING PRDTS: Automobile Polish
CLEANING PRDTS: Bleaches, Household, Dry Or Liquid
CLEANING PRDTS: Deodorants, Nonpersonal
CLEANING PRDTS: Disinfectants, Household Or Indl Plant
CLEANING PRDTS: Drain Pipe Solvents Or Cleaners
CLEANING PRDTS: Laundry Preparations
CLEANING PRDTS: Sanitation Preparations
CLEANING PRDTS: Sanitation Preps, Disinfectants/Deodorants
CLEANING PRDTS: Shoe Polish Or Cleaner
CLEANING PRDTS: Specialty
CLEANING SVCS: Industrial Or Commercial
CLIPPERS: Fingernail & Toenail
CLOSURES: Closures, Stamped Metal
CLOTHING & ACCESS, WOMEN, CHILDREN & INFANT, WHOL: Access
CLOTHING & ACCESS, WOMEN, CHILDREN & INFANT, WHOL: Uniforms
CLOTHING & ACCESS, WOMEN, CHILDREN/INFANT, WHOL: Baby Goods
CLOTHING & ACCESS, WOMEN, CHILDREN/INFANT, WHOL: Nightwear
CLOTHING & ACCESS: Handicapped
CLOTHING & ACCESS: Hospital Gowns
CLOTHING & ACCESS: Men's Miscellaneous Access
CLOTHING & ACCESS: Suspenders
CLOTHING & APPAREL STORES: Custom
CLOTHING & FURNISHINGS, MEN'S & BOYS', WHOLESALE: Shirts
CLOTHING & FURNISHINGS, MEN'S & BOYS', WHOLESALE: Uniforms
CLOTHING & FURNISHINGS, MENS & BOYS, WHOL: Sportswear/Work
CLOTHING STORES: T-Shirts, Printed, Custom
CLOTHING STORES: Uniforms & Work
CLOTHING STORES: Unisex
CLOTHING STORES: Work
CLOTHING: Academic Vestments
CLOTHING: Access, Women's & Misses'
CLOTHING: Anklets & Socks
CLOTHING: Aprons, Exc Rubber/Plastic, Women, Misses, Junior
CLOTHING: Aprons, Waterproof, From Purchased Materials
CLOTHING: Athletic & Sportswear, Men's & Boys'
CLOTHING: Athletic & Sportswear, Women's & Girls'
CLOTHING: Baker, Barber, Lab/Svc Ind Apparel, Washable, Men
CLOTHING: Bathing Suits & Swimwear, Knit
CLOTHING: Belts
CLOTHING: Blouses, Women's & Girls'
CLOTHING: Blouses, Womens & Juniors, From Purchased Mtrls
CLOTHING: Caps, Baseball
CLOTHING: Children & Infants'
CLOTHING: Children's, Girls'
CLOTHING: Coats & Jackets, Leather & Sheep-Lined
CLOTHING: Coats & Suits, Men's & Boys'
CLOTHING: Collar & Cuff Sets, Knit
CLOTHING: Costumes
CLOTHING: Disposable
CLOTHING: Dresses
CLOTHING: Dresses & Skirts
CLOTHING: Hats & Headwear, Knit
CLOTHING: Hosiery, Pantyhose & Knee Length, Sheer
CLOTHING: Hospital, Men's
CLOTHING: Jackets & Vests, Exc Fur & Leather, Women's
CLOTHING: Jeans, Men's & Boys'
CLOTHING: Leather
CLOTHING: Men's & boy's underwear & nightwear
CLOTHING: Mens & Boys Jackets, Sport, Suede, Leatherette
CLOTHING: Neckwear
CLOTHING: Outerwear, Knit
CLOTHING: Outerwear, Women's & Misses' NEC
CLOTHING: Panty Hose

PRODUCT INDEX

CLOTHING: Robes & Dressing Gowns
CLOTHING: Robes & Housecoats, Children's
CLOTHING: Service Apparel, Women's
CLOTHING: Shirts
CLOTHING: Shirts, Knit
CLOTHING: Shirts, Women's & Juniors', From Purchased Mtrls
CLOTHING: Socks
CLOTHING: Sportswear, Women's
CLOTHING: Sweaters & Sweater Coats, Knit
CLOTHING: Sweaters, Men's & Boys'
CLOTHING: Sweatshirts & T-Shirts, Men's & Boys'
CLOTHING: T-Shirts & Tops, Knit
CLOTHING: T-Shirts & Tops, Women's & Girls'
CLOTHING: Tailored Suits & Formal Jackets
CLOTHING: Tights, Exc Women's
CLOTHING: Trousers & Slacks, Men's & Boys'
CLOTHING: Underwear, Knit
CLOTHING: Underwear, Women's & Children's
CLOTHING: Uniforms & Vestments
CLOTHING: Uniforms, Ex Athletic, Women's, Misses' & Juniors'
CLOTHING: Uniforms, Firemen's, From Purchased Materials
CLOTHING: Uniforms, Men's & Boys'
CLOTHING: Uniforms, Military, Men/Youth, Purchased Materials
CLOTHING: Uniforms, Work
CLOTHING: Vests
CLOTHING: Work Apparel, Exc Uniforms
COAL & OTHER MINERALS & ORES WHOLESALERS
COAL MINING SERVICES
COAL MINING: Bituminous Coal & Lignite-Surface Mining
COATING COMPOUNDS: Tar
COATING SVC: Metals, With Plastic Or Resins
COATINGS: Epoxy
COATINGS: Polyurethane
COILS & TRANSFORMERS
COILS: Electric Motors Or Generators
COILS: Pipe
COLORS: Pigments, Inorganic
COMFORTERS & QUILTS, FROM MANMADE FIBER OR SILK
COMMERCIAL & OFFICE BUILDINGS RENOVATION & REPAIR
COMMERCIAL ART & GRAPHIC DESIGN SVCS
COMMERCIAL ART & ILLUSTRATION SVCS
COMMERCIAL CONTAINERS WHOLESALERS
COMMERCIAL EQPT WHOLESALERS, NEC
COMMERCIAL EQPT, WHOLESALE: Restaurant, NEC
COMMERCIAL EQPT, WHOLESALE: Scales, Exc Laboratory
COMMERCIAL EQPT, WHOLESALE: Store Fixtures & Display Eqpt
COMMERCIAL LAUNDRY EQPT
COMMERCIAL PHOTOGRAPHIC STUDIO
COMMERCIAL PRINTING & NEWSPAPER PUBLISHING
COMMON SAND MINING
COMMUNICATIONS EQPT WHOLESALERS
COMMUNICATIONS EQPT: Microwave
COMMUNICATIONS EQPT: Radio, Marine
COMMUNICATIONS SVCS
COMMUNICATIONS SVCS: Data
COMMUNICATIONS SVCS: Internet Connectivity Svcs
COMMUNICATIONS SVCS: Internet Host Svcs
COMMUNICATIONS SVCS: Online Svc Providers
COMMUNICATIONS SVCS: Signal Enhancement Network Svcs
COMMUTATORS: Electronic
COMPOSITION STONE: Plastic
COMPOST
COMPRESSORS: Air & Gas
COMPRESSORS: Air & Gas, Including Vacuum Pumps
COMPRESSORS: Refrigeration & Air Conditioning Eqpt
COMPUTER & COMPUTER SOFTWARE STORES
COMPUTER & COMPUTER SOFTWARE STORES: Peripheral Eqpt
COMPUTER & COMPUTER SOFTWARE STORES: Personal Computers
COMPUTER & COMPUTER SOFTWARE STORES: Software & Access
COMPUTER & COMPUTER SOFTWARE STORES: Software, Bus/Non-Game
COMPUTER & COMPUTER SOFTWARE STORES: Software, Computer Game

COMPUTER & DATA PROCESSING EQPT REPAIR & MAINTENANCE
COMPUTER & OFFICE MACHINE MAINTENANCE & REPAIR
COMPUTER FACILITIES MANAGEMENT SVCS
COMPUTER GRAPHICS SVCS
COMPUTER PERIPHERAL EQPT REPAIR & MAINTENANCE
COMPUTER PERIPHERAL EQPT, NEC
COMPUTER PERIPHERAL EQPT, WHOLESALE
COMPUTER PERIPHERAL EQPT: Encoders
COMPUTER PERIPHERAL EQPT: Input Or Output
COMPUTER PROCESSING SVCS
COMPUTER PROGRAMMING SVCS: Custom
COMPUTER RELATED MAINTENANCE SVCS
COMPUTER SOFTWARE DEVELOPMENT
COMPUTER SOFTWARE DEVELOPMENT & APPLICATIONS
COMPUTER SOFTWARE SYSTEMS ANALYSIS & DESIGN: Custom
COMPUTER STORAGE DEVICES, NEC
COMPUTER SYSTEMS ANALYSIS & DESIGN
COMPUTER TERMINALS
COMPUTERS, NEC
COMPUTERS, NEC, WHOLESALE
COMPUTERS, PERIPHERALS & SOFTWARE, WHOLESALE: Printers
COMPUTERS, PERIPHERALS & SOFTWARE, WHOLESALE: Software
COMPUTERS: Personal
CONCENTRATES, DRINK
CONCENTRATES, FLAVORING, EXC DRINK
CONCRETE BUILDING PRDTS WHOLESALERS
CONCRETE CURING & HARDENING COMPOUNDS
CONCRETE PLANTS
CONCRETE PRDTS
CONCRETE PRDTS, PRECAST, NEC
CONCRETE: Dry Mixture
CONCRETE: Ready-Mixed
CONDENSERS & CONDENSING UNITS: Air Conditioner
CONNECTORS: Electronic
CONSTRUCTION & MINING MACHINERY WHOLESALERS
CONSTRUCTION & ROAD MAINTENANCE EQPT: Drags, Road
CONSTRUCTION EQPT REPAIR SVCS
CONSTRUCTION EQPT: Attachments, Snow Plow
CONSTRUCTION EQPT: Cranes
CONSTRUCTION EQPT: Finishers & Spreaders
CONSTRUCTION EQPT: Graders, Road
CONSTRUCTION EQPT: Loaders, Shovel, Self-Propelled
CONSTRUCTION EQPT: Roofing Eqpt
CONSTRUCTION MATERIALS, WHOLESALE: Aggregate
CONSTRUCTION MATERIALS, WHOLESALE: Architectural Metalwork
CONSTRUCTION MATERIALS, WHOLESALE: Awnings
CONSTRUCTION MATERIALS, WHOLESALE: Brick, Exc Refractory
CONSTRUCTION MATERIALS, WHOLESALE: Building Stone, Marble
CONSTRUCTION MATERIALS, WHOLESALE: Building, Exterior
CONSTRUCTION MATERIALS, WHOLESALE: Building, Interior
CONSTRUCTION MATERIALS, WHOLESALE: Cement
CONSTRUCTION MATERIALS, WHOLESALE: Concrete Mixtures
CONSTRUCTION MATERIALS, WHOLESALE: Doors, Garage
CONSTRUCTION MATERIALS, WHOLESALE: Masons' Materials
CONSTRUCTION MATERIALS, WHOLESALE: Millwork
CONSTRUCTION MATERIALS, WHOLESALE: Molding, All Materials
CONSTRUCTION MATERIALS, WHOLESALE: Pallets, Wood
CONSTRUCTION MATERIALS, WHOLESALE: Paving Materials
CONSTRUCTION MATERIALS, WHOLESALE: Plywood
CONSTRUCTION MATERIALS, WHOLESALE: Prefabricated Structures
CONSTRUCTION MATERIALS, WHOLESALE: Roofing & Siding Material
CONSTRUCTION MATERIALS, WHOLESALE: Sand
CONSTRUCTION MATERIALS, WHOLESALE: Septic Tanks

CONSTRUCTION MATERIALS, WHOLESALE: Siding, Exc Wood
CONSTRUCTION MATERIALS, WHOLESALE: Stone, Crushed Or Broken
CONSTRUCTION MATERIALS, WHOLESALE: Veneer
CONSTRUCTION MATERIALS, WHOLESALE: Windows
CONSTRUCTION MATLS, WHOL: Doors, Combination, Screen-Storm
CONSTRUCTION SAND MINING
CONSTRUCTION: Agricultural Building
CONSTRUCTION: Athletic & Recreation Facilities
CONSTRUCTION: Bridge
CONSTRUCTION: Commercial & Office Building, New
CONSTRUCTION: Commercial & Office Buildings, Prefabricated
CONSTRUCTION: Dams, Waterways, Docks & Other Marine
CONSTRUCTION: Drainage System
CONSTRUCTION: Farm Building
CONSTRUCTION: Food Prdts Manufacturing or Packing Plant
CONSTRUCTION: Heavy Highway & Street
CONSTRUCTION: Indl Buildings, New, NEC
CONSTRUCTION: Indl Plant
CONSTRUCTION: Land Preparation
CONSTRUCTION: Marine
CONSTRUCTION: Oil & Gas Pipeline Construction
CONSTRUCTION: Parking Lot
CONSTRUCTION: Pipeline, NEC
CONSTRUCTION: Residential, Nec
CONSTRUCTION: Sewer Line
CONSTRUCTION: Single-Family Housing
CONSTRUCTION: Single-family Housing, New
CONSTRUCTION: Swimming Pools
CONSTRUCTION: Transmitting Tower, Telecommunication
CONSTRUCTION: Warehouse
CONSTRUCTION: Water & Sewer Line
CONSULTING SVC: Business, NEC
CONSULTING SVC: Educational
CONSULTING SVC: Human Resource
CONSULTING SVC: Management
CONSULTING SVCS, BUSINESS: Communications
CONSULTING SVCS, BUSINESS: Energy Conservation
CONSULTING SVCS, BUSINESS: Environmental
CONSULTING SVCS, BUSINESS: Safety Training Svcs
CONSULTING SVCS, BUSINESS: Sys Engnrg, Exc Computer/ Prof
CONSULTING SVCS, BUSINESS: Systems Analysis & Engineering
CONSULTING SVCS, BUSINESS: Testing, Educational Or Personnel
CONSULTING SVCS: Scientific
CONTACT LENSES
CONTACTS: Electrical
CONTAINERS, GLASS: Water Bottles
CONTAINERS: Foil, Bakery Goods & Frozen Foods
CONTAINERS: Food, Folding, Made From Purchased Materials
CONTAINERS: Food, Liquid Tight, Including Milk
CONTAINERS: Frozen Food & Ice Cream
CONTAINERS: Glass
CONTAINERS: Laminated Phenolic & Vulcanized Fiber
CONTAINERS: Metal
CONTAINERS: Plastic
CONTAINERS: Sanitary, Food
CONTAINERS: Shipping, Bombs, Metal Plate
CONTAINERS: Wood
CONTRACTOR: Dredging
CONTRACTOR: Framing
CONTRACTOR: Rigging & Scaffolding
CONTRACTORS: Acoustical & Insulation Work
CONTRACTORS: Asbestos Removal & Encapsulation
CONTRACTORS: Boiler Maintenance Contractor
CONTRACTORS: Carpentry Work
CONTRACTORS: Carpentry, Cabinet & Finish Work
CONTRACTORS: Carpentry, Finish & Trim Work
CONTRACTORS: Closet Organizers, Installation & Design
CONTRACTORS: Coating, Caulking & Weather, Water & Fire
CONTRACTORS: Commercial & Office Building
CONTRACTORS: Decontamination Svcs
CONTRACTORS: Directional Oil & Gas Well Drilling Svc
CONTRACTORS: Drywall
CONTRACTORS: Electric Power Systems
CONTRACTORS: Electronic Controls Installation
CONTRACTORS: Energy Management Control

PRODUCT INDEX

CONTRACTORS: Fence Construction
CONTRACTORS: Fiber Optic Cable Installation
CONTRACTORS: Fiberglass Work
CONTRACTORS: Gas Field Svcs, NEC
CONTRACTORS: General Electric
CONTRACTORS: Glass Tinting, Architectural & Automotive
CONTRACTORS: Heating & Air Conditioning
CONTRACTORS: Heating Systems Repair & Maintenance Svc
CONTRACTORS: Highway & Street Construction, General
CONTRACTORS: Highway & Street Paving
CONTRACTORS: Hydraulic Eqpt Installation & Svcs
CONTRACTORS: Kitchen Cabinet Installation
CONTRACTORS: Machine Rigging & Moving
CONTRACTORS: Machinery Installation
CONTRACTORS: Marble Installation, Interior
CONTRACTORS: Masonry & Stonework
CONTRACTORS: Office Furniture Installation
CONTRACTORS: Oil & Gas Wells Pumping Svcs
CONTRACTORS: Oil Field Pipe Testing Svcs
CONTRACTORS: Ornamental Metal Work
CONTRACTORS: Painting, Commercial
CONTRACTORS: Painting, Indl
CONTRACTORS: Petroleum Storage Tanks, Pumping & Draining
CONTRACTORS: Plumbing
CONTRACTORS: Process Piping
CONTRACTORS: Roustabout Svcs
CONTRACTORS: Septic System
CONTRACTORS: Sheet Metal Work, NEC
CONTRACTORS: Siding
CONTRACTORS: Structural Iron Work, Structural
CONTRACTORS: Structural Steel Erection
CONTRACTORS: Textile Warping
CONTRACTORS: Tile Installation, Ceramic
CONTRACTORS: Underground Utilities
CONTRACTORS: Warm Air Heating & Air Conditioning
CONTRACTORS: Water Well Drilling
CONTRACTORS: Windows & Doors
CONTRACTORS: Wood Floor Installation & Refinishing
CONTROL EQPT: Electric
CONTROL EQPT: Noise
CONTROLS & ACCESS: Indl, Electric
CONTROLS & ACCESS: Motor
CONTROLS: Automatic Temperature
CONTROLS: Electric Motor
CONTROLS: Environmental
CONTROLS: Thermostats, Built-in
CONVENIENCE STORES
CONVERTERS: Frequency
CONVERTERS: Rotary, Electrical
CONVEYOR SYSTEMS: Belt, General Indl Use
CONVEYOR SYSTEMS: Bulk Handling
CONVEYOR SYSTEMS: Pneumatic Tube
CONVEYORS & CONVEYING EQPT
COOKING & FOODWARMING EQPT: Commercial
COOKING EQPT, HOUSEHOLD: Ranges, Electric
COOKWARE, STONEWARE: Coarse Earthenware & Pottery
COOKWARE: Fine Earthenware
COOLING TOWERS: Metal
COPPER ORE MINING
COPPER PRDTS: Smelter, Primary
COPPER: Rolling & Drawing
CORD & TWINE
CORK & CORK PRDTS: Bottle
COSMETIC PREPARATIONS
COSMETICS & TOILETRIES
COSMETICS WHOLESALERS
COSMETOLOGY & PERSONAL HYGIENE SALONS
COUGH MEDICINES
COUNTER & SINK TOPS
COUNTERS OR COUNTER DISPLAY CASES, EXC WOOD
COUNTERS OR COUNTER DISPLAY CASES, WOOD
COUNTING DEVICES: Controls, Revolution & Timing
COUNTING DEVICES: Speedometers
COUPLINGS, EXC PRESSURE & SOIL PIPE
COUPLINGS: Hose & Tube, Hydraulic Or Pneumatic
COVERS: Automobile Seat
COVERS: Automotive, Exc Seat & Tire
CRANE & AERIAL LIFT SVCS
CRANES: Indl Plant
CRANES: Overhead
CREDIT CARD SVCS

CROWNS & CLOSURES
CULTURE MEDIA
CUPS & PLATES: Foamed Plastics
CURBING: Granite Or Stone
CURTAIN & DRAPERY FIXTURES: Poles, Rods & Rollers
CURTAIN WALLS: Building, Steel
CURTAINS: Window, From Purchased Materials
CUSHIONS & PILLOWS
CUSHIONS & PILLOWS: Bed, From Purchased Materials
CUSHIONS: Carpet & Rug, Foamed Plastics
CUSTOM COMPOUNDING OF RUBBER MATERIALS
CUT STONE & STONE PRODUCTS
CUTLERY
CUTLERY WHOLESALERS
CUTLERY: Carving Sets
CYCLIC CRUDES & INTERMEDIATES
CYLINDER & ACTUATORS: Fluid Power
CYLINDERS: Pump

D

DAIRY EQPT
DAIRY PRDTS STORE: Ice Cream, Packaged
DAIRY PRDTS STORES
DAIRY PRDTS: Acidophilus Milk
DAIRY PRDTS: Butter
DAIRY PRDTS: Canned Milk, Whole
DAIRY PRDTS: Cheese
DAIRY PRDTS: Dairy Based Desserts, Frozen
DAIRY PRDTS: Dietary Supplements, Dairy & Non-Dairy Based
DAIRY PRDTS: Ice Cream & Ice Milk
DAIRY PRDTS: Ice Cream, Bulk
DAIRY PRDTS: Ice Cream, Packaged, Molded, On Sticks, Etc.
DAIRY PRDTS: Milk & Cream, Cultured & Flavored
DAIRY PRDTS: Milk, Fluid
DAIRY PRDTS: Natural Cheese
DAIRY PRDTS: Processed Cheese
DAIRY PRDTS: Yogurt, Frozen
DATA PROCESSING & PREPARATION SVCS
DATA PROCESSING SVCS
DECORATIVE WOOD & WOODWORK
DEFENSE SYSTEMS & EQPT
DEGREASING MACHINES
DENTAL EQPT
DENTAL EQPT & SPLYS
DENTAL EQPT & SPLYS: Enamels
DENTAL EQPT & SPLYS: Orthodontic Appliances
DENTISTS' OFFICES & CLINICS
DEODORANTS: Personal
DEPARTMENT STORES
DEPARTMENT STORES: Country General
DEPILATORIES, COSMETIC
DERMATOLOGICALS
DESIGN SVCS, NEC
DESIGN SVCS: Commercial & Indl
DESIGN SVCS: Computer Integrated Systems
DETECTIVE & ARMORED CAR SERVICES
DIAGNOSTIC SUBSTANCES
DIAGNOSTIC SUBSTANCES OR AGENTS: Cytology & Histology
DIAGNOSTIC SUBSTANCES OR AGENTS: In Vitro
DIAGNOSTIC SUBSTANCES OR AGENTS: Microbiology & Virology
DIAGNOSTIC SUBSTANCES OR AGENTS: Radioactive
DIAGNOSTIC SUBSTANCES OR AGENTS: Veterinary
DIAMONDS, GEMS, WHOLESALE
DIE CUTTING SVC: Paper
DIE SETS: Presses, Metal Stamping
DIES & TOOLS: Special
DIES: Cutting, Exc Metal
DIES: Diamond, Metalworking
DIES: Extrusion
DIES: Plastic Forming
DIODES: Light Emitting
DIODES: Solid State, Germanium, Silicon, Etc
DIRECT SELLING ESTABLISHMENTS: Food Svcs
DISASTER SVCS
DISCOUNT DEPARTMENT STORES
DISKETTE DUPLICATING SVCS
DISPLAY FIXTURES: Wood
DISPLAY ITEMS: Corrugated, Made From Purchased Materials

DISTRIBUTORS: Motor Vehicle Engine
DOCUMENT STORAGE SVCS
DOOR FRAMES: Wood
DOORS & WINDOWS: Screen & Storm
DOORS & WINDOWS: Storm, Metal
DOORS: Garage, Overhead, Metal
DOORS: Garage, Overhead, Wood
DOORS: Glass
DOORS: Screen, Metal
DRAPERIES & CURTAINS
DRAPERIES: Plastic & Textile, From Purchased Materials
DRAPERY & UPHOLSTERY STORES: Draperies
DRILL BITS
DRILLING MACHINERY & EQPT: Oil & Gas
DRINKING PLACES: Bars & Lounges
DRINKING PLACES: Beer Garden
DRUG STORES
DRUGS & DRUG PROPRIETARIES, WHOLESALE
DRUGS & DRUG PROPRIETARIES, WHOLESALE: Bandages
DRUGS & DRUG PROPRIETARIES, WHOLESALE: Pharmaceuticals
DRUGS & DRUG PROPRIETARIES, WHOLESALE: Vitamins & Minerals
DRUGS ACTING ON THE CENTRAL NERVOUS SYSTEM & SENSE ORGANS
DRUGS AFFECTING NEOPLASMS & ENDOCRINE SYSTEMS
DRUGS: Parasitic & Infective Disease Affecting
DRUMS: Fiber
DRUMS: Shipping, Metal
DUCTING: Metal Plate
DUCTS: Sheet Metal
DUMPSTERS: Garbage
DUST OR FUME COLLECTING EQPT: Indl
DYES & PIGMENTS: Organic

E

EATING PLACES
EDUCATIONAL SVCS
ELECTRIC & OTHER SERVICES COMBINED
ELECTRIC MOTOR & GENERATOR AUXILIARY PARTS
ELECTRIC MOTOR REPAIR SVCS
ELECTRIC SERVICES
ELECTRIC SVCS, NEC: Power Generation
ELECTRIC WATER HEATERS WHOLESALERS
ELECTRICAL APPARATUS & EQPT WHOLESALERS
ELECTRICAL DISCHARGE MACHINING, EDM
ELECTRICAL EQPT REPAIR SVCS
ELECTRICAL EQPT REPAIR SVCS: High Voltage
ELECTRICAL EQPT: Automotive, NEC
ELECTRICAL GOODS, WHOLESALE: Batteries, Dry Cell
ELECTRICAL GOODS, WHOLESALE: Electrical Appliances, Major
ELECTRICAL GOODS, WHOLESALE: Electronic Parts
ELECTRICAL GOODS, WHOLESALE: Fittings & Construction Mat
ELECTRICAL GOODS, WHOLESALE: Generators
ELECTRICAL GOODS, WHOLESALE: Light Bulbs & Related Splys
ELECTRICAL GOODS, WHOLESALE: Modems, Computer
ELECTRICAL GOODS, WHOLESALE: Security Control Eqpt & Systems
ELECTRICAL GOODS, WHOLESALE: Semiconductor Devices
ELECTRICAL GOODS, WHOLESALE: Telephone & Telegraphic Eqpt
ELECTRICAL GOODS, WHOLESALE: Wire & Cable
ELECTRICAL GOODS, WHOLESALE: Wire & Cable, Electronic
ELECTRICAL SPLYS
ELECTRICAL SUPPLIES: Porcelain
ELECTROMEDICAL EQPT
ELECTROMEDICAL EQPT WHOLESALERS
ELECTRON TUBES
ELECTRONIC DEVICES: Solid State, NEC
ELECTRONIC EQPT REPAIR SVCS
ELECTRONIC LOADS & POWER SPLYS
ELECTRONIC PARTS & EQPT WHOLESALERS
ELECTRONIC SHOPPING
ELECTROPLATING & PLATING SVC
ELEVATORS & EQPT
ELEVATORS WHOLESALERS

PRODUCT INDEX

ELEVATORS: Installation & Conversion
EMBLEMS: Embroidered
EMBROIDERY ADVERTISING SVCS
EMBROIDERY KITS
EMERGENCY ALARMS
ENCLOSURES: Electronic
ENCLOSURES: Screen
ENDOCRINE PRDTS
ENGINE REBUILDING: Diesel
ENGINE REBUILDING: Gas
ENGINEERING SVCS
ENGINEERING SVCS: Chemical
ENGINEERING SVCS: Civil
ENGINEERING SVCS: Construction & Civil
ENGINEERING SVCS: Electrical Or Electronic
ENGINEERING SVCS: Machine Tool Design
ENGINEERING SVCS: Marine
ENGINEERING SVCS: Mechanical
ENGINES: Internal Combustion, NEC
ENGINES: Jet Propulsion
ENGINES: Marine
ENGRAVING SVC, NEC
ENGRAVING SVCS
ENVELOPES
ENVELOPES WHOLESALERS
ENZYMES
EPOXY RESINS
EQUIPMENT & VEHICLE FINANCE LEASING COMPANIES
EQUIPMENT: Pedestrian Traffic Control
EQUIPMENT: Rental & Leasing, NEC
ESCALATORS: Passenger & Freight
ETCHING & ENGRAVING SVC
ETHYLENE
ETHYLENE-PROPYLENE RUBBERS: EPDM Polymers
EXHAUST SYSTEMS: Eqpt & Parts
EXPANSION JOINTS: Rubber
EXPLOSIVES
EXTRACTS, FLAVORING

F

FABRIC STORES
FABRICS & CLOTH: Quilted
FABRICS & CLOTHING: Rubber Coated
FABRICS: Acetate, Broadwoven
FABRICS: Apparel & Outerwear, Broadwoven
FABRICS: Apparel & Outerwear, Cotton
FABRICS: Automotive, From Manmade Fiber
FABRICS: Basket Weave, Cotton
FABRICS: Bonded-Fiber, Exc Felt
FABRICS: Broad Woven, Goods, Cotton
FABRICS: Broadwoven, Wool
FABRICS: Cloth, Warp Knit
FABRICS: Cotton, Narrow
FABRICS: Denims
FABRICS: Dress, Cotton
FABRICS: Elastic, From Manmade Fiber Or Silk
FABRICS: Fiberglass, Broadwoven
FABRICS: Glass & Fiberglass, Broadwoven
FABRICS: Glass, Narrow
FABRICS: Jacquard Woven, Cotton
FABRICS: Jacquard Woven, From Manmade Fiber Or Silk
FABRICS: Lacings, Textile
FABRICS: Laundry, Cotton
FABRICS: Nonwoven
FABRICS: Nylon, Broadwoven
FABRICS: Pile, Circular Knit
FABRICS: Polyester, Broadwoven
FABRICS: Polypropylene, Broadwoven
FABRICS: Resin Or Plastic Coated
FABRICS: Rubber & Elastic Yarns & Fabrics
FABRICS: Rubberized
FABRICS: Scrub Cloths
FABRICS: Shoe Laces, Exc Leather
FABRICS: Specialty Including Twisted Weaves, Broadwoven
FABRICS: Spunbonded
FABRICS: Tickings
FABRICS: Trimmings, Textile
FABRICS: Upholstery, Cotton
FABRICS: Upholstery, Wool
FABRICS: Warp & Flat Knit Prdts
FABRICS: Weft Or Circular Knit
FABRICS: Wool, Broadwoven
FABRICS: Worsted fabrics, broadwoven

FAMILY CLOTHING STORES
FANS, BLOWING: Indl Or Commercial
FANS, VENTILATING: Indl Or Commercial
FANS: Ceiling
FARM & GARDEN MACHINERY WHOLESALERS
FARM PRDTS, RAW MATERIALS, WHOLESALE: Broomcorn
FARM SPLYS WHOLESALERS
FARM SPLYS, WHOLESALE: Fertilizers & Agricultural Chemicals
FARM SPLYS, WHOLESALE: Insecticides
FASTENERS WHOLESALERS
FASTENERS: Metal
FASTENERS: Metal
FASTENERS: Notions, Hooks & Eyes
FASTENERS: Wire, Made From Purchased Wire
FAUCETS & SPIGOTS: Metal & Plastic
FELDSPAR: Ground Or Otherwise Treated
FENCE POSTS: Iron & Steel
FENCES OR POSTS: Ornamental Iron Or Steel
FENCING MADE IN WIREDRAWING PLANTS
FENCING MATERIALS: Docks & Other Outdoor Prdts, Wood
FENCING: Chain Link
FERTILIZER MINERAL MINING
FERTILIZER, AGRICULTURAL: Wholesalers
FERTILIZERS: Nitrogen Solutions
FERTILIZERS: Nitrogenous
FERTILIZERS: Phosphatic
FIBER & FIBER PRDTS: Acrylic
FIBER & FIBER PRDTS: Polyester
FIBER & FIBER PRDTS: Vinyl
FIBER OPTICS
FIBER: Vulcanized
FIBERS: Carbon & Graphite
FILM BASE: Cellulose Acetate Or Nitrocellulose Plastics
FILTER CLEANING SVCS
FILTER ELEMENTS: Fluid & Hydraulic Line
FILTERING MEDIA: Pottery
FILTERS
FILTERS & SOFTENERS: Water, Household
FILTERS & STRAINERS: Pipeline
FILTERS: Air
FILTERS: Air Intake, Internal Combustion Engine, Exc Auto
FILTERS: General Line, Indl
FILTERS: Oil, Internal Combustion Engine, Exc Auto
FILTRATION DEVICES: Electronic
FINANCIAL SVCS
FINGERPRINT EQPT
FINISHING AGENTS
FINISHING AGENTS: Textile
FINISHING SVCS
FIRE ALARM MAINTENANCE & MONITORING SVCS
FIRE ARMS, SMALL: Guns Or Gun Parts, 30 mm & Below
FIRE ARMS, SMALL: Pistols Or Pistol Parts, 30 mm & below
FIRE ARMS, SMALL: Rifles Or Rifle Parts, 30 mm & below
FIRE CONTROL EQPT REPAIR SVCS, MILITARY
FIRE CONTROL OR BOMBING EQPT: Electronic
FIRE DETECTION SYSTEMS
FIRE EXTINGUISHERS, WHOLESALE
FIRE EXTINGUISHERS: Portable
FIRE OR BURGLARY RESISTIVE PRDTS
FIREARMS & AMMUNITION, EXC SPORTING, WHOLESALE
FIREFIGHTING APPARATUS
FIREPLACE EQPT & ACCESS
FIREPLACES: Concrete
FIRST AID SPLYS, WHOLESALE
FISH & SEAFOOD PROCESSORS: Canned Or Cured
FISH & SEAFOOD PROCESSORS: Fresh Or Frozen
FISH & SEAFOOD WHOLESALERS
FISHING EQPT: Lures
FITTINGS & ASSEMBLIES: Hose & Tube, Hydraulic Or Pneumatic
FITTINGS & SPECIALTIES: Steam
FITTINGS: Pipe
FITTINGS: Pipe, Fabricated
FIXTURES & EQPT: Kitchen, Metal, Exc Cast Aluminum
FIXTURES: Cut Stone
FLAGS: Fabric
FLAGSTONES
FLAKEBOARD
FLAT GLASS: Construction
FLAT GLASS: Float
FLAT GLASS: Window, Clear & Colored
FLOOR COVERING STORES

FLOOR COVERING STORES: Carpets
FLOOR COVERINGS WHOLESALERS
FLOOR COVERINGS: Rubber
FLOOR COVERINGS: Textile Fiber
FLOORING: Hardwood
FLOWERS, ARTIFICIAL, WHOLESALE
FLUID METERS & COUNTING DEVICES
FLUID POWER PUMPS & MOTORS
FLUID POWER VALVES & HOSE FITTINGS
FOAM RUBBER
FOAMS & RUBBER, WHOLESALE
FOIL & LEAF: Metal
FOIL: Aluminum
FOOD COLORINGS
FOOD PRDTS, BREAKFAST: Cereal, Oatmeal
FOOD PRDTS, CANNED OR FRESH PACK: Fruit Juices
FOOD PRDTS, CANNED: Baby Food
FOOD PRDTS, CANNED: Barbecue Sauce
FOOD PRDTS, CANNED: Fruit Juices, Fresh
FOOD PRDTS, CANNED: Fruits
FOOD PRDTS, CANNED: Fruits & Fruit Prdts
FOOD PRDTS, CANNED: Jams, Jellies & Preserves
FOOD PRDTS, CANNED: Mexican, NEC
FOOD PRDTS, CONFECTIONERY, WHOLESALE: Candy
FOOD PRDTS, CONFECTIONERY, WHOLESALE: Snack Foods
FOOD PRDTS, DAIRY, WHOLESALE: Frozen Dairy Desserts
FOOD PRDTS, FISH & SEAFOOD: Crabmeat, Frozen
FOOD PRDTS, FISH & SEAFOOD: Fish, Filleted
FOOD PRDTS, FROZEN: Ethnic Foods, NEC
FOOD PRDTS, FROZEN: Fruits, Juices & Vegetables
FOOD PRDTS, FRUITS & VEGETABLES, FRESH, WHOLESALE: Fruits
FOOD PRDTS, WHOLESALE: Beans, Field
FOOD PRDTS, WHOLESALE: Beverages, Exc Coffee & Tea
FOOD PRDTS, WHOLESALE: Chocolate
FOOD PRDTS, WHOLESALE: Coffee, Green Or Roasted
FOOD PRDTS, WHOLESALE: Condiments
FOOD PRDTS, WHOLESALE: Dried or Canned Foods
FOOD PRDTS, WHOLESALE: Flavorings & Fragrances
FOOD PRDTS, WHOLESALE: Flour
FOOD PRDTS, WHOLESALE: Grains
FOOD PRDTS, WHOLESALE: Natural & Organic
FOOD PRDTS, WHOLESALE: Salad Dressing
FOOD PRDTS, WHOLESALE: Specialty
FOOD PRDTS, WHOLESALE: Spices & Seasonings
FOOD PRDTS, WHOLESALE: Water, Distilled
FOOD PRDTS: Almond Pastes
FOOD PRDTS: Animal & marine fats & oils
FOOD PRDTS: Cheese Curls & Puffs
FOOD PRDTS: Chicken, Processed, Cooked
FOOD PRDTS: Chicken, Processed, Fresh
FOOD PRDTS: Chicken, Slaughtered & Dressed
FOOD PRDTS: Cocoa, Powdered
FOOD PRDTS: Coffee
FOOD PRDTS: Coffee Extracts
FOOD PRDTS: Cooking Oils, Refined Vegetable, Exc Corn
FOOD PRDTS: Corn Chips & Other Corn-Based Snacks
FOOD PRDTS: Corn Meal
FOOD PRDTS: Desserts, Ready-To-Mix
FOOD PRDTS: Dips, Exc Cheese & Sour Cream Based
FOOD PRDTS: Dough, Pizza, Prepared
FOOD PRDTS: Dressings, Salad, Raw & Cooked Exc Dry Mixes
FOOD PRDTS: Dried & Dehydrated Fruits, Vegetables & Soup Mix
FOOD PRDTS: Edible fats & oils
FOOD PRDTS: Edible Oil Prdts, Exc Corn Oil
FOOD PRDTS: Fish Oil
FOOD PRDTS: Flour
FOOD PRDTS: Flour & Other Grain Mill Products
FOOD PRDTS: Fruit Juices
FOOD PRDTS: Fruits & Vegetables, Pickled
FOOD PRDTS: Gelatin Dessert Preparations
FOOD PRDTS: Ice, Cubes
FOOD PRDTS: Mixes, Bread & Bread-Type Roll
FOOD PRDTS: Mixes, Gravy, Dry
FOOD PRDTS: Mixes, Pancake From Purchased Flour
FOOD PRDTS: Mixes, Sauces, Dry
FOOD PRDTS: Mixes, Seasonings, Dry
FOOD PRDTS: Mustard, Prepared
FOOD PRDTS: Oils & Fats, Marine
FOOD PRDTS: Olive Oil

PRODUCT INDEX

FOOD PRDTS: Pasta, Uncooked, Packaged With Other Ingredients
FOOD PRDTS: Peanut Butter
FOOD PRDTS: Pickles, Vinegar
FOOD PRDTS: Pork Rinds
FOOD PRDTS: Potato Chips & Other Potato-Based Snacks
FOOD PRDTS: Poultry, Processed, Cooked
FOOD PRDTS: Poultry, Processed, Frozen
FOOD PRDTS: Poultry, Slaughtered & Dressed
FOOD PRDTS: Raw cane sugar
FOOD PRDTS: Sandwiches
FOOD PRDTS: Seasonings & Spices
FOOD PRDTS: Soup Mixes
FOOD PRDTS: Starch, Indl
FOOD PRDTS: Syrup, Maple
FOOD PRDTS: Syrups
FOOD PRDTS: Tea
FOOD PRDTS: Tortilla Chips
FOOD PRDTS: Turkey, Slaughtered & Dressed
FOOD PRDTS: Vinegar
FOOD PRDTS: Wheat Flour
FOOD PRODUCTS MACHINERY
FOOD STORES: Convenience, Independent
FOOD STORES: Cooperative
FOOD STORES: Grocery, Independent
FOOD STORES: Supermarkets, Chain
FOOTWEAR, WHOLESALE: Athletic
FOOTWEAR, WHOLESALE: Boots
FOOTWEAR: Cut Stock
FORGINGS: Aircraft, Ferrous
FORGINGS: Aluminum
FORGINGS: Automotive & Internal Combustion Engine
FORGINGS: Construction Or Mining Eqpt, Ferrous
FORGINGS: Iron & Steel
FORGINGS: Nuclear Power Plant, Ferrous
FORGINGS: Plumbing Fixture, Nonferrous
FORMS: Concrete, Sheet Metal
FOUNDRIES: Aluminum
FOUNDRIES: Gray & Ductile Iron
FOUNDRIES: Nonferrous
FOUNDRIES: Steel
FRAMES & FRAMING WHOLESALE
FRAMES: Chair, Metal
FRANCHISES, SELLING OR LICENSING
FREIGHT FORWARDING ARRANGEMENTS
FRICTION MATERIAL, MADE FROM POWDERED METAL
FRUITS & VEGETABLES WHOLESALERS: Fresh
FUEL ADDITIVES
FUEL DEALERS: Coal
FUEL OIL DEALERS
FUEL TREATING
FUELS: Diesel
FUELS: Nuclear
FUELS: Nuclear, Uranium Slug, Radioactive
FULLER'S EARTH MINING
FUND RAISING ORGANIZATION, NON-FEE BASIS
FUNGICIDES OR HERBICIDES
FURNACES & OVENS: Indl
FURNACES: Warm Air, Electric
FURNITURE COMPONENTS: Porcelain Enameled
FURNITURE PARTS: Metal
FURNITURE REFINISHING SVCS
FURNITURE REPAIR & MAINTENANCE SVCS
FURNITURE STOCK & PARTS: Hardwood
FURNITURE STOCK & PARTS: Turnings, Wood
FURNITURE STORES
FURNITURE WHOLESALERS
FURNITURE, HOUSEHOLD: Wholesalers
FURNITURE, MATTRESSES: Wholesalers
FURNITURE, OFFICE: Wholesalers
FURNITURE, OUTDOOR & LAWN: Wholesalers
FURNITURE, WHOLESALE: Beds
FURNITURE, WHOLESALE: Beds & Bedding
FURNITURE, WHOLESALE: Chairs
FURNITURE, WHOLESALE: Lockers
FURNITURE, WHOLESALE: Racks
FURNITURE: Assembly Hall
FURNITURE: Bean Bag Chairs
FURNITURE: Bedroom, Wood
FURNITURE: Bedsprings, Assembled
FURNITURE: Box Springs, Assembled
FURNITURE: Cabinets & Filing Drawers, Office, Exc Wood
FURNITURE: Chairs & Couches, Wood, Upholstered
FURNITURE: Chairs, Household Upholstered
FURNITURE: Chairs, Household Wood
FURNITURE: Chairs, Household, Metal
FURNITURE: Chairs, Office Wood
FURNITURE: Church
FURNITURE: Couches, Sofa/Davenport, Upholstered Wood Frames
FURNITURE: Dining Room, Wood
FURNITURE: Fiberglass & Plastic
FURNITURE: Garden, Exc Wood, Metal, Stone Or Concrete
FURNITURE: Hotel
FURNITURE: Household, Metal
FURNITURE: Household, Upholstered, Exc Wood Or Metal
FURNITURE: Juvenile, Upholstered On Wood Frames
FURNITURE: Laboratory
FURNITURE: Lawn, Exc Wood, Metal, Stone Or Concrete
FURNITURE: Living Room, Upholstered On Wood Frames
FURNITURE: Mattresses & Foundations
FURNITURE: Mattresses, Box & Bedsprings
FURNITURE: Mattresses, Innerspring Or Box Spring
FURNITURE: Novelty, Wood
FURNITURE: Office, Exc Wood
FURNITURE: Office, Wood
FURNITURE: Recliners, Upholstered On Wood Frames
FURNITURE: School
FURNITURE: Sleep
FURNITURE: Stadium
FURNITURE: Storage Chests, Household, Wood
FURNITURE: Table Tops, Marble
FURNITURE: Tables, Household, Metal
FURNITURE: Tables, Office, Exc Wood
FURNITURE: Tables, Office, Wood
FURNITURE: Upholstered
FURNITURE: Wicker & Rattan
FUSES: Electric

G

GAMES & TOYS: Board Games, Children's & Adults'
GAMES & TOYS: Craft & Hobby Kits & Sets
GAMES & TOYS: Electronic
GAMES & TOYS: Erector Sets
GARBAGE CONTAINERS: Plastic
GAS & OIL FIELD EXPLORATION SVCS
GAS & OIL FIELD SVCS, NEC
GASES: Acetylene
GASES: Indl
GASES: Nitrogen
GASES: Oxygen
GASKETS
GASKETS & SEALING DEVICES
GASOLINE FILLING STATIONS
GASOLINE WHOLESALERS
GEARS
GEARS & GEAR UNITS: Reduction, Exc Auto
GEARS: Power Transmission, Exc Auto
GENERATION EQPT: Electronic
GENERATOR REPAIR SVCS
GENERATORS SETS: Steam
GIFT SHOP
GIFT, NOVELTY & SOUVENIR STORES: Gifts & Novelties
GLASS & GLASS CERAMIC PRDTS, PRESSED OR BLOWN: Tableware
GLASS PRDTS, FROM PURCHASED GLASS: Insulating
GLASS PRDTS, FROM PURCHASED GLASS: Mirrored
GLASS PRDTS, FROM PURCHASED GLASS: Windshields
GLASS PRDTS, FROM PURCHD GLASS: Strengthened Or Reinforced
GLASS PRDTS, PRESSED OR BLOWN: Scientific Glassware
GLASS PRDTS, PRESSED OR BLOWN: Yarn, Fiberglass
GLASS, AUTOMOTIVE: Wholesalers
GLASS: Broadwoven Fabrics
GLASS: Fiber
GLASS: Flat
GLASS: Leaded
GLASS: Optical
GLASS: Pressed & Blown, NEC
GLASS: Tempered
GLASSWARE: Laboratory
GLOVES: Safety
GLOVES: Work
GOLF EQPT
GOLF GOODS & EQPT
GOURMET FOOD STORES

GRADING SVCS
GRANITE: Crushed & Broken
GRANITE: Cut & Shaped
GRAPHIC ARTS & RELATED DESIGN SVCS
GRASSES: Artificial & Preserved
GRATINGS: Tread, Fabricated Metal
GRAVE VAULTS, METAL
GREENHOUSES: Prefabricated Metal
GRINDING SVC: Precision, Commercial Or Indl
GROCERIES, GENERAL LINE WHOLESALERS
GUIDANCE SYSTEMS & EQPT: Space Vehicle
GUIDED MISSILES & SPACE VEHICLES
GUM & WOOD CHEMICALS
GUTTERS: Sheet Metal
GYPSUM PRDTS

H

HAIR & HAIR BASED PRDTS
HAIR CARE PRDTS
HAIR DRESSING, FOR THE TRADE
HAMPERS: Solid Fiber, Made From Purchased Materials
HANDBAGS
HANDBAGS: Women's
HANDLES: Brush Or Tool, Plastic
HANDYMAN SVCS
HANG GLIDERS
HARDWARE
HARDWARE & BUILDING PRDTS: Plastic
HARDWARE & EQPT: Stage, Exc Lighting
HARDWARE STORES
HARDWARE STORES: Builders'
HARDWARE STORES: Pumps & Pumping Eqpt
HARDWARE STORES: Tools
HARDWARE STORES: Tools, Hand
HARDWARE WHOLESALERS
HARDWARE, WHOLESALE: Bolts
HARDWARE, WHOLESALE: Builders', NEC
HARDWARE, WHOLESALE: Furniture, NEC
HARDWARE, WHOLESALE: Power Tools & Access
HARDWARE, WHOLESALE: Security Devices, Locks
HARDWARE: Aircraft
HARDWARE: Builders'
HARDWARE: Door Opening & Closing Devices, Exc Electrical
HARDWARE: Furniture
HARDWARE: Furniture, Builders' & Other Household
HARDWARE: Parachute
HARNESS ASSEMBLIES: Cable & Wire
HARNESS WIRING SETS: Internal Combustion Engines
HEALTH AIDS: Exercise Eqpt
HEARING AIDS
HEAT TREATING: Metal
HEATERS: Swimming Pool, Electric
HEATING & AIR CONDITIONING UNITS, COMBINATION
HEATING EQPT: Complete
HEATING UNITS & DEVICES: Indl, Electric
HELICOPTERS
HELMETS: Athletic
HELMETS: Steel
HIGH ENERGY PARTICLE PHYSICS EQPT
HOBBY, TOY & GAME STORES: Arts & Crafts & Splys
HOBBY, TOY & GAME STORES: Ceramics Splys
HOBBY, TOY & GAME STORES: Toys & Games
HOISTS
HOISTS: Hand
HOLDING COMPANIES: Investment, Exc Banks
HOLDING COMPANIES: Personal, Exc Banks
HOME ENTERTAINMENT EQPT: Electronic, NEC
HOME FOR THE MENTALLY HANDICAPPED
HOME HEALTH CARE SVCS
HOMEFURNISHING STORES: Beddings & Linens
HOMEFURNISHING STORES: Lighting Fixtures
HOMEFURNISHING STORES: Pottery
HOMEFURNISHINGS, WHOLESALE: Blinds, Vertical
HOMEFURNISHINGS, WHOLESALE: Fireplace Eqpt & Access
HOMEFURNISHINGS, WHOLESALE: Floor Cushion & Padding
HOMEFURNISHINGS, WHOLESALE: Linens, Table
HOMEFURNISHINGS, WHOLESALE: Stainless Steel Flatware
HOMEFURNISHINGS, WHOLESALE: Wood Flooring
HOMES: Log Cabins
HOODS: Door, Aluminum

PRODUCT INDEX

HORSESHOES
HOSE: Automobile, Rubber
HOSE: Flexible Metal
HOSE: Plastic
HOSE: Rubber
HOSIERY DYEING & FINISHING
HOSPITALS: Medical & Surgical
HOT TUBS
HOT TUBS: Plastic & Fiberglass
HOUSEHOLD ARTICLES, EXC FURNITURE: Cut Stone
HOUSEHOLD ARTICLES: Metal
HOUSEHOLD FURNISHINGS, NEC
HOUSEHOLD SEWING MACHINES WHOLESALERS: Electric
HOUSEWARES, ELECTRIC, EXC COOKING APPLIANCES & UTENSILS
HOUSEWARES, ELECTRIC: Air Purifiers, Portable
HOUSEWARES, ELECTRIC: Heating Units, Electric Appliances
HUMIDIFIERS & DEHUMIDIFIERS
HYDRAULIC EQPT REPAIR SVC

I

ICE
ICE CREAM & ICES WHOLESALERS
IGNITION APPARATUS & DISTRIBUTORS
IGNITION SYSTEMS: High Frequency
INCUBATORS & BROODERS: Farm
INDL & PERSONAL SVC PAPER WHOLESALERS
INDL & PERSONAL SVC PAPER, WHOLESALE: Shipping Splys
INDL CONTRACTORS: Exhibit Construction
INDL EQPT SVCS
INDL GASES WHOLESALERS
INDL MACHINERY & EQPT WHOLESALERS
INDL PROCESS INSTRUMENTS: Control
INDL PROCESS INSTRUMENTS: Elements, Primary
INDL SPLYS WHOLESALERS
INDL SPLYS, WHOLESALE: Bearings
INDL SPLYS, WHOLESALE: Clean Room Splys
INDL SPLYS, WHOLESALE: Drums, New Or Reconditioned
INDL SPLYS, WHOLESALE: Gaskets
INDL SPLYS, WHOLESALE: Mill Splys
INDL SPLYS, WHOLESALE: Power Transmission, Eqpt & Apparatus
INDL SPLYS, WHOLESALE: Rubber Goods, Mechanical
INDL SPLYS, WHOLESALE: Tools
INDL SPLYS, WHOLESALE: Tools, NEC
INDL SPLYS, WHOLESALE: Valves & Fittings
INDL TRUCK REPAIR SVCS
INDUSTRIAL & COMMERCIAL EQPT INSPECTION SVCS
INFORMATION RETRIEVAL SERVICES
INFORMATION SVCS: Consumer
INFRARED OBJECT DETECTION EQPT
INK: Printing
INSECTICIDES
INSECTICIDES & PESTICIDES
INSPECTION & TESTING SVCS
INSTRUMENTS & METERS: Measuring, Electric
INSTRUMENTS, LABORATORY: Analyzers, Automatic Chemical
INSTRUMENTS, MEASURING & CNTRL: Geophysical & Meteorological
INSTRUMENTS, MEASURING & CNTRLG: Aircraft & Motor Vehicle
INSTRUMENTS, MEASURING & CONTROLLING: Ion Chambers
INSTRUMENTS, MEASURING & CONTROLLING: Transits, Surveyors'
INSTRUMENTS, OPTICAL: Mirrors
INSTRUMENTS, SURGICAL & MED: Needles & Syringes, Hypodermic
INSTRUMENTS, SURGICAL & MEDICAL: Blood & Bone Work
INSTRUMENTS, SURGICAL & MEDICAL: Blood Transfusion
INSTRUMENTS, SURGICAL & MEDICAL: Catheters
INSTRUMENTS, SURGICAL & MEDICAL: Inhalation Therapy
INSTRUMENTS, SURGICAL & MEDICAL: IV Transfusion
INSTRUMENTS, SURGICAL & MEDICAL: Muscle Exercise, Ophthalmic
INSTRUMENTS, SURGICAL & MEDICAL: Ophthalmic
INSTRUMENTS: Analytical
INSTRUMENTS: Combustion Control, Indl
INSTRUMENTS: Electrocardiographs
INSTRUMENTS: Endoscopic Eqpt, Electromedical
INSTRUMENTS: Flow, Indl Process
INSTRUMENTS: Indl Process Control
INSTRUMENTS: Infrared, Indl Process
INSTRUMENTS: Measurement, Indl Process
INSTRUMENTS: Measuring, Electrical Power
INSTRUMENTS: Medical & Surgical
INSTRUMENTS: Optical, Analytical
INSTRUMENTS: Power Measuring, Electrical
INSTRUMENTS: Pressure Measurement, Indl
INSTRUMENTS: Radio Frequency Measuring
INSTRUMENTS: Seismographs
INSTRUMENTS: Test, Electronic & Electric Measurement
INSTRUMENTS: Test, Electronic & Electrical Circuits
INSULATING COMPOUNDS
INSULATION & ROOFING MATERIALS: Wood, Reconstituted
INSULATION MATERIALS WHOLESALERS
INSULATION: Felt
INSULATION: Fiberglass
INSULATORS & INSULATION MATERIALS: Electrical
INSULATORS, PORCELAIN: Electrical
INSURANCE: Agents, Brokers & Service
INTEGRATED CIRCUITS, SEMICONDUCTOR NETWORKS, ETC
INTERIOR DESIGN SVCS, NEC
INVERTERS: Nonrotating Electrical
INVERTERS: Rotating Electrical
INVESTORS, NEC
INVESTORS: Real Estate, Exc Property Operators

J

JEWELRY & PRECIOUS STONES WHOLESALERS
JEWELRY REPAIR SVCS
JEWELRY STORES
JEWELRY STORES: Precious Stones & Precious Metals
JEWELRY, PRECIOUS METAL: Medals, Precious Or Semiprecious
JEWELRY, PRECIOUS METAL: Pins
JEWELRY, PRECIOUS METAL: Rings, Finger
JEWELRY, PRECIOUS METAL: Settings & Mountings
JEWELRY, WHOLESALE
JEWELRY: Precious Metal
JIGS & FIXTURES
JOB PRINTING & NEWSPAPER PUBLISHING COMBINED
JOISTS: Fabricated Bar
JOISTS: Long-Span Series, Open Web Steel

K

KITCHEN CABINETS WHOLESALERS
KITCHEN UTENSILS: Food Handling & Processing Prdts, Wood
KITCHENWARE STORES
KNIT OUTERWEAR DYEING & FINISHING, EXC HOSIERY & GLOVE
KNIVES: Agricultural Or Indl

L

LABELS: Cotton, Printed
LABELS: Paper, Made From Purchased Materials
LABELS: Woven
LABORATORIES, TESTING: Pollution
LABORATORIES, TESTING: Product Testing
LABORATORIES, TESTING: Product Testing, Safety/Performance
LABORATORIES: Biological Research
LABORATORIES: Biotechnology
LABORATORIES: Electronic Research
LABORATORIES: Medical
LABORATORIES: Physical Research, Commercial
LABORATORIES: Testing
LABORATORIES: Testing
LABORATORY APPARATUS & FURNITURE
LABORATORY APPARATUS, EXC HEATING & MEASURING
LABORATORY APPARATUS: Pipettes, Hemocytometer
LABORATORY CHEMICALS: Organic
LABORATORY EQPT, EXC MEDICAL: Wholesalers
LABORATORY EQPT: Clinical Instruments Exc Medical
LABORATORY EQPT: Incubators
LABORATORY EQPT: Measuring
LACE GOODS & WARP KNIT FABRIC DYEING & FINISHING
LADDERS: Permanent Installation, Metal
LAMINATED PLASTICS: Plate, Sheet, Rod & Tubes
LAMINATING SVCS
LAMP & LIGHT BULBS & TUBES
LAMP BULBS & TUBES, ELECTRIC: Glow Lamp
LAMP BULBS & TUBES, ELECTRIC: Health, Infrared/Ultraviolet
LAMP BULBS & TUBES, ELECTRIC: Light, Complete
LAMP BULBS & TUBES/PARTS, ELECTRIC: Generalized Applications
LAMP SHADES: Glass
LAMPS: Boudoir, Residential
LAMPS: Table, Residential
LAND SUBDIVIDERS & DEVELOPERS: Commercial
LASER SYSTEMS & EQPT
LASERS: Welding, Drilling & Cutting Eqpt
LATEX: Foamed
LAUNDRY EQPT: Commercial
LAUNDRY SVC: Work Clothing Sply
LAWN & GARDEN EQPT
LAWN & GARDEN EQPT: Blowers & Vacuums
LAWN & GARDEN EQPT: Grass Catchers, Lawn Mower
LAWN & GARDEN EQPT: Lawnmowers, Residential, Hand Or Power
LAWN & GARDEN EQPT: Tractors & Eqpt
LEAD PENCILS & ART GOODS
LEAF TOBACCO WHOLESALERS
LEASING & RENTAL: Construction & Mining Eqpt
LEASING & RENTAL: Medical Machinery & Eqpt
LEASING & RENTAL: Trucks, Without Drivers
LEASING: Passenger Car
LEATHER & CUT STOCK WHOLESALERS
LEATHER GOODS, EXC FOOTWEAR, GLOVES, LUGGAGE/ BELTING, WHOL
LEATHER GOODS: Card Cases
LEATHER GOODS: Garments
LEATHER GOODS: Holsters
LEATHER GOODS: Personal
LEATHER GOODS: Safety Belts
LEATHER GOODS: Wallets
LEATHER TANNING & FINISHING
LEATHER, LEATHER GOODS & FURS, WHOLESALE
LEATHER: Accessory Prdts
LICENSE TAGS: Automobile, Stamped Metal
LIFE SAVING & SURVIVAL EQPT REPAIR SVCS, NONMEDICAL
LIGHTING EQPT: Flashlights
LIGHTING EQPT: Motor Vehicle, NEC
LIGHTING FIXTURES WHOLESALERS
LIGHTING FIXTURES, NEC
LIGHTING FIXTURES: Arc
LIGHTING FIXTURES: Decorative Area
LIGHTING FIXTURES: Fluorescent, Commercial
LIGHTING FIXTURES: Fluorescent, Residential
LIGHTING FIXTURES: Indl & Commercial
LIGHTING FIXTURES: Motor Vehicle
LIGHTING FIXTURES: Residential, Electric
LIGHTING FIXTURES: Street
LIGHTING FIXTURES: Underwater
LIME ROCK: Ground
LIMESTONE: Crushed & Broken
LIMESTONE: Dimension
LINENS: Tablecloths, From Purchased Materials
LINERS & COVERS: Fabric
LINERS: Indl, Metal Plate
LININGS: Fabric, Apparel & Other, Exc Millinery
LIP BALMS
LIQUID CRYSTAL DISPLAYS
LITHIUM MINERAL MINING
LITHOGRAPHIC PLATES
LOADS: Electronic
LOCKERS
LOCKERS: Wood, Exc Refrigerated
LOCKS
LOCKS & LOCK SETS, WHOLESALE
LOCKS: Safe & Vault, Metal
LOCKSMITHS
LOGGING
LOGGING CAMPS & CONTRACTORS
LOGGING: Timber, Cut At Logging Camp
LOGGING: Wooden Logs
LOGS: Gas, Fireplace
LOTIONS OR CREAMS: Face
LOTIONS: SHAVING
LOZENGES: Pharmaceutical

PRODUCT INDEX

LUBRICATING OIL & GREASE WHOLESALERS
LUBRICATION SYSTEMS & EQPT
LUGGAGE & BRIEFCASES
LUMBER & BLDG MATLS DEALER, RET: Electric Constructn Matls
LUMBER & BLDG MATLS DEALER, RET: Garage Doors, Sell/Install
LUMBER & BLDG MATRLS DEALERS, RETAIL: Doors, Wood/Metal
LUMBER & BLDG MTRLS DEALERS, RET: Planing Mill Prdts/Lumber
LUMBER & BUILDING MATERIAL DEALERS, RETAIL: Roofing Material
LUMBER & BUILDING MATERIALS DEALER, RET: Door & Window Prdts
LUMBER & BUILDING MATERIALS DEALER, RET: Masonry Matls/Splys
LUMBER & BUILDING MATERIALS DEALERS, RETAIL: Brick
LUMBER & BUILDING MATERIALS DEALERS, RETAIL: Cement
LUMBER & BUILDING MATERIALS DEALERS, RETAIL: Sand & Gravel
LUMBER & BUILDING MATERIALS RET DEALERS: Millwork & Lumber
LUMBER & BUILDING MATLS DEALERS, RET: Screens, Door/Window
LUMBER: Dimension, Hardwood
LUMBER: Flooring, Dressed, Softwood
LUMBER: Hardboard
LUMBER: Hardwood Dimension
LUMBER: Hardwood Dimension & Flooring Mills
LUMBER: Kiln Dried
LUMBER: Plywood, Hardwood
LUMBER: Plywood, Hardwood or Hardwood Faced
LUMBER: Plywood, Prefinished, Hardwood
LUMBER: Rails, Fence, Round Or Split
LUMBER: Treated
LUMBER: Veneer, Softwood

M

MACHINE PARTS: Stamped Or Pressed Metal
MACHINE TOOL ACCESS: Drills
MACHINE TOOL ACCESS: Tools & Access
MACHINE TOOL ATTACHMENTS & ACCESS
MACHINE TOOLS & ACCESS
MACHINE TOOLS, METAL CUTTING: Drilling
MACHINE TOOLS, METAL CUTTING: Drilling & Boring
MACHINE TOOLS, METAL CUTTING: Home Workshop
MACHINE TOOLS, METAL CUTTING: Lathes
MACHINE TOOLS, METAL CUTTING: Numerically Controlled
MACHINE TOOLS, METAL CUTTING: Tool Replacement & Rpr Parts
MACHINE TOOLS, METAL FORMING: Bending
MACHINE TOOLS, METAL FORMING: Headers
MACHINE TOOLS, METAL FORMING: Mechanical, Pneumatic Or Hyd
MACHINE TOOLS, METAL FORMING: Punching & Shearing
MACHINE TOOLS, METAL FORMING: Rebuilt
MACHINE TOOLS: Metal Cutting
MACHINE TOOLS: Metal Forming
MACHINERY & EQPT, AGRICULTURAL, WHOLESALE: Agricultural, NEC
MACHINERY & EQPT, AGRICULTURAL, WHOLESALE: Lawn & Garden
MACHINERY & EQPT, INDL, WHOLESALE: Chemical Process
MACHINERY & EQPT, INDL, WHOLESALE: Conveyor Systems
MACHINERY & EQPT, INDL, WHOLESALE: Cranes
MACHINERY & EQPT, INDL, WHOLESALE: Engines & Parts, Diesel
MACHINERY & EQPT, INDL, WHOLESALE: Engines, Gasoline
MACHINERY & EQPT, INDL, WHOLESALE: Fans
MACHINERY & EQPT, INDL, WHOLESALE: Food Product Manufacturng
MACHINERY & EQPT, INDL, WHOLESALE: Hydraulic Systems
MACHINERY & EQPT, INDL, WHOLESALE: Indl Machine Parts
MACHINERY & EQPT, INDL, WHOLESALE: Instruments & Cntrl Eqpt
MACHINERY & EQPT, INDL, WHOLESALE: Machine Tools & Access
MACHINERY & EQPT, INDL, WHOLESALE: Machine Tools & Metalwork
MACHINERY & EQPT, INDL, WHOLESALE: Packaging
MACHINERY & EQPT, INDL, WHOLESALE: Safety Eqpt
MACHINERY & EQPT, INDL, WHOLESALE: Sewing
MACHINERY & EQPT, INDL, WHOLESALE: Textile & Leather
MACHINERY & EQPT, INDL, WHOLESALE: Trailers, Indl
MACHINERY & EQPT, WHOLESALE: Construction, General
MACHINERY & EQPT: Farm
MACHINERY & EQPT: Liquid Automation
MACHINERY, EQPT & SUPPLIES: Parking Facility
MACHINERY, FOOD PRDTS: Beverage
MACHINERY, FOOD PRDTS: Dairy & Milk
MACHINERY, FOOD PRDTS: Food Processing, Smokers
MACHINERY, FOOD PRDTS: Oilseed Crushing & Extracting
MACHINERY, FOOD PRDTS: Ovens, Bakery
MACHINERY, FOOD PRDTS: Packing House
MACHINERY, FOOD PRDTS: Processing, Poultry
MACHINERY, MAILING: Postage Meters
MACHINERY, PACKAGING: Canning, Food
MACHINERY, PAPER INDUSTRY: Converting, Die Cutting & Stampng
MACHINERY, PAPER INDUSTRY: Pulp Mill
MACHINERY, PRINTING TRADES: Plates
MACHINERY, TEXTILE: Creels
MACHINERY, TEXTILE: Finishing
MACHINERY, TEXTILE: Printing
MACHINERY, WOODWORKING: Sanding, Exc Portable Floor Sanders
MACHINERY: Ammunition & Explosives Loading
MACHINERY: Automotive Related
MACHINERY: Bridge Or Gate, Hydraulic
MACHINERY: Construction
MACHINERY: Cotton Ginning
MACHINERY: Custom
MACHINERY: Electronic Component Making
MACHINERY: Ice Making
MACHINERY: Kilns, Lumber
MACHINERY: Metalworking
MACHINERY: Mining
MACHINERY: Packaging
MACHINERY: Paint Making
MACHINERY: Plastic Working
MACHINERY: Recycling
MACHINERY: Road Construction & Maintenance
MACHINERY: Robots, Molding & Forming Plastics
MACHINERY: Rubber Working
MACHINERY: Semiconductor Manufacturing
MACHINERY: Textile
MACHINERY: Wire Drawing
MACHINERY: Woodworking
MACHINISTS' TOOLS & MACHINES: Measuring, Metalworking Type
MACHINISTS' TOOLS: Measuring, Precision
MACHINISTS' TOOLS: Precision
MACHINISTS' TOOLS: Scales, Measuring, Precision
MAGAZINES, WHOLESALE
MAGNESIUM
MAGNETIC INK & OPTICAL SCANNING EQPT
MAGNETIC SHIELDS, METAL
MAGNETIC TAPE, AUDIO: Prerecorded
MAGNETS: Permanent
MAIL-ORDER HOUSE, NEC
MAIL-ORDER HOUSES: Fitness & Sporting Goods
MAIL-ORDER HOUSES: Jewelry
MAIL-ORDER HOUSES: Women's Apparel
MAILBOX RENTAL & RELATED SVCS
MAILING LIST: Compilers
MAILING MACHINES WHOLESALERS
MAILING SVCS, NEC
MANAGEMENT CONSULTING SVCS: Administrative
MANAGEMENT CONSULTING SVCS: Automation & Robotics
MANAGEMENT CONSULTING SVCS: Business
MANAGEMENT CONSULTING SVCS: Business Planning & Organizing
MANAGEMENT CONSULTING SVCS: Construction Project
MANAGEMENT CONSULTING SVCS: Distribution Channels
MANAGEMENT CONSULTING SVCS: Food & Beverage
MANAGEMENT CONSULTING SVCS: General
MANAGEMENT CONSULTING SVCS: Hospital & Health
MANAGEMENT CONSULTING SVCS: Industrial
MANAGEMENT CONSULTING SVCS: Industrial & Labor
MANAGEMENT CONSULTING SVCS: Quality Assurance
MANAGEMENT CONSULTING SVCS: Training & Development
MANAGEMENT CONSULTING SVCS: Transportation
MANAGEMENT SERVICES
MANAGEMENT SVCS: Business
MANAGEMENT SVCS: Construction
MANAGEMENT SVCS: Restaurant
MANUFACTURING INDUSTRIES, NEC
MARBLE, BUILDING: Cut & Shaped
MARINE HARDWARE
MARINE RELATED EQPT
MARINE SPLYS WHOLESALERS
MARKETS: Meat & fish
MARKING DEVICES
MARKING DEVICES: Embossing Seals & Hand Stamps
MATERNITY WEAR STORES
MATS OR MATTING, NEC: Rubber
MATS, MATTING & PADS: Varnished Glass
MATTRESS PROTECTORS, EXC RUBBER
MEAT MARKETS
MEAT PRDTS: Bacon, Side & Sliced, From Purchased Meat
MEAT PRDTS: Bacon, Slab & Sliced, From Slaughtered Meat
MEAT PRDTS: Boxed Beef, From Slaughtered Meat
MEAT PRDTS: Ham, Smoked, From Purchased Meat
MEAT PRDTS: Prepared Beef Prdts From Purchased Beef
MEAT PRDTS: Sausages, From Purchased Meat
MEAT PRDTS: Snack Sticks, Incl Jerky, From Purchased Meat
MEAT PROCESSING MACHINERY
MEDIA: Magnetic & Optical Recording
MEDICAL & HOSPITAL EQPT WHOLESALERS
MEDICAL & SURGICAL SPLYS: Bandages & Dressings
MEDICAL & SURGICAL SPLYS: Braces, Orthopedic
MEDICAL & SURGICAL SPLYS: Clothing, Fire Resistant & Protect
MEDICAL & SURGICAL SPLYS: Cosmetic Restorations
MEDICAL & SURGICAL SPLYS: Gynecological Splys & Appliances
MEDICAL & SURGICAL SPLYS: Ligatures
MEDICAL & SURGICAL SPLYS: Limbs, Artificial
MEDICAL & SURGICAL SPLYS: Orthopedic Appliances
MEDICAL & SURGICAL SPLYS: Personal Safety Eqpt
MEDICAL & SURGICAL SPLYS: Prosthetic Appliances
MEDICAL CENTERS
MEDICAL EQPT REPAIR SVCS, NON-ELECTRIC
MEDICAL EQPT: CAT Scanner Or Computerized Axial Tomography
MEDICAL EQPT: Diagnostic
MEDICAL EQPT: Electromedical Apparatus
MEDICAL EQPT: Ultrasonic Scanning Devices
MEDICAL EQPT: Ultrasonic, Exc Cleaning
MEDICAL SVCS ORGANIZATION
MEMBERSHIP ORGANIZATIONS, BUSINESS: Growers' Association
MEMBERSHIP ORGANIZATIONS, RELIGIOUS: Baptist Church
MEN'S & BOYS' CLOTHING STORES
MEN'S & BOYS' CLOTHING WHOLESALERS, NEC
MEN'S & BOYS' HOSIERY WHOLESALERS
MERCHANDISING MACHINE OPERATORS: Vending
METAL & STEEL PRDTS: Abrasive
METAL COMPONENTS: Prefabricated
METAL FINISHING SVCS
METAL OXIDE SILICONE OR MOS DEVICES
METAL SERVICE CENTERS & OFFICES
METAL STAMPING, FOR THE TRADE
METAL STAMPINGS: Perforated
METAL: Battery
METALS SVC CENTERS & WHOLESALERS: Foundry Prdts
METALS SVC CENTERS & WHOLESALERS: Pipe & Tubing, Steel
METALS SVC CENTERS & WHOLESALERS: Steel
METALS: Precious NEC
METALS: Primary Nonferrous, NEC
METALWORK: Miscellaneous
METALWORK: Ornamental
METALWORKING MACHINERY WHOLESALERS
METERING DEVICES: Gasoline Dispensing
METERING DEVICES: Water Quality Monitoring & Control Systems
METERS: Turbine Flow, Indl Process

PRODUCT INDEX

MICROCIRCUITS, INTEGRATED: Semiconductor
MICROPROCESSORS
MICROWAVE COMPONENTS
MILITARY INSIGNIA
MILITARY INSIGNIA, TEXTILE
MILLWORK
MINE & QUARRY SVCS: Nonmetallic Minerals
MINERAL WOOL
MINERALS: Ground or Treated
MINIATURES
MINING EXPLORATION & DEVELOPMENT SVCS
MINING MACHINERY & EQPT WHOLESALERS
MIXTURES & BLOCKS: Asphalt Paving
MOBILE COMMUNICATIONS EQPT
MOBILE HOMES
MOBILE HOMES, EXC RECREATIONAL
MODELS: General, Exc Toy
MODULES: Computer Logic
MODULES: Solid State
MOLDED RUBBER PRDTS
MOLDING COMPOUNDS
MOLDINGS & TRIM: Metal, Exc Automobile
MOLDINGS & TRIM: Wood
MOLDINGS OR TRIM: Automobile, Stamped Metal
MOLDS: Indl
MONUMENTS & GRAVE MARKERS, WHOLESALE
MOPS: Floor & Dust
MOTION PICTURE & VIDEO DISTRIBUTION
MOTION PICTURE & VIDEO PRODUCTION SVCS: Educational
MOTOR & GENERATOR PARTS: Electric
MOTOR CONTROL CENTERS
MOTOR HOMES
MOTOR VEHICLE ASSEMBLY, COMPLETE: Ambulances
MOTOR VEHICLE ASSEMBLY, COMPLETE: Buses, All Types
MOTOR VEHICLE ASSEMBLY, COMPLETE: Fire Department Vehicles
MOTOR VEHICLE ASSEMBLY, COMPLETE: Military Motor Vehicle
MOTOR VEHICLE ASSEMBLY, COMPLETE: Motor Buses
MOTOR VEHICLE ASSEMBLY, COMPLETE: Universal Carriers, Mil
MOTOR VEHICLE ASSEMBLY, COMPLETE: Wreckers, Tow Truck
MOTOR VEHICLE DEALERS: Automobiles, New & Used
MOTOR VEHICLE PARTS & ACCESS: Acceleration Eqpt
MOTOR VEHICLE PARTS & ACCESS: Air Conditioner Parts
MOTOR VEHICLE PARTS & ACCESS: Ball Joints
MOTOR VEHICLE PARTS & ACCESS: Body Components & Frames
MOTOR VEHICLE PARTS & ACCESS: Brakes, Air
MOTOR VEHICLE PARTS & ACCESS: Clutches
MOTOR VEHICLE PARTS & ACCESS: Cylinder Heads
MOTOR VEHICLE PARTS & ACCESS: Electrical Eqpt
MOTOR VEHICLE PARTS & ACCESS: Engines & Parts
MOTOR VEHICLE PARTS & ACCESS: Engs & Trans,Factory, Rebuilt
MOTOR VEHICLE PARTS & ACCESS: Fuel Pumps
MOTOR VEHICLE PARTS & ACCESS: Fuel Systems & Parts
MOTOR VEHICLE PARTS & ACCESS: Gas Tanks
MOTOR VEHICLE PARTS & ACCESS: Gears
MOTOR VEHICLE PARTS & ACCESS: Lifting Mechanisms, Dump Truck
MOTOR VEHICLE PARTS & ACCESS: Mufflers, Exhaust
MOTOR VEHICLE PARTS & ACCESS: Power Steering Eqpt
MOTOR VEHICLE PARTS & ACCESS: Propane Conversion Eqpt
MOTOR VEHICLE PARTS & ACCESS: Tire Valve Cores
MOTOR VEHICLE PARTS & ACCESS: Tops
MOTOR VEHICLE PARTS & ACCESS: Transmissions
MOTOR VEHICLE PARTS & ACCESS: Universal Joints
MOTOR VEHICLE PARTS & ACCESS: Wiring Harness Sets
MOTOR VEHICLE RACING & DRIVER SVCS
MOTOR VEHICLE SPLYS & PARTS WHOLESALERS: New
MOTOR VEHICLE SPLYS & PARTS WHOLESALERS: Used
MOTOR VEHICLE: Hardware
MOTOR VEHICLE: Radiators
MOTOR VEHICLE: Shock Absorbers
MOTOR VEHICLE: Steering Mechanisms
MOTOR VEHICLE: Wheels
MOTOR VEHICLES & CAR BODIES
MOTOR VEHICLES, WHOLESALE: Fire Trucks
MOTOR VEHICLES, WHOLESALE: Truck tractors
MOTORCYCLE ACCESS
MOTORCYCLE DEALERS
MOTORCYCLES & RELATED PARTS
MOTORS: Electric
MOTORS: Fluid Power
MOTORS: Generators
MOUNTING SVC: Swatches & Samples
MULTIPLEXERS: Telephone & Telegraph
MUSIC DISTRIBUTION APPARATUS
MUSICAL INSTRUMENTS & ACCESS: Carrying Cases
MUSICAL INSTRUMENTS & ACCESS: NEC
MUSICAL INSTRUMENTS & SPLYS STORES: Pianos
MUSICAL INSTRUMENTS WHOLESALERS
MUSICAL INSTRUMENTS: Guitars & Parts, Electric & Acoustic

N

NAILS: Steel, Wire Or Cut
NAME PLATES: Engraved Or Etched
NATURAL GAS DISTRIBUTION TO CONSUMERS
NATURAL GAS LIQUIDS PRODUCTION
NATURAL GAS PRODUCTION
NATURAL PROPANE PRODUCTION
NAVIGATIONAL SYSTEMS & INSTRUMENTS
NEW & USED CAR DEALERS
NICKEL
NITRILE RUBBERS: Butadiene-Acrylonitrile
NONCURRENT CARRYING WIRING DEVICES
NONFERROUS: Rolling & Drawing, NEC
NOVELTIES
NOVELTIES & SPECIALTIES: Metal
NOVELTIES, PAPER, WHOLESALE
NOVELTIES: Paper, Made From Purchased Materials
NOVELTIES: Plastic
NOZZLES: Fire Fighting
NOZZLES: Spray, Aerosol, Paint Or Insecticide
NUCLEAR SHIELDING: Metal Plate
NURSERIES & LAWN & GARDEN SPLY STORES, RETAIL: Fertilizer
NUTRITION SVCS
NYLON FIBERS

O

OFFICE EQPT WHOLESALERS
OFFICE FURNITURE REPAIR & MAINTENANCE SVCS
OFFICE SPLY & STATIONERY STORES: Office Forms & Splys
OFFICE SPLYS, NEC, WHOLESALE
OFFICES & CLINICS OF DOCTORS OF MEDICINE: Radiologist
OIL & GAS FIELD MACHINERY
OIL FIELD SVCS, NEC
OILS & ESSENTIAL OILS
OILS: Mineral, Natural
OPHTHALMIC GOODS
OPHTHALMIC GOODS: Frames, Lenses & Parts, Eyeglasses
OPTICAL GOODS STORES
OPTICAL GOODS STORES: Eyeglasses, Prescription
OPTICAL GOODS STORES: Opticians
OPTICAL INSTRUMENTS & APPARATUS
OPTICAL INSTRUMENTS & LENSES
ORGANIZATIONS: Biotechnical Research, Noncommercial
ORGANIZATIONS: Medical Research
ORGANIZATIONS: Professional
ORGANIZATIONS: Religious
ORGANIZATIONS: Research Institute
ORIENTED STRANDBOARD
OVENS: Paint Baking & Drying

P

PACKAGE DESIGN SVCS
PACKAGING & LABELING SVCS
PACKAGING MATERIALS, WHOLESALE
PACKAGING MATERIALS: Paper
PACKAGING MATERIALS: Paper, Coated Or Laminated
PACKAGING MATERIALS: Plastic Film, Coated Or Laminated
PACKING & CRATING SVC
PACKING MATERIALS: Mechanical
PADS: Mattress
PAINTS & ADDITIVES
PAINTS & ALLIED PRODUCTS
PAINTS, VARNISHES & SPLYS WHOLESALERS
PAINTS, VARNISHES & SPLYS, WHOLESALE: Paints
PAINTS: Oil Or Alkyd Vehicle Or Water Thinned
PALLET LOADERS & UNLOADERS
PALLET REPAIR SVCS
PALLETS & SKIDS: Wood
PALLETS: Wood & Metal Combination
PANEL & DISTRIBUTION BOARDS & OTHER RELATED APPARATUS
PANELS: Building, Metal
PANELS: Building, Plastic, NEC
PAPER & BOARD: Die-cut
PAPER & PAPER PRDTS: Crepe, Made From Purchased Materials
PAPER PRDTS: Cleansing Tissues, Made From Purchased Material
PAPER PRDTS: Infant & Baby Prdts
PAPER PRDTS: Napkin Stock
PAPER PRDTS: Pressed & Molded Pulp & Fiber Prdts
PAPER PRDTS: Sanitary
PAPER PRDTS: Sanitary Tissue Paper
PAPER PRDTS: Toilet Paper, Made From Purchased Materials
PAPER PRDTS: Toilet Tissue, Stock
PAPER, WHOLESALE: Fine
PAPER, WHOLESALE: Printing
PAPER: Absorbent
PAPER: Adhesive
PAPER: Book
PAPER: Building Laminated, Made From Purchased Materials
PAPER: Building, Insulating & Packaging
PAPER: Cardboard
PAPER: Cigarette
PAPER: Coated & Laminated, NEC
PAPER: Coated, Exc Photographic, Carbon Or Abrasive
PAPER: Corrugated
PAPER: Fine
PAPER: Packaging
PAPER: Specialty
PAPER: Tissue
PAPER: Wrapping & Packaging
PAPERBOARD PRDTS: Folding Boxboard
PAPERBOARD PRDTS: Setup Boxboard
PARACHUTES
PARTICLEBOARD
PARTICLEBOARD: Laminated, Plastic
PARTITIONS & FIXTURES: Except Wood
PARTITIONS: Wood & Fixtures
PARTS: Metal
PATTERNS: Indl
PAVERS
PERFUME: Perfumes, Natural Or Synthetic
PERFUMES
PESTICIDES
PET SPLYS
PETROLEUM BULK STATIONS & TERMINALS
PHARMACEUTICAL PREPARATIONS: Adrenal
PHARMACEUTICAL PREPARATIONS: Druggists' Preparations
PHARMACEUTICAL PREPARATIONS: Pills
PHARMACEUTICAL PREPARATIONS: Proprietary Drug
PHARMACEUTICAL PREPARATIONS: Solutions
PHARMACEUTICAL PREPARATIONS: Tablets
PHARMACEUTICALS
PHONOGRAPH RECORDS WHOLESALERS
PHOSPHATE ROCK MINING
PHOSPHATES
PHOTOCOPYING & DUPLICATING SVCS
PHOTOGRAPHIC EQPT & SPLYS
PHOTOGRAPHIC EQPT & SPLYS, WHOLESALE: Printing Apparatus
PHOTOGRAPHIC EQPT & SPLYS: Film, Sensitized
PHOTOGRAPHIC EQPT & SPLYS: Printing Eqpt
PHOTOGRAPHY SVCS: Commercial
PHYSICIANS' OFFICES & CLINICS: Medical doctors
PICTURE FRAMES: Metal
PICTURE FRAMES: Wood
PIECE GOODS & NOTIONS WHOLESALERS
PIECE GOODS, NOTIONS & DRY GOODS, WHOL: Textiles, Woven
PIECE GOODS, NOTIONS & OTHER DRY GOODS, WHOLESALE: Cotton
PIECE GOODS, NOTIONS & OTHER DRY GOODS, WHOLESALE: Fabrics

PRODUCT INDEX

PIECE GOODS, NOTIONS/DRY GOODS, WHOL: Fabrics, Synthetic
PINS
PIPE & FITTINGS: Cast Iron
PIPE & FITTINGS: Soil, Cast Iron
PIPE FITTINGS: Plastic
PIPE SECTIONS, FABRICATED FROM PURCHASED PIPE
PIPE, SEWER: Concrete
PIPE: Concrete
PIPE: Plastic
PIPE: Sheet Metal
PIPELINE & POWER LINE INSPECTION SVCS
PIPELINE TERMINAL FACILITIES: Independent
PIPELINES: Natural Gas
PIPELINES: Refined Petroleum
PIPES & TUBES
PIPES & TUBES: Steel
PIPES & TUBES: Welded
PIPES: Steel & Iron
PLAQUES: Picture, Laminated
PLASMAS
PLASTIC WOOD
PLASTICIZERS, ORGANIC: Cyclic & Acyclic
PLASTICS FILM & SHEET
PLASTICS FILM & SHEET: Polyethylene
PLASTICS FILM & SHEET: Polyvinyl
PLASTICS FILM & SHEET: Vinyl
PLASTICS FINISHED PRDTS: Laminated
PLASTICS MATERIAL & RESINS
PLASTICS MATERIALS, BASIC FORMS & SHAPES WHOLESALERS
PLASTICS PROCESSING
PLASTICS SHEET: Packing Materials
PLASTICS: Blow Molded
PLASTICS: Extruded
PLASTICS: Finished Injection Molded
PLASTICS: Molded
PLASTICS: Polystyrene Foam
PLASTICS: Thermoformed
PLATES: Steel
PLATING & POLISHING SVC
PLATING SVC: Chromium, Metals Or Formed Prdts
PLAYGROUND EQPT
PLEATING & STITCHING SVC
PLUGS: Electric
PLUMBING FIXTURES
PLUMBING FIXTURES: Plastic
PLUMBING FIXTURES: Vitreous
POINT OF SALE DEVICES
POLE LINE HARDWARE
POLISHING SVC: Metals Or Formed Prdts
POLYESTERS
POLYETHYLENE RESINS
POLYMETHYL METHACRYLATE RESINS: Plexiglas
POLYSTYRENE RESINS
POLYTETRAFLUOROETHYLENE RESINS
POLYURETHANE RESINS
POLYVINYL CHLORIDE RESINS
POSTERS
POTASH MINING
POTPOURRI
POULTRY & SMALL GAME SLAUGHTERING & PROCESSING
POWDER: Aluminum Atomized
POWDER: Metal
POWER GENERATORS
POWER SUPPLIES: All Types, Static
POWER SWITCHING EQPT
POWER TOOLS, HAND: Chain Saws, Portable
PRECAST TERRAZZO OR CONCRETE PRDTS
PRECIOUS STONES & METALS, WHOLESALE
PRERECORDED TAPE, CD/RECORD STORES: Audio Tapes, Prerecorded
PRESSED FIBER & MOLDED PULP PRDTS, EXC FOOD
PRIMARY FINISHED OR SEMIFINISHED SHAPES
PRIMARY ROLLING MILL EQPT
PRINT CARTRIDGES: Laser & Other Computer Printers
PRINTED CIRCUIT BOARDS
PRINTERS & PLOTTERS
PRINTERS: Computer
PRINTERS: Magnetic Ink, Bar Code
PRINTING & BINDING: Books
PRINTING & ENGRAVING: Card, Exc Greeting
PRINTING & STAMPING: Fabric Articles
PRINTING & WRITING PAPER WHOLESALERS
PRINTING MACHINERY
PRINTING, COMMERCIAL: Business Forms, NEC
PRINTING, COMMERCIAL: Calendars, NEC
PRINTING, COMMERCIAL: Decals, NEC
PRINTING, COMMERCIAL: Envelopes, NEC
PRINTING, COMMERCIAL: Labels & Seals, NEC
PRINTING, COMMERCIAL: Letterpress & Screen
PRINTING, COMMERCIAL: Literature, Advertising, NEC
PRINTING, COMMERCIAL: Periodicals, NEC
PRINTING, COMMERCIAL: Promotional
PRINTING, COMMERCIAL: Screen
PRINTING, COMMERCIAL: Stationery, NEC
PRINTING, COMMERCIAL: Tags, NEC
PRINTING, LITHOGRAPHIC: Advertising Posters
PRINTING, LITHOGRAPHIC: Calendars
PRINTING, LITHOGRAPHIC: Forms, Business
PRINTING, LITHOGRAPHIC: Offset & photolithographic printing
PRINTING, LITHOGRAPHIC: Posters & Decals
PRINTING, LITHOGRAPHIC: Promotional
PRINTING, LITHOGRAPHIC: Souvenir Cards
PRINTING, LITHOGRAPHIC: Tickets
PRINTING: Books
PRINTING: Broadwoven Fabrics. Cotton
PRINTING: Checkbooks
PRINTING: Commercial, NEC
PRINTING: Flexographic
PRINTING: Gravure, Labels
PRINTING: Gravure, Rotogravure
PRINTING: Laser
PRINTING: Letterpress
PRINTING: Lithographic
PRINTING: Manmade Fiber & Silk, Broadwoven Fabric
PRINTING: Offset
PRINTING: Photo-Offset
PRINTING: Photolithographic
PRINTING: Rotogravure
PRINTING: Screen, Broadwoven Fabrics, Cotton
PRINTING: Screen, Fabric
PRINTING: Screen, Manmade Fiber & Silk, Broadwoven Fabric
PRINTING: Thermography
PROFESSIONAL EQPT & SPLYS, WHOLESALE: Engineers', NEC
PROFESSIONAL EQPT & SPLYS, WHOLESALE: Optical Goods
PROFESSIONAL INSTRUMENT REPAIR SVCS
PROFILE SHAPES: Unsupported Plastics
PROMOTION SVCS
PROPERTY DAMAGE INSURANCE
PROTECTION EQPT: Lightning
PROTECTIVE FOOTWEAR: Rubber Or Plastic
PUBLIC RELATIONS & PUBLICITY SVCS
PUBLIC RELATIONS SVCS
PUBLISHERS: Art Copy & Poster
PUBLISHERS: Music Book & Sheet Music
PUBLISHERS: Music, Sheet
PUBLISHERS: Telephone & Other Directory
PUBLISHING & BROADCASTING: Internet Only
PUBLISHING & PRINTING: Art Copy
PUBLISHING & PRINTING: Book Music
PUBLISHING & PRINTING: Books
PUBLISHING & PRINTING: Directories, NEC
PUBLISHING & PRINTING: Directories, Telephone
PUBLISHING & PRINTING: Magazines: publishing & printing
PUBLISHING & PRINTING: Music, Book
PUBLISHING & PRINTING: Newsletters, Business Svc
PUBLISHING & PRINTING: Newspapers
PUBLISHING & PRINTING: Pamphlets
PUBLISHING & PRINTING: Shopping News
PUBLISHING & PRINTING: Textbooks
PUBLISHING & PRINTING: Trade Journals
PUBLISHING & PRINTING: Yearbooks
PULLEYS: Power Transmission
PULP MILLS
PULP MILLS: Mechanical & Recycling Processing
PUMP JACKS & OTHER PUMPING EQPT: Indl
PUMPS & PARTS: Indl
PUMPS & PUMPING EQPT REPAIR SVCS
PUMPS & PUMPING EQPT WHOLESALERS
PUMPS: Domestic, Water Or Sump
PUMPS: Gasoline, Measuring Or Dispensing
PUMPS: Measuring & Dispensing
PUMPS: Oil, Measuring Or Dispensing
PURIFICATION & DUST COLLECTION EQPT

Q

QUILTING: Individuals

R

RACEWAYS
RACKS: Pallet, Exc Wood
RADIO BROADCASTING & COMMUNICATIONS EQPT
RADIO BROADCASTING STATIONS
RADIO COMMUNICATIONS: Airborne Eqpt
RAILINGS: Prefabricated, Metal
RAILINGS: Wood
RAILROAD EQPT
RAILROAD EQPT & SPLYS WHOLESALERS
RAILROAD EQPT, EXC LOCOMOTIVES
RAILROAD EQPT: Brakes, Air & Vacuum
RAILROAD EQPT: Cars & Eqpt, Train, Freight Or Passenger
RAILROAD MAINTENANCE & REPAIR SVCS
RAILROAD RELATED EQPT
RAILROAD RELATED EQPT: Railway Track
RAILS: Steel Or Iron
RAMPS: Prefabricated Metal
RAZORS, RAZOR BLADES
REAL ESTATE AGENCIES & BROKERS
REAL ESTATE AGENTS & MANAGERS
REAL ESTATE INVESTMENT TRUSTS
REAL ESTATE LISTING SVCS
RECEIVERS: Radio Communications
RECORDS & TAPES: Prerecorded
RECREATIONAL VEHICLE PARTS & ACCESS STORES
REFINING: Petroleum
REFRACTORIES: Alumina Fused
REFRACTORIES: Brick
REFRACTORIES: Clay
REFRACTORIES: Nonclay
REFRACTORY MATERIALS WHOLESALERS
REFRIGERATION & HEATING EQUIPMENT
REFRIGERATION EQPT & SPLYS WHOLESALERS
REFRIGERATION EQPT: Complete
REFRIGERATION SVC & REPAIR
REFUSE SYSTEMS
REGULATORS: Power
REHABILITATION CENTER, OUTPATIENT TREATMENT
REHABILITATION CTR, RESIDENTIAL WITH HEALTH CARE INCIDENTAL
RELAYS & SWITCHES: Indl, Electric
RELAYS: Control Circuit, Ind
REMOVERS & CLEANERS
REMOVERS: Paint
RENTAL SVCS: Electronic Eqpt, Exc Computers
RENTAL SVCS: Eqpt, Theatrical
RENTAL SVCS: Sign
RENTAL SVCS: Video Disk/Tape, To The General Public
RENTAL: Portable Toilet
REPRODUCTION SVCS: Video Tape Or Disk
RESEARCH & DEVELOPMENT SVCS, COMMERCIAL: Engineering Lab
RESEARCH, DEVELOPMENT & TESTING SVCS, COMMERCIAL: Business
RESEARCH, DEVELOPMENT & TESTING SVCS, COMMERCIAL: Energy
RESEARCH, DEVELOPMENT & TESTING SVCS, COMMERCIAL: Medical
RESINS: Custom Compound Purchased
RESPIRATORS
RESTAURANT EQPT: Carts
RESTAURANT EQPT: Sheet Metal
RESTAURANTS:Full Svc, American
RETAIL BAKERY: Cookies
RETAIL BAKERY: Doughnuts
RETAIL BAKERY: Pretzels
RETAIL STORES: Alcoholic Beverage Making Eqpt & Splys
RETAIL STORES: Audio-Visual Eqpt & Splys
RETAIL STORES: Business Machines & Eqpt
RETAIL STORES: Cleaning Eqpt & Splys
RETAIL STORES: Concrete Prdts, Precast
RETAIL STORES: Educational Aids & Electronic Training Mat
RETAIL STORES: Electronic Parts & Eqpt
RETAIL STORES: Foam & Foam Prdts

PRODUCT INDEX

RETAIL STORES: Hair Care Prdts
RETAIL STORES: Ice
RETAIL STORES: Medical Apparatus & Splys
RETAIL STORES: Orthopedic & Prosthesis Applications
RETAIL STORES: Perfumes & Colognes
RETAIL STORES: Pet Food
RETAIL STORES: Pet Splys
RETAIL STORES: Religious Goods
RETAIL STORES: Water Purification Eqpt
REUPHOLSTERY & FURNITURE REPAIR
RIVETS: Metal
ROAD CONSTRUCTION EQUIPMENT WHOLESALERS
ROBOTS: Assembly Line
ROLLING MILL ROLLS: Cast Steel
ROLLS & BLANKETS, PRINTERS': Rubber Or Rubberized Fabric
ROOFING GRANULES
ROOFING MATERIALS: Asphalt
ROOFING MEMBRANE: Rubber
RUBBER PRDTS: Appliance, Mechanical
RUBBER PRDTS: Medical & Surgical Tubing, Extrudd & Lathe-Cut
RUBBER PRDTS: Silicone
RUBBER PRDTS: Sponge
RUBBER STRUCTURES: Air-Supported
RUGS : Hand & Machine Made
RUGS : Tufted

S

SAFETY EQPT & SPLYS WHOLESALERS
SALES PROMOTION SVCS
SALT
SAMPLE BOOKS
SAND & GRAVEL
SAND MINING
SANDBLASTING EQPT
SANITARY SVC, NEC
SANITARY SVCS: Liquid Waste Collection & Disposal
SANITARY SVCS: Oil Spill Cleanup
SANITARY SVCS: Refuse Collection & Disposal Svcs
SANITARY SVCS: Rubbish Collection & Disposal
SANITARY SVCS: Waste Materials, Recycling
SASHES: Door Or Window, Metal
SATELLITES: Communications
SAWMILL MACHINES
SAWS & SAWING EQPT
SCAFFOLDS: Mobile Or Stationary, Metal
SCALES & BALANCES, EXC LABORATORY
SCIENTIFIC EQPT REPAIR SVCS
SCIENTIFIC INSTRUMENTS WHOLESALERS
SCRAP & WASTE MATERIALS, WHOLESALE: Ferrous Metal
SCRAP & WASTE MATERIALS, WHOLESALE: Metal
SCRAP & WASTE MATERIALS, WHOLESALE: Paper
SCREENS: Woven Wire
SCREW MACHINE PRDTS
SCREWS: Metal
SEALANTS
SEALING COMPOUNDS: Sealing, synthetic rubber or plastic
SEARCH & NAVIGATION SYSTEMS
SEAT BELTS: Automobile & Aircraft
SEATING: Stadium
SECURE STORAGE SVC: Household & Furniture
SECURITY CONTROL EQPT & SYSTEMS
SECURITY DEVICES
SECURITY SYSTEMS SERVICES
SEMICONDUCTOR & RELATED DEVICES: Random Access Memory Or RAM
SEMICONDUCTOR CIRCUIT NETWORKS
SEMICONDUCTOR DEVICES: Wafers
SEMICONDUCTORS & RELATED DEVICES
SENSORS: Infrared, Solid State
SEPTIC TANK CLEANING SVCS
SEPTIC TANKS: Concrete
SEWAGE & WATER TREATMENT EQPT
SEWING, NEEDLEWORK & PIECE GOODS STORES: Knitting Splys
SHADES: Window
SHAPES & PILINGS, STRUCTURAL: Steel
SHEET METAL SPECIALTIES, EXC STAMPED
SHEETS: Fabric, From Purchased Materials
SHELVING: Office & Store, Exc Wood
SHIP BUILDING & REPAIRING: Cargo Vessels
SHOCK ABSORBERS: Indl

SHOE STORES
SHOE STORES: Women's
SHOES: Canvas, Rubber Soled
SHOES: Men's
SHOES: Orthopedic, Children's
SHOES: Orthopedic, Men's
SHOES: Orthopedic, Women's
SHOES: Plastic Or Rubber
SHOES: Sandals, Rubber
SHOES: Women's
SHOT PEENING SVC
SHOWCASES & DISPLAY FIXTURES: Office & Store
SHOWER STALLS: Metal
SHOWER STALLS: Plastic & Fiberglass
SHREDDERS: Indl & Commercial
SHUTTERS, DOOR & WINDOW: Metal
SIDING MATERIALS
SIDING: Plastic
SIGN PAINTING & LETTERING SHOP
SIGNALING DEVICES: Sound, Electrical
SIGNALS: Traffic Control, Electric
SIGNS & ADVERTISING SPECIALTIES
SIGNS & ADVERTISING SPECIALTIES: Artwork, Advertising
SIGNS & ADVERTISING SPECIALTIES: Letters For Signs, Metal
SIGNS & ADVERTISING SPECIALTIES: Novelties
SIGNS & ADVERTISING SPECIALTIES: Scoreboards, Electric
SIGNS, ELECTRICAL: Wholesalers
SIGNS, EXC ELECTRIC, WHOLESALE
SIGNS: Electrical
SIGNS: Neon
SILICONES
SILK SCREEN DESIGN SVCS
SILO STAVES: Concrete Or Cast Stone
SILVERWARE & PLATED WARE
SINTER: Iron
SKILL TRAINING CENTER
SLINGS: Rope
SMOKE DETECTORS
SNIPS: Tinners'
SOFT DRINKS WHOLESALERS
SOFTWARE PUBLISHERS: Home Entertainment
SOFTWARE PUBLISHERS: Operating Systems
SOFTWARE TRAINING, COMPUTER
SOLAR CELLS
SOLAR HEATING EQPT
SOUND EQPT: Electric
SPACE PROPULSION UNITS & PARTS
SPAS
SPEAKER SYSTEMS
SPECIALTY FOOD STORES: Coffee
SPECIALTY FOOD STORES: Health & Dietetic Food
SPECIALTY FOOD STORES: Juices, Fruit Or Vegetable
SPECIALTY FOOD STORES: Vitamin
SPECIALTY OUTPATIENT CLINICS, NEC
SPORTING & ATHLETIC GOODS: Bowling Balls
SPORTING & ATHLETIC GOODS: Fishing Eqpt
SPORTING & ATHLETIC GOODS: Fishing Tackle, General
SPORTING & ATHLETIC GOODS: Gymnasium Eqpt
SPORTING & ATHLETIC GOODS: Hunting Eqpt
SPORTING & ATHLETIC GOODS: Racket Sports Eqpt
SPORTING & ATHLETIC GOODS: Rods & Rod Parts, Fishing
SPORTING & ATHLETIC GOODS: Shafts, Golf Club
SPORTING & ATHLETIC GOODS: Targets, Archery & Rifle Shooting
SPORTING & ATHLETIC GOODS: Team Sports Eqpt
SPORTING & ATHLETIC GOODS: Track & Field Athletic Eqpt
SPORTING & REC GOODS, WHOLESALE: Camping Eqpt & Splys
SPORTING & RECREATIONAL GOODS, WHOLESALE: Boat Access & Part
SPORTING FIREARMS WHOLESALERS
SPORTING GOODS STORES: Firearms
SPORTING GOODS STORES: Fishing Eqpt
SPORTING GOODS STORES: Specialty Sport Splys, NEC
SPORTING GOODS: Sleeping Bags
SPORTS APPAREL STORES
SPORTS CLUBS, MANAGERS & PROMOTERS
SPRINGS: Coiled Flat
SPRINGS: Furniture
SPRINGS: Mechanical, Precision
SPRINGS: Precision

SPRINGS: Steel
SPRINGS: Wire
STAINLESS STEEL
STAIRCASES & STAIRS, WOOD
STAMPINGS: Automotive
STAPLES: Steel, Wire Or Cut
STATIONARY & OFFICE SPLYS, WHOLESALE: Office Filing Splys
STATIONERY & OFFICE SPLYS WHOLESALERS
STATORS REWINDING SVCS
STATUARY & OTHER DECORATIVE PRDTS: Nonmetallic
STEEL & ALLOYS: Tool & Die
STEEL, COLD-ROLLED: Strip NEC, From Purchased HotRolled
STOKERS: Mechanical, Domestic Or Indl
STONE: Dimension, NEC
STONE: Quarrying & Processing, Own Stone Prdts
STONEWARE PRDTS: Pottery
STORE FIXTURES: Wood
STORES: Auto & Home Supply
STOVES: Wood & Coal Burning
STRAPS: Braids, Textile
STRAPS: Braids, Tubular Nylon Or Plastic
STRAPS: Webbing, Woven
STRUCTURAL SUPPORT & BUILDING MATERIAL: Concrete
STUDS & JOISTS: Sheet Metal
SUNDRIES & RELATED PRDTS: Medical & Laboratory, Rubber
SURFACE ACTIVE AGENTS
SURGICAL APPLIANCES & SPLYS
SURGICAL APPLIANCES & SPLYS
SURGICAL IMPLANTS
SUSPENSION SYSTEMS: Acoustical, Metal
SVC ESTABLISHMENT EQPT, WHOLESALE: Firefighting Eqpt
SVC ESTABLISHMENT EQPT, WHOLESALE: Laundry Eqpt & Splys
SWIMMING POOL ACCESS: Leaf Skimmers Or Pool Rakes
SWIMMING POOL EQPT: Filters & Water Conditioning Systems
SWITCHES: Electric Power, Exc Snap, Push Button, Etc
SWITCHES: Electronic
SWITCHES: Electronic Applications
SWITCHES: Time, Electrical Switchgear Apparatus
SWITCHGEAR & SWITCHBOARD APPARATUS
SWITCHGEAR & SWITCHGEAR ACCESS, NEC
SYNTHETIC RESIN FINISHED PRDTS, NEC
SYRUPS, DRINK
SYSTEMS ENGINEERING: Computer Related
SYSTEMS INTEGRATION SVCS
SYSTEMS INTEGRATION SVCS: Local Area Network
SYSTEMS SOFTWARE DEVELOPMENT SVCS

T

TABLE OR COUNTERTOPS, PLASTIC LAMINATED
TABLETS: Bronze Or Other Metal
TAGS & LABELS: Paper
TAGS: Paper, Blank, Made From Purchased Paper
TALLOW: Animal
TANK REPAIR & CLEANING SVCS
TANK TOWERS: Metal Plate
TANKS & OTHER TRACKED VEHICLE CMPNTS
TANKS: Lined, Metal
TANKS: Plastic & Fiberglass
TANKS: Standard Or Custom Fabricated, Metal Plate
TAPE DRIVES
TAPES, ADHESIVE: Masking, Made From Purchased Materials
TAPES: Fabric
TAPES: Pressure Sensitive
TAPES: Pressure Sensitive, Rubber
TARGET DRONES
TARPAULINS
TELECOMMUNICATION EQPT REPAIR SVCS, EXC TELEPHONES
TELEPHONE ANSWERING SVCS
TELEPHONE EQPT: NEC
TELEPHONE STATION EQPT & PARTS: Wire
TELEPHONE SVCS
TELEVISION BROADCASTING & COMMUNICATIONS EQPT
TELEVISION BROADCASTING STATIONS
TELEVISION: Closed Circuit Eqpt
TELEVISION: Monitors

PRODUCT INDEX

TEMPERING: Metal
TEMPORARY HELP SVCS
TEST KITS: Pregnancy
TESTERS: Physical Property
TESTING SVCS
TEXTILE & APPAREL SVCS
TEXTILE CONVERTERS: Knit Goods
TEXTILE DESIGNERS
TEXTILE FINISHING: Dyeing, Manmade Fiber & Silk, Broadwoven
TEXTILE: Finishing, Raw Stock NEC
TEXTILES: Bagging, Jute
TEXTILES: Linen Fabrics
TEXTILES: Mill Waste & Remnant
THEATRICAL PRODUCERS & SVCS
THERMOPLASTIC MATERIALS
THIN FILM CIRCUITS
THREAD: Cotton
THREAD: Sewing
TILE: Brick & Structural, Clay
TIN
TIRE & INNER TUBE MATERIALS & RELATED PRDTS
TIRE CORD & FABRIC
TIRES & INNER TUBES
TIRES & TUBES WHOLESALERS
TIRES & TUBES, WHOLESALE: Automotive
TOBACCO: Chewing
TOBACCO: Chewing & Snuff
TOBACCO: Cigarettes
TOBACCO: Cigars
TOBACCO: Smoking
TOILETRIES, WHOLESALE: Perfumes
TOILETRIES, WHOLESALE: Toilet Soap
TOILETRIES, WHOLESALE: Toiletries
TOOL & DIE STEEL
TOOLS & EQPT: Taxidermist
TOOLS: Hand
TOWELETTES: Premoistened
TOWERS, SECTIONS: Transmission, Radio & Television
TOYS: Dolls, Stuffed Animals & Parts
TOYS: Video Game Machines
TRAILER COACHES: Automobile
TRAILERS & PARTS: Boat
TRAILERS & PARTS: Horse
TRAILERS & TRAILER EQPT
TRAILERS: Camping, Tent-Type
TRAILERS: Truck, Chassis
TRANSDUCERS: Electrical Properties
TRANSFORMERS: Distribution
TRANSFORMERS: Distribution, Electric
TRANSFORMERS: Specialty
TRANSFORMERS: Voltage Regulating
TRANSMISSIONS: Motor Vehicle
TRANSPORTATION AGENTS & BROKERS
TRANSPORTATION BROKERS: Truck
TRANSPORTATION EQPT & SPLYS WHOLESALERS, NEC
TRAP ROCK: Crushed & Broken
TRAVEL TRAILERS & CAMPERS
TRAYS: Cable, Metal Plate
TRAYS: Plastic
TREAD RUBBER: Camelback For Tire Retreading
TROPHIES, NEC
TROPHIES, WHOLESALE
TROPHIES: Metal, Exc Silver
TRUCK & BUS BODIES: Beverage Truck
TRUCK & BUS BODIES: Bus Bodies
TRUCK & BUS BODIES: Garbage Or Refuse Truck
TRUCK & BUS BODIES: Motor Vehicle, Specialty
TRUCK & BUS BODIES: Truck Beds
TRUCK & BUS BODIES: Truck, Motor Vehicle
TRUCK & BUS BODIES: Utility Truck
TRUCK BODIES: Body Parts
TRUCK BODY SHOP
TRUCK GENERAL REPAIR SVC
TRUCK PARTS & ACCESSORIES: Wholesalers
TRUCKING & HAULING SVCS: Building Materials
TRUCKING & HAULING SVCS: Contract Basis
TRUCKING & HAULING SVCS: Heavy, NEC
TRUCKING & HAULING SVCS: Lumber & Log, Local
TRUCKING: Except Local
TRUCKING: Local, With Storage
TRUCKING: Local, Without Storage
TRUCKS & TRACTORS: Industrial
TRUCKS: Forklift
TRUCKS: Indl
TRUSSES & FRAMING: Prefabricated Metal
TRUSSES: Wood, Floor
TUBES: Steel & Iron
TUBES: Vacuum
TUBING: Rubber
TUNGSTEN CARBIDE POWDER
TURBINES & TURBINE GENERATOR SET UNITS, COMPLETE
TURBINES & TURBINE GENERATOR SETS
TURBINES & TURBINE GENERATOR SETS & PARTS
TURNKEY VENDORS: Computer Systems
TWINE: Binder & Baler
TYPESETTING SVC

U

UMBRELLAS & CANES
UNIFORM STORES
UNIVERSITY
UPHOLSTERY FILLING MATERIALS
UPHOLSTERY MATERIALS, BROADWOVEN
UPHOLSTERY WORK SVCS
USED CAR DEALERS
USED MERCHANDISE STORES
UTENSILS: Household, Cooking & Kitchen, Metal
UTILITY TRAILER DEALERS

V

VACUUM CLEANERS: Indl Type
VACUUM SYSTEMS: Air Extraction, Indl
VALUE-ADDED RESELLERS: Computer Systems
VALVES & PARTS: Gas, Indl
VALVES & PIPE FITTINGS
VALVES & REGULATORS: Pressure, Indl
VALVES: Aerosol, Metal
VALVES: Aircraft, Control, Hydraulic & Pneumatic
VALVES: Control, Automatic
VALVES: Fluid Power, Control, Hydraulic & pneumatic
VALVES: Indl
VALVES: Plumbing & Heating
VALVES: Regulating & Control, Automatic
VALVES: Regulating, Process Control
VALVES: Water Works
VAN CONVERSIONS
VARIETY STORES
VARNISHES, NEC
VEHICLES: Recreational
VENDING MACHINE OPERATORS: Sandwich & Hot Food
VENDING MACHINES & PARTS
VENTILATING EQPT: Metal
VETERINARY PHARMACEUTICAL PREPARATIONS
VIDEO & AUDIO EQPT, WHOLESALE
VIDEO PRODUCTION SVCS
VIDEO TAPE PRODUCTION SVCS
VIDEO TRIGGERS: Remote Control TV Devices
VISUAL COMMUNICATIONS SYSTEMS
VITAMINS: Natural Or Synthetic, Uncompounded, Bulk
VOCATIONAL REHABILITATION AGENCY
VOCATIONAL TRAINING AGENCY

W

WALLBOARD: Decorated, Made From Purchased Materials
WALLBOARD: Gypsum
WALLPAPER & WALL COVERINGS
WALLS: Curtain, Metal
WAREHOUSING & STORAGE FACILITIES, NEC
WAREHOUSING & STORAGE: Farm Prdts
WAREHOUSING & STORAGE: General
WAREHOUSING & STORAGE: Miniwarehouse
WAREHOUSING & STORAGE: Refrigerated
WARM AIR HEATING/AC EQPT/SPLYS, WHOL Warm Air Htg Eqpt/Splys
WASHERS
WASTE CLEANING SVCS
WATCH REPAIR SVCS
WATCHES
WATER HEATERS
WATER PURIFICATION EQPT: Household
WATER SUPPLY
WATER TREATMENT EQPT: Indl
WATER: Mineral, Carbonated, Canned & Bottled, Etc
WATER: Pasteurized & Mineral, Bottled & Canned
WATER: Pasteurized, Canned & Bottled, Etc
WATERPROOFING COMPOUNDS
WAVEGUIDES & FITTINGS
WAXES: Paraffin
WAXES: Petroleum, Not Produced In Petroleum Refineries
WEATHER STRIP: Sponge Rubber
WEIGHING MACHINERY & APPARATUS
WELDING & CUTTING APPARATUS & ACCESS, NEC
WELDING EQPT
WELDING EQPT & SPLYS WHOLESALERS
WELDING EQPT & SPLYS: Gas
WELDING EQPT & SPLYS: Generators, Arc Welding, AC & DC
WELDING EQPT REPAIR SVCS
WELDING EQPT: Electric
WELDING EQPT: Electrical
WELDING MACHINES & EQPT: Ultrasonic
WELDING REPAIR SVC
WELDING SPLYS, EXC GASES: Wholesalers
WELDING TIPS: Heat Resistant, Metal
WET CORN MILLING
WHEELCHAIR LIFTS
WHEELCHAIRS
WHEELS & PARTS
WHEELS: Disc, Wheelbarrow, Stroller, Etc, Stamped Metal
WHIRLPOOL BATHS: Hydrotherapy
WINCHES
WIND TUNNELS
WINDINGS: Coil, Electronic
WINDOW & DOOR FRAMES
WINDOW CLEANING SVCS
WINDOW FRAMES, MOLDING & TRIM: Vinyl
WINDOW SCREENING: Plastic
WINDOWS: Wood
WINE & DISTILLED ALCOHOLIC BEVERAGES WHOLESALERS
WIRE
WIRE & CABLE: Aluminum
WIRE & CABLE: Nonferrous, Aircraft
WIRE & CABLE: Nonferrous, Automotive, Exc Ignition Sets
WIRE & CABLE: Nonferrous, Building
WIRE & WIRE PRDTS
WIRE FABRIC: Welded Steel
WIRE MATERIALS: Copper
WIRE MATERIALS: Steel
WIRE PRDTS: Ferrous Or Iron, Made In Wiredrawing Plants
WIRE PRDTS: Steel & Iron
WIRE: Communication
WIRE: Mesh
WIRE: Nonferrous
WIRE: Nonferrous, Appliance Fixture
WOMEN'S & CHILDREN'S CLOTHING WHOLESALERS, NEC
WOMEN'S & GIRLS' SPORTSWEAR WHOLESALERS
WOMEN'S CLOTHING STORES
WOMEN'S CLOTHING STORES: Ready-To-Wear
WOMEN'S FULL & KNEE LENGTH HOSIERY DYEING & FINISHING
WOOD & WOOD BY-PRDTS, WHOLESALE
WOOD CHIPS, PRODUCED AT THE MILL
WOOD PRDTS: Applicators
WOOD PRDTS: Battery Separators
WOOD PRDTS: Laundry
WOOD PRDTS: Moldings, Unfinished & Prefinished
WOOD PRDTS: Mulch Or Sawdust
WOOD PRDTS: Mulch, Wood & Bark
WOOD PRDTS: Outdoor, Structural
WOOD PRDTS: Panel Work
WOOD PRDTS: Signboards
WOOD PRODUCTS: Reconstiiuted
WOOD TREATING: Millwork
WOOD TREATING: Structural Lumber & Timber
WOOD TREATING: Wood Prdts, Creosoted
WOODWORK & TRIM: Exterior & Ornamental
WOODWORK & TRIM: Interior & Ornamental
WOODWORK: Interior & Ornamental, NEC
WOVEN WIRE PRDTS, NEC

X

X-RAY EQPT & TUBES

Y

YARN & YARN SPINNING

PRODUCT INDEX

YARN MILLS: Texturizing, Throwing & Twisting
YARN WHOLESALERS
YARN: Combed, Spun
YARN: Cotton, Spun
YARN: Knitting, Spun
YARN: Manmade & Synthetic Fiber, Spun
YARN: Needle & Handicraft, Spun
YARN: Nylon, Spun Staple
YARN: Plastic Coated, Made From Purchased Yarn
YARN: Polyester, Spun From Purchased Staple
YARN: Wool, Spun
YARNS, INDL, WHOLESALE

PRODUCT SECTION

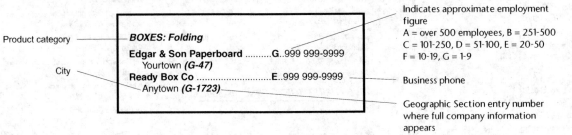

See footnotes for symbols and codes identification.
• Refer to the Industrial Product Index preceding this section to locate product headings.

ABRASIVE STONES, EXC GRINDING STONES: Ground Or Whole

His Glassworks Inc................................ G..... 828 254-2559
  Asheville *(G-653)*

ABRASIVES

Advanced Superabrasives Inc............... E..... 828 689-3200
  Mars Hill *(G-10191)*
Eagle Superabrasives Inc...................... F..... 828 261-7281
  Hickory *(G-8014)*
Farris Belt & Saw Company.................. F..... 704 527-6166
  Charlotte *(G-2748)*
Sia Abrasives Inc USA........................... D..... 704 587-7355
  Lincolnton *(G-9918)*
Starcke Abrasives Usa Inc..................... E..... 704 583-3338
  Charlotte *(G-3623)*
Sunbelt Abrasives Inc........................... G..... 336 882-6837
  High Point *(G-8557)*
Syntech Abrasives Inc........................... F..... 704 525-8030
  Charlotte *(G-3666)*

ABRASIVES: Coated

Klingspor Abrasives Inc......................... C..... 828 322-3030
  Hickory *(G-8078)*

ACCELERATION INDICATORS & SYSTEM COMPONENTS: Aerospace

Beyond Electronics Corp....................... G..... 919 231-8000
  Raleigh *(G-12553)*
Eco Building Corporation...................... G..... 910 736-1540
  Red Springs *(G-13499)*
New Phoenix Aerospace Inc.................. F..... 919 380-8500
  Raleigh *(G-13062)*
US Prototype Inc.................................. E..... 866 239-2848
  Wilmington *(G-16439)*

ACCELEROMETERS

Vinatoru Enterprises Inc....................... G..... 336 227-4300
  Graham *(G-6716)*

ACID RESIST: Etching

Chem-Tech Solutions Inc...................... E..... 704 829-9202
  Belmont *(G-980)*
Protek Services LLC.............................. G..... 910 556-4121
  Cameron *(G-1562)*

ACIDS: Sulfuric, Oleum

Southern States Chemical Inc............... E..... 910 762-5054
  Wilmington *(G-16411)*

ACOUSTICAL BOARD & TILE

Mid-Atlantic Specialties Inc.................. G..... 919 212-1939
  Raleigh *(G-13030)*

ACRYLIC RESINS

Evonik Superabsorber LLC..................... C..... 336 333-7540
  Greensboro *(G-7007)*
Phase II Creations Inc........................... G..... 336 249-0673
  Lexington *(G-9769)*

ACTUATORS: Indl, NEC

Aalberts Integrated Piping.................... E..... 704 841-6000
  Charlotte *(G-2121)*
Duff-Norton Company Inc..................... G..... 704 588-0510
  Charlotte *(G-2656)*
Shopbot Tools Inc................................. E..... 919 680-4800
  Durham *(G-5354)*

ADDITIVE BASED PLASTIC MATERIALS: Plasticizers

Tosaf Inc.. F..... 980 533-3000
  Bessemer City *(G-1087)*

ADHESIVES

Aggressive Adhesives Inc...................... G..... 910 270-3282
  Hampstead *(G-7635)*
Aldo Products Company Inc.................. G..... 704 932-3054
  Salisbury *(G-13918)*
American Acrylic Adhesives................... G..... 520 954-1700
  Mooresville *(G-10855)*
Avanti Coatings Inc.............................. G..... 908 723-4596
  Hendersonville *(G-7822)*
Beardowadams Inc............................... F..... 704 359-8443
  Charlotte *(G-2292)*
Coatings and Adhesives Corp................ C..... 910 371-3184
  Leland *(G-9537)*
Cohera Medical Inc.............................. G..... 800 641-7458
  Raleigh *(G-12632)*
Colquimica Adhesives Inc..................... E..... 704 318-4750
  Charlotte *(G-2525)*
Everkem Diversified Pdts Inc................. F..... 336 661-7801
  Winston Salem *(G-16701)*
GLS Products LLC................................ G..... 704 334-2425
  Charlotte *(G-2836)*
HB Fuller Co.. G..... 415 878-7202
  Morrisville *(G-11353)*
HB Fuller Company............................... G..... 336 294-5939
  Greensboro *(G-7079)*
Henkel US Operations Corp.................. G..... 704 799-0385
  Mooresville *(G-10972)*
Henkel US Operations Corp.................. E..... 704 647-3500
  Salisbury *(G-13977)*
Hexion Inc... G..... 336 884-8918
  High Point *(G-8384)*
Hickory Adchem Inc............................. G..... 828 327-0936
  Hickory *(G-8043)*

Ips Corporation..................................... E..... 919 598-2400
  Durham *(G-5164)*
Jowat Corporation................................ G..... 336 434-9356
  Archdale *(G-288)*
Jowat Corporation................................ D..... 336 434-9000
  Archdale *(G-289)*
Jowat International Corp....................... E..... 336 434-9000
  Archdale *(G-290)*
Jowat Properties Corp.......................... F..... 336 434-9000
  Archdale *(G-291)*
Kestrel I Acquisition Corporation........... A..... 919 990-7500
  Durham *(G-5180)*
Kleiberit Adhesives USA Inc................... F..... 704 843-3339
  Waxhaw *(G-15765)*
LD Davis Industries Inc........................ E..... 704 289-4551
  Monroe *(G-10756)*
Liquidating Reichhold Inc..................... A..... 919 990-7500
  Durham *(G-5191)*
Lord Corporation.................................. D..... 919 469-2500
  Cary *(G-1818)*
Lord Corporation.................................. B..... 919 468-5979
  Cary *(G-1817)*
Lord Far East Inc.................................. E..... 919 468-5979
  Cary *(G-1819)*
Natural Adhesive LLC........................... G..... 616 217-8392
  Wilmington *(G-16332)*
Phoenix Tapes Usa LLC......................... G..... 704 588-3090
  Charlotte *(G-3338)*
Power Adhesives Ltd............................ G..... 704 578-9984
  Charlotte *(G-3358)*
Pregis LLC... E..... 828 465-9197
  Conover *(G-4486)*
Psa Incorporated.................................. F..... 910 371-1115
  Belville *(G-1024)*
Robix America Inc................................ C..... 336 668-9555
  Greensboro *(G-7314)*
Rutland Fire Clay Company................... G..... 802 775-5519
  Chapel Hill *(G-2066)*
Sika Corporation.................................. E..... 704 810-0500
  Gastonia *(G-6510)*
STI Polymer Inc.................................... E..... 800 874-5878
  Sanford *(G-14194)*
Textile Rubber and Chem Co Inc............ G..... 704 376-3582
  Indian Trail *(G-8968)*
Udm Systems LLC................................ G..... 919 789-0777
  Raleigh *(G-13374)*
Udm Systems LLC................................ G..... 919 789-0777
  Raleigh *(G-13375)*
Unecol Adhesives N Amer LLC.............. G..... 888 963-8879
  Durham *(G-5419)*
Web-Don Incorporated......................... E..... 800 532-0434
  Charlotte *(G-3800)*
Weiss USA LLC.................................... G..... 704 282-4496
  Monroe *(G-10832)*

ADHESIVES & SEALANTS

Arclin USA LLC .... G 919 542-2526
  Moncure *(G-10614)*

Bonding Materials LLC .... G 704 277-6697
  Charlotte *(G-2332)*

Carroll-Baccari Inc .... G 561 585-2227
  Flat Rock *(G-5962)*

Dbt Coatings LLC .... G 336 834-9700
  Greensboro *(G-6961)*

Ddp Spclty Elctrnic Mtls US 9 .... D 336 547-7112
  Greensboro *(G-6962)*

Hexpol Compounding NC Inc .... A 704 872-1585
  Statesville *(G-14813)*

His Company Inc .... G 800 537-0351
  Wilmington *(G-16255)*

Knight Safety Coatings Co Inc .... F 910 458-3145
  Wilmington *(G-16290)*

Loba-Wakol LLC .... E 704 527-5919
  Wadesboro *(G-15515)*

Manning Fabrics Inc .... G 910 295-1970
  Pinehurst *(G-12228)*

Reichhold Holdings Us Inc .... A 919 990-7500
  Durham *(G-5323)*

Scott Bader Inc .... F 330 920-4410
  Mocksville *(G-10602)*

Slade Operating Company LLC .... E 704 873-1366
  Statesville *(G-14887)*

Southern Resin Inc .... E 336 475-1348
  Thomasville *(G-15279)*

Tailored Chemical Products Inc .... D 828 322-6512
  Hickory *(G-8173)*

ADHESIVES: Adhesives, plastic

Ips Structural Adhesives Inc .... E 919 598-2400
  Durham *(G-5165)*

ADHESIVES: Epoxy

Daystar Materials Inc .... E 919 734-0460
  Goldsboro *(G-6609)*

Laticrete International Inc .... F 910 582-2252
  Hamlet *(G-7626)*

ADRENAL DERIVATIVES

Founders Hemp LLC .... G 888 334-4367
  Asheboro *(G-436)*

ADVERTISING AGENCIES

822tees Inc .... G 910 822-8337
  Fayetteville *(G-5748)*

Advertising Design Systems Inc .... G 828 264-8060
  Boone *(G-1172)*

Clarks Printing Service Inc .... E 828 254-1432
  Asheville *(G-594)*

Creative Conquest LLC .... G 720 481-4372
  Shelby *(G-14304)*

Dale Advertising Inc .... G 704 484-0971
  Shelby *(G-14310)*

Embroidme Lake Norman .... G 704 987-9630
  Cornelius *(G-4543)*

Executive Promotions Inc .... F 704 663-4000
  Mooresville *(G-10940)*

Fit1media LLC .... G 919 925-2200
  Raleigh *(G-12770)*

Idea People Inc .... G 704 398-4437
  Huntersville *(G-8233)*

Ifpo - Ifmo/American Image Inc .... G 336 945-9867
  Hamptonville *(G-7672)*

JB II Printing LLC .... E 336 222-0717
  Burlington *(G-1439)*

Lomar Specialty Advg Inc .... F 704 788-4380
  Concord *(G-4307)*

Planet Logo Inc .... G 910 763-2554
  Wilmington *(G-16356)*

Shannon Media Inc .... F 919 933-1551
  Chapel Hill *(G-2071)*

Two24 Digital LLC .... G 910 475-7555
  Wilmington *(G-16437)*

Yp Advrtising Pubg LLC Not LLC .... C 704 522-5500
  Charlotte *(G-3847)*

ADVERTISING AGENCIES: Consultants

B&P Enterprise NC Inc .... G 727 669-6877
  Hickory *(G-7947)*

Ed Kemp Associates Inc .... G 336 869-2155
  High Point *(G-8336)*

Golf Associates Advertising Co .... E 828 252-6544
  Asheville *(G-637)*

Inspire Creative Studios Inc .... G 910 395-0200
  Wilmington *(G-16269)*

ADVERTISING CURTAINS

Autoverters Inc .... F 252 537-0426
  Roanoke Rapids *(G-13567)*

Blur Development Group LLC .... E 919 701-4213
  Cary *(G-1711)*

Dorian Corporation .... F 910 352-6939
  Wilmington *(G-16204)*

Impact Fulfillment Svcs LLC .... C 336 227-1130
  Burlington *(G-1434)*

Simontic Composite Inc .... E 336 897-9885
  Greensboro *(G-7340)*

ADVERTISING DISPLAY PRDTS

Ebony & Ivorys Unique Btq LLC .... G 704 324-4035
  Wingate *(G-16574)*

Web 4 Half LLC .... E 855 762-4638
  Asheboro *(G-509)*

ADVERTISING REPRESENTATIVES: Newspaper

Gatehouse Media LLC .... F 336 626-6103
  Asheboro *(G-439)*

Iwanna .... G 828 505-7319
  Asheville *(G-665)*

Latino Communications Inc .... F 919 645-1680
  Raleigh *(G-12959)*

ADVERTISING SPECIALTIES, WHOLESALE

B F I Industries Inc .... G 919 229-4509
  Wake Forest *(G-15529)*

Burlow Promotions Inc .... F 336 856-0500
  Greensboro *(G-6869)*

C & M Enterprise Inc .... G 704 545-1180
  Mint Hill *(G-10524)*

Carroll Signs & Advertising .... G 336 983-3415
  King *(G-9267)*

Causekeepers Inc .... E 336 824-2518
  Franklinville *(G-6167)*

Consumer Concepts .... F 252 247-7000
  Morehead City *(G-11164)*

Dale Advertising Inc .... G 704 484-0971
  Shelby *(G-14310)*

Daztech Inc .... G 800 862-6360
  Wilmington *(G-16196)*

Dicks Store .... G 336 548-9358
  Madison *(G-10073)*

Identify Yourself LLC .... F 252 202-1452
  Kitty Hawk *(G-9407)*

Ink n Stitches LLC .... G 336 633-3898
  Asheboro *(G-444)*

Markell Publishing Company Inc .... G 336 226-7148
  Burlington *(G-1454)*

Marketing One Sportswear Inc .... G 704 334-9333
  Charlotte *(G-3126)*

Memories of Orangeburg Inc .... G 803 533-0035
  Mooresville *(G-11020)*

Office Sup Svcs Inc Charlotte .... E 704 786-4677
  Concord *(G-4323)*

PSM Enterprises Inc .... F 336 789-8888
  Mount Airy *(G-11561)*

Silverlining Screen Prtrs Inc .... G 919 554-0340
  Youngsville *(G-17097)*

Sun Printing Company Inc .... G 336 773-1346
  Winston Salem *(G-16923)*

T & R Signs .... G 919 779-1185
  Garner *(G-6317)*

Tannis Root Productions Inc .... G 919 832-8552
  Raleigh *(G-13327)*

ADVERTISING SVCS: Direct Mail

Heritage Prtg & Graphics Inc .... G 704 551-0700
  Charlotte *(G-2905)*

Laser Ink Corporation .... E 919 361-5822
  Durham *(G-5186)*

Mb-F Inc .... D 336 379-9352
  Greensboro *(G-7192)*

Meredith - Webb Prtg Co Inc .... D 336 228-8378
  Burlington *(G-1460)*

Professional Laminating LLC .... E 919 465-0400
  Cary *(G-1862)*

William George Printing LLC .... E 910 221-2700
  Hope Mills *(G-8738)*

Yp Advrtising Pubg LLC Not LLC .... C 704 522-5500
  Charlotte *(G-3847)*

ADVERTISING SVCS: Display

Apple Rock Advg & Prom Inc .... E 336 232-4800
  Greensboro *(G-6811)*

RLM/Universal Packaging Inc .... F 336 644-6161
  Greensboro *(G-7312)*

ADVERTISING SVCS: Outdoor

Signlite Services Inc .... G 336 751-9543
  Mocksville *(G-10603)*

Sweatnet LLC .... G 847 331-7287
  Charlotte *(G-3658)*

AERIAL WORK PLATFORMS

Ken Garner Mfg - RHO Inc .... E 336 969-0416
  Rural Hall *(G-13844)*

Man Lift Mfg Co .... E 414 486-1760
  Shelby *(G-14344)*

Mid-Atlantic Crane and Eqp Co .... E 919 790-3535
  Raleigh *(G-13029)*

AEROSOLS

Ambro-Sol Usa LLC .... G 844 824-6959
  Rutherfordton *(G-13862)*

AGENTS, BROKERS & BUREAUS: Personal Service

Boramed Inc .... G 919 419-9518
  Durham *(G-4973)*

Carolina Connections Inc .... G 336 786-7030
  Mount Airy *(G-11488)*

Chicopee Inc .... G 919 894-4111
  Benson *(G-1032)*

Professnal Alterations EMB Inc .... G 910 577-8484
  Jacksonville *(G-9022)*

AGRICULTURAL DISINFECTANTS

Degesch America Inc .... E 800 548-2778
  Wilson *(G-16492)*

I Must Garden LLC..................................... G 919 929-2299
  Raleigh (G-12872)

AGRICULTURAL EQPT: BARN, SILO, POULTRY, DAIRY/LIVESTOCK MACH

Lock Drives Inc... G 704 588-1844
  Pineville (G-12281)

AGRICULTURAL EQPT: Fertilizing Machinery

General Fertilizer Eqp Inc........................... F 336 299-4711
  Greensboro (G-7035)

AGRICULTURAL EQPT: Fertilizng, Sprayng, Dustng/Irrigatn Mach

Spectrum Products Inc............................... F 919 556-7797
  Youngsville (G-17100)

AGRICULTURAL EQPT: Grounds Mowing Eqpt

Befco Inc.. E 252 977-9920
  Rocky Mount (G-13684)

AGRICULTURAL EQPT: Spreaders, Fertilizer

Sides Spreader and Eqp Co Inc................ F 336 978-6732
  Lexington (G-9779)

AGRICULTURAL EQPT: Turf & Grounds Eqpt

Carolina Golfco Inc.................................... G 704 525-7846
  Charlotte (G-2397)
Deere & Company...................................... B 919 567-6400
  Fuquay Varina (G-6195)

AGRICULTURAL MACHINERY & EQPT: Wholesalers

General Fertilizer Eqp Inc........................... F 336 299-4711
  Greensboro (G-7035)
Griffin Industries LLC................................. E 704 624-9140
  Marshville (G-10217)
North American Implements Inc................ G 336 476-2904
  Thomasville (G-15259)

AIR CLEANING SYSTEMS

Acculabs Technologies Inc........................ G 919 468-8780
  Morrisville (G-11276)
Cosatron... F 704 785-8145
  Concord (G-4244)
D J Enviro Solutions.................................. G 828 495-7448
  Taylorsville (G-15139)
Eas Incorporated....................................... G 704 734-4945
  Kings Mountain (G-9305)
Flanders/Csc LLC...................................... D 252 946-8081
  Washington (G-15702)
Nederman Mikropul LLC............................ G 704 998-2600
  Charlotte (G-3246)
Novaerus US Inc.. G 813 304-2468
  Charlotte (G-3273)
P & G Manufacturing Wash Inc................. G 252 946-9110
  Washington (G-15721)

AIR CONDITIONERS: Motor Vehicle

Southeast Air Control Inc.......................... E 704 392-0149
  Charlotte (G-3587)

AIR CONDITIONING & VENTILATION EQPT & SPLYS: Wholesales

Filtration Technology Inc........................... G 336 294-5655
  Greensboro (G-7014)

AIR CONDITIONING EQPT

Air System Components Inc..................... D 919 279-8868
  Sanford (G-14083)
Air System Components Inc..................... D 919 775-2201
  Sanford (G-14084)
Air System Components Inc..................... D 252 641-5900
  Tarboro (G-15093)
Air System Components Inc..................... C 252 641-0875
  Tarboro (G-15094)
Boles Holding Inc...................................... G 828 264-4200
  Boone (G-1178)
Carrier Corporation.................................... C 704 921-3800
  Charlotte (G-2415)
Eneco East Inc.. G 828 322-6008
  Hickory (G-8017)
NC Filtration of Florida LLC...................... D 704 822-4444
  Belmont (G-996)
Snap Rite Manufacturing Inc.................... E 910 897-4080
  Coats (G-4134)
Trane Company... E 704 398-4600
  Charlotte (G-3713)
Trane Technologies Company LLC.......... A 704 655-4000
  Davidson (G-4702)
Trane Technologies Mfg LLC................... F 704 655-4000
  Davidson (G-4703)
Transarctic North Carolina Inc.................. E 336 861-6116
  High Point (G-8574)

AIR CONDITIONING EQPT, WHOLE HOUSE: Wholesalers

Boles Holding Inc...................................... G 828 264-4200
  Boone (G-1178)
Heat Transfer Sales of The...................... E 336 294-3838
  Greensboro (G-7085)
Roofing Tools and Eqp Inc....................... G 252 291-1800
  Wilson (G-16534)

AIR CONDITIONING REPAIR SVCS

Diagnostic Shop Inc.................................. G 704 933-3435
  Kannapolis (G-9117)
Johnson Controls Inc................................ D 919 743-3500
  Raleigh (G-12920)

AIR CONDITIONING UNITS: Complete, Domestic Or Indl

Airboss Heating and Coolg Inc................. G 252 586-0500
  Littleton (G-9950)
Daikin Applied Americas Inc..................... G 704 588-0087
  Charlotte (G-2598)
Dynamic Air Engineering Inc.................... E 714 540-1000
  Claremont (G-3925)
Rifled Air Conditioning Inc........................ E 800 627-1707
  High Point (G-8511)
Trane US Inc... A 704 655-4000
  Davidson (G-4704)

AIR MATTRESSES: Plastic

Ace Plastics Inc.. G 704 527-5752
  Charlotte (G-2127)
Englishs All Wood Homes Inc.................. F 252 524-5000
  Grifton (G-7600)
Fiber Composites LLC.............................. D 704 463-7118
  New London (G-11869)
Global Packaging Inc................................ D 610 666-1608
  Hamlet (G-7622)
Laird Plastics Inc...................................... G 704 597-8555
  Charlotte (G-3070)
Molded Fibr GL Cmpny/Nrth Crli............. C 828 584-4974
  Morganton (G-11234)
Poppelmann Properties USA LLC............ G 828 466-9500
  Claremont (G-3934)
Pretium Packaging LLC............................ E 336 621-1891
  Greensboro (G-7280)
Tri-Star Plastics Corp............................... E 704 598-2800
  Denver (G-4810)

AIR POLLUTION MEASURING SVCS

Environmental Supply Co Inc................... F 919 956-9688
  Durham (G-5089)

AIR PURIFICATION EQPT

Absolent Inc... F 919 570-2862
  Raleigh (G-12465)
Air Control Inc... E 252 492-2300
  Henderson (G-7775)
Airbox LLC... G 855 927-1386
  Statesville (G-14743)
Associated Metal Works Inc..................... E 704 546-7002
  Harmony (G-7685)
Exquisite Air and Water............................ G 919 524-4625
  Raleigh (G-12757)
Ffi Holdings III Corp.................................. E 800 690-3650
  Charlotte (G-2755)
Flanders Filters Inc.................................... C 252 946-8081
  Washington (G-15701)
Global Plasma Solutions Inc.................... E 980 279-5622
  Charlotte (G-2833)
Kch Services Inc....................................... E 828 245-9836
  Forest City (G-6073)
Mikropor America Inc................................ F
  Charlotte (G-3178)
Schletter NA Inc.. F 704 595-4200
  Charlotte (G-3503)
SCR-Tech LLC... C 704 504-0191
  Charlotte (G-3513)
Staclean Diffuser Company LLC.............. F 704 636-8697
  Salisbury (G-14047)

AIRCRAFT & AEROSPACE FLIGHT INSTRUMENTS & GUIDANCE SYSTEMS

United States Dept of Navy...................... G 252 466-4514
  Cherry Point (G-3859)

AIRCRAFT & HEAVY EQPT REPAIR SVCS

Brant & Lassiter Septic Tank................... G 252 587-4321
  Potecasi (G-12395)
GE Aircraft Engs Holdings Inc.................. A 919 361-4400
  Durham (G-5111)

AIRCRAFT ASSEMBLY PLANTS

Adamantium Aerospace Inc...................... G 252 444-6265
  Havelock (G-7739)
Anuma Aerospace LLC............................. G 919 600-0142
  Raleigh (G-12511)
Atlas Aerospace Inc.................................. G 704 528-3356
  Cleveland (G-4067)
BEC-Faye LLC... G 252 714-8700
  Grimesland (G-7604)
Boeing Arospc Operations Inc.................. F 919 722-4351
  Goldsboro (G-6594)
Boeing Company....................................... G 704 572-8280
  Charlotte (G-2330)
CJ Partners LLC.. G 336 838-3080
  Wilkesboro (G-16018)
Cyberlux Corporation................................ F 984 363-6894
  Research Triangle Pa (G-13549)
Franklin Aerospace Inc............................. G 336 474-1960
  Thomasville (G-15225)
Gulfstream Plans & Design Inc................ G 704 641-2544
  Cornelius (G-4553)
Hawthorne Services................................... F 910 436-9013
  Fayetteville (G-5833)

AIRCRAFT ASSEMBLY PLANTS

Honda Aircraft Company LLC .... F 336 662-0246
   Greensboro *(G-7097)*

Honda Aircraft Company LLC .... F 336 662-0246
   Greensboro *(G-7098)*

Honda Aircraft Company LLC .... B 336 662-0246
   Greensboro *(G-7099)*

Lulaza Aerospace LLC .... G 919 371-4240
   Morrisville *(G-11384)*

Piedmont AVI Cmponent Svcs LLC .... C 336 423-5100
   Greensboro *(G-7255)*

Signature Flight Air Inc .... E 919 840-4400
   Morrisville *(G-11429)*

Sikora Aerospace Tech Inc .... G 336 870-6351
   Winston Salem *(G-16910)*

Spirit Aerosystems Inc .... A 252 208-4645
   Kinston *(G-9386)*

Summit Aviation Inc .... F 302 834-5400
   Greensboro *(G-7379)*

United States Dept of Navy .... G 252 464-7228
   Cherry Point *(G-3860)*

Vicki Vermont Aircraft Sale .... G 828 225-6517
   Asheville *(G-815)*

Wham Aviation LLC .... G 336 605-4663
   Summerfield *(G-14993)*

AIRCRAFT ENGINES & ENGINE PARTS: Air Scoops

GE Aircraft Engs Holdings Inc .... A 919 361-4400
   Durham *(G-5111)*

AIRCRAFT ENGINES & ENGINE PARTS: Airfoils

Pratt & Whitney Eng Svcs Inc .... G 860 565-4321
   Asheville *(G-740)*

AIRCRAFT ENGINES & ENGINE PARTS: Mount Parts

Hiab USA Inc .... F 704 896-9089
   Cornelius *(G-4555)*

Lord Corporation .... B 919 468-5979
   Cary *(G-1817)*

Lord Far East Inc .... E 919 468-5979
   Cary *(G-1819)*

AIRCRAFT ENGINES & ENGINE PARTS: Research & Development, Mfr

Ica(usa)inc .... G 704 798-3488
   Winston Salem *(G-16754)*

Triad Engines Parts & Svcs Inc .... G 800 334-6437
   Burlington *(G-1507)*

AIRCRAFT ENGINES & PARTS

Aero 8 Inc .... F 336 776-9165
   Winston Salem *(G-16592)*

Carolina Precision Tech LLC .... E 215 675-4590
   Mooresville *(G-10898)*

Christine N Honeywell PT .... G 802 496-6509
   Whispering Pines *(G-15953)*

Curtiss-Wright Controls Inc .... E 704 869-2300
   Shelby *(G-14305)*

Ek Air LLC .... G 704 881-1959
   Statesville *(G-14792)*

Goodrich Corporation .... C 704 423-7000
   Charlotte *(G-2847)*

Honda Aero Inc .... D 336 226-2376
   Burlington *(G-1430)*

Honeywell .... E 734 942-5823
   Charlotte *(G-2918)*

Honeywell International Inc .... G 910 436-5144
   Fort Bragg *(G-6090)*

Honeywell International Inc .... A 919 662-7539
   Raleigh *(G-12857)*

Honeywell International Inc .... A 704 627-6200
   Charlotte *(G-2919)*

James Tool Machine & Engrg Inc .... C 828 584-8722
   Morganton *(G-11224)*

Precision Metals LLC .... G 919 762-7481
   Benson *(G-1041)*

Smiths Aerospace Components .... G 828 274-4540
   Asheville *(G-774)*

Thermal Pane Inc .... G 336 722-9977
   Lexington *(G-9791)*

Unique Tool and Mfg Co .... E 336 498-2614
   Franklinville *(G-6171)*

AIRCRAFT EQPT & SPLYS WHOLESALERS

Ontic Engineering and Mfg Inc .... B 919 395-3908
   Creedmoor *(G-4619)*

AIRCRAFT FLIGHT INSTRUMENT REPAIR SVCS

T Air Inc .... D 980 595-2840
   Charlotte *(G-3668)*

AIRCRAFT LIGHTING

B/E Aerospace Inc .... E 336 747-5000
   Winston Salem *(G-16613)*

AIRCRAFT MAINTENANCE & REPAIR SVCS

D2 Government Solutions LLC .... E 662 655-4554
   New Bern *(G-11797)*

Haeco Cabin Solutions LLC .... D 336 862-1418
   Greensboro *(G-7074)*

Piedmont AVI Cmponent Svcs LLC .... C 336 423-5100
   Greensboro *(G-7255)*

Powerhouse Resources Intl LLC .... D 919 291-1783
   Raleigh *(G-13123)*

AIRCRAFT PARTS & AUXILIARY EQPT: Assemblies, Fuselage

Blue Force Technologies LLC .... D 919 443-1660
   Morrisville *(G-11305)*

AIRCRAFT PARTS & AUXILIARY EQPT: Assys, Subassemblies/Parts

Blanket Aero LLC .... F 704 591-2878
   Concord *(G-4209)*

Curtiss-Wright Controls Inc .... F 704 869-2320
   Gastonia *(G-6391)*

Curtiss-Wright Controls Inc .... E 704 869-4600
   Charlotte *(G-2587)*

Oro Manufacturing Company .... E 704 283-2186
   Monroe *(G-10783)*

AIRCRAFT PARTS & AUXILIARY EQPT: Bodies

Collins Aerospace .... F 704 423-7000
   Charlotte *(G-2524)*

AIRCRAFT PARTS & AUXILIARY EQPT: Body Assemblies & Parts

AMF-NC Enterprise Company LLC .... F 704 489-2206
   Denver *(G-4760)*

Gray Manufacturing Tech LLC .... F 704 489-2206
   Denver *(G-4778)*

AIRCRAFT PARTS & AUXILIARY EQPT: Military Eqpt & Armament

Safety & Security Intl Inc .... G 336 285-8673
   Greensboro *(G-7322)*

Tigerswan LLC .... C 919 439-7110
   Apex *(G-248)*

AIRCRAFT PARTS & AUXILIARY EQPT: Research & Development, Mfr

Weststar Precision Inc .... E 919 557-2820
   Cary *(G-1926)*

AIRCRAFT PARTS & AUXILIARY EQPT: Tanks, Fuel

Isometrics Inc .... F 336 342-4150
   Reidsville *(G-13527)*

Isometrics Inc .... E 336 349-2329
   Reidsville *(G-13528)*

AIRCRAFT PARTS & EQPT, NEC

A & A Drone Service LLC .... G 704 928-5054
   Statesville *(G-14733)*

AAR Key Enterprises Inc .... G 919 337-9706
   Morrisville *(G-11275)*

Acme Aerofab LLC .... G 704 806-3582
   Charlotte *(G-2129)*

Air-We-Go LLC .... E 704 289-6565
   Monroe *(G-10640)*

Aircraft Parts Solutions LLC .... G 843 300-1725
   Apex *(G-157)*

Ark Aviation Inc .... G 336 379-0900
   Greensboro *(G-6814)*

ASAP Components .... G 919 258-2230
   Raleigh *(G-12526)*

B/E Aerospace Inc .... G 336 841-7698
   High Point *(G-8261)*

B/E Aerospace Inc .... F 336 692-8940
   Winston Salem *(G-16612)*

B/E Aerospace Inc .... E 336 293-1823
   Winston Salem *(G-16614)*

B/E Aerospace Inc .... E 336 293-1823
   Winston Salem *(G-16615)*

B/E Aerospace Inc .... E 336 744-6914
   Winston Salem *(G-16616)*

B/E Aerospace Inc .... E 336 767-2000
   Winston Salem *(G-16617)*

B/E Aerospace Inc .... D 520 733-1719
   Winston Salem *(G-16618)*

B/E Aerospace Inc .... C 336 776-3500
   Winston Salem *(G-16619)*

B/E Aerospace Inc .... C 336 767-2000
   Winston Salem *(G-16620)*

B/E Aerospace Inc .... E 336 747-5000
   Winston Salem *(G-16613)*

Ballistic Recovery Systems Inc .... E 651 457-7491
   Pinebluff *(G-12213)*

Beta Fueling Systems LLC .... D 336 342-0306
   Reidsville *(G-13509)*

Brice Manufacturing Co Inc .... E 818 896-2938
   Greensboro *(G-6851)*

Carolina Ground Svc Eqp Inc .... F 252 565-0288
   New Bern *(G-11785)*

Carolina Metals Inc .... E 828 667-0876
   Asheville *(G-582)*

Curtiss-Wright Controls Inc .... E 704 869-2300
   Shelby *(G-14305)*

D2 Government Solutions LLC .... E 662 655-4554
   New Bern *(G-11797)*

DEB Manufacturing Inc .... G 704 703-6618
   Concord *(G-4253)*

Dt Aerospace Inc .... G 919 417-1895
   Hillsborough *(G-8648)*

PRODUCT SECTION

ALUMINUM: Rolling & Drawing

Equipment & Supply Inc .... E 704 289-6565
 Monroe *(G-10716)*
Esterline Technologies Corp .... G 910 814-1222
 Lillington *(G-9851)*
Firstmark Aerospace Corp .... G 919 956-4323
 Durham *(G-5098)*
Frisby Aerospace Inc .... G 336 712-8004
 Clemmons *(G-4040)*
GE Aviation Systems LLC .... C 828 210-5076
 Asheville *(G-631)*
General Electric Company .... A 910 675-5000
 Wilmington *(G-16230)*
Goaero LLC .... G 815 713-1190
 Greensboro *(G-7049)*
Goodrich Corporation .... G 704 282-2500
 Monroe *(G-10725)*
Goodrich Corporation .... C 704 282-2500
 Monroe *(G-10726)*
Goodrich Corporation .... C 704 423-7000
 Charlotte *(G-2847)*
Gounmanned LLC .... G 919 835-2140
 Raleigh *(G-12810)*
Honda Aircraft Company LLC .... F 336 662-0849
 Greensboro *(G-7096)*
Honeywell International Inc .... C 252 977-2100
 Rocky Mount *(G-13701)*
James Tool Machine & Engrg Inc .... C 828 584-8722
 Morganton *(G-11224)*
Kearfott Corporation .... B 828 350-5300
 Black Mountain *(G-1127)*
Kidde Technologies Inc .... D 252 237-4004
 Wilson *(G-16506)*
Legacy Aerospace and Def LLC .... G 828 398-0981
 Arden *(G-347)*
Logic Hydraulic Controls Inc .... E 910 791-9293
 Wilmington *(G-16304)*
Lord Corporation .... B 919 468-5979
 Cary *(G-1817)*
Lord Far East Inc .... E 919 468-5979
 Cary *(G-1819)*
PCC Airfoils LLC .... B 919 774-4300
 Sanford *(G-14164)*
Proedge Precision LLC .... E 704 872-3393
 Statesville *(G-14871)*
Purolator Facet Inc .... E 336 668-4444
 Greensboro *(G-7293)*
R S Skillen .... G 828 433-5353
 Morganton *(G-11244)*
Rockwell Collins Inc .... G 336 744-3288
 Winston Salem *(G-16886)*
Sierra Nevada Corporation .... D 919 595-8551
 Durham *(G-5355)*
Soisa Inc .... G 336 940-4006
 Mocksville *(G-10604)*
Southern Prestige Intl LLC .... F 704 872-9524
 Statesville *(G-14894)*
Specialty Perf LLC .... G 704 872-9980
 Statesville *(G-14897)*
Spirit Aerosystems Inc .... A 252 208-4645
 Kinston *(G-9386)*
Spirit Aerosystems NC Inc .... F 252 208-4645
 Raleigh *(G-13292)*
Starhgen Arospc Components LLC .... F 704 660-1001
 Mooresville *(G-11099)*
T Air Inc .... D 980 595-2840
 Charlotte *(G-3668)*
Tcom Limited Partnership .... B 252 330-5555
 Elizabeth City *(G-5575)*
Telair US LLC .... C 919 705-2400
 Goldsboro *(G-6665)*
Tempest Aero Group .... F 336 449-5054
 Burlington *(G-1505)*

Tempest Aero Group .... E 336 449-5054
 Gibsonville *(G-6571)*
Triumph Actuation Systems LLC .... C 336 766-9036
 Clemmons *(G-4064)*
Unison Engine Components Inc .... B 828 274-4540
 Asheville *(G-808)*
United States Dept of Navy .... E 252 466-4415
 Cherry Point *(G-3858)*
Vannoy Construction Arcft LLC .... G 336 846-7191
 Jefferson *(G-9093)*
Veritable Aerospace .... G 919 258-2230
 Raleigh *(G-13398)*
Vx Aerospace Corporation .... F 828 433-5353
 Morganton *(G-11266)*

AIRCRAFT PARTS WHOLESALERS

Carolina Ground Svc Eqp Inc .... F 252 565-0288
 New Bern *(G-11785)*

AIRCRAFT SEATS

B/E Aerospace Inc .... E 336 747-5000
 Winston Salem *(G-16613)*
Custom Products Inc .... D 704 663-4159
 Mooresville *(G-10920)*
Haeco Cabin Solutions LLC .... A 336 464-0122
 Winston Salem *(G-16731)*
Haeco Cabin Solutions LLC .... D 336 862-1418
 Greensboro *(G-7074)*

AIRCRAFT SERVICING & REPAIRING

Haeco Americas LLC .... A 336 668-4410
 Greensboro *(G-7073)*
Textron Aviation Inc .... C 336 605-7000
 Greensboro *(G-7398)*

AIRCRAFT: Airplanes, Fixed Or Rotary Wing

Boeing Company .... G 919 722-1983
 Sjafb *(G-14446)*
Charter Jet Transport Inc .... G 704 359-8833
 Charlotte *(G-2468)*
Marshall USA LLC .... G 301 481-1241
 Greensboro *(G-7183)*
Textron Aviation Inc .... C 336 605-7000
 Greensboro *(G-7398)*

AIRCRAFT: Motorized

Birds Eye View Aerial Drone .... G 828 691-1550
 Candler *(G-1571)*
Highlander Unmanned Drone .... G 828 776-6061
 Fairview *(G-5713)*
USA Drones .... G 937 830-1856
 Belmont *(G-1017)*

AIRCRAFT: Research & Development, Manufacturer

Southern Aero LLC .... G 336 476-9094
 Thomasville *(G-15278)*
Vx Aerospace Corporation .... F 828 433-5353
 Morganton *(G-11266)*

AIRPORTS, FLYING FIELDS & SVCS

Summit Aviation Inc .... F 302 834-5400
 Greensboro *(G-7379)*

ALARMS: Burglar

Carrier Fire SEC Americas Corp .... E 919 563-5911
 Mebane *(G-10404)*
Elk Products Inc .... E 828 397-4200
 Connelly Springs *(G-4400)*
Tektone Sound & Signal Mfg Inc .... D 828 524-9967
 Franklin *(G-6145)*

ALARMS: Fire

Kidde Technologies Inc .... B 252 237-7004
 Wilson *(G-16508)*
Safe Fire Detection Inc .... F 704 821-7920
 Monroe *(G-10801)*

ALCOHOL: Ethyl & Ethanol

Tyton NC Biofuels LLC .... E 910 878-7820
 Raeford *(G-12443)*

ALKALIES & CHLORINE

Albemarle Corporation .... A 980 299-5700
 Charlotte *(G-2152)*
Buckeye International Inc .... G 704 523-9400
 Charlotte *(G-2363)*
Global Ecosciences Inc .... G 252 631-6266
 Wake Forest *(G-15560)*
Occidental Chemical Corp .... G 910 675-7200
 Castle Hayne *(G-1958)*
Pavco Inc .... E 704 496-6800
 Charlotte *(G-3321)*
PPG Industries Inc .... G 919 772-3093
 Greensboro *(G-7272)*

ALTERNATORS: Automotive

Goldsboro Strter Altrntor Svc .... G 919 735-6745
 Goldsboro *(G-6620)*

ALUMINUM

3a Composites USA Inc .... C 704 872-8974
 Statesville *(G-14732)*
Alcoa Power Generating Inc .... E 704 422-5691
 Badin *(G-862)*
Essex Group Inc .... G 704 921-9605
 Charlotte *(G-2730)*
Muriel Harris Investments Inc .... F 800 932-3191
 Fayetteville *(G-5879)*

ALUMINUM PRDTS

Alfiniti Inc .... D 252 358-5811
 Winton *(G-17020)*
Aviation Metals NC Inc .... F 704 264-1647
 Charlotte *(G-2246)*
CCL Metal Science LLC .... D 910 299-0911
 Clinton *(G-4090)*
Container Products Corporation .... D 910 392-6100
 Wilmington *(G-16179)*
Hydro Extrusion Usa LLC .... D 336 227-8826
 Burlington *(G-1433)*
IPC Corporation .... F 704 821-7084
 Stallings *(G-14671)*
Owens Corning Sales LLC .... E 419 248-8000
 Roxboro *(G-13814)*
Pexco LLC .... D 336 493-7500
 Asheboro *(G-461)*
Seg Systems LLC .... F 704 579-5800
 Huntersville *(G-8896)*

ALUMINUM: Ingots & Slabs

AGM Carolina Inc .... G 336 431-4100
 High Point *(G-8236)*

ALUMINUM: Ingots, Primary

Kymera International LLC .... F 919 544-8090
 Durham *(G-5184)*

ALUMINUM: Rolling & Drawing

Design Specialties Inc .... E 919 772-6955
 Raleigh *(G-12678)*
Mitsubishi Chemical Amer Inc .... D 980 580-2839
 Charlotte *(G-3188)*

ALUMINUM: Rolling & Drawing

Southwire Company LLC .... F 704 379-9600
  Huntersville *(G-8898)*

AMMUNITION: Cartridges Case, 30 mm & Below

Interordnance Amer Ltd Partnr .... G 321 212-7801
  Monroe *(G-10740)*

AMMUNITION: Components

North American Trade LLC .... G 828 712-3004
  Fletcher *(G-6030)*
War Sport LLC .... G 910 948-2237
  Eagle Springs *(G-5462)*

AMMUNITION: Small Arms

Canis Lupus Enterprises LLC .... G 828 450-2074
  Hendersonville *(G-7832)*
Easy E Enterprises LLC .... G 704 763-7906
  Durham *(G-5075)*
Every Day Carry LLc .... F 203 231-0256
  Winnabow *(G-16580)*
Global Synergy Group Inc .... G 704 254-9886
  Matthews *(G-10318)*
Gridlock Enterprises LLC .... G 910 939-4867
  Jacksonville *(G-9006)*
Michael Ray McKinney .... G 828 765-7001
  Spruce Pine *(G-14650)*
North American Trade LLC .... G 828 712-3004
  Fletcher *(G-6030)*
R & S Precision Customs LLC .... G 704 984-3480
  Albemarle *(G-101)*
Riley Defense Inc .... G 704 507-9224
  Hickory *(G-8136)*
Sirius Tactical Entps LLC .... G 704 256-3660
  Waxhaw *(G-15775)*
SRI Gear LLC .... G 704 910-2751
  Charlotte *(G-3612)*
Stillwood Ammun Systems LLC .... G 919 721-9096
  Burlington *(G-1502)*

AMPLIFIERS

Acoustic Image LLC .... G 919 785-1280
  Raleigh *(G-12472)*
Carr Amplifers .... G 919 545-0747
  Pittsboro *(G-12334)*
Carr Amplifers Inc .... F 919 545-0747
  Pittsboro *(G-12335)*
Signal Path International LLC .... G 704 391-9337
  Matthews *(G-10290)*

AMPLIFIERS: RF & IF Power

Akoustis Technologies Inc .... C 704 997-5735
  Huntersville *(G-8787)*
Lcf Enterprise .... G 208 415-4300
  Hickory *(G-8085)*

AMUSEMENT & RECREATION SVCS: Art Gallery, Commercial

Clark Art Shop Inc .... G 919 832-8319
  Raleigh *(G-12625)*

AMUSEMENT ARCADES

Southland Amusements Vend Inc .... E 910 343-1809
  Wilmington *(G-16412)*

AMUSEMENT MACHINES: Coin Operated

Brian McGregor Enterprise .... G 919 732-2317
  Hillsborough *(G-8640)*
Southland Amusements Vend Inc .... E 910 343-1809
  Wilmington *(G-16412)*

AMUSEMENT PARK DEVICES & RIDES

Buy Smart Inc .... G 252 293-4700
  Wilson *(G-16482)*
Dynamic Machine Works LLC .... F 336 462-7370
  Clemmons *(G-4036)*
North Carolina Dept Labor .... F 919 807-2770
  Raleigh *(G-13068)*
Vortex USA Inc .... F 972 410-3619
  Cornelius *(G-4593)*

ANALGESICS

Nationwide Analgesics LLC .... G 704 651-5551
  Matthews *(G-10274)*
Specgx LLC .... C 919 878-4706
  Raleigh *(G-13286)*

ANALYZERS: Blood & Body Fluid

Biomerieux Inc .... B 919 620-2000
  Durham *(G-4960)*

ANALYZERS: Moisture

Cem Corporation .... C 704 821-7015
  Matthews *(G-10307)*
Cem Holdings Corporation .... E 704 821-7015
  Matthews *(G-10308)*

ANALYZERS: Network

Arris Technology Inc .... D 678 473-2907
  Hickory *(G-7944)*
Comtech Group Inc .... G 919 313-4800
  Durham *(G-5029)*
Infinity Communications LLC .... E 919 797-2334
  Durham *(G-5154)*
Jcv Communications Inc .... F 844 399-8282
  Wilmington *(G-16277)*
Joyce Heflin President .... G 919 451-0003
  Durham *(G-5173)*
Network Integrity Systems Inc .... G 828 322-2181
  Hickory *(G-8101)*

ANALYZERS: Respiratory

Polarean Inc .... F 919 206-7900
  Durham *(G-5293)*

ANESTHESIA EQPT

623 Medical LLC .... F 877 455-0112
  Morrisville *(G-11272)*
Cancer Diagnostics Inc .... E 877 846-5393
  Durham *(G-4997)*
Carolina Lquid Chmistries Corp .... E 336 722-8910
  Greensboro *(G-6888)*
Salem Professional Anesthesia .... G 336 998-3396
  Advance *(G-49)*
Suntech Medical Inc .... D 919 654-2300
  Morrisville *(G-11435)*

ANIMAL FEED & SUPPLEMENTS: Livestock & Poultry

A & B Milling Company .... G 252 445-3161
  Enfield *(G-5673)*
Bartlett Milling Company LP .... E 704 487-5061
  Shelby *(G-14288)*
Bartlett Milling Company LP .... D 704 872-9581
  Statesville *(G-14759)*
Bay State Milling Company .... E 704 664-4873
  Mooresville *(G-10870)*
Boggs Farm Center Inc .... G 704 538-7176
  Fallston *(G-5728)*
Boonville Flour Feed Mill Inc .... G 336 367-7541
  Boonville *(G-1253)*
Cargill Incorporated .... C 704 523-0414
  Charlotte *(G-2388)*
Cargill Incorporated .... G 704 278-2941
  Cleveland *(G-4069)*
Cargill Incorporated .... E 252 752-1879
  Greenville *(G-7496)*
Coker Feed Mill Inc .... F 919 778-3491
  Goldsboro *(G-6602)*
Darling Ingredients Inc .... F 704 864-9941
  Gastonia *(G-6395)*
Garland Farm Supply Inc .... F 910 529-9731
  Garland *(G-6244)*
Griffin Industries LLC .... E 704 624-9140
  Marshville *(G-10217)*
Ifta Usa Inc .... G 919 659-8393
  Durham *(G-5147)*
Linkone Src LLC .... E 252 206-0960
  Wilson *(G-16512)*
Midstate Mills Inc .... C 828 464-1611
  Newton *(G-11953)*
Monitor Roller Mill Inc .... G 336 591-4126
  Walnut Cove *(G-15634)*
Mountaire Farms Inc .... D 910 844-3126
  Maxton *(G-10361)*
Murphy-Brown LLC .... D 910 277-8999
  Laurinburg *(G-9490)*
Murphy-Brown LLC .... D 910 293-3434
  Rose Hill *(G-13779)*
Murphy-Brown LLC .... C 910 282-4264
  Rose Hill *(G-13780)*
Nutrien AG Solutions Inc .... F 252 977-2025
  Rocky Mount *(G-13670)*
Purina Mills LLC .... D 704 872-0456
  Statesville *(G-14873)*
Southeastern Minerals Inc .... E 252 492-0831
  Henderson *(G-7811)*
Southern States Coop Inc .... G 336 629-3977
  Asheboro *(G-484)*
Southern States Coop Inc .... G 336 246-3201
  Creedmoor *(G-4620)*
Southern States Coop Inc .... E 919 528-1516
  Creedmoor *(G-4621)*
Southern States Coop Inc .... E 336 786-7545
  Mount Airy *(G-11575)*
Southern States Coop Inc .... E 919 658-5061
  Mount Olive *(G-11669)*
Southern States Coop Inc .... E 919 693-6136
  Oxford *(G-12157)*
Southern States Coop Inc .... G 252 823-2520
  Princeville *(G-12406)*
Southern States Coop Inc .... F 336 599-2185
  Roxboro *(G-13824)*
Southern States Coop Inc .... E 704 872-6364
  Statesville *(G-14896)*
Southern States Coop Inc .... F 910 285-8213
  Wallace *(G-15628)*
Star Milling Company .... G 704 873-9561
  Statesville *(G-14900)*
Steelman Milling Company Inc .... G 336 463-5586
  Yadkinville *(G-17051)*
Valley Proteins (de) Inc .... C 336 333-3030
  Greensboro *(G-7435)*

ANIMAL FEED: Wholesalers

G & M Milling Co Inc .... E 704 873-5758
  Statesville *(G-14802)*
Mountaire Farms LLC .... B 910 974-3232
  Candor *(G-1596)*
Mountaire Farms Inc .... D 910 844-3126
  Maxton *(G-10361)*

ANIMAL FOOD & SUPPLEMENTS: Chicken Feeds, Prepared

Braswell Milling Company .... E 252 459-2143
  Nashville *(G-11736)*
Mountaire Farms LLC .... B 910 974-3232
  Candor *(G-1596)*

ANIMAL FOOD & SUPPLEMENTS: Dog

Barbaras Canine Catering Inc .... G 704 588-3647
  Charlotte *(G-2277)*
Carolina Prime Pet Inc .... E 888 370-2360
  Lenoir *(G-9595)*
Mars Petcare Us Inc .... D 252 438-1600
  Henderson *(G-7798)*

ANIMAL FOOD & SUPPLEMENTS: Dog & Cat

Braswell Milling Company .... E 252 459-2143
  Nashville *(G-11736)*
Carolina By-Products Co .... G 336 333-3030
  Greensboro *(G-6882)*
Crump Group USA Inc .... F 936 465-5870
  Nashville *(G-11742)*
Nestle Purina Petcare Company .... E 314 982-1000
  Eden *(G-5498)*

ANIMAL FOOD & SUPPLEMENTS: Feed Supplements

Apc LLC .... E 919 965-2051
  Selma *(G-14252)*
Darling Ingredients Inc .... F 704 694-3701
  Wadesboro *(G-15509)*
Nutrotonic LLC .... F 855 948-0008
  Charlotte *(G-3285)*
S P Co Inc .... G 919 848-3599
  Raleigh *(G-13222)*

ANIMAL FOOD & SUPPLEMENTS: Livestock

Mountaire Farms LLC .... C 704 978-3055
  Statesville *(G-14847)*

ANIMAL FOOD & SUPPLEMENTS: Meat Meal & Tankage

Protein For Pets Opco LLC .... E 252 206-0960
  Wilson *(G-16524)*

ANIMAL FOOD & SUPPLEMENTS: Pet, Exc Dog & Cat, Canned

Two Percent LLC .... G 301 401-2750
  Lincolnton *(G-9930)*

ANIMAL FOOD & SUPPLEMENTS: Pet, Exc Dog & Cat, Dry

Springmill Products Inc .... G 336 406-9050
  Lawsonville *(G-9504)*

ANIMAL FOOD & SUPPLEMENTS: Poultry

G & M Milling Co Inc .... E 704 873-5758
  Statesville *(G-14802)*
Goldsboro Milling Company .... C 919 778-3130
  Goldsboro *(G-6618)*
Johnson Nash & Sons Farms Inc .... B 910 289-3113
  Rose Hill *(G-13778)*
Pilgrims Pride Corporation .... B 704 624-2171
  Marshville *(G-10222)*

ANNEALING: Metal

By-Design Black Oxide & TI LLC .... F 828 874-0610
  Valdese *(G-15443)*

ANODIZING EQPT

Hockmeyer Equipment Corp .... D 252 338-4705
  Elizabeth City *(G-5548)*

ANODIZING SVC

Industrial Anodizing .... F 336 434-2110
  Trinity *(G-15346)*
Rodeco Company .... F 919 775-7149
  Sanford *(G-14175)*

ANTENNAS: Receiving

Eclipse Composite Engineering .... E 801 601-8559
  Mooresville *(G-10937)*
QMF Mtal Elctrnic Slutions Inc .... D 336 992-8002
  Kernersville *(G-9227)*
Tecworks Inc .... G 704 829-9700
  Belmont *(G-1015)*

ANTI-GLARE MATERIAL

Metal & Materials Proc LLC .... G 260 438-8901
  Aberdeen *(G-13)*

ANTIFREEZE

Camco Manufacturing Inc .... G 336 348-6609
  Reidsville *(G-13511)*

ANTIQUE REPAIR & RESTORATION SVCS, EXC FURNITURE & AUTOS

Dimill Enterprises LLC .... G 919 629-2011
  Raleigh *(G-12684)*

ANTISEPTICS, MEDICINAL

Esc Brands LLC .... G 888 331-8332
  Lexington *(G-9717)*

APPAREL ACCESS STORES

Sweet Room LLC .... G 336 567-1620
  High Point *(G-8560)*
Tafford Uniforms LLC .... D 888 823-3673
  Charlotte *(G-3670)*

APPAREL DESIGNERS: Commercial

LDR Designs .... G 252 375-4484
  Greenville *(G-7555)*

APPAREL FILLING MATERIALS: Cotton Waste, Kapok/Related Matl

Cumulus Fibres Inc .... B 704 394-2111
  Charlotte *(G-2586)*

APPLIANCE PARTS: Porcelain Enameled

Acme Aerofab LLC .... G 704 806-3582
  Charlotte *(G-2129)*
Allied Tool and Machine Co .... G 336 993-2131
  Kernersville *(G-9160)*
Custom Cnverting Solutions Inc .... E 336 292-2616
  Greensboro *(G-6949)*

APPLIANCES, HOUSEHOLD: Kitchen, Major, Exc Refrigs & Stoves

Big Vac .... G 910 947-3654
  Carthage *(G-1660)*
Crizaf Inc .... G 919 251-7661
  Durham *(G-5037)*
Psnc Energy .... G 919 367-2735
  Apex *(G-235)*
Smartway of Carolinas LLC .... F 704 900-7877
  Charlotte *(G-3566)*

APPLIANCES: Household, Refrigerators & Freezers

Bsh Home Appliances Corp .... B 252 672-9155
  New Bern *(G-11780)*
K2 Scientific LLC .... F 800 218-7613
  Charlotte *(G-3041)*

APPLIANCES: Major, Cooking

Electrolux Home Products Inc .... B 252 527-5100
  Kinston *(G-9363)*
Marshall Middleby Inc .... D 919 762-1000
  Fuquay Varina *(G-6212)*
Middleby Marshall Inc .... C 919 762-1000
  Fuquay Varina *(G-6216)*
Weber Stephen Products LLC .... F 704 662-0335
  Mooresville *(G-11125)*
Whaley Foodservice LLC .... D 704 529-6242
  Charlotte *(G-3809)*

APPLIANCES: Small, Electric

Aeroquip Corp .... G 828 286-4157
  Forest City *(G-6057)*
Carolina Water Jets .... G 704 853-3663
  Gastonia *(G-6371)*
Madison Manufacturing Company .... D 828 622-7500
  Hot Springs *(G-8745)*
Sculptural Arts Coating Inc .... G 336 379-7651
  Greensboro *(G-7328)*

APPLICATIONS SOFTWARE PROGRAMMING

Able Softsystems Corp .... G 919 241-7907
  Raleigh *(G-12463)*
Czechmate Enterprises LLC .... G 704 784-6547
  Concord *(G-4250)*
Fiestic Inc .... F 888 935-3999
  Raleigh *(G-12765)*
Information Tech Works LLC .... F 919 232-5332
  Raleigh *(G-12888)*
Innait Inc .... G 406 241-5245
  Charlotte *(G-2975)*
Inneroptic Technology Inc .... G 919 732-2090
  Hillsborough *(G-8656)*
Sato Global Solutions Inc .... F 954 261-3279
  Charlotte *(G-3494)*
School Directorease LLC .... G 240 206-6273
  Charlotte *(G-3505)*
Splendidcrm Software Inc .... G 919 604-1258
  Holly Springs *(G-8718)*
Tc2 Labs LLC .... G 919 380-2171
  Raleigh *(G-13329)*
Telephys Inc .... G 312 625-9128
  Davidson *(G-4699)*

AQUARIUM ACCESS, METAL

Truelove Fabrications Inc .... G 910 343-0195
  Wilmington *(G-16434)*

AQUARIUMS & ACCESS: Glass

All Glass Inc .... G 828 324-8609
  Hickory *(G-7931)*
Done-Gone Adios Inc .... F 336 993-7300
  Kernersville *(G-9192)*
Jackson Arts Market LLC .... G 415 659-0710
  Sylva *(G-15059)*
Merge Scientific Solutions LLC .... G 919 346-0999
  Fuquay Varina *(G-6215)*

ARCHITECTURAL SVCS

Carolina Timberworks LLC .... F 828 266-9663
  West Jefferson *(G-15936)*

ARCHITECTURAL SVCS

PRODUCT SECTION

Solid Holdings LLC .... F 704 423-0260
  Charlotte *(G-3578)*
Sterling Cleora Corporation .... E 919 563-5800
  Durham *(G-5374)*

ARMATURE REPAIRING & REWINDING SVC

3 D Sewing Contractors .... G 336 499-1619
  Winston Salem *(G-16585)*
Electrical Equipment Company .... E 910 276-2141
  Laurinburg *(G-9478)*
GE Vernova International LLC .... F 704 587-1300
  Charlotte *(G-2812)*
Snow Electric Co Inc .... G 336 723-2092
  Winston Salem *(G-16912)*

ARMATURES: Ind

Siemens Med Solutions USA Inc .... E 919 468-7400
  Cary *(G-1887)*

ARMOR PLATES

Lelantos Group Inc .... D 704 780-4127
  Mooresville *(G-11005)*

AROMATIC CHEMICAL PRDTS

Balanced Health Plus LLC .... F 704 604-9524
  Charlotte *(G-2271)*
Yanek LLC .... G 252 558-3757
  Snow Hill *(G-14512)*

ART DEALERS & GALLERIES

World Art Gallery Incorporated .... G 910 989-0203
  Jacksonville *(G-9047)*

ART GOODS, WHOLESALE

Cedar Hill Studio & Gallery .... G 828 456-6344
  Waynesville *(G-15797)*

ART MARBLE: Concrete

Henson Family Investments LLC .... E 910 817-9450
  Rockingham *(G-13628)*

ARTIFICIAL FLOWERS & TREES

Earth-Kind Inc .... G 701 751-4456
  Mooresville *(G-10934)*
Evergreen Silks NC Inc .... F 704 845-5577
  Matthews *(G-10248)*
Tree Masters Inc .... E 828 464-9443
  Newton *(G-11979)*

ARTISTS' MATERIALS, WHOLESALE

Speedball Art Products Co LLC .... D 800 898-7224
  Statesville *(G-14898)*

ARTS & CRAFTS SCHOOL

Stamping & Scrapbooking Rm Inc .... G 336 389-9538
  Greensboro *(G-7365)*

ARTWORK: Framed

Brett Salter .... G 828 252-4311
  Asheville *(G-572)*
Caldwell Hohl Artworks .... G 336 879-9090
  Seagrove *(G-14234)*
Historic Interpretations Inc .... G 919 339-1558
  Raleigh *(G-12847)*
Laura Gaskin .... G 828 628-5891
  Fairview *(G-5715)*
Marvin Saltzman .... G 919 942-7091
  Chapel Hill *(G-2037)*
Reeses Balloon Art .... G 919 303-2147
  Cary *(G-1867)*
Susan Strazzella .... G 828 676-1162
  Asheville *(G-792)*

Techscan Industries LLC .... G 704 843-4518
  Waxhaw *(G-15780)*
Watercolors By Mista .... G 828 775-7751
  Weaverville *(G-15868)*

ASPHALT & ASPHALT PRDTS

Barnhill Contracting Company .... F 336 584-1306
  Burlington *(G-1375)*
Blythe Construction Inc .... B 704 375-8474
  Charlotte *(G-2325)*
Boggs Materials Inc .... G 704 289-8482
  Monroe *(G-10664)*
Boggs Transport Inc .... E 704 289-8482
  Monroe *(G-10665)*
Cloverleaf Mixing Inc .... G 336 765-7900
  Winston Salem *(G-16655)*
D&S Asphalt Materials Inc .... G 828 894-2778
  Tryon *(G-15424)*
Garris Grading and Paving Inc .... F 252 749-1101
  Farmville *(G-5736)*
Highland Paving Co LLC .... D 910 482-0080
  Fayetteville *(G-5839)*

ASPHALT COATINGS & SEALERS

Axalta Coating Systems USA LLC .... F 336 802-5701
  High Point *(G-8259)*
C3 Sealcoating LLC .... G 919 880-5515
  Wake Forest *(G-15537)*
Carolina Solvents Inc .... E 828 322-1920
  Hickory *(G-7966)*
Rgpack Concrete LLC .... G 919 561-0855
  Chinquapin *(G-3893)*

ASPHALT MINING & BITUMINOUS STONE QUARRYING SVCS

Johnson Paving Company Inc .... F 828 652-4911
  Marion *(G-10154)*

ASPHALT MIXTURES WHOLESALERS

D&S Asphalt Materials Inc .... G 828 894-2778
  Tryon *(G-15424)*
Fsc II LLC .... F 919 783-5700
  Raleigh *(G-12785)*

ASPHALT PLANTS INCLUDING GRAVEL MIX TYPE

Apac-Atlantic Inc .... D 336 412-6800
  Raleigh *(G-12512)*
Barnhill Contracting Company .... F 252 527-8021
  Kinston *(G-9344)*
Cardinal Stone Company Inc .... E 336 846-7191
  Jefferson *(G-9087)*
Carolina Paving Hickory Inc .... G 828 328-3909
  Hickory *(G-7964)*
Carolina Paving Hickory Inc .... F 828 322-1706
  Hickory *(G-7965)*
Ferebee Corporation .... C 704 509-2586
  Charlotte *(G-2751)*
S T Wooten Corporation .... E 252 636-2568
  New Bern *(G-11842)*
S T Wooten Corporation .... E 919 965-7176
  Princeton *(G-12403)*
S T Wooten Corporation .... E 919 776-2736
  Sanford *(G-14178)*

ASSEMBLING SVC: Plumbing Fixture Fittings, Plastic

B & B Building Maintenance LLC .... G 910 494-2715
  Bunnlevel *(G-1329)*

Gods Son Plumbing Inc .... G 252 299-0983
  Wilson *(G-16501)*
H & H Representatives Inc .... G 704 596-6950
  Charlotte *(G-2877)*
Union Plastics Company .... G 704 624-2112
  Marshville *(G-10226)*

ASSOCIATIONS: Business

Kidde Technologies Inc .... B 252 237-7004
  Wilson *(G-16507)*

ASSOCIATIONS: Real Estate Management

Solarh2ot Ltd .... G 919 439-2387
  Raleigh *(G-13279)*

ASSOCIATIONS: Scientists'

International Society Automtn .... E 919 206-4176
  Durham *(G-5162)*

ATOMIZERS

Atlantic Group Usa Inc .... F 919 623-7824
  Raleigh *(G-12530)*
Biganodes LLC .... G 828 245-1115
  Forest City *(G-6060)*
Cambbro Manufacturing Company .... F 919 568-8506
  Mebane *(G-10402)*
Gallimore Fmly Investments Inc .... F 336 625-5138
  Asheboro *(G-438)*
Gentry Mills Inc .... D 704 983-5555
  Albemarle *(G-86)*
Kerdea Technologies Inc .... F 971 900-1113
  Greenville *(G-7552)*
Phillips Corporation .... E 336 665-1080
  Colfax *(G-4157)*
Qspac Industries Inc .... E 704 635-7815
  Monroe *(G-10791)*
Sewerkote LLC .... G 919 602-8002
  Durham *(G-5350)*
Stuart Ryan Kent & Co .... G 252 916-8226
  Winterville *(G-17014)*

ATTENUATORS

M2 Optics Inc .... G 919 342-5619
  Raleigh *(G-12985)*
Shallco Inc .... E 919 934-3135
  Smithfield *(G-14482)*

AUDIO & VIDEO EQPT, EXC COMMERCIAL

Advanced Tech Systems Inc .... F 336 299-6695
  Greensboro *(G-6782)*
Anthony Demaria Labs Inc .... F 845 255-4695
  Cary *(G-1683)*
Apple Inc .... F 516 318-6744
  Cary *(G-1685)*
Cablenc LLC .... G 919 307-9065
  Zebulon *(G-17124)*
Cco Holdings LLC .... C 828 414-4238
  Blowing Rock *(G-1155)*
Cco Holdings LLC .... C 828 355-4149
  Boone *(G-1186)*
Cco Holdings LLC .... C 910 292-4083
  Dunn *(G-4857)*
Cco Holdings LLC .... C 828 270-7016
  Hickory *(G-7973)*
Cco Holdings LLC .... C 919 502-4007
  Kenly *(G-9147)*
Cco Holdings LLC .... C 828 394-0635
  Lenoir *(G-9597)*
Cco Holdings LLC .... C 704 308-3361
  Lincolnton *(G-9880)*
Cco Holdings LLC .... C 828 528-4004
  Newland *(G-11883)*

PRODUCT SECTION — AUTOMOTIVE & TRUCK GENERAL REPAIR SVC

Cco Holdings LLC................................ C 919 200-6260
  Siler City *(G-14402)*
Cco Holdings LLC................................ C 828 368-4161
  Valdese *(G-15445)*
Evolution Technologies Inc.................. G 919 544-3777
  Raleigh *(G-12752)*
Fairfield Pro AV Inc.............................. G 214 375-8570
  Charlotte *(G-2746)*
Hartley Products Corp......................... G 910 392-0500
  Wilmington *(G-16249)*
Integrated Info Systems Inc................. F 919 488-5000
  Youngsville *(G-17086)*
JPS Communications Inc.................... D 919 534-1168
  Raleigh *(G-12923)*
Multi Technical Services Inc................ G 919 553-2995
  Clayton *(G-4000)*
Palmer Senn.. G 704 451-3971
  Charlotte *(G-3309)*
PC Satellite Solutions.......................... G 252 217-7237
  Roper *(G-13770)*
Wheatstone Corporation..................... D 252 638-7000
  New Bern *(G-11855)*

AUDIO COMPONENTS

Cary Audio Design LLC...................... E 919 355-0010
  Raleigh *(G-12605)*
East Coast Digital Inc......................... F 919 304-1142
  Mebane *(G-10408)*

AUDIO ELECTRONIC SYSTEMS

Eastern Sun Communications Inc........ G 704 408-7668
  Charlotte *(G-2674)*
Linor Technology Inc........................... F 336 485-6199
  Winston Salem *(G-16788)*
Moon Audio.. G 919 649-5018
  Cary *(G-1826)*

AUDIO-VISUAL PROGRAM PRODUCTION SVCS

Avcon Inc.. E 919 388-0203
  Cary *(G-1696)*
Cog Glbal Media/Consulting LLC........ E 980 239-8042
  Matthews *(G-10244)*

AUTO & HOME SUPPLY STORES: Auto & Truck Eqpt & Parts

Advance Stores Company Inc............. F 336 545-9091
  Greensboro *(G-6780)*
Prem Corp.. E 704 921-1799
  Charlotte *(G-3373)*
Satco Truck Equipment Inc................. G 919 383-5547
  Durham *(G-5340)*

AUTO & HOME SUPPLY STORES: Automotive Access

Boondock S Manufacturing Inc........... G 828 891-4242
  Etowah *(G-5691)*
Down East Offroad Inc....................... F 252 246-9440
  Wilson *(G-16493)*
Treadz LLC... G 704 664-0995
  Mooresville *(G-11114)*
Van Products Inc................................ E 919 878-7110
  Raleigh *(G-13392)*

AUTO & HOME SUPPLY STORES: Automotive parts

Heintz Bros Automotives Inc............... G 704 872-8081
  Statesville *(G-14809)*
Irvan-Smith Inc................................... F 704 788-2554
  Concord *(G-4290)*
Kerdea Technologies Inc.................... F 971 900-1113
  Greenville *(G-7552)*
Kgt Enterprises Inc............................. E 704 662-3272
  Mooresville *(G-10997)*
Roy Dunn... G 919 963-3700
  Four Oaks *(G-6111)*
Sika Corporation................................ E 704 810-0500
  Gastonia *(G-6510)*
Sparksmith LLC.................................. G 828 266-0152
  Waynesville *(G-15827)*

AUTO & HOME SUPPLY STORES: Batteries, Automotive & Truck

Alk Investments LLC.......................... G 984 233-5353
  Raleigh *(G-12488)*

AUTO & HOME SUPPLY STORES: Trailer Hitches, Automotive

Leonard Alum Utlity Bldngs Inc........... G 919 872-4442
  Raleigh *(G-12968)*

AUTO & HOME SUPPLY STORES: Truck Eqpt & Parts

Consolidated Truck Parts Inc............... G 704 279-5543
  Rockwell *(G-13650)*
Leonard Alum Utlity Bldngs Inc........... G 336 226-9410
  Burlington *(G-1450)*
Leonard Alum Utlity Bldngs Inc........... D 336 789-5018
  Mount Airy *(G-11538)*

AUTO SPLYS & PARTS, NEW, WHSLE: Exhaust Sys, Mufflers, Etc

Tri-City Mechanical Contrs Inc............. D 336 272-9495
  Greensboro *(G-7410)*

AUTOMATIC REGULATING CONTROL: Building Svcs Monitoring, Auto

Comp Environmental Inc..................... F 919 316-1321
  Durham *(G-5028)*
Delkote Machine Finishing Inc............. G 828 253-1023
  Asheville *(G-606)*
Nascent Technology LLC.................... F 704 654-3035
  Charlotte *(G-3232)*

AUTOMATIC REGULATING CONTROLS: AC & Refrigeration

Belham Management Ind LLC............. G 704 815-4246
  Charlotte *(G-2297)*
Dorsett Technologies Inc.................... E 855 387-2232
  Yadkinville *(G-17038)*
Thermik Corporation........................... E 252 636-5720
  New Bern *(G-11850)*
Trane US Inc...................................... A 704 655-4000
  Davidson *(G-4704)*

AUTOMATIC REGULATING CONTROLS: Appliance Regulators

Johnson Global Cmplnce Contrls........ G 704 552-1119
  Charlotte *(G-3032)*

AUTOMATIC REGULATING CONTROLS: Appliance, Exc AirCond/Refr

Pas USA Inc....................................... C 252 974-5500
  Washington *(G-15726)*

AUTOMATIC REGULATING CONTROLS: Hardware, Environmental Reg

Green Stream Technologies Inc.......... G 844 499-8880
  Wake Forest *(G-15563)*
Layer27.. G 919 909-9088
  Youngsville *(G-17088)*

AUTOMATIC REGULATING CONTROLS: Hydronic Pressure Or Temp

Icare Usa Inc...................................... G 919 877-9607
  Raleigh *(G-12874)*

AUTOMATIC REGULATING CONTROLS: Pneumatic Relays, Air-Cond

Ultratech Industries Inc....................... G 919 779-2004
  Benson *(G-1045)*

AUTOMATIC REGULATING CONTROLS: Refrig/Air-Cond Defrost

TRf Manufacturing NC Inc................... E 252 223-1112
  Newport *(G-11909)*

AUTOMATIC REGULATING CTRLS: Damper, Pneumatic Or Electric

Effikal LLC.. G 252 522-3031
  Kinston *(G-9361)*
Salice America Inc.............................. E 704 841-7810
  Charlotte *(G-3483)*

AUTOMATIC TELLER MACHINES

Buvic LLC... G 910 302-7950
  Fayetteville *(G-5776)*
Cisco Systems Inc.............................. F 919 392-2000
  Morrisville *(G-11323)*
Express Yourself................................. G 919 526-0611
  Raleigh *(G-12755)*
Extron Electronics............................... G 919 850-1000
  Raleigh *(G-12758)*
Noregon Systems Inc......................... C 336 615-8555
  Greensboro *(G-7223)*

AUTOMOBILES & OTHER MOTOR VEHICLES WHOLESALERS

Parker-Hannifin Corporation................ G 704 664-1922
  Mooresville *(G-11047)*
Pro-System Inc................................... F 704 799-8100
  Mooresville *(G-11064)*

AUTOMOBILES: Off-Road, Exc Recreational Vehicles

American Growler Inc.......................... E 352 671-5393
  Robbins *(G-13596)*
Crown Defense Ltd............................. G 202 800-8848
  Denver *(G-4769)*
Down East Offroad Inc....................... F 252 246-9440
  Wilson *(G-16493)*

AUTOMOTIVE & TRUCK GENERAL REPAIR SVC

Aiken-Black Tire Service Inc............... E 828 322-3736
  Hickory *(G-7930)*
B & B Welding Inc.............................. G 336 643-5702
  Oak Ridge *(G-12057)*
Barrs Competition............................... F 704 482-5169
  Shelby *(G-14287)*
Courtesy Ford Inc............................... E 252 338-4783
  Elizabeth City *(G-5537)*
Diagnostic Shop Inc............................ G 704 933-3435
  Kannapolis *(G-9117)*

Employee Codes: A=Over 500 employees, B=251-500
C=101-250, D=51-100, E=20-50, F=10-19, G=1-9

AUTOMOTIVE & TRUCK GENERAL REPAIR SVC

F & C Repair and Sales LLC .... F 704 907-2461
  Charlotte *(G-2741)*

Falls Automotive Service Inc .... G 336 723-0521
  Winston Salem *(G-16708)*

Greensboro Tire & Auto Service .... G 336 294-9495
  Greensboro *(G-7066)*

Haneys Tire Recapping Svc LLC .... F 910 276-2636
  Laurinburg *(G-9481)*

John West Auto Service Inc .... G 919 250-0825
  Raleigh *(G-12919)*

L & S Automotive Inc .... G 704 391-7657
  Charlotte *(G-3065)*

Lewis Brothers Tire & Algnmt .... G 919 359-9050
  Clayton *(G-3993)*

Mr Tire Inc .... G 828 262-3555
  Boone *(G-1225)*

Mr Tire Inc .... F 704 483-1500
  Denver *(G-4790)*

Mr Tire Inc .... F 828 322-8130
  Hickory *(G-8099)*

Mr Tire Inc .... G 704 739-6456
  Kings Mountain *(G-9319)*

Mr Tire Inc .... G 828 758-0047
  Lenoir *(G-9637)*

Mr Tire Inc .... G 704 735-8024
  Lincolnton *(G-9910)*

Mr Tire Inc .... G 704 484-0816
  Shelby *(G-14350)*

Mr Tire Inc .... G 704 872-4127
  Statesville *(G-14849)*

NC Diesel Performance LLC .... G 704 431-3257
  Salisbury *(G-14016)*

Quality Investments Inc .... E 252 492-8777
  Henderson *(G-7805)*

R & J Mechanical & Welding LLC .... G 919 362-6630
  Apex *(G-238)*

Snider Tire Inc .... F 336 691-5480
  Greensboro *(G-7347)*

Spring Repair Service Inc .... F 336 299-5660
  Greensboro *(G-7360)*

Stoltz Automotive Inc .... G 336 595-4218
  Walkertown *(G-15616)*

Sullivan Motorsports Inc .... G 252 923-2257
  Bath *(G-917)*

Team X-Treme LLC .... G 919 562-8100
  Rolesville *(G-13760)*

Universal Tire Service Inc .... G 919 779-8798
  Raleigh *(G-13383)*

Wooten John .... G 828 322-4031
  Hickory *(G-8210)*

Zickgraf Enterprises Inc .... G 828 524-2313
  Franklin *(G-6149)*

AUTOMOTIVE CUSTOMIZING SVCS, NONFACTORY BASIS

Specialty Trnsp Systems Inc .... G 828 464-9738
  Newton *(G-11971)*

AUTOMOTIVE GLASS REPLACEMENT SHOPS

A R Perry Corporation .... F 252 492-6181
  Henderson *(G-7774)*

Orare Inc .... G 919 742-1003
  Siler City *(G-14429)*

Rice S Glass Company Inc .... E 919 967-9214
  Carrboro *(G-1655)*

AUTOMOTIVE PARTS, ACCESS & SPLYS

Aerofabb LLC .... G 919 793-8487
  Raleigh *(G-12480)*

Agve Inc .... G 704 243-8300
  Matthews *(G-10231)*

American Racg Hders Exhust Inc .... E 631 608-1986
  Stanfield *(G-14674)*

Amsted Industries Incorporated .... G 704 226-5243
  Monroe *(G-10646)*

Amt .... G 617 549-4395
  Thomasville *(G-15186)*

Andreani USA Inc .... G 828 435-0125
  Hendersonville *(G-7819)*

Andrews Products Inc .... G 704 785-9715
  Concord *(G-4197)*

Auria Albemarle LLC .... B 704 983-5166
  Albemarle *(G-74)*

Auria Old Fort LLC .... C 828 668-7601
  Old Fort *(G-12098)*

Auria Old Fort II LLC .... D 828 668-3277
  Old Fort *(G-12099)*

Auria Troy LLC .... D 910 572-3721
  Troy *(G-15401)*

Ben Huffman Enterprises LLC .... G 704 724-4705
  Mooresville *(G-10872)*

Beulaville Wstn Auto Value Inc .... F 910 298-4246
  Beulaville *(G-1091)*

Billet Speed Inc .... G 828 226-8127
  Sylva *(G-15054)*

Bordeaux Dynocams .... G 910 655-9482
  Delco *(G-4718)*

Borg-Warner Automotive Inc .... G 828 684-3501
  Fletcher *(G-5990)*

Borgwarner Arden LLC .... F 248 754-9200
  Arden *(G-313)*

Bostrom Seating Inc .... A 704 596-0040
  Charlotte *(G-2338)*

Br549 Enterprises LLC .... G 704 799-0955
  Sherrills Ford *(G-14384)*

Brembo North America Inc .... G 704 799-0530
  Concord *(G-4214)*

Brucato Power Inc .... G 919 234-1776
  Apex *(G-173)*

BT America Inc .... G 704 434-8072
  Boiling Springs *(G-1158)*

Camco Manufacturing Inc .... G 336 348-6609
  Reidsville *(G-13511)*

Camcraft Performance Cams .... G 828 492-0950
  Canton *(G-1605)*

Carbotech USA Inc .... G 704 481-8500
  Concord *(G-4224)*

Carolina Cltch Brake Rbldrs In .... G 828 327-9358
  Hickory *(G-7962)*

Catlow Inc .... G 336 894-3367
  Greensboro *(G-6895)*

Certification Services International LLC G 828 458-1573
  Fletcher *(G-5993)*

City of Charlotte-Atando .... F 704 336-2722
  Charlotte *(G-2487)*

Classic Wood Manufacturing .... G 336 691-1344
  Greensboro *(G-6913)*

Coconut Paradise Inc .... G 704 662-3443
  Mooresville *(G-10908)*

Commercial Vehicle Group Inc .... E 704 886-6407
  Concord *(G-4238)*

Consolidated Metco Inc .... D 828 488-5126
  Bryson City *(G-1322)*

Consolidated Metco Inc .... C 828 488-5114
  Canton *(G-1611)*

Consolidated Metco Inc .... D 704 226-5246
  Monroe *(G-10693)*

Continental Auto Systems Inc .... B 828 654-2000
  Fletcher *(G-5996)*

Continental Auto Systems Inc .... D 828 584-4500
  Valdese *(G-15446)*

Cooper-Standard Automotive Inc .... D 919 735-5394
  Goldsboro *(G-6604)*

Corvac Inc .... G 772 692-5514
  Hayesville *(G-7764)*

Cox Machine Co Inc .... F 704 296-0118
  Monroe *(G-10696)*

Cummins Inc .... G 919 284-9111
  Kenly *(G-9150)*

Cummins Inc .... G 704 588-1240
  Pineville *(G-12264)*

Curtis L Maclean L C .... C 704 940-5531
  Mooresville *(G-10919)*

Cycle Pro LLC .... F 704 662-6682
  Mooresville *(G-10922)*

Daimler Truck North Amer LLC .... A 704 868-5700
  Gastonia *(G-6394)*

Dambach Lagersysteme Inc .... G 704 421-6425
  Charlotte *(G-2602)*

David Vizard Motortec Features .... G 865 850-0666
  Mount Holly *(G-11630)*

Dhollandia Us Llc .... G 909 251-7979
  Bessemer City *(G-1063)*

Dnj Engine Comp Onents .... G 704 855-5505
  China Grove *(G-3882)*

Doosan Bobcat North Amer Inc .... C 704 883-3500
  Statesville *(G-14789)*

Dover Power LLC .... G 704 485-2020
  Oakboro *(G-12072)*

East Coast Roadster .... G 336 624-5083
  Winston Salem *(G-16688)*

Eaton Corporation .... B 336 322-0696
  Roxboro *(G-13801)*

Elite Metal Performance LLC .... F 704 660-0006
  Statesville *(G-14793)*

Epic Restorations LLC .... G 866 597-2733
  Roxboro *(G-13802)*

Esta Extraction USA LP .... G 704 942-8844
  Charlotte *(G-2731)*

Five Star Bodies .... G 262 325-9126
  Troutman *(G-15377)*

Fox Factory Inc .... G 831 421-1791
  Mooresville *(G-10950)*

Gear Fx Driveline LLC .... G 704 799-9117
  Mooresville *(G-10955)*

GKN Driveline Newton LLC .... E 828 428-5292
  Newton *(G-11934)*

GKN Driveline North Amer Inc .... C 336 364-6200
  Timberlake *(G-15314)*

Global Products LLC .... G 336 227-7327
  Greensboro *(G-7046)*

GM Defense LLC .... D 800 462-8782
  Concord *(G-4275)*

Grede II LLC .... B 910 428-2111
  Biscoe *(G-1110)*

Grimme Services LLC .... G 828 490-6366
  Asheville *(G-645)*

Guilford Performance Textiles .... G 910 296-5362
  Kenansville *(G-9143)*

Hamilton Sundstrand Corp .... B 860 654-6000
  Charlotte *(G-2882)*

Hanak Enterprises .... G 704 315-5249
  Gastonia *(G-6413)*

Hanwha Advanced Mtls Amer LLC .... E 704 434-2271
  Shelby *(G-14325)*

Hendrens Racg Engs Chassis Inc .... G 828 286-0780
  Rutherfordton *(G-13879)*

Hickory Springs Mfg Co .... F 336 491-4131
  High Point *(G-8386)*

High Street Baptist Church .... G 336 234-0400
  Milton *(G-10515)*

Holman & Moody Inc .... G 704 394-4141
  Charlotte *(G-2914)*

PRODUCT SECTION — AUTOMOTIVE REPAIR SHOPS: Machine Shop

Hotchkis Bryde Incorporated .... G 704 660-3060
  Mooresville (G-10977)
Ignite Dirt Sports LLC .... G 704 770-7806
  Cornelius (G-4559)
Inter-Continental Gear & Brake .... G 704 599-3420
  Charlotte (G-2980)
Jri Development Group LLC .... F 704 660-8346
  Mooresville (G-10989)
Jri Shocks LLC .... F 704 660-8346
  Mooresville (G-10990)
Kck Holding Corp .... E 336 513-0002
  Burlington (G-1443)
Kessler Inc .... G 248 717-0027
  Indian Trail (G-8942)
Kgt Enterprises Inc .... E 704 662-3272
  Mooresville (G-10997)
Kooks Custom Headers .... G 704 838-1110
  Statesville (G-14833)
Lear Corporation .... E 919 552-5667
  Fuquay Varina (G-6208)
Lear Enterprises Inc .... G 704 321-0027
  Charlotte (G-3078)
Leonard Alum Utlty Bldngs Inc .... G 919 872-4442
  Raleigh (G-12968)
Leonard Alum Utlty Bldngs Inc .... G 910 392-4921
  Wilmington (G-16299)
Mack Trucks Inc .... A 336 291-9001
  Greensboro (G-7177)
Magna Composites LLC .... B 704 797-8744
  Salisbury (G-14008)
Mahle Motorsports Inc .... F 888 255-1942
  Fletcher (G-6020)
Mann+hmmel Prlator Filters LLC .... C 910 425-4181
  Fayetteville (G-5865)
Mann+hmmel Prlator Filters LLC .... C 704 869-3441
  Gastonia (G-6453)
Mann+hmmel Prlator Filters LLC .... E 910 425-4181
  Fayetteville (G-5864)
Mann+hummel Filtration Technol ...... D 704 869-3500
  Gastonia (G-6454)
Mann+hummel Filtration Technol ...... D 704 869-3501
  Gastonia (G-6456)
Marmon Engine Controls LLC .... E 843 701-5145
  Laurinburg (G-9487)
Mayflower Vehicle Systems LLC .... D 704 937-4400
  Kings Mountain (G-9318)
MB Marketing & Mfg Inc .... G 828 285-0882
  Asheville (G-697)
Meritor Inc .... F 910 844-9401
  Maxton (G-10359)
Meritor Inc .... D 910 844-9401
  Maxton (G-10360)
Meritor Inc .... C 828 433-4600
  Morganton (G-11232)
Metalcraft & Mech Svc Inc .... G 919 736-1029
  Goldsboro (G-6636)
Moores Mch Co Fayetteville Inc .... D 919 837-5354
  Bear Creek (G-941)
Motoring Inc .... G 704 809-1265
  Mooresville (G-11030)
Motorsport Innovations Inc .... G 704 728-7837
  Davidson (G-4686)
Motorsports Machining Tech LLC .... F 336 475-3742
  Thomasville (G-15254)
MSI Defense Solutions LLC .... D 704 660-8348
  Mooresville (G-11032)
NC Saturn Parts LLC .... G 704 802-5277
  Charlotte (G-3240)
Olivers Drive Shaft Repair .... G 719 539-1823
  Winston Salem (G-16829)
PCC Airfoils LLC .... B 919 774-4300
  Sanford (G-14164)

Poppelmann Plastics USA .... G 828 466-9500
  Claremont (G-3932)
Powerbrake Corporation .... G 704 804-2438
  Huntersville (G-8880)
Precision Pdts Prfmce Ctr Inc .... E 828 684-8569
  Arden (G-367)
Pro-Motor Engines Inc .... G 704 664-6800
  Mooresville (G-11063)
Race Technologies Concord NC .... G 704 799-0530
  Concord (G-4346)
Razor Motorsports .... G 704 517-0649
  Charlotte (G-3415)
Reuben James Auto Electric .... G 910 980-1056
  Falcon (G-5727)
Richardson Racing Products Inc .... G 704 784-2602
  Concord (G-4350)
Ripari Automotive LLC .... G 585 267-0228
  Charlotte (G-3452)
Roadactive Suspension Inc .... G 704 523-2646
  Charlotte (G-3454)
Rp Motor Sports Inc .... E 704 720-4200
  Concord (G-4353)
RTC Ventures LLC .... G 704 247-9781
  Charlotte (G-3470)
Saf-Holland Inc .... G 336 310-4595
  Kernersville (G-9230)
Save-A-Load Inc .... G 704 650-4947
  Charlotte (G-3495)
Schnitzer Group Usa Inc .... G 347 982-6880
  Charlotte (G-3504)
Scorpion Products Inc .... G 336 813-3241
  King (G-9281)
Siebenwurst US Inc .... G 704 333-7790
  Charlotte (G-3545)
Simrek Corporation .... G 336 497-5331
  Kernersville (G-9234)
SL Liquidation LLC .... D 910 353-3666
  Jacksonville (G-9031)
Spod Inc .... G 910 477-6297
  Southport (G-14584)
SRI Performance LLC .... E 704 662-6982
  Mooresville (G-11097)
Stanadyne Operating Co LLC .... D 910 353-3666
  Jacksonville (G-9040)
Studleys Independent Rods .... G 704 296-9036
  Monroe (G-10816)
Superfast Performance Pdts Inc .... G 828 980-8072
  Hudson (G-8781)
T & N Manufacturing Co Inc .... G 704 788-1418
  Davidson (G-4698)
Teijin Automotive Tech Inc .... C 828 754-8441
  Lenoir (G-9655)
Teijin Automotive Tech Inc .... D 828 466-7000
  Newton (G-11977)
Tenowo Inc .... A 704 732-3525
  Lincolnton (G-9926)
Thyssenkrupp Bilstein Amer Inc .... F 704 663-7563
  Mooresville (G-11112)
Tire Kountry LLC .... G 336 637-8320
  Reidsville (G-13542)
Trane Technologies Company LLC .... C 910 692-8700
  Southern Pines (G-14558)
Trend Performance Products .... G 828 862-8290
  Pisgah Forest (G-12329)
Trevira North America LLC .... G 704 910-0970
  Charlotte (G-3722)
Triangle Auto Components LLC .... F 704 848-4121
  Lilesville (G-9841)
Uchiyama Mfg Amer LLC .... B 919 731-2364
  Goldsboro (G-6668)
Ultimate Qm Inc .... G 704 500-9035
  Stanley (G-14710)

US Legend Cars Intl Inc .... E 704 455-3896
  Harrisburg (G-7732)
Visual Impact Prfmce Systems L .... G 704 278-3552
  Cleveland (G-4083)
Wenker Inc .... G 704 333-7790
  Charlotte (G-3804)
Wesley Leblanc Racing LLC .... G 336 560-7630
  Archdale (G-305)
Xceldyne LLC .... D 336 472-2242
  Thomasville (G-15306)
Zeta Performance Vhcl Tech LLC .... G 804 690-8979
  Cornelius (G-4596)
Zingerle Group Usa Inc .... G 704 312-1600
  Charlotte (G-3851)

AUTOMOTIVE PARTS: Plastic

Atlantic Automotive Entps LLC .... F 910 377-4108
  Tabor City (G-15077)
Auto Parts Fayetteville LLC .... G 910 889-4026
  Fayetteville (G-5766)
Borgwarner Turbo Systems LLC .... D 828 650-7515
  Arden (G-315)
Central Carolina Products Inc .... C 336 226-1449
  Burlington (G-1392)
Central Carolina Products Inc .... D 336 226-0005
  Burlington (G-1393)
Debotech Inc .... C 704 664-1361
  Mooresville (G-10927)
Thanet Inc .... E 704 483-4175
  Denver (G-4807)
Trelleborg Salisbury Inc .... E 704 797-8030
  Salisbury (G-14055)

AUTOMOTIVE PRDTS: Rubber

Hexpol Compounding NC Inc .... A 704 872-1585
  Statesville (G-14813)
Lgc Consulting Inc .... E 704 216-0171
  Salisbury (G-14003)
Maranz Inc .... D 336 996-7776
  Winston Salem (G-16799)

AUTOMOTIVE REPAIR SHOPS: Diesel Engine Repair

Cummins Atlantic LLC .... E 704 596-7690
  Charlotte (G-2584)
Cummins Atlantic LLC .... E 704 588-1240
  Charlotte (G-2585)
S Strickland Diesel Svc Inc .... G 252 291-6999
  Wilson (G-16536)

AUTOMOTIVE REPAIR SHOPS: Electrical Svcs

Goldsboro Strter Altrntor Svc .... G 919 735-6745
  Goldsboro (G-6620)
Mc Cullough Auto Elc & Assoc .... G 704 376-5388
  Charlotte (G-3148)
R S Integrators Inc .... G 704 588-8288
  Pineville (G-12294)

AUTOMOTIVE REPAIR SHOPS: Engine Rebuilding

Griffin Automotive Marine Inc .... G 252 940-0714
  Washington (G-15706)
Johnson Machine Co Inc .... G 252 638-2620
  New Bern (G-11814)

AUTOMOTIVE REPAIR SHOPS: Machine Shop

Broadsight Systems Inc .... G 336 837-1272
  Mebane (G-10401)

Employee Codes: A=Over 500 employees, B=251-500
C=101-250, D=51-100, E=20-50, F=10-19, G=1-9

AUTOMOTIVE REPAIR SHOPS: Machine Shop

Chiron America Inc .... D 704 587-9526
  Charlotte *(G-2478)*

G T Racing Heads Inc .... G 336 905-7988
  Sophia *(G-14517)*

Performance Entps & Parts Inc .... G 336 621-6572
  Greensboro *(G-7251)*

Subaru Folger Automotive .... E 704 531-8888
  Charlotte *(G-3645)*

AUTOMOTIVE REPAIR SHOPS: Rebuilding & Retreading Tires

Albemarle Tire Retreading Inc .... G 704 982-4113
  Albemarle *(G-71)*

Big Tire Outfitters .... G 919 568-9605
  Mc Leansville *(G-10383)*

Bridgestone Ret Operations LLC .... G 919 471-4468
  Durham *(G-4977)*

Bridgestone Ret Operations LLC .... G 910 864-4106
  Fayetteville *(G-5775)*

Bridgestone Ret Operations LLC .... F 704 861-8146
  Gastonia *(G-6360)*

Bridgestone Ret Operations LLC .... G 919 778-0230
  Goldsboro *(G-6597)*

Bridgestone Ret Operations LLC .... G 336 282-6646
  Greensboro *(G-6852)*

Bridgestone Ret Operations LLC .... F 336 852-8524
  Greensboro *(G-6853)*

Bridgestone Ret Operations LLC .... G 252 522-5126
  Kinston *(G-9347)*

Bridgestone Ret Operations LLC .... G 919 872-6402
  Raleigh *(G-12573)*

Bridgestone Ret Operations LLC .... G 919 872-6566
  Raleigh *(G-12574)*

Bridgestone Ret Operations LLC .... G 252 243-5189
  Wilson *(G-16480)*

Bridgestone Ret Operations LLC .... G 336 725-1580
  Winston Salem *(G-16636)*

Carolina Retread LLC .... F 910 642-4123
  Whiteville *(G-15961)*

Dunlop Aircraft Tyres Inc .... E 336 283-0979
  Mocksville *(G-10567)*

Piedmont Truck Tires Inc .... E 828 277-1549
  Asheville *(G-731)*

Piedmont Truck Tires Inc .... F 336 223-9412
  Graham *(G-6706)*

Piedmont Truck Tires Inc .... E 336 668-0091
  Greensboro *(G-7262)*

Tire Sls Svc Inc Fytteville NC .... E 910 485-1121
  Fayetteville *(G-5931)*

AUTOMOTIVE REPAIR SHOPS: Sound System Svc & Installation

Sonaron LLC .... G 808 232-6168
  Fayetteville *(G-5919)*

AUTOMOTIVE REPAIR SHOPS: Tire Recapping

Accel Discount Tire .... G 704 636-0323
  Salisbury *(G-13913)*

Aiken-Black Tire Service Inc .... E 828 322-3736
  Hickory *(G-7930)*

Avery County Recapping Co Inc .... E 828 733-0161
  Newland *(G-11881)*

Bill Martin Inc .... F 704 873-0241
  Statesville *(G-14764)*

Bray S Recapping Service Inc .... E 336 786-6182
  Mount Airy *(G-11486)*

Cecil Budd Tire Company LLC .... F 919 742-2322
  Siler City *(G-14403)*

Claybrook Tire Inc .... F 336 573-3135
  Stoneville *(G-14955)*

Crossroads Tire Store Inc .... G 704 888-2064
  Midland *(G-10465)*

Enfield Tire Service Inc .... G 252 445-5016
  Enfield *(G-5677)*

Foster Tire Sales Inc .... G 336 248-6726
  Lexington *(G-9719)*

Greensboro Tire & Auto Service .... G 336 294-9495
  Greensboro *(G-7066)*

Haneys Tire Recapping Svc LLC .... F 910 276-2636
  Laurinburg *(G-9481)*

John Conrad Inc .... G 336 475-8144
  Thomasville *(G-15239)*

M & R Retreading & Oil Co Inc .... F 704 474-4101
  Norwood *(G-12040)*

Merchants Inc .... G 252 447-2121
  Havelock *(G-7743)*

Mr Tire Inc .... G 828 262-3555
  Boone *(G-1225)*

Mr Tire Inc .... F 704 483-1500
  Denver *(G-4790)*

Mr Tire Inc .... F 828 322-8130
  Hickory *(G-8099)*

Mr Tire Inc .... G 704 739-6456
  Kings Mountain *(G-9319)*

Mr Tire Inc .... G 828 758-0047
  Lenoir *(G-9637)*

Mr Tire Inc .... G 704 735-8024
  Lincolnton *(G-9910)*

Mr Tire Inc .... G 704 484-0816
  Shelby *(G-14350)*

Mr Tire Inc .... G 704 872-4127
  Statesville *(G-14849)*

Oakie S Tire & Recapping Inc .... F 704 482-5629
  Shelby *(G-14353)*

Parrish Tire Company .... E 704 872-6565
  Jonesville *(G-9101)*

Parrish Tire Company .... D 800 849-8473
  Winston Salem *(G-16836)*

Perry Brothers Tire Svc Inc .... F 919 693-2128
  Oxford *(G-12140)*

Perry Brothers Tire Svc Inc .... E 919 775-7225
  Sanford *(G-14167)*

Phil S Tire Service Inc .... G 828 682-2421
  Burnsville *(G-1530)*

Richmond Investment .... E 910 410-8200
  Rockingham *(G-13640)*

Small Brothers Tire Co Inc .... G 704 289-3531
  Monroe *(G-10808)*

Snider Tire Inc .... D 704 373-2910
  Charlotte *(G-3571)*

Snider Tire Inc .... F 336 691-5480
  Greensboro *(G-7347)*

Snider Tire Inc .... G 828 324-9955
  Hickory *(G-8160)*

Super Retread Center Inc .... F 919 734-0073
  Goldsboro *(G-6663)*

Tires Incorporated of Clinton .... E 910 592-4741
  Clinton *(G-4114)*

Towel City Tire & Wheel LLC .... G 704 933-2143
  Kannapolis *(G-9136)*

White S Tire Svc Wilson Inc .... G 252 237-0770
  Wilson *(G-16559)*

White S Tire Svc Wilson Inc .... D 252 237-5426
  Wilson *(G-16560)*

Whites Tire Svc New Bern Inc .... G 252 633-1170
  New Bern *(G-11857)*

AUTOMOTIVE REPAIR SHOPS: Tire Repair Shop

A 1 Tire Service Inc .... G 828 684-1860
  Fletcher *(G-5978)*

Arenas Tires .... G 828 962-9422
  Hickory *(G-7940)*

Autosmart Inc .... G 919 210-7936
  Apex *(G-168)*

Burnett Darrill Stephen .... G 828 287-8778
  Spindale *(G-14604)*

Ed S Tire Laurinburg Inc .... G 910 277-0565
  Laurinburg *(G-9476)*

Elias Gonzalez .... G 910 271-9514
  Warsaw *(G-15667)*

Go Ev and Go Green Corp .... G 704 327-9040
  Charlotte *(G-2839)*

Hall Tire and Battery Co Inc .... F 336 275-3812
  Greensboro *(G-7075)*

Halls Auto Repair .... G 919 879-9946
  Dunn *(G-4874)*

Hardison Tire Co Inc .... F 252 745-4561
  Bayboro *(G-935)*

Johnnys Tire Sales and Svc Inc .... F 252 353-8473
  Greenville *(G-7551)*

Lewis Brothers Tire & Algnmt .... G 919 359-9050
  Clayton *(G-3993)*

Lexington Tire & Auto LLC .... G 336 249-2105
  Lexington *(G-9748)*

Mock Tire & Automotive Inc .... E 336 753-8473
  Mocksville *(G-10591)*

Mock Tire & Automotive Inc .... E 336 774-0081
  Winston Salem *(G-16812)*

Mock Tire & Automotive Inc .... E 336 768-1010
  Winston Salem *(G-16813)*

Pumpkin Pacific LLC .... G 704 226-4176
  Charlotte *(G-3397)*

Quality Investments Inc .... E 252 492-8777
  Henderson *(G-7805)*

Safe Tire & Autos LLC .... G 910 590-3101
  Clinton *(G-4107)*

Stoltz Automotive Inc .... G 336 595-4218
  Walkertown *(G-15616)*

Tbc Retail Group Inc .... G 336 540-8066
  Greensboro *(G-7392)*

Terrys Tires & Services LLC .... G 336 251-7366
  East Bend *(G-5469)*

Toe River Service Station LLC .... G 828 688-6385
  Bakersville *(G-890)*

Treadz LLC .... G 704 664-0995
  Mooresville *(G-11114)*

Vestal Buick Gmc Inc .... D 336 310-0261
  Kernersville *(G-9251)*

Village Tire Center Inc .... G 919 862-8500
  Raleigh *(G-13400)*

White Tire and Service LLC .... G 704 636-0323
  Salisbury *(G-14066)*

Wilson Tire and Automotive Inc .... G 336 584-9638
  Elon College *(G-5668)*

Woodlawn Tire and Algnmt Inc .... G 828 756-4212
  Marion *(G-10190)*

AUTOMOTIVE REPAIR SHOPS: Trailer Repair

Colfax Trailer & Repair LLC .... G 336 993-8511
  Colfax *(G-4144)*

Spring Repair Service Inc .... F 336 299-5660
  Greensboro *(G-7360)*

AUTOMOTIVE REPAIR SHOPS: Wheel Alignment

Claybrook Tire Inc .... F 336 573-3135
  Stoneville *(G-14955)*

Hall Tire and Battery Co Inc .... F 336 275-3812
  Greensboro *(G-7075)*

Whitaker S Tire Service Inc............................ F 704 786-6174
  Concord (G-4389)

AUTOMOTIVE REPAIR SVC

Anglers Marine NC.. G 919 585-7900
  Clayton (G-3953)
Avery County Recapping Co Inc..................... E 828 733-0161
  Newland (G-11881)
B S R-Hess Race Cars Inc................................ E 704 547-0901
  Charlotte (G-2254)
Carolina... F 919 851-0906
  Cary (G-1722)
Nichols Spdmtr & Instr Co Inc......................... G 336 273-2881
  Greensboro (G-7219)
One Source SEC & Sound Inc......................... G 281 850-9487
  Mooresville (G-11044)
Prevost Car (us) Inc... E 908 222-7211
  Greensboro (G-7281)
Pumpkin Pacific LLC... G 704 226-4176
  Charlotte (G-3397)
Scattered Wrenches Inc.................................... G 919 480-1605
  Raleigh (G-13236)
Treadz LLC... G 704 664-0995
  Mooresville (G-11114)

AUTOMOTIVE SPLYS & PARTS, NEW, WHOLESALE: Hardware

Mfi Products Inc.. F 910 944-2128
  Aberdeen (G-15)

AUTOMOTIVE SPLYS & PARTS, NEW, WHOLESALE: Testing Eqpt, Eng

RNS International Inc....................................... E 704 329-0444
  Charlotte (G-3453)

AUTOMOTIVE SPLYS & PARTS, NEW, WHOLESALE: Trailer Parts

A-1 Hitch & Trailors Sales Inc.......................... F 910 755-6025
  Supply (G-15005)

AUTOMOTIVE SPLYS & PARTS, NEW, WHOLESALE: Wheels

Te Wheel Inc... G 336 376-1364
  Graham (G-6712)
Wagon Wheel... G 828 689-4755
  Mars Hill (G-10198)
Wheel City Wholesale Inc................................ F 828 665-2442
  Asheville (G-819)
Wheel Pros LLC... G 336 851-6705
  Greensboro (G-7459)

AUTOMOTIVE SPLYS & PARTS, WHOLESALE, NEC

Auto Machine Shop Inc.................................... G 910 483-6016
  Fayetteville (G-5765)
Heintz Bros Automotives Inc........................... G 704 872-8081
  Statesville (G-14809)
Johnson Machine Co Inc.................................. G 252 638-2620
  New Bern (G-11814)
Lake Shore Radiator Inc.................................. G 336 271-2626
  Greensboro (G-7162)
Mann+hmmel Fltrtion Tech Group................. G 704 869-3300
  Gastonia (G-6449)
Mc Cullough Auto Elc & Assoc....................... G 704 376-5388
  Charlotte (G-3148)
Merchant 1 Marketing LLC.............................. G 888 853-9992
  Greensboro (G-7199)
Pfaff Molds Ltd Partnership............................. F 704 423-9484
  Charlotte (G-3334)

Pro-Motor Engines Inc..................................... G 704 664-6800
  Mooresville (G-11063)
Robert Blake... G 704 720-9341
  Concord (G-4351)
T & N Manufacturing Co Inc........................... G 704 788-1418
  Davidson (G-4698)

AUTOMOTIVE SVCS, EXC REPAIR & CARWASHES: Lubrication

Newfound Tire & Quick Lube Inc.................... G 828 683-3232
  Leicester (G-9516)

AUTOMOTIVE SVCS, EXC RPR/CARWASHES: High Perf Auto Rpr/Svc

Capital Value Center Sls & Svc...................... G 910 799-4060
  Wilmington (G-16153)
Pro-Motor Engines Inc..................................... G 704 664-6800
  Mooresville (G-11063)
Richard Chldress Racg Entps In.................... E 336 731-3334
  Welcome (G-15874)
Richard Chldress Racg Entps In.................... B 336 731-3334
  Welcome (G-15875)

AUTOMOTIVE TOWING SVCS

Bucks Wrecker Service..................................... G 704 776-0899
  Statesville (G-14767)

AUTOMOTIVE TRANSMISSION REPAIR SVC

Parrish Tire Company....................................... F 336 334-9979
  Greensboro (G-7246)

AUTOMOTIVE WELDING SVCS

Donald Auton... G 704 872-7528
  Statesville (G-14788)
Richards Welding and Repr Inc..................... G 828 396-8705
  Granite Falls (G-6753)
Technique Chassis LLC.................................... E 517 819-3579
  Concord (G-4374)
United Services Group LLC............................ G 980 237-1335
  Charlotte (G-3752)

AUTOMOTIVE: Bodies

Csi Armoring Inc... G 336 313-8561
  Lexington (G-9701)

AUTOMOTIVE: Seat Frames, Metal

Jeffrey Sheffer... G 919 861-9126
  Raleigh (G-12915)

AUTOMOTIVE: Seating

Clarios LLC.. E 866 589-8883
  Charlotte (G-2492)
Clarios LLC.. E 336 884-5832
  High Point (G-8296)
Clarios LLC.. B 336 761-1550
  Kernersville (G-9180)
Clarios LLC.. E 252 754-0782
  Winterville (G-16997)
Indiana Mills & Manufacturing........................ C 336 862-7519
  High Point (G-8407)
Johnson Controls Inc.. F 828 225-3200
  Asheville (G-673)
Johnson Controls Inc.. F 919 905-5745
  Durham (G-5172)
Johnson Controls Inc.. D 919 743-3500
  Raleigh (G-12920)
Johnson Controls Inc.. E 910 392-2372
  Wilmington (G-16281)
Johnson Controls Inc.. E 704 521-8889
  Charlotte (G-3031)

Joie of Seating Inc.. F 704 795-7474
  Concord (G-4295)

AWNINGS & CANOPIES

Hamlin Sheet Metal Company Inc.................. D 919 894-2224
  Benson (G-1036)
Raleigh Mechanical & Mtls Inc....................... F 919 598-4601
  Raleigh (G-13179)

AWNINGS & CANOPIES: Awnings, Fabric, From Purchased Matls

Accent Awnings Inc.. F 828 321-4517
  Andrews (G-123)
Alpha Canvas and Awning Co Inc.................. F 704 333-1581
  Charlotte (G-2167)
Clark Art Shop Inc.. G 919 832-8319
  Raleigh (G-12625)
Coastal Awnings Inc... F 252 222-0707
  Morehead City (G-11162)
Coastal Canvas Mfg Inc................................... G 252 728-4946
  Beaufort (G-950)
Colored Metal Products Inc............................. F 704 482-1407
  Shelby (G-14301)
CSC Awnings Inc... G 336 744-5006
  Winston Salem (G-16666)
Custom Canvas Works Inc............................... F 919 662-4800
  Garner (G-6270)
Rocky Mount Awning & Tent Co..................... F 252 442-0184
  Rocky Mount (G-13730)
Trivantage LLC... D 800 786-1876
  Burlington (G-1510)

AWNINGS & CANOPIES: Canopies, Fabric, From Purchased Matls

Custom Golf Car Supply Inc............................ C 704 855-1130
  Salisbury (G-13952)

AWNINGS: Fiberglass

Identigraph Signs & Awnings......................... G 704 635-7911
  Monroe (G-10736)

AWNINGS: Metal

Champion Win Co of Charlotte...................... F 704 398-0085
  Charlotte (G-2446)
Colored Metal Products Inc............................. F 704 482-1407
  Shelby (G-14301)
Midway Blind & Awning Co Inc...................... G 336 226-4532
  Burlington (G-1461)

AXLES

Meritor Inc... F 828 687-2000
  Fletcher (G-6023)
Meritor Inc... C 828 687-2000
  Fletcher (G-6024)
Meritor Inc... D 828 247-0440
  Forest City (G-6077)

AXLES: Rolled Or Forged, Made In Steel Mills

Meritor Inc... C 828 433-4600
  Morganton (G-11232)

BACKHOES

Bakchoe Services... G 828 321-3360
  Topton (G-15325)
Bares Backhoe & Septic System..................... G 336 352-3951
  Mount Airy (G-11480)
Bartleys Backhoe Service................................. G 910 918-1384
  Chadbourn (G-1974)
Darren Moretz Backhoe Ser............................ G 828 964-1006
  Boone (G-1193)

BACKHOES

East Cast Trckg Bckhoe Svcs LL................. G 919 209-0198
  Smithfield *(G-14459)*
Edd Loftis Backhoe Servic........................ G 919 971-5740
  Ocean Isle Beach *(G-12091)*
Ellis Backhoe Service Inc......................... G 336 451-6265
  Greensboro *(G-6994)*
Holder Backhoe & Hauling Inc................. F 336 622-7388
  Liberty *(G-9816)*
Kevins Backhoe Service.......................... G 336 591-7751
  Germanton *(G-6554)*
Melton Backhoe Service Inc.................... G 828 779-6728
  Black Mountain *(G-1130)*
Patrick... G 336 846-4759
  West Jefferson *(G-15947)*
Pittmanbac... G 252 430-4745
  Henderson *(G-7802)*
Robs Backhoe Service............................. G 910 295-3317
  Aberdeen *(G-25)*
Ronny D Phelps...................................... G 828 206-6339
  Hot Springs *(G-8746)*
Sain Grading & Backhoe......................... G 704 481-9179
  Shelby *(G-14362)*
Southern Trucking & Backhoe................. G 919 548-9723
  Siler City *(G-14432)*
Strickland Backhoe................................. G 910 893-5274
  Bunnlevel *(G-1331)*
T Simmons Backhoe................................ G 336 295-3100
  Browns Summit *(G-1317)*
T T Beckham Backhoe Service................ G 252 438-7620
  Henderson *(G-7812)*
Top Hat Bbcat Backhoe Svcs Inc............. G 336 382-0068
  Madison *(G-10089)*
Ward Backhoe Bulldozer Svc LLC........... G 252 446-5878
  Battleboro *(G-932)*

BAGS & BAGGING: Knit

Adele Knits Inc....................................... C 336 499-6010
  Winston Salem *(G-16589)*
Coville Inc.. F 336 759-0115
  Winston Salem *(G-16664)*
Griffin Tubing Company Inc.................... G 336 449-4822
  Gibsonville *(G-6560)*

BAGS & CONTAINERS: Textile, Exc Sleeping

Hdb Inc... G 800 403-2247
  Greensboro *(G-7080)*

BAGS & SACKS: Shipping & Shopping

Tsg2 Inc... G 704 347-4484
  Charlotte *(G-3733)*

BAGS: Canvas

Camoteck LLC.. G 910 590-3213
  Clinton *(G-4089)*
J Stahl Sales & Sourcing Inc................... E 828 645-3005
  Weaverville *(G-15849)*

BAGS: Duffle, Canvas, Made From Purchased Materials

Cross Canvas Company Inc..................... E 828 252-0440
  Asheville *(G-599)*

BAGS: Food Storage & Frozen Food, Plastic

Bioselect Inc... G 704 521-8585
  Charlotte *(G-2315)*

BAGS: Food Storage & Trash, Plastic

Reynolds Consumer Products Inc............ A 704 371-5550
  Huntersville *(G-8885)*

BAGS: Paper

Inplac North America Inc........................ G 704 587-1151
  Charlotte *(G-2976)*
Westrock Rkt LLC................................... C 828 464-5560
  Conover *(G-4512)*

BAGS: Paper, Made From Purchased Materials

Cardinal Bag & Envelope Co Inc.............. E 704 225-9636
  Monroe *(G-10672)*
Novolex Holdings LLC............................ D 980 498-4082
  Charlotte *(G-3277)*

BAGS: Plastic

Berry Global Films LLC.......................... C 704 821-2316
  Matthews *(G-10304)*
Bulk Sak International Inc....................... E 704 833-1361
  Gastonia *(G-6361)*
Classic Packaging Company................... D 336 922-4224
  Pfafftown *(G-12187)*
Cryovac Leasing Corporation.................. E 980 430-7000
  Charlotte *(G-2578)*
Dayton Bag & Burlap Co........................ E 704 873-7271
  Statesville *(G-14783)*
Hood Packaging Corporation.................. C 910 582-1842
  Hamlet *(G-7623)*
Printpack Inc.. C 828 693-1723
  Hendersonville *(G-7892)*
Rgees LLC... E 828 708-7178
  Arden *(G-372)*
Rubbermaid Commercial Pdts LLC......... A 540 667-8700
  Huntersville *(G-8888)*
Sealed Air Corporation........................... D 828 728-6610
  Hudson *(G-8779)*
Sonoco Hickory Inc................................ E 828 286-1356
  Forest City *(G-6081)*
Transcontinental Tvl LLC....................... D 336 476-3131
  Thomasville *(G-15294)*
Wastezero Inc.. E 919 322-1208
  Raleigh *(G-13413)*

BAGS: Plastic & Pliofilm

Sealed Air Corporation (us)................... A 201 791-7600
  Charlotte *(G-3518)*
Sealed Air LLC...................................... F 980 430-7000
  Charlotte *(G-3520)*

BAGS: Plastic, Made From Purchased Materials

Ice Box Company Inc............................. F 910 579-3273
  Ocean Isle Beach *(G-12092)*
Imaflex Usa Inc..................................... E 336 885-8131
  Thomasville *(G-15235)*
Liqui-Box Corporation........................... D 804 325-1400
  Charlotte *(G-3092)*
Novolex Holdings LLC........................... D 980 498-4082
  Charlotte *(G-3277)*
Poly Plastic Products NC Inc.................. D 704 624-2555
  Marshville *(G-10223)*

BAGS: Shipping

Automated Solutions LLC....................... F 828 396-9900
  Granite Falls *(G-6723)*
Hood Packaging Corporation.................. C 910 582-1842
  Hamlet *(G-7623)*
Pro Choice Contractors Corp................. F 919 696-7383
  Raleigh *(G-13146)*

BAGS: Shopping, Made From Purchased Materials

Downtown Graphics Network Inc............ G 704 637-0855
  Salisbury *(G-13954)*

BAKERIES, COMMERCIAL: On Premises Baking Only

Accidental Baker.................................... G 919 732-6777
  Hillsborough *(G-8632)*
Apple Baking Company Inc.................... E 704 637-6800
  Salisbury *(G-13922)*
Bimbo Bakeries Usa Inc........................ A 252 641-2200
  Tarboro *(G-15096)*
Bluebird Cupcakes................................ G 919 616-7347
  Raleigh *(G-12565)*
Burney Sweets & More Inc.................... G 910 862-2099
  Elizabethtown *(G-5587)*
Buttercreme Bakery Inc........................ G 336 722-1022
  Winston Salem *(G-16641)*
Casa Di Cupcakes................................ G 919 255-9994
  Raleigh *(G-12609)*
Cupcake A La Mo LLC.......................... G 919 322-8824
  Raleigh *(G-12660)*
Evelyn T Burney................................... G 336 473-9794
  Rocky Mount *(G-13697)*
Event Extravaganza LLC...................... F 252 679-7004
  Elizabeth City *(G-5544)*
Five Points Baking Company LLC......... G 919 349-2033
  Raleigh *(G-12771)*
Flowers Baking Co Newton LLC........... G 336 903-1345
  Wilkesboro *(G-16022)*
Flowers Bkg Co Jamestown LLC.......... G 252 492-1519
  Henderson *(G-7784)*
Flowers Bkg Co Jamestown LLC.......... G 704 296-1000
  Monroe *(G-10720)*
Flowers Bkg Co Jamestown LLC.......... E 336 744-3525
  Winston Salem *(G-16716)*
Franklin Baking Company LLC............. F 252 752-4600
  Greenville *(G-7529)*
Franklin Baking Company LLC............. F 910 425-5090
  Hope Mills *(G-8737)*
Franklin Baking Company LLC............. G 919 832-7942
  Raleigh *(G-12780)*
Franklin Baking Company LLC............. E 252 946-3340
  Washington *(G-15705)*
Fuquay-Varina Baking Co Inc............... G 919 557-2237
  Fuquay Varina *(G-6201)*
Harris Teeter LLC................................ D 704 846-7117
  Matthews *(G-10252)*
Harris Teeter LLC................................ D 919 859-0110
  Raleigh *(G-12831)*
Ingles Markets Incorporated................. D 704 434-0096
  Boiling Springs *(G-1161)*
Jps Cupcakery LLC............................... F 919 894-5000
  Benson *(G-1038)*
Kelley G Cupcakes............................... G 314 368-5316
  Durham *(G-5179)*
La Estrella Inc..................................... G 919 639-6559
  Angier *(G-144)*
La Farm Inc... E 919 657-0657
  Cary *(G-1805)*
Lc Foods LLC....................................... G 919 510-6688
  Raleigh *(G-12961)*
Martins Fmous Pstry Shoppe Inc.......... G 800 548-1200
  Charlotte *(G-3134)*
Mennel Mil & Bky Mix NC LLC.............. E 828 468-6015
  Newton *(G-11952)*
Novas Bakery Inc................................. F 704 333-5566
  Charlotte *(G-3275)*
Old Salem Incorporated....................... G 336 721-7305
  Winston Salem *(G-16828)*
Orange Bakery Inc............................... E 704 875-3003
  Huntersville *(G-8872)*

PRODUCT SECTION — BALERS

Simple Baking...G.....704 523-4962
  Charlotte (G-3555)
Sls Baking Company......................................G.....704 421-2763
  Charlotte (G-3564)
Spoons Bowls N Baking Pans LLC..............G.....919 662-0494
  Raleigh (G-13293)
Sunninghill Jill Baking Co LLC......................G.....704 894-9901
  Cornelius (G-4590)
Wildflour Bakery Inc.....................................G.....828 749-9224
  Saluda (G-14075)

BAKERIES: On Premises Baking & Consumption

Bakeboxx Company.......................................F.....336 861-1212
  High Point (G-8262)
Dewey S Bakery Inc......................................F.....336 748-0230
  Winston Salem (G-16677)
Ingles Markets Incorporated......................D.....704 434-0096
  Boiling Springs (G-1161)
Normandie Bakery Inc.................................G.....910 686-1372
  Wilmington (G-16340)
Novas Bakery Inc..F.....704 333-5566
  Charlotte (G-3275)
Sprinkle of Sugar LLC..................................G.....336 474-8620
  Thomasville (G-15281)
Wildflour Bakery Inc.....................................G.....828 749-9224
  Saluda (G-14075)

BAKERY MACHINERY

Baker Thermal Solutions LLC.....................E.....919 674-3750
  Clayton (G-3957)
M G Newell Corporation...............................D.....336 393-0100
  Greensboro (G-7173)
Stanza Machinery Inc...................................E.....704 599-0623
  Charlotte (G-3622)

BAKERY PRDTS, FROZEN: Wholesalers

Evelyn T Burney..G.....336 473-9794
  Rocky Mount (G-13697)

BAKERY PRDTS: Bagels, Fresh Or Frozen

Dewey S Bakery Inc......................................F.....336 748-0230
  Winston Salem (G-16677)

BAKERY PRDTS: Biscuits, Dry

Imperial Falcon Group Inc..........................G.....646 717-1128
  Charlotte (G-2953)

BAKERY PRDTS: Bread, All Types, Fresh Or Frozen

Bakkavor Foods Usa Inc.............................C.....704 522-1977
  Charlotte (G-2270)
Flowers Baking Co Newton LLC................D.....336 841-8840
  Jamestown (G-9049)
Flowers Bkg Co Jamestown LLC................E.....919 776-8932
  Sanford (G-14118)
Franklin Baking Company LLC...................F.....252 410-0255
  Roanoke Rapids (G-13574)
Franklin Baking Company LLC..................B.....919 735-0344
  Goldsboro (G-6614)

BAKERY PRDTS: Cakes, Bakery, Exc Frozen

A Taste of Heavenly Sweetness.................G.....336 825-7321
  Greensboro (G-6768)
Cupcake Stop Shop LLC............................G.....919 457-7900
  Raleigh (G-12661)
Delish Cakery Co..G.....704 724-7743
  Charlotte (G-2613)
Flowers Bakery of Winston-Salem LLC....C.....336 785-8700
  Winston Salem (G-16715)
Heavenly Cheesecakes...............................G.....336 577-9390
  Winston Salem (G-16741)
Premier Cakes LLC......................................G.....919 274-8511
  Raleigh (G-13137)
Scotts & Associates Inc..............................F.....336 581-3141
  Bear Creek (G-942)
Sweet Room LLC..G.....336 567-1620
  High Point (G-8560)

BAKERY PRDTS: Cakes, Bakery, Frozen

Big Bundts..G.....919 448-4184
  Chapel Hill (G-1990)
Hais Kookies & More...................................G.....980 819-8256
  Charlotte (G-2880)

BAKERY PRDTS: Cookies

Gracie Goodness Inc..................................G.....910 792-0800
  Wilmington (G-16238)
Kalo Foods LLC..G.....336 949-4802
  Stokesdale (G-14944)
Keebler Company...D.....919 774-6431
  Sanford (G-14143)
S-L Snacks National LLC...........................E.....704 554-1421
  Charlotte (G-3480)
Scotts & Associates Inc..............................F.....336 581-3141
  Bear Creek (G-942)
Snyders-Lance Inc.......................................G.....704 557-8013
  Charlotte (G-3573)
Snyders-Lance Inc.......................................A.....704 554-1421
  Charlotte (G-3574)

BAKERY PRDTS: Cookies & crackers

B&G Foods Inc..E.....336 849-7000
  Yadkinville (G-17032)
Burney Sweets & More Inc.........................G.....910 862-2099
  Elizabethtown (G-5587)
Dewey S Bakery Inc.....................................F.....336 748-0230
  Winston Salem (G-16677)
Flowers Bakery of Winston-Salem LLC....C.....336 785-8700
  Winston Salem (G-16715)
Grandmas Sugar Shack..............................G.....336 760-8822
  Winston Salem (G-16727)
Old Salem Incorporated..............................G.....336 721-7305
  Winston Salem (G-16828)
S-L Snacks Pa LLC......................................C.....704 554-1421
  Charlotte (G-3481)
Steven-Robert Originals LLC.....................C.....910 521-0199
  Pembroke (G-12184)

BAKERY PRDTS: Doughnuts, Exc Frozen

Donut Shop...G.....910 640-3317
  Whiteville (G-15962)
Dunkin Donuts..F.....919 217-9603
  Knightdale (G-9417)
Krispy Kreme Doughnut Corp....................E.....919 669-6151
  Gastonia (G-6440)
Krispy Kreme Doughnut Corp....................E.....336 854-8275
  Greensboro (G-7158)
Krispy Kreme Doughnut Corp....................E.....336 733-3780
  Winston Salem (G-16779)
Krispy Kreme Doughnut Corp....................C.....980 270-7117
  Charlotte (G-3062)
Krispy Kreme Doughnuts Inc....................C.....336 725-2981
  Winston Salem (G-16781)

BAKERY PRDTS: Dry

Divine South Baking Co LLC.....................G.....828 421-2042
  Highlands (G-8615)
Evelyn T Burney..G.....336 473-9794
  Rocky Mount (G-13697)
Lotus Bakeries Us LLC................................G.....415 956-8956
  Mebane (G-10417)

BAKERY PRDTS: Frozen

Bimbo Bakeries Usa Inc.............................A.....252 641-2200
  Tarboro (G-15096)
Kalo Foods LLC..G.....336 949-4802
  Stokesdale (G-14944)
Orange Bakery Inc.......................................E.....704 875-3003
  Huntersville (G-8872)
Stefano Foods Inc..C.....704 399-3935
  Charlotte (G-3628)

BAKERY PRDTS: Pastries, Exc Frozen

Carolina Foods LLC.....................................B.....704 333-9812
  Charlotte (G-2395)

BAKERY PRDTS: Pretzels

Chestnut Land Company............................G.....828 299-9108
  Asheville (G-590)
SE Co-Brand Ventures LLC........................G.....704 598-9322
  Charlotte (G-3514)

BAKERY PRDTS: Rolls, Bread Type, Fresh Or Frozen

Martins Fmous Pstry Shoppe Inc.............G.....800 548-1200
  Fayetteville (G-5867)
Martins Fmous Pstry Shoppe Inc.............G.....800 548-1200
  Kernersville (G-9214)

BAKERY PRDTS: Wholesalers

Krispy Kreme Doughnuts Inc....................C.....336 725-2981
  Winston Salem (G-16781)
Novas Bakery Inc..F.....704 333-5566
  Charlotte (G-3275)

BAKERY: Wholesale Or Wholesale & Retail Combined

All Baked Out Company..............................F.....336 861-1212
  High Point (G-8241)
Connectivity Group LLC.............................E.....910 799-9023
  Wilmington (G-16177)
Depalo Foods Inc...E.....704 827-0245
  Belmont (G-983)
Mon Macaron LLC..G.....984 200-1387
  Raleigh (G-13038)
Neomonde Baking Company.....................E.....919 469-8009
  Morrisville (G-11393)
Normandie Bakery Inc.................................G.....910 686-1372
  Wilmington (G-16340)
Northeast Foods Inc....................................F.....919 585-5178
  Clayton (G-4002)
Picassomoesllc..G.....216 703-4547
  Hillsborough (G-8665)
Queen City Pastry Llc.................................E.....704 660-5706
  Mooresville (G-11066)
Retail Market Place......................................G.....984 201-1948
  Smithfield (G-14480)
Simple Supplies LLC...................................G.....336 358-7704
  Greensboro (G-7341)
SMA Enterprise LLC....................................G.....980 616-0140
  Concord (G-4360)
Sprinkle of Sugar LLC.................................G.....336 474-8620
  Thomasville (G-15281)
Suarez Bakery Inc..F.....704 525-0145
  Charlotte (G-3644)
Underground Baking Co LLC.....................G.....828 674-7494
  Hendersonville (G-7910)

BALERS

Airborn Industries Inc.................................E.....704 483-5000
  Lincolnton (G-9869)
Hog Slat Incorporated.................................E.....800 949-4647
  Newton Grove (G-11989)

Employee Codes: A=Over 500 employees, B=251-500
C=101-250, D=51-100, E=20-50, F=10-19, G=1-9

BALERS

Jo-Mar Group LLC .... E
   Belmont *(G-993)*

BALLOONS: Hot Air

Fire Fly Ballons 2006 LLC .... F 704 878-9501
   Statesville *(G-14798)*

Firefly Balloons 2010 Inc .... F 704 878-9501
   Statesville *(G-14799)*

BALLOONS: Novelty & Toy

A Stitch In Time .... G 828 274-5193
   Asheville *(G-513)*

BANKS: Mortgage & Loan

GLG Corporation .... F 336 784-0396
   Winston Salem *(G-16722)*

BANNERS: Fabric

Downtown Graphics Network Inc ...... G 704 637-0855
   Salisbury *(G-13954)*

BANQUET HALL FACILITIES

Communitys Kitchen L3c .... G 828 817-2308
   Tryon *(G-15423)*

BAR

Williamson Mead & Brewing LLC ..... F 661 827-7290
   Glade Valley *(G-6573)*

BAR FIXTURES: Wood

Artisan Leaf LLC .... G 252 674-1223
   Wilson *(G-16468)*

B & L Custom Cabinets Inc .... F 704 857-1940
   Westfield *(G-15950)*

D & B Concepts Inc .... G 336 885-8292
   High Point *(G-8315)*

Holt Group Inc .... F 336 668-2770
   High Point *(G-8398)*

Interlam Corporation .... E 336 786-6254
   Mount Airy *(G-11523)*

BAR JOISTS & CONCRETE REINFORCING BARS: Fabricated

J F Fabricators LLC .... G 704 454-7224
   Harrisburg *(G-7713)*

BARBECUE EQPT

Jebco Inc .... E 919 557-2001
   Holly Springs *(G-8702)*

BARGES BUILDING & REPAIR

Edenton Boatworks LLC .... E 252 482-7600
   Edenton *(G-5514)*

BARRICADES: Metal

Barrier1 Systems Inc .... F 336 617-8478
   Greensboro *(G-6832)*

Control and Barricade LLC .... G 704 315-2138
   Durham *(G-5032)*

BARS & BAR SHAPES: Steel, Cold-Finished, Own Hot-Rolled

Muriel Harris Investments Inc .... F 800 932-3191
   Fayetteville *(G-5879)*

BARS: Concrete Reinforcing, Fabricated Steel

Composite Factory LLC .... F 484 264-3306
   Mooresville *(G-10910)*

Freedom Industries Inc .... C 252 984-0007
   Rocky Mount *(G-13698)*

Gastonia Ornamental Wldg Inc .... F 704 827-1146
   Mount Holly *(G-11635)*

Gorilla Offroad Company .... G 815 715-6003
   Rolesville *(G-13757)*

Low Country Steel SC LLC .... E 336 283-9611
   Winston Salem *(G-16793)*

Lowder Steel Inc .... E 336 431-9000
   Archdale *(G-293)*

Queen City Engrg & Design .... G 704 918-5851
   Concord *(G-4344)*

Underbrinks LLC .... G 866 495-4465
   Salisbury *(G-14059)*

Universal Steel NC LLC .... E 336 476-3105
   Thomasville *(G-15298)*

BASALT: Crushed & Broken

Mafic USA LLC .... F 704 967-8006
   Shelby *(G-14343)*

BASEBOARDS: Metal

Amarr Company .... G 336 936-0010
   Mocksville *(G-10553)*

Building Envlope Erction Svcs .... F 252 747-2015
   Snow Hill *(G-14499)*

Kindred Rolling Doors LLC .... G 704 905-3806
   Gastonia *(G-6439)*

BASEMENT WINDOW AREAWAYS: Concrete

David Allen Company Inc .... C 919 821-7100
   Raleigh *(G-12675)*

BASES, BEVERAGE

Prime Beverage Group LLC .... C 704 385-5451
   Concord *(G-4339)*

Prime Beverage Group LLC .... G 704 385-5450
   Concord *(G-4338)*

BASKETS: Steel Wire

Rack Works Inc .... E 336 368-1302
   Pilot Mountain *(G-12201)*

BATH SALTS

Burts Bees Inc .... B 919 998-5200
   Durham *(G-4994)*

BATHROOM ACCESS & FITTINGS: Vitreous China & Earthenware

Custom Marble Corporation .... G 910 215-0679
   Pinehurst *(G-12219)*

Division Eight Inc .... F 336 852-1275
   Greensboro *(G-6973)*

Tileware Global LLC .... G 828 322-9273
   Hickory *(G-8183)*

Welcome Industrial Corp .... D 336 329-9640
   Burlington *(G-1517)*

BATTERIES, EXC AUTOMOTIVE: Wholesalers

Exide Technologies LLC .... G 919 553-3578
   Clayton *(G-3977)*

L L C Batteries of N C .... G 919 331-0241
   Angier *(G-143)*

BATTERIES: Alkaline, Cell Storage

Spectrum Brands Inc .... G 704 658-2060
   Mooresville *(G-11095)*

BATTERIES: Lead Acid, Storage

Polypore International LP .... D 704 587-8409
   Charlotte *(G-3353)*

BATTERIES: Rechargeable

Enerjali LLC .... G 336 451-6479
   Kernersville *(G-9197)*

Saft America Inc .... B 828 874-4111
   Valdese *(G-15454)*

BATTERIES: Storage

Associated Battery Company .... F 704 821-8311
   Matthews *(G-10301)*

Clarios LLC .... B 336 761-1550
   Kernersville *(G-9180)*

East Penn Manufacturing Co .... F 336 771-1380
   Winston Salem *(G-16689)*

Energizer Holdings Inc .... E 336 672-3526
   Asheboro *(G-431)*

Exide .... G 704 357-9845
   Charlotte *(G-2737)*

Lexington Road Properties Inc .... C 336 650-7209
   Winston Salem *(G-16787)*

Magnevolt .... F 919 553-2202
   Clayton *(G-3995)*

Smith Utility Buildings .... G 336 957-8211
   Traphill *(G-15327)*

BATTERIES: Wet

Clarios LLC .... B 336 761-1550
   Kernersville *(G-9180)*

Edgewell Per Care Brands LLC .... G 336 672-4500
   Asheboro *(G-427)*

L L C Batteries of N C .... G 919 331-0241
   Angier *(G-143)*

Lexington Road Properties Inc .... C 336 650-7209
   Winston Salem *(G-16787)*

Saft America Inc .... B 828 874-4111
   Valdese *(G-15454)*

Spectrum Brands Inc .... G 800 854-3151
   Charlotte *(G-3599)*

BATTERY CASES: Plastic Or Plastics Combination

Fourshare LLC .... F 336 714-0448
   Clemmons *(G-4039)*

BATTERY CHARGERS

Exide Technologies LLC .... G 704 521-8016
   Charlotte *(G-2738)*

Exide Technologies LLC .... G 919 553-3578
   Clayton *(G-3977)*

BATTERY CHARGERS: Storage, Motor & Engine Generator Type

Alk Investments LLC .... G 984 233-5353
   Raleigh *(G-12488)*

Mikes Core & Battery Inc .... G 910 920-4490
   Fayetteville *(G-5874)*

BATTS & BATTING: Cotton

Kem-Wove Inc .... E 704 588-0080
   Charlotte *(G-3049)*

BEARINGS & PARTS Ball

Baldor Dodge Reliance .... F 828 652-0074
   Marion *(G-10141)*

Ketchie-Houston Inc .... E 704 786-5101
   Concord *(G-4300)*

Linamar Forgings Carolina Inc .... D 252 237-8181
   Wilson *(G-16511)*

PRODUCT SECTION

BEVERAGES, ALCOHOLIC: Applejack

Nn Inc .... G 980 264-4300
  Charlotte *(G-3264)*

Reich LLC .... C 828 651-9019
  Arden *(G-371)*

BEARINGS: Ball & Roller

Atlantic Bearing Co Inc .... G 252 243-0233
  Wilson *(G-16469)*

Coc USA Inc .... G 888 706-0059
  Matthews *(G-10243)*

Everything Industrial Supply .... G 743 333-2222
  Winston Salem *(G-16702)*

Hpc NC .... G 704 978-0103
  Statesville *(G-14817)*

Justice Bearing LLC .... G 800 355-2500
  Mooresville *(G-10993)*

Lincolnton Bearing Plant .... G 704 794-5964
  Iron Station *(G-8974)*

Ltlb Holding Company .... D 704 585-2908
  Hiddenite *(G-8223)*

Ltlb Holding Company .... F 828 624-1460
  Hickory *(G-8089)*

Pioneer Motor Bearing Company .... E 704 937-7000
  Kings Mountain *(G-9325)*

Timken Company .... C 704 736-2700
  Iron Station *(G-8977)*

BEARINGS: Plastic

Enpro Industries Inc .... C 704 731-1500
  Charlotte *(G-2713)*

BEARINGS: Roller & Parts

American Roller Bearing Inc .... C 828 624-1460
  Hiddenite *(G-8213)*

American Roller Bearing Inc .... F 828 624-1460
  Morganton *(G-11197)*

Urethane Innovators Inc .... E 252 637-7110
  New Bern *(G-11853)*

BEAUTY & BARBER SHOP EQPT

American Eagle Mfg LLC .... G 252 633-0603
  New Bern *(G-11767)*

Boyd Manufacturing Inc .... F 336 301-6433
  Siler City *(G-14400)*

Brandy Thompson .... F 321 252-2911
  Fayetteville *(G-5774)*

Buddy Cut Inc .... G 888 608-4701
  Pittsboro *(G-12333)*

Corsan LLC .... F 704 765-9979
  Huntersville *(G-8806)*

Cosmopros .... G 704 717-7420
  Charlotte *(G-2560)*

Equagen Engineers Pllc .... E 919 444-5442
  Raleigh *(G-12744)*

Hair Socety Inc .... G 919 588-1453
  Morrisville *(G-11350)*

Hanes Industries-Newton .... F 828 469-2000
  Newton *(G-11939)*

Mammoth Machine and Design LLC ... G 704 727-3330
  Mooresville *(G-11014)*

Nederman Manufacturing .... F 704 898-7945
  Charlotte *(G-3245)*

Pmb Industries Inc .... F 336 453-3121
  Lexington *(G-9771)*

Prezioso Ventures LLC .... G 704 793-1602
  Concord *(G-4337)*

Salon & Spa Design Services .... G 919 556-6380
  Wake Forest *(G-15587)*

Skidril Industries LLC .... F 800 843-3745
  Randleman *(G-13491)*

Sutton Scientifics Inc .... G 910 428-1600
  Star *(G-14723)*

Tribofilm Research Inc .... G 919 838-2844
  Raleigh *(G-13364)*

Ubora Dens LLC .... G 704 425-3560
  Concord *(G-4381)*

West Side Industries LLC .... G 980 223-8665
  Statesville *(G-14924)*

BEAUTY & BARBER SHOP EQPT & SPLYS WHOLESALERS

Cosmopros .... G 704 717-7420
  Charlotte *(G-2560)*

UGLy Essentials LLC .... F 910 319-9945
  Raleigh *(G-13376)*

BEAUTY SALONS

Gifted Hands Styling Salon .... G 828 781-2781
  Hickory *(G-8032)*

BEDDING, BEDSPREADS, BLANKETS & SHEETS

Js Royal Home Usa Inc .... E 704 542-2304
  Charlotte *(G-3038)*

R & D Weaving Inc .... F 828 248-1910
  Ellenboro *(G-5638)*

Velco Inc .... F 828 324-5440
  Hickory *(G-8202)*

BEDDING, FROM SILK OR MANMADE FIBER

Sunrise Development LLC .... F 828 453-0590
  Mooresboro *(G-10841)*

BEDS & ACCESS STORES

Perfect Fit Industries LLC .... C 800 864-7618
  Charlotte *(G-3330)*

BEDS: Institutional

Kci .... G 910 612-4914
  Wilmington *(G-16286)*

BEDSPREADS & BED SETS, FROM PURCHASED MATERIALS

Diane Britt .... G 910 763-9600
  Wilmington *(G-16200)*

Pacific Coast Feather LLC .... G 252 492-0051
  Henderson *(G-7801)*

Smith Draperies Inc .... E 336 226-2183
  Burlington *(G-1496)*

BEDSPREADS, COTTON

Lillys Interiors Cstm Quilting .... G 336 475-1421
  Thomasville *(G-15242)*

BEER & ALE WHOLESALERS

Glass Jug .... F 919 818-6907
  Durham *(G-5116)*

Glass Jug LLC .... F 919 813-0135
  Durham *(G-5117)*

Koi Pond Brewing Company LLC .... G 252 231-1660
  Rocky Mount *(G-13706)*

Salty Turtle Beer Company .... E 910 803-2019
  Surf City *(G-15016)*

White Street Brewing Co Inc .... E 919 647-9439
  Youngsville *(G-17115)*

BEER, WINE & LIQUOR STORES: Beer, Packaged

Aviator Brewing Company Inc .... G 919 601-5497
  Holly Springs *(G-8687)*

Koi Pond Brewing Company LLC .... G 252 231-1660
  Rocky Mount *(G-13706)*

Land of Sky Mobile Canning LLC .... G 303 880-1297
  Asheville *(G-679)*

BELLOWS

Nabell USA Corporation .... E 704 986-2455
  Albemarle *(G-98)*

BELTING: Rubber

Beltservice Corporation .... E 704 947-2264
  Huntersville *(G-8797)*

Forbo Belting .... E 704 948-0800
  Huntersville *(G-8822)*

Forbo Siegling LLC .... G 704 948-0800
  Huntersville *(G-8824)*

Forbo Siegling LLC .... B 704 948-0800
  Huntersville *(G-8825)*

BELTS & BELT PRDTS

All-State Industries Inc .... G 704 588-4081
  Charlotte *(G-2157)*

R/W Connection Inc .... G 252 446-0114
  Rocky Mount *(G-13726)*

BELTS: Conveyor, Made From Purchased Wire

Automated Solutions LLC .... F 828 396-9900
  Granite Falls *(G-6723)*

Belt Concepts America Inc .... F 888 598-2358
  Spring Hope *(G-14614)*

Belt Shop Inc .... F 704 865-3636
  Gastonia *(G-6352)*

Everything Industrial Supply .... G 743 333-2222
  Winston Salem *(G-16702)*

Forbo Movement Systems .... E 704 334-5353
  Charlotte *(G-2786)*

BELTS: Seat, Automotive & Aircraft

Aircraft Belts Inc .... E 919 956-4395
  Creedmoor *(G-4601)*

BEVERAGE BASES & SYRUPS

Freedom Beverage Company .... G 336 316-1260
  Greensboro *(G-7022)*

Herbalife Manufacturing LLC .... F 336 970-6400
  Winston Salem *(G-16744)*

BEVERAGE PRDTS: Malt, Barley

Whitehat Seed Farms Inc .... G 252 264-2427
  Hertford *(G-7925)*

BEVERAGES, ALCOHOLIC: Ale

Creative Brewing Company LLC .... G 919 297-8182
  Smithfield *(G-14458)*

Duck-Rabbit Craft Brewery Inc .... G 252 753-7745
  Farmville *(G-5734)*

Foothills Brewing .... G 336 997-9484
  Winston Salem *(G-16717)*

Goose and Monkey Brewhouse LLC ... F 336 239-0206
  Lexington *(G-9724)*

Heist Brewing Company LLC .... G 603 969-8012
  Charlotte *(G-2900)*

Highland Brewing Company Inc .... F 828 299-3370
  Asheville *(G-652)*

Innovation Brewing LLC .... G 828 586-9678
  Sylva *(G-15058)*

White Street Brewing Co Inc .... E 919 647-9439
  Youngsville *(G-17115)*

BEVERAGES, ALCOHOLIC: Applejack

Bold Rock Partners LP .... F 828 595-9940
  Mills River *(G-10501)*

BEVERAGES, ALCOHOLIC: Applejack

Mystic Farm & Distillery.................................G.....336 409-0131
  Durham *(G-5233)*
Warehouse Distillery LLC...........................G.....828 464-5183
  Newton *(G-11983)*

BEVERAGES, ALCOHOLIC: Beer

6 Brothers LLC...G.....706 662-2232
  Charlotte *(G-2110)*
Anheuser-Busch LLC....................................F.....704 321-9319
  Charlotte *(G-2194)*
Aviator Brewing Company Inc....................G.....919 601-5497
  Holly Springs *(G-8687)*
Beverage Innovation Corp..........................F.....425 222-4900
  Concord *(G-4208)*
Bombshell Beer Company LLC...................F.....919 823-1933
  Holly Springs *(G-8691)*
Bull Durham Beer Co LLC...........................G.....919 744-3568
  Durham *(G-4990)*
Cabarrus Brewing Company LLC................E.....704 490-4487
  Concord *(G-4216)*
Carolina Beverage Group LLC....................E.....704 799-2337
  Mooresville *(G-10896)*
Craft Brew Alliance Inc...............................G.....828 263-1111
  Boone *(G-1188)*
Dreamweavers Brewery LLC......................G.....704 507-7773
  Waxhaw *(G-15753)*
Eurisko Beer Company................................G.....828 774-5055
  Asheville *(G-618)*
Gingers Revenge LLC.................................F.....828 505-2462
  Asheville *(G-634)*
Glass Jug..F.....919 818-6907
  Durham *(G-5116)*
Glass Jug LLC..F.....919 813-0135
  Durham *(G-5117)*
Haw River Farmhouse Ales LLC................G.....336 525-9270
  Saxapahaw *(G-14217)*
High Branch Brewing Co LLC.....................G.....704 706-3807
  Concord *(G-4279)*
Hugger Mugger LLC.....................................F.....910 585-2749
  Sanford *(G-14134)*
Koi Pond Brewing Company LLC...............G.....252 231-1660
  Rocky Mount *(G-13706)*
Lake Norman Industries LLC......................G.....704 987-9048
  Cornelius *(G-4565)*
Monster Brewing Company LLC................D.....828 883-2337
  Brevard *(G-1280)*
Mordecai Beverage Co................................G.....919 831-9125
  Raleigh *(G-13042)*
Mother Earth Brewing LLC.........................G.....252 208-2437
  Kinston *(G-9377)*
Nachos & Beer LLC......................................G.....828 298-2280
  Asheville *(G-709)*
New Sarum Brewing Co LLC......................G.....704 310-5048
  Salisbury *(G-14018)*
Newgrass Brewing Company LLC..............G.....704 477-2795
  Shelby *(G-14352)*
Next Generation Beer Co............................G.....828 989-7662
  Asheville *(G-712)*
Ponysaurus Brewing LLC.............................E.....919 455-3737
  Durham *(G-5295)*
Preyer Brewing Company............................G.....336 420-0902
  Greensboro *(G-7282)*
Resident Culture Brewing LLC...................E.....704 333-1862
  Charlotte *(G-3438)*
Salty Turtle Beer Company.........................E.....910 803-2019
  Surf City *(G-15016)*
Salud LLC..E.....980 495-6612
  Charlotte *(G-3485)*
Southern Range Brewing LLC....................G.....704 289-4049
  Monroe *(G-10810)*
Spark716 LLC...G.....704 439-6864
  Wilmington *(G-16414)*

Stout Beverages LLC...................................E.....704 293-7640
  Kings Mountain *(G-9334)*
Sugar Creek Brewing Co LLC.....................E.....704 521-3333
  Charlotte *(G-3646)*
Sunstead Brewing LLC.................................G.....980 949-6200
  Charlotte *(G-3655)*
Sycamore Brewing LLC...............................E.....704 910-3821
  Charlotte *(G-3664)*
Triple C Brewing Company LLC.................F.....704 372-3212
  Charlotte *(G-3729)*
Trophy On Maywood LLC...........................F.....919 803-1333
  Raleigh *(G-13367)*
Wedge Brewing Co......................................F.....828 505-2792
  Asheville *(G-817)*
Weeping Radish Farm Brewry LLC............F.....252 491-5205
  Grandy *(G-6719)*
Wnc Craft Beer Export LLC........................G.....828 407-9444
  Asheville *(G-823)*

BEVERAGES, ALCOHOLIC: Beer & Ale

760 Craft Works LLC...................................F.....704 274-5216
  Huntersville *(G-8785)*
Adam Dalton Distillery LLC........................G.....828 785-1499
  Asheville *(G-514)*
Bearwaters Brewing Company...................G.....828 237-4200
  Canton *(G-1599)*
Beer Study..G.....919 240-5423
  Chapel Hill *(G-1989)*
Bite My Cookies Brewing Co Inc................G.....919 602-7636
  Pittsboro *(G-12332)*
Brew Masters of Goldsboro........................G.....919 288-2014
  Goldsboro *(G-6596)*
Brew Publik Incorporated...........................G.....704 231-2703
  Charlotte *(G-2352)*
Brewmasters Inc...F.....252 991-6035
  Wilson *(G-16479)*
Ekos Brewmaster LLC..................................G.....704 973-5640
  Charlotte *(G-2688)*
Fiddlin Fish Brewing Co...............................F.....336 999-8945
  Winston Salem *(G-16710)*
Good Bros Ginger Brew LLC......................G.....828 279-2512
  Mars Hill *(G-10195)*
Heckler Brewing Company.........................G.....910 748-0085
  Fayetteville *(G-5835)*
Hootenanny Brewing Company LLC..........G.....704 254-6190
  Mooresville *(G-10976)*
House of Hops...G.....919 819-0704
  Raleigh *(G-12863)*
Koolabrew LLC..G.....910 579-6711
  Shallotte *(G-14275)*
Shortway Brewing Company LLC...............G.....252 777-3065
  Newport *(G-11907)*
Side Hustle Ventures LLC...........................G.....919 816-2324
  Raleigh *(G-13253)*
Southern Wicked Distillery Inc..................G.....919 539-1620
  Raleigh *(G-13284)*
Sweet Taters LLC...G.....252 969-0229
  Rocky Mount *(G-13736)*

BEVERAGES, ALCOHOLIC: Bourbon Whiskey

Asheville Distilling Company.....................F.....828 575-2000
  Asheville *(G-535)*

BEVERAGES, ALCOHOLIC: Distilled Liquors

78c Spirits...G.....919 615-0839
  Raleigh *(G-12449)*
Blu Distilling Company LLC........................E.....919 999-6736
  Durham *(G-4965)*
Blu Distilling Company LLC........................G.....919 999-6736
  Raleigh *(G-12563)*

Blue Seas LLC..G.....828 245-2041
  Bostic *(G-1261)*
Bogue Sound Distillery Inc.........................G.....252 241-1606
  Newport *(G-11898)*
Broad Branch Distillery LLC.......................G.....336 602-2824
  Winston Salem *(G-16638)*
Buffalo City Distillery LLC..........................G.....252 256-1477
  Point Harbor *(G-12380)*
Call Family Distillers LLC............................G.....336 990-0708
  Wilkesboro *(G-16015)*
Chemist..G.....828 505-8778
  Asheville *(G-589)*
Chopin Vodka..G.....336 707-8305
  Greensboro *(G-6908)*
Copper Barrel Distillery LLC......................G.....336 262-6500
  North Wilkesboro *(G-12003)*
Dark Moon Distileries LLC.........................G.....704 222-8063
  Banner Elk *(G-895)*
Diablo Distilleries LLC.................................G.....910 467-5017
  Jacksonville *(G-8998)*
Doodle Sasser Distilling LLC.....................G.....704 806-6594
  Indian Trail *(G-8929)*
Durham Distillery Llc..................................G.....919 937-2121
  Durham *(G-5072)*
End of Days Distillery.................................F.....910 399-1133
  Wilmington *(G-16211)*
Fainting Goat Spirits LLC...........................G.....336 273-6221
  Greensboro *(G-7010)*
Foothills Distillery LLC................................G.....704 462-1055
  Conover *(G-4455)*
Founding Fathers Distillery........................G.....336 434-0149
  High Point *(G-8357)*
Four Hounds Distilling LLC.........................G.....757 717-9393
  Carolina Beach *(G-1637)*
Graybeard Distillery Inc..............................F.....919 361-9980
  Durham *(G-5126)*
Great Wagon Road Distlg Co LLC.............G.....704 246-8740
  Charlotte *(G-2860)*
Great Wagon Road Distlg Co LLC.............G.....704 469-9330
  Charlotte *(G-2861)*
Greensboro Distilling LLC..........................G.....336 273-6221
  Greensboro *(G-7062)*
H&H Distillery LLC.......................................G.....828 338-9779
  Asheville *(G-646)*
Howling Moon Distillery Inc.......................G.....828 208-1469
  Asheville *(G-655)*
Lake Norman Industries LLC......................G.....704 987-9048
  Cornelius *(G-4565)*
Lassiter Distilling Company.......................G.....919 295-0111
  Knightdale *(G-9419)*
Laws Distillery Inc..G.....828 726-3663
  Lenoir *(G-9623)*
Lizard Lick Brewing & Dist LLC.................G.....919 887-4369
  Zebulon *(G-17134)*
Mason Inlet Distillery LLC..........................G.....910 200-4584
  Wilmington *(G-16316)*
Mayberry Distillery......................................G.....336 719-6860
  Mount Airy *(G-11544)*
Muddy River Distillery LLC........................G.....336 516-4190
  Belmont *(G-995)*
New River Distilling Co LLC.......................G.....732 673-4852
  Deep Gap *(G-4710)*
Oak & Bull Distilling LLC............................G.....978 732-4531
  Raleigh *(G-13076)*
Oak & Grist Distilling Co LLC....................G.....914 450-0589
  Asheville *(G-713)*
Oak & Grist Distilling Co LLC....................F.....828 357-5750
  Black Mountain *(G-1131)*
Oak City Distilling Inc.................................G.....919 520-4102
  Raleigh *(G-13079)*
Outer Banks Craft Distlg LLC....................G.....252 423-3011
  Manteo *(G-10128)*

BEVERAGES, ALCOHOLIC: Wines

Pine Top Distillery LLC .... G 888 261-5287
  Raleigh *(G-13110)*
Pinnix Distillery Inc .... G 828 412-5441
  Asheville *(G-733)*
Seventy Eight C Inc .... G 919 602-0677
  Raleigh *(G-13245)*
Shipwreck Rum Inc .... G 215 896-6172
  Clayton *(G-4008)*
Southern Distilling Co LLC .... G 704 677-4069
  Statesville *(G-14891)*
Sutlers Spirit Company .... G 336 565-6006
  Winston Salem *(G-16926)*
Three Stacks Distilling Co LLC .... G 252 468-0779
  Kinston *(G-9388)*
Two Trees Distilling Co LLC .... G 803 767-1322
  Fletcher *(G-6046)*
Waltons Distillery Inc .... G 910 347-7770
  Jacksonville *(G-9045)*
Weldon Mills Distillery LLC .... G 252 220-4235
  Weldon *(G-15889)*
Wyoming Whiskey Inc .... G 561 573-5605
  Mooresville *(G-11132)*

BEVERAGES, ALCOHOLIC: Rum

Azure Skye Beverages Inc .... G 704 909-7394
  Charlotte *(G-2251)*

BEVERAGES, ALCOHOLIC: Wines

Adagio Vineyards .... G 336 258-2333
  Elkin *(G-5609)*
Aek Inc .... G 704 864-7968
  Gastonia *(G-6337)*
Alexander Crush Inc .... G 828 635-7136
  Taylorsville *(G-15128)*
American Alcohollery LLC .... G 704 960-7243
  Moravian Falls *(G-11141)*
Asheville Meadery LLC .... G 828 454-6188
  Asheville *(G-538)*
Autumn Creek Vineyards Inc .... G 336 548-9463
  Greensboro *(G-6823)*
B & C Winery .... G 828 550-3610
  Waynesville *(G-15794)*
B C Winery .... G 828 550-3610
  Maggie Valley *(G-10093)*
Banner Elk Winery Inc .... G 828 898-9090
  Banner Elk *(G-892)*
Banner Elk Winery Inc .... G 828 260-1790
  Banner Elk *(G-893)*
Belews Creek Vineyard .... G 904 345-1466
  Kernersville *(G-9168)*
Biltmore Estate Wine Co LLC .... C 828 225-6776
  Asheville *(G-560)*
Black Rock Landscaping LLC .... G 910 295-4470
  Carthage *(G-1661)*
Black Rock Winery LLC .... G 910 295-9511
  Carthage *(G-1662)*
Blue Zephry Vineyard .... G 336 366-5066
  Dobson *(G-4820)*
Botanist and Barrel .... G 919 644-7777
  Cedar Grove *(G-1970)*
Burntshirt Vineyards LLC .... F 828 685-2402
  Hendersonville *(G-7830)*
Cabo Winery LLC .... G 704 785-9463
  Concord *(G-4220)*
Cape Fear Vineyard Winery LLC .... G 844 846-3386
  Elizabethtown *(G-5589)*
Cape Fear Vinyrd & Winery LLC .... G 910 645-4292
  Elizabethtown *(G-5590)*
Carolina Coast Vineyard .... G 910 707-1777
  Carolina Beach *(G-1634)*
Carolina Heritg Vinyrd Winery .... G 336 448-4781
  Elkin *(G-5613)*

Cellar .... G 910 399-2997
  Wilmington *(G-16166)*
Cellar 4201 LLC .... G 336 699-6030
  East Bend *(G-5464)*
Chateau Jourdain LLC .... G 786 273-2869
  Jonesville *(G-9094)*
Chestnut Trail Vineyard LLC .... G 336 655-4755
  Mocksville *(G-10563)*
Childress Vineyards LLC .... E 336 236-9463
  Lexington *(G-9692)*
Childress Winery LLC .... G 336 775-0522
  Lexington *(G-9693)*
Coastal Carolina Winery .... G 843 443-9463
  Cornelius *(G-4536)*
Cougar Run Winery .... F 704 788-2746
  Concord *(G-4245)*
Cypress Bend Vineyards Inc .... G 910 369-0411
  Wagram *(G-15522)*
Davidson Wine Co LLC .... G 614 738-0051
  Davidson *(G-4671)*
Deep Creek Winery .... G 828 341-0592
  Bryson City *(G-1323)*
Divine Llama Vineyards LLC .... G 336 699-2525
  East Bend *(G-5466)*
Dove Vine LLC .... G 336 751-3794
  Mocksville *(G-10566)*
Doyles Vineyard .... G 919 544-6291
  Durham *(G-5061)*
Drink A Bull LLC .... G 919 818-3321
  Durham *(G-5065)*
Duplin Wine Cellars Inc .... E 910 289-3888
  Rose Hill *(G-13776)*
Elephants Corner Wines LLC .... G 336 782-7084
  Winston Salem *(G-16694)*
Elkin Creek Vineyard LLC .... G 336 526-5119
  Elkin *(G-5618)*
Far Niente LLC .... G 252 715-0154
  Kitty Hawk *(G-9404)*
First Miracle Vine & Wine LLC .... G 910 990-5681
  Garland *(G-6242)*
Grandfather Vinyrd Winery LLC .... G 828 963-2400
  Banner Elk *(G-898)*
Grassy Creek Vineyard & Winery .... G 336 835-2458
  State Road *(G-14726)*
Green Creek Winery LLC .... G 828 863-4176
  Columbus *(G-4174)*
Gregory Vineyards .... G 919 427-9409
  Angier *(G-139)*
Grimes Mill LLC .... G 336 470-6864
  Lexington *(G-9725)*
Haw River Valley Entps LLC .... G 336 584-4060
  Gibsonville *(G-6562)*
Haze Gray Vineyards LLC .... G 610 247-9387
  Dobson *(G-4824)*
Hilton Vineyards LLC .... G 704 776-9656
  Monroe *(G-10731)*
Honeygirl Meadery LLC .... G 919 399-3056
  Durham *(G-5139)*
Hooks Vineyard .... G 919 917-5658
  Raleigh *(G-12858)*
Hutton Vineyards LLC .... G 336 374-2321
  Dobson *(G-4827)*
Jackson Wine .... G 828 508-9292
  Brevard *(G-1277)*
James Michael Vineyards LLC .... G 704 539-4749
  Harmony *(G-7687)*
Jolo Winery & Vineyards LLC .... F 954 816-5649
  Pilot Mountain *(G-12199)*
Jones Vondrehle Vineyards LLC .... G 336 874-2800
  Thurmond *(G-15310)*
Kefi Winery Inc .... G 704 591-5791
  Monroe *(G-10751)*

Ladybug Vineyard LLC .... G 336 366-4701
  Dobson *(G-4828)*
Laurel Gray Vineyards Inc .... G 336 468-9463
  Hamptonville *(G-7673)*
Linville Falls Winery .... G 828 733-9021
  Newland *(G-11889)*
Longleaf Vineyard .... G 828 435-3555
  Marshall *(G-10204)*
Lucky Tusk .... G 704 985-1127
  Albemarle *(G-95)*
Maia LLC .... G 828 612-6109
  Morganton *(G-11230)*
McRitchie Wine Company LLC .... G 336 874-3003
  Thurmond *(G-15312)*
Medaloni Cellars LLC .... G 305 509-2004
  Lewisville *(G-9669)*
Melissae Meadery & Winery LLC .... G 336 207-7097
  Marion *(G-10165)*
Midnight Mndance Vineyards LLC .... G 336 835-6681
  Jonesville *(G-9100)*
My Wine Saver LLC .... G 828 595-2632
  Hendersonville *(G-7883)*
Nomacorc Holdings LLC .... G 919 460-2200
  Zebulon *(G-17137)*
Noni Bacca Winery .... G 910 397-7617
  Wilmington *(G-16338)*
Old Homeplace Vineyard LLC .... G 336 399-7293
  Winston Salem *(G-16827)*
Old North State Winery Inc .... F 336 789-9463
  Mount Airy *(G-11554)*
Parker-Binns Vineyard LLC .... G 828 894-0154
  Mill Spring *(G-10490)*
Parkway Vineyard & Winery LLC .... G 828 765-1400
  Newland *(G-11892)*
Patria Vineyard LLC .... G 336 407-8254
  Winston Salem *(G-16837)*
Pharmdawg Vineyards LLC .... G 770 596-0960
  State Road *(G-14728)*
Piccione Vinyards .... G 312 342-0181
  Ronda *(G-13767)*
Pilot Mountain Vineyards LLC .... G 828 400-9533
  Pinnacle *(G-12322)*
Pleb Urban Winery .... G 828 767-6445
  Asheville *(G-736)*
Queen of Wines LLC .... F 919 348-6630
  Durham *(G-5314)*
Raffaldini Vneyards Winery LLC .... F 336 835-9463
  Ronda *(G-13769)*
Raylen Vineyards Inc .... G 336 998-3100
  Winston Salem *(G-16881)*
Retro Meadery LLC .... G 910 622-7098
  Burgaw *(G-1348)*
Rickety Bridge Winery Inc USA .... G 336 781-0645
  High Point *(G-8510)*
Rise Over Run Inc .... G 303 819-1566
  Swannanoa *(G-15034)*
Rock Ages Winery & Vineyard .... G 336 364-7625
  Hendersonville *(G-7896)*
Rock Ages Winery & Vinyrd Inc .... G 336 364-7625
  Hurdle Mills *(G-8914)*
Rockfish Creek Winery LLC .... G 910 729-0648
  Raeford *(G-12436)*
Rocky River Vineyards LLC .... G 704 781-5035
  Midland *(G-10478)*
Roots Run Deep LLC .... G 919 909-9117
  Youngsville *(G-17094)*
Round Peak Vineyards LLC .... G 336 352-5595
  Mount Airy *(G-11568)*
Russian Chapel Hills Winery .... G 828 863-0541
  Columbus *(G-4180)*
Rustic Grape LLC .... G 828 319-7939
  Asheville *(G-761)*

BEVERAGES, ALCOHOLIC: Wines

Saint Paul Mountain Vineyards............ F 828 685-4002
   Hendersonville *(G-7897)*
Sanders Ridge Inc............................... G 336 677-1700
   Boonville *(G-1256)*
Seven Pines Vineyard Inc.................... G 252 717-2283
   Fountain *(G-6097)*
Shadow Line Vineyard LLC.................. E 828 234-5773
   Granite Falls *(G-6756)*
Shadow Springs Vineyard Inc............... G 336 998-6598
   Advance *(G-50)*
Shelton Vineyards Inc.......................... E 336 366-4818
   Dobson *(G-4831)*
Six Waterpots Vinyrd & Winery............ E 828 728-5099
   Hudson *(G-8780)*
Sommerville Enterprises LLC................ F 919 924-1594
   Hillsborough *(G-8668)*
Souther Williams Vineyard LLC............ G 828 651-8011
   Fletcher *(G-6042)*
Southern Range Brewing LLC................ G 704 289-4049
   Monroe *(G-10810)*
Stardust Cellars LLC............................ G 336 466-4454
   Winston Salem *(G-16916)*
Starrlight Mead LLC............................ G 919 672-1469
   Durham *(G-5371)*
Stonefield Cellars LLC.......................... G 336 632-2391
   Stokesdale *(G-14951)*
Sweet Hme Carolna Vinyrd & Win........ G 336 469-9905
   Yadkinville *(G-17053)*
Sweet Home Yadkin Inc....................... G 336 414-9822
   Yadkinville *(G-17054)*
Thistle Meadow Winery Inc.................. G 800 233-1505
   Laurel Springs *(G-9467)*
Tom Burgiss.. G 336 359-2995
   Laurel Springs *(G-9468)*
Tunnel Creek Venues LLC.................... G 336 322-3600
   Roxboro *(G-13828)*
Village At Duplin Winery LLC............... G 910 285-6814
   Wallace *(G-15629)*
Vineyard Bluffton LLC......................... G 704 307-2737
   Charlotte *(G-3778)*
Vineyard Hill Distributing LLC............... G 828 684-5113
   Fletcher *(G-6049)*
Vineyards On Scuppernong LLC............ G 252 796-4727
   Columbia *(G-4170)*
Vintners Hill.. G 704 737-8023
   Mint Hill *(G-10547)*
Weathervane Winery Inc...................... G 336 793-3366
   Lexington *(G-9802)*
Whitefin Vineyards LLC....................... G 219 902-6647
   Apex *(G-259)*
Willowcroft.. F 704 540-0367
   Charlotte *(G-3815)*
Windsor Run Cellars Inc...................... G 336 998-6598
   Advance *(G-53)*
Winery Assoc Southeast Inc................. G 919 219-1929
   Cary *(G-1927)*
Woodmill Winery Inc........................... G 704 276-9911
   Vale *(G-15473)*
Yadkin Valley Herbs Inc....................... G 336 468-4062
   Hamptonville *(G-7681)*
Yadkin Valley Wine Company............... G 336 467-0257
   Hamptonville *(G-7682)*

BEVERAGES, MALT

Craft Revolution LLC........................... F 347 924-7540
   Charlotte *(G-2568)*

BEVERAGES, NONALCOHOLIC: Bottled & canned soft drinks

Aberdeen Coca-Cola Btlg Co Inc........... E 910 944-2305
   Aberdeen *(G-1)*
Bebida Beverage Company.................. E 704 660-0226
   Statesville *(G-14760)*
Carolina Beverage Corporation............ E 704 636-2191
   Salisbury *(G-13932)*
Carolina Bottling Company.................. D 704 637-5869
   Salisbury *(G-13933)*
Ccbcc Inc.. A 704 557-4000
   Charlotte *(G-2425)*
Ccbcc Operations LLC......................... E 704 557-4038
   Charlotte *(G-2426)*
Ccbcc Operations LLC......................... E 910 582-3543
   Hamlet *(G-7619)*
Ccbcc Operations LLC......................... E 704 872-3634
   Statesville *(G-14774)*
Ccbcc Operations LLC......................... D 828 687-1300
   Arden *(G-319)*
Ccbcc Operations LLC......................... E 828 297-2141
   Boone *(G-1185)*
Ccbcc Operations LLC......................... E 828 488-2874
   Bryson City *(G-1321)*
Ccbcc Operations LLC......................... F 704 359-5600
   Charlotte *(G-2427)*
Ccbcc Operations LLC......................... E 704 399-6043
   Charlotte *(G-2429)*
Ccbcc Operations LLC......................... C 980 321-3226
   Charlotte *(G-2430)*
Ccbcc Operations LLC......................... D 919 359-2966
   Clayton *(G-3964)*
Ccbcc Operations LLC......................... D 910 483-6158
   Fayetteville *(G-5787)*
Ccbcc Operations LLC......................... D 336 664-1116
   Greensboro *(G-6896)*
Ccbcc Operations LLC......................... D 828 322-5097
   Hickory *(G-7972)*
Ccbcc Operations LLC......................... D 704 225-1973
   Monroe *(G-10678)*
Ccbcc Operations LLC......................... E 336 789-7111
   Mount Airy *(G-11494)*
Ccbcc Operations LLC......................... E 704 364-8728
   Charlotte *(G-2428)*
Choice USA Beverage Inc..................... G 704 487-6951
   Shelby *(G-14294)*
Coca Cola Bottling Co.......................... G 704 509-1812
   Charlotte *(G-2516)*
Coca-Cola Consolidated Inc................. G 704 398-2252
   Charlotte *(G-2517)*
Coca-Cola Consolidated Inc................. D 980 321-3001
   Charlotte *(G-2518)*
Coca-Cola Consolidated Inc................. C 919 550-0611
   Clayton *(G-3968)*
Coca-Cola Consolidated Inc................. D 252 334-1820
   Elizabeth City *(G-5535)*
Coca-Cola Consolidated Inc................. E 704 551-4500
   Kinston *(G-9354)*
Coca-Cola Consolidated Inc................. G 919 763-3172
   Leland *(G-9538)*
Coca-Cola Consolidated Inc................. E 828 322-5096
   Newton *(G-11920)*
Coca-Cola Consolidated Inc................. A 704 557-4400
   Charlotte *(G-2519)*
Durham Coca-Cola Bottling Co............ G 919 510-0574
   Raleigh *(G-12711)*
ICEE Company.................................... G 704 357-6865
   Charlotte *(G-2946)*
Independent Beverage Co LLC.............. F 704 399-2504
   Charlotte *(G-2959)*
McPherson Beverages Inc.................... E 252 537-3571
   Roanoke Rapids *(G-13579)*
Midas Spring Water Btlg Co LLC........... G 704 392-2150
   Davidson *(G-4685)*
Old Saratoga Inc................................. E 252 238-2175
   Saratoga *(G-14216)*
Original New York Seltzer LLC.............. E 323 500-0757
   Cornelius *(G-4573)*
Packo Bottling Inc............................... E 919 496-4286
   Louisburg *(G-9995)*
Pepsi Bottling Ventures LLC................. E 252 335-4355
   Elizabeth City *(G-5561)*
Pepsi Bottling Ventures LLC................. D 919 865-2388
   Garner *(G-6302)*
Pepsi-Cola Btlg Hickry NC Inc............... G 828 322-8090
   Granite Falls *(G-6749)*
Pepsi-Cola Btlg Hickry NC Inc............... E 828 497-1235
   Whittier *(G-16010)*
Piedmont Cheerwine Bottling Co.......... D 336 993-7733
   Colfax *(G-4158)*
Piedmont Coca-Cola Btlg Partnr........... C 252 752-2446
   Greenville *(G-7574)*
Piedmont Coca-Cola Btlg Partnr........... D 252 536-3611
   Halifax *(G-7611)*
Piedmont Coca-Cola Btlg Partnr........... C 252 637-3157
   New Bern *(G-11836)*
Piedmont Coca-Cola Btlg Partnr........... E 704 551-4400
   Charlotte *(G-3339)*
Quality Beverage LLC.......................... G 704 637-5881
   Salisbury *(G-14034)*
Sanford Coca-Cola Bottling Co............. E 919 774-4111
   Sanford *(G-14180)*
Summit Seltzer Company LLC.............. G 980 819-6416
   Charlotte *(G-3648)*
Suntory International.......................... F 917 756-2747
   Raleigh *(G-13316)*
Vortex Bottle Shop LLC....................... F 980 258-0827
   Harrisburg *(G-7734)*

BEVERAGES, NONALCOHOLIC: Carbonated

Central Carolina Btlg Co Inc................. G 919 542-3226
   Bear Creek *(G-937)*
Frito-Lay North America Inc................ G 980 224-3730
   Wilmington *(G-16223)*
Midland Bottling LLC........................... G 919 865-2300
   Raleigh *(G-13031)*
Pepsi Bottling Group........................... G 828 286-4406
   Rutherfordton *(G-13884)*
Pepsi Bottling Group Inc...................... G 704 507-4031
   Midland *(G-10473)*
Pepsi Bottling Ventures LLC................. E 800 879-8884
   Cary *(G-1849)*
Pepsi Bottling Ventures LLC................. G 919 863-4000
   Garner *(G-6301)*
Pepsi Bottling Ventures LLC................. D 919 778-8300
   Goldsboro *(G-6644)*
Pepsi Bottling Ventures LLC................. C 704 455-0800
   Harrisburg *(G-7720)*
Pepsi Bottling Ventures LLC................. E 252 451-1811
   Rocky Mount *(G-13719)*
Pepsi Bottling Ventures LLC................. D 910 865-1600
   Saint Pauls *(G-13907)*
Pepsi Bottling Ventures LLC................. E 704 873-0249
   Statesville *(G-14858)*
Pepsi Bottling Ventures LLC................. G 336 464-9227
   Winston Salem *(G-16840)*
Pepsi Bottling Ventures LLC................. E 336 464-9227
   Winston Salem *(G-16841)*
Pepsi Bottling Ventures LLC................. D 919 865-2300
   Raleigh *(G-13107)*
Pepsi Cola Bottling Co......................... C 828 650-7800
   Fletcher *(G-6031)*
Pepsi Cola Co...................................... G 704 357-9166
   Charlotte *(G-3328)*
Pepsi-Cola Btlg Hickry NC Inc............... E 828 322-8090
   Hickory *(G-8111)*
Pepsi-Cola Btlg New Bern Inc............... E 252 522-0232
   New Bern *(G-11834)*

PRODUCT SECTION

Pepsi-Cola Metro Btlg Co Inc................ G..... 980 581-1099
  Charlotte *(G-3329)*
Pepsi-Cola Metro Btlg Co Inc................ A..... 336 896-4000
  Winston Salem *(G-16843)*
Pepsico Inc.. G..... 828 756-4662
  Marion *(G-10171)*
Pepsico Inc.. G..... 914 253-2000
  Winston Salem *(G-16844)*
Raleigh Ventures Inc........................ G..... 910 350-0036
  Wilmington *(G-16377)*
Red Bull Distribution Co Inc............. F..... 910 500-1566
  Havelock *(G-7745)*

BEVERAGES, NONALCOHOLIC: Carbonated, Canned & Bottled, Etc

Asheville Kombucha Mamas LLC......... E..... 828 595-4340
  Asheville *(G-537)*
Asheville Kombucha Mamas LLC......... F..... 828 394-2360
  Marshall *(G-10199)*
Choice USA Beverage Inc.................. D..... 704 823-1651
  Lowell *(G-10007)*
Grins Enterprises LLC...................... G..... 336 831-0534
  Winston Salem *(G-16730)*
Pepsi-Cola Metro Btlg Co Inc............. E..... 704 736-2640
  Cherryville *(G-3874)*
Refresco Beverages US Inc............... G..... 252 234-0493
  Wilson *(G-16530)*
Waynesville Soda Jerks LLC............. G..... 828 278-8589
  Waynesville *(G-15832)*

BEVERAGES, NONALCOHOLIC: Cider

Red Clay Ciderworks......................... G..... 980 498-0676
  Charlotte *(G-3421)*
Urban Orchard Cider Company.......... G..... 828 779-6372
  Weaverville *(G-15866)*

BEVERAGES, NONALCOHOLIC: Flavoring extracts & syrups, nec

Bunge Oils Inc................................... E..... 910 293-7917
  Warsaw *(G-15665)*
Crude LLC... G..... 919 391-8185
  Raleigh *(G-12657)*
Fuji Foods Inc.................................... G..... 336 226-8817
  Burlington *(G-1416)*
Great Eastern Sun Trdg Co Inc.......... F..... 828 665-7790
  Asheville *(G-642)*
Larrys Beans Inc................................ E..... 919 828-1234
  Raleigh *(G-12958)*
Mary Macks Inc................................. G..... 770 234-6333
  Clinton *(G-4097)*
Only Bitters....................................... G..... 617 413-6571
  Raleigh *(G-13085)*
Sakun Inc.. G..... 919 255-2994
  Cary *(G-1878)*

BEVERAGES, NONALCOHOLIC: Fruit Drnks, Under 100% Juice, Can

Alamance Foods Inc.......................... C..... 336 226-6392
  Burlington *(G-1362)*

BEVERAGES, NONALCOHOLIC: Soft Drinks, Canned & Bottled, Etc

Choice USA Beverage Inc.................. E..... 704 861-1029
  Gastonia *(G-6377)*
Dr Pepper Co of Wilmington.............. G..... 910 792-5400
  Wilmington *(G-16205)*
Dr Pepper/Seven-Up Bottling............. F..... 828 322-8090
  Hickory *(G-8012)*
Dr Ppper Btlg W Jffrson NC In............ E..... 336 846-2433
  West Jefferson *(G-15939)*
Durham Coca-Cola Bottling Company... C..... 919 383-1531
  Durham *(G-5071)*
Ginger Supreme Inc........................... G..... 919 812-8986
  Apex *(G-195)*
Mae Rodgers Cola............................. G..... 252 797-4253
  Creswell *(G-4626)*
Minges Bottling Group....................... F..... 252 636-5898
  New Bern *(G-11823)*
Pepsi Bottling Ventures LLC.............. E..... 828 264-7702
  Deep Gap *(G-4711)*
Pepsi Bottling Ventures LLC.............. D..... 910 792-5400
  Wilmington *(G-16351)*
Pepsi Bottling Ventures LLC.............. C..... 336 724-4800
  Winston Salem *(G-16842)*
Pepsi-Cola Btlg Hickry NC Inc............ E..... 828 322-8090
  Hickory *(G-8110)*
Pepsi-Cola Metro Btlg Co Inc............. G..... 252 446-7181
  Rocky Mount *(G-13720)*
Quality Beverage LLC....................... E..... 910 371-3596
  Belville *(G-1025)*
Redux Beverages LLC....................... G..... 951 304-1144
  Hillsborough *(G-8666)*
Refresco Beverages US Inc............... F..... 252 234-0493
  Wilson *(G-16531)*
Sun-Drop Btlg Rocky Mt NC Inc.......... F..... 252 977-4586
  Rocky Mount *(G-13735)*
USa Wholesale and Distrg Inc............ F..... 888 484-6872
  Fayetteville *(G-5945)*

BEVERAGES, NONALCOHOLIC: Tea, Iced, Bottled & Canned, Etc

Brewitt & Dreenkupp Inc.................... G..... 704 525-3366
  Charlotte *(G-2353)*
S & D Coffee Inc............................... A..... 704 782-3121
  Concord *(G-4355)*

BEVERAGES, WINE & DISTILLED ALCOHOLIC, WHOLESALE: Wine

Drink A Bull LLC................................ G..... 919 818-3321
  Durham *(G-5065)*

BEVERAGES, WINE/DISTILLED ALCOHOLIC, WHOL: Bttlg Wine/Liquor

Outer Banks Craft Distlg LLC............. G..... 252 423-3011
  Manteo *(G-10128)*

BICYCLES, PARTS & ACCESS

Club The Nantahala Bicycle Inc.......... G..... 828 524-4900
  Franklin *(G-6119)*
Huck Cycles Corporation................... G..... 704 275-1735
  Cornelius *(G-4557)*
Industry Nine LLC............................. G..... 828 210-5113
  Asheville *(G-661)*
Rhoddie Bicycle Outfitters Inc........... G..... 828 414-9800
  Blowing Rock *(G-1156)*
Rinehart Racing Inc........................... E..... 828 350-7653
  Fletcher *(G-6035)*

BILLIARD & POOL TABLES & SPLYS

Mettech Inc....................................... G..... 919 833-9460
  Raleigh *(G-13023)*

BINDING SVC: Books & Manuals

Adpress Printing Incorporated........... G..... 336 294-2244
  Summerfield *(G-14975)*
American Multimedia Inc................... D..... 336 229-7101
  Burlington *(G-1364)*
Appalachian State University............. F..... 828 262-2047
  Boone *(G-1174)*
Arzberger Engravers Inc.................... E..... 704 376-1151
  Charlotte *(G-2224)*
Asheboro Piedmont Printing Inc......... F..... 336 899-7910
  Asheboro *(G-406)*
Atlantis Graphics Inc......................... E..... 919 361-5809
  Durham *(G-4933)*
Bennett & Associates Inc................... G..... 919 477-7362
  Durham *(G-4955)*
Boingo Graphics Inc.......................... E..... 704 527-4963
  Charlotte *(G-2331)*
BP Solutions Group Inc..................... E..... 828 252-4476
  Asheville *(G-570)*
Carter-Hubbard Publishing Co........... F..... 336 838-4117
  North Wilkesboro *(G-12000)*
Coastal Press Inc.............................. G..... 252 726-1549
  Morehead City *(G-11163)*
David Presnell.................................. G..... 336 372-5989
  Sparta *(G-14592)*
Docusource North Carolina LLC......... E..... 919 459-5900
  Morrisville *(G-11335)*
Dokja Inc.. G..... 336 852-5190
  Greensboro *(G-6975)*
Etherngton Cnservation Ctr Inc......... D..... 336 665-1317
  Greensboro *(G-7004)*
Flash Printing Company Inc.............. E..... 704 375-2474
  Charlotte *(G-2769)*
Free Will Bptst Press Fndtion............ F..... 252 746-6128
  Ayden *(G-852)*
Gik Inc... F..... 919 872-9498
  Raleigh *(G-12800)*
Hickory Printing Solutions LLC.......... C..... 828 465-3431
  Conover *(G-4464)*
Holt Sublimation Prtg Pdts Inc........... C..... 336 222-3600
  Burlington *(G-1429)*
Itek Graphics LLC............................. E..... 704 357-6002
  Concord *(G-4291)*
Jag Graphics Inc............................... G..... 828 259-9020
  Asheville *(G-668)*
Joseph C Woodard Prtg Co Inc.......... F..... 919 829-0634
  Raleigh *(G-12922)*
Leatherbound Book Works................ G..... 919 448-7847
  Durham *(G-5187)*
Lee County Industries Inc................. G..... 919 775-3439
  Sanford *(G-14148)*
Loftin & Company Inc....................... E..... 704 393-9393
  Charlotte *(G-3100)*
Measurement Incorporated............... C..... 919 683-2413
  Durham *(G-5213)*
Medlit Solutions LLC......................... D..... 919 878-6789
  Garner *(G-6287)*
Occasions Group Inc......................... E..... 252 321-5805
  Greenville *(G-7566)*
Ollis Enterprises Inc......................... E..... 828 265-0004
  Wilkesboro *(G-16037)*
Owen G Dunn Co Inc......................... G..... 252 633-3197
  New Bern *(G-11832)*
Pamela A Adams................................ G..... 919 876-5949
  Raleigh *(G-13096)*
Person Printing Company Inc............ E..... 336 599-2146
  Roxboro *(G-13818)*
Piedmont Business Forms Inc........... F..... 828 464-0010
  Newton *(G-11960)*
Postal Instant Press.......................... F..... 336 222-0717
  Burlington *(G-1477)*
Powell Ink Inc................................... F..... 828 253-6886
  Asheville *(G-739)*
Printing Svcs Greensboro Inc............ F..... 336 274-7663
  Greensboro *(G-7285)*
Quality Prtg Cartridge Fctry............... G..... 336 852-2505
  Greensboro *(G-7301)*
S Chamblee Incorporated.................. E..... 919 833-7561
  Raleigh *(G-13221)*

BINDING SVC: Books & Manuals　　　　　　　　　　　　　　　　　　　　　　　PRODUCT SECTION

S Ruppe Inc .... E 828 287-4936
　Rutherfordton (G-13889)
Three Trees Bindery .... G 704 724-9409
　Charlotte (G-3692)
Weber and Weber Inc .... F 336 722-4109
　Winston Salem (G-16968)

BINDINGS: Bias, Made From Purchased Materials

International Foam Pdts Inc .... G 704 588-0080
　Charlotte (G-2982)

BIOLOGICAL PRDTS: Agar Culture Media

Grifols Therapeutics LLC .... B 919 316-6300
　Durham (G-5127)

BIOLOGICAL PRDTS: Blood Derivatives

Grifols Therapeutics LLC .... F 919 316-6214
　Durham (G-5129)
Grifols Therapeutics LLC .... A 919 316-6612
　Raleigh (G-12821)
Immunotek Bio Centers LLC .... E 828 569-6264
　Hickory (G-8063)
Immunotek Bio Centers LLC .... E 336 781-4901
　High Point (G-8406)

BIOLOGICAL PRDTS: Exc Diagnostic

Anatech Ltd .... F 704 489-1488
　Denver (G-4761)
Astellas Gene Therapies Inc .... D 415 638-6561
　Sanford (G-14089)
Biologix of The Triangle Inc .... G 919 696-4544
　Cary (G-1703)
Boehrnger Inglheim Anmal Hlth .... D 919 577-9020
　Fuquay Varina (G-6185)
Bonap Inc .... G 919 967-6240
　Chapel Hill (G-1994)
Carolina Biological Supply Co .... C 336 446-7600
　Whitsett (G-15985)
Carolina Biological Supply Company .... G 336 584-0381
　Burlington (G-1384)
Cedarlane Laboratories USA .... E 336 513-5135
　Burlington (G-1391)
Chelsea Therapeutics International Ltd .... F 704 341-1516
　Charlotte (G-2469)
Cytonet LLC .... F
　Durham (G-5044)
Engaged Media Inc .... E 239 280-4202
　Durham (G-5087)
Genotech Inc .... G 919 369-4947
　Cary (G-1773)
Keranetics LLC .... F 336 725-0621
　Winston Salem (G-16778)
Microban Products Company .... D 704 766-4267
　Huntersville (G-8854)
Molecular Toxicology Inc .... F 828 264-9099
　Boone (G-1223)
Pfizer Inc .... C 919 775-7100
　Sanford (G-14168)
Prokidney LLC .... E 336 448-2857
　Winston Salem (G-16872)
Prokidney Corp .... D 336 999-7028
　Winston Salem (G-16873)
Serum Source International Inc .... F 704 588-6467
　Waxhaw (G-15774)
Tengion Inc .... E 336 722-5855
　Winston Salem (G-16938)

BIOLOGICAL PRDTS: Vaccines

Albion Medical Holdings Inc .... F 800 378-3906
　Lenoir (G-9571)

Avp Vaccines LLC .... G 704 799-0161
　Mooresville (G-10868)
Greer Laboratories Inc .... E 828 758-2388
　Lenoir (G-9614)
Greer Laboratories Inc .... C 828 754-5327
　Lenoir (G-9615)
International Ptnrshp For Vacc .... G 919 367-0379
　Cary (G-1792)

BIOLOGICAL PRDTS: Vaccines & Immunizing

Embrex LLC .... C 919 941-5185
　Durham (G-5080)
Novartis Vccnes Dagnostics Inc .... B 617 871-7000
　Holly Springs (G-8708)
Passport Health Triangle .... F 919 781-0053
　Cary (G-1842)
Seqirus Inc .... F 919 577-5000
　Holly Springs (G-8715)

BIOLOGICAL PRDTS: Veterinary

Epicypher Inc .... F 855 374-2461
　Durham (G-5092)
Quo Vademus LLC .... G 910 296-1632
　Kenansville (G-9145)

BIRTH CONTROL DEVICES: Rubber

Hygeia Marketing Corporation .... F 704 933-5190
　Kannapolis (G-9123)

BLADES: Knife

Daniel Winkler Knifemaker LLC .... G 828 262-3691
　Boone (G-1192)

BLADES: Saw, Hand Or Power

Raleigh Saw Co Inc .... G 919 832-2248
　Raleigh (G-13184)

BLANKBOOKS & LOOSELEAF BINDERS

American Sample House Inc .... G 704 276-1970
　Vale (G-15463)
Carolina Swatching Inc .... F 828 327-9499
　Hickory (G-7967)
E Feibusch Company Inc .... E 336 434-5095
　High Point (G-8333)
Swatchworks Inc .... G 336 626-9971
　Asheboro (G-490)
Visual Products Inc .... F 336 883-0156
　High Point (G-8596)

BLANKBOOKS: Checkbooks & Passbooks, Bank

Clarke Harland Corp .... G 210 697-8888
　High Point (G-8297)

BLANKETS & BLANKETING, COTTON

Riddle & Company LLC .... E 336 229-1856
　Burlington (G-1485)
Westpoint Home Inc .... B 910 369-2231
　Wagram (G-15524)

BLEACHING YARN & FABRICS: Wool Or Similar Fibers

Burlington Industries LLC .... G 336 379-6220
　Greensboro (G-6865)

BLINDS & SHADES: Vertical

Carolina Blind Outlet Inc .... G 828 697-8425
　Hendersonville (G-7834)

Decolux USA .... G 704 340-3532
　Charlotte (G-2611)
Raven Rock Manufacturing Inc .... G 910 308-8430
　Dunn (G-4880)
Vertical Solutions of NC Inc .... F 919 285-2251
　Holly Springs (G-8724)
Vista Products Inc .... D 910 582-0130
　Hamlet (G-7634)

BLINDS : Window

A Window Treatment Co Inc .... F 919 934-7100
　Smithfield (G-14447)
Bridgewater Blinds Interi .... G 910 408-1900
　Leland (G-9530)
Elite Textiles Fabrication Inc .... F 888 337-0977
　High Point (G-8341)
Empire Carpet & Blinds Inc .... F 704 541-3988
　Charlotte (G-2709)
Erics Cheesecakes LLC .... G 336 264-4303
　Burlington (G-1412)
First Rate Blinds .... G 800 655-1080
　Cornelius (G-4547)
H2h Blinds .... F 704 628-5084
　Matthews (G-10250)
Mountaintop Cheesecakes LLC .... G 336 391-9127
　Mocksville (G-10593)
My Favorite Cheesecake .... G 919 824-0782
　Durham (G-5232)
Newell Brands Inc .... G 336 812-8181
　High Point (G-8466)
Royal Cheesecake Varieties LLC .... G 919 670-8766
　Raleigh (G-13215)
Royal Textile Products Sw LLC .... G 602 276-4598
　Charlotte (G-3465)
Selective Enterprises Inc .... C 704 588-3310
　Charlotte (G-3525)
Synoptix Companies LLC .... F 910 790-3630
　Wilmington (G-16425)
Turnage Blind Co .... G 919 736-1809
　Goldsboro (G-6666)
USA Blind Inc .... G 704 309-5171
　Charlotte (G-3761)

BLOCKS & BRICKS: Concrete

Custom Brick Company Inc .... E 919 832-2804
　Raleigh (G-12663)
East Fork Pottery LLC .... G 828 575-2150
　Asheville (G-616)
Fayblock Materials Inc .... D 910 323-9198
　Fayetteville (G-5823)
General Shale Brick Inc .... E 919 775-2121
　Moncure (G-10622)
Oldcastle Adams .... F 336 310-0542
　Colfax (G-4156)
Oldcastle Retail Inc .... B 704 799-8083
　Cornelius (G-4572)
Southeastern Concrete Pdts Co .... D 704 873-2226
　Statesville (G-14890)
Southern Block Company .... F 910 293-7844
　Warsaw (G-15674)
Southern Hardscape Pdts Inc .... G 704 528-6726
　Statesville (G-14892)

BLOCKS: Landscape Or Retaining Wall, Concrete

Carolina Lawnscape Inc .... G 803 230-5570
　Charlotte (G-2398)
Dnl Services LLC .... G 910 689-8759
　Harrells (G-7692)
Global Stone Impex LLC .... G 336 609-1113
　Greensboro (G-7047)

PRODUCT SECTION

Good Earth Ministries............................. G 828 287-9826
  Rutherfordton *(G-13873)*
Helping Hands Concrete Llc.................. G 828 817-1288
  Mill Spring *(G-10486)*
Landsman Forest Lawn Guard................ G 828 898-3433
  Banner Elk *(G-901)*
Southern Elements Hardscapes.............. G 240 626-1586
  Sanford *(G-14188)*
Taylco Inc.. E 910 739-0405
  Lumberton *(G-10057)*
Top Dawg Landscape Inc..................... G 336 877-7519
  West Jefferson *(G-15949)*
Trademark Landscape Group Inc........... F 910 253-0560
  Supply *(G-15013)*

BLOCKS: Paving

Custom Brick Company Inc................... E 919 832-2804
  Raleigh *(G-12663)*

BLOCKS: Standard, Concrete Or Cinder

Adams Products Company..................... C 919 467-2218
  Morrisville *(G-11278)*
Argos USA LLC..................................... C 704 872-9566
  Statesville *(G-14752)*
Greystone Concrete Pdts Inc................. E 252 438-5144
  Henderson *(G-7785)*
Hefty Concrete Inc................................ G 910 483-1598
  Fayetteville *(G-5836)*
Johnson Concrete Company.................. E 704 786-4204
  Concord *(G-4294)*
Johnson Concrete Company.................. E 336 248-2918
  Lexington *(G-9736)*
Johnson Concrete Company.................. E 704 636-5231
  Willow Spring *(G-16079)*
Johnson Concrete Company.................. E 704 636-5231
  Salisbury *(G-13993)*
Leonard Block Company........................ F 336 764-0607
  Winston Salem *(G-16786)*
Motsinger Block Plant Inc...................... G 336 764-0350
  Winston Salem *(G-16818)*
Old Castle Apg South Inc..................... G 919 383-2521
  Durham *(G-5255)*
Union Masonry Inc................................ G 919 217-7806
  Raleigh *(G-13382)*

BLOWERS & FANS

Air Purification Inc................................. F 919 783-6161
  Raleigh *(G-12482)*
Bahnson Holdings Inc........................... D 336 760-3111
  Clemmons *(G-4029)*
Breezer Holdings LLC........................... D 844 233-5673
  Charlotte *(G-2351)*
Camfil Usa Inc...................................... E 828 465-2880
  Conover *(G-4429)*
Camfil Usa Inc...................................... D 252 975-1141
  Washington *(G-15685)*
Dynamic Air Engineering Inc................. E 714 540-1000
  Claremont *(G-3925)*
Environmental Specialties LLC............... D 919 829-9300
  Raleigh *(G-12742)*
Field Controls LLC................................ D 252 208-7300
  Kinston *(G-9366)*
Firefly Balloons Inc............................... G 704 878-9501
  Statesville *(G-14800)*
Greenheck Fan Corporation.................. G 704 476-3700
  Shelby *(G-14321)*
Hughs Sheet Mtal Sttsvlle LLC............... F 704 872-4621
  Statesville *(G-14818)*
Kirk & Blum Manufacturing Co.............. E 801 728-6533
  Greensboro *(G-7152)*
Kitchen Vntilation Systems LLC............. G 704 476-3565
  Kings Mountain *(G-9315)*

Meadows Mills Inc................................ E 336 838-2282
  North Wilkesboro *(G-12027)*
Nederman Inc....................................... D 336 821-0827
  Thomasville *(G-15255)*
Pamlico Air Inc..................................... F 252 995-6267
  Washington *(G-15724)*
Punker LLC... F 828 322-1951
  Lincolnton *(G-9913)*
Purolator Facet Inc............................... E 336 668-4444
  Greensboro *(G-7293)*
Universal Air Products Corp.................. G 704 374-0600
  Charlotte *(G-3755)*
WV Holdings Inc................................... G 704 853-8338
  Gastonia *(G-6544)*
Ziehl-Abegg Inc.................................... E 336 834-9339
  Greensboro *(G-7475)*
G Denver and Co LLC.......................... E 704 896-4000
  Davidson *(G-4675)*
Hunter Fan Company............................ G 704 896-9250
  Cornelius *(G-4558)*
Rotron Incorporated.............................. C 336 449-3400
  Whitsett *(G-16001)*

BLUEPRINTING SVCS

AEC Imaging & Graphics LLC............... G 910 693-1034
  Hope Mills *(G-8730)*
Copy King Inc....................................... G 336 333-9900
  Greensboro *(G-6936)*
Document Imaging Systems Inc............ G 919 460-9440
  Raleigh *(G-12693)*
Occasions Group Inc............................ G 919 751-2400
  Goldsboro *(G-6641)*
Richa Inc.. G 704 944-0230
  Charlotte *(G-3448)*
Richa Inc.. F 704 331-9744
  Charlotte *(G-3449)*

BOAT & BARGE COMPONENTS: Metal, Prefabricated

Gore S Mar Met Fabrication Inc............. G 910 763-6066
  Wilmington *(G-16237)*

BOAT BUILDING & REPAIR

2nd Shift Cycles LLC............................ G 336 462-3262
  Lexington *(G-9676)*
2topia Cycles Inc.................................. G 704 778-7849
  Charlotte *(G-2106)*
33rd Strike Group LLC.......................... G 910 371-9688
  Leland *(G-9523)*
A & J Canvas Inc.................................. E 252 244-1509
  Vanceboro *(G-15474)*
A Squared Pro Services LLC................ G 336 675-3546
  Burlington *(G-1360)*
Anglers Marine NC................................ G 919 585-7900
  Clayton *(G-3953)*
B&S Shingle Savers Inc........................ G 336 264-3898
  Burlington *(G-1374)*
Baja Marine Inc.................................... E 252 975-2000
  Washington *(G-15683)*
Bilge Masters Inc.................................. G 704 995-4293
  Charlotte *(G-2310)*
Black Oak Boat Works.......................... G 828 252-4997
  Asheville *(G-561)*
Blackbeards Boatworks......................... G 252 726-6161
  Morehead City *(G-11154)*
Brp US Inc.. G 828 766-1164
  Spruce Pine *(G-14630)*
C E Hicks Enterprises Inc..................... F 919 772-5131
  Garner *(G-6259)*
Cabarrus Cycling Company.................. G 704 938-8735
  Kannapolis *(G-9114)*

BOAT BUILDING & REPAIR

Cape Fear Boat Works Inc.................... F 910 371-3460
  Navassa *(G-11757)*
Certified Fiberglass Inc.......................... G 252 241-9641
  Cape Carteret *(G-1630)*
Coastal Trimworks Inc........................... G 910 231-8532
  Leland *(G-9536)*
Cote Timeworks LLC............................. G 910 246-1767
  Southern Pines *(G-14531)*
Croswait Custom Composites Inc.......... G 252 423-1245
  Wanchese *(G-15645)*
Crystal Coast Boatworks....................... G 252 723-9370
  Beaufort *(G-952)*
Crystal Coast Composites Inc............... F 252 838-0025
  Beaufort *(G-953)*
Crystal Coast Composites Inc............... G 252 838-0025
  Morehead City *(G-11165)*
Custom Boatworks Inc........................... G 252 235-2461
  Bailey *(G-869)*
Custom Marine Fabrication Inc.............. G 252 638-5422
  New Bern *(G-11795)*
Donzi Marine LLC................................. F 252 975-2000
  Washington *(G-15696)*
Egret Boats LLC.................................... G 252 948-0004
  Washington *(G-15698)*
Elite Marine LLC................................... E 919 495-6388
  Four Oaks *(G-6103)*
Fiberglass Fabrication Inc..................... G 828 685-0940
  Hendersonville *(G-7847)*
French Broad Boatworks....................... G 828 230-6600
  Asheville *(G-628)*
Gem Buoy Incorporated........................ G 252 469-3680
  Tarboro *(G-15105)*
Giant Wake Forest LLC......................... G 919 556-7433
  Wake Forest *(G-15559)*
Gillikin Marine Railways Inc.................. G 252 726-7284
  Beaufort *(G-958)*
Gunboat International Ltd..................... F 252 305-8700
  Wanchese *(G-15646)*
Gwg Boatworks LLC............................. G 252 422-0757
  Morehead City *(G-11173)*
Harding Enterprise Inc.......................... G 252 725-9785
  Beaufort *(G-960)*
Hc Composites LLC.............................. C 252 641-8000
  Tarboro *(G-15107)*
Hysucat USA LLC................................. G 919 345-0240
  Raleigh *(G-12871)*
Iconic Marine Group LLC...................... D 252 975-2000
  Chocowinity *(G-3895)*
Jabec Enterprise Inc............................. G 336 655-8441
  Winston Salem *(G-16768)*
Jarrett Bay Offshore.............................. G 919 803-1990
  Raleigh *(G-12913)*
JG Agnew Holdings Inc........................ G 704 594-0900
  Harrisburg *(G-7714)*
John Glen Alexander Corp.................... G 704 309-7258
  Huntersville *(G-8841)*
Johnson Custom Boats Inc.................... G 910 232-4594
  Wilmington *(G-16282)*
Kennys Fiberglass Restoration............... G 704 252-0979
  Mooresville *(G-10996)*
Lake House Enterprises Inc.................. G 919 424-3780
  Raleigh *(G-12952)*
Laytons Custom Boatworks LLC............ G 252 482-1504
  Edenton *(G-5518)*
Marinemax of North Carolina................ E 910 256-8100
  Wrightsville Beach *(G-17026)*
Mike Luszcz... G 252 717-6282
  Winterville *(G-17007)*
Moores Marine Yacht Center Inc........... F 252 504-7060
  Beaufort *(G-961)*
Mr Home Genius LLC........................... G 252 902-4663
  Winterville *(G-17009)*

BOAT BUILDING & REPAIR PRODUCT SECTION

Nomad Houseboats Inc.................................. G 252 288-5670
   New Bern *(G-11831)*

Obx Boatworks LLC.. G 336 878-9490
   High Point *(G-8469)*

Onslow Bay Boatworks & Marine................... G 910 270-3703
   Hampstead *(G-7653)*

Pacific Seacraft LLC..................................... G 252 948-1421
   Washington *(G-15722)*

Powers Boatworks.. G 910 762-3636
   Wilmington *(G-16364)*

Rent A Guy Now LLC..................................... G 919 637-1104
   Garner *(G-6309)*

Rings True LLC.. G 919 265-7600
   Carrboro *(G-1656)*

Salt Boatworks Inc... G 919 394-3795
   Newport *(G-11906)*

Sea Mark Boats Inc....................................... G 910 675-1877
   Rocky Point *(G-13749)*

Shm Jarrett Bay Trs LLC............................... G 972 488-1314
   Beaufort *(G-966)*

Specialty Boatworks Inc................................ G 910 251-5219
   Wilmington *(G-16415)*

Starflite Companies Inc................................. C 252 728-2690
   Beaufort *(G-968)*

Stroudcraft Marine LLC.................................. F 910 623-4055
   Rocky Point *(G-13751)*

Taylor Boat Works.. G 252 726-6374
   Morehead City *(G-11194)*

Taylor Manufacturing Inc............................... E 910 862-2576
   Elizabethtown *(G-5605)*

Triad Marine Center Inc................................ G 252 634-1880
   New Bern *(G-11851)*

U S Propeller Service Inc.............................. G 704 528-9515
   Troutman *(G-15396)*

Wanchese Dock and Haul LLC...................... G 252 473-6424
   Wanchese *(G-15651)*

Warrior Boats... G 336 885-2628
   High Point *(G-8601)*

Williams United LLC...................................... G 336 251-7355
   Kernersville *(G-9253)*

Winterville Machine Works Inc...................... D 252 756-2130
   Winterville *(G-17018)*

Xcelerator Boatworks Inc.............................. G 704 622-8978
   Statesville *(G-14930)*

BOAT BUILDING & REPAIRING: Fiberglass

Alb Boats... C 252 482-7600
   Edenton *(G-5505)*

Bayliss Boatworks Inc................................... E 252 473-9797
   Wanchese *(G-15641)*

Briggs Boat Works Incorporated................... F 252 473-2393
   Wanchese *(G-15643)*

Brooks Boatworks Inc................................... G 252 974-1005
   Bath *(G-914)*

Bryan Blake James....................................... G 252 729-8021
   Gloucester *(G-6574)*

Budsin Wood Craft.. G 252 729-1540
   Marshallberg *(G-10209)*

Custom Steel Boats Inc................................ F 252 745-7447
   Merritt *(G-10439)*

Grady-White Boats Inc.................................. C 252 752-2111
   Greenville *(G-7534)*

Kencraft Manufacturing Inc.......................... F 252 291-0271
   Wilson *(G-16505)*

Mann Custom Boats Inc................................ E 252 473-1716
   Manns Harbor *(G-10122)*

Marine Tooling Technology Inc..................... G 336 887-9577
   High Point *(G-8439)*

May-Craft Fiberglass Pdts Inc...................... E 919 934-3000
   Four Oaks *(G-6109)*

Pair Marine Inc.. F 252 717-7009
   Washington *(G-15723)*

Parker Marine Enterprises Inc...................... D 252 728-5621
   Beaufort *(G-964)*

Richard Scarborough Boat Works................. G 252 473-3646
   Wanchese *(G-15650)*

Shearline Boatworks LLC.............................. G 252 726-6916
   Morehead City *(G-11189)*

BOAT BUILDING & REPAIRING: Kayaks

Coastal Woodworking..................................... G 910 477-1330
   Bolivia *(G-1163)*

BOAT BUILDING & REPAIRING: Motorboats, Inboard Or Outboard

Barrs Competition.. F 704 482-5169
   Shelby *(G-14287)*

Brp US Inc... D 828 766-1100
   Spruce Pine *(G-14631)*

CC Boats Inc... F 252 482-3699
   Edenton *(G-5509)*

Fountain Powerboat Inds Inc........................ C 252 975-2000
   Washington *(G-15703)*

Fountain Powerboats Inc.............................. D 252 975-2000
   Washington *(G-15704)*

Jones Marine Inc... G 704 639-0173
   Salisbury *(G-13994)*

Rapid Response Technology LLC................. G 910 763-3856
   Wilmington *(G-16378)*

Smoky Mountain Jet Boats LLC.................... F 828 488-0522
   Bryson City *(G-1325)*

BOAT BUILDING & REPAIRING: Motorized

Craig & Sandra Blackwell Inc....................... G 252 473-1803
   Wanchese *(G-15644)*

Jones Brothers Marine Mfg Inc.................... F 252 240-1995
   Morehead City *(G-11178)*

M & J Marine LLC... F 252 249-0522
   Oriental *(G-12111)*

Todds Rv & Marine Inc................................. F 828 651-0007
   Hendersonville *(G-7908)*

BOAT BUILDING & REPAIRING: Non-Motorized

Custom Fiberglass Products......................... G 252 235-2461
   Bailey *(G-870)*

Sullivan Motorsports Inc............................... G 252 923-2257
   Bath *(G-917)*

BOAT BUILDING & REPAIRING: Yachts

Bennett Brothers Yachts Inc........................ E 910 772-9277
   Wilmington *(G-16135)*

Caison Yachts Inc... G 910 270-6394
   Hampstead *(G-7641)*

Daedalus Composites LLC............................ F 252 368-9000
   Edenton *(G-5512)*

Hatteras Yachts Inc...................................... A 252 633-3101
   New Bern *(G-11808)*

Knooosc Inc... G 415 640-0080
   Morehead City *(G-11179)*

Mass Enterprises Inc.................................... F 443 585-0732
   New Bern *(G-11821)*

White River Marine Group LLC..................... C 252 633-3101
   New Bern *(G-11856)*

BOAT BUILDING & RPRG: Fishing, Small, Lobster, Crab, Oyster

Bayliss Boatyard Inc..................................... F 252 473-9797
   Wanchese *(G-15642)*

Regulator Marine Inc.................................... D 252 482-3877
   Edenton *(G-5521)*

Spencer Yachts Inc....................................... F 252 473-2660
   Manns Harbor *(G-10123)*

Trawler Incorporated..................................... G 252 745-3751
   Lowland *(G-10015)*

True World Marine LLC.................................. G 252 728-2541
   Beaufort *(G-970)*

BOAT DEALERS

Anglers Marine NC.. G 919 585-7900
   Clayton *(G-3953)*

Cape Fear Yacht Works LLC......................... F 910 540-1685
   Wilmington *(G-16151)*

Kencraft Manufacturing Inc.......................... F 252 291-0271
   Wilson *(G-16505)*

M & J Marine LLC... G 252 249-0522
   Oriental *(G-12111)*

Mann Custom Boats Inc................................ E 252 473-1716
   Manns Harbor *(G-10122)*

BOAT DEALERS: Motor

Marinemax of North Carolina....................... E 910 256-8100
   Wrightsville Beach *(G-17026)*

Nomad Houseboats Inc.................................. G 252 288-5670
   New Bern *(G-11831)*

Todds Rv & Marine Inc................................. F 828 651-0007
   Hendersonville *(G-7908)*

Triad Marine Center Inc................................ G 252 634-1880
   New Bern *(G-11851)*

BOAT LIFTS

Boat Lift US Inc.. G 239 283-9040
   Leland *(G-9527)*

Boat Lift Warehouse LLC.............................. G 877 468-5438
   Snow Hill *(G-14498)*

Float Lifts of Carolinas LLC........................ G 919 972-1082
   Wilmington *(G-16218)*

Hl & Dri Boat Lift Systems Inc.................... G 704 663-5438
   Mooresville *(G-10973)*

Hydrohoist of North Carolina....................... G 704 799-1910
   Mooresville *(G-10979)*

Veon Inc.. F 252 623-2102
   Washington *(G-15736)*

BOAT REPAIR SVCS

Admiral Marine Pdts & Svcs Inc.................. G 704 489-8771
   Denver *(G-4758)*

BOATS & OTHER MARINE EQPT: Plastic

Brunson Marine Group LLC........................... E 252 291-0271
   Wilson *(G-16481)*

Hydroeye Marine Group LLC........................ G 828 394-4406
   Connelly Springs *(G-4404)*

Marine & Industrial Plastics........................ G 252 224-1000
   Pollocksville *(G-12393)*

BODIES: Truck & Bus

Bucks Wrecker Service................................. G 704 776-0899
   Statesville *(G-14767)*

Courtesy Ford Inc... E 252 338-4783
   Elizabeth City *(G-5537)*

Daimler Truck North Amer LLC..................... A 704 868-5700
   Gastonia *(G-6394)*

Designline Usa LLC....................................... E 704 494-7800
   Charlotte *(G-2622)*

Epv Corporation... G 704 494-7800
   Charlotte *(G-2723)*

Epv Corporation... E 704 494-7800
   Charlotte *(G-2724)*

Immixt LLC.. G 336 207-8679
   Siler City *(G-14415)*

Laurinburg Machine Company....................... G 910 276-0360
   Laurinburg *(G-9484)*

PRODUCT SECTION

BOXES: Corrugated

Matthews Spcialty Vehicles Inc............. D 336 297-9600
  Greensboro *(G-7189)*
Mdb Investors LLC................................... F 704 507-6850
  Charlotte *(G-3155)*
Meritor Inc.. C 828 433-4600
  Morganton *(G-11232)*
Mickey Truck Bodies Inc......................... G 336 882-6806
  High Point *(G-8454)*
Mickey Truck Bodies Inc......................... G 336 882-6806
  Thomasville *(G-15248)*
Prevost Car (us) Inc................................ E 908 222-7211
  Greensboro *(G-7281)*
Smithway Inc... G 828 628-1756
  Fairview *(G-5718)*
Volvo Logistics North America Inc.......... C 336 393-4746
  Greensboro *(G-7449)*

BODY PARTS: Automobile, Stamped Metal

AMF-NC Enterprise Company LLC......... F 704 489-2206
  Denver *(G-4760)*
Borgwarner Turbo Systems LLC............. D 828 650-7515
  Arden *(G-315)*
Continental Auto Systems Inc.................. B 828 654-2000
  Fletcher *(G-5996)*
Coopers Fayetteville Inc.......................... F 910 483-0606
  Fayetteville *(G-5796)*
Dutch Miller Charlotte Inc....................... E 704 522-8422
  Charlotte *(G-2660)*
Gray Manufacturing Tech LLC................ F 704 489-2206
  Denver *(G-4778)*
Harrah Enterprise Ltd............................. G 336 253-3963
  Cornelius *(G-4554)*
Irvan-Smith Inc.. F 704 788-2554
  Concord *(G-4290)*
Off Road Addiction.................................. G 910 620-4675
  Fayetteville *(G-5885)*
Performance Entps & Parts Inc............... G 336 621-6572
  Greensboro *(G-7251)*
Revmax Performance LLC..................... F 877 780-4334
  Charlotte *(G-3440)*

BOILER REPAIR SHOP

Chicago Tube and Iron Company........... D 704 781-2060
  Locust *(G-9956)*

BOILERS & BOILER SHOP WORK

Icon Boiler Inc... E 844 562-4266
  Greensboro *(G-7110)*

BOILERS: Low-Pressure Heating, Steam Or Hot Water

Marley-Wylain Company.......................... C 336 627-6000
  Eden *(G-5497)*

BOLTS: Metal

Cardinal America Inc.............................. G 704 810-1620
  Statesville *(G-14771)*
Derita Precision Mch Co Inc.................... F 704 392-7285
  Charlotte *(G-2620)*
Metal Processors Inc.............................. F 336 993-2181
  Kernersville *(G-9216)*
Moore S Welding Service Inc................. G 919 837-5769
  Bear Creek *(G-940)*

BOOK STORES

Dobbins Products.................................... G 919 580-0621
  Goldsboro *(G-6610)*
Free Will Bptst Press Fndtion.................. F 252 746-6128
  Ayden *(G-852)*
Good Will Publishers Inc........................ D 704 853-3567
  Gastonia *(G-6408)*
Grateful Steps Foundation...................... G 828 277-0998
  Asheville *(G-639)*

BOOK STORES: Children's

Idea People Inc...................................... G 704 398-4437
  Huntersville *(G-8833)*

BOOKS, WHOLESALE

Book Lover Search.................................. G 336 889-6127
  High Point *(G-8274)*
Cherokee Publications............................ G 828 627-2424
  Cherokee *(G-3854)*
Gryphon House Inc................................ E 800 638-0928
  Lewisville *(G-9667)*
Wisdom House Books Inc...................... G 919 883-4669
  Chapel Hill *(G-2098)*

BOOTHS: Spray, Sheet Metal, Prefabricated

Carolina Custom Booth Co LLC............. E 336 886-3127
  High Point *(G-8285)*
L6 Realty LLC... G 704 654-3000
  Charlotte *(G-3067)*
Production Systems Inc.......................... E 336 886-7161
  High Point *(G-8499)*
Standard Tools and Eqp Co.................... E 336 697-7177
  Greensboro *(G-7366)*
Superior Finishing Systems LLC............. G 336 956-2000
  Lexington *(G-9788)*
Triad Welding Contractors Inc................. G 336 882-3902
  Clemmons *(G-4063)*

BOOTS: Men's

McRae Industries Inc............................. E 910 439-6147
  Mount Gilead *(G-11606)*

BOTTLED GAS DEALERS: Liquefied Petro, Dlvrd To Customers

Euliss Oil Company Inc........................... G 336 622-3055
  Liberty *(G-9813)*

BOTTLED GAS DEALERS: Propane

Blossman Propane Gas & Appl.............. F 828 396-0144
  Hickory *(G-7950)*
Parker Gas Company Inc........................ F 800 354-7250
  Clinton *(G-4101)*

BOTTLES: Plastic

Amcor Phrm Packg USA LLC................. D 919 556-9715
  Youngsville *(G-17066)*
CKS Packaging Inc................................ D 336 578-5800
  Graham *(G-6685)*
Intertech Corporation.............................. D 336 621-1891
  Greensboro *(G-7120)*
Mesa International.................................. G 207 774-5946
  Thomasville *(G-15247)*
Precision Concepts Intl LLC.................... G 704 360-8923
  Mooresville *(G-11058)*
Sonoco Products Company.................... G 910 455-6903
  Jacksonville *(G-9034)*
Southeastern Container Inc.................... C 828 350-7200
  Enka *(G-5684)*
Vav Plastics Nc LLC............................... G 704 325-9322
  Charlotte *(G-3767)*

BOX & CARTON MANUFACTURING EQPT

W V Doyle Enterprises Inc...................... G 336 885-2035
  High Point *(G-8600)*

BOXES & CRATES: Rectangular, Wood

M O Deviney Lumber Co Inc.................. G 704 538-9071
  Casar *(G-1934)*
McBride Lumber Co Partnr LLC............. F 910 428-2747
  Star *(G-14721)*
Moorecraft Wood Proucts Inc.................. G 252 823-2510
  Tarboro *(G-15116)*

BOXES & SHOOK: Nailed Wood

Arcola Lumber Company Inc................. E 252 257-4923
  Warrenton *(G-15655)*
Arcola Sawmill.. G 252 257-1139
  Warrenton *(G-15656)*
Carolina WD Pdts Mrshville Inc.............. D 704 624-2119
  Marshville *(G-10211)*
Clemmons Pallet Skid Works Inc............ E 336 766-5462
  Clemmons *(G-4034)*
Spartacraft Inc... E 828 397-4630
  Connelly Springs *(G-4409)*
Timberline Acquisition LLC.................... E 252 492-6144
  Henderson *(G-7814)*
Universal Forest Products Inc................. F 252 338-0319
  Elizabeth City *(G-5580)*

BOXES: Cash & Stamp, Stamped Metal

Umi Company Inc.................................... G 704 479-6210
  Lincolnton *(G-9932)*

BOXES: Corrugated

3d Packaging LLC................................... F 336 625-0652
  Asheboro *(G-397)*
Archer Box Company.............................. F 336 788-1910
  Winston Salem *(G-16607)*
Axis Corrugated Container LLC.............. F 919 575-0500
  Butner *(G-1541)*
Carolina Container Company.................. D 336 883-7146
  High Point *(G-8284)*
Carolina Container LLC.......................... F 828 322-3380
  Hickory *(G-7963)*
Carolina Container LLC.......................... F 910 277-0400
  Laurinburg *(G-9471)*
Carolina Packaging & Sup Inc................ D 919 201-5592
  Raleigh *(G-12600)*
Corney Transportation Inc...................... E 800 354-9111
  Saint Pauls *(G-13904)*
Custom Corrugated Cntrs Inc.................. E 704 588-0371
  Charlotte *(G-2589)*
Ds Smith PLC... E 919 557-3148
  Holly Springs *(G-8696)*
Ferguson & Company LLC..................... G 704 332-4396
  Charlotte *(G-2752)*
Ferguson Box.. E 704 597-0310
  Charlotte *(G-2753)*
Ferguson Supply and Box Mfg Co.......... D 704 597-0310
  Charlotte *(G-2754)*
Freeman Container Company Inc........... G 704 922-7972
  Dallas *(G-4641)*
Georgia Pratt Box Inc.............................. C 919 872-3007
  Raleigh *(G-12796)*
Georgia-Pacific LLC................................ C 336 629-2151
  Asheboro *(G-440)*
Highland Containers Inc........................ C 336 887-5400
  Jamestown *(G-9054)*
Highland Containers Inc........................ C 336 887-5400
  Jamestown *(G-9053)*
Industrial Container Corp........................ F 336 886-7031
  High Point *(G-8408)*
Inter-Continental Corporation.................. D 828 464-8250
  Newton *(G-11945)*
International Paper Company.................. G 704 588-8522
  Charlotte *(G-2987)*
International Paper Company.................. D 910 738-6214
  Lumberton *(G-10041)*
International Paper Company.................. G 252 456-3111
  Manson *(G-10124)*

BOXES: Corrugated

International Paper Company............... G 252 633-7407
   New Bern *(G-11811)*

Jackson Corrugated LLC.................... D 828 608-0931
   Morganton *(G-11223)*

Lone Star Container Sales Corp............ D 704 588-1737
   Charlotte *(G-3102)*

Package Craft LLC............................... E 252 825-0111
   Bethel *(G-1090)*

Package Crafters Incorporated.............. D 336 431-9700
   High Point *(G-8473)*

Packaging Corporation America............. G 252 753-8450
   Farmville *(G-5741)*

Packaging Corporation America............. G 336 434-0600
   Goldsboro *(G-6642)*

Packaging Corporation America............. F 704 664-5010
   Mooresville *(G-11046)*

Packaging Corporation America............. D 828 584-1511
   Morganton *(G-11241)*

Packaging Corporation America............. E 828 286-9156
   Rutherfordton *(G-13881)*

Packaging Corporation America............. D 704 633-3611
   Salisbury *(G-14023)*

Packaging Corporation America............. D 336 434-0600
   Trinity *(G-15352)*

Packaging Unlimited NC Inc.................. D 704 732-7100
   Lincolnton *(G-9912)*

Paperworks Industries Inc.................... C 910 439-6137
   Mount Gilead *(G-11611)*

Paperworks Industries Inc.................... C 336 447-7278
   Whitsett *(G-15998)*

Piedmont Corrugated Specialty.............. D 828 874-1153
   Valdese *(G-15452)*

Piedmont Packaging Inc........................ G 336 886-5043
   High Point *(G-8482)*

Pratt (jet Corr) Inc............................... A 704 878-6615
   Statesville *(G-14865)*

Pratt Industries.................................... F 704 864-4022
   Gastonia *(G-6494)*

Pratt Industries Inc.............................. G 919 334-7400
   Raleigh *(G-13131)*

Pratt Industries Inc.............................. B 704 878-6615
   Statesville *(G-14866)*

Stronghaven Incorporated..................... D 770 739-6080
   Matthews *(G-10294)*

Sumter Packaging Corporation............... G 704 873-0583
   Statesville *(G-14908)*

Sun & Surf Containers Inc.................... G 910 754-9600
   Shallotte *(G-14279)*

Westrock - Southern Cont LLC............... D 704 662-8496
   Mooresville *(G-11128)*

Westrock Company............................... G 470 484-1183
   Claremont *(G-3943)*

Westrock Company............................... G 828 248-4815
   Forest City *(G-6087)*

Westrock Converting LLC...................... B 828 245-9871
   Forest City *(G-6088)*

Westrock Converting LLC...................... G 336 661-1700
   Winston Salem *(G-16972)*

Westrock Paper and Packg LLC.............. C 919 463-3100
   Morrisville *(G-11466)*

Westrock Rkt LLC................................ G 828 655-1303
   Marion *(G-10186)*

Westrock Rkt LLC................................ E 704 662-8494
   Mooresville *(G-11129)*

Westrock Rkt LLC................................ E 336 661-1700
   Winston Salem *(G-16973)*

Weyerhaeuser Company......................... G 253 924-2345
   Charlotte *(G-3808)*

Wilmington Box Company....................... E 910 259-0402
   Burgaw *(G-1358)*

Wrkco Inc... G 828 287-9430
   Rutherfordton *(G-13903)*

BOXES: Junction, Electric

Austin Company of Greensboro............... C 336 468-2851
   Yadkinville *(G-17031)*

BOXES: Paperboard, Folding

A Klein & Co Inc.................................. C 828 459-9261
   Claremont *(G-3899)*

Caraustar Brlngton Rgid Box In............... E 336 226-1616
   Burlington *(G-1383)*

Caraustar Cstm Packg Group Inc............. C 336 498-2631
   Randleman *(G-13455)*

Container Systems Incorporated............. D 919 496-6133
   Franklinton *(G-6153)*

Graphic Packaging Intl LLC..................... C 704 588-1750
   Charlotte *(G-2856)*

Graphic Packaging Intl LLC..................... D 336 744-1222
   Winston Salem *(G-16728)*

Kme Consolidated Inc........................... E 704 847-9888
   Matthews *(G-10260)*

Max Solutions Inc................................. E 203 683-8094
   Concord *(G-4311)*

Pactiv LLC... G 910 944-1800
   Aberdeen *(G-20)*

Snyder Packaging Inc............................ D 704 786-3111
   Concord *(G-4361)*

Specialized Packaging Radisson LLC........ D 336 574-1513
   Greensboro *(G-7357)*

Thomco Inc... G 336 292-3300
   Greensboro *(G-7401)*

Westrock Rkt LLC................................ C 828 459-8006
   Claremont *(G-3944)*

Westrock Rkt LLC................................ C 828 464-5560
   Conover *(G-4512)*

Westrock Rkt LLC................................ B 770 448-2193
   Marion *(G-10187)*

BOXES: Paperboard, Set-Up

A Klein & Co Inc.................................. C 828 459-9261
   Claremont *(G-3899)*

Caraustar Cstm Packg Group Inc............. C 336 498-2631
   Randleman *(G-13455)*

Caraustar Industries Inc........................ F 336 498-2631
   Randleman *(G-13456)*

Eastcoast Packaging Inc........................ E 919 562-6060
   Middlesex *(G-10447)*

Transylvnia Vcational Svcs Inc................ D 828 884-1548
   Fletcher *(G-6045)*

Transylvnia Vcational Svcs Inc................ C 828 884-3195
   Brevard *(G-1291)*

Westrock Rkt LLC................................ C 828 459-8006
   Claremont *(G-3944)*

Westrock Rkt LLC................................ E 704 662-8494
   Mooresville *(G-11129)*

BOXES: Plastic

Amesbury Group Inc.............................. D 704 978-2883
   Statesville *(G-14748)*

BOXES: Wooden

Carolina Crate & Pallet Inc.................... E 910 245-4001
   Vass *(G-15491)*

BRAKES & BRAKE PARTS

Ceco Friction Products Inc.................... F 704 857-1156
   Landis *(G-9450)*

Continental Auto Systems Inc................. B 828 584-4500
   Morganton *(G-11208)*

Haldex Inc.. C 828 652-9308
   Marion *(G-10150)*

Indian Head Industries Inc.................... D 704 547-7411
   Murphy *(G-11710)*

Indian Head Industries Inc.................... E 704 547-7411
   Charlotte *(G-2961)*

Mann+hmmel Fltrtion Tech Group........... G 704 869-3300
   Gastonia *(G-6449)*

BRAKES: Metal Forming

Delta Phoenix Inc................................. E 336 621-3960
   Greensboro *(G-6966)*

BRASS & BRONZE PRDTS: Die-casted

Carolina Foundry Inc............................ F 704 376-3145
   Charlotte *(G-2396)*

BRAZING: Metal

Zion Industries Inc............................... F 828 397-2701
   Hildebran *(G-8629)*

BRICK, STONE & RELATED PRDTS WHOLESALERS

Custom Brick Company Inc..................... E 919 832-2804
   Raleigh *(G-12663)*

Design Specialties Inc........................... E 919 772-6955
   Raleigh *(G-12678)*

General Shale Brick Inc........................ G 919 775-2121
   Sanford *(G-14124)*

General Shale Brick Inc........................ G 910 452-3498
   Wilmington *(G-16231)*

J&R SERvices/J&r Lumber Co................. G 956 778-7005
   Wilmington *(G-16276)*

Performnce Strl Con Sltons LLC.............. G 980 333-6414
   Davidson *(G-4690)*

Sid Jenkins Inc.................................... G 336 632-0707
   Greensboro *(G-7337)*

BRICKS & BLOCKS: Structural

Forterra Brick LLC............................... C 704 341-8750
   Charlotte *(G-2791)*

General Shale Brick Inc........................ F 704 937-7431
   Grover *(G-7607)*

BRICKS: Paving, Clay

Demilo Bros NC LLC.............................. G 704 771-0762
   Waxhaw *(G-15752)*

BRICKS: Clay

Dudley Inc.. G 704 636-8850
   Salisbury *(G-13955)*

General Shale Brick Inc........................ E 919 775-2121
   Moncure *(G-10622)*

General Shale Brick Inc........................ G 910 452-3498
   Wilmington *(G-16231)*

J L Anderson Co Inc............................. G 704 289-9599
   Monroe *(G-10744)*

Meridian Brick LLC............................... D 704 636-0131
   Salisbury *(G-14013)*

Nash Brick Company............................. E 252 443-4965
   Enfield *(G-5680)*

Statesville Brick Company..................... D 704 872-4123
   Statesville *(G-14901)*

BROADCASTING & COMMS EQPT: Antennas, Transmitting/Comms

CPI Satcom & Antenna Tech Inc.............. C 704 462-7330
   Conover *(G-4440)*

Lba Group Inc..................................... E 252 329-9243
   Greenville *(G-7553)*

Lba Technology Inc.............................. E 252 757-0279
   Greenville *(G-7554)*

Ni4I Antennas and Elec LLC................... G 828 738-6445
   Moravian Falls *(G-11146)*

PRODUCT SECTION

BUILDING PRDTS & MATERIALS DEALERS

Qualia Networks Inc.................................. G 805 637-2083
  Raleigh *(G-13162)*
Rf Das Systems Inc................................... G 980 279-2388
  Charlotte *(G-3446)*

BROADCASTING & COMMS EQPT: Trnsmttng TV Antennas/Grndng Eqpt

Raven Antenna Systems Inc................... C 919 934-9711
  Smithfield *(G-14478)*

BROADCASTING & COMMUNICATIONS EQPT: Cellular Radio Telephone

Serra Wireless Inc.................................... G 980 318-0873
  Charlotte *(G-3529)*

BROADCASTING & COMMUNICATIONS EQPT: Studio Eqpt, Radio & TV

Audio Advice Inc...................................... D 919 881-2005
  Raleigh *(G-12534)*

BROADCASTING STATIONS, RADIO: News

Wtvd Television LLC................................ C 919 683-1111
  Durham *(G-5451)*

BROKERS' SVCS

S P Co Inc... G 919 848-3599
  Raleigh *(G-13222)*

BROKERS: Food

Alta Foods llc... D 919 734-0233
  Goldsboro *(G-6588)*
La Tortilleria LLC..................................... C 336 773-0010
  Winston Salem *(G-16782)*
Value Clothing Inc................................... E 704 638-6111
  Salisbury *(G-14061)*

BROKERS: Printing

Creative Printers & Brks Inc.................... G 828 321-4663
  Andrews *(G-125)*
Esequence Inc... G 919 831-1995
  Raleigh *(G-12747)*
Fast Pro Media LLC................................ G 704 799-8040
  Cornelius *(G-4545)*
Gilmore Globl Lgstics Svcs Inc............... D 919 277-2700
  Morrisville *(G-11347)*
Mjt Us Inc... G 704 826-7828
  Charlotte *(G-3189)*
Randall Printing Inc................................. G 336 272-3333
  Greensboro *(G-7303)*

BRONZE FOUNDRY, NEC

Saueressig North America Inc................ E 336 395-6200
  Burlington *(G-1491)*

BROOMS

Newell Novelty Co Inc............................. G 336 597-2246
  Roxboro *(G-13808)*

BROOMS & BRUSHES

Carolina Brush Company........................ E 704 867-0286
  Gastonia *(G-6366)*
Quickie Manufacturing Corp.................... C 910 737-6500
  Lumberton *(G-10049)*
Shur Line Inc... E 317 442-8850
  Mooresville *(G-11085)*

BROOMS & BRUSHES: Household Or Indl

Carolina Brush Mfg Co............................ E 704 867-0286
  Gastonia *(G-6367)*

Zibra LLC... G 704 271-4503
  Mooresville *(G-11140)*

BROOMS & BRUSHES: Paint & Varnish

Renaissance Innovations LLC................ G 844 473-7246
  Apex *(G-239)*

BROOMS & BRUSHES: Paint Rollers

P&A Indstrial Fabrications LLC............... E 336 322-1766
  Roxboro *(G-13815)*

BROOMS & BRUSHES: Street Sweeping, Hand Or Machine

Tarheel Pavement Clg Svcs Inc.............. F 704 895-8015
  Cornelius *(G-4591)*

BUCKETS: Plastic

Rubbermaid Incorporated....................... A 888 859-8294
  Huntersville *(G-8889)*
Rubbermaid Incorporated....................... A 704 987-4339
  Huntersville *(G-8890)*

BUCKLES & PARTS

Ideal Fastener Corporation..................... C 919 693-3115
  Oxford *(G-12133)*

BUILDING & STRUCTURAL WOOD MEMBERS

C & C Chipping Inc................................. F 252 249-1617
  Grantsboro *(G-6764)*
Capitol Funds Inc.................................... F 910 439-5275
  Mount Gilead *(G-11599)*
Capitol Funds Inc.................................... E 704 487-8547
  Shelby *(G-14291)*
Idaho Timber NC LLC............................. D 252 430-0030
  Henderson *(G-7789)*
Nvr Inc... D 704 484-7170
  Kings Mountain *(G-9320)*
Rafters and Walls LLC............................ E 980 404-0209
  Shelby *(G-14359)*
Smokey Mountain Lumber Inc................ G 828 298-3958
  Asheville *(G-775)*
Trusses R US Inc.................................... G 704 361-7004
  Waxhaw *(G-15784)*
Universal Forest Products Inc................. F 252 338-0319
  Elizabeth City *(G-5580)*

BUILDING CLEANING & MAINTENANCE SVCS

A & B Chem-Dry..................................... F 919 878-0288
  Raleigh *(G-12451)*

BUILDING COMPONENTS: Structural Steel

Asheville Maintenance and C.................. E 828 687-8110
  Arden *(G-312)*
Bet-Mac Wilson Steel Inc........................ G 919 528-1540
  Creedmoor *(G-4606)*
Blacksand Metal Works LLC................... F 703 489-8282
  Fayetteville *(G-5771)*
H T Wade Enterprises Inc....................... F 336 375-8900
  Browns Summit *(G-1307)*
Hercules Steel Company Inc................... F 910 488-5110
  Fayetteville *(G-5837)*
Industrial Metal Products of.................... F 910 944-8110
  Aberdeen *(G-7)*
Maco Inc.. E 704 434-6800
  Shelby *(G-14342)*
McCombs Steel Company Inc................ E 704 873-7563
  Statesville *(G-14840)*

McCune Technology Inc.......................... F 910 424-2978
  Fayetteville *(G-5871)*
North State Steel Inc............................... F 919 496-2506
  Louisburg *(G-9994)*
Nucor Corporation................................... C 704 366-7000
  Charlotte *(G-3281)*
Peak Steel LLC....................................... F 919 362-5955
  Apex *(G-229)*
Performnce Strl Con Sltons LLC............. G 980 333-6414
  Davidson *(G-4690)*
Sanford Steel Corporation...................... F 919 898-4799
  Goldston *(G-6676)*
Southeastern Steel Cnstr Inc.................. F 910 346-4462
  Jacksonville *(G-9036)*
Specialty Manufacturing Inc.................... C 704 247-9300
  Charlotte *(G-3598)*
Steel Specialty Co Belmont Inc.............. E 704 825-4745
  Belmont *(G-1010)*
Steelfab Inc... B 704 394-5376
  Charlotte *(G-3627)*
Structural Steel Products Corp............... D 919 359-2811
  Clayton *(G-4013)*

BUILDING ITEM REPAIR SVCS, MISCELLANEOUS

Western Crlina Tl Mold Corp In............... E 828 890-4448
  Mills River *(G-10514)*

BUILDING MAINTENANCE SVCS, EXC REPAIRS

Asheville Maintenance and C.................. E 828 687-8110
  Arden *(G-312)*

BUILDING PRDTS & MATERIALS DEALERS

Authentic Iron LLC.................................. G 910 648-6989
  Bladenboro *(G-1143)*
Barber Furniture & Supply...................... F 704 278-9367
  Cleveland *(G-4068)*
Bfs Asset Holdings LLC.......................... C 303 784-4288
  Raleigh *(G-12554)*
Builders Firstsource Inc.......................... G 336 884-5454
  Greensboro *(G-6860)*
Builders Frstsrce - Rleigh LLC............... D 919 363-4956
  Apex *(G-174)*
C & R Building Supply Inc...................... E 910 567-6293
  Autryville *(G-840)*
Division 10.. G 919 661-1101
  Raleigh *(G-12689)*
E W Godwin S Sons Inc......................... E 910 762-7747
  Wilmington *(G-16208)*
General Wholesale Bldg Sup Co............ D 252 638-5861
  New Bern *(G-11806)*
GLG Corporation.................................... F 336 784-0396
  Winston Salem *(G-16722)*
Goodman Millwork Inc............................ E 704 633-2421
  Salisbury *(G-13972)*
Interrs-Exteriors Asheboro Inc................ F 336 629-2148
  Asheboro *(G-446)*
Jak Moulding & Supply Inc..................... F 252 753-5546
  Walstonburg *(G-15638)*
M O Deviney Lumber Co Inc.................. G 704 538-9071
  Casar *(G-1934)*
Robbinsville Cstm Molding Inc............... F 828 479-2317
  Robbinsville *(G-13610)*
Salt Wood Products Inc.......................... G 252 830-8875
  Greenville *(G-7581)*
Selectbuild Construction Inc................... E 208 331-4300
  Raleigh *(G-13244)*
Sipe Lumber Company Inc..................... E 828 632-4679
  Taylorsville *(G-15167)*

Employee Codes: A=Over 500 employees, B=251-500
C=101-250, D=51-100, E=20-50, F=10-19, G=1-9

2024 Harris North Carolina
Manufacturers Directory

BUILDING PRDTS & MATERIALS DEALERS — PRODUCT SECTION

Smith Companies Lexington Inc............ G 336 249-4941
  Lexington *(G-9781)*

Sorrells Cabinet Co Inc........................ G 919 639-4320
  Lillington *(G-9860)*

T E Johnson Lumber Co Inc................ F 919 963-2233
  Four Oaks *(G-6113)*

Thomas Concrete SC Inc..................... G 704 868-4545
  Gastonia *(G-6526)*

Yadkin Lumber Company Inc............... F 336 679-2432
  Yadkinville *(G-17064)*

BUILDING PRDTS: Concrete

Greystone Concrete Pdts Inc................ E 252 438-5144
  Henderson *(G-7785)*

BUILDING PRDTS: Stone

Carolina North Granite Corp................. D 336 719-2600
  Mount Airy *(G-11490)*

BUILDINGS & COMPONENTS: Prefabricated Metal

American Carports Structures.............. G 336 710-1091
  Mount Airy *(G-11476)*

American Carports Stuctures............... G 844 628-4973
  Mount Airy *(G-11477)*

Amt/Bcu Inc.. E 336 622-6200
  Liberty *(G-9807)*

Barnyard Utlity Bldngs-Strg/Tl.............. G 704 867-4700
  Gastonia *(G-6351)*

Barnyard Utlity Bldngs-Strg/Tl.............. G 704 226-9454
  Monroe *(G-10660)*

Bennett Buildings of Conover............... G 828 465-6117
  Conover *(G-4422)*

Bluescope Buildings N Amer Inc.......... G 336 996-4801
  Greensboro *(G-6843)*

Buildings R US.................................... G 828 382-0167
  Forest City *(G-6062)*

Carport Central Inc............................. D 980 321-9898
  Mount Airy *(G-11491)*

Carport Commander LLC..................... G 800 688-6151
  Mount Airy *(G-11492)*

Carport Direct Inc............................... G 336 715-8217
  Mount Airy *(G-11493)*

Central States Mfg Inc......................... C 336 719-3280
  Mount Airy *(G-11495)*

CF Steel LLC...................................... G 704 516-1750
  Midland *(G-10460)*

Direct Discount Carports...................... G 888 642-1910
  Mount Airy *(G-11502)*

E A Duncan Cnstr Co Inc..................... G 910 653-3535
  Tabor City *(G-15081)*

Eastcoast Carports.............................. G 336 755-3409
  Mount Airy *(G-11504)*

Express Carport LLC.......................... G 888 389-2485
  Asheville *(G-619)*

Friedrich Metal Pdts Co Inc.................. E 336 375-3067
  Browns Summit *(G-1303)*

Go Ask Erin LLC................................. G 336 747-3777
  Roxboro *(G-13804)*

Heritage Steel LLC.............................. F 704 431-4097
  Salisbury *(G-13978)*

J&J Outdoor Accessories..................... G 910 742-1969
  Delco *(G-4721)*

Lear Metal Carports LLC..................... G 877 219-4677
  Mount Airy *(G-11537)*

Mast Woodworks................................ F 336 468-1194
  Hamptonville *(G-7677)*

McGee Corporation............................. E 980 721-1911
  Matthews *(G-10269)*

McGee Corporation............................. D 704 882-1500
  Matthews *(G-10270)*

Metal Buildings Charlotte..................... G 980 365-6583
  Midland *(G-10471)*

Metallum Structures Inc....................... G 877 517-4422
  Mount Airy *(G-11545)*

Millennium Buildings Inc...................... G 866 216-8499
  Dobson *(G-4829)*

Millennium Mfg Structures LLC............ F 828 265-3737
  Boone *(G-1222)*

Milligan House Movers Inc.................. G 910 653-2272
  Tabor City *(G-15084)*

Morton Buildings Inc........................... G 252 291-1300
  Wilson *(G-16516)*

Nash Building Systems Inc.................. F 252 823-1905
  Tarboro *(G-15118)*

Neals Carpentry & Cnstr..................... G 910 346-6154
  Jacksonville *(G-9017)*

OSteel Buildings Inc........................... F 704 824-6061
  Gastonia *(G-6481)*

Pine View Buildings LLC..................... D 704 876-1501
  Statesville *(G-14860)*

Richfield Prtable Buildings Inc.............. G 704 463-1802
  Richfield *(G-13554)*

Storage System Solutions Inc.............. G 336 710-5600
  Mount Airy *(G-11578)*

T-N-T Carports Inc............................. G 336 789-3818
  Mount Airy *(G-11586)*

Triton Industries LLC........................... F 336 816-3794
  Mount Airy *(G-11591)*

Turner Equipment Company Inc.......... E 919 734-8328
  Goldsboro *(G-6667)*

Twin Carports LLC.............................. F 336 790-8284
  East Bend *(G-5470)*

Twin Carports LLC.............................. G 866 486-3924
  Pilot Mountain *(G-12203)*

Unrivaled Metal Buildings LLC............. G 844 848-8676
  Maiden *(G-10121)*

Viking Steel Structures LLC................. G 877 623-7549
  Boonville *(G-1258)*

Wholesale Direct Carports................... G 336 399-3221
  King *(G-9285)*

BUILDINGS: Mobile, For Commercial Use

Conway Entps Carteret Cnty LLC........ G 252 504-3518
  Beaufort *(G-951)*

BUILDINGS: Portable

Alaska Structures Inc.......................... D 910 323-0562
  Fayetteville *(G-5756)*

Betco Inc... D 704 872-2999
  Statesville *(G-14762)*

Boxman Studios LLC.......................... G 704 333-3733
  Charlotte *(G-2342)*

Camelot Rturn Intrmdate Hldngs.......... D 866 419-0042
  Cary *(G-1721)*

Cardinal Buildings LLC........................ G 919 422-5670
  Garner *(G-6261)*

Classic Steel Buildings Inc.................. G 252 465-4184
  Sunbury *(G-14995)*

Cornerstone Bldg Brands Inc............... B 281 897-7788
  Cary *(G-1736)*

Eagle Carports Inc.............................. E 800 579-8589
  Mount Airy *(G-11503)*

Harvest Homes and Handi Houses....... G 704 637-3878
  Salisbury *(G-13975)*

Harvest Homes and Handi Houses....... G 336 243-2382
  Lexington *(G-9728)*

Heritage Building Company LLC.......... F 704 431-4494
  Statesville *(G-14811)*

Manufacturing Structures LLC.............. G 828 264-6198
  Boone *(G-1217)*

Mayse Manufacturing Co Inc............... G 828 245-1891
  Forest City *(G-6076)*

Mobile Mini - Stor Tanks Pumps.......... G 919 365-0377
  Knightdale *(G-9421)*

Mobile Mini Inc................................... G 480 894-6311
  Knightdale *(G-9422)*

Mobile Mini Inc................................... G 919 365-3057
  Wendell *(G-15908)*

Rogers Manufacturing Company.......... G 910 259-9898
  Burgaw *(G-1349)*

Simonton Windows & Doors Inc.......... D 919 677-3938
  Cary *(G-1890)*

Sunshine Mnfctred Strctres Inc............ E 704 279-6600
  Rockwell *(G-13659)*

US Chemical Storage LLC................... E 828 264-6032
  Wilkesboro *(G-16050)*

Vinyl Structures LLC........................... G 336 468-4311
  Hamptonville *(G-7680)*

BUILDINGS: Prefabricated, Metal

Coastal Machine & Welding Inc........... G 910 754-6476
  Shallotte *(G-14272)*

Leonard Alum Utlity Bldngs Inc............ G 336 226-9410
  Burlington *(G-1450)*

Leonard Alum Utlity Bldngs Inc............ G 919 872-4442
  Raleigh *(G-12968)*

Leonard Alum Utlity Bldngs Inc............ G 910 392-4921
  Wilmington *(G-16299)*

Leonard Alum Utlity Bldngs Inc............ D 336 789-5018
  Mount Airy *(G-11538)*

Nci Group Inc..................................... G 919 926-4800
  Raleigh *(G-13059)*

Nucor Corporation............................... C 704 366-7000
  Charlotte *(G-3281)*

BUILDINGS: Prefabricated, Wood

Deltec Homes Inc............................... E 828 253-0483
  Asheville *(G-607)*

Glennstone Field Office....................... G 919 680-8700
  Durham *(G-5124)*

Johnston County Industries Inc............ C 919 743-8700
  Selma *(G-14257)*

Outlaw Step Co.................................. G 252 568-4384
  Deep Run *(G-4717)*

Quality Housing Corporation................ F 336 274-2622
  Greensboro *(G-7300)*

Tuff Shed Inc..................................... G 919 413-2494
  Morrisville *(G-11458)*

Ufp New London LLC.......................... E 704 463-1400
  New London *(G-11880)*

Wood Right Lumber Company............ G 910 576-4642
  Troy *(G-15420)*

BULLETPROOF VESTS

Arma Co LLC..................................... F 717 295-6805
  Wilmington *(G-16117)*

Greene Mountain Outdoors LLC.......... F 336 670-2186
  North Wilkesboro *(G-12011)*

Premier Body Armor LLC..................... F 704 750-3118
  Gastonia *(G-6497)*

BURIAL VAULTS: Concrete Or Precast Terrazzo

Arnold-Wilbert Corporation.................. D 919 735-5008
  Goldsboro *(G-6592)*

Asheville Vault Service Inc.................. E 828 665-6799
  Candler *(G-1568)*

Best Workers Company....................... G 336 665-0076
  Riegelwood *(G-13557)*

Bryant Grant Mutual Burial Asn........... G 828 524-2411
  Franklin *(G-6117)*

Carolina Cemetery Park Corp.............. G 704 528-5543
  Troutman *(G-15369)*

| PRODUCT SECTION | | BUSINESS FORMS WHOLESALERS |

Eastern Carolina Vault Co Inc.................. G 252 243-5614
  Wilson (G-16495)
Hairfield Wilbert Burial Vlt...................... E 828 437-4319
  Morganton (G-11218)
Imperial Vault Company........................ E 336 983-6343
  King (G-9273)
International Vault Inc.......................... E 919 742-3132
  Siler City (G-14417)
Neighborhood Union Burial Soc............ G 252 448-0581
  Trenton (G-15333)
Sentry Vault Service Inc....................... G 252 243-2241
  Elm City (G-5653)
Western Crlina Mutl Brial Assn.............. G 828 837-2577
  Murphy (G-11718)
Wilbert Burial Vault Company............... E 910 739-7276
  Lumberton (G-10060)
Wilbert Funeral Services Inc................. E 800 828-5879
  Greensboro (G-7461)
Wilbert Yates Vault Co Inc.................... F 704 399-8453
  Charlotte (G-3814)
Wilmington Mortuary Svc Inc................ F 910 791-9099
  Wilmington (G-16449)
WP Simmons Inc................................... F 336 789-3114
  Mount Airy (G-11597)
Yates Wilbert Vault LLC....................... F 704 399-8453
  Charlotte (G-3843)

BURNERS: Gas, Indl

Flynn Burner Corporation..................... E 704 660-1500
  Mooresville (G-10947)

BUS BARS: Electrical

M & M Electric Service Inc................... E 704 867-0221
  Gastonia (G-6448)

BUSHINGS & BEARINGS

ABB Motors and Mechanical Inc........... C 828 645-1706
  Weaverville (G-15836)
Zwz Bearing USA Inc........................... E 734 456-6206
  Lincolnton (G-9937)

BUSINESS ACTIVITIES: Non-Commercial Site

Abercrombie Textiles Inc..................... G 704 487-0935
  Shelby (G-14281)
Aj & Raine Scrubs & More LLC............ G 646 374-5198
  Charlotte (G-2149)
Allfuel Hst Inc...................................... F 919 868-9410
  Hampstead (G-7636)
Arisaka LLC... F 919 601-5629
  Apex (G-165)
C&A Hockaday Transport LLC.............. G 252 676-5956
  Roanoke Rapids (G-13570)
Carolina Coastal Coatings Inc............... F 910 346-9607
  Maple Hill (G-10131)
Champion Thread Company................. G 704 867-6611
  Gastonia (G-6375)
Charlies Heating & Cooling LLC........... G 336 260-1973
  Snow Camp (G-14495)
Council Trnsp & Logistics LLC.............. G 910 322-7588
  Fayetteville (G-5797)
Creative Brewing Company LLC.......... G 919 297-8182
  Smithfield (G-14458)
Cupcake Stop Shop LLC..................... G 919 457-7900
  Raleigh (G-12661)
Danby Barcoding LLC.......................... G 770 416-9845
  Kernersville (G-9187)
Davie Property Restoration LLC........... G 336 923-4018
  Advance (G-40)
Day 3 Lwncare Ldscpg Prfctnist.......... G 910 574-8422
  Fayetteville (G-5806)

DB CUSTOM CRAFTS LLC................. F 336 791-0940
  Winston Salem (G-16674)
DMD Logistics LLC............................... G 336 480-8149
  Winston Salem (G-16685)
Drs Transportation Inc.......................... G 919 215-2770
  Raleigh (G-12704)
Eatclub Inc... G 609 578-7942
  Chapel Hill (G-2011)
Elevated Cnstr Renovations LLC.......... G 910 301-4243
  Red Springs (G-13500)
Envirnmntal Cmfort Sltions Inc............. E 980 272-7327
  Kannapolis (G-9119)
Every Day Carry LLc............................ F 203 231-0256
  Winnabow (G-16580)
Exteriors Inc Ltd.................................. G 919 325-2251
  Spring Lake (G-14625)
Forward Dsptching Lgistics LLC........... G 252 907-9797
  Greenville (G-7527)
Frostie Bottom Tree Stand LLC........... G 828 466-1708
  Claremont (G-3927)
Galaxy Pressure Washing Inc.............. G 888 299-3129
  Pineville (G-12270)
Galvix Inc... G 925 434-6243
  Cary (G-1770)
Gentrys Cabnt Doors........................... G 336 957-8787
  Roaring River (G-13593)
Georges Sauces LLC.......................... G 252 459-3084
  Nashville (G-11745)
Go For Green Fleet Svcs LLC.............. G 803 306-3683
  Charlotte (G-2840)
Gracefully Broken LLC......................... G 980 474-0309
  Charlotte (G-2851)
Greenfield Energy LLC......................... F 910 509-1805
  Wrightsville Beach (G-17025)
Gt Rhyno Construction LLC................. G 919 737-3620
  Raleigh (G-12824)
Imperial Falcon Group Inc.................... G 646 717-1128
  Charlotte (G-2953)
Inspiration Leather Design Inc.............. G 336 420-2265
  Jamestown (G-9058)
Intersport Group Inc............................. G 814 968-3085
  Vilas (G-15496)
J &D Contractor Service Inc................ G 919 427-0218
  Angier (G-142)
J6 & Company LLC.............................. F 336 997-4497
  Winston Salem (G-16767)
Just Black LLC.................................... G 252 204-5437
  Gastonia (G-6436)
Kenn M LLC.. G 678 755-6607
  Raleigh (G-12935)
Klearoptics Inc.................................... G 760 224-6770
  Lattimore (G-9457)
Livengood Innovations LLC................. G 336 925-7604
  Linwood (G-9946)
Luxor Hydration LLC............................ F 919 568-5047
  Durham (G-5200)
Make Solutions Inc.............................. F 623 444-0098
  Asheville (G-694)
Merchant 1 Manufacturing LLC............ G 336 617-3008
  Summerfield (G-14989)
Modern Structure Solutions LLC.......... G 984 286-2447
  Hudson (G-8776)
Mountain Homes of Wnc LLC.............. F 828 216-2546
  Weaverville (G-15852)
N3xt Inc... G 704 905-2209
  Charlotte (G-3227)
Nafshi Enterprises LLC........................ G 910 986-9888
  Aberdeen (G-17)
NC Diesel Performance LLC................ G 704 431-3257
  Salisbury (G-14016)
Ni4I Antennas and Elec LLC................ G 828 738-6445
  Moravian Falls (G-11146)

North American Trade LLC.................. G 828 712-3004
  Fletcher (G-6030)
Northern Star Technologies Inc........... G 516 353-3333
  Indian Trail (G-8952)
Ocufii Inc... G 804 874-4036
  Huntersville (G-8869)
Pampering Moms Ntral Skin Care........ G 706 490-3083
  Raleigh (G-13098)
Paper Route Transportation LLC......... G 919 478-6615
  Sanford (G-14162)
Performance Additives LLC.................. F 215 321-4388
  Southern Pines (G-14543)
Performance Parts Intl LLC.................. F 704 660-1084
  Mooresville (G-11052)
Personal Xpressionz LLC..................... G 919 587-7462
  Durham (G-5282)
Power and Ctrl Solutions LLC.............. G 704 609-9623
  Charlotte (G-3359)
Prototech Manufacturing Inc................ F 508 646-8849
  Washington (G-15728)
Queen Wrist Bling Inc.......................... G 980 635-0287
  Concord (G-4345)
Quinlan Publishing Company................ G 229 886-7995
  Wilmington (G-16374)
Random & Kind LLC............................ G 919 249-8809
  Durham (G-5319)
Rebecca Trickey................................. G 910 584-5549
  Raeford (G-12435)
Richards Southern Soul Fd LLC........... G 919 210-8275
  Raleigh (G-13207)
Sakun Inc.. G 919 255-2994
  Cary (G-1878)
Scoggins Industrial Inc......................... F 252 977-9222
  Sharpsburg (G-14280)
Secured Shred..................................... G 443 288-6375
  Raleigh (G-13243)
Serenity Home Services LLC............... G 910 233-8733
  Troutman (G-15393)
Sg-Clw Inc... F 336 865-4980
  Winston Salem (G-16903)
Sign Shop of The Triangle Inc.............. G 919 363-3930
  Apex (G-242)
Smissons Inc....................................... G 660 537-3219
  Clayton (G-4009)
Sml Transportation LLC....................... G 704 402-6744
  Harmony (G-7689)
Sweet Treats By Treat Lady LLC......... G 336 831-3282
  Winston Salem (G-16928)
Tailored Visionz & Dreamz LLC............ G 919 340-3613
  Hollister (G-8677)
Three Ladies and A Male LLC.............. G 704 287-1584
  Charlotte (G-3691)
Triangle Prcsion Dgnostics Inc............. G 919 345-0110
  Durham (G-5409)
Tryhard Infinity LLC............................. G 252 269-0985
  New Bern (G-11852)
Viiv Healthcare Company..................... A 919 483-2100
  Durham (G-5434)
Vital Being.. G 828 964-5853
  Zionville (G-17149)
White Tiger Btq & Candle Co............... G 919 610-7244
  Sanford (G-14205)
WW&s Construction Inc...................... G 217 620-4042
  Dallas (G-4661)
Z Collection LLC.................................. G 919 247-1513
  Zebulon (G-17147)
Zelaya Bros LLC.................................. G 980 833-0099
  Charlotte (G-3850)
Zysense LLC....................................... G 215 485-1955
  Chapel Hill (G-2105)

Employee Codes: A=Over 500 employees, B=251-500
C=101-250, D=51-100, E=20-50, F=10-19, G=1-9

2024 Harris North Carolina Manufacturers Directory

BUSINESS FORMS WHOLESALERS

BUSINESS FORMS WHOLESALERS

Austin Business Forms Inc................... F 704 821-6165
Indian Trail *(G-8922)*

Consolidated Press Inc..................... G 704 372-6785
Charlotte *(G-2541)*

Gbf Inc................................... D 336 665-0205
High Point *(G-8363)*

S Ruppe Inc............................... E 828 287-4936
Rutherfordton *(G-13889)*

Taylor Business Forms Inc.................. G 336 667-0300
North Wilkesboro *(G-12034)*

BUSINESS FORMS: Printed, Manifold

American Forms Mfg Inc..................... E 704 866-9139
Gastonia *(G-6345)*

Apperson Inc............................... E 704 399-2571
Charlotte *(G-2203)*

Fain Enterprises Inc....................... F 336 724-0417
Winston Salem *(G-16705)*

Golf Associates Advertising Co.............. E 828 252-6544
Asheville *(G-637)*

Holley Selinda............................. G 919 351-9466
Raleigh *(G-12851)*

Print Haus Inc............................. G 828 456-8622
Waynesville *(G-15817)*

R R Donnelley & Sons Company............... G 704 864-5717
Gastonia *(G-6501)*

Reynolds and Reynolds Company............... G 321 287-3939
Charlotte *(G-3445)*

S Ruppe Inc............................... E 828 287-4936
Rutherfordton *(G-13889)*

Taylor Communications Inc................... F 336 841-7700
High Point *(G-8564)*

Taylor Communications Inc................... E 704 282-0989
Monroe *(G-10820)*

BUSINESS TRAINING SVCS

Training Industry Inc...................... D 919 653-4990
Raleigh *(G-13356)*

CABINETS & CASES: Show, Display & Storage, Exc Wood

Forbes Custom Cabinets LLC.................. E 919 362-4277
Apex *(G-192)*

Friedrich Metal Pdts Co Inc................. E 336 375-3067
Browns Summit *(G-1303)*

CABINETS: Bathroom Vanities, Wood

Allen & Son S Cabinet Shop Inc.............. G 919 963-2196
Four Oaks *(G-6099)*

American Woodmark Corporation............... G 540 665-9100
Stoneville *(G-14953)*

B & L Custom Cabinets Inc................... F 704 857-1940
Westfield *(G-15950)*

Designer Woodwork.......................... G 910 521-1252
Pembroke *(G-12182)*

Mike Powell Inc............................ F 910 792-6152
Wilmington *(G-16324)*

Oyama Cabinet Inc.......................... G 828 327-2668
Conover *(G-4477)*

Riverview Cabinet & Supply Inc.............. G 336 228-1486
Burlington *(G-1486)*

TS Woodworks & RAD Design Inc............... F 704 238-1015
Monroe *(G-10824)*

CABINETS: Entertainment

Distinctive Cabinets Inc.................... F 704 529-6234
Charlotte *(G-2642)*

Mountain Showcase Group Inc................. E 828 692-9494
Hendersonville *(G-7881)*

Quality Custom Woodworks Inc................ G 704 843-1584
Waxhaw *(G-15771)*

Wood Technology Inc........................ E 828 464-8049
Conover *(G-4515)*

CABINETS: Entertainment Units, Household, Wood

Ocean Woodworking Inc...................... G 910 579-2233
Ocean Isle Beach *(G-12094)*

Philip Brady............................... G 336 581-3999
Bennett *(G-1027)*

Sycamore Cabinetry Inc..................... G 704 375-1617
Dallas *(G-4659)*

CABINETS: Factory

Alligood Cabinet Shop...................... G 252 927-3201
Washington *(G-15681)*

AMG Casework LLC........................... F 919 462-9203
Morrisville *(G-11286)*

Bud Baumgarner............................. G 828 256-6230
Hickory *(G-7954)*

Contemporary Design Co LLC.................. F 704 375-6030
Gastonia *(G-6386)*

Drews Cabinets and Cases................... G 919 796-3985
Selma *(G-14254)*

Tice Kitchens & Interiors LLC............... F 919 366-4117
Raleigh *(G-13350)*

Woodsmiths Company......................... F 406 626-3102
Lenoir *(G-9661)*

CABINETS: Kitchen, Metal

Conestoga Wood Spc Corp.................... D 919 284-2258
Kenly *(G-9148)*

Greg Price................................. G 847 778-4426
Hampstead *(G-7648)*

CABINETS: Kitchen, Wood

A Plus Kitchen Bath Cabinets................ G 919 622-0515
Raleigh *(G-12452)*

ABC Cabinetry LLc.......................... G 704 307-8310
Monroe *(G-10633)*

Advance Cabinetry Inc...................... G 828 676-3550
Fletcher *(G-5982)*

Alco Custom Cabinets Inc................... G 919 363-9480
Cary *(G-1678)*

Alexanders Cbinets Countertops.............. G 336 774-2966
Winston Salem *(G-16595)*

American Cabinetry......................... G 704 502-4450
Huntersville *(G-8789)*

American Wood Reface Inc................... G 704 577-2948
Monroe *(G-10645)*

American Wood Reface of Triad............... G 336 345-2837
Kernersville *(G-9164)*

Anders Custom Cabinetry.................... G 828 342-4222
Franklin *(G-6115)*

Angell Crafted Cabinetry................... G 336 655-7735
Germanton *(G-6550)*

Artistic Kitchens & Baths LLC............... G 910 692-4000
Southern Pines *(G-14527)*

Asheville Custom Closets................... G 828 337-7539
Asheville *(G-534)*

Ashleys Kit Bath Dsign Stdio L............... F 828 669-5281
Black Mountain *(G-1119)*

Aspen Cabinetry Inc........................ G 828 466-0216
Conover *(G-4419)*

Atlantic Coast Cabinet Distrs............... E 919 554-8165
Youngsville *(G-17068)*

Barber Furniture & Supply................... F 704 278-9367
Cleveland *(G-4068)*

Bcac Holdings LLC.......................... G 910 754-5689
Supply *(G-15006)*

Belvedere Cabinets Inc..................... G 919 949-2005
Cary *(G-1701)*

Bill Truitt Wood Works Inc.................. G 704 398-8499
Charlotte *(G-2311)*

Black Rock Granite & Cabinetry............... G 828 787-1100
Highlands *(G-8612)*

Blue Ridge Cab Connection LLC............... G 828 891-2281
Mills River *(G-10500)*

Brandon Hilbert............................ F 704 243-5593
Waxhaw *(G-15747)*

Brown Cabinet Co........................... G 704 933-2731
Kannapolis *(G-9113)*

Burlington Distributing Co.................. G 336 292-1415
Greensboro *(G-6862)*

Busbin Cabinetry........................... G 704 560-4485
Belmont *(G-976)*

C & F Custom Cabinets Inc................... E 910 424-7475
Hope Mills *(G-8733)*

C and L Cabinets LLC....................... G 828 550-9820
Canton *(G-1604)*

Cabinet Connection of NC Inc................ G 919 653-1300
Apex *(G-175)*

Cabinet Creations Inc...................... G 919 542-3722
Moncure *(G-10616)*

Cabinet Door World LLC..................... F 877 929-2750
Hickory *(G-7958)*

Cabinet Doors For Less..................... G 828 351-3510
Conover *(G-4428)*

Cabinet Guy................................ G 919 375-4559
Zebulon *(G-17123)*

Cabinet King Refinishing................... G 704 241-6405
Mint Hill *(G-10525)*

Cabinet Makers Inc......................... E 704 876-2808
Statesville *(G-14769)*

Cabinet Man Cabinetry...................... G 336 382-0879
Denton *(G-4727)*

Cabinet Masters and More LLC................ G 828 396-1881
Granite Falls *(G-6725)*

Cabinet Plus............................... G 917 698-7708
Huntersville *(G-8799)*

Cabinet Sales LLC.......................... G 919 604-9536
Raleigh *(G-12583)*

Cabinet Shop Inc........................... G 252 726-6965
Morehead City *(G-11156)*

Cabinet Solutions Usa Inc................... E 828 358-2349
Hickory *(G-7959)*

Cabinet Transitions Inc.................... G 336 382-7154
Greensboro *(G-6874)*

Cabinetry Squared.......................... G 919 589-7253
Willow Spring *(G-16077)*

Cabinets 4 U LLC........................... G 919 291-4617
Hillsborough *(G-8641)*

Cabinets and Things........................ G 828 652-1734
Union Mills *(G-15439)*

Cabinets Plus Inc.......................... B 718 213-3300
Charlotte *(G-2373)*

Cabinets Trim and More..................... G 704 680-7076
Concord *(G-4219)*

Cabinetworks Group Mich LLC................. E 803 984-2285
Charlotte *(G-2374)*

Cabinetworks Group Mich LLC................. E 919 868-8174
Raleigh *(G-12584)*

Caldwell Cabinets NC LLC................... E 828 212-0000
Hudson *(G-8765)*

Cape Fear Cabinet Co Inc................... F 910 703-8760
Fayetteville *(G-5778)*

Capefear Woodworks......................... G 910 988-3306
Leland *(G-9533)*

Cardinal Cabinetworks Inc.................. G 919 829-3634
Raleigh *(G-12594)*

Carocraft Cabinets Inc..................... E 704 376-0022
Charlotte *(G-2391)*

PRODUCT SECTION

CABINETS: Kitchen, Wood

Carolina Cab Specialist LLC .... G 919 818-4375
　Cary *(G-1724)*

Carolina Cabinets of Cedar Pt .... G 252 393-6236
　Swansboro *(G-15042)*

Carolina Creative Cabinets Inc .... G 919 842-2060
　Sanford *(G-14097)*

Carolina Custom Cabinetry .... G 704 808-1225
　Waxhaw *(G-15750)*

Carolina Custom Cabinets .... G 910 525-3096
　Roseboro *(G-13783)*

Carolina Custom Cabinets Inc .... G 252 491-5475
　Powells Point *(G-12396)*

Carolina Surfaces LLC .... G 910 874-1335
　Elizabethtown *(G-5591)*

Carolinas Top Shelf Cust Cabn .... G 704 376-5844
　Charlotte *(G-2414)*

Case Green Cabinetry .... G 828 620-9730
　Asheville *(G-585)*

Casework Etc Inc .... G 910 763-7119
　Wilmington *(G-16160)*

Charlotte Cabinetry LLC .... G 704 966-2500
　Gastonia *(G-6376)*

Chesnick Corporation .... F 919 231-2899
　Raleigh *(G-12619)*

Clemmons Hardwoods Cabinet Sp .... G 336 773-0551
　Winston Salem *(G-16654)*

Coastal Cabinetry Inc .... G 910 367-8864
　Shallotte *(G-14271)*

Coastal Cabinets & Granite LLC .... G 252 717-0611
　Simpson *(G-14437)*

Coastal Cabinets of New Bern .... G 252 514-5030
　New Bern *(G-11789)*

Cold Mtn Cabinetry .... G 828 577-8582
　Horse Shoe *(G-8739)*

Colonial Cabinets LLC .... G 910 579-2954
　Calabash *(G-1553)*

Comm-Kab Inc .... F 336 873-8787
　Asheboro *(G-417)*

Commercial Property LLC .... E 336 818-1078
　North Wilkesboro *(G-12002)*

Concord Custom Cabinets .... G 704 773-0081
　Concord *(G-4239)*

Conestoga Wood Spc Corp .... D 919 284-2258
　Kenly *(G-9148)*

Corilam Fabricating Co .... E 336 993-2371
　Kernersville *(G-9182)*

Cornerstone Kitchens Inc .... G 919 510-4200
　Raleigh *(G-12648)*

Cotner Cabinet .... G 336 498-6199
　Randleman *(G-13460)*

Cotner Cabinet .... G 336 672-1560
　Sophia *(G-14514)*

Covenantmade LLC .... F 336 434-4725
　Archdale *(G-275)*

Craft Woodwork Inc .... G 252 237-7581
　Wilson *(G-16490)*

Craigscabinet .... G 919 219-3970
　Clayton *(G-3970)*

Creations Cabinetry Design LLC .... G 919 865-5979
　Raleigh *(G-12653)*

Creative Closets and Cabinetry .... G 570 952-1702
　Ocean Isle Beach *(G-12089)*

Creative Woodcrafters Inc .... G 828 252-9663
　Leicester *(G-9509)*

CTS Custom Cabinets .... G 704 376-5844
　Charlotte *(G-2582)*

Custom Cabinet Works .... G 828 396-6348
　Granite Falls *(G-6730)*

Custom Cabinets & Rmdlg Inc .... G 828 264-1806
　Boone *(G-1191)*

Custom Cabinets By Livengood .... G 704 279-3031
　Salisbury *(G-13950)*

Custom Marble Corporation .... G 910 215-0679
　Pinehurst *(G-12219)*

Custom Surfaces Corporation .... G 252 638-3800
　New Bern *(G-11796)*

Cut Above Construction .... G 828 758-8557
　Lenoir *(G-9602)*

Cynthia Saar .... G 910 480-2523
　Stedman *(G-14934)*

D & L Cabinets Inc .... F 336 376-6009
　Graham *(G-6687)*

Dante Cabinets .... G 919 306-3261
　Durham *(G-5046)*

Darrell Scott Carriker .... G 704 201-7465
　Midland *(G-10466)*

Dash Cabinet Company LLC .... G 704 746-7382
　Cornelius *(G-4538)*

Davis Cabinet Co Wilson Inc .... F 252 291-9052
　Sims *(G-14441)*

Davis Custom Cabinets .... G 336 961-2817
　Yadkinville *(G-17036)*

De Little Cabinet Inc .... G 704 888-5994
　Stanfield *(G-14677)*

Decima Corporation LLC .... E 734 516-1535
　Charlotte *(G-2610)*

Distinctive Cabinets Inc .... F 704 529-6234
　Charlotte *(G-2642)*

Doin It Rght Cbnetry More LLC .... G 980 297-3116
　Denver *(G-4774)*

Downeast Cabinets William Brya .... G 252 414-7730
　Winterville *(G-16999)*

Dublin Woodwork Shop .... G 910 862-2289
　Dublin *(G-4837)*

Duocraft Cabinets & Dist Co .... G 252 240-1476
　Morehead City *(G-11169)*

Eastcarolinacustomcabinets .... G 757 450-7385
　Moyock *(G-11696)*

Eastern Cabinet Company Inc .... G 252 237-5245
　Wilson *(G-16494)*

Eastern Cabinet Installers Inc .... G 336 774-2966
　Winston Salem *(G-16690)*

Eno Mt Cabinets James Ray .... G 919 644-1981
　Hillsborough *(G-8649)*

Eudys Cabinet Manufacturing .... E 704 888-4454
　Stanfield *(G-14678)*

Expressions Cabinetry LLC .... G 828 278-7999
　Fletcher *(G-6003)*

Ferguson Cabinet Works .... G 828 433-8710
　Morganton *(G-11213)*

Firehouse Cabinets .... G 704 689-5243
　Belmont *(G-990)*

Gate City Kitchens LLC .... G 336 378-0870
　Greensboro *(G-7031)*

Gentrys Cabnt Doors .... G 336 957-8787
　Roaring River *(G-13593)*

Goembel Inc .... F 919 303-0485
　Apex *(G-196)*

Gonzalez Cab Installers LLC .... G 336 897-1046
　Greensboro *(G-7052)*

Grove Cabinet LLC .... G 828 575-4463
　Fairview *(G-5711)*

H Brothers Fine Wdwkg LLC .... G 931 216-1955
　Zebulon *(G-17131)*

Hager Cabinet Works John E Hag .... G 704 799-8113
　Mooresville *(G-10969)*

Hans Krug .... E 704 370-0809
　Charlotte *(G-2884)*

Hargenrader Cstm Woodcraft LLC .... G 828 896-7182
　Hickory *(G-8038)*

Harris Custom Cabinetry LLC .... G 828 289-5620
　Rutherfordton *(G-13876)*

Henderson & Kirkland Inc .... G 252 355-0224
　Winterville *(G-17002)*

Heritage Cabinet Company Inc .... F 252 648-8151
　Morehead City *(G-11176)*

Hester Cabinets .... G 336 376-0186
　Graham *(G-6691)*

Hollingsworth Custom Shop .... G 910 251-8849
　Castle Hayne *(G-1951)*

Hollingswrth Cbnets Intrors LL .... F 910 251-1490
　Castle Hayne *(G-1952)*

Home Imprv Solutions NC LLC .... G 919 876-3230
　Raleigh *(G-12856)*

Hometown Cabinets Inc .... G 919 245-3554
　Hillsborough *(G-8654)*

Honeycutt Custom Cabinets Inc .... E 910 567-6766
　Autryville *(G-841)*

Idx Impressions LLC .... C 703 550-6902
　Washington *(G-15711)*

In Style Kitchen Cabinetry .... G 336 769-9605
　Winston Salem *(G-16756)*

Innovative Custom Cabinets Inc .... G 813 748-0655
　Kannapolis *(G-9124)*

Innovative Kitchens Baths Inc .... G 336 279-1188
　Greensboro *(G-7117)*

International Cabinetry Inc .... G 828 393-7998
　Hendersonville *(G-7866)*

Island Wood Crafts Ltd .... G 252 473-5363
　Wanchese *(G-15648)*

J & M Cabinet Installers LLC .... G 336 500-7148
　Greensboro *(G-7130)*

J B I Custom Cabinets .... G 910 538-3831
　Wilmington *(G-16274)*

Johnson Cabinet Co .... G 252 714-2051
　Simpson *(G-14438)*

Jon Mitchell Cabinets .... G 336 229-6261
　Burlington *(G-1442)*

Junes Craftmanship Inc .... G 704 230-0901
　Mooresville *(G-10992)*

Kay & Sons Woodworks Inc .... F 919 556-1060
　Wake Forest *(G-15566)*

KBK Cabinetry Inc .... G 704 506-0088
　Indian Trail *(G-8940)*

Kc Stone Enterprise Inc .... G 704 907-1361
　Indian Trail *(G-8941)*

Kc Stone Inc .... G 704 907-1361
　Matthews *(G-10327)*

Kd Cabinets Inc .... G 828 689-3848
　Marshall *(G-10203)*

Keep Stanly Beautiful Corp .... G 704 982-2649
　Albemarle *(G-92)*

Kens Custom Cabinets Inc .... G 252 637-3378
　New Bern *(G-11815)*

Kitchen Cabinet Designers LLC .... C 919 833-6532
　Raleigh *(G-12943)*

Kitchen Cabinets and Design .... G 828 779-4453
　Asheville *(G-676)*

Kitchen Cabinets of Raleigh .... G 919 291-4397
　Wake Forest *(G-15569)*

Kitchen Masters Charlotte LLC .... F 704 375-3320
　Salisbury *(G-14000)*

Kkb Biltmore Inc .... G 828 274-6711
　Asheville *(G-677)*

Kohnle Cabinetry .... G 828 640-2498
　Hickory *(G-8079)*

Krieger Cabinets Dewayne .... G 704 630-0609
　Salisbury *(G-14002)*

Laborie Sons Cstm Wodworks LLC .... G 910 769-2524
　Wilmington *(G-16293)*

Lakeshore Cabinet .... G 847 508-3594
　Huntersville *(G-8847)*

Larry S Cabinet Shop Inc .... G 252 442-4330
　Rocky Mount *(G-13707)*

Luxemark Company .... G 919 863-0101
　Raleigh *(G-12982)*

CABINETS: Kitchen, Wood

Markraft Cabinets Direct Sales............... G 910 762-1986
   Wilmington *(G-16314)*

Marsh Furniture Company...................... F 336 229-5122
   Graham *(G-6700)*

Marsh Furniture Company...................... F 336 273-8196
   Greensboro *(G-7182)*

Marsh Furniture Company...................... F 336 884-7393
   High Point *(G-8443)*

Marsh Furniture Company...................... G 336 765-7832
   Winston Salem *(G-16801)*

Marsh Furniture Company...................... B 336 884-7363
   High Point *(G-8444)*

Masterbrand Cabinets Inc .... D 252 523-4131
   Kinston *(G-9376)*

Masterbrand Cabinets Inc .... E 765 491-2385
   Lexington *(G-9754)*

McClellan Patric Michael...................... G 336 385-1878
   Creston *(G-4623)*

McDowell County Millwork LLC .... F 828 682-6215
   Marion *(G-10162)*

McFarlin Cabinets................................. G 828 310-9906
   Maiden *(G-10113)*

McLean Precision Cabinetry Inc .... G 910 327-9217
   Sneads Ferry *(G-14492)*

MDN Cabinets Inc................................. G 919 662-1090
   Garner *(G-6285)*

Metro Woodcrafter of Nc Inc .... E 704 394-9622
   Charlotte *(G-3169)*

Mid Carolina Cabinets Inc .... G 704 358-9950
   Matthews *(G-10273)*

Mike S Custom Cabinets Inc .... G 252 224-5351
   Pollocksville *(G-12394)*

Mint Hill Cabinet Shop Inc .... E 704 821-9373
   Monroe *(G-10770)*

Miters Touch Inc .... G 828 963-4445
   Banner Elk *(G-903)*

Morgans Cabinets Inc .... F 704 485-8693
   Oakboro *(G-12078)*

Mountain Cabinetry Closets LLC .... G 828 966-9000
   Brevard *(G-1281)*

Mountain Showcase Group Inc .... E 828 692-9494
   Hendersonville *(G-7881)*

Murphy S Custom Cabinetry Inc .... G 828 891-3050
   Hendersonville *(G-7882)*

Myricks Cabinet Shop Inc .... G 919 266-3720
   Knightdale *(G-9423)*

Nico Solid Maple Cabinets LLC .... G 602 319-2758
   Greensboro *(G-7220)*

Noble Bros Cabinets Mllwk LLC .... G 252 335-1213
   Elizabeth City *(G-5559)*

Noble Bros Cabinets Mllwk LLC .... G 252 482-9100
   Edenton *(G-5520)*

Noles Cabinets Inc................................ F 919 552-4257
   Fuquay Varina *(G-6217)*

Norcraft Companies LP .... C 336 622-4281
   Liberty *(G-9825)*

Normac Kitchens Inc............................. F 704 485-1911
   Oakboro *(G-12079)*

Norman Lake Cabinet Company.............. G 704 498-6647
   Davidson *(G-4688)*

Nuworks.. G 919 223-2587
   Goldsboro *(G-6640)*

Odell Custom Cabinets.......................... G 704 201-6975
   Monroe *(G-10782)*

Organized Cabinet LLC.......................... G 517 402-8639
   Morrisville *(G-11404)*

P R Sparks Enterprises Inc .... G 336 272-7200
   Greensboro *(G-7238)*

Pacific Cabinets................................... G 919 695-3640
   Durham *(G-5267)*

Pb & J Industries Inc .... F 919 661-2738
   Raleigh *(G-13103)*

Pioneer Cabinets Inc............................. G 828 688-2642
   Bakersville *(G-887)*

Port City Cabinets LLC .... G 910 622-0375
   Winnabow *(G-16583)*

Precision Cabinetry Inc.......................... G 828 465-3341
   Newton *(G-11962)*

Precision Cabinets Inc........................... G 828 262-5080
   Boone *(G-1228)*

Premier Kit & Cabinetry Design............... G 910 224-5018
   Aberdeen *(G-22)*

Prestige Millwork Inc............................. F 910 428-2360
   Star *(G-14722)*

Provision Cabinetry.............................. G 336 442-3537
   Archdale *(G-296)*

Quality Cabinets Woodworks.................. G 252 536-0568
   Halifax *(G-7612)*

Raleigh Cabinet Works .... G 919 412-7750
   Raleigh *(G-13174)*

Red House Cabinets LLC .... G 919 201-2101
   Raleigh *(G-13198)*

Robbinsville Cstm Molding Inc .... F 828 479-2317
   Robbinsville *(G-13610)*

Rowan Custom Cabinets Inc................... G 704 855-4778
   China Grove *(G-3888)*

Royal Maple LLC................................... G 704 900-5086
   Charlotte *(G-3464)*

Rugby Acquisition LLC .... D 336 993-8686
   Kernersville *(G-9229)*

S Banner Cabinets Incorporated.............. E 828 733-2031
   Newland *(G-11893)*

S Eudy Cabinet Shop Inc .... E 704 888-4454
   Stanfield *(G-14682)*

S Shelton Inc....................................... G 336 643-5916
   Stokesdale *(G-14948)*

S Zaytoun Custom Cabinets Inc .... F 252 638-8390
   New Bern *(G-11843)*

Sanford Kitchen & Bath Inc .... G 919 708-9080
   Sanford *(G-14181)*

Scotts Cabinet Store LLC .... G 919 725-2530
   Wake Forest *(G-15589)*

Seema Intl Custom Cabinetry................. G 917 703-9820
   Wake Forest *(G-15591)*

Selpro LLC... F 336 513-0550
   Greensboro *(G-7332)*

Signature Custom Cabinets LLC .... G 704 753-4874
   Monroe *(G-10807)*

Simmons Cstm Cbnetry Mllwk Inc .... G 252 240-1020
   Morehead City *(G-11190)*

Sjr Incorporated................................... E 828 254-8966
   Asheville *(G-773)*

Smiths Custom Kitchen Inc .... G 828 652-9033
   Marion *(G-10177)*

Sorrells Cabinet Co Inc.......................... G 919 639-4320
   Lillington *(G-9860)*

Southern Cabinet Co Inc .... F 704 373-2299
   Matthews *(G-10291)*

Southern Design Cabinetry LLC.............. F 919 340-1858
   Wake Forest *(G-15594)*

Stallings Cabinets Inc............................ G 252 338-6747
   Elizabeth City *(G-5571)*

Stella Cabinet Works............................. G 910 358-4248
   Maysville *(G-10375)*

Steves Cabinets Plus Inc .... G 919 351-0454
   Princeton *(G-12405)*

Stone Mountain Cabinetary.................... G 828 676-3600
   Arden *(G-381)*

Sundance Cstm Painted Cabinets............ G 704 500-3732
   Cornelius *(G-4589)*

Sunhs Warehouse LLC........................... G 919 908-1523
   Durham *(G-5380)*

Superior Custom Cabinets LLC .... G 919 778-1845
   Goldsboro *(G-6664)*

Tarheel Wood Designs Inc..................... G 910 395-2226
   Wilmington *(G-16427)*

Tarheel Woodcrafters Inc...................... G 252 432-3035
   Henderson *(G-7813)*

Tarlton Cabinet Shop............................ G 704 573-7064
   Mint Hill *(G-10545)*

Team Triangle Cabinets........................ G 919 609-1332
   Raleigh *(G-13332)*

Thomas Lcklars Cbnets Lrnburg.............. G 910 369-2094
   Laurinburg *(G-9499)*

Tice Kitchens & Interiors LLC .... F 919 366-4117
   Raleigh *(G-13350)*

Tombogancraftsman Com...................... G 919 932-9878
   Chapel Hill *(G-2081)*

Tommy W Smith Inc .... G 704 436-6616
   Mount Pleasant *(G-11678)*

Tonys Cabinets.................................... G 910 592-2028
   Clinton *(G-4115)*

Topline Cabinet Co Inc.......................... G 919 762-0045
   Holly Springs *(G-8722)*

Travis Alfrey Woodworking Inc................ G 910 639-3553
   Aberdeen *(G-33)*

Triangle Cabinet Company..................... G 336 869-6401
   High Point *(G-8576)*

Triangle Kitchen Supply........................ G 919 562-3888
   Youngsville *(G-17108)*

True Cabinet LLC.................................. F 828 855-9200
   Hickory *(G-8185)*

Tsquared Cabinets............................... G 336 655-0208
   Winston Salem *(G-16956)*

Twin City Custom Cabinets.................... G 336 773-7200
   Winston Salem *(G-16957)*

U S Cabinets Express LLC...................... G 336 875-4011
   High Point *(G-8582)*

US Precision Cabinetry LLC.................... D 828 351-2020
   Rutherfordton *(G-13900)*

V/N Woodwork..................................... G 704 277-6336
   Indian Trail *(G-8969)*

Verona Cabinets & Surfaces LLC............. G 704 755-5259
   Charlotte *(G-3773)*

Vine & Branch Woodworks LLC............... G 704 663-0077
   Mooresville *(G-11120)*

Vivas Custom Cabinets LLC.................... G 252 650-1103
   Elm City *(G-5654)*

Walker Woodworking Inc....................... E 704 434-0823
   Shelby *(G-14381)*

Watkins Cabinets LLC........................... G 704 634-1724
   Matthews *(G-10299)*

Windsors Cbnetry For Kit Baths.............. G 336 275-0190
   Greensboro *(G-7462)*

Winstons Woodworks............................ G 919 693-4120
   Oxford *(G-12161)*

Wnc Cabinetry LLC............................... G 828 400-6492
   Waynesville *(G-15835)*

Wood Done Right Inc........................... G 919 623-4557
   Chapel Hill *(G-2099)*

Wood Technology Inc........................... E 828 464-8049
   Conover *(G-4515)*

Woodmaster Custom Cabinets Inc........... F 919 554-3707
   Youngsville *(G-17116)*

Woodmasters Woodworking Inc.............. G 336 985-4000
   King *(G-9287)*

Woods Cabinet Company Inc .... G 919 207-1663
   Benson *(G-1046)*

Woods End LLC................................... G 910 470-0389
   Castle Hayne *(G-1962)*

Woodworking Unlimited........................ G 252 235-5285
   Bailey *(G-879)*

Xylem Inc.. G 919 772-4126
   Garner *(G-6328)*

Yadkin Valley Cabinet Co Inc.................. G 336 786-9860
   Mount Airy *(G-11598)*

PRODUCT SECTION — CANDLES

Your Cabinet Connection Inc............... G 919 641-2877
  Morrisville *(G-11468)*

CABINETS: Office, Wood

3c Store Fixtures Inc........................... D 252 291-5181
  Wilson *(G-16461)*

A R Byrd Company Inc....................... G 704 732-5675
  Lincolnton *(G-9864)*

Appalachian Cabinet Inc.................... G 828 265-0830
  Deep Gap *(G-4708)*

B&H Millwork and Fixtures Inc........... E 336 431-0068
  High Point *(G-8260)*

Custom Cabinets By Livengood.......... G 704 279-3031
  Salisbury *(G-13950)*

Dp Woodworks Inc.............................. G 704 821-7799
  Monroe *(G-10707)*

Element Designs Inc........................... D 704 332-3114
  Charlotte *(G-2691)*

Ocean Woodworking Inc..................... G 910 579-2233
  Ocean Isle Beach *(G-12094)*

Pridgen Woodwork Inc....................... E 910 642-7175
  Whiteville *(G-15975)*

Woodsmiths Company........................ F 406 626-3102
  Lenoir *(G-9661)*

CABINETS: Show, Display, Etc, Wood, Exc Refrigerated

Ajs Dezigns Inc................................... G 828 652-6304
  Marion *(G-10138)*

Davis Cabinet Co Wilson Inc.............. F 252 291-9052
  Sims *(G-14441)*

Harris Wood Products Inc................... G 704 550-5494
  New London *(G-11872)*

Hollingswrth Cbnets Intrors LL.......... F 910 251-1490
  Castle Hayne *(G-1952)*

Rowland Woodworking Inc................. E 336 887-0700
  High Point *(G-8516)*

Washington Cabinet Company............ G 252 946-3457
  Washington *(G-15738)*

CABLE & OTHER PAY TELEVISION DISTRIBUTION

M I Connection................................... F 704 662-3255
  Mooresville *(G-11013)*

CABLE TELEVISION

Cco Holdings LLC.............................. C 828 414-4238
  Blowing Rock *(G-1155)*

Cco Holdings LLC.............................. C 828 355-4149
  Boone *(G-1186)*

Cco Holdings LLC.............................. C 910 292-4083
  Dunn *(G-4857)*

Cco Holdings LLC.............................. C 828 270-7016
  Hickory *(G-7973)*

Cco Holdings LLC.............................. C 919 502-4007
  Kenly *(G-9147)*

Cco Holdings LLC.............................. C 828 394-0635
  Lenoir *(G-9597)*

Cco Holdings LLC.............................. C 704 308-3361
  Lincolnton *(G-9880)*

Cco Holdings LLC.............................. C 828 528-4004
  Newland *(G-11883)*

Cco Holdings LLC.............................. C 919 200-6260
  Siler City *(G-14402)*

Cco Holdings LLC.............................. C 828 368-4161
  Valdese *(G-15445)*

CABLE TELEVISION PRDTS

Edge Broadband Solutions LLC.......... E 828 785-1420
  Waynesville *(G-15803)*

CABLE: Coaxial

Commscope Technologies LLC............ F 919 934-9711
  Smithfield *(G-14457)*

Draka Communications Americas Inc.... B 828 459-8456
  Claremont *(G-3921)*

CABLE: Fiber

Fusion Fiber Optics LLC..................... G 252 933-5244
  Kinston *(G-9367)*

CABLE: Fiber Optic

Arris Solutions LLC........................... A 678 473-2000
  Hickory *(G-7943)*

Corning Incorporated......................... F 252 316-4500
  Tarboro *(G-15100)*

Crww Specialty Composites Inc.......... F 828 548-5002
  Claremont *(G-3917)*

Emtelle USA Inc................................. E 828 707-9970
  Fletcher *(G-6000)*

Opticoncepts Inc................................ G 828 320-0138
  Hickory *(G-8108)*

Tensor Fiber Optics Tech.................... G 828 322-8224
  Hickory *(G-8178)*

US Conec Ltd..................................... G 828 323-8883
  Hickory *(G-8197)*

US Conec Ltd..................................... D 828 323-8883
  Hickory *(G-8198)*

CABLE: Noninsulated

Coleman Cable LLC........................... E 828 389-8013
  Hayesville *(G-7762)*

Voltage LLC....................................... F 919 391-9405
  Chapel Hill *(G-2096)*

CABLE: Ropes & Fiber

Jhrg Manufacturing LLC..................... G 252 478-4977
  Spring Hope *(G-14619)*

Ls Cable & System USA Inc................ C 252 824-3553
  Tarboro *(G-15112)*

Moon Audio....................................... G 919 649-5018
  Cary *(G-1826)*

CABLE: Steel, Insulated Or Armored

Draka Elevator Products Inc............... C 252 984-5100
  Rocky Mount *(G-13690)*

CAFES

Cabarrus Brewing Company LLC........ E 704 490-4487
  Concord *(G-4216)*

Sugar Creek Brewing Co LLC............. E 704 521-3333
  Charlotte *(G-3646)*

CAFETERIAS

Wildflour Bakery Inc.......................... G 828 749-9224
  Saluda *(G-14075)*

CALCULATING & ACCOUNTING EQPT

Diebold Nixdorf Incorporated.............. F 704 599-3100
  Charlotte *(G-2632)*

One Source SEC & Sound Inc............. G 281 850-9487
  Mooresville *(G-11044)*

CALIBRATING SVCS, NEC

Broadwind Indus Solutions LLC.......... E 919 777-2907
  Sanford *(G-14096)*

Cross Technologies Inc....................... E 800 327-7927
  Greensboro *(G-6942)*

CAMPERS: Truck Mounted

Boondock S Manufacturing Inc........... G 828 891-4242
  Etowah *(G-5691)*

CAMSHAFTS

CAM Craft LLC.................................. G 828 681-5183
  Arden *(G-316)*

CANDLE SHOPS

Wildflwers Btq of Blowing Rock.......... G 828 295-9655
  Blowing Rock *(G-1157)*

CANDLES

131 Candle Co.................................... G 325 650-4903
  Durham *(G-4892)*

222 Dream Co LLC............................. G 919 803-9741
  Fayetteville *(G-5745)*

Amish Lights Candles......................... G 330 546-3900
  Concord *(G-4196)*

Anchored Scents LLC......................... G 910 709-1582
  Winterville *(G-16994)*

Apollonias Candles Things LLC........... G 910 408-2508
  Durham *(G-4921)*

Auralites Inc...................................... G 828 687-7990
  Fletcher *(G-5986)*

Ava Aliza Candle Co LLC.................... G 704 906-4328
  Charlotte *(G-2243)*

Beelite Inc... G 828 584-1488
  Morganton *(G-11201)*

Bell Book & Candle LLC..................... G 336 480-1422
  Clemmons *(G-4031)*

Bethany Small.................................... G 910 409-2167
  Southport *(G-14567)*

Brew Candle Company........................ G 980 275-9355
  Boone *(G-1182)*

Camera To Candle.............................. G 339 224-1073
  Huntersville *(G-8800)*

Candle Bar... G 704 497-6099
  Charlotte *(G-2383)*

Cardinal Creek Cndles Gfts LLC......... G 336 941-3158
  Advance *(G-39)*

Carolina Candle.................................. G 336 835-6020
  Elkin *(G-5612)*

Cat Daddy Ventures LLC.................... G 252 229-8617
  Arden *(G-318)*

Celebration Candles Inc..................... G 610 360-1545
  Leland *(G-9535)*

Charming Pot Candle Co LLC............. G 828 768-4827
  Candler *(G-1574)*

Coastal Tides Soap Candles LLC........ G 910 833-2132
  Wilmington *(G-16174)*

Craig Hart.. G 269 365-5568
  Greensboro *(G-6938)*

Cristal Dragon Candle Company......... G 336 997-4210
  Sandy Ridge *(G-14077)*

D & T Soy Candles............................. G 704 320-2804
  Polkton *(G-12386)*

Daisy Pink Co..................................... G 704 907-3526
  Charlotte *(G-2600)*

David Oreck Candle............................ F 336 375-8411
  Greensboro *(G-6959)*

Element Tree Essentials LLC............. G 828 707-0407
  Arden *(G-327)*

Ella B Candles LLC........................... E 980 339-8898
  Charlotte *(G-2697)*

Essence Candles................................ G 980 785-4309
  Troutman *(G-15375)*

Essence Noire LLC............................. G 704 351-8322
  Charlotte *(G-2728)*

Forage Soaps LLC.............................. G 828 737-9088
  Newland *(G-11886)*

Fragrant Passage Candle Co LP.......... E 336 375-8411
  Greensboro *(G-7020)*

Get Wickd Candles............................. G 704 437-9062
  Troutman *(G-15379)*

CANDLES

Glossy Wicks LLC .... G 980 349-5908
  Charlotte (G-2835)
Gold Canyon Candles .... G 828 358-5729
  Connelly Springs (G-4401)
Happy Wax .... G 888 400-3053
  Durham (G-5131)
Harmony Farm Candles .... G 919 698-5200
  Mebane (G-10414)
Hopperncleve Designs LLC .... G 919 721-4406
  Cameron (G-1561)
Isabellas Oils LLC .... G 828 221-4274
  Hickory (G-8069)
J Ali Candles .... G 910 603-2997
  West End (G-15927)
Jasmine Wade Co LLC .... G 704 345-8301
  Charlotte (G-3009)
JC Wicks LLC .... G 828 514-9788
  Charlotte (G-3013)
Kens Candles and Soaps .... G 919 207-2880
  Willow Spring (G-16080)
Litbywhit LLC .... G 704 293-5743
  Charlotte (G-3093)
Love Knot Candles .... G 336 456-1619
  Greensboro (G-7171)
Manda Pandas LLC .... G 919 452-7917
  Durham (G-5205)
Miahna Moon LLC .... G 704 449-9495
  Charlotte (G-3172)
Mommamade Scents LLC .... G 704 458-5901
  Charlotte (G-3194)
Moose Candle Company .... G 828 244-1384
  Conover (G-4473)
Moya Custom Designs LLC .... G 984 208-3118
  Siler City (G-14426)
Mvp Group International Inc .... E 336 527-2238
  Mount Airy (G-11549)
Mvp Group International Inc .... E 843 216-8380
  Elkin (G-5627)
Natives Rest Candles .... G 828 774-9838
  Hendersonville (G-7884)
Paul Hoge Creations Inc .... F 704 624-6860
  Marshville (G-10221)
Peak City Candles Inc .... G 919 601-8223
  Apex (G-228)
Perfect Match Candles LLC .... G 919 482-6649
  Apex (G-230)
Potterwyx Scnted Candles Soaps .... G 336 245-8560
  Lewisville (G-9671)
Pretty Honest LLC .... G 804 837-1038
  Charlotte (G-3378)
Scentual Candles .... G 252 281-4919
  Wilson (G-16540)
Shelby Candles .... G 336 804-4182
  Thomasville (G-15277)
Sincere Scents Co LLC .... G 910 616-4697
  Southport (G-14580)
Sniff N Rescue Candles LLC .... G 704 909-9853
  Mooresville (G-11091)
Sniff To Remember LLC .... G 210 373-2115
  Charlotte (G-3572)
Southern Elegance Candle LLC .... G 706 825-7658
  Raeford (G-12439)
Southern Made Candles LLC .... G 704 740-7748
  Weaverville (G-15863)
Soy Clever Candle Co LLC .... G 919 869-5360
  Clayton (G-4011)
Spring Rock Farms Inc .... G 336 973-1447
  Purlear (G-12413)
Stick Candles .... G 315 369-0011
  Cashiers (G-1937)
Strike & Flame Candles .... G 336 207-4487
  Greensboro (G-7375)
Sweet Wick Candle Company LLC .... G 770 687-1519
  Kernersville (G-9240)
Tinman Candles .... G 828 329-1140
  Etowah (G-5694)
Tobacco Outlet Products LLC .... G 704 341-9388
  Charlotte (G-3702)
Uncle Browns Scented Candles .... G 704 993-0409
  Monroe (G-10827)
Underground Renovations LLC .... G 202 316-9286
  Raleigh (G-13381)
Valley Run Candles LLC .... G 828 729-8652
  Durham (G-5431)
Waxhaw Candle Company LLC .... G 980 245-2827
  Charlotte (G-3798)
White Tiger Btq & Candle Co .... G 919 610-7244
  Sanford (G-14205)
Wicked Calm Candles LLc .... G 856 343-2499
  Clayton (G-4021)
Wildflwers Btq of Blowing Rock .... G 828 295-9655
  Blowing Rock (G-1157)
Wix By Mel .... G 973 479-0795
  Carolina Beach (G-1643)
World Wicks Candles .... G 919 791-6123
  Zebulon (G-17146)

CANDLES: Wholesalers

Tobacco Outlet Products LLC .... G 704 341-9388
  Charlotte (G-3702)

CANDY & CONFECTIONS: Candy Bars, Including Chocolate Covered

Best Bar Ever Inc .... G 910 508-3628
  Raleigh (G-12552)
French Broad Chocolates LLC .... G 828 252-4181
  Asheville (G-629)
Snyders-Lance Inc .... A 704 554-1421
  Charlotte (G-3574)

CANDY & CONFECTIONS: Chocolate Candy, Exc Solid Chocolate

Carolina Chocolatiers Inc .... G 828 652-4496
  Marion (G-10146)
Foiled Agin Choclat Coins LLC .... G 919 342-4601
  Sanford (G-14120)

CANDY & CONFECTIONS: Licorice

Lucky Country USA LLC .... E 828 428-8313
  Lincolnton (G-9903)

CANDY & CONFECTIONS: Nuts, Candy Covered

KLb Enterprises Incorporated .... F 336 605-0773
  Greensboro (G-7153)

CANDY & CONFECTIONS: Popcorn Balls/ Other Trtd Popcorn Prdts

Tastebuds LLC .... G 704 461-8755
  Belmont (G-1014)

CANDY, NUT & CONFECTIONERY STORES: Candy

Bilcat Inc .... E 828 295-3088
  Blowing Rock (G-1154)
Butterfields Candy LLC .... G 252 459-2577
  Nashville (G-11738)
Chocolate Smiles Village LLC .... G 919 469-5282
  Cary (G-1729)
French Broad Chocolates LLC .... G 828 252-4181
  Asheville (G-629)
Sugar Pops .... G 704 799-0959
  Mooresville (G-11107)

CANDY: Chocolate From Cacao Beans

Chocolate Fetish LLC .... G 828 258-2353
  Asheville (G-592)
Chocolate Smiles Village LLC .... G 919 469-5282
  Cary (G-1729)

CANDY: Soft

Morinaga America Foods Inc .... E 919 643-2439
  Mebane (G-10420)

CANNED SPECIALTIES

Ritas One Inc .... G 919 650-2415
  Cary (G-1871)
Stevens Foodservice .... G 919 322-5470
  Raleigh (G-13304)

CANS & TUBES: Ammunition, Board Laminated With Metal Foil

C L Rabb Inc .... E 704 865-0295
  Gastonia (G-6365)
Conitex Sonoco Usa Inc .... C 704 864-5406
  Gastonia (G-6384)
Mm Clayton LLC .... B 919 553-4113
  Clayton (G-3997)

CANS: Aluminum

Trivium Packaging USA Inc .... B 336 785-8500
  Winston Salem (G-16953)

CANS: Metal

Container Products Corporation .... D 910 392-6100
  Wilmington (G-16179)
Fleetgenius of Nc Inc .... C 828 726-3001
  Lenoir (G-9612)
Leisure Craft Holdings LLC .... D 828 693-8241
  Flat Rock (G-5967)
Leisure Craft Inc .... C 828 693-8241
  Flat Rock (G-5968)
Waste Container Services LLC .... G 910 257-4474
  Fayetteville (G-5950)

CANS: Tin

Tin Can Ventures LLC .... G 919 732-9078
  Cedar Grove (G-1973)
Tin Cans LLC .... G 910 322-2626
  Lillington (G-9861)

CANVAS PRDTS

A & J Canvas Inc .... E 252 244-1509
  Vanceboro (G-15474)
Allison Sails and Canvas LLC .... G 910 515-1381
  Carolina Beach (G-1631)
Camoteck LLC .... G 910 590-3213
  Clinton (G-4089)
Canvasmasters LLC .... G 828 369-0406
  Franklin (G-6118)
Cape Lookout Canvas & Customs .... G 252 726-3751
  Morehead City (G-11157)
Carol Williams .... G 252 883-7968
  Rocky Mount (G-13687)
Carteret Canvas Company .... G 252 247-9588
  Atlantic Beach (G-828)
Cdv LLC .... F 919 674-3460
  Morrisville (G-11316)
Cross Canvas Company Inc .... E 828 252-0440
  Asheville (G-599)
DLM Sales Inc .... F 704 399-2776
  Charlotte (G-2647)

PRODUCT SECTION — CASES: Shipping, Nailed Or Lock Corner, Wood

Dunn Manufacturing Corp.................... C 704 283-2147
  Monroe (G-10709)
Ernies Boat Canvas & Awning C........... G 252 491-8279
  Jarvisburg (G-9084)
Hatteras Hammocks Inc....................... C 252 758-0641
  Greenville (G-7537)
M & M Signs and Awnings Inc............. F 336 352-4300
  Mount Airy (G-11543)
OBrian Tarping Systems Inc................. F 252 291-6710
  Wilson (G-16520)
Prem Corp... E 704 921-1799
  Charlotte (G-3373)
Ricks Custom Marine Canvas............... G 937 623-1672
  Cornelius (G-4583)
Sawyers Sign Service Inc................... F
  Mount Airy (G-11571)
Trivantage... G 800 438-1061
  Statesville (G-14918)
Watkins Custom Sewing Inc................ G 252 996-0642
  Wanchese (G-15652)
WC&r Interests LLC.............................. C 828 684-9848
  Fletcher (G-6050)

CAPACITORS & CONDENSERS

Nwl Inc... E 252 747-5943
  Snow Hill (G-14505)

CAPACITORS: NEC

ABB Inc... D 919 856-2360
  Raleigh (G-12457)
Global Manufacturing Svcs Inc............. E 336 846-1674
  West Jefferson (G-15940)
Hitachi Energy USA Inc....................... F 919 324-5403
  Raleigh (G-12849)
Hitachi Energy USA Inc....................... C 919 856-2360
  Raleigh (G-12850)
Kemet Electronics Corporation............. E 864 963-6300
  Shelby (G-14334)
LLC Diamond Bell................................ G 704 806-4705
  Charlotte (G-3097)
M2 Optics Inc...................................... G 919 342-5619
  Raleigh (G-12985)
Nwl Inc.. E 252 747-5943
  Snow Hill (G-14505)
Reuel Inc... E 919 734-0460
  Goldsboro (G-6650)
United Chemi-Con Inc......................... B 336 384-6903
  Lansing (G-9456)

CAR WASH EQPT

Ferguson Companies........................... G
  Linwood (G-9945)
Jq Pro Detailing LLC............................ G 336 543-0663
  Greensboro (G-7141)
Majestic Xpress Handwash Inc............ G 919 440-7611
  Goldsboro (G-6633)

CARBIDES

Techmet Carbides Inc......................... D 828 624-0222
  Hickory (G-8176)

CARBON & GRAPHITE PRDTS, NEC

Asbury Graphite Mills.......................... G 910 671-4141
  Lumberton (G-10026)
Debotech Inc....................................... C 704 664-1361
  Mooresville (G-10927)
Energy Conversion Syste.................... G 910 892-8081
  Dunn (G-4864)
Morgan Advanced Mtls Tech Inc......... C 910 892-9677
  Dunn (G-4877)
Pbi Performance Products Inc............. D 704 554-3378
  Charlotte (G-3322)

Sgl Inc... G 910 790-3631
  Wilmington (G-16401)
Sgl Carbon LLC................................... G 828 437-3221
  Morganton (G-11251)
Sgl Carbon LLC................................... E 704 593-5100
  Charlotte (G-3533)
Sgl Composites Inc............................. E 704 593-5100
  Charlotte (G-3534)
Slade Operating Company LLC........... E 704 873-1366
  Statesville (G-14887)
Thanet Inc... E 704 483-4175
  Denver (G-4807)
Tokai Carbon GE LLC.......................... E 980 260-1130
  Charlotte (G-3705)

CARBON BLACK

Etmo TEC LLC..................................... G 704 878-9979
  Statesville (G-14795)

CARBURETORS

Bill Pink Carburetors LLC..................... G 704 575-1645
  Denver (G-4765)
Classic Carburetor Rebuilders............. G 336 613-5715
  Eden (G-5489)
Marvel-Schbler Arcft Crbrtors.............. F 336 446-0002
  Burlington (G-1456)
Robert Blake....................................... G 704 720-9341
  Concord (G-4351)

CARDS: Color

Copymatic United Cerebral................. F 252 695-6155
  Greenville (G-7507)

CARDS: Greeting

Walgreen Co.. F 704 525-2628
  Charlotte (G-3792)
Wit & Whistle...................................... G 919 609-5309
  Cary (G-1930)

CARDS: Identification

US One DOT Com Inc......................... G 704 587-0678
  Charlotte (G-3760)

CARDS: Jacquard, Made From Purchased Materials

Valdese Weavers LLC......................... B 828 874-2181
  Valdese (G-15461)

CARPET & UPHOLSTERY CLEANING SVCS

Bridgport Restoration Svcs Inc............ F 336 996-1212
  Kernersville (G-9169)

CARPETS & RUGS: Tufted

Karastan... G 336 627-7200
  Eden (G-5493)
Mohawk Industries Inc........................ F 919 661-5590
  Garner (G-6290)

CARPETS, RUGS & FLOOR COVERING

Anchored Home Inc............................ G 910 769-7092
  Wilmington (G-16111)
Bellaire Dynamik LLC.......................... G 704 779-3755
  Charlotte (G-2299)
Burlington Industries LLC.................... C 336 379-6220
  Greensboro (G-6865)
Columbia Forest Products Inc.............. G 336 605-0429
  Greensboro (G-6920)
Due Process Stable Trdg Co LLC......... E 910 608-0284
  Lumberton (G-10032)
Elevate Textiles Inc............................. G 336 379-6220
  Charlotte (G-2693)

Elevate Textiles Holding Corp.............. D 336 379-6220
  Charlotte (G-2694)
Flint Hill Textiles Inc........................... G 704 434-9331
  Shelby (G-14318)
Furniture Fair Inc................................ E 910 455-4044
  Jacksonville (G-9001)
Grund America LLC............................. E 704 287-1805
  Matthews (G-10319)
Hampton Capital Partners LLC............ A
  Aberdeen (G-6)
Horizon Home Imports Inc................... G 704 859-5133
  Clemmons (G-4046)
Itg Holdings Inc................................... A 336 379-6220
  Greensboro (G-7126)
Michaelian & Kohlberg Inc................... G 828 891-8511
  Horse Shoe (G-8741)
Mohawk Industries Inc........................ G 919 609-4759
  Garner (G-6289)
Raleigh Area Masters.......................... G 919 233-6713
  Raleigh (G-13173)
Royal Textile Mills Inc......................... D 336 694-4121
  Yanceyville (G-17065)
Shaw Industries Inc............................ B 828 369-1701
  Franklin (G-6143)
Shaw Industries Group Inc.................. E 877 996-5942
  Charlotte (G-3536)
Shaw Industries Group Inc.................. G 877 996-5942
  Charlotte (G-3537)
White Oak Carpet Mills Inc.................. G 828 287-8892
  Spindale (G-14611)

CARS: Electric

Ev Fleet Inc.. G 704 425-6272
  Charlotte (G-2734)
Lynn Jones Race Cars......................... G 252 522-0705
  Kinston (G-9374)
Performance Racing Whse Inc............ G 704 838-1400
  Mooresville (G-11053)
Solar Pack.. E 919 515-2194
  Raleigh (G-13277)

CARTS: Grocery

Technibilt Ltd..................................... E 828 464-7388
  Newton (G-11976)

CASES: Carrying

Case Smith Inc................................... F 336 969-9786
  Rural Hall (G-13836)

CASES: Carrying, Clothing & Apparel

Birddog Outdoor Co Inc...................... G 919 604-8134
  Cary (G-1706)
Bratz Playground LLC......................... F 704 858-1934
  Charlotte (G-2349)
Glaser Designs Inc............................. F 415 552-3188
  Raleigh (G-12803)
Highiq LLC.. G 704 956-8716
  Concord (G-4280)
Kute N Klassy By Jen LLc.................. G 828 755-5613
  Forest City (G-6074)
Paulas Pretty Things Inc..................... G 919 656-1163
  Pikeville (G-12193)
Picassomoesllc................................... G 216 703-4547
  Hillsborough (G-8665)
Random & Kind LLC............................ G 919 249-8809
  Durham (G-5319)

CASES: Plastic

Dexterity LLC..................................... F 919 524-7732
  Greenville (G-7514)

CASES: Shipping, Nailed Or Lock Corner, Wood

Carolina Crating Inc	E	910 276-7170
Laurinburg (G-9472)

Kontane Logistics Inc ..... G 828 397-5501
Hickory (G-8080)

Mc Gees Crating Inc ..... E 828 758-4660
Lenoir (G-9635)

CASINGS: Sheet Metal

Tfam Solutions LLC ..... G 910 637-0266
Aberdeen (G-31)

CAST STONE: Concrete

Custom Brick Company Inc ..... E 919 832-2804
Raleigh (G-12663)

Fletcher Limestone Company Inc ..... F 828 684-6701
Fletcher (G-6005)

CASTINGS GRINDING: For The Trade

Daily Grind ..... G 919 864-8775
Morrisville (G-11327)

Daily Grind LLC ..... G 910 541-0471
Surf City (G-15015)

Grind Athletics LLC ..... G 910 228-0035
Wilmington (G-16242)

McJast Inc ..... F 828 884-4809
Pisgah Forest (G-12326)

North Iredell Grinding Inc ..... F 704 902-4771
Statesville (G-14852)

Petteway Body Shop Inc ..... G 910 455-3272
Jacksonville (G-9020)

Social Grind Gourmet Cof LLC ..... G 919 937-9503
Durham (G-5363)

Stump and Grind LLC ..... G 704 488-2271
Charlotte (G-3643)

CASTINGS: Aerospace Investment, Ferrous

Cold Mountain Capital LLC ..... F 828 210-8129
Asheville (G-596)

CASTINGS: Aerospace, Aluminum

CAT Logistics Inc ..... F 252 447-2490
New Bern (G-11787)

CASTINGS: Aluminum

Briggs-Shaffner Acquisition Co ..... F 336 463-4272
Yadkinville (G-17034)

Consolidated Metco Inc ..... F 704 289-6492
Monroe (G-10691)

Consolidated Metco Inc ..... D 704 289-6491
Monroe (G-10692)

CASTINGS: Brass, NEC, Exc Die

Maiden Casting Company ..... G 704 735-6812
Maiden (G-10112)

CASTINGS: Bronze, NEC, Exc Die

Kayne & Son Custom Hdwr Inc ..... G 828 665-1988
Candler (G-1585)

CASTINGS: Die, Aluminum

Carolina Foundry Inc ..... F 704 376-3145
Charlotte (G-2396)

Cascade Die Casting Group Inc ..... C 336 882-0186
High Point (G-8289)

Cs Alloys ..... G 704 675-5810
Gastonia (G-6389)

Dynacast LLC ..... E 704 927-2790
Charlotte (G-2662)

Dynacast International LLC ..... G 704 927-2790
Charlotte (G-2663)

Ksm Castings USA Inc ..... E 704 751-0559
Shelby (G-14335)

Leggett & Platt Incorporated ..... G 704 380-6208
Statesville (G-14835)

Linamar Light Metal S-Mr LLC ..... A 828 348-4010
Mills River (G-10506)

RCM Industries Inc ..... C 828 286-4003
Rutherfordton (G-13886)

Sensus USA Inc ..... C 919 576-6185
Morrisville (G-11426)

Sensus USA Inc ..... E 919 845-4000
Morrisville (G-11425)

CASTINGS: Die, Nonferrous

Dynacast LLC ..... E 704 927-2790
Charlotte (G-2662)

Dynacast International LLC ..... G 704 927-2790
Charlotte (G-2663)

Dynacast US Holdings Inc ..... E 704 927-2786
Charlotte (G-2664)

CASTINGS: Gray Iron

Humber Street Facility Inc ..... E 919 775-3628
Sanford (G-14135)

Modacam Incorporated ..... G 704 489-8500
Denver (G-4789)

Southern Cast Inc ..... E 704 335-0692
Charlotte (G-3590)

Venture Products Intl Inc ..... G 828 285-0495
Asheville (G-814)

CASTINGS: Machinery, Aluminum

Advanced Machine Services ..... G 910 410-0099
Rockingham (G-13617)

Maiden Casting Company ..... G 704 735-6812
Maiden (G-10112)

CASTINGS: Precision

PCC Airfoils LLC ..... B 919 774-4300
Sanford (G-14164)

CASTINGS: Steel

Norca Engineered Products LLC ..... E 919 846-2010
Raleigh (G-13067)

CATALOG & MAIL-ORDER HOUSES

Cbdmd Inc ..... F 704 445-3060
Charlotte (G-2422)

Celtic Ocean International Inc ..... E 828 299-9005
Arden (G-320)

Glen Raven Custom Fabrics LLC ..... C 828 682-2142
Burnsville (G-1526)

Old Salem Incorporated ..... G 336 721-7305
Winston Salem (G-16828)

CATALOG SALES

Owen G Dunn Co Inc ..... G 252 633-3197
New Bern (G-11832)

Stump Printing Co Inc ..... C 260 723-5171
Wrightsville Beach (G-17028)

Trophy House Inc ..... F 910 323-1791
Fayetteville (G-5934)

CATALYSTS: Chemical

Advanced Marketing International Inc ..... F 910 392-0508
Wilmington (G-16095)

American Ripener LLC ..... G 704 527-8813
Charlotte (G-2183)

Clariant Corporation ..... D 704 331-7000
Charlotte (G-2491)

Coalogix Inc ..... C 704 827-8933
Charlotte (G-2510)

Innospec Inc ..... E 704 633-8028
Salisbury (G-13985)

Innospec Inc ..... E 704 633-8028
Salisbury (G-13986)

CATERERS

Over Rainbow Inc ..... F 704 332-5521
Charlotte (G-3307)

Sawmill Catering LLC ..... F 910 769-7455
Wilmington (G-16393)

Sweet Room LLC ..... G 336 567-1620
High Point (G-8560)

CAULKING COMPOUNDS

Dap Products Inc ..... F 704 799-9640
Mooresville (G-10924)

Firestopping Products Inc ..... F 336 661-0102
Winston Salem (G-16711)

CEMENT & CONCRETE RELATED PRDTS & EQPT: Bituminous

John Deere Kernersville LLC ..... A 336 996-8100
Kernersville (G-9207)

CEMENT ROCK: Crushed & Broken

Marietta Martin Materials Inc ..... G 910 743-6471
Maysville (G-10374)

Martin Marietta Materials Inc ..... F 360 424-3441
Raleigh (G-12999)

CEMENT: Asbestos, Siding

Plycem Usa LLC ..... D 336 696-2007
North Wilkesboro (G-12030)

CEMENT: Heat Resistant

3tex Inc ..... E 919 481-2500
Rutherfordton (G-13860)

Martin Marietta Materials Inc ..... C 919 781-4550
Raleigh (G-13001)

CEMENT: Hydraulic

Argos USA LLC ..... G 919 942-0381
Carrboro (G-1644)

Bonsal American Inc ..... G 704 848-4141
Lilesville (G-9835)

Giant Cement Co ..... G 704 583-1568
Charlotte (G-2828)

CEMENT: Masonry

Vega Construction Company Inc ..... E 336 756-3477
Pilot Mountain (G-12204)

CEMENT: Natural

Beazer East Inc ..... F 919 567-9512
Holly Springs (G-8688)

CHASSIS: Motor Vehicle

Direct Chassislink Inc ..... E 704 594-3800
Charlotte (G-2639)

Thomas Built Buses Inc ..... A 336 889-4871
High Point (G-8569)

CHASSIS: Travel Trailer

Elite Metal Performance LLC ..... F 704 660-0006
Statesville (G-14793)

CHEMICAL ELEMENTS

8th Elment Cndtning Prfmce LLC ..... G 828 298-1290
Asheville (G-512)

PRODUCT SECTION

CHEMICALS: Agricultural

Beauty Elements LLC .... G 910 333-9957
Jacksonville *(G-8990)*

Element Arbor Inc .... G 828 550-2250
Waynesville *(G-15804)*

Element Countertops Inc .... G 704 641-7145
Monroe *(G-10712)*

Element Strategy LLC .... G 704 997-5627
Davidson *(G-4674)*

Elements Imaging LLC .... F 504 258-3317
Candler *(G-1578)*

Natural Elements Bath and Body .... G 828 226-0853
Brevard *(G-1283)*

New Element .... G 704 890-7292
Charlotte *(G-3251)*

Tutcu-Farnam Custom Products .... E 828 684-3766
Arden *(G-388)*

CHEMICAL PROCESSING MACHINERY & EQPT

CVC Equipment Company .... G 704 300-6242
Cherryville *(G-3867)*

Envirotek Worldwide LLC .... F 704 285-6400
Charlotte *(G-2719)*

Indian Tff-Tank Greensboro Inc .... G 336 625-2629
Asheboro *(G-442)*

CHEMICALS & ALLIED PRDTS WHOLESALERS, NEC

American Chrome & Chem NA Inc .... G 910 675-7200
Castle Hayne *(G-1942)*

Arc3 Gases Inc .... F 336 275-3333
Greensboro *(G-6812)*

Arc3 Gases Inc .... F 704 220-1029
Monroe *(G-10650)*

Arc3 Gases Inc .... E 910 892-4016
Dunn *(G-4851)*

Chem-Tex Laboratories Inc .... E 706 602-8600
Concord *(G-4232)*

Coatings and Adhesives Corp .... C 910 371-3184
Leland *(G-9537)*

Jci Jones Chemicals Inc .... E 704 392-9767
Charlotte *(G-3014)*

Newell Novelty Co Inc .... G 336 597-2246
Roxboro *(G-13808)*

Pavco Inc .... E 704 496-6800
Charlotte *(G-3321)*

Pencco Inc .... F 252 235-5300
Middlesex *(G-10453)*

Reedy International Corp .... F 980 819-6930
Charlotte *(G-3424)*

Reichhold Holdings Us Inc .... A 919 990-7500
Durham *(G-5323)*

Textile Rubber and Chem Co Inc .... G 704 376-3582
Indian Trail *(G-8968)*

Universal Preservachem Inc .... D 732 568-1266
Mebane *(G-10434)*

CHEMICALS & ALLIED PRDTS, WHOLESALE: Adhesives

Jowat Corporation .... D 336 434-9000
Archdale *(G-289)*

Jowat International Corp .... E 336 434-9000
Archdale *(G-290)*

CHEMICALS & ALLIED PRDTS, WHOLESALE: Chemical Additives

Fil-Chem Inc .... G 919 878-1270
Raleigh *(G-12766)*

CHEMICALS & ALLIED PRDTS, WHOLESALE: Chemicals, Indl

Access Technologies LLC .... G 574 286-1255
Mooresville *(G-10847)*

Custom Nano Inc .... G 919 608-3540
Raleigh *(G-12665)*

Fortrans Inc .... G 919 365-8004
Wendell *(G-15902)*

Kymera International LLC .... F 919 544-8090
Durham *(G-5184)*

Leke LLC .... E 704 523-1452
Pineville *(G-12280)*

Polytec Inc .... E 704 277-3960
Mooresville *(G-11055)*

Sostram Corporation .... G 919 226-1195
Durham *(G-5364)*

T - Square Enterprises Inc .... G 704 846-8233
Charlotte *(G-3667)*

Umicore USA Inc .... E 919 874-7171
Raleigh *(G-13379)*

CHEMICALS & ALLIED PRDTS, WHOLESALE: Chemicals, Indl & Heavy

Advanced Marketing International Inc . F 910 392-0508
Wilmington *(G-16095)*

Kincol Industries Incorporated .... G 704 372-8435
Charlotte *(G-3055)*

Marlowe-Van Loan Sales Co .... F 336 882-3351
High Point *(G-8441)*

CHEMICALS & ALLIED PRDTS, WHOLESALE: Detergent/Soap

Ada Marketing Inc .... E 910 221-2189
Dunn *(G-4848)*

Lathers Skin Essentials .... G 828 449-9244
Hickory *(G-8084)*

CHEMICALS & ALLIED PRDTS, WHOLESALE: Detergents

Greenology Products LLC .... E 877 473-3650
Raleigh *(G-12815)*

South / Win LLC .... D 336 398-5650
Greensboro *(G-7350)*

CHEMICALS & ALLIED PRDTS, WHOLESALE: Indl Gases

Air & Gas Solutions LLC .... E 704 897-2182
Charlotte *(G-2146)*

CHEMICALS & ALLIED PRDTS, WHOLESALE: Oil Additives

Carolina Bg .... G 704 847-8840
Matthews *(G-10236)*

Qualice LLC .... F 910 419-6589
Hamlet *(G-7630)*

CHEMICALS & ALLIED PRDTS, WHOLESALE: Oxygen

Oxlife of NC LLC .... G 828 684-7353
Hendersonville *(G-7889)*

CHEMICALS & ALLIED PRDTS, WHOLESALE: Plastics Materials, NEC

Advanced Marketing International Inc . F 910 392-0508
Wilmington *(G-16095)*

CHEMICALS & ALLIED PRDTS, WHOLESALE: Plastics Prdts, NEC

Advanced Plastiform Inc .... D 919 404-2080
Zebulon *(G-17117)*

Eastn20 Holdings Llc .... G 919 313-2100
Greensboro *(G-6987)*

Mdsi Inc .... G 919 783-8730
Browns Summit *(G-1312)*

Tri-Star Plastics Corp .... E 704 598-2800
Denver *(G-4810)*

Wilbert Plstic Svcs Acqstion L .... E 704 455-5191
Harrisburg *(G-7735)*

CHEMICALS & ALLIED PRDTS, WHOLESALE: Plastics Sheets & Rods

Custom Extrusion Inc .... G 336 495-7070
Asheboro *(G-420)*

Endless Plastics LLC .... F 336 346-1839
Greensboro *(G-6998)*

Piedmont Plastics Inc .... D 704 597-8200
Charlotte *(G-3340)*

United Plastics Corporation .... C 336 786-2127
Mount Airy *(G-11592)*

CHEMICALS & ALLIED PRDTS, WHOLESALE: Resins

Reichhold Holdings Us Inc .... A 919 990-7500
Durham *(G-5323)*

CHEMICALS & ALLIED PRDTS, WHOLESALE: Spec Clean/Sanitation

Desco Equipment Company Inc .... G 704 873-2844
Statesville *(G-14787)*

CHEMICALS & ALLIED PRDTS, WHOLESALE: Syn Resin, Rub/Plastic

Fibex LLC .... G 336 605-9002
Colfax *(G-4150)*

CHEMICALS & OTHER PRDTS DERIVED FROM COKING

Thermochem Recovery Intl .... F 919 606-3282
Durham *(G-5399)*

CHEMICALS, AGRICULTURE: Wholesalers

AG Provision LLC .... E 910 296-0302
Kenansville *(G-9140)*

Coastal Agrobusiness Inc .... G 828 697-2220
Flat Rock *(G-5963)*

Coastal Agrobusiness Inc .... G 252 798-3481
Hamilton *(G-7613)*

Coastal Agrobusiness Inc .... D 252 238-7391
Greenville *(G-7503)*

Harvey Fertilizer and Gas Co .... E 252 526-4150
Kinston *(G-9369)*

Helena Agri-Enterprises LLC .... G 828 685-1182
Hendersonville *(G-7861)*

Industrial and Agricultural .... E 910 843-2121
Red Springs *(G-13501)*

Upl NA Inc .... E 610 491-2800
Durham *(G-5426)*

CHEMICALS: Agricultural

Aqua 10 Corporation .... G 252 726-5421
Morehead City *(G-11149)*

Arysta Lifescience Inc .... D 919 678-4900
Cary *(G-1690)*

CHEMICALS: Agricultural

Arysta Lifescience N Amer LLC .... E 919 678-4900
  Cary (G-1691)
Atticus LLC .... E 984 465-4754
  Cary (G-1694)
Chemours Company .... E 910 483-4681
  Fayetteville (G-5788)
Chemours Company Fc LLC .... C 910 678-1314
  Fayetteville (G-5789)
Dupont .... G 919 414-0089
  Raleigh (G-12710)
E I Du Pont De Nemours .... G 919 518-1332
  Raleigh (G-12712)
Fair Products Inc .... G 919 467-1599
  Cary (G-1767)
Harvey Fertilizer and Gas Co .... E 252 753-2063
  Farmville (G-5738)
Makhteshim Agan North Amer Inc .... E 919 256-9300
  Raleigh (G-12990)
Monsanto Company .... G 252 212-5421
  Battleboro (G-925)
Pro Farm Group Inc .... D 530 750-2800
  Raleigh (G-13147)
Southeastern Minerals Inc .... E 252 492-0831
  Henderson (G-7811)
Southern AG Insecticides Inc .... E 828 264-8843
  Boone (G-1238)
Southern AG Insecticides Inc .... E 828 692-2233
  Hendersonville (G-7902)
Trinity Manufacturing Inc .... D 910 582-5650
  Hamlet (G-7633)
Upl NA Inc .... E 610 491-2800
  Durham (G-5426)
Vpm Liquidating Inc .... F 336 292-1781
  Greensboro (G-7451)

CHEMICALS: Alcohols

Gee Spot Mobile Bar LLC .... G 910 581-1786
  Jacksonville (G-9002)

CHEMICALS: Bromine, Elemental

Albemarle Corporation .... A 980 299-5700
  Charlotte (G-2152)

CHEMICALS: Fire Retardant

Albemarle Corporation .... A 980 299-5700
  Charlotte (G-2152)
Fire Retardant Chem Tech LLC .... G 980 253-8880
  Matthews (G-10316)

CHEMICALS: High Purity Grade, Organic

Carbon Conversion Systems LLC .... G 919 883-4238
  Chapel Hill (G-1996)
Clariant Corporation .... D 704 331-7000
  Charlotte (G-2491)

CHEMICALS: Inorganic, NEC

Access Technologies LLC .... G 574 286-1255
  Mooresville (G-10847)
Airgas Usa LLC .... F 704 394-1420
  Charlotte (G-2147)
Airgas Usa LLC .... G 919 544-3773
  Durham (G-4909)
Airgas Usa LLC .... G 919 735-5276
  Goldsboro (G-6587)
Al-Tex Dyes Co LLC .... G 704 849-9727
  Matthews (G-10232)
Albemarle Corporation .... C 704 739-2501
  Kings Mountain (G-9290)
All Elements Incorporated .... G 919 641-9576
  Cary (G-1679)
Apollo Chemical Corp .... D 336 226-1161
  Burlington (G-1366)
Archroma US Inc .... E 704 353-4100
  Charlotte (G-2211)
Arkema Inc .... D 919 469-6700
  Cary (G-1688)
Baikowski International Corp .... F 704 587-7100
  Charlotte (G-2265)
Blue Nano Inc .... F 888 508-6266
  Cornelius (G-4527)
Bluestone Metals & Chem LLC .... G 704 662-8632
  Cornelius (G-4528)
Bluestone Specialty Chem LLC .... F 704 662-8632
  Cornelius (G-4529)
Borden Chemical .... G 828 584-3800
  Morganton (G-11202)
Bryson Industries Inc .... F 336 931-0026
  Thomasville (G-15191)
Carus LLC .... E 704 822-1441
  Belmont (G-977)
Celanese .... E 910 343-5000
  Wilmington (G-16165)
Chemol Company Inc .... E 336 333-3050
  Greensboro (G-6906)
Chemtrade Logistics (us) Inc .... E 773 646-2500
  Charlotte (G-2471)
Clift Industries Inc .... G 704 752-0031
  Mount Holly (G-11628)
Conference Inc .... G 704 349-0203
  Gastonia (G-6383)
Corrtrac Systems Corporation .... G 252 232-3975
  Currituck (G-4633)
Dupont Specialty Pdts USA LLC .... E 919 248-5109
  Durham (G-5070)
Dystar LP .... E 704 561-3000
  Charlotte (G-2668)
Eidp Inc .... D 910 483-4681
  Fayetteville (G-5819)
Eidp Inc .... D 252 522-6111
  Grifton (G-7599)
Eidp Inc .... G 910 371-4000
  Leland (G-9540)
Element West LLC .... G 336 853-6118
  Lexington (G-9713)
Elemental Bee .... G 336 471-9085
  High Point (G-8339)
Elements Brands LLC .... F 503 230-8008
  Charlotte (G-2692)
Elements In Focus LLC .... G 561 289-8641
  Cary (G-1756)
Fil-Chem Inc .... G 919 878-1270
  Raleigh (G-12766)
Fortrans Inc .... G 919 365-8004
  Wendell (G-15902)
Fuji Silysia Chemical USA Ltd .... E 252 413-0003
  Greenville (G-7531)
Geo Specialty Chemicals Inc .... G 252 793-2121
  Plymouth (G-12373)
Grace and Company LLC .... G 336 893-7511
  Winston Salem (G-16726)
Gresco Manufacturing Inc .... G 336 475-8101
  Thomasville (G-15228)
Highland International .... G 828 265-2513
  Boone (G-1206)
Industrial and Agricultural .... E 910 843-2121
  Red Springs (G-13501)
Invista Capital Management LLC .... A 316 828-1000
  Wilmington (G-16273)
Leke LLC .... E 704 523-1452
  Pineville (G-12280)
M & G Polymers Usa LLC .... G 910 509-4414
  Wilmington (G-16311)
Marlowe-Van Loan Corporation .... E 336 886-7126
  High Point (G-8440)
Metallix Refining Inc .... E 252 413-0346
  Greenville (G-7559)
Microban Products Company .... D 704 766-4267
  Huntersville (G-8854)
Mount Vernon Chemicals LLC .... D 336 226-1161
  Burlington (G-1463)
Mount Vernon Mills Inc .... B 336 226-1161
  Burlington (G-1464)
Netqem LLC .... G 919 544-4122
  Durham (G-5243)
Novalent Ltd .... F 336 375-7555
  Greensboro (G-7225)
Olin Black Enterprise LLC .... G 704 363-5675
  Midland (G-10472)
Oneh2 Inc .... E 844 996-6342
  Hickory (G-8107)
Pavco Inc .... E 704 496-6800
  Charlotte (G-3321)
Pencco Inc .... F 252 235-5300
  Middlesex (G-10453)
Piedmont Lithium Carolinas Inc .... F 434 664-7643
  Belmont (G-1002)
Pretinned Carbide Co Inc .... E 704 871-9644
  Statesville (G-14868)
Rockwood Lithium .... F 704 739-2501
  Kings Mountain (G-9330)
Sciepharm LLC .... C 307 352-9559
  Durham (G-5343)
Sciteck Diagnostics Inc .... G 828 650-0409
  Fletcher (G-6036)
Sibelco .... E 828 765-1114
  Spruce Pine (G-14655)
Solvay USA Inc .... C 919 786-4555
  Raleigh (G-13280)
Sostram Corporation .... G 919 226-1195
  Durham (G-5364)
Tecgrachem Inc .... G 336 993-6785
  Kernersville (G-9241)
Unichem IV Ltd .... F 336 578-5476
  Haw River (G-7758)
Venator Chemicals LLC .... D 704 454-4811
  Harrisburg (G-7733)

CHEMICALS: Lithium Compounds, Inorganic

Albemarle US Inc .... C 704 739-2501
  Kings Mountain (G-9291)
FMC Corporation .... E 704 868-5300
  Bessemer City (G-1067)
FMC Corporation .... B 704 426-5336
  Bessemer City (G-1068)

CHEMICALS: Magnesium Compounds Or Salts, Inorganic

Giles Chemical Corporation .... G 828 452-4784
  Waynesville (G-15805)
Giles Chemical Corporation .... E 828 452-4784
  Waynesville (G-15806)

CHEMICALS: NEC

Ae Technology Inc .... F 704 528-2000
  Troutman (G-15365)
American Chrome & Chem NA Inc .... G 910 675-7200
  Castle Hayne (G-1942)
American Phoenix Inc .... C 910 484-4007
  Fayetteville (G-5760)
Attl Products Inc .... G 336 475-8101
  Thomasville (G-15187)
Blast Off Intl Chem & Mfg Co .... G 509 885-4525
  Seaboard (G-14226)
Bnnano Inc .... F 844 926-6266
  Burlington (G-1377)

Bonsal American Inc.......................... D 704 525-1621
   Charlotte *(G-2334)*

Buckeye International Inc.................. G 704 523-9400
   Charlotte *(G-2363)*

Burlington Chemical Co LLC................ G 336 584-0111
   Greensboro *(G-6861)*

Camco Manufacturing LLC.................. C 800 334-2004
   Greensboro *(G-6876)*

Championx LLC.................................. G 704 506-4830
   Belmont *(G-979)*

Chem-Tex Laboratories Inc................. E 706 602-8600
   Concord *(G-4232)*

Chemtech North Carolina LLC............. E 910 514-9575
   Lillington *(G-9849)*

Clariant Corporation............................ D 704 331-7000
   Charlotte *(G-2489)*

Clean Solutions LLC........................... G 919 391-8047
   Charlotte *(G-2495)*

Copia Labs Inc................................... G 910 904-1000
   Raeford *(G-12417)*

Dst Manufacturing LLC....................... G 336 676-6096
   Randleman *(G-13465)*

Emerald Carolina Chemical LLC.......... D 704 393-0089
   Charlotte *(G-2706)*

Enviroserve Chemicals Inc................. F 910 892-1791
   Dunn *(G-4865)*

Eoncoat LLC....................................... G 941 928-9401
   Lenoir *(G-9606)*

Euclid Chemical Company................... G 704 283-2544
   Monroe *(G-10717)*

FMC Corporation................................. E 704 868-5300
   Bessemer City *(G-1067)*

FMC Corporation................................. B 704 426-5336
   Bessemer City *(G-1068)*

Freudenberg Prfmce Mtls LP.............. C 828 665-5000
   Candler *(G-1579)*

Gb Biosciences LLC............................ D 336 632-6000
   Greensboro *(G-7032)*

Global Bioprotect LLC......................... F 336 861-0162
   High Point *(G-8367)*

Goulston Technologies Inc.................. E 704 289-6464
   Monroe *(G-10727)*

Gtg Engineering Inc........................... G 877 569-8572
   Clarendon *(G-3946)*

Gtg Engineering Inc........................... G 910 457-0068
   Southport *(G-14571)*

Hexion Inc.. E 910 483-1311
   Fayetteville *(G-5838)*

Hospira Inc.. B 919 553-3831
   Clayton *(G-3988)*

Ifs Industries Inc................................ E 919 234-1397
   Morrisville *(G-11357)*

Ivm Chemicals Inc.............................. E 407 506-4913
   Charlotte *(G-3000)*

Jci Jones Chemicals Inc..................... E 704 392-9767
   Charlotte *(G-3014)*

Laticrete International Inc.................. F 910 582-2252
   Hamlet *(G-7626)*

LCI Corporation International.............. E 704 399-7441
   Charlotte *(G-3076)*

Lime-Chem Inc................................... G 910 843-2121
   Rockwell *(G-13655)*

Liquid Ice Corporation........................ F 704 882-3505
   Matthews *(G-10328)*

Lubrizol Global Management Inc......... D 704 865-7451
   Gastonia *(G-6447)*

Marlowe-Van Loan Sales Co............... F 336 882-3351
   High Point *(G-8441)*

Microban Products Company.............. D 704 766-4267
   Huntersville *(G-8854)*

Molecular Toxicology Inc.................... F 828 264-9099
   Boone *(G-1223)*

Novalent Ltd...................................... F 336 375-7555
   Greensboro *(G-7225)*

Nsi Lab Solutions Inc......................... F 919 789-3000
   Raleigh *(G-13075)*

Pavco Inc... E 704 496-6800
   Charlotte *(G-3321)*

Polytec Inc... E 704 277-3960
   Mooresville *(G-11055)*

Radiator Specialty Company............... D 704 688-2302
   Indian Trail *(G-8959)*

Riba Fairfield.................................... G 919 294-4819
   Durham *(G-5330)*

RSC Bio Solutions LLC....................... G 800 661-3558
   Charlotte *(G-3467)*

RSC Chemical Solutions LLC.............. E 704 821-7643
   Indian Trail *(G-8961)*

Rust911 Inc....................................... G 607 425-2882
   Hickory *(G-8144)*

Seacon Corporation............................ F 704 333-6000
   Charlotte *(G-3516)*

Sirchie Acquisition Co LLC................. C 800 356-7311
   Youngsville *(G-17098)*

Soto Industries LLC........................... E 706 643-5011
   Charlotte *(G-3582)*

Specgx LLC.. C 919 878-4706
   Raleigh *(G-13286)*

Sportsmans Supply Company Inc....... G 336 725-8791
   Winston Salem *(G-16913)*

Surry Chemicals Incorporated........... E 336 786-4607
   Mount Airy *(G-11580)*

Tribodyn Technologies Inc................. F 859 750-6299
   Mooresville *(G-11115)*

Unitex Chemical Corp......................... E 336 378-0965
   Greensboro *(G-7432)*

Venator Chemicals LLC...................... D 704 454-4811
   Harrisburg *(G-7733)*

Westrock Company............................. G 770 448-2193
   Winston Salem *(G-16971)*

Winton Products Company.................. F 704 399-5151
   Charlotte *(G-3818)*

Xelera Inc.. G 540 915-6181
   Denver *(G-4816)*

CHEMICALS: Phosphates, Defluorinated/Ammoniated, Exc Fertlr

Pcs Phosphate Company Inc.............. E 252 322-4111
   Aurora *(G-838)*

CHEMICALS: Reagent Grade, Refined From Technical Grade

Hemo Bioscience Inc.......................... G 919 313-2888
   Durham *(G-5135)*

Synnovator Inc................................... G 919 360-0518
   Durham *(G-5384)*

CHEMICALS: Silica Compounds

Applied Nano Solutions Inc................ G 336 687-6517
   Trinity *(G-15338)*

Fuji Silysia Chemical Ltd.................... F 919 484-4158
   Greenville *(G-7530)*

CHEMICALS: Water Treatment

Loy & Loy Inc.................................... G 919 942-6356
   Graham *(G-6699)*

Matchem Inc...................................... G 336 886-5000
   High Point *(G-8450)*

Moe Jt Enterprises Inc....................... F 423 512-1427
   Winston Salem *(G-16816)*

Pencco Inc... F 252 235-5900
   Middlesex *(G-10453)*

Second Earth Inc............................... G 336 740-9333
   Greensboro *(G-7329)*

Xelera Inc.. G 855 493-5372
   Charlotte *(G-3833)*

Xylem Water Solutions USA Inc........... E 704 409-9700
   Charlotte *(G-3841)*

CHICKEN SLAUGHTERING & PROCESSING

Game Processing Leonards Wild......... G 980 429-7042
   Lincolnton *(G-9894)*

Hopkins Poultry Company................... F 336 656-3361
   Browns Summit *(G-1308)*

CHILDREN'S & INFANTS' CLOTHING STORES

Aidleyco LLC..................................... G 704 782-0648
   Mooresville *(G-10851)*

Cannon & Daughters Inc................... D 828 254-9236
   Asheville *(G-579)*

Pashes LLC....................................... G 704 682-6535
   Statesville *(G-14857)*

CHILDREN'S WEAR STORES

W E Nixons Wldg & Hdwr Inc.............. G 252 221-4348
   Edenton *(G-5523)*

CHOCOLATE, EXC CANDY FROM BEANS: Chips, Powder, Block, Syrup

Mountain Bear & Co Inc..................... G 828 631-0156
   Dillsboro *(G-4817)*

CHOCOLATE, EXC CANDY FROM PURCH CHOC: Chips, Powder, Block

Barry Callebaut USA LLC.................... D 828 685-2443
   Hendersonville *(G-7823)*

Escazu Artisan Chocolate LLC............ F 919 832-3433
   Raleigh *(G-12745)*

Nutkao USA Inc.................................. E 252 595-1000
   Battleboro *(G-926)*

CHRISTMAS TREE LIGHTING SETS: Electric

Anndori Outdoor Art LLC.................... E 336 202-8400
   Greensboro *(G-6809)*

Posh Pad... G 910 988-4800
   Stedman *(G-14936)*

CHRISTMAS TREES: Artificial

Fisherman Creations Inc.................... E 252 725-0138
   Beaufort *(G-956)*

CHROMATOGRAPHY EQPT

Practichem LLC................................. G 919 714-8430
   Morrisville *(G-11411)*

Waters Corporation............................ G 910 270-3137
   Hampstead *(G-7664)*

CHUCKS

Tfam Solutions LLC............................ G 910 637-0266
   Aberdeen *(G-31)*

CIGARETTE & CIGAR PRDTS & ACCESS

E-Liquid Brands LLC.......................... E 828 385-5090
   Mooresville *(G-10933)*

Medallion Company Inc...................... C 919 990-3500
   Timberlake *(G-15315)*

Peak Level Media Solutions LLC......... G 919 917-8002
   Cary *(G-1846)*

Purilum LLC....................................... E 252 931-8020
   Greenville *(G-7577)*

CIGARETTE FILTERS

USa Wholesale and Distrg Inc............ F 888 484-6872
  Fayetteville *(G-5945)*

CIGARETTE FILTERS

Filtrona Filters Inc............ D 336 362-1333
  Greensboro *(G-7015)*

CIRCUIT BOARD REPAIR SVCS

Esco Electronic Services Inc............ F 252 753-4433
  Farmville *(G-5735)*

Protronics Inc............ F 919 217-0007
  Knightdale *(G-9427)*

CIRCUIT BOARDS: Wiring

Global Manufacturing Svcs Inc............ E 336 846-1674
  West Jefferson *(G-15940)*

CIRCUITS, INTEGRATED: Hybrid

X-Celeprint Inc............ F 919 248-0020
  Durham *(G-5453)*

CIRCUITS: Electronic

Acterna LLC............ F 919 388-5100
  Morrisville *(G-11277)*

Advanced Substrate............ F 336 285-5955
  Greensboro *(G-6781)*

Anuva Services Inc............ F 919 468-6441
  Morrisville *(G-11288)*

Carolina Elctrnic Assmblers In............ E 919 938-1086
  Smithfield *(G-14452)*

CCS International Circuits LLC............ G 704 907-1208
  Matthews *(G-10239)*

CMS Associates Inc............ G 919 365-0881
  Wendell *(G-15895)*

Cnc-Ke Inc............ D 704 333-0145
  Charlotte *(G-2509)*

Cooper Crouse-Hinds LLC............ E 252 566-3014
  La Grange *(G-9439)*

Crackle Holdings LP............ A 704 927-7620
  Charlotte *(G-2567)*

Duotech Services Inc............ E 828 369-5411
  Franklin *(G-6126)*

Edc Inc............ D 336 993-0468
  Kernersville *(G-9194)*

Ferguson Manufacturing Company............ F 336 661-1116
  Winston Salem *(G-16709)*

Finnord North America Corp............ F 704 723-4913
  Huntersville *(G-8820)*

Geotrak Incorporated............ F 919 303-1467
  Apex *(G-194)*

Innova-Con Incorporated............ G 919 303-1467
  Apex *(G-206)*

Mystery Circuits LLC............ G 919 942-4992
  Chapel Hill *(G-2045)*

Pt Marketing Incorporated............ G 412 471-8995
  Raleigh *(G-13157)*

Snap One LLC............ B 704 927-7620
  Charlotte *(G-3569)*

Snap One Holdings Corp............ D 704 927-7620
  Charlotte *(G-3570)*

Spruce Pine Mica Company............ F 828 765-4241
  Spruce Pine *(G-14659)*

Tresco............ C 361 985-3154
  Boone *(G-1242)*

Wieland Electric Inc............ F 910 259-5050
  Wilmington *(G-16442)*

CIRCULAR KNIT FABRICS DYEING & FINISHING

Carolina Mills Incorporated............ B 828 428-9911
  Maiden *(G-10102)*

Century Textile Mfg Inc............ F 704 869-6660
  Gastonia *(G-6373)*

Mocaro Dyeing & Finishing Inc............ D 704 878-6645
  Statesville *(G-14844)*

Sdfc LLC............ F 704 878-6645
  Monroe *(G-10804)*

South Fork Industries Inc............ D 828 428-9921
  Maiden *(G-10117)*

Unifour Finishers Inc............ E 828 322-9435
  Hickory *(G-8194)*

Unifour Finishers Inc............ E 828 322-9435
  Hickory *(G-8193)*

CLAMPS & COUPLINGS: Hose

Parker-Hannifin Corporation............ G 704 664-1922
  Mooresville *(G-11047)*

CLAMPS: Metal

Nuclamp System LLC............ G 336 643-1766
  Oak Ridge *(G-12061)*

CLAY, PETROLEUM REFINING: Chemically Processed

Carolina Stalite Co Ltd Partnr............ E 704 279-2166
  Gold Hill *(G-6581)*

CLAY: Filtering, Treated

Cormetech Inc............ C 919 620-3000
  Charlotte *(G-2554)*

CLEANING EQPT: Commercial

Anderson Living Center LLC............ G 828 229-3243
  Forest City *(G-6059)*

Galaxy Pressure Washing Inc............ G 888 299-3129
  Pineville *(G-12270)*

Green Waste Management LLC............ G 704 289-0720
  Charlotte *(G-2864)*

Legacy Commercial Service LLC............ G 757 831-5291
  Charlotte *(G-3080)*

Level Ten Facilities Svcs LLC............ G 704 759-6799
  Charlotte *(G-3083)*

Midsouth Power Eqp Co Inc............ F 336 389-0515
  Greensboro *(G-7201)*

Quality Cleaning Services LLC............ F 919 638-4969
  Durham *(G-5311)*

Skyview Commercial Cleaning............ G 704 858-0134
  Charlotte *(G-3562)*

Supreme Sweepers LLC............ G 888 698-9996
  Charlotte *(G-3657)*

CLEANING EQPT: Floor Washing & Polishing, Commercial

Amano Pioneer Eclipse Corp............ E 704 900-1352
  Charlotte *(G-2177)*

Amano Pioneer Eclipse Corp............ D 336 372-8080
  Sparta *(G-14588)*

Onyx Environmental Solutions Inc............ E 800 858-3533
  Stanley *(G-14705)*

CLEANING EQPT: High Pressure

Aquatic Pressure Washing............ G 910 232-3273
  Raleigh *(G-12516)*

B&C Xterior Cleaning Svc Inc............ G 919 779-7905
  Raleigh *(G-12540)*

Bk Seamless Gutters LLC............ G 252 955-5414
  Spring Hope *(G-14615)*

Butler Trieu Inc............ G 910 346-4929
  Jacksonville *(G-8992)*

Desco Equipment Company Inc............ G 704 873-2844
  Statesville *(G-14787)*

Painting By Colors LLC............ G 919 963-2300
  Clayton *(G-4005)*

CLEANING OR POLISHING PREPARATIONS, NEC

Ace Industries Inc............ G 336 427-5316
  Madison *(G-10069)*

Amano Pioneer Eclipse Corp............ D 336 372-8080
  Sparta *(G-14588)*

Awesome Products Inc............ G 336 374-5900
  Mount Airy *(G-11478)*

Busch Enterprises Inc............ G 704 878-2067
  Statesville *(G-14768)*

Cherryville Distrg Co Inc............ G 704 435-9692
  Cherryville *(G-3863)*

Elevate Cleaning Service............ G 347 928-4030
  Fayetteville *(G-5820)*

Elsco Inc............ G 509 885-4525
  Seaboard *(G-14228)*

Eminess Technologies Inc............ E 704 283-2600
  Monroe *(G-10713)*

Fresh As A Daisy Inc............ G 336 869-3002
  High Point *(G-8359)*

Harper Corporation of America............ C 704 588-3371
  Charlotte *(G-2890)*

Ice Companies Inc............ G 910 791-1970
  Wilmington *(G-16261)*

Organizer Llc............ G 336 391-7591
  Winston Salem *(G-16832)*

CLEANING PRDTS: Automobile Polish

Chrome Bubbles By Maurice............ G 704 224-8866
  Charlotte *(G-2479)*

Dings Etc............ G 252 933-0208
  Kinston *(G-9357)*

First Class Ridez LLC............ G 919 610-6043
  Zebulon *(G-17127)*

Unx Industries Inc............ G 252 355-8433
  Greenville *(G-7593)*

CLEANING PRDTS: Bleaches, Household, Dry Or Liquid

Unx Industries Inc............ D 252 756-8616
  Greenville *(G-7594)*

CLEANING PRDTS: Deodorants, Nonpersonal

Remodeez LLC............ F 704 428-9050
  Charlotte *(G-3431)*

CLEANING PRDTS: Disinfectants, Household Or Indl Plant

Enc Industrial Supply............ G 252 862-8300
  Ahoskie *(G-62)*

Patel Deepal............ G 704 634-5141
  Concord *(G-4330)*

CLEANING PRDTS: Drain Pipe Solvents Or Cleaners

Entrust Services LLC............ F 336 274-5175
  Greensboro *(G-7002)*

CLEANING PRDTS: Laundry Preparations

A Cleaner Tomorrow Dry Clg LLC............ G 919 639-6396
  Dunn *(G-4847)*

Dewill Inc............ G 919 426-9550
  Cary *(G-1749)*

Fresh-N-Mobile LLC............ G 704 251-4643
  Charlotte *(G-2797)*

PRODUCT SECTION   CLOTHING: Aprons, Exc Rubber/Plastic, Women, Misses, Junior

M and R Inc... G 704 332-5999
  Charlotte *(G-3114)*
Piece of Pie LLC....................................... F 919 286-7421
  Durham *(G-5289)*
Quail Dry Cleaning................................... G 704 947-7435
  Charlotte *(G-3401)*

CLEANING PRDTS: Sanitation Preparations

Mooresvlle Pub Wrks Snttion De............ G 704 664-4278
  Mooresville *(G-11029)*

CLEANING PRDTS: Sanitation Preps, Disinfectants/Deodorants

AEC Consumer Products LLC................ F 704 904-0578
  Fayetteville *(G-5754)*

CLEANING PRDTS: Shoe Polish Or Cleaner

Hickory Brands Inc.................................. D 828 322-2500
  Hickory *(G-8044)*

CLEANING PRDTS: Specialty

Autec Inc... E 704 871-9141
  Statesville *(G-14755)*
Buckeye International Inc....................... G 704 523-9400
  Charlotte *(G-2363)*
Ecolab Inc.. E 336 931-2289
  Greensboro *(G-6989)*
H & H Products Incorporated................. G 910 891-4276
  Dunn *(G-4873)*
Illinois Tool Works Inc.............................. C 336 996-7046
  Kernersville *(G-9206)*
Isana LLC.. G 704 439-6761
  Charlotte *(G-2997)*
Kay Chemical Company........................... A 336 668-7290
  Greensboro *(G-7144)*
Microban Products Company................... D 704 766-4267
  Huntersville *(G-8854)*
Mill-Chem Manufacturing Inc.................. E 336 889-8038
  Thomasville *(G-15251)*
Procter & Gamble Mfg Co........................ D 336 954-0000
  Greensboro *(G-7287)*
Rga Enterprises Inc................................. D 704 398-0487
  Charlotte *(G-3447)*
Solo Solutions Corporation...................... G 336 992-2585
  Kernersville *(G-9235)*
Speed Brite Inc.. G 704 639-9771
  Salisbury *(G-14046)*
Superior Envmtl Svcs LLC....................... G 919 717-1199
  Knightdale *(G-9429)*
W G of Southwest Raleigh Inc............... G 919 629-7327
  Holly Springs *(G-8725)*

CLEANING SVCS: Industrial Or Commercial

Darius All Access LLC.............................. E 910 262-8567
  Wilmington *(G-16194)*
Isana LLC.. G 704 439-6761
  Charlotte *(G-2997)*

CLIPPERS: Fingernail & Toenail

L Michelle LLC.. G 980 946-0204
  Mooresville *(G-11002)*

CLOSURES: Closures, Stamped Metal

Aquahut... G 704 335-8554
  Charlotte *(G-2207)*

CLOTHING & ACCESS, WOMEN, CHILDREN & INFANT, WHOL: Access

AC Valor Reyes LLC................................ G 910 431-3526
  Castle Hayne *(G-1941)*

Moon and Lola Inc.................................. G 919 306-2257
  Raleigh *(G-13040)*

CLOTHING & ACCESS, WOMEN, CHILDREN & INFANT, WHOL: Uniforms

Tresmc LLC... G 919 900-0868
  Knightdale *(G-9432)*

CLOTHING & ACCESS, WOMEN, CHILDREN/ INFANT, WHOL: Baby Goods

Sunrise Development LLC....................... F 828 453-0590
  Mooresboro *(G-10841)*

CLOTHING & ACCESS, WOMEN, CHILDREN/ INFANT, WHOL: Nightwear

Sanders Industries Inc............................ G 410 277-8565
  Waynesville *(G-15820)*

CLOTHING & ACCESS: Handicapped

Burlington Coat Fctry Whse Cor.............. E 919 468-9312
  Cary *(G-1718)*
Hinsons Typing & Printing........................ G 919 934-9036
  Smithfield *(G-14462)*

CLOTHING & ACCESS: Hospital Gowns

Belvoir Manufacturing Corp..................... D 252 746-1274
  Greenville *(G-7494)*
Health Supply Us LLC............................ F 888 408-1694
  Mooresville *(G-10971)*
Whitewood Contracts LLC...................... E 336 885-9300
  High Point *(G-8603)*

CLOTHING & ACCESS: Men's Miscellaneous Access

Apparel USA Inc....................................... E 212 869-5495
  Fairmont *(G-5700)*
Duck Head LLC...................................... F 855 457-1865
  Greensboro *(G-6983)*
Eagle Sportswear LLC........................... F 919 365-9805
  Wendell *(G-15900)*
Hanesbrands Export Canada LLC........... G 336 519-8080
  Winston Salem *(G-16733)*
Jestines Jewels Inc................................ G 704 904-0191
  Salisbury *(G-13991)*
Kayser-Roth Hosiery Inc........................ E 336 852-2030
  Greensboro *(G-7146)*
Lebos Shoe Store Inc............................ F 704 987-6540
  Cornelius *(G-4567)*
Military Products Inc.............................. G 910 637-0315
  West End *(G-15930)*
Mischief Makers Local 816 LLC............ E 336 763-2003
  Greensboro *(G-7202)*
MJ Soffe LLC... E 910 422-9002
  Rowland *(G-13791)*
Vanceboro Apparel Inc............................ G 252 244-2780
  Vanceboro *(G-15484)*

CLOTHING & ACCESS: Suspenders

Madison Company Inc............................ E 336 548-9624
  Madison *(G-10079)*
The Madison Company Inc...................... E 336 548-9624
  Madison *(G-10088)*

CLOTHING & APPAREL STORES: Custom

Brands Fashion US Inc............................ G 704 953-8246
  Charlotte *(G-2348)*
Carolina Shirt Company Inc................... G 910 575-4447
  Calabash *(G-1552)*
Ebony & Ivorys Unique Btq LLC.............. G 704 324-4035
  Wingate *(G-16574)*

Global Products & Mfg Svcs Inc.............. G 360 870-9876
  Charlotte *(G-2834)*
Ics North America Corp........................... E 704 794-6620
  Concord *(G-4283)*
Manna Corp North Carolina..................... G 828 696-3642
  Hendersonville *(G-7875)*

CLOTHING & FURNISHINGS, MEN'S & BOYS', WHOLESALE: Shirts

Associated Distributors Inc...................... G 910 895-5800
  Hamlet *(G-7616)*

CLOTHING & FURNISHINGS, MEN'S & BOYS', WHOLESALE: Uniforms

Bob Barker Company Inc....................... C 800 334-9880
  Fuquay Varina *(G-6184)*
Carolina Tailors Inc................................ F 252 247-6469
  Newport *(G-11899)*

CLOTHING & FURNISHINGS, MENS & BOYS, WHOL: Sportswear/Work

Ics North America Corp........................... E 704 794-6620
  Concord *(G-4283)*

CLOTHING STORES: T-Shirts, Printed, Custom

K Formula Enterprises Inc....................... G 910 323-3315
  Fayetteville *(G-5853)*
Screen Master... G 252 492-8407
  Henderson *(G-7810)*

CLOTHING STORES: Uniforms & Work

Gmg Group LLC..................................... G 252 441-8374
  Kill Devil Hills *(G-9258)*
McDaniel Delmar..................................... E 336 284-6377
  Mocksville *(G-10586)*

CLOTHING STORES: Unisex

Labonte Racing Inc................................... F 336 431-1004
  Trinity *(G-15348)*

CLOTHING STORES: Work

Kontoor Brands Inc................................ C 336 332-3400
  Greensboro *(G-7156)*

CLOTHING: Academic Vestments

Atlantic Trading LLC.............................. F
  Charlotte *(G-2233)*
Craftex Rework Inc................................ G 252 239-0123
  Lucama *(G-10016)*

CLOTHING: Access, Women's & Misses'

Apparel USA Inc....................................... E 212 869-5495
  Fairmont *(G-5700)*
Blacqueladi Styles LLC............................ G 877 977-7798
  Cary *(G-1707)*
Centric Brands LLC.................................. C 646 582-6000
  Greensboro *(G-6900)*
Live It Boutique LLC................................. G 704 492-2402
  Charlotte *(G-3095)*
Lm Shea LLC.. G 919 608-1901
  Raleigh *(G-12977)*
Vanceboro Apparel Inc............................ G 252 244-2780
  Vanceboro *(G-15484)*

CLOTHING: Anklets & Socks

Midpines Hosiery Inc............................. G 919 774-3888
  Sanford *(G-14153)*

CLOTHING: Aprons, Exc Rubber/Plastic, Women, Misses, Junior

J C Custom Sewing Inc............................G..... 336 449-4586
Gibsonville *(G-6563)*

CLOTHING: Aprons, Waterproof, From Purchased Materials

Drydog Barriers LLC................................G..... 704 334-8222
Indian Trail *(G-8930)*

CLOTHING: Athletic & Sportswear, Men's & Boys'

Badger Sportswear LLC............................C..... 704 871-0990
Statesville *(G-14758)*
Brand New Life Clothing LLC....................G..... 980 266-4788
Charlotte *(G-2345)*
Capefear Sportswear................................G..... 910 620-7844
Wilmington *(G-16152)*
Capstar Corporation................................C..... 704 878-2007
Statesville *(G-14770)*
Custom Spt & Imprintables LLC.................F..... 910 799-9914
Wilmington *(G-16193)*
Gfsi Holdings LLC...................................A..... 336 519-8080
Winston Salem *(G-16720)*
Ics North America Corp............................E..... 704 794-6620
Concord *(G-4283)*
Levi Strauss International........................G..... 828 665-2417
Asheville *(G-683)*
Mk Global Holdings LLC..........................E..... 704 334-1904
Charlotte *(G-3190)*
Ramco..G..... 704 794-6620
Concord *(G-4347)*
Walter Reynolds......................................G..... 704 735-6050
Lincolnton *(G-9935)*

CLOTHING: Athletic & Sportswear, Women's & Girls'

Alleson of Rochester Inc..........................D..... 585 272-0606
Statesville *(G-14744)*
Capstar Corporation................................C..... 704 878-2007
Statesville *(G-14770)*
Ican Clothes Company.............................F..... 910 670-1494
Fayetteville *(G-5840)*
Kayla Jonise Bernhardt Crutch..................G..... 252 457-5367
Elizabeth City *(G-5552)*
Old Dell Designs....................................G..... 910 532-6066
Magnolia *(G-10098)*
Walter Reynolds....................................G..... 704 735-6050
Lincolnton *(G-9935)*

CLOTHING: Baker, Barber, Lab/Svc Ind Apparel, Washable, Men

Criticore Inc...F..... 704 542-6876
Charlotte *(G-2570)*
White Knght Engineered Pdts Inc...............E..... 828 687-0940
Asheville *(G-820)*

CLOTHING: Bathing Suits & Swimwear, Knit

Wings Store 765....................................G..... 910 458-0278
Carolina Beach *(G-1642)*

CLOTHING: Belts

Belt Shop Inc...F..... 704 865-3636
Gastonia *(G-6352)*
Centric Brands LLC.................................C..... 646 582-6000
Greensboro *(G-6900)*
Hawk Distributors Inc..............................G..... 888 334-1407
Sanford *(G-14129)*

Madison Company Inc.............................E..... 336 548-9624
Madison *(G-10079)*
Military Products Inc...............................G..... 910 637-0315
West End *(G-15930)*
Point Blank Enterprises Inc.......................D..... 910 893-2071
Lillington *(G-9858)*
The Madison Company Inc.......................E..... 336 548-9624
Madison *(G-10088)*
Wentworth Corporation............................F..... 336 548-1802
Madison *(G-10091)*

CLOTHING: Blouses, Women's & Girls'

Custom Ink..E..... 704 935-5604
Charlotte *(G-2591)*
Grateful Union Family Inc.........................F..... 828 622-3258
Asheville *(G-640)*

CLOTHING: Blouses, Womens & Juniors, From Purchased Mtrls

Bon Worth Inc..E..... 800 355-5131
Hendersonville *(G-7829)*

CLOTHING: Caps, Baseball

Americap Co Inc....................................E..... 252 445-2388
Enfield *(G-5675)*

CLOTHING: Children & Infants'

Cannon & Daughters Inc.........................D..... 828 254-9236
Asheville *(G-579)*
Devil Dog Manufacturing Co Inc................C..... 919 269-7485
Zebulon *(G-17125)*
Justice..E..... 910 392-1581
Wilmington *(G-16284)*
Mulberry Street Inc.................................G..... 252 638-3195
New Bern *(G-11827)*
Tiara Inc...G..... 828 484-8236
Asheville *(G-800)*

CLOTHING: Children's, Girls'

M J Soffe Co..A..... 910 435-3138
Fayetteville *(G-5863)*
Mulberry Street Inc.................................G..... 252 638-3195
New Bern *(G-11827)*
Vanceboro Apparel Inc............................G..... 252 244-2780
Vanceboro *(G-15484)*

CLOTHING: Coats & Jackets, Leather & Sheep-Lined

Gerbings LLC..D..... 800 646-5916
Greensboro *(G-7039)*

CLOTHING: Coats & Suits, Men's & Boys'

American Safety Utility Corp.....................E..... 704 482-0601
Shelby *(G-14285)*
Centric Brands LLC.................................C..... 646 582-6000
Greensboro *(G-6900)*
Nbn Sports Inc.......................................G..... 919 824-5143
Durham *(G-5240)*
Trotters Sewing Company Inc...................D..... 336 629-4550
Asheboro *(G-501)*

CLOTHING: Collar & Cuff Sets, Knit

C & L Manufacturing...............................G..... 336 957-8359
Hays *(G-7773)*
Charlotte Trimming Company Inc...............D..... 704 529-8427
Charlotte *(G-2465)*

CLOTHING: Costumes

McCabes Costumes LLC..........................G..... 252 295-7691
Winterville *(G-17006)*

Morris Family Theatrical Inc.....................E..... 704 332-3304
Charlotte *(G-3203)*

CLOTHING: Disposable

Ddm Inc...G..... 910 686-1481
Wilmington *(G-16197)*
Pearl River Group LLC.............................G..... 704 283-4667
Monroe *(G-10785)*
Precept Medical Products Inc....................F..... 828 681-0209
Arden *(G-365)*

CLOTHING: Dresses

Crt Inc..G..... 704 905-9748
Charlotte *(G-2575)*
Gerson & Gerson Inc..............................E..... 252 235-2441
Middlesex *(G-10450)*
Granite Knitwear Inc...............................G..... 704 279-5526
Granite Quarry *(G-6760)*
Hugger Inc..C..... 704 735-7422
Lincolnton *(G-9895)*
Jestines Jewels Inc.................................G..... 704 904-0191
Salisbury *(G-13991)*
Patti Boo Inc..G..... 828 648-6495
Canton *(G-1621)*

CLOTHING: Dresses & Skirts

Contempora Fabrics Inc..........................C..... 910 345-0150
Lumberton *(G-10030)*

CLOTHING: Hats & Headwear, Knit

Slum Dog Head Gear LLC........................F..... 704 713-8125
Charlotte *(G-3565)*

CLOTHING: Hosiery, Pantyhose & Knee Length, Sheer

Acme - McCrary Corporation....................F..... 336 625-2161
Siler City *(G-14395)*
Acme-Mccrary Corporation......................C..... 336 625-2161
Asheboro *(G-398)*
Bossong Corporation..............................G..... 336 625-2175
Asheboro *(G-410)*
Cajah Corporation..................................C..... 828 728-7300
Hudson *(G-8764)*
Catawba Valley Finishing LLC..................E..... 828 464-2252
Newton *(G-11918)*
Central Carolina Hosiery Inc....................E..... 910 428-9688
Biscoe *(G-1106)*
Crawford Knitting Company Inc................D..... 336 824-1065
Ramseur *(G-13442)*
De Feet International Inc.........................E..... 828 397-7025
Hildebran *(G-8621)*
Felice Hosiery Co Inc..............................E..... 336 996-2371
Kernersville *(G-9200)*
Fine Line Hosiery Inc..............................F..... 336 498-8022
Asheboro *(G-435)*
Glen Raven Inc......................................G..... 336 227-6211
Altamahaw *(G-122)*
Goldtoemoretz LLC.................................B..... 828 464-0751
Newton *(G-11937)*
Hanesbrands Inc....................................G..... 336 789-6118
Mount Airy *(G-11515)*
Huffman Finishing Company Inc...............C..... 828 396-1741
Granite Falls *(G-6739)*
Kayser-Roth Corporation.........................C..... 336 852-2030
Greensboro *(G-7145)*
Mas Acme USA......................................G..... 336 625-2161
Asheboro *(G-456)*
Mayo Knitting Mill Inc..............................C..... 252 823-3101
Tarboro *(G-15114)*
Neat Feet Hosiery Inc.............................G..... 336 573-2177
Stoneville *(G-14962)*

PRODUCT SECTION — CLOTHING: Socks

North Carolina Sock Inc .... G 828 327-4664
  Hickory *(G-8104)*
Rogers Knitting Inc .... G 336 789-4155
  Mount Airy *(G-11567)*
Royal Hosiery Company Inc .... G 828 496-2200
  Granite Falls *(G-6755)*
Simmons Hosiery Mill Inc .... G 828 327-4890
  Hickory *(G-8157)*
Slane Hosiery Mills Inc .... C 336 883-4136
  High Point *(G-8538)*
Special T Hosiery Mills Inc .... G 336 227-2858
  Burlington *(G-1499)*
Surratt Hosiery Mill Inc .... F 336 859-4583
  Denton *(G-4751)*
Teamwork Inc .... G 336 578-3456
  Elon *(G-5662)*
Thorneburg Hosiery Mills Inc .... E 704 279-7247
  Rockwell *(G-13661)*
Thorneburg Hosiery Mills Inc .... E 704 838-6329
  Statesville *(G-14913)*
Zimmermann - Dynayarn Usa LLC .... E 336 222-8129
  Graham *(G-6717)*

CLOTHING: Hospital, Men's

Aj & Raine Scrubs & More LLC .... G 646 374-5198
  Charlotte *(G-2149)*
Dmg Manufacturing LLC .... E 828 855-1997
  Hickory *(G-8011)*
Ics North America Corp .... E 704 794-6620
  Concord *(G-4283)*
Keani Furniture Inc .... E 336 303-5484
  Asheboro *(G-448)*
Smissons Inc .... G 660 537-3219
  Clayton *(G-4009)*
Tafford Uniforms LLC .... D 888 823-3673
  Charlotte *(G-3670)*

CLOTHING: Jackets & Vests, Exc Fur & Leather, Women's

Fox Apparel Inc .... C 336 629-7641
  Asheboro *(G-437)*

CLOTHING: Jeans, Men's & Boys'

Brilliant You LLC .... G 336 343-5535
  Greensboro *(G-6855)*

CLOTHING: Leather

Inspiration Leather Design Inc .... G 336 420-2265
  Jamestown *(G-9058)*
Rmg Leather Usa LLC .... F 828 466-5489
  Conover *(G-4492)*

CLOTHING: Men's & boy's underwear & nightwear

Carolina Apparel Group Inc .... D 704 694-6544
  Wadesboro *(G-15506)*
Vanceboro Apparel Inc .... G 252 244-2780
  Vanceboro *(G-15484)*
Wilo Incorporated .... E 336 679-4440
  Yadkinville *(G-17063)*

CLOTHING: Mens & Boys Jackets, Sport, Suede, Leatherette

Fox Apparel Inc .... C 336 629-7641
  Asheboro *(G-437)*
Wrangler Apparel Corp .... B 336 332-3400
  Greensboro *(G-7468)*

CLOTHING: Neckwear

316 Print Company LLC .... G 919 454-6906
  Clayton *(G-3949)*
Angunique .... G 336 392-5866
  Greensboro *(G-6808)*
Bigred Krafts LLC .... G 919 480-2388
  Garner *(G-6257)*
Brown & Church Neck Wear Co .... E 336 368-5502
  Pilot Mountain *(G-12196)*
Hbb Global LLC .... G 615 306-1270
  Apex *(G-201)*
HL James LLC .... G 516 398-3311
  Durham *(G-5138)*
Lizzys Logos Inc .... G 704 321-2588
  Matthews *(G-10263)*
Logothreads Inc .... G 704 892-9433
  Cornelius *(G-4569)*
MEI Tai Baby LLC .... G 919 260-4022
  Chapel Hill *(G-2038)*
Mudgear LLC .... G 347 674-9102
  Charlotte *(G-3212)*
On The Inside LLC .... G 828 606-8483
  Asheville *(G-716)*
Polly & Crackers LLC .... G 716 680-2456
  Wilmington *(G-16358)*
Refined Outdoors LLC .... G 704 634-4027
  Monroe *(G-10794)*
Trueflies LLC .... G 828 337-9716
  Biltmore Lake *(G-1102)*
Venture Shades LLC .... G 804 240-2854
  Raleigh *(G-13396)*
Wicked Oceans .... G 252 269-0488
  Nags Head *(G-11729)*

CLOTHING: Outerwear, Knit

Blue Lagoon Inc .... G 828 324-2333
  Hickory *(G-7951)*
Diamond Apparel .... G 866 578-9708
  Advance *(G-41)*
Hanesbrands Inc .... G 910 462-2001
  Laurel Hill *(G-9460)*
Hillshire Brands Company .... G 336 519-8080
  Winston Salem *(G-16746)*
Park Shirt Company .... F 931 879-5894
  Fayetteville *(G-5894)*
Pitman Knits Inc .... G 704 276-3262
  Vale *(G-15470)*
Xtinguish LLC .... F 704 868-9500
  Charlotte *(G-3838)*

CLOTHING: Outerwear, Women's & Misses' NEC

Badger Sportswear LLC .... D 704 871-0990
  Statesville *(G-14757)*
Belvoir Manufacturing Corp .... D 252 746-1274
  Greenville *(G-7494)*
Bennett Uniform Mfg Inc .... F 336 232-5772
  Greensboro *(G-6835)*
Devil Dog Manufacturing Co Inc .... C 919 269-7485
  Zebulon *(G-17125)*
Divine Creations .... G 704 364-5844
  Morehead City *(G-11168)*
Eagle Sportswear LLC .... G 252 235-4082
  Middlesex *(G-10446)*
Formark Corporation .... F 704 922-9516
  Charlotte *(G-2789)*
Granite Knitwear Inc .... E 704 279-5526
  Granite Quarry *(G-6760)*
Levi Strauss International .... G 828 665-2417
  Asheville *(G-683)*
McDaniel Delmar .... E 336 284-6937
  Mocksville *(G-10586)*

Mitt S Nitts Inc .... E 919 596-6793
  Durham *(G-5229)*
MSE Beautyshapewear LLC .... G 910 500-0179
  Fayetteville *(G-5878)*
Patti Boo Inc .... G 828 648-6495
  Canton *(G-1621)*
Seafarer Inc .... G 704 624-3200
  Marshville *(G-10224)*

CLOTHING: Panty Hose

Acme-Mccrary Corporation .... C 919 663-2200
  Siler City *(G-14396)*
Acme-Mccrary Corporation .... B 336 625-2161
  Asheboro *(G-399)*
Commonwealth Hosiery Mills Inc .... D 336 498-2621
  Randleman *(G-13459)*
Concord Trading Inc .... E 704 375-3333
  Concord *(G-4241)*
Fine Sheer Industries Inc .... B 704 375-3333
  Concord *(G-4265)*
Hanesbrands Inc .... A 336 519-8080
  Winston Salem *(G-16734)*
Sue-Lynn Textiles Inc .... C 336 578-0871
  Haw River *(G-7757)*
Upel Inc .... E 336 519-8080
  Winston Salem *(G-16960)*

CLOTHING: Robes & Dressing Gowns

Sanders Industries Inc .... G 410 277-8565
  Waynesville *(G-15820)*

CLOTHING: Robes & Housecoats, Children's

Sanders Industries Inc .... G 410 277-8565
  Waynesville *(G-15820)*

CLOTHING: Service Apparel, Women's

Kontoor Brands Inc .... C 336 332-3400
  Greensboro *(G-7156)*

CLOTHING: Shirts

Custom Ink .... E 704 935-5604
  Charlotte *(G-2591)*
Devil Dog Manufacturing Co Inc .... C 919 269-7485
  Zebulon *(G-17125)*
Fun-Tees Inc .... G 704 788-3003
  Concord *(G-4269)*
Fun-Tees Inc .... D 704 788-3003
  Concord *(G-4270)*
Jensen Activewear .... G 704 982-3005
  Albemarle *(G-91)*
M J Soffe Co .... A 910 435-3138
  Fayetteville *(G-5863)*
MJ Soffe LLC .... E 910 422-9002
  Rowland *(G-13791)*
Royal Textile Mills Inc .... D 336 694-4121
  Yanceyville *(G-17065)*

CLOTHING: Shirts, Knit

Associated Distributors Inc .... G 910 895-5800
  Hamlet *(G-7616)*
L C Industries Inc .... C 919 596-8277
  Durham *(G-5185)*
Winstn-Slem Inds For Blind Inc .... B 336 759-0551
  Winston Salem *(G-16979)*

CLOTHING: Shirts, Women's & Juniors', From Purchased Mtrls

Kontoor Brands Inc .... D 336 332-3586
  Greensboro *(G-7155)*
Wrangler Apparel Corp .... B 336 332-3400
  Greensboro *(G-7468)*

CLOTHING: Socks

B & B Hosiery Mill .... G 336 368-4849
  Pinnacle (G-12319)
B & M Wholesale Inc .... G 336 789-3916
  Mount Airy (G-11479)
Beard Hosiery Co .... D 828 758-1942
  Lenoir (G-9580)
Bossong Hosiery Mills Inc .... C 336 625-2175
  Asheboro (G-411)
Cabarrus Hosiery Dist Inc .... G 704 436-3575
  Mount Pleasant (G-11672)
Cedar Valley Hosiery Mill Inc .... G 828 396-1804
  Hudson (G-8768)
Charlotte Sock Basket .... G 704 910-2388
  Charlotte (G-2463)
Commonwealth Hosiery Mills Inc .... D 336 498-2621
  Randleman (G-13459)
Concord Trading Inc .... E 704 375-3333
  Concord (G-4241)
Custom Socks Ink Inc .... E 828 695-9869
  Newton (G-11929)
De Feet International Inc .... E 828 397-7025
  Hildebran (G-8621)
Diabetic Sock Club .... G 800 214-0218
  Belmont (G-984)
Elder Hosiery Mills Inc .... F 336 226-0673
  Burlington (G-1409)
Farr Knitting Company Inc .... G 336 625-5561
  Asheboro (G-433)
Felice Hosiery Co Inc .... E 336 996-2371
  Kernersville (G-9200)
Fine Sheer Industries Inc .... B 704 375-3333
  Concord (G-4265)
Goldtoemoretz LLC .... B 828 464-0751
  Newton (G-11937)
Grady Distributing Co Inc .... F 919 556-5630
  Youngsville (G-17083)
Graham Dyeing & Finishing Inc .... D 336 228-9981
  Burlington (G-1426)
Hanesbrands Inc .... C 336 519-8080
  Rural Hall (G-13843)
Hanesbrands Inc .... A 336 519-8080
  Winston Salem (G-16734)
Harriss & Covington Hsy Mills .... G 336 882-6811
  High Point (G-8376)
Harriss Cvington Hsy Mills Inc .... C 336 882-6811
  High Point (G-8377)
Hill Hosiery Mill Inc .... F 336 472-7908
  Thomasville (G-15230)
Huitt Mills Inc .... E 828 322-8628
  Hildebran (G-8624)
Implus LLC .... F 828 485-3318
  Hickory (G-8064)
J R B and J Knitting Inc .... G 910 439-4242
  Mount Gilead (G-11601)
Jefferies Socks LLC .... E 336 226-7316
  Burlington (G-1440)
JI Hosiery LLC .... F 910 974-7156
  Candor (G-1593)
Just Sayin Socks LLC .... G 828 513-1517
  Flat Rock (G-5966)
Kayser-Roth Hosiery Inc .... E 336 229-2269
  Graham (G-6696)
Kayser-Roth Hosiery Inc .... E 336 852-2030
  Greensboro (G-7146)
KB Socks Inc .... E 336 719-8000
  Mount Airy (G-11529)
Kelly Hosiery Mill Inc .... G 828 324-6456
  Hickory (G-8073)
Knit Tech Inc .... G 336 584-8999
  Elon College (G-5665)

Legacy Knitting LLC .... G 844 762-2678
  Wilmington (G-16296)
Lyons Hosiery Inc .... F 336 789-2651
  Mount Airy (G-11542)
M Davis and Associates LLC .... G 336 337-7089
  Greensboro (G-7172)
Marcott Hosiery LLC .... E 704 485-8702
  Oakboro (G-12077)
Mayo Knitting Mill Inc .... C 252 823-3101
  Tarboro (G-15114)
NC Quality Sales LLC .... F 336 786-7211
  Mount Airy (G-11550)
Neat Feet Hosiery Inc .... G 336 573-2177
  Stoneville (G-14962)
Nester Hosiery Inc .... D 336 789-0026
  Mount Airy (G-11552)
Nester Hosiery LLC .... E 336 789-0026
  Mount Airy (G-11553)
North Carolina Sock Inc .... G 828 327-4664
  Hickory (G-8104)
O P S Holding Company LLC .... G 361 446-8376
  Pineville (G-12286)
Odd Sock Inc .... G 704 451-4298
  Davidson (G-4689)
On Foot Innovations LLC .... G 336 301-3732
  Charlotte (G-3295)
One Black Sock LLC .... G 919 967-6855
  Carrboro (G-1652)
Pickett Hosiery Mills Inc .... E 336 227-2716
  Burlington (G-1472)
R Evans Hosiery LLC .... E 828 397-3715
  Connelly Springs (G-4408)
Renfro LLC .... D 336 719-8290
  Mount Airy (G-11562)
Renfro LLC .... B 336 719-8000
  Mount Airy (G-11563)
Renfro Mexico Holdings LLC .... F 336 786-3501
  Mount Airy (G-11565)
Riverside Knitting Dept .... G 336 719-8252
  Mount Airy (G-11566)
Robinson Hosiery Mill Inc .... F 828 874-2228
  Valdese (G-15453)
Robinwood Enterprises .... G 910 571-0145
  Troy (G-15412)
Royce Too LLC .... E 212 356-1627
  Winston Salem (G-16891)
Russell-Fshion Foot Hsy Mlls I .... G 336 299-0741
  Troy (G-15413)
Sara Lee Socks .... G 336 789-6118
  Mount Airy (G-11570)
School Team Socks .... G 704 500-1738
  Charlotte (G-3507)
Serving Our Cmnty Kids Scks SC .... G 704 814-4704
  Charlotte (G-3530)
So & So Socks .... G 919 437-6458
  Raleigh (G-13274)
Sock Basket LLC .... G 828 251-7072
  Asheville (G-779)
Sock Factory Inc .... E 828 328-5207
  Hickory (G-8161)
Sock Inc .... G 561 254-2223
  Charlotte (G-3576)
Socks and Other Things LLC .... G 704 904-2472
  Charlotte (G-3577)
Socks Vterinary Hse Calls Pllc .... G 919 244-2826
  Cary (G-1898)
Special T Hosiery Mills Inc .... G 336 227-2858
  Burlington (G-1499)
Sports Solutions Inc .... F 336 368-1100
  Pilot Mountain (G-12202)
Step In Sock .... G 704 508-9966
  Belmont (G-1011)

Surratt Hosiery Mill Inc .... F 336 859-4583
  Denton (G-4751)
Teamwork Inc .... G 336 578-3456
  Elon (G-5662)
Thorneburg Hosiery Mills Inc .... E 704 279-7247
  Rockwell (G-13661)
Thorneburg Hosiery Mills Inc .... E 704 872-6522
  Statesville (G-14911)
Thorneburg Hosiery Mills Inc .... E 704 838-6329
  Statesville (G-14913)
Thorneburg Hosiery Mills Inc .... E 704 872-6522
  Statesville (G-14912)
Trimfit Inc .... C 336 476-6154
  Thomasville (G-15296)
Trinity Sock Group LLC .... F 336 226-0237
  Burlington (G-1508)
Tysinger Hosiery Mill Inc .... F 336 472-2148
  Lexington (G-9798)
Upel Inc .... E 336 519-8080
  Winston Salem (G-16960)
US Custom Socks Co LLC .... G 336 549-1088
  Greensboro (G-7433)
Wells Hosiery Mills Inc .... C 336 633-4881
  Asheboro (G-510)
Wilson Brown Inc .... F 336 226-0237
  Burlington (G-1518)
Woodland Hosiery Inc .... F 910 439-4843
  Mount Gilead (G-11616)

CLOTHING: Sportswear, Women's

G & G Enterprises .... G 336 764-2493
  Clemmons (G-4041)
Hanesbrands Inc .... G 910 462-2001
  Laurel Hill (G-9460)

CLOTHING: Sweaters & Sweater Coats, Knit

Mitt S Nitts Inc .... E 919 596-6793
  Durham (G-5229)

CLOTHING: Sweaters, Men's & Boys'

Home T LLC .... F 646 797-4768
  Charlotte (G-2917)

CLOTHING: Sweatshirts & T-Shirts, Men's & Boys'

Wrangler Apparel Corp .... B 336 332-3400
  Greensboro (G-7468)

CLOTHING: T-Shirts & Tops, Knit

Ba International LLC .... E 336 519-8080
  Winston Salem (G-16621)
Blue Bay Distributing Inc .... G 919 957-1300
  Durham (G-4966)
Hanesbrands Inc .... A 336 519-8080
  Winston Salem (G-16734)
Hbi Sourcing LLC .... F 336 519-8080
  Winston Salem (G-16739)
Hbi Wh Minority Holdings LLC .... F 336 519-8080
  Winston Salem (G-16740)
Hugger Inc .... C 704 735-7422
  Lincolnton (G-9895)
Kamp Usa Inc .... F 336 668-1169
  High Point (G-8421)
Noble Wholesalers Inc .... G 409 739-3803
  Clayton (G-4001)
Playtex Dorado LLC .... F 336 519-8080
  Winston Salem (G-16858)
Royal Textile Mills Inc .... D 336 694-4121
  Yanceyville (G-17065)
Upel Inc .... E 336 519-8080
  Winston Salem (G-16960)

CLOTHING: T-Shirts & Tops, Women's & Girls'

Fun-Tees Inc .... D 704 788-3003
  Concord *(G-4270)*
Patti Boo Inc .... G 828 648-6495
  Canton *(G-1621)*
Royce Apparel Inc .... E 704 933-6000
  Salisbury *(G-14038)*

CLOTHING: Tailored Suits & Formal Jackets

Tailored Designs LLC .... G 919 605-6349
  Charlotte *(G-3671)*

CLOTHING: Tights, Exc Women's

Central Carolina Hosiery Inc .... E 910 428-9688
  Biscoe *(G-1106)*
Star America Inc .... C 704 788-4700
  Concord *(G-4367)*

CLOTHING: Trousers & Slacks, Men's & Boys'

Centric Brands LLC .... C 646 582-6000
  Greensboro *(G-6900)*
Devil Dog Manufacturing Co Inc ...... C 919 269-7485
  Zebulon *(G-17125)*
Kontoor Brands Inc .... D 336 332-3586
  Greensboro *(G-7155)*
Ralph Lauren Corporation .... G 336 632-5000
  Greensboro *(G-7302)*
Wrangler Apparel Corp .... B 336 332-3400
  Greensboro *(G-7468)*

CLOTHING: Underwear, Knit

Hillshire Brands Company .... G 336 519-8080
  Winston Salem *(G-16746)*

CLOTHING: Underwear, Women's & Children's

Carolina International Inc .... E 336 472-7788
  Thomasville *(G-15197)*
Vanceboro Apparel Inc .... G 252 244-2780
  Vanceboro *(G-15484)*
Verena Designs Inc .... E 336 869-8235
  High Point *(G-8593)*

CLOTHING: Uniforms & Vestments

Remington 1816 Foundation .... G 866 686-7778
  Charlotte *(G-3430)*
Royal Park Uniforms Inc .... E 336 562-3445
  Prospect Hill *(G-12408)*
Spiritus Systems Company .... E 910 637-0196
  Aberdeen *(G-30)*

CLOTHING: Uniforms, Ex Athletic, Women's, Misses' & Juniors'

Bennett Uniform Mfg Inc .... F 336 232-5772
  Greensboro *(G-6835)*
Formark Corporation .... F 704 922-9516
  Charlotte *(G-2789)*

CLOTHING: Uniforms, Firemen's, From Purchased Materials

Salute Industries Inc .... E 844 937-2588
  Archdale *(G-298)*

CLOTHING: Uniforms, Men's & Boys'

McDaniel Delmar .... E 336 284-4677
  Mocksville *(G-10586)*

Tresmc LLC .... G 919 900-0868
  Knightdale *(G-9432)*

CLOTHING: Uniforms, Military, Men/Youth, Purchased Materials

Lelantos Group Inc .... D 704 780-4127
  Mooresville *(G-11005)*
Military Products Inc .... G 910 637-0315
  West End *(G-15930)*
Safety & Security Intl Inc .... G 336 285-8673
  Greensboro *(G-7322)*
US Patriot LLC .... F 803 787-9398
  Fort Bragg *(G-6091)*

CLOTHING: Uniforms, Work

Bennett Uniform Mfg Inc .... F 336 232-5772
  Greensboro *(G-6835)*
Brands Fashion US Inc .... G 704 953-8246
  Charlotte *(G-2348)*
Intersport Group Inc .... G 814 968-3085
  Vilas *(G-15496)*
S Loflin Enterprises Inc .... F 704 633-1159
  Salisbury *(G-14039)*
Tillery Accessories Inc .... G 704 474-3013
  Norwood *(G-12046)*

CLOTHING: Vests

London Garment Mfg LLC .... G 336 573-9300
  Stoneville *(G-14961)*

CLOTHING: Work Apparel, Exc Uniforms

Causa LLC .... G 866 695-7022
  Charlotte *(G-2421)*
Kontoor Brands Inc .... C 336 332-3400
  Greensboro *(G-7156)*

COAL & OTHER MINERALS & ORES WHOLESALERS

Daystar Materials Inc .... E 919 734-0460
  Goldsboro *(G-6609)*

COAL MINING SERVICES

Cowee Mountain Ruby Mine .... G 828 369-5271
  Franklin *(G-6123)*

COAL MINING: Bituminous Coal & Lignite-Surface Mining

Florida Progress Corporation .... C 704 382-3853
  Raleigh *(G-12775)*

COATING COMPOUNDS: Tar

Actega North America Inc .... G 704 736-9389
  Iron Station *(G-8973)*

COATING SVC: Metals, With Plastic Or Resins

Coating Concepts Inc .... G 704 391-0499
  Charlotte *(G-2511)*

COATINGS: Epoxy

New Finish Inc .... E 704 474-4116
  Norwood *(G-12041)*
Renner Wood Companies .... F 704 527-9261
  Charlotte *(G-3436)*
Verylak Inc .... F 812 442-7281
  Lewisville *(G-9675)*

COATINGS: Polyurethane

Axalta Coating Systems LLC .... F 855 629-2582
  Concord *(G-4202)*

Lord Corporation .... B 919 468-5979
  Cary *(G-1817)*
Lord Far East Inc .... E 919 468-5979
  Cary *(G-1819)*

COILS & TRANSFORMERS

Carolina Metals Inc .... E 828 667-0876
  Asheville *(G-582)*
Peak Demand Inc .... F 252 360-2777
  Wilson *(G-16522)*
Prolec-GE Waukesha Inc .... B 919 734-8900
  Goldsboro *(G-6646)*
Smart Wires Inc .... D 919 294-3999
  Durham *(G-5359)*

COILS: Electric Motors Or Generators

Lennox International Inc .... E 828 633-4805
  Candler *(G-1586)*
Sag Harbor Industries Inc .... E 252 753-7175
  Farmville *(G-5743)*

COILS: Pipe

Coil Masters LLC .... G 704 500-8341
  Mocksville *(G-10564)*

COLORS: Pigments, Inorganic

Americhem Inc .... E 704 782-6411
  Concord *(G-4195)*
Avient Colorants USA LLC .... D 704 331-7000
  Charlotte *(G-2248)*
Ultra Coatings Incorporated .... E 336 883-8853
  High Point *(G-8584)*

COMFORTERS & QUILTS, FROM MANMADE FIBER OR SILK

Premier Quilting Corporation .... F 919 693-1151
  Oxford *(G-12146)*

COMMERCIAL & OFFICE BUILDINGS RENOVATION & REPAIR

Exteriors Inc Ltd .... G 919 325-2251
  Spring Lake *(G-14625)*
International Tela-Com Inc .... F 828 651-9801
  Fletcher *(G-6013)*
Lock Drives Inc .... G 704 588-1844
  Pineville *(G-12281)*
Seashore Builders Inc .... E 910 259-3404
  Maple Hill *(G-10132)*

COMMERCIAL ART & GRAPHIC DESIGN SVCS

Barron Legacy Mgmt Group LLC ..... G 301 367-4735
  Charlotte *(G-2285)*
Big Fish Dpi .... G 704 545-8112
  Mint Hill *(G-10522)*
Blue Dog Graphics Inc .... G 252 291-9191
  Wilson *(G-16477)*
Boundless Inc .... G 919 622-9051
  Four Oaks *(G-6101)*
CD Dickie & Associates Inc .... F 704 527-9102
  Charlotte *(G-2433)*
Contract Printing & Graphics .... G 919 832-7178
  Raleigh *(G-12644)*
Creative Conquest LLC .... G 720 481-4372
  Shelby *(G-14304)*
Designs By Rachel .... G 828 783-0698
  Spruce Pine *(G-14639)*
Embroidme Lake Norman .... G 704 987-9630
  Cornelius *(G-4543)*

COMMERCIAL ART & GRAPHIC DESIGN SVCS

Family Industries Inc................................. F 919 875-4499
  Raleigh *(G-12762)*

Fast Pro Media LLC................................. G 704 799-8040
  Cornelius *(G-4546)*

Fieldsway Solutions LLC........................ G 984 920-7791
  Four Oaks *(G-6104)*

Fiestic Inc... F 888 935-3999
  Raleigh *(G-12765)*

Foundry A Print Cmmnctions LLC............ G 703 329-3300
  Apex *(G-193)*

Gmg Group LLC.................................... G 252 441-8374
  Kill Devil Hills *(G-9258)*

Heritage Prtg & Graphics Inc................... G 704 551-0700
  Charlotte *(G-2905)*

High Performance Marketing Inc............... G 919 870-9915
  Raleigh *(G-12843)*

Merge LLC.. G 919 832-3924
  Raleigh *(G-13016)*

Metro Productions Inc............................. F 919 851-6420
  Raleigh *(G-13022)*

Multi Packaging Solutions....................... A 336 855-7142
  Greensboro *(G-7207)*

NC Graphic Pros LLC............................. G 252 492-7326
  Kittrell *(G-9397)*

Prism Publishing Inc............................... F 919 319-6816
  Cary *(G-1860)*

Triangle Solutions Inc............................. G 919 481-1235
  Cary *(G-1912)*

Weathervane Creative Inc....................... G 828 542-0136
  Hickory *(G-8208)*

COMMERCIAL ART & ILLUSTRATION SVCS

Skipper Graphics.................................... G 910 754-8729
  Shallotte *(G-14278)*

COMMERCIAL CONTAINERS WHOLESALERS

Boxman Studios LLC.............................. G 704 333-3733
  Charlotte *(G-2342)*

COMMERCIAL EQPT WHOLESALERS, NEC

Dandy Light Traps Inc............................ G 980 223-2744
  Statesville *(G-14782)*

Heed Group Inc..................................... G 877 938-8853
  Stanley *(G-14696)*

Satco Truck Equipment Inc...................... F 919 383-5547
  Durham *(G-5340)*

COMMERCIAL EQPT, WHOLESALE: Restaurant, NEC

Bunzl Processor Dist LLC....................... G 910 738-8111
  Lumberton *(G-10028)*

Elxsi Corporation.................................... B 407 849-1090
  Charlotte *(G-2701)*

Government Sales LLC........................... G 252 726-6315
  Morehead City *(G-11172)*

Singer Equipment Company Inc............... E 910 484-1128
  Fayetteville *(G-5918)*

Thompson & Little Inc............................. E 910 484-1128
  Fayetteville *(G-5929)*

COMMERCIAL EQPT, WHOLESALE: Scales, Exc Laboratory

True Portion Inc..................................... F 336 362-6326
  High Point *(G-8579)*

COMMERCIAL EQPT, WHOLESALE: Store Fixtures & Display Eqpt

Riddley Retail Fixtures Inc....................... E 704 435-8829
  Kings Mountain *(G-9329)*

COMMERCIAL LAUNDRY EQPT

Leonard Automatics Inc.......................... E 704 483-9316
  Denver *(G-4788)*

Talley Machinery Corporation.................. G 336 664-0012
  Greensboro *(G-7388)*

COMMERCIAL PHOTOGRAPHIC STUDIO

Advertising Design Systems Inc................ G 828 264-8060
  Boone *(G-1172)*

COMMERCIAL PRINTING & NEWSPAPER PUBLISHING

Asian (korean) Herald Inc....................... G 704 332-5656
  Charlotte *(G-2227)*

Automail LLC... F 704 677-0152
  Mooresville *(G-10865)*

Carter Publishing Company Inc................ F 336 993-2161
  Kernersville *(G-9174)*

Carteret Publishing Company................... G 910 326-5066
  Swansboro *(G-15043)*

Charlotte Observer Pubg Co.................... A 704 358-5000
  Charlotte *(G-2456)*

Cooke Communications NC LLC............... F 252 329-9500
  Greenville *(G-7506)*

Dth Publishing Inc.................................. C 919 962-1163
  Chapel Hill *(G-2010)*

Duke Student Publishing Co Inc............... G 919 684-3811
  Durham *(G-5067)*

Fayetteville Publishing Co....................... D 910 323-4848
  Fayetteville *(G-5824)*

Foundry A Print Cmmnctions LLC............ G 703 329-3300
  Apex *(G-193)*

Gaston Gazette LLP............................... A 704 869-1700
  Gastonia *(G-6405)*

Halifax Media Holdings LLC.................... G 828 692-5763
  Hendersonville *(G-7857)*

High Country News Inc........................... F 828 264-2262
  Boone *(G-1205)*

High Point Enterprise Inc......................... F 336 472-9500
  Thomasville *(G-15229)*

High Point Enterprise Inc......................... C 336 888-3500
  High Point *(G-8389)*

Nash County Newspapers Inc.................. F 252 459-7101
  Nashville *(G-11747)*

New Bern Craven Co Bd of Educ............. G 252 635-1822
  New Bern *(G-11829)*

Rennasentient Inc................................... F 919 233-7710
  Cary *(G-1868)*

Sun-Journal Incorporated........................ E 252 638-8101
  New Bern *(G-11848)*

Taylorsville Times................................... F 828 632-2532
  Taylorsville *(G-15172)*

Times News Publishing Company............ E 336 226-4414
  Burlington *(G-1506)*

Times Printing Company......................... E 252 473-2105
  Manteo *(G-10130)*

Wen Biz Journal..................................... G 509 663-6730
  Marshall *(G-10208)*

Wilson Daily Times Inc........................... D 252 243-5151
  Wilson *(G-16561)*

COMMON SAND MINING

Bulk Transport Service Inc...................... G 910 329-0555
  Holly Ridge *(G-8680)*

Columbia Silica Sand LLC...................... F 803 755-1036
  Wilmington *(G-16175)*

Cumberland Grav & Sand Min Co............ F 828 686-3844
  Swannanoa *(G-15024)*

COMMUNICATIONS EQPT WHOLESALERS

Majorpower Corporation.......................... E 919 563-6610
  Mebane *(G-10418)*

Tellad Supply Company.......................... G 919 572-6700
  Durham *(G-5392)*

US Microwave Inc.................................. G 520 891-2444
  Pittsboro *(G-12353)*

COMMUNICATIONS EQPT: Microwave

Commscope Inc North Carolina............... G 828 459-5001
  Claremont *(G-3908)*

Commscope Inc North Carolina............... D 828 324-2200
  Claremont *(G-3909)*

Commscope Cnnctvity Sltons LLC............ F 828 324-2200
  Hickory *(G-7990)*

Commscope Technologies LLC................ F 919 934-9711
  Smithfield *(G-14457)*

Pendulum Electromagnetics Inc............... F 919 571-9970
  Raleigh *(G-13106)*

COMMUNICATIONS EQPT: Radio, Marine

Triton Marine Services Inc....................... G 252 728-9958
  Beaufort *(G-969)*

COMMUNICATIONS SVCS

Commscope Technologies LLC................ A 828 324-2200
  Claremont *(G-3916)*

COMMUNICATIONS SVCS: Data

Bluetick Inc... F 336 294-4102
  Greensboro *(G-6844)*

Gpx Intelligence Inc................................ E 888 260-0706
  Greensboro *(G-7055)*

Spectrasite Communications LLC............. E 919 468-0112
  Cary *(G-1900)*

COMMUNICATIONS SVCS: Internet Connectivity Svcs

Cengage Learning Inc............................ E 919 829-8181
  Raleigh *(G-12616)*

Charlotte Observer Pubg Co.................... A 704 358-5000
  Charlotte *(G-2456)*

Fastzone Dsl & Internet Servic................. G 828 963-1350
  Banner Elk *(G-897)*

Telit Wireless Solutions Inc..................... D 919 439-7977
  Durham *(G-5391)*

COMMUNICATIONS SVCS: Internet Host Svcs

Mountain Area Info Netwrk..................... F 828 255-0182
  Asheville *(G-707)*

COMMUNICATIONS SVCS: Online Svc Providers

M I Connection...................................... F 704 662-3255
  Mooresville *(G-11013)*

COMMUNICATIONS SVCS: Signal Enhancement Network Svcs

Commscope LLC.................................... C 828 324-2200
  Claremont *(G-3911)*

Commscope Holding Company Inc.......... A 828 459-5000
  Claremont *(G-3913)*

COMMUTATORS: Electronic

Ashbran LLC... G 919 215-3567
  Clayton *(G-3956)*

COMPOSITION STONE: Plastic

Fibreworks Composites LLC.................... E 704 696-1084
  Mooresville *(G-10944)*

PRODUCT SECTION

COMPUTER PERIPHERAL EQPT, NEC

COMPOST

Company	Code	Phone
Carolina Compost	G	252 202-6602
Camden *(G-1556)*		
Cmd Land Services LLC	G	919 554-2281
Wake Forest *(G-15543)*		
Crown Town Compost LLC	G	704 654-5689
Charlotte *(G-2573)*		
Eastern Compost LLC	G	252 446-3636
Elm City *(G-5649)*		
Tarheel Enviromental LLC	G	910 425-4939
Stedman *(G-14937)*		
Tryon Equine Compost LLC	G	914 774-7486
Columbus *(G-4181)*		
Wilmington Compost Company LLC	G	910 839-3011
Wilmington *(G-16445)*		
Wormfarmer	G	252 944-1012
Washington *(G-15741)*		

COMPRESSORS: Air & Gas

Company	Code	Phone
Air & Gas Solutions LLC	E	704 897-2182
Charlotte *(G-2146)*		
Atlas Copco Compressors LLC	F	704 525-0124
Charlotte *(G-2236)*		
Eagle Compressors Inc	E	336 370-4159
Greensboro *(G-6985)*		
Eagleair Inc	G	336 398-8000
Greensboro *(G-6986)*		
Fresh Air Technologies LLC	F	704 622-7877
Matthews *(G-10317)*		
Hayward Industries Inc	A	336 712-9900
Clemmons *(G-4044)*		
Hertz Kompressoren USA Inc	G	704 579-5900
Charlotte *(G-2907)*		
Ingersoll Rand Inc	E	704 774-4290
Charlotte *(G-2973)*		
Metal Impact East LLC	E	743 205-1900
Graham *(G-6703)*		
Nordson Corporation	G	724 656-5600
Hickory *(G-8103)*		
Pattons Medical LLC	E	704 529-5442
Charlotte *(G-3319)*		
Peco Inc	E	828 684-1234
Arden *(G-362)*		
Reddick Equipment Co NC LLC	G	252 792-1191
Williamston *(G-16068)*		
Trane Technologies Company LLC	B	336 751-3561
Mocksville *(G-10608)*		
Universal Air Products Corp	G	704 374-0600
Charlotte *(G-3755)*		

COMPRESSORS: Air & Gas, Including Vacuum Pumps

Company	Code	Phone
Backyard Entps & Svcs LLC	G	828 755-4960
Spindale *(G-14603)*		
Elgi Compressors USA Inc	G	704 943-7966
Charlotte *(G-2695)*		
G Denver and Co LLC	E	704 896-4000
Davidson *(G-4675)*		
INGERSOLL RAND INC	A	704 896-4000
Davidson *(G-4679)*		
Ingersoll-Rand Indus US Inc	D	704 896-4000
Davidson *(G-4680)*		
Safe Air Systems Inc	E	336 674-0749
Randleman *(G-13489)*		
Sub-Aquatics Inc	E	336 674-0749
Randleman *(G-13492)*		

COMPRESSORS: Refrigeration & Air Conditioning Eqpt

Company	Code	Phone
City Compressor Rebuilders	G	704 947-1811
Charlotte *(G-2485)*		

COMPUTER & COMPUTER SOFTWARE STORES

Company	Code	Phone
Coastal Office Eqp & Computers	G	252 335-9427
Elizabeth City *(G-5534)*		
Northstar Computer Tech Inc	G	980 272-1969
Monroe *(G-10780)*		

COMPUTER & COMPUTER SOFTWARE STORES: Peripheral Eqpt

Company	Code	Phone
Global Products & Mfg Svcs Inc	G	360 870-9876
Charlotte *(G-2834)*		
Preferred Data Corporation	G	336 886-3282
High Point *(G-8495)*		
Terarecon Inc	D	650 372-1100
Durham *(G-5395)*		

COMPUTER & COMPUTER SOFTWARE STORES: Personal Computers

Company	Code	Phone
Complete Comp St of Ralgh Inc	E	919 828-5227
Raleigh *(G-12635)*		

COMPUTER & COMPUTER SOFTWARE STORES: Software & Access

Company	Code	Phone
Infisoft Software	G	704 307-2619
Charlotte *(G-2969)*		
Information Tech Works LLC	F	919 232-5332
Raleigh *(G-12888)*		

COMPUTER & COMPUTER SOFTWARE STORES: Software, Bus/Non-Game

Company	Code	Phone
Barefoot Cnc Inc	G	828 438-5038
Morganton *(G-11199)*		
Payload Media Inc	G	919 367-2969
Cary *(G-1844)*		

COMPUTER & COMPUTER SOFTWARE STORES: Software, Computer Game

Company	Code	Phone
Grover Gaming Inc	D	252 329-7900
Greenville *(G-7536)*		
Ideacode Inc	G	919 341-5170
Greensboro *(G-7111)*		

COMPUTER & DATA PROCESSING EQPT REPAIR & MAINTENANCE

Company	Code	Phone
Artesian Future Technology LLC	F	919 904-4940
Chapel Hill *(G-1987)*		
Complete Comp St of Ralgh Inc	E	919 828-5227
Raleigh *(G-12635)*		
Innait Inc	G	406 241-5245
Charlotte *(G-2975)*		

COMPUTER & OFFICE MACHINE MAINTENANCE & REPAIR

Company	Code	Phone
Biz Technology Solutions LLC	E	704 658-1707
Mooresville *(G-10881)*		
Carolina Cartridge Systems Inc	E	704 347-2447
Charlotte *(G-2392)*		
Coastal Office Eqp & Computers	G	252 335-9427
Elizabeth City *(G-5534)*		
Comtech Group Inc	E	919 313-4800
Durham *(G-5029)*		
Northrop Grumman Systems Corp	E	252 225-0911
Atlantic *(G-827)*		

COMPUTER FACILITIES MANAGEMENT SVCS

Company	Code	Phone
Infobelt LLC	F	980 223-4000
Charlotte *(G-2971)*		

COMPUTER GRAPHICS SVCS

Company	Code	Phone
Big Fish Dpi	G	704 545-8112
Mint Hill *(G-10522)*		
Line Drive Sports Center Inc	G	336 824-1692
Ramseur *(G-13446)*		
Outer Banks Internet Inc	G	252 441-6698
Kill Devil Hills *(G-9259)*		
Richa Inc	G	704 944-0230
Charlotte *(G-3448)*		
Richa Inc	F	704 331-9744
Charlotte *(G-3449)*		
S & A Cherokee LLC	E	919 674-6020
Cary *(G-1876)*		
Stitchmaster LLC	G	336 852-6448
Greensboro *(G-7373)*		
Telepathic Graphics Inc	E	919 342-4603
Raleigh *(G-13337)*		

COMPUTER PERIPHERAL EQPT REPAIR & MAINTENANCE

Company	Code	Phone
St Investors Inc	D	704 969-7500
Charlotte *(G-3618)*		

COMPUTER PERIPHERAL EQPT, NEC

Company	Code	Phone
Adama US	G	919 817-7103
Durham *(G-4903)*		
Apple Inc	F	516 318-6744
Cary *(G-1685)*		
Axon Systems LLC	G	910 796-7872
Wilmington *(G-16128)*		
Black Box Corporation	G	704 248-6430
Pineville *(G-12255)*		
Brilliant Sole Inc	G	339 222-8528
Wilmington *(G-16143)*		
Cable Devices Incorporated	C	714 554-4370
Hickory *(G-7960)*		
Carlisle Corporation	G	704 501-1100
Charlotte *(G-2390)*		
Coastal Office Eqp & Computers	G	252 335-9427
Elizabeth City *(G-5534)*		
Commscope Technologies LLC	F	919 934-9711
Smithfield *(G-14457)*		
Ensinger Polytech Inc	G	704 992-8100
Huntersville *(G-8815)*		
Faith Computer Repairs	G	910 730-1731
Lumberton *(G-10036)*		
Hermes Medical Solutions Inc	G	252 355-4373
Greenville *(G-7539)*		
International Bus Mchs Corp	B	919 543-6919
Durham *(G-5161)*		
JPS Communications Inc	D	919 534-1168
Raleigh *(G-12923)*		
Monolith Corporation	E	919 878-1900
Wake Forest *(G-15572)*		
Oracle Corporation	D	919 205-6000
Morrisville *(G-11403)*		
Pro-Face America LLC	E	734 477-0600
Greensboro *(G-7286)*		
Revware Inc	G	919 790-0000
Raleigh *(G-13205)*		
Riverbed Technology LLC	E	415 247-8800
Durham *(G-5333)*		
Rsa Security LLC	F	704 847-4725
Matthews *(G-10287)*		
Savoye Solutions Inc	G	919 466-9784
Raleigh *(G-13232)*		
Sighttech LLC	G	855 997-4448
Charlotte *(G-3549)*		

COMPUTER PERIPHERAL EQPT, NEC

Southern Data Systems Inc............... F 919 781-7603
  Oxford *(G-12156)*
Technology Partners LLC................. D 704 553-1004
  Charlotte *(G-3677)*
Terarecon Inc............................. D 650 372-1100
  Durham *(G-5395)*
Xerox Corporation........................ E 919 428-9718
  Cary *(G-1932)*
Xeroxdata Center......................... G 704 329-7245
  Charlotte *(G-3835)*

COMPUTER PERIPHERAL EQPT, WHOLESALE

Vrush Industries Inc..................... F 336 886-7700
  High Point *(G-8597)*

COMPUTER PERIPHERAL EQPT: Encoders

Lea Aid Acquisition Company........... F 919 872-6210
  Raleigh *(G-12963)*
Lynn Electronics Corporation............ G 704 369-0093
  Concord *(G-4308)*
Vocollect Inc............................. E 980 279-4119
  Charlotte *(G-3781)*

COMPUTER PERIPHERAL EQPT: Input Or Output

Garrettcom Inc........................... D 510 438-9071
  Mooresville *(G-10954)*
Toshiba Globl Cmmrce Sltons In......... E 984 444-2767
  Durham *(G-5404)*

COMPUTER PROCESSING SVCS

Northrop Grumman Systems Corp......... E 252 225-0911
  Atlantic *(G-827)*

COMPUTER PROGRAMMING SVCS: Custom

Computer Task Group Inc................ G 919 677-1313
  Raleigh *(G-12636)*
Digital Designs Inc....................... E 704 790-7100
  Charlotte *(G-2634)*
Predatar Inc.............................. G 919 827-4516
  Raleigh *(G-13135)*

COMPUTER RELATED MAINTENANCE SVCS

NCR Voyix Corporation................... G 937 445-5000
  Cary *(G-1830)*
Sighttech LLC............................ G 855 997-4448
  Charlotte *(G-3549)*
VA Claims LLC........................... G 305 984-0936
  Greenville *(G-7596)*

COMPUTER SOFTWARE DEVELOPMENT

Add-On Technologies Inc................. F 704 882-2227
  Indian Trail *(G-8918)*
Advanced Digital Systems Inc........... F 919 485-4819
  Durham *(G-4904)*
Cmisolutions Inc.......................... E 704 759-9950
  Charlotte *(G-2505)*
Ideacode Inc.............................. G 919 341-5170
  Greensboro *(G-7111)*
Infisoft Software.......................... G 704 307-2619
  Charlotte *(G-2969)*
Insightsoftware LLC...................... G 919 872-7800
  Raleigh *(G-12892)*
Inspectionxpert Corporation............. F 919 249-6442
  Raleigh *(G-12893)*
Kdy Automation Solutions Inc........... G 888 219-0049
  Mooresville *(G-11364)*
Noregon Systems Inc.................... C 336 615-8555
  Greensboro *(G-7223)*
Novisystems Inc.......................... G 919 205-5005
  Raleigh *(G-13074)*
Pai Services LLC......................... G 856 231-4667
  Charlotte *(G-3308)*
Pogo Software Inc....................... F 407 267-4864
  Raleigh *(G-13118)*
Red Hat Inc.............................. A 919 754-3700
  Raleigh *(G-13196)*
Red Hat SA I LLC........................ E 919 754-3700
  Raleigh *(G-13197)*
Rvb Systems Group Inc.................. G 919 362-5211
  Garner *(G-6311)*
S C I A Inc.............................. G 919 387-7000
  Cary *(G-1877)*
USA Metal Structure LLP................ G 336 717-2884
  Dobson *(G-4832)*
Web 4 Half LLC.......................... E 855 762-4638
  Asheboro *(G-509)*

COMPUTER SOFTWARE DEVELOPMENT & APPLICATIONS

Aiken Development LLC................. G 828 572-4040
  Lenoir *(G-9568)*
Artibis Corporation....................... G 919 592-4794
  Cary *(G-1689)*
Bae Systems Info Elctrnic Syst......... E 919 323-5800
  Durham *(G-4941)*
Bluetick Inc.............................. F 336 294-4102
  Greensboro *(G-6844)*
Bravo Team LLC......................... E 704 309-1918
  Mooresville *(G-10887)*
Computational Engrg Intl Inc............ E 919 363-0883
  Apex *(G-176)*
Cyberlux Corporation.................... F 984 363-6894
  Research Triangle Pa *(G-13549)*
Flameoff Coatings Inc................... G 888 816-7468
  Raleigh *(G-12772)*
Inspire Creative Studios Inc............. G 910 395-0200
  Wilmington *(G-16269)*
Jasie Blanks LLC........................ F 910 485-0016
  Fayetteville *(G-5846)*
Lenovo (united States) Inc.............. A 855 253-6686
  Morrisville *(G-11376)*
Phononic Inc............................. C 919 908-6300
  Durham *(G-5286)*
Proctorfree Inc........................... F 704 759-6569
  Davidson *(G-4692)*
Tekelec Inc.............................. C
  Morrisville *(G-11442)*
Tekelec Global Inc....................... A 919 460-5500
  Morrisville *(G-11443)*
Vortant Technologies LLC............... G 828 645-1026
  Weaverville *(G-15867)*
Vortex Bottle Shop LLC.................. F 980 258-0827
  Harrisburg *(G-7734)*

COMPUTER SOFTWARE SYSTEMS ANALYSIS & DESIGN: Custom

27 Software US Inc...................... F 704 968-2879
  Mooresville *(G-10844)*
Applied Strategies Inc................... G 704 525-4478
  Charlotte *(G-2205)*
Camelot Computers Inc.................. F 704 554-1670
  Charlotte *(G-2378)*
Dynamac Corporation.................... E 919 544-6428
  Durham *(G-5073)*
Intelligent Apps LLC..................... G 919 628-6256
  Raleigh *(G-12897)*
International Bus Mchs Corp............ B 919 543-6919
  Durham *(G-5161)*
Iqe North Carolina LLC.................. F 336 609-6270
  Greensboro *(G-7121)*
Jctm LLC................................ D 252 571-8678
  Charlotte *(G-3015)*
Logicbit Software LLC................... E 888 366-2280
  Durham *(G-5194)*
Medicor Imaging Inc..................... E 704 332-5532
  Charlotte *(G-3159)*
Openfire Systems........................ G 336 251-3991
  Millers Creek *(G-10494)*
Terida LLC.............................. F 910 693-1633
  Pinehurst *(G-12238)*
Twork Technology Inc................... F 704 218-9675
  Charlotte *(G-3743)*
Xsport Global Inc........................ F 212 541-6222
  Charlotte *(G-3836)*

COMPUTER STORAGE DEVICES, NEC

Boy Scout Troop......................... G 704 643-8955
  Charlotte *(G-2343)*
Carolina Data Recovery LLC............. G 704 536-1717
  Charlotte *(G-2394)*
Christopher Ridley....................... G 919 291-9999
  Raleigh *(G-12621)*
Consolidated EMC Inc................... G 980 245-2859
  Matthews *(G-10310)*
Digiton Corp............................. G 919 601-4826
  Apex *(G-182)*
EMC Contractor LLC..................... G 910 576-7101
  Troy *(G-15405)*
EMC Corporation........................ G 720 341-3274
  Charlotte *(G-2705)*
EMC Corporation........................ F 919 851-3241
  Raleigh *(G-12735)*
Emergent Tech Solutions Inc............ G 704 777-1909
  Charlotte *(G-2707)*
Halifax EMC............................. F 252 445-5111
  Enfield *(G-5678)*
Ict/Data On Cd Inc...................... G 704 841-8404
  Charlotte *(G-2947)*
Inmylife Inc.............................. G 336 644-8856
  Greensboro *(G-7115)*
Jean Dupree............................. G 919 821-4020
  Salisbury *(G-13990)*
Netapp Inc.............................. E 919 476-4571
  Durham *(G-5242)*
Quantum Insulation Inc.................. G 252 752-7828
  Greenville *(G-7578)*
Quantum Newswire...................... G 919 439-8800
  Raleigh *(G-13166)*
Quantum Solutions...................... F 828 615-7500
  Hickory *(G-8130)*
Quantum Usa LLP....................... G 919 704-8266
  Chapel Hill *(G-2059)*
Queen City Event Mgmt Cnsltng......... G 704 780-7811
  Charlotte *(G-3404)*
Raleigh Ventures Inc.................... G 910 350-0036
  Wilmington *(G-16377)*
Seagate Technology LLC................. F 910 821-8310
  Wilmington *(G-16396)*
Verbatim Americas LLC.................. G 704 547-6551
  Charlotte *(G-3769)*
Verbatim Americas LLC.................. D 704 547-6500
  Charlotte *(G-3770)*
Verbatim Corporation.................... D 704 547-6500
  Charlotte *(G-3771)*
Walker and Associates Inc.............. C 336 731-6391
  Lexington *(G-9800)*

COMPUTER SYSTEMS ANALYSIS & DESIGN

Innait Inc............................... G 406 241-5245
  Charlotte *(G-2975)*

PRODUCT SECTION   CONCRETE PRDTS

International Bus Mchs Corp.............................. B 919 543-6919
   Durham *(G-5161)*

Meridian Zero Degrees LLC............................... E 866 454-6757
   Aberdeen *(G-12)*

COMPUTER TERMINALS

Apple Inc.. F 516 318-6744
   Cary *(G-1685)*

NCR Voyix Corporation....................................... G 937 445-5000
   Cary *(G-1830)*

Pro-Face America LLC....................................... E 734 477-0600
   Greensboro *(G-7286)*

COMPUTERS, NEC

Albert E Mann... G 919 497-0815
   Louisburg *(G-9979)*

Apple Branch Company....................................... G 910 859-8549
   Wilmington *(G-16112)*

Apple Inc... F 516 318-6744
   Cary *(G-1685)*

Barcovvsion LLC.. F 704 392-9371
   Charlotte *(G-2279)*

Clean-Sweep Solutions Inc................................. G 469 450-8317
   Raleigh *(G-12627)*

Digital Audio Corporation.................................... F 919 572-6767
   Hendersonville *(G-7844)*

Dimill Enterprises LLC.. G 919 629-2011
   Raleigh *(G-12684)*

Dramen of Raleigh LLC...................................... G 919 828-5464
   Raleigh *(G-12699)*

Fred L Brown.. G 336 643-7523
   Summerfield *(G-14983)*

General Dynmics Mssion Systems...................... F 910 497-7900
   Fort Bragg *(G-6089)*

Green Apple Studio... G 919 377-2239
   Cary *(G-1778)*

Hypernova Inc.. G 704 360-0096
   Charlotte *(G-2944)*

International Bus Mchs Corp.............................. B 919 543-6919
   Durham *(G-5161)*

Itron Inc.. D 919 876-2600
   Raleigh *(G-12905)*

K12 Computers... G 336 754-6111
   Lexington *(G-9738)*

Karwin Technologies Inc..................................... G 919 612-3974
   Clayton *(G-3991)*

Lenovo (united States) Inc................................. G 919 486-9627
   Morrisville *(G-11374)*

Lenovo (united States) Inc................................. D 919 237-8389
   Morrisville *(G-11375)*

Lenovo (united States) Inc................................. A 855 253-6686
   Morrisville *(G-11376)*

Lenovo US Fulfillment Ctr LLC........................... C 855 253-6686
   Morrisville *(G-11378)*

Litton Systems Inc.. G 704 588-2340
   Charlotte *(G-3094)*

Mason International... G 704 921-3407
   Charlotte *(G-3137)*

McKelvey Fulks.. G 704 357-1550
   Charlotte *(G-3152)*

Omnicell... G 910 538-2141
   Hampstead *(G-7652)*

Original Image... G 919 781-0064
   Raleigh *(G-13091)*

Q-Edge Corporation.. G 919 935-8167
   Durham *(G-5310)*

Salem Technologies Inc..................................... F 336 777-3652
   Winston Salem *(G-16895)*

Selex Es LLC.. D 336 379-7135
   Greensboro *(G-7331)*

Serra Wireless Inc.. G 980 318-0873
   Charlotte *(G-3529)*

Shiftwizard Inc.. F 866 828-3318
   Morrisville *(G-11427)*

Steve Brooks.. G 919 248-1458
   Raleigh *(G-13303)*

Teguar Corporation... E 704 960-1761
   Charlotte *(G-3678)*

Teradata Corporation... F 919 816-1900
   Raleigh *(G-13339)*

Usat LLC.. E 919 942-4214
   Chapel Hill *(G-2091)*

Utd Technology Corp.. G 704 612-0121
   Mint Hill *(G-10546)*

Walker and Associates Inc................................. C 336 731-6391
   Lexington *(G-9800)*

Zelaya Bros LLC... G 980 833-0099
   Charlotte *(G-3850)*

COMPUTERS, NEC, WHOLESALE

Reynolds and Reynolds Company...................... G 321 287-3939
   Charlotte *(G-3445)*

Smartway of Carolinas LLC................................ F 704 900-7877
   Charlotte *(G-3566)*

COMPUTERS, PERIPHERALS & SOFTWARE, WHOLESALE: Printers

Amt Datasouth Corp... E 704 523-8500
   Charlotte *(G-2192)*

Glover Corporation Inc....................................... E 919 821-5535
   Raleigh *(G-12807)*

Sato America LLC.. C 704 644-1650
   Charlotte *(G-3493)*

St Investors Inc.. D 704 969-7500
   Charlotte *(G-3618)*

COMPUTERS, PERIPHERALS & SOFTWARE, WHOLESALE: Software

Envirnmntal Systems RES Inst I......................... E 704 541-9810
   Charlotte *(G-2718)*

Iqe North Carolina LLC....................................... F 336 609-6270
   Greensboro *(G-7121)*

Medicor Imaging Inc... E 704 332-5532
   Charlotte *(G-3159)*

COMPUTERS: Personal

Apple Valley Cabin LLC...................................... G 828 513-1911
   Hendersonville *(G-7820)*

Artibis Corporation.. G 919 592-4794
   Cary *(G-1689)*

HP Inc.. G 704 523-3548
   Charlotte *(G-2927)*

Lenovo Holding Company Inc............................. F 855 253-6686
   Morrisville *(G-11377)*

Monolith Corporation.. E 919 878-1900
   Wake Forest *(G-15572)*

Novant Health Appel... G 704 316-5025
   Charlotte *(G-3274)*

CONCENTRATES, DRINK

Speed Energy Drink LLC.................................... F 704 949-1255
   Concord *(G-4364)*

CONCENTRATES, FLAVORING, EXC DRINK

Alternative Ingredients Inc.................................. G 336 378-5368
   Greensboro *(G-6794)*

CONCRETE BUILDING PRDTS WHOLESALERS

Adams Products Company.................................. C 919 467-2218
   Morrisville *(G-11278)*

Merchants Metals Inc... G 704 921-9192
   Charlotte *(G-3165)*

Old Castle Apg South Inc................................... G 919 383-2521
   Durham *(G-5255)*

CONCRETE CURING & HARDENING COMPOUNDS

Continental Manufacturing Co............................. G 336 697-2591
   Mc Leansville *(G-10386)*

CONCRETE PLANTS

S T Wooten Corporation..................................... E 919 363-3141
   Apex *(G-240)*

S T Wooten Corporation..................................... E 919 562-1851
   Franklinton *(G-6163)*

S T Wooten Corporation..................................... E 919 772-7991
   Fuquay Varina *(G-6227)*

S T Wooten Corporation..................................... E 252 393-2206
   Garner *(G-6312)*

S T Wooten Corporation..................................... E 919 779-6089
   Garner *(G-6313)*

S T Wooten Corporation..................................... E 919 779-7589
   Garner *(G-6314)*

S T Wooten Corporation..................................... E 252 291-5165
   Raleigh *(G-13224)*

S T Wooten Corporation..................................... E 910 762-1940
   Wilmington *(G-16391)*

S T Wooten Corporation..................................... E 252 291-5165
   Wilson *(G-16537)*

CONCRETE PRDTS

360 Ballistics LLC.. G 919 883-8338
   Cary *(G-1670)*

Adams Products Company.................................. C 919 467-2218
   Morrisville *(G-11278)*

Beazer East Inc.. G 919 380-2610
   Morrisville *(G-11301)*

Bonsal American Inc.. G 336 854-8200
   Greensboro *(G-6847)*

Bonsal American Inc.. G 704 848-4141
   Lilesville *(G-9835)*

Cast First Stone Ministry.................................... G 704 437-1053
   Troutman *(G-15373)*

Cast Stone Systems Inc..................................... E 252 257-1599
   Warrenton *(G-15657)*

Craven Tire Inc.. G 252 633-0200
   New Bern *(G-11792)*

Decocrete... G 910 358-4175
   Jacksonville *(G-8997)*

Fayblock Materials Inc....................................... D 910 323-9198
   Fayetteville *(G-5823)*

Gate Precast Company....................................... C 919 603-1633
   Oxford *(G-12129)*

Imagine That Creations LLC............................... F 480 528-6775
   Black Mountain *(G-1125)*

Merchants Metals Inc... G 704 921-9192
   Charlotte *(G-3165)*

Metromont Materials Corp.................................. G 828 253-9383
   Asheville *(G-700)*

Mid-Atlantic Concrete Pdts Inc........................... G 336 774-6544
   Winston Salem *(G-16810)*

Mitchell Concrete Products Inc........................... G 919 934-4333
   Smithfield *(G-14472)*

Oldcastle Infrastructure Inc................................ F 910 433-2931
   Fayetteville *(G-5887)*

Oldcastle Infrastructure Inc................................ E 919 772-6269
   Raleigh *(G-13082)*

Precast Solutions Inc... F 336 656-7991
   Browns Summit *(G-1313)*

Precast Terrazzo Entps Inc................................ E 919 231-6200
   Raleigh *(G-13132)*

CONCRETE PRDTS — PRODUCT SECTION

Quikrete Companies LLC .... E 704 272-7677
  Peachland *(G-12175)*

S T Wooten Corporation .... F 919 783-5507
  Raleigh *(G-13223)*

Speer Concrete Inc .... E 910 947-3144
  Carthage *(G-1666)*

Stay-Right Pre-Cast Concrete Inc ..... D 919 494-7600
  Franklinton *(G-6164)*

Techo-Bloc .... G 336 431-4133
  Archdale *(G-300)*

Troy Ready - Mix Inc .... G 910 572-1011
  Troy *(G-15418)*

Tru-Contour Inc .... F 704 455-8700
  Concord *(G-4379)*

CONCRETE PRDTS, PRECAST, NEC

A & D Precast Inc .... F 704 735-3337
  Lincolnton *(G-9863)*

B & C Concrete Products Inc .... G 336 838-4201
  North Wilkesboro *(G-11998)*

Ballistics Technology Intl Ltd .... G 252 360-1650
  Wilson *(G-16473)*

Carolina Precast Concrete .... F 910 230-0028
  Dunn *(G-4855)*

Carr Precast Concrete Inc .... E 910 892-1151
  Dunn *(G-4856)*

Cherry Contracting Inc .... D 336 969-1825
  Rural Hall *(G-13838)*

Coastal Precast Systems LLC .... C 910 444-4682
  Wilmington *(G-16173)*

Continental Stone Company .... G 336 951-2945
  Reidsville *(G-13514)*

Ideal Precast Inc .... F 919 801-8287
  Durham *(G-5146)*

International Precast Inc .... E 919 742-4241
  Siler City *(G-14416)*

Lucas Concrete Products Inc .... E 704 525-9622
  Charlotte *(G-3106)*

Mack Industries .... G 252 977-3733
  Elm City *(G-5651)*

MC Precast Concrete Inc .... D 919 367-3636
  Apex *(G-216)*

Merritts Pottery Inc .... F 910 862-3774
  Elizabethtown *(G-5600)*

Old Castle Apg South Inc .... E 919 383-2521
  Durham *(G-5255)*

Oldcastle Retail Inc .... F 704 525-1621
  Charlotte *(G-3292)*

P & D Archtectural Precast Inc .... F 252 566-9811
  La Grange *(G-9444)*

Prestress of Carolinas LLC .... F 704 587-4273
  Charlotte *(G-3376)*

Shoaf Precast Septic Tank Inc .... G 336 787-5826
  Lexington *(G-9778)*

Smith-Carolina Corporation .... E 336 349-2905
  Reidsville *(G-13540)*

Utility Precast Inc .... E 704 721-0106
  Concord *(G-4384)*

CONCRETE: Dry Mixture

Bonsal American Inc .... D 704 525-1621
  Charlotte *(G-2334)*

Jones Ornamental Concrete .... F 828 685-3740
  Hendersonville *(G-7867)*

CONCRETE: Ready-Mixed

Abhw Concrete Co .... G 252 940-1002
  Washington *(G-15679)*

Adams Oldcastle .... G 980 229-7678
  Charlotte *(G-2135)*

Allen-Godwin Concrete Inc .... F 910 686-4890
  Wilmington *(G-16107)*

Allie M Powell III .... G 252 535-9717
  Roanoke Rapids *(G-13565)*

Ameri-Con Materials Inc .... F 828 863-0444
  Mill Spring *(G-10483)*

Argos Ready Mix (carolinas) Corp .. B 919 790-1520
  Raleigh *(G-12519)*

Argos USA .... F 336 784-5181
  Winston Salem *(G-16608)*

Argos USA LLC .... E 910 675-1262
  Castle Hayne *(G-1943)*

Argos USA LLC .... G 704 679-9431
  Charlotte *(G-2214)*

Argos USA LLC .... E 910 299-5046
  Clinton *(G-4088)*

Argos USA LLC .... F 704 483-4013
  Denver *(G-4763)*

Argos USA LLC .... G 910 892-3188
  Dunn *(G-4852)*

Argos USA LLC .... G 919 552-2294
  Fuquay Varina *(G-6180)*

Argos USA LLC .... E 919 772-4188
  Garner *(G-6255)*

Argos USA LLC .... G 828 322-9325
  Hickory *(G-7941)*

Argos USA LLC .... E 336 841-3379
  High Point *(G-8253)*

Argos USA LLC .... G 919 732-7509
  Hillsborough *(G-8634)*

Argos USA LLC .... E 252 527-8008
  Kinston *(G-9343)*

Argos USA LLC .... G 704 872-9566
  Mooresville *(G-10862)*

Argos USA LLC .... G 252 223-4348
  Newport *(G-11897)*

Argos USA LLC .... F 919 828-3695
  Raleigh *(G-12520)*

Argos USA LLC .... F 919 775-5441
  Raleigh *(G-12521)*

Argos USA LLC .... G 919 790-1520
  Raleigh *(G-12522)*

Argos USA LLC .... G 252 443-5046
  Roanoke Rapids *(G-13566)*

Argos USA LLC .... G 252 291-8888
  Sims *(G-14439)*

Argos USA LLC .... C 704 872-9566
  Statesville *(G-14752)*

Argos USA LLC .... E 919 554-2087
  Wake Forest *(G-15528)*

Argos USA LLC .... G 252 946-4704
  Washington *(G-15682)*

Argos USA LLC .... G 252 792-3148
  Williamston *(G-16057)*

Argos USA LLC .... G 910 686-4890
  Wilmington *(G-16115)*

Argos USA LLC .... E 910 796-3469
  Wilmington *(G-16116)*

Argos USA LLC .... D 336 784-4888
  Winston Salem *(G-16609)*

Asheboro Ready-Mix Inc .... E 336 672-0957
  Asheboro *(G-407)*

B V Hedrick Gravel & Sand Co .... F 704 633-5982
  Salisbury *(G-13928)*

Black Concrete Inc .... F 336 243-1388
  Lexington *(G-9685)*

Blue DOT Readi-Mix LLC .... F 704 971-7676
  Mint Hill *(G-10523)*

Cabarrus Concrete Co .... F 704 788-3000
  Concord *(G-4217)*

Capital Rdymx Pittsboro LLC .... F 919 217-0222
  Moncure *(G-10617)*

Capital Ready Mix Concrete LLC .... E 919 217-0222
  Knightdale *(G-9414)*

Capitol Funds Inc .... F 910 439-5275
  Mount Gilead *(G-11599)*

Capitol Funds Inc .... E 704 487-8547
  Shelby *(G-14291)*

Carolina Concrete Inc .... F 704 596-6511
  Charlotte *(G-2393)*

Carolina Concrete Inc .... E 704 821-7645
  Matthews *(G-10237)*

Carolina Concrete Materials .... G 828 686-3040
  Swannanoa *(G-15022)*

Carolina Ready Mix & Build .... G 828 686-3041
  Swannanoa *(G-15023)*

Carolina Ready-Mix LLC .... G 704 225-1112
  Monroe *(G-10677)*

Carolina Sunrock LLC .... G 919 201-4201
  Creedmoor *(G-4609)*

Carolina Sunrock LLC .... E 252 433-4617
  Kittrell *(G-9395)*

Carolina Sunrock LLC .... E 919 861-1860
  Raleigh *(G-12601)*

Carolina Sunrock LLC .... E 919 554-0500
  Wake Forest *(G-15538)*

Carolina Sunrock LLC .... E 919 575-4502
  Butner *(G-1543)*

Cemex Cnstr Mtls ATL LLC .... G 704 873-3263
  Statesville *(G-14776)*

Cemex Materials LLC .... C 704 455-1100
  Harrisburg *(G-7704)*

Cemex Materials LLC .... D 800 627-2986
  Thomasville *(G-15202)*

Cemex Materials LLC .... D 252 243-6153
  Wilson *(G-16487)*

Central Carolina Concrete LLC .... E 336 315-0785
  Greensboro *(G-6899)*

CFI Ready Mix LLC .... G 910 814-4238
  Lillington *(G-9847)*

Chandler Con Pdts of Chrstnber ..... G 336 226-1181
  Burlington *(G-1394)*

Chandler Concrete Co .... G 919 742-2627
  Siler City *(G-14405)*

Chandler Concrete Co Inc .... G 910 974-4744
  Biscoe *(G-1107)*

Chandler Concrete Co Inc .... D 336 272-6127
  Burlington *(G-1395)*

Chandler Concrete High Co .... F 828 264-8694
  Boone *(G-1187)*

Chandler Concrete Inc .... F 336 625-1070
  Asheboro *(G-414)*

Chandler Concrete Inc .... G 336 982-8760
  Crumpler *(G-4628)*

Chandler Concrete Inc .... F 919 598-1424
  Durham *(G-5012)*

Chandler Concrete Inc .... G 336 342-5771
  Eden *(G-5488)*

Chandler Concrete Inc .... G 336 222-9716
  Graham *(G-6683)*

Chandler Concrete Inc .... F 336 297-1179
  Greensboro *(G-6902)*

Chandler Concrete Inc .... E 919 644-1058
  Hillsborough *(G-8644)*

Chandler Concrete Inc .... G 919 542-4242
  Pittsboro *(G-12336)*

Chandler Concrete Inc .... F 336 599-8343
  Roxboro *(G-13799)*

Chandler Concrete Inc .... D 704 636-4711
  Salisbury *(G-13939)*

Chandler Concrete Inc .... F 336 372-4348
  Sparta *(G-14591)*

Charlotte Block Inc .... G 704 399-4526
  Charlotte *(G-2450)*

Childers Concrete Company .... F 336 841-3111
  High Point *(G-8295)*

CONCRETE: Ready-Mixed

Commercial Ready Mix Pdts Inc................ G...... 252 332-3590
  Ahoskie *(G-58)*

Commercial Ready Mix Pdts Inc................ F...... 252 335-9740
  Elizabeth City *(G-5536)*

Commercial Ready Mix Pdts Inc................ F...... 252 232-1250
  Moyock *(G-11695)*

Commercial Ready Mix Pdts Inc................ F...... 252 585-1777
  Pendleton *(G-12185)*

Commercial Spclty Trck Hldngs................ C...... 859 234-1100
  Burlington *(G-1398)*

Concrete Service Co Inc................ E...... 910 483-0396
  Fayetteville *(G-5794)*

Concrete Service Company................ G...... 910 590-0035
  Clinton *(G-4093)*

Concrete Supply Co LLC................ G...... 864 517-4055
  Charlotte *(G-2537)*

Concrete Supply Holdings Inc................ B...... 704 372-2930
  Charlotte *(G-2538)*

Crete Solutions LLC................ E...... 910 726-1686
  Wilmington *(G-16189)*

Crh Americas Inc................ C...... 704 282-8443
  Monroe *(G-10699)*

Crmp Inc................ G...... 252 358-5461
  Winton *(G-17021)*

Dean S Ready Mixed Inc................ E...... 704 982-5520
  Albemarle *(G-82)*

DOT Blue Readi-Mix LLC................ E...... 704 391-3000
  Charlotte *(G-2652)*

DOT Blue Readi-Mix LLC................ E...... 704 247-2778
  Harrisburg *(G-7707)*

DOT Blue Readi-Mix LLC................ E...... 704 247-2777
  Monroe *(G-10706)*

DOT Blue Readi-Mix LLC................ E...... 704 978-2331
  Statesville *(G-14790)*

E & M Concrete Inc................ E...... 919 235-7221
  Fuquay Varina *(G-6197)*

Eagle Rock Concrete LLC................ E...... 919 596-7077
  Apex *(G-186)*

Eagle Rock Concrete LLC................ E...... 919 281-0120
  Raleigh *(G-12714)*

Eagle Rock Concrete LLC................ E...... 919 781-3744
  Raleigh *(G-12713)*

Eveready Mix Concrete Co Inc................ G...... 336 961-6688
  Yadkinville *(G-17039)*

Explosives Supply Company................ F...... 828 765-2762
  Spruce Pine *(G-14640)*

Forsyth Redi-Mix Inc................ F...... 336 969-0446
  Rural Hall *(G-13841)*

Greenville Ready Mix Concrete................ E...... 252 756-0119
  Winterville *(G-17001)*

Greystone Concrete Pdts Inc................ E...... 252 438-5144
  Henderson *(G-7785)*

Hamby Brother S Incorporated................ F...... 336 667-1154
  North Wilkesboro *(G-12013)*

Hamby Brothers Concrete Inc................ E...... 828 754-2176
  Lenoir *(G-9618)*

Hamrick Precast LLC................ G...... 704 434-6551
  Shelby *(G-14324)*

Hartley Ready Mix Con Mfg Inc................ G...... 336 294-5995
  Greensboro *(G-7077)*

Hartley Ready Mix Con Mfg Inc................ G...... 336 788-3928
  Winston Salem *(G-16737)*

Heidelberg Materials Us Inc................ E...... 252 235-4162
  Sims *(G-14443)*

Heidelberg Mtls Sthast Agg LLC................ E...... 919 556-4011
  Wake Forest *(G-15564)*

Heidelberg Mtls US Cem LLC................ G...... 919 682-5791
  Durham *(G-5134)*

Heritage Concrete Service Corp................ G...... 910 892-4445
  Dunn *(G-4875)*

Heritage Concrete Service Corp................ F...... 919 775-5014
  Sanford *(G-14131)*

Hildreth Ready Mix LLC................ G...... 704 694-2034
  Rockingham *(G-13629)*

I Mix 4 U LLC................ G...... 336 307-6297
  Thomasville *(G-15234)*

J S Myers Co Inc................ F...... 336 463-5572
  Yadkinville *(G-17042)*

Jab-C LLC................ G...... 704 507-6196
  Mineral Springs *(G-10517)*

Kerrs Hickry Ready-Mixed Con................ E...... 828 322-3157
  Hickory *(G-8074)*

Legacy Vulcan LLC................ G...... 828 963-7100
  Boone *(G-1213)*

Legacy Vulcan LLC................ G...... 704 788-7833
  Concord *(G-4301)*

Legacy Vulcan LLC................ G...... 252 338-2201
  Elizabeth City *(G-5554)*

Legacy Vulcan LLC................ G...... 336 835-1439
  Elkin *(G-5624)*

Legacy Vulcan LLC................ G...... 828 255-8561
  Enka *(G-5683)*

Legacy Vulcan LLC................ G...... 704 279-5566
  Gold Hill *(G-6583)*

Legacy Vulcan LLC................ G...... 252 438-3161
  Henderson *(G-7794)*

Legacy Vulcan LLC................ G...... 828 692-0254
  Hendersonville *(G-7873)*

Legacy Vulcan LLC................ G...... 828 754-5348
  Lenoir *(G-9624)*

Legacy Vulcan LLC................ G...... 828 437-2616
  Morganton *(G-11227)*

Legacy Vulcan LLC................ G...... 336 838-8072
  North Wilkesboro *(G-12021)*

Legacy Vulcan LLC................ G...... 910 895-2415
  Rockingham *(G-13633)*

Legacy Vulcan LLC................ F...... 336 767-0911
  Winston Salem *(G-16785)*

Lenoir Concrete Cnstr Co................ G...... 828 759-0449
  Lenoir *(G-9625)*

Loflin Concrete Co Inc................ E...... 336 904-2788
  Kernersville *(G-9209)*

Loflin Materials Inc................ G...... 336 993-2432
  Kernersville *(G-9210)*

Loven Ready Mix LLC................ G...... 828 265-4671
  Boone *(G-1215)*

Macleod Construction Inc................ C...... 704 483-3580
  Charlotte *(G-3116)*

Martin Marietta Materials Inc................ G...... 910 602-6058
  Castle Hayne *(G-1954)*

Martin Marietta Materials Inc................ G...... 919 929-7131
  Chapel Hill *(G-2036)*

Martin Marietta Materials Inc................ G...... 704 392-1333
  Charlotte *(G-3130)*

Martin Marietta Materials Inc................ G...... 919 557-7412
  Fuquay Varina *(G-6213)*

Martin Marietta Materials Inc................ F...... 704 932-4379
  Landis *(G-9451)*

Martin Marietta Materials Inc................ G...... 919 664-1700
  Raleigh *(G-13002)*

Martin Marietta Materials Inc................ G...... 910 324-7430
  Richlands *(G-13556)*

Massey Ready-Mix Concrete Inc................ G...... 336 221-8100
  Burlington *(G-1457)*

McDowell Cement Products Co................ G...... 828 765-2762
  Spruce Pine *(G-14646)*

McDowell Cement Products Co................ F...... 828 652-5721
  Marion *(G-10161)*

Monsted Mix Inc................ G...... 704 979-6911
  Charlotte *(G-3201)*

Mulls Con & Septic Tanks Inc................ G...... 828 437-0959
  Morganton *(G-11236)*

Northeastern Ready Mix................ G...... 252 335-1931
  Elizabeth City *(G-5560)*

Oldcastle Retail Inc................ B...... 704 799-8083
  Cornelius *(G-4572)*

Quality Concrete Co Inc................ F...... 910 483-7155
  Fayetteville *(G-5903)*

Quikrete Companies LLC................ E...... 704 272-7677
  Peachland *(G-12175)*

Ready Mix of Carolinas Inc................ E...... 704 888-3027
  Locust *(G-9967)*

Ready Mixed Concrete................ G...... 252 758-1181
  Ayden *(G-854)*

Ready When You Are................ G...... 828 243-7514
  Arden *(G-370)*

Redy Mix of Carolinas Inc................ G...... 704 888-2224
  Locust *(G-9969)*

Rinker Materials................ F...... 704 455-1100
  Harrisburg *(G-7724)*

Rinker Materials................ G...... 704 827-8175
  Mount Holly *(G-11650)*

Riverside Cement Co................ G...... 760 245-5321
  Raleigh *(G-13209)*

Roanoke Chowan Ready Mix Inc................ G...... 252 332-7995
  Ahoskie *(G-65)*

Robert S Concrete Service Inc................ G...... 910 391-3973
  Fayetteville *(G-5909)*

S & W Ready Mix Con Co LLC................ F...... 910 592-2191
  Clinton *(G-4105)*

S & W Ready Mix Con Co LLC................ G...... 910 645-6868
  Elizabethtown *(G-5603)*

S & W Ready Mix Con Co LLC................ F...... 910 864-0939
  Fayetteville *(G-5911)*

S & W Ready Mix Con Co LLC................ F...... 919 751-1796
  Goldsboro *(G-6653)*

S & W Ready Mix Con Co LLC................ F...... 910 329-1201
  Holly Ridge *(G-8685)*

S & W Ready Mix Con Co LLC................ F...... 252 527-1881
  Kinston *(G-9382)*

S & W Ready Mix Con Co LLC................ F...... 252 726-2566
  Morehead City *(G-11186)*

S & W Ready Mix Con Co LLC................ F...... 252 633-2115
  New Bern *(G-11841)*

S & W Ready Mix Con Co LLC................ F...... 910 496-3232
  Spring Lake *(G-14627)*

S & W Ready Mix Con Co LLC................ F...... 910 285-2191
  Wallace *(G-15625)*

S & W Ready Mix Con Co LLC................ F...... 910 592-1733
  Clinton *(G-4104)*

S T Wooten Corporation................ E...... 252 291-5165
  Wilson *(G-16538)*

Smyrna Ready Mix Concrete LLC................ G...... 252 447-5356
  Havelock *(G-7747)*

Smyrna Ready Mix Concrete LLC................ F...... 252 637-4155
  New Bern *(G-11847)*

Southern Concrete Incorporated................ F...... 919 906-4069
  Broadway *(G-1297)*

Southern Concrete Materials................ G...... 704 641-9604
  Concord *(G-4363)*

Southern Concrete Materials Inc................ C...... 828 253-6421
  Asheville *(G-783)*

Southern Concrete Mtls Inc................ E...... 828 684-3636
  Arden *(G-378)*

Southern Concrete Mtls Inc................ E...... 828 670-6450
  Asheville *(G-784)*

Southern Concrete Mtls Inc................ G...... 828 682-2298
  Burnsville *(G-1533)*

Southern Concrete Mtls Inc................ F...... 704 394-2346
  Charlotte *(G-3591)*

Southern Concrete Mtls Inc................ E...... 704 394-2344
  Charlotte *(G-3592)*

Southern Concrete Mtls Inc................ G...... 828 681-5178
  Fletcher *(G-6043)*

Southern Concrete Mtls Inc................ F...... 828 524-3555
  Franklin *(G-6144)*

Employee Codes: A=Over 500 employees, B=251-500
C=101-250, D=51-100, E=20-50, F=10-19, G=1-9

CONCRETE: Ready-Mixed

Southern Concrete Mtls Inc............... E..... 828 692-6517
  Hendersonville *(G-7903)*
Southern Concrete Mtls Inc............... F..... 877 788-3001
  Salisbury *(G-14045)*
Southern Concrete Mtls Inc............... F..... 828 586-5280
  Sylva *(G-15069)*
Southern Concrete Mtls Inc............... E..... 828 456-9048
  Waynesville *(G-15826)*
Southern Hldings Goldsboro Inc......... F..... 919 920-6998
  Goldsboro *(G-6658)*
Southern Ready Mix LLC................... G..... 919 988-8448
  Goldsboro *(G-6659)*
Speer Concrete Inc............................ E..... 910 947-3144
  Carthage *(G-1666)*
Star Ready-Mix Inc............................ F..... 336 725-9401
  Winston Salem *(G-16915)*
Sunrock Group Holdings Corp........... D..... 919 747-6400
  Raleigh *(G-13315)*
Thomas Concrete Carolina................ G..... 919 828-6923
  Raleigh *(G-13346)*
Thomas Concrete Carolina Inc.......... F..... 704 333-0390
  Charlotte *(G-3688)*
Thomas Concrete Carolina Inc.......... F..... 919 557-3144
  Fuquay Varina *(G-6233)*
Thomas Concrete Carolina Inc.......... F..... 919 460-5317
  Morrisville *(G-11447)*
Thomas Concrete Carolina Inc.......... F..... 919 832-0451
  Raleigh *(G-13347)*
Thomas Concrete SC Inc................... G..... 704 868-4545
  Gastonia *(G-6526)*
Three Sisters Ready Mix LLC............ F..... 919 217-0222
  Knightdale *(G-9430)*
Titan America LLC............................. G..... 336 754-0143
  Belews Creek *(G-973)*
TNT Services Inc............................... F..... 252 261-3073
  Kitty Hawk *(G-9408)*
Toxaway Concrete Inc....................... F..... 828 966-4270
  Cashiers *(G-1938)*
Tri City Concrete Co LLC................... E..... 828 245-2011
  Forest City *(G-6084)*
Tri-City Concrete LLC........................ G..... 704 372-2930
  Charlotte *(G-3723)*
Triangle Ready Mix LLC.................... E..... 919 859-4190
  Morrisville *(G-11454)*
Tyrrell Ready Mix Inc........................ G..... 252 796-0265
  Columbia *(G-4169)*
Vulcan Construction Mtls LLC........... F..... 828 754-3200
  Lenoir *(G-9658)*
Vulcan Construction Mtls LLC........... G..... 336 767-1201
  Winston Salem *(G-16965)*
Vulcan Construction Mtls LLC........... E..... 336 767-0911
  Winston Salem *(G-16966)*
Vulcan Materials Company................ G..... 828 963-7100
  Boone *(G-1246)*
Vulcan Materials Company................ G..... 704 545-5687
  Charlotte *(G-3784)*
Vulcan Materials Company................ G..... 704 549-1540
  Charlotte *(G-3785)*
Vulcan Materials Company................ G..... 828 692-0039
  Hendersonville *(G-7912)*
Vulcan Materials Company................ G..... 336 869-2148
  Kernersville *(G-9252)*
Watauga Ready Mixed...................... G..... 336 246-6441
  Boone *(G-1248)*
White Cap LP................................... G..... 704 921-4420
  Charlotte *(G-3810)*
Williams Ready Mix Pdts Inc............ F..... 704 283-1137
  Monroe *(G-10834)*
Wnc Material Sales........................... G..... 828 658-8368
  Weaverville *(G-15869)*

CONDENSERS & CONDENSING UNITS: Air Conditioner

Bally Refrigerated Boxes Inc............ C..... 252 240-2829
  Morehead City *(G-11151)*
Rheem Manufacturing Company........ C..... 336 495-6800
  Randleman *(G-13488)*

CONNECTORS: Electronic

Vrg Components Inc........................ F..... 980 244-3862
  Indian Trail *(G-8970)*

CONSTRUCTION & MINING MACHINERY WHOLESALERS

Gregory Poole Equipment Co........... F..... 919 872-2691
  Raleigh *(G-12818)*
James River Equipment.................... E..... 704 821-7399
  Monroe *(G-10747)*

CONSTRUCTION & ROAD MAINTENANCE EQPT: Drags, Road

VT Leeboy Inc.................................. C..... 704 966-3300
  Lincolnton *(G-9934)*

CONSTRUCTION EQPT REPAIR SVCS

S & S Repair Service Inc.................. F..... 252 756-5989
  Winterville *(G-17013)*

CONSTRUCTION EQPT: Attachments, Snow Plow

Root Spring Scraper Co................... F..... 269 382-2025
  Pinehurst *(G-12235)*

CONSTRUCTION EQPT: Cranes

Cavotec USA Inc.............................. E..... 704 873-3009
  Mooresville *(G-10900)*

CONSTRUCTION EQPT: Finishers & Spreaders

Rocky Springs Applicator................. G..... 704 546-7560
  Harmony *(G-7688)*

CONSTRUCTION EQPT: Graders, Road

Champion LLC.................................. F..... 704 392-1038
  Charlotte *(G-2445)*
Four Points Recycling LLC............... F..... 910 333-5961
  Jacksonville *(G-9000)*
Stone Supply Inc............................. G..... 828 678-9966
  Burnsville *(G-1534)*

CONSTRUCTION EQPT: Loaders, Shovel, Self-Propelled

Caterpillar Inc.................................. D..... 919 550-1100
  Clayton *(G-3963)*

CONSTRUCTION EQPT: Roofing Eqpt

Dimensional Metals Inc..................... G..... 704 279-9691
  Salisbury *(G-13953)*
Metal Roofing Systems LLC............. E..... 704 820-3110
  Stanley *(G-14702)*
Roofing Tools and Eqp Inc................ G..... 252 291-1800
  Wilson *(G-16534)*

CONSTRUCTION MATERIALS, WHOLESALE: Aggregate

Concrete Service Co Inc.................. E..... 910 483-0396
  Fayetteville *(G-5794)*

CONSTRUCTION MATERIALS, WHOLESALE: Architectural Metalwork

Design Specialties Inc...................... E..... 919 772-6955
  Raleigh *(G-12678)*

CONSTRUCTION MATERIALS, WHOLESALE: Awnings

DLM Sales Inc.................................. F..... 704 399-2776
  Charlotte *(G-2647)*
Harvest Homes and Handi Houses.... G..... 704 637-3878
  Salisbury *(G-13975)*
Innovative Awngs & Screens LLC..... F..... 833 337-4233
  Cornelius *(G-4561)*

CONSTRUCTION MATERIALS, WHOLESALE: Brick, Exc Refractory

General Shale Brick Inc................... G..... 919 828-0541
  Raleigh *(G-12793)*
Pine Hall Brick Co Inc...................... E..... 336 721-7500
  Winston Salem *(G-16857)*

CONSTRUCTION MATERIALS, WHOLESALE: Building Stone, Marble

Southern Marble Co LLC.................. G..... 704 982-4142
  Albemarle *(G-107)*
Tarheel Marble Company Inc........... F..... 704 888-6003
  Locust *(G-9975)*

CONSTRUCTION MATERIALS, WHOLESALE: Building, Exterior

Ace Marine Rigging & Supply Inc..... F..... 252 726-6620
  Morehead City *(G-11148)*
Albatross Supply LLC...................... G..... 336 488-1128
  Hamptonville *(G-7665)*
Four Jaks....................................... G..... 828 484-9545
  Weaverville *(G-15847)*
L G Sourcing Inc............................. E..... 704 758-1000
  Mooresville *(G-11001)*
Sipe Lumber Company Inc............... E..... 828 632-4679
  Taylorsville *(G-15167)*

CONSTRUCTION MATERIALS, WHOLESALE: Building, Interior

Southern Staircase Inc.................... D..... 704 357-1221
  Charlotte *(G-3597)*

CONSTRUCTION MATERIALS, WHOLESALE: Cement

Plycem Usa LLC............................... D..... 336 696-2007
  North Wilkesboro *(G-12030)*

CONSTRUCTION MATERIALS, WHOLESALE: Concrete Mixtures

Greenville Ready Mix Concrete......... E..... 252 756-0119
  Winterville *(G-17001)*
Jones Ornamental Concrete............. F..... 828 685-3740
  Hendersonville *(G-7867)*
Speer Concrete Inc......................... E..... 910 947-3144
  Carthage *(G-1666)*
Troy Ready - Mix Inc...................... G..... 910 572-1011
  Troy *(G-15418)*

CONSTRUCTION MATERIALS, WHOLESALE: Doors, Garage

Amarr Company............................... C..... 336 744-5100
  Winston Salem *(G-16602)*

PRODUCT SECTION

CONSTRUCTION: Heavy Highway & Street

Ultimate Products Inc................................ F 919 836-1627
  Raleigh *(G-13377)*

CONSTRUCTION MATERIALS, WHOLESALE: Masons' Materials

Motsinger Block Plant Inc......................... G 336 764-0350
  Winston Salem *(G-16818)*

CONSTRUCTION MATERIALS, WHOLESALE: Millwork

Ecmd Inc... D 336 667-5976
  North Wilkesboro *(G-12006)*
Harris Wood Products Inc......................... G 704 550-5494
  New London *(G-11872)*
Hunter Innovations Ltd............................. G 919 848-8814
  Raleigh *(G-12869)*
Mesa Quality Fenestration Inc................. G 828 393-0132
  Hendersonville *(G-7879)*

CONSTRUCTION MATERIALS, WHOLESALE: Molding, All Materials

Ornamental Mouldings LLC....................... F 336 431-9120
  Archdale *(G-295)*
Resinart East Inc...................................... F 828 687-0215
  Fletcher *(G-6034)*

CONSTRUCTION MATERIALS, WHOLESALE: Pallets, Wood

East Industries Inc................................... D 252 442-9662
  Rocky Mount *(G-13693)*
MAC Grading Co....................................... F 910 531-4642
  Autryville *(G-842)*
Steelman Lumber & Pallet LLC................. F 336 468-2757
  Hamptonville *(G-7678)*
Wood Country Creations LLC................... G 704 545-5966
  Mint Hill *(G-10549)*

CONSTRUCTION MATERIALS, WHOLESALE: Paving Materials

Asphalt Emulsion Inds LLC...................... G 252 726-0653
  Morehead City *(G-11150)*

CONSTRUCTION MATERIALS, WHOLESALE: Plywood

Weyerhaeuser Company........................... E 336 835-5100
  Elkin *(G-5633)*

CONSTRUCTION MATERIALS, WHOLESALE: Prefabricated Structures

Outlaw Step Co.. G 252 568-4384
  Deep Run *(G-4717)*
Woodland Logging Inc............................. G 910 298-3350
  Beulaville *(G-1099)*

CONSTRUCTION MATERIALS, WHOLESALE: Roofing & Siding Material

Triad Corrugated Metal Inc...................... E 336 625-9727
  Asheboro *(G-499)*
Union Corrugating Company.................... E 910 483-0479
  Fayetteville *(G-5937)*

CONSTRUCTION MATERIALS, WHOLESALE: Sand

Apac-Atlantic Inc...................................... D 336 412-6800
  Raleigh *(G-12512)*
Barnhill Contracting Company................. F 252 527-8021
  Kinston *(G-9344)*

CONSTRUCTION MATERIALS, WHOLESALE: Septic Tanks

Welbuilt Homes Inc.................................. F 910 323-0098
  Fayetteville *(G-5952)*

CONSTRUCTION MATERIALS, WHOLESALE: Septic Tanks

1st Choice Service Inc............................. F 704 913-7685
  Cherryville *(G-3861)*
Bobby Cahoon Construction Inc............... E 252 249-1617
  Grantsboro *(G-6763)*
Explosives Supply Company..................... F 828 765-2762
  Spruce Pine *(G-14640)*
Southern Concrete Mtls Inc..................... G 828 681-5178
  Fletcher *(G-6043)*
Southern Concrete Mtls Inc..................... E 828 692-6517
  Hendersonville *(G-7903)*

CONSTRUCTION MATERIALS, WHOLESALE: Siding, Exc Wood

Carolina Home Exteriors LLC.................... F 252 637-6599
  New Bern *(G-11786)*
Vinyl Windows & Doors Corp.................... F 910 944-2100
  Aberdeen *(G-35)*
Wake Supply Company............................. G 252 234-6012
  Wilson *(G-16557)*

CONSTRUCTION MATERIALS, WHOLESALE: Stone, Crushed Or Broken

Explosives Supply Company..................... F 828 765-2762
  Spruce Pine *(G-14640)*
Fletcher Limestone Company Inc............. F 828 684-6701
  Fletcher *(G-6005)*
Heidelberg Mtls Sthast Agg LLC.............. E 910 893-8308
  Bunnlevel *(G-1330)*
Lbm Industries Inc................................... F 828 966-4270
  Sapphire *(G-14213)*
Martin Marietta Materials Inc.................. G 336 674-0836
  Greensboro *(G-7185)*
Radford Quarries Inc................................ F 828 264-7008
  Boone *(G-1231)*
Surface Buff LLC...................................... G 919 341-2873
  Cary *(G-1906)*
Wake Stone Corporation.......................... E 919 775-7349
  Moncure *(G-10629)*

CONSTRUCTION MATERIALS, WHOLESALE: Veneer

Global Veneer Sales Inc........................... G 336 885-5061
  High Point *(G-8368)*
Sauers & Company Inc............................. F 336 956-1200
  Lexington *(G-9776)*
Southern Vneer Spclty Pdts LLC............... F 919 642-7004
  Moncure *(G-10626)*

CONSTRUCTION MATERIALS, WHOLESALE: Windows

Double Hung LLC..................................... E 888 235-8956
  Greensboro *(G-6976)*
Lookout Boat Window Frames LLC.......... G 252 723-2222
  Morehead City *(G-11182)*
Tompkins Industries Inc.......................... C 828 254-2351
  Asheville *(G-802)*
Vinyl Windows & Doors Corp.................... F 910 944-2100
  Aberdeen *(G-35)*

CONSTRUCTION MATLS, WHOL: Doors, Combination, Screen-Storm

Jeld-Wen Inc.. B 800 535-3936
  Charlotte *(G-3018)*

CONSTRUCTION SAND MINING

American Materials Company LLC........... G 252 752-2124
  Greenville *(G-7481)*
American Materials Company LLC........... E 910 532-6070
  Ivanhoe *(G-8979)*
B V Hedrick Gravel & Sand Co................. E 704 633-5982
  Salisbury *(G-13928)*
Glover Materials Inc................................ G 252 536-2660
  Pleasant Hill *(G-12364)*
Hedrick B V Gravel & Sand Co................. E 704 848-4165
  Lilesville *(G-9837)*
Welbuilt Homes Inc.................................. F 910 323-0098
  Fayetteville *(G-5952)*

CONSTRUCTION: Agricultural Building

United Visions Corp.................................. G 704 953-4555
  Davidson *(G-4705)*

CONSTRUCTION: Athletic & Recreation Facilities

Dimill Enterprises LLC............................. G 919 629-2011
  Raleigh *(G-12684)*

CONSTRUCTION: Bridge

Blythe Construction Inc........................... B 704 375-8474
  Charlotte *(G-2325)*

CONSTRUCTION: Commercial & Office Building, New

Atlantic Group Usa Inc............................. F 919 623-7824
  Raleigh *(G-12530)*
B V Hedrick Gravel & Sand Co................. E 704 633-5982
  Salisbury *(G-13928)*
M F C Inc.. E 252 322-5004
  Aurora *(G-836)*
Retail Installation Svcs LLC..................... G 336 818-1333
  Millers Creek *(G-10495)*
W T Humphrey Inc.................................... D 910 455-3555
  Jacksonville *(G-9044)*

CONSTRUCTION: Commercial & Office Buildings, Prefabricated

Robinsons Welding Service...................... G 336 622-3150
  Liberty *(G-9828)*

CONSTRUCTION: Dams, Waterways, Docks & Other Marine

Bobby Cahoon Construction Inc............... E 252 249-1617
  Grantsboro *(G-6763)*
Component Sourcing Intl LLC.................. E 704 843-9292
  Charlotte *(G-2534)*

CONSTRUCTION: Drainage System

Barnhill Contracting Company................. D 910 488-1319
  Fayetteville *(G-5769)*
Heath and Sons MGT Svcs LLC................ F 910 679-6142
  Rocky Point *(G-13747)*

CONSTRUCTION: Farm Building

American Builders Anson Inc................... E 704 272-7655
  Polkton *(G-12383)*
Hog Slat Incorporated.............................. B 800 949-4647
  Newton Grove *(G-11988)*

CONSTRUCTION: Food Prdts Manufacturing or Packing Plant

Herbal Innovations LLC........................... E 336 818-2332
  Wilkesboro *(G-16024)*

CONSTRUCTION: Heavy Highway & Street

CONSTRUCTION: Heavy Highway & Street

Crowder Trucking LLC .... G 910 797-4163
   Fayetteville *(G-5800)*

Dan Moore Inc .... G 336 475-8350
   Thomasville *(G-15210)*

Long Asp Pav Trckg of Grnsburg ..... F 336 643-4121
   Summerfield *(G-14986)*

S T Wooten Corporation .... E 919 965-9880
   Princeton *(G-12404)*

CONSTRUCTION: Indl Buildings, New, NEC

Ansgar Industrial LLC .... A 704 962-5249
   Charlotte *(G-2196)*

B V Hedrick Gravel & Sand Co .... E 704 633-5982
   Salisbury *(G-13928)*

Bwxt Investment Company .... E 704 625-4900
   Charlotte *(G-2369)*

Jbr Properties of Greenville Inc .... A 252 355-9353
   Winterville *(G-17004)*

TRC Acquisition LLC .... A 252 355-9353
   Winterville *(G-17015)*

CONSTRUCTION: Indl Plant

Bwxt Investment Company .... E 704 625-4900
   Charlotte *(G-2369)*

Wnc White Corporation .... E 828 477-4895
   Sylva *(G-15076)*

CONSTRUCTION: Land Preparation

United Visions Corp .... G 704 953-4555
   Davidson *(G-4705)*

CONSTRUCTION: Marine

Triton Marine Services Inc .... G 252 728-9958
   Beaufort *(G-969)*

CONSTRUCTION: Oil & Gas Pipeline Construction

Carlson Environmental Cons PC ...... D 704 283-9765
   Monroe *(G-10673)*

CONSTRUCTION: Parking Lot

Apac-Atlantic Inc .... D 336 412-6800
   Raleigh *(G-12512)*

Barnhill Contracting Company .... F 252 527-8021
   Kinston *(G-9344)*

Garris Grading and Paving Inc .... F 252 749-1101
   Farmville *(G-5736)*

CONSTRUCTION: Pipeline, NEC

Pipeline Plastics LLC .... G 817 693-4100
   Fair Bluff *(G-5699)*

CONSTRUCTION: Residential, Nec

Atlantic Group Usa Inc .... F 919 623-7824
   Raleigh *(G-12530)*

Merhi Glass Inc .... G 919 961-5930
   Raleigh *(G-13017)*

Seashore Builders Inc .... E 910 259-3404
   Maple Hill *(G-10132)*

Thompson Millwork LLC .... D 919 596-8236
   Mebane *(G-10433)*

United Visions Corp .... G 704 953-4555
   Davidson *(G-4705)*

CONSTRUCTION: Sewer Line

1st Choice Service Inc .... F 704 913-7685
   Cherryville *(G-3861)*

CONSTRUCTION: Single-Family Housing

Bennett Elec Maint & Cnstr LLC ...... G 910 231-0300
   Raeford *(G-12414)*

Brown Building Corporation .... F 919 782-1800
   Morrisville *(G-11308)*

Distinctive Bldg & Design Inc .... G 828 456-4730
   Waynesville *(G-15802)*

Downtown Graphics Network Inc .... G 704 637-0855
   Salisbury *(G-13954)*

GLG Corporation .... F 336 784-0396
   Winston Salem *(G-16722)*

Heidelberg Mtls Sthast Agg LLC ..... E 919 936-4221
   Princeton *(G-12400)*

J &D Contractor Service Inc .... G 919 427-0218
   Angier *(G-142)*

Merhi Glass Inc .... G 919 961-5930
   Raleigh *(G-13017)*

Mill Creek Post & Beam Co .... G 828 749-8000
   Saluda *(G-14072)*

Nuworks .... G 919 223-2587
   Goldsboro *(G-6640)*

RDc Debris Removal Cnstr LLC ...... E 323 614-2353
   Smithfield *(G-14479)*

Safe Home Pro Inc .... F 704 662-2299
   Cornelius *(G-4585)*

Selectbuild Construction Inc .... E 208 331-4300
   Raleigh *(G-13244)*

Zoetic Digital Development .... G 919 720-5945
   Raleigh *(G-13437)*

CONSTRUCTION: Single-family Housing, New

Champion Home Builders Inc .... C 910 893-5713
   Lillington *(G-9848)*

E A Duncan Cnstr Co Inc .... G 910 653-3535
   Tabor City *(G-15081)*

G A Lankford Construction .... G 828 254-2467
   Alexander *(G-118)*

High Cntry Tmbrframe Gllery WD .... G 828 264-8971
   Boone *(G-1204)*

Lewtak Pipe Organ Builders Inc ..... G 336 554-2251
   Mocksville *(G-10585)*

Lowder Steel Inc .... E 336 431-9000
   Archdale *(G-293)*

Mike Powell Inc .... F 910 792-6152
   Wilmington *(G-16324)*

Nobscot Construction Co Inc .... G 919 929-2075
   Chapel Hill *(G-2048)*

Nvr Inc .... D 704 484-7170
   Kings Mountain *(G-9320)*

Old Hickory Log Homes Inc .... G 704 489-8989
   Denver *(G-4791)*

Robbinsville Cstm Molding Inc .... F 828 479-2317
   Robbinsville *(G-13610)*

Ten Nails Construction Inc .... G 910 232-4883
   Hampstead *(G-7659)*

W T Humphrey Inc .... D 910 455-3555
   Jacksonville *(G-9044)*

CONSTRUCTION: Swimming Pools

Carolina Solar Structures Inc .... E 828 684-9900
   Asheville *(G-583)*

CONSTRUCTION: Transmitting Tower, Telecommunication

Spectrasite Communications LLC ... E 919 468-0112
   Cary *(G-1900)*

Wirenet Inc .... E 513 774-7759
   Huntersville *(G-8906)*

CONSTRUCTION: Warehouse

Hyman Furniture Warehouse LLC ... G 336 528-4950
   Winston Salem *(G-16752)*

CONSTRUCTION: Water & Sewer Line

Wnc White Corporation .... E 828 477-4895
   Sylva *(G-15076)*

CONSULTING SVC: Business, NEC

Airfield Solutions LLC .... G 919 348-4271
   Jacksonville *(G-8985)*

Alpha Theory LLC .... G 212 235-2180
   Charlotte *(G-2168)*

Alpha Theory LLC .... G 212 235-2180
   Charlotte *(G-2169)*

Atlantic Group Usa Inc .... F 919 623-7824
   Raleigh *(G-12530)*

Carolina Textile Services Inc .... G 910 843-3033
   Red Springs *(G-13496)*

Cleveland Compounding Inc .... G 704 487-1971
   Shelby *(G-14297)*

Competitive Solutions Inc .... E 919 851-0058
   Raleigh *(G-12634)*

Cycle Pro LLC .... F 704 662-6682
   Mooresville *(G-10922)*

Easter Seals Ucp NC & VA Inc .... D 919 856-0250
   Raleigh *(G-12717)*

Environmental Supply Co Inc .... F 919 956-9688
   Durham *(G-5089)*

Impact Fulfillment Svcs LLC .... C 336 227-1130
   Burlington *(G-1434)*

Kberg Productions LLC .... G 910 232-0342
   Raleigh *(G-12932)*

L Michelle LLC .... G 980 946-0204
   Mooresville *(G-11002)*

Lake Norman Industries LLC .... G 704 987-9048
   Cornelius *(G-4565)*

Piedmont Flight Inc .... E 336 776-6070
   Winston Salem *(G-16852)*

Security Consult Inc .... G 704 531-8399
   Charlotte *(G-3522)*

Spectrasite Communications LLC ... E 919 468-0112
   Cary *(G-1900)*

Sutton Scientifics Inc .... G 910 428-1600
   Star *(G-14723)*

CONSULTING SVC: Educational

Brightly Software Inc .... C 919 816-8237
   Cary *(G-1714)*

I-Leadr Inc .... F 910 431-5252
   Sherrills Ford *(G-14385)*

National Voctnl Tech Honor Soc ..... G 828 698-8011
   Flat Rock *(G-5970)*

Thinking Maps Inc .... G 919 678-8778
   Cary *(G-1908)*

CONSULTING SVC: Human Resource

National Ctr For Social Impact .... G 984 212-2285
   Raleigh *(G-13054)*

CONSULTING SVC: Management

Academy Association Inc .... F 919 544-0835
   Durham *(G-4899)*

Anew Look Homes LLC .... F 800 796-5152
   Hickory *(G-7935)*

Apex Analytix LLC .... C 336 272-4669
   Greensboro *(G-6810)*

Carolina By-Products Co .... G 336 333-3030
   Greensboro *(G-6882)*

Eco Building Corporation .... G 910 736-1540
   Red Springs *(G-13499)*

Educatrx Inc .... G 980 328-0013
   Monroe *(G-10711)*

PRODUCT SECTION

CONTAINERS: Wood

Go Energies LLC .... F 877 712-5999
 Wilmington *(G-16234)*
Go Energies Holdings Inc .... G 910 762-5802
 Wilmington *(G-16235)*
Intelligent Apps LLC .... G 919 628-6256
 Raleigh *(G-12897)*
Jestines Jewels Inc .... G 704 904-0191
 Salisbury *(G-13991)*
Make Solutions Inc .... F 623 444-0098
 Asheville *(G-694)*
Oberle Group .... G 336 399-6833
 Pfafftown *(G-12189)*
One Srce Dcument Solutions Inc .... E 800 401-9544
 Greensboro *(G-7234)*
Red Oak Sales Company .... G 704 483-8464
 Denver *(G-4798)*
Sonaron LLC .... G 808 232-6168
 Fayetteville *(G-5919)*
Wirenet Inc .... E 513 774-7759
 Huntersville *(G-8906)*

CONSULTING SVCS, BUSINESS: Communications

Amplified Elctronic Design Inc .... F 336 223-4811
 Greensboro *(G-6806)*
JPS Communications Inc .... D 919 534-1168
 Raleigh *(G-12923)*

CONSULTING SVCS, BUSINESS: Energy Conservation

Envirnmntal Cmfort Sltions Inc .... E 980 272-7327
 Kannapolis *(G-9119)*

CONSULTING SVCS, BUSINESS: Environmental

Carlson Environmental Cons PC .... D 704 283-9765
 Monroe *(G-10673)*

CONSULTING SVCS, BUSINESS: Safety Training Svcs

James King .... G 910 308-8818
 Fayetteville *(G-5845)*

CONSULTING SVCS, BUSINESS: Sys Engnrg, Exc Computer/ Prof

Aceyus Inc .... E 704 443-7900
 Charlotte *(G-2128)*
Avail Forensics LLC .... F 877 888-5895
 Wilmington *(G-16125)*
Bachstein Consulting LLC .... G 410 322-4917
 Youngsville *(G-17070)*
Camstar Systems Inc .... C 704 227-6600
 Charlotte *(G-2380)*
Ideacode Inc .... G 919 341-5170
 Greensboro *(G-7111)*
Qplot Corporation .... G 949 302-7928
 Raleigh *(G-13160)*

CONSULTING SVCS, BUSINESS: Systems Analysis & Engineering

Infinite Software Resorces LLC .... G 704 509-0431
 Charlotte *(G-2967)*

CONSULTING SVCS, BUSINESS: Testing, Educational Or Personnel

Emath360 LLC .... F 919 744-4944
 Cary *(G-1757)*

Learning Craftsmen Inc .... G 813 321-5003
 Apex *(G-213)*
Measurement Incorporated .... C 919 683-2413
 Durham *(G-5213)*

CONSULTING SVCS: Scientific

Prophysics Innovations Inc .... F 919 245-0406
 Cary *(G-1863)*
Qplot Corporation .... G 949 302-7928
 Raleigh *(G-13160)*
Tempest Environmental Corp .... G 919 973-1609
 Durham *(G-5393)*
Xona Microfluidics Inc .... G 951 553-6400
 Durham *(G-5456)*

CONTACT LENSES

Chentech Corp .... G 919 749-8765
 Holly Springs *(G-8694)*

CONTACTS: Electrical

Deringer-Ney Inc .... E 828 649-3232
 Marshall *(G-10201)*

CONTAINERS, GLASS: Water Bottles

CHI Resources .... G 828 835-7878
 Murphy *(G-11707)*

CONTAINERS: Foil, Bakery Goods & Frozen Foods

De Luxe Packaging Corp .... E 800 845-6051
 Charlotte *(G-2608)*

CONTAINERS: Food, Folding, Made From Purchased Materials

Pactiv LLC .... D 252 527-6300
 Kinston *(G-9380)*

CONTAINERS: Food, Liquid Tight, Including Milk

Caraustar Industries Inc .... F 336 498-2631
 Randleman *(G-13456)*

CONTAINERS: Frozen Food & Ice Cream

Candies Italian ICEE LLC .... G 980 475-7429
 Charlotte *(G-2382)*

CONTAINERS: Glass

Gerresheimer Glass Inc .... F 828 433-5000
 Morganton *(G-11215)*
Precision Concepts Intl LLC .... G 704 360-8923
 Mooresville *(G-11058)*

CONTAINERS: Laminated Phenolic & Vulcanized Fiber

Atlantic Custom Container Inc .... G 336 437-9302
 Graham *(G-6678)*

CONTAINERS: Metal

Carolina Expediters LLC .... G 888 537-5330
 Mount Airy *(G-11489)*
CSM Logistics LLC .... G 980 800-2621
 Charlotte *(G-2581)*
Jhrg Manufacturing LLC .... G 252 478-4977
 Spring Hope *(G-14619)*

CONTAINERS: Plastic

Altium Packaging LLC .... F 704 873-6729
 Statesville *(G-14746)*
Altium Packaging LLC .... D 336 472-1500
 Thomasville *(G-15183)*

Altium Packaging LP .... D 336 342-4749
 Reidsville *(G-13506)*
Berry Global Inc .... E 252 332-7270
 Ahoskie *(G-55)*
Berry Global Inc .... G 252 984-4100
 Battleboro *(G-918)*
Berry Global Inc .... C 704 664-3733
 Mooresville *(G-10873)*
Berry Global Inc .... D 252 984-4104
 Rocky Mount *(G-13664)*
C&K Plastics Nc LLC .... F 833 232-4848
 Mooresville *(G-10893)*
Cks Packaging .... E 704 663-6510
 Mooresville *(G-10904)*
CKS Packaging Inc .... D 336 578-5800
 Graham *(G-6685)*
CKS Packaging Inc .... E 704 663-6510
 Mooresville *(G-10905)*
Coltec Industries Inc .... A 704 731-1500
 Charlotte *(G-2527)*
Genpak LLC .... E 800 626-6695
 Charlotte *(G-2823)*
Great Pacific Entps US Inc .... E 980 256-7729
 Charlotte *(G-2859)*
Liqui-Box Corporation .... D 804 325-1400
 Charlotte *(G-3092)*
New Innovative Products Inc .... G 919 631-6759
 Pine Level *(G-12212)*
Plasgad Usa LLC .... E 704 775-6461
 Statesville *(G-14861)*
Plastic Ingenuity Inc .... D 919 693-2009
 Oxford *(G-12143)*
Proto Labs Inc .... C 833 245-8827
 Morrisville *(G-11413)*
Reynolds Consumer Products Inc .... A 704 371-5550
 Huntersville *(G-8885)*
Rubbermaid Commercial Pdts LLC .... A 540 667-8700
 Huntersville *(G-8888)*
Sealed Air Corporation .... D 828 728-6610
 Hudson *(G-8779)*
Sonoco Products Company .... D 828 245-0118
 Forest City *(G-6082)*
Sysmetric USA .... G 704 522-8778
 Mooresville *(G-11108)*
Technical Coating Intl Inc .... E 910 371-0860
 Belville *(G-1026)*
THEM International Inc .... G 336 855-7880
 Greensboro *(G-7399)*
Thomson Plastics Inc .... D 336 843-4255
 Lexington *(G-9793)*
Vault LLC .... F 336 698-3796
 High Point *(G-8590)*
Xceldyne Group LLC .... D 336 472-2242
 Thomasville *(G-15307)*

CONTAINERS: Sanitary, Food

CKS Packaging Inc .... E 704 663-6510
 Mooresville *(G-10905)*
Thomco Inc .... G 336 292-3300
 Greensboro *(G-7401)*

CONTAINERS: Shipping, Bombs, Metal Plate

Crown Case Co .... G 704 453-1542
 Charlotte *(G-2572)*
Worthington Cylinder Corp .... E 336 777-8600
 Winston Salem *(G-16985)*

CONTAINERS: Wood

Arcola Hardwood Company Inc .... F 252 257-4484
 Warrenton *(G-15654)*
Arcola Lumber Company Inc .... E 252 257-4923
 Warrenton *(G-15655)*

CONTAINERS: Wood

Arcola Sawmill .... G 252 257-1139
  Warrenton *(G-15656)*

Carolina Crate & Pallet Inc .... E 910 245-4001
  Vass *(G-15491)*

Carolina WD Pdts Mrshville Inc .... D 704 624-2119
  Marshville *(G-10211)*

Dac Products Inc .... E 336 969-9786
  Rural Hall *(G-13839)*

Elberta Crate & Box Co .... C 252 257-4659
  Warrenton *(G-15658)*

Kontane Logistics Inc .... G 828 397-5501
  Hickory *(G-8080)*

Lee County Industries Inc .... E 919 775-3439
  Sanford *(G-14148)*

CONTRACTOR: Dredging

Stone Supply Inc .... G 828 678-9966
  Burnsville *(G-1534)*

CONTRACTOR: Framing

Seashore Builders Inc .... E 910 259-3404
  Maple Hill *(G-10132)*

Selectbuild Construction Inc .... E 208 331-4300
  Raleigh *(G-13244)*

CONTRACTOR: Rigging & Scaffolding

Advantage Machinery Svcs Inc .... E 336 463-4700
  Yadkinville *(G-17030)*

CONTRACTORS: Acoustical & Insulation Work

Delve Interiors LLC .... C 336 274-4661
  Greensboro *(G-6968)*

Sika Corporation .... E 704 810-0500
  Gastonia *(G-6510)*

CONTRACTORS: Asbestos Removal & Encapsulation

Carlton Enterprizes LLC .... G 919 534-5424
  Rocky Point *(G-13743)*

CONTRACTORS: Boiler Maintenance Contractor

Riley Power Group LLC .... C 910 420-6999
  Pinehurst *(G-12234)*

CONTRACTORS: Carpentry Work

Artistic Southern Inc .... D 919 861-4695
  Charlotte *(G-2222)*

Athol Arbor Corporation .... F 919 643-1100
  Hillsborough *(G-8636)*

Classic Cleaning LLC .... E 800 220-7101
  Raleigh *(G-12626)*

Idx Impressions LLC .... C 703 550-6902
  Washington *(G-15711)*

White Robert Custom Wdwkg .... F 704 489-2005
  Denver *(G-4814)*

Wildwood Studios Inc .... G 828 299-8696
  Asheville *(G-822)*

CONTRACTORS: Carpentry, Cabinet & Finish Work

Cabinet Solutions Usa Inc .... E 828 358-2349
  Hickory *(G-7959)*

Comm-Kab Inc .... F 336 873-8787
  Asheboro *(G-417)*

Marsh Furniture Company .... F 336 273-8196
  Greensboro *(G-7182)*

Neals Carpentry & Cnstr .... G 910 346-6154
  Jacksonville *(G-9017)*

Riddley Retail Fixtures Inc .... E 704 435-8829
  Kings Mountain *(G-9329)*

Ullman Group LLC .... F 704 246-7333
  Charlotte *(G-3747)*

Vaughn Woodworking Inc .... G 828 963-6858
  Banner Elk *(G-905)*

Washington Cabinet Company .... G 252 946-3457
  Washington *(G-15738)*

CONTRACTORS: Carpentry, Finish & Trim Work

Interior Trim Creations Inc .... G 704 821-1470
  Charlotte *(G-2981)*

CONTRACTORS: Closet Organizers, Installation & Design

Closets By Design .... D 704 361-6424
  Charlotte *(G-2498)*

CONTRACTORS: Coating, Caulking & Weather, Water & Fire

Surface Renewal Systems LLC .... G 704 207-3596
  Matthews *(G-10348)*

CONTRACTORS: Commercial & Office Building

J &D Contractor Service Inc .... G 919 427-0218
  Angier *(G-142)*

Pro Choice Contractors Corp .... F 919 696-7383
  Raleigh *(G-13146)*

CONTRACTORS: Decontamination Svcs

Filtration Technology Inc .... G 336 294-5655
  Greensboro *(G-7014)*

Kberg Productions LLC .... G 910 232-0342
  Raleigh *(G-12932)*

Noble Oil Services Inc .... C 919 774-8180
  Sanford *(G-14159)*

CONTRACTORS: Directional Oil & Gas Well Drilling Svc

4d Directional Boring LLC .... G 614 348-1339
  Elizabeth City *(G-5529)*

NBC Enterprises Inc .... F 910 705-5781
  Fayetteville *(G-5880)*

Tim Hlley Excvtg Drctnal Drlg .... G 336 595-3320
  Walkertown *(G-15617)*

Vision Directional Drilling .... G 336 570-4621
  Burlington *(G-1514)*

CONTRACTORS: Drywall

Precision Walls Inc .... G 336 852-7710
  Greensboro *(G-7276)*

CONTRACTORS: Electric Power Systems

Power Integrity Corp .... E 336 379-9773
  Greensboro *(G-7269)*

CONTRACTORS: Electronic Controls Installation

Audio Vdeo Concepts Design Inc .... G 704 821-2823
  Indian Trail *(G-8921)*

Custom Controls Unlimited LLC .... F 919 812-6553
  Raleigh *(G-12664)*

International Tela-Com Inc .... F 828 651-9801
  Fletcher *(G-6013)*

Total Controls Inc .... G 704 821-6391
  Matthews *(G-10295)*

CONTRACTORS: Energy Management Control

Belham Management Ind LLC .... G 704 815-4246
  Charlotte *(G-2297)*

CONTRACTORS: Fence Construction

Afsc LLC .... D 704 523-4936
  Charlotte *(G-2142)*

Asheville Contracting Co Inc .... E 828 665-8900
  Candler *(G-1567)*

Automated Controls LLC .... F 704 724-7625
  Huntersville *(G-8796)*

Digger Specialties Inc .... G 336 495-1517
  Randleman *(G-13464)*

Englishs All Wood Homes Inc .... F 252 524-5000
  Grifton *(G-7600)*

Hamrick Fence Company .... F 704 434-5011
  Boiling Springs *(G-1160)*

Harrison Fence Inc .... G 919 244-6908
  Apex *(G-200)*

Invisible Fencing of Mtn Reg .... G 828 667-8847
  Candler *(G-1584)*

CONTRACTORS: Fiber Optic Cable Installation

NBC Enterprises Inc .... F 910 705-5781
  Fayetteville *(G-5880)*

Nkt Inc .... G 919 601-1970
  Cary *(G-1832)*

Telecmmnctons Resource MGT Inc ...... F 919 779-0776
  Raleigh *(G-13336)*

Unitape (usa) Inc .... F 828 464-5695
  Conover *(G-4507)*

CONTRACTORS: Fiberglass Work

Accel Wldg & Fabrication LLC .... G 980 722-7198
  Stanley *(G-14683)*

American Stainless Tubing LLC .... C 704 878-8823
  Troutman *(G-15366)*

Core Technology Molding Corp .... E 336 294-2018
  Greensboro *(G-6937)*

Gainsborough Baths LLC .... F 336 357-0797
  Lexington *(G-9722)*

Moores Fiberglass Inc .... F 252 753-2583
  Walstonburg *(G-15640)*

Piedmont Well Covers Inc .... F 704 664-8488
  Mount Ulla *(G-11685)*

S Kivett Inc .... E 910 592-0161
  Clinton *(G-4106)*

CONTRACTORS: Gas Field Svcs, NEC

Quick N Easy 12 Nc739 .... G 336 824-3832
  Ramseur *(G-13449)*

Trans-Tech Energy Inc .... G 252 446-4357
  Rocky Mount *(G-13674)*

TransMontaigne Terminaling Inc .... F 303 626-8200
  Selma *(G-14262)*

CONTRACTORS: General Electric

Cemco Electric Inc .... F 704 504-0294
  Charlotte *(G-2441)*

JA Smith Inc .... G 704 860-4910
  Lawndale *(G-9500)*

M & M Electric Service Inc .... E 704 867-0221
  Gastonia *(G-6448)*

Mc Controls LLC .... G 336 518-1303
  Yadkinville *(G-17045)*

Presley Group Ltd .... D 828 254-9971
  Asheville *(G-741)*

Southern Elc & Automtn Corp............ F 919 718-0122
Sanford *(G-14187)*

Watson Electrical Cnstr Co LLC........... D 252 756-4550
Greenville *(G-7597)*

CONTRACTORS: Glass Tinting, Architectural & Automotive

Tint Plus... G 910 229-5303
Fayetteville *(G-5930)*

CONTRACTORS: Heating & Air Conditioning

Chichibone Inc....................................... G 919 785-0090
Morrisville *(G-11321)*

Commercial Flter Svc of Triad................ G 336 272-1443
Greensboro *(G-6924)*

Envirnmntal Cmfort Sltions Inc............... E 980 272-7327
Kannapolis *(G-9119)*

Harco Air LLC.. G 252 491-5220
Powells Point *(G-12397)*

Jenkins Services Group LLC................ G 704 881-3210
Catawba *(G-1965)*

Mc Controls LLC................................... G 336 518-1303
Yadkinville *(G-17045)*

CONTRACTORS: Heating Systems Repair & Maintenance Svc

Hollingsworth Heating Air Cond............. G 252 824-0355
Tarboro *(G-15108)*

J & W Service Incorporated.................. G 336 449-4584
Whitsett *(G-15994)*

Kenny Fowler Heating and A Inc............ G 910 508-4553
Wilmington *(G-16288)*

Saab Barracuda LLC............................. E 910 814-3088
Lillington *(G-9859)*

CONTRACTORS: Highway & Street Construction, General

Brown Brothers Construction Co............ F 828 297-2131
Zionville *(G-17148)*

Brown Building Corporation................... F 919 782-1800
Morrisville *(G-11308)*

Carlton Enterprizes LLC........................ G 919 534-5424
Rocky Point *(G-13743)*

Ferebee Corporation.............................. C 704 509-2586
Charlotte *(G-2751)*

Heath and Sons MGT Svcs LLC............ G 910 679-6142
Rocky Point *(G-13747)*

Reliable Woodworks Inc........................ G 704 785-9663
Concord *(G-4349)*

S T Wooten Corporation........................ E 252 291-5165
Wilson *(G-16538)*

Stone Supply Inc................................... G 828 678-9966
Burnsville *(G-1534)*

CONTRACTORS: Highway & Street Paving

Apac-Atlantic Inc................................... D 336 412-6800
Raleigh *(G-12512)*

Barnhill Contracting Company................ G 704 721-7500
Concord *(G-4204)*

Barnhill Contracting Company................ E 252 752-7608
Greenville *(G-7493)*

Barnhill Contracting Company................ F 252 527-8021
Kinston *(G-9344)*

Blythe Construction Inc......................... E 336 854-9003
Greensboro *(G-6845)*

Blythe Construction Inc......................... B 704 375-8474
Charlotte *(G-2325)*

Dickerson Group Inc............................. G 704 289-3111
Charlotte *(G-2631)*

Highland Paving Co LLC....................... D 910 482-0080
Fayetteville *(G-5839)*

Johnson Paving Company Inc............... F 828 652-4911
Marion *(G-10154)*

Lane Construction Corporation.............. B 919 876-4550
Raleigh *(G-12956)*

Moretz & Sipe Inc.................................. G 828 327-8661
Hickory *(G-8098)*

Russell Standard Corporation................ G 336 292-6875
Greensboro *(G-7320)*

Young & McQueen Grading Co Inc........ D 828 682-7714
Burnsville *(G-1539)*

CONTRACTORS: Hydraulic Eqpt Installation & Svcs

Atlantic Hydraulics Svcs LLC................. E 919 542-2985
Sanford *(G-14091)*

Limitless Wldg Fabrication LLC.............. G 252 753-0660
Farmville *(G-5739)*

Satco Truck Equipment Inc.................... F 919 383-5547
Durham *(G-5340)*

CONTRACTORS: Kitchen Cabinet Installation

B & L Custom Cabinets Inc................... F 704 857-1940
Westfield *(G-15950)*

Cabinet Solutions Usa Inc..................... E 828 358-2349
Hickory *(G-7959)*

Sare Granite & Tile................................ G 828 676-2666
Arden *(G-374)*

Thomas Lcklars Cbnets Lrnburg............ G 910 369-2094
Laurinburg *(G-9499)*

CONTRACTORS: Machine Rigging & Moving

Advantage Machinery Svcs Inc.............. E 336 463-4700
Yadkinville *(G-17030)*

RPM Plastics LLC................................. E 704 871-0518
Statesville *(G-14881)*

CONTRACTORS: Machinery Installation

Alpha 3d LLC....................................... G 704 277-6300
Charlotte *(G-2166)*

Dustcontrol Inc..................................... F 910 395-1808
Wilmington *(G-16207)*

Johnson Industrial Mchy Svcs............... E 252 239-1944
Lucama *(G-10017)*

Mantissa Corporation............................ E 704 525-1749
Charlotte *(G-3122)*

CONTRACTORS: Marble Installation, Interior

Apex Marble and Granite Inc................. E 919 462-9202
Morrisville *(G-11289)*

CONTRACTORS: Masonry & Stonework

Stonemaster Inc.................................... F 704 333-0353
Charlotte *(G-3638)*

Vega Construction Company Inc............ E 336 756-3477
Pilot Mountain *(G-12204)*

CONTRACTORS: Office Furniture Installation

Ie Furniture Inc..................................... E 336 475-5050
Archdale *(G-284)*

Retail Installation Svcs LLC................... G 336 818-1333
Millers Creek *(G-10495)*

Unique Office Solutions Inc................... F 336 854-0900
Greensboro *(G-7430)*

CONTRACTORS: Oil & Gas Wells Pumping Svcs

Well Doctor LLC.................................... G 704 909-9258
Charlotte *(G-3803)*

CONTRACTORS: Oil Field Pipe Testing Svcs

Doble Engineering Company................. G 919 380-7461
Morrisville *(G-11333)*

CONTRACTORS: Ornamental Metal Work

Alamance Iron Works Inc...................... G 336 852-5940
Greensboro *(G-6788)*

Blue Mountain Metalworks Inc............... G 828 898-8582
Banner Elk *(G-894)*

Gastonia Ornamental Wldg Inc.............. F 704 827-1146
Mount Holly *(G-11635)*

J&P Metal Arts Inc................................. G 704 684-5140
Monroe *(G-10745)*

James Iron & Steel Inc.......................... E 704 283-2299
Monroe *(G-10746)*

CONTRACTORS: Painting, Commercial

Carlton Enterprizes LLC........................ G 919 534-5424
Rocky Point *(G-13743)*

Custom Steel Boats Inc........................ F 252 745-7447
Merritt *(G-10439)*

Yontz & Sons Painting Inc..................... G 336 784-7099
Winston Salem *(G-16990)*

CONTRACTORS: Painting, Indl

Auto Parts Fayetteville LLC................... G 910 889-4026
Fayetteville *(G-5766)*

High Rise Service Company Inc............ E 910 371-2325
Leland *(G-9548)*

CONTRACTORS: Petroleum Storage Tanks, Pumping & Draining

Volta Group Corporation LLC................. E 919 637-0273
Raleigh *(G-13408)*

CONTRACTORS: Plumbing

Fixed-NC LLC....................................... G 252 751-1911
Greenville *(G-7526)*

Go Green Services LLC........................ D 336 252-2999
Greensboro *(G-7048)*

Heath and Sons MGT Svcs LLC............ F 910 679-6142
Rocky Point *(G-13747)*

Prestige Cleaning Incorporated.............. F 704 752-7747
Charlotte *(G-3375)*

Prime Water Services Inc..................... G 919 504-1020
Raleigh *(G-13140)*

Spc Mechanical Corporation.................. C 252 237-9035
Wendell *(G-15919)*

CONTRACTORS: Process Piping

Ansonville Piping & Fabg Inc................. G 704 826-8403
Ansonville *(G-152)*

Hicks Wterstoves Solar Systems........... F 336 789-4977
Mount Airy *(G-11518)*

Southern Pdmont Pping Fbrction........... F 704 272-7936
Peachland *(G-12176)*

CONTRACTORS: Roustabout Svcs

Filter Srvcng of Chrltte 135.................... G 704 619-3768
Charlotte *(G-2761)*

CONTRACTORS: Septic System

Affordable Septic Tank.......................... G 910 417-9537
Hamlet *(G-7615)*

Inman Septic Tank Service Inc.............. G 910 763-1146
Wilmington *(G-16268)*

Leonard McSwain Sptic Tank Svc......... G 704 482-1380
Shelby *(G-14337)*

O R Prdgen Sons Sptic Tank I.............. G 252 442-3338
Rocky Mount *(G-13717)*

CONTRACTORS: Septic System

TNT Services Inc .... F 252 261-3073
  Kitty Hawk (G-9408)
Trane US Inc .... F 704 697-9006
  Charlotte (G-3715)

CONTRACTORS: Sheet Metal Work, NEC

Carolina Machining Fabrication .... G 919 554-9700
  Youngsville (G-17075)
Herman Reeves Tex Shtmtl Inc .... E 704 865-2231
  Gastonia (G-6415)
Hughs Sheet Mtal Sttsvlle LLC .... F 704 872-4621
  Statesville (G-14818)
Oak Ridge Industries LLC .... E 252 833-4061
  Washington (G-15720)
R E Bengel Sheet Metal Co .... E 252 637-3404
  New Bern (G-11839)
Raleigh Mechanical & Mtls Inc .... F 919 598-4601
  Raleigh (G-13179)
Taylorsville Precast Molds Inc .... G 828 632-4608
  Taylorsville (G-15171)

CONTRACTORS: Siding

Midway Blind & Awning Co Inc .... G 336 226-4532
  Burlington (G-1461)
Vinyl Windows & Doors Corp .... F 910 944-2100
  Aberdeen (G-35)

CONTRACTORS: Structural Iron Work, Structural

Apex Steel Corp .... E 919 362-6611
  Raleigh (G-12514)
Garden Metalwork .... G 828 733-1077
  Newland (G-11887)
Watson Steel & Iron Works LLC .... E 704 821-7140
  Matthews (G-10350)

CONTRACTORS: Structural Steel Erection

Ansonville Piping & Fabg Inc .... G 704 826-8403
  Ansonville (G-152)
Asheville Maintenance and C .... E 828 687-8110
  Arden (G-312)
Burton Steel Company .... F 910 675-9241
  Castle Hayne (G-1944)
Canalta Enterprises LLC .... E 919 615-1570
  Raleigh (G-12586)
King Stone Innovation LLC .... G 704 352-1134
  Charlotte (G-3056)
Roderick Mch Erectors Wldg Inc ...... G 910 343-0381
  Wilmington (G-16386)
Steel Supply and Erection Co .... F 336 625-4830
  Asheboro (G-487)
Williams Industries Inc .... C 919 604-1746
  Raleigh (G-13423)

CONTRACTORS: Textile Warping

American Yarn LLC .... F 919 614-1542
  Burlington (G-1365)

CONTRACTORS: Tile Installation, Ceramic

David Allen Company Inc .... C 919 821-7100
  Raleigh (G-12675)
Precision Walls Inc .... G 336 852-7710
  Greensboro (G-7276)
Sare Granite & Tile .... G 828 676-2666
  Arden (G-374)

CONTRACTORS: Underground Utilities

Batista Grading Inc .... F 919 359-3449
  Clayton (G-3958)
McLean Sbsrface Utlity Engrg L .... F 336 340-0024
  Greensboro (G-7194)

Zoetic Digital Development .... G 919 720-5945
  Raleigh (G-13437)

CONTRACTORS: Warm Air Heating & Air Conditioning

Envirnmntal Cmfort Sltions Inc .... E 980 272-7327
  Kannapolis (G-9119)
James M Pleasants Company Inc ..... E 336 275-3152
  Greensboro (G-7133)
Johnson Controls Inc .... E 704 521-8889
  Charlotte (G-3030)
Kenny Fowler Heating and A Inc ..... G 910 508-4553
  Wilmington (G-16288)
Ppa Industries Inc .... E 828 328-1142
  Hickory (G-8118)

CONTRACTORS: Water Well Drilling

Merrill Resources Inc .... F 828 877-4450
  Penrose (G-12186)

CONTRACTORS: Windows & Doors

Jewers Doors Us Inc .... E 888 510-5331
  Greensboro (G-7136)

CONTRACTORS: Wood Floor Installation & Refinishing

Creative Stone Fyetteville Inc .... F 910 491-1225
  Fayetteville (G-5799)

CONTROL EQPT: Electric

Abco Controls and Eqp Inc .... G 704 394-2424
  Charlotte (G-2123)
AC Corporation .... B 336 273-4472
  Greensboro (G-6775)
Fortech Inc .... F 704 333-0621
  Charlotte (G-2790)
ITT LLC .... F 704 716-7600
  Charlotte (G-2999)
ITT LLC .... G 336 662-0113
  Colfax (G-4152)
Masonite Corporation .... B 704 599-0235
  Charlotte (G-3138)
Pro-Tech Inc .... G 704 872-6227
  Statesville (G-14870)
Rockwell Automation Inc .... F 919 804-0200
  Cary (G-1872)
Rockwell Automation Inc .... D 704 665-6000
  Charlotte (G-3456)

CONTROL EQPT: Noise

Ambient Noise Control LLC .... G 919 477-6791
  Durham (G-4914)

CONTROLS & ACCESS: Indl, Electric

Cross Technologies Inc .... E 800 327-7727
  Greensboro (G-6942)
Custom Controls Unlimited LLC ...... F 919 812-6553
  Raleigh (G-12664)
Eaton Corporation .... B 910 677-5375
  Fayetteville (G-5817)
I C E S Gaston County Inc .... G 704 263-1418
  Stanley (G-14697)
Rockwell Automation Inc .... F 828 652-0074
  Marion (G-10174)
Textrol Laboratories Inc .... E 704 764-3400
  Monroe (G-10821)

CONTROLS & ACCESS: Motor

2391 Eatons Ferry Rd Assoc LLC ..... G 919 844-0565
  Raleigh (G-12446)

Eaton Corporation .... C 919 870-3000
  Raleigh (G-12720)
Griffin Motion LLC .... F 919 577-6333
  Apex (G-198)
Melltronics Industrial Inc .... G 704 821-6651
  Matthews (G-10335)

CONTROLS: Automatic Temperature

Hoffman Building Tech Inc .... C 336 292-8777
  Greensboro (G-7094)
JMS Southeast Inc .... E 704 873-1835
  Statesville (G-14825)

CONTROLS: Electric Motor

Eaton Corporation .... B 828 684-2381
  Arden (G-326)
Hubbell Industrial Contrls Inc .... C 336 434-2800
  Archdale (G-283)

CONTROLS: Environmental

Ademco Inc .... G 919 872-5556
  Raleigh (G-12476)
AMR Systems LLC .... G 704 980-9072
  Charlotte (G-2190)
Building Automation Svcs LLC .... F 336 884-4026
  High Point (G-8277)
Cooke Companies Intl .... F 919 968-0848
  Chapel Hill (G-2006)
Ditex LLC .... G 919 215-3773
  Durham (G-5054)
Dna Group Inc .... G 919 881-0889
  Raleigh (G-12690)
Dynamac Corporation .... E 919 544-6428
  Durham (G-5073)
Global Envmtl Ctrl III Inc .... G 704 603-6155
  Salisbury (G-13970)
Huber Usa Inc .... F 919 674-4266
  Raleigh (G-12865)
Industrial Heat LLC .... F 919 743-5727
  Raleigh (G-12885)
Mc Controls LLC .... G 336 518-1303
  Yadkinville (G-17045)
Miller Ctrl Mfg Inc Clinton NC .... G 910 592-5112
  Clinton (G-4098)
Qualia Networks Inc .... G 805 637-2083
  Raleigh (G-13162)
Ruskin LLC .... G 919 583-5444
  Goldsboro (G-6652)
Strandberg Engrg Labs Inc .... F 336 274-3775
  Greensboro (G-7374)
W A Brown & Son Incorporated .... E 704 636-5131
  Salisbury (G-14063)

CONTROLS: Thermostats, Built-in

Shelby Kendrion Inc .... C 704 482-9582
  Shelby (G-14366)

CONVENIENCE STORES

Amko Express Inc .... G 336 434-7192
  Archdale (G-266)
Coker Feed Mill Inc .... F 919 778-3491
  Goldsboro (G-6602)
J L Powell & Co Inc .... G 910 642-8989
  Whiteville (G-15967)

CONVERTERS: Frequency

Global Emssons Systems Inc-USA ... G 704 585-8490
  Troutman (G-15380)
Greenfield Energy LLC .... F 910 509-1805
  Wrightsville Beach (G-17025)

CONVERTERS: Rotary, Electrical

DCS USA Corporation.................................. G 919 535-8000
  Morrisville *(G-11329)*

CONVEYOR SYSTEMS: Belt, General Indl Use

Conveyor Technologies Inc....................... G 919 732-8291
  Efland *(G-5526)*
Industrial Sup Solutions Inc..................... E 704 636-4241
  Salisbury *(G-13983)*
Qcs Acquisition Corporation..................... G 252 446-5000
  Rocky Mount *(G-13725)*

CONVEYOR SYSTEMS: Bulk Handling

RSI Leasing Inc NS Tbt.............................. G 704 587-9300
  Charlotte *(G-3468)*

CONVEYOR SYSTEMS: Pneumatic Tube

Sunco Powder Systems Inc...................... E 704 545-3922
  Charlotte *(G-3651)*

CONVEYORS & CONVEYING EQPT

AC Corporation... B 336 273-4472
  Greensboro *(G-6775)*
Advance Conveying Tech LLC.................. E 704 710-4001
  Kings Mountain *(G-9289)*
Altec Industries Inc.................................... B 919 528-2535
  Creedmoor *(G-4603)*
Automated Lumber Handling Inc............. G 828 754-4662
  Lenoir *(G-9576)*
Basic Machinery Company Inc................ D 919 663-2244
  Siler City *(G-14399)*
Belt Concepts America Inc....................... F 888 598-2358
  Spring Hope *(G-14614)*
Beltservice Corporation............................ E 704 947-2264
  Huntersville *(G-8797)*
Conroll Corporation................................... F 910 202-4292
  Wilmington *(G-16178)*
Conveying Solutions LLC......................... F 704 636-4241
  Salisbury *(G-13947)*
Conveyor Tech LLC.................................... C 919 776-7227
  Goldston *(G-6674)*
Conveyor Technologies of Sa.................. D 919 776-7227
  Sanford *(G-14103)*
Davis Conveyor Components................... G 704 557-1742
  Charlotte *(G-2605)*
Esco Group LLC... G 919 900-8226
  Raleigh *(G-12746)*
Forbo Movement Systems........................ E 704 334-5353
  Charlotte *(G-2786)*
Forbo Siegling LLC.................................... B 704 948-0800
  Huntersville *(G-8825)*
Gardner Machinery Corporation.............. F 704 372-3890
  Charlotte *(G-2808)*
Goals In Service LLC................................. G 919 440-2656
  Seven Springs *(G-14267)*
Gough Econ Inc.. E 704 399-4501
  Charlotte *(G-2848)*
Greenline Corporation.............................. G 704 333-3377
  Charlotte *(G-2866)*
Interroll Corporation................................. C 910 799-1100
  Wilmington *(G-16271)*
Interroll USA Holding LLC........................ D 910 799-1100
  Wilmington *(G-16272)*
Ism Inc... E
  Arden *(G-342)*
Jayson Concepts Inc................................ E 828 654-8900
  Arden *(G-344)*
Lns Turbo Inc... G 704 739-7111
  Kings Mountain *(G-9316)*

Machinex Technologies Inc..................... E 773 867-8801
  High Point *(G-8437)*
Mantissa Corporation............................... E 704 525-1749
  Charlotte *(G-3122)*
Material Handling Technologies Inc...... D 919 388-0050
  Morrisville *(G-11388)*
Memios LLC... D 336 664-5256
  Greensboro *(G-7197)*
Movex Usa Inc... G 434 616-2590
  Raleigh *(G-13044)*
National Conveyors Company Inc.......... G 860 325-4011
  Charlotte *(G-3234)*
Niels Jorgensen Company Inc................ G 910 259-1624
  Burgaw *(G-1346)*
Nunn Probst Installations Inc.................. G 704 822-9443
  Belmont *(G-997)*
Process Automation Tech Inc.................. F 828 298-1055
  Asheville *(G-745)*
Production Systems Inc........................... E 336 886-7161
  High Point *(G-8499)*
Pteris Global (usa) Inc............................. F 980 253-3267
  Charlotte *(G-3395)*
Sherrill Contract Mfg Inc.......................... F 704 922-7871
  Dallas *(G-4657)*
Southco Industries Inc............................. C 704 482-1477
  Shelby *(G-14369)*
Superior Finishing Systems LLC............ G 336 956-2000
  Lexington *(G-9788)*
Transbotics Corporation.......................... G 704 362-1115
  Charlotte *(G-3716)*

COOKING & FOODWARMING EQPT: Commercial

Kuenz America Inc.................................... F 984 255-1018
  Raleigh *(G-12948)*
Marshall Air Systems Inc........................ D 704 525-6230
  Charlotte *(G-3129)*
Rasa Malaysia... G 919 601-1765
  Chapel Hill *(G-2062)*
Sinnovatek Inc... G 919 694-0974
  Raleigh *(G-13264)*

COOKING EQPT, HOUSEHOLD: Ranges, Electric

The Tarheel Electric Member.................. F 919 876-4603
  Raleigh *(G-13342)*

COOKWARE, STONEWARE: Coarse Earthenware & Pottery

Haand... F 336 350-7597
  Burlington *(G-1427)*
Jamie M Dollahan...................................... G 571 435-2060
  Maysville *(G-10373)*

COOKWARE: Fine Earthenware

Swiss Made Brands USA Inc................... F 704 900-6622
  Charlotte *(G-3663)*

COOLING TOWERS: Metal

Akg Nrth Amercn Operations Inc........... F 919 563-4286
  Mebane *(G-10397)*
Marley Company LLC............................... C 704 752-4400
  Charlotte *(G-3128)*
SPX Cooling Tech LLC.............................. E 630 881-9977
  Charlotte *(G-3606)*
SPX Corporation.. F 336 627-6020
  Eden *(G-5503)*

COPPER ORE MINING

Ames Copper Group LLC......................... F 860 622-7626
  Shelby *(G-14286)*

COPPER PRDTS: Smelter, Primary

Imc-Metalsamerica LLC............................ G 704 482-8200
  Shelby *(G-14330)*

COPPER: Rolling & Drawing

Essex Group Inc.. G 704 921-9605
  Charlotte *(G-2730)*
Manhattan Amrcn Terrazzo Strip........... C 336 622-4247
  Staley *(G-14667)*
Torpedo Specialty Wire Inc..................... D 252 977-3900
  Rocky Mount *(G-13737)*

CORD & TWINE

All American Braids Inc........................... E 704 852-4380
  Gastonia *(G-6339)*
Apex Skip-Its LLC..................................... G 919 270-1752
  Apex *(G-163)*
Dayton Bag & Burlap Co........................... G 704 873-7271
  Statesville *(G-14783)*
MHS Ltd... G 336 767-2641
  Winston Salem *(G-16807)*
Sackner Products Inc.............................. G 704 873-1086
  Statesville *(G-14883)*
Sgb13 LLC.. F 844 627-5381
  Burlington *(G-1492)*
Standard Tytape Company Inc................ F 828 693-6594
  Hendersonville *(G-7906)*
Yale Rope Technologies Inc.................... G 704 630-0331
  Salisbury *(G-14068)*

CORK & CORK PRDTS: Bottle

Vinventions Usa LLC................................ C 919 460-2200
  Zebulon *(G-17145)*

COSMETIC PREPARATIONS

A M P Laboratories Ltd............................ G 704 894-9721
  Cornelius *(G-4519)*
Active Concepts... G 704 276-7386
  Lincolnton *(G-9866)*
Active Concepts LLC................................ G 704 276-7372
  Lincolnton *(G-9867)*
Active Concepts LLC................................ E 704 276-7100
  Lincolnton *(G-9868)*
Armorri Cosmetics LLC............................ G 910 352-6209
  Durham *(G-4924)*
Burts Bees Inc... C 919 998-5200
  Durham *(G-4993)*
Eb5 Corporation... G 503 230-8008
  Charlotte *(G-2680)*
Ei LLC.. B 704 857-0707
  Winston Salem *(G-16692)*
Emage Medical LLC.................................. G 704 904-1873
  Charlotte *(G-2703)*
Keller Cosmetics Inc................................ G 704 399-2226
  Monroe *(G-10753)*
Litex Industries Inc.................................. G 704 799-3758
  Mooresville *(G-11010)*
Mommi & ME Kozmeticz LLC.................. G 704 620-0082
  Charlotte *(G-3195)*
Onixx Manufacturing LLC........................ G 828 298-4625
  Swannanoa *(G-15032)*
Revlon Inc.. C 919 603-2782
  Oxford *(G-12148)*
Revlon Inc.. E 919 603-2000
  Oxford *(G-12149)*
Revlon Consumer Products Corp........... D 919 603-2000
  Oxford *(G-12150)*

COSMETICS & TOILETRIES

A Matter of Scents............................. G 980 939-3285
  Charlotte *(G-2116)*
Adora... G 336 880-0342
  High Point *(G-8233)*
Adoratherapy Inc............................. F 917 297-8904
  Asheville *(G-515)*
Alywillow.. G 919 454-4826
  Raleigh *(G-12495)*
American Fiber & Finishing Inc........ E 704 984-9256
  Albemarle *(G-73)*
Aprinnova LLC................................. G 910 371-2234
  Leland *(G-9526)*
Artisan Aromatics............................ G 800 456-6475
  Burnsville *(G-1523)*
Body Butter Blends LLC................. G 704 307-9200
  Charlotte *(G-2329)*
Body Shop Inc................................. C 919 554-4900
  Wake Forest *(G-15534)*
Burts Bees Inc................................. B 919 238-6450
  Morrisville *(G-11310)*
Cheeky Lather LLC......................... G 919 672-8071
  Efland *(G-5525)*
Cindys Souther Scents.................... G 828 492-0562
  Canton *(G-1609)*
Clover Garden Soaps...................... G 828 970-7289
  Maiden *(G-10105)*
Common Scents.............................. G 704 780-2230
  Charlotte *(G-2530)*
Common Scents Solutions............... G 812 344-4312
  Wilmington *(G-16176)*
Conopco Inc.................................... B 910 875-4121
  Raeford *(G-12416)*
Coty Inc... D 919 895-5000
  Sanford *(G-14105)*
Cryogen LLC................................... F 919 649-7027
  Raleigh *(G-12658)*
Deb SBS Inc.................................... F 704 263-4240
  Stanley *(G-14690)*
Dexios Services LLC....................... G 704 946-5101
  Cornelius *(G-4540)*
Domimex.. G 919 602-3921
  Raleigh *(G-12695)*
Don Koons Inc................................. E 919 603-0948
  Oxford *(G-12128)*
Erythis Inc....................................... G 704 644-0963
  Huntersville *(G-8816)*
Filltech Inc....................................... F 704 279-4300
  Rockwell *(G-13652)*
Filltech USA LLC............................. F 704 279-4300
  Rockwell *(G-13653)*
Gent of Scent.................................. G 980 505-9903
  Charlotte *(G-2824)*
Giddy LLC.. G 813 767-1444
  Chapel Hill *(G-2021)*
Go Green Miracle Balm................... G 630 209-0226
  Cornelius *(G-4551)*
Greenwich Bay Trading Co Inc....... E 919 781-5008
  Raleigh *(G-12816)*
HFC Prestige Products Inc............. G 919 895-5300
  Sanford *(G-14133)*
Humble Tree Naturals..................... G 704 770-1007
  Charlotte *(G-2931)*
Hummingbird Naturals LLC............. G 774 276-0889
  Knightdale *(G-9418)*
Karess Krafters............................... G 919 961-5575
  Holly Springs *(G-8703)*
Koru Naturals LLC........................... G 800 253-7011
  Hillsborough *(G-8658)*
Little River Naturals LLC................. G 919 760-3708
  Zebulon *(G-17133)*

Lo & Behold LLC............................. G 336 988-0589
  Durham *(G-5193)*
Luxuriously Natural Products.......... G 919 345-9050
  Franklinton *(G-6158)*
Michelles Scrubs and More............ G 980 215-9461
  Stanley *(G-14703)*
Neet Scrubs.................................... G 704 431-5019
  Salisbury *(G-14017)*
Pampering Moms Ntral Skin Care... G 706 490-3083
  Raleigh *(G-13098)*
Parkdale Mills Incorporated............ D 704 874-5000
  Gastonia *(G-6486)*
Philosophy Inc................................ E 602 794-8701
  Sanford *(G-14169)*
Plm Inc.. G 336 788-7529
  Winston Salem *(G-16859)*
Pure Soy Scents.............................. G 980 722-1483
  Mount Holly *(G-11649)*
Raw Elements................................. G 704 307-8025
  Charlotte *(G-3413)*
S & B Scents Inc............................. G 828 287-9410
  Rutherfordton *(G-13888)*
Sawyer Creek Soaps LLC............... G 910 231-5013
  Wallace *(G-15626)*
Sephora Inside Jcpenney................ G 919 778-4800
  Goldsboro *(G-6656)*
Skin So Soft Spa Inc....................... G 800 674-7554
  Charlotte *(G-3560)*
Sleepy Bee Worx LLC..................... G 336 824-6998
  Franklinville *(G-6170)*
Southern Scents............................. G 910 431-6492
  Hampstead *(G-7656)*
Suds ME Up Buttercup.................... G 704 419-2075
  Kings Mountain *(G-9337)*
Taltic Properties LLC...................... G 731 656-2735
  Mooresville *(G-11109)*
Tea and Honey Blends LLC........... G 919 673-4273
  Raleigh *(G-13331)*
That Make Scents LLC................... G 919 283-0237
  Clayton *(G-4018)*
Traceymack Products...................... G 919 499-8459
  Cameron *(G-1564)*
Unilever... G 910 988-1054
  Raeford *(G-12444)*
Unique Body Blends Inc.................. G 910 302-5484
  Fayetteville *(G-5938)*
Universal Preservachem Inc........... D 732 568-1266
  Mebane *(G-10434)*
US Cotton LLC................................. C 216 676-6400
  Gastonia *(G-6535)*
Virtue Labs LLC............................... E 781 316-5437
  Winston Salem *(G-16963)*
Walex Products Company Inc......... F 910 371-2242
  Leland *(G-9565)*
Yentiyahs Naturals LLC................... G 919 295-4279
  Raleigh *(G-13434)*

COSMETICS WHOLESALERS

A M P Laboratories Ltd................... G 704 894-9721
  Cornelius *(G-4519)*
Keller Cosmetics Inc....................... G 704 399-2226
  Monroe *(G-10753)*
Philosophy Inc................................ E 602 794-8701
  Sanford *(G-14169)*

COSMETOLOGY & PERSONAL HYGIENE SALONS

Katchi Tees Incorporated................ G 252 315-4691
  Wilson *(G-16504)*

COUGH MEDICINES

Generics Bidco II LLC..................... C 980 389-2501
  Charlotte *(G-2819)*
Generics Bidco II LLC..................... E 704 612-8830
  Charlotte *(G-2820)*

COUNTER & SINK TOPS

AP Granite Installation LLC............. G 919 215-1795
  Clayton *(G-3954)*
Cutting Edge Stoneworks Inc......... G 704 799-1227
  Mooresville *(G-10921)*
Endeavour Fbrication Group Inc..... G 919 479-1453
  Durham *(G-5086)*
Hargrove Countertops & ACC Inc... E 919 981-0163
  Raleigh *(G-12830)*
Old Castle Service Inc.................... G 336 992-1601
  Kernersville *(G-9221)*
Sare Granite & Tile......................... G 828 676-2666
  Arden *(G-374)*
Stonery LLC.................................... G 704 662-8702
  Mooresville *(G-11104)*
William Stone & Tile Inc.................. G 910 353-0914
  Hubert *(G-8757)*

COUNTERS OR COUNTER DISPLAY CASES, EXC WOOD

Mijo Enterprises Inc........................ G 252 442-6806
  Rocky Mount *(G-13712)*

COUNTERS OR COUNTER DISPLAY CASES, WOOD

Carolina Countertops of Garner...... F 919 832-3335
  Raleigh *(G-12595)*
Prp Ventures Inc............................. F 919 554-8734
  Wake Forest *(G-15577)*

COUNTING DEVICES: Controls, Revolution & Timing

Dynapar Corporation....................... C 800 873-8731
  Elizabethtown *(G-5595)*

COUNTING DEVICES: Speedometers

Nichols Spdmtr & Instr Co Inc........ G 336 273-2881
  Greensboro *(G-7219)*

COUPLINGS, EXC PRESSURE & SOIL PIPE

Victaulic Company........................... E 910 371-5588
  Leland *(G-9564)*

COUPLINGS: Hose & Tube, Hydraulic Or Pneumatic

Anchor Coupling Inc........................ B 919 739-8000
  Goldsboro *(G-6590)*
Bulldog Hose Company LLC........... E 919 639-6151
  Angier *(G-134)*
Cross Technologies Inc.................. G 336 370-4673
  Greensboro *(G-6943)*
On-Site Hose Inc............................. G 919 303-3840
  Apex *(G-222)*

COVERS: Automobile Seat

Flint Hill Textiles Inc........................ G 704 434-9331
  Shelby *(G-14318)*

COVERS: Automotive, Exc Seat & Tire

Guilford Mills LLC............................ A 910 794-5810
  Wilmington *(G-16243)*
Lear Corporation.............................. A 910 794-5810
  Wilmington *(G-16294)*

PRODUCT SECTION

CRANE & AERIAL LIFT SVCS

CVC Equipment Company .... G 704 300-6242
Cherryville *(G-3867)*

Flores Crane Services LLC .... F 704 243-4347
Waxhaw *(G-15757)*

K-M Machine Company Inc .... D 910 428-2368
Biscoe *(G-1114)*

Moore S Welding Service Inc .... G 919 837-5769
Bear Creek *(G-940)*

Nashville Wldg & Mch Works Inc .... E 252 243-0113
Wilson *(G-16517)*

Piedmont Fiberglass Inc .... E 828 632-8883
Statesville *(G-14859)*

Service and Equipment Company ..... G 910 545-5886
Jacksonville *(G-9029)*

Steel Supply and Erection Co .... F 336 625-4830
Asheboro *(G-487)*

Tony D Hildreth .... F 910 276-1803
Laurel Hill *(G-9465)*

Watson Steel & Iron Works LLC .... E 704 821-7140
Matthews *(G-10350)*

CRANES: Indl Plant

Kuenz America Inc .... F 984 255-1018
Raleigh *(G-12948)*

CRANES: Overhead

Altec Industries Inc .... B 919 528-2535
Creedmoor *(G-4603)*

Altec Northeast LLC .... D 508 320-9041
Creedmoor *(G-4604)*

CREDIT CARD SVCS

Atlantic Bankcard Center Inc .... G 336 855-9250
Greensboro *(G-6821)*

CROWNS & CLOSURES

Assa Abloy ACC Door Cntrls Gro .... C 877 974-2255
Monroe *(G-10653)*

CULTURE MEDIA

Business Mogul LLC .... G 919 605-2165
Raleigh *(G-12578)*

Kdr Visuality LLC .... G 704 451-1290
Charlotte *(G-3046)*

Thw of Wilson Inc .... G 252 237-7100
Wilson *(G-16546)*

CUPS & PLATES: Foamed Plastics

Unified2 Globl Packg Group LLC ..... C 774 696-3643
Durham *(G-5420)*

CURBING: Granite Or Stone

Asp Distribution Inc .... F 336 375-5672
Greensboro *(G-6820)*

Century Stone LLC .... G 919 774-3334
Sanford *(G-14099)*

Georgia-Carolina Quarries Inc .... E 336 786-6978
Mount Airy *(G-11511)*

Grancreations Inc .... G 704 332-7625
Charlotte *(G-2852)*

CURTAIN & DRAPERY FIXTURES: Poles, Rods & Rollers

Locklear Cabinets Wdwrk Sp Inc ..... G 910 521-1463
Rowland *(G-13790)*

CURTAIN WALLS: Building, Steel

Central Steel Buildings Inc .... F 336 789-7896
Mount Airy *(G-11496)*

Cornerstone Bldg Brands Inc .... B 281 897-7788
Cary *(G-1736)*

Eagle Carports Inc .... E 800 579-8589
Mount Airy *(G-11503)*

Millennium Mfg Structures LLC .... F 828 265-3737
Boone *(G-1222)*

Williams Industries Inc .... C 919 604-1746
Raleigh *(G-13423)*

CURTAINS: Window, From Purchased Materials

National Mastercraft Inds Inc .... F 919 896-8858
Raleigh *(G-13055)*

CUSHIONS & PILLOWS

Arden Companies LLC .... E 919 258-3081
Sanford *(G-14087)*

Carolina Fairway Cushions LLC ...... G 336 434-4292
Thomasville *(G-15196)*

Dale Ray Fabrics LLC .... G 704 932-6411
Kannapolis *(G-9116)*

Fiber Cushioning Inc .... F 336 629-8442
Asheboro *(G-434)*

Glenoit Universal Ltd .... C 919 735-7111
Goldsboro *(G-6616)*

Hickory Springs Mfg Co .... D 336 861-4195
High Point *(G-8385)*

Innovative Cushions LLC .... F 336 861-2060
Archdale *(G-285)*

Js Fiber Co Inc .... D 704 871-1582
Statesville *(G-14828)*

North Carolina Lumber Company .... F 336 498-6600
Randleman *(G-13481)*

Perfect Fit Industries LLC .... C 800 864-7618
Charlotte *(G-3330)*

Royale Comfort Seating Inc .... D 828 352-9021
Taylorsville *(G-15162)*

Signature Seating Inc .... E 828 325-0174
Hickory *(G-8156)*

Snyder Paper Corporation .... F 336 884-1172
High Point *(G-8539)*

Stn Cushion Company .... D 336 476-9100
Thomasville *(G-15284)*

Trtl Inc .... G 844 811-5816
Raleigh *(G-13368)*

Wayne Industries Inc .... E 336 434-5017
Archdale *(G-304)*

CUSHIONS & PILLOWS: Bed, From Purchased Materials

Creative Textiles Inc .... G 919 693-4427
Oxford *(G-12123)*

Discover Night LLC .... F 888 825-6282
Raleigh *(G-12687)*

Hardin Manufacturing Co .... G 828 685-2008
Hendersonville *(G-7858)*

Premium Cushion Inc .... E 828 464-4783
Conover *(G-4487)*

Richard Shew .... G 828 781-3294
Conover *(G-4491)*

Sunrise Development LLC .... F 828 453-0590
Mooresboro *(G-10841)*

Tempo Products LLC .... E 336 434-8649
High Point *(G-8565)*

Tempur Sealy International Inc .... E 336 861-2900
Trinity *(G-15361)*

CUSHIONS: Carpet & Rug, Foamed Plastics

Enginred Plstic Components Inc ..... C 919 663-3141
Siler City *(G-14410)*

Fxi Inc .... D 336 431-1171
High Point *(G-8362)*

Reedy International Corp .... F 980 819-6930
Charlotte *(G-3424)*

Shaw Industries Group Inc .... E 877 996-5942
Charlotte *(G-3536)*

CUSTOM COMPOUNDING OF RUBBER MATERIALS

American Phoenix Inc .... C 910 484-4007
Fayetteville *(G-5760)*

CUT STONE & STONE PRODUCTS

Buechel Stone Corp .... D 800 236-4474
Marion *(G-10145)*

Chadsworth Incorporated .... E 910 763-7600
Wilmington *(G-16168)*

Clifford W Estes Co Inc .... E 336 622-6410
Staley *(G-14664)*

Conway Development Inc .... F 252 756-2168
Greenville *(G-7505)*

Custom Marble Corporation .... G 910 215-0679
Pinehurst *(G-12219)*

E T Sales Inc .... E 704 888-4010
Midland *(G-10467)*

FTM Enterprises Inc .... F 910 798-2045
Wilmington *(G-16224)*

Ginkgo Stone LLC .... G 704 451-8678
Charlotte *(G-2830)*

Granite Memorials Inc .... G 336 786-6596
Mount Airy *(G-11512)*

Ivey Ln Inc .... G 336 230-0062
Greensboro *(G-7129)*

John J Morton Company Inc .... F 704 332-6633
Charlotte *(G-3028)*

M & M Stone Sculpting & Engrv ..... G 336 877-3842
Todd *(G-15323)*

Modern Marble & Glass Inc .... G 336 668-4197
Greensboro *(G-7203)*

Quality Marble .... G 336 472-1000
Thomasville *(G-15268)*

Royal Baths Manufacturing Co .... E 704 837-1701
Charlotte *(G-3461)*

RSI Home Products Inc .... C 828 428-6300
Lincolnton *(G-9917)*

Sharp Stone Supply Inc .... F 336 659-7777
Winston Salem *(G-16904)*

Sid Jenkins Inc .... G 336 632-0707
Greensboro *(G-7337)*

Tserings LLC .... G 704 283-8811
Monroe *(G-10825)*

Wake Stone Corporation .... E 919 266-1100
Knightdale *(G-9434)*

Waycaster Nick Stone Co .... G 828 756-4011
Marion *(G-10185)*

World Stone Fabricators Inc .... E 704 372-9968
Charlotte *(G-3825)*

World Stone of Sanford LLC .... F 919 468-8450
Sanford *(G-14209)*

CUTLERY

Bic Corporation .... D 704 598-7700
Charlotte *(G-2308)*

Butchers Best Inc .... G 252 533-0961
Roanoke Rapids *(G-13569)*

Edge-Works Manufacturing Co .... G 910 455-9834
Burgaw *(G-1339)*

Fred Marvin and Associates Inc ...... G 330 784-9211
Greensboro *(G-7021)*

J Culpepper & Co .... G 828 524-6842
Otto *(G-12118)*

CUTLERY

Mother of Pearl Co Inc .... G 828 524-6842
  Franklin *(G-6140)*

Spartan Blades LLC .... G 910 757-0035
  Southern Pines *(G-14556)*

Sword Conservatory Inc .... G 919 557-4465
  Holly Springs *(G-8720)*

CUTLERY WHOLESALERS

Freud America Inc .... C 800 334-4107
  High Point *(G-8360)*

CUTLERY: Carving Sets

Pineland Cutlery Inc .... G 910 757-0035
  Southern Pines *(G-14548)*

CYCLIC CRUDES & INTERMEDIATES

Burlington Chemical Co LLC .... G 336 584-0111
  Greensboro *(G-6861)*

Dystar LP .... E 704 561-3000
  Charlotte *(G-2668)*

Marlowe-Van Loan Corporation .... E 336 886-7126
  High Point *(G-8440)*

Melatex Incorporated .... F 704 332-5046
  Charlotte *(G-3162)*

Tar Heel Landworks LLC .... F 336 941-3009
  Mocksville *(G-10607)*

Tar Heel Materials & Hdlg LLC .... F 704 659-5143
  Cleveland *(G-4082)*

CYLINDER & ACTUATORS: Fluid Power

Atlantic Hydraulics Svcs LLC .... E 919 542-2985
  Sanford *(G-14091)*

Curtiss-Wright Controls Inc .... E 704 481-1150
  Shelby *(G-14306)*

Duff-Norton Company Inc .... G 704 588-0510
  Charlotte *(G-2656)*

Indian Head Industries Inc .... E 704 547-7411
  Charlotte *(G-2961)*

Shelby Kendrion Inc .... C 704 482-9582
  Shelby *(G-14366)*

Triumph Actuation Systems LLC .... C 336 766-9036
  Clemmons *(G-4064)*

CYLINDERS: Pump

IMO Industries Inc .... C 704 289-6511
  Monroe *(G-10738)*

DAIRY EQPT

Dairy Services .... G 919 303-2442
  Raleigh *(G-12670)*

DAIRY PRDTS STORE: Ice Cream, Packaged

Bilcat Inc .... E 828 295-3088
  Blowing Rock *(G-1154)*

Goodberry Creamery Inc .... F 919 878-8870
  Wake Forest *(G-15562)*

Mooresville Ice Cream Company LLC .... E 704 664-5456
  Mooresville *(G-11024)*

Paletria La Mnrca McHacana LLC .... G 919 803-0636
  Raleigh *(G-13095)*

Tony S Ice Cream Company Inc .... F 704 867-7085
  Gastonia *(G-6528)*

DAIRY PRDTS STORES

Buffalo Creek Farm & Crmry LLC .... G 336 969-5698
  Germanton *(G-6552)*

Dewey S Bakery Inc .... F 336 748-0230
  Winston Salem *(G-16677)*

G & M Milling Co Inc .... E 704 873-5758
  Statesville *(G-14802)*

DAIRY PRDTS: Acidophilus Milk

Maola Milk and Ice Cream Co .... E 844 287-1970
  New Bern *(G-11817)*

DAIRY PRDTS: Butter

Michaels Creamery Inc .... G 910 292-4172
  Fayetteville *(G-5873)*

Village Creamery & Caf Inc .... G 336 447-4726
  Elon *(G-5663)*

Waxhaw Creamery LLC .... F 704 843-7927
  Waxhaw *(G-15789)*

DAIRY PRDTS: Canned Milk, Whole

Chef Martini LLC .... A 919 327-3183
  Raleigh *(G-12618)*

DAIRY PRDTS: Cheese

Celebrity Dairy LLC .... G 919 742-4931
  Siler City *(G-14404)*

Old Salem Incorporated .... G 336 721-7305
  Winston Salem *(G-16828)*

Stans Quality Foods Inc .... G 336 570-2572
  Burlington *(G-1500)*

Tin Can Ventures LLC .... G 919 732-9078
  Cedar Grove *(G-1973)*

DAIRY PRDTS: Dairy Based Desserts, Frozen

Antkar LLC .... G 919 322-4100
  Raleigh *(G-12509)*

Delizza LLC .... F 252 442-0270
  Battleboro *(G-919)*

Hunter Farms .... C 336 822-2300
  High Point *(G-8403)*

DAIRY PRDTS: Dietary Supplements, Dairy & Non-Dairy Based

Arms Race Nutrition LLC .... G 888 978-2332
  Statesville *(G-14753)*

Bestco LLC .... E 704 664-4300
  Mooresville *(G-10875)*

Bionutra Life Sciences LLC .... G 828 572-2838
  Lenoir *(G-9590)*

Blue Ridge Silver Inc .... G 828 729-8610
  Boone *(G-1177)*

BNC Nutrition LLC .... G 336 567-0104
  Burlington *(G-1376)*

Body Engineering Inc .... G 704 650-3434
  Matthews *(G-10234)*

Disruptive Enterprises LLC .... F 336 567-0104
  Burlington *(G-1407)*

Gold Star .... G 704 651-8186
  Mooresville *(G-10961)*

Herbalife Manufacturing LLC .... F 336 970-6400
  Winston Salem *(G-16744)*

Ka-Ex LLC .... G 704 343-5143
  Charlotte *(G-3042)*

merica Labz LLC .... G 844 445-5335
  Statesville *(G-14842)*

Muscadine Naturals Inc .... G 888 628-5898
  Clemmons *(G-4053)*

NPC Corporation .... F 336 998-2386
  Mocksville *(G-10595)*

Pave Wellness LLC .... G 919 335-3575
  Durham *(G-5275)*

Rainforest Nutritionals Inc .... G 919 847-2221
  Raleigh *(G-13171)*

Sapphire Innvtive Thrapies LLC .... G 877 402-4325
  Chapel Hill *(G-2067)*

DAIRY PRDTS: Ice Cream & Ice Milk

Goodberry Creamery Inc .... F 919 878-8870
  Wake Forest *(G-15562)*

Mooresville Ice Cream Company LLC .... E 704 664-5456
  Mooresville *(G-11024)*

Simply Natural Creamery LLC .... F 252 746-3334
  Ayden *(G-858)*

DAIRY PRDTS: Ice Cream, Bulk

Homeland Creamery LLC .... G 336 685-6455
  Julian *(G-9105)*

Maola Milk and Ice Cream Co .... E 252 756-3160
  Greenville *(G-7557)*

Meadows Frozen Custar .... G 336 298-7246
  Oak Ridge *(G-12060)*

Yo Zone .... G 336 270-5262
  Burlington *(G-1520)*

DAIRY PRDTS: Ice Cream, Packaged, Molded, On Sticks, Etc.

Bignisha Rgrts Chill Cream LLC .... G 910 528-8966
  Fayetteville *(G-5770)*

DAIRY PRDTS: Milk & Cream, Cultured & Flavored

Alamance Foods Inc .... C 336 226-6392
  Burlington *(G-1362)*

DAIRY PRDTS: Milk, Fluid

Carolina Yogurt Inc .... G 828 754-9685
  Lenoir *(G-9596)*

Dfa Dairy Brands Fluid LLC .... G 336 714-9032
  Tarboro *(G-15101)*

Maola Milk and Ice Cream Co .... E 252 756-3160
  Greenville *(G-7557)*

New Dairy Opco LLC .... E 336 725-8141
  Winston Salem *(G-16819)*

DAIRY PRDTS: Natural Cheese

Fading D Farm LLC .... G 704 633-3888
  Salisbury *(G-13962)*

Looking Glass Creamery LLC .... G 828 458-0088
  Columbus *(G-4177)*

Saputo Cheese USA Inc .... C 847 267-1100
  Troy *(G-15414)*

DAIRY PRDTS: Processed Cheese

Ethnicraft Usa LLC .... F 336 885-2055
  High Point *(G-8346)*

Kraft Cabin LLc .... G 224 409-4374
  Raleigh *(G-12946)*

DAIRY PRDTS: Yogurt, Frozen

Carolina Yogurt Inc .... G 828 754-9685
  Lenoir *(G-9596)*

DATA PROCESSING & PREPARATION SVCS

Computer Task Group Inc .... G 919 677-1313
  Raleigh *(G-12636)*

Mjt Us Inc .... G 704 826-7828
  Charlotte *(G-3189)*

NCR Voyix Corporation .... G 937 445-5000
  Cary *(G-1830)*

DATA PROCESSING SVCS

Checkfree Services Corporation .... B 919 941-2640
  Durham *(G-5014)*

Consultants In Data Proc Inc .... G 704 542-6339
  Charlotte *(G-2542)*

Infobelt LLC .... F 980 223-4000
  Charlotte *(G-2971)*

Innait Inc.. G 406 241-5245
 Charlotte *(G-2975)*
Quinsite LLC Fka Mile 5 Anlyti................ F 317 313-5152
 Chapel Hill *(G-2061)*
Raleigh Ventures Inc............................... G 910 350-0036
 Wilmington *(G-16377)*

DECORATIVE WOOD & WOODWORK

A M Moore and Company Inc................ G 336 294-6994
 Greensboro *(G-6767)*
Archdale Millworks Inc............................ G 336 431-9019
 Archdale *(G-268)*
Blind Nail and Company Inc................... G 919 967-0388
 Chapel Hill *(G-1992)*
Cormark International LLC..................... G 828 658-8455
 Weaverville *(G-15844)*
Cranberry Wood Works Inc.................... G 336 877-8771
 Fleetwood *(G-5974)*
Dean Company of North Carolina........... F 910 622-1012
 Holly Ridge *(G-8681)*
Design Surfaces Inc................................ F 919 781-0310
 Raleigh *(G-12679)*
G & G Management LLC......................... F 336 444-6271
 Greensboro *(G-7027)*
George R Hardie..................................... G 336 263-7920
 Liberty *(G-9815)*
H & P Wood Turnings Inc....................... F 910 675-2784
 Rocky Point *(G-13746)*
Leist Studios Inc..................................... G 828 262-5912
 Boone *(G-1214)*
Pro Custom Cabinets LLC...................... G 704 239-6054
 Salisbury *(G-14031)*
Reliable Woodworks Inc......................... G 704 785-9663
 Concord *(G-4349)*
Renner Usa Corp..................................... G 704 527-9261
 Charlotte *(G-3435)*
Saluda Mountain Products Inc................ F 828 696-2296
 Flat Rock *(G-5971)*
Square Peg Construction Inc.................. G 828 277-5164
 Asheville *(G-787)*
Treeforms Inc... E 336 292-8998
 Greensboro *(G-7409)*
Vintage Editions Inc................................ F 828 632-4185
 Taylorsville *(G-15175)*
White Robert Custom Wdwkg................. G 704 489-2005
 Denver *(G-4814)*
Worthyware Dsgns By D McHlle L........... G 803 565-0615
 Charlotte *(G-3828)*

DEFENSE SYSTEMS & EQPT

Armored Self Defense LLC..................... G 336 749-7556
 Winston Salem *(G-16610)*
Black Barrel Defense LLC....................... G 336 468-8102
 Hamptonville *(G-7668)*
Blue Diamond Defense LLC.................... G 334 905-0246
 Sylva *(G-15055)*
Blue Maiden Defense.............................. G 678 292-8342
 Pinebluff *(G-12214)*
Blue Ridge Armor LLC............................. G 844 556-6855
 Rutherfordton *(G-13866)*
Cyber Defense Advisors.......................... G 336 899-6072
 Greensboro *(G-6952)*
Damsel Dedicated To Defense................ G 910 546-5603
 Southport *(G-14570)*
Damsel In Defense.................................. E 919 362-5972
 Apex *(G-179)*
Damsel In Defense.................................. F 919 744-8776
 Clayton *(G-3972)*
Damsel In Defense.................................. G 919 901-9926
 Goldsboro *(G-6608)*
Dark City Defense................................... G 805 729-8400
 Black Mountain *(G-1123)*
Defense of Implicit.................................. G 919 554-2735
 Louisburg *(G-9985)*
Dodson Defense LLC.............................. G 336 421-9649
 Burlington *(G-1408)*
Dynamic Defense Tactics II LLC............. G 703 850-1103
 Canton *(G-1614)*
Empowered Defense LLC....................... G 919 624-1304
 Raleigh *(G-12736)*
Foothills Fire Defense LLC..................... G 828 381-3988
 Hickory *(G-8027)*
Foothills Fire Defense LLC..................... G 828 612-9575
 Hickory *(G-8028)*
Green Line Defense LLC......................... G 828 707-5236
 Leicester *(G-9512)*
High Velocity Defense............................. G 704 738-3574
 Salisbury *(G-13980)*
Kdh Defense Systems Inc....................... C 336 635-4158
 Eden *(G-5494)*
Lynx Defense Corporation...................... G 919 701-9411
 Four Oaks *(G-6108)*
Mas Defense LLC.................................... G 980 265-1005
 Charlotte *(G-3136)*
Northstar Computer Tech Inc................. G 980 272-1969
 Monroe *(G-10780)*
Personal Defense Trainin....................... G 910 455-4473
 Jacksonville *(G-9019)*
Plane Defense Ltd.................................. G 828 254-6061
 Hendersonville *(G-7891)*
Sash and Saber Castings....................... G 919 870-5513
 Raleigh *(G-13230)*
Sense and Defenseability LLC.............. G 704 880-0165
 Stony Point *(G-14973)*
Serio Self Defense School of................. G 225 245-0693
 Waynesville *(G-15822)*
Soul Defense LLC................................... G 704 726-7898
 Charlotte *(G-3583)*
Willis Defense LLC.................................. G 704 609-9953
 Iron Station *(G-8978)*

DEGREASING MACHINES

Cox Machine Co Inc................................ F 704 296-0118
 Monroe *(G-10696)*

DENTAL EQPT

Almore International Inc......................... G 503 643-6633
 Hickory *(G-7932)*
Anutra Medical Inc.................................. F 919 648-1215
 Morrisville *(G-11287)*
Pelton & Crane Company....................... B 704 588-2126
 Charlotte *(G-3326)*
Preventive Technologies Inc.................. G 704 684-1211
 Indian Trail *(G-8958)*

DENTAL EQPT & SPLYS

Amann Girrbach North Amer LP............. F 704 837-1404
 Charlotte *(G-2176)*
Cefla Dental Group America.................. F 704 731-5293
 Charlotte *(G-2436)*
Custom Smiles Inc.................................. F 919 331-2090
 Angier *(G-138)*
Dental Equipment LLC........................... B 704 588-2126
 Charlotte *(G-2617)*
Dentonics Inc.. F 704 238-0245
 Monroe *(G-10705)*
Dentsply Sirona Inc................................ A 844 848-0137
 Charlotte *(G-2618)*
Kavo Kerr Group..................................... F 704 927-0617
 Charlotte *(G-3045)*
Salvin Dental Specialties LLC................ D 704 442-5400
 Charlotte *(G-3486)*
Voco America Inc.................................... G 917 923-7698
 Waxhaw *(G-15788)*

DENTAL EQPT & SPLYS: Enamels

Nelson Rodriguez.................................... G 828 433-1223
 Morganton *(G-11238)*
Oasis Denistry.. G 704 332-8188
 Charlotte *(G-3287)*

DENTAL EQPT & SPLYS: Orthodontic Appliances

Bioventus Inc... E 919 474-6700
 Durham *(G-4962)*
Cdb Corporation...................................... E 910 383-6464
 Leland *(G-9534)*

DENTISTS' OFFICES & CLINICS

Fidelity Associates Inc........................... E 704 864-3766
 Gastonia *(G-6402)*
Preventive Technologies Inc.................. G 704 684-1211
 Indian Trail *(G-8958)*

DEODORANTS: Personal

Procter & Gamble Mfg Co...................... D 336 954-0000
 Greensboro *(G-7287)*

DEPARTMENT STORES

Belk Department Stores LP.................... C 704 357-4000
 Charlotte *(G-2298)*
Burlington Coat Fctry Whse Cor............. E 919 468-9312
 Cary *(G-1718)*
Gildan Activewear (eden) Inc................. C 336 623-9555
 Eden *(G-5491)*

DEPARTMENT STORES: Country General

Village Produce & Cntry Str In................ G 336 661-8685
 Winston Salem *(G-16962)*

DEPILATORIES, COSMETIC

Beauty 4 Love LLC.................................. G 704 802-2844
 Charlotte *(G-2294)*
Oakstone Associates LLC...................... F 704 946-5101
 Cornelius *(G-4571)*

DERMATOLOGICALS

Nvn Liquidation Inc................................. G 919 485-8080
 Pittsboro *(G-12343)*

DESIGN SVCS, NEC

Advanced Non-Lethal Tech Inc............... G 847 812-6450
 Raleigh *(G-12479)*
Ahlberg Cameras Inc.............................. F 910 523-5876
 Wilmington *(G-16097)*
Aria Designs LLC................................... F 828 572-4303
 Lenoir *(G-9575)*
Asheville Color & Imaging Inc................ G 828 774-5040
 Asheville *(G-533)*
Banner Signs Today Inc......................... G 704 525-2241
 Charlotte *(G-2275)*
By-Design Black Oxide & TI LLC............. F 828 874-0610
 Valdese *(G-15443)*
Evolution of Style LLC............................ G 914 329-3078
 Charlotte *(G-2735)*
Keel Labs Inc.. G 917 848-9066
 Morrisville *(G-11365)*
M&M Bioplastic LLC................................ G 877 366-5227
 Mill Spring *(G-10488)*
Next World Design Inc........................... F 800 448-1223
 Thomasville *(G-15256)*
Powerlyte Paintball Game Pdts.............. F 919 713-4317
 Raleigh *(G-13124)*
Riley Technologies LLC.......................... E 704 663-6319
 Mooresville *(G-11069)*

DESIGN SVCS, NEC

Salon & Spa Design Services............... G 919 556-6380
  Wake Forest *(G-15587)*
Sv Plastics LLC.................................. G 336 472-2242
  Thomasville *(G-15287)*
Weaveup Inc....................................... G 443 540-4201
  Durham *(G-5439)*

DESIGN SVCS: Commercial & Indl

AMP Agency....................................... G 704 430-2313
  Harrisburg *(G-7701)*
Bull City Designs LLC........................ E 919 908-6252
  Durham *(G-4986)*
Distinctive Furniture Inc..................... G 828 754-3947
  Lenoir *(G-9604)*
Fe26 LLC.. G 980 875-0170
  Charlotte *(G-2750)*
Sitzer & Spuria Inc............................. G 919 929-0299
  Chapel Hill *(G-2073)*
Wild Child Custom Graphics LLC....... G 910 762-5335
  Wilmington *(G-16443)*

DESIGN SVCS: Computer Integrated Systems

057 Technology LLC.......................... G 855 557-7057
  Hickory *(G-7926)*
Cicero Inc.. G 919 380-5000
  Cary *(G-1730)*
Computerway Food Systems Inc....... E 336 841-7289
  High Point *(G-8302)*
Extreme Networks Inc....................... B 408 579-2800
  Morrisville *(G-11339)*
General Dynmics Mssion Systems..... C 336 698-8000
  Mc Leansville *(G-10391)*
Infobelt LLC....................................... F 980 223-4000
  Charlotte *(G-2971)*
Juniper Networks Inc......................... F 888 586-4737
  Raleigh *(G-12928)*
Q T Corporation................................. G 252 399-7600
  Wilson *(G-16526)*
S C I A Inc... G 919 387-7000
  Cary *(G-1877)*
Sostram Corporation.......................... G 919 226-1195
  Durham *(G-5364)*
St Investors Inc.................................. D 704 969-7500
  Charlotte *(G-3618)*
Utd Technology Corp......................... G 704 612-0121
  Mint Hill *(G-10546)*

DETECTIVE & ARMORED CAR SERVICES

A&B Integrators LLC......................... F 919 371-0750
  Durham *(G-4897)*
Diebold Nixdorf Incorporated............. F 704 599-3100
  Charlotte *(G-2632)*

DIAGNOSTIC SUBSTANCES

AR Corp... G 910 763-8530
  Wilmington *(G-16113)*
Gbf Inc... D 336 665-0205
  High Point *(G-8363)*
Liebel-Flarsheim Company LLC......... C 919 878-2930
  Raleigh *(G-12969)*
Liposcience Inc.................................. C 919 212-1999
  Morrisville *(G-11381)*
Molecular Toxicology Inc................... F 828 264-9099
  Boone *(G-1223)*
Novartis Vccnes Dagnostics Inc......... B 617 871-7000
  Holly Springs *(G-8708)*
Sapere Bio Inc................................... G 919 260-2565
  Durham *(G-5337)*
Tripath Imaging Inc............................ D 336 222-9707
  Burlington *(G-1509)*

DIAGNOSTIC SUBSTANCES OR AGENTS: Cytology & Histology

Multigen Diagnostics LLC................... G 336 510-1120
  Greensboro *(G-7208)*

DIAGNOSTIC SUBSTANCES OR AGENTS: In Vitro

Baebies Inc.. D 919 891-0432
  Durham *(G-4942)*
Sciteck Diagnostics Inc..................... G 828 650-0409
  Fletcher *(G-6036)*

DIAGNOSTIC SUBSTANCES OR AGENTS: Microbiology & Virology

Celplor LLC.. G 919 961-1961
  Cary *(G-1726)*
Precision Genomics Inc..................... G 843 737-1911
  Wrightsville Beach *(G-17027)*
Thurston Genomics LLC.................... G 980 237-7547
  Charlotte *(G-3693)*

DIAGNOSTIC SUBSTANCES OR AGENTS: Radioactive

Cardinal Health 414 LLC................... G 704 644-7989
  Charlotte *(G-2387)*
Petnet Solutions Inc........................... G 919 572-5544
  Durham *(G-5283)*
Petnet Solutions Inc........................... G 865 218-2000
  Winston Salem *(G-16847)*

DIAGNOSTIC SUBSTANCES OR AGENTS: Veterinary

North Carolina Department of A......... G 828 684-8188
  Arden *(G-356)*

DIAMONDS, GEMS, WHOLESALE

Bengal-Protea Ltd.............................. G 336 299-0299
  Greensboro *(G-6834)*

DIE CUTTING SVC: Paper

Paper Specialties Inc......................... G 919 431-0028
  Raleigh *(G-13099)*

DIE SETS: Presses, Metal Stamping

Parker Industries Inc......................... D 828 437-7779
  Connelly Springs *(G-4407)*

DIES & TOOLS: Special

ABT Manufacturing LLC..................... E 704 847-9188
  Statesville *(G-14736)*
American Artworks............................. G 910 803-2525
  Holly Ridge *(G-8679)*
Ameritek Inc...................................... E 336 292-1165
  Greensboro *(G-6803)*
Ameritek Lasercut Dies Inc................ E 336 292-1165
  Greensboro *(G-6805)*
Atlantic Tool & Die Co Inc.................. G 910 270-2888
  Hampstead *(G-7638)*
Brooks of Dallas Inc........................... E 704 922-5219
  Dallas *(G-4635)*
Cascade Die Casting Group Inc......... E 336 882-0186
  High Point *(G-8290)*
Container Graphics Corp.................... F 919 481-4200
  Cary *(G-1733)*
Continental Tool Works Inc................ G 828 692-2578
  Hendersonville *(G-7839)*
Converting Technology Inc................. G 336 333-2886
  Greensboro *(G-6934)*
Die-Tech Inc....................................... F 336 475-9186
  Thomasville *(G-15213)*
Dura-Craft Die Inc.............................. G 828 632-1944
  Taylorsville *(G-15141)*
Elizabeth Carbide NC Inc................... E 336 472-5555
  Lexington *(G-9715)*
Fisk Tool Company............................ G 828 684-5454
  Arden *(G-329)*
Flat Rock Tool & Mold Inc.................. G 828 692-2578
  Hendersonville *(G-7852)*
Foot To Die For.................................. G 704 577-2822
  Charlotte *(G-2785)*
Gerald Hartsoe.................................. G 336 498-3233
  Randleman *(G-13471)*
H + M USA Management Co Inc......... E 704 599-9325
  Charlotte *(G-2878)*
Its A Snap... G 828 254-3456
  Asheville *(G-664)*
Jmk Tool & Die Inc............................ G 910 897-6373
  Coats *(G-4131)*
KAM Tool & Die Inc........................... E 919 269-5099
  Zebulon *(G-17132)*
Madern Usa Inc................................. E 919 363-4248
  Apex *(G-215)*
Modern Mold & Tool Company.......... G 704 377-2300
  Mount Holly *(G-11643)*
Northeast Tool and Mfg Company...... E 704 882-1187
  Matthews *(G-10337)*
Palmer Senn..................................... G 704 451-3971
  Charlotte *(G-3309)*
Precision Partners LLC..................... E 800 545-3121
  Charlotte *(G-3370)*
Precision Tool & Stamping Inc........... E 910 592-0174
  Clinton *(G-4102)*
Precision Tool Dye and Mold.............. F 828 687-2990
  Arden *(G-368)*
Progressive Service Die Co............... F 910 353-4836
  Jacksonville *(G-9023)*
Progressive Tool & Mfg Inc................ F 336 664-1130
  Greensboro *(G-7289)*
Prototype Tooling Co......................... G 704 864-7777
  Gastonia *(G-6498)*
Southeastern Die of NC..................... G 336 275-5212
  Greensboro *(G-7352)*
Specialty Machine Co Inc.................. E 704 853-2102
  Gastonia *(G-6511)*
Stafford Cutting Dies Inc.................... D 704 821-6330
  Indian Trail *(G-8965)*
Stampco Metal Products Inc............. E 828 645-4271
  Weaverville *(G-15864)*
Stratford Tool & Die Co Inc................ F 336 765-2030
  Winston Salem *(G-16921)*
Tgr Enterprises Incorporated............. G 828 665-4427
  Candler *(G-1590)*
Wirtz Wire Edm LLC.......................... F 828 696-0830
  Hendersonville *(G-7915)*
Wright Machine & Tool Co Inc........... E 828 298-8440
  Swannanoa *(G-15038)*

DIES: Cutting, Exc Metal

DCS USA Corporation........................ G 919 535-8000
  Morrisville *(G-11329)*
Marbach America Inc......................... E 704 644-4900
  Charlotte *(G-3124)*

DIES: Diamond, Metalworking

Meusburger Us Inc............................ F 704 526-0330
  Mint Hill *(G-10539)*

DIES: Extrusion

Industrial Mtal Flame Spryers............ G 919 596-9381
  Durham *(G-5152)*

PRODUCT SECTION

Qrmc Ltd.. E 828 696-2000
  Hendersonville (G-7893)

DIES: Plastic Forming

Emerald Tool and Mold Inc............... F 336 996-6445
  Kernersville (G-9195)
Superior Tooling Inc............................ F 919 570-9762
  Wake Forest (G-15600)

DIODES: Light Emitting

Creeled Inc.. B 919 313-5330
  Durham (G-5035)
Hiviz Led Lighting LLC...................... F 703 662-3458
  Hendersonville (G-7864)
Multisite Led LLC................................ G 650 823-7247
  Charlotte (G-3216)

DIODES: Solid State, Germanium, Silicon, Etc

Leviton Manufacturing Co Inc........... G 336 846-3246
  West Jefferson (G-15942)
Lullicoin LLC.. G 336 955-1159
  Charlotte (G-3108)
Powersecure Solar LLC..................... B 919 213-0798
  Durham (G-5299)

DIRECT SELLING ESTABLISHMENTS: Food Svcs

Lotus Bakeries Us LLC...................... G 415 956-8956
  Mebane (G-10417)
Over Rainbow Inc............................... F 704 332-5521
  Charlotte (G-3307)

DISASTER SVCS

Fixed-NC LLC...................................... G 252 751-1911
  Greenville (G-7526)
Infinity Communications LLC........... E 919 797-2334
  Durham (G-5154)

DISCOUNT DEPARTMENT STORES

Val-U-King Group Inc......................... G 980 306-5342
  Gastonia (G-6536)

DISKETTE DUPLICATING SVCS

Succession Solutions Inc.................. F 704 631-9004
  Pineville (G-12311)

DISPLAY FIXTURES: Wood

D & D Displays Inc............................. E 336 667-8765
  North Wilkesboro (G-12005)
Dac Products Inc................................ E 336 969-9786
  Rural Hall (G-13839)
Display Options Woodwork Inc........ G 704 599-6525
  Belmont (G-985)
Grice Showcase Display Mfg Inc..... G 704 423-8888
  Charlotte (G-2868)
Spartacraft Inc.................................... E 828 397-4630
  Connelly Springs (G-4409)

DISPLAY ITEMS: Corrugated, Made From Purchased Materials

Intermarket Technology Inc.............. E 252 623-2199
  Washington (G-15713)
Rocktenn In-Store Solutions Inc...... B 828 245-9871
  Forest City (G-6080)
Supplyone Rockwell Inc.................... C 704 279-5650
  Rockwell (G-13660)

DISTRIBUTORS: Motor Vehicle Engine

Ineos Automotive Americas LLC..... G 404 513-8577
  Raleigh (G-12887)

DOCUMENT STORAGE SVCS

Legalis Dms LLC................................ F 919 741-8260
  Raleigh (G-12965)

DOOR FRAMES: Wood

Cook & Boardman Group LLC......... D 336 768-8872
  Winston Salem (G-16658)
Dac Products Inc................................ E 336 969-9786
  Rural Hall (G-13839)
Double Hung LLC............................... E 888 235-8956
  Greensboro (G-6976)
Jeld-Wen Inc....................................... C 336 838-0292
  North Wilkesboro (G-12016)
Lj Cbg Acquisition Company............ A 336 768-8872
  Winston Salem (G-16790)
Lookout Boat Window Frames LLC.. G 252 723-2222
  Morehead City (G-11182)

DOORS & WINDOWS: Screen & Storm

Door Screen.. G 406 531-4516
  Kitty Hawk (G-9401)

DOORS & WINDOWS: Storm, Metal

Champion Win Co of Charlotte........ F 704 398-0085
  Charlotte (G-2446)
Energy Svers Windows Doors Inc... G 252 758-8700
  Greenville (G-7523)
Envirnmental Win Solutions LLC..... G 704 200-2001
  Charlotte (G-2717)
Moss Supply Company...................... C 704 596-8717
  Charlotte (G-3205)
Ramsey Industries Inc....................... E 704 827-3560
  Belmont (G-1005)
Vinyl Windows & Doors Corp........... F 910 944-2100
  Aberdeen (G-35)

DOORS: Garage, Overhead, Metal

Amarr Company.................................. G 704 599-5858
  Charlotte (G-2178)
Amarr Company.................................. C 336 744-5100
  Winston Salem (G-16602)

DOORS: Garage, Overhead, Wood

Amarr Company.................................. G 704 599-5858
  Charlotte (G-2178)
Amarr Company.................................. C 336 744-5100
  Winston Salem (G-16602)
Craft Doors Usa LLC......................... F 828 469-7029
  Newton (G-11927)
Custom Doors Incorporated............. F 704 982-2885
  Albemarle (G-79)

DOORS: Glass

Envision Glass Inc............................. F 336 283-9701
  Winston Salem (G-16698)

DOORS: Screen, Metal

Owens Corning Sales LLC................ E 419 248-8000
  Roxboro (G-13814)

DRAPERIES & CURTAINS

A Window Treatment Co Inc............ F 919 934-7100
  Smithfield (G-14447)
Chf Industries Inc.............................. E 212 951-7800
  Charlotte (G-2473)
Ferncrest Fashions Inc..................... D 704 283-6422
  Monroe (G-10719)
Guest Interiors................................... G 828 244-5738
  Hickory (G-8035)

DRINKING PLACES: Beer Garden

Lichtenberg Inc................................... G 336 949-9438
  Madison (G-10078)
Stage Decoration and Sups Inc....... F 336 621-5454
  Greensboro (G-7364)
Textile Products Inc.......................... E 704 636-6221
  Salisbury (G-14051)
Wildcat Territory Inc.......................... F 718 361-6726
  Thomasville (G-15301)

DRAPERIES: Plastic & Textile, From Purchased Materials

Atlantic Window Coverings Inc....... E 704 392-0043
  Charlotte (G-2234)
Carolina Custom Draperies Inc....... G 336 945-5190
  Winston Salem (G-16644)
Diane Britt... G 910 763-9600
  Wilmington (G-16200)
Patterson Custom Drapery............... G 910 791-4332
  Wilmington (G-16349)
Smith Draperies Inc.......................... E 336 226-2183
  Burlington (G-1496)
Walker Draperies Inc........................ F 919 220-1424
  Durham (G-5437)

DRAPERY & UPHOLSTERY STORES: Draperies

Bettys Drapery Design Workroom... G 828 264-2392
  Boone (G-1176)
Walker Draperies Inc........................ F 919 220-1424
  Durham (G-5437)

DRILL BITS

Irwin Industrial Tool Company......... C 704 987-4555
  Huntersville (G-8838)

DRILLING MACHINERY & EQPT: Oil & Gas

Lintons Gas Piping & Service.......... F 828 734-6259
  Canton (G-1620)

DRINKING PLACES: Bars & Lounges

Bearwaters Brewing Company......... F 828 237-4200
  Canton (G-1599)
Bold Rock Partners LP...................... F 828 595-9940
  Mills River (G-10501)
Booneshine Brewing Co Inc............ G 828 263-4305
  Boone (G-1180)
Highland Brewing Company Inc..... F 828 299-3370
  Asheville (G-652)
Innovation Brewing LLC................... G 828 586-9678
  Sylva (G-15058)
Koi Pond Brewing Company LLC..... G 252 231-1660
  Rocky Mount (G-13706)
Oklawaha Brewing Company LLC... F 828 595-9956
  Hendersonville (G-7888)
Resident Culture Brewing LLC........ E 704 333-1862
  Charlotte (G-3438)
Salty Turtle Beer Company.............. E 910 803-2019
  Surf City (G-15016)
Shortway Brewing Company LLC... G 252 777-3065
  Newport (G-11907)
Sweet Room LLC................................ G 336 567-1620
  High Point (G-8560)
Triple C Brewing Company LLC...... F 704 372-3212
  Charlotte (G-3729)
White Street Brewing Co Inc........... E 919 647-9439
  Youngsville (G-17115)

DRINKING PLACES: Beer Garden

Cabarrus Brewing Company LLC.... E 704 490-4487
  Concord (G-4216)

DRINKING PLACES: Beer Garden

Glass Jug... F 919 818-6907
  Durham *(G-5116)*
Glass Jug LLC....................................... F 919 813-0135
  Durham *(G-5117)*
High Branch Brewing Co LLC................ G 704 706-3807
  Concord *(G-4279)*
Sugar Creek Brewing Co LLC................ E 704 521-3333
  Charlotte *(G-3646)*
Sycamore Brewing LLC......................... E 704 910-3821
  Charlotte *(G-3664)*

DRUG STORES

Modoral Brands Inc............................... G 336 741-7230
  Winston Salem *(G-16815)*
Natures Pharmacy Inc........................... G 828 251-0094
  Asheville *(G-710)*
Walgreen Co.. F 704 525-2628
  Charlotte *(G-3792)*

DRUGS & DRUG PROPRIETARIES, WHOLESALE

V1 Pharma LLC..................................... G 919 338-5744
  Raleigh *(G-13388)*

DRUGS & DRUG PROPRIETARIES, WHOLESALE: Bandages

Ambra Le Roy LLC................................ G 704 392-7080
  Charlotte *(G-2179)*

DRUGS & DRUG PROPRIETARIES, WHOLESALE: Pharmaceuticals

Bioventus LLC....................................... D 800 396-4325
  Durham *(G-4963)*
Glaxosmithkline LLC.............................. G 252 315-9774
  Durham *(G-5121)*
Glaxosmithkline LLC.............................. F 919 483-2100
  Durham *(G-5122)*
Glenmark Phrmceuticals Inc USA.......... D 704 218-2600
  Monroe *(G-10723)*
King Bio Inc.. D 828 255-0201
  Asheville *(G-675)*
Pharmacutical Dimension...................... G 336 664-5287
  Greensboro *(G-7253)*
Purdue Pharmaceuticals LP................... F 252 265-1900
  Wilson *(G-16525)*
Stiefel Laboratories Inc......................... C 888 784-3335
  Durham *(G-5376)*
Stiefel Laboratories Inc......................... C 888 784-3335
  Durham *(G-5375)*

DRUGS & DRUG PROPRIETARIES, WHOLESALE: Vitamins & Minerals

Bartlett Milling Company LP.................. E 704 487-5061
  Shelby *(G-14288)*
Interntnal Agrclture Group LLC.............. F 908 323-3246
  Mooresville *(G-10983)*
Premex Inc.. F 561 962-4128
  Durham *(G-5304)*

DRUGS ACTING ON THE CENTRAL NERVOUS SYSTEM & SENSE ORGANS

Allergan Inc.. G 704 301-7790
  Raleigh *(G-12491)*
Grifols Therapeutics LLC....................... D 919 316-6668
  Durham *(G-5128)*

DRUGS AFFECTING NEOPLASMS & ENDOCRINE SYSTEMS

Alcami Carolinas Corporation................ G 910 619-3952
  Garner *(G-6251)*
Alcami Carolinas Corporation................ G 910 254-7000
  Morrisville *(G-11282)*
Alcami Carolinas Corporation................ G 910 254-7000
  Morrisville *(G-11283)*
Alcami Carolinas Corporation................ B 910 254-7000
  Wilmington *(G-16103)*

DRUGS: Parasitic & Infective Disease Affecting

Novartis Vccnes Dagnostics Inc............. B 617 871-7000
  Holly Springs *(G-8708)*

DRUMS: Fiber

Greif Inc... D 704 588-3895
  Charlotte *(G-2867)*

DRUMS: Shipping, Metal

General Steel Drum LLC....................... F 704 525-7160
  Charlotte *(G-2818)*
Mauser Usa LLC.................................. D 704 455-2111
  Harrisburg *(G-7718)*

DUCTING: Metal Plate

Nordfab LLC... C 336 821-0829
  Thomasville *(G-15258)*

DUCTS: Sheet Metal

APT Industries Inc................................ F 704 598-9100
  Charlotte *(G-2206)*
Dantherm Filtration Inc......................... F 336 889-5599
  Thomasville *(G-15211)*
Gray Flex Systems Inc.......................... D 910 897-3539
  Coats *(G-4130)*
Hamlin Sheet Metal Company............... E 919 772-8780
  Garner *(G-6274)*
Harco Air LLC....................................... G 252 491-5220
  Powells Point *(G-12397)*
Jacksonville Metal Mfg Inc.................... G 910 938-7635
  Jacksonville *(G-9010)*
McGill Corporation................................ G 919 467-1993
  Cary *(G-1822)*
Monroe Metal Manufacturing Inc........... D 800 366-1391
  Monroe *(G-10775)*
Southern Comfort A Systems LLC......... G 919 324-6336
  Morrisville *(G-11432)*
Suppliers To Wholesalers Inc................ F 704 375-7406
  Charlotte *(G-3656)*
W T Humphrey Inc................................ D 910 455-3555
  Jacksonville *(G-9044)*

DUMPSTERS: Garbage

Dumpster Mate LLC.............................. G 919 303-7402
  Apex *(G-184)*
Fleetgenius of Nc Inc............................ C 828 726-3001
  Lenoir *(G-9612)*
J & L Bckh/Nvrnmental Svcs Inc........... G 910 237-7351
  Eastover *(G-5481)*
Miller Dumpster Service LLC................ G 704 504-9300
  Charlotte *(G-3181)*
Moore Dumpster Service LLC............... G 704 560-4410
  Ocean Isle Beach *(G-12093)*
Mrr Southern LLC................................ F 919 436-3571
  Raleigh *(G-13049)*
Waste Container Repair Svcs................ G 910 257-4474
  Fayetteville *(G-5949)*
Waste Industries Usa LLC.................... D 919 325-3000
  Raleigh *(G-13412)*
Wastequip LLC..................................... F 704 366-7140
  Charlotte *(G-3796)*

Wastequip Manufacturing Co LLC......... G 704 504-7597
  Charlotte *(G-3797)*

DUST OR FUME COLLECTING EQPT: Indl

Air Craftsmen Inc................................. F 336 248-5777
  Statesville *(G-14742)*
Air Systems Mfg of Lenoir Inc............... E 828 757-3500
  Lenoir *(G-9569)*
Bruning and Federle Mfg Co................. E 704 873-7237
  Statesville *(G-14766)*
Dantherm Filtration Inc......................... F 336 889-5599
  Thomasville *(G-15211)*
Jorlink Usa Inc..................................... F 336 288-1613
  Greensboro *(G-7140)*

DYES & PIGMENTS: Organic

Clariant Corporation............................. D 704 331-7000
  Charlotte *(G-2489)*
Dystar LP... D 336 342-6631
  Reidsville *(G-13518)*

EATING PLACES

Chatham News Publishing Co............... G 919 663-4042
  Siler City *(G-14406)*
Cintoms Inc.. G 828 684-1317
  Asheville *(G-593)*
Donut Shop.. G 910 640-3317
  Whiteville *(G-15962)*
Emanuel Hoggard................................. F 252 794-3724
  Windsor *(G-16566)*
Jebco Inc.. E 919 557-2001
  Holly Springs *(G-8702)*
McDonalds... G 910 295-1112
  Pinehurst *(G-12229)*
Tonys Ice Cream Co Inc....................... G 704 853-0018
  Gastonia *(G-6529)*

EDUCATIONAL SVCS

Advanced Computer Lrng Co LLC......... E 910 779-2254
  Fayetteville *(G-5752)*
Center for Creative Leadership............. B 336 288-7210
  Greensboro *(G-6898)*
Communitys Kitchen L3c....................... G 828 817-2308
  Tryon *(G-15423)*
Lulu Technology Circus Inc................... E 919 459-5858
  Morrisville *(G-11385)*
National Ctr For Social Impact............... G 984 212-2285
  Raleigh *(G-13054)*

ELECTRIC & OTHER SERVICES COMBINED

Flexgen Power Systems Inc.................. G 855 327-5674
  Durham *(G-5100)*
Flexgen Power Systems Inc.................. F 855 327-5674
  Durham *(G-5101)*

ELECTRIC MOTOR & GENERATOR AUXILIARY PARTS

ABB Motors and Mechanical Inc............ B 704 734-2500
  Kings Mountain *(G-9288)*

ELECTRIC MOTOR REPAIR SVCS

A & W Electric Inc................................. E 704 333-4986
  Charlotte *(G-2113)*
American Rewinding of NC Inc.............. E 704 589-1020
  Monroe *(G-10643)*
Averitt Enterprises Inc.......................... F 910 276-1294
  Laurinburg *(G-9469)*
B & M Electric Motor Service................ G 828 267-0829
  Hickory *(G-7946)*
Blue Ridge Elc Mtr Repr Inc.................. G 828 258-0800
  Asheville *(G-564)*

Bowden Electric Motor Svc Inc................... G..... 252 446-4203
  Rocky Mount (G-13685)
Brigman Electric Motors Inc.......................... G..... 828 492-0568
  Canton (G-1603)
Brittenhams Rebuilding Service.................. F..... 252 332-3181
  Ahoskie (G-57)
Canipe & Lynn Elc Mtr Repr Inc................... G..... 828 322-9052
  Hickory (G-7961)
Clayton Electric Mtr Repr Inc....................... F..... 336 584-3756
  Elon College (G-5664)
Consolidated Truck Parts Inc....................... G..... 704 279-5543
  Rockwell (G-13650)
Custom Industries Inc.................................. E..... 336 299-2885
  Greensboro (G-6950)
Dixie Electro Mech Svcs Inc......................... F..... 704 332-1116
  Charlotte (G-2646)
Electric Motor Rewinding Inc...................... G..... 252 338-8856
  Elizabeth City (G-5543)
Electric Motor Svc Ahoskie Inc................... G..... 252 332-4364
  Ahoskie (G-61)
Electric Mtr Sls Svc Pitt Cnty....................... G..... 252 752-3170
  Greenville (G-7522)
Electric Mtr Sp Wake Frest Inc.................... E..... 252 446-4173
  Rocky Mount (G-13694)
Electric Mtr Sp Wake Frest Inc.................... E..... 919 556-3229
  Wake Forest (G-15552)
Elektran Inc.. F..... 910 997-6640
  Rockingham (G-13625)
Energetics Inc.. G..... 910 483-2581
  Fayetteville (G-5821)
Esco Electronic Services Inc....................... F..... 252 753-4433
  Farmville (G-5735)
General Motor Repair & Svc Inc.................. G..... 336 292-1715
  Greensboro (G-7036)
Hammond Electric Motor Company............. F..... 704 983-3178
  Albemarle (G-89)
Hanover Electric Motor Svc Inc................... G..... 910 762-3702
  Wilmington (G-16244)
High Country Electric Mtrs LLC.................. G..... 336 838-4808
  North Wilkesboro (G-12014)
Hill & Ferencz Elc Mtr Co Inc....................... G..... 919 736-7473
  Goldsboro (G-6625)
Jenkins Electric Company........................... D..... 800 438-3003
  Charlotte (G-3020)
Jordan Electric Motors Inc.......................... F..... 919 708-7010
  Sanford (G-14142)
Lake City Electric Motor Repr..................... G..... 336 248-2377
  Lexington (G-9744)
Lingle Electric Repair Inc............................. F..... 704 636-5591
  Salisbury (G-14004)
Maybin Emergency Power Inc..................... G..... 828 697-1195
  Zirconia (G-17154)
McKinney Electric & Mch Co Inc................. G..... 828 765-7910
  Spruce Pine (G-14648)
Motor Shop Inc... G..... 704 867-8488
  Gastonia (G-6471)
Omninvest LLC... G..... 336 623-1717
  Harrisburg (G-7719)
Presley Group Ltd....................................... D..... 828 254-9971
  Asheville (G-741)
Pumps Blowers & Elc Mtrs LLC.................. G..... 919 286-4975
  Durham (G-5309)
Purser Centl Rewinding Co Inc................... F..... 704 786-3131
  Concord (G-4343)
Randall Supply Inc....................................... E..... 704 289-6479
  Monroe (G-10792)
Rocky Mount Electric Motor LLC................ G..... 252 446-1510
  Rocky Mount (G-13732)
Sanders Electric Motor Svc Inc................... E..... 828 754-0513
  Lenoir (G-9651)
Southern Electric Motor Co........................ G..... 919 688-7879
  Durham (G-5365)

Stone Cllins Mtr Rewinding Inc................... G..... 910 347-2775
  Jacksonville (G-9041)
Surry Elc Mtr & Contrls Inc.......................... F..... 336 786-1717
  Mount Airy (G-11581)
Tencarva Machinery Company LLC............ F..... 336 665-1435
  Greensboro (G-7395)
Tigertek Industrial Svcs LLC....................... E..... 336 623-1717
  Stoneville (G-14970)
Watson Electrical Cnstr Co LLC.................. D..... 252 756-4550
  Greenville (G-7597)
Williams Electric Mtr Repr Inc.................... G..... 919 859-9790
  Sanford (G-14206)
XCEL Hrmetic Mtr Rewinding Inc............... G..... 704 694-6001
  Wadesboro (G-15520)

ELECTRIC SERVICES

Pike Electric LLC... B..... 336 316-7068
  Greensboro (G-7263)

ELECTRIC SVCS, NEC: Power Generation

Florida Progress Corporation..................... C..... 704 382-3853
  Raleigh (G-12775)
Panenergy Corp... F..... 704 594-6200
  Charlotte (G-3310)

ELECTRIC WATER HEATERS WHOLESALERS

McKenzie Supply Company......................... G..... 910 276-1691
  Laurinburg (G-9489)

ELECTRICAL APPARATUS & EQPT WHOLESALERS

Abb Inc... E..... 704 587-1362
  Charlotte (G-2122)
ABB Inc.. C..... 919 856-2360
  Cary (G-1674)
Ademco Inc.. G..... 704 525-8899
  Charlotte (G-2137)
Ademco Inc.. G..... 336 668-3644
  Greensboro (G-6779)
Ademco Inc.. G..... 919 872-5556
  Raleigh (G-12476)
Code LLC... E..... 828 328-6004
  Hickory (G-7987)
Dna Group Inc... E..... 919 881-0889
  Raleigh (G-12690)
Envirnmntal Cmfort Sltions Inc................... E..... 980 272-9327
  Kannapolis (G-9119)
Exide Technologies LLC............................. G..... 704 521-8016
  Charlotte (G-2738)
His Company Inc... G..... 800 537-0351
  Wilmington (G-16255)
Hubbell Industrial Contrls Inc..................... C..... 336 434-2800
  Archdale (G-283)
JA Smith Inc.. G..... 704 860-4910
  Lawndale (G-9500)
Jenkins Electric Company........................... D..... 800 438-3003
  Charlotte (G-3020)
Johnson Controls Inc.................................. E..... 704 521-8889
  Charlotte (G-3030)
Ls Cable & System USA Inc........................ C..... 252 824-3553
  Tarboro (G-15112)
Minka Lighting Inc...................................... D..... 704 785-9200
  Concord (G-4316)
Rotron Incorporated.................................... C..... 336 449-3400
  Whitsett (G-16001)
Smart Electric North Amer LLC................... G..... 828 323-1200
  Conover (G-4497)

ELECTRICAL DISCHARGE MACHINING, EDM

Max Daetwyler Corp.................................... E..... 704 875-1200
  Huntersville (G-8853)
Southern Prestige Intl LLC.......................... F..... 704 872-9524
  Statesville (G-14894)
Specialty Perf LLC...................................... G..... 704 872-9980
  Statesville (G-14897)

ELECTRICAL EQPT REPAIR SVCS

Eaton Corporation....................................... D..... 864 433-1603
  Raleigh (G-12721)
Eaton Corporation....................................... C..... 919 872-3020
  Raleigh (G-12722)
Eaton Power Quality Corp........................... C..... 919 872-3020
  Raleigh (G-12723)
Eaton Power Quality Group Inc.................. F..... 919 872-3020
  Raleigh (G-12724)
Electrical Equipment Company.................. E..... 910 276-2141
  Laurinburg (G-9478)

ELECTRICAL EQPT REPAIR SVCS: High Voltage

Trans East Inc... D..... 910 892-1081
  Dunn (G-4887)
Transformer Sales & Service...................... G..... 910 594-1495
  Newton Grove (G-11994)

ELECTRICAL EQPT: Automotive, NEC

Jmedic Inc... G..... 336 744-4444
  Winston Salem (G-16771)
Mc Cullough Auto Elc & Assoc................... G..... 704 376-5388
  Charlotte (G-3148)
Scattered Wrenches Inc............................. G..... 919 480-1605
  Raleigh (G-13236)

ELECTRICAL GOODS, WHOLESALE: Batteries, Dry Cell

Edgewell Per Care Brands LLC................... G..... 336 672-4500
  Asheboro (G-427)

ELECTRICAL GOODS, WHOLESALE: Electrical Appliances, Major

Psnc Energy.. G..... 919 367-2735
  Apex (G-235)

ELECTRICAL GOODS, WHOLESALE: Electronic Parts

Btc Electronic Components LLC................ E..... 919 229-2162
  Wake Forest (G-15536)
East West Manufacturing LLC.................... G..... 704 663-5975
  Mooresville (G-10936)
Huber + Suhner North Amer Corp............... D..... 704 790-7300
  Charlotte (G-2929)
Kuebler Inc.. F..... 704 705-4711
  Charlotte (G-3064)

ELECTRICAL GOODS, WHOLESALE: Fittings & Construction Mat

Eizi Group Llc... G..... 919 397-3638
  Raleigh (G-12729)
Sigma Engineered Solutions PC................. D..... 919 773-0011
  Garner (G-6315)

ELECTRICAL GOODS, WHOLESALE: Generators

Bolton Investors Inc................................... G..... 919 471-1197
  Durham (G-4971)
Cemco Electric Inc...................................... F..... 704 504-0294
  Charlotte (G-2441)

ELECTRICAL GOODS, WHOLESALE: Generators

Cummins Atlantic LLC .... E 704 596-7690
  Charlotte (G-2584)
Cummins Atlantic LLC .... E 704 588-1240
  Charlotte (G-2585)
Pcai Inc .... D 704 588-1240
  Charlotte (G-3323)

ELECTRICAL GOODS, WHOLESALE: Light Bulbs & Related Splys

Blue Sun Energy Inc .... G 336 218-6707
  Greensboro (G-6842)
Fintronx LLC .... F 919 324-3960
  Raleigh (G-12767)
Long Life Lighting Inc .... G 919 833-1292
  Raleigh (G-12979)

ELECTRICAL GOODS, WHOLESALE: Modems, Computer

Avail Forensics LLC .... F 877 888-5895
  Wilmington (G-16125)

ELECTRICAL GOODS, WHOLESALE: Security Control Eqpt & Systems

A&B Integrators LLC .... F 919 371-0750
  Durham (G-4897)
Alert Protection Systems Inc .... G 919 467-4357
  Raleigh (G-12487)
Cargotec Port Security LLC .... G 919 620-1763
  Durham (G-4998)
Edwards Electronic Systems Inc .... E 919 359-2239
  Clayton (G-3976)
Telecmmnctons Resource MGT Inc ..... F 919 779-0776
  Raleigh (G-13336)
Total Technologies LLC .... G 336 259-5541
  Gastonia (G-6530)

ELECTRICAL GOODS, WHOLESALE: Semiconductor Devices

Disco Hi-TEC America Inc .... G 919 468-6003
  Morrisville (G-11332)
Synopsys Inc .... F 919 941-6600
  Morrisville (G-11437)

ELECTRICAL GOODS, WHOLESALE: Telephone & Telegraphic Eqpt

Abacon Telecommunications LLC .... E 336 855-1179
  Greensboro (G-6771)

ELECTRICAL GOODS, WHOLESALE: Wire & Cable

Abl Electronics Supply Inc .... G 704 784-4225
  Concord (G-4186)
Iron Box LLC .... E 919 890-0025
  Raleigh (G-12901)
Wieland Electric Inc .... F 910 259-5050
  Wilmington (G-16442)

ELECTRICAL GOODS, WHOLESALE: Wire & Cable, Electronic

Lutze Inc .... E 704 504-0222
  Charlotte (G-3110)

ELECTRICAL SPLYS

Electrical Equipment Company .... E 910 276-2141
  Laurinburg (G-9478)
McKenzie Supply Company .... G 910 276-1691
  Laurinburg (G-9489)

McNaughton-Mckay Southeast Inc .... F 910 392-0940
  Wilmington (G-16318)
Power-Utility Products Company .... F 704 375-0776
  Charlotte (G-3361)
Southland Electrical Sup LLC .... C 336 227-1486
  Burlington (G-1498)
State Electric Supply Company .... F 336 855-8200
  Greensboro (G-7367)

ELECTRICAL SUPPLIES: Porcelain

Greenleaf Corporation .... E 828 693-0461
  East Flat Rock (G-5476)
Pyrotek Incorporated .... E 704 642-1993
  Salisbury (G-14033)
The Tarheel Electric Member .... F 919 876-4603
  Raleigh (G-13342)

ELECTROMEDICAL EQPT

Albemrle Orthotics Prosthetics .... G 252 332-4334
  Ahoskie (G-54)
Altaravision Inc .... G 919 342-5778
  Apex (G-158)
Medi Mall Inc .... G 877 501-6334
  Fletcher (G-6022)
Odin Technologies LLC .... G 408 309-1925
  Charlotte (G-3288)
Oxlife of NC LLC .... G 828 684-7353
  Hendersonville (G-7889)
Ribometrix .... G 919 744-9634
  Durham (G-5331)
Tearscience Inc .... D 919 459-4880
  Morrisville (G-11439)
United Mobile Imaging Inc .... G 800 983-9840
  Clemmons (G-4065)
Volumetrics Med Systems LLC .... G 800 472-0900
  Durham (G-5436)

ELECTROMEDICAL EQPT WHOLESALERS

Turbomed LLC .... F 973 527-5299
  Fayetteville (G-5936)

ELECTRON TUBES

Ecoatm LLC .... E 858 324-4111
  Boone (G-1195)

ELECTRONIC DEVICES: Solid State, NEC

Maxtronic Technologies LLC .... G 704 756-5354
  Charlotte (G-3147)

ELECTRONIC EQPT REPAIR SVCS

Advanced Electronic Svcs Inc .... D 336 789-0792
  Mount Airy (G-11473)
Anuva Services Inc .... F 919 468-6441
  Morrisville (G-11288)
Applied Drives Inc .... G 704 573-2324
  Charlotte (G-2204)
Duotech Services Inc .... E 828 369-5411
  Franklin (G-6126)
SCR Controls Inc .... F 704 821-6651
  Matthews (G-10342)

ELECTRONIC LOADS & POWER SPLYS

Emrise Corporation .... C 408 200-3040
  Durham (G-5084)
Entergy Group LLC .... G 866 988-8884
  Sanford (G-14116)
Parker-Hannifin Corporation .... E 704 588-3246
  Charlotte (G-3315)
US Prototype Inc .... E 866 239-2848
  Wilmington (G-16439)
Utility Solutions Inc .... G 828 323-8914
  Hickory (G-8200)

ELECTRONIC PARTS & EQPT WHOLESALERS

Acterna LLC .... F 919 388-5100
  Morrisville (G-11277)
Commscope Technologies LLC .... F 919 329-8700
  Garner (G-6266)
Dupont Specialty Pdts USA LLC .... E 919 248-5109
  Durham (G-5070)
His Company Inc .... G 800 537-0351
  Wilmington (G-16255)
Huber + Suhner Inc .... E 704 790-7300
  Charlotte (G-2928)
Interconnect Products and Services Inc E 336 667-3356
  Wilkesboro (G-16026)
Lutze Inc .... E 704 504-0222
  Charlotte (G-3110)
Tactical Support Equipment Inc .... F 910 425-3360
  Fayetteville (G-5924)
Vishay Measurements Group Inc .... G 919 365-3800
  Wendell (G-15923)
Walker and Associates Inc .... C 336 731-6391
  Lexington (G-9800)
Wieland Electric Inc .... F 910 259-5050
  Wilmington (G-16442)

ELECTRONIC SHOPPING

Buddy Cut Inc .... G 888 608-4701
  Pittsboro (G-12333)
Fireresq Incorporated .... F 888 975-0858
  Mooresville (G-10945)
Grailgame Inc .... G 804 517-3102
  Reidsville (G-13522)
Nutrotonic LLC .... F 855 948-0008
  Charlotte (G-3285)
Simple & Sentimental LLC .... G 252 320-9458
  Ayden (G-857)
Speed Utv LLC .... E 704 949-1255
  Concord (G-4365)

ELECTROPLATING & PLATING SVC

Amplate Inc .... E 704 607-0191
  Charlotte (G-2189)
Xceldyne Group LLC .... D 336 472-2242
  Thomasville (G-15307)

ELEVATORS & EQPT

Crockers Inc .... F 336 366-2005
  Elkin (G-5615)
Ecs Group-NC LLC .... G 919 830-1171
  Wake Forest (G-15550)
Home Elevators & Lift Pdts LLC .... E 910 427-0006
  Sunset Beach (G-14999)
Otis Elevator Company .... C 704 519-0100
  Charlotte (G-3306)
Park Manufacturing Company .... F 704 869-6128
  Gastonia (G-6483)
Southeastern Elevator LLC .... G 252 726-9983
  Morehead City (G-11192)
Vertical Access LLC .... G 800 325-1116
  Snow Hill (G-14509)

ELEVATORS WHOLESALERS

Ask Elevator Service Inc .... G 336 674-2715
  Pleasant Garden (G-12356)
Otis Elevator Company .... G 828 251-1248
  Asheville (G-718)
Otis Elevator Company .... C 704 519-0100
  Charlotte (G-3306)
Port City Elevator Inc .... E 910 790-9300
  Castle Hayne (G-1959)

PRODUCT SECTION

ENGINES: Internal Combustion, NEC

Tk Elevator Corporation .... C 336 272-4563
  Greensboro *(G-7404)*

ELEVATORS: Installation & Conversion

Home Elevators & Lift Pdts LLC .... E 910 427-0006
  Sunset Beach *(G-14999)*
Park Manufacturing Company .... F 704 869-6128
  Gastonia *(G-6483)*
Southeastern Elevator LLC .... G 252 726-9983
  Morehead City *(G-11192)*

EMBLEMS: Embroidered

Conrad Embroidery Company LLC .... E 828 645-3015
  Weaverville *(G-15842)*
Conrad Industries Inc .... E 828 645-3015
  Weaverville *(G-15843)*
Lake Norman EMB & Monogramming .... G 704 892-8450
  Cornelius *(G-4564)*
Mojo Sportswear Inc .... G 252 758-4176
  Greenville *(G-7562)*
Stitchery Inc .... G 336 248-5604
  Lexington *(G-9785)*

EMBROIDERY ADVERTISING SVCS

Marketing One Sportswear Inc .... G 704 334-9333
  Charlotte *(G-3126)*
Orlandos Cstm Design T-Shirts .... G 919 220-5515
  Durham *(G-5264)*
Patti Boo Inc .... G 828 648-6495
  Canton *(G-1621)*
Patti Boo Designs Inc .... G 828 648-6495
  Canton *(G-1622)*
Raleigh Tees .... G 919 850-3378
  Raleigh *(G-13187)*
Screen Printers Unlimited LLC .... G 336 667-8737
  Wilkesboro *(G-16039)*
US Logoworks LLC .... F 910 307-0312
  Fayetteville *(G-5944)*

EMBROIDERY KITS

Stitchmaster LLC .... G 336 852-6448
  Greensboro *(G-7373)*

EMERGENCY ALARMS

Ademco Inc .... G 704 525-8899
  Charlotte *(G-2137)*
Ademco Inc .... G 336 668-3644
  Greensboro *(G-6779)*
Ademco Inc .... G 919 872-5556
  Raleigh *(G-12476)*
C & S Antennas Inc .... F 828 324-2454
  Conover *(G-4427)*
General Dynmcs Mssion Systems .... C 336 698-8000
  Mc Leansville *(G-10391)*
Johnson Controls .... C 704 501-0500
  Charlotte *(G-3029)*
New Innovative Products Inc .... G 919 631-6759
  Pine Level *(G-12212)*
R & J Road Service Inc .... G 252 239-1404
  Lucama *(G-10018)*
Romeo Six LLC .... F 919 589-7150
  Holly Springs *(G-8713)*
Safeguard Medical Alarms Inc .... F 312 506-2900
  Harrisburg *(G-7727)*
Seal Innovation Inc .... G 919 302-7870
  Raleigh *(G-13240)*
Squarehead Technology LLC .... G 571 299-4849
  Hickory *(G-8167)*

ENCLOSURES: Electronic

Friedrich Metal Pdts Co Inc .... E 336 375-3067
  Browns Summit *(G-1303)*

Nederman Corporation .... F 704 399-7441
  Charlotte *(G-3244)*
Rfr Metal Fabrication Inc .... D 919 693-1354
  Oxford *(G-12151)*

ENCLOSURES: Screen

Carolina Solar Structures Inc .... E 828 684-9900
  Asheville *(G-583)*
Innovative Awngs & Screens LLC .... F 833 337-4233
  Cornelius *(G-4561)*
Lees Screen Enclosures & More .... G 843 283-7227
  Sunset Beach *(G-15000)*

ENDOCRINE PRDTS

Inneroptic Technology Inc .... G 919 732-2090
  Hillsborough *(G-8656)*

ENGINE REBUILDING: Diesel

Engine Systems Inc .... D 252 977-2720
  Rocky Mount *(G-13695)*
NC Diesel Performance LLC .... G 704 431-3257
  Salisbury *(G-14016)*

ENGINE REBUILDING: Gas

Holman Automotive Inc .... G 704 583-2888
  Charlotte *(G-2915)*

ENGINEERING SVCS

ABB Enterprise Software Inc .... C 919 582-3283
  Raleigh *(G-12455)*
ABB Inc .... C 919 856-2360
  Cary *(G-1674)*
Advanced Computer Lrng Co LLC .... E 910 779-2254
  Fayetteville *(G-5752)*
Belkoz Inc .... G 919 703-0694
  Raleigh *(G-12551)*
Boeing Arospc Operations Inc .... F 919 722-4351
  Goldsboro *(G-6594)*
Century Furniture LLC .... D 828 326-8535
  Hickory *(G-7977)*
Cross Technology Inc .... E 336 725-4700
  East Bend *(G-5465)*
Custom Controls Unlimited LLC .... F 919 812-6553
  Raleigh *(G-12664)*
Dronescape Pllc .... G 704 953-3798
  Charlotte *(G-2655)*
Electro Magnetic Research Inc .... G 919 365-3723
  Zebulon *(G-17126)*
Entropy Solar Integrators LLC .... G 704 936-5018
  Charlotte *(G-2716)*
Equagen Engineers Pllc .... E 919 444-5442
  Raleigh *(G-12744)*
Ferguson Manufacturing Company .... F 336 661-1116
  Winston Salem *(G-16709)*
Finnord North America Corp .... F 704 723-4913
  Huntersville *(G-8820)*
Flextronics Intl USA Inc .... C 919 998-4000
  Morrisville *(G-11341)*
Froehling & Robertson Inc .... E 804 264-2701
  Raleigh *(G-12783)*
General Dynmcs Mssion Systems .... C 336 698-8000
  Mc Leansville *(G-10391)*
Global Products & Mfg Svcs Inc .... G 360 870-9876
  Charlotte *(G-2834)*
JA Smith Inc .... G 704 860-4910
  Lawndale *(G-9500)*
John Deere Consumer Pdts Inc .... C 919 804-2000
  Cary *(G-1798)*
Kdy Automation Solutions Inc .... G 888 219-0049
  Morrisville *(G-11364)*
Keller Technology Corporation .... E 704 875-1605
  Huntersville *(G-8844)*

McLean Sbsrface Utlity Engrg L .... F 336 340-0024
  Greensboro *(G-7194)*
MSI Defense Solutions LLC .... D 704 660-8348
  Mooresville *(G-11032)*
Multi Technical Services Inc .... G 919 553-2995
  Clayton *(G-4000)*
Nederman Corporation .... F 704 399-7441
  Charlotte *(G-3244)*
Penske Racing South Inc .... C 704 664-2300
  Mooresville *(G-11050)*
Pratt Mller Engrg Fbrction LLC .... C 704 977-0642
  Huntersville *(G-8881)*
Precision Concepts Group LLC .... B 336 761-8572
  Winston Salem *(G-16863)*
Simon Industries Inc .... E 919 469-2004
  Raleigh *(G-13262)*
Ssi Services Inc .... G 919 867-1450
  Raleigh *(G-13295)*
Sunqest Inc .... G 828 325-4910
  Newton *(G-11975)*
Team Industries Inc .... C 828 837-5377
  Andrews *(G-128)*
VA Claims LLC .... G 305 984-0936
  Greenville *(G-7596)*
Volta Group Corporation LLC .... E 919 637-0273
  Raleigh *(G-13408)*
Walker and Associates Inc .... C 336 731-6391
  Lexington *(G-9800)*

ENGINEERING SVCS: Chemical

Abb Inc .... E 704 587-1362
  Charlotte *(G-2122)*

ENGINEERING SVCS: Civil

Comp Environmental Inc .... F 919 316-1321
  Durham *(G-5028)*

ENGINEERING SVCS: Construction & Civil

Young & McQueen Grading Co Inc .... D 828 682-7714
  Burnsville *(G-1539)*

ENGINEERING SVCS: Electrical Or Electronic

Acroplis Cntrls Engineers Pllc .... F 919 275-3884
  Raleigh *(G-12473)*
Doble Engineering Company .... G 919 380-7461
  Morrisville *(G-11333)*
Goshen Engineering Inc .... G 919 429-9798
  Mount Olive *(G-11661)*
SCR Controls Inc .... F 704 821-6651
  Matthews *(G-10342)*
Subsea Video Systems Inc .... G 252 338-1001
  Elizabeth City *(G-5572)*
Vortant Technologies LLC .... G 828 645-1026
  Weaverville *(G-15867)*

ENGINEERING SVCS: Machine Tool Design

Descher LLC .... G 919 828-7708
  Raleigh *(G-12677)*
Irsi Automation Inc .... G 336 303-5320
  Mc Leansville *(G-10393)*

ENGINEERING SVCS: Marine

Big Rock Industries Inc .... G 252 222-3618
  Morehead City *(G-11152)*

ENGINEERING SVCS: Mechanical

Airspeed LLC .... E 919 644-1222
  Hillsborough *(G-8633)*
Tdc International LLC .... G 704 875-1198
  Concord *(G-4372)*

ENGINES: Internal Combustion, NEC

Blue Gas Marine Inc .... F 919 238-3427
  Apex (G-172)
Caterpillar Inc .... D 919 777-2000
  Sanford (G-14098)
Cummins Atlantic LLC .... E 704 596-7690
  Charlotte (G-2584)
Cummins Atlantic LLC .... D 336 275-4531
  Greensboro (G-6946)
Cummins Atlantic LLC .... E 919 284-9111
  Kenly (G-9149)
Cummins Atlantic LLC .... E 704 588-1240
  Charlotte (G-2585)
Cummins Inc .... G 704 588-1240
  Pineville (G-12264)
Custom Engines Ltd .... G 910 532-4114
  Harrells (G-7691)
Daimler Truck North Amer LLC ... A 704 645-5000
  Cleveland (G-4071)
Holman & Moody Inc .... G 704 394-4141
  Charlotte (G-2914)
Patricks Small Engines .... G 910 653-2061
  Tabor City (G-15085)
Pcai Inc .... D 704 588-1240
  Charlotte (G-3323)
Southport NC .... G 910 524-7425
  Southport (G-14581)
Xre Performance Engines LLC .... G 704 663-3505
  Mooresville (G-11133)

ENGINES: Jet Propulsion

General Electric Company .... A 910 675-5000
  Wilmington (G-16230)

ENGINES: Marine

Ilmor Marine LLC .... E 704 360-1901
  Mooresville (G-10981)
John R Bell .... G 252 297-2499
  Belvidere (G-1022)
Jones Marine Inc .... G 704 639-0173
  Salisbury (G-13994)
Lehr LLC .... F 704 827-9368
  Huntersville (G-8849)
Outlet Marine Engines Inc .... G 919 279-3338
  Cary (G-1839)

ENGRAVING SVC, NEC

Anilox Roll Company Inc .... G 704 588-1809
  Charlotte (G-2195)
Arden Engraving US Inc .... G 704 547-4581
  Charlotte (G-2213)
Raleigh Engraving Co .... G 919 832-5557
  Raleigh (G-13177)
Two Engravers LLC .... G 919 526-0102
  Raleigh (G-13373)
Western Roto Engravers Incorporated .. E 336 275-9821
  Greensboro (G-7457)

ENGRAVING SVCS

Fines and Carriel Inc .... G 919 929-0702
  Chapel Hill (G-2018)
Signcaster Corporation .... G 336 712-2525
  Winston Salem (G-16908)

ENVELOPES

Blue Ridge Paper Products Inc ... A 828 646-2000
  Canton (G-1600)
S Ruppe Inc .... E 828 287-4936
  Rutherfordton (G-13889)
Westrock Mwv LLC .... G 919 334-3200
  Raleigh (G-13419)

ENVELOPES WHOLESALERS

Printing Press .... G 828 299-1234
  Asheville (G-743)

ENZYMES

Alltech Inc .... E 336 635-5190
  Eden (G-5486)
Enzyme Customs .... G 704 888-8278
  Locust (G-9959)
N-Zyme Specialist LLC .... G 919 349-2429
  Wake Forest (G-15573)
Novozymes North America Inc ... D 919 494-2014
  Franklinton (G-6160)

EPOXY RESINS

Kestrel I Acquisition Corporation .. A 919 990-7500
  Durham (G-5180)

EQUIPMENT & VEHICLE FINANCE LEASING COMPANIES

Vna Holding Inc .... A 336 393-4890
  Greensboro (G-7445)

EQUIPMENT: Pedestrian Traffic Control

Roadmasters Traffic Ctrl LLC ..... G 704 585-9635
  Statesville (G-14877)

EQUIPMENT: Rental & Leasing, NEC

Arc3 Gases Inc .... F 336 275-3333
  Greensboro (G-6812)
Arc3 Gases Inc .... F 704 220-1029
  Monroe (G-10650)
Arc3 Gases Inc .... E 910 892-4016
  Dunn (G-4851)
B V Hedrick Gravel & Sand Co ... E 704 633-5982
  Salisbury (G-13928)
Cherokee Instruments Inc .... F 919 552-0554
  Angier (G-137)
Classic Industrial Services .... E 919 209-0909
  Smithfield (G-14455)
Lynn Ladder Scaffolding Co Inc .. G 301 336-4700
  Charlotte (G-3111)
Medaccess Inc .... G 828 264-4085
  Robbinsville (G-13609)
Sharpe Co .... E 336 724-2871
  Winston Salem (G-16905)

ESCALATORS: Passenger & Freight

Rs Bostic Service Inc .... G 252 527-4781
  Kinston (G-9381)

ETCHING & ENGRAVING SVC

NC Graphic Pros LLC .... G 252 492-7326
  Kittrell (G-9397)
Professional Laminating LLC ...... G 919 465-0400
  Cary (G-1862)

ETHYLENE

Wpt LLC .... G 704 770-1311
  Monroe (G-10837)

ETHYLENE-PROPYLENE RUBBERS: EPDM Polymers

Axchem Solutions Inc .... G 919 742-9810
  Siler City (G-14398)
Custom Polymers Inc .... F 704 332-6070
  Charlotte (G-2593)
Dupont Electronic Polymers L P .. F 919 248-5135
  Durham (G-5069)
ERA Polymers Corporation .... F 704 931-3675
  Stanley (G-14693)

Indulor America LP .... E 336 578-6855
  Graham (G-6692)
M & P Polymers Inc .... G 910 246-6585
  Pinehurst (G-12227)
Tethis Inc .... E 919 808-2866
  Raleigh (G-13340)

EXHAUST SYSTEMS: Eqpt & Parts

B & B Fabrication Inc .... F 623 581-7600
  Mooresville (G-10869)
Cataler North America Corp .... C 828 970-0026
  Lincolnton (G-9879)

EXPANSION JOINTS: Rubber

Frenzelit Inc .... E 336 814-4317
  Lexington (G-9721)

EXPLOSIVES

Austin Powder Company .... F 828 645-4291
  Denton (G-4725)
Dyno Nobel Explosive Blasting ... G 919 771-1522
  Garner (G-6272)
K2 Solutions Inc .... B 910 692-6898
  Southern Pines (G-14538)
Maxam North America Inc .... F 214 736-8100
  Mooresville (G-11018)

EXTRACTS, FLAVORING

Blue Mountain Enterprises Inc ... E 252 522-1544
  Kinston (G-9345)
Flavor Sciences Inc .... E 828 758-2525
  Taylorsville (G-15142)
Fuji Foods Inc .... E 336 897-3373
  Browns Summit (G-1304)
Fuji Foods Inc .... E 336 375-3111
  Browns Summit (G-1305)
Mother Murphys Labs Inc .... E 336 273-1737
  Greensboro (G-7205)
Mother Murphys Labs Inc .... D 336 273-1737
  Greensboro (G-7206)
Specialty Products Intl Ltd .... G 910 897-4706
  Erwin (G-5688)

FABRIC STORES

Cloth Barn Inc .... F 919 735-3643
  Goldsboro (G-6601)
Composite Fabrics America LLC .. G 828 632-5220
  Taylorsville (G-15135)
Distinctive Furniture Inc .... G 828 754-3947
  Lenoir (G-9604)
Ledford Upholstery .... G 704 732-0233
  Lincolnton (G-9899)
McMurray Fabrics Inc .... D 704 732-9613
  Lincolnton (G-9906)
Quilt Shop .... G 828 263-8691
  Boone (G-1230)

FABRICS & CLOTH: Quilted

Fabric Services Hickory Inc .... F 828 397-7331
  Hildebran (G-8622)
High Point Quilting Inc .... F 336 861-4180
  High Point (G-8393)
Just Stitchin Quilts LLc .... G 828 644-3368
  Hayesville (G-7767)

FABRICS & CLOTHING: Rubber Coated

Trelleborg Ctd Systems US Inc ... C 828 286-9126
  Rutherfordton (G-13897)

FABRICS: Acetate, Broadwoven

Composite Fabrics America LLC .. G 828 632-5220
  Taylorsville (G-15135)

PRODUCT SECTION

FABRICS: Nonwoven

Crypton Mills LLC.................................. E 828 202-5875
  Cliffside (G-4085)
David Rothschild Co Inc....................... D 336 342-0035
  Reidsville (G-13516)
Hanes Companies Inc.......................... B 828 464-4673
  Conover (G-4460)
Kontoor Brands Inc.............................. D 336 332-3577
  Greensboro (G-7157)

FABRICS: Apparel & Outerwear, Broadwoven

Ivy Brand LLC...................................... G 980 225-7866
  Charlotte (G-3001)

FABRICS: Apparel & Outerwear, Cotton

Chaos Worldwide LLC.......................... G 336 558-5654
  Greensboro (G-6904)
Courtesy of Kamdyn LLC..................... G 706 831-5395
  Charlotte (G-2563)
Gracefully Broken LLC......................... G 980 474-0309
  Charlotte (G-2851)
Ivy Brand LLC...................................... G 980 225-7866
  Charlotte (G-3001)
Kimmys Customs LLC.......................... G 904 699-2933
  Rural Hall (G-13845)
M J E J Inc... F 910 399-3795
  Wilmington (G-16312)
Mfi Products Inc.................................. F 910 944-2128
  Aberdeen (G-15)
VF Corporation.................................... G 336 424-6000
  Greensboro (G-7438)
VF Corporation.................................... G 336 424-6000
  Greensboro (G-7439)

FABRICS: Automotive, From Manmade Fiber

Abercrombie Textiles I LLC.................. F 704 487-1245
  Shelby (G-14282)
Highland Industries Inc........................ E 336 855-0625
  Greensboro (G-7090)
Highland Industries Inc........................ E 336 547-1600
  Greensboro (G-7091)
P&A Indstrial Fabrications LLC............. E 336 322-1766
  Roxboro (G-13815)
Seiren North America LLC................... F 828 430-3456
  Morganton (G-11250)

FABRICS: Basket Weave, Cotton

American Fiber & Finishing Inc............. E 704 984-9256
  Albemarle (G-73)

FABRICS: Bonded-Fiber, Exc Felt

Glatfelter Inds Asheville Inc................. D 828 670-0041
  Candler (G-1580)

FABRICS: Broad Woven, Goods, Cotton

American Silk Mills LLC........................ F 570 822-7147
  High Point (G-8248)
Wade Manufacturing Company............. E 910 895-0276
  Rockingham (G-13646)
Wade Manufacturing Company............. C 704 694-2131
  Wadesboro (G-15519)

FABRICS: Broadwoven, Wool

Barrday Corp....................................... G 704 395-0311
  Charlotte (G-2284)
Carlisle Finishing LLC........................... D 864 466-4173
  Greensboro (G-6880)
Circa 1801... E 828 397-7003
  Connelly Springs (G-4399)
I T G Raeford..................................... G 910 875-3736
  Raeford (G-12424)
Lustar Dyeing and Finshg Inc............... G 828 274-2440
  Asheville (G-691)

Milliken & Company............................. E 828 247-4300
  Bostic (G-1265)
Voith Fabrics Inc................................. B 252 291-3800
  Wilson (G-16555)
Xtinguish LLC...................................... F 704 868-9500
  Charlotte (G-3838)

FABRICS: Cloth, Warp Knit

Guilford Mills LLC................................. A 910 794-5810
  Wilmington (G-16243)
Hornwood Inc...................................... E 704 694-3009
  Wadesboro (G-15512)
Hornwood Inc...................................... B 704 848-4121
  Lilesville (G-9838)
Lear Corporation................................. E 910 296-8671
  Kenansville (G-9144)
Lear Corporation................................. A 910 794-5810
  Wilmington (G-16294)
Mohican Mills Inc................................ B 704 735-3343
  Lincolnton (G-9908)

FABRICS: Cotton, Narrow

Dunn Manufacturing Corp.................... C 704 283-2147
  Monroe (G-10709)
Parkdale Mills Incorporated................. D 704 874-5000
  Gastonia (G-6486)
US Cotton LLC.................................... C 216 676-6400
  Gastonia (G-6535)

FABRICS: Denims

Burlington Industries LLC...................... C 336 379-6220
  Greensboro (G-6865)
Cone Denim LLC.................................. D 336 379-6165
  Greensboro (G-6928)
Elevate Textiles Inc............................. F 336 379-6220
  Charlotte (G-2693)
Elevate Textiles Holding Corp.............. D 336 379-6220
  Charlotte (G-2694)
Itg Holdings Inc................................... A 336 379-6220
  Greensboro (G-7126)
Raleigh Workshop Inc.......................... E 919 917-8969
  Raleigh (G-13188)

FABRICS: Dress, Cotton

Belk Department Stores LP................. C 704 357-4000
  Charlotte (G-2298)
Textile-Based Delivery Inc.................. E 866 256-8420
  Conover (G-4504)

FABRICS: Elastic, From Manmade Fiber Or Silk

Efa Inc.. C 336 275-9401
  Greensboro (G-6991)

FABRICS: Fiberglass, Broadwoven

Admiral Marine Pdts & Svcs Inc........... G 704 489-8771
  Denver (G-4758)
American Olympus Fibrgls Corp............ G 828 459-0444
  Claremont (G-3901)
Piedmont Cmposites Tooling LLC......... D 828 632-8883
  Taylorsville (G-15156)
Windsor Fiberglass Inc........................ F 910 259-0057
  Burgaw (G-1359)

FABRICS: Glass & Fiberglass, Broadwoven

Feinberg Enterprises Inc..................... F 704 822-2400
  Belmont (G-988)

FABRICS: Glass, Narrow

Nouveau Verre Holdings Inc................ F 336 545-0011
  Greensboro (G-7224)

Nvh Inc... G 336 545-0011
  Greensboro (G-7228)

FABRICS: Jacquard Woven, Cotton

Cone Jacquards LLC............................ E 336 379-6220
  Greensboro (G-6929)

FABRICS: Jacquard Woven, From Manmade Fiber Or Silk

Cone Jacquards LLC............................ E 336 379-6220
  Greensboro (G-6929)

FABRICS: Lacings, Textile

Spuntech Industries Inc....................... C 336 330-9000
  Roxboro (G-13825)

FABRICS: Laundry, Cotton

Trelleborg Ctd Systems US Inc............ C 828 286-9126
  Rutherfordton (G-13896)

FABRICS: Nonwoven

Advantage Nn-Wvens Cnvrting LL........ G 828 635-1880
  Taylorsville (G-15127)
Allyn International Trdg Corp................ G 877 858-2482
  Marshville (G-10210)
Avgol America Inc............................... C 336 936-2500
  Mocksville (G-10556)
Avintiv Inc.. C 704 697-5100
  Charlotte (G-2249)
Avintiv Specialty Mtls Inc.................... D 704 660-6242
  Mooresville (G-10867)
Avintiv Specialty Mtls Inc.................... A 704 697-5100
  Charlotte (G-2250)
Carolina Nonwovens LLC..................... F 704 735-5600
  Maiden (G-10104)
Chicopee Inc....................................... G 919 894-4111
  Benson (G-1032)
Cumulus Fibres Inc.............................. B 704 394-2111
  Charlotte (G-2586)
Dalco GF Technologies LLC................. D 828 459-2577
  Conover (G-4445)
Dalco Gft Nonwovens LLC................... D 828 459-2577
  Conover (G-4446)
Fiber Dynamics Inc.............................. D 336 886-7111
  High Point (G-8353)
Fibrix LLC... E 704 394-2111
  Charlotte (G-2758)
Fibrix LLC... E 704 872-5223
  Statesville (G-14796)
Fibrix LLC... E 704 878-0027
  Statesville (G-14797)
Freudenberg Nonwovens Limit............. A 919 620-3900
  Durham (G-5103)
Freudenberg Prfmce Mtls LP................ C 828 665-5000
  Candler (G-1579)
Freudenberg Prfmce Mtls LP................ D 919 479-7443
  Durham (G-5104)
Glatflter Sntara Old Hckry Inc.............. F 615 526-2100
  Charlotte (G-2832)
Hanes Companies Inc.......................... C 336 747-1600
  Winston Salem (G-16732)
Hendrix Batting Company.................... C 336 431-1181
  High Point (G-8382)
Kem-Wove Inc..................................... E 704 588-0080
  Charlotte (G-3049)
Lydall Inc.. G 336 468-8522
  Hamptonville (G-7674)
Lydall Inc.. G 336 468-1323
  Yadkinville (G-17044)
Mitt S Nitts Inc................................... E 919 596-6793
  Durham (G-5229)

FABRICS: Nonwoven

Mountain International LLC .... E 828 606-0194
  Brevard *(G-1282)*

Nutex Concepts NC Corp .... E 828 726-8801
  Lenoir *(G-9643)*

Polyvlies Usa Inc .... E 336 769-0206
  Winston Salem *(G-16860)*

Printcraft Company Inc .... E 336 248-2544
  Lexington *(G-9773)*

Saertex Usa LLC .... E 704 464-5998
  Huntersville *(G-8893)*

Scorpio Acquisition Corp .... E 704 697-5100
  Charlotte *(G-3511)*

Shalag US Inc .... D 919 690-0250
  Oxford *(G-12155)*

Tenowo Inc .... F 704 732-3525
  Lincolnton *(G-9925)*

Twe Nonwovens Us Inc .... E 336 431-7187
  High Point *(G-8581)*

Vitaflex LLC .... F 888 616-8848
  Burlington *(G-1515)*

Warm Products Inc .... F 425 248-2424
  Hendersonville *(G-7913)*

Westpoint Home Inc .... B 910 369-2231
  Wagram *(G-15524)*

Yanjan USA LLC .... C 704 380-6230
  Statesville *(G-14931)*

FABRICS: Nylon, Broadwoven

Kings Plush Inc .... C 704 739-9931
  Kings Mountain *(G-9314)*

Newgard Industries Inc .... F 704 283-6011
  Monroe *(G-10779)*

FABRICS: Pile, Circular Knit

Heritage Knitting Co LLC .... E 704 872-7653
  Statesville *(G-14812)*

Innofa Usa LLC .... E 336 635-2900
  Eden *(G-5492)*

Russ Knits Inc .... F 910 974-4114
  Candor *(G-1598)*

Toms Knit Fabrics .... G 704 867-4236
  Gastonia *(G-6527)*

FABRICS: Polyester, Broadwoven

Burlington Industries LLC .... C 336 379-6220
  Greensboro *(G-6865)*

Carriff Corporation Inc .... G 704 888-3330
  Midland *(G-10459)*

Elevate Textiles Inc .... F 336 379-6220
  Charlotte *(G-2693)*

Elevate Textiles Holding Corp .... D 336 379-6220
  Charlotte *(G-2694)*

Glen Raven Custom Fabrics LLC 828 682-2142
  Burnsville *(G-1526)*

Itg Holdings Inc .... A 336 379-6220
  Greensboro *(G-7126)*

Performance Fibers .... F 704 947-7193
  Huntersville *(G-8874)*

Wade Manufacturing Company .... E 910 895-0276
  Rockingham *(G-13646)*

Wade Manufacturing Company .... C 704 694-2131
  Wadesboro *(G-15519)*

FABRICS: Polypropylene, Broadwoven

Gale Pacific Usa Inc .... F 407 772-7900
  Charlotte *(G-2804)*

FABRICS: Resin Or Plastic Coated

Engineered Recycling Company LLC ... E 704 358-6700
  Charlotte *(G-2712)*

Tosaf Aw Inc .... D 980 533-3000
  Bessemer City *(G-1088)*

Uretek LLC .... E 203 468-0342
  Rutherfordton *(G-13899)*

FABRICS: Rubber & Elastic Yarns & Fabrics

Efa Inc .... C 336 275-9401
  Greensboro *(G-6991)*

McMichael Mills Inc .... E 336 584-0134
  Burlington *(G-1459)*

McMichael Mills Inc .... C 336 548-4242
  Mayodan *(G-10365)*

FABRICS: Rubberized

Contour Enterprises LLC .... D 828 328-1550
  Hildebran *(G-8620)*

FABRICS: Scrub Cloths

Mdkscrubs LLC .... G 980 250-4708
  Charlotte *(G-3156)*

Star Wipers Inc .... E 888 511-2656
  Gastonia *(G-6515)*

FABRICS: Shoe Laces, Exc Leather

Hickory Brands Inc .... D 828 322-2600
  Hickory *(G-8044)*

FABRICS: Specialty Including Twisted Weaves, Broadwoven

Fiber Company .... G 336 725-5277
  Lewisville *(G-9666)*

Weavexx LLC .... A 919 556-7235
  Youngsville *(G-17113)*

FABRICS: Spunbonded

Berry Global Inc .... A 704 697-5100
  Charlotte *(G-2302)*

Chicopee Inc .... E 704 697-5100
  Charlotte *(G-2476)*

Pgi Polymer Inc .... A 704 697-5100
  Charlotte *(G-3336)*

Providencia Usa Inc .... D 704 881-2837
  Statesville *(G-14872)*

FABRICS: Tickings

Bekaert Textiles USA Inc .... C 336 769-4300
  Winston Salem *(G-16624)*

Bekaertdeslee USA Inc .... B 336 747-4900
  Winston Salem *(G-16625)*

Ct-Nassau Ticking LLC .... E 336 570-0091
  Burlington *(G-1403)*

Culp Inc .... C 336 643-7751
  Stokesdale *(G-14941)*

FABRICS: Trimmings, Textile

Ramseur Inter-Lock Knitting Co 336 824-2427
  Asheboro *(G-470)*

FABRICS: Upholstery, Cotton

Carolina Mills Incorporated .... B 828 428-9911
  Maiden *(G-10102)*

Culp Inc .... E 662 844-7144
  Burlington *(G-1404)*

Cv Industries Inc .... G 828 328-1851
  Hickory *(G-8001)*

Heritage Classic Wovens LLC .... F 828 247-6010
  Forest City *(G-6070)*

Lantal Textiles Inc .... C 336 969-9551
  Rural Hall *(G-13847)*

Marlatex Corporation .... E 704 829-7797
  Charlotte *(G-3127)*

Swatchworks Inc .... G 336 626-9971
  Asheboro *(G-490)*

Theodore Alexander Uphl LLC .... G 336 472-7540
  Thomasville *(G-15288)*

Vlr LLC .... E 252 355-4610
  Morganton *(G-11265)*

FABRICS: Upholstery, Wool

Lantal Textiles Inc .... C 336 969-9551
  Rural Hall *(G-13847)*

FABRICS: Warp & Flat Knit Prdts

Innovaknits LLC .... G 828 536-9348
  Conover *(G-4467)*

Whiteville Fabrics LLC .... F 910 639-4444
  Whiteville *(G-15979)*

Whiteville Fabrics LLC .... F 910 914-0456
  Whiteville *(G-15978)*

FABRICS: Weft Or Circular Knit

Contempora Fabrics Inc .... C 910 345-0150
  Lumberton *(G-10030)*

Early Bird Hosiery Mills Inc .... F 828 324-6745
  Hickory *(G-8015)*

Innovaknits LLC .... G 828 536-9348
  Conover *(G-4467)*

Innovative Knitting LLC .... E 336 350-8122
  Burlington *(G-1438)*

Knit-Wear Fabrics Inc .... F 336 226-4342
  Burlington *(G-1444)*

McMurray Fabrics Inc .... C 910 944-2128
  Aberdeen *(G-11)*

New River Fabrics Inc .... G 704 462-1401
  Lawndale *(G-9502)*

Ramseur Inter-Lock Knitting Co .... G 336 824-2427
  Asheboro *(G-470)*

Tommys Tubing & Stockenettes .... F 336 449-6461
  Gibsonville *(G-6572)*

FABRICS: Wool, Broadwoven

National Spinning Co Inc .... C 910 298-3131
  Beulaville *(G-1097)*

FABRICS: Worsted fabrics, broadwoven

Burlington Industries III LLC .... G 336 379-2000
  Greensboro *(G-6864)*

Burlington Intl Svcs Co .... G 336 379-2000
  Greensboro *(G-6866)*

Burlington Investment II Inc .... G 336 379-2000
  Greensboro *(G-6867)*

Burlington Worsteds Inc .... G 336 379-2000
  Greensboro *(G-6868)*

Elevate Textiles Inc .... F 336 379-6220
  Charlotte *(G-2693)*

Elevate Textiles Holding Corp .... D 336 379-6220
  Charlotte *(G-2694)*

Itg Holdings Inc .... A 336 379-6220
  Greensboro *(G-7126)*

FAMILY CLOTHING STORES

Pdf and Associates .... G 252 332-7749
  Colerain *(G-4139)*

Raleigh Workshop Inc .... E 919 917-8969
  Raleigh *(G-13188)*

Ralph Lauren Corporation .... G 336 632-5000
  High Point *(G-8504)*

Secret Spot Inc .... G 252 441-4030
  Nags Head *(G-11725)*

FANS, BLOWING: Indl Or Commercial

Greenheck Fan Co .... F 336 852-5788
  Greensboro *(G-7061)*

PRODUCT SECTION — FIBER & FIBER PRDTS: Polyester

FANS, VENTILATING: Indl Or Commercial
Miller Ctrl Mfg Inc Clinton NC.................. G 910 592-5112
 Clinton *(G-4098)*
Nederman Corporation............................. F 704 399-7441
 Charlotte *(G-3244)*
Select Air Systems Usa Inc....................... E 704 289-1122
 Monroe *(G-10805)*
Trane US Inc.. A 704 655-4000
 Davidson *(G-4704)*

FANS: Ceiling
Minka Lighting Inc................................... D 704 785-9200
 Concord *(G-4316)*

FARM & GARDEN MACHINERY WHOLESALERS
Tar River Trading Post LLC....................... G 919 589-3618
 Youngsville *(G-17104)*

FARM PRDTS, RAW MATERIALS, WHOLESALE: Broomcorn
Barkleys Mill On Southern Cro.................. G 828 626-3344
 Weaverville *(G-15839)*

FARM SPLYS WHOLESALERS
C A Perry & Son Inc............................... G 252 330-2323
 Elizabeth City *(G-5532)*
C A Perry & Son Inc............................... E 252 221-4463
 Hobbsville *(G-8675)*
Southern States Coop Inc....................... E 704 872-6364
 Statesville *(G-14896)*
Southern States Coop Inc....................... F 910 285-8213
 Wallace *(G-15628)*
Thompson Sunny Acres Inc.................... G 910 206-1801
 Rockingham *(G-13644)*

FARM SPLYS, WHOLESALE: Fertilizers & Agricultural Chemicals
Helena Agri-Enterprises LLC.................... F 910 422-8901
 Rowland *(G-13789)*

FARM SPLYS, WHOLESALE: Insecticides
Southern AG Insecticides Inc................... E 828 264-8843
 Boone *(G-1238)*
Southern AG Insecticides Inc................... E 828 692-2233
 Hendersonville *(G-7902)*

FASTENERS WHOLESALERS
Dubose National Enrgy Svcs Inc.............. G 704 295-1060
 Waxhaw *(G-15754)*
Gesipa Fasteners Usa Inc....................... E 336 751-1555
 Mocksville *(G-10577)*
Gesipa Fasteners Usa Inc....................... F 609 208-1740
 Mocksville *(G-10578)*
Heico Fasteners Inc............................... E 828 261-0184
 Hickory *(G-8041)*
ND Southeastern Fastener..................... G 704 329-0033
 Charlotte *(G-3241)*

FASTENERS: Metal
Piranha Nail and Staple Inc..................... G 336 852-8358
 Greensboro *(G-7265)*
Wurth Revcar Fasteners Inc................... E 919 772-9930
 Garner *(G-6327)*
Oak City Metal LLC................................. G 919 375-4535
 Zebulon *(G-17138)*
Penn Engineering & Mfg Corp................. C 336 631-8741
 Winston Salem *(G-16839)*

FASTENERS: Notions, Hooks & Eyes
Aplix Inc.. B 704 588-1920
 Charlotte *(G-2201)*

FASTENERS: Wire, Made From Purchased Wire
Eastern Wholesale Fence LLC.................. D 631 698-0975
 Salisbury *(G-13957)*
Redtail Group LLC................................. G 828 539-4700
 Swannanoa *(G-15033)*

FAUCETS & SPIGOTS: Metal & Plastic
Masco Corporation................................ G 704 658-9646
 Mooresville *(G-11015)*

FELDSPAR: Ground Or Otherwise Treated
Quartz Corp USA................................... D 828 766-2104
 Spruce Pine *(G-14654)*

FENCE POSTS: Iron & Steel
Moes Hndy Svcs Fnce Instl Mno.............. G 910 712-1402
 Raeford *(G-12426)*

FENCES OR POSTS: Ornamental Iron Or Steel
Alamance Iron Works Inc....................... G 336 852-5940
 Greensboro *(G-6788)*
Garden Gate Ornamental Iron In............. G 704 922-1635
 Dallas *(G-4642)*

FENCING MADE IN WIREDRAWING PLANTS
Blue Ridge Metals Corporation................ C 828 687-2525
 Fletcher *(G-5989)*

FENCING MATERIALS: Docks & Other Outdoor Prdts, Wood
1st Time Contracting............................. G 774 289-3321
 Clemmons *(G-4023)*
4 Home Products Inc.............................. G 888 609-8222
 North Wilkesboro *(G-11996)*
Phelps Wood Products LLC.................... F 336 284-2149
 Cleveland *(G-4079)*
Universal Forest Products Inc.................. F 252 338-0319
 Elizabeth City *(G-5580)*

FENCING: Chain Link
Classic Cleaning LLC.............................. E 800 220-7101
 Raleigh *(G-12626)*
Harrison Fence Inc................................ G 919 244-6908
 Apex *(G-200)*
Merchants Metals LLC........................... D 704 878-8706
 Statesville *(G-14841)*
Turner & Reeves Fence Co LLC............... G 910 671-8851
 Clayton *(G-4020)*

FERTILIZER MINERAL MINING
Verdesian Life Science US LLC................ E 919 825-1901
 Cary *(G-1919)*

FERTILIZER, AGRICULTURAL: Wholesalers
Boggs Farm Center Inc.......................... G 704 538-7176
 Fallston *(G-5728)*
Clapp Fertilizer and Trckg Inc.................. G 336 449-6103
 Whitsett *(G-15986)*
Harvey Fertilizer and Gas Co................... E 252 753-2063
 Farmville *(G-5738)*
Harvey Fertilizer and Gas Co................... F 252 523-9090
 Kinston *(G-9368)*

Nutrien AG Solutions Inc........................ G 252 585-0282
 Conway *(G-4516)*

FERTILIZERS: Nitrogen Solutions
Farm Chemicals Inc............................... F 910 875-4277
 Raeford *(G-12420)*

FERTILIZERS: Nitrogenous
Carolina Eastern Inc.............................. G 252 795-3128
 Robersonville *(G-13615)*
Clapp Fertilizer and Trckg Inc.................. G 336 449-6103
 Whitsett *(G-15986)*
Harvey Fertilizer and Gas Co................... F 252 523-9090
 Kinston *(G-9368)*
Harvey Fertilizer and Gas Co................... E 252 526-4150
 Kinston *(G-9369)*
Kamlar Corporation............................... E 252 443-2576
 Rocky Mount *(G-13705)*
Mineral Springs Fertilizer Inc................... G 704 843-2683
 Mineral Springs *(G-10518)*
Nutrien AG Solutions Inc........................ G 252 235-4161
 Bailey *(G-876)*
Southern States Coop Inc....................... G 336 246-3201
 Creedmoor *(G-4620)*
Southern States Coop Inc....................... E 336 786-7545
 Mount Airy *(G-11575)*
Southern States Coop Inc....................... E 919 658-5061
 Mount Olive *(G-11669)*
Southern States Coop Inc....................... E 704 872-6364
 Statesville *(G-14896)*
Southern States Coop Inc....................... F 910 285-8213
 Wallace *(G-15628)*

FERTILIZERS: Phosphatic
Nutrien AG Solutions Inc........................ F 252 977-2025
 Rocky Mount *(G-13670)*
Pcs Phosphate Company Inc.................. E 252 322-4111
 Aurora *(G-838)*
Southern States Coop Inc....................... G 336 246-3201
 Creedmoor *(G-4620)*
Southern States Coop Inc....................... E 336 786-7545
 Mount Airy *(G-11575)*
Southern States Coop Inc....................... E 919 658-5061
 Mount Olive *(G-11669)*
Southern States Coop Inc....................... E 704 872-6364
 Statesville *(G-14896)*
Southern States Coop Inc....................... F 910 285-8213
 Wallace *(G-15628)*

FIBER & FIBER PRDTS: Acrylic
Coats HP Inc... B 704 824-9904
 Mc Adenville *(G-10377)*
Coats HP Inc... E 704 329-5800
 Charlotte *(G-2514)*
Mannington Mills Inc.............................. E 704 824-3551
 Mc Adenville *(G-10379)*
Pharr McAdenville Corporation................ D 704 824-3551
 Mc Adenville *(G-10380)*
Snp Inc.. E 919 598-0400
 Durham *(G-5361)*

FIBER & FIBER PRDTS: Polyester
Alpek Polyester Usa LLC........................ B 910 371-4000
 Wilmington *(G-16108)*
Auriga Polymers Inc.............................. C 864 579-5570
 Charlotte *(G-2239)*
Fibrix LLC... E 828 459-7064
 Conover *(G-4454)*
Polycor Holdings Inc.............................. D 828 459-7064
 Conover *(G-4483)*
Southern Fiber Inc................................ E 704 736-0011
 Lincolnton *(G-9919)*

FIBER & FIBER PRDTS: Polyester

Stein Fibers Ltd... E 704 599-2804
  Charlotte (G-3629)
Warp Technologies Inc................................. C 919 552-2311
  Holly Springs (G-8726)

FIBER & FIBER PRDTS: Vinyl

Military Wraps Inc.. F 910 671-0008
  Lumberton (G-10045)
Morbern LLC... E 336 883-4332
  High Point (G-8458)
Trelleborg Ctd Systems US Inc.................... C 828 286-9126
  Rutherfordton (G-13897)

FIBER OPTICS

Connexion Technologies............................... F 919 674-0036
  Cary (G-1732)
Corning Incorporated.................................... D 910 784-7200
  Wilmington (G-16184)
M2 Optics Inc.. G 919 342-5619
  Raleigh (G-12985)
Roblon US Inc... D 828 396-2121
  Granite Falls (G-6754)

FIBER: Vulcanized

Royale Comfort Seating Inc........................... D 828 352-9021
  Taylorsville (G-15162)

FIBERS: Carbon & Graphite

Nouveau Verre Holdings Inc.......................... F 336 545-0011
  Greensboro (G-7224)
Nvh Inc... G 336 545-0011
  Greensboro (G-7228)
Sgl Technologies LLC.................................... E 704 593-5100
  Charlotte (G-3535)

FILM BASE: Cellulose Acetate Or Nitrocellulose Plastics

Icons America LLC....................................... E 704 922-0041
  Dallas (G-4645)
Printpack Inc.. C 828 649-3800
  Marshall (G-10206)

FILTER CLEANING SVCS

Hlmf Logistics Inc.. G 704 782-0356
  Pineville (G-12273)

FILTER ELEMENTS: Fluid & Hydraulic Line

Main Filter LLC... E 704 735-0009
  Lincolnton (G-9904)

FILTERING MEDIA: Pottery

Daramic LLC.. D 704 587-8599
  Charlotte (G-2603)
Selee Corporation... C 828 693-0256
  Hendersonville (G-7898)

FILTERS

City of Morganton.. F 828 584-1460
  Morganton (G-11205)
Ddp Spclty Elctrnic Mtls US 9..................... D 336 547-7112
  Greensboro (G-6962)
Ffi Holdings III Corp.................................... E 800 690-3650
  Charlotte (G-2755)
Flanders Corporation................................... C 919 934-3020
  Smithfield (G-14460)
Flanders Filters Inc..................................... G 252 217-3978
  Smithfield (G-14461)
Global Filter Source LLC.............................. G 919 571-4945
  Raleigh (G-12804)
Liquid Process Systems Inc........................ G 704 821-1115
  Indian Trail (G-8945)
Ltd Industries LLC...................................... E 704 897-2182
  Charlotte (G-3105)
Mann+hummel Filtration Technol.............. G 704 869-3952
  Gastonia (G-6455)
NAPA Filters.. G 704 864-6748
  Gastonia (G-6474)
Ralph B Hall.. G 919 258-3634
  Sanford (G-14173)
Rubber Mill Inc... G 336 622-1680
  Conover (G-4494)
Rubber Mill Inc... E 336 622-1680
  Liberty (G-9830)
Southern Products Company Inc................ E 910 281-3189
  Hoffman (G-8676)
Textile Parts and Mch Co Inc..................... F 704 865-5003
  Gastonia (G-6524)
US Filter... G 828 274-8282
  Asheville (G-812)

FILTERS & SOFTENERS: Water, Household

Carolina Water Consultants LLC.................. G 828 251-2420
  Fletcher (G-5992)
Centaur Laboratories Inc............................ F 919 249-5072
  Oxford (G-12119)
City of Greensboro..................................... E 336 373-5855
  Greensboro (G-6911)
Greenstory Globl Gvrnment Mlta................ F 828 446-9278
  Terrell (G-15179)
I2m LLC.. G 984 202-0582
  Raleigh (G-12873)
Imagine One LLC.. G 828 324-6454
  Hickory (G-8061)
Water-Revolution LLC................................. G 336 525-1015
  Blanch (G-1153)

FILTERS & STRAINERS: Pipeline

Elxsi Corporation.. B 407 849-1090
  Charlotte (G-2701)
Hayward Industries Inc.............................. C 336 712-9900
  Clemmons (G-4043)
Hayward Industries Inc.............................. B 908 351-5400
  Charlotte (G-2894)

FILTERS: Air

Ffi Holdings III Corp................................... E 800 690-3650
  Charlotte (G-2755)
Nederman Mikropul LLC............................. G 704 998-2600
  Charlotte (G-3246)

FILTERS: Air Intake, Internal Combustion Engine, Exc Auto

Canvas Sx LLC.. C 980 474-3700
  Charlotte (G-2384)

FILTERS: General Line, Indl

Beacon Industrial Mfg LLC.......................... A 704 399-7441
  Charlotte (G-2290)
Drum Filter Media Inc................................ G 336 434-4195
  High Point (G-8332)
Erdle Perforating Holdings Inc................... F 704 588-4380
  Charlotte (G-2726)
Fuji America Inc... G 704 527-3854
  Charlotte (G-2800)
John W Foster Sales Inc............................ G 704 821-3822
  Matthews (G-10326)
Mann+hmmel Fltrtion Tech US LL.............. C 704 869-3300
  Gastonia (G-6452)
Mann+hummel Filtration Technol............. D 704 869-3501
  Gastonia (G-6456)
Reclaim Filters and Systems...................... G 919 528-1787
  Wake Forest (G-15582)

FILTERS: Oil, Internal Combustion Engine, Exc Auto

Centaur Laboratories Inc........................... F 919 249-5072
  Oxford (G-12119)

FILTRATION DEVICES: Electronic

Amiad Filtration Systems Ltd..................... E 805 377-0288
  Mooresville (G-10859)
Branford Filtration LLC.............................. D 704 394-2111
  Mooresville (G-10886)
Fueltec Systems LLC.................................. G 828 212-1141
  Granite Falls (G-6733)
Liquid Process Systems Inc...................... G 704 821-1115
  Indian Trail (G-8945)
Mann+hmmel Fltrtion Tech US LL............. C 704 869-3300
  Gastonia (G-6452)
Nederman Mikropul Canada Inc................ G 704 998-2606
  Charlotte (G-3247)
PSI Global USA.. G 704 544-1893
  Charlotte (G-3394)
Purolator Facet Inc................................... E 336 668-4444
  Greensboro (G-7293)

FINANCIAL SVCS

Apex Analytix LLC..................................... C 336 272-4669
  Greensboro (G-6810)
Katchi Tees Incorporated.......................... G 252 315-4691
  Wilson (G-16504)

FINGERPRINT EQPT

Tri-Tech Forensics Inc.............................. D 910 457-6600
  Leland (G-9562)

FINISHING AGENTS

Fine Line Hosiery Inc................................ F 336 498-8022
  Asheboro (G-435)
Lindley Laboratories Inc........................... F 336 449-7521
  Gibsonville (G-6567)

FINISHING AGENTS: Textile

Cross-Link Inc.. G 828 657-4477
  Cliffside (G-4084)
Surry Chemicals Incorporated................... E 336 786-4607
  Mount Airy (G-11580)

FINISHING SVCS

Blue Ridge Quick Print Inc....................... G 828 883-2420
  Brevard (G-1270)

FIRE ALARM MAINTENANCE & MONITORING SVCS

Automated Controls LLC........................... F 704 724-7625
  Huntersville (G-8796)
GNB Ventures LLC.................................... F 704 488-4468
  Charlotte (G-2837)
Integrated Roe Security LLC..................... G 919 297-8036
  Raleigh (G-12896)

FIRE ARMS, SMALL: Guns Or Gun Parts, 30 mm & Below

Arisaka LLC.. F 919 601-5625
  Apex (G-165)
Bachstein Consulting LLC......................... G 410 322-4917
  Youngsville (G-17070)
Grip Pod Systems Intl LLC....................... G 239 233-3694
  Raleigh (G-12822)
Remington Arms Company LLC................ B 800 544-8892
  Madison (G-10085)

PRODUCT SECTION   FLAGS: Fabric

Werywin Corporation................................ G..... 410 322-4917
   Youngsville (G-17114)

FIRE ARMS, SMALL: Pistols Or Pistol Parts, 30 mm & below

Microtech Defense Inds Inc.................... G..... 828 684-4355
   Fletcher (G-6026)

FIRE ARMS, SMALL: Rifles Or Rifle Parts, 30 mm & below

Remington Arms Company LLC............ C..... 800 544-8892
   Madison (G-10086)

FIRE CONTROL EQPT REPAIR SVCS, MILITARY

Rk Enterprises LLC................................. G..... 910 481-0777
   Fayetteville (G-5908)

FIRE CONTROL OR BOMBING EQPT: Electronic

Total Fire Systems Inc........................... E..... 919 556-9161
   Youngsville (G-17107)

FIRE DETECTION SYSTEMS

Argus Fire CONtrol-Pf&s Inc................. E..... 704 372-1228
   Charlotte (G-2215)

FIRE EXTINGUISHERS, WHOLESALE

Beco Holding Company Inc.................... C..... 800 826-3473
   Charlotte (G-2295)
GNB Ventures LLC................................. F..... 704 488-4468
   Charlotte (G-2837)
Walter Kidde Portable Eqp Inc............... B..... 919 563-5911
   Mebane (G-10435)

FIRE EXTINGUISHERS: Portable

Bonaventure Group Inc.......................... F..... 919 781-6610
   Raleigh (G-12568)
Bryants Fire Extinguisher Co.................. G..... 252 563-4111
   Tarboro (G-15098)
GNB Ventures LLC................................. F..... 704 488-4468
   Charlotte (G-2837)
Speer Operational Tech LLC.................. G..... 864 631-2512
   Marion (G-10179)

FIRE OR BURGLARY RESISTIVE PRDTS

International Vault Inc........................... E..... 919 742-3132
   Siler City (G-14417)
Mma Manufacturing Inc......................... E..... 828 692-0256
   East Flat Rock (G-5478)
North Star Fbrication Repr Inc............... G..... 704 393-5243
   Charlotte (G-3269)
Sinnovatek Inc....................................... G..... 919 694-0974
   Raleigh (G-13264)
West Side Industries LLC...................... G..... 980 223-8665
   Statesville (G-14924)

FIREARMS & AMMUNITION, EXC SPORTING, WHOLESALE

Consolidated Elec Distrs Inc.................. G..... 828 433-4689
   Morganton (G-11207)

FIREFIGHTING APPARATUS

Buckeye Fire Equipment Company........ E..... 704 739-7415
   Kings Mountain (G-9296)
Hurst Jaws of Life Inc........................... C..... 704 487-6961
   Shelby (G-14328)
Kenmar Inc.. F..... 336 884-8722
   High Point (G-8423)

Scott Technologies Inc.......................... B..... 704 291-8300
   Monroe (G-10803)

FIREPLACE EQPT & ACCESS

Avanti Hearth Products LLC.................. G..... 704 866-4342
   Belmont (G-975)
Hearth & Home Technologies LLC......... C..... 336 274-1663
   Greensboro (G-7082)
Woodlane Envmtl Tech Inc..................... E..... 828 894-8383
   Columbus (G-4182)

FIREPLACES: Concrete

Blue Rdge Elc Mmbers Fndtion I............ D..... 828 754-9071
   Lenoir (G-9591)

FIRST AID SPLYS, WHOLESALE

Project Bean LLC.................................. D..... 201 438-1598
   Harrisburg (G-7723)

FISH & SEAFOOD PROCESSORS: Canned Or Cured

Bay Breeze Seafood Rest Inc................. E..... 828 697-7106
   Hendersonville (G-7824)
Capt Neills Seafood Inc......................... C..... 252 796-0795
   Columbia (G-4166)
Carolina Seafood Company Inc.............. G..... 252 322-5455
   Aurora (G-833)
Lloyds Oyster House Inc....................... E..... 910 754-6958
   Shallotte (G-14276)
Quality Foods From Sea Inc.................. D..... 252 338-5455
   Elizabeth City (G-5565)
Quality Seafood Co Inc......................... F..... 252 338-2800
   Elizabeth City (G-5566)
Steve S Seafood Inc.............................. G..... 910 279-5711
   Leland (G-9560)

FISH & SEAFOOD PROCESSORS: Fresh Or Frozen

Bakkavor Foods Usa Inc....................... C..... 704 522-1977
   Charlotte (G-2270)
Hare Asian Trading Company LLC......... E..... 910 524-4667
   Burgaw (G-1340)

FISH & SEAFOOD WHOLESALERS

Atlantis Foods Inc................................ E..... 336 768-6101
   Clemmons (G-4027)
Bay Breeze Seafood Rest Inc................. E..... 828 697-7106
   Hendersonville (G-7824)
Janet W Whitbeck Inc............................ G..... 252 986-2800
   Hatteras (G-7737)
Pamlico Packing Co Inc........................ F..... 252 745-3688
   Vandemere (G-15489)
Pamlico Packing Co Inc........................ F..... 252 745-3688
   Grantsboro (G-6765)

FISHING EQPT: Lures

Barrys Custom Lures LLC..................... G..... 828 256-1792
   Hickory (G-7948)
Big Nics Lures LLC............................... G..... 910 805-1360
   Wilmington (G-16138)
Dobbins Products.................................. G..... 919 580-0621
   Goldsboro (G-6610)
Fish Getter Lure Co LLC....................... G..... 704 538-9863
   Casar (G-1933)
Hanta Rods and Lures LLC.................... G..... 919 480-5138
   Raleigh (G-12829)
Laceration Lures LLC........................... G..... 919 612-3368
   Raleigh (G-12951)
Lures Galore LLC................................. G..... 336 643-0948
   Summerfield (G-14987)

Total Limit Lures.................................. G..... 910 330-5786
   Concord (G-4378)

FITTINGS & ASSEMBLIES: Hose & Tube, Hydraulic Or Pneumatic

Bmrs Management Services Inc............ G..... 704 793-4319
   Concord (G-4212)
Carolina Components Group Inc........... E..... 919 635-8438
   Durham (G-5001)
Carolina Rubber & Spc Inc.................... G..... 336 744-5111
   Winston Salem (G-16647)
Cross Technologies Inc........................ E..... 800 327-7727
   Greensboro (G-6942)
Custom Hydraulics & Design................. F..... 704 347-0023
   Cherryville (G-3865)
Deetag USA Inc..................................... G..... 828 465-2644
   Conover (G-4447)
Dickie Jones... G..... 828 733-5084
   Newland (G-11885)
Eagle Assembly Unlimited Inc............... G..... 252 462-0408
   Castalia (G-1939)
Eaton Corporation................................ D..... 828 286-4157
   Forest City (G-6066)
Hydraulic Hose Depot Inc..................... G..... 252 356-1862
   Cofield (G-4135)
Metrohose Incorporated....................... G..... 252 329-9891
   Greenville (G-7560)
Talladega Mchy & Sup Co NC................ G..... 256 362-4124
   Fayetteville (G-5925)

FITTINGS & SPECIALTIES: Steam

Tlv Corporation..................................... E..... 704 597-9070
   Charlotte (G-3698)

FITTINGS: Pipe

Appalachian Pipe Distrs LLC................. F..... 704 688-5703
   Charlotte (G-2202)
Atlantic Tube & Fitting LLC................... G..... 704 545-6166
   Mint Hill (G-10520)
General Refrigeration Company............. G..... 919 661-4727
   Garner (G-6273)
Industrial Mgmt of Materials................. F..... 704 359-9928
   Charlotte (G-2963)
Triangle Pipe Ftting Sltons In................ G..... 919 696-8635
   Morrisville (G-11453)

FITTINGS: Pipe, Fabricated

Florida Fire Supply............................... E..... 336 885-5007
   Winston Salem (G-16714)

FIXTURES & EQPT: Kitchen, Metal, Exc Cast Aluminum

Henry & Rye Incorporated..................... F..... 919 365-7045
   Wendell (G-15904)
Metalfab of North Carolina LLC............. C..... 704 841-1090
   Matthews (G-10271)
Select Stainless Products LLC.............. E..... 888 843-2345
   Charlotte (G-3524)
Singer Equipment Company Inc............ E..... 910 484-1128
   Fayetteville (G-5918)
Thompson & Little Inc.......................... E..... 910 484-1128
   Fayetteville (G-5929)

FIXTURES: Cut Stone

Athena Marble Incorporated................. F..... 704 636-7810
   Salisbury (G-13924)
McAd Inc.. E..... 336 299-3030
   Greensboro (G-7193)

FLAGS: Fabric

FLAGSTONES

Dunn Manufacturing Corp................... C 704 283-2147
  Monroe *(G-10709)*

FLAGSTONES

Jacobs Creek Stone Company Inc........ F 336 857-2602
  Denton *(G-4738)*

FLAKEBOARD

Flakeboard America Limited................ G 910 569-7010
  Biscoe *(G-1109)*

FLAT GLASS: Construction

Four Jaks.. G 828 484-9545
  Weaverville *(G-15847)*
Grace Construction & Glass................. G 919 805-8380
  Clayton *(G-3982)*
James E Latta....................................... G 919 682-5793
  Durham *(G-5170)*

FLAT GLASS: Float

Cardinal Glass Industries Inc................ C 704 660-0900
  Mooresville *(G-10895)*

FLAT GLASS: Window, Clear & Colored

Tint Plus... G 910 229-5303
  Fayetteville *(G-5930)*

FLOOR COVERING STORES

Anderson Living Center LLC................. G 828 229-3243
  Forest City *(G-6059)*
Bfs Operations LLC.............................. A 919 431-1000
  Raleigh *(G-12555)*
Heartwood Pine Floors Inc.................... G 919 542-4394
  Moncure *(G-10624)*
Stock Building Supply Holdings LLC..... A 919 431-1000
  Raleigh *(G-13305)*

FLOOR COVERING STORES: Carpets

Interrs-Exteriors Asheboro Inc.............. F 336 629-2148
  Asheboro *(G-446)*

FLOOR COVERINGS WHOLESALERS

Freudenberg Nonwovens Limit............. A 919 620-3900
  Durham *(G-5103)*

FLOOR COVERINGS: Rubber

Core Technology Molding Corp............. E 336 294-2018
  Greensboro *(G-6937)*
Prototech Manufacturing Inc................. F 508 646-8849
  Washington *(G-15728)*

FLOOR COVERINGS: Textile Fiber

Rug & Home Inc................................... G 828 785-4480
  Asheville *(G-760)*

FLOORING: Hardwood

Bona USA... F 704 220-6943
  Monroe *(G-10666)*
Eskimo 7 Limited.................................. G 252 726-8181
  Morehead City *(G-11171)*
Green River Resource MGT................. F 828 697-0357
  Zirconia *(G-17153)*
Horizon Forest Products Co LP............ G 336 993-9663
  Colfax *(G-4151)*
Horizon Frest Pdts Wlmngton LP......... F 919 424-8265
  Raleigh *(G-12860)*
J & B Hardwood Inc.............................. G 828 226-2326
  Canton *(G-1619)*
J L Powell & Co Inc............................... G 910 642-8989
  Whiteville *(G-15967)*
Mannington Mills Inc............................. F 336 884-5600
  High Point *(G-8438)*

Mr Hardwood Floors Inc....................... G 919 369-8027
  Raleigh *(G-13046)*
Old Growth Riverwood Inc.................... G 910 762-4077
  Wilmington *(G-16343)*
Robert St Clair Co Inc........................... F 919 847-8611
  Raleigh *(G-13211)*
Vivet Inc... G 909 390-1039
  Greensboro *(G-7444)*

FLOWERS, ARTIFICIAL, WHOLESALE

Government Sales LLC........................ G 252 726-6315
  Morehead City *(G-11172)*
Jefferson Group Inc.............................. E 252 752-6195
  Greenville *(G-7549)*

FLUID METERS & COUNTING DEVICES

Danaher Indus Sensors Contrls............ G 910 862-5426
  Elizabethtown *(G-5592)*
Measurement Controls Inc.................... F 704 921-1101
  Charlotte *(G-3157)*
Phitech Laboratories Inc....................... G 910 420-1020
  Jackson Springs *(G-8983)*
Sensus... F 919 376-2617
  Cary *(G-1885)*
Vontier Corporation.............................. D 984 275-6000
  Raleigh *(G-13409)*

FLUID POWER PUMPS & MOTORS

Caterpillar Inc....................................... D 919 550-1100
  Clayton *(G-3963)*
E-Z Dumper Products LLC................... F 717 762-8432
  Southern Pines *(G-14534)*
Hurst Jaws of Life Inc.......................... C 704 487-6961
  Shelby *(G-14328)*
Hyde Park Partners Inc........................ C 704 587-4819
  Charlotte *(G-2939)*
Hydralic Engnered Pdts Svc Inc.......... G 704 374-1306
  Charlotte *(G-2940)*
Livingston & Haven LLC....................... C 704 588-3670
  Charlotte *(G-3096)*
Logic Hydraulic Controls Inc................ E 910 791-9293
  Wilmington *(G-16304)*
Mro Stop LLC....................................... F 704 587-5429
  Charlotte *(G-3210)*
Parker-Hannifin Corporation................. B 704 739-9781
  Kings Mountain *(G-9323)*
Schunk Intec Inc................................... D 919 572-2705
  Morrisville *(G-11420)*
SCI Sharp Controls Inc........................ C 704 394-1395
  Pineville *(G-12304)*

FLUID POWER VALVES & HOSE FITTINGS

Cross Technologies Inc........................ D 336 292-0511
  Whitsett *(G-15987)*
Dixon Valve & Coupling Co LLC........... F 704 334-9175
  Dallas *(G-4637)*
Engineered Controls Intl LLC............... C 828 466-2153
  Conover *(G-4451)*
George W Dahl Company Inc............... E 336 668-4444
  Greensboro *(G-7038)*
Hydac Technology Corp....................... D 610 266-0100
  Denver *(G-4783)*
Polyhose Incorporated......................... F 732 512-9141
  Wilmington *(G-16360)*
Romac Industries Inc........................... G 704 915-3317
  Dallas *(G-4656)*
SCI Sharp Controls Inc........................ G 704 394-1395
  Pineville *(G-12304)*

FOAM RUBBER

Bsci Inc.. G 704 664-3005
  Mooresville *(G-10890)*

Carolina Custom Rubber Inc................ G 704 636-6989
  Salisbury *(G-13934)*
Catawba Valley Fabrication Inc............ E 828 459-1191
  Conover *(G-4435)*
Craftsman Foam Fabricators Inc......... F 336 476-5655
  Thomasville *(G-15207)*
Elite Comfort Solutions LLC................. C 828 328-2201
  Conover *(G-4450)*
GP Foam Fabricators Inc..................... E 336 434-3600
  High Point *(G-8370)*
Hickory Springs Manufacturi................ D 828 328-2201
  Hickory *(G-8052)*
Hickory Springs Mfg Co....................... G 828 322-7994
  Hickory *(G-8053)*
Hickory Springs Mfg Co....................... G 828 728-9274
  Lenoir *(G-9619)*
Highland Foam Inc.............................. F 828 327-0400
  Conover *(G-4465)*
Hilliard Fabricators LLC....................... F 336 861-8833
  Thomasville *(G-15231)*
Interstate Foam & Supply Inc............... C 828 459-9700
  Conover *(G-4468)*
Marx Industries Incorporated............... G 828 396-6700
  Hudson *(G-8775)*
Ohio Foam Corporation........................ F 704 883-8402
  Statesville *(G-14854)*
Skelly Inc... F 828 433-7070
  Morganton *(G-11254)*

FOAMS & RUBBER, WHOLESALE

Olympic Products LLC.......................... D 336 378-9620
  Greensboro *(G-7231)*
Snyder Paper Corporation.................... G 828 464-1189
  Newton *(G-11969)*

FOIL & LEAF: Metal

Acme Liquidating Company LLC........... E 704 873-3731
  Statesville *(G-14739)*
Granges Americas Inc.......................... C 704 633-6020
  Salisbury *(G-13973)*
Kurz Transfer Products LP................... D 336 764-4128
  Lexington *(G-9742)*
Kurz Transfer Products LP................... D 704 927-3700
  Huntersville *(G-8845)*
Reynolds Consumer Products Inc........ A 704 371-5550
  Huntersville *(G-8885)*

FOIL: Aluminum

Granges Americas Inc.......................... C 704 633-6020
  Salisbury *(G-13973)*

FOOD COLORINGS

GNT Usa LLC....................................... E 914 524-0600
  Dallas *(G-4643)*

FOOD PRDTS, BREAKFAST: Cereal, Oatmeal

Post Consumer Brands LLC................ E 336 672-0124
  Asheboro *(G-464)*

FOOD PRDTS, CANNED OR FRESH PACK: Fruit Juices

Arcadia Beverage LLC......................... G 828 684-3556
  Arden *(G-310)*
Arcadia Farms LLC.............................. D 828 684-3556
  Arden *(G-311)*
Clement Pappas Nc LLC...................... G 856 455-1000
  Hendersonville *(G-7838)*
Dfa Dairy Brands Fluid LLC.................. G 704 341-2794
  Charlotte *(G-2625)*

FOOD PRDTS, CANNED: Baby Food

PRODUCT SECTION

FOOD PRDTS, WHOLESALE: Spices & Seasonings

Atlantic Natural Foods LLC .... D 888 491-0524
Nashville *(G-11734)*

FOOD PRDTS, CANNED: Barbecue Sauce

Baileys Sauces Inc .... G 252 756-7179
Greenville *(G-7491)*

Big Show Foods Inc .... F 919 920-1888
Fremont *(G-6172)*

Brookwood Farms Inc .... D 919 663-3612
Siler City *(G-14401)*

Mike DS Bbq LLC .... G 866 960-8652
Durham *(G-5225)*

Papa Lonnies Inc .... G 336 573-9313
Stoneville *(G-14964)*

T W Garner Food Company .... G 336 661-1550
Winston Salem *(G-16929)*

T W Garner Food Company .... E 336 661-1550
Winston Salem *(G-16930)*

FOOD PRDTS, CANNED: Fruit Juices, Fresh

Dole Food Company Inc .... E 818 874-4000
Charlotte *(G-2650)*

Goodstuff Juices LLC .... G 252 347-2341
Greenville *(G-7532)*

McF Operating LLC .... E 828 685-8821
Hendersonville *(G-7878)*

FOOD PRDTS, CANNED: Fruits

Blue Ridge Jams .... G 828 685-1783
Hendersonville *(G-7826)*

Carolina Canners Inc .... D 843 537-5281
Southern Pines *(G-14530)*

Goshen House & Trading LLC .... G 832 407-8153
Cary *(G-1776)*

Kraft Heinz Foods Company .... G 704 565-5500
Charlotte *(G-3060)*

Marie Sharps Usa LLC .... F 336 701-0377
Winston Salem *(G-16800)*

Welchs Recycling Inc .... G 336 638-9601
Greensboro *(G-7455)*

FOOD PRDTS, CANNED: Fruits & Fruit Prdts

Lc Foods LLC .... G 919 510-6688
Raleigh *(G-12961)*

FOOD PRDTS, CANNED: Jams, Jellies & Preserves

Dutch Kettle LLC .... G 336 468-8422
Hamptonville *(G-7669)*

Girlie Jams .... G 704 575-5815
Cornelius *(G-4549)*

Miss Kllys Jllies Jams Such LL .... G 910 988-8042
Southern Pines *(G-14542)*

Palace Green LLC .... G 919 827-7950
Raleigh *(G-13094)*

Pamela Stoeppelwerth .... G 828 837-7293
Marble *(G-10133)*

FOOD PRDTS, CANNED: Mexican, NEC

Plantation House Foods Inc .... G 919 381-5495
Durham *(G-5291)*

Tyson Mexican Original Inc .... D 919 777-9428
Sanford *(G-14201)*

FOOD PRDTS, CONFECTIONERY, WHOLESALE: Candy

Bilcat Inc .... E 828 295-3088
Blowing Rock *(G-1154)*

FOOD PRDTS, CONFECTIONERY, WHOLESALE: Snack Foods

Gold Medal Products Co .... G 336 665-4997
Greensboro *(G-7051)*

Lc America Inc .... F 336 676-5129
Colfax *(G-4153)*

Lotus Bakeries Us LLC .... G 415 956-8956
Mebane *(G-10417)*

Lrw Holdings Inc .... G 919 609-4172
Durham *(G-5196)*

Snyders-Lance Inc .... A 704 554-1421
Charlotte *(G-3574)*

FOOD PRDTS, DAIRY, WHOLESALE: Frozen Dairy Desserts

Celebrity Dairy LLC .... G 919 742-4931
Siler City *(G-14404)*

Queen City Pastry Llc .... E 704 660-5706
Mooresville *(G-11066)*

FOOD PRDTS, FISH & SEAFOOD: Crabmeat, Frozen

Sea Supreme Inc .... G 919 556-1188
Wake Forest *(G-15590)*

FOOD PRDTS, FISH & SEAFOOD: Fish, Filleted

Classic Seafood Group Inc .... C 252 746-2818
Ayden *(G-849)*

FOOD PRDTS, FROZEN: Ethnic Foods, NEC

Ricewrap Foods Corporation .... F 919 614-1179
Butner *(G-1549)*

FOOD PRDTS, FROZEN: Fruits, Juices & Vegetables

Alphin Brothers Inc .... E 910 892-8751
Dunn *(G-4850)*

Caseiro International LLC .... G 919 530-8333
Durham *(G-5007)*

Neighborhood Smoothie LLC .... G 919 845-5513
Raleigh *(G-13061)*

Nice Blends Corp .... D 910 640-1000
Whiteville *(G-15973)*

Seal Seasons Inc .... F 919 245-3535
Durham *(G-5347)*

Smoothie Fabrication LLC .... G 704 291-7728
Monroe *(G-10809)*

Smoothiesorg Inc .... G 704 906-4121
Charlotte *(G-3568)*

Southport Smoothies LLC .... G 910 363-4526
Southport *(G-14582)*

Triad Smoothies LLC .... G 336 972-1130
Winston Salem *(G-16949)*

FOOD PRDTS, FRUITS & VEGETABLES, FRESH, WHOLESALE: Fruits

Dole Food Company Inc .... E 818 874-4000
Charlotte *(G-2650)*

FOOD PRDTS, WHOLESALE: Beans, Field

Catawba Farms Enterprises LLC .... F 828 464-5780
Newton *(G-11917)*

FOOD PRDTS, WHOLESALE: Beverages, Exc Coffee & Tea

Coca-Cola Consolidated Inc .... C 919 550-0611
Clayton *(G-3968)*

FOOD PRDTS, WHOLESALE: Chocolate

Chocolate Fetish LLC .... G 828 258-2353
Asheville *(G-592)*

Chocolate Smiles Village LLC .... G 919 469-5282
Cary *(G-1729)*

Escazu Artisan Chocolate LLC .... F 919 832-3433
Raleigh *(G-12745)*

FOOD PRDTS, WHOLESALE: Coffee, Green Or Roasted

Dfa Dairy Brands Fluid LLC .... G 704 341-2794
Charlotte *(G-2625)*

Larrys Beans Inc .... E 919 828-1234
Raleigh *(G-12958)*

Royal Cup Inc .... F 704 597-5756
Charlotte *(G-3463)*

S & D Coffee Inc .... A 704 782-3121
Concord *(G-4355)*

Tradewinds Coffee Co Inc .... F 919 556-1835
Zebulon *(G-17144)*

FOOD PRDTS, WHOLESALE: Condiments

Vintage South Inc .... G 919 362-4079
Apex *(G-253)*

FOOD PRDTS, WHOLESALE: Dried or Canned Foods

Clay County Food Pantry Inc .... G 828 389-1657
Hayesville *(G-7761)*

FOOD PRDTS, WHOLESALE: Flavorings & Fragrances

Azure Skye Beverages Inc .... G 704 909-7394
Charlotte *(G-2251)*

FOOD PRDTS, WHOLESALE: Flour

Interntnal Agrclture Group LLC .... F 908 323-3246
Mooresville *(G-10983)*

FOOD PRDTS, WHOLESALE: Grains

C A Perry & Son Inc .... G 252 330-2323
Elizabeth City *(G-5532)*

C A Perry & Son Inc .... E 252 221-4463
Hobbsville *(G-8675)*

Celtic Ocean International Inc .... E 828 299-9005
Arden *(G-320)*

Clapp Fertilizer and Trckg Inc .... G 336 449-6103
Whitsett *(G-15986)*

Farm Chemicals Inc .... F 910 875-4277
Raeford *(G-12420)*

FOOD PRDTS, WHOLESALE: Natural & Organic

Celtic Ocean International Inc .... E 828 299-9005
Arden *(G-320)*

Chef Martini LLC .... A 919 327-3183
Raleigh *(G-12618)*

FOOD PRDTS, WHOLESALE: Salad Dressing

Tracys Gourmet LLC .... G 919 672-1731
Asheville *(G-804)*

FOOD PRDTS, WHOLESALE: Specialty

Tropical Nut & Fruit Co .... C 800 438-4470
Charlotte *(G-3731)*

FOOD PRDTS, WHOLESALE: Spices & Seasonings

Random Rues Botanical LLC .... G 252 214-2759
Greenville *(G-7579)*

FOOD PRDTS, WHOLESALE: Water, Distilled

Alamance Foods Inc .... C 336 226-6392
Burlington *(G-1362)*

Carolina Bottle Mfr LLC .... G 704 635-8759
Monroe *(G-10674)*

FOOD PRDTS: Almond Pastes

Herbal Innovations LLC .... E 336 818-2332
Wilkesboro *(G-16024)*

FOOD PRDTS: Animal & marine fats & oils

Carolina By-Products Co .... G 336 333-3030
Greensboro *(G-6882)*

Coastal Protein Products Inc .... G 910 567-6102
Godwin *(G-6577)*

Darling Ingredients Inc .... G 910 289-2083
Rose Hill *(G-13775)*

Valley Proteins .... F 252 348-4200
Lewiston Woodville *(G-9663)*

Valley Proteins (de) Inc .... C 336 333-3030
Greensboro *(G-7435)*

Valley Proteins (de) Inc .... C 540 877-2533
Oakboro *(G-12084)*

FOOD PRDTS: Cheese Curls & Puffs

Bakers Southern Traditions Inc .... G 252 344-2120
Roxobel *(G-13829)*

Ginny O s Inc .... F 919 816-7276
Warsaw *(G-15668)*

Lc America Inc .... F 336 676-5129
Colfax *(G-4153)*

Ripe Revival Produce LLC .... G 252 567-8305
Rocky Mount *(G-13728)*

Stormberg Foods LLC .... E 919 947-6011
Goldsboro *(G-6662)*

FOOD PRDTS: Chicken, Processed, Cooked

Filet of Chicken .... E 336 751-4752
Mocksville *(G-10571)*

FOOD PRDTS: Chicken, Processed, Fresh

Perdue Farms Inc .... E 252 348-4287
Ahoskie *(G-64)*

Perdue Farms Inc .... A 704 789-2400
Concord *(G-4331)*

Perdue Farms Inc .... D 336 366-2591
Elkin *(G-5628)*

FOOD PRDTS: Chicken, Slaughtered & Dressed

Pilgrims Pride Corporation .... E 704 721-3585
Concord *(G-4333)*

Pilgrims Pride Corporation .... B 704 624-2171
Marshville *(G-10222)*

Pilgrims Pride Corporation .... C 704 233-4047
Wingate *(G-16577)*

Sanderson Farms LLC Proc Div .... A 910 274-0220
Saint Pauls *(G-13909)*

FOOD PRDTS: Cocoa, Powdered

Celestial Cocoa Co .... G 704 871-2495
Statesville *(G-14775)*

FOOD PRDTS: Coffee

AC Imports LLC .... G 919 229-6650
Durham *(G-4898)*

Alamance Kaffee Werks LLC .... F 662 617-4573
Burlington *(G-1363)*

Anchor Coffee Co Inc .... G 336 265-7458
North Wilkesboro *(G-11997)*

High Noon Coffee Roasters LLC .... G 770 851-7004
Asheville *(G-651)*

Larrys Beans Inc .... E 919 828-1234
Raleigh *(G-12958)*

Royal Cup Inc .... F 704 597-5756
Charlotte *(G-3463)*

Sharewell Coffee Company LLC .... G 828 290-8188
Hendersonville *(G-7899)*

FOOD PRDTS: Coffee Extracts

Muddy Dog LLC .... G 919 371-2818
Cary *(G-1828)*

FOOD PRDTS: Cooking Oils, Refined Vegetable, Exc Corn

Whole Harvest Foods LLC .... E 910 293-7917
Warsaw *(G-15677)*

FOOD PRDTS: Corn Chips & Other Corn-Based Snacks

Frito-Lay North America Inc .... C 704 588-4150
Charlotte *(G-2798)*

KLb Enterprises Incorporated .... F 336 605-0773
Greensboro *(G-7153)*

FOOD PRDTS: Corn Meal

Atkinson Milling Company .... D 919 965-3547
Selma *(G-14253)*

House-Autry Mills Inc .... E 919 963-6200
Four Oaks *(G-6107)*

Lakeside Mills Inc .... F 828 286-4866
Spindale *(G-14607)*

FOOD PRDTS: Desserts, Ready-To-Mix

Sweet Treats By Treat Lady LLC .... G 336 831-3282
Winston Salem *(G-16928)*

FOOD PRDTS: Dips, Exc Cheese & Sour Cream Based

Apex Salsa Company .... G 919 363-1486
Apex *(G-162)*

Red Pepper Salsa .... G 503 799-9170
Winston Salem *(G-16882)*

Salsa Greensboro .... G 781 648-4140
Greensboro *(G-7324)*

FOOD PRDTS: Dough, Pizza, Prepared

Boonville Flour Feed Mill Inc .... G 336 367-7541
Boonville *(G-1253)*

Romanos Pizza .... G 704 782-5020
Concord *(G-4352)*

FOOD PRDTS: Dressings, Salad, Raw & Cooked Exc Dry Mixes

Jhonny Delgado .... G 704 218-9424
Charlotte *(G-3021)*

Pop Products LLC .... G 336 263-1884
Burlington *(G-1476)*

FOOD PRDTS: Dried & Dehydrated Fruits, Vegetables & Soup Mix

Dehydration LLC .... G 252 747-8200
Snow Hill *(G-14502)*

Naturesrules Inc .... G 336 427-2526
Madison *(G-10081)*

FOOD PRDTS: Edible fats & oils

American Cltvtion Extrction Sv .... G 336 544-1072
Greensboro *(G-6798)*

Bunge Oils Inc .... E 910 293-7917
Warsaw *(G-15665)*

FOOD PRDTS: Edible Oil Prdts, Exc Corn Oil

Herbs Gaia Inc .... D 828 884-4242
Brevard *(G-1276)*

FOOD PRDTS: Fish Oil

Odens Fish & Oil Co Inc .... G 252 588-0036
Ocracoke *(G-12097)*

FOOD PRDTS: Flour

Lindley Mills Inc .... F 336 376-6190
Graham *(G-6697)*

FOOD PRDTS: Flour & Other Grain Mill Products

Archer-Daniels-Midland Company .... E 704 332-3165
Charlotte *(G-2210)*

Archer-Daniels-Midland Company .... C 910 457-5011
Southport *(G-14565)*

Beaver Tooth Milling Inc .... G 910 262-4438
Bolivia *(G-1162)*

Smith Milling Company .... G 336 957-8108
Roaring River *(G-13595)*

FOOD PRDTS: Fruit Juices

Goodstuff Juices LLC .... G 252 347-2341
Greenville *(G-7532)*

Milkco Inc .... B 828 254-8428
Asheville *(G-702)*

Tropical Fruit Juice Bar .... G 910 426-5842
Fayetteville *(G-5935)*

FOOD PRDTS: Fruits & Vegetables, Pickled

Posh Pickle Company LLC .... G 336 870-6712
Greensboro *(G-7268)*

FOOD PRDTS: Gelatin Dessert Preparations

Pregel America Inc .... C 704 707-0300
Concord *(G-4336)*

FOOD PRDTS: Ice, Cubes

Ice Cube Recording Studios .... G 910 260-7616
Wilmington *(G-16262)*

FOOD PRDTS: Mixes, Bread & Bread-Type Roll

Proximity Foods Corporation .... G 336 691-1700
Greensboro *(G-7290)*

FOOD PRDTS: Mixes, Gravy, Dry

Bost Distributing Company Inc .... E 919 775-5931
Sanford *(G-14095)*

FOOD PRDTS: Mixes, Pancake From Purchased Flour

Julias Southern Foods LLC .... G 919 609-6745
Raleigh *(G-12927)*

Lovegrass Kitchen Inc .... G 919 234-7541
Fuquay Varina *(G-6210)*

FOOD PRDTS: Mixes, Sauces, Dry

American Miso Company Inc.............F.....828 287-2940
Rutherfordton (G-13863)

FOOD PRDTS: Mixes, Seasonings, Dry
Julias Southern Foods LLC.................G.....919 609-6745
Raleigh (G-12927)

FOOD PRDTS: Mustard, Prepared
Lusty Monk LLC..........................G.....828 645-5056
Asheville (G-692)

FOOD PRDTS: Oils & Fats, Marine
Neptune Hlth Wllness Innvtion............C.....888 664-9166
Conover (G-4475)

FOOD PRDTS: Olive Oil
Arba LLC..................................G.....302 946-0079
Charlotte (G-2208)
Corner Station Olive Oil Co...............G.....828 246-0218
Waynesville (G-15800)
Green Gate Olive Oils Inc.................G.....910 986-0880
Pinehurst (G-12225)
Olive Beaufort Oil Company...............G.....252 504-2474
Beaufort (G-962)
Olive Beaufort Oil Company...............G.....910 325-1556
Swansboro (G-15047)
Olive Euro Oil LLC........................G.....336 310-4624
Kernersville (G-9222)
Olive Pinehurst Oil Co....................G.....910 315-9923
Aberdeen (G-19)
Olive Wagon LLC...........................G.....919 559-0845
Raleigh (G-13083)
Oliventures Inc...........................G.....800 231-2619
Raleigh (G-13084)
Outer Banks Olive Oil Company............G.....252 449-8229
Kill Devil Hills (G-9260)

FOOD PRDTS: Pasta, Uncooked, Packaged With Other Ingredients
Lc Foods LLC..............................G.....919 510-6688
Raleigh (G-12961)

FOOD PRDTS: Peanut Butter
Morven Partners LP........................E.....252 482-2193
Edenton (G-5519)
Peanut Butter Fingers LLC.................G.....704 997-5787
Cornelius (G-4574)
Peanut Butter Project.....................G.....704 654-0212
Charlotte (G-3324)
Peanut Processors Inc.....................F.....910 862-2136
Dublin (G-4838)
Peanut Processors Sherman Inc.............G.....910 862-2136
Dublin (G-4839)
Universal Blanchers LLC...................D.....252 482-2112
Edenton (G-5522)

FOOD PRDTS: Pickles, Vinegar
Dana Fancy Foods..........................G.....828 685-2937
Hendersonville (G-7843)
Mount Olive Pickle Company................G.....704 867-5585
Gastonia (G-6472)
Mount Olive Pickle Company Inc............F.....704 867-5585
Gastonia (G-6473)
Mount Olive Pickle Company Inc............B.....919 658-2535
Mount Olive (G-11666)

FOOD PRDTS: Pork Rinds
American Skin Food Group LLC..............E.....910 259-2232
Burgaw (G-1332)
Julias Southern Foods LLC.................G.....919 609-6745
Raleigh (G-12927)

Skin Boys LLC.............................E.....910 259-2232
Burgaw (G-1350)

FOOD PRDTS: Potato Chips & Other Potato-Based Snacks
Golden Pop Shop LLC.......................G.....704 236-9455
Charlotte (G-2844)
Igh Enterprises Inc.......................E.....704 372-6744
Charlotte (G-2949)
Snyders-Lance Inc.........................A.....704 554-1421
Charlotte (G-3574)

FOOD PRDTS: Poultry, Processed, Cooked
Integra Foods LLC.........................F.....910 984-2007
Bladenboro (G-1149)

FOOD PRDTS: Poultry, Processed, Frozen
Advancepierre Foods Inc...................A.....828 459-7626
Claremont (G-3900)

FOOD PRDTS: Poultry, Slaughtered & Dressed
Johnson Nash & Sons Farms Inc.............B.....910 289-3113
Rose Hill (G-13778)
Perdue Farms Incorporated.................A.....910 997-8600
Rockingham (G-13638)
Tyson Foods Inc...........................C.....336 838-2171
Wilkesboro (G-16049)

FOOD PRDTS: Raw cane sugar
Dermasweet LLC............................G.....843 834-1413
Wilmington (G-16199)
Golding Farms Foods Inc...................D.....336 766-6161
Winston Salem (G-16723)

FOOD PRDTS: Sandwiches
Advancepierre Foods Inc...................A.....828 459-7626
Claremont (G-3900)

FOOD PRDTS: Seasonings & Spices
Cool Runnings Jamaican LLC................G.....919 818-9220
Raleigh (G-12645)
Indulgent Essential Spices LLC............G.....919 973-3069
Franklinton (G-6155)
Signature Seasonings LLC..................G.....252 746-1001
Ayden (G-856)

FOOD PRDTS: Soup Mixes
Anns House of Nuts........................G.....252 795-6500
Robersonville (G-13614)

FOOD PRDTS: Starch, Indl
Western Technology Inc....................F.....336 361-0402
Reidsville (G-13545)

FOOD PRDTS: Syrup, Maple
Syrup and More LLC........................G.....781 548-1346
Greensboro (G-7384)

FOOD PRDTS: Syrups
Sweets Syrup LLC..........................G.....704 989-2156
Charlotte (G-3660)

FOOD PRDTS: Tea
Kimbees Inc...............................G.....336 323-8773
Greensboro (G-7150)
Kloud Hemp Co.............................G.....336 740-2528
Greensboro (G-7154)
Natures Cup LLC...........................G.....910 795-2700
Raeford (G-12427)

Wallingford Coffee Mills Inc..............D.....513 771-3131
Concord (G-4387)

FOOD PRDTS: Tortilla Chips
Gruma Corporation.........................E.....919 778-5553
Goldsboro (G-6622)
R W Garcia Co Inc.........................E.....828 428-0115
Lincolnton (G-9914)

FOOD PRDTS: Turkey, Slaughtered & Dressed
House of Raeford Farms Inc................A.....912 222-4090
Rose Hill (G-13777)

FOOD PRDTS: Vinegar
Isabellas Fine Olive Oils & Vi............G.....704 237-4949
Huntersville (G-8839)
Johnson Harn Vngar Gee GL Pllc............G.....919 213-6163
Raleigh (G-12921)
Oil and Vinegar Market Inc................G.....919 491-9225
Durham (G-5253)
Virgilios Premium Vinegars................G.....919 717-3373
Wake Forest (G-15610)
Wagco Oil and Vinegar Taproom.............G.....919 295-6134
Knightdale (G-9433)

FOOD PRDTS: Wheat Flour
Bartlett Milling Company LP...............D.....704 872-9581
Statesville (G-14759)
Midstate Mills Inc........................C.....828 464-1611
Newton (G-11953)

FOOD PRODUCTS MACHINERY
AC Corporation............................B.....336 273-4472
Greensboro (G-6775)
AMF Automation Tech LLC...................G.....919 288-1523
Goldsboro (G-6589)
Are Management LLC........................E.....336 855-7800
High Point (G-8252)
Babington Technology Inc..................G.....252 984-0349
Rocky Mount (G-13683)
Buhler Inc................................C.....800 722-7483
Cary (G-1716)
Cates Mechanical Corporation..............G.....704 458-5163
Charlotte (G-2419)
Designtek Fabrication Inc.................F.....910 359-0130
Red Springs (G-13498)
Flagstone Foods LLC.......................B.....252 795-6500
Robersonville (G-13616)
Fmp Equipment Corp........................F.....336 621-2882
Browns Summit (G-1302)
Gea Intec LLC.............................E.....919 433-0131
Durham (G-5112)
Griffin Marketing Group...................G.....336 558-5802
Greensboro (G-7068)
Induction Food Systems Inc................G.....919 907-0179
Raleigh (G-12883)
Jbt Aerotech Services.....................G.....336 740-3737
Greensboro (G-7135)
Krispy Kreme Doughnut Corp................E.....336 726-8908
Winston Salem (G-16780)
Marshall Middleby Inc.....................D.....919 762-1000
Fuquay Varina (G-6212)
Meadows Mills Inc.........................E.....336 838-2282
North Wilkesboro (G-12027)
Sinnovatek Inc............................G.....919 694-0974
Raleigh (G-13264)
SPX Flow Inc..............................C.....704 752-4400
Charlotte (G-3607)
SPX Flow Tech Systems Inc.................A.....704 752-4400
Charlotte (G-3609)

FOOD STORES: Convenience, Independent

Utsey Duskie & Associates................... G..... 704 663-0036
  Mooresville *(G-11117)*

FOOD STORES: Convenience, Independent

B & D Enterprises Inc........................ F..... 704 739-2958
  Kings Mountain *(G-9293)*

Rose Ice & Coal Company................... F..... 910 762-2464
  Wilmington *(G-16387)*

FOOD STORES: Cooperative

Communitys Kitchen L3c.................... G..... 828 817-2308
  Tryon *(G-15423)*

Whole Harvest Foods LLC................... E..... 910 293-7917
  Warsaw *(G-15677)*

FOOD STORES: Grocery, Independent

Bluff Mountain Outfitters Inc............... G..... 828 622-7162
  Hot Springs *(G-8744)*

FOOD STORES: Supermarkets, Chain

Harris Teeter LLC............................ D..... 704 846-7117
  Matthews *(G-10252)*

Harris Teeter LLC............................ D..... 919 859-0110
  Raleigh *(G-12831)*

Ingles Markets Incorporated................ D..... 704 434-0096
  Boiling Springs *(G-1161)*

Ruddick Operating Company LLC........... A..... 704 372-5404
  Charlotte *(G-3472)*

FOOTWEAR, WHOLESALE: Athletic

Implus Footcare LLC......................... B..... 800 446-7587
  Durham *(G-5150)*

FOOTWEAR, WHOLESALE: Boots

McRae Industries Inc........................ C..... 910 439-6149
  Mount Gilead *(G-11605)*

FOOTWEAR: Cut Stock

Direct Action K-9 LLC........................ G..... 910 246-0806
  Southern Pines *(G-14533)*

Quarter Turn LLC............................ G..... 336 712-0811
  Clemmons *(G-4058)*

Upper Room.................................. G..... 910 540-7719
  Watha *(G-15742)*

FORGINGS: Aircraft, Ferrous

Chatham Steel Corporation.................. E..... 912 233-4182
  Durham *(G-5013)*

FORGINGS: Aluminum

Emmco Sport LLC............................ G..... 336 354-7244
  Kernersville *(G-9196)*

FORGINGS: Automotive & Internal Combustion Engine

Victory 1 Performance Inc................... F..... 704 799-1955
  Mooresville *(G-11118)*

FORGINGS: Construction Or Mining Eqpt, Ferrous

Northern Cres Ir / Matt Wldrop.............. G..... 828 848-8884
  Zirconia *(G-17156)*

Volvo Motor Graders Inc.................... D..... 704 609-3604
  Charlotte *(G-3782)*

FORGINGS: Iron & Steel

Component Sourcing Intl LLC............... E..... 704 843-9292
  Charlotte *(G-2534)*

FORGINGS: Nuclear Power Plant, Ferrous

Consolidated Pipe & Sup Co Inc............. F..... 336 294-8577
  Greensboro *(G-6930)*

FORGINGS: Plumbing Fixture, Nonferrous

Entrust Services LLC........................ F..... 336 274-5175
  Greensboro *(G-7002)*

FORMS: Concrete, Sheet Metal

Form Tech Concrete Forms Inc.............. F..... 704 395-9910
  Charlotte *(G-2787)*

M&N Construction Supply Inc............... G..... 336 996-7740
  Colfax *(G-4154)*

FOUNDRIES: Aluminum

Cascade Die Casting Group Inc............. C..... 336 882-0186
  High Point *(G-8289)*

Dynacast LLC................................ E..... 704 927-2790
  Charlotte *(G-2662)*

RCM Industries Inc.......................... C..... 828 286-4003
  Rutherfordton *(G-13886)*

FOUNDRIES: Gray & Ductile Iron

Ej Usa Inc................................... G..... 919 362-7744
  Apex *(G-188)*

FOUNDRIES: Nonferrous

Rim-TEC Castings Eastern LLC.............. E..... 336 302-0912
  Davidson *(G-4695)*

Tru-Cast Inc................................. E..... 336 294-2370
  Greensboro *(G-7420)*

United Brass Works Inc..................... C..... 336 498-2661
  Randleman *(G-13494)*

FOUNDRIES: Steel

Coder Foundry.............................. E..... 704 910-3077
  Charlotte *(G-2521)*

Harris Rebar Inc............................. F..... 919 528-8333
  Benson *(G-1037)*

Nucor Corporation........................... C..... 252 356-3700
  Cofield *(G-4136)*

Rim-TEC Castings Eastern LLC.............. E..... 336 302-0912
  Asheboro *(G-473)*

Seven Cast.................................. G..... 704 335-0692
  Charlotte *(G-3532)*

FRAMES & FRAMING WHOLESALE

Four Corners Frmng Gallery Inc............. G..... 704 662-7154
  Mooresville *(G-10949)*

T Distribution NC Inc........................ E..... 828 438-1112
  Morganton *(G-11259)*

FRAMES: Chair, Metal

Precision Partners LLC...................... G..... 704 560-6442
  Charlotte *(G-3369)*

FRANCHISES, SELLING OR LICENSING

Body Shop Inc............................... C..... 919 554-4900
  Wake Forest *(G-15534)*

Ohio Mat Lcnsing Cmpnnts Group.......... G..... 336 861-3500
  Trinity *(G-15349)*

FREIGHT FORWARDING ARRANGEMENTS

Elizabeth Logistic LLC....................... D..... 803 920-3931
  Indian Trail *(G-8931)*

Kendall E Krause............................ G..... 910 690-4119
  Vass *(G-15492)*

Rapid Run Transport LLC.................... F..... 704 615-3458
  Charlotte *(G-3410)*

FRICTION MATERIAL, MADE FROM POWDERED METAL

Em2 Machine Corporation................... G..... 336 707-8409
  Greensboro *(G-6996)*

FRUITS & VEGETABLES WHOLESALERS: Fresh

Aseptia Inc.................................. C..... 678 373-6751
  Raleigh *(G-12528)*

FUEL ADDITIVES

Carolina Bg.................................. G..... 704 847-8840
  Matthews *(G-10236)*

FUEL DEALERS: Coal

Herrin Bros Coal & Ice Co................... G..... 704 332-2193
  Charlotte *(G-2906)*

FUEL OIL DEALERS

Euliss Oil Company Inc...................... G..... 336 622-3055
  Liberty *(G-9813)*

Go Energies LLC............................. F..... 877 712-5999
  Wilmington *(G-16234)*

Go Energies Holdings Inc................... G..... 910 762-5802
  Wilmington *(G-16235)*

Herrin Bros Coal & Ice Co................... G..... 704 332-2193
  Charlotte *(G-2906)*

Hickman Oil & Ice Co Inc................... G..... 910 576-2501
  Troy *(G-15406)*

M & R Retreading & Oil Co Inc.............. F..... 704 474-4101
  Norwood *(G-12040)*

Parker Gas Company Inc.................... F..... 800 354-7250
  Clinton *(G-4101)*

Starflite Companies Inc..................... C..... 252 728-2690
  Beaufort *(G-968)*

FUEL TREATING

Opw Fueling Components Inc............... E..... 919 464-4569
  Smithfield *(G-14475)*

FUELS: Diesel

Sinowest Mfg LLC........................... G..... 919 289-9337
  Raleigh *(G-13266)*

FUELS: Nuclear

Ge-Hitchi Nclear Enrgy Amrcas.............. A..... 910 819-5073
  Castle Hayne *(G-1948)*

Ge-Hitchi Nclear Enrgy Intl LL.............. E..... 518 433-4338
  Wilmington *(G-16228)*

Global Laser Enrichment LLC................ E..... 910 819-7255
  Castle Hayne *(G-1949)*

Global Nuclear Fuel LLC..................... F..... 910 819-6181
  Wilmington *(G-16232)*

Global Nuclear Fuel-Americas LLC........... E..... 910 819-5950
  Castle Hayne *(G-1950)*

FUELS: Nuclear, Uranium Slug, Radioactive

General Electric Company.................... A..... 910 675-5000
  Wilmington *(G-16230)*

FULLER'S EARTH MINING

Profile Products LLC......................... E..... 828 327-4165
  Conover *(G-4489)*

FUND RAISING ORGANIZATION, NON-FEE BASIS

Ipas.. C..... 919 967-7052
  Durham *(G-5163)*

FUNGICIDES OR HERBICIDES

Scotts Company LLC......................... F..... 704 663-6088
  Mooresville *(G-11080)*

PRODUCT SECTION

FURNITURE, HOUSEHOLD: Wholesalers

Summit Agro Usa LLC .... G 984 260-0407
Durham *(G-5379)*

FURNACES & OVENS: Indl

Billy Rice .... G 828 691-4831
Mars Hill *(G-10193)*

Buhler Inc .... C 800 722-7483
Cary *(G-1716)*

Greenline .... G 704 333-3377
Charlotte *(G-2865)*

Industrial Prcess Slutions Inc .... G 336 926-1511
Wilkesboro *(G-16025)*

Radcon Inc .... G 919 806-5233
Durham *(G-5318)*

Southeastern Installation Inc .... E 704 352-7146
Lexington *(G-9783)*

FURNACES: Warm Air, Electric

Lennox International Inc .... E 828 633-4805
Candler *(G-1586)*

Thermo Products LLC .... E 800 348-5130
Denton *(G-4752)*

FURNITURE COMPONENTS: Porcelain Enameled

Hunt Country Component LLC .... G 336 475-7000
Thomasville *(G-15233)*

Vrush Industries Inc .... F 336 886-7700
High Point *(G-8597)*

FURNITURE PARTS: Metal

M & M Frame Company Inc .... G 336 859-8166
Denton *(G-4745)*

Problem Solver Inc .... F 919 596-5555
Raleigh *(G-13148)*

Timmerman Manufacturing Inc .... F 828 464-1778
Conover *(G-4505)*

FURNITURE REFINISHING SVCS

Barker and Martin Inc .... G 336 275-5056
Greensboro *(G-6831)*

FURNITURE REPAIR & MAINTENANCE SVCS

Brice Manufacturing Co Inc .... E 818 896-2938
Greensboro *(G-6851)*

Otto and Moore Inc .... F 336 887-0017
High Point *(G-8472)*

Touch Up Solutions Inc .... E 828 428-9094
Maiden *(G-10120)*

FURNITURE STOCK & PARTS: Hardwood

A C Furniture Company Inc .... B 336 623-3430
Eden *(G-5484)*

Appalachian Lumber Company Inc .... E 336 973-7205
Wilkesboro *(G-16013)*

Ariston Hospitality Inc .... E 626 458-8668
High Point *(G-8254)*

Bruex Inc .... E 828 754-1186
Lenoir *(G-9592)*

Carolina Leg Supply LLC .... G 828 446-6838
Lenoir *(G-9594)*

Curved Plywood Inc .... G 336 249-6901
Lexington *(G-9703)*

D & S Frames Inc .... G 828 241-5962
Claremont *(G-3918)*

Hughes Furniture Inds Inc .... G 336 498-8700
Randleman *(G-13473)*

Hyman Furniture Warehouse LLC .... G 336 528-4950
Winston Salem *(G-16752)*

Latham Inc .... G 336 857-3702
Denton *(G-4741)*

M & S Warehouse Inc .... E 828 728-3733
Lenoir *(G-9628)*

Mc Gees Crating Inc .... E 828 758-4660
Lenoir *(G-9635)*

Paul P Poovey Jr .... G 828 465-2975
Newton *(G-11958)*

Pilot View Wood Works Inc .... F 336 883-2511
High Point *(G-8484)*

Quality Fabricators .... G 336 622-3402
Staley *(G-14670)*

Rudisill Frame Shop Inc .... E 828 464-7020
Newton *(G-11965)*

Ruskin Inc .... F 828 324-6500
Hickory *(G-8143)*

Select Frame Shop Inc .... D 910 428-1225
Biscoe *(G-1116)*

Sure Wood Products Inc .... F 828 261-0004
Hickory *(G-8172)*

Valendrawers Inc .... E 336 956-2118
Lexington *(G-9799)*

Woodline Inc .... G 336 476-7100
Thomasville *(G-15304)*

Woodwright of Wilson Co Inc .... G 252 243-9663
Elm City *(G-5655)*

FURNITURE STOCK & PARTS: Turnings, Wood

Adams Wood Turning Inc .... G 336 882-0196
High Point *(G-8232)*

B & E Woodturning Inc .... F 828 758-2843
Lenoir *(G-9577)*

Caldwell WD Carving Turning Co .... G 828 758-0186
Lenoir *(G-9593)*

Ideaitlia Cntmporary Furn Corp .... E 828 464-1000
Conover *(G-4466)*

Traditions Wood Carving & Frms .... G 828 322-5625
Hickory *(G-8184)*

FURNITURE STORES

Aria Designs LLC .... F 828 572-4303
Lenoir *(G-9575)*

Bassett Furniture Inds Inc .... D 828 465-7700
Newton *(G-11915)*

Bernhardt Furniture Company .... F 828 759-6205
Lenoir *(G-9587)*

Burrough Furniture .... G 336 841-3129
Archdale *(G-271)*

Carolina Chair Inc .... F 828 459-1330
Conover *(G-4430)*

Distinctive Furniture Inc .... G 828 754-3947
Lenoir *(G-9604)*

Elite Wood Products .... G 828 994-4446
Newton *(G-11930)*

Ethan Allen Retail Inc .... E 828 428-9361
Maiden *(G-10107)*

Furniture Fair Inc .... E 910 455-4044
Jacksonville *(G-9001)*

Hfi Wind Down Inc .... C 828 438-5767
Morganton *(G-11220)*

Ideaitlia Cntmporary Furn Corp .... C 828 464-1000
Conover *(G-4466)*

Keani Furniture Inc .... E 336 303-5484
Asheboro *(G-448)*

Lexington Furniture Inds Inc .... C 336 474-5300
Thomasville *(G-15241)*

M & S Warehouse Inc .... E 828 728-3733
Lenoir *(G-9628)*

McNeillys Inc .... E 704 300-1712
Lawndale *(G-9501)*

Mitchell Gold Co LLC C
Taylorsville *(G-15153)*

Miters Touch Inc .... G 828 963-4445
Banner Elk *(G-903)*

Neil Allen Industries Inc .... G 336 887-6500
High Point *(G-8465)*

O Henry House Ltd .... E 336 431-5350
Archdale *(G-294)*

Olde Lexington Products Inc .... G 336 956-2355
Linwood *(G-9947)*

Royal Colony Furniture Inc .... G 336 472-8833
Thomasville *(G-15272)*

Sides Furniture Inc .... G 336 869-5509
High Point *(G-8524)*

Smartway of Carolinas LLC .... F 704 900-7877
Charlotte *(G-3566)*

Tatum Galleries Inc .... G 828 963-6466
Banner Elk *(G-904)*

Verellen Inc .... D 336 889-7379
High Point *(G-8592)*

Weathercraft Outdoor Furn Inc .... G 336 629-3939
Asheboro *(G-508)*

Woodwright of Wilson Co Inc .... G 252 243-9663
Elm City *(G-5655)*

World Art Gallery Incorporated .... G 910 989-0203
Jacksonville *(G-9047)*

Yukon Inc .... E 919 366-2001
Wendell *(G-15926)*

FURNITURE WHOLESALERS

Apollo Designs LLC .... E 336 886-0260
High Point *(G-8250)*

Ashley Furniture Inds LLC .... D 336 998-1066
Advance *(G-37)*

Brookline Furniture Co Inc .... D 336 841-8503
Archdale *(G-270)*

Funder America Inc .... F 336 751-3501
Mocksville *(G-10575)*

Furniture At Work .... F 336 472-6619
Trinity *(G-15341)*

Lexington Furniture Inds Inc .... C 336 474-5300
Thomasville *(G-15241)*

Lodging By Liberty Inc .... C 336 622-2201
Siler City *(G-14423)*

Minhas Furniture House Inc .... E 910 898-0808
Robbins *(G-13601)*

Prepac Manufacturing US LLC .... F 800 665-1266
Whitsett *(G-15999)*

Prime Mill LLC .... F 336 819-4300
High Point *(G-8498)*

Simplicity Sofas Inc .... G 800 813-2889
High Point *(G-8531)*

Stone Marble Co Inc .... G 773 227-1161
Thomasville *(G-15285)*

Vrush Industries Inc .... F 336 886-7700
High Point *(G-8597)*

Watauga Creek LLC .... G 828 369-7881
Franklin *(G-6147)*

FURNITURE, HOUSEHOLD: Wholesalers

Carolina Csual Otdoor Furn Inc .... F 252 491-5171
Jarvisburg *(G-9083)*

Elite Furniture Mfg Inc .... G 336 882-0406
High Point *(G-8340)*

French Heritage Inc .... F 336 882-3565
High Point *(G-8358)*

Magnussen Home Furnishings Inc .... G 336 841-4424
Greensboro *(G-7178)*

Mongoose LLC .... F 919 400-0772
Burlington *(G-1462)*

Rbc Inc .... C 336 889-7333
Sophia *(G-14521)*

Southandenglish LLC .... G 336 888-8333
High Point *(G-8543)*

Employee Codes: A=Over 500 employees, B=251-500
C=101-250, D=51-100, E=20-50, F=10-19, G=1-9

FURNITURE, HOUSEHOLD: Wholesalers

Woodwright of Wilson Co Inc......... G 252 243-9663
Elm City *(G-5655)*

FURNITURE, MATTRESSES: Wholesalers

Affordable Bedding Inc................ G 828 254-5555
Asheville *(G-516)*

Bekaert Textiles USA Inc............ C 336 769-4300
Winston Salem *(G-16624)*

Bekaertdeslee USA Inc............... B 336 747-4900
Winston Salem *(G-16625)*

Mattress Firm........................... G 910 868-0950
Fayetteville *(G-5870)*

Mattress Firm........................... G 252 443-1259
Rocky Mount *(G-13711)*

FURNITURE, OFFICE: Wholesalers

Con-Tab Inc............................... F 336 476-0104
Thomasville *(G-15206)*

Office Sup Svcs Inc Charlotte..... E 704 786-4677
Concord *(G-4323)*

Professinal Sales Associates...... F 336 210-2756
High Point *(G-8500)*

Unique Office Solutions Inc........ G 336 854-0900
Greensboro *(G-7430)*

FURNITURE, OUTDOOR & LAWN: Wholesalers

Outer Banks Hammocks Inc........ F 910 256-4001
Wilmington *(G-16347)*

FURNITURE, WHOLESALE: Beds

Stuart Ryan Kent & Co................ G 252 916-8226
Winterville *(G-17014)*

FURNITURE, WHOLESALE: Beds & Bedding

Amor Furniture and Bedding LLC... F 336 795-0044
Liberty *(G-9806)*

Welcome Industrial Corp............. D 336 329-9640
Burlington *(G-1517)*

FURNITURE, WHOLESALE: Chairs

Chateau DAx USA Ltd................. G 336 885-9777
High Point *(G-8294)*

Jerry Blevins............................. G 336 384-3726
Lansing *(G-9455)*

FURNITURE, WHOLESALE: Lockers

Penco Products Inc.................... C 252 798-4000
Hamilton *(G-7614)*

FURNITURE, WHOLESALE: Racks

Rack Works Inc.......................... E 336 368-1302
Pilot Mountain *(G-12201)*

Wood Technology Inc................. E 828 464-8049
Conover *(G-4515)*

FURNITURE: Assembly Hall

Beaufurn LLC............................. E 336 768-2544
Advance *(G-38)*

FURNITURE: Bean Bag Chairs

Looc Studio Inc.......................... G 336 472-6877
Newton *(G-11950)*

FURNITURE: Bedroom, Wood

Affordable Beds & Furniture........ G 336 988-1520
Greensboro *(G-6785)*

Gram Furniture........................... G 828 241-2836
Claremont *(G-3928)*

Homestead Country Built Furn.... G 910 799-6489
Wilmington *(G-16256)*

Hooker Furniture Corporation...... C 336 819-7200
High Point *(G-8401)*

Lea Industries Inc..................... C 336 294-5233
Hudson *(G-8774)*

Philip Brady............................... G 336 581-3999
Bennett *(G-1027)*

FURNITURE: Bedsprings, Assembled

Comfort Bay Home Fashions Inc.. G 843 442-7477
Hickory *(G-7988)*

FURNITURE: Box Springs, Assembled

Cotton Belt Inc........................... D 252 689-6847
Greenville *(G-7509)*

Ohio Mat Lcnsing Cmpnnts Group... G 336 861-3500
Trinity *(G-15349)*

FURNITURE: Cabinets & Filing Drawers, Office, Exc Wood

Blue-Hen Inc.............................. G 407 322-2262
Asheville *(G-567)*

L B Plastics Incorporated........... D 704 663-1543
Mooresville *(G-11000)*

Sdv Office Systems LLC............ F 844 968-9500
Fletcher *(G-6037)*

Sdv Office Systems LLC............ G 844 968-9500
Asheville *(G-767)*

FURNITURE: Chairs & Couches, Wood, Upholstered

Dal Leather Inc.......................... G 828 302-1667
Conover *(G-4444)*

Images of America Inc............... D 336 475-7106
Thomasville *(G-15237)*

Southfield Ltd............................ F 336 434-6220
High Point *(G-8546)*

Wise Living Inc.......................... F 336 991-5346
High Point *(G-8606)*

FURNITURE: Chairs, Household Upholstered

Aria Designs LLC....................... F 828 572-4303
Lenoir *(G-9575)*

Bradington-Young LLC................ C 704 435-5881
Hickory *(G-7953)*

Brookline Furniture Co Inc.......... D 336 841-8503
Archdale *(G-270)*

C R Laine Furniture Co Inc......... C 828 328-1831
Hickory *(G-7957)*

Century Furniture LLC............... C 828 326-8458
Hickory *(G-7978)*

Century Furniture LLC............... F 828 326-8495
Hickory *(G-7982)*

Custom Contract Furn LLC......... G 336 882-8565
High Point *(G-8312)*

D R Kincaid Chair Co Inc............ E 828 754-0255
Lenoir *(G-9603)*

Directional Buying Group Inc....... E 336 472-6187
Thomasville *(G-15214)*

Fairfield Chair Company............. E 828 785-5571
Lenoir *(G-9609)*

Fairfield Chair Company............. E 828 758-5571
Lenoir *(G-9610)*

Furniture Concepts.................... F 828 323-1590
Hickory *(G-8029)*

Grand Manor Furniture Inc.......... D 828 758-5521
Lenoir *(G-9613)*

Hdm Furniture Industries Inc...... A 800 349-4579
Hickory *(G-8039)*

International Furnishings Inc...... G 336 472-8422
Thomasville *(G-15238)*

Jack Cartwright Incorporated...... E 336 889-9400
High Point *(G-8414)*

Jessica Charles LLC................... D 336 434-2124
High Point *(G-8416)*

Keani Furniture Inc.................... E 336 303-5484
Asheboro *(G-448)*

Kellex Corp................................ C 828 874-0389
Valdese *(G-15449)*

Lee Industries LLC.................... C 828 464-8318
Newton *(G-11947)*

LLC Ferguson Copeland.............. C 828 584-0664
Morganton *(G-11229)*

McNeillys Inc............................. E 704 300-1712
Lawndale *(G-9501)*

Mitchell Gold Co LLC................. C
Taylorsville *(G-15153)*

Paul Robert Chair Inc................. D 828 632-7021
Taylorsville *(G-15155)*

Prominence Furniture Inc........... E 336 475-6505
Thomasville *(G-15267)*

Smith Novelty Company Inc....... G 704 982-7413
Albemarle *(G-105)*

Style Upholstering Inc................ G 828 322-4882
Hickory *(G-8171)*

Verellen Inc............................... D 336 889-7379
High Point *(G-8592)*

Whitewood Contracts LLC.......... E 336 885-9300
High Point *(G-8603)*

FURNITURE: Chairs, Household Wood

A C Furniture Company Inc........ B 336 623-3430
Eden *(G-5484)*

A E Nesbitt Woodwork............... G 828 625-2428
Black Mountain *(G-1118)*

Abbey Robert Inc....................... G 336 883-1078
High Point *(G-8230)*

Baker Interiors Furniture Co....... G 336 431-9115
High Point *(G-8263)*

Baker Interiors Furniture Co....... C 336 431-9115
Connelly Springs *(G-4397)*

Barber Furniture & Supply.......... F 704 278-9367
Cleveland *(G-4068)*

Barker and Martin Inc................ G 336 275-5056
Greensboro *(G-6831)*

Bassett Furniture Direct Inc....... F 704 979-5700
Concord *(G-4205)*

Bernhardt Furniture Company..... F 828 759-6652
Lenoir *(G-9584)*

Bernhardt Furniture Company..... F 828 758-9811
Lenoir *(G-9585)*

Bernhardt Furniture Company..... F 828 759-6205
Lenoir *(G-9587)*

Bernhardt Industries Inc............. C 828 758-9811
Lenoir *(G-9588)*

Boggs Collective Inc.................. G 828 398-9701
Asheville *(G-569)*

Bookcase Shop........................... G 919 683-1922
Durham *(G-4972)*

Bradington-Young LLC................ C 276 656-3335
Cherryville *(G-3862)*

Brown Cabinet Co...................... G 704 933-2731
Kannapolis *(G-9113)*

Cabinet Makers Inc.................... E 704 876-2808
Statesville *(G-14769)*

Carolina Business Furn Inc......... A 336 431-9400
Archdale *(G-272)*

Carolina Furniture Mfrs Inc........ G 336 873-7355
Seagrove *(G-14236)*

Carolina Woodcraft LLC............. G 919 585-2563
Clayton *(G-3961)*

Carrington Court Inc.................. G 828 396-1049
Granite Falls *(G-6727)*

PRODUCT SECTION

FURNITURE: Couches, Sofa/Davenport, Upholstered Wood Frames

Carroll Russell Mfg Inc.......................... E 919 779-2273
 Raleigh *(G-12604)*

Century Furniture LLC......................... D 828 326-8410
 Hickory *(G-7975)*

Century Furniture LLC......................... C 828 326-8201
 Hickory *(G-7976)*

Century Furniture LLC......................... D 828 326-8535
 Hickory *(G-7977)*

Century Furniture LLC......................... G 828 326-8300
 Hickory *(G-7981)*

Century Furniture LLC......................... G 336 889-8286
 High Point *(G-8292)*

Chf Industries Inc................................ E 212 951-7800
 Charlotte *(G-2473)*

Chris Isom Inc..................................... F 336 629-0240
 Asheboro *(G-415)*

Classic Leather Inc.............................. B 828 328-2046
 Conover *(G-4436)*

Councill Company LLC......................... C 336 859-2155
 Denton *(G-4731)*

Craftmaster Furniture Inc..................... A 828 632-8127
 Hiddenite *(G-8215)*

Cv Industries Inc................................. C 828 328-1851
 Hickory *(G-8001)*

Davis Furniture Industries Inc................ C 336 889-2009
 High Point *(G-8319)*

Design Workshop Incorporated.............. F 910 293-7329
 Warsaw *(G-15666)*

Drexel Heritage Furnishings.................. G 828 391-6400
 Lenoir *(G-9605)*

Easyglass Inc...................................... E 336 786-1800
 Mount Airy *(G-11505)*

Ethan Allen Retail Inc.......................... E 828 428-9361
 Maiden *(G-10107)*

Fairfield Chair Company....................... E 828 785-5571
 Lenoir *(G-9609)*

Fairfield Chair Company....................... C 828 758-5571
 Lenoir *(G-9610)*

Fulfords Restorations........................... G 252 243-7727
 Wilson *(G-16500)*

Furniture Company.............................. G 910 686-1937
 Wilmington *(G-16225)*

G A Lankford Construction.................... G 828 254-2467
 Alexander *(G-118)*

Goodson Enterprises Inc...................... G 410 303-5053
 Candler *(G-1581)*

Guy Chaddock and Company LLC......... C 828 584-0664
 Morganton *(G-11217)*

H & H Furniture Mfrs Inc....................... C 336 873-7245
 Seagrove *(G-14239)*

Hancock & Moore LLC......................... C 828 495-8235
 Taylorsville *(G-15145)*

Hdm Furniture Industries Inc................. A 800 349-4579
 Hickory *(G-8039)*

Hdm Furniture Industries Inc................. C 336 882-8135
 Hickory *(G-8040)*

Hfi Wind Down Inc............................... C 828 430-3355
 Morganton *(G-11221)*

Hickory Chair Company........................ D 800 225-0265
 Hickory *(G-8046)*

HM Frame Company Inc....................... E 828 428-3354
 Newton *(G-11940)*

Hollingswrth Cbnets Intrors LL.............. F 910 251-1490
 Castle Hayne *(G-1952)*

Home Meridian Group LLC................... D 336 819-7200
 High Point *(G-8399)*

Home Meridian Holdings Inc.................. C 336 887-1985
 High Point *(G-8400)*

Ibolili Natural Fibers............................. G 866 834-9857
 Greensboro *(G-7109)*

Jalco Inc... G 336 434-5909
 Trinity *(G-15347)*

Johnston Casuals Furniture Inc.............. D 336 838-5178
 North Wilkesboro *(G-12018)*

Kenzie Layne Company........................ G 704 485-2282
 Locust *(G-9961)*

Kincaid Furniture Company Inc.............. D 828 728-3261
 Hudson *(G-8773)*

Kolcraft Enterprises Inc........................ C 910 944-9345
 Aberdeen *(G-10)*

Kustom Kraft Wdwrks Mt Airy In............ G 336 786-2831
 Mount Airy *(G-11533)*

Lacquer Craft Hospitality Inc.................. C 336 822-8086
 High Point *(G-8428)*

Leisure Craft Holdings LLC................... D 828 693-8241
 Flat Rock *(G-5967)*

Leisure Craft Inc.................................. C 828 693-8241
 Flat Rock *(G-5968)*

Linwood Inc.. F 336 300-8307
 Lexington *(G-9750)*

Magnussen Home Furnishings Inc......... G 336 841-4424
 Greensboro *(G-7178)*

Martin Obrien Cabinetmaker.................. G 336 773-1334
 Winston Salem *(G-16802)*

Michael Parker Cabinetry...................... G 919 833-5117
 Raleigh *(G-13024)*

Murrah Woodcraft LLC......................... G 919 302-3661
 Bahama *(G-866)*

Nobscot Construction Co Inc................. G 919 929-2075
 Chapel Hill *(G-2048)*

Ofs Brands Inc.................................... F 800 763-0212
 High Point *(G-8470)*

One Furniture Group Corp..................... G 336 235-0221
 Greensboro *(G-7232)*

Phoenix Home Furnishings Inc............... C
 High Point *(G-8480)*

Precast Terrazzo Entps Inc................... E 919 231-6200
 Raleigh *(G-13132)*

Precision Materials LLC........................ F 828 632-8851
 Taylorsville *(G-15159)*

Quality Contemporary Furniture............. G 919 758-7277
 Raleigh *(G-13163)*

Robert Bergelin Company..................... E 828 437-6409
 Morganton *(G-11246)*

Royal Colony Furniture Inc................... G 336 472-8833
 Thomasville *(G-15272)*

Ruskin Inc... F 828 324-6500
 Hickory *(G-8143)*

Shelfgenie... G 704 705-0005
 Charlotte *(G-3540)*

Shelfgenie Coastal Carolinas................. G 910 547-9595
 Wilmington *(G-16402)*

Sherrill Furniture Company.................... B 828 322-2640
 Hickory *(G-8149)*

South Mountain Crafts.......................... G 828 433-2607
 Morganton *(G-11255)*

Southern Finishing Company Inc............ F 336 573-3741
 Stoneville *(G-14967)*

Southwood Furniture Corp..................... D 828 465-1776
 Hickory *(G-8165)*

Stanley Furniture Company LLC............. C 336 884-7700
 High Point *(G-8550)*

Stone Marble Co Inc............................. G 773 227-1161
 Thomasville *(G-15285)*

Style Upholstering Inc.......................... G 828 322-4882
 Hickory *(G-8171)*

Sullivan Workshop LLC......................... G 704 560-9900
 Charlotte *(G-3647)*

Superior Wood Products Inc.................. F 336 472-2237
 Thomasville *(G-15286)*

Sutter Street Manufacturing................... C 828 459-5598
 Claremont *(G-3940)*

Tatum Galleries Inc.............................. G 828 963-6466
 Banner Elk *(G-904)*

Thayer Coggin Inc............................... D 336 841-6000
 High Point *(G-8566)*

Thayer Coggin Furniture....................... G 336 841-6000
 High Point *(G-8567)*

Tiger Mountain Woodworks Inc.............. E 828 526-5577
 Highlands *(G-8618)*

Treeforms Inc..................................... E 336 292-8998
 Greensboro *(G-7409)*

Troutman Careconnect Corp.................. F 704 838-9389
 Troutman *(G-15394)*

Tsai Winddown Inc............................... E 704 873-3106
 Statesville *(G-14919)*

Turning Pges Pctrial Heirlooms............. G 704 634-2911
 Charlotte *(G-3740)*

Unigel Inc... G 828 228-2095
 Hickory *(G-8195)*

Universal Furniture Intl Inc.................... G 828 241-3191
 Claremont *(G-3941)*

Uwharrie Chair Company LLC............... G 336 431-2055
 High Point *(G-8587)*

Vaughan-Bassett Furn Co Inc................ A 336 835-2670
 Elkin *(G-5631)*

Vaughan-Bassett Furn Co Inc................ A 336 889-9111
 High Point *(G-8589)*

WB Frames Inc................................... G 828 459-2147
 Hickory *(G-8207)*

We Organize You LLC.......................... G 919 773-8990
 Apex *(G-258)*

Willow Creek Furniture Inc.................... G 336 889-0076
 High Point *(G-8604)*

Winston Concept Furniture.................... G 336 472-7839
 Thomasville *(G-15302)*

Wise Living Inc.................................... F 336 991-5346
 High Point *(G-8606)*

Wood Country Creations LLC................ G 704 545-5966
 Mint Hill *(G-10549)*

Wood N Things.................................... G 910 990-4448
 Clinton *(G-4119)*

Woodsmiths Company.......................... F 406 626-3102
 Lenoir *(G-9661)*

Xylem Inc.. G 919 772-4126
 Garner *(G-6328)*

Yorkshire House Inc............................. G 336 869-9714
 High Point *(G-8609)*

Yukon Inc... E 919 366-2001
 Wendell *(G-15926)*

FURNITURE: Chairs, Household, Metal

Powder River Technologies Inc.............. G 828 465-2894
 Newton *(G-11961)*

FURNITURE: Chairs, Office Wood

Carolina House Furniture Inc................ E 828 459-7400
 Claremont *(G-3903)*

Davis Furniture Industries Inc................ C 336 889-2009
 High Point *(G-8319)*

High Point Furniture Inds Inc................. D 336 431-7101
 High Point *(G-8391)*

Thomasville Upholstery Inc.................... C 828 345-6225
 Hickory *(G-8180)*

FURNITURE: Church

Gram Furniture.................................... G 828 241-2836
 Claremont *(G-3928)*

FURNITURE: Couches, Sofa/Davenport, Upholstered Wood Frames

4 Seasons Furniture Indust LLC............. F 336 873-7245
 Seagrove *(G-14231)*

Bernhardt Furniture Company................ C 828 758-9811
 Lenoir *(G-9586)*

Employee Codes: A=Over 500 employees, B=251-500
C=101-250, D=51-100, E=20-50, F=10-19, G=1-9

FURNITURE: Couches, Sofa/Davenport, Upholstered Wood Frames

Contemporary Furnishings Corp........... D 704 633-8000
  Salisbury *(G-13946)*
Craftmaster Furniture Inc................... A 828 632-8127
  Hiddenite *(G-8215)*
Craftmaster Furniture Inc................... B 828 632-9786
  Hiddenite *(G-8214)*
E J Victor Inc................................... C 828 437-1991
  Morganton *(G-11210)*
Framewright Inc................................ F 828 459-2284
  Conover *(G-4457)*
H W S Company Inc........................... B 828 322-8624
  Hickory *(G-8037)*
HM Liquidation Inc............................ G 828 495-8235
  Hickory *(G-8058)*
Joseph Halker................................... G 336 769-4734
  Winston Salem *(G-16772)*
King Hickory Furniture Company......... G 828 324-0472
  Hickory *(G-8075)*
King Hickory Furniture Company......... C 828 322-6025
  Hickory *(G-8076)*
Lee Industries LLC............................ C 828 464-8318
  Newton *(G-11948)*
Lee Industries LLC............................ B 828 464-8318
  Conover *(G-4470)*
N Style Living Inc............................. G 336 938-4014
  High Point *(G-8461)*
Sherrill Furniture Company................ B 828 322-2640
  Hickory *(G-8149)*
Southwood Furniture Corp................. D 828 465-1776
  Hickory *(G-8165)*
Temple Inc....................................... D 828 428-8031
  Maiden *(G-10119)*
Thomasville Upholstery Inc................ C 828 345-6225
  Hickory *(G-8180)*
Vanguard Furniture Co Inc................. B 828 328-5601
  Conover *(G-4510)*

FURNITURE: Dining Room, Wood

Bernhardt Furniture Company............ C 828 758-9811
  Lenoir *(G-9586)*
Designmaster Furniture Inc................ E 828 324-7992
  Hickory *(G-8008)*
E J Victor Inc................................... C 828 437-1991
  Morganton *(G-11210)*
Universal Furniture Limited................ D 336 822-8888
  High Point *(G-8586)*

FURNITURE: Fiberglass & Plastic

Built To Last NC LLC......................... F 252 232-0055
  Moyock *(G-11693)*
Keter Us Inc..................................... D 704 263-1967
  Stanley *(G-14699)*
Selenis North America LLC................. G 210 380-2723
  Fayetteville *(G-5914)*

FURNITURE: Garden, Exc Wood, Metal, Stone Or Concrete

Joseph Sotanski............................... E 407 324-6187
  Marion *(G-10155)*
Riverwood Inc................................... E 336 956-3034
  Lexington *(G-9774)*

FURNITURE: Hotel

Contemporary Furnishings Corp........... D 704 633-8000
  Salisbury *(G-13946)*
Distinction Hospitality Inc.................. F 336 875-3043
  High Point *(G-8325)*
Iv-S Metal Stamping Inc..................... E 336 861-2100
  Archdale *(G-286)*
Lee Industries LLC............................ B 828 464-8318
  Conover *(G-4470)*

Neil Allen Industries Inc..................... G 336 887-6500
  High Point *(G-8465)*

FURNITURE: Household, Metal

Biologics Inc.................................... G 919 546-9810
  Raleigh *(G-12558)*
Creative Metal and Wood Inc.............. F 336 475-9400
  Colfax *(G-4145)*
Leisure Craft Holdings LLC................. D 828 693-8241
  Flat Rock *(G-5967)*
Leisure Craft Inc............................... C 828 693-8241
  Flat Rock *(G-5968)*
Stiles Mfg Co Inc.............................. G 910 592-6344
  Clinton *(G-4113)*
Timmerman Manufacturing Inc............ F 828 464-1778
  Conover *(G-4505)*

FURNITURE: Household, Upholstered, Exc Wood Or Metal

Arnold B Cochrane Inc....................... G 336 294-8038
  Greensboro *(G-6815)*
Bull City Designs LLC........................ E 919 908-6252
  Durham *(G-4986)*
Creative Metal and Wood Inc.............. F 336 475-9400
  Colfax *(G-4145)*
French Heritage Inc........................... F 336 882-3565
  High Point *(G-8358)*

FURNITURE: Juvenile, Upholstered On Wood Frames

Kolcraft Enterprises Inc...................... C 910 944-9345
  Aberdeen *(G-10)*

FURNITURE: Laboratory

Kewaunee Scientific Corp................... A 704 873-7202
  Statesville *(G-14831)*

FURNITURE: Lawn, Exc Wood, Metal, Stone Or Concrete

Suncast Corporation.......................... E 704 274-5394
  Huntersville *(G-8902)*

FURNITURE: Living Room, Upholstered On Wood Frames

Berkeley Home Furniture LLC.............. G 336 882-0012
  High Point *(G-8271)*
Cedar Rock Home Furnishings............. G 828 396-2361
  Hudson *(G-8767)*
Cotton Belt Inc................................. D 252 689-6847
  Greenville *(G-7509)*
Hughes Furniture Inds Inc.................. C 336 498-8700
  Randleman *(G-13473)*
Key City Furniture Company Inc.......... C 336 818-1161
  Wilkesboro *(G-16035)*
March Furniture Manufacturing Inc...... C 336 824-4413
  Ramseur *(G-13447)*
Masterfield Furniture Co Inc............... E 828 632-8535
  Taylorsville *(G-15151)*
McCreary Modern Inc........................ B 828 464-6465
  Newton *(G-11951)*
Schnadig Corporation........................ E 336 389-5200
  Greensboro *(G-7327)*
Select Furniture Company Inc............. F 336 886-3572
  High Point *(G-8522)*
Swaim Inc.. C 336 885-6131
  High Point *(G-8559)*
Universal Furniture Intl Inc................. C 828 464-0911
  Conover *(G-4509)*
Violino USA Ltd................................ E 336 889-6623
  High Point *(G-8594)*

FURNITURE: Mattresses & Foundations

Comfort Sleep LLC............................ F 336 267-5853
  Thomasville *(G-15205)*
L C Industries Inc............................. C 919 596-8277
  Fayetteville *(G-5857)*
L C Industries Inc............................. C 919 596-8277
  Durham *(G-5185)*
Lin Wggins Mem Schlarship Fund......... G 919 749-2340
  Fuquay Varina *(G-6209)*
Mattress Warehouse........................... G 919 463-0329
  Cary *(G-1821)*
Tempur Sealy International Inc............ E 336 861-2900
  Trinity *(G-15361)*

FURNITURE: Mattresses, Box & Bedsprings

Affordable Bedding Inc...................... G 828 254-5555
  Asheville *(G-516)*
Arden Companies LLC........................ D 919 258-3081
  Sanford *(G-14088)*
Bjmf Inc... E 704 554-6333
  Charlotte *(G-2318)*
Carolina Mattress Guild Inc................ D 336 841-8529
  Thomasville *(G-15198)*
Caudle Bedding Supplies.................... G 336 498-2600
  Randleman *(G-13458)*
Culp Inc.. E 336 885-2800
  Stokesdale *(G-14940)*
Iredell Fiber Inc............................... D 704 878-0884
  Statesville *(G-14822)*
Jones Frame Inc................................ E 336 434-2531
  High Point *(G-8417)*
Leggett & Platt.................................. E 336 357-3641
  Lexington *(G-9746)*
Leggett & Platt Incorporated.............. C 336 379-7777
  Greensboro *(G-7166)*
Leggett & Platt Incorporated.............. D 336 884-4306
  High Point *(G-8429)*
Leggett & Platt Incorporated.............. F 336 622-0121
  Liberty *(G-9819)*
Leggett & Platt Incorporated.............. D 828 322-6855
  Conover *(G-4471)*
Leggett & Platt Incorporated.............. D 336 889-2600
  High Point *(G-8430)*
Mattress Firm.................................... G 910 868-0950
  Fayetteville *(G-5870)*
Mattress Firm.................................... G 252 443-1259
  Rocky Mount *(G-13711)*
Reliable Bedding Company................. G 336 886-7036
  High Point *(G-8508)*
Reliable Quilting Company.................. G 336 886-7036
  High Point *(G-8509)*
Stn Cushion Company........................ D 336 476-9100
  Thomasville *(G-15284)*
Timeless Bedding Inc......................... G 336 472-6603
  Lexington *(G-9794)*
Vaughan-Bassett Furn Co Inc.............. A 336 835-2670
  Elkin *(G-5631)*

FURNITURE: Mattresses, Innerspring Or Box Spring

Dilworth Mattress Company Inc........... G 704 333-6564
  Charlotte *(G-2638)*
Kingsdown Incorporated..................... E 919 563-3531
  Mebane *(G-10415)*
Ohio-Sealy Mattress Mfg Co................ C 336 861-3500
  Trinity *(G-15350)*
Reliable Bedding Company................. E 336 883-0648
  Archdale *(G-297)*
Riverside Mattress Co Inc................... E 910 483-0461
  Fayetteville *(G-5906)*

PRODUCT SECTION

FURNITURE: Upholstered

Royale Komfort Bedding Inc .... F 828 632-5631
 Taylorsville *(G-15163)*

Sealy Corporation .... C 336 861-3500
 Trinity *(G-15355)*

Sealy Mattress Co SW Virginia .... G 336 861-3500
 Trinity *(G-15356)*

Sealy Mattress Company .... C 336 861-3500
 Trinity *(G-15357)*

Spring Air Mattress Corp .... D 336 272-1141
 Greensboro *(G-7359)*

Ssb Manufacturing Company .... D 704 596-4935
 Charlotte *(G-3615)*

FURNITURE: Novelty, Wood

Artisans Guild Incorporated .... G 336 841-4140
 High Point *(G-8256)*

Riverview Cabinet & Supply Inc .... G 336 228-1486
 Burlington *(G-1486)*

FURNITURE: Office, Exc Wood

A C Furniture Company Inc .... B 336 623-3430
 Eden *(G-5484)*

Abercrombie Textiles I LLC .... F 704 487-1245
 Shelby *(G-14282)*

Baypointe Partners LLC .... G 336 882-5200
 Archdale *(G-269)*

Bernhardt Furniture Company .... F 828 759-6245
 Lenoir *(G-9583)*

Bernhardt Furniture Company .... F 828 759-6205
 Lenoir *(G-9587)*

Bernhardt Industries Inc .... C 828 758-9811
 Lenoir *(G-9588)*

Buzzispace Inc .... G 336 821-3150
 Winston Salem *(G-16642)*

Coriander Designs .... G 425 402-8001
 Lincolnton *(G-9884)*

Davidson House Inc .... F 704 791-0171
 Davidson *(G-4670)*

Davis Furniture Industries Inc .... C 336 889-2009
 High Point *(G-8319)*

Delve Interiors LLC .... C 336 274-4661
 Greensboro *(G-6968)*

Desmond Office Furniture Inc .... F 828 235-9400
 Canton *(G-1613)*

Frazier Holdings LLC .... G 919 868-8651
 Clayton *(G-3978)*

Haworth Inc .... E 828 328-5600
 Conover *(G-4461)*

Images of America Inc .... D 336 475-7106
 Thomasville *(G-15237)*

Intensa Inc .... F 336 884-4003
 High Point *(G-8412)*

Kn Furniture Inc .... E 336 953-3259
 Ramseur *(G-13444)*

Old Hickory Tannery Inc .... E 828 465-6599
 Newton *(G-11955)*

Sbfi-North America Inc .... F 828 236-3993
 Asheville *(G-764)*

Studio Tk LLC .... E 919 464-2920
 Clayton *(G-4014)*

Unique Office Solutions Inc .... F 336 854-0900
 Greensboro *(G-7430)*

Wheatstone Corporation .... D 252 638-7000
 New Bern *(G-11855)*

FURNITURE: Office, Wood

A C Furniture Company Inc .... B 336 623-3430
 Eden *(G-5484)*

Amcase Inc .... E 336 784-5992
 High Point *(G-8244)*

Baypointe Partners LLC .... G 336 882-5200
 Archdale *(G-269)*

Bernhardt Furniture Company .... F 828 759-6245
 Lenoir *(G-9583)*

Bernhardt Furniture Company .... F 828 758-9811
 Lenoir *(G-9585)*

Bernhardt Furniture Company .... F 828 759-6205
 Lenoir *(G-9587)*

Bernhardt Industries Inc .... C 828 758-9811
 Lenoir *(G-9588)*

Boss Design US Inc .... G 844 353-7834
 High Point *(G-8275)*

Bull City Designs LLC .... E 919 908-6252
 Durham *(G-4986)*

Carolina Furniture Mfrs Inc .... G 336 873-7455
 Seagrove *(G-14236)*

Century Furniture LLC .... C 828 267-8739
 Hickory *(G-7983)*

Classic Leather Inc .... B 828 328-2046
 Conover *(G-4436)*

Comm-Kab Inc .... F 336 873-8787
 Asheboro *(G-417)*

Corilam Fabricating Co .... E 336 993-2371
 Kernersville *(G-9182)*

Darran Furniture Inds Inc .... C 828 861-2400
 High Point *(G-8318)*

Delve Interiors LLC .... C 336 274-4661
 Greensboro *(G-6968)*

Geiger International Inc .... F 828 324-6500
 Hildebran *(G-8623)*

Hancock & Moore LLC .... C 828 495-8235
 Taylorsville *(G-15145)*

Harris House Furn Inds Inc .... E 336 431-2802
 Archdale *(G-282)*

Haworth Inc .... E 828 328-5600
 Conover *(G-4461)*

Hickory Business Furniture LLC .... B 828 328-2064
 Hickory *(G-8045)*

Idx Impressions LLC .... C 703 550-6902
 Washington *(G-15711)*

Ie Furniture Inc .... E 336 475-5050
 Archdale *(G-284)*

Jasper Seating Company Inc .... C 704 528-4506
 Troutman *(G-15384)*

Looc Studio Inc .... G 336 472-6877
 Newton *(G-11950)*

Michael Parker Cabinetry .... G 919 833-5117
 Raleigh *(G-13024)*

Ofm LLC .... D 919 303-6389
 Holly Springs *(G-8709)*

Parker Southern Inc .... F 336 428-3506
 Maiden *(G-10115)*

Precision Materials LLC .... F 828 632-8851
 Taylorsville *(G-15159)*

Precision Mtls - Blue Rdge LLC .... G 828 322-7990
 Hickory *(G-8119)*

Prestige Millwork Inc .... F 910 428-2360
 Star *(G-14722)*

Professinal Sales Associates .... F 336 210-2756
 High Point *(G-8500)*

Sbfi-North America Inc .... F 828 236-3993
 Asheville *(G-764)*

Sdv Office Systems LLC .... F 844 968-9500
 Fletcher *(G-6037)*

Sdv Office Systems LLC .... G 844 968-9500
 Asheville *(G-767)*

Triune Business Furniture Inc .... G 336 884-8341
 High Point *(G-8578)*

Upholstery Designs Hickory Inc .... E 828 324-2002
 Hickory *(G-8196)*

Wood Country Creations LLC .... G 704 545-5966
 Mint Hill *(G-10549)*

Xylem Inc .... G 919 772-4196
 Garner *(G-6328)*

FURNITURE: Recliners, Upholstered On Wood Frames

Joerns Healthcare Parent LLC .... B 800 966-6662
 Charlotte *(G-3027)*

FURNITURE: School

Artisans Guild Incorporated .... G 336 841-4140
 High Point *(G-8256)*

Custom Educational Furn LLC .... F 800 255-9189
 Taylorsville *(G-15137)*

Interior Wood Specialties Inc .... E 336 431-0068
 High Point *(G-8413)*

Krueger International Inc .... E 336 434-5011
 High Point *(G-8426)*

Precision Materials LLC .... F 828 632-8851
 Taylorsville *(G-15159)*

FURNITURE: Sleep

Hill-Rom Inc .... B 919 854-3600
 Cary *(G-1784)*

Roadmster Trck Conversions Inc .... G 252 412-3980
 Grifton *(G-7602)*

FURNITURE: Stadium

Artisan LLC .... G 855 582-3539
 Concord *(G-4199)*

Ken Staley Co Inc .... G 336 685-4294
 Franklinville *(G-6169)*

FURNITURE: Storage Chests, Household, Wood

Liberty Hse Utility Buildings .... G 828 209-3390
 Horse Shoe *(G-8740)*

FURNITURE: Table Tops, Marble

Nova Enterprises Inc .... E 828 687-8770
 Arden *(G-357)*

Russell Custom Stone LLC .... G 336 859-5755
 New London *(G-11877)*

Trade Venture Stones LLC .... G 919 803-3923
 Knightdale *(G-9431)*

Web-Don Incorporated .... E 800 532-0434
 Charlotte *(G-3800)*

Woodsmiths Company .... F 406 626-3102
 Lenoir *(G-9661)*

FURNITURE: Tables, Household, Metal

Swaim Inc .... C 336 885-6131
 High Point *(G-8559)*

FURNITURE: Tables, Office, Exc Wood

Con-Tab Inc .... F 336 476-0104
 Thomasville *(G-15206)*

FURNITURE: Tables, Office, Wood

Evelyn T Burney .... G 336 473-9794
 Rocky Mount *(G-13697)*

Ullmanique Inc .... G 336 885-5111
 High Point *(G-8583)*

FURNITURE: Upholstered

A C Furniture Company Inc .... B 336 623-3430
 Eden *(G-5484)*

AB New Beginnings Inc .... D 828 465-6953
 Conover *(G-4412)*

American of High Point Inc .... E 336 431-1513
 High Point *(G-8247)*

Amor Furniture and Bedding LLC .... F 336 795-0044
 Liberty *(G-9806)*

Archdale Furniture Distributor .... G 336 431-1081
 Archdale *(G-267)*

FURTHITURE: Upholstered

Baker Interiors Furniture Co.............. G 336 431-9115
High Point (G-8263)

Bassett Furniture Inds Inc.................... D 828 465-7700
Newton (G-11915)

Bernhardt Furniture Company............ F 828 572-4664
Lenoir (G-9582)

Bernhardt Furniture Company............ F 828 759-6652
Lenoir (G-9584)

Bernhardt Furniture Company............ F 828 758-9811
Lenoir (G-9585)

Bernhardt Furniture Company............ F 828 759-6205
Lenoir (G-9587)

Bernhardt Industries Inc..................... C 828 758-9811
Lenoir (G-9588)

Blackstone Furniture Inds Inc............. F 910 428-2833
Ether (G-5690)

Bradington-Young LLC......................... C 276 656-3335
Cherryville (G-3862)

Burrough Furniture................................ G 336 841-3129
Archdale (G-271)

Cargill & Pendleton Inc........................ E 336 882-5510
High Point (G-8283)

Carolina Chair Inc................................ F 828 459-1330
Conover (G-4430)

Carolina Mills Incorporated................ B 828 428-9911
Maiden (G-10102)

Carolina Tape & Supply Corp............. E 828 322-3991
Hickory (G-7968)

Carrington Court Inc............................ G 828 396-1049
Granite Falls (G-6727)

Century Furniture LLC........................ C 828 326-8201
Hickory (G-7976)

Century Furniture LLC........................ E 828 326-8410
Hickory (G-7979)

Century Furniture LLC........................ E 828 326-8650
Hickory (G-7980)

Century Furniture LLC........................ G 828 326-8300
Hickory (G-7981)

Chair Man.. G 610 809-0871
Manteo (G-10127)

Charles Stewart Co............................. C 828 322-9464
Hickory (G-7984)

Chateau DAx USA Ltd.......................... G 336 885-9777
High Point (G-8294)

Classic Leather Inc............................. B 828 328-2046
Conover (G-4436)

Contract Seating Inc........................... G 828 322-6662
Hickory (G-7994)

Councill Company LLC........................ C 336 859-2155
Denton (G-4731)

Country At Home Furniture Inc.......... F 828 464-7498
Newton (G-11926)

Cox Manufacturing Company Inc..... E 828 397-4123
Hickory (G-7997)

Craymer McElwee Holdings Inc......... F 828 326-6100
Hickory (G-7998)

Creations By Taylor.............................. G 410 269-6430
Mount Pleasant (G-11673)

Custom Designs and Upholstery........ F 336 882-1516
Thomasville (G-15208)

Cv Industries Inc.................................. G 828 328-1851
Hickory (G-8001)

Daniels Woodcarving Co Inc.............. F 828 632-7336
Taylorsville (G-15140)

Design Theory LLC.............................. F 336 912-0155
High Point (G-8322)

Dexter Inc.. E 828 459-7904
Claremont (G-3919)

Dexter Inc.. G 919 510-5050
Raleigh (G-12681)

Dfp Inc... D 336 841-3028
High Point (G-8323)

Distinctive Furniture Inc..................... G 828 754-3947
Lenoir (G-9604)

Domenicks Furniture Mfr LLC............. E 336 442-3348
High Point (G-8329)

Elite Furniture Mfg Inc......................... G 336 882-0406
High Point (G-8340)

England Inc... E 336 861-5266
High Point (G-8345)

Friendship Upholstery Co Inc............ E 828 632-9836
Taylorsville (G-15143)

Geiger International Inc..................... F 828 324-6500
Hildebran (G-8623)

Golden Rctangle Enteprises Inc........ G 828 389-3336
Hayesville (G-7766)

Hancock & Moore LLC......................... E 828 495-8235
Taylorsville (G-15145)

Hancock & Moore LLC......................... D 828 495-8235
Taylorsville (G-15144)

Hdm Furniture Industries Inc............. E 336 812-4434
High Point (G-8379)

Hester Enterprises Inc........................ E 704 865-4480
Gastonia (G-6416)

Hfi Wind Down Inc............................... E 828 438-5767
Morganton (G-11220)

HM Frame Company Inc...................... E 828 428-3354
Newton (G-11940)

Huddle Furniture Inc........................... E 828 874-8888
Valdese (G-15448)

Huntington House Inc......................... E 828 495-4400
Taylorsville (G-15147)

Huntington House Inc......................... E 828 495-4400
Hickory (G-8060)

Indiana Chair Frame Company........... E 574 825-9355
Liberty (G-9817)

Intensa Inc.. F 336 884-4003
High Point (G-8412)

Isenhour Furniture Company.............. D 828 632-8849
Taylorsville (G-15149)

Jarrett Brothers................................... G 828 433-8036
Morganton (G-11225)

Kincaid Furniture Company Inc......... D 828 728-3261
Hudson (G-8773)

King Hickory Furniture Company...... G 336 841-6140
High Point (G-8424)

Kn Furniture Inc................................... E 336 953-3259
Ramseur (G-13444)

Lancer Incorporated............................ C 910 428-2181
Star (G-14719)

Lazar Industries LLC........................... C 919 742-9303
Siler City (G-14420)

Lazar Industries East Inc................... F 919 742-9303
Siler City (G-14421)

Lexington Furniture Inds Inc.............. C 336 474-5300
Thomasville (G-15241)

Linrene Furniture Inc.......................... G 919 742-9391
Siler City (G-14422)

Lloyds Chatham Ltd Partnership....... F 919 742-4692
High Point (G-8433)

Lodging By Liberty Inc....................... C 336 622-2201
Siler City (G-14423)

M & M Frame Company Inc................ G 336 859-8166
Denton (G-4745)

Marquis Contract Corporation........... E 336 884-8200
High Point (G-8442)

Mastercraft Lamp Intl Furn................. G 336 882-1535
High Point (G-8449)

McKinley Leather Hickory Inc............ E 828 459-2884
Claremont (G-3931)

Minhas Furniture House Inc............... E 910 898-0808
Robbins (G-13601)

Mitchell Gold Co LLC.......................... D 828 632-7916
Taylorsville (G-15152)

Moores Upholstering Interiors........... G 704 240-8393
Lincolnton (G-9909)

NC Custom Leather Inc....................... F 828 404-2973
Conover (G-4474)

Nobscot Construction Co Inc............. G 919 929-2075
Chapel Hill (G-2048)

North Carolina Lumber Company...... F 336 498-6600
Randleman (G-13481)

O Henry House Ltd.............................. E 336 431-5350
Archdale (G-294)

Old Hickory Tannery Inc..................... E 828 465-6599
Newton (G-11955)

Paladin Industries Inc......................... D 828 635-0448
Hiddenite (G-8225)

Parker Southern Inc............................ F 828 428-3506
Maiden (G-10115)

Plat LLC... F 828 358-4564
Granite Falls (G-6750)

R & D Weaving Inc............................... F 828 248-1910
Ellenboro (G-5638)

Rbc Inc... G 336 889-7573
High Point (G-8506)

Rbc Inc... C 336 889-7333
Sophia (G-14521)

Restaurant Furniture Inc..................... F 828 459-9992
Claremont (G-3937)

Rhf Investments Inc............................. G 828 326-8350
Hickory (G-8135)

Richard Shew.. F 828 781-3294
Conover (G-4491)

Rowes... G 828 241-2609
Catawba (G-1967)

Rufco Inc... G 919 829-1332
Wake Forest (G-15585)

S Dorsett Upholstery Inc.................... G 336 472-7076
Thomasville (G-15275)

Seam-Craft Inc..................................... F 336 861-4156
High Point (G-8521)

Sherrill Furniture Company................ G 828 322-8624
Hickory (G-8147)

Sherrill Furniture Company................ F 828 328-5241
Hickory (G-8148)

Sherrill Furniture Company................ G 336 884-0974
High Point (G-8523)

Sherrill Furniture Company................ G 828 437-2256
Morganton (G-11252)

Sherrill Furniture Company................ D 828 465-0844
Newton (G-11967)

Sides Furniture Inc.............................. G 336 869-5509
High Point (G-8524)

Simplicity Sofas Inc............................ G 800 813-2889
High Point (G-8531)

Southandenglish LLC.......................... G 336 888-8333
High Point (G-8543)

Stone Marble Co Inc............................ G 773 227-1161
Thomasville (G-15285)

Superior Wood Products Inc.............. F 336 472-2237
Thomasville (G-15286)

Taylor King Furniture Inc................... C 828 632-7731
Taylorsville (G-15170)

Tb Arhaus LLC...................................... C 828 465-6953
Conover (G-4503)

TCS Designs Inc................................... F 828 324-9944
Hickory (G-8175)

Theodore Alexander.............................. G 336 689-4178
Greensboro (G-7400)

Tomlinson/Erwin-Lambeth Inc.......... D 336 472-5005
Thomasville (G-15293)

Universal Furniture Intnl Inc............... G 828 241-3191
Claremont (G-3941)

Universal Furniture Limited................ D 336 822-8888
High Point (G-8586)

PRODUCT SECTION

GEARS: Power Transmission, Exc Auto

Upholstery Designs Hickory Inc..................... E 828 324-2002
  Hickory *(G-8196)*
Vaughan-Bassett Furn Co Inc..................... A 336 835-2670
  Elkin *(G-5631)*
Watauga Creek LLC..................... G 828 369-7881
  Franklin *(G-6147)*
Woodmark Originals Inc..................... C 336 841-6409
  High Point *(G-8607)*

FURNITURE: Wicker & Rattan

Acacia Home & Garden Inc..................... F 828 465-1700
  Conover *(G-4413)*
Rbc Inc..................... C 336 889-7333
  Sophia *(G-14521)*

FUSES: Electric

Cooper Bussmann LLC..................... C 252 566-0278
  La Grange *(G-9438)*

GAMES & TOYS: Board Games, Children's & Adults'

Banilla Games Inc..................... G 252 329-7977
  Greenville *(G-7492)*
Cog In Games LLP..................... G 704 763-4609
  Charlotte *(G-2522)*

GAMES & TOYS: Craft & Hobby Kits & Sets

Bougiejones..................... G 704 492-3029
  Charlotte *(G-2340)*
Gracefully Gifted Hands LLC..................... G 845 248-8743
  Raleigh *(G-12812)*
Jasie Blanks LLC..................... F 910 485-0016
  Fayetteville *(G-5846)*
Kenson Parenting Solutions..................... G 919 637-1499
  Wake Forest *(G-15567)*
Personal Xpressionz LLC..................... G 919 587-7462
  Durham *(G-5282)*
Pridgen-Lucas Latisha..................... G 252 360-7866
  Wilson *(G-16523)*
South Mountain Crafts..................... G 828 433-2607
  Morganton *(G-11255)*

GAMES & TOYS: Electronic

Grailgame Inc..................... G 804 517-3102
  Reidsville *(G-13522)*
Wersunsllc..................... G 857 209-8701
  Winston Salem *(G-16969)*

GAMES & TOYS: Erector Sets

All Signs & Graphics LLC..................... G 910 323-3115
  Fayetteville *(G-5757)*

GARBAGE CONTAINERS: Plastic

All Source Security Cont Cal..................... F 704 504-9908
  Charlotte *(G-2156)*
Allstar Waste Systems Inc..................... G 252 343-5156
  Rocky Mount *(G-13680)*
County of Alexander..................... E 828 632-1101
  Taylorsville *(G-15136)*
Dons Disposal..................... G 919 542-2208
  Pittsboro *(G-12341)*
Duramax Holdings LLC..................... C 704 588-9191
  Charlotte *(G-2659)*
Robbins Beane Inc..................... G 336 953-5919
  Asheboro *(G-474)*
Schaefer Systems International Inc..................... C 704 944-4500
  Charlotte *(G-3499)*
Schaefer Systems Intl Inc..................... G 704 944-4500
  Charlotte *(G-3500)*
Schaefer Systems Intl Inc..................... G 704 944-4550
  Charlotte *(G-3501)*

Toter LLC..................... E 704 936-5610
  Charlotte *(G-3711)*
Toter LLC..................... D 800 424-0422
  Statesville *(G-14916)*

GAS & OIL FIELD EXPLORATION SVCS

3d Oil Inc..................... G 609 408-9159
  Swansboro *(G-15041)*
Blackhawk Diversified Svcs Inc..................... G 919 279-5679
  Raleigh *(G-12562)*
BP Oil Corp Distributors..................... G 828 264-8516
  Boone *(G-1181)*
Citi Energy LLC..................... F 336 379-0800
  Greensboro *(G-6910)*
Das Oil Werks LLC..................... G 919 267-5781
  New Hill *(G-11860)*
Energy and Entropy Inc..................... G 919 933-1365
  Chapel Hill *(G-2013)*
EP Nisbet Company..................... F 704 332-7755
  Charlotte *(G-2720)*
Funston Company..................... G 910 383-1425
  Leland *(G-9544)*
Maverick Biofuels..................... G 919 931-1434
  Durham *(G-5211)*
Mpv Morganton Pressu..................... F 828 652-3704
  Marion *(G-10167)*
Onward Energy Holdings LLC..................... G 980 294-0204
  Charlotte *(G-3304)*
Speer Oil Company LLC..................... G 910 947-5494
  Carthage *(G-1667)*
Wr Allen LLC..................... G 704 390-4032
  Charlotte *(G-3829)*

GAS & OIL FIELD SVCS, NEC

Hari Krupa Oil and Gas LLC..................... G 860 805-1704
  Winston Salem *(G-16736)*
Parker Oil Inc..................... G 828 253-7265
  Asheville *(G-722)*

GASES: Acetylene

Airgas Usa LLC..................... F 704 333-5475
  Charlotte *(G-2148)*
Andy-OXY Co Inc..................... E 828 258-0271
  Asheville *(G-518)*

GASES: Indl

Airgas Usa LLC..................... F 704 394-1420
  Charlotte *(G-2147)*
Airgas Usa LLC..................... G 919 544-3773
  Durham *(G-4909)*
Airgas Usa LLC..................... G 919 735-5276
  Goldsboro *(G-6587)*
Airgas Usa LLC..................... F 910 392-2711
  Wilmington *(G-16098)*
Arc3 Gases Inc..................... F 336 275-3333
  Greensboro *(G-6812)*
Arc3 Gases Inc..................... F 704 220-1029
  Monroe *(G-10650)*
Arc3 Gases Inc..................... E 910 892-4016
  Dunn *(G-4851)*
East Coast Oxygen Inc..................... G 828 252-7770
  Asheville *(G-613)*
James Oxygen and Supply Co..................... E 704 322-5438
  Hickory *(G-8071)*
Legacy Biogas LLC..................... G 713 253-9013
  Goldsboro *(G-6629)*

GASES: Nitrogen

Linde Gas & Equipment Inc..................... F 919 380-7411
  Cary *(G-1811)*
Linde Gas & Equipment Inc..................... F 704 587-7096
  Charlotte *(G-3090)*

Linde Gas & Equipment Inc..................... F 866 543-3427
  Whitsett *(G-15995)*
Linde Inc..................... G 910 343-0241
  Wilmington *(G-16302)*
Matheson Tri-Gas Inc..................... F 919 556-6461
  Wake Forest *(G-15571)*

GASES: Oxygen

Linde Gas & Equipment Inc..................... D 919 549-0633
  Durham *(G-5190)*
Messer LLC..................... E 704 583-0313
  Charlotte *(G-3167)*

GASKETS

Carolina Components Group Inc..................... E 919 635-8438
  Durham *(G-5001)*
CGR Products Inc..................... D 336 621-4568
  Greensboro *(G-6901)*
Michael Simmons..................... G 704 298-1103
  Concord *(G-4313)*
Mueller Die Cut Solutions Inc..................... E 704 588-3900
  Charlotte *(G-3213)*
SAS Industries Inc..................... F 631 727-1441
  Elizabeth City *(G-5570)*
Southern Rubber Company Inc..................... E 336 299-2456
  Greensboro *(G-7355)*
T & N Manufacturing Co Inc..................... G 704 788-1418
  Davidson *(G-4698)*
Tim P Krahulec..................... G 919 554-1331
  Wake Forest *(G-15603)*
Universal Rubber Products Inc..................... G 704 483-1249
  Denver *(G-4812)*

GASKETS & SEALING DEVICES

Coltec Industries Inc..................... A 704 731-1500
  Charlotte *(G-2527)*
Enpro Industries Inc..................... C 704 731-1500
  Charlotte *(G-2713)*
Henniges Automotive N Amer Inc..................... D 336 342-9300
  Reidsville *(G-13526)*
Pfaff Molds Ltd Partnership..................... F 704 423-9484
  Charlotte *(G-3334)*

GASOLINE FILLING STATIONS

College Sun Do..................... G 910 521-9189
  Pembroke *(G-12181)*
Murphy USA Inc..................... E 828 758-7055
  Lenoir *(G-9638)*

GASOLINE WHOLESALERS

Euliss Oil Company Inc..................... G 336 622-3055
  Liberty *(G-9813)*
Herrin Bros Coal & Ice Co..................... G 704 332-2193
  Charlotte *(G-2906)*

GEARS

Ketchie-Houston Inc..................... E 704 786-5101
  Concord *(G-4300)*
Tim Conner Enterprises Inc..................... E 704 629-4327
  Bessemer City *(G-1085)*

GEARS & GEAR UNITS: Reduction, Exc Auto

Perfection Gear Inc..................... D 828 253-0000
  Asheville *(G-726)*

GEARS: Power Transmission, Exc Auto

Carolina Keller LLC..................... C 252 237-8181
  Wilson *(G-16484)*
Linamar Forgings Carolina Inc..................... D 252 237-8181
  Wilson *(G-16511)*
Martin Sprocket & Gear Inc..................... F 817 258-3000
  Albemarle *(G-97)*

Employee Codes: A=Over 500 employees, B=251-500
C=101-250, D=51-100, E=20-50, F=10-19, G=1-9

GEARS: Power Transmission, Exc Auto

Martin Sprocket & Gear Inc .... F 704 394-9111
 Charlotte *(G-3133)*

Nord Gear Corporation .... G 888 314-6673
 Charlotte *(G-3266)*

GENERATION EQPT: Electronic

Ametek Electronics Systems .... E 800 645-9721
 Knightdale *(G-9411)*

Equagen Engineers Pllc .... E 919 444-5442
 Raleigh *(G-12744)*

Ifanatic LLC .... G 919 387-6062
 Apex *(G-203)*

Laird Thermal Systems Inc .... E 919 597-7300
 Morrisville *(G-11370)*

North Fork Electric Inc .... G 336 982-4020
 Crumpler *(G-4629)*

Power Integrity Corp .... G 336 379-9773
 Greensboro *(G-7269)*

Powergpu LLC .... F 919 702-6757
 Youngsville *(G-17092)*

Powersecure International Inc .... A 919 556-3056
 Wake Forest *(G-15576)*

Team Manufacturing - E W LLC .... D 336 554-2442
 Youngsville *(G-17105)*

GENERATOR REPAIR SVCS

Allan Drth Sons Gnrtor Sls Svc .... G 828 526-9325
 Highlands *(G-8611)*

Genelect Services Inc .... F 828 255-7999
 Asheville *(G-632)*

GENERATORS SETS: Steam

Catamount Energy Corporation .... F 802 773-6684
 Charlotte *(G-2418)*

GIFT SHOP

A Stitch In Time .... G 828 274-5193
 Asheville *(G-513)*

Burlington Outlet .... G 910 278-3442
 Oak Island *(G-12048)*

Carolina Perfumer Inc .... G 910 295-5600
 Pinehurst *(G-12217)*

James Lammers .... G 252 491-2303
 Powells Point *(G-12398)*

Jkl Inc .... F 252 355-6714
 Greenville *(G-7550)*

Michael S North Wilkesboro Inc .... G 336 838-5964
 North Wilkesboro *(G-12028)*

Oleksynprannyk LLC .... F 704 450-0182
 Mooresville *(G-11043)*

Poppies LLC .... G 704 896-3433
 Huntersville *(G-8879)*

Starflite Companies Inc .... C 252 728-2690
 Beaufort *(G-968)*

GIFT, NOVELTY & SOUVENIR STORES: Gifts & Novelties

Simple & Sentimental LLC .... G 252 320-9458
 Ayden *(G-857)*

GLASS & GLASS CERAMIC PRDTS, PRESSED OR BLOWN: Tableware

Bright Angle LLC .... G 828 771-6966
 Asheville *(G-573)*

GLASS PRDTS, FROM PURCHASED GLASS: Insulating

Press Glass Inc .... D 336 573-2393
 Stoneville *(G-14965)*

GLASS PRDTS, FROM PURCHASED GLASS: Mirrored

Cgmi Acquisition Company LLC .... F 919 533-6123
 Kernersville *(G-9176)*

Gardner Glass Products Inc .... F 336 838-2151
 North Wilkesboro *(G-12009)*

Gardner Glass Products Inc .... C 336 651-9300
 North Wilkesboro *(G-12010)*

Glass Works of Hickory Inc .... G 828 322-2122
 Hickory *(G-8033)*

Lenoir Mirror Company .... C 828 728-3271
 Lenoir *(G-9626)*

Slane O W Glass Co Inc .... F 704 872-4291
 Statesville *(G-14888)*

GLASS PRDTS, FROM PURCHASED GLASS: Windshields

Florida Marine Tanks Inc .... F 305 620-9030
 Henderson *(G-7783)*

GLASS PRDTS, FROM PURCHD GLASS: Strengthened Or Reinforced

PPG Industries Inc .... G 919 772-3093
 Greensboro *(G-7272)*

GLASS PRDTS, PRESSED OR BLOWN: Scientific Glassware

M 5 Scentific Glassblowing Inc .... G 704 663-0101
 Mooresville *(G-11012)*

GLASS PRDTS, PRESSED OR BLOWN: Yarn, Fiberglass

Spt Technology Inc .... F 612 332-1880
 Monroe *(G-10811)*

GLASS, AUTOMOTIVE: Wholesalers

Oldcastle Infrastructure Inc .... E 919 772-6269
 Raleigh *(G-13082)*

GLASS: Broadwoven Fabrics

Nouveau Verre Holdings Inc .... F 336 545-0011
 Greensboro *(G-7224)*

Nvh Inc .... G 336 545-0011
 Greensboro *(G-7228)*

GLASS: Fiber

Corning Incorporated .... F 828 465-0016
 Newton *(G-11925)*

Corning Incorporated .... F 252 316-4500
 Tarboro *(G-15100)*

Corning Incorporated .... F 336 771-8000
 Winston Salem *(G-16662)*

Mateenbar USA Inc .... E 704 662-2005
 Concord *(G-4310)*

Piedmont Well Covers Inc .... F 704 664-8488
 Mount Ulla *(G-11685)*

PPG Industries Inc .... G 919 772-3093
 Greensboro *(G-7272)*

GLASS: Flat

A R Perry Corporation .... F 252 492-6181
 Henderson *(G-7774)*

Corning Incorporated .... D 704 569-6000
 Midland *(G-10464)*

Pilkington .... G 828 357-8043
 Black Mountain *(G-1135)*

Pilkington Group Inc .... G 336 545-0425
 Greensboro *(G-7264)*

Pilkington North America Inc .... E 910 276-5630
 Laurinburg *(G-9492)*

PPG Industries Inc .... G 919 772-3093
 Greensboro *(G-7272)*

GLASS: Leaded

Custom Glass Works Inc .... G 704 597-0290
 Charlotte *(G-2590)*

GLASS: Optical

Optometric Eyecare Center Inc .... G 910 326-3050
 Swansboro *(G-15048)*

GLASS: Pressed & Blown, NEC

Corning Optcal Cmmncations LLC ..... A 336 771-8000
 Winston Salem *(G-16663)*

Easyglass Inc .... E 336 786-1800
 Mount Airy *(G-11505)*

Heraeus Quartz North Amer LLC .... G 910 799-6230
 Wilmington *(G-16250)*

Opticoncepts Inc .... G 828 874-0667
 Morganton *(G-11240)*

PPG-Devold LLC .... E 704 434-2261
 Shelby *(G-14356)*

Preformed Line Products Co .... E 704 983-6161
 Albemarle *(G-99)*

San Kawa LLC .... G 704 982-4527
 Albemarle *(G-103)*

Slane O W Glass Co Inc .... F 704 872-4291
 Statesville *(G-14888)*

Spruce Pine Batch Inc .... G 828 765-9876
 Spruce Pine *(G-14658)*

GLASS: Tempered

Cardinal CT Company .... C 336 719-6857
 Mount Airy *(G-11487)*

GLASSWARE: Laboratory

Norell Inc .... G 828 584-2600
 Morganton *(G-11239)*

Prism Research Glass Inc .... F 919 571-0078
 Raleigh *(G-13145)*

GLOVES: Safety

Gloves-Online Inc .... G 919 468-4244
 Cary *(G-1775)*

Ingle Protective Systems Inc .... F 704 788-3327
 Concord *(G-4285)*

GLOVES: Work

American Made Products Inc .... F 252 747-2010
 Hookerton *(G-8728)*

Carolina Glove Company .... E 828 464-1132
 Conover *(G-4432)*

Southern Glove Inc .... B 828 464-4884
 Newton *(G-11970)*

United Glove Inc .... E 828 464-2510
 Newton *(G-11981)*

GOLF EQPT

Arnold S Welding Service Inc .... E 910 323-3822
 Fayetteville *(G-5764)*

Bad Monkey Lures LLC .... G 910 433-5617
 Hope Mills *(G-8732)*

Custom Golf Car Supply Inc .... C 704 855-1130
 Salisbury *(G-13952)*

Golf Shop .... G 704 636-7070
 Salisbury *(G-13971)*

Revels Turf and Tractor LLC .... E 919 552-5697
 Fuquay Varina *(G-6226)*

Smith Holdings .... G 704 472-4937
 Shelby *(G-14368)*

GOLF GOODS & EQPT

I Must Garden LLC .... G 919 929-2299
  Raleigh *(G-12872)*
Land and Loft LLC .... G 315 560-7060
  Raleigh *(G-12953)*

GOURMET FOOD STORES

Bakers Southern Traditions Inc .... G 252 344-2120
  Roxobel *(G-13829)*
Blazing Foods LLC .... G 336 865-2933
  Charlotte *(G-2320)*
Blue Ridge Jams .... G 828 685-1783
  Hendersonville *(G-7826)*
Induction Food Systems Inc .... G 919 907-0179
  Raleigh *(G-12883)*
Ludlam Family Foods LLC .... G 919 805-6061
  Chapel Hill *(G-2035)*
Stormberg Foods LLC .... E 919 947-6011
  Goldsboro *(G-6662)*

GRADING SVCS

Barnhill Contracting Company .... D 910 488-1319
  Fayetteville *(G-5769)*
Carolina Paving Hickory Inc .... G 828 328-3909
  Hickory *(G-7964)*
Carolina Paving Hickory Inc .... F 828 322-1706
  Hickory *(G-7965)*
Cjc Enterprises .... E 919 266-3158
  Wake Forest *(G-15541)*
Haulco LLC .... G 336 781-0468
  Trinity *(G-15344)*
Macleod Construction Inc .... C 704 483-3580
  Charlotte *(G-3116)*

GRANITE: Crushed & Broken

Alamo North Texas Railroad Co .... G 919 787-9504
  Raleigh *(G-12485)*
Blue Rock Materials LLC .... F 828 479-3581
  Robbinsville *(G-13605)*
Charlotte Instyle Inc .... E 704 665-8880
  Charlotte *(G-2452)*
Georgia-Carolina Quarries Inc .... E 336 786-6978
  Mount Airy *(G-11511)*
Heidelberg Mtls Sthast Agg LLC .... E 910 893-8308
  Bunnlevel *(G-1330)*
Heidelberg Mtls Sthast Agg LLC .... E 910 893-2111
  Lillington *(G-9852)*
Heidelberg Mtls Sthast Agg LLC .... G 252 222-0812
  Morehead City *(G-11174)*
Legacy Vulcan LLC .... G 704 788-7833
  Concord *(G-4301)*
Legacy Vulcan LLC .... G 828 255-8561
  Enka *(G-5683)*
Luck Stone Corporation .... E 336 786-4693
  Mount Airy *(G-11541)*
Marietta Martin Materials Inc .... G 704 278-2218
  Woodleaf *(G-17023)*
Martin Marietta Materials Inc .... G 336 584-8875
  Burlington *(G-1455)*
Martin Marietta Materials Inc .... G 919 863-4305
  Raleigh *(G-13000)*
Martin Marietta Materials Inc .... C 919 781-4550
  Raleigh *(G-13001)*
Meridian Granite Company .... E 919 781-4550
  Raleigh *(G-13018)*
Wake Stone Corp .... F 252 985-4411
  Battleboro *(G-931)*
Wake Stone Corporation .... E 919 775-7450
  Moncure *(G-10629)*

GRANITE: Cut & Shaped

Amanzi Marble & Granite LLC .... G 336 993-9998
  Kernersville *(G-9162)*
Apex Marble and Granite Inc .... E 919 462-9202
  Morrisville *(G-11289)*
Bloomday Granite & Marble Inc .... E 336 724-0300
  Winston Salem *(G-16633)*
Carolina Quarries Inc .... D 704 633-0201
  Salisbury *(G-13936)*
Creative Stone Fyetteville Inc .... F 910 491-1225
  Fayetteville *(G-5799)*
King Stone Innovation LLC .... G 704 352-1134
  Charlotte *(G-3056)*
Kitchen Man Inc .... F 910 408-1322
  Winnabow *(G-16582)*
Mables Headstone & Monu Co LLP .... G 919 724-8705
  Creedmoor *(G-4618)*

GRAPHIC ARTS & RELATED DESIGN SVCS

A Plus Graphics Inc .... G 252 243-0404
  Wilson *(G-16463)*
Advertising Design Systems Inc .... G 828 264-8060
  Boone *(G-1172)*
Brandilly of Nc Inc .... F 919 278-7896
  Raleigh *(G-12572)*
Connected 2k LLC .... G 910 321-7446
  Fayetteville *(G-5795)*
Fast Pro Media LLC .... G 704 799-8040
  Cornelius *(G-4545)*
Graphic Components LLC .... E 336 542-2128
  Greensboro *(G-7057)*
Graphic Image of Cape Fear Inc .... G 910 313-6768
  Wilmington *(G-16239)*
Gulfstream Publications Inc .... G 252 449-2222
  Kitty Hawk *(G-9406)*
Idx Impressions LLC .... C 703 550-6902
  Washington *(G-15711)*
Kathie S Mc Daniel .... G 336 835-1544
  Elkin *(G-5622)*
Kreber .... D 336 861-2700
  High Point *(G-8425)*
Logo Wear Graphics LLC .... F 336 382-0455
  Summerfield *(G-14985)*
Mark/Trece Inc .... E 336 292-3424
  Whitsett *(G-15997)*
Signs Etc .... G 336 722-9341
  Winston Salem *(G-16909)*
Studio Displays Inc .... F 704 588-6590
  Pineville *(G-12310)*
Tannis Root Productions Inc .... G 919 832-8552
  Raleigh *(G-13327)*
Village Graphics .... G 252 745-4600
  Oriental *(G-12013)*
Wild Child Custom Graphics LLC .... G 910 762-5335
  Wilmington *(G-16443)*
Zebra Communications Inc .... E 919 314-3700
  Morrisville *(G-11469)*

GRASSES: Artificial & Preserved

Plantd Inc .... D 434 906-3445
  Oxford *(G-12142)*

GRATINGS: Tread, Fabricated Metal

Bill Slate Grating .... G 336 591-8607
  Walnut Cove *(G-15631)*

GRAVE VAULTS, METAL

Winston-Salem Casket Company .... G 336 661-1695
  Winston Salem *(G-16984)*

GREENHOUSES: Prefabricated Metal

Carolina Greenhouse Plants Inc .... F 252 523-9300
  Kinston *(G-9350)*

Lock Drives Inc .... G 704 588-1844
  Pineville *(G-12281)*
Van Wingerden Grnhse Co Inc .... E 828 891-7389
  Mills River *(G-10513)*
Williamson Greenhouses Inc .... F 910 592-7072
  Clinton *(G-4118)*

GRINDING SVC: Precision, Commercial Or Indl

Intelligent Tool Corp .... F 704 799-0449
  Concord *(G-4286)*

GROCERIES, GENERAL LINE WHOLESALERS

USa Wholesale and Distrg Inc .... F 888 484-6872
  Fayetteville *(G-5945)*

GUIDANCE SYSTEMS & EQPT: Space Vehicle

Firstmark Aerospace Corp .... D 919 956-4200
  Creedmoor *(G-4613)*

GUIDED MISSILES & SPACE VEHICLES

End Camp North .... G 980 337-4600
  Charlotte *(G-2710)*

GUM & WOOD CHEMICALS

Monticello Labs Inc .... G 919 623-6390
  Hurdle Mills *(G-8911)*
Soto Industries LLC .... E 706 643-5011
  Charlotte *(G-3582)*
Westrock Mwv LLC .... G 919 334-3200
  Raleigh *(G-13419)*

GUTTERS: Sheet Metal

Beacon Roofing Supply Inc .... G 704 886-1555
  Charlotte *(G-2291)*
Clt 2016 Inc .... D 704 886-1555
  Charlotte *(G-2501)*
Triangle Installation Svc Inc .... G 919 363-7637
  Apex *(G-252)*

GYPSUM PRDTS

Ng Operations LLC .... D 704 916-2082
  Charlotte *(G-3261)*
Precision Walls Inc .... G 336 852-7710
  Greensboro *(G-7276)*
Proform Finishing Products LLC .... E 704 398-3900
  Mount Holly *(G-11648)*
Proform Finishing Products LLC .... B 704 365-7300
  Charlotte *(G-3392)*

HAIR & HAIR BASED PRDTS

Brittany Smith .... G 912 313-0588
  Greensboro *(G-6858)*
Candypearls Hair LLC .... G 252 558-7202
  Raleigh *(G-12587)*
CCI Hair Boutique LLC .... F 407 216-9213
  Hope Mills *(G-8735)*
E Cache & Co LLC .... F 919 590-0779
  Charlotte *(G-2670)*
Fifty Combs LLC .... G 252 406-6242
  Tarboro *(G-15103)*
Gifted Hands Styling Salon .... G 828 781-2781
  Hickory *(G-8032)*
Johnny Slicks Inc .... G 910 803-2159
  Holly Ridge *(G-8683)*
Let It Flo LLC .... G 717 421-3754
  Fayetteville *(G-5860)*
Luxury Tresses Collection LLC .... G 910 501-4451
  Laurinburg *(G-9485)*

HAIR & HAIR BASED PRDTS

Marvica McLendon LLC .... G 704 965-9408
  Charlotte *(G-3135)*
Pashes LLC .... G 704 682-6535
  Statesville *(G-14857)*
Sassy Queen Collection LLC .... G 919 949-0085
  Durham *(G-5339)*
Tmcm Services LLC .... G 336 609-4378
  Greensboro *(G-7405)*
Z Collection LLC .... G 919 247-1513
  Zebulon *(G-17147)*

HAIR CARE PRDTS

Blaq Beauty Naturalz Inc .... G 252 326-5621
  Weldon *(G-15880)*
O Grayson Company .... E 704 932-6195
  Kannapolis *(G-9128)*
Peculiar Roots LLC .... G 845 379-4039
  Greensboro *(G-7250)*
Procter & Gamble Mfg Co .... A 336 954-0000
  Browns Summit *(G-1314)*
Rebecca Trickey .... G 910 584-5549
  Raeford *(G-12435)*
Salonexclusive Beauty LLC .... G 704 488-3909
  Charlotte *(G-3484)*
Virtue Labs LLC .... G 844 782-4247
  Raleigh *(G-13404)*

HAIR DRESSING, FOR THE TRADE

Ruth Hicks Enterprise Inc .... F 704 469-4741
  Waxhaw *(G-15773)*

HAMPERS: Solid Fiber, Made From Purchased Materials

Westrock Rkt LLC .... C 336 661-7180
  Winston Salem *(G-16974)*

HANDBAGS

Blacqueladi Styles LLC .... G 877 977-7798
  Cary *(G-1707)*

HANDBAGS: Women's

Glaser Designs Inc .... F 415 552-3188
  Raleigh *(G-12803)*
Grace & Glory Goods LLC .... G 828 575-2166
  Asheville *(G-638)*
R Riveter LLC .... G 406 321-2315
  Southern Pines *(G-14550)*

HANDLES: Brush Or Tool, Plastic

Balcrank Corporation .... E 800 747-5300
  Weaverville *(G-15838)*

HANDYMAN SVCS

Darius All Access LLC .... E 910 262-8567
  Wilmington *(G-16194)*

HANG GLIDERS

Ride Best LLC .... G 252 489-2959
  Rodanthe *(G-13756)*

HARDWARE

Alloy Fabricators Inc .... E 704 263-2281
  Alexis *(G-121)*
Amesbury Acqstion Hldngs 2 Inc ..... C 704 924-8586
  Statesville *(G-14747)*
Amesbury Group Inc .... E 704 924-7694
  Statesville *(G-14749)*
Appalchian Stove Fbrcators Inc .... F 828 253-0164
  Asheville *(G-525)*
Balcrank Corporation .... E 800 747-5300
  Weaverville *(G-15838)*

Blum Inc .... G 919 345-6214
  Oak Ridge *(G-12058)*
CSC Family Holdings Inc .... G 336 993-2680
  Colfax *(G-4147)*
Division 10 .... G 919 661-1101
  Raleigh *(G-12689)*
Endura Products LLC .... F 336 991-8818
  High Point *(G-8343)*
Hardware Ventures Inc .... G 919 818-9039
  Clayton *(G-3986)*
Industrial Metal Products of .... F 910 944-8110
  Aberdeen *(G-7)*
Kaba Ilco Corp .... B 336 725-1331
  Winston Salem *(G-16775)*
Kdy Automation Solutions Inc .... G 888 219-0049
  Morrisville *(G-11364)*
Kearfott Corporation .... B 828 350-5300
  Black Mountain *(G-1127)*
Ketchie-Houston Inc .... E 704 786-5101
  Concord *(G-4300)*
Nova Mobility Systems Inc .... G 800 797-9861
  Charlotte *(G-3272)*
Rize LLC .... G 910 487-9759
  Fayetteville *(G-5907)*
Royal Brass & Hose .... F 704 847-2156
  Charlotte *(G-3462)*
Seac Banche Usa Inc .... G 919 360-6442
  Chapel Hill *(G-2068)*
Skinner Company .... G 336 580-4716
  Greensboro *(G-7343)*
Stephen P Wolfe .... G 252 792-3001
  Jamesville *(G-9082)*
Success In Marketplace LLC .... G 919 608-1259
  Raleigh *(G-13311)*
Sunray Inc .... E 828 287-7030
  Rutherfordton *(G-13892)*
Triangle Biosystems Inc .... F 919 361-2663
  Durham *(G-5405)*
Village Produce & Cntry Str In .... G 336 661-8685
  Winston Salem *(G-16962)*
WaveTherm Corporation .... E 919 307-8071
  Raleigh *(G-13415)*
Wilmington Rbr & Gasket Co Inc ..... F 910 762-4262
  Wilmington *(G-16450)*
X-Jet Technologies Inc .... G 800 983-7467
  Raleigh *(G-13429)*

HARDWARE & BUILDING PRDTS: Plastic

Ashland Products Inc .... C 815 266-0250
  Huntersville *(G-8794)*
Caro-Polymers Inc .... F 704 629-5319
  Bessemer City *(G-1055)*
Chadsworth Incorporated .... E 910 763-7600
  Wilmington *(G-16168)*
Corner Stone Plastics Inc .... G 336 629-1828
  Asheboro *(G-418)*
Digger Specialties Inc .... F 919 255-2533
  Fuquay Varina *(G-6196)*
Digger Specialties Inc .... G 336 495-1517
  Randleman *(G-13464)*
Hayward Industries Inc .... C 336 712-9900
  Clemmons *(G-4043)*
Hayward Industries Inc .... B 908 351-5400
  Charlotte *(G-2894)*
L B Plastics Incorporated .... D 704 663-1543
  Mooresville *(G-11000)*
Manufacturing Services Inc .... E 704 629-4163
  Bessemer City *(G-1074)*
Performance Plastics Pdts Inc .... D 336 454-0350
  Jamestown *(G-9066)*
Tenn-Tex Plastics Inc .... F 336 931-1100
  Colfax *(G-4161)*

HARDWARE & EQPT: Stage, Exc Lighting

Stage Decoration and Sups Inc .... F 336 621-5454
  Greensboro *(G-7364)*

HARDWARE STORES

Ace Marine Rigging & Supply Inc ..... F 252 726-6620
  Morehead City *(G-11148)*
AGM Carolina Inc .... G 336 431-4100
  High Point *(G-8236)*
B&C Xterior Cleaning Svc Inc .... G 919 779-7905
  Raleigh *(G-12540)*
C & M Industrial Supply Co .... G 704 483-4001
  Mill Spring *(G-10484)*
Capitol Funds Inc .... F 910 439-5275
  Mount Gilead *(G-11599)*
Capitol Funds Inc .... E 704 487-8547
  Shelby *(G-14291)*
Discount Pallet Services LLC .... G 910 892-3760
  Dunn *(G-4862)*
Hudson S Hardware Inc .... G 919 553-3030
  Garner *(G-6276)*
Ledger Hardware Inc .... G 828 688-4798
  Bakersville *(G-885)*
Matthews Building Supply Co .... E 704 847-2106
  Matthews *(G-10268)*
W E Nixons Wldg & Hdwr Inc .... G 252 221-4348
  Edenton *(G-5523)*

HARDWARE STORES: Builders'

Bfs Operations LLC .... A 919 431-1000
  Raleigh *(G-12555)*
Castle Hayne Hardware LLC .... F 910 675-9205
  Castle Hayne *(G-1945)*
Gesipa Fasteners Usa Inc .... F 609 208-1740
  Mocksville *(G-10578)*
Stock Building Supply Holdings LLC .. A 919 431-1000
  Raleigh *(G-13305)*

HARDWARE STORES: Pumps & Pumping Eqpt

Merrill Resources Inc .... F 828 877-4450
  Penrose *(G-12186)*

HARDWARE STORES: Tools

Shopbot Tools Inc .... E 919 680-4800
  Durham *(G-5354)*
Snap-On Power Tools Inc .... C 828 835-4400
  Murphy *(G-11717)*
Triad Cutting Tools Inc .... G 336 873-8708
  Asheboro *(G-500)*

HARDWARE STORES: Tools, Hand

Joe Armstrong .... G 336 207-6503
  Greensboro *(G-7138)*

HARDWARE WHOLESALERS

AGM Carolina Inc .... G 336 431-4100
  High Point *(G-8236)*
Allegion Access Tech LLC .... E 704 789-7000
  Concord *(G-4191)*
Belwith Products LLC .... G 336 841-3899
  High Point *(G-8270)*
Con-Tab Inc .... F 336 476-0104
  Thomasville *(G-15206)*
Godwin Door & Hardware Inc .... G 919 580-0543
  Goldsboro *(G-6617)*
Grass America Inc .... C 336 996-4041
  Kernersville *(G-9203)*
Imperial Usa Ltd .... E 704 596-2444
  Charlotte *(G-2954)*

PRODUCT SECTION

HEATING UNITS & DEVICES: Indl, Electric

Restoration Hardware Inc................... F 919 544-4196
  Durham (G-5329)
Triangle Indus Sup Hldings LLC.......... G 704 395-0600
  Charlotte (G-3725)
Vista Products Inc............................ D 910 582-0130
  Hamlet (G-7634)

HARDWARE, WHOLESALE: Bolts

Bamal Corporation............................ F 980 225-7700
  Charlotte (G-2273)

HARDWARE, WHOLESALE: Builders', NEC

Sentinel Door Controls LLC................ F 704 921-4627
  Charlotte (G-3528)

HARDWARE, WHOLESALE: Furniture, NEC

Hickory Springs Manufacturi.............. D 828 328-2201
  Hickory (G-8052)
RPM Wood Finishes Group Inc........... D 828 261-0325
  Hickory (G-8142)
Salice America Inc........................... E 704 841-7810
  Charlotte (G-3483)

HARDWARE, WHOLESALE: Power Tools & Access

Greenworks North America LLC.......... D 704 658-0539
  Mooresville (G-10965)
TTI Floor Care North Amer Inc............ B 440 996-2000
  Charlotte (G-3736)
Yat Usa Inc..................................... G 480 584-4096
  Huntersville (G-8908)

HARDWARE, WHOLESALE: Security Devices, Locks

A&B Integrators LLC........................ F 919 371-0750
  Durham (G-4897)
Total Technologies LLC..................... G 336 259-5541
  Gastonia (G-6530)

HARDWARE: Aircraft

Jtec Radiowave............................... G 704 799-1658
  Mooresville (G-10991)
Sikorsky Aircraft Corporation.............. G 252 447-5050
  New Bern (G-11846)

HARDWARE: Builders'

Endura Products LLC........................ B 336 668-2472
  Colfax (G-4149)
Fix-A-Latch Usa LLC........................ E 435 901-4146
  Chapel Hill (G-2020)
Fix-A-Latch Usa LLC........................ G 435 901-4146
  Chapel Hill (G-2019)
Masonite Corporation........................ B 704 599-0235
  Charlotte (G-3138)
Stanley Black & Decker Inc............... G 704 509-0844
  Charlotte (G-3621)

HARDWARE: Door Opening & Closing Devices, Exc Electrical

Absolute Security & Lock Inc............. G 336 322-4598
  Roxboro (G-13792)
Sentinel Door Controls LLC................ F 704 921-4627
  Charlotte (G-3528)

HARDWARE: Furniture

Acme Rental Company...................... F 704 873-3731
  Statesville (G-14740)
Belwith Products LLC........................ G 336 841-3899
  High Point (G-8270)

Blum Inc... B 704 827-1345
  Stanley (G-14687)
Buie Manufacturing Company............. E 910 610-3504
  Laurinburg (G-9470)
Division Eight Inc............................. F 336 852-1275
  Greensboro (G-6973)
Fortress International Corp NC........... G 336 645-9365
  Conover (G-4456)
Hickory Springs California LLC............ A 828 328-2201
  Hickory (G-8051)
Hickory Springs Mfg Co.................... D 828 328-2201
  Hickory (G-8054)
Imperial Usa Ltd.............................. E 704 596-2444
  Charlotte (G-2954)
Jacob Holtz Company....................... E 828 328-1003
  Hickory (G-8070)
Mepla-Alfit Incorporated.................... E 336 289-2300
  Kernersville (G-9215)
Restoration Hardware Inc.................. F 919 544-4196
  Durham (G-5329)
Ultra-Mek Inc.................................. D 336 859-4552
  Denton (G-4754)

HARDWARE: Furniture, Builders' & Other Household

Custom Seatings.............................. G 828 879-1964
  Valdese (G-15447)
Grass America Inc............................ C 336 996-4041
  Kernersville (G-9203)
Ingersoll-Rand Indus US Inc............... D 704 896-4000
  Davidson (G-4680)

HARDWARE: Parachute

Sun Path Products Inc....................... D 910 875-9002
  Raeford (G-12442)

HARNESS ASSEMBLIES: Cable & Wire

Interconnect Products and Services Inc E 336 667-3356
  Wilkesboro (G-16026)
Iron Box LLC................................... E 919 890-0025
  Raleigh (G-12901)
Lutze Inc.. E 704 504-0222
  Charlotte (G-3110)
Protechnologies Inc.......................... E 336 368-1375
  Pilot Mountain (G-12200)
Suretech Assembly Inc..................... E 919 569-0346
  Youngsville (G-17103)

HARNESS WIRING SETS: Internal Combustion Engines

Suretech Assembly Inc..................... E 919 569-0346
  Youngsville (G-17103)

HEALTH AIDS: Exercise Eqpt

ABC Fitness Products LLC................. G 704 649-0000
  Raleigh (G-12461)
Advantage Fitness Products Inc.......... F 336 643-8810
  Kernersville (G-9159)
RSR Fitness Inc............................... F 919 255-1233
  Raleigh (G-13217)

HEARING AIDS

Carolina Ear Hring Aid Assoc L........... E 919 876-4327
  Raleigh (G-12596)

HEAT TREATING: Metal

American Metallurgy Inc.................... G 336 889-3277
  High Point (G-8246)
Atmo-TEC....................................... G 704 528-3935
  Troutman (G-15367)

Bodycote Thermal Proc Inc................ F 704 664-1808
  Mooresville (G-10884)
East Crlina Metal Treating Inc............ E 919 834-2100
  Raleigh (G-12716)
Furnace Rebuilders Inc..................... F 704 483-4025
  Denver (G-4777)
Industrial Prcess Slutions Inc.............. G 336 926-1511
  Wilkesboro (G-16025)
J F Heat Treating Inc........................ G 704 864-0998
  Gastonia (G-6433)
M-B Industries Inc............................ C 828 862-4201
  Rosman (G-13786)
Thermal Metal Treating Inc................ E 910 944-3636
  Aberdeen (G-32)
Tuff Temp Corp................................ F 252 398-3400
  Murfreesboro (G-11703)
United TI & Stamping Co NC Inc......... D 910 323-8588
  Fayetteville (G-5939)

HEATERS: Swimming Pool, Electric

Pentair Water Pool and Spa Inc........... F 919 463-4640
  Cary (G-1848)
Pentair Water Pool and Spa Inc........... A 919 566-8000
  Sanford (G-14166)

HEATING & AIR CONDITIONING UNITS, COMBINATION

American Coil Inc............................. F 310 515-1215
  Bostic (G-1259)
Charlies Heating & Cooling LLC.......... G 336 260-1973
  Snow Camp (G-14495)
Chichibone Inc................................. F 919 785-0090
  Kernersville (G-9177)
Firstsource Distributors LLC............... G 704 553-8510
  Charlotte (G-2767)
Go Green Services LLC..................... D 336 252-2999
  Greensboro (G-7048)
J&R Precision Heating and Air............ G 910 480-8322
  Fayetteville (G-5844)
Kenny Fowler Heating and A Inc......... G 910 508-4553
  Wilmington (G-16288)
Ppa Industries Inc............................ E 828 328-1142
  Hickory (G-8118)
Tier 1 Heating and Air LLC................ F 910 556-1444
  Vass (G-15494)
Trs-Sesco LLC.................................. D 336 996-2220
  Kernersville (G-9248)
Xp Climate Control LLC..................... G 828 266-2006
  Boone (G-1251)

HEATING EQPT: Complete

Bahnson Holdings Inc........................ D 336 760-3111
  Clemmons (G-4029)
Jenkins Services Group LLC............... G 704 881-3210
  Catawba (G-1965)
Man Around House........................... G 919 625-5933
  Durham (G-5204)
Trane US Inc................................... G 336 387-1735
  Greensboro (G-7408)

HEATING UNITS & DEVICES: Indl, Electric

ABB Installation Products Inc.............. E 828 322-1855
  Hickory (G-7928)
Custom Electric Mfg LLC.................... E 248 305-7700
  Concord (G-4249)
L F I Services Inc............................. G 215 343-0411
  Sanford (G-14145)
Lambda Technologies Inc................... E 919 462-1919
  Morrisville (G-11371)
Nutec Inc.. E 877 318-2430
  Huntersville (G-8867)

HEATING UNITS & DEVICES: Indl, Electric

Thermcraft Holding Co LLC .... D 336 784-4800
  Winston Salem *(G-16941)*
Tutco Inc .... D 828 654-1665
  Arden *(G-387)*

HELICOPTERS

Vx Aerospace Holdings Inc .... F 828 433-5353
  Morganton *(G-11267)*

HELMETS: Athletic

Kask America Inc .... E 704 960-4851
  Charlotte *(G-3043)*

HELMETS: Steel

Interactive Safety Pdts Inc .... E 704 664-7377
  Huntersville *(G-8835)*

HIGH ENERGY PARTICLE PHYSICS EQPT

Consolidated Elec Distrs Inc .... G 828 433-4689
  Morganton *(G-11207)*
Raw Earth Energy Corporation .... G 704 492-0793
  Charlotte *(G-3412)*

HOBBY, TOY & GAME STORES: Arts & Crafts & Splys

Grateful Union Family Inc .... F 828 622-3258
  Asheville *(G-640)*

HOBBY, TOY & GAME STORES: Ceramics Splys

Bright Angle LLC .... G 828 771-6966
  Asheville *(G-573)*

HOBBY, TOY & GAME STORES: Toys & Games

Burlington Outlet .... G 910 278-3442
  Oak Island *(G-12048)*

HOISTS

Columbus McKinnon Corporation ...... D 704 694-2156
  Wadesboro *(G-15507)*
Duff-Norton Company Inc .... G 704 588-0510
  Charlotte *(G-2656)*
Toter LLC .... D 800 424-0422
  Statesville *(G-14916)*

HOISTS: Hand

Service and Equipment Company ..... G 910 545-5866
  Jacksonville *(G-9029)*

HOLDING COMPANIES: Investment, Exc Banks

Alcami Holdings LLC .... A 910 254-7000
  Wilmington *(G-16105)*
Atticus LLC .... E 984 465-4754
  Cary *(G-1694)*
Interroll USA Holding LLC .... D 910 799-1100
  Wilmington *(G-16272)*
Ipi Acquisition LLC .... A 704 588-1100
  Charlotte *(G-2996)*
K&K Holdings Inc .... G 704 341-5567
  Charlotte *(G-3040)*
Pharr McAdenville Corporation .... D 704 824-3551
  Mc Adenville *(G-10380)*

HOLDING COMPANIES: Personal, Exc Banks

Hlm Legacy Group Inc .... C 704 878-8823
  Troutman *(G-15381)*

HOME ENTERTAINMENT EQPT: Electronic, NEC

Cymbal LLC .... G 877 365-9622
  Cary *(G-1744)*
Unique Home Theater Inc .... G 704 787-3239
  Concord *(G-4382)*

HOME FOR THE MENTALLY HANDICAPPED

Watauga Opportunities Inc .... E 828 264-5009
  Boone *(G-1247)*

HOME HEALTH CARE SVCS

Allotropica Technologies Inc .... G 919 522-4374
  Chapel Hill *(G-1982)*
Hap Innovations LLC .... E 919 650-6497
  Morrisville *(G-11351)*

HOMEFURNISHING STORES: Beddings & Linens

Dewoolfson Down Intl Inc .... G 828 963-2750
  Banner Elk *(G-896)*
Leighdeux LLC .... G 704 965-4889
  Charlotte *(G-3082)*

HOMEFURNISHING STORES: Lighting Fixtures

Interrs-Exteriors Asheboro Inc .... F 336 629-2148
  Asheboro *(G-446)*

HOMEFURNISHING STORES: Pottery

Ceder Creek Gallery & Pottery .... G 919 528-1041
  Creedmoor *(G-4610)*
Jugtown Pottery .... G 910 464-3266
  Seagrove *(G-14241)*

HOMEFURNISHINGS, WHOLESALE: Blinds, Vertical

Shutter Factory Inc .... G 252 974-2795
  Washington *(G-15731)*

HOMEFURNISHINGS, WHOLESALE: Fireplace Eqpt & Access

Appalchian Stove Fbrcators Inc .... F 828 253-0164
  Asheville *(G-525)*
Avanti Hearth Products LLC .... G 704 866-4342
  Belmont *(G-975)*

HOMEFURNISHINGS, WHOLESALE: Floor Cushion & Padding

Artisans Guild Incorporated .... G 336 841-4140
  High Point *(G-8256)*

HOMEFURNISHINGS, WHOLESALE: Linens, Table

Sanders Industries Inc .... G 410 277-8565
  Waynesville *(G-15820)*

HOMEFURNISHINGS, WHOLESALE: Stainless Steel Flatware

Wichard Inc .... G 704 597-1502
  Charlotte *(G-3811)*

HOMEFURNISHINGS, WHOLESALE: Wood Flooring

Green River Resource MGT .... F 828 697-0357
  Zirconia *(G-17153)*

HOMES: Log Cabins

Bear Creek Log Tmber Homes LLC .... G 336 751-6180
  Mocksville *(G-10557)*
Braswell Realty .... G 828 733-5800
  Newland *(G-11882)*
Dex n Dox .... G 910 576-4644
  Troy *(G-15404)*
Distinctive Bldg & Design Inc .... G 828 456-4730
  Waynesville *(G-15802)*
Fascoe Realty .... G 828 963-7600
  Boone *(G-1198)*
Gray Wolf Log Homes Inc .... G 828 586-4662
  Sylva *(G-15057)*
Log Cabin Homes Ltd .... G 252 454-1548
  Battleboro *(G-924)*
Log Cabin Homes Ltd .... D 252 454-1500
  Rocky Mount *(G-13708)*
Mast Woodworks .... F 336 468-1194
  Hamptonville *(G-7677)*
Mill Creek Post & Beam Co .... G 828 749-8000
  Saluda *(G-14072)*
Mountain Rcrtion Log Cbins LLC ...... G 828 387-6688
  Newland *(G-11890)*
Old Hickory Log Homes Inc .... G 704 489-8989
  Denver *(G-4791)*
South-East Lumber Company .... E 336 996-5322
  Kernersville *(G-9236)*
Southland Log Homes Inc .... G 336 449-5388
  Whitsett *(G-16002)*
Tree Craft Log Homes Inc .... G 828 689-2240
  Mars Hill *(G-10197)*

HOODS: Door, Aluminum

Envision Glass Inc .... F 336 283-9701
  Winston Salem *(G-16698)*

HORSESHOES

Blue Horseshoe .... G 980 312-8202
  Charlotte *(G-2321)*
H Horseshoe .... G 336 853-5913
  Lexington *(G-9727)*
Pierce Farrier Supply Inc .... G 704 753-4358
  Indian Trail *(G-8957)*

HOSE: Automobile, Rubber

Mmb One Inc .... F 704 523-8163
  Charlotte *(G-3191)*
Steele Rubber Products Inc .... D 704 483-9343
  Denver *(G-4803)*

HOSE: Flexible Metal

Hoser Inc .... F 704 989-7151
  Monroe *(G-10734)*
Titeflex Corporation .... G 647 638-7160
  Charlotte *(G-3697)*

HOSE: Plastic

Titeflex Corporation .... G 647 638-7160
  Charlotte *(G-3697)*

HOSE: Rubber

Alliance Hose & Tube Works Inc .... G 336 378-9736
  Greensboro *(G-6793)*
Flextrol Corporation .... F 704 888-1120
  Locust *(G-9960)*
Industrial Power Inc .... G 910 483-4230
  Fayetteville *(G-5841)*

HOSIERY DYEING & FINISHING

Huffman Finishing Company Inc .... C 828 396-1741
  Granite Falls *(G-6739)*

PRODUCT SECTION — INDL MACHINERY & EQPT WHOLESALERS

Lakeside Dyeing & Finshg Inc.................. G 336 229-0064
  Burlington *(G-1448)*
Ward Hosiery Company Inc.................. G 828 381-2346
  Hickory *(G-8206)*

HOSPITALS: Medical & Surgical
Statesville Med MGT Svcs LLC.................. F 704 996-6748
  Statesville *(G-14904)*

HOT TUBS
Aqua Doc Pool Sparkling S.................. G 828 231-9398
  Waynesville *(G-15793)*
Bradford Products LLC.................. D 910 791-2202
  Leland *(G-9529)*
Mountain Leisure Hot Tubs LLC.................. F 828 649-7727
  Arden *(G-353)*
Southern Home Spa and Wtr Pdts.................. G 336 286-3564
  Greensboro *(G-7354)*

HOT TUBS: Plastic & Fiberglass
Creekraft Cultured Marble Inc.................. F 252 636-5488
  New Bern *(G-11793)*

HOUSEHOLD ARTICLES, EXC FURNITURE: Cut Stone
Armen Stone LLC.................. G 743 228-3901
  Burlington *(G-1367)*
Capital Marble Creations Inc.................. F 910 893-2462
  Lillington *(G-9845)*
Piedmont Marble Inc.................. G 336 274-1800
  Oak Ridge *(G-12066)*

HOUSEHOLD ARTICLES: Metal
ARC Steel Fabrication LLC.................. F 980 533-8302
  Bessemer City *(G-1052)*
Artistic Ironworks LLC.................. G 919 908-6888
  Durham *(G-4927)*
Gray Manufacturing Co.................. F 615 841-3066
  Charlotte *(G-2858)*
Mecha Inc.................. F 919 858-0372
  Raleigh *(G-13012)*

HOUSEHOLD FURNISHINGS, NEC
American Fiber & Finishing Inc.................. E 704 984-9256
  Albemarle *(G-73)*
Arden Companies LLC.................. D 919 258-3081
  Sanford *(G-14088)*
Artisans Guild Incorporated.................. G 336 841-4140
  High Point *(G-8256)*
Blue Ridge Products Co Inc.................. E 828 322-7990
  Hickory *(G-7952)*
Bob Barker Company Inc.................. C 800 334-9880
  Fuquay Varina *(G-6184)*
Carpenter Co.................. E 828 632-7061
  Taylorsville *(G-15133)*
Chf Industries Inc.................. E 212 951-7800
  Charlotte *(G-2473)*
Deep River Fabricators Inc.................. E 336 824-8881
  Franklinville *(G-6168)*
Fiber Cushioning Inc.................. F 336 887-4782
  High Point *(G-8352)*
Manual Woodworkers Weavers Inc.................. C 828 692-7333
  Hendersonville *(G-7876)*
Party Tables Land Co LLC.................. F 919 596-3521
  Durham *(G-5272)*
Pure Country Inc.................. D 828 859-9916
  Lynn *(G-10063)*
Q C Apparel Inc.................. F 828 586-5663
  Sylva *(G-15065)*
Riddle & Company LLC.................. F 336 229-1856
  Burlington *(G-1485)*

Snyder Paper Corporation.................. G 828 464-1189
  Newton *(G-11969)*
Textile Products Inc.................. E 704 636-6221
  Salisbury *(G-14051)*
Westpoint Home Inc.................. B 910 369-2231
  Wagram *(G-15524)*
Wildcat Territory Inc.................. F 718 361-6726
  Thomasville *(G-15301)*

HOUSEHOLD SEWING MACHINES WHOLESALERS: Electric
Zibra LLC.................. G 704 271-4503
  Mooresville *(G-11140)*

HOUSEWARES, ELECTRIC, EXC COOKING APPLIANCES & UTENSILS
Grizzly Cookware LLC.................. G 704 322-3521
  Charlotte *(G-2870)*

HOUSEWARES, ELECTRIC: Air Purifiers, Portable
Airbox LLC.................. G 855 927-1386
  Statesville *(G-14743)*
Trick Tank Inc.................. G 980 406-3200
  Charlotte *(G-3726)*
TTI Floor Care North Amer Inc.................. D 440 996-2000
  Charlotte *(G-3735)*

HOUSEWARES, ELECTRIC: Heating Units, Electric Appliances
Blossman Propane Gas & Appl.................. F 828 396-0144
  Hickory *(G-7950)*

HUMIDIFIERS & DEHUMIDIFIERS
American Moistening Co Inc.................. F 704 889-7281
  Pineville *(G-12252)*

HYDRAULIC EQPT REPAIR SVC
Atlantic Hydraulics Svcs LLC.................. E 919 542-2985
  Sanford *(G-14091)*
Auto Parts Fayetteville LLC.................. G 910 889-4026
  Fayetteville *(G-5766)*

ICE
Carolina Ice Inc.................. E 252 527-3178
  Kinston *(G-9351)*
Dfa Dairy Brands Fluid LLC.................. G 704 341-2794
  Charlotte *(G-2625)*
Herrin Bros Coal & Ice Co.................. G 704 332-2193
  Charlotte *(G-2906)*
Hickman Oil & Ice Co Inc.................. G 910 576-2501
  Troy *(G-15406)*
Reddy Ice Group Inc.................. D 704 824-4611
  Gastonia *(G-6502)*
Robert D Starr.................. G 336 697-0286
  Greensboro *(G-7313)*
Rose Ice & Coal Company.................. F 910 762-2464
  Wilmington *(G-16387)*
Taylor Products Inc.................. G 910 862-2576
  Elizabethtown *(G-5606)*

ICE CREAM & ICES WHOLESALERS
Dfa Dairy Brands Fluid LLC.................. G 704 341-2794
  Charlotte *(G-2625)*
Tonys Ice Cream Co Inc.................. G 704 853-0018
  Gastonia *(G-6529)*

IGNITION APPARATUS & DISTRIBUTORS
Smart Start Inc.................. G 828 328-2822
  Hickory *(G-8159)*

IGNITION SYSTEMS: High Frequency
Lmg Holdings Inc.................. F 919 653-0910
  Durham *(G-5192)*

INCUBATORS & BROODERS: Farm
Smoky Mtn Nativ Plant Assn.................. G 828 479-8788
  Robbinsville *(G-13612)*
Upper Coastl Plain Bus Dev Ctr.................. F 252 234-5900
  Wilson *(G-16554)*

INDL & PERSONAL SVC PAPER WHOLESALERS
Atlantic Corp Wilmington Inc.................. E 910 259-3600
  Burgaw *(G-1333)*
Atlantic Corp Wilmington Inc.................. D 910 343-0624
  Wilmington *(G-16121)*
C L Rabb Inc.................. E 704 865-0295
  Gastonia *(G-6365)*
Gold Medal Products Co.................. G 336 665-4997
  Greensboro *(G-7051)*
Pactiv LLC.................. F 828 758-7580
  Lenoir *(G-9645)*
Veritiv Operating Company.................. E 336 834-3488
  Greensboro *(G-7437)*

INDL & PERSONAL SVC PAPER, WHOLESALE: Shipping Splys
Lls Investments Inc.................. F 919 662-7283
  Raleigh *(G-12976)*

INDL CONTRACTORS: Exhibit Construction
Exhibit World Inc.................. G 704 882-2272
  Indian Trail *(G-8933)*

INDL EQPT SVCS
GE Vernova International LLC.................. F 704 587-1300
  Charlotte *(G-2812)*
Hydro Service & Supplies Inc.................. E 919 544-3744
  Durham *(G-5142)*
Jly Invstmnts Inc Fka Nwman Mc.................. E 336 273-8261
  Browns Summit *(G-1310)*
Safe Air Systems Inc.................. E 336 674-0749
  Randleman *(G-13489)*
Sub-Aquatics Inc.................. E 336 674-0749
  Randleman *(G-13492)*
Waste Container Repair Svcs.................. G 910 257-4474
  Fayetteville *(G-5949)*
Westlift LLC.................. F 919 242-4379
  Goldsboro *(G-6670)*

INDL GASES WHOLESALERS
Airgas Usa LLC.................. F 704 394-1420
  Charlotte *(G-2147)*
Airgas Usa LLC.................. G 919 544-3773
  Durham *(G-4909)*
Airgas Usa LLC.................. G 919 735-5276
  Goldsboro *(G-6587)*

INDL MACHINERY & EQPT WHOLESALERS
American Linc Corporation.................. E 704 861-9242
  Gastonia *(G-6346)*
Arbon Equipment Corporation.................. F 414 355-2600
  Charlotte *(G-2209)*
Arc3 Gases Inc.................. F 704 220-1029
  Monroe *(G-10650)*
Arc3 Gases Inc.................. E 910 892-4016
  Dunn *(G-4851)*
Arnold S Welding Service Inc.................. E 910 323-3822
  Fayetteville *(G-5764)*
Bear Pages.................. G 828 837-0785
  Murphy *(G-11706)*

INDL MACHINERY & EQPT WHOLESALERS

PRODUCT SECTION

Birch Bros Southern Inc................. E 704 843-2111
  Waxhaw (G-15745)

Bunzl Processor Dist LLC.................. G 910 738-8111
  Lumberton (G-10028)

Burris Machine Company Inc................. G 828 322-6914
  Hickory (G-7955)

C R Onsrud Inc................. E 704 508-7000
  Troutman (G-15368)

Carotek Inc................. D 704 844-1100
  Matthews (G-10238)

Cross Technologies Inc................. D 336 292-0511
  Whitsett (G-15987)

Cummins Atlantic LLC................. E 704 596-7690
  Charlotte (G-2584)

Deurotech America Inc................. F 980 272-6827
  Charlotte (G-2623)

Drum Filter Media Inc................. G 336 434-4195
  High Point (G-8332)

Dwd Industries LLC................. E 336 498-6327
  Randleman (G-13466)

Encertec Inc................. G 336 288-7226
  Greensboro (G-6997)

Flanders/Csc LLC................. D 252 946-8081
  Washington (G-15702)

Gregory Poole Equipment Co................. F 919 872-2691
  Raleigh (G-12818)

Heat Transfer Sales of The................. E 336 294-3838
  Greensboro (G-7085)

His Glassworks Inc................. G 828 254-2559
  Asheville (G-653)

Huber Technology Inc................. E 704 949-1010
  Denver (G-4782)

J & P Entrprses of Crlinas Inc................. E 704 861-1867
  Gastonia (G-6431)

Ligna Machinery Inc................. E 336 584-0030
  Burlington (G-1451)

Lock Drives Inc................. G 704 588-1844
  Pineville (G-12281)

Machinex................. G 336 665-5030
  High Point (G-8436)

Mang Systems Inc................. E 704 292-1041
  Matthews (G-10330)

McDonald Services Inc................. G 704 753-9669
  Monroe (G-10769)

Mixon Mills Inc................. G 828 297-5431
  Vilas (G-15497)

Morris Machine Company Inc................. G 704 824-4242
  Gastonia (G-6470)

Northline Nc LLC................. F 336 283-4811
  Rural Hall (G-13850)

Oerlikon AM US Inc................. E 980 260-2827
  Huntersville (G-8870)

Oerlikon Metco (us) Inc................. F 713 715-6300
  Huntersville (G-8871)

Palmer Wahl Instruments Inc................. E 828 658-3131
  Asheville (G-721)

Pavco Inc................. E 704 496-6800
  Charlotte (G-3321)

Pharmaceutical Equipment Svcs................. G 239 699-9120
  Asheville (G-727)

Psi-Polymer Systems Inc................. E 828 468-2600
  Conover (G-4490)

RPM Plastics LLC................. E 704 871-0518
  Statesville (G-14881)

Russell Finex Inc................. F 704 588-9808
  Pineville (G-12299)

Rvb Systems Group Inc................. E 919 362-5211
  Garner (G-6311)

Schaefer Systems International Inc................. C 704 944-4500
  Charlotte (G-3499)

Schaefer Systems Intl Inc................. G 704 944-4550
  Charlotte (G-3501)

Vrg Components Inc................. F 980 244-3862
  Indian Trail (G-8970)

West Dynamics Us Inc................. E 704 735-0009
  Lincolnton (G-9936)

INDL PROCESS INSTRUMENTS: Control

Electro Magnetic Research Inc................. G 919 365-3723
  Zebulon (G-17126)

Hitech Controls Inc................. G 336 498-1534
  Randleman (G-13472)

Sure Trip Inc................. F 704 983-4651
  Albemarle (G-110)

INDL PROCESS INSTRUMENTS: Elements, Primary

Temposonics LLC................. G 470 380-5103
  Cary (G-1907)

INDL SPLYS WHOLESALERS

Allyn International Trdg Corp................. G 877 858-2482
  Marshville (G-10210)

Automated Designs Inc................. F 828 696-9625
  Flat Rock (G-5959)

Biganodes LLC................. G 828 245-1115
  Forest City (G-6060)

Carr Mill Supplies Inc................. G 336 883-0135
  High Point (G-8287)

Custom Hydraulics & Design................. F 704 347-0023
  Cherryville (G-3865)

D M & E Corporation................. E 704 482-8876
  Shelby (G-14309)

H-T-L Perma USA Ltd Partnr................. E 704 377-3100
  Charlotte (G-2879)

Holland Supply Company................. E 252 492-7541
  Henderson (G-7788)

Industrial Sup Solutions Inc................. E 704 636-4241
  Salisbury (G-13983)

Ips Corporation................. E 919 598-2400
  Durham (G-5164)

Justice Bearing LLC................. G 800 355-2500
  Mooresville (G-10993)

Machine Tool Components LLC................. G 866 466-0120
  Indian Trail (G-8948)

Mount Hope Machinery Co................. F
  Charlotte (G-3208)

Parker-Hannifin Corporation................. F 336 373-1761
  Greensboro (G-7245)

Person Printing Company Inc................. E 336 599-2146
  Roxboro (G-13818)

Purser Centl Rewinding Co Inc................. F 704 786-3131
  Concord (G-4343)

Ravenox Rope................. G 336 226-5260
  Burlington (G-1482)

Sanders Company Inc................. E 252 338-3995
  Elizabeth City (G-5569)

SAS Industries Inc................. F 631 727-1441
  Elizabeth City (G-5570)

Sherrill Contract Mfg Inc................. F 704 922-7871
  Dallas (G-4657)

Structural Materials Inc................. G 828 754-6413
  Lenoir (G-9653)

Triangle Indus Sup Hldings LLC................. G 704 395-0600
  Charlotte (G-3725)

INDL SPLYS, WHOLESALE: Bearings

Oiles America Corporation................. F 704 784-4500
  Concord (G-4324)

INDL SPLYS, WHOLESALE: Clean Room Splys

Murata Machinery Usa Inc................. C 704 875-9280
  Charlotte (G-3219)

INDL SPLYS, WHOLESALE: Drums, New Or Reconditioned

National Container Group LLC................. G 704 393-9050
  Charlotte (G-3233)

INDL SPLYS, WHOLESALE: Gaskets

Uchiyama Mfg Amer LLC................. B 919 731-2364
  Goldsboro (G-6668)

INDL SPLYS, WHOLESALE: Mill Splys

Laurinburg Machine Company................. G 910 276-0360
  Laurinburg (G-9484)

T P Supply Co Inc................. E 336 789-2337
  Mount Airy (G-11585)

Talladega Mchy & Sup Co NC................. G 256 362-4124
  Fayetteville (G-5925)

INDL SPLYS, WHOLESALE: Power Transmission, Eqpt & Apparatus

Alan R Williams Inc................. E 704 372-8281
  Charlotte (G-2151)

Altra Industrial Motion Corp................. G 704 588-5610
  Charlotte (G-2174)

Boston Gear LLC................. B 704 588-5610
  Charlotte (G-2337)

INDL SPLYS, WHOLESALE: Rubber Goods, Mechanical

Carolina Custom Rubber Inc................. G 704 636-6989
  Salisbury (G-13934)

Cinters Inc................. G 336 267-3051
  Raleigh (G-12622)

Easth20 Holdings Llc................. G 919 313-2100
  Greensboro (G-6987)

Novaflex Hose Inc................. D 336 578-2161
  Haw River (G-7755)

Oliver Rubber Company LLC................. B 336 629-1436
  Asheboro (G-459)

INDL SPLYS, WHOLESALE: Tools

B & M Wholesale Inc................. G 336 789-3916
  Mount Airy (G-11479)

INDL SPLYS, WHOLESALE: Tools, NEC

Loflin Handle Co Inc................. F 336 463-2422
  Yadkinville (G-17043)

Robert Bosch Tool Corporation................. E 704 735-7464
  Lincolnton (G-9915)

INDL SPLYS, WHOLESALE: Valves & Fittings

Bonomi North America Inc................. F 704 412-9031
  Charlotte (G-2333)

Consolidated Pipe & Sup Co Inc................. F 336 294-8577
  Greensboro (G-6930)

Flo-Tite Inc Valves & Contrls................. E 910 738-8904
  Lumberton (G-10038)

Fortiline LLC................. E 704 788-9800
  Concord (G-4266)

INDL TRUCK REPAIR SVCS

Whiteville Forklift & Eqp................. G 910 642-6642
  Whiteville (G-15980)

INDUSTRIAL & COMMERCIAL EQPT INSPECTION SVCS

SCR-Tech LLC................. C 704 504-0191
  Charlotte (G-3513)

PRODUCT SECTION   INSTRUMENTS: Analytical

INFORMATION RETRIEVAL SERVICES

Carolina Connections Inc .... G 336 786-7030
  Mount Airy *(G-11488)*
ID Pros LLC .... G 904 887-6210
  Gastonia *(G-6421)*
Vrush Industries Inc .... F 336 886-7700
  High Point *(G-8597)*

INFORMATION SVCS: Consumer

Telephys Inc .... G 312 625-9128
  Davidson *(G-4699)*

INFRARED OBJECT DETECTION EQPT

Spatial Light LLC .... G 617 213-0314
  Cary *(G-1899)*

INK: Printing

Actega Wit Inc .... C 704 735-8282
  Lincolnton *(G-9865)*
Allied Pressroom Products Inc .... E 954 920-0909
  Monroe *(G-10641)*
American Water Graphics Inc .... F 828 247-0700
  Forest City *(G-6058)*
Archie Supply LLC .... G 336 987-0895
  Greensboro *(G-6813)*
Arpro M-Tec LLC .... F 828 433-0699
  Morganton *(G-11198)*
Crossroads Fuel Service Inc .... E 252 426-5216
  Hertford *(G-7918)*
Doris E Inc .... G 919 858-5419
  Raleigh *(G-12697)*
DSM Desotech Inc .... G 704 862-5000
  Stanley *(G-14691)*
Environmental Inks and Coat .... C 828 433-1922
  Morganton *(G-11212)*
Flint Group Inc .... F 828 687-4363
  Arden *(G-330)*
Flint Group US LLC .... G 828 687-4309
  Arden *(G-331)*
Flint Group US LLC .... G 704 504-2626
  Charlotte *(G-2779)*
GSE Dispensing .... G 704 509-2651
  Charlotte *(G-2873)*
Hoffman Steinberg .... G 336 292-5501
  Greensboro *(G-7095)*
Hubergroup Usa Inc .... F 336 292-5501
  Greensboro *(G-7103)*
Ink Tec Inc .... F 828 465-6411
  Newton *(G-11944)*
INX International Ink Co .... F 704 372-2080
  Charlotte *(G-2990)*
Mirchandani Inc .... G 919 872-8871
  Raleigh *(G-13034)*
Mitsubishi Chemical Amer Inc .... D 980 580-2839
  Charlotte *(G-3188)*
RPM Wood Finishes Group Inc .... D 828 261-0325
  Hickory *(G-8141)*
RPM Wood Finishes Group Inc .... D 828 728-8266
  Hudson *(G-8777)*
Rutland Group Inc .... G 704 553-0046
  Charlotte *(G-3474)*
Siegwerk Eic LLC .... F 800 368-4657
  Morganton *(G-11253)*
Sun Chemical Corporation .... E 704 587-4531
  Charlotte *(G-3650)*
Wikoff Color Corporation .... E 704 392-4657
  Charlotte *(G-3813)*
Wikoff Color Corporation .... E 336 668-3423
  Greensboro *(G-7460)*
Xsys North America Corporation .... E 828 687-2485
  Arden *(G-394)*

INSECTICIDES

Amika LLC .... G 984 664-9804
  Cary *(G-1681)*
Cape Fear Chemicals Inc .... E 910 862-3139
  Elizabethtown *(G-5588)*
Jabb of Carolinas Inc .... G 919 965-9007
  Pine Level *(G-12211)*
Lanxess Corporation .... F 704 868-7200
  Gastonia *(G-6443)*
Mey Corporation .... G 919 932-5800
  Chapel Hill *(G-2043)*
Tyratech Inc .... E 919 415-4275
  Morrisville *(G-11459)*

INSECTICIDES & PESTICIDES

Vestaron Corporation .... D 919 694-1022
  Durham *(G-5432)*

INSPECTION & TESTING SVCS

Froehling & Robertson Inc .... E 804 264-2701
  Raleigh *(G-12783)*

INSTRUMENTS & METERS: Measuring, Electric

International Instrumentation .... G 919 496-4208
  Bunn *(G-1328)*

INSTRUMENTS, LABORATORY: Analyzers, Automatic Chemical

Parata Systems LLC .... F 919 363-2454
  Cary *(G-1841)*
Parata Systems LLC .... C 888 727-2821
  Durham *(G-5270)*
Sciteck Diagnostics Inc .... G 828 650-0409
  Fletcher *(G-6036)*

INSTRUMENTS, MEASURING & CNTRL: Geophysical & Meteorological

Allied Manufacturing Tech Inc .... F 704 276-8192
  Lincolnton *(G-9870)*
Russ Simmons .... G 910 686-1656
  Wilmington *(G-16389)*

INSTRUMENTS, MEASURING & CNTRLG: Aircraft & Motor Vehicle

Circor Pumps North America LLC .... D 704 289-6511
  Monroe *(G-10683)*
Dynisco Instruments LLC .... E 828 326-9888
  Hickory *(G-8013)*
IMO Industries Inc .... D 301 323-9000
  Monroe *(G-10737)*

INSTRUMENTS, MEASURING & CONTROLLING: Ion Chambers

Biomerieux Inc .... G 800 682-2666
  Raleigh *(G-12559)*

INSTRUMENTS, MEASURING & CONTROLLING: Transits, Surveyors'

Pretoria Transit Interiors Inc .... E 615 867-8515
  Charlotte *(G-3377)*

INSTRUMENTS, OPTICAL: Mirrors

Glass Works of Hickory Inc .... G 828 322-2122
  Hickory *(G-8033)*

INSTRUMENTS, SURGICAL & MED: Needles & Syringes, Hypodermic

Becton Dickinson and Company .... B 201 847-6800
  Durham *(G-4952)*

INSTRUMENTS, SURGICAL & MEDICAL: Blood & Bone Work

Accumed Corp .... D 800 278-6796
  Raleigh *(G-12468)*
Acw Technology Inc .... A
  Raleigh *(G-12474)*
Ascepi Medical Group LLC .... G 919 336-4246
  Raleigh *(G-12527)*
Healthlink Europe .... F 919 783-4142
  Raleigh *(G-12833)*
MTI Medical Cables LLC .... F 828 890-2888
  Fletcher *(G-6029)*
Sfp Research Inc .... G 336 622-5266
  Liberty *(G-9831)*
Wnyh LLC .... C 716 853-1800
  Mocksville *(G-10610)*

INSTRUMENTS, SURGICAL & MEDICAL: Blood Transfusion

Charter Medical Ltd .... D 336 768-6447
  Winston Salem *(G-16651)*

INSTRUMENTS, SURGICAL & MEDICAL: Catheters

Cook Incorporated .... A 336 744-0157
  Winston Salem *(G-16661)*
Mallinckrodt LLC .... G 919 878-2900
  Raleigh *(G-12992)*
Robling Medical LLC .... D 919 570-9605
  Youngsville *(G-17093)*
Teleflex Incorporated .... F 919 544-8000
  Morrisville *(G-11444)*
Zoes Kitchen Inc .... E 336 748-0587
  Winston Salem *(G-16991)*

INSTRUMENTS, SURGICAL & MEDICAL: Inhalation Therapy

Aromatherapy By Irene LLC .... G 404 457-1871
  Marston *(G-10229)*

INSTRUMENTS, SURGICAL & MEDICAL: IV Transfusion

Luxor Hydration LLC .... F 919 568-5047
  Durham *(G-5200)*

INSTRUMENTS, SURGICAL & MEDICAL: Muscle Exercise, Ophthalmic

Advantage Fitness Products LLC .... G 336 643-8810
  Archdale *(G-265)*
Healthlink International Inc .... F 877 324-2837
  Raleigh *(G-12834)*

INSTRUMENTS, SURGICAL & MEDICAL: Ophthalmic

Optopol Usa Inc .... G 833 678-6765
  Raleigh *(G-13087)*

INSTRUMENTS: Analytical

Apex Waves LLC .... G 919 809-5227
  Cary *(G-1684)*
Atrium Hlth Bspcmen Repository .... G 704 863-4001
  Mint Hill *(G-10521)*

Employee Codes: A=Over 500 employees, B=251-500
C=101-250, D=51-100, E=20-50, F=10-19, G=1-9

INSTRUMENTS: Analytical

Autom8 LLC .... G 704 252-3425
 Charlotte *(G-2240)*
Biofluidica Inc .... G 858 535-6493
 Raleigh *(G-12557)*
Biomerieux Inc .... B 919 620-2000
 Durham *(G-4960)*
Biorad .... G 919 463-7866
 Cary *(G-1705)*
Bmg Labtech Inc .... F 919 678-1633
 Cary *(G-1712)*
Box Scientific LLC .... G 408 361-8631
 Newton *(G-11916)*
Camag Scientific Inc .... G 910 343-1830
 Wilmington *(G-16148)*
Carolina Biological Supply Company .... C 336 584-0381
 Burlington *(G-1384)*
DOE & Ingalls Investors Inc .... E 919 598-1986
 Durham *(G-5056)*
DOE & Ingalls Management LLC ... F 919 598-1986
 Durham *(G-5057)*
DOE & Inglls Nrth Crlina Oprti .... E 919 282-1792
 Durham *(G-5058)*
Dog Black Services LLC .... G 336 266-0778
 Graham *(G-6688)*
Environmental Supply Co Inc .... F 919 956-9688
 Durham *(G-5089)*
Fisher Scientific Company LLC ...... D 800 252-7100
 Asheville *(G-623)*
Hamilton .... G 704 896-1427
 Davidson *(G-4676)*
Horiba Instruments Inc .... F 828 676-2801
 Fletcher *(G-6012)*
Htx Technologies LLC .... F 919 928-5688
 Carrboro *(G-1648)*
Institute For Resch Biotecnoly .... G 252 689-2205
 Greenville *(G-7544)*
Microsolv Technology Corp .... F 720 949-1302
 Leland *(G-9556)*
Phitonex Inc .... F 855 874-4866
 Durham *(G-5285)*
Precision Prtcle Msrements Inc ..... G 919 667-6960
 Mebane *(G-10426)*
Sapphire Tchncal Solutions LLC ... G 704 561-3100
 Pineville *(G-12302)*
Shimadzu Scientific Instrs Inc .... G 919 425-1010
 Durham *(G-5352)*
Thermo Elctron Scntfic Instrs .... G 828 281-2651
 Asheville *(G-797)*
Thermo Fisher Scientific Inc .... G 800 955-6288
 Durham *(G-5398)*
Thermo Fisher Scientific Inc .... F 252 707-7093
 Greenville *(G-7589)*
Thermo Fisher Scientific Inc .... G 800 955-6288
 High Point *(G-8568)*
Thermo Fisher Scientific Inc .... E 919 876-2352
 Raleigh *(G-13344)*
Thermo Fsher Scntfic Ashvlle L ..... B 828 658-2711
 Weaverville *(G-15865)*
Thermo Fsher Scntfic Ashvlle L ..... B 828 658-2711
 Asheville *(G-798)*
Trajan Inc .... G 919 435-1105
 Raleigh *(G-13357)*
Warren Oil Company LLC .... D 910 892-6456
 Dunn *(G-4890)*

INSTRUMENTS: Combustion Control, Indl

Delta Msrment Cmbstn Cntrls LL .. E 919 623-7133
 Cary *(G-1747)*

INSTRUMENTS: Electrocardiographs

US Prototype Inc .... E 866 239-2848
 Wilmington *(G-16439)*

INSTRUMENTS: Endoscopic Eqpt, Electromedical

Kyocera Precision Tools Inc .... G 800 823-7284
 Hendersonville *(G-7870)*

INSTRUMENTS: Flow, Indl Process

Diverse Flooring Systems .... G 910 425-8915
 Fayetteville *(G-5812)*
Hoffer Flow Controls Inc .... D 252 331-1997
 Elizabeth City *(G-5550)*

INSTRUMENTS: Indl Process Control

AC Corporation .... B 336 273-4472
 Greensboro *(G-6775)*
Acucal Inc .... G 252 337-9975
 Elizabeth City *(G-5530)*
Eng Solutions Inc .... F 919 831-1830
 Chapel Hill *(G-2014)*
Kdy Automation Solutions Inc .... G 888 219-0049
 Morrisville *(G-11364)*
Strandberg Engrg Labs Inc .... F 336 274-3775
 Greensboro *(G-7374)*
Thermaco Incorporated .... G 336 629-4651
 Asheboro *(G-497)*

INSTRUMENTS: Infrared, Indl Process

Tc2 Labs LLC .... G 919 380-2171
 Raleigh *(G-13329)*

INSTRUMENTS: Measurement, Indl Process

QMAX Industries LLC .... G 704 643-7299
 Pineville *(G-12293)*
Sapphire Tchncal Solutions LLC ... G 704 561-3100
 Pineville *(G-12302)*
Southstern Prcess Eqp Cntrls I ..... F 704 483-1141
 Denver *(G-4802)*
Triad Automation Group Inc .... E 336 767-1379
 Winston Salem *(G-16947)*

INSTRUMENTS: Measuring, Electrical Power

G B Technologies .... G 919 954-0721
 Raleigh *(G-12788)*
Hvte Inc .... F 919 274-8899
 Youngsville *(G-17084)*
Ndsl Inc .... F 919 790-7877
 Durham *(G-5241)*

INSTRUMENTS: Medical & Surgical

3shape Inc .... G 919 813-8694
 Morrisville *(G-11271)*
Acme United Corporation .... E 252 822-5051
 Rocky Mount *(G-13663)*
Adhezion Biomedical LLC .... G 828 728-6116
 Hudson *(G-8760)*
Alcon .... G 919 624-5868
 Raleigh *(G-12486)*
Alpha Medsource LLC .... G 704 408-8505
 Huntersville *(G-8788)*
Alveolus Inc .... E 704 921-2215
 Charlotte *(G-2175)*
Andersen Energy Inc .... G 336 376-0107
 Haw River *(G-7749)*
Andersen Products Inc .... E 336 376-3000
 Haw River *(G-7750)*
Andersen Sterilizers Inc .... E 336 376-8622
 Haw River *(G-7751)*
Angstrom Medica Inc .... F 781 933-6121
 Greenville *(G-7483)*
Applied Catheter Tech Inc .... G 336 817-1005
 Winston Salem *(G-16606)*
Bariatric Partners Inc .... F 704 542-2256
 Charlotte *(G-2280)*
Beacon Prosthetics & Orthotics .... G 919 231-6890
 Raleigh *(G-12548)*
Becton Dickinson and Company ... E 919 963-1307
 Four Oaks *(G-6100)*
Biogeniv Inc .... G 828 850-1007
 Lenoir *(G-9589)*
Biomerieux Inc .... B 919 620-2000
 Durham *(G-4960)*
Bioventus Inc .... E 919 474-6700
 Durham *(G-4962)*
Birth Tissue Recovery LLC .... E 336 448-1910
 Winston Salem *(G-16631)*
Brandel LLC .... G 704 525-4548
 Charlotte *(G-2346)*
Carefusion 303 Inc .... E 919 528-5253
 Creedmoor *(G-4608)*
Carolina Precision Tech LLC .... E 215 675-4590
 Mooresville *(G-10898)*
Colowrap LLC .... F 888 815-3376
 Durham *(G-5025)*
Contego Medical Inc .... E 919 606-3917
 Raleigh *(G-12642)*
Convatec Inc .... C 336 855-5500
 Greensboro *(G-6931)*
Convatec Inc .... C 336 297-3021
 Greensboro *(G-6932)*
Convatec Purchasing Department ... G 336 297-3021
 Greensboro *(G-6933)*
Cook Group Inc .... F 336 744-0157
 Winston Salem *(G-16660)*
Core Sound Imaging Inc .... E 919 277-0636
 Raleigh *(G-12647)*
Corning Incorporated .... C 919 620-6200
 Durham *(G-5034)*
Covidien Holding Inc .... C 919 878-2930
 Raleigh *(G-12650)*
Custom Assemblies Inc .... G 919 202-4533
 Pine Level *(G-12207)*
D R Burton Healthcare LLC .... F 252 228-7038
 Farmville *(G-5733)*
Diamond Orthopedic LLC .... G 704 585-8258
 Gastonia *(G-6397)*
East West Manufacturing LLC ...... G 704 663-5975
 Mooresville *(G-10936)*
Easy Light LLC .... G 972 313-5474
 Charlotte *(G-2676)*
Elite Metal Performance LLC .... F 704 660-0006
 Statesville *(G-14793)*
Emitbio Inc .... G 919 321-1726
 Morrisville *(G-11337)*
Fertility Tech Resources Inc .... G 404 626-9786
 Murphy *(G-11709)*
Genco .... G 919 963-4227
 Four Oaks *(G-6105)*
Gilero LLC .... C 919 595-8220
 Durham *(G-5115)*
Greg Goodwin PA .... G 828 657-5371
 Forest City *(G-6069)*
Greiner Bio-One North Amer Inc ... B 704 261-7800
 Monroe *(G-10728)*
H W Andersen Products Inc .... G 336 376-3000
 Haw River *(G-7752)*
Health Supply Us LLC .... F 888 408-1694
 Mooresville *(G-10971)*
Healthlink Europe .... F 919 368-2187
 Raleigh *(G-12832)*
Horizon Vision Research Inc .... F 910 796-8600
 Wilmington *(G-16257)*
Hyperbranch Medical Tech Inc ...... F 919 433-3325
 Durham *(G-5143)*

PRODUCT SECTION

INSURANCE: Agents, Brokers & Service

Innavasc Medical Inc .... F 813 902-2228
Durham *(G-5158)*

Intelligent Endoscopy LLC .... E 336 608-4375
Clemmons *(G-4048)*

Janus Development Group Inc .... F 252 551-9042
Greenville *(G-7548)*

Karamedica Inc .... G 919 302-1325
Raleigh *(G-12930)*

Kashif Mazhar .... G 919 314-2891
Durham *(G-5176)*

Kyocera Precision Tools Inc .... G 800 823-7284
Hendersonville *(G-7870)*

Logiksavvy Solutions LLC .... G 336 392-6149
Greensboro *(G-7167)*

Lucerno Dynamics LLC .... G 317 294-1395
Cary *(G-1820)*

Maplight Therapeutics Inc .... G 603 553-9013
Greenville *(G-7558)*

Martin Manufacturing Co LLC .... G 919 741-5439
Rocky Mount *(G-13710)*

Maximum Asp .... G 919 544-7900
Morrisville *(G-11389)*

Med Express/Medical Spc Inc .... F 919 572-2568
Durham *(G-5214)*

Medcor Inc .... G 888 579-1050
Lexington *(G-9757)*

Micell Technologies Inc .... E 919 313-2102
Durham *(G-5223)*

Mission Srgcal Innovations LLC .... G 810 965-7455
Raleigh *(G-13035)*

Murray Inc .... E 704 329-0400
Charlotte *(G-3221)*

Murray Inc .... E 847 620-7990
Charlotte *(G-3222)*

Ncontact Surgical LLC .... E
Morrisville *(G-11392)*

Next Safety Inc .... F 336 246-7700
Jefferson *(G-9092)*

Nocturnal Product Dev LLC .... F 919 321-1331
Durham *(G-5247)*

Nuvasive Inc .... F 336 430-3169
Greensboro *(G-7227)*

Oxlife of NC LLC .... G 828 684-7353
Hendersonville *(G-7889)*

Pattons Medical LLC .... E 704 529-5442
Charlotte *(G-3319)*

Perseus Intermediate Inc .... E 919 474-6700
Durham *(G-5281)*

Photonicare Inc .... E 866 411-3277
Durham *(G-5287)*

Pioneer Srgcal Orthblogics Inc .... F 252 355-4405
Greenville *(G-7575)*

Plexus Corp .... D 919 807-8000
Raleigh *(G-13116)*

Polyzen Inc .... F 919 319-9599
Cary *(G-1854)*

Precision Concepts Group LLC ...... B 336 761-8572
Winston Salem *(G-16863)*

Rdd Pharma Inc .... G 302 319-9970
Raleigh *(G-13191)*

React Innovations LLC .... G 704 773-1276
Charlotte *(G-3418)*

Retrofix Screws LLC .... G 980 432-8412
Salisbury *(G-14036)*

Retroject Inc .... G 919 619-3042
Chapel Hill *(G-2063)*

Rm Liquidation Inc .... D 828 274-7996
Asheville *(G-756)*

Safeguard Medical .... G 855 428-6074
Harrisburg *(G-7726)*

Sonablate Corp .... F 888 874-4384
Charlotte *(G-3580)*

Staclear Inc .... G 919 838-2844
Raleigh *(G-13296)*

Statesville Med MGT Svcs LLC ...... F 704 996-6748
Statesville *(G-14904)*

Strong Medical Partners LLC .... D 716 507-4476
Pineville *(G-12309)*

Strong Medical Partners LLC .... E 716 626-9400
Pineville *(G-12308)*

Stryker Corp .... G 919 455-6755
Raleigh *(G-13310)*

Stryker Corporation .... F 919 433-3325
Durham *(G-5378)*

Surgilum LLC .... G 910 202-2202
Wilmington *(G-16422)*

Technosoft Innovations Inc .... G 919 388-3360
Morrisville *(G-11441)*

Teleflex Incorporated .... G 919 433-2575
Durham *(G-5388)*

Teleflex Medical Incorporated .... G 336 498-4153
Asheboro *(G-496)*

Teleflex Medical Incorporated .... G 919 544-8000
Durham *(G-5390)*

Teleflex Medical Incorporated .... D 919 544-8000
Morrisville *(G-11445)*

Touchamerica Inc .... F 919 732-6968
Hillsborough *(G-8670)*

Transenterix Surgical Inc .... D 919 765-8400
Morrisville *(G-11450)*

Traumtic Drect Trnsfsion Dvcs ...... G 423 364-5828
Apex *(G-250)*

Trimed LLC .... G 919 615-2784
Raleigh *(G-13365)*

Tryton Medical Inc .... G 919 226-1490
Raleigh *(G-13370)*

Vasonova Inc .... F 650 327-1412
Morrisville *(G-11461)*

Visitech Systems Inc .... G 919 387-0524
Apex *(G-255)*

Webster Entps Jackson Cnty Inc .. E 828 586-8981
Sylva *(G-15074)*

Weslacova Corp .... G 704 607-1449
Mooresville *(G-11127)*

Wilson Outpatient Imaging .... G 252 399-7430
Wilson *(G-16563)*

Wilson-Cook Medical Inc .... G 336 744-0157
Winston Salem *(G-16976)*

INSTRUMENTS: Optical, Analytical

Sensory Analytics LLC .... E 336 315-6090
Greensboro *(G-7333)*

INSTRUMENTS: Power Measuring, Electrical

TTI Floor Care North Amer Inc ...... B 440 996-2000
Charlotte *(G-3736)*

INSTRUMENTS: Pressure Measurement, Indl

Eno Scientific LLC .... G 910 778-2660
Hillsborough *(G-8650)*

Trafag .... G 704 343-6339
Charlotte *(G-3712)*

Vishay Precision Group Inc .... F 919 374-5555
Raleigh *(G-13405)*

INSTRUMENTS: Radio Frequency Measuring

Langley & Huther Rf Tech .... G 919 880-4968
Raleigh *(G-12957)*

INSTRUMENTS: Seismographs

Geosonics Inc .... G 919 790-9500
Raleigh *(G-12797)*

INSTRUMENTS: Test, Electronic & Electric Measurement

Minipro LLC .... G 844 517-4776
Chapel Hill *(G-2044)*

MTS Systems Corporation .... C 919 677-2352
Cary *(G-1827)*

Tektronix Inc .... G 919 233-9490
Raleigh *(G-13335)*

Troxler Electronic Labs Inc .... D 919 549-8661
Durham *(G-5412)*

INSTRUMENTS: Test, Electronic & Electrical Circuits

Konica Mnlta Hlthcare Amrcas I ... E 919 792-6420
Garner *(G-6278)*

Viztek LLC .... E 919 792-6420
Garner *(G-6324)*

INSULATING COMPOUNDS

Gtg Engineering Inc .... G 877 569-8572
Clarendon *(G-3947)*

Tailored Chemical Products Inc .... D 828 322-6512
Hickory *(G-8173)*

INSULATION & ROOFING MATERIALS: Wood, Reconstituted

Attic Tent Inc .... G 704 892-5399
Mooresville *(G-10864)*

INSULATION MATERIALS WHOLESALERS

Mid-Atlantic Specialties Inc .... G 919 212-1939
Raleigh *(G-13030)*

INSULATION: Felt

Performance Goods LLC .... G 704 361-8600
Harrisburg *(G-7721)*

INSULATION: Fiberglass

Owens Corning Glass Metal Svcs .. D 704 721-2000
Concord *(G-4328)*

Wwj LLC .... E 704 871-8500
Statesville *(G-14929)*

INSULATORS & INSULATION MATERIALS: Electrical

Basalt Specialty Products Inc ...... G 336 835-5153
Elkin *(G-5610)*

Chase Corporation .... G 828 396-2121
Granite Falls *(G-6729)*

Chase Corporation .... G 828 726-6023
Lenoir *(G-9598)*

Essex Group Inc .... G 704 921-9605
Charlotte *(G-2730)*

Penn Compression Moulding Inc .. G 919 934-5144
Smithfield *(G-14476)*

INSULATORS, PORCELAIN: Electrical

Duco-SCI Inc .... E 704 289-9502
Monroe *(G-10708)*

Reuel Inc .... E 919 734-0460
Goldsboro *(G-6650)*

INSURANCE: Agents, Brokers & Service

Hinson Industries Inc .... G 252 937-7171
Rocky Mount *(G-13700)*

Katchi Tees Incorporated .... G 252 315-4691
Wilson *(G-16504)*

Motor Vhcles Lcense Plate Agcy .. G 252 338-6965
Elizabeth City *(G-5558)*

INTEGRATED CIRCUITS, SEMICONDUCTOR NETWORKS, ETC

INTEGRATED CIRCUITS, SEMICONDUCTOR NETWORKS, ETC

Advanced Micro Devices Inc.................... G 919 840-8080
  Morrisville *(G-11280)*

Agile Microwave Technology Inc............ G 984 228-8001
  Cary *(G-1677)*

Akoustis Inc... E 704 997-5735
  Huntersville *(G-8786)*

Amkor Technology Inc............................. G 919 248-1800
  Durham *(G-4916)*

Analog Devices Inc................................... G 336 202-6503
  Durham *(G-4918)*

Analog Devices Inc................................... E 336 668-9511
  Greensboro *(G-6807)*

Analog Devices Inc................................... G 919 831-2790
  Raleigh *(G-12504)*

Broadcom Corporation............................ D 919 865-2954
  Durham *(G-4981)*

Galaxy Electronics Inc.............................. F 704 343-9881
  Charlotte *(G-2803)*

Kyma Technologies Inc........................... G 919 789-8880
  Raleigh *(G-12949)*

Nokia of America Corporation................ G 919 850-6000
  Raleigh *(G-13066)*

Qorvo Us Inc.. D 336 931-8298
  Greensboro *(G-7299)*

Qualcomm Datacenter Tech Inc............. D 858 567-1121
  Raleigh *(G-13161)*

Qualia Networks Inc................................ G 805 637-2083
  Raleigh *(G-13162)*

Rfhic US Corporation............................... G 919 677-8780
  Morrisville *(G-11417)*

Rhino Networks LLC................................ E 855 462-9434
  Asheville *(G-755)*

Triad Semiconductor Inc......................... D 336 774-2150
  Winston Salem *(G-16948)*

Vrg Components Inc............................... F 980 244-3862
  Indian Trail *(G-8970)*

Wolfspeed Inc... C 919 407-5300
  Durham *(G-5444)*

INTERIOR DESIGN SVCS, NEC

Delve Interiors LLC................................... C 336 274-4661
  Greensboro *(G-6968)*

Tatum Galleries Inc.................................. G 828 963-6466
  Banner Elk *(G-904)*

Taylor Interiors LLC.................................. F 980 207-3160
  Charlotte *(G-3674)*

Textile Products Inc................................. E 704 636-6221
  Salisbury *(G-14051)*

INVERTERS: Nonrotating Electrical

Majorpower Corporation........................ E 919 563-6610
  Mebane *(G-10418)*

INVERTERS: Rotating Electrical

Everything Industrial Supply.................. G 743 333-2222
  Winston Salem *(G-16702)*

INVESTORS, NEC

Atlantic Caribbean LLC........................... F 910 343-0624
  Wilmington *(G-16120)*

Century Furniture LLC............................. C 828 267-8739
  Hickory *(G-7983)*

Igm Specialties Holding Inc.................... F 704 945-8702
  Charlotte *(G-2951)*

Rhf Investments Inc................................ G 828 326-8450
  Hickory *(G-8135)*

Solarbrook Water and Pwr Corp............ G 919 231-3205
  Raleigh *(G-13278)*

INVESTORS: Real Estate, Exc Property Operators

Lm Shea LLC.. G 919 608-1901
  Raleigh *(G-12977)*

JEWELRY & PRECIOUS STONES WHOLESALERS

Gma Creative Inc...................................... G 919 435-6984
  Wake Forest *(G-15561)*

Made By Custom LLC............................... G 704 980-9840
  Charlotte *(G-3117)*

NCSMJ Inc.. F 704 544-1118
  Pineville *(G-12285)*

JEWELRY REPAIR SVCS

D C Crsman Mfr Fine Jwly Inc................. G 828 252-9891
  Asheville *(G-601)*

Donald Haack Diamonds Inc.................. G 704 365-4400
  Charlotte *(G-2651)*

Dons Fine Jewelry Inc.............................. G 336 724-7826
  Clemmons *(G-4035)*

John Laughter Jewelry Inc...................... G 828 456-4772
  Waynesville *(G-15808)*

Made By Custom LLC............................... G 704 980-9840
  Charlotte *(G-3117)*

R Gregory Jewelers Inc........................... F 704 872-6669
  Statesville *(G-14874)*

Stonehaven Jewelry Gallery Ltd............ G 919 462-8888
  Cary *(G-1905)*

Sumpters Jwly & Collectibles................. G 704 399-5348
  Charlotte *(G-3649)*

JEWELRY STORES

Buchanan Gem Stone Mines Inc............ F 828 765-6130
  Spruce Pine *(G-14632)*

Byrd Designs Inc...................................... G 828 628-0151
  Fairview *(G-5709)*

Duncan Design Ltd.................................. G 919 834-7713
  Raleigh *(G-12709)*

Gma Creative Inc...................................... G 919 435-6984
  Wake Forest *(G-15561)*

Jewelry By Gail Inc................................... G 252 441-5387
  Nags Head *(G-11721)*

Jkl Inc... F 252 355-6714
  Greenville *(G-7550)*

Made By Custom LLC............................... G 704 980-9840
  Charlotte *(G-3117)*

NCSMJ Inc.. F 704 544-1118
  Pineville *(G-12285)*

R & B Partnership.................................... G 828 298-7988
  Asheville *(G-750)*

Speed Brite Inc... G 704 639-9771
  Salisbury *(G-14046)*

William Travis Jewelry Ltd...................... G 919 968-0011
  Chapel Hill *(G-2097)*

JEWELRY STORES: Precious Stones & Precious Metals

Barnes Dmnd Gllery Jwly Mfrs I............. G 910 347-4300
  Jacksonville *(G-8989)*

D C Crsman Mfr Fine Jwly Inc................. G 828 252-9891
  Asheville *(G-601)*

Donald Haack Diamonds Inc.................. G 704 365-4400
  Charlotte *(G-2651)*

Dons Fine Jewelry Inc.............................. G 336 724-7826
  Clemmons *(G-4035)*

Jewel Masters Inc.................................... F 336 243-2711
  Lexington *(G-9734)*

John Laughter Jewelry Inc...................... G 828 456-4772
  Waynesville *(G-15808)*

Michael S North Wilkesboro Inc............ G 336 838-5964
  North Wilkesboro *(G-12028)*

R Gregory Jewelers Inc........................... F 704 872-6669
  Statesville *(G-14874)*

Starcraft Diamonds Inc........................... F 252 717-2548
  Washington *(G-15733)*

Thomas Jewelers...................................... G 252 756-1641
  Greenville *(G-7590)*

JEWELRY, PRECIOUS METAL: Medals, Precious Or Semiprecious

Diamond Outdoor Entps Inc................... G 336 857-1450
  Denton *(G-4733)*

JEWELRY, PRECIOUS METAL: Pins

Engage2excel Inc...................................... D 704 872-5231
  Mooresville *(G-10939)*

JEWELRY, PRECIOUS METAL: Rings, Finger

Herff Jones LLC... G 704 962-1483
  Charlotte *(G-2902)*

Herff Jones LLC... G 704 873-5563
  Statesville *(G-14810)*

Jostens Inc... B 336 765-0070
  Winston Salem *(G-16773)*

JEWELRY, PRECIOUS METAL: Settings & Mountings

D C Crsman Mfr Fine Jwly Inc................. G 828 252-9891
  Asheville *(G-601)*

Donald Haack Diamonds Inc.................. G 704 365-4400
  Charlotte *(G-2651)*

JEWELRY, WHOLESALE

Duncan Design Ltd.................................. G 919 834-7713
  Raleigh *(G-12709)*

Soulku LLC... F 828 273-4278
  Asheville *(G-780)*

JEWELRY: Precious Metal

123 Precious Metal Ref LLC.................... G 910 228-5403
  Wilmington *(G-16087)*

Acme General Design Group LLC........... G 843 466-6000
  Benson *(G-1029)*

Alex and Ani LLC...................................... G 704 366-6029
  Charlotte *(G-2153)*

Barnes Dmnd Gllery Jwly Mfrs I............. G 910 347-4300
  Jacksonville *(G-8989)*

Byrd Designs Inc...................................... G 828 628-0151
  Fairview *(G-5709)*

Charles & Colvard Ltd............................. F 919 468-0399
  Morrisville *(G-11318)*

Charmed Wright LLC............................... G 704 850-8186
  Mooresville *(G-10902)*

Cindy Blackburn....................................... G 336 643-3822
  Kernersville *(G-9179)*

Dallas L Pridgen Inc................................. G 919 732-4422
  Carrboro *(G-1647)*

David Yurman Enterprises LLC............... G 704 366-7259
  Charlotte *(G-2604)*

Dons Fine Jewelry Inc.............................. G 336 724-7826
  Clemmons *(G-4035)*

Duncan Design Ltd.................................. G 919 834-7713
  Raleigh *(G-12709)*

Eurogold Art... G 336 989-6205
  Kernersville *(G-9198)*

Faerie Star Forge...................................... G 910 743-2862
  Maysville *(G-10372)*

LABORATORIES: Physical Research, Commercial

Gma Creative Inc .... G 919 435-6984
 Wake Forest *(G-15561)*

Goldsmith By Rudi Ltd .... G 828 693-1030
 Hendersonville *(G-7856)*

Jewelry By Gail Inc .... G 252 441-5387
 Nags Head *(G-11721)*

Jewelry Spoken Here .... G 828 225-8464
 Asheville *(G-671)*

Jkl Inc .... F 252 355-6714
 Greenville *(G-7550)*

John Laughter Jewelry Inc .... G 828 456-4772
 Waynesville *(G-15808)*

Michael S North Wilkesboro Inc .... G 336 838-5964
 North Wilkesboro *(G-12028)*

NCSMJ Inc .... F 704 544-1118
 Pineville *(G-12285)*

R & B Partnership .... G 828 298-7988
 Asheville *(G-750)*

R Gregory Jewelers Inc .... F 704 872-6669
 Statesville *(G-14874)*

Soulku LLC .... F 828 273-4278
 Asheville *(G-780)*

Starcraft Diamonds Inc .... F 252 717-2548
 Washington *(G-15733)*

Sumpters Jwly & Collectibles .... G 704 399-5348
 Charlotte *(G-3649)*

Thomas Jewelers .... G 252 756-1641
 Greenville *(G-7590)*

Vault of Forsyth Inc .... G 336 996-2044
 Kernersville *(G-9250)*

William Travis Jewelry Ltd .... G 919 968-0011
 Chapel Hill *(G-2097)*

JIGS & FIXTURES

Cross Technology Inc .... E 336 725-4700
 East Bend *(G-5465)*

Worth Products LLC .... F 252 747-9994
 Snow Hill *(G-14510)*

JOB PRINTING & NEWSPAPER PUBLISHING COMBINED

Boone Newspapers Inc .... E 252 332-2123
 Ahoskie *(G-56)*

Spring Hope Enterprise Inc .... G 252 478-3651
 Spring Hope *(G-14622)*

JOISTS: Fabricated Bar

Simpson Strong-Tie Company Inc .... E 336 841-1338
 High Point *(G-8532)*

JOISTS: Long-Span Series, Open Web Steel

Universal Steel NC LLC .... E 336 476-3105
 Thomasville *(G-15298)*

KITCHEN CABINETS WHOLESALERS

Dixon Custom Cabinetry LLC .... F 336 992-3306
 Kernersville *(G-9190)*

Mint Hill Cabinet Shop Inc .... E 704 821-9373
 Monroe *(G-10770)*

Murphy S Custom Cabinetry Inc .... G 828 891-3050
 Hendersonville *(G-7882)*

Nova Enterprises Inc .... E 828 687-8770
 Arden *(G-357)*

United Finishers Intl Inc .... G 336 883-3901
 High Point *(G-8585)*

KITCHEN UTENSILS: Food Handling & Processing Prdts, Wood

Ellismorris LLC .... G 646 538-1870
 Apex *(G-189)*

Pamlico Shores Inc .... E 252 926-0011
 Swanquarter *(G-15040)*

KITCHENWARE STORES

Ashdan Enterprises .... G 336 375-9698
 Greensboro *(G-6818)*

KNIT OUTERWEAR DYEING & FINISHING, EXC HOSIERY & GLOVE

Textile Piece Dyeing Co Inc .... C 704 732-4200
 Lincolnton *(G-9927)*

KNIVES: Agricultural Or indl

USA Made Blade .... G 704 798-6478
 Salisbury *(G-14060)*

LABELS: Cotton, Printed

Creative Label Solutions Inc .... G 828 320-5389
 Hickory *(G-7999)*

D & F Consolidated Inc .... G 704 664-6660
 Statesville *(G-14781)*

Minnewawa Inc .... F 865 522-8103
 Thomasville *(G-15252)*

US Label Corporation .... E 336 332-7000
 Greensboro *(G-7434)*

LABELS: Paper, Made From Purchased Materials

Bay Tech Label Inc .... G 828 296-8900
 Asheville *(G-557)*

Grand Encore Charlotte LLC .... E 513 482-7500
 Charlotte *(G-2854)*

J R Cole Industries Inc .... D 704 523-6622
 Charlotte *(G-3005)*

Label Line Ltd .... D 336 857-3115
 Asheboro *(G-450)*

Label Printing Systems Inc .... E 336 760-3271
 Winston Salem *(G-16783)*

Lpm Inc .... G 704 922-6137
 Gastonia *(G-6444)*

Rapid Response Inc .... G 704 588-8890
 Charlotte *(G-3409)*

Tarason Label Inc .... G 828 464-4743
 Hickory *(G-8174)*

LABELS: Woven

Minnewawa Inc .... F 865 522-8103
 Thomasville *(G-15252)*

LABORATORIES, TESTING: Pollution

Apex Instruments Incorporated .... E 919 557-7300
 Fuquay Varina *(G-6179)*

LABORATORIES, TESTING: Product Testing

Alcami Carolinas Corporation .... G 910 619-3952
 Garner *(G-6251)*

Alcami Carolinas Corporation .... B 910 254-7000
 Wilmington *(G-16103)*

Bachstein Consulting LLC .... G 410 322-4917
 Youngsville *(G-17070)*

Catalent Pharma Solutions LLC .... C 919 481-4855
 Morrisville *(G-11314)*

LABORATORIES, TESTING: Product Testing, Safety/Performance

Educated Design & Developme .... E 919 469-9434
 Cary *(G-1755)*

LABORATORIES: Biological Research

Alcami Carolinas Corporation .... G 910 619-3952
 Garner *(G-6251)*

Alcami Carolinas Corporation .... G 910 254-7000
 Morrisville *(G-11283)*

Alcami Carolinas Corporation .... B 910 254-7000
 Wilmington *(G-16103)*

Carolinas Cord Blood Bank .... G 919 668-1102
 Durham *(G-5006)*

LABORATORIES: Biotechnology

Cedarlane Laboratories USA .... E 336 513-5135
 Burlington *(G-1391)*

Epicypher Inc .... F 855 374-2461
 Durham *(G-5092)*

Hydromer Inc .... E 908 526-2828
 Concord *(G-4282)*

Neurametrix Inc .... G 408 507-2366
 Asheville *(G-711)*

Novex Innovations LLC .... G 336 231-6693
 Winston Salem *(G-16824)*

Praetego Inc .... G 919 237-7969
 Durham *(G-5301)*

Tengion Inc .... E 336 722-5855
 Winston Salem *(G-16938)*

Triangle Biosystems Inc .... F 919 361-2663
 Durham *(G-5405)*

LABORATORIES: Electronic Research

Nuvotronics Inc .... D 984 666-3543
 Durham *(G-5251)*

LABORATORIES: Medical

Alcami Carolinas Corporation .... F 910 254-7000
 Wilmington *(G-16100)*

Biomerieux Inc .... B 919 620-2000
 Durham *(G-4960)*

LABORATORIES: Physical Research, Commercial

Case Farms LLC .... D 919 735-5010
 Dudley *(G-4841)*

Case Farms LLC .... E 919 658-2252
 Goldsboro *(G-6599)*

Case Farms LLC .... F 704 528-4501
 Troutman *(G-15370)*

Cisco Systems Inc .... A 919 392-2000
 Morrisville *(G-11324)*

Core Technology Molding Corp .... E 336 294-2018
 Greensboro *(G-6937)*

Greer Laboratories Inc .... E 828 758-2388
 Lenoir *(G-9614)*

Health Supply Us LLC .... F 888 408-1694
 Mooresville *(G-10971)*

K2 Solutions Inc .... B 910 692-6898
 Southern Pines *(G-14538)*

King Phrmceuticals RES Dev LLC .... B 919 653-7001
 Cary *(G-1803)*

Lexitas Pharma Services Inc .... D 919 205-0012
 Durham *(G-5189)*

Linde Gas & Equipment Inc .... D 919 549-0633
 Durham *(G-5190)*

Lord Corporation .... D 919 469-2500
 Cary *(G-1818)*

Penske Racing South Inc .... C 704 664-2300
 Mooresville *(G-11050)*

Pharmagra Holding Company LLC ..... E 828 884-8656
 Brevard *(G-1284)*

Ppd Inc .... C 910 251-0081
 Wilmington *(G-16366)*

Propharma Group LLC .... D 888 242-0559
 Raleigh *(G-13153)*

LABORATORIES: Physical Research, Commercial

Qatch Technologies LLC .... G 678 908-3112
  Chapel Hill *(G-2058)*

Raybow Usa Inc .... F 828 884-8656
  Brevard *(G-1286)*

Scentair Technologies LLC .... D 704 504-2320
  Charlotte *(G-3498)*

Signalscape Inc .... E 919 859-4565
  Cary *(G-1889)*

Squarehead Technology LLC .... G 571 299-4849
  Hickory *(G-8167)*

Textile Manufacturing Tech LLC .... G 828 632-3012
  Taylorsville *(G-15173)*

Tribofilm Research Inc .... G 919 838-2844
  Raleigh *(G-13364)*

Vacs America Inc .... G 910 259-9854
  Burgaw *(G-1354)*

Venator Chemicals LLC .... D 704 454-4811
  Harrisburg *(G-7733)*

Walker and Associates Inc .... C 336 731-6391
  Lexington *(G-9800)*

LABORATORIES: Testing

Liposcience Inc .... C 919 212-1999
  Morrisville *(G-11381)*

Acterna LLC .... F 919 388-5100
  Morrisville *(G-11277)*

Albion Medical Holdings Inc .... F 800 378-3906
  Lenoir *(G-9571)*

American Safety Utility Corp .... E 704 482-0601
  Shelby *(G-14285)*

Avista Pharma Solutions Inc .... E 919 544-8600
  Durham *(G-4939)*

Dynisco Instruments LLC .... E 828 326-9888
  Hickory *(G-8013)*

Froehling & Robertson Inc .... E 804 264-2701
  Raleigh *(G-12783)*

Greer Laboratories Inc .... E 828 758-2388
  Lenoir *(G-9614)*

Greer Laboratories Inc .... C 828 754-5327
  Lenoir *(G-9615)*

Sapphire Tchncal Solutions LLC .... G 704 561-3100
  Pineville *(G-12302)*

SCR-Tech LLC .... C 704 504-0191
  Charlotte *(G-3513)*

Tergus Pharma LLC .... E 919 549-9700
  Durham *(G-5396)*

Unity Hlthcare Lab Billing LLP .... G 980 209-0402
  Charlotte *(G-3754)*

LABORATORY APPARATUS & FURNITURE

Air Control Inc .... E 252 492-2300
  Henderson *(G-7775)*

Carolina Biological Supply Company .... C 336 584-0381
  Burlington *(G-1384)*

Corilam Fabricating Co .... E 336 993-2371
  Kernersville *(G-9182)*

Diversified Woodcrafts Inc .... E 336 688-3114
  High Point *(G-8326)*

Dove Medical Supply LLC .... E 336 643-9367
  Summerfield *(G-14980)*

Ika-Works Inc .... D 910 452-7059
  Wilmington *(G-16264)*

Intensa Inc .... E 336 884-4096
  High Point *(G-8411)*

Parameter Generation Ctrl Inc .... E 828 669-8717
  Black Mountain *(G-1133)*

Research Instruments Inc .... G 919 383-2775
  Durham *(G-5327)*

Sarstedt Inc .... C 828 465-4000
  Newton *(G-11966)*

Thermo Fsher Scntfc Ashvlle L .... B 828 658-2711
  Asheville *(G-798)*

LABORATORY APPARATUS, EXC HEATING & MEASURING

Biovind LLC .... G 512 217-3077
  Charlotte *(G-2317)*

Xona Microfluidics Inc .... G 951 553-6400
  Durham *(G-5456)*

LABORATORY APPARATUS: Pipettes, Hemocytometer

Corning Incorporated .... C 919 620-6200
  Durham *(G-5034)*

LABORATORY CHEMICALS: Organic

Chirazyme Labs Inc .... G 252 717-1112
  Washington *(G-15687)*

Custom Nano Inc .... G 919 608-3540
  Raleigh *(G-12665)*

LABORATORY EQPT, EXC MEDICAL: Wholesalers

Carolina Biological Supply Co .... C 336 446-7600
  Whitsett *(G-15985)*

Carolina Biological Supply Company .... C 336 584-0381
  Burlington *(G-1384)*

Turbomed LLC .... F 973 527-5299
  Fayetteville *(G-5936)*

LABORATORY EQPT: Clinical Instruments Exc Medical

Clinicians Advocacy Group Inc .... G 704 751-9515
  Charlotte *(G-2497)*

Fisher Scientific Company LLC .... D 800 252-7100
  Asheville *(G-623)*

Primevigilance Inc .... G 781 703-5540
  Raleigh *(G-13141)*

LABORATORY EQPT: Incubators

Pacon Manufacturing Corp LLC .... C 732 764-9070
  Navassa *(G-11758)*

LABORATORY EQPT: Measuring

Aisthesis Products Inc .... G 828 627-6555
  Clyde *(G-4120)*

LACE GOODS & WARP KNIT FABRIC DYEING & FINISHING

McComb Industries Lllp .... D 336 229-9139
  Burlington *(G-1458)*

LADDERS: Permanent Installation, Metal

Ladder & Things .... G 704 779-7211
  Charlotte *(G-3069)*

LAMINATED PLASTICS: Plate, Sheet, Rod & Tubes

Bemis Manufacturing Company .... C 828 754-1086
  Lenoir *(G-9581)*

Clear Defense LLC .... E 336 370-1699
  Greensboro *(G-6916)*

Dynacast LLC .... E 704 927-2790
  Charlotte *(G-2662)*

Manning Fabrics Inc .... G 910 295-1970
  Pinehurst *(G-12228)*

Meyer Decorative Surfaces .... G 910 794-7225
  Wilmington *(G-16322)*

Rk Enterprises LLC .... G 910 481-0777
  Fayetteville *(G-5908)*

Robetex Inc .... F 910 671-8787
  Lumberton *(G-10053)*

Tech Medical Plastics Inc .... F 919 563-9272
  Mebane *(G-10432)*

Tekni-Plex Inc .... D 919 553-4151
  Clayton *(G-4017)*

Unilin North America LLC .... E 919 773-5900
  Garner *(G-6321)*

Upm Raflatac Inc .... B 828 651-4800
  Mills River *(G-10512)*

LAMINATING SVCS

Esco Industries Inc .... F 336 495-3772
  Randleman *(G-13469)*

LAMP & LIGHT BULBS & TUBES

Adams Wood Turning Inc .... G 336 882-0196
  High Point *(G-8232)*

Greenlights LLC .... E 919 766-8900
  Cary *(G-1779)*

Hiviz Lighting Inc .... G 703 382-5675
  Hendersonville *(G-7865)*

Robert Abbey Inc .... C 828 322-3480
  Hickory *(G-8137)*

Specialty Manufacturing Inc .... C 704 247-9300
  Charlotte *(G-3598)*

Sunnex Inc .... F 800 445-7869
  Charlotte *(G-3653)*

Traxon Technologies LLC .... E 201 508-1570
  Charlotte *(G-3719)*

LAMP BULBS & TUBES, ELECTRIC: Glow Lamp

Fixtures & More .... G 828 855-9093
  Hickory *(G-8026)*

LAMP BULBS & TUBES, ELECTRIC: Health, Infrared/Ultraviolet

Variety Consult LLC .... G 704 275-2284
  Shelby *(G-14380)*

LAMP BULBS & TUBES, ELECTRIC: Light, Complete

Alk Investments LLC .... G 984 233-5353
  Raleigh *(G-12488)*

Fintronx LLC .... F 919 324-3960
  Raleigh *(G-12767)*

LAMP BULBS & TUBES/PARTS, ELECTRIC: Generalized Applications

Arva LLC .... G 803 336-2230
  Charlotte *(G-2223)*

Invictus Lighting LLC .... G 828 855-9324
  Hickory *(G-8068)*

LAMP SHADES: Glass

Done-Gone Adios Inc .... F 336 993-7300
  Kernersville *(G-9192)*

Industrial Glass Tech LLC .... F 704 853-2429
  Gastonia *(G-6426)*

Orare Inc .... G 919 742-1003
  Siler City *(G-14429)*

Triangle Glass Service Inc .... G 919 477-9508
  Durham *(G-5408)*

LAMPS: Boudoir, Residential

Clarolux Inc .... E 336 378-6800
  Greensboro *(G-6912)*

Doug Bowman Galleries .... G 704 662-5620
  Chimney Rock *(G-3879)*

LAMPS: Table, Residential

Adams Wood Turning Inc .... G 336 882-0196
  High Point (G-8232)
Coast Lamp Manufacturing Inc .... E 828 648-7876
  Canton (G-1610)
Sapps Ventures .... G 910 824-0762
  Raeford (G-12438)
Sunnex Inc .... F 800 445-7869
  Charlotte (G-3653)
Wildwood Lamps & Accents Inc .... E 252 446-3266
  Rocky Mount (G-13741)

LAND SUBDIVIDERS & DEVELOPERS: Commercial

Capitol Funds Inc .... F 910 439-5275
  Mount Gilead (G-11599)
Capitol Funds Inc .... E 704 487-8547
  Shelby (G-14291)

LASER SYSTEMS & EQPT

Little Reds Engraving LLC .... G 910 599-7747
  Burgaw (G-1344)
Spectra Integrated Systems Inc .... G 919 876-3666
  Raleigh (G-13287)

LASERS: Welding, Drilling & Cutting Eqpt

Sonaspection International .... F 704 262-3384
  Concord (G-4362)

LATEX: Foamed

Earth Edge LLC .... F 828 624-0252
  Hickory (G-8016)
Sun Fabricators Inc .... E 336 885-0095
  High Point (G-8556)

LAUNDRY EQPT: Commercial

Hockmeyer Equipment Corp .... D 252 338-4705
  Elizabeth City (G-5548)
Laundry Svc Tech Ltd Lblty Co .... G 908 327-1997
  Matthews (G-10262)

LAUNDRY SVC: Work Clothing Sply

Ican Clothes Company .... F 910 670-1494
  Fayetteville (G-5840)

LAWN & GARDEN EQPT

Befco Inc .... E 252 977-9920
  Rocky Mount (G-13684)
Bosmere Inc .... F 704 784-1608
  Salisbury (G-13930)
Certified Lawnmower Inc .... G 704 527-2765
  Belmont (G-978)
Daphne Lawson Espino .... G 910 290-2762
  Beulaville (G-1093)
Deere & Company .... B 919 567-6400
  Fuquay Varina (G-6195)
Green Pastures Lawn Care .... G 828 758-9265
  Boomer (G-1170)
H & H Farm Machine Co Inc .... E 704 753-1555
  Monroe (G-10729)
Husqvrna Cnsmr Otdoor Pdts NA .... A 704 597-5000
  Charlotte (G-2937)
Husqvrna Cnsmr Otdoor Pdts NA .... D 704 597-5000
  Charlotte (G-2936)
John Deere Consumer Pdts Inc .... C 919 804-2000
  Cary (G-1798)
Miller Saws & Supplies Inc .... G 252 636-3437
  New Bern (G-11822)
Root Spring Scraper Co .... F 269 382-2025
  Pinehurst (G-12235)
S Duff Fabricating Inc .... G 910 298-3060
  Beulaville (G-1098)
Swell Home Solutions Inc .... G 919 440-4692
  Mount Olive (G-11670)
United Southern Industries Inc .... D 866 273-1810
  Forest City (G-6085)
Vegherb LLC .... F 800 914-9835
  Erwin (G-5689)

LAWN & GARDEN EQPT: Blowers & Vacuums

Peco Inc .... E 828 684-1234
  Arden (G-362)
Sunseeker US Inc .... G 443 253-1546
  Indian Trail (G-8966)

LAWN & GARDEN EQPT: Grass Catchers, Lawn Mower

New Peco Inc .... E 828 684-1234
  Arden (G-355)

LAWN & GARDEN EQPT: Lawnmowers, Residential, Hand Or Power

Darius All Access LLC .... E 910 262-8567
  Wilmington (G-16194)
Group 6 Holdings Inc .... F 888 804-5008
  Denver (G-4779)

LAWN & GARDEN EQPT: Tractors & Eqpt

Husqvrna Cnsmr Otdoor Pdts NA .... A 704 494-4810
  Charlotte (G-2938)

LEAD PENCILS & ART GOODS

Reissmann Entertainment Inc .... G 734 641-4434
  Statesville (G-14876)

LEAF TOBACCO WHOLESALERS

Pyxus International Inc .... C 252 753-8000
  Farmville (G-5742)

LEASING & RENTAL: Construction & Mining Eqpt

International Cnstr Eqp Inc .... E 704 821-8200
  Matthews (G-10322)
Stanly Tractor Company .... G 704 983-1106
  New London (G-11879)

LEASING & RENTAL: Medical Machinery & Eqpt

Medaccess Inc .... G 828 264-4085
  Robbinsville (G-13609)

LEASING & RENTAL: Trucks, Without Drivers

Chimneyrock Storage .... G 828 685-2893
  Hendersonville (G-7836)
Dutchman Creek Self-Storage .... G 919 363-8878
  Apex (G-185)
Security Self Storage .... G 919 544-3969
  Durham (G-5348)

LEASING: Passenger Car

Courtesy Ford Inc .... E 252 338-4783
  Elizabeth City (G-5537)

LEATHER & CUT STOCK WHOLESALERS

Leather Miracles LLC .... D 828 464-7448
  Hickory (G-8086)

LEATHER GOODS, EXC FOOTWEAR, GLOVES, LUGGAGE/ BELTING, WHOL

Carroll Companies Inc .... E 828 264-2521
  Boone (G-1184)

LEATHER GOODS: Card Cases

Pioneer Square Brands Inc .... G 360 733-5608
  High Point (G-8485)

LEATHER GOODS: Garments

Coast To Coast Lea & Vinyl Inc .... G 336 886-5050
  High Point (G-8298)

LEATHER GOODS: Holsters

Greene Mountain Outdoors LLC .... F 336 670-2186
  North Wilkesboro (G-12011)
Point Blank Enterprises Inc .... D 910 893-2071
  Lillington (G-9858)
Taylor Made Cases Inc .... F 919 209-0555
  Benson (G-1043)

LEATHER GOODS: Personal

Glaser Designs Inc .... F 415 552-3188
  Raleigh (G-12803)
Kyson Leather Incorporated .... G 919 245-0053
  Hurdle Mills (G-8909)
McKinley Leather Hickory Inc .... E 828 459-2884
  Claremont (G-3931)
Point Blank Enterprises Inc .... D 910 893-2071
  Lillington (G-9858)

LEATHER GOODS: Safety Belts

Ellison Company Inc .... C 704 889-7518
  Charlotte (G-2698)
VH Industries Inc .... E 704 743-2400
  Concord (G-4385)

LEATHER GOODS: Wallets

Wallets For Water .... G 704 564-0763
  Charlotte (G-3793)
Wobo Wallet LLC .... G 704 604-6041
  Harrisburg (G-7736)

LEATHER TANNING & FINISHING

Arcona Leather Company LLC .... G 828 396-7728
  Hudson (G-8761)
Carolina Fur Dressing Company .... E 919 231-0086
  Raleigh (G-12598)
Carroll Companies Inc .... F 828 466-5489
  Conover (G-4434)
Dani Leather USA Inc .... G 973 598-0890
  High Point (G-8317)
Leather Miracles LLC .... D 828 464-7448
  Hickory (G-8086)

LEATHER, LEATHER GOODS & FURS, WHOLESALE

Arcona Leather Company LLC .... G 828 396-7728
  Hudson (G-8761)
Carroll Companies Inc .... F 828 466-5489
  Conover (G-4434)
Jenkins Properties Inc .... E 336 667-4282
  North Wilkesboro (G-12017)

LEATHER: Accessory Prdts

Tasman Industries Inc .... G 502 587-0701
  High Point (G-8563)

LICENSE TAGS: Automobile, Stamped Metal

LICENSE TAGS: Automobile, Stamped Metal

City of Graham .... F 336 570-6811
  Graham *(G-6684)*

DMV Commissioners Office .... G 704 679-3914
  Charlotte *(G-2649)*

License Plate Agency .... G 910 763-7076
  Wilmington *(G-16300)*

NC License Plate .... G 336 889-8247
  High Point *(G-8462)*

NC License Plate Agency .... G 910 347-1000
  Jacksonville *(G-9016)*

NC Motor Vhcl Lcnse Plate Agcy .... G 336 228-7152
  Burlington *(G-1468)*

North Carolina Dept Trnsp. .... E 704 633-5873
  Salisbury *(G-14020)*

North Crlina Lcense Plate Agcy ...... G 910 485-1590
  Fayetteville *(G-5884)*

LIFE SAVING & SURVIVAL EQPT REPAIR SVCS, NONMEDICAL

Turbomed LLC .... F 973 527-5299
  Fayetteville *(G-5936)*

LIGHTING EQPT: Flashlights

Energizer Holdings Inc .... E 336 672-3526
  Asheboro *(G-431)*

LIGHTING EQPT: Motor Vehicle, NEC

Three GS Enterprises Inc .... F 828 696-2060
  Flat Rock *(G-5972)*

LIGHTING FIXTURES WHOLESALERS

Clarolux Inc .... E 336 378-6800
  Greensboro *(G-6912)*

Conservation Station Inc .... G 919 932-9201
  Chapel Hill *(G-2005)*

Egi Associates Inc .... F 704 561-3337
  Charlotte *(G-2687)*

LIGHTING FIXTURES, NEC

American Sports Lighting Inc .... G 910 520-1074
  Wilmington *(G-16110)*

Blue Sun Energy Inc .... G 336 218-6707
  Greensboro *(G-6842)*

Busiapp Corporation .... F 877 558-2518
  Morrisville *(G-11311)*

Dandy Light Traps Inc .... G 980 223-2744
  Statesville *(G-14782)*

Furnlite Inc .... E 704 538-3193
  Fallston *(G-5729)*

Led Integrations .... G 336 257-9935
  Burlington *(G-1449)*

Lightjunction .... G 919 607-9717
  Morrisville *(G-11380)*

Nexxus Lighting Inc .... E 407 857-9900
  Charlotte *(G-3257)*

Parhelion Incorporated .... F 866 409-1839
  Apex *(G-226)*

PDM Lighting LLC .... G 919 771-3230
  Raleigh *(G-13104)*

Pelican Ventures LLC .... G 919 518-8203
  Raleigh *(G-13105)*

Powertac Usa Inc .... G 919 239-4470
  Greensboro *(G-7270)*

Progress Solar Solutions LLC .... F 919 363-3738
  Raleigh *(G-13150)*

S C I A Inc .... G 919 387-7000
  Cary *(G-1877)*

Sels Smart ERA Ltg Systems .... G 336 661-8031
  Winston Salem *(G-16901)*

Solacure LLC .... G 336 601-2868
  Browns Summit *(G-1316)*

Specialty Manufacturing Inc .... C 704 247-9300
  Charlotte *(G-3598)*

Srb Technologies Inc .... E 336 659-2610
  Winston Salem *(G-16914)*

Sunnex Inc .... F 800 445-7869
  Charlotte *(G-3653)*

W F Harris Lighting Inc .... F 704 283-7477
  Monroe *(G-10830)*

LIGHTING FIXTURES: Arc

Cyberlux Corporation .... F 984 363-6894
  Research Triangle Pa *(G-13549)*

LIGHTING FIXTURES: Decorative Area

Light Source Usa Inc .... E 704 504-8399
  Charlotte *(G-3087)*

LIGHTING FIXTURES: Fluorescent, Commercial

Optimum Lighting LLC .... E 508 646-3324
  Henderson *(G-7800)*

W F Harris Lighting Inc .... F 704 283-7477
  Monroe *(G-10830)*

LIGHTING FIXTURES: Fluorescent, Residential

W F Harris Lighting Inc .... F 704 283-7477
  Monroe *(G-10830)*

LIGHTING FIXTURES: Indl & Commercial

A M Moore and Company Inc .... G 336 294-6994
  Greensboro *(G-6767)*

Arva LLC .... G 803 336-2230
  Charlotte *(G-2223)*

Atlas Lighting Products Inc .... C 336 222-9258
  Burlington *(G-1370)*

Avcon Inc .... E 919 388-0203
  Cary *(G-1696)*

B&M Donnelly Inc .... G 704 358-9229
  Charlotte *(G-2256)*

Biologcal Innvtion Optmztion S .... F 321 260-2467
  Wake Forest *(G-15533)*

Conservation Station Inc .... G 919 932-9201
  Chapel Hill *(G-2005)*

Enttec Americas LLC .... F 919 200-6468
  Durham *(G-5088)*

Idaho Wood Inc .... F 208 263-9521
  Oxford *(G-12132)*

Invictus Lighting LLC .... G 828 855-9324
  Hickory *(G-8068)*

Led Lighting Fixtures Inc .... G 919 991-0700
  Morrisville *(G-11373)*

Lighting .... G 919 828-0351
  Raleigh *(G-12970)*

Lumenfocus LLC .... F 252 430-6970
  Henderson *(G-7796)*

Progress Solar Solutions LLC .... F 919 363-3738
  Raleigh *(G-13150)*

Rapid Connector .... G 843 315-4700
  Manteo *(G-10129)*

Rsf Solid State Lighting Inc .... G 252 478-9915
  Spring Hope *(G-14621)*

Shat-R-Shield Lighting Inc .... D 800 223-0853
  Salisbury *(G-14042)*

Shield & Steel Enterprises LLC ...... G 704 607-0869
  Salisbury *(G-14043)*

Specialty Lighting LLC .... F 704 538-6522
  Fallston *(G-5730)*

Stevens Lighting Inc .... F 910 944-7187
  Carthage *(G-1668)*

LIGHTING FIXTURES: Motor Vehicle

B/E Aerospace Inc .... F 336 692-8940
  Winston Salem *(G-16612)*

Go Ev and Go Green Corp .... G 704 327-9040
  Charlotte *(G-2839)*

LIGHTING FIXTURES: Residential, Electric

Epl & Solar Corp .... G 201 577-8966
  Wake Forest *(G-15554)*

LIGHTING FIXTURES: Street

Curlee Machinery Company .... G 919 467-9311
  Cary *(G-1743)*

M-B Industries Inc .... C 828 862-4201
  Rosman *(G-13786)*

LIGHTING FIXTURES: Underwater

Pentair Water Pool and Spa Inc ..... F 919 463-4640
  Cary *(G-1848)*

Pentair Water Pool and Spa Inc ..... A 919 566-8000
  Sanford *(G-14166)*

LIME ROCK: Ground

Limestone Products Inc .... G 704 283-9492
  Monroe *(G-10758)*

LIMESTONE: Crushed & Broken

Boyd Stone & Quarries .... G 828 659-6862
  Marion *(G-10144)*

Buffalo Crushed Stone Inc .... F 919 688-6881
  Durham *(G-4985)*

Bwi Etn LLC .... G 828 682-2645
  Burnsville *(G-1525)*

Heidelberg Mtls Sthast Agg LLC .... E 919 936-4221
  Princeton *(G-12400)*

Marietta Martin Materials Inc .... D 704 525-7740
  Charlotte *(G-3125)*

Marietta Martin Materials Inc .... G 252 749-2641
  Fountain *(G-6095)*

Marietta Martin Materials Inc .... E 919 772-3563
  Garner *(G-6283)*

Marietta Martin Materials Inc .... F 336 668-3253
  Greensboro *(G-7180)*

Marietta Martin Materials Inc .... G 828 322-8386
  Hickory *(G-8091)*

Marietta Martin Materials Inc .... G 336 886-5015
  Jamestown *(G-9060)*

Marietta Martin Materials Inc .... G 336 769-3803
  Kernersville *(G-9213)*

Marietta Martin Materials Inc .... G 704 739-4761
  Kings Mountain *(G-9317)*

Marietta Martin Materials Inc .... G 704 283-4915
  Monroe *(G-10765)*

Marietta Martin Materials Inc .... F 919 788-4392
  Raleigh *(G-12994)*

Marietta Martin Materials Inc .... G 336 349-3333
  Reidsville *(G-13530)*

Marietta Martin Materials Inc .... F 704 636-6372
  Salisbury *(G-14009)*

Marietta Martin Materials Inc .... G 704 873-8191
  Statesville *(G-14839)*

Marietta Martin Materials Inc .... G 336 475-9134
  Thomasville *(G-15245)*

Marietta Martin Materials Inc .... G 704 278-2218
  Woodleaf *(G-17023)*

Martin Marietta Materia .... G 336 372-6311
  Sparta *(G-14596)*

Martin Marietta Materials Inc .... G 919 894-2003
  Benson *(G-1039)*

Martin Marietta Materials Inc .... G 336 584-8875
  Burlington *(G-1455)*

PRODUCT SECTION

LOGGING

Martin Marietta Materials Inc.................. G 910 675-2283
   Castle Hayne *(G-1953)*

Martin Marietta Materials Inc.................. G 704 547-9775
   Charlotte *(G-3131)*

Martin Marietta Materials Inc.................. G 704 588-1471
   Charlotte *(G-3132)*

Martin Marietta Materials Inc.................. G 704 932-4377
   China Grove *(G-3885)*

Martin Marietta Materials Inc.................. G 704 786-8415
   Concord *(G-4309)*

Martin Marietta Materials Inc.................. G 336 375-7584
   Greensboro *(G-7184)*

Martin Marietta Materials Inc.................. G 336 674-0836
   Greensboro *(G-7185)*

Martin Marietta Materials Inc.................. G 910 371-3848
   Leland *(G-9555)*

Martin Marietta Materials Inc.................. F 828 754-3077
   Lenoir *(G-9633)*

Martin Marietta Materials Inc.................. G 704 847-3087
   Matthews *(G-10267)*

Martin Marietta Materials Inc.................. G 252 633-5308
   New Bern *(G-11820)*

Martin Marietta Materials Inc.................. G 336 672-1501
   Randleman *(G-13477)*

Martin Marietta Materials Inc.................. G 336 672-1501
   Randleman *(G-13478)*

Martin Marietta Materials Inc.................. G 919 788-4391
   Sanford *(G-14149)*

Martin Marietta Materials Inc.................. C 919 781-4550
   Raleigh *(G-13001)*

Quarries Petroleum.............................. G 919 387-0986
   Apex *(G-236)*

Radford Quarries Inc............................ F 828 264-7008
   Boone *(G-1231)*

LIMESTONE: Dimension

Nantahala Talc & Limestone Co................ F 828 321-4239
   Topton *(G-15326)*

LINENS: Tablecloths, From Purchased Materials

Sanders Industries Inc.......................... G 410 277-8565
   Waynesville *(G-15820)*

Watson Party Tables Inc........................ F 919 294-9153
   Durham *(G-5438)*

LINERS & COVERS: Fabric

Howell & Sons Canvas Repairs................ G 704 892-7913
   Cornelius *(G-4556)*

Winstn-Slem Inds For Blind Inc................ B 336 759-0551
   Winston Salem *(G-16979)*

LINERS: Indl, Metal Plate

B&B Cap Liners LLC............................. G 585 598-1828
   Raleigh *(G-12539)*

LININGS: Fabric, Apparel & Other, Exc Millinery

Domestic Fabrics Blankets Corp............... E 252 523-7948
   Kinston *(G-9359)*

LIP BALMS

Lick er Lips Lip Balm LLC...................... G 702 355-5433
   Charlotte *(G-3084)*

LIQUID CRYSTAL DISPLAYS

Lxd Research & Display LLC................... F 919 600-6440
   Raleigh *(G-12984)*

Smallhd LLC..................................... E 919 439-2166
   Cary *(G-1895)*

LITHIUM MINERAL MINING

Piedmont Lithium Inc............................ G 704 461-8000
   Belmont *(G-1003)*

LITHOGRAPHIC PLATES

F C C LLC... G 336 883-7314
   High Point *(G-8349)*

Southern Lithoplate Inc......................... C 919 556-9400
   Youngsville *(G-17099)*

LOADS: Electronic

Vishay Transducers Ltd......................... E 919 365-3800
   Wendell *(G-15924)*

LOCKERS

Penco Products Inc.............................. E 252 917-5287
   Greenville *(G-7570)*

LOCKERS: Wood, Exc Refrigerated

Treeforms Inc.................................... E 336 292-8998
   Greensboro *(G-7409)*

LOCKS

Appalachian Technology LLC.................. E 828 210-8888
   Asheville *(G-524)*

Assa Abloy ACC Door Cntrls Gro............. C 877 974-2255
   Monroe *(G-10653)*

Norton Door Controls........................... E 704 233-4011
   Monroe *(G-10781)*

LOCKS & LOCK SETS, WHOLESALE

Norton Door Controls........................... E 704 233-4011
   Monroe *(G-10781)*

LOCKS: Safe & Vault, Metal

Kaba Ilco Corp.................................... B 336 725-1331
   Winston Salem *(G-16775)*

LOCKSMITHS

ACS Advnced Clor Solutions Inc.............. G 252 442-0098
   Rocky Mount *(G-13679)*

Ilco Unican Holding Corp....................... D 252 446-3321
   Rocky Mount *(G-13703)*

Kaba Ilco Corp.................................... A 252 446-3321
   Rocky Mount *(G-13704)*

Omnia Industries LLC.......................... G 704 707-6062
   Matthews *(G-10278)*

LOGGING

3 D Footprints Logging Inc..................... G 910 521-2640
   Maxton *(G-10353)*

A and J Ta Logging.............................. G 919 663-1110
   Siler City *(G-14394)*

ABB Logging LLC................................ G 252 809-0180
   Williamston *(G-16056)*

Allsbrook Logging LLC......................... G 252 567-1085
   Enfield *(G-5674)*

Appalachian Timber Company................ G 828 507-6505
   Sylva *(G-15052)*

Associated Artists Southport.................. G 910 457-5450
   Southport *(G-14566)*

Autry Logging Inc................................ G 910 303-4943
   Stedman *(G-14933)*

Backwoods Logging Pink Hl Inc.............. G 910 298-1284
   Pink Hill *(G-12315)*

Barry Lane Perry................................. G 252 799-4334
   Jamesville *(G-9078)*

Baur Logging LLC............................... G 757 535-5693
   Gatesville *(G-6547)*

Bh Logging.. G 980 330-0229
   Statesville *(G-14763)*

Black River Logging Inc........................ G 910 669-2850
   Ivanhoe *(G-8980)*

Boyles Logging LLC............................. G 910 206-7086
   Ellerbe *(G-5641)*

Bracey Bros Logging LLC...................... G 910 231-9543
   Delco *(G-4719)*

Bradley Todd Baugus............................ G 252 665-4901
   Maysville *(G-10369)*

Brett McHenry Logging LLC................... F 252 243-7285
   Wilson *(G-16478)*

Bruce Stanley..................................... G 828 683-1265
   Leicester *(G-9508)*

Buds Logging and Trucking.................... G 704 465-8016
   Wadesboro *(G-15505)*

Burgess Duke Hward Ktrina Kner............ G 704 732-0547
   Lincolnton *(G-9877)*

Calvin Laws Jay.................................. G 336 973-4318
   Ferguson *(G-5956)*

Carter Thomas Wayne Sr...................... G 336 623-2177
   Reidsville *(G-13513)*

Cbr Logging LLC................................. G 252 791-0494
   Plymouth *(G-12368)*

Coastal Carolina Loggin........................ G 252 474-2165
   Ernul *(G-5686)*

Conetoe Land & Timber LLC.................. F 252 717-4648
   Goldsboro *(G-6603)*

Country Roads Logging LLC.................. G 252 578-8191
   Margarettsville *(G-10136)*

Country Roads Logging LLC.................. G 252 398-4770
   Como *(G-4183)*

D & W Logging Inc.............................. F 919 820-0826
   Four Oaks *(G-6102)*

D J Logging Inc.................................. G 919 219-6853
   Raleigh *(G-12669)*

Dan Morton Logging............................. G 919 693-1898
   Oxford *(G-12126)*

Daniel A Malpass Logging..................... G 910 669-2823
   Kelly *(G-9137)*

David E Meiggs.................................. G 252 340-1640
   Hertford *(G-7919)*

David J Spain.................................... G 252 902-6900
   Washington *(G-15694)*

Douglas Temple & Son Inc.................... F 252 771-5676
   Elizabeth City *(G-5541)*

Dustin Ellis Logging............................. G 704 732-6027
   Lincolnton *(G-9891)*

Dustin Lynn Sink................................. G 336 442-5602
   Trinity *(G-15340)*

Duvall Timber LLC.............................. G 704 236-2211
   Waxhaw *(G-15755)*

East Coast Log & Timber Inc.................. G 252 568-4344
   Albertson *(G-115)*

Eddie Ta Mendenhall Logging................. G 919 718-9293
   Moncure *(G-10620)*

Edsel G Barnes Jr Inc.......................... G 252 793-4170
   Plymouth *(G-12372)*

Edwards Logging Inc........................... G 336 783-0833
   Mount Airy *(G-11506)*

Emanuel Hoggard................................ F 252 794-3724
   Windsor *(G-16566)*

Eric Martin Jermey.............................. G 704 692-0389
   Bostic *(G-1262)*

G&N Logging LLC............................... G 919 524-1555
   Middlesex *(G-10449)*

General Wood Preserving Co Inc............ F 910 371-3131
   Leland *(G-9546)*

George P Gatling Logging..................... G 252 465-8983
   Sunbury *(G-14996)*

Gmd Logging Inc................................ G 704 985-5460
   Albemarle *(G-87)*

Goodsons All Terrain Log...................... G 910 934-8451
   Jacksonville *(G-9005)*

LOGGING

Grassy Ridge Logging Co .... G 919 935-5355
  Robbins *(G-13598)*
Greenes Logging .... G 910 533-2021
  Roseboro *(G-13785)*
H & H Login .... G 704 272-8763
  Polkton *(G-12387)*
H&R Transport LLC .... G 910 588-4410
  Garland *(G-6245)*
Hardister Logging .... G 336 857-2397
  Denton *(G-4736)*
Hunt Logging Co .... G 919 853-2850
  Louisburg *(G-9991)*
I I G Logging Inc .... G 704 984-3175
  Morven *(G-11471)*
Ivey Icenhour DBA .... G 704 786-0676
  Mount Pleasant *(G-11674)*
J E Kerr Timber Co Corp .... F 252 537-0544
  Roanoke Rapids *(G-13576)*
J&D Logging Inc .... G 910 271-0750
  Warsaw *(G-15670)*
James Keith Nations .... G 828 421-5391
  Whittier *(G-16007)*
James L Johnson .... G 704 694-0103
  Wadesboro *(G-15514)*
Jds Logging LLC .... G 910 713-5980
  Ash *(G-395)*
Jennifer Niten Logging .... G 336 428-6245
  Elkin *(G-5621)*
Jimmie A Hogan .... G 910 428-2535
  Biscoe *(G-1112)*
Jj Hernandez Logging LLC .... G 919 742-3381
  Siler City *(G-14418)*
Jk Logging LLC .... G 910 648-5471
  Evergreen *(G-5698)*
Jmw Logging LLC .... G 919 934-4115
  Smithfield *(G-14466)*
Joseph and Jerry Curtis .... G 704 663-4811
  Mooresville *(G-10988)*
Josh Lane Logging LLC .... G 828 289-4052
  Union Mills *(G-15441)*
Jph III Logging Inc .... G 910 610-9338
  Laurinburg *(G-9482)*
Jrt Logging Inc .... G 704 322-0458
  Polkton *(G-12388)*
Juan J Hernandez .... G 919 742-3381
  Siler City *(G-14419)*
Justin Moretz & Greg Moretz Db .... G 828 263-8668
  Deep Gap *(G-4709)*
K & J Ashworth Logging LLC .... G 336 879-2388
  Seagrove *(G-14242)*
Keith Laws .... G 336 973-7220
  Wilkesboro *(G-16034)*
Kenneth Perkins .... G 919 267-9396
  Holly Springs *(G-8704)*
Kornegay Logging & Timber Co .... G 919 658-5716
  Mount Olive *(G-11665)*
Laceys Tree Service .... G 910 330-2868
  Jacksonville *(G-9012)*
Lannings Farming and Logging .... G 828 246-8938
  Clyde *(G-4125)*
Laws Logging .... G 336 973-4318
  Ferguson *(G-5958)*
Lees Logging Company .... F 910 385-7201
  Harrells *(G-7694)*
Lite Logging LLC .... G 252 560-8131
  La Grange *(G-9442)*
Logger Head Logging .... G 919 842-0249
  New Hill *(G-11862)*
Luxury Escapes LLC .... F 706 373-8500
  Raleigh *(G-12983)*
Lyon Logging .... G 336 957-3131
  Thurmond *(G-15311)*

M M & D Harvesting Inc .... G 252 793-4074
  Plymouth *(G-12376)*
Matthew Johnson Logging .... G 919 291-0197
  Sanford *(G-14150)*
McKoys Logging Company Inc .... G 910 862-2706
  Elizabethtown *(G-5598)*
McNeely Accounting & Tax Svc .... G 828 652-7405
  Marion *(G-10164)*
Mendoza Logging Inc .... G 252 935-5560
  Pantego *(G-12168)*
Mickey Blanton Logging .... G 828 289-9344
  Mooresboro *(G-10839)*
Mike Goodwin Logging .... G 704 848-8222
  Lilesville *(G-9840)*
Mini Semi Logging .... G 828 284-1360
  Burnsville *(G-1529)*
MN Logging LLC .... G 828 286-9262
  Rutherfordton *(G-13880)*
Montgomery Logging Inc .... G 910 572-2806
  Troy *(G-15409)*
Morgan & Son Logging .... G 828 389-9618
  Hayesville *(G-7769)*
Mountain Valley Logging LLC .... G 828 551-0861
  Zirconia *(G-17155)*
Myers Logging LLC .... G 919 496-0379
  Castalia *(G-1940)*
Nathan Beiler .... G 252 935-5141
  Pantego *(G-12169)*
NC Logging & Clearing LLC .... G 919 524-4878
  Sanford *(G-14157)*
New Vision Logging LLC .... G 910 594-0571
  Newton Grove *(G-11991)*
North Cape Fear Logging LLC .... G 910 876-3197
  Harrells *(G-7695)*
OBrien Logging Co .... G 910 655-3830
  Delco *(G-4723)*
Outkast Timber Harvesting LLC .... G 336 906-0962
  Randleman *(G-13482)*
P & C Logging LLC .... G 919 552-3420
  Fuquay Varina *(G-6221)*
Pack Brothers Logging .... G 828 894-2191
  Mill Spring *(G-10489)*
Piedmont Logging LLC .... G 919 562-1861
  Youngsville *(G-17091)*
Plan B Chipping and Logging .... G 336 942-2692
  Sophia *(G-14520)*
Preferred Logging .... G 910 471-4011
  Delco *(G-4724)*
Pritchard Logging LLC .... G 828 447-4354
  Rutherfordton *(G-13885)*
Randy Chappell Logging LLC .... G 910 439-6690
  Mount Gilead *(G-11612)*
Randy Smith and Sons Logging .... G 828 263-0574
  Deep Gap *(G-4712)*
Richard Lewis Von .... G 910 628-9292
  Orrum *(G-12117)*
Ricky Don Thornton .... G 910 271-2989
  Teachey *(G-15178)*
Ricky Wyatt Logging .... G 336 984-3145
  North Wilkesboro *(G-12032)*
Roberson Logging LLC .... F 252 799-7076
  Williamston *(G-16069)*
Roland Brothers LLC .... G 336 385-9013
  Warrensville *(G-15653)*
Ronnie A Mabe .... G 336 994-2257
  King *(G-9280)*
Ronnie L Poole .... G 336 657-3956
  Ennice *(G-5685)*
Rotens Logging LLC .... G 336 981-7019
  North Wilkesboro *(G-12033)*
Roundwood Logging Inc .... G 252 230-9980
  Sims *(G-14444)*

Rudys Logging LLC .... G 910 918-2993
  Leland *(G-9559)*
Shepherd Family Logging LLC .... G 910 572-4098
  Troy *(G-15415)*
Skj Moore Logging LLC .... G 828 642-5724
  Nakina *(G-11731)*
Southern Style Logging LLC .... G 910 259-9897
  Rocky Point *(G-13750)*
Spencer Logging .... G 910 638-4899
  Southern Pines *(G-14557)*
SSS Logging Inc .... G 828 467-1155
  Marion *(G-10180)*
Stafford Logging LLC .... G 828 635-8584
  Moravian Falls *(G-11147)*
Steve Whiteside Logging LLC .... G 828 287-5862
  Rutherfordton *(G-13891)*
Steven C Haddock DBA Haddock .... G 252 714-2431
  Vanceboro *(G-15483)*
Stroud Logging .... G 828 541-2721
  Marble *(G-10134)*
Stump Logging .... G 910 620-7000
  Supply *(G-15012)*
Sugg Logging LLC .... G 910 995-5728
  Ellerbe *(G-5645)*
Summit Logging LLC .... G 910 734-8787
  Lumberton *(G-10056)*
T and T Timber .... G 252 799-6077
  Roper *(G-13771)*
T W Hathcock Logging Inc .... G 704 485-9457
  Locust *(G-9974)*
T&L Nursery and Logging LLC .... G 828 387-0448
  Newland *(G-11895)*
Taylor Timber Co LLC .... G 910 588-6214
  Harrells *(G-7696)*
Ted M Hart Logging Inc .... G 919 776-7237
  Sanford *(G-14195)*
Thomas Gary Helton .... G 828 726-3694
  Lenoir *(G-9656)*
Thompson Timber Harvest LLC .... G 919 632-4326
  Franklinton *(G-6166)*
Timothy Kornegay .... G 919 222-3184
  Albertson *(G-116)*
Top Notch Log Homes Inc .... G 828 926-4300
  Waynesville *(G-15829)*
Triple E Equipment LLC .... G 252 448-1002
  Trenton *(G-15336)*
Tysinger Logging Inc .... G 910 220-5053
  Star *(G-14724)*
Vincent L Taylor .... G 252 792-2987
  Williamston *(G-16072)*
W H Bunting Thinning .... G 252 826-4025
  Scotland Neck *(G-14223)*
Walker Logging .... G 336 964-1380
  Denton *(G-4755)*
Wayne Dunn Logging LLC .... G 910 439-5478
  Mount Gilead *(G-11615)*
William Shawn Staley .... G 336 838-9193
  Millers Creek *(G-10496)*
Wolf Timber LLC .... G 252 799-0495
  Williamston *(G-16074)*
Wst Logging LLC .... G 336 857-0147
  Denton *(G-4756)*
Young Logging Company Inc .... G 919 552-9753
  Willow Spring *(G-16085)*

LOGGING CAMPS & CONTRACTORS

360 Forest Products Inc .... G 910 285-5838
  Wallace *(G-15618)*
A & S Logging LLC .... G 336 879-4364
  Seagrove *(G-14232)*
Alan Walsh Logging LLC .... G 828 234-7500
  Lenoir *(G-9570)*

PRODUCT SECTION — LOGGING CAMPS & CONTRACTORS

Allen Brothers Timber Company............ E 910 997-6412
  Rockingham *(G-13619)*
Allen R Goodson Logging Co................ G 910 455-4177
  Jacksonville *(G-8987)*
Alligood Brothers Logging..................... G 252 927-2358
  Washington *(G-15680)*
Alpha Logging Inc................................... G 252 568-2727
  Deep Run *(G-4715)*
Anthony B Andrews Logging Inc........... G 252 448-8901
  Trenton *(G-15332)*
Arcola Logging Co Inc............................ F 252 257-3205
  Macon *(G-10068)*
Arrants Logging Inc................................ F 252 792-1889
  Jamesville *(G-9077)*
Ashworth Logging.................................. G 910 464-2136
  Carthage *(G-1659)*
Atlantic Logging Inc................................ F 252 229-9997
  New Bern *(G-11772)*
Backwoods Logging LLC........................ G 910 298-3786
  Pink Hill *(G-12314)*
Barnes Logging Co Inc........................... F 252 799-6016
  Plymouth *(G-12365)*
Bateman Logging Co Inc........................ G 252 482-8959
  Edenton *(G-5508)*
Bill Ratliff Jr Logging I............................. G 704 694-5403
  Wadesboro *(G-15502)*
Billy Harrell Logging Inc......................... F 252 221-4995
  Tyner *(G-15433)*
Billy Harrell Logging Inc......................... G 252 426-1362
  Hertford *(G-7916)*
Blankenship Logging.............................. G 828 652-2250
  Nebo *(G-11759)*
Bobby A Herring Logging...................... G 919 658-9768
  Mount Olive *(G-11656)*
Boone Logging Company Inc................. G 252 443-7641
  Elm City *(G-5647)*
Broadway Logging Co Inc...................... E 252 633-2693
  New Bern *(G-11778)*
Brown Brothers Lumber.......................... G 828 632-6486
  Taylorsville *(G-15132)*
Brown Creek Timber Company Inc........ G 704 694-3529
  Wadesboro *(G-15504)*
Buck Lucas Logging Companies........... G 252 410-0160
  Roanoke Rapids *(G-13568)*
Bundy Logging Company Inc................. F 252 357-0191
  Gatesville *(G-6548)*
By Faith Logging Inc.............................. G 252 792-0019
  Williamston *(G-16058)*
Cahoon Brothers Logging LLC.............. F 252 943-9901
  Pinetown *(G-12245)*
Cahoon Logging Company Inc.............. G 252 943-6805
  Pinetown *(G-12246)*
Capps Noble Logging............................. G 828 696-9690
  Zirconia *(G-17150)*
Caraway Logging Inc............................. G 252 633-1230
  New Bern *(G-11783)*
Carolina East Timber Inc....................... G 252 638-1914
  New Bern *(G-11784)*
Cauley Construction Company.............. G 252 522-1078
  Kinston *(G-9353)*
Chapman Brothers Logging LLC........... G 828 437-6498
  Connelly Springs *(G-4398)*
Charles Ferguson Logging..................... G 336 921-3126
  Moravian Falls *(G-11144)*
CJ Stallings Logging Inc........................ F 252 297-2272
  Belvidere *(G-1021)*
Claybourn Walters Log Co Inc............... F 910 628-7075
  Fairmont *(G-5701)*
Corbett Timber Company....................... G 910 406-1129
  Hampstead *(G-7644)*
Cutting Up Logging LLC........................ G 910 389-3539
  Maysville *(G-10371)*

Cypress Creek Harvesting Inc............... G 805 462-9412
  Garland *(G-6241)*
D & M Logging of Wnc LLC.................. G 828 648-4366
  Canton *(G-1612)*
D T Bracy Logging Inc.......................... G 252 332-8332
  Ahoskie *(G-59)*
Dannies Logging Inc.............................. G 919 528-2370
  Creedmoor *(G-4612)*
Danny Huffman Logging LLC............... G 336 973-0555
  Purlear *(G-12410)*
Darrell T Bracy...................................... G 252 358-1432
  Ahoskie *(G-60)*
Dave Mulhollem Logging Inc................ G 919 796-8994
  Wendell *(G-15896)*
David Miller Logging LLC..................... G 336 831-4052
  Boonville *(G-1254)*
David Raynor Logging Inc..................... E 910 980-0129
  Linden *(G-9939)*
Delbert White Logging Inc.................... G 252 209-4779
  Windsor *(G-16564)*
Derick Cordon Logging Inc................... F 252 964-2009
  Bath *(G-915)*
Dockery Logging.................................... G 828 557-9149
  Murphy *(G-11708)*
Donald R Young Logging Inc................ G 910 934-6769
  Lillington *(G-9850)*
Down South Logging LLC..................... G 843 333-1649
  Tabor City *(G-15080)*
Dr Logging LLC...................................... G 910 417-9643
  Hamlet *(G-7620)*
Duncan Junior D.................................... G 336 871-3599
  Sandy Ridge *(G-14078)*
Duplin Forest Products Inc................... F 910 285-5381
  Wallace *(G-15621)*
E JS Logging Inc................................... G 252 927-3539
  Pinetown *(G-12248)*
East Coast Logging Inc......................... G 252 794-4054
  Windsor *(G-16565)*
Enterprise Loggers Company Inc.......... F 252 586-4805
  Littleton *(G-9951)*
Evans Logging Inc................................. F 252 792-3865
  Jamesville *(G-9080)*
Evergreen Forest Products Inc.............. G 910 762-9156
  Wilmington *(G-16213)*
Evergreen Logging LLC......................... G 910 654-1662
  Evergreen *(G-5697)*
Faith Logging.. G 828 446-5671
  Lenoir *(G-9611)*
Foster Jackson & Sons LLC.................. G 828 674-7941
  Saluda *(G-14070)*
Frankie York Logging Co...................... G 252 633-4825
  New Bern *(G-11804)*
Fred R Harrris Logging Inc................... G 919 853-2266
  Louisburg *(G-9989)*
Freeman Transport and Logging........... G 910 220-5358
  Star *(G-14715)*
Fuqua Logging Company Inc................ F 336 562-5178
  Leasburg *(G-9505)*
G & G Logging....................................... G 336 352-5586
  Lowgap *(G-10013)*
G & H Broadway Logging Inc............... G 252 229-4594
  New Bern *(G-11805)*
Glacier Forestry Inc.............................. G 704 902-2594
  Mooresville *(G-10959)*
Gladsons Logging LLC.......................... F 252 670-8813
  Aurora *(G-835)*
Glenn Trexler & Sons Log Inc............... G 704 694-5644
  Wadesboro *(G-15510)*
Gold Creek Inc....................................... G 336 468-4495
  Hamptonville *(G-7670)*
Goodson S All Terrain Log Inc.............. F 910 347-7919
  Jacksonville *(G-9004)*

Gouge Logging....................................... G 828 675-9216
  Burnsville *(G-1527)*
Grady & Son Atkins Logging................. G 919 934-7785
  Four Oaks *(G-6106)*
Greene Logging..................................... G 336 667-6960
  Purlear *(G-12412)*
H & L Logging Inc................................. F 252 793-2778
  Plymouth *(G-12374)*
H Clyde Moore Jr................................... G 910 642-3507
  Whiteville *(G-15965)*
Harris Logging LLC............................... G 336 859-2786
  Denton *(G-4737)*
Hofler Logging Inc................................ G 252 465-8921
  Sunbury *(G-14998)*
Holmes Logging - Wallace LLC............. F 910 271-1216
  Wallace *(G-15623)*
Htc Logging Inc..................................... G 828 625-1601
  Mill Spring *(G-10487)*
J & J Logging Inc.................................. E 252 430-1110
  Henderson *(G-7790)*
J E Carpenter Logging Co Inc.............. F 252 633-0037
  Trent Woods *(G-15328)*
J&R Cohoon Logging & Tidewater........ F 252 943-6300
  Pantego *(G-12165)*
Jackson Logging................................... G 919 658-2757
  Mount Olive *(G-11663)*
James Moore & Son Logging................ G 336 656-9858
  Browns Summit *(G-1309)*
Jared Sasnett Logging Co Inc.............. G 252 939-6289
  Kinston *(G-9370)*
Jeff Weaver Logging............................. G 864 909-1758
  Columbus *(G-4175)*
Jeffers Logging Inc............................... G 919 708-2193
  Sanford *(G-14139)*
Jerry Cox Logging................................. G 919 742-6089
  Ramseur *(G-13443)*
Jh Logging... G 336 599-0278
  Roxboro *(G-13805)*
Jif Logging Inc....................................... G 252 398-2249
  Murfreesboro *(G-11699)*
Jimmy D Nelms Logging Inc................ F 919 853-2597
  Louisburg *(G-9993)*
Johnny Daniel.. G 336 859-2480
  Denton *(G-4739)*
K L Butler Logging Inc......................... G 910 648-6016
  Bladenboro *(G-1150)*
Keck Logging & Chipping Inc.............. G 336 538-6903
  Gibsonville *(G-6564)*
Keck Logging Company......................... G 336 538-6903
  Gibsonville *(G-6565)*
Keith Call Logging LLC......................... G 336 262-3681
  Millers Creek *(G-10493)*
Ken Horton Logging LLC....................... G 336 789-2849
  Mount Airy *(G-11530)*
Ken Wood Corp...................................... G 252 792-6481
  Williamston *(G-16064)*
Lake Creek Logging & Trckg Inc........... F 910 532-2041
  Harrells *(G-7693)*
Lane Land & Timber Inc....................... G 252 443-1151
  Battleboro *(G-923)*
Ledford Logging Co Inc......................... G 828 644-5410
  Murphy *(G-11711)*
Leonard Logging Co.............................. G 336 857-2776
  Denton *(G-4743)*
Little Logging Inc.................................. F 704 201-8185
  Oakboro *(G-12076)*
M & K Logging LLC............................... G 252 349-8975
  New Bern *(G-11816)*
Mark III Logging Inc............................. G 910 862-4820
  Tar Heel *(G-15089)*
Mark Lindsay Looper............................. G 828 234-5453
  Lenoir *(G-9630)*

Employee Codes: A=Over 500 employees, B=251-500
C=101-250, D=51-100, E=20-50, F=10-19, G=1-9

2024 Harris North Carolina
Manufacturers Directory

LOGGING CAMPS & CONTRACTORS

McKay Logging Inc .... G 910 334-3448
   Rockingham *(G-13634)*

McKeel & Sons Logging Inc .... G 252 244-3903
   Vanceboro *(G-15480)*

McKenzies Tree Service & Log .... G 910 995-1576
   Hamlet *(G-7627)*

McLendon Logging Incorporated .... G 910 439-6223
   Mount Gilead *(G-11604)*

Meacham Logging Inc .... G 910 652-2794
   Ellerbe *(G-5642)*

Merritt Logging & Chipping Co .... F 910 862-4905
   Elizabethtown *(G-5599)*

Michael L Goodson Logging Inc .... G 910 346-8399
   Jacksonville *(G-9013)*

Micheal Langdon Logging Inc .... G 910 890-5295
   Erwin *(G-5687)*

Mike Atkins & Son Logging Inc .... G 919 965-8002
   Selma *(G-14258)*

Miller Logging Co Inc .... G 252 229-9860
   Vanceboro *(G-15481)*

Mud Duck Operations .... G 910 253-7669
   Bolivia *(G-1165)*

Myers Brothers Logging LLC .... G 828 432-9738
   Morganton *(G-11237)*

Nat Black Logging Inc .... F 704 826-8834
   Ansonville *(G-153)*

Noble Brothers Logging Company .... G 252 355-2587
   Winterville *(G-17010)*

Nrfp Logging LLC .... G 919 738-0989
   Goldsboro *(G-6639)*

OLT Logging Inc .... G 919 894-4506
   Smithfield *(G-14473)*

Phillip Dunn Logging Co Inc .... F 252 633-4577
   New Bern *(G-11835)*

Potter Logging .... G 704 483-2738
   Denver *(G-4795)*

Potts Logging Inc .... G 704 463-7549
   New London *(G-11875)*

Precision Log & Chipping LLC .... G 828 446-1592
   Taylorsville *(G-15158)*

Price Logging Inc .... G 252 792-5687
   Jamesville *(G-9081)*

Puett Trucking & Logging .... G 919 853-2071
   Louisburg *(G-9997)*

R & R Logging Inc .... G 704 483-5733
   Iron Station *(G-8976)*

R & S Logging Inc .... G 252 426-5880
   Hertford *(G-7923)*

R R Mickey Logging Inc .... G 910 205-0525
   Hamlet *(G-7631)*

R W Britt Logging Inc .... G 252 799-7682
   Pinetown *(G-12249)*

Rabbit Bottom Logging Co Inc .... F 252 257-3585
   Warrenton *(G-15660)*

Randolph Goodson Logging Inc .... G 910 347-5117
   Jacksonville *(G-9025)*

Red Maple Logging Company Inc .... G 704 279-6379
   Rockwell *(G-13657)*

Richard C Jones .... G 919 853-2096
   Louisburg *(G-10000)*

Robert L Rich Tmber Hrvstg Inc .... G 910 529-7321
   Garland *(G-6246)*

Rondol Cordon Logging Inc .... G 252 944-9220
   Washington *(G-15729)*

Ronnie Boyds Logging LLC .... G 336 613-0229
   Eden *(G-5501)*

Ronnie Garrett Logging .... G 828 894-8413
   Columbus *(G-4179)*

Ross Phelps Logging Co Inc .... F 252 356-2560
   Colerain *(G-4140)*

Russell Loudermilk Logging .... G 828 632-4968
   Taylorsville *(G-15164)*

S & K Logging Inc .... F 252 794-2045
   Windsor *(G-16569)*

Shelton Logging & Chipping Inc .... G 336 548-3860
   Stoneville *(G-14966)*

Simmons Logging & Trucking Inc .... F 910 287-6344
   Ash *(G-396)*

Smith Brothers Logging .... G 828 265-1506
   Deep Gap *(G-4713)*

Smiths Logging .... G 910 653-4422
   Tabor City *(G-15086)*

Snowbird Logging LLC .... G 828 479-6635
   Robbinsville *(G-13613)*

Southeast Wood Products Inc .... F 910 285-4359
   Wallace *(G-15627)*

Southern Logging Inc .... F 336 859-5057
   Denton *(G-4748)*

Squeaks Logging Inc .... G 252 794-1531
   Windsor *(G-16570)*

Steve Evans Logging Inc .... G 252 792-1836
   Williamston *(G-16071)*

Stone House Creek Logging .... G 252 586-4477
   Littleton *(G-9953)*

Swain & Temple Inc .... E 252 771-8147
   South Mills *(G-14525)*

SWB Logging LLC .... G 704 485-3411
   Oakboro *(G-12082)*

T E Garner Logging .... G 252 678-3836
   Gaston *(G-6332)*

TA Logging LLC .... G 704 485-8337
   Oakboro *(G-12083)*

Tar River Thinning Inc .... F 919 497-1647
   Louisburg *(G-10004)*

Terry Leggett Logging Co Inc .... E 252 927-4671
   Pinetown *(G-12250)*

Terry Logging Company .... G 919 477-9170
   Bahama *(G-867)*

Thomas Timber Inc .... F 910 532-4542
   Harrells *(G-7697)*

Tim Con Wood Products Inc .... E 252 793-4819
   Roper *(G-13772)*

Timber Harvester Inc .... G 910 346-9754
   Jacksonville *(G-9042)*

Timber Specialists LLC .... F 704 873-5756
   Statesville *(G-14915)*

Timber Stand Improvements Inc .... G 910 439-6121
   Mount Gilead *(G-11613)*

Tippett Logging LLC .... G 252 301-3170
   Whitakers *(G-15957)*

Trexler Logging Inc .... G 704 694-5272
   Wadesboro *(G-15517)*

Tucker Logging .... G 336 857-2674
   Denton *(G-4753)*

Vultare Logging LLC .... G 252 578-0377
   Roanoke Rapids *(G-13584)*

W & T Logging LLC .... G 252 209-4351
   Windsor *(G-16571)*

W R White Inc .... F 252 794-6577
   Windsor *(G-16572)*

Wade Biggs Logging Inc .... F 252 927-4470
   Pinetown *(G-12251)*

Wayne Lamb Logging Co .... G 910 529-1115
   Garland *(G-6247)*

Wetherington Logging Inc .... G 252 393-8435
   Stella *(G-14938)*

Williams & Son Logging LLC .... G 252 533-9201
   Roanoke Rapids *(G-13590)*

Williams Logging Inc .... G 919 542-2740
   Moncure *(G-10630)*

Wilson Bros Logging Inc .... G 252 445-5317
   Enfield *(G-5682)*

Wilson Logging Nc LLC .... G 336 280-8648
   Summerfield *(G-14994)*

Wood Logging .... G 910 866-4018
   White Oak *(G-15958)*

LOGGING: Timber, Cut At Logging Camp

Arauco - NA .... G 910 569-7020
   Biscoe *(G-1103)*

Cjc Enterprises .... E 919 266-3158
   Wake Forest *(G-15541)*

JM Williams Timber Company .... G 919 362-1333
   Apex *(G-209)*

Log Home Builders Inc .... G 704 638-0677
   Salisbury *(G-14007)*

Noralex Inc .... G 252 974-1253
   Vanceboro *(G-15482)*

Timber Specialists Inc .... G 704 902-5146
   Statesville *(G-14914)*

Wright & Hobbs Inc .... E 252 537-5817
   Roanoke Rapids *(G-13591)*

LOGGING: Wooden Logs

Ivp Forest Products LLC .... F 252 241-8126
   Morehead City *(G-11177)*

LOGS: Gas, Fireplace

Dna Services Inc .... G 910 279-2775
   Kure Beach *(G-9437)*

LOTIONS OR CREAMS: Face

3rd Phaze Bdy Oils Urban Lnks .... G 704 344-1138
   Charlotte *(G-2109)*

Clutch Inc .... F 919 448-8654
   Durham *(G-5022)*

Lash Out Inc .... G 919 342-0221
   Clayton *(G-3992)*

Love Thy Skin LLC .... G 910 703-2321
   Coats *(G-4133)*

Luxebright Skin Care LLC .... G 877 614-9128
   Matthews *(G-10264)*

Naturally ME Boutique Inc .... G 919 519-0783
   Durham *(G-5238)*

Product Quest Manufacturing Inc .... C 386 239-8787
   Winston Salem *(G-16869)*

Product Quest Manufacturing LLC ...... B 386 239-8787
   Winston Salem *(G-16870)*

SC Johnson Prof USA Inc .... D 704 263-4240
   Stanley *(G-14707)*

SC Johnson Prof USA Inc .... C 443 521-1606
   Charlotte *(G-3496)*

UGLy Essentials LLC .... F 910 319-9945
   Raleigh *(G-13376)*

LOTIONS: SHAVING

Floraleads Group .... G 919 303-1420
   Raleigh *(G-12773)*

Johnny Slicks Inc .... G 910 803-2159
   Holly Ridge *(G-8683)*

LOZENGES: Pharmaceutical

Bestco LLC .... C 704 664-4300
   Mooresville *(G-10879)*

LUBRICATING OIL & GREASE WHOLESALERS

Moroil Corp .... F 704 795-9595
   Concord *(G-4319)*

Warren Oil Company LLC .... D 910 892-6456
   Dunn *(G-4890)*

LUBRICATION SYSTEMS & EQPT

Balcrank Corporation .... E 800 747-5300
   Weaverville *(G-15838)*

PRODUCT SECTION LUMBER: Hardwood Dimension & Flooring Mills

Bijur Delimon Intl Inc .... E 919 465-4448
　Morrisville *(G-11302)*
Farval Lubrication Systems .... E 252 527-6001
　Kinston *(G-9364)*
Farval Lubrication Systems .... E 252 527-6001
　Kinston *(G-9365)*
Linter North America Corp .... G 828 645-4261
　Asheville *(G-687)*
Petroliance LLC .... C 336 472-3000
　Thomasville *(G-15263)*

LUGGAGE & BRIEFCASES

Cross Canvas Company Inc .... E 828 252-0440
　Asheville *(G-599)*
New Media Golf Inc .... F 828 533-9954
　Highlands *(G-8616)*
Saundra D Hall .... G 828 251-9859
　Asheville *(G-763)*
Tumi Store - Chrltte Dglas Int .... E 704 359-8771
　Charlotte *(G-3738)*
Tumi Store - Streets South Pt .... G 919 224-1028
　Durham *(G-5415)*

LUMBER & BLDG MATLS DEALER, RET: Electric Constructn Matls

Cummins Atlantic LLC .... E 704 588-1240
　Charlotte *(G-2585)*
Southern Concrete Materials Inc .... C 828 253-6421
　Asheville *(G-783)*
Southland Electrical Sup LLC .... C 336 227-1486
　Burlington *(G-1498)*

LUMBER & BLDG MATLS DEALER, RET: Garage Doors, Sell/Install

Amarr Company .... C 336 744-5100
　Winston Salem *(G-16602)*

LUMBER & BLDG MATRLS DEALERS, RETAIL: Doors, Wood/Metal

Carport Central Inc .... D 980 321-9898
　Mount Airy *(G-11491)*

LUMBER & BLDG MTRLS DEALERS, RET: Planing Mill Prdts/Lumber

Big Pine Log and Lumber Inc .... G 828 656-2754
　Marshall *(G-10200)*
Glenn Lumber Company Inc .... E 704 434-7873
　Shelby *(G-14320)*
Hewlin Brothers Lumber Co .... G 252 586-6473
　Enfield *(G-5679)*
Ronald Lee Fulbright Lbr Inc .... F 704 462-1421
　Vale *(G-15471)*
Walton Lumber Co .... G 919 563-6565
　Mebane *(G-10436)*

LUMBER & BUILDING MATERIAL DEALERS, RETAIL: Roofing Material

Triad Corrugated Metal Inc .... E 336 625-9727
　Asheboro *(G-499)*

LUMBER & BUILDING MATERIALS DEALER, RET: Door & Window Prdts

Atlantic Coastal Enterprises .... G 910 478-0777
　Jacksonville *(G-8988)*
Hunter Millwork Inc .... F 704 821-0144
　Matthews *(G-10321)*
Maxson & Associates .... G 336 632-0524
　Greensboro *(G-7190)*

Shutter Production Inc .... G 910 289-2620
　Rose Hill *(G-13781)*
TRf Manufacturing NC Inc .... E 252 223-1112
　Newport *(G-11909)*

LUMBER & BUILDING MATERIALS DEALER, RET: Masonry Matls/Splys

Glover Materials Inc .... G 252 536-2660
　Pleasant Hill *(G-12364)*
Leonard Block Company .... F 336 764-0607
　Winston Salem *(G-16786)*

LUMBER & BUILDING MATERIALS DEALERS, RETAIL: Brick

General Shale Brick Inc .... F 704 937-7431
　Grover *(G-7607)*
Pine Hall Brick Co Inc .... F 336 721-7500
　Madison *(G-10083)*
Triangle Brick Company .... E 704 695-1420
　Wadesboro *(G-15518)*
Triangle Brick Company .... E 919 544-1796
　Durham *(G-5406)*

LUMBER & BUILDING MATERIALS DEALERS, RETAIL: Cement

Concrete Service Company .... G 910 590-0035
　Clinton *(G-4093)*

LUMBER & BUILDING MATERIALS DEALERS, RETAIL: Sand & Gravel

Privette Enterprises Inc .... E 704 634-3291
　Monroe *(G-10789)*

LUMBER & BUILDING MATERIALS RET DEALERS: Millwork & Lumber

Bfs Operations LLC .... A 919 431-1000
　Raleigh *(G-12555)*
Builders Firstsource Inc .... G 919 562-6601
　Youngsville *(G-17072)*
Builders Firstsource - SE Grp .... G 910 313-3056
　Wilmington *(G-16144)*
Smokey Mountain Lumber Inc .... G 828 298-3958
　Asheville *(G-775)*
Stock Building Supply Holdings LLC .... A 919 431-1000
　Raleigh *(G-13305)*
Triad Prefinish & Lbr Sls Inc .... G 336 375-4849
　Greensboro *(G-7415)*

LUMBER & BUILDING MATLS DEALERS, RET: Screens, Door/Window

All Glass Inc .... G 828 324-8609
　Hickory *(G-7931)*

LUMBER: Dimension, Hardwood

Church & Church Lumber LLC .... D 336 973-5700
　Wilkesboro *(G-16017)*
J & D Wood Inc .... F 910 628-9000
　Fairmont *(G-5703)*
Powell Industries Inc .... D 828 926-9114
　Waynesville *(G-15815)*
Universal Forest Products Inc .... F 252 338-0319
　Elizabeth City *(G-5580)*

LUMBER: Flooring, Dressed, Softwood

Beasley Flooring Products Inc .... E 828 524-3248
　Bryson City *(G-1320)*
Unilin Flooring Nc LLC .... C 336 313-4000
　Thomasville *(G-15297)*

LUMBER: Hardboard

Custom Finishers Inc .... E 336 431-7141
　High Point *(G-8313)*
Louisiana-Pacific Corporation .... C 336 696-2751
　North Wilkesboro *(G-12024)*

LUMBER: Hardwood Dimension

Fortner Lumber Inc .... F 704 585-2383
　Hiddenite *(G-8216)*
North Carolina Lumber Company .... F 336 498-6600
　Randleman *(G-13481)*
Parton Lumber Company Inc .... D 828 287-4257
　Rutherfordton *(G-13883)*
Turn Bull Lumber Company .... E 910 862-4447
　Elizabethtown *(G-5607)*
W M Cramer Lumber Co .... D 828 397-7481
　Connelly Springs *(G-4411)*
Walton Lumber Co .... G 919 563-6565
　Mebane *(G-10436)*

LUMBER: Hardwood Dimension & Flooring Mills

Arcola Sawmill .... G 252 257-1139
　Warrenton *(G-15656)*
Associated Hardwoods Inc .... E 828 396-3321
　Granite Falls *(G-6722)*
Beasley Flooring Products Inc .... E 828 349-7000
　Franklin *(G-6116)*
Blue Ridge Lbr Log & Timber Co .... F 336 961-5211
　Yadkinville *(G-17033)*
Blue Ridge Products Co Inc .... E 828 322-7990
　Hickory *(G-7952)*
Braxton Sawmill Inc .... F 336 376-6798
　Graham *(G-6680)*
Cagle Frames LLC .... G 910 464-1170
　Seagrove *(G-14233)*
Cagle Sawmill Inc .... F 336 857-2274
　Denton *(G-4728)*
Chris Isom Inc .... F 336 629-0240
　Asheboro *(G-415)*
Church & Church Lumber LLC .... F 336 838-1256
　Millers Creek *(G-10492)*
Church & Church Lumber LLC .... D 336 973-4297
　Wilkesboro *(G-16016)*
Clary Lumber Company .... D 252 537-2558
　Gaston *(G-6330)*
Cleveland Lumber Company .... E 704 487-5263
　Shelby *(G-14298)*
Columbia Flooring .... G 304 239-2633
　Garner *(G-6264)*
Columbia Forest Products Inc .... C 336 605-0429
　Greensboro *(G-6920)*
Columbia Plywood Corporation .... B 828 724-4191
　Old Fort *(G-12100)*
Danbartex LLC .... G 704 323-8728
　Mooresville *(G-10923)*
David Raynor Logging Inc .... E 910 980-0129
　Linden *(G-9939)*
Dimension Milling Co Inc .... G 336 983-2820
　Denton *(G-4734)*
Edwards Wood Products Inc .... C 704 624-3624
　Marshville *(G-10216)*
Eekkohart Floors & Lbr Co Inc .... G 336 409-2672
　Mocksville *(G-10569)*
Ethan Allen Retail Inc .... E 828 428-9361
　Maiden *(G-10107)*
F L Turlington Lumber Co Inc .... E 910 592-7197
　Clinton *(G-4095)*
Framewright Inc .... F 828 459-2284
　Conover *(G-4457)*

LUMBER: Hardwood Dimension & Flooring Mills

Franklin Veneers Inc............................ E 919 494-2284
  Franklinton *(G-6154)*
Gates Custom Milling Inc..................... E 252 357-0116
  Gatesville *(G-6549)*
Glenn Lumber Company Inc................. E 704 434-7873
  Shelby *(G-14320)*
H T Jones Lumber Company................. F 252 332-4135
  Ahoskie *(G-63)*
Hfi Wind Down Inc............................... C 828 438-5767
  Morganton *(G-11220)*
HM Frame Company Inc....................... E 828 428-3354
  Newton *(G-11940)*
Hofler H S & Sons Lumber Co............... F 252 465-8603
  Sunbury *(G-14997)*
Hull Brothers Lumber Co Inc................. E 336 789-5252
  Mount Airy *(G-11519)*
Ideal Liquidation Inc............................ F 828 632-3771
  Taylorsville *(G-15148)*
Jones Frame Inc.................................. E 336 434-2531
  High Point *(G-8417)*
Josey Lumber Company Inc.................. E 252 826-5614
  Scotland Neck *(G-14219)*
L F Delp Lumber Co Inc........................ F 336 359-8202
  Laurel Springs *(G-9466)*
Leisure Craft Holdings LLC................... D 828 693-8241
  Flat Rock *(G-5967)*
Leisure Craft Inc.................................. C 828 693-8241
  Flat Rock *(G-5968)*
Lines Unlimited Inc.............................. G 336 996-6603
  Walnut Cove *(G-15632)*
Mac-Vann Inc...................................... G 919 577-0746
  Fuquay Varina *(G-6211)*
Maynard Frame Shop Inc..................... E 910 428-2033
  Star *(G-14720)*
Murdock Building Company.................. G 919 669-1859
  Rolesville *(G-13758)*
Oceania Hardwoods LLC...................... C 910 862-4447
  Elizabethtown *(G-5601)*
Palletone North Carolina Inc................ D 704 462-1882
  Siler City *(G-14430)*
Piedmont Hardwood Lbr Co Inc............ E 704 436-9311
  Mount Pleasant *(G-11676)*
Price Logging Inc................................ G 252 792-5687
  Jamesville *(G-9081)*
Ritch Face Veneer Company................ E 336 883-4184
  High Point *(G-8512)*
Ross Phelps Logging Co Inc................. F 252 356-2560
  Colerain *(G-4140)*
S E Board Inc...................................... G 336 885-7230
  High Point *(G-8518)*
Shaver Wood Products Inc.................. D 704 278-1482
  Cleveland *(G-4080)*
T & S Hardwoods Inc........................... D 828 586-4044
  Sylva *(G-15072)*
Unilin Flooring Nc LLC......................... C 336 313-4000
  Thomasville *(G-15297)*
United Finishers Intl Inc...................... G 336 883-3901
  High Point *(G-8585)*
Uwharrie Lumber Co............................ E 910 572-3731
  Troy *(G-15419)*
Veneer Technologies Inc..................... C 252 223-5600
  Newport *(G-11910)*
Weyerhaeuser Company....................... F 252 746-7200
  Grifton *(G-7603)*
Wright & Hobbs Inc............................. E 252 537-5817
  Roanoke Rapids *(G-13591)*
Zickgraf Enterprises Inc...................... G 704 369-1200
  Franklin *(G-6150)*

LUMBER: Kiln Dried

Jordan-Holman Lumber Co Inc............. D 828 396-3101
  Granite Falls *(G-6740)*

McCreary Modern Inc.......................... B 828 464-6465
  Newton *(G-11951)*
Pleasant Garden Dry Kiln..................... G 336 674-2863
  Pleasant Garden *(G-12359)*
Southeastern Hardwoods Inc............... G 828 581-0197
  Swannanoa *(G-15037)*
World Wood Company.......................... D 252 523-0021
  Cove City *(G-4599)*

LUMBER: Plywood, Hardwood

Adwood Corporation............................ E 336 884-1846
  High Point *(G-8235)*
Autumn House Inc............................... D 828 728-1121
  Granite Falls *(G-6724)*
Burke Veneers Inc............................... E 828 437-8510
  Morganton *(G-11203)*
Capitol Funds Inc................................ D 704 482-0645
  Shelby *(G-14292)*
Chesterfield Wood Products Inc........... F 828 433-0042
  Morganton *(G-11204)*
Columbia Panel Mfg Co Inc................. D 336 861-4100
  High Point *(G-8300)*
Esco Industries Inc.............................. F 336 495-3772
  Randleman *(G-13469)*
Gates Custom Milling Inc..................... E 252 357-0116
  Gatesville *(G-6549)*
Georgia-Pacific LLC............................. D 919 580-1078
  Dudley *(G-4843)*
HM Frame Company Inc....................... E 828 428-3354
  Newton *(G-11940)*
Superior Veneers Inc........................... F 828 433-6986
  Morganton *(G-11258)*
Tramway Veneers Inc.......................... E 919 776-7606
  Sanford *(G-14198)*
Ufp New London LLC............................ E 704 463-1400
  New London *(G-11880)*

LUMBER: Plywood, Hardwood or Hardwood Faced

Atlantic Veneer Company LLC............... C 252 728-3169
  Beaufort *(G-943)*
Columbia Plywood Corporation............. B 828 724-4191
  Old Fort *(G-12100)*
Georgia-Pacific LLC............................. E 910 642-5041
  Whiteville *(G-15963)*
North Carolina Plywood LLC................. G 850 948-2211
  Whiteville *(G-15974)*
Whiteville Plywood Inc......................... F 910 642-7114
  Whiteville *(G-15981)*

LUMBER: Plywood, Prefinished, Hardwood

Diply LLC.. G 828 495-4352
  Hickory *(G-8010)*
G & G Lumber Company Inc................. E 704 539-5110
  Harmony *(G-7686)*
Southern Vneer Spclty Pdts LLC........... F 919 642-7004
  Moncure *(G-10626)*

LUMBER: Rails, Fence, Round Or Split

Afsc LLC... D 704 523-4936
  Charlotte *(G-2142)*
Asheville Contracting Co Inc................ E 828 665-8900
  Candler *(G-1567)*

LUMBER: Treated

Atlantic Wood & Timber LLC................ F 704 390-7479
  Charlotte *(G-2235)*
Coastal Treated Products LLC.............. E 252 410-0180
  Roanoke Rapids *(G-13571)*
Culpeper Roanoke Rapids LLC.............. G 252 678-3804
  Roanoke Rapids *(G-13572)*

Durable Wood Preservers Inc............... G 704 537-3113
  Charlotte *(G-2658)*
Fiberon... G 704 463-2955
  Concord *(G-4264)*
Fortress Wood Products Inc................. F 336 854-5121
  High Point *(G-8356)*
Shenandoah Wood Preservers Inc........ E 252 826-4151
  Scotland Neck *(G-14221)*
Ufp Salisbury LLC................................ B 704 855-1600
  Salisbury *(G-14057)*
Ufp Salisbury LLC................................ F 704 855-1600
  Salisbury *(G-14058)*
Universal Forest Products Inc.............. F 252 338-0319
  Elizabeth City *(G-5580)*
Woodline Inc....................................... G 336 476-7100
  Thomasville *(G-15304)*
Woodtreaters Inc................................ G 910 675-0038
  Rocky Point *(G-13755)*

LUMBER: Veneer, Softwood

A-1 Face Inc....................................... F 336 248-5555
  Lexington *(G-9677)*
David R Webb Company Inc.................. G 336 605-3355
  Greensboro *(G-6960)*
Quality Veneer Company...................... F 336 622-2211
  Liberty *(G-9827)*

MACHINE PARTS: Stamped Or Pressed Metal

Bnp Inc... F 919 775-7070
  Sanford *(G-14094)*
Ceramco Incorporated......................... E 704 588-4814
  Charlotte *(G-2444)*
CMS Tool and Die Inc........................... F 910 458-3322
  Carolina Beach *(G-1636)*
Derita Precision Mch Co Inc................. F 704 392-7285
  Charlotte *(G-2620)*
Matt Bieneman Enterprises LLC............ G 704 856-0200
  Mooresville *(G-11017)*
Moores Mch Co Fayetteville Inc............ D 919 837-5354
  Bear Creek *(G-941)*
RC Investment Company...................... E 336 226-5511
  Burlington *(G-1483)*
Robinson Mch & Cutter Grinding.......... G 704 629-5591
  Bessemer City *(G-1080)*
Spruce Pine Mica Company.................. F 828 765-4241
  Spruce Pine *(G-14659)*
Stroup Machine & Mfg Inc................... G 704 394-0023
  Charlotte *(G-3641)*
Team 21st.. F 910 826-3676
  Fayetteville *(G-5928)*
Toner Machining Tech Inc.................... D 828 432-8007
  Morganton *(G-11261)*
Toolcraft Inc North Carolina................. F 828 659-7379
  Marion *(G-10183)*
Youngs Welding & Machine Svcs........... G 910 488-1190
  Fayetteville *(G-5955)*

MACHINE TOOL ACCESS: Drills

Dormer Pramet LLC.............................. B 800 877-3745
  Mebane *(G-10407)*
Robert Bosch Tool Corporation............. F 252 551-7512
  Greenville *(G-7580)*

MACHINE TOOL ACCESS: Tools & Access

21st Century Tech of Amer.................. F 910 826-3676
  Fayetteville *(G-5744)*
Creative Tooling Solutions Inc.............. G 704 504-5415
  Pineville *(G-12263)*
Tar Heel Tling Prcsion McHning............ E 919 965-6160
  Smithfield *(G-14486)*
Toolcraft Inc North Carolina................. F 828 659-7379
  Marion *(G-10183)*

PRODUCT SECTION — MACHINERY & EQPT, AGRICULTURAL, WHOLESALE: Lawn & Garden

Yat Usa Inc .... G 480 584-4096
  Huntersville (G-8908)

MACHINE TOOL ATTACHMENTS & ACCESS

Central Tool & Mfg Co Inc .... G 828 328-2383
  Hickory (G-7974)
Eversharp Saw & Tool Inc .... G 828 345-1200
  Hickory (G-8019)
Production Tool and Die Co Inc .... F 704 525-0498
  Charlotte (G-3390)

MACHINE TOOLS & ACCESS

C R Onsrud Inc .... E 704 508-7000
  Troutman (G-15368)
Calco Enterprises Inc .... F 910 695-0089
  Aberdeen (G-3)
Canvas Sx LLC .... C 980 474-3700
  Charlotte (G-2384)
Carbo-Cut Inc .... G 828 685-7890
  Hendersonville (G-7833)
Cooper Bussmann LLC .... C 252 566-0278
  La Grange (G-9438)
Disston Co Inc .... G 336 547-6300
  Greensboro (G-6972)
Em2 Machine Corp .... G 336 297-4110
  Summerfield (G-14981)
Frank G Shumate .... G 336 784-0828
  Kernersville (G-9201)
Freud America Inc .... C 800 334-4107
  High Point (G-8360)
Kennametal Inc .... D 252 492-4163
  Henderson (G-7791)
Kyocera Precision Tools Inc .... G 800 823-7284
  Hendersonville (G-7870)
Lns Turbo North America .... G 704 435-6370
  Cherryville (G-3871)
LS Starrett Company .... E 336 789-5141
  Mount Airy (G-11540)
North Carolina Mfg Inc .... E 919 734-1115
  Goldsboro (G-6638)
Putsch & Company Inc .... E 828 684-0671
  Fletcher (G-6033)
Rymon Company Inc .... G 704 519-5310
  Charlotte (G-3475)
Salice America Inc .... E 704 841-7810
  Charlotte (G-3483)
Sandvik Inc .... C 919 563-5008
  Mebane (G-10427)
Sandvik McHning Sltons USA LLC .... F 919 563-5008
  Mebane (G-10428)
Speedwell Machine Works Inc .... E 704 866-7418
  Gastonia (G-6512)
Stanley Black & Decker Inc .... G 704 293-9392
  Huntersville (G-8900)
Stanly Tractor Company .... G 704 983-1106
  New London (G-11879)
Toner Machining Tech Inc .... D 828 432-8007
  Morganton (G-11261)
United Machine & Metal Fab Inc .... E 828 464-5167
  Conover (G-4508)
W D Lee & Company .... E 704 864-0346
  Gastonia (G-6537)
W T Mander & Son Inc .... G 336 562-5755
  Prospect Hill (G-12409)
Wise Storage Solutions LLC .... E 336 789-5141
  Mount Airy (G-11596)

MACHINE TOOLS, METAL CUTTING: Drilling

Circor Precision Metering LLC .... A 919 774-7667
  Sanford (G-14102)
J & B Tool Making Inc .... G 704 827-4805
  Mount Holly (G-11639)

Sandvik Tooling .... G 919 563-5008
  Mebane (G-10429)

MACHINE TOOLS, METAL CUTTING: Drilling & Boring

Drill & Fill Mfg LLC .... G 252 937-4555
  Rocky Mount (G-13691)
Grindtec Enterprises Corp .... G 704 636-1825
  Salisbury (G-13974)

MACHINE TOOLS, METAL CUTTING: Home Workshop

Tactile Workshop LLC .... G 919 738-9924
  Raleigh (G-13323)

MACHINE TOOLS, METAL CUTTING: Lathes

L & R Specialties Inc .... F 704 853-3296
  Gastonia (G-6441)

MACHINE TOOLS, METAL CUTTING: Numerically Controlled

Casetec Precision Machine LLC .... G 704 663-6043
  Mooresville (G-10899)

MACHINE TOOLS, METAL CUTTING: Tool Replacement & Rpr Parts

Machine Tool Components LLC .... G 866 466-0120
  Indian Trail (G-8948)
Motion Control Integration .... G 704 608-1279
  Charlotte (G-3206)

MACHINE TOOLS, METAL FORMING: Bending

Surry Logistix LLC .... G 336 710-3446
  Mount Airy (G-11582)

MACHINE TOOLS, METAL FORMING: Headers

American Racg Hders Exhust Inc .... E 631 608-1986
  Stanfield (G-14674)

MACHINE TOOLS, METAL FORMING: Mechanical, Pneumatic Or Hyd

CPM Wolverine Proctor LLC .... F 336 479-2983
  Lexington (G-9699)
CPM Wolverine Proctor LLC .... D 336 248-5181
  Lexington (G-9700)

MACHINE TOOLS, METAL FORMING: Punching & Shearing

Murata Machinery Usa Inc .... C 704 875-9280
  Charlotte (G-3219)
Murata McHy USA Holdings Inc .... F 704 394-8331
  Charlotte (G-3220)

MACHINE TOOLS, METAL FORMING: Rebuilt

Moores Mch Co Fayetteville Inc .... D 919 837-5354
  Bear Creek (G-941)

MACHINE TOOLS: Metal Cutting

Accurate Fabrications Inc .... G 910 383-2140
  Leland (G-9524)
Amada America Inc .... G 877 262-3297
  High Point (G-8243)
Blue Inc Usa LLC .... E 828 346-8660
  Conover (G-4623)
Brown Equipment and Capitl Inc .... F 704 921-4644
  Monroe (G-10670)

C & J Machine Company Inc .... G 704 922-5913
  Dallas (G-4636)
Central Tool & Mfg Co Inc .... G 828 328-2383
  Hickory (G-7974)
Delta Phoenix Inc .... E 336 621-3960
  Greensboro (G-6966)
Exact Cut Inc .... F 336 207-4022
  Greensboro (G-7008)
Hamilton Indus Grinding Inc .... E 828 253-6796
  Asheville (G-647)
Kyocera Precision Tools Inc .... G 800 823-7284
  Hendersonville (G-7870)
Lynn Electronics Corporation .... G 704 369-0093
  Concord (G-4308)
Matcor Mtal Fbrction Wlcome In .... C 336 731-5700
  Lexington (G-9756)
Okuma America Corporation .... C 704 588-7000
  Charlotte (G-3290)
Putsch & Company Inc .... E 828 684-0671
  Fletcher (G-6033)
Schelling America Inc .... E 919 544-0430
  Morrisville (G-11418)
Schenck USA Corp .... G 704 529-5300
  Conover (G-4495)
Slack & Parr International .... G 704 527-2975
  Dallas (G-4658)
Superior Dry Kilns Inc .... E 828 754-7001
  Hudson (G-8782)
Tigra Usa Inc .... G 828 324-8227
  Hickory (G-8182)
Triad Cutting Tools Inc .... G 336 873-8708
  Asheboro (G-500)
Union Grove Saw & Knife Inc .... D 704 539-4442
  Union Grove (G-15438)
Whiteside Mch & Repr Co Inc .... E 828 459-2141
  Claremont (G-3945)
Wieland Electric Inc .... F 910 259-5050
  Wilmington (G-16442)
Windco LLC .... G 704 846-6029
  Indian Trail (G-8971)

MACHINE TOOLS: Metal Forming

Arnold S Welding Service Inc .... E 910 323-3822
  Fayetteville (G-5764)
Cyril Bath Company .... F 704 289-8531
  Monroe (G-10701)
E G A Products Inc .... F 704 664-1221
  Mooresville (G-10932)
Emery Corporation .... D 828 433-1536
  Morganton (G-11211)
Schunk Intec Inc .... D 919 572-2705
  Morrisville (G-11420)
Sona Autocomp USA LLC .... C 919 965-5555
  Selma (G-14260)
Sona Blw Precision Forge Inc .... C 919 828-3375
  Selma (G-14261)
Ultra Machine & Fabrication Inc .... C 704 482-1399
  Shelby (G-14379)
Wuko Inc .... G 980 938-0512
  Greensboro (G-7470)
Wysong and Miles Company .... E 336 621-3960
  Greensboro (G-7471)

MACHINERY & EQPT, AGRICULTURAL, WHOLESALE: Agricultural, NEC

Buy Smart Inc .... G 252 293-4700
  Wilson (G-16482)

MACHINERY & EQPT, AGRICULTURAL, WHOLESALE: Lawn & Garden

MACHINERY & EQPT, INDL, WHOLESALE: Chemical Process — PRODUCT SECTION

Southag Mfg Inc .... F 919 365-5111
  Wendell (G-15918)

MACHINERY & EQPT, INDL, WHOLESALE: Chemical Process

LCI Corporation International .... E 704 399-7441
  Charlotte (G-3076)
Nederman Corporation .... F 704 399-7441
  Charlotte (G-3244)

MACHINERY & EQPT, INDL, WHOLESALE: Conveyor Systems

Machinex Technologies Inc .... E 773 867-8801
  High Point (G-8437)
Mueller Die Cut Solutions Inc .... E 704 588-3900
  Charlotte (G-3213)

MACHINERY & EQPT, INDL, WHOLESALE: Cranes

Hiab USA Inc .... F 704 896-9089
  Cornelius (G-4555)
Rose Welding & Crane Service I .... G 252 796-9171
  Columbia (G-4167)
Thomas M Brown Inc .... F 704 597-0246
  Charlotte (G-3690)

MACHINERY & EQPT, INDL, WHOLESALE: Engines & Parts, Diesel

Cummins Atlantic LLC .... D 336 275-4531
  Greensboro (G-6946)
Cummins Atlantic LLC .... E 919 284-9111
  Kenly (G-9149)
Cummins Atlantic LLC .... E 704 588-1240
  Charlotte (G-2585)
Engine Systems Inc .... D 252 977-2720
  Rocky Mount (G-13695)
Pcai Inc .... D 704 588-1240
  Charlotte (G-3323)
S Strickland Diesel Svc Inc .... G 252 291-6999
  Wilson (G-16536)
Sound Heavy Machinery Inc .... G 910 782-2477
  Wilmington (G-16407)

MACHINERY & EQPT, INDL, WHOLESALE: Engines, Gasoline

Ledger Hardware Inc .... G 828 688-4798
  Bakersville (G-885)

MACHINERY & EQPT, INDL, WHOLESALE: Fans

Hunter Fan Company .... G 704 896-9250
  Cornelius (G-4558)

MACHINERY & EQPT, INDL, WHOLESALE: Food Product Manufacturng

Babington Technology Inc .... G 252 984-0349
  Rocky Mount (G-13683)
Sinnovatek Inc .... G 919 694-0974
  Raleigh (G-13264)
Stork United Corporation .... A 704 598-7171
  Charlotte (G-3639)

MACHINERY & EQPT, INDL, WHOLESALE: Hydraulic Systems

AP&t North America Inc .... F 704 292-2900
  Monroe (G-10648)
Apex Industrial Group LLC .... G 919 578-9039
  Sanford (G-14086)

Bosch Rexroth Corporation .... E 704 583-4338
  Charlotte (G-2336)
Custom Hydraulics & Design .... F 704 347-0023
  Cherryville (G-3865)
Deetag USA Inc .... G 828 465-2644
  Conover (G-4447)
Hawe North America Inc .... E 704 509-1599
  Huntersville (G-8828)
Hyde Park Partners Inc .... D 704 587-4819
  Charlotte (G-2939)
Hydralic Engnered Pdts Svc Inc .... G 704 374-1306
  Charlotte (G-2940)
Industrial Sup Solutions Inc .... E 704 636-4241
  Salisbury (G-13983)
Livingston & Haven LLC .... C 704 588-3670
  Charlotte (G-3096)
Mro Stop LLC .... F 704 587-5429
  Charlotte (G-3210)
Parker-Hannifin Corporation .... E 828 245-3233
  Forest City (G-6079)
Talladega Mchy & Sup Co NC .... G 256 362-4124
  Fayetteville (G-5925)

MACHINERY & EQPT, INDL, WHOLESALE: Indl Machine Parts

Cross Technologies Inc .... E 800 327-7727
  Greensboro (G-6942)
Machine Tool Components LLC .... G 866 466-0120
  Indian Trail (G-8948)

MACHINERY & EQPT, INDL, WHOLESALE: Instruments & Cntrl Eqpt

Grecon Inc .... F 503 641-7731
  Charlotte (G-2862)
Linor Technology Inc .... F 336 485-6199
  Winston Salem (G-16788)
Weathers Machine Mfg Inc .... F 919 552-5945
  Fuquay Varina (G-6238)

MACHINERY & EQPT, INDL, WHOLESALE: Machine Tools & Access

Chiron America Inc .... D 704 587-9526
  Charlotte (G-2478)
Container Graphics Corp .... E 704 588-7230
  Pineville (G-12261)
Okuma America Corporation .... C 704 588-7000
  Charlotte (G-3290)
Phillips Corporation .... E 336 665-1080
  Colfax (G-4157)
Stanza Machinery Inc .... E 704 599-0623
  Charlotte (G-3622)
Triangle Glass Service Inc .... G 919 477-9508
  Durham (G-5408)

MACHINERY & EQPT, INDL, WHOLESALE: Machine Tools & Metalwork

Alamo Distribution LLC .... C 704 398-5600
  Belmont (G-974)
Schunk Intec Inc .... D 919 572-2705
  Morrisville (G-11420)

MACHINERY & EQPT, INDL, WHOLESALE: Packaging

Automated Machine Technologies .... G 919 361-0121
  Morrisville (G-11297)
Chase-Logeman Corporation .... F 336 665-0754
  Greensboro (G-6905)
Glover Corporation Inc .... E 919 821-5835
  Raleigh (G-12807)

MACHINERY & EQPT, INDL, WHOLESALE: Safety Eqpt

Cintas Corporation No 2 .... D 336 632-4412
  Greensboro (G-6909)

MACHINERY & EQPT, INDL, WHOLESALE: Sewing

Hester Enterprises Inc .... E 704 865-4480
  Gastonia (G-6416)

MACHINERY & EQPT, INDL, WHOLESALE: Textile & Leather

Murata Machinery Usa Inc .... C 704 875-9280
  Charlotte (G-3219)
Petroleum Tank Corporation .... F 919 284-2418
  Kenly (G-9155)

MACHINERY & EQPT, INDL, WHOLESALE: Trailers, Indl

Kaufman Trailers Inc .... E 336 790-6800
  Lexington (G-9739)
Southag Mfg Inc .... F 919 365-5111
  Wendell (G-15918)

MACHINERY & EQPT, WHOLESALE: Construction, General

Berco of America Inc .... E 336 931-1415
  Greensboro (G-6836)

MACHINERY & EQPT: Farm

American Urns .... G 828 994-4239
  Conover (G-4414)
Case & Bear Great Homes LLC .... G 704 595-3832
  Charlotte (G-2417)
Case Basket Creations .... G 828 381-4908
  Granite Falls (G-6728)
Case By Case LLC .... G 910 814-3288
  Lillington (G-9846)
Case-Closed Investigations .... G 336 794-2274
  Morehead City (G-11160)
Cases For A Cause .... G 704 239-3269
  Rockwell (G-13648)
Deere & Company .... G 336 996-8100
  Kernersville (G-9189)
Evans Machinery Inc .... D 252 243-4006
  Wilson (G-16498)
Granville Equipment LLC .... F 919 693-1425
  Oxford (G-12130)
Gum Drop Cases LLC .... G 206 805-0818
  High Point (G-8373)
Hog Slat Incorporated .... E 252 209-0092
  Aulander (G-830)
Hog Slat Incorporated .... G 910 862-7081
  Elizabethtown (G-5596)
Hog Slat Incorporated .... E 919 663-3321
  Siler City (G-14414)
JM Innovations LLC .... G 704 495-4841
  Charlotte (G-3025)
Johnson Industrial Mchy Svcs .... E 252 239-1944
  Lucama (G-10017)
Madison Ave Cases .... G 843 214-0476
  Winston Salem (G-16797)
North American Implements Inc .... G 336 476-2904
  Thomasville (G-15259)
Pasture Management Systems Inc .... F 704 436-6401
  Mount Pleasant (G-11675)
Reddick & Reddick LLC .... G 919 845-7333
  Raleigh (G-13200)

PRODUCT SECTION — MACHINERY: Construction

Reddick Equipment Co NC LLC............ G 252 792-1191
  Williamston *(G-16068)*

Sound Heavy Machinery Inc................. G 910 782-2477
  Wilmington *(G-16407)*

Stanly Tractor Company...................... G 704 983-1106
  New London *(G-11879)*

Stiles Mfg Co Inc................................. G 910 592-6344
  Clinton *(G-4113)*

Stone Equipment Company Inc........... C 980 202-4448
  Lexington *(G-9786)*

Strickland Bros Entps Inc.................... F 252 478-3058
  Spring Hope *(G-14623)*

Tetac.. G 919 369-9106
  Franklinton *(G-6165)*

MACHINERY & EQPT: Liquid Automation

Abco Automation Inc.......................... C 336 375-6400
  Browns Summit *(G-1298)*

Industrial Automation Company........... F 877 727-8757
  Raleigh *(G-12884)*

Irsi Automation Inc............................. G 336 303-5420
  Mc Leansville *(G-10393)*

Peformance Chassis........................... G 919 319-3484
  Cary *(G-1847)*

MACHINERY, EQPT & SUPPLIES: Parking Facility

Autopark Logistics LLC....................... G 704 365-3544
  Charlotte *(G-2241)*

MACHINERY, FOOD PRDTS: Beverage

Community Brewing Ventures LLC........ G 800 579-6539
  Newton *(G-11923)*

Microthermics Inc............................... F 919 878-8045
  Raleigh *(G-13028)*

MACHINERY, FOOD PRDTS: Dairy & Milk

Corporate Place LLC.......................... E 704 808-3848
  Charlotte *(G-2559)*

Delaney Holdings Co.......................... E 704 808-3848
  Charlotte *(G-2612)*

SPX Flow Holdings Inc........................ E 704 808-3848
  Charlotte *(G-3608)*

SPX Flow Technology Usa Inc............. D 704 808-3848
  Charlotte *(G-3610)*

SPX Latin America Corporation........... E 704 808-3848
  Charlotte *(G-3611)*

MACHINERY, FOOD PRDTS: Food Processing, Smokers

Friedrich Metal Pdts Co Inc................. E 336 375-3067
  Browns Summit *(G-1303)*

Wins Smokehouse Services Ltd........... G 828 884-7476
  Pisgah Forest *(G-12330)*

MACHINERY, FOOD PRDTS: Oilseed Crushing & Extracting

East Crlina Olseed Prcssors LL............ D 252 935-5553
  Pantego *(G-12163)*

MACHINERY, FOOD PRDTS: Ovens, Bakery

Middleby Marshall Inc......................... C 919 762-1000
  Fuquay Varina *(G-6216)*

MACHINERY, FOOD PRDTS: Packing House

Carolina Packing House Sups.............. G 910 653-3438
  Tabor City *(G-15079)*

MACHINERY, FOOD PRDTS: Processing, Poultry

Embrex LLC....................................... C 919 941-5185
  Durham *(G-5080)*

Stork United Corporation.................... A 704 598-7171
  Charlotte *(G-3639)*

MACHINERY, MAILING: Postage Meters

Pitney Bowes Inc................................ F 336 805-3320
  Greensboro *(G-7266)*

Pitney Bowes Inc................................ G 919 785-3480
  Raleigh *(G-13112)*

MACHINERY, PACKAGING: Canning, Food

Land of Sky Mobile Canning LLC......... G 303 880-1297
  Asheville *(G-679)*

MACHINERY, PAPER INDUSTRY: Converting, Die Cutting & Stampng

Masterwork USA Inc........................... G 704 288-9506
  Charlotte *(G-3140)*

MACHINERY, PAPER INDUSTRY: Pulp Mill

Valmet Inc... G 803 289-4900
  Charlotte *(G-3764)*

MACHINERY, PRINTING TRADES: Plates

Container Graphics Corp..................... F 919 481-4200
  Cary *(G-1733)*

Digital Highpoint LLC.......................... C 336 883-7146
  High Point *(G-8324)*

Mark/Trece Inc.................................. E 336 292-3424
  Whitsett *(G-15997)*

MACHINERY, TEXTILE: Creels

Diversified Textile Mchy Corp............... G 704 739-2121
  Kings Mountain *(G-9304)*

MACHINERY, TEXTILE: Finishing

Fab-Con Machinery Dev Corp.............. E 516 883-3999
  Harrisburg *(G-7708)*

MACHINERY, TEXTILE: Printing

Spgprints America Inc........................ D 704 598-7171
  Charlotte *(G-3603)*

Stork United Corporation.................... A 704 598-7171
  Charlotte *(G-3639)*

MACHINERY, WOODWORKING: Sanding, Exc Portable Floor Sanders

Singley Specialty Co Inc..................... G 336 852-8581
  Greensboro *(G-7342)*

MACHINERY: Ammunition & Explosives Loading

Advanced Plastiform Inc..................... D 919 404-2080
  Zebulon *(G-17117)*

Birch Bros Southern Inc..................... E 704 843-2111
  Waxhaw *(G-15745)*

MACHINERY: Automotive Related

Autec Inc.. E 704 871-9141
  Statesville *(G-14755)*

Canvas Sx LLC.................................. C 980 474-3700
  Charlotte *(G-2384)*

Clean Green Inc................................ G 919 596-3500
  Durham *(G-5020)*

Enforge LLC...................................... E 704 983-4146
  Albemarle *(G-83)*

Global Resource Corporation.............. F 919 972-7803
  Morrisville *(G-11349)*

Keffer Auto Huntersville LLC............... G 877 260-4062
  Huntersville *(G-8842)*

NGK Ceramics Usa Inc....................... F 704 664-7000
  Mooresville *(G-11035)*

Williams Performance Inc................... G 704 603-4431
  Mount Ulla *(G-11688)*

MACHINERY: Bridge Or Gate, Hydraulic

Surelift Inc.. G 828 963-6899
  Boone *(G-1241)*

MACHINERY: Construction

Altec Industries Inc............................ D 828 678-5500
  Burnsville *(G-1521)*

American Attachments Inc.................. G 336 859-2002
  Lexington *(G-9679)*

Arrow Equipment LLC........................ G 803 765-2040
  Charlotte *(G-2218)*

Automated Designs Inc...................... F 828 696-9625
  Flat Rock *(G-5959)*

Beasley Contracting........................... G 828 479-3775
  Robbinsville *(G-13604)*

Berco of America Inc......................... E 336 931-1415
  Greensboro *(G-6836)*

Bobcat of Mount Airy......................... G 336 459-3844
  Mount Airy *(G-11484)*

Caterpillar Inc.................................... D 919 777-2000
  Sanford *(G-14098)*

Conjet Inc... G 636 485-4724
  Charlotte *(G-2540)*

Construction Attachments Inc............. D 828 758-2674
  Lenoir *(G-9601)*

Cutting Systems Inc.......................... D 704 592-2451
  Union Grove *(G-15436)*

Dan Moore Inc................................... G 336 475-8350
  Thomasville *(G-15210)*

Design Engnred Fbrications Inc.......... E 336 768-8260
  Winston Salem *(G-16675)*

Engcon North America....................... E 203 691-5920
  High Point *(G-8344)*

Engineered Attachments LLC.............. G 336 703-5266
  Winston Salem *(G-16697)*

Everything Attachments..................... G 828 464-0161
  Conover *(G-4452)*

Ferguson Highway Products Inc.......... G 704 320-3087
  Indian Trail *(G-8934)*

General Fertilizer Eqp Inc................... F 336 299-4711
  Greensboro *(G-7035)*

Hills Machinery Company LLC............ G 828 820-5265
  Mills River *(G-10504)*

Hockmeyer Equipment Corp............... D 252 338-4705
  Elizabeth City *(G-5548)*

Ingersoll-Rand Intl Holdg.................... B 704 655-4000
  Davidson *(G-4681)*

Instrotek Inc..................................... E 919 875-8371
  Durham *(G-5160)*

Linder Industrial Machinery Co........... G 980 777-8345
  Concord *(G-4304)*

Loflin Fabrication LLC........................ E 336 859-4333
  Denton *(G-4744)*

North American Implements Inc.......... G 336 476-2904
  Thomasville *(G-15259)*

Paladin Custom Works....................... F 336 996-2796
  Kernersville *(G-9223)*

Redi-Mix LP...................................... E 704 596-6511
  Charlotte *(G-3423)*

Roadsafe Traffic Systems Inc............. G 919 772-9401
  High Point *(G-8513)*

Roofing Supply.................................. G 919 779-6223
  Garner *(G-6310)*

Employee Codes: A=Over 500 employees, B=251-500
C=101-250, D=51-100, E=20-50, F=10-19, G=1-9

MACHINERY: Construction

Rut Manufacturing Inc .... F 336 859-0328
  Denton *(G-4747)*
Superior Dry Kilns Inc .... E 828 754-7001
  Hudson *(G-8782)*
Tandemloc Inc .... D 252 447-7155
  Havelock *(G-7748)*
Tom Rochester & Associates Inc ..... G 704 896-5805
  Charlotte *(G-3706)*
Vermeer Manufacturing Company .... F 410 285-0200
  Charlotte *(G-3772)*

MACHINERY: Cotton Ginning

Coastal Carolina Gin LLC .... F 252 943-6990
  Pantego *(G-12162)*

MACHINERY: Custom

Angels Path Ventures Inc .... G 828 654-9530
  Arden *(G-309)*
Appalachian Tool & Machine Inc ...... E 828 669-0142
  Swannanoa *(G-15017)*
Automated Machine Technologies .... G 919 361-0121
  Morrisville *(G-11297)*
Avail Forensics LLC .... F 877 888-5895
  Wilmington *(G-16125)*
Axccellus LLC .... F 919 589-9800
  Apex *(G-169)*
Betech Inc .... E 828 687-9917
  Fletcher *(G-5987)*
Brock and Triplett Machine Sp .... G 336 667-6951
  Moravian Falls *(G-11142)*
Bunting Equipment Company Inc ..... F 336 626-7300
  Sophia *(G-14513)*
Burlington Machine Service .... G 336 228-6758
  Burlington *(G-1381)*
Curti USA Corporation .... G 910 769-1977
  Belville *(G-1023)*
DSI Innovations LLC .... E 336 893-8385
  Thomasville *(G-15216)*
Erecto Mch & Fabrication Inc .... G 704 922-8621
  Dallas *(G-4639)*
General Machining Inc .... G 336 342-2759
  Reidsville *(G-13519)*
Gordon Enterprises .... G 919 776-8784
  Sanford *(G-14127)*
Gormac Custom Mfg Inc .... G 828 891-9984
  Arden *(G-334)*
Goshen Engineering Inc .... G 919 429-9798
  Mount Olive *(G-11661)*
Grandeur Manufacturing Inc .... G 336 526-2468
  Jonesville *(G-9098)*
Holder Machine & Mfg Co .... G 828 479-8627
  Robbinsville *(G-13608)*
I2e Group LLC .... G 336 884-2014
  High Point *(G-8404)*
Machine Builders & Design Inc .... G 704 482-3456
  Shelby *(G-14340)*
Mecha Inc .... F 919 858-0372
  Raleigh *(G-13012)*
Noxon Automation USA LLC .... G 919 390-1560
  Morrisville *(G-11400)*
Ora Inc .... G 540 903-7177
  Marion *(G-10170)*
Paul Norman Company Inc .... G 704 399-4221
  Charlotte *(G-3320)*
Precision Fabricators Inc .... G 336 835-4763
  Ronda *(G-13768)*
Production Wldg Fbrication Inc .... E 828 687-7466
  Arden *(G-369)*
Tar Heel Tling Prcsion McHning ...... E 919 965-6160
  Smithfield *(G-14486)*
Tdc International LLC .... G 704 875-1198
  Concord *(G-4372)*

Turnamics Inc .... E 828 254-1059
  Asheville *(G-807)*
Turnkey Technologies Inc .... G 704 245-6437
  Salisbury *(G-14056)*
Worth Products LLC .... F 252 747-9994
  Snow Hill *(G-14510)*

MACHINERY: Electronic Component Making

Atmosphric Plsma Solutions Inc ...... G 919 341-8325
  Cary *(G-1693)*
D M & E Corporation .... E 704 482-8876
  Shelby *(G-14309)*
Progressive Elc Greenville LLC .... F 252 413-6957
  Emerald Isle *(G-5671)*
Wispry Inc .... G 919 854-7500
  Cary *(G-1929)*

MACHINERY: Ice Making

Work Well Hydrtion Systems LLC .... G 704 853-7788
  Gastonia *(G-6543)*

MACHINERY: Kilns, Lumber

Kiln Drying Systems Cmpnnts In ..... E 828 891-8115
  Etowah *(G-5692)*
Southeastern Installation Inc .... E 704 352-7146
  Lexington *(G-9783)*
Superior Dry Kilns Inc .... E 828 754-7001
  Hudson *(G-8782)*

MACHINERY: Metalworking

Atlantic Hydraulics Svcs LLC .... E 919 542-2985
  Sanford *(G-14091)*
Efco USA Inc .... E 800 332-6872
  Charlotte *(G-2686)*
Feeder Innovations Corporation ...... G 910 276-3511
  Laurinburg *(G-9480)*
G T Racing Heads Inc .... G 336 905-7988
  Sophia *(G-14517)*
Gerringer Enterprises .... G 336 227-6535
  Burlington *(G-1420)*
High Definition Tool Corp .... E 828 397-2467
  Connelly Springs *(G-4403)*
IMS Fabrication Inc .... E 704 216-0255
  Salisbury *(G-13982)*
Joe and La Inc .... F 336 585-0313
  Burlington *(G-1441)*
Manufacturing Methods LLC .... E 910 371-1700
  Leland *(G-9554)*
Obi Machine & Tool Inc .... G 252 946-1580
  Chocowinity *(G-3896)*
Petty Machine Company Inc .... E 704 864-3254
  Gastonia *(G-6488)*
Rosendahl Nextrom USA Inc .... F 828 464-2543
  Claremont *(G-3938)*
Winston Steel Stair Co .... G 336 721-0020
  Winston Salem *(G-16983)*

MACHINERY: Mining

80 Acres Urban Agriculture Inc .... G 704 437-6115
  Granite Falls *(G-6720)*
Brunner & Lay Inc .... G 828 274-2770
  Flat Rock *(G-5961)*
Junaluska Mill Engineering .... G 828 321-3693
  Andrews *(G-127)*
Paschal Associates Ltd .... F 336 625-2535
  Raleigh *(G-13100)*

MACHINERY: Packaging

A Hartness Inc .... G 704 351-2323
  Charlotte *(G-2115)*
Abco Automation Inc .... C 336 375-6400
  Browns Summit *(G-1298)*

Alotech Inc .... E 919 774-1297
  Goldston *(G-6672)*
Automated Machine Technologies ... G 919 361-0121
  Morrisville *(G-11297)*
Awcnc LLC .... E 252 633-5757
  New Bern *(G-11773)*
Axon LLC .... E 919 772-8383
  Raleigh *(G-12538)*
Aylward Enterprises LLC .... E 252 639-9242
  New Bern *(G-11774)*
Bunzl Processor Dist LLC .... G 910 738-8111
  Lumberton *(G-10028)*
Cates Mechanical Corporation .... G 704 458-5163
  Charlotte *(G-2419)*
Chase-Logeman Corporation .... F 336 665-0754
  Greensboro *(G-6905)*
Chudy Group LLC .... D 262 279-5307
  Durham *(G-5018)*
Container Systems Incorporated .... D 919 496-6133
  Franklinton *(G-6153)*
Focke & Co Inc .... D 336 449-7200
  Whitsett *(G-15990)*
Groninger USA LLC .... G 704 588-3873
  Charlotte *(G-2871)*
Hycorr LLC .... G 216 570-7408
  Huntersville *(G-8832)*
Keymac USA LLC .... F 704 877-5137
  Charlotte *(G-3052)*
Korber Medipak Systems NA Inc .... E 727 538-4644
  Cary *(G-1804)*
Korber Medipak Systems NA Inc .... E 727 538-4644
  Morrisville *(G-11367)*
Krw Packaging Machinery Inc .... F 828 658-0912
  Weaverville *(G-15850)*
Ossid LLC .... D 252 446-6177
  Battleboro *(G-927)*
Petty Machine Company Inc .... E 704 864-3254
  Gastonia *(G-6488)*
Roberts Polypro Inc .... E 704 588-1794
  Charlotte *(G-3455)*
Syntegon Technology Svcs LLC ..... E 919 877-0886
  Raleigh *(G-13321)*
Windak Inc .... F 828 322-2292
  Conover *(G-4514)*

MACHINERY: Paint Making

Corob North America Inc .... F 704 588-8408
  Charlotte *(G-2558)*

MACHINERY: Plastic Working

Dymetrol Company Inc .... F 866 964-8632
  Bladenboro *(G-1148)*
Enplas Life Tech Inc .... G 828 633-2250
  Asheville *(G-617)*
Mdsi Inc .... G 919 783-8730
  Browns Summit *(G-1312)*
Petty Machine Company Inc .... E 704 864-3254
  Gastonia *(G-6488)*
Psi-Polymer Systems Inc .... E 828 468-2600
  Conover *(G-4490)*
Single Temperature Contrls Inc ...... G 704 504-4800
  Charlotte *(G-3556)*

MACHINERY: Recycling

Apb Wrecker Service LLC .... G 704 400-0857
  Charlotte *(G-2199)*
McDonald Services Inc .... E 704 597-0590
  Charlotte *(G-3149)*
McDonald Services Inc .... G 704 753-9669
  Monroe *(G-10769)*
Shred-Tech Usa LLC .... G 919 387-8220
  Raleigh *(G-13252)*

PRODUCT SECTION

MACHINERY: Road Construction & Maintenance

Power Curbers Inc .... D 704 636-5871
  Salisbury *(G-14027)*

MACHINERY: Robots, Molding & Forming Plastics

Ilsemann Corp .... G 610 323-4143
  Charlotte *(G-2952)*

MACHINERY: Rubber Working

Mono Plate Inc .... G 631 643-3100
  Apex *(G-220)*

MACHINERY: Semiconductor Manufacturing

Bayatronics LLC .... F 980 432-0438
  Concord *(G-4206)*
Gladiator Enterprises Inc .... G 336 944-6932
  Greensboro *(G-7044)*
Industry Choice Solutions LLC .... G 828 628-1991
  Fairview *(G-5714)*
Kanthal Thermal Process Inc .... D 704 784-3001
  Concord *(G-4298)*
Power Components Inc .... G 704 321-9481
  Charlotte *(G-3360)*

MACHINERY: Textile

A B Carter Inc .... D 704 865-1201
  Gastonia *(G-6334)*
Abercrombie Textiles Inc .... G 704 487-0935
  Shelby *(G-14281)*
American Linc Corporation .... E 704 861-9242
  Gastonia *(G-6346)*
American Trutzschler Inc .... D 704 399-4521
  Charlotte *(G-2187)*
Bowman-Hollis Manufacturing Co .... E 704 374-1500
  Charlotte *(G-2341)*
Briggs-Shaffner Acquisition Co .... F 336 463-4272
  Yadkinville *(G-17034)*
Burnett Machine Company Inc .... E 704 867-7786
  Gastonia *(G-6363)*
Carolina Loom Reed Company Inc ..... F 336 274-7631
  Greensboro *(G-6887)*
Carolina Tex Sls Gastonia Inc .... F 704 739-1646
  Kings Mountain *(G-9301)*
Carolina Textile Services Inc .... G 910 843-3033
  Red Springs *(G-13496)*
Custom Enterprises Inc .... G 336 226-8296
  Burlington *(G-1405)*
Custom Industries Inc .... F 704 825-3346
  Belmont *(G-981)*
D & S International Inc .... F 336 578-3800
  Mebane *(G-10406)*
D M & E Corporation .... E 704 482-8876
  Shelby *(G-14309)*
Ellerre Tech Inc .... E 704 524-9096
  Dallas *(G-4638)*
Excel Inc .... F 704 735-6535
  Lincolnton *(G-9892)*
Ferguson Companies .... G
  Linwood *(G-9945)*
Fletcher Industries Inc .... E 910 692-7133
  Southern Pines *(G-14536)*
Flint Group US LLC .... G 828 687-4291
  Arden *(G-333)*
French Apron Manufacturing Co .... G 704 865-7666
  Gastonia *(G-6403)*
Gastex LLC .... G 704 824-9861
  Gastonia *(G-6404)*
Imperial Machine Company Inc .... E 704 739-8038
  Bessemer City *(G-1071)*

International McHy Sls Inc .... G 336 759-9548
  Winston Salem *(G-16763)*
Itm Ltd South .... G 336 883-2400
  Greensboro *(G-7128)*
J & P Entrprses of Crlinas Inc .... E 704 861-1867
  Gastonia *(G-6431)*
J J Jenkins Incorporated .... E 704 821-6648
  Matthews *(G-10324)*
James T White Company .... E 704 865-9811
  Gastonia *(G-6434)*
Kern-Liebers USA Textile Inc .... E 704 329-7153
  Matthews *(G-10259)*
M-B Industries Inc .... C 828 862-4201
  Rosman *(G-13786)*
Mount Hope Machinery Co .... F
  Charlotte *(G-3208)*
Murata McHy USA Holdings Inc .... F 704 394-8331
  Charlotte *(G-3220)*
Parts and Systems Company Inc .... F 828 684-7070
  Arden *(G-361)*
Pinco Usa Inc .... G 704 895-5766
  Cornelius *(G-4575)*
Precision Comb Works Inc .... G 704 864-2761
  Gastonia *(G-6495)*
Precision Machine Products Inc .... D 704 865-7490
  Gastonia *(G-6496)*
Sam M Butler Inc .... E 910 277-7456
  Laurinburg *(G-9495)*
TCI Mobility Inc .... F 704 867-8331
  Gastonia *(G-6520)*
Textrol Laboratories Inc .... E 704 764-3400
  Monroe *(G-10821)*
Tri State Plastics Inc .... G 704 865-7431
  Gastonia *(G-6532)*
Tsg Finishing LLC .... G 828 328-5522
  Hickory *(G-8186)*
Tsg Finishing LLC .... E 828 328-5541
  Hickory *(G-8187)*
Tsg Finishing LLC .... E 828 328-5522
  Hickory *(G-8188)*
Tubular Textile Machinery .... G 336 956-6444
  Lexington *(G-9797)*

MACHINERY: Wire Drawing

Southern Steel and Wire Inc .... D 336 548-9611
  Madison *(G-10087)*

MACHINERY: Woodworking

Automated Lumber Handling Inc .... G 828 754-4662
  Lenoir *(G-9576)*
Carbide Saws Incorporated .... F 336 882-6835
  High Point *(G-8282)*
Caterpillar Inc .... D 919 550-1100
  Clayton *(G-3963)*
Etk International Inc .... G 704 819-1541
  Indian Trail *(G-8932)*
Eurohansa Inc .... G 336 885-1010
  High Point *(G-8347)*
Fletcher Machine Inds Inc .... D 336 249-6101
  Lexington *(G-9718)*
Grecon Dimter Inc .... F 828 397-5139
  Connelly Springs *(G-4402)*
Jly Invstmnts Inc Fka Nwman Mc ...... E 336 273-8261
  Browns Summit *(G-1310)*
Karl Ogden Enterprises Inc .... G 704 845-2785
  Matthews *(G-10258)*
Leitz Tooling Systems LP .... G 336 861-3367
  Archdale *(G-292)*
Mill Art Wood .... G 919 828-7376
  Raleigh *(G-13032)*
Ostwalt Leasing Co Inc .... G 704 528-4458
  Troutman *(G-15388)*

Otb Machinery Inc .... G 336 323-1035
  Thomasville *(G-15260)*
Peco Inc .... E 828 684-1234
  Arden *(G-362)*
Rfsprotech LLC .... E 704 845-2785
  Matthews *(G-10286)*
Rp Fletcher Machine Co Inc .... D 336 249-6101
  Lexington *(G-9775)*
Smith Woodturning Inc .... G 828 464-2230
  Newton *(G-11968)*
Venture Cabinets .... G 252 299-0051
  Fremont *(G-6175)*

MACHINISTS' TOOLS & MACHINES: Measuring, Metalworking Type

If Armor International LLC .... C 704 482-1399
  Shelby *(G-14329)*
Modern Tool Service .... F 919 365-7470
  Wendell *(G-15909)*

MACHINISTS' TOOLS: Measuring, Precision

Linamar North Carolina Inc .... F 828 348-5343
  Arden *(G-349)*

MACHINISTS' TOOLS: Precision

C & C Precision Machine Inc .... E 704 739-0505
  Kings Mountain *(G-9297)*
Cross Technology Inc .... E 336 725-4700
  East Bend *(G-5465)*
Diamond Dog Tools Inc .... D 828 687-3686
  Arden *(G-325)*
Kenmar Inc .... F 336 884-8722
  High Point *(G-8423)*
Penco Precision LLC .... E 910 292-6542
  Wilmington *(G-16350)*
Unique Tool and Mfg Co .... E 336 498-2614
  Franklinville *(G-6171)*

MACHINISTS' TOOLS: Scales, Measuring, Precision

Vishay Transducers Ltd .... E 919 365-3800
  Wendell *(G-15924)*

MAGAZINES, WHOLESALE

Comfort Publishing Svcs LLC .... G 704 907-7848
  Concord *(G-4236)*

MAGNESIUM

Mg12 LP .... G 828 440-1144
  Tryon *(G-15425)*

MAGNETIC INK & OPTICAL SCANNING EQPT

NCR Voyix Corporation .... G 937 445-5000
  Cary *(G-1830)*

MAGNETIC SHIELDS, METAL

Northsouth Biomagnetics Inc .... G 828 478-2277
  Sherrills Ford *(G-14389)*

MAGNETIC TAPE, AUDIO: Prerecorded

American Multimedia Inc .... D 336 229-7101
  Burlington *(G-1364)*

MAGNETS: Permanent

Docmagnet Inc .... G 919 788-7999
  Raleigh *(G-12691)*

MAIL-ORDER HOUSE, NEC

Employee Codes: A=Over 500 employees, B=251-500
C=101-250, D=51-100, E=20-50, F=10-19, G=1-9

2024 Harris North Carolina Manufacturers Directory

MAIL-ORDER HOUSES: Fitness & Sporting Goods

PRODUCT SECTION

Grateful Union Family Inc.................F..... 828 622-3258
  Asheville *(G-640)*

MAIL-ORDER HOUSES: Fitness & Sporting Goods

Advantage Fitness Products LLC............G..... 336 643-8810
  Archdale *(G-265)*

MAIL-ORDER HOUSES: Jewelry

Dallas L Pridgen Inc....................G..... 919 732-4422
  Carrboro *(G-1647)*

MAIL-ORDER HOUSES: Women's Apparel

Kayser-Roth Corporation.................C..... 336 852-2030
  Greensboro *(G-7145)*

MAILBOX RENTAL & RELATED SVCS

Bryan Austin............................F..... 336 841-6573
  High Point *(G-8276)*
King Business Service Inc...............G..... 910 610-1030
  Laurinburg *(G-9483)*

MAILING LIST: Compilers

Randall-Reilly LLC......................C..... 704 814-1390
  Charlotte *(G-3408)*

MAILING MACHINES WHOLESALERS

Bell and Howell LLC.....................E..... 919 767-6400
  Durham *(G-4954)*

MAILING SVCS, NEC

Alpha Mailing Service Inc...............E..... 704 484-1711
  Shelby *(G-14283)*
King Business Service Inc...............G..... 910 610-1030
  Laurinburg *(G-9483)*
Metro Productions Inc...................F..... 919 851-6420
  Raleigh *(G-13022)*
Mjt Us Inc..............................G..... 704 826-7828
  Charlotte *(G-3189)*
Salem One Inc...........................F..... 336 722-2886
  Kernersville *(G-9231)*

MANAGEMENT CONSULTING SVCS: Administrative

Reynolds Consumer Products Inc..........A..... 704 371-5550
  Huntersville *(G-8885)*

MANAGEMENT CONSULTING SVCS: Automation & Robotics

Goshen Engineering Inc..................G..... 919 429-9798
  Mount Olive *(G-11661)*
Irsi Automation Inc.....................G..... 336 303-5320
  Mc Leansville *(G-10393)*
Scott Systems Intl Inc..................F..... 704 362-1115
  Charlotte *(G-3512)*

MANAGEMENT CONSULTING SVCS: Business

Competitive Solutions Inc...............E..... 919 851-0058
  Raleigh *(G-12634)*

MANAGEMENT CONSULTING SVCS: Business Planning & Organizing

Emath360 LLC............................F..... 919 744-4944
  Cary *(G-1757)*

MANAGEMENT CONSULTING SVCS: Construction Project

Esequence Inc...........................G..... 919 831-1995
  Raleigh *(G-12747)*

MANAGEMENT CONSULTING SVCS: Distribution Channels

Triple Crown International LLC..........G..... 704 846-4983
  Charlotte *(G-3730)*

MANAGEMENT CONSULTING SVCS: Food & Beverage

Microthermics Inc.......................F..... 919 878-8045
  Raleigh *(G-13028)*

MANAGEMENT CONSULTING SVCS: General

K2 Solutions Inc........................B..... 910 692-6898
  Southern Pines *(G-14538)*

MANAGEMENT CONSULTING SVCS: Hospital & Health

UNC Campus Health Services..............D..... 919 966-2281
  Chapel Hill *(G-2087)*

MANAGEMENT CONSULTING SVCS: Industrial

Q T Corporation.........................G..... 252 399-7600
  Wilson *(G-16526)*

MANAGEMENT CONSULTING SVCS: Industrial & Labor

Archie Supply LLC.......................G..... 336 987-0895
  Greensboro *(G-6813)*

MANAGEMENT CONSULTING SVCS: Quality Assurance

Propharma Group LLC.....................D..... 888 242-0559
  Raleigh *(G-13153)*

MANAGEMENT CONSULTING SVCS: Training & Development

Camstar Systems Inc.....................C..... 704 227-6600
  Charlotte *(G-2380)*
Heed Group Inc..........................G..... 877 938-8853
  Stanley *(G-14696)*

MANAGEMENT CONSULTING SVCS: Transportation

Nexxt Level Trucking LLC................G..... 980 205-4425
  Charlotte *(G-3256)*

MANAGEMENT SERVICES

Allyn International Trdg Corp...........G..... 877 858-2482
  Marshville *(G-10210)*
Drew Roberts LLC........................G..... 336 497-1679
  Whitsett *(G-15988)*
Jebco Inc...............................E..... 919 557-2001
  Holly Springs *(G-8702)*
Kayser-Roth Corporation.................C..... 336 852-2030
  Greensboro *(G-7145)*
S & A Cherokee LLC......................E..... 919 674-6020
  Cary *(G-1876)*
Triangle Brick Company..................E..... 919 544-1796
  Durham *(G-5406)*
Volvo Logistics North America Inc.......C..... 336 393-4746
  Greensboro *(G-7449)*
W T Humphrey Inc........................D..... 910 455-3555
  Jacksonville *(G-9044)*

MANAGEMENT SVCS: Business

Bus Safety Inc..........................G..... 336 671-0838
  Mocksville *(G-10558)*
Competitive Solutions Inc...............E..... 919 851-0058
  Raleigh *(G-12634)*

MANAGEMENT SVCS: Construction

Carlson Environmental Cons PC...........D..... 704 283-9765
  Monroe *(G-10673)*
Equagen Engineers Pllc..................E..... 919 444-5442
  Raleigh *(G-12744)*
Trademark Landscape Group Inc...........F..... 910 253-0560
  Supply *(G-15013)*

MANAGEMENT SVCS: Restaurant

Xenial Inc..............................E..... 800 253-8664
  Charlotte *(G-3834)*

MANUFACTURING INDUSTRIES, NEC

26 Industries Inc.......................G..... 704 839-3218
  Concord *(G-4184)*
3-Oceans Mfg Inc........................G..... 919 600-4500
  Garner *(G-6248)*
89 Industries...........................G..... 303 681-3188
  Littleton *(G-9949)*
A Plus Five Star Trnsp LLC..............G..... 919 771-4820
  Clayton *(G-3950)*
Access Manufacturing Tech LLC...........G..... 224 610-0171
  Mooresville *(G-10846)*
Acu Trol Inc............................G..... 919 566-8332
  Sanford *(G-14082)*
Addendum LLC............................G..... 704 664-9898
  Mooresville *(G-10848)*
AIM Industries Inc......................G..... 336 656-9990
  Browns Summit *(G-1299)*
Ajc Craftworks Inc......................G..... 919 279-1621
  Raleigh *(G-12483)*
American Made Industries Inc............G..... 650 218-7608
  Concord *(G-4193)*
Andrews Industries LLC..................G..... 919 266-9656
  Raleigh *(G-12505)*
Andy Maylish Fabrication Inc............G..... 704 785-1491
  Denver *(G-4762)*
Angel Industries Inc....................G..... 919 264-0765
  Raleigh *(G-12507)*
Applied Components Mfg LLC..............G..... 828 323-8915
  Hickory *(G-7936)*
Applied Components Mfg LLC..............G..... 828 322-6535
  Hickory *(G-7937)*
Astroturf...............................G..... 336 528-5496
  Lexington *(G-9682)*
Astroturf Corp..........................G..... 336 238-9060
  Lexington *(G-9683)*
Atlantic Manufacturing LLC..............G..... 336 497-5500
  Kernersville *(G-9166)*
Atlantic Mfg & Fabrication Inc..........G..... 704 647-6200
  Salisbury *(G-13925)*
Bark House Supply Company...............G..... 828 765-9010
  Spruce Pine *(G-14629)*
Barry Lowe Fabrication..................G..... 828 776-7354
  Fairview *(G-5708)*
Bass Fabrications LLC...................G..... 252 312-8937
  Hobbsville *(G-8674)*
Beachbub USA............................G..... 336 965-5941
  Greensboro *(G-6833)*
Beast Chains............................G..... 336 346-9081
  High Point *(G-8268)*
Belev En U Water Mfg Co.................G..... 704 620-0450
  Cornelius *(G-4526)*
Blue Ridge Bracket Co...................G..... 828 242-8577
  Asheville *(G-563)*

PRODUCT SECTION

MANUFACTURING INDUSTRIES, NEC

Blue Ridge Bracket Inc...................... G 828 808-3273
  Fletcher (G-5988)
Boka Industries LLC......................... G 704 237-4692
  Cornelius (G-4530)
Boleef Industries............................... G 336 330-0404
  Roxboro (G-13796)
Boles Industries LLC........................ G 919 489-9254
  Durham (G-4970)
Bordchek Industries LLC.................. G 864 363-2117
  Cornelius (G-4531)
Borden Mfg Co Fund Inc................... G 919 734-4301
  Goldsboro (G-6595)
BR Lee Industries Inc....................... G 704 966-3317
  Lincolnton (G-9876)
Brand Art Manufacturing LLC............ G 704 241-1104
  Winston Salem (G-16635)
Brite Sky LLC.................................... G 757 589-4676
  Godwin (G-6576)
Brooks Manufacturing Solutions........ F 336 438-1280
  Graham (G-6681)
C J Manufacturing Inc....................... G 252 927-4913
  Pinetown (G-12244)
C6 Manufacturing.............................. G 704 896-3934
  Cornelius (G-4532)
Cambro.. G 919 563-0761
  Mebane (G-10403)
Carbon-Less Industries Inc............... G 704 361-1231
  Harrisburg (G-7703)
Caring For Body LLC........................ G 706 897-9904
  Arden (G-317)
Carolina Gyps Reclamation LLC........ G 704 895-4506
  Cornelius (G-4534)
Carolina Mfg Group LLC................... G 336 413-8335
  Winston Salem (G-16645)
Carolina Mnufactured Homes LLC..... G 910 374-6889
  Lumberton (G-10029)
CB Industries.................................... G 704 660-1955
  Mooresville (G-10901)
Chatter Free Tling Sltions Inc............ G 828 659-7379
  Marion (G-10148)
Cjm Industries LLC........................... G 704 506-5926
  Mooresville (G-10903)
Claremont Products LLC.................. G 704 325-3580
  Claremont (G-3907)
Clean Green Sustainable Lf LLC....... F 855 946-8785
  Greensboro (G-6915)
Cmw Mfg LLC................................... G 330 283-5551
  Charlotte (G-2507)
Cnc Creations................................... G 704 508-2668
  Troutman (G-15374)
Collier Industries NC......................... G 980 263-0510
  Stanley (G-14689)
Collin Manufacturing Inc................... G 919 917-5969
  Wake Forest (G-15544)
Collin Mfg Inc.................................... G 919 917-6264
  Oriental (G-12109)
Commdoor Inc................................... G 800 565-1851
  Concord (G-4237)
Component Manufacturing & Mch..... G 336 699-4204
  Lewisville (G-9665)
Concise Manufacturing Inc............... G 704 796-8419
  Salisbury (G-13945)
Conmech Industries LLC.................. G 919 306-6228
  Apex (G-177)
Continental Manufacturing Co........... G 336 697-2591
  Mc Leansville (G-10386)
Cooper Industries LLC...................... G 304 545-1482
  Greensboro (G-6935)
Coramdeo Lighting Industries........... G 704 906-8864
  Mooresville (G-10913)
Core Grip LLC.................................. G 252 341-7783
  Greenville (G-7508)

Cornerstone Mfg Co LLC.................. G 704 624-6145
  Marshville (G-10212)
CP Industries Inc.............................. G 704 816-0580
  Charlotte (G-2564)
Cr Appraisal Firm LLC...................... G 704 344-0909
  Charlotte (G-2566)
Creative Fish Company Inc............... G 203 515-8631
  Kernersville (G-9184)
Creative Lights.................................. G 336 209-8209
  Stoneville (G-14956)
Creek Industries Inc......................... F 828 319-7490
  Weaverville (G-15845)
Cross Manufacturing LLC................. G 336 269-6542
  Burlington (G-1401)
Cross Manufacturing LLC................. G 336 603-6926
  Gibsonville (G-6557)
Crown Town Industries LLC............. G 704 579-0387
  Concord (G-4248)
Cs Manufacturing Cs Mfg.................. G 704 837-1701
  Charlotte (G-2580)
Cutting Edge Industries.................... G 336 937-2129
  Greensboro (G-6951)
Cv Industries.................................... G 919 778-7280
  Goldsboro (G-6605)
Dale Reynolds Cabinets Inc............. G 704 890-5962
  Charlotte (G-2601)
Dauntless Mfg Solutions LLC............ G 757 870-2173
  Asheboro (G-423)
Devan Us Inc.................................... G 704 365-7111
  Charlotte (G-2624)
Direct Distribution Inds Inc................ G 910 217-0000
  Wagram (G-15523)
Dlss Mfg.. G 919 619-6184
  Pittsboro (G-12340)
Douglas Battery Mfg Co................... G 336 650-7000
  Winston Salem (G-16687)
Draxlor Industries Inc....................... G 757 274-6771
  Durham (G-5062)
Dynamic Mounting............................ G 704 978-8723
  Mooresville (G-10931)
E&G Industries Inc........................... G 347 665-3039
  Durham (G-5074)
Eagle Rock Industries LLC............... G 919 799-1021
  Siler City (G-14409)
Earnhardt Manufacturing.................. G 910 738-9426
  Lumberton (G-10033)
East West Diversified LLC............... G 919 671-0301
  Wake Forest (G-15549)
Eastern Carolina Mfg Co LLC........... G 252 824-3794
  Tarboro (G-15102)
Eastern Manufacturing LLC.............. G 919 580-2058
  Goldsboro (G-6611)
Echo Industries Inc.......................... G 704 921-2293
  Charlotte (G-2682)
Ellie Industries Inc............................ G 828 626-3935
  Barnardsville (G-909)
Enepay Corporation.......................... G 919 788-1454
  Raleigh (G-12738)
Energizer Battery Mfg...................... G 336 736-7936
  Asheboro (G-430)
Enoco LLC.. G 336 398-5650
  Greensboro (G-7001)
Fac Ette Manufacturing.................... G 910 599-7352
  Wilmington (G-16216)
Fiber Transport Systems Inc............ G 704 905-3549
  Charlotte (G-2757)
Fields Industries LLC........................ G 704 264-3872
  Charlotte (G-2760)
Flow Fabrication............................... G 704 376-8555
  Charlotte (G-2780)
Furniture Mfrs Claring Hse Inc.......... G 866 477-8468
  Thomasville (G-15226)

General Foam Plastics Corp............. G 757 857-0153
  Tarboro (G-15106)
Gfm Industries LLC.......................... G 614 439-5349
  Burlington (G-1421)
Give You Hope Industries Inc........... G 336 608-2774
  Winston Salem (G-16721)
Gratz Industries................................ G 828 467-6380
  Asheville (G-641)
Griffin Manufacturing LLC................. G 704 984-2070
  Albemarle (G-88)
Gw Industries LLC............................ G 919 608-1911
  Raleigh (G-12825)
Harris Industries LLC........................ G 410 924-3894
  Mint Hill (G-10536)
Health At Home Inc.......................... F 850 543-4482
  Charlotte (G-2896)
Heico Manufacturing Inc................... G 828 304-5499
  Hickory (G-8042)
Hensley Corporation......................... G 828 230-9447
  Fairview (G-5712)
Highlight Industries Inc..................... G 704 661-1734
  Concord (G-4281)
Hodge Industries Inc........................ G 704 491-0104
  Charlotte (G-2913)
Holten Industries LLC....................... G 919 810-8467
  Raleigh (G-12854)
Hudson Industries LLC..................... G 704 480-0014
  Shelby (G-14327)
Hughes Products Co Inc................... G 336 475-0091
  Winston Salem (G-16751)
Humboldt Mfg Co Inc........................ G 919 832-6509
  Raleigh (G-12867)
Idael Mfg Co..................................... G 919 480-1329
  Raleigh (G-12875)
IMS Intrnational Mfrs Showroom....... G 336 454-0388
  Jamestown (G-9057)
Innovative Technology Mfg LLC....... G 980 248-3731
  Mooresville (G-10982)
Insurrection Industries LLC.............. G 443 801-7356
  Winston Salem (G-16762)
Ironmex Fabrication Inc.................... G 336 937-1045
  Greensboro (G-7122)
Jacob Holm Industries Amer Inc....... G 828 490-6017
  Fletcher (G-6014)
Jag Industries LLC........................... G 704 655-2507
  Huntersville (G-8840)
Jepp Industries Inc........................... G 910 232-8715
  Wilmington (G-16279)
Joanna Division Ch F Inds................ G 704 522-5000
  Charlotte (G-3026)
Jochum Industries............................ G 336 288-7975
  Greensboro (G-7137)
Justrite Manufacturing...................... G 336 990-0918
  North Wilkesboro (G-12020)
K & K Industries LLC........................ G 336 689-4293
  Lexington (G-9737)
Karl RI Manufacturing....................... G 919 846-3801
  Raleigh (G-12931)
Kinetic Performance Llc................... G 910 248-2121
  Raeford (G-12425)
King Charles Industries LLC............. G 704 848-4121
  Lilesville (G-9839)
King Charles Industries LLC............. G 910 974-4114
  Candor (G-1594)
Kituwah Industries LLC..................... G 828 477-4616
  Whittier (G-16008)
Koonts Manufacturing Inc................. G 336 300-8009
  Lexington (G-9741)
Kwiatek Innovations LLC.................. G 919 455-8295
  Wilmington (G-16291)
La Oaxaquena.................................. G 336 274-0173
  Greensboro (G-7160)

Employee Codes: A=Over 500 employees, B=251-500
C=101-250, D=51-100, E=20-50, F=10-19, G=1-9

MANUFACTURING INDUSTRIES, NEC — PRODUCT SECTION

LA West Inc .... G 704 685-2833
  Sherrills Ford *(G-14387)*

Ladder Carry LLC .... G 704 245-2359
  Cary *(G-1806)*

Lady C E Crews LLC .... G 703 565-3687
  Hickory *(G-8082)*

Lamberts Industries .... G 980 244-0898
  Albemarle *(G-94)*

Lee Linear .... G 800 221-0811
  Southport *(G-14573)*

Lee Paving Solutions LLC .... G 828 302-0415
  Denver *(G-4787)*

Lexington Home Brands Mfg .... G 336 243-5740
  Lexington *(G-9747)*

Limitless Prfmce Fbrication LL .... G 910 799-5441
  Wilmington *(G-16301)*

LLC Stanton Gray .... G 704 975-9392
  Newton *(G-11949)*

Lr Manufacturing Inc .... G 910 399-1410
  Delco *(G-4722)*

Mammoth Industries LLC .... G 919 749-8183
  Raleigh *(G-12993)*

Manufactur LLC .... G 919 937-2090
  Durham *(G-5206)*

Manufacturing Analysis Inc .... G 919 434-3005
  Carrboro *(G-1649)*

Manufacturing Strategies LLC .... G 828 758-9092
  Lenoir *(G-9629)*

Maximizer Systems Inc .... F 828 345-6036
  Hickory *(G-8092)*

McKenzie Industries Inc .... G 336 870-9229
  Jamestown *(G-9061)*

Mdi Solutions LLC .... F 845 721-6758
  Salisbury *(G-14012)*

Mdm Mfg LLC .... G 919 908-6574
  Hillsborough *(G-8662)*

Meera Industries Usa LLC .... G 336 906-7570
  High Point *(G-8452)*

MGe Products LLC .... G 828 443-3214
  Morganton *(G-11233)*

Mikron Industries .... G 253 398-1382
  Durham *(G-5226)*

Minnewawa Inc .... G 865 522-8103
  Charlotte *(G-3184)*

Mint Hill Industries .... G 704 545-8852
  Mint Hill *(G-10540)*

Mizelle Industries LLC .... G 252 940-5506
  Washington *(G-15716)*

Moose-Tek Industries Inc .... G 336 416-7034
  New London *(G-11874)*

Morgan Manufacturing .... G 336 497-5763
  Kernersville *(G-9220)*

Mpx Manufacturing Inc .... G 704 762-9207
  Salisbury *(G-14014)*

N & N Industries Inc .... G 919 770-1311
  Sanford *(G-14156)*

Nacho Industries Inc .... G 919 937-9471
  Durham *(G-5236)*

Narricot Industries LLC .... G 215 322-3908
  Greensboro *(G-7212)*

NC Pallet Manufacturer LLC .... G 910 576-4902
  Troy *(G-15410)*

New River Mills .... G 336 385-1446
  Creston *(G-4624)*

Norcep Industries .... G 910 762-5933
  Castle Hayne *(G-1957)*

Norfield LLC .... G 530 879-3121
  Garner *(G-6297)*

Novak Industries LLC .... G 704 662-2982
  Maiden *(G-10114)*

Novem Industries Inc .... G 704 660-6460
  Charlotte *(G-3276)*

Oak Street Mfg .... G 877 465-4344
  Statesville *(G-14853)*

Obscura Mfg LLC .... G 336 419-5648
  Lenoir *(G-9644)*

Oleksynprannyk LLC .... F 704 450-0182
  Mooresville *(G-11043)*

One Packaging Excel Inc .... G 919 268-9330
  Wendell *(G-15910)*

Optimal Industries LLC .... G 601 530-5222
  Salisbury *(G-14021)*

Optomill Solutions LLC .... G 704 560-4037
  Matthews *(G-10338)*

P A Indl Fabrications .... D 252 329-8881
  Greenville *(G-7567)*

Pag Asb LLC .... G 336 883-4187
  High Point *(G-8474)*

Paps Performance & Machine LLC .... G 336 225-1877
  Lexington *(G-9767)*

Pate Industries .... G 704 889-2376
  Pineville *(G-12289)*

Payne Leather and Tool LLC .... G 336 391-8964
  Weaverville *(G-15858)*

Pendergast Industries LLC .... G 919 636-1621
  Chapel Hill *(G-2052)*

PL&e Sales Inc .... G 704 561-9650
  Charlotte *(G-3346)*

Pma Industries Inc .... G 704 575-6200
  Charlotte *(G-3350)*

Pnb Manufacturing .... G 336 883-0021
  High Point *(G-8488)*

Polypore Inc .... D 704 587-8409
  Charlotte *(G-3352)*

Posh Industries LLC .... G 919 596-8434
  Durham *(G-5296)*

Precision Boat Mfg .... G 336 395-8795
  Graham *(G-6707)*

Producers Gin Murfreesboro LLC .... G 252 398-3762
  Murfreesboro *(G-11702)*

Product Quest Mfg LLC .... G 321 255-3250
  Winston Salem *(G-16871)*

Progressive Industries Inc .... G 919 267-6948
  Apex *(G-233)*

Pullover Pal .... G 910 340-1801
  Jacksonville *(G-9024)*

Quadalupe Industries Inc .... G 786 241-0315
  Asheville *(G-748)*

Quadsaw Usa LLC .... G 980 339-8554
  Charlotte *(G-3400)*

Quality Salvage Industries .... G 336 884-4433
  Thomasville *(G-15269)*

Qualtech Industries Inc .... G 704 734-0345
  Kings Mountain *(G-9327)*

R3cycle Industries LLC .... F 404 754-4499
  Waxhaw *(G-15772)*

Rail-Scale-Models .... G 248 421-6276
  Garner *(G-6307)*

Ratoon Agroprocessing LLC .... G 828 273-9114
  Marion *(G-10173)*

RC Industries .... G 828 693-1953
  Hendersonville *(G-7895)*

Re-Crtion Sstainable Wdwkg LLC .... G 919 612-4791
  Raleigh *(G-13192)*

Red Wolfe Industries LLC .... G 336 570-2282
  Hurdle Mills *(G-8913)*

Renew Protect LLC .... G 828 318-5654
  Weaverville *(G-15859)*

Replar Mfg Inc .... G 919 622-5942
  Durham *(G-5326)*

Resolute Fabricators LLC .... G 704 728-1249
  Cornelius *(G-4582)*

Ritter Fab LLC .... G 336 879-2428
  Seagrove *(G-14246)*

Rothrock Industries .... G 336 454-4549
  Jamestown *(G-9070)*

Rq Industries Inc .... G 704 701-1071
  Concord *(G-4354)*

Rsk Industries LLC .... G 216 905-4014
  Wake Forest *(G-15584)*

Sapona Manufacturing Co Inc .... G 336 625-2161
  Asheboro *(G-477)*

Sas Industries Company LLC .... G 704 323-9098
  Pineville *(G-12303)*

Sawgrass Industries .... G 912 884-4008
  Saluda *(G-14074)*

Sbm Industries LLC .... G 919 625-3672
  Raleigh *(G-13235)*

Schueler Industries Inc .... G 847 613-0673
  Hickory *(G-8146)*

Sealco Manufacturing LLC .... G 704 662-2850
  Mooresville *(G-11082)*

Seneca Devices Inc .... G 301 412-3576
  Durham *(G-5349)*

Sesmfg LLC .... G 803 917-3248
  Charlotte *(G-3531)*

Sewerkote .... G 919 598-1974
  Chapel Hill *(G-2069)*

Sfd Industries Inc .... G 336 829-5796
  Winston Salem *(G-16902)*

Shealy Designed Wood Pdts LLC .... G 704 308-9435
  Cherryville *(G-3876)*

Shenk Industries Inc .... G 828 808-3327
  Asheville *(G-768)*

Shocktec Inc .... G 704 663-5678
  Mooresville *(G-11084)*

Shoffner Industries Inc .... G 336 226-9356
  Burlington *(G-1494)*

Shoreline Industries Inc .... G 910 571-0111
  Troy *(G-15416)*

Siggbey Industries LLC .... G 336 483-6035
  Greensboro *(G-7339)*

Sk Enterprises Mfg LLC .... G 919 721-1458
  Sanford *(G-14185)*

Skeeter Beaters .... G 919 285-6054
  Willow Spring *(G-16083)*

Ski Time Industries Inc .... G 704 455-3870
  Harrisburg *(G-7728)*

Snow On Go Trucking LLC .... G 980 892-1791
  Salisbury *(G-14044)*

Solara of Carolinas .... G 910 723-1270
  Linden *(G-9942)*

Southland Industries .... G 336 989-0944
  High Point *(G-8547)*

Spectre Custom Solutions LLC .... G 704 450-4428
  Mooresville *(G-11094)*

Speed King Manufacturing Inc .... G 910 457-1995
  Southport *(G-14583)*

Spire Industries Inc .... G 435 994-4756
  Raleigh *(G-13291)*

Spotless Industries LLC .... G 980 430-1560
  Charlotte *(G-3604)*

Ss Manufacturing Inc .... G 770 317-8121
  Kannapolis *(G-9134)*

Stansell Industries LLC .... G 864 371-2425
  Asheville *(G-788)*

Steri-Air LLC .... G 336 434-1166
  High Point *(G-8552)*

Stokes Mfg LLC .... G 336 270-8746
  Roxboro *(G-13826)*

Sung Industries Inc .... G 919 387-8550
  Apex *(G-246)*

Suntex Industries .... F 336 784-1000
  Winston Salem *(G-16924)*

Tag Stringing Service Inc .... G 336 294-9394
  Greensboro *(G-7387)*

PRODUCT SECTION MEAT PRDTS: Sausages, From Purchased Meat

Tagtraum Industries Inc.................................. G 919 809-7797
   Raleigh *(G-13325)*
Tak Manufacturing LLC................................. G 704 473-6391
   Shelby *(G-14372)*
Tcc Manufacturing.. G 828 970-7270
   Maiden *(G-10118)*
Tethis Manufacturing LLC............................. G 919 808-2866
   Raleigh *(G-13341)*
Texlon Industries LLC................................... G 252 292-6590
   Wilmington *(G-16428)*
Textile Manufacturing Tech LLC................... G 828 632-3012
   Taylorsville *(G-15173)*
Thomas B Brugh Mfg Rep.............................. G 858 385-8987
   Charlotte *(G-3687)*
Toolmarx LLC.. G 919 725-0122
   Winston Salem *(G-16945)*
Toque Industries LLC..................................... G 704 640-6232
   Charlotte *(G-3710)*
Tree Frog Industries LLC............................... G 919 986-2229
   Wendell *(G-15921)*
Twisted Fire Industires LLC.......................... G 704 652-8559
   Concord *(G-4380)*
Urban Industries Corp.................................... F 980 209-9471
   Pineville *(G-12313)*
Useable Products... G 919 870-6693
   Raleigh *(G-13387)*
Vaibas Industries LLC..................................... G 919 749-4422
   Raleigh *(G-13389)*
Vallee Industries Inc....................................... G 910 477-0092
   Oak Island *(G-12056)*
Vandilay Industries LLC................................ G 704 962-5140
   Charlotte *(G-3765)*
Velocita Inc... G 336 764-8513
   Clemmons *(G-4066)*
Vermont Designs Unlimited LLC................. G 910 846-4477
   Supply *(G-15014)*
Vibration Solutions.. G 704 754-3118
   Troutman *(G-15398)*
Vision Contract Mfg LLC................................ E 336 405-8784
   High Point *(G-8595)*
W & F Manufacturing LLC............................. G 336 665-4023
   Colfax *(G-4163)*
W Gamby C O Hanes Dye & Finish............. E 336 724-9020
   Winston Salem *(G-16967)*
W W Industries... G 336 312-1806
   Greensboro *(G-7452)*
Walflor Industries Inc..................................... G 360 899-8060
   Candler *(G-1592)*
War Sport Manufacturing LLC..................... G 252 220-6505
   Nashville *(G-11754)*
Wayne Trademark... G 336 887-3173
   Asheboro *(G-506)*
Wears Industries Inc...................................... G 828 575-9466
   Asheville *(G-816)*
Weaver Fabrication... G 336 877-3427
   Fleetwood *(G-5977)*
Whelan Industries LLC................................... G 704 506-9515
   Mint Hill *(G-10548)*
Worsham Sprinkler Co Inc............................ G 704 805-9700
   Charlotte *(G-3827)*
Wright Industries LLC.................................... G 919 824-2936
   Huntersville *(G-8907)*
Xtra Light Manufacturing............................... G 919 422-7281
   Apex *(G-261)*
Young & Son Mfg LLC................................... G 704 799-1658
   Mooresville *(G-11137)*
Zeal Industries LLC... G 828 575-9894
   Asheville *(G-825)*
Zengerle Industries Inc................................. G 919 240-5415
   Chapel Hill *(G-2104)*

MARBLE, BUILDING: Cut & Shaped

Beautimar Manufactured MBL Inc................. F 919 779-1181
   Raleigh *(G-12550)*
Caesarstone Tech USA Inc............................. G 818 779-0999
   Charlotte *(G-2376)*
Carolina Marble Products Inc....................... F 252 753-3020
   Farmville *(G-5731)*
Exquisite Granite and MBL Inc..................... G 336 851-8890
   Greensboro *(G-7009)*
Ketchie Marble Co Inc.................................... G 704 279-8377
   Salisbury *(G-13998)*
Lawing Marble Co Inc..................................... G 704 732-0360
   Lincolnton *(G-9898)*
Marion Cultured Marble Inc.......................... F 828 724-4782
   Marion *(G-10157)*
National Marble Products Inc...................... G 910 326-3005
   Emerald Isle *(G-5670)*
Natural Granite & Marble Inc....................... G 919 872-1508
   Raleigh *(G-13056)*
Southern Marble Co LLC............................... G 704 982-4142
   Albemarle *(G-107)*
Southern Stone Cutting................................. G 252 566-3116
   La Grange *(G-9446)*
Stoneworx Inc... G 252 937-8080
   Rocky Mount *(G-13734)*
Tarheel Marble Company Inc....................... F 704 888-6003
   Locust *(G-9975)*
Turmar Marble Inc.. F 704 391-1800
   Charlotte *(G-3739)*
USA Dreamstone LLC..................................... G 919 615-4329
   Garner *(G-6323)*

MARINE HARDWARE

Ace Marine Rigging & Supply Inc................. F 252 726-6620
   Morehead City *(G-11148)*
Carolina North Mfg Inc................................... G 336 992-0082
   Kernersville *(G-9173)*
Custom Industries Inc................................... E 336 299-2885
   Greensboro *(G-6950)*
Marine Tooling Technology Inc.................... G 336 887-9577
   High Point *(G-8439)*
Winterville Machine Works Inc..................... D 252 756-2130
   Winterville *(G-17018)*

MARINE RELATED EQPT

Allied Marine Contractors LLC..................... G 910 367-2159
   Hampstead *(G-7637)*
Sturdy Corporation... C 910 763-2500
   Wilmington *(G-16420)*
Tcom Ground Systems LP............................. F 252 338-3200
   Elizabeth City *(G-5576)*

MARINE SPLYS WHOLESALERS

Barbour S Marine Supply Co Inc................. F 252 728-2136
   Beaufort *(G-944)*
Trivantage LLC.. D 800 786-1876
   Burlington *(G-1510)*

MARKETS: Meat & fish

Ashe Hams Inc.. G 828 259-9426
   Asheville *(G-530)*
Mitchells Meat Processing............................ F 336 591-7420
   Walnut Cove *(G-15633)*

MARKING DEVICES

Ennis-Flint Inc.. G 800 331-8118
   Thomasville *(G-15220)*
Ennis-Flint Inc.. F 800 331-8118
   Greensboro *(G-7000)*
Flint Trading Inc... D 336 475-6600
   Thomasville *(G-15224)*

Stamp Approval - Anita White..................... G 910 433-2279
   Fayetteville *(G-5922)*

MARKING DEVICES: Embossing Seals & Hand Stamps

Bear Pages.. G 828 837-0785
   Murphy *(G-11706)*

MATERNITY WEAR STORES

Belevation LLC.. F 803 517-9030
   Biscoe *(G-1104)*

MATS OR MATTING, NEC: Rubber

Blachford Rbr Acquisition Corp.................... E 704 730-1005
   Kings Mountain *(G-9295)*
L B Plastics Incorporated............................... D 704 663-1543
   Mooresville *(G-11000)*

MATS, MATTING & PADS: Varnished Glass

Nouveau Verre Holdings Inc......................... F 336 545-0011
   Greensboro *(G-7224)*
Nvh Inc... G 336 545-0011
   Greensboro *(G-7228)*

MATTRESS PROTECTORS, EXC RUBBER

L C Industries Inc.. C 919 596-8277
   Durham *(G-5185)*

MEAT MARKETS

Acre Station Meat Farm Inc......................... F 252 927-3700
   Pinetown *(G-12243)*
Mt Airy Meat Center Inc............................... F 336 786-2023
   Mount Airy *(G-11548)*
Stevens Packing Inc...................................... G 336 274-6033
   Greensboro *(G-7371)*
Suncrest Farms Cntry Hams Inc................. E 336 667-4441
   Wilkesboro *(G-16044)*
Wells Jnkins Wells Mt Proc Inc................... G 828 245-5544
   Forest City *(G-6086)*

MEAT PRDTS: Bacon, Side & Sliced, From Purchased Meat

White Packing Co Inc -Va............................. G 540 373-9883
   Raleigh *(G-13422)*

MEAT PRDTS: Bacon, Slab & Sliced, From Slaughtered Meat

Murphy-Brown LLC.. D 910 293-3434
   Warsaw *(G-15671)*

MEAT PRDTS: Boxed Beef, From Slaughtered Meat

Smithfield Foods Inc...................................... D 252 208-4700
   Kinston *(G-9384)*

MEAT PRDTS: Ham, Smoked, From Purchased Meat

Ashe Hams Inc.. G 828 259-9426
   Asheville *(G-530)*

MEAT PRDTS: Prepared Beef Prdts From Purchased Beef

Harris-Robinette Inc...................................... G 252 813-5794
   Pinetops *(G-12242)*
Julian Freirich Company Inc........................ E 704 636-2621
   Salisbury *(G-13996)*

MEAT PRDTS: Sausages, From Purchased Meat

Carolina Packers Inc .... D 919 934-2181
Smithfield *(G-14453)*

Jenkins Foods Inc .... E 704 434-2347
Shelby *(G-14332)*

Larry S Sausage Company .... E 910 483-5148
Fayetteville *(G-5859)*

MEAT PRDTS: Snack Sticks, Incl Jerky, From Purchased Meat

Jerky Man Inc .... G 828 749-3685
Saluda *(G-14071)*

Patriot Jerky LLC .... G 828 850-9160
Conover *(G-4479)*

Shanes Carolina Jerky LLC .... G 336 653-3673
Thomasville *(G-15276)*

MEAT PROCESSING MACHINERY

Dean St Processing LLC .... G 252 235-0401
Bailey *(G-871)*

Tipper Tie Inc .... C 919 362-8811
Apex *(G-249)*

MEDIA: Magnetic & Optical Recording

Assa Abloy AB .... D 704 283-2101
Monroe *(G-10652)*

Legalis Dms LLC .... F 919 741-8260
Raleigh *(G-12965)*

Talking Devices Company .... G 828 658-0660
Asheville *(G-795)*

MEDICAL & HOSPITAL EQPT WHOLESALERS

Albemrle Orthotics Prosthetics ... E 252 338-3002
Elizabeth City *(G-5531)*

Colowrap LLC .... F 888 815-3376
Durham *(G-5025)*

Ddm Inc .... G 910 686-1481
Wilmington *(G-16197)*

Dove Medical Supply LLC .... E 336 643-9367
Summerfield *(G-14980)*

Fidelity Pharmaceuticals LLC ..... G 704 274-3192
Huntersville *(G-8819)*

Fla Orthopedics Inc .... D 800 327-4110
Charlotte *(G-2768)*

Janus Development Group Inc ... F 252 551-9042
Greenville *(G-7548)*

Kberg Productions LLC .... G 910 232-0342
Raleigh *(G-12932)*

RPM Products Inc .... F 704 871-0518
Statesville *(G-14882)*

Sg-Clw Inc .... F 336 865-4980
Winston Salem *(G-16903)*

MEDICAL & SURGICAL SPLYS: Bandages & Dressings

Ambra Le Roy LLC .... G 704 392-7080
Charlotte *(G-2179)*

Bar Squared Inc .... F 919 878-0578
Raleigh *(G-12543)*

Caromed International Inc .... F 919 878-0578
Raleigh *(G-12603)*

Scivolutions Inc .... E 704 853-0100
Kings Mountain *(G-9331)*

MEDICAL & SURGICAL SPLYS: Braces, Orthopedic

Artificial Funhouse .... G 919 423-4103
Hillsborough *(G-8635)*

Biologic Solutions LLC .... G 919 770-8266
Holly Springs *(G-8690)*

MEDICAL & SURGICAL SPLYS: Clothing, Fire Resistant & Protect

Jhrg LLC .... G 252 478-4997
Spring Hope *(G-14618)*

Precept Medical Products Inc .... F 828 681-0209
Arden *(G-365)*

United Protective Tech LLC .... E 704 888-2470
Locust *(G-9977)*

MEDICAL & SURGICAL SPLYS: Cosmetic Restorations

Random Rues Botanical LLC ..... G 252 214-2759
Greenville *(G-7579)*

MEDICAL & SURGICAL SPLYS: Gynecological Splys & Appliances

Ipas .... C 919 967-7052
Durham *(G-5163)*

MEDICAL & SURGICAL SPLYS: Ligatures

Trimed LLC .... G 919 615-2784
Raleigh *(G-13365)*

MEDICAL & SURGICAL SPLYS: Limbs, Artificial

Advanced Brace & Limb .... G 252 991-6109
Wilson *(G-16464)*

Advanced Brace & Limb Inc ...... G 910 483-5737
Fayetteville *(G-5751)*

Advanced Brace & Limb Inc ...... G 919 818-0359
Raleigh *(G-12478)*

Albemrle Orthotics Prosthetics ... E 252 338-3002
Elizabeth City *(G-5531)*

Biotech Prsthtics Orthtics Drh .... G 919 471-4994
Durham *(G-4961)*

Center For Orthotic & Prosthet ... D 919 585-4173
Clayton *(G-3965)*

Center For Orthtic Prsthtic CA ... E 919 797-1230
Durham *(G-5011)*

Delaby Brace and Limb Co .... G 910 484-2509
Fayetteville *(G-5810)*

East Carolina Brace Limb Inc ..... G 252 726-8068
Morehead City *(G-11170)*

Faith Prsthtc-Rthotic Svcs Inc .... F 704 782-0908
Concord *(G-4263)*

Floyd S Braces and Limbs Inc ... G 910 763-0821
Wilmington *(G-16219)*

Guilford Orthtic Prothetic Inc ..... G 336 676-5394
Greensboro *(G-7072)*

Skyland Prsthtics Orthtics Inc .... E 828 684-1644
Fletcher *(G-6040)*

MEDICAL & SURGICAL SPLYS: Orthopedic Appliances

Ability Orthopedics .... G 704 630-6789
Salisbury *(G-13912)*

Albemrle Orthotics Prosthetics ... G 252 332-4334
Ahoskie *(G-54)*

BSN Medical Inc .... C 704 554-9933
Charlotte *(G-2361)*

Comfortland International LLC ... F 866 277-3135
Mebane *(G-10405)*

Custom Rehabilitation Spc Inc ... G 910 471-2922
Wilmington *(G-16192)*

Fillauer North Carolina Inc .... E 828 658-8330
Weaverville *(G-15846)*

Ing Source LLC .... F 828 855-0481
Hickory *(G-8065)*

Kaye Products Inc .... E 919 732-6444
Hillsborough *(G-8657)*

Knit-Rite Inc .... C 910 557-5378
Hamlet *(G-7625)*

Medical Specialties Inc .... G 704 694-2434
Wadesboro *(G-15516)*

North Crlina Orthtics Prsthtic .... E 919 210-0906
Wake Forest *(G-15574)*

Orthopedic Appliance Company .. E 828 254-6305
Asheville *(G-717)*

Orthopedic Appliance Company .. E 828 348-1960
Hickory *(G-8109)*

Orthopedic Services .... G 336 716-3349
Winston Salem *(G-16833)*

Orthorx Inc .... G 919 929-5550
Chapel Hill *(G-2050)*

Performance Orthotics .... G 704 945-7790
Charlotte *(G-3331)*

R82 Inc .... E 704 882-0668
Matthews *(G-10284)*

Spenco Medical Corporation ..... E 919 544-7900
Durham *(G-5369)*

Structure Medical LLC .... D 704 799-3450
Mooresville *(G-11106)*

MEDICAL & SURGICAL SPLYS: Personal Safety Eqpt

Health Supply Us LLC .... F 888 408-1694
Mooresville *(G-10971)*

Jackson Products Inc .... F 704 598-4949
Wake Forest *(G-15565)*

MSA Safety Sales LLC .... D 910 353-1540
Jacksonville *(G-9015)*

Protection Products Inc .... E 828 324-2173
Hickory *(G-8127)*

Safewaze LLC .... D 704 262-7893
Concord *(G-4356)*

Spintech LLC .... E 704 885-4758
Statesville *(G-14899)*

Veon Inc .... F 252 623-2102
Washington *(G-15736)*

MEDICAL & SURGICAL SPLYS: Prosthetic Appliances

Adaptive Technologies LLC .... G 919 231-6890
Raleigh *(G-12475)*

Alternative Care Group LLC ...... G 336 499-5644
Kernersville *(G-9161)*

Atlantic Prosthetics Orthtcs .... G 919 806-3260
Durham *(G-4932)*

Bio-Tech Prosthetics .... G 336 768-3666
Winston Salem *(G-16630)*

Bio-Tech Prsthtics Orthtics In .... G 336 333-9081
Greensboro *(G-6839)*

Cape Fear Orthtics Prsthtics I ... G 910 483-0933
Fayetteville *(G-5780)*

Creative Prosthetics and Ortho .. G 828 994-4808
Conover *(G-4442)*

Paceline Inc .... E 704 290-5007
Matthews *(G-10280)*

Village Ceramics Inc .... G 828 685-9491
Hendersonville *(G-7911)*

MEDICAL CENTERS

Statesville Med MGT Svcs LLC .. F 704 996-6748
Statesville *(G-14904)*

PRODUCT SECTION
METALS SVC CENTERS & WHOLESALERS: Steel

MEDICAL EQPT REPAIR SVCS, NON-ELECTRIC

Trimed LLC... G 919 615-2784
   Raleigh (G-13365)

MEDICAL EQPT: CAT Scanner Or Computerized Axial Tomography

Mobius Imaging LLC........................ E 704 773-7652
   Charlotte (G-3192)

MEDICAL EQPT: Diagnostic

Mallinckrodt LLC................................. G 919 878-2900
   Raleigh (G-12992)
Total Sono LLC.................................. G 908 349-8610
   Cary (G-1910)

MEDICAL EQPT: Electromedical Apparatus

Fernel Therapeutics Inc.................. G 919 614-2375
   Apex (G-191)
Ori Diagnostic Instruments LLC......... G 919 864-8140
   Durham (G-5262)
Vald Group Inc................................. G 704 345-5145
   Charlotte (G-3762)
Vortant Technologies LLC.............. G 828 645-1026
   Weaverville (G-15867)

MEDICAL EQPT: Ultrasonic Scanning Devices

Cyberbiota Incorporated.................. G 919 308-3839
   Durham (G-5043)
Hemosonics LLC................................ E 800 280-5589
   Durham (G-5136)
Hemosonics LLC................................ D 800 280-5589
   Durham (G-5137)
Size Stream LLC................................ G 919 355-5708
   Cary (G-1893)
Trackx Technology LLC.................... F 888 787-2259
   Hillsborough (G-8671)

MEDICAL EQPT: Ultrasonic, Exc Cleaning

Bioventus LLC..................................... D 800 396-4325
   Durham (G-4963)
Inneroptic Technology Inc................ G 919 732-2090
   Hillsborough (G-8656)

MEDICAL SVCS ORGANIZATION

Annihilare Medical Systems Inc........ F 855 545-5677
   Lincolnton (G-9872)
Medaccess Inc................................. G 828 264-4085
   Robbinsville (G-13609)

MEMBERSHIP ORGANIZATIONS, BUSINESS: Growers' Association

US Tobacco Cooperative Inc............ D 919 821-4560
   Raleigh (G-13386)

MEMBERSHIP ORGANIZATIONS, RELIGIOUS: Baptist Church

Brookstone Baptist Church.............. E 828 658-9443
   Weaverville (G-15840)

MEN'S & BOYS' CLOTHING STORES

Hudson Overall Company Inc.......... G 336 314-5024
   Greensboro (G-7104)

MEN'S & BOYS' CLOTHING WHOLESALERS, NEC

Apparel USA Inc............................... E 212 869-5495
   Fairmont (G-5700)
Badger Sportswear LLC................... D 704 871-0990
   Statesville (G-14757)
Burlington Coat Fctry Whse Cor....... E 919 468-9312
   Cary (G-1718)
Gildan Activewear (eden) Inc............ C 336 623-9555
   Eden (G-5491)
Gold Toe Stores Inc......................... G 828 464-0751
   Newton (G-11936)
Madison Company Inc..................... E 336 548-9624
   Madison (G-10079)
Raleigh Workshop Inc....................... E 919 917-8969
   Raleigh (G-13188)
Seafarer LLC..................................... G 704 624-3200
   Marshville (G-10224)
Walter Reynolds................................. G 704 735-6050
   Lincolnton (G-9935)

MEN'S & BOYS' HOSIERY WHOLESALERS

Simmons Hosiery Mill Inc................. G 828 327-4890
   Hickory (G-8157)

MERCHANDISING MACHINE OPERATORS: Vending

Coca-Cola Consolidated Inc............. C 919 550-0611
   Clayton (G-3968)
Compass Group Usa Inc.................. A 704 398-6515
   Charlotte (G-2532)
Compass Group Usa Inc.................. B 919 381-9577
   Garner (G-6267)

METAL & STEEL PRDTS: Abrasive

Keselowski Advanced Mfg LLC........ E 704 799-0206
   Statesville (G-14830)
Tiger Steel Inc................................... G 336 624-4481
   Mount Airy (G-11588)

METAL COMPONENTS: Prefabricated

Component Sourcing Intl LLC........... E 704 843-9292
   Charlotte (G-2534)
Norwood Manufacturing Inc............. E 704 474-0505
   Norwood (G-12042)
Remedios LLC................................. G 203 453-6000
   Charlotte (G-3429)
RMC Advanced Technologies Inc........ D 704 325-7100
   Newton (G-11964)

METAL FINISHING SVCS

Fanuc America Corporation............. G 704 596-5121
   Huntersville (G-8818)
Fil-Chem Inc..................................... G 919 878-1270
   Raleigh (G-12766)

METAL OXIDE SILICONE OR MOS DEVICES

Altera Corporation............................. G 919 852-1004
   Raleigh (G-12494)

METAL SERVICE CENTERS & OFFICES

Allens Gutter Service........................ G 910 738-9509
   Lumberton (G-10025)
Biganodes LLC................................. G 828 245-1115
   Forest City (G-6060)
Iron Box LLC..................................... E 919 890-0025
   Raleigh (G-12901)
Pavco Inc.. E 704 496-6800
   Charlotte (G-3321)

METAL STAMPING, FOR THE TRADE

ABT Manufacturing LLC................... E 704 847-9188
   Statesville (G-14736)
Allred Metal Stamping Works Inc......... E 336 886-5221
   High Point (G-8242)
Carolina Stamping Company........... D 704 637-0260
   Salisbury (G-13938)
Col-Eve Metal Products Co.............. G 336 472-7039
   Lexington (G-9696)
Component Sourcing Intl LLC........... E 704 843-9292
   Charlotte (G-2534)
Dynamic Stampings of NC I.............. G 704 864-1572
   Gastonia (G-6399)
Gasser and Sons............................... G 910 471-6907
   Wilmington (G-16227)
Griffiths Corporation......................... D 704 552-6793
   Pineville (G-12271)
Griffiths Corporation......................... D 704 554-5657
   Pineville (G-12272)
Hi-Tech Fabrication Inc.................... C 919 781-6150
   Raleigh (G-12842)
Iv-S Metal Stamping Inc................... E 336 861-2100
   Archdale (G-286)
K & S Tool & Manufacturing Co........ E 336 410-7260
   High Point (G-8419)
M-B Industries Inc............................ C 828 862-4201
   Rosman (G-13786)
New Standard Corporation............... C 252 446-5481
   Rocky Mount (G-13714)
Parker Industries Inc........................ D 828 437-7779
   Connelly Springs (G-4407)
Precision Concepts Group LLC........ B 336 761-8572
   Winston Salem (G-16863)
Precision Partners LLC.................... E 800 545-3121
   Charlotte (G-3370)
Precision Stampers Inc.................... G 919 366-3333
   Wendell (G-15912)
SMC Holdco Inc................................ C 910 844-3956
   Laurinburg (G-9498)
Southern Spring & Stamping............ F 336 548-3520
   Stokesdale (G-14949)
Stamping School LLC....................... G 407 435-3135
   Hendersonville (G-7905)
United TI & Stamping Co NC Inc......... D 910 323-8588
   Fayetteville (G-5939)
Wolverine Mtal Stmping Sltons......... E 919 774-4729
   Sanford (G-14208)

METAL STAMPINGS: Perforated

Erdle Perforating Holdings Inc......... F 704 588-4380
   Charlotte (G-2726)

METAL: Battery

Aseptia Inc....................................... C 678 373-6751
   Raleigh (G-12528)
ATI Allvac... G 541 967-9000
   Monroe (G-10657)

METALS SVC CENTERS & WHOLESALERS: Foundry Prdts

Sanders Company Inc...................... E 252 338-3995
   Elizabeth City (G-5569)

METALS SVC CENTERS & WHOLESALERS: Pipe & Tubing, Steel

Advanced Drainage Systems Inc........ E 704 629-4151
   Bessemer City (G-1050)
Consolidated Pipe & Sup Co Inc......... F 336 294-8577
   Greensboro (G-6930)

METALS SVC CENTERS & WHOLESALERS: Steel

Employee Codes: A=Over 500 employees, B=251-500 C=101-250, D=51-100, E=20-50, F=10-19, G=1-9

METALS SVC CENTERS & WHOLESALERS: Steel

Alamo Distribution LLC................................ C 704 398-5600
   Belmont *(G-974)*

Aviation Metals NC Inc.............................. F 704 264-1647
   Charlotte *(G-2246)*

Bessemer City Machine Shop Inc............. E 704 629-4111
   Bessemer City *(G-1053)*

C & B Salvage Company Inc..................... G 336 374-3946
   Ararat *(G-263)*

Charter Dura-Bar Inc.................................. F 704 637-1906
   Salisbury *(G-13940)*

Chatham Steel Corporation....................... E 912 233-4182
   Durham *(G-5013)*

Chicago Tube and Iron Company.............. D 704 781-2060
   Locust *(G-9956)*

Dave Steel Company Inc........................... F 828 252-2771
   Asheville *(G-603)*

Dave Steel Company Inc........................... D 828 252-2771
   Asheville *(G-604)*

Dunavants Welding & Steel Inc................. G 252 338-6533
   Camden *(G-1557)*

Freedom Metals Inc................................... F 704 333-1214
   Charlotte *(G-2794)*

Harris Rebar Inc... F 919 528-8333
   Benson *(G-1037)*

Hercules Steel Company Inc..................... E 910 488-5110
   Fayetteville *(G-5837)*

Howard Steel Inc.. F 704 376-9631
   Charlotte *(G-2925)*

McCombs Steel Company Inc................... E 704 873-7563
   Statesville *(G-14840)*

McCune Technology Inc............................ F 910 424-2978
   Fayetteville *(G-5871)*

Schwartz Steel Service Inc........................ E 704 865-9576
   Gastonia *(G-6506)*

Steel and Pipe Corporation........................ E 919 776-0751
   Sanford *(G-14193)*

Sun Valley Stl Fabrication Inc.................... F 704 289-5830
   Monroe *(G-10817)*

METALS: Precious NEC

Alloyworks LLC.. F 704 645-0511
   Salisbury *(G-13920)*

KS Precious Metals LLC............................ G 910 687-0244
   Pinehurst *(G-12226)*

Metallix Refining Inc................................... E 252 413-0346
   Greenville *(G-7559)*

Omega Precious Metals............................. G 269 903-9330
   Youngsville *(G-17089)*

Sigma PM... G 269 903-9330
   Youngsville *(G-17096)*

METALS: Primary Nonferrous, NEC

Cvmr (usa) Inc... C 828 288-3768
   Union Mills *(G-15440)*

Parker-Hannifin Corporation...................... G 704 662-3500
   Statesville *(G-14856)*

METALWORK: Miscellaneous

Blue Mountain Metalworks Inc................... G 828 898-8582
   Banner Elk *(G-894)*

Canalta Enterprises LLC........................... E 919 615-1570
   Raleigh *(G-12586)*

Concept Steel Inc...................................... E 704 874-0414
   Gastonia *(G-6382)*

Custom Design Inc.................................... G 704 637-7110
   Salisbury *(G-13951)*

Dave Steel Company Inc........................... F 828 252-2771
   Asheville *(G-603)*

Dave Steel Company Inc........................... D 828 252-2771
   Asheville *(G-604)*

Davis Steel and Iron Co Inc....................... E 704 821-7676
   Matthews *(G-10311)*

Dwiggins Metal Masters Inc...................... G 336 751-2379
   Mocksville *(G-10568)*

Eland Industries Inc................................... E 910 304-5353
   Hampstead *(G-7646)*

Gerdau Ameristeel US Inc......................... E 919 833-9737
   Raleigh *(G-12798)*

Keypoint LLC... F 704 962-8110
   Waxhaw *(G-15764)*

Paul Charles Englert................................. G 704 824-2102
   Gastonia *(G-6487)*

Pigeon Rver Cstm Mtalworks LLC............ G 828 619-0559
   Canton *(G-1623)*

Protech Metals LLC................................... E 910 295-6905
   Pinehurst *(G-12232)*

Steel Smart Incorporated.......................... E 919 736-0681
   Pikeville *(G-12194)*

Steelfab Inc.. B 704 394-5376
   Charlotte *(G-3627)*

Steelfab of Virginia Inc.............................. E 919 828-9545
   Raleigh *(G-13301)*

Umi Company Inc...................................... G 704 479-6210
   Lincolnton *(G-9932)*

METALWORK: Ornamental

Apex Steel Corp.. E 919 362-6611
   Raleigh *(G-12514)*

Davis Steel and Iron Co Inc....................... E 704 821-7676
   Matthews *(G-10311)*

Esher LLC.. G 704 975-1463
   Huntersville *(G-8817)*

Oldcastle Buildingenvelope Inc................. F 704 504-0345
   Charlotte *(G-3291)*

Ornamental Specialties Inc....................... F 704 821-9154
   Matthews *(G-10339)*

Vann S Wldg & Orna Works Inc............... F 704 289-6056
   Monroe *(G-10829)*

METALWORKING MACHINERY WHOLESALERS

Amada America Inc................................... G 877 262-3287
   High Point *(G-8243)*

Ellison Technologies Inc............................ D 704 545-7362
   Charlotte *(G-2699)*

Rodeco Company...................................... F 919 775-7149
   Sanford *(G-14175)*

METERING DEVICES: Gasoline Dispensing

Triangle Microsystems Inc........................ F 919 878-1880
   Raleigh *(G-13359)*

METERING DEVICES: Water Quality Monitoring & Control Systems

Park Court Properties RE Inc.................... F 919 304-3110
   Mebane *(G-10423)*

METERS: Turbine Flow, Indl Process

Liburdi Turbine Services LLC.................... E 704 230-2510
   Mooresville *(G-11008)*

MICROCIRCUITS, INTEGRATED: Semiconductor

Cml Micro Circuit USA............................... E 336 744-5050
   Winston Salem *(G-16656)*

Memscap Inc.. E 919 248-4102
   Durham *(G-5217)*

Microchip Technology Inc.......................... F 919 844-7510
   Raleigh *(G-13027)*

Micross Advnced Intrcnnect TEC.............. E 919 248-1872
   Durham *(G-5224)*

Northstar Computer Tech Inc.................... G 980 272-1969
   Monroe *(G-10780)*

Rt Cardiac Systems Inc............................ G 954 908-1074
   Raleigh *(G-13218)*

Xilinx Inc.. F 919 846-3922
   Raleigh *(G-13431)*

MICROPROCESSORS

Ghost Hawk Intel LLC................................ G 910 235-0323
   Pinehurst *(G-12222)*

MICROWAVE COMPONENTS

Cem Corporation.. C 704 821-7015
   Matthews *(G-10307)*

Communications & Pwr Inds LLC.............. E 650 846-2900
   Conover *(G-4437)*

Huber + Suhner Inc................................... E 704 790-7300
   Charlotte *(G-2928)*

James W McManus Inc............................. G 828 688-2560
   Bakersville *(G-884)*

Nuvotronics Inc.. D 984 666-3543
   Durham *(G-5251)*

US Microwave Inc...................................... G 520 891-2444
   Pittsboro *(G-12353)*

MILITARY INSIGNIA

D & D Industries.. G 252 331-2528
   Elizabeth City *(G-5539)*

MILITARY INSIGNIA, TEXTILE

Cw Media Inc... G 910 302-3066
   Raeford *(G-12419)*

Dickson Elberton Mill Inc........................... G 336 226-3556
   Burlington *(G-1406)*

S Loflin Enterprises Inc............................. F 704 633-1159
   Salisbury *(G-14039)*

MILLWORK

648 Woodworks LLC................................. G 910 603-6286
   Fuquay Varina *(G-6177)*

Acorn Woodworks NC LLC........................ G 828 361-9953
   Murphy *(G-11704)*

Against Grain Woodworking Inc................ G 704 309-5750
   Charlotte *(G-2143)*

Against The Grain Woodworking............... G 704 969-5837
   Gastonia *(G-6338)*

Ajs Dezigns Inc.. G 828 652-6304
   Marion *(G-10138)*

American Wdwrkery Bnjmin Htchi............. G 910 302-5678
   Fayetteville *(G-5762)*

American Woodmark Corporation............. E 704 947-3280
   Huntersville *(G-8790)*

American Woodworkery Inc...................... G 910 916-8098
   Fayetteville *(G-5763)*

Andrew Bates... G 252 413-6988
   Greenville *(G-7482)*

Antler and Oak Joinery LLC...................... G 845 505-6185
   Raleigh *(G-12510)*

ARC Woodworking..................................... G 828 863-4994
   Tryon *(G-15421)*

Archdale Millworks Inc............................... G 336 431-9019
   Archdale *(G-268)*

Arthur Woodworking.................................. G 919 381-0329
   Durham *(G-4926)*

Artistic Woodworks Inc.............................. G 828 459-0178
   Claremont *(G-3902)*

Asheville Woodworks................................. G 828 734-0536
   Asheville *(G-543)*

Aspire Woodworks..................................... G 828 855-6811
   Hickory *(G-7945)*

Athol Arbor Corporation............................. F 919 643-1100
   Hillsborough *(G-8636)*

MILLWORK

Atlantic Woodworking .... G 704 680-8802
   Mooresville *(G-10863)*

AZ Faux .... G 704 279-0114
   Salisbury *(G-13926)*

B&H Millwork and Fixtures Inc .... E 336 431-0068
   High Point *(G-8260)*

B2rv2woodworks .... G 304 578-9881
   Youngsville *(G-17069)*

Baldwin Wood Works LLC .... G 828 974-2716
   Mills River *(G-10499)*

Ballash Woodworks LLC .... G 910 709-0717
   Fayetteville *(G-5768)*

Barewoodworking Inc .... F 828 758-0694
   Lenoir *(G-9578)*

Barnhardts Woodworking Co .... G 336 449-5564
   Whitsett *(G-15983)*

Beach Craft Woodworking LLC .... G 919 624-4463
   Cary *(G-1700)*

Bedard Custom Woodworks .... G 828 432-6556
   Morganton *(G-11200)*

Bent Creek Studio LLC .... G 336 692-6477
   Clemmons *(G-4032)*

Bfs Asset Holdings LLC .... C 303 784-4288
   Raleigh *(G-12554)*

Bfs Operations LLC .... A 919 431-1000
   Raleigh *(G-12555)*

Bg Woodworks .... G 919 656-2529
   Cary *(G-1702)*

Black River Woodwork LLC .... G 919 757-4559
   Angier *(G-132)*

Black Wolf Custom Woodworks .... G 828 925-0399
   Asheville *(G-562)*

Blue Heaven Woodworks .... G 704 743-6648
   Concord *(G-4210)*

Blue Stallion Woodworks .... G 919 766-2865
   Wilmington *(G-16139)*

Bo Taylor Custom Wdwkg LLC .... G 919 839-7175
   Raleigh *(G-12567)*

Bob Callahan LLC .... G 828 620-9730
   Asheville *(G-568)*

Bobby Barns Woodworking .... G 336 824-2821
   Ramseur *(G-13441)*

Bone Tred Beds Smmit Woodworks .... G 910 319-7583
   Wilmington *(G-16141)*

Born In A Barn Inc .... G 828 635-5808
   Taylorsville *(G-15131)*

Branched Out Wood Works LLC .... G 828 515-0377
   Leicester *(G-9507)*

Brookshire Woodworking Inc .... D 828 779-2119
   Barnardsville *(G-906)*

Brookshire Woodworking Inc .... G 828 779-2119
   Asheville *(G-574)*

Brun Millworks LLC .... G 704 989-3145
   Midland *(G-10458)*

Brushy Mtn Cstm Woodworks Inc .... G 336 921-3510
   Moravian Falls *(G-11143)*

Bucks Woodworks LLC .... G 336 764-3979
   Clemmons *(G-4033)*

Buffingtons Commercial Trim .... G 919 244-8848
   Cary *(G-1715)*

Builders Firstsource Inc .... G 919 562-6601
   Youngsville *(G-17072)*

Building Center Inc .... D 704 889-8182
   Pineville *(G-12257)*

Burdetts Custom Woodworks Inc .... G 919 592-9903
   Cary *(G-1717)*

Burris Woodworks .... G 336 746-5286
   Lexington *(G-9687)*

C&M Woodworks .... G 919 280-9896
   Raleigh *(G-12582)*

Capitol Woodworks .... G 919 703-9293
   Wilmington *(G-16154)*

Cardinal Millwork & Supply Inc .... E 336 665-9811
   Greensboro *(G-6878)*

Carolina Sheds LLC .... G 336 623-7433
   Eden *(G-5487)*

Carolina Urban Lumber .... G 704 755-5110
   Pineville *(G-12260)*

Carolina Woodwork & Stair Inc .... G 704 363-5114
   Charlotte *(G-2412)*

Carolina Woodworks Trim of NC .... G 252 492-9259
   Henderson *(G-7778)*

Carpathian Woodworks Inc .... G 919 669-7546
   Clayton *(G-3962)*

Cedar Fork Woodworks LLC .... G 910 340-0821
   Beulaville *(G-1092)*

Charles White Woodworking .... G 252 714-9124
   Winterville *(G-16996)*

Charlott Custom Woodworks .... G 704 634-0863
   Cornelius *(G-4535)*

Clark Co Cstm Trim & Wdwkg Inc .... G 704 905-7131
   Midland *(G-10462)*

Cleveland Lumber Company .... E 704 487-5263
   Shelby *(G-14298)*

Coastal Custom Wood Works LLC .... G 252 675-8732
   New Bern *(G-11790)*

Coastal Millwork Supply Co .... E 910 763-3300
   Wilmington *(G-16172)*

Coastal Woodworking .... G 910 477-1330
   Bolivia *(G-1163)*

Compass Woodworks Co .... G 704 232-0272
   Salisbury *(G-13944)*

Contemporary Design Co LLC .... F 704 375-6030
   Gastonia *(G-6386)*

Cook & Boardman Nc LLC .... E 336 768-8872
   Winston Salem *(G-16659)*

Cornerstone Woodworks LLC .... G 908 343-3708
   Charlotte *(G-2555)*

Crafted Hart Hand .... G 704 539-4808
   Union Grove *(G-15435)*

Creative Custom Wdwkg LLC .... G 910 431-8544
   Wilmington *(G-16185)*

Creative Custom Woodworks Inc .... G 910 431-8544
   Wilmington *(G-16186)*

Creative Woodworks .... G 910 233-3042
   Hampstead *(G-7645)*

Creativewoodworks Wilmington .... G 910 233-3042
   Wilmington *(G-16188)*

Credle Woodworks LLC .... G 919 353-4298
   Hillsborough *(G-8647)*

Cris Bifaro Woodworks Inc .... G 828 776-2453
   Asheville *(G-598)*

Crown Heritage Inc .... E 336 835-1424
   Elkin *(G-5616)*

Crowntown Tinker LLC .... G 843 614-9566
   Charlotte *(G-2574)*

Currier Woodworks Inc .... G 252 725-4233
   Beaufort *(G-954)*

Curvemakers Inc .... G 919 690-1121
   Oxford *(G-12125)*

Custom Decks and Woodworking .... G 828 699-2349
   Zirconia *(G-17152)*

Custom Wood Creations .... G 252 341-7923
   Greenville *(G-7511)*

Custom Wood Creations .... G 910 367-8747
   Leland *(G-9539)*

Dan Forrest Woodworks Wrap Up .... G 919 532-9190
   Raleigh *(G-12672)*

Daughtrys Creations LLC .... G 704 929-8717
   Newland *(G-11884)*

Davis Cabinet Co Wilson Inc .... F 252 291-9052
   Sims *(G-14441)*

Davis Mechanical Inc .... F 704 272-9366
   Peachland *(G-12173)*

Decarlo Woodworks .... G 919 327-3647
   Apex *(G-181)*

Decicco Woodshop LLC .... G 914 213-8553
   Cary *(G-1745)*

Dellinger Woodworks LLC .... G 980 245-6086
   Waxhaw *(G-15751)*

Distinctive Millworks LLC .... G 919 263-4337
   Wake Forest *(G-15547)*

Division Six Incorporated .... G 910 420-3305
   New Bern *(G-11801)*

DN Yager Woodworks .... G 704 236-3481
   Matthews *(G-10312)*

Douglas Duane Sniffen .... G 919 924-8337
   Garner *(G-6271)*

Downsouth Wood Working LLC .... G 910 259-4617
   Burgaw *(G-1337)*

Dragonfly Studios .... G 704 706-2910
   Concord *(G-4258)*

Drw Renovations & Custom Wdwkg ...... G 910 471-9367
   Wilmington *(G-16206)*

East Bay Woodworks .... G 503 313-4079
   Mooresville *(G-10935)*

East End Mllwk DBA Avvento Inc .... G 516 313-7739
   Ocean Isle Beach *(G-12090)*

Eastern Cornerstone Cnstr LLC .... G 919 702-3583
   Louisburg *(G-9986)*

Ecmd Inc .... C 336 835-1182
   Elkin *(G-5617)*

Edwards Mountain Woodworks LLC .... G 919 932-6050
   Chapel Hill *(G-2012)*

Elite Wood Classics Inc .... G 910 454-8745
   Oak Island *(G-12049)*

Endgrain Woodworks LLC .... G 980 237-2612
   Charlotte *(G-2711)*

Eric Leffingwell .... G 910 367-1928
   Wilmington *(G-16212)*

Ervin Woodworks LLC .... G 919 451-0652
   Efland *(G-5527)*

Extreme Scenes Inc .... F 336 687-3369
   High Point *(G-8348)*

Finely Finished Wdwkg LLC .... G 828 553-9549
   Hendersonville *(G-7849)*

Flat Iron Mill Works LLC .... G 828 768-7770
   Leicester *(G-9511)*

Fleming Wood & Rod LLC .... G 828 278-9194
   Vilas *(G-15495)*

Forest Millwork Inc .... F 828 251-5264
   Asheville *(G-624)*

Forged Timber Company .... G 704 351-7712
   Mooresville *(G-10948)*

Foundation Woodworks LLC .... G 828 713-9665
   Asheville *(G-625)*

Fox Briar Furniture & Wdwkg .... G 980 254-8433
   Mocksville *(G-10572)*

Frank Ficca Woodworking .... G 336 937-2985
   Summerfield *(G-14982)*

Franken Woodworking .... G 910 488-6931
   Fayetteville *(G-5828)*

Franklin Forest Products LLC .... G 336 982-5550
   Jefferson *(G-9088)*

Frederick and Frederick Entp .... F 252 235-4849
   Middlesex *(G-10448)*

Front Prch Cstm Frmng Wodworks .... G 252 717-2868
   Williamston *(G-16060)*

Funder America Inc .... C 336 751-3501
   Mocksville *(G-10574)*

Garner Woodworks LLC .... G 828 775-1790
   Swannanoa *(G-15026)*

Gary Forte Woodworking Inc .... G 704 780-0095
   Monroe *(G-10722)*

Gates Custom Milling Inc .... E 252 357-0116
   Gatesville *(G-6549)*

MILLWORK — PRODUCT SECTION

General Painting & Woodwork............ G 828 318-1252
  Asheville *(G-633)*
Ggs Woodworking............................... G 704 279-5482
  Salisbury *(G-13967)*
Giving Tree Woodworks LLc................ G 704 930-5847
  Mount Holly *(G-11636)*
GLG Corporation................................ F 336 784-0396
  Winston Salem *(G-16722)*
Goodman Millwork Inc....................... E 704 633-2421
  Salisbury *(G-13972)*
Grey Star Woodworks......................... G 919 903-8471
  Moncure *(G-10623)*
Griggs Custom Woodwork................... G 828 719-1503
  Banner Elk *(G-899)*
GTW Woodworks................................ G 704 640-5402
  Cleveland *(G-4072)*
H & H Woodworking LLC.................... G 336 676-6524
  Mc Leansville *(G-10392)*
H & H Woodworking Inc..................... G 336 884-5848
  High Point *(G-8374)*
H and H Woodworks........................... G 704 827-4506
  Stanley *(G-14695)*
H&M Woodworks Inc.......................... F 919 496-5993
  Louisburg *(G-9990)*
Hammer & Shaw Woodworks.............. G 336 339-4829
  Greensboro *(G-7076)*
Harley S Woodworks Inc.................... G 828 776-0120
  Barnardsville *(G-911)*
Harrison Woodworks Inc.................... G 919 632-3703
  Durham *(G-5132)*
Henderson & Kirkland Inc.................. G 252 355-0224
  Winterville *(G-17002)*
Herd Woodworking LLC..................... G 704 778-0556
  New London *(G-11873)*
Heritage Woodworks LLC................... G 919 774-1554
  Sanford *(G-14132)*
High Creek Woodworks...................... G 919 418-1210
  Hillsborough *(G-8653)*
Hos Woodworking Inc........................ G 712 298-1985
  Monroe *(G-10733)*
Hosmer Woodworks............................ G 415 730-5401
  Wilmington *(G-16258)*
Hunter Innovations Ltd..................... G 919 848-8814
  Raleigh *(G-12869)*
Idx Impressions LLC......................... C 703 550-6902
  Washington *(G-15711)*
Interior Trim Creations Inc............... G 704 821-1470
  Charlotte *(G-2981)*
Interior Wood Works LLC................... G 910 754-3987
  Bolivia *(G-1164)*
Intracoastal Woodworks LLC.............. G 910 270-5515
  Hampstead *(G-7649)*
Iron Forged Woodworks..................... G 910 581-6574
  Jacksonville *(G-9009)*
J & M Woodworking Inc..................... F 828 728-3253
  Hudson *(G-8770)*
J&J Millworks Inc............................. G 336 252-2868
  Winston Salem *(G-16766)*
J&J Woodworking LLC........................ G 704 941-9537
  Matthews *(G-10325)*
Jala Woodshop LLC........................... G 704 439-6119
  Cornelius *(G-4563)*
JDG Woodworks Inc........................... G 910 367-8806
  Wilmington *(G-16278)*
Jeld-Wen Holding Inc....................... B 704 378-5700
  Charlotte *(G-3019)*
Jenkins Millwork LLC......................... E 336 667-3344
  Wilkesboro *(G-16032)*
Jhons Wood Work LLC........................ G 828 231-6240
  Leicester *(G-9514)*
Joel Moretz...................................... G 828 355-9936
  Boone *(G-1211)*

Joeys Woodworking Gifts................... G 336 427-5263
  Madison *(G-10075)*
John H Peterson Jr............................ G 910 762-9957
  Rocky Point *(G-13748)*
John Lindenberger............................. G 919 337-6741
  Raleigh *(G-12918)*
Joines Custom Woodwork.................... G 336 984-7237
  Moravian Falls *(G-11145)*
Jones Doors & Windows Inc................ F 336 998-8624
  Mocksville *(G-10582)*
Jr S Custom Woodworks..................... G 336 643-1524
  Stokesdale *(G-14943)*
K&S Custom LLC................................ G 336 861-1607
  Sophia *(G-14519)*
K&S Rustic Woodworks....................... G 336 504-6988
  High Point *(G-8420)*
Kabinet Werks LLC............................. G 704 359-7311
  Harrisburg *(G-7715)*
Kauffman & Co.................................. G 716 969-2005
  Charlotte *(G-3044)*
Keglers Woodworks LLC..................... G 919 608-7220
  Raleigh *(G-12934)*
Kennedy Woodworking LLC................. G 704 278-9444
  Mount Ulla *(G-11684)*
Kettu Woodworks............................... G 919 699-4173
  Wake Forest *(G-15568)*
Kevs Woodworking LLC....................... G 850 559-3228
  Hubert *(G-8750)*
Kingdom Woodworks Inc..................... G 704 678-8134
  Kings Mountain *(G-9312)*
Knowlton Woodworking LLC................ G 336 588-3502
  Seagrove *(G-14243)*
KS Custom Woodworks Inc.................. G 252 714-3957
  Walstonburg *(G-15639)*
L & B Custom Woodworking................. G 252 578-8955
  Woodland *(G-17022)*
L & W GL Mirror & WD Works LLC........ G 336 562-2155
  Prospect Hill *(G-12407)*
Laborie Sons Cstm Wodworks LLC....... G 910 769-2524
  Wilmington *(G-16293)*
Lee Builder Mart Inc......................... E
  Sanford *(G-14147)*
Lets Build It Woodworking................. G 704 352-7131
  Concord *(G-4303)*
Libasci Woodworks Inc...................... G 828 524-7073
  Franklin *(G-6135)*
Liberty Wood Products Inc................. F 828 524-7958
  Franklin *(G-6136)*
Linkous Carpentry & Wdwkg LLC......... G 828 460-5610
  Swannanoa *(G-15028)*
Ln Woodworks................................... G 509 480-0263
  Fayetteville *(G-5861)*
Louisiana-Pacific Corporation............. C 336 599-8080
  Roxboro *(G-13806)*
Madison Woodworking......................... G 704 634-1143
  Charlotte *(G-3118)*
Maines Woodworks Cstm Mil LLC......... G 336 263-0799
  Hurdle Mills *(G-8910)*
Manhattan Woodworking Inc............... G 704 528-5733
  Statesville *(G-14838)*
Mark L Wood..................................... G 919 977-6507
  Raleigh *(G-12997)*
Mark T Galvin................................... G 828 627-0823
  Clyde *(G-4126)*
Markham Woodworks LLC................... G 252 492-5823
  Henderson *(G-7797)*
Martins Woodworking LLC................... F 704 473-7617
  Lattimore *(G-9458)*
Marvida Acres LLC............................. G 336 392-0414
  Greensboro *(G-7187)*
Master Kraft Inc................................ E 704 234-2673
  Matthews *(G-10332)*

Masters Craftsman............................. G 919 800-0096
  Raleigh *(G-13005)*
Masterwrap Inc................................. E 336 243-4515
  Lexington *(G-9755)*
Matthews Building Supply Co............. E 704 847-2106
  Matthews *(G-10268)*
Matthews Millwork Inc....................... G 704 821-4499
  Monroe *(G-10767)*
Mesa Quality Fenestration Inc............ G 828 393-0132
  Hendersonville *(G-7879)*
Metalfab of North Carolina LLC.......... C 704 841-1090
  Matthews *(G-10271)*
Metrolina Woodworks Inc................... F 704 821-9095
  Stallings *(G-14672)*
Metropolitan Woodworks Inc............... G 704 215-5018
  Gastonia *(G-6463)*
Metzgers Burl Wood Gallery................ G 828 452-2550
  Waynesville *(G-15810)*
Mh Libman Woodturning..................... G 828 360-5530
  Asheville *(G-701)*
Mike Powell Inc................................. F 910 792-6152
  Wilmington *(G-16324)*
Miter Point LLC................................ G 910 864-3645
  Fayetteville *(G-5876)*
Modern Workbench LLC...................... G 828 845-4466
  Horse Shoe *(G-8742)*
Moretz Bldg & Woodworks LLC........... G 828 406-4672
  Fleetwood *(G-5976)*
Morrison Mill Work............................ G 828 774-5415
  Asheville *(G-705)*
Moulding Millwork LLC....................... G 704 504-9880
  Charlotte *(G-3207)*
Mountain Top Woodworking................. G 336 982-4059
  West Jefferson *(G-15946)*
Muddy Creek Mill Works Inc............... G 828 659-5558
  Nebo *(G-11762)*
Mullis Millwork Inc............................ F 919 496-5993
  New Bern *(G-11828)*
Narron Woodworks.............................. G 252 258-2151
  Kinston *(G-9378)*
New England Wood Works................... G 706 491-5885
  Whittier *(G-16009)*
Nordic Custom Woodworks.................. G 203 209-5854
  Wilmington *(G-16339)*
Normac Kitchens Inc......................... F 704 485-1911
  Oakboro *(G-12079)*
North State Millwork......................... G 252 442-9090
  Rocky Mount *(G-13715)*
Northside Millwork Inc...................... E 919 732-6100
  Hillsborough *(G-8664)*
Oak & Axe Custom Woodworking......... G 919 434-1939
  Cary *(G-1835)*
Oak City Artisans LLC....................... G 347 738-1228
  Raleigh *(G-13077)*
Oak City Woodshop LLC..................... G 937 830-0808
  Cary *(G-1836)*
Oak City Woodworks.......................... G 919 247-5984
  Knightdale *(G-9424)*
Old Mill Precision Gun Works &.......... G 704 284-2832
  Bessemer City *(G-1076)*
Ole Pelicans Custom Wdwkg............... G 252 808-7633
  Newport *(G-11903)*
Orion Manufacturing LLC.................... G 714 633-5850
  Richfield *(G-13553)*
Osceola Custom Woodworks................ G 336 514-3720
  Reidsville *(G-13537)*
Overman Cabinet & Supply LLC.......... F 336 584-1349
  Burlington *(G-1469)*
Oyama Cabinet Inc........................... G 828 327-2668
  Conover *(G-4477)*
Pauls Custom Woodworking Inc.......... G 828 712-6234
  Black Mountain *(G-1134)*

PRODUCT SECTION — MILLWORK

Perusi Woodcarving .... G 828 734-6121
  Waynesville (G-15814)
Phillip Rice Woodworking LLC .... G 919 339-4543
  Oxford (G-12141)
Piedmont Stairworks LLC .... E 704 483-3721
  Denver (G-4794)
Piedmont Turning & Wdwkg Co .... G 336 475-7161
  Thomasville (G-15264)
Piedmont Wood Products Inc .... F 828 632-4077
  Taylorsville (G-15157)
Pine Creek Products LLC .... F 336 399-8806
  Winston Salem (G-16856)
Pitch & Burl LLC .... G 512 653-9413
  Charlotte (G-3345)
Pk Woodworks .... G 828 284-4570
  Burnsville (G-1531)
Ply Gem Holdings Inc .... D 919 677-3900
  Cary (G-1852)
Port City Wood Works Inc .... G 910 398-8274
  Wilmington (G-16363)
Porters Tavern Wood Works .... G 910 639-4519
  Robbins (G-13602)
Prestige Millwork Inc .... F 910 428-2360
  Star (G-14722)
Pro-Kay Supply Inc .... F 910 628-0882
  Orrum (G-12116)
R L Roten Woodworking LLC .... G 336 982-3830
  Crumpler (G-4630)
Rabbit Town Molding & Trim LLC .... G 336 688-2162
  Trinity (G-15354)
Raleigh Custom Woodwork Inc .... G 919 522-6621
  Raleigh (G-13175)
Raw Design Woodworks LLC .... G 516 477-1963
  Indian Trail (G-8960)
Red Shed Woodworks Inc .... G 828 768-3854
  Marshall (G-10207)
Reeb Millwork Corporation .... G 336 751-4650
  Mocksville (G-10601)
Refab Wood LLC .... G 919 272-2589
  Raleigh (G-13203)
Reliable Construction Co Inc .... E 704 289-1501
  Monroe (G-10795)
Rescued Wood Rehab LLC .... G 984 500-7904
  Fuquay Varina (G-6225)
Richmond Millwork LLC .... G 910 331-1009
  Rockingham (G-13641)
Ritchie Woodworks .... G 980 322-7779
  China Grove (G-3887)
Ritenis Woodworks .... G 336 643-6426
  Summerfield (G-14991)
Rivers Edge Woodworkers LLC .... G 252 443-5099
  Rocky Mount (G-13729)
Robert Wiggins Wood Work LLC .... G 828 254-5644
  Asheville (G-758)
Roots Originals LLC .... G 573 673-1669
  Winston Salem (G-16889)
Rowland Woodworking Inc .... E 336 887-0700
  High Point (G-8516)
Royal Impressions LLC .... G 910 340-5955
  Greensboro (G-7319)
Rustic Innovations LLC .... G 804 822-2492
  Raleigh (G-13219)
S Banner Cabinets Incorporated .... E 828 733-2031
  Newland (G-11893)
S H Woodworking .... G 336 463-2885
  Yadkinville (G-17049)
Sal and Sons Woodworking LLC .... G 910 489-5373
  Raeford (G-12437)
Salem Woodworking Company .... G 336 768-7443
  Winston Salem (G-16896)
Salisbury Millwork Inc .... G 704 603-4501
  Salisbury (G-14040)

Samswoodworks .... G 336 893-5499
  Winston Salem (G-16897)
Sandy Creek Woodworks .... G 919 853-3415
  Louisburg (G-10001)
Sauder Woodworking Co .... G 704 799-6782
  Mooresville (G-11079)
Scott Meek Woodworks .... G 828 283-0796
  Asheville (G-765)
Scott Woodworking .... G 828 550-4742
  Asheville (G-766)
Seaside Woodworks .... G 910 523-1377
  Bolivia (G-1166)
Select Stainless Products LLC .... E 888 843-2345
  Charlotte (G-3524)
Shaw Fine Woodworking .... G 336 529-4080
  Sparta (G-14599)
Shep Berryhill Woodworking .... G 828 242-3227
  Asheville (G-769)
Shower Glass LLC .... G 980 785-4030
  Indian Trail (G-8962)
Signature Custom Wdwkg Inc .... G 336 983-9905
  King (G-9282)
Simpson Sawmill LLC .... G 704 485-8814
  Oakboro (G-12081)
Skettis Woodworks .... G 336 671-9866
  Winston Salem (G-16911)
Skin Wellness By Patricia Inc .... G 704 634-6635
  Mooresville (G-11089)
Smith Companies Lexington Inc .... G 336 249-4941
  Lexington (G-9781)
Smith Creations LLC .... G 704 771-6749
  Swannanoa (G-15036)
Smith Woodworks Inc .... G 910 890-2923
  Dunn (G-4884)
Snyder Custom Creations LLC .... G 704 743-3386
  Mooresville (G-11092)
Solid Woodworker .... G 336 786-7385
  Mount Airy (G-11573)
Solutions In Wood .... G 828 696-2996
  Hendersonville (G-7901)
Sornig Cstm Wdwrks Thmas Srnig .... G 734 925-3905
  Advance (G-51)
Southern Custom Doors James NA .... G 919 986-6943
  Raleigh (G-13282)
Southern Custom Doors LLC .... G 919 889-5404
  Raleigh (G-13283)
Southern Mllwk By Design Inc .... G 704 309-8854
  Matthews (G-10345)
Southern Pine Woodworking LLC .... G 910 690-9800
  Southern Pines (G-14554)
Southern Roots Millwork .... G 336 736-8812
  Asheboro (G-483)
Southern Staircase Inc .... D 704 357-1221
  Charlotte (G-3597)
Southern Woodcraft Design LLC .... G 919 693-8995
  Oxford (G-12158)
Southern Woodworking Inc .... G 336 693-5892
  Burlington (G-1497)
Sparks Mill Works LLC .... G 512 779-5837
  Asheville (G-785)
Spartacraft Inc .... E 828 397-4630
  Connelly Springs (G-4409)
Spring Valley Carving Svcs LLC .... G 919 553-7906
  Clayton (G-4012)
Square One Woodworking .... G 828 277-5164
  Asheville (G-786)
St Lucie Woodworks Inc .... G 772 626-4778
  Raeford (G-12441)
Stairways From Heaven Inc .... G 828 627-3860
  Clyde (G-4128)
Stanleys Woodworking .... G 828 612-4286
  Newton (G-11973)

Stephenson Millwork Co Inc .... C 252 237-1141
  Wilson (G-16543)
Steve Noggle Turned Wood .... G 828 437-8017
  Morganton (G-11257)
Stevens Mill Woodworks LLC .... G 919 440-8834
  Goldsboro (G-6661)
Stevenson Woodworking .... G 919 362-9121
  Apex (G-245)
Stickler Woodworking Inc .... G 336 302-0683
  Asheboro (G-488)
Stock Building Supply Holdings LLC ..... A 919 431-1000
  Raleigh (G-13305)
Straight Edge Woodworks LLC .... G 704 456-7046
  Harrisburg (G-7729)
Straightline Woodworks .... G 336 469-7029
  Yadkinville (G-17052)
Strandh Woodworks LLC .... G 919 703-8056
  New Hill (G-11865)
Sugar Mountain Woodworks Inc .... G 423 292-6245
  Newland (G-11894)
Summit Peak Pens and WD Works .... G 336 404-8312
  Liberty (G-9832)
Susan Link Woodworks LLC .... G 828 492-8026
  Canton (G-1627)
Swanson Custom Wood Workin .... G 910 465-3199
  Wilmington (G-16423)
Swanson Custom Woodworking Inc .... G 910 465-3199
  Southport (G-14585)
Sylvester Artsan Woodworks LLC .... G 989 529-3573
  West End (G-15933)
T J S Woodworks .... G 336 299-5913
  Greensboro (G-7386)
Ta Lost Pines Woodwork .... G 828 367-7517
  Asheville (G-794)
Tallent Wood Works .... G 704 592-2013
  Statesville (G-14910)
Thompson Joinery LLC .... G 919 672-2770
  Durham (G-5401)
Thompson Millwork LLC .... D 919 596-8236
  Mebane (G-10433)
Tiger Mountain Woodworks Inc .... E 828 526-5577
  Highlands (G-8618)
Timber Wolf Forest Products .... F 828 728-7500
  Hudson (G-8783)
Timber Wolf Wood Creations Inc .... G 704 309-5118
  Charlotte (G-3694)
Tivoli Woodworks LLC .... G 336 602-3512
  Salisbury (G-14053)
Todrin Fine Woodwork Llc .... G 413 478-2818
  Chapel Hill (G-2080)
Tom Marsh Jr DBA Tm Woodworks ...... G 910 376-2760
  Hampstead (G-7660)
Travis Harrell .... G 828 279-2937
  Wilmington (G-16431)
Triangle Custom Woodworks LLC .... G 919 637-8857
  Fuquay Varina (G-6234)
Triangle Woodworks Inc .... G 919 570-0337
  Wake Forest (G-15605)
Trinity Woodworks LLC .... G 980 938-4765
  Gold Hill (G-6586)
True Blue Wdcrfting Lser Etchi .... G 609 784-2431
  Clayton (G-4019)
TS Woodworks & RAD Design Inc .... F 704 238-1015
  Monroe (G-10824)
Tuckers Farm Inc .... G 704 375-8199
  Charlotte (G-3737)
Two Green Thumbs and More Inc .... G 704 614-8703
  Hickory (G-8192)
United Finishers Intl Inc .... G 336 883-3901
  High Point (G-8585)
United Wood Products Inc .... G 336 626-2281
  Asheboro (G-502)

Employee Codes: A=Over 500 employees, B=251-500
C=101-250, D=51-100, E=20-50, F=10-19, G=1-9

MILLWORK

Van Duyn Woodwork .... G 919 760-0327
   Raleigh *(G-13391)*

Vision Woodworks LLC .... G 704 779-0734
   Huntersville *(G-8905)*

Visions Stairways and Millwork .... E 919 878-5622
   Raleigh *(G-13406)*

Walnut Woodworks .... G 828 290-6438
   Flat Rock *(G-5973)*

Waterdog Wood Works LLC .... G 252 808-7978
   Oriental *(G-12114)*

Wayne Woodworks .... G 910 298-5669
   Pink Hill *(G-12318)*

Wells Woodworks Gary Wells .... G 828 553-0177
   Brevard *(G-1292)*

Western Crlina Cstm Cswork Inc .... F 828 669-0459
   Black Mountain *(G-1141)*

Wheelhouse Builders LLC .... G 828 553-7519
   Brevard *(G-1293)*

Whitaker Mill Works LLC .... G 919 772-3030
   Raleigh *(G-13421)*

Wigal Wood Works .... G 580 890-9723
   Fayetteville *(G-5953)*

Willow Oak Woodworks .... G 919 906-1232
   Hurdle Mills *(G-8915)*

Winchester Woodworks .... G 828 421-2693
   Waynesville *(G-15833)*

Windsor Window Company .... G 704 283-7459
   Monroe *(G-10835)*

Winfield Woodworks .... G 828 808-9727
   Fletcher *(G-6053)*

Witherspoon Woodworks LLC .... G 919 669-9103
   Raleigh *(G-13425)*

Wizards Wood Werks .... G 252 813-3929
   Macclesfield *(G-10067)*

Wolphs Wood Works Ltd .... G 719 629-6350
   Trenton *(G-15337)*

Wood Surgeon .... G 252 728-5767
   Beaufort *(G-971)*

Wood Works .... G 336 580-4134
   Greensboro *(G-7466)*

Wood Works .... G 910 579-1487
   Sunset Beach *(G-15004)*

Wood Works of Ahoskie LLC .... G 252 287-7396
   Ahoskie *(G-67)*

Woodlake Wood Works .... G 919 972-1000
   Durham *(G-5446)*

Woodmaster Custom Cabinets Inc .... F 919 554-3707
   Youngsville *(G-17116)*

Woodtech/Interiors Inc .... G 704 332-7215
   Charlotte *(G-3820)*

Woodworking At Dinahs Landing .... G 252 402-2248
   Washington *(G-15740)*

Woodworking By Robt Wadde .... G 704 236-0883
   Matthews *(G-10352)*

Woodworking Unlimited Inc .... G 704 903-8080
   Olin *(G-12108)*

Work Custom LLC .... G 704 488-3113
   Charlotte *(G-3821)*

Wurtz Woodworks Llc .... G 704 657-6584
   Troutman *(G-15399)*

Wyatt Woodworks .... G 919 619-8593
   Fuquay Varina *(G-6239)*

Xl Paws Woodworking LLC .... G 336 309-1173
   Cameron *(G-1565)*

Young Wood Works LLC .... G 704 654-1722
   Charlotte *(G-3845)*

MINE & QUARRY SVCS: Nonmetallic Minerals

Triple B Stone LLC .... G 704 663-5860
   Terrell *(G-15180)*

MINERAL WOOL

Bunting Equipment Company Inc .... F 336 626-7300
   Sophia *(G-14513)*

Freudenberg Prfmce Mtls LP .... C 828 665-5000
   Candler *(G-1579)*

JPS Communications Inc .... D 919 534-1168
   Raleigh *(G-12923)*

Sharp Fiberglass LLC .... G 610 760-0638
   Kittrell *(G-9398)*

MINERALS: Ground or Treated

Covia Holdings LLC .... E 828 765-4283
   Spruce Pine *(G-14637)*

Imerys Clays Inc .... G 828 648-2668
   Canton *(G-1618)*

Imerys Mica Kings Mountain Inc .... E 704 739-3616
   Kings Mountain *(G-9309)*

Iperionx Limited .... E 704 578-3217
   Charlotte *(G-2993)*

Mathis Quarries Inc .... G 336 984-4010
   North Wilkesboro *(G-12026)*

Premier Magnesia LLC .... E 828 452-4784
   Waynesville *(G-15816)*

Quartz Corp USA .... C 828 765-8950
   Spruce Pine *(G-14653)*

Southeastern Minerals Inc .... E 252 492-0831
   Henderson *(G-7811)*

Southern Products Company Inc .... E 910 281-3189
   Hoffman *(G-8676)*

Vanderbilt Minerals LLC .... E 910 948-2266
   Robbins *(G-13603)*

MINIATURES

Marties Miniatures .... G 336 869-5952
   High Point *(G-8446)*

MINING EXPLORATION & DEVELOPMENT SVCS

Charah LLC .... C 704 731-2300
   Charlotte *(G-2447)*

Charah LLC .... C 502 873-6993
   Mount Holly *(G-11626)*

Iperionx Technology LLC .... G 704 578-3217
   Charlotte *(G-2994)*

RDc Debris Removal Cnstr LLC .... E 323 614-2353
   Smithfield *(G-14479)*

MINING MACHINERY & EQPT WHOLESALERS

Component Sourcing Intl LLC .... E 704 843-9292
   Charlotte *(G-2534)*

MIXTURES & BLOCKS: Asphalt Paving

Barnhill Contracting Company .... G 704 721-7500
   Concord *(G-4204)*

Barnhill Contracting Company .... D 910 488-1319
   Fayetteville *(G-5769)*

Barnhill Contracting Company .... E 252 752-7608
   Greenville *(G-7493)*

Blythe Construction Inc .... G 704 788-9733
   Concord *(G-4211)*

Blythe Construction Inc .... E 336 854-9003
   Greensboro *(G-6845)*

Brown Brothers Construction Co .... F 828 297-2131
   Zionville *(G-17148)*

Carolina Sunrock LLC .... E 919 575-4502
   Butner *(G-1543)*

Dickerson Group Inc .... G 704 289-3911
   Charlotte *(G-2631)*

Fsc Holdings Inc .... G 919 782-1247
   Raleigh *(G-12784)*

Gardner Asphalt Co .... F 336 784-8924
   Winston Salem *(G-16719)*

Gelder & Associates Inc .... C 919 772-6895
   Raleigh *(G-12792)*

Gem Asset Acquisition LLC .... E 919 851-0799
   Cary *(G-1772)*

Gem Asset Acquisition LLC .... E 704 697-9577
   Charlotte *(G-2815)*

Gem Asset Acquisition LLC .... G 336 854-8200
   Greensboro *(G-7033)*

Gem Asset Acquisition LLC .... G 704 225-3321
   Charlotte *(G-2814)*

Haulco LLC .... G 336 781-0468
   Trinity *(G-15344)*

Highway Maintenance Ofc .... G 252 534-4031
   Jackson *(G-8982)*

Hudson Paving Inc .... D 910 895-5910
   Rockingham *(G-13630)*

Johnson Paving Company Inc .... F 828 652-4911
   Marion *(G-10154)*

Krebs Corporation .... G 336 548-3250
   Madison *(G-10076)*

Lane Construction Corporation .... B 919 876-4550
   Raleigh *(G-12956)*

Long Asp Pav Trckg of Grnsburg .... F 336 643-4121
   Summerfield *(G-14986)*

Maymead Materials .... G 828 758-9299
   Lenoir *(G-9634)*

Russell Standard Corporation .... G 336 292-6875
   Greensboro *(G-7320)*

Russell Standard Nc LLC .... C 336 292-6875
   Greensboro *(G-7321)*

S T Wooten Corporation .... E 919 965-9880
   Princeton *(G-12404)*

Sunrock Group Holdings Corp .... D 919 747-6400
   Raleigh *(G-13315)*

Thorworks Industries Inc .... G 919 852-3714
   Raleigh *(G-13348)*

Vulcan Materials Company .... G 704 545-5687
   Charlotte *(G-3784)*

MOBILE COMMUNICATIONS EQPT

Dexterity LLC .... F 919 524-7732
   Greenville *(G-7514)*

Motorola Mobility LLC .... E 919 294-1289
   Morrisville *(G-11391)*

MOBILE HOMES

Alan Lane Wesley .... G 704 433-8338
   Salisbury *(G-13917)*

Brig Homes NC .... G 252 459-7026
   Nashville *(G-11737)*

Cavalier Home Builders LLC .... G 252 459-7026
   Nashville *(G-11741)*

Clayton Homes Inc .... G 828 667-8701
   Candler *(G-1575)*

Clayton Homes Inc .... G 828 684-1550
   Fletcher *(G-5994)*

Crest Capital LLC .... F 336 664-2400
   Greensboro *(G-6939)*

Daly Company Inc .... G 919 751-3625
   Goldsboro *(G-6607)*

Eco Modern Homes LLC .... G 252 833-4335
   Chocowinity *(G-3894)*

Elite Mountain Business LLC .... G 828 349-0403
   Franklin *(G-6128)*

Esco Industries Inc .... F 336 495-3772
   Randleman *(G-13469)*

Home City Ltd .... G 910 428-2196
   Biscoe *(G-1111)*

Phillips Mobile Home Vlg LLC............ G 704 298-4648
  Kannapolis (G-9130)
Platipus Anchors Ltd......................... G 919 662-0900
  Garner (G-6303)
Readilite & Barricade Inc................... F 919 231-8309
  Raleigh (G-13194)
Sunshine Mnfctred Strctres Inc.......... E 704 279-6600
  Rockwell (G-13659)
Wetherington S Mobile Home............. G 910 347-3664
  Jacksonville (G-9046)

MOBILE HOMES, EXC RECREATIONAL

Champion Home Builders Inc........... C 910 893-5713
  Lillington (G-9848)
CMH Manufacturing Inc.................... A 704 279-4659
  Rockwell (G-13649)
R-Anell Custom Homes Inc................ E 704 483-5511
  Denver (G-4797)
R-Anell Housing Group LLC............... D 704 445-9610
  Crouse (G-4627)

MODELS: General, Exc Toy

S Y Shop Inc...................................... G 704 545-7710
  Mint Hill (G-10544)

MODULES: Computer Logic

Iqe North Carolina LLC...................... F 336 609-6270
  Greensboro (G-7121)

MODULES: Solid State

Telit Wireless Solutions Inc................ D 919 439-7977
  Durham (G-5391)

MOLDED RUBBER PRDTS

Flint Group US LLC............................ G 828 687-2485
  Arden (G-332)
Longwood Industries Inc.................... F 336 272-3710
  Greensboro (G-7168)
Nu-Tech Enterprises Inc.................... E 336 725-1691
  Winston Salem (G-16825)
Patch Rubber Company..................... C 252 536-2574
  Weldon (G-15887)
Qrmc Ltd... E 828 696-2000
  Hendersonville (G-7893)
Rp Fletcher Machine Co Inc............... D 336 249-6101
  Lexington (G-9775)
Rubber Mill Inc................................... G 336 622-1680
  Conover (G-4494)
Rubber Mill Inc................................... E 336 622-1680
  Liberty (G-9830)

MOLDING COMPOUNDS

Wp Reidsville LLC.............................. C 336 342-1200
  Reidsville (G-13547)

MOLDINGS & TRIM: Metal, Exc Automobile

Airspeed LLC..................................... E 919 644-1222
  Hillsborough (G-8633)
Panels By Paith Inc........................... G 336 599-3437
  Roxboro (G-13816)

MOLDINGS & TRIM: Wood

Chesnick Corporation........................ F 919 231-2899
  Raleigh (G-12619)
Itc Millwork LLC................................. D 704 821-1470
  Matthews (G-10323)
Ornamental Mouldings LLC................ F 336 431-9120
  Archdale (G-295)
Trim Inc... F 336 751-3491
  Mocksville (G-10609)
Trimworks Inc.................................... G 704 753-4149
  Monroe (G-10823)

MOLDINGS OR TRIM: Automobile, Stamped Metal

Revolution Pd LLC............................. G 919 949-0241
  Pittsboro (G-12347)

MOLDS: Indl

Ameritech Die & Mold Inc.................. E 704 664-0801
  Mooresville (G-10857)
Ameritech Die & Mold South Inc........ F 704 664-0801
  Mooresville (G-10858)
Atlantic Mold Inc................................ G 919 832-8151
  Fuquay Varina (G-6182)
Bethlehem Manufacturing Co............. F 828 495-7731
  Hickory (G-7949)
Brooks Tool Inc.................................. G 704 283-0112
  Monroe (G-10669)
DEB Manufacturing Inc...................... G 704 703-6618
  Concord (G-4253)
Hasco America Inc............................ G 828 650-2631
  Fletcher (G-6010)
Mold Trans LLC................................. G 828 356-5181
  Fletcher (G-6027)
R A Serafini Inc................................. E 704 864-6763
  Gastonia (G-6500)
Select Mold Service Inc..................... F 910 323-1287
  Fayetteville (G-5913)
T D M Corporation............................. E
  Fletcher (G-6044)

MONUMENTS & GRAVE MARKERS, WHOLESALE

Conway Development Inc.................. F 252 756-2168
  Greenville (G-7505)

MOPS: Floor & Dust

E T C of Henderson N C Inc.............. G 252 492-4033
  Henderson (G-7781)
Lions Services Inc............................. B 704 921-1527
  Charlotte (G-3091)
Newell & Sons Inc............................. F 336 597-2248
  Roxboro (G-13807)
Quickie Manufacturing Corp.............. C 910 737-6500
  Lumberton (G-10049)

MOTION PICTURE & VIDEO DISTRIBUTION

AEC Consumer Products LLC........... F 704 904-0578
  Fayetteville (G-5754)
Pop Products LLC.............................. G 336 263-1884
  Burlington (G-1476)

MOTION PICTURE & VIDEO PRODUCTION SVCS: Educational

National Ctr For Social Impact........... G 984 212-2285
  Raleigh (G-13054)

MOTOR & GENERATOR PARTS: Electric

ABB Motors and Mechanical Inc........ G 479 646-4711
  Marion (G-10137)
Hlmf Logistics Inc.............................. G 704 782-0356
  Pineville (G-12273)
Motor Rite Inc.................................... F 919 625-3653
  Raleigh (G-13043)
SCR Controls Inc............................... F 704 821-6651
  Matthews (G-10342)
Siemens Energy Inc........................... C 919 365-2200
  Wendell (G-15916)

MOTOR CONTROL CENTERS

Siemens Industry Inc......................... C 919 365-2200
  Wendell (G-15917)

MOTOR HOMES

Hunckler Fabrication LLC.................. F 336 753-0905
  Mocksville (G-10581)
Van Products Inc............................... E 919 878-7110
  Raleigh (G-13392)

MOTOR VEHICLE ASSEMBLY, COMPLETE: Ambulances

First Prrity Emrgncy Vhcles In............ E 908 645-0788
  Wilkesboro (G-16021)
Halcore Group Inc............................. E 336 982-9824
  Jefferson (G-9089)
Halcore Group Inc............................. B 336 846-8010
  Jefferson (G-9090)
Matthews Spcialty Vehicles Inc......... D 336 297-9600
  Greensboro (G-7189)
RFH Tactical Mobility Inc................... F 910 916-0284
  Milton (G-10516)

MOTOR VEHICLE ASSEMBLY, COMPLETE: Buses, All Types

Bus Safety Inc................................... G 336 671-0838
  Mocksville (G-10558)
Designline Corporation...................... C 704 494-7800
  Charlotte (G-2621)
Jem Acres Inc.................................... G 252 823-3483
  Tarboro (G-15110)
Prevost Car (us) Inc.......................... E 908 222-7211
  Greensboro (G-7281)
Streets Auto Sales & Four WD.......... G 704 888-8686
  Locust (G-9973)

MOTOR VEHICLE ASSEMBLY, COMPLETE: Fire Department Vehicles

Trenton Emergency Med Svcs Inc..... F 252 448-2646
  Trenton (G-15335)
Your Fire Source Inc......................... F 828 669-9000
  Black Mountain (G-1142)

MOTOR VEHICLE ASSEMBLY, COMPLETE: Military Motor Vehicle

Fortem Genus Inc.............................. G 910 574-5214
  Fayetteville (G-5826)
James Tool Machine & Engrg Inc...... C 828 584-8722
  Morganton (G-11224)
Operating Shelby LLC Tag................ E 704 482-1399
  Shelby (G-14354)

MOTOR VEHICLE ASSEMBLY, COMPLETE: Motor Buses

Epv Corporation................................. G 704 494-7800
  Charlotte (G-2723)
Epv Corporation................................. E 704 494-7800
  Charlotte (G-2724)

MOTOR VEHICLE ASSEMBLY, COMPLETE: Universal Carriers, Mil

Lelantos Group Inc............................ D 704 780-4127
  Mooresville (G-11005)

MOTOR VEHICLE ASSEMBLY, COMPLETE: Wreckers, Tow Truck

Ashville Wrecker Service Inc............. G 828 252-2388
  Asheville (G-546)

Employee Codes: A=Over 500 employees, B=251-500
C=101-250, D=51-100, E=20-50, F=10-19, G=1-9

MOTOR VEHICLE DEALERS: Automobiles, New & Used

ABB Motors and Mechanical Inc	C	828 645-1706	
Weaverville *(G-15836)*			
Courtesy Ford Inc	E	252 338-4783	
Elizabeth City *(G-5537)*			
Daimler Truck North Amer LLC	A	704 645-5000	
Cleveland *(G-4071)*			
Dutch Miller Charlotte Inc	E	704 522-8422	
Charlotte *(G-2660)*			
Saab Barracuda LLC	E	910 814-3088	
Lillington *(G-9859)*			
Subaru Folger Automotive	E	704 531-8888	
Charlotte *(G-3645)*			
Vestal Buick Gmc Inc	D	336 310-0261	
Kernersville *(G-9251)*			
Volvo Trucks North America Inc	A	336 393-2000	
Greensboro *(G-7450)*			

MOTOR VEHICLE PARTS & ACCESS: Acceleration Eqpt

- Axle Holdings LLC .... E 800 895-3276
  Concord *(G-4203)*
- Bosch Rexroth Corporation .... E 704 583-4338
  Charlotte *(G-2336)*
- Cleveland Yutaka Corporation .... D 704 480-9290
  Shelby *(G-14299)*
- Hitch Crafters LLC .... G 336 859-3257
  Lexington *(G-9731)*
- Marmon Holdings Inc .... F 910 291-2571
  Laurinburg *(G-9488)*
- Rostra Precision Controls Inc .... D 910 291-2502
  Aberdeen *(G-27)*

MOTOR VEHICLE PARTS & ACCESS: Air Conditioner Parts

- Longs Machine & Tool Inc .... E 336 625-3844
  Asheboro *(G-454)*

MOTOR VEHICLE PARTS & ACCESS: Ball Joints

- Suspensions LLC .... F 704 809-1269
  Denver *(G-4804)*

MOTOR VEHICLE PARTS & ACCESS: Body Components & Frames

- Can-AM Custom Trucks Inc .... G 704 334-0322
  Charlotte *(G-2381)*
- Jenkins Properties Inc .... E 336 667-4282
  North Wilkesboro *(G-12017)*

MOTOR VEHICLE PARTS & ACCESS: Brakes, Air

- Atkinson International Inc .... D 704 865-7750
  Gastonia *(G-6349)*
- G-Loc Brakes LLC .... G 704 765-0213
  Mooresville *(G-10952)*

MOTOR VEHICLE PARTS & ACCESS: Clutches

- FCC (north Carolina) LLC .... C 910 462-4465
  Laurinburg *(G-9479)*
- Linnig Corporation .... D 704 482-9582
  Shelby *(G-14338)*

MOTOR VEHICLE PARTS & ACCESS: Cylinder Heads

- Moores Cylinder Heads LLC .... E 704 786-8412
  Concord *(G-4318)*

MOTOR VEHICLE PARTS & ACCESS: Electrical Eqpt

- Arrival Automotive USA Inc .... F 415 439-2002
  Charlotte *(G-2217)*

MOTOR VEHICLE PARTS & ACCESS: Engines & Parts

- Barrs Competition .... F 704 482-5169
  Shelby *(G-14287)*
- Clarcor Eng MBL Solutions LLC .... C 860 992-3496
  Washington *(G-15688)*
- Durham Racing Engines Inc .... G 336 471-1830
  Thomasville *(G-15217)*
- Holman Automotive Inc .... G 704 583-2888
  Charlotte *(G-2915)*
- Mann+hmmel Fltrtion Tech US LL .... D 704 869-3700
  Gastonia *(G-6451)*
- McCoy Motorsports .... G 704 929-8802
  Cleveland *(G-4075)*
- Stanadyne Jacksonville LLC .... C 860 683-4553
  Jacksonville *(G-9039)*
- US Prototype Inc .... E 866 239-2848
  Wilmington *(G-16439)*
- Xceldyne Technologies LLC .... D 336 475-0201
  Thomasville *(G-15308)*

MOTOR VEHICLE PARTS & ACCESS: Engs & Trans, Factory, Rebuilt

- Jasper Engine Exchange Inc .... E 704 664-2300
  Mooresville *(G-10987)*
- Truck Parts Inc .... F 704 332-7909
  Charlotte *(G-3732)*

MOTOR VEHICLE PARTS & ACCESS: Fuel Pumps

- SL Liquidation LLC .... B 860 525-0821
  Jacksonville *(G-9032)*
- Xtreme Fabrication Ltd .... F 336 472-4562
  Thomasville *(G-15309)*

MOTOR VEHICLE PARTS & ACCESS: Fuel Systems & Parts

- SL Liquidation LLC .... B 910 353-3666
  Jacksonville *(G-9033)*
- Stanadyne Intrmdate Hldngs LLC .... C 860 525-0821
  Jacksonville *(G-9038)*

MOTOR VEHICLE PARTS & ACCESS: Gas Tanks

- Edelbrock LLC .... D 919 718-9737
  Sanford *(G-14113)*
- Isometrics Inc .... F 336 342-4150
  Reidsville *(G-13527)*
- Isometrics Inc .... E 336 349-2329
  Reidsville *(G-13528)*

MOTOR VEHICLE PARTS & ACCESS: Gears

- Abundant Manufacturing Inc .... E 704 871-9911
  Statesville *(G-14737)*
- GKN Driveline Newton LLC .... A 828 428-3711
  Newton *(G-11933)*

MOTOR VEHICLE PARTS & ACCESS: Lifting Mechanisms, Dump Truck

- Diamondback Products Inc .... G 336 236-9800
  Lexington *(G-9708)*
- Godwin Manufacturing Co Inc .... C 910 897-4995
  Dunn *(G-4870)*
- Satco Truck Equipment Inc .... F 919 383-5547
  Durham *(G-5340)*

MOTOR VEHICLE PARTS & ACCESS: Mufflers, Exhaust

- AP Emissions Technologies LLC .... A 919 580-2000
  Goldsboro *(G-6591)*

MOTOR VEHICLE PARTS & ACCESS: Power Steering Eqpt

- Cjr Products Inc .... G 336 766-2710
  Winston Salem *(G-16653)*

MOTOR VEHICLE PARTS & ACCESS: Propane Conversion Eqpt

- Deuces Custom .... G 704 658-1777
  Mooresville *(G-10930)*
- Parker Gas Company Inc .... F 800 354-7250
  Clinton *(G-4101)*

MOTOR VEHICLE PARTS & ACCESS: Tire Valve Cores

- Dill Air Controls Products LLC .... C 919 692-2300
  Oxford *(G-12127)*

MOTOR VEHICLE PARTS & ACCESS: Tops

- Kee Auto Top Manufacturing Co .... E 704 332-8213
  Charlotte *(G-3047)*

MOTOR VEHICLE PARTS & ACCESS: Transmissions

- Aisin North Carolina Corp .... C 919 529-0951
  Creedmoor *(G-4602)*
- Aisin North Carolina Corp .... A 919 479-6400
  Durham *(G-4910)*
- Borgwarner Inc .... E 828 684-4000
  Arden *(G-314)*
- Eaton Corporation .... C 704 937-7411
  Kings Mountain *(G-9306)*

MOTOR VEHICLE PARTS & ACCESS: Universal Joints

- GKN Dna Inc .... G 919 304-7378
  Mebane *(G-10412)*
- GKN Driveline North Amer Inc .... E 919 304-7252
  Mebane *(G-10413)*

MOTOR VEHICLE PARTS & ACCESS: Wiring Harness Sets

- Ae Wiring LLC .... F 252 749-0195
  Fountain *(G-6092)*
- Dce Inc .... G 704 230-4649
  Mooresville *(G-10926)*
- Mr Tire Inc .... F 828 322-8130
  Hickory *(G-8099)*
- R M Gear Harness .... G 336 498-1169
  Randleman *(G-13486)*

MOTOR VEHICLE RACING & DRIVER SVCS

- Labonte Racing Inc .... F 336 431-1004
  Trinity *(G-15348)*

PRODUCT SECTION — MOTORS: Generators

Penske Racing South Inc............................ C 704 664-2300
  Mooresville (G-11050)

MOTOR VEHICLE SPLYS & PARTS WHOLESALERS: New

Camco Manufacturing Inc........................ G 336 348-6609
  Reidsville (G-13511)
Capitol Bumper.. G 919 772-7330
  Fayetteville (G-5782)
Cummins Atlantic LLC............................... D 336 275-4531
  Greensboro (G-6946)
Nichols Spdmtr & Instr Co Inc................. G 336 273-2881
  Greensboro (G-7219)
Prevost Car (us) Inc.................................... E 908 222-7211
  Greensboro (G-7281)
Vna Holding Inc... A 336 393-4890
  Greensboro (G-7445)
Volvo Group North America LLC........... A 336 393-2000
  Greensboro (G-7447)
Volvo Group North America LLC........... A 336 393-2000
  Greensboro (G-7446)
Volvo Trucks North America Inc............ A 336 393-2000
  Greensboro (G-7450)

MOTOR VEHICLE SPLYS & PARTS WHOLESALERS: Used

Tire Kountry LLC... G 336 637-8320
  Reidsville (G-13542)

MOTOR VEHICLE: Hardware

Blue Ridge Global Inc................................ G 828 252-5225
  Asheville (G-565)
Volvo Group North America LLC........... A 731 968-0151
  Greensboro (G-7448)

MOTOR VEHICLE: Radiators

Lake Shore Radiator Inc............................ F 336 271-2626
  Greensboro (G-7162)

MOTOR VEHICLE: Shock Absorbers

Fox Factory Inc... F 828 633-6840
  Asheville (G-627)
Lord Corporation... D 919 342-3380
  Cary (G-1816)
Ohlins Usa Inc... E 828 692-4525
  Hendersonville (G-7887)

MOTOR VEHICLE: Steering Mechanisms

Carolina Attachments LLC........................ F 336 474-7309
  Thomasville (G-15194)
ZF Chassis Components LLC................... C 828 468-3711
  Newton (G-11986)

MOTOR VEHICLE: Wheels

Accuride Corporation................................. G 336 393-0671
  Greensboro (G-6776)
Gracie & Lucas LLC..................................... G 704 707-3207
  Mooresville (G-10962)

MOTOR VEHICLES & CAR BODIES

Bucher Municipal N Amer Inc................. E 704 658-1333
  Mooresville (G-10891)
Carolina Movile Bus Systems.................. G 336 475-0983
  Thomasville (G-15199)
Daimler Truck North Amer LLC.............. A 704 645-5000
  Cleveland (G-4071)
Dej Holdings LLC... E 704 799-4800
  Mooresville (G-10928)
Ecovehicle Enterprises Inc....................... G 704 544-9907
  Charlotte (G-2685)

Elio Inc.. G 919 708-5554
  Sanford (G-14114)
Epk LLC... F 980 643-4787
  Salisbury (G-13958)
Force Protection Inc................................... F 336 597-2381
  Roxboro (G-13803)
Ford Division... G 336 838-4155
  North Wilkesboro (G-12008)
GM Defense LLC.. D 800 462-8782
  Concord (G-4275)
Holman Automotive Inc............................ G 704 583-2888
  Charlotte (G-2915)
Jasper Engine Exchange Inc.................... E 704 664-2300
  Mooresville (G-10987)
Jasper Penske Engines.............................. F 704 788-8996
  Concord (G-4292)
Jeff Anderson... G 910 481-8923
  Fayetteville (G-5848)
Labonte Racing Inc..................................... F 336 431-1004
  Trinity (G-15348)
Maxxdrive LLC.. G 704 600-8684
  Shelby (G-14345)
Mickey Truck Bodies Inc........................... B 336 882-6806
  High Point (G-8455)
Navistar Inc... G 704 596-3860
  Charlotte (G-3239)
Penske Racing South Inc.......................... C 704 664-2300
  Mooresville (G-11050)
Prevost Car (us) Inc.................................... F 336 812-3504
  High Point (G-8496)
Propane Trucks & Tanks Inc.................... F 919 362-5000
  Apex (G-234)
Rp Motor Sports Inc................................... E 704 720-4200
  Concord (G-4353)
Smith Fabrication Inc................................. G 704 660-5170
  Mooresville (G-11090)
Southco Industries Inc.............................. C 704 482-1477
  Shelby (G-14369)
Subaru Folger Automotive....................... E 704 531-8888
  Charlotte (G-3645)
Supreme Murphy Trck Bodies Inc.......... C 252 291-2191
  Wilson (G-16544)
Thomas of High Point................................ G 336 889-4871
  High Point (G-8570)
Toymakerz LLC... F 843 267-3477
  Reidsville (G-13543)
US Legend Cars Intl Inc............................ E 704 455-3896
  Harrisburg (G-7732)
Vision Motor Cars Inc................................ G 704 425-6271
  Concord (G-4386)

MOTOR VEHICLES, WHOLESALE: Fire Trucks

National Foam Inc....................................... E 919 639-6100
  Angier (G-147)

MOTOR VEHICLES, WHOLESALE: Truck tractors

Mack Trucks Inc... A 336 291-9001
  Greensboro (G-7177)

MOTORCYCLE ACCESS

Capital Value Center Sls & Svc............... G 910 799-4060
  Wilmington (G-16153)
Edelbrock LLC.. D 919 718-9737
  Sanford (G-14113)
Ironworks Motorcycles.............................. G 336 542-7868
  Greensboro (G-7123)
P P M Cycle and Custom........................... G 336 434-5289
  Trinity (G-15351)

MOTORCYCLE DEALERS

Barrs Competition....................................... F 704 482-5169
  Shelby (G-14287)
Ironworks Motorcycles.............................. G 336 542-7868
  Greensboro (G-7123)

MOTORCYCLES & RELATED PARTS

B & B Welding Inc....................................... G 336 643-5702
  Oak Ridge (G-12057)
Barrs Competition....................................... F 704 482-5169
  Shelby (G-14287)
C & S Custom.. G 336 242-9730
  Lexington (G-9688)
Choppers and Hotrods............................... G 336 993-3939
  Kernersville (G-9178)
Driver Distribution Inc.............................. G 984 204-2929
  Raleigh (G-12702)
Driver Distribution Inc.............................. G 984 204-2929
  Maiden (G-10106)
Hop A Chopper Inc..................................... G 704 624-6794
  Marshville (G-10219)
Indian Motorcycle Company.................... G 704 879-4560
  Lowell (G-10010)
John Jones DBA Grass Choppers............ G 336 413-6613
  Lewisville (G-9668)
Moto Group LLC.. F 828 350-7653
  Fletcher (G-6028)
Next World Design Inc.............................. F 800 448-1223
  Thomasville (G-15256)
Performance Parts Intl LLC..................... F 704 660-1084
  Mooresville (G-11052)
Suspension Experts LLC........................... E 855 419-3072
  Roxboro (G-13827)
Sv Plastics LLC... G 336 472-2242
  Thomasville (G-15287)

MOTORS: Electric

057 Technology LLC................................... G 855 557-7057
  Hickory (G-7926)
ABB Motors and Mechanical Inc............ G 336 272-6104
  Greensboro (G-6772)
Asmo North America LLC......................... A 704 872-2319
  Statesville (G-14754)
Buehler Motor Inc....................................... E 919 380-3333
  Morrisville (G-11309)
Ohio Electric Motors Inc........................... D 828 626-2901
  Barnardsville (G-912)
Petty Machine Company Inc................... E 704 864-3254
  Gastonia (G-6488)
Powertec Industrial Motors Inc.............. F 704 227-1580
  Charlotte (G-3363)
Xavier Power Systems............................... F 910 734-7813
  Lumberton (G-10061)

MOTORS: Fluid Power

Asmo Greenville of North Carolina Inc.. B 252 754-1000
  Greenville (G-7486)
Denso Manufacturing NC Inc................... B 252 754-1000
  Greenville (G-7513)

MOTORS: Generators

Allan Drth Sons Gnrtor Sls Svc............... G 828 526-9325
  Highlands (G-8611)
Alternative Pwr Sls & Rent LLP.............. G 919 467-8001
  Morrisville (G-11284)
Altom Fuel Cells LLC.................................. G 828 231-6889
  Leicester (G-9506)
Ao Smith Chatlotte..................................... G 704 597-8910
  Charlotte (G-2198)
Curtiss-Wright Corporation..................... B 704 869-4600
  Davidson (G-4669)

MOTORS: Generators

Denso Manufacturing NC Inc.............. B 704 878-6663
  Statesville *(G-14786)*
Dna Group Inc.............................. E 919 881-0889
  Raleigh *(G-12690)*
Eaton Corporation......................... B 828 684-2381
  Arden *(G-326)*
Elnik Systems LLC....................... E 973 239-6066
  Pineville *(G-12267)*
GE Vernova International LLC......... F 704 587-1300
  Charlotte *(G-2812)*
Genelect Services Inc................... F 828 255-7999
  Asheville *(G-632)*
Generator Supercenter Raleigh....... G 919 925-3434
  Raleigh *(G-12794)*
Hitachi Energy USA Inc................. G 919 856-2360
  Raleigh *(G-12850)*
Ini Power Systems Inc................... F 919 677-7112
  Morrisville *(G-11359)*
Li-Ion Motors Corp....................... G 704 662-0827
  Mooresville *(G-11006)*
Pinnacle Converting Eqp Inc.......... E 704 376-3855
  Pineville *(G-12291)*
R D Tillson & Associates Inc.......... G 336 454-1410
  Jamestown *(G-9069)*
Regal Rexnord Corporation............ F 800 825-6544
  Charlotte *(G-3426)*
Rotron Incorporated..................... C 336 449-3400
  Whitsett *(G-16001)*
Siemens Energy Inc..................... C 336 969-1351
  Rural Hall *(G-13853)*
Trane Technologies Company LLC... B 336 751-3561
  Mocksville *(G-10608)*

MOUNTING SVC: Swatches & Samples

American Sample House Inc........... G 704 276-1970
  Vale *(G-15463)*
Associated Printing & Svcs Inc....... F 828 286-9064
  Rutherfordton *(G-13864)*
Carolina Swatching Inc................. F 828 327-9499
  Hickory *(G-7967)*
Creative Services Usa Inc............. F 336 887-1958
  High Point *(G-8307)*
Custom Sample Service Inc........... G 336 861-2010
  Archdale *(G-277)*
E Feibusch Company Inc............... E 336 434-5095
  High Point *(G-8333)*
Kreber..................................... D 336 861-2700
  High Point *(G-8425)*
Sampletech Inc........................... F 336 882-1717
  High Point *(G-8519)*

MULTIPLEXERS: Telephone & Telegraph

Abacon Telecommunications LLC.... E 336 855-1179
  Greensboro *(G-6771)*
Alcatel Dunkermotoren.................. B 704 782-0691
  Concord *(G-4190)*
Arris Solutions LLC...................... A 678 473-2000
  Hickory *(G-7943)*
Avaya LLC................................. B 919 425-8268
  Research Triangle Pa *(G-13548)*
Conversant Products Inc............... F 919 465-3456
  Cary *(G-1734)*
Corning Incorporated.................... F 252 316-4500
  Tarboro *(G-15100)*
Corning Optcal Cmmncations LLC... A 828 901-5000
  Charlotte *(G-2556)*
Emrise Corporation...................... C 408 200-3040
  Durham *(G-5084)*
Extreme Networks Inc.................. B 408 579-2800
  Morrisville *(G-11339)*
Hatteras Networks Inc.................. E 919 991-5440
  Morrisville *(G-11352)*
JPS Communications Inc.............. D 919 534-1168
  Raleigh *(G-12923)*
Newton Instrument Company......... C 919 575-6426
  Butner *(G-1546)*
Nvent Thermal LLC...................... A 919 552-3811
  Fuquay Varina *(G-6218)*
Personal Communication Systems Inc.. D 336 722-4917
  Winston Salem *(G-16846)*
R E Mason Enterprises Inc............ G 910 483-5016
  Fayetteville *(G-5904)*
Siemens Corporation.................... G 919 465-1287
  Cary *(G-1886)*
Spectrasite Communications LLC... E 919 468-0112
  Cary *(G-1900)*
Tekelec Inc............................... C
  Morrisville *(G-11442)*
Tekelec Global Inc....................... A 919 460-5500
  Morrisville *(G-11443)*
Trimm International Inc................. E 847 362-3700
  Youngsville *(G-17110)*
Usat LLC.................................. E 919 942-4214
  Chapel Hill *(G-2091)*
Uteck....................................... F 910 483-5016
  Fayetteville *(G-5946)*

MUSIC DISTRIBUTION APPARATUS

Carolina Certif Mus Group LLC....... G 984 234-2073
  Durham *(G-5000)*
Worldwide Entrmt Mltimedia LLC.... G 704 208-6913
  Charlotte *(G-3826)*

MUSICAL INSTRUMENTS & ACCESS: Carrying Cases

Conn-Selmer Inc......................... D 704 289-6459
  Monroe *(G-10690)*

MUSICAL INSTRUMENTS & ACCESS: NEC

Appalachian Strings Inc................ G 828 712-8721
  Asheville *(G-523)*
Cape Fear Music Center LLC......... G 910 480-2362
  Fayetteville *(G-5779)*
Conn-Selmer Inc......................... D 704 289-6459
  Monroe *(G-10690)*
Engine Wellness Inc.................... G 503 231-0495
  Chapel Hill *(G-2015)*
Epi Centre Sundries..................... G 704 650-9575
  Charlotte *(G-2721)*
Fire Flutes................................ G 321 230-3878
  Wake Forest *(G-15556)*
Heartland Harps......................... G 828 329-6477
  Hendersonville *(G-7859)*
J L Smith & Co Inc...................... F 704 521-1088
  Charlotte *(G-3004)*
Lewtak Pipe Organ Builders Inc...... G 336 554-2251
  Mocksville *(G-10585)*
Lucky Man Inc............................ E 828 251-0090
  Asheville *(G-689)*
Luthiers Workshop LLC................ G 919 241-4578
  Hillsborough *(G-8660)*
Music & Arts............................. G 919 329-6069
  Garner *(G-6294)*
Saraz Musical Instruments............ G 828 782-8896
  Swannanoa *(G-15035)*
School of Rock Charlotte.............. G 704 842-3172
  Charlotte *(G-3506)*

MUSICAL INSTRUMENTS & SPLYS STORES: Pianos

MW Enterprises Inc..................... G 828 963-7083
  Vilas *(G-15498)*

MUSICAL INSTRUMENTS WHOLESALERS

J L Smith & Co Inc...................... F 704 521-1088
  Charlotte *(G-3004)*

MUSICAL INSTRUMENTS: Guitars & Parts, Electric & Acoustic

DAngelico Guitars....................... G 908 451-9606
  Lumberton *(G-10031)*
Kelhorn Corporation..................... G 828 837-5833
  Brasstown *(G-1266)*

NAILS: Steel, Wire Or Cut

Masonite Corporation................... B 704 599-0235
  Charlotte *(G-3138)*
Specialty Nails Company............... G 336 883-0135
  High Point *(G-8548)*

NAME PLATES: Engraved Or Etched

Acme Nameplate & Mfg Inc........... E 704 283-8175
  Monroe *(G-10635)*
Boyd Gmn Inc............................ C 206 284-2200
  Monroe *(G-10668)*
Product Identification Inc.............. E 919 544-4136
  Durham *(G-5305)*

NATURAL GAS DISTRIBUTION TO CONSUMERS

Blue Gas Marine Inc.................... F 919 238-3427
  Apex *(G-172)*

NATURAL GAS LIQUIDS PRODUCTION

Bi County Gas Producers LLC....... G 704 844-8990
  Charlotte *(G-2307)*
Green Power Producers................ G 704 844-8990
  Charlotte *(G-2863)*
Landfill Gas Producers................. F 704 844-8990
  Charlotte *(G-3072)*
Renewable Power Producers LLC... G 704 844-8990
  Charlotte *(G-3433)*

NATURAL GAS PRODUCTION

City of Lexington........................ E 336 248-3945
  Lexington *(G-9695)*
City of Shelby............................ E 704 484-6840
  Shelby *(G-14295)*
Renewco-Meadow Branch LLC...... G 404 584-3552
  Wake Forest *(G-15583)*
Srng-Liberty LLC........................ G 248 212-7209
  Charlotte *(G-3613)*
SRNg-T&w LLC.......................... G 704 271-9889
  Charlotte *(G-3614)*
Trans-Tech Energy LLC................ G 254 840-3355
  Rocky Mount *(G-13675)*

NATURAL PROPANE PRODUCTION

Diversified Energy LLC................. G 828 266-9800
  Boone *(G-1194)*
Euliss Oil Company Inc................ G 336 622-3055
  Liberty *(G-9813)*
South Central Oil and Prpn Inc....... G 704 982-2173
  Albemarle *(G-106)*

NAVIGATIONAL SYSTEMS & INSTRUMENTS

Garmin International Inc............... B 919 337-0116
  Cary *(G-1771)*

NEW & USED CAR DEALERS

Streets Auto Sales & Four WD....... G 704 888-8686
  Locust *(G-9973)*

PRODUCT SECTION

OPTICAL GOODS STORES: Eyeglasses, Prescription

Window Motor World Inc .... G 800 252-2649
  Boone (G-1250)

NICKEL

Haynes International Inc .... E 765 456-6000
  Mountain Home (G-11689)
Metal & Materials Proc LLC .... G 260 438-8901
  Aberdeen (G-13)
Stainless & Nickel Alloys LLC .... G 704 201-2898
  Charlotte (G-3619)
Wanda Nickel .... G 828 265-3246
  Deep Gap (G-4714)

NITRILE RUBBERS: Butadiene-Acrylonitrile

Kestrel I Acquisition Corporation .... A 919 990-7500
  Durham (G-5180)
Liquidating Reichhold Inc .... A 919 990-7500
  Durham (G-5191)

NONCURRENT CARRYING WIRING DEVICES

Erico .... G 704 846-5743
  Charlotte (G-2727)
Hydro Extrusion Usa LLC .... D 336 227-8826
  Burlington (G-1433)
Pcore .... F 919 734-0460
  Goldsboro (G-6643)
Preformed Line Products Co .... G 336 461-3513
  New London (G-11876)
Sigma Engineered Solutions PC .... D 919 773-0011
  Garner (G-6315)

NONFERROUS: Rolling & Drawing, NEC

Powerlab Inc .... E 336 650-0706
  Winston Salem (G-16861)
Southern Metals Company .... E 704 394-3161
  Charlotte (G-3594)

NOVELTIES

Encore Group Inc .... C 336 768-7859
  Winston Salem (G-16696)

NOVELTIES & SPECIALTIES: Metal

Vault of Forsyth Inc .... G 336 996-2044
  Kernersville (G-9250)

NOVELTIES, PAPER, WHOLESALE

Stump Printing Co Inc .... C 260 723-5171
  Wrightsville Beach (G-17028)

NOVELTIES: Paper, Made From Purchased Materials

Stump Printing Co Inc .... C 260 723-5171
  Wrightsville Beach (G-17028)

NOVELTIES: Plastic

Carolina Print Works Inc .... F 704 637-6902
  Salisbury (G-13935)

NOZZLES: Fire Fighting

Fireresq Incorporated .... F 888 975-0458
  Mooresville (G-10945)

NOZZLES: Spray, Aerosol, Paint Or Insecticide

Merchant 1 Manufacturing LLC .... G 336 617-3008
  Summerfield (G-14989)
Spraying Systems Co .... G 704 357-6499
  Charlotte (G-3605)

NUCLEAR SHIELDING: Metal Plate

Columbiana Hi Tech LLC .... D 336 497-3600
  Kernersville (G-9181)

NURSERIES & LAWN & GARDEN SPLY STORES, RETAIL: Fertilizer

Farm Services Inc .... G 336 226-7381
  Graham (G-6689)

NUTRITION SVCS

Premex Inc .... F 561 962-4128
  Durham (G-5304)

NYLON FIBERS

High Speed Gear Inc .... F 910 325-1000
  Swansboro (G-15045)

OFFICE EQPT WHOLESALERS

Branch Office Solutions Inc .... G 800 743-1047
  Indian Trail (G-8924)
Bryan Austin .... F 336 841-6573
  High Point (G-8276)
Digital Print & Imaging Inc .... G 910 341-3005
  Wilmington (G-16201)

OFFICE FURNITURE REPAIR & MAINTENANCE SVCS

Freedom Enterprise LLC .... G 502 510-7296
  Shallotte (G-14273)

OFFICE SPLY & STATIONERY STORES: Office Forms & Splys

American Forms Mfg Inc .... E 704 866-9139
  Gastonia (G-6345)
Carter Publishing Company Inc .... F 336 993-2161
  Kernersville (G-9174)
Coastal Press Inc .... G 252 726-1549
  Morehead City (G-11163)
Jofra Graphics Inc .... G 910 259-1717
  Burgaw (G-1342)
King Business Service Inc .... G 910 610-1030
  Laurinburg (G-9483)
L C Industries Inc .... C 919 596-8277
  Fayetteville (G-5857)
L C Industries Inc .... C 919 596-8277
  Durham (G-5185)
Lynchs Office Supply Co Inc .... F 252 537-6041
  Roanoke Rapids (G-13578)
M C C of Laurinburg Inc .... G 910 276-0519
  Laurinburg (G-9486)
Office Sup Svcs Inc Charlotte .... E 704 786-4677
  Concord (G-4323)
Owen G Dunn Co Inc .... G 252 633-3197
  New Bern (G-11832)
Print Management Group LLC .... F 704 821-0114
  Charlotte (G-3385)
Printing Press .... G 828 299-1234
  Asheville (G-743)
Southern Printing Company Inc .... G 910 259-4807
  Burgaw (G-1352)
Times Printing Company .... E 252 473-2105
  Manteo (G-10130)
Times Printing Company Inc .... G 252 441-2223
  Kill Devil Hills (G-9263)
W B Mason Co Inc .... E 888 926-2766
  Charlotte (G-3787)
Westmoreland Printers Inc .... F 704 482-9100
  Shelby (G-14382)
Wright Printing Service Inc .... G 336 427-4768
  Madison (G-10092)

OFFICE SPLYS, NEC, WHOLESALE

Acme United Corporation .... E 252 822-5051
  Rocky Mount (G-13663)
Fain Enterprises Inc .... F 336 724-0417
  Winston Salem (G-16705)

OFFICES & CLINICS OF DOCTORS OF MEDICINE: Radiologist

Telephys Inc .... G 312 625-9128
  Davidson (G-4699)

OIL & GAS FIELD MACHINERY

Patty Knio .... G 919 995-2670
  Raleigh (G-13102)

OIL FIELD SVCS, NEC

Apergy Artfl Lift Intl LLC .... F 919 934-1533
  Smithfield (G-14449)
Duke Energy Center .... E 919 464-0960
  Raleigh (G-12708)
Jordan Piping Inc .... G 336 818-9252
  North Wilkesboro (G-12019)
Petra Technologies Inc .... G 704 577-0687
  Indian Trail (G-8956)
Reservoir Group LLC .... G 610 764-0269
  Charlotte (G-3437)
Saybolt LP .... G 910 763-8444
  Wilmington (G-16394)
Tgi Incorporated .... G 336 768-0139
  Winston Salem (G-16939)

OILS & ESSENTIAL OILS

Old Belt Extracts LLC .... E 336 530-5784
  Roxboro (G-13811)
Silver Moon Nutraceuticals LLC .... G 828 698-5795
  Fletcher (G-6039)
Vital Being .... G 828 964-5853
  Zionville (G-17149)

OILS: Mineral, Natural

Native Naturalz Inc .... F 336 334-2984
  Greensboro (G-7213)

OPHTHALMIC GOODS

Clarity Vision of Smithfield .... G 919 938-6101
  Smithfield (G-14454)
Luxottica of America Inc .... G 910 867-0200
  Fayetteville (G-5862)
Luxottica of America Inc .... G 919 778-5692
  Goldsboro (G-6632)
O D Eyecarecenter P A .... G 252 443-7011
  Rocky Mount (G-13716)
Ocutech Inc .... G 919 967-6460
  Chapel Hill (G-2049)
Optical Place Inc .... E 336 274-1300
  Greensboro (G-7235)

OPHTHALMIC GOODS: Frames, Lenses & Parts, Eyeglasses

Eye Glass Lady LLC .... F 828 669-2154
  Black Mountain (G-1124)

OPTICAL GOODS STORES

O D Eyecarecenter P A .... G 252 443-7011
  Rocky Mount (G-13716)

OPTICAL GOODS STORES: Eyeglasses, Prescription

OPTICAL GOODS STORES: Eyeglasses, Prescription

Clarity Vision of Smithfield................ G 919 938-6101
  Smithfield (G-14454)
Luxottica of America Inc..................... G 910 867-0200
  Fayetteville (G-5862)
Luxottica of America Inc..................... G 919 778-5692
  Goldsboro (G-6632)

OPTICAL GOODS STORES: Opticians

Optical Place Inc.............................. E 336 274-1300
  Greensboro (G-7235)
Optics Inc...................................... G 336 288-9504
  Greensboro (G-7236)

OPTICAL INSTRUMENTS & APPARATUS

Advanced Photonic Crystals LLC......... G 803 547-0481
  Cornelius (G-4520)
ARW Optical Corp............................. G 910 452-7373
  Wilmington (G-16118)
Klearoptics Inc................................. G 760 224-6770
  Lattimore (G-9457)
Lightform Inc................................... G 908 281-9098
  Asheville (G-685)
Rk Enterprises LLC.......................... G 910 481-0777
  Fayetteville (G-5908)

OPTICAL INSTRUMENTS & LENSES

Corning Incorporated....................... D 910 784-7200
  Wilmington (G-16184)
Imagineoptix Corporation.................. F 919 757-4945
  Durham (G-5149)
M3 Products Com............................. G 631 938-1245
  Matthews (G-10329)
New Vision Investments Inc.............. G 336 757-1120
  Winston Salem (G-16820)
Optics Inc...................................... G 336 288-9504
  Greensboro (G-7236)
Optics Inc...................................... G 336 884-5677
  High Point (G-8471)
Opto Alignment Technology Inc......... E 704 893-0399
  Indian Trail (G-8954)
Precision Optics LLC....................... G 919 619-4468
  Chapel Hill (G-2055)
Roger D Thomas............................. G 919 258-3148
  Sanford (G-14176)
US Optics...................................... F 828 874-2242
  Connelly Springs (G-4410)

ORGANIZATIONS: Biotechnical Research, Noncommercial

Kbi Biopharma Inc........................... D 919 479-9898
  Durham (G-5177)

ORGANIZATIONS: Medical Research

King Phrmceuticals RES Dev LLC...... B 919 653-7001
  Cary (G-1803)

ORGANIZATIONS: Professional

American Inst Crtif Pub Accntn.......... B 919 402-0682
  Durham (G-4915)
Assoction Intl Crtif Prof Accn............ A 919 402-4500
  Durham (G-4930)

ORGANIZATIONS: Religious

Church Initiative Inc........................ E 919 562-2112
  Wake Forest (G-15540)
New Journey Now............................ G 336 234-1534
  Greensboro (G-7216)

ORGANIZATIONS: Research Institute

Fire Retardant Chem Tech LLC.......... G 980 253-8880
  Matthews (G-10316)

Parata Systems LLC........................ C 888 727-2821
  Durham (G-5270)

ORIENTED STRANDBOARD

Louisiana-Pacific Corporation............ G 336 696-2751
  Roaring River (G-13594)

OVENS: Paint Baking & Drying

Production Systems Inc.................... E 336 886-7161
  High Point (G-8499)
Superior Finishing Systems LLC........ G 336 956-2000
  Lexington (G-9788)

PACKAGE DESIGN SVCS

Piranha Industries Inc...................... G 704 248-7843
  Charlotte (G-3344)
Precision Concepts Intl LLC.............. C 704 360-8923
  Mooresville (G-11058)
St Johns Packaging Usa LLC............ C 336 292-9911
  Greensboro (G-7362)

PACKAGING & LABELING SVCS

J R Cole Industries Inc..................... D 704 523-6622
  Charlotte (G-3005)
Label & Printing Solutions Inc........... G 919 782-1242
  Raleigh (G-12950)
Lions Services Inc........................... B 704 921-1527
  Charlotte (G-3091)
Packaging Unlimited NC Inc.............. D 704 732-7100
  Lincolnton (G-9912)
Piranha Industries Inc...................... G 704 248-7843
  Charlotte (G-3344)
Royce Too LLC................................ E 212 356-1627
  Winston Salem (G-16891)
Salem One Inc................................ C 336 744-9990
  Winston Salem (G-16893)
Sanford Transition Company Inc........ E 919 775-4989
  Sanford (G-14182)
Thompson Printing & Packg Inc......... G 704 313-7323
  Mooresboro (G-10842)

PACKAGING MATERIALS, WHOLESALE

3d Packaging LLC............................ F 336 625-0652
  Asheboro (G-397)
Aseptia Inc..................................... C 678 373-6751
  Raleigh (G-12528)
Blue Stone Industries Ltd................. G 919 379-3986
  Cary (G-1709)
Cardinal Container Svcs Inc.............. D 336 249-6816
  Lexington (G-9689)
Conitex Sonoco Usa Inc................... C 704 864-5406
  Gastonia (G-6384)
Geami Ltd...................................... E 919 654-7700
  Raleigh (G-12791)
Global Packaging Inc....................... D 610 666-1608
  Hamlet (G-7622)
Interntnal Tray Pads Packg Inc.......... E 910 944-1800
  Aberdeen (G-8)
Loparex LLC................................... C 336 635-0192
  Eden (G-5496)
Mm Clayton LLC.............................. B 919 553-4113
  Clayton (G-3997)
Packaging Unlimited NC Inc.............. D 704 732-7100
  Lincolnton (G-9912)
Pactiv LLC..................................... G 910 944-1800
  Aberdeen (G-20)
Poly Packaging Systems Inc............. D 336 889-8334
  High Point (G-8489)
Pregis Innovative Packg LLC............. E 847 597-2200
  Granite Falls (G-6751)
Pretium Packaging LLC.................... E 336 621-1891
  Greensboro (G-7280)

RLM/Universal Packaging Inc............ F 336 644-6161
  Greensboro (G-7312)
Sonoco Hickory Inc.......................... D 828 328-2466
  Hickory (G-8163)
Storopack Inc.................................. G 800 827-7225
  Winston Salem (G-16918)
Tesa Tape Inc.................................. D 704 554-0707
  Charlotte (G-3682)
Thompson Printing & Packg Inc......... G 704 313-7323
  Mooresboro (G-10842)
Unified2 Globl Packg Group LLC....... C 774 696-3643
  Durham (G-5420)

PACKAGING MATERIALS: Paper

Abx Innvtive Pckg Slutions LLC......... D 980 443-1100
  Charlotte (G-2126)
Box Board Products Inc.................... C 336 668-3347
  Greensboro (G-6849)
Box Company of America LLC........... E 910 582-0100
  Hamlet (G-7617)
Challnge Prtg of Crlnas Inc Th.......... G 919 777-2820
  Sanford (G-14101)
Datamark Graphics Inc..................... G 336 629-0267
  Asheboro (G-422)
Ds Smith PLC.................................. E 919 557-3148
  Holly Springs (G-8696)
Dubose Strapping Inc....................... D 910 590-1020
  Clinton (G-4094)
Eastcoast Packaging Inc................... E 919 562-6060
  Middlesex (G-10447)
Graphic Packaging Intl LLC............... C 704 588-1750
  Charlotte (G-2856)
Induspac USA.................................. G 919 484-9484
  Durham (G-5151)
Interflex Acquisition Co LLC.............. C 336 921-3505
  Wilkesboro (G-16028)
Interntnal Tray Pads Packg Inc.......... E 910 944-1800
  Aberdeen (G-8)
Label Line Ltd................................. D 336 857-3115
  Asheboro (G-450)
Multi Packaging Solutions................. A 336 855-7142
  Greensboro (G-7207)
Npx One LLC.................................. C 910 997-2217
  Rockingham (G-13637)
NS Packaging LLC........................... F 800 688-7391
  Greensboro (G-7226)
Pactiv LLC..................................... D 252 527-6300
  Kinston (G-9380)
Poly Packaging Systems Inc............. D 336 889-8334
  High Point (G-8489)
Pregis Innovative Packg LLC............. E 847 597-2200
  Granite Falls (G-6751)
Printcraft Company Inc..................... E 336 248-2544
  Lexington (G-9773)
Quality Packaging Corp.................... G 336 881-5300
  High Point (G-8502)
R R Donnelley & Sons Company........ D 252 243-0337
  Wilson (G-16528)
Rgees LLC..................................... G 828 708-7178
  Arden (G-372)
Sealed Air Corporation (us)............... A 201 791-7600
  Charlotte (G-3518)
Sonoco Hickory Inc.......................... C 828 286-1356
  Forest City (G-6081)
St Johns Packaging Usa LLC............ C 336 292-9911
  Greensboro (G-7362)
Storopack Inc.................................. G 800 827-7225
  Winston Salem (G-16918)
Tarason Label Inc............................ G 828 464-4743
  Hickory (G-8174)
Valdese Packaging & Label Inc.......... E 828 879-9772
  Valdese (G-15456)

PRODUCT SECTION

PALLETS & SKIDS: Wood

Westrock Mwv LLC .... G 919 334-3200
Raleigh *(G-13419)*

PACKAGING MATERIALS: Paper, Coated Or Laminated

Atlantic Corporation .... D 910 343-0624
Wilmington *(G-16122)*

De Luxe Packaging Corp .... E 800 845-6051
Charlotte *(G-2608)*

PACKAGING MATERIALS: Plastic Film, Coated Or Laminated

Automated Solutions LLC .... F 828 396-9900
Granite Falls *(G-6723)*

Jbb Packaging LLC .... F 201 470-8501
Weldon *(G-15883)*

Jd2 Company LLC .... G 800 811-6441
Denver *(G-4786)*

Neopac Us Inc .... G 908 342-0990
Wilson *(G-16518)*

Paragon Films Inc .... F 828 632-5552
Taylorsville *(G-15154)*

Shurtech Brands LLC .... G 704 799-0779
Mooresville *(G-11086)*

PACKING & CRATING SVC

Broadwind Indus Solutions LLC .... E 919 777-2907
Sanford *(G-14096)*

Lls Investments Inc .... F 919 662-7283
Raleigh *(G-12976)*

PACKING MATERIALS: Mechanical

Interflex Acquisition Co LLC .... C 336 921-3505
Wilkesboro *(G-16031)*

Packaging Plus North Carolina .... F 336 643-4097
Summerfield *(G-14990)*

The Interflex Group Inc .... C 336 921-3505
Wilkesboro *(G-16045)*

PADS: Mattress

Bed In A Box .... G 800 588-5720
Mount Airy *(G-11482)*

Js Linens and Curtain Outlet .... F 704 871-1582
Statesville *(G-14829)*

Leggett & Platt Incorporated .... G 704 380-6208
Statesville *(G-14835)*

PAINTS & ADDITIVES

Auto Parts Fayetteville LLC .... G 910 889-4026
Fayetteville *(G-5766)*

Axalta Coating Systems Ltd .... E 336 802-4392
High Point *(G-8258)*

Crossroads Coatings Inc .... F 704 873-2244
Statesville *(G-14779)*

Highland International LLC .... F 828 265-2513
Boone *(G-1207)*

Keim Mineral Coatings Amer Inc .... F 704 588-4811
Charlotte *(G-3048)*

Paint Company of NC .... G 336 764-1648
Clemmons *(G-4054)*

Rack Works Inc .... E 336 368-1302
Pilot Mountain *(G-12201)*

Sherwin-Williams Company .... D 704 548-2820
Charlotte *(G-3541)*

Sherwin-Williams Company .... E 704 881-0245
Statesville *(G-14885)*

PAINTS & ALLIED PRODUCTS

Actega North America Inc .... G 704 736-9389
Iron Station *(G-8973)*

Akzo Nobel Coatings Inc .... E 336 841-5111
High Point *(G-8237)*

Americhem Inc .... E 704 782-6411
Concord *(G-4195)*

Axalta Coating Systems Ltd .... G 336 802-5701
High Point *(G-8257)*

Bay Painting Contractors .... G 252 435-5374
Moyock *(G-11692)*

Carolina Commercial Coatings .... G 910 279-6045
Wilmington *(G-16157)*

Cdv LLC .... F 919 674-3460
Morrisville *(G-11316)*

Electric Glass Fiber Amer LLC .... B 704 434-2261
Shelby *(G-14313)*

Ennis-Flint .... G 336 477-8439
Thomasville *(G-15219)*

Ennis-Flint Inc .... G 800 331-8118
Thomasville *(G-15220)*

Ennis-Flint Inc .... F 800 331-8118
Greensboro *(G-7000)*

Flint Acquisition Corp .... D 336 475-6600
Thomasville *(G-15222)*

Flint Ennis Inc .... G 800 331-8118
High Point *(G-8354)*

Flint Trading Inc .... F 336 308-3770
Thomasville *(G-15223)*

Kestrel I Acquisition Corporation .... A 919 990-7500
Durham *(G-5180)*

Liquidating Reichhold Inc .... A 919 990-7500
Durham *(G-5191)*

Lubrizol Global Management Inc .... D 704 865-7451
Gastonia *(G-6447)*

Matlab Inc .... F 336 629-4161
Asheboro *(G-457)*

Modern Recreational Tech .... E 847 272-2278
Hickory *(G-8096)*

Northwest Coatings Systems Inc .... G 336 924-1459
Pfafftown *(G-12188)*

Piedmont Indus Coatings Inc .... G 336 377-3399
Winston Salem *(G-16854)*

PPG Architectural Finishes Inc .... G 910 484-5161
Fayetteville *(G-5899)*

PPG Architectural Finishes Inc .... G 704 864-6783
Gastonia *(G-6493)*

PPG Architectural Finishes Inc .... G 336 273-9761
Greensboro *(G-7271)*

PPG Architectural Finishes Inc .... G 704 847-7251
Matthews *(G-10282)*

PPG Architectural Finishes Inc .... G 704 658-9250
Mooresville *(G-11056)*

PPG Architectural Finishes Inc .... G 828 438-9210
Morganton *(G-11242)*

PPG Architectural Finishes Inc .... G 919 981-0600
Raleigh *(G-13126)*

PPG Architectural Finishes Inc .... G 919 872-6500
Raleigh *(G-13127)*

PPG Architectural Finishes Inc .... G 919 779-5400
Raleigh *(G-13128)*

PPG Architectural Finishes Inc .... G 704 633-0673
Salisbury *(G-14028)*

PPG Industries Inc .... G 919 319-0113
Cary *(G-1857)*

PPG Industries Inc .... G 704 542-8880
Charlotte *(G-3364)*

PPG Industries Inc .... G 704 523-0888
Charlotte *(G-3365)*

PPG Industries Inc .... G 919 382-3100
Durham *(G-5300)*

PPG Industries Inc .... G 919 772-3093
Greensboro *(G-7272)*

PPG Industries Inc .... G 252 480-1970
Kill Devil Hills *(G-9262)*

PPG Industries Inc .... G 704 658-9250
Mooresville *(G-11057)*

PPG Industries Inc .... G 919 981-0600
Raleigh *(G-13129)*

PPG Industries Inc .... G 910 452-3289
Wilmington *(G-16368)*

PPG Industries Inc .... G 336 771-8878
Winston Salem *(G-16862)*

Renaissance Innovations LLC .... E 774 901-4642
Durham *(G-5324)*

Renaissance Innovations LLC .... G 844 473-7246
Apex *(G-239)*

Road Infrstrcture Inv Hldngs I .... E 336 475-6600
Thomasville *(G-15271)*

Rust-Oleum Corporation .... G 704 662-7730
Mooresville *(G-11077)*

S&F Products .... G 714 412-1298
Holly Springs *(G-8714)*

Sherwin-Williams Company .... G 919 436-2460
Raleigh *(G-13248)*

Sibelco North America Inc .... D 828 766-6050
Spruce Pine *(G-14656)*

PAINTS, VARNISHES & SPLYS WHOLESALERS

Keim Mineral Coatings Amer Inc .... F 704 588-4811
Charlotte *(G-3048)*

PAINTS, VARNISHES & SPLYS, WHOLESALE: Paints

Akzo Nobel Coatings Inc .... G 336 665-9897
Greensboro *(G-6787)*

Controlled Release Tech Inc .... G 704 487-0878
Shelby *(G-14303)*

Highland International LLC .... F 828 265-2513
Boone *(G-1207)*

Renaissance Innovations LLC .... G 844 473-7246
Apex *(G-239)*

Sherwin-Williams Company .... E 336 292-3000
Greensboro *(G-7335)*

PAINTS: Oil Or Alkyd Vehicle Or Water Thinned

Akzo Nobel Coatings Inc .... F 704 366-8435
Charlotte *(G-2150)*

Akzo Nobel Coatings Inc .... G 336 665-9897
Greensboro *(G-6787)*

Allied Pressroom Products Inc .... E 954 920-0909
Monroe *(G-10641)*

PALLET LOADERS & UNLOADERS

Kinston Neuse Corporation .... C 252 522-3088
Kinston *(G-9372)*

PALLET REPAIR SVCS

Gamble Associates Inc .... F 704 375-9301
Charlotte *(G-2806)*

MAC Grading Co .... F 910 531-4642
Autryville *(G-842)*

Neal S Pallet Company Inc .... E 704 393-8568
Charlotte *(G-3242)*

PALLETS & SKIDS: Wood

Alan Kimzey .... G 828 891-8720
Mills River *(G-10498)*

Clary Lumber Company .... D 252 537-2558
Gaston *(G-6330)*

Glenn Lumber Company Inc .... E 704 434-7873
Shelby *(G-14320)*

PALLETS & SKIDS: Wood

Johnston County Industries Inc............. C 919 743-8700
  Selma *(G-14257)*

McBride Lumber Co Partnr LLC............. F 910 428-2747
  Star *(G-14721)*

Pallets and More................................ G 919 815-6134
  Franklinton *(G-6162)*

Somers Lumber and Mfg Inc............... F
  Harmony *(G-7690)*

Steelman Lumber & Pallet LLC........... F 336 468-2757
  Hamptonville *(G-7678)*

Tri-County Industries Inc.................... C 252 977-3800
  Rocky Mount *(G-13676)*

Triple C Companies LLC..................... E 704 966-1999
  Denver *(G-4811)*

Universal Forest Products Inc............. F 252 338-0319
  Elizabeth City *(G-5580)*

PALLETS: Wood & Metal Combination

Propak Logistics................................ G 704 471-1070
  Shelby *(G-14358)*

T P Supply Co Inc............................... E 336 789-2337
  Mount Airy *(G-11585)*

PANEL & DISTRIBUTION BOARDS & OTHER RELATED APPARATUS

Elster Solutions LLC........................... B 919 212-4819
  Raleigh *(G-12733)*

PANELS: Building, Metal

Bonitz Inc.. E 803 799-0181
  Concord *(G-4213)*

PANELS: Building, Plastic, NEC

Whiteville Plywood Inc........................ F 910 642-7114
  Whiteville *(G-15981)*

PAPER & BOARD: Die-cut

Boingo Graphics Inc............................ E 704 527-4963
  Charlotte *(G-2331)*

Box Company of America LLC............ E 910 582-0100
  Hamlet *(G-7617)*

Lakebrook Corporation........................ G 207 947-4051
  Oak Island *(G-12052)*

Morrisette Paper Company Inc............ G 336 342-5570
  Reidsville *(G-13533)*

Mueller Die Cut Solutions Inc.............. E 704 588-3900
  Charlotte *(G-3213)*

Triangle Converting Corp.................... E 919 596-6656
  Durham *(G-5407)*

PAPER & PAPER PRDTS: Crepe, Made From Purchased Materials

Rgees LLC... G 828 708-7178
  Arden *(G-372)*

PAPER PRDTS: Cleansing Tissues, Made From Purchased Material

Cardinal Tissue LLC........................... D 815 503-2096
  Spindale *(G-14605)*

PAPER PRDTS: Infant & Baby Prdts

Shower ME With Love LLC.................. F 704 302-1555
  Charlotte *(G-3542)*

PAPER PRDTS: Napkin Stock

Nakos Paper Products Inc................... G 704 238-0717
  Charlotte *(G-3229)*

PAPER PRDTS: Pressed & Molded Pulp & Fiber Prdts

Reynolds Consumer Products Inc......... A 704 371-5550
  Huntersville *(G-8885)*

PAPER PRDTS: Sanitary

Attends Healthcare Pdts Inc................. G 252 752-1100
  Greenville *(G-7488)*

Attends Healthcare Products Inc.......... B 800 428-8363
  Raleigh *(G-12532)*

Edtech Systems LLC........................... G 919 341-0613
  Raleigh *(G-12727)*

Hygiene Systems Inc........................... E 910 462-2661
  Laurel Hill *(G-9461)*

Kimberly-Clark Corporation.................. C 828 698-5230
  Hendersonville *(G-7869)*

Livedo Usa Inc.................................... D 252 237-1373
  Wilson *(G-16513)*

Pacon Manufacturing Corp LLC............ C 732 764-9070
  Navassa *(G-11758)*

Sealed Air Corporation......................... D 828 728-6610
  Hudson *(G-8779)*

PAPER PRDTS: Sanitary Tissue Paper

Kimberly-Clark Corporation.................. C 828 698-5230
  Hendersonville *(G-7869)*

PAPER PRDTS: Toilet Paper, Made From Purchased Materials

Cascades Tissue Group - NC Inc........ C 910 895-4033
  Rockingham *(G-13622)*

PAPER PRDTS: Toilet Tissue, Stock

M Davis and Associates LLC.............. G 336 337-7089
  Greensboro *(G-7172)*

PAPER, WHOLESALE: Fine

McGrann Paper Corporation.................. E 800 240-9455
  Charlotte *(G-3151)*

PAPER, WHOLESALE: Printing

Jasie Blanks LLC................................ F 910 485-0016
  Fayetteville *(G-5846)*

PAPER: Absorbent

Abzorbit Inc.. F 828 464-9944
  Newton *(G-11911)*

Encertec Inc....................................... G 336 288-7226
  Greensboro *(G-6997)*

Evergreen Packaging LLC.................... B 828 454-0676
  Canton *(G-1615)*

PAPER: Adhesive

Avery Dennison Corporation................. G 336 553-2436
  Greensboro *(G-6825)*

T - Square Enterprises Inc.................. G 704 846-8233
  Charlotte *(G-3667)*

Tailored Chemical Products Inc........... D 828 322-6512
  Hickory *(G-8173)*

PAPER: Book

Annes Books and Papers..................... G 336 608-8612
  Winston Salem *(G-16605)*

Enriched Abundance Entp LLC............. F 704 369-6363
  Charlotte *(G-2715)*

Glatfelter Corporation.......................... A 704 885-2555
  Charlotte *(G-2831)*

PAPER: Building Laminated, Made From Purchased Materials

Acucote Inc....................................... C 336 578-1800
  Graham *(G-6677)*

Cdv LLC.. F 919 674-3460
  Morrisville *(G-11316)*

PAPER: Building, Insulating & Packaging

Hibco Plastics Inc.............................. E 336 463-2391
  Yadkinville *(G-17040)*

Technical Coating Intl Inc.................... E 910 371-0860
  Belville *(G-1026)*

PAPER: Cardboard

Sonoco Products Company.................. G 910 455-6903
  Jacksonville *(G-9034)*

PAPER: Cigarette

Filtrona Filters Inc............................... D 336 362-1333
  Greensboro *(G-7015)*

PAPER: Coated & Laminated, NEC

Avery Dennison Corporation................. D 336 621-2570
  Greensboro *(G-6824)*

Avery Dennison Rfid Company............. F 626 304-2000
  Greensboro *(G-6829)*

Datamark Graphics Inc........................ E 336 629-0267
  Asheboro *(G-422)*

Intertape Polymer Corp........................ D 980 907-4871
  Midland *(G-10469)*

J C Enterprises.................................. G 336 986-1688
  Winston Salem *(G-16765)*

LIflex LLC... C 336 777-5000
  Winston Salem *(G-16791)*

Oracle Flexible Packaging Inc.............. B 336 777-5000
  Winston Salem *(G-16831)*

R T Barbee Company Inc.................... F 704 375-4421
  Charlotte *(G-3406)*

TEC Graphics Inc................................ F 919 567-2077
  Fuquay Varina *(G-6232)*

Technical Coating Intl Inc.................... E 910 371-0860
  Belville *(G-1026)*

Tesa Tape Inc.................................... D 704 554-0707
  Charlotte *(G-3682)*

Upm Raflatac Inc................................ F 828 335-3289
  Fletcher *(G-6047)*

Upm Raflatac Inc................................ F 828 651-4800
  Fletcher *(G-6048)*

PAPER: Coated, Exc Photographic, Carbon Or Abrasive

Avery Dennison Corporation................. G 864 938-1400
  Greensboro *(G-6827)*

Avery Dennison Corporation................. F 336 665-6481
  Greensboro *(G-6828)*

Blue Ridge Paper Products LLC........... C 828 452-0834
  Waynesville *(G-15795)*

Loparex LLC...................................... D 919 678-7700
  Cary *(G-1814)*

PAPER: Corrugated

Box Company of America LLC............ E 910 582-0100
  Hamlet *(G-7617)*

Carolina Container Company............... D 336 883-7146
  High Point *(G-8284)*

Quality Packaging Corp....................... G 336 881-5300
  High Point *(G-8502)*

PAPER: Fine

PRODUCT SECTION — PET SPLYS

Blue Ridge Paper Products LLC............. C 828 235-3023
  Canton *(G-1602)*
Blue Ridge Paper Products LLC............. D 828 454-0676
  Canton *(G-1601)*

PAPER: Packaging

Ds Smith Packaging and Paper................ G 336 668-0871
  Greensboro *(G-6980)*
Geami Ltd... E 919 654-7700
  Raleigh *(G-12791)*
Ranpak Corp.. G 919 790-8225
  Raleigh *(G-13190)*
Westrock Shared Services LLC............. A 336 642-4165
  Rural Hall *(G-13855)*

PAPER: Specialty

Glatfelter Corporation........................... G 828 877-2110
  Pisgah Forest *(G-12323)*
Westrock Kraft Paper LLC..................... G 252 533-6000
  Roanoke Rapids *(G-13586)*

PAPER: Tissue

Cascades Tissue Group - NC Inc......... C 910 895-4033
  Rockingham *(G-13622)*
Laurel Hill Paper Co.............................. E 910 997-4526
  Cordova *(G-4518)*

PAPER: Wrapping & Packaging

Pregis LLC.. D 828 396-2373
  Granite Falls *(G-6752)*
Transcontinental AC US LLC................ F 704 847-9171
  Matthews *(G-10296)*

PAPERBOARD PRDTS: Folding Boxboard

Kme Consolidated Inc........................... E 704 847-9888
  Matthews *(G-10260)*
Printing & Packaging Inc....................... E 704 482-3866
  Shelby *(G-14357)*

PAPERBOARD PRDTS: Setup Boxboard

Napco Inc.. C 336 372-5214
  Sparta *(G-14597)*

PARACHUTES

Ballistic Recovery Systems Inc............. E 651 457-7491
  Pinebluff *(G-12213)*
Mills Manufacturing Corp....................... C 828 645-3061
  Asheville *(G-703)*
North Amercn Aerodynamics Inc........... D 336 599-9266
  Roxboro *(G-13809)*
Piedmont Parachute Inc....................... G 336 597-2225
  Roxboro *(G-13819)*
Saab Barracuda LLC............................ E 910 814-3088
  Lillington *(G-9859)*

PARTICLEBOARD

Aconcagua Timber Corp....................... B 919 542-2128
  Moncure *(G-10612)*
Arauco - NA.. G 910 569-7020
  Biscoe *(G-1103)*
Olon Industries Inc (us)........................ F 630 232-4705
  Mocksville *(G-10596)*

PARTICLEBOARD: Laminated, Plastic

Egger Wood Products LLC................... B 336 843-7000
  Linwood *(G-9943)*
Georgia-Pacific LLC.............................. D 919 580-1078
  Dudley *(G-4843)*

PARTITIONS & FIXTURES: Except Wood

B&H Millwork and Fixtures Inc.............. E 336 431-0068
  High Point *(G-8260)*

Chatsworth Products Inc....................... C 252 514-2779
  New Bern *(G-11788)*
Coregrp LLC... F 845 876-5109
  Mooresville *(G-10914)*
Cub Creek Kitchens & Baths Inc.......... F 336 651-8983
  North Wilkesboro *(G-12004)*
Ds Smith PLC....................................... E 919 557-3148
  Holly Springs *(G-8696)*
E G A Products Inc............................... F 704 664-1221
  Mooresville *(G-10932)*
Hemco Wire Products Inc..................... F 336 454-7280
  Jamestown *(G-9052)*
Idx Corporation..................................... C 252 948-2048
  Washington *(G-15710)*
Leisure Craft Holdings LLC................... D 828 693-8241
  Flat Rock *(G-5967)*
Leisure Craft Inc................................... C 828 693-8241
  Flat Rock *(G-5968)*
Madix.. G 804 456-3007
  Raleigh *(G-12986)*
Parker Brothers Incorporated................ G 910 564-4132
  Clinton *(G-4100)*
Sid Jenkins Inc..................................... G 336 632-0707
  Greensboro *(G-7337)*
Stanly Fixtures Company Inc................ F 704 474-3184
  Norwood *(G-12045)*
Technibilt Ltd.. E 828 464-7388
  Newton *(G-11976)*
Thomasvlle Mtal Fbricators Inc............. E 336 248-4992
  Lexington *(G-9792)*
Treeforms Inc.. E 336 292-8998
  Greensboro *(G-7409)*

PARTITIONS: Wood & Fixtures

3c Store Fixtures Inc............................ D 252 291-5181
  Wilson *(G-16461)*
Amcase Inc... E 336 784-5992
  High Point *(G-8244)*
Carolina Store Fixtures LLC................. G 252 508-0110
  Jamesville *(G-9079)*
Corilam Fabricating Co......................... E 336 993-2371
  Kernersville *(G-9182)*
Craft Woodwork Inc.............................. G 252 237-7581
  Wilson *(G-16490)*
Cub Creek Kitchens & Baths Inc.......... F 336 651-8983
  North Wilkesboro *(G-12004)*
E T Sales Inc.. E 704 888-4010
  Midland *(G-10467)*
Hardwood Store of NC Inc.................... F 336 449-9627
  Gibsonville *(G-6561)*
Marsh Furniture Company.................... F 336 273-8196
  Greensboro *(G-7182)*
Michael Parker Cabinetry..................... G 919 833-5117
  Raleigh *(G-13024)*
Normac Kitchens Inc............................ F 704 485-1911
  Oakboro *(G-12079)*
Reliable Construction Co Inc................ E 704 289-1501
  Monroe *(G-10795)*
Relic Wood LLC.................................... G 828 855-8924
  Taylorsville *(G-15160)*
Rugby Acquisition LLC.......................... D 336 993-8686
  Kernersville *(G-9229)*
Sheets Smith Wealth MGT Inc.............. E 336 765-2020
  Winston Salem *(G-16907)*
Thompson Millwork LLC....................... D 919 596-8236
  Mebane *(G-10433)*
Ullman Group LLC................................ F 704 246-7333
  Charlotte *(G-3747)*
Wilsonart LLC....................................... ..... 866 267-7360
  Fletcher *(G-6052)*

PARTS: Metal

Alloy Fabricators Inc............................. E 704 263-2281
  Alexis *(G-121)*
Classic Car Metal & Parts LLC............. G 919 567-0693
  Fuquay Varina *(G-6187)*
Lrs Technology Inc............................... G 336 669-5982
  Lexington *(G-9752)*
Royall Development Co Inc.................. C 336 889-2569
  High Point *(G-8517)*

PATTERNS: Indl

Lampe & Malphrus Lumber Co............ F 919 934-1124
  Smithfield *(G-14471)*
Pattern Box.. G 704 535-8743
  Charlotte *(G-3318)*
Sweet Tea Girls Patterns...................... G 843 907-2727
  Clayton *(G-4015)*

PAVERS

AAA Paver Care Inc............................. G 828 687-1669
  Fletcher *(G-5979)*
J & M Pavers LLC................................. G 704 776-6613
  Monroe *(G-10743)*
Young & McQueen Grading Co Inc...... D 828 682-7714
  Burnsville *(G-1539)*

PERFUME: Perfumes, Natural Or Synthetic

Coty US LLC... A 919 895-5374
  Sanford *(G-14106)*
Scentair Technologies LLC................... D 704 504-2320
  Charlotte *(G-3498)*
Up On Hill... G 704 664-7971
  Troutman *(G-15397)*

PERFUMES

Carolina Perfumer Inc........................... G 910 295-5600
  Pinehurst *(G-12217)*

PESTICIDES

Nutrien AG Solutions Inc...................... F 252 977-2025
  Rocky Mount *(G-13670)*

PET SPLYS

Asheville Pet Supply............................. G 828 252-2054
  Asheville *(G-540)*
Care A Lot Pet Supply.......................... G 757 457-9425
  Moyock *(G-11694)*
Fill Pac LLC.. F 828 322-1916
  Hickory *(G-8024)*
G H Group LLC..................................... G 919 264-0939
  Raleigh *(G-12789)*
Hudson S Hardware Inc........................ E 919 553-3030
  Garner *(G-6276)*
Kennel-Aire LLC.................................... E 704 459-0044
  Norwood *(G-12039)*
L & B Jandrew Enterprises................... G 828 687-8927
  Hendersonville *(G-7871)*
Legacy River Company......................... G 704 618-7260
  Charlotte *(G-3081)*
Lizmere Cavaliers................................. G 704 418-2543
  Shelby *(G-14339)*
Microfine Inc... G 336 768-1480
  Winston Salem *(G-16809)*
Protect Adoptable Labs........................ G 253 383-2733
  Asheville *(G-746)*
Stellar Innovations Inc.......................... G 704 746-2886
  Cornelius *(G-4588)*
Tarheel Old English Sheepdog............. G 336 499-6788
  Lewisville *(G-9674)*
Titan Land Group LLC.......................... G 704 400-1842
  Charlotte *(G-3696)*

Employee Codes: A=Over 500 employees, B=251-500
C=101-250, D=51-100, E=20-50, F=10-19, G=1-9

PET SPLYS

Walco International..................G..... 704 624-2473
  Marshville *(G-10228)*

PETROLEUM BULK STATIONS & TERMINALS

Warren Oil Company LLC............D..... 910 892-6456
  Dunn *(G-4890)*

PHARMACEUTICAL PREPARATIONS: Adrenal

Cell Microsystems Inc..............G..... 919 608-2035
  Durham *(G-5010)*
Daily Manufacturing Inc............F..... 704 782-0700
  Rockwell *(G-13651)*
Glenmark Phrmceuticals Inc USA....D..... 704 218-2600
  Monroe *(G-10723)*
M&M Bioplastic LLC.................G..... 877 366-5227
  Mill Spring *(G-10488)*

PHARMACEUTICAL PREPARATIONS: Druggists' Preparations

Cardioxyl Pharmaceuticals Inc......G..... 919 869-8586
  Chapel Hill *(G-1997)*
Gale Global Research Inc...........G..... 910 795-8595
  Leland *(G-9545)*
Hospira Inc........................F..... 704 335-1300
  Charlotte *(G-2923)*
Mylan Pharmaceuticals Inc..........E..... 336 271-6571
  Greensboro *(G-7211)*
Natures Pharmacy Inc...............G..... 828 251-0094
  Asheville *(G-710)*
New Paradigm Therapeutics Inc......G..... 919 259-0026
  Chapel Hill *(G-2047)*
Niras Inc..........................G..... 919 439-4562
  Cary *(G-1831)*
Patheon Manufacturing Svcs LLC.....D..... 252 758-3436
  Greenville *(G-7568)*
Pharmagra Holding Company LLC......E..... 828 884-8656
  Brevard *(G-1284)*
Raybow Usa Inc.....................F..... 828 884-8656
  Brevard *(G-1286)*
Synthonix Inc......................F..... 919 875-9277
  Wake Forest *(G-15601)*
Tavros Therapeutics Inc............E..... 919 602-2631
  Durham *(G-5387)*
V1 Pharma LLC......................G..... 919 338-5744
  Raleigh *(G-13388)*

PHARMACEUTICAL PREPARATIONS: Pills

Bayer Corporation..................E..... 800 242-5897
  Durham *(G-4949)*
Eppin Pharma Inc...................G..... 919 608-2984
  Chapel Hill *(G-2017)*

PHARMACEUTICAL PREPARATIONS: Proprietary Drug

Anelleo Inc........................G..... 919 448-4008
  Chapel Hill *(G-1984)*
Arrivo Management LLC..............G..... 919 460-9500
  Morrisville *(G-11292)*
Avior Inc..........................G..... 919 234-0068
  Cary *(G-1697)*
Camargo Phrm Svcs LLC..............G..... 513 618-0325
  Durham *(G-4995)*
Carolinas Cord Blood Bank..........G..... 919 668-1102
  Durham *(G-5006)*
Cornerstone Biopharma Inc..........F..... 919 678-6507
  Cary *(G-1735)*

PHARMACEUTICAL PREPARATIONS: Solutions

Fsc Therapeutics LLC...............F..... 704 941-2500
  Charlotte *(G-2799)*
Tripharm Services Inc..............F..... 984 243-0800
  Morrisville *(G-11457)*

PHARMACEUTICAL PREPARATIONS: Tablets

Nutraceutical Lf Sciences Inc......B..... 336 956-0800
  Lexington *(G-9765)*

PHARMACEUTICALS

A1 Biochem Labs LLC................G..... 315 299-4775
  Wilmington *(G-16090)*
A2a Integrated Logistics Inc.......G..... 800 493-3736
  Fayetteville *(G-5749)*
Abbott Enterprises.................B..... 252 757-1298
  Greenville *(G-7477)*
Abbott Laboratories................G..... 704 243-1832
  Waxhaw *(G-15743)*
Abbott Sales LLC...................G..... 919 523-5478
  Raleigh *(G-12460)*
Accord Healthcare Inc..............E..... 919 941-7878
  Raleigh *(G-12467)*
Aceragen Inc.......................G..... 919 271-1032
  Durham *(G-4900)*
Achelios Therapeutics LLC..........G..... 919 354-6233
  Durham *(G-4901)*
Aerami Therapeutics Inc............F..... 650 773-5926
  Durham *(G-4905)*
Aerami Thrpeutics Holdings Inc.....G..... 919 589-7495
  Durham *(G-4906)*
Aerie Pharmaceuticals Inc..........G..... 919 237-5300
  Durham *(G-4907)*
Albemarle Corporation..............A..... 980 299-5700
  Charlotte *(G-2152)*
Albion Medical Holdings Inc........F..... 800 378-3906
  Lenoir *(G-9571)*
Alcami Carolinas Corporation.......G..... 919 957-5500
  Durham *(G-4911)*
Alcami Carolinas Corporation.......G..... 910 254-7000
  Morrisville *(G-11281)*
Alcami Carolinas Corporation.......F..... 910 254-7000
  Wilmington *(G-16100)*
Alcami Carolinas Corporation.......G..... 910 254-7000
  Wilmington *(G-16101)*
Alcami Carolinas Corporation.......G..... 910 254-7000
  Wilmington *(G-16102)*
Alcami Corporation.................A..... 910 254-7000
  Wilmington *(G-16104)*
Alcami Holdings LLC................A..... 910 254-7000
  Wilmington *(G-16105)*
American Pharmaceutical Svcs.......G..... 828 328-1816
  Hickory *(G-7933)*
Arbor Pharmaceuticals Inc..........G..... 919 792-1700
  Raleigh *(G-12517)*
Areteia Therapeutics Inc...........F..... 973 985-0597
  Chapel Hill *(G-1985)*
Aristos Pharmaceuticals Inc........F..... 919 678-6592
  Cary *(G-1687)*
Array Biopharma Inc................D..... 303 381-6600
  Morrisville *(G-11291)*
Ascend Research Corp...............G..... 336 710-5793
  Winston Salem *(G-16611)*
Askbio.............................G..... 336 407-6217
  Durham *(G-4929)*
Asklepios Bopharmaceutical Inc.....C..... 919 561-6210
  Morrisville *(G-11294)*
Astrazeneca Pharmaceuticals LP.....D..... 919 647-4990
  Durham *(G-4931)*

Atsena Therapeutics Inc............E..... 352 273-9342
  Durham *(G-4935)*
Aurobindo Pharma USA Inc...........E..... 732 839-9400
  Durham *(G-4936)*
Aurolife Pharma LLC................E..... 732 839-9408
  Durham *(G-4937)*
Avadim Holdings Inc................E..... 877 677-2723
  Asheville *(G-551)*
Avadim Holdings Inc................E..... 877 677-2723
  Charlotte *(G-2244)*
Avient Protective Mtls LLC.........D..... 704 862-5100
  Stanley *(G-14684)*
Avista Pharma Solutions Inc........E..... 919 544-8600
  Durham *(G-4939)*
Axitare Corporation................G..... 919 256-8196
  Raleigh *(G-12537)*
B3 Bio Inc.........................G..... 919 226-3079
  Durham *(G-4940)*
Balanced Pharma Incorporated.......G..... 704 278-7054
  Cornelius *(G-4525)*
Bausch Health Americas Inc.........F..... 949 461-6000
  Durham *(G-4948)*
Baxter Healthcare Corporation......B..... 828 756-6600
  Marion *(G-10142)*
Baxter Healthcare Corporation......F..... 828 756-6623
  Marion *(G-10143)*
Bayer Corp.........................E..... 704 373-0991
  Charlotte *(G-2288)*
Bayer Cropscience Inc..............D..... 412 777-2000
  Durham *(G-4950)*
Bayer Healthcare LLC...............E..... 919 461-6525
  Morrisville *(G-11300)*
Bayer Hlthcare Pharmaceuticals.....G..... 602 469-6846
  Raleigh *(G-12546)*
Be Pharmaceuticals Inc.............G..... 704 560-1444
  Cary *(G-1699)*
Beaker Inc.........................F..... 919 803-7422
  Raleigh *(G-12549)*
Bestco LLC.........................E..... 704 664-4300
  Mooresville *(G-10876)*
Bestco LLC.........................C..... 704 664-4300
  Mooresville *(G-10877)*
Bestco LLC.........................C..... 704 664-4300
  Mooresville *(G-10878)*
Biocryst Pharmaceuticals Inc.......B..... 919 859-1302
  Durham *(G-4958)*
Biogen MA Inc......................C..... 919 941-1100
  Durham *(G-4959)*
Biogen Pharma......................G..... 919 993-1100
  Morrisville *(G-11303)*
Biomontr Labs......................G..... 919 650-1185
  Cary *(G-1704)*
Bioresource International Inc......G..... 919 267-3758
  Apex *(G-171)*
Bpc Plasma Inc.....................F..... 910 463-2603
  Jacksonville *(G-8991)*
Bpl Usa LLC........................F..... 919 354-8405
  Durham *(G-4975)*
Bright Path Laboratories Inc.......G..... 858 281-8121
  Kannapolis *(G-9112)*
Brii Biosciences Inc...............F..... 919 240-5605
  Durham *(G-4980)*
Bristol-Myers Squibb Company.......G..... 800 321-1335
  Charlotte *(G-2357)*
Bristol-Myers Squibb Company.......B..... 336 855-5500
  Greensboro *(G-6857)*
Cambrex High Point Inc.............D..... 336 841-5250
  High Point *(G-8281)*
Capnostics LLC.....................F..... 610 442-1363
  Concord *(G-4223)*
Cardinal Health 414 LLC............G..... 704 644-7989
  Charlotte *(G-2387)*

PHARMACEUTICALS

Cardiopharma Inc.................................F 910 791-1361
  Wilmington *(G-16156)*
Catalent Greenville Inc.......................E 732 537-6200
  Greenville *(G-7499)*
Catalent Greenville Inc.......................D 252 752-3800
  Greenville *(G-7500)*
Catalent Pharma Solutions LLC..........F 919 481-4855
  Morrisville *(G-11313)*
Catalent Pharma Solutions LLC..........C 919 481-4855
  Morrisville *(G-11314)*
Catalent Pharma Solutions Inc............F 919 465-8206
  Durham *(G-5008)*
Catalent Pharma Solutions Inc............F 919 481-2614
  Morrisville *(G-11315)*
Cem-102 Pharmaceuticals Inc.............G 919 576-2306
  Chapel Hill *(G-2000)*
Cempra Pharmaceuticals Inc...............F 919 803-6882
  Chapel Hill *(G-2001)*
Cenerx Biopharma Inc..........................G 919 234-4072
  Cary *(G-1727)*
Certirx Corporation...............................G 919 354-1029
  Rtp *(G-13830)*
Chemogenics Biopharma LLC.............G 919 323-8133
  Durham *(G-5015)*
Chimerix Inc..E 919 806-1074
  Durham *(G-5016)*
Civentichem Usa LLC..........................G 919 672-8865
  Cary *(G-1731)*
Cleveland Compounding Inc................G 704 487-1971
  Shelby *(G-14297)*
Closure Medical Corporation................C 919 876-7800
  Raleigh *(G-12630)*
Cloud Pharmaceuticals Inc...................G 919 558-1254
  Durham *(G-5021)*
Cmp Pharma Inc...................................E 252 753-7111
  Farmville *(G-5732)*
Cosette Pharmaceuticals Inc................C 704 735-5700
  Lincolnton *(G-9885)*
Cosette Phrmctcals NC Labs LLC........C 908 753-2000
  Lincolnton *(G-9886)*
Dataspectrum..G 919 341-3200
  Raleigh *(G-12673)*
Davospharma...G 919 662-8432
  Apex *(G-180)*
Delarrivo Inc..G 919 460-9500
  Morrisville *(G-11330)*
Diagnostic Devices................................G 704 599-5908
  Charlotte *(G-2627)*
Dignify Inc...G 336 500-8668
  Greensboro *(G-6971)*
Dignify Therapeutics LLC....................G 919 371-8138
  Durham *(G-5052)*
Diomorph Pharmaceuticals LP.............G 919 354-6233
  Chapel Hill *(G-2009)*
Docent Pharma Services LLC...............G 229 310-0111
  Apex *(G-183)*
Dova Pharmaceuticals Inc.....................F 919 748-5975
  Durham *(G-5060)*
Dpi Newco LLC......................................A 252 758-3436
  Greenville *(G-7516)*
Dsk Biopharma Inc................................G 919 465-9104
  Morrisville *(G-11336)*
DSM..G 408 582-2610
  Greenville *(G-7517)*
Dsm Inc...F 919 876-2802
  Raleigh *(G-12706)*
DSM Pharmaceuticals Inc.....................E 252 758-3436
  Greenville *(G-7518)*
DSM Pharmaceuticals Inc.....................A 252 758-3436
  Greenville *(G-7519)*
East Coast Biologics..............................G 717 919-9980
  Fayetteville *(G-5815)*

Ei LLC..B 704 857-0707
  Winston Salem *(G-16692)*
Eisai Inc...F 919 941-6920
  Raleigh *(G-12728)*
Elanco US Inc..F 812 230-2745
  Greensboro *(G-6992)*
Eli Company..G 908 242-3497
  Winston Salem *(G-16695)*
Eli Lilly and Company...........................F 317 296-1226
  Durham *(G-5078)*
Embrex Poultry Health LLC..................F 910 844-5566
  Maxton *(G-10355)*
Encube Ethicals Inc...............................F 984 439-2761
  Durham *(G-5085)*
Engineered Processing Eqp LLC..........G 919 321-6891
  Wilson *(G-16496)*
Environmental Science US LLC...........F 800 331-2867
  Cary *(G-1759)*
Envisia Therapeutics Inc.......................E 919 973-1440
  Durham *(G-5090)*
Eon Labs Inc..B 252 234-2222
  Wilson *(G-16497)*
Exela Drug Substance LLC...................E 828 758-5474
  Lenoir *(G-9607)*
Exela Pharma Sciences LLC................E 828 758-5474
  Lenoir *(G-9608)*
Exp Pharmaceuticals Inc........................F 336 631-2893
  Winston Salem *(G-16704)*
Fervent Pharmaceuticals LLC..............G 252 558-9700
  Greenville *(G-7525)*
Fidelity Pharmaceuticals LLC..............G 704 274-3192
  Huntersville *(G-8819)*
Fortovia Therapeutics Inc......................G 919 872-5578
  Raleigh *(G-12779)*
Fortrea Holdings Inc..............................E 877 495-0816
  Durham *(G-5102)*
Fresenius Kabi Usa LLC......................B 252 991-2692
  Wilson *(G-16499)*
Fujifilm Diosynth Biotechnolog............G 919 337-4400
  Durham *(G-5107)*
Fujifilm Dsynth Btchnlgies USA..........C 919 337-4400
  Morrisville *(G-11343)*
Furiex Pharmaceuticals LLC................E 919 456-7800
  Morrisville *(G-11344)*
G1 Therapeutics Inc...............................C 919 213-9835
  Durham *(G-5110)*
Gb Biosciences LLC..............................D 336 632-6000
  Greensboro *(G-7032)*
Genixus Corp...G 877 436-4987
  Concord *(G-4272)*
Genixus Corp...F 877 436-4987
  Kannapolis *(G-9120)*
George Clinical Inc................................G 919 789-2022
  Raleigh *(G-12795)*
Gilead Sciences Inc...............................G 650 574-3000
  Raleigh *(G-12801)*
Glaxosmithkline 69 Pharma...................G 612 719-4438
  Durham *(G-5118)*
Glaxosmithkline LLC..............................G 704 962-5786
  Cornelius *(G-4550)*
Glaxosmithkline LLC..............................E 919 483-5302
  Durham *(G-5119)*
Glaxosmithkline LLC..............................E 919 483-2100
  Durham *(G-5120)*
Glaxosmithkline LLC..............................G 252 315-9774
  Durham *(G-5121)*
Glaxosmithkline LLC..............................F 919 483-2100
  Durham *(G-5122)*
Glaxosmithkline LLC..............................G 336 392-3058
  Greensboro *(G-7045)*
Glaxosmithkline LLC..............................G 919 628-3690
  Morrisville *(G-11348)*

Glaxosmithkline LLC..............................E 919 483-5006
  Research Triangle Pa *(G-13551)*
Glaxosmithkline LLC..............................E 919 269-5000
  Zebulon *(G-17129)*
Glaxosmithkline Services Inc................B 919 483-2100
  Durham *(G-5123)*
Glycyx Pharmaceuticals Ltd.................G 919 862-1097
  Raleigh *(G-12808)*
GNH Pharmaceuticals USA LLC..........G 919 820-3077
  Charlotte *(G-2838)*
Gracili Therapeutics Inc........................G 617 331-4110
  Rtp *(G-13831)*
Greer Laboratories Inc..........................C 828 754-5327
  Lenoir *(G-9615)*
Grifols Inc..D 919 553-5011
  Clayton *(G-3983)*
Grifols Therapeutics LLC.....................D 919 359-7069
  Clayton *(G-3984)*
Grifols Therapeutics LLC.....................C 919 553-0172
  Clayton *(G-3985)*
Grifols Therapeutics LLC.....................B 919 316-6300
  Durham *(G-5127)*
Hammock Pharmaceuticals Inc............G 704 727-7926
  Charlotte *(G-2883)*
Hdh Pharma Inc.....................................G 919 462-1494
  Cary *(G-1780)*
Health Choice Pharmacy........................G 281 741-8358
  Arden *(G-337)*
Hendersonville Phrm RES.....................G 828 696-2483
  Hendersonville *(G-7863)*
High Point Pharmaceuticals LLC..........F 336 841-0300
  High Point *(G-8392)*
Hipra Scientific USA..............................F 919 605-8256
  Raleigh *(G-12846)*
Hospira Inc..E 252 977-5111
  Battleboro *(G-922)*
Hospira Inc..B 919 553-3831
  Clayton *(G-3988)*
Hospira Inc..C 252 977-5500
  Rocky Mount *(G-13669)*
Hospira Inc..A 252 977-5111
  Rocky Mount *(G-13702)*
Icagen LLC...D 919 941-5206
  Durham *(G-5144)*
Idexx Pharmaceuticals Inc....................E 336 834-6500
  Greensboro *(G-7112)*
Imbrium Therapeutics LP......................F 984 439-1075
  Morrisville *(G-11358)*
In Acorda Therapeutics.........................G 914 347-4300
  Raleigh *(G-12880)*
Indapharma LLC.....................................G 919 968-4500
  Chapel Hill *(G-2025)*
Indivior Manufacturing LLC..................D 804 594-0974
  Raleigh *(G-12882)*
Inhalon Biopharma Inc..........................G 650 439-0110
  Durham *(G-5155)*
Innobioactives LLC................................G 336 235-0838
  Greensboro *(G-7116)*
Innocrin Pharmaceuticals Inc...............G 919 467-8539
  Fuquay Varina *(G-6204)*
Inpernum Pharma Solutions LLC..........G 919 599-5501
  Durham *(G-5159)*
Intas Pharmaceuticals Limited..............D 919 941-7878
  Raleigh *(G-12895)*
Interpace Pharma Solutions Inc............G 919 678-7024
  Morrisville *(G-11361)*
Ioto Usa LLC...F 252 413-7343
  Greenville *(G-7545)*
Iqvia Pharma Inc....................................D 919 998-2000
  Durham *(G-5166)*
Ixc Discovery Inc...................................E 919 941-5206
  Durham *(G-5169)*

PHARMACEUTICALS

PRODUCT SECTION

Kbi Biopharma Inc .... G 919 479-9898
Durham *(G-5178)*

Kbi Biopharma Inc .... D 919 479-9898
Durham *(G-5177)*

Keranetics LLC .... F 336 725-0621
Winston Salem *(G-16778)*

King Bio Inc .... D 828 255-0201
Asheville *(G-675)*

King Phrmceuticals RES Dev LLC .... B 919 653-7001
Cary *(G-1803)*

Kintor Pharmaceuticals Inc .... G 984 208-1255
Chapel Hill *(G-2029)*

Kowa Research Institute Inc .... E 919 433-1600
Morrisville *(G-11368)*

Krenitsky Pharmaceuticals Inc .... G 919 493-4631
Chapel Hill *(G-2030)*

Krigen Pharmaceuticals LLC .... G 919 523-7530
Lillington *(G-9854)*

Krigen Pharmaceuticals LLC .... G 919 961-3751
Lillington *(G-9855)*

Ksep Systems LLC .... F 919 339-1850
Morrisville *(G-11369)*

Lexitas Pharma Services Inc .... D 919 205-0012
Durham *(G-5189)*

Lonza Rtp .... G 800 748-8979
Morrisville *(G-11382)*

Lq3 Pharmaceuticals Inc .... G 919 794-7391
Morrisville *(G-11383)*

Majorpharma US Inc .... G 919 799-2010
Raleigh *(G-12989)*

Mallinckrodt LLC .... F 919 878-2800
Raleigh *(G-12991)*

Mallinckrodt LLC .... G 919 878-2900
Raleigh *(G-12992)*

Mayne Pharma Commercial LLC .... B 984 242-1400
Raleigh *(G-13009)*

Mayne Pharma Ventures LLC .... G 252 752-3800
Raleigh *(G-13010)*

Melinta Therapeutics Inc .... G 919 313-6601
Chapel Hill *(G-2039)*

Merck .... G 919 423-4328
Chapel Hill *(G-2040)*

Merck & Co Inc .... E 908 423-3000
Charlotte *(G-3166)*

Merck Sharp & Dohme LLC .... C 919 425-4000
Durham *(G-5219)*

Merck Sharp & Dohme LLC .... B 252 243-2011
Wilson *(G-16515)*

Merck Teknika LLC .... E 919 620-7200
Durham *(G-5220)*

Merz Incorporated .... C 919 582-8196
Raleigh *(G-13019)*

Merz North America Inc .... F 919 582-8000
Raleigh *(G-13020)*

Merz Pharmaceuticals LLC .... D 919 582-8000
Raleigh *(G-13021)*

Millennium Pharmaceuticals Inc .... D 866 466-7779
Charlotte *(G-3180)*

Mixx-Point 5 Project LLC .... G 858 298-4625
Swannanoa *(G-15029)*

Musa Gold LLC .... F 704 579-7894
Charlotte *(G-3223)*

Nautilus Holdco Inc .... G 919 859-1302
Durham *(G-5239)*

Neuronex Inc .... G 919 460-9500
Morrisville *(G-11394)*

Neurotronik Inc .... F 919 883-4155
Durham *(G-5244)*

New Life Medicals Inc .... G 610 615-1483
Garner *(G-6195)*

None .... G 336 408-6008
Winston Salem *(G-16821)*

Nontoxic Pthgen Erdction Cons .... G 800 308-1094
Matthews *(G-10276)*

Nortria Inc .... F 919 440-3253
Raleigh *(G-13073)*

Novo Nordisk Phrm Inds LP .... D 919 820-9985
Clayton *(G-4003)*

Novo Nordisk Phrm Inds LP .... B 919 820-9985
Clayton *(G-4004)*

Novo Nordisk Phrm Inds LP .... E 919 550-2200
Durham *(G-5250)*

Nutra-Pharma Mfg Corp NC .... D 631 846-2500
Lexington *(G-9764)*

Oncoceutics Inc .... F 678 897-0563
Durham *(G-5257)*

OnTarget Labs Inc .... G 919 846-3877
Raleigh *(G-13086)*

Oriel Therapeutics Inc .... E 919 313-1290
Durham *(G-5263)*

Patheon Calculus Merger LLC .... G 919 226-3200
Morrisville *(G-11406)*

Patheon Inc .... G 919 226-3200
Durham *(G-5273)*

Patheon Inc .... A 919 226-3200
Durham *(G-5274)*

Patheon Pharmaceuticals Inc .... A 866 728-4366
High Point *(G-8475)*

Patheon Pharmaceuticals Inc .... D 919 226-3200
Morrisville *(G-11407)*

Patheon Phrmceuticals Svcs Inc .... E 919 226-3200
Morrisville *(G-11408)*

Paw Pharma Services LLC .... G 919 367-0413
Cary *(G-1843)*

Pfizer Inc .... G 252 382-3309
Battleboro *(G-928)*

Pfizer Inc .... F 919 941-5185
Durham *(G-5284)*

Pfizer Inc .... E 252 977-5111
Rocky Mount *(G-13721)*

Pfizer Inc .... C 919 775-7100
Sanford *(G-14168)*

Pharmaceutical Dimensions .... G 336 297-4851
Greensboro *(G-7252)*

Pharmaceutical Equipment Svcs .... G 239 699-9120
Asheville *(G-727)*

Pharmacutical Dimension .... G 336 664-5287
Greensboro *(G-7253)*

Pharmasone LLC .... G 910 679-8364
Wilmington *(G-16353)*

Piedmont Animal Health Inc .... E 336 544-0320
Greensboro *(G-7254)*

Pozen Inc .... F 919 913-1030
Raleigh *(G-13125)*

Ppd Inc .... C 910 251-0081
Wilmington *(G-16366)*

Ppd International Holdings LLC .... C 910 251-0081
Wilmington *(G-16367)*

Praetego Inc .... G 919 237-7969
Durham *(G-5301)*

Promethera Biosciences LLC .... D 919 354-1930
Durham *(G-5307)*

Promethera Biosciences LLC .... G 919 354-1933
Raleigh *(G-13151)*

Propella Therapeutics Inc .... G 703 631-7523
Pittsboro *(G-12345)*

PSI Pharma Support America Inc .... E 919 249-2660
Durham *(G-5308)*

Purdue Pharmaceuticals LP .... F 252 265-1900
Wilson *(G-16525)*

Qualicaps Inc .... C 336 449-3900
Whitsett *(G-16000)*

Quatrobio LLC .... G 919 460-9500
Morrisville *(G-11414)*

Rainforest Nutritionals Inc .... G 919 847-2221
Raleigh *(G-13171)*

Recipharm Laboratories Inc .... E 919 884-2064
Morrisville *(G-11416)*

Redhill Biopharma Inc .... D 984 444-7010
Raleigh *(G-13202)*

Sagent Pharmaceuticals Inc .... C 919 327-5500
Raleigh *(G-13227)*

Salubrent Phrma Solutions Corp .... G 301 980-7224
Kannapolis *(G-9131)*

Sandoz Inc .... B 252 234-2222
Wilson *(G-16539)*

Santarus Inc .... B 919 862-1000
Raleigh *(G-13228)*

Satsuma Pharmaceuticals Inc .... G 650 410-3200
Durham *(G-5341)*

Scipher Medicine Corporation .... G 781 755-2063
Durham *(G-5344)*

Scorpius Holdings Inc .... E 919 240-7133
Morrisville *(G-11423)*

Sobi Inc .... G 844 506-3682
Durham *(G-5362)*

Solvekta LLC .... G 336 944-4677
Greensboro *(G-7348)*

Sprout Pharmaceuticals Inc .... F 919 882-0850
Raleigh *(G-13294)*

Sterling Pharma Usa LLC .... E 919 678-0702
Cary *(G-1904)*

Stiefel Laboratories Inc .... C 888 784-3335
Durham *(G-5376)*

Stiefel Laboratories Inc .... E 888 784-3335
Durham *(G-5375)*

Sunstar Network LLC .... G 828 684-3571
Arden *(G-382)*

Syneos Health Consulting Inc .... D 866 462-7373
Morrisville *(G-11436)*

Synereca Pharmaceuticals Inc .... G 919 966-3929
Chapel Hill *(G-2077)*

Synthon Pharmaceuticals Inc .... E 919 493-6006
Durham *(G-5385)*

Tarheel Solutions LLC .... G 336 420-9265
Pleasant Garden *(G-12362)*

Tergus Pharma LLC .... E 919 549-9700
Durham *(G-5396)*

Tg Therapeutics Inc .... D 212 554-4484
Morrisville *(G-11446)*

Therapeutics .... G 919 695-7291
Raleigh *(G-13343)*

Transtech Pharma LLC .... C 336 841-0300
High Point *(G-8575)*

Umethod Health Inc .... F 984 232-6699
Raleigh *(G-13378)*

United Therapeutics Corp .... F 919 246-9389
Durham *(G-5422)*

United Therapeutics Corp .... D 919 361-6141
Durham *(G-5423)*

Universal Preservachem Inc .... D 732 568-1266
Mebane *(G-10434)*

Urovant Sciences Inc .... F 919 323-8528
Durham *(G-5428)*

Vascular Pharmaceuticals Inc .... G 919 345-7933
Chapel Hill *(G-2092)*

Viiv Healthcare Company .... G 919 445-2770
Chapel Hill *(G-2093)*

Viiv Healthcare Company .... A 919 483-2100
Durham *(G-5434)*

Vogenx Inc .... G 919 659-5677
Durham *(G-5435)*

Vtv Therapeutics Inc .... E 336 841-0300
High Point *(G-8598)*

Vtv Therapeutics LLC .... E 336 841-0300
High Point *(G-8599)*

PRODUCT SECTION

PIECE GOODS, NOTIONS/DRY GOODS, WHOL: Fabrics, Synthetic

West Pharmaceutical Svcs Inc.................. G 252 522-8956
  Kinston *(G-9392)*

Wyeth Holdings LLC................................... A 919 775-7100
  Sanford *(G-14210)*

Zoetis Inc... C 919 941-5185
  Durham *(G-5460)*

Zoetis Products LLC.................................. G 336 333-9356
  Greensboro *(G-7476)*

PHONOGRAPH RECORDS WHOLESALERS

Sony Music Holdings Inc............................ G 336 886-1807
  High Point *(G-8542)*

PHOSPHATE ROCK MINING

Lbm Industries Inc..................................... F 828 966-4270
  Sapphire *(G-14213)*

Pcs Phosphate... G 252 402-5779
  New Bern *(G-11833)*

Pcs Phosphate Company Inc..................... E 252 322-4111
  Aurora *(G-838)*

PHOSPHATES

Potash Corp Saskatchewan Inc.................. D 252 322-4111
  Aurora *(G-839)*

Scotts Company LLC.................................. F 704 663-6088
  Mooresville *(G-11080)*

PHOTOCOPYING & DUPLICATING SVCS

Accelerated Press Inc................................ G 248 524-1850
  Wilmington *(G-16092)*

Asheville Quickprint................................... G 828 252-7667
  Fletcher *(G-5984)*

Better Business Printing Inc....................... G 704 867-3366
  Gastonia *(G-6353)*

Branch Office Solutions Inc........................ G 800 743-1047
  Indian Trail *(G-8924)*

Carolina Copy Services Inc........................ F 704 375-9099
  Cornelius *(G-4533)*

Copycat Print Shop Inc............................... F 910 799-1500
  Wilmington *(G-16182)*

Gik Inc.. F 919 872-9498
  Raleigh *(G-12800)*

Kathie S Mc Daniel.................................... G 336 835-1544
  Elkin *(G-5622)*

Legalis Dms LLC....................................... F 919 741-8260
  Raleigh *(G-12965)*

Make An Impression Inc............................. G 919 557-7400
  Holly Springs *(G-8707)*

Moore Printing & Graphics Inc.................... E 919 821-3293
  Raleigh *(G-13041)*

Occasions Group Inc.................................. E 252 321-5805
  Greenville *(G-7566)*

Print Express Inc.. F 910 455-4554
  Jacksonville *(G-9021)*

Print Haus Inc... G 828 456-8622
  Waynesville *(G-15817)*

Printing Svcs Greensboro Inc..................... F 336 274-7663
  Greensboro *(G-7285)*

Quality Instant Printing Inc......................... F 919 544-1777
  Durham *(G-5313)*

Rite Instant Printing Inc.............................. G 336 768-5061
  Winston Salem *(G-16885)*

Sharpe Images Properties Inc.................... E 336 724-2871
  Winston Salem *(G-16906)*

Sillaman & Sons Inc................................... G 919 774-6324
  Sanford *(G-14184)*

SOS Printing Inc.. F 828 264-4262
  Boone *(G-1237)*

Steeds Service Co..................................... G 336 748-1587
  Thomasville *(G-15283)*

Triangle Solutions Inc................................ G 919 481-1235
  Cary *(G-1912)*

Unlimted Potential Sanford Inc................... E 919 852-1117
  Morrisville *(G-11460)*

Village Instant Printing Inc.......................... G 919 968-0000
  Chapel Hill *(G-2094)*

Weber and Weber Inc................................. F 336 722-4109
  Winston Salem *(G-16968)*

Zebra Communications Inc........................ E 919 314-3700
  Morrisville *(G-11469)*

PHOTOGRAPHIC EQPT & SPLYS

Applied Technologies Group...................... G 618 977-9872
  Cornelius *(G-4521)*

Dmarcian... E 828 767-7588
  Brevard *(G-1273)*

Geometry Workbook.................................. G 252 714-3327
  Charlotte *(G-2826)*

Jason Case Corp.. F 212 786-2288
  Durham *(G-5171)*

Kliersolutions... G 919 806-1287
  Apex *(G-211)*

Kodak.. G 919 559-7232
  Morrisville *(G-11366)*

M T Industries Inc...................................... F 828 697-2864
  Hendersonville *(G-7874)*

Mark Johnson.. G 919 834-1157
  Raleigh *(G-12996)*

Strong Global Entrmt Inc............................ C 704 471-6784
  Charlotte *(G-3640)*

Tehan Company Inc.................................... G 800 283-7290
  Burgaw *(G-1353)*

Zink Holdings LLC..................................... D 336 449-8000
  Whitsett *(G-16005)*

Zink Imaging Inc.. E 336 449-8000
  Whitsett *(G-16006)*

PHOTOGRAPHIC EQPT & SPLYS, WHOLESALE: Printing Apparatus

Creative Conquest LLC............................... G 720 481-4372
  Shelby *(G-14304)*

PHOTOGRAPHIC EQPT & SPLYS: Film, Sensitized

Nabell USA Corporation............................. E 704 986-2455
  Albemarle *(G-98)*

PHOTOGRAPHIC EQPT & SPLYS: Printing Eqpt

Digital Progressions Inc............................. F 336 676-6570
  Greensboro *(G-6970)*

Rb3 Enterprises Inc................................... G 919 795-5822
  Wake Forest *(G-15580)*

PHOTOGRAPHY SVCS: Commercial

Above Topsail LLC..................................... G 910 803-1759
  Holly Ridge *(G-8678)*

David Presnell.. G 336 372-5989
  Sparta *(G-14592)*

PHYSICIANS' OFFICES & CLINICS: Medical doctors

Herbs Gaia Inc... D 828 884-4242
  Brevard *(G-1273)*

Orthopedic Services................................... G 336 716-3349
  Winston Salem *(G-16833)*

PICTURE FRAMES: Metal

Chartreuse Shepherd................................. G 252 532-2708
  Weldon *(G-15881)*

Four Corners Frmng Gallery Inc................. G 704 662-7154
  Mooresville *(G-10949)*

Graphik Dimensions Limited...................... D 800 332-8884
  High Point *(G-8371)*

PICTURE FRAMES: Wood

Four Corners Frmng Gallery Inc................. G 704 662-7154
  Mooresville *(G-10949)*

G & G Moulding Inc.................................... E 828 438-1112
  Morganton *(G-11214)*

Graphik Dimensions Limited...................... D 800 332-8884
  High Point *(G-8371)*

L G Sourcing Inc.. E 704 758-1000
  Mooresville *(G-11001)*

Mirrormate LLC.. F 704 390-7377
  Charlotte *(G-3187)*

Quantico Tactical Incorporated................... E 910 944-5800
  Aberdeen *(G-23)*

William L Day Companies Inc.................... F 828 693-1333
  Tryon *(G-15431)*

World Art Gallery Incorporated................... G 910 989-0203
  Jacksonville *(G-9047)*

PIECE GOODS & NOTIONS WHOLESALERS

Adele Knits Inc... C 336 499-6010
  Winston Salem *(G-16589)*

Continental Ticking Corp Amer................... D 336 570-0091
  Alamance *(G-68)*

Culp Inc... E 662 844-7144
  Burlington *(G-1404)*

Domestic Fabrics Blankets Corp................. E 252 523-7948
  Kinston *(G-9359)*

Global Textile Alliance Inc.......................... G 336 217-1300
  Reidsville *(G-13520)*

Oakhurst Textiles Inc................................. E 336 668-0733
  Greensboro *(G-7229)*

Sam M Butler Inc....................................... E 704 364-8647
  Charlotte *(G-3487)*

Warm Products Inc.................................... F 425 248-2424
  Hendersonville *(G-7913)*

PIECE GOODS, NOTIONS & DRY GOODS, WHOL: Textiles, Woven

Gentry Mills Inc.. D 704 983-5555
  Albemarle *(G-86)*

Langenthal Corporation.............................. F 336 969-9551
  Rural Hall *(G-13846)*

Pearson Textiles Inc................................... G 919 776-8730
  Sanford *(G-14165)*

Svcm... G 305 767-3595
  Lincolnton *(G-9924)*

PIECE GOODS, NOTIONS & OTHER DRY GOODS, WHOLESALE: Cotton

Barnhardt Manufacturing Co....................... C 704 331-0657
  Charlotte *(G-2282)*

PIECE GOODS, NOTIONS & OTHER DRY GOODS, WHOLESALE: Fabrics

Cloth Barn Inc.. F 919 735-3643
  Goldsboro *(G-6601)*

Copland Industries Inc............................... B 336 226-0272
  Burlington *(G-1400)*

Freudenberg Prfmce Mtls LP...................... D 919 479-7443
  Durham *(G-5104)*

New River Fabrics Inc................................ G 704 462-1401
  Lawndale *(G-9502)*

Omnia LLC... G 919 696-2193
  Oxford *(G-12138)*

Ripstop By Roll LLC................................... F 877 525-7210
  Durham *(G-5332)*

PIECE GOODS, NOTIONS/DRY GOODS, WHOL: Fabrics, Synthetic

Polyvlies Usa Inc .... E 336 769-0206
  Winston Salem *(G-16860)*

PINS

Pins and Needles .... G 910 639-9662
  Pinebluff *(G-12216)*

PIPE & FITTINGS: Cast Iron

ABT Foam Inc .... F 800 433-1119
  Statesville *(G-14734)*
Florida Fire Supply .... E 336 885-5007
  Winston Salem *(G-16714)*

PIPE & FITTINGS: Soil, Cast Iron

Charlotte Pipe and Foundry Co .... C 704 372-5030
  Charlotte *(G-2457)*

PIPE FITTINGS: Plastic

Charlotte Pipe and Foundry Co .... C 704 372-5030
  Charlotte *(G-2457)*
Pipeline Plastics LLC .... G 817 693-4100
  Fair Bluff *(G-5699)*

PIPE SECTIONS, FABRICATED FROM PURCHASED PIPE

Ansgar Industrial LLC .... A 704 962-5249
  Charlotte *(G-2196)*

PIPE, SEWER: Concrete

Pipe Bridge Products Inc .... G 919 786-4499
  Raleigh *(G-13111)*

PIPE: Concrete

Advanced Drainage Systems Inc .... E 336 764-0341
  Winston Salem *(G-16591)*
Autry Con Pdts & Bldrs Sup Co .... G 704 504-8830
  Charlotte *(G-2242)*
Johnson Concrete Company .... E 704 636-5231
  Willow Spring *(G-16079)*
Johnson Concrete Company .... E 704 636-5231
  Salisbury *(G-13993)*
Oldcastle Infrastructure Inc .... E 704 788-4050
  Concord *(G-4326)*
Southeastern Concrete Pdts Co .... D 704 873-2226
  Statesville *(G-14890)*
Watson Concrete Pipe Company .... G 828 754-6476
  Lenoir *(G-9660)*

PIPE: Plastic

Advanced Drainage Systems Inc .... E 704 629-4151
  Bessemer City *(G-1050)*
Charlotte Pipe and Foundry Co .... B 704 348-5416
  Charlotte *(G-2458)*
Charlotte Pipe and Foundry Co .... A 704 372-3650
  Monroe *(G-10680)*
Charlotte Pipe and Foundry Co .... A 704 887-8015
  Oakboro *(G-12069)*
Charlotte Pipe and Foundry Co .... C 704 372-5030
  Charlotte *(G-2457)*
Charlotte Pipe and Foundry Com .... F 704 379-0700
  Charlotte *(G-2459)*
Charlotte Pipe Inc .... G 704 291-3269
  Monroe *(G-10681)*
Consolidated Pipe & Sup Co Inc .... F 336 294-8577
  Greensboro *(G-6930)*
Crumpler Plastic Pipe Inc .... D 910 525-4046
  Roseboro *(G-13784)*

Fitt Usa Inc .... F 866 348-8872
  Mooresville *(G-10946)*
Ipex USA LLC .... F 704 889-2431
  Pineville *(G-12276)*
Ipex USA LLC .... C 704 889-2431
  Pineville *(G-12275)*
J-M Manufacturing Company Inc .... D 919 575-6515
  Creedmoor *(G-4615)*
National Pipe & Plastics Inc .... C 336 996-2711
  Colfax *(G-4155)*
Opw Fling Cntnment Systems Inc .... E 919 209-2280
  Smithfield *(G-14474)*
Performance Plastics Pdts Inc .... D 336 454-0350
  Jamestown *(G-9066)*
Silver-Line Plastics LLC .... C 828 252-8755
  Asheville *(G-771)*
Southern Pipe Inc .... F 704 550-5935
  Albemarle *(G-108)*
Southern Pipe Inc .... E 704 463-5202
  New London *(G-11878)*
Teknor Apex Company .... E 401 642-3598
  Jamestown *(G-9074)*

PIPE: Sheet Metal

Muriel Harris Investments Inc .... F 800 932-3191
  Fayetteville *(G-5879)*

PIPELINE & POWER LINE INSPECTION SVCS

Appalachian Pipe Distrs LLC .... F 704 688-5703
  Charlotte *(G-2202)*
Dronescape Pllc .... G 704 953-3798
  Charlotte *(G-2655)*

PIPELINE TERMINAL FACILITIES: Independent

Speedway Link Inc .... F 704 338-2028
  Matthews *(G-10292)*

PIPELINES: Natural Gas

Panenergy Corp .... F 704 594-6200
  Charlotte *(G-3310)*

PIPELINES: Refined Petroleum

Panenergy Corp .... F 704 594-6200
  Charlotte *(G-3310)*

PIPES & TUBES

Saertex Multicom LP .... E 704 946-9229
  Huntersville *(G-8892)*
Saertex Multicom LP .... F 704 946-9229
  Huntersville *(G-8891)*

PIPES & TUBES: Steel

Allrail Inc .... G 828 287-3747
  Rutherfordton *(G-13861)*
Appalachian Pipe Distrs LLC .... F 704 688-5703
  Charlotte *(G-2202)*
Border Concepts Inc .... G 336 248-2419
  Lexington *(G-9686)*
Border Concepts Inc .... G 704 541-5509
  Charlotte *(G-2335)*
Buhlmann North America LP .... G 704 485-4144
  Oakboro *(G-12068)*
Fortiline LLC .... E 704 788-9800
  Concord *(G-4266)*
Maysteel Porters LLC .... B 704 864-1313
  Gastonia *(G-6459)*
NC River Riders LLC .... G 336 244-6220
  Ronda *(G-13766)*
Piedmont Pipe Mfg LLC .... G 704 489-0911
  Denver *(G-4793)*

Porters Group LLC .... B 704 864-1313
  Gastonia *(G-6490)*
Tricorn Usa Inc .... C 828 369-6682
  Franklin *(G-6146)*

PIPES & TUBES: Welded

Blacksand Metal Works LLC .... F 703 489-8282
  Fayetteville *(G-5771)*
Riley Power Group LLC .... C 910 420-6999
  Pinehurst *(G-12234)*

PIPES: Steel & Iron

Okaya Shinnichi Corp America .... E 704 588-3131
  Charlotte *(G-3289)*

PLAQUES: Picture, Laminated

Coates Designers & Craftsmen .... G 828 349-9700
  Franklin *(G-6120)*
Professional Laminating LLC .... G 919 465-0400
  Cary *(G-1862)*

PLASMAS

Kedplasma .... G 704 691-3287
  Gastonia *(G-6437)*
Plasma Games .... G 252 721-3294
  Raleigh *(G-13113)*
Plasma Games Inc .... E 919 627-1252
  Raleigh *(G-13114)*
Plasma Surgical .... G 704 608-6756
  Huntersville *(G-8875)*
Plasma Web Services Inc .... G 561 703-0485
  Charlotte *(G-3348)*
Sheffibilt Inc .... G 336 963-0086
  Asheboro *(G-480)*
Sir Plasma .... G 919 232-1961
  Raleigh *(G-13267)*

PLASTIC WOOD

Fiber Composites LLC .... B 704 463-7120
  New London *(G-11870)*

PLASTICIZERS, ORGANIC: Cyclic & Acyclic

Vpm Liquidating Inc .... F 336 292-1781
  Greensboro *(G-7451)*

PLASTICS FILM & SHEET

Abx Innvtive Pckg Slutions LLC .... D 980 443-1100
  Charlotte *(G-2126)*
Bright View Technologies Corp .... E 919 228-4370
  Durham *(G-4978)*
Desco Industries Inc .... E 919 718-0000
  Sanford *(G-14107)*
Liqui-Box Corporation .... D 804 325-1400
  Charlotte *(G-3092)*
Pacrim Inc .... E 919 363-7711
  Apex *(G-224)*
Piedmont Plastics Inc .... D 704 597-8200
  Charlotte *(G-3340)*
Ready Solutions Inc .... G 704 534-9221
  Davidson *(G-4693)*

PLASTICS FILM & SHEET: Polyethylene

Berry Global Films LLC .... C 704 821-2316
  Matthews *(G-10304)*
Daliah Plastics Corp .... E 336 629-0551
  Asheboro *(G-421)*
Inteplast Group Corporation .... E 704 504-3200
  Charlotte *(G-2979)*
Paragon Films Inc .... F 828 632-5552
  Taylorsville *(G-15154)*
Southern Film Extruders Inc .... C 336 885-8091
  High Point *(G-8545)*

PRODUCT SECTION

PLASTICS MATERIAL & RESINS

PLASTICS FILM & SHEET: Polyvinyl

Southern Prestige Intl LLC .... F 704 872-9524
  Statesville *(G-14894)*

Specialty Perf LLC .... G 704 872-9980
  Statesville *(G-14897)*

PLASTICS FILM & SHEET: Vinyl

Krs Plastics Inc .... F 910 653-3602
  Tabor City *(G-15083)*

Mikron Industries Inc .... D 713 961-4600
  Durham *(G-5227)*

Rays Classic Vinyl Repair Inc .... G 910 520-1626
  Hampstead *(G-7654)*

PLASTICS FINISHED PRDTS: Laminated

Ram Industries Inc .... F 704 982-4015
  Albemarle *(G-102)*

PLASTICS MATERIAL & RESINS

3a Composites Holding Inc .... E 704 658-3527
  Davidson *(G-4664)*

Abt Inc .... E 704 528-9806
  Troutman *(G-15364)*

Albemarle Corporation .... G 252 482-7423
  Edenton *(G-5506)*

Albemarle Corporation .... A 980 299-5700
  Charlotte *(G-2152)*

Allotropica Technologies Inc .... G 919 522-4374
  Chapel Hill *(G-1982)*

Alpek Polyester Miss Inc .... C 228 533-4000
  Charlotte *(G-2164)*

American Durafilm Co Inc .... G 704 895-7701
  Mooresville *(G-10856)*

Arclin USA LLC .... G 919 542-2526
  Moncure *(G-10614)*

Auriga Polymers Inc .... C 864 579-5570
  Charlotte *(G-2239)*

Aurora Plastics Inc .... F 336 775-2640
  Welcome *(G-15872)*

Avient Protective Mtls LLC .... D 252 707-2547
  Greenville *(G-7490)*

Bio-TEC Environmental LLC .... G 505 629-1777
  Charlotte *(G-2314)*

Bluesky Polymers LLC .... G 919 522-4374
  Cary *(G-1710)*

Carpenter Co .... D 828 464-9470
  Conover *(G-4433)*

Carpenter Co .... E 828 322-6545
  Hickory *(G-7969)*

Carpenter Co .... D 336 861-5730
  High Point *(G-8286)*

Carpenter Co .... E 828 632-7061
  Taylorsville *(G-15133)*

Celanese Intl Corp .... F 704 480-5798
  Grover *(G-7606)*

Celgard LLC .... D 704 588-5310
  Charlotte *(G-2439)*

Celgard LLC .... D 704 720-5200
  Concord *(G-4230)*

Celgard LLC .... C 800 235-4273
  Charlotte *(G-2440)*

Chase Corporation .... G 828 855-9316
  Hickory *(G-7985)*

Chase Corporation .... G 828 649-5578
  Hickory *(G-7986)*

Chroma Color Corporation .... D 336 629-9184
  Asheboro *(G-416)*

Chroma Color Corporation .... G 704 637-7000
  Salisbury *(G-13941)*

Cs Systems Company Inc .... F 800 525-9878
  Candler *(G-1576)*

Custom Polymers Inc .... F 704 332-6070
  Charlotte *(G-2593)*

Custom Polymers Pet LLC .... E 866 717-0716
  Charlotte *(G-2594)*

D2h Advanced Composites Inc .... G 336 239-9637
  Winston Salem *(G-16667)*

Darnel Inc .... G 704 625-9869
  Monroe *(G-10703)*

Ddp Spclty Elctrnic Mtls US 9 .... D 336 547-7112
  Greensboro *(G-6962)*

Delcor Polymers Inc .... G 704 847-0640
  Matthews *(G-10246)*

Dow Silicones Corporation .... D 336 547-7100
  Greensboro *(G-6978)*

Dupont Teijin Films .... G 910 433-8200
  Fayetteville *(G-5813)*

Eastern Plastics Company .... G 704 542-7786
  Charlotte *(G-2673)*

Eidp Inc .... G 252 522-6286
  Kinston *(G-9362)*

Essay Operations Inc .... G 252 443-6010
  Rocky Mount *(G-13696)*

Freudenberg Prfmce Mtls LP .... F 919 620-3900
  Durham *(G-5105)*

Future Foam Inc .... D 336 885-4121
  High Point *(G-8361)*

Genpak LLC .... D 704 588-6202
  Charlotte *(G-2822)*

Gersan Industries Incorporated .... G 336 886-5455
  High Point *(G-8365)*

Hanwha Advanced Mtls Amer LLC .... E 704 434-2271
  Shelby *(G-14325)*

Hexion Inc .... E 910 483-1211
  Fayetteville *(G-5838)*

Hexion Inc .... G 336 884-8918
  High Point *(G-8384)*

Hexion Inc .... E 828 584-3800
  Morganton *(G-11219)*

Huntsman Textile Effects .... E 704 587-5000
  Charlotte *(G-2935)*

Imaflex Usa Inc .... E 336 474-1190
  Thomasville *(G-15236)*

Ineo Usa Inc .... G 919 467-2199
  Cary *(G-1788)*

Intertape Polymer Corp .... D 252 792-2083
  Everetts *(G-5695)*

Invista Capital Management LLC .... A 316 828-1000
  Wilmington *(G-16273)*

Jpi Coastal .... F 704 310-5867
  Salisbury *(G-13995)*

JPS Composite Materials Corp .... C 704 872-9831
  Statesville *(G-14826)*

Kattermann Ventures Inc .... E 828 651-8737
  Fletcher *(G-6015)*

Kilop USA Inc .... G 336 297-4999
  Greensboro *(G-7149)*

Lanxess Corporation .... G 704 923-0121
  Dallas *(G-4647)*

Lanxess Corporation .... F 704 868-7200
  Gastonia *(G-6443)*

Liquidating Reichhold Inc .... G 919 990-7500
  Durham *(G-5191)*

Lkf Inc .... F 336 475-7400
  Thomasville *(G-15243)*

Mallard Creek Polymers LLC .... G 704 547-0622
  Charlotte *(G-3120)*

Mallard Creek Polymers LLC .... G 704 547-0622
  Harrisburg *(G-7716)*

Mallard Creek Polymers LLC .... G 704 547-0622
  Charlotte *(G-3121)*

Mdt Bromley LLC .... E 828 651-8737
  Fletcher *(G-6021)*

Mexichem Spcalty Compounds Inc .... D 704 889-7821
  Pineville *(G-12283)*

Modern Densifying Inc .... F 704 434-8335
  Shelby *(G-14348)*

Modern Polymers Inc .... G 704 435-5825
  Cherryville *(G-3872)*

Modern Polymers Inc .... E 704 435-5825
  Cherryville *(G-3873)*

Olympic Products LLC .... D 336 378-9620
  Greensboro *(G-7231)*

Olympic Products LLC .... D 336 378-9620
  Greensboro *(G-7230)*

Peninsula Polymers .... G 336 885-8185
  High Point *(G-8479)*

Performance Additives LLC .... F 215 321-4388
  Southern Pines *(G-14543)*

Plaskolite LLC .... C 704 588-3800
  Charlotte *(G-3347)*

Plastic Products Inc .... E 704 739-7463
  Bessemer City *(G-1078)*

Plastic Solutions Inc .... F 678 353-2100
  Ellenboro *(G-5637)*

Polychem Alloy Inc .... E 828 754-7570
  Lenoir *(G-9648)*

Polygal Inc .... F 704 588-3800
  Charlotte *(G-3351)*

Polyone Corporation .... G 704 838-0457
  Statesville *(G-14864)*

Polyquest Incorporated .... F 910 342-9554
  Wilmington *(G-16361)*

Poole Company LLC .... G 828 275-0460
  Fairview *(G-5717)*

Poppelmann Plastics USA LLC .... E 828 466-9500
  Claremont *(G-3933)*

PPG Industries Inc .... G 919 772-3093
  Greensboro *(G-7272)*

PQ Recycling LLC .... E 910 342-9554
  Wilmington *(G-16369)*

Pressure Washing Near Me LLC .... G 704 280-0351
  Waxhaw *(G-15770)*

Prototech Manufacturing Inc .... F 508 646-8849
  Washington *(G-15728)*

Reichhold Holdings Us Inc .... A 919 990-7500
  Durham *(G-5323)*

Resinall Corp .... C 252 585-1445
  Severn *(G-14269)*

Rugby Acquisition LLC .... D 336 993-8686
  Kernersville *(G-9229)*

Rutland Group Inc .... C 704 553-0046
  Pineville *(G-12300)*

Rutland Holdings LLC .... E 704 553-0046
  Pineville *(G-12301)*

Samos Polymers Corporation .... F 704 241-2065
  Stanley *(G-14706)*

Sanctuary Systems LLC .... D 305 989-0953
  Fremont *(G-6173)*

Scentair Technologies LLC .... D 704 504-2320
  Charlotte *(G-3498)*

Schlaadt Plastics Limited .... F 252 634-9494
  New Bern *(G-11844)*

Sealed Air Corporation .... A 980 221-3235
  Charlotte *(G-3517)*

Spt Technology Inc .... G 704 290-5007
  Monroe *(G-10812)*

Ssd Designs LLC .... F 980 245-2988
  Charlotte *(G-3616)*

Superskinsystems Inc .... G 336 601-6005
  Greensboro *(G-7380)*

Syncot Plastics Inc .... D 704 967-0010
  Belmont *(G-1012)*

Tosaf Inc .... G 704 396-7097
  Bessemer City *(G-1086)*

PLASTICS MATERIAL & RESINS — PRODUCT SECTION

Toter LLC .... D 800 424-0422
  Statesville *(G-14916)*

PLASTICS MATERIALS, BASIC FORMS & SHAPES WHOLESALERS

Ace Plastics Inc .... G 704 527-5752
  Charlotte *(G-2127)*

Advanced Technology Inc .... E 336 668-0488
  Greensboro *(G-6783)*

Cardinal Plastics Inc .... G 704 739-9420
  Kings Mountain *(G-9298)*

Interlam Corporation .... E 336 786-6254
  Mount Airy *(G-11523)*

Mdt Bromley LLC .... E 828 651-8737
  Fletcher *(G-6021)*

Mpe Usa Inc .... E 704 340-4910
  Pineville *(G-12284)*

Poly-Tech Industrial Inc .... E 704 948-8055
  Huntersville *(G-8878)*

PLASTICS PROCESSING

Carolina Base - Pac Corp .... E 828 728-7304
  Hudson *(G-8766)*

Dunstone Company Inc .... F 704 841-1380
  Charlotte *(G-2657)*

Fortron Industries LLC .... E 910 343-5000
  Wilmington *(G-16220)*

Inplac North America Inc .... G 704 587-1151
  Charlotte *(G-2976)*

Lamination Services Inc .... E 336 643-7369
  Stokesdale *(G-14945)*

Opw Fling Cntnment Systems Inc .... E 919 209-2280
  Smithfield *(G-14474)*

Salem Technologies Inc .... F 336 777-3652
  Winston Salem *(G-16895)*

Sealed Air Corporation (us) .... A 201 791-7600
  Charlotte *(G-3518)*

Stephen P Wolfe .... G 252 792-3001
  Jamesville *(G-9082)*

PLASTICS SHEET: Packing Materials

Bonset America Corporation .... C 336 375-0234
  Browns Summit *(G-1301)*

Dymetrol Company Inc .... F 866 964-8632
  Bladenboro *(G-1148)*

Plastic Ingenuity Inc .... D 919 693-2009
  Oxford *(G-12143)*

PLASTICS: Blow Molded

Eastn20 Holdings Llc .... G 919 313-2100
  Greensboro *(G-6987)*

Intertech Corporation .... D 336 621-1891
  Greensboro *(G-7120)*

PLASTICS: Extruded

Amesbury Group Inc .... E 704 924-7694
  Statesville *(G-14749)*

Carolina Extruded Plastics Inc .... E 336 272-1191
  Greensboro *(G-6884)*

Manning Fabrics Inc .... G 910 295-1970
  Pinehurst *(G-12228)*

Mikron Industries Inc .... D 713 961-4600
  Durham *(G-5227)*

Rowmark LLC .... G 252 448-9900
  Trenton *(G-15334)*

PLASTICS: Finished Injection Molded

Carlisle Corporation .... G 704 501-1100
  Charlotte *(G-2390)*

Cross Technology Inc .... E 336 725-4700
  East Bend *(G-5465)*

Gentry Plastics Inc .... E 704 864-4300
  Gastonia *(G-6407)*

Medical Cable Specialists Inc .... E 828 890-2888
  Mills River *(G-10507)*

Precise Technology Inc .... G 704 576-9527
  Charlotte *(G-3368)*

Rpp Acquisition LLC .... E 919 248-9001
  Kenly *(G-9157)*

Sonoco Hickory Inc .... D 828 328-2466
  Hickory *(G-8163)*

Tarheel Plastics LLC .... E
  Lexington *(G-9790)*

Tech Medical Plastics Inc .... F 919 563-9272
  Mebane *(G-10432)*

Volex Inc .... E 828 485-4500
  Hickory *(G-8204)*

Volex Inc .... E 828 485-4500
  Hickory *(G-8205)*

PLASTICS: Molded

Accu-Form Polymers Inc .... E 910 293-6961
  Warsaw *(G-15664)*

Aim Molding & Door LLC .... G 704 913-7211
  Charlotte *(G-2145)*

Amcor Tob Packg Americas Inc .... A 828 274-1611
  Asheville *(G-517)*

Aqua Plastics Inc .... E 828 324-6284
  Hickory *(G-7939)*

Beaufort Composite Tech Inc .... G 252 728-1547
  Beaufort *(G-946)*

Blue Ridge Molding LLC .... D 828 485-2017
  Conover *(G-4425)*

Bull Engineered Products Inc .... D 704 504-0300
  Charlotte *(G-2364)*

Centro Inc .... E 319 626-3200
  Claremont *(G-3905)*

Coats & Clark Inc .... D 704 542-5959
  Charlotte *(G-2512)*

Coats N Amer De Rpblica Dmncan .... C 800 242-8095
  Charlotte *(G-2515)*

Dynacast LLC .... E 704 927-2790
  Charlotte *(G-2662)*

Hoffman Plasti-Form Company .... G 336 431-2934
  High Point *(G-8396)*

Integrity Plastics .... G 828 247-8801
  Forest City *(G-6071)*

Leonard Alum Utlity Bldngs Inc .... G 919 872-4442
  Raleigh *(G-12968)*

Leonard Alum Utlity Bldngs Inc .... G 910 392-4921
  Wilmington *(G-16299)*

Nypro Oregon Inc .... A 541 753-4700
  Arden *(G-359)*

Penn Compression Moulding Inc .... G 919 934-5144
  Smithfield *(G-14476)*

Poly-Tech Industrial Inc .... E 704 948-8055
  Huntersville *(G-8878)*

Revolution Pd LLC .... G 919 949-0241
  Pittsboro *(G-12347)*

Sunray Inc .... E 828 287-7030
  Rutherfordton *(G-13892)*

PLASTICS: Polystyrene Foam

A Plus Service Inc .... G 828 324-4397
  Hickory *(G-7927)*

ABT Foam LLC .... F 704 508-1010
  Statesville *(G-14735)*

Amesbury Group Inc .... D 704 978-2883
  Statesville *(G-14748)*

Amesbury Group Inc .... E 704 924-7694
  Statesville *(G-14749)*

Armacell LLC .... D 828 464-5880
  Conover *(G-4417)*

Armacell LLC .... C 919 913-0555
  Chapel Hill *(G-1986)*

Armacell US Holdings LLC .... C 919 304-3846
  Mebane *(G-10399)*

Barnhardt Manufacturing Co .... C 704 331-0657
  Charlotte *(G-2282)*

Barnhardt Manufacturing Co .... C 336 789-9161
  Mount Airy *(G-11481)*

Barnhardt Manufacturing Company .... C 800 277-0377
  Charlotte *(G-2283)*

Bwh Foam and Fiber Inc .... F 336 498-6949
  Randleman *(G-13454)*

Crown Foam Products Inc .... F 336 434-4024
  High Point *(G-8309)*

Dart Container Corp Georgia .... C 336 495-1101
  Randleman *(G-13463)*

Deep River Fabricators Inc .... E 336 824-8881
  Franklinville *(G-6168)*

Ffnc Inc .... D 336 885-4121
  High Point *(G-8351)*

Frisby Technologies Inc .... F 336 998-6652
  Advance *(G-42)*

Future Foam Inc .... E 336 861-8095
  Archdale *(G-281)*

Gaylord Inc .... D 704 694-2434
  Mint Hill *(G-10533)*

Guilford Fabricators Inc .... F 336 434-3163
  High Point *(G-8372)*

Hickory Springs California LLC .... A 828 328-2201
  Hickory *(G-8051)*

Independence Holdings Inc .... G 704 588-6202
  Charlotte *(G-2958)*

Kidkusion Inc .... F 252 946-7162
  Washington *(G-15714)*

Marx LLC .... D 828 396-6700
  Granite Falls *(G-6743)*

Marx Industries Incorporated .... E 828 396-6700
  Hudson *(G-8775)*

Nomaco Inc .... B 919 269-6500
  Zebulon *(G-17136)*

Poly Packaging Systems Inc .... D 336 889-8334
  High Point *(G-8489)*

Prototech Manufacturing Inc .... F 508 646-8849
  Washington *(G-15728)*

Ritchie Foam Company Inc .... G 704 663-2533
  Mooresville *(G-11070)*

Sealed Air Corporation .... D 828 728-6610
  Hudson *(G-8779)*

Sealed Air Corporation (us) .... A 201 791-7600
  Charlotte *(G-3518)*

Swimways .... F 252 563-1101
  Tarboro *(G-15123)*

T Renee Severt LLC .... G 248 540-3741
  Chapel Hill *(G-2078)*

Trego Innovations LLC .... G 919 374-0089
  Wilson *(G-16550)*

Vpc Foam USA Inc .... D 704 622-0552
  Conover *(G-4511)*

PLASTICS: Thermoformed

American Wick Drain Corp .... E 704 296-5801
  Monroe *(G-10644)*

Douglas Fabrication & Mch Inc .... F 919 365-7553
  Wendell *(G-15898)*

Panel Wholesalers Incorporated .... F 336 765-4040
  Winston Salem *(G-16835)*

Prime Mill LLC .... F 336 819-4300
  High Point *(G-8498)*

Thermodynamx LLC .... G 704 622-1086
  Waxhaw *(G-15781)*

US Drainage Systems LLC .... G 828 855-1906
  Hickory *(G-8199)*

PRODUCT SECTION   POULTRY & SMALL GAME SLAUGHTERING & PROCESSING

Wilbert Plstic Svcs Acqstion L............... E 704 455-5191
  Harrisburg (G-7735)

PLATES: Steel

Cleveland-Cliffs Plate LLC..................... A 828 464-9214
  Newton (G-11919)

PLATING & POLISHING SVC

Advanced Motor Sports Coatings......... G 336 472-5518
  Thomasville (G-15181)
Advanced Plating Technologies............ G 704 291-9325
  Monroe (G-10637)
Dave Steel Company Inc...................... D 828 252-2771
  Asheville (G-604)
Malcolms Metal & More......................... G 828 286-1419
  Bostic (G-1263)
Paragon Navigator Inc......................... G 336 316-1206
  Greensboro (G-7243)
Prince Group LLC................................. E 828 681-8860
  Mills River (G-10509)
Scrappys Metal LLC............................. G 828 557-5861
  Murphy (G-11715)
Sterling Rack Inc................................. F 704 866-9131
  Gastonia (G-6516)
Te Connectivity Corporation................. C 336 665-4400
  Greensboro (G-7394)
United Tl & Stamping Co NC Inc........... D 910 323-8588
  Fayetteville (G-5939)
Yontz & Sons Painting Inc.................... G 336 784-7099
  Winston Salem (G-16990)

PLATING SVC: Chromium, Metals Or Formed Prdts

C & R Hard Chrome Service Inc............ G 704 861-8831
  Gastonia (G-6364)
Hi-Tech Fabrication Inc......................... C 919 781-6150
  Raleigh (G-12842)

PLAYGROUND EQPT

Brookhurst Associates......................... G 919 792-0987
  Raleigh (G-12576)
Family Industries Inc............................ F 919 875-4499
  Raleigh (G-12762)
Miracle Recreation Eqp Co................... B 704 875-6550
  Huntersville (G-8855)
Peggs Recreation Inc.......................... G 704 660-0007
  Mooresville (G-11048)
Playpower Inc..................................... D 704 949-1600
  Huntersville (G-8876)

PLEATING & STITCHING SVC

B&Lk Enterprises................................. G 910 395-5151
  Wilmington (G-16130)
Body Billboards Inc.............................. G 919 544-4540
  Durham (G-4969)
Consumer Concepts............................ F 252 247-7000
  Morehead City (G-11264)
Freeman Screen Printers Inc............... G 704 521-9148
  Charlotte (G-2795)
Gaston Screen Printing Inc.................. F 704 399-0459
  Charlotte (G-2810)
Logowear... G 336 969-0444
  Rural Hall (G-13849)
Monogram This................................... G 336 528-9980
  Mocksville (G-10592)
Pacific Coast Feather LLC.................... G 252 492-0051
  Henderson (G-7801)
Promos Inc... G 336 251-1434
  Winston Salem (G-16874)
Vocatnal Sltons Hndrson Cnty I............ E 828 692-9626
  East Flat Rock (G-5479)

PLUGS: Electric

Leviton Manufacturing Co Inc............... G 336 846-3246
  West Jefferson (G-15942)

PLUMBING FIXTURES

American Backflow Technologies......... G 252 714-8378
  Greenville (G-7480)
Brasscraft Manufacturing Co................ F 336 475-2131
  Thomasville (G-15190)
Clearwater Services LLC..................... G 704 995-9260
  Concord (G-4233)
Enviro-Companies LLC........................ G 919 758-6246
  Raleigh (G-12741)
Flologic Inc.. G 919 878-1808
  Morrisville (G-11342)
Key Gas Components Inc.................... E 828 655-1700
  Marion (G-10156)
Piedmont Well Covers Inc.................... F 704 664-8488
  Mount Ulla (G-11685)
Royal Baths Manufacturing Co.............. E 704 837-1701
  Charlotte (G-3461)
SL Liquidation LLC............................... B 910 353-3666
  Jacksonville (G-9033)
Victaulic Company.............................. E 910 371-5588
  Leland (G-9564)
Watts Drainage Products Inc................ F 828 288-2179
  Spindale (G-14609)

PLUMBING FIXTURES: Plastic

Custom Marble Corporation.................. G 910 215-0679
  Pinehurst (G-12219)
Fiberglass Fabrication Inc.................... G 828 685-0940
  Hendersonville (G-7847)
Jupiter Bathware Inc........................... F 800 343-8295
  Wilson (G-16503)
LL Cultured Marble Inc......................... F 336 789-3908
  Mount Airy (G-11539)
Marion Cultured Marble Inc.................. F 828 724-4782
  Marion (G-10157)
Moores Fiberglass Inc......................... F 252 753-2583
  Walstonburg (G-15640)
Plastic Oddities Inc............................. E 704 484-1830
  Shelby (G-14355)

PLUMBING FIXTURES: Vitreous

As America Inc................................... E 704 398-4602
  Charlotte (G-2225)
Athena Marble Incorporated................. F 704 636-7810
  Salisbury (G-13924)
R Jacobs Fine Plbg & Hdwr Inc............. F 919 720-4202
  Raleigh (G-13167)

POINT OF SALE DEVICES

Advanced Point SL Systems Inc........... G 877 381-6100
  Charlotte (G-2138)
NCR Voyix Corporation........................ G 937 445-5000
  Cary (G-1830)

POLE LINE HARDWARE

Preformed Line Products Co................. C 704 983-6161
  Albemarle (G-99)

POLISHING SVC: Metals Or Formed Prdts

Lees Polishing & Powdercoatin............. G 704 827-4309
  Stanley (G-14700)
Tico Polishing.................................... G 704 788-2466
  Concord (G-4377)

POLYESTERS

Spt Technology Inc............................. F 612 332-1880
  Monroe (G-10811)

Unifi Kinston LLC................................ E 252 522-6518
  Kinston (G-9389)

POLYETHYLENE RESINS

Alpek Polyester Usa LLC..................... B 910 371-4000
  Wilmington (G-16108)
Consolidated Pipe & Sup Co Inc............ F 336 294-8577
  Greensboro (G-6930)
Invista Capital Management LLC.......... D 704 636-6000
  Salisbury (G-13989)
Starpet Inc.. C 336 672-0101
  Asheboro (G-485)

POLYMETHYL METHACRYLATE RESINS: Plexiglas

Coates Designers & Craftsmen............. G 828 349-9700
  Franklin (G-6120)
Intrinsic Advanced Mtls LLC................. G 704 874-5000
  Gastonia (G-6430)

POLYSTYRENE RESINS

Huntsman Corporation......................... F 706 272-4020
  Charlotte (G-2933)
Huntsman International LLC................. E 704 588-6082
  Charlotte (G-2934)

POLYTETRAFLUOROETHYLENE RESINS

Alpek Polyester Usa LLC..................... C 910 433-8200
  Fayetteville (G-5758)
Norell Inc.. G 828 584-2600
  Morganton (G-11239)

POLYURETHANE RESINS

Tailored Chemical Products Inc............. D 828 322-6512
  Hickory (G-8173)

POLYVINYL CHLORIDE RESINS

J-M Manufacturing Company Inc........... D 919 575-6515
  Creedmoor (G-4615)
Robix America Inc.............................. C 336 668-9555
  Greensboro (G-7314)
W M Plastics Inc................................ F 704 599-0511
  Charlotte (G-3789)

POSTERS

Digital Printing Systems Inc................. E 704 525-0190
  Charlotte (G-2636)

POTASH MINING

Pcs Phosphate Company Inc............... E 252 322-4111
  Aurora (G-838)

POTPOURRI

Carolina Perfumer Inc......................... G 910 295-5600
  Pinehurst (G-12217)

POULTRY & SMALL GAME SLAUGHTERING & PROCESSING

Basic American Foods......................... G 336 887-3930
  High Point (G-8267)
Broomes Poultry Inc........................... G 704 983-0965
  Albemarle (G-75)
Calvin C Mooney Poultry...................... G 336 374-6690
  Ararat (G-264)
Carolina Egg Companies Inc................. D 252 459-2143
  Nashville (G-11739)
Carrol Poultry LLC.............................. G 347 203-9637
  Bladenboro (G-1145)
Case Farms LLC................................. D 919 735-5010
  Dudley (G-4841)

POULTRY & SMALL GAME SLAUGHTERING & PROCESSING

Case Farms LLC .... E 919 658-2252
  Goldsboro *(G-6599)*
Case Farms LLC .... D 919 635-2390
  Mount Olive *(G-11659)*
Case Farms LLC .... F 704 528-4501
  Troutman *(G-15370)*
Case Farms Processing Inc .... E 704 528-4501
  Troutman *(G-15371)*
Case Foods Inc .... C 919 736-4498
  Goldsboro *(G-6600)*
House of Raeford Farms Inc .... A 910 289-3191
  Raeford *(G-12423)*
House of Raeford Farms Inc .... A 910 763-0475
  Wilmington *(G-16259)*
House of Raeford Farms La LLC .... C 336 751-4752
  Mocksville *(G-10580)*
Mountaire Farms LLC .... C 910 843-5942
  Lumber Bridge *(G-10020)*
Mountaire Farms LLC .... C 910 843-3332
  Lumber Bridge *(G-10021)*
Mountaire Farms Inc .... C 919 663-1768
  Siler City *(G-14424)*
Mountaire Farms Inc .... A 910 843-5942
  Lumber Bridge *(G-10022)*
Mountaire Farms Inc .... B 919 663-0848
  Siler City *(G-14425)*
Mountaire Farms Inc .... F 704 978-3055
  Statesville *(G-14848)*
Perdue Farms Inc .... D 910 673-4148
  Candor *(G-1597)*
Perdue Farms Inc .... E 704 278-2228
  Cleveland *(G-4078)*
Perdue Farms Inc .... B 252 358-8245
  Cofield *(G-4137)*
Perdue Farms Inc .... E 252 338-1543
  Elizabeth City *(G-5562)*
Perdue Farms Inc .... G 252 758-2141
  Greenville *(G-7571)*
Perdue Farms Inc .... E 252 583-5731
  Halifax *(G-7610)*
Perdue Farms Inc .... D 919 284-2033
  Kenly *(G-9154)*
Perdue Farms Inc .... E 910 738-8581
  Lumberton *(G-10048)*
Perdue Farms Inc .... C 252 398-5112
  Murfreesboro *(G-11701)*
Perdue Farms Inc .... C 252 459-9763
  Nashville *(G-11748)*
Perdue Farms Inc .... E 336 896-9121
  Winston Salem *(G-16845)*
Perdue Farms Inc .... D 336 679-7733
  Yadkinville *(G-17046)*
Pilgrim LLC .... G 980 224-9567
  Charlotte *(G-3343)*
Pilgrims Pride Corporation .... E 919 774-7333
  Sanford *(G-14171)*
Pilgrims Pride Corporation .... E 336 622-4251
  Staley *(G-14669)*
Prestige Farms Inc .... E 919 861-8867
  Raleigh *(G-13139)*
Sanderson Farms Inc .... E 252 208-0036
  Kinston *(G-9383)*
Tyson Foods Inc .... F 910 483-3282
  Eastover *(G-5483)*
Tyson Foods Inc .... G 704 283-7571
  Monroe *(G-10826)*
Tyson Foods Inc .... F 336 838-2171
  Wilkesboro *(G-16048)*
Wayne Farms LLC .... A 336 386-8151
  Dobson *(G-4833)*
Wayne Farms LLC .... F 770 538-2120
  Newton *(G-11984)*

POWDER: Aluminum Atomized

Blue Ridge Metals Corporation .... C 828 687-2525
  Fletcher *(G-5989)*

POWDER: Metal

D Block Metals LLC .... G 980 238-2600
  Lincolnton *(G-9889)*
D Block Metals LLC .... F 704 705-5895
  Gastonia *(G-6393)*
Oerlikon Metco (us) Inc .... F 713 715-6300
  Huntersville *(G-8871)*
Quinn Powder Coating .... G 252 235-0200
  Middlesex *(G-10455)*
SCM Metal Products Inc .... E 919 544-8090
  Durham *(G-5345)*
Timothy W Gillespie .... G 919 567-2687
  Holly Springs *(G-8721)*

POWER GENERATORS

Bwx Technologies Inc .... D 980 365-4000
  Charlotte *(G-2368)*
Coastal Carolina Clean Pwr LLC .... F 910 296-1909
  Kenansville *(G-9141)*
Powersecure Inc .... G 919 818-8700
  Princeton *(G-12402)*
Xylem Lnc .... E 704 409-9700
  Charlotte *(G-3839)*

POWER SUPPLIES: All Types, Static

Asp Holdings Inc .... G 888 330-2538
  Zebulon *(G-17121)*
CD Snow Hill LLC .... D 252 747-5943
  Snow Hill *(G-14501)*
Matsusada Precision Inc .... G 704 496-2644
  Charlotte *(G-3142)*

POWER SWITCHING EQPT

Trimantec .... E 336 767-1379
  Winston Salem *(G-16952)*

POWER TOOLS, HAND: Chain Saws, Portable

Farm Services Inc .... G 336 226-7381
  Graham *(G-6689)*
John Deere Consumer Pdts Inc .... C 919 804-2000
  Cary *(G-1798)*

PRECAST TERRAZZO OR CONCRETE PRDTS

Concrete Pipe & Precast LLC .... E 910 892-6411
  Dunn *(G-4858)*
Concrete Pipe & Precast LLC .... E 704 485-4614
  Oakboro *(G-12070)*
Forterra Pipe & Precast LLC .... G 910 892-6411
  Dunn *(G-4867)*
High Point Precast Pdts Inc .... G 336 434-1815
  Lexington *(G-9730)*
Lindsay Precast Inc .... E 919 494-7600
  Franklinton *(G-6157)*
Oldcastle Infrastructure Inc .... G 919 552-5915
  Fuquay Varina *(G-6220)*
Precast Supply Company Inc .... F 704 784-2000
  Concord *(G-4335)*
Quality Precast Inc .... G 919 497-0660
  Louisburg *(G-9998)*

PRECIOUS STONES & METALS, WHOLESALE

Sumpters Jwly & Collectibles .... G 704 399-5348
  Charlotte *(G-3649)*

PRERECORDED TAPE, CD/RECORD STORES: Audio Tapes, Prerecorded

Song of Wood Ltd .... G 828 669-7675
  Black Mountain *(G-1139)*

PRESSED FIBER & MOLDED PULP PRDTS, EXC FOOD

Carpet Rentals Inc .... E 704 872-4461
  Statesville *(G-14773)*

PRIMARY FINISHED OR SEMIFINISHED SHAPES

Lee Controls LLC .... F 732 752-5200
  Southport *(G-14572)*

PRIMARY ROLLING MILL EQPT

Ew Jackson Transportation LLC .... G 919 586-2514
  Holly Springs *(G-8698)*

PRINT CARTRIDGES: Laser & Other Computer Printers

Ace Laser Recycling Inc .... G 919 775-5521
  Sanford *(G-14081)*
Branch Office Solutions Inc .... G 800 743-1047
  Indian Trail *(G-8924)*
Cartridge World .... G 336 885-0989
  High Point *(G-8288)*
Complete Comp St of Ralgh Inc .... E 919 828-5227
  Raleigh *(G-12635)*
Digital Highpoint LLC .... C 336 883-7146
  High Point *(G-8324)*
Drew Roberts LLC .... G 336 497-1679
  Whitsett *(G-15988)*
New East Cartridge Inc .... G 252 329-0837
  Greenville *(G-7563)*
Sato Global Solutions Inc .... F 954 261-3279
  Charlotte *(G-3494)*
Static Control Components Inc .... A 919 774-3808
  Sanford *(G-14191)*

PRINTED CIRCUIT BOARDS

615 Alton Place LLC .... G 336 431-4487
  High Point *(G-8228)*
Assembly Technologies Inc .... F 704 596-3903
  Charlotte *(G-2228)*
C-Tron Incorporated .... F 919 494-7811
  Franklinton *(G-6151)*
Circuit Board Assemblers Inc .... C 919 556-7881
  Youngsville *(G-17077)*
Cml Micro Circuit USA .... E 336 744-5050
  Winston Salem *(G-16656)*
Ferguson Manufacturing Company .... F 336 661-1116
  Winston Salem *(G-16709)*
Flextronics Corporation .... G 704 598-3300
  Charlotte *(G-2776)*
Flextronics Intl USA Inc .... B 704 509-8700
  Charlotte *(G-2777)*
Flextronics Intl USA Inc .... C 919 998-4000
  Morrisville *(G-11341)*
Galaxy Electronics Inc .... F 704 343-9881
  Charlotte *(G-2803)*
Hitech Circuits Inc .... E 336 838-3420
  Indian Trail *(G-8939)*
Jabil Inc .... E 828 684-3141
  Arden *(G-343)*
Jabil Inc .... G 828 209-4202
  Mills River *(G-10505)*
M & M Technology Inc .... E 704 882-9432
  Indian Trail *(G-8947)*

Mac Panel Company .... E 336 861-3100
High Point (G-8435)

Plexus Corp .... D 919 807-8000
Raleigh (G-13116)

S M Company Inc .... F 828 274-0827
Asheville (G-762)

SBS Diversified Tech Inc .... F 336 884-5564
Jamestown (G-9071)

Spectrum Integrity Inc .... F 805 426-4267
Trinity (G-15359)

Wolfspeed Inc .... C 919 407-5300
Durham (G-5444)

PRINTERS & PLOTTERS

Primesource Corporation .... E 336 661-3300
Winston Salem (G-16867)

Strategic 3d Solutions Inc .... F 919 451-5963
Raleigh (G-13307)

PRINTERS: Computer

Alterra Labs LLC .... G 704 770-7695
Morrisville (G-11285)

Amt Datasouth Corp .... E 704 523-8500
Charlotte (G-2192)

Branch Office Solutions Inc .... G 800 743-1047
Indian Trail (G-8924)

St Investors Inc .... D 704 969-7500
Charlotte (G-3618)

PRINTERS: Magnetic Ink, Bar Code

Covington Barcoding Inc .... G 336 996-5759
Kernersville (G-9183)

Sato Global Solutions Inc .... F 954 261-3279
Charlotte (G-3494)

Thomco Inc .... G 336 292-3300
Greensboro (G-7401)

Zebra Technologies Corporation . G 704 517-5271
Charlotte (G-3849)

PRINTING & BINDING: Books

Hf Group LLC .... E 336 931-0800
Greensboro (G-7088)

Tan Books and Publishers Inc .... G 704 731-0651
Charlotte (G-3672)

PRINTING & ENGRAVING: Card, Exc Greeting

Pinkston Properties LLC .... F 828 252-9867
Asheville (G-732)

PRINTING & STAMPING: Fabric Articles

Blue Dog Graphics Inc .... G 252 291-9191
Wilson (G-16477)

Broome Sign Company .... G 704 782-0422
Concord (G-4215)

F & H Print Sign Design LLC ..... G 252 335-0181
Elizabeth City (G-5545)

PSM Enterprises Inc .... F 336 789-8888
Mount Airy (G-11561)

Simple & Sentimental LLC .... G 252 320-9458
Ayden (G-857)

Weaveup Inc .... G 443 540-2201
Durham (G-5439)

PRINTING & WRITING PAPER WHOLESALERS

Archie Supply LLC .... G 336 987-0895
Greensboro (G-6813)

PRINTING MACHINERY

Anilox Roll Company Inc .... G 704 588-1809
Charlotte (G-2195)

Cary Manufacturing Corporation . G 704 527-4402
Charlotte (G-2416)

Cogent Dynamics Inc .... G 828 628-9025
Fletcher (G-5995)

Creative Printing Inc .... G 828 265-2800
Boone (G-1189)

CTX Builders Supply .... G 704 983-6748
Albemarle (G-78)

Diazit Company Inc .... G 919 556-5188
Wake Forest (G-15546)

Diversfied Prtg Techniques Inc ... E 704 583-9433
Charlotte (G-2644)

Encore Group Inc .... C 336 768-7859
Winston Salem (G-16696)

Harper Companies Intl Inc .... G 800 438-3111
Charlotte (G-2889)

Harper Corporation of America .. C 704 588-3371
Charlotte (G-2890)

Mark/Trece Inc .... F 973 884-1005
Greensboro (G-7181)

National Roller Supply Inc .... G 704 853-1174
Gastonia (G-6475)

Rotec North American .... G 828 681-0151
Arden (G-373)

Spgrints America Inc .... D 704 598-7171
Charlotte (G-3603)

Trio Labs Inc .... F 919 818-9646
Morrisville (G-11456)

PRINTING, COMMERCIAL: Business Forms, NEC

E R W Printing .... G 704 201-5642
Charlotte (G-2671)

Kalajdzic Inc .... F 855 465-4225
Clemmons (G-4052)

PRINTING, COMMERCIAL: Calendars, NEC

Timeplanner Calendars Inc .... C 704 377-0024
Charlotte (G-3695)

PRINTING, COMMERCIAL: Decals, NEC

Label & Printing Solutions Inc .... G 919 782-1242
Raleigh (G-12950)

Magnet America Intl Inc .... E 336 985-0320
King (G-9275)

Pro Cal Prof Decals Inc .... F 704 795-6090
Concord (G-4340)

PRINTING, COMMERCIAL: Envelopes, NEC

Vision Envelope Inc .... F 704 392-9090
Charlotte (G-3779)

PRINTING, COMMERCIAL: Labels & Seals, NEC

All Stick Label LLC .... G 336 659-4660
Winston Salem (G-16598)

American Label Tech Inc .... F 984 269-5078
Garner (G-6253)

CCL Label Inc .... F 919 713-0388
Raleigh (G-12613)

CCL Label Inc .... C 704 714-4800
Charlotte (G-2431)

CCL Label Inc .... E 919 713-0388
Raleigh (G-12614)

Datamark Graphics Inc .... E 336 629-0267
Asheboro (G-422)

Draft DOT International LLC ...... G 336 775-0525
Lexington (G-9710)

Hickory Printing Solutions LLC .. C 828 465-3431
Conover (G-4464)

Imprinting Systems Spcalty Inc . G 704 527-4545
Charlotte (G-2956)

Lots of Labels .... G 252 410-1611
Roanoke Rapids (G-13577)

Miller Products Inc .... E 704 587-1870
Charlotte (G-3182)

Multi Packaging Solutions .... A 336 855-7142
Greensboro (G-7207)

Multi-Color Corporation .... E 828 658-6800
Weaverville (G-15854)

Product Identification Inc .... E 919 544-4136
Durham (G-5305)

Sato Inc .... G 980 613-2022
Mooresville (G-11078)

Thomco Inc .... G 336 292-3300
Greensboro (G-7401)

PRINTING, COMMERCIAL: Letterpress & Screen

LDR Designs .... G 252 375-4484
Greenville (G-7555)

Logo Wear Graphics LLC .... F 336 382-0455
Summerfield (G-14985)

PRINTING, COMMERCIAL: Literature, Advertising, NEC

Carolina Classifiedscom LLC ..... D 704 246-0900
Monroe (G-10675)

M D C Graphics LLC .... G 336 454-6467
High Point (G-8434)

Southstern Edctl Toy Bk Dstrs ... E 919 954-0140
Raleigh (G-13285)

PRINTING, COMMERCIAL: Periodicals, NEC

Academy Association Inc .... F 919 544-0835
Durham (G-4899)

Aeroplantation .... G 704 843-2223
Waxhaw (G-15744)

American City Bus Journals Inc G 704 973-1100
Charlotte (G-2182)

Cmm Quarterly Inc .... G 704 995-3007
Charlotte (G-2506)

Duke University .... D 919 687-3600
Durham (G-5068)

Education Center LLC .... E 336 854-0309
Oak Ridge (G-12059)

Forrentcom .... G 336 420-9562
High Point (G-8355)

Jo Mangum .... G 919 271-8822
Asheville (G-672)

Jobs Magazine LLC .... G 919 319-6816
Cary (G-1797)

Lafauci .... G 919 244-5912
Holly Springs (G-8705)

Lift Equipment Inc .... G 704 799-3355
Mooresville (G-11009)

Mb-F Inc .... D 336 379-9352
Greensboro (G-7192)

Rapid River Magazine .... G 828 646-0071
Canton (G-1624)

Rapport Magazine Inc .... G 919 435-7690
Southport (G-14577)

Scalawag .... G 917 671-7240
Durham (G-5342)

Spectrum News .... F 919 882-4009
Raleigh (G-13288)

Tourist Baseball Inc .... E 828 258-0428
Asheville (G-803)

PRINTING, COMMERCIAL: Promotional

Up & Coming Magazine .... F 910 391-3859
  Fayetteville (G-5941)

PRINTING, COMMERCIAL: Promotional

Htm Concepts Martin Entps LLC .... G 252 789-0508
  Williamston (G-16063)
Identify Yourself LLC .... F 252 202-1452
  Kitty Hawk (G-9407)
Inspire Creative Studios Inc .... G 910 395-0200
  Wilmington (G-16269)
Kraftsman Tactical Inc .... G 336 465-3576
  Albemarle (G-93)
Magnet Guys .... G 816 259-5201
  Durham (G-5203)
Mass Connection Inc .... G 910 424-0940
  Fayetteville (G-5868)
McLamb Group Inc .... G 704 333-1171
  Charlotte (G-3153)
Valassis Communications Inc .... D 919 544-4511
  Durham (G-5429)
Valassis Communications Inc .... D 919 361-7900
  Durham (G-5430)

PRINTING, COMMERCIAL: Screen

2 Wishes Tees LLC .... G 919 621-1401
  Cary (G-1669)
3d Maternitees LLC .... G 704 778-0633
  Huntersville (G-8784)
822tees Inc .... G 910 822-8337
  Fayetteville (G-5748)
A A Logo Gear .... G 704 795-7100
  Concord (G-4185)
A B C Screenprinting and EMB .... G 704 937-3452
  Grover (G-7605)
A1 Awards & Promotions Inc .... G 252 321-7701
  Winterville (G-16993)
Aardvark Screen Printing .... G 919 829-9058
  Raleigh (G-12454)
ABC Tees Stuff .... G 828 287-7843
  Forest City (G-6056)
AC Valor Reyes LLC .... G 910 431-3256
  Castle Hayne (G-1941)
Acorn Printing .... G 704 868-4522
  Bessemer City (G-1048)
ADS N Art Screenprinting & EMB .... G 919 453-0400
  Wake Forest (G-15525)
Advantage Marketing .... G 919 872-8610
  Louisburg (G-9978)
Amped Events LLC .... F 888 683-4386
  Gastonia (G-6348)
Aquarius Designs & Logo Wear .... G 919 821-4646
  Raleigh (G-12515)
Armac Inc .... E 919 878-9836
  Raleigh (G-12524)
Art Enterprises Inc .... G 828 277-1211
  Asheville (G-528)
Art House .... G 919 552-7327
  Fuquay Varina (G-6181)
Asheville Promo LLC .... G 828 575-2767
  Asheville (G-542)
Ashton LLC .... F 336 447-4951
  Gibsonville (G-6556)
Atlantic Coast Screen Prtg LLC .... G 910 200-0818
  Burlington (G-1368)
Aunt Tee LLC .... G 336 269-9466
  Burlington (G-1371)
Benchmark Screen Ptg Design .... G 704 785-7826
  Midland (G-10457)
Bender Apparel & Signs Inc .... G 252 636-8337
  New Bern (G-11777)
Blp Products and Services Inc .... G 704 899-5505
  Pineville (G-12256)

Blue Lzard Cstm Scrnprnting In .... G 919 296-9041
  Durham (G-4967)
Body Billboards Inc .... G 919 544-4540
  Durham (G-4969)
Bradleys Inc .... E 704 484-2077
  Shelby (G-14289)
Carolina Sgns Grphic Dsgns Inc .... G 919 383-3344
  Durham (G-5004)
Carolina Tailors Inc .... F 252 247-6469
  Newport (G-11899)
Carolina Vinyl Shack LLC .... G 704 788-9493
  Concord (G-4226)
Castle Shirt Company LLC .... F 336 992-7727
  Kernersville (G-9175)
Causekeepers Inc .... G 336 824-2518
  Franklinville (G-6167)
Chesapeake Graphics Inc .... G 704 827-7172
  Stanley (G-14688)
Commonwealth Graphics Inc .... G 704 997-8501
  Mooresville (G-10909)
Consoldted Grphics - PBM Grphi .... G 919 544-6222
  Durham (G-5031)
Contagious Graphics Inc .... E 704 529-5600
  Charlotte (G-2543)
Cork Tee .... G 919 536-3200
  Durham (G-5033)
Cranford Silk Screen Prcess In .... F 336 434-6544
  Archdale (G-276)
Crazie Tees .... G 704 898-2272
  Mount Holly (G-11629)
Creative Printers Inc .... G 336 246-7746
  West Jefferson (G-15938)
Creative Screening .... G 919 467-5081
  Cary (G-1740)
Creative T-Shirts Imaging LLC .... G 919 828-0204
  Raleigh (G-12654)
Creative Tees .... G 919 828-0204
  Raleigh (G-12655)
Crystal Clear Images Inc .... G 704 708-5420
  Charlotte (G-2579)
Crystal Impressions Ltd .... F 704 821-7678
  Indian Trail (G-8928)
Custom Creations By Ellen .... G 509 480-0263
  Fayetteville (G-5802)
Custom Express .... G 704 845-0900
  Matthews (G-10245)
Custom Tees Lab .... G 704 804-8706
  Charlotte (G-2596)
Dale Advertising Inc .... G 704 484-0971
  Shelby (G-14310)
Daryl Duff Lockyer .... G 704 658-0695
  Mooresville (G-10925)
Davis Vogler Enterprises LLC .... G 402 257-7188
  Charlotte (G-2607)
DB CUSTOM CRAFTS LLC .... F 336 791-0940
  Winston Salem (G-16674)
Deep South Holding Company Inc .... D 336 427-0265
  Madison (G-10072)
Dia-Be-Tees LLC .... G 330 687-7792
  Mint Hill (G-10529)
Digital Print & Imaging Inc .... G 910 341-3005
  Wilmington (G-16201)
Digitaurus Inc .... G 910 794-9243
  Wilmington (G-16202)
Digitaurus EMB Screen Prtg Inc .... G 910 794-3275
  Wilmington (G-16203)
Dillon L Colter L C .... G 828 242-7750
  Chapel Hill (G-2008)
Dirty Dog Threads LLC .... G 704 240-3668
  Lincolnton (G-9890)
Dynagraphics Screenprintng .... G 919 212-2898
  Holly Springs (G-8697)

East Coast Designs LLC .... G 910 865-1070
  Fayetteville (G-5816)
Edge Promo Team LLC .... F 919 946-4218
  Clayton (G-3975)
Egads Printing Co .... G 252 335-1554
  Elizabeth City (G-5542)
Epic Apparel .... G 980 335-0463
  Charlotte (G-2722)
Expressive Screen Printing .... G 910 739-3221
  Lumberton (G-10035)
EZ Custom Screen Printing .... E 704 821-8488
  Matthews (G-10314)
EZ Custom Scrnprinting EMB Inc .... G 704 821-9641
  Matthews (G-10315)
Finch Industries Incorporated .... D 336 472-4499
  Thomasville (G-15221)
First Impressions Ltd .... F 704 536-3622
  Charlotte (G-2765)
Flutterby Embroidery .... G 980 225-6053
  Harrisburg (G-7709)
Funny Bone EMB & Screening .... G 704 663-4711
  Mooresville (G-10951)
Galloreecom .... G 704 644-0978
  Charlotte (G-2805)
Geographics Screenprinting Inc .... G 704 357-3300
  Charlotte (G-2825)
Get Stuck Inc .... G 336 698-3277
  Greensboro (G-7040)
Graphixx Screen Printing Inc .... G 919 736-3995
  Goldsboro (G-6621)
Happiteescom .... G 704 965-2507
  Charlotte (G-2885)
Have A Shirt Made .... G 910 201-9911
  Oak Island (G-12050)
High Cotton Screenprinting .... G 704 872-7630
  Statesville (G-14816)
Home Team Athletics Inc .... G 910 938-0862
  Jacksonville (G-9007)
Humbly Made Brand .... G 740 506-1554
  Raleigh (G-12866)
I Print Ttees LLC .... G 336 202-8148
  Greensboro (G-7108)
If Tees Could Talk LLC .... G 919 938-8031
  Clayton (G-3989)
Image 420 Screenprinting Inc .... G 828 253-9420
  Asheville (G-659)
Image Designs Ink LLC .... G 252 235-1964
  Bailey (G-875)
Infinity S End Inc .... F 704 900-8355
  Charlotte (G-2968)
Ink n Stitches LLC .... G 336 633-3898
  Asheboro (G-444)
Jamn Tees .... G 336 444-4327
  Pilot Mountain (G-12198)
Jax Brothers Inc .... G 704 732-3351
  Lincolnton (G-9897)
Jtc Awards and Printing .... G 910 346-9522
  Jacksonville (G-9011)
Jubilee Screen Printing Inc .... G 910 673-4240
  West End (G-15928)
Jumbo Co .... G 919 637-0313
  Wendell (G-15906)
K & K Stitch & Screen .... G 336 246-5477
  West Jefferson (G-15941)
Kahne Screen Print LLC .... G 704 662-8549
  Mooresville (G-10994)
Kannapolis Awards and Graphics .... G 704 224-3695
  Kannapolis (G-9125)
Katchi Tees Incorporated .... G 252 315-4691
  Wilson (G-16504)
Kelleys Sports and Awards Inc .... G 828 728-4600
  Hudson (G-8772)

PRINTING, COMMERCIAL: Stationery, NEC

Kerr Lake Cornhole & Printing............ G..... 252 430-7144
  Henderson *(G-7792)*

Kessel Development LLC................. G..... 704 752-4282
  Charlotte *(G-3051)*

Kimballs Screen Print Inc................. G..... 704 636-0488
  Salisbury *(G-13999)*

Kna... F..... 704 847-4280
  Charlotte *(G-3058)*

Kraken-Skulls.................................. F..... 910 500-9100
  Fayetteville *(G-5855)*

L & B Monograms Plus................... G..... 336 229-0152
  Burlington *(G-1445)*

Lake Nrman Screen Prtg Fctry L..... G..... 704 664-8337
  Mooresville *(G-11003)*

Lakeside Cstm Tees & Embroider.... G..... 704 274-3730
  Cornelius *(G-4566)*

Laniers Screen Printing................... G..... 336 857-2699
  Denton *(G-4740)*

Legend-Tees.................................... G..... 828 585-2066
  Arden *(G-348)*

Logo Dogz....................................... G..... 888 827-8866
  Monroe *(G-10760)*

Logo Label Printing Company......... G..... 919 309-0007
  Durham *(G-5195)*

Logonation Inc................................. E..... 704 799-0612
  Mooresville *(G-11011)*

Lsg LLC.. E..... 919 878-5500
  Wallace *(G-15624)*

Make An Impression Inc................. G..... 919 557-7400
  Holly Springs *(G-8707)*

Masters Imaging Screen PR........... G..... 704 500-1039
  Mooresville *(G-11016)*

Max B Smith Jr................................ G..... 828 434-0238
  Boone *(G-1219)*

Memories of Orangeburg Inc.......... G..... 803 533-0035
  Mooresville *(G-11020)*

Merch Inc... G..... 919 933-6037
  Carrboro *(G-1650)*

Merch Connect Studios Inc............ G..... 336 501-6722
  Greensboro *(G-7198)*

MI Screen Printing Inc.................... G..... 704 500-1039
  Mooresville *(G-11022)*

Michael D Pressley......................... G..... 828 652-8292
  Nebo *(G-11761)*

Motorsports Designs Inc................ E..... 336 454-1181
  High Point *(G-8460)*

Moving Screens Incorporated........ G..... 336 364-9259
  Rougemont *(G-13787)*

Mrs GS Tees.................................... G..... 704 372-0610
  Charlotte *(G-3211)*

Mrschis Sticker N Tees.................. G..... 919 606-1940
  Clayton *(G-3999)*

Mundo Uniformes LLC.................... G..... 704 287-1527
  Charlotte *(G-3218)*

National Sign & Decal Inc.............. G..... 828 478-2123
  Sherrills Ford *(G-14388)*

Nclogowearcom............................... G..... 919 821-4646
  Raleigh *(G-13060)*

Need T-Shirts Now......................... G..... 910 644-0455
  Fayetteville *(G-5881)*

New Directions Enterprises Inc..... G..... 980 428-1866
  Charlotte *(G-3249)*

New Directions Screen Prtrs Inc.... G..... 704 393-1769
  Charlotte *(G-3250)*

Nvizion Inc....................................... F..... 336 985-3862
  King *(G-9278)*

Omega Tees + Screen Prtg LLC..... G..... 828 268-0600
  Boone *(G-1226)*

Onc Tees.. G..... 252 671-7576
  Oriental *(G-12112)*

Orlandos Cstm Design T-Shirts..... G..... 919 220-5515
  Durham *(G-5264)*

Pages Screen Printing LLC............ G..... 336 759-7979
  Winston Salem *(G-16834)*

Paraclete Xp Sky Venture LLC...... F..... 910 848-2600
  Raeford *(G-12428)*

Paraclete Xp Skyventure LLC........ E..... 910 904-0027
  Raeford *(G-12429)*

Paradigm Solutions Inc.................. G..... 910 392-2611
  Wilmington *(G-16348)*

Paradise Printers............................ G..... 336 570-2922
  Burlington *(G-1471)*

Patti Boo Designs Inc.................... G..... 828 648-6495
  Canton *(G-1622)*

Pop Designs Mktg Solutions LLC.. G..... 336 444-4033
  Mount Airy *(G-11559)*

Poteet Printing Systems LLC........ D..... 704 588-0005
  Charlotte *(G-3357)*

Premier Printing & Apparel............ G..... 910 805-0545
  Wilmington *(G-16370)*

Print Zilla LLC................................. G..... 800 340-6120
  Charlotte *(G-3387)*

Promothreads Inc............................ G..... 704 248-0942
  Cornelius *(G-4579)*

Queensboro Industries Inc............ C..... 910 251-1251
  Wilmington *(G-16373)*

R R Donnelley & Sons Company... D..... 252 243-0337
  Wilson *(G-16528)*

R&R Custom Embroidery LLC....... G..... 336 693-5029
  Hurdle Mills *(G-8912)*

Ragg Co Inc..................................... G..... 336 838-4895
  North Wilkesboro *(G-12031)*

Raleigh Shirt Printer....................... G..... 919 261-6628
  Raleigh *(G-13185)*

Rdu Print Studio LLC..................... G..... 919 260-0173
  Durham *(G-5321)*

Reliance Management Group Inc.. F..... 704 282-2255
  Monroe *(G-10796)*

Rikki Tikki Tees.............................. G..... 828 454-0515
  Waynesville *(G-15818)*

Rogers Screenprinting EMB Inc.... G..... 910 738-6208
  Lumberton *(G-10054)*

RTS Screen Printing....................... G..... 252 972-3599
  Nashville *(G-11749)*

S & S Screenprinters LLC............ G..... 704 707-5497
  Charlotte *(G-3476)*

Screen It... G..... 919 581-9981
  Goldsboro *(G-6654)*

Screen Printers Unlimited LLC..... G..... 336 667-8737
  Wilkesboro *(G-16039)*

Screen Specialty Shop Inc............ G..... 336 982-4135
  West Jefferson *(G-15948)*

Screens Stitches & Stones LLC.... G..... 704 622-1660
  Mooresville *(G-11081)*

Sea & Tee Rsort Rsdntial Prpts.... G..... 910 231-8212
  Wilmington *(G-16395)*

Sewing Plus LLC............................ G..... 704 616-1750
  Bessemer City *(G-1083)*

Shirtails... G..... 910 277-0960
  Laurinburg *(G-9496)*

Silkscreen Specialists................... G..... 910 353-8859
  Jacksonville *(G-9030)*

Silverlining Screen Prtrs Inc.......... G..... 919 554-0340
  Youngsville *(G-17097)*

Simply TS Inc.................................. G..... 828 586-1113
  Sylva *(G-15068)*

Spectrum Screen Prtg Svc Inc...... F..... 919 481-9905
  Cary *(G-1901)*

Spiral Graphics Inc........................ G..... 919 571-3371
  Raleigh *(G-13290)*

Squeegee Tees & More Inc.......... G..... 704 888-0336
  Midland *(G-10480)*

Steves TS & Uniforms Inc............ G..... 919 554-4221
  Wake Forest *(G-15598)*

Stewart Sreen Printing.................. G..... 336 434-4444
  Trinity *(G-15360)*

Sticky Fingers Vinyl....................... G..... 336 859-0262
  Denton *(G-4749)*

STS Screen Printing Inc................ G..... 704 821-8488
  Matthews *(G-10347)*

Supreme T-Shirts & Apparel......... F..... 919 772-9040
  Raleigh *(G-13317)*

Sweet Tees Screen Printing LLC.. G..... 919 497-0500
  Louisburg *(G-10003)*

T S Designs Incorporated............. E..... 336 226-5694
  Burlington *(G-1504)*

T Shirt More.................................... G..... 828 389-3200
  Hayesville *(G-7772)*

T T S D Productions LLC............... G..... 704 829-6666
  Belmont *(G-1013)*

Tannis Root Productions Inc........ G..... 919 832-8552
  Raleigh *(G-13327)*

Team Connection............................ G..... 336 287-3892
  Winston Salem *(G-16936)*

TEC Graphics Inc............................ F..... 919 567-2077
  Fuquay Varina *(G-6232)*

Tees Pretty Things......................... G..... 704 674-0982
  Gastonia *(G-6521)*

Tef Inc... G..... 704 786-9577
  Concord *(G-4375)*

Third Street Screen Print Inc........ G..... 919 365-2725
  Wendell *(G-15920)*

Threesixty Graphix Inc.................. G..... 704 960-4467
  Salisbury *(G-14052)*

Thunderbolt Tees............................ G..... 828 855-1124
  Hickory *(G-8181)*

TLC Enterprises............................... G..... 336 454-4981
  Jamestown *(G-9075)*

TNT Web & Grafix LLC................... G..... 252 289-8846
  Nashville *(G-11751)*

Touch Tone Tees LLC.................... G..... 919 358-5536
  Raleigh *(G-13354)*

Travistees.. G..... 910 506-8827
  Wilmington *(G-16432)*

Trin-I-Tee Designz LLC.................. G..... 910 520-2032
  Rocky Point *(G-13754)*

True Southern Tees........................ G..... 919 604-6068
  Youngsville *(G-17111)*

Tshirts Made By U.......................... G..... 980 309-9749
  Charlotte *(G-3734)*

Twin City Sports LLC..................... G..... 336 765-5070
  Winston Salem *(G-16958)*

Two Little Birds Screen Ptg.......... G..... 336 988-7488
  Greensboro *(G-7422)*

Underground Printing..................... G..... 919 525-2029
  Chapel Hill *(G-2088)*

Unique Impressions....................... G..... 704 873-3241
  Statesville *(G-14921)*

Walk In Faith LLC........................... G..... 704 660-8337
  Mooresville *(G-11122)*

We Print T-Shirts Inc..................... G..... 910 822-8337
  Fayetteville *(G-5951)*

Westmoreland Printers Inc........... F..... 704 482-9100
  Shelby *(G-14382)*

Winso Dsgns Screenprinting LLC.. G..... 704 967-5776
  Charlotte *(G-3817)*

Wooten Graphics Inc..................... F..... 336 731-4650
  Welcome *(G-15878)*

Xpertees Prfmce Screen Prtg....... G..... 910 763-7703
  Wilmington *(G-16457)*

Yourlogowear................................... G..... 704 664-1290
  Cornelius *(G-4595)*

Zoom Apparel Inc............................ G..... 336 993-9666
  Winston Salem *(G-16992)*

Employee Codes: A=Over 500 employees, B=251-500
C=101-250, D=51-100, E=20-50, F=10-19, G=1-9

PRINTING, COMMERCIAL: Stationery, NEC

Blue Ridge Paper Products Inc.................. A 828 646-2000
  Canton *(G-1600)*

Devora Designs Inc........................... G 336 782-0964
  Winston Salem *(G-16676)*

Godglamit LLC................................ G 336 558-1097
  Charlotte *(G-2841)*

Kimberly Gordon Studios Inc................. E 980 287-6420
  Charlotte *(G-3054)*

Texpack USA Inc.............................. E 704 864-5406
  Gastonia *(G-6523)*

Westrock Mwv LLC............................. G 919 334-3200
  Raleigh *(G-13419)*

PRINTING, COMMERCIAL: Tags, NEC

C & M Enterprise Inc......................... G 704 545-1180
  Mint Hill *(G-10524)*

Printcraft Company Inc....................... D 336 248-2544
  Lexington *(G-9772)*

Printcraft Company Inc....................... E 336 248-2544
  Lexington *(G-9773)*

PRINTING, LITHOGRAPHIC: Advertising Posters

McGrann Paper Corporation.................... E 800 240-9455
  Charlotte *(G-3151)*

PRINTING, LITHOGRAPHIC: Calendars

Celestial Products Inc....................... G 540 338-4040
  Huntersville *(G-8801)*

PRINTING, LITHOGRAPHIC: Forms, Business

R T Barbee Company Inc....................... F 704 375-4421
  Charlotte *(G-3406)*

PRINTING, LITHOGRAPHIC: Offset & photolithographic printing

Glover Corporation Inc....................... E 919 821-5535
  Raleigh *(G-12807)*

Readable Communications Inc.................. G 919 876-5260
  Raleigh *(G-13193)*

Valdese Packaging & Label Inc................ E 828 879-9772
  Valdese *(G-15457)*

Valdese Packaging & Label Inc................ E 828 879-9772
  Valdese *(G-15456)*

PRINTING, LITHOGRAPHIC: Posters & Decals

Heritage Prtg & Graphics Inc................. G 704 551-0700
  Charlotte *(G-2905)*

PRINTING, LITHOGRAPHIC: Promotional

Ad Spice Marketing LLC....................... G 919 286-7110
  Durham *(G-4902)*

B F I Industries Inc......................... G 919 229-4509
  Wake Forest *(G-15529)*

PRINTING, LITHOGRAPHIC: Souvenir Cards

Fantasy Sports Breaks LLC.................... G 276 233-5204
  Dobson *(G-4823)*

PRINTING, LITHOGRAPHIC: Tickets

EDM Technology Inc........................... E 336 882-8115
  High Point *(G-8337)*

Tickets Plus Inc............................. E 616 222-4000
  Morrisville *(G-11448)*

PRINTING: Books

Goslen Printing Company...................... F 336 768-5775
  Winston Salem *(G-16725)*

Herff Jones LLC.............................. G 704 845-3355
  Charlotte *(G-2903)*

Lsc Communications Inc....................... F 704 889-5800
  Pineville *(G-12282)*

New Journey Now.............................. G 336 234-1534
  Greensboro *(G-7216)*

Rose Reprographics........................... G 336 222-0727
  Burlington *(G-1487)*

PRINTING: Broadwoven Fabrics. Cotton

Advanced Digital Textiles LLC................ E 704 226-9600
  Monroe *(G-10636)*

Holt Sublimation Prtg Pdts Inc............... C 336 222-3600
  Burlington *(G-1429)*

PRINTING: Checkbooks

Deluxe Corp.................................. G 704 969-5200
  Charlotte *(G-2616)*

Deluxe Corporation........................... F 336 851-4600
  Greensboro *(G-6967)*

Printing Press............................... G 828 299-1234
  Asheville *(G-743)*

PRINTING: Commercial, NEC

A Create Card Inc............................ G 631 584-2273
  Charlotte *(G-2114)*

Abe Entercom Holdings LLC.................... E 336 691-4337
  Greensboro *(G-6773)*

Action Specialties LLC....................... G 704 865-6699
  Gastonia *(G-6336)*

AEL Services LLC............................. E 704 525-3710
  Charlotte *(G-2140)*

Ambrose Signs Inc............................ G 252 338-8522
  Camden *(G-1555)*

American Multimedia Inc...................... D 336 229-7101
  Burlington *(G-1364)*

American Solutions For Bu.................... G 919 848-2442
  Raleigh *(G-12500)*

Appalachian State University................. F 828 262-2047
  Boone *(G-1174)*

Arzberger Engravers Inc...................... E 704 376-1151
  Charlotte *(G-2224)*

Asheville Color & Imaging Inc................ G 828 774-5040
  Asheville *(G-533)*

Austin Business Forms Inc.................... F 704 821-6165
  Indian Trail *(G-8922)*

Brunswick Screen Prtg & EMB.................. F 910 579-1234
  Ocean Isle Beach *(G-12087)*

Bryan Austin................................. F 336 841-6573
  High Point *(G-8276)*

Burlow Promotions Inc........................ G 336 856-0500
  Greensboro *(G-6869)*

Circle Graphics Inc.......................... C 919 864-4518
  Raleigh *(G-12623)*

Comedycd..................................... G 336 273-0077
  Greensboro *(G-6923)*

Consumer Concepts............................ F 252 247-7000
  Morehead City *(G-11164)*

Contract Printing & Graphics................. G 919 832-7178
  Raleigh *(G-12644)*

Creative Label Solutions..................... G 828 315-9500
  Newton *(G-11928)*

Creative Label Solutions Inc................. G 828 320-5389
  Hickory *(G-7999)*

Daniels Business Services Inc................ E 828 277-8250
  Asheville *(G-602)*

David Presnell............................... G 336 372-5989
  Sparta *(G-14592)*

Dbt Coatings LLC............................. G 336 834-9700
  Greensboro *(G-6961)*

Dime EMB LLC................................. F 336 765-0910
  Winston Salem *(G-16681)*

Document Directs Inc......................... G 919 829-8810
  Raleigh *(G-12692)*

Dtbtla Inc................................... E 336 769-0000
  Greensboro *(G-6981)*

Easter Seals Ucp NC & VA Inc................. D 919 856-0250
  Raleigh *(G-12717)*

Eatumup Lure Company Inc..................... G 336 218-0896
  Greensboro *(G-6988)*

Electronic Imaging Svcs Inc.................. F 704 587-3323
  Charlotte *(G-2690)*

Embroidme Lake Norman........................ G 704 987-9630
  Cornelius *(G-4543)*

F C C LLC.................................... G 336 883-7314
  High Point *(G-8349)*

Fabrix Inc................................... G 704 953-1239
  Charlotte *(G-2743)*

Fayetteville Publishing Co................... D 910 323-4848
  Fayetteville *(G-5824)*

Flexo Factor................................. G 704 962-5404
  Charlotte *(G-2775)*

Flint Group US LLC........................... G 828 687-2485
  Arden *(G-332)*

Gibraltar Packaging Inc...................... C 910 439-6137
  Mount Gilead *(G-11600)*

Gilmore Globl Lgstics Svcs Inc............... D 919 277-2700
  Morrisville *(G-11347)*

Gmg Group LLC................................ G 252 441-8374
  Kill Devil Hills *(G-9258)*

Go Postal In Boone Inc....................... F 828 262-0027
  Boone *(G-1200)*

Golf Associates Advertising Co............... E 828 252-6544
  Asheville *(G-637)*

Graphic Image of Cape Fear Inc............... G 910 313-6768
  Wilmington *(G-16239)*

Greenfield Printing Co....................... G 910 763-0647
  Wilmington *(G-16241)*

Herald Printing Inc.......................... G 252 726-3534
  Morehead City *(G-11175)*

High Performance Marketing Inc............... G 919 870-9915
  Raleigh *(G-12843)*

ID Images LLC................................ G 704 494-0444
  Charlotte *(G-2948)*

Interflex Acquisition Co LLC................. C 336 921-3505
  Wilkesboro *(G-16027)*

Interflex Acquisition Co LLC................. C 336 921-3505
  Wilkesboro *(G-16028)*

Iwanna....................................... G 828 505-7319
  Asheville *(G-665)*

J C Lawrence Co.............................. G 919 553-3044
  Oriental *(G-12110)*

Kathie S Mc Daniel........................... G 336 835-1544
  Elkin *(G-5622)*

Kdm Enterprise LLC........................... G 919 689-9720
  Goldsboro *(G-6628)*

Label Printing Systems Inc................... E 336 760-3271
  Winston Salem *(G-16783)*

Label Southeast LLC.......................... G 518 796-6320
  Charlotte *(G-3068)*

Labels Tags & Inserts Inc.................... F 336 227-8485
  Burlington *(G-1447)*

Lake Norman EMB & Monogramming............... G 704 892-8450
  Cornelius *(G-4564)*

M-Prints Inc................................. G 828 265-4929
  Boone *(G-1216)*

Masters Hand Print Works Inc................. G 828 652-5833
  Marion *(G-10159)*

Maxim Label Packg High Pt Inc................ F 336 861-1666
  High Point *(G-8451)*

PRODUCT SECTION — PRINTING: Lithographic

Mb-F Inc .... D 336 379-9352
 Greensboro *(G-7192)*

Measurement Incorporated .... C 919 683-2413
 Durham *(G-5213)*

Medlit Solutions LLC .... D 919 878-6789
 Garner *(G-6287)*

Napoleon James .... G 413 331-9560
 Charlotte *(G-3230)*

News & Record Commercial Prtg .... E 336 373-7300
 Greensboro *(G-7217)*

One Source Document Solutions .... G 336 482-2360
 Greensboro *(G-7233)*

Owen G Dunn Co Inc .... G 252 633-3197
 New Bern *(G-11832)*

Park Communications LLC .... G 919 852-1117
 Morrisville *(G-11405)*

Piedmont Business Forms Inc .... F 828 464-0010
 Newton *(G-11960)*

Plasticard Products Inc .... G 828 665-7774
 Asheville *(G-734)*

Prince Manufacturing Corp .... C 828 681-8860
 Mills River *(G-10510)*

Print Express Inc .... F 910 455-4554
 Jacksonville *(G-9021)*

Print Haus Inc .... G 828 456-8622
 Waynesville *(G-15817)*

Printful Inc .... F 818 351-7181
 Charlotte *(G-3388)*

Printing Press .... G 828 299-1234
 Asheville *(G-743)*

Printing Svcs Greensboro Inc .... F 336 274-7663
 Greensboro *(G-7285)*

Proforma Hanson Branding .... G 210 437-3061
 High Point *(G-8501)*

Quik Print Inc .... G 910 738-6775
 Lumberton *(G-10050)*

R R Donnelley & Sons Company .... E 919 596-8942
 Durham *(G-5316)*

Salem One Inc .... C 336 744-9990
 Winston Salem *(G-16893)*

Serigraph Techniques Inc .... G 336 454-5066
 Jamestown *(G-9072)*

Sharpe Images Properties Inc .... E 336 724-2871
 Winston Salem *(G-16906)*

Smart Play USA .... G 252 747-2587
 Snow Hill *(G-14508)*

Sml Raleigh LLC .... G 919 585-0100
 Clayton *(G-4010)*

SOS Printing Inc .... F 828 264-4262
 Boone *(G-1237)*

St Johns Packaging Usa LLC .... C 336 292-9911
 Greensboro *(G-7362)*

Steeds Service Co .... G 336 748-1587
 Thomasville *(G-15283)*

Stump Printing Co Inc .... C 260 723-5171
 Wrightsville Beach *(G-17028)*

Substance Incorporated .... F 800 985-9485
 Claremont *(G-3939)*

Tarason Label Inc .... G 828 464-4743
 Hickory *(G-8174)*

Tennessee Nedgraphics Inc .... F 704 414-4224
 Charlotte *(G-3681)*

Times Printing Company Inc .... G 252 441-2223
 Kill Devil Hills *(G-9263)*

Transformational Bible Inst .... G 702 218-3528
 Elizabeth City *(G-5578)*

Triad Printing NC Inc .... G 336 422-8752
 Greensboro *(G-7416)*

Uniforms Galore .... G 252 975-5878
 Washington *(G-15735)*

Visigraphix Inc .... G 336 882-1935
 Colfax *(G-4162)*

Walgreen Co .... F 704 525-2628
 Charlotte *(G-3792)*

Weathervane Creative Inc .... G 828 542-0136
 Hickory *(G-8208)*

Winston Printing Company .... D 336 896-7631
 Winston Salem *(G-16980)*

Workflowone .... G 252 215-8880
 Winterville *(G-17019)*

Wright of Thomasville Inc .... F 336 472-4200
 Thomasville *(G-15305)*

PRINTING: Flexographic

Valdese Packaging & Label Inc .... F 828 879-9772
 Valdese *(G-15457)*

Valdese Packaging & Label Inc .... E 828 879-9772
 Valdese *(G-15456)*

PRINTING: Gravure, Labels

Huntpack Inc .... G 704 986-0684
 Albemarle *(G-90)*

PRINTING: Gravure, Rotogravure

Arzberger Engravers Inc .... E 704 376-1151
 Charlotte *(G-2224)*

Big Fish Dpi .... G 704 545-8112
 Mint Hill *(G-10522)*

Business Wise Inc .... G 704 554-4112
 Charlotte *(G-2367)*

Executive Promotions Inc .... F 704 663-4000
 Mooresville *(G-10940)*

Linprint Company .... F 910 763-5103
 Wilmington *(G-16303)*

Sharpe Co .... E 336 724-2871
 Winston Salem *(G-16905)*

Synthomer Inc .... D 704 225-1872
 Monroe *(G-10819)*

PRINTING: Laser

Ics North America Corp .... E 704 794-6620
 Concord *(G-4283)*

Laser Ink Corporation .... E 919 361-5822
 Durham *(G-5186)*

Theo Davis Sons Incorporated .... E 919 269-7401
 Zebulon *(G-17143)*

PRINTING: Letterpress

Arrowhead Graphics Inc .... G 336 274-2419
 Greensboro *(G-6816)*

Artcraft Press Inc .... F 828 397-8612
 Icard *(G-8916)*

Carolina Printing Co .... G 919 834-0433
 Princeton *(G-12399)*

Carter Publishing Company Inc .... F 336 993-2161
 Kernersville *(G-9174)*

Coastal Press Inc .... G 252 726-1549
 Morehead City *(G-11163)*

Concord Printing Company Inc .... F 704 786-3717
 Concord *(G-4240)*

Hunsucker Printing Co Inc .... G 336 629-9125
 Asheboro *(G-441)*

Imagemark Business Svcs Inc .... G 704 865-4912
 Gastonia *(G-6423)*

Ingalls Alton .... G 252 975-2056
 Washington *(G-15712)*

Pharmaceutic Litho Label Inc .... E 336 785-4000
 Winston Salem *(G-16848)*

Poole Printing Company Inc .... G 919 876-5260
 Raleigh *(G-13120)*

Skipper Graphics .... G 910 754-8729
 Shallotte *(G-14278)*

Sun Printing Company Inc .... G 336 773-1346
 Winston Salem *(G-16923)*

Twyford Printing Company Inc .... G 910 892-3271
 Dunn *(G-4888)*

PRINTING: Lithographic

3 Kids Screen Printing .... G 910 212-0672
 Evergreen *(G-5696)*

3d Print Lodge LLC .... G 804 309-6028
 Roanoke Rapids *(G-13564)*

3d Upfitters LLC .... G 336 355-8673
 Greensboro *(G-6766)*

828 Custom Printing LLC .... G 828 586-1828
 Sylva *(G-15051)*

A & B Screen Prtg & EMB LLC .... G 252 245-0573
 Wilson *(G-16462)*

A & M Paper and Printing .... G 919 813-7852
 Durham *(G-4895)*

A-I Vnyl Grphics Prtg Slutions .... G 910 436-4880
 Spring Lake *(G-14624)*

ACe Cstm Kicks N Prints LLC .... G 336 457-9059
 Greensboro *(G-6777)*

Acta Print & Marketing LLC .... G 704 773-1493
 Stanfield *(G-14673)*

Additive Prtg & Robotics Inc .... G 704 375-6788
 Charlotte *(G-2136)*

Advance Printing Solutions .... G 301 919-7868
 Wilmington *(G-16094)*

AEC Imaging & Graphics LLC .... G 910 693-1034
 Hope Mills *(G-8730)*

AEL Services LLC .... E 704 525-3710
 Charlotte *(G-2140)*

Alexander Press Inc .... G 336 884-8063
 High Point *(G-8239)*

All Occasion Printing .... G 336 926-7766
 Winston Salem *(G-16597)*

All Star Printing .... G 252 689-6464
 Greenville *(G-7478)*

Alpha Printing & Mailing .... G 704 751-4930
 Shelby *(G-14284)*

AlphaGraphics .... G 704 887-3430
 Charlotte *(G-2171)*

AlphaGraphics .... G 336 759-8000
 Winston Salem *(G-16601)*

AlphaGraphics Downtown Raleigh .... F 919 832-2828
 Garner *(G-6252)*

AlphaGraphics North Raleigh .... G 919 322-2257
 Raleigh *(G-12493)*

AlphaGraphics Pineville .... F 704 541-3678
 Charlotte *(G-2172)*

American Lgacy Timeline Prints .... G 252 514-0225
 New Bern *(G-11769)*

AMP Pros LLC .... G 910 315-1620
 Southern Pines *(G-14526)*

Anav Yofi Inc .... G 828 217-7746
 Charlotte *(G-2193)*

Anthony Alexander Prints Inc .... G 704 870-7213
 Charlotte *(G-2197)*

Apidae Prints .... G 413 320-3839
 Durham *(G-4920)*

Appalachian State University .... F 828 262-2047
 Boone *(G-1174)*

Artesian Future Technology LLC .... F 919 904-4940
 Chapel Hill *(G-1987)*

Arzberger Engravers Inc .... E 704 376-1151
 Charlotte *(G-2224)*

Auten Reporting .... G 828 230-5035
 Asheville *(G-550)*

Babusci Crtive Prtg Imging LLC .... G 704 423-9864
 Charlotte *(G-2260)*

Ballantyne One .... G 704 926-7009
 Charlotte *(G-2272)*

Baseline Screen Printing .... G 336 857-0101
 Denton *(G-4726)*

PRINTING: Lithographic

Bennett & Associates Inc .... G 919 477-7362
Durham (G-4955)

Boundless Inc .... G 919 622-9051
Four Oaks (G-6101)

Brand Fuel Promotions .... G 704 256-4057
Waxhaw (G-15746)

Brandilly of Nc Inc .... F 919 278-7896
Raleigh (G-12572)

Brevard Business Ctr .... G 828 883-4363
Brevard (G-1272)

Brian Allen Artisan Printer .... G 919 609-8992
Durham (G-4976)

Brickfields Incorporated .... G 704 351-1524
Charlotte (G-2355)

Brown Printing Inc .... G 704 849-9292
Charlotte (G-2360)

Bull Cy Arts Collaborative LLC .... G 919 949-4847
Durham (G-4989)

C B C Printing .... G 828 497-5510
Cherokee (G-3853)

Canvas Giclee Printing .... G 910 458-4229
Carolina Beach (G-1632)

Carden Printing Company .... G 336 364-2923
Timberlake (G-15313)

Carolina Copy Services Inc .... F 704 375-9099
Cornelius (G-4533)

Carolina Newspapers Inc .... G 336 274-7829
Greensboro (G-6890)

Carolina Printing Associates .... G 704 477-0626
Shelby (G-14293)

Carolina Vinyl Printing .... G 910 603-3036
Pinehurst (G-12218)

Carroll Signs & Advertising .... G 336 983-3415
King (G-9267)

Cary Printing .... G 919 266-9005
Raleigh (G-12606)

Cascadas Nye Corporation .... F 919 834-8128
Raleigh (G-12610)

Cavu Printing Inc .... G 336 818-9790
Elkin (G-5614)

Chanmala Gallery Fine Art Prtg .... G 704 975-7695
Wake Forest (G-15539)

Check Printers Inc .... G 336 724-5980
Winston Salem (G-16652)

City Prints LLC .... G 404 273-5741
Matthews (G-10242)

Cjk Custom Printing and D .... G 910 488-1288
Fayetteville (G-5791)

Clondalkin Pharma & Healthcare .... F 336 292-4555
Greensboro (G-6918)

Coastal Fish Prints LLC .... G 910 200-7005
Hampstead (G-7643)

Coastal Press Inc .... G 252 726-1549
Morehead City (G-11163)

Coleys Printing .... G 704 785-8837
Concord (G-4235)

Commercial Prtg Co of Clinton .... G 910 592-8163
Clinton (G-4092)

Commercial Prtg Solututions .... G 828 764-4137
Morganton (G-11206)

CPS Resources Inc .... E 704 628-7678
Monroe (G-10697)

Currie Motorsports Inc .... G 910 580-1765
Raeford (G-12418)

Darla Ward .... G 252 340-1895
Elizabeth City (G-5540)

Davidson Printing & Machinery .... G 202 558-2055
Stantonsburg (G-14711)

Dbw Print & Promo .... G 704 906-8551
Concord (G-4252)

Ddi Print .... G 919 829-8810
Raleigh (G-12676)

Delfortgroup Printing Services .... G 336 272-9344
Greensboro (G-6965)

Design Printing Inc .... G 336 472-3333
Thomasville (G-15212)

Dg Printing Solutions .... G 919 779-0225
Raleigh (G-12682)

DH Screen Print Plus .... G 704 609-4823
Charlotte (G-2626)

Digital AP Prtg DBA F4mily Mtt .... G 980 939-8066
Charlotte (G-2633)

Distributech .... G 800 742-0141
Cary (G-1752)

Dma Design Print .... G 336 877-0068
Lansing (G-9454)

Dogwood Print .... G 919 906-0617
Wendell (G-15897)

Dokja Inc .... G 336 852-5190
Greensboro (G-6975)

Down East Screen Printing LLC .... G 252 808-7742
Beaufort (G-955)

Downtown Raleigh .... G 919 821-7897
Raleigh (G-12698)

E C U Univ Prtg & Graphics .... F 252 737-1301
Greenville (G-7520)

Earth Dog Enterprises LLC .... G 919 876-7768
Raleigh (G-12715)

East Coast Digital Prtg Inc .... G 919 465-3799
Cary (G-1754)

Ed Kemp Associates Inc .... G 336 869-2155
High Point (G-8336)

Erleclair Inc .... E 919 233-7710
Cary (G-1761)

Everhart Printinc Co .... G 336 764-3978
Winston Salem (G-16700)

Fast Pro Media LLC .... G 704 799-8040
Cornelius (G-4545)

Fast Pro Media LLC .... G 704 799-8040
Cornelius (G-4546)

Fayetteville Publishing Co .... D 910 323-4848
Fayetteville (G-5824)

Fieldproof Prints LLC .... G 270 313-8439
Fayetteville (G-5825)

Free Will Bptst Press Fndtion .... F 252 746-6128
Ayden (G-852)

Fully Involved Printing LLC .... G 980 521-2670
Concord (G-4268)

Future Prints Inc .... G 704 241-4164
Charlotte (G-2801)

Get Custom Print .... G 336 682-3891
Kernersville (G-9202)

Gik Inc .... F 919 872-9498
Raleigh (G-12800)

Gilmore Globl Lgstics Svcs Inc .... D 919 277-2700
Morrisville (G-11347)

Ginas Processing & Prtg Ctr .... G 910 476-0037
Raeford (G-12422)

Ginkgo Print Studio LLC .... G 828 275-6300
Asheville (G-635)

Graphx Printing Inc .... G 828 475-4970
Morganton (G-11216)

Greensboro News & Record LLC .... A 336 373-7000
Greensboro (G-7064)

Gso Printing Inc .... G 336 288-5778
Greensboro (G-7070)

Harrison Martha Print Studio .... G 949 290-8630
Claremont (G-3929)

Hashtag Screen Printing .... G 980 429-5447
Vale (G-15468)

Hasty Print Works .... G 704 964-6401
Mooresville (G-10970)

Heated Bed Printing LLC .... G 860 230-6912
Durham (G-5133)

Herff Jones .... G 910 399-2740
Wilmington (G-16251)

Hickory Printing Group Inc H .... F 828 465-3431
Conover (G-4463)

High Concepts LLC .... G 704 377-3467
Denver (G-4781)

Hollands Floor Covering LLC .... G 602 703-1951
New Bern (G-11809)

Holy Mountain Printing .... G 801 634-3462
Raleigh (G-12855)

Image 420 Screenprinting Inc .... G 828 253-9420
Asheville (G-659)

Industrial Motions Inc .... G 734 284-8944
Apex (G-205)

Industrial Sign & Graphics Inc .... E 704 371-4985
Charlotte (G-2965)

Infinity S End Inc .... F 704 900-8355
Charlotte (G-2968)

Ink City Screen Printing LLC .... G 347 729-5870
Waxhaw (G-15762)

Ink Well Inc .... G 919 682-8279
Durham (G-5156)

Ink Well Tatoo .... G 919 682-8279
Durham (G-5157)

Instant Imprints .... G 704 864-1510
Gastonia (G-6429)

Instant Imprints .... G 919 468-9808
Morrisville (G-11360)

Instant Imprints Greenville .... G 252 364-3254
Greenville (G-7543)

Integrated Print Services Inc .... G 704 307-4495
Charlotte (G-2978)

Interflex Acquisition Co LLC .... C 336 921-3505
Wilkesboro (G-16027)

Interflex Acquisition Co LLC .... C 336 921-3505
Wilkesboro (G-16028)

International Minute Press .... G 919 762-0054
Fuquay Varina (G-6205)

International Minute Press .... G 704 827-7173
Huntersville (G-8836)

International Minute Press .... G 336 231-3178
Winston Salem (G-16764)

Inventive Graphics Inc .... G 704 814-4900
Charlotte (G-2989)

J R Cole Industries Inc .... F 704 523-6622
Charlotte (G-3006)

Jag Graphics Inc .... G 828 259-9020
Asheville (G-668)

Jeans Printshop LLC .... G 704 564-4348
Charlotte (G-3017)

Jones Media .... F 828 264-3612
Boone (G-1212)

Keller Cres U To Be Phrmgraphi .... F 336 851-1150
Greensboro (G-7148)

Kieffer Starlite Company .... G 800 659-2493
Mount Airy (G-11531)

Kingdom Prints LLC .... G 828 894-8851
Columbus (G-4176)

Kristen Screen Printing & EMB .... G 980 256-4561
Charlotte (G-3063)

Label & Printing Solutions Inc .... G 919 782-1242
Raleigh (G-12950)

Lad Ways of Printing Inc .... G 252 814-9559
Fountain (G-6094)

Laser Ink Corporation .... E 919 361-5822
Durham (G-5186)

Little Stitches EMB & Prtg LLC .... G 828 352-7550
Taylorsville (G-15150)

Local Print .... G 919 620-9050
Bahama (G-864)

M & S Systems Inc .... G 336 996-7118
Kernersville (G-9211)

PRODUCT SECTION

PRINTING: Lithographic

Maxim Label Packg High Pt Inc............... F 336 861-1666
   High Point *(G-8451)*

Mb-F Inc... D 336 379-9352
   Greensboro *(G-7192)*

Mc Stitch & Print..................................... G 336 263-3677
   Graham *(G-6701)*

Medlit Solutions....................................... G 919 878-6789
   Garner *(G-6286)*

Meredith - Webb Prtg Co Inc.................. D 336 228-8378
   Burlington *(G-1460)*

Minuteman Press..................................... G 336 270-4426
   Graham *(G-6704)*

Minuteman Press of Gastonia................. G 704 867-3366
   Gastonia *(G-6467)*

Mjt Us Inc.. G 704 826-7828
   Charlotte *(G-3189)*

Mlb Screen Printing................................. G 704 363-6124
   Huntersville *(G-8856)*

Modern Information Svcs Inc.................. G 704 872-1020
   Statesville *(G-14846)*

Monk Lekeisha....................................... G 910 385-0361
   Goldsboro *(G-6637)*

Moores Printing....................................... G 336 856-0540
   Greensboro *(G-7204)*

More Than Billboards Inc........................ E 336 723-1018
   Kernersville *(G-9219)*

Motorsports Designs Inc......................... E 336 454-1181
   High Point *(G-8460)*

Mountaineer Inc...................................... F 828 452-0661
   Waynesville *(G-15811)*

Mpressive Shirt Works LLC.................... G 919 395-8295
   Raleigh *(G-13045)*

Multi Packaging Solutions....................... A 336 855-7142
   Greensboro *(G-7207)*

N2god Print Center LLC......................... G 910 318-4259
   Laurinburg *(G-9491)*

Natel Inc.. G 336 227-1227
   Burlington *(G-1466)*

NC Imprints Inc....................................... G 336 790-4546
   Lexington *(G-9759)*

Nerdpopprints.. G 910 514-2279
   Lillington *(G-9857)*

Nerdy Llama LLC.................................... G 571 431-8933
   Lenoir *(G-9640)*

News and Observer Pubg Co.................. A 919 829-4500
   Raleigh *(G-13063)*

Nine Thirteen LLC.................................. G 919 876-8070
   Raleigh *(G-13064)*

Noble Printers... G 877 786-6253
   Raleigh *(G-13065)*

Norman Lake Graphics Inc..................... G 704 896-8444
   Huntersville *(G-8861)*

Notepad Enterprises LLC....................... G 704 377-3467
   Charlotte *(G-3271)*

Nrs Printing & Displays LLC................... G 704 907-2887
   Charlotte *(G-3278)*

Observer News Enterprise Inc................ E 828 464-0221
   Newton *(G-11954)*

Occasions Group Inc.............................. G 919 751-2400
   Goldsboro *(G-6641)*

Office Sup Svcs Inc Charlotte................. E 704 786-4677
   Concord *(G-4323)*

Omega Studios Inc.................................. G 704 889-5800
   Pineville *(G-12287)*

On Demand Screen Printing LLC........... G 704 661-0788
   Concord *(G-4327)*

One Stop Shipg & Prtg Etc LLC.............. G 910 745-9733
   Fayetteville *(G-5888)*

Os Press LLC.. G 910 485-7955
   Fayetteville *(G-5890)*

Owen G Dunn Co Inc.............................. G 252 633-3197
   New Bern *(G-11832)*

Pamela A Adams..................................... G 919 876-5949
   Raleigh *(G-13096)*

Pamlico Screen Printing Inc.................... G 252 944-6001
   Washington *(G-15725)*

Perfect Cube LLC................................... G 970 481-5785
   Raleigh *(G-13108)*

Performance Print Services LLC............. G 919 957-9995
   Durham *(G-5280)*

Pharmaceutic Litho Label Inc.................. E 336 785-4000
   Winston Salem *(G-16848)*

Pics and Prints LLC................................ G 917 753-3542
   Harrisburg *(G-7722)*

Platesetterscom...................................... G 888 380-7483
   Greensboro *(G-7267)*

Plum Print Inc... F 828 633-5535
   Asheville *(G-737)*

PMG Acquisition Corp............................. D 828 758-7381
   Lenoir *(G-9647)*

Polly and Associates LLC....................... G 910 319-7564
   Wilmington *(G-16359)*

Polyprint Usa Inc..................................... G 888 389-8618
   Charlotte *(G-3354)*

Power Business Products LLC............... G 704 604-2844
   Matthews *(G-10281)*

Preiss Paper & Printing........................... G 919 325-3790
   Raleigh *(G-13136)*

Pressed Design & Printing Llc................ G 252 314-6036
   Rocky Mount *(G-13723)*

Print & Pack Sense LLC......................... G 336 394-6930
   Eden *(G-5500)*

Print 4 ME Inc... G 336 854-1589
   Greensboro *(G-7283)*

Print Advisors LLC.................................. G 704 385-4315
   Huntersville *(G-8882)*

Print Doc Pack and................................. G 910 454-9104
   Southport *(G-14576)*

Print Magic Transfers Llc....................... G 848 250-9906
   Charlotte *(G-3384)*

Print Mine Tees....................................... G 336 972-1245
   Winston Salem *(G-16868)*

Print Path.. G 843 615-7882
   Hickory *(G-8123)*

Print Path LLC.. G 828 855-9966
   Hickory *(G-8124)*

Print Social.. G 980 430-4483
   Huntersville *(G-8883)*

Printing.. G 770 815-7367
   Asheville *(G-742)*

Printing Pro... G 704 748-9396
   Iron Station *(G-8975)*

Prints On Parade LLC............................. G 713 387-9061
   Julian *(G-9107)*

Prints Plus... G 828 389-7190
   Hayesville *(G-7770)*

Private Label Digital Prtg LLC................ G 919 929-6053
   Chapel Hill *(G-2057)*

Pro Cal Prof Decals Inc.......................... F 704 795-6090
   Concord *(G-4340)*

Professional Bus Systems Inc................ G 704 333-2444
   Charlotte *(G-3391)*

Professional Laminating LLC.................. G 919 465-0400
   Cary *(G-1861)*

Proforma Tierney Printing....................... G 910 392-2611
   Wilmington *(G-16372)*

Promographix Inc.................................... F 919 846-1379
   Carolina Beach *(G-1640)*

Prostar Printing Prom Pro....................... G 704 839-0253
   Matthews *(G-10341)*

Quailwood Screen Prtg & EMB............... G 704 910-2385
   Mint Hill *(G-10543)*

R & D Label LLC..................................... G 336 889-2900
   Jamestown *(G-9068)*

R L Lasater Printing................................ G 919 639-6662
   Angier *(G-149)*

Raleigh Screen Print Inc......................... G 919 662-0358
   Aberdeen *(G-24)*

Red 5 Printing LLC................................. G 704 996-3848
   Cornelius *(G-4581)*

Revolution Screen Printing LLC.............. G 704 340-4406
   Charlotte *(G-3441)*

Rgf Printing... G 201 832-5233
   Snow Camp *(G-14497)*

Riverbank Screen Printing Co................. G 910 248-4647
   Lumberton *(G-10052)*

Rocco Marie Ventures LLC.................... G 704 341-8800
   Pineville *(G-12296)*

Rodney Tyler... G 336 629-0951
   Asheboro *(G-475)*

Roi Sales Solutions Inc........................... G 704 564-9748
   Charlotte *(G-3458)*

Rose of City Prints.................................. G 980 201-9133
   Charlotte *(G-3460)*

Roz Inc... G 704 737-7940
   Monroe *(G-10799)*

Salem One Inc.. F 336 722-2886
   Kernersville *(G-9231)*

Salem One Inc.. C 336 744-9990
   Winston Salem *(G-16893)*

Scriptorium Pubg Svcs Inc...................... G 919 481-2701
   Durham *(G-5346)*

Secure Bag Custom Prints...................... G 856 834-9037
   Concord *(G-4357)*

Sennett Security Products LLC............... D 336 375-1134
   Browns Summit *(G-1315)*

Simple & Sentimental LLC..................... G 252 320-9458
   Ayden *(G-857)*

Simple Graphx LLC................................ G 828 428-1567
   Maiden *(G-10116)*

Sir Speedy Printing................................. G 704 664-1911
   Mooresville *(G-11088)*

Sizemore Custom Jewelry Repair........... G 336 633-8979
   Pleasant Garden *(G-12360)*

Sizemore Printing.................................... G 910 228-8749
   Wilmington *(G-16406)*

Smith Family Screen Printing.................. G 336 317-4849
   Pleasant Garden *(G-12361)*

Stanfast... G 336 841-7700
   High Point *(G-8549)*

Stewart Screen Printing Inc.................... G 336 451-9636
   High Point *(G-8553)*

Succession Solutions Inc........................ F 704 631-9004
   Pineville *(G-12311)*

Sundrop Printing...................................... G 704 960-1592
   Kannapolis *(G-9135)*

Super G Print Lab LLC........................... G 919 864-9351
   Durham *(G-5381)*

Sweetgran Prints..................................... G 919 387-0711
   Apex *(G-247)*

Sylva Herald and Ruralite....................... E 828 586-2611
   Sylva *(G-15070)*

Tag-M Prints.. G 919 615-4222
   Raleigh *(G-13324)*

Taylor Business Forms Inc..................... G 336 667-0300
   North Wilkesboro *(G-12034)*

Teeshizzle Printing.................................. G 336 715-1113
   Clemmons *(G-4061)*

Thompson Printing & Packg Inc.............. G 704 313-7323
   Mooresboro *(G-10842)*

Time Warner Cable Inc........................... G 704 751-5207
   Shelby *(G-14373)*

Tm15 Printing Services........................... G 704 606-0112
   Charlotte *(G-3699)*

Triad Print Promo LLC............................ G 336 416-3488
   Yadkinville *(G-17057)*

PRINTING: Lithographic

Tryon Newsmedia LLC .... F 828 859-9151
  Tryon *(G-15430)*
Twigs Screen Printing .... G 910 770-1605
  Tabor City *(G-15088)*
Unique 3d Printing LLC .... G 704 843-7367
  Waxhaw *(G-15785)*
Valassis Communications Inc .... D 919 544-4511
  Durham *(G-5429)*
Valassis Communications Inc .... D 919 361-7900
  Durham *(G-5430)*
Vanilla Print Inc .... G 919 637-0745
  Cary *(G-1917)*
Village Graphics .... G 252 745-4600
  Oriental *(G-12113)*
Viovio Inc .... G 919 827-1932
  Raleigh *(G-13403)*
W B Mason Co Inc .... E 888 926-2766
  Charlotte *(G-3787)*
Weathervane Creative Inc .... G 828 542-0136
  Hickory *(G-8208)*
Weber & Weber Inc .... G 336 889-6322
  High Point *(G-8602)*
Weber and Weber Inc .... F 336 722-4109
  Winston Salem *(G-16968)*
Westrock - Graphics Inc .... F 610 392-0416
  Charlotte *(G-3806)*
Westrock Rkt LLC .... B 770 448-2193
  Marion *(G-10187)*
Whatever You Need Screen Print .... G 704 287-8603
  Concord *(G-4388)*
Whimsical Prints Paper & Gifts .... G 919 544-8491
  Durham *(G-5440)*
Whitney Screen Printing .... G 910 673-0309
  Eagle Springs *(G-5463)*
Wick Communications Co .... E 252 537-2505
  Roanoke Rapids *(G-13589)*
Wilmington Star-News Inc .... G 910 343-2000
  Wilmington *(G-16452)*
Wilsonepes Printing .... G 252 224-0248
  New Bern *(G-11858)*
Wilsons Planning & Consulting .... G 919 592-0935
  Garner *(G-6326)*
Xpres LLC .... E 336 245-1596
  Winston Salem *(G-16989)*
Xtreme Postcard Profits System .... G 919 894-8886
  Benson *(G-1047)*
Your Source For Printing .... G 704 957-5922
  Charlotte *(G-3846)*
Zeri Consulting Inc .... G 412 512-2027
  Sneads Ferry *(G-14494)*

PRINTING: Manmade Fiber & Silk, Broadwoven Fabric

Advanced Digital Textiles LLC .... E 704 226-9600
  Monroe *(G-10636)*
Holt Sublimation Prtg Pdts Inc .... C 336 222-3600
  Burlington *(G-1429)*
Printology Signs Graphics LLC .... G 843 473-4984
  Davidson *(G-4691)*
Weaveup Inc .... G 443 540-4201
  Durham *(G-5439)*

PRINTING: Offset

4 Over LLC .... F 919 875-3187
  Raleigh *(G-12447)*
A Better Image Printing Inc .... F 919 967-0319
  Durham *(G-4896)*
A Forbes Company .... F
  Lenoir *(G-9566)*
A Plus Graphics Inc .... G 252 243-0404
  Wilson *(G-16463)*

A&R Printing LLC .... G 336 971-7677
  Clemmons *(G-4024)*
Able Graphics Company LLC .... G 336 753-1812
  Mocksville *(G-10551)*
Abolder Image .... G 336 856-1300
  Greensboro *(G-6774)*
Accelerated Press Inc .... G 248 524-1850
  Wilmington *(G-16092)*
Acme Sample Books Inc .... E 336 883-4336
  High Point *(G-8231)*
Adpress Printing Incorporated .... G 336 294-2244
  Summerfield *(G-14975)*
Advanced Teo Corp .... G 305 278-4474
  Charlotte *(G-2139)*
Advantage Printing Inc .... F 828 252-7667
  Arden *(G-307)*
Advantage Printing & Design .... G 252 523-8133
  Kinston *(G-9341)*
Aesco Inc .... G 910 763-6612
  Wilmington *(G-16096)*
All In One Printing .... G 919 360-8092
  Raleigh *(G-12489)*
Allegra Marketing Print Mail .... G 828 698-7622
  Hendersonville *(G-7817)*
Allegra Marketing Print Mail .... G 919 373-0531
  Knightdale *(G-9410)*
Alpha and Omega Printing Inc .... G 336 778-1400
  Clemmons *(G-4025)*
America Printer .... G 336 465-0269
  Randleman *(G-13452)*
American Indian Printing Inc .... G 336 230-1551
  Greensboro *(G-6800)*
American Indian Printing Inc .... G 336 884-5442
  High Point *(G-8245)*
American Multimedia Inc .... D 336 229-7101
  Burlington *(G-1364)*
American Printers Inc .... G 252 977-7468
  Rocky Mount *(G-13681)*
American Printing Co Inc .... G 336 852-9894
  Greensboro *(G-6801)*
American Printing Services .... G 336 465-0199
  Asheboro *(G-401)*
American Speedy Printing Ctrs .... G 828 322-3981
  Hickory *(G-7934)*
Andrews Graphics LLC .... G 252 633-3199
  New Bern *(G-11771)*
Anitas Marketing Concepts Inc .... G 252 243-3993
  Wilson *(G-16465)*
Apex Printing Company .... G 919 362-9856
  Apex *(G-161)*
Archdale Printing Company Inc .... G 336 884-5312
  High Point *(G-8251)*
Arrowhead Graphics Inc .... G 336 274-2419
  Greensboro *(G-6816)*
Artcraft Press Inc .... F 828 397-8612
  Icard *(G-8916)*
Artech Graphics Inc .... G 704 545-9804
  New London *(G-11866)*
Arthur Demarest .... G 252 473-1449
  Manteo *(G-10126)*
Asheboro Piedmont Printing Inc .... F 336 899-7910
  Asheboro *(G-406)*
Asheville Print Shop .... G 828 214-5286
  Asheville *(G-541)*
Asheville Quickprint .... G 828 252-7667
  Fletcher *(G-5984)*
Associated Printing & Svcs Inc .... F 828 286-9064
  Rutherfordton *(G-13864)*
Atlantis Graphics Inc .... E 919 361-5809
  Durham *(G-4933)*
Austin Printing Company Inc .... G 704 289-1445
  Monroe *(G-10658)*

Automated Printing Services .... F 252 243-3993
  Wilson *(G-16470)*
Aztech Products Inc .... G 910 763-5599
  Wilmington *(G-16129)*
B P Printing and Copying Inc .... G 704 821-8219
  Matthews *(G-10303)*
Baicy Communications Inc .... G 336 722-7768
  Winston Salem *(G-16622)*
Baileys Quick Copy Shop Inc .... F 704 637-2020
  Salisbury *(G-13929)*
Bakeshot Prtg & Graphics LLC .... G 704 532-9326
  Charlotte *(G-2268)*
Barefoot Press Inc .... G 919 283-6396
  Raleigh *(G-12545)*
Barretts Printing House Inc .... G 252 243-2820
  Wilson *(G-16474)*
Bbf Printing Solutions .... G 336 969-2323
  Rural Hall *(G-13833)*
BEC-Car Printing Co Inc .... F 704 873-1911
  Statesville *(G-14761)*
Better Business Printing Inc .... G 704 867-3366
  Gastonia *(G-6353)*
Binders of Jhc LLC .... G 980 875-9274
  Charlotte *(G-2313)*
Blackleys Printing Co .... G 919 553-6813
  Clayton *(G-3959)*
Blue Ridge Printing Co Inc .... D 828 254-1000
  Asheville *(G-566)*
Blue Ridge Quick Print Inc .... G 828 883-2420
  Brevard *(G-1270)*
Boingo Graphics Inc .... E 704 527-4963
  Charlotte *(G-2331)*
BP Solutions Group Inc .... E 828 252-4476
  Asheville *(G-570)*
Brodie-Jones Printing Co Inc .... G 252 438-7992
  Louisburg *(G-9981)*
Budget Printing Co .... G 910 642-7306
  Whiteville *(G-15960)*
Burco International Inc .... F 828 252-4481
  Asheville *(G-575)*
Burco Promotional Printing Inc .... G 864 546-3443
  Asheville *(G-576)*
Burrow Family Corporation .... D 336 887-3173
  High Point *(G-8279)*
C D J & P Inc .... G 252 446-3611
  Rocky Mount *(G-13686)*
Call Printing & Copying .... G 704 821-6554
  Indian Trail *(G-8925)*
Cardinal Graphics Inc .... G 704 545-4144
  Mint Hill *(G-10526)*
Carolina Graphic Services LLC .... G 336 668-0871
  Greensboro *(G-6885)*
Carolina Print Mill .... G 919 607-9452
  Cary *(G-1725)*
Carolina Printing Co .... G 919 834-0433
  Princeton *(G-12399)*
Carolina Prtg Wilmington Inc .... G 910 762-2453
  Supply *(G-15007)*
Carter Printing .... G 919 373-0531
  Knightdale *(G-9415)*
Carter Printing & Graphics Inc .... E 919 266-5280
  Knightdale *(G-9416)*
Carter-Hubbard Publishing Co .... F 336 838-4117
  North Wilkesboro *(G-12000)*
Cashiers Printing Inc .... G 828 787-1324
  Highlands *(G-8613)*
Causekeepers Inc .... E 336 824-2518
  Franklinville *(G-6167)*
Central Carolina Printing LLC .... G 910 572-3344
  Asheboro *(G-413)*
Ceprint Solutions Inc .... E 336 956-6327
  Lexington *(G-9691)*

PRODUCT SECTION

PRINTING: Offset

Company	Emp	Phone
Charlotte Printing Company Inc	F	704 888-5181
Concord *(G-4231)*		
Charnel Inc	G	910 763-8476
Wilmington *(G-16169)*		
Choice Printing LLC	G	919 790-0680
Raleigh *(G-12620)*		
City Graphics Inc	G	704 529-6448
Charlotte *(G-2486)*		
Clarks Printing Service Inc	E	828 254-1432
Asheville *(G-594)*		
Cline Printing Inc	G	704 394-8144
Charlotte *(G-2496)*		
Clinton Press Inc	F	336 275-8491
Greensboro *(G-6917)*		
Coastal Impressions Inc	G	252 480-1717
Nags Head *(G-11719)*		
Coble Printing Co Inc	G	919 693-4622
Oxford *(G-12122)*		
Commercial Enterprises NC Inc	G	910 592-8163
Clinton *(G-4091)*		
Commercial Printing Company	E	919 832-2828
Garner *(G-6265)*		
Commercial Prtg Lincolnton NC	G	704 735-6831
Lincolnton *(G-9883)*		
Concord Printing Company Inc	F	704 786-3717
Concord *(G-4240)*		
Consolidated Press Inc	G	704 372-6785
Charlotte *(G-2541)*		
Cooper Thomas & Benton Prtg Co	G	336 698-0951
Mc Leansville *(G-10387)*		
Copy Cat Instant Prtg Chrltte	G	704 529-6606
Charlotte *(G-2550)*		
Copy Express Charlotte Inc	G	704 527-1750
Charlotte *(G-2551)*		
Copy King Inc	G	336 333-9900
Greensboro *(G-6936)*		
Copy That Business Services	G	980 297-7088
Charlotte *(G-2552)*		
Copy Works	G	828 698-7622
Hendersonville *(G-7840)*		
Copycat Print Shop Inc	F	910 799-1500
Wilmington *(G-16182)*		
Copymasters Printing Svcs Inc	G	828 324-0532
Hickory *(G-7995)*		
Cornerstone Custom Printi	G	919 524-7420
Clayton *(G-3969)*		
Craig S Printing LLC	G	336 786-2327
Dobson *(G-4822)*		
CRC Printing Co Inc	G	704 875-1804
Huntersville *(G-8808)*		
Creative Printers Inc	G	336 246-7746
West Jefferson *(G-15938)*		
Creative Printers & Brks Inc	G	828 321-4663
Andrews *(G-125)*		
Creative Printing Stanley Inc	G	704 732-6398
Lincolnton *(G-9887)*		
Creative Prtg Intrnet Svcs LLC	G	828 265-2800
Boone *(G-1190)*		
Crisp Printers Inc	G	704 867-6663
Gastonia *(G-6388)*		
CRS/Las Inc	E	910 392-0883
Wilmington *(G-16190)*		
Custom Marking & Printing Inc	G	704 866-8245
Gastonia *(G-6392)*		
Custom Printing Solutions Inc	F	336 992-1161
Kernersville *(G-9186)*		
D & B Printing Co	G	919 876-3530
Raleigh *(G-12668)*		
Dancing Moon Print Sltions Inc	G	828 689-9353
Mars Hill *(G-10194)*		
Daniels Business Services Inc	E	828 277-8250
Asheville *(G-602)*		
Davidson Printing Inc	G	336 357-0555
Lexington *(G-9704)*		
Deluxe Printing Co Inc	E	828 322-1329
Hickory *(G-8007)*		
Dew Group Enterprises Inc	E	919 585-0100
Clayton *(G-3974)*		
Dg Solutions LLC	G	864 605-3223
Arden *(G-324)*		
Digital Ink Technology Inc	G	603 707-7843
Charlotte *(G-2635)*		
Digital Printing	G	336 430-8011
Colfax *(G-4148)*		
Discount Printing Inc	G	704 365-3665
Charlotte *(G-2641)*		
Docu Source of NC	F	919 459-5900
Morrisville *(G-11334)*		
Dorsett Printing Company	G	910 895-3520
Rockingham *(G-13624)*		
Dove Communications Inc	G	336 855-5491
Greensboro *(G-6977)*		
Dtbtla Inc	E	336 769-0000
Greensboro *(G-6981)*		
Duncan-Parnell Inc	G	252 977-7832
Rocky Mount *(G-13692)*		
Eastern Offset Printing Co	G	252 247-6791
Atlantic Beach *(G-829)*		
Elledge Family Inc	F	919 876-2300
Raleigh *(G-12731)*		
Emerald Printing Inc	G	336 325-3522
Pinnacle *(G-12320)*		
Enterprint Corp	G	919 821-7897
Raleigh *(G-12740)*		
Fairway Printing Inc	G	919 779-4797
Raleigh *(G-12760)*		
First Due Prints Inc	G	704 320-1251
Indian Trail *(G-8935)*		
Flanagan Printing Company Inc	G	828 693-7380
Hendersonville *(G-7851)*		
Flash Printing Company Inc	E	704 375-2474
Charlotte *(G-2769)*		
Fletcher Printville	G	828 348-5126
Fletcher *(G-6006)*		
Forsyth Printing Company Inc	G	336 969-0383
Rural Hall *(G-13840)*		
Forward Design & Print Co Inc	G	704 776-9304
Monroe *(G-10721)*		
Foxfire Printing	G	252 329-8181
Greenville *(G-7528)*		
Freedom Mailing & Mktg Inc	G	336 595-6300
Winston Salem *(G-16718)*		
Galaxy Graphics Inc	G	704 724-9057
Matthews *(G-10249)*		
Gaston Printing and Signs LLC	G	702 267-5633
Belmont *(G-991)*		
Geo-Lin Inc	G	336 884-0648
Jamestown *(G-9050)*		
Gibraltar Packaging Inc	C	910 439-6137
Mount Gilead *(G-11600)*		
Gilley Printers Inc	G	910 295-6317
Pinehurst *(G-12223)*		
Goffstar Inc	G	704 895-3878
Charlotte *(G-2842)*		
Golf Associates Advertising Co	E	828 252-6544
Asheville *(G-637)*		
Goslen Printing Company	F	336 768-5775
Winston Salem *(G-16725)*		
Graphic Impressions Inc	E	704 596-4921
Charlotte *(G-2855)*		
Graphic Products Inc	G	919 894-3661
Benson *(G-1035)*		
Greybeard Printing Inc	G	828 252-3082
Asheville *(G-644)*		
Greyberry Printing	G	919 649-3187
Raleigh *(G-12819)*		
Griffin Printing Inc	G	919 832-6931
Raleigh *(G-12820)*		
Gso Printing	G	336 292-1601
Greensboro *(G-7069)*		
Haley Promotions Inc	G	336 402-7450
Raleigh *(G-12827)*		
Harco Printing Incorporated	G	336 771-0234
Winston Salem *(G-16735)*		
Hayes Print-Stamp Co Inc	G	336 667-1116
Wilkesboro *(G-16023)*		
Henco North	G	828 552-3671
Asheville *(G-650)*		
Herald Printing Inc	G	252 726-3534
Morehead City *(G-11175)*		
Heritage Prtg & Graphics Inc	G	704 551-0700
Charlotte *(G-2905)*		
Hill Printing Company	G	919 833-5934
Raleigh *(G-12845)*		
Hinson Industries Inc	G	252 937-7171
Rocky Mount *(G-13700)*		
Hinsons Typing & Printing	G	919 934-9036
Smithfield *(G-14462)*		
Hunsucker Printing Co Inc	G	336 629-9125
Asheboro *(G-441)*		
Ideal Printing	G	336 754-4050
Walkertown *(G-15614)*		
Ideal Printing Services Inc	G	336 784-0074
Kernersville *(G-9205)*		
Image Solutions	G	336 769-8403
Pilot Mountain *(G-12197)*		
Image Works Inc	G	336 668-3338
Jamestown *(G-9056)*		
Imagemark Business Svcs Inc	G	704 865-4912
Gastonia *(G-6423)*		
Impact Digital Printing Inc	G	704 609-7638
Cornelius *(G-4560)*		
Impact Printing and Design LLC	G	919 377-9747
Fuquay Varina *(G-6203)*		
Imperial Printing Pdts Co Inc	E	704 554-1188
Lowell *(G-10009)*		
Independence Printing	G	336 771-0234
Winston Salem *(G-16757)*		
Ingalls Alton	G	252 975-2056
Washington *(G-15712)*		
Ink Well	G	336 727-9750
Winston Salem *(G-16761)*		
Inkwell	G	919 433-7539
Fayetteville *(G-5843)*		
Inprimo Solutions Inc	G	919 390-7776
Raleigh *(G-12891)*		
Insta Copy Shop Ltd	F	704 376-1350
Charlotte *(G-2977)*		
International Minute Press	G	704 246-3758
Matthews *(G-10255)*		
Itek Graphics LLC	E	704 357-6002
Concord *(G-4291)*		
J & E Digital Printing Inc	G	919 803-8913
Raleigh *(G-12906)*		
James G Gouge	G	336 854-1551
High Point *(G-8415)*		
JB II Printing LLC	E	336 222-0717
Burlington *(G-1439)*		
JM Graphics Inc	G	704 375-1147
Charlotte *(G-3024)*		
Jofra Graphics Inc	G	910 259-1717
Burgaw *(G-1342)*		
Jones Printing Company Inc	F	919 774-9442
Sanford *(G-14141)*		
Joseph C Woodard Prtg Co Inc	F	919 829-0634
Raleigh *(G-12922)*		

Employee Codes: A=Over 500 employees, B=251-500
C=101-250, D=51-100, E=20-50, F=10-19, G=1-9

2024 Harris North Carolina Manufacturers Directory

PRINTING: Offset

Js Printing LLC .... G 919 773-1103
  Raleigh (G-12925)

Kathie S Mc Daniel .... G 336 835-1544
  Elkin (G-5622)

Kelly Printing LLC .... G 336 760-0505
  Winston Salem (G-16777)

Key Printing Inc .... F 252 459-4783
  Nashville (G-11746)

Kinston Office Supply Co Inc .... E 252 523-7654
  Kinston (G-9373)

Kolb Boyette & Assoc Inc .... E 919 544-7839
  Durham (G-5182)

Kudzu Printing Company Inc .... G 828 330-4887
  Black Mountain (G-1128)

Kwik Kopy Business .... G 704 987-0111
  Huntersville (G-8846)

Landmark Printing Inc .... G 919 833-5151
  Raleigh (G-12954)

Landmark Printing Co Inc .... G 919 833-5151
  Raleigh (G-12955)

Legacy Graphics Inc .... G 919 741-6262
  Garner (G-6281)

Lenoir Printing Inc .... G 828 758-7260
  Lenoir (G-9627)

Litho Priting Inc .... G 919 755-9542
  Raleigh (G-12975)

Loftin & Company Inc .... E 704 393-9393
  Charlotte (G-3100)

Lynchs Office Supply Co Inc .... F 252 537-6041
  Roanoke Rapids (G-13578)

M C C of Laurinburg Inc .... G 910 276-0519
  Laurinburg (G-9486)

Mail Management Services LLC ..... F 828 236-0076
  Asheville (G-693)

Markell Publishing Company Inc ..... G 336 226-7148
  Burlington (G-1454)

Master Marketing Group LLC .... G 870 932-4491
  Raleigh (G-13004)

Masters Hand Print Works Inc .... G 828 652-5833
  Marion (G-10159)

Measurement Incorporated .... C 919 683-2413
  Durham (G-5213)

Medlit Solutions LLC .... D 919 878-6789
  Garner (G-6287)

Mellineum Printing .... F 919 267-5752
  Apex (G-217)

Metro Productions Inc .... F 919 851-6420
  Raleigh (G-13022)

Minges Printing & Advg Co .... G 704 867-6791
  Gastonia (G-6466)

Minuteman Quick Copy Svc Inc ...... G 910 455-5353
  Jacksonville (G-9014)

Mj Printing .... G 336 992-3828
  Kernersville (G-9217)

Monarch Printers .... G 704 376-1533
  Charlotte (G-3198)

Monte Enterprises Inc .... G 252 637-5803
  New Bern (G-11825)

Moore Printing & Graphics Inc .... E 919 821-3293
  Raleigh (G-13041)

Morgan Printers Inc .... F 252 355-5588
  Winterville (G-17008)

Murphy Printing & Vinyl LLC .... G 828 835-4848
  Murphy (G-11714)

NC Printing LLC .... G 828 393-4615
  Hendersonville (G-7885)

New Hanover Printing and Pubg ..... G 910 520-7173
  Wilmington (G-16336)

Old Style Printing .... G 828 452-1122
  Waynesville (G-15813)

Ollis Enterprises Inc .... E 828 265-0004
  Wilkesboro (G-16037)

Pamor Fine Print .... G 919 559-2846
  Raleigh (G-13097)

PBM Graphics Inc .... C 919 544-6222
  Durham (G-5276)

PBM Graphics Inc .... C 336 664-5800
  Greensboro (G-7248)

PBM Graphics Inc .... C 919 544-6222
  Durham (G-5277)

Perlman Inc .... F 704 332-1164
  Charlotte (G-3332)

Person Printing Company Inc .... E 336 599-2146
  Roxboro (G-13818)

Piedmont Business Forms Inc .... F 828 464-0010
  Newton (G-11960)

Piedmont Graphics Inc .... E 336 230-0040
  Greensboro (G-7257)

Piedmont Triad Printing Inc .... G 336 235-3080
  Greensboro (G-7261)

Pilgrim Tract Society Inc .... G 336 495-1241
  Randleman (G-13483)

Pilot LLC .... D 910 692-7271
  Southern Pines (G-14546)

Pioneer Printing Company Inc .... G 336 789-4011
  Mount Airy (G-11558)

PIP Printing & Document Servic .... G 336 222-0717
  Burlington (G-1475)

Poole Printing Company Inc .... G 919 876-5260
  Raleigh (G-13120)

Pope Printing & Design Inc .... G 828 274-5945
  Asheville (G-738)

Postal Instant Press .... F 336 222-0717
  Burlington (G-1477)

Powell Ink Inc .... F 828 253-6886
  Asheville (G-739)

Precision Printing .... G 252 338-2450
  Elizabeth City (G-5564)

Precision Printing .... G 336 273-5794
  Greensboro (G-7275)

Prime Source Opc LLC .... E 336 661-3300
  Winston Salem (G-16866)

Primo Inc .... G 888 822-5815
  Cornelius (G-4578)

Print Charlotte Inc .... G 704 488-5896
  Charlotte (G-3383)

Print Express Enterprises Inc .... G 336 765-5505
  Clemmons (G-4055)

Print Express Inc .... F 910 455-4554
  Jacksonville (G-9021)

Print Express Plus .... G 252 541-4444
  Roanoke Rapids (G-13580)

Print Haus Inc .... G 828 456-8622
  Waynesville (G-15817)

Print Management Group LLC .... F 704 821-0114
  Charlotte (G-3385)

Print Media Associates Inc .... G 704 529-0555
  Charlotte (G-3386)

Print Professionals .... G 607 279-3335
  Pinehurst (G-12231)

Print Shoppe of Rocky Mt Inc .... F 252 442-9912
  Rocky Mount (G-13724)

Print Usa Inc .... G 910 485-2254
  Fayetteville (G-5901)

Print Works Fayetteville Inc .... G 910 864-8100
  Fayetteville (G-5902)

Printcrafters Incorporated .... G 704 873-7387
  Statesville (G-14869)

Printer Solutions Inc .... G 919 592-1077
  Raleigh (G-13142)

Printery .... F 336 852-9774
  Greensboro (G-7284)

Printing & Packaging Inc .... E 704 482-3866
  Shelby (G-14357)

Printing Partners Inc .... G 336 996-2268
  Kernersville (G-9225)

Printing Press .... G 828 299-1234
  Asheville (G-743)

Printing Svcs Greensboro Inc .... F 336 274-7663
  Greensboro (G-7285)

Printlogic Inc .... E 336 626-6680
  Asheboro (G-468)

Printmarketing LLC .... G 828 261-0063
  Hickory (G-8125)

Printsurge Incorporated .... G 919 854-4376
  Raleigh (G-13143)

Printville .... G 828 225-3777
  Asheville (G-744)

Priority Prtg Charlotte Inc .... G 802 374-8360
  Charlotte (G-3389)

Prism Printing & Design Inc .... G 919 706-5977
  Cary (G-1859)

Proforma Print Source .... G 919 383-2070
  Durham (G-5306)

Quad/Graphics Inc .... E 706 648-5456
  Charlotte (G-3399)

Quality Instant Printing Inc .... F 919 544-1777
  Durham (G-5313)

Quality Printing Solutions Inc .... G 919 261-9527
  Raleigh (G-13165)

Quality Prtg Cartridge Fctry .... G 336 852-2505
  Greensboro (G-7301)

Quick Color Solutions .... G 336 698-0951
  Mc Leansville (G-10395)

Quick Print of Concord .... G 704 782-6634
  Salisbury (G-14035)

Quik Print Inc .... G 910 738-6775
  Lumberton (G-10050)

Raleigh .... G 919 306-3208
  Raleigh (G-13172)

Raleigh Printing & Typing Inc .... G 919 662-8001
  Raleigh (G-13181)

Randall Printing Inc .... G 336 272-3333
  Greensboro (G-7303)

Redbird Screen Printing LLC .... G 919 946-0005
  Raleigh (G-13199)

Richa Inc .... G 704 944-0230
  Charlotte (G-3448)

Richa Inc .... F 704 331-9744
  Charlotte (G-3449)

Rite Instant Printing Inc .... G 336 768-5061
  Winston Salem (G-16885)

Roark Printing Inc .... G 704 889-5544
  Pineville (G-12295)

Ronald .... G 828 433-1377
  Morganton (G-11247)

Russell Printing Inc .... G 404 366-0552
  Burlington (G-1489)

S Chamblee Incorporated .... E 919 833-7561
  Raleigh (G-13221)

S Ruppe Inc .... E 828 287-4936
  Rutherfordton (G-13889)

S&A Marketing Inc .... G 704 376-0938
  Charlotte (G-3478)

Sdp Impress ME .... G 919 947-1197
  Goldsboro (G-6655)

Seaside Press Co Inc .... G 910 458-8156
  Carolina Beach (G-1641)

Seaway Printing Company .... G 910 457-6158
  Southport (G-14579)

Shelby Business Cards .... G 704 481-8341
  Shelby (G-14363)

Sign and Print Shop .... G 919 542-0727
  Pittsboro (G-12349)

Signature Mailings .... G 919 981-5736
  New Hill (G-11864)

PRODUCT SECTION

PROFILE SHAPES: Unsupported Plastics

Sillaman & Sons Inc .... G 919 774-6324
  Sanford *(G-14184)*

Sire Tees .... G 919 787-6843
  Raleigh *(G-13268)*

Smith & Fox Inc .... F 828 684-4512
  Arden *(G-377)*

Smith Printing Company LLC ..... G 704 575-9235
  Charlotte *(G-3567)*

SOS Printing Inc .... F 828 264-4262
  Boone *(G-1237)*

Southern Printing Company Inc .... G 910 259-4807
  Burgaw *(G-1352)*

Southport Graphics LLC .... G 919 650-3822
  Morrisville *(G-11433)*

Spee Dee Que Instant Prtg Inc .... G 919 683-1307
  Durham *(G-5367)*

SpeeDee Prints LLC .... G 704 366-1405
  Charlotte *(G-3601)*

Speediprint Inc .... F 910 483-2553
  Fayetteville *(G-5921)*

Stein-Palmer Printing Co .... G 740 633-3894
  Mooresville *(G-11101)*

Sun Printing Company Inc .... G 336 773-1346
  Winston Salem *(G-16923)*

T & R Signs .... G 919 779-1185
  Garner *(G-6317)*

Table Rock Printers LLC .... G 828 433-1477
  Morganton *(G-11260)*

Tarason Label Inc .... G 828 464-4743
  Hickory *(G-8174)*

Telepathic Graphics Inc .... F 919 342-4603
  Rocky Mount *(G-13672)*

Theo Davis Sons Incorporated .... E 919 269-7401
  Zebulon *(G-17143)*

Total Print Solutions .... G 336 841-5292
  High Point *(G-8573)*

Treva Mason LLC .... G 704 566-7973
  Charlotte *(G-3721)*

Triangle Solutions Inc .... G 919 481-1235
  Cary *(G-1912)*

Twyford Printing Company Inc .... G 910 892-3271
  Dunn *(G-4888)*

Unique Printer Solutions LLC ...... G 704 544-4822
  Charlotte *(G-3749)*

Unlimted Potential Sanford Inc .... E 919 852-1117
  Morrisville *(G-11460)*

Value Printing Inc .... G 919 380-9883
  Cary *(G-1916)*

Via Prnting Graphic Design Inc ... G 919 872-8688
  Youngsville *(G-17112)*

Victory Press LLC .... G 704 660-0348
  Mooresville *(G-11119)*

Village Instant Printing Inc .... G 919 968-0000
  Chapel Hill *(G-2094)*

Village Printing Co .... F 336 629-0951
  Asheboro *(G-505)*

VIP Print and Signs .... G 919 968-0000
  Chapel Hill *(G-2095)*

Vista Print .... G 919 400-2736
  Raleigh *(G-13407)*

Wallace Printing Inc .... F 828 466-3300
  Newton *(G-11982)*

Walter Printing Company Inc ...... G 704 982-8899
  Albemarle *(G-112)*

Wayne Trademark Prtg Packg LLC .... E 336 887-3173
  Asheboro *(G-507)*

Welloyt Enterprises Inc .... G 919 821-7897
  Raleigh *(G-13418)*

West Pointe Printing .... G 704 806-3670
  Charlotte *(G-3805)*

Whistle Stop Press Inc .... F 910 695-1403
  Southern Pines *(G-14560)*

William George Printing LLC ...... E 910 221-2700
  Hope Mills *(G-8738)*

Williams Printing Inc .... G 336 969-2733
  Rural Hall *(G-13856)*

Williams Printing Inc .... G 336 969-2733
  Rural Hall *(G-13857)*

Wright Printing Service Inc .... G 336 427-4768
  Madison *(G-10092)*

Young Graphics Inc .... G 336 249-3148
  Lexington *(G-9803)*

Zebra Communications Inc .... E 919 314-3700
  Morrisville *(G-11469)*

PRINTING: Photo-Offset

Occasions Group Inc .... E 252 321-5805
  Greenville *(G-7566)*

PRINTING: Photolithographic

Interflex Acquisition Co LLC .... C 336 921-3505
  Wilkesboro *(G-16029)*

PRINTING: Rotogravure

Master Screens South LLC .... G 704 226-9600
  Monroe *(G-10766)*

Shamrock Corporation .... C 336 574-4200
  Greensboro *(G-7334)*

PRINTING: Screen, Broadwoven Fabrics, Cotton

Barron Legacy Mgmt Group LLC .... G 301 367-4735
  Charlotte *(G-2285)*

Bread & Butter Custom Scrn Prt .... G 919 942-3198
  Chapel Hill *(G-1995)*

Daztech Inc .... G 800 862-6360
  Wilmington *(G-16196)*

Gaston Screen Printing Inc .... F 704 399-0459
  Charlotte *(G-2810)*

Graphic Attack Inc .... G 252 491-2174
  Harbinger *(G-7683)*

K Formula Enterprises Inc .... G 910 323-3315
  Fayetteville *(G-5853)*

Mojo Sportswear Inc .... G 252 758-4176
  Greenville *(G-7562)*

One Hundred Ten Percent Screen .... G 252 728-3848
  Beaufort *(G-963)*

Raleigh Tees .... G 919 850-3378
  Raleigh *(G-13187)*

S & L Creations Inc .... G 704 824-1930
  Lowell *(G-10011)*

Screen Master .... G 252 492-8407
  Henderson *(G-7810)*

Silverlining Screen Prtrs Inc .... G 919 554-0340
  Youngsville *(G-17097)*

T & R Signs .... G 919 779-1185
  Garner *(G-6317)*

Tryon Finishing Corporation .... F 828 859-5891
  Tryon *(G-15429)*

PRINTING: Screen, Fabric

A&M Screen Printing NC Inc .... G 910 792-1111
  Wilmington *(G-16089)*

Amy Smith .... G 828 352-1001
  Burnsville *(G-1522)*

Boardwalk Inc .... G 252 240-1095
  Morehead City *(G-11155)*

Brandrpm LLC .... D 704 225-1800
  Charlotte *(G-2347)*

Combintons Screen Prtg EMB Inc .... G 336 472-4420
  Thomasville *(G-15204)*

Dicks Store .... G 336 548-9358
  Madison *(G-10073)*

Freeman Screen Printers Inc ...... G 704 521-9148
  Charlotte *(G-2795)*

G & G Enterprises .... G 336 764-2493
  Clemmons *(G-4041)*

Grace Apparel Company Inc ...... G 828 242-8172
  Arden *(G-335)*

Hi-Tech Screens Inc .... F 828 452-5151
  Waynesville *(G-15807)*

Island Xprtees of Oter Bnks In .... E 252 480-3990
  Nags Head *(G-11720)*

Keiths Kustomz LLC .... G 704 524-8684
  Gastonia *(G-6438)*

Lee Marks .... G 919 493-2208
  Durham *(G-5188)*

Line Drive Sports Center Inc ...... G 336 824-1692
  Ramseur *(G-13446)*

M-Prints Inc .... G 828 265-4929
  Boone *(G-1216)*

Manna Corp North Carolina .... G 828 696-3642
  Hendersonville *(G-7875)*

Marketing One Sportswear Inc .... G 704 334-9333
  Charlotte *(G-3126)*

R & S Sporting Goods Ctr Inc ..... G 336 599-0248
  Roxboro *(G-13820)*

Regimental Flag & T Shirts .... G 919 496-2888
  Louisburg *(G-9999)*

Rogers Screenprinting EMB Inc .... G 910 628-1983
  Fairmont *(G-5705)*

Tapped Tees LLC .... G 919 943-9692
  Durham *(G-5386)*

Tarason Label Inc .... G 828 464-4743
  Hickory *(G-8174)*

Textile Printing Inc .... G 704 521-8099
  Charlotte *(G-3683)*

Torches Design Studio Inc .... G 704 966-4000
  Denver *(G-4808)*

PRINTING: Screen, Manmade Fiber & Silk, Broadwoven Fabric

Custom Screens Inc .... E 336 427-0265
  Madison *(G-10071)*

Gaston Screen Printing Inc .... F 704 399-0459
  Charlotte *(G-2810)*

Visigraphix Inc .... G 336 882-1935
  Colfax *(G-4162)*

PRINTING: Thermography

Beacon Thermography Inc .... G 727 470-1694
  Hampstead *(G-7640)*

Endaxi Company Inc .... E 919 467-8895
  Morrisville *(G-11338)*

Laru Industries Inc .... F 704 821-7503
  Indian Trail *(G-8944)*

PROFESSIONAL EQPT & SPLYS, WHOLESALE: Engineers', NEC

Sharpe Images Properties Inc .... E 336 724-2871
  Winston Salem *(G-16906)*

PROFESSIONAL EQPT & SPLYS, WHOLESALE: Optical Goods

Optical Place Inc .... E 336 274-1300
  Greensboro *(G-7235)*

PROFESSIONAL INSTRUMENT REPAIR SVCS

Measurement Controls Inc .... F 704 921-1101
  Charlotte *(G-3157)*

PROFILE SHAPES: Unsupported Plastics

American Extruded Plastics Inc........... E 336 274-1131
  Greensboro *(G-6799)*
Boramed Inc.. G 919 419-9518
  Durham *(G-4973)*
M2 Optics Inc..................................... G 919 342-5619
  Raleigh *(G-12985)*
Plastic Technology Inc...................... E 828 328-8570
  Conover *(G-4481)*
Plastic Technology Inc...................... F 828 328-2201
  Hickory *(G-8116)*
Precise Technology Inc..................... G 704 576-9527
  Charlotte *(G-3368)*
Robetex Inc.. F 910 671-8787
  Lumberton *(G-10053)*
Roechling Indus Gastonia LP............ C 704 922-7814
  Dallas *(G-4655)*
United Plastics Corporation............... C 336 786-2127
  Mount Airy *(G-11592)*
Weener Plastics Inc........................... D 252 206-1400
  Wilson *(G-16558)*

PROMOTION SVCS

822tees Inc.. G 910 822-8337
  Fayetteville *(G-5748)*
Apple Rock Advg & Prom Inc............ E 336 232-4800
  Greensboro *(G-6811)*

PROPERTY DAMAGE INSURANCE

Discovery Insurance Company........... D 800 876-1492
  Kinston *(G-9358)*

PROTECTION EQPT: Lightning

Capital Lghtning Prtection Inc........... G 919 832-5574
  Raleigh *(G-12590)*
Lightning Prtction Systems LLC......... D 252 213-9900
  Raleigh *(G-12971)*

PROTECTIVE FOOTWEAR: Rubber Or Plastic

Winstn-Slem Inds For Blind Inc......... B 336 759-0551
  Winston Salem *(G-16979)*

PUBLIC RELATIONS & PUBLICITY SVCS

Ed Kemp Associates Inc..................... G 336 869-2155
  High Point *(G-8336)*

PUBLIC RELATIONS SVCS

Inspire Creative Studios Inc............... G 910 395-0200
  Wilmington *(G-16269)*
S & A Cherokee LLC.......................... E 919 674-6020
  Cary *(G-1876)*

PUBLISHERS: Art Copy & Poster

Cedar Hill Studio & Gallery................ G 828 456-6344
  Waynesville *(G-15797)*
Klazzy Magazine Inc.......................... G 704 293-8321
  Charlotte *(G-3057)*

PUBLISHERS: Music Book & Sheet Music

Otter Publications............................... G 336 643-5387
  Oak Ridge *(G-12063)*
Ron Clearfield..................................... G 828 683-4425
  Leicester *(G-9519)*

PUBLISHERS: Music, Sheet

Money 4 Lyfe...................................... G 704 606-8671
  Charlotte *(G-3199)*

PUBLISHERS: Telephone & Other Directory

1 Click Web Solutions LLC................. E 910 790-9330
  Wilmington *(G-16086)*
School Directorease LLC.................... G 240 206-6273
  Charlotte *(G-3505)*
SRI Ventures Inc................................ G 919 427-1681
  Sanford *(G-14190)*
Tarheel Publishing Co........................ F 919 553-9042
  Clayton *(G-4016)*

PUBLISHING & BROADCASTING: Internet Only

3 Hungry Guys LLC............................ G 408 644-3119
  Chapel Hill *(G-1980)*
Beyond Normal Media LLC................ G 980 263-9921
  Charlotte *(G-2306)*
Black Business Universe LLC............ G 215 279-1509
  Louisburg *(G-9980)*
Datanyze LLC.................................... E 866 408-1633
  Durham *(G-5049)*
Domco Technology LLC..................... G 888 834-8541
  Barnardsville *(G-908)*
Finley Enterprises LLC...................... G 910 747-6679
  Durham *(G-5096)*
Fit1media LLC.................................... G 919 925-2200
  Raleigh *(G-12770)*
Hearsay Guides LLC.......................... G 336 584-1440
  Elon *(G-5659)*
Lookwhatqmade LLC......................... G 980 330-1995
  Charlotte *(G-3103)*
Mesurio Inc.. G 919 633-8773
  Chapel Hill *(G-2042)*
Norsan Media LLC............................. E 704 494-7181
  Charlotte *(G-3268)*
Online Memorial Services LLC........... G 914 471-6852
  Durham *(G-5258)*
Outer Banks Internet Inc................... G 252 441-6698
  Kill Devil Hills *(G-9259)*
Timberlake Ventures Inc.................... G 704 896-7499
  Wilmington *(G-16429)*
Training Industry Inc.......................... D 919 653-4990
  Raleigh *(G-13356)*
Two24 Digital LLC............................. G 910 475-7555
  Wilmington *(G-16437)*
Video Optimize LLC........................... G 818 421-1489
  Castle Hayne *(G-1960)*
Yeeka LLC.. G 919 308-9826
  Durham *(G-5457)*

PUBLISHING & PRINTING: Art Copy

Document Imaging Systems Inc........ G 919 460-9440
  Raleigh *(G-12693)*
Land and Loft LLC............................. G 315 560-7060
  Raleigh *(G-12953)*

PUBLISHING & PRINTING: Book Music

Landmark Music Group Inc................ G 919 800-7277
  Garner *(G-6280)*

PUBLISHING & PRINTING: Books

International Society Automtn............ E 919 206-4176
  Durham *(G-5162)*
Lulu Technology Circus Inc............... E 919 459-5858
  Morrisville *(G-11385)*
Mable Mullen...................................... G 252 599-1181
  Elizabeth City *(G-5555)*
Sticker Farm LLC............................... G 919 332-1342
  Charlotte *(G-3632)*
Tan Books and Publishers Inc........... G 704 731-0651
  Charlotte *(G-3672)*
Tower House Publishing LLC............. G 917 284-0619
  Sanford *(G-14197)*
Two of A Kind Publishing LLC........... G 704 497-2879
  Charlotte *(G-3742)*

PUBLISHING & PRINTING: Directories, NEC

Deverger Systems Inc........................ G 828 253-2255
  Asheville *(G-608)*
Strawbridge Studios Inc..................... D 919 286-9512
  Durham *(G-5377)*

PUBLISHING & PRINTING: Directories, Telephone

University Directories LLC.................. D 800 743-5556
  Durham *(G-5424)*

PUBLISHING & PRINTING: Magazines: publishing & printing

Carolina Publishing Company............. G 252 206-1633
  Wilson *(G-16485)*
Carolina Woman Inc........................... G 919 869-8200
  Chapel Hill *(G-1998)*
Greater Wilmington Business............. G 910 343-8600
  Wilmington *(G-16240)*
Knight Communications Inc............... F 704 568-7804
  Indian Trail *(G-8943)*
M&J Oldco Inc.................................... D 336 854-0309
  Greensboro *(G-7175)*
Magazine Nakia Lashawn................... G 919 875-1156
  Raleigh *(G-12987)*
New Bern Magazine........................... G 252 626-5812
  New Bern *(G-11830)*
News and Observer Pubg Co.............. A 919 829-4500
  Raleigh *(G-13063)*
Oasis Magazine LLC........................... G 888 559-7549
  Huntersville *(G-8868)*
Randall-Reilly LLC.............................. C 704 814-1390
  Charlotte *(G-3408)*
Red Hand Media LLC......................... F 704 523-6987
  Charlotte *(G-3422)*
Rose Media Inc................................... F 919 736-1154
  Goldsboro *(G-6651)*
Shannon Media Inc............................. F 919 933-1551
  Chapel Hill *(G-2071)*
Todays Charlotte Woman.................... G 704 521-6872
  Charlotte *(G-3703)*

PUBLISHING & PRINTING: Music, Book

Kindermusik International Inc............ E 800 628-5687
  Greensboro *(G-7151)*
Music Matters Inc............................... G 336 272-5303
  Greensboro *(G-7210)*

PUBLISHING & PRINTING: Newsletters, Business Svc

Ft Media Holdings LLC...................... F 336 605-0121
  Greensboro *(G-7024)*
Savvy - Discountscom News Ltr........ F 252 729-8691
  Smyrna *(G-14490)*

PUBLISHING & PRINTING: Newspapers

ACC Sports Journal............................ F 919 846-7502
  Raleigh *(G-12466)*
Acento Latino..................................... G 910 486-2760
  Fayetteville *(G-5750)*
Advantage Newspaper........................ E 910 323-0349
  Fayetteville *(G-5753)*
Alameen A Haqq................................. G 336 965-8339
  Greensboro *(G-6789)*
Annette Cameron................................ G 828 505-0404
  Asheville *(G-520)*
Anson Express.................................... G 704 694-2480
  Wadesboro *(G-15500)*

PUBLISHING & PRINTING: Newspapers

Apg/East LLC... C 252 329-9500
   Greenville (G-7484)
APS Hickory... G 828 323-1010
   Hickory (G-7938)
Asheville Citizen-Times................................. G 828 252-5611
   Asheville (G-532)
Asheville Global Report................................. G 828 236-3103
   Asheville (G-536)
Benmot Publishing Company Inc................... G 919 658-9456
   Mount Olive (G-11655)
Black Mountain News Inc.............................. G 828 669-8727
   Black Mountain (G-1120)
Burke Mill... G 336 774-2952
   Winston Salem (G-16640)
Business Journals.. D 704 371-3248
   Charlotte (G-2365)
C Alan Publications LLC............................... G 336 272-3920
   Greensboro (G-6870)
C York Law Pllc.. G 910 256-1235
   Wilmington (G-16146)
Camp Lejeune Globe..................................... G 910 939-0705
   Jacksonville (G-8993)
Cape Fear Newspapers Inc........................... G 910 285-2178
   Wallace (G-15620)
Carolina Trader... G 910 433-2229
   Fayetteville (G-5785)
Carolinian Pubg Group LLC........................... G 919 834-5558
   Raleigh (G-12602)
Carteret Publishing Company........................ D 252 726-7081
   Morehead City (G-11159)
Catawba Vly Youth Soccer Assoc................. G 828 234-7082
   Hickory (G-7971)
Catholic News and Herald............................. G 704 370-3333
   Charlotte (G-2420)
Champion Media LLC................................... C 910 506-3021
   Laurinburg (G-9473)
Charlotte Observer....................................... E 704 358-5000
   Charlotte (G-2453)
Charlotte Observer Pubg Co......................... E 704 987-3660
   Charlotte (G-2454)
Charlotte Observer Pubg Co......................... E 704 572-0747
   Charlotte (G-2455)
Charlotte Observer Pubg Co......................... E 704 358-6020
   Matthews (G-10241)
Charlotte Post Pubg Co Inc.......................... F 704 376-0496
   Charlotte (G-2461)
Charlotte Publishing Company..................... E 704 547-0900
   Charlotte (G-2462)
Charlotte Weekly.. G 704 849-2261
   Charlotte (G-2466)
Chatham News Publishing Co...................... G 919 663-4042
   Siler City (G-14406)
Chronicle Mill Land LLC................................ G 704 527-3227
   Gastonia (G-6378)
Chronicles.. G 252 617-1774
   Jacksonville (G-8995)
Community First Media Inc........................... G 704 482-4142
   Shelby (G-14302)
Community Newspapers Inc......................... G 828 743-5101
   Cashiers (G-1935)
Community Newspapers Inc......................... G 828 369-3430
   Franklin (G-6121)
Community Newspapers Inc......................... G 828 389-8431
   Hayesville (G-7763)
Community Newspapers Inc......................... G 828 479-3383
   Robbinsville (G-13606)
Community Newspapers Inc......................... G 828 765-7169
   Spruce Pine (G-14633)
County Press Inc.. G 919 894-2112
   Benson (G-1033)
Cox Nrth Crlina Pblcations Inc..................... G 252 482-4418
   Edenton (G-5510)

Cox Nrth Crlina Pblcations Inc..................... C 252 335-0841
   Elizabeth City (G-5538)
Cox Nrth Crlina Pblcations Inc..................... D 252 792-1181
   Williamston (G-16059)
Cox Nrth Crlina Pblcations Inc..................... C 252 329-9643
   Greenville (G-7510)
Cryotherapy of Pines LLC............................ G 910 988-0357
   Southern Pines (G-14532)
Cynthia Drew.. G 828 301-8697
   Barnardsville (G-907)
Daily Courier.. E 828 245-6431
   Rutherfordton (G-13871)
Daily Living Solutions Inc............................. G 704 614-0977
   Charlotte (G-2599)
Daily N-Gine LLC... G 336 285-8042
   Greensboro (G-6957)
Daily Victories Inc.. G 704 982-1341
   Albemarle (G-81)
Db North Carolina Holdings Inc.................... E 910 323-4848
   Fayetteville (G-5808)
Defy Hickory.. G 828 222-4144
   Hickory (G-8005)
Democracy Greensboro................................ G 336 635-7016
   Greensboro (G-6969)
Denton Orator.. G 336 859-3131
   Denton (G-4732)
Dolan LLC.. G 919 829-9333
   Raleigh (G-12694)
Ellis Publishing Company Inc....................... F 252 444-1999
   New Bern (G-11803)
Epi Group Llc... B 843 577-7111
   Durham (G-5091)
Epoch Times Nc Inc..................................... G 919 649-6014
   Cary (G-1760)
Fairfax Digital LLC....................................... F 407 822-2918
   Charlotte (G-2745)
Fairview Town Crier...................................... G 828 628-4547
   Fairview (G-5710)
Framers Cottage.. G 910 638-0100
   Whispering Pines (G-15954)
Franklin County Newspapers Inc.................. F 919 496-6503
   Louisburg (G-9988)
Future Endeavors Hickory LLC.................... G 828 256-5488
   Hickory (G-8030)
Gannett Media Corp...................................... G 828 649-1075
   Marshall (G-10202)
Gannett Media Corp...................................... F 919 467-1402
   Morrisville (G-11346)
Gastonia.. G 704 377-3687
   Gastonia (G-6406)
Good News Iphc Ministries Inc..................... G 919 906-2104
   Jacksonville (G-9003)
Granville Publishing Co Inc.......................... G 919 528-2393
   Creedmoor (G-4614)
Greensboro Drifters Inc............................... G 336 375-6743
   Greensboro (G-7063)
Greensboro News & Record LLC................. A 336 373-7000
   Greensboro (G-7064)
Greensboro Voice... F 336 255-1006
   Greensboro (G-7067)
Grey Area News.. G 919 637-6973
   Zebulon (G-17130)
Halifax Media Group..................................... F 704 869-1700
   Gastonia (G-6411)
Harley Owners Group Sttsvlle I.................... G 704 872-3883
   Statesville (G-14808)
Hendersnvlle Affrdbl Hsing Cor.................... F 828 692-6175
   Hendersonville (G-7862)
Henderson Newspapers Inc......................... D 252 436-2700
   Henderson (G-7786)
Herald A Pierre LLC..................................... G 919 730-2965
   Fairmont (G-5702)

Herald Huntersville.. G 704 766-2100
   Huntersville (G-8830)
Herald Printing Co Inc.................................. E 252 537-2505
   Roanoke Rapids (G-13575)
Herald Sanford Inc....................................... D 919 708-9000
   Sanford (G-14130)
Hickory Publishing Co Inc............................ E 828 322-4510
   Hickory (G-8049)
Hickory Youth Sports Inc............................. G 828 327-9550
   Hickory (G-8057)
High Country Media LLC.............................. G 828 733-2448
   Newland (G-11888)
High Point Enterprise Inc............................. G 336 434-2716
   High Point (G-8387)
High Point Enterprise Inc............................. F 336 883-2839
   High Point (G-8388)
Highcorp Incorporated.................................. E 910 642-4104
   Whiteville (G-15966)
Horizon Publications Inc.............................. F 828 464-0221
   Newton (G-11941)
Hpt Hitoms LLC... G 336 541-8093
   Greensboro (G-7102)
Hush Greensboro.. G 336 676-6133
   Greensboro (G-7106)
Indy Week.. G 919 832-8774
   Raleigh (G-12886)
Iodine Poetry Journal................................... G 704 595-9526
   Charlotte (G-2991)
Iredell Holding LLC...................................... G 828 506-2555
   Claremont (G-3930)
Iwanna.. G 828 505-7319
   Asheville (G-665)
Jamestown News.. G 336 841-4933
   Jamestown (G-9059)
Jesus Daily Group LLC................................ G 336 727-4781
   Winston Salem (G-16770)
Jim John... G 336 352-4650
   Mount Airy (G-11526)
Jones Media.. F 828 264-3612
   Boone (G-1212)
Journal Doctors Inc..................................... G 919 469-1438
   Cary (G-1799)
Journal Vacuum Science & Tech.................. G 919 361-2787
   Cary (G-1800)
JR Mooresville Inc....................................... G 973 434-6453
   Statesville (G-14827)
Kinston Free Press Company....................... C 252 527-3191
   Kinston (G-9371)
Ledger Publishing Company......................... F 919 693-2646
   Oxford (G-12135)
Lincoln Herald LLC...................................... G 704 735-3620
   Lincolnton (G-9901)
Lumina News.. G 910 256-6569
   Wilmington (G-16309)
Mc Clatchy Interactive USA.......................... F 919 861-1200
   Raleigh (G-13011)
McDowell Pressure Washing........................ G 828 620-2141
   Marion (G-10163)
Media Wilimington Co.................................. G 910 791-0688
   Wilmington (G-16319)
Mid South Management NC Inc................... E 336 835-1513
   Elkin (G-5625)
Montgomery Herald...................................... G 910 576-6051
   Troy (G-15408)
Mooresville NC... G 704 909-6459
   Mooresville (G-11025)
Mooresville Parlor LLC................................ G 704 450-1836
   Mooresville (G-11026)
Mooresville Tax Service Inc......................... G 704 360-1040
   Mooresville (G-11027)
Mooresville Tribune..................................... G 704 872-0148
   Hickory (G-8097)

Employee Codes: A=Over 500 employees, B=251-500
C=101-250, D=51-100, E=20-50, F=10-19, G=1-9

PUBLISHING & PRINTING: Newspapers

Mooresvlle Blue Dvil Band Bste............ G 704 787-2994
Mooresville *(G-11028)*

Morganton Service League Inc........... G 828 439-9525
Morganton *(G-11235)*

Mountain Times Inc.............................. G 336 246-6397
West Jefferson *(G-15945)*

Mountaineer Enterprise....................... G 828 670-5425
Biltmore Lake *(G-1101)*

Mullen Publications Inc...................... F 704 527-5111
Charlotte *(G-3214)*

News & Record..................................... F 336 627-1781
Reidsville *(G-13536)*

News 14 Carolina................................. F 704 973-5700
Charlotte *(G-3253)*

News and Observer Pubg Co.............. F 919 894-4170
Benson *(G-1040)*

News and Observer Pubg Co.............. F 919 419-6500
Durham *(G-5245)*

News and Observer Pubg Co.............. F 919 829-8903
Garner *(G-6296)*

News and Observer Pubg Co.............. A 919 829-4500
Raleigh *(G-13063)*

Next Magazine....................................... G 910 609-0638
Fayetteville *(G-5882)*

Norman E Clark..................................... G 336 573-9629
Stoneville *(G-14963)*

Norman Lake High................................ G 336 971-7348
Mooresville *(G-11039)*

Observer News Enterprise Inc............ E 828 464-0221
Newton *(G-11954)*

Old-Time Music Group Inc.................. G 919 286-2041
Durham *(G-5256)*

Our Daily Living..................................... G 919 220-8160
Durham *(G-5265)*

Owner Tryon Backdoor Dist................ G 864 237-1667
Tryon *(G-15426)*

Paxton Media Group............................. F 704 289-1541
Monroe *(G-10784)*

Perfect Square Music Inc.................... G 478 718-5702
Arden *(G-363)*

Pflag Hickory.. G 828 244-5578
Hickory *(G-8113)*

Philantrophy Journal............................. G 919 890-6240
Raleigh *(G-13109)*

Pilot LLC... G 864 430-6337
Southern Pines *(G-14545)*

Pilot LLC... D 910 692-7271
Southern Pines *(G-14546)*

PMG-DH Company................................ C 919 419-6500
Durham *(G-5292)*

Post Publishing Company................... D 704 633-8950
Salisbury *(G-14026)*

Post Voice LLC..................................... G 910 259-9111
Burgaw *(G-1347)*

Pride Publishing & Typsg Inc............. G 704 531-9988
Charlotte *(G-3380)*

Raleigh Downtowner............................ G 919 821-9000
Raleigh *(G-13176)*

Raysweathercom Inc............................ G 828 264-2030
Boone *(G-1233)*

Record Publishing Company............... E 910 230-1948
Dunn *(G-4881)*

Rhinoceros Times.................................. F 336 763-4170
Greensboro *(G-7310)*

Richard D Stewart................................. G 919 284-2295
Kenly *(G-9156)*

Richmond Observer LLP..................... G 910 817-3169
Rockingham *(G-13642)*

Robert Laskowski.................................. G 203 732-0846
New Bern *(G-11840)*

Rockingham Now.................................. G 336 349-4331
Reidsville *(G-13538)*

Rotary Club Statesville........................ F 704 872-6851
Statesville *(G-14878)*

Ryjak Enterprises LLC......................... F 910 638-0716
Southern Pines *(G-14551)*

Sandhills Sentinel Inc.......................... G 910 944-0992
Aberdeen *(G-28)*

Seaside Press Co Inc.......................... G 910 458-8156
Carolina Beach *(G-1641)*

Seven Lakes News Corporation......... G 910 685-0320
West End *(G-15932)*

Shelby Freedom Star Inc.................... C 704 484-7000
Shelby *(G-14365)*

Silver Miller Holdings Llc.................... G 828 652-6677
Marion *(G-10176)*

Snap Publications LLC......................... F 336 274-8531
Greensboro *(G-7346)*

Spectacular Publishing Inc................. F 919 672-0289
Durham *(G-5366)*

St of Greensboro LLC.......................... G 336 851-1600
Greensboro *(G-7363)*

Statesville High..................................... F 704 873-3491
Statesville *(G-14902)*

Statesville LLC...................................... G 704 872-3303
Statesville *(G-14903)*

Statesville Sandlot Basbal Inc........... G 704 880-1334
Statesville *(G-14905)*

Sudanese Cmnty Schl Greensboro.... G 336 763-7761
Greensboro *(G-7378)*

Surry Scene... G 336 786-4141
Mount Airy *(G-11583)*

Sylva Herald and Ruralite.................... E 828 586-2611
Sylva *(G-15070)*

Sylva Herald Pubg Co Incthe.............. F 828 586-2611
Sylva *(G-15071)*

Tallahassee Democrat.......................... G 919 832-9430
Raleigh *(G-13326)*

Times Journal Inc................................. G 828 682-4067
Burnsville *(G-1535)*

Topsail Voice LLC................................ G 910 270-2944
Hampstead *(G-7662)*

Triangle Tribune.................................... G 704 376-0496
Durham *(G-5411)*

Tribune Papers Inc............................... G 828 606-5050
Asheville *(G-806)*

Tryon Newsmedia LLC......................... F 828 859-9151
Tryon *(G-15430)*

Tucker Production Incorporated........ G 828 322-1036
Hickory *(G-8190)*

Twin Cy Kwnis Fndtion Wnstn-SL..... G 336 784-1649
Winston Salem *(G-16959)*

Up & Coming Magazine....................... F 910 391-3859
Fayetteville *(G-5941)*

Up and Coming Weekly....................... E 910 484-6200
Fayetteville *(G-5942)*

Urban News.. G 828 253-5585
Asheville *(G-810)*

Virginn-Plot Mdia Cmpanies LLC....... G 252 441-3628
Nags Head *(G-11728)*

Wake Forest Gazette............................ G 919 556-3409
Wake Forest *(G-15611)*

Want of ADS of Greensboro................ F 336 297-4300
Greensboro *(G-7454)*

Washington News Publishing Co...... F 252 946-2144
Washington *(G-15739)*

Wayne Printing Company Inc............. E 919 778-2211
Goldsboro *(G-6669)*

West Stkes Wldcat Grdron CLB I...... G 336 985-6152
King *(G-9284)*

Wick Communications Co.................. E 252 537-2505
Roanoke Rapids *(G-13589)*

Wilmington Journal Company............ G 910 762-5502
Wilmington *(G-16446)*

Wilmington Star-News Inc.................. D 910 343-2000
Wilmington *(G-16452)*

Winstn-Slem Chronicle Pubg Inc...... F 336 722-8624
Winston Salem *(G-16978)*

Winston Salem Journal....................... E 336 727-7211
Winston Salem *(G-16982)*

Womack Newspaper Inc..................... G 336 316-1231
Greensboro *(G-7465)*

World Newspaper Publishing............. G 704 548-1737
Charlotte *(G-3824)*

Wtvd Television LLC........................... C 919 683-1111
Durham *(G-5451)*

Yancy Common Times Journal.......... G 828 682-2120
Burnsville *(G-1538)*

PUBLISHING & PRINTING: Pamphlets

Readable Communications Inc........... G 919 876-5260
Raleigh *(G-13193)*

PUBLISHING & PRINTING: Shopping News

Health Wyze Media............................... G 336 528-4120
Mocksville *(G-10579)*

News and Observer Pubg Co.............. A 919 829-4500
Raleigh *(G-13063)*

PUBLISHING & PRINTING: Textbooks

Carson-Dellosa Publishing LLC......... D 336 632-0084
Greensboro *(G-6893)*

PUBLISHING & PRINTING: Trade Journals

Capre Omnimedia LLC......................... G 917 460-3572
Wilmington *(G-16155)*

Ft Media Holdings LLC........................ F 336 605-0121
Greensboro *(G-7024)*

PUBLISHING & PRINTING: Yearbooks

Herff Jones LLC.................................... G 704 845-3355
Charlotte *(G-2903)*

PULLEYS: Power Transmission

Cavotec USA Inc................................... E 704 873-3009
Mooresville *(G-10900)*

PULP MILLS

Arauco - NA... G 910 569-7020
Biscoe *(G-1103)*

Blue Ridge Paper Products Inc.......... A 828 646-2000
Canton *(G-1600)*

Broad River Forest Products.............. G 828 287-8003
Rutherfordton *(G-13868)*

Buckeye Technologies Inc.................. C 704 822-6400
Mount Holly *(G-11623)*

Ingram Woodyards Inc........................ F 910 556-1250
Sanford *(G-14138)*

North Carolina Converting LLC......... F 704 871-2912
Statesville *(G-14851)*

Westrock Mwv LLC.............................. G 919 334-3200
Raleigh *(G-13419)*

Westrock Paper and Packg LLC........ B 252 533-6000
Roanoke Rapids *(G-13587)*

Weyerhaeuser Company...................... E 252 633-7100
Vanceboro *(G-15485)*

Weyerhaueser Nr Co............................ G 252 633-7252
Vanceboro *(G-15488)*

PULP MILLS: Mechanical & Recycling Processing

Clear Path Recycling LLC................... G 877 387-3738
Fayetteville *(G-5792)*

Everyday Fix Cyclery........................... G 828 855-9989
Hickory *(G-8020)*

PRODUCT SECTION

Martin Materials Inc .... G 336 697-1800
  Greensboro *(G-7186)*

Old School Crushing Co Inc .... F 919 661-0011
  Garner *(G-6298)*

PUMP JACKS & OTHER PUMPING EQPT: Indl

Circor Precision Metering LLC .... A 919 774-7667
  Sanford *(G-14102)*

Enovis Corporation .... F 704 289-6511
  Monroe *(G-10715)*

Flowserve US Inc .... F 972 443-6500
  Raleigh *(G-12776)*

PUMPS & PARTS: Indl

1st Choice Service Inc .... F 704 913-7685
  Cherryville *(G-3861)*

Allied/Carter Machining Inc .... G 704 784-1253
  Concord *(G-4192)*

Clyde Union (us) Inc .... C 704 808-3000
  Charlotte *(G-2503)*

Colfax Pump Group .... C 704 289-6511
  Monroe *(G-10688)*

G Denver and Co LLC .... E 704 896-4000
  Davidson *(G-4675)*

Hurst Jaws of Life Inc .... C 704 487-6961
  Shelby *(G-14328)*

Kral USA Inc .... G 704 814-6164
  Matthews *(G-10261)*

Primax Usa Inc .... G 704 587-3377
  Charlotte *(G-3381)*

Stockholm Corporation .... E 704 552-9314
  Charlotte *(G-3637)*

Vooner Flogard LLC .... F 980 225-3277
  Charlotte *(G-3783)*

PUMPS & PUMPING EQPT REPAIR SVCS

McKinney Electric & Mch Co Inc .... G 828 765-7910
  Spruce Pine *(G-14648)*

Motor Shop Inc .... G 704 867-8488
  Gastonia *(G-6471)*

PUMPS & PUMPING EQPT WHOLESALERS

Air Control Inc .... E 252 492-2300
  Henderson *(G-7775)*

Bfs Industries LLC .... E 919 575-6711
  Butner *(G-1542)*

Bornemann Pumps Inc .... G 704 849-8636
  Matthews *(G-10235)*

Chichibone Inc .... G 919 785-0090
  Morrisville *(G-11321)*

Chichibone Inc .... F 919 785-0090
  Kernersville *(G-9177)*

Circor Precision Metering LLC .... D 704 289-6511
  Monroe *(G-10682)*

Circor Pumps North America LLC .... D 704 289-6511
  Monroe *(G-10683)*

Clydeunion Pumps Inc .... C 704 808-3848
  Charlotte *(G-2504)*

Colfax Amrcas Engnered Systems .... G 704 289-6511
  Monroe *(G-10687)*

Dynisco Instruments LLC .... E 828 326-9888
  Hickory *(G-8013)*

Fairbanks Nijhuis .... G 262 728-7449
  Cary *(G-1768)*

Flowserve Corporation .... E 704 494-0497
  Charlotte *(G-2782)*

Flowserve Corporation .... G 910 371-9011
  Leland *(G-9543)*

Haldex Inc .... C 828 652-9308
  Marion *(G-10150)*

Hayward Industries Inc .... C 336 712-9900
  Clemmons *(G-4043)*

Hayward Industries Inc .... A 336 712-9900
  Clemmons *(G-4044)*

Hayward Industries Inc .... B 908 351-5400
  Charlotte *(G-2894)*

IMO Industries Inc .... D 301 323-9000
  Monroe *(G-10737)*

INGERSOLL RAND INC .... A 704 896-4000
  Davidson *(G-4679)*

Ingersoll-Rand Company .... D 704 655-4836
  Charlotte *(G-2974)*

Ingersoll-Rand Indus US Inc .... D 704 896-4000
  Davidson *(G-4680)*

James M Pleasants Company Inc .... E 336 275-3152
  Greensboro *(G-7133)*

Maag Reduction Inc .... E 704 716-9000
  Charlotte *(G-3115)*

Marley Company LLC .... C 704 752-4400
  Charlotte *(G-3128)*

Merrill Resources Inc .... F 828 877-4450
  Penrose *(G-12186)*

Opw Fling Cntnment Systems Inc .... E 919 209-2280
  Smithfield *(G-14474)*

Raymond Brown Well Company Inc .... G 336 374-4999
  Danbury *(G-4663)*

SL Liquidation LLC .... B 910 353-3666
  Jacksonville *(G-9033)*

SPX Flow Inc .... C 704 752-4400
  Charlotte *(G-3607)*

Sundyne Corp .... F 303 249-5350
  Charlotte *(G-3652)*

Trs-Sesco LLC .... D 336 996-2220
  Kernersville *(G-9248)*

Xaloy Extrusion LLC .... E 828 326-9888
  Hickory *(G-8212)*

Xylem Water Solutions USA Inc .... D 704 409-9700
  Charlotte *(G-3840)*

PUMPS: Domestic, Water Or Sump

Camp S Well and Pump Co Inc .... G 828 453-7322
  Ellenboro *(G-5634)*

Pentair Water Pool and Spa Inc .... F 919 463-4640
  Cary *(G-1848)*

Pentair Water Pool and Spa Inc .... A 919 566-8000
  Sanford *(G-14166)*

PUMPS: Gasoline, Measuring Or Dispensing

Balcrank Corporation .... E 800 747-5300
  Weaverville *(G-15838)*

Gilbarco Inc .... A 336 547-5000
  Greensboro *(G-7043)*

PUMPS: Measuring & Dispensing

Aptargroup Inc .... C 828 970-6300
  Lincolnton *(G-9873)*

Circor Precision Metering LLC .... A 919 774-7667
  Sanford *(G-14102)*

Gasboy International Inc .... G 336 547-5000
  Greensboro *(G-7030)*

Marley Company LLC .... C 704 752-4400
  Charlotte *(G-3128)*

Nelson Holdings Nc Inc .... F 828 322-9226
  Hickory *(G-8100)*

PUMPS: Oil, Measuring Or Dispensing

Samoa Corporation .... E 828 645-2290
  Weaverville *(G-15861)*

PURIFICATION & DUST COLLECTION EQPT

Bwxt Investment Company .... E 704 625-4900
  Charlotte *(G-2369)*

Dustcontrol Inc .... F 910 395-1808
  Wilmington *(G-16207)*

Envirco Corporation .... E 919 775-2201
  Sanford *(G-14117)*

Filtration Technology Inc .... G 336 294-5655
  Greensboro *(G-7014)*

Mikropul LLC .... G 704 998-2600
  Charlotte *(G-3179)*

QUILTING: Individuals

Owens Quilting Inc .... G 828 695-1495
  Newton *(G-11956)*

Quilt Shop .... G 828 263-8691
  Boone *(G-1230)*

RACEWAYS

Bear Creek Raceway Inc .... G 336 367-4264
  Dobson *(G-4819)*

Motor Raceways Inc .... G 252 715-3990
  Nags Head *(G-11723)*

Sbrc Hobbies & Raceway LLC .... G 336 782-8420
  Rural Hall *(G-13852)*

RACKS: Pallet, Exc Wood

Wireway/Husky Corp .... C 704 483-1135
  Denver *(G-4815)*

RADIO BROADCASTING & COMMUNICATIONS EQPT

Arris Global Services Inc .... E 215 323-1000
  Hickory *(G-7942)*

Ascom (us) Inc .... C 877 712-7266
  Morrisville *(G-11293)*

CBS Radio Holdings Inc .... E 704 319-9369
  Charlotte *(G-2424)*

Lea Aid Acquisition Company .... F 919 872-6210
  Raleigh *(G-12963)*

T-Metrics Inc .... E 704 523-9583
  Charlotte *(G-3669)*

RADIO BROADCASTING STATIONS

Latino Communications Inc .... F 704 319-5044
  Charlotte *(G-3073)*

Latino Communications Inc .... F 919 645-1680
  Raleigh *(G-12959)*

Latino Communications Inc .... D 336 714-2823
  Winston Salem *(G-16784)*

RADIO COMMUNICATIONS: Airborne Eqpt

Amphenol Antenna Solutions .... E 828 324-6971
  Conover *(G-4415)*

RAILINGS: Prefabricated, Metal

Alamance Steel Fabricators .... G 336 887-3015
  High Point *(G-8238)*

RAILINGS: Wood

Piedmont Stairworks LLC .... G 704 697-0259
  Charlotte *(G-3341)*

RAILROAD EQPT

Frit Car Inc .... E 252 638-2675
  Bridgeton *(G-1294)*

Knorr Brake Truck Systems Co .... A 888 836-6922
  Salisbury *(G-14001)*

Ohilda Bombardier .... G 704 658-7134
  Locust *(G-9965)*

Twin Oaks Service South Inc .... G 704 914-7142
  Shelby *(G-14378)*

RAILROAD EQPT & SPLYS WHOLESALERS

Harsco Rail LLC .... G 980 960-2624
  Charlotte *(G-2893)*

Employee Codes: A=Over 500 employees, B=251-500
C=101-250, D=51-100, E=20-50, F=10-19, G=1-9

2024 Harris North Carolina Manufacturers Directory

RAILROAD EQPT, EXC LOCOMOTIVES

Kck Holding Corp......................... E..... 336 513-0002
  Burlington (G-1443)

RAILROAD EQPT, EXC LOCOMOTIVES

Railroad Friction Pdts Corp........... C..... 910 844-9709
  Maxton (G-10362)

RAILROAD EQPT: Brakes, Air & Vacuum

Kck Holding Corp......................... E..... 336 513-0002
  Burlington (G-1443)

New York Air Brake LLC.............. D..... 315 786-5200
  Salisbury (G-14019)

RAILROAD EQPT: Cars & Eqpt, Train, Freight Or Passenger

Freightpal Inc.............................. G..... 704 971-8183
  Charlotte (G-2796)

RAILROAD MAINTENANCE & REPAIR SVCS

Harsco Rail LLC......................... G..... 980 960-2624
  Charlotte (G-2893)

RAILROAD RELATED EQPT

Harsco Metro Rail LLC................ G..... 980 960-2624
  Charlotte (G-2892)

RAILROAD RELATED EQPT: Railway Track

Harsco Rail LLC......................... G..... 980 960-2624
  Charlotte (G-2893)

St Engineering Leeboy Inc........... G..... 704 966-3300
  Lincolnton (G-9921)

RAILS: Steel Or Iron

Steel City Services LLC............... F..... 919 698-2407
  Durham (G-5373)

RAMPS: Prefabricated Metal

Veon Inc.................................... F..... 252 623-2102
  Washington (G-15736)

RAZORS, RAZOR BLADES

Edgewell Per Care Brands LLC..... E..... 336 672-4500
  Asheboro (G-425)

Edgewell Per Care Brands LLC..... E..... 336 629-1581
  Asheboro (G-426)

Edgewell Per Care Brands LLC..... E..... 336 672-4500
  Asheboro (G-427)

Procter & Gamble Mfg Co............ D..... 336 954-0000
  Greensboro (G-7287)

REAL ESTATE AGENCIES & BROKERS

Fascoe Realty............................. G..... 828 963-7600
  Boone (G-1198)

Green Waste Management LLC.... G..... 704 289-0720
  Charlotte (G-2864)

Joe Robin Darnell........................ G..... 704 482-1186
  Shelby (G-14333)

L6 Realty LLC............................. G..... 704 654-3000
  Charlotte (G-3067)

REAL ESTATE AGENTS & MANAGERS

Brookhurst Associates................. G..... 919 792-0987
  Raleigh (G-12576)

Brunswick Beacon Inc................. F..... 910 754-6890
  Shallotte (G-14270)

Jdh Capital LLC.......................... F..... 704 357-1220
  Charlotte (G-3016)

Lindley Laboratories Inc.............. F..... 336 449-7521
  Gibsonville (G-6567)

Town of Maggie Valley Inc........... F..... 828 926-0145
  Maggie Valley (G-10096)

REAL ESTATE INVESTMENT TRUSTS

Anew Look Homes LLC................ F..... 800 796-5152
  Hickory (G-7935)

REAL ESTATE LISTING SVCS

Fathom Holdings Inc................... E..... 888 455-6040
  Cary (G-1769)

RECEIVERS: Radio Communications

JPS Intrprbility Solutions Inc........ F..... 919 332-5009
  Raleigh (G-12924)

RECORDS & TAPES: Prerecorded

Cda Inc..................................... C
  Charlotte (G-2434)

Digi Ronin Games LLC................. G..... 919 845-9960
  Raleigh (G-12683)

Digital Recorders Inc.................. C..... 919 361-2155
  Morrisville (G-11331)

Operable Inc.............................. G..... 757 617-0935
  Wake Forest (G-15575)

Puny Human LLC........................ F..... 919 420-4538
  Raleigh (G-13158)

Reel-Scout Inc........................... G..... 704 348-1484
  Charlotte (G-3425)

Robert Wrren MBL TV Prductions. G..... 910 483-4777
  Eastover (G-5482)

SMC Corporation of America........ F..... 704 947-7556
  Huntersville (G-8897)

Snowman Software...................... G..... 888 918-4384
  Durham (G-5360)

Sony Music Holdings Inc.............. G..... 336 886-1807
  High Point (G-8542)

Technolio Inc.............................. G..... 919 481-4454
  Morrisville (G-11440)

Turnsmith LLC........................... G..... 919 667-9804
  Chapel Hill (G-2085)

Virscidian Inc............................. G..... 919 809-7651
  Cary (G-1921)

Xdri Inc..................................... G..... 919 361-2155
  Durham (G-5454)

Yellow Rubber Ball LLC............... G..... 919 357-6307
  Durham (G-5458)

RECREATIONAL VEHICLE PARTS & ACCESS STORES

Derrow Enterprises Inc................ G..... 252 635-3375
  New Bern (G-11800)

REFINING: Petroleum

Harvey Fertilizer and Gas Co....... E..... 919 731-2474
  Goldsboro (G-6624)

Murphy USA Inc.......................... E..... 828 758-7055
  Lenoir (G-9638)

Pbf LLC..................................... G..... 828 252-1742
  Asheville (G-724)

Sg-Clw Inc................................. F..... 336 865-4980
  Winston Salem (G-16903)

Stop N Go LLC........................... F..... 919 523-7355
  Morrisville (G-11434)

Volta Group Corporation LLC....... E..... 919 637-0273
  Raleigh (G-13408)

Warren Oil Company LLC............ D..... 910 892-6456
  Dunn (G-4890)

REFRACTORIES: Alumina Fused

Vesuvius Nc LLC......................... D..... 336 578-7728
  Graham (G-6715)

REFRACTORIES: Brick

Skamol Americas Inc................... G..... 704 544-1015
  Charlotte (G-3559)

REFRACTORIES: Clay

Harbisonwalker Intl Inc............... G..... 704 599-6540
  Charlotte (G-2887)

Oldcastle Retail Inc.................... B..... 704 799-8083
  Cornelius (G-4572)

Pyrotek Incorporated.................. E..... 704 642-1993
  Salisbury (G-14033)

Resco Products Inc.................... F..... 336 299-1441
  Greensboro (G-7306)

REFRACTORIES: Nonclay

General Electric Company........... A..... 910 675-5000
  Wilmington (G-16230)

Vesuvius USA Corporation........... D..... 412 429-1800
  Charlotte (G-3775)

Virginia Carolina Refr Inc............ G..... 704 216-0223
  Salisbury (G-14062)

REFRACTORY MATERIALS WHOLESALERS

Harbisonwalker Intl Inc............... G..... 704 599-6540
  Charlotte (G-2887)

REFRIGERATION & HEATING EQUIPMENT

Aqua Logic Inc........................... E..... 858 292-4773
  Monroe (G-10649)

Beverage-Air Corporation............ E..... 336 245-6400
  Winston Salem (G-16628)

Buhler Inc.................................. C..... 800 722-7483
  Cary (G-1716)

Carolina Products Inc................. E..... 704 364-9029
  Charlotte (G-2403)

Carrier Carolinas....................... G..... 336 292-0909
  Greensboro (G-6892)

Carrier Corporation.................... G..... 704 494-2600
  Morrisville (G-11312)

Cbg Draft Services Lc LLC.......... G..... 704 727-3300
  Charlotte (G-2423)

City Compressor Rebuilders........ E..... 704 947-1811
  Charlotte (G-2484)

Culligan Water Conditioning........ G..... 252 646-3800
  Morehead City (G-11166)

Dienes Apparatus Inc.................. G..... 704 525-3770
  Pineville (G-12265)

Heat Transfer Sales LLC............. F..... 336 292-8777
  Greensboro (G-7084)

James M Pleasants Company Inc.. E..... 336 275-3152
  Greensboro (G-7133)

Lennox Stores (partsplus)........... G..... 910 660-7070
  Wilmington (G-16298)

Lenox Birkdale LLC.................... G..... 704 997-8116
  Huntersville (G-8850)

Lenox Land................................ G..... 704 507-4877
  Huntersville (G-8851)

Morris & Associates Inc.............. D..... 919 582-9200
  Garner (G-6292)

NSi Holdings Inc......................... F..... 914 664-3542
  Huntersville (G-8864)

Parameter Generation Ctrl Inc..... E..... 828 669-8717
  Black Mountain (G-1133)

Supreme Murphy Trck Bodies Inc. C..... 252 291-2191
  Wilson (G-16544)

Thermo King Corporation............ C..... 732 652-6774
  Davidson (G-4700)

Trane Export LLC....................... E..... 608 788-0569
  Davidson (G-4701)

Trane US Inc.............................. G..... 828 277-8664
  Asheville (G-805)

Trane US Inc.............................. D..... 704 525-9600
  Charlotte (G-3714)

PRODUCT SECTION RETAIL BAKERY: Cookies

Trane US Inc .... F 704 697-9006
  Charlotte (G-3715)
Trane US Inc .... G 336 273-6353
  Greensboro (G-7406)
Trane US Inc .... F 336 378-0670
  Greensboro (G-7407)
Trane US Inc .... G 919 781-0458
  Morrisville (G-11449)
United Air Filter Company Corp .... E 704 334-5311
  Charlotte (G-3750)
Wen Bray Heating & AC .... G 828 267-0635
  Hickory (G-8209)

REFRIGERATION EQPT & SPLYS WHOLESALERS

Bally Refrigerated Boxes Inc .... C 252 240-2829
  Morehead City (G-11151)

REFRIGERATION EQPT: Complete

Afe Victory Inc .... C 856 428-4200
  Winston Salem (G-16593)
Arneg LLC .... D 336 956-5300
  Lexington (G-9680)
Middleby Marshall Inc .... C 919 762-1000
  Fuquay Varina (G-6216)
Pro Refrigeration Inc .... E 336 283-7281
  Mocksville (G-10599)
W A Brown & Son Incorporated .... E 704 636-5131
  Salisbury (G-14063)

REFRIGERATION SVC & REPAIR

Chichibone Inc .... F 919 785-0090
  Kernersville (G-9177)
Daikin Applied Americas Inc .... G 704 588-0087
  Charlotte (G-2598)
Environmental Specialties LLC .... D 919 829-9300
  Raleigh (G-12742)
Trs-Sesco LLC .... D 336 996-2220
  Kernersville (G-9248)

REFUSE SYSTEMS

Eastern Crlina Vctonal Ctr Inc .... D 252 758-4188
  Greenville (G-7521)
Global Ecosciences Inc .... G 252 631-6266
  Wake Forest (G-15560)
Parkdale Mills Incorporated .... F 704 825-2529
  Belmont (G-1000)
Wastezero Inc .... E 919 322-1208
  Raleigh (G-13413)

REGULATORS: Power

Elster American Meter Company LLC ..... F 402 873-8200
  Charlotte (G-2700)

REHABILITATION CENTER, OUTPATIENT TREATMENT

Transylvnia Vcational Svcs Inc .... D 828 884-1548
  Fletcher (G-6045)
Transylvnia Vcational Svcs Inc .... C 828 884-3195
  Brevard (G-1291)

REHABILITATION CTR, RESIDENTIAL WITH HEALTH CARE INCIDENTAL

Gladiator Enterprises Inc .... G 336 944-6932
  Greensboro (G-7044)

RELAYS & SWITCHES: Indl, Electric

Dozier Industrial Electric Inc .... F 252 451-0020
  Rocky Mount (G-13666)

Stay Online LLC .... E 888 346-4688
  Creedmoor (G-4622)
Te Connectivity Corporation .... G 828 338-1000
  Fairview (G-5720)

RELAYS: Control Circuit, Ind

Aiken Development LLC .... G 828 572-4040
  Lenoir (G-9568)
General Electric Company .... F 919 563-7445
  Mebane (G-10410)
General Electric Company .... B 919 563-5561
  Mebane (G-10411)

REMOVERS & CLEANERS

Delta Contractors Inc .... F 817 410-9481
  Linden (G-9940)

REMOVERS: Paint

Electric Glass Fiber Amer LLC .... C 336 357-8151
  Lexington (G-9712)

RENTAL SVCS: Electronic Eqpt, Exc Computers

Tarheel Monitoring LLC .... G 910 763-1490
  Wilmington (G-16426)

RENTAL SVCS: Eqpt, Theatrical

Stage Decoration and Sups Inc .... F 336 621-5454
  Greensboro (G-7364)

RENTAL SVCS: Sign

R O Givens Signs Inc .... G 252 338-6578
  Elizabeth City (G-5567)

RENTAL SVCS: Video Disk/Tape, To The General Public

Wen Bray Heating & AC .... G 828 267-0635
  Hickory (G-8209)

RENTAL: Portable Toilet

Comer Sanitary Service Inc .... F 336 629-8311
  Lexington (G-9697)
Readilite & Barricade Inc .... F 919 231-8309
  Raleigh (G-13194)

REPRODUCTION SVCS: Video Tape Or Disk

American Multimedia Inc .... D 336 229-7101
  Burlington (G-1364)
Robert Wrren MBL TV Prductions .... G 910 483-4777
  Eastover (G-5482)

RESEARCH & DEVELOPMENT SVCS, COMMERCIAL: Engineering Lab

Advanced Non-Lethal Tech Inc .... G 847 812-6450
  Raleigh (G-12479)
Vortant Technologies LLC .... G 828 645-1026
  Weaverville (G-15867)

RESEARCH, DEVELOPMENT & TESTING SVCS, COMMERCIAL: Business

Konica Mnlta Hlthcare Amrcas I .... E 919 792-6420
  Garner (G-6278)
Viztek LLC .... E 919 792-6420
  Garner (G-6324)

RESEARCH, DEVELOPMENT & TESTING SVCS, COMMERCIAL: Energy

Centaur Laboratories Inc .... F 919 249-5072
  Oxford (G-12119)

RESEARCH, DEVELOPMENT & TESTING SVCS, COMMERCIAL: Medical

Alcami Carolinas Corporation .... G 910 254-7000
  Wilmington (G-16101)
Alcami Carolinas Corporation .... G 910 254-7000
  Wilmington (G-16102)
Birth Tissue Recovery LLC .... E 336 448-1910
  Winston Salem (G-16631)
Gale Global Research Inc .... G 910 795-8595
  Leland (G-9545)

RESINS: Custom Compound Purchased

Avient Colorants USA LLC .... D 704 331-7000
  Charlotte (G-2248)
Borealis Compounds Inc .... E 908 798-7497
  Taylorsville (G-15130)
Crp Usa LLC .... G 704 660-0258
  Mooresville (G-10918)
Hexpol Compounding NC Inc .... A 704 872-1585
  Statesville (G-14813)
Lubrizol Global Management Inc .... D 704 865-7451
  Gastonia (G-6447)
Phoenix Epoxy Systems LLC .... G 252 747-3735
  Hookerton (G-8729)
Premix North Carolina LLC .... G 704 412-7922
  Belmont (G-1004)
Rutland Group Inc .... C 704 553-0046
  Pineville (G-12300)
Rutland Holdings LLC .... E 704 553-0046
  Pineville (G-12301)
Sealed Air Corporation .... D 828 728-6610
  Hudson (G-8779)
Sealed Air Corporation (us) .... A 201 791-7600
  Charlotte (G-3518)
Teknor Apex Company .... E 401 642-3598
  Jamestown (G-9074)
Tru-Contour Inc .... F 704 455-8700
  Concord (G-4379)
Zeon Technologies Inc .... G 704 680-9160
  Salisbury (G-14069)

RESPIRATORS

North Crlina Soc For Rsprtory .... G 919 619-4206
  Hillsborough (G-8663)
Oxlife of NC LLC .... G 828 684-7353
  Hendersonville (G-7889)

RESTAURANT EQPT: Carts

Holders Restaurant Furniture .... G 828 754-8383
  Lenoir (G-9620)

RESTAURANT EQPT: Sheet Metal

Captive-Aire Systems Inc .... G 704 843-7215
  Waxhaw (G-15748)
Captive-Aire Systems Inc .... C 919 887-2721
  Youngsville (G-17074)
Captive-Aire Systems Inc .... C 919 882-2410
  Raleigh (G-12593)
Custom Industries Inc .... E 336 299-2885
  Greensboro (G-6950)
E C L Inc .... G 919 365-7101
  Wendell (G-15899)

RESTAURANTS: Full Svc, American

Booneshine Brewing Co Inc .... G 828 263-4305
  Boone (G-1180)
Sistas 4 Life Food Svcs LLC .... G 704 957-6437
  Charlotte (G-3557)
Vortex Bottle Shop LLC .... F 980 258-0827
  Harrisburg (G-7734)

RETAIL BAKERY: Cookies

Swirl Oakhurst LLC .... G 704 258-1209
  Charlotte (G-3662)

RETAIL BAKERY: Doughnuts

Dunkin Donuts .... F 919 217-9603
  Knightdale (G-9417)
Krispy Kreme Doughnut Corp .... E 919 669-6151
  Gastonia (G-6440)
Krispy Kreme Doughnut Corp .... E 336 854-8275
  Greensboro (G-7158)
Krispy Kreme Doughnut Corp .... E 336 733-3780
  Winston Salem (G-16779)
Krispy Kreme Doughnut Corp .... E 336 726-8908
  Winston Salem (G-16780)
Krispy Kreme Doughnut Corp .... C 980 270-7117
  Charlotte (G-3062)
Krispy Kreme Doughnuts Inc .... C 336 725-2981
  Winston Salem (G-16781)

RETAIL BAKERY: Pretzels

Chestnut Land Company .... G 828 299-9108
  Asheville (G-590)
SE Co-Brand Ventures LLC .... G 704 598-9322
  Charlotte (G-3514)

RETAIL STORES: Alcoholic Beverage Making Eqpt & Splys

DNB Humidifier Mfg Inc .... F 336 764-2076
  Winston Salem (G-16686)
Js Linens and Curtain Outlet .... F 704 871-1582
  Statesville (G-14829)

RETAIL STORES: Audio-Visual Eqpt & Splys

Integrated Info Systems Inc .... F 919 488-5000
  Youngsville (G-17086)
Moon Audio .... G 919 649-5018
  Cary (G-1826)
Utd Technology Corp .... G 704 612-0121
  Mint Hill (G-10546)

RETAIL STORES: Business Machines & Eqpt

Danbartex LLC .... G 704 323-8728
  Mooresville (G-10923)
Lynchs Office Supply Co Inc .... F 252 537-6041
  Roanoke Rapids (G-13578)

RETAIL STORES: Cleaning Eqpt & Splys

Busch Enterprises Inc .... G 704 878-2067
  Statesville (G-14768)

RETAIL STORES: Concrete Prdts, Precast

Craven Tire Inc .... G 252 633-0200
  New Bern (G-11792)

RETAIL STORES: Educational Aids & Electronic Training Mat

Learning Craftsmen Inc .... G 813 321-5003
  Apex (G-213)

RETAIL STORES: Electronic Parts & Eqpt

Applied Drives Inc .... G 704 573-2324
  Charlotte (G-2204)

RETAIL STORES: Foam & Foam Prdts

Carpenter Co .... D 828 464-9470
  Conover (G-4433)
Guilford Fabricators Inc .... F 336 434-3163
  High Point (G-8372)

Pregis LLC .... D 828 396-2373
  Granite Falls (G-6752)

RETAIL STORES: Hair Care Prdts

Luxebright Skin Care LLC .... G 877 614-9128
  Matthews (G-10264)

RETAIL STORES: Ice

Airgas Usa LLC .... G 919 544-1056
  Durham (G-4908)
Herrin Bros Coal & Ice Co .... G 704 332-2193
  Charlotte (G-2906)

RETAIL STORES: Medical Apparatus & Splys

All 4 U Home Medical LLC .... G 828 437-0684
  Morganton (G-11196)
Custom Rehabilitation Spc Inc .... G 910 471-2962
  Wilmington (G-16192)
Legend Compression Wear .... G 877 711-5343
  Denton (G-4742)
Medi Mall Inc .... G 877 501-6334
  Fletcher (G-6022)
Rm Liquidation Inc .... D 828 274-7996
  Asheville (G-756)
Safeguard Medical Alarms Inc .... F 312 506-2900
  Harrisburg (G-7727)
Tekni-Plex Inc .... D 919 553-4151
  Clayton (G-4017)
United Mobile Imaging Inc .... G 800 983-9840
  Clemmons (G-4065)

RETAIL STORES: Orthopedic & Prosthesis Applications

Bio-Tech Prosthetics .... G 336 768-3666
  Winston Salem (G-16630)
Bio-Tech Prsthtics Orthtics In .... G 336 333-9081
  Greensboro (G-6839)
Cape Fear Orthtics Prsthtics I .... G 910 483-0933
  Fayetteville (G-5780)
Faith Prsthtc-Rthotic Svcs Inc .... F 704 782-0908
  Concord (G-4263)

RETAIL STORES: Perfumes & Colognes

Body Shop Inc .... C 919 554-4900
  Wake Forest (G-15534)

RETAIL STORES: Pet Food

Wholesale Kennel Supply Co .... G 919 742-2515
  Siler City (G-14434)

RETAIL STORES: Pet Splys

Kennel-Aire LLC .... E 704 459-0044
  Norwood (G-12039)

RETAIL STORES: Religious Goods

Free Will Bptst Press Fndtion .... F 252 746-6128
  Ayden (G-852)

RETAIL STORES: Water Purification Eqpt

Carolina Water Consultants LLC .... G 828 251-2420
  Fletcher (G-5992)
Evoqua Water Technologies LLC .... F 919 477-2161
  Durham (G-5094)
Scaltrol Inc .... G 678 990-0858
  Charlotte (G-3497)
Second Earth Inc .... G 336 740-9333
  Greensboro (G-7329)
Solarbrook Water and Pwr Corp .... G 919 231-3205
  Raleigh (G-13278)

REUPHOLSTERY & FURNITURE REPAIR

Bedex LLC .... E 336 617-6755
  High Point (G-8269)
S Dorsett Upholstery Inc .... G 336 472-7076
  Thomasville (G-15275)
S Kivett Inc .... E 910 592-0161
  Clinton (G-4106)
Stone Marble Co Inc .... G 773 227-1161
  Thomasville (G-15285)
Unique Office Solutions Inc .... F 336 854-0900
  Greensboro (G-7430)

RIVETS: Metal

Gesipa Fasteners Usa Inc .... E 336 751-1555
  Mocksville (G-10577)

ROAD CONSTRUCTION EQUIPMENT WHOLESALERS

Carolina Traffic Devices Inc .... F 704 588-7055
  Charlotte (G-2410)

ROBOTS: Assembly Line

Fanuc America Corporation .... G 704 596-5121
  Huntersville (G-8818)
Keller Technology Corporation .... E 704 875-1605
  Huntersville (G-8844)
Southern Machine Services .... G 919 658-9300
  Mount Olive (G-11668)

ROLLING MILL ROLLS: Cast Steel

American Builders Anson Inc .... E 704 272-7655
  Polkton (G-12383)

ROLLS & BLANKETS, PRINTERS': Rubber Or Rubberized Fabric

Andritz Fabrics and Rolls Inc .... F 919 556-7235
  Youngsville (G-17067)
Andritz Fabrics and Rolls Inc .... D 919 526-1400
  Raleigh (G-12506)
Perma-Flex Rollers Inc .... D 704 633-1201
  Salisbury (G-14025)

ROOFING GRANULES

3M Company .... D 919 642-0006
  Moncure (G-10611)

ROOFING MATERIALS: Asphalt

Exteriors Inc Ltd .... G 919 325-2251
  Spring Lake (G-14625)
Roofing Tools and Eqp Inc .... G 252 291-1800
  Wilson (G-16534)

ROOFING MEMBRANE: Rubber

Daramic LLC .... D 704 587-8599
  Charlotte (G-2603)

RUBBER PRDTS: Appliance, Mechanical

Essay Operations Inc .... G 252 443-6010
  Rocky Mount (G-13696)

RUBBER PRDTS: Medical & Surgical Tubing, Extrudd & Lathe-Cut

Surgical Guide Systems LLC .... G 919 244-4463
  Chapel Hill (G-2076)

RUBBER PRDTS: Silicone

Seal It Services Inc .... F 919 777-0374
  Sanford (G-14183)

RUBBER PRDTS: Sponge

PRODUCT SECTION   SATELLITES: Communications

Rempac LLC.. E 910 737-6557
  Lumberton *(G-10051)*

RUBBER STRUCTURES: Air-Supported

East West Manufacturing LLC................ G..... 704 663-5975
  Mooresville *(G-10936)*

RUGS : Hand & Machine Made

Sorrells Sheree White............................... G..... 828 452-4864
  Waynesville *(G-15825)*

RUGS : Tufted

Glenoit Universal Ltd................................ C..... 919 735-7111
  Goldsboro *(G-6616)*

SAFETY EQPT & SPLYS WHOLESALERS

American Safety Utility Corp.................... E..... 704 482-0601
  Shelby *(G-14285)*
Speer Operational Tech LLC.................... G..... 864 631-2512
  Marion *(G-10179)*
VH Industries Inc...................................... E..... 704 743-2400
  Concord *(G-4385)*

SALES PROMOTION SVCS

UGLy Essentials LLC............................... F..... 910 319-9945
  Raleigh *(G-13376)*

SALT

Barker Industries Inc................................ G..... 704 391-1023
  Charlotte *(G-2281)*
Giles Chemical Corporation..................... G..... 828 452-4784
  Waynesville *(G-15805)*
Giles Chemical Corporation..................... E..... 828 452-4784
  Waynesville *(G-15806)*
S A L T Soak Away Lfes Trubles.............. G..... 910 238-2695
  Jacksonville *(G-9027)*
Schoenberg Salt Co................................. F..... 336 766-0600
  Winston Salem *(G-16899)*

SAMPLE BOOKS

Custom Sample Service Inc.................... G..... 336 861-2010
  Archdale *(G-277)*
Design Concepts Incorporated................. F..... 336 887-1932
  High Point *(G-8321)*
Sample House Inc.................................... F..... 828 327-4786
  Hickory *(G-8145)*

SAND & GRAVEL

American Materials Company LLC........... F..... 910 799-1411
  Wilmington *(G-16109)*
Aquadale Query.. G..... 704 474-3165
  Norwood *(G-12036)*
Ashley Taylor... G..... 828 230-2953
  Candler *(G-1569)*
Atmax Engineering................................... G..... 910 233-4881
  Wilmington *(G-16124)*
B E R Trucking and Gravel...................... G..... 919 738-5928
  Mount Olive *(G-11654)*
B V Hedrick Gravel & Sand Co................ G..... 336 337-0706
  Asheville *(G-555)*
B V Hedrick Gravel & Sand Co................ G..... 828 738-0332
  Marion *(G-10140)*
B V Hedrick Gravel & Sand Co................ C..... 704 827-8114
  Stanley *(G-14686)*
B V Hedrick Gravel & Sand Co................ E..... 828 686-3844
  Swannanoa *(G-15020)*
B V Hedrick Gravel & Sand Co................ E..... 828 645-5460
  Weaverville *(G-15837)*
Beazer East Inc.. F..... 919 567-9512
  Holly Springs *(G-8688)*
Black Sand Company Inc......................... G..... 336 788-6411
  Winston Salem *(G-16632)*

Blue Ridge Quarry.................................... G..... 828 693-0025
  Flat Rock *(G-5960)*
Blue Rock Materials LLC.......................... F..... 828 479-3581
  Robbinsville *(G-13605)*
Bob Harrington Assoc............................... G..... 336 855-7252
  Greensboro *(G-6846)*
Bobby Cahoon Construction Inc............... E..... 252 249-1617
  Grantsboro *(G-6763)*
Bonsal American Inc................................ D..... 704 525-1621
  Charlotte *(G-2334)*
Carolina Stone LLC.................................. F..... 252 208-1633
  Dover *(G-4834)*
Clifford W Estes Co Inc........................... E..... 336 622-6410
  Staley *(G-14664)*
Crowder Trucking LLC.............................. G..... 910 797-4163
  Fayetteville *(G-5800)*
Cumberland Gravel & Sand Co................. F..... 704 633-4241
  Salisbury *(G-13949)*
Cumberland Sand and Gravel................... G..... 704 474-3165
  Norwood *(G-12038)*
D&J Sand & Gravel................................... F..... 919 584-8267
  Goldsboro *(G-6606)*
Garland Langley Gravel............................ G..... 252 450-9022
  Rocky Mount *(G-13699)*
Garland Langley Sand and Grav............... G..... 252 235-2812
  Bailey *(G-873)*
Gravel Monkey Geodes LLC..................... G..... 224 848-0401
  Dunn *(G-4871)*
Grits and Gravel Services LLC................. G..... 919 758-8975
  Apex *(G-199)*
Harrins Sand & Gravel Inc........................ G..... 828 254-2744
  Asheville *(G-648)*
Jason Culbertson...................................... G..... 910 733-6794
  Maxton *(G-10357)*
Long Branch Partners LLC....................... G..... 828 837-1400
  Brasstown *(G-1267)*
Long J E & Sons Grading Inc................... F..... 336 228-9706
  Burlington *(G-1452)*
Martin Marietta Materials Inc.................... F..... 360 424-3441
  Raleigh *(G-12999)*
Martin Marietta Materials Inc.................... C..... 919 781-4550
  Raleigh *(G-13001)*
Mother Sand Fathers Black Sons............. G..... 919 301-8161
  Garner *(G-6293)*
Mugo Gravel & Grading Inc...................... E..... 704 782-3478
  Concord *(G-4320)*
NC Sand and Rock Inc............................. G..... 919 538-9001
  Willow Spring *(G-16081)*
Parrish Contracting LLC........................... G..... 828 524-9100
  Franklin *(G-6141)*
Rogers Group Inc..................................... G..... 828 657-9331
  Mooresboro *(G-10840)*
S & K Sand LLC....................................... G..... 252 964-3144
  Bath *(G-916)*
Soundside Recycling & Mtls Inc................ G..... 252 491-8666
  Jarvisburg *(G-9086)*
Southside Materials LLC........................... G..... 336 388-5613
  Pelham *(G-12178)*
Tar Heel Enddntic Edctl Fndtio.................. G..... 207 843-6703
  Raleigh *(G-13328)*
Tarheel Sand & Stone Inc......................... G..... 336 468-4003
  Hamptonville *(G-7679)*
Thrills Hauling LLC................................... F..... 407 383-3483
  Arden *(G-383)*
Triple M Consolidated Inc........................ G..... 910 484-1303
  Fayetteville *(G-5933)*

SAND MINING

A-1 Sandrock Inc...................................... E..... 336 855-8195
  Greensboro *(G-6770)*
G S Materials Inc...................................... E..... 336 584-1745
  Burlington *(G-1418)*

Landsdown Mining Corporation................. F..... 704 753-5400
  Monroe *(G-10755)*
Prize Management LLC............................ G..... 252 532-1939
  Garysburg *(G-6329)*

SANDBLASTING EQPT

Hess Manufacturing Inc............................ E..... 704 637-3300
  Salisbury *(G-13979)*

SANITARY SVC, NEC

Carlson Environmental Cons PC............... D..... 704 283-9765
  Monroe *(G-10673)*

SANITARY SVCS: Liquid Waste Collection & Disposal

RDc Debris Removal Cnstr LLC............... E..... 323 614-2353
  Smithfield *(G-14479)*

SANITARY SVCS: Oil Spill Cleanup

Global Ecosciences Inc............................ G..... 252 631-6266
  Wake Forest *(G-15560)*
Noble Oil Services Inc............................. C..... 919 774-8180
  Sanford *(G-14159)*

SANITARY SVCS: Refuse Collection & Disposal Svcs

Alleghany Garbage Service Inc................. G..... 336 372-4413
  Sparta *(G-14587)*
National Container Group LLC.................. G..... 704 393-9050
  Charlotte *(G-3233)*

SANITARY SVCS: Rubbish Collection & Disposal

Waste Industries Usa LLC........................ D..... 919 325-3000
  Raleigh *(G-13412)*

SANITARY SVCS: Waste Materials, Recycling

A-1 Sandrock Inc...................................... E..... 336 855-8195
  Greensboro *(G-6770)*
Clean Green Inc.. G..... 919 596-3500
  Durham *(G-5020)*
Crizaf Inc.. G..... 919 251-7661
  Durham *(G-5037)*
Custom Polymers Inc................................ F..... 704 332-6070
  Charlotte *(G-2593)*
Duramax Holdings LLC............................. C..... 704 588-9191
  Charlotte *(G-2659)*
Elan Trading Inc.. E..... 704 342-1696
  Charlotte *(G-2689)*
Fiber Composites LLC.............................. D..... 704 463-7118
  New London *(G-11869)*
Noble Oil Services Inc.............................. C..... 919 774-8180
  Sanford *(G-14159)*
Soundside Recycling & Mtls Inc................ G..... 252 491-8666
  Jarvisburg *(G-9086)*
Steelman Lumber & Pallet LLC................. F..... 336 468-2757
  Hamptonville *(G-7678)*

SASHES: Door Or Window, Metal

Amesbury Group Inc................................. D..... 704 978-2883
  Statesville *(G-14748)*
Amesbury Group Inc................................. E..... 704 924-7694
  Statesville *(G-14749)*
Garden Metalwork..................................... G..... 828 733-1077
  Newland *(G-11887)*
YKK AP America Inc................................. F..... 336 665-1963
  Greensboro *(G-7474)*

SATELLITES: Communications

SATELLITES: Communications

5 Star Satellite Inc.................................. G 910 584-4354
  Fayetteville *(G-5747)*
Carolina Unplugged................................ G 336 965-4443
  Greensboro *(G-6891)*
Lunar International Tech LLC.................. F 800 975-7153
  Charlotte *(G-3109)*
McShan Inc... G 980 355-9790
  Charlotte *(G-3154)*
Sbg Digital Inc....................................... G 828 476-0030
  Waynesville *(G-15821)*
Thompson Sunny Acres Inc.................... G 910 206-1801
  Rockingham *(G-13644)*

SAWMILL MACHINES

Bmi Wood Products Inc........................... G 919 829-9505
  Raleigh *(G-12566)*
Edmiston Hydrlic Swmill Eqp In.............. E 336 921-2304
  Boomer *(G-1169)*
Ligna Machinery Inc............................... E 336 584-0030
  Burlington *(G-1451)*
Meadows Mills Inc.................................. E 336 838-2282
  North Wilkesboro *(G-12027)*

SAWS & SAWING EQPT

Bolton Investors Inc............................... G 919 471-1197
  Durham *(G-4971)*
Ledger Hardware Inc.............................. G 828 688-4798
  Bakersville *(G-885)*
Quality Equipment LLC........................... G 919 493-3545
  Durham *(G-5312)*

SCAFFOLDS: Mobile Or Stationary, Metal

Grady F Smith & Co Inc.......................... F 866 900-0983
  Greenville *(G-7533)*

SCALES & BALANCES, EXC LABORATORY

Computerway Food Systems Inc............. E 336 841-7289
  High Point *(G-8302)*
Vishay Transducers Ltd.......................... E 919 365-3800
  Wendell *(G-15924)*

SCIENTIFIC EQPT REPAIR SVCS

Cherokee Instruments Inc....................... F 919 552-0554
  Angier *(G-137)*

SCIENTIFIC INSTRUMENTS WHOLESALERS

Fisher Scientific Company LLC................ D 800 252-7100
  Asheville *(G-623)*

SCRAP & WASTE MATERIALS, WHOLESALE: Ferrous Metal

Allyn International Trdg Corp.................. G 877 858-2482
  Marshville *(G-10210)*
Elan Trading Inc..................................... E 704 342-1696
  Charlotte *(G-2689)*
Renew Recycling LLC.............................. D 919 550-8012
  Clayton *(G-4007)*

SCRAP & WASTE MATERIALS, WHOLESALE: Metal

S Foil Incorporated................................. F 704 455-5134
  Harrisburg *(G-7725)*
Umicore USA Inc..................................... E 919 874-7171
  Raleigh *(G-13379)*

SCRAP & WASTE MATERIALS, WHOLESALE: Paper

Piedmont Paper Stock LLC...................... G 336 285-8592
  Greensboro *(G-7259)*

SCREENS: Woven Wire

Aluminum Screen Manufacturing............. G 336 605-8080
  Greensboro *(G-6795)*

SCREW MACHINE PRDTS

Abbott Products Inc................................ E 336 463-3135
  Yadkinville *(G-17029)*
Accuking Inc... G 252 649-2323
  New Bern *(G-11765)*
Angels Path Ventures Inc....................... G 828 654-9530
  Arden *(G-309)*
B & Y Machining Co Inc.......................... G 252 235-2180
  Bailey *(G-868)*
Barefoot Cnc Inc..................................... G 828 438-5038
  Morganton *(G-11199)*
Black Mtn Mch Fabrication Inc................ E 828 669-9557
  Black Mountain *(G-1121)*
Bravo Team LLC..................................... E 704 309-1918
  Mooresville *(G-10887)*
Carolina Screw Products......................... G 336 760-7400
  Winston Salem *(G-16648)*
Conner Brothers Machine Co Inc............. D 704 864-6084
  Bessemer City *(G-1056)*
Curtis L Maclean L C............................... C 704 940-5531
  Mooresville *(G-10919)*
Edward Heil Screw Products................... G 828 345-6140
  Conover *(G-4449)*
Ellison Technologies Inc......................... D 704 545-7362
  Charlotte *(G-2699)*
Gary J Younts Machine Company............ F 336 476-7930
  Thomasville *(G-15227)*
Griffiths Corporation............................... D 704 554-5657
  Pineville *(G-12272)*
IMS Usa LLC.. G 910 796-2040
  Wilmington *(G-16265)*
M & W Industries Inc.............................. E 704 837-0331
  Charlotte *(G-3113)*
Manufacturing Services Inc.................... E 704 629-4163
  Bessemer City *(G-1074)*
Tomarjo Corp.. G 336 762-0065
  Thomasville *(G-15291)*
West Side Industries LLC........................ G 980 223-8665
  Statesville *(G-14924)*

SCREWS: Metal

C E Smith Co Inc..................................... E 336 273-0166
  Greensboro *(G-6872)*
Pan American Screw LLC........................ D 828 466-0060
  Conover *(G-4478)*

SEALANTS

Capital City Sealants LLC........................ G 919 427-4077
  Raleigh *(G-12589)*
Carolina Solvents Inc.............................. E 828 322-1920
  Hickory *(G-7966)*
Impact Technologies LLC........................ G 704 400-5364
  Concord *(G-4284)*
Pyramid Cement Products Inc................ F 704 373-2529
  Pineville *(G-12292)*
Sensus USA Inc....................................... C 919 576-6185
  Morrisville *(G-11426)*
Sensus USA Inc....................................... E 919 845-4000
  Morrisville *(G-11425)*

SEALING COMPOUNDS: Sealing, synthetic rubber or plastic

Tosaf Inc... F 980 533-3000
  Bessemer City *(G-1087)*
Wholeseal International......................... G 919 346-0788
  Pittsboro *(G-12355)*

SEARCH & NAVIGATION SYSTEMS

Airfield Solutions LLC.............................. G 844 478-6929
  Hubert *(G-8747)*
Airfield Solutions LLC.............................. G 919 348-4271
  Jacksonville *(G-8985)*
Assa Abloy Accessories and.................... B 704 233-4011
  Monroe *(G-10654)*
Bae Systems Inc..................................... D 855 223-8363
  Charlotte *(G-2263)*
Btc Electronic Components LLC.............. E 919 229-2162
  Wake Forest *(G-15536)*
Commscope Inc North Carolina.............. D 828 324-2200
  Claremont *(G-3909)*
Commscope Technologies LLC................ F 919 934-9711
  Smithfield *(G-14457)*
Curtiss-Wright Controls Inc.................... E 704 869-2300
  Shelby *(G-14305)*
Defense Logistics Services LLC.............. C 703 449-1620
  Fayetteville *(G-5809)*
Fil-Chem Inc... G 919 878-1270
  Raleigh *(G-12766)*
General Dynmics Mssion Systems.......... C 336 698-8000
  Mc Leansville *(G-10391)*
General Electric Company...................... A 910 675-5000
  Wilmington *(G-16230)*
Honeywell International Inc................... C 252 977-2100
  Rocky Mount *(G-13701)*
Ickler Manufacturing LLC........................ G 704 658-1195
  Mooresville *(G-10980)*
James W McManus Inc........................... G 828 688-2560
  Bakersville *(G-884)*
JMS Southeast Inc.................................. E 704 873-1835
  Statesville *(G-14825)*
Kearfott Corporation............................... B 828 350-5300
  Black Mountain *(G-1127)*
Kidde Technologies Inc.......................... B 252 237-7004
  Wilson *(G-16507)*
Navelite LLC.. G 336 509-9924
  Jamestown *(G-9062)*
Northrop Grmman Gdnce Elec Inc.......... E 704 588-2340
  Charlotte *(G-3270)*
Northrop Grmman Tchncal Svcs I........... E 252 447-7575
  Havelock *(G-7744)*
Northrop Grumman Systems Corp......... E 252 225-0911
  Atlantic *(G-827)*
Northrop Grumman Systems Corp......... D 252 447-7557
  Cherry Point *(G-3857)*
Northrop Grumman Systems Corp......... D 919 465-5020
  Morrisville *(G-11398)*
Ping Gps Inc... G 704 806-7945
  Cornelius *(G-4576)*
Rockwell Collins Inc............................... G 336 776-3444
  Winston Salem *(G-16887)*
Rockwell Collins Inc............................... G 336 744-1097
  Winston Salem *(G-16888)*
Roy Bridgmohan..................................... G 804 426-9652
  Henderson *(G-7808)*
Sierra Nevada Corporation..................... D 919 595-8551
  Durham *(G-5355)*
Sierra Nevada Corporation..................... G 910 307-0362
  Fayetteville *(G-5915)*
Sierra Nevada Corporation..................... F 775 331-0222
  Southern Pines *(G-14553)*
Tempest Aero Group............................... E 336 449-5054
  Gibsonville *(G-6571)*
Ultra Elec Ocean Systems Inc................ G 781 848-3400
  Wake Forest *(G-15608)*
Usat LLC... E 919 942-4214
  Chapel Hill *(G-2091)*

PRODUCT SECTION

SEAT BELTS: Automobile & Aircraft

Aircraft Belts Inc.................................. E 919 956-4395
  Creedmoor *(G-4601)*

SEATING: Stadium

4topps LLC .... G 704 281-8451
  Winston Salem *(G-16586)*

Legions Stadium .... G 910 341-4604
  Wilmington *(G-16297)*

SECURE STORAGE SVC: Household & Furniture

Ideaitlia Cntmporary Furn Corp .... C 828 464-1000
  Conover *(G-4466)*

SECURITY CONTROL EQPT & SYSTEMS

A&B Integrators LLC .... F 919 371-0750
  Durham *(G-4897)*

American Physcl SEC Group LLC .... G 919 363-1894
  Apex *(G-159)*

Audio Vdeo Concepts Design Inc .... G 704 821-2823
  Indian Trail *(G-8921)*

Automated Controls LLC .... F 704 724-7625
  Huntersville *(G-8796)*

Cargotec Port Security LLC .... G 919 620-1763
  Durham *(G-4998)*

Diverse Security Systems Inc .... G 919 848-9599
  Raleigh *(G-12688)*

Integrated Roe Security LLC .... G 919 297-8036
  Raleigh *(G-12896)*

Leonine Protection Systems LLC .... G 704 296-2675
  Mount Holly *(G-11640)*

Pathway Technologies Inc .... G 919 847-2680
  Raleigh *(G-13101)*

Plan B Enterprises LLC .... G 919 387-4856
  New Hill *(G-11863)*

Security Consult Inc .... G 704 531-8399
  Charlotte *(G-3522)*

SECURITY DEVICES

Alert Protection Systems Inc .... G 919 467-4357
  Raleigh *(G-12487)*

Campus Safety Products LLC .... G 919 321-1477
  Durham *(G-4996)*

Carolina Growler Inc .... E 910 948-2114
  Robbins *(G-13597)*

Crowdguard Inc .... G 919 605-1948
  Cary *(G-1742)*

Edwards Electronic Systems Inc .... E 919 359-2239
  Clayton *(G-3976)*

Hamrick Fence Company .... F 704 434-5011
  Boiling Springs *(G-1160)*

Public Safety UAS LLC .... G 336 601-7578
  Gibsonville *(G-6570)*

Total Technologies LLC .... G 336 259-5541
  Gastonia *(G-6530)*

SECURITY SYSTEMS SERVICES

Advanced Detection Tech LLC .... E 704 663-1949
  Mooresville *(G-10850)*

Diebold Nixdorf Incorporated .... F 704 599-3100
  Charlotte *(G-2632)*

Integrated Info Systems Inc .... F 919 488-5000
  Youngsville *(G-17086)*

Lunar International Tech LLC .... F 800 975-7453
  Charlotte *(G-3109)*

One Source SEC & Sound Inc .... G 281 850-9487
  Mooresville *(G-11044)*

Security Consult Inc .... G 704 531-8399
  Charlotte *(G-3522)*

Tektone Sound & Signal Mfg Inc .... D 828 524-9967
  Franklin *(G-6145)*

Teletec Corporation .... F 919 954-7300
  Raleigh *(G-13338)*

SEMICONDUCTOR & RELATED DEVICES: Random Access Memory Or RAM

Memoryc Inc .... G 980 224-2875
  Charlotte *(G-3164)*

SEMICONDUCTOR CIRCUIT NETWORKS

Silanna Semicdtr N Amer Inc .... D 984 444-6500
  Raleigh *(G-13261)*

SEMICONDUCTOR DEVICES: Wafers

Brumley/South Inc .... G 704 664-9251
  Mooresville *(G-10889)*

Hoffman Materials LLC .... F 717 243-2011
  Granite Falls *(G-6736)*

SEMICONDUCTORS & RELATED DEVICES

Air Control Inc .... E 252 492-2300
  Henderson *(G-7775)*

Amalfi Semiconductor Inc .... G 336 664-1233
  Greensboro *(G-6796)*

Arva LLC .... G 803 336-2230
  Charlotte *(G-2223)*

ATI Industrial Automation Inc .... C 919 772-0115
  Apex *(G-167)*

Avago Technology .... G 704 887-7735
  Charlotte *(G-2245)*

Convergent Integration Inc .... G 704 516-5922
  Charlotte *(G-2547)*

Corning Incorporated .... F 252 316-4500
  Tarboro *(G-15100)*

Cortina Systems .... G 919 226-1800
  Morrisville *(G-11325)*

Disco Hi-TEC America Inc .... G 919 468-6003
  Morrisville *(G-11332)*

Flexgen Power Systems Inc .... G 855 327-5674
  Durham *(G-5100)*

Flexgen Power Systems Inc .... F 855 327-5674
  Durham *(G-5101)*

Gainspan Corporation .... D 408 627-6500
  Morrisville *(G-11345)*

Harris Solar Inc .... G 704 490-8374
  Concord *(G-4277)*

Hexatech Inc .... F 919 481-4412
  Morrisville *(G-11354)*

Hexatech Inc .... G 919 633-0583
  Raleigh *(G-12839)*

Hoffman Materials LLC .... F 828 212-1669
  Granite Falls *(G-6738)*

Kidde Technologies Inc .... D 252 237-7004
  Wilson *(G-16506)*

Kidsvidz Productions .... G 704 663-4487
  Mooresville *(G-10998)*

Larry Shackelford .... G 919 467-8817
  Cary *(G-1807)*

Macom Technology Solutions Inc .... E 919 807-9100
  Morrisville *(G-11386)*

Marvell Semiconductor Inc .... C 408 222-2500
  Morrisville *(G-11387)*

Nexperia USA Inc .... G 919 740-6235
  Durham *(G-5246)*

Nhanced Semiconductors Inc .... E 630 561-6813
  Morrisville *(G-11396)*

Nitronex LLC .... E 919 807-9100
  Morrisville *(G-11397)*

North Crlina Rnwable Prpts LLC .... G 407 536-5846
  Raleigh *(G-13071)*

Nvidia Corporation .... F 408 486-2000
  Durham *(G-5252)*

Nxp Usa Inc .... G 919 468-3251
  Cary *(G-1834)*

Phononic Inc .... C 919 908-6300
  Durham *(G-5286)*

Poweramerica Institute .... F 919 515-6013
  Raleigh *(G-13122)*

Qorvo Inc .... B 336 664-1233
  Greensboro *(G-7294)*

Qorvo Inc .... A 336 664-1233
  Greensboro *(G-7295)*

Qorvo International Holdg Inc .... G 336 664-1233
  Greensboro *(G-7296)*

Qorvo International Svcs Inc .... E 336 664-1233
  Greensboro *(G-7297)*

Qorvo Us Inc .... G 336 662-1150
  Greensboro *(G-7298)*

Qorvo Us Inc .... G 503 615-9000
  Jamestown *(G-9067)*

Reuel Inc .... E 919 734-0460
  Goldsboro *(G-6650)*

Rf Micro Devices Inc .... A 336 664-1233
  Greensboro *(G-7308)*

Rfmd LLC .... F 336 664-1233
  Greensboro *(G-7309)*

Rfmd Infrstrcture PDT Group In .... E 704 996-2997
  Raleigh *(G-13206)*

Samsung Semiconductor Inc .... G 919 380-8483
  Cary *(G-1879)*

Sarda Technologies Inc .... G 919 757-6825
  Durham *(G-5338)*

Skan US Inc .... F 919 354-6380
  Raleigh *(G-13270)*

Skyworks Solutions Inc .... E 336 291-4200
  Greensboro *(G-7344)*

Tfs Inc .... G 919 556-9161
  Wake Forest *(G-15602)*

Thunderbird Technologies Inc .... G 919 481-3239
  Raleigh *(G-13349)*

Viavi Solutions Inc .... G 919 388-5100
  Morrisville *(G-11464)*

Wolfspeed Inc .... G 919 407-5300
  Durham *(G-5443)*

Wolfspeed Employee Services Co .... F 919 313-5300
  Durham *(G-5445)*

Xylem Lnc .... E 704 409-9700
  Charlotte *(G-3839)*

Ziptronix Inc .... F 919 459-2400
  Morrisville *(G-11470)*

SENSORS: Infrared, Solid State

AMS USA Inc .... E 919 755-2889
  Raleigh *(G-12502)*

Northrop Grmman Gdnce Elec Inc .... E 704 588-2340
  Charlotte *(G-3270)*

SEPTIC TANK CLEANING SVCS

Autry Con Pdts & Bldrs Sup Co .... G 704 504-8830
  Charlotte *(G-2242)*

Dellinger Precast Inc .... E 704 483-2868
  Denver *(G-4771)*

Inman Septic Tank Service Inc .... G 910 763-1146
  Wilmington *(G-16268)*

Mulls Con & Septic Tanks Inc .... G 828 437-0959
  Morganton *(G-11236)*

SEPTIC TANKS: Concrete

Affordable Septic Tank .... G 910 417-9537
  Hamlet *(G-7615)*

Argos USA LLC .... C 704 872-9566
  Statesville *(G-14752)*

SEPTIC TANKS: Concrete

Brant & Lassiter Septic Tank............ G 252 587-4321
   Potecasi *(G-12395)*
Dellinger Precast Inc.................... E 704 483-2868
   Denver *(G-4771)*
Erader Mills Septic Tank Inc............ F 252 478-5960
   Spring Hope *(G-14617)*
Futrell Precasting LLC................... G 252 568-3481
   Deep Run *(G-4716)*
Garners Septic Tank Inc................. G 919 718-5181
   Raeford *(G-12421)*
Inman Septic Tank Service Inc.......... G 910 763-1146
   Wilmington *(G-16268)*
Leonard McSwain Sptic Tank Svc...... G 704 482-1380
   Shelby *(G-14337)*
Moretz & Sipe Inc........................ G 828 327-8661
   Hickory *(G-8098)*
Northeastern Ready Mix................. G 252 335-1931
   Elizabeth City *(G-5560)*
O R Prdgen Sons Sptic Tank I.......... G 252 442-3338
   Rocky Mount *(G-13717)*
Southern Block Company................ F 910 293-7844
   Warsaw *(G-15674)*
TNT Services Inc......................... F 252 261-3073
   Kitty Hawk *(G-9408)*

SEWAGE & WATER TREATMENT EQPT

Abernethy Welding & Repair Inc....... G 828 324-7361
   Vale *(G-15462)*
Allens Environmental Cnstr LLC....... G 407 774-7100
   Brevard *(G-1269)*
Amerochem Corporation................. E 252 634-9344
   New Bern *(G-11770)*
Aqwa Inc................................... G 252 243-7693
   Wilson *(G-16467)*
County of Dare........................... C 252 475-5990
   Kill Devil Hills *(G-9255)*
Lely Manufacturing Inc.................. F 252 291-7050
   Wilson *(G-16510)*
Mann+hmmel Fltrtion Tech US LL..... C 704 869-3300
   Gastonia *(G-6452)*
Xelaqua Inc................................ G 919 964-4181
   Raleigh *(G-13430)*

SEWING, NEEDLEWORK & PIECE GOODS STORES: Knitting Splys

Innovaknits LLC.......................... G 828 536-9348
   Conover *(G-4467)*
Meridian Spcalty Yrn Group Inc........ B 828 874-2151
   Valdese *(G-15450)*
Uwharrie Knits Inc....................... F 704 474-4123
   Norwood *(G-12047)*

SHADES: Window

Penrock LLC............................... E 704 800-6722
   Mooresville *(G-11049)*

SHAPES & PILINGS, STRUCTURAL: Steel

ABB Installation Products Inc.......... E 828 322-1855
   Hickory *(G-7928)*
P & S Welding Inc........................ G 910 285-3126
   Willard *(G-16055)*
Structural Materials Inc.................. G 828 754-6413
   Lenoir *(G-9653)*

SHEET METAL SPECIALTIES, EXC STAMPED

Able Metal Fabricators Inc.............. E 704 394-8972
   Charlotte *(G-2124)*
Advanced Mfg Solutions NC Inc........ E 828 633-2633
   Candler *(G-1566)*
Afi Capital Inc............................. C 919 212-6400
   Raleigh *(G-12481)*
Allied Sheet Metal Works Inc........... F 704 376-8469
   Charlotte *(G-2161)*
Byers Prcision Fabricators Inc......... E 828 693-4088
   Hendersonville *(G-7831)*
Gray Metal South Inc.................... C 910 892-2119
   Dunn *(G-4872)*
Griffiths Corporation..................... D 704 554-5657
   Pineville *(G-12272)*
Kirk & Blum Manufacturing Co......... E 801 728-6533
   Greensboro *(G-7152)*
Len Corporation.......................... F 919 876-2964
   Knightdale *(G-9420)*
Loflin Fabrication LLC................... E 336 859-4333
   Denton *(G-4744)*
New Peco Inc............................. E 828 684-1234
   Arden *(G-355)*
Oak Ridge Industries LLC.............. E 252 833-4061
   Washington *(G-15720)*
QMF Mtal Elctrnic Slutions Inc......... D 336 992-8002
   Kernersville *(G-9227)*
Rfr Metal Fabrication Inc............... D 919 693-1354
   Oxford *(G-12151)*
S and R Sheet Metal Inc................ G 336 476-1069
   Thomasville *(G-15274)*
S K Bowling Inc.......................... F 252 243-1803
   Wilson *(G-16535)*
Swanson Sheetmetal Inc................ F 704 283-3955
   Monroe *(G-10818)*
Triangle Stainless Inc................... G 919 596-1335
   Butner *(G-1550)*
USA Dutch Inc............................ G 919 732-6956
   Efland *(G-5528)*

SHEETS: Fabric, From Purchased Materials

Babine Lake Corporation................ E 910 285-7955
   Hampstead *(G-7639)*
Quality Home Fashions Inc............. G 704 983-5906
   Albemarle *(G-100)*

SHELVING: Office & Store, Exc Wood

Innovative Design Tech LLC........... G 919 331-0204
   Angier *(G-141)*

SHIP BUILDING & REPAIRING: Cargo Vessels

Yang Ming America Corporation....... G 704 357-3817
   Charlotte *(G-3842)*

SHOCK ABSORBERS: Indl

F-N-D Machinery Services Inc......... G 336 906-2817
   Denton *(G-4735)*

SHOE STORES

Polyhose Incorporated................... F 732 512-9141
   Wilmington *(G-16360)*

SHOE STORES: Women's

W E Nixons Wldg & Hdwr Inc.......... G 252 221-4348
   Edenton *(G-5523)*

SHOES: Canvas, Rubber Soled

Vans Inc................................... G 704 364-3811
   Charlotte *(G-3766)*

SHOES: Men's

Allbirds Inc................................ F 980 296-0006
   Charlotte *(G-2158)*

SHOES: Orthopedic, Children's

Century Hosiery Inc...................... C 336 859-3806
   Denton *(G-4729)*

SHOES: Orthopedic, Men's

Century Hosiery Inc...................... C 336 859-3806
   Denton *(G-4729)*

SHOES: Orthopedic, Women's

Century Hosiery Inc...................... C 336 859-3806
   Denton *(G-4729)*

SHOES: Plastic Or Rubber

Vans Inc................................... G 919 792-2555
   Raleigh *(G-13393)*

SHOES: Sandals, Rubber

CBA Productions Inc..................... G 703 568-4758
   Fayetteville *(G-5786)*

SHOES: Women's

McRae Industries Inc.................... E 910 439-6147
   Mount Gilead *(G-11606)*
Unplugged Incorporated................. G 704 726-0614
   Charlotte *(G-3756)*

SHOT PEENING SVC

Metal Improvement Company LLC.... D 704 525-3818
   Charlotte *(G-3168)*
Metal Improvement Company LLC.... E 414 536-1573
   Gastonia *(G-6461)*
National Peening Inc..................... F 704 872-0113
   Statesville *(G-14850)*

SHOWCASES & DISPLAY FIXTURES: Office & Store

Amcase Inc................................ E 336 784-5992
   High Point *(G-8244)*
Grice Showcase Display Mfg Inc...... G 704 423-8888
   Charlotte *(G-2868)*
Master Displays Inc...................... D 336 884-5575
   High Point *(G-8448)*

SHOWER STALLS: Metal

Carolina Shower Door Inc............... G 910 343-0009
   Wilmington *(G-16158)*
Tubs-Usa LLC............................. F 336 884-5737
   High Point *(G-8580)*

SHOWER STALLS: Plastic & Fiberglass

Moen Incorporated....................... E 252 638-3300
   New Bern *(G-11824)*

SHREDDERS: Indl & Commercial

Piedmont Paper Stock LLC............. F 336 285-8592
   Greensboro *(G-7259)*
Secured Shred............................ G 443 288-6375
   Raleigh *(G-13243)*

SHUTTERS, DOOR & WINDOW: Metal

Atlantic Coastal Shutters LLC.......... G 252 441-4358
   Kill Devil Hills *(G-9254)*
Charlotte Shutter and Shades.......... G 336 351-3391
   Westfield *(G-15951)*
East Coast Hurricane Shutters........ G 910 352-5717
   Burgaw *(G-1338)*
Jeld-Wen Inc.............................. B 800 535-3936
   Charlotte *(G-3018)*
Plantation Shutter Pros Inc............ G 843 591-6834
   Midland *(G-10474)*
Shutter Factory Inc...................... G 252 974-2795
   Washington *(G-15731)*
Shutterhutch............................. G 704 918-7852
   Charlotte *(G-3544)*

PRODUCT SECTION

SIGNS & ADVERTISING SPECIALTIES

SIDING MATERIALS

Ply Gem Holdings Inc .... D 919 677-3900
  Cary (G-1852)
Texture Plus Inc .... E 631 218-9200
  Lincolnton (G-9928)
Wake Supply Company .... G 252 234-6012
  Wilson (G-16557)

SIDING: Plastic

Certainteed LLC .... C 828 459-0556
  Claremont (G-3906)
Variform Inc .... D 828 277-6420
  Asheville (G-813)

SIGN PAINTING & LETTERING SHOP

Broome Sign Company .... G 704 782-0422
  Concord (G-4215)
Creative Printers Inc .... G 336 246-7746
  West Jefferson (G-15938)
Fitch Sign Company Inc .... G 704 482-2916
  Shelby (G-14317)
Goldsboro Neon Sign Co Inc .... G 919 735-2035
  Goldsboro (G-6619)
JKS Motorsports Inc .... G 336 722-4129
  Lexington (G-9735)
Signs Etc .... G 336 722-9341
  Winston Salem (G-16909)

SIGNALING DEVICES: Sound, Electrical

Magnum Enterprize Inc .... G 252 524-5391
  Grifton (G-7601)
Marpac LLC .... D 910 602-1421
  Wilmington (G-16315)

SIGNALS: Traffic Control, Electric

Carolina Pwr Signalization LLC .... E 910 323-5589
  Fayetteville (G-5784)
Fulcher Elc Fayetteville Inc .... E 910 483-7772
  Fayetteville (G-5829)
Wilmongton Trffic Neighborhood .... G 910 341-7888
  Wilmington (G-16455)

SIGNS & ADVERTISING SPECIALTIES

310 Sign Company .... G 704 910-2242
  Charlotte (G-2107)
910 Sign Co LLC .... G 910 353-2298
  Jacksonville (G-8984)
A Greeting On Green LLC .... G 919 607-0966
  Cary (G-1671)
A To Z Signs & Engraving Inc .... G 828 456-6337
  Waynesville (G-15791)
AAA Mobile Signs LLC .... G 919 463-9768
  Morrisville (G-11274)
AAA Mobile Signs LLC .... G 252 446-9777
  Rocky Mount (G-13678)
ABC Signs .... G 252 223-5900
  Newport (G-11896)
Acsm Inc .... G 704 910-0243
  Charlotte (G-2131)
Action Graphics and Signs Inc .... G 919 690-1260
  Bullock (G-1326)
Action Installs LLC .... G 704 787-3828
  Wilkesboro (G-16012)
Actionsigncom .... G 828 572-2308
  Hudson (G-8759)
Ad Runner MBL Outdoor Advg Inc .... G 336 945-1190
  Lewisville (G-9664)
Aditi 108 Inc .... G 704 763-3741
  Mooresville (G-10849)
Advance Signs & Service Inc .... E 919 639-4666
  Angier (G-130)

Adventure Sign and Ltg LLC .... G 336 401-3410
  Mount Airy (G-11474)
Affordable Signs & Awnings .... G 910 237-1323
  Hope Mills (G-8731)
All Star Sign Company .... G 214 862-6797
  Franklin (G-6114)
Alltech Sign Service LLC .... G 803 548-9787
  Charlotte (G-2163)
Alpha Signs & Embroidery Inc .... G 704 878-8870
  Statesville (G-14745)
Alpha Signs & Lighting Inc .... F 910 567-5813
  Newton Grove (G-11987)
Altitude Sign Company LLC .... G 980 339-8160
  Matthews (G-10233)
American Sign Shop Inc .... G 704 527-6100
  Charlotte (G-2185)
American Signs By Tomorrow .... G 910 484-2313
  Fayetteville (G-5761)
Ancient Mariner Inc .... F 704 635-7911
  Monroe (G-10647)
Andark Graphics Inc .... G 704 882-1400
  Indian Trail (G-8919)
Anderson Designs .... G 919 489-1514
  Durham (G-4919)
Apple Rock Advg & Prom Inc .... E 336 232-4800
  Greensboro (G-6811)
Art Sign Co .... G 919 596-8681
  Durham (G-4925)
Artcraft Sign Co .... G 919 841-7686
  Spring Hope (G-14612)
Artisan Direct LLC .... G 704 655-9100
  Cornelius (G-4523)
Artistic Images Inc .... G 704 332-6225
  Charlotte (G-2221)
Asi Signage Innovations .... G 336 508-4668
  Greensboro (G-6819)
Asi Signage North Carolina .... F 919 362-9669
  Holly Springs (G-8686)
Atlantic Pinstriping ATL Wraps .... G 704 201-4406
  Matthews (G-10302)
Atlantic Pnstriping Greensboro .... G 910 880-3717
  Charlotte (G-2232)
Atlas Signs .... G 919 238-5078
  Morrisville (G-11296)
Auto Trim Design .... G 336 747-3309
  Burlington (G-1372)
AWC Sign & Light Inc .... G 910 279-0493
  Wilmington (G-16127)
B-Led Inc .... G 828 680-1444
  Mars Hill (G-10192)
Baac Business Solutions Inc .... G 704 333-4321
  Charlotte (G-2257)
Baldwin Sign & Awning .... G 910 642-8812
  Whiteville (G-15959)
Barracuda Displays .... G 704 322-0971
  Midland (G-10456)
Beane Signs Inc .... G 336 629-6748
  Asheboro (G-409)
Beaty Corporation .... G 704 599-4949
  Charlotte (G-2293)
Belk Construction Inc .... G 704 507-6327
  Mooresville (G-10871)
Bender Signs .... G 252 631-5144
  Pollocksville (G-12392)
Big Fish Digital Signs LLC .... G 252 363-1600
  Wilson (G-16476)
Blue Light Images Company Inc .... E 336 983-4986
  King (G-9264)
Bordentown Highway Sign LLC .... G 919 870-8116
  Raleigh (G-12570)
Boyd Gmn Inc .... C 206 284-2200
  Monroe (G-10668)

Boyles Sign Shop Inc .... G 336 782-1189
  Germanton (G-6551)
BP Signs Inc .... G 704 531-8000
  Charlotte (G-2344)
Burchette Services Corporation .... G 919 225-2890
  Durham (G-4992)
Burchette Sign Company Inc .... F 336 996-6501
  Colfax (G-4143)
Buzz Saw Inc .... G 910 321-7446
  Fayetteville (G-5777)
Camco Manufacturing Inc .... G 336 348-6609
  Reidsville (G-13511)
Capital Sign Solutions LLC .... E 919 789-1452
  Raleigh (G-12591)
Carmel By D3sign LLC .... G 336 617-6383
  Greensboro (G-6881)
Carolina Cstm Signs & Graphics .... G 336 681-4337
  Greensboro (G-6883)
Carolina Sgns Grphic Dsgns Inc .... G 919 383-3344
  Durham (G-5004)
Carolina Sign Co Inc .... G 704 399-3995
  Charlotte (G-2404)
Carolina Sign Svc .... G 919 247-0927
  Angier (G-136)
Carolina Signs .... G 704 622-1939
  Gastonia (G-6369)
Carolina Signs & Lighting Inc .... G 336 399-1400
  King (G-9266)
Carolina Signs and Wonders Inc .... F 704 286-1343
  Charlotte (G-2405)
Carolina Stickers & Signs LLC .... G 704 649-7318
  Charlotte (G-2408)
Casco Signs Inc .... E 704 788-9055
  Concord (G-4228)
Cbr Signs LLC .... G 910 794-8243
  Wilmington (G-16163)
Ccbs & Sign Shop Inc .... G 252 728-4866
  Beaufort (G-949)
CD Dickie & Associates Inc .... F 704 527-9102
  Charlotte (G-2433)
Chameleon Wraps & Designs .... G 910 544-9801
  Orrum (G-12115)
Charlotte Aarrow LLC .... G 704 909-7692
  Charlotte (G-2449)
Cheadles Auto Art & Sign .... G 828 254-2600
  Arden (G-321)
Classic Address Signs .... G 919 734-4482
  Dudley (G-4842)
Classic Sign Services LLC .... G 704 401-1466
  Monroe (G-10685)
CMA Signs LLC .... F 919 245-8339
  Hillsborough (G-8645)
Coates Designers & Crafstmen .... G 828 349-9700
  Franklin (G-6120)
Cobb Clark Richard II .... G 704 274-5479
  Huntersville (G-8804)
Cobb Sign Company Incorporated .... F 336 227-0181
  Burlington (G-1396)
Color Spot .... G 336 778-3982
  Winston Salem (G-16657)
Connected 2k LLC .... G 910 321-7446
  Fayetteville (G-5795)
Consumer Concepts .... F 252 247-7000
  Morehead City (G-11164)
Contagious Graphics Inc .... E 704 529-5600
  Charlotte (G-2543)
Cook Group Inc .... G 336 605-5557
  Mooresville (G-10911)
Cornhole Stop .... G 704 728-1550
  Cornelius (G-4537)
Cranky Creative Group .... G 877 775-9727
  Raleigh (G-12651)

Employee Codes: A=Over 500 employees, B=251-500
C=101-250, D=51-100, E=20-50, F=10-19, G=1-9

2024 Harris North Carolina
Manufacturers Directory

SIGNS & ADVERTISING SPECIALTIES — PRODUCT SECTION

Creative Images Inc .... G 919 467-2188
  Cary (G-1739)
Creative Signs Inc .... G 910 395-0100
  Wilmington (G-16187)
Custom Signage Company .... G 909 215-2404
  Charlotte (G-2595)
Custom Signs .... G 336 847-7700
  High Point (G-8314)
Darren Lee Depalo .... G 252 259-4515
  Havelock (G-7741)
Davcom Enterprises Inc .... G 919 872-9522
  Raleigh (G-12674)
Dem Party Gurls Entrmt LLC .... G 910 964-3599
  Fayetteville (G-5811)
Dert Sign Co .... G 336 225-1800
  Lexington (G-9706)
Desena Commercial Services LLC .... G 336 786-1111
  Mount Airy (G-11500)
Desena Commercial Svc .... G 336 786-1111
  Mount Airy (G-11501)
Designelement .... F 919 383-5561
  Raleigh (G-12680)
Digital Printing Systems Inc .... E 704 525-0190
  Charlotte (G-2636)
Direct Wholesale Signs LLC .... G 704 750-2842
  Kings Mountain (G-9303)
Display Techs LLC .... G 704 966-0679
  Denver (G-4773)
Display Your Graphics LLC .... G 828 489-2282
  Hendersonville (G-7845)
Diversified Signs & Graphics .... G 704 392-8165
  Charlotte (G-2645)
Dize Company .... D 336 722-5181
  Winston Salem (G-16684)
East Coast Signs .... G 910 462-2632
  Laurinburg (G-9475)
Embroidme .... G 919 316-1538
  Durham (G-5081)
Embroidme Lake Norman .... G 704 987-9630
  Cornelius (G-4543)
Engaging Signs & Graphics .... G 919 371-0885
  Raleigh (G-12739)
Eternal Wraps .... G 704 756-1914
  Cornelius (G-4544)
Excel Signs and Lighting .... G 336 257-9225
  Winston Salem (G-16703)
Exhibit World Inc .... G 704 882-2272
  Indian Trail (G-8933)
Expogo Inc .... G 910 452-3976
  Wilmington (G-16214)
EZ Sign Service .... G 919 604-3508
  Wake Forest (G-15555)
EZ Sign Service .... G 919 554-4300
  Youngsville (G-17080)
Fairway Outdoor Advg LLC .... F 919 755-1900
  Raleigh (G-12759)
Famous Amos Signs .... G 919 820-2211
  Dunn (G-4866)
Fast Lane Signs .... G 336 745-5257
  Mocksville (G-10570)
Fastsigns .... G 252 364-8745
  Greenville (G-7524)
Fastsigns .... G 704 360-3805
  Mooresville (G-10943)
Ferguson Design Inc .... E 704 394-0120
  Belmont (G-989)
Fines and Carriel Inc .... G 919 929-0702
  Chapel Hill (G-2018)
Fisher Signs Murals & Frames .... G 919 286-0591
  Durham (G-5099)
Foto Grafix .... G 336 570-1885
  Burlington (G-1415)

Franchise Signs International .... G 704 209-1087
  Rockwell (G-13654)
Franken Signs .... G 704 339-0059
  Charlotte (G-2793)
Frazees Trophies .... G 910 892-6722
  Dunn (G-4869)
Furr Signs .... G 704 455-5849
  Harrisburg (G-7710)
Global Resource NC Inc .... G 910 793-4770
  Wilmington (G-16233)
Gmg Group LLC .... G 252 441-8374
  Kill Devil Hills (G-9258)
Gogopanels .... G 702 800-1941
  Raleigh (G-12809)
Goins Signs Inc .... G 336 427-5783
  Stoneville (G-14959)
Grafix Unlimited LLC .... G 919 291-9035
  Wendell (G-15903)
Graphic Productions Inc .... G 336 765-9335
  Winston Salem (G-16729)
Graphix Solution Inc .... F 919 213-0371
  Apex (G-197)
Greene Imaging & Design Inc .... G 919 787-3737
  Raleigh (G-12814)
Greer and Associates Inc .... G 919 383-3500
  Raleigh (G-12817)
Guerrero Enterprises Inc .... G 828 286-4900
  Rutherfordton (G-13875)
Hand 2 Hand Signs .... G 919 401-2420
  Durham (G-5130)
Happy Sign Surprise LLC .... G 704 341-3359
  Charlotte (G-2886)
Hatleys Signs & Service Inc .... G 704 723-4027
  Concord (G-4278)
Headrick Otdoor Mdia of Crlnas .... F 704 487-5971
  Shelby (G-14326)
Heed Group Inc .... G 877 938-8853
  Stanley (G-14696)
Hello Signs LLC .... G 704 572-4853
  Charlotte (G-2901)
Heritage Custom Signs & Disp .... F 704 655-1465
  Charlotte (G-2904)
Hertford Printing Signs .... G 252 426-5505
  Elizabeth City (G-5547)
High Tech Signs Inc .... G 919 859-3206
  Raleigh (G-12844)
Holland Sign Plus Engrv Sltons .... G 252 339-5389
  Edenton (G-5516)
Icon Sign Systems Inc .... G 828 253-4266
  Asheville (G-657)
Identity Custom Signage Inc .... F 336 882-7446
  High Point (G-8405)
Image Design .... F 910 862-8988
  Elizabethtown (G-5597)
Image360 North Raleigh NC .... G 919 307-4119
  Raleigh (G-12879)
Industrial Sign & Graphics Inc .... E 704 371-4985
  Charlotte (G-2965)
Infinity S End Inc .... F 704 900-8355
  Charlotte (G-2968)
Island Xprtees of Oter Bnks In .... E 252 480-3990
  Nags Head (G-11720)
J & D Thorpe Enterprises Inc .... G 919 553-0918
  Clayton (G-3990)
J Morgan Signs Inc .... F 336 274-6509
  Greensboro (G-7131)
J R Craver & Associates Inc .... E 336 769-3330
  Clemmons (G-4049)
Jantec Sign Group LLC .... F 336 429-5010
  Mount Airy (G-11525)
Jaxonsigns .... G 910 467-3409
  Holly Ridge (G-8682)

JB II Printing LLC .... E 336 222-0717
  Burlington (G-1439)
JC Signs Charlotte .... G 704 370-2725
  Charlotte (G-3012)
Jeremy Weitzel .... G 919 878-4474
  Raleigh (G-12916)
Jester-Crown Inc .... G 919 872-1070
  Raleigh (G-12917)
Jj Led Solution Inc .... G 704 261-4279
  Charlotte (G-3023)
Jka Idustries .... G 980 225-5350
  Salisbury (G-13992)
JKS Motorsports Inc .... G 336 722-4129
  Lexington (G-9735)
Jones Sign .... G 828 478-4780
  Sherrills Ford (G-14386)
Jr Signs LLC .... G 980 255-3083
  Concord (G-4296)
K & D Signs LLC .... F 336 786-1111
  Mount Airy (G-11527)
K&K Holdings Inc .... G 704 341-5567
  Charlotte (G-3040)
Kathys Signs For Less .... G 910 840-1447
  Chadbourn (G-1977)
KB Sign Solutions LLC .... G 217 474-5861
  Concord (G-4299)
Kelly Signs .... G 828 778-4146
  Hendersonville (G-7868)
Kenneth Moore Signs .... G 910 458-6428
  Wilmington (G-16287)
Ki Agency LLC .... G 919 977-7075
  Raleigh (G-12937)
King Tutt Graphics .... G 919 977-6901
  Raleigh (G-12938)
King Tutt Graphics LLC .... G 877 546-4888
  Raleigh (G-12939)
Kingtuttgraphics .... G 919 748-0843
  Raleigh (G-12940)
Kranken Signs Vehicle Wraps .... G 704 339-0059
  Pineville (G-12279)
La Signs Inc .... G 919 779-1185
  Garner (G-6279)
Laws Sign Group LLC .... G 919 755-3632
  Raleigh (G-12960)
Legacy Designs & Graphx LLC .... G 910 237-2916
  Angier (G-145)
Legacy National Installers LLC .... G 336 804-1990
  Pleasant Garden (G-12357)
Liberty Sign and Lighting LLC .... G 336 703-7465
  Lexington (G-9749)
Lighthouse Led .... G 252 756-1158
  Winterville (G-17005)
Lighthouse Led Inc .... G 252 916-0998
  Greenville (G-7556)
Lights-Lights LLC .... G 919 798-2317
  Coats (G-4132)
Ls of Raleigh .... G 919 457-0340
  Raleigh (G-12980)
Main Street Vinyl LLC .... G 336 585-3089
  Burlington (G-1453)
Matthews Mobile Media LLC .... G 336 303-4982
  Greensboro (G-7188)
Melendez Signs LLC .... G 980 298-4057
  Concord (G-4312)
Mercury Signs Inc .... G 919 808-1205
  Apex (G-218)
Meredith Media Co .... F 919 748-4808
  Durham (G-5221)
Metro Print Inc .... F 704 827-3796
  Mount Holly (G-11642)
Metrolina Sign Co .... G 704 343-0885
  Charlotte (G-3170)

PRODUCT SECTION

SIGNS & ADVERTISING SPECIALTIES

Metrolina Sign Supply LLC .... G 704 343-0885
  Charlotte *(G-3171)*

Mistretta Laser Engraving .... G 704 418-5786
  Forest City *(G-6078)*

Moretz Signs Inc .... G 828 387-4600
  Beech Mountain *(G-972)*

Morningstar Signs and Banners .... G 704 861-0020
  Gastonia *(G-6469)*

Motorsports Designs Inc .... E 336 454-1181
  High Point *(G-8460)*

Mp Digital Print & Signs Inc .... G 571 315-1562
  Cornelius *(G-4570)*

NC Sign and Lighting Svc LLC .... F 586 764-0563
  Jamestown *(G-9063)*

Newton Sign Co Inc .... G 910 347-1661
  Jacksonville *(G-9018)*

Nomadic Display LLC .... F 800 336-5019
  Greensboro *(G-7221)*

North State Signs Inc .... G 919 977-7053
  Raleigh *(G-13072)*

Oak City Sign Solutions Inc .... G 919 792-8077
  Raleigh *(G-13080)*

Ocean Road Graphics Signs .... G 919 404-1444
  Four Oaks *(G-6110)*

Onsight Inc .... G 704 747-4168
  Charlotte *(G-3301)*

Optimum Sign Age .... G 919 372-8018
  Cary *(G-1838)*

Oramental Post .... F 704 376-8111
  Pineville *(G-12288)*

Outside Lines .... G 919 327-3041
  Garner *(G-6299)*

PC Signs & Graphics LLC .... G 919 661-5801
  Garner *(G-6300)*

Peaches Enterprises Inc .... G 910 868-5800
  Fayetteville *(G-5895)*

Pegasus Art and Signs LLC .... G 704 588-4948
  Charlotte *(G-3325)*

Phoenix Sign Pros Inc .... G 252 756-5685
  Winterville *(G-17011)*

Piedmont Directional Signs Inc .... G 704 607-6809
  Belmont *(G-1001)*

Piedmont Mediaworks Inc .... F 828 575-2250
  Asheville *(G-730)*

Piedmont Signs .... G 704 291-2345
  Monroe *(G-10787)*

Planet Logo Inc .... G 910 763-2554
  Wilmington *(G-16356)*

Playrace Inc .... E 828 251-2211
  Asheville *(G-735)*

Poblocki Sign Company LLC .... D 919 354-3800
  Morrisville *(G-11410)*

Point Harbor Art .... G 804 852-3633
  Point Harbor *(G-12381)*

Port City Signs & Graphics Inc .... G 910 350-8242
  Wilmington *(G-16362)*

Portable Displays LLC .... E 919 544-6504
  Cary *(G-1855)*

Print Management Group LLC .... F 704 821-0114
  Charlotte *(G-3385)*

Printology Signs Graphics LLC .... G 843 473-4984
  Davidson *(G-4691)*

Professional Bus Systems Inc .... G 704 333-2444
  Charlotte *(G-3391)*

Professional Laminating LLC .... G 919 465-0400
  Cary *(G-1862)*

Prosign .... G 919 222-6907
  Goldsboro *(G-6647)*

Proveer .... G 800 542-9941
  Raleigh *(G-13155)*

Purple Star Graphics Inc .... G 704 723-4020
  Concord *(G-4342)*

Qasioun LLC .... G 704 531-8000
  Charlotte *(G-3398)*

Qi Signs LLC .... G 336 625-0938
  Asheboro *(G-469)*

R and L Collision Center Inc .... F 704 739-2500
  Kings Mountain *(G-9328)*

R O Givens Signs Inc .... G 252 338-6578
  Elizabeth City *(G-5567)*

Ra Printing & Sign LLC .... G 704 393-0264
  Charlotte *(G-3407)*

Rags Signs + Graphics LLC .... G 910 793-9087
  Wilmington *(G-16376)*

Raleigh Sign Design .... G 919 244-1802
  Holly Springs *(G-8711)*

Raleigh Sign Solutions LLC .... G 919 578-7255
  Raleigh *(G-13186)*

Rama Sadri .... G 919 875-8088
  Raleigh *(G-13189)*

Readilite & Barricade Inc .... F 919 231-8309
  Raleigh *(G-13194)*

Rec Plus Inc .... E 704 375-9098
  Charlotte *(G-3419)*

Rena Sales .... G 704 364-3006
  Charlotte *(G-3432)*

Retail Installation Svcs LLC .... G 336 818-1333
  Millers Creek *(G-10495)*

Ricky Locklair & Randy Locklai .... G 910 470-3222
  Wilmington *(G-16383)*

RLM/Universal Packaging Inc .... F 336 644-6161
  Greensboro *(G-7312)*

Robbins Sign Supply Inc .... F 828 758-1954
  Lenoir *(G-9650)*

Routh Sign Service .... G 336 272-0895
  Greensboro *(G-7318)*

Rustic Oak Sign Co .... G 919 619-4452
  Raleigh *(G-13220)*

Salem Sports Inc .... G 336 722-2444
  Winston Salem *(G-16894)*

Sawyers Sign Service Inc .... F
  Mount Airy *(G-11571)*

Seaward Action Inc .... G 252 671-1684
  Wilmington *(G-16397)*

Shutterbug Grafix & Signs .... G 910 315-1556
  Pinehurst *(G-12237)*

Shytle Sign and Ltg Svcs LLC .... G 828 429-4120
  Ellenboro *(G-5639)*

Sidney Perry Cooper III .... G 252 257-3886
  Warrenton *(G-15661)*

Sign A Rama Inc .... G 336 893-8042
  Lewisville *(G-9673)*

Sign and Doodle .... G 704 763-7501
  Concord *(G-4358)*

Sign Company of Wilmington Inc .... F 910 392-1414
  Wilmington *(G-16405)*

Sign Gypsies Hickory .... G 828 244-3085
  Conover *(G-4496)*

Sign O Rama .... G 704 443-0092
  Matthews *(G-10289)*

Sign On Time .... G 704 507-2486
  Mooresville *(G-11087)*

Sign Resources of NC .... G 336 310-4611
  Kernersville *(G-9233)*

Sign Scientist LLC .... G 919 685-7641
  Raleigh *(G-13254)*

Sign Shop of The Triangle Inc .... G 919 363-3930
  Apex *(G-242)*

Sign Shoppe Inc .... G 910 754-5144
  Supply *(G-15011)*

Sign Solutions LLC .... G 828 687-9789
  Arden *(G-375)*

Sign Systems Inc .... G 828 785-1722
  Asheville *(G-770)*

Sign Technology Inc .... G 336 887-3211
  High Point *(G-8527)*

Sign With Anderson LLC .... G 704 599-6977
  Gastonia *(G-6508)*

Sign With Ease Inc .... G 919 285-3224
  Holly Springs *(G-8716)*

Sign Worxpress .... G 336 437-9889
  Burlington *(G-1495)*

Sign-A-Rama .... G 919 383-5561
  Raleigh *(G-13255)*

Signage Innovations Group LLC .... G 704 392-8165
  Charlotte *(G-3551)*

Signarama of Roxboro .... G 336 322-1663
  Roxboro *(G-13823)*

Signarc of Matthews LLC .... G 704 209-4444
  Matthews *(G-10343)*

Signergy LLC .... G 919 876-1370
  Raleigh *(G-13256)*

Signfactory Direct Inc .... G 336 903-0300
  Wilkesboro *(G-16041)*

Significant Others .... G 919 539-7551
  Raleigh *(G-13257)*

Signify It Inc .... F 910 678-8111
  Fayetteville *(G-5916)*

Signlogic Inc .... G 910 862-8965
  Elizabethtown *(G-5604)*

Signs By Design .... G 919 217-8000
  Raleigh *(G-13258)*

Signs By Design .... G 919 217-8000
  Raleigh *(G-13259)*

Signs By Tomorrow .... G 704 527-6100
  Charlotte *(G-3552)*

Signs Designed LLC .... G 704 332-4800
  Indian Trail *(G-8963)*

Signs Done Right .... G 910 384-2007
  Laurinburg *(G-9497)*

Signs Etc .... G 336 722-9341
  Winston Salem *(G-16909)*

Signs Now .... G 410 923-3534
  Fayetteville *(G-5917)*

Signs Now .... G 919 546-0006
  Raleigh *(G-13260)*

Signs Now 103 LLC .... G 252 355-0768
  Greenville *(G-7583)*

Signs Now Charlotte .... G 704 844-0552
  Pineville *(G-12306)*

Signs Now of Greenville .... G 252 382-0020
  Nashville *(G-11750)*

Signs Plus .... G 704 219-0290
  Wingate *(G-16578)*

Signs Sealed Delivered .... G 919 213-1280
  Durham *(G-5357)*

Signsations Ltd .... G 571 340-3330
  Chapel Hill *(G-2072)*

Signz Inc .... G 704 824-7446
  Gastonia *(G-6509)*

Siqnarama Pinevillw .... G 704 835-1123
  Pineville *(G-12307)*

Southern Signworks .... G 828 683-8726
  Leicester *(G-9521)*

Speedcal Graphics Inc .... G 704 412-3321
  Charlotte *(G-3600)*

Speedgraphics Sign Design Inc .... G 828 771-0322
  Arden *(G-380)*

Speedpro Imaging .... G 704 321-1200
  Charlotte *(G-3602)*

Speedpro Imaging .... G 704 799-8040
  Cornelius *(G-4587)*

Speedpro Imaging .... G 704 495-6749
  Mooresville *(G-11096)*

Speedpro Imaging .... G 919 578-4338
  Raleigh *(G-13289)*

Employee Codes: A=Over 500 employees, B=251-500
C=101-250, D=51-100, E=20-50, F=10-19, G=1-9

SIGNS & ADVERTISING SPECIALTIES

Speedpro Imaging Durham...................... G 919 278-7964
  Durham *(G-5368)*
Srb Technologies Inc............................... E 336 659-2610
  Winston Salem *(G-16914)*
Stay Alert Safety Services Inc.................. E 919 828-5399
  Raleigh *(G-13300)*
Sterling Products Corporation.................. G 646 423-3175
  Greensboro *(G-7370)*
Sticky Life.. G 910 817-4531
  Newton Grove *(G-11993)*
Studio Displays Inc................................. F 704 588-6590
  Pineville *(G-12310)*
Syd Inc... G 336 294-8807
  Greensboro *(G-7383)*
Talking Devices Company........................ G 828 658-0660
  Asheville *(G-795)*
Tebo Displays LLC................................... G 919 832-8525
  Raleigh *(G-13333)*
TEC Graphics Inc..................................... F 919 567-2077
  Fuquay Varina *(G-6232)*
Three Gypsies LLC.................................. G 843 337-7799
  Wingate *(G-16579)*
TNT Signs & Graphics.............................. G 704 460-5050
  Shelby *(G-14374)*
Tommy Signs.. G 704 877-1234
  Waxhaw *(G-15782)*
Tomorrow Cell LLC................................... G 704 378-8555
  Charlotte *(G-3707)*
Triangle Inner Vision Company................. G 919 460-6013
  Morrisville *(G-11452)*
Triangle Sign Solutions............................. G 919 302-2482
  Wake Forest *(G-15604)*
Triangle Solutions Inc............................... G 919 481-1235
  Cary *(G-1912)*
Twinvision North America Inc................... C 919 361-2155
  Durham *(G-5416)*
United Group Graphics Inc....................... G 919 596-3932
  Durham *(G-5421)*
US Logoworks LLC................................... F 910 307-0312
  Fayetteville *(G-5944)*
Veteran Safety Solutions LLC................... G 980 339-2721
  Southmont *(G-14562)*
Vic Inc... E 336 545-1124
  Greensboro *(G-7443)*
Victory Signs LLC..................................... G 919 642-3091
  Fuquay Varina *(G-6236)*
Vintage Editions Inc.................................. F 828 632-4185
  Taylorsville *(G-15175)*
Vittro Sign Studio...................................... G 917 698-1594
  Apex *(G-256)*
Vivid Pro Signs... G 919 352-8485
  Sanford *(G-14204)*
Warden Signs & Service LLC................... G 336 416-4029
  Yadkinville *(G-17062)*
Web 4 Half LLC.. E 855 762-4638
  Asheboro *(G-509)*
Webb of Wnc LLC..................................... G 828 648-2670
  Canton *(G-1628)*
Weddles Signs.. G 276 779-9218
  Mount Airy *(G-11593)*
Whats Your Sign LLC................................ G 919 274-5703
  Raleigh *(G-13420)*
Wicked Rooster Signs Inc......................... G 828 844-0404
  Hendersonville *(G-7914)*
Wild Child Custom Graphics LLC.............. G 910 762-5435
  Wilmington *(G-16443)*
Williams Signs... G 828 321-2438
  Andrews *(G-129)*
Wilson Billboard Advg Inc......................... G 919 934-2421
  Smithfield *(G-14489)*
Xo Signs.. G 919 328-9110
  Durham *(G-5455)*
Xtreme Graphix.. G 704 746-5744
  Mooresville *(G-11134)*

SIGNS & ADVERTISING SPECIALTIES: Artwork, Advertising

Awning Innovations................................... G 336 831-8996
  Clemmons *(G-4028)*
Graphic Components LLC........................ E 336 542-2128
  Greensboro *(G-7057)*
Merge LLC.. G 919 832-3924
  Raleigh *(G-13016)*
Ruth Arnold Graphics & Signs.................. G 910 793-9087
  Wilmington *(G-16390)*
Shop Dawg Signs LLC.............................. G 919 556-2672
  Wake Forest *(G-15592)*
Signal Signs of Ga Inc.............................. G 828 494-4913
  Murphy *(G-11716)*

SIGNS & ADVERTISING SPECIALTIES: Letters For Signs, Metal

Custom Metal Creation LLC...................... G 828 302-0623
  Vale *(G-15464)*
NC Graphic Pros LLC............................... G 252 492-7326
  Kittrell *(G-9397)*

SIGNS & ADVERTISING SPECIALTIES: Novelties

Image Matters Inc..................................... G 336 940-3000
  Clemmons *(G-4047)*
Promographix Inc...................................... F 919 846-1379
  Carolina Beach *(G-1640)*

SIGNS & ADVERTISING SPECIALTIES: Scoreboards, Electric

Major Display Inc...................................... G 800 260-1067
  Franklin *(G-6137)*

SIGNS, ELECTRICAL: Wholesalers

Kenneth Moore Signs................................ G 910 458-6428
  Wilmington *(G-16287)*
Southeastern Sign Works Inc.................... F 336 789-5516
  Mount Airy *(G-11574)*

SIGNS, EXC ELECTRIC, WHOLESALE

Darren Lee Depalo.................................... G 252 259-4515
  Havelock *(G-7741)*
Frazees Trophies...................................... G 910 892-6722
  Dunn *(G-4869)*
Signature Signs Inc.................................. G 336 431-2072
  High Point *(G-8528)*
Trivantage LLC... D 800 786-1876
  Burlington *(G-1510)*
Wild Child Custom Graphics LLC.............. G 910 762-5435
  Wilmington *(G-16443)*

SIGNS: Electrical

ABC Signs and Graphics LLC................... G 252 652-6620
  Havelock *(G-7738)*
Action Sign Company Lenoir Inc............... F 828 754-4116
  Lenoir *(G-9567)*
Ad-Art Signs Inc....................................... G 704 377-5369
  Charlotte *(G-2133)*
All Signs & Graphics LLC......................... G 910 323-3115
  Fayetteville *(G-5757)*
Allen Industries Inc................................... C 336 294-4777
  Greensboro *(G-6792)*
Allen Industries Inc................................... D 336 668-2791
  Greensboro *(G-6791)*
Anthem Displays LLC............................... F 910 746-8988
  Elizabethtown *(G-5583)*
Anthem Displays LLC............................... F 910 862-3550
  Elizabethtown *(G-5584)*
Aoa Signs Inc.. G 336 679-3344
  Wilson *(G-16466)*
B&P Enterprise NC Inc............................. G 727 669-6877
  Hickory *(G-7947)*
Beeson Sign Co Inc.................................. G 336 993-5617
  Kernersville *(G-9167)*
Blashfield Sign Company Inc.................... G 910 485-7200
  Fayetteville *(G-5772)*
Broach Custom Signs NC LLC.................. G 919 876-8380
  Wendell *(G-15893)*
Creativeminds Design LLC....................... G 678 457-6148
  Monroe *(G-10698)*
Ebert Sign Company Inc........................... G 336 768-2867
  Lexington *(G-9711)*
Ever Glo Sign Co Inc................................ G 704 633-3324
  Salisbury *(G-13959)*
Goldsboro Neon Sign Co Inc.................... G 919 735-2035
  Goldsboro *(G-6619)*
Grandwell Industries Inc.......................... E 919 557-1221
  Fuquay Varina *(G-6202)*
Interstate Sign Company Inc..................... E 336 789-3069
  Mount Airy *(G-11524)*
JC Signs Inc.. G 704 995-0988
  Charlotte *(G-3011)*
Lockwood Identity Inc............................... C 704 597-9801
  Charlotte *(G-3099)*
McCorkle Sign Company Inc.................... E 919 687-7080
  Durham *(G-5212)*
Moss Sign Company Inc........................... F 828 299-7766
  Asheville *(G-706)*
Parish Sign & Service Inc......................... E 910 875-6121
  Raeford *(G-12430)*
PFC Group LLC.. D 704 393-4040
  Charlotte *(G-3335)*
Powersigns Inc... G 910 343-1789
  Wilmington *(G-16365)*
Prismaflex Usa Inc................................... F 910 862-3550
  Elizabethtown *(G-5602)*
Reese Sign Service Inc............................ G 919 580-0705
  Goldsboro *(G-6649)*
Sensational Signs..................................... G 704 358-1099
  Charlotte *(G-3527)*
September Signs & Graphics LLC............ G 910 791-9084
  Wilmington *(G-16399)*
Sign & Awning Systems Inc...................... F 919 892-5900
  Dunn *(G-4883)*
Sign Connection Inc.................................. E 704 868-4500
  Gastonia *(G-6507)*
Sign Here of Lake Norman Inc.................. G 704 483-6454
  Denver *(G-4801)*
Sign Medic Inc.. G 336 789-5972
  Mount Airy *(G-11572)*
Sign World Inc.. F 704 529-4440
  Charlotte *(G-3550)*
Signature Signs Inc.................................. G 336 431-2072
  High Point *(G-8528)*
Signs Etc of Charlotte............................... F 704 522-8860
  Charlotte *(G-3553)*
Signs Unlimited Inc................................... F 919 596-7612
  Durham *(G-5358)*
Southeastern Sign Works Inc.................... F 336 789-5516
  Mount Airy *(G-11574)*
Stonetree Signs.. G 336 625-0938
  Denton *(G-4750)*
Yesco Sign Lighting Service..................... G 336 285-0795
  Greensboro *(G-7473)*

SIGNS: Neon

Custom Neon & Graphics Inc.................... G 704 344-1715
  Charlotte *(G-2592)*

PRODUCT SECTION

SPORTING & ATHLETIC GOODS: Rods & Rod Parts, Fishing

Mount Airy Signs & Letters Inc............... F 336 786-5777
  Mount Airy *(G-11547)*
Superior Sign Company Inc.................... G 336 454-2226
  High Point *(G-8558)*

SILICONES

Momentive Performance Mtls Inc............. C 704 805-6252
  Charlotte *(G-3193)*
Momentive Performance Mtls Inc............. D 704 805-6200
  Huntersville *(G-8857)*
Silicones Inc.. G 336 886-5018
  High Point *(G-8530)*
Xona Microfluidics Inc............................. G 951 553-6400
  Durham *(G-5456)*

SILK SCREEN DESIGN SVCS

Body Billboards Inc................................. G 919 544-4540
  Durham *(G-4969)*
Moving Screens Incorporated................. G 336 364-9259
  Rougemont *(G-13787)*
Rapp Productions Inc............................. F 919 913-0270
  Carrboro *(G-1654)*

SILO STAVES: Concrete Or Cast Stone

Cava Di Pietra Inc................................... G 910 338-5024
  Wilmington *(G-16161)*

SILVERWARE & PLATED WARE

D Winchester Designs............................. G 704 607-0678
  Monroe *(G-10702)*
Trinkets and Whimsey............................. G 919 368-6044
  Hendersonville *(G-7909)*

SINTER: Iron

GKN Sinter Metals LLC........................... C 828 464-0642
  Conover *(G-4459)*

SKILL TRAINING CENTER

Webster Entps Jackson Cnty Inc............. E 828 586-8981
  Sylva *(G-15074)*

SLINGS: Rope

Ace Marine Rigging & Supply Inc............. F 252 726-6620
  Morehead City *(G-11148)*

SMOKE DETECTORS

3 Alarm Smoke Detector Svcs................. G 757 636-6773
  Currituck *(G-4632)*
Walter Kidde Portable Eqp Inc................. B 919 563-5911
  Mebane *(G-10435)*

SNIPS: Tinners'

Irwin Industrial Tool Company................. C 704 987-4555
  Huntersville *(G-8838)*

SOFT DRINKS WHOLESALERS

Choice USA Beverage Inc....................... G 704 487-6951
  Shelby *(G-14294)*
Pepsi Bottling Ventures LLC................... C 336 724-4800
  Winston Salem *(G-16842)*
Pepsi-Cola Btlg Hickry NC Inc................. G 828 322-8090
  Granite Falls *(G-6749)*
Pepsi-Cola Btlg Hickry NC Inc................. E 828 322-8090
  Hickory *(G-8110)*
Pepsi-Cola Btlg Hickry NC Inc................. G 828 322-8090
  Hickory *(G-8111)*
Zeskp LLC.. G 910 762-8300
  Wilmington *(G-16460)*

SOFTWARE PUBLISHERS: Home Entertainment

Boss Key Productions Inc....................... D 919 659-5704
  Raleigh *(G-12571)*
Ientertainment Network Inc.................... G 919 238-4090
  Burnsville *(G-1528)*
Micronova Systems Inc........................... F 910 202-0564
  Wilmington *(G-16323)*
Utd Technology Corp.............................. G 704 612-0121
  Mint Hill *(G-10546)*
Wave Front Computers LLC.................... G 919 896-6121
  Raleigh *(G-13414)*

SOFTWARE PUBLISHERS: Operating Systems

Feedtrail Incorporated............................. F 757 618-7760
  Raleigh *(G-12763)*
Innait Inc.. G 406 241-5245
  Charlotte *(G-2975)*

SOFTWARE TRAINING, COMPUTER

Academy Association Inc....................... F 919 544-0835
  Durham *(G-4899)*
Camstar Systems Inc.............................. C 704 227-6600
  Charlotte *(G-2380)*
Ideacode Inc... G 919 341-5170
  Greensboro *(G-7111)*

SOLAR CELLS

510nano Inc.. F 919 521-5982
  Durham *(G-4894)*
Entropy Solar Integrators LLC................. G 704 936-5018
  Charlotte *(G-2716)*
Micro-OHM Corporation.......................... G 800 845-5167
  Raleigh *(G-13026)*

SOLAR HEATING EQPT

Entropy Solar Integrators LLC................. G 704 936-5018
  Charlotte *(G-2716)*
Low Impact Tech USA Inc....................... G 828 428-6310
  Fletcher *(G-6019)*
Solar Connection LLC............................. G 828 484-9163
  Marion *(G-10178)*
Solar Hot Limited.................................... G 919 439-2387
  Raleigh *(G-13276)*
Solarh2ot Ltd.. G 919 439-2387
  Raleigh *(G-13279)*
Sunqest Inc.. G 828 325-4910
  Newton *(G-11975)*

SOUND EQPT: Electric

Custom Light and Sound Inc................... E 919 286-1122
  Durham *(G-5040)*

SPACE PROPULSION UNITS & PARTS

James Tool Machine & Engrg Inc............ C 828 584-8722
  Morganton *(G-11224)*

SPAS

Southern Home Spa and Wtr Pdts.......... G 336 286-3564
  Greensboro *(G-7354)*

SPEAKER SYSTEMS

Hartley Loudspeakers Inc....................... F 910 392-1200
  Wilmington *(G-16248)*

SPECIALTY FOOD STORES: Coffee

Tradewinds Coffee Co Inc....................... F 919 556-1835
  Zebulon *(G-17144)*
Well-Bean Coffee & Crumbs LLC............ G 833 777-2326
  Wake Forest *(G-15612)*

SPECIALTY FOOD STORES: Health & Dietetic Food

Nutrotonic LLC....................................... F 855 948-0008
  Charlotte *(G-3285)*
Suntory International............................... F 917 756-2747
  Raleigh *(G-13316)*

SPECIALTY FOOD STORES: Juices, Fruit Or Vegetable

Goodstuff Juices LLC.............................. G 252 347-2341
  Greenville *(G-7532)*

SPECIALTY FOOD STORES: Vitamin

Daily Manufacturing Inc.......................... F 704 782-0700
  Rockwell *(G-13651)*

SPECIALTY OUTPATIENT CLINICS, NEC

Cape Fear Orthtics Prsthtics I................. G 910 483-0933
  Fayetteville *(G-5780)*

SPORTING & ATHLETIC GOODS: Bowling Balls

Thunder Alley Enterprises....................... G 910 371-0119
  Leland *(G-9561)*

SPORTING & ATHLETIC GOODS: Fishing Eqpt

Fathom Offshore Holdings LLC............... G 910 399-6882
  Wilmington *(G-16217)*

SPORTING & ATHLETIC GOODS: Fishing Tackle, General

Sea Striker Inc.. E 252 247-4113
  Morehead City *(G-11187)*

SPORTING & ATHLETIC GOODS: Gymnasium Eqpt

Carolina Gym Supply Corp...................... G 919 732-6999
  Hillsborough *(G-8642)*

SPORTING & ATHLETIC GOODS: Hunting Eqpt

Deerhunter Tree Stands Inc.................... G 704 462-1116
  Hickory *(G-8004)*
Frostie Bottom Tree Stand LLC............... G 828 466-1708
  Claremont *(G-3927)*
Hawk Distributors Inc............................. G 888 334-1307
  Sanford *(G-14129)*
Hughes Products Co Inc........................ G 336 769-3788
  Winston Salem *(G-16750)*
Kol Incorporated..................................... G 919 872-2340
  Raleigh *(G-12945)*
Rigem Right.. F 252 726-9508
  Newport *(G-11905)*
Rufton Brewhouse................................... G 828 289-8060
  Rutherfordton *(G-13887)*
Sports Products LLC.............................. G 919 562-4074
  Wake Forest *(G-15595)*

SPORTING & ATHLETIC GOODS: Racket Sports Eqpt

Syntech of Burlington Inc....................... E 336 570-2035
  Burlington *(G-1503)*

SPORTING & ATHLETIC GOODS: Rods & Rod Parts, Fishing

SPORTING & ATHLETIC GOODS: Shafts, Golf Club

Lees Tackle Inc.................................. E..... 910 386-5100
  Wilmington (G-16295)

SPORTING & ATHLETIC GOODS: Shafts, Golf Club

Thomas Golf Inc................................... G..... 704 461-1342
  Charlotte (G-3689)
VA Composites Inc.............................. G..... 844 474-2387
  Aberdeen (G-34)

SPORTING & ATHLETIC GOODS: Targets, Archery & Rifle Shooting

McKenzie Sports Products LLC............ C..... 704 279-7985
  Salisbury (G-14011)

SPORTING & ATHLETIC GOODS: Team Sports Eqpt

Parker Athletic Products LLC................ G..... 704 370-0400
  Charlotte (G-3312)

SPORTING & ATHLETIC GOODS: Track & Field Athletic Eqpt

Ucs Inc... D..... 704 732-9922
  Lincolnton (G-9931)
United Canvas & Sling Inc................... E..... 704 732-9922
  Lincolnton (G-9933)

SPORTING & REC GOODS, WHOLESALE: Camping Eqpt & Splys

Trivantage LLC..................................... D..... 800 786-1876
  Burlington (G-1510)

SPORTING & RECREATIONAL GOODS, WHOLESALE: Boat Access & Part

Custom Marine Fabrication Inc............. G..... 252 638-5422
  New Bern (G-11795)
Iconic Marine Group LLC..................... D..... 252 975-2000
  Chocowinity (G-3895)

SPORTING FIREARMS WHOLESALERS

Every Day Carry LLc............................. F..... 203 231-0256
  Winnabow (G-16580)
North American Trade LLC................... G..... 828 712-3004
  Fletcher (G-6030)

SPORTING GOODS STORES: Firearms

Sturm Ruger & Company Inc............... B..... 336 427-0286
  Mayodan (G-10368)

SPORTING GOODS STORES: Fishing Eqpt

Custom Marine Fabrication Inc............. G..... 252 638-5422
  New Bern (G-11795)
Fathom Offshore Holdings LLC............ G..... 910 399-6882
  Wilmington (G-16217)

SPORTING GOODS STORES: Specialty Sport Splys, NEC

Millers Sports and Trophies.................. G..... 252 792-2050
  Williamston (G-16067)

SPORTING GOODS: Sleeping Bags

Lomar Specialty Advg Inc..................... F..... 704 788-4380
  Concord (G-4307)
Treklite Inc.. G..... 919 610-1788
  Raleigh (G-13358)

SPORTS APPAREL STORES

Happy Jack Incorporated...................... G..... 252 747-2911
  Snow Hill (G-14503)
New Media Golf Inc.............................. F..... 828 533-9954
  Highlands (G-8616)
Rec Plus Inc.. E..... 704 375-9098
  Charlotte (G-3419)

SPORTS CLUBS, MANAGERS & PROMOTERS

Richard Chldress Racg Entps In........... B..... 336 731-3334
  Welcome (G-15875)

SPRINGS: Coiled Flat

Matthew Warren Inc............................. E..... 704 837-0331
  Charlotte (G-3143)

SPRINGS: Furniture

Leggett & Platt Incorporated................. G..... 704 380-6208
  Statesville (G-14835)

SPRINGS: Mechanical, Precision

Lee Spring Company LLC..................... E..... 336 275-3631
  Greensboro (G-7165)
Northeast Tool and Mfg Company......... E..... 704 882-1187
  Matthews (G-10337)

SPRINGS: Precision

Cox Precision Springs Inc.................... F..... 336 629-8500
  Asheboro (G-419)

SPRINGS: Steel

Lee Spring Company LLC..................... E..... 336 275-3631
  Greensboro (G-7165)
Southern ATL Spring Mfg Sls LL........... E..... 704 279-1331
  Granite Quarry (G-6762)
Stabilus Inc... D..... 704 865-7444
  Gastonia (G-6513)
Stable Holdco Inc................................ B..... 704 866-7140
  Gastonia (G-6514)

SPRINGS: Wire

Lee Spring Company............................ G..... 336 275-3631
  Greensboro (G-7164)
Leggett & Platt Incorporated................. G..... 704 380-6208
  Statesville (G-14835)
M-B Industries Inc............................... C..... 828 862-4201
  Rosman (G-13786)
Magnarep Incorporated........................ G..... 919 949-5488
  Durham (G-5202)
N C Coil Inc.. G..... 336 983-4440
  King (G-9277)
Newcomb Spring Corp......................... E..... 704 588-2043
  Gastonia (G-6477)
Southern Precision Spring Inc............... E..... 704 392-4393
  Charlotte (G-3595)

STAINLESS STEEL

American Stainless Tubing LLC............ C..... 704 878-8823
  Troutman (G-15366)
Davis Equipment Handlers Inc.............. G..... 704 792-9176
  Charlotte (G-2606)
Old Hickory Stainless Stl Inc................. E..... 910 567-6751
  Godwin (G-6579)
Quality Mechanical Contrs LLC............. D..... 336 228-0638
  Burlington (G-1480)
Stainless Steel Countertops NC............ G..... 919 935-0835
  Cameron (G-1563)

STAIRCASES & STAIRS, WOOD

Andronics Construction Inc.................. E..... 704 400-9562
  Indian Trail (G-8920)

Carolina Stairs Inc............................... F..... 704 664-5032
  Mount Ulla (G-11681)
Convert-A-Stair LLC............................. G..... 888 908-5657
  Wilmington (G-16181)
Masterpiece Staircase LLC................... G..... 704 806-2894
  Matthews (G-10333)
Royal Oak Stairs Inc............................ F..... 919 855-8988
  Raleigh (G-13216)
Southern Staircase Inc........................ G..... 704 363-2123
  Charlotte (G-3596)
Wood Barn Inc.................................... F..... 252 826-5538
  Scotland Neck (G-14225)
Wood Barn Inc.................................... E..... 919 496-6714
  Louisburg (G-10006)

STAMPINGS: Automotive

Belwith Products LLC.......................... G..... 336 841-3899
  High Point (G-8270)
Shiloh Products Inc............................. G..... 336 548-6035
  Mayodan (G-10367)
Vibration Solutions LLC....................... G..... 704 896-7535
  Charlotte (G-3776)

STAPLES: Steel, Wire Or Cut

Schafer Manufacturing Co LLC............. G..... 704 528-5321
  Troutman (G-15392)

STATIONARY & OFFICE SPLYS, WHOLESALE: Office Filing Splys

Cartridge World................................... G..... 336 885-0989
  High Point (G-8288)
Sdv Office Systems LLC...................... F..... 844 968-9500
  Fletcher (G-6037)
Sdv Office Systems LLC...................... G..... 844 968-9500
  Asheville (G-767)

STATIONERY & OFFICE SPLYS WHOLESALERS

Archie Supply LLC.............................. G..... 336 987-0895
  Greensboro (G-6813)
Bic Corporation................................... D..... 704 598-7700
  Charlotte (G-2308)
Digital Print & Imaging Inc................... G..... 910 341-3005
  Wilmington (G-16201)
Person Printing Company Inc.............. E..... 336 599-2146
  Roxboro (G-13818)

STATORS REWINDING SVCS

Leonard Electric Mtr Repr Inc............... G..... 336 625-2375
  Asheboro (G-453)

STATUARY & OTHER DECORATIVE PRDTS: Nonmetallic

Cairn Studio Ltd.................................. G..... 704 892-3581
  Davidson (G-4667)

STEEL & ALLOYS: Tool & Die

Greene Precision Products Inc............. G..... 828 262-0116
  Boone (G-1202)

STEEL, COLD-ROLLED: Strip NEC, From Purchased HotRolled

Sandvik Inc.. C..... 919 563-5008
  Mebane (G-10427)

STOKERS: Mechanical, Domestic Or Indl

Machining Technology Services........... G..... 704 282-1071
  Monroe (G-10763)

STONE: Dimension, NEC

Carolina Quarries Inc .... D 704 633-0201
  Salisbury (G-13936)
Carolina Sunrock LLC .... E 919 575-4502
  Butner (G-1543)
Lbm Industries Inc .... G 828 631-1227
  Sylva (G-15062)
Lbm Industries Inc .... F 828 966-4270
  Sapphire (G-14214)
McNeely Trucking Co .... E 828 966-4270
  Sapphire (G-14215)
Monkey Jct Mulch & Stone Inc ..... F 910 793-9111
  Wilmington (G-16326)
Rouse Custom Stone .... G 336 655-1613
  Lewisville (G-9672)
Sunrock Group Holdings Corp ..... D 919 747-6400
  Raleigh (G-13315)
Tarheel Sand & Stone Inc .... G 336 468-4003
  Hamptonville (G-7679)
Waycaster Nick Stone Co .... G 828 756-4011
  Marion (G-10185)

STONE: Quarrying & Processing, Own Stone Prdts

American Stone Company .... D 919 929-7131
  Chapel Hill (G-1983)
B V Hedrick Gravel & Sand Co ..... E 828 645-5560
  Weaverville (G-15837)
Boone-Woody Mining Company Inc .. G 828 675-5188
  Micaville (G-10442)
Lbm Industries Inc .... F 828 966-4270
  Sapphire (G-14213)
Midcoastal Development Corp ..... G 336 622-3091
  Staley (G-14668)
Stonemaster Inc .... F 704 333-0353
  Charlotte (G-3638)
Wake Stone Corporation .... E 919 677-0050
  Cary (G-1923)

STONEWARE PRDTS: Pottery

East Fork Pottery LLC .... G 828 237-7200
  Asheville (G-614)
East Fork Pottery LLC .... F 828 237-7200
  Asheville (G-615)

STORE FIXTURES: Wood

Idx Impressions LLC .... C 703 550-6902
  Washington (G-15711)
Ivey Fixture & Design Inc .... G 704 283-4398
  Monroe (G-10742)
Oyama Cabinet Inc .... G 828 327-2668
  Conover (G-4477)
Rusco Fixture Company Inc .... E 704 474-3184
  Norwood (G-12043)
Stanly Fixs Acquisition LLC .... E 704 474-3184
  Norwood (G-12044)
Sterling Cleora Corporation .... E 919 563-5800
  Durham (G-5374)

STORES: Auto & Home Supply

Courtesy Ford Inc .... E 252 338-4783
  Elizabeth City (G-5537)
Cummins Atlantic LLC .... D 336 275-4531
  Greensboro (G-6946)
L L C Batteries of N C .... G 919 331-0241
  Angier (G-143)
Piedmont Truck Tires Inc .... F 828 277-1549
  Asheville (G-731)
Piedmont Truck Tires Inc .... F 336 223-9412
  Graham (G-6706)
Piedmont Truck Tires Inc .... E 336 668-0091
  Greensboro (G-7262)
Trick Karts Inc .... G 704 883-0089
  Statesville (G-14917)
Williams Electric Mtr Repr Inc ..... G 919 859-9790
  Sanford (G-14206)

STOVES: Wood & Coal Burning

Appalchian Stove Fbrcators Inc ... F 828 253-0164
  Asheville (G-525)
Taylor Manufacturing Inc .... E 910 862-2576
  Elizabethtown (G-5605)

STRAPS: Braids, Textile

All American Braids Inc .... E 704 852-4380
  Gastonia (G-6339)
Standard Tytape Company Inc .... F 828 693-6594
  Hendersonville (G-7906)

STRAPS: Braids, Tubular Nylon Or Plastic

Newgard Industries Inc .... F 704 283-6011
  Monroe (G-10779)

STRAPS: Webbing, Woven

Hickory Springs Mfg Co .... F 336 491-4131
  High Point (G-8386)
Murdock Webbing Company Inc .. E 252 823-1131
  Tarboro (G-15117)
Tcu Industries Inc .... G 602 369-7270
  Harrisburg (G-7730)

STRUCTURAL SUPPORT & BUILDING MATERIAL: Concrete

Four Jaks .... G 828 484-9545
  Weaverville (G-15847)

STUDS & JOISTS: Sheet Metal

H&S Autoshot LLC .... E 847 662-8500
  Mooresville (G-10968)

SUNDRIES & RELATED PRDTS: Medical & Laboratory, Rubber

Custom Assemblies Inc .... E 919 202-4533
  Pine Level (G-12207)
Mount Hope Machinery Co .... F
  Charlotte (G-3208)

SURFACE ACTIVE AGENTS

Cht R Beitlich Corporation .... E 704 523-4242
  Charlotte (G-2481)
Diarkis LLC .... G 704 888-5244
  Locust (G-9957)
Henkel Corporation .... D 704 633-1731
  Salisbury (G-13976)
Syntha Group Inc .... D 336 885-5131
  High Point (G-8562)

SURGICAL APPLIANCES & SPLYS

Carolon Company .... D 336 969-6001
  Rural Hall (G-13835)
Teleflex Incorporated .... G 919 433-2575
  Durham (G-5388)
Teleflex Incorporated .... G 919 433-2575
  Durham (G-5389)
410 Medical Inc .... F 919 241-7900
  Durham (G-4893)
Allyn International Trdg Corp ...... G 877 858-2482
  Marshville (G-10210)
American Fiber & Finishing Inc ... E 704 984-9256
  Albemarle (G-73)
American Prosthetics .... G 704 782-0908
  Concord (G-4194)
Amtai Medical Equipment Inc ..... F 919 872-1803
  Raleigh (G-12503)
Andersen Products Inc .... E 336 376-3000
  Haw River (G-7750)
Andersen Sterilizers Inc .... E 336 376-8622
  Haw River (G-7751)
Beacon Prosthetics & Orthotics .. G 919 231-6890
  Raleigh (G-12548)
Beocare Inc .... C 828 728-7300
  Hudson (G-8762)
Biomedical Innovations Inc .... G 910 603-0267
  Southern Pines (G-14529)
Coastal Machine & Welding Inc .. G 910 754-6476
  Shallotte (G-14272)
Cranial Technologies Inc .... G 336 760-5530
  Winston Salem (G-16665)
Custom Medical Specialties Inc .. F 919 202-8462
  Pine Level (G-12208)
Ethicon Inc .... G 919 234-2124
  Cary (G-1762)
Hollister Incorporated .... G 919 792-2095
  Raleigh (G-12852)
Hyperbranch Medical Tech Inc ... F 919 433-3325
  Durham (G-5143)
Kayser-Roth Corporation .... C 336 852-2030
  Greensboro (G-7145)
Lifespan Incorporated .... D 336 838-2614
  North Wilkesboro (G-12022)
Lifespan Incorporated .... E 704 944-5100
  Charlotte (G-3086)
Medical Device Bus Svcs Inc ..... F 704 423-0033
  Charlotte (G-3158)
Medical Spclties of Crlnas Inc .... G 910 575-4542
  Sunset Beach (G-15001)
Mign Inc .... G 609 304-1617
  Charlotte (G-3177)
Mool Law Firm LLC .... G 217 496-3355
  Boone (G-1224)
Nonwoven Medical Tech LLC ..... G 888 978-6199
  Charlotte (G-3265)
Nufabrx LLC .... G 888 683-2279
  Charlotte (G-3284)
Pacon Manufacturing Corp LLC .. C 732 764-9070
  Navassa (G-11758)
Safe Home Pro Inc .... F 704 662-2299
  Cornelius (G-4585)
Soundside Orthtics Prsthtics L ... G 910 238-2026
  Jacksonville (G-9035)
Stryker Corporation .... F 919 433-3325
  Durham (G-5378)
Test ME Out Inc .... G 252 635-6770
  New Bern (G-11849)
U-Hear of Hickory .... G 704 434-2062
  Mooresboro (G-10843)
VH Industries Inc .... E 704 743-2400
  Concord (G-4385)

SURGICAL IMPLANTS

Medtrnic Sofamor Danek USA Inc .. G 919 457-9982
  Cary (G-1823)
Novex Innovations LLC .... G 336 231-6693
  Winston Salem (G-16824)

SUSPENSION SYSTEMS: Acoustical, Metal

Hotchkis Performance Mfg Inc ... G 704 660-3060
  Mooresville (G-10978)
Leo Gaev Metalworks Inc .... F 919 883-4666
  Chapel Hill (G-2031)

SVC ESTABLISHMENT EQPT, WHOLESALE: Firefighting Eqpt

Beco Holding Company Inc .... C 800 826-3473
  Charlotte (G-2295)
Fireresq Incorporated .... F 888 975-0858
  Mooresville (G-10945)
Lightning X Products Inc .... G 704 295-0299
  Charlotte (G-3088)

SVC ESTABLISHMENT EQPT, WHOLESALE: Laundry Eqpt & Splys

Gardner Machinery Corporation .... F 704 372-3890
  Charlotte (G-2808)
Laundry Svc Tech Ltd Lblty Co .... G 908 327-1997
  Matthews (G-10262)
Talley Machinery Corporation .... G 336 664-0012
  Greensboro (G-7388)

SWIMMING POOL ACCESS: Leaf Skimmers Or Pool Rakes

Hayward Industries Inc .... C 336 712-9900
  Clemmons (G-4043)
Hayward Industries Inc .... B 908 351-5400
  Charlotte (G-2894)

SWIMMING POOL EQPT: Filters & Water Conditioning Systems

Caldwells Water Conditioning .... G 828 253-6605
  Asheville (G-578)
Hayward Industries Inc .... C 336 712-9900
  Clemmons (G-4043)
Hayward Industries Inc .... A 336 712-9900
  Clemmons (G-4044)
Hayward Industries Inc .... B 908 351-5400
  Charlotte (G-2894)
Pentair Water Pool and Spa Inc .... F 919 463-4640
  Cary (G-1848)
Pentair Water Pool and Spa Inc .... A 919 566-8000
  Sanford (G-14166)

SWITCHES: Electric Power, Exc Snap, Push Button, Etc

Electro Switch Corp .... C 919 833-0707
  Raleigh (G-12730)
Shallco Inc .... E 919 934-3135
  Smithfield (G-14482)
Siemens Power Transmission .... A 919 463-8702
  Cary (G-1888)

SWITCHES: Electronic

Applied Drives Inc .... G 704 573-2324
  Charlotte (G-2204)
Silanna Semicdtr N Amer Inc .... D 984 444-6500
  Raleigh (G-13261)

SWITCHES: Electronic Applications

Silanna Semicdtr N Amer Inc .... D 984 444-6500
  Raleigh (G-13261)

SWITCHES: Time, Electrical Switchgear Apparatus

Precision Time Systems Inc .... F 910 253-9850
  Supply (G-15008)

SWITCHGEAR & SWITCHBOARD APPARATUS

Abb Inc .... E 704 587-1362
  Charlotte (G-2122)
ABB Enterprise Software Inc .... C 919 582-3283
  Raleigh (G-12455)
ABB Inc .... A 252 827-2121
  Pinetops (G-12239)
ABB Inc .... D 919 856-2360
  Raleigh (G-12457)
ABB Inc .... C 919 856-2360
  Cary (G-1674)
Carolina Elctrnc Assmblers In .... E 919 938-1086
  Smithfield (G-14452)
Carolina Products Inc .... E 704 364-9029
  Charlotte (G-2403)
Dna Group Inc .... E 919 881-0889
  Raleigh (G-12690)
General Electric Company .... G 704 561-5700
  Charlotte (G-2817)
General Electric Company .... B 919 563-5561
  Mebane (G-10411)
Grecon Inc .... F 503 641-7731
  Charlotte (G-2862)
JA Smith Inc .... G 704 860-4910
  Lawndale (G-9500)
JMS Southeast Inc .... E 704 873-1835
  Statesville (G-14825)
Miller Ctrl Mfg Inc Clinton NC .... G 910 592-5112
  Clinton (G-4098)
Precision Mch Fabrication Inc .... D 919 231-8648
  Raleigh (G-13134)
Reuel Inc .... E 919 734-0460
  Goldsboro (G-6650)
Schneider Electric Usa Inc .... C 919 266-3671
  Knightdale (G-9428)
Schneider Electric Usa Inc .... C 888 778-2733
  Morrisville (G-11419)
Shelby Kendrion Inc .... C 704 482-9582
  Shelby (G-14366)
Short Circuit Audio LLC .... G 908 868-7077
  Greensboro (G-7336)

SWITCHGEAR & SWITCHGEAR ACCESS, NEC

Eaton Corporation .... B 828 684-2381
  Arden (G-326)
Southern Electrical Eqp Co Inc .... G 704 392-1396
  Indian Trail (G-8964)

SYNTHETIC RESIN FINISHED PRDTS, NEC

American Composites Engrg .... F 252 641-9866
  Tarboro (G-15095)
Hornet Capital LLC .... G 252 641-8000
  Tarboro (G-15109)

SYRUPS, DRINK

Choice USA Beverage Inc .... D 704 823-1651
  Lowell (G-10007)
Little Beekeeper LLC .... G 704 215-9690
  Lincolnton (G-9902)

SYSTEMS ENGINEERING: Computer Related

Avail Forensics LLC .... F 877 888-5895
  Wilmington (G-16125)
Custom Controls Unlimited LLC .... F 919 812-6553
  Raleigh (G-12664)
Fieldsway Solutions LLC .... G 984 920-7791
  Four Oaks (G-6104)
Qplot Corporation .... G 949 302-7928
  Raleigh (G-13160)

SYSTEMS INTEGRATION SVCS

Esequence Inc .... G 919 831-1995
  Raleigh (G-12747)
Science Applications Intl Corp .... G 910 822-2100
  Fayetteville (G-5912)

SYSTEMS INTEGRATION SVCS: Local Area Network

Blue Wolf Technologies LLP .... G 919 810-1508
  Raleigh (G-12564)
Romeo Six LLC .... F 919 589-7150
  Holly Springs (G-8713)

SYSTEMS SOFTWARE DEVELOPMENT SVCS

Billsoft Inc .... E 913 859-9674
  Durham (G-4957)
Medicor Imaging Inc .... E 704 332-5532
  Charlotte (G-3159)
Twork Technology Inc .... F 704 218-9675
  Charlotte (G-3743)
Worden Brothers Inc .... D 919 202-8555
  Wilmington (G-16456)

TABLE OR COUNTERTOPS, PLASTIC LAMINATED

Buffalo Inv Group NC LLC .... G 252 522-0050
  Kinston (G-9348)
Custom Surfaces Corporation .... G 252 638-3800
  New Bern (G-11796)
McAd Inc .... E 336 299-3030
  Greensboro (G-7193)
Mkc85 Inc .... F 910 762-1986
  Wilmington (G-16325)
TS Woodworks & RAD Design Inc .... F 704 238-1015
  Monroe (G-10824)

TABLETS: Bronze Or Other Metal

Penco Products Inc .... C 252 798-4000
  Hamilton (G-7614)

TAGS & LABELS: Paper

Abx Innvtive Pckg Slutions LLC .... D 980 443-1100
  Charlotte (G-2126)
Genie Trcking Sltons Lbels LLC .... G 919 201-2600
  Clayton (G-3981)
Graphic Finshg Solutions LLC .... G 336 255-7857
  Greensboro (G-7058)
Label & Printing Solutions Inc .... G 919 782-1242
  Raleigh (G-12950)

TAGS: Paper, Blank, Made From Purchased Paper

Wright of Thomasville Inc .... F 336 472-4200
  Thomasville (G-15305)

TALLOW: Animal

Darling Ingredients Inc .... F 910 483-0473
  Fayetteville (G-5804)
Darling Ingredients Inc .... F 704 864-9941
  Gastonia (G-6395)

TANK REPAIR & CLEANING SVCS

High Rise Service Company Inc .... E 910 371-2325
  Leland (G-9548)
Noble Oil Services Inc .... C 919 774-8180
  Sanford (G-14159)
Petroleum Tank Corporation .... F 919 284-2418
  Kenly (G-9155)

PRODUCT SECTION

TANK TOWERS: Metal Plate
Agility Fuel Systems LLC..................G.....704 870-3520
Salisbury *(G-13915)*

TANKS & OTHER TRACKED VEHICLE CMPNTS
Carolina Custom Tank LLC..................F.....980 406-3200
Gastonia *(G-6368)*
Parker Gas Company Inc..................F.....800 354-7250
Clinton *(G-4101)*

TANKS: Lined, Metal
Friedrich Metal Pdts Co Inc..................E.....336 375-3067
Browns Summit *(G-1303)*
M M M Inc..................G.....252 527-0229
La Grange *(G-9443)*

TANKS: Plastic & Fiberglass
Asmo North America LLC..................A.....704 872-2319
Statesville *(G-14754)*

TANKS: Standard Or Custom Fabricated, Metal Plate
Adamson Global Technology Corp.....G.....252 523-5200
Kinston *(G-9339)*
Bendel Tank Heat Exchanger LLC.....F.....704 596-5112
Charlotte *(G-2300)*
Bthec Inc..................E.....704 596-5112
Charlotte *(G-2362)*
Florida Marine Tanks Inc..................F.....305 620-9030
Henderson *(G-7783)*
Gaston County Dyeing Machin.....D.....704 822-5000
Mount Holly *(G-11634)*
General Industries Inc..................E.....919 751-1791
Goldsboro *(G-6615)*
Highland Tank NC Inc..................C.....336 218-0801
Greensboro *(G-7092)*
Ind Fab Inc..................F.....252 977-0811
Elm City *(G-5650)*
Industrial Air Inc..................C.....336 292-1030
Greensboro *(G-7113)*
NC Diesel Performance LLC..................G.....704 431-3257
Salisbury *(G-14016)*
Tank Fab Inc..................F.....910 675-8999
Rocky Point *(G-13753)*
Ward Vessel and Exchanger Corp.....D.....704 568-3001
Charlotte *(G-3795)*

TAPE DRIVES
EMC Corporation..................F.....919 767-0641
Durham *(G-5082)*
Memoryc Inc..................G.....980 224-2875
Charlotte *(G-3164)*

TAPES, ADHESIVE: Masking, Made From Purchased Materials
Cdv LLC..................F.....919 674-3460
Morrisville *(G-11316)*

TAPES: Fabric
Carolina Narrow Fabric Company.....C.....336 631-3000
Winston Salem *(G-16646)*
Custom Fabric Samples Inc..................G.....336 472-1854
Thomasville *(G-15209)*
Spanset Inc..................E.....919 774-6316
Sanford *(G-14189)*
US Label Corporation..................E.....336 332-7000
Greensboro *(G-7434)*

TAPES: Pressure Sensitive
Carolina Tape & Supply Corp..................E.....828 322-3991
Hickory *(G-7968)*

TAPES: Pressure Sensitive, Rubber
Achem Industry America Inc..................G.....704 283-6144
Monroe *(G-10634)*
Draft DOT International LLC..................G.....336 775-0525
Lexington *(G-9710)*
Granite Tape Co..................G.....828 396-5614
Granite Falls *(G-6735)*
Lakebrook Corporation..................G.....207 947-4051
Oak Island *(G-12052)*
Neptco Incorporated..................C.....828 313-0149
Granite Falls *(G-6747)*
Neptco Incorporated..................C.....828 728-5951
Lenoir *(G-9639)*
Polymask Corporation..................C.....828 465-3053
Conover *(G-4484)*
Shurtape Technologies LLC..................G.....704 553-9441
Charlotte *(G-3543)*
Shurtape Technologies LLC..................G.....828 304-8302
Hickory *(G-8153)*
Shurtape Technologies LLC..................G.....828 322-2700
Hickory *(G-8154)*
Stm Industries Inc..................E.....828 322-2700
Hickory *(G-8170)*

TARGET DRONES
Cyberlux Corporation..................F.....984 363-6894
Research Triangle Pa *(G-13549)*
Dronescape Pllc..................G.....704 953-3798
Charlotte *(G-2655)*

TARPAULINS
Diamond Brand Gear Company..................E.....828 684-9848
Fletcher *(G-5998)*
Dize Company..................D.....336 722-5181
Winston Salem *(G-16684)*
OBrian Tarping Systems Inc..................F.....252 291-2141
Wilson *(G-16521)*
Trelleborg Ctd Systems US Inc..................C.....828 286-9126
Rutherfordton *(G-13896)*

TELECOMMUNICATION EQPT REPAIR SVCS, EXC TELEPHONES
Edge Broadband Solutions LLC..................E.....828 785-1420
Waynesville *(G-15803)*

TELEPHONE ANSWERING SVCS
Daniels Business Services Inc..................E.....828 277-8250
Asheville *(G-602)*

TELEPHONE EQPT: NEC
Atcom Inc..................F.....704 357-7900
Charlotte *(G-2230)*
Commscope Technologies LLC..................A.....828 324-2200
Claremont *(G-3916)*
Lba Group Inc..................E.....252 329-9243
Greenville *(G-7553)*
Lba Technology Inc..................E.....252 757-0279
Greenville *(G-7554)*
Nexans USA Inc..................B.....828 323-2660
Hickory *(G-8102)*
Siemens Airport..................E.....704 359-5551
Charlotte *(G-3546)*
Tellad Supply Company..................G.....919 572-6700
Durham *(G-5392)*

TELEPHONE STATION EQPT & PARTS: Wire
Code LLC..................E.....828 328-6004
Hickory *(G-7987)*

TELEPHONE SVCS
Fastzone Dsl & Internet Servic..................G.....828 963-1350
Banner Elk *(G-897)*
M I Connection..................F.....704 662-3255
Mooresville *(G-11013)*

TELEVISION BROADCASTING & COMMUNICATIONS EQPT
Bahakel Communications Ltd LLC..................B.....704 372-4434
Charlotte *(G-2264)*
Lets Talk Some Shit..................G.....704 264-6212
Paw Creek *(G-12172)*

TELEVISION BROADCASTING STATIONS
News 14 Carolina..................F.....704 973-5700
Charlotte *(G-3253)*
Robert Wrren MBL TV Prductions..................G.....910 483-4777
Eastover *(G-5482)*
Wtvd Television LLC..................C.....919 683-1111
Durham *(G-5451)*

TELEVISION: Closed Circuit Eqpt
Crest Electronics Inc..................F.....336 855-6422
Greensboro *(G-6940)*

TELEVISION: Monitors
Flexview Systems LLC..................G.....704 644-3079
Charlotte *(G-2778)*

TEMPERING: Metal
Hhh Tempering Resources Inc..................F.....336 201-5396
Winston Salem *(G-16745)*
Powerlyte Paintball Game Pdts..................F.....919 713-4317
Raleigh *(G-13124)*

TEMPORARY HELP SVCS
Delta Contractors Inc..................F.....817 410-9481
Linden *(G-9940)*

TEST KITS: Pregnancy
Gateway Campus..................G.....919 833-0096
Raleigh *(G-12790)*
Pregnancy Support Services..................G.....919 490-0203
Chapel Hill *(G-2056)*
Your Choice Pregnancy Clinic..................G.....919 577-9050
Fuquay Varina *(G-6240)*

TESTERS: Physical Property
Efco USA Inc..................G.....800 332-6872
Charlotte *(G-2686)*
Roehrig Engineering Inc..................E.....336 956-3800
Greensboro *(G-7316)*

TESTING SVCS
Te Connectivity Corporation..................C.....336 727-5122
Winston Salem *(G-16935)*

TEXTILE & APPAREL SVCS
Brands Fashion US Inc..................G.....704 953-8246
Charlotte *(G-2348)*
Crypton Mills LLC..................E.....828 202-5875
Cliffside *(G-4085)*
Rogers Knitting Inc..................G.....336 789-4155
Mount Airy *(G-11567)*

TEXTILE CONVERTERS: Knit Goods
Badger Sportswear LLC..................D.....704 871-0990
Statesville *(G-14757)*

TEXTILE DESIGNERS

Quiknit Crafting Inc .... F 704 861-1030
   Gastonia *(G-6499)*

TEXTILE DESIGNERS

Jubilee Screen Printing Inc .... G 910 673-4240
   West End *(G-15928)*

TEXTILE FINISHING: Dyeing, Manmade Fiber & Silk, Broadwoven

Hanes Companies Inc .... C 336 747-1600
   Winston Salem *(G-16732)*

Upper South Studio Inc .... F 336 724-5480
   Winston Salem *(G-16961)*

TEXTILE: Finishing, Raw Stock NEC

Carolina Yarn Processors Inc .... C 828 859-5891
   Tryon *(G-15422)*

Unifi Inc .... D 336 348-6539
   Reidsville *(G-13544)*

TEXTILES: Bagging, Jute

Kids Playhouse LLC .... G 704 299-4449
   Charlotte *(G-3053)*

TEXTILES: Linen Fabrics

Leighdeux LLC .... G 704 965-4889
   Charlotte *(G-3082)*

Opulence of Southern Pine .... G 919 467-1781
   Raleigh *(G-13088)*

TEXTILES: Mill Waste & Remnant

Firestone Fibers Textiles LLC .... A 704 734-2110
   Kings Mountain *(G-9308)*

S & S Samples Inc .... G 336 472-0402
   Thomasville *(G-15273)*

William Barnet & Son LLC .... C 252 522-2418
   Kinston *(G-9393)*

THEATRICAL PRODUCERS & SVCS

Royal Faires Inc .... F 704 896-5555
   Huntersville *(G-8887)*

THERMOPLASTIC MATERIALS

Alpek Polyester Usa LLC .... D 704 940-7500
   Charlotte *(G-2165)*

Aqua Plastics Inc .... E 828 324-6284
   Hickory *(G-7939)*

Calsak Plastics Inc .... G 704 597-8555
   Charlotte *(G-2377)*

Microban Products Company .... D 704 766-4267
   Huntersville *(G-8854)*

Poly One Distribution .... G 704 872-8168
   Statesville *(G-14863)*

Polyone Distribution .... G 919 413-4547
   Rolesville *(G-13759)*

THIN FILM CIRCUITS

Industrial Hard Carbon LLC .... E 704 489-1488
   Denver *(G-4785)*

THREAD: Cotton

Coats & Clark Inc .... D 704 542-5959
   Charlotte *(G-2512)*

Coats American Inc .... C 800 242-8095
   Charlotte *(G-2513)*

Coats N Amer De Rpblica Dmncan .... C 800 242-8095
   Charlotte *(G-2515)*

Ruddick Operating Company LLC .... A 704 372-5404
   Charlotte *(G-3472)*

THREAD: Sewing

American & Efird LLC .... F 704 823-2501
   Mount Holly *(G-11620)*

Ctc Holdings LLC .... G 704 867-6611
   Gastonia *(G-6390)*

Invista Capital Management LLC .... D 704 636-6000
   Salisbury *(G-13989)*

J Charles Saunders Co Inc .... E 704 866-9156
   Gastonia *(G-6432)*

TILE: Brick & Structural, Clay

Clay Taylor Products Inc .... D 704 636-2411
   Salisbury *(G-13942)*

Cunningham Brick Company .... C 336 248-8541
   Lexington *(G-9702)*

General Shale Brick Inc .... G 919 828-0541
   Raleigh *(G-12793)*

General Shale Brick Inc .... G 919 775-2121
   Sanford *(G-14124)*

Pine Hall Brick Co Inc .... E 336 721-7500
   Winston Salem *(G-16857)*

Triangle Brick Company .... D 919 387-9257
   Moncure *(G-10627)*

Triangle Brick Company .... E 704 695-1420
   Wadesboro *(G-15518)*

Triangle Brick Company .... E 919 544-1796
   Durham *(G-5406)*

TIN

Tin Shed LLc .... G 919 928-0600
   Chapel Hill *(G-2079)*

TIRE & INNER TUBE MATERIALS & RELATED PRDTS

Gerrard Family LLC .... G 704 545-5117
   Mint Hill *(G-10534)*

Mr Tire Inc .... G 704 735-8024
   Lincolnton *(G-9910)*

TIRE CORD & FABRIC

Tex-Tech Coatings LLC .... D 336 992-7500
   Kernersville *(G-9242)*

Tex-Tech Coatings LLC .... F 336 992-7500
   Kernersville *(G-9243)*

TIRES & INNER TUBES

Black Tire Service Inc .... G 919 908-6347
   Durham *(G-4964)*

Carolina Giant Tires Inc .... F 919 609-9077
   Henderson *(G-7777)*

Derrow Enterprises Inc .... G 252 635-3375
   New Bern *(G-11800)*

Goodyear Tire & Rubber Company .... G 919 552-9340
   Holly Springs *(G-8700)*

Oliver Rubber Company LLC .... B 336 629-1436
   Asheboro *(G-459)*

Roll-Tech Molding Products LLC .... E 828 431-4515
   Hickory *(G-8139)*

Too Hott Customs LLC .... G 336 722-4919
   Winston Salem *(G-16944)*

Wmb of Wake County Inc .... F 919 782-0419
   Raleigh *(G-13426)*

TIRES & TUBES WHOLESALERS

Derrow Enterprises Inc .... G 252 635-3375
   New Bern *(G-11800)*

Dunlop Aircraft Tyres Inc .... E 336 283-0979
   Mocksville *(G-10567)*

Mr Tire Inc .... F 704 483-1500
   Denver *(G-4790)*

Mr Tire Inc .... F 828 322-8130
   Hickory *(G-8099)*

Mr Tire Inc .... G 704 739-6456
   Kings Mountain *(G-9319)*

Mr Tire Inc .... G 828 758-0047
   Lenoir *(G-9637)*

Mr Tire Inc .... G 704 735-8024
   Lincolnton *(G-9910)*

Mr Tire Inc .... G 704 484-0816
   Shelby *(G-14350)*

Mr Tire Inc .... G 704 872-4127
   Statesville *(G-14849)*

Parrish Tire Company .... E 704 872-6565
   Jonesville *(G-9101)*

Wmb of Wake County Inc .... F 919 782-0419
   Raleigh *(G-13426)*

TIRES & TUBES, WHOLESALE: Automotive

A 1 Tire Service Inc .... G 828 684-1860
   Fletcher *(G-5978)*

Accel Discount Tire .... G 704 636-0323
   Salisbury *(G-13913)*

Aiken-Black Tire Service Inc .... E 828 322-3736
   Hickory *(G-7930)*

Albemarle Tire Retreading Inc .... G 704 982-4113
   Albemarle *(G-71)*

Avery County Recapping Co Inc .... E 828 733-0161
   Newland *(G-11881)*

Bill Martin Inc .... F 704 873-0241
   Statesville *(G-14764)*

Bray S Recapping Service Inc .... E 336 786-6182
   Mount Airy *(G-11486)*

Bridgestone Ret Operations LLC .... G 919 471-4468
   Durham *(G-4977)*

Bridgestone Ret Operations LLC .... G 910 864-4106
   Fayetteville *(G-5775)*

Bridgestone Ret Operations LLC .... G 704 861-8146
   Gastonia *(G-6360)*

Bridgestone Ret Operations LLC .... G 919 778-0230
   Goldsboro *(G-6597)*

Bridgestone Ret Operations LLC .... G 336 282-6646
   Greensboro *(G-6852)*

Bridgestone Ret Operations LLC .... G 336 852-8524
   Greensboro *(G-6853)*

Bridgestone Ret Operations LLC .... G 252 522-5126
   Kinston *(G-9347)*

Bridgestone Ret Operations LLC .... G 919 872-6402
   Raleigh *(G-12573)*

Bridgestone Ret Operations LLC .... G 919 872-6566
   Raleigh *(G-12574)*

Bridgestone Ret Operations LLC .... G 252 243-5189
   Wilson *(G-16480)*

Bridgestone Ret Operations LLC .... G 336 725-1580
   Winston Salem *(G-16636)*

Cecil Budd Tire Company LLC .... F 919 742-2322
   Siler City *(G-14403)*

Claybrook Tire Inc .... F 336 573-3135
   Stoneville *(G-14955)*

Colony Tire Corporation .... G 252 973-0004
   Rocky Mount *(G-13688)*

Crossroads Tire Store Inc .... G 704 888-2064
   Midland *(G-10465)*

Diagnostic Shop Inc .... G 704 933-3435
   Kannapolis *(G-9117)*

Ed S Tire Laurinburg Inc .... G 910 277-0565
   Laurinburg *(G-9476)*

Enfield Tire Service Inc .... G 252 445-5016
   Enfield *(G-5677)*

Foster Tire Sales Inc .... G 336 248-6726
   Lexington *(G-9719)*

Goodyear Tire & Rubber Company .... G 919 552-9340
   Holly Springs *(G-8700)*

Goodyear Tire & Rubber Company .... G 336 794-0035
   Winston Salem *(G-16724)*

PRODUCT SECTION

TOILETRIES, WHOLESALE: Toiletries

Greensboro Tire & Auto Service............ G 336 294-9495
  Greensboro *(G-7066)*
Hall Tire and Battery Co Inc.................. F 336 275-3812
  Greensboro *(G-7075)*
Haneys Tire Recapping Svc LLC........... F 910 276-2636
  Laurinburg *(G-9481)*
John Conrad Inc..................................... G 336 475-8144
  Thomasville *(G-15239)*
Johnnys Tire Sales and Svc Inc............ F 252 353-8473
  Greenville *(G-7551)*
M & M Tire and Auto Inc........................ G 336 643-7877
  Summerfield *(G-14988)*
M & R Retreading & Oil Co Inc.............. F 704 474-4101
  Norwood *(G-12040)*
McCarthy Tire Service Company........... G 910 791-0132
  Wilmington *(G-16317)*
Merchants Inc... G 252 447-2121
  Havelock *(G-7743)*
Mock Tire & Automotive Inc.................. E 336 753-8473
  Mocksville *(G-10591)*
Mock Tire & Automotive Inc.................. E 336 774-0081
  Winston Salem *(G-16812)*
Mock Tire & Automotive Inc.................. E 336 768-1010
  Winston Salem *(G-16813)*
Moss Brothers Tires & Svc Inc.............. G 910 895-4572
  Rockingham *(G-13635)*
Mr Tire Inc.. G 828 262-3555
  Boone *(G-1225)*
Mr Tire Inc.. F 704 483-1500
  Denver *(G-4790)*
Mr Tire Inc.. F 828 322-8130
  Hickory *(G-8099)*
Mr Tire Inc.. G 704 739-6456
  Kings Mountain *(G-9319)*
Mr Tire Inc.. G 828 758-0047
  Lenoir *(G-9637)*
Mr Tire Inc.. G 704 735-8024
  Lincolnton *(G-9910)*
Mr Tire Inc.. G 704 484-0816
  Shelby *(G-14350)*
Mr Tire Inc.. G 704 872-4127
  Statesville *(G-14849)*
Oakie S Tire & Recapping Inc............... F 704 482-5629
  Shelby *(G-14353)*
Parrish Tire Company............................ E 704 372-2013
  Charlotte *(G-3317)*
Parrish Tire Company............................ F 336 334-9979
  Greensboro *(G-7246)*
Parrish Tire Company............................ E 704 872-6565
  Jonesville *(G-9101)*
Parrish Tire Company............................ D 800 849-8473
  Winston Salem *(G-16836)*
Perry Brothers Tire Svc Inc................... F 919 693-2128
  Oxford *(G-12140)*
Perry Brothers Tire Svc Inc................... E 919 775-7225
  Sanford *(G-14167)*
Phil S Tire Service Inc........................... G 828 682-2421
  Burnsville *(G-1530)*
Piedmont Truck Tires Inc...................... F 828 202-5437
  Conover *(G-4480)*
Quality Investments Inc......................... E 252 492-8777
  Henderson *(G-7805)*
Richmond Investment............................ E 910 410-8200
  Rockingham *(G-13640)*
Roosevelt Tire Service Inc.................... F 704 864-5464
  Gastonia *(G-6504)*
Small Brothers Tire Co Inc.................... G 704 289-3531
  Monroe *(G-10808)*
Snider Tire Inc....................................... D 704 373-2910
  Charlotte *(G-3571)*
Snider Tire Inc....................................... F 336 691-5480
  Greensboro *(G-7347)*

Snider Tire Inc....................................... G 828 324-9955
  Hickory *(G-8160)*
Super Retread Center Inc..................... F 919 734-0073
  Goldsboro *(G-6663)*
Team X-Treme LLC................................ G 919 562-8100
  Rolesville *(G-13760)*
Thrifty Tire... G 919 220-7800
  Durham *(G-5402)*
Tire Sls Svc Inc Fyttevilie NC................ E 910 485-1121
  Fayetteville *(G-5931)*
Tires Incorporated of Clinton................. E 910 592-4741
  Clinton *(G-4114)*
Towel City Tire & Wheel LLC................. G 704 933-2143
  Kannapolis *(G-9136)*
Turn Key Tire Service Inc...................... G 919 836-8473
  Garner *(G-6319)*
Universal Tire Service Inc..................... G 919 779-8798
  Raleigh *(G-13383)*
Village Tire Center Inc........................... G 919 862-8500
  Raleigh *(G-13400)*
Whitaker S Tire Service Inc................... F 704 786-6174
  Concord *(G-4389)*
White S Tire Svc Wilson Inc.................. E 252 237-0770
  Wilson *(G-16559)*
White S Tire Svc Wilson Inc.................. D 252 237-5426
  Wilson *(G-16560)*
Whites Tire Svc New Bern Inc............... G 252 633-1170
  New Bern *(G-11857)*
Wilson Tire and Automotive Inc............. G 336 584-9638
  Elon College *(G-5668)*

TOBACCO: Chewing

American Snuff Company LLC.............. C 336 768-4630
  Winston Salem *(G-16603)*

TOBACCO: Chewing & Snuff

Cres Tobacco Company LLC................ E 336 983-7727
  King *(G-9268)*
Ioto Usa LLC... F 252 413-7343
  Greenville *(G-7545)*
Itg Holdings USA Inc............................. E 954 772-9000
  Greensboro *(G-7127)*
Tobacco Rag Processors Inc................. E 252 265-0081
  Wilson *(G-16548)*
Tobacco Rag Processors Inc................. E 252 237-8180
  Wilson *(G-16549)*
Tobacco Rag Processors Inc................. E 252 265-0081
  Wilson *(G-16547)*

TOBACCO: Cigarettes

A W Spears Research Ctr..................... G 336 335-6724
  Greensboro *(G-6769)*
Alternative Brands Inc........................... B 336 751-4818
  Mocksville *(G-10552)*
Commonwealth Brands Inc.................... C 336 634-4200
  Greensboro *(G-6925)*
Fontem Us Inc....................................... G 888 207-4588
  Charlotte *(G-2784)*
Happy Shack Smoke Shop..................... G 980 833-8053
  Gastonia *(G-6414)*
Itg Brands.. D 336 335-6600
  Greensboro *(G-7124)*
Itg Brands.. D 919 366-0220
  Raleigh *(G-12904)*
Itg Brands LLC...................................... D 336 335-7000
  Greensboro *(G-7125)*
Liggett Group LLC................................. B 919 304-7700
  Mebane *(G-10416)*
Lorillard LLC.. E 336 741-2000
  Winston Salem *(G-16792)*
Lorillard Q-Tech Inc............................... G 877 703-0386
  Greensboro *(G-7169)*

Lorillard Tobacco Company LLC........... A 336 335-6600
  Greensboro *(G-7170)*
Medallion Company Inc......................... C 919 990-3500
  Timberlake *(G-15315)*
Modoral Brands Inc............................... G 336 741-7230
  Winston Salem *(G-16815)*
Mr Tobacco.. G 919 747-9052
  Raleigh *(G-13047)*
On Demand Hemp Company LLC......... G 336 757-0320
  Tobaccoville *(G-15318)*
Philip Morris USA Inc............................ D 336 744-4401
  Winston Salem *(G-16849)*
R J Reynolds Tobacco Company........... D 919 366-0220
  Wendell *(G-15913)*
R J Reynolds Tobacco Company........... C 336 741-2132
  Winston Salem *(G-16876)*
R J Reynolds Tobacco Company........... D 336 741-5000
  Winston Salem *(G-16878)*
Rai Services Company.......................... F 336 741-6774
  Winston Salem *(G-16879)*
Reynolds American Inc......................... E 336 741-2000
  Winston Salem *(G-16884)*
Santa Fe Ntural Tob Foundation........... C 919 690-0880
  Oxford *(G-12154)*
Triaga Inc.. G 919 412-6019
  Wilson *(G-16551)*
US Tobacco Cooperative Inc................. D 919 821-4560
  Raleigh *(G-13386)*
Vector Tobacco Inc................................ E 919 990-3500
  Morrisville *(G-11463)*
Wainwright Warehouse.......................... G 252 237-5121
  Wilson *(G-16556)*

TOBACCO: Cigars

Modoral Brands Inc............................... G 336 741-7230
  Winston Salem *(G-16815)*
North Carolina Tobacco Mfg LLC........... F 252 238-6514
  Stantonsburg *(G-14712)*
Reynolds American Inc......................... E 336 741-2000
  Winston Salem *(G-16884)*
Santa Fe Natural Tob Co Inc................. F 919 690-1905
  Oxford *(G-12153)*

TOBACCO: Smoking

Alnamer Inc... G 252 215-0323
  Greenville *(G-7479)*
Modoral Brands Inc............................... G 336 741-7230
  Winston Salem *(G-16815)*
R J Reynolds Tobacco Company........... D 336 741-0400
  Tobaccoville *(G-15319)*
R J Reynolds Tobacco Company........... C 336 741-2132
  Winston Salem *(G-16876)*
R J Reynolds Tobacco Company........... D 336 741-5000
  Winston Salem *(G-16877)*
Reynolds American Inc......................... E 336 741-2000
  Winston Salem *(G-16884)*
Santa Fe Natural Tobacco Co................ C 800 332-5595
  Winston Salem *(G-16898)*
Top Tobacco LP..................................... C 910 646-3014
  Lake Waccamaw *(G-9449)*

TOILETRIES, WHOLESALE: Perfumes

Mvp Group International Inc.................. E 843 216-8380
  Elkin *(G-5627)*

TOILETRIES, WHOLESALE: Toilet Soap

Old Town Soap Co................................. F 704 796-8775
  China Grove *(G-3886)*

TOILETRIES, WHOLESALE: Toiletries

Bob Barker Company Inc...................... C 800 334-9880
  Fuquay Varina *(G-6184)*

Employee Codes: A=Over 500 employees, B=251-500
C=101-250, D=51-100, E=20-50, F=10-19, G=1-9

TOOL & DIE STEEL

PRODUCT SECTION

TOOL & DIE STEEL
Competition Tooling Inc..................G..... 336 887-4414
High Point *(G-8301)*

TOOLS & EQPT: Taxidermist
McKenzie Sports Products LLC.........C..... 704 279-7985
Salisbury *(G-14011)*

TOOLS: Hand
Everkem Diversified Pdts Inc..............F..... 336 661-7801
Winston Salem *(G-16701)*

TOWELETTES: Premoistened
Albaad Usa Inc..................................B..... 336 634-0091
Reidsville *(G-13504)*

TOWERS, SECTIONS: Transmission, Radio & Television
Towerco LLC.......................................F..... 919 653-5700
Cary *(G-1911)*

TOYS: Dolls, Stuffed Animals & Parts
PCS Collectibles LLC..........................G..... 805 306-1140
Huntersville *(G-8873)*

TOYS: Video Game Machines
Game Box LLC....................................G..... 866 241-1882
Greensboro *(G-7029)*

TRAILER COACHES: Automobile
Allison Globl Mnufacturing Inc............F..... 704 392-7883
Charlotte *(G-2162)*
Southag Mfg Inc..................................F..... 919 365-5111
Wendell *(G-15918)*

TRAILERS & PARTS: Boat
Long Trailer Co Inc..............................G..... 252 823-8828
Tarboro *(G-15111)*

TRAILERS & PARTS: Horse
Gore S Trlr Manufacturer S Inc............F..... 910 642-2246
Whiteville *(G-15964)*

TRAILERS & TRAILER EQPT
A-1 Hitch & Trailors Sales Inc.............F..... 910 755-6025
Supply *(G-15005)*
BOB Trailers Inc..................................E..... 208 375-5171
Charlotte *(G-2328)*
Colfax Trailer & Repair LLC................G..... 336 993-8511
Colfax *(G-4144)*
Faith Farm Inc....................................F..... 704 431-4566
Salisbury *(G-13963)*
Kaufman Trailers Inc..........................E..... 336 790-6800
Lexington *(G-9739)*
North Carolina Dept Trnsp..................G..... 828 733-9002
Newland *(G-11891)*

TRAILERS: Camping, Tent-Type
Cold Mountain Capital LLC.................F..... 828 210-8129
Asheville *(G-596)*
Inka Outdoor LLC................................G..... 828 539-0842
Gastonia *(G-6428)*

TRAILERS: Truck, Chassis
Ecovehicle Enterprises Inc.................G..... 704 544-9907
Charlotte *(G-2685)*

TRANSDUCERS: Electrical Properties
MTS Systems Corporation..................C..... 919 677-2352
Cary *(G-1827)*

Smith Systems Inc..............................E..... 828 884-3490
Brevard *(G-1289)*

TRANSFORMERS: Distribution
ABB Inc..D..... 919 856-2360
Raleigh *(G-12457)*

TRANSFORMERS: Distribution, Electric
ABB Power T & D Company Inc.........A..... 919 856-3806
Raleigh *(G-12459)*
Ced Incorporated................................F..... 336 378-0044
Greensboro *(G-6897)*
Pennsylvania Trans Tech Inc..............D..... 910 875-7600
Raeford *(G-12431)*

TRANSFORMERS: Specialty
Instrument Trans Eqp Corp.................D..... 704 282-4331
Monroe *(G-10739)*

TRANSFORMERS: Voltage Regulating
Abundant Power Solutions LLC..........F..... 704 271-9890
Charlotte *(G-2125)*

TRANSMISSIONS: Motor Vehicle
Unique Tool and Mfg Co.....................E..... 336 498-2614
Franklinville *(G-6171)*

TRANSPORTATION AGENTS & BROKERS
D C Custom Freight LLC.....................E..... 843 658-6484
Marshville *(G-10213)*

TRANSPORTATION BROKERS: Truck
Deliveright Logistics Inc....................C..... 862 279-7332
Lexington *(G-9705)*

TRANSPORTATION EQPT & SPLYS WHOLESALERS, NEC
At Your Service Express LLC.............E..... 704 270-9918
Charlotte *(G-2229)*
Foxster Opco LLC...............................E..... 910 297-6996
Hampstead *(G-7647)*
Haeco Americas LLC..........................A..... 336 668-4410
Greensboro *(G-7073)*

TRAP ROCK: Crushed & Broken
Carolina Sunrock LLC.........................E..... 919 575-4502
Butner *(G-1543)*
Heidelberg Mtls Sthast Agg LLC........F..... 252 235-4162
Bailey *(G-874)*
Sunrock Group Holdings Corp............D..... 919 747-6400
Raleigh *(G-13315)*

TRAVEL TRAILERS & CAMPERS
Alossi Renewal Spa LLC....................G..... 406 338-7700
Raleigh *(G-12492)*
Derrow Enterprises Inc......................G..... 252 635-3375
New Bern *(G-11800)*

TRAYS: Cable, Metal Plate
Mono Systems Inc..............................G..... 914 934-2075
Waxhaw *(G-15766)*

TRAYS: Plastic
Sherri Gossett....................................G..... 910 367-0099
Wilmington *(G-16403)*

TREAD RUBBER: Camelback For Tire Retreading
White S Tire Svc Wilson Inc...............G..... 252 237-0770
Wilson *(G-16559)*

White S Tire Svc Wilson Inc...............D..... 252 237-5426
Wilson *(G-16560)*

TROPHIES, NEC
DWM INTERNATIONAL INC.................E..... 646 290-7448
Charlotte *(G-2661)*

TROPHIES, WHOLESALE
Trophy House Inc...............................F..... 910 323-1791
Fayetteville *(G-5934)*

TROPHIES: Metal, Exc Silver
Contemporary Products Inc................G..... 919 779-4228
Garner *(G-6268)*

TRUCK & BUS BODIES: Beverage Truck
Mickey Truck Bodies Inc....................B..... 336 882-6806
High Point *(G-8455)*
R J Yeller Distribution Inc..................G..... 800 944-2589
Charlotte *(G-3405)*

TRUCK & BUS BODIES: Bus Bodies
Thomas Built Buses Inc.....................A..... 336 889-4871
High Point *(G-8569)*

TRUCK & BUS BODIES: Garbage Or Refuse Truck
Waste Container Repair Svcs.............G..... 910 257-4474
Fayetteville *(G-5949)*

TRUCK & BUS BODIES: Motor Vehicle, Specialty
Anchor-Richey Emergency Vehicl......E..... 828 495-8145
Taylorsville *(G-15129)*
Vna Holding Inc..................................A..... 336 393-4890
Greensboro *(G-7445)*
Volvo Group North America LLC........A..... 336 393-2000
Greensboro *(G-7447)*
Volvo Group North America LLC........A..... 336 393-2000
Greensboro *(G-7446)*

TRUCK & BUS BODIES: Truck Beds
John Jenkins Company.......................E..... 336 375-3717
Browns Summit *(G-1311)*

TRUCK & BUS BODIES: Truck, Motor Vehicle
American Scale Company LLC...........F..... 704 921-4556
Charlotte *(G-2184)*

TRUCK & BUS BODIES: Utility Truck
Satco Truck Equipment Inc................F..... 919 383-5547
Durham *(G-5340)*

TRUCK BODIES: Body Parts
Cabarrus Plastics Inc........................C..... 704 784-2100
Concord *(G-4218)*
Can-AM Custom Trucks Inc...............G..... 704 334-0322
Charlotte *(G-2381)*
Carroll Co..F..... 919 779-1900
Garner *(G-6262)*
Fontaine Modification Company........F..... 704 392-8502
Charlotte *(G-2783)*
Osprea Logistics Usa LLC.................E..... 704 504-1677
Charlotte *(G-3305)*
Volvo Trucks North America Inc.........A..... 336 393-2000
Greensboro *(G-7450)*

TRUCK BODY SHOP
Mickey Truck Bodies Inc....................B..... 336 882-6806
High Point *(G-8455)*

PRODUCT SECTION

TRUSSES: Wood, Floor

Quality Trck Bodies & Repr Inc............... E 252 245-5100
Elm City *(G-5652)*

Triangle Body Works Inc......................... F 336 788-0631
Winston Salem *(G-16951)*

TRUCK GENERAL REPAIR SVC

Container Technology Inc........................ G 910 350-1303
Wilmington *(G-16180)*

Mack Trucks Inc...................................... A 336 291-9001
Greensboro *(G-7177)*

Satco Truck Equipment Inc..................... F 919 383-5547
Durham *(G-5340)*

TRUCK PARTS & ACCESSORIES: Wholesalers

Consolidated Truck Parts Inc.................. G 704 279-5543
Rockwell *(G-13650)*

Fontaine Modification Company............. F 704 392-8502
Charlotte *(G-2783)*

Truck Parts Inc.. F 704 332-7909
Charlotte *(G-3732)*

Venture Products Intl Inc........................ G 828 285-0495
Asheville *(G-814)*

TRUCKING & HAULING SVCS: Building Materials

Fixtures & More....................................... G 828 855-9093
Hickory *(G-8026)*

TRUCKING & HAULING SVCS: Contract Basis

J & L Bckh/Nvrnmental Svcs Inc............. G 910 237-7351
Eastover *(G-5481)*

Southeast Wood Products Inc................ F 910 285-4359
Wallace *(G-15627)*

TRUCKING & HAULING SVCS: Heavy, NEC

Advantage Machinery Svcs Inc.............. E 336 463-4700
Yadkinville *(G-17030)*

TRUCKING & HAULING SVCS: Lumber & Log, Local

Raleigh Road Box Corporation............... G 252 438-7401
Henderson *(G-7806)*

TRUCKING: Except Local

Bundy Logging Company Inc................. F 252 357-0191
Gatesville *(G-6548)*

Firm Ascend LLC.................................... G 704 464-3024
Charlotte *(G-2763)*

RSI Leasing Inc NS Tbt........................... G 704 587-9300
Charlotte *(G-3468)*

T H Blue Inc... E 910 673-3033
Eagle Springs *(G-5461)*

TRUCKING: Local, With Storage

Bundy Logging Company Inc................. F 252 357-0191
Gatesville *(G-6548)*

Comer Sanitary Service Inc.................... F 336 629-8311
Lexington *(G-9697)*

Elizabeth Logistic LLC............................ D 803 920-3931
Indian Trail *(G-8931)*

Loflin Concrete Co Inc............................ E 336 904-2788
Kernersville *(G-9209)*

Lunar International Tech LLC................. F 800 975-7153
Charlotte *(G-3109)*

Wheeler Industries Inc............................ F 919 736-4256
Pikeville *(G-12195)*

TRUCKING: Local, Without Storage

Bobby Cahoon Construction Inc............ E 252 249-1617
Grantsboro *(G-6763)*

Central Carolina Concrete LLC.............. E 336 315-0785
Greensboro *(G-6899)*

Crowder Trucking LLC............................ G 910 797-4163
Fayetteville *(G-5800)*

Fayblock Materials Inc........................... D 910 323-9198
Fayetteville *(G-5823)*

New Finish Inc.. E 704 474-4116
Norwood *(G-12041)*

Stone Supply Inc.................................... G 828 678-9966
Burnsville *(G-1534)*

T H Blue Inc... E 910 673-3033
Eagle Springs *(G-5461)*

TRUCKS & TRACTORS: Industrial

Altec Industries Inc................................. B 919 528-2535
Creedmoor *(G-4603)*

Basic Machinery Company Inc............... D 919 663-2244
Siler City *(G-14399)*

Bromma Inc... E 919 620-8039
Durham *(G-4982)*

Caterpillar Inc... D 919 777-2000
Sanford *(G-14098)*

Cutting Systems Inc............................... D 704 592-2451
Union Grove *(G-15436)*

Daimler Truck North Amer LLC.............. A 704 645-5000
Cleveland *(G-4071)*

General Electric Company...................... F 919 563-7445
Mebane *(G-10410)*

General Electric Company...................... B 919 563-5561
Mebane *(G-10411)*

Gregory Poole Equipment Co................. G 252 931-5100
Greenville *(G-7535)*

Hanging C Farms.................................... F 704 239-6691
Kannapolis *(G-9121)*

Kaufman Trailers Inc.............................. E 336 790-6800
Lexington *(G-9739)*

Master Tow Inc....................................... E 910 630-2000
Fayetteville *(G-5869)*

McIntyre Manufacturing Group Inc........ D 336 476-3646
Thomasville *(G-15246)*

Nmhg... G 252 229-0071
Greenville *(G-7564)*

Nolan Manufacturing LLC...................... G 336 490-0086
Denton *(G-4746)*

Propane Trucks & Tanks Inc.................. F 919 362-5000
Apex *(G-234)*

Smithway Inc.. G 828 628-1756
Fairview *(G-5718)*

Sterling Rack Inc.................................... F 704 866-9131
Gastonia *(G-6516)*

Superior Dry Kilns Inc............................ E 828 754-7001
Hudson *(G-8782)*

TCI Mobility Inc...................................... F 704 867-8331
Gastonia *(G-6520)*

Tcom Limited Partnership..................... B 252 330-5555
Elizabeth City *(G-5575)*

Wastequip LLC....................................... F 704 366-7140
Charlotte *(G-3796)*

TRUCKS: Forklift

Central Carolina Forklift LLC.................. G 919 545-9749
Moncure *(G-10618)*

Combilift USA LLC.................................. F 336 378-8884
Greensboro *(G-6922)*

Crown Equipment Corporation............... B 252 522-3088
Kinston *(G-9355)*

Forklift Network...................................... G 877 327-7260
Cornelius *(G-4548)*

Forklift Pro Inc.. F 704 716-3636
Pineville *(G-12269)*

Hc Forklift America Corp........................ F 980 888-8335
Charlotte *(G-2895)*

Hyster-Yale Group Inc............................ F 252 931-5100
Greenville *(G-7541)*

Hyster-Yale Group Inc............................ D 252 931-5100
Greenville *(G-7542)*

Parkers Equipment Company................. G 252 560-0088
Snow Hill *(G-14506)*

Scootatrailertm....................................... G 336 671-0444
Lexington *(G-9777)*

Westlift LLC.. F 919 242-4379
Goldsboro *(G-6670)*

Whiteville Forklift & Eqp........................ G 910 642-6642
Whiteville *(G-15980)*

Wlc Forklift Services LLC....................... G 336 345-2571
Reidsville *(G-13546)*

TRUCKS: Indl

Batchlers LLC... G 910 619-4042
Wilmington *(G-16133)*

Bottomley Enterprises Inc..................... D 336 657-6400
Mount Airy *(G-11485)*

C&A Hockaday Transport LLC................ G 252 676-5956
Roanoke Rapids *(G-13570)*

Cbj Transit LLC....................................... D 252 417-9972
Garner *(G-6263)*

D&E Freight LLC..................................... F 704 977-4847
Charlotte *(G-2597)*

Drs Transportation Inc........................... G 919 215-2770
Raleigh *(G-12704)*

Elektrikredd LLC..................................... G 704 805-0110
Matthews *(G-10313)*

Forward Dsptching Lgistics LLC............ G 252 907-9797
Greenville *(G-7527)*

Go For Green Fleet Svcs LLC................. G 803 306-3683
Charlotte *(G-2840)*

Harrell Proper Transport LLC................. G 336 202-7135
Whitsett *(G-15992)*

Ksw Logistics & Transport LLC.............. G 919 578-5788
Raleigh *(G-12947)*

Mlg Trnscndent Trckg Trnsp Svc............ G 336 905-1192
High Point *(G-8457)*

MMS Logistics Incorporated.................. G 336 214-3552
Mc Leansville *(G-10394)*

Nexxt Level Trucking LLC...................... G 980 205-4425
Charlotte *(G-3256)*

No1 Can Do It Betta Trckg LLC.............. G 336 858-7693
High Point *(G-8467)*

Paper Route Transportation LLC........... G 919 478-6615
Sanford *(G-14162)*

Rucker Intrgrted Logistics LLC.............. G 704 352-2018
Charlotte *(G-3471)*

Sml Transportation LLC......................... G 704 402-6744
Harmony *(G-7689)*

Swing Kurve Logistic Trckg LLC............ G 704 506-7371
Charlotte *(G-3661)*

Three Ladies and A Male LLC................ G 704 287-1584
Charlotte *(G-3691)*

Triple H Hauling LLC.............................. G 984 220-4676
Elizabeth City *(G-5579)*

V M Trucking Inc.................................... G 984 239-4853
Morehead City *(G-11195)*

TRUSSES & FRAMING: Prefabricated Metal

Arboles NC Incorporated........................ F 828 675-4882
Clayton *(G-3955)*

Toza Truss LLC....................................... G 336 301-6338
Bennett *(G-1028)*

TRUSSES: Wood, Floor

Ufp New London LLC .... E 704 463-1400
   New London *(G-11880)*

Ufp Site Built LLC .... D 704 781-2520
   Locust *(G-9976)*

TUBES: Steel & Iron

AD Tubi Usa Inc .... E 919 930-3023
   Siler City *(G-14397)*

Southeast Tubular Products Inc .... E 704 883-8883
   Statesville *(G-14889)*

TUBES: Vacuum

Communications & Pwr Inds LLC .... E 650 846-2900
   Conover *(G-4437)*

Vintage Vacuum Tubes LLC .... G 336 688-7443
   Burlington *(G-1513)*

TUBING: Rubber

C & M Industrial Supply Co .... G 704 483-4001
   Mill Spring *(G-10484)*

Tekni-Plex Inc .... D 919 553-4151
   Clayton *(G-4017)*

TUNGSTEN CARBIDE POWDER

Betek Tools Inc .... F 980 498-2523
   Charlotte *(G-2303)*

TURBINES & TURBINE GENERATOR SET UNITS, COMPLETE

Bwxt Investment Company .... E 704 625-4900
   Charlotte *(G-2369)*

Leistriz Advanced Turbine C .... C 336 969-1352
   Rural Hall *(G-13848)*

TURBINES & TURBINE GENERATOR SETS

Babcock Wlcox Eqity Invstmnts .... E 704 625-4900
   Charlotte *(G-2258)*

Babcock Wlcox Intl Sls Svc Cor .... F 704 625-4900
   Charlotte *(G-2259)*

Caterpillar Inc .... D 919 777-2000
   Sanford *(G-14098)*

Diamond Power Intl LLC .... F 704 625-4900
   Charlotte *(G-2628)*

Diamond Pwr Astrlia Hldngs Inc .... G 704 625-4900
   Charlotte *(G-2629)*

Diamond Pwr Eqity Invstmnts In .... G 704 625-4900
   Charlotte *(G-2630)*

Grand Coulee Consortium .... G 704 943-4343
   Charlotte *(G-2853)*

Megtec India Holdings LLC .... G 704 625-4900
   Charlotte *(G-3160)*

Megtec Turbosonic Tech Inc .... F 704 625-4900
   Charlotte *(G-3161)*

Revloc Reclamation Service Inc .... G 704 625-4900
   Charlotte *(G-3439)*

Siemens Energy Inc .... C 704 551-5100
   Charlotte *(G-3547)*

Siemens Energy Inc .... C 336 969-1351
   Rural Hall *(G-13853)*

Windlift Inc .... G 919 490-8575
   Durham *(G-5442)*

Xylem Lnc .... E 704 409-9700
   Charlotte *(G-3839)*

TURBINES & TURBINE GENERATOR SETS & PARTS

Industrial Sup Solutions Inc .... E 704 636-4241
   Salisbury *(G-13983)*

Powermolekul Inc .... G 919 264-8487
   Cary *(G-1856)*

TURNKEY VENDORS: Computer Systems

Acroplis Cntrls Engineers Pllc .... F 919 275-3884
   Raleigh *(G-12473)*

TWINE: Binder & Baler

Ravenox Rope .... G 336 226-5260
   Burlington *(G-1482)*

TYPESETTING SVC

Advertising Design Systems Inc .... G 828 264-8060
   Boone *(G-1172)*

American Multimedia Inc .... D 336 229-7101
   Burlington *(G-1364)*

Appalachian State University .... F 828 262-2047
   Boone *(G-1174)*

Asheboro Piedmont Printing Inc .... F 336 899-7910
   Asheboro *(G-406)*

Atlantis Graphics Inc .... G 919 361-5809
   Durham *(G-4933)*

Austin Printing Company Inc .... G 704 289-1445
   Monroe *(G-10658)*

Bennett & Associates Inc .... G 919 477-7362
   Durham *(G-4955)*

Boingo Graphics Inc .... E 704 527-4963
   Charlotte *(G-2331)*

BP Solutions Group Inc .... E 828 252-4476
   Asheville *(G-570)*

Carter-Hubbard Publishing Co .... F 336 838-4117
   North Wilkesboro *(G-12000)*

Coastal Press Inc .... E 252 726-1549
   Morehead City *(G-11163)*

CPS Resources Inc .... E 704 628-7678
   Monroe *(G-10697)*

Creative Printing Inc .... G 828 265-2800
   Boone *(G-1189)*

Dokja Inc .... G 336 852-5190
   Greensboro *(G-6975)*

F C C LLC .... G 336 883-7314
   High Point *(G-8349)*

Fayetteville Publishing Co .... D 910 323-4848
   Fayetteville *(G-5824)*

Flash Printing Company Inc .... E 704 375-2474
   Charlotte *(G-2769)*

Free Will Bptst Press Fndtion .... F 252 746-6128
   Ayden *(G-852)*

Gik Inc .... F 919 872-9498
   Raleigh *(G-12800)*

Greensboro News & Record LLC .... A 336 373-7000
   Greensboro *(G-7064)*

Hickory Printing Solutions LLC .... C 828 465-3431
   Conover *(G-4464)*

Ips .... G 704 788-3327
   Concord *(G-4289)*

Jag Graphics Inc .... E 828 259-9020
   Asheville *(G-668)*

Jones Media .... F 828 264-3612
   Boone *(G-1212)*

Joseph C Woodard Prtg Co Inc .... F 919 829-0634
   Raleigh *(G-12922)*

Kathie S Mc Daniel .... G 336 835-1544
   Elkin *(G-5622)*

Loftin & Company Inc .... E 704 393-9393
   Charlotte *(G-3100)*

Measurement Incorporated .... C 919 683-2413
   Durham *(G-5213)*

Medlit Solutions LLC .... D 919 878-6789
   Garner *(G-6287)*

Ollis Enterprises Inc .... E 828 265-0004
   Wilkesboro *(G-16037)*

Owen G Dunn Co Inc .... G 252 633-3197
   New Bern *(G-11832)*

Pamela A Adams .... G 919 876-5949
   Raleigh *(G-13096)*

Person Printing Company Inc .... E 336 599-2146
   Roxboro *(G-13818)*

Pilot LLC .... D 910 692-7271
   Southern Pines *(G-14546)*

Powell Ink Inc .... F 828 253-6886
   Asheville *(G-739)*

Printery .... F 336 852-9774
   Greensboro *(G-7284)*

Printing & Packaging Inc .... E 704 482-3866
   Shelby *(G-14357)*

Printing Partners Inc .... G 336 996-2268
   Kernersville *(G-9225)*

Printing Svcs Greensboro Inc .... F 336 274-7663
   Greensboro *(G-7285)*

Quality Prtg Cartridge Fctry .... G 336 852-2505
   Greensboro *(G-7301)*

Raleigh Engraving Co .... G 919 832-5557
   Raleigh *(G-13177)*

Richard D Stewart .... G 919 284-2295
   Kenly *(G-9156)*

S Chamblee Incorporated .... E 919 833-7561
   Raleigh *(G-13221)*

S Ruppe Inc .... E 828 287-4936
   Rutherfordton *(G-13889)*

Tseng Information Systems Inc .... G 919 682-9197
   Durham *(G-5414)*

Weber and Weber Inc .... F 336 722-4109
   Winston Salem *(G-16968)*

UMBRELLAS & CANES

Arden Companies LLC .... E 919 258-3081
   Sanford *(G-14087)*

UNIFORM STORES

Kimmys Customs LLC .... G 904 699-2933
   Rural Hall *(G-13845)*

Tresmc LLC .... G 919 900-0868
   Knightdale *(G-9432)*

UNIVERSITY

Appalachian State University .... F 828 262-2047
   Boone *(G-1174)*

Appalachian State University .... G 828 262-7497
   Boone *(G-1175)*

North Carolina State Univ .... G 919 515-2760
   Raleigh *(G-13070)*

University NC At Chapel Hl .... G 919 962-0369
   Chapel Hill *(G-2089)*

UPHOLSTERY FILLING MATERIALS

A Land of Furniture Inc .... G 336 882-3866
   High Point *(G-8229)*

Prime Syntex LLC .... E 828 324-5496
   Thomasville *(G-15266)*

Spuntech Industries Inc .... C 336 330-9000
   Roxboro *(G-13825)*

Wind Defender LLC .... G 410 913-4660
   Statesville *(G-14926)*

Zonkd LLC .... E 919 977-6463
   Raleigh *(G-13438)*

UPHOLSTERY MATERIALS, BROADWOVEN

Carolina Mills Incorporated .... B 828 428-9911
   Maiden *(G-10102)*

Culp Inc .... F 336 889-5161
   High Point *(G-8310)*

Dicey Mills Inc .... F 704 487-6324
   Shelby *(G-14312)*

PRODUCT SECTION

Hickory Heritage of Falling Creek Inc..... E
 Hickory (G-8048)
Ledford Upholstery................................ G 704 732-0233
 Lincolnton (G-9899)
Valdese Weavers LLC........................ B 828 874-2181
 Valdese (G-15461)

UPHOLSTERY WORK SVCS

Davidson House Inc......................... F 704 791-0171
 Davidson (G-4670)
Hughes Furniture Inds Inc................. C 336 498-8700
 Randleman (G-13473)
Ledford Upholstery............................ G 704 732-0233
 Lincolnton (G-9899)

USED CAR DEALERS

Courtesy Ford Inc............................... E 252 338-4783
 Elizabeth City (G-5537)

USED MERCHANDISE STORES

Etherngton Cnservation Ctr Inc........... D 336 665-1317
 Greensboro (G-7004)
J C Lawrence Co................................ G 919 553-3044
 Oriental (G-12110)
Microtronic Us LLC........................... F 336 869-0429
 High Point (G-8456)

UTENSILS: Household, Cooking & Kitchen, Metal

Ashdan Enterprises............................ G 336 375-9698
 Greensboro (G-6818)
Kessebohmer USA Inc....................... F 910 338-5080
 Wilmington (G-16289)

UTILITY TRAILER DEALERS

A-1 Hitch & Trailors Sales Inc............. F 910 755-6025
 Supply (G-15005)
Gore S Trlr Manufacturer S Inc........... F 910 642-2246
 Whiteville (G-15964)
Kaufman Trailers Inc.......................... E 336 790-6800
 Lexington (G-9739)
Kraftsman Inc..................................... D 336 824-1114
 Ramseur (G-13445)
Leonard Alum Utlty Bldngs Inc........... G 919 872-4442
 Raleigh (G-12968)
Road King Trailers Inc....................... E 828 670-8012
 Candler (G-1588)

VACUUM CLEANERS: Indl Type

Cary Manufacturing Corporation........... G 704 527-4402
 Charlotte (G-2416)
Dustcontrol Inc................................... F 910 395-1808
 Wilmington (G-16207)
Vacs America Inc............................... G 910 259-9854
 Burgaw (G-1354)

VACUUM SYSTEMS: Air Extraction, Indl

Schmalz Inc....................................... C 919 713-0880
 Raleigh (G-13237)

VALUE-ADDED RESELLERS: Computer Systems

Trimech Solutions LLC...................... G 704 503-6444
 Charlotte (G-3727)

VALVES & PARTS: Gas, Indl

Key Gas Components Inc................... E 828 655-1700
 Marion (G-10156)

VALVES & PIPE FITTINGS

Aalberts Integrated Piping.................. E 704 841-6000
 Charlotte (G-2121)
Controls Southeast Inc....................... C 704 644-5000
 Pineville (G-12262)
Engineered Controls Intl LLC.............. C 336 226-3244
 Burlington (G-1411)
Engineered Controls Intl LLC.............. C 828 466-2153
 Conover (G-4451)
Engineered Controls Intl LLC.............. C 336 449-7706
 Whitsett (G-15989)
Hayward Industries Inc...................... C 336 712-9900
 Clemmons (G-4043)
Hayward Industries Inc...................... B 908 351-5400
 Charlotte (G-2894)
James M Pleasants Company Inc........ F 888 902-8324
 Greensboro (G-7134)
James M Pleasants Company Inc........ E 336 275-3152
 Greensboro (G-7133)
Key Gas Components Inc................... E 828 655-1700
 Marion (G-10156)
Mosack Group LLC........................... D 888 229-2874
 Mint Hill (G-10541)
National Foam Inc.............................. C 919 639-6151
 Angier (G-148)
Romac Industries Inc......................... D 704 915-3317
 Dallas (G-4656)
SCI Sharp Controls Inc...................... G 704 394-1395
 Pineville (G-12304)
Spc Mechanical Corporation............... C 252 237-9035
 Wendell (G-15919)
Thomas Mfg Co Inc Thomasville........ G 336 474-6030
 Thomasville (G-15289)
Titan Flow Control Inc........................ E 910 735-0000
 Lumberton (G-10058)
United Brass Works Inc..................... C 336 498-2661
 Randleman (G-13494)

VALVES & REGULATORS: Pressure, Indl

Eizi Group Llc................................... G 919 397-3638
 Raleigh (G-12729)
Engineered Controls Intl LLC.............. C 336 449-7707
 Elon (G-5657)
Mpv Mrgnton Prssure Vssels NC....... C 828 652-3704
 Marion (G-10168)
Watts Regulator Co............................ A 828 286-4151
 Spindale (G-14610)

VALVES: Aerosol, Metal

AP&t North America Inc..................... F 704 292-2900
 Monroe (G-10648)
Blue Mountain Metalworks Inc........... G 828 898-8582
 Banner Elk (G-894)
Cyrco Inc... E 336 668-0977
 Greensboro (G-6954)
Epic Enterprises Inc........................... E 910 692-5750
 Southern Pines (G-14535)
Ism Inc... E
 Arden (G-342)
Metal Works High Point Inc............... D 336 886-4612
 High Point (G-8453)
Metal-Cad Stl Frmng Systems In........ D 910 343-3338
 Wilmington (G-16321)
Werner Co... G 704 235-5660
 Mooresville (G-11126)
Zurn Industries LLC........................... E 919 775-2255
 Sanford (G-14212)

VALVES: Aircraft, Control, Hydraulic & Pneumatic

Flo-Tite Inc Valves & Contrls.............. E 910 738-8904
 Lumberton (G-10038)

VALVES: Control, Automatic

ADC Industries Inc............................. G 919 550-9515
 Clayton (G-3952)
Robert H Wager Company Inc............ F 336 969-6909
 Rural Hall (G-13851)

VALVES: Fluid Power, Control, Hydraulic & pneumatic

Hawe North America Inc.................... E 704 509-1599
 Huntersville (G-8828)
Logic Hydraulic Controls Inc............... E 910 791-9293
 Wilmington (G-16304)
McC Holdings Inc............................... C 828 724-4000
 Marion (G-10160)
Stanadyne Intrmdate Hldngs LLC....... C 860 525-0821
 Jacksonville (G-9038)

VALVES: Indl

Asco LP... G 919 460-5200
 Cary (G-1692)
Bonomi North America Inc................. F 704 412-9031
 Charlotte (G-2333)
Burkert USA Corporation.................... C 800 325-1405
 Huntersville (G-8798)
Carolina Conveying Inc...................... G 828 235-1005
 Canton (G-1608)
Celeros Flow Technology LLC............ D 704 752-3100
 Charlotte (G-2438)
Circor Pumps North America LLC....... C 877 853-7867
 Monroe (G-10684)
Curtiss-Wright Corporation................. G 704 481-1150
 Shelby (G-14307)
Curtiss-Wright Corporation................. B 704 869-4600
 Davidson (G-4669)
David Conrad..................................... G 336 253-6966
 Greensboro (G-6958)
Engineered Controls Intl LLC.............. C 336 226-3244
 Burlington (G-1411)
Engineered Controls Intl LLC.............. C 336 449-7706
 Whitsett (G-15989)
Engineering Mfg Svcs Co................... F 704 821-7325
 Monroe (G-10714)
Equilibar LLC..................................... E 828 650-6590
 Fletcher (G-6001)
General Control Equipment Co............ F 704 588-0484
 Charlotte (G-2816)
Hersey Meters Co LLC...................... E 704 278-2221
 Cleveland (G-4073)
Hydrant Mechanics............................ G 919 922-3829
 Princeton (G-12401)
Mueller Steam Specialty.................... D 910 865-8241
 Saint Pauls (G-13906)
Romac Industries Inc......................... D 704 915-3317
 Dallas (G-4656)
Sensus USA Inc................................ C 919 576-6185
 Morrisville (G-11426)
Sensus USA Inc................................ E 919 845-4000
 Morrisville (G-11425)
Spanglercv Inc................................... G 910 794-5547
 Wilmington (G-16413)
SPX Flow Inc..................................... C 704 752-4400
 Charlotte (G-3607)
United Brass Works Inc..................... C 336 498-2661
 Randleman (G-13494)
Watts Regulator................................. G 978 689-6066
 Saint Pauls (G-13910)
Zurn Elkay Wtr Solutions Corp........... F 910 501-1853
 Lumberton (G-10062)

VALVES: Plumbing & Heating

Employee Codes: A=Over 500 employees, B=251-500
C=101-250, D=51-100, E=20-50, F=10-19, G=1-9

VALVES: Plumbing & Heating

American Valve Inc.................................. D 336 668-0554
  Greensboro *(G-6802)*
Bonomi North America Inc..................... F 704 412-9031
  Charlotte *(G-2333)*
Mid-Atlantic Drainage Inc....................... F 828 324-0808
  Conover *(G-4472)*

VALVES: Regulating & Control, Automatic

Brasscraft... C 336 475-2131
  Thomasville *(G-15189)*
Huber Technology Inc............................. E 704 949-1010
  Denver *(G-4782)*
Parker-Hannifin Corporation.................... E 828 245-3233
  Forest City *(G-6079)*

VALVES: Regulating, Process Control

Tvl International LLC................................ G 704 814-0930
  Matthews *(G-10297)*

VALVES: Water Works

Zurn Elkay Wtr Solutions Corp................ G 855 663-9876
  Sanford *(G-14211)*

VAN CONVERSIONS

Matthews Spcialty Vehicles Inc............... D 336 297-9600
  Greensboro *(G-7189)*

VARIETY STORES

Atlantic Trading LLC................................ F
  Charlotte *(G-2233)*
Brasingtons Inc....................................... G 704 694-5191
  Wadesboro *(G-15503)*
Infinity S End Inc.................................... F 704 900-8355
  Charlotte *(G-2968)*

VARNISHES, NEC

Valspar Corporation................................ G 704 897-5700
  Davidson *(G-4706)*

VEHICLES: Recreational

Naarva... G 704 333-3070
  Charlotte *(G-3228)*
Xxxtreme Motorsport............................... G 704 663-1500
  Mooresville *(G-11135)*

VENDING MACHINE OPERATORS: Sandwich & Hot Food

Durham Coca-Cola Bottling Company..... C 919 383-1531
  Durham *(G-5071)*

VENDING MACHINES & PARTS

Country Corner.. G 919 444-9663
  Pittsboro *(G-12337)*
Jb-Isecurity LLC...................................... G 910 824-7601
  Fayetteville *(G-5847)*
Microtronic Us LLC.................................. F 336 869-0429
  High Point *(G-8456)*

VENTILATING EQPT: Metal

Northern Star Technologies Inc.............. G 516 353-3333
  Indian Trail *(G-8952)*
WV Holdings Inc..................................... G 704 853-8338
  Gastonia *(G-6544)*

VETERINARY PHARMACEUTICAL PREPARATIONS

Happy Jack Incorporated........................ G 252 747-2911
  Snow Hill *(G-14503)*
Huvepharma Inc...................................... F 910 506-4649
  Maxton *(G-10356)*

Pharmgate Animal Health LLC................ G 910 679-8364
  Wilmington *(G-16354)*
Pharmgate Inc.. F 910 679-8364
  Wilmington *(G-16355)*
Wholesale Kennel Supply Co.................. G 919 742-2515
  Siler City *(G-14434)*

VIDEO & AUDIO EQPT, WHOLESALE

Lea Aid Acquisition Company.................. F 919 872-6210
  Raleigh *(G-12963)*

VIDEO PRODUCTION SVCS

Inspire Creative Studios Inc.................... G 910 395-0200
  Wilmington *(G-16269)*
Metro Productions Inc............................. F 919 851-6420
  Raleigh *(G-13022)*

VIDEO TAPE PRODUCTION SVCS

Palmer Senn... G 704 451-3971
  Charlotte *(G-3309)*

VIDEO TRIGGERS: Remote Control TV Devices

522 Flipper LLC...................................... G 919 785-3417
  Raleigh *(G-12448)*

VISUAL COMMUNICATIONS SYSTEMS

Flat Water Corp...................................... G 704 584-7764
  Charlotte *(G-2771)*
Simplyhome LLC..................................... F 828 684-8441
  Arden *(G-376)*

VITAMINS: Natural Or Synthetic, Uncompounded, Bulk

Interntnal Agrclture Group LLC............... F 908 323-3246
  Mooresville *(G-10983)*
Natsol LLC... F 704 302-1246
  Matthews *(G-10275)*

VOCATIONAL REHABILITATION AGENCY

Lee County Industries Inc....................... E 919 775-3439
  Sanford *(G-14148)*
Tri-County Industries Inc........................ C 252 977-3800
  Rocky Mount *(G-13676)*
Vocatnal Sltons Hndrson Cnty I.............. E 828 692-9626
  East Flat Rock *(G-5479)*
Watauga Opportunities Inc..................... E 828 264-5009
  Boone *(G-1247)*

VOCATIONAL TRAINING AGENCY

Eastern Crlina Vctonal Ctr Inc................. D 252 758-4188
  Greenville *(G-7521)*
Hope Renovations................................... F 919 960-1957
  Chapel Hill *(G-2024)*

WALLBOARD: Decorated, Made From Purchased Materials

National Gyps Receivables LLC.............. E 704 365-7300
  Charlotte *(G-3235)*
Ng Corporate LLC................................... F 704 365-7300
  Charlotte *(G-3259)*
Ng Operations LLC.................................. G 704 365-7300
  Charlotte *(G-3260)*
Proform Finishing Products LLC............. B 704 365-7300
  Charlotte *(G-3392)*

WALLBOARD: Gypsum

Esco Industries Inc................................. F 336 495-3772
  Randleman *(G-13469)*

Proform Finishing Products LLC............. E 910 799-3954
  Wilmington *(G-16371)*
United States Gypsum Company........... F 828 765-9481
  Spruce Pine *(G-14660)*

WALLPAPER & WALL COVERINGS

Paperworks... G 704 548-9057
  Charlotte *(G-3311)*
Reliable Wallcovering LLC...................... G 980 565-5224
  Concord *(G-4348)*
Wallworx.. G 919 422-8604
  Apex *(G-257)*

WALLS: Curtain, Metal

3a Composites USA Inc.......................... C 704 872-8974
  Statesville *(G-14732)*

WAREHOUSING & STORAGE FACILITIES, NEC

Cairn Studio Ltd..................................... E 704 664-7128
  Mooresville *(G-10894)*
Trimfit Inc... C 336 476-6154
  Thomasville *(G-15296)*

WAREHOUSING & STORAGE: Farm Prdts

C A Perry & Son Inc................................ G 252 330-2323
  Elizabeth City *(G-5532)*
C A Perry & Son Inc................................ E 252 221-4463
  Hobbsville *(G-8675)*
High Rise Service Company Inc............. E 910 371-2325
  Leland *(G-9548)*

WAREHOUSING & STORAGE: General

Ashley Furniture Inds LLC...................... D 336 998-1066
  Advance *(G-37)*
Fishel Steel Company............................. G 336 788-2880
  Winston Salem *(G-16712)*
Metrohose Incorporated......................... G 252 329-9891
  Greenville *(G-7560)*
Pactiv LLC... G 828 396-2373
  Granite Falls *(G-6748)*
Parkdale Mills Incorporated.................... F 704 825-2529
  Belmont *(G-1000)*
Patheon Softgels Inc.............................. F 336 812-8700
  Greensboro *(G-7247)*

WAREHOUSING & STORAGE: Miniwarehouse

Warehouse Distillery LLC....................... G 828 464-5183
  Newton *(G-11983)*

WAREHOUSING & STORAGE: Refrigerated

Smith Utility Buildings............................. G 336 957-8211
  Traphill *(G-15327)*

WARM AIR HEATING/AC EQPT/SPLYS, WHOL Warm Air Htg Eqpt/Splys

Appalchian Stove Fbrcators Inc............. F 828 253-0164
  Asheville *(G-525)*
Ultimate Products Inc............................. F 919 836-1627
  Raleigh *(G-13377)*

WASHERS

Power Washer Pros................................ G 252 446-4643
  Rocky Mount *(G-13722)*

WASTE CLEANING SVCS

Valley Proteins (de) Inc......................... C 336 333-3030
  Greensboro *(G-7435)*

PRODUCT SECTION

WATCH REPAIR SVCS
Southern Digital Watch Repair............... G 336 299-6718
 Greensboro (G-7353)

WATCHES
Orbita Corporation...................................... E 910 256-5300
 Wilmington (G-16346)

WATER HEATERS
Prime Water Services Inc....................... G 919 504-1020
 Raleigh (G-13140)
State Industries Inc................................. G 704 597-8910
 Charlotte (G-3625)

WATER PURIFICATION EQPT: Household
Aquapro Solutions LLC............................ G 828 255-0772
 Asheville (G-527)
Columbus Industries LLC....................... E 910 872-1625
 Bladenboro (G-1146)
Mikropor America Inc.............................. F
 Charlotte (G-3178)
Scaltrol Inc... G 678 990-0858
 Charlotte (G-3497)
Tempest Envmtl Systems Inc................. F 919 973-1609
 Durham (G-5394)

WATER SUPPLY
County of Anson..................................... G 704 848-4849
 Lilesville (G-9836)
Prime Water Services Inc....................... G 919 504-1020
 Raleigh (G-13140)
Quantico Water & Sewer LLC................ G 336 528-9299
 Clemmons (G-4057)
Tempest Environmental Corp................. G 919 973-1609
 Durham (G-5393)

WATER TREATMENT EQPT: Indl
A3-Usa Inc... G 724 871-7170
 Chinquapin (G-3891)
Adr Hydro-Cut Inc.................................... G 919 388-2251
 Morrisville (G-11279)
Alpha-Advantage Inc............................... G 252 441-3766
 Kitty Hawk (G-9399)
Amiad Filtration Systems Ltd.................. E 805 377-0288
 Mooresville (G-10859)
Amiad USA Inc.. F 704 662-3133
 Mooresville (G-10860)
County of Anson..................................... G 704 848-4849
 Lilesville (G-9836)
Drch Inc... G 919 383-9421
 Durham (G-5063)
Eizi Group Llc.. G 919 397-3638
 Raleigh (G-12729)
Entex Technologies Inc........................... F 919 933-1380
 Chapel Hill (G-2016)
Envirnmntal Prcess Systems Inc............ G 704 827-0740
 Mount Holly (G-11632)
Ew2 Environmental Inc........................... G 704 542-2444
 Charlotte (G-2736)
Hoh Corporation...................................... F 336 723-9274
 Winston Salem (G-16747)
Hydro Service & Supplies Inc................. E 919 544-3744
 Durham (G-5142)
Imagine One Resources LLC................. G 828 328-1142
 Hickory (G-8062)
Jim Myers & Sons Inc............................. D 704 554-8397
 Charlotte (G-3022)
Living Water Filter Co Inc....................... G 252 438-6600
 Henderson (G-7795)
Meco Inc.. G 919 557-7330
 Fuquay Varina (G-6214)

Miller S Utility MGT Inc............................ G 910 298-3847
 Beulaville (G-1096)
Nala Membranes Inc............................... G 540 230-5606
 Durham (G-5237)
North Drham Wtr Rclmtion Fclty............. G 919 560-4384
 Durham (G-5248)
Pauls Water Treatment LLC................... G 336 886-5600
 High Point (G-8477)
Pep Filters Inc... E 704 662-3133
 Mooresville (G-11051)
Protect Plus Pro LLC.............................. G 828 328-1142
 Hickory (G-8126)
Pure Flow Inc.. D 336 532-0300
 Graham (G-6709)
Semper Fi Water LLC............................. G 910 381-3569
 Jacksonville (G-9028)
Solarbrook Water and Pwr Corp............. G 919 231-3205
 Raleigh (G-13278)
Tempest Environmental Corp................. G 919 973-1609
 Durham (G-5393)
Town of Jonesville................................... G 336 835-2250
 Jonesville (G-9102)
Town of Maggie Valley Inc..................... F 828 926-0145
 Maggie Valley (G-10096)
Town of Tarboro...................................... E 252 641-4284
 Tarboro (G-15124)
Town of Waynesville............................... G 828 456-8497
 Waynesville (G-15830)
Wedeco Uv Technologies Inc................. D 704 716-7600
 Charlotte (G-3802)

WATER: Mineral, Carbonated, Canned & Bottled, Etc
Milkco Inc.. B 828 254-8428
 Asheville (G-702)
Unix Packaging LLC............................... E 310 877-7979
 Morganton (G-11263)

WATER: Pasteurized & Mineral, Bottled & Canned
Pure Water Innovations Inc.................... G 919 301-8189
 Spring Hope (G-14620)

WATER: Pasteurized, Canned & Bottled, Etc
Ice River Springs Usa Inc....................... F 519 925-2929
 Morganton (G-11222)
Le Bleu Corporation................................ G 828 254-5105
 Arden (G-346)
Niagara Bottling LLC.............................. G 909 815-6310
 Mooresville (G-11036)
Zeskp LLC... G 910 762-8300
 Wilmington (G-16460)

WATERPROOFING COMPOUNDS
Carlisle Corporation................................ G 704 501-1100
 Charlotte (G-2390)
Hzo Inc.. D 919 439-0505
 Morrisville (G-11355)

WAVEGUIDES & FITTINGS
Commscope Inc North Carolina.............. D 828 324-2200
 Claremont (G-3909)
Commscope Technologies LLC.............. F 919 934-9711
 Smithfield (G-14457)

WAXES: Paraffin
Qualice LLC... F 910 419-6589
 Hamlet (G-7630)

WAXES: Petroleum, Not Produced In Petroleum Refineries
Carolina Golfco Inc.................................. G 704 525-7846
 Charlotte (G-2397)

WEATHER STRIP: Sponge Rubber
Comfort Tech Inc..................................... F 910 428-1779
 Biscoe (G-1108)
Mustang Reproductions Inc.................... F 704 786-0990
 Concord (G-4321)

WEIGHING MACHINERY & APPARATUS
True Portion Inc....................................... F 336 362-6326
 High Point (G-8579)
Vision Metals Inc..................................... F 336 622-7300
 Liberty (G-9834)

WELDING & CUTTING APPARATUS & ACCESS, NEC
Liburdi Dimetrics Corporation................. E 704 230-2510
 Mooresville (G-11007)
Modlins Anonized Aluminum Wldg......... G 252 753-7274
 Farmville (G-5740)

WELDING EQPT
Burco Welding & Cutng Pdts Inc............ G 336 887-6100
 High Point (G-8278)
Hanson Systems Inc............................... G 828 687-3701
 Fletcher (G-6009)

WELDING EQPT & SPLYS WHOLESALERS
Airgas Usa LLC....................................... F 704 394-1420
 Charlotte (G-2147)
Airgas Usa LLC....................................... F 704 333-5475
 Charlotte (G-2148)
Airgas Usa LLC....................................... G 919 544-3773
 Durham (G-4909)
Airgas Usa LLC....................................... G 919 735-5276
 Goldsboro (G-6587)
Airgas Usa LLC....................................... G 704 636-5049
 Salisbury (G-13916)
Airgas Usa LLC....................................... F 910 392-2711
 Wilmington (G-16098)
Andy-OXY Co Inc.................................... E 828 258-0271
 Asheville (G-518)
Burco Welding & Cutng Pdts Inc............ G 336 887-6100
 High Point (G-8278)
James Oxygen and Supply Co............... E 704 322-5438
 Hickory (G-8071)
Matheson Tri-Gas Inc.............................. F 919 556-6461
 Wake Forest (G-15571)

WELDING EQPT & SPLYS: Gas
American Welding & Gas Inc.................. G 984 222-2600
 Raleigh (G-12501)
Kincol Industries Incorporated................ G 704 372-8435
 Charlotte (G-3055)

WELDING EQPT & SPLYS: Generators, Arc Welding, AC & DC
Van Welder LLC...................................... G 919 495-2902
 Graham (G-6714)

WELDING EQPT REPAIR SVCS
Accel Wldg & Fabrication LLC................ G 980 722-7198
 Stanley (G-14683)
Spring Repair Service Inc....................... F 336 299-5660
 Greensboro (G-7360)

WELDING EQPT: Electric

Techsouth Inc.................................... G 704 334-1100
  Matthews (G-10349)

WELDING EQPT: Electric

Fanuc America Corporation................ G 704 596-5121
  Huntersville (G-8818)
Qws LLC.. E 252 723-2106
  Morehead City (G-11185)

WELDING EQPT: Electrical

Accurate Weld LLC............................. G 828 310-1517
  Taylorsville (G-15126)

WELDING MACHINES & EQPT: Ultrasonic

Hanson Systems Inc........................... G 828 687-3701
  Fletcher (G-6009)

WELDING REPAIR SVC

277 Metal Inc..................................... G 704 372-4513
  Gastonia (G-6333)
A&W Welding Inc................................ G 252 482-3233
  Edenton (G-5504)
AA Welding and Fabricatio.................. G 919 272-5433
  Clayton (G-3951)
Acme Welding Co............................... G 770 841-4335
  Harrisburg (G-7699)
Advanced Machine Services LLC....... G 910 410-0099
  Rockingham (G-13618)
Affordable Welding Specialists........... G 828 446-4436
  Hickory (G-7929)
Airgas Usa LLC.................................. G 704 636-5049
  Salisbury (G-13916)
Alamance Electric & Wldg Inc............. G 336 584-9339
  Elon (G-5656)
All Pro Fabrication & Wldg LLC.......... G 336 953-4082
  Lexington (G-9678)
Alloy Fabricators Inc.......................... E 704 263-2281
  Alexis (G-121)
Allsteel Welding LLC.......................... G 919 429-0468
  Middlesex (G-10444)
Aluminum Barges com LLC................ G 239 272-4857
  Boone (G-1173)
Anchor Welding LLC.......................... G 919 747-1926
  Knightdale (G-9412)
Ansonville Piping & Fabg Inc.............. G 704 826-8403
  Ansonville (G-152)
Arc3 Gases Inc................................... F 336 275-3333
  Greensboro (G-6812)
Arc3 Gases Inc................................... F 704 220-1029
  Monroe (G-10650)
Arc3 Gases Inc................................... E 910 892-4016
  Dunn (G-4851)
Archie S Steel Service Inc.................. G 252 355-5007
  Greenville (G-7485)
Arrow Glazing Fabrication Inc............ G 704 926-1509
  Charlotte (G-2219)
Ashevlle Prcsion Mch Rblding I.......... G 828 254-0884
  Asheville (G-544)
Avery Machine & Welding Co............. G 828 733-4944
  Fayetteville (G-5767)
B & D Enterprises Inc......................... F 704 739-2958
  Kings Mountain (G-9293)
B&A Welding Miscellaneous LLC....... G 980 287-9187
  Charlotte (G-2255)
Badger Welding Incorporated............. G 828 863-2078
  Rutherfordton (G-13865)
Banks Welding.................................... G 828 586-2258
  Sylva (G-15053)
Bentons Wldg Repr & Svcs Inc.......... G 910 343-8322
  Wilmington (G-16136)
Black Rver Wldg Fbrication LLC........ G 910 471-7434
  Atkinson (G-826)

Blacksand Metal Works LLC............... F 703 489-8282
  Fayetteville (G-5771)
Bladen Fabricators LLC...................... G 910 866-5225
  Bladenboro (G-1144)
Blands Welding.................................. G 704 932-1864
  Davidson (G-4666)
Blue ARC Fabrication Mech LLC........ G 336 693-7878
  Graham (G-6679)
Blue Light Welding of Triad................ G 336 442-9140
  Winston Salem (G-16634)
Boyd Welding and Mfg Inc.................. F 828 247-0630
  Forest City (G-6061)
Brafford Welding................................ G 336 318-5436
  Liberty (G-9808)
Brasingtons Inc.................................. G 704 694-5191
  Wadesboro (G-15503)
Braswell Welding................................ G 252 838-0089
  Beaufort (G-947)
Bright Fabrication LLC....................... G 704 660-3151
  Mooresville (G-10888)
Brightleaf Wldg & Mch Repr LLC....... G 919 934-3300
  Smithfield (G-14451)
Bumgarners Welding........................... G 704 764-7041
  Monroe (G-10671)
Burnett Welding................................. G 803 360-7406
  Elizabethtown (G-5586)
Burns Welding Services LLC.............. G 336 908-5716
  Germanton (G-6553)
C & B Welding & Fab Inc.................... G 704 435-6942
  Bessemer City (G-1054)
C & J Welding Inc............................... G 919 552-0275
  Holly Springs (G-8693)
C & M Welding Inspections Inc.......... G 919 762-7345
  Willow Spring (G-16076)
C and D Welders LLC......................... G 910 552-3294
  Wallace (G-15619)
Calhoun Welding Inc.......................... G 252 281-1455
  Macclesfield (G-10064)
Carer Welding..................................... G 336 558-3906
  Randleman (G-13457)
Carolina Tractor & Eqp Co.................. G 828 251-2500
  Asheville (G-584)
Carolina Welding & Cnstr.................... G 252 814-8740
  Kinston (G-9352)
Carotek Inc... D 704 844-1100
  Matthews (G-10238)
Central ARC Wldg Solutions LLC....... G 704 858-1614
  Huntersville (G-8802)
Chapman Welding LLC....................... G 919 951-8131
  Efland (G-5524)
CJS Welding....................................... G 252 972-7511
  Elm City (G-5648)
Clayton Welding................................. G 252 717-5909
  Washington (G-15689)
CM Welding.. G 704 791-0572
  Midland (G-10463)
Coastal Machine & Welding Inc.......... G 910 754-6476
  Shallotte (G-14272)
Coastal Sales Inc................................ G 252 717-3542
  Washington (G-15691)
Collins Fabrication & Wldg LLC......... G 704 861-9326
  Gastonia (G-6380)
Colt Welding...................................... G 361 244-2513
  Fuquay Varina (G-6190)
Combs Welding LLC........................... G 336 984-3832
  Roaring River (G-13592)
Combs Welding LLC........................... G 336 452-1386
  Ronda (G-13765)
Container Technology Inc................... G 910 350-1303
  Wilmington (G-16180)
Coomers Welding LLC........................ G 919 708-8087
  Sanford (G-14104)

Costin Welding and Fabrication.......... G 910 789-7961
  Burgaw (G-1336)
Crawfords Forge................................ G 828 280-2555
  Hendersonville (G-7841)
Creasmans Welding............................ G 828 667-1875
  Asheville (G-597)
Custom Enterprises Inc...................... G 336 226-8296
  Burlington (G-1405)
Custom Machine Company Inc.......... F 704 629-5326
  Bessemer City (G-1059)
Cutting Edge Piping Svcs LLC............ G 704 419-3995
  Shelby (G-14308)
Cwi Services LLC............................... G 704 560-9755
  Southport (G-14568)
D & D Welding & Repair LLC............. G 336 648-1393
  Mount Airy (G-11499)
Da Welding LLC.................................. G 336 231-7691
  Winston Salem (G-16669)
Dah Inc.. G 910 887-3675
  Southport (G-14569)
Dales Welding Service........................ G 919 872-6969
  Raleigh (G-12671)
David Beasley..................................... G 910 891-2557
  Dunn (G-4860)
David Bennett..................................... F 919 798-3424
  Fuquay Varina (G-6194)
David West... G 910 271-0757
  Willard (G-16054)
Davis Davis Mch & Wldg Co Inc......... F 252 443-2652
  Rocky Mount (G-13689)
Delgados Welding Inc........................ G 910 588-4762
  Elizabethtown (G-5593)
Deohges Welding Service LLC........... G 828 396-2770
  Granite Falls (G-6731)
Diversified Welding and Steel............ G 704 504-1111
  Pineville (G-12266)
Donalds Welding Inc.......................... F 910 298-5234
  Chinquapin (G-3892)
Double R Welding & Fabrication........ G 704 340-5825
  Concord (G-4257)
Dunavants Welding & Steel Inc.......... G 252 338-6533
  Camden (G-1557)
Duncan Joseph E & Duncan Billy....... G 828 299-8464
  Swannanoa (G-15025)
Dutchman Creek Self-Storage............ G 919 363-8878
  Apex (G-185)
Dynamic Fabrication & Wldg Inc........ G 828 390-8377
  Morganton (G-11209)
Ecomarc LLC...................................... G 828 226-4780
  Sylva (G-15056)
Ed Majka LLC..................................... G 570 985-9677
  Shiloh (G-14391)
Eddies Welding Inc............................. G 704 585-2024
  Stony Point (G-14972)
Edwards Lawnmower & Wldg Repr.... G 919 235-7173
  Wake Forest (G-15551)
Elite Wldg & Fabrications LLC........... G 919 224-6007
  Warrenton (G-15659)
Elmore Welding Inc............................ G 919 584-7460
  Durham (G-5079)
Estes Machine Co.............................. F 336 786-7680
  Mount Airy (G-11507)
Everettes Industrial Repr Svc............ F 252 527-4269
  Goldsboro (G-6613)
Evident Fab LLC................................. G 973 294-4507
  Havelock (G-7742)
Evolution Mobile Welding LLC........... G 336 383-9277
  Greensboro (G-7005)
Extreme Stud Welding LLC................ G 828 217-2587
  Vale (G-15466)
EZ Fabrication Inc.............................. G 828 674-0661
  Claremont (G-3926)

PRODUCT SECTION

WELDING REPAIR SVC

Fabrication Associates Inc .... D 704 535-8050
   Charlotte *(G-2742)*

Filer Micro Welding .... G 828 248-1813
   Forest City *(G-6068)*

Flores Welding Inc .... F 919 838-1060
   Raleigh *(G-12774)*

Franklin Industrial Contrs Inc .... G 252 670-6682
   Aurora *(G-834)*

Franks Millwright Services .... G 336 248-6692
   Lexington *(G-9720)*

Freedom Steel Welding LLC .... G 704 884-1277
   Cherryville *(G-3869)*

Freeman Custom Welding Inc .... G 919 210-6267
   Raleigh *(G-12781)*

Full Throttle Fabrication LLC .... G 910 770-1180
   Chadbourn *(G-1976)*

Fusion Fabrication & Wldg LLC .... G 704 240-9416
   Vale *(G-15467)*

Fusion Welding .... G 508 320-3525
   Rocky Point *(G-13745)*

Garcia Brothers Welding LLC .... G 919 207-8190
   Bailey *(G-872)*

Gary Tucker .... G 919 837-5724
   Bear Creek *(G-938)*

General Mch Wldg of Burlington .... G 336 227-5400
   Burlington *(G-1419)*

General Refrigeration Company .... G 919 661-4727
   Garner *(G-6273)*

Genesis Wldg & Fabrication LLC .... G 336 622-9533
   Liberty *(G-9814)*

George F Wlson Wldg Fbrication .... G 828 262-1668
   Boone *(G-1199)*

Gibbs Machine Company Incorporated . E 336 856-1907
   Greensboro *(G-7042)*

Gibbs Performance Spc Inc .... G 704 746-2225
   Concord *(G-4274)*

Glovers Welding LLC .... F 252 586-7692
   Littleton *(G-9952)*

Godfrey Industrial Welding .... G 919 604-0498
   Sanford *(G-14126)*

Gonzalez Welding Inc .... G 336 270-8179
   Graham *(G-6690)*

Gordon Wldg & Fabrication LLC .... G 336 406-7471
   Greensboro *(G-7054)*

Gore S Mar Met Fabrication Inc .... G 910 763-6066
   Wilmington *(G-16237)*

GS Fab Inc .... G 704 799-1227
   Mooresville *(G-10966)*

Gunmar Machine Corporation .... F 910 738-6295
   Lumberton *(G-10039)*

Guns Welding LLC .... G 336 786-1020
   Mount Airy *(G-11514)*

H & C Erectors and Welding LLC .... G 704 615-9849
   Charlotte *(G-2875)*

Hales Welding and Fabrication .... G 252 907-5508
   Macclesfield *(G-10065)*

Hancock & Grandson Inc .... G 252 728-2416
   Beaufort *(G-959)*

Harbor Welding Inc .... G 252 473-3777
   Wanchese *(G-15647)*

Harris Welding .... G 336 514-6640
   High Point *(G-8375)*

Hartman Welding .... G 336 372-2220
   Sparta *(G-14594)*

Hayes Welding .... G 336 989-6171
   Sophia *(G-14518)*

Heat Transfer Sales of The .... E 336 294-3838
   Greensboro *(G-7085)*

High Cotton Fabrication LLC .... G 910 408-6961
   Wilmington *(G-16252)*

High Rise Service Company Inc .... E 910 371-2325
   Leland *(G-9548)*

High Speed Welding LLC .... F 910 632-4427
   Wilmington *(G-16253)*

Highs Welding Shop .... G 704 624-5707
   Marshville *(G-10218)*

Hillsville Welding .... G 336 861-0732
   Trinity *(G-15345)*

His Specialty Fab LLC .... G 704 279-1638
   Salisbury *(G-13981)*

Hohn Welding Services LLC .... G 336 870-9617
   High Point *(G-8397)*

Holmes Welding LLC .... G 919 779-8844
   Raleigh *(G-12853)*

Hughes Welding & Crane Svc LLC ...... G 910 895-9767
   Rockingham *(G-13631)*

Idustrial Burkett Services .... F 252 244-0143
   Vanceboro *(G-15478)*

Imagination Fabrication .... G 919 280-4430
   Apex *(G-204)*

Industrial Metal Maint Inc .... G 910 285-3240
   Teachey *(G-15177)*

Industrial Welding & .... G 910 309-8540
   Fayetteville *(G-5842)*

Integrity Welding LLC .... G 919 556-5144
   Louisburg *(G-9992)*

Iron Men Fabrication .... G 336 929-6263
   Randleman *(G-13474)*

Iv-S Metal Stamping Inc .... E 336 861-2100
   Archdale *(G-286)*

J & D Welding & Fabg Corp .... G 704 393-9115
   Charlotte *(G-3002)*

J A King .... F 800 327-7727
   Raleigh *(G-12907)*

J R Nixon Welding .... G 252 221-4574
   Tyner *(G-15434)*

J&B Welding LLC .... G 910 316-5838
   Lumberton *(G-10042)*

J&C Welding and Fabrication .... G 704 654-8253
   Charlotte *(G-3007)*

Jax Specialty Welding LLC .... G 704 380-3548
   Statesville *(G-14823)*

JC Welding and Machine LLC .... G 336 306-2026
   Lexington *(G-9733)*

Joe Robin Darnell .... G 704 482-1186
   Shelby *(G-14333)*

Jones Fab LLC .... G 336 940-2769
   Advance *(G-45)*

Jones Welding .... G 828 508-0080
   Sylva *(G-15061)*

JP Mechanic & Welding Inc .... G 919 650-7438
   Staley *(G-14666)*

K & W Welding LLC .... G 910 895-9220
   Rockingham *(G-13632)*

K & W Welding LLC .... G 910 844-2288
   Maxton *(G-10358)*

K P Welding Inc .... G 540 250-7187
   Jonesville *(G-9099)*

Kenny Robinson S Wldg Svc Inc .... G 760 213-6454
   Liberty *(G-9818)*

Kinetic Sltons Fabrication LLC .... G 607 749-0946
   Holly Ridge *(G-8684)*

Kings Prtble Wldg Fbrction LLC .... G 336 789-2372
   Mount Airy *(G-11532)*

Krieg Corp .... G 704 361-1223
   Charlotte *(G-3061)*

Kurrent Wldg & Fabrication Inc .... G 800 738-6114
   Stoneville *(G-14960)*

Larry D Troxler .... G 336 585-1141
   Gibsonville *(G-6566)*

Laying Dimes Welding & Fab LLC .... G 704 677-5521
   Lexington *(G-9745)*

Leons Welding & Decking LLC .... G 919 923-7321
   Chapel Hill *(G-2032)*

Liberty Welding .... G 336 964-0640
   Liberty *(G-9823)*

Limitless Wldg Fabrication LLC .... G 252 753-0660
   Farmville *(G-5739)*

Lloyds Fabricating Solutions .... G 336 250-0154
   Thomasville *(G-15244)*

Lowes Welding and Camper Repr .... G 336 214-9058
   Graham *(G-6698)*

Luck Fabrication Incorporated .... G 336 498-0905
   Randleman *(G-13476)*

Lumsden Welding Company .... G 910 791-6336
   Wilmington *(G-16310)*

Lyerlys Wldg & Fabrication Inc .... G 704 680-2317
   Gold Hill *(G-6584)*

Magnum Mobile Welding Wrap Up ...... G 910 372-3380
   Beulaville *(G-1095)*

Marc Machine Works Inc .... F 704 865-3625
   Gastonia *(G-6458)*

Marine Fabrications LLC .... G 252 473-4767
   Wanchese *(G-15649)*

Marsh Welding .... G 919 335-5332
   Durham *(G-5209)*

Martin Welding Inc .... G 919 436-8805
   Garner *(G-6284)*

Matthews Welding Service .... G 828 862-4510
   Brevard *(G-1279)*

Maverick Metalworks LLC .... G 919 609-1274
   Raleigh *(G-13008)*

Max Patterson .... G 910 947-2524
   Sanford *(G-14151)*

Maynard S Fabricators Inc .... G 336 230-1048
   Greensboro *(G-7191)*

MCS of Fayetteville .... G 252 234-6001
   Wilson *(G-16514)*

Mechanical Maintenance Inc .... F 336 676-7133
   Climax *(G-4087)*

Medley S Garage Welding .... G 336 674-0422
   Pleasant Garden *(G-12358)*

Mendez Welding LLC .... G 336 618-9337
   Mocksville *(G-10588)*

Metal ARC .... G 910 770-1180
   Whiteville *(G-15971)*

Metal Solutions LLC .... G 252 702-7523
   Snow Hill *(G-14504)*

Micronics Tig-Welding .... G 828 691-0755
   Fletcher *(G-6025)*

Mike Beasley Services Inc .... G 910 892-6216
   Dunn *(G-4876)*

Mikes Welding & Fabricating .... G 336 472-5804
   Thomasville *(G-15249)*

Mikes Welding Service of Conc .... G 704 786-9795
   Concord *(G-4315)*

Miller Sheet Metal Co Inc .... G 336 751-2304
   Mocksville *(G-10590)*

Mitchell Welding Inc .... E 828 765-2620
   Spruce Pine *(G-14651)*

Modern Machine and Metal Fa .... D 336 993-4808
   Winston Salem *(G-16814)*

Modlins Anonized Aluminum Wldg ...... G 252 753-7274
   Farmville *(G-5740)*

Monical Enterprises Inc .... G 757 692-1345
   Hampstead *(G-7651)*

Montys Welding & Fabrication .... G 919 337-7859
   Garner *(G-6291)*

Moore S Welding Service Inc .... G 919 837-5769
   Bear Creek *(G-940)*

Moores Mch Co Fayetteville Inc .... D 919 837-5354
   Bear Creek *(G-941)*

MR Fabrications LLC .... G 980 785-3943
   Marshville *(G-10220)*

MTS Holdings Corp Inc .... E 336 227-0151
   Burlington *(G-1465)*

WELDING REPAIR SVC — PRODUCT SECTION

Mtz Welding Inc .... G 919 708-8288
  Sanford (G-14155)
Mullis Mechanical Inc .... G 704 254-5229
  Monroe (G-10776)
Nashville Wldg & Mch Works Inc .... E 252 243-0113
  Wilson (G-16517)
Newriverwelding .... G 336 413-3040
  Mocksville (G-10594)
Nic Nac Welding Co .... G 704 502-5178
  Charlotte (G-3262)
Nigoche Welding Services LLC .... G 252 373-8306
  Wilson (G-16519)
Ninos Wldg & Cnstr Svcs LLC .... G 980 214-5804
  Huntersville (G-8860)
Nucon Welding Inc .... G 980 253-9369
  Charlotte (G-3279)
OHerns Welding Inc .... G 910 484-2087
  Fayetteville (G-5886)
Olive HI Wldg Fabrication Inc .... E 336 597-0737
  Roxboro (G-13812)
Olympian Welding .... G 919 608-3829
  Franklinton (G-6161)
Parrish Welding .... G 336 707-3878
  Oak Ridge (G-12064)
Pats Mobile Welding .... G 910 891-9581
  Dunn (G-4879)
Paul Casper Inc .... G 919 269-5362
  Zebulon (G-17139)
Perkins Fabrications Inc .... G 828 688-3157
  Bakersville (G-886)
Peter J Hamann .... G 910 484-7877
  Fayetteville (G-5897)
Peterson Welding Inc .... G 336 480-4152
  Lewisville (G-9670)
Pg Technichians .... G 910 742-1017
  Wilmington (G-16352)
Piedmont Weld & Pipe Inc .... G 704 782-7774
  Concord (G-4332)
Pine State Welding .... G 910 639-3631
  Whispering Pines (G-15955)
Powell Welding Inc .... G 828 433-0831
  Drexel (G-4836)
Precise Mobile Welding .... G 980 785-7085
  Charlotte (G-3367)
Precision Fabricators Inc .... G 336 835-4763
  Ronda (G-13768)
Precision Welding Mntnc .... G 336 504-5894
  Oxford (G-12145)
Precision Wldg Fbrication Svcs .... G 704 243-1929
  Waxhaw (G-15769)
Quality Welding .... G 910 754-3232
  Shallotte (G-14277)
Quillen Welding Services LLC .... G 252 269-4908
  Morehead City (G-11184)
Quilt Shop .... G 828 263-8691
  Boone (G-1230)
R & H Welding LLC .... G 919 763-7955
  Garner (G-6306)
R & J Mechanical & Welding LLC .... G 919 362-6630
  Apex (G-238)
R Jones Fabrication LLC .... G 937 779-0826
  Mooresville (G-11067)
R S Welding LLC .... G 828 437-0768
  Morganton (G-11245)
Ram Welding & Fabrication Inc .... G 704 985-8486
  Mount Pleasant (G-11677)
Rcr Welding LLC .... G 704 200-8527
  Charlotte (G-3416)
Recap Inc .... G 336 299-8794
  Greensboro (G-7305)
Reeves Indus Wldg Fabrication .... G 910 399-7127
  Riegelwood (G-13562)

Relentless Wldg & Fabrication .... G 336 402-3749
  High Point (G-8507)
Rhythms Welding LLC .... G 910 477-7150
  Supply (G-15009)
Richards Wldg Met Fbrction LLC .... F 919 626-0134
  Wendell (G-15914)
Rickys Welding Inc .... G 252 336-4437
  Shiloh (G-14392)
Riley Power Group LLC .... C 910 420-6999
  Pinehurst (G-12234)
Robert Gregory .... G 919 821-9188
  Raleigh (G-13210)
Robert Raper Welding Inc .... G 252 399-0598
  Wilson (G-16533)
Robinson Mch & Cutter Grinding .... G 704 629-5591
  Bessemer City (G-1080)
Robinsons Welding Service .... G 336 622-3150
  Liberty (G-9828)
Rocas Welding LLC .... G 252 290-2233
  Durham (G-5334)
Rock Creek Welding Inc .... G 828 385-1554
  Bakersville (G-888)
Roderick Mch Erectors Wldg Inc .... G 910 343-0381
  Wilmington (G-16386)
Rodriguez Welding LLC .... G 980 299-9449
  Charlotte (G-3457)
Rose Welding & Crane Service I .... G 252 796-9171
  Columbia (G-4167)
Roxboro Welding .... G 336 364-2307
  Roxboro (G-13821)
Royal Welding LLC .... G 704 750-9353
  Pineville (G-12298)
Rugers Welding .... G 919 471-8795
  Rougemont (G-13788)
Ruppards Welding Service LLC .... G 828 386-8191
  Boone (G-1235)
S Boyd Welding .... G 336 349-8349
  Reidsville (G-13539)
S Oakley Machine Shop Inc .... G 336 599-6105
  Roxboro (G-13822)
S&S Welding .... G 828 408-2794
  Morganton (G-11248)
Sgr Welding & Fabrication LLC .... G 252 299-3629
  Zebulon (G-17142)
Skyline Welding LLC .... G 336 479-0166
  Lexington (G-9780)
Smiths Mower Marine & Wldg LLC .... G 919 729-0070
  Louisburg (G-10002)
South East Welding .... G 980 428-0742
  Charlotte (G-3585)
Southeast Wldg Fabrication LLC .... G 828 385-1380
  Bakersville (G-889)
Southeastern MBL Wldg Repr LLC .... G 919 521-7039
  Raleigh (G-13281)
Southeastern Mch & Wldg Co Inc .... E 910 791-6661
  Wilmington (G-16410)
Southern Star Cstm Fbrction LL .... G 704 880-8948
  Statesville (G-14895)
Sowers Welding Service .... G 704 929-5617
  Mooresville (G-11093)
Specialty Welding .... G 828 248-6229
  Forest City (G-6083)
Stackz Welding .... G 336 564-5481
  Stokesdale (G-14950)
Stafford Welding .... G 704 774-1837
  Monroe (G-10813)
State of ARC Welding .... G 336 341-9780
  Winston Salem (G-16917)
Steel Supply and Erection Co .... F 336 625-4830
  Asheboro (G-487)
Stewarts Garage and Welding Co .... G 336 983-5563
  Tobaccoville (G-15321)

Storybook Farm Metal Shop Inc .... G 919 967-9491
  Chapel Hill (G-2074)
Strickland Bros Entps Inc .... F 252 478-3058
  Spring Hope (G-14623)
Tatums Trucking & Welding LLC .... G 919 697-6913
  Mebane (G-10430)
That Welder Guy .... G 252 342-0391
  Newport (G-11908)
Think Welding .... G 980 230-2842
  Charlotte (G-3686)
Thompson Welding & Mechcl Svc .... G 252 536-9431
  Roanoke Rapids (G-13582)
Thompson Wldg & Mech Svc LLC .... G 252 535-4269
  Roanoke Rapids (G-13583)
Thornburg Machine & Sup Co Inc .... E 704 735-5421
  Lincolnton (G-9929)
Thurman Toler .... G 252 758-4082
  Greenville (G-7591)
Tobaccoville Welding LLC .... G 336 287-7323
  Tobaccoville (G-15322)
Tool-Weld LLC .... G 843 986-4931
  Rutherfordton (G-13893)
Trefena Welds .... G 203 551-1370
  Browns Summit (G-1318)
Trinweld Welding Services LLC .... G 704 721-5944
  Mount Pleasant (G-11679)
Triplett & Coffey Inc .... F 828 263-0561
  Boone (G-1243)
Tristate Welding & Fabrication .... G 336 899-5206
  High Point (G-8577)
Two Brothers Wldg Miscellane .... G 704 488-9845
  Charlotte (G-3741)
Tyler Walston .... G 919 269-9300
  Wilson (G-16552)
United Technical Services LLC .... F 980 237-1335
  Charlotte (G-3753)
United TI & Stamping Co NC Inc .... D 910 323-8588
  Fayetteville (G-5939)
United Welding and Iron Work .... G 704 281-3706
  Mooresville (G-11116)
Vernons Mobile Welding LLC .... G 336 388-0415
  Pelham (G-12179)
Villabona Iron Works Inc .... F 252 522-4005
  Kinston (G-9391)
W D Lee & Company .... E 704 864-0346
  Gastonia (G-6537)
W E Nixons Wldg & Hdwr Inc .... G 252 221-4348
  Edenton (G-5523)
Wallace Welding Inc .... F 919 934-2488
  Smithfield (G-14488)
Walrath Welding .... G 704 771-6640
  Sneads Ferry (G-14493)
Warsaw Welding Service Inc .... F 910 293-4261
  Warsaw (G-15676)
Waste Container Repair Svcs .... G 910 257-4474
  Fayetteville (G-5949)
Watkins Wldg Fabrications LLC .... G 828 429-2369
  Rutherfordton (G-13901)
Webb S Maint & Piping Inc .... F 252 972-2616
  Battleboro (G-933)
Welders Log .... G 919 473-3045
  Cary (G-1925)
Welding - Fbrcation - Repr Inc .... G 828 963-9372
  Boone (G-1249)
Welding Company .... G 336 667-0265
  Wilkesboro (G-16051)
Welding Needs .... G 252 902-4082
  Greenville (G-7598)
Welding Solutions LLC .... E 828 665-4363
  Fletcher (G-6051)
Weldingart4u LLC .... G 252 220-0294
  Nashville (G-11755)

PRODUCT SECTION — WIRE & WIRE PRDTS

Wells Mechanical Services LLC............. G..... 252 532-2632
 Roanoke Rapids *(G-13585)*
Wells Welding Svc................................ G..... 252 519-2808
 Enfield *(G-5681)*
West Stanly Fabrication Inc................. G..... 704 254-2967
 Oakboro *(G-12085)*
Wicked Welds LLC............................... G..... 704 907-5531
 Charlotte *(G-3812)*
Wilkes Welding and Mch Co Inc........... G..... 336 670-2742
 Mc Grady *(G-10382)*
Williams Mech & Wldg Svcs LLC........... G..... 919 820-5287
 Dunn *(G-4891)*
Wilson Mold & Machine Corp................ D..... 252 243-1831
 Wilson *(G-16562)*
Wilson Wldg & Line Boring LLC............ G..... 828 406-2078
 Vilas *(G-15499)*
Wldg Honeycutt & Fabrication.............. G..... 252 413-8754
 Columbia *(G-4171)*
Woodys Welding LLC............................ G..... 828 391-1484
 Morganton *(G-11270)*
Young Fabrication................................ G..... 828 776-3203
 Leicester *(G-9522)*
Youngs Welding & Machine Svcs........... G..... 910 488-1190
 Fayetteville *(G-5955)*
Zickgraf Enterprises Inc..................... G..... 828 524-2313
 Franklin *(G-6149)*

WELDING SPLYS, EXC GASES: Wholesalers

A R Perry Corporation.......................... F..... 252 492-6181
 Henderson *(G-7774)*
Airgas Usa LLC.................................... F..... 704 394-1420
 Charlotte *(G-2147)*
Airgas Usa LLC.................................... G..... 919 544-3773
 Durham *(G-4909)*
Airgas Usa LLC.................................... G..... 919 735-5276
 Goldsboro *(G-6587)*

WELDING TIPS: Heat Resistant, Metal

Babco Inc.. G..... 888 376-5083
 Ayden *(G-848)*

WET CORN MILLING

Pbrandecom... G..... 336 294-9771
 Greensboro *(G-7249)*

WHEELCHAIR LIFTS

Ask Elevator Service Inc....................... G..... 336 674-2715
 Pleasant Garden *(G-12356)*
Meghan Blake Industries Inc................ E..... 704 462-2988
 Vale *(G-15469)*
Specialty Trnsp Systems Inc................ G..... 828 464-9738
 Newton *(G-11971)*
Tk Elevator Corporation....................... C..... 336 272-4563
 Greensboro *(G-7404)*
Veon Inc.. F..... 252 623-2102
 Washington *(G-15736)*

WHEELCHAIRS

Affordable Wheelchair Vans LLC........... G..... 910 443-6989
 Greensboro *(G-6786)*
All 4 U Home Medical LLC................... G..... 828 437-0684
 Morganton *(G-11196)*
Carolina Tarwheels Whlchair Bs............ G..... 704 791-5803
 Concord *(G-4225)*
Carolina Whelchair Basktbl Co.............. G..... 828 248-2055
 Forest City *(G-6063)*
Ms Whlchair N CA AM State Coor......... G..... 828 230-1129
 Weaverville *(G-15853)*
Operation Wheelchair........................... G..... 910 391-1945
 Fayetteville *(G-5889)*
Safe Ride Wheelchair Tran.................... G..... 336 995-7529
 Winston Salem *(G-16892)*

Safety Wheelchair Company.................. G..... 919 819-3775
 Raleigh *(G-13226)*
The Wheelchair Place LLC.................... G..... 828 855-9099
 Hickory *(G-8179)*

WHEELS & PARTS

Goodyear Tire & Rubber Company........ G..... 919 552-9340
 Holly Springs *(G-8700)*

WHEELS: Disc, Wheelbarrow, Stroller, Etc, Stamped Metal

Oro Manufacturing Company................ E..... 704 283-2186
 Monroe *(G-10783)*

WHIRLPOOL BATHS: Hydrotherapy

Royal Baths Manufacturing Co.............. E..... 704 837-1701
 Charlotte *(G-3461)*

WINCHES

Ingersoll-Rand Indus US Inc................. D..... 704 896-4000
 Davidson *(G-4680)*

WIND TUNNELS

Wind Shear Inc.................................... F..... 704 788-9463
 Concord *(G-4390)*

WINDINGS: Coil, Electronic

Albatross Supply LLC.......................... G..... 336 488-1128
 Hamptonville *(G-7665)*
Electronic Products Design Inc............. G..... 919 365-9199
 Wendell *(G-15901)*
Kwik Elc Mtr Sls & Svc Inc.................... G..... 252 335-2524
 Elizabeth City *(G-5553)*

WINDOW & DOOR FRAMES

Atrium Extrusion Systems Inc.............. E..... 336 764-6400
 Welcome *(G-15871)*
Godwin Door & Hardware Inc.............. E..... 919 580-0543
 Goldsboro *(G-6617)*

WINDOW CLEANING SVCS

W G of Southwest Raleigh Inc.............. G..... 919 629-7327
 Holly Springs *(G-8725)*

WINDOW FRAMES, MOLDING & TRIM: Vinyl

Beacon Roofing Supply Inc.................. G..... 704 886-1555
 Charlotte *(G-2291)*
Clt 2016 Inc.. D..... 704 886-1555
 Charlotte *(G-2501)*
Jeld-Wen Inc....................................... C..... 336 838-0292
 North Wilkesboro *(G-12016)*
Ramsey Industries Inc.......................... E..... 704 827-3560
 Belmont *(G-1005)*

WINDOW SCREENING: Plastic

Carolina Home Exteriors LLC................ F..... 252 637-6599
 New Bern *(G-11786)*

WINDOWS: Wood

Ply Gem Industries Inc........................ D..... 919 677-3900
 Cary *(G-1853)*

WINE & DISTILLED ALCOHOLIC BEVERAGES WHOLESALERS

Aviator Brewing Company Inc.............. G..... 919 601-5497
 Holly Springs *(G-8687)*

WIRE

Fishel Steel Company.......................... G..... 336 788-2880
 Winston Salem *(G-16712)*

Haynes Wire Company......................... D..... 828 692-5791
 Mountain Home *(G-11690)*
Lee Spring Company LLC..................... E..... 336 275-3631
 Greensboro *(G-7165)*
Torpedo Specialty Wire Inc.................. D..... 252 977-3900
 Rocky Mount *(G-13737)*

WIRE & CABLE: Aluminum

Mark Stoddard..................................... G..... 910 797-7214
 Fayetteville *(G-5866)*
Nkt Inc... G..... 919 601-1970
 Cary *(G-1832)*
Trimantec.. E..... 336 767-1379
 Winston Salem *(G-16952)*

WIRE & CABLE: Nonferrous, Aircraft

CNA Technology LLC........................... G..... 954 312-1200
 Greenville *(G-7502)*
Ls Cable & System USA Inc.................. C..... 252 824-3553
 Tarboro *(G-15112)*
Unitape (usa) Inc................................ F..... 828 464-5695
 Conover *(G-4507)*

WIRE & CABLE: Nonferrous, Automotive, Exc Ignition Sets

C O Jelliff Corporation......................... G..... 828 428-3672
 Maiden *(G-10100)*
Draka Transport USA LLC.................... G..... 828 459-8895
 Claremont *(G-3923)*

WIRE & CABLE: Nonferrous, Building

Abl Electronics Supply Inc................... G..... 704 784-4225
 Concord *(G-4186)*
Essex Group Inc.................................. G..... 704 921-9605
 Charlotte *(G-2730)*

WIRE & WIRE PRDTS

American Fabricators........................... G..... 252 637-2600
 New Bern *(G-11768)*
Cavert Wire Company Inc.................... E..... 800 969-2601
 Rural Hall *(G-13837)*
Chatsworth Products Inc..................... C..... 252 514-2779
 New Bern *(G-11788)*
Dradura USA Corp............................... D..... 252 637-9660
 New Bern *(G-11802)*
Essex Group Inc.................................. G..... 704 921-9605
 Charlotte *(G-2730)*
Express Wire Services Inc.................... G..... 704 393-5156
 Charlotte *(G-2739)*
Fuller Specialty Company Inc............... F..... 336 226-3446
 Burlington *(G-1417)*
Hemco Wire Products Inc.................... F..... 336 454-7280
 Jamestown *(G-9052)*
I & I Sling Inc..................................... G..... 336 323-1532
 Greensboro *(G-7107)*
Ica Mid-Atlantic Inc............................. C..... 336 447-4546
 Whitsett *(G-15993)*
Leggett & Platt Incorporated................ D..... 336 889-2600
 High Point *(G-8431)*
M-B Industries Inc............................... C..... 828 862-4201
 Rosman *(G-13786)*
McIntyre Manufacturing Group Inc........ D..... 336 476-3646
 Thomasville *(G-15246)*
McJast Inc... F..... 828 884-4809
 Pisgah Forest *(G-12326)*
Merchants Metals LLC.......................... G..... 919 598-8471
 Raleigh *(G-13015)*
Merchants Metals LLC.......................... D..... 704 878-8706
 Statesville *(G-14841)*
Preformed Line Products Co................. C..... 704 983-6161
 Albemarle *(G-99)*

WIRE & WIRE PRDTS

Prysmian Cbles Systems USA LLC............. E 828 322-9473
  Hickory (G-8128)
Rack Works Inc................................... E 336 368-1302
  Pilot Mountain (G-12201)
Rolf Koerner LLC................................. G 704 714-8866
  Charlotte (G-3459)
Royal Wire Products Inc......................... E 704 596-2110
  Charlotte (G-3466)
Sid Jenkins Inc................................... E 336 632-0707
  Greensboro (G-7337)
Unified Scrning Crshing - NC I.................. G 336 824-2151
  Ramseur (G-13451)
Wieland Electric Inc.............................. F 910 259-5050
  Wilmington (G-16442)

WIRE FABRIC: Welded Steel

A B Carter Inc.................................... D 704 865-1201
  Gastonia (G-6334)
Insteel Wire Products Company................ C 336 719-9000
  Mount Airy (G-11521)
Van Blake Dixon.................................. F 336 282-1861
  Greensboro (G-7436)
Wireway/Husky Corp............................. C 704 483-1135
  Denver (G-4815)

WIRE MATERIALS: Copper

Hickory Wire Inc.................................. F 828 322-9473
  Hickory (G-8056)

WIRE MATERIALS: Steel

Coleman Cable LLC............................. E 828 389-8013
  Hayesville (G-7762)
Granite Falls Furnaces LLC..................... E 828 324-4394
  Granite Falls (G-6734)
ISS.. G 919 317-8314
  Durham (G-5168)
Southern Steel and Wire Inc.................... D 336 548-9611
  Madison (G-10087)
Williams Industries Inc........................... C 919 604-1746
  Raleigh (G-13423)

WIRE PRDTS: Ferrous Or Iron, Made In Wiredrawing Plants

Cavert Wire Company Inc........................ E 800 969-2601
  Rural Hall (G-13837)
Sandvik Inc....................................... C 919 563-5008
  Mebane (G-10427)

WIRE PRDTS: Steel & Iron

Interntonal Specialty Pdts Inc................... G 828 326-9053
  Hickory (G-8067)

WIRE: Communication

Commscope Inc North Carolina................ A 828 459-5000
  Claremont (G-3910)
Commscope Inc North Carolina................ D 828 324-2200
  Claremont (G-3909)
Commscope Technologies LLC................. A 828 324-2200
  Claremont (G-3916)
Corning Optcal Cmmncations LLC............. A 828 327-5290
  Hickory (G-7996)
Draka Holdings Usa Inc......................... A 828 383-0020
  Claremont (G-3922)
Nexans USA Inc.................................. B 828 323-2660
  Hickory (G-8102)
Rave Networx Inc................................ G 910 808-9346
  Fuquay Varina (G-6223)
Sumitomo Elc Lightwave Corp.................. C 919 541-8100
  Raleigh (G-13313)
Superior Essex Intl LP........................... C 252 823-5111
  Tarboro (G-15122)

WIRE: Mesh

Ashley Sling Inc.................................. E 704 347-0071
  Charlotte (G-2226)

WIRE: Nonferrous

AFL Network Services Inc....................... E 704 289-5522
  Monroe (G-10639)
AFL Network Services Inc....................... E 919 658-2311
  Mount Olive (G-11653)
Batt Fabricators Inc.............................. F 336 431-9334
  Trinity (G-15339)
Coleman Cable LLC............................. E 828 389-8013
  Hayesville (G-7762)
Corning Incorporated............................ D 704 569-6000
  Midland (G-10464)
Draka Elevator Products Inc.................... C 252 984-5100
  Rocky Mount (G-13690)
Draka Usa Inc.................................... F 828 459-9787
  Claremont (G-3924)
Frenzelit Inc...................................... E 336 814-4317
  Lexington (G-9721)
Huber + Suhner Inc.............................. E 704 790-7300
  Charlotte (G-2928)
Huber + Suhner North Amer Corp.............. D 704 790-7300
  Charlotte (G-2929)
Leviton Manufacturing Co Inc................... E 828 584-1611
  Morganton (G-11228)
Neptco Incorporated............................. C 828 728-5951
  Lenoir (G-9639)
Superior Essex Inc............................... D 252 823-5111
  Tarboro (G-15121)
Transcendent Technologies LLC............... G 704 334-1258
  Charlotte (G-3717)
Tyco Electronics Corporation................... G 717 986-5311
  Greensboro (G-7423)

WIRE: Nonferrous, Appliance Fixture

Cordset Designs Inc............................. E 252 568-4001
  Pink Hill (G-12316)

WOMEN'S & CHILDREN'S CLOTHING WHOLESALERS, NEC

Apparel USA Inc.................................. E 212 869-5495
  Fairmont (G-5700)
Badger Sportswear LLC......................... D 704 871-0990
  Statesville (G-14757)
Burlington Coat Fctry Whse Cor................ E 919 468-9312
  Cary (G-1718)
Gerson & Gerson Inc............................ E 252 235-2441
  Middlesex (G-10450)
Raleigh Workshop Inc............................ E 919 917-8969
  Raleigh (G-13188)
Seafarer LLC..................................... G 704 624-3200
  Marshville (G-10224)
Sorbe Ltd... G 704 562-2991
  Matthews (G-10344)
Walter Reynolds................................. G 704 735-6050
  Lincolnton (G-9935)

WOMEN'S & GIRLS' SPORTSWEAR WHOLESALERS

Ics North America Corp.......................... E 704 794-6920
  Concord (G-4283)
Marketing One Sportswear Inc.................. G 704 334-9333
  Charlotte (G-3126)

WOMEN'S CLOTHING STORES

Live It Boutique LLC............................. G 704 492-2402
  Charlotte (G-3095)

Pine State Corporate AP LLC................... F 336 789-9437
  Mount Airy (G-11557)
W E Nixons Wldg & Hdwr Inc.................... G 252 221-4348
  Edenton (G-5523)

WOMEN'S CLOTHING STORES: Ready-To-Wear

Grace Apparel Company Inc.................... G 828 242-8172
  Arden (G-335)

WOMEN'S FULL & KNEE LENGTH HOSIERY DYEING & FINISHING

Star America Inc................................. C 704 788-4700
  Concord (G-4367)
Ward Hosiery Company Inc..................... G 828 381-2346
  Hickory (G-8206)

WOOD & WOOD BY-PRDTS, WHOLESALE

Decima Corporation LLC........................ E 734 516-1535
  Charlotte (G-2610)

WOOD CHIPS, PRODUCED AT THE MILL

Godfrey Lumber Company Inc.................. F 704 872-6366
  Statesville (G-14804)
Jordan Lumber & Supply Inc.................... G 910 428-9048
  Star (G-14717)
Keener Wood Products Inc...................... G 828 428-1562
  Maiden (G-10111)
Powell Industries Inc............................ D 828 926-9114
  Waynesville (G-15815)
Valwood Corporation............................ F 828 321-4717
  Marble (G-10135)
Yildiz Entegre Usa Inc........................... G 910 763-4733
  Wilmington (G-16458)

WOOD PRDTS: Applicators

Alcorns Custom Woodworking Inc............... G 336 342-0908
  Reidsville (G-13505)
Gilbert Hardwoods Inc........................... F 336 431-2127
  Trinity (G-15342)
Heartwood Pine Floors Inc...................... G 919 542-4394
  Moncure (G-10624)
National Salvage & Svc Corp................... E 919 739-5633
  Dudley (G-4845)
Robert Hamms LLC.............................. G 704 605-8057
  Monroe (G-10797)

WOOD PRDTS: Battery Separators

Daramic LLC...................................... D 704 587-8599
  Charlotte (G-2603)

WOOD PRDTS: Laundry

C & D Woodworking Inc.......................... G 336 476-8722
  Thomasville (G-15193)
Ges Industries.................................... E 252 430-8851
  Kittrell (G-9396)

WOOD PRDTS: Moldings, Unfinished & Prefinished

Carter Millwork Inc............................... D 800 861-0734
  Lexington (G-9690)
Dwelling NC Inc.................................. G 252 619-0226
  Edenton (G-5513)
Ecmd Inc.. D 336 667-5976
  North Wilkesboro (G-12006)
Freedom Enterprise LLC........................ G 502 510-7296
  Shallotte (G-14273)
H & H Wood Products Inc....................... G 704 233-4148
  Wingate (G-16575)

PRODUCT SECTION — YARN & YARN SPINNING

H T Jones Lumber Company .... F 252 332-4135
  Ahoskie *(G-63)*

Moulding Source Incorporated .... G 704 658-1111
  Mooresville *(G-11031)*

Olde Lexington Products Inc .... G 336 956-2355
  Linwood *(G-9947)*

Profilform Us Inc .... E 252 430-0392
  Henderson *(G-7803)*

Robbinsville Cstm Molding Inc .... F 828 479-2317
  Robbinsville *(G-13610)*

Smokey Mountain Lumber Inc .... G 828 298-3958
  Asheville *(G-775)*

WOOD PRDTS: Mulch Or Sawdust

D C Custom Freight LLC .... E 843 658-6484
  Marshville *(G-10213)*

Gates Custom Milling Inc .... E 252 357-0116
  Gatesville *(G-6549)*

Martin Lumber & Mulch LLC .... F 252 935-5294
  Pantego *(G-12167)*

Mulch Solutions LLC .... G 704 893-5302
  Indian Trail *(G-8950)*

Turn Bull Lumber Company .... E 910 862-4447
  Elizabethtown *(G-5607)*

WOOD PRDTS: Mulch, Wood & Bark

A & J Pallets Inc .... G 336 969-0265
  Rural Hall *(G-13832)*

American Soil and Mulch Inc .... F 919 460-1349
  Raleigh *(G-12499)*

Carolina Bark Products LLC .... G 252 589-1324
  Seaboard *(G-14227)*

Garick LLC .... G 704 455-6418
  Harrisburg *(G-7712)*

Highland Craftsmen Inc .... F 828 765-9010
  Spruce Pine *(G-14642)*

Kamlar Corporation .... E 252 443-2576
  Rocky Mount *(G-13705)*

Mulch Masters of NC Inc .... F 919 676-0031
  Raleigh *(G-13050)*

North Carolina Mulch Inc .... G 252 478-4609
  Middlesex *(G-10452)*

Privette Enterprises Inc .... E 704 634-3291
  Monroe *(G-10789)*

Soundside Recycling & Mtls Inc .... G 252 491-8666
  Jarvisburg *(G-9086)*

WOOD PRDTS: Outdoor, Structural

Appalachian Getaways .... G 828 243-3105
  Asheville *(G-521)*

Vida Wood Us Inc .... G 919 934-9904
  Smithfield *(G-14487)*

WOOD PRDTS: Panel Work

Appalachian Lumber Company Inc .... E 336 973-7205
  Wilkesboro *(G-16013)*

Funder America Inc .... F 336 751-3501
  Mocksville *(G-10575)*

WOOD PRDTS: Signboards

Cw Media Inc .... G 910 302-3066
  Raeford *(G-12419)*

Kenneth Moore Signs .... G 910 458-6428
  Wilmington *(G-16287)*

WOOD PRODUCTS: Reconstituted

Arauco North America Inc .... D 919 542-2128
  Moncure *(G-10613)*

Atc Panels Inc .... G 888 200-7955
  Moncure *(G-10615)*

Atc Panels Inc .... F 919 653-6053
  Morrisville *(G-11295)*

Huber Engineered Woods LLC .... E 800 933-9220
  Charlotte *(G-2930)*

Industrial Timber LLC .... D 704 919-1215
  Hiddenite *(G-8220)*

Industrial Timber LLC .... D 704 919-1215
  Charlotte *(G-2966)*

J R Craver & Associates Inc .... E 336 769-3330
  Clemmons *(G-4049)*

Louisiana-Pacific Corporation .... C 336 599-8080
  Roxboro *(G-13806)*

Uniboard USA LLC .... C 919 542-2128
  Moncure *(G-10628)*

Weyerhaeuser Company .... E 336 835-5100
  Elkin *(G-5633)*

WOOD TREATING: Millwork

Jak Moulding & Supply Inc .... F 252 753-5546
  Walstonburg *(G-15638)*

Ufp Biscoe LLC .... F 910 294-8179
  Biscoe *(G-1117)*

Ufp Rockwell LLC .... G 704 279-0744
  Rockwell *(G-13662)*

WOOD TREATING: Structural Lumber & Timber

Albemarle Wood Prsv Plant Inc .... G 704 982-2516
  Albemarle *(G-72)*

Blue Ridge Lbr Log & Timber Co ...... F 336 961-5211
  Yadkinville *(G-17033)*

Boise Cascade Wood Pdts LLC .... G 336 598-3001
  Roxboro *(G-13795)*

Carolina Square Inc .... G 336 793-3222
  Mocksville *(G-10562)*

Hoover Treated Wood Pdts Inc .... E 866 587-8761
  Weldon *(G-15882)*

Soha Holdings LLC .... E 828 264-2314
  Boone *(G-1236)*

Tarheel Wood Treating Company ...... F 919 467-9176
  Morrisville *(G-11438)*

Tom Kleeberg .... G 336 516-2363
  High Point *(G-8572)*

Tri-H Molding Co .... G 252 491-8530
  Harbinger *(G-7684)*

WOOD TREATING: Wood Prdts, Creosoted

Wood-N-Boats Etc Inc .... G 828 682-7470
  Burnsville *(G-1536)*

WOODWORK & TRIM: Exterior & Ornamental

Triad Prefinish & Lbr Sls Inc .... G 336 375-4849
  Greensboro *(G-7415)*

WOODWORK & TRIM: Interior & Ornamental

Bakers Quality Trim Inc .... G 919 552-3621
  Willow Spring *(G-16075)*

Chadsworth Incorporated .... E 910 763-7600
  Wilmington *(G-16168)*

Exley Custom Woodwork Inc .... G 910 763-5445
  Castle Hayne *(G-1946)*

Hedrick Construction .... G 336 362-3443
  Kernersville *(G-9204)*

Jody Stowe .... G 704 519-6560
  Matthews *(G-10256)*

WOODWORK: Interior & Ornamental, NEC

Browns Woodworking LLC .... G 704 983-5917
  Albemarle *(G-76)*

Carraways Sign & WD Crafts LLC .... G 252 292-7141
  Wilson *(G-16486)*

Idaho Wood Inc .... F 208 263-9521
  Oxford *(G-12132)*

Martin Wood Products Inc .... G 336 548-3470
  Madison *(G-10080)*

Max Woodworks Inc .... G 786 286-2668
  Black Mountain *(G-1129)*

Miters Touch Inc .... G 828 963-4445
  Banner Elk *(G-903)*

Onsite Woodwork Corporation .... F 704 523-1380
  Charlotte *(G-3302)*

Tailored Visionz & Dreamz LLC .... G 919 340-3613
  Hollister *(G-8677)*

Trimsters Inc .... F 919 639-3126
  Angier *(G-150)*

Woodwizards Inc .... G 336 427-7698
  Stokesdale *(G-14952)*

WOVEN WIRE PRDTS, NEC

Ceramawire .... G 252 335-7411
  Elizabeth City *(G-5533)*

Davis Newell Company Inc .... F 910 762-3500
  Wilmington *(G-16195)*

X-RAY EQPT & TUBES

Digitome Corporation .... G 860 651-5560
  Davidson *(G-4672)*

Flow X Ray Corporation .... D 631 242-9729
  Battleboro *(G-920)*

Wolf X-Ray Corporation .... D 631 242-9729
  Battleboro *(G-934)*

Xinray Systems Inc .... F 919 701-4100
  Chapel Hill *(G-2101)*

YARN & YARN SPINNING

American & Efird LLC .... F 704 864-0977
  Gastonia *(G-6343)*

American & Efird LLC .... F 828 754-9066
  Lenoir *(G-9572)*

Aquafil OMara Inc .... C 828 874-2100
  Rutherford College *(G-13858)*

Carolina Mills Warehouse .... G 828 428-9911
  Maiden *(G-10103)*

Cs Carolina Inc .... G 336 578-0110
  Burlington *(G-1402)*

Cumins Machinery Corp .... G 336 622-1000
  Liberty *(G-9809)*

Dawn Processing Company Inc .... G 704 629-5321
  Bessemer City *(G-1062)*

Filtec Precise Inc .... E 910 653-5200
  Tabor City *(G-15082)*

Frontier Yarns Inc .... E 919 776-9940
  Sanford *(G-14121)*

Gildan Yarns LLC .... G 704 633-5133
  Salisbury *(G-13968)*

Grateful Union Family Inc .... F 828 622-3258
  Asheville *(G-640)*

Hampton Art Inc .... C 252 975-7207
  Washington *(G-15709)*

Hickory Dyg & Winding Co Inc .... F 828 322-1550
  Hickory *(G-8047)*

Hickory Throwing Company .... E 828 322-1158
  Hickory *(G-8055)*

Invista Capital Management LLC .... D 704 636-6000
  Salisbury *(G-13989)*

Krodsa USA Inc .... G 910 462-2041
  Laurel Hill *(G-9463)*

Marilyn Cook .... G 704 735-4414
  Lincolnton *(G-9905)*

Milliken & Company .... E 828 247-4300
  Bostic *(G-1265)*

Milliken & Company .... F 336 548-5680
  Mayodan *(G-10366)*

National Spinning Co Inc .... C 910 298-3131
  Beulaville *(G-1097)*

*Employee Codes: A=Over 500 employees, B=251-500
C=101-250, D=51-100, E=20-50, F=10-19, G=1-9*

YARN & YARN SPINNING

Normtex Incorporated.................................. G 828 428-3363
  Wilmington *(G-16341)*
North Crlina Spnning Mills Inc................... E 704 732-1171
  Lincolnton *(G-9911)*
Oakdale Cotton Mills................................... G 336 454-1144
  Jamestown *(G-9065)*
Parkdale Mills Incorporated..................... F 704 825-2529
  Belmont *(G-1000)*
Parkdale Mills Incorporated..................... E 704 739-7411
  Kings Mountain *(G-9322)*
Parkdale Mills Incorporated..................... E 704 855-3164
  Landis *(G-9452)*
Parkdale Mills Incorporated..................... E 704 292-1255
  Mineral Springs *(G-10519)*
Parkdale Mills Incorporated..................... D 919 774-7401
  Sanford *(G-14163)*
Parkdale Mills Incorporated..................... D 336 476-3181
  Thomasville *(G-15261)*
Parkdale Mills Incorporated..................... D 336 591-4644
  Walnut Cove *(G-15635)*
Patrick Yarn Mill Inc................................. C 704 739-4119
  Kings Mountain *(G-9324)*
Richmond Specialty Yarns LLC................ C 910 652-5554
  Ellerbe *(G-5643)*
Sgrtex LLC.. D 336 635-9420
  Eden *(G-5502)*
Shuford Yarns LLC.................................... D 828 324-4265
  Hickory *(G-8151)*
Shuford Yarns Management Inc............. G 828 324-4265
  Hickory *(G-8152)*
Spinrite Yarns LP....................................... G 252 833-4970
  Washington *(G-15732)*
Supreme Elastic Corporation................... E 828 302-3836
  Conover *(G-4502)*
Unifi Inc... D 336 348-6539
  Reidsville *(G-13544)*
Unifi Inc... C 336 679-3830
  Yadkinville *(G-17058)*
Unifi Manufacturing Inc........................... A 336 427-1515
  Yadkinville *(G-17059)*
World Elastic Corporation....................... E 704 786-9508
  Concord *(G-4391)*
Zimmermann - Dynayarn Usa LLC......... E 336 222-8129
  Graham *(G-6717)*

YARN MILLS: Texturizing, Throwing & Twisting

C S America Inc.. E
  Burlington *(G-1382)*
Glen Raven Inc... G 336 227-6211
  Altamahaw *(G-122)*
Hickory Dyg & Winding Co Inc.............. F 828 322-1550
  Hickory *(G-8047)*
Parkdale Mills Incorporated..................... F 704 825-2529
  Belmont *(G-1000)*
Premiere Fibers LLC................................ C 704 826-8321
  Ansonville *(G-155)*
Sam M Butler Inc..................................... E 704 364-8647
  Charlotte *(G-3487)*

Sam M Butler Inc..................................... E 910 276-2360
  Laurinburg *(G-9494)*
Sapona Manufacturing Co Inc................ C 336 873-8700
  Asheboro *(G-476)*
Sapona Manufacturing Co Inc................ E 336 625-2727
  Cedar Falls *(G-1969)*

YARN WHOLESALERS

Freudenberg Prfmce Mtls LP.................. C 828 665-5000
  Candler *(G-1579)*
Normtex Incorporated.............................. G 828 428-3363
  Wilmington *(G-16341)*

YARN: Combed, Spun

Parkdale America LLC............................. E 704 739-7411
  Kings Mountain *(G-9321)*

YARN: Cotton, Spun

Coats & Clark Inc..................................... D 704 542-5959
  Charlotte *(G-2512)*
Coats N Amer De Rpblica Dmncan........ C 800 242-8095
  Charlotte *(G-2515)*
Grp Inc.. G 919 776-9940
  Sanford *(G-14128)*
Parkdale Mills Incorporated..................... E 704 825-5324
  Belmont *(G-998)*
Parkdale Mills Incorporated..................... D 704 913-3917
  Belmont *(G-999)*
Parkdale Mills Incorporated..................... E 704 822-0778
  Mount Holly *(G-11646)*
Parkdale Mills Incorporated..................... D 704 874-5000
  Gastonia *(G-6486)*
Parkdale Mills Incorporated..................... E 704 857-3456
  Landis *(G-9453)*
Rocky Mount Mill LLC............................. F 919 890-6000
  Raleigh *(G-13213)*
Unifi Inc... G 919 774-7401
  Sanford *(G-14202)*

YARN: Knitting, Spun

Carolina Mills Incorporated..................... B 828 428-9911
  Maiden *(G-10102)*
National Spinning Co Inc........................ C 910 642-4181
  Whiteville *(G-15972)*
Pearson Textiles Inc................................. G 919 776-8730
  Sanford *(G-14165)*
Tuscarora Yarns Inc.................................. B 704 436-6527
  Mount Pleasant *(G-11680)*
World Fibers Inc....................................... G 704 788-3017
  Concord *(G-4392)*
World Fibers Inc....................................... G 704 788-3017
  Concord *(G-4393)*

YARN: Manmade & Synthetic Fiber, Spun

Charles Craft Inc...................................... G 910 844-3521
  Laurinburg *(G-9474)*
Coats HP Inc... B 704 824-9904
  Mc Adenville *(G-10377)*
Coats HP Inc... E 704 329-5800
  Charlotte *(G-2514)*

Fiber-Line LLC... D 828 326-8700
  Hickory *(G-8023)*
Glen Raven Inc... C 336 227-6211
  Burlington *(G-1423)*
Glen Rven Tchnical Fabrics LLC............ C 336 229-5576
  Burlington *(G-1425)*
Mannington Mills Inc............................... E 704 824-3551
  Mc Adenville *(G-10379)*
Pharr McAdenville Corporation............. D 704 824-3551
  Mc Adenville *(G-10380)*
Shuford Yarns LLC.................................... C 828 396-2342
  Granite Falls *(G-6757)*
Unifi Inc... C 336 427-1890
  Madison *(G-10090)*

YARN: Needle & Handicraft, Spun

Summit Yarn LLC..................................... A 704 874-5000
  Gastonia *(G-6517)*

YARN: Nylon, Spun Staple

Kordsa Inc... C 910 462-2051
  Laurel Hill *(G-9462)*
Unifi Inc... D 336 294-4410
  Greensboro *(G-7427)*
Unifi Manufacturing Inc........................... A 336 679-8891
  Yadkinville *(G-17060)*
Unifi Manufacturing Inc........................... C 336 294-4410
  Greensboro *(G-7428)*

YARN: Plastic Coated, Made From Purchased Yarn

Sam M Butler Inc..................................... E 910 277-7456
  Laurinburg *(G-9495)*

YARN: Polyester, Spun From Purchased Staple

Parkdale Incorporated.............................. C 704 874-5000
  Gastonia *(G-6484)*
Parkdale America LLC............................. A 704 874-5000
  Gastonia *(G-6485)*
Parkdale Mills Incorporated..................... E 336 243-2141
  Lexington *(G-9768)*
Universal Fibers Inc.................................. C 336 672-2600
  Asheboro *(G-503)*

YARN: Wool, Spun

National Spinning Co Inc........................ C 336 226-0141
  Burlington *(G-1467)*
National Spinning Co Inc........................ C 252 975-7111
  Washington *(G-15717)*
National Spnning Oprations LLC........... F 252 975-7111
  Washington *(G-15718)*

YARNS, INDL, WHOLESALE

Fibex LLC.. G 336 605-9002
  Colfax *(G-4150)*